New American Standard Bible

THE FOUNDATION PRESS PUBLICATIONS

Box 277, La Habra, Calif. 90631

Publisher
for
THE LOCKMAN FOUNDATION

E1-1

A Corporation Not for Profit

La Habra, Calif.

Producers of Amplified Translations

First Edition

Printed in the United States of America

FOREWORD

The New American Standard Bible has been produced with the conviction that the words of Scripture as originally penned in the Hebrew and Greek were inspired by God. Since they are the eternal Word of God, the Holy Scriptures speak with fresh power to each generation, to give wisdom that leads to salvation, that men may serve God to the glory of Christ.

The Editorial Board had a two-fold purpose in making this translation to adhere as closely as possible to the original language of the Holy Scriptures. To make the translation in a fluent and readable style according to current English usage. (This translation follows the principles used in the American Standard Version 1901 known as the Rock of Biblical Honesty.)

IMPORTANT

THE FOLLOWING INFORMATION

SHOULD BE READ

SCRIPTURAL PROMISE

"The grass withers, the flower fades, but the Word of our God shall stand forever." Isaiah 40:8

THE FOURFOLD AIM

OF

THE LOCKMAN FOUNDATION

1. These publications shall be true to the original Hebrew and Greek.
2. They shall be grammatically correct.
3. They shall be understandable to the masses.
4. They shall give the Lord Jesus Christ His proper place, the place which the Word gives Him; no work will ever be personalized.

PREFACE TO THE NEW AMERICAN STANDARD BIBLE
A. D. 1963

The producers of this translation were imbued with the conviction that interest in the American Standard Version 1901 should be renewed and increased. They have labored with prayerful seriousness to this end. This great responsibility was assumed only after the need was thoroughly established in the minds of many. That which is forever settled in heaven (Psa. 119:89) must ever be available on earth. Such availability is contingent upon (1) clarity of language in its current understanding and (2) the most appealing form of presentation contemporary facilities afford.

All that exists has a cause from which it springs, and this important undertaking was born of no light impulses. It was inspired and encouraged by wholesome and meaningful reasons. The chief inducement, of course, was the recognized value of the version of 1901 which deserves and demands perpetuation. The following observations are advanced as justifiable encouragement:

1. The American Standard Version of 1901 has been in a very real sense the standard for many translations.
2. It is a monumental product of applied scholarship, assiduous labor and thorough procedure.
3. It has enjoyed universal endorsement as a trustworthy translation of the original text.
4. The British and American organizations were governed by rules of procedure which assured accuracy in the completed work.
5. The American Standard Version, itself a revision of the 1881-1885 edition, is the product of international collaboration, invaluable for perspective, accuracy and finesse.
6. Unlike many modern translations of the Scriptures, the American Standard Version 1901 retains its acceptability for pulpit reading and for personal memorization.

Perhaps the most weighty impetus for this undertaking can be attributed to a disturbing awareness that the American Standard Version of 1901 was fast disappearing from the scene. As a generation "which knew not Joseph" was born, even so a generation unacquainted with this great and important work has come into being. Recognizing a responsibility to posterity, The Lockman Foundation felt an urgency to rescue this noble achievement from an inevitable demise, to preserve it as a heritage for coming generations, and to do so in such a form as the demands of passing time dictate.

THE FOUNDATION, a corporation not for profit in the State of California, took the initiative in the work of revision, engaging consultants to lay the groundwork for text arrangement, textual revision, linguistic accuracy and editorial finalizing.

1. TEXT ARRANGEMENT: This initial step was taken with caution and concern. Page construction registers the first impression when attention is given to a volume. But appearance is not the only consideration in designing a format of the printed page; utility is a major factor! Whatever tends to make the reading easier and more enjoyable is the desirable design. To develop this format it was found best to place cross references and marginal notes in a column alongside the text. References are noted by letters and marginal notes by numerals. (See explanation of format.)
2. TEXTUAL REVISION: Words are the vehicle of thought, and most languages, especially the English, have a flexibility which economic and cultural progress utilizes. Passing time with myriads of inventions and innovations automatically renders obsolete and inexpressive words that once were in acceptable usage. The ever-present danger of stripping divine Truth of its dignity and original intent was prominently before the minds of the producers at all times. An editorial board composed of linguists, Greek and Hebrew scholars and pastors undertook the responsibilities of translation.

PRINCIPLES OF REVISION

Greek Text: In revising the ASV, consideration was given to the latest available manuscripts with a view to determining the best Greek text. In most instances the 23rd edition of the Nestle Greek New Testament was followed.

Modern English Usage: The attempt has been made to render the grammar and terminology of the ASV in contemporary English. When it was felt that the word-for-word literalness of the ASV was unacceptable to the modern reader, a change was made in the direction of a more current English idiom. In the instances where this has been done, the more literal rendering has been indicated in the margin.

Marginal Readings: In addition to the more literal renderings, the marginal notations have been made to include alternate translations, readings of variant manuscripts and explanatory equivalents of the text. Only such notations have been used as have been felt justified in assisting the reader's comprehension of the terms used by the original author.

It is enthusiastically anticipated that the general public will be grateful to learn of the availability and value of the New American Standard Bible. It is released with strong confidence that those who seek a knowledge of the Scriptures will find herein a source of genuine satisfaction for a clear and accurate rendering of divinely-revealed truth.

Hebrew Text: In the present translation the latest edition of Rudolph Kittel's BIBLIA HEBRAICA has been employed together with the most recent light from lexicography, cognate languages, and the Dead Sea Scrolls.

Hebrew Tenses: Consecution of tenses in Hebrew remains a puzzling factor in translation. The translators have been guided by the requirements of a literal translation, the sequence of tenses, and the immediate and broad contexts.

Greek Tenses:

1. A careful distinction has been made in the treatment of the Greek aorist tense (usually translated as the English past, "He did") and the Greek imperfect tense (rendered either as English past progressive, "He was doing"; or, if inceptive, as "He *began* to do" or He started to do"); or else if customary past, as "He used to do." "Began" is italicized if it renders an imperfect tense, in order to distinguish it from the Greek verb for "begin."

2. On the other hand, not all aorists have been rendered as English pasts ("He did"), for some of them are clearly to be rendered as English perfects ("He has done"), or even as past perfects ("He had done"), judging from the context in which they occur. Such aorists have been rendered as perfects or past perfects in this version.

3. As for the distinction between aorist and present imperatives, the Board has usually rendered these imperatives in the customary manner, rather than attempting any such fine distinction as, "Begin to do!" (for the aorist imperative), or "Continually do!" (for the present imperative).

4. As for sequence of tenses, the Board took care to follow English rules rather than Greek in translating Greek presents, imperfects and aorists. Thus, where English says, "We knew that he was doing," Greek puts it, "We knew that he does"; similarly, "We knew that he had done," is the Greek, "We knew that he did." Likewise, the English, "When he had come, they met him," is represented in Greek by: "When he came, they met him." In all cases a consistent transfer has been made from the Greek tense in the subordinate clause to the appropriate tense in English.

5. In the rendering of negative questions introduced by the particle **mē** (which always expects the answer, "No") the wording has been altered from a mere, "Will he not do this?" to a more accurate, "He will not do this, will he?"

The Proper Name for God: To professing Christians, whether of conservative or liberal persuasion, the name of God is most significant and understandably so. It is inconceivable to think of spiritual matters without a proper designation for the Supreme Deity. Thus the most common name for deity is God, a translation of the original Elohim. The normal word for Master is Lord, a rendering of Adonai. There is yet another name which is particularly assigned to God as His special or proper name, that is, the four letters YHWH. See Exodus 3 and Isaiah 42:8. This name has not been pronounced by the Jews because of reverence for the great sacredness of the divine name. Therefore, it was consistently pronounced and translated LORD. The only exception to this translation of YHWH is when it occurs in immediate proximity to the word Lord, that is, Adonai. In that case it is regularly translated GOD in order to avoid confusion.

It is known that for many years YHWH has been transliterated as Yahweh. No complete certainty attaches to this pronunciation. However, it is felt by many who are in touch with the laity of our churches that this name conveys no religious or spiritual overtones. It is strange, uncommon, and without sufficient religious and devotional background. No amount of scholarly debate can overcome this deficiency. Hence, it was decided to avoid the use of this name in the translation proper.

Editorial Board
The Lockman Foundation

EXPLANATION OF GENERAL FORMAT

MARGINAL NOTES AND CROSS REFERENCES are placed in a column on the outer edge of the page and listed under verse numbers to which they refer. Superior numbers refer to literal renderings, alternate translations, or explanations. Superior letters refer to cross references. Cross references in italics are parallel passages.

PARAGRAPHS are designated by bold face numbers or letters.

QUOTATION MARKS are used in the text in accordance with modern English usage.

PUNCTUATION CHANGES have been made in order to conform with modern practice.

"THOU, THY AND THEE" are changed to "you" except in the language of prayer when addressing Deity.

PERSONAL PRONOUNS are capitalized when pertaining to Deity.

ITALICS are used in the text to indicate words which are not found in the original Hebrew or Greek but implied by it. Italics are used in the marginal notes to signify alternate readings for the text.

SMALL CAPS in the New Testament are used in the text to indicate Old Testament quotes.

ASTERISK—In regard to the use in Greek of the historical present, the Board recognized that in some contexts the present tense seems more unexpected and unjustified to the English reader than a past tense would have been. But Greek authors frequently used the present tense for the sake of heightened vividness, thereby transporting their readers in imagination to the actual scene at the time of occurrence. However, the Board felt that it would be wise to change these historical presents into English past tenses. Therefore verbs marked with an asterisk (*) represent historical presents in the Greek which have been translated with an English past tense in order to conform to modern usage.

ABBREVIATIONS: The Old Testament margins use the following abbreviations: DSS—Dead Sea Scrolls. Gk.—Septuagint (LXX) text. Heb.—Hebrew text, usually Masoretic. M.T.—Masoretic text.

New American Standard Bible

Old Testament

The Names and Order of the Books of The Old Testament

The Names and Order of the Books of The New Testament

GENESIS

The Creation.

[a]IN the beginning [b]God [c]created the heavens and the earth.
2 And the earth was [1a]formless and void, and [b]darkness
was over the [2]surface of the deep; and [c]the Spirit of God [d]was
[3]moving over the [2]surface of the waters.
3 Then [a]God said, "Let there be light"; and there was
light.
4 And God saw that the light was [a]good; and God [b]sepa-
rated the light from the darkness.
5 And [a]God called the light day, and the darkness He
called night. And [b]there was evening and there was morning,
one day.
6 Then God said, "Let there be an [1a]expanse in the midst
of the waters, and let it separate the waters from the waters."
7 And God made the [1]expanse, and separated [a]the waters
which were below the [1]expanse from the waters [b]which were
above the [1]expanse; and it was so.
8 And God called the [1]expanse heaven. And there was
evening and there was morning, a second day.
9 Then God said, "[a]Let the waters below the heavens be
gathered into one place, and let [b]the dry land appear"; and it
was so.
10 And God called the dry land earth, and the [a]gathering
of the waters He called seas; and God saw that it was good.
11 Then God said, "Let the earth sprout [1a]vegetation,
[2]plants yielding seed, *and* fruit trees bearing fruit after [3]their
kind, [4]with seed in them, on the earth"; and it was so.
12 And the earth brought forth [1]vegetation, [2]plants yielding seed after [3]their kind, and trees bearing fruit, [4]with seed in
them, after [3]their kind; and God saw that it was good.
13 And there was evening and there was morning, a third
day.
14 Then God said, "Let there be [1a]lights in the [2b]expanse
of the heavens to separate the day from the night, and let them
be for [c]signs, and for [d]seasons, and for days and years;
15 and let them be for [1]lights in the [2]expanse of the heavens to give light on the earth"; and it was so.
16 And God made the two [1]great lights; the [a]greater [2]light
[3]to govern the day, and the lesser [2]light [3]to govern the night;
He made [b]the stars also.
17 [a]And God placed them in the [1]expanse of the heavens
to give light on the earth,
18 and [1]to govern the day and the night, and to separate
the light from the darkness; and God saw that it was good.
19 And there was evening and there was morning, a fourth
day.
20 Then God said, "Let the waters [1]teem with swarms of
living creatures, and let birds fly above the earth [2]in the open
[3]expanse of the heavens."
21 And God created [a]the great sea monsters, and every
living creature that moves, with which the waters swarmed

1 [a]Ps. 102:25; Is. 40:21; John 1:1, 2 [b]Ps. 89:11; 90:2; Acts 17:24 [c]Is. 42:5; 45:18

2 [1]Or, *a waste and emptiness* [2]Lit., *face of* [3]Or, *hovering*
[a]Jer. 4:23 [b]Job 38:9 [c]Ps. 104:30 [d]Deut. 32:11; Is. 31:5

3 [a]Ps. 33:6, 9; 2 Cor. 4:6

4 [a]Ps. 145:9, 10 [b]Is. 45:7

5 [a]Ps 74:16 [b]Ps. 65:8

6 [1]Or, *firmament*
[a]Is. 40:22

7 [1]Or, *firmament*
[a]Job 38:8-11 [b]Ps. 148:4

8 [1]Or, *firmament*

9 [a]Ps. 104:6-9; Jer. 5:22; 2 Pet. 3:5 [b]Ps. 24:1, 2; 95:5

10 [a]Ps. 33:7; 95:5; 146:6

11 [1]Or, *grass* [2]Or, *herbs* [3]Lit., *its* [4]Lit., *in which is its seed*
[a]Ps. 65:9-13; 104:14

12 [1]Or, *grass* [2]Or, *herbs* [3]Lit., *its* [4]Lit., *in which is its seed*

14 [1]Or, *luminaries, light-bearers* [2]Or, *firmament*
[a]Ps. 74:16; 136:7 [b]Ps. 19:1; 150:1 [c]Jer. 10:2 [d]Ps. 104:19

15 [1]Or, *luminaries, light-bearers* [2]Or, *firmament*

16 [1]Or, *luminaries, light-bearers* [2]Or, *luminary, light-bearer* [3]Lit., *for the dominion of*
[a]Ps. 136:8, 9 [b]Job 38:7; Ps 8:3; Is. 40:26

17 [1]Or, *firmament*
[a]Jer. 33:20, 25

18 [1]Lit., *for the dominion of*

20 [1]Or, *swarm* [2]Lit., *on the face of* [3]Or, *firmament*

21 [a]Ps. 104:25-28

24 [1]Lit., *its*
[a]Gen. 2:19

25 [1]Lit., *its*
[a]Gen. 7:21, 22; Jer. 27:5

26 [1]Lit., *heavens*
[a]Gen. 3:22; 11:7; 19:24 [b]Gen. 5:1; 9:6 [c]Ps. 8:6-8

27 [a]1 Cor. 11:7 [b]Matt. 19:4, Mark 10:6

28 [1]Lit., *heavens* [2]Or, *creeps*
[a]Gen. 9:1, 7; Ps. 127:3, 5

29 [1]Lit., *face of* [2]Lit., *in which is the fruit of a tree yielding seed*
[a]Ps. 104:14; 136:25

30 [1]Lit., *heavens* [2]Or, *creeps* [3]Lit, *in which is a living soul*
[a]Ps. 145:15

31 [a]Ps. 104:24, 28; 119:68

1 [a]Deut. 4:19; 17:3

2 [a]Ex. 20:8-11 [b]Heb. 4:4

3 [1]Lit., *to make*

4 [1]Lit., *These are the generations*
[a]Job 38:4-11 [b]Gen. 1:3-31

5 [1]Lit., *work, serve*
[a]Gen. 1:11 [b]Jer. 10:12, 13

6 [1]Or, *flow* [2]Lit., *face of*

after their kind, and every winged bird after its kind; and God
saw that it was good.
22 And God blessed them, saying, "Be fruitful and multiply, and fill the waters in the seas, and let birds multiply on
the earth."
23 And there was evening and there was morning, a fifth
day.
24 [a]Then God said, "Let the earth bring forth living creatures after [1]their kind: cattle and creeping things and beasts of
the earth after [1]their kind"; and it was so.
25 And God made the [a]beasts of the earth after [1]their
kind, and the cattle after [1]their kind, and every thing that
creeps on the ground after its kind; and God saw that it was
good.
26 Then God said, "Let [a]us make [b]man in our image,
according to our likeness; and let them [c]rule over the fish of
the sea and over the birds of the [1]sky and over the cattle and
over all the earth, and over every creeping thing that creeps on
the earth."
27 And God created man [a]in His own image, in the image
of God He created him; [b]male and female He created them.
28 And God blessed them; and God said to them, "[a]Be
fruitful and multiply, and fill the earth, and subdue it; and rule
over the fish of the sea and over the birds of the [1]sky, and over
every living thing that [2]moves on the earth."
29 Then God said, "Behold, [a]I have given you every plant
yielding seed that is on the [1]surface of all the earth, and every
tree [2]which has fruit yielding seed; it shall be food for you;
30 and [a]to every beast of the earth and to every bird of the
[1]sky and to every thing that [2]moves on the earth [3]which has
life, *I have given* every green plant for food"; and it was so.
31 And God saw all that He had made, and behold, it was
very [a]good. And there was evening and there was morning, the
sixth day.

Chapter 2

THUS the heavens and the earth were completed, and all
[a]their hosts.
2 And by [a]the seventh day God completed His work
which He had done; and [b]He rested on the seventh day from
all His work which He had done.
3 Then God blessed the seventh day and sanctified it,
because in it He rested from all His work which God had
created [1]and made.
4 [1a]This is the account of the heavens and the earth when
they were created, in [b]the day that the LORD God made earth
and heaven.
5 [a]Now no shrub of the field was yet in the earth, and no
plant of the field had yet sprouted, [b]for the LORD God had not
sent rain upon the earth; and there was no man to [1]cultivate
the ground.
6 But a [1]mist used to rise from the earth and water the
whole [2]surface of the ground.

7 [a]Then the LORD God formed man of dust from the
ground, and breathed into his nostrils the breath of life; and
[b]man became a living [1]being.
8 And the LORD God planted a [a]garden toward the east,
in Eden; and there He placed the man whom He had formed.
9 [a]And out of the ground the LORD God caused to grow
every tree that is pleasing to the sight and good for food; [b]the
tree of life also in the midst of the garden, and the tree of the
knowledge of good and evil.
10 Now a river [1]flowed out of Eden to water the garden;
and from there it divided and became four [2]rivers.
11 The name of the first is Pishon; it [1]flows around the
whole land of Havilah, where there is gold.
12 And the gold of that land is good; the bdellium and the
onyx stone are there.
13 And the name of the second river is Gihon; it [1]flows
around the whole land of Cush.
14 And the name of the third river is [1a]Tigris; it [2]flows east
of Assyria. And the fourth [b]river is the [3]Euphrates.
15 Then the LORD God took the man and put him into
the garden of Eden to cultivate it and keep it.
16 And the LORD God [a]commanded the man, saying,
"From any tree of the garden you may eat freely;
17 but from the tree of the knowledge of good and evil
you shall not [1]eat, for in the day that you eat from it [a]you shall
surely die."
18 Then the LORD God said, "It is not good for the man
to be alone; [a]I will make him a helper [1]suitable for him."
19 And [a]out of the ground the LORD God formed every
beast of the field and every bird of the [1]sky, and brought *them*
[b]to the man to see what he would call them; and whatever the
man called a living creature, that was its name.
20 And the man gave names to all the cattle, and to the
birds of the [1]sky, and to every beast of the field, but for [2]Adam
there was not found [a]a helper [3]suitable for him.
21 So the LORD God caused a deep sleep to fall upon the
man, and he slept; then He took one of his ribs, and closed up
the flesh at that place.
22 And the LORD God [1]fashioned into a woman [a]the rib
which He had taken from the man, and brought her to the
man.
23 And the man said,
"[a]This is now bone of my bones,
And flesh of my flesh;
[1]She shall be called [2]Woman,
Because [1]she was taken out of [3]Man."
24 [a]For this cause a man shall leave his father and his
mother, and shall cleave to his wife; and they shall become one
flesh.
25 [a]And the man and his wife were both naked and were
not ashamed.

CHAPTER 3

NOW [a]the serpent was more crafty than any beast of the
field which the LORD God had made. And he said to the

7 [1]Lit., *soul* [a]Gen. 3:19 [b]1 Cor. 15:45

8 [a]Gen. 13:10; Is. 51:3; Ezek. 28:13

9 [a]Ezek. 47:12 [b]Gen. 3:22 Rev. 2:7; 22:2, 14

10 [1]Lit., *was going out* [2]Lit., *heads*

11 [1]Lit., *surrounds*

13 [1]Lit., *is the one surrounding*

14 [1]Heb., *Hiddekel* [2]Lit., *is the one going* [3]Heb., *Perath* [a]Dan. 10:4 [b]Gen. 15:18

16 [a]Gen. 3:2, 3

17 [1]Lit., *eat from it* [a]Deut. 30:15, 19, 20; Rom. 6:23; 1 Tim. 5:6; James 1:15

18 [1]Lit., *corresponding to* [a]1 Cor. 11:9

19 [1]Lit., *heavens* [a]Gen. 1:24 [b]Gen. 1:26

20 [1]Lit., *heavens* [2]Or, *man* [3]Lit., *corresponding to* [a]Gen. 2:18

22 [1]Lit., *built* [a]1 Cor. 11:8, 9

23 [1]Lit., *This one* [2]Heb., *Isshah* [3]Heb., *Ish* [a]Eph. 5:28, 29

24 [a]Matt. 19:5; Mark 10:7, 8; 1 Cor. 6:16; Eph. 5:31

25 [a]Gen. 3:7, 10, 11

1 [a]2 Cor. 11:3; Rev. 12:9; 20:2

woman, "Indeed, has God said, 'You shall not eat from [1]any
tree of the garden'?"
2 And the woman said to the serpent, "[a]From the fruit of
the trees of the garden we may eat;
3 but from the fruit of the tree which is in the middle of
the garden, God has said, 'You shall not eat from it or touch it,
lest you die.'"
4 [a]And the Serpent said to the woman, "You surely shall
not die!
5 "For God knows that in the day you eat from it your
eyes will be opened, and [a]you will be like God, knowing good
and evil."
6 [a]When the woman saw that the tree was good for food,
and that it was a delight to the eyes, and that the tree was
desirable to make *one* wise, she took from its fruit and ate; and
she gave also to her husband with her, and he ate.
7 Then the eyes of both of them were opened, and they
[a]knew that they were naked; and they sewed fig leaves together
and made themselves [1]loin coverings.
8 And they heard the sound of [a]the LORD God walking in
the garden in the [1]cool of the day, [b]and the man and his wife
hid themselves from the presence of the LORD God among the
trees of the garden.
9 Then the LORD God called to the man, and said to
him, "[a]Where are you?"
10 And he said, "[a]I heard the sound of Thee in the garden,
and I was afraid because I was naked; so I hid myself."
11 And He said, "Who told you that you were naked?
Have you eaten from the tree of which I commanded you not
to eat?"
12 [a]And the man said, "The woman whom Thou gavest *to
be* with me, she gave me from the tree, and I ate."
13 Then the LORD God said to the woman, "What is this
you have done?" And the woman said, "[a]The serpent deceived
me, and I ate."
14 And the LORD God said to the serpent,
"[a]Because you have done this,
Cursed are you more than all cattle,
And more than every beast of the field;
On your belly shall you go,
And [b]dust shall you eat
All the days of your life;
15 And I will put enmity
Between you and the woman,
And between your seed and her seed;
[a]He shall bruise you on the head,
And you shall bruise him on the heel."
16 To the woman He said,
"I will greatly multiply
Your pain [1]in childbirth,
[a]In pain you shall bring forth children;
Yet your desire shall be for your husband,
And [b]he shall rule over you."
17 Then to Adam He said, "Because you have listened to
the voice of your wife, and have eaten from the tree about
which I commanded you, saying, 'You shall not eat from it';

1 [1]Or, *every*
2 [a]Gen. 2:16, 17
4 [a]John 8:44
5 [a]Is. 14:14; Ezek. 28:2, 12-17
6 [a]1 Tim. 2:14; James 1:14, 15; 1 John 2:16
7 [1]Or, *girdles* [a]Is. 47:3; Lam. 1:8
8 [1]Lit., *wind, breeze* [a]Gen. 18:33; Lev. 26:12; Deut. 23:14 [b]Hos. 10:8; Rev. 6:15-17
9 [a]Gen. 4:9; 18:9
10 [a]Ex. 20:18, 19; Deut. 5:25
12 [a]Job 31:33; Prov. 28:13
13 [a]2 Cor. 11:3; 1 Tim. 2:14
14 [a]Deut. 28:15-20 [b]Is. 65:25; Mic. 7:17
15 [a]Rom. 16:20
16 [1]Lit., *and your pregnancy, conception* [a]1 Tim. 2:15 [b]1 Cor. 14:34

[a]Cursed is the ground because of you;
[b]In [1]toil you shall eat of it
All the days of your life.
18 Both thorns and thistles it shall grow for you;
And you shall eat the [1]plants of the field;
19 By the sweat of your face
You shall eat bread,
Till you [a]return to the ground,
Because [b]from it you were taken;
For you are dust,
And to dust you shall return."
20 Now the man called his wife's name [1a]Eve, because she
was the mother of all *the* living.
21 And the LORD God made garments of skin for Adam
and his wife, and clothed them.
22 Then the LORD God said, "Behold, the man has become like one of [a]Us, knowing good and evil; and now, lest he
stretch out his hand, and take also from [b]the tree of life, and
eat, and live forever"—
23 therefore the LORD God sent him out from the garden
of Eden, to cultivate the ground from which he was taken.
24 So [a]He drove the man out; and at the east of the garden of Eden He stationed the [b]cherubim, and the flaming
sword which turned every direction, to guard the way to [c]the
tree of life.

CHAPTER 4

NOW the man [1]had relations with his wife Eve, and she
conceived and gave birth to Cain, and she said, "I have gotten
a [2]manchild with *the help of* the LORD."
2 And again, she gave birth to his brother Abel. And
[a]Abel was [b]a keeper of flocks, but Cain was a tiller of the
ground.
3 So it came about [1]in the course of time that Cain
brought an offering to the LORD of the fruit of the ground.
4 And [a]Abel, on his part also brought of the firstlings of
his flock and of their fat portions. And [b]the LORD had regard
for Abel and for his offering;
5 but [a]for Cain and for his offering He had no regard. So
[b]Cain became very angry and his countenance fell.
6 Then the LORD said to Cain, "[a]Why are you angry?
And why has your countenance fallen?
7 "[a]If you do well, [1]will not *your countenance* be lifted
up? [b]And if you do not do well, sin is crouching at the door;
and its desire is for you, [c]but you must master it."
8 And Cain [1]told Abel his brother. And it came about
when they were in the field, that Cain rose up against Abel his
brother and [a]killed him.
9 Then the LORD said to Cain, "[a]Where is Abel your
brother?" And he said, "I do not know. Am I my brother's
keeper?"
10 And He said, "What have you done? [a]The voice of
your brother's blood is crying to Me from the ground.

17 [1]Or, *sorrow* [a]Gen. 5:29; Rom. 8:20-22 [b]Job 5:7; 14:1

18 [1]Lit., *plant*

19 [a]Ps. 90:3; 104:29; Eccles. 12:7 [b]Gen. 2:7

20 [1]Lit., *Living, or Life* [a]2 Cor. 11:3; 1 Tim. 2:13

22 [a]Gen. 1:26 [b]Gen. 2:9

24 [a]Ezek. 31:11 [b]Ex. 25:18-22; Ezek. 10:1-20 [c]Gen. 2:9

1 [1]Lit., *knew* [2]Or, *man, the LORD*

2 [a]Luke 11:50, 51 [b]Gen. 46:32; 47:3

3 [1]Lit., *at the end of days*

4 [a]Heb. 11:4 [b]1 Sam. 15:22

5 [a]Num. 16:15; 1 Sam. 16:7 [b]Is 3:9; Jude 11

6 [a]Jonah 4:4

7 [1]Or, *surely you will be accepted* [a]Jer. 3:12; Mic. 7:18 [b]Num. 32:23 [c]Job 11:14, 15; Rom. 6:12, 16

8 [1]Lit., *said to* [a]Matt. 23:35; 1 John 3:12

9 [a]Gen. 3:9

10 [a]Num. 35:33; Deut. 21:1-9; Heb. 12:24; Rev. 6:9, 10

11 "And now [a]you are cursed from the ground, which has opened its mouth to receive your brother's blood from your hand.

12 "[a]When you cultivate the ground, it shall no longer yield its strength to you; [b]you shall be a vagrant and a wanderer on the earth."

13 And Cain said to the LORD, "My punishment is too great to bear!

14 "Behold, Thou hast [a]driven me this day from the face of the ground; and from Thy face I shall be hidden, and [b]I shall be a vagrant and a wanderer on the earth, and it will come about that [c]whoever finds me will kill me."

15 [a]So the LORD said to him, "Therefore whoever kills Cain, vengeance will be taken on him [b]sevenfold." And the LORD [1]appointed a sign for Cain, lest anyone finding him should slay him.

16 Then Cain went out from the presence of the LORD, and [1]settled in the land of [2]Nod, east of Eden.

17 And Cain [1]had relations with his wife and she conceived, and gave birth to Enoch; and he built a city, and called the name of the city Enoch, after the name of his son.

18 Now to Enoch was born Irad; and Irad [1]became the father of Mehujael; and Mehujael [1]became the father of Methushael; and Methushael [1]became the father of Lamech.

19 And Lamech took to himself [a]two wives: the name of the one was Adah, and the name of the other, Zillah.

20 And Adah gave birth to Jabal; he was the father of those who dwell in tents and *have* livestock.

21 And his brother's name was Jubal; he was the father of all those who play the lyre and pipe.

22 As for Zillah, she also gave birth to Tubal-cain, the forger of all implements of bronze and iron; and the sister of Tubal-cain was Naamah.

23 And Lamech said to his wives,
"Adah and Zillah,
Listen to my voice,
You wives of Lamech,
Give heed to my speech,
[a]For I [1]have killed a man for wounding me;
And a boy for striking me;
24 If Cain is avenged [a]sevenfold,
Then Lamech seventy-sevenfold."

25 And [a]Adam [1]had relations with his wife again; and she gave birth to a son, and named him [2]Seth, for, *she said,* "God [3]has appointed me another [4]offspring in place of Abel; [b]for Cain killed him."

26 And to Seth, to him also [a]a son was born; and he called his name Enosh. Then *men* began [b]to call [1]upon the name of the LORD.

CHAPTER 5

THIS is the book of the generations of Adam. In the day when God created man, He made him [a]in the likeness of God.

2 He created them [a]male and female, and He [b]blessed

11 [a]Gen. 3:14

12 [a]Deut. 28:15-24; Joel 1:10-20 [b]Lev. 26:17, 36

14 [a]Gen. 3:24; Jer. 52:3 [b]Deut. 28:64-67 [c]Num. 35:19

15 [1]Or, *set a mark on* [a]Rom. 2:4 [b]Gen. 4:24

16 [1]Lit., *dwelt* [2]I.e., Wandering

17 [1]Lit., *knew*

18 [1]Lit., *begot*

19 [a]Gen. 2:24

23 [1]Or, *kill* [a]Ex. 20:13; Lev. 19:18; Deut. 32:35; Ps. 94:1

24 [a]Gen. 4:15

25 [1]Lit., *knew* [2]Heb., *Sheth* [3]Heb., *shath* [4]Lit., *seed* [a]Gen. 5:3 [b]Gen. 4:8

26 [1]Or, *by* [a]Luke 3:38 [b]Gen. 12:8; 26:25

1 [a]Gen. 1:27

2 [a]Mark 10:6 [b]Gen. 1:28

them and named them [1]Man in the day when they were
created.
3 When Adam had lived one hundred and thirty years,
he [1]became the father of *a son* in his own likeness, according
to his image, and named him Seth.
4 Then the days of Adam after he became the father of
Seth were eight hundred years, and he had *other* sons and
daughters.
5 So all the days that Adam lived were nine hundred and
thirty years, and he died.
6 And Seth lived one hundred and five years, and became
the father of Enosh.
7 Then Seth lived eight hundred and seven years after he
became the father of Enosh, and he had *other* sons and
daughters.
8 So all the days of Seth were nine hundred and twelve
years, and he died.
9 And Enosh lived ninety years, and became the father of
Kenan.
10 Then Enosh lived eight hundred and fifteen years after
he became the father of Kenan, and he had *other* sons and
daughters.
11 So all the days of Enosh were nine hundred and five
years, and he died.
12 And Kenan lived seventy years, and became the father
of Mahalalel.
13 Then Kenan lived eight hundred and forty years after
he became the father of Mahalalel, and he had *other* sons and
daughters.
14 So all the days of Kenan were nine hundred and ten
years, and he died.
15 And Mahalalel lived sixty-five years, and became the
father of Jared.
16 Then Mahalalel lived eight hundred and thirty years
after he became the father of Jared, and he had *other* sons and
daughters.
17 So all the days of Mahalalel were eight hundred and
ninety-five years, and he died.
18 And Jared lived one hundred and sixty-two years, and
became the father of Enoch.
19 Then Jared lived eight hundred years after he became
the father of Enoch, and he had *other* sons and daughters.
20 So all the days of Jared were nine hundred and sixty-
two years, and he died.
21 And Enoch lived sixty-five years, and became the father
of Methuselah.
22 Then Enoch [a]walked with God three hundred years
after he became the father of Methuselah, and he had *other*
sons and daughters.
23 So all the days of Enoch were three hundred and sixty-
five years.
24 And Enoch walked with God; and he was not, for God
[a]took him.
25 And Methuselah lived one hundred and eighty-seven
years, and became the father of Lamech.

2 [1]Lit., *Adam*

3 [1]Lit., *begot*, and so throughout the chap.

22 [a]Gen. 6:9; 17:1; 24:40; 48:15

24 [a]2 Kin. 2:10; Ps. 49:15; 73:24; Heb. 11:5

26 Then Methuselah lived seven hundred and eighty-two
years after he became the father of Lamech, and he had *other*
sons and daughters.
27 So all the days of Methuselah were nine hundred and
sixty-nine years, and he died.
28 And Lamech lived one hundred and eighty-two years,
and became the father of a son.
29 Now he called his name Noah, saying, "This one shall
[1]give us rest from our work and from the toil of our hands
arising from [a]the ground which the LORD has cursed."
30 Then Lamech lived five hundred and ninety-five years
after he became the father of Noah, and he had *other* sons and
daughters.
31 So all the days of Lamech were seven hundred and
seventy-seven years, and he died.
32 And Noah was [a]five hundred years old, and Noah became the father of Shem, Ham, and Japheth.

CHAPTER 6

NOW it came about, when men began to multiply on the
face of the land, and daughters were born to them,
2 that the sons of God saw that the daughters of men
were [1]beautiful; and they took wives for themselves, whomever
they chose.
3 Then the LORD said, "[a]My Spirit shall not [1]strive with
man forever, [2]because he also is flesh; [3]nevertheless his days
shall be one hundred and twenty years."
4 The Nephilim were on the earth in those days, and also
afterward, when the sons of God came in to the daughters of
men, and they bore *children* to them. Those were the mighty
men who *were* of old, men of renown.
5 Then the LORD saw that the wickedness of man was
great on the earth, and that [a]every intent of the thoughts of his
heart was only evil continually.
6 And [a]the LORD was sorry that He had made man on the
earth, and He was grieved [1]in His heart.
7 And the LORD said, "[a]I will blot out man whom I have
created from the face of the land, from man to animals to
creeping things and to birds of the [1]sky; for [b]I am sorry that I
have made them."
8 But Noah [a]found favor in the eyes of the LORD.
9 These are *the records of* the generations of Noah.
Noah was a [a]righteous man, [1b]blameless in his [2]time; Noah
[c]walked with God.
10 And Noah [1]became the father of three sons: Shem,
Ham, and Japheth.
11 Now the earth was [a]corrupt in the sight of God, and
the earth was [b]filled with violence.
12 And God looked on the earth, and behold, it was corrupt; for [a]all flesh had corrupted their way upon the earth.
13 Then God said to Noah, "[a]The end of all flesh has
come before Me; for the earth is filled with violence because
of them; and behold, I am about to destroy them with the
earth.

29 [1]Lit., *comfort us in* [a]Gen. 3:17-19

32 [a]Gen. 7:6

2 [1]Lit., *good*

3 [1]Or, *rule in*, some ancient versions read, *abide in* [2]Or, *in his going astray he is flesh* [3]Or, *therefore* [a]1 Pet. 3:20

5 [a]Gen. 8:21; Ps. 14:1-3

6 [1]Lit., *to* [a]Jer. 18:7-10

7 [1]Lit., *heavens* [a]Deut. 28:63; 29:20 [b]Amos 7:3, 6

8 [a]Ex. 33:17

9 [1]Lit., *complete, perfect;* or, *having integrity* [2]Lit., *generations* [a]Ps. 37:39 [b]Gen. 17:1; Deut. 18:13; Job 1:1 [c]Gen. 5:24

10 [1]Lit., *begot*

11 [a]Deut. 31:29; Judg. 2:19 [b]Ezek. 8:17

12 [a]Ps. 14:1-3

13 [a]Is. 34:1-4; Ezek. 7:2, 3

14 "Make for yourself an ark of gopher wood; you shall
make the ark with rooms, and shall [1]cover it inside and out
with pitch.
15 "And this is how you shall make it: the length of the ark
three hundred [1]cubits, its breadth fifty [1]cubits, and its height
thirty [1]cubits.
16 "You shall make a [1]window for the ark, and finish it to a
cubit from [2]the top; and set the door of the ark in the side of
it; you shall make it with lower, second, and third decks.
17 "And behold, I, even I am bringing the flood of water
upon the earth, to destroy all flesh in which is the breath of
life, from under heaven; everything that is on the earth shall
perish.
18 "But I will establish [a]My covenant with you; and [b]you
shall enter the ark—you and your sons and your wife, and your
sons' wives with you.
19 "[a]And of every living thing of all flesh, you shall bring
two of every *kind* into the ark, to keep *them* alive with you;
they shall be male and female.
20 "[a]Of the birds after their kind, and of the animals after
their kind, of every creeping thing of the ground after its kind,
two of every *kind* shall come to you to keep *them* alive.
21 "And as for you, take for yourself some of all food which
is edible, and gather *it* to yourself; and it shall be for food for
you and for them."
22 [a]Thus Noah did; according to all that God had commanded him, so he did.

Chapter 7

THEN the LORD said to Noah, "Enter the ark, you and all
your household; for you *alone* I have seen *to be* [a]righteous
before Me in this [1]time.
2 "You shall take [1]with you of every [a]clean animal [2]seven
pairs, a male and his female; and of the animals that are not
clean two, a male and his female;
3 also of the birds of the [1]sky, [2]seven pairs, male and
female, to keep [3]offspring alive on the face of all the earth.
4 "For after [a]seven more days, I will send rain on the earth
[b]forty days and forty nights; and I will blot out from the face
of the land [c]every living thing that I have made."
5 [a]And Noah did according to all that the LORD had
commanded him.
6 Now Noah was [a]six hundred years old when the flood
of water [1]came upon the earth.
7 Then [a]Noah and his sons and his wife and his sons'
wives with him entered the ark because of the water of the
flood.
8 [a]Of clean animals and animals that are not clean and
birds and everything that creeps on the ground,
9 there went into the ark to Noah two by two, male and
female, as God had commanded Noah.
10 And it came about after [a]the seven days, that the water
of the flood [1]came upon the earth.

14 [1]Or, *pitch*

15 [1]I.e., one cubit equals approx. 18 inches

16 [1]Or, *roof* [2]Lit., *above*

18 [a]Gen. 9:9-16; 17:7 [b]Gen. 7:7

19 [a]Gen. 7:2, 14, 15

20 [a]Gen. 7:3

22 [a]Gen. 7:5

1 [1]Lit., *generation* [a]Gen. 6:9

2 [1]Lit., *to* [2]Lit., *seven seven* [a]Lev. 11:1-31; Deut. 14:3-20

3 [1]Lit., *heavens* [2]Lit., *seven seven* [3]Lit., *seed*

4 [a]Gen. 7:10 [b]Gen. 7:12, 17 [c]Gen. 6:7, 13

5 [a]Gen. 6:22

6 [1]Lit., *was* [a]Gen. 5:32

7 [a]Gen. 7:13; Gen. 6:18

8 [a]Gen 7:2, 3; Gen. 6:19, 20

10 [1]Lit., *were* [a]Gen. 7:4

11 In the [a]six hundredth year of Noah's life, in the second
month, on the seventeenth day of the month, on the same day
all [b]the fountains of the great deep burst open, and the [1]flood-
gates of the sky were opened.
12 And [a]the rain [1]fell upon the earth for forty days and
forty nights.
13 On the very same day [a]Noah and Shem and Ham and
Japheth, the sons of Noah, and Noah's wife and the three
wives of his sons with them, entered the ark,
14 they and every beast after its kind, and all the cattle
after [1]their kind, and every creeping thing that creeps on the
earth after its kind, and every bird after its kind, [2]all sorts of
birds.
15 So they went into the ark to Noah, [a]two by two of all
flesh in which was the breath of life.
16 And those that entered, male and female of all flesh,
entered as God had commanded him; and the LORD closed *it*
behind him.
17 Then the flood [1]came upon the earth for [a]forty days;
and the water increased and lifted up the ark, so that it rose
above the earth.
18 And the water prevailed and increased greatly upon the
earth; and the ark [1]floated on the [2]surface of the water.
19 And the water prevailed more and more upon the
earth, so that all the high mountains [1]everywhere under the
heavens were covered.
20 The water prevailed fifteen [1]cubits higher, [a]and the
mountains were covered.
21 [a]And all flesh that [1]moved on the earth perished, birds
and cattle and beasts and every swarming thing that swarms
upon the earth, and all mankind;
22 of all that was on the dry land, all in whose nostrils was
the breath of the spirit of life, died.
23 Thus He blotted out [1]every living thing that was upon
the face of the land, from man to animals to creeping things
and to birds of the [2]sky, and they were blotted out from the
earth; and only [a]Noah was left, together with those that were
with him in the ark.
24 [a]And the water prevailed upon the earth one hundred
and fifty days.

CHAPTER 8

BUT God remembered Noah and all the beasts and all the
cattle that were with him in the ark; and [a]God caused a wind to
pass over the earth, and the water subsided.
2 Also [a]the fountains of the deep and the [1]floodgates of
the [2]sky were closed, and [b]the rain from the [2]sky was
restrained;
3 and the water receded steadily from the earth, and at
the end [a]of one hundred and fifty days the water decreased.
4 And in the seventh month, on the seventeenth day of
the month, [a]the ark rested upon the mountains of Ararat.
5 And the water decreased steadily until the tenth

11 [1]Or, *windows of the heavens* [a]Gen. 7:6 [b]Gen. 8:2

12 [1]Lit., *was* [a]Gen. 7:4, 17

13 [a]Gen. 7:7; 6:18

14 [1]Lit., *its* [2]Lit., *every bird, every wing*

15 [a]Gen. 7:9; 6:19

17 [1]Lit., *was* [a]Gen. 7:4

18 [1]Lit., *went* [2]Lit., *face*

19 [1]Lit., *which were under all the heavens*

20 [1]I.e., one cubit equals 18 inches [a]Gen. 8:4

21 [1]Or, *crept* [a]Gen. 7:4; 6:7, 13, 17

23 [1]Lit., *all existence* [2]Lit., *heavens* [a]Matt. 24:38, 39; Luke 17:26, 27; 1 Pet. 3:20; 2 Pet. 2:5

24 [a]Gen. 8:3

1 [a]Job 12:15; Ps. 29:10; Is. 44:27; Nah. 1:4

2 [1]Or, *windows of the heavens* [2]Lit., *heavens* [a]Gen. 7:11 [b]Gen. 7:4, 12

3 [a]Gen. 7:24

4 [a]Gen. 7:20

month; in the tenth month, on the first day of the month, the
tops of the mountains became visible.
6 Then it came about at the end of forty days, that Noah
opened the window of the ark which he had made;
7 and he sent out a raven, and it [1]flew here and there
until the water was dried up [2]from the earth.
8 Then he sent out a dove from him, to see if the water
was abated from the face of the land;
9 but the dove found no resting place for the sole of her
foot, so she returned to him into the ark; for the water was on
the [1]surface of all the earth. Then he put out his hand and
took her, and brought her into the ark to himself.
10 So he waited yet another seven days; and again he sent
out the dove from the ark.
11 And the dove came to him toward [1]evening; and behold, in her [2]beak was a freshly picked olive leaf. So Noah
knew that the water was abated from the earth.
12 Then he waited yet another seven days, and sent out
[a]the dove; but she did not return to him again.
13 Now it came about in the [a]six hundred and first year, in
the first *month,* on the first of the month, the water was dried
up [1]from the earth. Then Noah removed the covering of the
ark, and looked, and behold, the [2]surface of the ground was
dried up.
14 And in the second month, on the twenty-seventh day of
the month, the earth was dry.
15 Then God spoke to Noah, saying,
16 "Go out of the ark, you and your wife and your sons and
your sons' wives with you.
17 "Bring out with you every living thing of all flesh that is
with you, birds and animals and every creeping thing that
creeps on the earth, that they may [1a]breed abundantly on the
earth, and be fruitful and multiply on the earth."
18 So Noah went out, and his sons and his wife and his
sons' wives with him.
19 Every beast, every creeping thing, and every bird, everything that moves on the earth, went out [1]by their families
from the ark.
20 Then Noah built [a]an altar to the LORD, and took of
every [b]clean animal and of every clean bird and offered [c]burnt
offerings on the altar.
21 And the LORD [a]smelled the soothing aroma; and the
LORD said [1]to Himself, "I will never again [b]curse the ground on
account of man, for [c]the [2]intent of man's heart is evil from his
youth; [d]and I will never again [3]destroy every living thing, as I
have done.
22 "While the earth remains,
Seedtime and harvest,
And cold and heat,
And [a]summer and winter,
And day and night
Shall not cease."

CHAPTER 9

1 AND God blessed Noah and his sons and said to them, "[a]Be
fruitful and multiply, and fill the earth.

7 [1]Lit., *went out, going and returning* [2]Lit., *from upon*

9 [1]Lit., *face*

11 [1]Lit., *time of evening* [2]Lit., *mouth*

12 [a]Jer. 48:28

13 [1]Lit., *from upon* [2]Lit., *face* [a]Gen. 7:6

17 [1]Or, *swarm* [a]Gen. 1:22, 28

19 [1]Or, *according to their kind*

20 [a]Gen. 12:7, 8; 13:18; 22:9 [b]Gen. 7:2 [c]Gen. 22:2; Ex. 10:25

21 [1]Lit., *to His heart* [2]Or, *inclination* [3]Lit., *smite* [a]Ex. 29:18, 25 [b]Gen. 6:7, 13 [c]Gen. 6:5 [d]Gen. 9:11

22 [a]Ps. 74:17; Jer. 33:20, 25

1 [a]Gen. 9:7; 1:28

God's Blessing and the Covenant of the Rainbow.

2 "And the fear of you and the terror of you shall be on
every beast of the earth and on every bird of the [1]sky; with
everything that creeps on the ground, and all the fish of the
sea, into your hand they are given.
3 "Every moving thing that is alive shall be food for you; I
give all to you, [a]as *I gave* the green plant.
4 "Only you shall not eat flesh with its life, *that is,* [a]its
blood.
5 "And surely I will require [1a]your lifeblood; [2b]from every
beast I will require it. And [2]from *every* man, [2]from every man's
brother I will require the life of man.
6 "[a]Whoever sheds man's blood,
By man his blood shall be shed,
For in the image of God
He made man.
7 "And as for you, [a]be fruitful and multiply;
[1]Populate the earth abundantly and multiply in it."
8 Then God spoke to Noah and to his sons with him,
saying,
9 "Now behold, [a]I Myself do establish My covenant with
you, and with your [1]descendants after you;
10 and with every living creature that is with you, the
birds, the cattle, and every beast of the earth with you; of all
that comes out of the ark, even every beast of the earth.
11 "And I establish My covenant with you; and all flesh
shall [a]never again be cut off by the water of the flood, [b]neither
shall there again be a flood to destroy the earth."
12 And God said, "This is [a]the sign of the covenant which
I am making between Me and you and every living creature
that is with you, for [1]all successive generations;
13 I set My [a]bow in the cloud, and it shall be for a sign of a
covenant between Me and the earth.
14 "And it shall come about, when I bring a cloud over the
earth, that the bow shall be seen in the cloud,
15 and [a]I will remember My covenant, which is between
Me and you and every living creature of all flesh; and [b]never
again shall the water become a flood to destroy all flesh.
16 "When the bow is in the cloud, then I will look upon it,
to remember the everlasting covenant between God and every
living creature of all flesh that is on the earth."
17 And God said to Noah, "This is the sign of the covenant
which I have established between Me and all flesh that is
on the earth."
18 Now the sons of Noah who came out of the ark were
Shem and Ham and Japheth; and [a]Ham was the father of
Canaan.
19 These three *were* the sons of Noah; and [a]from these
the whole earth was [1]populated.
20 Then Noah began [1]farming and planted a vineyard.
21 And he drank of the wine and became drunk, and uncovered himself inside his tent.
22 And [a]Ham, the father of Canaan, saw the nakedness of
his father, and told his two brothers outside.
23 But Shem and Japheth took a garment and laid it upon
both their shoulders and walked backward and covered the

2 [1]Lit., *heavens*

3 [a]Gen. 1:29

4 [a]Lev. 17:10-16; Deut. 12:16, 23

5 [1]Lit., *your blood of your lives* [2]Lit., *from the hand of* [a]Ex. 20:13; 21:12 [b]Ex. 21:28, 29

6 [a]Num. 35:33

7 [1]Lit., *swarm in the earth* [a]Gen. 9:1

9 [1]Lit., *seed* [a]Gen. 6:18

11 [a]Gen. 8:21 [b]Is. 54:9

12 [1]Or, *everlasting generations* [a]Gen. 9:13, 17; 17:11

13 [a]Ezek. 1:28

15 [a]Deut. 7:9 [b]Gen. 9:11

18 [a]Gen. 9:25-27

19 [1]Lit., *scattered* [a]Gen. 9:1, 7; 10:32

20 [1]Lit., to be *a farmer*

22 [a]Hab. 2:15

nakedness of their father; and their faces were [1]turned away, so
that they did not see their father's nakedness.
24 When Noah awoke from his wine, he knew what his
youngest son had done to him.
25 So he said,
"[a]Cursed be Canaan;
[1]A servant of servants
He shall be to his brothers."
26 He also said,
"[a]Blessed be the LORD,
The God of Shem;
And let Canaan be [1]his servant.
27 "[a]May God enlarge Japheth,
And let him dwell in the tents of Shem;
And let Canaan be [1]his servant."
28 And Noah lived three hundred and fifty years after the
flood.
29 So all the days of Noah were nine hundred and fifty
years, and he died.

CHAPTER 10

NOW these are *the records of* the generations of Shem,
Ham, and Japheth, the sons of Noah; and sons were born to
them after the flood.
2 [a]The sons of Japheth *were* [b]Gomer and Magog and
[c]Madai and [d]Javan and Tubal and [e]Meshech and Tiras.
3 And the sons of Gomer *were* [a]Ashkenaz and [b]Riphath
and [c]Togarmah.
4 And the sons of Javan *were* Elishah and [a]Tarshish, Kittim and [b]Dodanim.
5 From these the coastlands of the nations [1]were separated into their lands, every one according to his language,
according to their families, into their nations.
6 [a]And the sons of Ham *were* Cush and Mizraim and Put
and Canaan.
7 And the sons of Cush *were* [a]Seba and Havilah and
Sabtah and [b]Raamah and Sabteca; and the sons of Raamah
were [b]Sheba and [c]Dedan.
8 Now Cush [1]became the father of Nimrod; he [2]became
a mighty one on the earth.
9 He was a mighty hunter before the LORD; therefore it is
said, "Like Nimrod a mighty hunter before the LORD."
10 And the beginning of his kingdom was [1a]Babel and
Erech and Accad and Calneh, in the land of [b]Shinar.
11 From that land he went forth [a]into Assyria, and built
Nineveh and Rehoboth-Ir and Calah,
12 and Resen between Nineveh and Calah; that is the
great city.
13 And Mizraim [1]became the father of [a]Ludim and Ana-
mim and Lehabim and Naphtuhim
14 and Pathrusim and Casluhim (from which came the
Philistines) and Caphtorim.

23 [1]Lit., *backward*

25 [1]I.e., The lowest of servants [a]Deut. 27:16

26 [1]Or, *their* [a]Gen. 14:20; 24:27

27 [1]Or, *their* [a]Gen. 10:2-5; Is. 66:19

2 [a]1 Chr. 1:5-7 [b]Ezek. 38:2, 6 [c]2 Kin. 17:6 [d]Is. 66:19 [e]Ezek. 38:2

3 [a]Jer. 51:27 [b]1 Chr. 1:6 *Diphath,* [c]Ezek. 27:14

4 [a]Ezek. 27:12, 25 [b]1 Chr. 1:7, *Rodanim*

5 [1]Or, *separated themselves*

6 [a]1 Chr. 1:8-10

7 [a]Is. 43:3 [b]Ezek. 27:22 [c]Ezek. 27:15, 20

8 [1]Lit., *begot* [2]Lit., *began to be*

10 [1]Or, *Babylon* [a]Gen. 11:9 [b]Gen. 11:2; 14:1

11 [a]Mic. 5:6

13 [1]Lit., *begot* [a]Jer. 46:9

15 And Canaan [1]became the father of [a]Sidon, his first-
born, and [b]Heth
16 and [a]the Jebusite and the Amorite and the Girgashite
17 and the Hivite and the Arkite and the Sinite
18 and the Arvadite and the Zemarite and the Hamathite;
and afterward the families of the Canaanite were spread
abroad.
19 And the territory of the Canaanite [1]extended from Sidon as you go toward Gerar, as far as Gaza; as you go toward
[a]Sodom and Gomorrah and Admah and Zeboiim, as far as
Lasha.
20 These are the sons of Ham, according to their families,
according to their languages, by their lands, by their nations.
21 And also to Shem, the father of all the children of
Eber, *and* the [1]older brother of Japheth, children were born.
22 [a]The sons of Shem *were* [b]Elam and [c]Asshur and [d]Ar-
pachshad and [e]Lud and Aram.
23 And the sons of Aram *were* [a]Uz and Hul and Gether
and Mash.
24 And Arpachshad [1]became the father of [a]Shelah; and
Shelah [1]became the father of Eber.
25 And two sons were born to Eber; the name of the one
was [1]Peleg, for in his days the earth was divided; and his brother's name *was* Joktan.
26 And Joktan [1]became the father of Almodad and Sheleph and Hazarmaveth and Jerah
27 and Hadoram and Uzal and Diklah
28 and [1]Obal and Abimael and Sheba
29 and Ophir and Havilah and Jobab; all these were the
sons of Joktan.
30 Now their [1]settlement [2]extended from Mesha as you
go toward Sephar, the hill country of the east.
31 These are the sons of Shem, according to their families,
according to their languages, by their lands, according to their
nations.
32 These are the families of the sons of Noah, according
to their genealogies, by their nations; and [a]out of these the
nations were separated on the earth after the flood.

Chapter 11

NOW the whole earth [1]used the same language and [2]the
same words.
2 And it came about as they journeyed east, that they
found a plain in the land [a]of Shinar and [1]settled there.
3 And they said to one another, "Come, let us make
bricks and burn *them* thoroughly." And they used brick for
stone, and they used [a]tar for mortar.
4 And they said, "Come, let us build for ourselves a city,
and a tower whose top [a]*will reach* into heaven, and let us make
for ourselves [b]a name; lest we [c]be scattered abroad over the
face of the whole earth."
5 [a]And the LORD came down to see the city and the tower
which the sons of men had built.

15 [1]Lit., *begot* [a]1 Chr. 1:13; Jer. 47:4 [b]Gen. 23:3
16 [a]Gen. 15:19-21
19 [1]Lit., *was* [a]Gen. 14:2, 3
21 [1]Or, *the brother of Japheth the elder*
22 [a]1 Chr. 1:17 [b]Gen. 14:1, 9 [c]2 Kin. 15:29 [d]Gen. 11:10 [e]Is. 66:19
23 [a]Job 1:1; Jer. 25:20
24 [1]Lit., *begot* [a]Luke 3:35
25 [1]I.e., Division
26 [1]Lit., *begot*
28 [1]In 1 Chr. 1:22, *Ebal*
30 [1]Lit., *dwelling* [2]Lit., *was*
32 [a]Gen. 9:19
1 [1]Lit., *was one lip* [2]Or, *few; or, one set of words*
2 [1]Lit., *dwelt* [a]Gen. 10:10; 14:1
3 [a]Gen. 14:10
4 [a]Deut. 1:28; 9:1; Ps. 107:26 [b]Gen. 6:4; 2 Sam. 8:13 [c]Deut. 4:27
5 [a]Gen. 18:21; Ex. 3:8; 19:11, 18, 20

6 And the LORD said, "Behold, they are one people, and
they all have [1a]the same language. And this is what they began
to do, and now nothing which they purpose to do will be
[2]impossible for them.
7 "Come, [a]let Us go down and there [b]confuse their [1]lan-
guage, that they may not understand one another's [1]speech."
8 So the LORD [a]scattered them abroad from there over
the face of the whole earth; and they stopped building the city.
9 Therefore its name was called [1a]Babel, because there
the LORD confused the [2]language of the whole earth; and from
there the LORD scattered them abroad over the face of the
whole earth.
10 [a]These are *the records of* the generations of Shem.
Shem was one hundred years old, and [1]became the father of
Arpachshad two years after the flood;
11 and Shem lived five hundred years after he became the
father of Arpachshad, and he had *other* sons and daughters.
12 And Arpachshad lived thirty-five years, and became
the father of Shelah;
13 and Arpachshad lived four hundred and three years
after he became the father of Shelah, and he had *other* sons
and daughters.
14 And Shelah lived thirty years, and became the father
of Eber;
15 and Shelah lived four hundred and three years after
he became the father of Eber, and he had *other* sons and
daughters.
16 And Eber lived thirty-four years, and became the father
of Peleg;
17 and Eber lived four hundred and thirty years after he
became the father of Peleg, and he had *other* sons and
daughters.
18 And Peleg lived thirty years, and became the father of
Reu;
19 and Peleg lived two hundred and nine years after he
became the father of Reu, and he had *other* sons and
daughters.
20 And Rue lived thirty-two years, and became the father
of Serug;
21 and Reu lived two hundred and seven years after he
became the father of Serug, and he had *other* sons and
daughters.
22 And Serug lived thirty years, and became the father of
Nahor;
23 And Serug lived two hundred years after he became
the father of Nahor, and he had *other* sons and daughters.
24 And Nahor lived twenty-nine years, and became the
father of [a]Terah;
25 and Nahor lived one hundred and nineteen years after
he became the father of Terah, and he had *other* sons and
daughters.
26 And Terah lived seventy years, and became the father
of Abram, Nahor and Haran.
27 Now these are *the records of* the generations of Terah.
Terah became the father of Abram, Nahor and Haran; and
[a]Haran became the father of Lot.

6 [1]Lit., *one lip* [2]Lit., *withheld from* [a]Gen. 11:1

7 [1]Lit., *lip* [a]Gen. 1:26 [b]Ex. 4:11; Is. 33:19

8 [a]Gen. 11:4

9 [1]Or, *Babylon;* cf. Heb., *balal,* confuse [2]Lit., *lip* [a]Gen. 10:10

10 [1]Lit., *begot,* and so throughout the chap. [a]Gen. 10:22-25

24 [a]Josh. 24:2

27 [a]Gen. 11:31; 12:4

28 And Haran died [1]in the presence of his father Terah in
the land of his birth, in [a]Ur of the Chaldeans.
29 And Abram and [a]Nahor took wives for themselves. The
name of Abram's wife was [b]Sarai; and the name of Nahor's
wife was [c]Milcah, the daughter of Haran, the father of Milcah
[1]and Iscah.
30 And [a]Sarai was barren; she had no child.
31 And Terah took Abram his son, and Lot the son of
Haran, his grandson, and Sarai his daughter-in-law, his son
Abram's wife; and they went out [1]together from [a]Ur of the
Chaldeans in order to enter the land of Canaan; and they went
as far as Haran, and [2]settled there.
32 And the days of Terah were two hundred and five
years; and Terah died in Haran.

Chapter 12

Now [a]the Lord said to Abram,
"[1]Go forth from your country,
And from your relatives
And from your father's house,
To the land which I will show you;
2 And [a]I will make you a great nation,
And [b]I will bless you,
And make your name great;
And so [1c]you shall be a blessing;
3 And [a]I will bless those who bless you,
And the one who [1]curses you I will [2]curse.
[b]And in you all the families of the earth shall be blessed."
4 So Abram went forth as the Lord had spoken to him;
and [a]Lot went with him. Now Abram was seventy-five years
old when he departed from Haran.
5 And Abram took Sarai his wife and Lot his nephew,
and all their [a]possessions which they had accumulated, and
[b]the [1]persons which they had acquired in Haran; and they [2]set
out for the land of Canaan, [c]thus they came to the land of
Canaan.
6 And Abram passed through the land as far as the site
[a]of Shechem, to the [1]oak of Moreh. Now the Canaanite *was*
then in the land.
7 And the Lord [a]appeared to Abram and said, "[b]To your
[1]descendants I will give this land." So he built [c]an altar there to
the Lord who had appeared to him.
8 Then he proceeded from there to the mountain on the
east of Bethel, and pitched his tent, with [a]Bethel on the west
and Ai on the east; and there he built an altar to the Lord and
[b]called upon the name of the Lord.
9 And Abram journeyed on, continuing toward [a]the
[1]Negev.
10 Now there was a famine in the land; so Abram went
down to Egypt to sojourn there, for the famine was severe in
the land.
11 And it came about when he [1]came near to Egypt, that
he said to Sarai his wife, "See now, I know that you are a
[2a]beautiful woman;

28 [1]Or, *during the lifetime of* [a]Gen. 11:31

29 [1]Lit., *and the father of* [a]Gen. 24:10 [b]Gen. 20:12 [c]Gen. 22:20, 23; 24:15

30 [a]Gen. 16:1

31 [1]Lit., *with them* [2]Lit., *dwelt* [a]Gen. 15:7; Neh. 9:7

1 [1]Lit., *Go for yourself* [a]Acts 7:3; Heb. 11:8

2 [1]Lit., *be a blessing* [a]Gen. 17:4, 5; 18:18 [b]Gen. 22:17 [c]Zech. 8:13

3 [1]Or, *reviles* [2]Or, *bind under a curse* [a]Gen. 27:29 [b]Acts 3:25; Gal. 3:8

4 [a]Gen. 11:27, 31

5 [1]Lit., *souls* [2]Lit., *went forth to go to* [a]Gen. 13:6 [b]Gen. 14:14; Lev. 22:11 [c]Gen. 11:31

6 [1]Or, *terebinth* [a]Gen. 35:4; Deut. 11:30

7 [1]Lit., *seed* [a]Gen. 17:1; 18:1 [b]Gen. 13:15; 15:18; Gal. 3:16 [c]Gen. 13:18; 22:9

8 [a]Josh. 8:9, 12 [b]Gen. 4:26; 21:33

9 [1]I.e., South country [a]Gen. 13:1, 3; 20:1; 24:62

11 [1]Lit., *drew near to enter* [2]Lit., *a woman of beautiful appearance* [a]Gen. 26:7; 29:17

12 [a]and it will come about when the Egyptians see you,
that they will say, 'This is his wife'; and they will kill me, but
they will let you live.
13 "Please say that you are [a]my sister so that it may go well
with me because of you, and that [1b]I may live on account of
you."
14 And it came about when Abram came into Egypt, the
Egyptians [1]saw that the woman was very beautiful.
15 And Pharaoh's officials saw her and praised her to Pharaoh; and [a]the woman was taken into Pharaoh's house.
16 Therefore [a]he treated Abram well for her sake; and
[1b]gave him sheep and oxen and donkeys and male and female
servants and female donkeys and camels.
17 But the LORD [a]struck Pharaoh and his house with great
plagues because of Sarai, Abram's wife.
18 Then Pharaoh called Abram and said, "[a]What is this
you have done to me? Why did you not tell me that she was
your wife?
19 "Why did you say, 'She is my sister,' so that I took her
for my wife? Now then [1]here is your wife, take her and go."
20 And Pharaoh commanded *his* men concerning him;
and they [1]escorted him away, with his wife and all that belonged to him.

CHAPTER 13

SO Abram went up from Egypt to [a]the [1]Negev, he and his
wife and all that belonged to him; and Lot with him.
2 Now Abram was very rich in livestock, in silver and in
gold.
3 And he went [1]on his journeys from the [2]Negev as far as
Bethel, to the place where his tent had been at the beginning,
[a]between Bethel and Ai,
4 to the place of the altar, which he had made there
formerly; and there Abram called on the name of the LORD.
5 Now [a]Lot, who went with Abram, also had flocks and
herds and tents.
6 And [a]the land could not [1]sustain them [2]while dwelling
together; [b]for their possessions were so great that they were not
able [b]to remain together.
7 [a]And there was strife between the herdsmen of Abram's
livestock and the herdsmen of Lot's livestock. Now [b]the Canaanite and the Perizzite were dwelling then in the land.
8 [a]Then Abram said to Lot, "Please let there be no strife
between you and me, nor between my herdsmen and your
herdsmen, for we are brothers.
9 "Is not the whole land before you? Please separate from
me: if *to* the left, then I will go to the right; or if *to* the right,
then I will go to the left."
10 And Lot lifted up his eyes and saw all the [1a]valley of the
Jordan, that it was well watered everywhere—*this was* before
the LORD destroyed Sodom and Gomorrah—like [b]the garden
of the LORD, [c]like the land of Egypt as you go to [d]Zoar.
11 So Lot chose for himself all the [1]valley of the Jordan;
and Lot journeyed eastward. Thus they separated from each
other.

12 [a]Gen. 20:11
13 [1]Lit., *my soul* [a]Gen. 20:2, 5, 12 [b]Jer. 38:17, 20
14 [1]Lit., *saw the woman that she was*
15 [a]Gen. 20:2
16 [1]Lit., *he had* [a]Gen. 20:14 [b]Gen. 13:2
17 [a]Ps. 105:14
18 [a]Gen. 20:9, 10
19 [1]Or, *behold*
20 [1]Lit., *sent*
1 [1]I.e., South country [a]Gen. 12:9
3 [1]Lit., *by his stages* [2]I.e., South country [a]Gen. 12:8
5 [a]Gen. 12:5
6 [1]Lit., *bear* [2]Lit., *to dwell* [a]Gen. 36:7 [b]Gen. 13:2; 12:5, 16
7 [a]Gen. 26:20 [b]Gen. 12:6; 15:19-21
8 [a]Prov. 15:18; 20:3
10 [1]Lit., *circle* [a]Gen. 19:17-29; Deut. 34:3 [b]Gen. 2:8 [c]Gen. 47:6 [d]Gen. 14:8; Deut. 34:3
11 [1]Lit., *circle*

12 Abram [1]settled in the land of Canaan, while Lot [1]settled in [a]the cities of the [2]valley, and moved his tents as far as Sodom.

13 Now the men of Sodom were wicked [1]exceedingly and [a]sinners against the LORD.

14 And the LORD said to Abram, after Lot had separated from him, "[a]Now lift up your eyes and look from the place where you are, northward and southward and eastward and westward;

15 [a]for all the land which you see, [b]I will give it to you and to your [1]descendants forever.

16 "And I will make your [1]descendants [a]as the dust of the earth; so that if anyone can number the dust of the earth, then your [1]descendants can also be numbered.

17 "Arise, [a]walk about the land through its length and breadth; for [b]I will give it to you."

18 Then Abram moved his tent and came and dwelt by the [1]oaks of [a]Mamre, which are in Hebron, and there he built [b]an altar to the LORD.

CHAPTER 14

AND it came about in the days of Amraphel king of [a]Shinar, Arioch king of Ellasar, Chedorlaomer king of [b]Elam, and Tidal King of [1]Goiim,

2 *that* they made war with Bera king of Sodom, and with Birsha king of Gomorrah, Shinab king of [a]Admah, and Shemeber king of [b]Zeboiim, and the king of Bela (that is, [c]Zoar).

3 All these [1]came as allies to [a]the valley of Siddim (that is, [b]the Salt Sea).

4 Twelve years they had served Chedorlaomer, but the thirteenth year they rebelled.

5 And in the fourteenth year Chedorlaomer and the kings that were with him, came and [1]defeated the [a]Rephaim in [b]Ashteroth-karnaim and the Zuzim in Ham and the Emim in [2c]Shaveh-kiriathaim,

6 and the [a]Horites in their Mount Seir, as far as [b]El-paran, which is by the wilderness.

7 Then they turned back and came to En-mishpat (that is [a]Kadesh), and [1]conquered all the country of the Amalekites, and also the Amorites, who lived in [b]Hazazon-tamar.

8 And the king of Sodom and the king of Gomorrah and the king of Admah and the king of Zeboiim and the king of Bela (that is, Zoar) came out; and they arrayed for battle against them in [a]the valley of Siddim,

9 against Chedorlaomer king of Elam and Tidal king of [1]Goiim and Amraphel King of Shinar and Arioch king of Ellasar—four kings against five.

10 Now the valley of Siddim was full of tar pits; and [a]the kings of Sodom and Gomorrah fled, and they fell [1]into them. But those who survived fled to the hill country.

11 Then they took all the goods of Sodom and Gomorrah and all their food supply, and departed.

12 And they also took Lot, [a]Abram's nephew and his possessions and departed, [b]for he was living in Sodom.

13 Then [1]a fugitive came and told Abram the [a]Hebrew.

12 [1]Lit., *dwelt* [2]Lit., *circle* [a]Gen. 14:2; 19:24, 25

13 [1]Lit., *wicked and sinners exceedingly* [a]Gen. 39:9, Num. 32:23; 2 Pet. 2:7, 8

14 [a]Deut. 3:27; 34:1-4

15 [1]Lit., *seed* [a]Gen. 12:7 [b]Gen. 13:17; 15:7, 8; 17:8

16 [1]Lit., *seed* [a]Gen. 16:10; 28:14; Num. 23:10

17 [a]Num. 13:17-24 [b]Gen. 13:15

18 [1]Or, *terebinths* [a]Gen. 14:13 [b]Gen. 8:20; 12:7, 8

1 [1]Or, *nations* [a]Gen. 10:10; 11:2 [b]Gen. 10:22; Dan. 8:2

2 [a]Gen. 10:19 [b]Deut. 29:23 [c]Gen. 13:10

3 [1]Lit., *joined together* [a]Gen. 14:8, 10 [b]Deut. 3:17; Josh 3:16

5 [1]Lit., *smote* [2]Or, *the plain of Kiriathaim* [a]Deut. 3:11, 13 [b]Deut. 1:4; Josh. 9:10 [c]Num. 32:37

6 [a]Gen. 36:20; Deut. 2:12, 22 [b]Gen. 21:21; Num. 10:12

7 [1]Lit., *smote* [a]Num. 13:26 [b]2 Chr. 20:2

8 [a]Gen. 14:3

9 [1]Or, *nations*

10 Lit., *there* [a]Gen. 14:17, 21, 22

12 [a]Gen. 11:27 [b]Gen. 13:12

13 [1]Lit., *the* [a]Gen., 40:15; Ex. 3:18

Now he was [2]living by the [3]oaks of [b]Mamre the Amorite,
brother of Eshcol and brother of Aner, and these were [4c]allies
with Abram.
14 And when Abram heard that [a]his [1]relative had been
taken captive, he [2]led out his trained men, [b]born in his house,
three hundred and eighteen, and went in pursuit as far as [c]Dan.
15 And [a]he divided [1]his forces against them by night, he
and his servants, and [2]defeated them, and pursued them as far
as Hobah, which is [3]north of [b]Damascus.
16 And he brought back all the goods, and also brought
back [a]his [1]relative Lot with his possessions, and also the wom-
en, and the people.
17 Then after his return from the [1]defeat of Chedorlaomer and the kings who were with him, [a]the king of Sodom
went out to meet him at the valley of Shaveh (that is, [b]the
King's valley).
18 And [a]Melchizedek king of Salem brought out [b]bread
and wine; now he was a [c]priest of [1]God Most High.
19 And he blessed him and said,
"Blessed be Abram of [1]God Most High,
[2a]Possessor of heaven and earth;
20 And blessed be [1]God Most High,
Who has delivered your enemies into your hand."
[a]And he gave him a tenth of all.
21 And the King of Sodom said to Abram, "Give the
[1]people to me and take the goods for yourself."
22 And Abram said to the king of Sodom, "I have [1]sworn
to the LORD [2a]God Most High, [3]possessor of heaven and earth,
23 that [a]I will not take a thread or a sandal thong or
anything that is yours, lest you should say, 'I have made Abram
rich.'
24 "[1]I will take nothing except what the young men have
eaten, and the share of the men who went with me, [a]Aner,
Eshcol, and Mamre; let them take their share."

CHAPTER 15

AFTER these things [a]the word of the LORD came to Abram
in a vision, saying,
"[b]Do not fear, Abram,
I am [c]a shield to you;
[1]Your [d]reward shall be very great."
2 And Abram said, "O Lord [1]God, what wilt Thou give
me, since I [2]am childless, and the [3]heir of my house is Eliezer
of Damascus?"
3 And Abram said, "[1]Since Thou hast given no [2]offspring
to me, [3]one [a]born in my house is my heir."
4 Then behold, the word of the LORD came to him,
saying, "This man will not be your heir; [a]but one who shall
come forth from your own [1]body, he shall be your heir."
5 And He took him outside and said, "Now look toward
the heavens, and [a]count the stars, if you are able to count
them." And He said to him, "[b]So shall your [1]descendants be."
6 [a]Then he believed in the LORD; and He reckoned it to
him as righteousness.
7 And He said to him, "I am the LORD who brought you

13 [2]Lit., *abiding* [3]Or, *terebinths* [4]Lit., *possessors of the covenant* [b]Gen. 13:18 [c]Gen. 21:27, 32

14 [1]Lit., *brother* [2]Or, *mustered* [a]Gen. 14:12 [b]Gen. 12:5; Eccles. 2:7 [c]1 Kin. 15:20

15 [1]Lit., *himself* [2]Lit., *smote* [3]Lit., *on the left* [a]Judg. 7:16 [b]Gen. 15:2

16 [1]Lit., *brother* [a]Gen. 14:12, 14

17 [1]Lit., *smiting* [a]Gen. 14:10 [b]2 Sam. 18:18

18 [1]Heb., *El Elyon* [a]Heb. 7:1 [b]Ps. 104:15 [c]Ps. 110:4; Heb. 5:6, 10

19 [1]Heb., *El Elyon* [2]Or, *Creator* [a]Gen. 14:22

20 [1]Heb., *El Elyon* [a]Heb. 7:4

21 [1]Lit., *soul*

22 [1]Lit., *lifted up my hand* [2]Heb. *El Elyon* [3]Or, *Creator* [a]Gen. 14:19

23 [a]2 Kin. 5:16

24 [1]Lit., *not to me except* [a]Gen. 14:13

1 [1]Or, *your very great reward* [a]Gen. 15:4; 1 Sam. 15:10 [b]Gen. 21:17; 26:24 [c]Deut. 33:29 [d]Num. 18:20

2 [1]YHWH, usually rendered LORD [2]Lit., *go* [3]Lit., *son of acquisition*

3 [1]Lit., *Behold* [2]Lit., *seed* [3]Lit., *and behold, a son of* [a]Gen. 14:14

4 [1]Lit., *inward parts* [a]Gal. 4:28

5 [1]Lit., *seed* [a]Gen. 22:17; 26:4; Deut. 1:10 [b]Ex. 32:13; Rom. 4:18

6 [a]Rom. 4:3; Gal. 3:6; James 2:23

out of [a]Ur of the Chaldeans, to [b]give you this land to [1]possess
it."
8 And he said, "O Lord [1]God, [a]how may I know that I
shall [2]possess it?"
9 So He said to him, "[1]Bring Me a three year old heifer,
and a three year old female goat, and a three year old ram, and
a turtledove, and a young pigeon."
10 Then he [1]brought all these to Him and [a]cut them [2]in
two, and laid each half opposite the other; but he did not cut
[b]the birds.
11 And the birds of prey came down upon the carcasses,
and Abram drove them away.
12 Now when the sun was going down, [a]a deep sleep fell
upon Abram; and behold, [1]terror *and* great darkness fell upon
him.
13 And God said to Abram, "Know for certain that [a]your
[1]descendants will be strangers in a land that is not theirs,
[2]where [b]they will be enslaved and oppressed [c]four hundred
years.
14 "But I will also judge the nation whom they will serve;
and afterward they will come out [a]with [1]many possessions.
15 "And as for you, [a]you shall go to your fathers in peace;
you shall be buried at a good old age.
16 "Then in [a]the fourth generation they shall return here,
for [b]the iniquity of the Amorite is not yet complete."
17 And it came about when the sun had set, that it was
very dark, and behold, *there appeared* a smoking oven and a
flaming torch which [a]passed between these pieces.
18 On that day the LORD made a covenant with Abram,
saying,
"To your [1]descendants I have given this land,
From [a]the river of Egypt as far as the great river, the
river Euphrates:
19 [a]the Kenite and the Kenizzite and the Kadmonite
20 and the Hittite and the Perizzite and the Rephaim
21 and the Amorite and the Canaanite and the Girgashite
and the Jebusite."

CHAPTER 16

NOW [a]Sarai, Abram's wife had borne him no *children,* and
she had [b]an Egyptian maid whose name was Hagar.
2 So Sarai said to Abram, "Now behold, the LORD has
prevented me from bearing *children.* [a]Please go in to my maid;
perhaps I shall [1]obtain children through her." And Abram
listened to the voice of Sarai.
3 And after Abram had [1]lived [a]ten years in the land of
Canaan, Abram's wife Sarai took Hagar the Egyptian, her
maid, and gave her to her husband Abram as his wife.
4 And he went in to Hagar, and she conceived; and when
she saw that she had conceived, her mistress was despised in
her sight.
5 And Sarai said to Abram, "[a]May the wrong done me be
upon you. I gave my maid into your [1]arms; but when she saw
that she had conceived, I was despised in her [2]sight. [b]May the
LORD judge between [3]you and me."

7 [1]Or, *inherit* [a]Gen. 11:31 [b]Gen. 13:15,17

8 [1]YHWH, usually rendered LORD [2]Or, *inherit* [a]Luke 1:18

9 [1]Lit., *Take*

10 [1]Lit., *took* [2]Lit., *in the midst* [a]Gen. 15:17 [b]Lev. 1:17

12 [1]Or, *a terror of great darkness* [a]Gen. 2:21; 28:11; Job 33:15

13 [1]Lit., *seed* [2]Lit., *and shall serve them; and they shall afflict them* [a]Acts 7:6, 17 [b]Deut. 5:15 [c]Gal. 3:17; Ex. 12:40

14 [1]Lit., *great* [a]Ex. 12:32-38

15 [a]Gen. 25:8; 47:30

16 [a]Gen. 15:13 [b]Lev. 18:24-28

17 [a]Jer. 34:18, 19

18 [1]Lit., *seed* [a]Ex. 23:31; Num. 34:1-15; Deut. 1:7, 8

19 [a]Ex. 3:17; 23:28; Josh 21:43; 24:11

1 [a]Gen. 11:30 [b]Gen. 12:16

2 [1]Lit., *be built from her* [a]Gen. 30:3, 4, 9, 10

3 [1]Lit., *dwelt* [a]Gen. 12:4

5 [1]Lit., bosom [2]Lit., *eyes* [3]Lit., *me and you* [a]Jer. 51:35 [b]Gen. 31:53

me to bury my dead out of my sight, hear me, and approach
[a]Ephron the son of Zohar for me,
9 that he may give me the cave of Machpelah which he
owns, which is at the end of his field; for the full price let him
give it to me in [1]your presence for a [2]burial site."
10 Now Ephron was sitting among the sons of Heth; and
Ephron the Hittite answered Abraham in the hearing of the
sons of Heth; *even* [a]of all who went in at the gate of his city,
saying,
11 "No, my lord, hear me; I give you the field, and I give
you the cave that is in it. In the presence of the sons of my
people I give it to you; bury your dead."
12 And Abraham bowed before the people of the land.
13 And he spoke to Ephron in the hearing of the people of
the land, saying, "If you will only please listen to me; I will give
the price of the field, accept *it* from me, that I may bury my
dead there."
14 Then Ephron answered Abraham, saying to him,
15 "My lord, listen to me; a piece of land worth four
hundred [a]shekels of silver, what is that between me and you?
So bury your dead."
16 And Abraham listened to Ephron; and Abraham
[a]weighed out for Ephron the silver which he had named in the
[1]hearing of the sons of Heth, four hundred shekels of silver,
[2]commercial standard.
17 So [a]Ephron's field, which was in Machpelah, which
faced Mamre, the field and cave which was in it, and all the
trees which were in the field, that were [1]within all the confines
of its border, [2]were deeded over
18 to Abraham for a possession [a]in the presence of the
sons of Heth, before all who went in at the gate of his city.
19 And after this, Abraham buried Sarah his wife in the
cave of the field at Machpelah facing Mamre (that is, Hebron)
in the land of Canaan.
20 So the field, and the cave that is in it, [1]were deeded
over to Abraham for a [2]burial site by the sons of Heth.

CHAPTER 24

NOW Abraham was old, advanced in age; and the LORD had
[a]blessed Abraham in every way.
2 And Abraham said to his servant, the oldest of his household, who had charge of all that he owned, "[a]Please place
your hand under my thigh,
3 and I will make you swear by the LORD, [a]the God of
heaven and the God of earth, that you shall not take a wife for
my son from the daughters of [b]the Canaanites, among whom I
live,
4 but you shall go to [a]my country and to my relatives,
and take a wife for my son Isaac."
5 And the servant said to him, "Suppose the woman will
not be willing to follow me to this land; should I take your son
back to the land from where you came?"
6 Then Abraham said to him, "[a]Beware lest you take my
son back there!
7 "[a]The LORD, the God of heaven, who took me from my

8 [a]Gen. 25:9

9 [1]Lit., *in the midst of you* [2]Lit., *possession of a burial place*

10 [a]Gen. 23:18; 34:20, 24; Ruth 4:1, 11

15 [a]Ex. 30:13

16 [1]Lit., *ears* [2]Lit., *current according to the merchant* [a]2 Sam. 14:26; Jer. 32:9; Zech. 11:12

17 [1]Lit., *in all its border around* [2]Or, *were ratified* [a]Gen. 25:9; 49:29, 30; 50:13

18 [a]Gen. 23:10

20 [1]Or, *were ratified* [2]Lit., *possession of a burial place*

1 [a]Gen. 24:35; 12:2

2 [a]Gen. 47:29

3 [a]Gen. 14:19, 22 [b]Gen. 10:18, 19; 26:34, 35; 28:1, 2, 8

4 [a]Gen. 12:1; Heb. 11:15

6 [a]Gen. 24:8

7 [a]Gen. 24:3

father's house and from the land of my birth, and who spoke
to me, and who swore to me, saying, '[b]To your [1]descendants I
will give this land', He will send [c]His angel before you, and you
will take a wife for my son from there.
8 "But if the woman is not willing to follow you, then you
will be free from this my oath; [a]only do not take my son back
there."
9 So the servant [a]placed his hand under the thigh of Abraham his master, and swore to him concerning this matter.
10 Then the servant took ten camels from the camels of
his master, and set out with a variety of [a]good things of his
master's in his hand; and he arose, and went to [1]Mesopotamia,
to [b]the city of Nahor.
11 And he made the camels kneel down outside the city
by [a]the well of water at evening time, [b]the time when women
go out to draw water.
12 And he said, "[a]O LORD, the God of my master Abraham, [b]please [1]grant me success today, and show lovingkindness
to my master Abraham.
13 "Behold, [a]I am standing by the [1]spring, and the daughters of the men of the city are coming out to draw water;
14 now may it be that the girl to whom I say, 'Please let
down your jar so that I may drink,' and [1]who answers, 'Drink,
and I will water your camels also';—*may* she *be the one* whom
Thou hast appointed for Thy servant Isaac; and by this I shall
know that Thou hast shown lovingkindness to my master."
15 And it came about [a]before he had finished speaking,
that behold, [b]Rebekah who was born to Bethuel the son of
Milcah, the wife of Abraham's brother Nahor, came out with
her jar on her shoulder.
16 And the girl was [a]very beautiful, a virgin, and no man
had [1]had relations with her; and she went down to the spring
and filled her jar, and came up.
17 Then the servant ran to meet her, and said, "Please let
me drink a little water from your jar."
18 And [a]she said, "Drink, my lord"; and she quickly lowered her jar to her hand, and gave him a drink.
19 Now when she had finished giving him a drink, [a]she
said, "I will draw also for your camels until they have finished
drinking."
20 So she quickly emptied her jar into the trough, and ran
back to the well to draw, and she drew for all his camels.
21 [a]Meanwhile, the man was gazing at her [1]in silence, to
know whether the LORD had made his journey successful or
not.
22 Then it came about, when the camels had finished
drinking, that the man took a [a]gold ring weighing a half-shekel
and two bracelets for her [1]wrists weighing ten shekels in gold,
23 and said, "Whose daughter are you? Please tell me, is
there room for us to lodge in your father's house?"
24 And she said to him, "[a]I am the daughter of Bethuel,
the son of Milcah, whom she bore to Nahor."
25 Again she said to him, "We have plenty of both straw
and feed, and room to lodge in."
26 Then the man [a]bowed low and worshiped the LORD.
27 And he said, "[a]Blessed be the LORD, the God of my

7 [1]Lit., *seed* [b]Gen. 12:7; 13:15; 15:18 [c]Gen. 16:7; 21:17; 22:11; Ex. 23:20, 23

8 [a]Gen. 24:6

9 [a]Gen. 24:2

10 [1]Heb., *Aram-na-haraim, Aram of the two rivers* [a]Gen. 24:22, 53 [b]Gen. 11:31, 32

11 [a]Gen. 24:42 [b]1 Sam. 9:11

12 [1]Lit., *cause to occur for me* [a]Gen. 24:27, 42, 48 [b]Gen. 27:20

13 [1]Lit., *fountain of water* [a]Gen. 24:43

14 [1]Lit., *she will say*

15 [a]Gen. 24:45 [b]Gen. 22:20, 23

16 [1]Lit., *known* [a]Gen. 12:11; 29:17

18 [a]Gen. 24:14, 46

19 [a]Gen. 24:14

21 [1]Lit., *keeping silent* [a]Gen. 24:12-14, 27, 52

22 [1]Lit., *hands* [a]Gen. 24:47

24 [a]Gen. 24:15

26 [a]Gen. 24:48, 52

27 [a]Gen. 24:12, 42, 48

master Abraham, who has not forsaken His lovingkindness and
His truth toward my master; as for me, [b]the LORD has guided
me in the way to the house of my master's brothers."
28 Then [a]the girl ran and told her mother's household
about these things.
29 Now Rebekah had a brother whose name was [a]Laban;
and Laban ran outside to the man at the spring.
30 And it came about that when he saw the ring, and the
bracelets on his sister's [1]wrists, and when he heard the words of
Rebekah his sister, saying, "[2]This is what the man said to me,"
he went to the man; and behold, he was standing by the camels
at the spring.
31 And he said, "[a]Come in, blessed of the LORD! Why do
you stand outside since [b]I have prepared the house, and a place
for the camels?"
32 So the man entered the house. Then [1]Laban unloaded
the camels, and he gave straw and feed to the camels, and
water to wash his feet and the feet of the men who were with
him.
33 But when *food* was set before him to eat, he said, "I
will not eat until I have told my business." And he said, "Speak
on."
34 So he said, "I am [a]Abraham's servant.
35 "And [a]the LORD has greatly blessed my master, so that
he has become [1]rich; and He has given him [b]flocks and herds,
and silver and gold, and servants and maids, and camels and
donkeys.
36 "[a]Now Sarah my master's wife bore a son to my master
[1]in her old age; [b]and he has given him all that he has.
37 "[a]And my master made me swear, saying, 'You shall not
take a wife for my son from the daughters of the Canaanites,
in whose land I [1]live;
38 but you shall go to my father's house, and to my relatives, and take a wife for my son.'
39 "[a]And I said to my master, 'Suppose the woman does
not follow me.'
40 "And he said to me, '[a]The LORD, before whom I have
walked, will send His angel with you to make your journey
successful, and you will take a wife for my son from my relatives, and from my father's house;
41 [a]then you will be free from my oath, when you come to
my relatives; and if they do not give her to you, you will be free
from my oath.'
42 "So [a]I came today to the spring, and said, 'O LORD, the
God of my master Abraham, if now Thou wilt make my journey on which I go successful;
43 [a]behold, I am standing by the [1]spring, and may it be
that the maiden who comes out to draw, and to whom I say,
"[b]Please let me drink a little water from your jar";
44 and she will say to me, "You drink, and I will draw for
your camels also"; let her be the woman whom the LORD has
appointed for my master's son.'
45 "Before I had finished [a]speaking in my heart, behold,
[b]Rebekah came out with her jar on her shoulder, and went
down to the spring and drew; and [c]I said to her, 'Please let me
drink.'

27 [b]Gen. 24:21
28 [a]Gen. 29:12
29 [a]Gen. 29:13
30 [1]Lit., *hands* [2]Lit., *Thus the man*
31 [a]Gen. 29:14 [b]Gen. 18:3-5; 19:2, 3
32 [1]Lit., *he*
34 [a]Gen. 24:2
35 [1]Lit., *great* [a]Gen. 24:1 [b]Gen. 13:2
36 [1]Lit., *after she was old* [a]Gen. 21:1-7 [b]Gen. 25:5
37 [1]Lit., *dwell* [a]Gen. 24:2-4
39 [a]Gen. 24:5
40 [a]Gen. 24:7
41 [a]Gen. 24:8
42 [a]Gen. 24:11, 12
43 [1]Lit., *fountain of water* [a]Gen. 24:13 [b]Gen. 24:14
45 [a]1 Sam. 1:13 [b]Gen. 24:15 [c]Gen. 24:17

46 "And she quickly lowered her jar from her *shoulder*, and
said, '[a]Drink, and I will water your camels also'; so I drank, and
she watered the camels also.
47 "[a]Then I asked her, and said, 'Whose daughter are you?'
And she said, 'The daughter of Bethuel, Nahor's son, whom
Milcah bore to him'; and I put the ring on her nose, and the
bracelets on her [1]wrists.
48 "And [a]I bowed low and worshiped the LORD, and blessed
the LORD, the God of my master Abraham, [b]who had guided
me in the right way to take the daughter of my master's [1]kins-
men for his son.
49 "So now if you are going to [1a]deal kindly and truly with
my master, tell me; and if not, let me know, that I may turn to
the right hand or the left."
50 Then Laban and Bethuel answered and said, "The
matter comes from the LORD; [a]*so* we cannot speak to you bad
or good.
51 "Behold, Rebekah is before you, take *her* and go, and let
her be the wife of your master's son, as the LORD has spoken."
52 And it came about when Abraham's servant heard their
words, that he [a]bowed himself to the ground [1]before the LORD.
53 And the servant brought out [a]articles of silver and articles of gold, and garments, and gave them to Rebekah; he
also gave precious things to her brother and to her mother.
54 Then he and the men who were with him ate and drank
and spent the night. When they arose in the morning, he said
"[a]Send me away to my master."
55 But her brother and her mother said, "[a]Let the girl stay
with us *a few* days, say ten; afterward she may go."
56 And he said to them, "Do not delay me, since the LORD
has prospered my way. Send me away that I may go to my
master."
57 And they said, "We will call the girl and [1]consult her
wishes."
58 Then they called Rebekah and said to her, "Will you
go with this man?" And she said, "I will go."
59 Thus they sent away their sister Rebekah and [a]her
nurse with Abraham's servant and his men.
60 And they blessed Rebekah and said to her,

"May you, our sister,
[a]Become thousands of ten thousands,
And may [b]your [1]descendants possess
The gate of those who hate them."

61 Then Rebekah arose with her maids, and they
mounted the camels and followed the man. So the servant
took Rebekah and departed.
62 Now Isaac had come from going to [a]Beer-lahai-roi; for
he [1]was living in [2b]the Negev.
63 And Isaac went out [a]to [1]meditate in the field toward
evening; and [b]he lifted up his eyes and looked, and behold,
camels were coming.
64 And Rebekah lifted up her eyes, and when she saw
Isaac she dismounted from the camel.
65 And she said to the servant, "Who is that man walking
in the field to meet us?" And the servant said, "He is my
master." Then she took her [1]veil and covered herself.

46 [a]Gen. 24:18

47 [1]Lit., *hands* [a]Gen. 24:23, 24

48 [1]Lit., *brother* [a]Gen. 24:26, 52 [b]Gen. 24:27

49 [1]Lit., *show lovingkindness and truth* [a]Gen. 47:29; Josh. 2:14

50 [a]Gen. 31:24, 29

52 [1]Lit., *to* [a]Gen. 24:26, 48

53 [a]Gen. 24:10, 22

54 [a]Gen. 24:56; 30:25

55 [a]Judg. 19:4

57 [1]Lit., *ask her mouth*

59 [a]Gen. 35:8

60 [1]Lit., *seed* [a]Gen. 17:16 [b]Gen. 22:17

62 [1]Lit., *was dwelling* [2]I.e., South country [a]Gen. 16:14; 25:11 [b]Gen. 20:1

63 [1]Or, *stroll*, Meaning uncertain. [a]Ps. 119:15, 27, 48; 143:5; 145:5 [b]Gen. 18:2

65 [1]Or, *shawl*

66 And the servant told Isaac all the things that he had done.

67 Then Isaac brought her into his mother Sarah's tent, and he took Rebekah, and she became his wife; and [a]he loved her; thus Isaac was comforted after [b]his mother's death.

Chapter 25

NOW Abraham took another wife, [1]whose name was Keturah.

2 And [a]she bore to him Zimran and Jokshan and Medan and Midian and Ishbak and Shuah.

3 And Jokshan [1]became the father of Sheba and Dedan. And the sons of Dedan were Asshurim and Letushim and Leummim.

4 And the sons of Midian *were* Ephah and Epher and Hanoch and Abida and Eldaah. All these *were* the sons of Keturah.

5 [a]Now Abraham gave all that he had to Isaac;

6 but to the sons of [1]his concubines, Abraham gave gifts while he was still living, and sent them away from his son Isaac eastward, to the land of the East.

7 And these are [1]all the years of Abraham's life that he lived, [a]one hundred and seventy-five years.

8 And Abraham breathed his last and died [a]in a [1]ripe old age, an old man and satisfied with *life;* and he was [b]gathered to his people.

9 Then his sons Isaac and Ishmael buried him in [a]the cave of Machpelah, in the field of Ephron the son of Zohar the Hittite, facing Mamre,

10 the field which Abraham purchased from the sons of Heth; there Abraham was buried with Sarah his wife.

11 And it came about after the death of Abraham, that [a]God blessed his son Isaac; and Isaac [1]lived by [b]Beer-lahai-roi.

12 Now these are *the records of* the generations of [a]Ishmael, Abraham's son, whom Hagar the Egyptian, Sarah's maid, bore to Abraham;

13 and these are the names of [a]the sons of Ishmael, by their names, [1]in the order of their birth: Nebaioth, the firstborn of Ishmael, and Kedar and Adbeel and Mibsam

14 and Mishma and Dumah and Massa,

15 Hadad and Tema, Jetur, Naphish and Kedemah.

16 These are the sons of Ishmael and these are their names, by their villages, and by their camps; [a]twelve princes according to their [1]tribes.

17 And these are the years of the life of Ishmael, [a]one hundred and thirty-seven years; and he breathed his last and died, and was [b]gathered to his people.

18 And they [1]settled from Havilah to [a]Shur which is [2]east of Egypt [3]as one goes toward Assyria; [b]he [4]settled in defiance of all his [5]relatives.

19 Now these are *the records of* the generations of Isaac, Abraham's son: Abraham [1]became the father of Isaac;

20 and Isaac was forty years old when he took [a]Rebekah, the daughter of Bethuel the [1]Syrian of Paddan-aram, the sister of Laban the [1]Syrian, to be his wife.

67 [a]Gen. 29:18 [b]Gen. 23:1, 2; 25:20

1 [1]Lit., *and her name*

2 [a]1 Chr. 1:32, 33

3 [1]Lit., *begot*

5 [a]Gen. 24:35, 36

6 [1]Lit., *concubines which belonged to Abraham*

7 [1]Lit., *the days of* [a]Gen. 12:4

8 [1]Lit., *good* [a]Gen. 15:15 [b]Gen. 25:17; 35:29; 49:29, 33

9 [a]Gen. 23:17, 18

11 [1]Lit., *dwelt* [a]Gen. 12:2, 3; 22:17; 26:3 [b]Gen. 24:62

12 [a]Gen. 16:15

13 [1]Lit., *in regard to their generations* [a]1 Chr. 1:29-31

16 [1]Or, *peoples,* [a]Gen. 17:20

17 [a]Gen. 16:16 [b]Gen. 25:8

18 [1]Lit., *dwelt* [2]Lit., *before* [3]Lit., *as you go* [4]Lit., *fell over against* [5]Lit., *brothers* [a]Gen. 20:1 [b]Gen. 16:12

19 [1]Lit., *begot*

20 [1]Heb., *Aramean* [a]Gen. 24:15, 29

21 And Isaac prayed to the LORD on behalf of his wife,
because she was barren; and [a]the LORD [1]answered him and
Rebekah his wife conceived.
22 But the children struggled together within her; and she
said, "If it is so, why then am I *this way?*" So she went to
inquire of the LORD.
23 And the LORD said to her,
"[a]Two nations are in your womb;
[b]And two peoples shall be separated from your body;
And one people shall be stronger than the other;
And [c]the older shall serve the younger."
24 When her days to be delivered were fulfilled, behold,
there were twins in her womb.
25 Now the first came forth red, all over like a hairy garment; and they named him Esau.
26 And afterward his brother came forth with [a]his hand
holding on to Esau's heel, so his name was called [1]Jacob; and
Isaac was [b]sixty years old when she gave birth to them.
27 When the boys grew up, Esau became a skillful hunter,
a man of the field; but Jacob was a [1]peaceful man, [2]living in
tents.
28 Now Isaac loved Esau, because [1]he had a taste for
game; but Rebekah loved Jacob.
29 And when Jacob had cooked [a]stew, Esau came in from
the field and he was [1]famished;
30 and Esau said to Jacob, "Please let me have a swallow
of [1]that red stuff there, for I am [2]famished." Therefore his
name was called [3]Edom.
31 But Jacob said, "[1]First sell me your [a]birthright."
32 And Esau said, "Behold, I am about to die; so of what
use then is the birthright to me?"
33 And Jacob said, "[1]First swear to me"; so he swore to
him, and [a]sold his birthright to Jacob.
34 Then Jacob gave Esau bread and lentil stew; and he ate
and drank, and rose and went on his way. Thus Esau despised
his birthright.

CHAPTER 26

NOW there was [a]a famine in the land, besides the previous
famine that had occurred in the days of Abraham. So Isaac
went to Gerar, to [b]Abimelech king of the Philistines.
2 And the LORD [a]appeared to him and said, "Do not go
down to Egypt; [1b]stay in the land of which I shall tell you.
3 "Sojourn in this land and [a]I will be with you and bless
you, for [b]to you and to your [1]descendants I will give all these
lands, and I will establish [c]the oath which I swore to your
father Abraham.
4 "And [a]I will multiply your [1]descendants as the stars of
heaven, and will give your [1]descendants all these lands; and [b]by
your [1]descendants all the nations of the earth [2]shall be blessed;
5 because Abraham [1]obeyed Me and kept My charge,
My commandments, My statutes and My laws."
6 So Isaac [1]lived in Gerar.
7 When the men of the place asked about his wife, he
said, "[a]She is my sister," for he was afraid to say, "My wife,"

21 [1]Lit., *was entreated of him* [a]Ps. 127:3; 1 Sam. 1:17

23 [a]Gen. 17:4-6, 16; Num. 20:14; Deut. 2:4, 8 [b]Gen. 27:29 [c]Gen. 27:40; Mal. 1:2, 3; Rom. 9:12

26 [1]I.e., One who takes by the heel or supplants [a]Hos. 12:3 [b]Gen. 25:20

27 [1]Lit., *complete* [2]Lit., *dwelling*

28 [1]Lit., *game was in his mouth*

29 [1]Lit., *weary* [a]2 Kin. 4:38

30 [1]Lit., *the red, this red* [2]Lit., *weary* [3]Or, *Red*

31 [1]Lit., *Today* [a]Deut. 21:16, 17; 1 Chr. 5:1, 2

33 [1]Lit., *Today* [a]Heb. 12:16

1 [a]Gen. 12:10 [b]Gen. 20:1,2

2 [1]Lit., *dwell* [a]Gen. 12:7; 17:1; 18:1 [b]Gen. 12:1

3 [1]Lit., *seed* [a]Gen. 26:24; 28:15; 31:3 [b]Gen. 12:7; 13:15; 15:18 [c]Gen. 22:16-18

4 [1]Lit., *seed* [2]Or, *bless themselves* [a]Gen. 15:5; 22:17; Ex. 32:13 [b]Gen. 22:18; Gal. 3:8

5 [1]Lit., *hearkened to My voice*

6 [1]Lit., *dwelt*

7 [a]Gen. 12:13; 20:2, 12

thinking, "[1]the men of the place might kill me on account of
Rebekah, for she is [b]beautiful."
8 And it came about, when he had been there a long
time, that Abimelech king of the Philistines looked out
through a window, and saw, and behold, Isaac was caressing his
wife Rebekah.
9 Then Abimelech called Isaac and said, "Behold, certainly she is your wife! How then did you say, 'She is my sister'?
And Isaac said to him, "Because I said, 'Lest I die on account
of her.'"
10 And [a]Abimelech said, "What is this you have done to
us? One of the people might easily have lain with your wife,
and you would have brought guilt upon us."
11 So Abimelech charged all the people, saying, "He who
touches this man or his wife shall surely be put to death."
12 Now Isaac sowed in that land, and [1]reaped in the same
year a hundredfold. And [a]the LORD blessed him,
13 and the man became rich, and continued to grow [1]rich-
er until he became very [1]wealthy;
14 for [a]he had possessions of flocks [1]and herds and a great
household, so that the Philistines envied him.
15 Now [a]all the wells which his father's servants had dug in
the days of Abraham his father, the Philistines stopped up [1]by
filling them with earth.
16 Then Abimelech said to Isaac, "Go away from us, for
you are [1]too powerful for us."
17 And Isaac departed from there and camped in the valley of Gerar, and [1]settled there.
18 Then Isaac dug again the wells of water which [1]had
been dug in the days of his father Abraham, for the Philistines
had stopped them up after the death of Abraham; and he
[2]gave them the same names which his father had [3]given them.
19 But when Isaac's servants dug in the valley and found
there a well of [1]flowing water,
20 the herdsmen of Gerar quarreled with the herdsmen of
Isaac, saying, "The water is ours!" So he named the well [1]Esek,
because they contended with him.
21 Then they dug another well, and they quarreled over it
too, so he named it [1]Sitnah.
22 And he moved away from there and dug another well,
and they did not quarrel over it; so he named it [1]Rehoboth, for
he said, "[2a]At last the LORD has made [3]room for us, and we
shall be fruitful in the land."
23 Then he went up from there to [a]Beersheba.
24 And the LORD [a]appeared to him the same night and
said,

"[b]I am the God of your father Abraham;
Do not fear, for I am with you.
I [c]will bless you, and multiply your [1]descendants,
For the sake of My servant Abraham."

25 So he built an [a]altar there, and called upon the name of
the LORD, and pitched his tent there; and there Isaac's servants
dug a well.
26 Then [a]Abimelech came to him from Gerar [1]with his
adviser Ahuzzath, and Phicol the commander of his army.

7 [1]Lit., *lest . . . place* [b]Gen. 12:11; 29:17

12 [1]Lit., *found* [a]Gen. 26:3

13 [1]Lit., *great*

14 [1]Lit., *and possessions of herds* [a]Gen. 24:35; 25:5

15 [1]Lit., *and filled them* [a]Gen. 21:25, 30

16 [1]Lit., *much mightier than we*

17 [1]Lit., *dwelt*

18 [1]Lit., *they had dug* [2]Lit., *called their names as the names* [3]Lit., *called*

19 [1]Lit., *living*

20 [1]I.e., contention

21 [1]I.e., enmity

22 [1]I.e., broad places [2]Lit., *Truly now* [3]Or, *broad* [a]Ps. 4:1; Is. 54:2

23 [a]Gen. 22:19

24 [1]Lit., *seed* [a]Gen. 26:2 [b]Gen. 17:7, 8;24:12; Ex. 3:6 [c]Gen. 26:3; 22:17

25 [a]Gen. 12:7, 8; 13:4

26 [1]Lit., *and his confidential friend* [a]Gen. 21:22

27 And Isaac said to them, "Why have you come to me,
since you hate me, and have sent me away from you?"
28 And they said, "We see plainly [a]that the LORD has been
with you; so we said, 'Let there now be an oath between us,
even between [1]you and us, and let us make a covenant with
you,
29 that you will do us no harm, just as we have not
touched you [1]and have done to you nothing but good, and
have sent you away in peace. You are now the blessed of the
LORD.' "
30 Then he made them a feast, and they ate and drank.
31 And in the morning they arose early and [1a]exchanged
oaths; then Isaac sent them away and they departed from him
in peace.
32 Now it came about on the same day, that Isaac's servants came in and told him about the well which they had dug,
and said to him, "We have found water."
33 So he called it [a]Shibah; therefore the name of the city is
Beersheba to this day.
34 And when Esau was forty years old [a]he [1]married Judith
the daughter of Beeri the Hittite, and Basemath the daughter
of Elon the Hittite;
35 and [a]they [1]made life miserable for Isaac and Rebekah.

CHAPTER 27

NOW it came about, when Isaac was old, and [a]his eyes were
too dim to see, that he called his [b]older son Esau and said to
him, "My son." And he said to him, "Here I am."
2 [a]And [1]Isaac said, "Behold now, I am old *and* I do not
know the day of my death.
3 "Now then, please take your gear, your quiver and your
bow, and go out to the field and [a]hunt game for me;
4 and prepare a savory dish for me such as I love, and
bring it to me that I may eat, so that [a]my soul may bless you
before I die."
5 And Rebekah was listening while Isaac spoke to his son
Esau. So when Esau went to the field to hunt for game to
bring *home,*
6 [a]Rebekah said to her son Jacob, "Behold, I heard your
father speak to your brother Esau, saying,
7 'Bring me *some* game and prepare a savory dish for me,
that I may eat, and bless you in the presence of the LORD
before my death.'
8 "Now therefore, my son, [a]listen to [1]me [2]as I command
you.
9 "Go now to the flock and [1]bring me from there two
choice [2]kids, and I will prepare them a savory dish for your
father, such as he loves.
10 "Then you shall bring *it* to your father, that he may eat,
so that he may bless you before his death."
11 And Jacob [1]answered his mother Rebekah, "Behold,
Esau my brother is a [a]hairy man and I am a smooth man.
12 "[a]Perhaps my father will feel me, then I shall be as a
[1]deceiver in his sight; and I shall bring upon myself a curse and
not a blessing."

28 [1]Lit., *us and you* [a]Gen. 21:22, 23
29 [1]Lit., *and just as we*
31 [1]Lit., *swore one to another* [a]Gen. 21:31
33 [a]Gen. 21:31
34 [1]Lit., *took as wife* [a]Gen. 28:8; 36:2
35 [1]Lit., *were a bitterness of spirit to* [a]Gen. 27:46
1 [a]Gen. 48:10; 1 Sam. 3:2 [b]Gen. 25:25, 33, 34
2 [1]Lit., *he* [a]Gen. 47:29
3 [a]Gen. 25:28
4 [a]Gen. 27:19, 25, 31
6 [a]Gen. 25:28
8 [1]Lit., *my voice* [2]Lit., *according to what* [a]Gen. 27:13, 43
9 [1]Lit., *take* [2]Lit., *kids of goats*
11 [1]Lit., *said to* [a]Gen. 25:25
12 [1]Lit., *mocker* [a]Gen. 27:21, 22

13 But his mother said to him, "Your curse be on me, my
son; only [a]obey my voice, and go, get *them* for me."
14 So he went and got *them*, and brought *them* to his
mother; and his mother made savory food such as his father
loved.
15 Then Rebekah took the [1]best [a]garments of Esau her
elder son, which were with her in the house, and put them on
Jacob her younger son.
16 And she put the skins of the [1]kids on his hands and on
the smooth part of his neck.
17 She also gave the savory food and the bread, which she
had made, [1]to her son Jacob.
18 Then he came to his father and said, "My father." And
he said, "Here I am. Who are you, my son?"
19 And Jacob said to his father, "I am Esau your first-
born; I have done as you told me. [a]Get up, please, sit and eat
of my game, that [1b]you may bless me."
20 And Isaac said to his son, "How is it that you have *it* so
quickly, my son?" And he said, "[a]Because the LORD your God
caused *it* to happen to me."
21 Then Isaac said to Jacob, "Please come close, that [a]I
may feel you, my son, whether you are really my son Esau or
not."
22 So Jacob came close to Isaac his father, and he felt him
and said, "The voice is the voice of Jacob, but the hands are
the hands of Esau."
23 And he did not recognize him, because his hands were
[a]hairy like his brother Esau's hands; so he blessed him.
24 And he said, "Are you really my son Esau?" And he
said, "I am."
25 So he said, "Bring *it* to me, and I will eat of my son's
game, that [1a]I may bless you." And he brought *it* to him, and
he ate; he also brought him wine and he drank.
26 Then his father Isaac said to him, "Please come close
and kiss me, my son."
27 So he came close and kissed him; and when he smelled
the smell of his garments, he [a]blessed him and said,

"See, [b]the smell of my son
Is like the smell of a field [c]which the LORD has blessed;
28 Now may [a]God give you of the dew of heaven,
And of the fatness of the earth,
And an abundance of grain and new wine;
29 [a]May peoples serve you,
And nations bow down to you;
[b]Be master of your brothers,
[c]And may your mother's sons bow down to you.
[d]Cursed be those who curse you,
And blessed be those who bless you."

30 Now it came about, as soon as Isaac had finished blessing Jacob, and Jacob had hardly gone out from the presence
of Isaac his father, that Esau his brother came in from his
hunting.
31 Then he also made savory food, and brought it to his
father; and he said to his father, "[a]Let my father arise, and eat
of his son's game, that [1b]you may bless me."

13 [a]Gen. 27:8

15 [1]Lit., *desirable;* or, *choice* [a]Gen. 27:27

16 [1]Lit., *kids of the goats*

17 [1]Lit., *into the hand of*

19 [1]Lit., *your soul* [a]Gen. 27:31 [b]Gen. 27:4

20 [a]Gen. 24:12

21 [a]Gen. 27:12

23 [a]Gen. 27:16

25 [1]Lit., *my soul* [a]Gen. 27:4

27 [a]Heb. 11:20 [b]Song of Sol. 4:11 [c]Ps. 65:10

28 [a]Gen. 27:39; Deut. 33:13, 28; Prov. 3:20; Zech. 8:12

29 [a]Gen. 25:23; Is. 45:14; 49:7, 23; 60:12, 14 [b]Gen. 27:37; 9:26, 27 [c]Gen. 37:7, 10 [d]Gen. 12:3; Num. 24:9

31 [1]Lit., *your soul* [a]Gen. 27:19 [b]Gen. 27:4

32 And Isaac his father said to him, "[a]Who are you?" And
he said, "I am your son, [b]your first-born, Esau."
33 Then Isaac [1]trembled violently, and said, "[a]Who was
he then that hunted game and brought *it* to me, so that I ate
of all *of it* before you came, and blessed him? [b]Yes, and he
shall be blessed."
34 When Esau heard the words of his father, [a]he cried out
with an exceedingly great and bitter cry, and said to his father,
"Bless me, *even* me also, O my father!"
35 And he said, "[a]Your brother came deceitfully, and has
taken away your blessing."
36 Then he said, "[1]Is he not rightly named [a]Jacob, for he
has supplanted me these two times? He took away my birthright, and behold, now he has taken away my blessing." And
he said, "Have you not reserved a blessing for me?"
37 But Isaac answered and said to Esau, "Behold, I have
made him [a]your master, and all his [1]relatives I have given to
him [2]as servants; and with grain and new wine I have sustained
him. Now as for you then, what can I do, my son?"
38 And Esau said to his father, "Do you have only one
blessing, my father? Bless me, *even* me also, O my father." So
Esau lifted his voice and [a]wept.
39 Then Isaac his father answered and [a]said to him,
"Behold, [1b]away from the [2]fertility of the earth shall
be your dwelling,
And [1]away from the dew of heaven from above.
40 "And by your sword you shall live,
And your brother [a]you shall serve;
But it shall come about [b]when you become restless,
That you shall [1]break his yoke from your neck."
41 So Esau [a]bore a grudge against Jacob because of the
blessing with which his father had blessed him; and Esau said
[1]to himself, "The days of mourning for my father are near;
then I will kill my brother Jacob."
42 Now when the words of her elder son Esau were reported to Rebekah, she sent and called her younger son Jacob,
and said to him, "Behold your brother Esau is consoling himself concerning you, *by planning* to kill you.
43 "Now therefore, my son, [a]obey my voice, and arise, [1]flee
to Haran, to my brother [b]Laban!
44 "And stay with him [a]a few days, until your brother's fury
[1]subsides,
45 until your brother's anger [1]against you subsides, and he
forgets [a]what you did to him. Then I shall send and get you
from there. Why should I be bereaved of you both in one
day?"
46 And Rebekah said to Isaac, "I am tired of [1]living because of [a]the daughters of Heth; if Jacob takes a wife from the
daughters of Heth, like these, from the daughters of the land,
what good will my life be to me?"

Chapter 28

So Isaac called Jacob and blessed him and charged him, and
said to him, "[a]You shall not take a wife from the daughters of
Canaan.

32 [a]Gen. 27:18 [b]Gen. 25:33, 34

33 [1]Lit., *trembled with a very great trembling* [a]Gen. 27:35 [b]Gen. 25:23

34 [a]Heb. 12:17

35 [a]Gen. 27:19

36 [1]Or, *Was he then named Jacob that he has . . .* [a]Gen. 25:26, 32-34

37 [1]Lit., *brothers* [2]Lit., *for* [a]Gen. 27:28, 29

38 [a]Heb. 12:17

39 [1]Or, *of* [2]Lit., *fatness* [a]Heb. 11:20 [b]Gen. 27:28; Deut. 33:13, 28

40 [1]Lit., *tear off* [a]Gen. 27:29 [b]2 Kin. 8:20-22

41 [1]Lit., *in his heart* [a]Gen. 32:3-11

43 [1]Lit., *flee for yourself* [a]Gen. 27:8, 13 [b]Gen. 24:29

44 [1]Lit., *turns away* [a]Gen. 31:41

45 [1]Lit., *turns away from you* [a]Gen. 27:12, 19, 35

46 [1]Lit., *my life* [a]Gen. 26:34, 35

1 [a]Gen. 24:3, 4

2 "Arise, go to Paddan-aram, to the house of [a]Bethuel
your mother's father; and from there take to yourself a wife
from the daughters of Laban your mother's brother.
3 "And may [1a]God Almighty [b]bless you and [c]make you
fruitful and [d]multiply you, that you may become a [e]company
of peoples.
4 "May He also give you the blessing of Abraham, to you
and to your [1]descendants with you; that you may [a]possess the
land of your sojournings, which God gave to Abraham."
5 Then [a]Isaac sent Jacob away, and he went to Paddan-
aram to Laban, son of Bethuel the [1]Syrian, the brother of
Rebekah, the mother of Jacob and Esau.
6 Now Esau saw that Isaac had blessed Jacob and sent
him away to Paddan-aram, to take to himself a wife from
there, *and that* when he blessed him he charged him, saying,
"[a]You shall not take a wife from the daughters of Canaan,"
7 and that Jacob had obeyed his father and his mother
and had gone to Paddan-aram.
8 So Esau saw that [a]the daughters of Canaan displeased
[1]his father Isaac;
9 and Esau went to Ishmael, and [1]married, [a]besides the
wives that he had, Mahalath the daughter of Ishmael, Abraham's son, the sister of Nebaioth.
10 Then Jacob departed from [a]Beersheba and went toward [b]Haran.
11 And he [1]came to [2]a [a]certain place and spent the night
there, because the sun had set; and he took one of the stones
of the place and put it [3]under his head, and lay down in that
place.
12 And [a]he had a dream, and behold, a ladder was set on
the earth with its top reaching to heaven; and behold, [b]the
angels of God were ascending and descending on it.
13 And behold, [a]the LORD stood [1]above it and said, "I am
the LORD, [b]the God of your father Abraham and the God of
Isaac; the land on which you lie, I will give it [c]to you and to
[d]your [2]descendants.
14 "Your [1]descendants shall also be like [a]the dust of the
earth, and you shall [2]spread out [b]to the west and to the east
and to the north and to the south; and [c]in you and in your
[1]descendants shall all the families of the earth be blessed.
15 "And behold, [a]I am with you, and [b]will keep you wherever
you go, and [c]will bring you back to this land; for [d]I will not
leave you until I have done what I have [1]promised you."
16 Then Jacob [a]awoke from his sleep and said, "[b]Surely
the LORD is in this place, and I did not know it."
17 And he was afraid and said, "[a]How awesome is this
place! This is none other than the house of God, and this is the
gate of heaven."
18 So Jacob rose early in the morning, and took [a]the stone
that he had put [1]under his head and set it up as a pillar, and
poured oil on its top.
19 And he called the name of that place [1]Bethel; however,
[2]previously the name of the city had been [a]Luz.
20 Then Jacob [a]made a vow, saying, "[b]If God will be with
me and will keep me on this journey that I [1]take, and will give
me [2]food to eat and garments to wear,

2 [a]Gen. 25:20

3 [1]Heb., *El Shaddai* [a]Gen. 17:1; 35:11; 48:3 [b]Gen. 22:17 [c]Gen. 17:6, 20 [d]Gen. 17:2; 26:4, 24 [e]Gen. 35:11; 48:4

4 [1]Lit., *seed* [a]Gen. 15:7, 8

5 [1]Lit., *Aramean* [a]Gen. 27:43

6 [a]Gen. 28:1

8 [1]Lit., *in the eyes of his* [a]Gen. 26:34, 35; 27:46

9 [1]Lit., *took for his wife* [a]Gen. 26:34; 36:2

10 [a]Gen. 26:23 [b]Gen. 12:4, 5; 27:43

11 [1]Lit., *lighted on* [2]Lit., *the place* [3]Lit., *at his head-place* [a]Gen. 28:19

12 [a]Num. 12:6 [b]John 1:51

13 [1]Or, *beside him* [2]Lit., *seed* [a]Amos 7:7; Gen. 35:1 [b]Gen. 26:3, 24 [c]Gen. 13:15, 17; 26:3 [d]Gen. 12:7; 15:18

14 [1]Lit., *seed* [2]Lit., *break through* [a]Gen. 13:16; 22:17 [b]Gen. 13:14, 15 [c]Gen. 12:3; 18:18; 22:18; 26:4

15 [1]Lit., *spoken to* [a]Gen. 26:3 [b]Num. 6:24; Ps. 121:7, 8 [c]Gen. 48:21; Deut. 30:3 [d]Deut. 7:9; 31:6, 8

16 [a]1 Kin. 3:15; Jer. 31:26 [b]Ps. 139:7-12

17 [a]Ps. 68:35

18 [1]Lit., *at his head-place* [a]Gen. 28:11; 35:14

19 [1]I.e., the house of God [2]Lit., *at the first* [a]Gen. 35:6; 48:3

20 [1]Lit., *go* [2]Lit., *bread* [a]Gen. 31:13 [b]Gen. 28:15

21 and I return to my father's house in [1]safety, then the
LORD will be my God.
22 "And this stone, which I have set up as a pillar, [a]will be
God's house; and [b]of all that Thou dost give me I will surely
give a tenth to Thee."

CHAPTER 29

THEN Jacob [1]went on his journey, and came to the land of
[a]the sons of the east.
2 And he looked, and [1]saw [a]a well in the field, and behold, three flocks of sheep were lying there beside it, for from
that well they watered the flocks. Now the stone on the mouth
of the well was large.
3 When all the flocks were gathered there, they would
then roll the stone from the mouth of the well, and water the
sheep, and put the stone back in its place on the mouth of the
well.
4 And Jacob said to them, "My brothers, where are you
from?" And they said, "We are from [a]Haran."
5 And he said to them, "Do you know Laban the [a]son of
Nahor?" And they said, "We know *him.*"
6 And he said to them, "Is it well with him?" And they
said, "It is well, and behold, [a]Rachel his daughter is coming
with the sheep."
7 And he said, "Behold, it is still high day; it is not time
for the livestock to be gathered. Water the sheep, and go,
pasture them."
8 But they said, "We cannot, until all the flocks are gathered, and they roll the stone from the mouth of the well; then
we water the sheep."
9 While he was still speaking with them, Rachel came
with her father's sheep, for she was a shepherdess.
10 And it came about, when Jacob saw Rachel the daughter of Laban his mother's brother, and the sheep of Laban his
mother's brother, that Jacob went up, and rolled the stone
from the mouth of the well, and watered the flock of Laban
his mother's brother.
11 Then Jacob kissed Rachel, and lifted his voice and
wept.
12 And Jacob told Rachel that he was a [1a]relative of her
father and that he was Rebekah's son, and [b]she ran and told
her father.
13 So it came about, when [a]Laban heard the news of Jacob his sister's son, that he ran to meet him, and [b]embraced
him and kissed him, and brought him to his house. Then he
related to Laban all these things.
14 And Laban said to him, "Surely you are [a]my bone and
my flesh." And he stayed with him a month.
15 Then Laban said to Jacob, "Because you are my [1]rela-
tive, should you therefore serve me for nothing? Tell me, what
shall [a]your wages be?"
16 Now Laban had two daughters; the name of the older
was Leah, and the name of the younger was Rachel.
17 And Leah's eyes were weak, but Rachel was [a]beautiful
of form and [1]face.

21 [1]Lit., *peace*
22 [a]Gen. 35:7 [b]Deut. 14:22
1 [1]Lit., *lifted up his feet* [a]Judg. 6:3, 33
2 [1]Lit., *behold* [a]Gen. 24:10, 11; Ex. 2:15, 16
4 [a]Gen. 28:10
5 [a]Gen. 24:24, 29
6 [a]Ex. 2:16
12 [1]Lit., *brother* [a]Gen. 28:5 [b]Gen. 24:28
13 [a]Gen. 24:29-31 [b]Gen. 33:4
14 [a]Judg. 9:2
15 [1]Lit., *brother* [a]Gen. 31:41
17 [1]Lit., *beautiful of appearance* [a]Gen. 12:11, 14; 26:7

18 Now Jacob [a]loved Rachel, so he said, "[b]I will serve you
seven years for your younger daughter Rachel."
19 And Laban said, "It is better that I give her to you than
that I should give her to another man; stay with me."
20 So Jacob served seven years for Rachel and they
seemed to him but a few days because of his love for her.
21 Then Jacob said to Laban, "Give *me* my wife, for my
[1]time is completed, that I may go in to her."
22 And Laban gathered all the men of the place, and
made a feast.
23 Now it came about in the evening that he took his
daughter Leah, and brought her to him; and *Jacob* went in to
her.
24 Laban also gave his maid Zilpah to his daughter Leah
as a maid.
25 So it came about in the morning that, behold, it was
Leah! And he said to Laban, "[a]What is this you have done to
me? Was it not for Rachel that I served with you? Why then
have you [b]deceived me?"
26 But Laban said, "It is not [1]the practice in our place, to
[2]marry off the younger before the first-born.
27 "[a]Complete the bridal week of this one, and we will give
you the other also for the service which [b]you shall serve with
me for another seven years."
28 And Jacob did so and completed her week, and he gave
him his daughter Rachel as his wife.
29 Laban also gave his maid Bilhah to his daughter Rachel
as her maid.
30 So *Jacob* went in to Rachel also, and indeed [a]he loved
Rachel more than Leah, and he served with [1]Laban for another
seven years.
31 Now the LORD saw that Leah was [1]unloved, and He
opened her womb, but Rachel was barren.
32 And Leah conceived and bore a son and named him
[1]Reuben, for she said, "Because the LORD has [2a]seen my affliction; surely now my husband will love me."
33 Then she conceived again and bore a son and said,
"[a]Because the LORD has [1]heard that I am [2]unloved, He has
therefore given me this *son* also." So she named him Simeon.
34 And she conceived again and bore a son and said,
"Now this time my husband will become [1]attached to me,
because I have borne him three sons." Therefore he was
named [a]Levi.
35 And she conceived again and bore a son and said, "This
time I will [1a]praise the LORD." Therefore she named him [2]Ju-
dah. Then she stopped bearing.

CHAPTER 30

NOW when Rachel saw that she bore Jacob no children,
[1]she became jealous of her sister; and she said to Jacob, "[a]Give
me children, or else I die."
2 Then Jacob's anger burned against Rachel, and he said,
"Am I in the place of God, who has [a]withheld from you the
fruit of the womb?"

18 [a]Gen. 24:67 [b]Hos. 12:12

21 [1]Lit., *days*

25 [a]Gen. 12:18; 20:9; 26:10 [b]1 Sam. 28:12

26 [1]Lit., *done thus in* [2]Lit., *give*

27 [a]Judg. 14:12 [b]Gen. 31:41

30 [1]Lit., *him* [a]Gen. 29:17, 18

31 [1]Lit., *hated*

32 [1]I.e., See, a son [2]Lit., *looked upon* [a]Gen. 16:11; 31:42

33 [1]Heb., *shama*, related to Simeon [2]Lit., *hated* [a]Deut. 21:15

34 [1]Heb., *lavah*, related to Levi [a]Gen. 49:5

35 [1]From Heb., *Jadah*, related to Judah [2]Heb., *Jehudah* [a]Gen. 49:8; Matt. 1:2

1 [1]Lit., *Rachel* [a]1 Sam. 1:5, 6

2 [a]Gen. 20:18; 29:31

3 And she said, "[a]Here is my maid Bilhah, go in to her,
that she may bear on my knees, that [1]through her I too may
have children."
4 So [a]she gave him her maid Bilhah as a wife, and Jacob
went in to her.
5 And Bilhah conceived and bore a son.
6 Then Rachel said, "God has [1]vindicated me, and has
indeed heard my voice and has given me a son." Therefore she
named him [2]Dan.
7 And Rachel's maid Bilhah conceived again and bore
Jacob a second son.
8 So Rachel said, "With [1]mighty wrestlings I have
[2]wrestled with my sister, *and* I have indeed prevailed." And she
named him Naphtali.
9 When Leah saw that she had stopped bearing, she took
her maid Zilpah and gave her to Jacob as a wife.
10 And Leah's maid Zilpah bore Jacob a son.
11 Then Leah said, "[1]How fortunate!" So she named him
[2]Gad.
12 And Leah's maid Zilpah bore Jacob a second son.
13 Then Leah said, "[1]Happy am I! For women will call
me happy." So she named him [2]Asher.
14 Now in the days of wheat harvest Reuben went and
found [a]mandrakes in the field, and brought them to his mother Leah. Then Rachel said to Leah, "Please give me some of
your son's mandrakes."
15 But she said to her, "Is it a small matter for you to take
my husband? And would you take my son's mandrakes also?"
So Rachel said, "Therefore he may lie with you tonight in
return for your son's mandrakes."
16 When Jacob came in from the field in the evening,
then Leah went out to meet him and said, "You must come in
to me, for I have surely hired you with my son's mandrakes."
So he lay with her that night.
17 And God gave heed to Leah, and she conceived and
bore Jacob a fifth son.
18 Then Leah said, "God has given me my [1]wages, because I gave my maid to my husband." So she named him
Issachar.
19 And Leah conceived again and bore a sixth son to
Jacob.
20 Then Leah said, "God has endowed me with a good
gift; now my husband [1]will dwell with me, because I have
borne him six sons." So she named him Zebulun.
21 And afterward she bore a daughter and named her
Dinah.
22 Then [a]God remembered Rachel, and God gave heed
to her and opened her womb.
23 So she conceived and bore a son and said, "God has
taken away my reproach."
24 And she named him Joseph, saying, "[a]May the LORD
[1]give me another son."
25 Now it came about when Rachel had borne Joseph,
that Jacob said to Laban, "[a]Send me away, that I may go to my
own place and to my own country.

3 [1]Lit., *from her I too may be built* [a]Gen. 16:2
4 [a]Gen. 16:3, 4
6 [1]Lit., *judged* [2]I.e., He judged
8 [1]Lit., *wrestlings of God* [2]From Heb., *niphtal*, related to Naphtali
11 [1]Lit., *"With fortune!"* Some versions read, *Fortune has come* [2]I.e., Fortune
13 [1]Lit., *"With my happiness!"* [2]I.e., Happy
14 [a]Song of Sol. 7:13
18 [1]Heb., *sachar*, related to Issachar
20 [1]Heb., *zabal*, related to Zebulun. Some translate *will honor*
22 [a]1 Sam. 1:19, 20
24 [1]Lit., *add to me;* Heb., *Joseph* [a]Gen. 35:17
25 [a]Gen. 24:54, 56

26 "Give *me* my wives and my children [a]for whom I have
served you, and let me depart; for you yourself know my service which I have [1]rendered you."
27 But Laban said to him, "If now [1]it pleases you, *stay*
with me; I have divined [a]that the LORD has blessed me on your
account."
28 And he [1]continued, "[a]Name me your wages, and I will
give it."
29 But he said to him, "You yourself know how I have
served you and how your cattle have [1]fared with me.
30 "For you had little before [1]I came, and it has [2]increased
to a multitude; and the LORD has blessed you [3]wherever I
turned. But now, when shall I provide for my own household
also?"
31 So he said, "What shall I give you?" And Jacob said,
"You shall not give me anything. If you will do this *one* thing
for me, I will again pasture *and* keep your flock:
32 let me pass through your entire flock today, removing
from there every [a]speckled and spotted sheep, and every black
one among the lambs, and the spotted and speckled among
the goats; and *such* shall be my wages.
33 "So my [1]honesty will answer for me later, when you
come concerning my [2]wages. Every one that is not speckled
and spotted among the goats and black among the lambs, *if*
found with me, will be considered stolen."
34 And Laban said, "[1]Good, let it be according to your
word."
35 So he removed on that day the striped and spotted
male goats and all the speckled and spotted female goats,
every one with white in it, and all the black ones among the
sheep, and gave them into the [1]care of his sons.
36 And he put *a distance of* three days' journey between
himself and Jacob, and Jacob fed the rest of Laban's flocks.
37 Then Jacob [1]took fresh rods of poplar and almond and
plane trees, and peeled white stripes in them, exposing the
white which *was* [2]in the rods.
38 And he set the rods which he had peeled in front of the
flocks in the gutters, *even* in the watering troughs, where the
flocks came to drink; and they [1]mated when they came to
drink.
39 So the flocks [1]mated by the rods, and the flocks
brought forth striped, speckled, and spotted.
40 And Jacob separated the lambs, and [1]made the flocks
face toward the striped and all the black in the flock of Laban;
and he put his own herds apart, and did not put them with
Laban's flock.
41 Moreover, it came about whenever the [1]stronger of the
flock [2]were mating, that Jacob would place the rods in the
sight of the flock in the gutters, so that they might [3]mate by
the rods;
42 but when the flock was feeble, he did not put *them* in;
so the feebler were Laban's and the [1]stronger Jacob's.
43 So [a]the man [1]became exceedingly prosperous, and had
large flocks and female and male servants and camels and
donkeys.

26 [1]Lit., *served* [a]Gen. 29:18, 27; Hos. 12:12

27 [1]Lit., *I have found favor in your eyes* [a]Gen. 39:5

28 [1]Lit., *said* [a]Gen. 29:15; 31:7, 41

29 [1]Lit., *been*

30 [1]Lit., *me* [2]Lit., *broken forth* [3]Lit., *at my foot*

32 [a]Gen. 31:8

33 [1]Lit., *righteousness* [2]Lit., *wages which are before you*

34 [1]Lit., *Behold, would that it might be*

35 [1]Lit., *hand*

37 [1]Lit., *took to himself* [2]Lit., *on*

38 [1]Or, *conceived*

39 [1]Or, *conceived*

40 [1]Lit., *set the faces of*

41 [1]Lit., *bound ones;* i.e., firm and compact [2]Or, *conceived* [3]Or, *conceive*

42 [1]Lit., *bound ones;* i.e., firm and compact

43 [1]Lit., *broke forth* [a]Gen. 12:16; 13:2; 24:35; 26:13, 14

Chapter 31

NOW [1]Jacob heard the words of Laban's sons, saying, "Jacob has taken away all that was our father's, and from what
belonged to our father he has made all this [2]wealth."
2 And Jacob saw the [1]attitude of Laban, and behold, it
was not *friendly* toward him as formerly.
3 Then the LORD said to Jacob, "Return to the land of
your fathers and to your relatives, and [a]I will be with you."
4 So Jacob sent and called Rachel and Leah to his flock
in the field,
5 and said to them, "I see your father's [1]attitude, that it is
not *friendly* toward me as formerly, but [a]the God of my father
has been with me.
6 "And you know that I have served your father with all
my strength.
7 "Yet your father has [a]cheated me and [b]changed my
wages ten times; however, [c]God did not allow him to hurt me.
8 "If he spoke thus, 'The speckled shall be your wages,'
then all the flock brought forth speckled; and if he spoke thus,
'The striped shall be your wages,' then all the flock brought
forth striped.
9 "Thus God has taken away your father's livestock and
given *them* to me.
10 "And it came about at the time when the flock were
[1]mating that I lifted up my eyes and saw in a dream, and
behold, the male goats which were [2]mating *were* striped,
speckled and mottled.
11 "Then [a]the angel of God said to me in the dream, 'Jacob,' and I said, 'Here I am.'
12 "And he said, 'Lift up, now, your eyes and see *that* all
the male goats which are [1]mating are striped, speckled, and
mottled; for I have seen all that Laban has been doing to you.
13 'I am [a]the God *of* Bethel, where you [b]anointed a pillar,
where you made a vow to Me; now arise, [1]leave this land, and
[c]return to the land of your birth.' "
14 And Rachel and Leah answered and said to him, "Do
we still have any portion or inheritance in our father's house?
15 "Are we not reckoned by him as foreigners? For [a]he has
sold us, and has also [1]entirely consumed [2]our purchase price.
16 "Surely all the wealth which God has taken away from
our father belongs to us and our children; now then, do whatever
God has said to you."
17 Then Jacob arose and put his children and his wives
upon camels;
18 and he drove away all his livestock and all his property
which he had gathered, his acquired livestock which he had
gathered in Paddan-aram, [a]to go to the land of Canaan to his
father Isaac.
19 When Laban had gone to shear his flock, then Rachel
stole the [1a]household idols that were her father's.
20 And Jacob [1]deceived Laban the Syrian, by not telling
him that he was fleeing.
21 So he fled with all that he had; and he arose and
crossed the *Euphrates* River, and set his face toward the hill
country of [a]Gilead.

1 [1]Lit., *he* [2]Lit., *glory*

2 [1]Lit., *face*

3 [a]Gen. 28:15

5 [1]Lit., *face*
[a]Gen. 31:29, 42, 53; 28:13, 15

7 [a]Gen. 29:25 [b]Gen. 31:41
[c]Gen. 31:29

10 [1]Or, *conceiving* [2]Lit., *leaping upon the flock*

11 [a]Gen. 31:13; 16:7-11; 22:11, 15

12 [1]Lit., *leaping upon the flock*

13 [1]Lit., *go out from*
[a]Gen. 28:13 [b]Gen. 28:18, 20
[c]Gen. 28:15

15 [1]I.e., enjoyed the benefit of [2]Lit., *our money*
[a]Gen. 29:20, 23, 27

18 [a]Gen. 35:27-29

19 [1]Heb., *teraphim*
[a]Gen. 31:30, 34; Judg. 17:5; 1 Sam. 19:13; Hos. 3:4

20 [1]Lit., *stole the heart of Laban the Aramean*

21 [a]Gen. 37:25

22 When it was told Laban on the third day that Jacob
had fled,
23 then he took his [1]kinsmen with him, and pursued him *a*
distance of seven days' journey; and he overtook him in the
hill country of Gilead.
24 And [a]God came to Laban the [1]Syrian in a [b]dream of
the night, and said to him, "[2c]Be careful that you do not speak
to Jacob either good or bad."
25 And Laban caught up with Jacob. Now Jacob had
pitched his tent in the hill country, and Laban with his [1]kins-
men camped in the hill country of Gilead.
26 Then Laban said to Jacob, "What have you done [1]by
deceiving me and carrying away my daughters like captives of
the sword?
27 "Why did you flee secretly and [1]deceive me, and did not
tell me, so that I might have sent you away with joy and with
songs, with [a]timbrel and with [b]lyre;
28 and did not allow me [a]to kiss my sons and my daughters? Now you have done foolishly.
29 "It is in [1]my power to do you harm, but [a]the God of
your father spoke to me last night, saying, '[2b]Be careful not to
speak either good or bad to Jacob.'
30 "And now you have indeed gone away because you
longed greatly for your father's house; *but* why did you steal
[a]my gods?"
31 Then Jacob answered and said to Laban, "Because I
was afraid, for I said, 'Lest you would take your daughters
from me by force.'
32 "[a]The one with whom you find your gods shall not live;
in the presence of our [1]kinsmen [2]point out what is yours
[3]among my belongings and take *it* for yourself." For Jacob did
not know that Rachel had stolen them.
33 So Laban went into Jacob's tent, and into Leah's tent,
and into the tent of the two maids, but he did not find *them.*
Then he went out of Leah's tent and entered Rachel's tent.
34 Now Rachel had taken the [1]household idols and put
them in the camel's saddle, and she sat on them. And Laban
felt through all the tent, but did not find *them.*
35 And she said to her father, "Let not my lord be angry
that I cannot rise before you, for the manner of women is
upon me." So he searched, but did not find the [1]household
idols.
36 Then Jacob became angry and contended with Laban;
and Jacob answered and said to Laban, "What is my transgression? What is my sin, that you have hotly pursued me?
37 "Though you have felt through all my goods, what have
you found of all your household goods? Set *it* here before my
[1]kinsmen and your [1]kinsmen, that they may decide between us
two.
38 "These twenty years I *have been* with you; your ewes
and your female goats have not miscarried, nor have I eaten
the rams of your flocks.
39 "That which was torn *of beasts* I did not bring to you; I
bore the loss of it myself. You required it of my hand *whether*
stolen by day or stolen by night.

23 [1]Lit., *brothers*

24 [1]Lit., *Aramean* [2]Lit., *Take heed to yourself* [a]Gen. 31:29 [b]Gen. 31:11; 20:3, 6 [c]Gen. 31:7, 29

25 [1]Lit., *brothers*

26 [1]Lit., *and have stolen my heart*

27 [1]Lit., *steal me* [a]Ex. 15:20 [b]Gen. 4:21

28 [a]Gen. 31:55

29 [1]Lit., *the power of my hand* [2]Lit., *Take heed to yourself* [a]Gen. 31:5, 42, 53 [b]Gen. 31:24

30 [a]Gen. 31:19

32 [1]Lit., *brothers* [2]Lit. *recognize* [3]Lit., *with me* [a]Gen. 44:9

34 [1]Heb., *teraphim*

35 [1]Heb., *teraphim*

37 [1]Lit., *brothers*

40 "*Thus* I was: by day the [1]heat consumed me, and the
frost by night, and my sleep fled from my eyes.
41 "These twenty years I have been in your house; [a]I served
you fourteen years for your two daughters, and six years for
your flock, and you [b]changed my wages ten times.
42 "If [a]the God of my father, the God of Abraham, and the
fear of Isaac, had not been for me, surely now you would have
sent me away empty-handed. [b]God has seen my affliction and
the toil of my hands, so He [c]rendered judgment last night."
43 Then Laban answered and said to Jacob, "The daughters are my daughters, and the children are my children, and
[a]the flocks are my flocks, and all that you see is mine. But what
can I do this day to these my daughters or to their children
whom they have borne?
44 "So now come, let us [a]make a covenant, [1]you and I, and
let it be a witness between [2]you and me."
45 Then Jacob took [a]a stone and set it up *as* a pillar.
46 And Jacob said to his [1]kinsmen, "Gather stones." So
they took stones and made a heap, and they ate there by the
heap.
47 Now Laban [a]called it [1]Jegar-sahadutha, but Jacob
called it [2]Galeed.
48 And Laban said, "This heap is a witness between [1]you
and me this day." Therefore it was named Galeed;
49 and [1a]Mizpah, for he said, "May the LORD watch between [2]you and me when we are [3]absent one from the other.
50 "If you mistreat my daughters, or if you take wives besides my daughters, *although* no man is with us, see, [a]God is
witness between [1]you and me."
51 And Laban said to Jacob, "Behold this heap and behold the pillar which I have set between [1]you and me.
52 "This heap is a witness, and the pillar is a witness, that I
will not pass by this heap to you for harm, and you will not
pass by this heap and this pillar to me, for harm.
53 "[a]The God of Abraham and the God of Nahor, the God
of their father, judge between us." So Jacob swore by [b]the fear
of his father Isaac.
54 [a]Then Jacob offered a sacrifice on the mountain, and
called his [1]kinsmen to [2]the meal; and they ate [3]the meal and
spent the night on the mountain.
55 [1]And early in the morning Laban arose, and [a]kissed his
sons and his daughters and blessed them. Then Laban departed and returned to his place.

CHAPTER 32

NOW as Jacob went on his way, [a]the angels of God met him.
2 And Jacob said when he saw them, "This is God's
[1]camp." So he named that place [2a]Mahanaim.
3 Then Jacob [a]sent messengers before him to his brother
Esau in the land of [b]Seir, the [1]country of [c]Edom.
4 He also commanded them saying, "Thus you shall say
to my lord Esau: 'Thus says your servant Jacob, "I have sojourned with Laban, and [a]stayed until now;
5 and [a]I have oxen and donkeys *and* flocks and male

---

40 [1]Or, *drought*

41 [a]Gen. 29:27, 30 [b]Gen. 31:7

42 [a]Gen. 31:5, 29, 53 [b]Gen. 29:32 [c]Gen. 31:24, 29

43 [a]Gen. 31:1

44 [1]Lit., *I and you* [2]Lit., *me and you* [a]Gen. 21:27, 32

45 [a]Gen. 28:18; Josh. 24:26, 27

46 [1]Lit., *brothers*

47 [1]I.e., The heap of witness, in Aramaic [2]I.e., The heap of witness, in Hebrew [a]Josh. 22:34

48 [1]Lit., *me and you*

49 [1]Lit., *The Mizpah*, i.e., The watchtower [2]Lit., *me and you* [3]Lit., *hidden* [a]Judg. 11:29

50 [1]Lit., *me and you* [a]Jer. 29:23; 42:5

51 [1]Lit., *me and you*

53 [a]Gen. 28:13 [b]Gen. 31:42

54 [1]Lit., *brothers* [2]Lit., *eat bread* [3]Lit., *bread* [a]Ex. 18:12

55 [1]Chap. 32:1 in Hebrew [a]Gen. 31:28, 43

1 [a]2 Kin. 6:16, 17; Ps. 34:7

2 [1]Or, *company* [2]I.e., Two Camps, or, Two Companies [a]Josh. 21:38; 2 Sam. 2:8

3 [1]Lit., *field* [a]Gen. 32:7, 11; Gen. 27:41, 42 [b]Gen. 14:6 [c]Gen. 25:30; 36:8, 9

4 [a]Gen. 31:41

5 [a]Gen. 30:43

and female servants; and I have sent to tell my lord, that I may
find favor in your sight." ' "
6 And the messengers returned to Jacob, saying, "We
came to your brother Esau, and furthermore he is coming to
meet you, and four hundred men are with him."
7 Then Jacob was [a]greatly afraid and distressed; and he
divided the people who were with him, and the flocks and the
herds and the camels, into two companies;
8 for he said, "If Esau comes to the one company and
[1]attacks it, then the company which is left will escape."
9 And Jacob said, "O [a]God of my father Abraham and
God of my father Isaac, O LORD, who didst say to me, '[b]Re-
turn to your country and to your relatives, and I will [1]prosper
you,'
10 [1]I am unworthy [a]of all the lovingkindness and of all the
[2]faithfulness which Thou hast shown to Thy servant; for with
my staff *only* I crossed this Jordan, and now I have become
two companies.
11 "Deliver me, I pray, [a]from the hand of my brother, from
the hand of Esau; for I fear him, lest he come and [1]attack me,
mother with children.
12 "For Thou didst say, '[a]I will surely [1]prosper you, and
[b]make your [2]descendants as the sand of the sea, which cannot
be numbered for multitude.' "
13 So he spent the night there. Then he [1]selected from
what [2]he had with him a present for his brother Esau:
14 two hundred female goats and twenty male goats, two
hundred ewes and twenty rams,
15 thirty milking camels and their colts, forty cows and ten
bulls, twenty female donkeys and ten male donkeys.
16 And he delivered *them* into the hand of his servants,
every drove by itself, and said to his servants, "Pass on before
me, and put a space between droves."
17 And he commanded the [1]one in front, saying, "When
my brother Esau meets you and asks you, saying, 'To whom do
you belong, and where are you going, and to whom do these
animals in front of you belong?'
18 then you shall say, '*These* belong to your servant Jacob;
it is a present sent to my lord Esau. And behold, he also is
behind us.' "
19 Then he commanded also the second and the third,
and all those who followed the droves, saying, "After this manner you shall speak to Esau when you find him;
20 and you shall say, 'Behold, your servant Jacob also is
behind us.' " For he said, "I will appease him with the present
that goes before me. Then afterward I will see his face; perhaps he will accept me."
21 So the present passed on before him, while he himself
spent that night in the camp.
22 Now he arose that same night and took his two wives
and his two maids and his eleven children, and crossed the ford
of the [a]Jabbok.
23 And he took them and sent them across the stream.
And he sent across whatever he had.
24 Then Jacob was left alone, and a man [a]wrestled with
him until daybreak.

7 [a]Gen. 32:11

8 [1]Lit., *smites*

9 [1]Lit., *do good with you* [a]Gen. 31:42 [b]Gen. 28:15; 31:13

10 [1]Lit., *I am less than all* [2]Or, *truth* [a]Gen. 24:27

11 [1]Lit., *smite* [a]Gen. 27:41, 42; 33:4

12 [1]Lit., *do good with* [2]Lit., *seed* [a]Gen. 28:14 [b]Gen. 22:17

13 [1]Lit., *took* [2]Lit., *had come to his hand*

17 [1]Lit., *first*

22 [a]Deut. 3:16; Josh. 12:2

24 [a]Hos. 12:3, 4

25 And when he saw that he had not prevailed against him, he touched the socket of his thigh; so the socket of Jacob's thigh was dislocated while he wrestled with him.

26 Then he said, "Let me go, for the dawn is breaking." But he said, "I will not let you go unless you bless me."

27 So he said to him, "What is your name?" And he said, "Jacob."

28 And [a]he said, "Your name shall no longer be Jacob, but [1]Israel; for you have striven with God and with me and have prevailed."

29 Then [a]Jacob asked him and said, "Please tell me your name." But he said, "Why is it that you ask my name?" And he blessed him there.

30 So Jacob named the place [1]Peniel, for *he said*, "[a]I have seen God face to face, yet my [2]life has been preserved."

31 Now the sun rose upon him just as he crossed over [a]Penuel, and he was limping on his thigh.

32 Therefore, to this day the sons of Israel do not eat the sinew of the hip which is on the socket of the thigh, because he touched the socket of Jacob's thigh in the sinew of the hip.

Chapter 33

THEN Jacob lifted his eyes and looked, and behold, [a]Esau was coming, and four hundred men with him. So he divided the children [1]among Leah and Rachel and the two maids.

2 And he put the maids and their children [1]in front, and Leah and her children [2]next, and Rachel and Joseph [2]last.

3 But he himself passed on ahead of them and bowed down to the ground seven times, until he came near to his brother.

4 Then Esau ran to meet him and embraced him, and [a]fell on his neck and kissed him, and they wept.

5 And he lifted his eyes and saw the women and the children, and said, "[1]Who are these with you?" So he said, "[a]The children whom God has graciously given your servant."

6 Then the maids came near [1]with their children, and they bowed down.

7 And Leah likewise came near with her children, and they bowed down; and afterward Joseph came near with Rachel, and they bowed down.

8 And he said, "What do you mean by [a]all this company which I have met?" And he said, "To find favor in the sight of my lord."

9 But Esau said, "[a]I have plenty, my brother; let what you have be your own."

10 And Jacob said, "No, please, if now I have found favor in your sight, then take my present from my hand, [1]for I see your face as one sees the face of God, and you have received me favorably.

11 "Please take my [1]gift which has been brought to you, [a]because God has dealt graciously with me, and because I have [2]plenty." Thus he urged him and he took *it*.

12 Then [1]Esau said, "Let us take our journey and go, and I will go before you."

13 But he said to him, "My lord knows that the children

28 [1]I.e., He who strives with God, or, God strives [a]Gen. 35:10; 1 Kin. 18:31

29 [a]Judg. 13:17, 18

30 [1]I.e., The face of God [2]Lit., *soul* [a]Gen. 16:13; Ex. 33:20; Num. 12:8; Judg. 6:22; 13:22

31 [a]Judg. 8:8

1 [1]Or, *to* [a]Gen. 32:6

2 [1]Lit., *first* [2]Lit., *behind*

4 [a]Gen. 45:14, 15

5 [1]Or, *"What relation are these to you?"* [a]Gen. 48:9

6 [1]Lit., *they and*

8 [a]Gen. 32:14-16

9 [a]Gen. 27:39, 40

10 [1]Lit., *for therefore I have seen your face like seeing God's face*

11 [1]Lit., *blessing* [2]Lit., *all* [a]Gen. 30:43

12 [1]Lit., *he*

are frail and that the flocks and herds which are nursing are [1]a
care to me. And if they are driven hard one day, all the flocks
will die.
14 "Please let my lord pass on before his servant; and I will
proceed at my leisure, according to the pace of the cattle that
are before me and according to the pace of the children, until I
come to my lord at [a]Seir."
15 And Esau said, "Please let me leave with you some of
the people who are with me." But he said, "[1]What need is
there? Let me find favor in the sight of my lord."
16 So Esau returned that day on his way to Seir.
17 And Jacob journeyed to [1a]Succoth; and built for himself a house, and made booths for his livestock, therefore the
place is named Succoth.
18 Now Jacob came safely to the city of [a]Shechem, which
is in the land of Canaan, when he came from [b]Paddan-aram,
and camped before the city.
19 And [a]he bought the piece of land where he had pitched
his tent, from the hand of the sons of Hamor, Shechem's
father, for one hundred [1]pieces of money.
20 Then he erected there an altar, and called it [1]El-Elohe-
Israel.

CHAPTER 34

NOW [a]Dinah the daughter of Leah, whom she had borne to
Jacob, went out to [1]visit the daughters of the land.
2 And when Shechem the son of Hamor [a]the Hivite, the
prince of the land, saw her, he took her and lay with her [1]by
force.
3 And [1]he was deeply attracted to Dinah the daughter of
Jacob, and he loved the girl and [2]spoke tenderly to her.
4 So Shechem spoke to his father Hamor, saying, "Get
me this young girl for a wife."
5 Now Jacob heard that he had defiled Dinah his daughter; but his sons were with his livestock in the field, so Jacob
kept silent until they came in.
6 Then Hamor the father of Shechem went out to Jacob
to speak with him.
7 Now the sons of Jacob came in from the field when
they heard *it;* and the men were grieved, and they were very
angry because he had done a [1a]disgraceful thing in Israel [2]by
lying with Jacob's daughter, for such a thing ought not to be
done.
8 But Hamor spoke with them, saying, "The soul of my
son Shechem longs for your daughter; please give her to him
[1]in marriage.
9 "And intermarry with us; give your daughters to us, and
take our daughters for yourselves.
10 "Thus you shall [1]live with us, and [a]the land shall be *open*
before you; [1]live and trade in it, and acquire property in it."
11 Shechem also said to her father and to her brothers, "If
I find favor in your sight, then I will give whatever you say to
me.
12 "Ask me ever so much bridal payment and gift, and I

13 [1]Lit., *upon me*
14 [a]Gen. 32:3
15 [1]Lit., *"Why this?"*
17 [1]I.e., Booths [a]Judg. 8:5, 14; Ps. 60:6
18 [a]Gen. 12:6; Josh. 24:1; Judg. 9:1 [b]Gen. 25:20; 28:2
19 [1]Heb., *qesitah* [a]Josh. 24:32; John 4:5
20 [1]I.e., God, the God of Israel
1 [1]Lit., *see* [a]Gen. 30:21
2 [1]Lit., *and humbled her* [a]Gen. 34:30
3 [1]Lit., *his soul clung* [2]Lit., *spoke to the heart of the girl*
7 [1]Lit., *senseless* [2]Lit., *to lie* [a]Deut. 22:21; Judg. 20:6; 2 Sam. 13:12
8 [1]Lit., *for a wife*
10 [1]Lit., *dwell* [a]Gen. 13:9; 20:15

will give according as you say to me; but give me the girl [1]in marriage."

13 But Jacob's sons answered Shechem and his father Hamor, with deceit, and spoke to them, because he had defiled Dinah their sister.

14 And they said to them, "We cannot do this thing, to give our sister to [a]one who is uncircumcised, for that would be a disgrace to us.

15 "Only on this *condition* will we consent to you: if you will become like us, in that every male of you be circumcised,

16 then we will give our daughters to you, and we will take your daughters for ourselves, and we will [1]live with you and become one people.

17 "But if you will not listen to us to be circumcised, then we will take our daughter and go."

18 Now their words seemed [1]reasonable to Hamor and Shechem, Hamor's son.

19 And the young man did not delay to do the thing, because he was delighted with Jacob's daughter. Now he was more respected than all the household of his father.

20 So Hamor and his son, Shechem, came to the gate of their city, and spoke to the men of their city, saying,

21 "These men are [1]friendly with us; therefore let them [2]live in the land and trade in it, for behold, the land is [3]large enough for them. Let us take their daughters [4]in marriage, and give our daughters to them.

22 "Only on this *condition* will the men consent to us to [1]live with us, to become one people: that every male among us be circumcised as they are circumcised.

23 "Will not their livestock and their property and all their animals be ours? Only let us consent to them, and they will [1]live with us."

24 And [a]all who went out of the gate of his city listened to Hamor and to his son Shechem, and every male was circumcised, all who went out of the gate of his city.

25 Now it came about on the third day, when they were in pain, that two of Jacob's sons, [a]Simeon and Levi, Dinah's brothers, each took his sword and came upon the city unawares, and killed every male.

26 And they killed Hamor and his son Shechem with the edge of the sword, and took Dinah from Shechem's house, and went forth.

27 Jacob's sons came upon the slain and looted the city, because they had defiled their sister.

28 They took their flocks and their herds and their donkeys, and that which was in the city and that which was in the field;

29 and they captured and looted all their wealth and all their little ones and their wives, even all that *was* in the houses.

30 Then Jacob said to Simeon and Levi, "You have brought trouble on me, [a]by making me odious among the inhabitants of the land, among [b]the Canaanites and the Perizzites; and [1c]my men being few in number, they will gather together against me and [2]attack me and I shall be destroyed, I and my household."

31 But they said, "Should he [1]treat our sister as a harlot?"

12 [1]Lit., *for a wife*

14 [a]Gen. 17:14

16 [1]Lit., *dwell*

18 [1]Lit., *good*

21 [1]Lit., *peaceful* [2]Lit., *dwell* [3]Lit., *wide of hands before them* [4]Lit., *to us for wives*

22 [1]Lit., *dwell*

23 [1]Lit., *dwell*

24 [a]Gen. 23:10

25 [a]Gen. 49:5-7

30 [1]Lit., *I, few in number* [2]Lit., *smite* [a]Ex. 5:21; 2 Sam. 10:6 [b]Gen. 34:2; Gen. 13:7 [c]Gen. 46:26, 27; 1 Chr. 16:19

31 [1]Or, *make*

CHAPTER 35

THEN God said to Jacob, "Arise, go up to [a]Bethel, and [1]live
there; and make an altar there to [b]God, who appeared to you
when you fled [2]from your brother Esau."
2 So Jacob said to his household and to all who were with
him, "Put away [a]the foreign gods which are among you, and
[b]purify yourselves, and change your garments;
3 and let us arise and go up to Bethel; and I will make [a]an
altar there to God, who answered me in the day of my distress,
and [b]has been with me [1]wherever I have gone."
4 So they gave to Jacob all the foreign gods which [1]they
had, and the rings which were in their ears; and Jacob hid them
under the [2]oak which was near Shechem.
5 As they journeyed, there was [1a]a great terror upon the
cities which were around them, and they did not pursue the
sons of Jacob.
6 So Jacob came to [a]Luz (that is, Bethel), which is in the
land of Canaan, he and all the people who were with him.
7 And [a]he built an altar there, and called the place [1]El-
bethel, because there God had revealed Himself to him, when
he fled [2]from his brother.
8 Now [a]Deborah, Rebekah's nurse, died, and she was
buried below Bethel under the oak; it was named [1]Allon-
bacuth.
9 Then God appeared to Jacob again when he came
from Paddan-aram, and He [a]blessed him.
10 And [a]God said to him,
"Your name is Jacob;
[1]You shall no longer be called Jacob,
But Israel shall be your name."
Thus He called [2]him Israel.
11 God also said to him,
"I am [1a]God Almighty;
[b]Be fruitful and multiply;
A nation and a [c]company of nations shall [2]come
from you,
And [d]kings shall [2]come forth from [3]you.
12 "And [a]the land which I gave to Abraham and Isaac,
I will give it to you,
And I will give the land to your [1]descendants after
you."
13 Then [a]God went up from him in the place where He
had spoken with him.
14 And Jacob set up [a]a pillar in the place where He had
spoken with him, a pillar of stone, and he poured out a [1]liba-
tion on it; he also poured oil on it.
15 So Jacob named the place where God had spoken with
him, [1]Bethel.
16 Then they journeyed from Bethel; and when there was
still some distance to go to [a]Ephrath, Rachel began to give
birth and she [1]suffered severe labor.
17 And it came about when she was in severe labor that
the midwife said to her, "Do not fear, for now [a]you have
another son."
18 And it came about as her soul was departing (for she

1 [1]Lit., *dwell* [2]Lit., *from the face of* [a]Gen. 28:19 [b]Gen. 28:13

2 [a]Gen. 31:19, 30 [b]Ex. 19:10, 14

3 [1]Lit., *in the way which* [a]Gen. 28:20-22 [b]Gen. 28:15

4 [1]Lit., *in their hand* [2]Or, *terebinth*

5 [1]Or, *a terror of God* [a]Ex. 15:16; Deut. 2:25

6 [a]Gen. 28:19; 48:3

7 [1]I.e., the God of Bethel [2]Lit., *from the face of* [a]Gen. 35:3

8 [1]I.e., Oak of weeping [a]Gen. 24:59

9 [a]Gen. 32:29

10 [1]Lit., *Your name* [2]Lit., *his name* [a]Gen. 32:28

11 [1]Heb., *El Shaddai* [2]Or, *come into being* [3]Lit., *your loins* [a]Gen. 17:1; 28:3 [b]Gen. 9:1, 7 [c]Gen. 48:4 [d]Gen. 17:6, 16; 36:31

12 [1]Lit., *seed* [a]Gen. 13:15; 26:3; 28:13

13 [a]Gen. 17:22; 18:33

14 [1]Or, *drink offering* [a]Gen. 28:18, 19; 31:45

15 [1]I.e., the house of God

16 [1]Lit., *had difficulty in her giving birth* [a]Gen. 35:19; Ruth 4:11; Mic. 5:2

17 [a]Gen. 30:24

died), that she named him [1]Ben-oni; but his father called him
[2]Benjamin.
19 So [a]Rachel died and was buried on the way to Ephrath
(that is, Bethlehem).
20 And Jacob set up a pillar over her grave; that is the
[a]pillar of Rachel's grave to this day.
21 Then Israel journeyed on and pitched his tent beyond
the [1]tower of [2]Eder.
22 And it came about while Israel was dwelling in that
land, that [a]Reuben went and lay with Bilhah his father's concubine; and Israel heard *of it.*
Now there were twelve sons of Jacob—
23 [a]the sons of Leah: Reuben, Jacob's first-born, then Simeon and Levi and Judah and Issachar and Zebulun;
24 [a]the sons of Rachel: Joseph and Benjamin;
25 and [a]the sons of Bilhah, Rachel's maid: Dan and
Naphtali;
26 and [a]the sons of Zilpah, Leah's maid: Gad and Asher.
These are the sons of Jacob who were born to him in Paddan-
aram.
27 And Jacob came to his father Isaac at [a]Mamre of
Kiriath-arba (that is, Hebron), where Abraham and Isaac had
sojourned.
28 Now the days of Isaac were [a]one hundred and eighty
years.
29 And Isaac breathed his last and died, and was [a]gathered
to his people, an [b]old man [1]of ripe age; and his sons Esau and
Jacob buried him.

CHAPTER 36

NOW these are *the records of* the generations of [a]Esau (that
is, Edom).
2 Esau took [a]his wives from the daughters of Canaan:
Adah the daughter of Elon the Hittite, and Oholibamah the
daughter of Anah, the [b]granddaughter of Zibeon the Hivite;
3 also Basemath, Ishmael's daughter, the sister of
Nebaioth.
4 And Adah bore Eliphaz to Esau, and Basemath bore
Reuel,
5 and Oholibamah bore Jeush and Jalam and Korah.
These are the sons of Esau who were born to him in the land
of Canaan.
6 [a]Then Esau took his wives and his sons and his daughters and all [1]his household, and his livestock and all his cattle
and all his goods which he had acquired in the land of Canaan,
and went to *another* land away from his brother Jacob.
7 [a]For their property had become too great for them to
[1]live together, and the land where they sojourned could not
sustain them because of their livestock.
8 So Esau lived in the hill country of [a]Seir; Esau is
[b]Edom.
9 These then are *the records of* the generations of Esau
the father of [1]the Edomites in the hill country of Seir.
10 These are the names of Esau's sons: Eliphaz the son of
Esau's wife Adah, Reuel the son of Esau's wife Basemath.

18 [1]I.e., the son of my sorrow [2]I.e., the son of the right hand

19 [a]Gen. 48:7

20 [a]1 Sam. 10:2

21 [1]Heb., *Migdal-eder* [2]Or, *flock*

22 [a]Gen. 49:4; 1 Chr. 5:1

23 [a]Gen. 29:31-35; 30:18-20

24 [a]Gen. 30:22-24; 35:18

25 [a]Gen. 30:5-8

26 [a]Gen. 30:10-13

27 [a]Gen. 18:1; 23:19

28 [a]Gen. 25:26

29 [1]Lit., *and satisfied with days* [a]Gen. 25:8 [b]Gen. 15:15

1 [a]Gen. 25:30

2 [a]Gen. 26:34; 28:9 [b]Gen. 36:24

6 [1]Lit., *the souls of his house* [a]Gen. 12:5

7 [1]Lit., *dwell* [a]Gen. 13:6

8 [a]Gen. 32:3 [b]Gen. 36:1, 19

9 [1]Lit., *Edom*

11 And the sons of Eliphaz were Teman, Omar, [1]Zepho
and Gatam and Kenaz.
12 And Timna was a concubine of Esau's son Eliphaz and
she bore Amalek to Eliphaz. These are the sons of Esau's wife
Adah.
13 And these are the sons of Reuel: Nahath and Zerah,
Shammah and Mizzah. These were the sons of Esau's wife
Basemath.
14 And these were the sons of Esau's wife Oholibamah,
the daughter of Anah, the daughter of Zibeon: [1]she bore to
Esau, Jeush and Jalam and Korah.
15 These are the chiefs of the sons of Esau. The sons of
Eliphaz, the first-born of Esau, are chief Teman, chief Omar,
chief Zepho, chief Kenaz,
16 chief Korah, chief Gatam, chief Amalek. These are the
chiefs [1]descended from Eliphaz in the land of Edom; these are
the sons of Adah.
17 And these are the sons of Reuel, Esau's son: chief Nahath, chief Zerah, chief Shammah, chief Mizzah. These are
the chiefs [1]descended from Reuel in the land of Edom; these
are the sons of Esau's wife Basemath.
18 And these are the sons of Esau's wife Oholibamah:
chief Jeush, chief Jalam, chief Korah. These are the chiefs
[1]descended from Esau's wife Oholibamah, the daughter of
Anah.
19 These are the sons of Esau (that is, Edom), and these
are their chiefs.
20 These are the sons of Seir [a]the Horite, the inhabitants
of the land: Lotan and Shobal and Zibeon and Anah,
21 and Dishon and Ezer and Dishan. These are the chiefs
[1]descended from the Horites, the sons of Seir in the land of
Edom.
22 And the sons of Lotan were Hori and [1]Hemam; and
Lotan's sister was Timna.
23 And these are the sons of Shobal: [1]Alvan and Manahath and Ebal, [2]Shepho and Onam.
24 And these are the sons of Zibeon: Aiah and Anah—he
is the Anah who found the hot springs in the wilderness when
he was pasturing the donkeys of his father Zibeon.
25 And these are the children of Anah: Dishon, and Oholibamah, the daughter of Anah.
26 And these are the sons of [1]Dishon: [2]Hemdan and Eshban and Ithran and Cheran.
27 These are the sons of Ezer: Bilhan and Zaavan and
[1]Akan.
28 These are the sons of Dishan: Uz and Aran.
29 These are the chiefs [1]descended from the Horites:
chief Lotan, chief Shobal, chief Zibeon, chief Anah,
30 chief Dishon, chief Ezer, chief Dishan. These are the
chiefs [1]descended from the Horites, according to their *various*
chiefs in the land of Seir.
31 Now these are the kings who reigned in the land of
Edom before any [a]king reigned over the sons of Israel.
32 [1]Bela the son of Beor reigned in Edom, and the name
of his city was Dinhabah.

11 [1]In 1 Chr. 1:36, *Zephi*

14 [1]Lit., *and she*

16 [1]Lit., *of Eliphaz*

17 [1]Lit., *of Reuel*

18 [1]Lit., *of Oholibamah, Esau's wife*

20 [a]Gen. 14:6; Deut. 2:12, 22; 1 Chr. 1:38-42

21 [1]Lit., *of the Horites*

22 [1]In 1 Chr. 1:39, *Homam*

23 [1]In 1 Chr. 1:40, *Alian* [2]In 1 Chr. 1:40, *Shephi*

26 [1]Heb., *Dishan*, but cf. 1 Chr. 1:41 [2]In 1 Chr. 1:41, *Hamran*

27 [1]In 1 Chr. 1:42, *Jaakan*

29 [1]Lit., *of the Horites*

30 [1]Lit., *of the Horites*

31 [a]Gen. 17:6, 16; 35:11; 1 Chr. 1:43

32 [1]Lit., *And Bela*

33 Then Bela died, and Jobab the son of Zerah of Bozrah
became king in his place.
34 Then Jobab died, and Husham of the land of the Te-
manites became king in his place.
35 Then Husham died, and Hadad the son of Bedad, who
[1]defeated Midian in the field of Moab, became king in his
place; and the name of his city was Avith.
36 Then Hadad died, and Samlah of Masrekah became
king in his place.
37 Then Samlah died, and Shaul of Rehoboth on the
Euphrates River became king in his place.
38 Then Shaul died, and Baalhanan the son of Achbor
became king in his place.
39 Then Baalhanan the son of Achbor died, and [1]Hadar
became king in his place; and the name of his city was [2]Pau;
and his wife's name was Mehetabel, the daughter of Matred,
daughter of Me-zahab.
40 Now these are the names of the chiefs [1]descended from
Esau, according to their families *and* their localities, by their
names: chief Timna, chief [2]Alvah, chief Jetheth,
41 chief Oholibamah, chief Elah, chief Pinon,
42 chief Kenaz, chief Teman, chief Mibzar,
43 chief Magdiel, chief Iram. These are the chiefs of
Edom (that is, Esau, the father of the [1]Edomites), according
to their habitations in the land of their possession.

Chapter 37

NOW Jacob lived in [a]the land [1]where his father had sojourned, in the land of Canaan.
2 These are *the records of* the generations of Jacob.
Joseph, when [a]seventeen years of age, was pasturing the
flock with his brothers while he was *still* a youth, along with
[b]the sons of Bilhah and the sons of Zilpah, his father's wives.
And Joseph brought back a bad report about them to their
father.
3 Now Israel loved Joseph more than all his sons, because he was [a]the son of his old age; and he made him a
[1b]varicolored tunic.
4 And his brothers saw that their father loved him more
than all his brothers; and *so* they hated him and could not
speak to him [1]on friendly terms.
5 Then Joseph [1a]had a dream, and when he told it to his
brothers, they hated him even more.
6 And he said to them, "Please listen to this dream which
I have [1]had;
7 for behold, we were binding sheaves in the field, and lo,
my sheaf rose up and also stood erect; and behold, your
sheaves gathered around and [a]bowed down to my sheaf."
8 Then his brothers said to him, "[a]Are you actually going
to reign over us? Or are you really going to rule over us?" So
they hated him even more for his dreams and for his words.
9 Now he [1]had still another dream, and related it to his
brothers, and said, "Lo, I have [1]had still another dream; and
behold, the sun and the moon and eleven stars were bowing
down to me."

35 [1]Or, *smote*

39 [1]In 1 Chr. 1:50, *Hadad* [2]In 1 Chr. 1:50, *Pai*

40 [1]Lit., *of Esau* [2]In 1 Chr. 1:51, *Aliah*

43 [1]Heb., *Edom*

1 [1]Lit., *of his father's sojournings* [a]Gen. 17:8; 28:4

2 [a]Gen. 41:46 [b]Gen. 35:25, 26

3 [1]Or, *full-length robe* [a]Gen. 44:20 [b]Gen. 37:23, 32

4 [1]Lit., *in peace*

5 [1]Lit., *dreamed* [a]Gen. 28:12; 31:10, 11, 24

6 [1]Lit., *dreamed*

7 [a]Gen. 42:6, 9; 43:26; 44:14

8 [a]Gen. 49:26; Deut. 33:16

9 [1]Lit., *dreamed*

10 And he related *it* to his father and to his brothers; and
his father rebuked him and said to him, "What is this dream
that you have [1]had? Shall I and your mother and [a]your brothers actually come to bow ourselves down before you to the
ground?"
11 And [a]his brothers were jealous of him, but his father
kept the saying *in mind*.
12 Then his brothers went to pasture their father's flock in
Shechem.
13 And Israel said to Joseph, "Are not your brothers pasturing *the flock* in [a]Shechem? Come, and I will send you to
them." And he said to him, "[1]I will go."
14 Then he said to him, "Go now and see about the welfare of your brothers and the welfare of the flock; and bring
word back to me." [a]So he sent him from the valley of Hebron,
and he came to Shechem.
15 And a man found him, and behold, he was wandering
in the field; and the man asked him, [1]"What are you looking
for?"
16 And he said, "I am looking for my brothers; please tell
me where they are pasturing *the flock*."
17 Then the man said, "They have moved from here; for I
heard *them* say, 'Let us go to [a]Dothan.'" So Joseph went after
his brothers and found them at Dothan.
18 [1]When they saw him from a distance and before he
came close to them, they plotted against him to put him to
death.
19 And they said to one another, "[1]Here comes this
dreamer!
20 "Now then, come and let us kill him and throw him into
one of the pits; and [a]we will say, 'A wild beast devoured him.'
Then let us see what will become of his dreams!"
21 But [a]Reuben heard *this* and rescued him out of their
hands and said, "Let us not [1]take his life."
22 Reuben further said to them, "Shed no blood. Throw
him into this pit that is in the wilderness, but do not lay hands
on him"—that he might rescue him out of their hands, to
restore him to his father.
23 So it came about, when Joseph [1]reached his brothers,
that they stripped Joseph of his [2]tunic, the varicolored tunic
that was on him;
24 and they took him and threw him into the pit. Now the
pit was empty, without any water in it.
25 Then they sat down to eat [1]a meal. And as they raised
their eyes and looked, behold, a caravan of [a]Ishmaelites was
coming from Gilead, with their camels bearing [2b]aromatic
gum and [3c]balm and [4]myrrh, [5]on their way to bring *them* down
to Egypt.
26 And Judah said to his brothers, "What profit is it for us
to kill our brother and [a]cover up his blood?
27 "[a]Come and let us sell him to the Ishmaelites and not
lay our hands on him; for he is our brother, our *own* flesh."
And his brothers listened *to him*.
28 Then some [a]Midianite traders passed by, so they pulled
him up and lifted Joseph out of the pit, and [b]sold [1]him to the

10 [1]Lit., *dreamed* [a]Gen. 27:29

11 [a]Acts 7:9

13 [1]Lit., *"Behold me."* [a]Gen. 33:18-20

14 [a]Gen. 35:27

15 [1]Lit., *saying, "What*

17 [a]2 Kin. 6:13

18 [1]Or, *And*

19 [1]Lit., *Behold, this master of dreams comes*

20 [a]Gen. 37:32

21 [1]Lit., *smite his soul* [a]Gen. 42:22

23 [1]Lit., *came to* [2]Or, *full-length robe*

25 [1]Lit., *bread* [2]Or, *ladanum spice* [3]Or, *mastic* [4]Or, *resinous bark* [5]Lit., *going* [a]Gen. 37:28; 16:12; 39:1 [b]Gen. 43:11 [c]Jer. 8:22; 46:11

26 [a]Gen. 37:20

27 [a]Gen. 42:21

28 [1]Lit., *Joseph* [a]Gen. 37:25; Judg. 6:1; 8:22, 24 [b]Gen. 45:4; Acts 7:9

Ishmaelites for twenty *shekels* of silver. Thus [c]they brought
Joseph into Egypt.
29 Now Reuben returned to the pit, and behold, Joseph
was not in the pit; so he [a]tore his garments.
30 And he returned to his brothers and said, "[a]The boy is
not *there;* as for me, where am I to go?"
31 So [a]they took Joseph's tunic, and slaughtered a male
goat, and dipped the tunic in the blood;
32 and they sent the varicolored tunic and brought it to
their father and said, "We found this; please [1]examine *it* to *see*
whether it is your son's tunic or not."
33 Then he [1]examined it and said, "It is my son's tunic. [a]A
wild beast has devoured him; Joseph has surely been torn to
pieces!"
34 So Jacob [a]tore his clothes, and put sackcloth on his
loins, and mourned for his son many days.
35 Then all his sons and all his daughters arose to comfort
him, but he refused to be comforted. And he said, "Surely I
will go down to [a]Sheol in mourning for my son." So his father
wept for him.
36 Meanwhile, the [1]Midianites [a]sold him in Egypt to Potiphar, Pharaoh's officer, the captain of the bodyguard.

Chapter 38

AND it came about at that time, that Judah [1]departed from
his brothers, and [2]visited a certain [a]Adullamite, whose name
was Hirah.
2 And Judah saw there a daughter of a certain Canaanite
whose name was Shua; and he took her and went in to her.
3 So she conceived and bore a son and he named him
[a]Er.
4 Then she conceived again and bore a son and named
him Onan.
5 And she bore still another son and named him Shelah;
and it was at Chezib [1]that she bore him.
6 Now Judah took a wife for Er his first-born, and her
name *was* Tamar.
7 But [a]Er, Judah's first-born, was evil in the sight of the
LORD, so the LORD took his life.
8 Then Judah said to Onan, "[a]Go in to your brother's
wife, and perform your duty as a brother-in-law to her, and
raise up [1]offspring for your brother."
9 And Onan knew that the [1]offspring would not be his; so
it came about that when he went in to his brother's wife, he
[2]wasted his seed on the ground, in order not to give [1]offspring
to his brother.
10 But what he did was displeasing in the sight of the
LORD; so He took his life also.
11 Then Judah said to his daughter-in-law Tamar, "[a]Re-
main a widow in your father's house until my son Shelah grows
up"; for he [1]thought, "[2]*I am afraid* that he too may die like his
brothers." So Tamar went and lived in her father's house.
12 Now [1]after a considerable time Shua's daughter, the
wife of Judah, died; and when [2]the time of mourning was

28 [c]Gen. 39:1

29 [a]Gen. 37:34; 44:13

30 [a]Gen. 42:13, 36

31 [a]Gen. 37:3, 23

32 [1]Or, *recognize*

33 [1]Or, *recognized* [a]Gen. 37:20

34 [a]Gen. 37:29

35 [a]Gen. 37:33; 25:8; 35:29; 42:38; 44:29, 31

36 [1]Lit., *Medanites* [a]Gen. 39:1

1 [1]Lit., *went down* [2]Lit., *turned aside to* [a]Josh. 15:35; 1 Sam. 22:1

3 [a]Gen. 46:12; Num. 26:19

5 [1]Lit., *when*

7 [a]1 Chr. 2:3

8 [1]Lit., *seed* [a]Deut. 25:5, 6; Matt. 22:24

9 [1]Lit., *seed* [2]Lit., *spilled on the ground*

11 [1]Lit., *said* [2]Lit., *Lest he also die* [a]Ruth 1:12, 13

12 [1]Lit., *the days became many and* [2]Lit., *Judah was comforted, he*

ended, Judah went up to his sheep-shearers at [a]Timnah, he and
his friend Hirah the Adullamite.
13 And it was told to Tamar, "[1]Behold, your father-in-law
is going up to Timnah to shear his sheep."
14 So she [1]removed her widow's garments and [a]covered
herself with a [2]veil, and wrapped herself, and sat in the gateway
of [b]Enaim, which is on the road to Timnah; for she saw that
Shelah had grown up, and she had not been given to him as a
wife.
15 When Judah saw her, he thought she *was* a harlot, for
she had covered her face.
16 So he turned aside to her by the road, and said, "[1]Here
now, let me come in to you"; for he did not know that she was
his daughter-in-law. And she said, "What will you give me, that
you may come in to me?"
17 He said, therefore, "I will send you a [1]kid from the
flock." She said, moreover, "[2]Will you give a pledge until you
send *it?*"
18 And he said, "What pledge shall I give you?" And she
said, "[a]Your seal and your cord, and your staff that is in your
hand." So he gave *them* to her, and went in to her, and she
conceived by him.
19 Then she arose and departed, and [1]removed her [2]veil
and put on her widow's garments.
20 When Judah sent the [1]kid by his friend the Adullamite,
to receive the pledge from the woman's hand, he did not find
her.
21 And he asked the men of her place, saying, "Where is
the temple prostitute who was by the road at Enaim?" But
they said, "There has been no temple prostitute here."
22 So he returned to Judah, and said, "I did not find her;
and furthermore, the men of the place said, 'There has been
no temple prostitute here.' "
23 Then Judah said, "Let her [1]keep them, lest we become
a laughingstock. [2]After all, I sent this kid, but you did not find
her."
24 Now it was about three months later that Judah was
informed, "[1]Your daughter-in-law Tamar has played the harlot, and behold, she is also with child by harlotry." Then Judah
said, "Bring her out and [a]let her be burned!"
25 It was while she was being brought out that she sent to
her father-in-law, saying, "I am with child by the man to whom
these things belong." And she said, "Please examine and see,
whose signet ring and cords and staff are these?"
26 And Judah recognized *them,* and said, "She is more
righteous than I, inasmuch as I did not give her to my son
Shelah." And he did not [1]have relations with her again.
27 And it came about at the time she was giving birth, that
behold, there were [a]twins in her womb.
28 Moreover, it took place while she was giving birth, one
put out a hand, and the midwife took and tied a scarlet *thread*
on his hand, saying, "This one came out first."
29 But it came about as he drew back his hand, that behold, his brother came out. Then she said, "What a breach
you have made for yourself!" So he was named [1a]Perez.

12 [a]Josh. 15:10, 57

13 [1]Lit., *saying, Behold*

14 [1]Lit., *removed from herself* [2]Or, *shawl* [a]Gen. 24:65 [b]Josh. 15:34

16 [1]Or, *Come, now . . .*

17 [1]Lit., *Kid of goats* [2]Or, *Will you give . . . ?*

18 [a]Gen. 41:42

19 [1]Lit., *removed from herself* [2]Or, *shawl*

20 [1]Lit., *kid of goats by the hand of*

23 [1]Lit., *take for herself* [2]Lit., *Behold*

24 [1]Lit., *saying, Your* [a]Lev. 21:9

26 [1]Lit., *know her yet again*

27 [a]Gen. 25:24-26

29 [1]I.e., A breach [a]Gen. 46:12; Ruth 4:12

30 And afterward his brother came out who had the scarlet *thread* on his hand; and he was named [1a]Zerah.

Chapter 39

Now Joseph had been taken down to Egypt; and Potiphar, an Egyptian officer of Pharaoh, the captain of the bodyguard, bought him [1]from the [a]Ishmaelites, who had taken him down there.

2 And [a]the Lord was with Joseph, so he became a [1]successful man. And he was in the house of his master the Egyptian.

3 Now his master [a]saw that the Lord was with him and *how* the Lord [b]caused all that he did to prosper in his hand.

4 So Joseph found favor in his sight, and [1]became his personal servant; and he made him overseer over his house, and [a]all that he owned he put in his [2]charge.

5 And it came about that from the time he made him overseer in his house, and over all that he owned, the Lord [a]blessed the Egyptian's house on account of Joseph; thus [b]the Lord's blessing was upon all that he owned, in the house and in the field.

6 So he left everything he owned in Joseph's [1]charge; and with him *around* he did not [2]concern himself with anything except the [3]food which he [4]ate. Now Joseph was [a]handsome in form and appearance.

7 And it came about after these events [a]that his master's wife [1]looked with desire at Joseph, and she said, "Lie with me."

8 But [a]he refused and said to his master's wife, "Behold, with me *around*, my master [1]does not concern himself with anything in the house, and he has put all that he owns in my [2]charge.

9 "[1a]There is no one greater in this house than I, and he has withheld nothing from me except you, because you are his wife. How then could I do this great evil, and [b]sin against God?"

10 And it came about as she spoke to Joseph day after day, that he did not listen to her to *lie* beside her, *or* be with her.

11 Now it happened [1]one day that he went into the house to do his work, and none of the men of the household was there inside.

12 And she caught him by his garment, saying, "Lie with me!" And he left his garment in her hand and fled, and went outside.

13 [1]When she saw that he had left his garment in her hand, and had fled outside,

14 she called to the men of her household, and said to them, "See, he has brought in a [1]Hebrew to us to make sport of us; he came in to me to lie with me, and I [2]screamed.

15 And it came about when he heard that I raised my voice and [1]screamed, that he left his garment beside me and fled, and went outside."

16 So she [1]left his garment beside her until his master came home.

17 Then she spoke to him [1]with these words, "[2]The Hebrew

30 [1]I.e., A dawning or brightness [a]1 Chr. 2:5

1 [1]Lit., *from the hand of* [a]Gen. 37:25, 28, 36; Ps. 105:17

2 [1]Or, *prosperous* [a]Gen. 39:3, 21, 23

3 [a]Gen. 21:22; 26:28 [b]Ps. 1:3

4 [1]Or, *ministered to him* [2]Lit., *hand* [a]Gen. 39:8, 22

5 [a]Gen. 30:27 [b]Deut. 28:3, 4, 11

6 [1]Lit., *hand* [2]Lit., *know* [3]Lit., *bread* [4]Or, *used to eat* [a]Gen. 29:17

7 [1]Lit., *lifted up her eyes at* [a]Prov. 7:15-20

8 [1]Lit., *does not know what is in the house* [2]Lit., *hand* [a]Prov. 6:23, 24

9 [1]Or, *He is not greater* [a]Gen. 41:40 [b]Gen. 42:18; 2 Sam. 12:13

11 [1]Lit., *about this day*

13 [1]Lit., *And it came about when*

14 [1]Lit., *Hebrew man* [2]Lit., *called with a great voice.*

15 [1]Lit., *called out*

16 [1]Lit., *let . . . lie beside*

17 [1]Lit, *according to* [2]Lit., *saying, "The*

slave, whom you brought to us, came in to me to make
sport of me;
18 and it happened as I raised my voice and [1]screamed,
that he left his garment beside me and fled outside."
19 Now it came about when his master heard the words of
his wife, which she spoke to him, saying, "[1]This is what your
slave did to me"; that his anger burned.
20 So Joseph's master took him and [a]put him into the jail,
the place where the king's prisoners were confined; and he was
there in the jail.
21 But [a]the LORD was with Joseph and extended kindness
to him, and gave him favor in the sight of the chief jailer.
22 And the chief jailer [a]committed to Joseph's [1]charge all
the prisoners who were in the jail; so that whatever was done
there, he was [2]responsible *for it*.
23 [a]The chief jailer did not supervise anything under
[1]Joseph's charge because [b]the LORD was with him; and whatever
he did, [c]the LORD made to prosper.

CHAPTER 40

THEN it came about after these things [a]the cupbearer and
the baker of the king of Egypt offended their lord, the king of
Egypt.
2 And Pharaoh was furious with his two officials, the
chief cupbearer and the chief baker.
3 So he put them in confinement in the house of the
[a]captain of the bodyguard, in the jail, the *same* place where
Joseph was imprisoned.
4 And the captain of the bodyguard put Joseph in charge
of them, and he [1]took care of them; and they were in confinement for [2]some time.
5 Then the cupbearer and the baker of the king of Egypt,
who were confined in jail, they both had a dream the same
night, each man with his *own* dream *and* each dream with its
own interpretation.
6 [1]When Joseph came to them in the morning and observed them, [2]behold, they were dejected.
7 And he asked Pharaoh's officials who were with him in
confinement in his master's house, "[1a]Why are your faces so
sad today?"
8 Then they said to him, "[a]We have [1]had a dream and
there is no one to interpret it." Then Joseph said to them,
"[b]Do not interpretations belong to God? Tell *it* to me,
please."
9 So the chief cupbearer told his dream to Joseph, and
said to him, "In my dream, [1]behold, *there was* a vine in front
of me;
10 and on the vine *were* three branches. And as it was
budding, its blossoms came out, *and* its clusters produced ripe
grapes.
11 "Now Pharaoh's cup was in my hand; so I took the
grapes and squeezed them into Pharaoh's cup, and I put the
cup into Pharaoh's [1]hand."
12 Then Joseph said to him, "This is the interpretation of
it: the three branches are three days;

18 [1]Lit., *called out*
19 [1]Lit., *According to these things your slave*
20 [a]Ps. 105:18
21 [a]Gen. 39:2; Ps. 105:19; Acts 7:9
22 [1]Lit., *hand* [2]Lit., *the doer* [a]Gen. 39:4
23 [1]Lit., *his hand* [a]Gen. 39:3, 8 [b]Gen. 39:2 [c]Gen. 39:3
1 [a]Gen. 40:11, 13
3 [a]Gen. 39:1, 20
4 [1]Lit., *ministered to* [2]Lit., *days*
6 [1]Or, *And* [2]Lit., *and behold*
7 [1]Lit., *saying, Why* [a]Neh. 2:2
8 [1]Lit., *dreamed* [a]Gen. 41:15 [b]Gen. 41:16; Dan. 2:27, 28
9 [1]Lit., *and behold*
11 [1]Lit., *palm*

13 within three more days Pharaoh will [1]lift up your head
and restore you to your [2]office; and you will put Pharaoh's cup
into his hand according to your former custom when you were
his cupbearer.
14 "Only [1]keep me in mind when it goes well with you, and
please do me a kindness [2]by mentioning me to Pharaoh, and
get me out of this house.
15 "For [a]I was in fact kidnapped from the land of the Hebrews, and even here I have done nothing that they should have
put me into the [1]dungeon."
16 When the chief baker saw that he had interpreted favorably, he said to Joseph, "I also *saw* in my dream, and behold,
there were three baskets of white bread on my head;
17 and in the top basket *there were* some of all [1]sorts of
baked food for Pharaoh, and the birds were eating them out of
the basket on my head."
18 Then Joseph answered and said, "This is its interpretation: the three baskets are three days;
19 within three more days Pharaoh will lift up your head
from you and will hang you on a tree; and the birds will eat
your flesh off you."
20 Thus it came about on the third day, *which was* Pharaoh's birthday, that he made a feast for all his servants; [a]and
he lifted up the head of the chief cupbearer and the head of
the chief baker among his servants.
21 And he restored the chief cupbearer to his [1]office, and
[a]he put the cup into Pharaoh's [2]hand;
22 but [a]he hanged the chief baker, just as Joseph had interpreted to them.
23 Yet the chief cupbearer did not remember Joseph, but
forgot him.

Chapter 41

NOW it happened at the end of two full years that Pharaoh
had a dream, and behold, he was standing by the Nile.
2 And lo, from the Nile there came up seven cows, sleek
and [1]fat; and they grazed in the [a]marsh grass.
3 Then behold, seven other cows came up after them
from the Nile, ugly and [1]gaunt, and they stood by the *other*
cows on the bank of the Nile.
4 And the ugly and [1]gaunt cows ate up the seven sleek
and fat cows. Then Pharaoh awoke.
5 And he fell asleep and dreamed a second time; and
behold, seven ears of grain came up on a single stalk, plump
and good.
6 Then behold, seven ears, thin and scorched by the east
wind, sprouted up after them.
7 And the thin ears swallowed up the seven plump and
full ears. Then Pharaoh awoke, and behold, *it was* a dream.
8 Now it came about in the morning that [a]his spirit was
troubled, so he sent and called for all the [1b]magicians of Egypt,
and all its wise men. And Pharaoh told them his [2]dreams, but
[c]there was no one who could interpret them to Pharaoh.
9 Then the chief cupbearer spoke to Pharaoh, saying, "I
would make mention today of [a]my *own* [1]offenses.

13 [1]Or possibly, *forgive you* [2]Lit., *place*
14 [1]Lit., *remember me with yourself* [2]Lit., *and mention*
15 [1]Or, *pit* [a]Gen. 37:26-28
17 [1]Lit., *food for Pharaoh made by a baker*
20 [a]2 Kin. 25:27; Jer. 52:31
21 [1]Lit., *wine-pouring* [2]Lit., *palm* [a]Gen. 40:13
22 [a]Gen. 40:19
2 [1]Lit., *fat of flesh* [a]Job 8:11; Is. 19:6, 7
3 [1]Lit., *lean of flesh*
4 [1]Lit., *lean of flesh*
8 [1]Or, *sooth-sayer priests* [2]Lit., *dream* [a]Dan. 2:1, 3 [b]Ex. 7:11, 22 [c]Dan. 2:27; 4:7
9 [1]Or, *sins* [a]Gen. 40:23

10 "Pharaoh was furious with his servants, and he put me in
confinement in the house of the captain of the bodyguard,
both me and the chief baker.
11 "And we had a dream on [1]the same night, [2]he and I;
each of us dreamed according to the interpretation of his *own*
dream.
12 "Now a Hebrew youth *was* with us there, a servant of
the captain of the bodyguard, and we related *them* to him, and
he interpreted our dreams for us. To each one he interpreted
according to his *own* dream.
13 "And it came about that just [a]as he interpreted for us, so
it happened; he restored me in my [1]office, but he hanged
him."
14 [a]Then Pharaoh sent and called for Joseph, and they
[b]hurriedly brought him out of the dungeon; and when he had
shaved himself and changed his clothes, he came to Pharaoh.
15 And Pharaoh said to Joseph, "I have had a dream, [a]but
no one can interpret it; and I have heard [1]it said about you,
that [2]when you hear a dream you can interpret it."
16 Joseph then answered Pharaoh, saying, "[1a]It is not in
me; [b]God will [2]give Pharaoh a favorable answer."
17 So Pharaoh spoke to Joseph, "In my dream, behold, I
was standing on the bank of the Nile;
18 and behold, seven cows, [1]fat and sleek came up out of
the Nile; and they grazed in the marsh grass.
19 "And lo, seven other cows came up after them, poor and
very ugly and [1]gaunt, such as I had never seen for [2]ugliness in
all the land of Egypt;
20 and the lean and [1]ugly cows ate up the first seven fat
cows.
21 "Yet when they had [1]devoured them, it could not be
[2]detected that they had [1]devoured them; [3]for they were just as
ugly as [4]before. Then I awoke.
22 "I saw also in my dream, and behold, seven ears, full and
good, came up on a single stalk;
23 and lo, seven ears, withered, thin, *and* scorched by the
east wind, sprouted up after them;
24 and the thin ears swallowed the seven good ears. Then I
told it to the [1]magicians, but there was no one who could
explain it to me."
25 Now Joseph said to Pharaoh, "Pharaoh's [1]dreams are
one *and the same;* [a]God has told to Pharaoh what He is about
to do.
26 "The seven good cows are seven years; and the seven
good ears are seven years; the [1]dreams are one *and the same.*
27 "And the seven lean and ugly cows that came up after
them are seven years, and the seven thin ears scorched by the
east wind [a]shall be seven years of famine.
28 "[1]It is as I have spoken to Pharaoh: [a]God has shown to
Pharaoh what He is about to do.
29 "Behold, [a]seven years of great abundance are coming in
all the land of Egypt;
30 and after them [a]seven years of famine will [1]come, and
all the abundance will be forgotten in the land of Egypt; and
the famine will [2]ravage the land.

11 [1]Lit., *one night* [2]Lit., *I and he*

13 [1]Lit., *place* [a]Gen. 40:21, 22

14 [a]Ps. 105:20 [b]Dan. 2:25

15 [1]Lit., *about you, saying* [2]Lit., *you hear a dream to interpret it* [a]Gen. 41:8

16 [1]Lit., *apart from me* [2]Lit., *answer the peace of Pharaoh* [a]Dan. 2:30; Zech. 4:6; Acts 3:12; 2 Cor. 3:5 [b]Gen. 41:25, 28, 32; Gen. 40:8

18 [1]Lit., *fat of flesh*

19 [1]Lit., *lean of flesh* [2]Lit., *badness*

20 [1]Lit., *bad*

21 [1]Lit., *entered their inward parts* [2]Or, *known* [3]Lit., *and* [4]Lit., *in the beginning*

24 [1]Or, *sooth-sayer priests*

25 [1]Lit., *dream is* [a]Gen. 41:28, 32

26 [1]Lit., *dream is*

27 [a]2 Kin. 8:1

28 [1]Lit., *That is the thing which I spoke* [a]Gen. 41:25, 32

29 [a]Gen. 41:47

30 [1]Lit., *arise* [2]Lit., *destroy* [a]Gen. 41:54, 56; Gen. 47:13

31 "So the abundance will be unknown in the land because of that [1]subsequent famine; for it *will be* very severe.

32 "[a]Now as for the repeating of the dream to Pharaoh twice, *it means* that the matter is determined by God, and God will quickly bring it about.

33 "And now let Pharaoh look for a man [a]discerning and wise, and set him over the land of Egypt.

34 "Let Pharaoh take action to appoint overseers [1]in charge of the land, and let him exact a fifth *of the produce* of the land of Egypt in the seven years of abundance.

35 "Then [a]let them gather all the food of these good years that are coming, and store up the grain for food in the cities under Pharaoh's authority, and let them guard *it*.

36 "And let the food become as a reserve for the land for the seven years of famine which will occur in the land of Egypt, so that the land may not perish during the famine."

37 Now the [1]proposal seemed good [2]to Pharaoh and [2]to all his servants.

38 Then Pharaoh said to his servants, "Can we find a man like this, [a]in whom is a divine spirit?"

39 So Pharaoh said to Joseph, "Since God has informed you of all this, [a]there is no one so discerning and wise as you are.

40 "[a]You shall be over my house, and according to your [1]command all my people shall [2]do homage; only in the throne I will be greater than you."

41 And Pharaoh said to Joseph, "See I have set you [a]over all the land of Egypt."

42 Then Pharaoh [a]took off his signet ring from his hand, and put it on Joseph's hand, and clothed him in garments of fine linen, and [b]put the gold necklace around his neck.

43 And he had him ride in [1]his second chariot; and they proclaimed before him, "[2]Bow the knee!" And he set him over all the land of Egypt.

44 Moreover, Pharaoh said to Joseph, "*Though* I am Pharaoh, yet [a]without [1]your permission no one shall raise his hand or foot in all the land of Egypt."

45 Then Pharaoh named Joseph [1]Zaphenath-paneah; and he gave him Asenath, the daughter of Potiphera priest of [2a]On, as his wife. And Joseph went forth over the land of Egypt.

46 Now Joseph was [a]thirty years old when he [1]stood before Pharaoh, king of Egypt. And Joseph went out from the presence of Pharaoh, and went through all the land of Egypt.

47 And during the seven years of plenty the land brought forth [1]abundantly.

48 So he gathered all the food of *these* seven years which occurred in the land of Egypt, and placed the food in the cities; he placed in every city the food from its own surrounding fields.

49 Thus Joseph stored up grain [1]in great abundance like the sand of the sea, until he stopped [2]measuring *it*, for it was [3]beyond measure.

50 Now before the year of famine came, two sons were born to Joseph, whom Asenath, the daughter of Potiphera priest of [1]On, bore to him.

51 And Joseph named the first-born [1]Manasseh, "For," *he*

---

31 [1]Lit., *afterwards*

32 [a]Gen. 41:25, 28

33 [a]Gen. 41:39

34 [1]Lit., *over*

35 [a]Gen. 41:48

37 [1]Lit., *word* [2]Lit., *in the sight of*

38 [a]Dan. 4:8, 9, 18; 5:11, 14

39 [a]Gen. 41:33

40 [1]Lit., *mouth* [2]Lit., *kiss* [a]Ps. 105:21, 22; Acts 7:10

41 [a]Gen. 42:6

42 [a]Esther 3:10 [b]Dan. 5:7, 16, 29

43 [1]Lit., *the second . . . which was his* [2]Text: *Abreck; "Attention"*

44 [1]Lit., *you no one* [a]Ps. 105:22

45 [1]Probably Egyptian for "God Speaks; he lives" [2]Or, *Heliopolis* [a]Jer. 43:13; Ezek. 30:17

46 [1]Or, *entered the service of* [a]Gen. 37:2

47 [1]Lit., *by handfuls*

49 [1]Lit., *very much* [2]Lit., *numbering* [3]Or, *without number*

50 [1]Or, *Heliopolis*

51 [1]I.e., Making to forget

said, "God has made me forget all my trouble and all my
father's household."
52 And he named the second [1]Ephraim, "For," *he said,*
"[a]God has made me fruitful in the land of my affliction."
53 When the seven years of plenty which had been in the
land of Egypt came to an end,
54 and [a]the seven years of famine began to come, just as
Joseph had said, then there was famine in all the lands; but in
all the land of Egypt there was bread.
55 So when all the land of Egypt was famished, the people
cried out to Pharaoh for bread; and Pharaoh said to all the
Egyptians, "Go to Joseph; whatever he says to you, you shall
do."
56 When the famine was *spread* over all the face of the
earth, then Joseph opened all [1]the storehouses, and sold to the
Egyptians; and the famine was severe in the land of Egypt.
57 And *the people of* all the earth came to Egypt to buy
grain from Joseph, because the famine was severe in all the
earth.

Chapter 42

Now [a]Jacob saw that there was grain in Egypt, and Jacob
said to his sons, "Why are you staring at one another?"
2 And he said, "Behold, I have heard that there is grain in
Egypt; go down there and buy *some* for us [1]from that place, [a]so
that we may live and not die."
3 Then ten brothers of Joseph went down to buy grain
from Egypt.
4 But Jacob did not send Joseph's brother [a]Benjamin
with his brothers, for he said, "[1]I am afraid that harm may
befall him."
5 So the sons of Israel came to buy *grain* among those
who were coming, [a]for the famine was in the land of Canaan
also.
6 Now [a]Joseph was the ruler over the land; he was the
one who sold to all the people of the land. And Joseph's brothers came and [b]bowed down to him with *their* faces to the
ground.
7 When Joseph saw his brothers he recognized them, but
he disguised himself to them and [a]spoke to them harshly. And
he said to them, "Where have you come from?" And they
said, "From the land of Canaan, to buy food."
8 But Joseph had recognized his brothers, although [a]they
did not recognize him.
9 And Joseph [a]remembered the dreams which he [1]had
about them, and said to them, "You are spies; you have come
to look at the [2]undefended parts of our land."
10 Then they said to him, "No, [a]my lord, but your servants have come to buy food.
11 "We are all sons of one man; we are [a]honest men, your
servants are not spies."
12 Yet he said to them, "No, but you have come to look
at the [1]undefended parts of our land!"
13 But they said, "Your servants are twelve brothers *in all,*

52 [1]I.e., fruitfulness [a]Gen. 17:6; 28:3; 49:22

54 [a]Gen. 41:30; Ps. 105:16; Acts 7:11

56 [1]Lit., *that which was in them*

1 [a]Acts 7:12

2 [1]Lit., *from there* [a]Gen. 43:8

4 [1]Lit., *Lest harm* [a]Gen. 35:24

5 [a]Gen. 41:57; Acts 7:11

6 [a]Gen. 41:41, 55 [b]Gen. 37:8-10; 41:43

7 [a]Gen. 42:30

8 [a]Gen. 37:2; 41:46, 53

9 [1]Lit., *had dreamed* [2]Lit., *nakedness of the land* [a]Gen. 37:6-9

10 [a]Gen. 37:8

11 [a]Gen. 42:16, 19, 31, 34

12 [1]Lit., *nakedness of the land*

13 [a]Gen. 43:7 [b]Gen. 42:32; 37:30; 44:20

14 [1]Lit., *to you, saying*

16 [a]Gen. 42:11

17 [a]Gen. 40:4, 7

18 [a]Gen. 39:9

19 [1]Lit., *the house of your prison*

20 [a]Gen. 42:34

21 [a]Gen. 37:26-28; 45:3

22 [1]Lit., *you saying* [2]Lit., *And behold, his blood also is required*
[a]Gen. 37:22 [b]Gen. 9:5-6

24 [a]Gen. 43:30; 45:14, 15 [b]Gen. 43:14, 23

25 [a]Gen. 44:1

28 [1]Lit., *went out* [2]Lit., *trembled*
[a]Gen. 43:23

31 [a]Gen. 42:11

the sons of one man in the land of Canaan; and behold, the
youngest is with [a]our father today, and [b]one is no more."
14 And Joseph said to them, "It is as I said [1]to you, you
are spies;
15 by this you will be tested: by the life of Pharaoh, you
shall not go from this place unless your youngest brother
comes here!
16 "Send one of you that he may get your brother, while
you remain confined, that your words may be tested, whether
there is [a]truth in you. But if not, by the life of Pharaoh, surely
you are spies."
17 So he put them all together in [a]prison for three days.
18 Now Joseph said to them on the third day, "Do this
and live, for [a]I fear God:
19 if you are honest men, let one of your brothers be
confined in [1]your prison; but as for *the rest of* you, go, carry
grain for the famine of your households,
20 and [a]bring your youngest brother to me, so your words
may be verified, and you will not die." And they did so.
21 Then they said to one another, "[a]Truly we are guilty
concerning our brother, because we saw the distress of his soul
when he pleaded with us, yet we would not listen; therefore
this distress has come upon us."
22 And Reuben answered them, saying, "[a]Did I not tell
[1]you, 'Do not sin against the boy'; and you would not listen?
[2b]Now comes the reckoning for his blood."
23 They did not know, however, that Joseph understood,
for there was an interpreter between them.
24 And he turned away from them and [a]wept. But when
he returned to them and spoke to them, he [b]took Simeon from
them and bound him before their eyes.
25 [a]Then Joseph gave orders to fill their bags with grain
and to restore every man's money in his sack, and to give them
provisions for the journey. And thus it was done for them.
26 So they loaded their donkeys with their grain, and departed from there.
27 And as one *of them* opened his sack to give his donkey
fodder at the lodging place, he saw his money; and behold, it
was in the mouth of his sack.
28 Then he said to his brothers, "My money has been
returned, and behold, it is even in my sack." And their hearts
[1]sank, and they *turned* [2]trembling to one another, saying,
"[a]What is this that God has done to us?"
29 When they came to their father Jacob in the land of
Canaan, they told him all that had happened to them, saying,
30 "The man, the lord of the land, spoke harshly with us,
and took us for spies of the country.
31 "But we said to him, 'We are [a]honest men; we are not
spies.
32 'We are twelve brothers, sons of our father; one is no
more, and the youngest is with our father today in the land of
Canaan.'
33 "And the man, the lord of the land, said to us, 'By this I
shall know that you are honest men: leave one of your brothers
with me and take *grain for* the famine of your households, and
go.

34 'But bring your youngest brother to me that I may
know that you are not spies, but [1]honest men. I will give your
brother to you, and you may trade in the land.' "
35 Now it came about as they were emptying their sacks,
that behold, [a]every man's bundle of money *was* in his sack; and
when they and their father saw their bundles of money, they
were dismayed.
36 And their father Jacob said to them, "You have bereaved me of my children: Joseph is no more, and Simeon is no
more, and you would take Benjamin; all these things are
against me."
37 Then Reuben spoke to his father, saying, "You may
put my two sons to death if I do not bring him *back* to you;
put him in my [1]care, and I will return him to you."
38 But [1]Jacob said, "My son shall not go down with you;
for his brother is dead, and he alone is left. If harm should
befall him on the journey [2]you are taking, then you will [a]bring
my gray hair down to Sheol in sorrow."

Chapter 43

[a]NOW the famine was severe in the land.
2 So it came about when they had finished eating the
grain which they had brought from Egypt, that their father
said to them, "Go back, buy us a little food."
3 Judah spoke to him, however, saying, "[a]The man solemnly warned [1]us, 'You shall not see my face unless your
brother is with you.'
4 "If you send our brother with us, we will go down and
buy you food.
5 "But if you do not send *him*, we will not go down; for
the man said to us, 'You shall not see my face unless your
brother is with you.' "
6 Then Israel said, "Why did you treat me so badly [1]by
telling the man whether you still had *another* brother?"
7 But they said, "The man questioned particularly about
us and our relatives, saying, '[a]Is your father still alive? Have
you *another* brother?' So we [1]answered his questions. Could
we possibly know that he would say, 'Bring your brother
down'?"
8 And Judah said to his father Israel, "Send the lad with
me, and we will arise and go, [a]that we may live and not die, we
as well as you and our little ones.
9 "[a]I myself will be surety for him; [1]you may hold me
responsible for him. If I do not bring him *back* to you and set
him before you, then [2]let me bear the blame before you
forever.
10 "For if we had not delayed, surely by now we could have
returned twice."
11 Then their father Israel said to them, "If *it must be* so,
then do this: take some of the best products of the land in your
[1]bags, and carry down to the man [a]as a present, a little [2b]balm
and a little honey, [3]aromatic gum and [4]myrrh, pistachio nuts
and almonds.
12 "And take double *the* money in your hand, and take

34 [1]Lit., *you are honest*

35 [a]Gen. 43:12, 15

37 [1]Lit., *hand*

38 [1]Lit., *he* [2]Lit., *on which you are going* [a]Gen. 37:35; 44:29, 31

1 [a]Gen. 41:56, 57

3 [1]Lit., *us, saying* [a]Gen. 43:5; Gen. 44:23

6 [1]Lit., *to tell*

7 [1]Lit., *told him according to these words* [a]Gen. 43:27; 42:13

8 [a]Gen. 42:2

9 [1]Lit., *from my hand you may require him* [2]Lit., *I shall have sinned before you all the days* [a]Gen. 42:37

11 [1]Or, *vessels* [2]Or, *mastic* [3]Or, *ladanum spice* [4]Or, *resinous bark* [a]Gen. 43:25, 26 [b]Gen. 37:25

back in your hand [a]the money that was returned in the mouth
of your sacks; perhaps it was a mistake.
13 "Take your brother also, and arise, return to the man;
14 and may [1a]God Almighty [b]grant you compassion in the
sight of the man, that he may release to you [c]your other brother and Benjamin. And as for me, [d]if I am bereaved of my
children, I am bereaved."
15 So the men took [a]this present, and they took double
the money in their hand, and Benjamin; then they arose and
went down to Egypt and stood before Joseph.
16 When Joseph saw Benjamin with them, he said to his
house steward, "Bring the men into the house, and slay *an*
animal and make ready; for the men are to dine with me at
noon."
17 So the man did as Joseph said, and [1]brought the men to
Joseph's house.
18 Now the men were afraid, because they were brought
to Joseph's house; and they said, "*It is* because of the money
that was returned in our sacks the first time that we are being
brought in, that he may [1]seek occasion against us and fall upon
us, and take us for slaves with our donkeys."
19 So they came near to Joseph's house steward, and
spoke to him at the entrance of the house,
20 and said, "Oh, my lord, we indeed came down the first
time to buy food,
21 and it came about when we came to the lodging place,
that we opened our sacks, and behold, [a]each man's money was
in the mouth of his sack, our money in [1]full. So [b]we have
brought it back in our hand.
22 "We have also brought down other money in our hand
to buy food; we do not know who put our money in our sacks."
23 And he said, "[1]Be at ease, do not be afraid. [a]Your God
and the God of your father has given you treasure in your
sacks; [2]I had your money." Then [b]he brought Simeon out to
them.
24 Then the man brought the men into Joseph's house
and [a]gave them water, and they washed their feet; and he gave
their donkeys fodder.
25 So they prepared [a]the present [1]for Joseph's coming at
noon; for they had heard that they were to eat [2]a meal there.
26 When Joseph came home, they brought into the house
to him the present which was in their hand and [a]bowed to the
ground before him.
27 Then he asked them about their welfare, and said, "[a]Is
your old father well, of whom you spoke? Is he still alive?"
28 And they said, "Your servant our father is well; he is
still alive." [a]And they bowed down [1]in homage.
29 As he lifted his eyes and saw his brother Benjamin, his
mother's son, he said, "Is this [a]your youngest brother, of whom
you spoke to me?" And he said, "[b]May God be gracious to
you, my son."
30 And Joseph hurried *out* for [1]he was deeply stirred over
his brother, and he sought *a place* to weep; and he entered his
chamber and [a]wept there.
31 Then he washed his face, and came out; and he [a]con-
trolled himself and said, "[1]Serve the meal."

12 [a]Gen. 43:21, 22

14 [1]Heb., *El Shaddai* [a]Gen. 17:1; 28:3; 35:11 [b]Ps. 106:46 [c]Gen. 42:24 [d]Gen. 42:36

15 [a]Gen. 43:11

17 [1]Lit., *the man brought*

18 [1]Lit., *roll himself upon us*

21 [1]Lit., *its weight* [a]Gen. 42:35 [b]Gen. 43:12, 15

23 [1]Lit., *Peace be to you* [2]Lit., *your money had come to me* [a]Gen. 42:28 [b]Gen. 42:24

24 [a]Gen. 18:4; 19:2; 24:32

25 [1]Lit., *until* [2]Lit., *bread* [a]Gen. 43:11, 15

26 [a]Gen. 37:7, 10

27 [a]Gen. 43:7; 45:3

28 [1]Lit., *and prostrated themselves* [a]Gen. 37:7, 10

29 [a]Gen. 42:13 [b]Num. 6:25; Ps. 67:1

30 [1]Lit., *his compassion grew warm* [a]Gen. 42:24; 45:2, 14, 15; 46:29

31 [1]Lit., *"Set on bread."* [a]Gen. 45:1

32 So they served him by himself, and them by themselves, and the Egyptians, who ate with him, by themselves; because the Egyptians could not eat bread with the Hebrews, for that is [1a]loathsome to the Egyptians.
33 Now they [1]were seated before him, [a]the first-born according to his birthright and the youngest according to his youth, and the men looked at one another in astonishment.
34 And he took portions to them from [1]his own table; [a]but Benjamin's portion was five times as much as any of theirs. So they feasted and drank freely with him.

Chapter 44

[a]THEN he commanded his house steward, saying, "Fill the men's sacks with food, as much as they can carry, and put each man's money in the mouth of his sack.
2 "And put my cup, the silver cup, in the mouth of the sack of the youngest, and his money for the grain." And he did [1]as Joseph had told *him*.
3 [1]As soon as it was light, the men were sent away, they with their donkeys.
4 They had *just* gone out of [a]the city, *and* were not far off, when Joseph said to his house steward, "Up, follow the men; and when you overtake them, say to them, 'Why have you repaid evil for good?
5 'Is not this the one from which my lord drinks, and which he indeed uses for [a]divination? You have done wrong in doing this.' "
6 So he overtook them and spoke these words to them.
7 And they said to him, "Why does my lord speak such words as these? Far be it from your servants to do such a thing.
8 "Behold, [a]the money which we found in the mouth of our sacks we have brought back to you from the land of Canaan. How then could we steal silver or gold from your lord's house?
9 "[a]With whomever of your servants it is found, let him die, and we also will be my lord's [b]slaves."
10 So he said, "Now let it also be according to your words; he with whom it is found shall be my slave, and *the rest of* you shall be innocent."
11 Then they hurried, each man lowered his sack to the ground, and each man opened his sack.
12 And he searched, beginning with the oldest and ending with the youngest, and [a]the cup was found in Benjamin's sack.
13 Then they [a]tore their clothes, and when each man loaded his donkey, they returned to [b]the city.
14 When Judah and his brothers came to Joseph's house, he was still there, and [a]they fell to the ground before him.
15 And Joseph said to them, "What is this deed that you have done? Do you not know that such a man as I can indeed practice [a]divination?"
16 So Judah said, "What can we say to my lord? What can we speak? And how can we justify ourselves? God has found out the iniquity of your servants; behold, we are my lord's [a]slaves, both we and the one in whose [1]possession the cup has been found."

32 [1]Lit., *an abomination* [a]Gen. 46:34
33 [1]Lit., *sat* [a]Gen. 42:7
34 [1]Lit., *his face* [a]Gen. 35:24
1 [a]Gen. 42:25
2 [1]Or, *according to the word*
3 [1]Lit., *The morning was light*
4 [a]Gen. 44:13
5 [a]Gen. 44:15; 30:27; Lev. 19:26; Deut. 18:10-14
8 [a]Gen. 43:21
9 [a]Gen. 31:32 [b]Gen. 44:16
12 [a]Gen. 44:2
13 [a]Gen. 37:29, 34 [b]Gen. 44:4
14 [a]Gen. 37:7, 10
15 [a]Gen. 44:5
16 [1]Lit., *hand* [a]Gen. 44:9

17 [1]Lit., *hand*

17 But he said, "Far be it from me to do this. The man in
whose [1]possession the cup has been found, he shall be my
slave; but as for you, go up in peace to your father."

18 [1]Lit., *let not your anger burn against* [a]Gen. 37:7, 8; 41:40-44

18 Then Judah approached him, and said, "Oh my lord,
may your servant please speak a word in my lord's ears, and [1]do
not be angry with your servant; for [a]you are equal to Pharaoh.

19 [a]Gen. 43:7

19 "[a]My lord asked his servants, saying, 'Have you a father
or a brother?'

20 [a]Gen. 44:30; 43:8 [b]Gen. 37:33; 42:13, 38

20 "And we said to my lord, 'We have an old father and [a]a
little child of *his* old age. Now his brother [b]is dead, so he alone
is left of his mother, and his father loves him.'
21 "Then you said to your servants, 'Bring him down to me,
that I may set my eyes on him.'

22 [1]Lit., *he*

22 "But we said to my lord, 'The lad cannot leave his father,
for if he should leave his father, [1]his father would die.'

23 [a]Gen. 43:3

23 "You said to your servants, however, '[a]Unless your
youngest brother comes down with you, you shall not see my
face again.'
24 "Thus it came about when we went up to your servant
my father, we told him the words of my lord.
25 "And our father said, 'Go back, buy us a little food.'
26 "But we said, 'We cannot go down. If our youngest
brother is with us, then we will go down; for we cannot see the
man's face unless our youngest brother is with us.'
27 "And your servant my father said to us, 'You know that
my wife bore me two sons;

28 [a]Gen. 37:31-35

28 and the one went out from me, and [a]I said, "Surely he
is torn in pieces," and I have not seen him since.

29 [1]Lit., *my face* [2]Lit., *evil* [a]Gen. 44:31; 42:38

29 'And if you take this one also from [1]me, and harm
befalls him, you will [a]bring my gray hair down to Sheol in
[2]sorrow.'

30 [1]Lit., *his soul is bound with his soul* [a]1 Sam 18:1

30 "Now, therefore, when I come to your servant my father,
and the lad is not with us, since [1a]his life is bound up in the
lad's life,

31 [a]Gen. 44:29

31 it will come about when he sees that the lad is not *with
us,* that he will die. Thus your servants will [a]bring the gray hair
of your servant our father down to Sheol in sorrow.

32 [1]Lit., *and I shall have sinned for all the days before my father* [a]Gen. 43:9

32 "For your servant [a]became surety for the lad to my father,
saying, 'If I do not bring him *back* to you, then [1]let me
bear the blame before my father forever.'
33 "Now, therefore, please let your servant remain instead
of the lad a slave to my lord, and let the lad go up with his
brothers.

34 [1]Lit., *find*

34 "For how shall I go up to my father if the lad is not with
me, lest I see the evil that would [1]overtake my father?"

Chapter 45

1 [1]Lit., *stood* [a]Acts 7:13

THEN Joseph could not control himself before all those
who stood by him, and he cried, "Have everyone go out from
me." So there [1]was no man with him [a]when Joseph made
himself known to his brothers.

2 [1]Lit., *gave forth his voice in weeping* [a]Gen. 45:14, 15; 46:29

2 And [a]he [1]wept so loudly that the Egyptians heard *it,*
and the household of Pharaoh heard *of it.*

3 [a]Gen. 43:27

3 Then Joseph said to his brothers, "I am Joseph! [a]Is my

father still alive?" But his brothers could not answer him, for
[b]they were dismayed at his presence.
4 Then Joseph said to his brothers, "Please come [1]closer
to me." And they came [1]closer. And he said, "I am your brother Joseph, whom you sold into Egypt.
5 "And now do not be grieved or angry [1]with yourselves,
because [a]you sold me here; for [b]God sent me before you to preserve life.
6 "For the famine *has been* in the land [a]these two years,
and there are still five years in which there will be neither plowing nor harvesting.
7 "And [a]God sent me before you to preserve for you a
remnant in the earth, and to keep you alive by a great [1]deliverance.
8 "Now, therefore, it was not you who sent me here, but
God; and He has made me a father to Pharaoh and lord of all his household and ruler over all the land of Egypt.
9 "Hurry and go up to my father, and [a]say to him, 'Thus
says your son Joseph, "God has made me lord of all Egypt; come down to me, do not delay.
10 "And you shall [1]live in the land of [a]Goshen, and you
shall be near me, you and your children and your children's children and your flocks and your herds and all that you have.
11 "There I will also [a]provide for you, for there are still five
years of famine *to come*, lest you and your household and all that you have be impoverished." '
12 "And behold, your eyes see, and the eyes of my brother
Benjamin *see*, that it is my mouth which is speaking to you.
13 "Now you must tell my father of all my splendor in
Egypt, and all that you have seen; and you must hurry and [a]bring my father down here."
14 Then he fell on his brother Benjamin's neck and [a]wept;
and Benjamin wept on his neck.
15 And he kissed all his brothers and wept on them, and
afterward his brothers talked with him.
16 Now when [a]the [1]news was heard in Pharaoh's house
[2]that Joseph's brothers had come, it [3]pleased Pharaoh and his servants.
17 Then Pharaoh said to Joseph, "Say to your brothers,
'Do this: load your beasts and [1]go to the land of Canaan,
18 and take your father and your households and come to
me, and [a]I will give you the [1]best of the land of Egypt and you shall eat the fat of the land.'
19 "Now you are ordered, 'Do this: [1]take [a]wagons from the
land of Egypt for your little ones and for your wives, and bring your father and come.
20 'And do not [1]concern yourselves with your goods, for
the [2]best of all the land of Egypt is yours.' "
21 Then the sons of Israel did so; and Joseph gave them
[a]wagons according to the [1]command of Pharaoh, and gave them provisions for the journey.
22 To [1]each of them he gave [a]changes of garments, but to
Benjamin he gave three hundred *pieces of* silver and [b]five changes of garments.
23 And to his father he sent [1]as follows: ten donkeys
loaded with the [2]best things of Egypt, and ten female donkeys

3 [b]Gen. 37:20-28; 42:21, 22

4 [1]Lit., *near*

5 [1]Lit., *in your eyes* [a]Gen. 37:28; 44:20 [b]Gen. 45:7, 8; 50:20

6 [a]Gen. 37:2; 41:46, 53

7 [1]Lit., *escaped company* [a]Gen. 45:5

9 [a]Acts 7:14

10 [1]Lit., *dwell* [a]Gen. 46:28, 34

11 [a]Gen. 47:12

13 [a]Acts 7:14

14 [a]Gen. 45:2

16 [1]Lit., *voice* [2]Lit., *saying, "Joseph's brothers have come."* [3]Lit., *was good in the eyes of* [a]Acts 7:13

17 [1]Lit., *come, go*

18 [1]Lit., *good* [a]Gen. 27:28

19 [1]Lit., *take for yourselves* [a]Gen. 45:21, 27; 46:5; Num. 7:3-8

20 [1]Lit., *let your eye look with regret upon your vessels* [2]Lit., *good*

21 [1]Lit., *mouth* [a]Gen. 45:19

22 [1]Lit., *all of them he gave each man* [a]2 Kin. 5:5 [b]Gen. 43:34

23 [1]Lit., *like this* [2]Lit., *good*

loaded with grain and bread and sustenance for his father [3]on
the journey.
24 So he sent his brothers away, and [1]as they departed, he
said to them, "Do not [2]quarrel on the journey."
25 Then they went up from Egypt, and came to the land
of Canaan to their father Jacob.
26 And they told him, saying, "Joseph is still alive, and
indeed he is ruler over all the land of Egypt." But [1]he was
stunned, for [a]he did not believe them.
27 When they told him all the words of Joseph that he
had spoken to them, and when he saw the [a]wagons that Joseph
had sent to carry him, the spirit of their father Jacob revived.
28 Then Israel said, "It is enough; my son Joseph is still
alive. I will go and see him before I die."

Chapter 46

So Israel set out with all that he had, and came to [a]Beer-
sheba, and offered sacrifices to the [b]God of his father Isaac.
2 And [a]God spoke to Israel [1]in visions of the night and
said, "[b]Jacob, Jacob." And he said, "Here I am."
3 And He said, "[a]I am God, the God of your father; do
not be afraid to go down to Egypt, for I will make you a great
nation there.
4 "[a]I will go down with you to Egypt, and [b]I will also
surely bring you up again; and [c]Joseph will [1]close your eyes."
5 Then Jacob arose from Beersheba; and the sons of
Israel carried their father Jacob and their little ones and their
wives, in the [a]wagons which Pharaoh had sent to carry him.
6 And they took their livestock and their property, which
they had acquired in the land of Canaan, and [a]came to Egypt,
Jacob and all his [1]descendants with him:
7 his sons and his grandsons with him, his daughters and
his granddaughters, and all his [1]descendants he brought with
him to Egypt.
8 Now these are the [a]names of the sons of Israel, Jacob
and his sons, who went to Egypt: Reuben, Jacob's first-born.
9 And the sons of Reuben: Hanoch and Pallu and Hezron and Carmi.
10 And the sons of Simeon: [1]Jemuel and Jamin and Ohad
and [2]Jachin and [3]Zohar and Shaul the son of a Canaanite
woman.
11 And the sons of Levi: [1]Gershon, Kohath, and Merari.
12 And the sons of Judah: Er and Onan and Shelah and
Perez and Zerah (but Er and Onan died in the land of Canaan). And the sons of Perez were Hezron and Hamul.
13 And the sons of Issachar: Tola and [1]Puvvah and [2]Iob
and Shimron.
14 And the sons of Zebulun: Sered and Elon and Jahleel.
15 These are the sons of Leah, whom she bore to Jacob in
Paddan-aram, with his daughter Dinah; [1]all his sons and his
daughters *numbered* thirty-three.
16 And the sons of Gad: [1]Ziphion and Haggi, Shuni and
[2]Ezbon, Eri and [3]Arodi and Areli.
17 And the sons of Asher: Imnah and Ishvah and Ishvi and

23 [3]Lit., *for*

24 [1]Lit., *they departed; and he said* [2]Lit., *be agitated*

26 [1]Lit., *his heart grew numb* [a]Gen. 37:31-35

27 [a]Gen. 45:19

1 [a]Gen. 28:10 [b]Gen. 26:24; 28:13

2 [1]Lit., *in the visions* [a]Num. 12:6; Job 33:14, 15 [b]Gen. 22:11; 31:11

3 [a]Gen. 17:1; 28:13

4 [1]Lit., *put his hand on* [a]Gen. 28:15 [b]Gen. 50:24; Ex. 3:8 [c]Gen. 50:1

5 [a]Gen. 45:21

6 [1]Lit., *seed* [a]Acts 7:15

7 [1]Lit., *seed*

8 [a]Num. 26:5; 1 Chr. 2:1 ff.

10 [1]Num. 26:12; In 1 Chr. 4:24, *Nemuel* [2]In 1 Chr. 4:24, *Jarib* [3]In Num. 26:13; and 1 Chr. 4:24, *Zerah*

11 [1]In 1 Chr. 6:16, *Gershom*

13 [1]In Num. 26:23, *Puvah;* in 1 Chr. 7:1, *Puah;* [2]Num. 26:24; In 1 Chr. 7:1, *Jashub*

15 [1]Lit., *all the souls of*

16 [1]In Num. 26:15, *Zephon* [2]In Num. 26:16, *Ozni* [3]In Num. 26:17, *Arod*

Beriah and their sister Serah. And the sons of Beriah: Heber
and Malchiel.
18 These are the sons of Zilpah, whom Laban gave to his
daughter Leah; and she bore to Jacob these sixteen persons.
19 The sons of Jacob's wife Rachel: Joseph and Benjamin.
20 Now to Joseph in the land of Egypt were born Manasseh and Ephraim, whom Asenath, the daughter of Potiphera,
priest of On, bore to him.
21 And the sons of Benjamin: Bela and Becher and Ashbel, Gera and Naaman, [1]Ehi and Rosh, [2]Muppim and [3]Hup-
pim and Ard.
22 These are the sons of Rachel, who were born to Jacob;
there were fourteen persons in all.
23 And the sons of Dan: [1]Hushim.
24 And the sons of Naphtali: [1]Jahzeel and Guni and Jezer
and [2]Shillem.
25 These are the sons of Bilhah, whom Laban gave to his
daughter Rachel, and she bore these to Jacob; *there were* sev-
en persons in all.
26 All the persons belonging to Jacob, who came to Egypt,
[1]his direct descendants, not including the wives of Jacob's sons,
were sixty-six persons in all,
27 and the sons of Joseph, who were born to him in Egypt
were [1]two; [a]all the persons of the house of Jacob, who came to
Egypt, *were* seventy.
28 Now he sent Judah before him to Joseph, to point out
the way before him to [a]Goshen; and they came into the land
of Goshen.
29 And Joseph [1]prepared his chariot and went up to Goshen
to meet his father Israel; as soon as he appeared [2]before
him, he fell on his neck and [a]wept on his neck a long time.
30 Then Israel said to Joseph, "Now let me die, since I
have seen your face, that you are still alive."
31 And Joseph said to his brothers and to his father's household, "[a]I will go up and tell Pharaoh, and will say to him,
'My brothers and my father's household, who *were* in the land
of Canaan, have come to me;
32 and the men are shepherds, for they have been [1]keepers
of livestock; and they have brought their flocks and their herds
and all that they have.'
33 "And it shall come about when Pharaoh calls you and
says, 'What is your occupation?'
34 that you shall say, 'Your servants have been [1]keepers of
livestock from our youth even until now, both we [a]and our
fathers,' that you may [2]live in the land of [b]Goshen; for every
shepherd is [3]loathsome to the Egyptians."

Chapter 47

THEN Joseph went in and told Pharoah, and said, "My
father and my brothers and their flocks and their herds and all
that they have, have come out of the land of Canaan; and
behold, they are in the land of Goshen."
2 And he took five men from among his brothers, and
presented them to Pharaoh.
3 Then Pharaoh said to his brothers, "What is your

21 [1]In Num. 26:38, *Ahiram* [2]In Num. 26:39, *Shephupham;* 1 Chr. 7:12, *Shuppim* [3]In Num. 26:39, *Hupham*

23 [1]In Num. 26:42, *Shuham*

24 [1]In 1 Chr. 7:13, *Jahziel* [2]In 1 Chr. 7:13, *Shallum*

26 [1]Lit., *who came out of his loins*

27 [1]Lit., *two souls* [a]Ex. 1:5; Deut. 10:22; Acts 7:14

28 [a]Gen. 45:10

29 [1]Lit., *tied, harnessed* [2]Lit., *to* [a]Gen. 45:14, 15

31 [a]Gen. 47:1

32 [1]Lit., *men.*

34 [1]Lit., *men* [2]Lit., *dwell* [3]Lit., *an abomination* [a]Gen. 13:7, 8; 26:20; 37:2 [b]Gen. 45:10, 18; 47:6, 11; Ex. 3:22

occupation?" So they said to Pharaoh, "Your servants are [a]shepherds, both we and our fathers."

4 And they said to Pharaoh, "We have come to sojourn in the land, for there is no pasture for your servants' flocks, for the famine is severe in the land of Canaan. Now, therefore, please let your servants [1]live in the land of Goshen."

5 Then Pharaoh said to [1]Joseph, "Your father and your brothers have come to you.

6 "The land of Egypt is [1]at your disposal; [2]settle your father and your brothers in [a]the best of the land, let them [3]live in the land of Goshen; and if you know any [b]capable men among them, then [4]put them in charge of my livestock."

7 Then Joseph brought his father Jacob and [1]presented him to Pharaoh; and Jacob [a]blessed Pharaoh.

8 And Pharaoh said to Jacob, "How many [1]years have you lived?"

9 So Jacob said to Pharaoh, "The [1]years of my sojourning are one hundred and [2]thirty; few and [3]unpleasant have been the [1]years of my life, nor have [a]they [4]attained the [1]years [5]that my fathers lived during the days of their sojourning."

10 And Jacob [a]blessed Pharaoh, and went out from [1]his presence.

11 So Joseph [1]settled his father and his brothers, and gave them a possession in the land of Egypt, in [a]the best of the land, in the land of Rameses, as Pharaoh had ordered.

12 And Joseph provided his father and his brothers and all his father's household with [1]food, according to their [a]little ones.

13 Now there was no [1]food in all the land, because the famine was very severe, so that the land of Egypt and the land of Canaan languished because of the famine.

14 And Joseph gathered all the money that was found in the land of Egypt and in the land of Canaan for the grain which they bought, and Joseph brought the money into Pharaoh's house.

15 And when the money was all spent in the land of Egypt and in the land of Canaan, all the Egyptians came to Joseph [1]and said, "Give us [2]food, for why should we die in your presence? For *our* money [3]is gone."

16 Then Joseph said, "Give up your livestock, and I will give you *food* for your livestock, since *your* money [1]is gone."

17 So they brought their livestock to Joseph, and Joseph gave them [1]food in exchange for the horses and the [2]flocks and the herds and the donkeys; and he [3]fed them with [1]food in exchange for all their livestock [4]that year.

18 And when that year was ended, they came to him the [1]next year and said to him, "We will not hide from my lord that our money is all spent, and the [2]cattle are my lord's. There is nothing left [3]for my lord except our bodies and our lands.

19 "Why should we die before your eyes, both we and our land? Buy us and our land for [1]food, and we and our land will be slaves to Pharaoh. So give us seed, that we may live and not die, and that the land may not be desolate."

20 So Joseph bought all the land of Egypt for Pharaoh, for

---

3 [a]Gen. 46:34

4 [1]Lit., *dwell*

5 [1]Lit., *Joseph, saying*

6 [1]Lit., *before you* [2]Lit., *cause them to dwell* [3]Lit., *dwell* [4]Lit., *appoint them rulers* [a]Gen. 47:11; 45:10, 18 [b]Ex. 18:21, 25

7 [1]Lit., *set him before* [a]Gen. 47:10; 2 Sam. 14:22; 1 Kin. 8:66

8 [1]Lit., *are the days of the years of your life*

9 [1]Lit., *days of the years* [2]Lit., *thirty years* [3]Lit., *evil* [4]Lit., *reached* [5]Lit., *of the life of my fathers* [a]Gen. 25:7; 35:28

10 [1]Lit., *Pharaoh's* [a]Gen. 47:7

11 [1]Lit., *caused to dwell* [a]Gen. 47:6, 27

12 [1]Or, *bread* [a]Gen. 45:11

13 [1]Or, *bread*

15 [1]Lit., *saying* [2]Or, *bread* [3]Lit., *ceases*

16 [1]Lit., *ceases*

17 [1]Or, *bread* [2]Lit., *livestock of the flocks and livestock of the herds* [3]Lit., *led them as a shepherd* [4]Lit., *in that year*

18 [1]Lit., *second* [2]Lit., *livestock of the cattle* [3]Lit., *in the presence of*

19 [1]Or, *bread*

[1]every Egyptian sold his field, because the famine was severe
upon them. Thus the land became Pharaoh's.
21 And as for the people, he removed them to the cities
from one end of Egypt's border to the other.
22 Only the land of the priests he did not buy, for the
priests had an allotment from Pharaoh, and they [1]lived off the
allotment which Pharaoh gave them. Therefore, they did not
sell their land.
23 Then Joseph said to the people, "Behold, I have today
bought you and your land for Pharaoh; now, *here* is seed for
you, and you may sow the land.
24 "And [1]at the harvest you shall give a [a]fifth to Pharaoh,
and four fifths shall be your own for seed of the field and for
your food and for those of your households and as food for
your little ones."
25 So they said, "You have saved our lives! Let us find
favor in the sight of my lord, and we will be Pharaoh's slaves."
26 And Joseph made it a statute concerning the land of
Egypt *valid* to this day, that Pharaoh should have the fifth;
only the land of the priests [1]did not become Pharaoh's.
27 Now Israel [1]lived in the land of Egypt, in [2]Goshen, and
they acquired [a]property in it and [b]were fruitful and became
very numerous.
28 And Jacob lived in the land of Egypt [a]seventeen years;
so the [1]length of Jacob's life was one hundred and forty-seven
years.
29 When [1]the time for Israel to die drew near, he called
his son Joseph and said to him, "Please, if I have found favor
in your sight, [a]place now your hand under my thigh and [b]deal
with me in kindness and [2]faithfulness. Please do not bury me
in Egypt,
30 but when I lie down [a]with my fathers, you shall carry
me out of Egypt and bury me in [b]their burial place." And he
said, "I will do as you have said."
31 And he said, "[a]Swear to me." So he swore to him. Then
Israel bowed *in worship* at the head of the bed.

Chapter 48

NOW it came about after these things that [1]Joseph was told,
"Behold, your father is sick." So he took his two sons [a]Manas-
seh and Ephraim with him.
2 When [1]it was told to Jacob, "Behold, your son Joseph
has come to you," Israel [2]collected his strength and sat [3]up in
the bed.
3 Then Jacob said to Joseph, "[1a]God Almighty appeared
to me at [b]Luz in the land of Canaan and blessed me,
4 and He said to me, 'Behold, I will make you fruitful
and numerous, and I will make you a company of peoples, and
will give this land to your [1]descendants after you for an everlasting possession.'
5 "And now your two sons, who were born to you in the
land of Egypt before I came to you in Egypt, are mine; [a]Ephra-
im and Manasseh shall be mine, as [b]Reuben and Simeon
are.
6 "But your offspring that [1]have been born after them

20 [1]Lit., *Egypt, every man*

22 [1]Lit., *ate their allotment*

24 [1]Lit., *it shall come about . . . that you shall* [a]Gen. 41:34

26 [1]Lit., *alone did*

27 [1]Lit., *dwelt* [2]Lit., *in the land of Goshen* [a]Gen. 47:11 [b]Gen. 35:11; Ex. 1:7

28 [1]Lit., *the days of Jacob, the years of his life* [a]Gen. 47:9

29 [1]Lit., *the days of Israel to die drew near* [2]Lit., *truth* [a]Gen. 24:2 [b]Gen. 24:49

30 [a]Gen. 15:15; Deut. 31:16 [b]Gen. 23:17-20; 49:29-32

31 [a]Gen. 21:23, 24; 24:3, 31:53; 50:25

1 [1]Lit., *one said to Joseph* [a]Gen. 41:51, 52

2 [1]Lit., *one told Jacob and said* [2]Lit., *strengthened himself* [3]Lit., *upon the bed*

3 [1]Heb., *El Shaddai* [a]Gen. 35:9-12 [b]Gen. 28:19; 35:6

4 [1]Lit., *seed*

5 [a]Gen. 48:1 [b]1 Chr. 5:1, 2

6 [1]Lit., *you have begotten*

shall be yours; they shall be called by the [2]names of their
brothers in their inheritance.
7 "Now as for me, when I came from [a]Paddan, [b]Rachel
died, [1]to my sorrow, in the land of Canaan on the journey,
when there was still some distance to go to Ephrath; and I
buried her there on the way to Ephrath (that is, Bethlehem)."
8 When Israel [a]saw Joseph's sons, he said, "Who are
these?"
9 And Joseph said to his father, "[a]They are my sons,
whom God has given me here." So he said, "Bring them to me,
please, that I may bless them."
10 Now [a]the eyes of Israel were *so* dim from age *that* he
could not see. Then [1]Joseph brought them close to him, and
he kissed them and embraced them.
11 And Israel said to Joseph, "I never [1]expected to see
your face, and behold, God has let me see your [2]children as
well."
12 Then Joseph [1]took them from his knees, and bowed
with [a]his face to the ground.
13 And Joseph took them both, Ephraim with his right
hand toward Israel's left, and Manasseh with his left hand
toward Israel's right, and brought them close to him.
14 But Israel stretched out his right hand and laid it on the
head of Ephraim, who was the younger, and his left hand on
Manasseh's head, [1]crossing his hands, [2]although [a]Manasseh
was the first-born.
15 And he blessed Joseph, and said,
"[a]The God before whom my fathers Abraham and
Isaac walked,
[b]The God who has been my shepherd [1]all my life to
this day,
16 [a]The angel who has redeemed me from all evil,
Bless the lads;
And may my name [1]live on in them,
And the [2]names of my fathers Abraham and Isaac;
And [b]may they grow into a multitude in the midst of
the earth."
17 When Joseph saw that his father laid his right hand on
Ephraim's head, it displeased him; and he grasped his father's
hand to remove it from Ephraim's head to Manasseh's head.
18 And Joseph said to his father, "Not so, my father, for
this one is the first-born. Place your right hand on his head."
19 But his father refused and said, "I know, my son, I
know; he also shall become a people and he also shall be great.
However, his younger brother shall be greater than he, and [a]his
[1]descendants shall become a [2]multitude of nations."
20 And he blessed them that day, saying,
"By you Israel shall pronounce blessing, saying,
'May God make you like Ephraim and Manasseh!' "
Thus he put Ephraim before Manasseh.
21 Then Israel said to Joseph, "Behold, I am about to die,
but [a]God will be with you, and [b]bring you back to the land of
your fathers.
22 "And I give you one [1]portion more than your brothers,
[a]which I took from the hand of the Amorite with my sword
and my bow."

6 [2]Lit., *name*

7 [1]Lit., *upon me*
[a]Gen. 33:18 [b]Gen. 35:19, 20

8 [a]Gen. 48:10

9 [a]Gen. 33:5

10 [1]Lit., *he*
[a]Gen. 27:1

11 [1]Lit., *meditated, judged* [2]Lit., *seed*

12 [1]Lit., *made them come out*
[a]Gen. 42:6

14 [1]Or, *consciously directing* [2]Lit., *when*
[a]Gen. 41:51, 52

15 [1]Lit., *from the continuance of me*
[a]Gen. 17:1 [b]Gen. 49:24

16 [1]Lit., *be called* [2]Lit., *name*
[a]Gen. 22:11, 15-18; 28:13-15; 31:11 [b]Gen. 28:14; 46:3

19 [1]Lit., *seed* [2]Lit., *fullness*
[a]Gen. 28:14; 46:3

21 [a]Gen. 26:3 [b]Gen. 28:15; 46:4; 50:24

22 [1]Or, *ridge;* lit., *shoulder;* Heb., *Shechem*
[a]Josh. 24:32; John 4:5

CHAPTER 49

THEN Jacob summoned his sons and said, "Assemble yourselves that I may tell you what shall befall you [a]in the [1]days to
come.
2 "Gather together and hear, O sons of Jacob;
And listen to Israel your father.

3 "Reuben, you are my first-born;
My might and [a]the beginning of my strength,
[1]Preeminent in dignity and [1]preeminent in power.
4 "[1]Uncontrolled as water, you shall not have preeminence,
[a]Because you went up to your father's bed;
Then you defiled *it*—he went up to my couch.

5 "[a]Simeon and Levi are brothers;
Their swords are implements of violence.
6 "[a]Let my soul not enter into their council;
Let not my glory be united with their assembly;
Because in their anger they slew [1]men,
And in their self-will they lamed [2]oxen.
7 "Cursed be their anger, for it is fierce;
And their wrath, for it is cruel.
[a]I will [1]disperse them in Jacob,
And scatter them in Israel.

8 "Judah, your brothers shall praise you;
Your hand shall be on the neck of your enemies;
[a]Your father's sons shall bow down to you.
9 "Judah is a [a]lion's whelp;
From the prey, my son, you have gone up.
He [1]couches, he lies down as a lion,
And as a [2]lion, who [3]dares rouse him up?
10 "[a]The scepter shall not depart from Judah,
Nor the ruler's staff from between his feet,
[1]Until Shiloh comes,
And [b]to him *shall be* the obedience of the peoples.
11 "[1a]He ties *his* foal to the vine,
And his donkey's colt to the choice vine;
[b]He washes his garments in wine,
And his robes in the blood of grapes.
12 "His eyes are [1]dull from wine,
And his teeth [2]white from milk.

13 "[a]Zebulun shall dwell at the seashore;
And he *shall be* [1]a haven for ships,
And his flank *shall be* toward Sidon.

14 "Issachar is [1]a strong donkey,
[a]Lying down between the [2]sheepfolds.
15 "When he saw that a resting place was good
And that the land was pleasant,
He bowed his shoulder to bear *burdens*,
And became a slave at forced labor.

1 [1]Lit., *end of the days*
[a]Num. 24:14

3 [1]Lit., *preeminence*
[a]Deut. 21:17; Ps. 78:51; 105:36

4 [1]Or, *Boiling over;* lit., *wrecklessness*
[a]Gen. 35:22; Deut. 27:20

5 [a]Gen. 34:25-30

6 [1]Lit., *a man* [2]Lit., *an ox*
[a]Ps. 64:2

7 [1]Lit., *divide*
[a]Josh. 19:1, 9;21:1-42

8 [a]Gen. 27:29; 1 Chr. 5:2

9 [1]Lit., *bows down* [2]Or, *lioness* [3]Lit., *shall*
[a]Ezek. 19:5-7; Mic. 5:8

10 [1]Or, *Until he comes to Shiloh;* or *Until he comes to whom it belongs*
[a]Num. 24:17; Ps. 60:7; 108:8
[b]Ps. 2:6-9; 72:8-11

11 [1]Lit., *Binding of*
[a]Deut. 8:7, 8; 2 Kin. 18:32
[b]Is. 63:2

12 [1]Or, *darker than* [2]Or, *whiter than*

13 [1]Lit., *for a shore of ships*
[a]Deut. 33:18, 19

14 [1]Lit., *a donkey of bone* [2]Or, *saddlebags*
[a]Judg. 5:16; Ps. 68:13

16 [a]Deut. 33:22; Judg. 18:26, 27 [b]Gen. 30:6

18 [a]Ex. 15:2; Ps. 25:5; 40:1-3; 119:166, 174; Is. 25:9; Mic. 7:7

19 [1]Lit., *a raiding band* [2]Lit., *heel* [a]Deut. 33:20

20 [1]Lit., *From* [2]Or, *bread* [3]Lit., *fat* [a]Deut. 33:24, 25 [b]Gen. 30:13

21 [a]Deut. 33:23

22 [1]Lit., *son* [2]Lit., *daughters* [a]Deut. 33:13-17

24 [1]I.e., in an unyielding position [2]Lit., *the arms of his hands* [a]Ps. 18:34; 73:23; Is. 41:10 [b]Ps. 132:2, 5; Is. 1:24; 49:26 [c]Ps. 23:1; 80:1 [d]Ps. 118:22; Is. 28:16; 1 Pet. 2:6-8

25 [1]Or, *with* [2]Heb., *Shaddai* [a]Gen. 28:13; 32:9 [b]Gen. 28:3; 48:3 [c]Gen. 27:28

26 [1]Lit., *limit or desire* [a]Deut. 33:15, 16

27 [1]Lit., *a wolf that tears*

28 [1]Lit., *and* [2]Lit., *according to his blessing*

29 [a]Gen. 25:8 [b]Gen. 23:16-20

30 [1]Lit., *possession of a burial place*

31 [a]Gen. 25:9 [b]Gen. 23:19 [c]Gen. 35:29

16 "[a]Dan shall [b]judge his people,
As one of the tribes of Israel.
17 "Dan shall be a serpent in the way,
A horned snake in the path,
That bites the horse's heels,
So that his rider falls backward.
18 "[a]For Thy salvation I wait, O LORD.

19 "[a]As for Gad, [1]raiders shall raid him,
But he shall raid *at* their [2]heels.

20 "[1a]As for [b]Asher, his [2]food shall be [3]rich,
And he shall yield royal dainties.

21 "[a]Naphtali is a doe let loose,
He gives beautiful words.

22 "[a]Joseph is a fruitful [1]bough,
A fruitful [1]bough by a spring;
Its [2]branches run over a wall.
23 "The archers bitterly attacked him,
And shot *at him* and harassed him;
24 "But his bow remained [1]firm,
And [2a]his arms were agile,
From the hands of the [b]Mighty One of Jacob
(From there is [c]the Shepherd, [d]the Stone of Israel),
25 "From [a]the God of your father who helps you,
And [1b]by the [2]Almighty who blesses you
[c]*With* blessings of heaven above,
Blessings of the deep that lies beneath,
Blessings of the breasts and of the womb.
26 "The blessings of your father
Have surpassed the blessings of my ancestors
Up to the [1]utmost bound of [a]the everlasting hills;
May they be on the head of Joseph,
And on the crown of the head of the one distinguished among his brothers.

27 Benjamin is a [1]ravenous wolf;
In the morning he devours the prey,
And in the evening he divides the spoil."

28 All these are the twelve tribes of Israel, and this is what
their father said to them [1]when he blessed them. He blessed
them, every one [2]with the blessing appropriate to him.
29 Then he charged them and said to them, "I am about
to be [a]gathered to my people; bury me with my fathers in the
cave that is in [b]the field of Ephron the Hittite,
30 in the cave that is in the field of Machpelah, which is
before Mamre, in the land of Canaan, which Abraham bought
along with the field from Ephron the Hittite for a [1]burial site.
31 "There they buried [a]Abraham and his wife [b]Sarah, there
they buried [c]Isaac and his wife Rebekah, and there I buried
Leah—
32 the field and the cave that is in it, purchased from the
sons of Heth."
33 When Jacob finished charging his sons, he drew his feet

into the bed and [a]breathed his last, and was [b]gathered to his
people.

Chapter 50

THEN Joseph fell on his father's face, and wept over him
and kissed him.
2 And Joseph commanded his servants the physicians to
embalm his father. So the physicians [a]embalmed Israel.
3 Now forty days were [1]required for [2]it, for [3]such is the
period required for embalming. And the Egyptians [a]wept for
him seventy days.
4 And when the days of [1]mourning for him were past,
Joseph spoke to the household of Pharaoh, saying, "If now I
have found favor in your sight, please speak [2]to Pharaoh,
saying,
5 '[a]My father made me swear, saying, "Behold, I am
about to die; in my grave which I dug for myself in the land of
Canaan, there you shall bury me." Now therefore, please let
me go up and bury my father; then I will return.' "
6 And Pharaoh said, "Go up and bury your father, as he
made you swear."
7 So Joseph went up to bury his father, and with him
went up all the servants of Pharaoh, the elders of his household and all the elders of the land of Egypt,
8 and all the household of Joseph and his brothers and
his father's household; they left only their little ones and their
flocks and their herds in the land of Goshen.
9 There also went up with him both chariots and horsemen; and it was a very great company.
10 When they came to the [1]threshing floor of Atad, which
is beyond the Jordan, they lamented there with a very great
and [2]sorrowful lamentation; and he [3]observed seven days
mourning for his father.
11 Now when the inhabitants of the land, the Canaanites,
saw the mourning at [1]the threshing floor of Atad, they said,
"This is a [2]grievous [3]mourning for the Egyptians." Therefore it
was named [4]Abel-mizraim, which is beyond the Jordan.
12 And thus his sons did for him as he had charged them;
13 for his sons carried him to the land of Canaan, and
buried him in [a]the cave of the field of Machpelah before
Mamre, which Abraham had bought along with the field for a
[1]burial site from Ephron the Hittite.
14 And after he had buried his father, Joseph returned to
Egypt, he and his brothers, and all who had gone up with him
to bury his father.
15 When Joseph's brothers saw that their father was dead,
they said, "[a]What if Joseph should bear a grudge against us
and pay us back in full for all the wrong which we did to him!"
16 So they [1]sent *a message* to Joseph, saying, "Your father
charged before he died, saying,
17 'Thus you shall say to Joseph, "Please forgive, I beg
you, the transgression of your brothers and their sin, for they
did you wrong." And now, please forgive the transgression of
the servants of the God of your father.' " And Joseph wept
when they spoke to him.

33 [a]Gen. 25:8; Acts 7:15 [b]Gen. 49:29

2 [a]Gen. 50:26

3 [1]Lit., *fulfilled* [2]Or, *him* [3]Lit., *so are fulfilled the days of embalming* [a]Gen. 50:10; Num. 20:29; Deut. 34:8

4 [1]Lit., *weeping* [2]Lit., *In the ears of*

5 [a]Gen. 47:29-31

10 [1]Heb., *Goren ha-Atad* [2]Lit., *heavy* [3]Lit., *made a mourning for seven days*

11 [1]Heb., *Goren ha-Atad* [2]Lit., *heavy* [3]Heb., *ebel* [4]I.e., the meadow (or mourning) of Egypt

13 [1]Lit., *possession of a burial place* [a]Gen. 23:16-20

15 [a]Gen. 37:28; 42:21, 22

16 [1]Lit., *commanded*

18 Then his brothers also came and [a]fell down before him
and said, "Behold, we are your servants."
19 But Joseph said to them, "Do not be afraid, for am I in
God's place?
20 "And as for you, [a]you meant evil against me, *but* God
meant it for good in order to bring about [1]this present result,
to preserve many people alive.
21 "So therefore, do not be afraid; [a]I will provide for you
and your little ones." So he comforted them and spoke [1]kindly
to them.
22 Now Joseph stayed in Egypt, he and his father's household, and Joseph lived one hundred and ten years.
23 And Joseph saw the third generation of Ephraim's sons;
also the sons of Machir, the son of Manasseh, were born [a]on
Joseph's knees.
24 And Joseph said to his brothers, "I am about to die, but
[a]God will surely [1]take care of you, and bring you up from this
land to the land which He [2]promised on oath to [b]Abraham, to
[c]Isaac and [d]to Jacob."
25 Then Joseph made the sons of Israel swear, saying,
"God will surely [1]take care of you, and [a]you shall carry my
bones up from here."
26 So Joseph died at the age of one hundred and ten years;
and [1]he was [a]embalmed and placed in a coffin in Egypt.

18 [a]Gen. 37:8-10; 41:43
20 [1]Lit., *as it is this day* [a]Gen. 37:26, 27; 45:5, 7
21 [1]Lit., *to their heart* [a]Gen. 45:11; 47:12
23 [a]Gen. 30:3
24 [1]Or, *visit* [2]Lit., *swore* [a]Gen. 48:21; Heb. 11:22 [b]Gen. 13:15, 17; 15:7, 8 [c]Gen. 26:3 [d]Gen. 28:13; 35:12
25 [1]Or, *visit* [a]Ex. 13:19; Josh. 24:32; Heb. 11:22
26 [1]Lit., *they embalmed him* [a]Gen. 50:2

EXODUS

Israel's Expansion in Egypt. Hard Bondage. Murder of Male Infants.

1 NOW these are the [a]names of the sons of Israel who came to
Egypt with Jacob; they came each one [1]with his household:
2 Reuben, Simeon, Levi and Judah;
3 Issachar, Zebulun and Benjamin;
4 Dan and Naphtali, Gad and Asher.
5 And all the [1]persons who came from the loins of Jacob
were [a]seventy [2]in number, but Joseph was *already* in Egypt.
6 And [a]Joseph died, and all his brothers and all that
generation.
7 But the sons of Israel [a]were fruitful and [1]increased
greatly, and multiplied, and became exceedingly [2]mighty, so
that the land was filled with them.
8 Now a new [a]king arose over Egypt, who did not know
Joseph.
9 And [a]he said to his people, "Behold, the people of the
sons of Israel are [1]more and mightier than we.
10 "Come, let us deal wisely with them, lest they multiply
and [1]in the event of war, they also join themselves to those
who hate us, and fight against us, and [2]depart from the land."
11 So they appointed [a]taskmasters over them to afflict
them with [1]hard labor. And they built for Pharaoh [b]storage
cities, Pithom and Raamses.

1 [1]Lit., *and* [a]Gen. 46:8-27
5 [1]Lit., *souls* [2]Lit., *as to souls* [a]Gen. 46:26, 27; Deut. 10:22
6 [a]Gen. 50:26
7 [1]Lit., *swarmed* [2]Or, *numerous* [a]Gen. 12:2; 28:3; 35:11; 46:3; 47:27; 48:4; Acts 7:17
8 [a]Acts 7:18, 19
9 [1]Or, *too many and too mighty for us* [a]Ps. 105:24, 25
10 [1]Lit., *it came about when war befalls that* [2]Lit., *go up from*
11 [1]Lit., *their burdens* [a]Ex. 3:7; 5:6 [b]1 Kin. 9:19; 2 Chr. 8:4

12 But the more they afflicted them, [a]the more they multiplied and the more they [1]spread out, so that they were in
dread of the sons of Israel.
13 And the Egyptians compelled the sons of Israel [a]to
labor rigorously;
14 and they made their lives bitter with hard labor in mortar and bricks and at *all kinds* of labor in the field, all their
labors which they rigorously [1]imposed on them.
15 Then the king of Egypt spoke to the Hebrew midwives,
one of whom [1]was named Shiphrah, and the other [1]was named
Puah;
16 and he said, "When you are helping the Hebrew wom-
en to give birth and see *them* upon the birthstool, [a]if it is a
son, then you shall put him to death; but if it is a daughter,
then she shall live."
17 But the midwives [1a]feared God, and did not do as the
king of Egypt had [2]commanded them, but let the boys live.
18 So the king of Egypt called for the midwives, and said
to them, "Why have you done this thing, and let the boys
live?"
19 And the midwives said to Pharaoh, "Because the Hebrew
women are not as the Egyptian women; for they are vigorous, and they give birth before the midwife [1]can get to them."
20 So God was good to the midwives, and [a]the people
multiplied, and became very [1]mighty.
21 And it came about because the midwives [1a]feared God,
that He [2]established [3]households for them.
22 Then Pharaoh commanded all his people, saying, "[a]Ev-
ery son who is born [1]you are to cast into [b]the Nile, and every
daughter you are to keep alive."

CHAPTER 2

NOW a man from [a]the house of Levi went and [1]married a
daughter of Levi.
2 And the woman conceived and bore a son; and when
she saw [1]that he was [2a]beautiful, she hid him for three months.
3 But when she could hide him no longer, she got him a
[1a]wicker [2]basket and covered it over with tar and pitch. Then
she put the child into it, and set *it* among the [b]reeds by the
bank of the Nile.
4 And [a]his sister stood at a distance to [1]find out what
would [2]happen to him.
5 Then the daughter of Pharaoh came down [a]to bathe at
the Nile, with her maidens walking alongside the Nile; and she
saw the [1]basket among the reeds and sent her maid, and she
brought it *to her*.
6 When she opened *it*, she [1]saw the child, and behold,
the [2]boy was crying. And she had pity on him and said, "This is
one of the Hebrews' children."
7 Then his sister said to Pharaoh's daughter, "Shall I go
and call [1]a nurse for you from the Hebrew women, that she
may nurse the child for you?"
8 And Pharaoh's daughter said to her, "Go *ahead*." So
the girl went and called the child's mother.
9 Then Pharaoh's daughter said to her, "Take this child

12 [1]Lit., *broke forth* [a]Ex. 1:7

13 [a]Gen. 15:13; Deut. 4:20

14 [1]Lit., *worked through them*

15 [1]Lit., *the name was*

16 [a]Acts 7:19

17 [1]Or, *revered* [2]Lit., *spoken to* [a]Ex. 1:21

19 [1]Lit., *comes to*

20 [1]Or, *numerous* [a]Ex. 1:12; Is. 3:10

21 [1]Or, *revered* [2]Lit., *made* [3]Or, *families* [a]Ex. 1:17

22 [1]Some versions insert, *to the Hebrews* [a]Acts 7:19 [b]Gen. 41:1

1 [1]Lit., *took* [a]Ex. 6:16, 18, 20

2 [1]Lit., *him that* [2]Lit., *good* [a]Acts 7:20; Heb. 11:23

3 [1]I.e., of papyrus reeds [2]Or, *chest* [a]Is. 18:2 [b]Is. 19:6

4 [1]Lit., *know* [2]Lit., *be done* [a]Ex. 15:20; Num. 26:59

5 [1]Or, *chest* [a]Ex. 7:15, 8:20

6 [1]Heb., *saw it, the child* [2]Or, *lad*

7 [1]Lit., *a woman giving suck*

away and nurse him for me and I shall give *you* your wages."
So the woman took the child and nursed him.
10 And the child grew, and she brought him to Pharaoh's
daughter, and [a]he became her son. And she named him
[1]Moses, and said, "Because I [2]drew him out of the water."
11 Now it came about in those days, [a]when Moses had
grown up, that he went out to his brethren and looked on their
[1b]hard labors; and [c]he saw an Egyptian beating a Hebrew, one
of his brethren.
12 So he [1]looked this way and that, and when he saw there
was no one *around*, he [a]struck down the Egyptian and hid him
in the sand.
13 And he went out [a]the next day, and behold, two Hebrews
were [1]fighting with each other; and he said to the [2]offend-
er, "Why are you striking your companion?"
14 But he said, "[a]Who made you a [1]prince or a judge over
us? Are you [2]intending to kill me, as you killed the Egyptian?"
Then Moses was afraid, and said, "Surely the matter has become known."
15 When Pharaoh heard of this matter, he tried to kill
Moses. But [a]Moses fled from the presence of Pharaoh and
[1]settled in the land of Midian; and he sat down [b]by a well.
16 Now [a]the priest of Midian had seven daughters; and
[b]they came to draw water, and filled the troughs to water their
father's flock.
17 Then the shepherds came and drove them away, but
[a]Moses stood up and helped them, and watered their flock.
18 When they came to [a]Reuel their father, he said, "Why
have you come *back* so soon today?"
19 So they said, "An Egyptian delivered us from the hand
of the shepherds; and what is more, he even drew the water for
us and watered the flock."
20 And he said to his daughters, "Where is he then? Why
is it that you have left the man behind? Invite him [1]to have
something to eat."
21 [a]And Moses was willing to dwell with the man, and he
gave his daughter [b]Zipporah to Moses.
22 Then she gave birth to [a]a son, and he named him [1]Ger-
shom, for he said, "I have been [b]a [2]sojourner in a foreign
land."
23 Now it came about in *the course of* [a]those many days
that the king of Egypt died. And the sons of Israel [b]sighed
because of the bondage, and they cried out; and [c]their cry for
help because of *their* bondage rose up to God.
24 So God heard their groaning; and God remembered
[a]His covenant with Abraham, Isaac, and Jacob.
25 And God saw the sons of Israel, and God [1]took notice
of them.

CHAPTER 3

NOW Moses was pasturing the flock of [a]Jethro his father-in-
law, the priest of Midian; and he led the flock to the [1]west side
of the wilderness, and came to [b]Horeb, the [c]mountain of God.
2 And [a]the angel of the LORD appeared to him in a blazing fire from the midst of [1]a [b]bush; and he looked, and be-

10 [1]Heb., *Mosheh,* from *mashah* [2]Heb., *mashah* [a]Acts 7:21

11 [1]Lit., *burdens* [a]Acts 7:23; Heb. 11:24-26 [b]Ex. 1:11; 5:4, 5; 6:6, 7

12 [1]Lit., *turned* [a]Acts 7:24, 25

13 [1]Or, *quarreling* [2]Or, *the guilty one* [a]Acts 7:26-28

14 [1]Lit., *man, a prince* [2]Lit., *saying in your heart* [a]Gen. 19:9; Acts 7:27, 28

15 [1]Lit., *dwelt* [a]Acts 7:29 [b]Gen. 24:11; 29:2

16 [a]Ex. 3:1; 18:12 [b]Gen. 24:13, 19

17 [a]Gen. 29:3, 10

18 [a]Ex. 3:1; Num. 10:29

20 [1]Lit., *that he may eat bread*

21 [a]Acts 7:29 [b]Ex. 4:25; 18:2

22 [1]Cf. Heb. *ger sham, a stranger there* [2]Heb. *ger* [a]Ex. 4:20; 18:3, 4 [b]Gen. 23:4; Heb. 11:13, 14

23 [a]Acts 7:30 [b]Ex. 6:5, 9 [c]Ex. 3:7, 9; Deut. 26:7; James 5:4

24 [a]Gen. 22:16-18; 26:2-5; 28:13-15; Ps. 105:8, 42

25 [1]Lit., *knew* them

1 [1]Or, *rear part* [a]Ex. 2:18; 4:18; 18:12; Num. 10:29 [b]Ex. 3:12; 17:6; 33:6 [c]Ex. 4:27; 18:5; 24:13

2 [1]Lit., *the* [a]Ex. 3:4-11, 16; Gen. 22:11, 15 [b]Deut. 33:16; Mark 12:26; Luke 20:37; Acts 7:30

hold, the bush was burning with fire, yet the bush was not
consumed.
3 So Moses said, "[1a]I must turn aside now, and see this
[2]marvelous sight, why the bush is not burned up."
4 When the LORD saw that he turned aside to look, [a]God
called to him from the midst of the bush, and said, "Moses,
Moses!" And he said, "Here I am."
5 Then He said, "Do not come near here; [a]remove your
sandals from your feet, for the place on which you are standing
is holy ground."
6 He said also, "[a]I am the God of your father, the God of
Abraham, the God of Isaac, and the God of Jacob." [b]Then
Moses hid his face, for he was afraid to look at God.
7 And the LORD said, "I have surely [a]seen the affliction of
My people who are in Egypt, and have given heed to their cry
because of their taskmasters, for I am aware of their sufferings.
8 "So I have come down [a]to deliver them from the [1]power
of the Egyptians, and to bring them up from that land to a
good and spacious land, to a land [b]flowing with milk and
honey, to the place of [c]the Canaanite and the Hittite and the
Amorite and the Perizzite and the Hivite and the Jebusite.
9 "And now, behold, [a]the cry of the sons of Israel has
come to Me; furthermore, I have seen the oppression with
which the Egyptians are oppressing them.
10 "Therefore, come now, and I will send you to Pharaoh,
[a]so that you may bring My people, the sons of Israel, out of
Egypt."
11 But Moses said to God, "[a]Who am I, that I should go
to Pharaoh, and that I should bring the sons of Israel out of
Egypt?"
12 And He said, "Certainly [a]I will be with you, and this
shall be the sign to you that it is I who have sent you: [b]when
you have brought the people out of Egypt, [c]you shall [1]worship
God at this mountain."
13 Then Moses said to God, "Behold, I am going to the
sons of Israel, and I shall say to them, 'The God of your
fathers has sent me to you.' Now they may say to me, 'What is
His name?' What shall I say to them?"
14 And God said to Moses, "[1a]I AM WHO [1]I AM"; and
He said, "Thus you shall say to the sons of Israel, '[1]I AM has
sent me to you.'"
15 And God, furthermore, said to Moses, "Thus you shall
say to the sons of Israel, '[a]The LORD, the God of your fathers,
the God of Abraham, the God of Isaac, and the God of Jacob,
has sent me to you.' This is My name forever, and this is My
[b]memorial-name [1]to all generations.
16 "Go and gather the elders of Israel together, and say to
them, '[a]The LORD, the God of your fathers, the God of Abraham, Isaac and Jacob, has appeared to me, saying, "[1]I am
indeed concerned about you and what has been done to you in
Egypt.
17 "So [a]I said, I will bring you up out of the affliction of
Egypt to the land of [b]the Canaanite and the Hittite and the
Amorite and the Perizzite and the Hivite and the Jebusite, to a
land [c]flowing with milk and honey."'
18 "And [a]they will [1]pay heed to what you say; and [b]you with

3 [1]Lit., *Let me turn* [2]Lit., *great*
[a]Acts 7:31

4 [a]Ex. 4:5

5 [a]Josh. 5:15; Acts 7:33

6 [a]Matt. 22:31, 32; Mark 12:26; Luke 20:37 [b]Acts 7:32

7 [a]Ex. 2:25; Neh. 9:9; Is. 63:9; Acts 7:34

8 [1]Lit., *hand*
[a]Gen. 15:13-16; 46:4; 50:24, 25 [b]Ex. 3:17; 13:5 Jer. 11:5 [c]Gen. 15:19-21; Josh. 24:11

9 [a]Ex. 2:23

10 [a]Gen. 15:13; Ex. 12:40, 41; Acts 7:6, 7

11 [a]Ex. 4:10; 6:12

12 [1]Or, *serve*
[a]Ex. 4:12, 15; 33:14-16; Gen. 31:3; Josh. 1:5 [b]Ex. 19:1 [c]Ex. 19:2, 3; Acts 7:7

14 [1]Related to the name of God, *YHWH*, rendered LORD, which is derived from the verb *HAYAH, to be*
[a]Ex. 6:3; John 8:58; Heb. 13:8; Rev. 1:8; 4:8

15 [1]Lit., *to generation of generation*
[a]Ex. 3:6, 13 [b]Ps. 30:4; 97:12; 102:12; 135:13; Hos. 12:5

16 [1]Lit., *Visiting I have visited*
[a]Ex. 3:2

17 [a]Gen. 15:13-21; 46:4; 50:24, 25 [b]Josh. 24:11 [c]Ex. 3:8

18 [1]Lit., *hear your voice*
[a]Ex. 4:31 [b]Ex. 5:1

the elders of Israel will come to the king of Egypt, and you
will say to him, 'The LORD, the God of the Hebrews, has met
with us. So now, please, let us go a [c]three days' journey into the
wilderness, that we may sacrifice to the LORD our God.'
19 "But I know that the king of Egypt [a]will not permit you
to go, [b]except [1]under compulsion.
20 "So I will stretch out [a]My hand, and strike Egypt with all
My [b]miracles which I shall do in the midst of it; and [c]after that
he will let you go.
21 "And I will grant this people [a]favor in the sight of the
Egyptians; and it shall be that when you go, you will not go
empty-handed.
22 "But every woman [a]shall ask of her neighbor and the
woman who lives in her house, articles of silver and articles of
gold, and for clothing; and you will put them on your sons and
daughters. Thus you will plunder the Egyptians."

CHAPTER 4

THEN Moses answered and said, "What if they will not
believe me, or [a]listen [1]to what I say? For they may say, '[b]The
LORD has not appeared to you.'"
2 And the LORD said to him, "What is that in your
hand?" And he said, "[a]A staff."
3 Then He said, "Throw it on the ground." So he threw
it on the ground, and [a]it became a serpent; and Moses fled
from it.
4 But the LORD said to Moses, "Stretch out your hand
and grasp *it* by its tail"—so he stretched out his hand and
caught it, and it became a staff in his [1]hand—
5 "that they may believe that the LORD, the God of their
fathers, the God of Abraham, the God of Isaac, and the God
of Jacob, has appeared to you."
6 And the LORD furthermore said to him, "Now put your
hand into your bosom." So he put his hand into his bosom,
and when he took it out, behold, his hand was [a]leprous like
snow.
7 Then He said, "Put your hand into your bosom again."
So he put his hand into his bosom again; and when he took it
out of his bosom, behold, [a]it was restored like *the rest of* his
flesh.
8 "And it shall come about that if they will not believe
you or [1]heed the [2]witness of the first sign, they may believe the
[2]witness of the last sign.
9 "But it shall be that if they will not believe even these
two signs or heed what you say, then you shall take some water
from the Nile and pour it on the dry ground; and the water
which you take from the Nile [a]will become blood on the dry
ground."
10 Then Moses said to the LORD, "Please, Lord, [a]I have
never been [1]eloquent, neither [2]recently nor in time past, nor
since Thou hast spoken to Thy servant; for I am [3]slow of
speech and [3]slow of tongue."
11 And the LORD said to him, "Who has made man's
mouth? Or [a]who makes *him* dumb or deaf, or seeing or blind?
Is it not I, the LORD?

18 [c]Ex. 5:3; 8:27

19 [1]Lit., *by a strong hand* [a]Ex. 5:2 [b]Ex. 6:1

20 [a]Ex. 6:1; 7:4, 5; 9:15; 13:3, 9, 14 [b]Ex. 15:11; Deut. 6:22; Neh. 9:10 [c]Ex. 11:1; 12:31-33

21 [a]Ex. 11:3; 12:36

22 [a]Ex. 11:2; 12:35

1 [1]Lit., *to my voice* [a]Ex. 3:18; 6:30 [b]Ex. 3:15, 16

2 [a]Ex. 4:17, 20

3 [a]Ex. 7:10-12

4 [1]Lit., *palm*

6 [a]Num. 12:10; 2 Kin. 5:27

7 [a]Num. 12:13-15; Deut. 32:39; 2 Kin. 5:14; Matt. 8:3; Luke 17:12-14

8 [1]Lit., *listen to* [2]Lit., *voice*

9 [a]Ex. 7:19, 20

10 [1]Lit., *a man of words* [2]Lit., *yesterday* [3]Lit., *heavy* [a]Ex. 4:1; 3:11; 6:12; Jer. 1:6

11 [a]Ps. 94:9; 146:8; Matt. 11:5; Luke 1:20, 64

12 "Now then go, and [a]I, even I, will be with your mouth,
and [b]teach you what you are to say."
13 But he said, "Please, Lord, now [1]send the *message* by
whomever Thou wilt."
14 Then the anger of the LORD burned against Moses, and
He said, "Is there not your brother Aaron the Levite? I know
that he speaks [1]fluently. And moreover, behold, [a]he is coming
out to meet you; when he sees you, he will be glad in his heart.
15 "And you are to speak to him and [a]put the words in his
mouth; and I, even I, will be with your mouth and his mouth,
and I will teach you what you are to do.
16 "Moreover, [a]he shall speak for you to the people; and it
shall come about that he shall be as a mouth for you, and you
shall be as God to him.
17 "And you shall take in your hand [a]this staff, [b]with which
you shall perform the signs."
18 Then Moses departed and returned to [1]Jethro [a]his
father-in-law, and said to him, "Please, let me go, that I may
return to my brethren who are in Egypt, and see if they are still
alive." And Jethro said to Moses, "Go in peace."
19 Now the LORD said to Moses in Midian, "Go [1]back to
Egypt, for [a]all the men who were seeking your life are dead."
20 So Moses took his wife and his [a]sons and mounted
them on a donkey, and he returned to the land of Egypt.
Moses also took the [b]staff of God in his hand.
21 And the LORD said to Moses, "When you go [1]back to
Egypt see that you perform before Pharaoh all [a]the wonders
which I have put in your [2]power; but [b]I will harden his heart so
that he will not let the people go.
22 "Then you shall say to Pharaoh, 'Thus says the LORD,
"[a]Israel is My son, My first-born.
23 "So I said to you, '[a]Let My son go, that he may serve
Me'; but you have refused to let him go. Behold, [b]I will kill
your son, your first-born."' "
24 Now it came about at the lodging-place on the way
that the LORD met him and [a]sought to put him to death.
25 Then Zipporah took [a]a flint and cut off her son's
foreskin and [1]threw *it* at Moses' feet, and she said, "You are
indeed a bridegroom of blood to me."
26 So He let him alone. At that time she said, "*You are* a
bridegroom of blood"—[1]because of the circumcision.
27 [a]Now the LORD said to Aaron, "Go to meet Moses in
the wilderness." So he went and met him at the mountain of
God, and he kissed him.
28 And Moses told Aaron all the words of the LORD with
which He had sent him, and all the signs that He had commanded him *to do*.
29 Then Moses and Aaron went and [a]assembled all the
elders of the sons of Israel;
30 and [a]Aaron spoke all the words which the LORD had
spoken to Moses. He then performed the [b]signs in the sight of
the people.
31 So [a]the people believed; and when they heard that the
LORD [1]was concerned about the sons of Israel and that He had
seen their affliction, then [b]they bowed low and worshiped.

12 [a]Ex. 4:15, 16; Deut. 18:18; Is. 50:4; Jer. 1:9 [b]Matt. 10:19, 20; Mark 13:11; Luke 12:11, 12; 21:14, 15

13 [1]Lit., *send by the hand which Thou sendest*

14 [1]Lit., *speaking he speaks* [a]Ex. 4:27

15 [a]Ex. 4:12, 30; Num. 23:5, 12, 16; Is. 51:16; 59:21; Jer. 1:9

16 [a]Ex. 7:1, 2

17 [a]Ex. 4:2, 20; 17:9 [b]Ex. 7:9-20; 14:16

18 [1]Heb., *Jether* [a]Ex. 2:21; 3:1

19 [1]Lit., *return* [a]Ex. 2:15, 23

20 [a]Ex. 18:3, 4; Acts 7:29 [b]Ex. 4:17; 17:9; Num. 20:8

21 [1]Lit., *to return* [2]Lit., *hand* [a]Ex. 11:9, 10 [b]Ex. 7:3, 13; 9:12; 9:35; 10:1, 20, 27; 14:4, 8; Deut. 2:30; John 12:40; Rom. 9:18

22 [a]Is. 63:16; 64:8; Jer. 31:9; Hos. 11:1

23 [a]Ex. 5:1; 6:11; 7:16 [b]Ex. 12:29

24 [a]Num. 22:22

25 [1]Lit., *made it touch at his feet* [a]Gen. 17:14; Josh. 5:2, 3

26 [1]Lit., *with reference to*

27 [a]Ex. 4:14

29 [a]Ex. 3:16

30 [a]Ex. 4:15, 16 [b]Ex. 4:1-9

31 [1]Lit., *had visited* [a]Ex. 3:18 [b]Ex. 12:27

CHAPTER 5

AND afterward Moses and Aaron came and said to Pharaoh, "[a]Thus says the LORD, the God of Israel, '[b]Let My people go that they may celebrate a feast to Me in the wilderness.' "

2 But Pharaoh said, "[a]Who is the LORD that I should obey His voice to let Israel go? I do not know the LORD, and besides, [b]I will not let Israel go."

3 Then they said, "[a]The God of the Hebrews has met with us. Please, let us go a three days' journey into the wilderness that we may sacrifice to the LORD our God, lest He fall upon us with pestilence or with the sword."

4 But the king of Egypt said to them, "Moses and Aaron, why do you [1]draw the people away from their [2]work? Get *back* to your [3a]labors!"

5 Again Pharaoh said, "Look, [a]the people of the land are now many, and you would have them cease from their labors!"

6 So the same day Pharaoh commanded [a]the taskmasters over the people and their [b]foremen, saying,

7 "You are no longer to give the people straw to make brick as previously; let them go and gather straw for themselves.

8 "But the quota of bricks which they were making previously, you shall impose on them; you are not to reduce any of it. Because they are [a]lazy, therefore they cry out, '[1]Let us go and sacrifice to our God.'

9 "Let the labor be heavier on the men, and let them work at it that they may pay no attention to false words."

10 So [a]the taskmasters of the people and their foremen went out and spoke to the people, saying, "Thus says Pharaoh, 'I am not going to give you *any* straw.

11 'You go *and* get straw for yourselves wherever you can find *it;* but none of your labor will be reduced.' "

12 So the people scattered through all the land of Egypt to gather stubble for straw.

13 And the taskmasters pressed them, saying, "Complete your [1]work quota, [2]*your* daily amount, just as when [3]you had straw."

14 Moreover, [a]the foremen of the sons of Israel, whom Pharaoh's taskmasters had set over them, [b]were beaten [1]and were asked, "Why have you not completed your required amount either yesterday or today in making brick as previously?"

15 Then the foremen of the sons of Israel came and cried out to Pharaoh, saying, "Why do you deal this way with your servants?

16 "There is no straw given to your servants, yet they keep saying to us, 'Make bricks!' And behold, your servants are being beaten; but it is the fault of your *own* people."

17 But he said, "You are [a]lazy, *very* lazy; therefore you say, 'Let us go *and* sacrifice to the LORD.'

18 "So go now *and* work; for you shall be given no straw, yet must deliver the quota of bricks."

19 And the foremen of the sons of Israel saw that they were in trouble [1]because they were told, "You must not reduce [2]*your* daily amount of bricks."

1 [a]Ex. 3:18 [b]Ex. 4:23

2 [a]Job 21:15 [b]Ex. 3:19

3 [a]Ex. 3:18

4 [1]Lit., *loose* [2]Lit., *works* [3]Lit., *burdens* [a]Ex. 1:11; 2:11; 6:5-7

5 [a]Ex. 1:7, 9

6 [a]Ex. 5:10, 13, 14; 1:11; 3:7 [b]Ex. 5:10, 14, 15, 19

8 [1]Lit., *saying, 'Let* [a]Ex. 5:17

10 [a]Ex. 5:6

13 [1]Lit., *works* [2]Lit., *the matter of a day in its day* [3]Lit., *there was*

14 [1]Lit., *saying* [a]Ex. 5:6 [b]Is. 10:24

17 [a]Ex. 5:8

19 [1]Lit., *saying* [2]Lit., *from your bricks the matter of a day in its day*

20 When they left Pharaoh's presence, they met Moses
and Aaron as they were [1]waiting for them.
21 And [a]they said to them, "[b]May the LORD look upon
you and judge *you,* for you have [c]made [1]us odious in Pharaoh's
sight and in the sight of his servants, to put a sword in their
hand to kill us."
22 Then Moses returned to the LORD and said, "[a]O LORD,
why hast Thou brought harm to this people? Why didst Thou
ever send me?
23 "Ever since I came to Pharaoh to speak in Thy name, he
has done harm to this people; [a]and Thou hast not delivered
Thy people at all."

CHAPTER 6

THEN the LORD said to Moses, "Now you shall see what I
will do to Pharaoh; for [1a]under compulsion he shall let them
go, and [1]under compulsion he shall drive them out of his
land."
2 God spoke further to Moses and said to him, "I am
[a]the LORD;
3 and I appeared to Abraham, Isaac, and Jacob, as [1]God
Almighty, [a]but *by* My name, [2]LORD, I did not make Myself
known to them.
4 "And I also established [a]My covenant with them, to give
them the land of Canaan, the [1]land in which they sojourned.
5 "And furthermore I have [a]heard the groaning of the sons
of Israel, because the Egyptians are holding them in bondage;
and I have remembered My covenant.
6 "Say, therefore, to the sons of Israel, '[a]I am the LORD,
and [b]I will bring you out from under the burdens of the Egyptians, and I will deliver you from their bondage. I will also
redeem you with [c]an outstretched arm and with great
judgments.
7 'Then I will take you [1a]for My people, and I will be
[2]your God; and [b]you shall know that I am the LORD your God,
who brought you out from under the burdens of the
Egyptians.
8 'And I will bring you to the land which [a]I [1]swore to give
to Abraham, Isaac, and Jacob, and [b]I will give it to you *for* a
possession; [c]I am the LORD.' "
9 So Moses spoke thus to the sons of Israel, but they did
not listen to Moses on [a]account of *their* [1]despondency and
cruel bondage.
10 Now the LORD spoke to Moses, saying,
11 "[a]Go, [1]tell Pharaoh king of Egypt [2]to let the sons of
Israel go out of his land."
12 But Moses spoke before the LORD, saying, "Behold, the
sons of Israel have not listened to me; [a]how then will Pharaoh
listen to me, for I am [1]unskilled in speech?"
13 Then the LORD spoke to Moses and to Aaron, and gave
them a charge to the sons of Israel and to Pharaoh king of
Egypt, to bring the sons of Israel out of the land of Egypt.
14 These are the heads of their fathers' households. [a]The
sons of Reuben, Israel's first-born: Hanoch and Pallu, Hezron
and Carmi; these are the families of Reuben.

20 [1]Lit., *standing to meet*

21 [1]Lit., *our savor to stink* [a]Ex. 14:11; 15:24; 16:2 [b]Gen. 16:5; 31:53 [c]Gen. 34:30; 1 Sam. 27:12

22 [a]Num. 11:11; Jer. 4:10

23 [a]Ex. 3:8

1 [1]Lit., *by a strong hand* [a]Ex. 3:19, 20; 7:4, 5; 12:31, 33, 39; 13:3

2 [a]Ex. 3:14, 15

3 [1]Heb., *El Shaddai* [2]YHWH, usually rendered LORD [a]Is. 52:6; Jer. 16:21; Ezek. 37:6, 13; Ps. 68:4; 83:18

4 [1]Lit., *land of their sojournings in which . . .* [a]Gen. 12:7; 15:18; 26:3, 4; 28:4, 13

5 [a]Ex. 2:24

6 [a]Ex. 13:3, 14; 20:2; Deut. 6:12 [b]Ex. 12:51; 16:6; 18:1 [c]Deut. 4:34; 5:15; 26:8

7 [1]Lit., *to Me for a people* [b]Lit., *to you for a God* [a]Deut. 4:20 [b]Ex. 16:12; Is. 41:20; 49:23, 26; 60:16

8 [1]Lit., *lifted up My hand* [a]Gen. 15:18; Num. 14:30; Neh. 9:15; Ezek. 20:5, 6 [b]Josh. 24:13; Ps. 136:21, 22 [c]Ex. 6:6

9 [1]Lit., *shortness of spirit* [a]Ex. 2:23

11 [1]Lit., *speak to* [2]Lit., *that he let* [a]Ex. 4:22, 23

12 [1]Lit., *uncircumcised of lips* [a]Ex. 6:30; 4:1, 10

14 [a]Gen. 46:9; Num. 26:5-11

15 And the sons of Simeon: Jemuel and Jamin and Ohad
and Jachin and Zohar and Shaul the son of a Canaanite woman; these are the families of Simeon.
16 And these are the names of [a]the sons of Levi according
to their generations: Gershon and Kohath and Merari; and the
[1]length of Levi's life was one hundred and thirty-seven years.
17 [a]The sons of Gershon; Libni and Shimei, according to
their families.
18 And [a]the sons of Kohath: Amram and Izhar and Hebron
and Uzziel; and the [1]length of Kohath's life was one
hundred and thirty-three years.
19 And the sons of Merari: Mahli and Mushi. These are
the families of the Levites according to their generations.
20 And [a]Amram [1]married his father's sister Jochebed, and
she bore him Aaron and Moses; and the [2]length of Amram's
life was one hundred and thirty-seven years.
21 And [a]the sons of Izhar: Korah and Nepheg and Zichri.
22 [a]And the sons of Uzziel: Mishael and [1]Elzaphan and
Sithri.
23 And Aaron [1]married Elisheba, the daughter of [a]Ammin-
adab, the sister of [b]Nahshon, and she bore him [c]Nadab and
Abihu, Eleazar and Ithamar.
24 And the [a]sons of Korah: Assir and Elkanah and [1]Abia-
saph; these are the families of the Korahites.
25 And Aaron's son [a]Eleazar [1]married one of the daughters of Putiel, and she bore him [b]Phinehas. These are the
heads of the fathers' *households* of the Levites according to
their families.
26 It was *the same* Aaron and Moses to whom the LORD
said, "[a]Bring out the sons of Israel from the land of Egypt
according to their hosts."
27 They were the ones [a]who spoke to Pharaoh king of
Egypt [1]about bringing out the sons of Israel from Egypt; it was
the same Moses and Aaron.
28 Now it came about on the day when the LORD spoke to
Moses in the land of Egypt,
29 that the LORD spoke to Moses, saying, "[a]I am the LORD;
[b]speak to Pharaoh king of Egypt all that I speak to you."
30 But Moses said before the LORD, "Behold, I am [1a]un-
skilled in speech; how then will Pharaoh listen to me?"

CHAPTER 7

THEN the LORD said to Moses, "[a]See, I make you *as* God to
Pharaoh, and your brother Aaron shall be your prophet.
2 "You shall speak all that I command you, and your
brother Aaron shall speak to Pharaoh that he let the sons of
Israel go out of his land.
3 "But [a]I will harden Pharaoh's heart that I may multiply
My signs and My wonders in the land of Egypt.
4 "When [a]Pharaoh will not listen to you, then I will lay
My hand on Egypt, and [b]bring out My hosts, My people the
sons of Israel, from the land of Egypt by [c]great judgments.
5 "And [a]the Egyptians shall know that I am the LORD,
when I stretch out My hand on Egypt and bring out the sons
of Israel from their midst."

---

16 [1]Lit., *years* [a]Gen. 46:11; Num. 3:17; 1 Chr. 6:1

17 [a]Num. 3:18-20; 1 Chr. 6:17

18 [1]Lit., *years* [a]Num. 3:19

20 [1]Lit., *took to him to wife* [2]Lit., *years* [a]Ex. 2:1, 2; Num. 26:59

21 [a]Num. 16:1; 1 Chr. 6:37, 38

22 [1]In Num. 3:30, *Elizaphen* [a]Lev. 10:4; Num. 3:30

23 [1]Lit., *took to him to wife* [a]Ruth 4:19, 20; 1 Chr. 2:10 [b]Num. 1:7; 2:3 [c]Lev. 10:1; Num. 3:2

24 [1]In 1 Chr. 6:23 and 9:19, *Ebiasaph* [a]1 Chr. 6:22, 23, 37

25 [1]Lit., *took to him to wife* [a]Josh. 24:33 [b]Num. 25:7, 11; Ps. 106:30

26 [a]Ex. 6:13

27 [1]Lit., *to bring out* [a]Ex. 5:1

29 [a]Ex. 6:2, 6, 8 [b]Ex. 6:11; 7:2

30 [1]Lit., *uncircumcised of lips* [a]Ex. 4:10; 6:12

1 [a]Ex. 4:16

2 [a]Ex. 4:15

3 [a]Ex. 4:21

4 [a]Ex. 3:19, 20; 11:9 [b]Ex. 12:51; 13:3, 9 [c]Ex. 6:6

5 [a]Ex. 7:17; 8:19; 10:7

6 So Moses and Aaron did *it;* [a]as the LORD commanded
them, thus they did.
7 And Moses was [a]eighty years old and Aaron [1]eighty-
three, when they spoke to Pharaoh.
8 Now the LORD spoke to Moses and Aaron, saying,
9 "When Pharaoh speaks to you, saying, '[1a]Work a miracle'; then you shall say to Aaron, 'Take your staff and throw
it down before Pharaoh, *that* it may become a serpent.' "
10 So Moses and Aaron came to Pharaoh, and thus they
did just as the LORD had commanded; and Aaron threw his
staff down before Pharaoh and [1]his servants, and it [a]became a
serpent.
11 Then Pharaoh also called for *the* wise men and *the*
sorcerers, and they also, the [1a]magicians of Egypt, [b]did [2]the
same with their secret arts.
12 For each one threw down his staff and they turned into
serpents. But Aaron's staff swallowed up their staffs.
13 Yet Pharaoh's heart was [1]hardened, and [a]he did not
listen to them, as the LORD had said.
14 Then the LORD said to Moses, "Pharaoh's heart is
[1]stubborn; he refuses to let the people go.
15 "Go to Pharaoh in the morning [1]as [a]he is going out to
the water, and station yourself to meet him on the bank of the
Nile; and you shall take in your hand [b]the staff that was turned
into a serpent.
16 "[a]And you will say to him, 'The LORD, the God of the
Hebrews, sent me to you, saying, "[b]Let My people go, that
they may serve Me in the wilderness. But behold, you have
not listened until now."
17 'Thus says the LORD, "[a]By this you shall know that I am
the LORD: behold, I will strike [1]the water that is in the Nile
with the staff that is in My hand, and [b]it shall be turned to
blood.
18 "And [a]the fish that are in the Nile will die, and the Nile
will [1]become foul; and the Egyptians will [2b]find difficulty in
drinking water from the Nile." ' "
19 Then the LORD said to Moses, "Say to Aaron, 'Take
your staff and [a]stretch out your hand over the waters of Egypt,
over their rivers, over their [1]streams, and over their pools, and
over all their reservoirs of water, that they may become blood;
and there shall be blood throughout all the land of Egypt,
both in *vessels of* wood and in *vessels of* stone.' "
20 So Moses and Aaron did even as the LORD had commanded. And he lifted up [1]the staff and struck the water that
was in the Nile, in the sight of Pharaoh and in the sight of his
servants, and [a]all the water that *was* in the Nile was turned to
blood.
21 And the fish that *were* in the Nile died, and the Nile
[1]became foul, so that the Egyptians could not drink water
from the Nile. And the blood was through all the land of
Egypt.
22 [a]But the [1]magicians of Egypt did [2]the same with their
secret arts; and Pharaoh's heart was [3]hardened, and he did not
listen to them, as the LORD had said.
23 Then Pharaoh turned and went into his house [1]with no
concern even for this.

6 [a]Gen. 6:22; 7:5; Ex. 7:2

7 [1]Lit., *83 years old* [a]Deut. 34:7; Acts 7:23, 30

9 [1]Lit., *Show a wonder for yourselves* [a]Is. 7:11; John 2:18

10 [1]Lit., *before his* [a]Ex. 4:3; 7:9

11 [1]Or, *soothsayer priests* [2]Lit., *thus* [a]Gen. 41:8 [b]Ex. 7:22; 8:7, 18; 2 Tim. 3:9

13 [1]Lit., *strong* [a]Ex. 7:4; 8:15

14 [1]Or, *hard;* lit., *heavy*

15 [1]Lit., *behold* [a]Ex. 2:5; 8:20 [b]Ex. 4:2, 3; 7:10

16 [a]Ex. 3:13, 18; 4:22; 5:1 [b]Ex. 4:23; 5:1, 3

17 [1]Lit., *upon the waters* [a]Ex. 5:2; 7:5; 10:2 [b]Ex. 4:9; 7:20; Rev. 11:6; 16:4, 6

18 [1]I.e., have a bad smell [2]Or, *be weary of* [a]Ex. 7:21 [b]Ex. 7:21, 24

19 [1]Or, *canals* [a]Ex. 8:5, 6, 16; 9:22; 10:12, 21; 14:21, 26

20 [1]Lit., *with the staff* [a]Ps. 78:44; 105:29

21 [1]I.e., had a bad smell

22 [1]Or, *soothsayer priests* [2]Lit., *thus* [3]Lit., *strong* [a]Ex. 7:11; 8:7

23 [1]Lit., *and he did not set his heart even to this*

24 So all the Egyptians dug around the Nile for water to drink, for they could not drink of the water of the Nile.

25 And seven days [1]passed after the LORD had struck the Nile.

CHAPTER 8

1 THEN the LORD said to Moses, "Go to Pharaoh and say to him, 'Thus says the LORD, "[a]Let My people go, that they may serve Me.

2 "But if you refuse to let *them* go, behold, I will smite your whole territory with frogs;

3 "And the Nile will swarm with frogs, which will come up and go into your house and into your bedroom and on your bed, and into the houses of your servants and on your people, and into your ovens and into your kneading bowls.

4 "So the frogs will come up on you and your people and all your servants." ' "

5 [1]Then the LORD said to Moses, "Say to Aaron, '[a]Stretch out your hand with your staff over the rivers, over the [2]streams and over the pools, and make frogs come up on the land of Egypt.' "

6 So Aaron stretched out his hand over the waters of Egypt, and the [1a]frogs came up and covered the land of Egypt.

7 [a]And the [1]magicians did [2]the same with their secret arts, [3]making frogs come up on the land of Egypt.

8 Then Pharaoh [a]called for Moses and Aaron and said, "[b]Entreat the LORD that He remove the frogs from me and from my people; and [c]I will let the people go, that they may sacrifice to the LORD."

9 And Moses said to Pharaoh, "[1]The honor is yours to tell me: when shall I entreat for you and your servants and your people, that the frogs be [2]destroyed from you and your houses, *that* they may be left only in the Nile?"

10 Then he said, "Tomorrow." So he said, "*May it be* according to your word, that you may know that there is [a]no one like the LORD our God.

11 "And the [a]frogs will depart from you and your houses and your servants and your people; they will be left only in the Nile."

12 Then Moses and Aaron went out from Pharaoh, and [a]Moses cried to the LORD concerning the frogs which He had [1]inflicted upon Pharaoh.

13 And the LORD did according to the word of Moses, and the frogs died out of the houses, the courts, and the fields.

14 So they piled them in heaps, and the land [1]became foul.

15 But when Pharaoh saw that there was relief, he [1]hardened his heart and [a]did not listen to them, as the LORD had said.

16 Then the LORD said to Moses, "Say to Aaron, 'Stretch out your staff and strike the dust of the earth, that it may become [1]gnats through all the land of Egypt.' "

17 And they did so; and Aaron stretched out his hand with his staff, and struck the dust of the earth, and there were [1]gnats

25 [1]Lit., *were fulfilled*

1 [1]Chap. 7:26 in Heb. [a]Ex. 3:18; 4:23; 5:1, 3

5 [1]Chap. 8:1 in Heb. [2]Or, *canals* [a]Ex. 7:19

6 [1]Lit., *frog* [a]Ps. 78:45; 105:30

7 [1]Or, *soothsayer priests* [2]Lit., *thus* [3]Lit., *and made* [a]Ex. 7:11, 22

8 [a]Ex. 8:25; 9:27; 10:16 [b]Ex. 8:28 [c]Ex. 8:15, 29

9 [1]Lit., *Glory over me* [2]Lit., *cut off*

10 [a]Ex. 9:14; Deut. 4:35, 39; 33:26; Ps. 86:8; Is. 46:9; Jer. 10:6, 7

11 [a]Ex. 8:13

12 [1]Lit., *placed* [a]Ex. 8:30; 9:33; 10:18

14 [1]I.e., had a bad smell

15 [1]Lit., *made heavy* [a]Ex. 7:4

16 [1]Or, *lice*

17 [1]Or, *lice*

on man and beast. All the dust of the earth became [1a]gnats through all the land of Egypt.

18 And the [1]magicians tried with their secret arts to bring forth [2]gnats, but [a]they could not; so there were [2]gnats on man and beast.

19 Then the [1]magicians said to Pharaoh, "[a]This is the finger of God." But Pharaoh's heart was [2]hardened, and he did not listen to them, as the LORD had said.

20 Now the LORD said to Moses, "[a]Rise early in the morning and present yourself before Pharaoh, [1]as [b]he comes out to the water, and say to him, 'Thus says the LORD, "[c]Let My people go, that they may serve Me.

21 "For if you will not let My people go, behold, I will send swarms of insects on you and on your servants and on your people and into your houses; and the houses of the Egyptians shall be full of swarms of insects, and also the ground on which they *dwell.*

22 "[a]But on that day I will set apart the land of Goshen, where My people are [1]living, so that no swarms of insects will be there, in order that you may know that [2b]I, the LORD, am in the midst of the land.

23 "And I will [1]put a division between My people and your people. Tomorrow this sign shall occur." ' "

24 Then the LORD did so. And there came [1]great swarms of insects into the house of Pharaoh and the houses of his servants and the land was [a]laid waste because of the swarms of insects in all the land of Egypt.

25 And Pharaoh [a]called for Moses and Aaron and said, "[b]Go, sacrifice to your God within the land."

26 But Moses said, "It is not right to do so, for we shall sacrifice to the LORD our God [1]what is an abomination to the Egyptians. If we sacrifice [1]what is an abomination to the Egyptians before their eyes, will they not then stone us?

27 "We must go a [a]three days' journey into the wilderness and sacrifice to the LORD our God as He [1]commands us."

28 And Pharaoh said, "[a]I will let you go, that you may sacrifice to the LORD your God in the wilderness; only you shall not go very far away. [b]Make supplication for me."

29 Then Moses said, "Behold, I am going out from you, and I shall make supplication to the LORD that the swarms of insects may depart from Pharaoh, from his servants, and from his people tomorrow; only do not let Pharaoh [a]deal deceitfully again in not letting the people go to sacrifice to the LORD."

30 So Moses went out from Pharaoh and made supplication to the LORD.

31 And the LORD did [1]as Moses asked, and removed the swarms of insects from Pharaoh, from his servants and from his people; not one remained.

32 But Pharaoh [1]hardened his heart this time also, and [a]he did not let the people go.

CHAPTER 9

THEN the LORD said to Moses, "Go to Pharaoh and speak to him, 'Thus says the LORD, the God of the Hebrews, "[a]Let My people go, that they may serve Me.

---

17 [1]Or, *lice* [a]Ps. 105:31

18 [1]Or, *soothsayer priests* [2]Or, *lice* [a]Ex. 8:7; 7:11, 12; 9:11

19 [1]Or, *soothsayer priests* [2]Lit., *strong* [a]Ex. 7:5; 10:7

20 [1]Lit., *behold* [a]Ex. 9:13 [b]Ex. 2:5; 7:15 [c]Ex. 3:18; 4:23; 5:1, 3

22 [1]Lit., *standing* [2]Or, *I am the LORD in the midst of the earth* [a]Ex. 9:4, 6, 24; 10:23; 11:7 [b]Ex. 9:29; 19:5; 20:11

23 [1]Lit., *set a ransom*

24 [1]Lit., *heavy* [a]Ps. 78:45; 105:31

25 [a]Ex. 8:8; 9:27; 10:16 [b]Ex. 9:28; 10:8, 24; 12:31

26 [1]Lit., *the abomination of Egypt*

27 [1]Lit., *says to us* [a]Ex. 3:18; 5:3

28 [a]Ex. 8:8, 15, 29, 32 [b]Ex. 8:8

29 [a]Ex. 8:8, 15

31 [1]Lit., *according to the word of Moses*

32 [1]Lit., *made heavy* [a]Ex. 4:21; 8:8, 15

1 [a]Ex. 4:23; 8:1

2 "For if you refuse to let *them* go, and [1]continue to hold them,

3 behold, the hand of the LORD [1]will come *with* a very severe pestilence on your livestock which are in the field, on the horses, on the donkeys, on the camels, on the herds, and on the flocks.

4 "[a]But the LORD will make a distinction between the livestock of Israel and the livestock of Egypt, so that [b]nothing will die of all that belongs to the sons of Israel." ' "

5 And the LORD set a definite time, saying, "Tomorrow the LORD will do this thing in the land."

6 So the LORD did this thing on the morrow, and [a]all the livestock of Egypt died; [b]but of the livestock of the sons of Israel, not one died.

7 And Pharaoh sent, and behold, there was not even one of the livestock of Israel dead. But the heart of Pharaoh was [1]hardened, and he did not let the people go.

8 Then the LORD said to Moses and Aaron, "Take for yourselves handfuls of soot from a kiln, and let Moses throw it toward the sky in the sight of Pharaoh.

9 "And it will become fine dust over all the land of Egypt, and will become boils breaking out with [a]sores on man and beast through all the land of Egypt."

10 So they took soot from a kiln, and stood before Pharaoh; and Moses threw it toward the sky, and it became boils breaking out with sores on man and beast.

11 [a]And the magicians could not stand before Moses because of the boils, for the boils were on the [1]magicians [2]as well as on all the Egyptians.

12 And [a]the LORD [1]hardened Pharaoh's heart, and he did not listen to them, just as the LORD had spoken to Moses.

13 Then the LORD said to Moses, "[a]Rise up early in the morning and stand before Pharaoh and say to him, 'Thus says the LORD, the God of the Hebrews, "[b]Let My people go, that they may serve Me.

14 "For this time I will send all My plagues [1]on you and your servants and your people, so that you may know that there is [a]no one like Me in all the earth.

15 "For *if by* now I had put forth My hand and struck you and your people with pestilence, you would then have been cut off from the earth.

16 "But, indeed, [a]for this cause I have allowed you to [1]remain, in order to show you My power, and in order to proclaim My name through all the earth.

17 "Still you exalt yourself against My people [1]by not letting them go.

18 "Behold, about this time tomorrow, [a]I will [1]send a very heavy hail, such as has not been *seen* in Egypt from the day it was founded [2]until now.

19 "Now therefore send, bring [a]your livestock and whatever you have in the field to safety. [b]Every man and beast that is found in the field and is not brought home, when the hail comes down on them, will die." ' "

20 [a]The one among the servants of Pharaoh who [1]feared the word of the LORD made his servants and his livestock flee into the houses;

2 [1]Lit., *still hold*

3 [1]Lit., *will be*

4 [a]Ex. 8:22 [b]Ex. 9:6

6 [a]Ex. 9:19, 20, 25 [b]Ex. 9:4

7 [1]Lit., *heavy* [a]Ex. 7:14; 8:32

9 [a]Rev. 16:2

11 [1]Or, *soothsayer priests* [2]Lit., *and on all* [a]Ex. 8:18

12 [1]Lit., *made strong* [a]Ex. 4:21

13 [a]Ex. 8:20 [b]Ex. 4:23

14 [1]Lit., *to your heart* [a]Ex. 8:10

16 [1]Lit., *stand* [a]Rom. 9:17

17 [1]Lit., *so as not to let*

18 [1]Lit., *cause to rain* [2]Lit., *and until now* [a]Ex. 9:23, 24

19 [a]Ex. 9:6 [b]Ex. 9:25

20 [1]Or, *revered* [a]Prov. 13:13

21 but he who [1]paid no regard to the word of the LORD
[2]left his servants and his livestock in the field.
22 Now the LORD said to Moses, "Stretch out your hand
toward the sky, that [1a]hail may fall on all the land of Egypt, on
man and on beast and on every plant of the field, throughout
the land of Egypt."
23 And Moses stretched out his staff toward the sky, and
the LORD [1]sent [2]thunder and hail, and fire ran down to the
earth. And [a]the LORD rained hail on the land of Egypt.
24 So there was hail, and fire [1]flashing continually in the
midst of the hail, very severe, such as had not been in all the
land of Egypt since it became a nation.
25 And [a]the hail struck all that was in the field through all
the land of Egypt, both man and beast; the hail also struck
every plant of the field and shattered every tree of the field.
26 [a]Only in the land of Goshen, where the sons of Israel
were there was no hail.
27 Then Pharaoh [1a]sent for Moses and Aaron, and said to
them, "[b]I have sinned this time; the LORD is the righteous one,
and I and my people are the wicked ones.
28 "[a]Make supplication to the LORD, for there has been
enough of God's [1]thunder and hail; and [b]I will let you go, and
you shall stay no longer."
29 And Moses said to him, "As soon as I go out of the city,
I will spread out my [1]hands to the LORD; the [2]thunder will
cease, and there will be hail no longer, that you may know that
[a]the earth is the LORD's.
30 "[a]But as for you and your servants, I know that you do
not yet [1]fear [2]the LORD God."
31 (Now the flax and the barley were [1]ruined, for the
barley was in the ear and the flax was in bud.
32 But the wheat and the spelt were not [1]ruined, for they
ripen late.)
33 So Moses went out of the city from Pharaoh, and
spread out his [1]hands to the LORD; and the [2]thunder and the
hail ceased, and rain [3]no longer poured on the earth.
34 But when Pharaoh saw that the rain and the hail and
the [1]thunder had ceased, he sinned again and [2]hardened his
heart, he and his servants.
35 And Pharaoh's heart was [1]hardened, and he did not let
the sons of Israel go, just as the [a]LORD had spoken through
Moses.

CHAPTER 10

THEN the LORD said to Moses, "Go to Pharaoh, for [a]I have
[1]hardened his heart and the heart of his servants, that I may
[2]perform these signs of Mine [3]among them,
2 and [a]that you may tell in the [1]hearing of your son, and
of your grandson, how I made a mockery of the Egyptians, and
how I [2]performed My signs among them; [b]that you may know
that I am the LORD."
3 And Moses and Aaron went to Pharaoh and said to
him, "Thus says the LORD, the God of the Hebrews, 'How long
will you refuse to humble yourself before Me? [a]Let My people
go, that they may serve Me.

21 [1]Lit., *did not set his heart to* [2]Lit., *then left*

22 [1]Lit., *there may be hail* [a]Rev. 16:21

23 [1]Lit., *gave* [2]Lit., *sounds* [a]Gen. 19:24; Josh. 10:11; Is. 30:30; Ezek. 38:22; Rev. 8:7

24 [1]Lit., *taking hold of itself*

25 [a]Ex. 9:19; Ps. 78:47, 48; 105:32

26 [a]Ex. 8:22

27 [1]Lit., *sent and called* [a]Ex. 8:8 [b]Ex. 10:16, 17; 2 Chr. 12:6; Ps. 129:4

28 [1]Lit., *sounds* [a]Ex. 8:8 [b]Ex. 8:25; 10:8, 24

29 [1]Lit., *palms* [2]Lit., *sounds* [a]Ex. 8:22; 19:5; 20:11; Ps. 24:1

30 [1]Or, *reverence* [2]Lit., *before the LORD* [a]Ex. 8:29

31 [1]Lit., *smitten*

32 [1]Lit., *smitten*

33 [1]Lit., *palms* [2]Lit., *sounds* [3]Lit., *was not poured*

34 [1]Lit., *sounds* [2]Lit., *made heavy*

35 [1]Lit., *strong* [a]Ex. 4:21

1 [1]Lit., *made heavy* [2]Lit., *put* [3]Lit., *in his midst* [a]Ex. 4:21; 7:13

2 [1]Lit., *ears* [2]Lit., *put* [a]Ex. 12:26, 27; 13:8, 14, 15; Deut. 4:9; Ps. 44:1 [b]Ex. 7:5, 17

3 [a]Ex. 4:23

6 [1]Lit., *were*
7 [1]Lit., *know* [a]Ex. 7:5; 8:19; 12:33
8 [1]Lit., *who and who are* [a]Ex. 8:8 [b]Ex. 8:25
9 [1]Lit., *have a feast* [a]Ex. 12:37, 38 [b]Ex. 5:1; 10:26
10 [1]Lit., *when I* [2]Lit., *before your face*
11 [1]Lit., *you desire it* [a]Ex. 10:28
13 [1]Lit., *carried* [a]Ps. 78:46; 105:34
14 [1]Lit., *heavy* [2]Lit., *locusts like them before them* [3]Lit., *after them* [a]Joel 1:4, 7; 2:1-11
15 [a]Ex. 10:5
16 [a]Ex. 8:8 [b]Ex. 9:27
17 [a]Ex. 8:8, 28
19 [1]Lit., *Sea of Reeds*

4 'For if you refuse to let My people go, behold, tomorrow I will bring locusts into your territory.
5 'And they shall cover the surface of the land, so that no
one shall be able to see the land. They shall also eat the rest of
what has escaped—what is left to you from the hail—and they
shall eat every tree which sprouts for you out of the field.
6 'Then your houses shall be filled, and the houses of all
your servants and the houses of all the Egyptians, *something*
which neither your fathers nor your grandfathers have seen,
from the day that they [1]came upon the earth until this day.' "
And he turned and went out from Pharaoh.
7 And [a]Pharaoh's servants said to him, "How long will
this man be a snare to us? Let the men go, that they may serve
the LORD their God. Do you not [1]realize that Egypt is
destroyed?"
8 So Moses and Aaron [a]were brought back to Pharaoh,
and he said to them, "[b]Go, serve the LORD your God! [1]Who
are the ones that are going?"
9 And Moses said, "[a]We shall go with our young and our
old; with our sons and our daughters, [b]with our flocks and our
herds we will go, for we [1]must hold a feast to the LORD."
10 Then he said to them, "Thus may the LORD be with
you, [1]if ever I let you and your little ones go! Take heed, for
evil is [2]in your mind.
11 "Not so! Go now, the men *among you*, and serve the
LORD, for [1]that is what you desire." So [a]they were driven out
from Pharaoh's presence.
12 Then the LORD said to Moses, "[a]Stretch out your hand
over the land of Egypt for the locusts, that they may come up
on the land of Egypt, and eat every plant of the land, *even* all
that the hail has left."
13 So Moses stretched out his staff over the land of Egypt,
and the LORD directed an east wind on the land all that day
and all the night; and when it was morning, the east wind
[1]brought the [a]locusts.
14 And [a]the locusts came up over all the land of Egypt and
settled in all the territory of Egypt; *they were* very [1]numerous.
There had never been so *many* [2]locusts, nor would there be so
many [3]again.
15 For they covered the surface of the whole land, so that
the land was darkened; and they [a]ate every plant of the land
and all the fruit of the trees that the hail had left. Thus nothing green was left on tree or plant of the field through all the
land of Egypt.
16 Then Pharaoh hurriedly [a]called for Moses and Aaron,
and he said, "[b]I have sinned against the LORD your God and
against you.
17 "Now therefore, please forgive my sin only this once,
and [a]make supplication to the LORD your God, that He would
only remove this death from me."
18 And he went out from Pharaoh and made supplication
to the LORD.
19 So the LORD shifted *the wind* to a very strong west wind
which took up the locusts and drove them into the [1]Red Sea;
not one locust was left in all the territory of Egypt.

20 But [a]the LORD [1]hardened Pharaoh's heart, and he did
not let the sons of Israel go.
21 Then the LORD said to Moses, "Stretch out your hand
toward the sky, that there may be darkness over the land of
Egypt, even a darkness [a]which may be felt."
22 So Moses stretched out his hand toward the sky, and
there was [a]thick darkness in all the land of Egypt for three
days.
23 They did not see one another, nor did anyone rise from
his place for three days, [a]but all the sons of Israel had light in
their dwellings.
24 Then Pharaoh [a]called to Moses, and said, "Go, serve
the LORD; only let your flocks and your herds be detained.
Even your little ones may go with you."
25 But Moses said, "You must also [1]let us have sacrifices
and burnt offerings, that we may [2]sacrifice *them* to the LORD
our God.
26 "[a]Therefore, our livestock, too, will go with us; not a
hoof will be left behind, for we shall take some of them to
serve the LORD our God. And until we arrive there, we ourselves do not know with what we shall serve the LORD."
27 But [a]the LORD [1]hardened Pharaoh's heart, and he was
not willing to let them go.
28 Then Pharaoh said to him, "[a]Get away from me! [1]Be-
ware, do not see my face again, for in the day you see my face
you shall die!"
29 And Moses said, "You are right; [a]I shall never see your
face again!"

CHAPTER 11

NOW the LORD said to Moses, "One more plague I will
bring on Pharaoh and on Egypt; [a]after that he will let you go
from here. When he lets you go, he will surely drive you out
from here completely.
2 "Speak now in the [1]hearing of the people that [a]each man
ask from his neighbor and each woman from her neighbor for
articles of silver and articles of gold."
3 [a]And the LORD gave the people favor in the sight of the
Egyptians. [b]Furthermore, the man Moses *himself* was [1]greatly
esteemed in the land of Egypt, *both* in the sight of Pharaoh's
servants and in the sight of the people.
4 And Moses said, "Thus says the LORD, 'About [a]mid-
night I am going out into the midst of Egypt,
5 and [a]all the first-born in the land of Egypt shall die,
from the first-born of the Pharaoh who sits on his throne, even
to the first-born of the slave girl who is behind the millstones;
all the first-born of the cattle as well.
6 'Moreover, there shall be [a]a great cry in all the land of
Egypt, such as there has not been *before* and such as shall
never be again.
7 '[a]But against any of the sons of Israel a dog shall not
even [1]bark, whether against man or beast, that you may [2]under-
stand how the LORD makes a distinction between Egypt
and Israel.'

20 [1]Lit., *made strong* [a]Ex. 4:21; 11:10
21 [a]Deut. 28:29
22 [a]Ps. 105:28
23 [a]Ex. 8:22
24 [a]Ex. 8:8, 25
25 [1]Lit., *give into our hand* [2]Lit., *make*
26 [a]Ex. 10:9
27 [1]Lit., *made strong* [a]Ex. 10:20
28 [1]Lit., *Take heed to yourself* [a]Ex. 10:11
29 [a]Ex. 11:8; Heb. 11:27
1 [a]Ex. 12:31, 33, 39
2 [1]Lit., *ears* [a]Ex. 3:22; 12:35, 36
3 [1]Lit., *very great* [a]Ex. 3:21; 12:36 [b]Deut. 34:10-12
4 [a]Ex. 12:29
5 [a]Ex. 12:12, 29; Ps. 73:51; 105:36; 135:8; 136:10
6 [a]Ex. 12:30
7 [1]Lit., *sharpen his tongue* [2]Lit., *know* [a]Ex. 8:22

8 "And [a]all these your servants will come down to me and
bow themselves [1]before me, saying, 'Go out, you and all the
people who [2]follow you,' and after that I will go out." [b]And he
went out from Pharaoh in hot anger.
9 Then the LORD said to Moses, "[a]Pharaoh will not listen
to you, so that My wonders will be multiplied in the land of
Egypt."
10 And [a]Moses and Aaron performed all these wonders
before Pharaoh; yet the LORD [1]hardened Pharaoh's heart, and
he did not let the sons of Israel go out of his land.

CHAPTER 12

NOW the LORD said to Moses and Aaron in the land of
[1]Egypt,
2 "[a]This month shall be the beginning of months for you;
it is to be the first month of the year to you.
3 "Speak to all the congregation of Israel, saying, 'On the
tenth of this month they are each one to take a [1]lamb for
themselves, according to their fathers' households, a [1]lamb for
[2]each household.
4 'Now if the household is too small for a [1]lamb, then he
and his neighbor nearest to his house are to take one according
to the [2]number of persons *in them;* according to [3]what each
man should eat, you are to [4]divide the lamb.
5 'Your [1]lamb shall be [a]an unblemished male a year old;
you may take it from the sheep or from the goats.
6 'And [1]you shall keep it until the [a]fourteenth day of the
same month, then the whole assembly of the congregation of
Israel is to kill it [2b]at twilight.
7 '[a]Moreover, they shall take some of the blood and put it
on the two doorposts and on the lintel [1]of the houses in which
they eat it.
8 'And they shall eat the flesh [a]that *same* night, [b]roasted
with fire, and they shall eat it with [c]unleavened bread [1d]and
bitter herbs.
9 'Do not eat any of it raw or boiled at all with water, but
rather [a]roasted with fire, *both* its head and its legs along with
[b]its entrails.
10 '[a]And you shall not leave any of it over until morning,
but whatever is left of it until morning, you shall burn with
fire.
11 'Now you shall eat it in this manner: *with* your loins
girded, your sandals on your feet, and your staff in your hand;
and you shall eat it in haste—it is [a]the LORD's Passover.
12 'For I will go through the land of Egypt on that night,
and will strike down all the first-born in the land of Egypt,
both man and beast; and [a]against all the gods of Egypt I will
execute judgments—I am the LORD.
13 'And the blood shall be a sign for you on the houses
where you [1]live; and when I see the blood I will pass over you,
and no plague will befall you [2]to destroy *you* when I strike the
land of Egypt.

8 [1]Lit., *to* [2]Lit., *are at your feet* [a]Ex. 12:31-33 [b]Heb. 11:27

9 [a]Ex. 7:4

10 [1]Lit., *made strong* [a]Ex. 4:21; 10:20, 27

1 [1]Lit., *Egypt, saying*

2 [a]Ex. 13:4; 23:15; 34:18; Deut. 16:1

3 [1]Or, *kid* [2]Lit., *the*

4 [1]Or, *kid* [2]Or, *amount* [3]Lit., *each man's eating* [4]Lit., *compute for*

5 [1]Or, *kid* [a]Lev. 22:18-20

6 [1]Lit., *it shall be to you for a guarding* [2]Lit., *between the two evenings* [a]Ex. 12:14, 17; Lev. 23:5; Num. 9:1-3, 11 [b]Deut. 16:4, 6

7 [1]Lit., *upon* [a]Ex. 12:22

8 [1]Lit., *in addition to* [a]Ex. 34:25; Num. 9:12 [b]Deut. 16:7 [c]Deut. 16:3, 4 [d]Num. 9:11

9 [a]Ex. 12:8 [b]Ex. 29:13, 17, 22

10 [a]Ex. 16:19; 23:18; 34:25

11 [a]Ex. 12:13, 21, 27, 43

12 [a]Num. 33:4

13 [1]Lit., *are* [2]Lit., *for destruction*

14 'Now [a]this day will be [b]a memorial to you, and you shall celebrate it *as* a feast to the LORD; throughout your generations you are to celebrate it *as* [c]a [1]permanent ordinance.

15 '[a]Seven days you shall eat unleavened bread, but on the first day you shall [1]remove leaven from your houses; for whoever eats anything leavened from the first day until the seventh day, [b]that [2]person shall be cut off from Israel.

16 'And [a]on the first day you shall have a holy assembly, and *another* holy assembly on the seventh day; no work at all shall be done on them, except what must be eaten [1]by every person, that alone may be [2]prepared by you.

17 'You shall also observe the *Feast of* Unleavened Bread, for on this [a]very day I brought your hosts out of the land of Egypt; therefore you shall observe this day throughout your generations as [b]a [1]permanent ordinance.

18 '[a]In the first *month,* on the fourteenth day of the month at evening, you shall eat unleavened bread, until the twenty-first day of the month at evening.

19 '[a]Seven days there shall be no leaven found in your houses; for whoever eats what is leavened, that [1]person shall be cut off from the congregation of Israel, whether *he is* an alien or a native of the land.

20 'You shall not eat anything leavened; in all your dwellings you shall eat unleavened bread.' "

21 Then [a]Moses called for all the elders of Israel, and said to them, "[1]Go and take for yourselves [2]lambs according to your families, and slay [b]the Passover *lamb.*

22 "[a]And you shall take a bunch of hyssop and dip it in the blood which is in the basin, and [1]apply some of the blood that is in the basin to the lintel and the two doorposts; and none of you shall go outside the door of his house until morning.

23 "For [a]the LORD will pass through to smite the Egyptians; and when He sees the blood on the lintel and on the two doorposts, the LORD will pass over the door and will not allow the destroyer to come in to your houses to smite *you.*

24 "And [a]you shall observe this event as an ordinance for you and your children forever.

25 "And it will come about when you enter the land which the LORD will give you, as He has [1]promised, that you shall observe this [2]rite.

26 "[a]And it will come about when your children will say to you, '[1]What does this rite mean to you?'

27 that you shall say, 'It is a Passover sacrifice to [a]the LORD [1]who passed over the houses of the sons of Israel in Egypt when He smote the Egyptians, but [2]spared our homes.' " [b]And the people bowed low and worshiped.

28 Then the sons of Israel went and did *so;* just as the LORD had commanded Moses and Aaron, so they did.

29 Now it came about at [a]midnight that the LORD struck all [b]the first-born in the land of Egypt, from the first-born of Pharaoh who sat on his throne to the first-born of the captive who was in the dungeon, and all the first-born of [c]cattle.

30 And Pharaoh arose in the night, he and all his servants and all the Egyptians; and there was [a]a great cry in Egypt, for there was no home where there was not someone dead.

14 [1]Or, *eternal*
[a]Ex. 12:6 [b]Ex. 13:9 [c]Ex. 12:17, 24; 13:10

15 [1]Lit., *cause to cease* [2]Lit., *soul*
[a]Ex. 23:15; 34:18; Deut. 16:3 [b]Ex. 12:19

16 [1]Lit., *pertaining to* [2]Lit., *done*
[a]Lev. 23:7, 8

17 [1]Or, *eternal*
[a]Ex. 12:41 [b]Ex. 12:14; 13:3, 10

18 [a]Ex. 12:2; Lev. 23:5-8; Num. 28:16-25

19 [1]Lit., *soul*
[a]Ex. 12:15

21 [1]Lit., *Draw out* [2]Lit., *sheep*
[a]Heb. 11:28 [b]Ex. 12:11

22 [1]Lit., *cause to touch*
[a]Ex. 12:7

23 [a]Ex. 12:12, 13; 11:4

24 [a]Ex. 12:14, 17; 13:5, 10

25 [1]Lit., *spoken* [2]Lit., *service*

26 [1]Lit., *What is this service to you?*
[a]Ex. 10:2; 13:14, 15; Josh. 4:6

27 [1]Lit., *because He* [2]Lit., *delivered*
[a]Ex. 12:11 [b]Ex. 4:31

29 [a]Ex. 11:4, 5 [b]Ex. 4:23; Ps. 78:51; 105:36 [c]Ex. 9:6

30 [a]Ex. 11:6

31 Then [a]he called for Moses and Aaron at night and said, "Rise up, [b]get out from among my people, both you and the sons of Israel; and go, [1]worship the LORD, as you have said.

32 "Take [a]both your flocks and your herds, as you have said, and go, and bless me also."

33 And [a]the Egyptians urged the people, to send them out of the land in haste, for they said, "We shall all be dead."

34 So the people took [a]their dough before it was leavened, *with* their kneading bowls bound up in the clothes on their shoulders.

35 [a]Now the sons of Israel had done according to the word of Moses, for they had requested from the Egyptians articles of silver and articles of gold, and clothing;

36 and the LORD had given the people favor in the sight of the Egyptians, so that they let them have their request. Thus they [a]plundered the Egyptians.

37 Now the sons of Israel journeyed from [a]Rameses to Succoth, about [b]six hundred thousand men on foot, aside from children.

38 And a [a]mixed multitude also went up with them, [1]along with flocks and herds, a [b]very large number of livestock.

39 And they baked the dough which they had brought out of Egypt into cakes of unleavened bread. For it had not become leavened, since they were [a]driven out of Egypt and could not delay, nor had they [1]prepared any provisions for themselves.

40 Now the time [1]that the sons of Israel lived in Egypt was [a]four hundred and thirty years.

41 And it came about at the end of four hundred and thirty years, [1]to [a]the very day, that [b]all the hosts of the LORD went out from the land of Egypt.

42 [a]It is a night [1]to be observed for the LORD for having brought them out from the land of Egypt; this night is for the LORD, [1]to be observed [2]by all the sons of Israel throughout their generations.

43 And the LORD said to Moses and Aaron, "This is the ordinance of [a]the Passover: no [1b]foreigner is to eat of it;

44 but every man's [a]slave purchased with money, after you have circumcised him, then he may eat of it.

45 "A sojourner or a hired servant shall not eat of it.

46 "It is to be eaten in a single house; you are not to bring forth any of the flesh outside of the house, [a]nor are you to break any bone of it.

47 "[a]All the congregation of Israel are to [1]celebrate this.

48 "But if a [1]stranger sojourns with you, and [2]celebrates the Passover to the LORD, let all his males be circumcised, and then let him come near to [3]celebrate it; and he shall be like a native of the land. But no uncircumcised person may eat of it.

49 "[1a]The same law shall [2]apply to the native as to the [3]stranger who sojourns among you."

50 Then all the sons of Israel did *so;* they did just as the LORD had commanded Moses and Aaron.

51 And it came about on that same day that [a]the LORD brought the sons of Israel out of the land of Egypt [1]by their hosts.

31 [1]Or, *serve* [a]Ex. 8:8 [b]Ex. 8:25

32 [a]Ex. 10:9, 26

33 [a]Ex. 12:39; 10:7; 11:1; Ps. 105:38

34 [a]Ex. 12:39

35 [a]Ex. 3:21, 22; 11:2, 3; Ps. 105:37

36 [a]Ex. 3:22

37 [a]Num. 33:3, 4 [b]Ex. 38:26; Num. 1:46; 2:32; 11:21; 26:51

38 [1]Lit., *and* [a]Num. 11:4 [b]Ex. 17:3; Num. 20:19; 32:1; Deut. 3:19

39 [1]Lit., *made* [a]Ex. 12:31-33; 11:1

40 [1]Or, *of the sons of Israel who dwelt* [a]Gen. 15:13, 16; Acts 7:6; Gal. 3:17

41 [1]Lit., *that it happened on this very day* [a]Ex. 12:17 [b]Ex. 3:8, 10; 6:6

42 [1]Or, *of vigil* [2]Lit., *to the sons* [a]Ex. 13:10; 34:18; Deut. 16:1

43 [1]Lit., *son of a stranger* [a]Ex. 12:11 [b]Ex. 12:48

44 [a]Gen. 17:12, 13; Lev. 22:11

46 [a]Num. 9:12; John 19:33, 36

47 [1]Lit., *do* [a]Num. 9:13, 14

48 [1]Lit., *sojourner* [2]Lit., *does* [3]Lit., *do*

49 [1]Lit., *One law* [2]Lit., *be* [3]Lit., *sojourner* [a]Lev. 24:22; Num. 15:15, 16, 29

51 [1]Lit., *according to* [a]Ex. 12:41

CHAPTER 13

THEN the LORD spoke to Moses, saying,
2 "[a]Sanctify to Me every first-born, the first [1]offspring of
every womb among the sons of Israel, both of man and beast;
it belongs to Me."
3 And Moses said to the people, "Remember this day in
which you went out from Egypt, from the house of [1]slavery;
for [a]by [2]a powerful hand the LORD brought you out from this
place. [b]And nothing leavened shall be eaten.
4 "On this day in the [a]month of Abib, you are about to go
forth.
5 "And it shall be when the LORD [a]brings you to the land
of the Canaanite, the Hittite, the Amorite, the Hivite and the
Jebusite, which He swore to your fathers to give you, a land
flowing with milk and honey, [b]that you shall [1]observe this rite
in this month.
6 "For [a]seven days you shall eat unleavened bread, and on
the seventh day there shall be a feast to the LORD.
7 "Unleavened bread shall be eaten throughout the seven
days; and nothing leavened shall be seen [1]among you, nor shall
any leaven be seen [1]among you in all your borders.
8 "[a]And you shall tell your son on that day, saying, 'It is
because of what the LORD did for me when I came out of
Egypt.'
9 "And [a]it shall [1]serve as a sign to you on your hand, and as
a reminder [2]on your forehead, that the law of the LORD may be
in your mouth; for with [b]a powerful hand the LORD brought
you out of Egypt.
10 "Therefore, you shall [a]keep this ordinance at its appointed time from [1]year to year.
11 "Now it shall come about when [a]the LORD brings you to
the land of the Canaanite, as He swore to you and to your
fathers, and gives it to you,
12 that [a]you shall [1]devote to the LORD the first [2]offspring
of every womb, and [3]the first offspring of every beast that you
own; the males belong to the LORD.
13 "But [a]every first [1]offspring of a donkey you shall redeem
with a lamb, but if you do not redeem *it*, then you shall break
its neck; and every first-born of man among your sons you shall
redeem.
14 "[a]And it shall be when your son asks you in time to
come, saying, 'What is this?' then you shall say to him, '[b]With
a [1]powerful hand the LORD brought us out of Egypt, from the
house of [2]slavery.
15 'And it came about, when Pharaoh was stubborn about
letting us go, that the LORD killed every first-born in the land
of Egypt, both the first-born of man and the first-born of
beast. Therefore, I sacrifice to the LORD the males, the first
[1]offspring of every womb, but every first-born of my sons I
redeem.'
16 "So [a]it shall [1]serve as a sign on your hand, and as [2]phy-
lacteries [3]on your forehead, for with a [4]powerful hand the
LORD brought us out of Egypt."
17 Now it came about when Pharaoh had let the people
go, that God did not lead them by the way of the land of the

2 [1]Lit., *opening* [a]Ex. 13:12, 13, 15; 22:29; Luke 2:23

3 [1]Lit., *slaves* [2]Lit., *strength of hand* [a]Ex. 3:20; 6:1 [b]Ex. 12:19

4 [a]Ex. 12:22

5 [1]Lit., *serve this service* [a]Ex. 3:8, 17; Josh. 24:11 [b]Ex. 12:25

6 [a]Ex. 12:15-20

7 [1]Lit., *to*

8 [a]Ex. 13:14; 10:2

9 [1]Lit., *be for* [2]Lit., *between your eyes* [a]Ex. 13:16; 12:14; Deut. 6:8; 11:18 [b]Ex. 13:3

10 [1]Lit., *days to days* [a]Ex. 13:5; 12:24, 25

11 [a]Ex. 13:5

12 [1]Lit., *cause to pass over* [2]Lit., *opening* [3]Lit., *every issue the offspring of a beast* [a]Ex. 13:1, 2

13 [1]Lit., *opening* [a]Ex. 34:20

14 [1]Lit., *strength of hand* [2]Lit., *slaves* [a]Ex. 13:8; 10:2; 12:26, 27; Deut. 6:20 [b]Ex. 13:3, 9

15 [1]Lit., *opening*

16 [1]Lit., *be for* [2]Or, *frontlet-bands* [3]Lit., *between your eyes* [4]Lit., *strength of hand* [a]Ex. 13:9

17 [a]Ex. 14:11, 12; Num. 14:1-4; Deut. 17:16

18 [1]Lit., *Sea of Reeds* [a]Josh. 1:14; 4:12, 13

19 [1]Lit., *visit* [a]Gen. 50:24, 25; Josh. 24:32; Acts 7:15, 16

20 [a]Ex. 12:37; Num. 33:6

21 [1]Lit., *go* [a]Ex. 14:19, 24; 33:9, 10; Ps. 78:14; 99:7; 105:39; 1 Cor. 10:1

22 [1]Or, *the pillar of cloud by day and the pillar of fire by night did not depart*

2 [a]Num. 33:7

4 [1]Lit., *make strong* [a]Ex. 14:17; 4:21 [b]Ex. 14:17, 23 [c]Ex. 7:5; 14:25

5 [1]Lit., *the heart of Pharaoh . . . was changed*

8 [1]Lit., *made strong* [2]Lit., *with a high hand* [a]Ex. 14:4 [b]Num. 33:3; Acts 13:17

9 [a]Ex. 14:2

10 [1]Lit., *lifted up their eyes* [a]Neh. 9:9

11 [1]Lit., *so as to bring* [a]Ex. 5:21; 15:24; 16:2; Ps. 106:7, 8

Philistines, even though it was near; for God said, "[a]Lest the people change their minds when they see war, and they return to Egypt."

18 Hence God led the people around by the way of the wilderness to the [1]Red Sea; and the sons of Israel went up [a]in martial array from the land of Egypt.

19 And Moses took [a]the bones of Joseph with him, for he had made the sons of Israel solemnly swear, saying, "God shall surely [1]take care of you; and you shall carry my bones from here with you."

20 Then they set out from [a]Succoth and camped in Etham on the edge of the wilderness.

21 And [a]the LORD was going before them in a pillar of cloud by day to lead them on the way, and in a pillar of fire by night to give them light, that they might [1]travel by day and by night.

22 [1]He did not take away the pillar of cloud by day, nor the pillar of fire by night, from before the people.

CHAPTER 14

NOW the LORD spoke to Moses, saying,

2 "Tell the sons of Israel to turn back and camp before [a]Pi-hahiroth, between Migdol and the sea; you shall camp in front of Baal-zephon, opposite it, by the sea.

3 "For Pharaoh will say of the sons of Israel, 'They are wandering aimlessly in the land; the wilderness has shut them in.'

4 "Thus [a]I will [1]harden Pharaoh's heart, and [b]he will chase after them; and I will be honored through Pharaoh and all his army, and [c]the Egyptians will know that I am the LORD." And they did so.

5 When the king of Egypt was told that the people had fled, [1]Pharaoh and his servants had a change of heart toward the people, and they said, "What is this we have done, that we have let Israel go from serving us?"

6 So he made his chariot ready and took his people with him;

7 and he took six hundred select chariots, and all the *other* chariots of Egypt with officers over all of them.

8 And [a]the LORD [1]hardened the heart of Pharaoh, king of Egypt, and he chased after the sons of Israel as the sons of Israel were going out [2b]boldly.

9 Then the Egyptians chased after them *with* all the horses *and* chariots of Pharaoh, his horsemen and his army, and they overtook them camping by the sea, [a]beside Pi-hahiroth, in front of Baal-zephon.

10 And as Pharaoh drew near, the sons of Israel [1]looked, and behold, the Egyptians were marching after them, and they became very frightened; [a]so the sons of Israel cried out to the LORD.

11 Then [a]they said to Moses, "Is it because there were no graves in Egypt that you have taken us away to die in the wilderness? Why have you dealt with us in this way, [1]bringing us out of Egypt?

12 "Is this not the word that we spoke to you in Egypt,

saying, '[1]Leave us alone that we may serve the Egyptians'? For
it would have been better for us to serve the Egyptians than to
die in the wilderness."
13 But Moses said to the people, "[a]Do not fear! [1]Stand by
and see [b]the salvation of the LORD which He will accomplish
for you today; for the Egyptians whom you have seen today,
you will never see them again forever.
14 "[a]The LORD will fight for you while [b]you keep silent."
15 Then the LORD said to Moses, "Why are you crying
out to me? Tell the sons of Israel to go forward.
16 "And as for you, lift up [a]your staff and stretch out your
hand over the sea and divide it, and the sons of Israel shall [1]go
through the midst of the sea on dry land.
17 "And as for Me, behold, [a]I will [1]harden the hearts of the
Egyptians so that they will go in after them; and I will be
honored through Pharaoh and all his army, through his chariots and his horsemen.
18 "[a]Then the Egyptians will know that I am the LORD,
when I am honored through Pharaoh, through his chariots and
his horsemen."
19 And [a]the angel of God, who had been going before the
camp of Israel, moved and went behind them; and the pillar of
cloud moved from before them and stood behind them.
20 So it came between the camp of Egypt and the camp of
Israel; and there was the cloud [1]along with the darkness, yet it
gave light at night. Thus the one did not come near the other
all night.
21 [a]Then Moses stretched out his hand over the sea; and
the LORD [1]swept the sea *back* by a strong east wind all night,
and turned the sea into [b]dry land, so [c]the waters were divided.
22 [a]And the sons of Israel [1]went through the midst of the
sea on the dry land, and [b]the waters *were like* a wall to them on
their right hand and on their left.
23 Then [a]the Egyptians took up the pursuit, and all Pharaoh's horses, his chariots and his horsemen went in after them
into the midst of the sea.
24 And it came about at the morning watch, that [a]the
LORD looked down on the [1]army of the Egyptians [2]through the
pillar of fire and cloud and brought the [1]army of the Egyptians
into confusion.
25 And He [1]caused their chariot wheels to swerve, and He
made them drive with difficulty; so the Egyptians said, "Let
[2]us flee from Israel, [a]for the LORD is fighting for them against
the Egyptians."
26 Then the LORD said to Moses, "[a]Stretch out your hand
over the sea so that the waters may come back over the Egyptians, over their chariots and their horsemen."
27 So Moses stretched out his hand over the sea, and the
sea returned to its normal state at daybreak, while the Egyptians were fleeing [1]right into it; then the LORD [2a]overthrew the
Egyptians in the midst of the sea.
28 And the waters returned and covered the chariots and
the horsemen, [1]even Pharaoh's entire army that had gone into
the sea after them; [a]not even one of them remained.
29 But the sons of Israel walked on [a]dry land through the

12 [1]Lit., *Cease from us*

13 [1]Or, *take your stand* [a]Ex. 20:20; Gen. 15:1; 46:3 [b]Ex. 14:30; 15:2

14 [a]Ex. 15:3; Deut. 1:30; 3:22 [b]Is. 30:15

16 [1]Lit., *enter the* [a]Ex. 4:17, 20; 17:5, 6; Num. 20:8, 9, 11; Is. 10:26

17 [1]Lit., *make strong* [a]Ex. 14:4

18 [a]Ex. 14:25

19 [a]Ex. 13:21, 22

20 [1]Lit., *and the darkness*

21 [1]Lit., *caused to go* [a]Ex. 14:16; 7:19 [b]Ps. 106:9; 136:13, 14 [c]Ps. 78:13; 114:3, 5; Is. 63:12, 13

22 [1]Lit., *entered the* [a]Josh. 3:17; 4:22; Neh. 9:11; Heb. 11:29 [b]Ex. 14:29; 15:8

23 [a]Ex. 14:4, 17

24 [1]Lit., *camp* [2]Or, *in* [a]Ex. 13:21

25 [1]Or, *removed* [2]Lit., *me* [a]Ex. 14:4, 18

26 [a]Ex. 14:16

27 [1]Lit., *to meet it* [2]Lit., *shook off* [a]Ex. 15:1, 7

28 [1]Lit., *in respect to* [a]Ps. 78:53; 106:11

29 [a]Ex. 14:22; Ps. 66:6; Is. 11:15

midst of the sea, and the waters *were like* a wall to them on
their right hand and on their left.
30 [a]Thus the LORD saved Israel that day from the hand of
the Egyptians, and Israel saw the Egyptians dead on the
seashore.
31 And when Israel saw the great [1]power which the LORD
had [2]used against the Egyptians, the people [3]feared the LORD,
and [a]they believed in the LORD and in His servant Moses.

CHAPTER 15

[a] THEN Moses and the sons of Israel sang this song to the
LORD, [1]and said,

"[2b]I will sing to the LORD, for He [3]is highly exalted;
[c]The horse and its rider He has hurled into the sea.
2 "[1a]The LORD is my strength and song,
And He has become my salvation;
[b]This is my God, and I will praise Him;
[c]My father's God, and I will extol Him.
3 "[a]The LORD is a warrior;
[1b]The LORD is His name.
4 "[a]Pharaoh's chariots and his army He has cast into the sea;
And the choicest of his officers are [1]drowned in the [2]Red Sea.
5 "The deeps cover them;
[a]They went down into the depths like a stone.
6 "[a]Thy right hand, O LORD, is majestic in power,
[b]Thy right hand, O LORD, shatters the enemy.
7 "And in the greatness of Thine [1]excellence Thou [a]dost overthrow those who rise up against Thee;
[b]Thou dost send forth Thy burning anger, *and* it consumes them as chaff.
8 "[a]And at the blast of Thy nostrils the waters were piled up,
[b]The flowing waters stood up like a heap;
The deeps were congealed in the heart of the sea.
9 "[a]The enemy said, 'I will pursue, I will overtake, I will divide the spoil;
My [1]desire shall be [2]gratified against them;
I will draw out my sword, my hand shall [3]destroy them.'
10 "[a]Thou didst blow with Thy wind, the sea covered them;
[b]They sank like lead in the [1]mighty waters.
11 "[a]Who is like Thee among the gods, O LORD?
Who is like Thee, [b]majestic in holiness,
[c]Awesome in praises, [d]working wonders?
12 "[a]Thou didst stretch out Thy right hand,
The earth swallowed them.
13 "In Thy lovingkindness Thou hast [a]led the people whom Thou hast [b]redeemed;
In Thy strength Thou has guided *them* [c]to Thy holy habitation.
14 "[a]The peoples have heard, they tremble;
Anguish has gripped the inhabitants of Philistia.
15 "Then the [a]chiefs of Edom were dismayed;
[b]The leaders of Moab, trembling grips them;

30 [a]Ex. 14:13; Ps. 106:8, 10, 21, 22; Is. 63:8, 11

31 [1]Lit., *hand* [2]Lit., *done* [3]Or, *revered* [a]Ps. 106:12

1 [1]Lit., *and said, saying* [2]Or, *"Let me sing* [3]Or, *triumphed gloriously* [a]Ps. 106:12; Rev. 15:3 [b]Is. 12:5; 42:10-12 [c]Jer. 51:21

2 [1]Heb., *YAH* [a]Is. 12:2 [b]Ps. 48:14 [c]Ex. 3:6, 15, 16

3 [1]YHWH, usually rendered LORD [a]Ex. 14:14 [b]Ex. 3:15; 6:2, 7, 8; Ps. 24:8

4 [1]Lit., *sunk* [2]Lit., *Sea of Reeds* [a]Ex. 14:6, 7, 17, 28

5 [a]Ex. 14:10; Neh. 9:11

6 [a]Ex. 3:20; 6:1 [b]Ps. 118:15, 16

7 [1]Or, *exaltation* [a]Ex. 14:27 [b]Ps. 78:49, 50

8 [a]Ex. 14:22, 29 [b]Ps. 78:13

9 [1]Lit., *soul* [2]Lit., *be filled with them* [3]Or, *disposses, bring to ruin* [a]Ex. 14:5, 8, 9

10 [1]Or, *majestic* [a]Ex. 14:27, 28 [b]Ex. 15:5

11 [a]Ex. 8:10; 9:14; Deut. 3:24; Ps. 71:19; Mic. 7:18 [b]Is. 6:3; Rev. 4:8 [c]Ps. 22:23 [d]Ps. 72:18; 136:4

12 [a]Ex. 15:6

13 [a]Neh. 9:12; Ps. 77:20 [b]Ex. 15:16; Ps. 77:15 [c]Ex. 15:17; Ps. 78:54

14 [a]Deut. 2:25; Hab. 3:7

15 [a]Gen. 36:15 [b]Num. 22:3, 4; Ps. 114:5, 7

[c]All the inhabitants of Canaan have melted away.
16 "[a]Terror and dread fall upon them;
[b]By the greatness of Thine arm they are motionless as stone;
Until Thy people pass over, O LORD,
Until the people pass over whom Thou [c]hast purchased.
17 "[a]Thou wilt bring them and [b]plant them in [c]the mountain of Thine inheritance,
[d]The place, O LORD, which Thou hast made for Thy dwelling,
[e]The sanctuary, O LORD, which Thy hands have established.
18 "[a]The LORD shall reign forever and ever."
19 [a]For the horses of Pharaoh with his chariots and his
horsemen went into the sea, and the LORD brought back the
waters of the sea on them; but the sons of Israel walked on [b]dry
land through the midst of the sea.
20 And [a]Miriam the prophetess, Aaron's sister, took the
[b]timbrel in her hand, and all the women went out after her
with timbrels and with [1c]dancing.
21 And Miriam answered them,
"[a]Sing to the LORD, for He [1]is highly exalted;
The horse and his rider He has hurled into the sea."
22 [a]Then Moses [1]led Israel from the [2]Red Sea, and they
went out into the [b]the wilderness of [c]Shur; and they went three
days in the wilderness and found no water.
23 And when they came to [a]Marah, they could not drink
the waters [1]of Marah, for they were [2]bitter; therefore it was
named [3]Marah.
24 So the people [a]grumbled at Moses, saying, "What shall
we drink?"
25 Then he [a]cried out to the LORD, and the LORD showed
him [b]a tree; and he threw *it* into the waters, and the waters
became sweet. There He made for them a statute and regulation, and there He [c]tested them.
26 And He said, "[a]If you will give earnest heed to the
voice of the LORD your God, and do what is right in His sight,
and give ear [b]to His commandments, and keep all His statutes,
[c]I will put none of the diseases on you which I have put on the
Egyptians; for I, [d]the LORD, am your healer."
27 Then they came to [a]Elim where there *were* twelve
springs of water and seventy date palms, and they camped
there beside the waters.

CHAPTER 16

THEN they set out from Elim, and all the congregation of
the sons of Israel came to the wilderness of [a]Sin, which is
between Elim and Sinai, on [b]the fifteenth day of the second
month after their departure from the land of Egypt.
2 And the whole congregation of the sons of Israel [a]grum-
bled against Moses and Aaron in the wilderness.
3 And the sons of Israel said to them, "[a]Would that we
had died by the LORD's hand in the land of Egypt, [b]when we
sat by the pots of [1]meat, when we ate bread to the full; for you

15 [c]Josh. 2:9, 11, 24

16 [a]Ex. 23:27 [b]Ex. 15:5, 6 [c]Ex. 15:13; Ps. 74:2

17 [a]Ex. 23:20; 32:34 [b]Ps. 44:2; 80:8, 15 [c]Ps. 2:6; 78:54, 68 [d]Ps. 68:16; 76:2; 132:13, 14 [e]Ps. 78:69

18 [a]Ps. 10:16; 29:10

19 [a]Ex. 14:23, 28 [b]Ex. 14:22, 29

20 [1]Lit., *dances* [a]Ex. 2:4; 6:20; Num. 26:59 [b]Ps. 81:2; 149:3 [c]Ps. 30:11; 150:4

21 [1]Or, *has triumphed gloriously* [a]Ex. 15:1

22 [1]Lit., *caused Israel to journey* [2]Lit., *Sea of Reeds* [a]Ps. 77:20; 78:52, 53 [b]Num. 33:8 [c]Gen. 16:7; 20:1

23 [1]Lit., *from* [2]Heb., *Marim* [3]I.e., Bitterness [a]Num. 33:8

24 [a]Ex. 14:11; Ps. 106:13

25 [a]Ex. 14:10 [b]Ezek. 47:7, 8 [c]Ex. 16:4

26 [a]Ex. 19:5, 6 [b]Ex. 20:2-17 [c]Deut. 7:15; 28:58, 60 [d]Deut. 32:39; Ps. 103:3

27 [a]Num. 33:9

1 [a]Num. 33:10, 11 [b]Ex. 12:6, 51; 19:1

2 [a]Ex. 14:11; 1 Cor. 10:10

3 [1]Or, *flesh* [a]Ex. 17:3; Num. 14:2, 3; 20:3 [b]Num. 11:4, 5

have brought us out into this wilderness to kill this whole
assembly with hunger."
4 Then the LORD said to Moses, "Behold, [a]I will rain
bread from heaven for you; and the people shall go out and
gather a day's portion every day, that I may [b]test them, whether or not they will walk in My [1]instruction.
5 "And it will come about [a]on the sixth day, when they
prepare what they bring in, it will be twice as much as they
gather daily."
6 So Moses and Aaron said to all the sons of Israel, "At
evening [1]you will know that the LORD has brought you out of
the land of Egypt;
7 and in the morning [1]you will see [a]the glory of the LORD,
for [b]He hears your grumblings against the LORD; and [c]what are
we, that you grumble against us?"
8 And Moses said, "*This will happen* when the LORD
gives you [1]meat to eat in the evening, and bread to the full in
the morning; for the LORD hears your grumblings which you
grumble against Him. And what are we? Your grumblings are
not against us but against the LORD."
9 Then Moses said to Aaron, "Say to all the congregation
of the sons of Israel, '[a]Come near before the LORD, for He has
heard your grumblings.' "
10 And it came about as Aaron spoke to the whole congregation of the sons of Israel, that they [1]looked toward the wilderness, and behold, [a]the glory of the LORD appeared in the
cloud.
11 And the LORD spoke to Moses, saying,
12 "I have heard the grumblings of the sons of Israel; speak
to them, saying, '[1]At twilight you shall eat [2]meat, and in the
morning you shall be filled with bread; and you shall know that
I am the LORD your God.' "
13 So it came about at evening that [a]the quails came up
and covered the camp, and in the morning there was a layer of
dew around the camp.
14 [a]When the layer of dew [1]evaporated, behold, on the
[2]surface of the wilderness [b]there was a fine flake-like thing, fine
as the hoarfrost on the ground.
15 When the sons of Israel saw *it*, they said to one another,
"[1]What is it?" For they did not know what it was. And
Moses said to them, "[a]It is the bread which the LORD has given
you to eat.
16 "This is [1]what the LORD has commanded, 'Gather of it
every man [2]as much as he should eat; you shall take [3]an omer
apiece according to the number of persons each of you has in
his tent.' "
17 And the sons of Israel did so, and *some* gathered much
and *some* little.
18 When they measured it with an omer, [a]he who had
gathered much had no excess, and he who had gathered little
had no lack; every man gathered [1]as much as he should eat.
19 And Moses said to them, "[a]Let no man leave any of it
until morning."
20 But they did not listen to Moses, and some left part of
it until morning, and it bred worms and became foul; and
Moses was angry with them.

4 [1]Or, *law*
[a]John 6:31; Neh. 9:15; Ps. 78:23-25; 105:40; 1 Cor. 10:3
[b]Ex. 15:25; Deut. 8:2, 16

5 [a]Ex. 16:22

6 [1]Lit., *and you*

7 [1]Lit., *and you*
[a]Ex. 16:12 [b]Num. 14:27; 17:5
[c]Num. 16:11

8 [1]Or, *flesh*

9 [a]Num. 16:16

10 [1]Lit., *turned*
[a]Ex. 16:7; Num. 16:19

12 [1]Lit., *Between the two evenings* [2]Or, *flesh*

13 [a]Num. 11:31; Ps. 78:27-29; 105:40

14 [1]Lit., *had gone up* [2]Lit., *face of*
[a]Num. 11:7-9 [b]Ex. 16:31

15 [1]Heb., *Man hu*, cf. vs. 31
[a]Ex. 16:4

16 [1]Lit., *the thing which* [2]Lit., *according to his eating* [3]Lit., *an omer for a head*

18 [1]Lit., *according to his eating*
[a]2 Cor. 8:15

19 [a]Ex. 16:23; 12:10; 23:18

21 And they gathered it morning by morning, every man
[1]as much as he should eat; but when the sun grew hot, it would
melt.
22 [a]Now it came about on the sixth day they gathered
twice as much bread, two omers for each one. When all the
[b]leaders of the congregation came and told Moses,
23 then he said to them, "This is what the LORD [1]meant:
[a]Tomorrow is a sabbath observance, a holy sabbath to the
LORD. Bake what you will bake and boil what you will boil, and
[b]all that is left over [2]put aside to be kept until morning."
24 So they [1]put it aside until morning, as Moses had ordered, and [a]it did not become foul, nor was there any worm in
it.
25 And Moses said, "Eat it today, for today is a sabbath to
the LORD; today you will not find it in the field.
26 "Six days you shall gather it, but on the seventh day, *the*
sabbath, there will be [1]none."
27 And it came about on the seventh day that some of the
people went out to gather, but they found none.
28 Then the LORD said to Moses, "[a]How long do you
refuse to keep My commandments and My [1]instructions?
29 "See, [1]the LORD has given you the sabbath, therefore He
gives you bread for two days on the sixth day. Remain every
man in his place; let no man go out of his place on the seventh
day."
30 So the people rested on the seventh day.
31 And the house of [a]Israel named it [1]manna, and it was
like [b]coriander seed, white; and its taste was like wafers with
honey.
32 Then Moses said, "This is [1]what the LORD has commanded, 'Let an omerful of it be kept throughout your generations, that they may see the bread that I fed you in the wilderness, when I brought you out of the land of Egypt.' "
33 And Moses said to Aaron, "[a]Take a jar and put an
omerful of manna in it, and place it before the LORD, to be
kept throughout your generations."
34 As the LORD commanded Moses, so Aaron placed it
before [a]the Testimony, to be kept.
35 [a]And the sons of Israel ate the manna forty years, until
they came to an inhabited land; they ate the manna until they
came to the border of the land of Canaan.
36 (Now an omer is a tenth of an ephah.)

CHAPTER 17

THEN all the congregation of the sons of Israel journeyed
by [1]stages from the wilderness of [a]Sin, according to the [2]command of the LORD, and camped at [b]Rephidim, and there was
no water for the people to drink.
2 Therefore the people [a]quarreled with Moses and said,
"Give us water that we may drink." And Moses said to them,
"[b]Why do you quarrel with me? Why do you test the LORD?"
3 But the people thirsted there for water; and [1]they
grumbled against Moses and said, "[a]Why, now, have you
brought us up from Egypt, to kill [2]us and [3]our children and
[3b]our livestock with thirst?"

21 [1]Lit., *according to his eating*

22 [a]Ex. 16:5 [b]Ex. 34:31

23 [1]Lit., *spoke* [2]Lit., *lay up for you* [a]Ex. 20:8; 23:12; Neh. 9:13, 14 [b]Ex. 16:19

24 [1]Lit., *laid it up* [a]Ex. 16:20

26 [1]Lit., *none on it*

28 [1]Or, *laws* [a]Ps. 78:10

29 [1]Lit., *for the LORD*

31 [1]Heb., *man,* cf. v. 15 [a]Num. 11:7-9; Deut. 8:3, 16 [b]Ex. 16:14

32 [1]Lit., *the thing which*

33 [a]Heb. 9:4; Rev. 2:17

34 [a]Ex. 25:16; 27:21

35 [a]Josh. 5:12; Neh. 9:20, 21

1 [1]Lit., *their journeyings* [2]Lit., *mouth* [a]Ex. 16:1 [b]Ex. 19:2; Num. 33:14

2 [a]Ex. 14:11; Num. 20:2, 3, 13 [b]Ex. 16:8

3 [1]Lit., *the people* [2]Lit., *me* [3]Lit., *my* [a]Ex. 16:3 [b]Ex. 12:38

4 So Moses cried out to the LORD, saying, "What shall I do to this people? A [a]little more and they will stone me."

5 Then the LORD said to Moses, "Pass before the people and take with you some of [a]the elders of Israel; and take in your hand your staff with which [b]you struck the Nile, and go.

6 "Behold, I will stand before you there on the rock at [a]Horeb; and [b]you shall strike the rock, and water will come out of it, that the people may drink." And Moses did so in the sight of the elders of Israel.

7 And he named the place [1a]Massah and [2b]Meribah because of the quarrel of the sons of Israel, and because they [c]tested the LORD, saying, "Is the LORD among us, or not?"

8 Then [a]Amalek came and fought against Israel at [b]Rephidim.

9 So Moses said to [a]Joshua, "Choose men for us, and go out, fight against Amalek. Tomorrow I will station myself on the top of the hill with [b]the staff of God in my hand."

10 And Joshua did as Moses [1]told him, [2]and fought against Amalek; and Moses, Aaron, and [a]Hur went up to the top of the hill.

11 So it came about when Moses held his hand up, that Israel prevailed, and when he let his hand [1]down, Amalek prevailed.

12 But Moses' hands were heavy. Then they took a stone and put it under him, and he sat on it; and Aaron and Hur [a]supported his hands, one on one side and one on the other. Thus his hands were steady until the sun set.

13 So Joshua [1]overwhelmed Amalek and his people with the edge of the sword.

14 Then the LORD said to Moses, "[a]Write this in [1]a book as a memorial, and [2]recite it to Joshua, [3]that [b]I will utterly blot out the memory of Amalek from under heaven."

15 And Moses built an [a]altar, and named it [b]The LORD is My Banner;

16 and he said, "[1a]The LORD has sworn; the LORD will have war against Amalek from generation to generation."

CHAPTER 18

NOW [a]Jethro, the priest of Midian, Moses' father-in-law, heard of all that God had done for Moses and for Israel His people, how the LORD had brought Israel out of Egypt.

2 And Jethro, Moses' father-in-law, took Moses' wife [a]Zipporah, after he had sent her away,

3 and her [a]two sons, of whom [1]one was named Gershom, for he said, "I have been [b]a [2]sojourner in a foreign land."

4 And [1]the other was named [2]Eliezer, for *he said*, "[a]The God of my father was my help, and delivered me from the sword of Pharaoh."

5 Then Jethro, Moses' father-in-law, came with his sons and his wife to Moses [1]in the wilderness where he was camped, at [a]the mount of God.

6 And he [1]sent word to Moses, "I, your father-in-law Jethro, am coming to you with your wife and her two sons with her."

7 Then Moses went out to meet his father-in-law, and [a]he

4 [a]Num. 14:10; 1 Sam. 30:6

5 [a]Ex. 3:16, 18 [b]Ex. 7:20

6 [a]Ex. 3:1 [b]Deut. 8:15; Neh. 9:15; Ps. 78:15; 105:41; 1 Cor. 10:4

7 [1]I.e., Test [2]I.e., Quarrel [a]Deut. 6:16; 9:22; Ps. 95:8 [b]Num. 20:13, 24; 27:14; Ps. 81:7 [c]Num. 14:22; Deut. 33:8

8 [a]Num. 24:20; Deut. 25:17-19 [b]Ex. 17:1

9 [a]Ex. 24:13 [b]Ex. 4:20

10 [1]Lit., *said to* [2]Lit., *to fight* [a]Ex. 24:14; 31:2

11 [1]Lit., *rest*

12 [a]Is. 35:3

13 [1]Lit., *weakened*

14 [1]Lit., *the book* [2]Lit., *place it in the ears of* [3]Or, *for* [a]Ex. 24:4; 34:27; Num. 33:2 [b]Deut. 25:19

15 [a]Ex. 24:4 [b]Gen. 22:14

16 [1]Or, *Because a hand is against the throne of the* LORD; lit., *a hand upon the throne of YAH* [a]Gen. 22:16

1 [a]Ex. 2:16, 18; 3:1

2 [a]Ex. 2:21; 4:25

3 [1]Lit., *the name of the one was* [2]Heb., *ger* [a]Ex. 2:22; 4:20; Acts 7:29 [b]Ex. 2:22

4 [1]Lit., *the name of the other was* [2]Heb., *El-ezer*; i.e., My God is help [a]Gen. 49:25

5 [1]Lit., *unto* [a]Ex. 3:1, 12; 4:27; 24:13

6 [1]Lit., *said*

7 [a]Gen. 43:26, 28

bowed down and [b]kissed him; and they asked [c]each other of
their welfare, and went into the tent.
8 And Moses told his father-in-law all that the LORD had
done to Pharaoh and to the Egyptians [a]for Israel's sake, all the
[b]hardship that had befallen them on the journey, and *how* [c]the
LORD had delivered them.
9 And Jethro rejoiced over all [a]the goodness which the
LORD had done to Israel, [1]in delivering [2]them from the hand of
the Egyptians.
10 So Jethro said, "[a]Blessed be the LORD who delivered
you from the hand of the Egyptians and from the hand of
Pharaoh, *and* who delivered the people from under the hand
of the Egyptians.
11 "Now I know that [a]the LORD is greater than all the gods;
[1]indeed, it was proven when they dealt proudly against [2]the
people."
12 [a]Then Jethro, Moses' father-in-law, took a burnt offering and sacrifices for God, and Aaron came with all the elders
of Israel to eat [1]a meal with Moses' father-in-law before God.
13 And it came about the next day that Moses sat to judge
the people, and the people stood about Moses from the morning until the evening.
14 Now when Moses' father-in-law saw all that he was
doing for the people, he said, "What is this thing that you are
doing for the people? Why do you alone sit *as judge* and all
the people stand about you from morning until evening?"
15 And Moses said to his father-in-law, "Because the
people come to me [a]to inquire of God.
16 "When they have a [1]dispute, it comes to me, and I judge
between a man and his neighbor, and make known the statutes
of God and His laws."
17 And Moses' father-in-law said to him, "The thing that
you are doing is not good.
18 "[a]You will surely wear out, both yourself and [1]these
people who are with you, for the [2]task is too heavy for you; you
cannot do it alone.
19 "Now listen to [1]me: I shall give you counsel, and God be
with you. [2]You be the people's representative before God, and
you bring the [3]disputes to God,
20 [a]then teach them the statutes and the laws, and make
known to them the way in which they are to walk, and the
work they are to do.
21 "Furthermore, you shall [1]select out of all the people
[a]able men who fear God, men of truth, those who hate dishonest gain; and you shall place *these* over them, *as* leaders of thousands, [2]of hundreds, [2]of fifties and [2]of tens.
22 "And let them judge the people at all times; and let it be
[a]that every major [1]dispute they will bring to you, but every
minor [1]dispute they themselves will judge. So it will be easier
for you, and they will bear *the burden* with you.
23 "If you do this thing and God *so* commands you, then
you will be able to [1]endure, and all [2]these people also will go to
[3]their place in peace."
24 So Moses listened [1]to his father-in-law, and did all that
he had said.
25 And Moses chose [a]able men out of all Israel, and made

7 [b]Ex. 4:27 [c]Gen. 43:27

8 [a]Ex. 4:23; 7:4, 5 [b]Num. 20:14; Neh. 9:32 [c]Ex. 15:6, 16

9 [1]Lit., *in that He had delivered* [2]Lit., *him*
[a]Is. 63:7-14

10 [a]1 Kin. 8:56; Ps. 68:19, 20

11 [1]Lit., *indeed, in the thing in which they* [2]Lit., *them*
[a]Ex. 12:12; 15:11

12 [1]Lit., *bread*
[a]Ex. 24:5; Gen. 31:54

15 [a]Num. 9:6, 8; 27:5; Deut. 17:8-13

16 [1]Lit., *matter*

18 [1]Lit., *this* [2]Lit., *matter*
[a]Num. 11:14, 17; Deut. 1:12

19 [1]Lit., *my voice* [2]Lit., *You be for the people in front of God* [3]Lit., *matters*

20 [a]Deut. 1:18

21 [1]Lit., *see* [2]Lit., *leaders of*
[a]Ex. 18:25; Deut. 1:13, 15; Ps. 15:1-5

22 [1]Lit., *matter*
[a]Deut. 1:17, 18

23 [1]Lit., *stand* [2]Lit., *this* [3]Lit., *his*

24 [1]Lit., *to the voice of*

25 [a]Ex. 18:21

them heads over the people, leaders of thousands, [1]of hundreds, [1]of fifties and [1]of tens.
26 And they judged the people at all times; [a]the difficult
[1]dispute they would bring to Moses, but every minor [1]dispute
they themselves would judge.
27 Then Moses [1a]bade his father-in-law farewell, and he
went his way into his own land.

[a] Chapter 19

IN the third month after the sons of Israel had gone out of
the land of Egypt, [1]on that very day they came into the wilderness of [b]Sinai.
2 When they set out from [a]Rephidim, they came to the
wilderness of Sinai, and camped in the wilderness; and there
Israel camped in front of [b]the mountain.
3 And Moses went up to God, and the LORD called to
him from the mountain, saying, "Thus you shall say to the
house of Jacob and tell the sons of Israel:
4 'You yourselves have seen what I did to the Egyptians,
and *how* I bore you on [a]eagles' wings, and brought you to
Myself.
5 'Now then, [a]if you will indeed obey My voice and [b]keep
My covenant, then you shall be [c]My [1]own possession among
all the peoples, for [d]all the earth is Mine;
6 and you shall be to Me [a]a kingdom of priests and [b]a
holy nation.' These are the words that you shall speak to the
sons of Israel."
7 [a]So Moses came and called the elders of the people,
and set before them all these words which the LORD had commanded him.
8 [a]And all the people answered together and said, "All
that the LORD has spoken we will do!" And Moses brought
back the words of the people to the LORD.
9 And the LORD said to Moses, "Behold, I shall come to
you in [a]a thick cloud, in order that the people may hear when I
speak with you, and may also believe in you forever." Then
Moses told the words of the people to the LORD.
10 The LORD also said to Moses, "Go to the people and
consecrate them today and tomorrow, and let them [a]wash
their garments;
11 and let them be ready for the third day, for on [a]the
third day the LORD will come down on Mount Sinai in the
sight of all the people.
12 "And you shall set bounds for the people all around,
saying, '[1]Beware that you do not go up on the mountain or
touch the border of it; whoever touches the mountain shall
surely be put to death.
13 'No hand shall touch him, but [a]he shall surely be stoned
or [1]shot through; whether beast or man, he shall not live.'
When the ram's horn sounds a long blast, they shall come up
to [b]the mountain."
14 So Moses went down from the mountain to the people
and consecrated the people, and they washed their garments.
15 And he said to the people, "Be ready for the third day;
do not go near a woman."

25 [1]Lit., *leaders of*

26 [1]Lit., *matter*
[a]Ex. 18:22

27 [1]Lit., *sent off his father-in-law*
[a]Num. 10:29, 30

1 [1]Lit., *on this day*
[a]Ex. 12:6, 51; 16:1 [b]Deut. 1:6; 4:10, 15; 5:2

2 [a]Ex. 17:1; Num. 33:15
[b]Ex. 18:5

4 [a]Deut. 32:11

5 [1]Or, *special treasure*
[a]Ex. 15:26 [b]Ps. 78:10 [c]Deut. 7:6; 14:2 [d]Ex. 9:29

6 [a]1 Pet. 2:5, 9; Rev. 1:6; 5:10 [b]Deut. 14:21; 26:19

7 [a]Ex. 4:29, 30

8 [a]Ex. 4:31; 24:3, 7; Deut. 5:27

9 [a]Ex. 19:16; 24:15, 16; Ps. 99:7

10 [a]Gen. 35:2; Num. 8:7; 19:19; Rev. 22:14

11 [a]Ex. 19:16

12 [1]Lit., *Take heed to yourselves*

13 [1]I.e., with arrows
[a]Heb. 12:20 [b]Ex. 19:17

16 [a]So it came about on the third day, when it was morning, that there were [1]thunder and lightning flashes and a thick
cloud upon the mountain and a very loud trumpet sound, so
that all the people who *were* in the camp trembled.
17 And Moses brought the people out of the camp to
meet God, and they stood at the [1]foot of the mountain.
18 [a]Now Mount Sinai *was* all in smoke because the LORD
descended upon it [b]in fire; and its smoke ascended like [c]the
smoke of a furnace, and [d]the whole mountain [1]quaked
violently.
19 When the sound of the trumpet grew louder and louder, Moses spoke and God answered him with [1]thunder.
20 [a]And the LORD came down on Mount Sinai, to the top
of the mountain; and the LORD called Moses to the top of the
mountain, and Moses went up.
21 Then the LORD spoke to Moses, "Go down, [1]warn the
people, lest [a]they break through to the LORD to gaze, and
many of them [2]perish.
22 "And also let the [a]priests who come near to the LORD
consecrate themselves, lest the LORD break out against them."
23 And Moses said to the LORD, "The people cannot
come up to Mount Sinai, for Thou didst [1]warn us, saying, '[a]Set
bounds about the mountain and consecrate it.' "
24 Then the LORD said to him, "[1]Go down and come up
again, [a]you and Aaron with you; but do not let the [b]priests and
the people break through to come up to the LORD, lest He
break forth upon them."
25 So Moses went down to the people and told them.

CHAPTER 20

THEN God spoke all these words, saying,
2 "I am the LORD your God, [a]who brought you out of the
land of Egypt, out of the house of [1]slavery.
3 "You shall have no other [a]gods [1]before Me.
4 "[a]You shall not make for yourself [1]an idol, or any likeness of what is in heaven above or on the earth beneath or in
the water under the earth.
5 "[a]You shall not worship them or serve them; for I, the
LORD your God, am a [b]jealous God, [c]visiting the iniquity of
the fathers on the children, on the third and the fourth *generations* of those who hate Me,
6 but showing lovingkindness to [a]thousands, to those
who love Me and keep My commandments.
7 "[a]You shall not take the name of the LORD your God in
vain, for the LORD will not [1]leave him unpunished who takes
His name in vain.
8 "Remember [a]the sabbath day, to keep it holy.
9 "Six days you shall labor and [a]do all your work,
10 but the seventh day is a sabbath of the LORD your God;
in it you shall not do any work, you or your son or your
daughter, your male servant or your female servant or your
cattle or your sojourner who [1]stays with you.
11 "[a]For in six days the LORD made the heavens and the
earth, the sea and all that is in them, and rested on the seventh

16 [1]Lit., *sounds* [a]Heb. 12:18, 19
17 [1]Lit., *lower part*
18 [1]Or, *trembled* [a]Ps. 104:32; 144:5 [b]Deut. 5:4; Heb. 12:18 [c]Gen. 19:28 [d]Ps. 68:7, 8
19 [1]Or, *a voice;* lit., *a sound*
20 [a]Neh. 9:13
21 [1]Lit., *testify to* [2]Lit., *fall* [a]Ex. 3:5; 1 Sam. 6:19
22 [a]Ex. 19:24; 24:5; Lev. 10:3; 21:6-8
23 [1]Lit., *testify to* [a]Ex. 19:12
24 [1]Lit., Go, *descend* [a]Ex. 24:1, 9, 12 [b]Ex. 19:22
2 [1]Lit., *slaves* [a]Ex. 15:13, 16; Deut. 5:6; 7:8
3 [1]Or, *besides Me* [a]Ex. 20:23; 15:11
4 [1]Or, *a graven image* [a]Lev. 26:1; Deut. 4:15-19; 27:15
5 [a]Ex. 23:24 [b]Ex. 34:14; Deut. 4:24 [c]Ex. 34:6, 7; Deut. 5:9, 10
6 [a]Deut. 7:9
7 [1]Or, *hold him guiltless* [a]Lev. 19:12; Deut. 6:13; 10:20
8 [a]Ex. 23:12; 31:15
9 [a]Ex. 34:21; 35: 2, 3
10 [1]Lit., *is in your gates*
11 [a]Ex. 31:17; Gen. 2:2, 3

day; therefore the LORD blessed the sabbath day and made it
holy.
12 "[a]Honor your father and your mother, that your [b]days
may be prolonged in the land which the LORD your God gives
you.
13 "[a]You shall not murder.
14 "[a]You shall not commit adultery.
15 "[a]You shall not steal.
16 "[a]You shall not bear false witness against your
[b]neighbor.
17 "[a]You shall not covet your neighbor's house; you shall
not covet your neighbor's wife or his male servant or his female
servant or his ox or his donkey or anything that belongs to your
neighbor."
18 [a]And all the people perceived the [1]thunder and the
lightning flashes and the sound of the trumpet and the mountain smoking; and when the people saw *it,* they trembled and
stood at a distance.
19 [a]Then they said to Moses, "Speak [1]to us yourself and
we will listen; but let not God speak [1]to us, lest we die."
20 And Moses said to the people, "[a]Do not be afraid; for
God has come in order [b]to test you, and in order that [c]the fear
of Him may [1]remain with you, so that you may not sin."
21 So the people stood at a distance, while Moses approached [a]the thick cloud where God *was.*
22 Then the LORD said to Moses, "Thus you shall say to
the sons of Israel, 'You yourselves have seen that [a]I have spoken [1]to you from heaven.
23 '[a]You shall not make *other gods* besides Me; [b]gods of
silver or gods of gold, you shall not make for yourselves.
24 'You shall make [a]an altar of earth for Me, and you shall
sacrifice on it your [b]burnt offerings and your [c]peace offerings,
your sheep and your oxen; in every place [d]where I cause My
name to be remembered, I will come to you and bless you.
25 'And if you make an altar of stone for Me, you shall not
build it of [a]cut stones, for if you wield your tool on it, you will
profane it.
26 'And you shall not go up by steps to My altar, that [a]your
nakedness may not be exposed on it.'

CHAPTER 21

"NOW these are the ordinances which you are to set before
them.
2 "If you buy [a]a Hebrew slave, he shall serve for six years;
but on the seventh he shall go out as a free man without
payment.
3 "If he comes [1]alone, he shall go out [1]alone; if he is the
husband of a wife, then his wife shall go out with him.
4 "If his master gives him a wife, and she bears him sons or
daughters, the wife and her children shall belong to her master,
and he shall go out [1]alone.
5 "But if the slave plainly says, 'I love my master, my wife
and my children; I will not go out as a free man,'
6 then his master shall bring him to [1a]God, then he shall

12 [a]Lev. 19:3; Matt. 15:4; 19:19; Eph. 6:2 [b]Deut. 5:16, 33; 6:2; 11:8, 9

13 [a]Ex. 21:12; Matt. 19:18; Rom. 13:9

14 [a]Lev. 20:10; Matt. 19:18; Rom. 13:9

15 [a]Ex. 21:16; Lev. 19:11, 13; Matt. 19:18; Rom. 13:9

16 [a]Ex. 23:1, 7; Matt. 19:18 [b]Lev. 19:18

17 [a]Rom. 7:7; 13:9

18 [1]Lit., *sounds* [a]Ex. 19:16, 18

19 [1]Lit., *with* [a]Deut. 5:5, 23-27; Heb. 12:19

20 [1]Lit., *be before* [a]Ex. 14:13 [b]Ex. 15:25 [c]Deut. 4:10; 6:24

21 [a]Ex. 19:16; Deut. 5:22

22 [1]Lit., *with* [a]Deut. 4:36; 5:24, 26; Neh. 9:13

23 [a]Ex. 20:3 [b]Deut. 29:17; Ex. 32:1, 2, 4

24 [a]Ex. 20:25; 27:1-8 [b]Ex. 10:25; 18:12 [c]Ex. 24:5 [d]Deut. 12:5; 26:2

25 [a]Deut. 27:5, 6

26 [a]Ex. 28:42, 43

2 [a]Lev. 25:39-43; Deut. 15:12-18

3 [a]Lit., *by himself*

4 [1]Lit., *by himself*

6 [1]Or, *the judges who acted in God's name* [a]Ex. 22:8, 9, 28

bring him to the door or the doorpost. And his master shall pierce his ear with an awl; and he shall serve him permanently.

7 "[a]And if a man sells his daughter as a female slave, she is not to [1]go free [b]as the male slaves [1]do.

8 "If she is [1]displeasing in the eyes of her master [2]who designated her for himself, then he shall let her be redeemed. He does not have authority to sell her to a foreign people because of his [3]unfairness to her.

9 "And if he designates her for his son, he shall deal with her according to the custom of daughters.

10 "If he takes to himself another woman, he may not reduce her [1]food, her clothing, or [a]her conjugal rights.

11 "And if he will not do these three *things* for her, then she shall go out for nothing, without *payment of* money.

12 "[a]He who strikes a man so that he dies shall surely be put to death.

13 "[a]But [1]if he did not lie in wait *for him*, but God let *him* fall into his hand, then I will appoint you a place to which he may flee.

14 "[a]If, however, a man acts presumptuously toward his neighbor, so as to kill him craftily, you are to take him *even* from My altar, that he may die.

15 "And he who strikes his father or his mother shall surely be put to death.

16 "[a]And he who [1]kidnaps a man, whether he sells him or he is found in his [2]possession, shall surely be put to death.

17 "[a]And he who curses his father or his mother shall surely be put to death.

18 "And if men have a quarrel and one strikes the other with a stone or with *his* fist, and he does not die but [1]remains in bed;

19 if he gets up and walks around outside on his staff, then he who struck him shall go unpunished; he shall only pay for his [1]loss of time, and [2]shall take care of him until he is completely healed.

20 "And if a man strikes his male or female slave with a rod and he dies [1]at his hand, he shall [2]be punished.

21 "If, however, he [1]survives a day or two, no vengeance shall be taken; [a]for he is his [2]property.

22 "And *if* men struggle with each other and strike a woman with child so that [1]she has a miscarriage, yet there is no *further* injury, he shall surely be fined as the woman's husband [2]may demand of him; and he shall pay [3]as the judges *decide*.

23 "But if there is *any further* injury, [a]then you shall appoint *as a penalty* life for life,

24 [a]eye for eye, tooth for tooth, hand for hand, foot for foot,

25 burn for burn, wound for wound, [1]bruise for bruise.

26 "And if a man strikes the eye of his male or female slave, and destroys it, he shall let him go free on account of his eye.

27 "And if he [1]knocks out a tooth of his male or female slave, he shall let him go free on account of his tooth.

28 "And if an ox gores a man or a woman [1]to death, [a]the ox shall surely be stoned and its flesh shall not be eaten; but the owner of the ox shall go unpunished.

29 "If, however, an ox was previously in the habit of goring,

7 [1]Lit., *go out* [a]Neh. 5:5 [b]Ex. 21:2, 3

8 [1]Lit., *bad* [2]Another reading is, *so that he did not designate her* [3]Lit., *dealing treacherously*

10 [1]Lit., *flesh* [a]1 Cor. 7:3, 5

12 [a]Gen. 9:6; Lev. 24:17

13 [1]Lit., *he who* [a]Num. 35:10-34; Deut. 19:1-13; Josh. 20:1-9

14 [a]1 Kin. 2:28-34

16 [1]Lit., *steals* [2]Lit., *hand* [a]Deut. 24:7

17 [a]Lev. 20:9; Matt. 15:4; Mark 7:10

18 [1]Lit., *lies*

19 [1]Lit., *his sitting* [2]Lit., *healing, he shall cause to be healed*

20 [1]Lit., *under* [2]Lit., *suffer vengeance*

21 [1]Lit., *stands* [2]Lit., *money* [a]Lev. 25:44-46

22 [1]Lit., *her children come out* [2]Lit., *lays on him* [3]Lit., *by arbitration*

23 [a]Lev. 24:19; Deut. 19:21

24 [a]Lev. 24:20; Matt. 5:38

25 [1]Lit., *welt*

27 [1]Lit., *causes to fall*

28 [1]Lit., *so that he dies* [a]Gen. 9:5

and its owner has been warned, yet he does not confine it, and
it kills a man or a woman, the ox shall be stoned and its owner
also shall be put to death.
30 "If a ransom is [1]demanded of him, then he shall give for
the redemption of his life whatever is [1]demanded of him.
31 "Whether it gores a son or [1]a daughter, it shall be done
to him according to [2]the same rule.
32 "If the ox gores a male or female slave, the [1]owner shall
give his *or her* master [a]thirty shekels of silver, and the ox shall
be stoned.
33 "And if a man opens a pit, or [1]digs a pit and does not
cover it over, and an ox or a donkey falls into it,
34 the owner of the pit shall make restitution; he shall
[1]give money to its owner, and the dead *animal* shall become
his.
35 "And if one man's ox hurts another's so that it dies, then
they shall sell the live ox and divide its price equally; and also
they shall divide the dead *ox*.
36 "Or *if* it is known that the ox was previously in the habit
of goring, yet its owner has not confined it, he shall surely pay
ox for ox, and the dead *animal* shall become his.

CHAPTER 22

"[1]IF a man steals an ox or a sheep, and slaughters it or sells it,
he shall pay five oxen for the ox and [a]four sheep for the sheep.
2 "[1]If the thief is [2]caught while breaking in, and is struck
so that he dies, there will be no bloodguiltiness on his account.
3 "*But* if the sun has risen on him, there will be [1]blood-
guiltiness on his account. He shall surely make restitution; if
he owns nothing, then he shall be sold for his theft.
4 "If what he stole is actually found alive in his [1]posses-
sion, whether an ox or a donkey or a sheep, he shall pay
double.
5 "If a man lets a field or vineyard be grazed *bare* and lets
his animal loose so that it grazes in another man's field, he
shall make restitution from the best of his own field and the
best of his own vineyard.
6 "If a fire breaks out and spreads to thorn bushes, so that
stacked grain or the standing grain or the field *itself* is consumed, he who started the fire shall surely make restitution.
7 "[a]If a man gives his neighbor money or goods to keep *for
him,* and it is stolen from the man's house, if the thief is
[1]caught, he shall pay double.
8 "If the thief is not [1]caught, then the owner of the house
shall [2]appear before [3a]the judges, *to* determine whether he
[4]laid his hands on his neighbor's property.
9 "For every [1]breach of trust, *whether it is* for ox, for
donkey, for sheep, for clothing, *or* for any lost thing about
which one says, "This is it," the [2]case of both parties shall
come before [3a]the judges; he whom [3]the judges condemn shall
pay double to his neighbor.
10 "If a man gives his neighbor a donkey, an ox, a sheep, or
any animal to keep *for him,* and it dies or is hurt or is driven
away while no one is looking,
11 an oath before the LORD shall be made by the two of

30 [1]Lit., *laid on him*

31 [1]Lit., *gores a daughter* [2]Lit., *this judgment*

32 [1]Lit., *he* [a]Zech. 11:12; Matt. 26:15

33 [1]Lit., *if a man digs*

34 [1]Lit., *give back*

1 [1]Ch. 21:37 in Heb. [a]2 Sam. 12:6; Luke 19:8

2 [1]Ch. 22:1 in Heb. [2]Lit., *found*

3 [1]I.e., if he is killed

4 [1]Lit., *hand*

7 [1]Lit., *found* [a]Lev. 6:1-7

8 [1]Lit., *found* [2]Lit., *approach to* [3]Or, *God* [4]Lit., *stretched his hand* [a]Ex. 22:9, 28; 21:6; Deut. 17:8, 9; 19:17

9 [1]Or, *matter of transgression* [2]Lit., *matter* [3]Or, *God* [a]Ex. 22:8,28

them, [1]that he has not [2]laid hands on his neighbor's property;
and its owner shall accept *it*, and he shall not make restitution.
12 "But if it is actually stolen from him, he shall make
restitution to its owner.
13 "If it is all torn to pieces, let him bring it as evidence; he
shall not make restitution for what has been torn to pieces.
14 "And if a man [1]borrows *anything* from his neighbor, and
it is injured or dies while its owner is not with it, he shall make
full restitution.
15 "If its owner is with it, he shall not make restitution; if it
is hired, it came for its hire.
16 "[a]And if a man seduces a virgin who is not engaged, and
lies with her, he must pay a dowry for her *to be* his wife.
17 "If her father absolutely refuses to give her to him, he
shall [1]pay money equal to the dowry for virgins.
18 "You shall not allow a [a]sorceress to live.
19 "[a]Whoever lies with an animal shall surely be put to
death.
20 "[a]He who sacrifices to [1]any god, other than to the LORD
alone, shall be [2b]utterly destroyed.
21 "And you shall not wrong [a]a stranger or oppress him, for
you were strangers in the land of Egypt.
22 "[a]You shall not afflict any widow or orphan.
23 "If you afflict him at all, *and* [a]if he does cry out to Me,
[b]I will surely hear his cry;
24 and My anger will be kindled, and I will kill you with
the sword; [a]and your wives shall become widows and your
children fatherless.
25 "[a]If you lend money to My people, to the poor [1]among
you, you are not to [2]act as a creditor to him; you shall
not [3]charge him [b]interest.
26 "If you ever take your neighbor's cloak as a pledge, you
are to return it to him before the sun sets,
27 for that is his only covering; it is his cloak for his [1]body.
What else shall he sleep in? And it shall come about that
[a]when he cries out to Me, I will hear *him*, for I am gracious.
28 "You shall not [1a]curse God, [b]nor curse a ruler of your
people.
29 "[a]You shall not delay *the offering from* [1]your harvest
and your vintage. [b]The first-born of your sons you shall give to
Me.
30 "You shall do the same with your oxen *and* with your
sheep. It shall be with its mother seven days; [a]on the eighth day
you shall give it to Me.
31 "[a]And you shall be holy men to Me, therefore [b]you shall
not eat *any* flesh torn to pieces in the field; you shall throw it
to the dogs.

CHAPTER 23

"[a]YOU shall not carry a false rumor; do not join your hand
with a wicked man to be a [b]malicious witness.
2 "You shall not follow [1]a multitude in doing evil, nor
shall you [2]testify in a dispute so as to turn aside after [1]a multitude in order to [a]pervert *justice*;
3 [a]nor shall you [1]be partial to a poor man in his dispute.

11 [1]Lit., *whether* [2]Lit., *stretched his hand*

14 [1]Lit., *asks*

16 [a]Deut. 22:28, 29

17 [1]Lit., *weigh out silver*

18 [a]Lev. 20:27; Deut. 18:10; Jer. 27:9, 10

19 [a]Lev. 18:23; 20:15, 16; Deut. 27:21

20 [1]Lit., *the gods* [2]Lit., *put under the ban* [a]Ex. 32:8; 34:15; Lev. 17:7

21 [a]Lev. 19:33, 34; Deut. 1:16; 27:19

22 [a]Deut. 24:17, 18; Prov. 23:10, 11; Jer. 7:6, 7; 23:3

23 [a]Deut. 15:9; Luke 18:7; [b]Deut. 10:18; Ps. 10:14, 17, 18; 68:5

24 [a]Ps. 109:2, 9

25 [1]Lit., *with* [2]Lit., *be* [3]Lit., *lay upon* [a]Lev. 25:35-37 [b]Deut. 23:19, 20

27 [1]Lit., *skin* [a]Ex. 22:23

28 [1]Or, *revile* [a]Lev. 24:15, 16 [b]Acts 23:5

29 [1]Lit., *your fullness and your tears* [a]Ex. 23:16, 19; Deut. 26:2-11 [b]Ex. 13:2

30 [a]Gen. 17:12; Lev. 12:3

31 [a]Ex. 19:6; Lev. 11:44 [b]Lev. 7:24; 17:15

1 [a]Ex. 20:16 [b]Deut. 19:16-21; Ps. 35:11

2 [1]Lit., *many men* [2]Or, *answer* [a]Deut. 16:19; 24:17

3 [1]Lit., *honor* [a]Ex. 23:6; Lev. 19:15; Deut. 1:17; 16:19

4 "[a]If you meet your enemy's ox or his donkey wandering away, you shall surely return it to him.

5 "If you see the donkey of one who hates you lying *helpless* under its load, you shall refrain from leaving it to him, you shall surely release *it* with him.

6 "[a]You shall not pervert the justice *due* to your needy *brother* in his dispute.

7 "[a]Keep far from a false charge, and do not [b]kill the innocent or the righteous, for [c]I will not acquit the guilty.

8 "[a]And you shall not take a bribe, for a bribe blinds the clear-sighted and [1]subverts the cause of the just.

9 "[a]And you shall not oppress a [1]stranger, since you yourselves know the [2]feelings of a [1]stranger, for you *also* were [1]strangers in the land of Egypt.

10 "[a]And you shall sow your land for six years and gather in its yield,

11 but *on* the seventh year you shall let it [1]rest and lie fallow, so that the needy of your people may eat; and whatever they leave the beast of the field may eat. You are to do the same with your vineyard *and* your olive *grove*.

12 "[a]Six days you are to do your work, but on the seventh day you shall cease *from labor;* in order that your ox and your donkey may rest, and the son of your female slave, as well as [1]your stranger, may refresh themselves.

13 "Now [a]concerning everything which I have said to you, be on your guard; and [b]do not mention the name of other gods, nor let *them* be heard [1]from your mouth.

14 "[a]Three times a year you shall celebrate a feast to Me.

15 "You shall observe the Feast of Unleavened Bread; for seven days you are to eat unleavened bread, as I commanded you, at the appointed time in the [a]month Abib, for in it you came out of Egypt. And [1b]none shall appear before Me empty-handed.

16 "Also *you shall observe* [a]the Feast of the Harvest *of* the first fruits of your labors *from* what you sow in the field; also the Feast of the Ingathering at the end of the year when you gather in *the fruit of* your labors from the field.

17 "[a]Three times a year all your males shall appear before the Lord [1]GOD.

18 "[a]You shall not offer the blood of My sacrifice with leavened bread; [b]nor is the fat of My [1]feast to remain overnight until morning.

19 "You shall bring [a]the choice first fruits of your soil into the house of the LORD your God. [b]You are not to boil a kid in the milk of its mother.

20 "Behold, I am going to send [a]an angel before you to guard you along the way, and [b]to bring you into the place which I have prepared.

21 "Be on your guard before him and obey his voice; [a]do not be rebellious toward him, for he will not pardon your transgression, since [b]My name is in him.

22 "But if you will truly obey his voice and do all that I say, then [a]I will be an enemy to your enemies and an adversary to your adversaries.

23 "[a]For My angel will go before you and bring you in to *the* land of the Amorites, the Hittites, the Perizzites, the Ca-

4 [a]Deut. 22:1-4

6 [a]Ex. 23:2, 3

7 [a]Ex. 20:16; Ps. 119:29 [b]Ex. 20:13; Deut. 27:25 [c]Ex. 34:7; Deut. 25:1; Rom. 1:18

8 [1]Or, *distorts the words* [a]Deut. 10:17; 16:19; Prov. 17:23; Is. 5:22, 23

9 [1]Or, *sojourner(s)* [2]Lit., *soul* [a]Ex. 22:21

10 [a]Lev. 25:1-7; Ex. 23:29

11 [1]Lit., *drop*

12 [1]Lit., *the sojourner* [a]Ex. 20:8-11; 31:15; 35:2, 3

13 [1]Lit., *on* [a]Deut. 4:9, 23 [b]Josh. 23:7; Ps. 16:4

14 [a]Ex. 34:22-24; Deut. 16:16

15 [1]Lit., *they . . . not* [a]Ex. 12:2; 13:4 [b]Ex. 22:29; 34:20

16 [a]Ex. 34:22

17 [1]YHWH usually rendered LORD [a]Ex. 23:14

18 [1]Or, *festival* [a]Ex. 34:25; Lev. 2:11 [b]Ex. 12:10; Lev. 7:15

19 [a]Ex. 22:29; 34:26 [b]Deut. 14:21

20 [a]Ex. 23:23; 3:2; 14:19; 32:34; 33:2 [b]Ex. 15:16, 17

21 [a]Deut. 9:7 [b]Ex. 3:14; 6:3; 34:5-7

22 [a]Gen. 12:3; Num. 24:9; Deut. 30:7

23 [a]Josh. 24:11

naanites, the Hivites and the Jebusites; and I will completely
destroy them.
24 "[a]You shall not worship their gods, nor serve them, nor
do according to their deeds; [b]but you shall utterly overthrow
them, and break their [c]sacred pillars in pieces.
25 "[a]But you shall serve the LORD your God, [1]and He will
bless your bread and your water; and [b]I will remove sickness
from your midst.
26 "There shall be no one miscarrying or [a]barren in your
land; [b]I will fulfill the number of your days.
27 "I will [a]send My terror ahead of you, and throw into
confusion all the people among whom you come, and I will
make all your enemies turn *their* backs to you.
28 "And I will send [a]hornets ahead of you, that they may
[b]drive out the Hivites, the Canaanites, and the Hittites before
you.
29 "I will not drive them out before you in a single year,
that the land may not become desolate, and the beasts of the
field become too numerous for you.
30 "I will drive them out before you [a]little by little, until
you become fruitful and take possession of the land.
31 "[a]And I will fix your boundary from the [1]Red Sea to the
sea of the Philistines, and from the wilderness to the River
Euphrates; [b]for I will deliver the inhabitants of the land into
your hand, and [c]you will drive them out before you.
32 "[a]You shall [1]make no covenant with them [b]or with their
gods.
33 "[a]They shall not live in your land, lest they make you sin
against Me; for *if* you serve their gods, it will surely be a snare
to you."

CHAPTER 24

THEN He said to Moses, "[a]Come up to the LORD, you and
Aaron, [b]Nadab and Abihu and seventy of the elders of Israel,
and you shall worship at a distance.
2 "Moses alone, however, shall come near to the LORD,
but they shall not come near, nor shall the people come up
with him."
3 Then Moses came and recounted to the people all the
words of the LORD and all the [1]ordinances; and all the people
answered with one voice, and said, "[a]All the words which the
LORD has spoken we will do!"
4 And [a]Moses wrote down all the words of the LORD.
Then he arose early in the morning, and built an [b]altar [1]at the
foot of the mountain with twelve pillars for the twelve tribes of
Israel.
5 And he sent young men of the sons of Israel, [a]and they
offered burnt offerings and sacrificed young bulls as peace
offerings to the LORD.
6 And [a]Moses took half of the blood and put *it* in basins,
and the *other* half of the blood he sprinkled on the altar.
7 Then he took [a]the Book of the Covenant and read *it* in
the hearing of the people; and they said, "[b]All that the LORD
has spoken we will do, and we will be obedient!"
8 So [a]Moses took the blood and sprinkled *it* on the

24 [a]Ex. 23:13, 33; 20:5 [b]Num. 33:52; Deut. 7:5; 12:3; 2 Kin. 18:4 [c]Ex. 34:13; Lev. 26:1; 2 Kin. 3:2

25 [1]Or, *that He may bless* [a]Lev. 26:3-13; Deut. 28:1-14 [b]Ex. 15:26; Deut. 7:15

26 [a]Deut. 7:14 [b]Deut. 4:40; Job 5:26

27 [a]Ex. 15:16 [b]Deut. 7:23

28 [a]Deut. 7:20; Josh. 24:12 [b]Ex. 33:2; 34:11

30 [a]Deut. 7:22

31 [1]Lit., *Sea of Reeds* [a]Gen. 15:18; Deut. 1:7, 8 [b]Deut. 2:36; Josh. 21:44 [c]Josh. 24:12, 18

32 [1]Lit., *cut* [a]Ex. 34:12; Deut. 7:2 [b]Ex. 23:13, 24

33 [a]Deut. 7:1-5, 16

1 [a]Ex. 19:24 [b]Ex. 6:23; Lev. 10:1, 2

3 [1]Or, *judgments* [a]Ex. 24:7; 19:8

4 [1]Lit., *under* [a]Ex. 17:14; 34:27 [b]Ex. 17:15

5 [a]Ex. 18:12

6 [a]Ps. 99:6

7 [a]Ex. 24:4 [b]Ex. 24:3

8 [a]Heb. 9:19, 20

people, and said, "Behold, [b]the blood of the covenant, which
the LORD has [1]made with you [2]in accordance with all these
words."

9 Then Moses went up [1]with Aaron, [a]Nadab and Abihu,
and seventy of the elders of Israel,

10 and [a]they saw the God of Israel; and under His feet
[1b]there appeared to be a pavement of sapphire, [2]as clear as the
sky itself.

11 Yet He did not stretch out His hand against the nobles
of the sons of Israel; and [a]they beheld God, and they ate and
drank.

12 Now the LORD said to Moses, "Come up to Me on the
mountain and [1]remain there, and [a]I will give you the stone
tablets [2]with the law and the commandment which I have
written for their instruction."

13 So Moses arose [1]with [a]Joshua his [2]servant, and Moses
went up to [b]the mountain of God.

14 But to the elders he said, "[a]Wait here for us until we
return to you. And behold, [b]Aaron and Hur are with you;
whoever [1]has a legal matter, let him approach them."

15 Then Moses went up to the mountain, and [a]the cloud
covered the mountain.

16 And the glory of the LORD [1]rested on Mount Sinai, and
the cloud covered it for six days; and on the seventh day He
[a]called to Moses from the midst of the cloud.

17 [a]And to the eyes of the sons of Israel the appearance of
the glory of the LORD was like a [b]consuming fire on the mountain top.

18 And Moses entered the midst of the cloud [1]as he went
up to the mountain; and Moses was on the mountain [a]forty
days and forty nights.

Chapter 25

THEN the LORD spoke to Moses, saying,

2 "[a]Tell the sons of Israel to [1]raise a [2]contribution for Me;
[b]from every man whose heart moves him you shall [1]raise My
[2]contribution.

3 "And this is the [1]contribution which you are to [2]raise
from them: gold, silver and bronze,

4 [1]blue, purple and scarlet *material,* fine linen, goat *hair,*

5 rams' skins dyed red, [1]porpoise skins, acacia wood,

6 oil for lighting, spices for the anointing oil and for the
fragrant incense,

7 onyx stones and setting stones, for the ephod and for
the [1]breastpiece.

8 "And let them construct a sanctuary for Me, [a]that I may
dwell among them.

9 "[a]According to all that I am going to show you, *as* the
pattern of the tabernacle and the pattern of all its furniture,
just so you shall construct *it.*

10 "[a]And they shall construct an ark of acacia wood two
and a half [1]cubits [2]long, and one and a half cubits [3]wide, and
one and a half cubits [4]high.

11 "And you shall [a]overlay it with pure gold, inside and out

8 [1]Lit., *cut* [2]Lit., *on all* [b]Matt. 26:28; Luke 22:20; 1 Cor. 11:25; Zech. 9:11

9 [1]Lit., *and* [a]Ex. 24:1

10 [1]Lit., *like a pavement* [2]Lit., *and as* [a]Ex. 24:11; Num. 12:8; Is. 6:5; John 1:18; 6:46 [b]Ezek. 1:26; Matt. 17:2; Rev. 4:3

11 [a]Ex. 24:10

12 [1]Lit., *be* [2]Lit., *and* [a]Ex. 31:18

13 [1]Lit., *and* [2]Or, *minister* [a]Ex. 17:9-14; 33:11 [b]Ex. 3:1

14 [1]Lit., *is a master of matters* [a]Gen. 22:5 [b]Ex. 17:10, 12

15 [a]Ex. 19:9

16 [1]Lit., *dwelt* [a]Ps. 99:7

17 [a]Ex. 3:2; Ezek. 1:28 [b]Deut. 4:24; 9:3; Heb. 12:29

18 [1]Lit., *and* [a]Ex. 34:28; Deut. 9:9; 10:10

2 [1]Lit., *take* [2]Or, *heave offering* [a]Ex. 35:4-9 [b]Ex. 35:5, 21; 2 Cor. 8:11, 12

3 [1]Or, *heave offering* [2]Lit., *take*

4 [1]Or, *violet*

5 [1]Or, *dolphin*

7 [1]Or, *pouch*

8 [a]Ex. 29:45, 46; Num. 5:3; Deut. 12:11; Rev. 21:3

9 [a]Ex. 25:40; 26:30; Acts 7:44; Heb. 8:2, 5

10 [1]A cubit was about 18 in. [2]Lit., *its length* [3]Lit., *its width* [4]Lit., *its height* [a]Ex. 37:1-9

11 [a]Heb. 9:4

you shall overlay it, and you shall make a gold molding
[1]around it.
12 "And you shall cast four gold rings for it, and [1]fasten
them on its four feet, and two rings shall be on one side of it
and two rings on the other side of it.
13 "And you shall make poles of acacia wood and overlay
them with gold.
14 "And you shall put the poles into the rings on the sides
of the ark, to carry the ark with them.
15 "The poles shall [1]remain in the rings of the ark; they
shall not be removed from it.
16 "And you shall [a]put into the ark the testimony which I
shall give you.
17 "And you shall make a [1]mercy seat of pure gold, two and
a half [2]cubits [3]long and one and a half cubits [4]wide.
18 "And you shall make two cherubim of gold, make them
of hammered work [1]at the two ends of the mercy seat.
19 "And make one cherub [1]at one end and one cherub [1]at
the other end; you shall make the cherubim *of one piece* with
the mercy seat at its two ends.
20 "And [a]the cherubim shall have *their* wings spread upward, covering the mercy seat with their wings and [1]facing one
another; the faces of the cherubim are to be *turned* toward the
mercy seat.
21 "And you shall put the mercy seat [1]on top of the ark,
and in the ark you shall put the testimony which I shall give to
you.
22 "And [a]there I will meet with you, and from above the
mercy seat, from between the two cherubim which are upon
the ark of the testimony, I will speak to you about all that I
will give you in commandment for the sons of Israel.
23 "[a]And you shall make a table of acacia wood, two cubits
[1]long and one cubit [2]wide and one and a half cubits [3]high.
24 "And you shall overlay it with pure gold and make a gold
[a]border around it.
25 "And you shall make for it a rim of a handbreadth
around *it;* and you shall make a gold border for the rim around
it.
26 "And you shall make four gold rings for it and put rings
on the four corners which are on its four feet.
27 "The rings shall be close to the rim as holders for the
poles to carry the table.
28 "And you shall make the poles of acacia wood and overlay them with gold, so that with them the table may be carried.
29 "And you shall make its [1]dishes and its pans and its jars
and its [2]bowls, with which to pour libations; you shall make
them of pure gold.
30 "And you shall set [a]the bread of the [1]Presence on the
table before Me [2]at all times.
31 "[a]Then you shall make a lampstand of pure gold. The
lampstand *and* its base and its shaft are to be made of hammered work; its cups, its [1]bulbs and its flowers shall be *of one
piece* with it.
32 "And six branches shall go out from its sides; three
branches of the lampstand from its one side, and three
branches of the lampstand from its [1]other side.

11 [1]Lit., *on it round about*

12 [1]Or, *put*

15 [1]Lit., *be*

16 [a]Heb. 9:4

17 [1]Lit., *propitiatory;* and so through v. 22 [2]I.e., one cubit equals approximately 18 inches [3]Lit., *its length* [4]Lit., *its width*

18 [1]Lit., *from*

19 [1]Lit., *from*

20 [1]Lit., *their faces to* [a]1 Kin. 8:7; Heb. 9:5

21 [1]Lit., *above, upon*

22 [a]Ex. 29:42, 43; 30:6, 36

23 [1]Lit., *its length* [2]Lit., *its width* [3]Lit., *its height* [a]Ex. 37:10-16

24 [a]Ex. 25:11

29 [1]Or, *platters* [2]Lit., *libation bowls*

30 [1]Lit., *face* [2]Or, *continually* [a]Ex. 39:36; 40:23; Lev. 24:5-9

31 [1]Or, *calyx* [a]Ex. 37:17-24

32 [1]Lit., *second*

33 [1]Or, *calyx* [2]Lit., *one branch*

34 [1]Or, *calyxes*

35 [1]Or, *calyx*

36 [1]Or, *calyxes*

37 [1]Lit., *raise up*

38 [1]Lit., *its snuff dishes*

40 [a]Heb. 8:5 [b]Ex. 25:9

1 [1]Or, *violet* [a]Ex. 36:8-19

2 [1]I.e., One cubit equals approximately 18 inches [2]Lit., *one measure*

3 [1]Or, *coupled*

4 [1]Or, *violet* [2]Lit., *one curtain from the end in the coupling* [3]Lit., *coupling*

5 [1]Lit., *end* [2]Lit., *coupling*

6 [1]Or, *couple* [2]Or, *dwelling place,* and so throughout the chap.

8 [1]I.e., one cubit equals approximately 18 inches [2]Lit., *one measure*

9 [1]Or, *couple* [2]Lit., *toward the front of the face of the tent*

10 [1]Lit., *one curtain* [2]Lit., *coupling*

11 [1]Or, *copper*

33 "Three cups *shall be* shaped like almond *blossoms* in the
one branch, a [1]bulb and a flower, and three cups shaped like
almond *blossoms* in the [2]other branch, a [1]bulb and a flower—
so for six branches going out from the lampstand;
34 and in the lampstand four cups shaped like almond
blossoms, its [1]bulbs and its flowers.
35 "And a [1]bulb shall be under the *first* pair of branches
coming out of it, and a [1]bulb under the *second* pair of
branches *coming* out of it, and a [1]bulb under the *third* pair of
branches *coming* out of it, for the six branches coming out of
the lampstand.
36 "Their [1]bulbs and their branches *shall be of one piece*
with it; all of it shall be one piece of hammered work of pure
gold.
37 "Then you shall make its lamps seven *in number;* and
they shall [1]mount its lamps so as to shed light on the space in
front of it.
38 "And its snuffers and [1]their trays *shall be* of pure gold.
39 "It shall be made from a talent of pure gold, with all
these utensils.
40 "And [a]see that you make *them* [b]after the pattern for
them, which was shown to you on the mountain.

Chapter 26

"[a]MOREOVER you shall make the tabernacle with ten
curtains of fine twisted linen and [1]blue and purple and scarlet
material; you shall make them with cherubim, the work of a
skillful workman.
2 "The length of each curtain shall be twenty-eight [1]cu-
bits, and the width of each curtain four [1]cubits; all the curtains
shall have [2]the same measurements.
3 "Five curtains shall be [1]joined to one another; and *the
other* five curtains *shall be* [1]joined to one another.
4 "And you shall make loops of [1]blue on the edge of the
[2]outermost curtain in the *first* set, and likewise you shall make
it on the edge of the curtain that is outermost in the second
[3]set.
5 "You shall make fifty loops in the one curtain, and you
shall make fifty loops on the [1]edge of the curtain that is in the
second [2]set; the loops shall be opposite each other.
6 "And you shall make fifty clasps of gold, and [1]join the
curtains to one another with the clasps, that the [2]tabernacle
may be a unit.
7 "Then you shall make curtains of goats' *hair* for a tent
over the tabernacle; you shall make eleven curtains in all.
8 "The length of each curtain *shall be* thirty [1]cubits, and
the width of each curtain four cubits; the eleven curtains shall
have [2]the same measurements.
9 "And you shall [1]join five curtains by themselves, and the
other six curtains by themselves, and you shall double over the
sixth curtain [2]at the front of the tent.
10 "And you shall make fifty loops on the edge of the
[1]curtain that is outermost in the *first* [2]set, and fifty loops on
the edge of the curtain *that is outermost in* the second [2]set.
11 "And you shall make fifty clasps of [1]bronze, and you

shall put the clasps into the loops and [2]join the tent together,
that it may be [3]a unit.
12 "And the [1]overlapping part that is left over in the curtains of the tent, the half curtain that is left over, shall lap over
the back of the tabernacle.
13 "And the cubit on one side and the cubit on the other,
of what is left over in the length of the curtains of the tent,
shall lap over the sides of the tabernacle on one side and on
the other, to cover it.
14 "And you shall make a covering for the tent of rams'
skins [1]dyed red, and a covering of [2]porpoise skins above.
15 "Then you shall make [a]the boards for the tabernacle of
acacia wood, standing upright.
16 "Ten cubits *shall be* the length of [1]each board, and one
and a half cubits the width of each board.
17 "There *shall be* two tenons for each board, [1]fitted to
one another; thus you shall do for all the boards of the
tabernacle.
18 "And you shall make the boards for the tabernacle:
twenty boards [1]for the south side.
19 "And you shall make forty [1]sockets of silver under the
twenty boards, two [1]sockets under one board for its two tenons
and two [1]sockets under another board for its two tenons;
20 and for the second side of the tabernacle, on the north
side, twenty boards,
21 and their forty [1]sockets of silver; two [1]sockets under
one board and two [1]sockets under another board.
22 "And for the [1]rear of the tabernacle, to the west, you
shall make six boards.
23 "And you shall make two boards for the corners of the
tabernacle at the [1]rear.
24 "And they shall be double beneath, and together they
shall be complete [1]to its top [2]to the first ring; thus it shall be
with both of them: they shall form the two corners.
25 "And there shall be eight boards with their [1]sockets of
silver, sixteen [1]sockets; two [1]sockets under one board and two
[1]sockets under another board.
26 "Then you shall make bars of acacia wood, five for the
boards of one side of the tabernacle,
27 and five bars for the boards of the [1]other side of the
tabernacle, and five bars for the boards of the side of the
tabernacle for the [2]rear *side* to the west.
28 "And the middle bar in the [1]center of the boards shall
pass through from end to end.
29 "And you shall overlay the boards with gold and make
their rings of gold *as* holders for the bars; and you shall overlay
the bars with gold.
30 "Then you shall erect the tabernacle [a]according to its
plan which you have been shown in the mountain.
31 "And you shall make [a]a veil of [1]blue and purple and
scarlet *material* and fine twisted linen; it shall be made with
cherubim, the work of a skillful workman.
32 "And you shall [1]hang it on four pillars of acacia overlaid
with gold, their hooks *also being of* gold, on four [2]sockets of
silver.
33 "And you shall [1]hang up the veil under the clasps, and

11 [2]Or, *couple* [3]Lit., *one*

12 [1]Lit., *excess*

14 [1]Or, *tanned* [2]Or, *dolphin*

15 [a]Ex. 36:20-34

16 [1]Lit., *the*

17 [1]Lit., *bound*

18 [1]Lit., *toward the side of the Negev to the south*

19 [1]Or, *bases*

21 [1]Or, *bases*

22 [1]Lit., *extreme parts*

23 [1]Lit., *extreme parts*

24 [1]Or, *at its head* [2]Or, *with reference to*

25 [1]Or, *bases*

27 [1]Lit., *second* [2]Lit., *extreme parts*

28 [1]Lit., *midst*

30 [a]Ex. 25:9

31 [1]Or, *violet* [a]Ex. 36:35, 36; Matt. 27:51; Heb. 9:3

32 [1]Lit., *put* [2]Or, *bases*

33 [1]Lit., *put*

shall bring in the ark of the testimony there within the veil; and
the veil shall [2]serve for you as a partition between the holy
place and the holy of holies.
34 "And you shall put the mercy seat on the ark of the
testimony in the holy of holies.
35 "And you shall set the table outside the veil, and the
lampstand opposite the table on the side of the tabernacle
toward the south; and you shall put the table on the north side.
36 "And you shall make a screen for the doorway of the
tent of [1]blue and purple and scarlet *material* and fine twisted
linen, the work of a [2]weaver.
37 "And you shall make five pillars of acacia for the screen,
and overlay them with gold, their hooks *also being of* gold; and
you shall cast five [1]sockets of [2]bronze for them.

Chapter 27

"AND you shall make [a]the altar of acacia wood, five [1]cubits
long and five cubits wide; the altar shall be square, and its
height shall be three cubits.
2 "And you shall make its horns on its four corners; its
horns shall be of one piece with it, and you shall overlay it with
[1]bronze.
3 "And you shall make its pails for removing its ashes, and
its shovels and its basins and its forks and its fire pans; you shall
make all its utensils of bronze.
4 "And you shall make for it a grating of network of
bronze, and on the net you shall make four bronze rings [1]at its
four corners.
5 "And you shall put it beneath, under the ledge of the
altar, that the net may reach halfway up the altar.
6 "And you shall make poles for the altar, poles of acacia
wood, and overlay them with bronze.
7 "And its poles shall be inserted into the rings, so that the
poles shall be on the two sides of the altar when it is carried.
8 "You shall make it hollow with planks; as it was shown
to you in the mountain, so they shall make *it*.
9 "And you shall make [a]the court of the [1]tabernacle. [2]On
the south side *there shall be* hangings for the court of fine
twisted linen one hundred cubits long for one side;
10 and its pillars *shall be* twenty, with their twenty [1]sock-
ets of bronze; the hooks of the pillars and their [2]bands *shall
be* of silver.
11 "And likewise for the north side in length *there shall be*
hangings one hundred *cubits* long, and its twenty pillars with
their twenty [1]sockets of bronze; the hooks of the pillars and
their bands *shall be* of silver.
12 "And *for* the width of the court on the west side *shall be*
hangings of fifty cubits *with* their ten pillars and their ten
[1]sockets.
13 "And the width of the court on the [1]east side *shall be*
fifty cubits.
14 "The hangings for the *one* [1]side *of the gate shall be*
fifteen cubits *with* their three pillars and their three [2]sockets.
15 "And for the [1]other [2]side *shall be* hangings of fifteen
cubits *with* their three pillars and their three [3]sockets.

33 [2]Lit., *separate for you between*

36 [1]Or, *violet* [2]Lit., *variegator;* i.e., a weaver in colors

37 [1]Or, *bases* [2]Or, *copper*

1 [1]I.e., one cubit equals approximately 18 inches [a]Ex. 38:1-7

2 [1]Or, *copper,* and so for *bronze* throughout the chap.

4 [1]Lit., *on*

9 [1]Or, *dwelling place* [2]Lit., *For the side of the Negev to the south* [a]Ex. 38:9-20

10 [1]Or, *bases* [2]Or, *fillets, rings*

11 [1]Or, *bases*

12 [1]Or, *bases*

13 [1]Lit., *east side eastward*

14 [1]Lit., *shoulder* [2]Or, *bases*

15 [1]Lit., *second* [2]Lit., *shoulder* [3]Or, *bases*

16 "And for the gate of the court there *shall be* a screen of
twenty cubits, of [1]blue and purple and scarlet *material* and
fine twisted linen, the work of a [2]weaver, *with* their four pillars
and their four [3]sockets.
17 "All the pillars around the court shall be furnished with
silver bands *with* their hooks of silver and their [1]sockets of
bronze.
18 "The length of the court *shall be* one hundred cubits,
and the width fifty throughout, and the height five cubits of
fine twisted linen, and their [1]sockets of bronze.
19 "All the utensils of the tabernacle *used* in all its service,
and all its pegs, and all the pegs of the court, *shall be* of
bronze.
20 "And you shall charge the sons of Israel, that they bring
you [a]clear oil of beaten olives for the [1]light, to make a lamp
[2]burn continually.
21 "In the [a]tent of meeting, outside the veil which is before
the testimony, Aaron and his sons shall keep it in order from
evening to morning before the LORD; *it shall be* a perpetual
statute throughout their generations [1]for the sons of Israel.

CHAPTER 28

"THEN [a]bring near to yourself Aaron your brother, and his
sons with him, from among the sons of Israel, to minister as
priest to Me—Aaron, [b]Nadab and Abihu, Eleazar and Ithamar, Aaron's sons.
2 "And you shall make holy garments for Aaron your brother, for glory and for beauty.
3 "And you shall speak to all the [1]skillful persons whom I
have endowed with [2]the spirit of wisdom, that they make Aaron's garments to consecrate him, that he may minister as
priest to Me.
4 "And these are the garments which they shall make: a
[1]breastpiece and an ephod and a robe and a tunic of checkered
work, a turban and a sash, and they shall make holy garments
for Aaron your brother and his sons, that he may minister as
priest to Me.
5 "And they shall take [a]the gold and the [1]blue and the
purple and the scarlet *material* and the fine linen.
6 "They shall also make [a]the ephod of gold, of [1]blue and
purple *and* scarlet *material* and fine twisted linen, the work of
the skillful workman.
7 "It shall have two shoulder pieces joined to its two ends,
that it may be joined.
8 "And the skillfully woven band, which is on it, shall be
like its workmanship, [1]of the same material: of gold, of [2]blue
and purple and scarlet *material* and fine twisted linen.
9 "And you shall take two onyx stones and engrave on
them the names of the sons of Israel,
10 six of their names on the one stone, and the names of
the remaining six on the [1]other stone, according to their birth.
11 "[1]As a jeweler engraves a signet, you shall engrave the
two stones according to the names of the sons of Israel; you
shall [2]set them in filigree *settings* of gold.
12 "And you shall put the two stones on the shoulder pieces

16 [1]Or, *violet* [2]Lit., *variegator;* i.e., a weaver in colors [3]Or, *bases*

17 [1]Or, *bases*

18 [1]Or, *bases*

20 [1]Or, *luminary* [2]Lit., *ascend* [a]Ex. 35:8, 28; Lev. 24:1-4

21 [1]Lit., *from* [a]Ex. 25:22; 29:42; 30:36

1 [a]Ps. 99:6; Heb. 5:4 [b]Ex. 24:1, 9

3 [1]Lit., *wise of heart* [2]I.e., artistic skill

4 [1]Or, *pouch*

5 [1]Or, *violet* [a]Ex. 25:3

6 [1]Or, *violet* [a]Ex. 39:2-7

8 [1]Lit., *from it* [2]Or, *violet*

10 [1]Lit., *second*

11 [1]Lit., *A work of a lapidary, engravings of a seal* [2]Lit., *make them to be surrounded*

of the ephod, *as* stones of memorial for the sons of Israel, and
Aaron shall bear their names before the LORD on his two shoulders for a memorial.
13 "[a]And you shall make filigree *settings* of gold,
14 and two chains of pure gold; you shall make them of
twisted cordage work, and you shall put the corded chains on
the filigree *settings*.
15 "And you shall make a [1]breastpiece of judgment, the
work of a skillful workman; like the work of the ephod you
shall make it: of gold, of [2]blue and purple and scarlet *material*
and fine twisted linen you shall make it.
16 "It shall be square *and* folded double, a span [1]in length
and a span [1]in width.
17 "And you shall [1]mount on it four rows of stones; the first
row *shall be* a row of ruby, topaz and emerald;
18 and the second row a turquoise, a sapphire and a
diamond;
19 and the third row a jacinth, an agate and an amethyst;
20 and the fourth row a beryl and an onyx and a jasper;
they shall be [1]set in gold filigree.
21 "And the stones shall be according to the names of the
sons of Israel: twelve, according to their names; they shall be
like the engravings of a seal, each according to his name for the
twelve tribes.
22 "And you shall make on the [1]breastpiece chains of
twisted cordage work in pure gold.
23 "And you shall make on the breastpiece two rings of
gold, and shall put the two rings on the two ends of the
breastpiece.
24 "And you shall put the two cords of gold on the two
rings at the ends of the breastpiece.
25 "And you shall put the *other* two ends of the two cords
on the two filigree *settings*, and put them on the shoulder
pieces of the ephod, at the front of it.
26 "And you shall make two rings of gold and shall place
them on the two ends of the breastpiece, on the edge of it,
which is toward the inner side of the ephod.
27 "And you shall make two rings of gold and put them on
the bottom of the two shoulder pieces of the ephod, on the
front of it close to the place where it is joined, above the
skillfully woven band of the ephod.
28 "And they shall bind the breastpiece by its rings to the
rings of the ephod with a [1]blue cord, that it may be on the
skillfully woven band of the ephod, and that the breastpiece
may not come loose from the ephod.
29 "And Aaron shall carry the names of the sons of Israel in
the breastpiece of judgment over his heart when he enters the
holy place, for a memorial before the LORD continually.
30 "And you shall put in the breastpiece of judgment the
[1]Urim and the Thummim, and they shall be over Aaron's
heart when he goes in before the LORD; and Aaron shall carry
the judgment of the sons of Israel over his heart before the
LORD continually.
31 "[a]And you shall make the robe of the ephod all of [1]blue.
32 "And there shall be an opening [1]at its top in the middle
of it; around its opening there shall be a binding of woven

13 [a]Ex. 39:16-18

15 [1]Or, *pouch* [2]Or, *violet*

16 [1]Lit., *its*

17 [1]Lit., *fill in a setting of stones, four rows of stones*

20 Lit., *inwoven with gold in their settings*

22 [1]Or, *pouch*, and so through vs. 30

28 [1]Or, *violet*

30 [1]I.e., lights and the perfections

31 [1]Or, *violet*
[a]Ex. 39:22-26

32 [1]Or, *for his head*

work, as *it were* the opening of a coat of mail, that it may not
be torn.
33 "And you shall make on its hem pomegranates of blue
and purple and scarlet *material*, all around on its hem, and
bells of gold between them all around:
34 a golden bell and a pomegranate, a golden bell and a
pomegranate, all around on the hem of the robe.
35 "And it shall be on Aaron [1]when he ministers; and [2]its
tinkling may be heard when he enters and [3]leaves the holy
place before the LORD, that he may not die.
36 "You shall also make [a]a plate of pure gold and shall
engrave on it, like the engravings of a seal, 'Holy to the LORD.'
37 "And you shall [1]fasten it on a [2]blue cord, and it shall be
on the turban; it shall be at the front of the turban.
38 "And it shall be on Aaron's forehead, and Aaron shall
[1]take away [a]the iniquity of the holy things which the sons of
Israel consecrate, with regard to all their holy gifts; and it shall
always be on his forehead, that they may be accepted before
the LORD.
39 "And you shall weave [a]the tunic of checkered work of
fine linen, and shall make a turban of fine linen, and you shall
make a sash, the work of a [1]weaver.
40 "And for Aaron's sons you shall make tunics; you shall
also make sashes for them, and you shall make [1a]caps for them,
for glory and for beauty.
41 "And you shall put them on Aaron your brother and on
his sons with him; and you shall anoint them and [1]ordain them
and consecrate them, that they may serve Me as priests.
42 "And you shall make for them [a]linen breeches to cover
their bare flesh; they shall [1]reach from the loins even to the
thighs.
43 "And they shall be on Aaron and on his sons when they
enter the tent of meeting, or [a]when they approach the altar to
minister in the holy place, so that they do not incur [1]guilt and
die. It *shall be* a statute forever to him and to his [2]descendants
after him.

CHAPTER 29

"[a]NOW this is [1]what you shall do to them to consecrate
them to minister as priests to Me: take one young bull and two
rams without blemish;
2 and [a]unleavened bread and unleavened cakes mixed
with oil, and unleavened wafers [1]spread with oil, you shall
make them of fine wheat flour.
3 "And you shall put them in one basket, and present
them in the basket along with the bull and the two rams.
4 "Then you shall bring Aaron and his sons to the doorway of the tent of meeting, and wash them with water.
5 "And you shall take the garments, and put on Aaron the
[a]tunic and [b]the robe of the ephod and [c]the ephod and [d]the
[1]breastpiece, and gird him with the skillfully [e]woven band of
the ephod;
6 and you shall set the [a]turban on his head, and put [b]the
holy crown on the turban.

35 [1]Lit., *for ministering* [2]Lit., *its sound* [3]Lit., *comes out* from

36 [a]Ex. 39:30, 31

37 [1]Lit., *place* [2]Or, *violet*

38 [1]Or, *bear* [a]Lev. 10:17; 22:16; Num.18:1

39 [1]Lit., *variegator;* i.e., a weaver in colors [a]Ex. 39:27-29

40 [1]Lit., *headgear* [a]Ex. 29:9; 39:28; Lev.8:13

41 [1]Lit., *fill their hand*

42 [1]Lit., *be* [a]Ex. 39:28

43 [1]Or, *iniquity* [2]Lit., *seed* [a]Ex. 20:26

1 [1]Lit., *the thing which* [a]Lev. 8:1-34

2 [1]Or, *anointed* [a]Lev. 6:19-23

5 [1]Or, *pouch* [a]Ex. 28:39 [b]Ex. 28:31 [c]Ex. 28:6 [d]Ex. 28:15 [e]Ex. 28:8

6 [a]Ex. 28:4, 39 [b]Ex. 28:36, 37; Lev. 8:9

7 “Then you shall take [a]the anointing oil, and pour it on
his head and anoint him.
8 “And you shall bring his sons and put [a]tunics on them.
9 “And you shall gird them with [a]sashes, Aaron and his
sons, and bind [1]caps on them, and they shall have [b]the priesthood by a perpetual statute. So you shall [2]ordain Aaron and
his sons.
10 “Then you shall bring the bull before the tent of meeting, and Aaron and his sons shall lay their hands on the head
of the bull.
11 “And you shall slaughter the bull before the LORD at the
doorway of the tent of meeting.
12 “And you shall take some of the blood of the bull and
put *it* on the horns of the altar with your finger; and you shall
pour out all the blood at the base of the altar.
13 “And you shall take all the fat that covers the entrails
and the [1]lobe of the liver and the two kidneys and the fat that
is on them, and offer them up in smoke on the altar.
14 “But the flesh of the bull and its hide and its refuse, you
shall burn with fire outside the camp; it is a sin offering.
15 “You shall also take the one ram, and Aaron and his sons
shall lay their hands on the head of the ram;
16 and you shall slaughter the ram and shall take its blood
and sprinkle it around on the altar.
17 “Then you shall cut the ram into its pieces, and wash its
entrails and its legs, and put *them* [1]with its pieces and [2]its head.
18 “And you shall offer up in smoke the whole ram on the
altar; it is a burnt offering to the LORD: it is a soothing aroma,
an offering by fire to the LORD.
19 “Then you shall take the [1]other ram, and Aaron and his
sons shall lay their hands on the head of the ram.
20 “And you shall slaughter the ram, and take some of its
blood and put *it* on the lobe of Aaron’s right ear and on the
lobes of his sons’ right ears and on the thumbs of their right
hands and on the big toes of their right feet, and sprinkle the
rest of the blood around on the altar.
21 “Then you shall take some of the blood that is on the
altar and some of the anointing oil, and sprinkle *it* on Aaron
and on his garments, and on his sons and on his sons’ garments
with him; so he and his garments shall be consecrated, as well
as his sons and his sons’ garments with him.
22 “You shall also take the fat from the ram and the fat
tail, and the fat that covers the entrails and the [1]lobe of the
liver and the two kidneys, and the fat that is on them and the
right thigh (for it is a ram of [2]ordination),
23 and one cake of bread and one cake of bread *mixed
with* oil and one wafer from the basket of unleavened bread
which is *set* before the LORD;
24 and you shall put [1]all these [2]in the [3]hands of Aaron and
[2]in the [3]hands of his sons, and shall wave them as a wave
offering before the LORD.
25 “And you shall take them from their hands, and offer
them up in smoke on the altar on the burnt offering for a
soothing aroma before the LORD; it is an offering by fire to the
LORD.
26 “Then you shall take [a]the breast of Aaron’s ram of [1]ordi-

7 [a]Ps. 133:2

8 [a]Ex. 28:39, 40

9 [1]Lit., *headgear* [2]Lit., *fill the hand of* [a]Ex. 28:40 [b]Ex. 40:15; Num. 3:10; 18:7; 25:13; Deut. 18:5

13 [1]Or, *appendage on*

17 [1]Lit., *on* [2]Lit., *on its*

19 [1]Lit., *second*

22 [1]Or, *appendage on* [2]Lit., *filling*

24 [1]Lit., *the whole* [2]Lit., *on* [3]Lit., *palms*

26 [1]Lit., *filling* [a]Lev. 7:31-34

nation, and wave it as a wave offering before the LORD; and it
shall be your portion.
27 "And you shall consecrate the breast of the wave offering and the thigh of the heave offering which was waved and
which was [1]offered from the ram of [2]ordination, from the one
which was for Aaron and from the one which was for his sons.
28 "And it shall be for Aaron and his sons as *their* portion
forever from the sons of Israel, for it is a heave offering; and it
shall be a heave offering from the sons of Israel from the
sacrifices of their peace offerings, *even* their heave offering to
the LORD.
29 "And the holy garments of Aaron shall be for his sons
after him, [1]that in them they may be anointed and ordained.
30 "For seven days the one of his sons who is priest in his
stead shall put them on, when he enters the tent of meeting to
minister in the holy place.
31 "And you shall take the ram of [1]ordination and boil its
flesh in a holy place.
32 "And Aaron and his sons shall eat the flesh of the ram,
and the bread that is in the basket, at the doorway of the tent
of meeting.
33 "Thus they shall eat [1]those things by which atonement
was made [2]at their ordination *and* consecration; but a [3a]lay-
man shall not eat *them*, because they are holy.
34 "And [a]if any of the flesh of [1]ordination or any of the
bread remains until morning, then you shall burn the remainder with fire; it shall not be eaten, because it is holy.
35 "And thus you shall do to Aaron and to his sons, according to all that I have commanded you; you shall [1]ordain them
through [a]seven days.
36 "And each day you shall offer a bull as a sin offering for
atonement, and you shall [1]purify the altar when you make
atonement [2]for it; and you shall anoint it to consecrate it.
37 "For seven days you shall make atonement [1]for the altar
and consecrate it; then the altar shall be most holy, *and* whatever
touches the altar shall be holy.
38 "Now [a]this is what you shall offer on the altar: two one
year old lambs each day, continuously.
39 "The one lamb you shall offer in the morning, and the
[1]other lamb you shall offer at [2]twilight;
40 and there *shall be* one-tenth *of an ephah* of fine flour
mixed with one-fourth of a hin of beaten oil, and one-fourth of
a hin of wine for a libation for one lamb.
41 "And the [1]other lamb you shall offer at [2]twilight, and
shall offer as the grain offering of the morning, with its libation, for a soothing aroma, an offering by fire to the LORD.
42 "It shall be a continual burnt offering throughout your
generations at the doorway of the tent of meeting before the
LORD, where I will meet with you, to speak to you there.
43 "And I will meet there with the sons of Israel, and it
shall be consecrated by My glory.
44 "And I will consecrate the tent of meeting and the altar;
I will also consecrate Aaron and his sons to minister as priests
to Me.
45 "And [a]I will dwell among the sons of Israel and will be
their God.

27 [1]Lit., *heaved or lifted up* [2]Lit., *filling*

29 [1]Lit., *for anointing in them and filling their hand in them*

31 [1]Lit., *filling*

33 [1]Lit., *them* [2]Lit., *to fill their hand to sanctify them* [3]Lit., *stranger* [a]Lev. 22:10, 13

34 [1]Lit., *filling* [a]Ex. 12:10; 23:18; 34:25

35 [1]Lit., *fill their hand* [a]Lev. 8:33

36 [1]Or, *offer a sin offering on the altar* [2]Lit., *upon*

37 [1]Lit., *upon*

38 [a]Num. 28:3-31; 29:6-38

39 [1]Lit., *second* [2]Lit., *between the two evenings*

41 [1]Lit., *second* [2]Lit., *between the two evenings*

45 [a]Ex. 25:8; Num. 5:3; Deut. 12:11

46 "And they shall know that I am the LORD their God who
brought them out of the land of Egypt, that I might dwell
among them; I am the LORD their God.

CHAPTER 30

"MOREOVER, you shall make [a]an altar as a place for
burning incense; you shall make it of acacia wood.
2 "Its length *shall be* a [1]cubit, and its width a cubit, it shall
be square, and its height *shall be* two cubits; its horns *shall be*
[2]of one piece with it.
3 "And you shall overlay it with pure gold, its top and its
[1]sides all around, and its horns; and you shall make a gold
molding all around for it.
4 "And you shall make two gold rings for it under its
molding; you shall make *them* on its two sides—on [1]opposite
sides—and [2]they shall be holders for poles with which to carry
it.
5 "And you shall make the poles of acacia wood and overlay them with gold.
6 "And you shall put [1]this ark in front of the veil that is
[2]near the ark of the testimony, in front of the [3]mercy seat that
is over *the ark of* the testimony, where I will meet with you.
7 "And Aaron shall burn fragrant incense on it; he shall
burn it every morning when he trims the lamps.
8 "And when Aaron [1]trims the lamps at [2]twilight, he shall
burn incense. *There shall be* perpetual incense before the
LORD throughout your generations.
9 "You shall not offer any strange incense on [1]this altar, or
burnt offering or meal offering; and you shall not pour out a
libation on it.
10 "And Aaron shall make atonement on its horns once a
year; he shall make atonement on it with the blood of the sin
offering of atonement once a year throughout your generations. It is most holy to the LORD."
11 The LORD also spoke to Moses, saying,
12 "When you take [a]a [1]census of the sons of Israel [2]to
number them, then each one of them shall give a ransom for
[3]himself to the LORD, when you [4]number them, that there may
be no plague among them when you [4]number them.
13 "This is what everyone who [1]is numbered shall give: half
a shekel according to the shekel of the sanctuary (the shekel is
twenty gerahs), half a shekel as a [2]contribution to the LORD.
14 "Everyone who [1]is numbered, from twenty years old and
over, shall give the [2]contribution to the LORD.
15 "The rich shall not pay more, and the poor shall not pay
less than the half shekel, when you give the [1]contribution to
the LORD to make atonement for [2]yourselves.
16 "And you shall take the atonement money from the sons
of Israel, and shall give it for the service of the tent of meeting,
that it may be a memorial for the sons of Israel before the
LORD, to make atonement for [1]yourselves."
17 And the LORD spoke to Moses, saying,
18 "You shall also make [a]a laver of bronze, with its base of
bronze, for washing; and you shall put it between the tent of
meeting and the altar, and you shall put water in it.

1 [a]Ex. 37:25-29

2 [1]I.e., a cubit equals approx. 18 inches [2]Lit., *from itself*

3 [1]Lit., *walls*

4 [1]Lit., *its two* [2]Lit., *it*

6 [1]Lit., *it* [2]Lit., *upon, or over* [3]Lit., *propitiatory*

8 [1]Lit., *causes to ascend* [2]Lit., *between the two evenings*

9 [1]Lit., *it*

12 [1]Lit., *sum* [2]Lit., *for their being mustered* [3]Lit., *his soul* [4]Lit., *muster* [a]Ex. 38:25, 26; Num. 1:2; 26:2

13 [1]Lit., *passes over to those who are mustered* [2]Lit., *heave offering*

14 [1]Note 1, vs. 13 [2]Lit., *heave offering of the LORD*

15 [1]Lit., *heave offering of the LORD* [2]Lit., *your souls*

16 [1]Lit., *your souls*

18 [1]Or, *copper* [a]Ex. 38:8

19 "And Aaron and his sons shall wash their hands and their
feet from it;
20 when they enter the tent of meeting, they shall wash
with water, that they may not die; or when they approach the
altar to minister, by offering up in smoke a fire *sacrifice* to the
LORD.
21 "So they shall wash their hands and their feet, that they
may not die; and it shall be a perpetual statute for them, for
[1]Aaron and his [2]descendants throughout their generations."
22 Moreover, the LORD spoke to Moses, saying,
23 "Take also for yourself the finest of spices: of flowing
myrrh five hundred *shekels*, and of fragrant cinnamon half as
much, two hundred and fifty, and of fragrant cane two
hundred and fifty,
24 and of cassia five hundred, according to the shekel of
the sanctuary, and of olive oil a hin.
25 "And you shall make [1]of these a holy anointing oil, a
perfume mixture, the work of a perfumer; it shall be [a]a holy
anointing oil.
26 "And with it you shall anoint the tent of meeting and
the ark of the testimony,
27 and the table and all its utensils, and the lampstand and
its utensils, and the altar of incense,
28 and the altar of burnt offering and all its utensils, and
the laver and its stand.
29 "You shall also consecrate them, that they may be most
holy; whatever touches them shall be holy.
30 "And you shall anoint Aaron and his sons, and consecrate
them, that they may minister as priests to Me.
31 "And you shall speak to the sons of Israel, saying, 'This
shall be a holy anointing oil to Me throughout your
generations.
32 'It shall not be poured on [1]anyone's body, nor shall you
make *any* like it, in [2]the same proportions; it is holy, *and* it
shall be holy to you.
33 'Whoever shall mix *any* like it, or whoever puts any of it
on a [1]layman, [2]shall be cut off from his people.' "
34 Then the LORD said to Moses, "Take for yourself
spices, stacte and onycha and galbanum, spices with pure frankincense; there shall be an equal part of each.
35 "And with it you shall make incense, a perfume, the
work of a perfumer, salted, pure, *and* holy.
36 "And you shall beat some of it very fine, and put part of
it before the testimony in the tent of meeting, where I shall
meet with you; it shall be most holy to you.
37 "And the incense which you shall make, you shall not
make in [1]the same proportions for yourselves, it shall be holy
to you for the LORD.
38 "Whoever shall make *any* like it, to [1]use as perfume,
[2]shall be cut off from his people."

CHAPTER 31

[a]NOW the LORD spoke to Moses, saying,
2 "See, I have called by name Bezalel, the son of Uri, the
son of Hur, of the tribe of Judah.

21 [1]Lit., *him* [2]Lit., *seed*

25 [1]Lit., *it*
[a]Ex. 37:29; 40:9; Lev. 8:10

32 [1]Lit., *the flesh of man*
[2]Lit., *its proportion*

33 [1]Lit., *stranger* [2]Lit., *even he shall*

37 [1]Lit., *its proportion*

38 [1]Lit., *smell of it* [2]Lit., *even he shall*

1 [a]Ex. 35:30-36:1

3 "And I have filled him with the Spirit of God in wisdom,
in understanding, in knowledge, and in all *kinds of*
[1]craftsmanship,
4 to [1]make artistic designs for work in gold, in silver, and
in [2]bronze,
5 and in the cutting of stones [1]for settings, and in the
carving of wood, that he may work in all *kinds of*
[2]craftsmanship.
6 "And behold, I Myself have [1]appointed with him Oholiab, the son of Ahisamach, of the tribe of Dan; and in the
hearts of all who are [2]skillful I have put [3]skill, that they may
make all that I have commanded you:
7 the tent of meeting, and the ark of testimony, and the
[1]mercy seat upon it, and all the furniture of the tent,
8 the table also and its [1]utensils, and the [a]pure *gold* lampstand with all its [1]utensils, and the altar of incense,
9 the altar of burnt offering also with all its [1]utensils, and
the laver and its stand,
10 the [1]woven garments as well, and the holy garments for
Aaron the priest, and the garments of his sons, *with which* to
[2]carry on their priesthood;
11 the anointing oil also, and the fragrant incense for the
holy place, they are to make *them* according to all that I have
commanded you."
12 And the LORD spoke to Moses, saying,
13 "But as for you, speak to the sons of Israel, saying, '[a]You
shall surely observe My sabbaths; for *this* is [b]a sign between Me
and you throughout your generations, that you may know that
I am the LORD who sanctifies you.
14 'Therefore you are to observe the sabbath, for it is holy
to you. [a]Everyone who profanes it shall surely be put to death;
for whoever does any work on it, that person shall be cut off
from among his people.
15 'For six days work may be done, but on the seventh day
there is a [a]sabbath of complete rest, holy to the LORD; [b]whoever
does any work on the sabbath day shall surely be put to
death.
16 'So the sons of Israel shall observe the sabbath, to [1]cele-
brate the sabbath throughout their generations as a perpetual covenant.'
17 "[a]It is a sign between Me and the sons of Israel forever;
[b]for in six days the LORD made heaven and earth, but on the
seventh day He ceased *from labor*, and was refreshed."
18 And when He had finished speaking with him upon
Mount Sinai, He gave Moses [a]the two tablets of the testimony,
tablets of stone, [b]written by the finger of God.

CHAPTER 32

NOW when the people saw that Moses [a]delayed to come
down from the mountain, the people assembled about Aaron,
and said to him, "Come, [b]make us [1]a god who will go before
us; as for [c]this Moses, the man who brought us up from the
land of Egypt, we do not know what has become of him."
2 And Aaron said to them, "[a]Tear off the gold rings

3 [1]Or, *workmanship*

4 [1]Lit., *devise devices* [2]Or, *copper*

5 [1]Lit., *to fill in (for a setting)* [2]Or, *workmanship*

6 [1]Lit., *given* [2]Lit., *wise of heart* [3]Lit., *wisdom*

7 [1]Lit., *propitiatory*

8 [1]Or, *vessels* [a]Lev. 24:4

9 [1]Or, *vessels*

10 [1]Or, *service garments* [2]Lit., *minister as priests*

13 [a]Ex. 20:8 [b]Ex. 31:17; Ezek. 20:12, 20

14 [a]Ex. 31:15; 35:2; Num. 15:32, 35; John 7:23

15 [a]Ex. 16:23; 35:2, 3 [b]Ex. 31:14

16 [1]Lit., *do*

17 [a]Ex. 31:13 [b]Ex. 20:11; Gen. 2:2, 3

18 [1]Ex. 24:12 [b]Ex. 32:15, 16; 34:1, 28

1 [1]Or, *gods* [a]Ex. 24:18; Deut. 9:11, 12 [b]Acts 7:40 [c]Ex. 14:11

2 [a]Ex. 35:22

which are in the ears of your wives, your sons, and your daughters, and bring *them* to me."
3 Then all the people tore off the gold rings which were
in their ears, and brought *them* to Aaron.
4 And he took *this* from their hand, and fashioned it with
a graving tool, and made it into a [a]molten calf; and they said,
"[1]This is your god, O Israel, who brought you up from the land
of Egypt."
5 Now when Aaron saw *this*, he built an altar before it;
and Aaron made proclamation and said, "Tomorrow *shall be* a
feast to the LORD."
6 So the next day they rose early and [a]offered burnt offerings, and brought peace offerings; and [b]the people sat down
to eat and to drink, and rose up [c]to play.
7 Then the LORD spoke to Moses, "Go [1]down at once,
for your people, whom [a]you brought up from the land of
Egypt, have corrupted *themselves*.
8 "They have quickly turned aside from the way which I
commanded them. They have made for themselves a molten
calf, and have worshiped it, and [a]have sacrificed to it, and said,
'This is your god, O Israel, who brought you up from the land
of Egypt!' "
9 [a]And the LORD said to Moses, "I have seen this people,
and behold, they are [1b]an obstinate people.
10 "Now then [a]let Me alone, that My anger may burn
against them, and that I may destroy them; and I will make of
you a great nation."
11 Then [a]Moses entreated the LORD his God, and said, "O
LORD, why doth Thine anger burn against Thy people whom
Thou has brought out from the land of Egypt with great power and with a mighty hand?
12 "Why should [a]the Egyptians speak, saying, 'With evil
intent He brought them out to kill them in the mountains and
to destroy them from the face of the earth'? Turn from Thy
burning anger and change Thy mind about *doing* harm to Thy
people.
13 "Remember Abraham, Isaac, and Israel, Thy servants to
whom Thou didst [a]swear by Thyself, and didst say to them, 'I
will multiply your [1]descendants [2]as the stars of the heavens,
and [c]all this land of which I have spoken I will give to your
[1]descendants, and they shall inherit *it* forever.' "
14 [a]So the LORD changed His mind about the harm which
He said He would do to His people.
15 [a]Then Moses turned and went down from the mountain with the two tablets of the testimony in his hand, [b]tablets
which were written on both [1]sides; they were written on one
side and the other.
16 And the tablets were God's work, and the writing was
God's writing engraved on the tablets.
17 Now when Joshua heard the sound of the people [1]as
they shouted, he said to Moses, "There is a sound of war in the
camp."
18 But he said,
"It is not the sound of the cry of triumph,
Nor is it the sound of the cry of defeat;
But the sound of singing I hear."

4 [1]Or, "*These are your gods*
[a]Deut. 9:16; Acts 7:41

6 [a]Acts 7:41 [b]1 Cor. 10:7
[c]Ex. 32:17-19; Num. 25:2

7 [1]Lit., *go down*
[a]Ex.32:4, 11; Deut. 9:12

8 [1]Or, *these are your gods*
[a]Ex. 22:20; 34:15; Deut. 32:17

9 [1]Or, *a stiff-necked*
[a]Num. 14:11-20 [b]Ex. 33:3, 5; 34:9; Acts 7:51

10 [a]Deut. 9:14

11 [a]Deut. 9:18

12 [a]Deut. 9:28; Josh. 7:9

13 [1]Lit., *seed*
[a]Gen. 22:16-18 [b]Gen. 15:5; 26:4 [c]Ex. 13:5, 11; 33:1

14 [a]Ps. 106:45

15 [1]Lit., *their sides*
[a]Deut. 9:15 [b]Ex. 31:18

17 [1]Lit., *in its shouting*

19 And it came about, as soon as [1]Moses came near the
camp, that he saw the calf and *the* [a]dancing; and Moses' anger
burned, and [b]he threw the tablets from his hands and shattered
them [2]at the foot of the mountain.
20 [a]And he took the calf which they had made and burned
it with fire, and ground it to powder, and scattered it over the
surface of the water, and made the sons of Israel drink *it*.
21 Then Moses said to Aaron, "What did this people do
to you, that you have brought *such* great sin upon them?"
22 And Aaron said, "Do not let the anger of my lord burn;
you know the people yourself, [a]that they are [1]prone to evil.
23 "For [a]they said to me, 'Make [1]a god for us who will go
before us; for this Moses, the man who brought us up from the
land of Egypt, we do not know what has become of him.'
24 "And I said to them, 'Whoever has any gold, let them
tear it off.' So they gave *it* to me, and [a]I threw it into the fire,
and out came this calf."
25 Now when Moses saw that the people were [1]out of
control—for [a]Aaron had let them [2]get out of control to be a
derision among [2]their enemies—
26 then Moses stood in the gate of the camp, and said,
"Whoever is for the LORD, *come* to me!" And all the sons of
Levi gathered together to him.
27 And he said to them, "Thus says the LORD, the God of
Israel, 'Every man *of you* put his sword upon his thigh, and go
back and forth from gate to gate in the camp, and kill every
man his brother, and every man his friend, and every man his
[1]neighbor.' "
28 So [a]the sons of Levi did [1]as Moses instructed, and
about three thousand men of the people fell that day.
29 Then Moses said, "[1]Dedicate yourselves today to the
LORD—for every man has been against his son and against his
brother—in order that He may bestow a blessing upon you
today."
30 And it came about on the next day that Moses said to
the people, "You yourselves have [1]committed a great sin; and
now I am going up to the LORD, perhaps I can make atonement for your sin."
31 Then Moses returned to the LORD, and said, "Alas, this
people has [1]committed a great sin, and they have made [2]a [a]god
of gold for themselves.
32 "But now, if Thou wilt forgive their sin—and if not,
please blot me out from Thy [a]book which Thou has written!"
33 And the LORD said to Moses, "Whoever has sinned
against Me, [a]I will blot him out of My book.
34 "But go now, lead the people [a]where I told you. Behold,
[b]My angel shall go before you; nevertheless in the day when I
[1]punish, [c]I will [2]punish them for their sin."
35 [a]Then the LORD smote the people, because of what
[b]they did with the calf which Aaron had made.

CHAPTER 33

THEN the LORD spoke to Moses, "Depart, go up from here,
you and the people whom you have brought up from the land

19 [1]Lit., *he* [2]Lit., *beneath* [a]Ex. 32:6 [b]Deut. 9:17

20 [a]Deut. 9:21

22 [1]Lit., *in evil* [a]Deut. 9:24

23 [1]Or, *gods* [a]Ex. 32:1-4

24 [a]Ex. 32:4

25 [1]Lit., *let loose* [2]Lit., *go loose* [3]Lit., *those who rise against them* [a]1 Kin. 12:28-30; 14:16

27 [1]Or, *kin*

28 [1]Lit., *according to Moses' word* [a]Num. 25:7-13; Deut. 33:9

29 [1]Lit., *"Fill your hand*

30 [1]Lit., *sinned*

31 [1]Lit., *sinned* [2]Or, *gods* [a]Ex. 20:23

32 [a]Ps. 69:28; Is. 4:3; Dan. 12:1; Mal. 3:16, 17

33 [a]Ex. 17:14; Deut. 29:20; Ps. 9:5

34 [1]Lit., *visit* [2]Lit., *visit their sin upon them* [a]Ex. 3:17 [b]Ex. 23:20 [c]Ps. 99:8

35 [a]Ex. 32:28 [b]Ex. 32:4, 24

of Egypt, to the land of which [a]I swore to Abraham, Isaac, and
Jacob, saying, 'To your [1]descendants I will give it':
2 "And I will send [a]an angel before you and [b]I will drive
out the Canaanite, the Amorite, the Hittite, the Perizzite, the
Hivite and the Jebusite—
3 to a land [a]flowing with milk and honey; for I will not go
up in your midst, because you are [1b]an obstinate people, lest [c]I
destroy you on the way."
4 When the people heard this [1]sad word, [a]they went into
mourning, and none of them put on his ornaments.
5 For the LORD had said to Moses, "Say to the sons of
Israel, 'You are [1a]an obstinate people; should I go up in your
midst for one moment, I would destroy you. Now therefore
put off your ornaments from you, that I may know what I will
do with you.' "
6 So the sons of Israel stripped themselves of their ornaments from Mount Horeb *onward.*
7 Now Moses used to take [a]the tent and pitch it outside
the camp, a good distance from the camp, and he called it the
tent of meeting. And it came about, that everyone who sought
the LORD would go out to the tent of meeting which was
outside the camp.
8 And it came about, whenever Moses went out to the
tent, that all the people would arise and stand, each at the
entrance of his tent, and gaze after Moses until he entered the
tent.
9 And it came about, whenever Moses entered the tent,
[a]the pillar of cloud would descend and stand at the entrance of
the tent; [b]and [1]the LORD would speak with Moses.
10 When all the people saw the pillar of cloud standing at
the entrance of the tent, all the people would arise and worship, each at the entrance of his tent.
11 Thus [a]the LORD used to speak to Moses face to face,
just as a man speaks to his friend. When [1]Moses returned to
the camp, his servant Joshua, the son of Nun, a young man,
would not depart from the tent.
12 Then Moses said to the LORD, "See, Thou dost say to
me, '[a]Bring up this people!' But Thou Thyself hast not let me
know [b]whom Thou wilt send with me. [c]Moreover, Thou hast
said, 'I have known you by name, and you have also found
favor in My sight.'
13 "Now therefore, I pray Thee, if I have found favor in
Thy sight, let me know [a]Thy ways, that I may know Thee,
so that I may find favor in Thy sight. [b]Consider too, that this
nation is Thy people."
14 And He said, "[a]My presence shall go *with you,* and [b]I
will give you rest."
15 Then he said to Him, "[a]If Thy presence does not go
with us, do not lead us up from here.
16 "For how then can it be known that I have found favor
in Thy sight, I and Thy people? Is it not by Thy going with us,
so that [a]we, I and Thy people, may be distinguished from all
the *other* people who are upon the face of the [1]earth?"
17 And the LORD said to Moses, "I will also do this thing
of which you have spoken; [a]for you have found favor in My
sight, and I have known you by name."

1 [1]Lit., *seed* [a]Ex. 32:13

2 [a]Ex. 32:34 [b]Ex. 23: 27-31

3 [1]Lit., *a stiff-necked* [a]Ex. 3:8, 17 [b]Ex. 33:5; 32:9 [c]Ex. 32:10

4 [1]Lit., *evil* [a]Num. 14:39

5 [1]Lit., *a stiff-necked* [a]Ex. 33:3

7 [a]Ex. 18:7, 12-16

9 [1]Lit., *He* [a]Ex. 13:21 [b]Ps. 99:7

11 [1]Lit., *he* [a]Num. 12:8; Deut. 34:10

12 [a]Ex. 3:10; 32:34 [b]Ex. 33:2 [c]Ex. 33:17

13 [a]Ps. 25:4; 51:13 [b]Ex. 3:7, 10; 5:1; 32:12, 14

14 [a]Deut. 4:37; Is. 63:9 [b]Deut. 12:10; 25:19; Josh. 22:4

15 [a]Ps. 80:3, 7, 19

16 [1]Lit., *ground* [a]Lev. 20:24, 26

17 [a]Ex. 33:12

18 [a]Then [1]Moses said, "I pray Thee, show me Thy glory!"
19 And He said, "[a]I Myself will make all My goodness pass
before you, and will proclaim the name of the LORD before
you; and [b]I will be gracious to whom I will be gracious, and will
show compassion on whom I will show compassion."
20 But He said, "You cannot see My face, [a]for no man
can see Me and live!"
21 Then the LORD said, "Behold, there is a place [1]by Me,
and [a]you shall stand *there* on the rock;
22 and it will come about, while My glory is passing by,
that I will put you in the cleft of the rock and [a]cover you with
My hand until I have passed by.
23 "Then I will take My hand away and you shall see My
back, but My face shall not be seen."

CHAPTER 34

NOW the LORD said to Moses, "Cut out for yourself [a]two
stone tablets like the former ones, and I will write on the
tablets the words that were on the former tablets which you
shattered.
2 "So be ready by morning, and come up in the morning
to [a]Mount Sinai, and [1]present yourself there to Me on the top
of the mountain.
3 "And [a]no man is to come up with you, nor let any man
be seen [1]anywhere on the mountain; even the flocks and the
herds may not graze in front of that mountain."
4 So he cut out [a]two stone tablets like the former ones,
and Moses rose up early in the morning and went up to Mount
Sinai, as the LORD had commanded him, and he took two
stone tablets in his hand.
5 And [a]the LORD descended in the cloud and stood there
with him as [1]he called upon the name of the LORD.
6 Then the LORD passed by in front of him and proclaimed, "The LORD, the LORD God, [a]compassionate and
gracious, slow to anger, and abounding in lovingkindness
and [1]truth;
7 who [a]keeps lovingkindness for thousands, who forgives
iniquity, transgression and sin; yet He [b]will by no means leave
the guilty unpunished, visiting the iniquity of fathers on the
children and on the grandchildren to the third and fourth
generations."
8 And Moses made haste [1]to bow low toward the earth
and worship.
9 And he said, "[a]If now I have found favor in Thy sight,
O LORD, I pray, [b]let the LORD go along in our midst, even
though [1c]the people are so obstinate; and do Thou [d]pardon
our iniquity and our sin, and [e]take us as Thine own
[2]possession."
10 Then [1]God said, "Behold, [a]I am going to make a covenant. Before all your people [b]I will perform miracles which
have not been [2]produced in all the earth, nor among any of the
nations; and all the people [3]among whom you live will see the
working of the LORD, for it is a fearful thing that I am going to
perform with you.

---

18 [1]Lit., *he* [a]Ex. 33:20-23

19 [a]Ex. 34:6, 7 [b]Rom. 9:15

20 [a]Is. 6:5

21 [1]Lit., *with* [a]Ps. 18:2, 46; 27:5; 61:2; 62:7

22 [a]Is. 49:2; 51:16

1 [a]Ex. 24:12; 31:18

2 [1]Or, *place yourself before* [a]Ex. 19:11, 18, 20

3 [1]Lit., *on all* [a]Ex. 19:12, 13

4 [a]Ex. 34:1

5 [1]Or, *He called out with the name of the LORD* [a]Ex. 19:9; 33:9

6 [1]Or, *faithfulness* [a]Num. 14:18; Deut. 4:31; Neh. 9:17; Ps. 86:15; 103:8; 145:8

7 [a]Ex. 20:5, 6 [b]Ex. 23:7

8 [1]Lit., *and bowed*

9 [1]Lit., *it is a people stiff-necked* [2]Or, *inheritance* [a]Ex. 33:13 [b]Ex. 33:12 [c]Ex. 32:9 [d]Ex. 34:7 [e]Deut. 4:20; 9:26, 29; 32:9; Ps. 33:12

10 [1]Lit., He *said* [2]Lit., *created* [3]Lit., *in whose midst you are* [a]Ex. 34:27, 28 [b]Ps. 72:18; 136:4

11 "[1]Be sure to observe what I am commanding you this
day: behold, [a]I am going to drive out the Amorite before you,
and the Canaanite, the Hittite, the Perizzite, the Hivite and
the Jebusite.
12 "[a]Watch yourself that you make no covenant with the
inhabitants of the land into which you are going, lest it become a snare in your midst.
13 "[a]But *rather,* you are to tear down their altars and smash
their sacred pillars and cut down their [1b]Asherahs
14 —for [a]you shall not worship any other god, for the
LORD, whose name is Jealous, is a jealous God—
15 lest you make a covenant with the inhabitants of the
land and they play the harlot with their gods, and [a]sacrifice to
their gods, and someone [b]invite you [1]to eat of his sacrifice;
16 and [a]you take some of his daughters for your sons, and
his daughters play the harlot with their gods, and cause your
sons *also* to play the harlot with their gods.
17 "[a]You shall make for yourself no molten gods.
18 "You shall observe [a]the Feast of Unleavened Bread. For
[b]seven days you are to eat unleavened bread, [1]as I commanded
you, at the appointed time in the [c]month of Abib, for in the
month of Abib you came out of Egypt.
19 "[a]The [1]first offspring from every womb belongs to Me,
and all your male livestock, the [1]first offspring from [2]cattle and
sheep.
20 "[a]And you shall redeem with a lamb the [1]first offspring
from a donkey; and if you do not redeem *it,* then you shall
break its neck. You shall redeem [b]all the first-born of your
sons. And [2c]none shall appear before Me empty-handed.
21 "You shall work [a]six days, but on the seventh day you
shall rest; *even* during plowing time and harvest you shall rest.
22 "And you shall celebrate [a]the Feast of Weeks, *that is,*
the first fruits of the wheat harvest, and the Feast of Ingathering at the turn of the year.
23 "[a]Three times a year all your males are to appear before
the Lord [1]GOD, the God of Israel.
24 "For I will [1]drive out nations before you and enlarge
your borders, and no man shall covet your land when you go
up three times a year to appear before the LORD your God.
25 "[a]You shall not [1]offer the blood of My sacrifice with
leavened bread, [b]nor is the sacrifice of the Feast of the Passover
to [2]be left over until morning.
26 "You shall bring [a]the very first of the first fruits of your
soil into the house of the LORD your God. You shall not boil a
kid in its mother's milk."
27 Then the LORD said to Moses, "[a]Write [1]down these
words, [b]for in accordance with these words I have made a
covenant with you and with Israel."
28 So he was there with the LORD [a]forty days and forty
nights; he did not eat bread or drink water. And [b]he wrote on
the tablets the words of the covenant, [c]the Ten
[1]Commandments.
29 And it came about when Moses was coming down from
Mount Sinai (and the two tablets of the testimony *were* in
Moses' hand as he was coming down from the mountain), that

11 [1]Lit., *Observe for yourself* [a]Ex. 33:2

12 [a]Ex. 23:32, 33

13 [1]I.e., wooden symbols of a female deity [a]Ex. 23:24 [b]Judg. 6:25, 26

14 [a]Ex. 20:3, 5; Deut. 4:24

15 [1]Lit., *and you eat* [a]Ex. 22:20; 32:8 [b]Num. 25:1, 2; Deut. 32:37, 38

16 [a]Deut. 7:3; Josh. 23:12, 13

17 [a]Ex. 20:23

18 [1]Or, *which* [a]Ex. 12:17 [b]Ex. 12:15, 16 [c]Ex. 12:2; 13:4

19 [1]Lit., *Every* [2]Or, *oxen* [a]Ex. 13:2

20 [1]Lit., *first opening of* [2]Lit., *they shall not* [a]Ex. 13:13 [b]Ex. 13:15; Num. 3:45 [c]Ex. 22:29

21 [a]Ex. 31:15; 35:2

22 [a]Ex. 23:16; Lev. 23:15

23 [1]YHWH, usually rendered LORD [a]Ex. 23:14-17

24 [1]Or, *dispossess*

25 [1]Lit., *slaughter* [2]Lit., *remain overnight* [a]Ex. 23:18 [b]Ex. 12:10

26 [a]Ex. 23:19

27 [1]Lit., *for yourself* [a]Ex. 17:14; 24:4 [b]Ex. 34:10

28 [1]Lit., *Words* [a]Ex. 24:18 [b]Ex. 31:18; 34:1 [c]Deut. 4:13; 10:4

Moses did not know that the skin of his face shone because of
his speaking with Him.
30 So when Aaron and all the sons of Israel saw Moses,
behold, the skin of his face shone, and [a]they were afraid to
come near him.
31 Then Moses called to them, and Aaron and all [a]the
rulers in the congregation returned to him; and Moses spoke
to them.
32 And afterward all the sons of Israel came near, and he
commanded them *to do* everything that the LORD had spoken
[1]to him on Mount Sinai.
33 When Moses had finished speaking with them, [a]he put
a veil over his face.
34 But whenever Moses went in before the LORD to speak
with Him, [a]he would take off the veil until he came out; and
whenever he came out and spoke to the sons of Israel what he
had been commanded,
35 the sons of Israel would see the face of Moses, that the
skin of Moses' face shone. So Moses would replace the veil
over his face until he went in to speak with Him.

CHAPTER 35

THEN Moses assembled all the congregation of the sons of
Israel, and said to them, "These are the things that the LORD
has commanded *you* to [1]do.
2 "[a]For six days work may be done, but on the seventh day
you shall have a holy *day*, [b]a sabbath of complete rest to the
LORD; [c]whoever does any work on it shall be put to death.
3 "[a]You shall not kindle a fire in any of your dwellings on
the sabbath day."
4 And Moses spoke to all the congregation of the sons of
Israel, saying, "This is the thing which the LORD has commanded, saying,
5 '[a]Take from among you a [1]contribution to the LORD;
whoever is of a willing heart, let him bring it as the LORD's
[1]contribution: gold, silver, and [2]bronze,
6 and [1]blue, purple and scarlet *material,* fine linen, goats'
hair,
7 and rams' skins [1]dyed red, and [2]porpoise skins, and
acacia wood,
8 and oil for lighting, and spices for the anointing oil, and
for the fragrant incense,
9 and onyx stones and setting stones, for the ephod and
for the [1]breastpiece.
10 'And let every skillful man among you come, and make
all that the LORD has commanded:
11 the [1]tabernacle, its tent and its covering, its hooks and
its boards, its bars, its pillars, and its [2]sockets;
12 the ark and its poles, the [1]mercy seat, and the curtain of
the screen;
13 the table and its poles, and all its [1]utensils, and the
[a]bread of the [2]Presence;

30 [a]2 Cor. 3:7
31 [a]Ex. 16:22
32 [1]Lit., *with*
33 [a]2 Cor. 3:13
34 [a]2 Cor. 3:16
1 [1]Lit., *do them.*
2 [a]Ex. 31:15 [b]Ex. 16:23 [c]Num. 15:32-36
3 [a]Ex. 12:16
5 [1]Or, *heave offering* [2]Or, *copper* [a]Ex. 25:1-9
6 [1]Or, *violet*
7 [1]Or, *tanned* [2]Or, *dolphin*
9 [1]Or, pouch
11 [1]Lit., *dwelling place* [2]Or, *bases*
12 [1]Lit., *propitiatory*
13 [1]Or, *vessels* [2]Lit., *Face* [a]Ex. 25:30

14 the lampstand also for the light and its utensils and its
lamps and the oil for the light;
15 and the altar of incense and its poles, and the anointing
oil and the fragrant incense, and the screen for the doorway at
the [1]entrance of the tabernacle;
16 the altar of burnt offering with its [1]bronze grating, its
poles, and all its [2]utensils, the [3]basin and its stand;
17 the hangings of the court, its pillars and its [1]sockets,
and the screen for the gate of the court;
18 the pegs of the tabernacle and the pegs of the court and
their cords;
19 the [1a]woven garments, for ministering in the holy place,
the holy garments for Aaron the priest, and the garments of his
sons, to minister as priests.' "
20 Then all the congregation of the sons of Israel departed from Moses' presence.
21 And [a]everyone whose heart [1]stirred him and everyone
whose spirit [2]moved him came *and* brought the LORD's [3]contri-
bution for the work of the tent of meeting and for all its
service and for the holy garments.
22 Then all [1]whose hearts moved them, both men and
women, came *and* brought brooches and [2]earrings and signet
rings and bracelets, all articles of gold; so *did* every man who
[3]presented an offering of gold to the LORD.
23 And every man, [1]who had in his possession [2]blue and
purple and scarlet *material* and fine linen and goats' *hair* and
rams' skins [3]dyed red and [4]seal skins, brought them.
24 Everyone who could make a [1]contribution of silver and
[2]bronze brought the LORD's [1]contribution; and every man,
[3]who had in his possession acacia wood for any work of the
service, brought it.
25 And all the [1]skilled women spun with their hands, and
brought what they had spun, *in* [2]blue and purple *and* scarlet
material and *in* fine linen.
26 And all the women whose heart [1]stirred with a skill
spun the goats' *hair*.
27 And the rulers brought the onyx stones and the stones
for setting for the ephod and for the [1]breastpiece;
28 and the spice and the oil for the light and for the
anointing oil and for the fragrant incense.
29 The [1]Israelites, all the men and women, whose heart
[2]moved them to bring *material* for all the work, which the
LORD had commanded through Moses to be done, brought a
freewill offering to the LORD.
30 [a]Then Moses said to the sons of Israel, "See, the LORD
has called by name Bezalel the son of Uri, the son of Hur, of
the tribe of Judah.
31 "And He has filled him with the Spirit of God, in wisdom, in understanding and in knowledge and in all
[1]craftsmanship;
32 [1]to make designs for working in gold and in silver and
in [2]bronze,
33 and in the cutting of stones for settings, and in the
carving of wood, so as to perform in every inventive work.
34 "He also has put in his heart to teach, both he and
Oholiab, the son of Ahisamach, of the tribe of Dan.

14 [1]Or, *luminary*
15 [1]Or, *doorway*
16 [1]Or, *copper* [2]Or, *vessels* [3]Or, *laver*
17 [1]Or, *bases*
19 [1]Or, *service garments* [a]Ex. 31:10
21 [1]Lit., *lifted up* [2]Or, *made him willing* [3]Or, *heave offering* [a]Ex. 25:2
22 [1]Or, *who were willing-hearted* [2]Or, *nose rings* [3]Lit., *waved a wave offering*
23 [1]Lit., *with whom was found* [2]Or, *violet* [3]Or, *tanned* [4]Or, *porpoise skins*
24 [1]Or, *heave offering* [2]Or, *copper* [3]Lit., *with whom was found*
25 [1]Lit., *women wise of heart* [2]Or, *violet*
26 [1]Lit., *lifted them up in wisdom*
27 [1]Or, *pouch*
29 [1]Lit., *sons of Israel* [2]Lit., *made them willing*
30 [a]Ex. 31:1-6
31 [1]Or, *work*
32 [1]Lit., *devise devices* [2]Or, *copper*

35 "He has filled them with [1]skill to perform every work of
an engraver and of a designer and of an embroiderer, in [2]blue
and in purple *and* in scarlet *material,* and in fine linen, and of
a weaver, as performers of every work and makers of designs.

CHAPTER 36

"NOW Bezalel and Oholiab and every [1]skillful person in
whom the LORD has put [2]skill and understanding to know how
to perform all the work [3]in the construction of the sanctuary
shall perform in accordance with all that the LORD has
commanded."
2 Then Moses called Bezalel and Oholiab and every [1]skill-
ful person in [2]whom the LORD had put [3]skill, everyone whose
heart stirred him, to come to the work to perform it.
3 And they received from Moses all the [1]contributions
which the sons of Israel had brought [2]to perform the work [3]in
the construction of the sanctuary. And they still *continued*
bringing to him freewill offerings every morning.
4 And all the [1]skillful men who were performing all the
work of the sanctuary came, each from [2]the work which [3]he
was performing,
5 and they said to [1]Moses, "[a]The people are bringing
much more than enough for the [2]construction work which the
LORD commanded *us* to [3]perform."
6 So Moses issued a command, and a [1]proclamation was
circulated throughout the camp, saying, "Let neither man nor
woman any longer perform work for the [2]contributions of the
sanctuary." Thus the people were restrained from bringing *any
more.*
7 [a]For the [1]material they had was sufficient and more
than enough for all the work, to perform it.
8 [a]And all the [1]skillful men among those who were performing the work made the [2]tabernacle with ten curtains; of
fine twisted linen and [3]blue and purple and scarlet *material,*
with cherubim, the work of a skillful workman, [4]Bezalel made
them.
9 The length of each curtain was twenty-eight [1]cubits,
and the width of each curtain four [1]cubits; all the curtains had
[2]the same measurements.
10 And he [1]joined five curtains to one another, and *the
other* five curtains he [1]joined to one another.
11 And he made loops of [1]blue on the edge of the [2]outer-
most curtain in the first [3]set; he did likewise on the edge of the
curtain that was [2]outermost in the second [3]set.
12 He made fifty loops in the one curtain and he made
fifty loops on the [1]edge of the curtain that was in the second
[2]set; the loops were opposite each other.
13 And he made fifty clasps of gold, and [1]joined the curtains to one another with the clasps, so the tabernacle was [2]a
unit.
14 Then he made curtains of goats' *hair* for a tent over the
tabernacle; he made eleven curtains [1]in all.
15 The length of each curtain was thirty cubits, and four
cubits the width of each curtain; the eleven curtains had [1]the
same measurements.

35 [1]Lit., *wisdom of heart* [2]Or, *violet*

1 [1]Lit., *man wise of heart* [2]Lit., *wisdom* [3]Or, *connected with the service of;* lit., *of the service of*

2 [1]Lit., *man wise of heart* [2]Lit., *whose heart* [3]Lit., *wisdom*

3 [1]Lit., *lifted offering* [2]Lit., *to perform it for the work* [3]Lit., *of the service of*

4 [1]Lit., *wise* [2]Lit., *his* [3]Lit., *they were*

5 [1]Lit., *Moses, saying,* [2]Lit., *service for the work* [3]Lit., *perform it*
[a]2 Chr. 24:14; 31:6-10

6 [1]Lit., *voice* [2]Lit., *heave offering*

7 [1]Lit., *work*
[a]1 Kin. 8:64

8 [1]Lit., *wise of heart* [2]Lit., *dwelling place* [3]Or, *violet* [4]Lit., *he*
[a]Ex. 26:1-14

9 [1]I.e., one cubit equals approximately 18 inches. [2]Lit., *one measure*

10 [1]Or, *coupled*

11 [1]Or, *violet* [2]Lit., *one curtain from the end in the coupling* [3]Lit., *coupling*

12 [1]Lit., *end* [2]Lit., *coupling*

13 [1]Or, *coupled* [2]Lit., *one*

14 [1]Lit., *them*

15 [1]Lit., *one measure*

16 And he [1]joined five curtains by themselves, and *the*
other six curtains by themselves.
17 Moreover, he made fifty loops on the edge of the curtain that was outermost in the *first* [1]set, and he made fifty
loops on the edge of the curtain *that was outermost in* the
second [1]set.
18 And he made fifty clasps of [1]bronze to [2]join the tent
together, that it might be [3]a unit.
19 And he made a covering for the tent of rams' skins
[1]dyed red, and a covering of [2]porpoise skins above.
20 [a]Then he made the boards for the tabernacle of acacia
wood, standing upright.
21 Ten cubits was the length of [1]each board, and one and
a half cubits the width of each board.
22 There were two tenons for each board, [1]fitted to one
another; thus he did for all the boards of the tabernacle.
23 And he made the boards for the tabernacle: twenty
boards [1]for the south side;
24 and he made forty [1]sockets of silver under the twenty
boards; two [1]sockets under one board for its two tenons and
two [1]sockets under another board for its two tenons.
25 Then for the second side of the tabernacle, on the
north side, he made twenty boards,
26 and their forty [1]sockets of silver; two [1]sockets under
one board and two [1]sockets under another board.
27 And for the [1]rear of the tabernacle, to the west, he
made six boards.
28 And he made two boards for the corners of the [1]taber-
nacle at the [2]rear.
29 And they were double beneath and together they were
complete to its [1]top [2]to the first ring; thus he did with both of
them for the two corners.
30 And there were eight boards with their [1]sockets of silver, sixteen [1]sockets, [2]two under every board.
31 Then he made bars of acacia wood, five for the boards
of one side of the tabernacle,
32 and five bars for the boards of the [1]other side of the
tabernacle, and five bars for the boards of the tabernacle for
the [2]rear *side* to the west.
33 And he made the middle bar to pass through in the
[1]center of the boards from end to end.
34 And he overlaid the boards with gold and made their
rings of gold *as* holders for the bars, and overlaid the bars with
gold.
35 [a]Moreover, he made the veil of [1]blue and purple and
scarlet *material,* and fine twisted linen; he made it with cherubim, the work of a skillful workman.
36 And he made four pillars of acacia for it, and overlaid
them with gold, with their hooks of gold; and he cast four
[1]sockets of silver for them.
37 And he made a screen for the doorway of the tent, of
[1]blue and purple and scarlet *material,* and fine twisted linen,
the work of a [2]weaver;
38 and *he made* its five pillars with their hooks, and he
overlaid their tops and their [1]bands with gold; but their five
[2]sockets were of [3]bronze.

16 [1]Or, *coupled*

17 [1]Lit., *coupling*

18 [1]Or, *copper* [2]Or, *couple* [3]Lit., *one*

19 [1]Or, *tanned* [2]Or, *dolphin skins*

20 [a]Ex 26:15-29

21 [1]Lit., *the*

22 [1]Lit., *bound*

23 [1]Lit., *toward the side of Negev to the south*

24 [1]Or, *bases*

26 [1]Or, *bases*

27 [1]Lit., *extreme parts*

28 [1]Lit., *dwelling place* [2]Lit., *extreme parts*

29 [1]Or, *head* [2]Or, *with reference to*

30 [1]Or, *bases* [2]Lit., *two sockets*

32 [1]Or, *second* [2]Lit., *extreme parts*

33 [1]Lit., *midst*

35 [1]Or, *violet* [a]Ex. 26:31-37

36 [1]Or, *bases*

37 [1]Or, *violet* [2]Lit., *variegator;* i.e., a weaver in colors

38 [1]Or, *fillets, rings* [2]Or, *bases* [3]Or, *copper*

Chapter 37

[a]NOW Bezalel made the ark of acacia wood; its length was two and a half [1]cubits, and its width one and a half cubits, and its height one and a half cubits;

2 and he overlaid it with pure gold inside and out, and made a gold molding for it all around.

3 And he cast four rings of gold for it on its four feet; even two rings on one side of it, and two rings on the [1]other side of it.

4 And he made poles of acacia wood and overlaid them with gold.

5 And he put the poles into the rings on the sides of the ark, to carry [1]it.

6 And he made a [1]mercy seat of pure gold, two and a half cubits [2]long, and one and a half cubits [3]wide.

7 And he made two cherubim of gold; he made them of hammered work, [1]at the two ends of the mercy seat;

8 one cherub [1]at the one end, and one cherub [1]at the other end; he made the cherubim *of one piece* with the mercy seat [1]at the two ends.

9 And the cherubim had *their* wings spread upward, covering the [1]mercy seat with their wings, with their faces toward each other; the faces of the cherubim were toward the mercy seat.

10 [a]Then he made the table of acacia wood, two [1]cubits [2]long and a cubit [3]wide and one and a half cubits [4]high.

11 And he overlaid it with pure gold, and made a gold molding for it all around.

12 And he made a rim for it of a hand breadth all around, and made a gold molding for its rim all around.

13 And he cast four gold rings for it and put the rings on the four corners that were on its four feet.

14 Close by the rim were the rings, the holders for the poles to carry the table.

15 And he made the poles of acacia wood and overlaid them with gold, to carry the table.

16 And he made the utensils which were on the table, its [1]dishes and its pans and its [2]bowls and its jars, with which to pour out libations, of pure gold.

17 [a]Then he made the lampstand of pure gold. He made the lampstand of hammered work, its base and its shaft; its cups, its [1]bulbs and its flowers were *of one piece* with it.

18 And there were six branches going out of its sides; three branches of the lampstand from the one side of it, and three branches of the lampstand from the [1]other side of it;

19 three cups shaped like almond *blossoms*, a [1]bulb and a flower in one branch, and three cups shaped like almond *blossoms*, a [1]bulb and a flower in the other branch—so for the six branches going out of the lampstand.

20 And in the lampstand *there were* four cups shaped like almond *blossoms*, its [1]bulbs and its flowers;

21 and a [1]bulb was under the *first* pair of branches *coming* out of it, and a [1]bulb under the *second* pair of branches *coming* out of it, and a [1]bulb under the *third* pair of branches

1 [1]I.e., one cubit equals approximately 18 inches [a]Ex. 25:10-20

3 [1]Lit., *second*

5 [1]Lit., *the ark*

6 [1]Lit., *propitiatory* [2]Lit., *its length* [3]Lit., *its width*

7 [1]Lit., *from*

8 [1]Lit., *from*

9 [1]Lit., *propitiatory*

10 [1]I.e., one cubit equals approximately 18 inches [2]Lit., *its length* [3]Lit., *its width* [4]Lit., *its height* [a]Ex. 25:23-29

16 [1]Or, *platters* [2]Lit., *libation bowls*

17 [1]Or, *calyxes* [a]Ex. 25:31-39

18 [1]Lit., *second*

19 [1]Or, *calyx*

20 [1]Or, *calyxes*

21 [1]Lit., *from it*

coming out of it, for the six branches coming out of the
lampstand.
22 Their [1]bulbs and their branches were *of one piece* with
it; the whole of it *was* a single hammered work of pure gold.
23 And he made its seven lamps with its snuffers and its
[1]trays of pure gold.
24 He made it and all its utensils from a talent of pure
gold.
25 [a]Then he made the altar of incense of acacia wood: a
cubit [1]long and a cubit [2]wide, square, and two cubits [3]high; its
horns were *of one piece* with it.
26 And he overlaid it with pure gold, its top and its [1]sides
all around, and its horns; and he made a gold molding for it all
around.
27 And he made two golden rings for it under its molding,
on its two sides—on opposite sides—as holders for poles with
which to carry it.
28 And he made the poles of acacia wood and overlaid
them with gold.
29 [a]And he made the holy anointing oil and the pure,
fragrant incense of spices, the work of a perfumer.

Chapter 38

[a]
THEN he made the altar of burnt offering of acacia wood,
five [1]cubits [2]long, and five cubits [3]wide, square, and three cubits [4]high.
2 And he made its horns on its four corners, its horns
[1]being *of one piece* with it, and he overlaid it with [2]bronze.
3 And he made all the utensils of the altar, the pails and
the shovels and the basins, the flesh hooks and the fire pans; he
made all its utensils of bronze.
4 And he made for the altar a grating of bronze network
beneath, under its ledge, reaching halfway up.
5 And he cast four rings on the four ends of the bronze
grating *as* holders for the poles.
6 And he made the poles of acacia wood and overlaid
them with bronze.
7 And he inserted the poles into the rings on the sides of
the altar, with which to carry it. He made it hollow with
planks.
8 [a]Moreover, he made the laver of bronze with its base of
bronze, [1]from the mirrors of the serving women who served at
the doorway of the tent of meeting.
9 [a]Then he made the court: for the [1]south side the hangings of the court were of fine twisted linen, one hundred
cubits;
10 their twenty pillars, and their twenty sockets, *made* of
bronze; the hooks of the pillars and their bands *were* of silver.
11 And for the north side *there were* one hundred cubits;
their twenty pillars and their twenty [1]sockets *were* of bronze,
the hooks of the pillars and their [2]bands *were* of silver.
12 And for the west side *there were* hangings of fifty cubits *with* their ten pillars and their ten [1]sockets; the hooks of
the pillars and their [2]bands *were* of silver.
13 And for the [1]east side fifty cubits.

22 [1]Or, *calyxes*

23 [1]Lit., *snuff dishes*

25 [1]Lit., *its length* [2]Lit., *its width* [3]Lit., *its height* [a]Ex. 30:1-5

26 [1]Lit., *walls*

29 [a]Ex. 30:23-25, 34, 35

1 [1]I.e., one cubit equals approximately 18 inches [2]Lit., *its length* [3]Lit., *its width* [4]Lit., *its height* [a]Ex. 27:1-8

2 [1]Lit., *were* [2]Or, *copper*, and so for *bronze* throughout the chap.

8 [1]Lit., *with* [a]Ex. 30:18

9 [1]Lit., *to the side of the Negev, to the south* [a]Ex. 27:9-19

10 [1]Or, *bases* [2]Or, *fillets, rings*

11 [1]Or, *bases* [2]Or, *fillets, rings*

12 [1]Or, *bases* [2]Or, *fillets, rings*

13 [1]Lit., *east side, eastward*

14 The hangings for the *one* [1]side *of the gate were* fifteen
cubits, *with* their three pillars and their three [2]sockets,
15 and so for the [1]other [2]side. [3]On both sides of the gate
of the court *were* hangings of fifteen cubits, *with* their three
pillars and their three [4]sockets.
16 All the hangings of the court all around *were* of fine
twisted linen.
17 And the [1]sockets for the pillars *were* of [2]bronze, the
hooks of the pillars and their [3]bands, of silver; and the overlaying of their tops, of silver, and all the pillars of the court
were furnished with silver [3]bands.
18 And the screen of the gate of the court was the work of
the [1]weaver, of [2]blue and purple and scarlet *material,* and fine
twisted linen. And the length was twenty cubits and the [3]height
was five cubits, corresponding to the hangings of the court.
19 And their four pillars and their four [1]sockets *were* of
bronze; their hooks *were* of silver, and the overlaying of their
tops and their [2]bands *were* of silver.
20 And all the pegs of the [1]tabernacle and of the court all
around *were* of bronze.
21 [1]This is the number of *the things for* the [2]tabernacle,
the [2]tabernacle of the testimony, as they were [3]numbered according to the [4]command of Moses, for the service of the
Levites, by the hand of Ithamar, the son of Aaron the priest.
22 Now Bezalel, the son of Uri the son of Hur, of the tribe
of Judah, made all that the LORD had commanded Moses.
23 And with him was Oholiab, the son of Ahisamach, of
the tribe of Dan, an engraver and a skillful workman and a
[1]weaver in [2]blue and in purple and in scarlet *material,* and fine
linen.
24 All the gold that was used for the work, in all the work
of the sanctuary, even the gold of the wave offering, was 29
talents and 730 shekels, according to the shekel of the
sanctuary.
25 [a]And the silver of those of the congregation who were
[1]numbered was 100 talents and 1,775 shekels, according to the
shekel of the sanctuary;
26 a beka a head (*that is,* half a shekel according to the
shekel of the sanctuary), for each one who passed over to those
who were [1]numbered, from twenty years old and upward, for
[a]603,550 men.
27 And the hundred talents of silver were for casting the
[1]sockets of the sanctuary and the [1]sockets of the veil; one
hundred [1]sockets for the hundred talents, a talent for a
[1]socket.
28 And of the 1,775 *shekels,* he made hooks for the pillars
and overlaid their tops and made [1]bands for them.
29 And the bronze of the wave offering was 70 talents, and
2,400 shekels.
30 And with it he made the [1]sockets to the doorway of the
tent of meeting, and the bronze altar and its bronze grating,
and all the utensils of the altar,
31 and the [1]sockets of the court all around and the [1]sock-
ets of the gate of the court, and all the pegs of the [2]tabernacle
and all the pegs of the court all around.

14 [1]Lit., *shoulder* [2]Or, *bases*

15 [1]Lit., *second* [2]Lit., *shoulder* [3]Lit., *on this side and on that side* [4]Or, *bases*

17 [1]Or, *bases* [2]Or, *copper* [3]Or, *fillets, rings*

18 [1]Lit., *variegator;* i.e., a weaver in colors [2]Or, *violet* [3]Lit., *height in width*

19 [1]Or, *bases* [2]Or, *fillets, rings*

20 [1]Lit., *dwelling place*

21 [1]Lit., *These are the appointed things of the tabernacle* [2]Lit., *dwelling place* [3]Lit., *appointed* [4]Lit., *mouth*

23 [1]Lit., *variegator;* i.e., a weaver in colors [2]Or, *violet*

25 [1]Lit., *mustered* [a]Ex. 30:11-16

26 [1]Lit., *mustered* [a]Ex. 12:37; Num. 1:46; 26:51

27 [1]Or, *bases*

28 [1]Or, *fillets, rings*

30 [1]Or, *bases*

31 [1]Or, *bases* [2]Lit., *dwelling place*

CHAPTER 39

MOREOVER, from the [1]blue and purple and scarlet *mate-*
rial, they made finely woven garments for ministering in the
holy place, [2]as well as the holy garments which were for Aaron,
just as the LORD had commanded Moses.
2 [a]And he made the ephod of gold, *and* of [1]blue and
purple and scarlet *material,* and fine twisted linen.
3 Then they hammered out gold sheets and cut *them*
into threads [1]to be woven in *with* the [2]blue and the purple and
the scarlet *material,* and the fine linen, the work of a skillful
workman.
4 They made attaching shoulder pieces for [1]the ephod; it
was attached at its two *upper* ends.
5 And the skillfully woven band which was on it was like
its workmanship, [1]of the same material: of gold *and* of [2]blue
and purple and scarlet *material,* and fine twisted linen, just as
the LORD had commanded Moses.
6 And they made the onyx stones, set in gold filigree
settings; they were engraved *like* the engravings of a signet,
according to the names of the sons of Israel.
7 And he placed them on the shoulder pieces of the ephod,
as memorial stones for the sons of Israel, just as the LORD
had commanded Moses.
8 [a]And he made the breastpiece, the work of a skillful
workman, like the workmanship of the ephod: of gold *and* of
[1]blue and purple and scarlet *material* and fine twisted linen.
9 It was square; they made the breastpiece folded
double, a span [1]long and a span [2]wide when folded double.
10 And they [1]mounted four rows of stones on it. The first
row *was* a row of ruby, topaz, and emerald;
11 and the second row, a turquoise, a sapphire and a
diamond;
12 and the third row, a jacinth, an agate, and an amethyst;
13 and the fourth row, a beryl, an onyx, and a jasper. They
were set in gold filigree *settings* when they were [1]mounted.
14 And the stones were corresponding to the names of the
sons of Israel; they were twelve, corresponding to their names,
engraved with the engravings of a signet, each with its name
for the twelve tribes.
15 And they made on the breastpiece chains like cords, of
twisted cordage work in pure gold.
16 And they made two gold filigree *settings* and two gold
rings, and put the two rings on the two ends of the breastpiece.
17 Then they put the two gold cords in the two rings at
the ends of the breastpiece.
18 And they put the *other* two ends of the two cords on
the two filigree *settings,* and put them on the shoulder pieces
of the ephod at the front of it.
19 And they made two gold rings and placed *them* on the
two ends of the breastpiece, on its inner edge which was next
to the ephod.
20 Furthermore, they made two gold rings and placed
them on the bottom of the two shoulder pieces of the ephod,
on the front of it, close to the place where it joined, above the
woven band of the ephod.

1 [1]Or, *violet* [2]Lit., *and they made*

2 [1]Or, *violet*
[a]Ex. 28:6-12

3 [1]Lit., *to work* [2]Or, *violet*

4 [1]Lit., *it*

5 [1]Lit., *from it* [2]Or, *violet*

8 [1]Or, *violet*
[a]Ex. 28:15-28

9 [1]Lit., *its length* [2]Lit., *its width*

10 [1]Lit., *filled*

13 [1]Lit., *filled*

21 And they bound the breastpiece by its rings to the rings of the ephod with a [1]blue cord, that it might be on the woven band of the ephod, and that the breastpiece might not come loose from the ephod, just as the LORD had commanded Moses.

22 [a]Then he made the robe of the ephod of woven work, all of [1]blue;

23 [a]and the opening of the robe was *at the top* in the center, as the opening of a coat of mail, with a binding all around its opening, that it might not be torn.

24 And they made pomegranates of [1]blue and purple and scarlet *material and* twisted *linen* on the hem of the robe.

25 They also made bells of pure gold, and put the bells between the pomegranates all around on the hem of the [1]robe,

26 [1]alternating a bell and a pomegranate all around on the hem of the robe, for the service, just as the LORD had commanded Moses.

27 [a]And they made the tunics of finely woven linen for Aaron and his sons,

28 and the turban of fine linen, and the decorated [1]caps of fine linen, and the linen breeches of fine twisted linen,

29 and the sash of fine twisted linen, and [1]blue and purple and scarlet *material*, the work of the [2]weaver, just as the LORD had commanded Moses.

30 [a]And they made the plate of the holy crown of pure gold, and [1]inscribed it like the engravings of a signet, "Holy to the LORD."

31 And they [1]fastened a [2]blue cord to it, to [1]fasten it on the turban above, just as the LORD had commanded Moses.

32 Thus all the work of the [1]tabernacle of the tent of meeting was completed; and the sons of Israel did according to all that the LORD had commanded Moses; so they did.

33 And they brought the tabernacle to Moses, the tent and all its [1]furnishings: its clasps, its boards, its bars, and its pillars and its [2]sockets;

34 and the covering of rams' skins [1]dyed red, and the covering of [2]porpoise skins, and the screening veil;

35 the ark of the testimony and its poles and the [1]mercy seat;

36 the table, all its utensils, and the bread of the [1]Presence;

37 the pure *gold* lampstand, [1]with its arrangement of lamps and all its utensils, and the oil for the light;

38 and the gold altar, and the anointing oil and the fragrant incense, and the veil for the doorway of the tent;

39 the [1]bronze altar and its [1]bronze grating, its poles and all its utensils, the laver and its stand;

40 the hangings for the court, its pillars and its [1]sockets, and the screen for the gate of the court, its cords and its pegs and all the [2]equipment for the service of the tabernacle, for the tent of meeting;

41 the woven garments for ministering in the holy place and the holy garments for Aaron the priest and the garments of his sons, to minister as priests.

42 So the sons of Israel did all the work according to all that the LORD had commanded Moses.

21 [1]Or, *violet*

22 [1]Or, *violet* [a]Ex. 28:31-34

24 [1]Or, *violet*

25 [a]Lit., *robe, between the pomegranates*

26 [1]Lit., *a bell and a pomegranate, a bell . . .*

27 [a]Ex. 28:39, 40, 42

28 [1]Lit., *headgear*

29 [1]Or, *violet* [2]Lit., *variegator* i.e., a weaver in colors

30 [1]Lit., *wrote on it a writing* [a]Ex. 28:36, 37

31 [1]Lit., *put* [2]Or, *violet*

32 [1]Lit., *dwelling place*

33 [1]Or, *utensils* [2]Or, *bases*

34 [1]Or, *tanned* [2]Or, *dolphin*

35 [1]Lit., *propitiatory*

36 [1]Lit., *Face*

37 [1]Lit., *its lamps, the lamps set in order*

39 [1]Or, *copper*

40 [1]Or, *bases* [2]Or, *utensils*

43 And Moses [1]examined all the work and behold, they
had done it; just as the LORD had commanded, this they had
done. So Moses blessed them.

CHAPTER 40

THEN the LORD spoke to Moses, saying,
2 "[a]On the first day of the first month you shall set up the
[1]tabernacle of the tent of meeting.
3 "And you shall place the ark of the testimony there, and
you shall screen the ark with the veil.
4 "And you shall bring in the table and [1]arrange what
belongs on it; and you shall bring in the lampstand and [2]mount
its lamps.
5 "Moreover, you shall set the gold altar of incense before
the ark of the testimony, and set up the veil for the doorway to
the tabernacle.
6 "And you shall set the altar of burnt offering in front of
the doorway of the tabernacle of the tent of meeting.
7 "And you shall set the laver between the tent of meeting
and the altar, and put water [1]in it.
8 "And you shall set up the court all around and [1]hang up
the veil for the gateway of the court.
9 "Then you shall take the anointing oil and anoint the
tabernacle and all that is in it, and shall consecrate it and all its
[1]furnishings; and it shall be holy.
10 "And you shall anoint the altar of burnt offering and all
its utensils, and consecrate the altar; and the altar shall be most
holy.
11 "And you shall anoint the laver and its stand, and consecrate it.
12 "Then you shall bring Aaron and his sons to the doorway of the tent of meeting and wash them with water.
13 "And you shall put the holy garments on Aaron and
anoint him and consecrate him, that he may minister as a
priest to Me.
14 "And you shall bring his sons and put tunics on them;
15 and you shall anoint them even as you have anointed
their father, that they may minister as priests to Me; and their
anointing shall [1]qualify them for a [a]perpetual priesthood
throughout their generations."
16 Thus Moses did; according to all that the LORD had
commanded him, so he did.
17 Now it came about [a]in the first month [1]of the second
year, on the first day of the month, that the [2]tabernacle was
erected.
18 And Moses erected the tabernacle and [1]laid its [2]sock-
ets, and set up its boards, and [1]inserted its bars and erected its
pillars.
19 And he spread the tent over the tabernacle and put the
covering of the tent [1]on top of it, just as the LORD had commanded Moses.
20 Then he took [a]the testimony and put *it* into the ark,
and [1]attached the poles to the ark, and put the [2]mercy seat [3]on
top of the ark.
21 And he brought the ark into the tabernacle, and set up

43 [1]Lit., *saw*

2 [1]Lit., *dwelling place*
[a]Ex. 40:17; 19:1; Num. 1:1

4 [1]Lit., *arrange its arrangement* [2]Or, *light*

7 [1]Lit., *there*

8 [1]Lit., *put the screen*

9 [1]Or, *utensils*

15 [1]Lit., *be for them*
[a]Ex. 29:9

17 [1]Lit., *in* [2]Lit., *dwelling place*
[a]Ex. 40:2

18 [1]Lit., *put* [2]Or, *bases*

19 [1]Lit., *over it above*

20 [1]Lit., *set* [2]Lit., *propitiatory* [3]Lit., *over the ark above*
[a]Deut. 10:5; 1 Kin. 8:9; 2 Chr. 5:10; Heb. 9:4

23 [a]Ex. 25:30; Lev. 24:5, 6

a veil for the screen, and screened off the ark of the testimony,
just as the LORD had commanded Moses.
22 Then he put the table in the tent of meeting, on the
north side of the tabernacle, outside the veil.
23 And he set the arrangement of [a]bread in order on it
before the LORD, just as the LORD had commanded Moses.
24 Then he placed the lampstand in the tent of meeting,
opposite the table, on the south side of the tabernacle.
25 And he lighted the lamps before the LORD, just as the
LORD had commanded Moses.
26 Then he placed the gold altar in the tent of meeting in
front of the veil;

28 [1]Or, *screen*

27 and he burned fragrant incense on it, just as the LORD
had commanded Moses.
28 Then he set up the [1]veil for the doorway of the
tabernacle.
29 And he set the altar of burnt offering *before* the doorway of the tabernacle of the tent of meeting, and offered on it
the burnt offering and the meal offering, just as the LORD had
commanded Moses.
30 And he placed the laver between the tent of meeting
and the altar, and put water in it for washing.

31 [a]Ex. 30:19, 20

31 [a]And from it Moses and Aaron and his sons washed
their hands and their feet.
32 When they entered the tent of meeting, and when they
approached the altar, they washed, just as the LORD had commanded Moses.
33 And he erected the court all around the [1]tabernacle
and the altar, and [2]hung up the veil for the gateway of the
court. Thus Moses finished the work.
34 [a]Then the cloud covered the tent of meeting, and the
glory of the LORD filled the tabernacle.

33 [1]Or, *dwelling place*
[2]Lit., *put the screen*

35 And Moses was not able to enter the tent of meeting
because the cloud had settled on it, and the glory of the LORD
filled the tabernacle.
36 And throughout all their journeys whenever the cloud
was taken up from over the tabernacle, the sons of Israel would
set out;
37 but if the cloud was not taken up, then they did not set
out until the day when it was taken up.
38 For throughout all their journeys, the cloud of the
LORD was on the tabernacle by day, and there was fire in it by
night, in the sight of all the house of Israel.

34 [a]Num. 9:15-23

LEVITICUS

The Law of Burnt Offerings.

THEN [a]the LORD called to Moses and spoke to him from the
tent of meeting, saying,
2 "Speak to the sons of Israel and say to them, 'When any
man of you brings an [1a]offering to the LORD, you shall bring
your [1]offering of animals from [b]the herd or the flock.
3 'If his offering is a [a]burnt offering from the herd, he
shall offer it a male [b]without defect; he shall offer it [c]at the
doorway of the tent of meeting, that he may be accepted
before the LORD.
4 '[a]And he shall lay his hand on the head of the burnt
offering, that it may be accepted for him to make [b]atonement
on his behalf.
5 'And [a]he shall slay the [1]young bull before the LORD; and
Aaron's sons, the priests, shall offer up [b]the blood and [c]sprinkle
the blood around on the altar that is at the doorway of the tent
of meeting.
6 '[a]He shall then skin the burnt offering and cut it into its
pieces.
7 '[a]And the sons of Aaron the priest shall put fire on the
altar and arrange wood on the fire.
8 'Then Aaron's sons, the priests, shall arrange the pieces,
the head, and the [a]suet over the wood which is on the fire that
is on the altar.
9 'Its entrails, however, and its legs he shall wash with
water. And [a]the priest shall offer up in smoke all of it on the
altar for a burnt offering, an offering by fire of [b]a soothing
aroma to the LORD.
10 'But if his offering is from the flock, of the sheep or of
the goats, for a burnt offering, he shall offer it a male without
defect.
11 'And he shall slay it on the side of the altar [a]northward
before the LORD, and Aaron's sons, the priests, shall sprinkle its
blood around on the altar.
12 'He shall then cut it into its pieces with its head and its
[a]suet, and the priest shall arrange them on the wood which is
on the fire that is on the altar.
13 'The entrails, however, and the legs he shall wash with
water. And [a]the priest shall offer all of it, and offer it up in
smoke on the altar; it is a burnt offering, an offering by fire of
a soothing aroma to the LORD.
14 'But if his offering to the LORD is a burnt offering of
birds, then he shall bring his offering from the [a]turtledoves or
from young pigeons.
15 'And the priest shall bring it to the altar and wring off its
head, and offer it up in smoke on the altar; and its blood is to
be drained out [a]on the side of the altar.
16 'He shall also take away its crop with its feathers, and
cast it beside the altar eastward, to the place of the [1]ashes.
17 'Then [a]he shall tear it by its wings, *but* shall not sever *it*.
And the priest shall offer it up in smoke on the altar on the
wood which is on the fire; it is a burnt offering, an offering by
fire of a soothing aroma to the LORD.

1 [a]Num. 7:89; Ex. 25:22

2 [1]Heb., *qorban* [a]Mark 7:11 [b]Lev. 22:19

3 [a]Lev. 6:8-13 [b]Lev. 22:20-24; Deut. 15:21; 17:1 [c]Lev. 17:8, 9; Deut. 12:6, 11

4 [a]Ex. 29:10, 15, 19 [b]Lev. 4:20, 26, 31; 2 Chr. 29:23, 24

5 [1]Or, *one of the herd;* lit., *son of the herd* [a]Ex. 29:11, 16, 20 [b]Lev. 17:11 [c]Lev. 1:11; 3:2, 8, 13

6 [a]Lev. 7:8

7 [a]Lev. 6:8-13

8 [a]Lev. 3:3, 4

9 [a]Num. 15:8-10; 28:12, 14 [b]Gen. 8:21; Ex. 29:18, 25; Eph. 5:2

11 [a]Lev. 1:5

12 [a]Lev. 3:3, 4

13 [a]Num. 15:4-7; 28:12-14

14 [a]Gen. 15:9

15 [a]Lev. 5:9

16 [1]Or, *fat ashes*

17 [a]Lev. 5:8; Gen. 15:10

E22-1

1 [a]Lev. 6:14-18
2 [a]Lev. 5:12; 6:15 [b]Lev. 2:9, 16; 5:12
3 [a]Lev. 6:16 [b]Lev. 10:12, 13
4 [1]Lit., *anointed*
7 [1]Lit., *lidded cooking pan*
9 [a]Lev. 2:2
10 [a]Lev. 2:3
11 [1]Lit., *up from it* [a]Lev. 6:16, 17; Ex. 23:18; 34:25
12 [a]Lev. 7:13; 23:17, 18
13 [a]Num. 18:19; 2 Chr. 13:5; Ezek. 43:24
14 [a]Lev. 23:14
16 [a]Lev. 2:2
1 [a]Lev. 7:11-34 [b]Lev. 22:21

Chapter 2

'NOW when anyone presents a [a]grain offering as an offering
to the LORD, his offering shall be of fine flour, and he shall
pour oil on it and put frankincense on it.
2 'He shall then bring it to Aaron's sons, the priests; and
shall take from it [a]his handful of its fine flour and of its oil with
all of its frankincense. And the priest shall offer *it* up in smoke
as its [b]memorial portion on the altar, an offering by fire of a
soothing aroma to the LORD.
3 'And [a]the remainder of the grain offering belongs to
[b]Aaron and his sons: a thing most holy of the offerings of the
LORD by fire.
4 'Now when you bring an offering of a grain offering
baked in an oven, *it shall be* unleavened cakes of fine flour
mixed with oil, or unleavened wafers [1]spread with oil.
5 'And if your offering is a grain offering *made* on the
griddle, *it shall be* of fine flour, unleavened, mixed with oil;
6 you shall break it into bits, and pour oil on it; it is a
grain offering.
7 'Now if your offering is a grain offering *made* in a [1]pan,
it shall be made of fine flour with oil.
8 'When you bring in the grain offering which is made of
these things to the LORD, it shall be presented to the priest and
he shall bring it to the altar.
9 'The priest then shall take up from the grain offering
[a]its memorial portion, and shall offer *it* up in smoke on the
altar *as* an offering by fire of a soothing aroma to the LORD.
10 'And [a]the remainder of the grain offering belongs to
Aaron and his sons: a thing most holy, of the offerings of the
LORD by fire.
11 '[a]No grain offering, which you bring to the LORD, shall
be made with leaven, for you shall not offer [1]up in smoke any
leaven or any honey as an offering by fire to the LORD.
12 '[a]As an offering of first fruits, you shall bring them to
the LORD, but they shall not ascend for a soothing aroma on
the altar.
13 'Every grain offering of yours, moreover, you shall season with salt, so that [a]the salt of the covenant of your God
shall not be lacking from your grain offering; with all your
offerings you shall offer salt.
14 'Also if you bring a grain offering of early ripened things
to the LORD, you shall bring [a]fresh heads of grain roasted in the
fire, grits of new growth, for the grain offering of your early
ripened things.
15 'You shall then put oil on it and lay incense on it; it is a
grain offering.
16 'And the priest shall offer up in smoke [a]its memorial
portion, part of its grits and its oil with all its incense as an
offering by fire to the LORD.

Chapter 3

'NOW if this offering is a [a]sacrifice of peace offerings, if he
is going to offer out of the herd, whether male or female, he
shall offer it [b]without defect before the LORD.

2 ‘[a]And he shall lay his hand on the head of his offering
and [b]slay it at the doorway of the tent of meeting, and Aaron’s
sons, the priests, shall sprinkle the blood around on the altar.
3 ‘And from the sacrifice of the peace offerings, he shall
present an offering by fire to the LORD, the fat that covers the
entrails and all the fat that is on the entrails,
4 and the two kidneys with the fat that is on them, which
is on the loins, and the [1]lobe of the liver, which he shall remove
with the kidneys.
5 ‘Then [a]Aaron’s sons shall offer up in smoke on the altar
[b]on the burnt offering, which is on the wood that is on the fire;
[c]it is an offering by fire of a soothing aroma to the LORD.
6 ‘But if his offering for a sacrifice of peace offerings to
the LORD is from the flock, he shall offer it, male or female,
[a]without defect.
7 ‘If he is going to offer [a]a lamb for his offering, then he
shall offer it [b]before the LORD,
8 and [a]he shall lay his hand on the head of his offering,
and [b]slay it before the tent of meeting; and Aaron’s sons shall
[c]sprinkle its blood around on the altar.
9 ‘And from the sacrifice of peace offerings he shall bring
as an offering by fire to the LORD, its fat, [1]the entire fat tail
which he shall remove close to the backbone, and the fat that
covers the entrails and all the fat that is on the entrails,
10 and the two kidneys with the fat that is on them, which
is on the loins, and the [1]lobe of the liver, which he shall remove
[a]with the kidneys.
11 ‘Then the priest shall offer up in smoke [a]on the altar, *as*
[b]food, an offering by fire to the LORD.
12 ‘Moreover, if his offering is [a]a goat, then he shall offer it
before the LORD,
13 and he shall lay his hand on its head and slay it before
the tent of meeting; and the sons of Aaron shall sprinkle its
blood around on the altar.
14 ‘And from it he shall present his offering as an offering
by fire to the LORD, the fat that covers the entrails and all the
fat that is on the entrails,
15 and the two kidneys with the fat that is on them, which
is on the loins, and the [1]lobe of the liver, which he shall remove
[a]with the kidneys.
16 ‘And the priest shall offer them up in smoke on the altar
as food, an offering by fire for a soothing aroma; [a]all fat is the
LORD’s.
17 ‘It is a perpetual statute throughout your generations in
all your dwellings: you shall not eat any fat [a]or any blood.’ ”

CHAPTER 4

THEN the LORD spoke to Moses, saying,
2 “Speak to the sons of Israel, saying, ‘If a person sins
[a]unintentionally in any of the [1]things which the LORD has commanded not to be done, and commits any of them,
3 [a]if the anointed priest who sins so as to bring guilt on
the people, then let him offer to the LORD a [1]bull without
defect as a sin offering for the sin he has [2]committed.

2 [a]Lev. 1:4 [b]Ex. 29:11, 16, 20
4 [1]Or, *appendage on*
5 [a]Lev. 7:28-34 [b]Ex. 29:38, 42; Num. 28:3-10 [c]Num. 15:8-10; 28:12-14
6 [a]Lev. 3:1
7 [a]Num. 15:4, 5; 28:5-7 [b]Lev. 17:8, 9
8 [a]Lev. 1:4 [b]Lev. 3:2 [c]Lev. 1:5
9 [1]Lit., *the fat tail, entire*
10 [1]Or, *appendage on* [a]Lev. 3:4
11 [a]Lev. 3:5 [b]Lev. 3:16; 21:6, 8, 17
12 [a]Num. 15:6-11
15 [1]Or, *appendage on* [a]Lev. 3:4
16 [a]Lev. 7:23-25
17 [a]Lev. 17:10-16
2 [1]Lit., *commands of the LORD which are not to be done* [a]Lev. 4:22, 27; 5:15-18; 22:14
3 [1]Or, *bull of the herd* [2]Lit., *sinned* [a]Lev. 4:14, 23, 28

4 'And he shall bring the bull to the doorway of the tent of meeting before the LORD, and [a]he shall lay his hand on the head of the bull, and slay the bull before the LORD.

5 'Then the [a]anointed priest is to take some of the blood of the bull and bring it to the tent of meeting,

6 and the priest shall dip his finger in the blood, and sprinkle some of the blood seven times before the LORD, in front of [a]the veil of the sanctuary.

7 'The priest shall also put some of the blood on the horns of [a]the altar of fragrant incense before the LORD, which is in the tent of meeting; and all the blood of the bull he shall pour out at the base of the altar of burnt offering which is at the doorway of the tent of meeting.

8 [1a]And he shall remove from it all the fat of the bull of the sin offering: the fat that covers the entrails, and all the fat which is on the entrails,

9 and the two kidneys with the fat that is on them, which is on the loins, and the [1]lobe of the liver, which he shall remove [a]with the kidneys

10 (just as it is removed from the ox of the sacrifice of peace offerings), and the priest is to offer them up in smoke on the altar of burnt offering.

11 'But the hide of the bull and all its flesh with its head and its legs and its entrails and its refuse,

12 [1]that is, all *the rest of* the bull, he is to bring out to [a]a clean place outside the camp where the [2]ashes are poured out, and burn it on wood with fire; where the [2]ashes are poured out it shall be burned.

13 '[a]Now if the whole congregation of Israel commits error, and the matter [1]escapes the notice of the assembly, and they commit any of the [2]things which the LORD has commanded not to be done, and they become guilty;

14 [a]when the sin [1]which they have [2]committed becomes known, then the assembly shall offer [b]a [3]bull of the herd for a sin offering, and bring it before the tent of meeting.

15 'Then [a]the elders of the congregation shall lay their hands on the head of the bull before the LORD, and the bull shall be slain [b]before the LORD.

16 'Then the anointed priest is to bring some of the blood of the bull to the tent of meeting;

17 and [a]the priest shall dip his finger in the blood, and sprinkle *it* seven times before the LORD, in front of the veil.

18 'And he shall put some of the blood on the horns of [a]the altar which is before the LORD [1]in the tent of meeting; and all the blood he shall pour out at the base of the altar of burnt offering which is at the doorway of the tent of meeting.

19 '[a]And he shall remove all its fat from it and offer it up in smoke on the altar.

20 'He shall also do with the bull just as he did with [a]the bull of the sin offering; thus he shall do with it. So the priest shall make atonement for them, and they shall be forgiven.

21 'Then he is to bring out the bull to *a place* outside the camp, and burn it as he burned the first bull; it is [a]the sin offering for the assembly.

22 'When [a]a leader [b]sins and unintentionally does any one

4 [a]Lev. 1:4

5 [a]Lev. 4:3

6 [a]Ex. 40:21, 26

7 [a]Lev. 4:18, 25, 30, 34

8 [a]Lev. 3:3, 4

9 [1]Or, *appendage on* [a]Lev. 3:4

12 [1]Lit., *and* [2]Or, *fat ashes are* [a]Lev. 6:10, 11

13 [1]Lit., *is hidden from the eyes of* [2]Lit., *commands of the LORD which are not to be done* [a]Num. 15:24-26

14 [1]Lit., *concerning which* [2]Lit., *sinned* [3]Or, *bull of the herd;* lit., *son of the herd* [a]Lev. 4:3 [b]Lev. 4:3, 23, 28

15 [a]Lev. 8:14, 18, 22; Num. 8:10, 12 [b]Lev. 1:3

17 [a]Lev. 4:6

18 [1]Lit., *which is in* [a]Lev. 4:7, 25, 30, 34

19 [a]Lev. 4:8

20 [a]Lev. 4:8, 21

21 [a]Lev. 4:13; 16:15-17; Num. 15:24-26

22 [a]Num. 31:13; 32:2 [b]Lev. 4:2

of all the [1]things which the LORD God has commanded not to
be done, and he becomes guilty,
23 [1a]if his sin [2]which he has committed is made known to
him, he shall bring for his offering a [3b]goat, [c]a male without
defect.
24 'And he shall lay his hand on the head of the male goat,
and slay it in the place where [1]they slay the burnt offering
before the LORD; it is a sin offering.
25 'Then the priest is to take some of the blood of the sin
offering with his finger, and put it on [a]the horns of the altar of
burnt offering; and *the rest of* its blood he shall pour out at the
base of the altar of burnt offering.
26 '[a]And all its fat he shall offer up in smoke on the altar *in
the case of* the fat of the sacrifice of peace offerings. Thus the
priest shall make atonement for him in regard to his sin, and
he shall be forgiven.
27 'Now if [1]anyone of [2]the common people sins [a]uninten-
tionally in doing any of the [3]things which the LORD has commanded not to be done, and becomes guilty,
28 [1a]if his sin, which he has [2]committed is made known to
him, then he shall bring for his offering a [3b]goat, a [c]female
without defect, for his sin which he has [2]committed.
29 'And [a]he shall lay his hand on the head of the sin offering, and [b]slay the sin offering at the place of the burnt
offering.
30 'And the priest shall take some of its blood with his
finger and put it on the horns of [a]the altar of burnt offering;
and [b]all *the rest of* its blood he shall pour out at the base of the
altar.
31 '[a]Then he shall remove all its fat, just as the fat was
removed from the sacrifice of peace offerings; and the priest
shall offer it up in smoke on the altar for a soothing aroma to
the LORD. Thus the priest shall make atonement for him, [1]and
he shall be forgiven.
32 'But if he brings [a]a lamb as his offering for a sin offering, he shall bring it, a female without defect.
33 'And [a]he shall lay his hand on the head of the sin offering, and slay it for a sin offering [b]in the place where [1]they slay
the burnt offering.
34 'And the priest is to take some of the blood of the sin
offering with his finger and put it on the horns of [a]the altar of
burnt offering; and [b]all *the rest of* its blood he shall pour out at
the base of the altar.
35 'Then he shall remove [a]all its fat, just as the fat of the
lamb is removed from the sacrifice of the peace offerings, and
the priest shall offer them up in smoke on the altar, on the
offerings by fire to the LORD. Thus the priest shall make atonement for him in regard to his sin which he has [1]committed, and
he shall be forgiven.

CHAPTER 5

'NOW if a person sins, after he hears a [1]public [a]adjuration
to testify, when he is a witness, whether he has seen or *otherwise* known, if he does not tell *it,* then he will bear his [2]guilt.

22 [1]Lit., *commands of the LORD which are not to be done*

23 [1]Lit., *or* [2]Lit., *in which he has sinned* [3]Lit., *buck of the goats*
[a]Lev. 4:3 [b]Lev. 4:3, 14, 28 [c]Lev. 4:28

24 [1]Lit., *one slays*

25 [a]Lev. 4:7, 18, 30, 34

26 [a]Lev. 4:19

27 [1]Lit., *one soul* [2]Lit., *the people of the land* [3]Lit., *commands of the LORD which are not to be done*
[a]Lev. 4:2

28 [1]Lit., *or* [2]Lit., *sinned* [3]Or, *female goat*
[a]Lev. 4:3 [b]Lev. 4:3, 14, 23, 32 [c]Lev. 4:23

29 [a]Lev. 1:4 [b]Lev. 1:5, 11

30 [a]Lev. 4:7, 18, 25, 34 [b]Lev. 4:7

31 [1]Or, *so that he may be*
[a]Lev. 4:8

32 [a]Lev. 4:28

33 [1]Lit., *one slays*
[a]Lev. 1:4, 5 [b]Lev. 4:29

34 [a]Lev. 4:7, 18, 25, 30 [b]Lev. 4:7

35 [1]Lit., *sinned*
[a]Lev. 4:31

1 [1]Lit., *voice of an oath* [2]Or, *iniquity*
[a]Prov. 29:24; Jer. 23:10

2 ‘Or if a person touches [a]any unclean thing, whether a
carcass of an unclean beast, or the carcass of unclean cattle, or
a carcass of unclean swarming things, though it is hidden from
him, and he is unclean, then he will be guilty.
3 ‘Or if he touches human uncleanness, of whatever *sort*
his uncleanness *may* be with which he becomes unclean, and it
is hidden from him, and then he comes to know *it*, he will be
guilty.
4 ‘Or if a person swears thoughtlessly with his lips to do
evil or to do good, in whatever matter a man may speak
thoughtlessly with an oath, and it is hidden from him, and then
he comes to know *it*, he will be guilty in one of these.
5 ‘So it shall be when he becomes guilty in one of these,
that he shall [a]confess that in which he has sinned.
6 ‘He shall also bring his guilt offering to the LORD for his
sin which he has [1]committed, [a]a female from the flock, a lamb
or a [2]goat as a sin offering.
7 ‘But if [1]he cannot afford a lamb, then he shall bring to
the LORD his guilt offering for that in which he has sinned, two
turtledoves or two young pigeons, [a]one for a sin offering and
the other for a burnt offering.
8 ‘And he shall bring them to the priest, who shall offer
first that which is for the sin offering and shall nip its head at
the front of its neck, but he [a]shall not sever *it*.
9 He shall also sprinkle some of the blood of the sin
offering [a]on the side of the altar, while the rest of the blood
shall be drained out [b]at the base of the altar: it is a sin offering.
10 ‘The second he shall then prepare as a burnt offering
[a]according to the ordinance. So the priest shall make atonement on his behalf for his sin which he has [1]committed, and it
shall be forgiven him.
11 ‘But [a]if his [1]means are insufficient for two turtledoves
or two young pigeons, then for his offering for that which he
has sinned, he shall bring the tenth of an [2]ephah of fine flour
for a sin offering; [b]he shall not put oil on it or place incense on
it, for it is a sin offering.
12 ‘And he shall bring it to the priest, and the priest shall
take his handful of it as its memorial portion and offer *it* up in
smoke on the altar, [1]with the offerings of the LORD by fire: it is
a sin offering.
13 ‘So the priest shall make atonement for him concerning
his sin which he has [1]committed from [a]one of these, and it
shall be forgiven him; then [b]*the rest* shall become the priest’s,
like the grain offering.’ ”
14 Then the LORD spoke to Moses, saying,
15 “[a]If a person acts unfaithfully and sins [b]unintentionally
against the LORD’s holy things, then he shall bring his [c]guilt
offering to the LORD: [d]a ram without defect from the flock,
according to your valuation in silver by shekels, in *terms of* the
[e]shekel of the sanctuary, for a guilt offering.
16 “[a]And he shall make restitution for that which he has
sinned against the holy thing, and shall add to it a fifth part of
it, and give it to the priest. [b]The priest shall then make atonement for him with the ram of the guilt offering, and it shall be
forgiven him.

2 [a]Lev. 11:8, 11, 24-39; Num. 19:11-16; Deut. 14:8
5 [a]Lev. 16:21; 26:40; Num. 5:7; Prov. 28:13
6 [1]Lit., *sinned* [2]Lit., *female goat* [a]Lev. 4:28, 32
7 [1]Lit., *his hand does not reach enough for* [a]Lev. 12:6, 8; 14:22, 30, 31
8 [a]Lev. 1:17
9 [a]Lev. 1:15 [b]Lev. 4:7
10 [1]Lit., *sinned* [a]Lev. 1:14-17
11 [1]Lit., *hand does not reach* [2]I.e., approximately one bushel [a]Lev. 14:21-32; 27:8 [b]Lev. 2:1, 2
12 [1]Lit., *upon*
13 [1]Lit., *sinned* [a]Lev. 5:4-5 [b]Lev. 2:3
15 [a]Num. 5:5-8 [b]Lev. 4:2; 22:14 [c]Lev. 7:1-10 [d]Lev. 6:6 [e]Ex. 30:13
16 [a]Lev. 6:5; 22:14; Num. 5:7, 8 [b]Lev. 7:2-7

17 "Now if a person sins and does any of the things [1]which
the LORD has commanded not to be done, [a]though he was
unaware, still he is guilty, and shall bear his punishment.
18 "He is then to bring to the priest [a]a ram without defect
from the flock, according to your valuation, for a guilt offering. So the priest shall make atonement for him concerning
his error in which he sinned [b]unintentionally and did not know
it, and it shall be forgiven him.
19 "It is a guilt offering; he was certainly guilty before the
LORD."

CHAPTER 6

1
THEN the LORD spoke to Moses, saying,
2 "[a]When a person sins and acts unfaithfully against the
LORD, and deceives his companion in regard to a deposit or a
security entrusted *to him*, or through robbery, or *if* he has
extorted from his companion,
3 or has found what was lost and lied about it and sworn
falsely, so that he sins in regard to any one of the things a man
may do;
4 then it shall be, when he sins and becomes guilty, that
he shall restore what he took by robbery, or what he got by
extortion, or the deposit which was [1]entrusted to him, or the
lost thing which he found,
5 or anything about which he swore falsely; [a]he shall
make restitution for it [1]in full, and add to it one-fifth more.
[b]He shall give it to the one to whom it belongs on the day *he
presents* his guilt offering.
6 "Then he shall bring to the priest his guilt offering to
the LORD, [a]a ram from the flock without defect, according to
your valuation, for a guilt offering,
7 and [a]the priest shall make atonement for him before
the LORD; and he shall be forgiven for any one of the things
which he may have done to incur guilt."
8 [1]Then the LORD spoke to Moses, saying,
9 "Command Aaron and his sons, saying, 'This is [a]the law
for the burnt offering: the burnt offering itself *shall remain* on
the hearth on the altar all night until the morning, and [b]the
fire on the altar is to be kept burning on it.
10 'And the priest is to put on [a]his linen robe, and he shall
put on undergarments next to his flesh; and he shall take up
the [1]ashes *to* which the fire [2]reduces the burnt offering on the
altar, and place them beside the altar.
11 'Then he shall take off his garments and put on other
garments, and carry the [1]ashes outside the camp to a clean
place.
12 'And the fire on the altar shall be kept burning on it. It
shall not go out, but the priest shall burn wood on it every
morning; and he shall lay out the burnt offering on it, and
offer up in smoke the fat portions of the peace offerings [a]on it.
13 'Fire shall be kept burning continually on the altar; it is
not to go out.
14 'Now this is the law of the grain offering: the sons of
Aaron shall present it before the LORD in front of the altar.

17 [1]Lit., *the commands of the LORD which are* [a]Lev. 5:19; 4:2

18 [a]Lev. 5:15 [b]Lev. 5:17

1 [1]In Heb. text, 5:20

2 [a]Ex. 22:7-15

4 [1]Or, *deposited with*

5 [1]Lit., *in its sum* [a]Lev. 5:16 [b]Num. 5:8

6 [a]Lev. 5:15

7 [a]Lev. 7:2-5

8 [1]In Heb. text, 6:1

9 [a]Ex. 29:38-42; Num. 28:3-10 [b]Lev. 6:12, 13

10 [1]Or, *fat ashes* [2]Lit., *consumes* [a]Ex. 28:39, 42; 27, 28

11 [1]Or, *fat ashes*

12 [a]Lev. 3:5

15 '[a]Then one *of them* shall lift up from it a handful of the
fine flour of the grain offering, [1]with its oil and all the incense
that is on the grain offering, and he shall offer *it* up in smoke
on the altar, a soothing aroma, as its memorial offering to the
LORD.
16 '[a]And what is left of it Aaron and his sons are to eat. It
shall be eaten as unleavened cakes in a holy place; they are to
eat it in the court of the tent of meeting.
17 '[a]It shall not be baked with leaven. I have given it as
their share from My offerings by fire; [b]it is most holy, like the
sin offering and [c]the guilt offering.
18 '[a]Every male among the sons of Aaron may eat it; it is a
permanent ordinance throughout your generations, from the
offerings by fire to the LORD. [b]Whoever touches them shall
become consecrated.' "
19 Then the LORD spoke to Moses, saying,
20 "This is the offering which Aaron and his sons are to
present to the LORD on the day when he is anointed; the tenth
of an ephah of fine flour as [a]a [1]regular grain offering, half of it
in the morning and half of it in the evening.
21 "It shall be prepared with oil on a [a]griddle. When it is
well stirred, you shall bring it. You shall present the grain
offering in baked pieces as a soothing aroma to the LORD.
22 "And the anointed priest who will be in his place
[1]among his sons shall [2]offer it. By a permanent ordinance it
shall be entirely offered up in smoke to the LORD.
23 "So every grain offering of the priest shall be burned
entirely. It shall not be eaten."
24 Then the LORD spoke to Moses, saying,
25 "Speak to Aaron and to his sons, saying, 'This is the law
of the sin offering: [a]in the place where the burnt offering is
slain the sin offering shall be slain before the LORD; it is most
holy.
26 '[a]The priest who offers it for sin shall eat it. It shall be
eaten in a holy place, in the court of the tent of meeting.
27 '[a]Anyone who touches its flesh shall become consecrated; and when any of its blood [1]splashes on a garment, in a
holy place you shall wash what was splashed on.
28 'Also [a]the earthenware vessel in which it was boiled shall
be broken; and if it was boiled in a bronze vessel, then it shall
be scoured and rinsed in water.
29 '[a]Every male among the priests may eat of it; it is most
holy.
30 'But no sin offering [a]of which any of the blood is
brought into the tent of meeting to make atonement [b]in the
holy place shall be eaten; [c]it shall be burned with fire.

CHAPTER 7

'NOW this is the law of the [a]guilt offering: it is most holy,
2 in [a]the place where they slay the burnt offering they are
to slay the guilt offering, and he shall sprinkle its blood around
on the altar.

15 [1]Lit., *and some of* [a]Lev. 2:2
16 [a]Lev. 2:3; 10:12-14
17 [a]Lev. 2:11 [b]Lev. 6:26, 29, 30 [c]Lev. 7:7; 10:16-18
18 [a]Lev. 6:29; 1 Cor. 9:13 [b]Lev. 6:27
20 [1]Lit., *grain offering continually* [a]Num. 4:16
21 [a]Lev. 2:5
22 [1]Lit., *from among* [2]Lit., *do*
25 [a]Lev. 1:11
26 [a]Lev. 6:29
27 [1]Lit., *one sprinkles* [a]Lev. 7:19
28 [a]Lev. 11:33; 15:12
29 [a]Lev. 6:18
30 [a]Lev. 4:1-21 [b]Lev. 4:7, 18 [c]Lev. 4:11, 12, 21
1 [a]Lev. 5:14-6:7
2 [a]Lev. 1:11

3 'Then he shall offer from it all its fat: the [a]fat tail and
the fat that covers the entrails,
4 and the two kidneys with the fat that is on them, which
is on the loins, and the lobe on the liver he shall remove [a]with
the kidneys.
5 'And the priest shall offer them up in smoke on the altar
as an offering by fire to the LORD; it is a guilt offering.
6 '[a]Every male among the priests may eat of it. It shall be
eaten in a holy place; it is most holy.
7 '[a]The guilt offering is like the sin offering, there is one
law for them; the [b]priest who makes atonement with it [1]shall
have it.
8 'Also the priest who presents any man's burnt offering,
[1]that priest shall have for himself the skin of the burnt offering
which he has presented.
9 'Likewise, every grain offering that is baked in the oven,
and everything prepared in a [1]pan or on a [a]griddle, [2]shall belong to the priest who presents it.
10 'And every grain offering mixed with oil, or dry, shall
[1]belong to all the sons of Aaron, [2]to all alike.
11 'Now this is the law of the sacrifice of peace offerings
which shall be presented to the LORD.
12 'If he offers it by way of [a]thanksgiving, then along with
the sacrifice of thanksgiving he shall offer unleavened cakes
mixed with oil, and unleavened wafers [1]spread with oil, and
cakes *of well* stirred fine flour mixed with oil.
13 'With the sacrifice of his peace offerings for thanksgiving, he shall present his offering with cakes of [a]leavened
bread.
14 'And of [1]this he shall present one of every offering as a
[2]contribution to the LORD; it shall [3]belong to the priest who
sprinkles the blood of the peace offerings.
15 '[a]Now *as for* the flesh of the sacrifice of his thanksgiving
peace offerings, it shall be eaten on the day of his offering; he
shall not leave any of it over until morning.
16 'But if the sacrifice of his offering is a [a]votive or a
freewill offering, it shall be eaten on the day that he offers his
sacrifice; and on the [1]next day what is left of it may be eaten;
17 [a]but what is left over from the flesh of the sacrifice on
the third day shall be burned with fire.
18 'So if any of the flesh of the sacrifice of his peace offerings should *ever* be eaten on the third day, he who offers it
shall not be accepted, *and* it shall not be reckoned to his
benefit. It shall be an offensive thing, and the person who eats
of it shall bear his *own* iniquity.
19 'Also the flesh that touches anything unclean shall not
be eaten; it shall be burned with fire. [1]As for *other* flesh,
anyone who is clean may eat *such* flesh.
20 '[a]But the person who eats the flesh of the sacrifice of
peace offerings which belong to the LORD, [1]in his uncleanness,
that person shall be cut off from his people.
21 '[a]And when anyone touches anything unclean, whether
human uncleanness, or an unclean animal, or any unclean [1]de-
testable thing, and eats of the flesh of the sacrifice of peace
offerings which belong to the LORD, that person shall be cut
off from his people.' "

3 [a]Lev. 3:9

4 [a]Lev. 3:4

6 [a]Lev. 6:18, 29

7 [1]Lit., *it shall be for him* [a]Lev. 6:30 [b]1 Cor. 9:13; 10:18

8 [1]Lit., *for the priest, it shall be for him*

9 [1]Lit., *lidded cooking pan* [2]Lit., *for the priest, it shall be for him* [a]Lev. 2:5

10 [1]Lit., *be* [2]Lit., *a man as his brother*

12 [1]Or, *anointed* [a]Lev. 7:15

13 [a]Lev. 2:12; 23:17, 18

14 [1]Lit., *it* [2]Or, *heave offering* [3]Lit., *be for*

15 [a]Lev. 22:29, 30

16 [1]Lit., *morrow and what* [a]Lev. 19:5-8

17 [a]Ex. 12:10

19 [1]Lit., *And the flesh*

20 [1]Lit., *and his uncleanness is on him* [a]Lev. 22:3-7; Num. 19:13

21 [1]Some mss. read, *swarming thing* [a]Lev. 5:2, 3

23 [a]Lev. 3:17

24 [a]Ex. 22:31; Lev. 17:15; 22:8

25 [1]Lit., *he offers an offering by fire*

26 [a]Lev. 17:10-16

30 [1]Lit., *waved*

31 [a]Num. 18:11; Deut. 18:3

32 [1]Or, *heave offering*

34 [1]Or, *heave offering*

35 [1]Lit., *the anointed portion of* [a]Num. 18:8

36 [1]Lit., *which*

37 [a]Lev. 8:22-23; Ex. 29:22-34

38 [1]Or, *offer* [a]Lev. 1:1; 26:46; 27:34; Deut. 4:5

2 [a]Ex. 28:1 [b]Lev. 6:10 [c]Ex. 30:25

22 Then the LORD spoke to Moses, saying,
23 "Speak to the sons of Israel, saying, 'You shall not eat
[a]any fat *from* an ox, a sheep, or a goat.
24 'Also the fat of *an animal* which dies, and the fat of an
animal [a]torn *by beasts,* may be put to any other use, but you
must certainly not eat it.
25 'For whoever eats the fat of the animal from which [1]an
offering by fire is offered to the LORD, even the person who
eats shall be cut off from his people.
26 '[a]And you are not to eat any blood, either of bird or
animal, in any of your dwellings.
27 'Any person who eats any blood, even that person shall
be cut off from his people.' "
28 Then the LORD spoke to Moses, saying,
29 "Speak to the sons of Israel, saying, 'He who offers the
sacrifice of his peace offerings to the LORD shall bring his
offering to the LORD from the sacrifice of his peace offerings.
30 'His own hands are to bring offerings by fire to the
LORD. He shall bring the fat with the breast, that the breast
may be [1]presented as a wave offering before the LORD.
31 'And the priest shall offer up the fat in smoke on the
altar; but [a]the breast shall belong to Aaron and his sons.
32 'And you shall give the right thigh to the priest as a
[1]contribution from the sacrifices of your peace offerings.
33 'The one among the sons of Aaron who offers the blood
of the peace offerings and the fat, the right thigh shall be his as
his portion.
34 'For I have taken the breast of the wave offering and
the thigh of the [1]contribution from the sons of Israel from the
sacrifices of their peace offerings, and have given them to
Aaron the priest and to his sons as *their* due forever from the
sons of Israel.
35 'This is [1]that which is consecrated to Aaron and [1]that
[a]which is consecrated to his sons from the offerings by fire to
the LORD, in that day when he presented them to serve as
priests to the LORD.
36 '[1]These the LORD had commanded to be given them
from the sons of Israel in the day that He anointed them. It is
their due forever throughout their generations.' "
37 This is the law of the burnt offering, the grain offering
and the sin offering and the guilt offering and [a]the ordination
offering and the sacrifice of peace offerings,
38 [a]which the LORD commanded Moses at Mount Sinai in
the day that He commanded the sons of Israel to [1]present
their offerings to the LORD in the wilderness of Sinai.

CHAPTER 8

THEN the LORD spoke to Moses, saying,
2 "[a]Take Aaron and his sons with him, and the [b]garments
and [c]the anointing oil and the bull of the sin offering, and the
two rams and the basket of unleavened bread;

3 and assemble all the congregation to the doorway of
the tent of meeting."
4 So Moses did just as the LORD commanded him. When
the congregation was assembled to the doorway of the tent of
meeting,
5 Moses said to the congregation, "This is the thing
which the LORD has commanded to do."
6 Then [a]Moses had Aaron and his sons come near, and
washed them with water.
7 And he put the tunic on him and girded him with the
sash, and clothed him with the robe, and put the ephod on
him; and he girded him with the artistic band of the ephod,
[1]with which he tied *it* to him.
8 He then placed the [1]breastpiece on him, and in the
[1]breastpiece he put [2a]the Urim and the Thummim.
9 He also placed the turban on his head, and on the
turban, at its front, he placed [a]the golden plate, the holy
crown, just as the LORD had commanded Moses.
10 Moses then took [a]the anointing oil and anointed the
[1]tabernacle and all that was in it, and consecrated them.
11 And he sprinkled some of it on the altar seven times
and anointed the altar and all its utensils, and the basin and its
stand, to [a]consecrate them.
12 Then he poured some of the [a]anointing oil on Aaron's
head and anointed him, to consecrate him.
13 [a]Next Moses had Aaron's sons come near and clothed
them with tunics, and girded them with sashes, and bound
[1]caps on them, just as the LORD had commanded Moses.
14 Then he brought [a]the bull of the sin offering, and Aaron and his sons laid their hands on the head of the bull of the
sin offering.
15 Next [1]Moses slaughtered *it* and took the blood and
with his finger [a]put *some of it* around on the horns of the altar,
and purified the altar. Then he poured out *the rest of* the
blood at the base of the altar and consecrated it, to make
atonement for it.
16 He also took all the fat that was on the entrails and the
[1]lobe of the liver, and the two kidneys and their fat; and Moses
offered it up in smoke on the altar.
17 [a]But the bull and its hide and its flesh and its refuse, he
burned in the fire outside the camp, just as the LORD had
commanded Moses.
18 Then he presented [a]the ram of the burnt offering, and
Aaron and his sons laid their hands on the head of the ram.
19 And [1]Moses slaughtered *it* and sprinkled the blood
around on the altar.
20 When he had cut the ram into its pieces, Moses [a]offered
up the head and the pieces and the suet in smoke.
21 After he had washed the entrails and the legs with water, Moses offered up the whole ram in smoke on the altar. It
was a burnt offering for a soothing aroma; it was an offering by
fire to the LORD, just as the LORD had commanded Moses.
22 Then he presented the second ram, [a]the ram of [1]ordi-
nation; and Aaron and his sons laid their hands on the head of
the ram.

6 [a]Ex. 29:4-6
7 [1]Lit., *and with it*
8 [1]Lit., *pouch* [2]I.e., the Lights and Perfections [a]Ex. 28:30
9 [a]Ex. 28:36
10 [1]Or, *dwelling place* [a]Lev. 8:2
11 [a]Ex. 29:36, 37; 30:29
12 [a]Ex. 30:30
13 [1]Lit., *headgear* [a]Ex. 29:8, 9
14 [a]Ex. 29:10
15 [1]Lit., *he slaughtered it and Moses took* [a]Lev. 4:7
16 [1]Or, *appendage on*
17 [a]Lev. 4:11, 12
18 [a]Lev. 8:2
19 [1]Lit., *he slaughtered it and Moses sprinkled*
20 [a]Lev. 1:8
22 [1]Lit., *filling*, and so throughout the chap. [a]Lev. 8:2

23 [1]Lit., *he slaughtered it and Moses took* [a]Ex. 29:20, 21

23 And [1]Moses slaughtered *it* and took some of its blood and [a]put it on the lobe of Aaron's right ear, and on the thumb of his right hand, and on the big toe of his right foot.

24 He also had Aaron's sons come near; and Moses put some of the blood on the lobe of their right ear, and on the thumb of their right hand, and on the big toe of their right foot. Moses then sprinkled *the rest of* the blood around on the altar.

25 And he took the fat, and the fat tail, and all the fat that was on the entrails, and the [1]lobe of the liver and the two kidneys and their fat and the right thigh.

25 [1]Or, *appendage on*

26 And from the basket of unleavened bread that was before the LORD, he took one unleavened cake and one cake of bread *mixed with* oil and one wafer, and placed *them* on the portions of fat and on the right thigh.

27 He then put all *these* on the hands of Aaron and on the hands of his sons, and presented them as a wave offering before the LORD.

28 Then Moses took them from their hands and offered them up in smoke on the altar with the burnt offering. They were an ordination offering for a soothing aroma; it was an offering by fire to the LORD.

29 [a]Lev. 7:31-34 [b]Ps. 99:6

29 Moses also took [a]the breast and presented it for a wave offering before the LORD; it was [b]Moses' portion of the ram of ordination, just as the LORD had commanded Moses.

30 So Moses took some of the anointing oil and some of the blood which was on the altar, and sprinkled it on Aaron, on his garments, on his sons, and on the garments of his sons with him; and he consecrated Aaron, his garments, and his sons, and the garments of his sons with him.

31 Then Moses said to Aaron and to his sons, "[a]Boil the flesh at the doorway of the tent of meeting, and eat it there together with the bread which is in the basket of the ordination offering, just as I commanded, [b]saying, 'Aaron and his sons shall eat it.'

31 [a]Ex. 29:31 [b]Ex. 29:32

32 "And the remainder of the flesh and of the bread you shall burn in the fire.

33 "[a]And you shall not go outside the doorway of the tent of meeting for seven days, until the day that the period of your ordination is fulfilled; for he will [1]ordain you through seven days.

34 "The LORD has commanded to do as has been done this day, to make atonement on your behalf.

33 [1]Lit., *fill your hands* [a]Ex. 29:35

35 "At the doorway of the tent of meeting, moreover, you shall remain day and night for seven days, and keep the charge of the LORD, that you may not die, for so I have been commanded."

36 Thus Aaron and his sons did all the things which the LORD had commanded through Moses.

CHAPTER 9

NOW it came about on the eighth day that Moses called Aaron and his sons and the elders of Israel;

2 and he said to Aaron, "Take for yourself a calf, a bull,
for a sin offering and a ram for a burnt offering, *both* without
defect, and offer *them* before the LORD.
3 "Then to the sons of Israel you shall speak, saying, 'Take
a male goat for a sin offering, and a calf and a lamb, both one
year old, without defect, for a burnt offering,
4 and an ox and a ram for peace offerings, to sacrifice
before the LORD, and a grain offering mixed with oil; for today
the LORD shall appear to you.' "
5 So they took what Moses had commanded to the front
of the tent of meeting, and the whole congregation came near
and stood before the LORD.
6 And Moses said, "This is the thing which the LORD has
commanded you to do, that [a]the glory of the LORD may appear
to you."
7 Moses then said to Aaron, "Come near to the altar and
[1]offer your sin offering and your burnt offering, that you may
make atonement for yourself and for the people; then make
the offering [2]for the people, that you may make atonement for
them, just as the LORD has commanded."
8 [a]So Aaron came near to the altar and slaughtered the
calf of the sin offering which was for himself.
9 [a]And Aaron's sons presented the blood to him; and he
dipped his finger in the blood, and put *some* on the horns of
the altar, and poured out *the rest of* the blood at the base of
the altar.
10 The fat and the kidneys and the [1]lobe of the liver of the
sin offering, he then offered up in smoke on the altar just as
the LORD had commanded Moses.
11 The flesh and the skin, however, he burned with fire
outside the camp.
12 Then he slaughtered the burnt offering; and Aaron's
sons handed the blood to him and he sprinkled it around on
the altar.
13 And they handed the burnt offering to him in [1]pieces
with the head, and he offered *them* up in smoke on the altar.
14 He also washed the entrails and the legs, and offered
them up in smoke with the burnt offering on the altar.
15 Then he presented the people's offering, and took the
[a]goat of the sin offering which was for the people, and slaughtered it and offered it for sin, like the first.
16 He also presented the burnt offering, and [1]offered it
according to [a]the ordinance.
17 Next he presented [a]the grain offering, and filled his
[1]hand with some of it and offered *it* up in smoke on the altar,
[b]besides the burnt offering of the morning.
18 Then [a]he slaughtered the ox and the ram, the sacrifice
of peace offerings which was for the people; and Aaron's sons
handed the blood to him and he sprinkled it around on the
altar.
19 As for the portions of fat from the ox and from the
ram, the fat tail, and the *fat* [a]covering, and the kidneys and the
[1]lobe of the liver,
20 they now placed the portions of fat on the breasts; and
he offered [1]them up in smoke on the altar.

6 [a]Lev. 8:23
7 [1]Lit., *make* [2]Lit., *of*
8 [a]Lev. 4:1-12
9 [a]Lev. 9:12, 18
10 [1]Or, *appendage on*
13 [1]Lit., *its pieces*
15 [a]Lev. 4:27-31
16 [1]Lit., *made* [a]Lev. 1:1-13
17 [1]Lit., *palm* [a]Lev. 2:1-3 [b]Lev. 3:5
18 [a]Lev. 3:1-11
19 [1]Or, *appendage on* [a]Lev. 3:9
20 [1]Lit., *the portions of fat*

21 But [a]the breasts and the right thigh Aaron [1]presented as a wave offering before the LORD, just as Moses had commanded.

22 Then Aaron lifted up his hands toward the people and blessed them, and he stepped down after making the sin offering and the burnt offering and the peace offerings.

23 And Moses and Aaron went into the tent of meeting. When they came out and blessed the people, [a]the glory of the LORD appeared to all the people.

24 [a]Then fire came out from before the LORD and consumed the burnt offering and the portions of fat on the altar; and when all the people saw *it,* they shouted and fell on their faces.

CHAPTER 10

NOW [a]Nadab and Abihu, the sons of Aaron, took their respective [b]firepans, and after putting fire in them, placed incense on it and offered strange fire before the LORD, which He had not commanded them.

2 [a]And fire came out from the presence of the LORD and consumed them, and they died before the LORD.

3 Then Moses said to Aaron, "It is what the LORD spoke, saying,

'By those who [a]come near Me I [1b]will be treated as holy,
And before all the people I will [c]be honored.'

So Aaron, therefore, kept silent.

4 Moses called also to [a]Mishael and Elzaphan, the sons of Aaron's uncle Uzziel, and said to them, "Come forward, carry your [1]relatives away from the front of the sanctuary to the outside of the camp."

5 So they came forward and carried them still in their [a]tunics to the outside of the camp, as Moses had said.

6 Then Moses said to Aaron and to his sons Eleazar and Ithamar, "[a]Do not [1]uncover your heads nor tear your clothes, so that you may not die, and that He may not [b]become wrathful against all the congregation. But your [2]kinsmen, the whole house of Israel, shall bewail the burning which the LORD has [3]brought about.

7 "You shall not even go out from the doorway of the tent of meeting, lest you die; for [a]the LORD's anointing oil is upon you." So they did according to the word of Moses.

8 The Lord then spoke to Aaron, saying,

9 "[a]Do not drink wine or strong drink, neither you nor your sons with you, when you come into the tent of meeting, so that you may not die—it is a perpetual statute throughout your generations—

10 and [a]so as to make a distinction between the holy and the profane, and between the unclean and the clean,

11 and [a]so as to teach the sons of Israel all the statutes which the LORD has spoken to them through Moses."

12 Then Moses spoke to Aaron, and to his surviving sons, [a]Eleazar and Ithamar, "[b]Take the grain offering that is left

21 [1]Lit., *waved* [a]Lev. 7:30-34
23 [a]Lev. 9:6
24 [a]1 Kin. 18:38
1 [a]Ex. 24:1, 9; Num. 3:2 [b]Lev. 16:12
2 [a]Num. 3:4; 26:61
3 [1]Or, *will show Myself holy* [a]Lev. 21:6; [b]Ezek. 38:16; Ex. 30:30 [c]Ex. 14:4, 17
4 [1]Lit., *brothers* [a]Ex. 6:18, 22
5 [a]Lev. 8:13; Ex. 29:5
6 [1]Lit., *unbind* [2]Lit., *brothers* [3]Lit., *burned* [a]Lev. 21:1-5, 10-12 [b]Num. 1:53; 16:22, 46; 18:5; Josh. 7:1; 22:18, 20; 2 Sam. 24:1
7 [a]Lev. 21:12
9 [a]Ezek. 44:21
10 [a]Lev. 11:47; 20:25; Ezek. 22:26
11 [a]Deut. 17:10, 11; 33:10
12 [a]Ex. 6:23; Num. 3:2 [b]Lev. 6:14-18

over from the LORD's offerings by fire and eat it unleavened
beside the altar, for it is most holy.
13 "You shall eat it, moreover, in a holy place, because it is
your due and your sons' due out of the LORD's offerings by fire;
for thus I have been commanded.
14 "[a]The breast of wave offering, however, and the thigh of
the offering you may eat in a clean place, you and your sons
and your daughters with you; for they have been given as your
due and your sons' due out of the sacrifices of the peace
offerings of the sons of Israel.
15 "[a]The thigh offered by lifting up and the breast offered
by waving, they shall bring along with the offerings by fire of
the portions of fat, to present as a wave offering before the
LORD; so it shall be a thing perpetually due you and your sons
with you, just as the LORD has commanded."
16 But Moses searched carefully for the [a]goat of the sin
offering, and behold, it had been burned up! So he was angry
with Aaron's surviving sons Eleazar and Ithamar, saying,
17 "Why [a]did you not eat the sin offering at the holy place?
For it is most holy, and [1]He gave it to you to bear away [b]the
guilt of the congregation, to make atonement for them before
the LORD.
18 "Behold, [a]since its blood had not been brought inside,
into the sanctuary, you should certainly have [b]eaten it in the
sanctuary, just as I commanded."
19 But Aaron spoke to Moses, "Behold, this very day they
presented their sin offering and their burnt offering before the
LORD. When [1]things like these happened to me, if I had eaten
a sin offering today, would it have been good in the sight of
the LORD?"
20 And when Moses heard *that*, it seemed good in his
sight.

CHAPTER 11

THE LORD spoke again to Moses and to Aaron, saying to
them,
2 "Speak to the sons of Israel, saying, '[a]These are the creatures which you may eat from all the animals that are on the
earth.
3 'Whatever divides a hoof, thus making split hoofs, *and*
chews the cud, among the animals, that you may eat.
4 'Nevertheless, [a]you are not to eat of these, among those
which chew the cud, or among those which divide the hoof:
the camel, for though it chews cud, it does not divide the hoof,
it is unclean to you.
5 'Likewise, the rock badger, for though it chews cud, it
does not divide the hoof, it is unclean to you;
6 the [1]rabbit also, for though it chews cud, it does not
divide the hoof, it is unclean to you;
7 and the pig, for though it divides the hoof, thus making
a split hoof, it does not chew cud, it is unclean to you.
8 'You shall not eat of their flesh nor touch their carcasses; they are unclean to you.
9 'These you may eat, whatever is in the water: all that

14 [a]Lev. 7:30-34
15 [a]Lev. 7:34
16 [a]Lev. 9:3, 15
17 [1]Or, *was given* [a]Lev. 6:24-30 [b]Lev. 22:16; Ex. 28:38; Num. 18:1
18 [a]Lev. 6:30 [b]Lev. 6:26
19 [1]Cf. vs. 1-4
2 [a]Deut. 14:3-21
4 [a]Acts 10:14
6 [1]Or, *hare*

have fins and scales, those in the water, in the seas or in the
rivers, you may eat.
10 'But whatever is in the seas and in the rivers, that do not
have fins and scales among all the teeming life of the water,
and among all the living creatures that are in the water, they
are detestable things to you,
11 and they shall be [1]abhorrent to you; you may not eat of
their flesh, and their carcasses you shall detest.
12 'Whatever in the water does not have fins and scales is
[1]abhorrent to you.
13 'These, moreover, you shall detest among the birds;
they are [1]abhorrent, not to be eaten: the [2]eagle and the vulture
and the [3]buzzard,
14 and the kite and the falcon in its kind,
15 every raven in its kind,
16 and the ostrich and the owl and the sea gull and the
hawk in its kind,
17 and the little owl and the cormorant and the [1]great owl,
18 and the white owl and the [1]pelican and the carrion-
vulture,
19 and the stork, the heron in its kinds, and the hoopoe,
and the bat.
20 'All the [1]winged insects that walk on *all* fours are detestable to you.
21 'Yet these you may eat among all the [1]winged insects
which walk on *all* fours: those which have above their feet
jointed legs with which to jump on the earth.
22 'These of them you may eat: the locust in its kinds, and
the devastating locust in its kinds, and the cricket in its kinds,
and the grasshopper in its kinds.
23 'But all other [1]winged insects which are four-footed are
detestable to you.
24 'By these, moreover, you will be made unclean: whoever
touches their carcasses becomes unclean until evening,
25 and [a]whoever picks up any of their carcasses shall wash
his clothes and be unclean until evening.
26 'Concerning all the animals which divide the hoof, but
do not make a split *hoof,* or which do not chew cud, they are
unclean to you: whoever touches them becomes unclean.
27 'Also whatever walks on its paws, among all the creatures that walk on *all* fours, are unclean to you; whoever
touches their carcasses becomes unclean until evening,
28 and the one who picks up their carcasses shall wash his
clothes and be unclean until evening; they are unclean to you.
29 'Now these are to you the unclean among the swarming
things which swarm on the earth: the mole, and the mouse,
and the [1]great lizard in its kinds,
30 and the gecko, and the [1]crocodile, and the lizard, and
the [2]sand reptile, and the chameleon.
31 'These are to you the unclean among all the swarming
things; whoever touches them when they are dead becomes
unclean until evening.
32 'Also anything on which one of them may fall when
they are dead, becomes unclean, including any wooden article,
or clothing, or a skin, or a sack—any article [1]of which use is

11 [1]Lit., *detestable things*

12 [1]Lit., *detestable things*

13 [1]Lit., *a detestable thing* [2]Or, *vulture* [3]Or, *black vulture*

17 [1]Specifically, *great horned owl*

18 [1]Or, *owl;* or, *jackdaw*

20 [1]Lit., *swarming things with wings*

21 [1]Note v. 20

23 [1]Note v. 20

25 [a]Lev. 11:40

29 [1]Or, *thorn-tailed lizard*

30 [1]Or, *lizard* [2]Species as yet undefined

32 [1]Lit., *with which work is done*

made—it shall be put in the water and be unclean until evening, then it becomes clean.
33 'As for any [a]earthenware vessel into which one of them
may fall, whatever is in it becomes unclean and you shall break
[1]the vessel.
34 'Any of the [1]food which may be eaten on which water
comes shall become unclean; and any [1]liquid which may be
drunk in every vessel shall become unclean.
35 'Everything, moreover, on which part of their carcass
may fall becomes unclean; an oven or a [1]stove shall be
smashed; they are unclean and shall continue as unclean to
you.
36 'Nevertheless a spring or a cistern [1]collecting water shall
be clean, though the one who touches their carcass shall be
unclean.
37 'And if a part of their carcass falls on any seed for
sowing which is to be sown, it is clean.
38 'Though if water is put on the seed, and a part of their
carcass falls on it, it is unclean to you.
39 'Also if one of the animals dies which you have for food,
the one who touches its carcass becomes unclean until
evening.
40 '[a]He too, who eats some of its carcass shall wash his
clothes and be unclean until evening; and the one who picks
up its carcass shall wash his clothes and be unclean until
evening.
41 '[a]Now every swarming thing that swarms on the earth is
detestable, not to be eaten.
42 'Whatever crawls on its belly, and whatever walks on *all*
fours, whatever has many feet, in respect to every swarming
thing that swarms on the earth, you shall not eat them, for
they are detestable.
43 '[a]Do not render [1]yourselves detestable through any of
the swarming things that swarm; and you shall not make yourselves unclean with them so that you become unclean.
44 'For [a]I am the LORD your God. Consecrate yourselves
therefore, and [b]be holy; for I am holy. And you shall not make
yourselves unclean with any of the swarming things that swarm
on the earth.
45 '[a]For I am the LORD, who brought you up from the land
of Egypt, to be your God; thus you shall be holy for I am
holy.' "
46 This is the law regarding the animal, and the bird, and
every living thing that moves in the waters, and everything that
swarms on the earth,
47 [a]to make a distinction between the unclean and the
clean, and between the edible creature and the creature which
is not to be eaten.

CHAPTER 12

THEN the LORD spoke to Moses, saying,
2 "Speak to the sons of Israel, saying, 'When a woman
[1]gives birth and bears a male *child*, then she shall be unclean
for seven days, [a]as in the days of [2]her menstruation she shall be
unclean.

33 [1]Lit., *it*
[a]Lev. 6:28; 15:12

34 [1]I.e., if touched by a carcass; cf. 29-32

35 [1]Lit., *hearth for supporting (two) pots*

36 [1]Lit., *of a gathering of*

40 [a]Lev. 17:15; 22:8

41 [a]Lev. 11:29

43 [1]Lit., *your souls*
[a]Lev. 20:25

44 [a]Ex. 6:7; 16:12; 23:25
[b]1 Pet. 1:16

45 [a]Lev. 22:33; 25:38; 26:45

47 [a]Lev. 10:10

2 [1]Lit., *produces seed*
[2]Lit., *the impurity of her sickness*
[a]Lev. 15:19; 18:19

3 ‘And on [a]the eighth day the flesh of his foreskin shall
be circumcised.
4 ‘Then she shall remain in the blood of *her* purification
for thirty-three days; she shall not touch any consecrated thing,
nor enter the sanctuary, until the days of her purification are
completed.
5 ‘But if she bears a female *child*, then she shall be unclean for two weeks, as in her [1]menstruation; and she shall
remain in the blood of *her* purification for sixty-six days.
6 ‘And [a]when the days of her purification are completed,
for a son or for a daughter, she shall bring to the priest at the
doorway of the tent of meeting, a one year old lamb for a
burnt offering, and a young pigeon or a turtledove [b]for a sin
offering.
7 ‘Then he shall offer it before the LORD and make atonement for her; and she shall be cleansed from the [1]flow of her
blood. This is the law for her who bears *a child, whether* a
male or a female.
8 ‘But if [1]she cannot afford a lamb, then she shall take
[a]two turtledoves or two young pigeons, [b]the one for a burnt
offering and the other for a sin offering; and the priest shall
make atonement for her, and she shall be clean.’ ”

CHAPTER 13

THEN the LORD spoke to Moses and to Aaron, saying,
2 “When a man has on the skin of his [1]body a swelling or a
scab or a bright spot, and it becomes [2]an infection of leprosy
on the skin of his [1]body, [a]then he shall be brought to Aaron the
priest, or to one of his sons the priests.
3 “And the priest shall look at the mark on the skin of the
[1]body, and if the hair in the infection has turned white and the
infection appears to be deeper than the skin of his [1]body, it is
an infection of leprosy; when the priest has looked at him, he
shall pronounce him unclean.
4 “But if the bright spot is white on the skin of his [1]body,
and [2]it does not appear to be deeper than the skin, and the hair
on it has not turned white, then the priest shall [3]isolate *him*
who has the infection for seven days.
5 “And the priest shall look at him on the seventh day, and
if in his eyes the infection [1]has not changed, *and* the infection
has not spread on the skin, then the priest shall [2]isolate him for
seven more days.
6 “And the priest shall look at him again on the seventh
day; and if the infection has faded, and the mark has not
spread on the skin, then the priest shall pronounce him clean;
it is *only* a scab. And he shall wash his clothes and be clean.
7 “But if the scab spreads farther on the skin, after he has
shown himself to the priest for his cleansing, he shall appear
again to the priest.
8 “And the priest shall look, and if the scab has spread on
the skin, then the priest shall pronounce him unclean; it is
leprosy.
9 “When the infection of leprosy is on a man, then he
shall be brought to the priest.
10 “The priest shall then look, and if there is a [a]white swell-

3 [a]Gen. 17:12
5 [1]Lit., *impurity*
6 [a]Luke 2:22 [b]Lev. 5:7
7 [1]Lit., *fountain*
8 [1]Lit., *her hand does not find a sufficiency of a lamb* [a]Luke 2:22-24 [b]Lev. 5:7
2 [1]Lit., *flesh* [2]Lit., *a mark, stroke* and so throughout the chap. [a]Deut. 24:8
3 [1]Lit., *flesh*
4 [1]Lit., *flesh* [2]Lit., *the appearance of it is not deeper* [3]Lit., *shut up*
5 [1]Lit., *has stood* [2]Lit., *shut up*
10 [a]Num. 12:10; 2 Kin. 5:27; 2 Chr. 26:19, 20

ing in the skin, and it has turned the hair white, and there is
quick raw flesh in the swelling,
11 it is [1]a chronic leprosy on the skin of his [2]body, and the
priest shall pronounce him unclean; he shall not [3]isolate him,
for he is unclean.
12 "And if the leprosy breaks out farther on the skin, and
the leprosy covers all the skin of *him who has* the infection
from his head even to his feet, [1]as far as the priest can see,
13 then the priest shall look, and behold, *if* the leprosy has
covered all his [1]body, he shall pronounce clean *him who has*
the infection; it has all turned white *and* he is clean.
14 "But whenever raw flesh appears on him, he shall be
unclean.
15 "And the priest shall look at the raw flesh, and he shall
pronounce him unclean; the raw flesh is unclean, it is leprosy.
16 "Or if the raw flesh turns again and is changed to white,
then he shall come to the priest,
17 and the priest shall look at him, and behold, *if* the
infection has turned to white, then the priest shall pronounce
clean *him who has* the infection; he is clean.
18 "And when the [1]body has a boil on its skin, and it is
healed,
19 and in the place of the boil there is a white swelling or a
reddish-white, bright spot, then it shall be shown to the priest;
20 and the priest shall look, and behold, *if* [1]it appears to
be lower than the skin, and the hair on it has turned white,
then the priest shall pronounce him unclean; it is the infection
of leprosy, it has broken out in the boil.
21 "But if the priest looks at it, and behold, there are no
white hairs in it and it is not lower than the skin and is faded,
then the priest shall [1]isolate him for seven days;
22 and if it spreads farther on the skin, then the priest shall
pronounce him unclean; it is an infection.
23 "But if the bright spot remains in its place, and does not
spread, it is *only* the scar of the boil; and the priest shall
pronounce him clean.
24 "Or if the [1]body sustains in its skin a burn by fire, and
the raw *flesh* of the burn becomes a bright spot, reddish-white,
or white,
25 then the priest shall look at it. And if the hair in the
bright spot has turned white, and it appears to be deeper than
the skin, it is leprosy; it has broken out in the burn. Therefore,
the priest shall pronounce him unclean; it is an infection of
leprosy.
26 "But if the priest looks at it, and indeed, there is no
white hair in the bright spot, and it is no [1]deeper than the skin,
but is dim, then the priest shall [2]isolate him for seven days;
27 and the priest shall look at him on the seventh day. If it
spreads farther in the skin, then the priest shall pronounce him
unclean; it is an infection of leprosy.
28 "But if the bright spot remains in its place, and has not
spread in the skin, but is dim, it is the swelling from the burn;
and the priest shall pronounce him clean, for it is *only* the scar
of the burn.
29 "Now if a man or woman has an infection on the head
or on the beard,

11 [1]Lit., *an old* [2]Lit., *flesh* [3]Lit., *shut up*

12 [1]Lit., *with regard to the whole sight of the priest's eyes*

13 [1]Lit., *flesh*

18 [1]Lit., *flesh*

20 [1]Lit., *the appearance of it is lower*

21 [1]Lit., *shut up*

24 [1]Lit., *flesh*

26 [1]Lit., *lower* [2]Lit., *shut up*

30 then the priest shall look at the infection, and if it
appears to be deeper than the skin, and there is thin yellowish
hair in it, then the priest shall pronounce him unclean; it is a
scale, it is leprosy of the head or of the beard.
31 "But if the priest looks at the infection of the scale, and
indeed, it appears to be no deeper than the skin, and there is
no black hair in it, then the priest shall [1]isolate *the person* with
the scaly infection for seven days.
32 "And on the seventh day the priest shall look at the
infection, and if the scale has not spread, and no yellowish hair
has [1]grown in it, and the appearance of the scale is no deeper
than the skin,
33 then he shall shave himself, but he shall not shave the
scale; and the priest shall [1]isolate *the person* with the scale
seven more days.
34 "Then on the seventh day the priest shall look at the
scale, and if the scale has not spread in the skin, and it appears
to be no deeper than the skin, the priest shall pronounce him
clean; and he shall wash his clothes and be clean.
35 "But if the scale spreads farther in the skin after his
cleansing,
36 then the priest shall look at him, and if the scale has
spread in the skin, the priest need not seek for the yellowish
hair; he is unclean.
37 "If in his sight the scale has remained, however, and
black hair has grown in it, the scale has healed, he is clean; and
the priest shall pronounce him clean.
38 "And when a man or a woman has bright spots on the
skin of the [1]body, *even* white bright spots,
39 then the priest shall look, and if the bright spots on the
skin of their [1]bodies are a faint white, it is [2]eczema that has
broken out on the skin; he is clean.
40 "Now if a [1]man loses the hair of his head, he is bald; he
is clean.
41 "And if his head becomes bald at the [1]front and sides, he
is bald on the forehead; he is clean.
42 "But if on the bald head or the bald forehead, there
occurs a reddish-white infection, it is leprosy breaking out on
his bald head or on his bald forehead.
43 "Then the priest shall look at him; and if the swelling of
the infection is reddish-white on his bald head or on his bald
forehead, like the appearance of leprosy in the skin of the
[1]body,
44 he is a leprous man, he is unclean. The priest shall
surely pronounce him unclean; his infection is on his head.
45 "As for the leper who has the infection, his clothes shall
be torn, and [a]the hair of his head shall be [1]uncovered, and he
shall [b]cover his mustache and cry '[c]Unclean! Unclean!'
46 "He shall remain unclean all the days during which he
has the infection; he is unclean. He shall live alone; his dwelling shall be [a]outside the camp.
47 "When a garment has a [1]mark of leprosy in it, whether it
is a wool garment or a linen garment,
48 whether in [1]warp or woof, of linen or of wool, whether
in leather or in any article made of leather,
49 if the mark is greenish or reddish in the garment or in

31 [1]Lit., *shut up*

32 [1]Lit., *been*

33 [1]Lit., *shut up*

38 [1]Lit., *flesh*

39 [1]Lit., *flesh* [2]Lit., *tetter*

40 [1]Lit., *man's head becomes bald*

41 [1]Lit., *border of his face*

43 [1]Lit., *flesh*

45 [1]Or, *disheveled* [a]Lev. 10:6 [b]Ezek. 24:17, 22; Mic. 3:7 [c]Lam. 4:15

46 [a]Num. 5:1-4; 12:14

47 [1]Lit., *infection*, and so throughout the chap.

48 [1]Or, *weaving or texture*

the leather, or in the [1]warp or in the woof, or in any article of
leather, it is a leprous mark and shall be shown to the priest.
50 "Then the priest shall look at the mark, and shall [1]quar-
antine the article with the mark for seven days.
51 "He shall then look at the mark on the seventh day; if
the mark has spread in the garment, whether in the warp or in
the woof, or in the leather, whatever the purpose for which the
leather is used, the mark is a [1]leprous malignancy, it is unclean.
52 "So he shall burn the garment, whether the warp or the
woof, in wool or in linen, or any article of leather in which the
mark occurs, for it is a [1]leprous malignancy; it shall be burned
in the fire.
53 "But if the priest shall look, and indeed, the mark has
not spread in the garment, either in the warp or in the woof, or
in any article of leather,
54 then the priest shall order them to wash the thing in
which the mark occurs, and he shall [1]quarantine it for seven
more days.
55 "After the article with the mark has been washed, the
priest shall again look, and if the mark has not changed its
appearance, even though the mark has not spread, it is
unclean; you shall burn it in the fire, [1]whether an eating away
has produced bareness on the top or on the front of it.
56 "Then if the priest shall look, and if the mark has faded
after it has been washed, then he shall tear it out of the garment or out of the leather, whether from the warp or from the
woof;
57 and if it appears again in the garment, whether in the
warp or in the woof, or in any article of leather, it is an out-
break; the article with the mark shall be burned in the fire.
58 "And the garment, whether the warp or the woof, or any
article of leather from which the mark has departed when you
washed it, it shall then be washed a second time and shall be
clean."
59 This is the law for the mark of leprosy in a garment of
wool or linen, whether in the warp or in the woof, or in any
article of leather, for pronouncing it clean or unclean.

Chapter 14

THEN the LORD spoke to Moses, saying,
2 "This shall be the law of the leper in the day of his
cleansing. [a]Now he shall be brought to the priest,
3 and the priest shall go [a]out to the outside of the camp.
Thus the priest shall look, and if the [1]infection of leprosy has
been healed in the leper,
4 then the priest shall give orders to take two live clean
birds and [a]cedar wood and a [1]scarlet string and hyssop for the
one who is to be cleansed.
5 "The priest shall also give orders to slay the one bird in
an earthenware vessel over [1]running water.
6 "*As for* the live bird, he shall take it, together with [a]the
cedar wood and the [1]scarlet string and the [b]hyssop, and shall
dip them and the live bird in the blood of the bird that was
slain over the [2]running water.
7 "He shall then sprinkle seven times the one who is to be

49 [1]Or, *weaving or texture*

50 [1]Lit., *shut up*

51 [1]Lit., *malignant leprosy*

52 [1]Lit., *malignant leprosy*

54 [1]Lit., *shut up*

55 [1]Lit., *it is*

2 [a]Matt. 8:4; Mark 1:44; Luke 5:14; 17:14

3 [1]Lit., *mark, stroke,* and so throughout the chap. [a]Lev. 13:46

4 [1]Lit., *scarlet color and* [a]Lev. 14:6, 49, 51, 52; Num. 19:6

5 [1]Lit., *living*

6 [1]Lit., *scarlet color and* [2]Lit., *living* [a]Lev. 14:4 [b]Ps. 51:7

cleansed from the leprosy, and shall pronounce him clean, and
shall let the live bird go free over the open field.
8 "[a]The one to be cleansed shall then wash his clothes and
shave off all his hair, and bathe in water and [b]be clean. Now
afterward, he may enter the camp, but he shall stay outside his
tent for seven days.
9 "And it will be on the seventh day that he shall shave off
all his hair: he shall shave his head and his beard and his
eyebrows, even all his hair. He shall then wash his clothes and
bathe his [1]body in water and [a]be clean.
10 "Now on the eighth day he is to take two male lambs
without defect, and a yearling ewe lamb without defect, and
three-tenths *of* [1]*a bushel* of fine flour mixed with oil for a grain
offering, and one [2a]log of oil;
11 and the priest who pronounces him clean shall present
the man to be cleansed and the [1]aforesaid before the LORD at
the doorway of the tent of meeting.
12 "Then the priest shall take the one male lamb and bring
it for a [a]guilt offering, with the [1b]log of oil, and present them as
a wave offering before the LORD.
13 "Next he shall slaughter the male lamb in [a]the place
where they slaughter the sin offering and the burnt offering, at
the place of the sanctuary—for the guilt offering, [b]like the sin
offering, belongs to the priest; it is most holy.
14 "The priest shall then take some of the blood of the
[a]guilt offering, and the priest shall put *it* on [b]the lobe of the
right ear of the one to be cleansed, and on the thumb of his
right hand, and on the big toe of his right foot.
15 "The priest shall also take some of the [1a]log of oil, and
pour *it* into his left palm;
16 the priest shall then dip his right-hand finger into the
oil that is in his left palm, and with his finger sprinkle some of
the oil seven times before the LORD.
17 "And of the remaining oil which is in his palm, the priest
shall put some on the right earlobe of the one to be cleansed,
and on the thumb of his right hand, and on the big toe of his
right foot, on the blood of the guilt offering;
18 while the rest of the oil that is in the priest's palm, he
shall put on the head of the one to be cleansed. So the priest
shall make atonement on his behalf before the LORD.
19 "The priest shall next offer the [a]sin offering and make
atonement for the one to be cleansed from his uncleanness.
Then afterward, he shall slaughter the burnt offering.
20 "And the priest shall offer up the burnt offering and the
grain offering on the altar. Thus the priest shall make atonement for him, and [a]he shall be clean.
21 "[a]But if he is poor, and his [1]means are insufficient, then
he is to take one male lamb for a [b]guilt offering as a wave
offering to make atonement for him, and one-tenth of [2]*a bushel* of fine flour mixed with oil for a grain offering, and a [3c]log
of oil,
22 and two turtledoves or two young pigeons which [1]are
within his means, [a]the one shall be a [b]sin offering and the other
a burnt offering.
23 "[a]Then the eighth day he shall bring them for his cleans-

8 [a]Num. 8:7 [b]Lev. 14:9, 20

9 [1]Lit., *flesh* [a]Lev. 14:8, 20

10 [1]An ephah is assumed, cf. Lev. 6:20 [2]Approx. one pint [a]Lev. 14:12, 15, 21, 24

11 [1]Lit., *them*

12 [1]Approx. one pint [a]Lev. 14:19 [b]Lev. 14:10

13 [a]Lev. 1:11 [b]Lev. 6:24-30

14 [a]Lev. 14:19 [b]Lev. 8:23, 24

15 [1]Approx. one pint [a]Lev. 14:10

19 [a]Lev. 14:12

20 [a]Lev. 14:8, 9

21 [1]Lit., *hand is not reaching* [2]An ephah is assumed; cf. Lev. 6:20 [3]Approx. one pint [a]Lev. 5:11; 27:8 [b]Lev. 14:22 [c]Lev. 14:10

22 [1]Lit., *his hand reaches* [a]Lev. 5:7 [b]Lev. 14:21, 24, 25

23 [a]Lev. 14:10, 11

ing to the priest, at the doorway of the tent of meeting, before the LORD.

24 "And the priest shall take the lamb of the guilt offering, and [a]the [1]log of oil, and the priest shall offer them for a wave offering before the LORD.

25 "Next he shall slaughter the lamb of the guilt offering; and the priest is to take some of the blood of the guilt offering and put *it* on [a]the lobe of the right ear of the one to be cleansed and on the thumb of his right hand, and on the big toe of his right foot.

26 "The priest shall also pour some of the oil into his left palm;

27 and with his right-hand finger the priest shall sprinkle some of the oil that is in his left palm seven times before the LORD.

28 "The priest shall then put some of the oil that is in his palm on the lobe of the right ear of the one to be cleansed, and on the thumb of his right hand, and on the big toe of his right foot, on the place of the blood of the guilt offering.

29 "Moreover, the rest of the oil that is in the priest's palm he shall put on the head of the one to be cleansed, to make atonement on his behalf before the LORD.

30 "He shall then offer one of the turtledoves or young pigeons, [1]which are within his means.

31 "*He shall offer* what [1]he can afford, [a]the one for a sin offering, and the other for a burnt offering, together with the grain offering. So the priest shall make atonement before the LORD on behalf of the one to be cleansed.

32 "This is the law *for him* in whom there is an infection of leprosy, whose [1]means are limited for his cleansing."

33 The LORD further spoke to Moses and to Aaron, saying,

34 "When you enter the land of Canaan, which I give you for a possession, and I put a mark of leprosy on a house in the land of your possession,

35 then the one who owns the house shall come and tell the priest, saying, '*something* like [a]a mark *of leprosy* has become visible to me in the house.'

36 "The priest shall then order that they empty the house before the priest goes in to look at the mark, so that everything in the house need not become unclean; and afterward the priest shall go in to look at the house.

37 "So he shall look at the mark, and if the mark on the walls of the house has greenish or reddish depressions, and appears deeper than the [1]surface;

38 then the priest shall come out of the house, to the [1]doorway, and [2]quarantine the house for seven days.

39 "And the priest shall return on the seventh day and [1]make an inspection. If the mark has indeed spread in the walls of the house,

40 then the priest shall order them to tear out the stones with the mark in them and throw them away [1]at an unclean place outside the city.

41 "And he shall have the house scraped all around [1]inside, and they shall dump the plaster that they scrape off at an unclean place outside the city.

24 [1]Approx. one pint [a]Lev. 14:10

25 [a]Lev. 14:14

30 [1]Lit., *from those which his hand can reach*

31 [1]Lit., *his hand can reach* [a]Lev. 5:7

32 [1]Lit., *hand does not reach*

35 [a]Ps. 91:10

37 [1]Lit., *wall*

38 [1]Lit., *doorway of the house* [2]Lit., *shut up*

39 [1]Lit., *look*

40 [1]Lit., *to*

41 [1]Lit., *from the house around*

42 "Then they shall take other stones and replace *those*
stones; and he shall take other plaster and replaster the house.
43 "If, however, the mark breaks out again in the house,
after he has torn out the stones and scraped the house, and
after it has been replastered,
44 then the priest shall come in and [1]make an inspection.
If he sees that the mark has indeed spread in the house, it is a
malignant mark in the house; it is unclean.
45 "He shall therefore tear down the house, its stones, and
its timbers, and all the plaster of the house, and he shall take
them outside the city to an [a]unclean place.
46 "Moreover, whoever goes into the house during the time
that he has [1]quarantined it, becomes unclean until evening.
47 "Likewise, whoever lies down in the house shall wash his
clothes, and whoever eats in the house shall wash his clothes.
48 "If, on the other hand, the priest comes in and [1]makes
an inspection, and the mark has not indeed spread in the house
after the house has been replastered, then the priest shall pronounce the house clean because the mark has [2]not reappeared.
49 "To cleanse the house then, he shall take [a]two birds and
cedar wood and a [1]scarlet string and hyssop,
50 and he shall slaughter the one bird in an earthenware
vessel over [1]running water.
51 "Then he shall take the cedar wood and the hyssop and
the [1]scarlet string, with the live bird, and dip them in the blood
of the slain bird, as well as in the [2]running water, and sprinkle
the house seven times.
52 "He shall thus cleanse the house with the blood of the
bird and with the [1]running water, along with the live bird and
with the cedar wood and with the hyssop and with the [2]scarlet
string.
53 "However, he shall let the live bird go free outside the
city into the open field. So he shall make atonement for the
house, and it shall be clean."
54 This is the law for any mark of leprosy—even for a
scale,
55 and for the leprous garment or house,
56 and for a swelling, and for a scab, and for a bright
spot—
57 to teach [1]when they are unclean, and [1]when they are
clean. This is the law of leprosy.

Chapter 15

THE LORD also spoke to Moses and to Aaron, saying,
2 "Speak to the sons of Israel, and say to them, '[a]When
any man has a discharge from his [1]body, [2]his discharge is
unclean.
3 'This, moreover, shall be his uncleanness in his discharge: it is his uncleanness whether his body allows its discharge to flow, or whether his body obstructs its discharge.
4 'Every bed on which the person with the discharge lies
becomes unclean, and everything on which he sits becomes
unclean.
5 'Anyone, moreover, who touches his bed shall wash his
clothes and bathe in water and be unclean until evening;

44 [1]Lit., *look*

45 [a]Lev. 14:41

46 [1]Lit., *shut up*

48 [1]Lit., *looks* [2]Lit., *healed*

49 [1]Lit., *scarlet color* [a]Lev. 14:4

50 [1]Lit., *living*

51 [1]Lit., *scarlet color* [2]Lit., *living*

52 [1]Lit., *living* [2]Lit., *scarlet color*

57 [1]Lit., *in the day of*

2 [1]Lit., *flesh,* and so throughout the chap. [2]Or, *by his discharge, he is unclean* [a]Lev. 22:4; Num. 5:2; 2 Sam. 3:29

6 and whoever sits on the thing on which the man with
the discharge has been sitting, shall wash his clothes and bathe
in water and be unclean until evening.
7 'Also whoever touches the [1]person with the discharge
shall wash his clothes and bathe in water and be unclean until
evening.
8 'Or if the man with the discharge spits on one who is
clean, he too shall wash his clothes and bathe in water and be
unclean until evening.
9 'And every saddle on which the person with the discharge rides becomes unclean.
10 'Whoever then touches any of the things which were
under him shall be unclean until evening, and he who carries
them shall wash his clothes and bathe in water and be unclean
until evening.
11 'Likewise, whomever the one with the discharge touches
without having rinsed his hands in water shall wash his clothes
and bathe in water and be unclean until evening.
12 'However, an [a]earthenware vessel which the person with
the discharge touches shall be broken, and every wooden vessel
shall be rinsed in water.
13 'Now when the man with the discharge becomes
cleansed from his discharge, then he shall count off for himself
seven days for his cleansing; he shall then wash his clothes and
bathe his body in [1]running water and shall become clean.
14 'Then on the eighth day he shall take for himself two
turtledoves or two young pigeons, and come before the LORD
to the doorway of the tent of meeting, and give them to the
priest;
15 and the priest shall offer them, [a]one for a sin offering,
and the other for a burnt offering. So the priest shall make
atonement on his behalf before the LORD because of his
discharge.
16 '[a]Now if a [1]man has a seminal emission, he shall bathe
all his body in water and be unclean until evening.
17 'As for any garment or any leather on which there is
seminal emission, it shall be washed with water and be unclean
until evening.
18 'If a man lies with a woman *so that* there is a seminal
emission, they shall both bathe in water and be [a]unclean until
evening.
19 'When a woman has a discharge *if* her discharge in her
body is blood, she shall continue in her menstrual impurity for
seven days; and whoever touches her shall be unclean until
evening.
20 'Everything also on which she lies during her menstruation impurity shall be unclean, and everything on which she
sits shall be unclean.
21 'And anyone who touches her bed shall wash his clothes
and bathe in water and be unclean until evening.
22 'And whoever touches any thing on which she sits shall
wash his clothes and bathe in water and be unclean until
evening.
23 'Whether it be on the bed or on the thing on which she
is sitting, when he touches it, he shall be unclean until evening.
24 '[a]And if a man actually lies with her, so that her menstru-

7 [1]Lit., *flesh*

12 [a]Lev. 6:28; 11:33

13 [1]Lit., *living*

15 [a]Lev. 5:7

16 [1]Lit., *man's, goes out from him*
[a]Lev. 22:4; Deut. 23:10, 11

18 [a]1 Sam. 21:4

24 [a]Lev. 18:19; 20:18

al impurity is on him, he shall be unclean seven days, and
every bed on which he lies shall be unclean.
25 ‘[a]Now if a woman has a discharge of her blood many
days, not at the period of her menstrual impurity, or if she has
a discharge beyond [1]that period, all the days of her impure
discharge she shall continue as though [2]in her menstrual impurity; she is unclean.
26 ‘Any bed on which she lies all the days of her discharge
shall be to her like [1]her bed at menstruation; and every thing
on which she sits shall be unclean, like [2]her uncleanness at that
time.
27 ‘Likewise, whoever touches them shall be unclean and
shall wash his clothes and bathe in water and be unclean until
evening.
28 ‘When she becomes clean from her discharge, she shall
count off for herself seven days; and afterward she shall be
clean.
29 ‘Then on the eighth day she shall take for herself two
turtledoves or two young pigeons, and bring them in to the
priest, to the doorway of the tent of meeting.
30 ‘And the priest shall offer the [a]one for a sin offering and
the other for a burnt offering. So the priest shall make atonement on her behalf before the LORD because of her impure
discharge.’
31 “Thus you shall keep the sons of Israel separated from
their uncleanness, lest they die in their uncleanness by their
[a]defiling My [1]tabernacle that is among them.”
32 This is the law for the one with a discharge, and for the
man [1]who has a seminal emission so that he is unclean by it,
33 and for the woman who is ill because of menstrual
impurity, and for the one who has a discharge, whether a male
or a female, or a man who lies with an unclean woman.

CHAPTER 16

NOW the LORD spoke to Moses after [a]the death of the two
sons of Aaron, when they had approached the presence of the
LORD and died.
2 And the LORD said to Moses, “Tell your brother Aaron
that he shall not enter [a]at any time into the holy place inside
the veil, before the [1]mercy seat which is on the ark, lest he die;
for [b]I will appear in the cloud over the [1]mercy seat.
3 “Aaron shall enter the holy place with this: with a [1]bull
for a [a]sin offering and a ram for a burnt offering.
4 “He shall put on the [a]holy linen tunic, and the linen
undergarments shall be next to his [1]body, and he shall be
girded with the linen sash, and attired with the linen turban
(these are holy garments). Then he shall [b]bathe his [1]body in
water and put them on.
5 “And he shall take from the congregation of the sons of
Israel [a]two male goats for a sin offering and one ram for a
burnt offering.
6 “Then [a]Aaron shall offer the bull for the sin offering
which is for himself, that he may make atonement for himself
and for his household.

25 [1]Lit., *her menstrual impurity* [2]Lit., *in the days of* [a]Matt. 9:20; Mark 5:25; Luke 8:43

26 [1]Lit., *the bed of her menstrual impurity* [2]Lit., *the uncleanness of her menstrual impurity*

30 [a]Lev. 5:7

31 [1]Or, *dwelling place* [a]Lev. 20:3; Num. 19:13, 20; Ezek. 36:17

32 [1]Lit., *whose seminal emission goes out from him*

1 [a]Lev. 10:1, 2

2 [1]Lit., *propitiatory* [a]Ex. 30:10; Heb. 9:7, 25 [b]Ex. 25:21, 22

3 [1]Or, *bull of the herd* [a]Lev. 16:6; 4:1-12

4 [1]Lit., *flesh* [a]Ex. 28:39, 42 [b]Lev. 16:24

5 [a]Lev. 4:13-21

6 [a]Heb. 5:3

7 "And he shall take the two goats and present them before the LORD at the doorway of the tent of meeting.
8 "And Aaron shall cast lots for the two goats, one lot for
the LORD and the other lot for the [1]scapegoat.
9 "Then Aaron shall offer the goat on which the lot for
the LORD fell, and make it a sin offering.
10 "But the goat on which the lot for the [1]scapegoat fell,
shall be presented alive before the LORD, to make atonement
upon it, to send it into the wilderness as the [1]scapegoat.
11 "Then Aaron shall offer the bull of the sin offering
[a]which is for himself, and make atonement for himself and [b]for
his household, and he shall slaughter the bull of the sin offering which is for himself.
12 "And he shall take a [a]firepan full of coals of fire from
upon the altar before the LORD, and [1]two handfuls of finely
ground [b]sweet incense, and bring *it* inside the veil.
13 "And he shall put the incense on the fire before the
LORD, that the cloud of incense may cover the [1]mercy seat that
is on *the ark of* the testimony, [a]lest he die.
14 "Moreover [a]he shall take some of the blood of the bull
and sprinkle *it* [b]with his finger on the [1]mercy seat on the east
side; also in front of the [1]mercy seat he shall sprinkle some of
the blood with his finger seven times.
15 "Then he shall slaughter the goat of the sin offering
[a]which is for the people, and bring its blood inside the veil, and
do with its blood as he did with the blood of the bull, and
sprinkle it on the [1]mercy seat and in front of the [1]mercy seat.
16 "And [a]he shall make atonement for the holy place, because of the impurities of the sons of Israel, and because of
their transgressions, in regard to all their sins; and thus he shall
do for the tent of meeting which abides with them in the midst
of their impurities.
17 "When he goes in to make atonement in the holy place,
no one shall be in the tent of meeting until he comes out, that
he may make atonement for himself and for his household and
for all the assembly of Israel.
18 "Then he shall go out to the altar that is before the
LORD and make atonement for it, and shall take some of the
blood of the bull and of the blood of the goat, and [a]put it on
the horns of the altar on all sides.
19 "And [a]with his finger he shall sprinkle some of the blood
on it seven times, and cleanse it, and from the impurities of the
sons of Israel consecrate it.
20 "When he finishes atoning for the holy place, and the
tent of meeting and the altar, he shall offer the live goat.
21 "Then Aaron shall lay both of his hands on the head of
the live goat, and [a]confess over it all the iniquities of the sons
of Israel, and all their transgressions [1]in regard to all their sins;
and he shall lay them on the head of the goat and send *it* away
into the wilderness by the hand of a man who *stands* in
readiness.
22 "And the goat shall bear on itself all their iniquities to a
solitary land; and he shall release the goat in the wilderness.
23 "Then Aaron shall come into the tent of meeting, and
take off [a]the linen garments which he put on when he went
into the holy place, and shall leave them there.

8 [1]Lit., *goat of removal*, or else a name: *Azazel*

10 [1]Lit., *goat of removal*, or else a name: *Azazel*

11 [a]Heb. 7:27; 9:7 [b]Lev. 16:33

12 [1]Lit., *the filling of the hollow of his hands* [a]Lev. 10:1 [b]Ex. 30:34-38

13 [1]Lit., *propitiatory* [a]Lev. 22:9; Ex. 28:43; Num. 4:15, 20

14 [1]Lit., *propitiatory* [a]Heb. 9:25 [b]Lev. 4:6, 17

15 [1]Lit., *propitiatory* [a]Heb. 7:27; 9:7

16 [a]Ex. 29:36, 37; 30:10; Heb. 2:17

18 [a]Lev. 4:25; Ezek. 43:20, 22

19 [a]Lev. 16:14

21 [1]Lit., *in addition to* [a]Lev. 5:5

23 [a]Lev. 16:4

24 "And [a]he shall bathe his [1]body with water in a holy place and put on [b]his clothes, and come forth and offer his burnt offering and the burnt offering of the people, and make atonement for himself and for the people.

25 "Then he shall offer up in smoke the fat of the sin offering on the altar.

26 "And the one who released the goat as the [1]scapegoat [a]shall wash his clothes and bathe his [2]body with water; then afterward he shall come into the camp.

27 "But the bull of the sin offering and the goat of the sin offering, [a]whose blood was brought in to make atonement in the holy place, shall be taken outside the camp, and they shall burn their hides, their flesh, and their refuse in the fire.

28 "Then the [a]one who burns them shall wash his clothes and bathe his body with water, then afterward he shall come into the camp.

29 "And *this* shall be a permanent statute for you: [a]in the seventh month, on the tenth day of the month, you shall humble your souls, and not [b]do any work, whether the native, or the alien who sojourns among you;

30 for it is on this day that [1]atonement shall be made for you to cleanse you; you shall be clean from all your sins before the LORD.

31 "It is to be a sabbath of solemn rest for you, that you may [a]humble your souls; it is a permanent statute.

32 "So the priest who is anointed and [1]ordained to serve as priest in his father's place shall make atonement: he shall thus put on [a]the linen garments, the holy garments,

33 and make atonement for the holy sanctuary; and he shall make atonement for the tent of meeting and for the altar. He shall also make atonement for [a]the priests and for all the people of the assembly.

34 "Now you shall have this as a permanent statute, to [a]make atonement for the sons of Israel for all their sins once every year." And just as the LORD had commanded Moses, *so* he did.

CHAPTER 17

THEN the LORD spoke to Moses, saying,

2 "Speak to Aaron and to his sons, and to all the sons of Israel, and say to them, 'This is what the LORD has commanded, saying,

3 "Any man from the house of Israel who slaughters an ox, or a lamb, or a goat in the camp, or who slaughters it outside the camp,

4 and [a]has not brought it to the doorway of the tent of meeting to present *it* as an offering to the LORD before the [1]tabernacle of the LORD, bloodguiltiness is to be reckoned to that man. He has shed blood and that man shall be cut off from among his people.

5 "[1]The reason is so that the sons of Israel may bring their sacrifices which they were sacrificing in the open field, that they may bring them in to the LORD, at the doorway of the tent of meeting to the priest, and sacrifice them as sacrifices of peace offerings to the LORD.

24 [1]Lit., *flesh* [a]Lev. 16:4 [b]Ex. 28:40, 41

26 [1]Lit., *goat of removal*, or else a name: *Azazel* [2]Lit., *flesh* [a]Lev. 11:25, 40

27 [a]Heb. 13:11

28 [a]Num. 19:8

29 [a]Lev. 23:27 [b]Ex. 31:14, 15

30 [1]Lit., *he shall make*

31 [a]Lev. 23:32; Ezra 8:21; Is. 58:3, 5; Dan. 10:12

32 [1]Lit., *whose hand is filled* [a]Lev. 16:4

33 [a]Lev. 16:11

34 [a]Heb. 9:7

4 [1]Lit., *dwelling place* [a]Deut. 12:5-21

5 [1]Lit., *In order that*

6 "And the priest shall sprinkle the blood on the altar of
the LORD at the doorway of the tent of meeting, and offer up
the fat in smoke as a soothing aroma to the LORD.
7 "And [a]they shall no longer sacrifice their sacrifices to the
[1]goat demons with which they play the harlot. This shall be a
permanent statute to them throughout their generations." '
8 "Then you shall say to them, 'Any man from the house
of Israel, or from the aliens who sojourn among them, who
offers a burnt offering or sacrifice,
9 and [a]does not bring it to the doorway of the tent of
meeting to [1]offer it to the LORD, that man also shall be cut off
from his people.
10 '[a]And any man from the house of Israel, or from the
aliens who sojourn among them, who eats any blood, [b]I will set
My face against that person who eats blood, and will cut him
off from among his people.
11 'For [a]the [1]life of the flesh is in the blood, and I have
given it to you on the altar to make atonement for your souls;
for it is the blood by reason of the [1]life that makes atonement.'
12 "Therefore I said to the sons of Israel, 'No person
among you may eat blood, nor may any alien who sojourns
among you eat blood.'
13 "So when any man from the sons of Israel, or from the
aliens who sojourn among them, [1]in hunting catches a beast or
a bird which may be eaten, [a]he shall pour out its blood and
cover it with earth.
14 "[a]For *as for the* [1]life of all flesh, its blood is *identified*
with its [1]life. Therefore I said to the sons of Israel, 'You are
not to eat the blood of any flesh, for the [1]life of all flesh is its
blood; whoever eats it shall be cut off.'
15 "[a]And when any person eats *an animal* which dies, or is
torn *by beasts,* whether he is a native or an alien, he shall wash
his clothes and bathe in water, and remain unclean until evening; then he will become clean.
16 "But if he does not wash *them* or bathe his body, then
he shall bear his [1]guilt."

CHAPTER 18

THEN the LORD spoke to Moses, saying,
2 "Speak to the sons of Israel and say to them, '[a]I am the
LORD your God.
3 'You shall not do [1]what is [a]done in the land of Egypt
where you lived, nor are you to do [1]what is [b]done in the land of
Canaan where I am bringing you; you shall not walk in their
statutes.
4 'You are to perform My judgments and keep My statutes, [1]to live in accord with them; [a]I am the LORD your God.
5 'So you shall keep My statutes and My judgments, [a]by
which a man may live if he does them; I am the LORD.
6 'None of you shall approach any blood relative [1]of his
to uncover nakedness; I am the LORD.
7 '[a]You shall not uncover the nakedness of your father,
that is, the nakedness of your mother. She is your mother; you
are not to uncover her nakedness.

7 [1]Or, *goat-idols* [a]Ex. 22:20; 32:8; 34:15; Deut. 32:17; 2 Chr. 11:15

9 [1]Lit., *do* [a]Lev. 17:4; Ex. 20:24

10 [a]Lev. 3:17; 7:26, 27; Deut. 12:16, 23-25 [b]Lev. 20:3, 6

11 [1]Lit., *soul* [a]Lev. 17:14; Gen. 9:4

13 [1]Lit., *who in hunting* [a]Deut. 12:16

14 [1]Lit., *soul* [a]Lev. 17:11

15 [a]Lev. 7:24; 22:8; Ex. 22:31

16 [1]Or, *iniquity*

2 [a]Lev. 11:44

3 [1]Lit., *according to the deed of* [a]Ezek. 20:7, 8 [b]Lev. 18:24-30; 20:23

4 [1]Lit., *to walk in them* [a]Lev. 18:2

5 [a]Gal. 3:12; Luke 10:28; Rom. 10:5; Ezek. 20:11

6 [1]Lit., *of his flesh*

7 [a]Lev. 20:11; Deut. 27:20; Ezek. 22:10

8 'You shall not uncover the nakedness of your father's
wife; it is your father's nakedness.
9 '[a]The nakedness of your sister, *either* your father's daughter or your mother's daughter, whether born at home or born
outside, their nakedness you shall not uncover.
10 'The nakedness of your son's daughter or your daughter's daughter, their nakedness you shall not uncover; for
[1]their nakedness is yours.
11 'The nakedness of your father's wife's daughter, [1]born
to your father, she is your sister, you shall not uncover her
nakedness.
12 '[a]You shall not uncover the nakedness of your father's
sister; she is your father's blood relative.
13 'You shall not uncover the nakedness of your mother's
sister, for she is your mother's blood relative.
14 '[a]You shall not uncover the nakedness of your father's
brother; you shall not approach his wife, she is your aunt.
15 '[a]You shall not uncover the nakedness of your daughter-
in-law; she is your son's wife, you shall not uncover her
nakedness.
16 '[a]You shall not uncover the nakedness of your brother's
wife; it is your brother's nakedness.
17 '[a]You shall not uncover the nakedness of a woman and
of her daughter, nor shall you take her son's daughter or her
daughter's daughter, to uncover her nakedness; they are blood
relatives. It is [1]lewdness.
18 'And you shall not [1]marry a woman in addition to [2]her
sister [3]as a rival while she is alive, to uncover her nakedness.
19 '[a]Also you shall not approach a woman to uncover her
nakedness during her [b]menstrual impurity.
20 '[a]And you shall not have intercourse with your neighbor's wife, to be defiled with her.
21 'Neither shall you give any of your offspring [a]to [1]offer
them to Molech, nor shall you [b]profane the name of your
God; I am the LORD.
22 '[a]You shall not lie with a male as [1]one lies with a female;
it is an abomination.
23 '[a]Also you shall not have intercourse with any animal to
be defiled with it, nor shall any woman stand before an animal
to [1]mate with it; it is a perversion.
24 'Do not defile yourselves by any of these things; for by
all these [a]the nations which I am casting out before you have
become defiled.
25 'For the land has become defiled, [a]therefore I have visited its [1]punishment upon it, so the land [b]has spewed out its
inhabitants.
26 'But as for you, you are to keep My statutes and My
judgments, and shall not do any of these abominations, *neither*
the native, nor the alien who sojourns among you;
27 (for the men of the land who have been before you
have done all these abominations, and the land has become
defiled);
28 so that the land may not spew you out should you
defile it, as it has spewed out the nation which has been before
you.

9 [a]Lev. 18:11; 20:17; Deut. 27:22
10 [1]Lit., *they are your nakedness*
11 [1]Lit., *begotten of*
12 [a]Lev. 20:19
14 [a]Lev. 20:20
15 [a]Lev. 20:12
16 [a]Lev. 20:21
17 [1]Or, *wickedness* [a]Lev. 20:14
18 [1]Lit., *take a wife* [2]Or, *another* [3]Lit., *to be*
19 [a]Lev. 15:24; 20:18 [b]Lev. 12:2
20 [a]Lev. 20:10
21 [1]Lit., *cause to pass over* [a]Lev. 20:2-5; Deut. 12:31 [b]Lev. 19:12; 20:3; 21:6
22 [1]Lit., *those who* [a]Lev. 20:13; Deut. 23:18
23 [1]Or, *lie* [a]Ex. 22:19; Lev. 20:15, 16; Deut. 27:21
24 [a]Lev. 18:3
25 [1]Lit., *iniquity* [a]Lev. 20:23; Deut. 9:5; 18:12 [b]Lev. 18:28; 20:22

29 'For whoever does any of these abominations, [1]those
persons who do *so* shall be cut off from among their people.
30 'Thus you are to keep [a]My charge, that you do not
practice any of the abominable customs which have been practiced before you, so as not to defile yourselves with them; [b]I
am the LORD your God.' "

CHAPTER 19

THEN the LORD spoke to Moses, saying,
2 "Speak to all the congregation of the sons of Israel and
say to them, '[a]You shall be holy, for I the LORD your God am
holy.
3 'Every one of you shall reverence his mother and his
father, and you shall keep [a]My sabbaths; [b]I am the LORD your
God.
4 'Do not turn to [a]idols or make for yourselves molten
[b]gods; I am the LORD your God.
5 'Now when you offer a sacrifice of peace offerings to
the LORD, you shall offer it so that you may be accepted.
6 'It shall be eaten the same day you offer *it*, and the next
day; but what remains until the third day shall be burned with
fire.
7 'So if it is eaten at all on the third day, it is an offense; it
will not be accepted.
8 'And everyone who eats it will bear his iniquity, for he
has profaned the holy thing of the LORD; and that person shall
be cut off from his people.
9 '[a]Now when you reap the harvest of your land, you shall
not reap to the very corners of your field, neither shall you
gather the gleanings of your harvest.
10 'Nor shall you glean your vineyard, nor shall you gather
the fallen fruit of your vineyard; you shall leave them for the
needy and for the stranger. I am the LORD your God.
11 '[a]You shall not steal, nor deal falsely, nor lie to one
another.
12 '[a]And you shall not swear falsely by My name, so as to
[b]profane the name of your God; I am the LORD.
13 '[a]You shall not oppress your neighbor, nor rob *him*.
[b]The wages of a hired man are not to remain with you all night
until morning.
14 'You shall not curse a deaf man, nor [a]place a stumbling
block before the blind, but you shall revere your God; I am the
LORD.
15 '[a]You shall do no injustice in judgment; you shall not be
partial to the poor nor defer to the great, but you are to judge
your neighbor fairly.
16 'You shall not go about as [a]a slanderer among your
people, and you are not to [1]act against the [2b]life of your neighbor; I am the LORD.
17 'You [a]shall not hate your [1]fellow-countryman in your
heart; you [b]may surely reprove your neighbor, but shall not
incur sin because of him.
18 '[a]You shall not take vengeance, [b]nor bear any grudge
against the sons of your people, but [c]you shall love your neighbor as yourself; I am the LORD.

29 [1]Or, *and the*

30 [1]Lev. 22:9; Deut. 11:1 [b]Lev. 18:2

2 [a]1 Pet. 1:16

3 [a]Ex. 20:8 [b]Lev. 11:44

4 [a]Lev. 26:1; Ps. 96:5; 115:4-7 [b]Ex. 20:23; 34:17

9 [a]Lev. 23:22; Deut. 24:20-22

11 [a]Ex. 20:15, 16

12 [a]Ex. 20:7 [b]Lev. 18:21

13 [a]Ex. 22:7-15, 21-27 [b]Deut. 24:15

14 [a]Deut. 27:18

15 [a]Ex. 23:3, 6; Deut. 1:17; 10:17

16 [1]Lit., *stand* [2]Lit., *blood* [a]Ps. 15:3; Jer. 6:28; 9:4; Ezek. 22:9 [b]Ex. 23:7; Deut. 27:25

17 [1]Lit., *brother* [a]1 John 2:9, 11; 3:15 [b]Matt. 18:15; Luke 17:3

18 [a]Deut. 32:35; Rom. 12:19; Heb. 10:30 [b]Ps. 103:9 [c]Matt. 19:19; Mark 12:31; Luke 10:27; Rom. 13:9

19 'You are to keep My statutes. You shall not breed together two kinds of your cattle; [a]you shall not sow your field with
two kinds of seed, nor wear a garment upon you of two kinds
of material mixed together.
20 '[a]Now if a man lies carnally with a woman who is a slave
acquired for *another* man, but who has in no way been redeemed, nor given her freedom, there shall be punishment;
they shall not, *however,* be put to death, because she was not
free.
21 'And he shall bring his guilt offering to the LORD to the
doorway of the tent of meeting, [a]a ram for a guilt offering.
22 'The priest shall also make atonement for him with the
ram of the guilt offering before the LORD for his sin which he
has committed, and the sin which he has committed shall be
forgiven him.
23 'And when you enter the land and plant all kinds of
trees for food, then you shall count their fruit as [1]forbidden.
Three years it shall be [1]forbidden to you; *it* shall not be eaten.
24 'But in the fourth year all its fruit shall be holy, an
offering of praise to the LORD.
25 'And in the fifth year you are to eat of its fruit, that its
yield may increase for you; I am the LORD your God.
26 'You shall not eat *anything* [a]with the blood, nor practice [b]divination or soothsaying.
27 '[a]You shall not round off the side-growth of your heads,
nor harm the edges of your beard.
28 'You shall not make any cuts in your [1]body for the
[2]dead, nor make any tattoo marks on yourselves: I am the
LORD.
29 '[a]Do not [1]profane your daughter by making her a harlot, so that the land may not fall to harlotry, and the land
become full of lewdness.
30 'You shall [a]keep My sabbaths and [b]revere My sanctuary;
I am the LORD.
31 '[a]Do not turn to [a]mediums or spiritists; do not seek
them out to be defiled by them. I am the LORD your God.
32 '[a]You shall rise up before the grayheaded, and honor
the [1]aged, and you shall revere your God; I am the LORD.
33 '[a]When a stranger resides with you in your land, you
shall not do him wrong.
34 'The stranger who resides with you shall be to you as the
native among you, and [a]you shall love him as yourself; for you
were aliens in the land of Egypt: I am the LORD your God.
35 '[a]You shall do no wrong in judgment, in measurement
of weight, or capacity.
36 'You shall have just balances, just weights, a just [1]ephah,
and a just [2]hin: I am the LORD your God, who brought you out
from the land of Egypt.
37 'You shall thus observe all My statutes, and all My
ordinances, and do them: I am the LORD.' "

CHAPTER 20

THEN the LORD spoke to Moses, saying,
2 "You shall also say to the sons of Israel, 'Any man from
the sons of Israel or from the aliens sojourning in Israel, [a]who

19 [a]Deut. 22:9, 11
20 [a]Deut. 22:23-27
21 [a]Lev. 6:1-7
23 [1]Lit., *uncircumcised*
26 [a]Lev. 17:10 [b]Deut. 18:10
27 [a]Lev. 21:5
28 [1]Lit., *flesh* [2]Lit., *soul*
29 [1]Or, *degrade* [a]Lev. 21:9; Deut. 22:21; 23:17, 18
30 [a]Lev. 19:3 [b]Lev. 26:2
31 [1]Or, *ghosts or spirits* [a]Lev. 20:6, 27; Deut. 18:11
32 [1]Lit., *face of the aged* [a]Lam. 5:12
33 [a]Ex. 22:21
34 [a]Lev. 19:18
35 [a]Deut. 25:13-16
36 [1]Approx. one bushel [2]Approx. one gallon
2 [a]Lev. 18:21

gives any of his [1]offspring to Molech, shall surely be put to
death; [b]the people of the land shall stone him with stones.
3 'I will also set My face against that man and will cut him
off from among his people, because he has given some of his
[1]offspring to Molech, [a]so as to defile My sanctuary and [b]to
profane My holy name.
4 'If the people of the land, however, [1]should ever disregard
that man when he gives any of his [2]offspring to Molech,
so as not to put him to death,
5 then I Myself will set My face against that man and
against his family; and I will cut off from among their people
both him and all those who play the harlot after him, by
playing the harlot after Molech.
6 'As for the person who turns to [1a]mediums and to spiritists, to play the harlot after them, I will also set My face
against that person and will cut him off from among his
people.
7 'You shall consecrate yourselves therefore and [a]be holy,
for I am the LORD your God.
8 'And you shall keep My statutes and practice them; I
am the LORD who sanctifies you.
9 '[a]If *there* is anyone who curses his father or his mother,
he shall surely be put to death; he has cursed his father or his
mother, his bloodguiltiness is upon him.
10 '[a]If *there is* a man who commits adultery with another
man's wife, one who commits adultery with his friend's wife,
the adulterer and the adulteress shall surely be put to death.
11 '[a]If *there is* a man who lies with his father's wife he has
uncovered his father's nakedness; both of them shall surely be
put to death, their bloodguiltiness is upon them.
12 '[a]If *there is* a man who lies with his daughter-in-law,
both of them shall surely be put to death; they have committed [1]incest, their bloodguiltiness is upon them.
13 '[a]If *there is* a man who lies with a male as those who lie
with a woman, both of them have committed a detestable act;
they shall surely be put to death. Their bloodguiltiness is upon
them.
14 '[a]If *there is* a man who [1]marries a woman and her mother, it is immorality; both he and they shall be burned with
fire, that there may be no immorality in your midst.
15 '[a]If *there is* a man who lies with an animal, he shall
surely be put to death; you shall also kill the animal.
16 'If *there is* a woman who approaches any animal to
[1]mate with it, you shall kill the woman and the animal; they
shall surely be put to death. Their bloodguiltiness is upon
them.
17 '[a]If *there is* a man who takes his sister, his father's daughter or his mother's daughter, so that he sees her nakedness
and she sees his nakedness, it is a disgrace; and they shall be cut
off in the sight of the sons of their people. He has uncovered
his sister's nakedness; he bears his guilt.
18 '[a]If *there is* a man who lies with a [1]menstruous woman
and uncovers her nakedness, he has laid bare her flow, and she
has [2]exposed the flow of her blood; thus both of them shall be
cut off from among their people.
19 '[a]You shall also not uncover the nakedness of your moth-

2 [1]Lit., *seed* [b]Lev. 20:27; 24:14-23; Num. 15:35, 36; Deut. 21:21

3 [1]Lit., *seed* [a]Lev. 15:31 [b]Lev. 18:21

4 [1]Lit., *hiding they hide their eyes from* [2]Lit., *seed*

6 [1]Or, *ghosts and spirits* [a]Lev. 19:31

7 [a]1 Pet. 1:16

9 [a]Ex. 21:17; Deut. 27:16

10 [a]Lev. 18:20; Ex. 20:14; Deut. 5:18

11 [a]Lev. 18:7, 8

12 [1]Lit., *confusion;* i.e., a violation of divine order [a]Lev. 18:15

13 [a]Lev. 18:22

14 [1]Lit., *takes* [a]Deut. 27:23

15 [a]Lev. 18:23

16 [1]Lit., *lie*

17 [a]Lev. 18:9

18 [1]Lit., *sick* [2]Or, *uncovered* [a]Lev. 15:24; 18:19

19 [a]Lev. 18:12, 13

er's sister or of your father's sister, for such a one has made
naked his [1]blood relative; they shall bear their guilt.
20 '[a]If *there is* a man who lies with his uncle's wife he has
uncovered his uncle's nakedness; they shall bear their sin. They
shall die childless.
21 '[a]If *there is* a man who takes his brother's wife, it is
[1]abhorrent; he has uncovered his brother's nakedness. They
shall be childless.
22 'You are therefore to keep all My statutes and all My
ordinances and do them, so that the land to which I am bringing you to [1]live will not [a]spew you out.
23 'Moreover, you shall not [1]follow [a]the customs of the
nation which I shall drive out before you, for they did all these
things, and [b]therefore I have abhorred them.
24 'Hence I have said to you, "[a]You are to possess their
land, and I Myself will give it to you to possess it, a land
flowing with milk and honey." I am the LORD your God, who
has [b]separated you from the peoples.
25 '[a]You are therefore to make a distinction between the
clean animal and the unclean, and between the unclean bird
and the clean; and you shall not make [1]yourselves detestable
by animal or by bird or by anything [2]that creeps on the ground,
which I have separated for you as unclean.
26 'Thus you are to be holy to Me, for I the LORD am holy;
and I [a]have set you apart from the peoples to be Mine.
27 'As for a man or a woman, [a]if there is a [1]medium or a
spiritist among them, they shall surely be put to death; they
shall be stoned with stones, their bloodguiltiness is upon
them.' "

CHAPTER 21

THEN the LORD said to Moses, "Speak to the priests, the
sons of Aaron, and say to them, '[a]No one shall defile himself
for a *dead* person among his people,
2 [a]except for his relatives who are nearest to him, his
mother and his father and his son and his daughter and his
brother,
3 also for his virgin sister, who is near to him [1]because she
has had no husband; for her he may defile himself.
4 'He shall not defile himself as a [1]relative by marriage
among his people, and so profane himself.
5 '[a]They shall not make any baldness on their heads, [b]nor
shave off the edges of their beards, [c]nor make any cuts in their
flesh.
6 'They shall be holy to their God and [a]not profane the
name of their God, for they present the offerings by fire [1]to
the LORD, [b]the bread of their God; so they shall be holy.
7 '[a]They shall not take a woman who is profaned by harlotry, nor shall they take a woman divorced from her husband;
for he is holy to his God.
8 'You shall consecrate him, therefore, for he offers [a]the
bread of your God; he shall be holy to you; for I the LORD,
who sanctifies you, am holy.
9 '[a]Also the daughter of any priest, if she profanes herself

19 [1]Lit., *flesh*
20 [a]Lev. 18:14
21 [1]Or, *an impure deed* [a]Lev. 18:16
22 [1]Lit., *dwell in it* [a]Lev. 18:28
23 [1]Lit., *walk in the statutes* [a]Lev. 18:3 [b]Lev. 18:25
24 [a]Ex. 13:5; 33:3 [b]Lev. 20:26; Ex. 33:16
25 [1]Lit., *your souls* [2]Lit., *with which the ground creeps* [a]Lev. 10:10; 11:1-47; Deut. 14:3-21
26 [a]Lev. 20:24
27 [1]Or, *ghost or familiar spirit with them* [a]Lev. 19:31
1 [a]Lev. 19:28; Ezek. 44:25
2 [a]Lev. 21:11
3 [1]Or, *whom no man has had*
4 [1]Lit., *husband among*
5 [a]Deut. 14:1; Ezek. 44:20 [b]Lev. 19:27 [c]Deut. 14:1
6 [1]Lit., of [a]Lev. 18:21 [b]Lev. 3:11
7 [a]Lev. 21:13, 14
8 [a]Lev. 21:6
9 [a]Lev. 19:29

by harlotry, she profanes her father; she shall be burned with
fire.
10 'And the priest who is the highest among his brothers,
on whose head the anointing oil has been poured, and [1]who
has been consecrated to wear the garments, [a]shall not [2]uncover
his head, nor tear his clothes;
11 [a]nor shall he approach any dead person, nor defile himself *even* for his father or his mother;
12 [a]nor shall he go out of the sanctuary, nor profane the
sanctuary of his God; for [b]the consecration of the anointing oil
of his God is on him: I am the LORD.
13 'And he shall take a wife in her virginity.
14 '[a]A widow, or a divorced woman, or one who is profaned by harlotry, these he may not take; but rather he is to
[1]marry a virgin of his own people;
15 that he may not profane his [1]offspring among his
people: for I am the LORD who sanctifies him.' "
16 Then the LORD spoke to Moses, saying,
17 "Speak to Aaron, saying, 'No man of your [1]offspring
throughout their generations who has a defect shall approach
to offer the [a]bread of his God.
18 '[a]For no one who has a defect shall approach: a blind
man, or a lame man, or he who has a [a]disfigured *face*, or any
deformed *limb*,
19 or a man who has a broken foot or broken hand,
20 or a hunchback or a dwarf, or *one who has* a [1]defect in
his eye or eczema or scabs or [a]crushed testicles.
21 'No man among the [1]descendants of Aaron the priest,
who has a defect, is to come near to offer the LORD's offerings
by fire; *since* he has a defect, he shall not come near to offer
[a]the bread of his God.
22 'He may eat [a]the bread of his God, *both* of the most
holy and of the holy,
23 only he shall not go in to the veil or come near the altar
because he has a defect, that he may not profane My sanctuaries. For I am the LORD who sanctifies them.' "
24 So Moses spoke to Aaron and to his sons and to all the
sons of Israel.

CHAPTER 22

THEN the LORD spoke to Moses, saying,
2 "Tell Aaron and his sons to be careful with the holy *gifts*
of the sons of Israel, which they dedicate to Me, so as not to
profane My holy name; I am the LORD.
3 "Say to them, '[a]If any man among all your [1]descendants
throughout your generations approaches the holy *gifts* which
the sons of Israel dedicate to the LORD, while he has an uncleanness, that person shall be cut off from before Me. I am
the LORD.
4 '[a]No man of the [1]descendants of Aaron who is a leper,
or who has a discharge, may eat of the holy *gifts* until he is
clean. [b]And if one touches anything made unclean by a corpse
or if [c]a man has a seminal emission,
5 or [a]if a man touches any teeming things, by which he is

10 [1]Lit., *whose hand has been filled* [2]Lit., *unbind* [a]Lev. 10:6, 7
11 [a]Lev. 19:28
12 [a]Lev. 10:7 [b]Ex. 29:6, 7
14 [1]Lit., *take as wife* [a]Lev. 21:7; Ezek. 44:22
15 [1]Lit., *seed*
17 [1]Lit., *seed* [a]Lev. 21:6
18 [1]Lit., *slit* [a]Lev. 22:19-25
20 [1]Lit., *obscurity* [a]Deut. 23:1; Is. 56:3-5
21 [1]Lit., *seed* [a]Lev. 21:6
22 [a]1 Cor. 9:13
3 [1]Lit., *seed* [a]Lev. 7:20, 21; Num. 19:13
4 [1]Lit., *seed* [a]Lev. 14:1-32 [b]Lev. 11:24-28, 39, 40 [c]Lev. 15:16, 17
5 [a]Lev. 11:24-28

made unclean, or any man by whom he is made unclean,
whatever his uncleanness;
6 a [1]person who touches any such shall be unclean until
evening, and shall not eat of the holy *gifts,* unless he has
bathed his [2]body in water.
7 'But when the sun sets, he shall be clean, and afterward
he shall eat of the holy *gifts,* for it is his [1]food.
8 'He shall not eat [a]*an animal* which dies or is torn *by*
beasts, becoming unclean by it; I am the LORD.
9 'They shall therefore keep [a]My charge, so that [b]they
may not bear sin because of it, and die thereby because they
profane it; I am the LORD who sanctifies them.
10 '[a]No [1]layman, however, is to eat the holy *gift;* a sojourner with the priest or a hired man shall not eat of the holy *gift.*
11 '[a]But if a priest buys a [1]slave as *his* property with his
money, [2]that one may eat of it, and those who are born in his
house may eat of his [3]food.
12 'And if a priest's daughter is married to a [1]layman, she
shall not eat of the [2]offering of the *gifts.*
13 'But if a priest's daughter becomes a widow or divorced,
and has no child and returns to her father's house as in her
youth, she shall eat of her father's [1]food; [a]but no [2]layman shall
eat of it.
14 '[a]But if a man eats a holy *gift* unintentionally, then he
shall add to it a fifth of it and shall give the holy *gift* to the
priest.
15 'And they shall not profane the holy *gifts* of the sons of
Israel which they offer to the LORD,
16 and *so* cause them [a]to bear [1]punishment for guilt by
eating their holy *gifts;* for I am the LORD who sanctifies
them.' "
17 Then the LORD spoke to Moses, saying,
18 "Speak to Aaron and to his sons and to all the sons of
Israel, and say to them, 'When any man of the house of Israel
or of the aliens in Israel, who presents his offering, whether it is
any of their [1]votive or any of their freewill offerings, which
they present to the LORD for a burnt offering,
19 [a]for you to be accepted, *it must be* a male without
defect from the cattle, the sheep, or the goats.
20 'Whatever has a defect, you shall not offer, for it will
not be accepted for you.
21 'And when a man offers a sacrifice of peace offerings to
the LORD to [1]fulfill a special vow, or for a freewill offering, of
the herd or of the flock, it must be perfect to be accepted;
there shall be no defect in it.
22 'Those *that are* blind or fractured or maimed or having
a running sore or eczema or scabs, you shall not offer to the
LORD, nor make of them an offering by fire on the altar to the
LORD.
23 'In respect to an ox or a lamb which has an [1]overgrown
or stunted *member,* you may present it for a freewill offering,
but for a vow it shall not be accepted.
24 'Also [a]anything *with its testicles* bruised or crushed or
torn or cut, you shall not offer to the Lord, or [1]sacrifice in your
land,
25 nor shall you accept any such from the hand of a foreign-

6 [1]Lit., *soul* [2]Lit., *flesh*
7 [1]Lit., *bread*
8 [a]Lev. 7:24; 11:39, 40; 17:15
9 [a]Lev. 18:30 [b]Lev. 22:16
10 [1]Lit., *stranger* [a]Lev. 22:13; Ex. 29:33
11 [1]Lit., *soul* [2]Lit., *he may* [3]Lit., *bread* [a]Gen. 17:13; Ex. 12:44
12 [1]Lit., *stranger* [2]Lit., *heave offering*
13 [1]Lit., *bread* [2]Lit., *stranger* [a]Lev. 22:10
14 [a]Lev. 5:15, 16
16 [1]Or, *iniquity requiring a guilt offering* [a]Lev. 22:9; 10:17
18 [1]Lit., *vows*
19 [a]Lev. 21:18-21; Deut. 15:21
21 [1]Or, *make a special votive offering*
23 [1]Or, *deformed*
24 [1]Lit., *do* [a]Lev. 21:20

er for offering [a]as the [1]food of your God; for their corruption
is in them, they have a defect, they shall not be accepted for
you.' "
26 Then the LORD spoke to Moses, saying,
27 "When an ox or a sheep or a goat is born, it shall [1]re-
main [a]seven days [2]with its mother, and from the eighth day on
it shall be accepted as a sacrifice of an offering by fire to the
LORD.
28 "[a]But, *whether* it is an ox or a sheep, you shall not kill
both it and its young in one day.
29 "And when you sacrifice [a]a sacrifice of thanksgiving to
the LORD, you shall sacrifice it so that you may be accepted.
30 "It shall be eaten on the same day, you shall leave none
of it until morning: I am the LORD.
31 "So you shall keep My commandments, and do them: I
am the LORD.
32 "And you shall not profane My holy name, but I will be
sanctified among the sons of Israel: I am the LORD who sanctifies you,
33 [a]who brought you out from the land of Egypt, to be
your God: I am the LORD."

CHAPTER 23

THE LORD spoke again to Moses, saying,
2 "Speak to the sons of Israel, and say to them, '[a]The
LORD's appointed times which you shall [b]proclaim as holy convocations—My appointed times are these:
3 '[a]For six days work may be done; but on the seventh day
there is a sabbath of complete rest, a holy convocation. You
shall not do any work; it is a sabbath to the LORD in all your
dwellings.
4 'These are the [a]appointed times of the LORD, holy convocations which you shall proclaim at the times appointed for
them.
5 '[a]In the first month, on the fourteenth day of the
month [1]at twilight is the LORD's Passover.
6 'Then on the fifteenth day of the same month there is
the Feast of Unleavened Bread to the LORD; for seven days
you shall eat unleavened bread.
7 'On the first day you shall have a holy convocation; you
shall [a]not do any laborious work.
8 'But for seven days you shall present an offering by fire
to the LORD. On the seventh day is a holy convocation; you
shall not do any laborious work.' "
9 Then the LORD spoke to Moses, saying,
10 "Speak to the sons of Israel, and say to them, 'When
you enter the land which I am going to give to you and [a]reap
its harvest, then you shall bring in the sheaf of the first fruits of
your harvest to the priest.
11 'And he shall wave the sheaf before the LORD for you to
be accepted; on the day after the sabbath the priest shall wave
it.
12 'Now on the day when you wave the sheaf, you shall
offer a male lamb one year old without defect for a burnt
offering to the LORD.

25 [1]Lit., *bread* [a]Lev. 21:22

27 [1]Lit., *be* [2]Lit., *under* [a]Ex. 22:30

28 [a]Deut. 22:6, 7

29 [a]Lev. 7:12

33 [a]Lev. 11:45

2 [a]Lev. 23:4, 37, 44; Num. 29:39 [b]Lev. 23:21

3 [a]Lev. 19:3; Ex. 31:13-17; 35:2,3

4 [a]Lev. 23:2

5 [1]Lit., *between the two evenings* [a]Ex. 12:18, 19; Num. 28:16-25

7 [a]Lev. 23:8, 21, 25, 35, 36

10 [a]Ex. 23:19; 34:26

13 [1]Approx. one gallon [a]Lev. 6:20

14 [a]Ex. 34:26; Num. 15:20, 21

15 [a]Num. 28:26-31; Deut. 16:9-12

16 [a]Num. 28:26

17 [1]An ephah is assumed [a]Lev. 2:12; 7:13

19 [a]Num. 28:30

21 [a]Lev. 23:2, 4 [b]Lev. 23:7

22 [a]Lev. 19:9

24 [1]Lit., *sabbath rest* [a]Num. 29:1 [b]Num. 10:9, 10

25 [a]Lev. 23:21

27 [a]Lev. 16:29; 25:9; Num. 29:7 [b]Lev. 23:28

28 [a]Lev. 23:27 [b]Lev. 16:34

29 [1]Lit., *soul*

13 'Its [a]grain offering shall then be two-tenths *of an ephah* of fine flour mixed with oil, an offering by fire to the LORD *for* a soothing aroma, with its libation, a fourth of a [1]hin of wine.

14 'Until this same day, until you have brought in the offering of your God, [a]you shall eat neither bread nor roasted grain nor new growth. It is to be a perpetual statute throughout your generations in all your dwelling places.

15 '[a]You shall also count for yourselves from the day after the sabbath, from the day when you brought in the sheaf of the wave offering; there shall be seven complete sabbaths.

16 'You shall count fifty days to the day after the seventh sabbath; then you shall present a [a]new grain offering to the LORD.

17 'You shall bring in from your dwelling places two *loaves* of bread for a wave offering, made of two-tenths *of a* [1]*bushel*; they shall be of a fine flour, baked [a]with leaven as first fruits to the LORD.

18 'Along with the bread, you shall present seven one year old male lambs without defect, and a bull of the herd, and two rams; they are to be a burnt offering to the LORD, with their grain offering and their libations, an offering by fire of a soothing aroma to the LORD.

19 'You shall also offer [a]one male goat for a sin offering and two male lambs one year old for a sacrifice of peace offerings.

20 'The priest shall then wave them with the bread of the first fruits for a wave offering with two lambs before the LORD; they are to be holy to the LORD for the priest.

21 'On this same day you shall [a]make a proclamation as well; you are to have a holy convocation. You shall do no laborious [b]work. It is to be a perpetual statute in all your dwelling places throughout your generations.

22 '[a]When you reap the harvest of your land, moreover, you shall not reap to the very corners of your field, nor gather the gleaning of your harvest; you are to leave them for the needy and the alien. I am the LORD your God.' "

23 Again the LORD spoke to Moses, saying,

24 "Speak to the sons of Israel, saying, '[a]In the seventh month on the first of the month, you shall have a [1]rest, a [b]reminder by blowing *of trumpets*, a holy convocation.

25 'You shall [a]not do any laborious work, but you shall present an offering by fire to the LORD.' "

26 And the LORD spoke to Moses, saying,

27 "On exactly [a]the tenth day of this seventh month is [b]the day of atonement; it shall be a holy convocation for you, and you shall humble your souls and present an offering by fire to the LORD.

28 "Neither shall you do any work on this same day, for it is a [a]day of atonement, [b]to make atonement on your behalf before the LORD your God.

29 "If there is any [1]person who will not humble himself on this same day, he shall be cut off from his people.

30 "As for any person who does any work on this same day, that person I will destroy from among his people.

31 "You shall do no work at all. It is to be a perpetual

statute throughout your generations in all your dwelling places.
32 "It is to be a sabbath of complete rest to you, and you
shall humble your soul; on the ninth of the month at evening,
from evening until evening you shall keep your sabbath."
33 Again the LORD spoke to Moses, saying,
34 "Speak to the sons of Israel, saying, 'On [a]the fifteenth of
this seventh month is the Feast [b]of Booths for seven days to
the LORD.
35 'On the first day is a holy convocation; you shall do [a]no
laborious work of any kind.
36 '[a]For seven days you shall present an offering by fire to
the LORD. On [b]the eighth day you shall have a holy convocation and present an offering by fire to the LORD; it is an assembly. You shall do no laborious work.
37 'These are [a]the appointed times of the LORD which you
shall proclaim as holy convocations, to present offerings by fire
to the LORD—burnt offerings and grain offerings, sacrifices
and libations, [b]*each* day's matter on its own day—
38 besides *those of* the sabbaths of the LORD, and besides
your gifts, and besides all your [1]votive and freewill offerings,
which you give to the LORD.
39 'On exactly the fifteenth day of the seventh month,
when you have gathered in the crops of the land, you shall
celebrate the feast of the LORD for seven days, with a [1]rest on
the first day and a [1]rest on the eighth day.
40 'Now on the first day you shall take for yourselves the
[1]foliage of beautiful trees, palm branches and boughs of leafy
trees and willows of the brook; and you shall rejoice before the
LORD your God for seven days.
41 'You shall thus celebrate it *as* a feast to the LORD for
seven days in the year. It *shall be* a perpetual statute throughout your generations; you shall celebrate it in the seventh
month.
42 'You shall [1]live [a]in booths for seven days; all the native-
born in Israel shall [1]live in booths,
43 so that your generations may know that I had the sons
of Israel live in booths when I brought them out from the land
of Egypt. I am the LORD your God.' "
44 So Moses declared to the sons of Israel [a]the appointed
times of the LORD.

CHAPTER 24

THEN the LORD spoke to Moses, saying,
2 "Command the sons of Israel that they bring to you
[a]clear oil from beaten olives for the [1]light, to make a lamp
[2]burn continually.
3 "Outside the veil of testimony in the tent of meeting,
Aaron shall keep it in order from evening to morning before
the LORD continually; *it shall be* a perpetual statute throughout your generations.
4 "He shall keep the lamps in order on the [a]pure *gold*
lampstand before the LORD continually.
5 "[a]Then you shall take fine flour and bake twelve cakes
with it; two-tenths *of an ephah* shall be *in* each cake.

34 [a]Num. 29:12 [b]Lev. 23:42, 43; Deut. 16:13, 16
35 [a]Lev. 23:25
36 [a]Num. 29:12-34 [b]Num. 29:35-38
37 [a]Lev. 23:2 [b]Num. 28:1-29, 38
38 [1]Lit., *vows, and besides all your*
39 [1]Lit., *sabbath rest*
40 [1]Lit., *products, fruit*
42 [1]Lit., *dwell* [a]Lev. 23:34
44 [a]Lev. 23:37
2 [1]Or, *luminary* [2]Lit., *ascend* [a]Ex. 27:20, 21
4 [a]Ex. 25:31; 31:8; 37:17
5 [a]Ex. 25:30; 39:36; 40:23

6 "And you shall set them *in* two rows, six *to* a row, on the
[a]pure *gold* table before the LORD.
7 "And you shall put pure frankincense on each row, that
it may be [a]a memorial portion for the bread, *even* an offering
by fire to the LORD.
8 "[a]Every sabbath day he shall set it in order before the
LORD [b]continually; it is an everlasting covenant [1]for the sons of
Israel.
9 "[a]And it shall be for Aaron and his sons, and they shall
eat it in a holy place; for it is most holy to him from the LORD's
offerings by fire, *his* portion forever."
10 Now the son of an Israelite woman, whose father was
an Egyptian, went out among the sons of Israel; and the Israelite woman's son and a man of Israel struggled with each other
in the camp.
11 And the son of the Israelite woman blasphemed the
[a]Name and cursed. So they brought him to Moses. (Now his
mother's name was Shelomith, the daughter of Dibri, of the
tribe of Dan.)
12 And they put him in [1]custody [2]so that [a]the command
of the LORD might be made clear to them.
13 Then the LORD spoke to Moses, saying,
14 "Bring the one who has cursed outside the camp, and let
all who heard him [a]lay their hands on his head; then [b]let all the
congregation stone him.
15 "And you shall speak to the sons of Israel, saying, '[a]If
anyone curses his God, then he shall bear his sin.
16 'Moreover, the one who blasphemes the name of the
LORD shall surely be put to death; all the congregation shall
certainly stone him. The alien as well as the native, when he
blasphemes the Name, shall be put to death.
17 '[a]And if a man [1]takes the life of any human being, he
shall surely be put to death.
18 'And [a]the one who [1]takes the life of an animal shall
make it good, life for life.
19 'And if a man [1]injures his neighbor, just as he has done,
so it shall be done to him:
20 [a]fracture for fracture, [b]eye for eye, tooth for tooth; just
as he has [1]injured a man, so it shall be [2]inflicted on him.
21 '[a]Thus the one who [1]kills an animal shall make it good,
but the one who [1]kills a man shall be put to death.
22 'There shall be [a]one [1]standard for you; it shall be for the
stranger as well as the native, for I am the LORD your God.' "
23 Then Moses spoke to the sons of Israel, and they
brought the one who had cursed outside the camp and stoned
him with stones. Thus the sons of Israel did, just as the LORD
had commanded Moses.

CHAPTER 25

THE LORD then spoke to Moses [1]at Mount Sinai, saying,
2 "Speak to the sons of Israel, and say to them, 'When
you come into the land which I shall give you, then the land
shall have a sabbath to the LORD.
3 '[a]Six years you shall sow your field, and six years you
shall prune your vineyard and gather in its crop,

6 [a]Ex. 25:24

7 [a]Lev. 2:2, 9, 16

8 [1]Lit., *from* [a]Matt. 12:5 [b]Ex. 25:30; Num. 4:7

9 [a]Matt. 12:4; Mark 2:26; Luke 6:4

11 [a]Ex. 3:15; 22:28

12 [1]Or, *prison* [2]Lit., *to declare distinctly to them according to the mouth of the LORD* [a]Ex. 18:15

14 [a]Deut. 13:9; 17:7 [b]Lev. 20:2, 27; Deut. 21:21

15 [a]Ex. 22:28

17 [1]Lit., *smites* [a]Ex. 21:12; Num. 35:30, 31; Deut. 27:24

18 [1]Lit., *smites* [a]Lev. 24:21

19 [1]Lit., *gives a blemish*

20 [1]Lit., *given a blemish* [2]Lit., *given* [a]Ex. 21:23; Deut. 19:21 [b]Matt. 5:38

21 [1]Lit., *smites* [a]Lev. 24:17

22 [1]Lit., *judgment* [a]Ex. 12:49; Num. 9:14; 15:15, 16, 29

1 [1]Or, *on*

3 [a]Ex. 23:10, 11

4 but during [a]the seven th year the land shall have a sabbath rest, a sabbath to the LORD; you shall not sow your field
nor prune your vineyard.
5 'Your harvest's [1]aftergrowth you shall not reap, and
your grapes of trimmed vines you shall not gather; the land
shall have a sabbatical year.
6 '[a]And all of you shall have the sabbath *products* of the
land for food: yourself, and your male and female slaves, and
your hired man and your foreign resident, those who live as
aliens with you.
7 'Even your cattle and the animals that are in your land
shall have all its crops to eat.
8 'You are also to count off seven sabbaths of years for
yourself, seven times seven years, so that you have the time of
the seven sabbaths of years, *namely,* forty-nine years.
9 'You shall then sound a ram's horn abroad on [a]the tenth
day of the seventh month; on the day of atonement you shall
sound a horn all through your land.
10 'You shall thus consecrate the fiftieth year and proclaim
[1]a release through the land to all its inhabitants. It shall be a
jubilee for you, [2]and [a]each of you shall return to his own
property, [2]and each of you shall return to his family.
11 'You shall have the fiftieth year as a jubilee: you shall
not sow, nor reap its aftergrowth, nor gather in *from* its un-
trimmed vines.
12 'For it is a jubilee; it shall be holy to you. You shall eat
its crops out of the field.
13 '[a]On this year of jubilee each of you shall return to his
own property.
14 'If you make a sale, moreover, to your friend, or buy
from your friend's hand, [a]you shall not wrong one another.
15 'Corresponding to the number of years after the jubilee,
you shall buy from your [1]friend; he is to sell to you according
to the number of years of crops.
16 '[a]In proportion to the [1]extent of the years you shall
increase its price, and in proportion to the fewness of the years,
you shall diminish its price; for *it is* a number of crops he is
selling to you.
17 'So [a]you shall not wrong one another, but you shall [1]fear
your God; for I am the LORD your God.
18 'You shall thus observe My statutes, and keep My judgments, so as to carry them out, that [a]you may live securely on
the land.
19 'Then the land will yield its produce, so that you can eat
your fill and live securely on it.
20 'But if you say, "[a]What are we going to eat on the
seventh year [1]if we do not sow or gather in our crops?"
21 then I will so order My blessing for you in the sixth year
that it will bring forth the crop for three years.
22 'When you are sowing the eighth year, you can still eat
[a]old things from the crop, eating *the old* until the ninth year
when its crop comes in.
23 'The land, moreover, shall not be sold permanently, for
[a]the land is Mine; for [b]you are *but* aliens and sojourners with
Me.

4 [a]Lev. 25:20
5 [1]Lit., *growth from spilled kernels*
6 [a]Lev. 25:20, 21
9 [a]Lev. 23:27
10 [1]Or, *liberty* [2]Or, *when* [a]Lev. 25:13, 28, 54
13 [a]Lev. 25:10
14 [a]Lev. 25:17
15 [1]Lit., *friend's hands*
16 [1]Lit., *multiplied* [a]Lev. 25:27, 51, 52
17 [1]Or, *reverence* [a]Lev. 25:14
18 [a]Lev. 26:4, 5
20 [1]Or, *behold* [a]Lev. 25:4
22 [a]Lev. 26:10
23 [a]Ex. 19:5 [b]Gen. 23:4; 1 Chr. 29:15; Ps. 39:12; Heb. 11:13; 1 Pet. 2:11

24 'Thus for every [1]piece of your property, you are to provide for the redemption of the land.
25 '[a]If a [1]fellow countryman of yours becomes so poor he
has to sell part of his property, then his nearest kinsman is to
come and buy back what his [1]relative has sold.
26 'Or in case a man has no kinsman, but so [1]recovers his
means as to find sufficient for its redemption,
27 [a]then he shall calculate the years since its sale and refund the balance to the man to whom he sold it, and so return
to his property.
28 'But if [1]he has not found sufficient means to get it back
for himself, then what he has sold shall remain in the hands of
its purchaser until the year of jubilee; but at the jubilee it shall
[2]revert, that [a]he may return to his property.
29 'Likewise, if a man sells a dwelling house in a walled
city, then his redemption right remains valid until a full year
from its sale; his right of redemption lasts a full year.
30 'But if it is not bought back for him within the space of
a full year, then the house that is in the walled city passes
permanently to its purchaser throughout his generations; it
does not [1]revert in the jubilee.
31 'The houses of the villages, however, which have no
surrounding wall shall be considered [1]as open fields; they have
redemption rights and [2]revert in the jubilee.
32 'As for [a]cities of the Levites, the Levites have a permanent right of redemption for the houses of the cities which are
their possession.
33 'What, therefore, [1]belongs to the Levites may be redeemed and a house sale [2]in the city of this possession [3]reverts
in the jubilee, for the houses of the Levites are their possession
among the sons of Israel.
34 '[a]But pasture fields of their cities shall not be sold, for
that is their perpetual possession.
35 '[a]Now in case a [1]countryman of yours becomes poor
and his [2]means with regard to you falter, then you are to
sustain him, like a stranger or a sojourner, that he may live with
you.
36 '[a]Do not take [1]usurious interest from him, but revere
your God, that your [2]countryman may live with you.
37 'You shall not give him your silver at interest, nor your
food for gain.
38 '[a]I am the LORD your God, who brought you out of the
land of Egypt to give you the land of Canaan *and* [b]to be your
God.
39 '[a]And if a [1]countryman of yours becomes so poor with
regard to you that he sells himself to you, you shall not subject
him to a slave's service.
40 'He shall be with you as a hired man, as [a]if he were a
sojourner with you, until the year of jubilee.
41 'He shall then go out from you, he and his sons with
him, and shall go back to his family, that he may return to the
property of his forefathers.
42 'For they are My servants whom I brought out from the
land of Egypt; they are not to be sold *in* a slave sale.
43 '[a]You shall not rule over him with severity, but are to
revere your God.

24 [1]Lit., *land*

25 [1]Lit., *brother* [a]Ruth 2:20; 4:4, 6

26 [1]Lit., *his hand reaches*

27 [a]Lev. 25:16

28 [1]Lit., *his hand has not found sufficient to* [2]Lit., *go out* [a]Lev. 25:10, 13

30 [1]Lit., *go out*

31 [1]Lit., *according to* [2]Lit., *go out*

32 [a]Num. 35:1-8

33 [1]Lit., *is from* [2]Lit., *and* [3]Lit., *goes out*

34 [a]Num. 35:2-5

35 [1]Lit., *brother* [2]Lit., *hand* [a]Deut. 15:7-11; 24:14, 15

36 [1]Lit., *interest and usury* [2]Lit., *brother* [a]Ex. 22:25; Deut. 23:19, 20

38 [a]Lev. 11:45 [b]Gen. 17:7

39 [1]Lit., *brother* [a]Ex. 21:2-6; Deut. 15:12-18

40 [a]Ex. 21:2

43 [a]Lev. 25:46, 53; Ex. 1:13, 14; Ezek. 34:4

44 'As for your male and female slaves whom you may
have—you may acquire male and female slaves from the pagan
nations that are around you.
45 'Then, too, *it is* out of the sons of the sojourners who
live as aliens among you that you may gain acquisition, and
out of their families who are with you, whom they will have
[1]produced in your land; they also may become your
possession.
46 'You may even bequeath them to your sons after you,
to receive as a possession; you can use them as permanent
slaves. [a]But in respect to your [1]countrymen, the sons of Israel,
you shall not rule with severity over one another.
47 'Now if the [1]means of a stranger or of a sojourner with
you becomes sufficient, and a [2]countryman of yours becomes
so poor with regard to him as to sell himself to a stranger who
is sojourning with you, or to the descendants of a stranger's
family,
48 then he shall have redemption right after he has been
sold. One of his brothers may redeem him,
49 or his uncle, or his uncle's son, may redeem him, or one
of his blood relatives from his family may redeem him; or [1a]if
he prospers, he may redeem himself.
50 'He then with his purchaser shall calculate from the
year when he sold himself to him up to the year of jubilee; and
the price of his sale shall correspond to the number of years. *It*
is like the days of a hired man *that* he shall be with him.
51 'If there are still many years, [a]he shall refund part of his
purchase price in proportion to them for his own redemption;
52 and if few years remain until the year of jubilee, he
shall so calculate with him. In proportion to his years he is to
refund *the amount for* his redemption.
53 'Like a man hired year by year he shall be with him; [a]he
shall not rule over him with severity in your sight.
54 'Even if he is not redeemed by [1]these *means*, [a]he shall
still go out in the year of jubilee, he and his sons with him.
55 'For the sons of Israel are My servants; they are My
servants whom I brought out from the land of Egypt. I am the
LORD your God.

CHAPTER 26

'YOU shall not make for yourselves [a]idols, nor shall you set
up for yourselves [b]an image or [c]a *sacred* pillar, nor shall you
place a [d]figured stone in your land to bow down [1]to it; for I am
the LORD your God.
2 '[a]You shall keep My sabbaths and reverence My sanctuary; I am the LORD.
3 '[a]If you walk in My statutes and keep My commandments so as to carry them out,
4 then I shall give you rains in their season, so that the
land will yield its produce and the trees of the field will bear
their fruit.
5 '[a]Indeed, your threshing will last for you until grape
gathering, and grape gathering will last until sowing time. You
will thus eat your [1]food to the full and [b]live securely in your
land.

45 [1]Lit., *begotten*
46 [1]Lit., *brother* [a]Lev. 25:43
47 [1]Lit., *hand . . . reaches* [2]Lit., *brother*
49 [1]Lit., *his hand has reached* [a]Lev. 25:26, 27
51 [a]Lev. 25:16
53 [a]Lev. 25:43
54 [1]Or, *these years* [a]Lev. 25:10, 13, 28
1 [1]Lit., *over* [a]Lev. 19:4 [b]Ex. 20:4 [c]Ex. 23:24 [d]Num. 33:52
2 [a]Lev. 19:30
3 [a]Deut. 7:12-26; 28:1-14
5 [1]Lit., *bread* [a]Amos 9:13 [b]Lev. 25:18, 19

6 ‘[a]I shall also grant peace in the land, so that [b]you may lie down with no one making *you* tremble. [c]I shall also eliminate harmful beasts from the land, and [d]no sword will pass through your land.

7 ‘But you will chase your enemies, and they will fall before you by the sword;

8 [a]five of you will chase a hundred, and a hundred of you will chase ten thousand, and your enemies will fall before you by the sword.

9 ‘So I will turn toward you and [a]make you fruitful and multiply you, and I will [b]confirm My covenant with you.

10 ‘[a]And you will eat the old supply and clear out the old because of the new.

11 ‘[a]Moreover, I will make My [1]dwelling among you, and My soul will not [2]reject you.

12 ‘[a]I will also walk among you and be your God, and you shall be My people.

13 ‘[a]I am the LORD your God, who brought you out of the land of Egypt so that *you* should not be their slaves, and [b]I broke the bars of your yoke and made you walk erect.

14 ‘[a]But if you do not obey Me and do not carry out all these commandments,

15 if, instead, you reject My statutes, and if [a]your soul abhors My ordinances so as not to carry out all My commandments, *and* so [a]break My covenant,

16 I, in turn, will do this to you: I will appoint over you a [a]sudden terror, consumption and fever that shall waste away the eyes and cause the [b]soul to pine away; also, [c]you shall sow your seed uselessly, for your enemies shall eat it up.

17 ‘And I will set My face against you so that you shall be struck down before your enemies; and [a]those who hate you shall rule over you, and [b]you shall flee when no one is pursuing you.

18 ‘If also after these things, you do not obey Me, then I will punish you [a]seven times more for your sins.

19 ‘And I will also [a]break down your pride of power; I will also make your sky like iron and your earth like bronze.

20 ‘And [a]your strength shall be spent uselessly, for your land shall not yield its produce and the trees of the land shall not yield their fruit.

21 ‘If then, you [1a]act with hostility against Me and are unwilling to obey Me, I will increase the plague on you [b]seven times according to your sins.

22 ‘And I will let loose among you the beasts of the field, which shall bereave you of your children and destroy your cattle and reduce your number so that your roads lie deserted.

23 ‘[a]And if by these things you are not turned to Me, but act with hostility against Me,

24 then I will [a]act with hostility against you; and I, even I, will strike you [b]seven times for your sins.

25 ‘I will also bring upon you a sword which will execute [a]vengeance for the covenant; and when you gather together into your cities, I will send [b]pestilence among you, so that you shall be delivered into enemy hands.

26 ‘[a]When I break your staff of bread, ten women will bake your bread in one oven, and they will bring back your

6 [a]Ps. 29:11; 85:8; 147:14 [b]Zeph. 3:13 [c]Lev. 26:22 [d]Lev. 26:25

8 [a]Deut. 32:30

9 [a]Gen. 17:6; 22:17; 48:4 [b]Gen. 17:7

10 [a]Lev. 25:22

11 [1]Or, *tabernacle* [2]Lit., *abhor* [a]Ex. 25:8; 29:45, 46

12 [a]2 Cor. 6:16; Gen. 3:8; Deut. 23:14

13 [a]Ex. 20:2 [b]Ezek. 34:27

14 [a]Deut. 28:15-68; Josh. 23:15

15 [a]Lev. 26:11 [b]Lev. 26:9

16 [a]Ps. 78:33 [b]Ezek. 24:23; 33:10 [c]Judg. 6:3-6

17 [a]Ps. 106:41 [b]Lev. 26:36, 37; Ps. 53:5; Prov. 28:1

18 [a]Lev. 26:21, 24, 28

19 [a]Is. 28:1-3; Ezek. 24:21

20 [a]Is. 17:10, 11; Jer. 12:13

21 [1]Lit., *walk*, and so throughout the chap.

22 [a]Lev. 26:23, 27, 40 [b]Lev. 26:18

23 [a]Lev. 26:21

24 [a]Lev. 26:28, 41 [b]Lev. 26:21

25 [a]Jer. 50:28; 51:11 [b]Num. 14:12

26 [a]Is. 3:1; Ezek. 4:16, 17; 5:16

bread [1]in rationed amounts, so that you will eat and not be
satisfied.
27 Yet if in spite of this, you do not obey Me, but act with
hostility against Me,
28 then [a]I will act with wrathful hostility against you; and
I, even I, will punish you seven times for your sins.
29 'Further, you shall eat the flesh of your sons and the
flesh of your daughters you shall eat.
30 'I then [a]will destroy your high places, and cut down your
[b]incense altars, and heap your [1]remains on the [1]remains of
your idols; for My soul shall abhor you.
31 'I will [1]lay [a]waste your cities as well, and will make your
[b]sanctuaries desolate; and I will not [c]smell your soothing
aromas.
32 'And I will make [a]the land desolate [b]so that your enemies
who settle in it shall be appalled over it.
33 'You, however, I [a]will scatter among the nations and
will draw out a sword after you, as your land becomes desolate
and your cities become waste.
34 '[a]Then the land will [1]enjoy its sabbaths all the days of
the desolation, while you are in your enemies' land; then the
land will rest and [1]enjoy its sabbaths.
35 'All the days of *its* desolation it will observe the rest
which it did not observe on your sabbaths, while you were
living on it.
36 'As for those of you who may be left, I will also bring
[a]weakness into their hearts in the lands of their enemies. And
the sound of a driven leaf will chase them and even when no
one is pursuing, they will flee [1]as though from the sword, and
they will fall.
37 '[a]They will therefore stumble over each other as if *running* from the sword, although no one is pursuing; and you will
have *no strength* [1]to stand up before your enemies.
38 'But [a]you will perish among the nations, and your enemies' land will consume you.
39 '[a]So those of you who may be left will rot away because
of their iniquity in the lands of your enemies; and also because
of the iniquities of their forefathers they will rot away with
them.
40 '[a]If they confess their iniquity and the iniquity of their
forefathers, in their unfaithfulness which they committed
against Me, and also in their acting with hostility against Me—
41 I also was acting with hostility against them, to bring
them into the land of their enemies—[a]or if their uncircumcised heart becomes humbled so that [b]they then make amends
for their iniquity,
42 then I will remember [a]My covenant with Jacob, and I
will remember also My covenant [b]with Isaac, and [c]My covenant
with Abraham as well, and I will remember the land.
43 '[a]For the land shall be abandoned by them, and shall
make up for its sabbaths while it is made desolate without
them. They, meanwhile, shall be making amends for their iniquity, [1]because they rejected My ordinances and their [b]soul
abhorred My statutes.
44 'Yet in spite of this, when they are in the land of their
enemies, I will not reject them, nor will I [a]so [b]abhor them as to

26 [1]Lit., *by weight*

28 [a]Lev. 26:24, 41

30 [1]Lit., *corpses* [a]2 Kin. 23:20; Ezek. 6:3, 6; Amos 7:9 [b]2 Chr. 34:4, 7; Is. 27:9

31 [1]Lit., *give desolation to* [a]Jer. 44:2, 6, 22 [b]Is. 63:18; Lam. 2:7 [c]Amos 5:21

32 [a]Jer. 12:11; 33:10 [b]Jer. 18:16; 19:8

33 [a]Ps. 44:11; 106:27; Jer. 31:10; Ezek. 12:15

34 [1]Lit., *satisfy* [a]Lev. 26:43; 2 Chr. 36:21

36 [1]Lit., *the flight of the sword* [a]Is. 30:17; Lam. 1:3, 6; 4:19

37 [1]Lit., *you will stand* [a]Jer. 6:21; Nah. 3:3

38 [a]Deut. 4:26

39 [a]Ezek. 4:17; 33:10

40 [a]Jer. 3:12-15; 14:20; Hos. 5:15

41 [a]Jer. 4:4; 9:25, 26; Ezek. 44:9 [b]Ezek. 20:43

42 [a]Gen. 28:13-15; 35:11, 12 [b]Gen. 26:2-5 [c]Gen. 22:15-18

43 [1]Lit., *because and by the cause* [a]Lev. 26:34 [b]Lev. 26:11

44 [a]Deut. 4:31; Jer. 30:11 [b]Lev. 26:11

destroy them, [c]breaking My covenant with them; for I am the
LORD their God.
45 'But I will remember for them the [a]covenant with their
ancestors, whom I brought out of the land of Egypt in the
sight of the nations, that [b]I might be their God. I am the
LORD.' "
46 [a]These are the statutes and ordinances and laws which
the LORD established between Himself and the sons of Israel
[1]through Moses at Mount Sinai.

Chapter 27

AGAIN, the LORD spoke to Moses, saying,
2 "Speak to the sons of Israel, and say to them, 'When a
man makes a difficult vow, he *shall be valued* according to
your valuation of persons, belonging to the LORD.
3 'If your valuation is of the male from twenty years even
to sixty years old, then your valuation shall be fifty shekels of
silver, after [a]the shekel of the sanctuary.
4 'Or if it is a female, then your valuation shall be thirty
shekels.
5 'And if it be from five years even to twenty years old
then your valuation for the male shall be twenty shekels, and
for the female ten shekels.
6 'But if *they are* from a month even up to five years old,
then your valuation shall be [a]five shekels of silver for the male,
and for the female your valuation shall be three shekels of
silver.
7 'And if *they are* from sixty years old and upward, if it is
a male, then your valuation shall be fifteen shekels, and for the
female ten shekels.
8 'But if he is poorer than your valuation, then he shall be
placed before the priest, and the priest shall value him; [a]accord-
ing to [1]the means of the one who vowed, the priest shall value
him.
9 'Now if it is an animal of the kind which [1]men can
present as an offering to the LORD, any such that one gives to
the LORD shall be holy.
10 '[a]He shall not replace it or exchange it, a good for a bad,
or a bad for a good; or if he does exchange animal for animal,
then both it and its substitute shall become holy.
11 'If, however, it is any unclean animal of the kind which
[1]men do not present as an offering to the LORD, then he shall
place the animal before the priest.
12 'And the priest shall value it [1]as either good or bad: as
you, the priest, value it, so it shall be.
13 'But if he should ever *wish to* redeem it, then he shall
add one-fifth of it to your valuation.
14 'Now if a man consecrates his house as holy to the
LORD, then the priest shall value it [1]as either good or bad; as
the priest values it, so it shall stand.
15 'Yet if the one who consecrates it should *wish to* redeem his house, then he shall add one-fifth of your valuation
price to it, so that it may be his.
16 'Again, if a man consecrates to the LORD part of the
fields of his own property, then your valuation shall be

44 [c]Jer. 33:20-26

45 [a]Ex. 6:6-8 [b]Gen. 17:7

46 [1]Lit., *by the hand of* [a]Lev. 7:38; 27:34; Deut. 4:5; 29:1

3 [a]Lev. 27:25; Ex. 30:13

6 [a]Num. 18:16

8 [1]Lit., *what the hand reaches* [a]Lev. 5:11; 14:21-24

9 [1]Lit., *they*

10 [a]Lev. 27:33

11 [1]Lit., *they*

12 [1]Lit., *between*

14 [1]Lit., *between good*

[1]proportionate to the seed needed for it: a homer of barley
seed at fifty shekels of silver.
17 'If he consecrates his field as of the year of jubilee,
according to your valuation it shall stand.
18 'If he consecrates his field after the jubilee, however,
then the priest shall calculate the price for [1]him [2]proportionate
to the years that are left until the year of jubilee; and it shall be
deducted from your valuation.
19 'And if the one who consecrates it should ever wish to
redeem the field, then he shall add one-fifth of your valuation
price to it, so that it may pass to him.
20 'Yet if he will not redeem the field, [1]but has sold the
field to another man, it may no longer be redeemed;
21 and when it [1]reverts in the jubilee, the field shall be
holy to the LORD, like a field [2]set apart; it shall be for the priest
as his [3]property.
22 'Or if he consecrates to the LORD a field which he has
bought, which is not a part of the field of his own [1]property,
23 then the priest shall calculate for [1]him the amount of
your valuation up to the year of jubilee; and he shall on that
day give your valuation as holy to the LORD.
24 'In the year of jubilee the field shall return to the one
from whom he bought it, to whom the possession of the land
belongs.
25 'Every valuation of yours, moreover, shall be after [a]the
shekel of the sanctuary. The shekel shall be twenty gerahs.
26 '[a]However, a first-born among animals, which as a first-
born belongs to the LORD, no man may consecrate it; whether
ox or sheep, it is the LORD's.
27 'But if *it is* among the unclean animals, then he shall
[1]redeem it according to your valuation, and add to it one-fifth
of it; and if it is not redeemed, then it shall be sold according
to your valuation.
28 'Nevertheless, any [a]proscribed thing which a man [1]sets
apart to the LORD out of all that he has, of man or animal or of
the fields of his own property, shall not be sold or redeemed.
Every proscribed thing is most holy to the LORD.
29 'No proscribed *person* who may have been [1]set apart
among men shall be ransomed; he shall surely be put to death.
30 Thus all the tithe of the land, of the seed of the land or
of the fruit of the tree, is the LORD's; it is holy to the LORD.
31 'If, therefore, a man wishes to redeem part of his tithe,
he shall add to it one-fifth of it.
32 'And for every tenth part of herd or flock, whatever
passes under the rod, the tenth one shall be holy to the LORD.
33 '[a]He is not to be concerned whether *it is* good or bad,
nor shall he exchange it; or if he does exchange it, then both it
and its substitute shall become holy. It shall not be
redeemed.' "
34 [a]These are the commandments which the LORD commanded Moses for the sons of Israel at Mount Sinai.

16 [1]Lit., *according to its seed*

18 [1]Or, *it* [2]Lit., *according to the years*

20 [1]Or, *if he*

21 [1]Lit., *goes out* [2]Or, *devoted, banned* [3]Lit., *possession*

22 [1]Lit., *possession*

23 [1]Or, *it*

25 [a]Lev. 27:3

26 [a]Ex. 13:2

27 [1]Or, *ransom*

28 [1]Or, *puts under bans* [a]Num. 18:14; Josh. 6:17-19

29 [1]Or, *puts under the ban*

33 [a]Lev. 27:10

34 [a]Lev. 26:46; Deut. 4:5

NUMBERS

The Census of Israel's Warriors.

THEN the LORD spoke to Moses in the wilderness of Sinai, in the tent of meeting, on [a]the first of the second month, in the second year after they had come out of the land of Egypt, saying,

2 "[a]Take a [1]census of all the congregation of the sons of Israel, by their families, by their fathers' households, according to the number of names, every male, head by head

3 from [a]twenty years old and upward, whoever *is able to* go out to war in Israel, you and Aaron shall [1]number them by their armies.

4 "With you, moreover, there shall be a man of each tribe, [a]each one head of his father's household.

5 "These then are the names of the men who shall stand with you: of Reuben, Elizur the son of Shedeur;

6 of Simeon, Shelumiel the son of Zurishaddai;

7 of Judah, Nahshon the son of Amminadab;

8 of Issachar, Nethanel the son of Zuar;

9 of Zebulun, Eliab the son of Helon;

10 of the sons of Joseph: of Ephraim, Elishama the son of Ammihud; of Manasseh, Gamaliel the son of Pedahzur;

11 of Benjamin, Abidan the son of Gideoni;

12 of Dan, Ahiezer the son of Ammishaddai;

13 of Asher, Pagiel the son of Ochran;

14 of Gad, Eliasaph the son of Deuel;

15 of Naphtali, Ahira the son of Enan.

16 "These are they who were [a]called of the congregation, the leaders of their fathers' tribes; they were the heads of [1]divisions of Israel."

17 So Moses and Aaron took these men who had been designated by name,

18 and they assembled all the congregation together on the [a]first of the second month. Then they registered by ancestry in their families, by their fathers' households, according to the number of names, from twenty years old and upward, head by head,

19 just as the LORD had commanded Moses. So he numbered them in the wilderness of Sinai.

20 [a]Now the sons of Reuben, Israel's first-born, their genealogical registration by their families, by their fathers' households, according to the number of names, head by head, every male from twenty years old and upward, whoever *was able to go* out to war,

21 their numbered men, of the tribe of Reuben, *were* 46,500.

22 [a]Of the sons of Simeon, their genealogical registration by their families, by their fathers' households, its numbered men, according to the number of names, head by head, every male from twenty years old and upward, whoever was able to go out to war,

1 [a]Ex. 40:2, 17

2 [1]Lit., *sum* [a]Num. 26:2; Ex. 12:37; 38:25, 26

3 [1]Lit., *muster*, and so throughout the chap. [a]Ex. 30:14; 38:26

4 [a]Num. 1:16; Ex. 18:21, 24; Deut. 1:15

16 [1]Lit., *thousands*, or, *clans* [a]Num. 16:2; 26:9

18 [a]Num. 1:1

20 [a]Num. 26:5-11

22 [a]Num. 26:12-14

23 their numbered men, of the tribe of Simeon, *were*
59,300.
24 [a]Of the sons of Gad, their genealogical registration by
their families, by their fathers' households, according to the
number of names, from twenty years old and upward, whoever
was able to go out to war,
25 their numbered men, of the tribe of Gad, were 45,650.
26 [a]Of the sons of Judah, their genealogical registration by
their families, by their fathers' households, according to the
number of names, from twenty years old and upward, whoever
was able to go out to war,
27 their numbered men, of the tribe of Judah, *were*
74,600.
28 [a]Of the sons of Issachar, their genealogical registration
by their families, by their fathers' households, according to the
number of names, from twenty years old and upward, whoever
was able to go out to war,
29 their numbered men, of the tribe of Issachar, *were*
54,400.
30 [a]Of the sons of Zebulun, their genealogical registration
by their families, by their fathers' households, according to the
number of names, from twenty years old and upward, whoever
was able to go out to war,
31 their numbered men, of the tribe of Zebulun, *were*
57,400.
32 [a]Of the sons of Joseph, *namely,* of the sons of Ephraim, their genealogical registration by their families, by their
fathers' households, according to the number of names, from
twenty years old and upward, whoever *was able to* go out to
war,
33 their numbered men, of the tribe of Ephraim, *were*
40,500.
34 [a]Of the sons of Manasseh, their genealogical registration by their families, by their fathers' households, according
to the number of names, from twenty years old and upward,
whoever *was able to* go out to war,
35 their numbered men, of the tribe of Manasseh, *were*
32,200.
36 [a]Of the sons of Benjamin, their genealogical registration by their families, by their fathers' households, according
to the number of names, from twenty years old and upward,
whoever *was able to* go out to war,
37 their numbered men, of the tribe of Benjamin, *were*
35,400.
38 [a]Of the sons of Dan, their genealogical registration by
their families, by their fathers' households, according to the
number of names, from twenty years old and upward, whoever
was able to go out to war,
39 their numbered men, of the tribe of Dan, *were* 62,700.
40 [a]Of the sons of Asher, their genealogical registration by
their families, by their fathers' households, according to the
number of names, from twenty years old and upward, whoever
was able to go out to war,
41 their numbered men, of the tribe of Asher, *were*
41,500.

24 [a]Num. 26:15-18
26 [a]Num. 26:19-22
28 [a]Num. 26:23-25
30 [a]Num. 26:26, 27
32 [a]Num. 26:35-37
34 [a]Num. 26:28-34
36 [a]Num. 26:38-41
38 [a]Num. 26:42, 43
40 [a]Num. 26:44-47

42 [a]Of the sons of Naphtali, their genealogical registration
by their families, by their fathers' households, according to the
number of names, from twenty years old and upward, whoever
was able to go out to war,
43 their numbered men, of the tribe of Naphtali, *were*
53,400.
44 These are the ones who were numbered, whom Moses
and Aaron numbered, with the leaders of Israel, twelve men,
each of whom was of his father's household.
45 So all the numbered men of the sons of Israel by their
fathers' households, from twenty years old and upward, whoever
was able to go out to war in Israel,
46 even all the numbered men were [a]603,550.
47 [a]The Levites, however, were not numbered among
them by their fathers' tribe.
48 For the LORD had spoken to Moses, saying,
49 "Only the tribe of Levi you shall not number, nor shall
you take their [1]census among the sons of Israel.
50 "But you shall [a]appoint the Levites over the [1]tabernacle
of the testimony, and over all its furnishings and over all that
belongs to it. They shall carry the tabernacle and all its furnishings, and they shall take care of it; they shall also camp
around the [1]tabernacle.
51 "[a]So when the tabernacle is to set out, the Levites shall
take it down; and when the tabernacle encamps, the Levites
shall set it up. But [b]the [1]layman who comes near shall be put to
death.
52 "[a]And the sons of Israel shall camp, each man by his own
camp, and each man by his own standard, according to their
armies.
53 "[a]But the Levites shall camp around the tabernacle of
the testimony, that there may be no wrath on the congregation
of the sons of Israel. So the Levites shall keep charge of the
tabernacle of the testimony."
54 Thus the sons of Israel did; according to all which the
LORD had commanded Moses, so they did.

CHAPTER 2

NOW the LORD spoke to Moses and to Aaron, saying,
2 "[a]The sons of Israel shall camp, each by his own standard, with the [1]banners of their fathers' households; they shall
camp around the tent of meeting [2]at a distance.
3 "Now those who camp on the east side toward the sunrise *shall be* of the standard of the camp of Judah, by their
armies, and the leader of the sons of Judah: [a]Nahshon the son
of Amminadab,
4 and his army, even their [1]numbered men, 74,600.
5 "And those who camp next to him *shall be* the tribe of
Issachar, and the leader of the sons of Issachar: [a]Nethanel the
son of Zuar,
6 and his army, even their numbered men, 54,400.

42 [a]Num. 26:48-50

46 [a]Num. 2:32; 26:51; Ex. 12:37; 38:26

47 [a]Num. 2:33; 3:14-39; 4:49; 26:57-64

49 [1]Lit., *sum*

50 [1]Lit., *dwelling place,* and so throughout the chap. [a]Num. 3:25-37

51 [1]Lit., *stranger* [a]Num. 4:1-33 [b]Num. 3:10, 38; 4:15, 19, 20

52 [a]Num. 2:2

53 [a]Num. 3:23, 29, 35

2 [1]Lit., *signs* [2]Or, *facing it* [a]Num. 1:52

3 [a]Num. 1:7

4 [1]Lit., *mustered,* and so throughout the chap.

5 [a]Num. 1:8

7 "Then *comes* the tribe of Zebulun, and the leader of the
sons of Zebulun: [a]Eliab the son of Helon,
8 and his army, even his numbered men, 57,400.
9 "The total of the numbered men of the camp of Judah:
186,400, by their armies. They shall set out first.
10 "On the south side *shall be* the standard of the camp of
Reuben by their armies, and the leader of the sons of Reuben:
[a]Elizur the son of Shedeur,
11 and his army, even their numbered men, 46,500.
12 "And those who camp next to him *shall be* the tribe of
Simeon, and the leader of the sons of Simeon: [a]Shelumiel the
son of Zurishaddai,
13 and his army, even their numbered men, 59,300.
14 "Then *comes* the tribe of Gad, and the leader of the
sons of Gad: Eliasaph the son of [1a]Deuel,
15 and his army, even their numbered men, 45,650.
16 "The total of the numbered men of the camp of Reuben: 151,450 by their armies. And they shall set out second.
17 "[a]Then the tent of meeting shall set out *with* the camp
of the Levites in the midst of the camps; just as they camp, so
they shall set out, every man in his place, by their standards.
18 "On the west side *shall be* the standard of the camp of
Ephraim by their armies, and the leader of the sons of Ephraim *shall be* [a]Elishama the son of Ammihud,
19 and his army, even their numbered men, 40,500.
20 "And next to him *shall be* the tribe of Manasseh, and
the leader of the sons of Manasseh: [a]Gamaliel the son of
Pedahzur,
21 and his army, even their numbered men, 32,200.
22 "Then *comes* the tribe of Benjamin, and the leader of
the sons of Benjamin: [a]Abidan the son of Gideoni,
23 and his army, even their numbered men, 35,400.
24 "The total of the numbered men of the camp of Ephraim: 108,100, by their armies. And they shall set out third.
25 "On the north side *shall be* the standard of the camp of
Dan by their armies, and the leader of the sons of Dan: [a]Ahie-
zer the son of Ammishaddai,
26 and his army, even their numbered men, 62,700.
27 "And those who camp next to him *shall be* the tribe of
Asher, and the leader of the sons of Asher: [a]Pagiel the son of
Ochran,
28 and his army, even their numbered men, 41,500.
29 "Then *comes* the tribe of Naphtali, and the leader of
the sons of Naphtali: [a]Ahira the son of Enan,
30 and his army, even their numbered men, 53,400.
31 "The total of the numbered men of the camp of Dan,
were 157,600. They shall set out last by their standards."
32 These are the numbered men of the sons of Israel by
their fathers' households; the total of the numbered men of
the camps by their armies, [a]603,550.
33 [a]The Levites, however, were not numbered among the
sons of Israel, just as the LORD had commanded Moses.
34 Thus the sons of Israel did; according to all that the
LORD commanded Moses, so they camped by their standards,
and so they set out, every one by his family, according to his
father's household.

7 [a]Num. 1:9
10 [a]Num. 1:5
12 [a]Num. 1:6
14 [1]Many mss. read, *Reuel* [a]Num. 1:14
17 [a]Num. 1:53
18 [a]Num. 1:10
20 [a]Num. 1:10
22 [a]Num. 1:11
25 [a]Num. 1:12
27 [a]Num. 1:13
29 [a]Num. 1:15
32 [a]Num. 1:46
33 [a]Num. 1:47

CHAPTER 3

[a]NOW these are *the records of* the generations of Aaron and
Moses at the time when the LORD spoke with Moses on Mount
Sinai.
2 [a]These then are the names of the sons of Aaron: Nadab
the first-born, and Abihu, Eleazar and Ithamar.
3 These are the names of the sons of Aaron, the anointed
priests, whom he [1]ordained to serve as priests.
4 [a]But Nadab and Abihu died before the LORD when
they offered strange fire before the LORD in the wilderness of
Sinai; and they had no children. So Eleazar and Ithamar served
as priests [1]in the lifetime of their father Aaron.
5 Then the LORD spoke to Moses, saying,
6 "[a]Bring the tribe of Levi near and set them before Aaron
the priest, that they may serve him.
7 "And they shall perform the duties for [1]him and for the
whole congregation before the tent of the meeting, to do the
service of the tabernacle.
8 "They shall also keep all the furnishings of the tent of
meeting, along with the duties of the sons of Israel, to do the
service of the tabernacle.
9 "You shall thus [a]give the Levites to Aaron and to his
sons; they are wholly given to him from among the sons of
Israel.
10 "So you shall appoint Aaron and his sons that [a]they may
keep their priesthood, but [b]the [1]layman who comes near shall
be put to death."
11 Again the LORD spoke to Moses, saying,
12 "Now, behold, I [a]have taken the Levites from among
the sons of Israel instead of every [b]first-born, the first issue of
the womb among the sons of Israel. So the Levites shall be
Mine.
13 "For all the first-born are Mine; on the day that I struck
down all the first-born in the land of Egypt, I sanctified to
Myself all the first-born in Israel, from man to beast. They
shall be Mine; I am the LORD."
14 Then the LORD spoke to Moses in the wilderness of
Sinai, saying,
15 "[1a]Number the sons of Levi by their fathers' households,
by their families; every male from a month old and upward
you shall number."
16 So Moses numbered them according to the [1]word of
the LORD, just as he had been commanded.
17 [a]These then are the sons of Levi by their names: Gershon and Kohath and Merari.
18 And these are the names of the sons of Gershon by
their families: Libni and Shimei;
19 and the sons of Kohath by their families: Amram and
Izhar, Hebron and Uzziel;
20 and the sons of Merari by their families: Mahli and
Mushi. These are the families of the Levites according to their
fathers' households.
21 Of Gershon *was* the family of the Libnites and the
family of the Shimeites; these *were* the families of the
Gershonites.

1 [a]Ex. 6:20-27
2 [a]Num. 26:60
3 [1]Lit., *filled their hand*
4 [1]Lit., *before the face* [a]Num. 26:61; Lev. 10:1, 2
6 [a]Num. 8:6-22; 18:1-7; Deut. 10:8
7 [1]Lit., *him and the duties of the whole congregation*
9 [a]Num. 18:6
10 [1]Lit., *stranger* [a]Ex. 29:9 [b]Num. 1:51
12 [a]Num. 3:45; 8:14 [b]Ex. 13:2
15 [1]Lit., *muster*, and so throughout the chap. [a]Num. 1:47
16 [1]Lit., *mouth*
17 [a]Ex. 6:16-22

22 Their numbered men, in the numbering of every male
from a month old and upward, *even* their numbered men *were*
7,500.
23 The families of the Gershonites were to camp behind
the [1]tabernacle westward,
24 and the leader of the fathers' households of the Gershonites *was* Eliasaph the son of Lael.
25 Now the duties of the sons of Gershon in the tent of
meeting *involved* the tabernacle and the tent, its covering, and
the screen for the doorway of the tent of meeting,
26 and the hangings of the court, and the screen for the
doorway of the court, which is around the tabernacle and the
altar, and its cords, according to all the service [1]concerning
them.
27 And of Kohath *was* the family of the Amramites and
the family of the Izharites and the family of the Hebronites
and the family of the Uzzielites; these were the families of the
Kohathites.
28 In the numbering of every male from a month old and
upward, *there were* 8,600, performing the duties of the
sanctuary.
29 The families of the sons of Kohath were to camp on
the southward side of the tabernacle,
30 and the leader of the fathers' households of the Kohathite families was Elizaphan the son of Uzziel.
31 Now their duties *involved* the ark, the table, the lampstand, the altars, and the utensils of the sanctuary with which
they minister, and the screen, and all the service [1]concerning
them;
32 and Eleazar the son of Aaron the priest *was* the chief of
the leaders of Levi, *and had* the oversight of those who perform the duties of the sanctuary.
33 Of Merari *was* the family of the Mahlites and the family of the Mushites; these *were* the families of Merari.
34 Their numbered men in the numbering of every male
from a month old and upward, *were* 6,200.
35 And the leader of the fathers' households of the families
of Merari *was* Zuriel the son of Abihail. They *were* to
camp on the northward side of the tabernacle.
36 Now the appointed duties of the sons of Merari involved the frames of the tabernacle, its bars, its pillars, its
sockets, all its equipment, and the service concerning them,
37 and the pillars around the court with their sockets and
their pegs and their cords.
38 Now those who were to camp before the tabernacle
eastward, before the tent of meeting toward the sunrise, are
Moses and Aaron and his sons, performing the duties of the
sanctuary for the obligation of the sons of Israel; but [a]the
[1]layman coming near was to be put to death.
39 All the numbered men of the Levites, whom Moses
and Aaron numbered at the [1]command of the LORD by their
families, every male from a month old and upward, *were*
[a]22,000.
40 Then the LORD said to Moses, "Number every first-
born male of the sons of Israel from a month old and upward,
and [1]make a list of their names.

23 [1]Lit., *dwelling place,* and so throughout the chap.

26 [1]Lit., *of it*

31 [1]Lit., *of it*

38 [1]Lit., *stranger*
[a]Num. 1:51

39 [1]Lit., *word*
[a]Num. 3:43; 4:48; 26:62

40 [1]Lit., *take the number*

41 "And you shall take the Levites for Me, I am the LORD,
instead of all the first-born among the sons of Israel, and the
cattle of the Levites instead of all the first-born among the
cattle of the sons of Israel."
42 So Moses numbered all the first-born among the sons
of Israel, just as the LORD had commanded him;
43 and all the first-born males by the number of names
from a month old and upward, for their numbered men were
[a]22,273.
44 Then the LORD spoke to Moses, saying,
45 "[a]Take the Levites instead of all the first-born among
the sons of Israel and the cattle of the Levites. And the Levites
shall be Mine; I am the LORD.
46 "[a]And for the ransom of the 273 of the first-born of the
sons of Israel who are in excess beyond the Levites,
47 you shall take five shekels apiece, per head; you shall
take *them* in [a]terms of the shekel of the sanctuary (the shekel
is twenty [1]gerahs),
48 and give the money, the ransom of those who are in
excess among them, to Aaron and to his sons."
49 So Moses took the ransom money from those who were
in excess, beyond those ransomed by the Levites;
50 from the first-born of the sons of Israel he took the
money in terms of the shekel of the sanctuary, 1,365.
51 Then Moses gave the ransom money to Aaron and to
his sons, at the [1]command of the LORD, just as the LORD had
commanded Moses.

CHAPTER 4

THEN the LORD spoke to Moses and to Aaron, saying,
2 "Take [1]a census of the [2]descendants of Kohath from
among the sons of Levi, by their families, by their fathers'
households,
3 from [a]thirty years and upward, even to fifty years old,
all who enter the service to do the work in the tent of meeting.
4 "This is the work of the [1]descendants of Kohath in the
tent of meeting, *concerning* the most holy things.
5 "When the camp sets out, Aaron and his sons shall go in
and they shall take down [a]the veil of the screen and cover the
ark of the testimony with it;
6 and they shall lay a [a]covering of [1]porpoise skin on it,
and shall spread over *it* a cloth of pure [2]blue, and shall insert its
poles.
7 "Over the table of the bread of the Presence they shall
also spread a cloth of [1]blue and put on it the dishes and the
spoons and the sacrificial bowls and the jars for the libation,
and [a]the continual bread shall be on it.
8 "And they shall spread over them a cloth of scarlet *material,* and cover the same with a covering of dolphin skin, and
they shall insert its poles.
9 "Then they shall take a [1]blue cloth and cover the lampstand for the light, along with its lamps and its snuffers, and its
[2]trays and all its oil vessels, by which they serve it;
10 and they shall put it and all its utensils in a covering of
dolphin skin, and shall put it on the carrying bars.

43 [a]Num. 3:39
45 [a]Num. 3:12
46 [a]Num. 18:15, 16; Ex. 13:13, 15
47 [1]I.e., A gerah equals approx. one-fortieth ounce [a]Ex. 30:13
51 [1]Lit., *mouth*
2 [1]Lit., *the sum* [2]Lit., *sons*
3 [a]Num. 4:23, 30, 35; 8:24
4 [1]Lit., *sons*
5 [a]Ex. 40:5
6 [1]Or, *dolphin* [2]Or, *violet* [a]Num. 4:25
7 [1]Or, *violet* [a]Ex. 25:30; Lev. 24:5-9
9 [1]Or, *violet* [2]Lit., *snuff dishes*

11 "And over the golden altar they shall spread a [1]blue
cloth and cover it with a covering of dolphin skin, and shall
insert its poles;
12 and they shall take all the utensils of service, with which
they serve in the sanctuary, and put them in a [1]blue cloth and
cover them with a covering of dolphin skin, and put them on
the carrying bars.
13 "Then they shall take away the [1]ashes from the [a]altar,
and spread a purple cloth over it.
14 "They shall also put on it all its utensils by which they
serve in connection with it: the firepans, the forks and shovels
and the basins, all the utensils of the altar; and they shall
spread a cover of [1]porpoise skin over it and insert its poles.
15 "And when Aaron and his sons have finished covering
the holy *objects* and all the furnishings of the sanctuary, when
the camp is to set out, after that the sons of Kohath shall come
to carry *them,* so that they may not touch the holy *objects*
[a]and die. These are the [1]things in the tent of meeting which
the sons of Kohath are to carry.
16 "And the responsibility of Eleazar the son of Aaron the
priest is [a]the oil for the light and the [b]fragrant incense and [c]the
continual grain offering and [d]the anointing oil—the responsibility of all the [1]tabernacle and of all that is in it, with the
sanctuary and its furnishings."
17 Then the LORD spoke to Moses and to Aaron, saying,
18 "Do not let the tribe of the families of the Kohathites
be cut off from among the Levites.
19 "But do this to them that they may live and [a]not die
when they approach the most holy *objects:* Aaron and his sons
shall go in and assign each of them to his work and to his load;
20 but they shall not go in to see the holy *objects* even for
a moment, lest they die."
21 Then the LORD spoke to Moses, saying,
22 "Take [1]a census of the sons of Gershon [2]also, by their
fathers' households, by their families;
23 from [a]thirty years and upward to fifty years old, you
shall [1]number them; all who enter to perform the service to do
the work in the tent of meeting.
24 "This is the service of the families of the Gershonites, in
serving and in carrying:
25 they shall carry the curtains of the tabernacle and the
tent of meeting *with* its covering and [a]the covering of [1]por-
poise skin that is on top of it, and the screen for the doorway
of the tent of meeting,
26 and the hangings of the court, and the screen for the
doorway of the gate of the court which is around the tabernacle and the altar, and their cords and all the equipment for
their service; and all that is to be done, [1]they shall perform.
27 "All the service of the sons of the Gershonites, in all
their loads and in all their work, shall be *performed* at the
[1]command of Aaron and his sons; and you shall assign to them
as a duty all their loads.
28 "This is the service of the families of the sons of the
Gershonites in the tent of meeting, and their duties *shall be*
[1]under the direction of Ithamar the son of Aaron the priest.

11 [1]Or, *violet*

12 [1]Or, *violet*

13 [1]Or, *fat ashes;* i.e., soaked with fat [a]Ex. 27:1-8

14 [1]Or, *dolphin*

15 [1]Lit., *burden . . . of the sons* [a]Num. 4:19, 20; 1:51; 2 Sam. 6:6, 7

16 [1]Lit., *dwelling place,* and so throughout the chap. [a]Lev. 24:1-3 [b]Ex. 30:34-38 [c]Lev. 6:20 [d]Ex. 30:22-33

19 [a]Num. 4:15

22 [1]Lit., *the sum* [2]Lit., *also them*

23 [1]Lit., *muster,* and so throughout the chap. [a]Num. 4:3

25 [1]Or, *dolphin* [a]Num. 4:6; Ex. 26:14

26 [1]Lit., *so they shall serve*

27 [1]Lit., *mouth*

28 [1]Lit., *in the hand*

29 "*As for* the sons of Merari, you shall number them by
their families, by their fathers' households;
30 from [1]thirty years and upward even to fifty years old,
you shall number them, everyone who enters the service to do
the work of the tent of meeting.
31 "Now this is the duty of their loads, for all their service
in the tent of meeting: the boards of the tabernacle and its bars
and its pillars and its [1]sockets,
32 and the pillars around the court and their [1]sockets and
their pegs and their cords, with all their equipment and with all
their service; and you shall assign *each man* by name the items
[2]he is to carry.
33 "This is the service of the families of the sons of Merari,
according to all their service in the tent of meeting, [1]under the
direction of Ithamar the son of Aaron the priest."
34 So Moses and Aaron and the leaders of the congregation numbered the sons of the Kohathites by their families,
and by their fathers' households,
35 from thirty years and upward even to fifty years old,
everyone who entered the service for work in the tent of
meeting.
36 And their numbered men by their families were 2,750.
37 These are the numbered men of the Kohathite families,
everyone who was serving in the tent of meeting, whom
Moses and Aaron numbered according to the [1]commandment
of the LORD [2]through Moses.
38 And the numbered men of the sons of Gershon by their
families, and by their fathers' households,
39 from thirty years and upward even to fifty years old,
everyone who entered the service for work in the tent of
meeting.
40 And their numbered men by their families, by their
fathers' households, were 2,630.
41 These are the numbered men of the families of the
sons of Gershon, everyone who was serving in the tent of
meeting, whom Moses and Aaron numbered according to the
[1]commandment of the LORD.
42 And the numbered men of the families of the sons of
Merari by their families, by their fathers' households,
43 from thirty years and upward even to fifty years old,
everyone who entered the service for work in the tent of
meeting.
44 And their numbered men by their families were 3,200.
45 These are the numbered men of the families of the
sons of Merari, whom Moses and Aaron numbered according
to the [1]commandment of the LORD [2]through Moses.
46 All the numbered men of the Levites, whom Moses
and Aaron and the leaders of Israel numbered, by their families
and by their fathers' households,
47 from thirty years and upward even to fifty years old,
everyone who could enter to do the work of service and the
work of carrying in the tent of meeting.
48 And their numbered men were [a]8,580.
49 According to the [1]commandment of the LORD
[2]through Moses, they [a]were numbered, everyone by his serving

30 [a]Num. 4:3

31 [1]Or, *bases*

32 [1]Or *bases* [2]Lit., *of the duty of their loads.*

33 [1]Lit., *in the hand*

37 [1]Lit., *mouth* [2]Lit., *by the hand of*

41 [1]Lit., *mouth*

45 [1]Lit., *mouth* [2]Lit., *by the hand*

48 [a]Num. 3:39

49 [1]Lit., *mouth* [2]Lit., *by the hand of*
[a]Num. 1:47

or carrying; thus these were his numbered men, just as the
LORD had commanded Moses.

CHAPTER 5

[a]THEN the LORD spoke to Moses, saying,
2 "Command the sons of Israel that they send away from
the camp every leper and everyone having a discharge and
everyone who is [a]unclean because of a *dead* person.
3 "You shall send away both male and female; you shall
send them outside the camp so that they will not defile their
camp where I dwell [a]in their midst."
4 And the sons of Israel did so and sent them outside the
camp; just as the LORD had spoken to Moses, thus the sons of
Israel did.
5 Then the LORD spoke to Moses, saying,
6 "Speak to the sons of Israel, '[a]When a man or woman
commits any of the sins of mankind, acting unfaithfully
against the LORD, and that person is guilty,
7 then [1]he shall [a]confess [2]his sins which [3]he has committed, and he shall make restitution in full for his wrong, and
add to it one-fifth of it, and give *it* to him whom he has
wronged.
8 'But if the man has no [1]relative to whom restitution
may be made for the wrong, the restitution which is made for
the wrong *must go* to the LORD for the priest, besides the ram
of atonement, by which atonement is made for him.
9 '[a]Also every [1]contribution pertaining to all the holy *gifts*
of the sons of Israel, which they offer to the priest, shall be his.
10 'So every man's holy *gifts* shall be his; whatever any man
gives to the priest, it becomes his.' "
11 Then the LORD spoke to Moses, saying,
12 "Speak to the sons of Israel, and say to them, 'If any
man's wife [a]goes astray and is unfaithful to him,
13 and a man has intercourse with her and it is hidden
from the eyes of her husband and she is [1]undetected, although
she has defiled herself, and there is no witness against her and
she has not been caught in the act,
14 [1]if a spirit of jealousy comes over him and he is jealous
of his wife when she has defiled herself, or if a spirit of jealousy
comes over him and he is jealous of his wife when she has not
defiled herself,
15 the man shall then bring his wife to the priest, and shall
bring *as* [1]an offering for her one-tenth of an [2]ephah of barley
meal; he shall not pour oil on it, nor put frankincense on it, for
it is a grain offering of jealousy, a grain offering of memorial,
[a]a reminder of iniquity.
16 'Then the priest shall bring her near and have her stand
before the LORD,
17 and the priest shall take holy water in an earthenware
vessel; and [1]he shall take some of the dust that is on the floor
of the tabernacle and put *it* into the water.
18 'The priest shall then have the woman stand before the
LORD and let *the hair of* the woman's head go loose, and place
the grain offering of memorial [1]in her hands, which is the grain

1 [a]Num. 12:15; Lev. 13:46

2 [a]Num. 19:11

3 [a]Num. 35:34; Lev. 26:12

6 [a]Lev. 5:14-6:7

7 [1]Lit., *they* [2]Lit., *their* [3]Lit., *they have* [a]Lev. 5:5

8 [1]Lit., *redeemer*

9 [1]Lit., *heave offering* [a]Lev. 7:32, 34; 10:14, 15

12 [a]Num. 5:19, 20, 29

13 [1]Lit., *concealed*

14 [1]Lit., *and*

15 [1]Lit., *her* [2]I.e., approx. one bushel [a]Ezek. 29:16

17 [1]Lit., *the priest*

18 [1]Lit., *on her palms*

offering of jealousy, and in the hand of the priest is to be the
water of bitterness that brings a curse.
19 'And the priest shall have her take an oath and shall say
to the woman, "If no man has lain with you and if you have
not [a]gone astray into uncleanness, *being* under *the authority
of* your husband, be [1]immune to this water of bitterness that
brings a curse;
20 if you, however, have [a]gone astray, *being* under *the
authority of* your husband, and if you have defiled yourself
and a man other than your husband has had intercourse with
you,"
21 then the priest shall have the woman swear with the
oath of the curse, and the priest shall say to the woman, "The
LORD make you a curse and an oath among your people by the
LORD's making your thigh [1]waste away and your abdomen
swell;
22 and this water that brings a curse shall go into your
[1]stomach, and make your abdomen swell and your thigh
[2]waste away." And the woman shall say, "Amen, Amen."
23 'The priest shall then write these curses on a scroll, and
he shall [1]wash them off into the water of bitterness.
24 'Then he shall make the woman drink the water of
bitterness that brings a curse, so that the water which brings a
curse will go into her [1]and *cause* bitterness.
25 'And the priest shall take the grain offering of jealousy
from the woman's hand, and he shall wave the grain offering
before the LORD and bring it to the altar;
26 and the priest shall take a handful of the grain offering
as its memorial offering and offer *it* up in smoke on the altar,
and afterward he shall make the woman drink the water.
27 'When he has made her drink the water, then it shall
come about, if she has defiled herself and has been unfaithful
to her husband, that the water which brings a curse shall go
into her [1]and *cause* bitterness, and her abdomen will swell and
her thigh will [2]waste away, and the woman will become [a]a
curse among her people.
28 'But if the woman has not defiled herself and is clean,
she will then be free and conceive [1]children.
29 'This is the law of jealousy: when a wife, *being* under
the authority of her husband, [a]goes astray and defiles herself,
30 or when a spirit of jealousy comes over a man and he is
jealous of his wife, he shall then make the woman stand before
the LORD, and the priest shall apply all this law to her.
31 'Moreover, the man shall be free from [1]guilt, but that
woman shall bear her [1]guilt.' "

CHAPTER 6

AGAIN the LORD spoke to Moses, saying,
2 "Speak to the sons of Israel, and say to them, 'When a
man or woman makes a [1]special vow, the vow of [a]a [2]Nazirite,
to [3]dedicate himself to the LORD,
3 he shall abstain from wine and strong drink; he shall
drink no vinegar, whether made from wine or strong drink,
neither shall he drink any grape juice, nor eat fresh or dried
grapes.

19 [1]Lit., *free from* [a]Num. 5:12
20 [a]Num. 5:12
21 [1]Lit., *fall*
22 [1]Or, *inward parts* [2]Lit., *fall*
23 [1]Lit., *wipe*
24 [1]Lit., *to*
27 [1]Lit., *to* [2]Lit., *fall* [a]Jer. 29:18; 42:18; 44:12
28 [1]Lit., *seed*
29 [a]Num. 5:12
31 [1]Or, *iniquity*
2 [1]Or, *difficult* [2]I.e., one separated [3]Or, *live as a Nazirite* [a]Judg. 13:5; 16:17; Amos 2:11, 12

4 'All the days of his [1]separation he shall not eat anything
that is produced by the grape vine, from *the* seeds even to *the*
skin.
5 'All the days of his vow of separation [a]no razor shall pass
over his head. He shall be holy until the days are fulfilled for
which he separated himself to the LORD; he shall let the locks
of hair on his head grow long.
6 '[a]All the days of his separation to the LORD he shall not
go near to a dead person.
7 'He shall not make himself unclean for his father or for
his mother, for his brother or for his sister, when they die,
because his separation to God is on his head.
8 'All the days of his separation he is holy to the LORD.
9 'But if a man dies very suddenly beside him and he
defiles his dedicated head *of hair,* then [a]he shall shave his head
on the day when he becomes clean; [b]he shall shave it on the
seventh day.
10 'Then on the eighth day he shall bring two turtle-doves
or two young pigeons to the priest, to the doorway of the tent
of meeting.
11 'And the priest shall offer [a]one for a sin offering and *the*
other for a burnt offering, and make atonement for him [1]con-
cerning his sin because of the *dead* person. And that same day
he shall consecrate his head,
12 and shall [1]dedicate to the LORD his days [2]as a Nazirite,
and shall bring a male lamb a year old for a guilt offering; but
the former days shall be void because his separation was
defiled.
13 'Now this is the law of the Nazirite when the days of his
separation are fulfilled, he shall bring [1]the offering to the doorway of the tent of meeting.
14 'And he shall present his offering to the LORD: one male
lamb a year old without defect for a burnt offering and one
[a]ewe-lamb a year old without defect for a sin offering and one
ram without defect for a peace offering,
15 and a basket of unleavened cakes of fine flour mixed
with oil and unleavened wafers spread with oil, along with
[a]their grain offering and their libations.
16 'Then the priest shall present *them* before the LORD and
shall offer his sin offering and his burnt offering.
17 'He shall also offer the ram for a sacrifice of peace
offerings to the LORD, together with the basket of unleavened
cakes; the priest shall likewise offer its grain offering and its
libation.
18 '[a]The Nazirite shall then shave his dedicated head *of*
hair at the doorway of the tent of meeting, and take the dedicated hair of his head and put *it* on the fire which is under the
sacrifice of peace offerings.
19 '[a]And the priest shall take the ram's shoulder *when it*
has been boiled, and one unleavened cake out of the basket,
and one unleavened wafer, and shall put *them* on the [1]hands of
the Nazirite after he has shaved his [2]dedicated *hair*.
20 'Then the priest shall wave them for a wave offering
before the LORD. It is holy, for the priest, together with the
breast offered by waving and the thigh offered by lifting up;
and afterward the Nazirite may drink wine.'

4 [1]Or, *living as a Nazirite,* and so through v. 21

5 [a]1 Sam. 1:11

6 [a]Num. 19:11-22; Lev. 21:1-3

9 [a]Lev. 14:8, 9 [b]Num. 6:18

11 [1]Lit., *because of that which he sinned* [a]Lev. 5:7

12 [1]Or, *of dedication* [2]I.e., one separated

13 [1]Lit., *it*

14 [a]Num. 15:27; Lev. 14:10

15 [a]Num 15:1-7

18 [a]Num. 6:9

19 [1]Lit., *palms* [2]Or, *separated* [a]Lev. 7:28-34

21 "This is the law of the Nazirite who vows his offering to
the LORD according to his separation, in addition to what *else*
[1]he can afford; according to his vow which he takes, so he shall
do according to the law of his separation."
22 Then the LORD spoke to Moses, saying,
23 "Speak to Aaron and to his sons, saying, 'Thus [a]you shall
bless the sons of Israel. You shall say to them:
24 The LORD [a]bless you, and [b]keep you;
25 The LORD [a]make His face shine on you,
And [b]be gracious to you;
26 The LORD [a]lift up His countenance on you,
And [b]give you peace.'
27 "So they shall [1a]invoke My name on the sons of Israel,
and I then will bless them."

CHAPTER 7

NOW it came about on [a]the day that Moses had finished
setting up the tabernacle, he [b]anointed it and consecrated it
with all its furnishings and the altar and all its utensils, he
anointed them and consecrated them also.
2 Then [a]the leaders of Israel, the heads of their fathers'
households, made an offering (they were the leaders of the
tribes; they were the ones who [1]were over the [2]numbered
men).
3 When they brought their offering before the Lord, six
[a]covered carts and twelve oxen, a cart for *every* two of the
leaders and an ox for each one, then they presented them
before the tabernacle.
4 Then the LORD spoke to Moses, saying,
5 "Accept *these things* from them, that they may be [1]used
in the service of the tent of meeting, and you shall give them
to the Levites, *to* each man according to his service."
6 So Moses took the carts and the oxen, and gave them
to the Levites.
7 Two carts and four oxen he gave to the sons of Gershon, according to [a]their service,
8 and four carts and eight oxen he gave to the sons of
Merari, according to [a]their service, under the [1]direction of
Ithamar the son of Aaron the priest.
9 But he did not give *any* to the sons of Kohath because
theirs *was* [a]the service of the holy *objects, which* they carried
on the shoulder.
10 And the leaders offered the dedication *offering* [1]for the
altar [2]when [a]it was anointed, so the leaders offered their offering before the altar.
11 Then the LORD said to Moses, "Let them present their
offering, one leader each day, for the dedication of the altar."
12 Now the one who presented his offering on the first
day *was* Nahshon the son of Amminadab, of the tribe of
Judah;
13 and his offering *was* one silver [1a]dish whose weight *was*
one hundred and thirty *shekels*, one silver bowl of seventy
shekels, [b]according to [2]the shekel of the sanctuary, both of
them full of fine flour mixed with oil for a grain offering;
14 one gold pan of ten *shekels*, full of incense;

21 [1]Lit., *his hand can reach*

23 [a]1 Chr. 23:13

24 [a]Deut. 28:3-6; Ps. 28:9 [b]1 Sam. 2:9; Ps. 17:8

25 [a]Ps. 80:3, 7, 19 [b]Ps. 86:16

26 [a]Ps. 4:6; 44:3 [b]Ps. 29:11; 37:11, 37

27 [1]Lit., *put* [a]2 Sam. 7:23

1 [a]Ex. 40:17 [b]Num. 7:10, 84, 88; Ex. 40:9-11

2 [1]Lit., *stood* [2]Lit., *mustered* [a]Num. 1:5-16

3 [a]Is. 66:20

5 [1]Lit., *for serving*

7 [a]Num. 4:24-26

8 [1]Lit., *hand* [a]Num. 4:31, 32

9 [a]Num. 4:5-15

10 [1]Lit., *of* [2]Lit., *in the day that* [a]Num. 7:1; 2 Chr. 7:9

13 [1]Or, *platter*, and so through v. 85 [2]I.e., approx. one-half ounce, and so through v. 86 [a]Ex. 25:29; 37:16 [b]Num. 3:47

15 one [1]bull, one ram, one male lamb one year old, for a
burnt offering;
16 one male goat for a sin offering;
17 and for the sacrifice of peace offerings, two oxen, five
rams, five male goats, five male lambs one year old. This *was*
the offering of Nahshon the son of Amminadab.
18 On the second day Nethanel the son of Zuar, leader of
Issachar, presented *an offering;*
19 he presented as his offering one silver dish whose
weight *was* one hundred and thirty *shekels,* one silver bowl of
seventy shekels, according to the shekel of the sanctuary, both
of them full of fine flour mixed with oil for a grain offering;
20 one gold pan of ten *shekels,* full of incense;
21 one bull, one ram, one male lamb one year old, for a
burnt offering;
22 one male goat for a sin offering;
23 and for the sacrifice of peace offerings, two oxen, five
rams, five male goats, five male lambs one year old. This *was*
the offering of Nethanel the son of Zuar.
24 On the third day *it was* Eliab the son of Helon, leader
of the sons of Zebulun;
25 his offering was one silver dish whose weight *was* one
hundred and thirty *shekels,* one silver bowl of seventy shekels,
according to the shekel of the sanctuary, both of them full of
fine flour mixed with oil for a grain offering;
26 one gold pan of ten *shekels,* full of incense;
27 one young bull, one ram, one male lamb one year old,
for a burnt offering;
28 one male goat for a sin offering;
29 and for the sacrifice of peace offerings, two oxen, five
rams, five male goats, five male lambs one year old. This *was*
the offering of Eliab the son of Helon.
30 On the fourth day *it was* Elizur the son of Shedeur,
leader of the sons of Reuben;
31 his offering was one silver dish whose weight *was* one
hundred and thirty *shekels,* one silver bowl of seventy shekels,
according to the shekel of the sanctuary, both of them full of
fine flour mixed with oil for a grain offering;
32 one gold pan of ten *shekels,* full of incense;
33 one bull, one ram, one male lamb one year old, for a
burnt offering;
34 one male goat for a sin offering;
35 and for the sacrifice of peace offerings, two oxen, five
rams, five male goats, five male lambs one year old. This *was*
the offering of Elizur the son of Shedeur.
36 On the fifth day *it was* Shelumiel the son of Zurishaddai, leader of the children of Simeon;
37 his offering was one silver dish whose weight *was* one
hundred and thirty *shekels,* one silver bowl of seventy shekels,
according to the shekel of the sanctuary, both of them full of
fine flour mixed with oil for a grain offering;
38 one gold pan of ten *shekels,* full of incense;
39 one bull, one ram, one male lamb one year old, for a
burnt offering;
40 one male goat for a sin offering;
41 and for the sacrifice of peace offerings, two oxen, five

15 [1]Or, *bull of the herd,* and so through vs. 81

rams, five male goats, five male lambs one year old. This *was*
the offering of Shelumiel the son of Zurishaddai.
42 On the sixth day *it was* Eliasaph the son of Deuel,
leader of the sons of Gad;
43 his offering was one silver dish whose weight *was* one
hundred and thirty *shekels,* one silver bowl of seventy shekels,
according to the shekel of the sanctuary, both of them full of
fine flour mixed with oil for a grain offering;
44 one gold pan of ten *shekels,* full of incense;
45 one bull, one ram, one male lamb one year old, for a
burnt offering;
46 one male goat for a sin offering;
47 and for the sacrifice of peace offerings, two oxen, five
rams, five male goats, five male lambs one year old. This *was*
the offering of Eliasaph the son of Deuel.
48 On the seventh day *it was* Elishama the son of Ammihud, leader of the sons of Ephraim;
49 his offering was one silver dish whose weight *was* one
hundred and thirty *shekels,* one silver bowl of seventy shekels,
according to the shekel of the sanctuary, both of them full of
fine flour mixed with oil for a grain offering;
50 one gold pan of ten *shekels,* full of incense;
51 one bull, one ram, one male lamb one year old, for a
burnt offering;
52 one male goat for a sin offering;
53 and for the sacrifice of peace offerings, two oxen, five
rams, five male goats, five male lambs one year old. This *was*
the offering of Elishama the son of Ammihud.
54 On the eight day *it was* Gamaliel the son of Pedahzur,
leader of the sons of Manasseh;
55 his offering was one silver dish whose weight *was* one
hundred and thirty *shekels,* one silver bowl of seventy shekels,
according to the shekel of the sanctuary, both of them full of
fine flour mixed with oil for a grain offering;
56 one gold pan of ten *shekels,* full of incense;
57 one bull, one ram, one male lamb one year old, for a
burnt offering;
58 one male goat for a sin offering;
59 and for the sacrifice of peace offerings, two oxen, five
rams, five male goats, five male lambs one year old. This *was*
the offering of Gamaliel the son of Pedahzur.
60 On the ninth day *it was* Abidan the son of Gideoni,
leader of the sons of Benjamin;
61 his offering *was* one silver dish whose weight *was* one
hundred and thirty *shekels,* one silver bowl of seventy shekels,
according to the shekel of the sanctuary, both of them full of
fine flour mixed with oil for a grain offering;
62 one gold pan of ten *shekels,* full of incense;
63 one bull, one ram, one male lamb one year old, for a
burnt offering;
64 one male goat for a sin offering;
65 and for the sacrifice of peace offerings, two oxen, five
rams, five male goats, five male lambs one year old. This *was*
the offering of Abidan the son of Gideoni.
66 On the tenth day *it was* Ahiezer the son of Ammishaddai, leader of the sons of Dan;

67 his offering was one silver dish whose weight *was* one
hundred and thirty *shekels*, one silver bowl of seventy shekels,
according to the shekel of the sanctuary, both of them full of
fine flour mixed with oil for a grain offering;
68 one gold pan of ten *shekels*, full of incense;
69 one bull, one ram, one male lamb one year old, for a
burnt offering;
70 one male goat for a sin offering;
71 and for the sacrifice of peace offerings, two oxen, five
rams, five male goats, five male lambs one year old. This *was*
the offering of Ahiezer the son of Ammishaddai.
72 On the eleventh day *it was* Pagiel the son of Ochran,
leader of the sons of Asher;
73 his offering *was* one silver dish whose weight *was* one
hundred and thirty *shekels*, one silver bowl of seventy shekels,
according to the shekel of the sanctuary, both of them full of
fine flour mixed with oil for a grain offering;
74 one gold pan of ten *shekels*, full of incense;
75 one bull, one ram, one male lamb one year old, for a
burnt offering;
76 one male goat for a sin offering;
77 and for the sacrifice of peace offerings, two oxen, five
rams, five male goats, five male lambs one year old. This *was*
the offering of Pagiel the son of Ochran.
78 On the twelfth day *it was* Ahira the son of Enan, leader
of the sons of Naphtali;
79 his offering *was* one silver dish whose weight *was* one
hundred and thirty *shekels*, one silver bowl of seventy shekels,
according to the shekel of the sanctuary, both of them full of
fine flour mixed with oil for a grain offering.
80 one gold pan of ten *shekels*, full of incense;
81 one bull, one ram, one male lamb one year old, for a
burnt offering;
82 one male goat for a sin offering;
83 and for the sacrifice of peace offerings, two oxen, five
rams, five male goats, five male lambs one year old. This *was*
the offering of Ahira the son of Enan.
84 This *was* [a]the dedication *offering* [1]for the altar from
the leaders of Israel [2]when [b]it was anointed: twelve silver
dishes, twelve silver bowls, twelve gold pans,
85 each silver dish *weighing* one hundred and thirty *shekels* and each bowl seventy; all the silver of the utensils *was*
2,400 *shekels*, according to the shekel of the sanctuary;
86 the twelve gold pans, full of incense, *weighing* ten *shekels* apiece, according to the shekel of the sanctuary, all the
gold of the pans 120 *shekels*;
87 all the oxen for the burnt offering twelve bulls, *all* the
rams twelve, the male lambs one year old with their grain
offering twelve, and the male goats for a sin offering twelve;
88 and all the oxen for the sacrifice of peace offerings 24
bulls, *all* the rams 60, the male goats 60, the male lambs one
year old 60. [a]This *was* the dedication *offering* for the altar
after it was anointed.
89 Now when [a]Moses went into the tent of meeting to
speak with Him, he heard the voice speaking to him from

84 [1]Lit., *of* [2]Lit., *in the day that* [a]Num. 7:10 [b]Num. 7:1

88 [a]Num. 7:1, 10

89 [a]Ex. 40:34, 35

above [b]the [1]mercy seat that was on the ark of the testimony,
from [c]between the two cherubim, so He spoke to him.

Chapter 8

THEN the LORD spoke to Moses, saying,
2 "Speak to Aaron and say to him, 'When you [1]mount the
lamps, the seven lamps will [a]give light in the front of the
lampstand.' "
3 Aaron therefore did so: he [1]mounted its lamps at the
front of the lampstand, just as the LORD had commanded
Moses.
4 [a]Now this was the workmanship of the lampstand,
hammered work of gold; from its base to its flowers, it was
hammered work; [b]according to the pattern which the LORD
had showed Moses, so he made the lampstand.
5 Again the LORD spoke to Moses, saying,
6 "Take the Levites from among the sons of Israel and
cleanse them.
7 "And thus you shall do to them, for their [1]cleansing:
sprinkle [2]purifying [a]water on them, and let them [3b]use a razor
over their whole [4]body, and [c]wash their clothes, and they shall
be clean.
8 "Then let them take a [1]bull with [a]its grain offering, fine
flour mixed with oil; and a second [1]bull you shall take for a sin
offering.
9 "So you shall present the Levites before the tent of
meeting. You shall also assemble the whole congregation of
the sons of Israel,
10 and present the Levites before the LORD; and the sons
of Israel shall lay their hands on the Levites.
11 "Aaron then shall [1]present the Levites before the LORD
as a [a]wave offering from the sons of Israel, that they may
[2]qualify to perform the service of the LORD.
12 "Now the Levites shall lay their hands on the heads of
the bulls; then offer the one for a sin offering and the other for
a burnt offering to the LORD, to make atonement for the
Levites.
13 "And you shall have the Levites stand before Aaron and
before his sons so as to present them as a wave offering to the
LORD.
14 "Thus you shall separate the Levites from among the
sons of Israel, and [a]the Levites shall be Mine.
15 "Then after that the Levites may go in to serve the tent
of meeting. But you shall cleanse them and present them as a
wave offering;
16 for they are [a]wholly given to Me from among the sons
of Israel. I have taken them for Myself [b]instead of every first
issue of the womb, the first-born of all the sons of Israel.
17 "For every first-born among the sons of Israel are Mine,
among the men and among the animals; on the day that I
struck down all the first-born in the land of Egypt I sanctified
them for Myself.
18 "But I have taken the Levites instead of every first-born
among the sons of Israel.

89 [1]Lit., *propitiatory* [b]Ex. 25:21, 22 [c]Ps. 80:1; 99:1

2 [1]Lit., *raise up* [a]Ex. 25:37; Lev. 24:2, 4

3 [1]Lit., *raised up*

4 [a]Ex. 25:31-40 [b]Ex. 25:9, 40; 26:30

7 [1]Lit., *water of sin* [2]Lit., *this their cleansing* [3]Lit., *cause to pass* [4]Lit., *flesh* [a]Num. 19:9, 13, 20 [b]Lev. 14:8, 9 [c]Num. 8:21

8 [1]Or, *bull of the herd* [a]Num. 15:8-10

11 [1]Lit., *wave,* and so throughout the chap. [2]Lit., *be able* [a]Lev. 7:30, 34

14 [a]Num. 3:12

16 [a]Num. 3:9 [b]Ex. 13:2

19 "And I have given the Levites as [1]a gift to Aaron and to his sons from among the sons of Israel, to perform the service of the sons of Israel at the tent of meeting, and to make atonement on behalf of the sons of Israel, and there may be no [a]plague among the sons of Israel by [2]their coming near to the sanctuary."

20 Thus did Moses and Aaron and all the congregation of the sons of Israel to the Levites: according to all that the LORD had commanded Moses concerning the Levites, so the sons of Israel did to them.

21 [a]The Levites, too, purified themselves from sin and washed their clothes; and Aaron presented them as a wave offering before the LORD. Aaron also made atonement for them to cleanse them.

22 Then after that the Levites went in to perform their service in the tent of meeting before Aaron and before his sons; just as the LORD had commanded Moses concerning the Levites, so they did to them.

23 Now the LORD spoke to Moses, saying,

24 "This is what *applies* to the Levites: from [a]twenty-five years old and upward [1]they shall enter to perform service in the work of the tent of meeting.

25 "But at the age of fifty years they shall [1]retire from service in the work and not work any more.

26 "They may, however, [1]assist their brothers in the tent of meeting, to keep an obligation; but they *themselves* shall do no work. Thus you shall deal with the Levites concerning their obligations."

CHAPTER 9

THUS the LORD spoke to Moses in the wilderness of Sinai, in [a]the first month of the second year after they had come out of the land of Egypt, saying,

2 "Now, let the sons of Israel observe the Passover at [a]its appointed time.

3 "On the fourteenth day of this month, [1]at twilight, you shall observe it at its appointed time; you shall observe it according to all its statutes and according to all its ordinances."

4 So Moses [1]told the sons of Israel, to observe the Passover.

5 And they observed the Passover in the first *month*, on the fourteenth day of the month, at twilight, in the wilderness of Sinai; according to all that the LORD had commanded Moses, so the sons of Israel did.

6 But there were *some* men who were [a]unclean because of *the* [1]dead person, so that they could not observe the Passover on that day; so they came before Moses and Aaron on that day.

7 And those men said to him. "*Though* we are unclean because of *the* [1]dead person, why are we restrained from presenting the offering of the LORD at its appointed time among the sons of Israel?"

19 [1]Lit., *given ones* [2]Lit., *the sons of Israel's* [a]Num. 1:53

21 [a]Num. 8:7

24 [1]Lit., *he* [a]Num. 4:3

25 [1]Lit., *return*

26 [1]Lit., *serve*

1 [a]Num. 1:1; Ex. 40:2, 17

2 [a]Ex. 12:6

3 [1]Lit., *between the two evenings*, and so throughout the chap.

4 [1]Lit., *spoke to*

6 [1]Lit., *soul of man* [a]Num. 19:11-22

7 [1]Lit., *soul of man*

8 Moses therefore said to them, "[1a]Wait, and I will listen to what the LORD will command concerning you."

9 Then the LORD spoke to Moses, saying,

10 "Speak to the sons of Israel, saying, 'If any one of you or of your generations becomes unclean because of a *dead* [1]person, or is on a distant journey, he may, however, observe the Passover to the LORD.

11 'In the second month on the fourteenth day at twilight, they shall observe it; they shall eat it with unleavened bread and bitter herbs.

12 'They shall leave none of it until morning, [a]nor break a bone of it; according to all the statute of the Passover they shall observe it.

13 '[a]But the man who is clean and is not on a journey, and yet [1]neglects to observe the Passover, that [2]person shall then be cut off from his people, for he did not present the offering of the LORD at its appointed time. That man shall bear his sin.

14 '[a]And if an alien sojourns among you and [1]observes the Passover to the LORD, according to the statute of the Passover and according to its ordinance, so he shall do; you shall have [b]one statute, both for the alien and for the native of the land.' "

15 Now on [a]the day that the tabernacle was erected [b]the cloud covered the tabernacle, the [c]tent of the testimony, and [d]in the evening it was like the appearance of fire over the tabernacle, until morning.

16 So it was continuously; the cloud would cover it *by day*, and the appearance of fire by night.

17 [a]And whenever the cloud was lifted from over the tent, afterward the sons of Israel would then set out; and in the place where the cloud settled down, there the sons of Israel would camp.

18 At the [1]command of the LORD the sons of Israel would set out, and at the [1]command of the LORD they would camp; as long as the cloud settled over the tabernacle, they remained camped.

19 Even when the cloud lingered over the tabernacle for many days, [1]the sons of Israel would keep the LORD's charge and not set out.

20 If [1]sometimes the cloud remained a few days over the tabernacle, according to the [2]command of the LORD they remained camped. Then according to the [2]command of the LORD they set out.

21 If [1]sometimes the cloud [2]remained from evening until morning, when the cloud was lifted in the morning, they would move out; or *if it remained* in the daytime and at night, whenever the cloud was lifted, they would set out.

22 Whether it was two days or a month or a year that the cloud lingered over the tabernacle, staying above it, the sons of Israel remained camped and did not set out; but when it was lifted, they did set out.

23 At the [1]command of the LORD they camped, and at the [1]command of the LORD they set out; they kept the LORD's charge, according to the [1]command of the LORD through Moses.

8 [1]Lit., *stand* [a]Ex. 18:15
10 [1]Lit., *soul*
12 [a]John 19:36; Ex. 12:46
13 [1]Or, *ceases* [2]Lit., *soul* [a]Ex. 12:47
14 [1]Or, *would observe* [a]Ex. 12:48 [b]Num. 15:15, 16, 29; Ex. 12:49; Lev 24:22
15 [a]Ex 40:1, 17 [b]Ex. 40:34 [c]Num. 17:7 [d]Ex. 13:21, 22
17 [a]Num. 10:11, 12; Ex. 40:36-38
18 [1]Lit., *mouth*
19 [1]Lit., *and the*
20 [1]Lit., *it was that* [2]Lit., *mouth*
21 [1]Lit., *it was that* [2]Lit., *was*
23 [1]Lit., *mouth*

CHAPTER 10

THE LORD spoke further to Moses, saying,

2 "Make yourself two trumpets of silver, of hammered work you shall make them; and you shall use them for summoning the congregation and for having the camps set out.

3 "And when both are blown, all the congregation shall gather themselves to you at the doorway of the tent of meeting.

4 "Yet if *only* one is blown, then the leaders, the heads of the [1]divisions of Israel, shall assemble before you.

5 "But when you blow an alarm, the camps that are pitched [a]on the east side shall set out.

6 "And when you blow an alarm the second time, the camps that are pitched on [a]the south side shall set out; an alarm is to be blown for them to set out.

7 "When convening the assembly, however, you shall blow without sounding an alarm.

8 "[a]The priestly sons of Aaron, moreover, shall blow the trumpets; and [1]this shall be for you a perpetual statute throughout your generations.

9 "And when you go to war in your land against the adversary who attacks you, then you shall sound an alarm with the trumpets, that you may be remembered before the LORD your God, and be saved from your enemies.

10 "Also in the day of your gladness and in your appointed [1]feasts, and on the first *days* of your months, [a]you shall blow the trumpets over your burnt offerings, and over the sacrifices of your peace offerings; and they shall be as a reminder of you before your God. I am the LORD your God."

11 Now it came about in [a]the second year, in the second month, on the twentieth of the month, that the cloud was lifted from over the [1]tabernacle of the testimony;

12 and the sons of Israel set out on their journeys from the wilderness of Sinai. Then the cloud settled down in the wilderness of Paran.

13 [a]So they moved out for the first time according to the [1]commandment of the LORD through Moses.

14 And the standard of the camp of the sons of Judah, according to their armies, [a]set out first, with Nahshon the son of Amminadab, over its army,

15 and Nethanel the son of Zuar, over the tribal army of the sons of Issachar;

16 and Eliab the son of Helon over the tribal army of the sons of Zebulun.

17 [a]Then the tabernacle was taken down; and the sons of Gershon and the sons of Merari, who were carrying the tabernacle, set out.

18 Next [a]the standard of the camp of Reuben, according to their armies, set out with Elizur the son of Shedeur, over its army,

19 and Shelumiel the son of Zurishaddai over the tribal army of the sons of Simeon,

20 and Eliasaph the son of Deuel was over the tribal army of the sons of Gad.

4 [1]Lit., *thousands*, or, *clans*
5 [a]Num. 10:14
6 [a]Num. 10:18
8 [1]Lit., *it* [a]Num. 31:6
10 [1]Or, *times* [a]Ps. 81:3-5
11 [1]Lit., *dwelling place* and so throughout the chap. [a]Ex. 40:17
13 [1]Lit., *mouth* [a]Deut. 1:6
14 [a]Num. 2:3-9
17 [a]Num. 4:21-32
18 [a]Num. 2:10-16

21 [a]Then the Kohathites set out, carrying the holy *objects;* and [b]the tabernacle was set up before their arrival.

22 [a]Next the standard of the camp of the sons of Ephraim, according to their armies, was set out, with Elishama the son of Ammihud over its army,

23 and Gamaliel the son of Pedahzur over the tribal army of the sons of Manasseh;

24 and Abidan the son of Gideoni over the tribal army of the sons of Benjamin.

25 [a]Then the standard of the camp of the sons of Dan, according to their armies, *which formed* the [b]rear guard for all the camps, set out, with Ahiezer the son of Ammishaddai over its army,

26 and Pagiel the son of Ochran over the tribal army of the sons of Asher;

27 and Ahira the son of Enan over the tribal army of the sons of Naphtali.

28 [1]This was the order of march of the sons of Israel by their armies as they set out.

29 Then Moses said to [a]Hobab the son of [b]Reuel the Midianite, Moses' father-in-law, "We are setting out to the place of which the LORD said, '[c]I will give it to you'; [d]come with us and we will do you good, for the LORD [e]has [1]promised good concerning Israel."

30 But he said to him, "[a]I will not come, but rather will go to my *own* land and relatives."

31 Then he said, "Please do not leave us, inasmuch as you know where we should camp in the wilderness, and you will be as eyes for us.

32 "So it will be, if you go with us, it will come about that [1a]whatever good the LORD [2]does for us, [b]we will [3]do for you."

33 [a]Thus they set out from the mount of the LORD three days' journey, with [b]the ark of the covenant of the LORD journeying in front of them for the [1]three days, to seek out [c]a resting place for them.

34 [a]And the cloud of the LORD was over them by day, when they set out from the camp.

35 Then it came about when the ark set out that Moses said,

"[a]Rise up, O LORD!
And let Thine enemies be scattered,
And let those [b]who hate Thee flee [1]before Thee."

36 And when it came to rest, he said,
"[a]Return Thou, O LORD
To the myriad [b]thousands of Israel."

CHAPTER 11

NOW the people became like [a]those who complain of adversity [b]in the hearing of the LORD; and when the LORD heard *it,* His anger was kindled, and the fire of the LORD burned among them and consumed *some* of the outskirts of the camp.

2 [a]The people therefore cried out to Moses, and Moses prayed to the LORD, and the fire [1]died out.

3 So the name of that place was called [1a]Taberah, because the fire of the LORD burned among them.

21 [a]Num. 4:4-20 [b]Num. 10:17

22 [a]Num. 2:18-24

25 [a]Num. 2:25-31 [b]Josh. 6:9, 13

28 [1]Lit., *These are the settings out of the sons*

29 [1]Lit., *spoken* [a]Judg. 4:11 [b]Ex. 2:18; 3:1; 18:12 [c]Gen. 12:7; Ex. 6:4-8 [d]Ps. 95:1-7; 100:1-5 [e]Deut. 4:40; 30:5

30 [a]Matt. 21:28, 29; Judg. 1:16

32 [1]Lit., *that good which* [2]Lit., *does good* [3]Lit., *do good* [a]Ps. 22:27-31; 67:5-7 [b]Lev. 19:34; Deut. 10:18

33 [1]Lit., *three days' journey* [a]Num. 10:11 [b]Deut. 1:33 [c]Is. 11:10

34 [a]Num. 9:15-23

35 [1]Or, *from Thy presence* [a]Ps. 68:1, 2; Is. 17:12-14 [b]Deut. 7:10; 32:41

36 [a]Is. 63:17 [b]Deut. 1:10

1 [a]Num. 14:2; 16:11; 17:5 [b]Num. 11:18; 14:28

2 [1]Lit., *sank down* [a]Num. 12:11, 13; 21:7

3 [1]I.e., Burning [a]Deut. 9:22

4 And the [a]rabble who were among them [1]had greedy
desires; and also the sons of Israel wept again and said, "[b]Who
will give us [2]meat to eat?
5 "[a]We remember the fish which we used to eat free in
Egypt, the cucumbers and the melons and the leeks and the
onions and the garlic,
6 but now [a]our [1]appetite is gone. There is nothing at all
[2]to look at except this manna."
7 [a]Now the manna was like coriander seed, and its appearance like that of bdellium.
8 The people would go about and gather *it* and grind *it*
[1]between two millstones or beat *it* in the mortar, and boil *it* in
the pot and make cakes with it; and its taste was as the taste of
[2]cakes baked with oil.
9 [a]And when the dew fell on the camp at night, the
manna would fall [1]with it.
10 Now Moses heard the people weeping throughout
their families, each man at the doorway of his tent; and the
anger of the LORD was kindled greatly, and [1]Moses was
displeased.
11 [a]So Moses said to the LORD, "Why hast Thou [1]been so
hard on Thy servant? And why have I not found favor in Thy
sight, that Thou hast laid the burden of all this people on me?
12 "Was it I who conceived all this people? Was it I who
brought them forth, that Thou shouldest say to me, 'Carry
them in your bosom as a [1a]nurse carries a nursing infant, to the
land which [b]Thou didst swear to their fathers'?
13 "Where am I to get [1]meat to give to [a]all this people? For
they weep before me, saying, 'Give us [1]meat that we may eat!'
14 "[a]I alone am not able to carry all this people, because it
is too [1]burdensome for me.
15 "[a]So if Thou art going to deal thus with me, please kill
me at once, if I have found favor in Thy sight, and do not let
me see my wretchedness."
16 The LORD therefore said to Moses, "Gather for Me
seventy men from the elders of Israel, [a]whom you know to be
the elders of the people and their officers and bring them to
the tent of meeting, and let them take their stand there with
you.
17 "[a]Then I will come down and speak with you there, and
I will take of the Spirit who is upon you, and will put *Him*
upon them; and they shall bear the burden of the people with
you, so that you shall not bear *it* all alone.
18 "And say to the people, '[a]Consecrate yourselves for tomorrow, and you shall eat meat; for you have wept [b]in the ears
of the LORD, saying, "Oh that someone would give us meat to
eat! For we were well-off in Egypt." Therefore the LORD will
give you meat and you shall eat.
19 'You shall eat, not one day, nor two days, nor five days,
nor ten days, nor twenty days,
20 [1]but a whole month, until it comes out of your nostrils
and becomes loathsome to you; because [a]you have rejected the
LORD who is among you and have wept before Him, saying,
"Why did we ever leave Egypt?"' "
21 But Moses said, "The people, among whom I am, are

4 [1]Lit., *desired a desire* [2]Lit., *flesh*, and so throughout the chap. [a]Ex. 12:38; 1 Cor. 10:6 [b]Ps. 78:20

5 [a]Ex. 16:3

6 [1]Lit., *soul is dried up* [2]Lit., *for our eyes* [a]Num. 21:5

7 [a]Ex. 16:31

8 [1]Lit., *with* [2]Lit., *juice of oil*

9 [1]Lit., *on* [a]Ex. 16:13, 14

10 [1]Lit., it was *evil in Moses' sight*

11 [1]Lit., *dealt ill with* [a]Ex. 5:22

12 [1]Or, *foster-father* [a]2 Kin. 10:1, 5; Is. 49:23 [b]Gen. 24:7; Ex. 13:5, 11; 33:1

13 [1]Lit., *flesh* [a]Num. 11:21, 22; John 6:5-9

14 [1]Lit., *heavy* [a]Ex. 18:18; Deut. 1:12

15 [a]Ex. 32:32

16 [a]Ex. 18:25

17 [a]Num. 11:25

18 [a]Ex. 19:10, 22 [b]Num. 11:1

20 [1]Lit., *until* [a]Josh. 24:27; 1 Sam. 10:19

600,000 on foot; yet Thou hast said, 'I will give them meat in
order that they may eat for a whole month.'
22 "Should flocks and herds be slaughtered for them, to be
sufficient for them? Or should all the fish of the sea be gathered together for them, to be sufficient for them?"
23 And the LORD said to Moses, "Is [a]the LORD's [1]power
limited? Now you shall see whether My word will [2]come true
for you or not."
24 So Moses went out and [a]told the people the words of
the LORD. Also, he gathered seventy men of the elders of the
people, and stationed them around the tent.
25 [a]Then the LORD came down in the cloud and spoke to
him; and He took of the Spirit who was upon him and placed
Him upon the seventy elders. And it came about that when the
Spirit rested upon them, they prophesied. But they did not do
it again.
26 But two men had remained in the camp; the name of
one was Eldad and the name of the [1]other Medad. And [a]the
Spirit rested upon them (now they were among those who had
been registered, but had not gone out to the tent), and they
prophesied in the camp.
27 So a young man ran and told Moses and said, "Eldad
and Medad are prophesying in the camp."
28 Then [a]Joshua the son of Nun, the attendant of Moses
from his youth, answered and said, "[b]Moses, my lord, restrain
them."
29 But Moses said to him, "Are you jealous for my sake?
Would that all the LORD's people were prophets, that the
LORD would put His Spirit upon them!"
30 Then Moses [1]returned to the camp, *both* he and the
elders of Israel.
31 [a]Now there went forth a wind from the LORD, and it
brought quail from the sea, and let *them* fall beside the camp,
about a day's journey on this side and a day's journey on the
other side, all around the camp, and [1]about two [2]cubits *deep*
on the surface of the ground.
32 And the people [1]spent all day and all night and all the
next day, and gathered the quail (he who gathered least gathered ten [2]homers) and they spread *them* out for themselves
all around the camp.
33 [a]While the meat was still between their teeth, before it
was chewed, the anger of the LORD was kindled against the
people, and the LORD struck the people with a very severe
plague.
34 So the name of that place was called [1a]Kibroth-hatta-
avah, because there they buried the people who had been
greedy.
35 From Kibroth-hattaavah the people set out for Hazeroth, and they [1]remained at Hazeroth.

CHAPTER 12

THEN Miriam and Aaron spoke against Moses because of
the Cushite woman whom he had married (for he had married
a [a]Cushite woman);
2 [a]and they said, "Has the LORD indeed spoken only

23 [1]Lit., *hand short* [2]Lit., *befall you* [a]Is. 50:2; 59:1

24 [a]Num. 11:16

25 [a]Num. 11:17; 12:5

26 [1]Lit., *second* [a]Num. 24:2; 1 Sam. 10:6; 2 Chr. 15:1; Neh. 9:30

28 [a]Ex. 33:11; Josh. 1:1 [b]Mark 9:38-40

30 [1]Lit., *removed himself*

31 [1]Or, from *about two cubits above* [2]I.e., one cubit equals 18 inches [a]Ex. 16:13; Ps. 78:26-28; 105:40

32 [1]Lit., *rose* [2]I.e., one homer equals about 11 bushels

33 [a]Ps. 78:29-31; 106:15

34 [1]I.e., The graves of greediness [a]Deut. 9:22

35 [1]Lit., *were*

1 [a]Ex. 2:21

2 [a]Num. 16:3

through Moses? Has He not spoken through us as well?" And
the LORD heard it.
3 (Now the man Moses was [a]very humble, more than any
man who was on the face of the earth.)
4 And suddenly the LORD said to Moses and Aaron and
to Miriam, "You three come out to the tent of meeting." So
the three of them came out.
5 [a]Then the LORD came down in a pillar of cloud and
stood at the doorway of the tent, and He called [1]Aaron and
Miriam. When they had both come forward,
6 He said,

"Hear now My words:
If there is a prophet among you,
I the LORD shall make Myself known to him in a [a]vision.
I shall speak with him in a [b]dream.

7 "Not so, with [a]My servant Moses,
[b]He is faithful in all My household;
8 [a]With him I speak mouth to mouth,
Even openly, and not in dark sayings,
And he beholds [b]the form of the LORD.
Why then were you not afraid
To speak against My servant, against Moses?"

9 So the anger of the LORD burned against them and [a]He
departed.
10 But when the cloud had withdrawn from over the tent,
behold, [a]Miriam *was* leprous, as [b]*white as* snow. As Aaron
turned toward Miriam, behold, she *was* leprous.
11 Then Aaron said to Moses, Oh, my lord, I beg you, [a]do
not account *this* sin to us, in which we have acted foolishly and
in which we have sinned.
12 "Oh do not let her be like one dead, whose flesh is half
eaten away when he comes from his mother's womb!"
13 And Moses cried out to the LORD, saying, "Oh God,
[a]heal her, I pray!"
14 But the LORD said to Moses, "If her father had but [a]spit
in her face, would she not bear her shame for seven days? Let
her be shut up for seven days [b]outside the camp, and afterward
she may be received again."
15 So Miriam was shut up outside the camp for seven
days, and the people did not move on until Miriam was received again.
16 Afterward, however, the people moved out from Hazeroth and camped in the wilderness of Paran.

CHAPTER 13

THEN [a]the LORD spoke to Moses saying,
2 "Send out for yourself men so that they may spy out the
land of Canaan, which I am going to give to the sons of Israel;
you shall send a man from each of their fathers' tribes, every
one a leader among them."
3 So Moses sent them from the wilderness of Paran at
the [1]command of the LORD, all of them men who were heads
of the sons of Israel.

12:3 [a]Matt. 11:29
12:5 [1]Or, *"Aaron and Miriam!"* [a]Ex. 19:9; 34:5
12:6 [a]Gen. 46:2; 1 Sam. 3:15 [b]Gen. 31:11; 1 Kin. 3:5, 15
12:7 [a]Josh. 1:1 [b]Heb. 3:2, 5
12:8 [a]Deut. 34:10; Hos. 12:13 [b]Ex. 20:4; 24:10, 11; Deut. 5:8; Ps. 17:15
12:9 [a]Gen. 17:22; 18:33
12:10 [a]Deut. 24:9 [b]Ex. 4:6; 2 Kin. 5:27
12:11 [a]2 Sam. 19:19; 24:10
12:13 [a]Ps. 30:2; 41:4; Is. 30:26; Jer. 17:14
12:14 [a]Deut. 25:9; Job 17:6; 30:10; Is. 50:6 [b]Num. 5:1-4
13:1 [a]Deut. 1:22, 23
13:3 [1]Lit., *mouth*

4 These then *were* their names: from the tribe of Reuben, Shammua the son of Zaccur;
5 from the tribe of Simeon, Shaphat the son of Hori;
6 from the tribe of Judah, Caleb the son of Jephunneh;
7 from the tribe of Issachar, Igal the son of Joseph;
8 from the tribe of Ephraim, [a]Hoshea the son of Nun;
9 from the tribe of Benjamin, Palti the son of Raphu;
10 from the tribe of Zebulun, Gaddiel the son of Sodi;
11 from the tribe of Joseph, from the tribe of Manasseh,
Gaddi the son of Susi;
12 from the tribe of Dan, Ammiel the son of Gemalli;
13 from the tribe of Asher, Sethur the son of Michael;
14 from the tribe of Naphtali, Nahbi the son of Vophsi;
15 from the tribe of Gad, Geuel the son of Machi.
16 These are the names of the men whom Moses sent to
spy out the land; but Moses called [a]Hoshea the son of Nun,
Joshua.
17 When Moses sent them to spy out the land of Canaan,
he said to them, "Go up [1]there into [a]the [2]Negev; then go up
into the hill country.
18 "And see what the land is like, and whether the people
who live in it are strong *or* weak, whether they are few or many.
19 "And how is the land in which they live, is it good or
bad? And how are the cities in which they live, are *they* [1]like
open camps or with fortifications?
20 "And [a]how is the land, is it fat or lean? Are there trees in
it or not? [1]Make an [b]effort then to get some of the fruit of the
land." Now the time was the time of the first ripe grapes.
21 So they went up and spied out the land from [a]the
wilderness of Zin as far as Rehob, [1b]at Lebo-hamath.
22 When they had gone up into [a]the Negev, [1]they came to
Hebron where [b]Ahiman, Sheshai and Talmai, the [2]descen-
dants of [c]Anak were. (Now Hebron was built seven years before [d]Zoan in Egypt.)
23 Then they came to the [1]valley of [2a]Eshcol and from
there cut down a branch with a single cluster of grapes; and
they carried it on a pole between two *men*, with some of the
pomegranates and the figs.
24 That place was called the valley of [1]Eshcol, because of
the cluster which the sons of Israel cut down from there.
25 When they returned from spying out the land, at the
end of forty days,
26 they proceeded to come to Moses and Aaron and to all
the congregation of the sons of Israel [1]in the wilderness of
Paran, at [a]Kadesh; and they brought back word to them and to
all the congregation and showed them the fruit of the land.
27 Thus they told him, and said, "We went in to the land
where you sent us; and [a]it certainly does flow with milk and
honey, and [b]this is its fruit.
28 "Nevertheless, the people who live in the land are
strong, and the cities are fortified *and* very large; and moreover
we saw [a]the [1]descendants of Anak there.
29 "Amalek is living in the land of [a]the Negev and the
Hittites and the Jebusites and [b]the Amorites are living in the
hill country, and [c]the Canaanites are living by the sea and by
the side of the Jordan."

8 [a]Num. 13:16; Deut. 32:44

16 [a]Num. 13:8; Deut. 32:44

17 [1]Lit., *here* [2]I.e., South country, and so throughout the chap. [a]Gen. 12:9; 13:1, 3

19 [1]Lit., *in*

20 [1]Lit., *use your strength* [a]Deut. 1:24, 25 [b]Deut. 31:6, 23

21 [1]Or, *to the entrance of Hamath* [a]Num. 20:1; 27:14; 33:36 [b]Josh. 13:5

22 [1]Lit., Most mss. read, *one came* [2]Lit., *children* [a]Num. 13:17 [b]Josh. 15:14 [c]Num. 13:28, 33 [d]Ps. 78:12, 43

23 [1]Or, *wadi* [2]I.e., cluster [a]Num. 13:24; 32:9; Gen. 14:13; Deut. 1:24

24 [1]I.e., Cluster

26 [1]Lit., *to* [a]Num. 20:1, 14; 32:8

27 [a]Ex. 3:8, 17; 13:5 [b]Deut. 1:25

28 [1]Lit., *born ones* [a]Num. 13:33

29 [a]Num. 13:17; 14: 25, 45 [b]Josh. 10:6 [c]Num. 14:43, 45

30 Then Caleb quieted the people [1]before Moses, and
said, "We should by all means go up and take possession of it,
for we shall surely overcome it."
31 But the men who had gone up with him said, "[a]We are
not able to go up against the people, for they are too strong for
us."
32 So they gave out to the sons of Israel [a]a bad report of
the land which they had spied out, saying, "The land through
which we have gone, in spying it out, is [b]a land that devours
its [1]inhabitants; and [c]all the people whom we saw in it are men
of *great* size.
33 "There also we saw the [a]Nephilim (the sons of Anak are
part of the Nephilim); and [b]we became like grasshoppers in
our own sight, and so we were in their sight."

CHAPTER 14

THEN all the congregation [1]lifted up their voice and cried,
and the people wept [2]that night.
2 And all the sons of Israel [a]grumbled against Moses and
Aaron; and the whole congregation said to them, "[b]Would
that we had died in the land of Egypt! Or would that we had
died in this wilderness!
3 "And why is the LORD bringing us into this land, [a]to fall
by the sword? [b]Our wives and our little ones will become plunder; would it not be better for us to return to Egypt?"
4 So they said to one another, "Let us appoint a leader
and return to Egypt."
5 [a]Then Moses and Aaron fell on their faces in the presence of all the assembly of the congregation of the sons of
Israel.
6 And Joshua the son of Nun and Caleb the son of Jephunneh, of those who had spied out the land, tore their
clothes;
7 and they spoke to all the congregation of the sons of
Israel, saying, "[a]The land which we passed through to spy out
is an exceedingly good land.
8 "[a]If the LORD is pleased with us, then He will bring us
into this land, and give it to us—[b]a land which flows with milk
and honey.
9 "Only [a]do not rebel against the LORD; and do not [b]fear
the people of the land, for they shall be our [1]prey. Their
[2]protection has been removed from them, and the LORD is
with us; do not fear them."
10 [a]But all the congregation said to stone them with
stones. Then [b]the glory of the LORD appeared in the tent of
meeting to all the sons of Israel.
11 [a]And the LORD said to Moses, "How long will this
people spurn Me? And how long will [b]they not believe in Me,
despite all the signs which I have performed in their midst?
12 "I will smite them with [1a]pestilence and dispossess them,
and I [b]will make you into a nation greater and mightier than
they."
13 [a]But Moses said to the LORD, "Then the Egyptians will
hear of it, for by Thy strength Thou didst bring up this people
from their midst,

30 [1]Lit., *toward*

31 [a]Deut. 1:28; 9:1-3

32 [1]Or, *settlers*
[a]Num. 14:36, 37; Ps. 106:24
[b]Ezek. 36:13, 14 [c]Amos 2:9

33 [a]Gen. 6:4 [b]Deut. 1:28; 9:2 John 11:21

1 [1]Lit., *lifted and gave their voice* [2]Lit., *in that*

2 [a]Num. 11:1 [b]Num. 11:5; 16:13; 20:3, 4; 21:5

3 [a]Ex. 5:21; 16:3 [b]Num. 14:31; Deut. 1:39

5 [a]Num. 16:4

7 [a]Num. 13:27; Deut. 1:25

8 [a]Deut. 10:15 [b]Num. 13:27; Ex. 3:8

9 [1]Lit., *food* [2]Lit., *shadow*
[a]Deut. 1:26; 9:23, 24 [b]Deut. 1:21, 29

10 [a]Ex. 17:4 [b]Ex. 16:10; Lev. 9:23

11 [a]Ex. 32:9-13 [b]Ps. 106:24

12 [1]Lit., *the pestilence*
[a]Lev. 26:25; Deut. 28:21 [b]Ex. 32:10

13 [a]Ps. 106:23

14 and they will tell *it* to the inhabitants of this land. They
have heard that Thou, O LORD, art in the midst of this people,
for [a]Thou, O LORD, art seen eye to eye, while Thy cloud stands
over them; and Thou dost go before them in a pillar of cloud
by day and in a pillar of fire by night.
15 "Now if Thou dost slay this people as one man, [a]then
the nations who have heard of Thy fame will [1]say,
16 'Because the LORD could not bring this people into the
land which He promised them by oath, therefore He slaughtered them in the wilderness.'
17 "But now, I pray, let the power of the Lord be great, just
as Thou hast [1]declared,
18 '[a]The LORD is slow to anger and abundant in lovingkindness, forgiving iniquity and transgression; but He will by no
means clear *the guilty;* visiting the iniquity of the fathers on
the children [1]to the third and the fourth *generations.*'
19 "[a]Pardon, I pray, the iniquity of this people according to
the greatness of Thy lovingkindness, just as Thou also hast
forgiven this people, from Egypt even until now."
20 So the LORD said, "[a]I have pardoned *them* according to
your word;
21 but indeed, [a]as I live, [1b]all the earth will be filled with
the glory of the LORD.
22 "Surely [a]all the men who have seen My glory and My
signs, which I performed in Egypt and in the wilderness, yet
have put Me to the test these [b]ten times and have not listened
to My voice,
23 [a]shall by no means see the land which I swore to their
fathers, nor shall any of those who spurned Me see it.
24 "But My servant Caleb, [a]because he has had a different
spirit and has followed Me fully, [1b]I will bring into the land
[2]which he entered, and his [3]descendants shall take possession
of it.
25 "[a]Now the Amalekites and the Canaanites live in the
valleys; turn tomorrow and set out to the wilderness by the way
of the [1]Red Sea."
26 And the LORD spoke to Moses and Aaron, saying,
27 "How long *shall I bear* with this evil congregation who
are [a]grumbling against Me? I have heard the complaints of the
sons of Israel, which they are [1]making against Me.
28 "Say to them '[a]As I live,' says the LORD, 'just as [b]you
have spoken in My hearing, so I will surely do to you;
29 your corpses shall fall in this wilderness, even all [a]your
[1]numbered men, according to your complete number from
twenty years old and upward, who have grumbled against Me.
30 'Surely you shall not come into the land in which I
[1]swore to settle you, [a]except Caleb the son of Jephunneh and
Joshua the son of Nun.
31 '[a]Your children, however, whom you said would become a prey—I will bring them in, and they shall know the
land which you have rejected.
32 '[a]But as for you, your corpses shall fall in this wilderness.
33 'And your sons shall be shepherds for [a]forty years in the
wilderness, and they shall [1]suffer *for* your [2]unfaithfulness, until
your corpses [3]lie in the wilderness.
34 'According to the number of days which you spied out

14 [a]Ex. 13:21; Deut. 5:4

15 [1]Lit., *speak, saying* [a]Ex. 32:12

17 [1]Lit., *spoken, saying,*

18 [1]Lit., *on* [a]Ex. 34:6, 7

19 [a]Ex. 32:32; 34:9

20 [a]Mic. 7:18-20

21 [1]Lit., *and all* [a]Num. 14:28; Deut. 32:40; Is. 49:18 [b]Is. 6:3; Hab. 2:14

22 [a]1 Cor. 10:5 [b]Ex. 5:21; 14:11; 15:24; 16:2; 17:2, 3; 32:1; Num. 11:1, 4; 12:1; 14:2

23 [a]Num. 26:65; 32:11

24 [1]Lit., *him I* [2]Lit., *where* [3]Lit., *seed* [a]Num. 14:7-9 [b]Num. 26:65; 32:12; Deut. 1:36; Josh. 14:6-15

25 [1]Lit., *Sea of Reeds* [a]Num. 13:29

27 [1]Lit., *complaining* [a]Num. 11:1

28 [a]Num. 14:21 [b]Num. 14:2; Deut. 2:14, 15; Heb. 3:17

29 [1]Lit., *mustered* [a]Num. 1:45, 46

30 [1]Lit., *raised My hand* [a]Num. 14:24

31 [a]Num. 14:3

32 [a]Num. 26:64, 65; 32:13; 1 Cor. 10:5

33 [1]Lit., *bear* [2]Lit., *fornications* [3]Lit., *are finished* [a]Deut. 2:7; 8:2, 4; 29:5

the land, forty days, for every day you shall bear your [1]guilt a
year, *even* forty years, and you shall know My opposition.
35 'I the LORD have spoken, surely this I will do to all this
evil congregation who are gathered together against Me. In
this wilderness they shall be destroyed, and there they shall
die.'"
36 [a]As for the men whom Moses sent to spy out the land
and who returned and made all the congregation grumble
against him by bringing out a bad report concerning the land,
37 even those men who brought out the very bad report of
the land died by a [a]plague before the LORD.
38 But Joshua the son of Nun and Caleb the son of Jephunneh remained alive out of those men who went to spy out
the land.
39 And when Moses spoke [a]these words to all the sons of
Israel, [b]the people mourned greatly.
40 In the morning, however, they rose up early and went
up to the [1]ridge of the hill country, saying, "[a]Here we are; [2]we
have indeed sinned, but we will go up to the place which the
LORD has promised."
41 But Moses said, "Why then are you transgressing the
[1]commandment of the LORD, when it will not succeed?
42 "Do not go up, lest you be struck down before your
enemies, for the LORD is not among you.
43 "For the Amalekites and the Canaanites will be there in
front of you, and you will fall by the sword, inasmuch as you
have turned back from following the LORD. And the LORD will
not be with you."
44 But they went up heedlessly to the [1]ridge of the hill
country; neither [a]the ark of the covenant of the LORD nor
Moses left the camp.
45 Then the Amalekites and the Canaanites who lived in
that hill country came down, and struck them and beat them
down as far as [a]Hormah.

CHAPTER 15

NOW the LORD spoke to Moses, saying,
2 "Speak to the sons of Israel, and say to them, 'When
you enter the land [1]where you are to live, which I am giving
you,
3 then make an offering by fire to the LORD, a burnt
offering or a sacrifice to [1]fulfill a special vow, or as a freewill
offering or in your [a]appointed times, to make a soothing
aroma to the LORD, from the herd or from the flock.
4 '[a]And the one who presents his offering shall present to
the LORD a grain offering of one-tenth *of an ephah* of fine
flour mixed with one-fourth of a [1]hin of oil,
5 and you shall prepare wine for the libation, one-fourth
of a hin, with the burnt offering or for the sacrifice, for [a]each
lamb.
6 'Or for a ram you shall prepare as a grain offering two-
tenths *of an ephah* of fine flour mixed with one-third of a hin
of oil;
7 and for the libation you shall offer one-third of a hin of
wine as a soothing aroma to the LORD.

34 [1]Or, *iniquities*
36 [a]Num. 13:4-16, 32
37 [a]Num. 16:49
39 [a]Num. 14:28-35 [b]Ex. 33:4
40 [1]Or, *top of the mountain* [2]Or, *and we will go up . . . for we have sinned* [a]Deut. 1:41-44
41 [1]Lit., *mouth*
44 [1]Or, *top of the mountain* [a]Num. 31:6
45 [a]Num. 21:3
2 [1]Lit., *of your dwellings*
3 [1]Or, *make a special votive offering* [a]Lev. 23:1-44
4 [1]I.e., approx. one gallon, and so through v. 10 [a]Num. 28:1-29, 40
5 [a]Num. 15:11; Lev. 1:10; 3:6

8 [1]Or, *make a special votive offering* [a]Lev. 1:3; 3:1

15 [a]Num. 15:29; 9:14

19 [1]Lit., *bread* [2]Or, *heave offering*

20 [1]Or, *coarse meal* [2]Or, *heave offering* [a]Ex. 34:26; Lev. 23:14 [b]Deut. 14:22, 23; 16:13

21 [1]Or, *coarse meal* [2]Or, *offering lifted up*

23 [1]Lit., *by the hand of*

24 [1]Lit., *from the eyes of the congregation* [a]Lev. 4:2, 22, 27; 5:15, 18 [b]Num. 15:8-10

26 [a]Num. 15:24

8 'And when you prepare [a]a bull as a burnt offering or a
sacrifice, to [1]fulfill a special vow, or for peace offerings to the
LORD,
9 then he shall offer with the bull a grain offering of
three-tenths *of an ephah* of fine flour mixed with one-half a
hin of oil;
10 and you shall offer as the libation one-half a hin of
wine as an offering by fire, as a soothing aroma to the LORD.
11 'Thus it shall be done for each ox, or for each ram, or
for each of the male lambs, or of the goats.
12 'According to the number that you prepare, so you shall
do for everyone according to their number.
13 'All who are native shall do these things in this manner,
in presenting an offering by fire, as a soothing aroma to the
LORD.
14 'And if an alien sojourns with you, or one who may be
among you throughout your generations, and he *wishes to*
make an offering by fire, as a soothing aroma to the LORD, just
as you do, so he shall do.
15 '*As for* the assembly, there shall be [a]one statute for you
and for the alien who sojourns *with you*, a perpetual statute
throughout your generations; as you are, so shall the alien be
before the LORD.
16 'There is to be one law and one ordinance for you and
for the alien who sojourns with you.' "
17 Then the LORD spoke to Moses, saying,
18 "Speak to the sons of Israel, and say to them, 'When
you enter the land where I bring you,
19 then it shall be, that when you eat of the [1]food of the
land, you shall lift up an [2]offering to the LORD.
20 '[a]Of the first of your [1]dough you shall lift up a cake as
an [2]offering; as [b]the [2]offering of the threshing floor, so you
shall lift it up.
21 'From the first of your [1]dough you shall give to the
LORD an [2]offering throughout your generations.
22 'But when you unwillingly fail and do not observe all
these commandments, which the LORD has spoken to Moses,
23 *even* all that the LORD has commanded you [1]through
Moses, from the day when the LORD gave commandment and
onward throughout your generations,
24 then it shall be, if it is done [a]unintentionally, [1]without
the knowledge of the congregation, that all the congregation
shall offer one bull for a burnt offering, as a soothing aroma to
the LORD, [b]with its grain offering, and its libation, according to
the ordinance, and one male goat for a sin offering.
25 'Then the priest shall make atonement for all the congregation of the sons of Israel, and they shall be forgiven; for it
was an error, and they have brought their offering, an offering
by fire to the LORD, and their sin offering before the LORD, for
their error.
26 'So all the congregation of the sons of Israel will be
forgiven, with the alien who sojourns among them, for *it happened* to all the people through [a]error.
27 'Also if one person sins unintentionally, then he shall
offer a one year old female goat for a sin offering.
28 'And the priest shall make atonement before the LORD

for the person who goes astray when he sins unintentionally,
making atonement for him [1]that he may be forgiven.
29 'You shall have one law for him who does *anything*
unintentionally, for him who is native among the sons of Israel
and for the alien who sojourns among them.
30 'But the person who does *anything* [a]defiantly, whether
he is native or an alien, that one is blaspheming the LORD; and
that person shall be cut off from among his people.
31 'Because he has despised the word of the LORD and has
broken His commandment, that person shall be completely
cut off; his [1]guilt *shall be* on him.' "
32 Now while the sons of Israel were in the wilderness,
they found a man [a]gathering wood on the sabbath day.
33 And those who found him gathering wood brought him
to Moses and Aaron, and to all the congregation;
34 and they put him in [1]custody [a]because it had not been
[2]declared what should be done to him.
35 Then the LORD said to Moses, "The man shall surely
be put to death; [a]all the congregation shall stone him with
stones outside the camp."
36 So all the congregation brought him outside the camp,
and stoned him [1]to death with stones, just as the LORD had
commanded Moses.
37 The LORD also spoke to Moses, saying,
38 "Speak to the sons of Israel, and tell them that they shall
make for themselves [a]tassels on the corners of their garments
throughout their generations, and that they shall put on the
tassel of each corner a cord of blue.
39 "And it shall be a tassel for you [1]to look at and [a]remem-
ber all the commandments of the LORD, so as to do them and
not [2]follow after your own heart and your own eyes, after
which you played the harlot,
40 in order that you may remember to do all My commandments, and be holy to your God.
41 "I am the LORD your God who brought you out from
the land of Egypt to be your God; I am the LORD your God."

CHAPTER 16

NOW [a]Korah the son of Izhar, the son of Kohath, the son of
Levi, with [b]Dathan and Abiram, the sons of Eliab, and On the
son of Peleth, sons of Reuben, took *action*,
2 and they rose up before Moses, [1]together with some of
the sons of Israel, two hundred and fifty leaders of the congregation, [2a]chosen in the assembly, men of renown.
3 And they assembled together [a]against Moses and Aaron, and said to them, "[1b]You have gone far enough, for all the
congregation are holy, every one of them, and [c]the LORD is in
their midst; so why do you exalt yourselves above the assembly
of the LORD?"
4 When Moses heard *this*, [a]he fell on his face;
5 and he spoke to Korah and all his company, saying,
"Tomorrow morning the LORD will show who is His, and [a]who
is holy, and will bring *him* near to Himself; even [b]the one
whom He will choose, He will bring near to Himself.

28 [1]Or, *and he shall*
30 [a]Num. 14:40-44; Deut. 1:43, 17:12, 13
31 [1]Or, *iniquity*
32 [a]Ex. 31:14, 15; 35:2, 3
34 [1]Or, *prison* [2]Lit., *declared distinctly* [a]Num. 9:8
35 [a]Lev. 20:2, 27; 24:14-23; Deut. 21:21
36 [1]Lit., *with stones and he died*
38 [a]Deut. 22:12, Matt. 23:5
39 [1]Lit., *and you shall look at it* [2]Lit., *seek* [a]Deut. 4:23; 6:12; 8:11, 14, 19
1 [a]Ex. 6:21; Jude 11 [b]Num. 26:9; Deut. 11:6
2 [1]Lit., *and men from* [2]Lit., *called ones of* [a]Num. 1:16; 26:9
3 [1]Lit., *It is much for you* [a]Num. 12:2; Ps. 106:16 [b]Num. 16:7 [c]Num. 5:3
4 [a]Num. 14:5
5 [a]Lev. 10:3; Ps. 65:4 [b]Num. 17:5, 8

6 "Do this: take censers for yourselves, Korah and all
[1]your company,
7 and put fire in them, and lay incense upon them in the
presence of the LORD tomorrow; and the man whom the LORD
chooses *shall be* the one who is holy. [1a]You have gone far
enough, you sons of Levi!"
8 Then Moses said to Korah, "Hear now, you sons of
Levi,
9 is it [1]not enough for you that the God of Israel has
separated you from the *rest of* the congregation of Israel, [a]to
bring you near to Himself, to do the service of the tabernacle
of the LORD, and to stand before the congregation to minister
to them;
10 and that He has brought you near, *Korah*, and all your
brothers, sons of Levi, with you? And are you [a]seeking for the
priesthood also?
11 "Therefore you and all your company are gathered together [a]against the LORD; but as for Aaron, [1]who is he that [b]you
grumble against him?"
12 Then Moses sent [1]a summons to Dathan and Abiram,
the sons of Eliab; but they said, "We will not come up.
13 "Is it [1]not enough that you have brought us up out of a
[a]land flowing with milk and honey [b]to have us die in the wilderness, but you would also lord it over us?
14 "Indeed, you have not brought us [a]into a land flowing
with milk and honey, nor have you given us an inheritance of
[b]fields and vineyards. Would you [1c]put out the eyes of [2]these
men? We will not come up!"
15 Then Moses became very angry and said to the LORD,
"[a]Do not regard their offering! [b]I have not taken a single donkey from them, nor have I done harm to any of them."
16 And Moses said to Korah, "You and all your company
be present before the LORD tomorrow, both you and they
along with Aaron.
17 "And each of you take his firepan and put incense on [1]it,
and each of you bring his censer before the LORD, two hundred
and fifty firepans; also you and Aaron *shall* each *bring* his
firepan."
18 So they each took his *own* censer and put fire on [1]it,
and laid incense on [1]it; and they stood at the doorway of the
tent of meeting, with Moses and Aaron.
19 Thus Korah assembled all the congregation against
them at the doorway of the tent of meeting. And [a]the glory of
the LORD appeared to all the congregation.
20 Then the LORD spoke to Moses and Aaron, saying,
21 "[a]Separate yourselves from among this congregation,
[b]that I may consume them instantly."
22 But they fell on their faces, and said, "O God, [a]Thou
God of the spirits of all flesh, [b]when one man sins, wilt Thou
be angry with the entire congregation?"
23 Then the LORD spoke to Moses, saying,
24 "Speak to the congregation, saying, '[a]Get back from
around the dwellings of Korah, Dathan and Abiram.' "
25 Then Moses arose and went to Dathan and Abiram,
with the elders of Israel following him,
26 and he spoke to the congregation, saying, "Depart now

6 [1]Lit., *his*

7 [1]Lit., *It is much for you* [a]Num. 16:3

9 [1]Or, *too little for you* [a]Num. 3:6, 9

10 [a]Num. 3:10; 18:1-7

11 [1]Lit., *what* [a]Ex. 16:7 [b]1 Cor. 10:10

12 [1]Lit., *to call*

13 [1]Lit., *a little thing* [a]Num. 11:4-6; Ex. 16:3 [b]Num. 14:2, 3

14 [1]Lit., *bore out* [2]Lit., *those* [a]Num. 13:27; 14:8 [b]Num. 20:5; Ex. 22:5; 23:11 [c]Judg. 16:21; 1 Sam. 11:2

15 [a]Gen. 4:4, 5 [b]1 Sam. 12:3

17 [1]Lit., *them*

18 [1]Lit., *them*

19 [a]Num. 16:42; 14:10; 20:6

21 [a]Num. 16:45 [b]Ex. 32:10, 12

22 [a]Num. 27:16 [b]Gen. 18:23-32; Lev. 4:3

24 [a]Num. 16:45

from the tents of these wicked men, and touch nothing that
belongs to them, [a]lest you be swept away in all their sin."
27 So they got back from around the dwellings of Korah,
Dathan and Abiram; and Dathan and Abiram came out *and*
stood at the doorway of their tents, along with their wives and
[a]their sons and their little ones.
28 And Moses said, "By this you shall know that [a]the
LORD has sent me to do all these deeds; for [1]this is not my
doing.
29 "If these men die [1]the death of all men, or [2]if they suffer
the fate of all men, *then* the LORD has not sent me.
30 "But if the LORD [1]brings about an entirely new thing and
the ground opens its mouth and swallows them up with all that
is theirs, and they descend alive into [2]Sheol, then you will
understand that these men have spurned the LORD."
31 Then it came about as he finished speaking all these
words, that the ground that was under them split open;
32 and [a]the earth opened its mouth and swallowed them
up, and their households, and [b]all the men who belonged to
Korah, with *their* possessions.
33 So they and all that belonged to them went down alive
to [1]Sheol; and the earth closed over them, and they perished
from the midst of the assembly.
34 And all Israel who *were* around them fled at their [1]out-
cry, for they said, "[2]The earth may swallow us up!"
35 [a]Fire also came forth from the LORD and consumed the
[b]two hundred and fifty men who were offering the incense.
36 [1]Then the LORD spoke to Moses, saying,
37 "Say to Eleazar, the son of Aaron the priest, that he shall
take up the censers out of the midst of the [1]blaze, for they are
holy; and you scatter the [2]burning coals abroad.
38 "As for the censers of these [1]men who have sinned at the
cost of their lives, let them be made into hammered sheets for
a plating of the altar, since they did present them before the
LORD and they are holy; and they shall be for a sign to the sons
of Israel."
39 So Eleazar the priest took the bronze censers which the
men who were burned had offered; and they hammered them
out as a plating for the altar,
40 as a [1]reminder to the sons of Israel that [a]no [2]layman
who is not of the [3]descendants of Aaron should come near [b]to
burn incense before the LORD; that he might not become like
Korah and his company—just as the LORD had spoken to him
[4]through Moses.
41 But on the next day all the congregation of the sons of
Israel [a]grumbled against Moses and Aaron, saying, "You are
the ones who have caused the death of the LORD's people."
42 It came about, however, when the congregation had
assembled against Moses and Aaron, that they turned toward
the tent of meeting, and behold, the cloud covered it and [a]the
glory of the LORD appeared.
43 Then Moses and Aaron came to the front of the tent of
meeting,
44 and the LORD spoke to Moses, saying,
45 "[1a]Get away from among this congregation, that I may
consume them instantly." Then they fell on their faces.

26 [a]Gen. 19:15, 17
27 [a]Num. 26:11
28 [1]Lit., *not from my heart* [a]Ex. 3:12-15; 4:12, 15
29 [1]Lit., *like the death* [2]Lit., *the visitation of all men be visited upon them*
30 [1]Lit., *creates a new creation* [2]I.e., the nether world
32 [a]Num. 26:10; Deut. 11:6; Ps. 106:17 [b]Num. 26:11
33 [1]I.e., the nether world
34 [1]Or, *voice* [2]Lit., *Lest the earth*
35 [a]Num. 11:1-3; 26:10 [b]Num. 16:2
36 [1]Chap. 17:1 in Heb.
37 [1]Or, *place of burning* [2]Lit., *the fire*
38 [1]Lit., *sinners against their lives*
40 [1]Or, *memorial* [2]Lit., *stranger* [3]Lit., *seed* [4]Lit., *by the hand of* [a]Num. 1:51 [b]Ex. 30:7-10
41 [a]Num. 16:3
42 [a]Num. 16:19
45 [1]Or, *Arise* [a]Num. 16:21, 24

46 And Moses said to Aaron, "Take your censer and put
in it fire from the altar, and lay incense *on it;* then bring it
quickly to the congregation and [a]make atonement for them,
for [b]wrath has gone forth from the LORD, the plague has
begun!"
47 Then Aaron took *it* as Moses had spoken, and ran into
the midst of the assembly, for behold, the plague had begun
among the people. [a]So he put *on* the incense and made atonement for the people.
48 And he took his stand between the dead and the living,
so that the plague was checked.
49 [a]But those who died by the plague were 14,700, besides
those who [b]died on account of Korah.
50 Then Aaron returned to Moses at the doorway of the
tent of meeting, for the plague had been checked.

CHAPTER 17

1 THEN the LORD spoke to Moses, saying,
2 "Speak to the sons of Israel, and get from them a rod for
each father's household: twelve rods, from all their leaders
according to their fathers' households. You shall write each
name on his rod,
3 and write Aaron's name on the rod of Levi; for there is
one rod for the head *of each* of their fathers' households.
4 "You shall then deposit them in the tent of meeting in
front of [a]the testimony, where I meet with you.
5 "And it will come about that the rod of [a]the man whom
I choose will sprout. Thus I shall lessen from upon Myself the
grumblings of the sons of Israel, who are grumbling against
you."
6 Moses therefore spoke to the sons of Israel, and all
their leaders gave him a rod apiece, for each leader according
to their fathers' housholds, twelve rods, with the rod of Aaron
among their rods.
7 So Moses deposited the rods before the LORD in [a]the
tent of the testimony.
8 Now it came about on the next day that Moses went
into the tent of the testimony; and behold, [a]the rod of Aaron
for the house of Levi had sprouted and put forth buds and
produced blossoms, and it bore ripe almonds.
9 Moses then brought out all the rods from the presence
of the LORD to all the sons of Israel; and they looked, and each
man took his rod.
10 But the LORD said to Moses, "Put back the rod of
Aaron [a]before the testimony [1]to be kept as a sign against the
[2b]rebels, that you may put an end to their grumblings against
Me, so that they should not die."
11 Thus Moses did; just as the LORD had commanded
him, so he did.
12 Then the sons of Israel spoke to Moses, saying, "[a]Be-
hold, we perish, we are dying, we are all dying!
13 "[a]Everyone who comes near, who comes near to the
tabernacle of the LORD, must die. Are we to perish
completely?"

46 [a]Num. 25:13; Is. 6:6, 7 [b]Num. 18:5; Deut. 9:22
47 [a]Num. 25:7, 8, 13
49 [a]Num. 25:9 [b]Num. 16:32, 35
1 [1]In Heb., chap. 17:16
4 [a]Num. 17:7; Ex. 25:16, 21, 22
5 [a]Num. 16:5
7 [a]Num. 1:50, 53; 9:15
8 [a]Heb. 9:4
10 [1]Lit., *for preserving* [2]Lit., *sons of rebellion* [a]Num. 17:4 [b]Deut. 9:7, 24
12 [a]Is. 6:5
13 [a]Num. 1:51

Chapter 18

So the Lord said to Aaron, "You and your sons and your
father's household with you shall [a]bear the guilt [1]in connection
with the sanctuary; and you and your sons with you shall bear
the guilt [2]in connection with your priesthood.
2 "But bring with you also your brothers, the tribe of Levi,
the tribe of your father, that they may be [a]joined with you and
serve you, while you and your sons with you are before the tent
of the testimony.
3 "And they shall thus attend to your obligation and the
obligation of all the tent, but [a]they shall not come near to the
furnishings of the sanctuary and [b]the altar, lest both they and
you die.
4 "And they shall be joined with you and attend to the
obligations of the tent of meeting, for all the service of the
tent; but an [1]outsider may not come near you.
5 "So you shall attend to the obligations of the sanctuary
and the obligations of the altar, [a]that there may no longer be
wrath on the sons of Israel.
6 "And behold, I Myself have taken your [1]fellow-Levites
from among the sons of Israel; they are [a]a gift to you, [2]dedi-
cated to the Lord, to perform the service for the tent of
meeting.
7 "But you and your sons with you shall [a]attend to your
priesthood for everything concerning the altar and inside the
veil, and you are to perform service. I am giving you the priesthood as [b]a [1]bestowed service, but [c]the [2]outsider who comes
near shall be put to death."
8 Then the Lord spoke to Aaron, "Now behold, I Myself
have given you charge of My [1a]offerings, even all the holy gifts
of the sons of Israel, I have given them to you as a portion, and
to your sons as a perpetual allotment.
9 "This shall be yours from the most holy *gifts, reserved*
from the fire; every offering of theirs, even [a]every grain offering and every [b]sin offering and every guilt offering, which they
shall render to Me, shall be most holy for you and for your
sons.
10 "As the most holy *gifts* you shall eat it; every male shall
eat it. It shall be holy to you.
11 "This also is yours, [a]the offering of their gift, even all the
wave offerings of the sons of Israel; I have [b]given them to you
and to your sons and daughters with you, as a perpetual allotment. Everyone of your household who is clean may eat it.
12 "[a]All the [1]best of the fresh oil and all the [1]best of the
fresh wine and of the grain, the first fruits of those which they
give to the Lord, I give them to you.
13 "[a]The first ripe fruits of all that is in their land, which
they bring to the Lord, shall be yours; everyone of your household who is clean may eat it.
14 "[a]Every devoted thing in Israel shall be yours.
15 "[1a]Every first issue of the womb of all flesh, whether
man or animal, which they offer to the Lord, shall be yours;
nevertheless the first-born of man you shall surely redeem, and
the first-born of unclean animals you shall redeem.
16 "And as to their redemption price, from a month old

1 [1]Lit., *of the sanctuary* [2]Lit., *of your priesthood* [a]Ex. 28:38; Lev. 10:17; 22:16

2 [a]Num. 3:5-10

3 [a]Num. 4:15-20 [b]Num. 18:7; 1:51

4 [1]Lit., *stranger*

5 [a]Num. 16:46

6 [1]Lit., *brethren the* [2]Lit., *given* [a]Num. 3:9

7 [1]Lit., *service of gift* [2]Lit., *stranger* [a]Ex. 29:9 [b]Num. 18:20; Deut. 18:2; Matt. 10:8; 1 Pet. 5:2, 3 [c]Num. 1:51

8 [1]Lit., *heave offerings*, and so throughout the chap. [a]Lev. 7:28-34

9 [a]Lev. 2:1-16 [b]Lev. 6:30

11 [a]Num. 18:1; Deut. 18:3 [b]Lev. 22:1-16

12 [1]Lit., *fat* [a]Deut. 18:4; 32:14; Ps. 81:16; 147:14

13 [a]Ex. 22:29; 23:19; 34:26

14 [a]Lev. 27:1-33

15 [1]Lit., *Everything that opens* [a]Num. 3:46; Ex. 13:13, 15

you shall redeem them, by your valuation, five [1]shekels in
silver, according to the [1]shekel of the sanctuary, which is
twenty gerahs.
17 "But the first-born of an ox or the first-born of a sheep
or the first-born of a goat, you shall not redeem; they are holy.
You shall sprinkle their blood on the altar and shall offer up
their fat in smoke *as* an offering by fire, for a soothing aroma
to the LORD.
18 "And their [1]meat shall be yours; it shall be yours like the
breast of a wave offering and like the right thigh.
19 "[a]All the offerings of the holy *gifts,* which the sons of
Israel offer to the LORD, I have given to you and your sons and
your daughters with you, as a perpetual allotment. It is [b]an
everlasting covenant of salt before the LORD to you and your
[1]descendants with you."
20 Then the LORD said to Aaron, "[a]You shall have no
inheritance in their land, nor own any portion among them; [b]I
am your portion and your inheritance among the sons of
Israel.
21 "And to the sons of Levi, behold, I have given all the
[a]tithe in Israel for an inheritance, in return for their service
which they perform, the service of the tent of meeting.
22 "And [a]the sons of Israel shall not come near the tent of
meeting again, lest they bear sin and die.
23 "Only the Levites shall perform the service of the tent of
meeting, and they shall [a]bear their iniquity; it shall be a perpetual statute throughout your generations, and among the sons
of Israel [b]they shall have no inheritance.
24 "For the tithe of the sons of Israel, which they offer as
an offering to the LORD, I have given to the Levites for an
inheritance; therefore I have said concerning them, 'They shall
have no inheritance among the sons of Israel.' "
25 Then the LORD spoke to Moses, saying,
26 "Moreover, you shall speak to the Levites and say to
them, 'When you take from the sons of Israel [a]the tithe which
I have given you from them for your inheritance, then you
shall present an offering from it to the LORD, a [b]tithe of the
tithe.
27 'And your offering shall be reckoned to you as the grain
from the threshing floor or the full produce from the wine vat.
28 'So you shall also present an offering to the LORD from
your tithes, which you receive from the sons of Israel; and
from it you shall give the LORD's offering to Aaron the priest.
29 'Out of all your gifts you shall present every offering
due to the LORD, from all the [1]best of them, [2]the sacred part
from them.'
30 "And you shall say to them, 'When you have [1]offered
from it the best of it, then *the rest* shall be reckoned to the
Levites as the product of the threshing floor, and as the product of the wine vat.
31 'And you may eat it anywhere, you and your households, for it is your compensation in return for your service in
the tent of meeting.
32 'And you shall bear no sin by reason of it, when you
have [1]offered the [2]best of it. But you shall not [a]profane the
sacred gifts of the sons of Israel, lest you die.' "

16 [1]A shekel equals approx. one-half ounce.

18 [1]Lit., *flesh*

19 [1]Lit., *seed* [a]Num. 18:11 [b]2 Chr. 13:5

20 [a]Deut. 10:9; 12:12; 14:27, 29 [b]Deut. 18:2; Josh. 13:33; Ezek. 44:28

21 [a]Lev. 27:30-33

22 [a]Num. 1:51

23 [a]Num. 18:1 [b]Num. 18:20

26 [a]Num. 18:21 [b]Neh. 10:38

29 [1]Lit., *fat* [2]Lit., *its*

30 [1]Lit., *lifted*

32 [1]Lit., *lifted* [2]Lit., *fat* [a]Lev. 22:15, 16

Chapter 19

THEN the LORD spoke to Moses and Aaron, saying,
2 "This is the statute of the law which the LORD has commanded, saying, 'Speak to the sons of Israel that they bring
you an [a]unblemished red heifer in which is no defect, *and* [b]on
which a yoke has never [1]been placed.
3 'And you shall give it to [a]Eleazar the priest, and it shall
[b]be brought outside the camp and be slaughtered in his
presence.
4 'Next Eleazar the priest shall take some of its blood
with his finger, and [a]sprinkle some of its blood toward the
front of the tent of meeting seven times.
5 'Then the heifer shall be burned in his sight; its hide and
its flesh and its blood, with its refuse, shall be burned.
6 'And the priest shall take [a]cedar wood and hyssop and
scarlet *material*, and cast it into the midst of the [1]burning
heifer.
7 'The priest [a]shall then wash his clothes and bathe his
[1]body in water, and afterward come into the camp, but the
priest shall be unclean until evening.
8 'The one who burns it shall also wash his clothes in
water and bathe his [1]body in water, and shall be unclean until
evening.
9 'Now a man who is clean shall gather up the ashes of the
heifer and deposit them outside the camp in a clean place, and
[1]the congregation of the sons of Israel shall keep it as [a]water to
remove impurity; it is [2]purification from sin.
10 'And the one who gathers the ashes of the heifer [a]shall
wash his clothes and be unclean until evening; and it shall be a
perpetual statute to the sons of Israel and to the alien who
sojourns among them.
11 '[a]The one who touches the corpse of any [1]person shall
be unclean for seven days.
12 'That one shall [a]purify himself from uncleanness with
[1]the water on the third day and on the seventh day, *and then*
he shall be clean; but if he does not purify himself on the third
day and on the seventh day, he shall not be clean.
13 '[a]Anyone who touches a corpse, the [1]body of a man who
has died, and does not purify himself, [b]defiles the [2]tabernacle
of the LORD; and that person shall be cut off from Israel.
Because the water for impurity was not [3][c]sprinkled on him, he
shall be unclean; his uncleanness is still on him.
14 'This is the law when a man dies in a tent: everyone who
comes into the tent and everyone who is in the tent shall be
unclean for seven days.
15 'And every open vessel, which has no covering [1]tied
down on it, shall be unclean.
16 '[a]Also, anyone who in the open field touches one who
has been slain with a sword or who has died *naturally*, or a
human bone or a grave, shall be unclean for seven days.
17 'Then for the unclean *person* they shall take some of
the [1]ashes of the [2]burnt [3][a]purification from sin and [4]flowing
water shall be [5]added to them in a vessel.
18 'And a clean person shall take hyssop and dip *it* in the

2 [1]Lit., *come up* [a]Lev. 22:20-25 [b]Deut. 21:3

3 [a]Num. 3:4 [b]Num. 19:9; Lev. 4:11, 12, 21

4 [a]Lev. 4:6, 17

6 [1]Lit., *burning of the heifer* [a]Lev. 14:4

7 [1]Lit., *flesh* [a]Lev. 16:26, 28; 22:6

8 [1]Lit., *flesh*

9 [1]Lit., *it shall be to the congregation . . . Israel, for a guarding as water of impurity* [2]Or, *sin offering* [a]Num. 8:7

10 [a]Num. 19:7

11 [1]Lit., *soul of man* [a]Num. 5:2; 6:6; Lev. 21:1, 11; Acts 21:26, 27

12 [1]Lit., *it* [a]Num. 19:19

13 [1]Lit., *soul* [2]Lit., *dwelling place* [3]Or, *thrown* [a]Lev. 7:20, 21; 22:3-7 [b]Num. 19:20; Lev. 15:31; 20:3 [c]Num. 19:19

15 [1]Lit., *cord*

16 [a]Num. 31:19

17 [1]Lit., *dust* [2]Lit., *burning of the* [3]Or, *sin offering* [4]Lit., *living* [5]Lit., *put* [a]Num. 19:9

water, and sprinkle *it* on the tent and on all the furnishings and
on the persons who were there, and on the one who touched
the bone or the one slain or the one dying *naturally* or the
grave.
19 'Then the clean *person* [a]shall sprinkle on the unclean on
the third day and on the seventh day; and on the seventh day
he shall purify him from uncleanness, and he shall wash his
clothes and bathe *himself* in water and shall be clean by
evening.
20 'But the man who is unclean and does not purify himself from uncleanness, that person shall be cut off from the
midst of the assembly, because he has [a]defiled the sanctuary of
the LORD; the water for impurity has not been sprinkled on
him, he is unclean.
21 'So it shall be a perpetual statute for them. And he [a]who
sprinkles the water for impurity shall wash his clothes, and he
who touches the water for impurity shall be unclean until
evening.
22 '[a]Furthermore, anything that the unclean *person*
touches shall be unclean; and the person who touches *it* shall
be unclean until evening.' "

CHAPTER 20

THEN the sons of Israel, the whole congregation, came to
the [a]wilderness of Zin in the first month; and the people
stayed at Kadesh. Now Miriam died there and was buried
there.
2 [a]And there was no water for the congregation; and they
assembled themselves against Moses and Aaron.
3 [a]The people thus contended with Moses and spoke,
saying, "[b]If only we had perished [c]when our brothers perished
before the LORD!
4 "Why then have you brought the LORD's assembly into
this wilderness, for us and our beasts to die [1]here?
5 "And why have you made us come up from Egypt, to
bring us in to this wretched place? [a]It is not a place of [1]grain or
figs or vines or pomegranates, nor is there water to drink."
6 Then Moses and Aaron came in from the presence of
the assembly to the doorway of the tent of meeting, and fell
on their faces. Then the glory of the LORD appeared to them;
7 and the LORD spoke to Moses, saying,
8 "Take [a]the rod; and you and your brother Aaron assemble the congregation and speak to the rock before their
eyes, that it may yield its water. You shall thus bring forth
water for them out of the rock and let the congregation and
their beasts drink."
9 So Moses took the rod from before the LORD, just as
He had commanded him;
10 and Moses and Aaron gathered the assembly before the
rock. And he said to them, "Listen now, you rebels; shall we
bring forth water for you out of this rock?"
11 Then Moses lifted up his hand and struck the rock

19 [a]Ezek. 36:25; Heb. 10:22
20 [a]Num. 19:13
21 [a]Num. 19:7
22 [a]Lev. 5:2, 3; 7:21; 22:5, 6
1 [a]Num. 13:21; 27:14; 33:36
2 [a]Ex. 17:1
3 [a]Ex. 17:2 [b]Num. 14:2, 3 [c]Num. 16:31-35
4 [1]Lit., *there*
5 [1]Lit., *seed* [a]Num. 16:14
8 [a]Ex. 4:17, 20; 17:5, 6

twice with his rod; and [a]water came forth abundantly, and the
congregation and their beasts drank.
12 But the LORD said to Moses and Aaron, "[a]Because you
have not believed Me, to treat Me as holy in the sight of the
sons of Israel, therefore you shall not bring this assembly into
the land which I have given them."
13 Those *were* the waters of [1a]Meribah, [2]because the sons
of Israel contended with the LORD, and He proved Himself
holy among them.
14 From Kadesh Moses then sent messengers to [a]the king
of Edom: "Thus your brother Israel has said, 'You [b]know all
the hardship that has befallen us;
15 that our fathers went down to Egypt, and we stayed in
Egypt a long time, and the Egyptians treated us and our fathers
badly.
16 'But when we cried out to the LORD, He heard our voice
and sent [a]an angel and brought us out from Egypt; now behold, we are at Kadesh, a town on the edge of your territory.
17 'Please let us pass through your land. We shall not pass
through field or through vineyard; we shall not even drink
water from a well. We shall go along the king's highway, not
turning to the right or left, until we pass through your
territory.' "
18 [a]Edom, however, said to him, "You shall not pass
through [1]us, lest I come out with the sword against you."
19 Again, the sons of Israel said to him, "We shall go up
by the highway, and if I and [a]my livestock do drink any of your
water, then I will [1]pay its price. Let me only pass through on
my feet, [2]nothing *else*."
20 But he said, "You shall not pass through." And Edom
came out against him with a heavy [1]force, and with a strong
hand.
21 [a]Thus Edom refused to allow Israel to pass through his
territory; [b]so Israel turned away from him.
22 Now when they set out from [a]Kadesh, the sons of Israel, the whole congregation, came to Mount Hor.
23 Then the LORD spoke to Moses and Aaron at [a]Mount
Hor by the border of the land of Edom, saying,
24 "Aaron shall be [a]gathered to his people; for he shall not
enter the land which I have given to the sons of Israel, because
[b]you rebelled against My [1]command at the waters of Meribah.
25 "Take Aaron and his son [a]Eleazar, and bring them up to
Mount Hor;
26 and strip Aaron of his garments and put them on his
son Eleazar. So Aaron will be [a]gathered *to his people*, and will
die there."
27 So Moses did just as the LORD had commanded, and
they went up to Mount Hor in the sight of all the
congregation.
28 And after Moses had stripped Aaron of his garments
and put them on his son Eleazar, [a]Aaron died there on the
mountain top. Then Moses and Eleazar came down from the
mountain.
29 And when all the congregation saw that Aaron had
died, all the house of Israel wept for Aaron thirty days.

11 [a]Ps. 78:16; Is. 48:21; 1 Cor. 10:4
12 [a]Num. 20:24; 27:14; Deut. 1:37; 3:26, 27
13 [1]I.e., Contention [2]Or, *where* [a]Ex. 17:7
14 [a]Gen. 36:31-39; Deut. 2:4 [b]Josh. 2:9, 10; 9:9, 10, 24
16 [a]Ex. 14:19
18 [1]Lit., *me* [a]Num. 24:18
19 [1]Lit., *give* [2]Or, *no great thing* [a]Ex. 12:38
20 [1]Lit., *people*
21 [a]Judg. 11:17 [b]Deut. 2:8
22 [a]Num. 20:1, 14
23 [a]Num. 33:37
24 [1]Lit., *mouth* [a]Gen. 25:8 [b]Num. 20:5, 10
25 [a]Num. 3:4
26 [a]Num. 20:24
28 [a]Num. 33:38; Deut. 10:6; 32:50

CHAPTER 21

WHEN the Canaanite, the king of [a]Arad, who lived in the
[1]Negev, heard that Israel was coming by the way of [2]Atharim;
then he fought against Israel, and took some of them captive.
2 So Israel made a vow to the LORD, and said, "If Thou
wilt indeed deliver this people into my hand, then I will [1]ut-
terly destroy their cities."
3 And the LORD heard the voice of Israel, and delivered
up the Canaanites; then they [1]utterly destroyed them and their
cities. Thus the name of the place was called [2a]Hormah.
4 Then they set out from Mount Hor by the way of the
[1]Red Sea, to [a]go around the land of Edom; and the [2]people
became impatient because of the journey.
5 And the people spoke against God and Moses, "[a]Why
have you brought us up out of Egypt to die in the wilderness?
For there is no [1]food and no water, and [2b]we loathe this miserable food."
6 [a]And the LORD sent fiery serpents among the people
and [b]they bit the people, so that [c]many people of Israel died.
7 [a]So the people came to Moses and said, "We have
sinned, because we have spoken against the LORD and you;
intercede with the LORD, that He may remove the serpents
from us." And Moses interceded for the people.
8 Then the LORD said to Moses, "[1]Make a [a]fiery *serpent*,
and set it on a standard; and it shall come about, that everyone
who is bitten, when he looks at it, he shall live."
9 And Moses made a [a]bronze serpent and set it on the
standard; and it came about, that if a serpent bit any man,
when he looked to the bronze serpent, he lived.
10 [a]Now the sons of Israel moved out and camped in
Oboth.
11 And they journeyed from Oboth, and camped at Iye-
abarim, in the wilderness which is opposite Moab, to the [1]east.
12 [a]From there they set out and camped in [1]Wadi Zered.
13 From there they journeyed and camped on the other
side of the Arnon, which is in the wilderness that comes out of
the border of the Amorites, for the Arnon is the border of
Moab, between Moab and the Amorites.
14 Therefore it is said in the Book of the Wars of the
LORD,

"Waheb in Suphah,
And the wadis of the Arnon,
15 And the slope of the wadis
That extends to the site of [a]Ar,
And leans to the border of Moab."

16 [a]And from there *they continued* to [1]Beer, that is the
well where the LORD said to Moses, "Assemble the people, that
I may give them water."
17 Then Israel sang this song:

"Spring up, O well! Sing to it!
18 "The well, which the leaders sank,
Which the nobles of the people dug,
With the sceptre *and* with their staffs."

And from the wilderness *they continued* to Mattanah,

1 [1]I.e., South country [2]Or, *of the spies* [a]Num. 33:40; Josh. 12:14; Judg. 1:16

2 [1]Lit., *devote to destruction*

3 [1]Lit., *devoted to destruction* [2]I.e., A devoted thing; or, Destruction [a]Num. 14:45

4 [1]Lit., *Sea of Reeds* [2]Lit., *soul of the people was short* [a]Deut. 2:8

5 [1]Lit., *bread* [2]Lit., *our soul* [a]Num. 14:2, 3 [b]Num. 11:6

6 [a]Deut. 8:15 [b]Jer. 8:17 [c]1 Cor. 10:9

7 [a]Num. 11:2

8 [1]Lit., *Make for yourself* [a]Is. 14:29; 30:6; John 3:14

9 [a]2 Kin. 18:4; John 3:14, 15

10 [a]Num. 33:43, 44

11 [1]Lit., *sunrise*

12 [1]I.e., a dry ravine except during rainy season [a]Num. 33:45

15 [a]Num. 21:28; Deut. 2:9, 18, 29

16 [1]I.e., A well [a]Num. 33:46-49

19 and from Mattanah to Nahaliel, and from Nahaliel to
Bamoth,
20 and from Bamoth to the valley that is in the land of
Moab, at the top of Pisgah which overlooks the [1]wasteland.
21 [a]Then Israel sent messengers to Sihon, king of the
Amorites, saying,
22 "[a]Let me pass through your land. We will not turn off
into field or vineyard; we will not drink water from wells. We
will go by the king's highway until we have passed through
your border."
23 [a]But Sihon would not permit Israel to pass through his
border. So Sihon gathered all his people and went out against
Israel in the wilderness, and came to [b]Jahaz and fought against
Israel.
24 Then Israel [1]struck him with the edge of the sword, and
took possession of his land from the Arnon to the Jabbok, as
far as the sons of Ammon; for the [a]border of the sons of
Ammon *was* [2]Jazer.
25 And Israel took all these cities and [a]Israel lived in all
the cities of the Amorites, in Heshbon, and in all her [1]villages.
26 For Heshbon was the city of Sihon, king of the Amorites, who had fought against the former king of Moab and had
taken all his land out of his hand, as far as the Arnon.
27 Therefore those who use proverbs say,
"Come to Heshbon! Let it be built!
So let the city of Sihon be established.
28 "[a]For a fire went forth from Heshbon,
A flame from the town of Sihon;
It devoured [b]Ar of Moab,
The [1c]dominant [2]heights of the Arnon.
29 "[a]Woe to you, O Moab!
You are ruined, O people of [b]Chemosh!
[c]He has given his sons as fugitives,
[d]And his daughters into captivity,
To an Amorite king, Sihon.
30 "But we have cast them down,
Heshbon is ruined as far as [a]Dibon,
Then we have laid waste even to Nophah,
Which *reaches* to Medeba."
31 Thus Israel lived in the land of the Amorites.
32 And Moses sent to spy out [a]Jazer, and they captured its
villages and dispossessed the Amorites who *were* there.
33 [a]Then they turned and went up by the way of Bashan,
and Og the king of Bashan went out [1]with all his people, for
battle at Edrei.
34 But the LORD said to Moses, "Do not fear him, for I
have given him into your hand, and all his people and his land;
and you shall do to him as you did to Sihon, king of the
Amorites, who lived at Heshbon."
35 So they [1]killed him and his sons and all his people, until
there was no remnant left him; and they possessed his land.

CHAPTER 22

[a]THEN the sons of Israel journeyed, and camped in the
plains of Moab beyond the Jordan *opposite* Jericho.

20 [1]Or, *Jeshimon*

21 [a]Deut. 2:26-37

22 [a]Num. 20:16, 17

23 [a]Num. 20:21 [b]Deut. 2:32

24 [1]Lit., *smote*, so with Gk. and Latin [2]M.T. reads *strong* [a]Deut. 2:37

25 [1]Lit., *daughters* [a]Amos 2:10

28 [1]Lit., *lords of the* [2]Or, *Bamoth* [a]Jer. 48:45 [b]Num. 21:15 [c]Num. 22:41; Is. 15:2; 16:12

29 [a]Jer. 48:46 [b]Judg. 11:24; 1 Kin. 11:33; 2 Kin. 23:13 [c]Is. 15:5 [d]Is. 16:2

30 [a]Num. 32:3, 34

32 [a]Num. 32:1, 3, 35

33 [1]Lit., *he and* [a]Deut. 3:1-7

35 [1]Lit., *smote*

1 [a]Num. 33:48, 49

2 Now Balak the son of Zippor saw all that Israel had
done to the Amorites.
3 [a]So Moab was in great fear because of the people, for
they were numerous; and Moab was in dread of the sons of
Israel.
4 And Moab said to the elders of [a]Midian, "Now this
[1]horde will lick up all that is around us, as the ox licks up the
grass of the field." And Balak the son of Zippor was king of
Moab at that time.
5 [a]So he sent messengers to Balaam the son of Beor, at
[b]Pethor, which is near the [1]River, *in* the land of the sons of his
people, to call him, saying, "Behold, a people came out of
Egypt; behold, they cover the surface of the land, and they are
living opposite me.
6 "[a]Now, therefore, please come, [b]curse this people for
me since they are too [1]mighty for me; perhaps I may be able to
[2]defeat them and drive them out of the land. For I know that
he whom you bless is blessed, and he whom you curse is
cursed."
7 So the elders of Moab and the elders of Midian departed with the *fees for* [a]divination in their hand; and they
came to Balaam and [1]repeated Balak's words to him.
8 And he said to them, "Spend the night here, and I will
bring word back to you as the LORD may speak to me." And
the leaders of Moab stayed with Balaam.
9 Then God came to Balaam and said, "Who are these
men with you?"
10 And Balaam said to God, "Balak the son of Zippor,
king of Moab, has sent *word* to me,
11 'Behold, there is a people who came out of Egypt and
they cover the surface of the land; now come, curse them for
me; perhaps I may be able to fight against them, and drive
them out.' "
12 And God said to Balaam, "Do not go with them; [a]you
shall not curse the people; for they are blessed."
13 So Balaam arose in the morning and said to Balak's
leaders, "Go back to your land, for the LORD has refused to let
me go with you."
14 And the leaders of Moab arose and went to Balak, and
said, "Balaam refused to come with us."
15 Then Balak again sent leaders, more numerous and
more distinguished than [1]the former.
16 And they came to Balaam and said to him, "Thus says
Balak the son of Zippor, 'Let nothing, I beg you, hinder you
from coming to me;
17 for I will indeed honor you richly, and I will do whatever
you say to me. [a]Please come then, curse this people for
me.' "
18 And Balaam answered and said to the servants of Balak, "[a]Though Balak were to give me his house full of silver
and gold, I could not do anything, either small or great, contrary to the [1]command of the LORD my God.
19 "And now please, you also stay here tonight, and I will
find out what else the LORD will speak to me."
20 And God came to Balaam at night and said to him, "If

3 [a]Ex. 15:15

4 [1]Lit., *assembly* [a]Num. 25:15-18; 31:1-3

5 [1]I.e., Euphrates [a]Josh. 24:9 [b]Num. 23:7; Deut. 23:4

6 [1]Or, *humorous* [2]Lit., *smite* [a]Num. 22:17; 23:7, 8 [b]Num. 22:12; 24:9

7 [1]Lit., *spoke* [a]Num. 23:23; 24:1; Josh. 13:22

12 [a]Num. 23:8; 24:9

15 [1]Lit., *these*

17 [a]Num. 22:6

18 [1]Lit., *mouth* [a]Num. 22:38; 24:13

the men have come to call you, rise up *and* go with them; but
[a]only the word which I speak to you shall you do."
21 [a]So Balaam arose in the morning, and saddled his donkey, and went with the leaders of Moab.
22 But God was angry because he was going, and the angel
of the LORD took his stand in the way as an adversary against
him. Now he was riding on his donkey and his two servants
were with him.
23 When the donkey saw the angel of the LORD standing
in the way with his drawn sword in his hand, the donkey turned
off from the way and went into the field; but Balaam struck
the donkey to turn her back into the way.
24 Then the angel of the LORD stood in a narrow path of
the vineyards, *with* a wall on this side and a wall on that side.
25 When the donkey saw the angel of the LORD, she
pressed herself to the wall and pressed Balaam's foot against
the wall, so he struck her again.
26 And the angel of the LORD went further, and stood in a
narrow place where there was no way to turn to the right hand
or the left.
27 When the donkey saw the angel of the LORD, she lay
down under Balaam; so Balaam was angry and struck the donkey with his stick.
28 And [a]the LORD opened the mouth of the donkey, and
she said to Balaam, "What have I done to you, that you have
struck me these three times?"
29 Then Balaam said to the donkey, "Because you have
made a mockery of me! If there had been a sword in my hand,
I would have killed you by now."
30 And the donkey said to Balaam, "Am I not your donkey on which you have ridden all your life to this day? Have I
ever been accustomed to do so to you?" And he said, "No."
31 Then the LORD opened the eyes of Balaam, and he saw
[a]the angel of the LORD standing in the way with his drawn
sword in his hand; and he bowed [1]all the way to the ground.
32 And the angel of the LORD said to him, "Why have you
struck your donkey these three times? Behold, I have come out
as an adversary, because your way was [1]contrary to me.
33 "But the donkey saw me and turned aside from me these
three times. If she had not turned aside from me, I would
surely have killed you just now, and let her live."
34 And Balaam said to the angel of the LORD, "[a]I have
sinned, for I did not know that you were standing in the way
against me. Now then, if it is displeasing to you, I will turn
back."
35 But the angel of the LORD said to Balaam, "Go with
the men, but [a]you shall speak only the word which I shall [1]tell
you." So Balaam went along with the leaders of Balak.
36 When Balak heard that Balaam was coming, he went
out to meet him at the city of Moab, which is on the Arnon
border, [1]at the extreme end of the border.
37 Then Balak said to Balaam, "Did I not urgently send
to you to call you? Why did you not come to me? Am I really
unable to honor you?"
38 So Balaam said to Balak, "Behold, I have come now to

20 [a]Num. 22:35; 23:5, 12, 16, 26; 24:13
21 [a]2 Pet. 2:15
28 [a]2 Pet. 2:16
31 [1]Lit., *and prostrated himself to his face* [a]Josh. 5:13-15
32 [1]Lit., *reckless*
34 [a]Num. 14:40
35 [1]Or, *speak to* [a]Num. 22:20
36 [1]Lit., *which is at*

you! [a]Am I able to speak anything at all? The word that God
puts in my mouth, that I shall speak."
39 And Balaam went with Balak, and they came to
Kiriath-huzoth.
40 And Balak sacrificed oxen and sheep, and sent *some* to
Balaam and the leaders who were with him.
41 Then it came about in the morning that Balak took
Balaam, and brought him up to [1a]the high places of Baal; and
he saw from there [2]a [b]portion of the people.

Chapter 23

THEN Balaam said to Balak, "Build seven altars for me
here, and prepare seven bulls and seven rams for me here."
2 And Balak did just as Balaam had spoken, and Balak
and Balaam offered up a bull and a ram on each altar.
3 Then Balaam said to Balak, "Stand beside your burnt
offering, and I will go; perhaps the LORD will come to me, and
whatever He shows me I will tell you." So he went to a bare
hill.
4 Now God met Balaam, and he said to Him, "I have set
up the seven altars, and I have offered up a bull and a ram on
each altar."
5 Then the LORD [a]put a word in Balaam's mouth and
said, "Return to Balak, and you shall speak thus."
6 So he returned to him, and behold, he was standing
beside his burnt offering, he and all the leaders of Moab.
7 And he took up his [1]discourse and said,
"From [a]Aram Balak has brought me,
Moab's king from the mountains of the East,
'[b]Come curse Jacob for me,
And come, denounce Israel!'
8 "[a]How shall I curse, whom God has not cursed?
And how can I denounce, whom the LORD has not
denounced?
9 "As I see him from the top of the rocks,
And I look at him from the hills;
[a]Behold, a people *who* dwells apart,
And shall not be reckoned among the nations.
10 "[a]Who can count the dust of Jacob,
Or number the fourth part of Israel?
[b]Let [1]me die the death of the upright,
[c]And let my end be like his!"
11 Then Balak said to Balaam, "What have you done to
me? I took you to curse my enemies, but behold, you have
actually blessed them!"
12 And he answered and said, "Must I not be careful to
speak [a]what the LORD puts in my mouth?"
13 Then Balak said to him, "Please come with me to another
place from where you may see them, although you will
only see the extreme end of them, and will not see all of them;
and curse them for me from there."
14 So he took him to the field of Zophim, to the top of
Pisgah, and built seven altars and offered a bull and a ram on
each altar.

38 [a]Num. 22:18

41 [1]Or, *Bamoth-baal* [2]Lit., *the end of the camp* [a]Num. 21:28 [b]Num. 23:13

5 [a]Num. 22:20

7 [1]Lit., *parable* [a]Num. 22:5; Deut. 23:4 [b]Num. 22:6

8 [a]Num. 22:12

9 [a]Deut. 32:8; 33:28

10 [1]Lit., *my soul* [a]Gen. 13:16; 28:14 [b]Is. 57:1 [c]Ps. 37:37

12 [a]Num. 22:20

15 And he said to Balak, "Stand here beside your burnt
offering, while I myself meet *the* LORD yonder."
16 Then the LORD met Balaam and [a]put a word in his
mouth and said, "Return to Balak, and thus you shall speak."
17 And he came to him, and behold, he was standing beside his burnt offering, and the leaders of Moab with him. And
Balak said to him, "What has the LORD spoken?"
18 Then he took up his [1]discourse and said,
"Arise, O Balak, and hear;
Give ear to me, O son of Zippor!
19 "[a]God is not a man, that He should lie,
Nor a son of man, that He should repent;
[b]Has He said, and will He not do it?
Or has He spoken, and will He not make it good?
20 "Behold, I have received *a command* to bless;
When He has blessed, then [a]I cannot revoke it.
21 "[a]He has not observed [1]misfortune in Jacob;
[b]Nor has He seen trouble in Israel;
[c]The LORD his God is with him,
[d]And the shout of a king is among them.
22 "[a]God brings them out of Egypt,
He is for them like the horns of the wild ox.
23 "[a]For there is no omen against Jacob,
Nor is there any divination against Israel;
At the proper time it shall be said to Jacob
And to Israel, what God has done.
24 "[a]Behold, a people rises like a lioness,
And as a lion it lifts itself;
It shall not lie down until it devours the prey,
And drinks the blood of the slain."
25 Then Balak said to Balaam, "Do not curse them at all
nor bless them at all!"
26 But Balaam answered and said to Balak, "Did I not tell
you, '[1a]Whatever the LORD speaks, that I must do'?"
27 Then Balak said to Balaam, "Please come, I will take
you to another place; perhaps it will be [1]agreeable with God
that you curse them for me from there."
28 So Balak took Balaam to the top of Peor which overlooks the [1]wasteland.
29 And Balaam said to Balak, "Build seven altars for me
here and prepare seven bulls and seven rams for me here."
30 And Balak did just as Balaam had said, and offered up
a bull and a ram on *each* altar.

CHAPTER 24

WHEN Balaam saw that it [1]pleased the LORD to bless Israel,
he did not go as at other times to [2]seek [a]omens but he set his
face toward the [b]wilderness.
2 And Balaam lifted up his eyes and saw Israel [1]camping
tribe by tribe; and [a]the Spirit of God came upon him.
3 And he took up his [1]discourse and said,
"[a]The oracle of Balaam the son of Beor,
And the oracle of the man whose eye is opened;
4 The oracle of him who [a]hears the [1]words of God,
Who sees the [b]vision of [2]the Almighty,

16 [a]Num. 22:20

18 [1]Lit., *parable*

19 [a]1 Sam. 15:29 [b]Is. 40:8; 55:11

20 [a]Is. 43:13

21 [1]Or, *iniquity* [a]Num. 14:18, 19, 34; Ps. 32:2, 5 [b]Deut. 9:24; 32:5; Jer. 50:20 [c]Ex. 3:12; Deut. 31:23 [d]Deut. 33:5; Ps. 89:15-18

22 [a]Num. 24:8

23 [a]Num. 22:7; 24:1; Josh. 13:22

24 [a]Gen. 49:9; Nah. 2:11, 12

26 [1]Lit., *saying, 'Whatever* [a]Num. 22:18

27 [1]Lit., *right in the sight of God*

28 [1]Or, *Jeshimon*

1 [1]Lit., *was good in the eyes of* [2]Lit., *encounter* [a]Num. 22:7; 23:23 [b]Num. 23:28

2 [1]Lit., *dwelling* [a]Num. 11:26

3 [1]Lit., *parable*, and so throughout the chap. [a]Num. 24:15, 16

4 [1]Lit., *sayings* [2]Heb., *Shaddai* [a]Num. 22:20 [b]Num. 12:6; Gen. 15:1

Falling down, yet having his eyes uncovered,
5 How fair are your tents, O Jacob,
Your dwellings, O Israel!
6 "Like [1]valleys that stretch out,
Like gardens beside the river,
Like [a]aloes planted by the LORD,
Like [b]cedars beside the waters.
7 "Water shall flow from his buckets,
And his seed *shall be* by many waters,
And his king shall be higher than [a]Agag,
[b]And his kingdom shall be exalted.
8 "[a]God brings him out of Egypt,
He is for him like the horns of the wild ox.
[b]He shall devour the nations *who are* his adversaries,
And shall crush their bones in pieces,
And shatter his [c]arrows.
9 "[a]He [1]couches, he lies down as a lion,
And as a [2]lion; who [3]dares rouse him?
[b]Blessed is everyone who blesses you,
And cursed is everyone who curses you."
10 Then Balak's anger burned against Balaam, and he
struck his [1]hands together; and Balak said to Balaam, "I called
you to curse my enemies, but behold, you have persisted in
blessing them these three times!
11 "Therefore, [1]flee to your place now. I said I would hon-
or you greatly, but behold, the LORD has held you back from
honor."
12 And Balaam said to Balak, "[a]Did I not tell your messengers whom you had sent to me, saying,
13 'Though Balak were to give me his house full of silver
and gold, I could not do anything contrary to the [1]command
of the LORD, either good or bad, [a]of my own [2]accord. [b]What
the LORD speaks, that I will speak'?
14 "And now behold, [a]I am going to my people; come, *and*
I will advise you what this people will do to your people in the
[1]days to come."
15 And he took up his discourse and said,
"[a]The oracle of Balaam the son of Beor,
And the oracle of the man whose eye is opened,
16 The oracle of him who hears the [1]words of God,
And knows the knowledge of the [2]Most High,
Who sees the vision of [3]the Almighty,
Falling down, yet having his eyes uncovered.
17 "I see him, but not now;
I behold him, but not near;
A star shall come forth from Jacob,
[a]And a scepter shall rise from Israel,
[b]And shall crush through the [1]forehead of Moab,
And [2]tear down all the sons of [3]Sheth.
18 "[a]And Edom shall be a possession,
[b]Seir, its enemies, also shall be a possession;
While Israel performs valiantly.
19 "[a]One from Jacob shall have dominion,
And shall destroy the remnant from the city."
20 And he looked at Amalek and took up his discourse
and said,

6 [1]Or possibly, *palm trees* [a]Ps. 45:8 [b]Ps. 1:3

7 [a]Num. 24:20; 1 Sam. 15:8 [b]Ps. 145:11-13

8 [a]Num. 23:22 [b]Num. 23:24; Ps. 2:9 [c]Ps. 45:5

9 [1]Lit., *bows down* [2]Or, *lioness* [3]Lit., *shall* [a]Num. 23:24; Gen. 49:9 [b]Gen. 12:3; 27:29

10 [1]Lit., *palms*

11 [1]Lit., *flee for yourself*

12 [a]Num. 22:18

13 [1]Lit., *mouth* [2]Lit., *heart* [a]Num. 16:28 [b]Num. 22:20

14 [1]Lit., *end of the days* [a]Num. 31:8, 16; Josh. 13:22

15 [a]Num. 24:3, 4

16 [1]Lit., *sayings* [2]Heb., *Elyon* [3]Heb., *Shaddai*

17 [1]Lit., *corners* [2]Another reading is, *the crown of the head of* [3]I.e., tumult [a]Gen. 49:10 [b]Num. 21:29; Is. 15:1-16:14

18 [a]Gen. 27:29 [b]Gen. 32:3

19 [a]Amos 9:11, 12

"Amalek was the first of the nations,
[a]But his end *shall be* [1]destruction."
21 And he looked at the [a]Kenite, and took up his discourse and said,
"Your dwelling place is enduring,
And your nest is set in the cliff.
22 "Nevertheless Kain shall be consumed,
How long shall [a]Asshur [1]keep you captive?"
23 And he took up his discourse and said,
"Alas, who can live except God has ordained it?
24 "But ships *shall come* from the coast of [a]Kittim,
And they shall afflict Asshur and shall afflict [b]Eber;
[c]So they also *shall come* to destruction."
25 Then Balaam arose and departed and returned to [a]his
place, and Balak also went his way.

Chapter 25

WHILE Israel remained at [a]Shittim, the people began [b]to
play the harlot with the daughters of Moab.
2 For [a]they invited the people to the sacrifices of their
gods, and the people ate and bowed down to their gods.
3 So [a]Israel joined themselves to [1]Baal of Peor, and the
LORD was angry against Israel.
4 And the LORD said to Moses, "Take all the leaders of
the people and execute them [1]in broad daylight before the
LORD, so that the fierce anger of the LORD may turn away from
Israel."
5 So Moses said to the judges of Israel, "Each of you
slay his men who have joined themselves to [1]Baal of Peor."
6 Then behold, one of the sons of Israel came and
brought to his [1]relatives a [a]Midianite woman, in the sight of
Moses and in the sight of all the congregation of the sons of
Israel, while they were weeping at the doorway of the tent of
meeting.
7 [a]When Phinehas the son of Eleazar, the son of Aaron
the priest, saw it, he arose from the midst of the congregation,
and took a spear in his hand;
8 and he went after the man of Israel into the [1]tent, and
pierced both of them through, the man of Israel and the woman, through the [2]body. So the plague on the sons of Israel
was checked.
9 [a]And those who died by the plague were 24,000.
10 Then the LORD spoke to Moses, saying,
11 "Phinehas the son of Eleazar, the son of Aaron the
priest, has turned away My wrath from the sons of Israel, in
that he was jealous with My jealousy among them, so that I
did not destroy the sons of Israel in My jealousy.
12 "Therefore say, '[a]Behold, I give him My [b]covenant of
peace;
13 and it shall be for him and his [1]descendants after him, a
covenant of a [a]perpetual priesthood, because he was jealous
for his God, and [b]made atonement for the sons of Israel.'"
14 Now the name of the [1]slain man of Israel who was
[1]slain with the Midianite woman, was Zimri the son of Salu, a
leader of a father's household among the Simeonites.

20 [1]Lit., *to destroying* [a]Num. 24:24
21 [a]Gen. 15:19
22 [1]Lit., *take* [a]Gen. 10:21, 22
24 [a]Gen. 10:4; Ezek. 27:6 [b]Gen. 10:21 [c]Num. 24:20
25 [a]Num. 24:14
1 [a]Num. 33:49; Josh. 2:1 [b]Num. 31:16; 1 Cor. 10:8; Rev. 2:14
2 [a]Ex. 34:15; Deut. 32:38
3 [1]Or, *Baal-peor* [a]Ps. 106:28, 29; Hos. 9:10
4 [1]Lit., *in front of the sun*
5 [1]Or, *Baal-peor*
6 [1]Lit., *brothers* [a]Num. 22:4
7 [a]Num. 16:46-48; Ps. 106:30
8 [1]Or, *inner rooms* [2]Or, *belly*
9 [a]Num. 14:37; 16:48-50; 31:16
12 [a]Ps. 106:31 [b]Is. 54:10; Ezek. 34:25; 37:26
13 [1]Lit., *seed* [a]Ex. 29:9 [b]Num. 16:46
14 [1]Lit., *smitten*

15 And the name of the Midianite woman who was [1]slain
was [a]Cozbi the daughter of [b]Zur, [2]who was head of the people
of a father's household in Midian.
16 Then the LORD spoke to Moses, saying,
17 "[a]Be hostile to the Midianites and strike them;
18 for they have been hostile to you with their tricks, with
which they have deceived you in the affair of Peor, and in the
affair of Cozbi, the daughter of the leader of Midian, their
sister who was slain on the day of the plague because of Peor."

CHAPTER 26

1 THEN it came about after the [a]plague, [2]that the LORD spoke
to Moses and to Eleazar the son of Aaron the priest, saying,
2 "[a]Take a [1]census of all the congregation of the sons of
Israel from twenty years old and upward, by their fathers'
households, whoever is able to go out to war in Israel."
3 So Moses and Eleazar the priest spoke with them in the
plains of Moab by the Jordan at Jericho, saying,
4 "*Take a census of the people* from twenty years old and
upward, as the LORD has commanded Moses."
Now the sons of Israel who came out of the land of Egypt
were:
5 Reuben, Israel's first-born, the sons of Reuben: *of* Hanoch, the family of the Hanochites; of Pallu, the family of the
Palluites;
6 of Hezron, the family of the Hezronites; of Carmi, the
family of the Carmites.
7 These are the families of the Reubenites, and those
who were numbered of them were [a]43,730.
8 And the son of Pallu: Eliab.
9 And the sons of Eliab: Nemuel and Dathan and Abiram. These are the Dathan and Abiram who were [a]called by
the congregation, who contended against Moses and against
Aaron in the company of Korah, when they contended against
the LORD,
10 and [a]the earth opened its mouth and swallowed them
up along with Korah, when that company died, [b]when the fire
devoured 250 men, so that they became a [1]warning.
11 [a]The sons of Korah, however, did not die.
12 The sons of Simeon according to their families: of
[1]Nemuel, the family of the Nemuelites; of Jamin, the family
of the Jaminites; of [2]Jachin, the family of the Jachinites;
13 of [1]Zerah, the family of the Zerahites; of Shaul, the
family of the Shaulites.
14 These are the families of the Simeonites, [a]22,200.
15 The sons of Gad according to their families: of [1]Zephon,
the family of the Zephonites; of Haggi, the family of the
Haggites; of Shuni, the family of the Shunites;
16 of [1]Ozni, the family of the Oznites; of Eri, the family
of the Erites;
17 of [1]Arod, the family of the Arodites; of Areli, the family of the Arelites.
18 These are the families of the sons of Gad according to
those who were numbered of them, [a]40,500.

15 [1]Lit., *smitten* [2]Lit., *he* [a]Num. 25:18 [b]Num. 31:8

17 [a]Num. 25:1; 31:1-3

1 [1]In Heb. 25:1 [2]In Heb. 26:1 [a]Num. 25:9

2 [1]Lit., *sum* [a]Num. 1:2; Ex. 30:11-16; 38:25, 26

7 [a]Num. 1:21

9 [a]Num. 1:16; 16:2

10 [1]Lit., *sign* [a]Num. 16:32 [b]Num. 16:35, 38

11 [a]Num. 16:27, 33; Deut. 24:16

12 [1]In Gen. 46:10; Ex. 6:15, *Jemuel* [2]In 1 Chr. 4:24, *Jarib*

13 [1]In Gen. 46:10 *Zohar*

14 [a]Num. 1:23

15 [1]In Gen. 46:16, *Ziphion*

16 [1]In Gen. 46:16, *Ezbon*

17 [1]In Gen. 46:16, *Arodi*

18 [a]Num. 1:25

19 The sons of Judah *were* Er and Onan, but Er and Onan
died in the land of Canaan.
20 And the sons of Judah according to their families were:
of Shelah, the family of the Shelanites; of Perez, the family of
the Perezites; of Zerah, the family of the Zerahites.
21 And the sons of Perez were: of Hezron, the family of
the Hezronites; of Hamul, the family of the Hamulites.
22 These are the families of Judah according to those who
were numbered of them, [a]76,500.
23 The sons of Issachar according to their families: *of*
Tola, the family of the Tolaites; of Puvah, the family of the
Punites;
24 of [1]Jashub, the family of the Jashubites; of Shimron,
the family of the Shimronites.
25 These are the families of Issachar according to those
who were numbered of them, [a]64,300.
26 The sons of Zebulun according to their families: of
Sered, the family of the Seredites; of Elon, the family of the
Elonites; of Jahleel, the family of the Jahleelites.
27 These are the families of the Zebulunites according to
those who were numbered of them, [a]60,500.
28 The sons of Joseph according to their families: Manasseh and Ephraim.
29 The sons of Manasseh: of Machir, the family of the
Machirites; and Machir [1]became the father of Gilead: of Gilead, the family of the Gileadites.
30 These are the sons of Gilead: *of* [1]Iezer, the family of
the Iezerites; of Helek, the family of the Helekites;
31 and *of* Asriel, the family of the Asrielites; and *of* Shechem, the family of the Shechemites;
32 and *of* Shemida, the family of the Shemidaites; and *of*
Hepher, the family of the Hepherites.
33 Now Zelophehad the son of Hepher had no sons, but
only daughters; and [a]the names of the daughters of Zelophehad were Mahlah, Noah, Hoglah, Milcah and Tirzah.
34 These are the families of Manasseh; and those who
were numbered of them were [a]52,700.
35 These are the sons of Ephraim according to their families: of Shuthelah, the family of the Shuthelaites; of [1]Becher,
the family of the Becherites; of Tahan, the family of the
Tahanites.
36 And these are the sons of Shuthelah: of Eran, the family of the Eranites.
37 These are the families of the sons of Ephraim according to those who were numbered of them, [a]32,500. These are
the sons of Joseph according to their families.
38 The sons of Benjamin according to their families: of
Bela, the family of the Belaites; of Ashbel, the family of the
Ashbelites; of [1]Ahiram, the family of the Ahiramites;
39 of [1]Shephupham, the family of the Shuphamites; of
[2]Hupham, the family of the Huphamites.
40 And the sons of Bela were [1]Ard and Naaman: *of Ard,*
the family of the Ardites; of Naaman, the family of the
Naamites.
41 These are the sons of Benjamin according to their families; and those who were numbered of them were [a]45,600.

22 [a]Num. 1:27

24 [1]In Gen. 46:13, *Iob*

25 [a]Num. 1:29

27 [a]Num. 1:31

29 [1]Lit., *begot*

30 [1]In. Josh. 17:2, *Abiezer* cf. Judg. 6:11, 24, 34

33 [a]Num. 27:1

34 [a]Num. 1:35

35 [1]In 1 Chr. 7:20, *Bered*

37 [a]Num. 1:33

38 [1]In Gen. 46:21, *Ehi;* in 1 Chr. 8:1, *Aharah*

39 [1]In Gen. 46:21, *Muppim;* in 1 Chr. 7:12, *Shuppim* [2]In Gen. 46:21, *Muppim* and *Huppim*

40 [1]In 1 Chr. 8:3, *Addar*

41 [a]Num. 1:37

42 [1]In Gen. 46:23, *Hushim*

43 [a]Num. 1:39

47 [a]Num. 1:41

50 [a]Num. 1:43

51 [a]Ex. 12:37; 38:26; Num. 1:46; 11:21

53 [1]Lit., *To*

54 [a]Num. 33:54

55 [1]Lit., *inherit according to* [a]Num. 33:54; 34:13

58 [1]Lit., *begot* [a]Ex. 6:20

60 [a]Num. 3:2

61 [a]Num. 3:4; Lev. 10:1, 2

62 [a]Num. 3:39 [b]Num. 1:47 [c]Num. 18:23, 24

42 These are the sons of Dan according to their families: of [1]Shuham, the family of the Shuhamites. These are the families of Dan according to their families.
43 All the families of the Shuhamites, according to those who were numbered of them, were [a]64,400.
44 The sons of Asher according to their families: of Imnah, the family of the Imnites; of Ishvi, the family of the Ishvites; of Beriah, the family of the Beriites.
45 Of the sons of Beriah: of Heber, the family of the Heberites; of Malchiel, the family of the Malchielites.
46 And the name of the daughter of Asher *was* Serah.
47 These are the families of the sons of Asher according to those who were numbered of them, [a]53,400.
48 The sons of Napthtali according to their families: of Jahzeel, the family of the Jahzeelites; of Guni, the family of the Gunites;
49 of Jezer, the family of the Jezerites; of Shillem, the family of the Shillemites.
50 These are the families of Napthtali according to their families; and those who were numbered of them were [a]45,400.
51 These are those who were numbered of the sons of Israel, [a]601,730.
52 Then the LORD spoke to Moses, saying,
53 "[1]Among these the land shall be divided for an inheritance according to the number of names.
54 "[a]To the larger *group* you shall increase their inheritance, and to the smaller *group* you shall diminish their inheritance; each shall be given their inheritance according to those who were numbered of them.
55 "But the land shall be [a]divided by lot. They shall [1]receive their inheritance according to the names of the tribes of their fathers.
56 "According to the selection by lot, their inheritance shall be divided between the larger and the smaller *groups*."
57 And these are those who were numbered of the Levites according to their families: of Gershon, the family of the Gershonites; of Kohath, the family of the Kohathites; of Merari, the family of the Merarites.
58 These are the families of Levi: the family of the Libnites, the family of the Hebronites, the family of the Mahlites, the family of the Mushites, the family of the Korahites. [a]And Kohath [1]became the father of Amram.
59 And the name of Amram's wife was Jochebed, the daughter of Levi, who was born to Levi in Egypt; and she bore to Amram: Aaron and Moses and their sister Miriam.
60 [a]And to Aaron were born Nadab and Abihu, Eleazar and Ithamar.
61 [a]But Nadab and Abihu died when they offered strange fire before the LORD.
62 And those who were numbered of them were [a]23,000, every male from a month old and upward, for [b]they were not numbered among the sons of Israel [c]since no inheritance was given to them among the sons of Israel.
63 These are those who were numbered by Moses and Eleazar the priest, who numbered the sons of Israel in the plains of Moab by the Jordan at Jericho.

64 [a]But among these there was not a man of those who
were numbered by Moses and Aaron the priest, who numbered
the sons of Israel in the wilderness of Sinai.
65 For the LORD had said [1]of them, "They shall surely die
in the wilderness." And not a man was left of them, except
Caleb the son of Jephunneh, and Joshua the son of Nun.

CHAPTER 27

THEN [a]the daughters of Zelophehad, the son of Hepher,
the son of Gilead, the son of Machir, the son of Manasseh, of
the families of Manasseh the son of Joseph, came near; and
these are [b]the names of his daughters: Mahlah, Noah and
Hoglah and Milcah and Tirzah.
2 And they stood before Moses and before Eleazar the
priest and before the leaders and all the congregation, at the
doorway of the tent of meeting, saying,
3 "Our father died in the wilderness, yet he was not
among the company of those who gathered themselves together against the LORD in the company of Korah; but [a]he died in
his own sin, and [b]he had no sons.
4 "Why should the name of our father be withdrawn from
among his family because he had no son? Give us a possession
among our father's brothers."
5 [a]And Moses brought their case before the LORD.
6 Then the LORD spoke to Moses, saying,
7 "[a]The daughters of Zelophehad are right in *their* statements. You shall surely give them a hereditary possession
among their father's brothers, and you shall transfer the inheritance of their father to them.
8 "Further, you shall speak to the sons of Israel, saying, 'If
a man dies and has no son, then you shall transfer his inheritance to his daughter.
9 'And if he has no daughter, then you shall give his inheritance to his brothers.
10 'And if he has no brothers, then you shall give his inheritance to his father's brothers.
11 'And if his father has no brothers, than you shall give his
inheritance to his nearest relative in his own family, and he
shall possess it; and it shall be a statutory ordinance to the sons
of Israel, just as the LORD commanded Moses.'"
12 [a]Then the LORD said to Moses, "Go up to this [b]moun-
tain of Abarim, and see the land which I have given to the sons
of Israel.
13 "And when you have seen it, you too [a]shall be gathered
to your people, as Aaron your brother [1]was;
14 for in the wilderness of Zin, during the strife of the
congregation, [a]you rebelled against My [1]command [2]to treat
Me as holy before their eyes at the water." (These are the
waters of Meribah of Kadesh in the wilderness of Zin.)
15 Then Moses spoke to the LORD, saying,
16 "[a]May the LORD, the God of the spirits of all flesh,
appoint a man over the congregation,
17 who will go out [1]and come in before them, and who
will lead them out and [2]bring them in, that the congregation of
the LORD may not be like sheep which have no shepherd."

64 [a]Num. 14:29-35; Deut. 2:14-16; Heb. 3:17

65 [1]Or, *too*

1 [a]Num. 26:33; 36:1 [b]Num. 26:33

3 [a]Num. 26:64, 65 [b]Num. 26:33

5 [a]Num. 27:21; 9:8

7 [a]Num. 36:2; Josh. 17:4

12 [a]Deut. 32:48-52 [b]Num. 33:47, 48

13 [1]Lit., *was gathered* [a]Num. 31:2

14 [1]Lit., *mouth* [2]Lit., *for My sanctity* [a]Num. 20:12

16 [a]Num. 16:22

17 [1]Lit., *before them and who will* [2]Lit., *who will bring*

18 So the LORD said to Moses, "[1]Take Joshua the son of
Nun, a man [a]in whom is the Spirit, and [b]lay your hand on him;
19 and have him stand before Eleazar the priest and before all the congregation; and [a]commission him in their sight.
20 "And you shall put some of your [1]authority on him, in
order that all the congregation of the sons of Israel may obey
him.
21 "Moreover, he shall stand before Eleazar the priest, who
shall inquire for him [a]by the judgment of the Urim before the
LORD. At his [1]command they shall go out and at his [1]command
they shall come in, *both* he and the sons of Israel with him,
even all the congregation."
22 And Moses did just as the LORD commanded him; and
he took Joshua and set him before Eleazar the priest, and
before all the congregation.
23 Then he laid his hands on him and commissioned him,
just as the LORD had spoken [1]through Moses.

CHAPTER 28

THEN the LORD spoke to Moses, saying,
2 "Command the sons of Israel and say to them, 'You
shall [1]be careful to present My offering, My [a]food for My
offerings by fire, of a soothing aroma to Me, at their
appointed time.'
3 "[a]And you shall say to them, 'This is the offering by fire
which you shall offer to the LORD; two male lambs one year
old without defect *as* a continual burnt offering every day.
4 'You shall offer the one lamb in the morning, and the
other lamb you shall offer [1]at twilight.
5 'Also a tenth of an ephah of fine flour for a grain offering, mixed with a fourth of a hin of beaten oil.
6 'It is a continual burnt offering which was ordained in
Mount Sinai as a soothing aroma, an offering by fire to the
LORD.
7 'Then the libation with it *shall be* a fourth of a hin for
each lamb, in the holy place you shall pour out a libation of
strong drink to the LORD.
8 'And the other lamb you shall offer [1]at twilight; as the
grain offering of the morning and as its libation, you shall offer
it, an offering by fire, a soothing aroma to the LORD.
9 "Then on the sabbath day two male lambs one year old
without defect, and two-tenths *of a measure* of fine flour
mixed with oil as a grain offering, and its libation.
10 'The burnt offering of every sabbath is in addition to
the [a]continual burnt offering and its libation.
11 'Then [a]at the beginning of each of your months you
shall present a burnt offering to the LORD; two [1]bulls and one
ram, seven male lambs one year old without defect,
12 [a]and three-tenths *of a measure* of fine flour for a grain
offering, mixed with oil, for each bull; and two-tenths of fine
flour for a grain offering, mixed with oil, for the one ram;
13 and a tenth *of a measure* of fine flour mixed with oil
for a grain offering for each lamb, for a burnt offering of a
soothing aroma, an offering by fire to the LORD.
14 'And their libations shall be half a hin of wine for a bull

18 [1]Lit., *Take for yourself* [a]Num. 11:25-29; Deut. 34:9 [b]Num. 27:23
19 [a]Deut. 3:28; 31:3, 7, 8, 23
20 [1]Lit., *majesty*
21 [1]Lit., *mouth* [a]1 Sam. 28:6
23 [1]Lit., *by the hand of*
2 [1]Lit., *watch* [a]Lev. 3:11
3 [a]Ex. 29:38-42
4 [1]Lit., *between the two evenings*
8 [1]Lit., *between the two evenings*
10 [a]Num. 28:3
11 [1]Lit., *bull of the herd* [a]Num. 10:10; Ezek. 46:6, 7
12 [a]Num. 15:4-12

and a third of a hin for the ram and a fourth of a hin for a
lamb; this is the burnt offering of each month throughout the
months of the year.
15 'And one male goat for a sin offering to the LORD; it
shall be offered with its libation in addition to the [a]continual
burnt offering.
16 '[a]Then on the fourteenth day of the first month shall be
the LORD's Passover.
17 'And on the fifteenth day of this month *shall be* a feast,
unleavened bread *shall be* eaten for seven days.
18 'On the first day *shall be* a holy convocation, you shall
do no laborious work.
19 'And you shall present an offering by fire, a burnt offering to the LORD; two [1]bulls and one ram and seven male lambs
one year old, having them without defect.
20 'And for their grain offering, you shall offer fine flour
mixed with oil; three-tenths *of a measure* for a bull and two-
tenths for the ram.
21 A tenth *of a measure* you shall offer for [1]each of the
seven lambs,
22 and one male goat for a sin offering, to make atonement for you.
23 'You shall present these besides [a]the burnt offering of
the morning, which is for a continual burnt offering.
24 'After this manner you shall present daily, for seven
days, [a]the food of the offering by fire, of a soothing aroma to
the LORD; it shall be presented with its libation in addition to
the [b]continual burnt offering.
25 'And on the seventh day you shall have a holy convocation, [a]you shall do no laborious work.
26 'Also on [a]the day of the first fruits, when you present a
new grain offering to the LORD in your *Feast of* Weeks, you
shall have a holy convocation; [b]you shall do no laborious work.
27 'And you shall offer a burnt offering for a soothing
aroma to the LORD, two young bulls, one ram, seven male
lambs one year old,
28 and their grain offering, fine flour mixed with oil,
three-tenths *of a measure* for each bull, two-tenths for the one
ram,
29 a tenth for [1]each of the seven lambs,
30 one male goat to make atonement for you.
31 '[a]Besides the continual burnt offering and its grain offering, you shall present *them* with their libations. They shall be
[1]without defect.

CHAPTER 29

[a]
NOW in the seventh month, on the first day of the month,
you shall also have a holy convocation, [b]you shall do no laborious work. It will be to you a day for blowing trumpets.
2 'And you shall offer a burnt offering as a soothing
aroma to the LORD; one [1]bull, one ram, *and* seven male lambs
one year old without defect;
3 also their grain offering, fine flour mixed with oil,
three-tenths *of a measure* for the bull, two-tenths for the ram,
4 and one-tenth for [1]each of the seven lambs.

15 [a]Num. 28:3

16 [a]Ex. 12:14-20; Lev. 23:5-8; Deut. 16:1-8

19 [1]Or, *bulls of the herd*

21 [1]Lit., *each lamb*

23 [a]Num. 28:3

24 [a]Lev. 3:11 [b]Num. 28:3

25 [a]Num. 28:18

26 [a]Ex. 23:16; 34:22; Lev. 23:15-21; Deut. 16:9-12 [b]Num. 28:18

29 [1]Lit., *each lamb*

31 [1]Lit., *without defect to you* [a]Num. 28:3

1 [a]Ex. 23:16; 34:22; Lev. 23:23-25 [b]Num. 28:26

2 [1]Or, *bull of a herd,* and so throughout the chap.

4 [1]Lit., *each lamb,* and so throughout the chap.

5 'And *offer* one male goat for a sin offering, to make
atonement for you,
6 [a]besides the burnt offering of the new moon, and its
grain offering, and the [b]continual burnt offering and its grain
offering, and their libations, according to their ordinance, for a
soothing aroma, an offering by fire to the LORD.
7 'Then on [a]the tenth day of this seventh month you shall
have a holy convocation, and you shall humble yourselves; you
shall not do any work.
8 'And you shall present a burnt offering to the LORD *as* a
soothing aroma; one [1]bull, one ram, seven male lambs one year
old, having them without defect;
9 and their grain offering, fine flour mixed with oil,
three-tenths *of a measure* for the bull, two-tenths for the one
ram,
10 a tenth for each of the seven lambs;
11 one male goat for a sin offering, besides the sin offering
of atonement and [a]the continual burnt offering and its grain
offering, and their libations.
12 'Then on [a]the fifteenth day of the seventh month you
shall have a holy convocation; you [b]shall do no laborious work,
and you shall observe a feast to the LORD for seven days.
13 'And you shall present a burnt offering, an offering by
fire as a soothing aroma to the LORD: thirteen bulls, two rams,
fourteen male lambs one year old, which are without defect,
14 and their grain offering, fine flour mixed with oil,
three-tenths *of a measure* for [1]each of the thirteen bulls, two-
tenths for [2]each of the two rams,
15 and a tenth for each of the fourteen lambs;
16 and one male goat for a sin offering, [a]besides the continual burnt offering, its grain offering and its libation.
17 'Then on [a]the second day: twelve bulls, two rams, fourteen male lambs one year old without defect;
18 and their grain offering and their libations for the bulls,
for the rams and for the lambs, by their number according to
the ordinance;
19 and one male goat for a sin offering, [a]besides the continual burnt offering and its grain offering, and their libations.
20 'Then on the third day: eleven bulls, two rams, fourteen
male lambs one year old without defect;
21 and their grain offering and their libations for the bulls,
for the rams and for the lambs, their number according to the
ordinance;
22 and one male goat for a sin offering, besides the continual burnt offering and its grain offering and its libation.
23 'Then on the fourth day: ten bulls, two rams, fourteen
male lambs one year old without defect;
24 their grain offering and their libations for the bulls, for
the rams and for the lambs, by their number according to the
ordinance;
25 and one male goat for a sin offering, besides the continual burnt offering, its grain offering and its libation.
26 'Then on the fifth day: nine bulls, two rams, fourteen
male lambs one year old without defect;
27 and their grain offering and their libations for the bulls,

6 [a]Num. 28:27 [b]Num. 28:3
7 [a]Lev. 16:29-34; 23:26-32
11 [a]Num. 28:3
12 [a]Lev. 23:33-35 [b]Num. 29:1
14 [1]Lit., *each bull* [2]Lit., *each ram.*
16 [a]Num. 28:3
17 [a]Lev. 23:36
19 [a]Num. 28:8

for the rams and for the lambs, by their number according to
the ordinance;
28 and one male goat for a sin offering, besides the continual burnt offering and its grain offering and its libation.
29 'Then on the sixth day: eight bulls, two rams, fourteen
male lambs one year old without defect;
30 and their grain offering and their libations for the bulls,
for the rams and for the lambs, by their number according to
the ordinance;
31 and one male goat for a sin offering, besides the continual burnt offering, its grain offering and its libations.
32 'Then on the seventh day seven bulls, two rams, fourteen male lambs one year old without defect;
33 and their grain offering and their libations for the bulls,
for the rams and for the lambs, by their number according to
the ordinance;
34 and one male goat for a sin offering, besides the continual burnt offering, its grain offering and its libation.
35 '[a]On the eighth day you shall have a solemn assembly;
you shall do no laborious work.
36 'But you shall present a burnt offering, an offering by
fire, as a soothing aroma to the LORD: one bull, one ram, seven
male lambs one year old without defect;
37 their grain offering and their libations for the bull, for
the ram and for the lambs, by their number according to the
ordinance;
38 and one male goat for a sin offering, besides the continual burnt offering and its grain offering and its libation.
39 'You shall present these to the LORD at your [a]appointed
times, besides your [1]votive offerings and your freewill offerings, for your burnt offerings and for your grain offerings and
for your libations and for your peace offerings.' "
40 [1]And Moses spoke to the sons of Israel in accordance
with all that the LORD had commanded Moses.

CHAPTER 30

THEN Moses spoke to the heads of the tribes of the sons of
Israel, saying, "This is the word which the LORD has
commanded.
2 "[a]If a man makes a vow to the LORD, or takes an oath to
bind himself with a binding obligation, he shall not violate his
word; he shall do according to all that proceeds out of his
mouth.
3 "Also if a woman makes a vow to the LORD, and binds
herself by an obligation in her father's house in her youth,
4 and her father hears her vow and her obligation by
which she has bound herself, and her father [1]says nothing to
her, then all her vows shall stand, and every obligation by
which she has bound herself shall stand.
5 "But if her father should forbid her on the day he hears
of it, none of her vows or her obligations by which she has
bound herself shall stand; and the LORD will forgive her because her father had forbidden her.

35 [a]Lev. 23:36

39 [1]Lit., *vows*
[a]Lev. 23:2

40 [1]Chap. 30:1 in Heb.

2 [a]Deut. 23:21-23; Matt. 5:33

4 [1]Lit., *is silent to her,* and so throughout the chap.

6 [1]Lit., *be to a husband* [2]Lit., *her vows are on her*

6 "However, if she should [1]marry while [2]under her vows or
the rash statement of her lips by which she has bound herself,
7 and her husband hears of it and says nothing to her on
the day he hears *it*, then her vows shall stand and her obligations by which she has bound herself shall stand.
8 "But if on the day her husband hears *of it*, he forbids
her, then he shall annul her vow which [1]she is under and the
rash statement of her lips by which she has bound herself; and
the LORD will forgive her.

8 [1]Lit., *is on her*

9 "But the vow of a widow or of a divorced woman, everything by which she has bound herself, shall stand against her.
10 "However, if she vowed in her husband's house, or
bound herself by an obligation with an oath,
11 and her husband heard *it*, but said nothing to her *and*
did not forbid her, then all her vows shall stand, and every
obligation by which she bound herself shall stand.
12 "But if her husband indeed annuls them on the day he
hears *them*, then whatever proceeds out of her lips concerning
her vows or concerning the obligation of herself, shall not
stand; her husband has annulled them, and the LORD will forgive her.
13 "Every vow and every binding oath to humble herself,
her husband may confirm it or her husband may annul it.
14 "But if her husband indeed says nothing to her from day
to day, then he confirms all her vows or all her obligations
which are on her; he has confirmed them, because he said
nothing to her on the day he heard them.
15 "But if he indeed annuls them after he has heard them,
then he shall bear her guilt."
16 These are the statutes which the LORD commanded
Moses, *as* between a man and his wife, *and as* between a father
and his daughter, *while she is* in her youth in her father's
house.

CHAPTER 31

2 [a]Num. 25:1, 16, 17 [b]Num. 20:24, 26; 27:13

THEN the LORD spoke to Moses, saying,
2 "[a]Take full vengeance for the sons of Israel on the Midianites; afterward you will be [b]gathered to your people."
3 And Moses spoke to the people, saying, "Arm men
from among you for the war, that they may [1]go against Midian, to execute [a]the LORD's vengeance on Midian.

3 [1]Lit., *be* [a]Lev. 26:25

4 "A thousand from each tribe of all the tribes of Israel
you shall send to the war."
5 So there were [1]furnished from the thousands of Israel,
a thousand from each tribe, twelve thousand armed for war.

5 [1]Lit., *delivered*

6 And Moses sent them, a thousand from each tribe, to
the war, and Phinehas the son of Eleazar the priest, to the war
with them, [a]and the holy vessels and [b]the trumpets for the
alarm in his hand.

6 [a]Num. 14:44 [b]Num. 10:8, 9

7 So they made war against Midian, just as the LORD had
commanded Moses, and they killed every male.
8 And they killed the kings of Midian along with the *rest*
of their slain: [a]Evi and Rekem and [b]Zur and Hur and Reba,

8 [a]Josh. 13:21 [b]Num. 25:15

the five kings of Midian; [c]they also killed Balaam the son of
Beor with the sword.
9 And the sons of Israel captured the women of Midian
and their little ones; and all their cattle and all their flocks and
all their goods, they plundered.
10 Then they burned all their cities where they lived and
all their camps with fire.
11 And they took all the spoil and all the prey, both of
man and of beast.
12 And they brought the captives and the prey and the
spoil to Moses, and to Eleazar the priest and to the congregation of the sons of Israel, to the camp at the plains of Moab,
which are by the Jordan opposite Jericho.
13 And Moses and Eleazar the priest and all the leaders of
the congregation went out to meet them outside the camp.
14 And Moses was angry with the officers of the army, the
captains of thousands and the captains of hundreds, who had
come from service in the war.
15 And Moses said to them, "Have you [1]spared all the
women?
16 "[a]Behold, these [1]caused the sons of Israel, through the
[2]counsel of [b]Balaam, to [3]trespass against the LORD in the matter of Peor, so the plague was among the congregation of the
LORD.
17 "[a]Now therefore kill every male among the little ones,
and kill every woman who has known man [1]intimately.
18 "But all the [1]girls who have not known man [2]intimately,
[3]spare for yourselves.
19 "[a]And you, camp outside the camp seven days; whoever
has killed any person, and whoever has touched any slain,
purify yourselves, you and your captives, on the third day and
on the seventh day.
20 "And you shall purify for yourselves every garment and
every article of [1]leather and all the work of goats' *hair*, and all
articles of wood."
21 Then Eleazar the priest said to the men of war who had
gone to battle, "This is the statute of the law which the LORD
has commanded Moses:
22 only the gold and the silver, the bronze, the iron, the
tin and the lead,
23 everything that can stand the fire, you shall pass
through the fire, and it shall be clean, but it shall be purified
with water for impurity. But whatever cannot stand the fire
you shall pass through the water.
24 "And you shall wash your clothes on the seventh day and
be clean, and afterward you may enter the camp."
25 Then the LORD spoke to Moses, saying,
26 "You and Eleazar the priest and the heads of the fathers'
households of the congregation, take a count of the
booty [1]that was captured, both of man and of animal;
27 and divide the booty between the warriors who went
out to battle and all the congregation.
28 "[a]And levy a tax for the LORD from the men of war who
went out to battle, one [1]in five hundred of the persons and of
the cattle and of the donkeys and of the sheep;

8 [c]Num. 31:16; Josh. 13:22

15 [1]Lit., *let . . . live*

16 [1]Lit., *were to* [2]Lit., *word* [3]Possibly, *defect from the Lord* [a]Num. 25:1-9 [b]Num. 31:8

17 [1]Lit., *by lying with* [a]Deut. 7:2; 20:16-18

18 [1]Lit., *female children* [2]Lit., *by lying with a man* [3]Lit., *keep alive*

19 [a]Num. 19:11-22

20 [1]Or, *skin*

26 [1]Lit., *of captives*

28 [1]Lit., *soul from* [a]Num. 18:21-30

29 [1]Lit., *heave offering,* and so throughout the chap.

32 [1]Lit., *people*

35 [1]Lit., *by lying with man*

42 [1]Or, *divided*

53 [a]Num. 31:32

29 take it from their half and give it to Eleazar the priest,
as an [1]offering to the LORD.
30 "And from the sons of Israel's half, you shall take one
drawn out of every fifty of the persons, of the cattle, of the
donkeys and of the sheep, from all the animals, and give them
to the Levites who keep charge of the tabernacle of the LORD."
31 And Moses and Eleazar the priest did just as the LORD
had commanded Moses.
32 Now the booty that remained from the spoil which the
[1]men of war had plundered was 675,000 sheep,
33 and 72,000 cattle,
34 and 61,000 donkeys,
35 and of human beings, of the women who had not
known man [1]intimately, all the persons are 32,000.
36 And the half, the portion of those who went out to war,
was *as follows:* the number of sheep was 337,500,
37 and the LORD's levy of the sheep was 675,
38 and the cattle were 36,000, from which the LORD's levy
was 72.
39 And the donkeys were 30,500, from which the LORD's
levy was 61.
40 And the human beings were 16,000, from whom the
LORD's levy was 32 persons.
41 And Moses gave the levy *which was* the LORD's offering
to Eleazar the priest, just as the LORD had commanded Moses.
42 As for the sons of Israel's half, which Moses [1]separated
from the men who had gone to war—
43 now the congregation's half was 337,500 sheep,
44 and 36,000 cattle,
45 and 30,500 donkeys,
46 and the human beings were 16,000—
47 and from the sons of Israel's half, Moses took one
drawn out of every fifty, both of man and of animals, and gave
them to the Levites, who kept charge of the tabernacle of the
LORD, just as the LORD had commanded Moses.
48 Then the officers who were over the thousands of the
army, the captains of thousands and the captains of hundreds,
approached Moses;
49 and they said to Moses, "Your servants have taken a
census of men of war who are in our charge, and no man of us
is missing.
50 "So we have brought as an offering to the LORD what
each man found, articles of gold, armlets and bracelets, signet
rings, earrings and necklaces, to make atonement for ourselves
before the LORD."
51 And Moses and Eleazar the priest took the gold from
them, all kinds of wrought articles.
52 And all the gold of the offering which they offered up
to the LORD, from the captains of thousands and the captains
of hundreds, was 16,750 shekels.
53 [a]The men of war had taken booty, every man for
himself.
54 So Moses and Eleazar the priest took the gold from the
captains of thousands and of hundreds, and brought it to the
tent of meeting as a memorial for the sons of Israel before the
LORD.

CHAPTER 32

NOW the sons of Reuben and the sons of Gad had an
[a]exceedingly large number of livestock. So when they saw the
land of [b]Jazer and the land of Gilead, that [1]it was indeed a
place suitable for livestock,
2 the sons of Gad and the sons of Reuben came and
spoke to Moses and to Eleazar the priest and to the leaders of
the congregation, saying,
3 "[a]Ataroth, Dibon, Jazer, Nimrah, Heshbon, Elealeh, Se-
bam, Nebo and Beon,
4 the land which the LORD [1]conquered before the congregation of Israel, is a land for livestock; and your servants have
livestock."
5 And they said, "If we have found favor in your sight, let
this land be given to your servants as a possession; do not take
us across the Jordan."
6 But Moses said to the sons of Gad and to the sons of
Reuben, "Shall your brothers go to war while you yourselves
sit here?
7 "[a]Now why [1]are you discouraging the sons of Israel from
crossing over into the land which the LORD has given them?
8 "[1]This is what your fathers did when I sent them from
[a]Kadesh-barnea to see the land.
9 "For when they went up to the [1]valley of Eshcol and saw
the land, they [2]discouraged the sons of Israel so that they did
not go into the land which the LORD had given them.
10 "So the LORD's anger burned in that day, and He swore,
saying,
11 '[a]None of the men who came up from Egypt, from
twenty years old and upward, shall see the land which I swore
to Abraham, to Isaac and to Jacob; for they did not follow Me
fully,
12 except Caleb the son of Jephunneh the Kenizzite and
Joshua the son of Nun, for they have followed the LORD
fully.'
13 "[a]So the LORD's anger burned against Israel, and He
made them wander in the wilderness forty years, until the
entire generation of those who had done evil in the sight of the
LORD was destroyed.
14 "Now behold, you have risen up in your fathers' place, a
brood of sinful men, to add still more to the burning anger of
the LORD against Israel.
15 "For if you turn away from following Him, He will once
more abandon them in the wilderness; and you will destroy all
these people."
16 Then they came near to him and said, "We will build
here sheepfolds for our livestock and cities for our little ones;
17 [a]but we ourselves will be armed ready *to go* before the
sons of Israel, until we have brought them to their place, while
our little ones live in the fortified cities because of the inhabitants of the land.
18 "[a]We will not return to our homes until every one of the
sons of Israel has possessed his inheritance.
19 "For we will not have an inheritance with them on the

1 [1]Lit., *behold, the place, a place for* [a]Ex. 12:38 [b]Num. 21:32

3 [a]Num. 32:34-38

4 [1]Lit., *smote*

7 [1]Lit., *restraining the heart* [a]Num. 13:27-14:4

8 [1]Lit., *Thus your fathers* [a]Num. 13:3, 26; Deut. 1:19-25

9 [1]Or, *wadi* [2]Lit., *restrained the heart*

11 [a]Num. 14:28-30

13 [a]Num. 14:33-35

17 [a]Josh. 4:12, 13

18 [a]Josh. 22:1-4

other side of the Jordan and beyond, because our inheritance
has fallen to us on this side of Jordan toward the east."
20 [a]So Moses said to them, "If you will do [1]this, if you will
arm yourselves before the LORD for the war,
21 and all of you armed men cross over the Jordan before
the LORD until He has driven His enemies out from before
Him,
22 [a]and the land is subdued before the LORD, then afterward you shall return and be free of obligation toward the
LORD and toward Israel, and this land shall be yours for a
possession before the LORD.
23 "But if you will not do so, behold, you have sinned
against the LORD, and be sure your sin will find you out.
24 "Build yourselves cities for your little ones, and sheepfolds for your sheep; and [a]do [1]what you have promised."
25 And the sons of Gad and the sons of Reuben spoke to
Moses, saying, "Your servants will do just as my lord
commands.
26 "Our little ones, our wives, our livestock and all our
cattle shall [1]remain there in the cities of Gilead;
27 while your servants, everyone who is armed for war, will
cross over in the presence of the LORD to battle, just as my lord
says."
28 So Moses gave command concerning them to Eleazar
the priest, and to Joshua the son of Nun, and to the heads of
the fathers' *households* of the tribes of the sons of Israel.
29 And Moses said to them, "If the sons of Gad and the
sons of Reuben, everyone who is armed for battle, will cross
with you over the Jordan in the presence of the LORD, and the
land will be subdued before you, then you shall give them the
land of Gilead for a possession;
30 but if they will not cross over with you armed, they
shall have possessions among you in the land of Canaan."
31 And the sons of Gad and the sons of Reuben answered,
saying, "As the LORD has said to your servants, so we will do.
32 "We ourselves will cross over armed in the presence of
the LORD into the land of Canaan, and the possession of our
inheritance *shall remain* with us across the Jordan."
33 [a]So Moses gave to them, to the sons of Gad and to the
sons of Reuben and to the half-tribe of Joseph's son Manasseh,
the kingdom of Sihon king of the Amorites and the kingdom
of Og the king of Bashan, the land with its cities with *their*
[1]territories, the cities of the surrounding land.
34 And the sons of Gad built Dibon and Ataroth and
Aroer,
35 and Atroth-shophan and Jazer and Jogbehah,
36 and Beth-nimrah and Beth-haran as fortified cities, and
sheepfolds for sheep.
37 And the sons of Reuben built Heshbon and Elealeh
and Kiriathaim,
38 and Nebo and Baal-meon—*their* names being
changed—and Sibmah, and they gave *other* names to the cities
which they built.
39 And the sons of Machir the son of Manasseh went to
Gilead and took it, and dispossessed the Amorites who were in
it.

20 [1]Lit., *this thing*
[a]Deut. 3:18

22 [a]Deut. 3:20

24 [1]Lit., *that which has come out of your mouth*
[a]Num. 30:2

26 [1]Lit., *be*

33 [1]Lit., *borders*
[a]Deut. 3:8-17; Josh. 12:1-6

40 So Moses gave Gilead to Machir the son of Manasseh,
and he lived in it.
41 And Jair the son of Manasseh went and took its [1]towns,
and called them [2a]Havvoth-jair.
42 And Nobah went and took Kenath and its villages, and
called it Nobah after his own name.

Chapter 33

THESE are the journeys of the sons of Israel, by which they
came out from the land of Egypt by their armies under [a]the
[1]leadership of Moses and Aaron.
2 And Moses recorded their starting places according to
their journeys by the [1]command of the LORD, and these are
their journeys according to their starting places.
3 [a]And they journeyed from Rameses in the first month,
on the fifteenth day of the first month; on the [1]next day after
the Passover the sons of Israel [b]started out [2]boldly in the sight
of all the Egyptians,
4 while the Egyptians were burying all their first-born
whom the LORD had struck down among them. The LORD had
also executed judgments [a]on their gods.
5 Then the sons of Israel journeyed from Rameses, and
camped in Succoth.
6 [a]And they journeyed from Succoth, and camped in
Etham, which is on the edge of the wilderness.
7 [a]And they journeyed from Etham, and turned back to
Pi-hahiroth, which faces Baal-zephon; and they camped before
Migdol.
8 [a]And they journeyed [1]from before Hahiroth, and
passed through the midst of the sea into the wilderness; and
[b]they went three days' journey in the wilderness of Etham, and
camped at Marah.
9 [a]And they journeyed from Marah, and came to Elim;
and in Elim there were twelve springs of water and seventy
palm trees; and they camped there.
10 And they journeyed from Elim, and camped by the
[1]Red Sea.
11 And they journeyed from the [1]Red Sea, and camped in
[a]the wilderness of Sin.
12 And they journeyed from the wilderness of Sin, and
camped at Dophkah.
13 And they journeyed from Dophkah, and camped at
Alush.
14 And they journeyed from Alush, and camped [a]at Rephidim; now it was there that the people had no water to drink.
15 And they journeyed from Rephidim, and camped in
[a]the wilderness of Sinai.
16 And they journeyed from the wilderness of Sinai, and
camped at [a]Kibroth-hattaavah.
17 And they journeyed from Kibroth-hattaavah, and
camped at [a]Hazeroth.
18 And they journeyed from Hazeroth, and camped at
Rithmah.
19 And they journeyed from Rithmah, and camped at
Rimmon-perez.

41 [1]Lit., *tent villages* [2]I.e., the towns of Jair [a]Deut. 3:14; Judg. 10:4

1 [1]Lit., *hand* [a]Ps. 77:20; 105:26; Mic. 6:4

2 [1]Lit., *mouth*

3 [1]Lit., *morrow* [2]Lit., *with a high hand* [a]Ex. 12:37 [b]Ex. 14:8

4 [a]Ex. 12:12

6 [a]Ex. 13:20

7 [a]Ex. 14:1, 2

8 [1]Many mss. read, *from Pi-hahiroth* [a]Ex. 14:22 [b]Ex. 15:22

9 [a]Ex. 15:27

10 [1]Lit., *Sea of Reeds*

11 [1]Lit., *Sea of Reeds* [a]Ex. 16:1

14 [a]Ex. 17:1

15 [a]Ex. 19:1

16 [a]Num. 11:34

17 [a]Num. 11:35

30 [a]Deut. 10:6 **20** And they journeyed from Rimmon-perez, and camped
at Libnah.
21 And they journeyed from Libnah, and camped at
Rissah.
22 And they journeyed from Rissah, and camped in
Kehelathah.
33 [a]Deut. 10:7 **23** And they journeyed from Kehelathah, and camped at
Mount Shepher.
24 And they journeyed from Mount Shepher, and camped
at Haradah.
25 And they journeyed from Haradah, and camped at
Makheloth.
26 And they journeyed from Makheloth, and camped at
35 [a]Deut. 2:8 Tahath.
27 And they journeyed from Tahath, and camped at
Terah.
28 And they journeyed from Terah, and camped at
Mithkah.
29 And they journeyed from Mithkah, and camped at
36 [a]Num. 20:1 Hashmonah.
30 And they journeyed from Hashmonah, and camped at
[a]Moseroth.
31 And they journeyed from Moseroth, and camped at
Bene-jaakan.
32 And they journeyed from Bene-jaakan, and camped at
Hor-haggidgad.
37 [a]Num. 20:22 [b]Num. 20:16 **33** And they journeyed from Hor-haggidgad, and camped
at [a]Jotbathah.
34 And they journeyed from Jotbathah, and camped at
Abronah.
35 And they journeyed from Abronah, and camped at
[a]Ezion-geber.
38 [1]Lit., *mouth* [a]Num. 20:28 **36** And they journeyed from Ezion-geber, and camped in
the wilderness of [a]Zin, that is, Kadesh.
37 And they journeyed from Kadesh, and camped at
[a]Mount Hor, [b]at the edge of the land of Edom.
38 [a]Then Aaron the priest went up to Mount Hor at the
[1]command of the LORD, and died there, in the fortieth year
after the sons of Israel had come from the land of Egypt on
the first *day* in the fifth month.
40 [1]Lit., *and he* [2]I.e., South country [a]Num. 21:1 **39** And Aaron was one hundred twenty-three years old
when he died on Mount Hor.
40 Now the Canaanite, the king of [a]Arad [1]who lived in the
[2]Negev in the land of Canaan, heard of the coming of the sons
of Israel.
41 Then they journeyed from Mount Hor, and camped at
Zalmonah.
43 [a]Num. 21:10, 11 **42** And they journeyed from Zalmonah, and camped at
Punon.
43 And they journeyed from Punon, and camped at
[a]Oboth.
44 And they journeyed from Oboth, and camped at Iye-
abarim, at the border of Moab.
45 And they journeyed from Iyim, and camped at Dibon-
gad.

46 And they journeyed from Dibon-gad, and camped at
Almon-diblathaim.
47 And they journeyed from Almon-diblathaim, and
camped in the mountains of [a]Abarim, before Nebo.
48 And they journeyed from the mountains of Abarim,
and [a]camped in the plains of Moab by the Jordan *opposite*
Jericho.
49 And they camped by the Jordan, from Beth-jeshimoth
as far as [a]Abel-shittim in the plains of Moab.
50 Then the LORD spoke to Moses in the plains of Moab
by the Jordan *opposite* Jericho, saying,
51 "Speak to the sons of Israel and say to them, 'When you
cross over the Jordan into the land of Canaan,
52 then you shall drive out all the inhabitants of the land
from before you, and [a]destroy all their *figured stones*, and
destroy all their molten images and demolish all their high
places;
53 [a]and you shall take possession of the land and live in it,
for I have given the land to you to possess it.
54 '[a]And you shall inherit the land by lot according to your
families; to the larger you shall give more inheritance, and to
the smaller you shall give less inheritance. Wherever the lot
falls to anyone, that shall be his. You shall inherit according to
the tribes of your fathers.
55 'But if you do not drive out the inhabitants of the land
from before you, then it shall come about that those whom
you let remain of them *will become* [a]as pricks in your eyes and
as thorns in your sides, and they shall trouble you in the land in
which you live.
56 'And it shall come about that as I plan to do to them, so
I will do to you.' "

CHAPTER 34

THEN the LORD spoke to Moses, saying,
2 "Command the sons of Israel and say to them, 'When
you enter the land of Canaan, this is the land that shall fall to
you as an inheritance, *even the* land of Canaan according to its
borders.
3 '[a]Your southern [1]sector shall [2]extend from the wilderness of Zin along the side of Edom, and your southern border
shall [2]extend from the end of the Salt Sea [b]eastward.
4 'Then your border shall turn *direction* from the south
to the ascent of Akrabbim, and [1]continue to Zin, and its [2]ter-
mination shall be to the south of Kadesh-barnea; and it shall
[3]reach Hazaraddar, and [1]continue to Azmon.
5 'And the border shall turn *direction* from Azmon to the
brook of Egypt, and its termination shall be at [a]the sea.
6 'As for the western border, you shall have the Great Sea,
that is, *its* [1]coastline; this shall be your west border.
7 '[a]And this shall be your north border: you shall draw
your *border* line from the Great Sea to Mount Hor.
8 'You shall draw a line from Mount Hor to [a]the [1]Lebo-
hamath, and the termination of the border shall be at Zedad;
9 and the border shall proceed to Ziphron, and its termination shall be at Hazer-enan. This shall be your north border.

47 [a]Num. 27:12
48 [a]Num. 22:1
49 [a]Num. 25:1
52 [a]Ex. 23:24; Lev 26:1; Deut. 7:5; 12:3, 30; Ps. 106:34
53 [a]Deut. 11:31; 17:14; Josh. 21:43
54 [a]Num. 26:53-56
55 [a]Josh 23:13
3 [1]Lit., *side* [2]Lit., *be* [a]Josh. 15:1-3 [b]Josh. 15:5
4 [1]Lit., *pass along* [2]Lit., *goings out*, and so throughout the chap. [3]Lit., *go forth to*
5 [a]Josh. 15:4
6 [1]Lit., *border*
7 [a]Ezek. 47:15-17
8 [1]Or, *entrance of Hamath* [a]Josh. 13:5

11 [1]Lit., *shoulder* [a]2 Kin. 23:33 [b]Deut. 3:17; Josh. 13:27

10 'For your eastern border you shall also draw a line from
Hazer-enan to Shepham,
11 and the border shall go down from Shepham to [a]Riblah
on the east side of Ain; and the border shall go down and reach
to the [1]slope on the east side of the sea of [b]Chinnereth.
12 'And the border shall go down to the Jordan and its
termination shall be at the Salt Sea. This shall be your land
according to its borders all around.' "
13 So Moses commanded the sons of Israel, saying, "[a]This
is the land that you are to apportion by lot among you as a
possession, which the LORD has commanded to give to the nine
and a half tribes.

13 [a]Gen. 15:18; Deut. 11:24

14 "[a]For the tribe of the sons of Reuben have received
theirs according to their fathers' households, and the tribe of
the sons of Gad according to their fathers' households, and the
half-tribe of Manasseh have received their possession.
15 "The two and a half tribes have received their possession
across the Jordan opposite Jericho, eastward toward the sun-
rising."
16 Then the LORD spoke to Moses, saying,
17 "[a]These are the names of the men who shall apportion
the land to you for inheritance: Eleazar the priest and Joshua
the son of Nun.

14 [a]Num. 32:33

18 "And you shall take one leader of every tribe to apportion the land for inheritance.
19 "And these are the names of the men: of the tribe of
Judah, Caleb the son of Jephunneh.
20 "And of the tribe of the sons of Simeon, Samuel the son
of Ammihud.
21 "Of the tribe of Benjamin, Elidad the son of Chislon.
22 "And of the tribe of the sons of Dan a leader, Bukki the
son of Jogli.
23 "Of the sons of Joseph: of the tribe of the sons of Manasseh a leader, Hanniel the son of Ephod.

17 [a]Josh. 14:1, 2

24 "And of the tribe of the sons of Ephraim a leader, Kemuel the son of Shiphtan.
25 "And of the tribe of the sons of Zebulun a leader, Elizaphan the son of Parnach.
26 "And of the tribe of the sons of Issachar a leader, Paltiel
the son of Azzan.
27 "And of the tribe of the sons of Asher a leader, Ahihud
the son of Shelomi.
28 "And of the tribe of the sons of Naphtali a leader, Peda-
hel the son of Ammihud."

1 [a]Lev. 25:32-34

29 These are those whom the LORD commanded to apportion the inheritance to the sons of Israel in the land of Canaan.

[a] Chapter 35

NOW the LORD spoke to Moses in the plains of Moab by
the Jordan opposite Jericho, saying,
2 "Command the sons of Israel that they give to the Levites from the inheritance of their possession, cities to live in;
and you shall give to the Levites pasture lands around the
cities.
3 "And the cities shall be theirs to live in; and their pasture

lands shall be for their cattle and for their herds and for all
their beasts.
4 "And the pasture lands of the cities which you shall give
to the Levites *shall extend* from the wall of the city [1]outward a
thousand cubits around.
5 "You shall also measure outside the city on the east side
two thousand cubits, and on the south side two thousand cubits, and on the west side two thousand cubits, and on the
north side two thousand cubits, with the city in the center.
This shall become theirs as pasture lands for the cities.
6 "And the cities which you shall give to the Levites *shall*
be the [a]six cities of refuge, which you shall give for the manslayer to flee to; and in addition to them you shall give forty-
two cities.
7 "All the cities which you shall give to the Levites *shall be*
forty-eight cities, [1]together with their pasture lands.
8 "[a]As for the cities which you shall give from the possession of the sons of Israel, you shall take more from the larger
and you shall take less from the smaller; each shall give some
of his cities to the Levites in proportion to his possession which
he inherits."
9 Then the LORD spoke to Moses, saying,
10 "Speak to the sons of Israel and say to them, 'When you
cross the Jordan into the land of Canaan,
11 [a]then you shall select for yourselves cities to be your
cities of refuge, that the manslayer who has [1]killed any person
[b]unintentionally may flee there.
12 'And the cities shall be to you as a refuge from the
avenger, so that the manslayer may not die until he stands
before the congregation for [1]trial.
13 'And the cities which you are to give shall be your six
cities of refuge.
14 'You shall give three cities across the Jordan and three
cities [1]in the land of Canaan, they are to be cities of refuge.
15 'These six cities shall be for refuge for the sons of Israel,
and for the alien and for the sojourner among them; that
anyone who [1]kills a person [a]unintentionally may flee there.
16 '[a]But if he struck him down with an iron object, so that
he died, he is a murderer; the murderer shall surely be put to
death.
17 'And if he struck him down with a stone in the hand, by
which he may die, and *as a result* he died, he is a murderer; the
murderer [a]shall surely be put to death.
18 'Or if he struck him with a wooden object in the hand,
by which he may die, and *as a result* he died, he is a murderer;
the murderer shall surely be put to death.
19 'The blood avenger himself shall put the murderer to
death; he shall put him to death when he meets him.
20 'And if he pushed him of hatred, or threw something at
him lying in wait and *as a result* he died,
21 or if he struck him down with his hand in enmity, and
as a result he died, the one who struck him shall surely be put
to death, he is a murderer; the blood avenger shall put the
murderer to death when he meets him.
22 '[a]But if he pushed him suddenly without enmity, or
threw something at him without lying in wait,

4 [1]Lit., *and outward*

6 [a]Josh. 20:7-9

7 [1]Lit., *them*

8 [a]Num. 26:54; 33:54; Lev. 25:32-34; Josh. 21:1-42

11 [1]Lit., *smote* [a]Deut. 19:1-13 [b]Num. 35:22; Ex. 21:13; Lev. 4:2, 22

12 [1]Lit., *judgment*

14 [1]Lit., *you shall give in*

15 [1]Lit., *smites* [a]Num. 35:11

16 [a]Ex. 21:12, 14; Lev. 24:17

17 [a]Num. 35:31

22 [a]Num. 35:11

23 or with any [1]deadly object of stone, and without seeing it dropped on him so that he died, while he was not his enemy nor seeking his injury,

24 then the congregation shall judge between the slayer and the blood avenger according to these ordinances.

25 'And the congregation shall deliver the manslayer from the hand of the blood avenger, and the congregation shall restore him to his city of refuge to which he fled; and he shall live in it until the death of the high priest who was anointed with the holy oil.

26 'But if the manslayer shall at any time go beyond the border of his city of refuge to which he may flee,

27 and the blood avenger finds him outside the border of his city of refuge, and the blood avenger kills the manslayer, he shall not be guilty of blood

28 because he should have remained in his city of refuge until the death of the high priest. But after the death of the high priest the manslayer shall return to the land of his possession.

29 'And these things shall be for a statutory ordinance to you throughout your generations in all your dwellings.

30 '[a]If anyone kills a person, the murderer shall be put to death at the [1]evidence of witnesses, but [b]no person shall be put to death on the testimony of one witness.

31 'Moreover you shall not take ransom for the life of a murderer who is guilty of death, but he shall surely be put to death.

32 'And you shall not take ransom for him who has fled to his city of refuge, that he may return to live in the land [1]before the death of the priest.

33 '[a]So you shall not pollute the land in which you are; for blood pollutes the land and no expiation can be made for the land for the blood that is shed on it, except [b]by the blood of him who shed it.

34 'And you shall not [a]defile the land in which you live, in the midst of which [b]I dwell; for I the LORD am dwelling in the midst of the sons of Israel.' "

[a] CHAPTER 36

AND the heads of the fathers' *households* of the family of the sons of Gilead, the son of Machir, the son of Manasseh, of the families of the sons of Joseph, came near and spoke before Moses and before the leaders, the heads of the fathers' *households* of the sons of Israel,

2 and they said, "The LORD commanded my lord to give the land by lot to the sons of Israel as an inheritance, and my lord [a]was commanded by the LORD to give the inheritance of Zelophehad our brother to his daughters.

3 "But if they [1]marry one of the sons of the *other* tribes of the sons of Israel, their inheritance will be withdrawn from the inheritance of our fathers and will be added to the inheritance of the tribe to which they belong; thus it will be withdrawn from our allotted inheritance.

4 "And when the [a]jubilee of the sons of Israel [1]comes, then their inheritance will be added to the inheritance of the

23 [1]Lit., *by which he may die*

30 [1]Lit., *mouth* [a]Num. 35:16 [b]Deut. 17:6; 19:15; Matt. 18:16; John 7:51; 8:17, 18

32 [1]Or, *until*

33 [a]Deut. 21:7, 8; Ps. 106:38 [b]Gen. 9:6

34 [a]Lev. 18:24, 25 [b]Num. 5:3

1 [a]Num. 27:1

2 [a]Num. 27:5, 6

3 [1]Lit., *become wives to*, and so throughout the chap.

4 [1]Lit., *shall be* [a]Lev. 25:10

tribe to which they belong; so their inheritance will be withdrawn from the inheritance of the tribe of our fathers."
5 Then Moses commanded the sons of Israel according
to the [1]word of the LORD, saying, "The tribe of the sons of
Joseph are right in *their* statements.
6 "This is [1]what the LORD has commanded concerning
the daughters of Zelophehad, saying, 'Let them marry [2]whom
they wish; only they must marry within the family of the tribe
of their father.'
7 "Thus no inheritance of the sons of Israel shall [1]be transferred from tribe to tribe, for the sons of Israel shall each
[2]hold to the inheritance of the tribe of his fathers.
8 "[a]And every daughter who comes into possession of an
inheritance of any tribe of the sons of Israel, shall be wife to
one of the family of the tribe of her father, so that the sons of
Israel each may possess the inheritance of his fathers.
9 "Thus no inheritance shall [1]be transferred from one
tribe to another tribe, for the tribes of the sons of Israel shall
each [2]hold to his own inheritance."
10 Just as the LORD had commanded Moses, so the daughters of Zelophehad did,
11 and for [a]Mahlah, Tirzah, and Hoglah and Milcah and
Noah, the daughters of Zelophehad married their uncles' sons.
12 They married *those* from the families of the sons of
Manasseh the sons of Joseph, and their inheritance [1]remained
with the tribe of the family of their father.
13 [a]These are the commandments and the ordinances
which the LORD commanded to the sons of Israel through
Moses in the plains of Moab by the Jordan *opposite* Jericho.

5 [1]Lit., *mouth*

6 [1]Lit., *the thing which* [2]Lit., *to the good one in their eyes*

7 [1]Lit., *turn about* [2]Lit., *cleave*

8 [a]1 Chr. 23:22

9 [1]Lit., *turn about* [2]Lit., *cleave*

11 [a]Num. 26:33

12 [1]Lit., *was*

13 [a]Num. 22:1; Lev. 26:46; 27:34

DEUTERONOMY

God's Command to Possess the Land.

THESE are the words which Moses spoke to all Israel [a]across
the Jordan in the wilderness, in the [b]Arabah opposite [1]Suph,
between Paran and Tophel and Laban and Hazeroth and Di-
zahab.
2 It is eleven days' *journey* from [a]Horeb by the way of
Mount [b]Seir to [c]Kadesh-barnea.
3 And it came about in the [a]fortieth year, on the first day
of the eleventh month, that Moses spoke to the children of
Israel, [b]according to all that the LORD had commanded him *to
give* to them,
4 after he had [1a]defeated Sihon the king of the Amorites,
who lived in Heshbon, and Og the king of Bashan, who lived in
Ashtaroth [2]and Edrei.
5 Across the Jordan in the land of Moab, Moses undertook to expound this law, saying,
6 "The LORD our God [a]spoke to us at Horeb, saying, 'You
have [1]stayed long enough at this mountain.

1 [1]Perhaps Red Sea [a]Deut. 4:46 [b]Deut. 2:8

2 [a]Ex. 3:1; 17:6 [b]Gen. 32:3 [c]Num. 32:8

3 [a]Num. 33:38 [b]Deut. 4:1, 2

4 [1]Lit., *smitten* [2]So with ancient versions. M.T. omits *and;* cf. also Josh. 12:4 [a]Num. 21:24, 25

6 [1]Lit., *dwelt* [a]Num. 10:11-13

7 ‘Turn and set your journey, and go to [a]the hill country
of the Amorites, and to all their neighbors in the Arabah, in
the hill country and in the lowland and in [1b]the Negev and by
the seacoast, the land of the Canaanites, and Lebanon, as far
as the great river, the river Euphrates.
8 ‘See, I have placed the land before you; go in and possess the land which the LORD [a]swore to give to your fathers, to
Abraham, to Isaac, and to Jacob, to them and their [1]descen-
dants after them.’
9 “And I spoke to you at that time, saying, ‘[a]I am not able
to bear *the burden* of you alone.
10 ‘The LORD your God has [a]multiplied you, and behold,
you are this day as the stars of heaven for multitude.
11 ‘May the LORD, the God of your fathers, increase you a
thousand-fold more than you are, and bless you, just as He has
[1]promised you!
12 ‘How can I alone bear the load and burden of you and
your strife?
13 ‘[1a]Choose wise and discerning and experienced men
from your tribes, and I will appoint them as your heads.’
14 “And you answered me and said, ‘The thing which you
have said to do is good.’
15 “So I took the heads of your tribes, wise and experienced men, and [1]appointed them heads over you, leaders of
thousands, and [2]of hundreds, [2]of fifties and [2]of tens, and officers for your tribes.
16 “Then I charged our judges at that time, saying, ‘Hear
the cases between your [1]fellow countrymen, and judge righteously between a man and his [2]fellow countryman, or the
alien who is with him.
17 ‘[a]You shall not show partiality in judgment; you shall
hear the small and the great alike. You shall not fear [1]man, for
the judgment is God’s. And [b]the case that is too hard for you,
you shall bring to me, and I will hear it.’
18 “[a]And I commanded you at that time all the things that
you should do.
19 “Then we set out from [a]Horeb, and went through all
that [b]great and terrible wilderness which you saw, on the way
to the [c]hill country of the Amorites, just as the LORD our God
had commanded us; and we came to [d]Kadesh-barnea.
20 “And I said to you, ‘You have come to the hill country
of the Amorites which the LORD our God is about to give us.
21 ‘See, the LORD your God has placed the land before
you; go up, take possession, as the LORD, the God of your
fathers, has spoken to you. Do not fear or be dismayed.’
22 “[a]Then all of you approached me and said, ‘Let us send
men before us, that they may search out the land for us, and
bring back to us word of the way by which we should go up,
and the cities which we shall enter.’
23 “And the thing pleased me and I took twelve of your
men, one man for each tribe.
24 “And [a]they turned and went up into the hill country,
and came to the valley of Eshcol, and spied it out.
25 “Then they took *some* of the fruit of the land in their
hands and brought it down to us; and they brought us back a

7 [1]I.e., South country [a]Deut. 11:24; Gen. 15:18; Josh. 10:40 [b]Gen. 12:9

8 [1]Lit., *seed* [a]Gen. 26:3; Ex. 33:1; Num. 14:23; 32:11

9 [a]Ex. 18:18, 24

10 [a]Deut. 10:22; 26:5; Gen. 15:5; 22:17

11 [1]Lit., *spoken to*

13 [1]Lit., *give for yourselves* [a]Ex. 18:21

15 [1]Lit., *gave* [2]Lit., *leaders of*

16 [1]Lit., *brothers* [2]Lit., *brother*

17 [1]Lit., *because of man* [a]Deut. 10:17; 16:19; 24:17 [b]Ex. 18:19, 23

18 [a]Ex. 18:20

19 [a]Deut. 1:2 [b]Deut. 2:7; 8:15; 32:10 [c]Deut. 1:7 [d]Deut. 1:2

22 [a]Num. 13:1-3

24 [a]Num. 13:21-25

report and said, 'It is a good land which the LORD our God is
about to give us.'
26 "[a]Yet you were not willing to go up, but rebelled against
the [1]command of the LORD your God;
27 and [a]you grumbled in your tents and said, 'Because the
LORD hates us, He has brought us out of the land of Egypt to
deliver us into the hand of the Amorites to destroy us.
28 'Where can we go up? Our brethren have made our
hearts melt, saying, "The people are bigger and taller than we;
the cities are large and fortified to heaven. And besides, we saw
[a]the sons of the Anakim there." '
29 "Then I said to you, 'Do not be shocked, nor fear them.
30 'The LORD your God who goes before you will [a]Himself
fight on your behalf, [1]just as He did for you in Egypt before
your eyes,
31 and in the wilderness where you saw how [a]the LORD
your God carried you, just as a man carries his son, in all the
way which you have walked, until you came to this place.'
32 "But [1]for all this, you did not trust the LORD your God,
33 [a]who goes before you on *your* way, to seek out a place
for you to encamp, in fire by night and cloud by day, to show
you the way in which you should go.
34 "Then the LORD heard the sound of your words, and He
was angry and [a]took an oath, saying,
35 'Not one of these men, this evil generation, shall see the
good land which I swore to give your fathers,
36 except Caleb the son of Jephunneh; he shall see it, and
[a]to him and to his sons I will give the land on which he has set
foot, because he has followed the LORD fully.'
37 "[a]The LORD was angry with me also on your account,
saying, '[b]Not even you shall enter there.
38 'Joshua the son of Nun, who stands before you, [a]he shall
enter there; encourage him, for [b]he shall cause Israel to inherit
it.
39 'Moreover, [a]your little ones who you said would become a prey, and your sons, who this day have no knowledge
of good or evil, shall enter there, and I will give it to them, and
they shall possess it.
40 'But as for you, [a]turn around and set out for the wilderness by the way to the [1]Red Sea.'
41 "[a]Then you answered and said to me, 'We have sinned
against the LORD; we will indeed go up and fight, just as the
LORD our God commanded us.' And every man of you girded
on his weapons of war, and regarded it as easy to go up into the
hill country.
42 "[a]And the LORD said to me, 'Say to them, "Do not go
up, nor fight, for I am not among you; lest you be [1]defeated
before your enemies." '
43 "So I spoke to you, but you would not listen. Instead
[a]you rebelled against the [1]command of the LORD, and acted
presumptuously and went up into the hill country.
44 "[a]And the Amorites who [1]lived in that hill country came
out against you, and chased you as bees do, and crushed you
from Seir to Hormah.
45 "Then you returned and wept before the LORD; but the
LORD did not listen to your voice, nor give ear to you.

26 [1]Lit., *mouth* [a]Num. 14:1-4
27 [a]Ps. 106:25
28 [a]Deut. 9:2; Num. 13:28, 33
30 [1]Lit., *according to all that* [a]Deut. 3:22; 20:4; Ex. 14:14
31 [a]Acts 13:18
32 [1]Lit., *in this matter*
33 [a]Num. 9:15-23
34 [a]Num. 14:28-30
36 [a]Num. 14:24; Josh. 14:9
37 [a]Num. 20:12 [b]Num. 27:13, 18
38 [a]Num. 14:20 [b]Deut. 3:28; 31:7; Num. 34:17; Josh. 11:23
39 [a]Num. 14:3, 31
40 [1]Or, *Sea of Reeds* [a]Num. 14:25
41 [a]Num. 14:40
42 [1]Lit., *smitten* [a]Num. 14:41-43
43 [1]Lit., *mouth* [a]Num. 14:40
44 [1]Lit., *dwelt* [a]Num. 14:45

46 "So you remained in Kadesh [a]many days, [1]the days that
you spent *there*.

Chapter 2

"[a]THEN we turned and set out for the wilderness by the
way to the [1]Red Sea, as the LORD spoke to me, and circled
[b]Mount Seir for many days.
2 "And the LORD spoke to me, saying,
3 'You have circled this mountain long enough. Now turn
north,
4 [a]and command the people, saying, "You will pass
through the territory of your brothers the sons of Esau who
live in Seir; and [b]they will be afraid of you. So be very careful;
5 do not [1]provoke them, for I will not give you any of
their land, even *as little as* a [2]footstep because I have given
Mount Seir to Esau as a possession.
6 "You shall buy food from them with money so that you
may eat, and you shall also purchase water from them with
money so that you may drink.
7 "For the LORD your God has blessed you in all [1]that you
have done; He has known your [2]wanderings through this [a]great
wilderness. These [b]forty years the LORD your God has been
with you; you have not lacked a thing." '
8 "So we passed beyond our brothers the sons of Esau,
who live in Seir, away from the [a]Arabah road, away from Elath
and from Ezion-geber. And we turned and passed through by
the way of the wilderness of Moab.
9 "Then the LORD said to me, 'Do not harass Moab, nor
provoke them to war, for I will not give you any of [1]their land
as a possession, because I have given [a]Ar to [b]the sons of Lot as
a possession.
10 (The Emim lived there formerly, a people as great,
numerous, and tall as the Anakim.
11 Like the Anakim, they are also regarded as [a]Rephaim,
but the Moabites call them Emim.
12 [a]The Horites formerly lived in Seir, but the sons of
Esau dispossessed them and destroyed them from before them
and settled in their place, [b]just as Israel did to the land of
[1]their possession which the LORD gave to them.)
13 'Now arise and cross over the [1]brook Zered yourselves.'
So we crossed over the [1]brook Zered.
14 "Now the [1]time that it took for us to come from Kadesh-barnea, until we crossed over the [2]brook Zered, was [a]thir-
ty-eight years; until [b]all the generation of the men of war
perished from within the camp, as the LORD had sworn to
them.
15 "[a]Moreover the hand of the LORD was against them, to
destroy them from within the camp, until they all perished.
16 "So it came about when [a]all the men of war had finally
perished from among the people,
17 that the LORD spoke to me, saying,
18 'You shall cross over [a]Ar, the border of Moab, today.
19 'And when you come opposite the sons of Ammon, do
not harass them nor provoke them, for I will not give you any

46 [1]Lit., *as the days* [a]Deut. 2:7, 14

1 [1]Or, *Sea of Reeds* [a]Num. 21:4 [b]Deut. 1:2

4 [a]Num. 20:14-21 [b]Ex. 15:15

5 [1]Or, *engage in strife with* [2]Lit., *treading of a sole of a foot*

7 [1]Lit., *the work of your hand* [2]Lit., *goings* [a]Deut. 1:19 [b]Deut. 2:14; Num. 14:33, 34; 32:13

9 [1]Lit., *his* [a]Deut. 2:18, 29; Num. 21:15, 28 [b]Gen. 19:36, 37

11 [a]Deut. 2:20; Gen. 14:5

12 [1]Lit., *his* [a]Deut. 2:22 [b]Num. 21:25, 35

13 [1]Or, *wadi*

14 [1]Lit., *days in which we went* [2]Or, *wadi* [a]Deut. 2:7 [b]Num. 14:29-35; 26:64, 65; Ps. 106:26; 1 Cor. 10:5

15 [a]Jude 5

16 [a]Deut. 2:14

18 [a]Deut. 2:9

of the land of the sons of Ammon as a possession, because I
have given it to [a]the sons of Lot as a possession.'
20 (It is also regarded as the land of the [a]Rephaim, *for*
Rephaim formerly lived in it, but the Amorites call them
Zamzummin,
21 a people as great, numerous, and tall as the Anakim,
but the LORD destroyed them before them. And they dispossessed them and settled in their place,
22 just as He did for the sons of Esau, who live in Seir,
when He destroyed [a]the Horites from before them; and they
dispossessed them, and settled in their place even to this day.
23 And the [a]Avvim, who lived in villages as far as Gaza, the
[1b]Caphtorim who came from [2c]Caphtor, destroyed them and
lived in their place.)
24 'Arise, set out, and pass through the [1]valley of Arnon.
Look! I have given Sihon the Amorite, king of Heshbon, and
his land into your hand; begin to take possession and contend
with him in battle.
25 'This day I will begin to put [a]the dread and fear of you
[1]upon the peoples [2]everywhere under the heavens, who, when
they hear the report of you, [b]shall tremble and be in anguish
because of you.'
26 "[a]So I sent messengers from the wilderness of Kedemoth
to Sihon king of Heshbon with words of peace, saying,
27 'Let me pass through your land, I will [1]travel only on
the highway; I will not turn aside to the right or to the left.
28 'You will sell me food for money so that I may eat, and
give me water for money so that I may drink, only let me pass
through on [1]foot,
29 just as the sons of Esau who live in Seir and the Moabites who live in [a]Ar, did for me, until I cross over the Jordan
into the land which the LORD our God is giving to us.'
30 "But Sihon king of Heshbon was not willing for us to
pass [1]through his land; for the LORD your God hardened his
spirit and made his heart obstinate, in order to deliver him into
your hand, as *he is* today.
31 "And the LORD said to me, 'See, I have begun to deliver
Sihon and his land [1]over to you. Begin to [2]occupy, that you
may possess his land.'
32 "Then Sihon [1]with all his people came out to meet us in
battle at Jahaz.
33 "And the LORD our God delivered him [1]over to us; and
we [2]defeated him with his sons and all his people.
34 "So we captured all his cities at that time, and [1a]utterly
destroyed [2]the men, women and children of every city. We left
no survivor.
35 "We took [a]only the animals as our booty and the spoil
of the cities which we had captured.
36 "From [a]Aroer which is on the edge of the [1]valley of
Arnon and *from* the city which is in the [1]valley, even to Gilead,
there was no city that was too high for us; the LORD our God
delivered all [2]over to us.
37 "[a]Only you did not go near to the land of the sons of
Ammon, all along the [1]river Jabbok and the cities of the hill
country, and wherever the LORD our God had commanded us.

19 [a]Deut. 2:9

20 [a]Deut. 2:11

22 [a]Deut. 2:12

23 [1]I.e., Philistines [2]I.e., Crete [a]Josh. 13:3 [b]Gen. 10:14; 1 Chr. 1:12 [c]Jer. 47:4; Amos 9:7

24 [1]Or, *wadi*

25 [1]Lit., *in front of* [2]Lit., *under all the heavens* [a]Deut. 11:25; Ex. 23:27; Josh. 2:9 [b]Ex. 15:14-16

26 [a]Num. 21:21-32

27 [1]Lit., *go by the way*

28 [1]Lit., *my feet*

29 [a]Deut. 2:9

30 [1]Lit., *by him*

31 [1]Lit., *before you* [2]Lit., *possess*

32 [1]Lit., *he and*

33 [1]Lit., *before us* [2]Lit., *smote*

34 [1]Or, *put under the ban* [2]Lit., *every city of man . . .* [a]Deut. 3:6

35 [a]Deut. 3:7

36 [1]Or, *wadi* [2]Lit., *before us* [a]Deut. 3:12; 4:48

37 [1]Or, *wadi* [a]Deut. 2:19

Chapter 3

"[a]THEN we turned and went up the road to Bashan, and
Og, king of Bashan, [1]with all his people came out to meet us in
battle.
2 "But the LORD said to me, 'Do not fear him, for I have
delivered him and all his people and his land into your hand;
and you shall do to him just as you did to Sihon king of the
Amorites, who lived at Heshbon.'
3 "So the LORD our God delivered Og also, king of Bashan,
with all his people into our hand, and we smote [1]them
until no survivor was [2]left.
4 "And we captured all his cities at that time; there was
not a city which we did not take from them: sixty cities, all the
region of [a]Argob, the kingdom of Og in Bashan.
5 "All these were cities fortified with high walls, gates and
bars, besides a great many [1]unwalled towns.
6 "And we [1]utterly destroyed them, as we did to Sihon
king of Heshbon, [2a]utterly destroying [3]the men, women and
children of every city.
7 "[a]But all the animals and the spoil of the cities we took
as our booty.
8 "[a]Thus we took the land at that time from the hand of
the two kings of the Amorites who were beyond the Jordan,
from the [1]valley of Arnon to Mount Hermon
9 (Sidonians [a]call Herman [b]Sirion, and the Amorites call
it Senir):
10 all the cities of the tableland and all Gilead and all
Bashan, as far as Salecah and Edrei, cities of the kingdom of
Og in Bashan.
11 (For only Og king of Bashan was left of the remnant of
the [a]Rephaim. Behold, his [1]bedstead was an iron [1]bedstead; it
is in [b]Rabbah of the sons of Ammon. Its length was nine cubits
and its width four cubits [2]by ordinary cubit.)
12 "So we took possession of this land at that time. From
[a]Aroer, which is by the [1]valley of Arnon, and half the hill
country of [b]Gilead and its cities, I gave to the Reubenites and
to the Gadites.
13 "And the rest of Gilead, and all Bashan, the kingdom of
Og, I gave to the half-tribe of Manasseh, all the region of
Argob concerning all Bashan, it is called the land of Rephaim.
14 [a]Jair the son of Manasseh took all the region of Argob
as far as the border of the Geshurites and the Maacathites, and
called [1]it, *that is,* Bashan, after his own name, [2]Havvothjair, *as
it is* to this day.)
15 "[a]And to Machir I gave Gilead.
16 "And to the Reubenites and to the Gadites, I gave from
Gilead even as far as the [1]valley of Arnon, the middle of the
[1]valley [2]as *a* border and as far as the [1]river Jabbok, the border
of the sons of Ammon;
17 the Arabah also, with the Jordan [1]as *a* border, from
[2a]Chinnereth even as far as the sea of the Arabah, the Salt Sea,
[3]at the foot of the slopes of Pisgah on the east.
18 "Then I commanded you at that time, saying, 'The
LORD your God has given you this land to possess it; [a]all you

1 [1]Lit., *he and* [a]Num. 21:33-35
3 [1]Lit., *him* [2]Lit., *left to him*
4 [a]Deut. 2:13, 14; 1 Kin. 4:13
5 [1]Or, *rural*
6 [1]Or, *put them under the ban* [2]Or, *putting under the ban* [3]Lit., *every city of men . . .* [a]Deut. 2:34
7 [a]Deut. 2:35
8 [1]Or, *wadi* [a]Num. 32:33; Josh. 12:1-7; 13:8-12
9 [a]Deut. 4:48; Josh. 11:17; Ps. 42:6; 133:3 [b]Ps. 29:6
11 [1]Or, *couch* [2]Lit., *by a man's forearm* [a]Deut. 2:11, 20 [b]2 Sam. 11:1; 12:26; Jer. 49:2
12 [1]Or, *wadi* [a]Deut. 2:36 [b]Num. 32:32-38; Josh. 13:8-13
14 [1]Lit., *them* [2]I.e., the towns of fair [a]Num. 32:41; 1 Chr. 2:22
15 [a]Num. 32:40
16 [1]Or, *wadi* [2]Lit., *and*
17 [1]Lit., *under* [2]I.e., The Sea of Galilee [3]Lit., *under* [a]Num. 34:11; Josh. 13:27
18 [a]Num. 32:20; Josh. 4:12, 13

aliant men shall cross over armed before your brothers, the ons of Israel.

19 'But your wives and your little ones and your livestock I know that you have [a]much livestock), shall remain in your ities which I have given you,

20 until the LORD gives rest to your fellow countrymen as o you, and they also possess the land which the LORD your God will give them beyond the Jordan. [a]Then you may return every man to his possession, which I have given you.'

21 "And I commanded Joshua at that time, saying, 'Your eyes have seen all that the LORD your God has done to these two kings; so the LORD shall do to all the kingdoms into which you are about to cross.

22 'Do not fear them, for the LORD your God [a]is the one fighting for you.'

23 "I also pleaded with the LORD at that time, saying,

24 'O LORD [1]God, Thou hast begun to show Thy servant Thy greatness and Thy strong hand; for what god is there in heaven or on earth who can do such works and mighty acts as Thine?

25 'Let me, I pray, cross over and see the fair land that is beyond the Jordan, [1]that good hill country and Lebanon.'

26 "But [a]the LORD was angry with me on your account, and would not listen to me; and the LORD said to me, '[1]Enough! Speak to Me no more of this matter.

27 'Go up to the top of [a]Pisgah and lift up your eyes to the west and north and south and east, and see *it* with your eyes, [b]for you shall not cross over this Jordan.

28 '[a]But charge Joshua and encourage him and strengthen him; [b]for he shall go across [1]at the head of this people, and he shall give them as an inheritance the land which you will see.'

29 "So we remained in the valley opposite [a]Beth-peor.

CHAPTER 4

1 "AND now, O Israel, listen to the statutes and the judgments which [a]I am teaching you to perform, in order that [b]you may live and go in and take possession of the land which the LORD, the God of your fathers, is giving you.

2 "[a]You shall not add to the word which [b]I am commanding you, nor take away from it, that you may keep the commandments of the LORD your God which I command you.

3 "[a]Your eyes have seen what the LORD has done in the case of Baal-peor, for all the men who followed Baal-peor, the LORD your God has destroyed [1]them from among you.

4 "But you who held fast to the LORD your God are alive today, every one of you.

5 "See, I have taught you statutes and judgments [a]just as the LORD my God commanded me, that you should do thus in the land where you are entering to possess it.

6 "So keep and do *them,* [a]for that is your wisdom and your understanding in the sight of the peoples who will hear all these statutes and say, 'Surely this great nation is a wise and understanding people.'

7 "For what great nation is there that has a god [a]so near to it as is the LORD our God [b]whenever we call on Him?

19 [a]Ex. 12:38

20 [a]Josh. 22:4

22 [a]Deut. 1:30

24 [1]YHWH, usually rendered LORD

25 [1]Lit., *this*

26 [1]Lit., *Enough for you* [a]Deut. 1:37

27 [a]Num. 23:14; 27:12 [b]Deut. 1:37

28 [1]Lit., *before this people* [a]Deut. 31:3, 7, 8, 23; Num. 27:18 [b]Deut. 1:38

29 [a]Deut. 4:46; 34:6; Num. 25:1-3

1 [a]Deut. 1:3 [b]Deut. 5:33; 8:1; 16:20; 30:16, 19

2 [a]Deut. 12:32 [b]Deut. 4:5, 14, 40

3 [1]Lit., *him* [a]Num. 25:1-9

5 [a]Lev. 26:46; 27:34

6 [a]Deut. 30:19, 20; 32:46, 47

7 [a]Ps. 148:14 [b]Ps. 34:18; 85:9

8 "Or what great nation is there that has [a]statutes and judgments as righteous as this whole law which I am setting before you today?

9 "Only [a]give heed to yourself and keep your soul diligently, lest you forget the things which your eyes have seen, and lest they depart from your heart [b]all the days of your life; but [c]make them known to your sons and your grandsons.

10 "*Remember* the day you stood before the LORD your God at Horeb, when the LORD said to me, 'Assemble the people to Me, that I may let them hear My words [a]so they may learn to [1]fear Me all the days they live on the earth, and that they may [b]teach their children.'

11 "And you came near and stood at the foot of the mountain, [a]and the mountain burned with fire to the *very* heart of the heavens, darkness, cloud and thick gloom.

12 "Then the LORD spoke to you from the midst of the fire; you heard the sound of words, but you saw no form—only a voice.

13 "So He declared to you His covenant which He commanded you to perform, *that is*, [a]the ten [1]commandments; and [b]He wrote them on two tablets of stone.

14 "And the LORD commanded me at that time to teach you statutes and judgments, that you might perform them in the land where you are going over to possess it.

15 "So watch yourselves carefully, since you did not see any form on the day the LORD spoke to you at Horeb from the midst of the fire;

16 lest you [a]act corruptly and [b]make a graven image for yourselves in the form of any figure, the likeness of male or female,

17 the likeness of any animal that is on the earth, the likeness of any winged bird that flies in the sky,

18 the likeness of anything that creeps on the ground, the likeness of any fish that is in the water below the earth.

19 "And *beware*, lest you lift up your eyes to heaven and see the sun and the moon and the stars, all the host of heaven, [a]and be drawn away and worship them and serve them, those which the LORD your God has allotted to all the peoples under the whole heaven.

20 "But the LORD has taken you and brought you out of [a]the iron furnace, from Egypt, to be a people for His own possession, as today.

21 "[a]Now the LORD was angry with me on your account, and swore that I should not cross the Jordan, and that I should not enter the good land which the LORD your God is giving you as an inheritance.

22 "For [a]I shall die in this land, I shall not cross the Jordan, but you shall cross and take possession of this good land.

23 "So watch yourselves, [a]lest you forget the covenant of the LORD your God, which He made with you, and [b]make for yourselves a graven image in the form of anything *against* which the LORD your God has commanded you.

24 "For the LORD your God is a [a]consuming fire, a [b]jealous God.

25 "When you [1]become the father of children and children's children and have remained long in the land, and [a]act

8 [a]Ps. 89:14; 97:2; 119:144, 160, 172

9 [a]Deut. 4:23; 6:12; 8:11, 14, 19 [b]Deut. 6:2; 12:1; 16:3 [c]Deut. 4:10; 6:7, 20-25; 11:19; 32:46

10 [1]Or, *reverence* [a]Deut. 14:23; 17:19; 31:12, 13 [b]Deut. 4:9

11 [a]Ex. 19:18; Heb. 12:18, 19

13 [1]Lit., *words* [a]Deut. 10:4; Ex. 34:28 [b]Ex. 31:18; 34:1, 28

16 [a]Deut. 4:25; 9:12; 31:29 [b]Deut. 5:8, 9

19 [a]Deut. 13:5, 10

20 [a]1 Kin. 8:51; Jer. 11:4

21 [a]Deut. 1:37

22 [a]Num. 27:13, 14

23 [a]Deut. 4:9 [b]Deut. 4:16

24 [a]Deut. 9:3; Ex. 24:17; Heb. 12:29 [b]Deut. 5:9; 6:15

25 [1]Lit., *beget* [a]Deut. 4:16

corruptly, and [b]make an [2]idol in the form of anything, and do
that which is evil in the sight of the LORD your God *so as* to
provoke Him to anger,
26 I [a]call heaven and earth to witness against you today,
that you shall [b]surely perish quickly from the land where you
are going over the Jordan to possess it. You shall not [1]live long
on it, but shall be utterly destroyed.
27 "And the LORD will [a]scatter you among the peoples, and
you shall be left few in number among the nations, where the
LORD shall drive you.
28 "And there you will serve gods, the work of man's hands,
[a]wood and stone, [b]which neither see nor hear nor eat nor smell.
29 "[a]But from there you will seek the LORD your God, and
you will find *Him* if you search for Him [b]with all your heart
and all your soul.
30 "When you [a]are in distress and all these things have
come upon you, in the latter days, you will return to the LORD
your God and listen to His voice.
31 "For the LORD your God is a [a]compassionate God; [b]He
will not fail you nor [c]destroy you nor [d]forget the covenant with
your fathers which He swore to them.
32 "Indeed, [a]ask now concerning the former days which
were before you, since the [b]day that God created [1]man on the
earth, and *inquire* [c]from one end of the heavens to the other.
Has *anything* been done like this great thing, or has *anything*
been heard like it?
33 "[a]Has *any* people heard the voice of God speaking from
the midst of the fire, as you have heard *it*, and survived?
34 "[a]Or has a god tried to go to take for himself a nation
from within *another* nation [b]by trials, by signs and wonders
and by war and [c]by a mighty hand and by an outstretched arm
and by great terrors, [1]as the LORD your God did for you in
Egypt before your eyes?
35 "To you it was shown that you might know that the
LORD, He is God; [a]there is no other besides Him.
36 "[a]Out of the heavens He let you hear His voice to discipline you; and on earth He let you see His great fire, and
you heard His words from the midst of the fire.
37 "[1a]Because He loved your fathers, therefore He chose
[2]their descendants after them. And He [3b]personally brought
you from Egypt by His great power,
38 driving out from before you nations greater and mightier than you, to bring you in *and* [a]to give you their land for
an inheritance, as it is today.
39 "Know therefore today, and take it to your heart, that
the LORD, He is God in heaven above and on the earth below;
[a]there is no other.
40 "[a]So you shall keep His statutes and His commandments which I am [1]giving you today, that [b]it may go well with
you and with your children after you, and [c]that you may [2]live
long on the land which the LORD your God is giving you for all
time."
41 [a]Then Moses set apart three cities across the Jordan to
the [1]east,
42 that a manslayer might flee there, who unintentionally

25 [2]Or, *a graven image* [b]Deut. 4:23
26 [1]Lit., *prolong your days* [a]Deut. 30:19; 31:28; 32:1 [b]Deut. 7:4; 8:19, 20
27 [a]Deut. 28:64; 29:28
28 [a]Deut. 28:36, 64; 29:17 [b]Ps. 115:4-8
29 [a]Deut. 30:1-3, 10 [b]Deut. 6:5; 10:12
30 [a]Ps. 18:6; 59:16; 107:6, 13
31 [a]Ex. 34:6 [b]Deut. 31:6, 8; Josh. 1:5; 1 Chr. 28:20; Heb. 13:5 [c]Jer. 30:11 [d]Lev. 26:45
32 [1]Or, *Adam* [a]Deut. 32:7 [b]Gen. 1:27; Is. 45:12 [c]Deut. 28:64
33 [a]Deut. 5:24, 26; Ex. 20:22
34 [1]Lit., *according to all that* [a]Deut. 33:29; Ex. 14:30 [b]Deut. 7:19 [c]Deut. 5:15; 6:21; Ps. 136:12
35 [a]Deut. 4:39; Ex. 8:10; 9:14; Mark 12:32
36 [a]Deut. 4:33; 8:5; Neh. 9:13; Heb. 12:25
37 [1]Lit., *And instead, because* [2]Lit., *his seed* [3]Lit., *with His presence* [a]Deut. 7:7, 8; 10:15; 33:3 [b]Ex. 33:14; Is. 63:9
38 [a]Num. 32:4; 34:14, 15
39 [a]Deut. 4:35
40 [1]Lit., *commanding* [2]Lit., *prolong your days* [a]Deut. 4:2; Ps. 105:45 [b]Deut. 5:16, 29, 33 [c]Deut. 32:47; Ex. 23:26
41 [1]Lit., *sunrise* [a]Deut. 19:2-13; Num. 35:6; Josh. 20:7-9

slew his neighbor without having enmity toward him in time past; and by fleeing to one of these cities he might live:

43 Bezer in the wilderness on the plateau for the Reubenites, and Ramoth in Gilead for the Gadites, and Golan in Bashan for the Manassites.

44 Now this is the law which Moses set before the sons of Israel;

45 these are the testimonies and the statutes and the ordinances which Moses spoke to the sons of Israel, when they came out from Egypt,

46 across the Jordan, in the valley [a]opposite Bethpeor, in the land of [b]Sihon king of the Amorites who lived at Heshbon, whom Moses and the sons of Israel [1]defeated when they came out from Egypt.

47 And they took possession of his land and the land of Og king of Bashan, the two kings of the Amorites, *who were* across the Jordan to the [1]east,

48 from [a]Aroer, which is on the edge of the [1]valley of Arnon, even as far as [b]Mount Sion (that is, Hermon),

49 with all the Arabah across the Jordan to the east, even as far as the sea of the Arabah, [1]at the foot of the slopes of Pisgah.

Chapter 5

THEN Moses summoned all Israel, and said to them, "Hear, O Israel, the statutes and the ordinances which I am speaking today in your [1]hearing, that you may learn them and observe [2]them carefully.

2 "The LORD our God made [a]a covenant with us at Horeb.

3 "[a]The LORD did not make this covenant with our fathers, but with us, *with* all those of [1]us alive here today.

4 "The LORD spoke to you [a]face to face at the mountain [b]from the midst of the fire,

5 *while* I was standing between the LORD and you at that time, to declare to you the word of the LORD; [a]for you were afraid because of the fire and did not go up the mountain. [1]He said,

6 '[a]I am the LORD your God, who brought you out of the land of Egypt, out of the house of [1]slavery.

7 'You shall have no other gods [1]before Me.

8 'You shall not make for yourself [1]an idol, *or* any likeness *of* what is in heaven above [2]or on the earth beneath [2]or in the water under the earth.

9 'You shall not worship them or serve them; for I, the LORD your God, am a jealous God, visiting the iniquity of the fathers on the children, and on the third and the fourth *generations* of those who hate Me,

10 but showing lovingkindness to thousands, to those who love Me and keep My commandments.

11 '[a]You shall not take the name of the LORD your God in vain, for the LORD will not [1]leave him unpunished who takes His name in vain.

12 'Observe the sabbath day to keep it holy, as the LORD your God commanded you.

13 'Six days you shall labor and do all your work,

46 [1]Lit., *smote* [a]Deut. 3:29 [b]Num. 21:21-25

47 [1]Lit., *sunrise*

48 [1]Or, *wadi* [a]Deut. 2:36 [b]Deut. 3:9

49 [1]Lit., *under*

1 [1]Lit., *ears* [2]Lit., *to do them*

2 [a]Ex. 19:5; Mal. 4:4

3 [1]Lit., *us ourselves* [a]Num. 26:63-65

4 [a]Num. 14:14 [b]Deut. 4:33

5 [1]Lit., *saying* [a]Ex. 19:16, 21-24

6 [1]Lit., *slaves* [a]Ex. 20:2-17

7 [1]Or, *besides*

8 [1]Or, *a graven image* [2]Lit., *or what is*

11 [1]Or, *hold him guiltless* [a]Deut. 6:13; 10:20

14 but the seventh day is a sabbath of the LORD your God;
in it you shall not do any work, you or your son or your
daughter or your male servant or your female servant or your
ox or your donkey or any of your cattle or your sojourner who
[1]stays with you, so that your male servant and your female
servant may rest as well as you.
15 '[a]And you shall remember that you were a slave in the
land of Egypt, and the LORD your God brought you out of
there by a mighty hand and by an outstretched arm; therefore
the LORD your God commanded you to observe the sabbath
day.
16 'Honor your father and your mother, as the LORD your
God has commanded you, that your days may be prolonged,
and that it may go well with you on the land which the LORD
your God gives you.
17 'You shall not murder.
18 'You shall not commit adultery.
19 'You shall not steal.
20 'You shall not bear false witness against your neighbor.
21 '[a]You shall not covet your neighbor's wife, and you shall
not desire your neighbor's house, his field or his manservant,
his ox or his donkey or anything that belongs to your
neighbor.'
22 "These words the LORD spoke to all your assembly at the
mountain from the midst of the fire, *of* the cloud and *of* the
thick gloom, with a great voice, and He added no more. And
[a]He wrote them on two tablets of stone and gave them to me.
23 "And it came about, when you heard the voice from the
midst of the darkness, while the mountain was burning with
fire, that you came near to me, all the heads of your tribes and
your elders.
24 "And you said, 'Behold, the LORD our God has shown us
His glory and His greatness, and we have heard His voice from
the midst of the fire; we have seen today that God speaks with
man, yet he lives.
25 '[a]Now then why should we die? For this great fire will
consume us; if we hear the voice of the LORD our God any
longer, then we shall die.
26 'For who is there of all flesh, who has heard the voice of
the living God speaking from the midst of the fire, as we *have*,
and lived?
27 '[1]Go near and hear all that the LORD our God says; then
speak to us all that the LORD our God will speak to you, and we
will hear and do *it*.'
28 "And the LORD heard the voice of your words when you
spoke to me, [a]and the LORD said to me, 'I have heard the voice
of the words of this people which they have spoken to you.
They have done well in all that they have spoken.
29 '[a]Oh that they had such a heart in them, that they
would fear Me, and keep all My commandments always, that
[b]it may be well with them and with their sons forever!
30 'Go, say to them, "Return to your tents."
31 '[a]But as for you, stand here by Me, that I may speak to
you all the commandment and the statutes and the judgments
which you shall teach them, that they may observe *them* in the
land which I give them to possess.'

14 [1]Lit., *is in your gates*
15 [a]Ex. 20:11
21 [a]Rom. 7:7; 13:9
22 [a]Deut. 4:13; Ex. 31:18
25 [a]Deut. 18:16; Ex. 20:18, 19
27 [1]Lit., *Go yourself*
28 [a]Deut. 18:17
29 [a]Ps. 81:13; Is. 48:18 [b]Deut. 5:16, 33
31 [a]Ex. 24:12

32 "So you shall observe to do just as the LORD your God
has commanded you; [a]you shall not turn aside to the right or
to the left.
33 "You shall walk in all the way which the LORD your God
has commanded you, [a]that you may live, and that it may be
well with you, and that you may prolong *your* days in the land
which you shall possess.

CHAPTER 6

"NOW this is the commandment, the statutes and the judgments which the LORD your God has commanded *me* to
teach you, that you might do *them* in the land where you are
going over to possess it,
2 so that you and your son and your grandson might [a]fear
the LORD your God, to keep all His statutes and His commandments, which I command you, [b]all the days of your life, and
that your days may be prolonged.
3 "O Israel, you should listen and [1]be careful to do *it*, that
[a]it may be well with you and that you may multiply greatly,
just as the LORD, the God of your fathers, has promised you, *in*
[b]a land flowing with milk and honey.
4 "[a]Hear, O Israel! The LORD is our God, the [b]LORD is
one!
5 "And you shall love the LORD your God with all your
heart and with all your soul and with all your might.
6 "And these words, which I am commanding you today,
shall be on your heart;
7 and [a]you shall teach them diligently to your sons and
shall talk of them when you sit in your house and when you
walk by the way and when you lie down and when you rise up.
8 "[a]And you shall bind them as a sign on your hand and
they shall be as [1]frontals [2]on your forehead.
9 "[a]And you shall write them on the doorposts of your
house and on your gates.
10 "Then it shall come about when the LORD your God
brings you into the land which He swore to your fathers, Abraham, Isaac and Jacob, to give you, [a]great and splendid cities
which you did not build,
11 and houses full of all good things which you did not fill,
and hewn cisterns which you did not dig, vineyards and olive
trees which you did not plant, and [a]you shall eat and be
satisfied,
12 then watch yourself, lest [a]you forget the LORD who
brought you from the land of Egypt, out of the house of
[1]slavery.
13 "[a]You shall [1]fear *only* the LORD your God; and you shall
[2]worship Him, and [b]swear by His name.
14 "You shall not follow other gods, any of the gods of the
peoples who surround you,
15 for the LORD your God in the midst of you is a [a]jealous
God; otherwise the anger of the LORD your God will be
kindled against you, and He will [1]wipe you off the face of the
earth.
16 "[a]You shall not put the LORD your God to the test, [b]as
you tested *Him* at Massah.

32 [a]Deut. 17:20; 28:14; Josh. 1:7; 23:6
33 [a]Deut. 4:1, 40
2 [a]Deut. 10:12 [b]Deut. 4:9
3 [1]Lit., *keep* [a]Deut. 5:33 [b]Ex. 3:8, 17
4 [a]Matt. 22:37; Mark 12:29, 30; Luke 10:27 [b]Deut. 4:35, 39
7 [a]Deut. 4:9
8 [1]Or, *frontlet bands* [2]Lit., *between your eyes* [a]Deut. 11:18; Ex. 12:14; 13:9, 16
9 [a]Deut. 11:20
10 [a]Deut. 9:1; 19:1; Josh. 24:13
11 [a]Deut. 8:10; 11:15; 14:29
12 [1]Lit., *slaves* [a]Deut. 4:9
13 [1]Or, *reverence* [2]Or, *serve* [a]Matt. 4:10; Luke 4:8 [b]Deut. 5:11; 10:20
15 [1]Lit., *destroy* [a]Deut. 4:24; 5:9
16 [a]Matt. 4:7; Luke 4:12 [b]Ex. 17:7

17 "[a]You should diligently keep the commandments of the
LORD your God, and His testimonies and His statutes which
He has commanded you.
18 "And you shall do what is right and good in the sight of
the LORD, that [a]it may be well with you and that you may go in
and possess the good land which the LORD swore to *give* your
fathers,
19 by driving out all your enemies from before you, as the
LORD has spoken.
20 "[a]When your son asks you in time to come, saying,
'What *do* the testimonies and the statutes and the judgments
mean which the LORD commanded you?'
21 then you shall say to your son, 'We were slaves to
Pharaoh in Egypt; and the LORD brought us from Egypt with a
mighty hand.
22 'Moreover, the LORD showed great and distressing signs
and wonders before our eyes against Egypt, Pharaoh and all his
household;
23 and He brought us out from there in order to bring us
in, to give us the land which He had sworn to our fathers.'
24 "So the LORD commanded us to observe all these statutes, [a]to fear the LORD our God for our good always and for
our survival, as *it is* today.
25 "And [a]it will be righteousness for us if we [1]are careful to
observe all this commandment before the LORD our God, just
as He commanded us.

CHAPTER 7

"[a]WHEN the LORD your God shall bring you into the land
where you are entering to possess it, and shall clear away many
nations before you, the Hittites and the Girgashites and the
Amorites and the Canaanites and the Perizzites and the Hivites and the Jebusites, [b]seven nations greater and stronger
than you;
2 and when the LORD your God shall deliver them before
you, and you shall [1]defeat them, [a]then you shall [2]utterly destroy
them. [b]You shall make no covenant with them [c]and show
no favor to them.
3 "Furthermore, [a]you shall not intermarry with them; you
shall not give your [1]daughters to [2]their sons, nor shall you take
[3]their daughters for your [4]sons.
4 "For [1]they will turn your [2]sons away from [3]following Me
to serve other gods; then the anger of the LORD will be kindled
against you, and [a]He will quickly destroy you.
5 "But thus you shall do to them: [a]you shall tear down
their altars, and smash their sacred pillars, and hew down their
[1]Asherim, and burn their graven images with fire.
6 "For you are [a]a holy people to the LORD your God; the
LORD your God has chosen you to be [b]a people for His [1]own
possession out of all the peoples who are on the face of
the [2]earth.
7 "[a]The LORD did not set His love on you nor choose you
because you were more in number than any of the peoples, for
you were the fewest of all peoples,
8 but because the LORD loved you and kept the oath

17 [a]Deut. 11:22

18 [a]Deut. 4:40

20 [a]Ex. 13:8, 14

24 [a]Deut. 10:12

25 [1]Lit., *keep*
[a]Deut. 24:13

1 [a]Deut. 20:16-18 [b]Acts 13:19

2 [1]Lit., *smite* [2]Lit., *surely devote*
[a]Num. 31:17 [b]Ex. 23:32
[c]Deut. 7:16; 13:8

3 [1]Lit., *daughter* [2]Lit., *his son* [3]Lit., *his daughter* [4]Lit., *son*
[a]Ex. 34:15, 16

4 [1]Lit., *he* [2]Lit., *son* [3]Lit., *after*
[a]Deut. 4:26

5 [1]I.e., wooden symbols of a female deity
[a]Deut. 12:3; Ex. 23:24; 34:13

6 [1]Or, *special treasure*
[2]Lit., *ground*
[a]Deut. 14:2, 21; Ex. 19:6
[b]Deut. 14:2; 26:18; Ex. 19:5

7 [a]Deut. 4:37

which He swore to your forefathers, the LORD brought you out
by a mighty hand, and redeemed you from the house of [1]slav-
ery, from the hand of Pharaoh king of Egypt.
9 "Know therefore that the LORD your God, [a]He is God,
the faithful God, who keeps [1]His covenant and [1]His lovingkindness to a thousandth generation with those who [b]love Him
and keep His commandments;
10 but repays those who hate Him to [1]their faces, to destroy
[2]them; He will not delay [3]with him who hates Him, He
will repay him to his face.
11 "Therefore, you shall keep the commandment and the
statutes and the judgments which I am commanding you today, to do them.
12 "[a]Then it shall come about, because you listen to these
judgments and keep and do them, that the LORD your God will
keep with you [1]His covenant and [1]His lovingkindness which
He swore to your forefathers.
13 "And He will love you and bless you and [a]multiply you;
He will also bless the fruit of your womb and the fruit of your
ground, your grain and your new wine and your oil, the
increase of your herd and the young of your flock, [1]in the land
which He swore to your forefathers to give you.
14 "You shall be blessed above all peoples; there shall be no
male or female [a]barren among you or among your cattle.
15 "And [a]the LORD will remove from you all sickness; and
He will not put on you any of the harmful diseases of Egypt
which you have known, but He will lay them on all who hate
you.
16 "And you shall consume all the peoples whom the LORD
your God will deliver to you; [a]your eye shall not pity them,
neither shall you serve their gods, for that *would be* [b]a snare to
you.
17 "If you should say in your heart, 'These nations are
greater than I; how can I dispossess them?'
18 you shall not be afraid of them; you shall well remember what the LORD your God did to Pharaoh and to all Egypt:
19 [a]the great trials which your eyes saw and the signs and
the wonders and the mighty hand and the outstretched arm by
which the LORD your God brought you out. So shall the LORD
your God do to all the peoples of whom you are afraid.
20 "Moreover, the LORD your God will send [a]the hornet
against them, until those who are left and hide themselves
from you, perish.
21 "You shall not dread [1]them, for [a]the LORD your God is
in your midst, a great and awesome God.
22 "[a]And the LORD your God will clear away these nations
before you little by little; you will not be able to put an end to
them quickly, lest the [1]wild beasts grow too numerous for you.
23 "[a]But the LORD your God shall deliver them before you,
and will [1]throw them into great confusion until they are
destroyed.
24 "[a]And He will deliver their kings into your hand so that
you shall make their name perish from under heaven; [b]no man
will be able to stand before you until you have destroyed them.
25 "[a]The graven images of their gods you are to burn with
fire; you shall not covet the silver or the gold that is on them,

8 [1]Lit., *slaves*
9 [1]Lit., *the* [a]Deut. 4:35, 39 [b]Deut. 5:10
10 [1]Lit., *his face* [2]Lit., *him* [3]Lit., *to*
12 [1]Lit., *the* [a]Deut. 28:1-14; Lev. 26:3-13
13 [1]Lit., *on* [a]Deut. 13:17; 30:5; Lev. 26:9
14 [a]Ex. 23:26
15 [a]Ex. 15:26
16 [a]Deut. 7:2 [b]Ex. 23:33
19 [a]Deut. 4:34
20 [a]Ex. 23:28; Josh. 24:12
21 [1]Lit., *from before them* [a]Ex. 29:45
22 [1]Lit., *beasts of the field* [a]Ex. 23:29, 30
23 [1]Lit., *confuse them with* [a]Ex. 23:27; Josh. 10:10
24 [a]Josh. 6:2; 10:23 [b]Deut. 11:25; Josh. 1:5; 10:8; 23:9
25 [a]Deut. 7:2

nor take it for yourselves, lest you be snared by it, for it is an
abomination to the LORD your God.
26 "And you shall not bring an abomination into your
house, and become a [1]devoted thing like it; you shall utterly
detest it and you shall utterly abhor it, for it is a [1]devoted
thing.

CHAPTER 8

"ALL the commandment that I am commanding you today
you shall be careful to do, that you [a]may live and multiply, and
go in and possess the land which the LORD swore *to give* to
your forefathers.
2 "[a]And you shall remember all the way which the LORD
your God has led you in the wilderness these forty years, that
He might humble you, [b]testing you, to know what was in your
heart, whether you would keep His commandments or not.
3 "And He humbled you and let you be hungry, and fed
you with manna which you did not know, nor did your fathers
know, that He might make you [1]understand that [a]man does
not live by bread alone, but man lives by everything that proceeds out of the mouth of the LORD.
4 "[a]Your clothing did not wear out on you, nor did your
foot swell these forty years.
5 "[a]Thus you are to know in your heart that the LORD your
God was disciplining you just as a man disciplines his son.
6 "Therefore, you shall keep the commandments of the
LORD your God, to walk in His ways and to [1]fear Him.
7 "For [a]the LORD your God is bringing you into a good
land, a land of brooks of water, of fountains and springs, flowing forth in valleys and hills;
8 a land of wheat and barley, of vines and fig trees and
pomegranates, a land of olive oil and honey;
9 a land where you shall eat food without scarcity, in
which you shall not lack anything; a land whose stones are iron,
and out of whose hills you can dig copper.
10 "When [a]you have eaten and are satisfied, you shall bless
the LORD your God for the good land which He has given you.
11 "[1]Beware lest you [a]forget the LORD your God by not
keeping His commandments and His ordinances and His statutes which I am commanding you today;
12 lest, when you have eaten and are satisfied, and have
built good houses and lived *in them*,
13 and when your herds and your flocks multiply, and
your silver and gold multiply, and all that you have multiplies,
14 then your heart becomes [1]proud, and you [a]forget the
LORD your God who brought you out from the land of Egypt,
out of the house of [2]slavery.
15 "He led you through [a]the great and terrible wilderness,
with its [b]fiery serpents and scorpions and thirsty ground where
there was no water; He [c]brought water for you out of the rock
of flint.
16 "In the wilderness He fed you manna [a]which your fathers
did not know, that He might humble you and that He
might [b]test you, to do good for you [1]in the end.

26 [1]Or, *banned*

1 [a]Deut. 4:1

2 [a]Deut. 8:16 [b]Ex. 15:25; 20:20

3 [1]Lit., *know* [a]Matt. 4:4; Luke 4:4

4 [a]Deut. 29:5; Neh. 9:21

5 [a]Deut. 4:36; Prov. 3:12; Heb. 12:6

6 [1]Or, *reverence*

7 [a]Deut. 11:9-12; Jer. 2:7

10 [a]Deut. 6:11

11 [1]Lit., *take heed to yourself* [a]Deut. 4:9

14 [1]Lit., *lifted up* [2]Lit., *slaves* [a]Deut. 8:11

15 [a]Deut. 1:19 [b]Num. 21:6 [c]Deut. 32:13; Ex. 17:6; Num. 20:11; Ps. 78:15; 114:8

16 [1]Lit., *at your end* [a]Ex. 16:15 [b]Deut. 8:2

17 "Otherwise, you may say in your heart, 'My power and
the strength of my hand made me this wealth.'
18 "But you shall remember the LORD your God, for [a]it is
He who is giving you power to make wealth, that He may
confirm His covenant which He swore to your fathers, as *it is*
this day.
19 "And it shall come about if you ever forget the LORD
your God, and go after other gods and serve them and worship
them, [a]I testify against you today that you shall surely perish.
20 "Like the nations that the LORD makes to perish before
you, so you shall perish; because you would not listen to the
voice of the LORD your God.

CHAPTER 9

"HEAR, O Israel! You are crossing over the Jordan today to
go in to dispossess nations greater and mightier than you, great
cities [1]fortified to heaven,
2 a people great and tall, the sons of the Anakim, whom
you know and of whom you have heard *it said*, '[a]Who can
stand before the sons of Anak?'
3 "Know therefore today that it is the LORD your God
who is crossing over before you as [a]a consuming fire. He will
destroy them and He will subdue them before you, so that you
may drive them out and destroy them quickly, just as the LORD
has spoken to you.
4 "Do not say in your heart when the LORD your God has
driven them out before [1]you, '[a]Because of my righteousness
the LORD has brought me in to possess this land,' but *it is*
[b]because of the wickedness of these nations *that* the LORD is
dispossessing them before you.
5 "It is not for your righteousness or for the uprightness of
your heart that you are going to possess their land, but *it is*
because of the wickedness of these nations *that* the LORD your
God is driving them out before you, in order to confirm the
[1]oath which the LORD swore to your fathers, to Abraham, Isaac
and Jacob.
6 "Know, then, *it is* not because of your righteousness
that the LORD your God is giving you this good land to possess,
for you are [a]a [1]stubborn people.
7 "Remember, do not forget how you provoked the LORD
your God to wrath in the wilderness; [a]from the day that you
left the land of Egypt until you arrived at this place, you have
been rebellious against the LORD.
8 "Even [a]at Horeb you provoked the LORD to wrath, and
the LORD was so angry with you that He would have destroyed
you.
9 "When I went up to the mountain to receive the tablets
of stone, the tablets of the covenant which the LORD had made
with you, then I remained on the mountain forty days and
nights; [a]I neither ate bread nor drank water.
10 "And the LORD gave me the two tablets of stone [a]written
by the finger of God; and on them *were* all the words which
the LORD had spoken with you at the mountain from the midst
of the fire on the day of the assembly.
11 "And it came about [a]at the end of forty days and nights

18 [a]Prov. 10:22; Hos. 2:8
19 [a]Deut. 4:26; 30:18
1 [1]Lit., *and fortified*
2 [a]Num. 13:22, 28, 33; Josh. 11:21, 22
3 [a]Deut. 4:24
4 [1]Lit., *you saying*, [a]Deut. 7:24; 31:27 [b]Deut. 12:31; 18:9-14; Lev. 18:3, 24-30
5 [1]Lit., *word*
6 [a]Or, *stiffnecked* [a]Deut. 9:13; 10:16; 31:27
7 [a]Num. 14:22
8 [a]Ex. 32:7-10
9 [a]Deut. 9:18; 8:3; Ex. 24:18
10 [a]Deut. 4:13
11 [a]Deut. 9:9

that the LORD gave me the two tablets of stone, the tablets of
the covenant.
12 "[a]Then the LORD said to me, 'Arise, go down from here
quickly, for your people whom you brought out of Egypt have
acted corruptly. They have quickly turned aside from the way
which I commanded them; they have made a molten image for
themselves.'
13 "The LORD spoke further to me, saying, 'I have seen this
people, and indeed, it is a [1]stubborn people.
14 '[a]Let Me alone, that I may destroy them and blot out
their name from under heaven; and I will make of you a nation
mightier and greater than they.'
15 "[a]So I turned and came down from the mountain while
the mountain was burning with fire, and the two tablets of the
covenant were in my two hands.
16 "And I saw that you had indeed sinned against the LORD
your God. You had made for yourselves a molten calf; you had
turned aside quickly from the way which the LORD had commanded you.
17 "And I took hold of the two tablets and threw them
from my hands, and smashed them before your eyes.
18 "[a]And I fell down before the LORD, [b]as at the first, forty
days and nights; [c]I neither ate bread nor drank water, [d]because
of all your sin which you had committed in doing what was evil
in the sight of the LORD to provoke him to anger.
19 "For [a]I was afraid of the anger and hot displeasure with
which the LORD was wrathful against you in order to destroy
you, [b]but the LORD listened to me that time also.
20 "And the LORD was angry enough with Aaron to destroy
him; so I also prayed for Aaron at the same time.
21 "[a]And I took your [1]sinful *thing*, the calf which you had
made, and burned it with fire and crushed it, grinding it very
small until it was as fine as dust; and I threw its dust into the
brook that came down from the mountain.
22 "Again at [a]Taberah and at [b]Massah and at [c]Kibroth-
hattaavah you provoked the LORD to wrath.
23 "And when the LORD sent you from Kadesh-barnea,
saying, 'Go up and possess the land which I have given you,'
then you rebelled against the [1]command of the LORD your
God; you neither believed Him nor listened to His voice.
24 "[a]You have been rebellious against the LORD from the
day I knew you.
25 "[a]So I fell down before the LORD the forty days and
nights, which I [1]did because the LORD had said He would
destroy you.
26 "[a]And I prayed to the LORD, and said, 'Oh Lord God do
not destroy Thy people, even Thine inheritance, whom Thou
hast redeemed through Thy greatness, whom Thou hast
brought out of Egypt with a mighty hand.
27 'Remember Thy servants, Abraham, Isaac, and Jacob;
do not look at the stubbornness of this people or at their
wickedness or their sin.
28 'Otherwise the land from which Thou didst bring us
may say, "Because the LORD was not able to bring them into
the land which He had [1]promised them and because He hated

12 [a]Ex. 32:7, 8
13 [1]Or, *stiffnecked*
14 [a]Ex. 32:10
15 [a]Ex. 32:15-19
18 [a]Ex. 34:28 [b]Deut. 10:10 [c]Deut. 9:9 [d]Ex. 34:9
19 [a]Heb. 12:21 [b]Ex. 34:10
21 [1]Lit., *sin* [a]Ex. 32:20
22 [a]Num. 11:3 [b]Ex. 17:7 [c]Num. 11:34
23 [1]Lit., *mouth*
24 [a]Deut. 9:7
25 [1]Lit., *fell down* [a]Deut. 9:18
26 [a]Ex. 32:11-13
28 [1]Lit., *spoken to*

E 30-1

them He has brought them out to slay them in the
wilderness."
29 'Yet they are Thy people, even [a]Thine inheritance,
whom Thou hast brought out by Thy [b]great power and Thine
outstretched arm.'

Chapter 10

"AT that time the LORD said to me, '[a]Cut out for yourself
two tablets of stone like the former ones, and come up to Me
on the mountain, and [b]make an ark of wood for yourself.
2 'And [a]I will write on the tablets the words that were on
the former tablets which you shattered, and [b]you shall put
them in the ark.'
3 "So [a]I made an ark of acacia wood and [b]cut out two
tablets of stone like the former ones, and went up on the
mountain with the two tablets in my hand.
4 "And He wrote on the tablets, like the former writing,
[a]the Ten [1]Commandments which the LORD had spoken to you
on the mountain from the midst of the fire on the day of the
assembly; and the LORD gave them to me.
5 "Then I turned and came down from the mountain, and
[a]put the tablets in the ark which I had made; and there they
are, as the LORD commanded me."
6 (Now the sons of Israel set out from [1]Beeroth [a]Bene-
jaakan to Moserah. [b]There Aaron died and there he was buried
and Eleazar his son ministered as priest in his place.
7 [a]From there they set out to Gudgodah; and from Gudgodah to Jotbathah, a land of brooks of water.
8 [a]At that time the LORD set apart the tribe of Levi to
carry the ark of the covenant of the LORD, to stand before the
LORD [b]to serve Him and to bless in His name until this day.
9 [a]Therefore, Levi does not have a portion or inheritance with his brothers; the LORD is his inheritance, just as the
LORD your God spoke to him.)
10 "[a]I, moreover, stayed on the mountain forty days and
forty nights like the first time, and the LORD listened to me
that time also; the LORD was not willing to destroy you.
11 "Then the LORD said to me, 'Arise, proceed on your
journey ahead of the people, that they may go in and possess
the land which I swore to their fathers to give them.'
12 "[a]And now, Israel, what does the LORD your God require
from you, but to [1]fear the LORD your God, to walk in all His
ways and [b]love Him, and to serve the LORD your God with [c]all
your heart and with all your soul,
13 *and* to keep the LORD's commandments and His statutes which I am commanding you today for your good?
14 "Behold, [a]to the LORD your God belong heaven and the
[1]highest heavens, the earth and all that is in it.
15 "[a]Yet on your fathers did the LORD set His affection to
love them, and He chose their [1]descendants after them, *even*
you above all peoples, as *it is* this day.
16 "[a]Circumcise then [1]your heart, and [b]stiffen no more.
17 "[a]For the LORD your God is the God of gods and the
LORD of lords, the great, the mighty, and the awesome God
[b]who does not show partiality, nor [c]take a bribe.

29 [a]Ps. 106:40 [b]Deut. 4:34

1 [a]Ex. 34:1 [b]Ex. 25:10

2 [a]Deut. 4:13 [b]Ex. 25:16

3 [a]Ex. 37:1-9 [b]Ex. 34:4

4 [1]Lit., *Words*
[a]Deut. 4:13; Ex. 34:28

5 [a]Ex. 40:20

6 [1]Or, *the wells of the sons of Jaakan*
[a]Num. 33:30, 31 [b]Num. 20:25-28

7 [a]Num. 33:33, 34

8 [a]Deut. 31:9; Num. 3:6; 18:1-7 [b]Deut. 17:12; 18:5; 21:5

9 [a]Num. 18:20, 24

10 [a]Deut. 9:18

12 [1]Or, *reverence*
[a]Mic. 6:8 [b]Deut. 6:5 [c]Deut. 4:29

14 [1]Lit., *heaven of heavens*
[a]1 Kin. 8:27; Neh. 9:6; Ps. 68:33; 115:16

15 [1]Lit., *seed*
[a]Deut. 4:37

16 [1]Lit., *the foreskin of your heart*
[a]Jer. 4:4 [b]Deut. 9:6

17 [a]Josh. 22:22; Ps. 136:2
[b]Deut. 1:17 [c]Deut. 16:19

18 "He executes justice for [a]the orphan and the widow, and
shows His love for the alien by giving him food and clothing.
19 "[a]So show your love for the alien, for you were aliens in
the land of Egypt.
20 "You shall fear the LORD your God; you shall serve Him
and [a]cling to Him, and [b]you shall swear by His name.
21 "He is [a]your praise and He is your God, who has done
these great and awesome things for you which your eyes have
seen.
22 "[a]Your fathers went down to Egypt seventy persons in
all, [b]and now the LORD your God has made you as numerous
as the stars of heaven.

CHAPTER 11

"YOU shall therefore [a]love the LORD your God, and always
[b]keep His charge, His statutes, His ordinances, and His
commandments.
2 "And know this day [a]that I *am* not *speaking* with your
sons who have not known and who have not seen the [1]discipline
of the LORD your God—His Greatness, His mighty hand,
and His outstretched arm,
3 and His signs and His works which He did in the midst
of Egypt to Pharaoh the king of Egypt and to all his land;
4 and what He did to Egypt's army, to its horses and its
chariots, [a]when He made the water of the [1]Red Sea to [2]engulf
them while they were pursuing you, and the LORD [3]completely
destroyed them;
5 and what He did to you in the wilderness until you
came to this place;
6 and [a]what He did to Dathan and Abiram, the sons of
Eliab, the son of Reuben, when the earth opened its mouth
and swallowed them, their households, their tents, and [b]every
living thing that [1]followed them, among Israel—
7 but your own eyes have seen all the great work of the
LORD which He did.
8 "You shall therefore keep every commandment which I
am commanding you today, [a]so that you may be strong and go
in and possess the land into which you are about to cross to
possess it;
9 [a]so that you may prolong *your* days on the land which
the LORD swore to your fathers to give to them and to their
[1]descendants, a land flowing with milk and honey.
10 "For the land, into which you are entering to possess it,
is not like the land of Egypt from which you came, where you
used to sow your seed and water it with your [1]foot like a
vegetable garden.
11 "But the land into which you are about to cross to possess it, a land of hills and valleys, drinks water from the rain of
heaven,
12 a land for which the LORD your God cares; the eyes of
the LORD your God are always on it, from the [1]beginning even
to the end of the year.
13 "And it shall come about, if you listen obediently to my
commandments which I am commanding you today, [a]to love

18 [a]Ex. 22:22-24; Ps. 68:5

19 [a]Lev. 19:34; Ezek. 47:22, 23

20 [a]Deut. 11:22; 13:4 [b]Deut. 5:11; 6:13

21 [a]Ps. 109:1; 148:14

22 [a]Gen. 46:27 [b]Deut. 1:10

1 [a]Deut. 6:5; 10:12 [b]Lev. 18:30; 22:9

2 [1]Or, *instruction* [a]Deut. 4:34

4 [1]Lit., *Sea of Reeds* [2]Lit., *flow over their faces* [3]Lit., *to this day* [a]Ex. 14:28 Deut. 1:40; 2:1

6 [1]Lit., *was at their feet* [a]Num. 16:31-33 [b]Num. 26:10, 11

8 [a]Deut. 31:6, 7, 23

9 [1]Lit., *seed* [a]Deut. 4:40; 5:33; 6:2

10 [1]I.e., probably a treadmill

12 [1]Lit., *beginning of the year*

13 [a]Deut. 11:1

the LORD your God and to serve Him [b]with all your heart and
all your soul,
14 that '[1a]I will give the rain for your land in its season, the
[2]early and [3]late rain, that you may gather in your grain and
your new wine and your oil.
15 'And I will give grass in your fields for your cattle, and
[a]you shall eat and be satisfied.'
16 "[1]Beware, lest your hearts be deceived and you turn
away and serve other gods and worship them.
17 "Or the anger of the LORD will be kindled against you,
and He will shut up the heavens [a]so that there will be no rain
and the ground will not yield its fruit; and [b]you will perish
quickly from the good land which the LORD is giving you.
18 "[a]You shall therefore [1]impress these words of mine on
your heart and on your soul; and you shall bind them as a sign
on your hand, and they shall be as [2]frontals [3]on your forehead.
19 "[a]And you shall teach them to your sons, talking of them
when you sit in your house and when you walk along the road
and when you lie down and when you rise up.
20 "[a]And you shall write them on the doorposts of your
house and on your gates,
21 so that your days and the days of your sons may be
multiplied on the land which the LORD swore to your fathers to
give them, as [1]long as the heavens *remain* above the earth.
22 "For if you are [a]careful to keep all this commandment
which I am commanding you, to do it, [b]to love the LORD your
God, to walk in all His ways and [c]hold fast to Him;
23 then the LORD will drive out all these nations from
before you, and you will dispossess nations greater and mightier than you.
24 "[a]Every place on which the sole of your foot shall tread
shall be yours; [b]your border shall be from the wilderness to
Lebanon, *and* from the river, the River Euphrates, as far as
[1]the Western Sea.
25 "[a]There shall no man be able to stand before you; the
LORD your God shall lay the dread of you and the fear of you
on all the land on which you set foot, as He has spoken to you.
26 "[a]See, I am setting before you today a blessing and a
curse:
27 the blessing, if you listen to the commandments of the
LORD your God, which I am commanding you today;
28 and the curse, if you do not listen to the commandments of the LORD your God, but turn aside from the way
which I am commanding you today, [1]by following other gods
which you have not known.
29 "And it shall come about, when the LORD your God
brings you into the land where you are entering to possess it,
[a]that you shall place the blessing on Mount Gerizim and the
curse on Mount Ebal.
30 "Are they not across the Jordan, west of the way toward
the sunset, in the land of the Canaanites who live in the Arabah, opposite [a]Gilgal, beside [b]the [1]oaks of Moreh?
31 "For you are about to cross the Jordan to go in to possess the land which the LORD your God is giving you, and [a]you
shall possess it and live in it,

13 [b]Deut. 4:29
14 [1]Some ancient versions read. *He* [2]I.e., autumn [3]I.e., spring [a]Deut. 28:12
15 [a]Deut. 6:11
16 [1]Lit., *watch yourselves*
17 [a]Deut. 28:24 [b]Deut. 4:26
18 [1]Lit., *put* [2]Lit., *frontlet bands* [3]Lit., *between your eyes* [a]Deut. 6:8; Ex. 12:14; 13:9, 16
19 [a]Deut. 4:9, 10; 6:7
20 [a]Deut. 6:9
21 [1]Lit., *the days of the heavens*
22 [a]Deut. 6:17 [b]Deut. 11:1 [c]Deut. 10:20
24 [1]I.e., the Mediterranean [a]Josh. 1:3 [b]Deut. 1:7, 8; Gen. 15:18; Ex. 23:31
25 [a]Deut. 7:24; Ex. 23:27
26 [a]Deut. 30:1, 19
28 [1]Lit., *to follow*
29 [a]Deut. 27:12; Josh. 8:33
30 [1]Lit., *terebinths* [a]Josh. 4:19 [b]Gen. 12:6
31 [a]Deut. 17:14; Josh. 21:43

32 and you shall be careful to do all the statutes and the
judgments which I am setting before you today.

CHAPTER 12

"THESE are the statutes and the judgments which you shall
carefully observe in the land which the LORD, the God of your
fathers, has given you to possess [1a]as long as you live on the
[2]earth.
2 "You shall utterly destroy all the places where the nations whom you shall dispossess serve their gods, on the high
mountains and on the hills and under every green tree.
3 "And [a]you shall tear down their altars and smash their
sacred pillars and burn their [1]Asherim with fire, and you shall
cut down the engraved images of their gods, and you shall
obliterate their name from that place.
4 "You shall not act like this toward the LORD your God.
5 "[a]But you shall seek *the* LORD at the place which the
LORD your God shall choose from all your tribes, to establish
His name there for His dwelling, and there you shall come.
6 "And there you shall bring your burnt offerings, your
sacrifices, your tithes, the [1]contribution of your hand, your
votive offerings, your freewill offerings, and the first-born of
your herd and of your flock.
7 "There also you and your households shall eat before
the LORD your God, and [a]rejoice in all [1]your undertakings in
which the LORD your God has blessed you.
8 "You shall not do at all what we are doing here today,
every man *doing* whatever is right in his own eyes;
9 for you have not as yet come to [a]the resting place and
the [b]inheritance which the LORD your God is giving you.
10 "When you cross the Jordan and live in the land which
the LORD your God is giving you to inherit, and [a]He gives you
rest from all your enemies around *you* so that you live in
security,
11 [a]then it shall come about that the place in which the
LORD your God shall choose for His name to dwell, there you
shall bring all that I command you: your burnt offerings and
your sacrifices, your tithes and the [1]contribution of your hand,
and all your choice votive offerings which you will vow to the
LORD.
12 "And you shall [a]rejoice before the LORD your God, you
and your sons and daughters, your male and female servants,
and the [b]Levite who is within your gates, since [c]he has no
portion or inheritance with you.
13 "[a]Be careful that you do not offer your burnt offerings
in every *cultic* place you see,
14 but in the place which the LORD chooses in one of your
tribes, there you shall offer your burnt offerings, and there you
shall do all that I command you.
15 "[a]However, you may slaughter and eat meat within any
of your gates, [1]whatever you desire, according to the blessing
of the LORD your God which He has given you; the unclean
and the clean may eat of it, as of [b]the gazelle and the deer.

1 [1]Lit., *all the days* [2]Lit., *ground*
[a]Deut. 4:9

3 [1]I.e., wooden symbols of a female deity
[a]Deut. 7:5

5 [a]Deut. 12:11, 13; Ex. 20:24

6 [1]Or, *heave-offering*

7 [1]Lit., *the putting forth of your hand*
[a]Deut. 12:12, 18; 14:26; 28:47

9 [a]Deut. 3:20; 25:19; 95:11 [b]Deut. 4:21

10 [a]Josh, 11:23

11 [1]Or, *heave offering*
[a]Deut. 12:5

12 [a]Deut. 12:7 [b]Deut. 12:18, 19; 26:11-13 [c]Deut. 10:9

13 [a]Deut. 12:5, 11

15 [1]Lit., *in every desire of your soul*
[a]Deut. 12:20-23 [b]Deut. 12:22; 14:5

16 "[a]Only you shall not eat the blood; [b]you are to pour it
out on the ground like water.
17 "[a]You are not allowed to eat within your gates the tithe
of your grain, or new wine, or oil, or the first-born of your herd
or flock, or any of your votive offerings which you vow, or your
freewill offerings, or the [1]contribution of your hand.
18 "But you shall eat them before the LORD your God in
[a]the place which the LORD your God will choose, you and your
son and daughter, and your male and female servants, and the
[b]Levite who is within your gates; and you shall [c]rejoice before
the LORD your God in all [1]your undertakings.
19 "Be careful that you do not forsake the Levite [1]as long
as you live in your land.
20 "When the LORD your God extends your border as He
has promised you, and you say, 'I will eat meat,' because [1]you
desire to eat meat, *then* you may eat meat, whatever [2]you
desire.
21 "If the place which the LORD your God chooses to put
His name is too far from you, then you may slaughter of your
herd and flock which the LORD has given you, as I have commanded you; and you may eat within your gates [1]whatever you
desire.
22 "Just as a gazelle or a deer is eaten, so you shall eat it;
the unclean and the clean alike may eat of it.
23 "Only be sure [a]not to eat the blood, for the blood is the
[1]life, and you shall not eat the [1]life with the flesh.
24 "You shall not eat it; you shall pour it out on the ground
like water.
25 "You shall not eat it, in order that [a]it may be well with
you and your sons after you, for you will be doing what is right
in the sight of the LORD.
26 "[a]Only your holy things which you may have and your
votive offerings, you shall take and go to the place which the
LORD chooses.
27 "And you shall offer your burnt offerings, the flesh and
the blood, on the altar of the LORD your God; and the blood of
your sacrifices shall be poured out on the altar of the LORD
your God, and [a]you shall eat the flesh.
28 "Be careful to listen to all these words which I command
you, in order that [a]it may be well with you and your sons after
you forever, for you will be doing what is good and right in the
sight of the LORD your God.
29 "When the LORD your God cuts off before you the
nations which you are going in to dispossess, and you dispossess them and dwell in their land,
30 beware that you are not ensnared [1]to follow them, after
they are destroyed before you, and that you do not inquire
after their gods, saying, 'How do these nations serve their gods,
that I also may do likewise?'
31 "[a]You shall not behave thus toward the LORD your God,
for every abominable act which the LORD hates they have done
for their gods; for [b]they even burn their sons and daughters in
the fire to their gods.
32 "[1a]Whatever I command you, you shall be careful to do;
you shall not add to nor take away from it.

16 [a]Lev. 17:10-12 [b]Deut. 15:23

17 [1]Lit., *heave-offering* [a]Deut. 12:26

18 [1]Lit., *the putting forth of your hand* [a]Deut. 12:5 [b]Deut. 12:12 [c]Deut. 12:7

19 [1]Lit., *all your days upon your land*

20 [1]Lit., *your soul* [2]Lit., *every desire of your soul*

21 [1]Lit., *in every desire of your soul*

23 [1]Lit., *soul* [a]Deut. 12:16

25 [a]Deut. 4:40

26 [a]Deut. 12:17

27 [a]Lev. 3:1-17

28 [a]Deut. 4:40

30 [1]Lit., *after them*

31 [a]Deut. 9:5 [b]Deut. 18:10; Lev. 18:21; Ps. 106:37

32 [1]Lit., *All the thing that* [a]Deut. 4:2

Chapter 13

“[1a]IF a prophet or a dreamer of dreams arises among you
and gives you a sign or a wonder,
2 and the sign or the wonder comes true, concerning
which he spoke to you, saying, ‘[a]Let us go after other gods
(whom you have not known) and let us serve them,’
3 you shall not listen to the words of that prophet or that
dreamer of dreams; for the LORD your God is [a]testing you to
find out if [b]you love the LORD your God with all your heart
and with all your soul.
4 “You shall follow the LORD your God and fear Him; and
you shall keep His commandments, listen to His voice, serve
Him, and [a]cling to Him.
5 “But that prophet or that dreamer of dreams shall be
[a]put to death, because he has [1]counseled [2]rebellion against the
LORD your God who brought you from the land of Egypt and
redeemed you from the house of [3]slavery, [b]to seduce you from
the way in which the LORD your God commanded you to walk.
So you shall purge the evil from among you.
6 “[a]If your brother, your mother’s son, or your son or
daughter, or the wife [1]you cherish, or your friend who is as
your own soul, entice you secretly, saying, ‘[b]Let us go and serve
other gods’ (whom neither you nor your fathers have known),
7 of the gods of the peoples who are around you, near
you or far from you, from one end of the earth to the other
end),
8 you shall not yield to him or listen to him; [a]and your
eye shall not pity him, nor shall you spare or conceal him.
9 “[a]But you shall surely kill him; [b]your hand shall be first
against him to put him to death, and afterwards the hand of all
the people.
10 “So you shall stone him [1]to death because he has sought
[a]to seduce you from the LORD your God who brought you out
from the land of Egypt, out of the house of [2]slavery.
11 “Then all Israel will hear and be afraid, and will never
again do such a wicked thing among you.
12 “If you hear in one of your cities which the LORD your
God is giving you to live in *anyone* saying *that*
13 some worthless men have gone out from among you
and have seduced the inhabitants of their city, saying, ‘[a]Let us
go and serve other gods’ (whom you have not known),
14 then you shall investigate and search out and inquire
thoroughly. And if it is true and the matter established that
this abomination has been done among you,
15 [a]you shall surely strike the inhabitants of that city with
the edge of the sword, [1]utterly destroying it and all that is in it
and its cattle with the edge of the sword.
16 “[a]Then you shall gather all its booty into the middle of
its open square and burn the city and all its booty with fire as a
whole burnt offering to the LORD your God; and it shall be a
[1]ruin forever. It shall never be rebuilt.
17 “And nothing from that which is put under the ban shall
cling to your hand, in order that the LORD may turn from [a]His
burning anger and [b]show mercy to you, and have compassion

1 [1]In Heb., 13:2 [a]Matt. 24:24; Mark 13:22
2 [a]Deut. 13:6, 13
3 [a]Deut. 8:2, 16; Ex. 20:20 [b]Deut. 6:5
4 [a]Deut. 10:20
5 [1]Lit., *spoken* [2]Lit., *turning aside* [3]Lit., *slaves* [a]Deut. 13:9, 15; 17:5 [b]Deut. 13:10; 4:19
6 [1]Lit., *of your bosom* [a]Deut. 17:2-7; 29:18 [b]Deut. 13:2
8 [a]Deut. 7:2
9 [a]Deut. 13:5 [b]Deut. 17:7; Lev. 24:14
10 [1]Lit., *with stones so that he dies* [2]Lit., *slaves* [a]Deut. 13:5
13 [a]Deut. 13:2
15 [1]Or, *putting it under the ban* [a]Deut. 13:5
16 [1]Lit., *mound* [a]Deut. 7:25, 26
17 [a]Ex. 32:12; Num. 25:4 [b]Deut. 30:3

on you and [c]make you increase, just as He has sworn to your
fathers,
18 [1]if you will listen to the voice of the LORD your God
[2]keeping all His commandments which I am commanding you
today, [3]and doing what is right in the sight of the LORD your
God.

CHAPTER 14

"You are the sons of the LORD your God; [a]you shall not cut
yourselves nor [1]shave your forehead for the sake of the dead.
2 "For you are [a]a holy people to the LORD your God; and
the LORD has chosen you to be a people for His [1]own possession out of all the peoples who are on the face of the earth.
3 "You shall not eat any detestable thing.
4 "[a]These are the animals which you may eat: the ox, the
sheep, the goat,
5 [1]the deer, the gazelle, the roebuck, the wild goat, the
ibex, the antelope and the mountain sheep.
6 And any animal that divides the hoof and has the hoof
split in [1]two *and* [2]chews the cud, among the animals, that you
may eat.
7 "Nevertheless, you are not to eat of these among those
which [1]chew the cud, or among those that divide the hoof in
[2]two: the camel and the [3]rabbit and the rock-badger, for
though they [1]chew the cud, they do not divide the hoof; they
are unclean for you.
8 "And the pig, because it divides the hoof but *does* not
chew the cud, it is unclean for you. You shall not eat any of
their flesh nor touch their carcasses.
9 "These you may eat of all that are in water: anything
that has fins and scales you may eat.
10 but anything that does not have fins and scales you
shall not eat; it is unclean for you.
11 "You may eat any clean bird.
12 "But these are the ones which you shall not eat: the
[1]eagle and the vulture and the [2]buzzard,
13 and the red kite, the falcon, and the kite in their kinds,
14 and every raven in its kind,
15 and the ostrich, the owl, the sea gull, and the hawk in
their kinds,
16 the little owl, the [1]great owl, the white owl,
17 the pelican, the carrion vulture, the cormorant,
18 the stork, and the heron in their kinds, and the hoopoe
and the bat.
19 "And all the [1]teeming life with wings are unclean to you;
they shall not be eaten.
20 "You may eat any clean bird.
21 "You shall not eat anything which dies *of itself.* You
may give it to the alien who is in your [1]town, so that he may
eat it, or you may sell it to a foreigner, for you are [a]a holy
people to the LORD your God. [b]You shall not boil a kid in its
mother's milk.
22 "You shall surely tithe all the produce from [1]what you
sow, which comes out of the field every year.
23 "And you shall eat in the presence of the LORD your

13:17 [c]Deut. 7:13

13:18 [1]Or, *for* [2]Lit., *to keep* [3]Lit., *to do*

1 [1]Lit., *make a baldness between your eyes* [a]Lev. 21:5

2 [1]Or, *special treasure* [a]Deut. 7:6

4 [a]Lev. 11:1-45; Acts 10:14

5 [1]Exact identification of these animals is uncertain

6 [1]Lit., *two hoofs* [2]Lit., *brings up*

7 [1]Lit., *brings up* [2]Lit., *a cleaving* [3]Or, *hare*

12 [1]Or, *vulture* [2]Or, *black vulture*

16 [1]Or, *great horned owl*

19 [1]I.e., flying insects

21 [1]Lit., *gates* [a]Deut. 14:2 [b]Ex. 23:19; 34:26

22 [1]Lit., *your seed*

God, [a]at the place where He chooses to establish His name, the tithe of your grain, your new wine, your oil, and the first-born of your herd and your flock, in order that you may [b]learn to fear the LORD your God always.

24 "And if the [1]distance is so great for you that you are not able to [2]bring *the tithe,* since the place where the LORD your God chooses [a]to set His name is too far away from you when the LORD your God blesses you,

25 then you shall [1]exchange *it* for money, and bind the money in your hand and go to the place which the LORD your God chooses.

26 "And you may spend the money for whatever your [1]heart desires, for oxen, or sheep, or wine, or strong drink, or whatever your [1]heart [2]desires; and [a]there you shall eat in the presence of the LORD your God and rejoice, you and your household.

27 "Also you shall not neglect [a]the Levite who is in your [1]town, [b]for he has no portion or inheritance among you.

28 "[a]At the end of every third year you shall bring out all the tithe of your produce in that year, and shall deposit *it* in your [1]town.

29 "And the Levite, [a]because he has no portion or inheritance among you, and [b]the alien, the [1]orphan and the widow who are in your [2]town, shall come and [c]eat and be satisfied, in order that the LORD your God may bless you in all the work of your hand which you do.

CHAPTER 15

"[a]AT the end of *every* seven years you shall [1]grant a remission *of debts.*

2 "And this is the manner of remission: every creditor shall release what he has loaned to his neighbor; he shall not exact it of his neighbor and his brother, because the LORD's remission has been proclaimed.

3 "From a foreigner you may exact *it,* but your hand shall release whatever of yours is with your brother.

4 "However, there shall be no poor among you, since the LORD will surely bless you in the land which the LORD your God is giving you as an inheritance to possess,

5 if only you listen obediently to the voice of the LORD your God, to carefully observe all this commandment which I am commanding you today.

6 "[a]For the LORD your God shall bless you as He has promised you, and you will lend to many nations, but you will not borrow; and you will rule over many nations, but they will not rule over you.

7 "If there is [a]a poor man with you, one of your brothers, in any of your [1]towns in your land which the LORD your God is giving you, you shall not harden your heart, nor close your hand from your poor brother;

8 but you shall freely open your hand to him, and shall generously lend him sufficient for his need *in* whatever he lacks.

9 "Beware, lest there is a base [1]thought in your heart, saying, '[a]The seventh year, the year of remission, is near,' and

23 [a]Deut. 12:5 [b]Deut. 4:10

24 [1]Lit., *way* [2]Lit., *carry it* [a]Deut. 12:5

25 [1]Lit., *give in money*

26 [1]Lit., *soul* [2]Lit., *asks of you* [a]Deut. 12:7

27 [1]Lit., *gates* [a]Deut. 12:12 [b]Deut. 10:9

28 [1]Lit., *gates* [a]Deut. 26:12

29 [1]Or, *fatherless* [2]Lit., *gates* [a]Deut. 10:9 [b]Deut. 16:11, 14; 24:19-21; 26:12 [c]Deut. 6:11

1 [1]Lit., *make a release* [a]Deut. 31:10

6 [a]Deut. 28:12, 13

7 [1]Lit., *gates* [a]Deut. 15:11

9 [1]Lit., *word* [a]Deut. 15:1

your eye is hostile toward your poor brother, and you give him
nothing; then he [b]may cry to the LORD against you, and it will
be a sin in you.
10 "You shall generously give to him, and your heart shall
not be grieved when you give to him, because for this thing the
LORD your God will bless you in all your work and in all [1]your
undertakings.
11 "[a]For the poor will never cease *to be* [1]in the land; therefore I command you, saying, 'You shall freely open your hand
to your brother, to your needy and poor in your land.'
12 "[a]If your [1]kinsman, a Hebrew man or woman, is sold to
you, then he shall serve you six years, but in the seventh year
you shall set him [2]free.
13 "And when you set him [1]free, you shall not send him
away empty-handed.
14 "You shall furnish him liberally from your flock and
from your threshing floor and from your wine vat; you shall
give to him as the LORD your God has blessed you.
15 "And you shall remember that you were a slave in the
land of Egypt, and the LORD your God redeemed you; therefore I command you [1]this today.
16 "And it shall come about if he says to you, 'I will not go
out from you,' because he loves you and your household, since
he fares well with you;
17 then you shall take an awl and pierce it through his ear
into the door, and he shall be your servant forever. And also
you shall do likewise to your maid servant.
18 "It shall not seem hard to you when you set him [1]free,
for he has given you six years *with* [2]double the service of a
hired man; so the LORD your God will bless you in whatever
you do.
19 "[a]You shall consecrate to the LORD your God all the
first-born males that are born of your herd and of your flock;
you shall not work with the first-born of your herd, nor shear
the first-born of your flock.
20 "[a]You and your household shall eat it every year before
the LORD your God in the place which the LORD chooses.
21 "[a]But if it has any [1]defect, *such as* lameness or blindness,
or any serious [1]defect, you shall not sacrifice it to the LORD
your God.
22 "You shall eat it within your gates; the unclean and the
clean alike *may eat it,* as [a]a gazelle or a deer.
23 "Only you shall not eat its blood; you are to pour it out
on the ground like water.

CHAPTER 16

"OBSERVE [a]the month of Abib and [1]celebrate the Passover
to the LORD your God, for in the month of Abib the LORD
your God brought you out of Egypt by night.
2 "And you shall sacrifice the Passover to the LORD your
God from the flock and the herd, in the place where the LORD
chooses to establish His name.
3 "[a]You shall not eat leavened bread with it; seven days
you shall eat with it unleavened bread, the bread of affliction
(for you came out of the land of Egypt in haste), in order that

9 [b]Deut. 24:15; Ex. 22:23

10 [1]Lit., *the putting forth of your hand*

11 [1]Lit., *in the midst of* [a]Matt. 26:11; Mark 14:7; John 12:8

12 [1]Lit., *brother* [2]Lit., *free from you* [a]Ex. 21:2-6; Lev. 25:39-43

13 [1]Lit., *free from you*

15 [1]Lit., *this thing*

18 [1]Lit., *free from you* [2]Lit., *double the amount*

19 [a]Ex. 13:2

20 [a]Lev. 7:15-18

21 [1]Lit., *blemish* [a]Lev. 22:19-25

22 [a]Deut. 12:15, 16

1 [1]Lit., *perform* [a]Ex. 12:2

3 [a]Ex. 12:8, 15

you may remember [b]all the days of your life the day when you
came out of the land of Egypt.
4 "For seven days no leaven shall be seen with you in all
your territory, and none of the flesh which you sacrifice on the
evening of the first day shall remain overnight until morning.
5 "You are not allowed to sacrifice the Passover in any of
your [1]towns which the LORD your God is giving you;
6 but [a]at the place where the LORD your God chooses to
establish His name, you shall sacrifice the Passover in the evening at sunset, at the time that you came out of Egypt.
7 "And you shall cook and eat *it* in the place which the
LORD your God chooses. And in the morning you are to return
to your tents.
8 "Six days you shall eat unleavened bread, and on the
seventh day there shall be [a]a solemn assembly to the LORD
your God; you shall do no work *on it*.
9 "[a]You shall count seven weeks for yourself; you shall
begin to count seven weeks from the time you begin to put the
sickle to the standing grain.
10 "Then you shall [1]celebrate the Feast of Weeks to the
LORD your God with a tribute of a freewill offering of your
hand, which you shall give just as the LORD your God blesses
you;
11 and you shall [a]rejoice before the LORD your God, you
and your son and your daughter and your male and female
servants and [b]the Levite who is in your [1]town, and [c]the stranger
and the [2]orphan and the widow who are in your midst, in the
place where the LORD your God chooses to establish His name.
12 "And you shall remember that you were a slave in
Egypt, and you shall be careful to observe these statutes.
13 "[a]You shall [1]celebrate the Feast of Booths seven days
after you have gathered in from your threshing floor and your
wine vat;
14 and you shall [a]rejoice in your feast, you and your son
and your daughter and your male and female servants and the
Levite and the stranger and the [1]orphan and the widow who
are in your [2]towns.
15 "Seven days you shall celebrate a feast to the LORD your
God in the place which the LORD chooses, because the LORD
your God will bless you in all your produce and in all the work
of your hands, so that you shall be altogether joyful.
16 "[a]Three times in a year all your males shall appear before the LORD your God in the place which He chooses, at the
Feast of Unleavened Bread and at the Feast of Weeks and at
the Feast of Booths, and [b]they shall not appear before the
LORD empty-handed.
17 "Every man [1]shall give as he is able, according to the
blessing of the LORD your God which He has given you.
18 "You shall appoint for yourself judges and officers in all
your [1]towns which the LORD your God is giving you, according
to your tribes, and they shall judge the people with righteous
judgment.
19 "[a]You shall not distort justice; you shall not [1]be partial,
and you shall not take a bribe, for a bribe blinds the eyes of the
wise and perverts the words of the righteous.
20 "Justice, *and only* justice, you shall pursue, that [a]you

3 [b]Deut. 4:9

5 [1]Lit., *gates*

6 [a]Deut. 12:5

8 [a]Lev. 23:36

9 [a]Ex. 23:16; 34:22; Lev. 23:15; Num. 28:26

10 [1]Lit., *perform*

11 [1]Lit., *gates* [2]Or, *fatherless* [a]Deut. 12:7 [b]Deut. 12:12 [c]Deut. 14:29

13 [1]Lit., *perform* [a]Lev. 23:34-43

14 [1]Or, *fatherless* [2]Lit., *gates* [a]Deut. 16:11

16 [a]Ex. 23:14-17; 34:23, 24 [b]Ex. 22:29; 34:20

17 [1]Lit., *according to the gift of his hand,*

18 [1]Lit., *gates*

19 [1]Lit., *regard persons* [a]Deut. 1:17; 10:17

20 [a]Deut. 4:1

may live and possess the land which the LORD your God is
giving you.
21 "[a]You shall not plant for yourself an [1]Asherah of any
kind of tree beside the altar of the LORD your God, which you
shall make for yourself.
22 "Neither shall you set up for yourself a sacred pillar
which the LORD your God hates.

CHAPTER 17

"[a]YOU shall not sacrifice to the LORD your God an ox or a
sheep which has a blemish or any [1]defect, for that is a detestable thing to the LORD your God.
2 "[a]If there is found in your midst, in any of your [1]towns,
which the LORD your God is giving you, a man or a woman
who does what is evil in the sight of the LORD your God, by
transgressing His covenant,
3 and has gone and served other gods and worshiped
them, or the sun or the moon or any of the heavenly host,
which I have not commanded;
4 and if it is told you and you have heard of it, then you
shall inquire thoroughly. And behold, if it is true and the thing
certain that this detestable thing has been done in Israel,
5 then you shall bring out that man or that woman who
has done this evil deed, to your gates, *that is,* the man or the
woman, and you shall stone them to [1]death.
6 "[a]On the [1]evidence of two witnesses or three witnesses,
he who is to die shall be put to death; he shall not be put to
death on the [1]evidence of one witness.
7 "[a]The hand of the witnesses shall be first against him to
put him to death, and afterward the hand of all the people. So
you shall purge the evil from your midst.
8 "If any case is too difficult for you to decide, between
[1]one kind of homicide or another, between [2]one kind of lawsuit or another, and between [3]one kind of assault or another,
being cases of dispute in your [4]courts, then you shall arise and
go up to [a]the place which the LORD your God chooses.
9 "So you shall come to [a]the Levitical priest or the judge
who is *in office* in those days, and you shall inquire *of them,*
and they will declare to you the verdict in the case.
10 "And you shall do according to the [1]terms of the verdict
which they declare to you from that place which the LORD
chooses; and you shall be careful to observe according to all
that they teach you.
11 "[a]According to the [1]terms of the law which they teach
you, and according to the verdict which they tell you, you shall
do; you shall not turn aside from the word which they declare
to you, to the right or the left.
12 "And the man who acts [a]presumptuously by not listening to the priest who stands there to serve the LORD your
God, nor to the judge, that man shall die; thus you shall purge
the evil from Israel.
13 "Then all the people will hear and be afraid, and will not
act [a]presumptuously again.
14 "When you enter the land which the LORD your God

21 [1]I.e., wooden symbols of a female deity [a]Deut. 7:5

1 [1]Lit., *evil thing* [a]Deut. 15:21

2 [1]Lit., *gates* [a]Deut. 13:6-11

5 [1]Lit., *death with stones*

6 [1]Lit., *mouth* [a]Deut. 19:15; Num. 35:30

7 [a]Deut. 13:9; Lev. 24:14

8 [1]Lit., *blood to blood* [2]Lit., *judgment to judgment* [3]Lit., *stroke to stroke* [4]Lit., *gates* [a]Deut. 12:5

9 [a]Deut. 19:17

10 [1]Lit., *mouth*

11 [1]Lit., *mouth* [a]Deut. 25:1

12 [a]Deut. 17:13; 1:43; 18:20

13 [a]Deut. 17:12

gives you, and you [a]possess it and live in it, and you say, '[b]I will
set a king over me like all the nations who are around me,'
15 you shall surely set a king over you whom the LORD
your God chooses, *one* from among your [1]countrymen you
shall set as king over yourselves; you may not put a foreigner
over yourselves who is not your [1]countryman.
16 "[a]Moreover, he shall not multiply horses for himself, nor
shall he [b]cause the people to return to Egypt to multiply
horses, since the LORD has said to you, 'You shall never again
return that way.'
17 "[a]Neither shall he multiply wives for himself, [1]lest his
heart turn away; nor shall he greatly increase silver and gold for
himself.
18 "Now it shall come about when he sits on the throne of
his kingdom, he shall write for himself a copy of this law on a
scroll [1a]in the presence of the Levitical priests.
19 "And it shall be with him, and he shall read it [a]all the
days of his life, that he may learn to fear the LORD his God, [1]by
carefully observing all the words of this law and these statutes,
20 that his heart may not be lifted up above his [1]country-
men [a]and that he may not turn aside from the commandment,
to the right or the left; in order that he and his sons may
continue long in his kingdom in the midst of Israel.

CHAPTER 18

"[a]THE Levitical priests, the whole tribe of Levi, shall have
no portion or inheritance with Israel; they shall eat the LORD's
offerings by fire and His [1]portion.
2 "And they shall have no inheritance among their [1]country-
men; the LORD is their inheritance, as He [2]promised them.
3 "[a]Now this shall be the priests' due from the people,
from those who offer a sacrifice, either an ox or a sheep, of
which they shall give to the priest the shoulder and the two
cheeks and the stomach.
4 "You shall give him the first fruits of your grain, your
new wine, and your oil, and the first shearing of your sheep.
5 "[a]For the LORD your God has chosen him and his sons
from all your tribes, to stand [1]and serve in the name of the
LORD forever.
6 "Now if a Levite comes from any of your [1]towns throughout Israel where he resides, and comes [2]whenever he desires
to the place which the LORD chooses,
7 then he shall serve in the name of the LORD his God,
like all his fellow Levites who stand there before the LORD.
8 "[a]They shall eat [1]equal portions, except *what they receive* from the sale of their fathers' *estates*.
9 "When you enter the land which the LORD your God
gives you, you shall not learn to [1a]imitate the detestable things
of those nations.
10 "There shall not be found among you anyone [a]who
makes his son or his daughter pass through the fire, one who
uses divination, one [b]who practices witchcraft, or one who
interprets omens, or a sorcerer,
11 or one who casts a spell, or a medium, or a spiritist, or
one who calls up the dead.

14 [a]Deut. 11:31; Josh. 21:43 [b]1 Sam. 8:5, 19, 20

15 [1]Lit., *brother(s)*

16 [a]1 Kin. 4:26; 10:26-29 [b]Is. 31:1; Ezek. 17:15

17 [1]Lit., *nor* [a]2 Sam. 5:13; 12:11; 1 Kin. 11:3, 4

18 [1]Lit., *from before* [a]Deut. 31:24-26

19 [1]Lit., *to keep to do them* [a]Deut. 4:9, 10

20 [1]Lit., *brothers* [a]Deut. 5:32

1 [1]Or, *inheritance* [a]Deut. 10:9; 1 Cor. 9:13

2 [1]Lit., *brothers* [2]Lit., *spoke to*

3 [a]Lev. 7:32-34; Num. 18:11, 12

5 [1]Lit., *to* [a]Ex. 29:9

6 [1]Lit., *gates* [2]Lit., *with all the desire of his soul*

8 [1]Lit., *portion like portion* [a]Lev. 27:30-33; Num. 18:21-24

9 [1]Lit., *do according to* [a]Deut. 9:5

10 [a]Deut. 12:31 [b]Ex. 22:18; Lev. 19:26, 31; 20:6; Jer. 27:9, 10; Mal. 3:5

12 "For whoever does these things is detestable to the
LORD; and because of these detestable things the LORD your
God will drive them out before you.
13 "[a]You shall be [1]blameless before the LORD your God.
14 "For those nations which you shall dispossess, listen to
those who practice witchcraft and to diviners, but as for you,
the LORD your God has not allowed you *to do* so.
15 "[a]The LORD your God will raise up for you a prophet
like me from among you, from your [1]countrymen, you shall
listen to him.
16 "This is [a]according to all that you asked of the LORD
your God in Horeb on the day of the assembly, saying, 'Let me
not hear again the voice of the LORD my God, let me not see
this great fire any more, lest I die.'
17 "[a]And the LORD said to me, 'They have [1]spoken well.
18 'I will raise up a prophet from among their [1]countrymen
like you, and I will put My words in his mouth, and he shall
speak to them all that I command him.
19 '[a]And it shall come about that whoever will not listen to
My words which he shall speak in My name, I Myself will
require *it* of him.
20 'But the prophet who shall speak a word [a]presump-
tuously in My name which I have not commanded him to
speak, or [b]which he shall speak in the name of other gods, [1]that
prophet shall die.'
21 "And [1]you may say in your heart, 'How shall we know
the word which the LORD has not spoken?'
22 "When a prophet speaks in the name of the LORD, if the
thing does not come about or come true, that is the thing
which the LORD has not spoken. The prophet has spoken it
[a]presumptuously; you shall not be afraid of him.

Chapter 19

"[a]WHEN the LORD your God cuts off the nations, whose
land the LORD your God gives you, and you dispossess them
and settle in their cities and in their houses,
2 [a]you shall set aside three cities for yourself in the midst
of your land, which the LORD your God gives you to [1]possess.
3 "You shall prepare the [1]roads for yourself, and divide
into three parts the territory of your land, which the LORD your
God will give you as a possession, [2]so that any manslayer may
flee there.
4 "[a]Now this is the case of the manslayer who may flee
there and live: when he [1]kills his friend [2]unintentionally, [3]not
hating him previously—
5 as when *a man* goes into the forest with his friend to
cut wood, and his hand [1]swings the axe to cut down the tree,
and the iron *head* slips off the [2]handle and [3]strikes his friend so
that he dies—he may flee to one of these cities and live;
6 lest the avenger of blood pursue the manslayer [1]in the
heat of his anger, and overtake him, because the way is long,
and [2]take his life, though he was not deserving of death, since
he had not hated him previously.

13 [1]Lit., *complete, perfect;* or, *having integrity* [a]Matt. 5:48; Gen. 6:9; 17:1

15 [1]Lit., *brothers* [a]Acts 3:22; 7:37; John 1:21, 25

16 [a]Deut. 5:23-27; Ex. 20:18, 19

17 [1]Lit., *done well what they have spoken* [a]Deut. 5:28

18 [1]Lit., *brothers*

19 [a]Acts 3:23; Heb. 12:25

20 [1]Lit., *and that* [a]Deut. 17:12 [b]Deut. 13:1, 2

21 [1]Lit., *if you say*

22 [a]Deut. 18:20

1 [a]Deut. 6:10, 11

2 [1]Lit., *possess it* [a]Deut. 4:41

3 [1]Lit., *road* [2]Lit., *and it shall be for every manslayer to flee there*

4 [1]Lit., *smites* [2]Lit., *without knowledge* [3]Lit., *and he was not hating him previously* [a]Num. 35:9-34

5 [1]Lit., *is thrust with* [2]Lit., *wood* [3]Lit., *finds*

6 [1]Lit., *while his heart is hot* [2]Lit., *smite him in the soul*

7 "Therefore, I command you, saying, 'You shall set aside
three cities for yourself.'
8 "And if the LORD your God enlarges your territory, just
as He has sworn to your fathers, and gives you all the land
which He [1]promised to give your fathers—
9 if you [1]carefully observe all this commandment, which
I command you today, [a]to love the LORD your God, and to
walk in His ways always—then you shall add three more cities
for yourself, besides these three.
10 "So innocent blood will not be shed in the midst of your
land which the LORD your God gives you as an inheritance, and
[a]bloodguiltiness be on you.
11 "But if there is a man who hates his neighbor and lies in
wait for him and rises up against him and strikes [1]him so that
he dies, and he flees to one of these cities,
12 then the elders of his city shall send and take him from
there and deliver him into the hand of the avenger of blood,
that he may die.
13 "[1a]You shall not pity him, but you shall purge the blood
of the innocent from Israel, that it may go well with you.
14 "[a]You shall not move your neighbor's boundary mark,
which the ancestors have set, in your inheritance which you
shall inherit in the land that the LORD your God gives you to
[1]possess.
15 "[a]A single witness shall not rise up against a man on
account of any iniquity or any sin [1]which he has committed;
on the [2]evidence of two or three witnesses a matter shall be
confirmed.
16 "[a]If a malicious witness rises up against a man to [1]accuse
him of [2]wrongdoing,
17 then both the men who have the dispute shall stand
[a]before the LORD, before the priests and the judges who will be
in office in those days.
18 "And the judges [a]shall investigate thoroughly; and if the
witness is a false witness *and* he has [1]accused his brother
falsely,
19 then you shall do to him just as he had intended to do
to his brother. Thus you shall purge the evil from among you.
20 "And the rest will hear and be afraid, and will never
again do such an evil thing among you.
21 "Thus [1a]you shall not show pity: [b]life for life, [c]eye for
eye, tooth for tooth, hand for hand, foot for foot.

CHAPTER 20

"WHEN you go out to battle against your enemies and see
horses and chariots *and* people more numerous than you, [a]do
not be afraid of them; for the LORD your God, who brought
you up from the land of Egypt, is with you.
2 "Now it shall come about that when you are approaching the battle, the priest shall come near and speak to the
people.
3 "And he shall say to them, 'Hear, O Israel, you are
approaching the battle against your enemies today. Do not be

8 [1]Lit., *spoke*

9 [1]Lit., *keep . . . to do it* [a]Deut. 6:5

10 [a]Deut. 21:1-9; Num. 35:33

11 [1]Lit., *him in the soul*

13 [1]Lit., *Your eye* [a]Deut. 7:2

14 [1]Lit., *possess it* [a]Deut. 27:17

15 [1]Lit., *in any sin, which he sins* [2]Lit., *mouth of two witnesses, or by the mouth of three* [a]Deut. 17:6; Num. 35:30; Matt. 18:16; 2 Cor. 13:1

16 [1]Lit., *testify against* [2]Lit., *turning aside* [a]Ex. 23:1

17 [a]Deut. 17:9

18 [1]Lit., *testified against* [a]Deut. 25:1

21 [1]Lit., *your eye* [a]Deut. 19:13 [b]Ex. 21:23; Lev. 24:20 [c]Matt. 5:38

1 [a]Deut. 3:22; 7:18; 31:6, 8

fainthearted. [a]Do not be afraid, or panic, or tremble before
them,
4 for the LORD your God [a]is the one who goes with you
to fight for you against your enemies, to save you.'
5 "The officers also shall speak to the people, saying,
'Who is the man that has built a new house and has not
dedicated it? Let him depart and return to his house, lest he
die in the battle and another man dedicate it.
6 'And who is the man that has planted a vineyard and has
not [1]begun to use its fruit? Let him depart and return to his
house, lest he die in the battle and another man [1]begin to use
its fruit.
7 '[a]And who is the man that is engaged to a woman and
has not [1]married her? Let him depart and return to his house,
lest he die in the battle and another man [2]marry her.'
8 "Then the officers shall speak further to the people, and
they shall say, '[a]Who is the man that is afraid and fainthearted? Let him depart and return to his house, so that [1]he
might not make his brothers' hearts melt like his heart.'
9 "And it shall come about that when the officers have
finished speaking to the people, they shall appoint commanders of armies at the head of the people.
10 "When you approach a city to fight against it, you shall
[1]offer it terms of peace.
11 "And it shall come about, if it [1]agrees to make peace
with you and opens to you, then it shall be that all the people
who are found in it shall become your forced labor and shall
serve you.
12 "However, if it does not make peace with you, but
makes war against you, then you shall besiege it.
13 "When the LORD your God gives it into your hand, you
shall strike all the [1]men in it with the edge of the sword.
14 "Only the women and the children and the animals and
all that is in the city, all its spoil, you shall take as booty for
yourself; and you shall [1]use the spoil of your enemies which
the LORD your God has given you.
15 "Thus you shall do to all the cities that are very far from
you, which are not of the cities of these nations [1]nearby.
16 "[a]Only in the cities of these peoples that the LORD your
God is giving you as an inheritance, you shall not leave alive
anything that breathes.
17 "But you shall [1]utterly destroy them, the Hittite and the
Amorite, the Canaanite and the Perizzite, the Hivite and the
Jebusite, as the LORD your God has commanded you,
18 in order that they may not teach you to do [a]according
to all their detestable things which they have done for their
gods, so that you would sin against the LORD your God.
19 "When you besiege a city a long time, to make war
against it in order to capture it, you shall not destroy its trees
by swinging an axe against them; for you may eat from them,
and you shall not cut them down. [1]For is the tree of the field a
man, that it should [2]be besieged by you?
20 "Only the trees which you know [1]are not fruit trees you
shall destroy and cut down, that you may construct siegeworks
against the city that is making war with you until it falls.

3 [a]Deut. 20:1; Josh. 23:10

4 [a]Deut. 1:30

6 [1]Lit., *treat(ed) it as common*

7 [1]Lit., *taken* [2]Lit., *take* [a]Deut. 24:5

8 [1]So with Gk. and other ancient versions. [a]Judg. 7:3

10 [1]Lit., *call to it for peace*

11 [1]Lit., *answer peace*

13 [1]Lit., *males*

14 [1]Lit., *eat*

15 [1]Lit., *here*

16 [a]Deut. 7:1-5; Ex. 23:31-33

17 [1]Or, *put them under the ban*

18 [a]Deut. 9:5

19 [1]Read as interrogative with ancient versions [2]Lit., *come before you in the siege*

20 [1]Lit., *they are not trees for food*

Chapter 21

'If a slain person is found lying in the open country in the
and which the Lord your God gives you to [1]possess, *and* it is
not known who has struck him,
2 then your elders and your judges shall go out and measure *the distance* to the cities which are around the slain one.
3 "And it shall be that the city which is nearest to the slain
man, that is, the elders of that city, shall take a heifer of the
herd, which has not been worked and which has not pulled in a
yoke;
4 and the elders of that city shall bring the heifer down to
a valley with running water, which has not been plowed or
sown, and shall break the heifer's neck there in the valley.
5 "Then [a]the priests, the sons of Levi, shall come near, for
the Lord your God has chosen them to serve Him and to bless
in the name of the Lord; and every dispute and every [1]assault
[2]shall be settled by them.
6 "And all the elders of that city [1]which is nearest to the
slain man shall wash their hands over the heifer whose neck
was broken in the valley;
7 and they shall answer and say, 'Our hands have not
shed this blood, nor did our eyes see *it*.
8 '[1]Forgive Thy people Israel whom Thou hast redeemed,
O Lord, and do not place the guilt of [a]innocent blood in the
midst of Thy people Israel.' And the bloodguiltiness shall be
[2]forgiven them.
9 "[a]So you shall remove the guilt of innocent blood from
your midst, when you do what is right in the eyes of the Lord.
10 "When you go out to battle against your enemies, and
the Lord your God delivers them into your hands, and you
take them away captive,
11 and see among the captives a beautiful woman, and
have a desire for her and would take her as a wife for yourself,
12 then you shall bring her home to your house, and she
shall [a]shave her head and [1]trim her nails.
13 "She shall also [1]remove the clothes of her captivity and
shall remain in your house, and mourn her father and mother a
full month; and after that you may go in to her and be her
husband and she shall be your wife.
14 "And it shall be, if you are not pleased with her, then
you shall let her go [1]wherever she wishes; but you shall certainly not sell her for money, you shall not [2]mistreat her, because you have humbled her.
15 "If a man has two wives, the one loved and the other
[1]unloved, and *both* the loved and the [1]unloved have borne him
sons, if the first-born son belongs to the [1]unloved,
16 then it shall be in the day he [1]wills what he has to his
sons, he cannot make the son of the loved the first-born before
the son of the [2]unloved, who is the first-born.
17 "But he shall acknowledge the first-born, the son of the
[1]unloved, by giving him a double portion of all that [2]he has, for
he is the [a]beginning of his strength; to him belongs the right of
the first-born.
18 "If any man has a stubborn and rebellious son who will

1 [1]Lit., *possess it*

5 [1]Lit., *stroke* [2]Lit., *shall be according to their mouth* [a]Deut. 17:9-11; 19:17

6 [1]Lit., *who are*

8 [1]Lit., *Cover over, atone for* [2]Lit., *covered over, atoned for* [a]Num. 35:33, 34

9 [a]Deut. 19:13

12 [1]Lit., *do* [a]Lev. 14:8, 9; Num. 6:9

13 [1]Lit., *remove from her*

14 [1]Lit., *according to her soul* [2]Or, *enslave*

15 [1]Lit., *hated*

16 [1]Lit., *makes to inherit* [2]Lit., *hated*

17 [1]Lit., *hated* [2]Lit., *is found with him* [a]Gen. 49:3

not obey his father or his mother, and when they chastise him
he will not even listen to them,
19 then his father and mother shall seize him, and bring
him out to the elders of his city [1]at the gateway of his home
town.
20 "And they shall say to the elders of his city, 'This son of
ours is stubborn and rebellious, he will not obey us, he is a
glutton and a drunkard.'
21 "[a]Then all the men of his city shall stone him to death;
so you shall remove the evil from your midst, and all Israel
shall hear *of it* and fear.
22 "And if a man has committed a sin [a]worthy of death,
and he is put to death, and you hang him on a tree,
23 [a]his corpse shall not hang all night on the tree, but you
shall surely bury him on the same day (for [b]he who is hanged is
[1]accursed of God), so that you do not define your land which
the LORD your God gives you as an inheritance.

CHAPTER 22

"[a]YOU shall not see your countryman's ox or his sheep
straying away, and [1]pay no attention to them; you shall certainly bring them back to your countryman.
2 "And if your countryman is not near you, or if you do
not know him, then you shall bring it home to your house, and
it shall remain with you until your countryman looks for it;
then you shall restore it to him.
3 "And thus you shall do with his donkey, and you shall do
the same with his garment, and you shall do likewise with
anything lost by your countryman, which he has lost and you
have found. You are not allowed to [1]neglect *them.*
4 "You shall not see your countryman's donkey or his ox
fallen down on the way, and [1]pay no attention to them; you
shall certainly help him to raise *them* up.
5 "A woman shall not wear man's clothing, nor shall a
man put on a woman's clothing; for whoever does these things
is an abomination to the LORD your God.
6 "If you happen to come upon a bird's nest along the
way, in any tree or on the ground, with young ones or eggs, and
the mother sitting on the young or on the eggs, [a]you shall not
take the mother with the young;
7 you shall certainly let the mother go, but the young you
may take for yourself, [a]in order that it may be well with you,
and that you may prolong your days.
8 "When you build a new house, you shall make a parapet
for your roof, that you may not bring blood-guilt on your
house if anyone falls from it.
9 "[a]You shall not sow your vineyard with two kinds of
seed, lest [1]all the produce of the seed which you have sown,
and the increase of the vineyard become defiled.
10 "You shall not plow with an ox and a donkey together.
11 "[a]You shall not wear a material mixed of wool and linen
together.
12 "[a]You shall make yourself tassels on the four corners of
your garment with which you cover yourself.
13 "[a]If any man takes a wife and goes in to her and *then*
[1]turns against her,

19 [1]Lit., *and to the gate of his place*

21 [a]Lev. 20:2, 27; 24:14-23; Num. 15:25, 36

22 [a]Matt. 26:66; Mark 14:64

23 [1]Lit., *the curse of God* [a]Josh. 8:29; 10:26, 27; John 19:31 [b]Gal. 3:13

1 [1]Lit., *hide yourself from them* [a]Ex. 23:4, 5

3 [1]Lit., *hide yourself*

4 [1]Lit., *hide yourself from them*

6 [a]Lev. 22:28

7 [a]Deut. 4:40

9 [1]Lit., *the fullness, seed* [a]Lev. 19:19

11 [a]Lev. 19:19

12 [a]Num. 15:37-41; Matt. 23:5

13 [1]Lit., *hates her* [a]Deut. 24:1

14 and charges her with shameful deeds and [1]publicly de-
fames her, and says, 'I took this woman, *but* when I came near
her, I did not find her a virgin.'
15 Then the girl's father and her mother shall take and
bring out the *evidence* of the girl's virginity to the elders of the
city at the gate.
16 "And the girl's father shall say to the elders, 'I gave my
daughter to this man for a wife, but he [1]turned against her;
17 and behold, he has charged her with shameful deeds,
saying, "I did not find your daughter a virgin." But [1]this is the
evidence of my daughter's virginity.' And they shall spread the
garment before the elders of the city.
18 "So the elders of that city shall take the man and chastise him,
19 and they shall fine him a hundred *shekels* of silver and
give it to the girl's father, because he [1]publicly defamed a
virgin of Israel. And she shall remain his wife; he cannot [2]di-
vorce her all his days.
20 "But if this [1]charge is true, that the girl was not found a
virgin,
21 then they shall bring out the girl to the doorway of her
father's house, and the men of her city shall stone her [1]to
death because she has [a]committed an act of folly in Israel, by
playing the harlot in her father's house; thus you shall purge
the evil from among you.
22 "[a]If a man is found lying with a married woman, then
both of them shall die, the man who lay with the woman, and
the woman; thus you shall purge the evil from Israel.
23 "[a]If there is a girl who is a virgin engaged to a man, and
another man finds her in the city and lies with her,
24 then you shall bring them both out to the gate of that
city and you shall stone them [1]to death; the girl, because she
did not cry out in the city, and the man, because he has violated his neighbor's wife. Thus you shall purge the evil from
among you.
25 "But if in the field the man finds the girl who is engaged,
and the man forces her and lies with her, then only the man
who lies with her shall die.
26 "But you shall do nothing to the girl; there is no sin in
the girl worthy of death, for just as a man rises against his
neighbor and murders him, so is this case.
27 "When he found her in the field, the engaged girl cried
out, but there was no one to save her.
28 "[a]If a man finds a girl who is a virgin, who is not engaged, and seizes her and lies with her and they are discovered,
29 then the man who lay with her shall give to the girl's
father fifty *shekels* of silver, and she shall become his wife
because he has violated her; he cannot divorce her all his days.
30 "[1a]A man shall not take his father's wife so that he shall
not uncover his father's skirt.

Chapter 23

"[a]No one who is [1]emasculated, or has his male organ cut
off, shall enter the assembly of the Lord.

14 [1]Lit., *causes an evil name to go out against her*

16 [1]Lit., *hated her*

17 [1]Lit., *these are*

19 [1]Lit., *caused an evil name to go out against a virgin* [2]Lit., *send her away*

20 [1]Lit., *matter*

21 [1]Lit., *with stones so that she dies* [a]Deut. 23:17, 18; Lev. 19:29; 21:9

22 [a]Lev. 20:10; Ezek. 16:38; John 8:5

23 [a]Lev. 19:20-22

24 [1]Lit., *with stones so that they die*

28 [a]Ex. 22:16

30 [1]Ch. 23:1 in Heb. [a]Deut. 27:20

1 [1]Lit., *wounded by crushing* of testicles [a]Lev. 21:20; 22:24

4 [1]Lit., *bread* [2]Heb. *Aram-naharaim*
[a]Num. 22:5; 23:7; 2 Pet. 2:15; Jude 11

5 [a]Deut. 4:37

9 [1]Or, *camp*

10 [1]Lit., *come to the midst of*
[a]Lev. 15:16

11 [1]Lit., *come to the midst of*

13 [1]Lit., *peg* [2]Lit., *and*

14 [1]Lit., *give up* [2]Lit., *nakedness of anything* [3]Lit., *and*
[a]Lev. 26:12

15 [1]Lit., *delivered himself*

16 [1]Lit., *gates*

17 [a]Deut. 22:21

18 [1]I.e., male prostitute, sodomite
[a]Lev. 18:22; 20:13

19 [1]Lit., *brothers*
[a]Ex. 22:25; Lev. 25:35-37

20 [1]Lit., *brother* [2]Lit., *the putting forth of your hand* [3]Lit., *possess it*
[a]Deut. 28:12

21 [a]Num. 30:1, 2; Matt. 5:33

2 "No one of illegitimate birth shall enter the assembly of
the LORD; none of his *descendants,* even to the tenth generation, shall enter the assembly of the LORD.
3 "No Ammonite or Moabite shall enter the assembly of
the LORD; none of their *descendants,* even to the tenth generation, shall ever enter the assembly of the LORD,
4 because they did not meet you with [1]food and water on
the way when you came out of Egypt, and because they hired
against you [a]Balaam the son of Beor from Pethor of [2]Mesopo-
tamia, to curse you.
5 "Nevertheless, the LORD your God was not willing to
listen to Balaam, but the LORD your God turned the curse into
a blessing for you because the LORD your God [a]loves you.
6 "You shall never seek their peace or their prosperity all
your days.
7 "You shall not detest an Edomite, for he is your brother;
you shall not detest an Egyptian, because you were an alien in
his land.
8 "The sons of the third generation who are born to them
may enter the assembly of the LORD.
9 "When you go out as an [1]army against your enemies,
then you shall keep yourself from every evil thing.
10 "[a]If there is among you any man who is unclean because
of a nocturnal emission, then he must go outside the camp; he
may not [1]reenter the camp.
11 "But it shall be when evening approaches, he shall bathe
himself with water, and at sundown he may [1]reenter the camp.
12 "You shall also have a place outside the camp and go
out there,
13 and you shall have a [1]spade among your tools, and it
shall be when you sit down outside, you shall dig with it and
shall turn [2]to cover up your excrement.
14 "Since [a]the LORD your God walks in the midst of your
camp to deliver you and to [1]defeat your enemies before you,
therefore your camp must be holy; and He must not see [2]any-
thing indecent among you [3]lest He turn away from you.
15 "You shall not hand over to his master a slave who has
[1]escaped from his master to you.
16 "He shall live with you in your midst, in the place which
he shall choose in one of your [1]towns where it pleases him; you
shall not mistreat him.
17 "[a]None of the daughters of Israel shall be a cult prostitute, nor shall any of the sons of Israel be a cult prostitute.
18 "You shall not bring the hire of a harlot or the wages of
a [1a]dog into the house of the LORD your God for any votive
offering, for both of these are an abomination to the LORD
your God.
19 "[a]You shall not charge interest to your [1]countrymen:
interest on money, food, *or* anything that may be loaned at
interest.
20 "[a]You may charge interest to a foreigner, but to your
[1]countryman you shall not charge interest, so that the LORD
your God may bless you in all [2]that you undertake in the land
which you are about to enter to [3]possess.
21 "[a]When you make a vow to the LORD your God, you

shall not delay to pay it, for it would be sin in you, [1]and the
LORD your God will surely require it of you.
22 "However, if you refrain from vowing, it would not be
sin in you.
23 "You shall be careful to perform what goes out from
your lips, just as you have voluntarily vowed to the LORD your
God, what you have [1]promised.
24 "When you enter your neighbor's vineyard, then you
may eat grapes [1]until you are fully satisfied, but you shall not
put any in your [2]basket.
25 "[a]When you enter your neighbor's standing grain, then
you may pluck the heads with your hand, but you shall not
wield a sickle in your neighbor's standing grain.

CHAPTER 24

"WHEN a man takes a wife and marries her, and it happens [1]that she finds no favor in his eyes because he has found
some [a]indecency in her, and [b]he writes her a certificate of
divorce and puts *it* in her hand and sends her out from his
house,
2 and she leaves his house and goes and becomes another
man's *wife,*
3 and if the latter husband [1]turns against her and writes
her a certificate of divorce and puts *it* in her hand and sends
her out of his house, or if the latter husband dies who took her
to be his wife,
4 *then* her former husband who sent her away is not
allowed to take her again to be his wife, since she has been
defiled; for that is an abomination before the LORD, and you
shall not bring sin on the land which the LORD your God gives
you as an inheritance.
5 "[a]When a man takes a new wife, he shall not go out with
the army, nor be charged with any duty; he shall be free at
home one year and shall give happiness to his wife whom he
has taken.
6 "No one shall take a handmill or an upper millstone in
pledge, for he would be taking a life in pledge.
7 "[a]If a man is [1]caught kidnapping any of his [2]countrymen
of the sons of Israel, and he deals with him violently, or sells
him, then that thief shall die; so you shall purge the evil from
among you.
8 "[a]Be careful against [1]an infection of leprosy, that you
diligently observe and do according to all that the Levitical
priests shall teach you; as I have commanded them, so you
shall be careful to do.
9 "Remember what the LORD your God did [a]to Miriam on
the way as you came out of Egypt.
10 "[a]When you make your neighbor a loan of any sort, you
shall not enter his house to take his pledge.
11 "You shall remain outside, and the man to whom you
make the loan shall bring the pledge out to you.
12 "And if he is a poor man, you shall not sleep with his
pledge.

21 [1]Lit., *for*

23 [1]Lit., *spoken with your mouth*

24 [1]Lit., *according to your satisfaction of your soul* [2]Or, *vessel*

25 [a]Matt. 12:1; Mark 2:23; Luke 6:1

1 [1]Lit., *if* [a]Deut. 22:13-21; Num. 5:12, 28 [b]Matt. 5:31; 19:7-9; Mark 10:4, 5

3 [1]Lit., *hates her*

5 [a]Deut. 20:7

7 [1]Lit., *found stealing* [2]Lit., *brothers* [a]Ex. 21:16

8 [1]Lit., *a mark or stroke* [a]Lev. 13:1-14, 57

9 [a]Num. 12:10

10 [a]Ex. 22:26, 27

13 "When the sun goes down you shall surely return the
pledge to him, that he may sleep in his cloak and bless you;
and [a]it will be righteousness for you before the LORD your
God.
14 "[a]You shall not oppress a hired servant *who is* poor and
needy, whether *he is* one of your [1]countrymen or one of your
aliens who is in your land in your [2]towns.
15 "[a]You shall give him his wages on his day [1]before the sun
sets, for he is poor and sets his [2]heart on it; so that [b]he may not
cry against you to the LORD and it become sin in you.
16 "[a]Fathers shall not be put to death [1]for *their* sons, nor
shall sons be put to death [1]for *their* fathers; everyone shall be
put to death for his own sin.
17 "[a]You shall not pervert the justice [1]due an alien *or* an
[2]orphan, nor take a widow's garment in pledge.
18 "But you shall remember that you were a slave in Egypt,
and that the LORD your God redeemed you from there; therefore I am commanding you to do this thing.
19 "[a]When you reap your harvest in your field and have
forgotten a sheaf in the field, you shall not go back to get it; it
shall be [b]for the alien, for the [1]orphan, and for the widow, in
order that the LORD your God may bless you in all the work of
your hands.
20 "[a]When you beat your olive tree, you shall not go over
the boughs [1]again; it shall be [b]for the alien, for the [2]orphan,
and for the widow.
21 "When you gather the grapes of your vineyard, you shall
not [1]go over it again; it shall be for the alien, for the [2]orphan,
and for the widow.
22 "And you shall remember that you were a slave in the
land of Egypt; therefore I am commanding you to do this
thing.

CHAPTER 25

"[a]IF there is a dispute between men and they go to [1]court,
and [2]the judges decide their case, [b]and they justify the righteous and condemn the wicked,
2 then it shall be if the wicked man [1]deserves to be beat-
en, the judge shall then make him lie down and be beaten in
his presence with the number of stripes according to his [2]guilt.
3 "[a]He may beat him forty times *but* no more, lest he beat
him with many more stripes than these, and your brother be
degraded in your eyes.
4 "[a]You shall not muzzle the ox while he is threshing.
5 "When brothers live together and one of them dies and
has no son, the wife of the deceased shall not be *married*
outside *the family* to a strange man. [a]Her husband's brother
shall go in to her and take her to himself as wife and perform
the duty of a husband's brother to her.
6 "And it shall be that the first-born whom she bears shall
[1]assume the name of his dead brother, that [a]his name may not
be blotted out from Israel.
7 "[a]But if the man does not desire to take his brother's

13 [a]Deut. 6:25

14 [1]Lit., *brothers* [2]Lit., *gates* [a]Deut. 15:7-18; Lev. 25:35-43; 1 Tim. 5:18

15 [1]Lit., *that the sun shall not go down on it* [2]Lit., *soul* [a]Lev. 19:13; James 5:4 [b]Deut. 15:9; Ex. 22:23

16 [1]Or, *with* [a]2 Kin. 14:6; 2 Chr. 25:4; Jer. 31:29, 30; Ezek. 18:20

17 [1]Lit., *of* [2]Or, *fatherless* [a]Deut. 1:17; 10:17; 16:19

19 [1]Or, *fatherless* [a]Lev. 19:9, 10; 23:22 [b]Deut. 14:29

20 [1]Lit., *after yourself* [2]Or, *fatherless* [a]Lev. 19:10 [b]Deut. 24:19

21 [1]Lit., *glean it after yourself* [2]Or, *fatherless*

1 [1]Lit., *the judgment* [2]Lit., *they judge them* [a]Deut. 17:8-13; 19:17 [b]Deut. 1:16, 17

2 [1]Lit., *is a son of beating* [2]Or, *wickedness*

3 [a]2 Cor. 11:24

4 [a]1 Cor. 9:9; 1 Tim. 5:18

5 [a]Matt. 22:24; Mark 12:19; Luke 20:28

6 [1]Lit., *stand on* [a]Ruth 4:5, 10

7 [a]Ruth 4:1, 2

wife, then his brother's wife shall go up to the gate to the
elders and say, 'My husband's brother refuses to establish a
name for his brother in Israel; he is not willing to perform the
duty of a husband's brother to me.'
8 "Then the elders of his city shall summon him and speak
to him. And *if* he persists and says, 'I do not desire to take her,'
9 [a]then his brother's wife shall come to him in the sight
of the elders, and pull his sandal off his foot and [b]spit in his
face; and she shall [1]declare, 'Thus it is done to the man who
does not build up his brother's house.'
10 "And in Israel his name shall be called, 'The house of
him whose sandal is removed.'
11 "If *two* men, a man and his [1]countryman, are struggling
together, and the wife of one comes near to deliver her husband from the hand of the one who is striking him, and puts
out her hand and seizes his genitals,
12 then you shall cut off her [1]hand; [2a]you shall not show
pity.
13 "[a]You shall not have in your bag [1]differing weights, a
large and a small.
14 "You shall not have in your house [1]differing measures, a
large and a small.
15 "You shall have a full and just weight; you shall have a
full and just [1]measure, that your days may be prolonged in the
[2]land which the LORD your God gives you.
16 "For everyone who does these things, everyone who acts
unjustly is an abomination to the LORD your God.
17 "[a]Remember what Amalek did to you along the way
when you came out from Egypt,
18 how he met you along the way and attacked among you
all the stragglers at your rear when you were faint and weary;
and he did not [1]fear God.
19 "Therefore it shall come about when the LORD your
God has given you [a]rest from all your surrounding enemies, in
the land which the LORD your God gives you as an inheritance
to [1]possess, you shall blot out the memory of Amalek from
under heaven; you must not forget.

CHAPTER 26

"THEN it shall be, when you enter the land which the LORD
your God gives you as an inheritance, and you possess it and
live in it,
2 that you shall take some of [a]the first of all the produce
of the ground which you shall bring in from your land that the
LORD your God gives you, and you shall put *it* in a basket and
go to the place where the LORD your God chooses to establish
His name.
3 "And you shall go to the priest who is in office at that
time, and say to him, 'I declare this day to the LORD [1]my God
that I have entered the land which the LORD swore to our
fathers to give us.'
4 "Then the priest shall take the basket from your hand
and set it down before the altar of the LORD your God.
5 "And you shall answer and say before the LORD your
God, '[a]My father was a [1]wandering Aramean, and he went

9 [1]Lit., *answer and say* [a]Ruth 4:7, 8 [b]Num. 12:14

11 [1]Lit., *brother*

12 [1]Lit., *palm* [2]Lit., *your eye* [a]Deut. 7:2

13 [1]Lit., *a stone and a stone* [a]Lev. 19:35-37

14 [1]Lit., *an ephah and an ephah*

15 [1]Lit., *ephah* [2]Lit., *ground*

17 [a]Ex. 17:8-16

18 [1]Or, *reverence*

19 [1]Lit., *possess it* [a]Deut. 12:9

2 [a]Ex. 22:29; 23:16, 19

3 [1]So with Gk; Heb., *your*

5 [1]Or, *perishing* [a]Gen. 25:30; 31:40-42; 43:1-14

down to Egypt and [2]sojourned there, [b]few in number; but
there he became a [c]great, mighty and populous nation.
6 'And the Egyptians treated us harshly and afflicted us,
and imposed hard labor on us.
7 'Then we cried to the LORD, the God of our fathers, and
the LORD heard our voice and saw our affliction and our toil
and our oppression;
8 [a]and the LORD brought us out of Egypt with a mighty
hand and an outstretched arm and with great terror and with
signs and wonders;
9 and He has brought us to this place, and has given us
this land, [a]a land flowing with milk and honey.
10 'And now behold, I have brought the first of the produce of the ground which Thou, O LORD hast given me.' And
you shall set it down before the LORD your God, and worship
before the LORD your God;
11 and you and [a]the Levite and the alien who is among
you shall [b]rejoice in all the good which the LORD your God has
given you and your household.
12 "[a]When you have finished [1]paying all the tithe of your
increase in the third year, the year of tithing, then you shall
give it to the Levite, to the stranger, to the [2]orphan and to the
widow, that they may eat in your [3]towns, and be satisfied.
13 "And you shall say before the LORD your God, 'I have
removed the sacred *portion* from *my* house, and also have
given it to the Levite and the alien, the [1]orphan and the widow, according to all Thy commandments which Thou hast
commanded me; I have not transgressed or forgotten any of
Thy commandments.
14 'I have not eaten of it [1]while mourning, nor have I
removed any of it while I was unclean, nor offered any of it to
the dead. I have listened to the voice of the LORD my God; I
have done according to all that Thou hast commanded me.
15 'Look down from Thy holy habitation, from heaven,
and bless Thy people Israel, and the ground which Thou hast
given us, [a]a land flowing with milk and honey, as Thou didst
swear to our fathers.'
16 "This day the LORD your God commands you to do
these statutes and ordinances. You shall therefore be careful to
do them [a]with all your heart and with all your soul.
17 "You have today declared the LORD to be your God, and
[1]that you would walk in His ways and keep His statutes, His
commandments and His ordinances, and listen to His voice.
18 "And the LORD has today declared you to be [a]His
people, a treasured possession, as He promised you, and [1]that
you should keep all His commandments;
19 and [1]that He shall [a]set you high above all nations which
He has made, for praise, fame, and honor; and that you shall
be [b]a consecrated people to the LORD your God, as He has
spoken."

CHAPTER 27

THEN Moses and the elders of Israel charged the people,
saying, "Keep all the commandments which I command you
today.

5 [2]Or, *lived as an alien* [b]Gen. 46:27 [c]Deut. 1:10; 10:22
8 [a]Deut. 4:34
9 [a]Ex. 3:8, 17
11 [a]Deut. 12:12 [b]Deut. 12:7
12 [1]Lit., *tithing* [2]Or, *fatherless* [3]Lit., *gates* [a]Deut. 14:28, 29; Heb. 7:5, 9, 10
13 [1]Or, *fatherless*
14 [1]Lit., *while in my*
15 [a]Deut. 26:9
16 [a]Deut. 4:29
17 [1]Lit., *to walk in*
18 [1]Lit., *to keep all* [a]Deut. 7:6
19 [1]Lit., *to set you* [a]Deut. 28:1, 13 [b]Deut. 7:6

2 "[a]So it shall be on the day when you shall cross the
Jordan to the land which the LORD your God gives you, that
you shall set up for yourself large stones, and coat them with
lime
3 and write on them all the words of this law, when you
cross over, in order that you may enter the land which the
LORD your God gives you, [a]a land flowing with milk and honey, as the LORD, the God of your fathers, [1]promised you.
4 "So it shall be when you cross the Jordan, you shall set
up on Mount Ebal, these stones, [1]as I am commanding you
today, and you shall coat them with lime.
5 "Moreover, you shall build there an altar to the LORD
your God, an altar of stones; you shall not [1]wield an iron *tool*
on them.
6 "You shall build the altar of the LORD your God of
[1]uncut stones; and you shall offer on it burnt offerings to the
LORD your God;
7 and you shall sacrifice peace offerings and eat there,
and you shall [a]rejoice before the LORD your God.
8 "And you shall write on the [1]stones all the words of this
law very distinctly."
9 Then Moses and the Levitical priests spoke to all
Israel, saying, "Be silent and listen, O Israel! This day you have
become a people for the LORD your God.
10 "You shall therefore [1]obey the LORD your God, and do
His commandments and His statutes which I command you
today."
11 Moses also charged the people on that day, saying,
12 "When you cross the Jordan, these shall stand on
Mount Gerizim to bless the people: [a]Simeon, Levi, Judah,
Issachar, Joseph, and Benjamin.
13 "And for the curse, these shall stand on Mount Ebal:
Reuben, Gad, Asher, Zebulun, Dan, and Naphtali.
14 "The Levites shall then answer and say to all the men of
Israel with a loud voice,
15 'Cursed is the man who makes [1a]an idol or a molten
image, an abomination to the LORD, the work of the hands of
the craftsman, and sets *it* up in secret.' And all the people shall
answer and say, 'Amen.'
16 '[a]Cursed is he who dishonors his father or mother.' And
all the people shall say, 'Amen.'
17 '[a]Cursed is he who moves his neighbor's boundary
mark.' And all the people shall say, 'Amen.'
18 '[a]Cursed is he who misleads a blind *person* on the road.'
And all the people shall say, 'Amen.'
19 '[a]Cursed is he who distorts the justice due an alien,
[1]orphan, and widow.' And all the people shall say, 'Amen.'
20 '[a]Cursed is he who lies with his father's wife, because he
has uncovered his father's skirt.' And all the people shall say,
'Amen.'
21 '[a]Cursed is he who lies with any animal.' And all the
people shall say, 'Amen.'
22 '[a]Cursed is he who lies with his sister, the daughter of his
father or of his mother.' And all the people shall say, 'Amen.'
23 '[a]Cursed is he who lies with his mother-in-law.' And all
the people shall say, 'Amen.'

2 [a]Josh. 8:30-32
3 [1]Lit., *spoke to* [a]Deut. 26:9
4 [1]Lit., *which*
5 [1]Lit., *lift up*
6 [1]Lit., *whole*
7 [a]Deut. 26:11
8 [1]I.e., stones coated with lime, cf. vs. 4
10 [1]Lit., *listen to the voice of*
12 [a]Josh. 8:33-35
15 [1]Or, *a graven image* [a]Ex. 20:4, 23; 34:17
16 [a]Ex. 21:17; Lev. 20:9; Ezek. 22:7
17 [a]Deut. 19:14
18 [a]Lev. 19:14
19 [1]Or, *fatherless* [a]Deut. 14:17
20 [a]Deut. 22:30; Lev. 18:8; 20:11
21 [a]Ex. 22:19; Lev. 18:23
22 [a]Lev. 18:9; 20:17
23 [a]Lev. 20:14

24 '[a]Cursed is he who strikes his neighbor in secret.' And all
the people shall say, 'Amen.'
25 '[a]Cursed is he who accepts a bribe to strike down an
innocent person.' And all the people shall say, 'Amen.'
26 '[a]Cursed is he who does not confirm the words of this
law by doing them.' And all the people shall say, 'Amen.'

Chapter 28

"[a]Now it shall be, if you will diligently [1]obey the Lord
your God, being careful to do all His commandments which I
command you today, the Lord your God [b]will set you high
above all the nations of the earth.
2 "And all these blessings shall come upon you and overtake you, if you will [1]obey the Lord your God.
3 "Blessed *shall* you *be* in the city, and blessed *shall* you
be in the [1]country.
4 "Blessed *shall be* the [1]offspring of your [2]body and the
[1]produce of your ground and the [1]offspring of your beasts, the
increase of your herd and the young of your flock.
5 "Blessed *shall be* your basket and your kneading bowl.
6 "Blessed *shall* you *be* when you come in, and blessed
shall you *be* when you go out.
7 "The Lord will cause your enemies who rise up against
you to be [1]defeated before you; they shall come out against
you one way and shall flee before you seven ways.
8 "The Lord will command the blessing upon you in your
barns and in all that you put your hand to, and He will bless
you in the land which the Lord your God gives you.
9 "The Lord will establish you as a holy people to Himself, as He swore to you, if you will keep the commandments
of the Lord your God, and walk in His ways.
10 "So all the peoples of the earth shall see that [1]you are
called by the name of the Lord; and they shall be afraid of
you.
11 "[a]And the Lord will make you abound in prosperity, in
the [1]offspring of your [2]body and in the [1]offspring of your beast
and in the [1]produce of your ground, in the land which the
Lord swore to your fathers to give you.
12 "The Lord will open for you His good storehouse, the
heavens, to give rain to your land in its season and to bless all
the work of your hand; and [a]you shall lend to many nations,
but you shall not borrow.
13 "[a]And the Lord shall make you the head and not the
tail, and you only shall be above, and you shall not be underneath, if you will listen to the commandments of the Lord
your God, which I charge you today, to [1]observe *them*
carefully,
14 and [a]do not turn aside from any of the words which I
command you today, to the right or to the left, to go after
other gods to serve them.
15 "[a]But it shall come about, if you will not [1]obey the Lord
your God, to observe to do all His commandments and His

24 [a]Ex. 21:12; Lev. 24:17; Num. 35:30, 31
25 [a]Ex. 23:7
26 [a]Gal. 3:10
1 [1]Lit., *listen to the voice of* [a]Deut. 7:12-26; Ex. 23:22-27 Lev. 26:3-13 [b]Deut. 28:13; 26:19
2 [1]Lit., *listen to the voice of*
3 [1]Or, *field*
4 [1]Lit., *fruit* [2]Lit., *womb*
7 [1]Lit., *smitten*
10 [1]Lit., *the name of the* Lord *is called upon you*
11 [1]Lit., *fruit* [2]Or, *womb* [a]Deut. 28:4
12 [a]Deut. 23:20
13 [1]Lit., *keep and do* [a]Deut. 28:1, 44
14 [a]Deut. 5:32
15 [1]Lit., *listen to the voice of* [a]Lev. 26:14-43; Josh. 23:15

statutes which I charge you today, that all these curses shall
come upon you and overtake you.
16 "[a]Cursed *shall* you *be* in the city, and cursed *shall* you be
in the [1]country.
17 "[a]Cursed *shall be* your basket and your kneading bowl.
18 "[a]Cursed *shall be* the [1]offspring of your [2]body and the
[1]produce of your ground, the increase of your herd and the
young of your flock.
19 "[a]Cursed *shall* you *be* when you come in, and cursed
shall you *be* when you go out.
20 "[a]The LORD will send upon you curses, confusion, and
rebuke, in all [1]you undertake to do, until you are destroyed
and until [b]you perish quickly, on account of the evil of your
deeds, because you have forsaken Me.
21 "[a]The LORD will make the pestilence cling to you until
He has consumed you from the land, where you are entering
to possess it.
22 "The LORD will smite you with consumption and with
fever and with inflammation and with fiery heat and with [1]the
sword and [a]with blight and with mildew, and they shall pursue
you until [b]you perish.
23 "And [1]the heaven which is over your head shall be
bronze, and the earth which is under you, iron.
24 "[a]The LORD will make the rain of your land powder and
dust; from heaven it shall come down on you until you are
destroyed.
25 "[a]The LORD will cause you to be [1]defeated before your
enemies; you shall go out one way against them, but you shall
flee seven ways before them, and you shall [b]be *an example of*
terror to all the kingdoms of the earth.
26 "[a]And your carcasses shall be food to all birds of the sky
and to the beasts of the earth, and there shall be no one to
frighten *them* away.
27 "[a]The LORD will smite you with the boils of Egypt and
with hemorrhoids and with the scab and with the itch, from
which you cannot be healed.
28 "The LORD will smite you with madness and with blindness and with bewilderment of heart;
29 and you shall [1a]grope at noon, as the blind man gropes
in darkness, and you shall not prosper in your ways; but you
shall only be oppressed and robbed continually, with none to
save you.
30 "You shall betroth a wife, but another man shall violate
her; [a]you shall build a house, but you shall not live in it; you
shall plant a vineyard, but you shall not [1]use its fruit.
31 "Your ox shall be slaughtered before your eyes, but you
shall not eat of it; your donkey shall be torn away from you,
and shall not be restored to you; your sheep shall be given to
your enemies, and you shall have none to save you.
32 "[a]Your sons and your daughters shall be given to another
people, while your eyes shall look on and yearn for them
continually; but there shall be nothing [1]you can do.
33 "A people whom you do not know shall eat up the produce of your ground and all your labors, and you shall never be
anything but oppressed and crushed continually.

16 [1]Or, *field* [a]Deut. 28:3

17 [a]Deut. 28:5

18 [1]Lit., *fruit* [2]Or, *womb* [a]Deut. 28:4

19 [a]Deut. 28:6

20 [1]Lit., *the putting forth of your hand which you do* [a]Deut. 28:8 [b]Deut. 4:26

21 [a]Lev. 26:25; Num. 14:12

22 [1]Another reading is, *drought* [a]Amos 4:9 [b]Deut. 4:29

23 [1]Lit., *your*

24 [a]Deut. 28:12; 11:17

25 [1]Lit., *smitten* [a]Deut. 28:7 [b]2 Chr. 29:8; Jer. 15:4

26 [a]Jer. 7:33; 16:4; 19:7; 34:20

27 [a]Deut. 28:60, 61; 7:15

29 [1]Lit., *be groping* [a]Ex. 10:21

30 [1]Lit., *begin it* [a]Amos 5:11

32 [1]Lit., *in the power of your hand* [a]Deut. 28:41

34 “And you shall be driven mad by the sight of [1]what you
see.
35 “[a]The LORD will strike you on the knees and legs with
sore boils, from which you cannot be healed, from the sole of
your foot to the crown of your head.
36 “[a]The LORD will bring you and your king whom you
shall set over you to a nation which neither you nor your
fathers have known, and there you shall serve other gods,
[b]wood and stone.
37 “And [a]you shall become a horror, a proverb, and a taunt
among all the people where the LORD will drive you.
38 “[a]You shall bring out much seed to the field but you
shall gather in little, for [b]the locust shall consume it.
39 “[a]You shall plant and cultivate vineyards, but you shall
neither drink of the wine nor gather *the grapes*, for the worm
shall devour them.
40 “[a]You shall have olive trees throughout your territory
but you shall not anoint yourself with the oil, for your olives
shall drop off.
41 “[a]You shall [1]have sons and daughters but they shall not
be yours, for they shall go into captivity.
42 “[a]The cricket shall possess all your trees and the produce
of your ground.
43 “[a]The alien who is among you shall rise above you higher and higher, but you shall go down lower and lower.
44 “[a]He shall lend to you, but you shall not lend to him;
[b]he shall be the head, and you shall be the tail.
45 “So all these curses shall come on you and pursue you
and overtake you [a]until you are destroyed, because you would
not [1]obey the LORD your God by keeping His commandments
and His statutes which He commanded you.
46 “And they shall become a sign and a wonder on you and
your [1]descendants forever.
47 “[a]Because you did not serve the LORD your God with joy
and a glad heart, for the abundance of all things;
48 therefore you shall serve your enemies whom the LORD
shall send against you, [a]in hunger, in thirst, in nakedness, and
in the lack of all things; and He [b]will put an iron yoke on your
neck until He has destroyed you.
49 “[a]The LORD will bring a nation against you from afar,
from the end of the earth, as the eagle swoops down, a nation
whose language you shall not understand,
50 a nation of fierce countenance who shall have no respect
for the old, nor show favor to the young.
51 “Moreover, it shall eat the [1]offspring of your herd and
the produce of your ground until you are destroyed, who also
leaves you no grain, new wine, or oil, nor the increase of your
herd or the young of your flock until they have caused you to
perish.
52 “[a]And it shall besiege you in all your [1]towns until your
high and fortified walls in which you trusted come down
throughout your land, and it shall besiege you in all your
[1]towns throughout your land which the LORD your God has
given you.
53 “[a]Then you shall eat the [1]offspring of your own body,
the flesh of your sons and of your daughters whom the LORD

34 [1]Lit., *your eyes which you*

35 [a]Deut. 28:27

36 [a]2 Kin. 17:4, 6; 24:12, 14; 25:7, 11 [b]Deut. 4:28

37 [a]Jer. 19:8; 29:18

38 [a]Is. 5:10; Mic. 6:15 [b]Joel 1:4

39 [a]Is. 5:10; 17:10, 11

40 [a]Jer. 11:16; Mic. 6:15

41 [1]Lit., *beget* [a]Deut. 28:32

42 [a]Deut. 28:38

43 [a]Deut. 28:13

44 [a]Deut. 28:12 [b]Deut. 28:13

45 [1]Lit., *listen to the voice of* [a]Deut. 4:25, 26

46 [1]Lit., *seed*

47 [a]Deut. 12:7

48 [a]Lam. 4:4-6 [b]Jer. 28:13, 14

49 [a]Is. 5:26-30; 7:18-20

51 [1]Lit., *fruit*

52 [1]Lit., *gates* [a]Jer. 10:17, 18; Zeph. 1:15, 16

53 [1]Lit., *fruit* [a]Lev. 26:29; Jer. 19:9; Lam. 2:20

your God has given you, during the siege and the distress by
which your enemy shall [2]oppress you.
54 "The man who is [1]refined and very delicate among you
[2]shall be hostile toward his brother and toward the wife [3]he
cherishes and toward the rest of his children who remain,
55 so that he will not give *even* one of them any of the
flesh of his children which he shall eat, since he has nothing
else left, during the siege and the distress by which your enemy
shall [1]oppress you in all your [2]towns.
56 "[a]The [1]refined and delicate woman among you, who
would not venture to set the sole of her foot on the ground for
delicateness and [2]refinement, [3]shall be hostile toward the husband [4]she cherishes and toward her son and daughter,
57 and toward her afterbirth which issues from between
her [1]legs and toward her children whom she bears; for she shall
eat them secretly for lack of anything *else*, during the siege and
the distress by which your enemy shall [2]oppress you in your
[3]towns.
58 "If you are not careful to observe all the words of this
law which are written in this book, to [1]fear this honored and
awesome name, [2]the LORD your God,
59 then the LORD will bring extraordinary plagues on you
and [1]your descendants, even [2]severe and lasting plagues, and
miserable and chronic sicknesses.
60 "[a]And He will bring back on you all the diseases of
Egypt of which you were afraid, and they shall cling to you.
61 "Also every sickness and every plague which, not written
in the book of this law, the LORD will bring them on you [a]until
you are destroyed.
62 "Then you shall be left few in number, [a]whereas you
were as the stars of heaven for multitude, because you did not
[1]obey the LORD your God.
63 "And it shall come about that as the LORD delighted
over you to prosper you, and multiply you, so the LORD will
delight over you to make you perish and destroy you; and you
shall be [a]torn from the land where you are entering to possess
it.
64 "Moreover, the LORD will [a]scatter you among all
peoples, from one end of the earth to the other end of the
earth; and there you shall [b]serve other gods, wood and stone,
which you or your fathers have not known.
65 "And [a]among those nations you shall find no rest, and
there shall be no resting place for the sole of your foot; but
there the LORD will give you a trembling heart, failing of eyes,
and despair of soul.
66 "So your life shall [1]hang in doubt before you; and you
shall be in dread night and day, and shall have no assurance of
your life.
67 "In the morning you shall say, 'Would that it were evening!' And at evening you shall say, 'Would that it were morning!' because of the dread of your heart which you dread, and
for the sight of your eyes which you shall see.
68 "And the LORD will bring you back to Egypt in ships, by
the way about which [a]I spoke to you, 'You will never see it
again!' And there you shall offer yourselves for sale to your
enemies as male and female slaves, but there will be no buyer."

53 [2]Or, *distress*

54 [1]Lit., *tender* [2]Lit., *his eye shall be evil toward* [3]Lit., *of his bosom*

55 [1]Or, *distress* [2]Lit., *gates*

56 [1]Lit., *tender* [2]Lit., *tenderness* [3]Lit., *her eye shall be evil toward* [4]Lit., *of her bosom* [a]Lam. 4:10

57 [1]Lit., *feet* [2]Or, *distress* [3]Lit., *gates*

58 [1]Or, *reverence* [2]YHWH, or Yahweh

59 [1]Lit., *plague on your seed* [2]Lit., *great*

60 [a]Deut. 28:27

61 [a]Deut. 4:25, 26

62 [1]Lit., *listen to the voice of* [a]Deut. 1:10

63 [a]Jer. 12:14; 45:4

64 [a]Deut. 4:27 [b]Deut. 4:28; 29:26; 32:17

65 [a]Lam. 1:3

66 [1]Lit., *be hung for you in front;*

68 [a]Ex. 13:14

1 [1]Chap. 28:69 in Heb. [a]Lev. 26:46; 27:34 [b]Deut. 5:2, 3
2 [1]Chap. 29:1 in Heb.
4 [a]Rom. 11:8; Is. 6:9, 10; Acts 28:26, 27
5 [a]Deut. 8:4
6 [a]Deut. 8:3
7 [1]Lit., *came to* [2]Lit., *smote* [a]Deut. 2:26-3:17; Num. 21:21-24, 33, 35
8 [a]Deut. 3:12, 13; Num. 32:32
9 [a]Deut. 4:6 [b]Josh. 1:7
11 [a]Josh. 9:21, 23, 27
13 [a]Gen. 17:7; Ex. 6:7
17 [a]Deut. 4:28; 28:36; Ex. 20:23
18 [a]Deut. 13:6 [b]Deut. 32:32; Heb. 12:15

Chapter 29

1[a] THESE are the words of the covenant which the LORD commanded Moses to make with the sons of Israel in the land of
Moab, besides the [b]covenant which He had made with them at
Horeb.
2 [1]And Moses summoned all Israel and said to them,
"You have seen all that the LORD did before your eyes in the
land of Egypt to Pharaoh and all his servants and all his land;
3 the great trials which your eyes have seen, those great
signs and wonders.
4 "Yet to this day [a]the LORD has not given you a heart to
know, nor eyes to see, nor ears to hear.
5 "And I have led you forty years in the wilderness; [a]your
clothes have not worn out on you, and your sandal has not
worn out on your foot.
6 "[a]You have not eaten bread, nor have you drunk wine or
strong drink, in order that you might know that I am the LORD
your God.
7 "[a]When you [1]reached this place, Sihon the king of Heshbon and Og the king of Bashan came out to meet us for
battle, but we [2]defeated them;
8 and we took their land and [a]gave it as an inheritance to
the Reubenites, the Gadites, and the half-tribe of the
Manassites.
9 "[a]So keep the words of this covenant to do them, [b]that
you may prosper in all that you do.
10 "You stand today, all of you, before the LORD your God:
your chiefs, your tribes, your elders and your officers, *even* all
the men of Israel,
11 your little ones, your wives, and the alien who is within
your camps, from [a]the one who chops your wood to the one
who draws your water,
12 that you may enter into the covenant with the LORD
your God, and into His oath which the LORD your God is
making with you today,
13 in order that He may establish you today as His people
and that [a]He may be your God, just as He spoke to you and as
He swore to your fathers, to Abraham, Isaac, and Jacob.
14 "Now not with you alone am I making this covenant
and this oath,
15 but both with those who stand here with us today in the
presence of the LORD our God and with those who are not with
us here today
16 (for you know how we lived in the land of Egypt, and
how we came through the midst of the nations through which
you passed.
17 "Moreover, you have seen their abominations and their
idols *of* [a]wood, stone, silver, and gold, which *they had* with
them);
18 [a]lest there shall be among you a man or woman, or
family or tribe, whose heart turns away today from the LORD
our God, to go and serve the gods of those nations; lest there
shall be among you [b]a root bearing poisonous fruit and
wormwood.
19 "And it shall be when he hears the words of this curse,

that he will [1]boast, saying, 'I have peace though I walk in the
stubbornness of my heart in order [2]to destroy the watered *land*
with the dry.'
20 "The LORD shall never be willing to forgive him, but
rather the anger of the LORD and His jealousy will [1a]burn
against that man, and every curse which is written in this book
will [2]rest on him, and the LORD will [b]blot out his name from
under heaven.
21 "Then the LORD will single him out for [1]adversity from
all the tribes of Israel, according to all the curses of the covenant
[a]which are written in this book of the law.
22 "Now the generation to come, your sons who rise up
after you and [a]the foreigner who comes from a distant land,
when they see the plagues of the land and the diseases with
which the LORD has [1]afflicted it, will say,
23 'All its land is [a]brimstone and salt, [b]a burning waste,
[1]unsown and unproductive, and no grass grows in it, like the
overthrow of Sodom and Gomorrah, Admah and Zeboiim,
which the LORD overthrew in His anger and in His wrath.'
24 "And all the nations shall say, 'Why has the LORD done
thus to this land? Why this great [1]outburst of anger?'
25 "Then *men* shall say, '[a]Because they forsook the covenant
of the LORD, the God of their fathers, which He made
with them when He brought them out of the land of Egypt.
26 'And they went and served other gods and worshiped
them, gods whom they have not known and whom He had not
[1]allotted to them.
27 'Therefore, the anger of the LORD burned against that
land, to bring upon it every curse which is written in this book;
28 and [a]the LORD uprooted them from their land in anger
and in fury and in great wrath, and cast them into another
land, as *it is* this day.'
29 "The secret things belong to the LORD our God, but the
things revealed belong to us and to our sons forever, that we
may observe all the words of this law.

CHAPTER 30

"So it shall become when all of these things have come
upon you, [a]the blessing and the curse which I have set before
you, and you [1]call *them* to mind [b]in all nations where the LORD
your God has banished you,
2 and you [a]return to the LORD your God and [1]obey Him
[b]with all your heart and soul according to all that I command
you today, you and your sons,
3 then the LORD your God will [a]restore [1]you from captivity, and have compassion on you, and will gather you again
from all the peoples where the LORD your God has [b]scattered
you.
4 "If your outcasts are at the ends of the [1]earth, [a]from
there the LORD your God will gather you, and from there He
will [2]bring you back.
5 "And [a]the LORD your God will bring you into the land
which your fathers possessed, and you shall possess it; and He
will prosper you and [b]multiply you more than your fathers.
6 "Moreover the LORD your God will circumcise your

19 [1]Lit., *bless himself in his heart* [2]I.e., to destroy everything

20 [1]Lit., *smoke* [2]Lit., *lie down*
[a]Ps. 74:1; 80:4 [b]Deut. 9:14; Ex. 32:33; 2 Kin. 14:27

21 [1]Lit., *evil*
[a]Deut. 30:10

22 [1]Lit., *made it sick*
[a]Jer. 19:8; 49:17; 50:13

23 [1]Lit., *it is not sown and does not cause to sprout*
[a]Gen. 19:24; Is. 34:9 [b]Is. 1:7; 64:11

24 [1]Lit., *heat*

25 [a]2 Kin. 17:9-23; 2 Chr. 36:13-21

26 [1]Lit., *portioned*

28 [a]Ezek. 19:12, 13

1 [1]Lit., *cause them to return to your heart*
[a]Deut. 30:15, 19; 11:26
[b]Deut. 28:64; 29:28; Lev. 26:40-45

2 [1]Lit., *listen to His voice*
[a]Deut. 4:29, 30 [b]Deut. 4:29

3 [1]Lit., *your captivity*
[a]Gen. 28:15; 48:21 [b]Deut. 4:27

4 [1]Lit., *sky* [2]Lit., *take you*
[a]Neh. 1:9; Is. 43:6; 48:20; 62:11

5 [a]Jer. 29:14; 30:3 [b]Deut. 7:13; 13:17

heart and the heart of your [1]descendants, [a]to love the LORD
your God with all your heart and with all your soul, in order
that you may live.
7 "[a]And the LORD your God will [1]inflict all these curses on
your enemies and on those who hate you, who persecuted you.
8 "And you shall again [1]obey the LORD, and observe all
His commandments which I command you today.
9 "[a]Then the LORD your God will [1]prosper you abundantly in all the work of your hand, in the [2]offspring of your [3]body
and in the [2]offspring of your cattle and in the [2]produce of your
ground, for the LORD will again rejoice over you for good, just
as He rejoiced over your fathers;
10 [1]if you [2]obey the LORD your God to keep His commandments and His statutes which [a]are written in this book of the
law, [1]if you turn to the LORD your God [b]with all your heart and
soul.
11 "For this commandment which I command you today is
not too difficult for you, nor is it [1]out of reach.
12 "It is not in heaven, [1]that you should say, '[a]Who will go
up to heaven for us to get it for us and make us hear it, that we
may observe it?'
13 "Nor is it beyond the sea, [1]that you should say, 'Who
will cross the sea for us to get it for us and make us hear it, that
we may observe it?'
14 "But the word is very near you, in your mouth and in
your heart, that you may observe it.
15 "See, I have set before you today life and [1]prosperity,
and death and [2]adversity;
16 in that I command you today [a]to love the LORD your
God, to walk in His ways and to keep His commandments and
His statutes and His judgments, that you [b]may live and multiply, and that the LORD your God may bless you in the land
where you are entering to possess it.
17 "But if your heart turns away and you will not obey, but
are drawn away and worship other gods and serve them,
18 I declare to you today that [a]you shall surely perish. You
shall not prolong *your* days in the land where you are crossing
the Jordan to enter [1]and possess it.
19 "[a]I call heaven and earth to witness against you today,
that I have set before you life and death, [b]the blessing and the
curse. So choose life in order that you may live, you and your
[1]descendants,
20 [a]by loving the LORD your God, by obeying His voice,
and [b]by holding fast to Him; [c]for [1]this is your life and the
length of your days, [2]that you may live in the land which the
LORD swore to your fathers, to Abraham, Isaac, and Jacob, to
give them."

CHAPTER 31

SO Moses went and spoke these words to all Israel.
2 And he said to them, "I am [a]a hundred and twenty
years old today; I am no longer able to come and go, and the
LORD has said to me, '[b]You shall not cross this Jordan.'
3 "It is the LORD your God who will cross ahead of you;
He will destroy these nations before you, and you shall dispos-

6 [1]Lit., *seed* [a]Deut. 7:15

7 [1]Lit., *put* [a]Deut. 7:15

8 [1]Lit., *listen to the voice of*

9 [1]Lit., *make you have excess for good* [2]Lit., *fruit* [3]Lit., *womb* [a]Jer. 31:27, 28

10 [1]Or, *for you will* [2]Lit., *listen to the voice of* [a]Deut. 29:21 [b]Deut. 4:29

11 [1]Lit., *far off*

12 [1]Lit., *to say* [a]Rom. 10:6-8

13 [1]Lit., *to say*

15 [1]Lit., *good* [2]Lit., *evil*

16 [a]Deut. 6:5 [b]Deut. 30:19; 4:1

18 [1]Lit., *to* [a]Deut. 4:26

19 [1]Lit., *seed* [a]Deut. 4:26 [b]Deut. 30:1

20 [1]Lit., *that* [2]Lit., *to dwell* [a]Deut. 6:5 [b]Deut. 10:20 [c]Deut. 4:1; 32:47

2 [a]Deut. 34:7 [b]Deut. 1:37

sess them. [a]Joshua is the one who will cross ahead of you, just
as the LORD has spoken.
4 "And the LORD will do to them just as He did to Sihon
and Og, the kings of the Amorites, and to their land, when He
destroyed them.
5 "And the LORD will deliver them up before you, and you
shall do to them according to all the commandment which I
have commanded you.
6 "Be strong and courageous, [a]do not be afraid or tremble
at them, for the LORD your God is the one who goes with you.
[b]He will not fail you or forsake you."
7 Then Moses called to Joshua and said to him in the
sight of all Israel, "[a]Be strong and courageous, for you shall go
with this people into the land which the LORD has sworn to
their fathers to give them, and you shall give it to them as an
inheritance.
8 "And the LORD is the one who goes ahead of you; He
will be with you. [a]He will not fail you or forsake you. Do not
fear, or be dismayed."
9 So Moses wrote this law and gave it to the priests, the
sons of Levi [a]who carried the ark of the covenant of the LORD,
and to all the elders of Israel.
10 Then Moses commanded them, saying, "At the end of
every seven years, at the time of [a]the year of remission of
debts, at the Feast of Booths,
11 when all Israel comes to appear before the LORD your
God at [a]the place which He will choose, you shall read this law
in front of all Israel in their hearing.
12 "Assemble the people, the men and the women and
children and [1]the alien who is in your [2]town, in order that they
may hear and [a]learn and fear the LORD your God, and be
careful to observe all the words of this law.
13 "And their children, who have not known will hear and
learn to fear the LORD your God, as long as you live on the
land where you are about to cross over the Jordan to possess
it."
14 Then the LORD said to Moses, "Behold, [1a]the time for
you to die is near; call Joshua, and present yourselves at the
tent of meeting, that I may commission him." [b]So Moses and
Joshua went and presented themselves at the tent of meeting.
15 [a]And the LORD appeared in the tent in a pillar of cloud,
and the pillar of cloud stood at the doorway of the tent.
16 And the LORD said to Moses, "Behold, [a]you are about
to lie down with your fathers; and [b]this people will arise and
play the harlot with the strange gods of the land, into the
midst of which they are going, and [c]will forsake Me and break
My covenant which I have made with them.
17 "[a]Then My anger will be kindled against them in that
day, and I will forsake them and hide My face from them, and
they shall be consumed, and many evils and troubles shall
come upon them; so that they will say in that day, 'Is it not
because our God is not among us that these evils have come
upon us?'
18 "But I will surely hide My face in that day because of all
the evil which they will do, for they will turn to other gods.
19 "Now therefore [a]write this song for yourselves, and

3 [a]Num. 27:18
6 [a]Deut. 20:1 [b]Heb. 13:5
7 [a]Deut. 1:38; 3:28
8 [a]Deut. 31:6
9 [a]Deut. 31:25, 26; 10:8; Num. 4:5, 6, 15
10 [a]Deut. 15:1, 2
11 [a]Deut. 12:5
12 [1]Lit., *your alien* [2]Lit., *gates* [a]Deut. 4:10
14 [1]Lit., *your days to die are* [a]Deut. 4:22; 32:50; Num. 27:12, 13 [b]Ex. 33:9-11
15 [a]Ex. 33:9
16 [a]Gen. 15:15 [b]Deut. 4:25-28; Judg. 2:11, 12 [c]Judg. 10:6
17 [a]Judg. 2:14; 6:13
19 [a]Deut. 31:22

19 [1]Lit., *in their mouth*

teach it to the sons of Israel; put it [1]on their lips, in order that this song may be a witness for Me against the sons of Israel.

20 [1]Lit., *fat* [a]Deut. 6:10-12; 8:10, 19; 11:16, 17 [b]Deut. 32:15-17

20 "[a]For when I bring them into the land flowing with milk and honey, which I swore to their fathers, and they have eaten and are satisfied and [b]become [1]prosperous, then they will turn to other gods and serve them, and spurn Me and break My covenant.

21 [1]Lit., *mouth of its seed* [2]Lit., *making* [a]Deut. 4:30; Lev. 26:41

21 "Then it shall come about, [a]when many evils and troubles have come upon them, that this song will testify before them as a witness (for it shall not be forgotten from the [1]lips of their descendants); for I know their intent which they are [2]developing today, before I have brought them into the land which I swore."

22 [a]Deut. 31:19

22 [a]So Moses wrote this song the same day, and taught it to the sons of Israel.

23 [a]Deut. 31:7 [b]Ex. 3:12

23 [a]Then He commissioned Joshua the son of Nun, and said, "Be strong and courageous, for you shall bring the sons of Israel into the land which I swore to them, and [b]I will be with you."

24 And it came about, when Moses finished writing the words of this law in a book until they were complete,

25 [a]Deut. 31:9

25 that Moses commanded the Levites [a]who carried the ark of the covenant of the LORD, saying,

26 [1]Lit., *be*

26 "Take this book of the law and place it beside the ark of the covenant of the LORD your God, that it may [1]remain there as a witness against you.

27 [1]Lit., *stiff neck* [a]Deut. 9:7 [b]Deut. 9:6, 13

27 "For I know [a]your rebellion and [b]your [1]stubbornness; behold, while I am still alive with you today, you have been rebellious against the LORD; how much more, then, after my death?

28 [a]Deut. 4:26

28 "Assemble to me all the elders of your tribes and your officers, that I may speak these words in their hearing and [a]call the heavens and the earth to witness against them.

29 "For I know that after my death you will act corruptly and turn from the way which I have commanded you; and evil will befall you in the latter days, for you will do that which is evil in the sight of the LORD, provoking Him to anger with the work of your hands."

30 Then Moses spoke in the hearing of all the assembly of Israel the words of this song, until they were complete:

CHAPTER 32

1 [a]Deut. 4:26; Is. 1:2

"[a]GIVE ear, oh heavens, and let me speak;
And let the earth hear the words of my mouth.

2 [a]Is. 55:10, 11

2 "[a]Let my teaching drop as the rain,
My speech distill as the dew,
As the droplets on the fresh grass
And as the showers on the herb.

3 [a]Ex. 33:19; 34:5, 6 [b]Deut. 3:24; 5:24

3 "[a]For I proclaim the name of the LORD;
[b]Ascribe greatness to our God!

4 [1]Or, *judgment* [a]Deut. 32:15, 18, 30 [b]Gen. 18:25 [c]Deut. 7:9

4 "[a]The Rock! His work is perfect,
[b]For all His ways are [1]just;
[c]A God of faithfulness and without injustice,
Righteous and upright is He.

5 "[1a]They have acted corruptly toward Him,
They are not His children, because of their defect;
[b]*But are* a perverse and crooked generation.
6 "Do you thus repay the LORD,
[a]O foolish and unwise people?
[b]Is not He your Father who has bought you?
[c]He has made you and established you.
7 "Remember the days of old,
Consider the years of all generations.
[a]Ask your father, and he will inform you,
Your elders, and they will tell you.
8 "When the Most High gave the nations their inheritance,
When He separated the sons of [1]man,
He set the boundaries of the peoples
[a]According to the number of the sons of Israel.
9 "[a]For the LORD's portion is His people;
Jacob is the allotment of His inheritance.
10 "[a]He found him a desert land,
And in the howling waste of a wilderness;
He encircled him, He cared for him,
He guarded him as [b]the pupil of His eye.
11 "[a]Like an eagle that stirs up its nest,
That hovers over its young,
[b]He spread His wings and caught them,
He carried them on His pinions.
12 "[a]The LORD alone guided him,
[b]And there was no foreign god with him.
13 "[a]He made him ride on the high places of the earth,
And he ate the produce of the field;
[b]And he made him suck honey from the rock,
And oil from the flinty rock,
14 Curds of cows, and milk of the flock,
With fat of lambs,
And rams, the breed of Bashan, and goats,
[a]With the finest of the wheat—
And of the blood of grapes you drank wine.

15 "[a]But [1]Jeshurun grew fat and kicked—
You are grown fat, thick, and sleek—
[b]Then he forsook God [c]who made him,
And scorned [d]the Rock of his salvation.
16 "[a]They made Him jealous with strange *gods;*
[b]With abominations they provoked Him to anger.
17 "[a]They sacrificed to demons *who were* not God,
[b]*To gods* whom they have not known,
[c]New *gods* who came lately,
Whom your fathers did not dread.
18 "You neglected [a]the Rock who begot you,
[b]And forgot the God who gave you birth.

19 "[a]And the LORD saw *this,* and spurned *them*
[b]Because of the provocation of His sons and daughters.
20 "Then he said, 'I will hide My face from them,
[a]I will see what their end *shall be;*

5 [1]Lit., *It has*
[a]Deut. 4:25; 31:29 [b]Matt. 17:17

6 [a]Deut. 32:28 [b]Deut. 1:31
[c]Deut. 32:15

7 [a]Ex. 12:26; Ps. 78:5-8

8 [1]Or, *Adam*
[a]Deut. 33:28; Num. 23:9

9 [a]1 Kin. 8:51, 53; Jer. 10:16

10 [a]Deut. 1:19 [b]Ps. 17:8; Zech. 2:8

11 [a]Deut. 33:12; Ex. 19:4
[b]Ps. 18:10-18

12 [a]Deut. 4:35, 39 [b]Deut. 32:39; Is. 43:12

13 [a]Is. 58:14 [b]Deut. 8:8; Ps. 81:16

14 [a]Ps. 81:16; 147:14

15 [1]I.e., Israel
[a]Deut. 31:20 [b]Judg. 10:6
[c]Deut. 32:6 [d]Deut. 32:4

16 [a]Ps. 78:58 [b]Ps. 106:29

17 [a]Lev. 17:7; 1 Cor. 10:20
[b]Deut. 28:64
[c]Judg. 5:8

18 [a]Deut. 32:4 [b]Ps. 106:21

19 [a]Lev. 26:30; Ps. 106:40
[b]Jer. 44:21-23

20 [a]Deut. 31:29

20 [b]Deut. 32:5 [c]Deut. 9:23

[b]For they are a perverse generation,
[c]Sons in whom is no faithfulness.

21 [1]Lit., *vanities* [a]Deut. 32:16 [b]Deut. 32:17; 1 Kin. 16:13, 26 [c]Rom. 10:19

21 '[a]They have made Me jealous with *what* is not God;
They have provoked Me to anger with their [1b]idols.
[c]So I will make them jealous with *those who* are not a people;
I will provoke them to anger with a foolish nation,

22 [1]I.e., the nether world [a]Num. 16:33-35; Ps. 18:7, 8 [b]Lev. 26:20

22 [a]For a fire is kindled in My anger,
And burns to the lowest part of [1]Sheol,
[b]And consumes the earth with its yield,
And sets on fire the foundations of the mountains.

23 [a]Deut. 29:21 [b]Ps. 18:14; 45:5

23 '[a]I will heap misfortunes on them;
[b]I will use My arrows on them.

24 [1]Lit., *burning heat* [a]Deut. 28:22, 48 [b]Ps. 91:6 [c]Lev. 26:22 [d]Amos 5:18, 19

24 '[a]*They shall be* wasted by famine, and consumed by [1]plague
[b]And bitter destruction;
[c]And the teeth of beasts I will send upon them,
[d]With the venom of crawling things of the dust.

25 [a]Lam. 1:20; Ezek. 7:15 [b]2 Chr. 36:17; Lam. 2:21

25 '[a]Outside the sword shall bereave,
And inside terror;
[b]*It shall destroy* both young man and virgin,
The nursling with the man of gray hairs.

26 [a]Deut. 4:27; 28:64 [b]Deut. 9:14

26 'I said, "[a]I will cleave them in pieces,
[b]I will make the memory of them to cease from among men."

27 [1]Lit., *high* [a]Deut. 9:26 [b]Num. 15:30

27 '[a]Had I not feared the provocation by the enemy,
Lest their adversaries should misjudge,
Lest they should say, "[b]Our hand is [1]triumphant,
And the LORD has not done all this." '

28 [1]Lit., *perishing* [a]Deut. 32:6

28 "[a]For they are a nation [1]lacking in counsel,
And there is no understanding in them.

29 [1]Or, *latter end* [a]Deut. 5:29 [b]Deut. 31:29

29 "[a]Would that they were wise, that they understood this,
[b]That they would discern their [1]future!

30 [a]Lev. 26:7, 8 [b]Deut. 32:4

30 "[a]How could one chase a thousand,
And two put ten thousand to flight,
Unless their [b]Rock had sold them,
And the LORD had given them up?

31 [1]Lit., *are judges* [a]Ex. 14:25

31 "Indeed their rock is not like our Rock,
[a]Even our enemies [1]themselves judge this.

32 [a]Deut. 29:18

32 "For their vine is from the vine of Sodom,
And from the fields of Gomorrah;
Their grapes are grapes of [a]poison,
Their clusters, bitter.

33 [1]Lit., *dragons* [2]Lit., *cruel*

33 "Their wine is the venom of [1]serpents,
And the [2]deadly poison of cobras.

34 [a]Jer. 44:21

34 '[a]Is it not laid up in store with Me,
Sealed up in My treasuries?

35 [a]Rom. 12:19 [b]Jer. 23:12 [c]Ezek. 7:5-10

35 '[a]Vengeance is Mine, and retribution,
[b]In due time their foot will slip;
[c]For the day of their calamity is near,
And the impending things are hastening upon them.'

36 "[a]For the LORD will vindicate His people,
[b]And will have compassion on His servants;
When He sees that *their* [1]strength is gone,
And there is none *remaining*, bond or free.
37 "And He will say, '[a]Where are their gods,
The rock in which they sought refuge?
38 '[a]Who ate the fat of their sacrifices,
And drank the wine of their libation?
[b]Let them rise up and help you,
Let them be your hiding place!
39 '[a]See now that I, I am He,
[b]And there is no god besides Me;
[c]It is I who put to death and give life.
[d]I have wounded, and it is I who heal;
[e]And there is no one who can deliver from My hand.
40 'Indeed, [a]I lift up My hand to heaven,
And say, as I live forever,
41 "[a]If I sharpen My [1]flashing sword,
And my hand takes hold on justice,
[b]I will render vengeance on My adversaries,
And I will repay those who hate Me.
42 '[a]I will make My arrows drunk with blood,
[b]And My sword shall devour flesh,
With the blood of the slain and the captives,
From the long-haired [1]leaders of the enemy.'
43 "[a]Rejoice, O nations, *with* His people;
[b]For He will avenge the blood of His servants,
[c]And will render vengeance on His adversaries,
[d]And will atone for His land *and* His people."
44 Then Moses came and spoke all the words of this song
in the hearing of the people, he, with [1a]Joshua the son of Nun.
45 When Moses had finished speaking all these words to
all Israel,
46 he said to them, "[a]Take to your heart all the words with
which I am warning you today, which you shall command
[b]your sons to observe [1]carefully, *even* all the words of this law.
47 "For it is not an idle word for you; indeed [a]it is your life.
And [b]by this word you shall prolong your days in the land,
where you are about to cross over the Jordan to possess it."
48 And the LORD spoke to Moses that very same day,
saying,
49 "[a]Go up to this mountain of the Abarim, Mount Nebo,
which is in the land of Moab [1]opposite Jericho, and look at the
land of Canaan, which I am giving to the sons of Israel for a
possession.
50 "Then die on the mountain where you ascend, and be
[a]gathered to your people, as Aaron your brother died on
Mount Hor and was gathered to his people,
51 [a]because you broke faith with Me in the midst of the
sons of Israel at the waters of Meribah-Kadesh, in the [b]wilder-
ness of Zin, because you did not treat Me as holy in the midst
of the sons of Israel.
52 "[a]For you shall see the land at a distance, but [b]you shall
not go there, into the land which I am giving the sons of
Israel."

36 [1]Lit., *hand*
[a]Heb. 10:30 [b]Deut. 30:1-3; Lev. 26:43-45

37 [a]Jer. 2:28

38 [a]Num. 25:1, 2 [b]Jer. 11:12

39 [a]Is. 41:4; 43:10 [b]Deut. 32:12 [c]1 Sam. 2:6 [d]Ps. 51:8 [e]Ps. 50:22

40 [a]Ezek. 20:5, 6

41 [1]Or, *lightning*
[a]Is. 34:6-8 [b]Jer. 50:28-32

42 [1]Lit., *head*
[a]Deut. 32:23
[b]Jer. 12:12; 46:10, 14

43 [a]Rom. 15:10 [b]2 Kin. 9:7 [c]Is. 1:24, 25 [d]Ps. 65:3; 79:9

44 [1]Lit., *Hoshea*
[a]Num. 13:8, 16

46 [1]Lit., *to do*
[a]Ezek. 40:4; 44:5 [b]Deut. 4:9

47 [a]Deut. 8:3; 30:20 [b]Deut. 4:40; 33:25

49 [1]Lit., *which is opposite*
[a]Deut. 3:27; Num. 27:12-14

50 [a]Gen. 25:8

51 [a]Num. 20:12 [b]Num. 27:14

52 [a]Deut. 34:1-3 [b]Deut. 1:37; 3:27

1 [a]Josh. 14:6

2 [1]Lit., *rose to* [2]Lit., *myriads of holiness* [3]Or, *a fiery law* [a]Ex. 19:18, 20; Ps. 68:8, 17 [b]Judg. 5:4 [c]Num. 10:12; Hab. 3:3 [d]Dan. 7:10 [e]Ex. 23:20-22

3 [1]Lit., *peoples* [2]Lit., *His* [3]Or, *lie down at Thy feet* [a]Deut. 4:37 [b]Deut. 7:6; 14:2 [c]Deut. 6:1-9

4 [a]Deut. 4:2 [b]Deut. 8:3; Ps. 119:111

5 [a]Num. 23:21

6 [a]Gen. 49:3, 4

7 [1]Lit., *him* [a]Gen. 49:8-12

8 [1]Lit., *him* [a]Lev. 8:8 [b]Ps. 106:16 [c]Deut. 6:16; Ex. 17:7; Num. 20:13, 24

9 [a]Ex. 32:27-29

10 [1]Lit., *in Thy nostrils* [a]Deut. 31:9-13; Lev. 10-11 [b]Lev. 16:12, 13

12 [a]Deut. 4:37; 12:10

CHAPTER 33

NOW this is the blessing with which Moses [a]the man of God blessed the sons of Israel before his death.
2 And he said,
"[a]The LORD came from Sinai,
[b]And [1]dawned on them from Seir;
[c]He shone forth from Mount Paran,
And He came from [d]the [2]midst of ten thousand holy ones;
[e]At His right hand there was [3]flashing lightning for them.
3 "[a]Indeed, He loves [1]the people;
[b]All [2]Thy holy ones are in Thy hand,
[c]And they [3]followed in Thy steps;
Everyone receives of Thy words.
4 "[a]Moses charged us with a law,
[b]A possession for the assembly of Jacob.
5 "[a]And He was king in Jeshurun,
When the heads of the people were gathered,
The tribes of Israel together.

6 "[a]May Reuben live and not die,
Nor his men be few."

7 [a]And this regarding Judah; so he said,
"Hear, O LORD, the voice of Judah,
And bring him to his people.
With his hands he contended for [1]them;
And mayest Thou be a help against his adversaries."

8 And of Levi he said,
"*Let* Thy [a]Thummim and Thy Urim *belong* to [1]Thy [b]godly man,
[c]Whom Thou didst prove at Massah,
With whom Thou didst contend at the waters of Meribah;
9 [a]Who said of his father and his mother,
'I did not consider them';
And he did not acknowledge his brothers,
Nor did he regard his own sons,
For they observed Thy word,
And kept Thy covenant.
10 "[a]They shall teach Thine ordinances to Jacob,
And Thy law to Israel.
[b]They shall put incense [1]before Thee,
And whole burnt offerings on Thine altar.
11 "O LORD, bless his substance,
And accept the work of his hands;
Shatter the loins of those who rise up against him,
And those who hate him, so that they may not rise *again*."

12 Of Benjamin he said,
"[a]May the beloved of the LORD dwell in security by Him,

[b]Who shields him all the day,
[c]And he dwells between His shoulders."

13 And of Joseph he said,
"[a]Blessed of the LORD *be* his land,
With the choice things of heaven, with the dew,
And from the deep lying beneath,
14 And with the choice yield of the sun,
And with the choice produce of the months.
15 "And with the [1]best things of the ancient mountains,
And with the choice things of the everlasting hills,
16 And with the choice things of the earth and its fulness,
And the favor [a]of Him who dwelt in the bush.
Let it come to the head of Joseph,
And to the crown of the head of the one distinguished among his brothers.
17 "As the first-born of his ox, majesty is his,
And his horns are the horns of [a]the wild ox;
With them he shall [b]push the peoples,
All [1]at once, *to* the ends of the earth.
And those are the ten thousands of Ephraim,
And those are the thousands of Manasseh."

18 [a]And of Zebulun he said,
"Rejoice, Zebulun, in your going forth,
And, Issachar, in your tents.
19 "[a]They shall call peoples *to* the mountain;
There they shall offer righteous [b]sacrifices;
For they shall [1]draw out [c]the abundance of the seas,
And the hidden treasures of the sand."

20 [a]And of Gad he said,
"Blessed is the one who enlarges Gad;
He lies down [b]as a [1]lion,
And tears the arm, also the crown of the head.
21 "[a]Then he [1]provided the first *part* for himself,
[b]For there the ruler's portion was [2]reserved;
[c]And he came *with* the leaders of the people;
[d]He executed the justice of the LORD,
And His ordinances with Israel."

22 [a]And of Dan he said,
"Dan is [b]a lion's whelp,
That leaps forth from Bashan."

23 And of Naphtali he said,
"[a]O Naphtali, satisfied with favor,
And full of the blessing of the LORD.
Take possession of the sea and the south."

24 [a]And of Asher he said,
"More blessed than sons is Asher;
May he be favored by his brothers,
[b]And may he dip his foot in oil.
25 "[a]Your locks shall be iron and bronze,

12 [b]Deut. 32:11 [c]Ex. 28:12
13 [a]Gen. 27:27, 28; 49:22-26
15 [1]Or, *chief*
16 [a]Ex. 2:2-6
17 [1]Or, *together* [a]Num. 23:22 [b]Ps. 44:5
18 [a]Gen. 49:13-15
19 [1]Lit., *suck* [a]Ex. 15:17; Ps. 2:6; Is. 2:3 [b]Ps. 4:5; 51:19 [c]Is. 60:5
20 [1]Or, *lioness* [a]Gen. 49:19 [b]Gen. 49:9
21 [1]Lit., *saw* [2]Or, *covered up* [a]Num. 32:1-5 [b]Num. 34:14 [c]Josh. 4:12 [d]Josh. 22:1-3
22 [a]Gen. 49:16 [b]Ezek. 19:2, 3
23 [a]Gen. 49:21
24 [a]Gen. 49:20 [b]Job 29:6
25 [a]Ps. 147:13

[b]And according to your days, so shall your leisurely walk be.

26 "[a]There is none like the God of [1]Jeshurun,
[b]Who rides the heavens [2]to your help,
And through the skies in His majesty.
27 "[a]The eternal God is a [1]dwelling place,
[b]And underneath are the everlasting arms;
[c]And He drove out the enemy from before you,
[d]And said, 'Destroy!'
28 "[a]So Israel dwells in security,
[b]The fountain of Jacob secluded,
[c]In a land of grain and new wine;
[d]His heavens also drop down dew.
29 "[a]Blessed are you, O Israel;
[b]Who is like you, a people saved by the LORD,
[c]Who is the shield of your help,
[d]And the sword of your majesty!
"[e]So your enemies shall cringe before you,
[f]And you shall tread upon their high places."

CHAPTER 34

[a]NOW Moses went up from the plains of Moab to Mount
Nebo, to the top of Pisgah, which is opposite Jericho. And the
LORD [b]showed him all the land, Gilead as far as Dan,
2 and all Naphtali and the land of Ephraim and Manasseh, and all the land of Judah as far as the [1]Western Sea,
3 and the [1]Negev and the Plain in the valley of Jericho,
the city of palm trees, as far as Zoar.
4 Then the LORD said to him, "This is the land which [a]I
swore to Abraham, Isaac, and Jacob, saying, 'I will give it to
your [1]descendants'; I have let you see *it* with your eyes, but you
shall not go over there."
5 So Moses [a]the servant of the LORD [b]died there in the
land of Moab, according to the [1]word of the LORD.
6 And He buried him in the valley in the land of Moab,
[a]opposite Beth-peor; but no man knows his burial place to this
day.
7 Although Moses was [a]one hundred and twenty years
old when he died, his eye was not dim, nor his vigor abated.
8 So the sons of Israel wept for Moses in the plains of
Moab [a]thirty days; then the days of weeping *and* mourning for
Moses came to an end.
9 Now Joshua the son of Nun was [a]filled with the spirit
of wisdom, for Moses had laid his hands on him; and the sons
of Israel listened to him and did as the LORD had commanded
Moses.
10 Since then no prophet has risen in Israel like Moses,
whom [a]the LORD knew face to face,
11 for all the signs and wonders which the LORD sent him
to perform in the land of Egypt against Pharaoh, all his servants, and all his land,
12 and for all the mighty [1]power and for all the great
terror which Moses performed in the sight of all Israel.

25 [b]Deut. 4:40; 32:47
26 [1]I.e., Israel [2]Lit., *in* [a]Deut. 4:35 [b]Deut. 10:14; Ps. 68:33, 34
27 [1]Or, *refuge* [a]Ps. 90:1, 2 [b]Gen. 49:24 [c]Ex. 34:11; Josh. 24:18 [d]Deut. 7:2
28 [a]Deut. 33:12 [b]Deut. 32:8; Num. 23:9 [c]Gen. 27:28, 37 [d]Deut. 33:13
29 [a]Ps. 1:1; 32:1, 2 [b]Deut. 4:32 [c]Gen. 15:1; Ps. 33:20; 115:9-11 [d]Ps. 68:34 [e]Ps. 66:3 [f]Deut. 32:13; Num. 33:52
1 [a]Deut. 32:49 [b]Deut. 32:52
2 [1]I.e., Mediterranean Sea
3 [1]I.e., South country
4 [1]Lit., *seed* [a]Gen. 12:7; 26:3; 28:13
5 [1]Lit., *mouth* [a]Num. 12:7 [b]Deut. 32:50
6 [a]Deut. 3:29; 4:46
7 [a]Deut. 31:2
8 [a]Deut. 1:3; Josh. 4:19
9 [a]Num. 27:18, 23
10 [a]Num. 12:8
12 [1]Lit., *hand*

THE BOOK OF JOSHUA

GOD'S Charge to Joshua. Preparations to Cross Jordan.

NOW it came about after the death of Moses the servant of
the LORD that the LORD spoke to Joshua the son of Nun,
Moses' [1]servant, saying,
2 "Moses [a]My servant is dead; now therefore arise, [b]cross
this Jordan, you and all this people, to the land which I am
giving to them, to the sons of Israel.
3 "[a]Every place on which the sole of your foot treads, I
have given it to you, just as I spoke to Moses.
4 "From the wilderness and this Lebanon, even as far as
the great river, the river Euphrates, all the land of the Hittites,
and as far as the Great Sea toward the setting of the sun, will
be your territory.
5 "[a]No man will *be able to* stand before you all the days of
your life. Just as I have been with Moses, I will be with you; [b]I
will not fail you or forsake you.
6 "Be strong and courageous, for you shall give this people
possession of the land which I swore to their fathers to give
them.
7 "[a]Only be strong and very courageous, to [1]be careful to
do according to all the law which Moses My servant commanded you; do not turn from it to the right or to the left, so
that you may [2]have success wherever you go.
8 "[a]This book of the law shall not depart from your
mouth, but you shall meditate on it day and night, so that you
may [1]be careful to do according to all that is written in it; [b]for
then you will make your way prosperous, and then you will
[2]have success.
9 "Have I not commanded you? [a]Be strong and courageous! Do not tremble or be dismayed, [b]for the LORD your
God is with you wherever you go."
10 Then Joshua commanded the officers of the people,
saying,
11 "Pass through the midst of the camp and command the
people, saying, 'Prepare provisions for yourselves, for within
[a]three days you are to cross this Jordan, to go in to possess the
land which the LORD your God is giving you, to possess it.' "
12 [a]And to the Reubenites and to the Gadites and to the
half-tribe of Manasseh, Joshua [1]said,
13 "Remember the word which Moses the servant of the
LORD commanded you, saying, '[a]The LORD your God gives you
rest, and will give you this land.'
14 "Your wives, your little ones, and your cattle shall remain in the land which Moses gave you beyond the Jordan,
but you shall cross before your brothers in battle array, all your
valiant warriors, and shall help them,
15 until the LORD gives your brothers rest, as *He gives* you,
and they also possess the land which the LORD your God is
giving them. [a]Then you shall return to [1]your own land, and

1 [1]Or, *minister*

2 [a]Num. 12:7; Deut. 34:5 [b]Josh. 1:11; Deut. 11:24

3 [a]Deut. 11:24

5 [a]Deut. 7:24; Heb. 13:5 [b]Deut. 31:6, 7

7 [1]Lit., *observe* [2]Or, *act wisely* [a]Deut. 5:32

8 [1]Lit., *observe* [2]Or, *act wisely* [a]Josh. 8:34; Deut. 31:24 [b]Deut. 29:9; Ps. 1:1-3

9 [a]Josh. 1:7 [b]Deut. 31:8

11 [a]Josh. 3:2

12 [1]Lit., *said, saying* [a]Num. 32:20-22

13 [a]Deut. 3:18-20

15 [1]Lit., *the land of your possession* [a]Josh. 22:4

possess [2]that which Moses [b]the servant of the LORD gave you
beyond the Jordan toward the sunrise."
16 And they answered Joshua, saying, "All that you have
commanded us we will do, and wherever you send us we will
go.
17 "Just as we obeyed Moses in all things, so we will obey
you; [a]only may the LORD your God be with you, as He was
with Moses.
18 "Anyone who rebels against your [1]command and does
not obey your words in all that you command him, shall be put
to death; only be strong and courageous."

CHAPTER 2

THEN Joshua the son of Nun sent two men as spies secretly
from [a]Shittim, saying, "Go, view the land, especially Jericho."
So they went and came into the house of [b]a harlot whose name
was Rahab, and [1]lodged there.
2 And it was told the king of Jericho, saying, "Behold,
men from the sons of Israel have come here tonight to search
out the land."
3 And the king of Jericho sent *word* to Rahab, saying,
"Bring out the men who have come to you, who have entered
your house, for they have come to search out all the land."
4 But the woman had taken the two men and hidden
them, and she said, "Yes, the men came to me, but I did not
know where they were from.
5 "And it came about when *it was time* to shut the gate, at
dark, that the men went out; I do not know where the men
went. Pursue them quickly, for you will overtake them."
6 [a]But she had brought them up to the roof and hidden
them in the stalks of flax which she had laid in order on the
roof.
7 So the men pursued them on the road to the Jordan to
the fords; and as soon as those who were pursuing them had
gone out, they shut the gate.
8 Now before they lay down, [1]she came up to them on
the roof,
9 and said to the men, "[a]I know that the LORD has given
you the land, and that the [b]terror of you has fallen on us, and
that all the inhabitants of the land have [1]melted away before
you.
10 "[a]For we have heard how the LORD dried up the water of
the [1]Red Sea before you when you came out of Egypt, and
what you did to the two kings of the Amorites who were
beyond the Jordan, to Sihon and Og, whom you [2]utterly
destroyed.
11 "And when we heard *it*, our hearts melted and no [1]cour-
age remained in any man any longer because of you; for the
LORD your God, He is God in heaven above and on earth
beneath.
12 "Now therefore, please swear to me by the LORD, since I
have dealt kindly with you, that you also will deal kindly with
my father's household, and give me a [a]pledge of [1]truth,
13 and [1]spare my father and my mother and my brothers

15 [2]Lit., *it* [b]Josh. 1:1
17 [a]Josh. 1:5, 9
18 [1]Lit., *mouth*
1 [1]Lit., *lay down* [a]Josh. 3:1; Num. 25:1 [b]Heb. 11:31; Jas. 2:25
6 [a]Jas. 2:25
8 [1]Lit., *then she*
9 [1]Or, *become demoralized* [a]Josh. 9:9, 10, 24; Num. 20:24 [b]Ex. 23:27; Deut. 2:25
10 [1]Lit., *Sea of Reeds* [2]Or, *put under the ban* [a]Num. 23:22
11 [1]Lit., *spirit arose*
12 [1]Or, *faithfulness* [a]Josh. 2:18
13 [1]Lit., *let live*

and my sisters, with all who belong to them, and deliver our
[2]lives from death."
14 So the men said to her, "Our [1]life [2]for yours if you do
not tell this business of ours; and it shall come about when the
LORD gives us the land that we will [a]deal kindly and [3]faithfully
with you."
15 Then she let them down by a rope through the window,
for her house was on the city wall, so that she was living on the
wall.
16 And she said to them, "[a]Go to the hill country, lest the
pursuers happen upon you, and hide yourselves there for three
days, until the pursuers return. Then afterward you may go on
your way."
17 And the men said to her, "[a]We *shall be* free from this
oath [1]to you which you have made us swear,
18 [1]unless, when we come into the land, you tie this cord
of scarlet thread in the window through which you let us down,
and [a]gather to yourself into the house your father and your
mother and your brothers and all your father's household.
19 "And it shall come about that anyone who goes out of
the doors of your house into the street, his blood *shall be* on
his own head, and we *shall be* free; but anyone who is with you
in the house, his blood *shall be* on our head, if a hand is *laid* on
him.
20 "But if you tell this business of ours, then we shall be
free from the oath which you have made us swear."
21 And she said, "According to your words, so be it." So
she sent them away, and they departed; and she tied the scarlet
cord in the window.
22 And they departed and came to the hill country, and
remained there for three days until the pursuers returned. Now
the pursuers had sought *them* [1]all along the road, but had not
found *them*.
23 Then the two men returned and came down from the
hill country and crossed over and came to Joshua the son of
Nun, and they related to him all that had happened to them.
24 And they said to Joshua, "Surely the LORD has given all
the land into our hands, and [a]all the inhabitants of the land,
moreover, have [1]melted away before us."

CHAPTER 3

THEN Joshua rose early in the morning; and he and all the
sons of Israel set out from [a]Shittim and came to the Jordan,
and they lodged there before they crossed.
2 And it came about [a]at the end of three days that the
officers went through the midst of the camp;
3 and they commanded the people, saying, "When you
see the [a]ark of the covenant of the LORD your God with the
Levitical priests carrying it, then you shall set out from your
place and go after it.
4 "However, there shall be between you and it a distance
of about 2,000 [1]cubits by measure. Do not come near it, that
you may know the way by which you shall go, for you have not
passed this way before."
5 Then Joshua said to the people, "[a]Consecrate

13 [2]Lit., *souls*
14 [1]Lit., *soul* [2]Lit., *instead of you to die* [3]Or, *truly* [a]Gen. 24:49
16 [a]Jas. 2:25
17 [1]Lit., *of yours* [a]Gen. 24:8
18 [1]Lit., *behold* [a]Josh. 2:12
22 [1]Lit., *through all the road*
24 [1]Or, *become demoralized* [a]Josh. 2:9
1 [a]Josh. 2:1
2 [a]Josh. 1:11
3 [a]Deut. 31:9
4 [1]I.e., one cubit equals approximately 18 inches
5 [a]Josh. 7:13; Ex. 19:10, 11

7 [a]Josh. 4:14

12 [a]Josh. 4:2

13 [1]Lit., *going* [2]Lit., *and they shall* [a]Ex. 15:8

16 [1]Lit., *going* [a]Ps. 66:6; 74:15; 114:3, 5 [b]Josh. 3:13 [c]Deut. 1:1

17 [a]Ex. 14:21, 22, 29

2 [a]Josh. 3:12

yourselves, for tomorrow the LORD will do wonders among you."

6 And Joshua spoke to the priests, saying, "Take up the ark of the covenant and cross over ahead of the people." So they took up the ark of the covenant and went ahead of the people.

7 Now the LORD said to Joshua, "This day I will begin to [a]exalt you in the sight of all Israel, that they may know that just as I have been with Moses, I will be with you.

8 "You shall, moreover, command the priests who are carrying the ark of the covenant, saying, 'When you come to the edge of the waters of the Jordan, you shall stand *still* in the Jordan.' "

9 Then Joshua said to the sons of Israel, "Come here, and hear the words of the LORD your God."

10 And Joshua said, "By this you shall know that the living God is among you, and that He will assuredly dispossess from before you the Canaanite, the Hittite, the Hivite, the Perizzite, the Girgashite, the Amorite, and the Jebusite.

11 "Behold, the ark of the covenant of the Lord of all the earth is crossing over ahead of you into the Jordan.

12 "[a]Now then, take for yourselves twelve men from the tribes of Israel, one man for each tribe.

13 "And it shall come about when the soles of the feet of the priests who carry the ark of the LORD, the Lord of all the earth, shall rest in the waters of the Jordan, the waters of the Jordan shall be cut off, *and* the waters which are [1]flowing down from above [2]shall [a]stand in one heap."

14 So it came about when the people set out from their tents to cross the Jordan with the priests carrying the ark of the covenant before the people,

15 and when those who carried the ark came into the Jordan, and the feet of the priests carrying the ark were dipped in the edge of the water (for the Jordan overflows all its banks all the days of harvest),

16 [a]that the waters which were [1]flowing down from above stood *and* rose up in [b]one heap, a great distance away at Adam, the city that is beside Zarethan; and those which were [1]flowing down toward the sea of the [c]Arabah, the Salt Sea, were completely cut off. So the people crossed opposite Jericho.

17 And the priests who carried the ark of the covenant of the LORD stood firm [a]on dry ground in the middle of the Jordan while all Israel crossed on dry ground, until all the nation had finished crossing the Jordan.

CHAPTER 4

NOW it came about when all the nation had finished crossing the Jordan, that the LORD spoke to Joshua, saying,

2 "[a]Take for yourselves twelve men from the people, one man from each tribe,

3 and command them, saying, 'Take up for yourselves twelve stones from here out of the middle of the Jordan, from the place where the priests' feet are standing firm, and carry

them over with you, and lay them down in [a]the lodging place
where you will lodge tonight.' "
4 So Joshua called the twelve men whom he had appointed from the sons of Israel, one man from each tribe;
5 and Joshua said to them, "[1]Cross again to the ark of the
LORD your God into the middle of the Jordan, and each of you
take up a stone on his shoulder, according to the number of
the tribes of the sons of Israel.
6 "[1]Let this be a sign among you, so that [a]when your
children ask [2]later, saying, 'What do these stones mean to
you?'
7 then you shall say to them, 'Because the waters of the
Jordan were cut off before the ark of the covenant of the
LORD; when it crossed the Jordan, the waters of the Jordan
were cut off.' So these stones shall become a memorial to the
sons of Israel forever."
8 And thus the sons of Israel did, as Joshua commanded,
and took up twelve stones from the middle of the Jordan, just
as the LORD spoke to Joshua, according to the number of the
tribes of the sons of Israel; and they carried them over with
them to [a]the lodging place, and put them down there.
9 Then Joshua set up twelve stones in the middle of the
Jordan at the place where the feet of the priests who carried
the ark of the covenant were standing, and they are there to
this day.
10 For the priests who carried the ark were standing in the
middle of the Jordan until everything was completed that the
LORD had commanded Joshua to speak to the people, according to all that Moses had commanded Joshua. And the
people hurried and crossed;
11 and it came about when all the people had finished
crossing, that the ark of the LORD and the priests crossed before the people.
12 [a]And the sons of Reuben and the sons of Gad and the
half-tribe of Manasseh crossed over in battle array before the
sons of Israel, just as Moses had spoken to them;
13 about 40,000, equipped for war, crossed for battle before the LORD to the desert plains of Jericho.
14 [a]On that day the LORD exalted Joshua in the sight of all
Israel; so that they [1]revered him, just as they had [1]revered
Moses all the days of his life.
15 Now the LORD said to [1]Joshua,
16 "Command the priests who carry the ark of the testimony that they come up from the Jordan."
17 So Joshua commanded the priests, saying, "Come up
from the Jordan."
18 And it came about when the priests who carried the ark
of the covenant of the LORD had come up from the middle of
the Jordan, and the soles of the priests' feet were [1]lifted up to
the dry ground, that the waters of the Jordan returned to their
place, and went over all its banks as before.
19 Now the people came up from the Jordan on the
[a]tenth of the first month and camped at Gilgal on the eastern
edge of Jericho.
20 [a]And [1]those twelve stones which they had taken from
the Jordan, Joshua set up [b]at Gilgal.

3 [a]Josh. 4:20

5 [1]Lit., *Cross before the ark*

6 [1]Lit., *That this may be* [2]Lit., *tomorrow* [a]Josh. 4:21; Ex. 12:26; 13:4

8 [a]Josh. 4:20

12 [a]Num. 32:17

14 [1]Or, *feared* [a]Josh. 3:7

15 [1]Lit., *Joshua, saying*

18 [1]Lit., *drawn out*

19 [a]Deut. 1:3

20 [1]Lit., *these* [a]Josh. 4:8 [b]Josh. 4:3, 8

21 And he said to the sons of [1]Israel, "When your children
ask their fathers in time to come, saying, 'What are these
stones?'
22 then you shall inform your children, saying, 'Israel
crossed this Jordan on [a]dry ground.'
23 "For the LORD your God dried up the waters of the
Jordan before you until you had crossed, just as the LORD your
God had done to the [1]Red Sea, which He dried up before us
until we had crossed;
24 that all the peoples of the earth may know that the
hand of the LORD is mighty, so that you may [1]fear the LORD
your God [2]forever."

CHAPTER 5

NOW it came about when all the kings of the Amorites who
were beyond the Jordan to the west, and all the kings of the
Canaanites [a]who *were* by the sea, [b]heard how the LORD had
dried up the waters of the Jordan before the sons of Israel until
[1]they had crossed, that their hearts melted, and there was no
spirit in them any longer, because of the sons of Israel.
2 At that time the LORD said to Joshua, "Make for yourself flint [a]knives and circumcise again the sons of Israel the
second time."
3 So Joshua made himself flint knives and circumcised
the sons of Israel at [1]Gibeath-haaraloth.
4 And this is the reason why Joshua circumcised them:
[a]all the people who came out of Egypt who were males, all the
men of war, died in the wilderness along the way, after they
came out of Egypt.
5 For all the people who came out were circumcised, but
all the people who were born in the wilderness along the way as
they came out of Egypt had not been circumcised.
6 For the sons of Israel walked [a]forty years in the wilderness, until all the nation, *that is,* the men of war who came out
of Egypt, [1]perished because they did not listen to the voice of
the LORD, [b]to whom the LORD had sworn that He would not let
them see the land which the LORD had sworn to their fathers to
give us, a land flowing with milk and honey.
7 And their children whom He raised up in their place,
Joshua [1]circumcised; for they were uncircumcised, because
they had not circumcised them along the way.
8 Now it came about when they had finished circumcis-
ing all the nation, that they remained in their places in the
camp until they were [1]healed.
9 Then the LORD said to Joshua, "Today I have rolled
away [a]the reproach of Egypt from you." So the name of that
place is called [1]Gilgal to this day.
10 While the sons of Israel camped at Gilgal, [a]they observed the Passover on the evening of the [b]fourteenth day of
the month on the desert plains of Jericho.
11 And on the [1]day after the Passover, on [2]that very day,
they ate some of the produce of the land, unleavened cakes
and parched grain.

21 [1]Lit., *Israel, saying,*

22 [a]Josh. 3:17

23 [1]Lit., *Sea of Reeds*

24 [1]Or, *reverence* [2]Lit., *all the days*

1 [1]Other mss. read, *we* [a]Num. 13:29 [b]Josh. 2:10, 11

2 [a]Ex. 4:25

3 [1]I.e., the hill of the foreskins

4 [a]Deut. 2:14

6 [1]Lit., *were finished* [a]Deut. 2:7, 14 [b]Num. 14:29-35; 26:63-65

7 [1]Lit., *circumcised them*

8 [1]Lit., *revived*

9 [1]I.e., Rolling [a]Zeph. 2:8

10 [a]Ex. 12:18 [b]Josh. 4:19

11 [1]Lit., *morrow* [2]Lit., *this*

12 And [a]the manna ceased on the [1]day after they had
eaten some of the produce of the land, so that the sons of
Israel no longer had manna, but they ate some of the yield of
the land of Canaan during that year.
13 Now it came about when Joshua was by Jericho, that
he lifted up his eyes and looked, and behold, [a]a man was
standing opposite him with his sword drawn in his hand, and
Joshua went to him and said to him, "Are you for us or for our
adversaries?"
14 And he said, "No, rather I indeed come now *as* captain
of the host of the LORD." And Joshua fell on his face to the
earth, and bowed down, and said to him, "What has my lord
to say to his servant?"
15 And the captain of the LORD's host said to Joshua,
"[a]Remove your sandals from your feet, for the place where
you are standing is holy." And Joshua did so.

12 [1]Lit., *morrow* [a]Ex. 16:35

13 [a]Gen. 18:1, 2; 32:24, 30; Num. 22:31

15 [a]Ex. 3:5

CHAPTER 6

NOW Jericho was tightly shut because of the sons of Israel;
no one went out and no one came in.
2 And the LORD said to Joshua, "See, I have given Jericho
into your hand, with [a]its king *and* the valiant warriors.
3 "And you shall march around the city, all the men of
war circling the city once. You shall do so for six days.
4 "Also seven priests shall carry seven [a]trumpets of rams'
horns before the ark; then on the seventh day you shall march
around the city seven times, and the priests shall blow the
trumpets.
5 "And it shall be that when they make a long blast with
the ram's horn, and when you hear the sound of the trumpet,
all the people shall shout with a great shout; and the wall of
the city will fall down [1]flat, and the people will go up every
man straight [2]ahead."
6 So Joshua the son of Nun called the priests and said to
them, "Take up the ark of the covenant, and let seven priests
carry seven trumpets of rams' horns before the ark of the
LORD."
7 Then [1]he said to the people, "Go forward, and march
around the city, and let the armed men go on before the ark of
the LORD."
8 And it was *so*, that when Joshua had spoken to the
people, the seven priests carrying the seven trumpets of rams'
horns before the LORD went forward and blew the trumpets;
and the ark of the covenant of the LORD followed them.
9 And the armed men went before the priests who blew
the trumpets, and [a]the rear guard came after the ark, while
they continued to blow the trumpets.
10 But Joshua commanded the people, saying, "You shall
not shout nor let your voice be heard, nor let a word proceed
out of your mouth, until the day I tell you, 'Shout!' Then you
shall shout!"
11 So he had the ark of the LORD [1]taken around the city,
circling *it* once; then they came into the camp and spent the
night in the camp.

2 [a]Deut. 7:24

4 [a]Lev. 25:9

5 [1]Lit., *in its place* [2]Lit., *before himself*

7 [1]Or, *they*

9 [a]Josh. 6:13; Is. 52:12

11 [1]Lit., *to go around*

12 Now Joshua rose early in the morning, and the priests
took up the ark of the LORD.
13 And [a]the seven priests carrying the seven trumpets of
rams' horns before the ark of the LORD went on continually,
and blew the trumpets; and the armed men went before them,
and [b]the rear guard came after the ark of the LORD, while they
continued to blow the trumpets.
14 Thus the second day they marched around the city
once and returned to the camp; they did so for six days.
15 Then it came about on the seventh day that they rose
early at the dawning of the day and marched around the city in
the same manner seven times, only on that day they marched
around the city seven times.
16 And it came about at the seventh time, when the
priests blew the trumpets, Joshua said to the people, "Shout!
For the LORD has given you the city.
17 "And the city shall be [a]under the ban, it and all that is in
it belongs to the LORD; only Rahab the harlot [1]and all who are
with her in the house shall live, because she hid the messengers
whom we sent.
18 "But as for you, only keep yourselves from the things
under the ban, lest you [1]covet *them* and take some of the
things under the ban, [a]so you would make the camp of Israel
accursed and bring trouble on it.
19 "[a]But all the silver and gold and articles of bronze and
iron are holy to the LORD; they shall go into the treasury of the
LORD."
20 So the people shouted, and [1]*priests* blew the trumpets;
and it came about, when the people heard the sound of the
trumpet, that the people shouted with a great shout and the
[a]wall fell down [2]flat, so that the people went up into the city,
every man straight [3]ahead, and they took the city.
21 [a]And they [1]utterly destroyed everything in the city,
both man and woman, young and old, and ox and sheep and
donkey, with the edge of the sword.
22 And Joshua said to the two men who had spied out the
land, "[a]Go into the harlot's house and bring the woman and all
she has out of there, as you have sworn to her."
23 So the young men who were spies went in and [a]brought
out Rahab and her father and her mother and her brothers and
all she had; they also brought out all her relatives, and placed
them outside the camp of Israel.
24 [a]And they burned the city with fire, and all that was in
it. Only the silver and gold and articles of bronze and iron,
they put into the treasury of the [1]house of the LORD.
25 [a]However, Rahab the harlot and her father's household
and all she had, Joshua [1]spared; and she has lived in the midst
of Israel to this day, for [b]she hid the messengers whom Joshua
sent to spy out Jericho.
26 Then Joshua made them take an oath at that time,
saying, "[a]Cursed before the LORD is the man who rises up and
builds this city Jericho; with *the loss of* his first-born he shall
lay its foundation, and with *the loss of* his youngest son he
shall set up its gates."
27 So the LORD was with Joshua, and his fame was in all
the land.

13 [a]Josh. 6:4 [b]Josh. 6:9
17 [1]Lit., *she and all* [a]Lev. 27:28; Deut. 20:17
18 [1]Lit., *devote* [a]Josh. 7:1
19 [a]Num. 31:11, 12, 21-23
20 [1]Or, *they* [2]Lit., *in its place* [3]Lit., *before himself* [a]Heb. 11:30
21 [1]Or, *put under the ban* [a]Deut. 20:16
22 [a]Josh. 2:12-19
23 [a]Heb. 11:31
24 [1]I.e., tabernacle [a]Deut. 20:16-18
25 [1]Lit., *let live* [a]Heb. 11:31 [b]Josh. 2:6
26 [a]1 Kin. 16:34

Chapter 7

[a]BUT the sons of Israel acted unfaithfully in regard to the
things under the ban, for Achan, the son of Carmi, the son of
Zabdi, the son of Zerah, from the tribe of Judah, took some of
the things under the ban, therefore the anger of the LORD
burned against the sons of Israel.
2 Now Joshua sent men from Jericho to Ai, which is near
[a]Beth-aven, east of Bethel, and said to them, [1]"Go up and spy
out the land." So the men went up and spied out Ai.
3 And they returned to Joshua and said to him, "Do not
let all the people go up; *only* about two or three thousand men
need go up [1]to Ai; do not make all the people toil up there, for
they are few."
4 So about three thousand men from the people went up
there, but they fled [1]from the men of Ai.
5 And the men of Ai struck down about thirty-six of their
men, and pursued them [1]*from* the gate as far as Shebarim, and
struck them down on the descent, so the hearts of the people
melted and became as water.
6 Then Joshua [a]tore his clothes and fell to the earth on
his face before the ark of the LORD until the evening, *both* he
and the elders of Israel; and [b]they put dust on their heads.
7 And Joshua said, "Alas, O LORD [1]God, why didst Thou
ever bring this people over the Jordan, *only* to deliver us into
the hand of the Amorites, to destroy us? If only we had been
willing [2]to dwell beyond the Jordan!
8 "Oh Lord, what can I say since Israel has turned *their*
[1]back before their enemies?
9 "[a]For the Canaanites and all the inhabitants of the land
will hear of it, and they will surround us and cut off our name
from the earth. And what wilt Thou do for Thy great name?"
10 So the LORD said to Joshua, "Rise up! Why is it that
you have fallen on your face?
11 "Israel has sinned, and [a]they have also transgressed My
covenant which I commanded them. And they have even tak-
en some of the things under the ban and have both stolen and
deceived. Moreover, they have also put *them* among their own
things.
12 "Therefore the sons of Israel cannot stand before their
enemies; they turn *their* [1]backs before their enemies, for they
have become accursed. I will not be with you any more unless
you destroy the things under the ban from your midst.
13 "Rise up! [a]Consecrate the people and say, 'Consecrate
yourselves for tomorrow, for thus the LORD, the God of Israel,
has said, "[b]There are things under the ban in your midst, O
Israel. You cannot stand before your enemies until you have
removed the things under the ban from your midst."
14 'In the morning then you shall come near by your
tribes. And it shall be that the tribe which the LORD takes *by
lot* shall come near by families, and the family which the LORD
takes shall come near by households, and the household which
the LORD takes shall come near man by man.
15 'And it shall be that the one who is taken with the things
under the ban shall be burned with fire, he and all that belongs

1 [a]Josh. 6:17-19

2 [1]Lit., *saying*, "Go [a]Josh. 18:12; 1 Sam. 13:5; 14:23

3 [1]Lit., *and smite*

4 [1]Lit., *before*

5 [1]Lit., *before*

6 [a]Job 2:12; 42:6 [b]Lam. 2:10; Rev. 18:19

7 [1]Lit., YHWH, usually rendered LORD [2]Lit., *and had dwelt*

8 [1]Lit., *neck*

9 [a]Ex. 32:12; Deut. 9:28

11 [a]Josh. 6:18, 19

12 [1]Lit., *necks*

13 [a]Josh. 3:5 [b]Josh. 6:18

16 [1]Lit., *its tribes*
20 [1]Lit., *thus and thus I did*
24 [1]Or, *cattle* [2]I.e., trouble [a]Josh. 15:7
25 [1]Lit., *him* [2]Lit., *and they stoned* [a]Josh. 6:18
26 [1]I.e., Trouble [a]Is. 65:10; Hos. 2:15
1 [a]Josh. 1:9; 10:8 [b]Josh. 6:2
2 [1]Lit., *Set for yourself* [a]Josh. 8:27; Deut. 20:14

to him, because he has transgressed the covenant of the LORD,
and because he has committed a disgraceful thing in Israel.' "
16 So Joshua arose early in the morning and brought Israel
near by [1]tribes, and the tribe of Judah was taken.
17 And he brought the family of Judah near, and he took
the family of the Zerahites; and he brought the family of the
Zerahites near man by man, and Zabdi was taken.
18 And he brought his household near man by man; and
Achan, son of Carmi, son of Zabdi, son of Zerah, from the
tribe of Judah, was taken.
19 Then Joshua said to Achan, "My son, I implore you,
give glory to the LORD, the God of Israel, and give praise to
Him; and tell me now what you have done. Do not hide it
from me."
20 So Achan answered Joshua and said, "Truly, I have
sinned against the LORD, the God of Israel, and [1]this is what I
did;
21 when I saw among the spoil a beautiful mantle from
Shinar and two hundred shekels of silver and a bar of gold fifty
shekels in weight, then I coveted them and took them; and
behold, they are concealed in the earth inside my tent with the
silver underneath it."
22 So Joshua sent messengers, and they ran to the tent;
and behold, it was concealed in his tent with the silver underneath it.
23 And they took them from inside the tent and brought
them to Joshua and to all the sons of Israel, and they poured
them out before the LORD.
24 Then Joshua and all Israel with him, took Achan the
son of Zerah, the silver, the mantle, the bar of gold, his sons,
his daughters, his [1]oxen, his donkeys, his sheep, his tent and all
that belonged to him; and they brought them up to [a]the valley
of [2]Achor.
25 And Joshua said, "Why have you [a]troubled us? The
LORD will trouble you this day." And all Israel stoned [1]them
with stones; and they burned them with fire [2]after they had
stoned them with stones.
26 And they raised over him a great heap of stones that
stands to this day, and the LORD turned from the fierceness of
His anger. Therefore the name of that place has been called
[a]the Valley of [1]Achor to this day.

CHAPTER 8

NOW the LORD said to Joshua, "[a]Do not fear or be
dismayed. Take all the people of war with you and arise, go up
to Ai; see, [b]I have given into your hand the king of Ai, his
people, his city, and his land.
2 "And you shall do to Ai and its king just as you did to
Jericho and its king; you shall take [a]only its spoil and its cattle
as plunder for yourselves. [1]Set an ambush for the city behind
it."
3 So Joshua rose with all the people of war to go up to Ai;
and Joshua chose 30,000 men, valiant warriors, and sent them
out at night.
4 And he commanded them, saying, "See, you are going

to ambush the city from behind [1]it. Do not go very far from
the city, but all of you be ready.
5 "Then I and all the people who are with me will approach the city. And it will come about when they come out to
meet us as at the first, that we will flee before them.
6 "And they will come out after us until we have drawn
them away from the city, for they will say, '*They* are fleeing
before us as at the first.' So we will flee before them.
7 "And you shall rise from *your* ambush and take possession of the city, for the LORD your God will deliver it into your
hand.
8 "Then it will be when you have seized the city, that you
shall set the city on fire. You shall do *it* [a]according to the word
of the LORD. See, I have commanded you."
9 So Joshua sent them away, and they went to the place
of ambush and remained between Bethel and Ai, on the west
side of Ai; but Joshua spent that night among the people.
10 Now Joshua rose early in the morning and mustered
the people, and he went up with the elders of Israel before the
people to Ai.
11 Then all the people of war who *were* with him went up
and drew near and arrived in front of the city, and camped on
the north side of Ai. Now *there was* a valley between him and
Ai.
12 And he took about 5,000 men and set them in ambush
between Bethel and Ai, on the west side of the [1]city.
13 So they stationed the people, all the army that was on
the north side of the city, and its rear guard on the west side of
the city, and Joshua spent that night in the midst of the valley.
14 And it came about when the king of Ai saw *it*, that the
men of the city hurried and rose up early and went out to meet
Israel in battle, he and all his people at the appointed place
before the [a]desert plain. But he did not know that *there was* an
ambush against him behind the city.
15 And Joshua and all Israel pretended to be beaten before them, and fled by the way of the wilderness.
16 And all the people who were in the city were called
together to pursue them, and they pursued Joshua, and were
drawn away from the city.
17 So not a man was left in Ai or Bethel who had not gone
out after Israel, and they left the city [1]unguarded and pursued
Israel.
18 Then the LORD said to Joshua, "[a]Stretch out the javelin
that is in your hand toward Ai, for I will give it into your
hand." So Joshua stretched out the javelin that was in his hand
toward the city.
19 And the *men in* ambush rose quickly from their place,
and when he had stretched out his hand, they ran and entered
the city and captured it; and they quickly set the city on fire.
20 When the men of Ai turned [1]back and looked, behold,
the smoke of the city ascended to the sky, and they had no
place to flee this way or that, for the people who had been
fleeing to the wilderness turned against the pursuers.
21 When Joshua and all Israel saw that the *men in*
ambush had captured the city and that the smoke of the city
ascended, they turned back and [1]slew the men of Ai.

4 [1]Lit., *the city*

8 [a]Josh. 8:2; Deut. 20:16-18

12 [1]I.e., Ai

14 [a]Josh. 3:16

17 [1]Lit., *open*

18 [a]Josh. 8:26; Ex. 14:16; 17:9-13

20 [1]Lit., *behind them*

21 [1]Lit., *smote*

22 [1]Lit., *these came* [2]Lit., *these . . . those* [3]Lit., *smote* [4]Lit., *for it* [a]Josh. 8:8
25 [1]Lit., *men* [a]Deut. 20:16-18
26 [1]Or, *put under the ban* [a]Ex. 17:11, 12
27 [a]Josh. 8:2
29 [a]Deut. 21:22, 23
30 [a]Deut. 27:2-8
31 [a]Ex. 20:25
32 [1]I.e., Moses
33 [a]Deut. 27:11-14
34 [a]Josh. 1:8
35 [1]Lit., *walking*
1 [a]Josh. 3:10; Num. 13:29

22 And [1]the others came out from the city to encounter
them, so that they were *trapped* in the midst of Israel, [2]some
on this side and some on that side; and they [3]slew them [a]until
no one was left [4]of those who survived or escaped.
23 But they took alive the king of Ai and brought him to
Joshua.
24 Now it came about when Israel had finished killing all
the inhabitants of Ai in the field in the wilderness where they
pursued them, and all of them were fallen by the edge of the
sword until they were destroyed, then all Israel returned to Ai
and struck it with the edge of the sword.
25 [a]And all who fell that day, both men and women, were
12,000—all the [1]people of Ai.
26 For Joshua did not withdraw his hand with which [a]he
stretched out the javelin until he had [1]utterly destroyed all the
inhabitants of Ai.
27 [a]Israel took only the cattle and the spoil of that city as
plunder for themselves, according to the word of the LORD
which He had commanded Joshua.
28 So Joshua burned Ai and made it a heap forever, a
desolation until this day.
29 [a]And he hanged the king of Ai on a tree until evening;
and at sunset Joshua gave command and they took his body
down from the tree, and threw it at the entrance of the city
gate, and raised over it a great heap of stones *that stands* to
this day.
30 Then Joshua built an altar to the LORD, the God of
Israel, in [a]Mount Ebal,
31 just as Moses the servant of the LORD had commanded
the sons of Israel, as it is written in the Book of the Law of
Moses, [a]an altar of uncut stones, on which no man had wielded
an iron *tool;* and they offered burnt offerings on it to the
LORD, and sacrificed peace offerings.
32 And he wrote there on the stones a copy of the Law of
Moses, which [1]he had written, in the presence of the sons of
Israel.
33 [a]And all Israel with their elders and officers and their
judges were standing on both sides of the ark before the Levitical priests who carried the ark of the covenant of the LORD, the
stranger as well as the native. Half of them *stood* in front of
Mount Gerizim and half of them in front of Mount Ebal, just
as Moses the servant of the LORD had given command at first
to bless the people of Israel.
34 Then afterward he read all the words of the law, the
blessing and the curse, according to all that is written in [a]the
Book of the Law.
35 There was not a word of all that Moses had commanded which Joshua did not read before all the assembly of
Israel with the women and the little ones and the strangers
who were [1]living among them.

CHAPTER 9

NOW it came about when [a]all the kings who were beyond
the Jordan, in the hill-country and in the lowland and on all
the coast of the Great Sea toward Lebanon, the Hittite and

the Amorite, the Canaanite, the Perizzite, the Hivite and the
Jebusite, heard of it,
2 that they gathered themselves together with [1]one accord to fight with Joshua and with Israel.
3 When the inhabitants of [a]Gibeon heard what Joshua
had done to Jericho and to Ai,
4 they also acted craftily and [1]set out as envoys, and took
worn-out sacks on their donkeys, and wineskins, worn-out and
torn and [2]mended,
5 and worn-out and patched sandals on their feet, and
worn-out clothes on themselves; and all the bread of their
provision was dry *and* had become crumbled.
6 And they went to Joshua to the camp at Gilgal, and
said to him and to the men of Israel, "We have come from a
far country; now therefore, make a covenant with us."
7 And the men of Israel said to the [a]Hivites, "Perhaps
you are living [1]within our land; [b]how then shall we make a
covenant with you?"
8 But they said to Joshua, "We are your servants." Then
Joshua said to them, "Who are you, and where do you come
from?"
9 And they said to him, "Your servants have come from
[a]a very far country because of the [1]fame of the LORD your
God; for [b]we have heard the report of Him and all that He did
in Egypt,
10 and all that He did to the two kings of the Amorites
who were beyond the Jordan, to Sihon king of Heshbon and to
Og king of Bashan who was at Ashtaroth.
11 "So our elders and all the inhabitants of our country
spoke to us, saying, 'Take provisions in your hand for the
journey, and go to meet them and say to them, "We are your
servants; now then, make a covenant with us."'
12 "This our bread *was* warm *when* we took it for our
provisions out of our houses on the day that we left to come to
you; but now behold, it is dry and has become crumbled.
13 "And these wineskins which we filled were new, and
behold, they are torn; and these our clothes and our sandals
are worn out because of the very long journey."
14 So the men of Israel took some of their provisions, and
[a]did not ask for the [1]counsel of the LORD.
15 [a]And Joshua made peace with them and made a covenant with them, to let them live; and the leaders of the congregation swore *an oath* to them.
16 And it came about at the end of three days after they
had made a covenant with them, that they heard that they
were neighbors and that they were living [1]within their land.
17 Then the sons of Israel set out and came to their cities
on the third day. Now their cities *were* Gibeon and Chephirah
and Beeroth and Kiriath-jearim.
18 And the sons of Israel did not strike them because the
leaders of the congregation had sworn to them by the LORD
the God of Israel. And the whole congregation grumbled
against the leaders.
19 But all the leaders said to the whole congregation, "We
have sworn to them by the LORD, the God of Israel, and now
we cannot touch them.

2 [1]Lit., *one mouth*

3 [a]Josh. 9:17, 22; 10:2; 21:17

4 [1]Lit., *went and traveled as envoys* [2]Lit., *tied up*

7 [1]Lit., *among us* [a]Josh. 9:2; 11:19 [b]Ex. 23:32

9 [1]Or, *name* [a]Josh. 9:16, 17 [b]Josh. 9:24; 2:9

14 [1]Lit., *mouth* [a]Num. 27:21

15 [a]Ex. 23:32

16 [1]Lit., *among them*

20 "This we will do to them, even let them live, lest wrath
be upon us for the oath which we swore to them."
21 And the leaders said to them, "Let them live." So they
became hewers of wood and drawers of water for the whole
congregation, just as the leaders had spoken to them.
22 Then Joshua called for them and spoke to them,
saying, "Why have you deceived us, saying, 'We are very far
from you,' [a]when you are living [1]within our land?
23 "Now therefore, you are cursed, and [1]you shall never
cease being slaves, both hewers of wood and drawers of water
for the house of my God."
24 So they answered Joshua and said, "[a]Because it was
certainly told your servants that the LORD your God had commanded his servant Moses to give you all the land, and to
destroy all the inhabitants of the land before you; therefore we
feared greatly for our lives because of you, and have done this
thing.
25 "And now behold, we are in your hands; do as it seems
good and right in your sight to do to us."
26 Thus he did to them, and delivered them from the
hands of the sons of Israel, and they did not kill them.
27 But Joshua made them that day hewers of wood and
drawers of water for the congregation and for the altar of the
LORD, to this day, [a]in the place which He would choose.

CHAPTER 10

NOW it came about when Adoni-zedek king of Jerusalem
heard that Joshua had captured Ai, and had [1]utterly destroyed
it (just as he had done to Jericho and its king, so he had done
to Ai and its king), and that the inhabitants of Gibeon had
made peace with Israel and were [2]within their land,
2 that [1]he feared greatly, because Gibeon *was* a great
city, like one of the royal cities, and because it was greater than
Ai, and all its men *were* mighty.
3 Therefore Adoni-zedek of Jerusalem sent *word* [a]to Ho-
ham king of Hebron and to Piram king of Jarmuth and to
Japhia king of Lachish and to Debir king of Eglon, saying,
4 "Come up to me and help me, and let us [1]attack Gibeon, for it has made peace with Joshua and with the sons of
Israel."
5 So the five kings of [a]the Amorites, the king of Jerusalem, the king of Hebron, the king of Jarmuth, the king of
Lachish, *and* the king of Eglon, gathered together and went
up, they with all their armies, and camped by Gibeon and
fought against it.
6 Then the men of Gibeon sent *word* to Joshua to the
camp at Gilgal, saying, "Do not [1]abandon your servants; come
up to us quickly and save us and help us, for all the kings of the
Amorites that live in the hill country have assembled against
us."
7 So Joshua went up from Gilgal, he and all the people of
war with him and all the valiant warriors.
8 And the LORD said to Joshua, "[a]Do not fear them, for I
have given them into your hands; not [1]one of them shall stand
before you."

22 [1]Lit., *among us* [a]Josh. 9:17
23 [1]Lit., *a servant shall not be cut off from you*
24 [a]Josh. 9:9
27 [a]Deut. 12:5
1 [1]Or, *put under the ban* [2]Lit., *among them*
2 [1]Lit., *they*
3 [a]Josh. 10:23
4 [1]Lit., *smite*
5 [a]Num. 13:29
6 [1]Lit., *slacken your hands from*
8 [1]Lit., *a man* [a]Josh. 1:5, 9

9 So Joshua came upon them suddenly [1]by marching all
night from Gilgal.
10 [a]And the LORD confounded them before Israel, and He
[1]slew them with a great slaughter at Gibeon, and pursued them
by the way of the ascent of Beth-horon, and struck them as far
as Azekah and Makkedah.
11 And it came about as they fled from before Israel,
while they were at the descent of Beth-horon, that the LORD
threw large stones from heaven on them as far as Azekah, and
they died; *there were* more who died [1]from the hailstones than
those whom the sons of Israel killed with the sword.
12 Then Joshua spoke to the LORD in the day when the
LORD delivered up the Amorites before the sons of Israel, and
he said in the sight of Israel,

"O sun, stand still at Gibeon,
And O moon in the valley of Aijalon."
13 [a]So the sun stood still, and the moon stopped,
Until the nation avenged themselves of their enemies.

Is it not written in the Book of [b]Jashar? And [c]the sun stopped
in the middle of the sky, and did not hasten to go *down* for
about a whole day.
14 And there was no day like that before it or after it,
when the LORD listened to the voice of a man; for [a]the LORD
fought for Israel.
15 Then Joshua and all Israel with him returned to the
camp to Gilgal.
16 Now these [a]five kings had fled and hidden themselves
in the cave at Makkedah.
17 And it was told Joshua, saying, "The five kings have
been found hidden in the cave at Makkedah."
18 And Joshua said, "Roll large stones against the mouth
of the cave, and assign men by it to guard them,
19 but do not stay *there* yourselves; pursue your enemies
and [1]attack them in the rear. Do not allow them to enter their
cities, for the LORD your God has delivered them into your
hand."
20 And it came about when Joshua and the sons of Israel
had finished [1]slaying them with a very great slaughter, [a]until
they were destroyed, and the survivors *who* remained of them
[2]had entered the fortified cities,
21 that all the people returned to the camp to Joshua at
Makkedah in peace. No one [1]uttered a word against any of the
sons of Israel.
22 Then Joshua said, "Open the mouth of the cave and
bring these five kings out to me from the cave."
23 And they did so, and [a]brought these five kings out to
him from the cave: the king of Jerusalem, the king of Hebron,
the king of Jarmuth, the king of Lachish, *and* the king of
Eglon.
24 And it came about when they brought these kings out
to Joshua, that Joshua called for all the men of Israel, and said
to the chiefs of the men of war who had gone with him,
"Come near, put your feet on the necks of these kings." So
they came near and put their feet on their necks.
25 Joshua then said to them, "[a]Do not fear or be

9 [1]Lit., *he went up*

10 [1]Lit., *struck*
[a]Deut. 7:23

11 [1]Lit., *with*

13 [a]Hab. 3:11 [b]2 Sam. 1:18
[c]Is. 38:8

14 [a]Josh 10:42; Ex. 14:14; Deut. 1:30

16 [a]Josh. 10:5

19 [1]Lit., *smite their tail*

20 [1]Lit., *striking* [2]Lit., *and had*
[a]Deut. 20:16

21 [1]Lit., *sharpened his tongue*

23 [a]Deut. 7:24

25 [a]Josh. 10:8

dismayed! Be strong and courageous, for thus the LORD will do
to all your enemies with whom you fight."
26 So afterward Joshua struck them and put them to
death, and he [a]hung them on five trees; and they hung on the
trees until evening.
27 And it came about at [1]sunset that Joshua commanded,
and [a]they took them down from the trees and threw them into
the cave where they had hidden themselves, and put large
stones over the mouth of the cave, to this very day.
28 Now Joshua captured Makkedah on that day, and
struck it and its king with the edge of the sword; [a]he [1]utterly
destroyed [2]it and every [3]person who was in it. He left no
survivor. Thus he did to the king of Makkedah [b]just as he had
done to the king of Jericho.
29 Then Joshua and all Israel with him passed on from
Makkedah to Libnah, and fought against Libnah.
30 And the LORD gave it also with its king into the hands
of Israel, and he struck it and every person who *was* in it with
the edge of the sword. He left no survivor in it. Thus he did to
its king just as he had done to the king of Jericho.
31 And Joshua and all Israel with him passed on from
Libnah to Lachish, and they camped by it and fought against
it.
32 And the LORD gave Lachish into the hands of Israel;
and he captured it on the second day, and struck it and every
person who *was* in it with the edge of the sword, according to
all that he had done to Libnah.
33 Then Horam king of Gezer came up to help Lachish,
and Joshua [1]defeated him and his people until he had left him
no survivor.
34 And Joshua and all Israel with him passed on from
Lachish to Eglon, and they camped by it and fought against it.
35 And they captured it on that day and struck it with the
edge of the sword; and he [1]utterly destroyed that day every
person who *was* in it, according to all that he had done to
Lachish.
36 Then Joshua and all Israel with him went up from
Eglon to Hebron, and they fought against it.
37 And they captured it and struck it and its king and all
its cities and all the persons who *were* in it with the edge of the
sword. He left no survivor, according to all that he had done to
Eglon. And he [1]utterly destroyed it and every person who *was*
in it.
38 Then Joshua and all Israel with him returned to Debir,
and they fought against it.
39 And he captured it and its king and all its cities, and
they struck them with the edge of the sword, and [1]utterly
destroyed every person *who was* in it. He left no survivor. Just
as he had done to Hebron, so he did to Debir and its king, as
he had also done to Libnah and its king.
40 Thus Joshua struck all the land, [a]the hill country and
the [1]Negev and the lowland and the slopes and [b]all their kings.
He left no survivor, but [c]he [2]utterly destroyed all who
breathed, just as the LORD, the God of Israel, had
commanded.
41 And Joshua struck them from Kadesh-barnea even as

26 [a]Josh. 8:29

27 [1]Lit., *the time of the going of the sun* [a]Deut. 21:22, 23

28 [1]Or, *put under the ban* [2]Some mss. read *them* [3]Lit., *soul,* and so throughout the chap. [a]Deut. 20:16 [b]Josh. 6:21

33 [1]Lit., *smote*

35 [1]Or, *put under the ban*

37 [1]Or, *put it under the ban*

39 [1]Or, *put it under the ban*

40 [1]I.e., South country [2]Or, *put it under the ban* [a]Deut. 1:7 [b]Deut. 7:24 [c]Deut. 20:16

far as Gaza, and all the country of [a]Goshen even as far as
Gibeon.
42 And Joshua captured all these kings and their lands at
one time, because the LORD, the God of Israel, [a]fought for
Israel.
43 So Joshua and all Israel with him returned to the camp
to Gilgal.

CHAPTER 11

THEN it came about, when Jabin king of [a]Hazor heard *of it,*
that he sent to Jobab king of Madon and to the king of Shimron and to the king of Achshaph,
2 and to the kings who were of the north in the hill
country, and in the [a]Arabah—south of [1]Chinneroth and in the
lowland and on the [2]heights of Dor on the west—
3 to the Canaanite on the east and on the west, and the
Amorite and the Hittite and the Perizzite and the Jebusite in
the hill country, and the Hivite [1]at the foot of Hermon in the
land of Mizpeh.
4 And they came out, they and all their armies with
them, *as* many people *as* [a]the sand that is on the seashore, with
very many horses and chariots.
5 So all of these kings having agreed to meet, came and
encamped together at the waters of Merom, to fight against
Israel.
6 Then the LORD said to Joshua, "[a]Do not be afraid because of them, for tomorrow at this time I will deliver all of
them slain before Israel; you shall [b]hamstring their horses and
burn their chariots with fire."
7 So Joshua and all the people of war with him came
upon them suddenly by the waters of Merom, and attacked
them.
8 And the LORD delivered them into the hand of Israel,
so that they [1]defeated them, and pursued them as far as great
Sidon and [a]Misrephoth-maim and the valley of [b]Mizpeh to the
east; and they struck them until no survivor was left to them.
9 And Joshua did to them as the LORD had told him; he
[a]hamstrung their horses, and burned their chariots with fire.
10 Then Joshua turned back at that time, and captured
[a]Hazor and struck its king with the sword; for Hazor formerly
was the head of all these kingdoms.
11 [a]And they struck every person who was in it with the
edge of the sword, [1]utterly destroying *them;* there was no one
left who breathed. And he burned Hazor with fire.
12 And Joshua captured all the cities of these kings, and
all their kings, and he struck them with the edge of the sword,
and utterly destroyed them; just as Moses the servant of the
LORD had commanded.
13 However, Israel did not burn any cities that stood on
their mounds, except Hazor alone, *which* Joshua burned.
14 [a]And all the spoil of these cities and the cattle, the sons
of Israel took as their plunder; but they struck every man with
the edge of the sword, until they had destroyed them. They
left no one who breathed.
15 Just as the LORD had commanded Moses his servant, so

41 [a]Josh. 11:16; 15:51

42 [a]Josh. 10:14

1 [a]Josh 11:10

2 [1]I.e., Sea of Galilee [2]Or, *Naphoth-dor* [a]Josh. 12:3-13:27

3 [1]Lit., *under*

4 [a]Judg. 7:12

6 [a]Josh. 10:8 [b]2 Sam. 8:4

8 [1]Lit., *smote* [a]Josh. 13:6 [b]Josh. 11:3

9 [a]Josh. 11:6

10 [a]Josh. 11:1

11 [1]Or, *putting them under the ban.* So throughout the chapter [a]Deut. 20:16

14 [a]Num. 31:11, 12

Moses commanded Joshua, and so Joshua did; he left nothing
undone of all that the LORD had commanded Moses.

16 [1]I.e., South country [a]Josh. 10:40, 41 [b]Josh. 11:2

16 Thus Joshua took all that land: [a]the hill country and all
the [1]Negev, all that land of Goshen, the lowland, [b]the Arabah,
the hill country of Israel and its lowland

17 [1]Lit., *under* [a]Josh. 12:7 [b]Deut. 7:24

17 from [a]Mount Halak, that rises toward Seir, even as far
as Baal-gad in the valley of Lebanon [1]at the foot of Mount
Hermon. And he captured [b]all their kings and struck them
down and put them to death.
18 Joshua waged war a long time with all these kings.

19 [a]Josh. 9:3, 7

19 There was not a city which made peace with the sons of
Israel except [a]the Hivites living in Gibeon; they took them all
in battle.

20 [1]Lit., *make strong* [2]Lit., *have* [a]Ex. 14:17

20 [a]For it was of the LORD to [1]harden their hearts, to meet
Israel in battle in order that he might utterly destroy them,
that they might [2]receive no mercy, but that he might destroy
them, just as the LORD had commanded Moses.

21 [a]Num. 13:33; Deut. 9:2

21 Then Joshua came at that time and cut off [a]the Anakim from the hill country, from Hebron, from Debir, from
Anab and from all the hill country of Judah and from all the
hill country of Israel. Joshua utterly destroyed them with their
cities.
22 There were no Anakim left in the land of the sons of
Israel; only in Gaza, in Gath, and in Ashdod some remained.

23 [a]Deut. 1:38 [b]Deut. 12:9, 10; 25:19; Heb. 4:8

23 So Joshua took the whole land, according to all that the
LORD had spoken to Moses, and [a]Joshua gave it for an inheritance to Israel according to their divisions by their tribes.
[b]Thus the land had rest from war.

1 [1]Lit., *smote* [a]Num. 32:33; Deut. 3:8-17

CHAPTER 12

[a]NOW these are the kings of the land whom the sons of Israel
[1]defeated, and whose land they possessed beyond the Jordan
toward the sunrise, from the valley of the Arnon as far as
Mount Hermon, and all the Arabah to the east:

2 [a]Deut. 2:36

2 Sihon king of the Amorites, who lived in Heshbon, *and*
ruled from Aroer, which is on the edge of the valley of the
Arnon, both [a]the middle of the valley and half of Gilead, even
as far as the brook Jabbok, the border of the sons of Ammon;

3 [1]I.e., Galilee [2]Lit., *the way of* [3]Lit., *under* [a]Josh. 11:2 [b]Josh. 13:20

3 and the [a]Arabah as far as the Sea of [1]Chinneroth toward the east, and as far as the sea of the Arabah, *even* the Salt
Sea, eastward [2]toward [b]Beth-jeshimoth, and on the south, [3]at
the foot of the slopes of Pisgah;

4 [a]Deut. 3:11

4 and the territory of Og king of Bashan, one of [a]the
remnant of Rephaim, who lived at Ashtaroth and at Edrei,
5 and ruled over Mount Hermon and Salecah and all
Bashan, as far as the border of the Geshurites and the Maacathites, and half of Gilead, *as far as* the border of Sihon king of
Heshbon.

6 [1]Lit., *smote*

6 Moses the servant of the LORD and the sons of Israel
[1]defeated them; and Moses the servant of the LORD gave it to
the Reubenites and the Gadites, and the half-tribe of Manasseh as a possession.

7 [1]Lit., *smote*

7 Now these are the kings of the land whom Joshua and
the sons of Israel [1]defeated beyond the Jordan toward the
west, from Baal-gad in the valley of Lebanon even as far as

[a]Mount Halak, which rises toward Seir; and Joshua gave it to
the tribes of Israel as a possession according to their divisions,
8 [a]in the hill country, in the lowland, in the Arabah, on
the slopes, and in the wilderness, and in the [1]Negev; the Hittite, the Amorite and the Canaanite, the Perizzite, the Hivite
and the Jebusite:
9 the king of Jericho, one; the king of Ai, which is beside
Bethel, one;
10 the king of Jerusalem, one; the king of Hebron, one;
11 the king of Jarmuth, one; the king of Lachish, one;
12 the king of Eglon, one; the king of Gezer, one;
13 the king of Debir, one; the king of Geder, one;
14 the king of Horman, one; the king of [a]Arad, one;
15 the king of Libnah, one; the king of Adullam, one
16 the king of Makkedah, one; the king of Bethel, one;
17 the king of Tappuah, one; the king of Hepher, one;
18 the king of Aphek, one; the king of Lasharon, one;
19 the king of Madon, one; the king of Hazor, one;
20 the king of Shimron-meron, one; the king of Achshaph,
one;
21 the king of Taanach, one; the king of Megiddo, one;
22 the king of Kedesh, one; the king of Jokneam in Carmel, one;
23 the king of Dor in the [1]heights of Dor, one; the king of
Goiim in Gilgal, one;
24 the king of Tirzah, one: [a]in all thirty-one kings.

CHAPTER 13

[a]NOW Joshua was old *and* advanced in years when the LORD
said to him, "You are old *and* advanced in years, and very
much of the land remains to be possessed.
2 "This is the land that remains: all the regions *of* the
Philistines and all *those of* the Geshurites;
3 from the Shihor which is [1]east of Egypt, even as far as
the border of Ekron to the north (it is counted as Canaanite);
the five lords of the Philistines: the Gazite, the Ashdodite, the
Ashkelonite, the Gittite, the Ekronite; and the Avvite
4 [1]to the south, all the land of the Canaanite, and Mea-
rah that belongs to the Sidonians, as far as Aphek, to the
border of the Amorite;
5 and the land of the Gebalite, and all of Lebanon, toward the [1]east, from Baal-gad below Mount Hermon as far as
[2]Lebo-hamath.
6 "All the inhabitants of the hill country from Lebanon as
far as [a]Misrephoth-maim, all the Sidonians, I will [1]drive them
out from before the sons of Israel; only allot it to Israel for an
inheritance as I have commanded you.
7 "Now therefore apportion this land for an inheritance
to the nine tribes, and the half-tribe of Manasseh."
8 With [1]the other half-tribe, the Reubenites and the Gadites received their inheritance which Moses gave them
[a]beyond the Jordan to the east, just as Moses the servant of the
LORD gave to them;
9 from Aroer, which is on the edge of the valley of the

7 [a]Josh. 11:17

8 [1]I.e., South country [a]Josh. 11:16

14 [a]Num. 21:1

23 [1]Or, *Naphath-dor*

24 [a]Deut. 7:24

1 [a]Josh. 14:10

3 [1]Lit., *on the face of*

4 [1]Or, *from the Teman*

5 [1]Lit., *sunrise* [2]Or, *the entrance of Hamath*

6 [1]Or, *dispossess* [a]Josh. 11:8

8 [1]Lit., *it, the* [a]Josh. 12:1-6

Arnon, with the city which is in the middle of the valley, and
all the plain of Medeba, as far as Dibon;
10 and all the cities of Sihon king of the Amorites, who
reigned in Heshbon, as far as the border of the sons of
Ammon;
11 and Gilead, and the [1]territory of the Geshurites and
Maacathites, and all Mount Hermon, and all Bashan as far as
Salecah;
12 all the kingdom of Og in Bashan, who reigned in Ashtaroth and in Edrei (he alone was left of the remnant of the
Rephaim); for Moses struck them and dispossessed them.
13 But the sons of Israel did not dispossess the Geshurites
or the Maacathites; for Geshur and Maacath live among Israel
until this day.
14 [a]Only to the tribe of Levi he did not give an inheritance; the offerings by fire to the LORD, the God of Israel, are
[1]their inheritance, as He spoke to him.
15 So Moses gave *an inheritance* to the tribe of the sons
of Reuben according to their families.
16 And their [1]territory was from [a]Aroer, which is on the
edge of the valley of the Arnon, with the city which is in the
middle of the valley and all the plain by Medeba;
17 Heshbon, and all its cities which are on the plain: Dibon and Bamoth-baal and Beth-baal-meon,
18 and Jahaz and Kedemoth and Mephaath,
19 and Kiriathaim and Sibmah and Zereth-shahar on the
hill of the valley,
20 and Beth-peor and the slopes of Pishgah and Beth-
jeshimoth,
21 even all the cities of the plain and all the kingdom of
Sihon king of the Amorites who reigned in Heshbon, whom
Moses struck with the chiefs of Midian, [a]Evi and Rekem and
Zur and Hur and Reba, the princes of Sihon, who lived in the
land.
22 The sons of Israel also killed [a]Balaam the son of Beor,
the diviner, with the sword among *the rest of* their slain.
23 And the border of the sons of Reuben was the [1]Jordan.
This was the inheritance of the sons of Reuben according to
their families, the cities and their villages.
24 Moses also gave *an inheritance* to the tribe of Gad, to
the sons of Gad, according to their families.
25 And their territory was Jazer, and all the cities of Gilead, and half the land of the sons of Ammon, as far as Aroer
which is before Rabbah;
26 and from Heshbon as far as Ramath-mizpeh and Beto-
nim, and from Mahanaim as far as the border of [1]Debir;
27 and in the valley, Beth-haram and Beth-nimrah and
Succoth and Zaphon, the rest of the kingdom of Sihon king of
Heshbon, with the Jordan [1]as a border, as far as the *lower* end
of the Sea of [2a]Chinnereth beyond the Jordan to the east.
28 This is the inheritance of the sons of Gad according to
their families, the cities and their villages.
29 Moses also gave *an inheritance* to the half-tribe of
Manasseh; and it was for the half-tribe of the sons of Manasseh
according to their families.
30 And their territory was from Mahanaim, all Bashan, all

11 [1]Or, *border*

14 [1]Lit., *his*
[a]Deut. 18:1, 2

16 [1]Or, *border*
[a]Josh. 13:9

21 [a]Num. 31:8

22 [a]Num. 31:8

23 [1]Lit., *Jordan and border*

26 [1]Or, *Lidebir*

27 [1]Lit., *and border* [2]I.e., Galilee
[a]Num. 34:11; Deut. 3:17

the kingdom of Og king of Bashan, and all [a]the [1]towns of Jair,
which are in Bashan, sixty cities;
31 also half of Gilead, with Ashtaroth and Edrei, the cities
of the kingdom of Og in Bashan, *were* for the sons of Machir
the son of Manasseh, for half of the sons of Machir according
to their families.
32 These are *the territories* which Moses apportioned for
an inheritance in the plains of Moab, beyond the Jordan at
Jericho to the east.
33 [a]But to the tribe of Levi Moses did not give an inheritance; the LORD, the God of Israel, is their inheritance, as He
had [1]promised to them.

30 [1]Lit., *tent villages* [a]Num. 32:41

33 [1]Lit., *spoken to* [a]Josh. 13:14

CHAPTER 14

NOW these are *the territories* which the sons of Israel inherited in the land of Canaan, which [a]Eleazar the priest, and
Joshua the son of Nun, and the heads of the [1]households of
the tribes of the sons of Israel apportioned to them for an
inheritance,
2 by the lot of their inheritance, as the LORD commanded
[1]through Moses, for the nine tribes and the half-tribe.
3 [a]For Moses had given the inheritance of the two tribes
and the half-tribe beyond the Jordan; [b]but he did not give an
inheritance to the the Levites among them.
4 For the sons of Joseph were two tribes, Manasseh and
Ephraim, and they did not give a portion to the Levites in the
land, except cities to live in, with their pasture lands for their
livestock and for their property.
5 Thus the sons of Israel did just as the LORD had commanded Moses, and they divided the land.
6 Then the sons of Judah drew near to Joshua in Gilgal,
and [a]Caleb the son of Jephunneh the Kenizzite said to him,
"You know the word which the LORD spoke to Moses the man
of God concerning [1]you and me in Kadesh-barnea.
7 "I was forty years old when Moses the servant of the
LORD sent me from Kadesh-barnea to spy out the land, and I
brought word back to him as *it was* in my heart.
8 "Nevertheless my brethren who went up with me made
the heart of the people [1]melt with fear; but I followed the
LORD my God fully.
9 "[a]So Moses swore on that day, saying, 'Surely the land
on which your foot has trodden shall be an inheritance to you
and to your children forever, because you have followed the
LORD my God fully.'
10 "And now behold, the LORD has let me live, just as He
spoke, these forty-five years, from the time that the LORD
spoke this word to Moses, when Israel walked in the wilderness; and now behold, I am eighty-five years old today.
11 "I am still as strong today as I was in the day Moses sent
me; as my strength was then, so my strength is now, for war
and for going out and coming in.
12 "Now then, give me this hill country about which the
LORD spoke on that day, for you heard on that day that [a]Anakim
were there, with great fortified cities; perhaps the LORD

1 [1]Lit., *fathers'* [a]Num. 34:16-29

2 [1]Lit., *by the hand of*

3 [a]Num. 32:33 [b]Josh. 13:14

6 [1]Lit., *me and concerning you* [a]Num. 13:6, 30; 14:6, 24, 30

8 [1]Lit., *become demoralized*

9 [a]Deut. 1:36

12 [a]Num. 13:33

12 [1]Or, *dispossess*

will be with me, and I shall [1]drive them out as the LORD has
spoken."
13 So Joshua blessed him, and gave Hebron to Caleb the
son of Jephunneh for an inheritance.
14 Therefore, Hebron became the inheritance of Caleb
the son of Jephunneh the Kenizzite until this day, because he
followed the LORD God of Israel fully.

15 [1]I.e., the city of Arba
[a]Josh. 11:23

15 Now the name of Hebron was formerly [1]Kiriath-arba;
for Arba was the greatest man among the Anakim. [a]Then the
land had rest from war.

CHAPTER 15

1 [1]Lit., *was to*
[a]Num. 34:3, 4 [b]Num. 20:16
[c]Deut. 32:51

[a] NOW the lot for the tribe of the sons of Judah according to
their families [1]reached the [b]border of Edom, southward to the
wilderness of [c]Zin at the extreme south.
2 And their south border was from the lower end of the
Salt Sea, from the bay that turns to the south.
3 Then it proceeded southward to the ascent of Akrabbim and continued to Zin, then went up by the south of
Kadesh-barnea and continued to Hezron, and went up to Addar and turned about to Karka.

4 [1]Or, *wadi* [2]Lit., *goings out of the border were*

4 And it continued to Azmon and proceeded to the
[1]brook of Egypt; and the [2]border ended at the sea. This shall
be your south border.

5 [1]Lit., *end*
[a]Num. 34:3 [b]Josh. 18:15-19

5 [a]And the east border *was* the Salt Sea, as far as the
[1]mouth of the Jordan. [b]And the border of the north side was
from the bay of the sea at the [1]mouth of the Jordan.
6 Then the border went up to Beth-hoglah, and continued on the north of Beth-arabah, and the border went up to
the stone of Bohan the son of Reuben.

7 [1]Lit., *the goings out of it were*
[a]Deut. 7:24

7 And the border went up to Debir from [a]the valley of
Achor, and turned northward toward Gilgal which is opposite
the ascent of Adummim, which is on the south of the valley;
and the border continued to the waters of En-shemesh, and [1]it
ended at En-rogel.

8 [a]Josh. 15:63

8 Then the border went up the valley of Ben-Hinnom to
the slope of the [a]Jebusite on the south (that is, Jerusalem); and
the border went up to the top of the mountain which is before
the valley of Hinnom to the west, which is at the end of the
valley Rephaim toward the north.
9 And from the top of the mountain the border curved
to the spring of the waters of Nephtoah and proceeded to the
cities of Mount Ephron, then the border curved to Baalah
(that is, Kiriath-jearim).
10 And the border turned about from Baalah westward to
Mount Seir, and continued to the slope of Mount Jearim on
the north (that is, Chesalon), and went down to Beth-shemesh
and continued through Timnah.

11 [1]Lit., *goings out . . . were*

11 And the border proceeded to the side of Ekron northward. Then the border curved to Shikkeron and continued to
Mount Baalah and proceeded to Jabneel, and the [1]border
ended at the sea.

12 [1]Lit., *border*

12 And the west border *was* at the Great Sea, even *its*
[1]coastline. This is the border around the sons of Judah according to their families.

13 [a]Now he gave to Caleb the son of Jephunneh a portion
[b]among the sons of Judah, according to the [1]command of the
LORD to Joshua, *namely,* [2]Kiriath-arba, *Arba being* the father
of Anak (that is, Hebron).
14 And [a]Caleb [1]drove out from there the three sons of
Anak: Sheshai and Ahiman and Talmai, the children of Anak.
15 Then he went up from there against the inhabitants of
Debir; now the name of Debir formerly was Kiriath-sepher.
16 And Caleb said, "The one who [1]attacks Kiriath-sepher
and captures it, [2]I will give him Achsah my daughter as a wife."
17 [a]And Othniel the son of Kenaz, the brother of Caleb,
captured it; so he gave him Achsah his daughter as a wife.
18 And it came about that when she came *to him,* she
persuaded him to ask her father for a field. So she alighted
from the donkey, and Caleb said to her, "What do you want?"
19 Then she said, "Give me a blessing; since you have
given me the land of the [1]Negev, give me also springs of water." So he gave her the upper springs and the lower springs.
20 This is the inheritance of the tribe of the sons of Judah
according to their families.
21 Now the cities at the extremity of the tribe of the sons
of Judah toward the border of Edom in the south were Kabzeel and [a]Eder and Jagur,
22 and Kinah and Dimonah and Adadah,
23 and Kedesh and Hazor and Ithnan,
24 Ziph and Telem and Bealoth,
25 and Hazor-hadattah and Kerioth-hezron (that is,
Hazor),
26 Amam and Shema and Moladah,
27 and Hazar-gaddah and Heshmon and Beth-pelet,
28 and Hazar-shual and [a]Beer-sheba and Biziothiah,
29 Baalah and Iim and Ezem,
30 and Eltolad and Chesil and Hormah,
31 and [a]Ziklag and Madmannah and Sansannah,
32 and Lebaoth and Shilhim and Ain and Rimmon; in all,
twenty-nine cities with their villages.
33 In the lowland: [a]Eshtaol and Zorah and Ashnah,
34 and Zanoah and En-gannim, Tappuah and Enam,
35 Jarmuth and [a]Adullam, Socoh and Azekah,
36 and Shaaraim and Adithaim and Gederah and Gedero-
thaim; fourteen cites with their villages.
37 Zenan and Hadashah and Migdal-gad,
38 and Dilean and Mizpeh and Joktheel,
39 [a]Lachish and Bozkath and Eglon,
40 and Cabbon and Lahmas and Chitlish,
41 and Gederoth, Beth-dagon and Naamah and Makkedah; sixteen cities with their villages.
42 Libnah and Ether and Ashan,
43 and Iphtah and Ashnah and Nezib,
44 and Keilah and Achzib and Mareshah; nine cities with
their villages.
45 Ekron, with its towns and its villages;
46 from Ekron even to the sea, all that were by the [1]side of
Ashdod, with their villages.
47 Ashdod, its towns and its villages; Gaza, its towns and

13 [1]Lit., *mouth* [2]I.e., the city of Arba [a]Josh. 14:13-15 [b]Num. 13:6

14 [1]Or, *dispossessed* [a]Josh. 11:21, 22; Num. 13:33; Deut. 9:2

16 [1]Lit., *smites* [2]Lit., *and I*

17 [a]Judg. 1:13; 3:9

19 [1]I.e., South country

21 [a]Gen. 35:21

28 [a]Gen. 21:31

31 [a]1 Sam. 27:6; 30:1

33 [a]Judg. 13:25; 16:31

35 [a]1 Sam. 22:1

39 [a]Josh. 10:3; 2 Kin. 14:19

46 [1]Lit., *hand*

47 [1]Or, *wadi* [2]Lit., *border*
[a]Josh. 13:3

63 [1]Or, *dispossess them*
[a]Judg. 1:21; 2 Sam. 5:6

1 [a]Josh. 8:15; 18:12

3 [1]Lit., *goings out of it were*
[a]Josh. 18:13; 1 Kin. 9:17
[b]Josh. 10:33

5 [a]Josh. 18:13

6 [a]Josh. 17:7

7 [a]1 Chr. 7:28

8 [1]Or, *wadi* [2]Lit., *goings out of it were*
[a]Josh. 17:8

10 [1]Or, *dispossess*
[a]Judg. 1:29; 1 Kin. 9:16
[b]Josh. 17:12, 13

its villages; as far as [a]the [1]brook of Egypt and the Great Sea,
even *its* [2]coastline.
48 And in the hill country: Shamir and Jattir and Socoh,
49 and Dannah and Kiriath-sannah (that is, Debir),
50 and Anab and Eshtemoh and Anim,
51 and Goshen and Holon and Giloh; eleven cities with
their villages.
52 Arab and Dumah and Eshan,
53 and Janum and Beth-tappuah and Aphekah,
54 and Humtah and Kiriath-arba (that is, Hebron), and
Zior; nine cities with their villages.
55 Maon, Carmel and Ziph and Juttah,
56 and Jezreel and Jokdeam and Zanoah,
57 Kain, Gibeah and Timnah; ten cities with their villages.
58 Halhul, Beth-zur and Gedor,
59 and Maarath and Beth-anoth and Eltekon; six cities
with their villages.
60 Kiriath-baal (that is, Kiriath-jearim), and Rabbah; two
cities with their villages.
61 In the wilderness: Beth-arabah, Middin and Secacah,
62 and Nibshan and the City of Salt and Engedi; six cities
with their villages.
63 Now as for the [a]Jebusites, the inhabitants of Jerusalem,
the sons of Judah could not [1]drive them out; so the Jebusites
live with the sons of Judah at Jerusalem until this day.

Chapter 16

THEN the lot for the sons of Joseph went from the Jordan at
Jericho to the waters of Jericho on the east into [a]the wilderness, going up from Jericho through the hill country to Bethel.
2 And it went from Bethel to Luz, and continued to the
border of the Archites at Ataroth.
3 And it went down westward to the territory of the Japh-
letites, as far as the territory of lower [a]Beth-horon even to
[b]Gezer, and [1]it ended at the sea.
4 And the sons of Joseph, Manasseh and Ephraim, received their inheritance.
5 Now *this* was the territory of the sons of Ephraim according to their families: the border of their inheritance eastward was [a]Ataroth-addar, as far as upper Beth-horon.
6 Then the border went westward at [a]Michmethath on
the north, and the border turned about eastward to Taanath-
shiloh, and continued *beyond* it to the east of Janoah.
7 And it went down from Janoah to Ataroth and to [a]Na-
arah, then reached Jericho and came out at the Jordan.
8 From [a]Tappuah the border continued westward to the
[1]brook of Kanah, and [2]it ended at the sea. This is the inheritance of the tribe of the sons of Ephraim according to their
families,
9 *together* with the cities which were set apart for the
sons of Ephraim in the midst of the inheritance of the sons of
Manasseh, all the cities with their villages.
10 [a]But they did not [1]drive out the Canaanites who lived
in Gezer, so [b]the Canaanites live in the midst of Ephraim to
this day, and they became forced laborers.

CHAPTER 17

NOW *this* was the lot for the tribe of Manasseh, for he was
the first-born of Joseph. To Machir the first-born of Manasseh, the father of Gilead, [1]was allotted Gilead and Bashan,
because he was a man of war.
2 So *the lot* was *made* for the rest of the sons of Manasseh according to their families: for the sons of Abiezer and for
the sons of Helek and for the sons of Asriel and for the sons of
Shechem and for the sons of Hepher and for the sons of
Shemida; these *were* the male *descendants* of Manasseh the
son of Joseph according to their families.
3 [a]However, Zelophehad, the son of Hepher, the son of
Gilead, the son of Machir, the son of Manasseh, had no sons,
only daughters; and these are the names of his daughters: Mahlah and Noah, Hoglah, Milcah and Tirzah.
4 And they came near before Eleazar the priest and before Joshua the son of Nun and before the leaders, saying,
"The LORD commanded Moses to give us an inheritance
among our brothers." So [a]according to the [1]command of the
LORD he gave them an inheritance among their father's
brothers.
5 Thus there fell ten portions to Manasseh, besides the
land of Gilead and Bashan, which is beyond the Jordan,
6 because the daughters of Manassesh received an inheritance among his sons. And the [a]land of Gilead belonged to the
rest of the sons of Manasseh.
7 And the border of Manasseh [1]ran from Asher to Mich-
methath which was east of Shechem; then the border went
[2]southward to the inhabitants of En-tappuah.
8 The land of Tappuah belonged to Manasseh, but Tappuah on the border of Manasseh *belonged* to the sons of
Ephraim.
9 And the border went down to the [1]brook of Kanah,
southward of the [1]brook (these cities *belonged* to Ephraim
among the cities of Manasseh), and the border of Manasseh
was on the north side of the [1]brook, and [2]it ended at the sea.
10 The south side *belonged* to Ephraim and the north side
to Manasseh, and the sea was [1]their border; and they reached
to Asher on the north and to Issachar on the east.
11 And in Issachar and in Asher, [a]Manasseh had Beth-
shean and its towns and Ibleam and its towns, and the inhabitants of Dor and its towns, and the inhabitants of En-dor and
its towns, and the inhabitants of Taanach and its towns, and
the inhabitants of Megiddo and its towns, the third is
[b]Napheth.
12 [a]But the sons of Manasseh could not take possession of
these cities, because the Canaanites persisted in living in that
land.
13 And it came about when the sons of Israel became
strong, [a]they put the Canaanites to forced labor, but they did
not [1]drive them out completely.
14 Then the sons [a]of Joseph spoke to Joshua, saying,
"Why have you given me only one lot and one portion for an
inheritance, since I am a numerous people whom the LORD has
thus far blessed?"

1 [1]Lit., *and there was to him*
3 [a]Num. 26:33; 27:1-7
4 [1]Lit., *mouth* [a]Num. 27:5-7
6 [a]Josh. 13:30, 31
7 [1]Lit., *was* [2]Lit., *to the right hand*
9 [1]Or, *wadi* [2]Lit., *goings out of it were*
10 [1]Lit., *its*
11 [a]1 Chr. 7:29 [b]Josh. 11:2; 12:23
12 [a]Judg. 1:27
13 [1]Or, *dispossess* [a]Josh. 16:10
14 [a]Num. 13:8

15 And Joshua said to them, "If you are a numerous
people, go [1]up to the forest and [2]clear a place for yourself
there in the land of the Perizzites and of the Rephaim, since
the hill country of Ephraim is too narrow for you."
16 And the sons of Joseph said, "The hill country is not
enough for us, and all the Canaanites who live in the valley
land have [a]chariots of iron, both those who are in Beth-shean
and its towns, and those who are in the valley of Jezreel."
17 And Joshua spoke to the house of Joseph, to Ephraim
and Manasseh, saying, "You are a numerous people and have
great power; you shall not have one lot *only*,
18 but the hill country shall be yours. For though it is a
forest, you shall [1]clear it, and to its [2]farthest borders it shall be
yours; for you shall [3]drive out the Canaanites, even though
they have [a]chariots of iron *and* though they are strong."

CHAPTER 18

THEN the whole congregation of the sons of Israel
assembled themselves at [a]Shiloh, and set up the tent of meeting there; and the land was subdued before them.
2 And there remained among the sons of Israel seven
tribes who had not divided their inheritance.
3 So Joshua said to the sons of Israel, "How long will you
put off entering to take possession of the land which the LORD,
the God of your fathers, has given you?
4 "Provide for yourselves three men from [1]each tribe that
I may send them, and that they may arise and walk through
the land and write a description of it according to their inheritance; then they shall [2]return to me.
5 "And they shall divide it into seven portions; Judah shall
stay in its territory on the south, and the house of Joseph shall
stay in their territory on the north.
6 "And you shall describe the land in seven divisions, and
bring *the description* here to me. And I will cast lots for you
here before the LORD our God.
7 "For [a]the Levites have no portion among you, because
the priesthood of the LORD is [1]their inheritance. Gad and Reuben and the half-tribe of Manasseh also have received their
inheritance eastward beyond the Jordan, which Moses the servant of the LORD gave them."
8 Then the men arose and went, and Joshua commanded
those who went to describe the land, saying, "Go and walk
through the land and describe it, and return to me; then I will
cast lots for you here before the LORD in [a]Shiloh."
9 So the men went and passed through the land, and
described it by cities in seven divisions in a book; and they
came to Joshua to the camp at Shiloh.
10 [a]And Joshua cast lots for them in Shiloh before the
LORD, and there Joshua divided the land to the sons of Israel
according to their divisions.
11 Now the lot of the tribe of the sons of Benjamin came
up according to their families, and the territory of their lot [1]lay
between the sons of Judah and the sons of Joseph.
12 And their border on the north side was from the Jordan, then the border went up to the side of Jericho on the

15 [1]Lit., *up for yourself* [2]Lit., *cut down*

16 [a]Josh. 17:18; Judg. 1:19; 4:3, 13

18 [1]Lit., *cut down* [2]Lit., *goings out* [3]Or, *dispossess* [a]Josh. 17:16

1 [a]Judg. 21:19; Jer. 7:12; 26:6, 9

4 [1]Lit., *the* [2]Lit., *come*

7 [1]Lit., *his* [a]Josh. 13:33; Num. 18:7, 20

8 [a]Josh. 18:1

10 [a]Josh. 19:51; Num. 34:16-29

11 [1]Lit., *went out*

north, and went up through the hill country westward; and [1]it
ended at the wilderness of Beth-aven.
13 And from there the border continued to Luz, to the
side of Luz (that is, Bethel) southward; and the border went
down to Ataroth-addar, near the hill which *lies* on the south of
lower Beth-horon.
14 And the border extended *from there*, and turned round
on the west side southward, from the hill which *lies* before
Beth-horon southward; and [1]it ended at Kiriath-baal (that is,
Kiriath-jearim), a city of the sons of Judah. This *was* the west
side.
15 [a]Then the south side *was* from the edge of Kiriath-
jearim, and the border went westward and went to the fountain of the waters of Nephtoah.
16 And the border went down to the edge of the hill which
is in the valley of Ben-Hinnom, which is in the vale of Rephaim northward; and it went down to the valley of Hinnom, to
the slope of the Jebusite southward, and went down to En-
rogel.
17 And it extended northward and went to En-shemesh
and went to Geliloth, which is opposite the ascent of Adummim, and it went down to the stone of Bohan the son of
Reuben.
18 And it continued to the side in front of the Arabah
northward, and went down to the Arabah.
19 And the border continued to the side of Beth-hoglah
northward; and the [1]border ended at the north bay of the Salt
Sea, at the south end of the Jordan. This *was* the south border.
20 Moreover, the Jordan was its border on the east side.
This *was* the inheritance of the sons of Benjamin, according to
their families *and* according to its borders all around.
21 Now the cities of the tribe of the sons of Benjamin
according to their families were Jericho and Beth-hoglah and
Emek-keziz,
22 and Beth-arabah and Zemaraim and Bethel,
23 and Avvim and Parah and Ophrah,
24 and Chephar-ammoni and Ophni and Geba; twelve
cities with their villages.
25 Gibeon and Ramah and Beeroth,
26 and Mizpeh and Chephirah and Mozah,
27 and Rekem and Irpeel and Taralah,
28 and Zelah, Haeleph and the Jebusite (that is, Jerusalem), Gilbeath, Kiriath; fourteen cities with their villages. This
is the inheritance of the sons of Benjamin according to their
families.

Chapter 19

THEN the second lot [1]fell to Simeon, to the tribe of the sons
of Simeon according to their families, and their inheritance
was in the midst of the inheritance of the sons of Judah.
2 So they had as their inheritance Beersheba and [1]Sheba
and Moladah,
3 and Hazar-shual and Balah and Ezem,
4 and Eltolad and Bethul and Hormah,

12 [1]Lit., *goings out of it were*

14 [1]Lit., *goings out of it were*

15 [a]Josh. 15:5-9

19 [1]Lit., *goings out of the border were*

1 [1]Lit., *came out*

2 [1]Or, *Shema*, cf. Josh. 15:26

5 and Ziklag and Beth-marcaboth and Hazar-susah,
6 and Beth-lebaoth and Sharuhen, thirteen cities with
their villages;
7 Ain, Rimmon and Ether and Ashan, four cities with
their villages;
8 and all the villages which *were* around these cities as far
as Baalath-beer, Ramah of the [1]Negev. This *was* the inheritance of the tribe of the sons of Simeon according to their
families.
9 The inheritance of the sons of Simeon *was taken* from
the portion of the sons of Judah, for the share of the sons of
Judah was too large for them; so the sons of Simeon received
an inheritance in the midst of [1]Judah's inheritance.
10 Now the third lot came up for the sons of Zebulun
according to their families. And the territory of their inheritance was as far as Sarid.
11 Then their border went up to the west and Marealah, it
then [1]touched Dabbesheth, and reached to the [2]brook that is
before Jokneam.
12 Then it turned from Sarid to the east toward the sunrise as far as the border of Chisloth-tabor, and it proceeded to
Daberath and [1]up to Japhia.
13 And from there it continued eastward toward the sunrise to Gath-hepher, to Eth-kazin, and it proceeded to Rimmon [1]which stretches to Neah.
14 And the border circled around it on the north to Han-
nothon, and [1]it ended at the valley of Iphtahel.
15 *Included* also *were* Kattah and Nahalal and Shimron
and Idalah and Bethlehem; twelve cities with their villages.
16 This *was* the inheritance of the sons of Zebulun according to their families, these cities with their villages.
17 The fourth lot [1]fell to Issachar, to the sons of Issachar
according to their families.
18 And their territory was to Jezreel and *included* Chesul-
loth and Shunem,
19 and Hapharaim and Shion and Anaharath,
20 and Rabbith and Kishion and Ebez,
21 and Remeth and En-gannim and En-haddah and Beth-
pazzez.
22 And the border reached to Tabor and Shahazumah and
Beth-shemesh, and [1]their border ended at the Jordan; sixteen
cities with their villages.
23 This *was* the inheritance of the tribe of the sons of
Issachar according to their families, the cities with their
villages.
24 Now the fifth lot [1]fell to the tribe of the sons of Asher
according to their families.
25 And their territory was Helkath and Hali and Beten
and Achshaph,
26 and Allammelech and Amad and Mishal; and it
reached to Carmel on the west and to Shihor-libnath.
27 And it turned toward the [1]east to Beth-dagon, and
reached to Zebulun, and to the valley of Iphtahel northward
to Beth-emek and Neiel; then it proceeded on [2]north to
Cabul,

8 [1]I.e., South country
9 [1]Lit., *their*
11 [1]Or, *reached to* [2]Or, *wadi*
12 [1]Lit., *went up*
13 [1]Or, *and is marked off*
14 [1]Lit., *goings out of it were*
17 [1]Lit., *came out*
22 [1]Lit., *goings out of their border were*
24 [1]Lit., *came out*
27 [1]Lit., *sunrise* [2]Lit., *from the left hand*

28 and Ebron and Rehob and Hammon and Kanah, as far
as Great Sidon.
29 And the border turned to Ramah, and to the fortified
city of Tyre; then the border turned to Hosah, and [1]it ended at
the sea by the region of Achzib.
30 *Included* also *were* Ummah, and Aphek and Rehob;
twenty-two cities with their villages.
31 This *was* the inheritance of the tribe of the sons of
Asher according to their families, these cities with their
villages.
32 The sixth lot [1]fell to the sons of Naphtali; to the sons
of Naphtali according to their families.
33 And their border was from Heleph, from the oak in
Zaanannim and Adami-nekeb and Jabneel, as far as Lakkum;
and [1]it ended at the Jordan.
34 Then the border turned westward to Aznoth-tabor, and
proceeded from there to Hukkok; and it reached to Zebulun
on the south and [1]touched Asher on the west, and to Judah at
the Jordan toward the [2]east.
35 And the fortified cities *were* Ziddim, Zer and Hammath, Rakkath and Chinnereth,
36 and Adamah and Ramah and Hazor,
37 and Kedesh and Edrei and En-hazor,
38 and Yiron and Migdal-el, Horem and Beth-anath and
Beth-shemesh; nineteen cities with their villages.
39 This *was* the inheritance of the tribe of the sons of
Naphtali according to their families, the cities with their
villages.
40 The seventh lot [1]fell to the tribe of the sons of Dan
according to their families.
41 And the territory of their inheritance was Zorah and
Eshtaol and Ir-shemesh,
42 and Shaalabbin and Aijalon and Ithlah,
43 and Elon and Timnah and Ekron,
44 and Eltekeh and Gibbethon and Baalath,
45 and Jehud and Bene-berak and Gath-rimmon,
46 and Me-jarkon and Rakkon, with the territory over
against [1]Joppa.
47 And the territory of the sons of Dan proceeded
[1]beyond them; for the sons of Dan went up and fought with
Leshem and captured it. Then they struck it with the edge of
the sword and possessed it and [2]settled in it; and they called
Leshem Dan after the name of Dan their father.
48 This *was* the inheritance of the tribe of the sons of Dan
according to their families, these cities with their villages.
49 When they finished apportioning the land for inheritance by its borders, the sons of Israel gave an inheritance in
their midst to Joshua the son of Nun.
50 In accordance with the [1]command of the LORD they
gave him the city for which he asked, [a]Timnath-serah in the
hill country of Ephraim. So he built the city and [2]settled in it.
51 [a]These are the inheritances which Eleazar the priest
and Joshua the son of Nun and the heads of the [1]households
of the tribes of the sons of Israel distributed by lot in Shiloh
before the LORD, at the doorway of the tent of meeting. So
they finished dividing the land.

29 [1]Lit., *goings out of it were*

32 [1]Lit., *came out*

33 [1]Lit., *goings out of it were*

34 [1]Or, *reached to* [2]Lit., *sunrise*

40 [1]Lit., *came out*

46 [1]Heb., *Japho*

47 [1]Lit., *from* [2]Lit., *dwelt*

50 [1]Lit., *mouth* [2]Lit., *dwelt*
[a]Josh. 24:30; Num. 13:8

51 [1]Lit., *fathers*
[a]Josh. 18:10

Chapter 20

THEN the Lord spoke to Joshua, saying,
2 "Speak to the sons of Israel, saying, '[1]Designate [a]the
cities of refuge, of which I spoke to you [2]through Moses,
3 that the manslayer who [1]kills any person unintentionally, without premeditation, may flee there, and they shall
become your refuge from the avenger of blood.
4 'And he shall flee to one of these cities, and shall stand
at the entrance of the gate of the city and state his case in the
hearing of the elders of that city; and they shall [1]take him into
the city to them and give him a place, so that he may dwell
among them.
5 'Now if the avenger of blood pursues him, then they
shall not deliver the manslayer into his hand, because he struck
his neighbor without premeditation and did not hate him
beforehand.
6 'And he shall dwell in that city until he stands before
the congregation for judgment, until the death of the one who
is high priest in those days. Then the manslayer shall [1]return to
his own city and to his own house, to the city from which he
fled.' "
7 So they [1]set apart [a]Kedesh in [2]Galilee in the hill country of Naphtali and Shechem in the hill country of Ephraim,
and Kiriath-arba (that is, Hebron) in [b]the hill country of
Judah.
8 And beyond the Jordan east of Jericho, they [1]desig-
nated Bezer in the wilderness on the plain from the tribe of
Reuben, and Ramoth in Gilead from the tribe of Gad, and
Golan in Bashan from the tribe of Manasseh.
9 These were the appointed cities for all the sons of Israel and for the stranger who sojourns among them, that whoever [1]kills any person unintentionally may flee there, and not
die by the hand of the avenger of blood until he stands before
the congregation.

Chapter 21

THEN the heads of [1]households [a]of the Levites approached
Eleazar the priest and Joshua the son of Nun and the heads of
[1]households of the tribes of the sons of Israel.
2 And they spoke to them at Shiloh in the land of Canaan, saying, "[a]The Lord commanded [1]through Moses to give
us cities to live in, with their pasture lands for our cattle."
3 So the sons of Israel gave the Levites from their inheritance these cities with their pasture lands, according to the
[1]command of the Lord.
4 Then the lot came out for the families of the Kohathites. And the sons of Aaron the priest, who were of the Levites, [1]received thirteen cities by lot from the tribe of Judah
and from the tribe of the Simeonites and from the tribe of
Benjamin.
5 And the rest of the sons of Kohath [1]received ten cities
by lot from the families of the tribe of Ephraim and from the
tribe of Dan and from the half-tribe of Manasseh.
6 And the sons of Gershon [1]received thirteen cities by lot

20:2 [1]Lit., *set for yourselves* [2]Lit., *by the hand of* [a]Num. 35:6-34; Deut. 4:41; 19:2
3 [1]Lit., *smites*
4 [1]Lit., *gather*
6 [1]Lit., *return and come*
7 [1]Lit., *sanctified* [2]Heb. *Galil* [a]Josh. 21:32; 1 Chr. 6:76 [b]Josh. 21:11; Luke 1:39
8 [1]Lit., *set*
9 [1]Lit., *smites*

21:1 [1]Lit., *fathers* [a]Num. 35:1-8
2 [1]Lit., *by the hand of* [a]Num. 35:2
3 [1]Lit., *mouth*
4 [1]Lit., *had*
5 [1]Lit., *had*
6 [1]Lit., *had*

from the families of the tribe of Issachar and from the tribe of
Asher and from the tribe of Naphtali and from the half-tribe
of Manasseh in Bashan.
7 The sons of Merari according to their families [1]re-
ceived twelve cities from the tribe of Reuben and from the
tribe of Gad and from the tribe of Zebulun.
8 Now the sons of Israel gave by lot to the Levites these
cities with their pasture lands, as the LORD had commanded
[1]through Moses.
9 And they gave these cities which are *here* mentioned by
name from the tribe of the sons of Judah and from the tribe of
the sons of Simeon;
10 and they were for the sons of Aaron, one of the families
of the Kohathites, of the sons of Levi, for the lot was theirs
first.
11 Thus they gave them Kirath-arba, *Arba being* the father
of Anak (that is, Hebron), in the hill country of Judah,
with its surrounding pasture lands.
12 But the fields of the city and its villages, they gave to
Caleb the son of Jephunneh as his possession.
13 So to the sons of Aaron the priest they gave Hebron,
the city of refuge for the manslayer, with its pasture lands, and
Libnah with its pasture lands,
14 and Jattir with its pasture lands and Eshtemoa with its
pasture lands,
15 and Holon with its pasture lands and Debir with its
pasture lands,
16 and Ain with its pasture lands and Juttah with its pasture lands *and* Beth-shemesh with its pasture lands; nine cities
from these two tribes.
17 And from the tribe of Benjamin, Gibeon with its pasture lands, Geba with its pasture lands,
18 Anathoth with its pasture lands and Almon with its
pasture lands; four cities.
19 All the cities of the sons of Aaron, the priests, were
thirteen cities with their pasture lands.
20 Then the cities from the tribe of Ephraim were allotted
to the families of the sons of Kohath, the Levites, *even to* the
rest of the sons of Kohath.
21 And they gave them Shechem, the city of refuge for
the manslayer, with its pasture lands, in the hill country of
Ephraim, and Gezer with its pasture lands,
22 and Kibzaim with its pasture lands and Beth-horon
with its pasture lands; four cities.
23 And from the tribe of Dan, Eltekе with its pasture
lands, Gibbethon with its pasture lands,
24 Aijalon with its pasture lands, Gath-rimmon with its
pasture lands; four cities.
25 And from the half-tribe of Manasseh, *they allotted*
Taanach with its pasture lands and Gath-rimmon with its pasture lands; two cities.
26 All the cities with their pasture lands for the families of
the rest of the sons of Kohath were ten.
27 And to the sons of Gershon, one of the families of the
Levites, from the half-tribe of Manasseh, *they gave* Golan in

7 [1]Lit., *had*

8 [1]Lit., *by the hand of*

Bashan, the city of refuge for the manslayer, with its pasture
lands, and Be-eshterah with its pasture lands; two cities.
28 And from the tribe of Issachar, *they gave* Kishion with
its pasture lands, Daberath with its pasture lands,
29 Jarmuth with its pasture lands, En-gannim with its pasture lands; four cities.
30 And from the tribe of Asher, *they gave* Mishal with its
pasture lands, Abdon with its pasture lands,
31 Helkath with its pasture lands and Rehob with its pasture lands; four cities.
32 And from the tribe of Naphtali, *they gave* Kedesh in
Galilee, the city of refuge for the manslayer, with its pasture
lands and Hammoth-dor with its pasture lands and Kartan
with its pasture lands; three cities.
33 All the cities of the Gershonites according to their families were thirteen cities with their pasture lands.
34 And to the families of the sons of Merari, the rest of
the Levites, *they gave* from the tribe of Zebulun, Jokneam
with its pasture lands and Kartah with its pasture lands.
35 Dimnah with its pasture lands, Nahalal with its pasture
lands; four cities.
36 And from the tribe of Reuben, *they gave* Bezer with its
pasture lands and Jahaz with its pasture lands,
37 Kedemoth with its pasture lands and Mephaath with its
pasture lands; four cities.
38 And from the tribe of Gad, *they gave* Ramoth in Gilead, the city of refuge for the manslayer, with its pasture lands
and Mahaniam with its pasture lands,
39 Heshbon with its pasture lands, Jazer with its pasture
lands; four cities in all.
40 All *these were* the cities of the sons of Merari according
to their families, the rest of the families of the Levites; and
their lot was twelve cities.
41 [a]All the cities of the Levites in the midst of the possession of the sons of Israel were forty-eight cities with their
pasture lands.
42 These cities each had its surrounding pasture lands;
thus *it was* with all these cities.
43 [a]So the LORD gave Israel all the land which He had
sworn to give to their fathers, and [b]they possessed it and lived
in it.
44 And the LORD [a]gave them rest on every side, according
to all that He had sworn to their fathers, and [b]no one of all
their enemies stood before them; [c]the LORD gave all their enemies into their hand.
45 [a]Not [1]one of the good [2]promises which the LORD had
[3]made to the house of Israel failed; all came to pass.

Chapter 22

[a]THEN Joshua summoned the Reubenites and the Gadites
and the half-tribe of Manasseh,
2 and said to them, "You have kept all that Moses the
servant of the LORD commanded you, [a]and have listened to my
voice in all that I commanded you.
3 "You have not forsaken your brothers these many days

41 [a]Num. 35:7

43 [a]Deut. 34:4 [b]Num. 33:53; Deut. 11:31; 17:14

44 [a]Josh. 1:13; 23:1 [b]Deut. 7:24 [c]Ex. 23:31

45 [1]Lit., *a word* [2]Lit., *words* [3]Lit., *spoken* [a]Josh. 23:14; 1 Kin. 8:56

1 [a]Num. 32:30-22

2 [a]Josh. 1:12-18

to this day, but have kept the charge of the commandment of
the LORD your God.
4 "[a]And now the LORD your God has given rest to your
brothers, as He spoke to them; therefore turn now and go to
your tents, to the land of your possession, which Moses the
servant of the LORD gave you beyond the Jordan.
5 "[a]Only be very careful to observe the commandment
and the law which Moses the servant of the LORD commanded
you, to love the LORD your God and walk in all His ways and
keep His commandments and hold fast to Him and serve Him
[b]with all your heart and with all your soul."
6 So Joshua blessed them and sent them away, and they
went to their tents.
7 [a]Now to the one half-tribe of Manasseh Moses had
given *a possession* in Bashan, [b]but to the other half Joshua
gave *a possession* among their brothers westward beyond the
Jordan. So when Joshua sent them away to their tents, he
blessed them,
8 and said to [1]them, "Return to your tents with great
riches and with very much livestock, with silver, gold, bronze,
iron, and with very many clothes; divide the spoil of your
enemies with your brothers."
9 And the sons of Reuben and the sons of Gad and the
half-tribe of Manasseh returned *home* and departed from the
sons of Israel at Shiloh which is in the land of Canaan, to go to
the land of Gilead, to the land of their possession which they
had possessed, according to the [1]command of the LORD
[2]through Moses.
10 And when they came to the region of the Jordan which
is in the land of Canaan, the sons of Reuben and the sons of
Gad and the half-tribe of Manasseh built an altar there by the
Jordan, a large altar in appearance.
11 And the sons of Israel heard *it* [1]said, "Behold, the sons
of Reuben and the sons of Gad and the half-tribe of Manasseh
have built [a]an altar at the [2]frontier of the land of Canaan, in
the region of the Jordan, on the side *belonging to* the sons of
Israel."
12 And when the sons of Israel heard *of it*, the whole
congregation of the sons of Israel gathered themselves at [a]Shi-
loh, to go up against them in war.
13 Then the sons of Israel sent to the sons of Reuben and
to the sons of Gad and to the half-tribe of Manasseh, into the
land of Gilead, [a]Phinehas the son of Eleazar the priest,
14 and with him ten chiefs, one chief for each father's
household from each of the tribes of Israel; and each one of
them *was* the head of his father's household among the [1]thou-
sands of Israel.
15 And they came to the sons of Reuben and to the sons
of Gad and to the half-tribe of Manasseh, to the land of Gilead, and they spoke with them saying,
16 "Thus says the whole congregation of the LORD, 'What
is this unfaithful act which you have committed against the
God of Israel, turning away from following the LORD this day,
by building yourselves [a]an altar, to rebel against the LORD this
day?
17 'Is not [a]the [1]iniquity of Peor enough for us, from which

4 [a]Num. 32:18; Deut. 3:20

5 [a]Deut. 5:10 [b]Deut. 4:29

7 [a]Num. 32:33 [b]Josh. 17:1-13

8 [1]Lit., *them, saying,* "*Return*

9 [1]Lit., *mouth* [2]Lit., *by the hand of*

11 [1]Lit., *saying* [2]Lit., *front* [a]Josh. 22:19; Deut. 12:5

12 [a]Josh. 18:1

13 [a]Num. 25:7, 11; 31:6

14 [1]Or, *families*

16 [a]Josh. 22:11

17 [1]Lit., *the iniquity . . . little for us* [a]Num. 25:1-9

19 [1]Lit., *cross for yourselves* [2]Lit., *abides* [a]Josh. 22:11

we have not cleansed ourselves to this day, although a plague
came on the congregation of the LORD,
18 that you must turn away this day from following the
LORD? And it will come about if you rebel against the LORD
today, that He will be angry with the whole congregation of
Israel tomorrow.
19 'If, however, the land of your possession is unclean then
[1]cross into the land of the possession of the LORD, where the
LORD's [a]tabernacle [2]stands, and take possession among us.
Only do not rebel against the LORD, or rebel against us by
building an altar for yourselves, besides the altar of the LORD
our God.

20 [a]Josh. 7:1-26

20 'Did not [a]Achan the son of Zerah act unfaithfully in the
things under the ban, and wrath fall on all the congregation of
Israel? And that man did not perish alone in his iniquity.' "

21 [1]Lit., *thousands*

21 Then the sons of Reuben and the sons of Gad and the
half-tribe of Manasseh answered, and spoke to the heads of the
[1]families of Israel.
22 "The Mighty One, God, the LORD, the Mighty One,
God, the LORD! He knows, and may Israel itself know. If *it was*
in rebellion, or if in an unfaithful act against the LORD do not
Thou save us this day!

23 [a]Deut. 12:11

23 "If we have built us an altar to turn away from following
the LORD, or [a]if to offer a burnt offering or grain offering on it,
or if to offer sacrifices of peace offerings on it, may the LORD
Himself require it.

24 [1]Lit., *from* [2]Lit., *sons, saying*

24 "But truly we have done this out of concern, [1]for a
reason, saying, 'In time to come your sons may say to our
[2]sons, "What have you to do with the LORD, the God of Israel?
25 "For the LORD has made the Jordan a border between us
and you, *you* sons of Reuben and sons of Gad; you have no
portion in the LORD." So your sons may make our sons stop
fearing the LORD.'

26 [1]Lit., *prepare to build for ourselves*

26 "Therefore we said, 'Let us [1]build an altar, not for burnt
offering or for sacrifice;
27 rather it shall be a witness between us and you and
between our generations after us, that we are to perform the
service of the LORD before Him with our burnt offerings, and
with our sacrifices and with our peace offerings, that your sons
may not say to our sons in time to come, "You have no portion in the LORD." '

29 [1]Lit., *dwelling place*

28 "Therefore we said, 'It shall also come about if they say
this to us or to our generations in time to come, then we shall
say, "See the copy of the altar of the LORD which our fathers
made, not for burnt offering or for sacrifice; rather it is a
witness between us and you." '
29 "Far be it from us that we should rebel against the LORD
and turn away from following the LORD this day, by building
an altar for burnt offering, for grain offering or for sacrifice,
besides the altar of the LORD our God which is before His
[1]tabernacle."

30 [1]Lit., *thousands*

30 So when Phinehas the priest and the leaders of the
congregation, even the heads of the [1]families of Israel who
were with him, heard the words which the sons of Reuben and
the sons of Gad and the sons of Manasseh spoke, it pleased
them.

31 And Phinehas the son of Eleazar the priest said to the
sons of Reuben and to the sons of Gad and to the sons of
Manasseh, "Today we know that the LORD is in our midst,
because you have not committed this unfaithful act against
the LORD; now you have delivered the sons of Israel from the
hand of the LORD."
32 Then Phinehas the son of Eleazar the priest and the
leaders returned from the sons of Reuben and from the sons of
Gad, from the land of Gilead, to the land of Canaan, to the
sons of Israel, and brought back word to them.
33 And the word pleased the sons of Israel, and the sons of
Israel blessed God; and they did not speak of going up against
them in war, to destroy the land in which the sons of Reuben
and the sons of Gad were living.
34 And the sons of Reuben and the sons of Gad [a]called
the altar *Witness;* "For," *they said,* "it is a witness between us
that the LORD is God."

CHAPTER 23

NOW it came about after many days, when the LORD had
given [a]rest to Israel from all their enemies [1]on every side, and
Joshua was old, advanced in years,
2 [a]that Joshua called for all Israel, for their elders and
their heads and their judges and their officers, and said to
them, "I am old, advanced in years.
3 "And you have seen all that the LORD your God has
done to all these nations because of you, for [a]the LORD your
God is He who has been fighting for you.
4 "See, [a]I have apportioned to you these nations which
remain as an inheritance for your tribes, with all the nations
which I have cut off, from the Jordan even to the Great Sea
toward the setting of the sun.
5 "And the LORD your God, He shall thrust them out
from before you and [1]drive them from before you; and [a]you
shall possess their land, just as the LORD your God [2]promised
you.
6 "[a]Be very firm, then, to keep and do [b]all that is written
in the book of the law of Moses, so that you may not turn
aside from it to the right hand or to the left,
7 in order that you may not [1]associate with these nations,
these which remain among you, [a]or mention the name of their
gods, or [b]make *anyone* swear *by them,* or [c]serve them, or bow
down to them.
8 "But you are to cling to the LORD your God, as you have
done to this day.
9 "[a]For the LORD has [1]driven out great and strong nations
from before you; and as for you, [b]no man has stood before you
to this day.
10 "[a]One of your men puts to flight a thousand, for the
LORD your God is [b]He who fights for you, just as He [1]promised
you.
11 "So take diligent heed to yourselves to love the LORD
your God.
12 "For if you ever go back and [a]cling to the rest of these

34 [a]Gen. 31:47-49

1 [1]Lit., *from round about* [a]Josh. 21:44

2 [a]Josh. 24:1

3 [a]Deut. 1:30

4 [a]Ex. 23:30

5 [1]Or, *dispossess* [2]Lit., *spoke to* [a]Num. 33:53

6 [a]Deut. 5:32 [b]Josh. 1:7

7 [1]Lit., *go among* [a]Ex. 23:13; Ps. 16:4 [b]Deut. 6:13; 10:20 [c]Ex. 20:5

9 [1]Or, *dispossessed* [a]Ex. 23:23, 30 [b]Deut. 7:24

10 [1]Lit., *spoke to* [a]Lev. 26:8; Deut. 28:7 [b]Josh. 23:3

12 [a]Ex. 34:15, 16; Ps. 106:34, 35

nations, these which remain among you, and [b]intermarry with
them, so that you [1]associate with them and they with you,
13 know with certainty that the LORD your God will not
continue to [1]drive these nations out from before you; but they
[a]shall be a snare and a trap to you, and a whip on your sides
and thorns in your eyes, until you perish from off this good
land which the LORD your God has given you.
14 "Now behold, today [a]I am going the way of all the earth,
and you know in all your hearts and in all your souls [b]that not
one word of all the good words which the LORD your God
spoke concerning you has failed; all have [1]been fulfilled for
you, not [2]one of them has failed.
15 "And it shall come about that just as all the good words
which the LORD your God spoke to you have come upon you,
[a]so the LORD will bring upon you all the threats, until He has
destroyed you from off this good land which the LORD your
God has given you.
16 "[a]When you transgress the covenant of the LORD your
God, which He commanded you, and go and serve other gods,
and bow down to them, then the anger of the LORD will burn
against you, and you shall perish quickly from off the good
land which He has given you."

CHAPTER 24

[a]THEN Joshua gathered all the tribes of Israel to Shechem,
and called for the elders of Israel and for their heads and their
judges and their officers; and they presented themselves before
God.
2 And Joshua said to all the people, "Thus says the LORD,
the God of Israel, 'From ancient times your fathers lived
beyond the [1]River, *namely*, [a]Terah, the father of Abraham and
the father of Nabor, and they served other gods.
3 '[a]Then I took your father Abraham from beyond the
[1]River, and led him through all the land of Canaan, and [b]mul-
tiplied his [2]descendants and gave him [c]Isaac.
4 'And to Isaac I gave [a]Jacob and Esau, and to Esau [b]I
gave Mount Seir, to possess it; but [c]Jacob and his sons went
down to Egypt.
5 'Then [a]I sent Moses and Aaron, and I plagued Egypt
[1]by what I did in its midst; and afterward I brought you out.
6 'And I brought your fathers out of Egypt, and [a]you
came to the sea; and Egypt pursued your fathers with chariots
and horsemen to the [1]Red Sea.
7 'But when they cried out to the LORD, He put darkness
between you and the Egyptians, and brought the sea upon
them and covered them; and your own eyes saw what I did in
Egypt. And [a]you lived in the wilderness for a long time.
8 'Then [a]I brought you into the land of the Amorites who
lived beyond the Jordan, and they fought with you; and I gave
them into your hand, and you took possession of their land
when I destroyed them before you.
9 'Then [a]Balak the son of Zippor, king of Moab, arose
and fought against Israel, and he sent and summoned Balaam
the son of Beor to curse you.

12 [1]Lit., *go among* [b]Deut. 7:3, 4; Ezra 9:2; Neh. 13:25

13 [1]Or, *dispossess* [a]Ex. 23:33; 34:12; Deut. 7:16

14 [1]Lit., *come* [2]Lit., *one word* [a]1 Kin. 2:2 [b]Josh. 21:45

15 [a]Lev. 26:14-33; Deut. 28:15

16 [a]Deut. 4:25, 26

1 [a]Josh. 23:2

2 [1]I.e., Euphrates [a]Gen. 11:27-32

3 [1]I.e., Euphrates [2]Lit., *seed* [a]Gen. 12:1; 24:7 [b]Gen. 15:5 [c]Gen. 21:3

4 [a]Gen. 25:25, 26 [b]Deut. 2:5 [c]Gen. 46:6, 7

5 [1]Lit., *according to* [a]Ex. 4:14-17

6 [1]Lit., *Sea of Reeds* [a]Ex. 14:2-31

7 [a]Deut. 1:46; 2:14

8 [a]Num. 21:21-35

9 [a]Num. 22:2

10 'But I was not willing to listen to Balaam. So he had to
bless you, and I delivered you from his hand.
11 'And [a]you crossed the Jordan and came to Jericho; and
the citizens of Jericho fought against you, *and* [b]the Amorite
and the Perizzite and the Canaanite and the Hittite and the
Girgashite, the Hivite and the Jebusite. Thus [c]I gave them into
your hand.
12 'Then I [a]sent the hornet before you and it [1]drove out
the two kings of the Amorites from before you, [b]*but* not by
your sword or your bow.
13 '[a]And I gave you a land on which you had not labored,
and cities which you had not built, and you have lived in them;
you are eating of vineyards and oliveyards which you did not
plant.'
14 "[a]Now, therefore, [1]fear the LORD and serve Him in sincerity and [2]truth; and put away the gods which your fathers
served beyond the [3]River and in Egypt, and serve the LORD.
15 "And if it is disagreeable in your sight to serve the LORD,
choose for yourselves today whom you will serve: whether the
gods which your fathers served which were beyond the River,
or the Gods of the Amorites in whose land you are living; but
as for me and my house, we will serve the LORD."
16 And the people answered and said, "Far be it from us
that we should forsake the LORD to serve other gods;
17 for the LORD our God is He who brought us and our
fathers up out of the land of Egypt, from the house of [1]bond-
age, and who did these great signs in our sight and preserved
us through all the way in which we went and among all the
peoples through whose midst we passed.
18 "And the LORD drove out from before us all the peoples,
even the Amorites who lived in the land. We also will serve the
LORD, for He is our God."
19 Then Joshua said to the people, "You will not be able
to serve the LORD, [a]for He is a holy God. He is [b]a jealous God;
[c]He will not forgive your transgression or your sins.
20 "[a]If you forsake the LORD and serve foreign gods, then
He will turn and do you harm and consume you after He has
done good to you."
21 And the people said to Joshua, "No, but we will serve
the LORD."
22 And Joshua said to the people, "You are witnesses
against yourselves that you have chosen for yourselves the
LORD, to serve Him." And they said, "We are witnesses."
23 "Now therefore, put away the foreign gods which are in
your midst, and [a]incline your hearts to the LORD, the God of
Israel."
24 [a]And the people said to Joshua, "We will serve the
LORD our God and we will [1]obey His voice."
25 [a]So Joshua made a covenant with the people that day,
and made for them a statute and an ordinance in Shechem.
26 And Joshua wrote these words in the book of the law of
God; and he took a large stone and set it up there under the
oak that was by the sanctuary of the LORD.
27 And Joshua said to all the people, "Behold, [a]this stone
shall be for a witness against us, for it has heard all the words of

11 [a]Josh. 3:16, 17 [b]Ex. 23:23, 28; Deut. 7:1 [c]Ex. 23:31

12 [1]Lit., *drove them out* [a]Ex. 23:28; Deut. 7:20 [b]Ps. 44:3

13 [a]Deut. 6:10, 11

14 [1]Or, *reverence* [2]Or, *faithfulness* [3]I.e., Euphrates [a]Deut. 10:12; 18:13; 1 Sam. 12:24

17 [1]Lit., *bondmen*

19 [a]Lev. 19:2; 20:7, 26 [b]Ex. 20:5; 34:14 [c]Ex. 23:21

20 [a]Deut. 4:25, 26

23 [a]1 Kin. 8:57, 58; Ps. 119:36; 141:4

24 [1]Lit., *listen to* [a]Ex. 19:8; 24:3, 7; Deut. 5:27

25 [a]Ex. 24:8

27 [a]Josh. 22:27, 34

the LORD which he spoke [1]to us; thus it shall be for a witness
against you, lest you deny your God."
28 Then Joshua dismissed the people, each to his
inheritance.
29 And it came about after these things that Joshua the
son of Nun, the servant of the LORD, died, being one hundred
and ten years old.
30 And they buried him in the territory of his inheritance
in [a]Timnath-serah, which is in the hill country of Ephraim, on
the north of Mount Gaash.
31 And Israel served the LORD all the days of Joshua and
all the days of the elders who [1]survived Joshua, and had known
all the deeds of the LORD which He had done for Israel.
32 [a]Now they buried the bones of Joseph, which the sons
of Israel brought up from Egypt, at Shechem, in the piece of
ground [b]which Jacob had bought from the sons of Hamor the
father of Shechem for one hundred [1]pieces of money; and they
became the inheritance of Joseph's sons.
33 And Eleazar the son of Aaron died; and they buried
him [1]at Gibeah of [a]Phinehas his son, which was given him in
the hill country of Ephraim.

THE BOOK OF JUDGES

Jerusalem Captured.

NOW it came about after the death of Joshua that the sons
of Israel [a]inquired of the LORD, saying, "Who shall go up first
for us [b]against the Canaanites, to fight against them?"
2 And the LORD said, "Judah shall go up; behold, I have
given the land into his hand."
3 Then Judah said to Simeon his brother, "Come up
with me into [1]the territory allotted me, that we may fight
against the Canaanites; and [2]I in turn will go with you into [3]the
territory allotted you."
4 And Judah went up, and the LORD gave the Canaanites
and the Perizzites into their hands; and they [1]defeated ten
thousand men at Bezek.
5 And they found Adoni-bezek in Bezek and fought
against him and they [1]defeated the Canaanites and the
Perizzites.
6 But Adoni-bezek fled; and they pursued him and
caught him and cut off his [1]thumbs and big toes.
7 And Adoni-bezek said, "Seventy kings with their
thumbs and their big toes cut off used to gather up *scraps*
under my table; as I have done, so God has repaid me." So
they brought him to Jerusalem and he died there.
8 Then the sons of Judah fought against [a]Jerusalem and
captured it and struck it with the edge of the sword and set the
city on fire.

27 [1]Lit., *with*

30 [a]Josh. 19:50

31 [1]Lit., *prolonged days after*

32 [1]Heb. *qesitah* [a]Gen. 50:24, 25; Ex. 13:19; Acts 7:15, 16 [b]Gen. 33:19

33 [1]Or, *on the hill* [a]Josh. 22:13

1 [a]Num. 27:21 [b]Judg. 1:27; 2:21-23; 3:1-6

3 [1]Lit., *my lot* [2]Lit., *I, even I* [3]Lit., *your lot*

4 [1]Lit., *smote them*

5 [1]Lit., *smote*

6 [1]Lit., *thumbs of his hands and his feet*

8 [a]Judg. 1:21; Josh. 15:63

9 And afterward the sons of Judah went down to fight
against the Canaanites living in the hill country and in the
[1]Negev and in the lowland.
10 [a]So Judah went against the Canaanites who lived in
Hebron (now the name of Hebron formerly *was* Kiriath-arba);
and they struck Sheshai and Ahiman and Talmai.
11 Then from there he went against the inhabitants of
Debir (now the name of Debir formerly *was* Kiriath-sepher).
12 And Caleb said, "The one who attacks Kiriath-sepher
and captures it, I will even give him my daughter Achsah for a
wife."
13 And [a]Othniel the son of Kenaz, Caleb's younger brother, captured it; so he gave him his daughter Achsah for a wife.
14 Then it came about when she came *to him*, that she
persuaded him to ask her father for a field. Then she alighted
from [1]her donkey, and Caleb said to her, "What [2]do you
want?"
15 And she said to him, "Give me a blessing, since you
have given me the land of the [1]Negev, give me also springs of
water." So Caleb gave her the upper springs and the lower
springs.
16 And the [1]descendants of [a]the Kenite, Moses' father-in-
law, went up from the [b]city of palms with the sons of Judah, to
the wilderness of Judah which is in the south of [c]Arad; and
they went and lived with the people.
17 Then Judah went with Simeon his brother, and they
struck the Canaanites living in Zephath, and utterly destroyed
it. So the name of the city was called [a]Hormah.
18 And Judah took Gaza with its territory and Ashkelon
with its territory and Ekron with its territory.
19 Now the LORD was with Judah, and they took possession of the hill country; but they could not [1]drive out the
inhabitants of the valley because they had [a]iron chariots.
20 Then they gave Hebron to Caleb, [a]as Moses had [1]prom-
ised; and he drove out from there [b]the three sons of Anak.
21 [a]But the sons of Benjamin did not drive out the Jebusites who lived in Jerusalem; so the Jebusites have lived with
the sons of Benjamin in Jerusalem to this day.
22 Likewise the house of Joseph went up against Bethel,
and the LORD was with them.
23 And the house of Joseph spied out Bethel ([a]now the
name of the city was formerly Luz).
24 And the spies saw a man coming out of the city, and
they said to him, "Please show us the entrance to the city and
we will treat you kindly."
25 So he showed them the entrance to the city, and they
struck the city with the edge of the sword, [a]but they let the
man and all his family go free.
26 And the man went into the land of the Hittites and
built a city and named it Luz [1]which is its name to this day.
27 [a]But Manasseh did not take possession of Bethshean
and its villages, or Taanach and its villages, or the inhabitants
of Dor and its villages, or the inhabitants of Ibleam and its
villages, or the inhabitants of Megiddo and its villages; so [b]the
Canaanites persisted in living in that land.
28 And it came about when Israel became strong, that

9 [1]I.e., South country
10 [a]Josh. 15:13-19
13 [a]Judg. 3:9
14 [1]Lit., *the* [2]Lit., *for yourself*
15 [1]I.e., South country
16 [1]Lit., *sons* [a]Judg. 4:11; Num. 10:20-32 [b]Judg. 3:13; Deut. 34:3 [c]Num. 21:1
17 [a]Num. 21:3
19 [1]Or, *dispossess* [a]Judg. 4:3, 13; Josh. 17:16
20 [1]Lit., *spoken* [a]Josh. 14:9 [b]Judg. 1:10; Josh. 15:14
21 [a]Judg. 1:8; Josh. 15:63
23 [a]Gen. 28:19
25 [a]Josh. 6:25
26 [1]Lit., *it*
27 [a]Josh. 17:12 [b]Judg. 1:1

they put the Canaanites to forced labor, but they did not drive
them out completely.
29 [a]Neither did Ephraim drive out the Canaanites who
were living in Gezer; so the Canaanites lived in Gezer among
them.
30 Zebulun did not drive out the inhabitants of Kitron, or
the inhabitants of Nahalol; so the Canaanites lived among
them and became subject to forced labor.
31 Asher did not drive out the inhabitants of Acco, or the
inhabitants of Sidon, or of Ahlab, or of Achzib, or of Helbah,
or of Aphik, or of Rehob.
32 So the Asherites lived among the Canaanites, the inhabitants of the land; for they did not drive them out.
33 Naphtali did not drive out the inhabitants of Beth-
shemesh, or the inhabitants of Beth-anath, but lived among
the Canaanites, the inhabitants of the land; and the inhabitants of Beth-shemesh and Beth-anath became forced labor for
them.
34 Then the Amorites [1]forced the sons of Dan into the
hill country, for they did not allow them to come down to the
valley;
35 yet the Amorites persisted in [1]living in Mount Heres, in
Aijalon and in Shaalbim; but when the [2]power of the house of
Joseph [3]grew strong, they became forced labor.
36 And the border of the Amorites ran from the [a]ascent of
Akrabbim, from Sela and upward.

Chapter 2

NOW [a]the angel of the LORD came up from Gilgal to [b]Bo-
chim. And he said, "[c]I brought you up out of Egypt and led
you into the land which I have sworn to your fathers; and I
said, '[d]I will never break My covenant with you,
2 and as for you, [a]you shall make no covenant with the
inhabitants of this land; [b]you shall tear down their altars.' But
you have not [1]obeyed Me; what is this you have done?
3 "Therefore [a]I also said, 'I will not drive them out before
you; but they shall [1]become [b]*as thorns* in your sides, and their
gods shall be a snare to you.' "
4 And it came about when the angel of the LORD spoke
these words to all the sons of Israel, that the people lifted up
their voices and wept.
5 So they named that place [1]Bochim; and there they
sacrificed to the LORD.
6 [a]When Joshua had dismissed the people, the sons of
Israel went each to his inheritance to possess the land.
7 And the people served the LORD all the days of Joshua,
and all the days of the elders who [1]survived Joshua, who had
seen all the great work of the LORD which He had done for
Israel.
8 Then Joshua the son of Nun, the servant of the LORD,
died at the age of one hundred and ten.
9 And they buried him in the territory of his inheritance
in Timnath-heres, in the hill country of Ephraim, north of
Mount Gaash.
10 And all that generation also were gathered to their

29 [a]Josh. 16:10

34 [1]Lit., *pressed*

35 [1]Lit., *dwelling* [2]Lit., *hand* [3]Lit., *was heavy*

36 [a]Josh. 15:3

1 [a]Judg. 6:11; 13:2-21 [b]Judg. 2:5 [c]Ex. 20:2 [d]Gen. 17:7, 8; Lev. 26:42, 44; Deut. 7:9

2 [1]Lit., *listened to My voice* [a]Ex. 23:32 [b]Ex. 34:12, 13

3 [1]Some ancient mss. read *be adversaries, and* [a]Josh. 23:13 [b]Num. 33:55

5 [1]I.e., Weepers

6 [a]Josh. 24:28-31

7 [1]Lit., *prolonged days after*

fathers; and there arose another generation after them who
did not know the LORD, nor yet the work which He had done
for Israel.
11 Then the sons of Israel did [a]evil in the sight of the
LORD, and [1]served the [b]Baals,
12 and [a]they forsook the LORD, the God of their fathers,
who had brought them out of the land of Egypt, and followed
other gods from *among* the gods of the peoples who were
around them, and bowed themselves down to them; thus they
provoked the LORD to anger.
13 So they forsook the LORD and [a]served Baal and the
Astartes.
14 [a]And the anger of the LORD burned against Israel, and
He gave them into the hands of plunderers who plundered
them; and [b]He sold them into the hands of their enemies
around *them,* so that they could no longer stand before their
enemies.
15 Wherever they went, the hand of the LORD was against
them for evil, as the LORD had spoken and as the LORD had
sworn to them, so that they were severely distressed.
16 [a]Then the LORD raised up judges [1]who delivered them
from the hands of those who plundered them.
17 And yet they did not listen to their judges, for they
played the harlot after other gods and bowed themselves down
to them. They turned aside quickly from the way [a]in which
their fathers had walked in obeying the commandments of the
LORD; they did not do as *their fathers.*
18 And when the LORD raised up judges for them, the
LORD was with the judge and delivered them from the hand of
their enemies all the days of the judge; for the LORD was
moved to pity by their groaning because of those who oppressed and afflicted them.
19 But it came about when the judge died, that they
would turn back and act more corruptly than their fathers, in
following other gods to serve them and bow down to them;
they did not abandon their practices or their stubborn ways.
20 [a]So the anger of the LORD burned against Israel, and
He said, "Because this nation has transgressed My covenant
which I commanded their fathers, and has not listened to My
voice,
21 [a]I also will no longer drive out before them any of the
nations which Joshua left when he died,
22 in order to test Israel by them, whether they will keep
the way of the LORD to walk in it as their fathers [1]did, or not."
23 So the LORD allowed those nations to remain, not driving them out quickly; and He did not give them into the hand
of Joshua.

CHAPTER 3

[a]NOW these are the nations which the LORD left, to test
Israel by them (*that is,* all who had not [1]experienced any of the
wars of Canaan;
2 only in order that the generations of the sons of Israel
might [1]be taught war, [2]those who had not [3]experienced it
formerly).

11 [1]Or, *worshiped* [a]Judg. 3:7, 12; 4:1; 6:1 [b]Judg. 6:25; 8:33; 10:6

12 [a]Deut. 31:16

13 [a]Judg. 10:6

14 [a]Deut. 31:17; Ps. 106:40-42 [b]Deut. 28:25; 32:30

16 [1]Lit., *and they* [a]Ps. 106:43-45

17 [a]Judg. 2:7

20 [a]Judg. 2:14

21 [a]Josh. 23:4, 5, 13

22 [1]Lit., *kept*

1 [1]Lit., *known* [a]Judg. 1:1

2 [1]Lit., *know, to teach them* [2]Lit., *only* [3]Lit., *known*

3 *These nations are*: the five lords of the Philistines and
all the Canaanites and the Sidonians and [a]the Hivites who
lived in Mount Lebanon, from Mount Baal-hermon as far as
[1]Lebo-hamath.
4 And they were for [1a]testing Israel, to find out if they
would [2]obey the commandments of the LORD, which He had
commanded their fathers [3]through Moses.
5 And the sons of Israel lived among the Canaanites, the
Hittites, the Amorites, the Perizzites, the Hivites, and the
Jebusites;
6 and [a]they took their daughters for themselves as wives,
and gave their own daughters to their sons, and served their
gods.
7 And the sons of Israel did [a]what was evil in the sight of
the LORD, and [b]forgot the LORD their God, and [c]served the
Baals and the [1]Asheroth.
8 Then the anger of the LORD was kindled against Israel,
so that He sold them into the hands of Cushan-rishathaim king
of [1]Mesopotamia; and the sons of Israel served Cushan-rishathaim eight years.
9 And when the sons of Israel cried to the LORD, the
LORD raised up a deliverer for the sons of Israel to deliver
them, [a]Othniel the son of Kenaz, Caleb's younger brother.
10 And [a]the Spirit of the LORD came upon him, and he
judged Israel. When he went out to war, the LORD gave Cushan-
rishathaim king of [1]Mesopotamia into his hand, so that
[2]he prevailed over Cushan-rishathaim.
11 Then the land had rest forty years. And Othniel the son
of Kenaz died.
12 Now the sons of Israel again [a]did evil in the sight of the
LORD. So [b]the LORD strengthened Eglon the king of Moab
against Israel, because they had done evil in the sight of the
LORD.
13 And he gathered to himself the sons of Ammon and
Amalek; and he went and [1]defeated Israel, and they possessed
[a]the city of the palm trees.
14 And the sons of Israel served Eglon the king of Moab
eighteen years.
15 But when the sons of Israel cried to the LORD, the LORD
raised up a deliverer for them, Ehud the son of Gera, the
Benjamite, a left-handed man. And the sons of Israel sent
tribute by [1]him to Eglon the king of Moab.
16 And Ehud made himself a sword which had two edges,
a cubit in length; and he bound it on his right thigh under his
cloak.
17 And he presented the tribute to Eglon king of Moab.
Now Eglon was a very fat man.
18 And it came about when he had finished presenting the
tribute, that he sent away the people who had carried the
tribute.
19 But he himself turned back from the idols which were
at Gilgal, and said, "I have a secret message for you, O king."
And he said, "Keep silence." And all who attended him left
him.
20 And Ehud came to him while he was sitting alone in his

3 [1]Or, *the entrance of Hamath*
[a]Josh. 9:3, 7; 11:19

4 [1]Lit., *testing by them* [2]Lit., *hear* [3]Lit., *by the hand of*
[a]Deut. 8:2

6 [a]Ex. 34:15, 16; Deut. 7:3, 4; Josh. 23:12

7 [1]I.e., wooden symbol of a female deity
[a]Judg. 2:11 [b]Deut. 4:9 [c]Judg. 2:13

8 [1]Heb., *Aram-naharaim*

9 [a]Judg. 1:13

10 [1]Heb., *Aram* [2]Lit., *his hand was strong*
[a]Num. 11:25-29; 24:2

12 [a]Judg. 2:11 [b]Judg. 2:14

13 [1]Lit., *smote*
[a]Judg. 1:16; Deut. 34:3

15 [1]Lit., *his hand*

cool roof chamber. And Ehud said, "I have a message from
God for you." And he arose from his seat.
21 And Ehud stretched out his left hand, took the sword
from his right thigh and thrust it into his belly.
22 The handle also went in after the blade, and the fat
closed over the blade, for he did not draw the sword out of his
belly; and the refuse came out.
23 Then Ehud went out into the vestibule and shut the
doors of the roof chamber behind him, and locked *them*.
24 When he had gone out, his servants came and looked,
and behold, the doors of the roof chamber were locked; and
they said, "[a]He is only [1]relieving himself in the cool room."
25 And they waited [a]until they [1]became anxious; but behold, he did not open the doors of the roof chamber. Therefore they took the key and opened them, and behold, their
master had fallen to the [2]floor dead.
26 Now Ehud escaped while they were delaying, and he
passed by the idols and escaped to Seirah.
27 And it came about when he had arrived, that he blew
the horn in the hill country of Ephraim; and the sons of Israel
went down with him from the hill country, and he *was* in front
of them.
28 And he said to them, "Pursue *them*, for the LORD has
given your enemies the Moabites into your hands." So they
went down after him and seized [a]the fords of the Jordan opposite Moab, and did not allow anyone to cross.
29 And they struck down at that time about ten thousand
Moabites, all robust and valiant men; and no one escaped.
30 So Moab was subdued that day under the hand of
Israel. And the land was undisturbed for eighty years.
31 And after him came [a]Shamgar the son of Anath, who
struck down six hundred Philistines with an oxgoad; and he
also saved Israel.

CHAPTER 4

THEN the sons of Israel again did evil in the sight of the
LORD, after Ehud died.
2 And the LORD sold them into the hand of [a]Jabin king of
Canaan, who reigned in Hazor; and the commander of his
army was Sisera, who lived in [b]Harosheth-hagoyim.
3 And the sons of Israel cried to the LORD; for he had
[a]nine hundred iron chariots, and he oppressed the sons of
Israel severely for twenty years.
4 Now Deborah, a [1]prophetess, the wife of Lappidoth,
was judging Israel at that time.
5 And she used to [1]sit under the palm tree of Deborah
between Ramah and Bethel in the hill country of Ephraim;
and the sons of Israel came up to her for judgment.
6 Now she sent and summoned [a]Barak the son of Abinoam from Kedesh-naphtali, and said to him, "[1]Behold, the
LORD, the God of Israel, has commanded, 'Go and march to
Mount Tabor, and take with you ten thousand men from the
sons of Naphtali and from the sons of Zebulun.
7 'And I will draw out to you Sisera, the commander of

24 [1]Lit., *covering his feet* [a]1 Sam. 24:3

25 [1]Lit., *were ashamed* [2]Lit., *earth* [a]2 kin. 2:17; 8:11

28 [a]Judg. 7:24; 12:5

31 [a]Judg. 5:6

2 [a]Josh. 11:1, 10 [b]Judg. 4:13, 16

3 [a]Judg. 1:19

4 [1]Lit., *woman prophetess*

5 [1]Or, *live*

6 [1]Or, "*Has not . . . commanded . . . ?* [a]Heb. 11:32

Jabin's army, with his chariots and his [1]many *troops* to the
river Kishon; and [a]I will give him into your hand.' "
8 Then Barak said to her, "If you will go with me, then I
will go; but if you will not go with me, I will not go."
9 And she said, "I will surely go with you; nevertheless,
the honor shall not be yours on the journey that you are about
to take, [a]for the LORD will sell Sisera into the hands of a
woman." Then Deborah arose and went with Barak to
Kedesh.
10 And Barak called [a]Zebulun and Naphtali together to
Kedesh, and ten thousand men went up [1b]with him; Deborah
also went up with him.
11 Now Heber [a]the Kenite had separated himself from
the Kenites, from the sons of Hobab the father-in-law of
Moses, and had pitched his tent as far away as the [1]oak in
[b]Zaanannim, which is near Kedesh.
12 Then they told Sisera that Barak the son of Abinoam
had gone up to Mount Tabor.
13 And Sisera called together all his chariots, [a]nine
hundred iron chariots, and all the people who *were* with him,
from [b]Harosheth-hagoyim to the river Kishon.
14 And Deborah said to Barak, "Arise! For this is the day
in which the LORD has given Sisera into your hands; [1]behold,
the LORD has gone out before you." So Barak went down from
Mount Tabor with ten thousand men following him.
15 [a]And the LORD [1]routed Sisera and all *his* chariots and
all *his* army, with the edge of the sword before Barak; and
Sisera alighted from *his* chariot and fled away on foot.
16 But Barak pursued the chariots and the army as far as
Harosheth-hagoyim, and all the army of Sisera fell by the edge
of the sword; [a]not even one was left.
17 Now Sisera fled away on foot to the tent of Jael the
wife of Heber the Kenite, for *there was* peace between Jabin
the king of Hazor and the house of Heber the Kenite.
18 And Jael went out to meet Sisera, and said to him,
"Turn aside, my master, turn aside to me! Do not be afraid."
And he turned aside to her into the tent, and she covered him
with a [1]rug.
19 [a]And he said to her, "Please give me a little water to
drink, for I am thirsty." So she opened a [1]bottle of milk and
gave him a drink; then she covered him.
20 And he said to her, "Stand in the doorway of the tent,
and it shall be if anyone comes and inquires of you, and says,
'Is there anyone here?' that you shall say, 'No.' "
21 But Jael, Heber's wife, took a tent peg and [1]seized a
hammer in her hand, and went secretly to him and drove the
peg into his temple, and it went through into the ground; for
he was sound asleep and exhausted. So he died.
22 And behold, as Barak pursued Sisera, Jael came out to
meet him and said to him, "Come, and I will show you the
man whom you are seeking." And he entered [1]with her, and
behold Sisera was lying dead with the tent peg in his temple.
23 So God subdued on that day Jabin the king of Canaan
before the sons of Israel.
24 And the hand of the sons of Israel pressed heavier and

7 [1]Lit., *multitude*
[a]Ps. 83:9

9 [a]Judg. 4:21

10 [1]Lit., *at his feet*
[a]Judg. 5:18 [b]Judg. 4:14; 5:15; 8:5

11 [1]Or, *terebinth*
[a]Judg. 1:16 [b]Josh. 19:33

13 [a]Judg. 4:3 [b]Judg. 4:2

14 [1]Or, *has not the LORD gone. . . ?*

15 [1]Lit., *confused*
[a]Deut. 7:23; Josh. 10:10

16 [a]Ex. 14:28; Ps. 83:9

18 [1]Or, *blanket*

19 [1]I.e., skin container
[a]Judg. 5:24-27

21 [1]Lit., *placed*

22 [1]Lit., *to*

heavier upon Jabin the king of Canaan, until they had
[1]destroyed Jabin the king of Canaan.

CHAPTER 5

THEN Deborah and Barak the son of Abinoam sang on that
day, saying,
2 "[a]That [1]the leaders led in Israel,
That [b]the people volunteered,
Bless the LORD!
3 "Hear, O kings; give ear, O rulers!
[a]I—to the LORD, I will sing,
I will sing praise to the LORD, the God of Israel.
4 "[a]LORD, when Thou didst go out from Seir,
When Thou didst march from the field of Edom,
[b]The earth quaked, the heavens also dripped,
Even the clouds dripped water.
5 "[a]The mountains [1]quaked at the presence of the LORD,
[b]This Sinai, at the presence of the LORD, the God of
Israel.

6 "In the days of [a]Shamgar the son of Anath,
In the days of [b]Jael, the highways [1]were deserted,
And [2]travelers went by [3]roundabout ways.
7 "The peasantry ceased, they ceased in Israel,
Until I, Deborah, arose,
Until I arose, a mother in Israel.
8 "[a]New gods were chosen;
[b]Then war *was* in the gates.
Not a shield or a spear was seen
Among forty thousand in Israel.
9 "My heart *goes out* to [a]the commanders of Israel,
The volunteers among the people;
Bless the LORD!
10 "[a]You who ride on [1]white donkeys,
You who sit on *rich* carpets,
And you who travel on the road—[2]sing!
11 "At the sound of those who divide *flocks* among [a]the
watering places,
There they shall recount [b]the righteous deeds of the
LORD,
The righteous deeds for His [1]*peasantry* in Israel.
Then the people of the LORD went down [c]to the gates.

12 "[a]Awake, awake, Deborah;
Awake, awake, [1]sing a song!
Arise, Barak, and [b]take away your captives, O son of
Abinoam.
13 "Then survivors came down to the nobles;
The people of [a]the LORD came down to me as warriors.
14 "From Ephraim those whose root is [a]in Amalek *came
down*,
Following you, Benjamin, with your peoples;
From Machir commanders came down,
And from Zebulun those who wield the staff of [1]office.
15 "And the [1]princes of Issachar *were* with Deborah;

4:24 [1]Lit., *cut off*
5:1 [a]Ex. 15:1
2 [1]Or, *locks hung loose in* [a]Judg. 5:9 [b]Ps. 110:3
3 [a]Ps. 27:6
4 [a]Deut. 33:2; Ps. 68:7; Hab. 3:3 [b]Ps. 68:8, 9
5 [1]Lit., *flowed* [a]Ex. 19:18 [b]Ps. 68:8
6 [1]Lit., *had ceased* [2]Lit., *walked* [3]Lit., *twisted* [a]Judg. 3:31 [b]Judg. 4:17
8 [a]Deut. 32:17 [b]Judg. 5:11
9 [a]Judg. 5:2
10 [1]Or, *tawny* [2]Or, *declare it* [a]Judg. 10:4; 12:14
11 [1]Or, *rural dwellers* [a]Gen. 24:11; 29:2, 3 [b]1 Sam. 12:7; Mic. 6:5 [c]Judg. 5:8
12 [1]Or, *utter* [a]Ps. 57:8 [b]Ps. 68:18; Eph. 4:8
13 [a]Judg. 5:23; Ps. 18:9
14 [1]Lit., *the scribe* [a]Judg. 12:15
15 [1]So with ancient versions, Heb., *My princes*

15 [2]Lit., *feet* [a]Judg. 5:10 [b]Is. 15:6-9

16 [1]Or, *saddlebags* [a]Num. 32:1, 2, 24, 36

17 [1]Or, *dwelt* [a]Josh. 22:9

18 [a]Judg. 4:6, 10

19 [a]Judg. 4:13; Josh. 11:1, 2 [b]Judg. 1:27 [c]Judg. 5:30

20 [a]Josh. 10:12-14

21 [a]Ex. 15:2; Ps. 44:5

22 [1]Lit., *mighty ones* [a]Job 39:19-25

23 [a]Judg. 5:13

24 [a]Judg. 4:19-21

27 [1]Lit., *devastated*

28 [1]Or, *window* [2]Lit., *steps* [a]Prov. 7:6

30 [a]Ex. 15:9

As *was* Issachar, so *was* Barak;
Into the valley they rushed [a]at his [2]heels;
[b]Among the divisions of Reuben
There were great resolves of heart.
16 "Why did you sit among [a]the [1]sheepfolds,
To hear the piping for the flocks?
Among the divisions of Reuben
There were great searchings of heart.
17 "[a]Gilead [1]remained across the Jordan;
And why did Dan stay in ships?
Asher sat at the seashore,
And [1]remained by its landings.
18 "[a]Zebulun *was* a people who despised their lives *even* to death,
And Naphtali also, on the high places of the field.

19 "[a]The kings came *and* fought;
Then fought the kings of Canaan
[b]At Taanach near the waters of Megiddo;
[c]They took no plunder in silver.
20 "[a]The stars fought from heaven,
From their courses they fought against Sisera.
21 "The torrent of Kishon swept them away,
The ancient torrent, the torrent Kishon.
[a]O my soul, march on with strength.
22 "[a]Then the horses' hoofs beat
From the dashing, the dashing of his [1]valiant steeds.
23 'Curse Meroz,' said the angel of the LORD,
'Utterly curse its inhabitants;
[a]Because they did not come to the help of the LORD,
To the help of the LORD against the warriors.'

24 "[a]Most blessed of women is Jael,
The wife of Heber the Kenite;
Most blessed is she of women in the tent.
25 "He asked for water *and* she gave him milk;
In a magnificent bowl she brought him curds.
26 "She reached out her hand for the tent peg,
And her right hand for the workmen's hammer.
Then she struck Sisera, she smashed his head;
And she shattered and pierced his temple.
27 "Between her feet he bowed, he fell, he lay;
Between her feet he bowed, he fell;
Where he bowed, there he fell [1]dead.

28 "[a]Out of the window she looked and lamented,
The mother of Sisera through the [1]lattice,
'Why does his chariot delay in coming?
Why do the [2]hoofbeats of his chariots tarry?'
29 "Her wise princesses would answer her,
Indeed she repeats her words to herself,
30 '[a]Are they not finding, are they not dividing the spoil?
A maiden, two maidens for every warrior;
To Sisera a spoil of dyed work,
A spoil of dyed work embroidered,

Dyed work of double embroidery on the [1]neck of the
spoiler?'
31 "[a]Thus let all Thine enemies perish, O LORD;
[b]But let those who love Him be like the rising of the
sun in its might."
And the land was undisturbed for forty years.

CHAPTER 6

THEN the sons of Israel [a]did what was evil in the sight of the
LORD; and the LORD gave them into the hands of [b]Midian
seven years.
2 And the [1]power of Midian prevailed against Israel. Because of Midian the sons of Israel made for themselves the
dens which were in the mountains and the caves and the
strongholds.
3 For it was when Israel had sown, that the Midianites
would come up with the Amalekites and the sons of the east
and [1]go against them.
4 So they would camp against them and [a]destroy the
produce of the earth [1]as far as Gaza, and [b]leave no sustenance
in Israel as well as no sheep, ox, or donkey.
5 For they would come up with their livestock and their
tents, they would come in [a]like locusts for number, both they
and their camels were innumerable; and they came into the
land to devastate it.
6 So Israel was brought [a]very low because of Midian, and
the sons of Israel cried to the LORD.
7 Now it came about when the sons of Israel cried to the
LORD on account of Midian,
8 that the LORD sent a prophet to the sons of Israel, and
[a]he said to them, "Thus says the LORD, the God of Israel, 'It
was I who brought you up from Egypt, and brought you out
from the house of [1]slavery.
9 'And I delivered you from the hands of the Egyptians
and from the hands of all your oppressors, and dispossessed
them before you and gave you their land,
10 and I said to you, "I am the LORD your God; you shall
not fear the gods of the Amorites in whose land you live. But
you have not [1]obeyed Me." ' "
11 Then [a]the angel of the LORD came and sat under the
[1]oak that was in Ophrah, which belonged to Joash the [b]Abiez-
rite as his son [c]Gideon was beating out wheat in the winepress
in order to save *it* from the Midianites.
12 And the angel of the LORD appeared to him and said to
him, "The LORD is with you, O valiant warrior."
13 Then Gideon said to him, "Oh my lord, if the LORD is
with us, why then has all this happened to us? And where are
all His miracles which our fathers told us about, saying, 'Did
not the LORD bring us up from Egypt?' But [a]now the LORD has
abandoned us and given us into the hand of Midian."
14 And the LORD [1]looked at him and said, "Go in this your
strength and deliver Israel from the hand of Midian. Have I
not sent you?"
15 [a]And he said to him, "O Lord, [1]how shall I deliver

30 [1]Lit., *necks of the spoil*
31 [a]Ps. 68:2; 92:9 [b]Ps. 19:4-6; 89:36, 37
1 [a]Judg. 2:11 [b]Num. 22:4; 25:15-18; 31:1-3
2 [1]Lit., *hand*
3 [1]Lit., *go up*
4 [1]Lit., *until your coming* [a]Lev. 26:16 [b]Deut. 28:31
5 [a]Judg. 7:12; 8:10
6 [a]Deut. 28:43
8 [1]Lit., *slaves* [a]Judg. 2:1, 2
10 [1]Lit., *listened to my voice*
11 [1]Or, *terebinth* [a]Judg. 6:14; Judg. 2:1; 13:3 [b]Judg. 6:15; Josh. 17:2 [c]Heb. 11:32
13 [a]Judg. 6:1 Ps. 44:9
14 [1]Or, *turned toward*
15 [1]Lit., *with what* [a]Ex. 3:11

15 [b]Judg. 6:11

16 [1]Lit., *smite* [a]Ex. 3:12; Josh. 1:5

17 [1]Lit., *he* [a]Josh. 6:37 Is. 38:7, 8

19 [1]I.e., approx. one bushel [2]Lit., *and he put* [3]Or, *terebinth* [a]Gen. 10:6-8

21 [1]Or, departed [a]Lev. 9:24

22 [1]Lit., *Gideon* [2]YHWH, usually rendered LORD [a]Judg. 13:21, 22; Gen. 32:30; Ex. 33:20

24 [1]Heb., Yahweh-shalom

25 [1]Or, *even* [2]I.e., wooden symbol of a female deity. Also vss. 26, 28, 30 [a]Ex. 34:13

31 [1]Or, *contend*

Israel? Behold, my family is the least in [b]Manasseh, and I am
the youngest in my father's house."
16 [a]But the LORD said to him, "Surely I will be with you,
and you shall [1]defeat Midian as one man."
17 So [1]Gideon said to Him, "If now I have found favor in
Thy sight, then show me [a]a sign that it is Thou who speakest
with me.
18 "Please do not depart from here, until I come *back* to
Thee, and bring out my offering and lay it before Thee." And
He said, "I will remain until you return."
19 Then Gideon went in and [a]prepared a kid and unleavened bread from an [1]ephah of flour; he put the meat in a
basket [2]and the broth in a pot, and brought *them* out to him
under the [3]oak, and presented *them*.
20 And the angel of God said to him, "Take the meat and
the unleavened bread and lay them on this rock, and pour out
the broth." And he did so.
21 Then the angel of the LORD put out the end of the staff
that was in his hand and touched the meat and the unleavened
bread; and [a]fire sprang up from the rock and consumed the
meat and the unleavened bread. Then the angel of the LORD
[1]vanished from his sight.
22 [a]When Gideon saw that he was the angel of the LORD,
[1]he said, "Alas, O Lord [2]GOD! For now I have seen the angel of
the LORD face to face."
23 And the LORD said to him, "Peace to you, do not fear;
you shall not die."
24 Then Gideon built an altar there to the LORD and
named it [1]The LORD is Peace. To this day it is still in Ophrah
of the Abiezrites.
25 Now the same night it came about that the LORD said
to him, "Take your father's bull [1]and a second bull seven years
old, and pull down the altar of Baal which belongs to your
father, and cut down the [2a]Asherah that is beside it;
26 and build an altar to the LORD your God on the top of
this stronghold in an orderly manner, and take a second bull
and offer a burnt offering with the wood of the Asherah which
you shall cut down."
27 Then Gideon took ten men of his servants and did as
the LORD had spoken to him; and it came about, because he
was too afraid of his father's household and the men of the city
to do it by day, that he did it by night.
28 When the men of the city arose early in the morning,
behold, the altar of Baal was torn down, and the Asherah
which was beside it was cut down, and the second bull was
offered on the altar which had been built.
29 And they said to one another, "Who did this thing?"
And when they searched about and inquired, they said, "Gideon the son of Joash did this thing."
30 Then the men of the city said to Joash, "Bring out your
son, that he may die, for he has torn down the altar of Baal,
and indeed, he has cut down the Asherah which was beside it."
31 But Joash said to all who stood against him, "Will you
contend for Baal, or will you deliver him? Whoever will [1]plead
for him shall be put to death by morning. If he is a god, let him

contend for himself, because someone has torn down his
altar."
32 Therefore on that day he named him [a]Jerubbaal, that is
to say, "Let Baal contend against him," because he has torn
down his altar.
33 Then all the Midianites and the Amalekites and the
sons of the east assembled themselves; and they crossed over
and camped in [a]the valley of Jezreel.
34 So [a]the Spirit of the LORD [1]came upon Gideon; and he
[b]blew a trumpet, and the Abiezerites were called together to
follow him.
35 And he sent messengers throughout Manasseh, and
they also were called together to follow him; and he sent messengers to Asher, [a]Zebulun, and Naphtali, and [b]they came up
to meet them.
36 Then Gideon said to God, "[a]If Thou wilt deliver Israel
[1]through me, as Thou hast spoken,
37 behold, I will put a fleece of wool on the threshing
floor. If there is dew on the fleece only, and it is dry on all the
ground, then I will know that Thou wilt deliver Israel [1]through
me, as Thou hast spoken."
38 And it was so. When he arose early the next morning
and squeezed the fleece, he drained the dew from the fleece, a
bowl full of water.
39 Then Gideon said to God, "[a]Do not let Thine anger
burn against me that I may speak once more; please let me
make a test once more with the fleece, let it now be dry only
on the fleece, and let there be dew on all the ground."
40 And God did so that night; for it was dry only on the
fleece, and dew was on all the ground.

CHAPTER 7

THEN [a]Jerubbaal (that is, Gideon) and all the people who
were with him, rose early and camped beside [1]the spring [b]of
Harod; and the camp of Midian was on the north side of
[2]them by the hill of [c]Moreh in the valley.
2 And the LORD said to Gideon, "The people who are
with you are too many for Me to give Midian into their hands,
[a]lest Israel [1]become boastful, saying, 'My own [2]power has delivered me.'
3 "Now therefore [1]come, proclaim in the hearing of the
people, saying, '[a]Whoever is afraid and trembling, let him return and depart from Mount Gilead.' " So 22,000 people returned, but 10,000 remained.
4 [a]Then the LORD said to Gideon, "The people are still
too many; bring them down to the water and I will test them
for you there. Therefore it shall be that he of whom I say to
you, 'This one shall go with you,' he shall go with you; but
everyone of whom I say to you, 'This one shall not go with
you,' he shall not go."
5 So he brought the people down to the water. And the
LORD said to Gideon, "You shall separate everyone who laps
the water with his tongue, as a dog laps, as well as everyone
who kneels to drink."
6 Now the number of those who lapped, putting their

32 [a]Judg. 7:1

33 [a]Josh. 17:16

34 [1]Lit., *clothed* [a]Judg. 3:10 [b]Judg. 3:27

35 [a]Judg. 4:6, 10; 5:18 [b]Judg. 7:3

36 [1]Lit., *by my hand* [a]Judg. 6:14, 16, 17

37 [1]Lit., *by my hand*

39 [a]Gen. 18:32

1 [1]Or, *En-Harod* [2]Lit., *him* [a]Judg. 6:32 [b]Judg. 7:3 [c]Gen. 12:6; Deut. 11:30

2 [1]Lit., *glorify itself against me* [2]Lit., *hand* [a]Deut. 8:17, 18

3 [1]Or, *please* [a]Deut. 20:8

4 [a]1 Sam. 14:6

hand to their mouth, was 300 men; but all the rest of the
people kneeled to drink water.
7 And the LORD said to Gideon, "I will deliver you with
the 300 men who lapped and will give the Midianites into your
hands; so let all the *other* people go, each man to his [1]home."
8 So [1]the 300 men took the people's provisions and their
trumpets into their hands. And [2]Gideon sent all the *other* men
of Israel, each to his tent, but retained the 300 men; and the
camp of Midian was below him in the valley.
9 Now the same night it came about that the LORD said
to him, "Arise, go down against the camp, [a]for I have given it
into your hands.
10 "But if you are afraid to go down, go with Purah your
servant down to the camp,
11 and you will hear what they say; and [a]afterward your
hands will be strengthened that you may go down against the
camp." So he went with Purah his servant down to the [1]out-
posts of the army that was in the camp.
12 Now the Midianites and the Amalekites and all the
sons of the east were lying in the valley [a]as numerous as locusts;
and their camels were without number, [b]as numerous as the
sand on the seashore.
13 When Gideon came, behold, a man was relating a
dream to his friend. And he said, "Behold, I [1]had a dream; [2]a
loaf of barley bread was tumbling into the camp of Midian,
and it came to the tent and struck it so that it fell, and turned
it [3]upside down so that the tent lay flat."
14 And his friend answered and said, "This is nothing less
than the sword of Gideon the son of Joash, a man of Israel;
God has given Midian and all the camp [a]into his hand."
15 And it came about when Gideon heard the account of
the dream and its interpretation, that he bowed in worship. He
returned to the camp of Israel and said, "Arise, for the LORD
has given the camp of Midian into your hands."
16 And he divided the 300 men into three [1]companies,
and he put trumpets and empty pitchers into the hands of all
of them, with torches inside the pitchers.
17 And he said to them, "Look at me, and do likewise.
And behold, when I come to the outskirts of the camp, [1]do as I
do.
18 "When I and all who are with me blow the trumpet,
then you also blow the trumpets all around the camp, and say,
'For the LORD and for Gideon.' "
19 So Gideon and the hundred men who were with him
came to the outskirts of the camp at the beginning of the
middle watch, when they had just posted the watch; and they
blew the trumpets and smashed the pitchers that were in their
hands.
20 When the three [1]companies blew the trumpets and
broke the pitchers, they held the torches in their left hands and
the trumpets in their right hands for blowing, and cried, "A
sword for the LORD and for Gideon!"
21 And each stood in his place around the camp; and all
the [1]army ran, crying out as they fled.
22 And when they blew 300 trumpets, the [a]LORD set the
sword of one against another even throughout the whole

7 [1]Lit., *place*

8 [1]Lit., *they* [2]Lit., *he*

9 [a]Josh. 2:24; 10:8; 11:6

11 [1]Lit., *extremity of the battle array*
[a]Judg. 7:15

12 [a]Judg. 6:5; 8:10
[b]Josh. 11:4

13 [1]Lit., *dreamed* [2]Lit., *and behold, a loaf* [3]Lit., *upwards*

14 [a]Josh. 2:9

16 [1]Lit., *heads*

17 [1]Lit., *it shall come about that just as I do, so you shall do.*

20 [1]Lit., *heads*

21 [1]Or, camp

22 [a]1 Sam. 14:20

[1]army; and the [1]army fled as far as Beth-shittah toward Zererah,
as far as the edge of [b]Abel-meholah, by Tabbath.
23 And the men of Israel were summoned from [a]Naphtali
and Asher and all Manasseh, and they pursued Midian.
24 And Gideon sent messengers throughout all the hill
country of Ephraim, saying, "Come down [1]against Midian and
[a]take the waters before them, as far as Beth-barah and the
Jordan." So all the men of Ephraim were summoned, and they
took the waters as far as Beth-barah and the Jordan.
25 And [a]they captured the two leaders of Midian, Oreb
and Zeeb, and they killed Oreb at the rock of Oreb, and they
killed Zeeb at the wine press of Zeeb, while they pursued
Midian; and they brought the heads of Oreb and Zeeb to
Gideon [b]from across the Jordan.

Chapter 8

THEN the men of Ephraim said to him, "[a]What is this thing
you have done to us, not calling us when you went to fight
against Midian?" And they contended with him vigorously.
2 But he said to them, "What have I done now in comparison with you? Is not the gleaning *of the grapes* of Ephraim
better than the vintage of Abiezer?
3 "God has given the leaders of Midian, Oreb and Zeeb
into your hands; and what was I able to do in comparison with
you?" Then their [1]anger toward him subsided when he said
[2]that.
4 Then Gideon and the 300 men who were with him
came [a]to the Jordan *and* crossed over, weary yet pursuing.
5 And he said to the men of [a]Succoth, "Please give loaves
of bread to the people who are following me, for they are
weary, and I am pursuing Zebah and Zalmunna, the kings of
Midian."
6 And the leaders of Succoth said, "[1a]Are the hands of
Zebah and Zalmunna already in your hands, that we should
give bread to your army?"
7 And Gideon said, "[1]All right, [a]when the LORD has given
Zebah and Zalmunna into my hand, then I will [2]thrash your
[3]bodies with the thorns of the wilderness and with briers."
8 And he went up from there to [a]Penuel, and spoke similarly to them; and the men of Penuel answered him just as the
men of Succoth had answered.
9 So he spoke also to the men of Penuel, saying, "When
I return safely, [a]I will tear down this tower."
10 Now Zebah and Zalmunna were in Karkor, and their
[1]armies with them, about 15,000 men, all who were left of the
entire [2]army of the sons of the east; [a]for the fallen were
120,000 [3]swordsmen.
11 And Gideon went up by the way of those who lived in
tents on the east of Nobah and Jogbehah, and [1]attacked the
camp, when the camp was [2]unsuspecting.
12 When Zebah and Zalmunna fled, he pursued them
and captured the two kings of Midian, Zebah and Zalmunna,
and routed the whole [1]army.
13 Then Gideon the son of Joash returned from the battle
[1]by the ascent of Heres.

22 [1]Or, *camp* [b]1 Kin. 4:12; 19:16

23 [a]Judg. 6:35

24 [1]Lit., *to meet* [a]Judg. 3:28

25 [a]Ps. 83:11; Is. 10:26 [b]Judg. 8:4

1 [a]Judg. 12:1

3 [1]Lit., *spirit* [2]Lit., *this thing*

4 [a]Judg. 7:25

5 [a]Gen. 33:17

6 [1]Lit., *Is the palm* [a]Judg. 8:15

7 [1]Lit., *For thus* [2]Or, *trample* [3]Lit., *flesh* [a]Judg. 7:15

8 [a]Gen. 32:30, 31

9 [a]Judg. 8:17

10 [1]Or, camps [2]Or, *camp* [3]Lit., *men who drew sword* [a]Judg. 6:5; 7:12; Ps. 83:9; Is. 9:4

11 [1]Lit., *smote* [2]Or, *secure*

12 [1]Or, *camp*

13 [1]Or, *from*

14 And he captured a youth [1]from Succoth and questioned him. Then *the youth* wrote down for him the princes of
Succoth and its elders, seventy-seven men.
15 And he came to the men of Succoth and said, "Behold
Zebah and Zalmunna, concerning whom you taunted me,
saying, '[1][a]Are the hands of Zebah and Zalmunna already in
your hand, that we should give bread to your men who are
weary?' "
16 And he took the elders of the city, and thorns of the
wilderness and briers, and he [1]disciplined the men of Succoth
with them.
17 [a]And he tore down the tower of Penuel and killed the
men of the city.
18 Then he said to Zebah and Zalmunna, "What kind of
men *were* they whom you killed at Tabor?" And they said,
"They were like you, each one [1]resembling the son of a king."
19 And he said, "They *were* my brothers, the sons of my
mother. *As* the LORD lives, if only you had let them live, I
would not kill you."
20 So he said to Jether his first-born, "Rise, kill them."
But the youth did not draw his sword, for he was afraid, because he was still a youth.
21 Then Zebah and Zalmunna said, "Rise up yourself,
and fall on us; for as the man, so is his strength." [a]So Gideon
arose and killed Zebah and Zalmunna, and [b]took the crescent
ornaments which were on their camels' necks.
22 Then the men of Israel said to Gideon, "Rule over us,
both you and your son, also your son's son, for you have delivered us from the hand of Midian."
23 But Gideon said to them, "I will not rule over you, nor
shall my son rule over you; the LORD shall rule over you."
24 Yet Gideon said to them, "I would [1]request of you,
that each of you give me [2]an earring from his spoil." (For they
had gold earrings, because they were Ishmaelites.)
25 And they said, "We will surely give *them.*" So they
spread out a garment, and every one of them threw an earring
there from his spoil.
26 And the weight of the gold earrings that he requested
was 1,700 *shekels* of gold, besides the crescent ornaments and
the pendants and the purple robes which *were* on the kings of
Midian, and besides the neck bands that *were* on their camels'
necks.
27 And Gideon made it into [a]an ephod, and placed it in
his city, Ophrah, and all Israel played the harlot with it there,
so that it became a snare to Gideon and his household.
28 So Midian was subdued before the sons of Israel, and
they did not lift up their heads any more. And the land was
undisturbed for forty years in the days of Gideon.
29 Then [a]Jerubbaal the son of Joash went and lived in his
own house.
30 Now Gideon had [a]seventy sons who [1]were his direct
descendants, for he had many wives.
31 And his concubine who was in Shechem also bore him
a son, and he [1]named him Abimelech.
32 And Gideon the son of Joash died at a ripe old age and

14 [1]Lit., *of the men of*

15 [1]Lit., *Is the palm* [a]Judg. 8:6

16 [1]Lit., *made the men . . . to know*

17 [a]Judg. 8:9

18 [1]Lit., *like the form of the sons*

21 [a]Judg. 17:5; 18:14-20; Ex. 28:6-35 [b]Judg. 8:26

24 [1]Lit., *request a request* [2]Or, *a nosering*

27 [a]Judg. 17:5; 18:14-20; Ex. 28:6-35

29 [a]Judg. 7:1

30 [1]Lit., *came from his loins* [a]Judg. 9:2, 5

31 [1]Lit., *appointed his name*

was buried in the tomb of his father Joash, in Ophrah of the
Abiezrites.
33 Then it came about, as soon as Gideon was dead, [a]that
the sons of Israel again played the harlot with the Baals, and
made [b]Baal-berith their god.
34 Thus the sons of Israel [a]did not remember the LORD
their God, who had delivered them from the hands of all their
enemies on every side;
35 nor did they show kindness to the household of Jerubbaal (*that is,* Gideon), in accord with all the good that he had
done to Israel.

CHAPTER 9

AND [a]Abimelech the son of Jerubbaal went to Shechem to
his mother's [1]relatives, and spoke to them and to the whole
clan of the household of his mother's father, saying,
2 "Speak, now, in the hearing of all the leaders of Shechem,
'Which is better for you, that [a]seventy men, all the sons
of Jerubbaal, rule over you, or that one man rule over you?'
Also, remember that I am [b]your bone and your flesh.' "
3 And his mother's [1]relatives spoke all these words on his
behalf in the hearing of all the leaders of Shechem; and [2]they
were inclined to follow Abimelech, for they said, "He is our
[3]relative."
4 And they gave him seventy *pieces* of silver from the
house of [a]Baal-berith with which Abimelech hired worthless
and reckless fellows, and they followed him.
5 Then he went to his father's house at Ophrah, and
killed his brothers the sons of Jerubbaal, [a]seventy men, on one
stone. But Jotham the youngest son of Jerubbaal was left, for
he hid himself.
6 And all the men of Shechem and all [1]Beth-millo assembled together, and they went and made Abimelech king,
by the [2]oak of the pillar which was in Shechem.
7 Now when they told Jotham, he went and stood on the
top of [a]Mount Gerizim, and lifted his voice and called out.
Thus he said to them, "Listen to me, O men of Shechem, that
God may listen to you.
8 "Once the trees went forth to anoint a king over them,
and they said to the olive tree, 'Reign over us!'
9 "But the olive tree said to them, 'Shall I leave my fatness
with [1]which God and men are honored, and go to wave over
the trees?'
10 Then the trees said to the fig tree, 'You come, reign
over us!'
11 "But the fig tree said to them, 'Shall I leave my sweetness and my good [1]fruit, and go to wave over the trees?'
12 "Then the trees said to the vine, 'You come, reign over
us!'
13 "But the vine said to them, 'Shall I leave my new wine,
which cheers God and men, and go to wave over the trees?'
14 "Finally all the trees said to the bramble, 'You come,
reign over us!'
15 "And the bramble said to the trees, 'If in [1]truth you are
anointing me as king over you, come and take refuge in my

33 [a]Judg. 2:11, 12 [b]Judg. 9:4, 27, 46
34 [a]Judg. 3:7; Deut. 4:9
1 [1]Lit., *brothers* [a]Judg. 8:31, 35
2 [a]Judg. 8:30 [b]Gen. 29:14
3 [1]Lit., *brothers* [2]Lit., *their hearts inclined after* [3]Lit., *brother*
4 [a]Judg. 8:33
5 [a]Judg. 9:2
6 [1]Or, *the house of Millo* [2]Or, *terebinth*
7 [a]Deut. 11:29, 30
9 [1]Lit., *which by me*
11 [1]Or, *produce*
15 [1]Or, *sincerity*

shade; but if not, may fire come out from the bramble and
consume the cedars of Lebanon.'
16 "Now therefore, if you have dealt in [1]truth and integrity
in making Abimelech king, and if you have dealt well with
[a]Jerubbaal and his house, and [2]have dealt with him [3]as he
deserved—
17 for my father fought for you and [1]risked his life and
delivered you from the hand of Midian;
18 but you have risen against my father's house today and
have killed [a]his sons, seventy men, on one stone, and have
made Abimelech, [b]the son of his maidservant, king over the
men of Shechem, because he is your [1]relative—
19 if then you have dealt in [1]truth and integrity with Jerubbaal and his house this day, rejoice in Abimelech, and let
him also rejoice in you.
20 "But if not, let fire come out from Abimelech and consume the men of Shechem and [1]Beth-millo; and let fire come
out from the men of Shechem and from [1]Beth-millo, and
consume Abimelech."
21 Then Jotham escaped and fled, and went to Beer and
remained there because of Abimelech his brother.
22 Now Abimelech ruled over Israel three years.
23 [a]Then God sent an evil spirit between Abimelech and
the men of Shechem; and the men of Shechem dealt treacherously with Abimelech,
24 [a]in order that the violence [1]done to the seventy sons of
Jerubbaal might come, and [b]their blood might be laid on Abimelech their brother, who killed them, and on the men of
Shechem, who strengthened his hands to kill his brothers.
25 And the men of Shechem set [1]men in ambush against
him on the tops of the mountains, and they robbed all who
might pass by them along the road; and it was told to
Abimelech.
26 Now Gaal the son of Ebed came with his [1]relatives, and
crossed over into Shechem; and the men of Shechem put their
trust in him.
27 And they went out into the field and gathered *the
grapes of* their vineyards and trod *them*, and held a [1]festival;
and they went into the house of [a]their god, and ate and drank
and cursed Abimelech.
28 Then Gaal the son of Ebed said, "Who is Abimelech,
and who is Shechem, that we should serve him? Is he not the
son of Jerubbaal, and *is* Zebul *not* his [1]lieutenant? Serve the
men of Hamor the father of Shechem; but why should we
serve him?
29 "[1a]Would, therefore, that this people were under authority! Then I would remove Abimelech." And he said to Abimelech, "Increase your army, and come out."
30 And when Zebul the ruler of the city heard the words
of Gaal the son of Ebed, his anger burned.
31 And he sent messengers to Abimelech [1]deceitfully,
saying, "Behold, Gaal the son of Ebed and his [2]relatives have
come to Shechem; and behold, they are [3]stirring up the city
against you.
32 "Now therefore, arise by night, you and the people who
are with you, and lie in wait in the field.

16 [1]Or, *sincerity* [2]Lit., *if you have* [3]Lit., *according to the dealing of his hands* [a]Judg. 8:35

17 [1]Lit., *cast his soul in front*

18 [1]Lit., *brother* [a]Judg. 9:5 [b]Judg. 8:31

19 [1]Or, *sincerity*

20 [1]Or, *the house of Millo*

23 [a]1 Sam. 16:14

24 [1]Lit., *of the seventy* [2]Lit., *come* [a]Judg. 9:56, 57; Deut. 27:25 [b]Num. 35:33

25 [1]Lit., *liers-in-wait for*

26 [1]Lit., *brothers*

27 [1]Lit., *rejoicing* [a]Judg. 9:46; 8:33

28 [1]Lit., *overseer*

29 [1]Lit., *And who will give this people into my hand*

31 [1]Or, *in Tormah* [2]Lit., *brothers* [3]Lit., *besieging*

33 "And it shall come about in the morning, as soon as the
sun is up, that you shall rise early and rush upon the city; and
behold, when he and the people who are with him come out
against you, you shall [a]do to them [1]whatever you can."
34 So Abimelech and all the people who *were* with him
arose by night and lay in wait against Shechem in four
[1]companies.
35 Now Gaal the son of Ebed went out and stood in the
entrance of the city gate; and Abimelech and the people who
were with him arose from the ambush.
36 And when Gaal saw the people, he said to Zebul,
"[1]Look, people are coming down from the tops of the mountains." But Zebul said to him, "You are seeing the shadow of
the mountains as *if they were* men."
37 And Gaal spoke again and said, "Behold, people are
coming down from [a]the [1]highest part of the land, and one
[2]company comes by the way of [3]the diviners' [4]oak."
38 Then Zebul said to him, "Where is your [1]boasting now
with which you said, 'Who is Abimelech that we should serve
him?' Is this not the people whom you despised? Go out now
and fight with them!"
39 So Gaal went out before the leaders of Shechem and
fought with Abimelech.
40 And Abimelech chased him, and he fled before him;
and many fell wounded up to the entrance of the gate.
41 Then Abimelech remained at Arumah, but Zebul
drove out Gaal and his [1]relatives so that they could not remain
in Shechem.
42 Now it came about the next day, that the people went
out to the field, and it was told to Abimelech.
43 So he took [1]his people and divided them into three
[2]companies, and lay in wait in the field; when he looked and
[3]saw the people coming out from the city, he arose against
them and [4]slew them.
44 Then Abimelech and the [1]company who was with him
dashed forward and stood in the entrance of the city gate; the
other two [2]companies then dashed against all who *were* in the
field and [3]slew them.
45 And Abimelech fought against the city all that day, and
he captured the city and killed the people who *were* in it; then
he razed the city and sowed it with salt.
46 When all the leaders of the tower of Shechem heard of
it, they entered the inner chamber of the [1]temple of [a]Elberith.
47 And it was told Abimelech that all the leaders of the
tower of Shechem were gathered together.
48 So Abimelech went up to Mount [a]Zalmon, he and all
the people who *were* with him; and Abimelech took [1]an axe in
his hand and cut down a branch from the trees, and lifted it
and laid *it* on his shoulder. Then he said to the people who
were with him, "What you have seen me do, hurry *and* do
[2]likewise."
49 And all the people also cut down each one his branch
and followed Abimelech, and put *them* on the inner chamber
and set the inner chamber on fire over those *inside*, so that all
the men of the tower of Shechem also died, about a thousand
men and women.

33 [1]Lit., *as your hand can find* [a]1 Sam. 10:7

34 [1]Lit., *heads*

36 [1]Lit., *Behold*

37 [1]Or, *center* [2]Lit., *head* [3]Heb., *Elommeonenim* [4]Or, *terebinth* [a]Ezek. 38:12

38 [1]Lit., *mouth*

41 [1]Lit., *brothers*

43 [1]Lit., *the* [2]Lit., *heads* [3]Lit., *behold* [4]Lit., *smote*

44 [1]Singular with Gk; Heb. plural, *heads* [2]Lit., *heads* [3]Lit., *smote*

46 [1]Lit., *house* [a]Judg. 8:33

48 [1]Lit., *the axes* [2]Lit., *like me* [a]Ps. 68:14

53 [a]2 Sam. 11:21

54 [1]Lit., *his*

55 [1]Lit., *place*

57 [1]Lit., *to*

4 [1]Lit., *which are in* [2]I.e., the towns of Jair [a]Num. 32:41

6 [1]Heb., *Aram* [a]Judg. 2:13 [b]Judg. 11:24 [c]Deut. 31:16, 17; 32:15

8 [1]Lit., *shattered* [2]Lit., *in that* [3]Lit., *which is in*

50 Then Abimelech went to Thebez, and he camped against Thebez and captured it.
51 But there was a strong tower in the center of the city, and all the men and women with all the leaders of the city fled there and shut themselves in; and they went up on the roof of the tower.
52 So Abimelech came to the tower and fought against it, and approached the entrance of the tower to burn it with fire.
53 But [a]a certain woman threw an upper millstone on Abimelech's head, crushing his skull.
54 Then he called quickly to the young man, his armor bearer, and said to him, "Draw your sword and kill me, lest it be said of me, 'A woman slew him.'" So [1]the young man pierced him through, and he died.
55 And when the men of Israel saw that Abimelech was dead, each departed to his [1]home.
56 Thus God repaid the wickedness of Abimelech, which he had done to his father, in killing his seventy brothers.
57 Also God returned all the wickedness of the men of Shechem on their heads, and the curse of Jotham the son of Jerubbaal came [1]upon them.

Chapter 10

NOW after Abimelech died, Tola the son of Puah, the son of Dodo, a man of Issachar, arose to save Israel; and he lived in Shamir in the hill country of Ephraim.
2 And he judged Israel twenty-three years. Then he died and was buried in Shamir.
3 And after him, Jair the Gileadite arose, and judged Israel twenty-two years.
4 And he had thirty sons who rode on thirty donkeys, and they had thirty cities [1]in the land of Gilead [a]that are called [2]Havveth-jair to this day.
5 And Jair died and was buried in Kamon.
6 Then the sons of Israel again did evil in the sight of the LORD, [a]served the Baals and the Ashtaroth, the gods of [1]Syria, the gods of Sidon, the gods of Moab, [b]the gods of the sons of Ammon, and the gods of the Philistines; thus [c]they forsook the LORD and did not serve Him.
7 And the anger of the LORD burned against Israel, and He sold them into the hands of the Philistines, and into the hands of the sons of Ammon.
8 And they [1]afflicted and crushed the sons of Israel [2]that year; for eighteen years they *afflicted* all the sons of Israel who were beyond the Jordan [3]in Gilead in the land of the Amorites.
9 And the sons of Ammon crossed the Jordan to fight also against Judah, Benjamin, and the house of Ephraim, so that Israel was greatly distressed.
10 Then the sons of Israel cried out to the LORD, saying, "We have sinned against Thee, for indeed, we have forsaken our God and served the Baals."
11 And the LORD said to the sons of Israel, "*Did I* not *deliver you* from the Egyptians, the Amorites, the sons of Ammon, and the Philistines?
12 "Also when the Sidonians, the Amalekites and the Maun-

ites oppressed you, you cried out to Me, and I delivered you
from their hands.
13 "Yet you have forsaken Me and served other gods; therefore I will deliver you no more.
14 "[a]Go and cry out to the gods which you have chosen; let
them deliver you in the time of your distress."
15 And the sons of Israel said to the LORD, "We have
sinned, do to us whatever seems good to Thee; only please
deliver us this day."
16 [a]So they put away the foreign gods from among them,
and served the LORD; and [1b]He could bear the misery of Israel
no longer.
17 Then the sons of Ammon were summoned, and they
camped in Gilead. And the sons of Israel gathered together,
and camped in [a]Mizpah.
18 And the people, the leaders of Gilead, said to one another, "Who is the man who will begin to fight against the sons
of Ammon? He shall become head over all the inhabitants of
Gilead."

CHAPTER 11

NOW [a]Jephthah the Gileadite was a [1]valiant warrior, but he
was the son of a harlot. And Gilead [2]was the father of
Jephthah.
2 And Gilead's wife bore him sons; and when his wife's
sons grew up, they drove Jephthah out and said to him, "You
shall not have an inheritance in our father's house, for you are
the son of another woman."
3 So Jephthah fled from his brothers and lived in the
land of [a]Tob; and worthless fellows gathered themselves
[1]about Jephthah, and they went out with him.
4 And it came about after a while that [a]the sons of Ammon fought against Israel.
5 And it happened when the sons of Ammon fought
against Israel that the elders of Gilead went to get Jephthah
from the land of Tob;
6 and they said to Jephthah, "Come and be our chief
that we may fight against the sons of Ammon."
7 Then Jephthah said to the elders of Gilead, "Did you
not hate me and drive me from my father's house? So why
have you come to me now when you are in trouble?"
8 And the elders of Gilead said to Jephthah, "For this
reason we have now returned to you, that you may go with us
and fight with the sons of Ammon and [a]become head over all
the inhabitants of Gilead."
9 So Jephthah said to the elders of Gilead, "If you take
me back to fight against the sons of Ammon and the LORD
gives them up [1]to me, will I become your head?"
10 And the elders of Gilead said to Jephthah, "[a]The LORD
is [1]witness between us; surely we will do [2]as you have said."
11 Then Jephthah went with the elders of Gilead, and the
people made him head and chief over them; and Jephthah
spoke all his words before the LORD at [a]Mizpah.
12 Now Jephthah sent messengers to the king of the sons

14 [a]Deut. 32:37

16 [1]Lit., *His soul was short with the misery* [a]Josh. 24:23 [b]Deut. 32:36

17 [a]Judg. 11:29

1 [1]Or, *mighty man of valor* [2]Lit., *begat* [a]Heb. 11:32

3 [1]Lit., *to* [a]2 Sam. 10:6, 8

4 [a]Judg. 10:9, 17

8 [a]Judg. 10:18

9 [1]Lit., *before*

10 [1]Lit., *hearer* [2]Lit., *according to your word* [a]Gen. 31:50

11 [a]Judg. 11:29

of Ammon, saying, "What is between you and me, that you
have come to me to fight against my land?"
13 And the king of the sons of Ammon said to the messengers of Jephthah, "Because Israel took away my land when
they came up from Egypt, from the Arnon as far as the Jabbok
and the Jordan; therefore, return them peaceably now."
14 But Jephthah sent messengers again to the king of the
sons of Ammon,
15 and he said to him, "Thus says Jephthah, 'Israel did not
take away the land of Moab, nor the land of the sons of
Ammon.
16 'For when they came up from Egypt, and Israel went
through the wilderness to the [1]Red Sea and [a]came to Kadesh,
17 then Israel sent messengers to the king of Edom,
saying, "Please let us pass through your land," but the king of
Edom would not listen. [a]And they also sent to the king of
Moab, but he would not consent. So Israel remained at
Kadesh.
18 'Then they went through the wilderness and [a]around
the land of Edom and the land of Moab, and came to the east
side of the land of Moab, and they camped beyond the Arnon;
but they [b]did not enter the territory of Moab, for the Arnon
was the border of Moab.
19 'And Israel sent [a]messengers to Sihon king of the Amorites, the king of Heshbon, and Israel said to him, "Please let
us pass through your land to our place."
20 'But Sihon did not trust Israel to pass through his territory; so Sihon gathered all his people and camped in Jahaz,
and fought with Israel.
21 'And the LORD, the God of Israel, gave Sihon and all his
people into the hand of Israel, and they [1]defeated them; so
Israel possessed all the land of the Amorites, the inhabitants of
that country.
22 '[a]So they possessed all the territory of the Amorites,
from the Arnon as far as the Jabbok, and from the wilderness
as far as the Jordan.
23 'Since now the LORD, the God of Israel, drove out the
Amorites from before His people Israel, are you then to possess it?
24 'Do you not possess what [a]Chemosh your god gives you
to possess? So whatever the LORD our God has driven out
before us, we will possess it.
25 'And now are you any better than [a]Balak the son of
Zippor, king of Moab? Did he ever strive with Israel, or did he
ever fight against them?
26 '[a]While Israel lived in Heshbon and its villages, and in
Aroer and its villages, and in all the cities that are on the banks
of the Arnon, three hundred years, why did you not recover
them within that time?
27 'I therefore have not sinned against you, but you are
doing me wrong by making war against me; [a]may the LORD, the
Judge, judge today between the sons of Israel and the sons of
Ammon.' "
28 But the king of the sons of Ammon [1]disregarded the
message which Jephthah sent him.

16 [1]Lit., *Sea of Reeds* [a]Num. 20:1, 4-21
17 [a]Josh. 24:9
18 [a]Num. 21:4; Deut. 2:8 [b]Deut. 2:9, 18, 19
19 [a]Num. 21:21-32; Deut. 2:26-36
21 [1]Lit., *smote*
22 [a]Deut. 2:37
24 [a]Num. 21:29 1 Kin. 11:7
25 [a]Num. 22:2; Josh. 24:9; Mic. 6:5
26 [a]Num. 21:25, 26; Deut. 2:36
27 [a]Gen. 16:5; 18:25; 31:53; 1 Sam. 24:12, 15
28 [1]Lit., *did not listen to the words*

29 Now [a]the Spirit of the LORD came upon Jephthah, so
that he passed through Gilead and Manasseh, then he passed
through Mizpah of Gilead, and from Mizpah of Gilead he
went on to the sons of Ammon.
30 And Jephthah made a vow to the LORD and said, "If
Thou wilt indeed give the sons of Ammon into my hand,
31 then it shall be that whatever comes out of the doors of
my house to meet me when I return in peace from the sons of
Ammon, it shall be the LORD'S, [1]or I will offer it up as a burnt
offering."
32 So Jephthah crossed over to the sons of Ammon to
fight against them; and the LORD gave them into his hand.
33 And he struck them with a very great slaughter from
Aroer to the entrance of [a]Minnith, twenty cities, and as far as
Abel-keramin. So the sons of Ammon were subdued before the
sons of Israel.
34 When Jephthah came to his house at [a]Mizpah, behold,
his daughter was coming out to meet him [b]with tambourines
and with dancing. Now she was his one *and* only child; besides
her he had neither son nor daughter.
35 And it came about when he saw her, that he tore his
clothes and said, "Alas, my daughter! You have brought me
very low, and you are among those who trouble me; for I have
[1]given my word to the LORD, and [a]I cannot take *it* back."
36 So she said to him, "My father, you have [1]given your
word to the LORD; do to me [2]as you have said, since the LORD
has avenged you of your enemies, the sons of Ammon."
37 And she said to her father, "Let this thing be done for
me; let me alone two months, that I may [1]go to the mountains
and weep because of my virginity, I and my companions."
38 Then he said, "Go." So he sent her away for two
months; and she left with her companions, and wept on the
mountains because of her virginity.
39 And it came about at the end of two months that she
returned to her father, who did to her according to the vow
which he had made; and she [1]had no relations with a man.
Thus it became a custom in Israel,
40 that the daughters of Israel went yearly to [1]commemo-
rate the daughter of Jephthah the Gileadite four days in the
year.

CHAPTER 12

THEN the men of Ephraim were summoned, and they
crossed [1]to Zaphon and [a]said to Jephthah, "Why did you cross
over to fight against the sons of Ammon without calling us to
go with you? We will burn your house down on you."
2 And Jephthah said to them, "I and my people were at
great strife with the sons of Ammon; when I called you, you
did not deliver me from their hand.
3 "And when I saw that you would not deliver *me*, I [1a]took
my life in my hands and crossed over against the sons of Ammon, and the LORD gave them into my hand. Why then have
you come up to me this day, to fight against me?"

29 [a]Judg. 3:10

31 [1]Or, *and*

33 [a]Ezek. 27:15

34 [a]Judg. 11:11; 10:17 [b]Ex. 15:20; 1 Sam. 18:6; Jer. 31:4

35 [1]Lit., *opened my mouth* [a]Num. 30:2; Eccles. 5:4, 5

36 [1]Lit., *opened your mouth* [2]Lit., *according to what has proceeded from your mouth*

37 [1]Lit., *go and go down on*

39 [1]Lit., *knew no man*

40 [1]Lit., *recount:* ancient versions, *lament*

1 [1]Or, *northward* [a]Judg. 8:1

3 [1]Lit., *put my soul in my palm* [a]1 Sam. 19:5; 28:21 Job 13:14

4 Then Jephthah gathered all the men of Gilead and
fought Ephraim; and the men of Gilead [1]defeated Ephraim,
because they said, "You are fugitives of Ephraim, O Gileadites, in the midst of Ephraim *and* in the midst of Manasseh."
5 And the Gileadites [a]captured the fords of the Jordan
opposite Ephraim. And it happened when *any of* the fugitives
of Ephraim said, "Let me cross over," the men of Gilead
would say to him, "Are you an Ephraimite?" If he said, "No,"
6 then they would say to him, "Say now 'Shibboleth.'"
But he said "Sibboleth," for he could not [1]pronounce it correctly. Then they seized him and slew him at the fords of the
Jordan. Thus there fell at that time 42,000 of Ephraim.
7 And Jephthah judged Israel six years. Then Jephthah
the Gileadite died and was buried in *one of* the cities of
Gilead.
8 Now Ibzan of Bethlehem judged Israel after him.
9 And he had thirty sons, and thirty daughters *whom* he
[1]gave in marriage outside *the family,* and he brought in thirty
daughters from outside for his sons. And he judged Israel seven
years.
10 Then Ibzan died and was buried in Bethlehem.
11 Now Elon the Zebulunite judged Israel after him; and
he judged Israel ten years.
12 Then Elon the Zebulunite died and was buried at Aijalon
in the land of Zebulun.
13 Now Abdon the son of Hillel the Pirathonite judged
Israel after him.
14 And he had forty sons and thirty grandsons who rode
on seventy donkeys; and he judged Israel eight years.
15 Then Abdon the son of Hillel the Pirathonite died and
was buried at Pirathon in the land of Ephraim, in the hill
country of the Amalekites.

Chapter 13

NOW the sons of Israel [a]again did evil in the sight of the
LORD, so that the LORD gave them into the hands of the Philistines forty years.
2 And there was a certain man of [a]Zorah, of the family of
the Danites, whose name was Manoah; and his wife was barren
and had borne no *children.*
3 [a]Then the angel of the LORD appeared to the woman,
and said to her, "Behold now, you are barren and have borne
no *children,* but you shall conceive and give birth to a son.
4 "Now therefore, be careful not to drink wine or strong
drink, nor eat any unclean thing.
5 "[a]For behold, you shall conceive and give birth to a son,
and no razor shall come upon his head, for the boy shall be a
[b]Nazirite to God from the womb; and he shall begin to deliver
Israel from the hands of the Philistines."
6 Then the woman came and told her husband, saying,
"[a]A man of God came to me and his appearance was like the
appearance of the angel of God, very awesome. And I did not
ask him where he *came* from, nor did he tell me his name.

4 [1]Lit., *smote*

5 [a]Judg. 3:28

6 [1]Lit., *speak so*

9 [1]Lit., *sent outside*

1 [a]Judg. 2:11

2 [a]Josh. 19:41

3 [a]Judg. 12:6, 8, 10, 11; 6:11, 14; Luke 1:11-13

5 [a]Luke 1:15 [b]Num. 6:2

6 [a]Judg. 13:8, 10, 11; 6:11

7 "But he said to me, 'Behold, you shall conceive and give
birth to a son, and now you shall not drink wine or strong drink
nor eat any unclean thing, for the boy shall be a Nazirite to
God from the womb to the day of his death.' "
8 Then Manoah entreated the LORD and said, "O Lord,
please let [a]the man of God whom Thou hast sent come to us
again that he may teach us what to do for the boy who is to be
born."
9 And God listened to the voice of Manoah; and [a]the
angel of God came again to the woman as she was sitting in the
field, but Manoah her husband was not with her.
10 So the woman ran quickly and told her [1]husband, "Behold, [a]the man who [2]came the *other* day has appeared to me."
11 Then Manoah arose and followed his wife, and when
he came to the man he said to him, "Are you [a]the man who
spoke to the woman?" And he said, "I am."
12 And Manoah said, "Now when your words come *to*
pass, what shall be the boy's mode of life and his vocation?"
13 So [a]the angel of the LORD said to Manoah, "[b]Let the
woman pay attention [1]to all that I said.
14 "She should not eat anything that comes from the [a]vine
nor drink wine or strong drink, nor eat any unclean thing; let
her observe all that I commanded."
15 Then Manoah said to [a]the angel of the LORD, "Please
let us detain you so that we may prepare a kid for you."
16 And the angel of the LORD said to Manoah, "Though
you detain me, [a]I will not eat your [1]food, but if you prepare a
burnt offering, *then* offer it to the LORD." For Manoah did not
know that he was the angel of the LORD.
17 And Manoah said to the angel of the LORD, "[a]What is
your name, so that when your words come *to pass*, we may
honor you?"
18 But the angel of the LORD said to him, "Why do you
ask my name, seeing it is [1a]wonderful?"
19 So [a]Manoah took the kid with the grain offering and
offered it on the rock to the LORD, and He performed wonders
while Manoah and his wife looked on.
20 For it came about when the flame went up from the
altar toward heaven, that the angel of the LORD ascended in
the flame of the altar. When Manoah and his wife saw *this*,
they fell on their faces to the ground.
21 Now the angel of the LORD appeared no more to Manoah or his wife. [a]Then Manoah knew that he was the angel of
the LORD.
22 So Manoah said to his wife, "[a]We shall surely die, for
we have seen God."
23 But his wife said to him, "If the LORD had desired to
kill us, He would not have accepted a burnt offering and a
grain offering from our hands, nor would He have showed us
all these things, nor would He have let us hear *things* like this
at this time."
24 Then the woman gave birth to a son and named him
Samson; and the child grew up and the LORD blessed him.
25 And [a]the Spirit of the LORD began to stir him in [1b]Ma-
haneh-dan, between Zorah and Eshtaol.

8 [a]Judg. 13:3, 7

9 [a]Judg. 13:8

10 [1]Lit., *husband, and said to him* [2]Lit., *came to me* [a]Judg. 13:9

11 [a]Judg. 13:8

13 [1]Lit., *from* [a]Judg. 13:11 [b]Judg. 13:4

14 [a]Num. 6:4

15 [a]Judg. 13:3

16 [1]Lit., *bread* [a]Judg. 6:20

17 [a]Gen. 32:29

18 [1]I.e., incomprehensible [a]Is. 9:6

19 [a]Judg. 6:20, 21

21 [a]Judg. 13:16

22 [a]Judg. 6:22

25 [1]I.e., the camp of Dan [a]Judg. 3:10 [b]Judg. 18:11, 12

CHAPTER 14

2 [1]Lit., *up* [2]Lit., *mother, saying,*

THEN Samson went down to Timnah and saw a woman in
Timnah, *one* of the daughters of the Philistines.
2 So he came [1]back and told his father and [2]mother, "I
saw a woman in Timnah, *one* of the daughters of the Philistines; now therefore, get her for me as a wife."

3 [1]Lit., *brothers* [2]Lit., *my* [3]Lit., *is right in my eyes*

3 Then his father and his mother said to him, "Is there
no woman among the daughters of your [1]relatives, or among
all [2]our people, that you go to take a wife from the uncircumcised Philistines?" But Samson said to his father, "Get her for
me, for she [3]looks good to me."
4 However, his father and mother did not know that it
was of the LORD, [a]for He was seeking an occasion against the

4 [a]Josh. 11:20

Philistines. Now at that time the Philistines were ruling over
Israel.
5 Then Samson went down to Timnah with his father
and mother, and came as far as the vineyards of Timnah; and
behold, a young lion *came* roaring toward him.
6 And [a]the spirit of the LORD [1]came upon him mightily,
so that [b]he tore him as one tears a kid though he had nothing

6 [1]Lit., *rushed upon* [a]Judg. 3:10 [b]1 Sam. 17:34-36

in his hand; but he did not tell his father or mother what he
had done.
7 So he went down and talked to the woman; and she
[1]looked good to Samson.
8 When he returned later to take her, he turned aside to
look at the carcass of the lion; and behold, a swarm of bees and

7 [1]Lit., *was right in Samson's eyes*

honey were in the body of the lion.
9 So he scraped [1]the honey into his [2]hands and went on,
eating as he went. When he came to his father and mother, he
gave *some* to them and they ate *it;* but he did not tell them
that he had scraped the honey out of the body of the lion.
10 Then his father went down to the woman; and Samson
made a feast there, for the young men customarily did this.

9 [1]Lit., *it* [2]Lit., *palms*

11 And it came about when they saw him that they
brought thirty companions to be with him.
12 Then Samson said to them, "Let me now [a]propound a
riddle to you; if you will indeed tell it to me within the [b]seven
days of the feast, and find it out, then I will give you thirty
linen wraps and thirty changes of clothes.

12 [a]Ezek. 17:2 [b]Gen. 29:27

13 "But if you are unable to tell me, then you shall give me
thirty linen wraps and thirty changes of clothes." And they said
to him, "Propound your riddle, that we may hear it."
14 So he said to them,

"Out of the eater came something to eat,
And out of the strong came something sweet."

But they could not tell the riddle in three days.

15 [1]So with some ancient versions. Heb., *seventh*

15 Then it came about on the [1]fourth day that they said to
Samson's wife, "Entice your husband, that he may tell us the
riddle, lest we burn you and your father's house with fire. Have
you invited us to impoverish us? Is this not *so?*"
16 And Samson's wife wept before him and said, "You
only hate me, and you do not love me; you have propounded a
riddle to the sons of my people, and have not told *it* to me."
And he said to her, "Behold, I have not told *it* to my father or
mother; so should I tell you?"

17 However she wept before him seven days while their
feast lasted. And it came about on the seventh day that he told
her because she pressed him so hard. She then told the riddle
to the sons of her people.
18 So the men of the city said to him on the seventh day
before the sun went down,
"What is sweeter than honey?
And what is stronger than a lion?"
And he said to them,
"If you had not plowed with my heifer,
You would not have found out my riddle."
19 Then [a]the Spirit of the LORD [1]came upon him mightily,
and he went down to Ashkelon and killed thirty of them and
took their spoil, and gave the changes *of clothes* to those who
told the riddle. And his anger burned, and he went up to his
father's house.
20 But Samson's wife was *given* to his companion who had
been his [1]friend.

CHAPTER 15

BUT after a while, in the time of wheat harvest, it came
about that Samson visited his wife [a]with a young goat; and
said, "I will go in to my wife in *her* room." But her father did
not let him enter.
2 And her father said, "I really thought that you hated
her intensely; so I gave her to your companion. Is not her
younger sister [1]more beautiful than she? Please let her be yours
[2]instead."
3 Samson then said to them, "This time I shall be blameless in regard to the Philistines when I do them harm."
4 And Samson went and caught three hundred foxes, and
took torches, and turned *them* tail to tail, and put one torch in
the middle between two tails.
5 When he had set fire to the torches, he released [1]the
foxes into the standing grain of the Philistines, thus burning up
both the shocks and the standing grain, along with the vineyards *and* groves.
6 Then the Philistines said, "Who did this?" And they
said, "Samson, the son-in-law of the Timnite, because [1]he took
his wife and gave her to his companion." So the Philistines
came up and [a]burned her and her father with fire.
7 And Samson said to them, "Since you act like this, I
will surely take revenge on you, but after that I will quit."
8 And he struck them [1]ruthlessly with a great slaughter;
and he went down and lived in the cleft of the rock of Etam.
9 Then the Philistines went up and camped in Judah,
and spread out in Lehi.
10 And the men of Judah said, "Why have you come up
against us?" And they said, "We have come up to bind Samson
in order to do to him as he did to us."
11 Then 3,000 men of Judah went down to the cleft of the
rock of Etam and said to Samson, "Do you not know [a]that the
Philistines are rulers over us? What then is this that you have
done to us?" And he said to them, "As they did to me, so I
have done to them."

19 [1]Lit., *rushed upon* [a]Judg. 3:10

20 [1]Or, *best man*

1 [a]Gen. 38:17

2 [1]Lit., *better* [2]Lit., *instead of her*

5 [1]Lit., *them*

6 [1]I.e., the Timnite [a]Judg. 14:15

8 [1]Lit., *leg on thigh*

11 [a]Judg. 13:1; 14:4

12 And they said to him, "We have come down to bind
you so that we may give you into the hands of the Philistines."
And Samson said to them, "Swear to me that you will not [1]kill
me."
13 So they said to [1]him, "No, but we will bind you fast and
give you into their hands; yet surely we will not kill you." Then
they bound him with two new ropes and brought him up from
the rock.
14 When he came to Lehi, the Philistines shouted as they
met him. And [a]the Spirit of the LORD [1]came upon him mightily so that the ropes that were on his arms were as flax that is
burned with fire, and his bonds [2]dropped from his hands.
15 And he found a fresh jawbone of a donkey, so he
[1]reached out and took it and [2]killed a thousand men with it.
16 Then Samson said,

"With the jawbone of a donkey,
[1]Heaps upon heaps,
With the jawbone of a donkey
I have [2]killed a thousand men."

17 And it came about when he had finished speaking, that
he threw the jawbone from his hand; and he named that place
[1]Ramath-lehi.
18 Then he became very thirsty, and he [a]called to the
LORD and said, "Thou hast given this great deliverance by the
hand of Thy servant, and now [1]shall I die of thirst [2]and fall
into the hands of the uncircumcised?"
19 But God split the hollow place that is in Lehi so that
water came out of it. When he drank, his [1]strength returned
and he revived. Therefore, he named it [2]En-hakkore, which is
in Lehi to this day.
20 So [a]he judged Israel twenty years in [b]the days of the
Philistines.

CHAPTER 16

NOW Samson went to [a]Gaza and saw a harlot there, and
went in to her.
2 *When it was told* to the Gazites, saying, "Samson has
come here," they surrounded *the place* and lay in wait for him
all night at the gate of the city. And they kept silent all night,
saying, "*Let us wait* until the morning light, then we will kill
him."
3 Now Samson lay until midnight, and at midnight he
arose and took hold of the doors of the city gate and the two
posts and pulled them up along with the bars; then he put
them on his shoulders and carried them up to the top of the
mountain which is opposite Hebron.
4 After this it came about that he loved a woman in the
valley of Sorek, whose name was Delilah.
5 And the [a]lords of the Philistines came up to her, and
said to her, "[b]Entice him, and see where his great strength *lies*
and [1]how we may overpower him that we may bind him to
afflict him. Then we will each give you eleven hundred *pieces*
of silver."
6 So Delilah said to Samson, "Please tell me where your
great strength is and [1]how you may be bound to afflict you."

12 [1]Lit., *fall upon me yourselves*

13 [1]Lit., *him, saying*

14 [1]Lit., *rushed upon* [2]Lit., *were melted* [a]Judg. 14:19; 1 Sam. 11:6

15 [1]Lit., *stretched out his hand* [2]Lit., *smote*

16 [1]Lit., *Heap, two heaps;* Heb. is same root as donkey [2]Lit., *smitten*

17 [1]I.e., The high place of the jawbone

18 [1]Or, *I shall . . . circumcised* [2]Or, *or* [a]Judg. 16:28

19 [1]I.e., the spring of him who called [2]Lit., *spirit*

20 [a]Heb. 11:32 [b]Judg. 13:1; 16:31

1 [a]Josh. 15:47

5 [1]Lit., *by what* [a]Josh. 13:3 [b]Judg. 14:15

6 [1]Lit., *by what*

7 And Samson said to her, "If they bind me with seven
fresh cords that have not been dried, then I shall become weak
and be like any *other* man."
8 Then the lords of the Philistines brought up to her
seven fresh cords that had not been dried, and she bound him
with them.
9 Now she had *men* lying in wait in an inner room. And
she said to him, "The Philistines are upon you, Samson!" But
he snapped the cords as a string of tow snaps when it [1]touches
fire. So his strength was not discovered.
10 Then Delilah said to Samson, "Behold, you have deceived me and told me lies; now please tell me, [1]how you may
be bound."
11 And he said to her, "If they bind me tightly with new
ropes [1]which have not been used, then I shall become weak
and be like any *other* man."
12 So Delilah took new ropes and bound him with them
and said to him, "The Philistines are upon you, Samson!" For
the *men* were lying in wait in the inner room. But he snapped
[1]the ropes from his arms like a thread.
13 Then Delilah said to Samson, "Up to now you have
deceived me and told me lies; tell me [1]how you may be
bound." And he said to her, "If you weave the seven locks of
my [2]hair with the web [3][and fasten it with a pin, then I shall
become weak and be like any other man."
14 So while he slept, Delilah took the seven locks of his
[1]hair and wove them into the web.] And she fastened *it* with
the pin, and said to him, "The Philistines are upon you, Samson!" But he awoke from his sleep and pulled out the pin of
the loom and the web.
15 Then she said to him, "[a]How can you say, 'I love you,'
when your heart is not with me? You have deceived me these
three times and have not told me where your great strength is."
16 And it came about when she pressed him daily with her
words and urged him, that his soul was [1]annoyed to death.
17 So he told her all *that was* in his heart and said to her,
"A razor has never come on my head, for I have been a [a]Nazi-
rite to God from my mother's womb. If I am shaved, then my
strength will leave me and I shall become weak and be like any
other man."
18 When Delilah saw that he had told her all *that was* in
his heart, she sent and called the lords of the Philistines,
saying, "Come up once more, for he has told me all *that is* in
his heart." Then the lords of the Philistines came up to her,
and brought the money in their hands.
19 And she made him sleep on her knees, and called for a
man and had him shave off the seven locks of his [1]hair. Then
she began to afflict him, and his strength left him.
20 And she said, "The Philistines are upon you, Samson!"
And he awoke from his sleep and said, "I will go out as at other
times and shake myself free." But he did not know that the
LORD had departed from him.
21 Then the Philistines seized him and gouged out his
eyes; and they brought him down to Gaza and bound him with
bronze chains, and he was a grinder in the prison.

9 [1]Lit., *smells*

10 [1]Lit., *by what*

11 [1]Lit., *with which work has not been done*

12 [1]Lit., *them*

13 [1]Lit., *by what* [2]Lit., *head* [3]The passage in brackets is found in Gk. but not in any Heb. mss.

14 [1]Lit., *head*

15 [a]Judg. 14:16

16 [1]Lit., *impatient to the point of*

17 [a]Judg. 13:5; Num. 6:5

19 [1]Lit., *head*

22 However, the hair of his head began to grow again after
it was shaved off.
23 Now the lords of the Philistines assembled to offer a
great sacrifice to [a]Dagon their god, and to rejoice, for they
said,

"Our god has given Samson our enemy into our hands."

24 When the people saw him, they praised their god, for
they said,

"Our god has given our enemy into our hands,
Even the destroyer of our country,
Who has slain many of us."

25 It so happened when [1]they were in high spirits, that
they said, "Call for Samson, that he may amuse us." So they
called for Samson from the prison, and he [2]entertained them.
And they made him stand between the pillars.
26 Then Samson said to the boy who was holding his
hand, "Let me feel the pillars on which the house rests, that I
may lean against them."
27 Now the house was full of men and women, and all the
lords of the Philistines were there. And about 3,000 men and
women were on the roof looking on while Samson was amus-
ing *them*.
28 [a]Then Samson called to the LORD and said, "O Lord
[1]GOD, please remember me and please strengthen me just this
time, O God, that I may at once be avenged of the Philistines
for my two eyes."
29 And Samson grasped the two middle pillars on which
the house rested, and braced himself against them, the one
with his right hand and the other with his left.
30 And Samson said, "Let me die with the Philistines!"
And he bent with [1]all his might so that the house fell on the
lords and all the people who were in it. So the dead whom he
killed at his death were more than those whom he killed in his
life.
31 Then his brothers and all his father's household came
down, took him, brought him up, and buried him between
Zorah and Eshtaol in the tomb of Manoah his father. [a]Thus
he had judged Israel twenty years.

CHAPTER 17

NOW there was a man of the hill country of Ephraim whose
name was Micah.
2 And he said to his mother, "The eleven hundred *pieces*
of silver which were taken from you, about which you uttered
a curse [1]in my hearing, behold, the silver is with me; I took it."
And his mother said, "Blessed be my son by the LORD."
3 He then returned the eleven hundred *pieces* of silver to
his mother, and his mother said, "I wholly dedicate the silver
from my hand to the LORD for my son [a]to make a graven image
and a molten image; now therefore, I will return [1]them to
you."
4 So when he returned the silver to his mother, his mother took two hundred *pieces* of silver and gave them to the
silversmith who made [1]them into a graven image and a molten
idol, and [2]they were in the house of Micah.

23 [a]1 Sam. 5:2

25 [1]Lit., *their heart was pleasant* [2]Lit., *made sport before them*

28 [1]YHWH, usually rendered LORD [a]Judg. 15:18

30 [1]Lit., *strength*

31 [a]Judg. 15:20

2 [1]Lit., *and also spoke it in my ears*

3 [1]Lit., *it* [a]Ex. 20:4, 23; 34:17

4 [1]Lit., *it* [2]Lit., *it was*

5 And the man Micah had a [1]shrine and he made an
[a]ephod and [2a]household idols and [3]consecrated one of his sons,
[c]that he might become his priest.
6 In those days [a]there was no king in Israel; [b]every man
did what was right in his own eyes.
7 Now there was a young man from [a]Bethlehem in Judah, of the family of Judah, who was a Levite; and he was
[1]staying there.
8 Then the man departed from the city, from Bethlehem
in Judah, to [1]stay wherever he might find *a place;* and as he
made his journey, he came to the [a]hill country of Ephraim to
the house of Micah.
9 And Micah said to him, "Where do you come from?"
And he said to him, "I am a Levite from Bethlehem in Judah,
and I am going to [1]stay wherever I may find *a place.*"
10 Micah then said to him, "Dwell with me and be [a]a
father and a priest to me, and I will give you ten *pieces* of silver
a year, a suit of clothes, and your maintenance." So the Levite
went *in.*
11 And the Levite agreed to live with the man; and the
young man became to him like one of his sons.
12 So Micah [1]consecrated the Levite, and the young man
[a]became his priest and [2]lived in the house of Micah.
13 Then Micah said, "Now I know that the LORD will
prosper me, seeing I have a Levite as priest."

CHAPTER 18

[a]
IN those days there was no king of Israel; and [b]in those days
the tribe of the Danites was seeking an inheritance for themselves to live in, for until that day [1]an inheritance had not
[2]been allotted to them as a possession among the tribes of
Israel.
2 So the sons of Dan sent from their family five men out
of their whole number, [1]valiant men from [a]Zorah and Eshtaol,
to spy out the land and to search it; and they said to them,
"Go, search the land." And they came to [b]the hill country of
Ephraim, to the house of Micah, and lodged there.
3 When they were near the house of Micah, they recognized the voice of the young man, the Levite; and they turned
aside there, and said to him, "Who brought you here? And
what are you doing in this *place?* And what do you have here?"
4 And he said to them, "Thus and so has Micah done to
me, and he has hired me, and [a]I have become his priest."
5 And they said to him, "Inquire of God, please, that we
may know whether our way on which we are going will be
prosperous."
6 And the priest said to them, "Go in peace; your way in
which you are going [1]has the LORD's approval."
7 Then the five men departed and came to [a]Laish and
saw the people who were in it living in security, after the
manner of the Sidonians, quiet and secure; for there was no
[1]ruler humiliating *them* for anything in the land, and they were
far from the Sidonians and had no dealings with anyone.
8 When they came back to their brothers at Zorah and
Eshtaol, their brothers said to them, "What *do you report?*"

5 [1]Lit., *house of gods* [2]Heb., *teraphim* [3]Lit., *filled the hand of* [a]Judg. 18:24 [b]Judg. 8:27; 18:14 [c]Gen. 31:19

6 [a]Judg. 18:1; 19:1 [b]Deut. 12:8

7 [1]Or, *sojourning* [a]Judg. 19:1; Ruth 1:1, 2; Mic. 5:2; Matt. 2:1

8 [1]Or, *sojourn* [a]Josh. 24:33

9 [1]Or, *sojourn*

10 [a]Judg. 18:19

12 [1]Lit., *filled the hand of* [2]Lit., *was* [a]Num. 16:10; 18:1-7

1 [1]Lit., *it* [2]Lit., *fallen* [a]Judg. 17:6; 19:1 [b]Josh. 19:40-48

2 [1]Lit., *men, sons of valor* [a]Judg. 13:25 [b]Judg. 17:1

4 [a]Judg. 17:12

6 [1]Lit., *is before the* LORD

7 [1]Lit., *a possessor of restraint* [a]Judg. 18:29; Josh. 19:47

9 [1]Lit., *be*
12 [1]I.e., the camp of Dan [2]Lit., *behind* [a]Judg. 13:25
14 [1]Heb. *teraphim* [a]Judg. 17:5
17 [1]Heb., *teraphim*
18 [1]Heb., *teraphim*
19 [a]Judg. 17:10
20 [1]Heb., *teraphim*
23 [1]Lit., *their faces*
25 [1]Lit., *bitter of soul* [2]Lit., *gather*

9 And they said, "Arise, and let us go up against them; for
we have seen the land, and behold, it is very good. And will you
[1]sit still? Do not delay to go, to enter, to possess the land.
10 "When you enter, you shall come to a secure people
with a spacious land; for God has given it into your hand, a
place where there is no lack of anything that is on the earth."
11 Then from the family of the Danites, from Zorah and
from Eshtaol, six hundred men armed with weapons of war set
out.
12 And they went up and camped at Kiriath-jearim in
Judah. Therefore they called that place [1a]Mahaneh-dan to this
day; behold, it is [2]west of Kiriath-jearim.
13 And they passed from there to the hill country of Ephraim and came to the house of Micah.
14 Then the five men who went to spy out the country of
Laish answered and said to their kinsmen, "Do you know that
there are in these houses [a]an ephod and [1]household idols and a
graven image and a molten image? Now therefore, consider
what you should do."
15 And they turned aside there and came to the house of
the young man, the Levite, to the house of Micah, and asked
him of his welfare.
16 And the six hundred men armed with their weapons of
war, who were of the sons of Dan, stood by the entrance of the
gate.
17 Now the five men who went to spy out the land went
up *and* entered there, *and* took the graven image and the
ephod and [1]household idols and the molten image, while the
priest stood by the entrance of the gate with the six hundred
men armed with weapons of war.
18 And when these went into Micah's house and took the
graven image, the ephod and [1]household idols and the molten
image, the priest said to them, "What are you doing?"
19 And they said to him, "Be silent, put your hand over
your mouth and come with us, and be to us [a]a father and a
priest. Is it better for you to be a priest to the house of one
man, or to be priest to a tribe and a family in Israel?"
20 And the priest's heart was glad, and he took the ephod
and [1]household idols and the graven image, and went among
the people.
21 Then they turned and departed, and put the little ones
and the livestock and the valuables in front of them.
22 When they had gone some distance from the house of
Micah, the men who *were* in the houses near Micah's house
assembled and overtook the sons of Dan.
23 And they cried to the sons of Dan, who turned [1]around
and said to Micah, "What is *the matter* with you, that you
have assembled together?"
24 And he said, "You have taken away my gods which I
made, and the priest, and have gone away, and what do I have
besides? So how can you say to me, 'What is *the matter* with
you?' "
25 And the sons of Dan said to him, "Do not let your
voice be heard among us, lest [1]fierce men fall upon you and
you [2]lose your life, with the lives of your household."
26 So the sons of Dan went on their way; and when Micah

saw that they were too strong for him, he turned and went
back to his house.
27 Then they took what Micah had made and the priest
who had belonged to him, and came to [a]Laish, to a people
quiet and secure, and struck them with the edge of the sword;
and they burned the city with fire.
28 And there was no one to deliver *them*, because it was
far from Sidon and they had no dealings with anyone, and it
was in the valley which is near [a]Beth-rehob. And they rebuilt
the city and lived in it.
29 And they called the name of the city Dan, after the
name of Dan their father who was born in Israel; however, the
name of the city formerly was Laish.
30 And the sons of Dan set up for themselves [a]the graven
image; and Jonathan, the son of [b]Gershom, the son of [1]Manas-
seh, [c]he and his sons were priests to the tribe of the Danites
until the day of the captivity of the land.
31 So they set up for themselves Micah's graven image
which he had made, all the time that the house of God was at
Shiloh.

Chapter 19

NOW it came about in those days, when [a]there was no king
in Israel, that there was a certain Levite [1]staying in the remote
part of the hill country of Ephraim, who took a concubine for
himself from Bethlehem in Judah.
2 But his concubine played the harlot against him, and
she went away from him to her father's house in Bethlehem in
Judah, and was there for a period of four months.
3 Then her husband arose and went after her to [a]speak
[1]tenderly to her in order to bring her back, [2]taking with him his
servant and a pair of donkeys. So she brought him into her
father's house, and when the girl's father saw him, he was glad
to meet him.
4 And his father-in-law, the girl's father, detained him;
and he remained with him three days. So they ate and drank
and lodged there.
5 Now it came about on the fourth day that they got up
early in the morning, and he [1]prepared to go; and the girl's
father said to his son-in-law, "[a]Sustain [2]yourself with a piece of
bread, and afterward you may go."
6 So both of them sat down and ate and drank together;
and the girl's father said to the man, "Please be willing to
spend the night, and [a]let your heart be merry."
7 Then the man arose to go, but his father-in-law urged
him so that he spent the night there again.
8 And on the fifth day he arose to go early in the morning, and the girl's father said, "Please sustain [1]yourself, and
wait until [2]afternoon"; so both of them ate.
9 When the man arose to go along with his concubine
and servant, his father-in-law, the girl's father, said to him,
"Behold now, the day has drawn to a close; please spend the
night. Lo, the day is [2]coming to an end; spend the night here
that your heart may be merry. Then tomorrow you may arise
early for your journey so that you may go [3]home."

27 [a]Judg. 18:7; Josh. 19:47

28 [a]2 Sam. 10:6

30 [1]Some ancient versions read, *Moses* [a]Judg. 17:3, 5 [b]Ex. 2:22; 18:3 [c]Judg. 17:3, 5

1 [1]Or, sojourning [a]Judg. 18:1

3 [1]Lit., *to her heart* [2]Lit., *and* [a]Gen. 34:3; 50:21

5 [1]Lit., *arose* [2]Lit., *your heart* [a]Judg. 19:8; Gen. 18:5

6 [a]Judg. 19:9, 22; Judg. 16:25; Ruth 3:7; 1 Kin. 21:7; Esth. 1:10

8 [1]Lit., *your heart* [2]Lit., *the day declines*

9 [1]Lit., *toward evening* [2]Lit., *declining* [3]Lit., *to your tent*

10 But the man was not willing to spend the night, so he
arose and departed and came to *a place* opposite [a]Jebus (that
is, Jerusalem). And there were with him a pair of saddled
donkeys; his concubine also was with him.
11 When they *were* near Jebus, the day was almost gone;
and [a]the servant said to his master, "Please come, and let us
turn aside into this city of the Jebusites and spend the night in
it."
12 However, his master said to him, "We will not turn
aside into the city of foreigners who are not of the sons of
Israel; but we will go on as far as Gibeah."
13 And he said to his servant, "Come and let us approach
one of these places; and we will spend the night in Gibeah or
Ramah."
14 So they passed along and went their way, and the sun
set on them near Gibeah which belongs to Benjamin.
15 And they turned aside there in order to enter *and* lodge
in Gibeah. When [1]they entered, [1]they sat down in the open
square of the city, for no one took them into *his* house to
spend the night.
16 Then behold, an old man was coming out of the field
from his work at evening. Now the man was from [a]the hill
country of Ephraim, and he was [1]staying in Gibeah, but the
men of the place [b]were Benjamites.
17 And he lifted up his eyes and saw the traveler in the
open square of the city; and the old man said, "Where are you
going, and where do you come from?"
18 And he said to him, "We are passing from Bethlehem
in Judah to the remote part of the hill country of Ephraim, *for*
I am from there, and I went to Bethlehem in Judah. But I am
now going to [1]my house, and no man will take me into his
house.
19 "Yet there is both straw and fodder for our donkeys, and
also bread and wine for me, [1]your maidservant, and [a]the young
man who is with your servants; there is no lack of anything."
20 And the old man said, "Peace to you. Only let me *take
care of* all your needs; however, do not spend the night in the
open square."
21 [a]So he took him into his house and gave the donkeys
fodder, and they washed their feet and ate and drank.
22 While they were [1]making merry, behold, [a]the men of
the city, certain [2b]worthless fellows, surrounded the house,
pounding the door; and they spoke to the owner of the house,
the old man, saying, "Bring out the man who came into your
house that we may have [3]relations with him."
23 Then the man, the owner of the house, went out to
them and said to them, "No, my fellows, please do not act so
wickedly; since this man has come into my house, [a]do not
commit this act of folly.
24 "[a]Here is my virgin daughter and his concubine. Please
let me bring them out that you may ravish them and do to
them [1]whatever you wish. But do not commit such an act of
folly against this man."
25 But the men would not listen to him, so the man seized
his concubine and brought *her* out to them. And they raped

10 [a]1 Chr. 11:4, 5

11 [a]Judg. 19:19

15 [1]So with Gk.; M.T., *he*

16 [1]Or, *sojourning* [a]Judg. 19:1 [b]Judg. 19:14

18 [1]Heb., *the house of the Lord*, cf. vs. 29

19 [1]I.e., my concubine [a]Judg. 19:11

21 [a]Gen. 24:32, 33

22 [1]Lit., *making their hearts merry* [2]Lit., *sons of Belial* [3]Lit., *intercourse* [a]Gen. 19:4, 5; Ezek. 16:46-48 [b]Deut. 13:13; 1 Sam. 2:12; 1 Kin. 21:10; 2 Cor. 6:15

23 [a]Judg. 20:6; Gen. 34:7; Deut. 22:21; 2 Sam. 13:12

24 [1]Lit., *the good in your eyes* [a]Gen. 19:8

her and abused her all night until morning, then let her go at
the approach of dawn.
26 [1]As the day began to dawn, the woman came and fell
down at the doorway of the man's house where her master was,
until *full* daylight.
27 When her master arose in the morning and opened the
doors of the house and went out to go on his way, then behold,
his concubine was lying at the doorway of the house, with her
hands on the threshold.
28 And he said to her, "Get up and let us go," [a]but there
was no answer. Then he placed her on the donkey; and the
man arose and went to his [1]home.
29 When he entered his house, he took a knife and laid
hold of his concubine and [a]cut her in twelve pieces, limb by
limb, and sent her throughout the territory of Israel.
30 And it came about that all who saw *it* said, "Nothing
like this has *ever* happened or been seen from the day when
the sons of Israel came up from the land of Egypt to this day.
Consider it, take counsel and speak up!"

Chapter 20

THEN all the sons of Israel from Dan to Beersheba, including the land of Gilead, came out, and the congregation assembled as one man to the LORD at [a]Mizpah.
2 And the [1]chiefs of all the people, *even* of all the tribes
of Israel, took their stand in the assembly of the people of
God, 400,000 foot [2]soldiers who drew the sword.
3 (Now the sons of Benjamin heard that the sons of
Israel had gone up to Mizpah.) And the sons of Israel said,
"Tell *us*, how did this wickedness take place?"
4 So the Levite, the husband of the woman who was
murdered, answered and said, "I came with my concubine to
spend the night at Gibeah which belongs to Benjamin.
5 "But the men of Gibeah rose up against me and surrounded the house at night because of me. They intended to
kill me; instead, they ravished my concubine so that she died.
6 "And I took hold of my concubine and cut her in pieces
and sent her throughout the land of Israel's inheritance; for
they have committed a lewd and disgraceful act in Israel.
7 "Behold, all you sons of Israel, give your advice and
counsel here."
8 Then all the people arose as one man, saying, "Not one
of us will go to his tent, nor will any of us return to his house.
9 "But now this is the thing which we will do to Gibeah;
we will go up against it by lot.
10 "And we will take 10 men out of 100 throughout the
tribes of Israel, and 100 out of 1,000, and 1,000 out of 10,000
to [1]supply food for the people, that when they come to [2]Gib-
eah of Benjamin, they may [3]punish *them* for all the disgraceful acts that they have committed in Israel."
11 Thus all the men of Israel were gathered against the
city, united as one man.
12 Then the tribes of Israel sent men through the entire
[1]tribe of Benjamin, saying, "What is this wickedness that has
taken place among you?

26 [1]Lit., *At the turning of the morning*

28 [1]Lit., *place*
[a]Judg. 20:5

29 [a]1 Sam. 11:12

1 [a]1 Sam. 7:5

2 [1]Lit., *cornerstones* [2]Lit., *men*

10 [1]Lit., *take* [2]Heb., *Geba* [3]Lit., *do*

12 [1]Lit., *tribes*

13 "Now then, deliver up the men, the [1a]worthless fellows
in Gibeah, that we may put them to death and remove *this*
wickedness from Israel." But the sons of Benjamin would not
listen to the voice of their brothers, the sons of Israel.
14 And the sons of Benjamin gathered from the cities to
Gibeah, to go out to battle against the sons of Israel.
15 And from the cities on that day the sons of Benjamin
were [1]numbered, [a]26,000 men who draw the sword, besides the
inhabitants of Gibeah who were [1]numbered 700 choice men.
16 Out of all these people 700 choice men were left-
handed; each one could sling a stone at a hair and not miss.
17 Then the men of Israel besides Benjamin were [1]num-
bered, 400,000 men who draw the sword; all these were men of
war.
18 Now the sons of Israel arose, went up to Bethel, and
[a]inquired of God, and said, "Who shall go up first for us to
battle against the sons of Benjamin?" Then the LORD said,
"Judah *shall go up* first."
19 So the sons of Israel arose in the morning and camped
against Gibeah.
20 And the men of Israel went out to battle against Benjamin, and the men of Israel arrayed for battle against them at
Gibeah.
21 Then the sons of Benjamin came out of Gibeah and
[1a]felled to the ground on that day 22,000 men of Israel.
22 But the people, the men of Israel, encouraged themselves and arrayed for battle again in the place where they had
arrayed themselves the first day.
23 [a]And the sons of Israel went up and wept before the
LORD until evening, and [b]inquired of the LORD, saying, "Shall
we again draw near for battle against the sons of my brother
Benjamin?" And the LORD said, "Go up against him."
24 Then the sons of Israel [1]came against the sons of Benjamin the second day.
25 And Benjamin went out [1]against them from Gibeah
the second day and [2a]felled to the ground again 18,000 men of
the sons of Israel; all these drew the sword.
26 Then [a]all the sons of Israel and all the people went up
and came to Bethel and wept; thus they remained there before
the LORD and fasted that day until evening. And they offered
burnt offerings and peace offerings before the LORD.
27 And the sons of Israel [a]inquired of the LORD (for the
ark of the covenant of God *was* there in those days,
28 and Phinehas the son of Eleazar, Aaron's son, stood
before it to *minister* in those days), saying, "Shall I yet again
go out to battle against the sons of my brother Benjamin, or
shall I cease?" And the LORD said, "Go up, [a]for tomorrow I
will deliver them into your hand."
29 [a]So Israel set men in ambush around Gibeah.
30 And the sons of Israel went up against the sons of
Benjamin on the third day and arrayed themselves against
Gibeah, as at other times.
31 [a]And the sons of Benjamin went out [1]against the
people and were drawn away from the city, and they began to
strike [2]and kill some of the people, as at other times, on the

13 [1]Lit., *sons of Belial* [a]2 Cor. 6:15
15 [1]Or, *mustered* [a]Num. 1:36, 37; 2:23; 26:41
17 [1]Or, *mustered*
18 [a]Judg. 20:23, 27; Num. 27:21
21 [1]Lit., *destroyed* [a]Judg. 20:25
23 [a]Josh. 7:6, 7 [b]Judg. 20:18
24 [1]Lit., *approached*
25 [1]Lit., *to meet* [2]Lit., *destroyed*
26 [a]Judg. 20:23; 21:2
27 [a]Judg. 20:18
28 [a]Judg. 7:9
29 [a]Josh. 8:4
31 [1]Lit., *to meet* [2]Lit., *slain ones* [a]Josh. 8:16

highways, one of which goes up to Bethel and the other to
Gibeah, *and* in the field, about thirty men of Israel.
32 And the sons of Benjamin said, "They are struck down
before us, as at the first." But the sons of Israel said, "Let us
flee that we may draw them away from the city to the
highways."
33 Then all the men of Israel arose from their place and
arrayed themselves at Baal-tamar; [a]and the men of Israel in
ambush broke out of their place, even out of Maareh-geba.
34 When ten thousand choice men from all Israel came
against Gibeah, the battle became [1]fierce; but [2]Benjamin did
not know that [3]disaster was [4]close to them.
35 And the LORD struck Benjamin before Israel, so that
the sons of Israel destroyed 25,100 men of Benjamin that day,
all [1]who draw the sword.
36 So the sons of Benjamin saw that they were [1]defeated.
When the men of Israel gave [2]ground to Benjamin because
they relied on the men in ambush whom they had set against
Gibeah,
37 the men in ambush hurried and rushed against Gibeah;
the men in ambush also deployed and struck all the city with
the edge of the sword.
38 Now the appointed sign between the men of Israel and
the men in ambush was [a]that they should make a great cloud
of smoke rise from the city.
39 Then the men of Israel turned in the battle, and Benjamin began to strike [1]and kill about thirty men of Israel, [a]for
they said, "Surely they are [2]defeated before us, as in the first
battle."
40 But when the cloud began to rise from the city in a
column of smoke, Benjamin looked behind them; and behold,
the whole city was going up *in smoke* to heaven.
41 Then the men of Israel turned, and the men of Benjamin were terrified; for they saw that [1]disaster was [2]close to
them.
42 Therefore, they turned their backs before the men of
Israel [a]toward the direction of the wilderness, but the battle
overtook them while those who came out of the cities
destroyed them in the midst of them.
43 They surrounded Benjamin, pursued them without rest
and trod them down opposite Gibeah toward the [1]east.
44 Thus 18,000 men of Benjamin fell; all these were valiant warriors.
45 [1]The rest turned and fled toward the wilderness to the
rock of [a]Rimmon, but they [2]caught 5,000 of them on the
highways and overtook them [3]at Gidom and [4]killed 2,000 of
them.
46 So all of Benjamin who fell that day were 25,000 men
who draw the sword; all these were valiant warriors.
47 But 600 men turned and fled toward the wilderness to
the rock of Rimmon, and they remained at the rock of Rimmon four months.
48 The men of Israel then turned back against the sons of
Benjamin and struck them with the edge of the sword, both
the entire city with the cattle and all that they found; they also
set on fire all the cities which they found.

33 [a]Josh. 8:19

34 [1]Lit., *heavy* [2]Lit., *they* [3]Lit., *evil* [4]Lit., *touching*

35 [1]Lit., *these*

36 [1]Lit., *smitten* [2]Lit., *place*

38 [a]Josh. 8:20

39 [1]Lit., *slain ones* [2]Lit., *smitten* [a]Judg. 20:32

41 [1]Lit., *evil* [2]Lit., *touching*

42 [a]Josh. 8:15, 24

43 [1]Lit., *sunrise*

45 [1]So with Gk.; Heb., *And they* [2]Lit., *gleaned* [3]Lit., *as far as* [4]Lit., *smote* [a]Judg. 21:13

1 [1]Lit., *for a wife*
[a]Judg. 21:7, 18

2 [1]Lit., *with great weeping*
[a]Judg. 20:26

4 [a]Deut. 12:5
2 Sam. 24:25

5 [1]Lit., *there was a great oath*

7 [a]Judg. 21:1

9 [1]Or, *mustered*

10 [a]Num. 31:17

11 [1]Lit., *known lying with*

12 [1]Lit., *a male*

13 [a]Deut. 20:10

14 [1]Lit., *did not find so*

18 [a]Judg. 21:1

CHAPTER 21

NOW the men of Israel [a]had sworn in Mizpah, saying,
"None of us shall give his daughter to Benjamin [1]in marriage."
2 [a]So the people came to Bethel and sat there before
God until evening, and lifted up their voices and wept
[1]bitterly.
3 And they said, "Why, O LORD, God of Israel, has this
come about in Israel, so that one tribe should be *missing* today
in Israel?"
4 And it came about the next day that the people arose
early and built [a]an altar there, and offered burnt offerings and
peace offerings.
5 Then the sons of Israel said, "Who is there among all
the tribes of Israel who did not come up in the assembly to the
LORD?" For [1]they had taken a great oath concerning him who
did not come up to the LORD at Mizpah, saying, "He shall
surely be put to death."
6 And the sons of Israel were sorry for their brother Benjamin and said, "One tribe is cut off from Israel today.
7 "What shall we do for wives for those who are left, since
we have [a]sworn by the LORD not to give them any of our
daughters in marriage?"
8 And they said, "What one is there of the tribes of Israel
who did not come up to the LORD at Mizpah?" And behold, no
one had come to the camp from Jabesh-gilead to the assembly.
9 For when the people were [1]numbered, behold, not one
of the inhabitants of Jabesh-gilead was there.
10 And the congregation sent 12,000 of the valiant warriors there, and commanded them, saying, "Go and [a]strike the
inhabitants of Jabesh-gilead with the edge of the sword, with
the women and the little ones.
11 "And this is the thing that you shall do: you shall utterly
destroy every man and every woman who has [1]lain with a
man."
12 And they found among the inhabitants of Jabesh-gilead
400 young virgins who had not known a man by lying with
[1]him; and they brought them to the camp at Shiloh, which is in
the land of Canaan.
13 Then the whole congregation sent *word* and spoke to
the sons of Benjamin who were at the rock of Rimmon, and
[a]proclaimed peace to them.
14 And Benjamin returned at that time, and they gave
them the women whom they had kept alive from the women
of Jabesh-gilead; yet they [1]were not enough for them.
15 And the people were sorry for Benjamin because the
LORD had made a breach in the tribes of Israel.
16 Then the elders of the congregation said, "What shall
we do for wives for those who are left, since the women are
destroyed out of Benjamin?"
17 And they said, "*There must be* an inheritance for the
survivors of Benjamin, that a tribe may not be blotted out
from Israel.
18 "But we cannot give them wives of our daughters." For
the sons of Israel [a]had sworn, saying, "Cursed is he who gives a
wife to Benjamin."

19 So they said, "Behold, there is a feast of the LORD from
year to year in [a]Shiloh, which is on the north side of Bethel,
on the east side of the highway that goes up from Bethel to
Shechem, and on the south side of Lebonah."
20 And they commanded the sons of Benjamin, saying,
"Go and lie in wait in the vineyards,
21 and watch; and behold, if the daughters of Shiloh come
out to [1a]take part in the dances, then you shall come out of the
vineyards and each of you shall catch his wife from the daughters of Shiloh, and go to the land of Benjamin.
22 "And it shall come about, when their fathers or their
brothers come to complain to us, that we shall say to them,
'Give them to us voluntarily, because we did not take for each
man of Benjamin [1]a wife in battle, [2]nor did you give *them* to
them, [a]*else* you would now be guilty.' "
23 And the sons of Benjamin did so, and took wives according to their number from those who danced, whom they
carried away. And they went and returned to their inheritance,
and [a]rebuilt the cities and lived in them.
24 And the sons of Israel departed from there at that time,
every man to his tribe and family, and each one of them went
out from there to his inheritance.
25 [a]In those days there was no king in Israel; everyone did
what was right in his own eyes.

19 [a]Judg. 18:31; Josh. 18:1; 1 Sam. 1:3
21 [1]Lit., *dance* [a]Judg. 11:34; Ex. 15:20
22 [1]Lit., *his* [2]Lit., *because* [a]Judg. 21:1, 18
23 [a]Judg. 20:48
25 [a]Judg. 17:6; 18:1; 19:1

THE BOOK OF RUTH

Naomi Widowed.

NOW it came about in the days [a]when the judges [1]governed,
that there was a famine in the land. And a certain man of
Bethlehem in Judah went to sojourn in the land of Moab [2]with
his wife and his two sons.
2 And the name of the man *was* Elimelech, and the
name of his wife, Naomi; and the names of his two sons *were*
Mahlon and Chilion, Ephrathites of Bethlehem in Judah.
Now they entered the land of Moab and remained there.
3 Then Elimelech, Naomi's husband, died; and she was
left with her two sons.
4 And they took for themselves Moabite women *as*
wives; the name of the one was Orpah and the name of the
other Ruth. And they lived there about ten years.
5 Then [1]both Mahlon and Chilion also died; and the
woman was bereft of her two children and her husband.
6 Then she arose with her daughters-in-law that she
might return from the land of Moab, for she had heard in the
land of Moab that the LORD had [a]visited His people in giving
them food.
7 So she departed from the place where she was, and her
two daughters-in-law with her; and they went on the way to
return to the land of Judah.
8 And Naomi said to her two daughters-in-law, "Go,

1 [1]Or, *judged* [2]Lit., *he, and* [a]Judg. 2:16-18
5 [1]Lit., *both of them*
6 [a]Ex. 4:31

return each of you to her mother's house. May the LORD deal
kindly with you as you have dealt with the dead and with me.
9 "May the LORD grant that you may find rest, each in the
house of her husband." Then she kissed them, and they lifted
up their voices and wept.
10 And they said to her, "*No*, but we will surely return
with you to your people."
11 But Naomi said, "Return, my daughters. Why should
you go with me? Have I yet sons in my womb, that they may
be your husbands?
12 "Return, my daughters! Go, for I am too old to have a
husband. If I said I have hope, if I should even have a husband
tonight and also bear sons,
13 would you therefore wait until they were grown?
Would you therefore refrain from marrying? No, my daughters; for it is [1]harder for me than for you, for the hand of the
LORD has gone forth against me."
14 And they lifted up their voices and wept again; and
Orpah kissed her mother-in-law, but Ruth clung to her.
15 Then she said, "Behold, your sister-in-law has gone
back to her people and her gods; return after your sister-in-
law."
16 But Ruth said, "Do not urge me to leave you *or* turn
back from following you; for where you go, I will go, and
where you lodge, I will lodge. Your people *shall be* my people,
and your God, my God.
17 "Where you die, I will die, and there I will be buried.
Thus may the LORD do to me, and worse, if *anything but*
death parts you and me."
18 When she saw that she was determined to go with her,
she [1]said no more to her.
19 So they both went until they came to Bethlehem. And
it came about when they had come to Bethlehem, that all the
city was stirred because of them, and [1]the women said, "Is this
Naomi?"
20 And she said to them, "Do not call me [1]Naomi; call me
[2]Mara, for [3][a]the Almighty has dealt very bitterly with me.
21 "I went out full, but the LORD has brought me back
empty. Why do you call me Naomi, since the LORD has witnessed against me and [1]the Almighty has afflicted me?"
22 So Naomi returned, and with her Ruth the Moabitess,
her daughter-in-law, who returned from the land of Moab.
And they came to Bethlehem at [a]the beginning of barley
harvest.

CHAPTER 2

NOW Naomi had [1]a kinsman of her husband, a [2]man of
great wealth, of the family of [a]Elimelech, whose name was
Boaz.
2 And Ruth the Moabitess said to Naomi, "Please let me
go to the field and [a]glean among the ears of grain after one in
whose sight I may find favor." And she said to her, "Go, my
daughter."
3 So she departed and went and gleaned in the field after

13 [1]Lit., *more bitter*

18 [1]Lit., *ceased to speak*

19 [1]Lit., *they*

20 [1]I.e., Pleasant [2]I.e., Bitter [3]Heb., *Shaddai* [a]Ex. 6:3; Job 6:4

21 [1]Heb., *Shaddai*

22 [a]Ex. 9:31; Lev. 23:10, 11

1 [1]Or, *an acquaintance* [2]Or, *mighty, valiant man* [a]Ruth 1:2

2 [a]Ruth 2:7; Lev. 19:9, 10; 23:22

the reapers; and [1]she happened to come to the portion of the
field belonging to Boaz, who was of the family of Elimelech.
4 Now behold, Boaz came from Bethlehem and said to
the reapers, "May the LORD be with you." And they said to
him, "May the LORD bless you."
5 Then Boaz said to his servant who was [1]in charge of the
reapers, "Whose young woman is this?"
6 And the servant [1]in charge of the reapers answered and
said, "She is the young Moabite woman who returned with
Naomi from the land of Moab.
7 "And she said, 'Please let me glean and gather after the
reapers among the sheaves.' Thus she came and has remained
from the morning until now; she has been sitting in the house
for a little while."
8 Then Boaz said to Ruth, "[1]Listen carefully, my daughter. Do not go to glean in another field; furthermore, do not
go on from this one, but stay here with my maids.
9 "Let your eyes be on the field which they reap, and go
after them. Indeed, I have commanded the servants not to
touch you. When you are thirsty, go to the [1]water jars and
drink from what the servants draw."
10 Then she fell on her face, bowing to the ground and
said to him, "Why have I found favor in your sight that you
should take notice of me, since I am a foreigner?"
11 And Boaz answered and said to her, "All that you have
done for your mother-in-law after the death of your husband
has been fully reported to me, and how you left your father
and your mother and the land of your birth, and came to a
people that you did not previously know.
12 "May the LORD reward your work, and your wages be
full from the LORD, the God of Israel, [a]under whose wings you
have come to seek refuge."
13 Then she said, "I have found favor in your sight, my
lord, for you have comforted me and indeed have spoken
[1]kindly to your maidservant, though I am not like one of your
maidservants."
14 And at mealtime Boaz said to her, "[1]Come here, that
you may eat of the bread and dip your piece of bread in the
vinegar." So she sat beside the reapers; and he [2]served her
roasted grain, and she ate and was satisfied [a]and had some left.
15 When she rose to glean, Boaz commanded his servants,
saying, "Let her glean even among the sheaves, and do not
insult her.
16 "And also you shall purposely pull out for her *some*
grain from the bundles and leave *it* that she may glean, and do
not rebuke her."
17 So she gleaned in the field until evening. Then she beat
out what she had gleaned, and it was about an ephah of barley.
18 And she took *it* up and went into the city, and her
mother-in-law saw what she had gleaned. She also took *it* out
and [a]gave [1]Naomi what she had left after [2]she was satisfied.
19 Her mother-in-law then said to her, "Where did you
glean today and where did you work? May he who took notice
of you be blessed." So she told her mother-in-law with whom
she had worked and said, "The name of the man with whom I
worked today is Boaz."

3 [1]Lit., *her chance chanced upon*

5 [1]Lit., *who was appointed over*

6 [1]Lit., *who was appointed over*

8 [1]Lit., *Have you not heard*

9 [1]Lit., *vessels*

12 [a]Ruth 1:16

13 [1]Lit., *to the heart of your*

14 [1]Lit., *Draw near* [2]Lit., *held out to*
[a]Ruth 2:18

18 [1]Lit., *her* [2]Lit., *her satiety*
[a]Ruth 2:14

20 And Naomi said to her daughter-in-law, "May he be
blessed of the LORD who has not withdrawn his kindness to the
living and to the dead." Again Naomi said to her, "The man is
[1]our relative, he is one of our [2]closest relatives."
21 Then Ruth the Moabitess said, "[1]Furthermore, he said
to me, 'You should stay close to my servants until they have
finished all my harvest.' "
22 And Naomi said to Ruth her daughter-in-law, "It is
good, my daughter, that you go out with his maids, lest *others*
fall upon you in another field."
23 So she stayed close by the maids of Boaz in order to
glean until [a]the end of the barley harvest and the wheat harvest. And she lived with her mother-in-law.

CHAPTER 3

THEN Naomi her mother-in-law said to her, "My daughter,
shall I not seek [1]security for you, that it may be well with you?
2 "And now is not Boaz [a]our [1]kinsman, with whose maids
you were? Behold, he winnows barley at the threshing floor
tonight.
3 "Wash yourself therefore, and anoint yourself and put
on your *best* clothes, and go down to the threshing floor; *but*
do not make yourself known to the man until he has finished
eating and drinking.
4 "And it shall be when he lies down, that you shall [1]notice
the place where he lies, and you shall go and uncover his feet
and lie down; then he will tell you what you shall do."
5 And she said to her, "All that you say I will do."
6 So she went down to the threshing floor and did according to all that her mother-in-law had commanded her.
7 When Boaz had eaten and drunk and his heart was
merry, he went to lie down at the end of the heap of grain; and
she came secretly, and uncovered his feet and lay down.
8 And it happened in the middle of the night that the
man was startled and [1]bent forward; and behold, a woman was
lying at his feet.
9 And he said, "Who are you?" And she answered, "I am
Ruth your maid. So spread your covering over your maid, for
you are a [1]close relative.
10 Then he said, "May you be blessed of the LORD, my
daughter. You have shown your last kindness to be better than
the first by not going after young men, whether poor or rich.
11 "And now, my daughter, do not fear. I will do for you
whatever you [1]ask, for all my people in the [2]city know that you
are [a]a woman of excellence.
12 "And now it is true I am a [1]close relative; however, there
is a [1]relative closer than I.
13 "Remain this night, and when morning comes, if he will
[1]redeem you, good; let him redeem you. But if he does not
wish to [1]redeem you, then I will redeem you, as the LORD lives.
Lie down until morning."
14 So she lay at his feet until morning and rose before one
could recognize another; and he said, "Let it not be known
that the woman came to the threshing floor."
15 Again he said, "Give me the cloak that is on you and

20 [1]Lit., *near to us* [2]Lit., *redeemers*
21 [1]Lit., *Also that*
23 [a]Deut. 16:9
1 [1]Lit., *rest*
2 [1]Or, *acquaintance* [a]Deut. 25:5-10
4 [1]Lit., *know*
8 [1]Lit., *twisted himself*
9 [1]Or, *redeemer*
11 [1]Lit., *say* [2]Lit., *gate* [a]Prov. 31:10
12 [1]Or, *redeemer*
13 [1]Or, *act as close relative to*

hold it." So she held it, and he measured six *measures* of barley
and laid *it* on her. Then [1]she went into the city.
16 And when she came to her mother-in-law, she said,
"[1]How did it go, my daughter?" And she told her all that the
man had done for her.
17 And she said, "These six *measures* of barley he gave to
me, for he said, 'Do not go to your mother-in-law empty-
handed.'"
18 Then she said, "Wait, my daughter, until you know
how the matter [1]turns out; for the man will not rest until he
has [2]settled it today."

Chapter 4

Now Boaz went up to the gate and sat down there, and
behold, [a]the [1]close relative of whom Boaz spoke was passing
by, so he said, "Turn aside, [2]friend, sit down here." And he
turned aside and sat down.
2 And he took ten men of the elders of the city and said,
"Sit down here." So they sat down.
3 Then he said to the [1]closest relative, "Naomi, who has
come back from the land of Moab, has to sell the piece of land
[a]which belonged to our brother Elimelech.
4 "So I thought to [1]inform you, saying, 'Buy *it* before
those who are sitting *here*, and before the elders of my people.
If you will redeem *it*, redeem *it*; but if [2]not, tell me that I may
know; for there is no one but you to redeem *it*, and I am after
you.'" And he said, "I will redeem *it*."
5 Then Boaz said, "On the day you buy the field from
the hand of Naomi, you must also acquire Ruth the Moabitess, the widow of the deceased, in order to raise up the name
of the deceased on his inheritance."
6 And [a]the [1]closest relative said, "I cannot redeem it for
myself, lest I [2]jeopardize my own inheritance. Redeem *it* for
yourself; you *may have* my right of redemption, for I cannot
redeem *it*."
7 Now this was [a]*the custom* in former times in Israel
concerning the redemption and the exchange *of land* to confirm any matter: a man removed his sandal and gave it to
another; and this was the *manner of* attestation in Israel.
8 So the [1]closest relative said to Boaz, "Buy *it* for yourself." And he removed his sandal.
9 Then Boaz said to the elders and all the people, "You
are witnesses today that I have bought from the hand of
Naomi all that belonged to Elimelech and all that belonged to
Chilion and Mahlon.
10 "Moreover, I have acquired Ruth the Moabitess, the
widow of Mahlon, to be my wife in order to raise up the name
of the deceased on his inheritance, so that the name of the
deceased may not be cut off from his brothers or from the
[1]court of his *birth-place*; you are witnesses today."
11 And all the people who were in the [1]court, and the
elders, said, "*We are* witnesses. May the Lord make the woman who is coming into your home [a]like Rachel and Leah,
both of whom built the house of Israel; and may you achieve
[2]wealth in Ephrathah and [3]become famous in Bethlehem.

15 [1]So with many mss.; M.T., *he*

16 [1]Lit., *Who are you?*

18 [1]Lit., *falls* [2]Lit., *finish the matter*

1 [1]Or, *redeemer* [2]Lit., *a certain one*
[a]Ruth 3:12

3 [1]Lit., *redeemer*
[a]Lev. 25:25

4 [1]Lit., *uncover your ear*
[2]Lit., *no one will redeem*

6 [1]Lit., *redeemer* [2]Lit., *ruin*
[a]Lev. 25:25

7 [a]Deut. 25:8-10

8 [1]Lit., *redeemer*

10 [1]Lit., *gate*

11 [1]Lit., *gate* [2]Or, *power*
[3]Lit., *call the name in*
[a]Gen. 29:25-30

12 [1]Lit., *seed* [a]Ruth 4:18; Gen. 38:29; 46:12

13 [1]Lit., *gave her conception*

14 [1]Or, *closest relative* [2]Lit., *be called in*

15 [1]Lit., *who* [a]Ruth 1:16, 17; 2:11, 12

16 [1]I.e., as her own

18 [1]Lit., *begot* and so through v. 22 [a]Matt. 1:4-6

12 "Moreover, may your house be like the house of [a]Perez
whom Tamar bore to Judah, through the [1]offspring which the
LORD shall give you by this young woman."
13 So Boaz took Ruth, and she became his wife, and he
went in to her. And the LORD [1]enabled her to conceive, and she
gave birth to a son.
14 Then the women said to Naomi, "Blessed is the LORD
who has not left you without a [1]redeemer today, and may his
name [2]become famous in Israel.
15 "May he also be to you a restorer of life and a sustainer
of your old age; for your daughter-in-law, who loves you [1a]and
is better to you than seven sons, has given birth to him."
16 Then Naomi took the child [1]and laid him in her lap,
and became his nurse.
17 And the neighbor women gave him a name, saying, "A
son has been born to Naomi!" So they named him Obed. He is
the father of Jesse, the father of David.
18 Now these are the generations of Perez: [a]to Perez [1]was
born Hezron,
19 and to Hezron was born Ram, and to Ram
Amminadab,
20 and to Amminadab was born Nahshon, and to Nahshon, Salmon,
21 and to Salmon was born Boaz, and to Boaz, Obed,
22 and to Obed was born Jesse, and to Jesse, David.

THE FIRST BOOK OF SAMUEL

Elkanah and His Wives.

1 [a]1 Sam. 1:19 [b]Josh. 17:17, 18 [c]1 Chr. 6:22-28, 33-38

2 [a]Deut. 21:15-17 [b]Luke 2:36

3 [a]1 Sam. 1:21; Ex. 34:23; Luke 2:41 [b]Deut. 12:5-7 [c]Josh. 18:1

4 [a]Deut. 12:17, 18

5 [a]Gen. 43:34 [b]Gen. 16:1; 30:1

6 [a]Job. 24:21

NOW there was a certain man from [a]Ramathaim-zophim
from the [b]hill country of Ephraim, and his name was [c]Elkanah
the son of Jeroham, the son of Elihu, the son of Tohu, the son
of Zuph, an Ephraimite.
2 And he had [a]two wives: the name of one was [b]Hannah
and the name of the other Peninnah; and Peninnah had children, but Hannah had no children.
3 Now this man would go up from his city [a]yearly [b]to
worship and to sacrifice to the LORD of hosts in [c]Shiloh. And
the two sons of Eli, Hophni and Phinehas were priests to the
LORD there.
4 And when the day came that Elkanah sacrificed, he
[a]would give portions to Peninnah his wife and to all her sons
and her daughters;
5 but to Hannah he would give [a]a double portion, for he
loved Hannah, [b]but the LORD had closed her womb.
6 Her rival, however, [a]would provoke her bitterly to irri-
tate her, because the LORD had closed her womb.
7 And it happened year after year, as often as she went

up to the house of the LORD, she would provoke her, so she
wept and would not eat.
8 Then Elkanah her husband said to her, "Hannah, why
do you weep and why do you not eat and why is your heart
sad? [a]Am I not better to you than ten sons?"
9 Then Hannah rose after eating and drinking in Shiloh.
Now Eli the priest was sitting on the seat by the doorpost of
[a]the temple of the LORD.
10 And she, [1]greatly distressed, prayed to the LORD and
wept bitterly.
11 And she [a]made a vow and said, "O LORD of hosts, if
Thou wilt indeed [b]look on the affliction of Thy maidservant
and remember me, and not forget Thy maidservant, but wilt
give Thy maidservant a [1]son, then I will give him to the LORD
all the days of his life, and [c]a razor shall never come on his
head."
12 Now it came about, as she [1]continued praying before
the LORD, that Eli was watching her mouth.
13 As for Hannah, [a]she was speaking in her heart, only her
lips were moving, but her voice was not heard. So Eli thought
she was drunk.
14 Then Eli said to her, "[a]How long will you make
yourself drunk? Put away your wine from you."
15 But Hannah answered and said, "No, my lord, I am a
woman [1]oppressed in spirit; I have drunk neither wine nor
strong drink, but I [a]have poured out my soul before the LORD.
16 "Do not [1]consider your maidservant as a worthless woman; for I have spoken until now [a]out of my great concern and
[2]provocation."
17 Then Eli answered and said, "[a]Go in peace; and may
the God of Israel [b]grant your petition that you have asked of
Him."
18 And she said, "[a]Let your maidservant find favor in your
sight." So the woman went her way and ate, and [b]her face was
no longer *sad*.
19 Then they arose early in the morning and worshiped
before the LORD, and returned again to their house in [a]Ramah.
And Elkanah [1]had relations with Hannah his wife, and [b]the
LORD remembered her.
20 And it came about [1]in due time, after Hannah had
conceived, that she gave birth to a son; and she named him
Samuel, *saying*, "[a]Because I have asked him of the LORD."
21 Then the man Elkanah [a]went up with all his household
to offer to the LORD the yearly sacrifice and *pay* his vow.
22 But Hannah did not go up, for she said to her husband,
"*I will not go up* until the child is weaned; then I will [a]bring
him, that he may appear before the LORD and [b]stay there
forever."
23 And [a]Elkanah her husband said to her, "Do what seems
best [1]to you. Remain until you have weaned him; only [b]may
the LORD confirm His word." So the woman remained and
nursed her son until she weaned him.
24 Now when she had weaned him, [a]she took him up with
her, with a three-year-old bull and one ephah of flour and a jug
of wine, and brought him to [b]the house of the LORD in Shiloh,
although the child was young.

8 [a]Ruth 4:15
9 [a]1 Sam. 3:3
10 [1]Lit., *bitter of soul*
11 [1]Lit., *seed of men* [a]Num. 30:6-11 [b]Gen. 29:32 [c]Num. 6:5; Judg. 13:5; Luke 1:15
12 [1]Lit., *multiplied*
13 [a]Gen. 24:42-45
14 [a]Acts 2:4, 13
15 [1]Lit., *severe* [a]Ps. 62:8
16 [1]Lit., *give* [2]Lit., *my provocation* [a]Luke 6:45
17 [a]1 Sam. 25:35; 2 Kin. 5:19; Mark 5:34 [b]Ps. 20:3-5
18 [a]Ruth 2:13 [b]Rom. 15:13
19 [1]Lit., *knew* [a]1 Sam. 1:1; 2:11 [b]Gen. 21:1; 30:22
20 [1]Lit., *at the circuit of the days* [a]Gen. 41:51, 52; Ex. 2:10, 22; Matt. 1:21
21 [a]1 Sam. 1:3; Deut. 12:11
22 [a]Luke 2:22 [b]1 Sam. 1:11, 28
23 [1]Lit., *in your eyes* [a]Num. 30:10, 11 [b]1 Sam. 1:17
24 [a]Num. 15:9, 10; Deut. 12:5, 6 [b]1 Sam. 4:3, 4; Josh. 18:1

25 Then [a]they slaughtered the bull, and [b]brought the boy
to Eli.
26 And she said, "Oh, my lord! [a]As your soul lives, my
lord, I am the woman who stood here beside you, praying to
the LORD.
27 "[a]For this boy I prayed, and the LORD has given me my
petition which I asked of Him.
28 "[a]So I have also [1]dedicated him to the LORD; as long as
he lives he is [1]dedicated to the LORD." And he worshiped the
LORD there.

CHAPTER 2

THEN Hannah [a]prayed and said,
"My heart exults in the LORD:
[b]My [1]horn is exalted in the LORD,
My mouth [2]speaks boldly against my enemies,
Because [c]I rejoice in Thy salvation.
2 "[a]There is no one holy like the LORD,
Indeed, [b]there is no one besides Thee,
[c]Nor is there any rock like our God.
3 "[1]Boast no more so very proudly,
[a]Do not let arrogance come out of your mouth;
[b]For the LORD is a God of knowledge,
[c]And with Him actions are weighed.
4 "[a]The bows of the mighty are shattered,
[b]But the feeble gird on strength.
5 "Those who were full hire themselves out for bread,
But those who were hungry cease *to hunger*.
[a]Even the barren gives birth to seven,
But [b]she who has many children languishes.
6 "[a]The LORD kills and makes alive;
[b]He brings down to [1]Sheol and raises up.
7 "[a]The LORD makes poor and rich;
[b]He brings low, He also exalts.
8 "[a]He raises the poor from the dust,
[b]He lifts the needy from the ash heap.
[c]To make them sit with nobles,
And inherit a seat of honor;
[d]For the pillars of the earth are the LORD's,
And He set the world on them.
9 "[a]He keeps the feet of His godly ones,
[b]But the wicked ones are silenced in darkness;
[c]For not by might shall a man prevail.
10 "[a]Those who contend with the LORD will be shattered;
[b]Against them He will thunder in the heavens,
[c]The LORD will judge the ends of the earth;
[d]And He will give strength to His king,
[e]And will exalt the [1]horn of His anointed."
11 Then Elkanah went to his home at [a]Ramah. [b]But the
boy ministered to the LORD before Eli the priest.
12 Now the sons of Eli were [1a]worthless men; they did not
know the LORD
13 [a]and the custom of the priests with the people. When
any man was offering a sacrifice, the priest's servant would

25 [a]Lev. 1:5 [b]Luke 2:22

26 [a]2 King. 2:2, 4, 6

27 [a]1 Sam. 1:11-13

28 [1]Lit., *lent*
[a]1 Sam. 1:11, 22

1 [1]I.e., strength [2]Lit., *is enlarged*
[a]Hab. 3:1; Ps. 72:20; 1 Sam. 2:1-10; Luke 1:46-55
[b]Deut. 33:17; Job. 16:15; Ps. 89:17 [c]Is. 12:2, 3

2 [a]Ex. 15:11 [b]2 Sam. 22:32 [c]Deut. 32:30, 31

3 [1]Lit., *Talk much*
[a]Prov. 8:13 [b]1 Sam. 16:7; 1 Kin. 8:39 [c]Prov. 16:2; 24:12

4 [a]Ps. 37:15; 46:9
[b]Ps. 18:39; Heb. 11:32-34

5 [a]Ps. 113:9; Ruth 4:15
[b]Jer. 15:9

6 [1]I.e., the nether world
[a]Deut. 32:39; 2 Kin. 5:7; Rev. 1:18 [b]Is. 26:19

7 [a]Deut. 8:17, 18
[b]Job. 5:11; James 4:10

8 [a]Job. 42:10-12; Ps. 75:7
[b]2 Sam. 7:8; Dan. 2:48; James 2:5 [c]Job. 36:7
[d]Job. 38:4-6; Ps. 75:3

9 [a]Ps. 91:11, 12; 1 Pet. 1:5
[b]Matt. 8:12 [c]Ps. 33:16, 17

10 [1]I.e., strength
[a]Ex. 15:6; Ps. 2:9
[b]1 Sam. 7:10; Ps. 18:13, 14
[c]Ps. 96:13; 98:9; Matt. 25:31, 32 [d]Ps. 21:1, 7 [e]Ps. 89:24

11 [a]1 Sam. 1:1, 19
[b]1 Sam. 2:18; 1 Sam. 1:28

12 [1]Lit., *sons of Belial*
[a]Jer. 2:8; 9:3, 6; 2 Cor. 6:15

13 [a]Lev. 7:29-34

come while the meat was boiling, with a three-pronged fork in
his hand.
14 Then he would thrust it into the pan, or kettle, or
caldron, or pot; all that the fork brought up the priest would
take for himself. Thus they did in Shiloh to all the Israelites
who came there.
15 Also, before [a]they burned the fat, the priest's servant
would come and say to the man who was sacrificing, "Give the
priest meat for roasting, as he will not take boiled meat from
you, only raw."
16 And if the man said to him, "They must surely [1]burn
the fat [2]first, and then take as much as [3]you desire," then he
would say, "No, but you shall give *it to me* now; and if not, I
will take it by force."
17 Thus the sin of the young men was very great before
the LORD, for the men [a]despised the offering of the LORD.
18 Now [a]Samuel was ministering before the LORD, *as* a
boy [1b]wearing a linen ephod.
19 And his mother would make him a little [a]robe and
bring it to him from year to year when she would come up with
her husband to offer [b]the yearly sacrifice.
20 Then Eli would [a]bless Elkanah and his wife and say,
"May the LORD give you [1]children from this woman in place of
[2]the one she [b]dedicated to the LORD." And they went to their
own [3]home.
21 And [a]the LORD visited Hannah; and she conceived and
gave birth to three sons and two daughters. And [b]the boy
Samuel grew before the LORD.
22 Now Eli was very old; and he heard [a]all that his sons
were doing to all Israel, and how they lay with [b]the women
who served at the doorway of the tent of meeting.
23 And he said to them, "Why do you do such things, the
evil things that I hear from all these people?
24 "No, my sons; for the report is not good [a]which I hear
[1]the LORD's people circulating.
25 "If one man sins against another, [a]God will mediate for
him; but [b]if a man sins against the LORD, who can intercede for
him?" But they would not listen to the voice of their father,
for the [c]LORD desired to put them to death.
26 Now the boy [a]Samuel [1]was growing in stature and in
favor both with the LORD and with men.
27 Then [a]a man of God came to Eli and said to him,
"Thus says the LORD, '[b]Did I *not* indeed reveal Myself to the
house of your father when they were in Egypt *in bondage* to
Pharaoh's house?
28 'And [a]did I *not* choose them from all the tribes of Israel
to be My priests, to go up to My altar, to burn incense, to carry
an ephod before Me; and did I *not* give to the house of your
father all the fire *offerings* of the sons of Israel?
29 'Why do you [a]kick at My sacrifice and at My offering
[b]which I have commanded *in My* [c]dwelling, and [d]honor your
sons above Me, by making yourselves fat with the [1]choicest of
every offering of My people Israel?'
30 "Therefore the LORD God of Israel declares, '[a]I did
indeed say that your house and the house of your father should

15 [a]Lev. 3:3-5, 16

16 [1]Lit., *offer up in smoke* [2]Lit., *like the day* [3]Lit., *your soul*

17 [a]Mal. 2:7-9

18 [1]Lit., *girded with* [a]1 Sam. 2:11; 3:1 [b]1 Sam. 2:28, 22:18

19 [a]Ex. 28:31 [b]1 Sam. 1:3, 21

20 [1]Lit., *seed* [2]Lit., *the one asked for which was lent* [3]Lit., *place* [a]Luke 2:34 [b]1 Sam. 1:11, 27, 28

21 [a]Gen. 21:1 [b]1 Sam. 2:26; 3:19-21; Luke 2:40

22 [a]1 Sam. 2:13-17 [b]Ex. 38:8

24 [1]Or, *making the LORD's people transgress* [a]1 Kin. 15:26

25 [a]Deut. 1:17 [b]1 Sam. 3:14; Num. 15:30; Heb. 10:26, 27 [c]Ex. 4:21; Josh. 11:20

26 [1]Lit., *was going on both great and good* [a]1 Sam. 2:21; Luke 2:52

27 [a]Deut. 33:1; Judg. 13:6 [b]Ex. 4:14-16; 12:1, 43

28 [a]Ex. 28:1-4; 30:7, 8; Lev. 8:7, 8

29 [1]Or, *first* [a]1 Sam. 2:13-17 [b]Deut. 12:5-9 [c]Ps. 26:8 [d]Matt. 10:37

30 [a]Ex. 29:9; Num. 25:13

walk before Me forever'; but now the LORD declares, 'Far be it from Me—for [b]those who honor Me I will honor, and those [c]who despise Me will be lightly esteemed.

31 'Behold, [a]the days are coming when I will break your [1]strength and the [1]strength of your father's house so that there will not be an old man in your house.

32 'And you will see [a]the distress of *My* dwelling, in *spite of* all that [1]I do good for Israel; and an [b]old man will not be in your house forever.

33 'Yet I will not cut off every man of yours from My altar [1]that your eyes may fail *from weeping* and your soul grieve, and all the increase of your house will die [2]in the prime of life.

34 'And this will be [a]the sign to you which shall come concerning your two sons, Hophni and Phinehas: [b]on the same day both of them shall die.

35 'But [a]I will raise up for Myself a faithful priest who will do according to what is in My heart and in My soul; and [b]I will build him an enduring house, and he will walk before [c]My anointed always.

36 'And it shall come about that everyone who is left in your house shall come and bow down to him for a [1]piece of silver or a loaf of bread, and say, "Please [2]assign me to one of the priest's offices so that I may eat a piece of bread." ' "

CHAPTER 3

NOW [a]the boy Samuel was ministering to the LORD before Eli. And [b]word from the LORD was rare in those days, [1]visions were infrequent.

2 And it happened at that time as Eli was lying down in his place (now [a]his eyesight had begun to grow dim *and* he could not see well),

3 and [a]the lamp of God had not yet gone out, and Samuel was lying down in the temple of the LORD where the ark of God *was*,

4 that the LORD called Samuel; and he said, "[a]Here I am."

5 Then he ran to Eli and said, "Here I am, for you called me." But he said, "I did not call, lie down again." So he went and lay down.

6 And the LORD called yet again, "Samuel!" So Samuel arose and went to Eli, and said, "Here I am, for you called me." But he [1]answered, "I did not call, my son, lie down again."

7 [a]Now Samuel did not yet know the LORD, nor had the word of the LORD yet been revealed to him.

8 So the LORD called Samuel again for the third time. And he arose and went to Eli, and said, "Here I am, for you called me." Then Eli discerned that the LORD was calling the boy.

9 And Eli said to Samuel, "Go lie down, and it shall be if He calls you, that you shall say, 'Speak, LORD, for Thy servant is listening.' " So Samuel went and lay down in his place.

10 Then the LORD came and stood and called as at other

30 [b]Ps. 50:23 [c]Mal. 2:9

31 [1]Or, *arm* [a]1 Sam. 4:11-18; 22:17-20

32 [1]Lit., *he* [a]1 Kin. 2:26, 27 [b]Zech. 8:4

33 [1]Lit., *to waste away your eyes and to grieve your soul* [2]Lit., *as men*

34 [a]1 Sam. 10:7-9; 1 Kin. 13:3 [b]1 Sam. 4:11, 17

35 [a]1 Sam. 3:1; 7:9; 9:12, 13 [b]1 Sam. 8:3-5; 1 King. 11:38 [c]1 Sam. 10:9, 10; 12:3; 16:13

36 [1]Or, *payment* [2]Lit., *attach*

1 [1]Lit., *no vision spread abroad* [a]1 Sam. 2:11, 18 [b]Ps. 74:9; Ezek. 7:26; Amos 8:11, 12

2 [a]1 Sam. 4:15

3 [a]Ex. 25:31-37; Lev. 24:3

4 [a]Is. 6:8

6 [1]Lit., *said*

7 [a]1 Cor. 13:11

times, "Samuel! Samuel!" And Samuel said, "Speak, for Thy
servant is listening."
11 And the LORD said to Samuel, "Behold, [a]I am about to
do a thing in Israel at which both ears of everyone who hears it
will tingle.
12 "In that day [a]I will carry out against Eli all that I have
spoken concerning his house, from beginning to end.
13 "For [a]I have told him that I am about to judge his house
forever for [b]the iniquity which he knew, because [c]his sons
brought a curse on themselves and [d]he did not rebuke them.
14 "And therefore I have sworn to the house of Eli that
[a]the iniquity of Eli's house shall not be atoned for by sacrifice
or offering forever."
15 So Samuel lay down until morning. Then he [a]opened
the doors of the house of the LORD. But Samuel was afraid to
tell [b]the vision to Eli.
16 Then Eli called Samuel and said, "Samuel, my son."
And he said, "Here I am."
17 And he said, "What is the word that He spoke to you?
Please do not hide it from me. [a]May God do so to you, and
more also, if you hide anything from me of all the words that
He spoke to you."
18 So Samuel told him everything and hid nothing from
him. And he said, "[a]It is the LORD; let Him do what seems
good to Him."
19 Thus [a]Samuel grew and [b]the LORD was with him and
[c]let none of his words [1]fail.
20 And all Israel [a]from Dan even to Beersheba knew that
Samuel was confirmed as a prophet of the LORD.
21 And the LORD appeared again at Shiloh, [a]because the
LORD revealed Himself to Samuel at Shiloh by the word of the
LORD.

CHAPTER 4

THUS the word of Samuel came to all Israel. Now Israel
went out to meet the Philistines in battle and camped beside
[a]Ebenezer while the Philistines camped in [b]Aphek.
2 And the Philistines drew up in battle array to meet
Israel. When the battle spread, Israel was [1]defeated before the
Philistines who killed about four thousand men on the
battlefield.
3 When the people came into the camp, the elders of
Israel said, "[a]Why has the LORD defeated us today before the
Philistines? [b]Let us take to ourselves from Shiloh the ark of the
covenant of the LORD, that [1]it may come among us and deliver
us from the power of our enemies."
4 So the people sent to Shiloh, and from there they
carried the ark of the covenant of the LORD of hosts [a]who sits
above the cherubim; and the two sons of Eli, Hophni and
Phinehas, *were* there with the ark of the covenant of God.
5 And it happened as the ark of the covenant of the LORD
came into the camp, that [a]all Israel shouted with a great shout,
so that the earth resounded.

11 [a]2 Kin. 21:12; Jer. 19:3
12 [a]1 Sam. 2:27-36
13 [a]1 Sam. 2:29-31 [b]1 Sam. 2:22 [c]1 Sam. 2:12, 17, 22 [d]Deut. 17:12; 21:18
14 [a]Lev. 15:31; Is. 22:14
15 [a]1 Chr. 15:23 [b]1 Sam. 3:10
17 [a]2 Sam. 3:35
18 [a]Ex. 34:5-7; Lev. 10:3; Job 2:10; Is. 39:8
19 [1]Lit., *fall to the ground* [a]1 Sam. 2:21 [b]Gen. 21:22; 28:15 [c]1 Sam. 9:6
20 [a]Judg. 20:1
21 [a]1 Sam. 3:10
1 [a]1 Sam. 7:12 [b]1 Sam. 29:1; Josh. 12:18
2 [1]Lit., *smitten*
3 [1]Or, *he* [a]Josh. 7:7, 8 [b]Num. 10:35; Josh. 6:6
4 [a]2 Sam. 6:2
5 [a]Josh. 6:5, 20

6 And when the Philistines heard the noise of the shout,
they said, "What *does* the noise of this great shout in the camp
of the Hebrews *mean?*" Then they understood that the ark of
the LORD had come into the camp.
7 And the Philistines were afraid, for they said, "God has
come into the camp." And they said, "[a]Woe to us! For nothing like this has happened before.
8 "Woe to us! Who shall deliver us from the hand of
these mighty gods? These are the gods who smote the Egyptians with all *kinds of* plagues in the wilderness.
9 "[a]Take courage and be men, O Philistines, lest you become slaves to the Hebrews, [b]as they have been slaves to you;
therefore, be men and fight."
10 So the Philistines fought and [a]Israel was [1]defeated, and
[b]every man fled to his tent, and the slaughter was very great;
for there fell of Israel thirty thousand foot soldiers.
11 And the ark of God was taken; and [a]the two sons of Eli,
Hophni and Phinehas, died.
12 Now a man of Benjamin ran from the battle line and
came to Shiloh the same day with [a]his clothes torn and [1]dust
on his head.
13 When he came, behold, [a]Eli was sitting on *his* seat [1]by
the road eagerly watching, because his heart was trembling for
the ark of God. So the man came to tell *it* in the city, and all
the city cried out.
14 When Eli heard the noise of the outcry, he said,
"What *does* the noise of this commotion *mean?*" Then the
man came hurriedly and told Eli.
15 Now Eli was ninety-eight years old, and [a]his eyes were
set so that he could not see.
16 And the man said to Eli, "I am the one who came from
the battle line. Indeed, I escaped from the battle line today."
And he said, "[a]How did things go, my son?"
17 Then the one who brought the news answered and said,
"Israel has fled before the Philistines and there has also been a
great slaughter among the people, and your two sons also,
Hophni and Phinehas, are dead, and the ark of God has been
taken."
18 And it came about when he mentioned the ark of God
that [1a]Eli fell off the seat backward beside the gate, and his
neck was broken and he died, for [2]he was old and heavy. Thus
he judged Israel forty years.
19 Now his daughter-in-law, Phinehas' wife, was pregnant
and about to give birth; and when she heard the news that the
ark of God was taken and that her father-in-law and her husband had died, she kneeled down and gave birth, for her pains
came upon her.
20 And about the time of her death the women who stood
by her said to her, "[a]Do not be afraid, for you have given birth
to a son." But she did not answer or pay attention.
21 And she called the boy [1]Ichabod, saying, "[a]The glory
has departed from Israel," because [b]the ark of God was taken
and because of her father-in-law and her husband.
22 And she said, "The glory has departed from Israel, for
the ark of God was taken."

7 [a]Ex. 15:14

9 [a]1 Cor. 16:13
[b]1 Sam. 14:21; Judg. 13:1

10 [1]Lit., *smitten*
[a]1 Sam. 4:2; Deut. 28:15, 25
[b]2 Sam. 18:17; 2 Kin. 14:12

11 [a]1 Sam. 2:34; Ps. 78:56-64

12 [1]Lit., *ground*
[a]Josh. 7:6; 2 Sam. 1:2; Neh. 9:1

13 [1]Gk. version reads, *beside the gate watching the road;* see v. 18
[a]1 Sam. 4:18, 1:9

15 [a]1 Kin. 14:4

16 [a]2 Sam. 1:4

18 [1]Lit., *he* [2]Lit., *the man*
[a]1 Sam. 4:13

20 [a]Gen. 35:16-19

21 [1]I.e., No glory
[a]Ps. 26:8; Jer. 2:11
[b]1 Sam. 4:11

Chapter 5

NOW the Philistines took the ark of God and [a]brought it
from Ebenezer to [b]Ashdod.
2 Then the Philistines took the ark of God and brought
it to [a]the house of Dagon, and set it by Dagon.
3 When the Ashdodites arose early the next morning,
behold, [a]Dagon had fallen on his face to the ground before the
ark of the LORD. So they took Dagon and [b]set him in his place
again.
4 But when they arose early the next morning, behold,
Dagon had fallen on his face to the ground before the ark of
the LORD. And the head of Dagon and both the palms of his
hands *were* cut off on the threshold; [1]only the trunk of Dagon
was left to him.
5 Therefore neither the priests of Dagon nor all who
enter Dagon's house tread on the threshold of Dagon in Ashdod to this day.
6 Now [a]the hand of the LORD was heavy on the Ashdodites, and [b]He ravaged them and smote them with [c]hemor-
rhoids, both Ashdod and its territories.
7 When the men of Ashdod saw that it was so, they said,
"The ark of the God of Israel must not remain with us, for His
hand is severe on us and on Dagon our god."
8 So they sent and [a]gathered all the lords of the Philistines to them and said, "What shall we do with the ark of the
God of Israel?" And they said, "Let the ark of the God of
Israel be brought around to Gath." And they brought the ark
of the God of Israel *around*.
9 And it came about that after they had brought it
around, [a]the hand of the LORD was against the city with very
great confusion; and He smote the men of the city, both
young and old, so that [b]hemorrhoids broke out on them.
10 So they sent the ark of God to Ekron. And it happened
as the ark of God came to Ekron that the Ekronites cried out,
saying, "They have brought the ark of the God of Israel
around to [1]us, to kill [1]us and [2]our people."
11 They [a]sent therefore and gathered all the lords of the
Philistines and said, "Send away the ark of the God of Israel,
and let it return to its own place, that it may not kill [1]us and
[2]our people." For there was a deadly confusion throughout the
city; [b]the hand of God was very heavy there.
12 And the men who did not die were smitten with hemorrhoids and [a]the cry of the city went up to heaven.

Chapter 6

NOW the ark of the LORD had been in the [1]country of the
Philistines seven months.
2 And [a]the Philistines called for the priests and the diviners, saying, "What shall we do with the ark of the LORD? Tell
us [1]how we shall send it to its place."
3 And they said, "If you send away the ark of the God of
Israel, [a]do not send it empty; but you shall surely [b]return to
Him a guilt offering. Then you shall be healed and it shall be
known to you why His hand is not removed from you."

1 [a]1 Sam. 4:1; 7:12 [b]Josh. 13:3
2 [a]Judg. 16:23-30; 1 Chr. 10:8-10
3 [a]Is. 19:1; 46:1, 2 [b]Is. 46:7
4 [1]So with ancient versions; Heb., *only Dagon.*
6 [a]1 Sam. 5:7, 11; Ex. 9:3 [b]1 Sam. 6:5 [c]Deut. 28:27; Ps. 78:66
8 [a]1 Sam. 5:11; 29:6-11
9 [a]1 Sam. 5:11; 7:13 [b]1 Sam. 5:6
10 [1]Lit., *me* [2]Lit., *my*
11 [1]Lit., *me* [2]Lit., *my* [a]1 Sam. 5:8 [b]1 Sam. 5:6, 9
12 [a]Ex. 12:30
1 [1]Lit., *field*
2 [1]Or, *with what* [a]Gen. 41:8; Ex. 7:11; Is. 2:6
3 [a]Ex. 23:15; Deut. 16:16 [b]Lev. 5:15, 16

4 Then they said, "What shall be the guilt offering which
we shall return to Him?" And they said, "Five golden [a]hemor-
rhoids and five golden mice [b]*according to* the number of the
lords of the Philistines, for one plague was on all of [1]you and
on your lords.
5 "So you shall make likenesses of your hemorrhoids and
likenesses of your mice that ravage the land, and [a]you shall give
glory to the God of Israel; perhaps [b]He will ease His hand
from you, [c]your gods, and your land.
6 "Why then do you harden your hearts [a]as the Egyptians
and Pharaoh hardened their hearts? When He had severely
dealt with them, [b]did they not allow [1]the people to go, and
they departed?
7 "Now therefore take and [a]prepare a new cart and two
milch cows on which there [b]has never been a yoke; and hitch
the cows to the cart and take their calves home, away from
them.
8 "And take the ark of the LORD and place it on the cart;
and put [a]the articles of gold which you return to Him as [b]a
guilt offering in a box by its side. Then send it away that it may
go.
9 "And watch, if it goes up by the way of its own territory
to [a]Bethshemesh, then He has done us this great evil. But if
not, then [b]we shall know that it was not His hand that struck
us; it happened to us by chance."
10 Then the men did so, and took two milch cows and
hitched them to the cart, and shut up their calves at home.
11 And they put the ark of the LORD on the cart, and the
box with the golden mice and the likenesses of their
hemorrhoids.
12 And the cows took the straight way in the [1]direction of
[a]Bethshemesh; they went along [b]the highway, lowing as they
went, and did not turn aside to the right or to the left. And the
lords of the Philistines followed them to the border of
Bethshemesh.
13 Now *the people of* Bethshemesh were reaping their
wheat harvest in the valley, and they raised their eyes and saw
the ark and were glad to see *it*.
14 And the cart came into the field of Joshua the Bethshemite and stood there where there *was* a large stone; and they
split the wood of the cart and [a]offered the cows as a burnt
offering to the LORD.
15 And [a]the Levites took down the ark of the LORD and
the box that was with it, in which were the articles of gold, and
put them on the large stone; and the men of Bethshemesh
offered burnt offerings and sacrificed sacrifices that day to the
LORD.
16 And when the five lords of the Philistines saw it, they
returned to Ekron that day.
17 And [a]these are the golden hemorrhoids which the Philistines returned for a guilt offering to the LORD: one for Ashdod, one for Gaza, one for Ashkelon, one for Gath, one for
Ekron;
18 and the golden mice, *according* to the number of all
the cities of the Philistines belonging to the five lords, [a]both of
fortified cities and of country villages. [b]The large [1]stone on

4 [1]Lit., *them*
[a]1 Sam. 6:17; 5:6, 9, 12
[b]1 Sam. 6:17, 18; Judg. 3:3

5 [a]Josh. 7:19; Is. 42:12
[b]1 Sam. 5:6, 11 [c]1 Sam. 5:3, 4, 7

6 [1]Lit., *them*
[a]Ex. 8:15, 32; 9:34 [b]Ex. 12:31

7 [a]2 Sam. 6:3 [b]Num. 19:2; Deut. 21:3, 4

8 [a]1 Sam. 6:4, 5
[b]1 Sam. 6:3

9 [a]Josh. 15:10; 21:16
[b]1 Sam. 6:3

12 [1]Lit., *way*
[a]1 Sam. 6:9 [b]Num. 20:19

14 [a]2 Sam. 24:22; 2 Kin. 19:21

15 [a]Ex. 4:14; Josh. 3:3

17 [a]1 Sam. 6:4

18 [1]So some mss. and versions. Heb., *Abel*
[a]Deut. 3:5 [b]1 Sam. 14:15

which they set the ark of the LORD *is a witness* to this day in
the field of Joshua the Bethshemite.
19 And [a]he struck down some of the men of Bethshemesh
because they had looked into the ark of the LORD. He struck
down of all the people, 50,070 men, and the people mourned
because the LORD had struck the people with a great slaughter.
20 And the men of Bethshemesh said, "[a]Who is able to
stand before the LORD, this holy God? And to whom shall He
go up from us?"
21 So they sent messengers to the inhabitants of [a]Kiriath-
jearim, saying, "The Philistines have brought back the ark of
the LORD; come down and take it up to you."

CHAPTER 7

AND the men of Kiriath-jearim came and took the ark of the
LORD and [a]brought it into the house of Abinadab on the hill,
and consecrated Eleazar his son to keep the ark of the LORD.
2 And it came about from the day that the ark remained
at Kiriath-jearim that the time was long, for it was twenty
years; and all the house of Israel lamented after the LORD.
3 Then Samuel spoke to all the house of Israel, saying,
"[a]If you return to the LORD with all your heart, [b]remove the
foreign gods and the [c]Ashtaroth from among you and [d]direct
your hearts to the LORD and [e]serve Him alone; and He will
deliver you from the hand of the Philistines."
4 So the sons of Israel removed the Baals and the Ashtaroth and served the LORD alone.
5 Then Samuel said, "Gather all Israel to [a]Mizpah, and
[b]I will pray to the LORD for you."
6 And they gathered to Mizpah, and drew water and
[a]poured it out before the LORD, and [b]fasted on that day, and
said there, "[c]We have sinned against the LORD." And Samuel
judged the sons of Israel at Mizpah.
7 Now when the Philistines heard that the sons of Israel
had gathered to Mizpah, the lords of the Philistines went up
against Israel. And when the sons of Israel heard it, [a]they were
afraid of the Philistines.
8 Then the sons of Israel said to Samuel, "[a]Do not cease
to cry to the LORD our God for us, that He may save us from
the hand of the Philistines."
9 And Samuel took [a]a suckling lamb and offered it for a
whole burnt offering to the LORD; and Samuel cried to the
LORD for Israel and [b]the LORD answered him.
10 Now Samuel was offering up the burnt offering, and
the Philistines drew near to battle against Israel. But [a]the LORD
thundered with a great [1]thunder on that day against the Philistines and [b]confused them, so that they were [2]routed before
Israel.
11 And the men of Israel went out of Mizpah and pursued
the Philistines, and struck them down as far as below Bethcar.
12 Then Samuel [a]took a stone and set it between Mizpah
and Shen, and named it [1]Ebenezer, saying, "Thus far the LORD
has helped us."
13 [a]So the Philistines were subdued and [b]they did not

19 [a]Num. 4:5, 15, 20; 2 Sam. 6:7
20 [a]Lev. 11:44, 45; 2 Sam. 6:9
21 [a]Josh. 9:17; 15:9, 60
1 [a]2 Sam. 6:3, 4
3 [a]Joel 2:12-14 [b]Josh. 24:14, 23; Judg. 10:16 [c]1 Sam. 31:10; Judg. 2:13 [d]Deut. 13:4; 2 Chr. 19:3 [e]Deut. 6:13; Matt. 4:10
5 [a]Judg. 20:1 [b]1 Sam. 8:6; 12:17-19
6 [a]1 Sam. 1:15; Ps. 62:8; Lam. 2:19 [b]Lev. 16:29; Neh. 9:1 [c]Judg. 10:10
7 [a]1 Sam. 13:6; 17:11
8 [a]1 Sam. 12:19-24; Is. 37:4
9 [a]Lev. 22:27 [b]Ps. 99:6; Jer. 15:1
10 [1]Lit., *voice* [2]Lit., *smitten* [a]1 Sam. 2:10; Ps. 29:3, 4; 2 Sam. 22:14, 15 [b]Josh. 10:10; Ps. 18:14
12 [1]I.e., The stone of help [a]Gen. 35:14; Josh. 4:9; 24:26
13 [a]Judg. 13:1-15 [b]1 Sam. 13:5

come any more within the border of Israel. And the hand of
the LORD was against the Philistines all the days of Samuel.
14 And the cities which the Philistines had taken from
Israel were restored to Israel, from Ekron even to Gath; and
Israel delivered their territory from the hand of the Philistines.
So there was peace between Israel and [a]the Amorites.
15 Now Samuel [a]judged Israel all the days of his life.
16 And he used to go annually on circuit to [a]Bethel and
[b]Gilgal and [c]Mizpah, and he judged Israel in all these places.
17 Then his return *was* to [a]Ramah, for his house *was*
there, and there he judged Israel; and he built there an altar to
the LORD.

CHAPTER 8

AND it came about when Samuel was old that [a]he appointed
his sons judges over Israel.
2 Now the name of his first-born was Joel, and the name
of his second, Abijah; *they* were judging in [a]Beersheba.
3 His sons, however, did not walk in his ways, but turned
aside after dishonest gain and [a]took bribes and perverted
justice.
4 Then all the elders of Israel gathered together and
came to Samuel at [a]Ramah;
5 and they said to him, "Behold, you have grown old, and
your sons do not walk in your ways. Now [a]appoint a king for us
to judge us like all the nations."
6 But the thing was [1a]displeasing in the sight of Samuel
when they said, "Give us a king to judge us." And [b]Samuel
prayed to the LORD.
7 And the LORD said to Samuel, "Listen to the voice of
the people in regard to all that they say to you, for [a]they have
not rejected you, but they have rejected Me from being king
over them.
8 "Like all the deeds which they have done since the day
that I brought them up from Egypt even to this day—in that
they have forsaken Me and served other gods—so they are
doing to you also.
9 "Now then, listen to their voice; [a]however, you shall
solemnly [1]warn them and tell them of [b]the [2]procedure of the
king who will reign over them."
10 So Samuel spoke all the words of the LORD to [a]the
people who had asked of him a king.
11 And he said, "[a]This will be the [1]procedure of the king
who will reign over you: [b]he will take your sons and place *them*
for himself in his chariots and among his horsemen and [c]they
will run before his chariots.
12 "And [a]he will appoint for himself commanders of thousands and of fifties, and *some* to [1]do his plowing and to reap
his harvest and to make his weapons of war and equipment for
his chariots.
13 "He will also take your daughters for perfumers and
cooks and bakers.
14 "And [a]he will take the best of your fields and your vineyards and your olive groves, and give *them* to his servants.

14 [a]Num. 13:29; Josh. 10:5-10
15 [a]1 Sam. 7:6; 12:11
16 [a]Gen. 28:19; 35:6 [b]Josh. 5:9, 10 [c]1 Sam. 7:5
17 [a]1 Sam. 1:1, 19; 2:11
1 [a]Deut. 16:18, 19
2 [a]Gen. 22:19; 1 Kin. 19:3; Amos 5:5
3 [a]Ex. 23:6, 8; Deut. 16:19
4 [a]1 Sam. 7:17
5 [a]Deut. 17:14, 15
6 [1]Or, *evil* [a]1 Sam. 12:17 [b]1 Sam. 15:11
7 [a]1 Sam. 10:19; Ex. 16:8
9 [1]Lit., *testify to* [2]Lit., *custom* [a]Ezek. 3:18 [b]1 Sam. 8:11-18; 10:25
10 [a]1 Sam. 8:4
11 [1]Lit., *custom* [a]1 Sam. 10:25; Deut. 17:14-20 [b]1 Sam. 14:52 [c]2 Sam. 15:1
12 [1]Lit., *plow his plowing* [a]1 Sam. 22:7; Num. 31:14
14 [a]1 Kin. 21:7; Ezek. 46:18

15 "And he will take a tenth of your seed and of your
vineyards, and give to his officers and to his servants.
16 "He will also take your male servants and your female
servants and your best young men and your donkeys, and [1]use
them for his work.
17 "He will take a tenth of your flocks, and you yourselves
will become his servants.
18 "Then [a]you will cry out in that day because of your king
whom you have chosen for yourselves, but [b]the LORD will not
answer you in that day."
19 Nevertheless, the people refused to listen to the voice
of Samuel, and they said, "No, but there shall be a king over
us,
20 [a]that we also may be like all the nations, that our king
may judge us and go out before us and fight our battles."
21 Now after Samuel had heard all the words of the
people, [a]he repeated them in the LORD's hearing.
22 And the LORD said to Samuel, "[a]Listen to their voice,
and [1]appoint them a king." So Samuel said to the men of
Israel, "Go every man to his city."

CHAPTER 9

NOW there was a man of Benjamin whose name was [a]Kish
the son of Abiel, the son of Zeror, the son of Becorath, the son
of Aphiah, the son of a Benjamite, a mighty man of [1]valor.
2 And he had a son whose name was Saul, a [a]choice and
handsome *man*, and there was not a more handsome person
than he among the sons of Israel; [b]from his shoulders and up
he was taller than any of the people.
3 Now the donkeys of Kish, Saul's father, were lost. So
Kish said to his son Saul, "Take now with you one of the
servants, and arise, go search for the donkeys."
4 And he passed through [a]the hill country of Ephraim
and passed through the land of [b]Shalishah, but they did not
find *them*. Then they passed through the land of [c]Shaalim, but
they were not *there*. Then he passed through the land of the
Benjamites, but they did not find *them*.
5 When they came to the land of [a]Zuph, Saul said to his
servant who was with him, "Come, and let us return, [b]lest my
father cease *to be concerned* about the donkeys and become
anxious for us."
6 And he said to him, "Behold now, there is [a]a man of
God in this city, and the man is held in honor; [b]all that he says
surely comes true. Now let us go there, [c]perhaps he can tell us
about our journey on which we have set out."
7 Then Saul said to his servant, "But behold, if we go,
what shall we bring the man? For the bread is gone from our
sack and there is [a]no present to bring to the man of God.
What do we have?"
8 And the servant answered Saul again and said, "Behold,
I have in my hand a fourth of a shekel of silver; I will give *it* to
the man of God and he will [a]tell us our way."
9 (Formerly in Israel, when a man went to inquire of
God, he used to say, "Come, and let us go to the seer"; for *he
who is called* a prophet now was formerly called [a]a seer.)

16 [1]Lit., *make*

18 [a]Is. 8:21 [b]Prov. 1:25-28; Mic. 3:4

20 [a]1 Sam. 8:5

21 [a]Judg. 11:11

22 [1]Lit., *cause a king to reign for them* [a]1 Sam. 8:7

1 [1]Or, *wealth,* or, *influence* [a]1 Sam. 14:51; 1 Chr. 9:36-39

2 [a]1 Sam. 10:24 [b]1 Sam. 10:23

4 [a]Josh. 24:33 [b]2 Kin. 4:42 [c]Josh. 19:42

5 [a]1 Sam. 1:1 [b]1 Sam. 10:2

6 [a]Deut. 33:1; 2 Kin. 5:8 [b]2 Sam. 3:19 [c]Gen. 24:42

7 [a]1 Kin. 14:3; 2 Kin. 5:15; 8:8, 9; Ezek. 13:19

8 [a]1 Sam. 9:6

9 [a]2 Sam. 24:11; 1 Chr. 9:22; 26:28; Is. 30:10

10 Then Saul said to his servant, "Well said; come, let us
go." So they went to the city where the man of God was.
11 As they went up the slope to the city, [a]they found
young women going out to draw water, and said to them, "Is
the seer here?"
12 And they answered them and said, "He is; [1]see, *he is*
ahead of you. Hurry now, for he has come into the city today,
for [a]the people have a sacrifice on [b]the high place today.
13 "As soon as you enter the city you will find him before
he goes up to the high place to eat, for the people will not eat
until he comes, because [a]he must bless the sacrifice; afterward
those who are invited will eat. Now therefore go up for you
will find him at once."
14 So they went up to the city. As they came into the city,
behold, Samuel was coming out toward them to go up to the
high place.
15 Now a day before Saul's coming, [a]the LORD had [1]re-
vealed *this* to Samuel saying,
16 "About this time tomorrow I will send you a man from
the land of Benjamin, and [a]you shall anoint him to be prince
over My people Israel; and he shall deliver My people from
the hand of the Philistines. For [b]I have regarded My people,
because their cry has come to Me."
17 When Samuel saw Saul, the LORD [1]said to him, "[a]Be-
hold, the man of whom I spoke to you! This one shall rule over
My people."
18 Then Saul approached Samuel in the gate, and said,
"Please tell me where the seer's house is."
19 And Samuel answered Saul and said, "I am the seer. Go
up before me to the high place, for you shall eat with me
today; and in the morning I will let you go, and will tell you all
that is on your mind.
20 "And [a]as for your donkeys which were lost three days
ago, do not set your mind on them, for they have been found.
And [b]for whom is all that is desirable in Israel? Is it not for you
and for all your father's household?"
21 And Saul answered and said, "[a]Am I not a Benjamite,
of [b]the smallest of the tribes of Israel, and my family the least
of all the families of the [1]tribe of Benjamin? Why then do you
speak to me in this way?"
22 Then Samuel took Saul and his servant and brought
them into the hall, and gave them a place at the head of those
who were invited, who were about thirty men.
23 And Samuel said to the cook, "[1]Bring the portion that I
gave you, concerning which I said to you, 'Set it [2]aside.' "
24 Then the cook [a]took up the leg with what was on it and
set *it* before Saul. And *Samuel* said, "Here is what has been
reserved! Set *it* before you *and* eat, because it has been kept
for you until the appointed time, [1]since I said, I have invited
the people." So Saul ate with Samuel that day.
25 When they came down from the high place into the
city, *Samuel* spoke with Saul [a]on the roof.[1]
26 And they arose early; and it came about at daybreak
that Samuel called to Saul on the roof, saying, "Get up, that I
may send you away." So Saul arose, and both he and Samuel
went out into the street.

11 [a]Gen. 24:15; 29:9 Ex. 2:16

12 [1]Or, *behold* [a]Num. 28:11-15 [b]1 Sam. 7:17; 10:5

13 [a]Luke 9:16; John 6:11

15 [1]Lit., *uncovered the ear* [a]1 Sam. 15:1; Acts 13:21

16 [a]1 Sam. 10:1 [b]Ex. 3:7, 9

17 [1]Lit., *answered* [a]1 Sam. 16:12

20 [a]1 Sam. 9:3 [b]1 Sam. 8:5; 12:13

21 [1]So some ancient versions; Heb., *tribes* [a]1 Sam. 15:17 [b]Judg. 20:46-48

23 [1]Lit., *Give* [2]Lit., *with you*

24 [1]Lit., *saying* [a]Ex. 29:22, 27; Lev. 7:32, 33; Num. 18:18

25 [1]Gk. adds, *and they spread a bed for Saul on the roof and he slept.* [a]Deut. 22:8; Acts 10:9

27 As they were going down to the edge of the city, Samuel said to Saul, "Say to the servant that he might go ahead
of us and pass on, but you remain standing now, that I may
proclaim the word of God to you."

CHAPTER 10

THEN [a]Samuel took the flask of oil, poured it on his head,
[b]kissed him and said, "Has not [c]the LORD anointed you a ruler
over [d]His inheritance?
2 "When you go from me today, then you will find two
men close to [a]Rachel's tomb in the territory of Benjamin at
Zelzah; and they will say to you, '[b]The donkeys which you
went to look for have been found. Now behold, your father
has [1]ceased to be concerned about the donkeys and is anxious
for you, saying, "What shall I do about my son?" '
3 "Then you will go on further from there, and you will
come as far as the [1a]oak of Tabor, and there three men going
up [b]to God at Bethel will meet you, one carrying three kids,
another carrying three loaves of bread, and another carrying a
jug of wine;
4 and they will greet you and give you two *loaves* of
bread, which you will accept from their hand.
5 "Afterward you will come to [1a]the hill of God where the
Philistine garrison is; and it shall be as soon as you have come
there to the city, that you will meet [b]a group of prophets
coming down from the high place with harp, tambourine,
flute, and a lyre before them, and [c]they will be prophesying.
6 "Then [a]the Spirit of the LORD will come upon you mightily, and [b]you shall prophesy with them and be changed into
another man.
7 "And it shall be when these signs come to you, [a]do for
yourself what [1]the occasion requires; for [b]God is with you.
8 "And [a]you shall go down before me to Gilgal; and behold, I will come down to you to offer burnt offerings and
[b]sacrifice peace offerings. [c]You shall wait seven days until I
come to you and show you what you should do."
9 Then it happened when he turned his back to leave
Samuel, God [a]changed [1]his heart; and all those signs came
about on that day.
10 [a]When they came to [1]the hill there, behold, a group of
prophets met him; and the Spirit of God came upon him
mightily, so that he prophesied among them.
11 And it came about, when all who knew him previously
saw that he prophesied now with the prophets, that the people
said to one another, "What has happened to the son of Kish?
[a]Is Saul also among the prophets?"
12 And a man there answered and said, "Now, who is their
father?" Therefore it became a proverb: "Is Saul also among
the prophets?"
13 When he had finished prophesying, he came to the
high place.
14 Now [a]Saul's uncle said to him and his servant, "Where
did you go?" And he said, "[b]To look for the donkeys. When
we saw that they could not be found, we went to Samuel."

1 [a]1 Sam. 16:13; Ex. 30:23-33; 2 Kin. 9:3, 6 [b]Ps. 2:12 [c]1 Sam. 10:9, 10; 16:13; 26:9; 2 Sam. 1:14 [d]Deut. 32:9; Ps. 78:71

2 [1]Lit., *abandoned the matter of* [a]Gen. 35:16-20; 48:7 [b]1 Sam. 9:3-5

3 [1]Or, *terebinth* [a]Gen. 35:8 [b]Gen. 28:16, 22; 35:1, 3, 7

5 [1]Or, *Gibeath-haelohim* [a]1 Sam. 13:2, 3 [b]1 Sam. 19:20; 2 Kin. 2:3, 5, 15 [c]2 Kin. 3:15; 1 Chr. 25:1-6

6 [a]Num. 11:25, 29; Judg. 14:6 [b]1 Sam. 10:10; 19:23, 24

7 [1]Lit., *your hand finds* [a]Eccles. 9:10 [b]Josh. 1:5

8 [a]1 Sam. 13:8 [b]1 Sam. 11:15 [c]1 Sam. 13:8

9 [1]Lit., *for him another heart* [a]1 Sam. 10:6

10 [1]Or, *Gibeath* [a]1 Sam. 10:5, 6

11 [a]1 Sam. 19:24; Amos 7:14, 15; Matt. 13:54-57

14 [a]1 Sam. 14:50 [b]1 Sam. 9:4-6

16 [a]1 Sam. 9:20

17 [a]1 Sam. 7:5

18 [1]Lit., *hand*
[a]Judg. 6:8, 9

19 [1]So with several mss. and versions M.T. *to Him*
[a]1 Sam. 8:6, 7 [b]Josh. 7:14-17; 24:1; Prov. 16:33

22 [a]1 Sam. 23:2, 4, 9-11; Ex. 28:30; Num. 27:21

23 [a]1 Sam. 9:2

24 [1]Lit., *May the king live*
[a]Deut. 17:15; 2 Sam. 21:6
[b]1 Kin. 1:25, 34, 39

25 [a]1 Sam. 8:11-18; Deut. 17:14-20 [b]Deut. 31:26

26 [a]1 Sam. 11:4; 15:34

27 [1]Lit., *sons of Belial*, cf. 2 Cor. 6:15
[a]1 Kin. 10:25; 2 Chr. 17:5

1 [1]Lit., *camped against*
[a]1 Sam. 12:12 [b]Judg. 21:8; 1 Sam. 31:11 [c]1 Kin. 20:34; Ezek. 17:13

2 [a]Num. 16:14
[b]1 Sam. 17:26; Ps. 44:13

3 [a]1 Sam. 8:4

4 [a]1 Sam. 10:26; 15:34

15 And Saul's uncle said, "Please tell me what Samuel said
to you."
16 So Saul said to his uncle, "[a]He told us plainly that the
donkeys had been found." But he did not tell him about the
matter of the kingdom which Samuel had mentioned.
17 Thereafter Samuel called the people together to the
LORD [a]at Mizpah;
18 and he said to the sons of Israel, "[a]Thus says the LORD,
the God of Israel, 'I brought Israel up from Egypt, and I
delivered you from the hand of the Egyptians, and from the
[1]power of all the kingdoms that were oppressing you.'
19 "But you [a]today rejected your God, who delivers you
from all your calamities and your distresses; yet you have said,
'[1]No, but set a king over us!' Now therefore [b]present yourselves before the LORD by your tribes and by your clans."
20 Thus Samuel brought all the tribes of Israel near, and
the tribe of Benjamin was taken by lot.
21 Then he brought the tribe of Benjamin near by its
families, and the Matrite family was taken. And Saul the son
of Kish was taken; but when they looked for him, he could not
be found.
22 Therefore [a]they inquired further of the LORD, "Has the
man come here yet?" So the LORD said, "Behold, he is hiding
himself by the baggage."
23 So they ran and took him from there, and when he
stood among the people, [a]he was taller than any of the people
from his shoulders upward.
24 And Samuel said to all the people, "Do you see him
[a]whom the LORD has chosen? Surely there is no one like him
among all the people." So all the people shouted and said,
"[1][b]Long live the king!"
25 Then Samuel told the people [a]the ordinances of the
kingdom, and wrote *them* in the book and [b]placed *it* before
the LORD. And Samuel sent all the people away, each one to
his house.
26 And Saul also went [a]to his house at Gibeah; and the
valiant *men* whose hearts God had touched went with him.
27 But certain [1]worthless men said, "How can this one
deliver us?" And they despised him and [a]did not bring him any
present. But he kept silent.

CHAPTER 11

NOW [a]Nahash the Ammonite came up and [1]besieged
[b]Jabesh-gilead; and all the men of Jabesh said to Nahash,
"Make [c]a covenant with us and we will serve you."
2 But Nahash the Ammonite said to them, I will make *it*
with you on this condition, [a]that I will gouge out the right eye
of every one of you, thus I will make it [b]a reproach on all
Israel."
3 And [a]the elders of Jabesh said to him, "Let us alone for
seven days, that we may send messengers throughout the territory of Israel. Then, if there is no one to deliver us, we will
come out to you."
4 Then the messengers came [a]to Gibeah of Saul and

spoke these words in the hearing of the people, and all the
people [b]lifted up their voices and wept.
5 Now behold, Saul was coming from the field [a]behind
the oxen; and [1]he said, "What is *the matter* with the people
that they weep?" So they related to him the words of the men
of Jabesh.
6 Then [a]the Spirit of God came upon Saul mightily when
he heard these words, and [1]he became very angry.
7 And he took a yoke of oxen and [a]cut them in pieces,
and sent *them* throughout the territory of Israel by the hand of
messengers, saying, "[b]Whoever does not come out after Saul
and after Samuel, so shall it be done to his oxen." Then the
dread of the LORD fell on the people, and they came out [c]as
one man.
8 And he [1]numbered them in [a]Bezek; and the sons of
Israel were [b]300,000, and the men of Judah 30,000.
9 And they said to the messengers who had come, "Thus
you shall say to the men of Jabesh-gilead, 'Tomorrow, by the
time the sun is hot, you shall have deliverance.' " So the messengers went and told the men of Jabesh; and they were glad.
10 Then the men of Jabesh said, "[a]Tomorrow we will
come out to you, and you may do to us whatever seems good
[1]to you."
11 And it happened the next morning that Saul put the
people [a]in three companies; and they came into the midst of
the camp at the morning watch, and struck down the Ammonites until the heat of the day. And it came about that those
who survived were scattered, so that no two of them were left
together.
12 Then the people said to Samuel, "[a]Who is he that said,
'Shall Saul reign over us?' [1b]Bring the men, that we may put
them to death."
13 But Saul said, "[a]Not a man shall be put to death this
day, for today [b]the LORD has accomplished deliverance in
Israel."
14 Then Samuel said to the people, "Come and let us go
to [a]Gilgal and [b]renew the kingdom there."
15 So all the people went to Gilgal, and there they made
Saul king [a]before the LORD in Gilgal. There they also [b]offered
sacrifices of peace offerings before the LORD; and there Saul
and all the men of Israel rejoiced greatly.

CHAPTER 12

THEN Samuel said to all Israel, "Behold, [a]I have listened to
your voice in all that you said to me, and I [b]have [1]appointed a
king over you.
2 "And now, [a]here is the king walking before you, but [b]I
am old and gray, and behold [c]my sons are with you. And [d]I
have walked before you from my youth even to this day.
3 "Here I am; bear witness against me before the LORD
and [a]His anointed. [b]Whose ox have I taken, or whose donkey
have I taken, or whom have I defrauded? Whom have I oppressed, or [c]from whose hand have I taken a bribe to blind my
eyes with it? I will restore *it* to you."

4 [b]1 Sam. 30:4 Gen. 27:38; Judg. 2:4

5 [1]Lit., *Saul*
[a]1 Kin. 19:19

6 [1]Lit., *his anger burned exceedingly*
[a]1 Sam. 10:10; 16:13; Judg. 3:10; 6:34; 13:25; 14:6

7 [a]Judg. 19:29 [b]Judg. 21:5, 8, 10 [c]Judg. 20:1

8 [1]Lit., *mustered*
[a]Judg. 1:5 [b]Judg. 20:2

10 [1]Lit., *in your sight*
[a]1 Sam. 11:3

11 [a]Judg. 7:16

12 [1]Lit., *Give*
[a]1 Sam. 10:27 [b]Luke 19:27

13 [a]1 Sam. 10:27; 2 Sam. 19:22 [b]1 Sam. 19:5; Ex. 14:13

14 [a]1 Sam. 7:16; 10:8
[b]1 Sam. 10:25

15 [a]1 Sam. 10:17
[b]1 Sam. 10:8

1 [1]Lit., *made*
[a]1 Sam. 8:7, 9, 22
[b]1 Sam. 10:24; 11:14, 15

2 [a]1 Sam. 8:20
[b]1 Sam. 8:1, 5 [c]1 Sam. 8:3, 5
[d]1 Sam. 3:10, 19, 20

3 [a]1 Sam. 10:1; 24:6; 2 Sam. 1:14 [b]Ex. 20:17; Num. 16:15; Acts 20:33
[c]Ex. 23:8; Deut. 16:19

4 And they said, "You have not defrauded us, or oppressed us, or taken anything from any man's hand."
5 And he said to them, "The LORD is witness against you,
and His anointed is witness this day that [a]you have found
nothing [b]in my hand." And they said, "*He is* witness."
6 Then Samuel said to the people, "It is the LORD who
[1a]appointed Moses and Aaron and who brought your fathers
up from the land of Egypt.
7 "So now, take your stand, [a]that I may plead with you
before the LORD concerning all the righteous acts of the LORD
which He did for you and your fathers.
8 "When Jacob went into Egypt and [a]your fathers cried
out to the LORD, then [b]the LORD sent Moses and Aaron [1c]who
brought your fathers out of Egypt and settled them in this
place.
9 "But [a]they forgot the LORD their God, so [b]He sold them
into the hand of Sisera, captain of the army of Hazor, and
[c]into the hand of the Philistines and [d]into the hand of the king
of Moab, and they fought against them.
10 "And [a]they cried out to the LORD and said, 'We have
sinned because we have forsaken the LORD and have served
[b]the Baals and the Ashtaroth; but [c]now deliver us from the
hands of our enemies, and we will serve Thee.'
11 "Then the LORD sent [a]Jerubbaal and [1b]Bedan and Jephthah and Samuel, and delivered you from the hands of your
enemies all around, so that you lived in security.
12 "When you saw [a]that Nahash the king of the sons of
Ammon came against you, you said to me, '[b]No, but a king
shall reign over us,' [c]although the LORD your God *was* your
king.
13 "Now therefore, [a]here is the king whom you have chosen, [b]whom you have asked for, and behold, the LORD has set a
king over you.
14 "[a]If you will fear the LORD and serve Him, and listen to
His voice and not rebel against the [1]command of the LORD,
then both you and also the king who reigns over you will
follow the LORD your God.
15 "And [a]if you will not listen to the voice of the LORD, but
rebel against the [1]command of the LORD, then [b]the hand of
the LORD will be against you, [c]*as it was* against your fathers.
16 "Even now, [a]take your stand and see this great thing
which the LORD will do before your eyes.
17 "[a]Is it not the wheat harvest today? [b]I will call to the
LORD, that He may send [1]thunder and rain. Then you will
know and see that [c]your wickedness is great which you have
done in the sight of the LORD by asking for yourselves a king."
18 So Samuel called to the LORD, and the LORD sent
[1]thunder and rain that day; and [a]all the people greatly feared
the LORD and Samuel.
19 Then all the people said to Samuel, "[a]Pray for your
servants to the LORD your God, so that we may not die, for we
have added to all our sins [b]*this* evil by asking for ourselves a
king."
20 And Samuel said to the people, "Do not fear. You have
committed all this evil, yet [a]do not turn aside from following
the LORD, but serve the LORD with all your heart.

5 [a]Acts 23:9; 24:20 [b]Ex. 22:4
6 [1]Lit., *made* [a]Ex. 6:26
7 [a]Ezek. 20:35; Mic. 6:1-5
8 [1]Lit., *and they brought* [a]Ex. 2:23-25 [b]Ex. 3:10; 4:14-16 [c]1 Sam. 10:18
9 [a]Deut. 32:18; Judg. 3:7 [b]Judg. 4:2 [c]Judg. 3:31; 10:7; 13:1 [d]Judg. 3:12-30
10 [a]Judg. 10:10 [b]Judg. 2:13; 3:7 [c]Judg. 10:15, 16
11 [1]Gk. and Syr. read *Barak* [a]Judg. 6:31, 32 [b]Judg. 4:6; 11:1
12 [a]1 Sam. 11:1, 2 [b]1 Sam. 8:6, 19 [c]1 Sam. 8:7; Judg. 8:23
13 [a]1 Sam. 10:24 [b]1 Sam. 12:17, 19; 8:5; Hos. 13:11
14 [1]Lit., *mouth* [a]Josh. 24:14
15 [1]Lit., *mouth* [a]Josh. 24:20; Is. 1:20 [b]1 Sam. 5:9 [c]1 Sam. 12:9
16 [a]Ex. 14:13, 31
17 [1]Lit., *sounds* [a]Prov. 26:1 [b]1 Sam. 7:9, 10 [c]1 Sam. 8:7
18 [1]Lit., *sounds* [a]Ex. 14:31
19 [a]1 Sam. 12:23; Ex. 9:28; Jer. 15:1 [b]1 Sam. 12:17, 20
20 [a]Deut. 11:16

21 "And you must not turn aside, for *then you would go*
after [a]futile things which can not profit or deliver, because
they are futile.
22 "For [a]the LORD will not abandon His people [b]on account of His great name, because the LORD [c]has been pleased
to make you a people for Himself.
23 "Moreover, as for me, [a]far be it from me that I should
sin against the LORD by ceasing to pray for you; but [b]I will
instruct you in the good and right way.
24 "[a]Only [1]fear the LORD and serve Him in truth with all
your heart; for consider [b]what great things He has done for
you.
25 "[a]But if you still do wickedly, [b]both you and your king
[c]shall be swept away."

CHAPTER 13

SAUL was *forty* years old when he began to reign, and he
reigned *thirty*-two years over Israel.
2 Now Saul chose for himself 3,000 men of Israel, of
which 2,000 were with Saul in [a]Michmash and in the hill country of Bethel, while 1,000 were with Jonathan at [b]Gibeah of
Benjamin. But he sent away the rest of the people, each to his
tent.
3 And Jonathan smote [a]the garrison of the Philistines
that was in [b]Geba, and the Philistines heard of *it*. Then Saul
[c]blew the trumpet throughout the land, saying, "Let the Hebrews hear."
4 And all Israel heard [1]the news that Saul had smitten the
garrison of the Philistines, and also that Israel [a]had become
odious to the Philistines. The people were then summoned [2]to
Saul at Gilgal.
5 Now the Philistines assembled to fight with Israel,
30,000 chariots and 6,000 horsemen, and [a]people like the sand
which is on the seashore in abundance; and they came up and
camped in Michmash, east of [b]Beth-aven.
6 When the men of Israel saw that they were in a strait
(for the people were hard pressed), then [a]the people hid themselves in caves, in thickets, in cliffs, in cellars, and in pits.
7 Also *some of* the Hebrews crossed the Jordan into the
land of [a]Gad and Gilead. But as for Saul, he *was* still in Gilgal,
and all the people followed him trembling.
8 Now [a]he waited seven days, according to the appointed
time [1]set by Samuel, but Samuel did not come to Gilgal; and
the people were scattering from him.
9 So Saul said, "Bring to me the burnt offering and the
peace offerings." And [a]he offered the burnt offering.
10 And it came about as soon as he finished offering the
burnt offering, that behold, Samuel came; and [a]Saul went out
to meet him *and* to [1]greet him.
11 But Samuel said, "What have you done?" And Saul
said, "Because I saw that the people were scattering from me,
and that you did not come within the appointed days, and that
[a]the Philistines were assembling at Michmash,
12 therefore I said, 'Now the Philistines will come down

21 [a]Is. 41:29; Hab. 2:18
22 [a]Deut. 31:6; 1 Kin. 6:13 [b]Ex. 32:12; Num. 14:13 [c]Deut. 7:6-11; 1 Pet. 2:9
23 [a]Rom. 1:9; Col. 1:9; 1 Thess. 3:10; 2 Tim. 1:3 [b]1 Kin. 8:36; Prov. 4:11
24 [1]Or, *reverence* [a]Eccles. 12:13 [b]Deut. 10:21
25 [a]Is. 1:20; 3:11 [b]Josh. 24:20 [c]1 Sam. 31:1-5; Hos. 10:3
2 [a]1 Sam. 13:5; 14:31 [b]1 Sam. 10:26
3 [a]1 Sam. 10:5 [b]1 Sam. 13:16; 14:5 [c]Judg. 3:27; 6:34
4 [1]Lit., *saying* [2]Lit., *after* [a]Gen. 34:30; Ex. 5:21; 2 Sam. 10:6
5 [a]Josh. 11:4 [b]1 Sam. 14:23
6 [a]Judg. 6:2
7 [a]Num. 32:33
8 [1]Lit., *which* [a]1 Sam. 10:8
9 [a]2 Sam. 24:25; 1 Kin. 3:4
10 [1]Lit., *bless* [a]1 Sam. 15:13
11 [a]1 Sam. 2:5, 16, 23

against me at Gilgal, and I have not asked the favor of the
LORD.' So I forced myself and offered the burnt offering."
13 And Samuel said to Saul, "[a]You have acted foolishly;
[b]you have not kept the commandment of the LORD your God,
which He commanded you, for now the LORD would have
established your kingdom [1]over Israel [c]forever.
14 "But [a]now your kingdom shall not endure. [b]The LORD
has sought out for Himself a man after His own heart, and the
LORD has appointed him as ruler over His people, because you
have not kept what the LORD commanded you."
15 Then Samuel arose and went up from Gilgal to [a]Gib-
eah of Benjamin. And Saul [1]numbered the people who were
present with him, [b]about six hundred men.
16 Now Saul and his son Jonathan and the people who
were present with them were staying in [a]Geba of Benjamin
while the Philistines camped at Michmash.
17 And [a]the [1]raiders came from the camp of the Philistines in three [2]companies: one [3]company turned [4]toward [b]Oph-
rah, to the land of Shual,
18 and another [1]company turned [2]toward [a]Beth-horon,
and another [1]company turned [2]toward the border which overlooks the valley of [b]Zeboim toward the wilderness.
19 Now [a]no blacksmith could be found in all the land of
Israel, for the Philistines said, "Lest the Hebrews make [1]swords
or spears."
20 So all Israel went down to the Philistines, each to sharp-
en his plowshare, his mattock, his axe, and his goad,
21 [1]whenever they had to sharpen the edge of the goads,
of the mattocks, of the forks, and of the axes, and to fix the
goad points.
22 So it came about on the day of battle that [a]neither
sword nor spear was found in the hands of any of the people
who *were* with Saul and Jonathan, but they were found with
Saul and his son Jonathan.
23 And [a]the garrison of the Philistines went out to [b]the
pass of Michmash.

CHAPTER 14

NOW the day came that Jonathan, the son of Saul, said to
the young man who was carrying his armor, "Come and let us
cross over to the Philistines' garrison that is on yonder side."
But he did not tell his father.
2 And Saul was staying in the outskirts of [a]Gibeah under
the pomegranate tree which is in [b]Migron. And the people
who *were* with him *were* [c]about six hundred men,
3 and [a]Ahijah, the son of Ahitub, [b]Ichabod's brother, the
son of Phinehas, the son of Eli, the priest of the LORD at
[c]Shiloh, [d]was [1]wearing an ephod. And the people did not know
that Jonathan had gone.
4 And [a]between the passes by which Jonathan sought to
cross over to the Philistines' garrison, there was a sharp crag on
the one side, and a sharp crag on the other side, and the name
of the one was Bozez, and the name of the other Seneh.
5 The one crag rose on the north opposite Michmash,
and the other on the south opposite Geba.

---

13 [1]Lit., *to* [a]2 Chr. 16:9 [b]1 Sam. 15:22, 28 [c]1 Sam. 1:22

14 [a]1 Sam. 15:28 [b]Acts 13:22

15 [1]Lit., *mustered* [a]1 Sam. 13:2 [b]1 Sam. 13:2, 6, 7; 14:2

16 [a]1 Sam. 13:2, 3

17 [1]Lit., *destroyers* [2]Lit., *heads* [3]Lit., *head* [4]Lit., *toward the direction of* [a]1 Sam. 14:15 [b]Josh. 18:23

18 [1]Lit., *head* [2]Lit., *the direction of* [a]Josh. 18:13, 14 [b]Neh. 11:34

19 [1]Lit., *sword or spear* [a]Judg. 5:8; 2 Kin. 24:14

21 [1]Lit., *and there was a bluntness of edge*

22 [a]Judg. 5:8

23 [a]1 Sam. 14:1; 2 Sam. 23:14 [b]1 Sam. 14:4, 5; Is. 10:28

2 [a]1 Sam. 13:15, 16 [b]Is. 10:28 [c]1 Sam. 13:15

3 [1]Lit., *carrying* [a]1 Sam. 22:9-12, 20 [b]1 Sam. 4:21 [c]1 Sam. 1:3 [d]1 Sam. 2:28

4 [a]1 Sam. 13:23

6 Then Jonathan said to the young man who was carrying his armor, "Come and let us cross over to the garrison of
[a]these uncircumcised; perhaps the LORD will work for us, for
[b]the LORD is not restrained to save by many or by few."
7 And his armor bearer said to him, "Do all that is in
your heart; turn yourself, *and* here I am with you according to
your [1]desire."
8 Then Jonathan said, "[a]Behold, we will cross over to the
men and reveal ourselves to them.
9 "If they [1]say to us, 'Wait until we come to you'; then we
will stand in our place and not go up to them.
10 "But if they [1]say, 'Come up to us,' then we will go up,
for the LORD has given them into our hands; and [a]this shall be
the sign to us."
11 And when both of them revealed themselves to the
garrison of the Philistines, the Philistines said, "Behold, [a]He-
brews are coming out of the holes where they have hidden
themselves."
12 So the men of the garrison [1]hailed Jonathan and his
armor bearer and said, "Come up to us and [a]we will tell you
something." And Jonathan said to his armor bearer, "Come up
after me, for [b]the LORD has given them into the hands of
Israel."
13 Then Jonathan climbed up on his hands and feet, with
his armor bearer behind him; and they fell before Jonathan,
and his armor bearer put some to death after him.
14 And that first slaughter which Jonathan and his armor
bearer made was about twenty men within about half a furrow
in an acre of land.
15 And there was a trembling in the camp, in the field,
and among all the people. Even the garrison and [a]the raiders
trembled, and [b]the earth quaked so [c]that it became a [1]great
trembling.
16 Now Saul's watchmen in Gibeah of Benjamin looked,
and behold, the multitude melted away; and they went here
and *there*.
17 And Saul said to the people who *were* with him,
"[1]Number now and see who has gone from us." And when
they had [1]numbered, behold, Jonathan and his armor bearer
were not *there*.
18 Then Saul said to Ahijah, "[a]Bring the ark of God here."
For the ark of God was at that time [1]with the sons of Israel.
19 And it happened [a]while Saul talked to the priest, that
the commotion in the camp of the Philistines continued and
increased; so Saul said to the priest, "Withdraw your hand."
20 Then Saul and all the people who *were* with him rallied
and came to the battle; and behold, [a]every man's sword was
against his fellow, *and there was* very great confusion.
21 Now the Hebrews *who* were with the Philistines previously, who went up with them all around in the camp, even
[a]they also *turned* to be with the Israelites who *were* with Saul
and Jonathan.
22 When all the [a]men of Israel who had hidden themselves in the hill country of Ephraim heard that the Philistines
had fled, even they also pursued them closely in the battle.

6 [a]1 Sam. 17:26, 36; Jer. 9:25, 26 [b]1 Sam. 17:46, 47; Judg. 7:4, 7; Heb. 11:34

7 [1]Lit., *heart*

8 [a]Judg. 7:9-14

9 [1]Lit., *say thus*

10 [1]Lit., *say thus*
[a]Gen. 24:14; Judg. 6:36

11 [a]1 Sam. 14:22; 13:6

12 [1]Lit., *answered*
[a]1 Sam. 17:43, 44; Judg. 8:16
[b]2 Sam. 5:24

15 [1]Lit., *trembling of God*
[a]1 Sam. 13:17, 18
[b]1 Sam. 7:10 [c]2 Kin. 7:6

17 [1]Lit., *mustered*

18 [1]Lit., *and*
[a]1 Sam. 23:9; 30:7

19 [a]Num. 27:21

20 [a]Judg. 7:22; 2 Chr. 20:23

21 [a]1 Sam. 29:4

22 [a]1 Sam. 13:6

23 So [a]the LORD delivered Israel that day, and the battle
[1]spread beyond [b]Beth-aven.
24 Now the men of Israel were hard pressed on that day,
for Saul had [a]put the people under oath, saying, "Cursed be
the man who eats food [1]before evening, and until I have
avenged myself on my enemies." So none of the people tasted
food.
25 And all *the people of* the land entered the forest, and
there was honey on the ground.
26 When the people entered the forest, behold, [a]*there
was* a flow of honey; but no man put his hand to his mouth, for
the people feared the oath.
27 But Jonathan had not heard when his father put the
people under oath; therefore, [a]he put out the end of the staff
that *was* in his hand and dipped it in the honeycomb, and put
his hand to his mouth, and [b]his eyes brightened.
28 Then one of the people answered and said, "Your father
strictly put the people under oath, saying, 'Cursed be the
man who eats food today.'" And the people were weary.
29 Then Jonathan said, "[a]My father has troubled the land.
See now, how my eyes have brightened because I tasted a little
of this honey.
30 "How much more, if only the people had eaten freely
today of the spoil of their enemies which they found! For now
the slaughter among the Philistines has not been great."
31 And they struck among the Philistines that day from
[a]Michmash to [b]Aijalon. And the people were very weary.
32 And [a]the people [1]rushed greedily upon the spoil, and
took sheep and oxen and calves, and slew *them* on the ground;
and the people ate *them* [b]with the blood.
33 Then they told Saul, saying, "Behold, the people are
sinning against the LORD by eating with the blood." And he
said, "You have acted treacherously; roll a great stone to me
today."
34 And Saul said, "Disperse yourselves among the people
and say to them, 'Each one of you bring me his ox or his sheep,
and slaughter *it* here and eat; and do not sin against the LORD
by eating with the blood.'" So all the people that night
brought each one his ox [1]with him, and slaughtered *it* there.
35 And [a]Saul built an altar to the LORD; it was the first
altar that he built to the LORD.
36 Then Saul said, "Let us go down after the Philistines by
night and take spoil among them until the morning light, and
let us not leave a man of them." And they said, "Do whatever
seems good [1]to you." So [a]the priest said, "Let us draw near to
God here."
37 And [a]Saul inquired of God, "Shall I go down after the
Philistines? Wilt Thou give them into the hand of Israel?" But
[b]He did not answer him on that day.
38 And Saul said, "[a]Draw near here, all you [1]chiefs of the
people, and investigate and see how this sin has happened
today.
39 "For [a]as the LORD lives, who delivers Israel, though it is
in Jonathan my son, he shall surely die." But not one of all the
people answered him.
40 Then he said to all Israel, "You shall be on one side

23 [1]*passed over*
[a]Ex. 14:30; 2 Chr. 32:22
[b]1 Sam. 13:5

24 [1]Lit., *until*
[a]Josh. 6:26

26 [a]Matt. 3:4

27 [a]1 Sam. 14:43
[b]1 Sam. 30:12

29 [a]Josh. 7:25; 1 Kin. 18:18

31 [a]1 Sam. 14:5
[b]Josh. 10:12

32 [1]Lit., *did with regard to the spoil*
[a]1 Sam. 15:19 [b]Gen. 9:4; Lev. 17:10-14; Acts 15:20

34 [1]Lit., *in his hand*

35 [a]1 Sam. 7:12, 17

36 [1]Lit., *in your eyes*
[a]1 Sam. 14:3, 18, 19

37 [a]1 Sam. 10:22
[b]1 Sam. 28:6

38 [1]Lit., *corners*
[a]1 Sam. 10:19, 20; Josh. 7:11, 12

39 [a]1 Sam. 14:24, 44

and I and Jonathan my son will be on the other side." And the
people said to Saul, "Do what seems good [1]to you."
41 Therefore, Saul said to the LORD, the God of Israel,
"[a]Give a perfect *lot*." And Jonathan and Saul were taken, but
the people escaped.
42 And Saul said, "Cast *lots* between me and Jonathan my
son." And Jonathan was taken.
43 Then Saul said to Jonathan, "[a]Tell me what you have
done." So Jonathan told him and said, "[b]I indeed tasted a little
honey with the end of the staff that was in my hand. Here I
am, I must die!"
44 And Saul said, "[a]May God do [1]this *to me* and more
also, for [b]you shall surely die, Jonathan."
45 But the people said to Saul, "Must Jonathan die, who
has [1]brought about this great deliverance in Israel? Far from it!
As the LORD lives, [a]there shall not one hair of his head fall to
the ground, for he has worked with God this day." So the
people [2]rescued Jonathan and he did not die.
46 Then Saul went up from [1]pursuing the Philistines, and
the Philistines went to their own place.
47 Now when Saul had taken the kingdom over Israel, he
fought against all his enemies on every side, against Moab, [a]the
sons of Ammon, Edom, [b]the kings of Zobah, and [c]the Philistines; and wherever he turned, he [1]inflicted punishment.
48 And he acted valiantly and [1a]defeated the Amalekites,
and delivered Israel from the hands of [2]those who plundered
them.
49 Now [a]the sons of Saul were Jonathan and Ishvi and
Malchishua; and the names of his two daughters *were these*:
the name of the first-born [b]Merab and the name of the
younger [c]Michal.
50 And the name of Saul's wife was Ahinoam the daughter
of Ahimaaz. And [a]the name of the captain of his army was
Abner the son of Ner, Saul's uncle.
51 [a]And Kish *was* the father of Saul, and Ner the father of
Abner *was* the son of Abiel.
52 Now the war against the Philistines was severe all the
days of Saul; and when Saul saw any mighty man or any valiant
man, he [1a]attached him to [2]his staff.

CHAPTER 15

THEN Samuel said to Saul, "[a]The LORD sent me to anoint
you as king over His people, over Israel; now therefore listen to
the [1]words of the LORD.
2 "Thus says the LORD of hosts, 'I will [1]punish Amalek [a]*for*
what he did to Israel, how he set himself against him on the
way while he was coming up from Egypt.
3 'Now go and strike Amalek and [a]utterly destroy all that
he has, and do not spare him; but [b]put to death both man and
woman, child and infant, ox and sheep, camel and donkey.' "
4 Then Saul summoned the people and [1]numbered them
in [a]Telaim, 200,000 foot soldiers and 10,000 men of Judah.
5 And Saul came to the city of Amalek, and set an ambush in the valley.
6 And Saul said to [a]the Kenites, "Go, depart, go down

40 [1]Lit., *in your eyes*

41 [a]Acts 1:24

43 [a]Josh. 7:19 [b]1 Sam. 14:27

44 [1]Lit., *thus* [a]1 Sam. 25:22 [b]1 Sam. 14:39

45 [1]Lit., *worked* [2]Lit., *ransomed* [a]2 Sam. 14:11; 1 Kin. 1:52; Acts 27:34

46 [1]Lit., *after*

47 [1]Or, *condemned* [a]1 Sam. 11:1-13 [b]2 Sam. 8:3-10 [c]1 Sam. 14:52

48 [1]Lit., *smote* [2]Lit., *its plunderers* [a]1 Sam. 15:3,7

49 [a]1 Sam. 31:2; 1 Chr. 10:2 [b]1 Sam. 18:17-19 [c]1 Sam. 18:20, 27; 19:12; 2 Sam. 6:20-23

50 [a]2 Sam. 2:8

51 [a]1 Sam. 9:1, 21

52 [1]Lit., *gathered* [2]Lit., *himself* [a]1 Sam. 8:11

1 [1]Lit., *sound of the words* [a]1 Sam. 9:16

2 [1]Or, *visit* [a]Ex. 17:8-16; Num. 24:20; Deut. 25:17-19

3 [a]Num. 24:20; Deut. 20:16-18; Josh. 6:17-21 [b]1 Sam. 22:19

4 [1]Lit., *mustered* [a]Josh. 15:24

6 [a]Judg. 1:16; 4:11

from among the Amalekites, lest I destroy you with them; for
[b]you showed kindness to all the sons of Israel when they came
up from Egypt." So the Kenites departed from among the
Amalekites.
7 So [a]Saul [1]defeated the Amalekites, from [b]Havilah as
you go to [c]Shur, which is [2]east of Egypt.
8 And he captured [a]Agag the king of the Amalekites
alive, and [b]utterly destroyed all the people with the edge of the
sword.
9 But Saul and the people [a]spared Agag and the best of
the sheep, the oxen, the fatlings, the lambs, and all that was
good, and were not willing to destroy them utterly; but everything despised and worthless, that they utterly destroyed.
10 Then the word of the LORD came to Samuel, saying,
11 "[a]I regret that I have made Saul king, for [b]he has turned
back from [1]following Me, and has not carried out My commands." And Samuel was distressed and [c]cried out to the LORD
all night.
12 And Samuel rose early in the morning to meet Saul;
and it was told Samuel, saying, "Saul came to [a]Carmel, and
behold, he set up a monument for himself, then turned and
proceeded on [1]down to [b]Gilgal."
13 And Samuel came to Saul, and Saul said to him, "[a]Bless-
ed are you of the LORD! I have carried out the command of
the LORD."
14 But Samuel said, "[a]What then is this [1]bleating of the
sheep in my ears, and the [1]lowing of the oxen which I hear?"
15 And Saul said, "They have brought them from the
Amalekites, for [a]the people spared the best of the sheep and
oxen, to sacrifice to the LORD your God; but the rest we have
utterly destroyed."
16 Then Samuel said to Saul, "Wait, and let me tell you
what the LORD said to me last night." And he said to him,
"Speak!"
17 And Samuel said, "Is it not true, [a]though you were little
in your own eyes, you were *made* the head of the tribes of
Israel? And the LORD anointed you king over Israel,
18 and the LORD sent you on a [1]mission, and said, '[a]Go
and utterly destroy the sinners, the Amalekites, and fight
against them until they are exterminated.'
19 "Why then did you not obey the voice of the LORD, [a]but
rushed upon the spoil and did what was evil in the sight of the
LORD?"
20 Then Saul said to Samuel, "[a]I did obey the voice of the
LORD, and went on the [1]mission on which the LORD sent me,
and have brought back Agag the king of Amalek, and have
utterly destroyed the Amalekites.
21 "But [a]the people took *some* of the spoil, sheep and
oxen, the choicest of the things devoted to destruction, to
sacrifice to the LORD your God at Gilgal."
22 And Samuel said,
"[a]Has the LORD as much delight in burnt offerings
and sacrifices
As in obeying the voice of the LORD?
Behold, [b]to obey is better than sacrifice,
And to heed than the fat of rams.

6 [b]Ex. 18:9, 10, 19; Num. 10:29-32

7 [1]Lit., *smote* [2]Lit., *before* [a]1 Sam. 14:48 [b]Gen. 16:7; 25:17, 18 [c]1 Sam. 27:8; Ex. 15:22

8 [a]Num. 24:7; Esth. 3:1 [b]1 Sam. 27:8; 30:1; 2 Sam. 8:12

9 [a]1 Sam. 15:3, 15, 19

11 [1]Lit., *after* [a]Gen. 6:6, 7; Ex. 32:14; 2 Sam. 24:16 [b]1 Kin. 9:6, 7 [c]Ex. 32:11-13; Luke 6:12

12 [1]Lit., *and went down* [a]1 Sam. 25:2; Josh. 15:55 [b]1 Sam. 13:13, 14

13 [a]Gen. 14:19; 2 Sam. 2:5

14 [1]Lit., *sound* [a]Ex. 32:21-24

15 [a]1 Sam. 15:9, 21; Gen. 3:12, 13; Ex. 32:22, 23

17 [a]1 Sam. 9:21; 10:22

18 [1]Lit., *way* [a]1 Sam. 15:3

19 [a]1 Sam. 14:32

20 [1]Lit., *way* [a]1 Sam. 15:13

21 [a]1 Sam. 15:15; Ex. 32:22, 23

22 [a]Ps. 40:6-8; 51:16, 17; Is. 1:11-15; Mic. 6:6-8 [b]Jer. 7:22, 23; Hos. 6:6; Mark 12:33

23 "For rebellion is as the sin of [a]divination,
And insubordination is as [b]iniquity and idolatry.
Because you have rejected the word of the LORD,
[c]He has also rejected you from *being* king."
24 Then Saul said to Samuel, "[a]I have sinned; [b]I have
indeed transgressed the [1]command of the LORD and your
words, because I feared the people and listened to their voice.
25 "Now therefore, [a]please pardon my sin and return with
me, that I may worship the LORD."
26 But Samuel said to Saul, "I will not return with you; for
[a]you have rejected the word of the LORD, and the LORD has
rejected you from being king over Israel."
27 And as Samuel turned to go, [a]*Saul* seized the edge of
his robe, and it tore.
28 So Samuel said to him, "[a]The LORD has torn the kingdom of Israel from you today, and has given it to your neighbor who is better than you.
29 "And also the [1a]Glory of Israel [b]will not lie or change
His mind; for He is not a man that He should change His
mind."
30 Then he said, "I have sinned; [a]*but* please honor me
now before the elders of my people and before Israel, and go
back with me, [b]that I may worship the LORD your God."
31 So Samuel went back following Saul, and Saul worshiped the LORD.
32 Then Samuel said, "Bring me Agag, the king of the
Amalekites." And Agag came to him [1]cheerfully. And Agag
said, "Surely the bitterness of death is past."
33 But Samuel said, "[a]As your sword has made women
childless, so shall your mother be childless among women."
And Samuel hewed Agag to pieces before the LORD at Gilgal.
34 Then Samuel went to [a]Ramah, but Saul went up to his
house at [b]Gibeah of Saul.
35 And [a]Samuel did not see Saul again until the day of his
death; for Samuel [b]grieved over Saul. And the LORD regretted
that He had made Saul king over Israel.

CHAPTER 16

NOW the LORD said to Samuel, "[a]How long will you grieve
over Saul, since [b]I have rejected him from being king over
Israel? [c]Fill your horn with oil, and go; I will send you to [d]Jesse
the Bethlehemite, for I have selected a king for Myself among
his sons."
2 But Samuel said, "How can I go? When Saul hears *of*
it, he will kill me." And the LORD said, "[a]Take a heifer with
you, and say, 'I have come to sacrifice to the LORD.'
3 "And you shall invite Jesse to the sacrifice, and [a]I will
show you what you shall do; and [b]you shall anoint for Me the
one whom I [1]designate you."
4 So Samuel did what the LORD said, and came to [a]Beth-
lehem. And the elders of the city came trembling to meet
him and said, "[b]Do you come in peace?"
5 And he said, "In peace; I have come to sacrifice to the
LORD. [a]Consecrate yourselves and come with me to the

23 [a]Deut. 18:10 [b]Gen. 31:19, 34 [c]1 Sam. 13:14

24 [1]Lit., *mouth* [a]Num. 22:34; 2 Sam. 12:13; Ps. 51:4 [b]Prov. 29:25; Is. 51:12, 13

25 [a]Ex. 10:17

26 [a]1 Sam. 13:14; 16:1

27 [a]1 Kin. 11:30, 31

28 [a]1 Sam. 28:17, 18

29 [1]Or, *Eminence* [a]1 Chr. 29:11; Ps. 18:1, 2 [b]Num. 23:19; Ezek. 24:14

30 [a]John 12:43 [b]Is. 29:13

32 [1]Or, *in bonds*

33 [a]Gen. 9:6; Judg. 1:7; Matt. 7:2

34 [a]1 Sam. 7:17 [b]1 Sam. 11:4

35 [a]1 Sam. 19:24 [b]1 Sam. 16:1

1 [a]1 Sam. 15:35 [b]1 Sam. 13:13, 14; 15:23 [c]1 Sam. 9:16; 10:1; 2 Kin. 9:1 [d]Ruth 4:18-22

2 [a]1 Sam. 20:29

3 [1]Lit., *say to you* [a]Ex. 4:15; Acts 9:6 [b]1 Sam. 9:16; Deut. 17:14, 15

4 [a]Gen. 48:7; Luke 2:4 [b]1 Kin. 2:13; 2 Kin. 9:22; 1 Chr. 12:17, 18

5 [a]Gen. 35:2; Ex. 19:10

sacrifice." He also consecrated Jesse and his sons, and invited
them to the sacrifice.
6 Then it came about when they entered, that he looked
at [a]Eliab and thought, "Surely the LORD's anointed is before
Him."
7 But the LORD said to Samuel, "Do not look at his
appearance or at the height of his stature, because I have
rejected him; for [1]God *sees* not as man sees, for man looks at
the *outward* appearance, [a]but the LORD looks at the heart."
8 Then Jesse called [a]Abinadab, and made him pass before Samuel. And he said, "Neither has the LORD chosen this
one."
9 Next Jesse made [a]Shammah pass by. And he said,
"Neither has the LORD chosen this one."
10 Thus Jesse made seven of his sons pass before Samuel.
But Samuel said to Jesse, "The LORD has not chosen these."
11 And Samuel said to Jesse, "Are these all the children?"
And he said, "[a]There remains yet the youngest, and behold, he
is tending the sheep." Then Samuel said to Jesse, "Send and
[1]bring him; for we will not sit down until he comes here."
12 So he sent and brought him in. Now he was ruddy, with
[a]beautiful eyes and a handsome appearance. And the LORD
said, "[b]Arise, anoint him; for this is he."
13 Then Samuel took the horn of oil and [a]anointed him in
the midst of his brothers; and [b]the Spirit of the LORD came
mightily upon David from that day forward. And Samuel arose
and went to Ramah.
14 [a]Now the Spirit of the LORD departed from Saul, and
[b]an evil spirit from the LORD terrorized him.
15 Saul's servants then said to him, "Behold now, an evil
spirit from God is terrorizing you.
16 "Let our lord now command your servants who are before you. Let them seek a man who is a skillful player on the
harp; and it shall come about when the evil spirit from God is
on you, that [a]he shall play *the harp* with his hand, and you will
be well."
17 So Saul said to his servants, "Provide for me now a man
who can play well, and bring *him* to me."
18 Then one of the young men answered and said, "Behold, I have seen a son of Jesse the Bethlehemite who is a
skillful musician, [a]a mighty man of valor, a warrior, one prudent in speech, and a handsome man; and [b]the LORD is with
him."
19 So Saul sent messengers to Jesse, and said, "Send me
your son David who is with the flock."
20 And Jesse [a]took a donkey *loaded with* bread and a jug
of wine and a young goat, and sent *them* to Saul by David his
son.
21 Then David came to Saul and [1a]attended him, and
[2]Saul loved him greatly; and he became his armor bearer.
22 And Saul sent to Jesse, saying, "Let David now stand
before me; for he has found favor in my sight."
23 So it came about whenever [a]the *evil* spirit from God
came to Saul, David would take the harp and play *it* with his
hand; and Saul would be refreshed and be well, and the evil
spirit would depart from him.

6 [a]1 Sam. 17:13
7 [1]So with Gk., Heb., *He sees not what man sees* [a]1 Sam. 2:3; 1 Kin. 8:39; 1 Chr. 28:9; Luke 16:15
8 [a]1 Sam. 17:13
9 [a]1 Sam. 17:13
11 [1]Lit., *take* [a]1 Sam. 17:12; 2 Sam. 13:3
12 [a]Gen. 39:6; Ex. 2:2; Acts 7:20 [b]1 Sam. 9:17
13 [a]1 Sam. 10:1 [b]1 Sam. 10:6, 9, 10
14 [a]1 Sam. 11:6; 18:12; 28:15 [b]1 Sam. 16:15, 16; 18:10; 19:9; 1 Kin. 22:19-22
16 [a]1 Sam. 18:10; 19:9; 2 Kin. 3:15
18 [a]1 Sam. 17:32-36 [b]1 Sam. 3:19
20 [a]1 Sam. 10:4, 27; Prov. 18:16
21 [1]Lit., *stood before him* [2]Lit., *he* [a]Gen. 41:46; Prov. 22:29
23 [a]1 Sam. 16:14-16

CHAPTER 17

NOW [a]the Philistines gathered their armies for battle; and
they were gathered at Socoh which belongs to Judah, and they
camped between [b]Socoh and [c]Azekah, in [d]Ephes-dammim.
2 And Saul and the men of Israel were gathered, and
camped in [a]the valley of Elah, and drew up in battle array to
encounter the Philistines.
3 And the Philistines stood on the mountain on one side
while Israel stood on the mountain on the other side, with the
valley between them.
4 Then a champion came out from the armies of the
Philistines named [a]Goliath, from [b]Gath, whose height was six
[1]cubits and a span.
5 And *he had* a bronze helmet on his head, and he was
clothed with scale armor [1]which weighed five thousand shekels
of bronze.
6 *He* also *had* bronze [1]greaves on his legs and a [a]bronze
javelin *slung* between his shoulders.
7 And [a]the shaft of his spear was like a weaver's beam,
and the head of his spear *weighed* six hundred shekels of iron;
[b]his shield-carrier also walked before him.
8 And he stood and shouted to the ranks of Israel, and
said to them, "Why do you come out to draw up in battle
array? Am I not the Philistine and you [a]servants of Saul?
Choose a man for yourselves and let him come down to me.
9 "[a]If he is able to fight with me and [1]kill me, then we will
become your servants; but if I prevail against him and [1]kill
him, then you shall become our servants and serve us."
10 Again the Philistine said, "[a]I defy the ranks of Israel
this day; give me a man that we may fight together."
11 When Saul and all Israel heard these words of the
Philistine, they were dismayed and greatly afraid.
12 Now David was [a]the son of [1]the [b]Ephrathite of Bethlehem in Judah, whose name was Jesse, and [c]he had eight sons.
And [2]Jesse was old in the days of Saul, advanced *in years*
among men.
13 And the three older sons of Jesse had [1]gone after Saul
to the battle. And [a]the names of his three sons who went to the
battle were Eliab the first-born, and the second to him Abinadab, and the third Shammah.
14 And [a]David was the youngest. Now the three oldest
followed Saul,
15 [a]but David went back and forth from Saul to tend his
father's flock at Bethlehem.
16 And the Philistine came [1]forward morning and evening
for forty days, and took his stand.
17 Then Jesse said to David his son, "[a]Take now for your
brothers an ephah of this roasted grain and these ten loaves,
and run to the camp to your brothers.
18 "[a]Bring also these ten cuts of cheese to the commander
of *their* thousand, [b]and look into the welfare of your brothers,
and bring back [1]news of them.
19 "For Saul and they and all the men of Israel are in the
valley of Elah, fighting with the Philistines."
20 So David arose early in the morning and left the flock

1 [a]1 Sam. 13:5 [b]2 Chr. 28:18 [c]Josh. 10:10 [d]1 Chr. 11:13

2 [a]1 Sam. 21:9

4 [1]One cubit equals approx. 18 inches [a]2 Sam. 21:19 [b]Josh. 11:21, 22

5 [1]Lit., *and the weight of the armor* was

6 [1]Or, *shin guards* [a]1 Sam. 17:45

7 [a]2 Sam. 21:19; 1 Chr. 11:23 [b]1 Sam. 17:41

8 [a]1 Sam. 8:17

9 [1]Lit., *smite* [a]2 Sam. 2:12-16

10 [a]1 Sam. 17:26, 36, 45

12 [1]Lit., *this* [2]Lit., *The man* [a]1 Sam. 16:18; Ruth 4:22 [b]Gen. 35:19 [c]1 Sam. 16:10, 11; 1 Chr. 2:13-15

13 [1]Lit., *gone; they went* [a]1 Sam. 16:6, 8, 9

14 [a]1 Sam. 16:11

15 [a]1 Sam. 16:21-23

16 [1]Lit., *near*

17 [a]1 Sam. 25:18

18 [1]Lit., *their pledge* [a]1 Sam. 16:20 [b]Gen. 37:13, 14

20 [a]1 Sam. 26:5, 7

22 [1]Lit., *hand*
[a]Judg. 18:21; Is. 10:28

23 [a]1 Sam. 17:8-10

25 [1]I.e., free from taxes and public service
[a]Josh. 15:16 [b]1 Sam. 8:11

26 [a]1 Sam. 11:2
[b]1 Sam. 17:36; 14:6;
Jer. 9:25, 26 [c]1 Sam. 17:10
[d]Deut. 5:26; 2 Kin. 19:4

27 [1]Lit., *said to*
[a]1 Sam. 17:25

28 [a]Gen. 37:4, 8-36

29 [1]Lit., *word*
[a]1 Sam. 17:17

30 [1]Lit., *from beside him*
[2]Lit., *the former word*
[a]1 Sam. 17:26, 27

31 [1]Lit., *before*

32 [a]Deut. 20:1-4
[b]1 Sam. 16:18

35 [1]Lit., *smote*
[a]Amos 3:12

36 [1]Lit., *smitten*

with a keeper and took *the supplies* and went as Jesse had
commanded him. And he came to the [a]circle of the camp
while the army was going out in battle array shouting the war
cry.
21 And Israel and the Philistines drew up in battle array,
army against army.
22 Then David left his [a]baggage in the [1]care of the baggage keeper, and ran to the battle line and entered in order to
greet his brothers.
23 As he was talking with them, behold, the champion, the
Philistine from Gath named Goliath, was coming up from the
army of the Philistines, and he spoke [a]these same words; and
David heard *them*.
24 When all the men of Israel saw the man, they fled from
him and were greatly afraid.
25 And the men of Israel said, "Have you seen this man
who is coming up? Surely he is coming up to defy Israel. And it
will be that the king will enrich the man who kills him with
great riches and [a]will give him his daughter [b]and make his
father's house [1]free in Israel."
26 Then David spoke to the men who were standing by
him, saying, "What will be done for the man who kills this
Philistine, and takes away [a]the reproach from Israel? For who
is this [b]uncircumcised Philistine, that he should [c]taunt the
armies of [d]the living God?"
27 And the people [1]answered him in accord with this
word, saying, "[a]Thus it will be done for the man who kills
him."
28 Now Eliab his oldest brother heard when he spoke to
the men; and [a]Eliab's anger burned against David and he said,
"Why have you come down? And with whom have you left
those few sheep in the wilderness? I know your insolence and
the wickedness of your heart; for you have come down in order
to see the battle."
29 But David said, "What have I done now? [a]Was it not
just a [1]question?"
30 Then he turned [1]away from him to another and [a]said
the same thing; and the people answered the same thing as
[2]before.
31 When the words which David spoke were heard, they
told *them* [1]to Saul, and he sent for him.
32 And David said to Saul, "[a]Let no man's heart fail on
account of him; [b]your servant will go and fight with this
Philistine."
33 Then Saul said to David, "You are not able to go
against this Philistine to fight with him; for you are *but* a
youth while he has been a warrior from his youth."
34 But David said to Saul, "Your servant was tending his
father's sheep. When a lion or a bear came and took a lamb
from the flock,
35 I went out after him and [1]attacked him, and [a]rescued *it*
from his mouth; and when he rose up against me, I seized *him*
by his beard and [1]struck him and killed him.
36 "Your servant has [1]killed both the lion and the bear; and
this uncircumcised Philistine will be like one of them, since he
has taunted the armies of the living God."

37 And David said, "[a]The LORD who delivered me from
the paw of the lion and from the paw of the bear, He will
deliver me from the hand of this Philistine." And Saul said to
David, "[b]Go, and may the LORD be with you."
38 Then Saul clothed David with his garments and put a
bronze helmet on his head, and he clothed him with armor.
39 And David girded his sword over his armor and tried to
walk, for he had not tested *them*. So David said to Saul, "I
cannot go with these, for I have not tested *them*." And David
took them [1]off.
40 And he took his stick in his hand and chose for himself
five smooth stones from the brook, and put them in the shepherd's bag which he had, even in *his* pouch, and [a]his sling was
in his hand; and he approached the Philistine.
41 Then the Philistine came on and approached David,
with the shield-bearer in front of him.
42 When the Philistine looked and saw David, [a]he disdained him; for he was *but* a youth, and [b]ruddy, with a handsome appearance.
43 And the Philistine said to David, "[a]Am I a dog, that
you come to me with sticks?" And [b]the Philistine cursed David
by his gods.
44 The Philistine also said to David, "Come to me, and I
will give your flesh [a]to the birds of the sky and the beasts of the
field."
45 Then David said to the Philistine, "You come to me
with a sword, a spear, and a javelin, [a]but I come to you in the
name of the LORD of hosts, the God of the armies of Israel,
whom you have taunted.
46 "This day the LORD will deliver you up into my hands,
and I will strike you down and remove your head from you.
And I will give the dead bodies of the army of the Philistines
this day to the birds of the sky and the wild beasts of the earth,
[a]that all the earth may know that there is a God in Israel,
47 and that all this assembly may know that [a]the LORD
does not deliver by sword or by spear; for the battle is the
LORD's and He will give you into our hands."
48 Then it happened when the Philistine rose and came
and drew near to meet David, that [a]David ran quickly toward
the battle line to meet the Philistine.
49 And David put his hand into his bag and took from it a
stone and slung *it*, and struck the Philistine on his forehead.
And the stone sank into his forehead, so that he fell on his face
to the ground.
50 Thus David prevailed over the Philistine with a sling
and a stone, and he struck the Philistine and killed him; but
there was no sword in David's hand.
51 Then David ran and stood over the Philistine and [a]took
his sword and drew it out of its sheath and killed him, and cut
off his head with it. [b]When the Philistines saw that their champion was dead, they fled.
52 And the men of Israel and Judah arose and shouted
and pursued the Philistines as far as [1]the entrance to the valley,
and to the gates of [a]Ekron. And the slain Philistines [2]lay along
the way to [b]Shaaraim, even to Gath and Ekron.

37 [a]2 Tim. 4:17 [b]1 Sam. 20:13
39 [1]Lit., *off from himself*
40 [a]Judg. 20:16
42 [a]Prov. 16:18 [b]1 Sam. 16:12
43 [a]1 Sam. 24:14; 2 Sam. 3:8 [b]1 Kin. 20:10
44 [a]1 Sam. 17:46
45 [a]2 Chr. 32:8; Ps. 124:8; Heb. 11:34
46 [a]1 Kin. 18:36; 2 Kin. 19:19; Is. 37:20
47 [a]1 Sam. 14:6; 2 Chr. 14:11; 20:15; Ps. 44:6
48 [a]Ps. 27:3
51 [a]1 Sam. 21:9; 2 Sam. 23:21 [b]Heb. 11:34
52 [1]Lit., *your coming* [2]Lit., *fell* [a]Josh. 15:11 [b]Josh. 15:36

53 And the sons of Israel returned from chasing the Philistines and plundered their camps.
54 Then David took the Philistine's head and brought it
to Jerusalem, but he put his weapons in his tent.
55 Now when Saul saw David going out against the Philistine, he said to Abner the commander of the army, "Abner,
whose son is [a]this young man?" And Abner said, "By your life,
O king, I do not know."
56 And the king said, "You inquire whose son the youth
is."
57 So when David returned from killing the Philistine,
Abner took him and [a]brought him before Saul with the Philistine's head in his hand.
58 And Saul said to him, "Whose son are you, young
man?" And David answered, "[a]*I am* the son of your servant
Jesse the Bethlehemite."

Chapter 18

1 Now it came about when he had finished speaking to Saul,
that [a]the soul of Jonathan was knit to the soul of David, and
[b]Jonathan loved him as himself.
2 And Saul took him that day and [a]did not let him return
to his father's house.
3 Then [a]Jonathan made a covenant [1]with David because
he loved him as himself.
4 And [a]Jonathan stripped himself of the robe that was on
him and gave it to David, with his armor, including his sword
and his bow and his belt.
5 So David went out wherever Saul sent him, *and* [1]pros-
pered; and Saul set him over the men of war. And it was
pleasing in the sight of all the people and also in the sight of
Saul's servants.
6 And it happened as they were coming, when David
returned from killing the Philistine, that [a]the women came
out of all the cities of Israel, singing and dancing, to meet
King Saul, with tambourines, with joy and with [1]musical
instruments.
7 And the women [a]sang as they [1]played, and said,
"[b]Saul has slain his thousands,
[c]And David his ten thousands."
8 Then Saul became very angry, for this saying [1]dis-
pleased him; and he said, "They have ascribed to David ten
thousands, but to me they have ascribed thousands. Now [a]what
more can he have but the kingdom?"
9 And Saul looked at David with suspicion from that day
on.
10 Now it came about on the next day that [a]an evil spirit
from God came mightily upon Saul, and [b]he raved in the midst
of the house, while David was playing *the harp* with his hand,
[1][c]as usual; and [2][d]a spear *was* in Saul's hand.
11 And [a]Saul hurled the spear for he thought, "I will [1]pin
David to the wall." But David [2]escaped from his presence
twice.
12 Now [a]Saul was afraid of David, [b]for the Lord was with
him but [c]had departed from Saul.

---

55 [a]1 Sam. 16:12, 21, 22
57 [a]1 Sam. 17:54
58 [a]1 Sam. 17:12
1 [a]Gen. 44:30 [b]1 Sam. 20:17; Deut. 13:6; 2 Sam. 1:26
2 [a]1 Sam. 17:15
3 [1]Lit., *and* [a]1 Sam. 20:8-17
4 [a]1 Sam. 17:38; Gen. 41:42; Esth. 6:8
5 [1]Or, *acted wisely*
6 [1]I.e., triangles, or, three-stringed instruments [a]Ex. 15:20, 21; Judg. 11:34; Ps. 68:25; 149:3
7 [1]Or, *danced* [a]1 Sam. 21:11; 29:5; Ex. 15:21 [b]1 Sam. 21:11 [c]2 Sam. 18:3
8 [1]Lit., *was evil in his eyes* [a]1 Sam. 15:28
10 [1]Lit., *day by day* [2]Lit., *the* [a]1 Sam. 16:14 [b]1 Sam. 19:23, 24 [c]1 Sam. 16:23 [d]1 Sam. 19:9
11 [1]Lit., *strike David and the wall* [2]Lit., *turned about* [a]1 Sam. 19:10; 20:33
12 [a]1 Sam. 18:15, 29 [b]1 Sam. 16:13, 18 [c]1 Sam. 16:14; 28:15

13 Therefore Saul removed him from [1]his presence, and
appointed him as his commander of a thousand; and [a]he went
out and came in before the people.
14 And David was [1]prospering in all his ways for [a]the LORD
was with him.
15 When Saul saw that he was [1]prospering greatly, he
dreaded him.
16 But [a]all Israel and Judah loved David, and he went out
and came in before them.
17 Then Saul said to David, "[a]Here is my older daughter
Merab; I will give her to you as a wife, only be a valiant man
for me and fight [b]the LORD's battles." For Saul thought, "My
hand shall not be against him, but [c]let the hand of the Philistines be against him."
18 But David said to Saul, "[a]Who am I, and what is my
life *or* my father's family in Israel, that I should be the king's
son-in-law?"
19 So it came about at the time when Merab, Saul's daughter, should have been given to David, that she was given to
[a]Adriel [b]the Meholathite for a wife.
20 Now [a]Michal, Saul's daughter, loved David. When
they told Saul, the thing was agreeable [1]to him.
21 And Saul thought, "I will give her to him that she may
become a snare to him, and [a]that the hand of the Philistines
may be against him." Therefore Saul said to David, "[b]For a
second time you may be my son-in-law today."
22 Then Saul commanded his servants, "Speak to David
secretly, saying, 'Behold, the king delights in you, and all his
servants love you; now therefore, become the king's son-in-
law.' "
23 So Saul's servants spoke these words [1]to David. But
David said, "Is it trivial in your sight to become the king's son-
in-law, [a]since I am a poor man and lightly esteemed?"
24 And the servants of Saul reported to him [1]according to
these words *which* David spoke.
25 Saul then said, "Thus you shall say to David, 'The king
does not desire any [a]dowry except a hundred foreskins of the
Philistines, [b]to take vengeance on the king's enemies.' " Now
[c]Saul planned to make David fall by the hand of the
Philistines.
26 When his servants told David these words, [1]it pleased
David to become the king's son-in-law. [2a]Before the days had
expired
27 David rose up and went, [a]he and his men, and struck
down two hundred men among the Philistines. Then [b]David
brought their foreskins, and they gave them in full number to
the king, that he might become the king's son-in-law. So Saul
gave him Michal his daughter for a wife.
28 When Saul saw and knew that the LORD was with David, and *that* Michal, Saul's daughter, loved him,
29 then Saul was even more afraid of David. Thus Saul
was David's enemy continually.
30 Then the commanders of the Philistines went out *to
battle*, and it happened as often as they went out, that David
[a]behaved himself more wisely than all the servants of Saul. So
his name was highly esteemed.

13 [1]Lit., *with him* [a]1 Sam. 18:16; 2 Sam. 5:2

14 [1]Or, *acting wisely* [a]1 Sam. 16:18

15 [1]Or, *acting very wisely*

16 [a]1 Sam. 18:5

17 [a]1 Sam. 17:25 [b]1 Sam. 17:36, 47; 25:28; Num. 21:14 [c]1 Sam. 18:21, 25

18 [a]1 Sam. 18:23; 9:21; 2 Sam. 7:18

19 [a]2 Sam. 21:8 [b]Judg. 7:22; 1 Kin. 19:16

20 [1]Lit., *in his sight* [a]1 Sam. 18:28

21 [a]1 Sam. 18:17 [b]1 Sam. 18:26

23 [1]Lit., *in the ears of* [a]Gen. 34:12; 29:20

24 [1]Lit., *by saying according*

25 [a]Ex. 22:17 [b]1 Sam. 14:24 [c]1 Sam. 18:17

26 [1]Lit., *it was agreeable in the sight of* [2]Lit., *And the days had not expired* [a]1 Sam. 18:21

27 [a]1 Sam. 18:17 [b]2 Sam. 3:14

30 [a]1 Sam. 18:5

1 [a]1 Sam. 18:8, 9 [b]1 Sam. 18:1-3
3 [1]Lit. *see* [a]1 Sam. 20:9, 13
4 [1]Lit., *good* [a]1 Sam. 20:32 [b]Gen. 42:22
5 [a]1 Sam. 17:49, 50 [b]1 Sam. 11:13 [c]Deut. 19:10-13; Ps. 94:21
7 [a]1 Sam. 16:21; 18:2, 10, 13
8 [1]Lit., *smote*
9 [a]1 Sam. 16:14; 18:10, 11 [b]1 Sam. 18:10 [c]1 Sam. 16:16
10 [1]Lit., *strike David and the wall* [a]1 Sam. 18:11; 20:33
11 [a]Ps. 59:title; Judg. 16:2
12 [a]Josh. 2:15; 2 Cor. 11:33
13 [1]Heb., *teraphim* [a]Gen. 31:19; Judg. 18:14, 17
14 [a]Josh. 2:5
15 [1]Lit., *the*
16 [1]Heb., *teraphim*
18 [a]1 Sam. 7:17 [b]2 Kin. 6:1, 2

CHAPTER 19

NOW Saul told Jonathan his son and all his servants [a]to put
David to death. But [b]Jonathan, Saul's son, greatly delighted in
David.
2 So Jonathan told David, saying "Saul my father is seeking to put you to death. Now therefore, please be on guard in
the morning, and stay in a secret place and hide yourself.
3 "And I will go out and stand beside my father in the
field where you are, and I will speak with my father about you;
[a]if I [1]find out anything, then I shall tell you."
4 Then Jonathan [a]spoke well of David to Saul his father,
and said to him, "[b]Do not let the king sin against his servant
David, since he has not sinned against you, and since his deeds
have been very [1]beneficial to you.
5 "For [a]he took his life in his hand and struck the Philistine, and [b]the LORD brought about a great deliverance for all
Israel; you saw *it* and rejoiced. [c]Why then will you sin against
innocent blood, by putting David to death without a cause?"
6 And Saul listened to the voice of Jonathan, and Saul
vowed, "As the LORD lives, he shall not be put to death."
7 Then Jonathan called David, and Jonathan told him all
these words. And Jonathan brought David to Saul, and he was
in his presence as [a]formerly.
8 When there was war again, David went out and fought
with the Philistines, and [1]defeated them with great slaughter,
so that they fled before him.
9 Now there was [a]an evil spirit from the LORD on Saul as
he was sitting in his house [b]with his spear in his hand, [c]and
David was playing *the harp* with *his* hand.
10 [a]And Saul tried to [1]pin David to the wall with the spear,
but he slipped away out of Saul's presence, so that he struck
the spear into the wall. And David fled and escaped that night.
11 Then [a]Saul sent messengers to David's house to watch
him, in order to put him to death in the morning. But Michal,
David's wife, told him, saying, "If you do not save your life
tonight, tomorrow you will be put to death."
12 [a]So Michal let David down through a window, and he
went out and fled and escaped.
13 And Michal took [a]the [1]household idol and laid *it* on
the bed, and put a quilt of goats' *hair* at its head, and covered
it with clothes.
14 When Saul sent messengers to take David, she said,
"[a]He is sick."
15 Then Saul sent messengers to see David, saying, "Bring
him up to me on [1]his bed, that I may put him to death."
16 When the messengers entered, behold, the [1]household
idol *was* on the bed with the quilt of goats' *hair* at its head.
17 So Saul said to Michal, "Why have you deceived me
like this and let my enemy go, so that he has escaped?" And
Michal said to Saul, "He said to me, 'Let me go! Why should I
put you to death?' "
18 Now David fled and escaped and came [a]to Samuel at
Ramah, and told him all that Saul had done to him. And he
and Samuel went and stayed in [b]Naioth.

19 And it was told Saul, saying, "Behold, David is at
Naioth in Ramah."
20 Then [a]Saul sent messengers to take David, but when
they saw [b]the company of the prophets prophesying, with Samuel standing *and* presiding over them, the Spirit of God
came upon the messengers of Saul; and [c]they also prophesied.
21 And when it was told Saul, he sent other messengers,
and they also prophesied. So Saul sent messengers again the
third time, and they also prophesied.
22 Then he himself went to Ramah, and came as far as the
large well that is in Secu; and he asked and said, "Where are
Samuel and David?" And *someone* said, "Behold, they are at
Naioth in Ramah."
23 And he [1]proceeded there to Naioth in Ramah; and [a]the
Spirit of God came upon him also, so that he went along
prophesying continually until he came to Naioth in Ramah.
24 And he also stripped off his clothes, and he too prophesied before Samuel and [1]lay down [2a]naked all that day and all
that night. Therefore they say, "[b]Is Saul also among the
prophets?"

Chapter 20

THEN David fled from Naioth in Ramah, and came and
[a]said [1]to Jonathan, "What have I done? What is my iniquity?
And what is my sin before your father, that he is seeking my
life?"
2 And he said to him, "Far from it, you shall not die.
Behold, my father does nothing either great or small [1]without
disclosing it to me. So why should my father hide this thing
from me? It is not so!"
3 Yet David [a]vowed again, [1]saying, "Your father knows
well that I have found favor in your sight, and he has said, 'Do
not let Jonathan know this, lest he be grieved.' But truly [b]as the
LORD lives and as your soul lives, there is [2]hardly a step between
me and death."
4 Then Jonathan said to David, "Whatever [1]you say, I
will do for you."
5 So David said to Jonathan, "Behold, tomorrow is [a]the
new moon, and I ought [b]to sit down to eat with the king. But
let me go, [c]that I may hide myself in the field until the third
evening.
6 "If your father misses me at all, then say, 'David earnestly asked *leave* of me to run to [a]Bethlehem his city, because it
is [b]the yearly sacrifice there for the whole family.'
7 "If he [1]says, 'It is good,' your servant *shall be* safe; but if
he is very angry, know that he has decided on evil.
8 "Therefore deal kindly with your servant, for [a]you have
brought your servant into a covenant of the LORD with you.
But [b]if there is iniquity in me, put me to death yourself; for
why then should you bring me to your father?"
9 And Jonathan said, "Far be it from you! For if I should
indeed learn that evil has been decided by my father to come
upon you, then would I not tell you about it?"
10 Then David said to Jonathan, "Who will tell me [1]if
your father answers you harshly?"

20 [a]1 Sam. 19:11, 14 [b]1 Sam. 10:5, 6, 10 [c]Num. 11:25

23 [1]Lit., *went* [a]1 Sam. 10:10

24 [1]Lit., *fell* [2]I.e., without outward garments [a]Is. 20:2 [b]1 Sam. 10:10-12

1 [1]Lit., *before* [a]1 Sam. 24:9

2 [1]Lit., *and he does not uncover my ear*

3 [1]Lit., *and said* [2]Lit., *about* [a]Deut. 6:13 [b]1 Sam. 25:26; 2 Kin. 2:6

4 [1]Lit., *your soul says*

5 [a]Num. 10:10; 28:11-15; Amos 8:5 [b]1 Sam. 20:24, 27 [c]1 Sam. 19:2

6 [a]1 Sam. 17:58 [b]Deut. 12:5

7 [1]Lit., *says thus*

8 [a]1 Sam. 18:3; 23:18 [b]2 Sam. 14:32

10 [1]Lit., *or what*

12 [1]Lit., *uncover your ear*

13 [1]Lit., *uncover your ear*
[a]1 Sam. 3:17; Ruth 1:17
[b]1 Sam. 18:12

15 [a]2 Sam. 9:1

16 [a]Deut. 23:21

17 [a]1 Sam. 18:1

18 [a]1 Sam. 20:5, 25

21 [1]Lit., *there is nothing*

22 [1]Lit., *say thus*
[a]1 Sam. 20:37

23 [1]Lit., *word*
[a]1 Sam. 20:14, 15
[b]Gen. 31:49, 53

25 [a]1 Sam. 20:18

26 [a]1 Sam. 16:5; Lev. 7:20, 21

28 [a]1 Sam. 20:6

29 [1]Lit., *send me away*

11 And Jonathan said to David, "Come, and let us go out
into the field." So both of them went out to the field.
12 Then Jonathan said to David, "The LORD, the God of
Israel, *be witness*! When I have sounded out my father about
this time tomorrow, *or* the third day, behold, if there is good
feeling toward David, shall I not then send to you and [1]make it
known to you?
13 "If it please my father to do you harm, [a]may the LORD
do so to Jonathan and more also, if I do not [1]make it known to
you and send you away, that you may go in safety. And [b]may
the LORD be with you as He has been with my father.
14 "And if I am still alive, will you not show me the lovingkindness of the LORD, that I may not die?
15 "And [a]you shall not cut off your lovingkindness from my
house forever, not even when the LORD cuts off every one of
the enemies of David from the face of the earth."
16 So Jonathan made a *covenant* with the house of David,
saying, "[a]May the LORD require *it* at the hands of David's
enemies."
17 And Jonathan made David vow again because of his
love for him, because [a]he loved him as he loved his own life.
18 Then Jonathan said to him, "[a]Tomorrow is the new
moon, and you will be missed because your seat will be empty.
19 "When you have stayed for three days, you shall go
down quickly and come to the place where you hid yourself on
that eventful day, and you shall remain by the stone Ezel.
20 "And I will shoot three arrows to the side, as though I
shot at a target.
21 "And behold, I will send the lad, *saying*, 'Go, find the
arrows.' If I specifically say to the lad, 'Behold, the arrows are
on this side of you, get them!' Then come; for there is safety
for you and [1]no harm, as the LORD lives.
22 "But if I [1]say to the youth, '[a]Behold, the arrows are
beyond you,' go, for the LORD has sent you away.
23 "[a]As for the [1]agreement of which you and I have spoken,
behold, [b]the LORD is between you and me forever."
24 So David hid in the field; and when the new moon
came, the king sat down to eat food.
25 And the king sat on his seat as usual, the seat by the
wall; then Jonathan rose up and Abner sat down by Saul's side,
but [a]David's place was empty.
26 Nevertheless Saul did not speak anything that day, for
he thought, "It is an accident, [a]he is not clean, surely *he is* not
clean."
27 And it came about the next day, the second *day* of the
new moon, that David's place was empty; so Saul said to Jonathan
his son, "Why has the son of Jesse not come to the meal,
either yesterday or today?"
28 Jonathan then answered Saul, "[a]David earnestly asked
leave of me *to go* to Bethlehem,
29 for he said, 'Please [1]let me go, since our family has a
sacrifice in the city, and my brother has commanded me to
attend. And now, if I have found favor in your sight, please let
me get away that I may see my brothers.' For this reason he
has not come to the king's table."
30 Then Saul's anger burned against Jonathan and he said

to him, "You son of a perverse, rebellious woman! Do I not
know that you are choosing the son of Jesse to your own shame
and to the shame of your mother's nakedness?
31 "For [1]as long as the son of Jesse lives on the earth,
neither you nor your kingdom will be established. Therefore
now, send and bring him to me, for [a]he [2]must surely die."
32 But Jonathan answered Saul his father and said to him,
"[a]Why should he be put to death? What has he done?"
33 Then [a]Saul hurled his spear at him to strike him down;
[b]so Jonathan knew that his father had decided to put David to
death.
34 Then Jonathan arose from the table in fierce anger,
and did not eat food on the second day of the new moon, for
he was grieved over David because his father had dishonored
him.
35 Now it came about in the morning that Jonathan went
out into the field for the appointment with David, and a little
lad *was* with him.
36 And he said to his lad, "[a]Run, find now the arrows
which I am about to shoot." As the lad was running, he shot
[1]an arrow past him.
37 When the lad reached the place of the arrow which
Jonathan had shot, Jonathan called after the lad, and said, "[a]Is
not the arrow beyond you?"
38 And Jonathan called after the lad, "Hurry, be quick, do
not stay!" And Jonathan's lad picked up the arrow and came to
his master.
39 But the lad was not aware of anything; only Jonathan
and David knew about the matter.
40 Then Jonathan gave his weapons to his lad and said to
him, "Go, bring *them* to the city."
41 When the lad was gone, David rose from the south side
and fell on his face to the ground, and [a]bowed three times.
And they kissed each other and wept together, but [b]David
more.
42 And Jonathan said to David, "[a]Go in safety! Inasmuch
as we have sworn to each other in the name of the LORD,
saying, '[b]The LORD will be between me and you, and between
my [1]descendants and your [1]descendants forever,' " [2]Then he
rose and departed, while Jonathan went into the city.

CHAPTER 21

THEN David came to [a]Nob to [b]Ahimelech the priest; and
[c]Ahimelech came trembling to meet David, and said to him,
"Why are you alone and no one with you?"
2 And David said to Ahimelech the priest, "The king has
commissioned me with a matter, and has said to me, 'Let no
one know anything about the matter on which I am sending
you and with which I have commissioned you; and I have
[1]directed the young men to a certain place.'
3 "Now therefore, what [1]do you have on hand? Give [2]me
five loaves of bread, or whatever can be found."
4 And the priest answered David and said, "There is no
ordinary bread [1]on hand, but there is [a]consecrated bread; if
only the young men have kept themselves from women."

31 [1]Lit., *all the days which* [2]Lit., *is a son of death* [a]2 Sam. 12:5

32 [a]1 Sam. 19:5

33 [a]1 Sam. 18:11; 19:10 [b]1 Sam. 20:7

36 [1]Lit., *the* [a]1 Sam. 20:20, 21

37 [a]1 Sam. 20:22

41 [a]Gen. 42:6 [b]1 Sam. 18:3

42 [1]Lit., *seed* [2]Chap. 21:1 in Heb. [a]1 Sam. 20:22 [b]1 Sam. 20:15, 16, 23

1 [a]1 Sam. 22:19 [b]1 Sam. 14:3; Mark 2:26 [c]1 Sam. 16:4

2 [1]Lit., *caused to know*

3 [1]Lit., *is under your hand?* [2]Lit., *in my hand*

4 [1]Lit., *under my hand* [a]Lev. 24:5-9; Matt. 12:4

5 And David answered the priest and said to him, "[a]Sure-
ly women have been kept from us as previously when I set
out and the vessels of the young men were holy, though it was
an ordinary journey; how much more then today will [1]their
vessels *be holy?*"
6 So [a]the priest gave him consecrated *bread;* for there
was no bread there but the bread of the Presence which was
removed from before the LORD, in order to put hot bread *in its
place* when it was taken away.
7 Now one of the servants of Saul was there that day,
detained before the LORD; and his name was [a]Doeg the Edomite, the [b]chief of Saul's shepherds.
8 And David said to Ahimelech, "Now is there not a
spear or a sword [1]on hand? For I brought neither my sword nor
my weapons [2]with me, because the king's matter was urgent."
9 Then the priest said, "[a]The sword of Goliath the Philistine, whom you [1]killed [b]in the valley of Elah, behold, it is
wrapped in a cloth behind the ephod; if you would take it for
yourself, take *it.* For there is no other except it here." And
David said, "There is none like it; give it to me."
10 Then David arose and fled that day from Saul, and
went to [a]Achish king of Gath.
11 But the [a]servants of Achish said to him, "Is this not
David the king of the land? [b]Did they not sing of this one as
they danced, saying,

'Saul has slain his thousands,
And David his ten thousands'?"

12 And David [a]took these words [1]to heart, and greatly
feared Achish king of Gath.
13 So he [a]disguised his sanity before them, and acted insane-
ly in their hands, and scribbled on the doors of the gate, and
let his saliva run down into his beard.
14 Then Achish said to his servants, "Behold, you see the
man behaving as a madman. Why do you bring him to me?
15 "Do I lack madmen, that you have brought this one to
get the madman in my presence? Shall this one come into my
house?"

CHAPTER 22

SO David departed from there and [a]escaped to [b]the cave of
Adullam; and when his brothers and all his father's household
heard *of it,* they went down there to him.
2 And everyone who was in distress, and everyone who
[1]was in debt, and everyone who was [2]discontented, gathered to
him; and he became captain over them. Now there were
[a]about four hundred men with him.
3 And David went from there to Mizpah of Moab; and
he said to the king of Moab, "Please let my father and my
mother come *and stay* with you until I know what God will do
for me."
4 Then he left them with the king of Moab; and they
stayed with him all the time that David was in the stronghold.
5 And [a]the prophet Gad said to David, "Do not stay in
the stronghold; depart, and go into the land of Judah." So
David departed and went into the forest of Hereth.

5 [1]Lit., *it be holy in the vessel* [a]Ex. 19:14, 15

6 [a]Matt. 12:3, 4; Mark 2:25

7 [a]1 Sam. 14:47; 22:9; Ps. 52: title [b]1 Chr. 27:29, 31

8 [1]Lit., *under your hand* [2]Lit., *in my hand*

9 [1]Lit., *smote* [a]1 Sam. 17:54 [b]1 Sam. 17:2

10 [a]Ps. 34:title

11 [a]Ps. 56:title [b]1 Sam. 18:7; 29:5

12 [1]Lit., *in his* [a]Luke 2:19

13 [a]Ps. 34:title

1 [a]Ps. 57:title; 142:title [b]Josh. 12:15; 15:35; 2 Sam. 23:13

2 [1]Lit., *had a creditor* [2]Lit., *bitter of soul* [a]1 Sam. 23:13; 25:13

5 [a]2 Sam. 24:11; 1 Chr. 29:29; 2 Chr. 29:25

6 Then Saul heard that David and the men who were
with him had been discovered. Now [a]Saul was sitting in Gibeah, under the tamarisk tree on the height with his spear in
his hand, and all his servants were standing around him.
7 And Saul said to his servants who stood around him,
"Hear now, O Benjamites! Will the son of Jesse also give to all
of you fields and vineyards? [a]Will he make you all commanders of thousands and commanders of hundreds?
8 For all of you have conspired against me so that there is
no one who [1]discloses to me [a]when my son makes *a covenant*
with the son of Jesse, and there is none of you [b]who is sorry for
me or [1]discloses to me that my son has stirred up my servant
against me to lie in ambush, as *it is* this day."
9 Then [a]Doeg the Edomite, who was [1]standing by the
servants of Saul, answered and said, "[b]I saw the son of Jesse
coming to Nob, to [c]Ahimelech the son of Ahitub.
10 "And [a]he inquired of the LORD for him, [b]gave him provisions, and [c]gave him the sword of Goliath the Philistine."
11 Then the king sent someone to summon Ahimelech
the priest, the son of Ahitub, and all his father's household, the
priests who were in Nob; and all of them came to the king.
12 And Saul said, "Listen now, son of Ahitub." And he
[1]answered, "Here I am, my lord."
13 Saul then said to him, "Why have you and the son of
Jesse conspired against me, in that you have given him bread
and a sword and have inquired of God for him, that he should
rise up against me [a]by lying in ambush as *it is* this day?"
14 [a]Then Ahimelech answered the king and said, "And
who among all your servants is as faithful as David, even the
king's son-in-law, who [1]is captain over your guard, and is honored in your house?
15 "Did I *just* begin [a]to inquire of God for him today? Far
be it from me! Do not let the king impute anything to his
servant *or* to any of the household of my father, for your
servant knows nothing [1]at all of this whole affair."
16 But the king said, "You shall surely die, Ahimelech,
you and all your father's household!"
17 And [a]the king said to the [1]guards who were attending
him, "Turn around and put the priests of the LORD to death,
because their hand also is with David and because they knew
that he was fleeing and did not [2]reveal it to me." But the
servants of the king were not willing to put forth their hands to
[3]attack the priests of the LORD.
18 Then the king said to Doeg, "You turn around and
[1]attack the priests." And Doeg the Edomite turned around
and [2]attacked the priests, and [a]he killed that day eighty-five
men [b]who wore the linen ephod.
19 And [a]he struck Nob the city of the priests with the edge
of the sword, both men and women, children and infants; also
oxen, donkeys, and sheep, *he struck* with the edge of the
sword.
20 But [a]one son of Ahimelech, the son of Ahitub named
Abiathar, [b]escaped and fled after David.
21 And Abiathar told David that Saul had killed the
priests of the LORD.
22 Then David said to Abiathar, "I knew on that day,

6 [a]1 Sam. 14:2; Judg. 4:5

7 [a]1 Sam. 8:14; 1 Chr. 12:16-18

8 [1]Lit., *uncovers my ear* [a]1 Sam. 18:3; 20:16 [b]1 Sam. 23:21

9 [1]Or, *set over* [a]Ps. 52:title [b]1 Sam. 21:1 [c]1 Sam. 14:3; 21:1

10 [a]1 Sam. 10:22 [b]1 Sam. 21:6, 9 [c]1 Sam. 21:9

12 [1]Lit., *said*

13 [a]1 Sam. 22:8

14 [1]So with Gk., Heb., *turns aside to* [a]1 Sam. 19:4, 5; 20:32

15 [1]Lit., *small or great* [a]2 Sam. 5:19, 23

17 [1]Lit., *runners* [2]Lit., *uncover my ear* [3]Lit., *fall upon* [a]2 Kin. 10:25; 2 Chr. 12:10

18 [1]Lit., *smite* [2]Lit., *smote* [a]1 Sam. 2:31 [b]1 Sam. 2:18

19 [a]1 Sam. 15:3

20 [a]1 Sam. 23:9; 30:7; 2 Sam. 2:1; 1 Kin. 2:26, 27 [b]1 Sam. 2:33

when [a]Doeg the Edomite was there, that he would surely tell Saul. I have brought about *the death* of every person in your father's household.

23 "Stay with me, do not be afraid, for [a]he who seeks my life seeks your life; for you are [1]safe with me."

Chapter 23

THEN they told David, saying, "Behold, the Philistines are fighting against [a]Keilah, and are plundering the threshing floors."

2 So David [a]inquired of the LORD, saying, "Shall I go and [1]attack these Philistines?" And the LORD said to David, "Go and [1]attack the Philistines, and deliver Keilah."

3 But David's men said to him, "Behold, we are afraid here in Judah. How much more then if we go to Keilah against the ranks of the Philistines?"

4 Then David inquired of the LORD once more. And the LORD answered him and said, "Arise, go down to Keilah, for [a]I will give the Philistines into your hand."

5 So David and his men went to Keilah and fought with the Philistines; and he led away their livestock and struck them with a great slaughter. Thus David delivered the inhabitants of Keilah.

6 Now it came about, when Abiathar the son of Ahimelech [a]fled to David at Keilah, *that* he came down *with* an ephod in his hand.

7 When it was told Saul that David had come to Keilah, Saul said, "God has [1]delivered him into my hand, for he shut himself in by entering a city with double gates and bars."

8 So Saul summoned all the people for war, to go down to Keilah to besiege David and his men.

9 Now David knew that Saul was plotting evil against him; so he said to [a]Abiathar the priest, "[b]Bring the ephod here."

10 Then David said, "O LORD God of Israel, Thy servant has heard for certain that Saul is seeking to come to Keilah to destroy the city on my account.

11 "Will the men of Keilah surrender me into his hand? Will Saul come down just as Thy servant has heard? O LORD God of Israel, I pray, tell Thy servant." And the LORD said, "He will come down."

12 Then David said, "Will the men of Keilah surrender me and my men into the hand of Saul?" And the LORD said, "[a]They will surrender you."

13 Then David and his men, [a]about six hundred, arose and departed from Keilah, and they went [b]wherever they could go. When it was told Saul that David had escaped from Keilah, he [1]gave up the pursuit.

14 And David stayed in the wilderness in the strongholds, and remained in the hill country in the wilderness of [a]Ziph. And Saul sought him every day, but [b]God did not deliver him into his hand.

15 Now David [1]became aware that Saul had come out to seek his life while David was in the wilderness of Ziph at Horesh.

22 [a]1 Sam. 21:7

23 [1]Lit., *a charge* [a]1 Kin. 2:26

1 [a]Josh. 15:44; Neh. 3:17, 18

2 [1]Lit., *smite* [a]1 Sam. 23:4, 6, 9-12; 2 Sam. 5:19, 23

4 [a]Josh. 8:7; Judg. 7:7

6 [a]1 Sam. 22:20

7 [1]Lit., *alienated*

9 [a]1 Sam. 22:20 [b]1 Sam. 23:6; 30:7

12 [a]1 Sam. 23:20; Judg. 15:10-13

13 [1]Lit., *ceased going out* [a]1 Sam. 22:2; 25:13 [b]2 Sam. 15:20

14 [a]Josh. 15:55; 2 Chr. 11:8 [b]Ps. 32:7

15 [1]Lit., *saw*

16 And Jonathan, Saul's son, arose and went to David at
Horesh, and [1a]encouraged him in God.
17 Thus he said to him, "Do not be afraid, because the
hand of Saul my father shall not find you, and you will be king
over Israel and I will be next to you; and [a]Saul my father knows
that also."
18 So [a]the two of them made a covenant before the LORD;
and David stayed at Horesh while Jonathan went to his house.
19 Then [a]Ziphites came up to Saul at Gibeah, saying, "Is
David not hiding with us in the strongholds at Horesh, on [b]the
hill of Hachilah, which is on the [1]south of [2]Jeshimon.
20 "Now then, O king, come down according to all the
desire of your soul to [1]do so; and [a]our part *shall be* to surrender him into the king's hand."
21 And Saul said, "May you be blessed of the LORD; [a]for
you have had compassion on me.
22 "Go now, make more sure, and investigate and see his
place where his [1]haunt is, *and* who has seen him there; for I am
told that he is very cunning.
23 "So look, and learn about all the hiding places where he
hides himself, and return to me with certainty, and I will go
with you; and it shall come about if he is in the land that I will
search him out among all the thousands of Judah."
24 Then they arose and went to Ziph before Saul. Now
David and his men were in the wilderness of [a]Maon, in the
Arabah to the [1]south of [2]Jeshimon.
25 When Saul and his men went to seek *him,* they told
David, and he came down to the rock and stayed in the wilderness of Maon. And when Saul heard *it,* he pursued David in
the wilderness of Maon.
26 And Saul went on one side of the mountain, and David
and his men on the other side of the mountain; and David was
hurrying to get away from Saul, for Saul and his men [a]were
surrounding David and his men to seize them.
27 But a messenger came to Saul, saying, "Hurry and
come, for the Philistines have made a raid on the land."
28 So Saul returned from pursuing David, and went to
meet the Philistines; therefore they called that place [1]the Rock
of Escape.
29 [1]And David went up from there and stayed in the strongholds of [a]Engedi.

CHAPTER 24

NOW it came about [a]when Saul returned from pursuing the
Philistines, [b]he was told, saying, "Behold, David is in the wilderness of Engedi."
2 Then [a]Saul took three thousand chosen men from all
Israel, and went to seek David and his men in front of the
Rocks of the Wild Goats.
3 And he came to the sheepfolds on the way, where there
was a cave; and Saul [a]went in to [1]relieve himself. Now [b]David
and his men were sitting in the inner recesses of the cave.
4 And the men of David said to him, "Behold, [a]*this is* the
day of which the LORD said to you, 'Behold; I am about to give
your enemy into your hand, and you shall do to him as it seems

16 [1]Lit., *strengthened his hand* [a]1 Sam. 30:6; Neh. 2:18

17 [a]1 Sam. 20:31; 24:20

18 [a]1 Sam. 18:3; 20:12-17; 2 Sam. 9:1

19 [1]Lit., *right side* [2]Or, *the desert* [a]1 Sam. 26:1; Ps. 51:title [b]1 Sam. 26:3

20 [1]Lit., *come down* [a]1 Sam. 23:12

21 [a]1 Sam. 22:8

22 [1]Lit., *foot*

24 [1]Lit., *right side* [2]Or, *the desert* [a]1 Sam. 25:2; Josh. 15:55

26 [a]Ps. 17:9

28 [1]Heb., *Sela-hammahlekoth*

29 [1]Chap. 24:1 in Heb. [a]Josh. 15:62; 2 Chr. 20:2

1 [a]1 Sam. 23:28, 29 [b]1 Sam. 23:19

2 [a]1 Sam. 26:2

3 [1]Lit., *cover his feet* [a]Judg. 3:24 [b]Ps. 57:title; 142:title

4 [a]1 Sam. 23:17; 25:28-30

good [1]to you.' " Then David arose and cut off the edge of
Saul's robe secretly.
5 And it came about afterward that [a]David's [1]conscience
bothered him because he had cut off the edge of Saul's *robe*.
6 So he said to his men, "[a]Far be it from me because of
the LORD that I should do this thing to my lord, the LORD's
anointed, to stretch out my hand against him, since he is the
LORD's anointed."
7 And David [1]persuaded his men with *these* words and
did not allow them to rise up against Saul. And Saul arose, [2]left
the cave, and went on *his* way.
8 Now afterward David arose and went out of the cave
and called after Saul, saying, "My lord the king!" And when
Saul looked behind him, [a]David bowed with his face to the
ground and prostrated himself.
9 And David said to Saul, "Why do you listen to the
words of men, saying, 'Behold, David seeks [1]to harm you'?
10 "[a]Behold, this day your eyes have seen that the LORD
had given you today into my hand in the cave, and [b]some said
to kill you, but *my eye* had pity on you; and I said, 'I will not
stretch out my hand against my lord, for he is the LORD's
anointed.'
11 "Now, [a]my father, see! Indeed, see the edge of your robe
in my hand! For in that I cut off the edge of your robe and did
not kill you, know and perceive that there is no evil or [1]rebel-
lion in my hands, and I have not sinned against you, though
you [b]are lying in wait for my life to take it.
12 "[a]May the LORD judge between [1]you and me, and may
the LORD avenge me on you; but my hand shall not be against
you.
13 "As the proverb of the ancients says, '[a]Out of the wicked
comes forth wickedness'; but my hand shall not be against you.
14 "After whom has the king of Israel come out? After
whom are you pursuing? After a dead dog, [a]after a single flea?
15 "[a]The LORD therefore be judge and decide between
[1]you and me; and may He see and [b]plead my cause, and [2]deliv-
er me from your hand."
16 Now it came about when David had finished speaking
these words to Saul, that Saul said, "[a]Is this your voice, my son
David?" Then Saul lifted up his voice and wept.
17 [a]And he said to David, "You are more righteous than I;
for [b]you have dealt well with me, while I have dealt wickedly
with you.
18 "And you have declared today that you have done good
to me, that [a]the LORD delivered me into your hand and *yet* you
did not kill me.
19 "For if a man [a]finds his enemy, will he let him go away
[1]safely? May the LORD therefore reward you with good in
return for what you have done to me this day.
20 "And now, behold, [a]I know that you shall surely be king,
and that [b]the kingdom of Israel shall be established in your
hand.
21 "So now [a]swear to me by the LORD that you will not cut
off my [1]descendants after me, and that you will not destroy my
name from my father's household."

4 [1]Lit., *in your sight*

5 [1]Lit., *heart struck* [a]2 Sam. 24:10

6 [a]1 Sam. 26:11

7 [1]Lit., *tore apart* [2]Lit., *from*

8 [a]1 Sam. 25:23, 24; 1 Kin. 1:31

9 [1]Lit., *your hurt*

10 [a]Ps. 7:3, 4 [b]1 Sam. 24:4

11 [1]Lit., *transgression* [a]2 Kin. 5:13 [b]1 Sam. 23:14, 23; 26:20

12 [1]Lit., *me and you* [a]1 Sam. 26:10, 23; Gen. 31:53; Judg. 11:27

13 [a]Matt. 7:16-20

14 [a]1 Sam. 26:20

15 [1]Lit., *me and you* [2]Lit., *vindicate* [a]1 Sam. 24:12 [b]Ps. 35:1

16 [a]1 Sam. 26:17

17 [a]1 Sam. 26:21 [b]Matt. 5:44

18 [a]1 Sam. 26:23

19 [1]Lit., *on a good road* [a]1 Sam. 23:17

20 [a]1 Sam. 23:17 [b]1 Sam. 13:14

21 [1]Lit., *seed* [a]1 Sam. 20:14-17; Gen. 21:23; 2 Sam. 21:6-8

22 And David swore to Saul. And Saul went to his home,
but David and his men went up to [a]the stronghold.

Chapter 25

[a]THEN Samuel died; and all Israel gathered together and
[b]mourned for him, and [c]buried him at his house in Ramah.
And David arose and went down to the [d]wilderness of Paran.
2 Now *there was* a man in [a]Maon whose business was in
[b]Carmel; and the man was [c]very [1]rich, and he had three thousand sheep and a thousand goats. And it came about while [d]he
was shearing his sheep in Carmel
3 (now the man's name was Nabal, and his wife's name
was Abigail. And the woman was [1]intelligent and beautiful in
appearance, but the man was harsh and evil in *his* dealings, and
he was [a]a Calebite),
4 that David heard in the wilderness that Nabal was shearing his sheep.
5 So David sent ten young men, and David said to the
young men, "Go up to Carmel, [1]visit Nabal and greet him in
my name;
6 and thus you shall say, '[1]Have a long life, [a]peace be to
you, and peace be to your house, and peace be to all that you
have.
7 'And now I have heard [a]that you have shearers; now
your shepherds have been with us and we have not insulted
them, [b]nor have they missed anything all the days they were in
Carmel.
8 'Ask your young men and they will tell you. Therefore
let *my* young men find favor in your eyes, for we have come on
[a]a [1]festive day. Please give whatever you find at hand to your
servants and to your son David.' "
9 When David's young men came, they spoke to Nabal
according to all these words in David's name; then they waited.
10 But Nabal answered David's servants, and said, "[a]Who
is David? And who is the son of Jesse? There are many servants
today who are each breaking away from his master.
11 "Shall I then take my bread and my water and my meat
that I have slaughtered for my shearers, and give it to men
[1]whose origin I do not know?"
12 So David's young men retraced their way and went
back; and they came and told him according to all these words.
13 And David said to his men, "Each *of you* gird on his
sword." So each man girded on his sword. And David also
girded on his sword, and about [a]four hundred men went up
behind David while two hundred [b]stayed with the baggage.
14 But one of the young men told Abigail, Nabal's wife,
saying, "Behold, David sent messengers from the wilderness to
[1a]greet our master, and he scorned them.
15 "Yet the men were very good to us, and we were not
[a]insulted, nor did we miss anything [1]as long as we went about
with them, while we were in the fields.
16 "[a]They were a wall to us both by night and by day, all
the time we were with them tending the sheep.
17 "Now therefore know and [1]consider what you should
do, for evil is plotted against our master and against all his

22 [a]1 Sam. 23:29

1 [a]1 Sam. 28:3 [b]Deut. 34:8 [c]2 Kin. 21:18; 2 Chr. 33:20 [d]Gen. 21:21; Num. 10:12; 13:3

2 [1]Lit., *great*
[a]1 Sam. 23:24 [b]Josh. 15:55 [c]2 Sam. 19:32 [d]2 Sam. 13:23

3 [1]Lit., *of good understanding*
[a]1 Sam. 30:14; Josh. 15:13

5 [1]Lit., *go into*

6 [1]Lit., *to life*
[a]1 Chr. 12:18

7 [a]2 Sam. 13:23, 24 [b]1 Sam. 15:21

8 [1]Lit., *good*
[a]Neh. 8:10-12

10 [a]Judg. 9:28

11 [1]Lit., *from where they are*

13 [a]1 Sam. 23:13 [b]1 Chr. 30:24

14 [1]Lit., *bless*
[a]1 Sam. 13:10; 15:13

15 [1]Lit., *all the days*
[a]1 Sam. 25:7, 21

16 [a]Ex. 14:22

17 [1]Lit., *see*

household; and he is such a [2]worthless man that no one can
speak to him."
18 Then Abigail hurried and [a]took two hundred *loaves* of
bread and two jugs of wine and five sheep already prepared
and five measures of roasted grain and a hundred clusters of
raisins and two hundred cakes of figs, and loaded *them* on
donkeys.
19 And she said to her young men, "[a]Go on before me;
behold, I am coming after you." But she did not tell her
husband Nabal.
20 And it came about as she was riding on her donkey and
coming down by the hidden part of the mountain, that behold,
David and his men were coming down toward her; so she met
them.
21 Now David had said, "Surely in vain I have guarded all
that this *man* has in the wilderness, so that nothing was missed
of all that belonged to him; and he has returned me evil for
good.
22 "[a]May God do so to the enemies of David, and more
also, [b]if by morning I leave *as much as* one [1]male of any who
belong to him."
23 When Abigail saw David, she hurried and dismounted
from her donkey, and fell on her face before David, [a]and
bowed herself to the ground.
24 And she fell at his feet and said, "On me [1]alone, my
lord, be the blame. And please let your maidservant speak [2]to
you, and listen to the words of your maidservant.
25 "Please do not let my lord [1]pay attention to this [2]worth-
less man, Nabal, for as his name is, so is he. [3]Nabal is his
name and folly is with him; but I your maidservant did not see
the young men of my lord whom you sent.
26 "Now therefore, my lord, as the LORD lives, and as your
soul lives, since the LORD has restrained you from [1]shedding
blood, and [a]from [2]avenging yourself by your own hand, now
then [b]let your enemies, and those who seek evil against my
lord, be as Nabal.
27 "And now let [a]this [1]gift which your maidservant has
brought to my lord be given to the young men who [2]accom-
pany my lord.
28 "Please forgive [a]the transgression of your maidservant;
for [b]the LORD will certainly make for my lord an enduring
house, because my lord is [c]fighting the battles of the LORD, and
[d]evil shall not be found in you all your days.
29 "And should anyone rise up to pursue you and to seek
your [1]life, then the [1]life of my lord shall be bound in the
bundle of the living with the LORD your God; but the [1]lives of
your enemies [a]He will sling out [2]as from the hollow of a sling.
30 "And it shall come about when the LORD shall do for my
lord according to all the good that He has spoken concerning
you, and [a]shall appoint you ruler over Israel,
31 that this will not [1]cause grief or a troubled heart to my
lord, both by having shed blood without cause and by my lord
having [2]avenged himself. [a]When the LORD shall deal well with
my lord, then remember your maidservant."
32 Then David said to Abigail, "[a]Blessed be the LORD
God of Israel, who sent you this day to meet me,

17 [2]Lit., *son of Belial*

18 [a]2 Sam. 16:1; 1 Chr. 12:40

19 [a]Gen. 32:16, 20

22 [1]Lit., *who urinates against the wall* [a]1 Sam. 3:17; 20:13 [b]1 Kin. 14:10

23 [a]1 Sam. 20:41

24 [1]Lit., *even me* [2]Lit., *in your ears*

25 [1]Lit., *set his heart to* [2]Lit., *man of Belial* [3]I.e., Fool

26 [1]Lit., *coming in with blood* [2]Lit., *saving* [a]Heb. 10:30 [b]2 Sam. 18:32

27 [1]Lit., *blessing* [2]Lit., *walk at the feet of* [a]1 Sam. 30:26; Gen. 33:11

28 [a]1 Sam. 25:24 [b]1 Sam. 22:14; 2 Sam. 7:16 [c]1 Sam. 18:17 [d]1 Sam. 24:11; Ps. 7:3

29 [1]Lit., *soul* [2]Lit., *in the midst* [a]Jer. 10:18

30 [a]1 Sam. 13:14

31 [1]Lit., *become staggering to you or a stumbling of the heart* [2]Lit., *saved* [a]1 Sam. 25:30; Gen. 40:14

32 [a]Ex. 18:10

33 and blessed be your discernment, and blessed be you,
[a]who have kept me this day from [1]bloodshed, and from [2]aveng-
ing myself by my own hand.
34 "Nevertheless, as the LORD God of Israel lives, [a]who has
restrained me from harming you, unless you had come quickly
to meet me, surely there would not have been left to Nabal
until the morning light *as much as* one [1]male."
35 So David received from her hand what she had brought
him, and he said to her, "[a]Go up to your house in peace. See, I
have listened to [1]you and [2b]granted your request."
36 Then Abigail came to Nabal, and behold, he was holding [a]a feast in his house, like the feast of a king. And Nabal's
heart was merry within him, for he was very drunk; so [b]she did
not tell him anything [1]at all until the morning light.
37 But it came about in the morning, when the wine had
gone out of Nabal, that his wife told him these things, and his
heart died within him so that he became *as* a stone.
38 And about ten days later, it happened that [a]the LORD
struck Nabal, and he died.
39 When David heard that Nabal was dead, he said,
"Blessed be the LORD, who has [a]pleaded the cause of my reproach
from the hand of Nabal, and [b]has kept back His servant
from evil. [c]The LORD has also returned the evil doing of Nabal
on his own head." Then David sent [1d]a proposal to Abigail, to
take her as his wife.
40 When the servants of David came to Abigail at Carmel, they spoke to her, saying, "David has sent us to you, to
take you as his wife."
41 And she arose [a]and bowed with her face to the ground
and said, "Behold, your maidservant is a maid [b]to wash the
feet of my lord's servants."
42 Then [a]Abigail quickly arose, and rode on a donkey,
with her five maidens who [1]attended her; and she followed the
messengers of David, and became his wife.
43 David had also taken Ahinoam of [a]Jezreel, and they
both became his wives.
44 Now Saul had given [a]Michal his daughter, David's wife,
to Palti the son of Laish, who was from [b]Gallim.

CHAPTER 26

THEN the Ziphites came to Saul at Gibeah, saying, "[a]Is not
David hiding on the hill of Hachilah, *which is* before
[1]Jeshimon?"
2 So Saul arose and went down to the wilderness of Ziph,
having with him [a]three thousand chosen men of Israel, to
search for David in the wilderness of Ziph.
3 And Saul camped in the hill of Hachilah, which is before [1]Jeshimon, [a]beside the road, and David was staying in the
wilderness. When [b]he saw that Saul came after him into the
wilderness,
4 David sent out spies, and he knew that Saul was definitely coming.
5 David then arose and came to the place where Saul had
camped. And David saw the place where Saul lay, and [a]Abner
the son of Ner, the commander of his army; and Saul was lying

33 [1]Lit., *coming in with blood* [2]Lit., *saying*
[a]1 Sam. 25:26

34 [1]Lit., *who urinates against the wall*
[a]1 Sam. 25:26

35 [1]Lit., *your voice* [2]Lit., *lifted up your face*
[a]1 Sam. 20:42; 2 Kin. 5:19 [b]Gen. 19:21

36 [1]Lit., *small or large*
[a]2 Sam. 13:23 [b]1 Sam. 25:19

38 [a]1 Sam. 26:10

39 [1]Lit., *and spoke*
[a]1 Sam. 24:15 [b]1 Sam. 26:34 [c]2 Sam. 3:28, 29 [d]Song of Sol. 8:8

41 [a]1 Sam. 25:23 [b]Mark 1:7

42 [1]Lit., *walked at her feet*
[a]Gen. 24:61-67

43 [a]Josh. 15:56

44 [a]1 Sam. 18:27; 2 Sam. 3:14 [b]Is. 10:31

1 [1]Or, *the desert*
[a]1 Sam. 23:19; Ps. 54:title

2 [a]1 Sam. 13:2; 24:2

3 [1]Or, *the desert*
[a]1 Sam. 24:3 [b]1 Sam. 23:15

5 [a]1 Sam. 14:50, 51; 17:55

in the circle of the camp, and the people were camped around
him.
6 Then David answered and said to Ahimelech [a]the Hittite and to [b]Abishai the son of Zeruiah, Joab's brother, saying,
"Who [c]will go down with me to Saul in the camp?" And
Abishai said, "I will go down with you."
7 So David and Abishai came to the people by night, and
behold, Saul lay sleeping inside the circle of the camp, with his
spear stuck in the ground at his head; and Abner and the
people were lying around him.
8 Then Abishai said to David, "Today God has delivered
your enemy into your hand; now therefore, please let me strike
him with the spear [1]to the ground with one stroke, and I will
not [2]strike him the second time."
9 But David said to Abishai, "Do not destroy him, for
[a]who can stretch out his hand against the LORD's anointed and
be without guilt?"
10 David also said, "As the LORD lives, [a]surely the LORD
will strike him, or [b]his day will come that he dies, or [c]he will go
down into battle and perish.
11 "[a]The LORD forbid that I should stretch out my hand
against the LORD's anointed; but now please take the spear that
is at his head and the jug of water, and let us go."
12 So David took the spear and the jug of water from
beside Saul's head, and they went away, but no one saw or
knew *it*, nor did any awake, for they were all asleep, because [a]a
sound sleep from the LORD had fallen on them.
13 Then David crossed over to the other side, and stood
on top of the mountain at a distance *with* a large area between
them.
14 And David called to the people and to Abner the son
of Ner, saying, "Will you not answer, Abner?" Then Abner
answered and said, "Who are you who calls to the king?"
15 So David said to Abner, "Are you not a man? And who
is like you in Israel? Why then have you not guarded your lord
the king? For one of the people came to destroy the king your
lord.
16 "This thing that you have done is not good. As the LORD
lives, *all* of you [1a]must surely die, because you did not guard
your lord, the LORD's anointed. And now, see where the king's
spear is, and the jug of water that was at his head."
17 Then Saul recognized David's voice and said, "[a]Is this
your voice, my son David?" And David said, "It is my voice,
my lord the king."
18 He also said, "[a]Why then is my lord pursuing his servant? For what have I done? Or what evil is in my hand?
19 "Now therefore, please let my lord the king listen to the
words of his servant. If [a]the LORD has stirred you up against
me, [b]let Him [1]accept an offering; but [c]if it is [2]men, cursed are
they before the LORD, for [d]they have driven me out today that
I should have no attachment with the inheritance of the LORD,
saying, 'Go, serve other gods.'
20 "Now then, do not let my blood fall to the ground away
from the presence of the LORD; for the king of Israel has come
out to search for [a]a single flea, just as one hunts a partridge in
the mountains."

6 [a]Gen. 23:3; 26:34; Josh. 3:10; 1 Kin. 10:29; 2 Kin. 7:6 [b]1 Chr. 2:15, 16 [c]Judg. 7:10, 11

8 [1]Lit., *even into* [2]Lit., *repeat with respect to him*

9 [a]1 Sam. 24:6, 7; 2 Sam. 1:14, 16

10 [a]1 Sam. 25:26, 38 [b]Deut. 31:14 [c]1 Sam. 31:6

11 [a]1 Sam. 24:6, 12

12 [a]Gen. 2:21; 15:12

16 [1]Lit., *are surely sons of death* [a]1 Sam. 20:31

17 [a]1 Sam. 24:16

18 [a]1 Sam. 24:9, 11-14

19 [1]Lit., *smell* [2]Lit., *sons of men* [a]2 Sam. 16:11; [b]Gen. 8:21 [c]1 Sam. 24:9 [d]Josh. 22:25-27

20 [a]1 Sam. 24:14

21 Then Saul said, "[a]I have sinned. Return, my son David, for I will not harm you again because my life was precious in your sight this day. Behold, I have played the fool and have committed a serious error."

22 And David answered and said, "Behold the spear of the king! Now let one of the young men come over and take it.

23 "And [a]the LORD will repay each man *for* his righteousness and his faithfulness; for the LORD delivered you into *my* hand today, but [b]I refused to stretch out my hand against the LORD's anointed.

24 "Now behold, as your life was [a]highly valued in my sight this day, so may my life be highly valued in the sight of the LORD, and may He [b]deliver me from all distress."

25 Then Saul said to David, "[a]Blessed are you, my son David; you will both accomplish much and surely prevail." So [b]David went on his way, and Saul returned to his place.

CHAPTER 27

THEN David said [1]to himself, "Now I will perish one day by the hand of Saul. [a]There is nothing better for me than [2]to escape into the land of the Philistines. Saul then will despair of searching for me any more in all the territory of Israel, and I will escape from his hand."

2 So David arose and crossed over, he and [a]the six hundred men who were with him, to [b]Achish the son of Maoch, king of Gath.

3 And David lived with Achish at Gath, he and his men, [a]each with his household, *even* David with [b]his two wives, Ahinoam the Jezreelitess, and Abigail the Carmelitess, Nabal's [1]widow.

4 Now it was told Saul that David had fled to Gath, so he no longer searched for him.

5 Then David said to Achish, "If now I have found favor in your sight, let them give me a place in one of the cities in the country, that I may live there; for why should your servant live in the royal city with you?"

6 So Achish gave him Ziklag that day; therefore [a]Ziklag has belonged to the kings of Judah to this day.

7 And the number of days that David lived in the country of the Philistines was [a]a year and four months.

8 Now David and his men went up and raided [a]the Geshurites and the Girzites and [b]the Amalekites; for they were the inhabitants of the land from ancient times, as you come to [c]Shur even as far as the land of Egypt.

9 And David [1]attacked the land and did not leave a man or a woman alive, and he [a]took away the sheep, the cattle, the donkeys, the camels, and the clothing. Then he returned and came to Achish.

10 Now Achish said, "Where have you [a]made a raid today?" And David said, "Against the [1]Negev of Judah and against the [1]Negev of [b]the Jerahmeelites and against the [1]Negev of [c]the Kenites."

11 And David did not leave a man or a woman alive, to bring to Gath, saying, "Lest they should tell about us, saying,

21 [a]1 Sam. 15:24, 30; 24:17

23 [a]1 Sam. 24:19 [b]1 Sam. 24:12

24 [a]1 Sam. 18:30 [b]Ps. 54:7

25 [a]1 Sam. 24:19 [b]1 Sam. 24:22

1 [1]Lit., *in his heart* [2]Lit., *that I should surely escape* [a]1 Sam. 26:19

2 [a]1 Sam. 25:13 [b]1 Sam. 21:10; 1 Kin. 2:39

3 [1]Lit., *wife* [a]1 Sam. 30:3; 2 Sam. 2:3 [b]1 Sam. 25:42, 43

6 [a]Josh. 15:31; 19:5; Neh. 11:28

7 [a]1 Sam. 29:3

8 [a]Josh. 13:2, 13 [b]1 Sam. 15:7, 8; Ex. 17:8 [c]Ex. 15:22

9 [1]Lit., *smote* [a]1 Sam. 15:3; Job 1:3

10 [1]I.e., South country [a]1 Sam. 23:27 [b]1 Sam. 30:29; 1 Chr. 2:9, 25 [c]Judg. 1:16; 4:11

'So has David done and so *has been* his practice all the time he
has lived in the country of the Philistines.' "
12 So Achish believed David, saying, "He has surely made
himself odious among his people Israel; therefore he will become my servant forever."

Chapter 28

1 NOW it came about in those days that [a]the Philistines gathered their armed camps for war, to fight against Israel. And
Achish said to David, "Know assuredly that you will go out
with me in the camp, you and your men."
2 And David said to Achish, "Very well, you shall know
what your servant can do." So Achish said to David, "Very
well, I will make you [1]my bodyguard [a]for life."
3 Now [a]Samuel was dead, and all Israel had lamented
him and buried him [b]in Ramah his own city. And Saul had
removed from the land those who [c]were mediums and
spiritists.
4 So the Philistines gathered together and came and
camped [a]in Shunem; and Saul gathered all Israel together and
they camped in [b]Gilboa.
5 When Saul saw the camp of the Philistines, he was
afraid and his heart trembled greatly.
6 [a]When Saul inquired of the LORD, [b]the LORD did not
answer him, either by [c]dreams or by [d]Urim or by prophets.
7 Then Saul said to his servants, "Seek for me a woman
who is a medium, that I may go to her and inquire of her."
And his servants said to him, "Behold, [a]there is a woman who
is a medium at [b]En-dor."
8 Then Saul [a]disguised himself by putting on other
clothes, and went, he and two men with him, and they came to
the woman by night; and he said, "[b]Conjure up for me, please,
and [c]bring up for me whom I shall [1]name to you."
9 But the woman said to him, "Behold, you know [a]what
Saul has done, how he has cut off those who are mediums and
spiritists from the land. Why are you then laying a snare for
my life to bring about my death?"
10 And Saul vowed to her by the LORD, saying, "As the
LORD lives, there shall no punishment come upon you for this
thing."
11 Then the woman said, "Whom shall I bring up for
you?" And he said, "Bring up Samuel for me."
12 When the woman saw Samuel, she cried out with a
loud voice; and the woman spoke to Saul, saying, "Why have
you deceived me? For you are Saul."
13 And the king said to her, "Do not be afraid; but what
do you see?" And the woman said to Saul, "I see a [1]divine
being coming up out of the earth."
14 And he said to her, "What is his form?" And she said,
"An old man is coming up, and [a]he is wrapped with a robe."
And Saul knew that it was Samuel, and [b]he bowed with his face
to the ground and did homage.
15 Then Samuel said to Saul, "Why have you disturbed
me by bringing me up?" And Saul answered, "I am greatly
distressed; for the Philistines are waging war against me, and

1 [a]1 Sam. 29:1
2 [1]Lit., *keeper of my head* [a]1 Sam. 1:22, 28
3 [a]1 Sam. 25:1 [b]1 Sam. 7:17 [c]1 Sam. 15:23; Lev. 19:31; Deut. 18:10
4 [a]1 Kin. 1:3; 2 Kin. 4:8 [b]1 Sam. 31:1
6 [a]1 Chr. 10:13, 14 [b]Prov. 1:24-31 [c]Num. 12:6; Joel 2:28 [d]Ex. 28:30; 2 Sam. 8:17
7 [a]Acts 16:16 [b]Josh. 17:1; Ps. 83:10
8 [1]Lit., *say* [a]2 Chr. 18:29; 35:22 [b]Is. 8:19 [c]Deut. 18:10, 11
9 [a]1 Sam. 28:3
13 [1]Or, *god*
14 [a]1 Sam. 15:27 [b]1 Sam. 24:8

[a]God has departed from me and [b]answers me no more, either
through prophets or by dreams; therefore I have called you,
that you may make known to me what I should do."
16 And Samuel said, "Why then do you ask me, since the
LORD has departed from you and has become your adversary?
17 "And the LORD has done [1]accordingly [a]as He spoke
through me; for the LORD has torn the kingdom out of your
hand and given it to your neighbor, to David.
18 "As [a]you did not [1]obey the LORD and did not execute
His fierce wrath on Amalek, so the LORD has done this thing to
you this day.
19 "Moreover the LORD will also give over Israel along with
you into the hands of the Philistines, therefore tomorrow [a]you
and your sons will be with me. Indeed the LORD will give over
the army of Israel into the hands of the Philistines!"
20 Then Saul immediately fell full length upon the
ground and was very afraid because of the words of Samuel;
also there was no strength in him, for he had eaten no [1]food all
day and all night.
21 And the woman came to Saul and saw that he was
terrified, and said to him, "Behold, your maidservant has
[1]obeyed you, and [a]I have [2]taken my life in my hand, and have
listened to your words which you spoke to me.
22 "So now also, please listen to the voice of your maidservant, and let me set a piece of bread before you that *you may*
eat and have strength when you go on *your* way."
23 But he refused and said, "I will not eat." [a]However, his
servants together with the woman urged him, and he listened
to [1]them. So he arose from the ground and sat on [b]the bed.
24 And the woman had a fattened calf in the house, and
[a]she quickly slaughtered it; and she took flour, kneaded it, and
baked unleavened bread from it.
25 And she brought *it* before Saul and his servants, and
they ate. Then they arose and went away that night.

CHAPTER 29

NOW [a]the Philistines gathered together all their armies to
[b]Aphek, while the Israelites were camping by the spring which
is in [c]Jezreel.
2 And the lords of the Philistines were proceeding on by
hundreds and by thousands, and [a]David and his men were
proceeding on in the rear with Achish.
3 Then the commanders of the Philistines said, "What
are these Hebrews *doing here*?" And Achish said to the commanders of the Philistines, "Is this not David, the servant of
Saul the king of Israel, [a]who has been with me these days, or
rather these years, and [b]I have found no fault in him from the
day he [1]deserted *to me* to this day?"
4 But the commanders of the Philistines were angry with
him, and the commanders of the Philistines said to him,
"Make the man go back, that he may return [a]to his place
where you have assigned him, and do not let him go down to
battle with us, [b]lest in the battle he become an adversary to us.
For with what could this *man* make himself acceptable to his
lord? *Would it* not *be* with the heads of [1]these men?

15 [a]1 Sam. 16:13, 14; 18:12 [b]1 Sam. 28:6

17 [1]Lit., *for himself* [a]1 Sam. 15:28

18 [1]Lit., *listen to the voice of* [a]1 Sam. 15:9, 20, 26

19 [a]1 Sam. 31:2; Job 3:17-19

20 [1]Lit., *bread*

21 [1]Lit., *listened to your voice* [2]Lit., *put* [a]1 Sam. 19:5

23 [1]Lit., *their voices* [a]2 Kin. 5:13 [b]Esth. 1:6; Ezek. 23:41

24 [a]Gen. 18:6, 7

1 [a]1 Sam. 28:1, 2 [b]1 Sam. 4:1; Josh. 12:18 [c]1 Kin. 18:19; 21:1; 2 Kin. 9:30

2 [a]1 Sam. 28:1, 2

3 [1]Lit., *fell* [a]1 Sam. 27:7 [b]1 Sam. 27:1-6; 1 Chr. 12:19, 20

4 [1]Lit., *those* [a]1 Sam. 27:6 [b]1 Sam. 14:21

5 "Is this not David, [a]of whom they sing in the dances,
saying,
'Saul has slain his thousands,
And David his ten thousands'?"
6 Then Achish called David and said to him, "*As* the
LORD lives, you *have been* upright, and your going out and
your coming in with me in the army are pleasing in my sight;
[a]for I have not found evil in you from the day of your coming
to me to this day. Nevertheless, you are not pleasing in the
sight of the lords.
7 "Now therefore return, and go in peace, that you may
not displease the lords of the Philistines."
8 And David said to Achish, "[a]But what have I done?
And what have you found in your servant from the day when I
came before you to this day, that I may not go and fight
against the enemies of my lord the king?"
9 But Achish answered and said to David, "I know that
you are pleasing in my sight, [a]like an angel of God; nevertheless [b]the commanders of the Philistines have said, 'He must
not go up with us to the battle.'
10 "Now then arise early in the morning [a]with the servants
of your lord who have come with you, and as soon as you have
arisen early in the morning and have light, depart."
11 So David arose early, he and his men, to depart in the
morning, to return to the land of the Philistines. And the
Philistines went up to Jezereel.

CHAPTER 30

THEN it happened when David and his men came to [a]Zik-
lag on the third day, that [b]the Amalekites had made a raid on
the [1]Negev and on [c]Ziklag, and had [2]overthrown Ziklag and
burned it with fire;
2 and they took captive the women *and all* who were in
it, both small and great, [1a]without killing anyone, and carried
them off and went their way.
3 And when David and his men came to the city, behold,
it was burned with fire, and their wives and their sons and their
daughters had been taken captive.
4 Then David and the people who were with him lifted
their voices and wept until there was no strength in them to
weep.
5 Now [a]David's two wives had been taken captive, Ahinoam the Jezreelitess and Abigail the [1]widow of Nabal the
Carmelite.
6 Moreover David was greatly distressed because [a]the
people spoke of stoning him, for all the people were [1]embittered,
each one because of his sons and his daughters. But
[b]David strengthened himself in the LORD his God.
7 Then [a]David said to Abiathar the priest, the son of
Ahimelech, "Please bring me the ephod." So Abiathar brought
the ephod to David.
8 And [a]David inquired of the LORD, saying, "[b]Shall I
pursue this band? Shall I overtake them?" And He said to him,
"Pursue, for you shall surely overtake them, [c]and you shall
surely rescue *all*."

5 [a]1 Sam. 18:7; 21:11
6 [a]1 Sam. 29:3; 27:8-12
8 [a]1 Sam. 27:10-12
9 [a]2 Sam. 14:17, 20; 19:27 [b]1 Sam. 29:4
10 [a]1 Chr. 12:19, 22
1 [1]I.e., South country [2]Lit., *smote* [a]1 Sam. 29:4, 11 [b]1 Sam. 15:7; 27:8-10 [c]1 Sam. 27:6, 8
2 [1]Lit., *they did not kill* [a]1 Sam. 27:11
5 [1]Lit., *wife* [a]1 Sam. 25:42, 43
6 [1]Lit., *bitter in soul* [a]Ex. 17:4 [b]1 Sam. 23:16; Ps. 18:2; 27:14
7 [a]1 Sam. 23:9
8 [a]1 Sam. 23:2, 4 [b]Ex. 15:9 [c]1 Sam. 30:18

9 So David went, [a]he and the six hundred men who were
with him, and came to the brook Besor, *where* those left behind remained.
10 But David pursued, he and four hundred men, for [a]two
hundred who were too exhausted to cross the brook Besor,
remained *behind*.
11 Now they found an Egyptian in the field and brought
him to David, and gave him bread and he ate, and they provided him water to drink.
12 And they gave him a piece of fig cake and two clusters
of raisins, and he ate; [a]then his spirit [1]revived. For he had not
eaten bread or drunk water for three days and three nights.
13 And David said to him, "To whom do you belong? And
where are you from?" And he said, "I am a young man of
Egypt, a servant of an Amalekite; and my master left me behind when I fell sick three days ago.
14 "We made a raid on [a]the [1]Negev of the Cherethites, and
on that which belongs to Judah, and on [b]the [1]Negev of Caleb,
and [c]we burned Ziklag with fire."
15 Then David said to him, "Will you bring me down to
this band?" And he said, "Swear to me by God that you will
not kill me or deliver me into the hands of my master, and I
will bring you down to this band."
16 And when he had brought him down, behold, they
were [1]spread over all the land, eating and drinking and [2]danc-
ing because of [a]all the great spoil that they had taken from
the land of the Philistines and from the land of Judah.
17 And David [1]slaughtered them [a]from the twilight [2]until
the evening of [3]the next day; and not a man of them escaped,
except four hundred young men who rode on [b]camels and fled.
18 So David recovered all that the Amalekites had taken,
and [1]rescued his two wives.
19 But nothing of theirs was missing, whether small or
great, sons or daughters, spoil or anything that they had taken
for themselves; [a]David brought *it* all back.
20 So David had [1]captured all the sheep and the cattle
which the people drove ahead of [2]the *other* livestock, and they
said, "[a]This is David's spoil."
21 When [a]David came to the two hundred men who were
too exhausted to follow David, who had also been left at the
brook Besor, and they went out to meet David and to meet the
people who were with him, then David approached the people
and greeted them.
22 Then all the wicked and worthless men among those
who went with David answered and said, "Because they did
not go with [1]us, we will not give them any of the spoil that we
have recovered, except to every man his wife and his children,
that they may lead *them* away and depart."
23 Then David said, "You must not do so, my brothers,
with what the LORD has given us, who has kept us and delivered
into our hand the band that came against us.
24 "And who will listen to you in this matter? For [a]as his
share is who goes down to the battle, so shall his share be who
stays by the baggage; they shall share alike."
25 And so it has been from that day forward, that he made
it a statute and an ordinance for Israel to this day.

9 [a]1 Sam. 27:2

10 [a]1 Sam. 30:9, 21

12 [1]Lit., *returned to him* [a]Judg. 15:19

14 [1]I.e., South country [a]1 Sam. 1:16; 2 Sam. 8:18; Ezek. 25:16 [b]Josh. 14:13; 21:11, 12 [c]1 Sam. 30:1

16 [1]Lit., *left* [2]Lit., *keeping a pilgrim-feast* [a]1 Sam. 30:14

17 [1]Lit., *smote* [2]Lit., *even until* [3]Lit., *their* [a]1 Sam. 11:11 [b]1 Sam. 15:3; Judg. 7:12

18 [1]Lit., *David rescued*

19 [a]1 Sam. 30:8

20 [1]Lit., *taken* [2]Lit., *those livestock* [a]1 Sam. 30:26-31

21 [a]1 Sam. 30:10

22 [1]Lit., *me*

24 [a]Num. 31:27; Josh. 22:8

26 Now when David came to Ziklag, he sent *some* of the
spoil to the elders of Judah, to his friends, saying, "Behold, [a]a
[1]gift for you from the spoil of [b]the enemies of the LORD:
27 to those who were in [a]Bethel, and to those who were in
[b]Ramoth of the South, and to those who were in [c]Jattir,
28 and to those who were in [a]Aroer, and to those who were
in [b]Siphmoth, and to those who were in [c]Eshtemoa,
29 and to those who were in Racal, and to those who were
in the cities of [a]the Jerahmeelites, and to those who were in the
cities of [b]the Kenites,
30 and to those who were in [a]Hormah, and to those who
were in [b]Bor-ashan, and to those who were in Athach,
31 and to those who were in [a]Hebron, and to all the places
where David himself and his men were accustomed to [b]go."

[a]CHAPTER 31

NOW the Philistines were fighting against Israel, and the
men of Israel fled from before the Philistines and fell slain [b]on
Mount Gilboa.
2 And the Philistines overtook Saul and his sons; and the
Philistines [1]killed Jonathan and Abinadab and Malchishua the
sons of Saul.
3 And [a]the battle went heavily against Saul, and the archers [1]hit him; and he was badly wounded by the archers.
4 [a]Then Saul said to his armor bearer, "Draw your sword
and pierce me through with it, lest [b]these uncircumcised come
and pierce me through and make sport of me." But his armor
bearer would not, for he was greatly afraid. [c]So Saul took his
sword and fell on it.
5 And when his armor bearer saw that Saul was dead, he
also fell on his sword and died with him.
6 Thus Saul died with his three sons, his armor bearer,
and all his men on that day together.
7 And when the men of Israel who were on the other side
of the valley, with those who were beyond the Jordan saw that
the men of Israel had fled and that Saul and his sons were
dead, they abandoned the cities and fled; then the Philistines
came and lived in them.
8 And it came about on the [1]next day when the Philistines came to strip the slain, that they found Saul and his three
sons fallen on Mount Gilboa.
9 And they cut off his head, and stripped off his weapons,
and sent *them* [1]throughout the land of the Philistines, [a]to carry
the good news [b]to the house of their idols and to the people.
10 And they put his weapons in the [1]temple of [a]Ash-
taroth, and [b]they fastened his body to the wall of [c]Beth-shan.
11 Now when [a]the inhabitants of Jabesh-gilead heard
[1]what the Philistines had done to Saul,
12 [a]all the valiant men rose and walked all night, and took
the body of Saul and the bodies of his sons from the wall of
Beth-shan, and they came to Jabesh, and [b]burned them there.
13 And they took their bones and [a]buried them under [b]the
tamarisk tree at Jabesh, and [c]fasted seven days.

26 [1]Lit., *blessing* [a]1 Sam. 25:27 [b]1 Sam. 18:17; 25:28

27 [a]Josh. 15:30; 19:4 [b]Josh. 19:8 [c]Josh. 15:48; 21:14

28 [a]1 Chr. 11:44 [b]1 Chr. 27:27 [c]Josh. 15:50

29 [a]1 Sam. 27:10 [b]1 Sam. 15:6

30 [a]Josh. 12:14; 15:30; 19:4 [b]Josh. 15:42; 19:7

31 [a]Josh. 14:13-15; 21:11-13; Num. 13:22 [b]1 Sam. 23:22

1 [a]1 Chr. 10:1-12 [b]1 Sam. 28:4

2 [1]Lit., *smote*

3 [1]Lit., *found* [a]2 Sam. 1:6

4 [a]Judg. 9:54 [b]Judg. 14:3 [c]2 Sam. 1:6, 10

8 [1]Lit., *morrow*

9 [1]Lit., *to . . . around* [a]2 Sam. 1:20 [b]Judg. 16:23, 24

10 [1]Lit., *house* [a]1 Sam. 7:3; Judg. 2:13 [b]1 Sam. 31:12; 2 Sam. 21:14 [c]Josh. 17:11

11 [1]Lit., *about him what* [a]1 Sam. 11:1-13

12 [a]2 Sam. 2:4-7 [b]2 Chr. 16:14

13 [a]2 Sam. 21:12-14 [b]1 Sam. 22:6 [c]2 Sam. 1:12

THE SECOND BOOK OF SAMUEL

David Learns of the Battle of Gilboa.

NOW it came about after [a]the death of Saul, when David
had returned from [b]the slaughter of the Amalekites, that David remained two days in Ziklag.
2 And it happened on the third day, that behold, [a]a man
came out of the camp from Saul, [b]with his clothes torn and
[1]dust on his head. And it came about when he came to David
that [c]he fell to the ground and prostrated himself.
3 Then David said to him, "From where do you come?"
And he said to him, "I have escaped from the camp of Israel."
4 And David said to him, "[a]How did things go? Please
tell me." And he said, "The people have fled from the battle,
and also many of the people have fallen and are dead; and Saul
and Jonathan his son are dead also."
5 So David said to the young man who told him, "How
do you know that Saul and his son Jonathan are dead?"
6 And the young man who told him said, "By chance I
happened to be on [a]Mount Gilboa, and behold, [b]Saul was
leaning on his spear. And behold, the chariots and the horsemen pursued him closely.
7 "And when he looked behind him, he saw me and called
to me. And I said, 'Here I am.'
8 "And he said to me, 'Who are you?' And I [1]answered
him, '[a]I am an Amalekite.'
9 "Then he said to me, 'Please stand beside me and kill
me; for agony has seized me because my [1]life still lingers in
me.'
10 "So I stood beside him [a]and killed him, because I knew
that he could not live after he had fallen. And [b]I took the
crown which *was* on his head and the bracelet which *was* on his
arm, and I have brought them here to my lord."
11 Then [a]David took hold of his clothes and tore them,
and *so* also *did* all the men who *were* with him.
12 And they mourned and wept and [a]fasted until evening
for Saul and his son Jonathan and for the people of the LORD
and the house of Israel, because they had fallen by the sword.
13 And David said to the young man who told him,
"Where are you from?" And he [1]answered, "[a]I am the son of
an alien, an Amalekite."
14 Then David said to him, "How is it you were not afraid
[a]to stretch out your hand to destroy the LORD's anointed?"
15 And David called one of the young men and said, "Go,
[1]cut him down." [a]So he struck him and he died.
16 And David said to him, "[a]Your blood is on your head,
for [b]your mouth has testified against you, saying, 'I have killed
the LORD's anointed.' "
17 Then [a]David chanted with this lament over Saul and
Jonathan his son
18 and he told *them* to teach the sons of Judah *the song of*
the bow; behold, it is written in [a]the book of Jashar.

1 [a]1 Sam. 31:6 [b]1 Sam. 30:1, 17, 26
2 [1]Lit., *ground* [a]2 Sam. 4:10 [b]1 Sam. 4:12 [c]1 Sam. 25:23
4 [a]1 Sam. 4:16
6 [a]1 Sam. 28:4; 31:6 [b]1 Sam. 31:2-4
8 [1]Lit., *said to* [a]1 Sam. 15:3; 30:1, 13, 17
9 [1]Lit., *whole life is still in me*
10 [a]Judg. 9:54 [b]2 Kin. 11:12
11 [a]Gen. 37:29, 34
12 [a]2 Sam. 3:35
13 [1]Lit., *said* [a]2 Sam. 1:8
14 [a]1 Sam. 24:6; 26:9, 11, 16
15 [1]Lit., *fall upon him* [a]2 Sam. 4:10, 12
16 [a]2 Sam. 3:28, 29 [b]2 Sam. 1:10; Luke 19:22
17 [a]2 Chr. 35:25
18 [a]Josh. 10:13

19 "[1]Your beauty, O Israel, is slain on your high places!
[a]How have the mighty fallen!
20 "[a]Tell *it* not in Gath,
Proclaim it not in the streets of Ashkelon;
Lest [b]the daughters of the Philistines rejoice,
Lest the daughters of [c]the uncircumcised exult.
21 "[a]O mountains of Gilboa,
[b]Let not dew or rain be on you, nor fields of offerings;
For there the shield of the mighty was defiled,
The shield of Saul, not [c]anointed with oil.
22 "[a]From the blood of the slain, from the fat of the mighty,
[b]The bow of Jonathan did not turn back,
And the sword of Saul did not return empty.
23 "Saul and Jonathan, beloved and pleasant in their life,
And in their death they were not parted;
[a]They were swifter than eagles,
[b]They were stronger than lions.
24 "O daughters of Israel, weep over Saul,
Who clothed you luxuriously in scarlet,
Who put ornaments of gold on your apparel.
25 "[a]How have the mighty fallen in the midst of the battle!
Jonathan is slain on your high places.
26 "I am distressed for you, my brother Jonathan;
You have been very pleasant to me.
[a]Your love to me was more wonderful
Than the love of women.
27 "[a]How have the mighty fallen,
And [b]the weapons of war perished!"

Chapter 2

THEN it came about afterwards that [a]David inquired of the
LORD, saying, "Shall I go up to one of the cities of Judah?"
And the LORD said to him, "Go up." So David said, "Where
shall I go up?" And He said, "[b]To Hebron."
2 So David went up there, and [a]his two wives also, Ahinoam the Jezreelitess and Abigail the [1]widow of Nabal the
Carmelite.
3 And [a]David brought up his men who *were* with him,
each with his household; and they lived in the cities of Hebron.
4 Then the men of Judah came and there [a]anointed David king over the house of Judah.
And they told David, saying, "It was [b]the men of Jabesh-
gilead who buried Saul."
5 And David sent messengers to the men of Jabesh-gilead, and said to them, "[a]May you be blessed of the LORD
because you have [1]shown this kindness to Saul your lord, and
have buried him.
6 "And now [a]may the LORD [1]show lovingkindness and
truth to you; and I also will [1]show this goodness to you, because you have done this thing.
7 "Now therefore let your hands be strong, and be [1]val-
iant; for Saul your lord is dead, and also the house of Judah
has anointed me king over them."
8 But [a]Abner the son of Ner, commander of Saul's army,

19 [1]Lit., *The* [a]2 Sam. 1:25, 27
20 [a]1 Sam. 31:8-13; Mic. 1:10 [b]Ex. 15:20, 21; 1 Sam. 18:6 [c]1 Sam. 14:6
21 [a]1 Sam. 31:1 [b]Ezek. 31:15 [c]Is. 21:5
22 [a]Deut. 32:42; Is. 34:6 [b]1 Sam. 18:4
23 [a]Jer. 4:13 [b]Judg. 14:18
25 [a]2 Sam. 1:19, 27
26 [a]1 Sam. 18:1-4
27 [a]2 Sam. 1:19, 25 [b]Is. 13:5
1 [a]1 Sam. 23:2, 4, 9-12 [b]Josh. 14:13; 1 Sam. 30:31
2 [1]Lit., *wife* [a]1 Sam. 25:42, 43
3 [a]1 Sam. 30:9; 1 Chr. 12:1
4 [a]2 Sam. 5:3, 5; 1 Sam. 16:13 [b]1 Sam. 31:11-13
5 [1]Lit., *done* [a]1 Sam. 23:21
6 [1]Lit., *do* [a]Ex. 34:6
7 [1]Lit., *sons of valor*
8 [a]1 Sam. 14:50

had taken [1]Ish-bosheth the son of Saul, and brought him over
to [b]Mahanaim.
9 And he made him king over [a]Gilead, over the [b]Ashur-
ites, over [c]Jezreel, over Ephraim, and over Benjamin, even
over all Israel.
10 Ish-bosheth, Saul's son, was forty years old when he
became king over Israel, and he was king for two years. The
house of Judah, however, followed David.
11 And [a]the [1]time that David was king in Hebron over the
house of Judah was seven years and six months.
12 Now Abner the son of Ner, went out from Mahanaim
to [a]Gibeon with the servants of Ish-bosheth the son of Saul.
13 And [a]Joab the son of Zeruiah and the servants of David
went out and met [1]them by the pool of Gibeon; and they sat
down, [2]one on the one side of the pool and [2]the other on the
other side of the pool.
14 Then Abner said to Joab, "Now let the young men
arise and [1a]hold a contest before us." And Joab said, "Let them
arise."
15 So they arose and went over by count, twelve for Benjamin and Ish-bosheth the son of Saul, and twelve of the servants
of David.
16 And each one of them seized his [1]opponent by the
head, and *thrust* his sword in his [2]opponent's side; so they
fell down together. Therefore that place was called [3]Helkath-
hazzurim, which is in Gibeon.
17 And that day the battle was very severe, and [a]Abner and
the men of Israel were beaten before the servants of David.
18 Now [a]the three sons of Zeruiah were there, Joab and
Abishai and Asahel; and Asahel *was* [b]*as* [1]swift-footed as one of
the gazelles which is in the field.
19 And Asahel pursued Abner and did not [1]turn to the
right or to the left from following Abner.
20 Then Abner looked behind him and said, "Is that you,
Asahel?" And he answered, "It is I."
21 So Abner said to him, "[1]Turn to your right or to your
left, and take hold of one of the young men for yourself, and
take for yourself his spoil." But Asahel was not willing to turn
aside from following him.
22 And Abner repeated again to Asahel, "Turn [1]aside
from following me. Why should I strike you to the ground?
[a]How then could I lift up my face to your brother Joab?"
23 However, he refused to turn aside; therefore Abner
struck him in the belly [a]with the butt end of the spear, so that
the spear came out at his back. And he fell there and died on
the spot. And it came about that all who came to the place
where [b]Asahel had fallen and died, stood still.
24 But Joab and Abishai pursued Abner, and when the sun
was going down, they came to the hill of Ammah, which is in
front of Giah by the way of the wilderness of Gibeon.
25 And the sons of Benjamin gathered together behind
Abner and became one band, and they stood on the top of a
certain hill.
26 Then Abner called to Joab and said, "Shall the sword
devour forever? Do you not know that it will be bitter in the

8 [1]I.e., Man of Shame; cf. 1 Chr. 8:33, *Eshbaal* [b]2 Sam. 17:24; Gen. 32:2, 10

9 [a]Josh. 22:9 [b]Judg. 1:32 [c]1 Sam. 29:1

11 [1]Lit., *number of days* [a]2 Sam. 5:5

12 [a]Josh. 10:12; 18:25

13 [1]Lit., *them together* [2]Lit., *these* [a]2 Sam. 8:16; 1 Chr. 2:16; 11:6

14 [1]Lit., *make sport* [a]2 Sam. 2:16, 17

16 [1]Lit., *fellow* [2]Lit., *fellow's* [3]I.e., the Field of Sword-edges

17 [a]2 Sam. 3:1

18 [1]Lit., *light in his feet* [a]1 Chr. 2:16 [b]1 Chr. 12:8; Hab. 3:19

19 [1]Lit., *turn to go to*

21 [1]Lit., *Turn for yourself*

22 [1]Lit., *aside for yourself* [a]2 Sam. 3:27

23 [a]1 Sam.26:7 [b]2 Sam. 20:12

end? How long will you [1]refrain from telling the people to turn
back from following their brothers?"
27 And Joab said, "As God lives, [a]if you had not spoken,
surely then the people would have gone away in the morning,
each from following his brother."
28 So Joab blew the trumpet; and all the people halted
and pursued Israel no longer, [a]nor did they continue to fight
any more.
29 Abner and his men then went through the Arabah all
that night; so they crossed the Jordan, walked all morning, and
came to [a]Mahanaim.
30 Then Joab returned from following Abner; when he
had gathered all the people together, [1]nineteen of David's
servants besides Asahel were missing.
31 But the servants of David had struck down many of
Benjamin and Abner's men, *so that* three hundred and sixty
men died.
32 And they took up Asahel and buried him in his father's
tomb which was in Bethlehem. Then Joab and his men went
all night until the day [1]dawned at Hebron.

Chapter 3

Now [a]there was a long war between the house of Saul and
the house of David; and David grew steadily stronger, but the
house of Saul grew weaker continually.
2 [a]Sons were born to David at Hebron: his first-born was
Amnon, by [b]Ahinoam the Jezreelitess;
3 and his second, Chileab, by Abigail the [1]widow of Nabal the Carmelite; and the third, Absalom the son of [a]Maacah,
the daughter of Talmai, [b]king of Geshur;
4 and the fourth, [a]Adonijah the son of Haggith; and the
fifth, Shephatiah the son of Abital;
5 and the sixth, Ithream, by David's wife Eglah. These
were born to David at Hebron.
6 And it came about while there was war between the
house of Saul and the house of David that Abner was making
himself strong in the house of Saul.
7 Now Saul had a concubine whose name was [a]Rizpah,
the daughter of Aiah; and [1]Ish-bosheth said to Abner, "Why
have you gone in to my father's concubine?"
8 Then Abner was very angry over the words of Ish-bosheth
and said, "[a]Am I a dog's head that belongs to Judah?
Today I show kindness to the house of Saul your father, to his
brothers and to his friends, and have not delivered you into the
hands of David; and yet today you charge me with a guilt
concerning the woman.
9 "[a]May God do so to Abner, and more also, if [b]as the
LORD has sworn to David, I do not accomplish this for him,
10 to transfer the kingdom from the house of Saul, and to
establish the throne of David over Israel and over Judah, [a]from
Dan even to Beersheba."
11 And he could no longer answer Abner a word, because
he was afraid of him.
12 Then Abner sent messengers to David in his place,
saying, "Whose is the land? Make your covenant with me, and

26 [1]Lit., *not tell the people*
27 [a]2 Sam. 2:14
28 [a]2 Sam. 3:1
29 [a]2 Sam. 2:8
30 [1]Lit., *nineteen men*
32 [1]Lit., *lighted on them*
1 [a]1 Kin. 14:30
2 [a]1 Chr. 3:1-3 [b]1 Sam. 25:42, 43
3 [1]Lit., *wife* [a]1 Sam. 27:8 [b]2 Sam. 14:32; 15:8
4 [a]1 Kin. 1:5
7 [1]So some ancient mss and versions M.T., *he* [a]2 Sam. 21:8-11
8 [a]2 Sam. 9:8; 1 Sam. 24:14
9 [a]1 Kin. 19:2 [b]1 Sam. 15:28; 25:28-31
10 [a]1 Sam. 3:20

behold, my hand shall be with you to bring all Israel over to
you."
13 And he said, "Good! I will make a covenant with you,
but I demand one thing of you, [1]namely, [a]you shall not see my
face unless you [b]first bring Michal, Saul's daughter, when you
come to see [2]me."
14 So David sent messengers to Ish-bosheth, Saul's son,
saying, "Give me my wife Michal, to whom I was betrothed
[a]for a hundred foreskins of the Philistines."
15 And Ish-bosheth sent and took her from *her* husband,
from [1]Paltiel the son of Laish.
16 But her husband went with her, weeping as he went,
and followed her as far as [a]Bahurim. Then Abner said to him,
"Go, return." So he returned.
17 Now Abner had [1]consultation with [a]the elders of Israel,
saying, "In times past you were seeking for David to be king
over you.
18 "Now then, do *it*! For the LORD has spoken of David,
saying, '[a]By the hand of My servant David [1]I will save My
people Israel from the hand of the Philistines and from the
hand of all their enemies.' "
19 And Abner also spoke in the hearing of Benjamin; and
in addition Abner went to speak in the hearing of David in
Hebron all that seemed good to Israel and to [a]the whole house
of Benjamin.
20 Then Abner and twenty men with him came to David
at Hebron. And David made a feast for Abner and the men
who were with him.
21 And Abner said to David, "Let me arise and go, and
[a]gather all Israel to my lord the king that they may make a
covenant with you, and that [b]you may be king over all that
your soul desires." So David sent Abner away, and he went in
peace.
22 And behold, [a]the servants of David and Joab came
from a raid and brought much spoil with them; but Abner was
not with David in Hebron, for he had sent him away, and he
had gone in peace.
23 When Joab and all the army that was with him arrived,
they told Joab, saying, "Abner the son of Ner came to the
king, and he has sent him away, and he has gone in peace."
24 Then Joab came to the king and said, "What have you
done? Behold, Abner came to you; why then have you sent
him away and he is already gone?
25 "You know Abner the son of Ner, that he came to deceive you and to learn of [a]your going out and coming in, and
to find out all that you are doing."
26 When Joab came out from David, he sent messengers
after Abner, and they brought him back from the well of Sirah;
but David did not know *it*.
27 So when Abner returned to Hebron, Joab took him
aside into the middle of the gate to speak with him privately,
and there [a]he struck him in the belly so that he died on
account of the blood of Asahel his brother.
28 And afterward when David heard it, he said, "I and my
kingdom are innocent before the LORD forever of the blood of
Abner the son of Ner.

13 [1]Lit. *saying* [2]Lit., *my face* [a]Gen. 43:3 [b]1 Sam. 18:20; 19:11

14 [a]1 Sam. 18:25, 27

15 [1]I.e., Palti; 1 Sam. 25:44

16 [a]2 Sam. 16:5

17 [1]Lit., *a word* [a]1 Sam. 8:4

18 [1]So many ancient mss and versions M.T., *he* [a]1 Sam. 9:16; 15:28

19 [a]1 Sam. 10:20, 21

21 [a]2 Sam. 3:10, 12 [b]1 Kin. 11:37

22 [a]1 Sam. 27:8

25 [a]Deut. 28:6; 1 Sam. 29:6

27 [a]2 Sam. 2:23; 20:9, 10; 1 Kin. 2:5

29 "[a]May it [1]fall on the head of Joab and on all his father's
house; and may there not fail from the house of Joab [b]one who
has a discharge, or who is a leper, or who takes hold of a
distaff, or who falls by the sword, or who lacks bread."
30 So Joab and Abishai his brother killed Abner [a]because
he had put their brother Asahel to death in the battle at
Gibeon.
31 Then David said to Joab and to all the people who
were with him, "[a]Tear your clothes and gird on sackcloth and
lament before Abner." And King David walked behind the
bier.
32 Thus they buried Abner in Hebron; and the king lifted
up his voice and wept at the grave of Abner, and all the people
wept.
33 And [a]the king chanted a *lament* for Abner and said,
"Should Abner die as a fool dies?
34 "Your hands were not bound, nor your feet put in
fetters;
As one falls before the [1]wicked, you have fallen."
And all the people wept again over him.
35 Then all the people came [a]to [1]persuade David to eat
bread while it was still day; but David vowed, saying, "[b]May
God do so to me, and more also, if I taste bread or anything
else [c]before the sun goes down."
36 Now all the people took note *of it*, and it [1]pleased
them, just as everything the king did [2]pleased all the people.
37 So all the people and all Israel understood that day that
it had not been *the will* of the king to put Abner the son of
Ner to death.
38 Then the king said to his servants, "Do you not know
that a prince and a great man has fallen this day in Israel?
39 "And I am [a]weak today, though anointed king; and these
men [b]the sons of Zeruiah are too difficult for me. [c]May the
LORD repay the evildoer according to his evil."

Chapter 4

Now when [1]Ish-bosheth, Saul's son, heard that [a]Abner had
died in Hebron, [2b]he lost courage, and all Israel was disturbed.
2 And Saul's son *had* two men who were commanders of
bands: the name of the one was Baanah and the name of the
other Rechab, sons of Rimmon the Beerothite, of the sons of
Benjamin (for [a]Beeroth is also considered [b]*part* of Benjamin,
3 and the Beerothites fled to [a]Gittaim, and have been
aliens there until this day).
4 Now [a]Jonathan, Saul's son, had a son crippled in his
feet. He was five years old when the [b]report of Saul and Jonathan came from Jezreel, and his nurse took him up and fled.
And it happened that in her hurry to flee, he fell and became
lame. And his name was [1]Mephibosheth.
5 So the sons of Rimmon the Beerothite, Rechab and
Baanah, departed and came [a]to the house of Ish-bosheth in the
heat of the day while he was taking his midday rest.
6 [1]And they came to the middle of the house as [2]if to get
wheat, and [a]they struck him in the belly; and Rechab and
Baanah his brother escaped.

29 [1]Lit., *whirl* [a]Deut. 21:6-9; 1 Kin. 2:31-33 [b]Lev. 13:46

30 [a]2 Sam. 2:23

31 [a]Gen. 37:34; Judg. 11:35

33 [a]2 Sam. 1:17; 2 Chr. 35:25

34 [1]Lit., *sons of wickedness*

35 [1]Lit., *cause* [a]2 Sam. 12:17 [b]1 Sam. 3:17 [c]2 Sam. 1:12

36 [1]Lit., *was good in their eyes* [2]Lit., *was good in the eyes of all*

39 [a]1 Chr. 29:1; 2 Chr. 13:7 [b]2 Sam. 19:5-7 [c]1 Kin. 2:32-34

1 [1]So some ancient mss.; M.T., *he* [2]Lit., *his hands dropped* [a]2 Sam. 3:27 [b]Ezra 4:4

2 [a]Josh. 9:17 [b]Josh. 18:25

3 [a]Neh. 11:33

4 [1]I.e., Merib-baal, 1 Chr. 8:34; 9:40 [a]2 Sam. 9:3, 6 [b]1 Sam. 31:1-4

5 [a]2 Sam. 2:8

6 [1]Lit., *And here* [2]Lit., *takers of wheat* [a]2 Sam. 2:23

7 Now when they came into the house, as he was lying on
his bed in his bedroom, they struck him and killed him and
beheaded him. And they took his head and [1a]traveled by way
of Arabah all night.
8 Then they brought the head of Ish-bosheth to David at
Hebron, and said to the king, "Behold, the head of Ish-bosheth,
[a]the son of Saul, your enemy, who sought your life; thus
the LORD has given my lord the king vengeance this day on
Saul and his [1]descendants."
9 And David answered Rechab and Baanah his brother,
sons of Rimmon the Beerothite, and said to them, "As the
LORD lives, [a]who has redeemed my life from all distress,
10 [a]when one told me, saying, 'Behold, Saul is dead,' and
[1]thought he was bringing good news, I seized him and killed
him in Ziklag, which was the reward I gave him for *his* news.
11 "How much more, when wicked men have killed a righteous man in his own house on his bed, shall I not now
[a]require his blood from your hand, and [1]destroy you from the
earth?"
12 Then [a]David commanded the young men, and they
killed them and cut off their hands and feet, and hung them
up beside the pool in Hebron. But they took the head of Ish-
bosheth [b]and buried it in the grave of Abner in Hebron.

CHAPTER 5

[a]THEN all the tribes of Israel came to David at Hebron and
[1]said, "Behold, we are [b]your bone and your flesh.
2 "Previously, when Saul was king over us, [a]you were the
one who led Israel out and in. And the LORD said to you, '[b]You
will shepherd My people Israel, and you will be [c]a ruler over
Israel.' "
3 So all the elders of Israel came to the king at Hebron,
and King David [a]made a covenant with them before the LORD
at Hebron; then [b]they anointed David king over Israel.
4 David was [a]thirty years old when he became king, *and*
[b]he reigned forty years.
5 At Hebron [a]he reigned over Judah seven years and six
months, and in Jerusalem he reigned thirty-three years over all
Israel and Judah.
6 [a]Now the king and his men went to [b]Jerusalem against
the Jebusites, the inhabitants of the land, and they said to
[1]David, "You shall not come in here, but the blind and lame
shall turn you away"; [2]thinking, "David cannot enter here."
7 Nevertheless, David captured the stronghold of Zion,
that is [a]the city of David.
8 And David said on that day, "Whoever would strike
the Jebusites, let him reach the lame and the blind who are
hated by David's soul through the water tunnel." Therefore
they say, "The blind or the lame shall not come into the
house."
9 So David lived in the stronghold, and called it [a]the city
of David. And David built all around from [1b]Millo and inward.
10 And [a]David became greater and greater, for the LORD
God of hosts was with him.
11 [a]Then Hiram king of Tyre sent messengers to David

7 [1]Lit., *went*
[a]2 Sam. 2:29

8 [1]Lit., *seed*
[a]1 Sam. 24:4; 25:29

9 [a]1 Kin. 1:29

10 [1]Lit., *he was as a bearer of good news in his own eyes*
[a]2 Sam. 1:2, 4, 15

11 [1]Lit., *burn*
[a]Gen. 9:5; Ps. 9:12

12 [a]2 Sam. 1:15
[b]2 Sam. 3:32

1 [1]Lit., *said, saying*
[a]1 Chr. 11:1-3 [b]2 Sam. 19:13

2 [a]1 Sam. 18:5, 13, 16
[b]2 Sam. 7:7; Gen. 49:24
[c]1 Sam. 25:30

3 [a]2 Sam. 3:21
[b]2 Sam. 2:4; 1 Sam. 16:13

4 [a]Gen. 41:46; Num. 4:3; Luke 3:23 [b]1 Kin. 2:11; 1 Chr. 26:31

5 [a]2 Sam. 2:11

6 [1]Lit., *David, saying*
[2]Lit., *saying*
[a]1 Chr. 11:4-9 [b]Josh. 15:63; 18:28; Judg. 1:21

7 [a]2 Sam. 6:12, 16; 1 Kin. 2:10; 9:24

9 [1]I.e., citadel
[a]2 Sam. 5:7 [b]1 Kin. 9:15, 24

10 [a]2 Sam. 3:1

11 [a]1 Chr. 14:1; 1 Kin. 5:2, 10, 18

with cedar trees and carpenters and stonemasons; and [b]they
built a house for David.
12 And David realized that the LORD had established him
as king over Israel, and that He had exalted his kingdom for
the sake of His people Israel.
13 Meanwhile [a]David took more concubines and wives
from Jerusalem, after he came from Hebron; and more sons
and daughters were born to David.
14 Now [a]these are the names of those who were born to
him in Jerusalem: Shammua, Shobab, Nathan, Solomon,
15 Ibhar, Elishua, Nepheg, Japhia,
16 Elishama, Eliada and Eliphelet.
17 When the Philistines heard that they had anointed David king over Israel, [a]all the Philistines went up to seek out
David; and when David heard *of it*, he went down to the
[b]stronghold.
18 Now the Philistines came and spread themselves out in
[a]the valley of Rephaim.
19 Then [a]David inquired of the LORD, saying, "Shall I go
up against the Philistines? Wilt Thou give them into my
hand?" And [b]the LORD said to David, "Go up, for I will certainly give the Philistines into your hand."
20 So David came to [a]Baal-perazim, and [1]defeated them
there; and he said, "The LORD has broken through my enemies
before me like the break-through of waters." Therefore he
named that place [2]Baal-perazim.
21 And they abandoned their idols there, so [a]David and
his men carried them away.
22 Now [a]the Philistines came up once again and spread
themselves out in the valley of Rephaim.
23 And when [a]David inquired of the LORD, He said, "You
shall not go *directly* up; circle around behind them and come
at them in front of the [1]balsam trees.
24 "And it shall be, when [a]you hear the sound of marching
in the tops of the [1]balsam trees, then you shall act promptly,
for then [b]the LORD will have gone out before you to strike the
army of the Philistines."
25 Then David did so, just as the LORD had commanded
him, and struck down the Philistines from [a]Geba until you
come to [b]Gezer.

CHAPTER 6

[a]NOW David again gathered all the chosen men of Israel,
thirty thousand.
2 And David arose and went with all the people who
were with him to [a]Baale-judah, to bring up from there the ark
of God which is called by the [b]Name, the very name of the
LORD of hosts who [c]is [1]enthroned *above* the cherubim.
3 And they [1]placed the ark of God on [a]a new cart that
they might bring it from the house of Abinadab which was on
the hill; and Uzzah and Ahio, the sons of Abinadab, were
leading the new cart.
4 So [a]they brought it with the ark of God from the house
of Abinadab, which was on the hill; and Ahio was walking
ahead of the ark.

11 [b]Ps. 30:title
13 [a]Deut. 17:17; 1 Chr. 3:9
14 [a]1 Chr. 3:5-8
17 [a]1 Sam. 29:1 [b]2 Sam. 23:14; 1 Chr. 11:16
18 [a]Gen. 14:5; Josh. 15:8; 17:15; 18:16
19 [a]1 Sam. 23:2 [b]1 Sam. 2:1
20 [1]Lit., *David smote* [2]I.e., the master of break-through [a]Is. 28:21
21 [a]1 Chr. 14:12
22 [a]2 Sam. 5:18
23 [1]Or, *baka-shrubs* [a]2 Sam. 5:19
24 [1]Or, *baka-shrubs* [a]2 Kin. 7:6 [b]Judg. 4:14
25 [a]Is. 28:21 [b]Josh. 12:12; 21:21
1 [a]1 Chr. 13:5-14
2 [1]Lit., *sitting* [a]Josh. 15:9, 10; 1 Sam. 7:1 [b]Lev. 24:16 [c]Ex. 25:22
3 [1]Lit., *caused to ride* [a]1 Sam. 6:7
4 [a]1 Sam. 7:1

5 Meanwhile, David and all the house of Israel [a]were
celebrating before the LORD [b]with all kinds of *instruments*
made of [1]fir wood, and with lyres, harps, tambourines, casta-
nets and cymbals.
6 But when they came to the threshing floor of [a]Nacon,
Uzzah [b]reached out toward the ark of God and took hold of it,
for the oxen nearly upset *it*.
7 And the anger of the LORD burned against Uzzah, and
[a]God struck him down there for [1]his irreverence; and he died
there by the ark of God.
8 And David became angry because [1]of the LORD's outburst against Uzzah, and that place is called [2]Perez-uzzah to
this day.
9 So David was afraid of the LORD that day; and he said,
"How can the ark of the LORD come to me?"
10 And David was unwilling to move the ark of the LORD
into the city of David with him; but David took it aside to the
house of [a]Obed-edom the Gittite.
11 Thus the ark of the LORD remained in the house of
Obed-edom the Gittite three months, and the LORD blessed
Obed-edom and all his household.
12 Now it was told King David, saying, "The LORD has
blessed the house of Obed-edom and all that belongs to him,
on account of the ark of God." [a]And David went and brought
up the ark of God from the house of Obed-edom into [b]the city
of David with gladness.
13 And so it was, that when the bearers of the ark of the
LORD had gone six paces, he sacrificed an ox and a fatling.
14 And [a]David was dancing before the LORD with all *his*
might, and David was [1b]wearing a linen ephod.
15 So David and all the house of Israel were bringing up
the ark of the LORD with shouting and the sound of the
trumpet.
16 Then it happened *as* the ark of the LORD came into the
city of David that [a]Michal the daughter of Saul looked out of
the window and saw King David leaping and dancing before
the LORD; and she despised him in her heart.
17 So they brought in the ark of the LORD and set it [a]in its
place inside the tent which David had pitched for it; and [b]Da-
vid offered burnt offerings and peace offerings before the
LORD.
18 And when David had finished offering the burnt offering and the peace offering, [a]he blessed the people in the name
of the LORD of hosts.
19 Further, he distributed to all the people, to all the
multitude of Israel, both to men and women, a cake of bread
and one of dates and one of raisins to each one. Then all the
people departed each to his house.
20 But when David returned to bless his household, Michal
the daughter of Saul came out to meet David and said,
"How the king of Israel distinguished himself today! [1a]He uncovered himself today in the eyes of his servants' maids as one
of the foolish ones shamelessly uncovers himself!"
21 So David said to Michal, "[a]*It was* before the LORD,
who chose me above your father and above all his house, to

5 [1]Or, *cypress*
[a]1 Sam. 18:6, 7
[b]1 Chr. 13:7, 8

6 [a]1 Chr. 13:9
[b]Num. 4:15, 19, 20

7 [1]Lit., *the*
[a]1 Sam. 6:19

8 [1]Lit., *the LORD broke through a break-through*
[2]I.e., the break-through of Uzzah

10 [a]1 Chr. 26:4-8

12 [a]1 Chr. 15:25-16:3
[b]1 Kin. 8:1

14 [1]Lit., *girded with*
[a]Ex. 15:20, 21; Judg. 11:34
[b]Ex. 19:6; 1 Sam. 2:18, 28

16 [a]2 Sam. 3:14

17 [a]1 Chr. 15:1; 2 Chr. 1:4
[b]1 Kin. 8:62-65

18 [a]1 Kin. 8:14, 15

20 [1]Lit., *who*
[a]2 Sam. 6:14, 16

21 [a]1 Sam. 13:14; 15:28

appoint me ruler over the people of the LORD, over Israel;
therefore I will celebrate before the LORD.
22 "And I will be more lightly esteemed than this and will
be humble in my own eyes, but with the maids of whom you
have spoken, with them I will be distinguished."
23 And Michal the daughter of Saul had no child to the
day of her death.

CHAPTER 7

[a]NOW it came about when the king lived in his house, and
the LORD had given him rest on every side from all his enemies,
2 that the king said to [a]Nathan the prophet, "See now, I
dwell in [b]a house of cedar, but the ark of God [c]dwells within
tent curtains."
3 And Nathan said to the king, "[a]Go, do all that is in
your mind, for the LORD is with you."
4 But it came about in the same night that the word of
the LORD came to Nathan, saying,
5 "Go and say to My servant David, 'Thus says the LORD:
"[a]Are you the one who should build Me a house to dwell in?
6 "For [a]I have not dwelt in a house since the day I brought
up the sons of Israel from Egypt, even to this day; but I have
been moving about [b]in a tent, even in a [1]tabernacle.
7 "[a]Wherever I have gone with all the sons of Israel, did I
speak a word with one of the tribes of Israel, [b]which I commanded to shepherd My people Israel, saying, 'Why have you
not built Me a house of cedar?' " '
8 "Now therefore, thus you shall say to My servant David,
'Thus says the LORD of hosts, "[a]I took you from the pasture,
from following the sheep, [b]that you should be ruler over My
people Israel.
9 "And [a]I have been with you wherever you have gone and
[b]have cut off all your enemies from before you; and I will
make you a great name, like the names of the great men who
are on the earth.
10 "I will also appoint a place for My people Israel and
[a]will plant them, that they may live in their own place and not
be disturbed again, [b]nor will the [1]wicked afflict them any more
as formerly,
11 even [a]from the day that I commanded judges to be
over My people Israel; and [b]I will give you rest from all your
enemies. The LORD also declares to you that [c]the LORD will
make a house for you.
12 "[a]When your days are complete and you lie down with
your fathers, I will raise up your [1]descendant after you, who
will come forth from [2]you, and I will establish his kingdom.
13 "[a]He shall build a house for My name, and [b]I will establish the throne of his kingdom forever.
14 "[a]I will be a father to him and he will be a son to Me;
[b]when he commits iniquity, I will correct him with the rod of
men and the strokes of the sons of men,
15 but My lovingkindness shall not depart from him, [a]as I
took *it* away from Saul, whom I removed from before you.
16 "And [a]your house and your kingdom shall endure before
[1]Me forever; your throne shall be established forever." ' "

1 [a]1 Chr. 17:1-27

2 [a]2 Sam. 6:17; 12:1; 1 Kin. 1:22; 1 Chr. 29:29; 2 Chr. 9:29 [b]2 Sam. 5:11 [c]Ex. 26:1

3 [a]1 Kin. 8:17, 18

5 [a]1 Kin. 5:3, 4; 8:19

6 [1]Lit., *dwelling place* [a]Josh. 18:1; 1 Kin. 8:16 [b]Ex. 40:18, 34

7 [a]Lev. 26:11, 12 [b]2 Sam. 5:2

8 [a]1 Sam. 16:11, 12; Ps. 78:70, 71 [b]1 Sam. 6:21

9 [a]1 Sam. 5:10 [b]Ps. 18:37-42

10 [1]Lit., *sons of wickedness* [a]Ex. 15:17; Is. 5:2, 7 [b]Ps. 89:22, 23; Is. 60:18

11 [a]Judg. 2:14-16; 1 Sam. 12:9-11 [b]2 Sam. 7:1 [c]1 Sam. 7:27; 1 Sam. 25:28

12 [1]Lit., *seed* [2]Lit., *your bowels* [a]1 Kin. 2:1

13 [a]1 Kin. 6:12; 8:19 [b]Is. 9:7; 49:8

14 [a]Heb. 1:5; Ps. 89:26, 27 [b]1 Kin. 11:34; Ps. 89:30-33

15 [a]1 Sam. 15:23; 16:14

16 [1]So with Gk. and some ancient mss.; M.T. *you* [a]2 Sam. 7:13; Ps. 89:36, 37

17 In accordance with all these words and all this vision, so
Nathan spoke to David.
18 Then David the king went in and sat before the LORD,
and he said, "[a]Who am I, O Lord [1]GOD, and what is my house,
that Thou hast brought me this far?
19 "And yet this was insignificant in Thine eyes, O Lord
GOD, [a]for Thou hast spoken also of the house of Thy servant
concerning the distant future. And [b]this is the [1]custom of man,
O Lord GOD.
20 "And again what more can David say to Thee? For [a]Thou
knowest Thy servant, O Lord GOD!
21 "[a]For the sake of Thy word, and according to Thine
own heart, Thou hast done all this greatness to let Thy servant
know.
22 "For this reason [a]Thou art great, O Lord GOD; for [b]there
is none like Thee, and there is no God besides Thee, [c]according
to all that we have heard with our ears.
23 "And [a]what one nation on the earth is like Thy people
Israel, whom God went to redeem for Himself as a people and
to make a name for Himself, and [b]to do a great thing for Thee
and awesome things for Thy land, before [c]Thy people whom
[d]Thou hast redeemed for Thyself from Egypt, *from* nations
and their gods?
24 "For [a]Thou hast established for Thyself Thy people Israel
as Thine own people forever, and [b]Thou, O LORD, hast
become their God.
25 "Now therefore, O LORD God, the word that Thou hast
spoken concerning Thy servant and his house, confirm *it* forever,
and do as Thou hast spoken,
26 [a]that Thy name may be magnified forever, by saying,
'The LORD of hosts is God over Israel'; and may the house of
Thy servant David be established before Thee.
27 "For Thou, O LORD of hosts, the God of Israel, hast
[1]made a revelation to Thy servant, saying, '[a]I will build you a
house'; therefore Thy servant has found [2]courage to pray this
prayer to Thee.
28 "And now, O Lord GOD, Thou art God, and [a]Thy words
are truth, and Thou hast [1]promised this good thing to Thy
servant.
29 "Now therefore may it please Thee to bless the house of
Thy servant, that it may continue forever before Thee. For
Thou, O Lord GOD, hast spoken; and [a]with Thy blessing may
the house of Thy servant be blessed forever."

CHAPTER 8

[a]NOW after this it came about that David [1]defeated the
Philistines and subdued them; and David took [2]control of the
chief city from the hand of the Philistines.
2 And [a]he [1]defeated [b]Moab, and measured them with the
line, making them lie down on the ground; and he measured
two lines to put to death and one full line to keep alive. And
[c]the Moabites became servants to David, [d]bringing tribute.
3 Then David [1]defeated [a]Hadadezer the son of Rehob
king of Zobah, as [b]he went to restore his [2]rule at the [3]River.
4 And David captured from him 1,700 horsemen and

18 [1]YHWH, usually rendered LORD and so throughout the chap. [a]Ex. 3:11; 1 Sam. 18:18

19 [1]Or, *law* [a]2 Sam. 7:11-16; 1 Chr. 17:17 [b]Is. 55:8, 9

20 [a]1 Sam. 16:7; John 21:17

21 [a]1 Chr. 17:19

22 [a]Deut. 3:24; Ps. 48:1; 86:10 [b]Ex. 15:11; 1 Sam. 2:2 [c]Ex. 10:2; Ps. 44:1

23 [a]Deut. 4:32-38 [b]Deut. 10:21 [c]Deut. 15:15 [d]Deut. 9:26

24 [a]Deut. 32:6 [b]Gen. 17:7, 8; Ex. 6:7

26 [a]Ps. 72:18, 19

27 [1]Lit., *uncovered the ear of* [2]Lit., *his heart* [a]2 Sam. 7:13

28 [1]Or, *spoken* [a]Ex. 34:6; John 17:17

29 [a]Num. 6:24-26

1 [1]Lit., *smote* [2]Lit., *the bridle of the mother city* [a]1 Chr. 18

2 [1]Lit., *smote* [a]Num. 24:17 [b]1 Sam. 22:3, 4 [c]2 Sam. 8:6; 1 Kin. 4:21; 2 Kin. 3:4 [d]2 Kin. 17:3

3 [1]Lit., *smote* [2]Lit., *hand* [3]I.e., Euphrates [a]2 Kin. 10:16, 19; 1 Sam. 14:47 [b]2 Kin. 10:15-19

20,000 foot soldiers; and David [a]hamstrung the chariot horses,
but reserved *enough* of them for 100 chariots.
5 And when [1a]the Syrians of Damascus came to help
Hadadezer, king of Zobah, David [2]killed 22,000 men of [1]the
Syrians.
6 Then David put garrisons in [1]Syria of Damascus, and
[1a]the Syrians became servants to David, bringing tribute. And
[b]the LORD helped David wherever he went.
7 And David took the shields of gold which were [1]carried
by the servants of Hadadezer, and brought them to Jerusalem.
8 And from [1]Betah and from [a]Berothai, cities of Hadadezer, King David took a very large amount of bronze.
9 Now when Toi king of [a]Hamath heard that David had
[1]defeated all the army of Hadadezer,
10 Toi sent [1]Joram his son to King David to [2]greet him
and bless him, because he had fought against Hadadezer and
[3]defeated him; for Hadadezer [4]had been at war with Toi. And
[5]*Joram* brought with him articles of silver, of gold and of
bronze.
11 King David also dedicated [a]these to the LORD, with the
silver and gold that he had dedicated from all the nations
which he had subdued:
12 from [1]Syria and [a]Moab and [b]the sons of Ammon and
[c]the Philistines and [d]Amalek, and from the spoil of Hadadezer,
son of Rehob, king of Zobah.
13 So [a]David made a name *for himself* when he returned
from [1]killing 18,000 [2]Syrians in [b]the Valley of Salt.
14 And he put garrisons in Edom. In all Edom he put
garrisons, and [a]all the Edomites became servants to David.
And [b]the LORD helped David wherever he went.
15 So David reigned over all Israel; and David [1]adminis-
tered justice and righteousness for all his people.
16 And Joab the son of Zeruiah *was* over the army, and
[a]Jehoshaphat the son of Ahilud *was* [b]recorder.
17 And [a]Zadok the son of Ahitub and Ahimelech the son
of Abiathar *were* [b]priests, and Seraiah *was* [c]secretary.
18 And [a]Benaiah the son of Jehoiada [1]was over the [b]Cher-
ethites and the Pelethites; and David's sons were [2c]chief
ministers.

CHAPTER 9

THEN David said, "Is there yet [1]anyone left of the house of
Saul, [a]that I may show him kindness for Jonathan's sake?"
2 Now there was a servant of the house of Saul whose
name was Ziba, and they called him to David; and the king
said to him, "Are you [a]Ziba?" And he said, "*I am* your
servant."
3 And the king said, "Is there not yet anyone of the
house of Saul to whom I may show the [a]kindness of God?"
And Ziba said to the king, "[b]There is still a son of Jonathan
who is crippled in both feet."
4 So the king said to him, "Where is he?" And Ziba said
to the king, "Behold, he is [a]in the house of Machir the son of
Ammiel in Lo-debar."

4 [a]Josh. 11:6, 9

5 [1]Heb., *Aram* [2]Lit., *smote* [a]1 Kin. 11:23-25; 15:18

6 [1]Heb., *Aram* [a]2 Sam. 8:2 [b]2 Sam. 3:18

7 [1]Lit., *on*

8 [1]Or, *Tibhath*, 1 Chr. 18:8 [a]Ezek. 47:16

9 [1]Lit., *smitten* [a]1 Kin. 8:65; 2 Chr. 8:4

10 [1]Or, *Hadoram*, 1 Chr. 18:10 [2]Lit., *ask him of his welfare* [3]Lit., *smitten* [4]Lit., *was a man of wars* [5]Lit., *there were in his hand*

11 [a]1 Kin. 7:51

12 [1]Heb., *Aram;* some mss. read, *Edom* [a]2 Sam. 8:2 [b]2 Sam. 10:14 [c]2 Sam. 5:17-25 [d]1 Sam. 27:8; 30:17-20

13 [1]Lit., *smiting* [2]Heb., *Aram;* some mss. read, *Edom* [a]2 Sam. 7:9 [b]2 Kin. 14:7

14 [a]Gen. 27:37-40; Num. 24:17, 18 [b]2 Sam. 8:6

15 [1]Lit., *was doing*

16 [a]1 Kin. 4:3 [b]2 Kin. 18:18, 37

17 [a]1 Chr. 6:4-8 [b]1 Chr. 16:39, 40 [c]2 Kin. 18:18

18 [1]Lit., *and the Cherethites* [2]Lit., *priests* [a]1 Kin. 4:4 [b]2 Sam. 15:18; 20:7, 23; 1 Sam. 30:14; 1 Kin. 1:38, 44 [c]1 Chr. 18:17

1 [1]Lit., *he who is* [a]1 Sam. 20:14-17, 42

2 [a]2 Sam. 16:1-4; 19:17, 29

3 [a]1 Sam. 20:14 [b]2 Sam. 4:4

4 [a]1 Sam. 17:27-29

5 Then King David sent and brought him from the house
of Machir the son of Ammiel, from Lo-debar.
6 And [a]Mephibosheth, the son of Jonathan the son of
Saul, came to David and [b]fell on his face and prostrated himself. And David said, "Mephibosheth." And he said, "Here is
your servant!"
7 And David said to him, "Do not fear, for [a]I will surely
show kindness to you for the sake of your father Jonathan, and
[b]will restore to you all the [1]land of your [2]grandfather Saul; and
[c]you shall [3]eat at my table regularly."
8 Again he prostrated himself and said, "What is your
servant, that you should regard [a]a dead dog like me?"
9 Then the king called Saul's servant Ziba, and said to
him, "[a]All that belonged to Saul and to all his house I have
given to your master's [1]grandson.
10 "And you and your sons and your servants shall cultivate
the land for him, and you shall bring in *the produce* so that
your master's grandson may have food; nevertheless [a]Mephib-
osheth your master's grandson [b]shall [1]eat at my table regularly." Now Ziba had fifteen sons and twenty servants.
11 Then Ziba said to the king, "According to all that my
lord the king commands his servant so your servant will do."
So Mephibosheth ate at [1]David's table as one of the king's
sons.
12 And Mephibosheth had a young son whose name was
[a]Mica. And all who lived in the house of Ziba were servants to
Mephibosheth.
13 So Mephibosheth lived in Jerusalem, for [a]he ate at the
king's table regularly. Now [b]he was lame in both feet.

Chapter 10

[a]NOW it happened afterwards that [b]the king of the Ammonites died, and Hanun his son became king in his place.
2 Then David said, "I will show kindness to Hanun the
son of [a]Nahash, just as his father showed kindness to me." So
David sent [1]some of his servants to console him concerning his
father. But when David's servants came to the land of the
Ammonites,
3 the princes of the Ammonites said to Hanun their lord,
"[1]Do you think that David is honoring your father because he
has sent consolers to you? [a]Has David not sent his servants to
you in order to search the city, to spy it out and overthrow it?"
4 So Hanun took David's servants and [a]shaved off half of
their beards, and [b]cut off their garments in the middle as far as
their hips, and sent them away.
5 When they told *it* to David, he sent to meet them, for
the men were greatly humiliated. And the king said, "[1]Stay at
Jericho until your beards grow, and then return."
6 Now when the sons of Ammon saw that [a]they had
become odious to David, the sons of Ammon sent and [b]hired
[1]the Syrians of [c]Beth-rehob and [1]the [d]Syrians of Zobah, 20,000
foot soldiers, and the king of [e]Maacah with 1,000 men, and the
men of Tob with 12,000 men.
7 When David heard *of it*, he sent Joab and all the army,
the mighty men.

6 [a]2 Sam. 16:4; 19:24-30 [b]1 Sam. 25:23

7 [1]Lit., *field* [2]Lit., *father* [3]Lit., *eat bread* [a]2 Sam. 9:1, 3 [b]2 Sam. 12:8 [c]2 Sam. 19:28; 1 Kin. 2:7; 2 Kin. 25:29

8 [a]2 Sam. 16:9

9 [1]Lit., *son* [a]2 Sam. 16:4; 19:29

10 [1]Lit., *eat bread* [a]2 Sam. 9:7, 11, 13 [b]2 Sam. 19:28; 1 Kin. 2:7

11 [1]Lit., *my*

12 [a]1 Chr. 8:34

13 [a]2 Sam. 9:7, 11 [b]2 Sam. 9:3

1 [a]1 Chr. 19:1-19 [b]1 Sam. 11:1

2 [1]Lit., *by the hand of* [a]1 Sam. 11:1

3 [1]Lit., *"In your eyes is David honoring* [a]Gen. 42:9, 16

4 [a]Is. 15:2; Jer. 41:5 [b]Is. 20:4

5 [1]Lit., *Return to*

6 [1]Heb., *Aram* (vss. 6-19) [a]Gen. 34:30; 1 Sam. 27:12 [b]2 Sam. 8:3, 5; 2 Kin. 7:6 [c]Gen. 36:37; Judg. 18:28 [d]2 Sam. 8:3 [e]Deut. 3:14

8 [1]Lit., *gate*
[a]1 Chr. 19:9 [b]Judg. 11:3, 5 [c]Josh. 13:9, 16

9 [1]Lit., *the faces of the battle were against*

12 [a]Deut. 31:6; Josh. 1:6 [b]1 Cor. 16:13 [c]1 Sam. 3:18

13 [a]1 Kin. 20:13-21

14 [a]2 Sam. 11:1

15 [1]Lit., *smitten before*

16 [1]I.e., Euphrates [2]Lit., *before*
[a]2 Sam. 8:3-8 [b]1 Chr. 19:16

18 [a]1 Chr. 19:18

19 [1]Lit., *smitten before*
[a]2 Sam. 8:6

1 [1]Lit., *at the return of the year*
[a]1 Chr. 20:1 [b]2 Sam. 10:14; 1 Kin. 20:22, 26
[c]2 Sam. 12:26-28; Jer. 49:2, 3; Amos 1:14

2 [a]2 Sam. 4:5, 7
[b]Deut. 22:8; 1 Sam. 9:25; Matt. 24:17; Acts 10:9

3 [a]1 Chr. 3:5 [b]1 Chr. 23:39

4 [a]Ps. 51:title; James 1:14, 15 [b]Lev. 12:2-5; 15:19-28; 18:19

8 And the sons of Ammon came out and drew up in
battle array [a]at the entrance of the [1]city, while the Syrians of
Zobah and of Rehob and the men of [b]Tob and Maacah *were*
by themselves [c]in the field.
9 Now when Joab saw that [1]the battle was set against him
in front and in the rear, he selected from all the choice men of
Israel, and arrayed *them* against the Syrians.
10 But the remainder of the people he placed in the hand
of Abishai his brother, and he arrayed *them* against the sons of
Ammon.
11 And he said, "If the Syrians are too strong for me, then
you shall help me, but if the sons of Ammon are too strong for
you, then I will come to help you.
12 "[a]Be strong, and [b]let us show ourselves courageous for
the sake of our people and for the cities of our God; and [c]may
the LORD do what is good in His sight."
13 So Joab and the people who were with him drew near
to the battle against the Syrians, and [a]they fled before him.
14 When the sons of Ammon saw that the Syrians fled,
they *also* fled before Abishai and entered the city. [a]Then Joab
returned from *fighting* against the sons of Ammon and came
to Jerusalem.
15 When the Syrians saw that they had been [1]defeated by
Israel, they gathered themselves together.
16 [a]And Hadadezer sent and brought out the Syrians who
were beyond the [1]River, and they came to Helam; and [b]Sho-
bach the commander of the army of Hadadezer [2]led them.
17 Now when it was told David, he gathered all Israel
together and crossed the Jordan, and came to Helam. And the
Syrians arrayed themselves to meet David and fought against
him.
18 But the Syrians fled before Israel, and David killed [a]700
charioteers of the Syrians and 40,000 horsemen and struck
down Shobach the commander of their army, and he died
there.
19 When all the kings, servants of Hadadezer, saw that
they were [1]defeated by Israel, [a]they made peace with Israel
and served them. So the Syrians feared to help the sons of
Ammon any more.

[a]CHAPTER 11

THEN it happened [1b]in the spring, at the time when kings go
out *to battle*, that David sent Joab and his servants with him
and all Israel, and they destroyed the sons of Ammon and
[c]besieged Rabbah. But David stayed at Jerusalem.
2 Now when evening came [a]David arose from his bed
and walked around on [b]the roof of the king's house, and from
the roof he saw a woman bathing; and the woman was very
beautiful in appearance.
3 So David sent and inquired about the woman. And one
said, "Is this not [a]Bathsheba, the daughter of Eliam, the wife
of [b]Uriah the Hittite?"
4 And David sent messengers and took her, and when she
came to him, [a]he lay with her; [b]and when she had purified
herself from her uncleanness, she returned to her house.

5 And the woman conceived; and she sent and told David, and said, "[a]I am pregnant."
6 Then David sent to Joab, *saying*, "Send me Uriah the
Hittite." So Joab sent Uriah to David.
7 When Uriah came to him, [a]David asked concerning
the welfare of Joab and [1]the people and the state of the war.
8 Then David said to Uriah, "Go down to your house,
and [a]wash your feet." And Uriah went out of the king's house,
and [b]a present from the king [1]was sent out after him.
9 But Uriah slept [a]at the door of the king's house with all
the servants of his lord, and did not go down to his house.
10 Now when they told David, saying, "Uriah did not go
down to his house," David said to Uriah, "Have you not come
from a journey? Why did you not go down to your house?"
11 And Uriah said to David, "[a]The ark and Israel and
Judah are staying in [1]temporary shelters, and my lord Joab and
[b]the servants of my lord are camping in the open field. Shall I
then go to my house to eat and to drink and to lie with my
wife? [c]By your life and the life of your soul, I will not do this
thing."
12 Then David said to Uriah, "Stay here today also, and
tomorrow I will let you go." So Uriah remained in Jerusalem
that day and the [1]next.
13 Now David called him, and he ate and drank before
him, and he made him drunk; and in the evening he went out
to lie on his bed [a]with his lord's servants, but he did not go
down to his house.
14 Now it came about in the morning that David [a]wrote a
letter to Joab, and sent *it* by the hand of Uriah.
15 And he had written in the letter, saying, "[1]Place Uriah
in the front line of the [2]fiercest battle and withdraw from him,
[a]so that he may be struck down and die."
16 So it was as Joab kept watch on the city, that he put
Uriah at the place where he knew there *were* valiant men.
17 And the men of the city went out and fought against
Joab, and some of the people among David's servants fell; and
[a]Uriah the Hittite also died.
18 Then Joab sent and reported to David all the events of
the war.
19 And he charged the messenger, saying, "When you
have finished telling all the events of the war to the king,
20 and if it happens that the king's wrath rises and he says
to you, 'Why did you go so near to the city to fight? Do you
not know that they would shoot from the wall?
21 'Who [a]struck down Abimelech the son of Jerubbesheth?
Did not a woman throw an upper millstone on him from
the wall so that he died at Thebez? Why did you go so near
the wall?'—then you shall say, 'Your servant Uriah the Hittite
is dead also.'"
22 So the messenger departed and came and reported to
David all that Joab had sent him *to tell*.
23 And the messenger said to David, "The men prevailed
against us and came out against us in the field, but we [1]pressed
them as far as the entrance of the gate.
24 "Moreover, the archers shot at your servants from the

5 [a]Lev. 20:10; Deut. 22:22

7 [1]Lit., *welfare of*
[a]Gen. 37:14; 1 Sam. 17:22

8 [1]Lit., *went out*
[a]Gen. 43:24; Luke 7:44
[b]Gen. 43:34

9 [a]1 Kin. 14:27, 28

11 [1]Or, *booths*
[a]2 Sam. 7:2, 6 [b]2 Sam. 20:6
[c]2 Sam. 4:9; 14:19

12 [1]Lit., *morrow*

13 [a]2 Sam. 11:9

14 [a]1 Kin. 21:8-10

15 [1]Lit., *Give* [2]Lit., *strong*
[a]2 Sam. 12:9

17 [a]2 Sam. 11:21

21 [a]Judg. 9:50-54

23 [1]Lit., *were upon*

25 [1]Lit., *be evil in your sight*

26 [a]Gen. 50:10; Deut. 34:8; 1 Sam. 31:13

27 [1]Lit., *gathered* [a]Gen. 12:9 [b]Ps. 51:4, 5

1 [1]Lit., *said to him* [a]2 Sam. 7:2, 4, 17 [b]Ps. 51:title [c]2 Sam. 14:4-7; 1 Kin. 20:35-41

3 [1]Lit., *morsel* [a]2 Sam. 11:3

4 [1]Lit., *spared*

5 [1]Lit., *is a son of death* [a]1 Kin.20:39, 40 [b]1 Sam. 26:16

6 [a]Ex. 22:1

7 [a]1 Kin. 20:42 [b]1 Sam. 16:13

8 [1]Lit., *bosom* [a]2 Sam. 9:7

9 [a]1 Sam. 15:23, 26 [b]2 Sam. 11:14-17, 27 [c]2 Sam. 11:27

10 [a]2 Sam. 13:28; 18:14; 1 Kin. 2:25

11 [1]Lit., *the sight of this sun* [a]2 Sam. 16:21, 22

wall; so some of the king's servants are dead, and your servant
Uriah the Hittite is also dead."
25 Then David said to the messenger, "Thus you shall say
to Joab, 'Do not let this thing [1]displease you, for the sword
devours one as well as another; make your battle against the
city stronger and overthrow it;' and *so* encourage him."
26 Now when the wife of Uriah heard that Uriah her
husband was dead, [a]she mourned for her husband.
27 When the *time of* mourning was over, David sent and
[1]brought her to his house and [a]she became his wife; then she
bore him a son. But [b]the thing that David had done was evil in
the sight of the LORD.

CHAPTER 12

THEN the LORD sent [a]Nathan to David. And [b]he came to
him, and [1c]said,

"There were two men in one city, the one rich and the other poor.
2 "The rich man had a great many flocks and herds.
3 "But the poor man had nothing except [a]one little ewe lamb
Which he bought and nourished;
And it grew up together with him and his children.
It would eat of his [1]bread and drink of his cup and lie in his bosom,
And was like a daughter to him.
4 "Now a traveler came to the rich man,
And he [1]was unwilling to take from his own flock or his own herd,
To prepare for the wayfarer who had come to him;
Rather he took the poor man's ewe lamb and prepared it for the man who had come to him."

5 [a]Then David's anger burned greatly against the man,
and he said to Nathan, "As the LORD lives, surely the man who
has done this [1b]deserves to die.
6 "And he must make restitution for the lamb [a]fourfold,
because he did this thing and had no compassion."
7 Nathan then said to David, "[a]You are the man! Thus
says the LORD God of Israel, '[b]It is I who anointed you king
over Israel and it is I who delivered you from the hand of Saul.
8 'I also gave you [a]your master's house and your master's
wives into your [1]care, and I gave you the house of Israel and
Judah; and if *that had been* too little, I would have added to
you many more things like these!
9 'Why [a]have you despised the word of the LORD by
doing evil in His sight? [b]You have struck down Uriah the
Hittite with the sword, [c]have taken his wife to be your wife,
and have killed him with the sword of the sons of Ammon.
10 'Now therefore, [a]the sword shall never depart from your
house, because you have despised Me and have taken the wife
of Uriah the Hittite to be your wife.'
11 "Thus says the LORD, 'Behold, I will raise up evil against
you from your own household; [a]I will even take your wives
before your eyes, and give *them* to your companion, and he
shall lie with your wives in [1]broad daylight.

12 'Indeed [a]you did it secretly, but [b]I will do this thing
before all Israel, and [1]under the sun.' "
13 Then David said to Nathan, "[a]I have sinned against the
LORD." And Nathan said to David, "The LORD also has [1b]taken
away your sin; you shall not die.
14 "However, because by this deed you have [a]given occasion
to the enemies of the LORD to blaspheme, the child also
that is born to you shall surely die."
15 So Nathan went to his house.
Then [a]the LORD struck the child that Uriah's [1]widow bore
to David, so that he was *very* sick.
16 David therefore inquired of God for the child; and
David fasted and went and [a]lay all night on the ground.
17 And [a]the elders of his household stood beside him in
order to raise him up from the ground, but he was unwilling
and would not eat food with them.
18 Then it happened on the seventh day that the child
died. And the servants of David were afraid to tell him that the
child was dead, for they said, "Behold, while the child was *still*
alive, we spoke to him and he did not listen to our voice. How
then can we tell him that the child is dead, since he might do
himself harm!"
19 But when David saw that his servants were whispering
together, David perceived that the child was dead; so David
said to his servants, "Is the child dead?" And they said, "He is
dead."
20 So David arose from the ground, [a]washed, anointed
himself, and changed his clothes; and he came into the house
of the LORD and worshiped. Then he came to his own house,
and when he requested, they set food before him and he ate.
21 Then his servants said to him, "What is this thing that
you have done? [1]While the child was alive, you fasted and
wept; but when the child died, you arose and ate food."
22 And he said, "While the child was *still* alive, [a]I fasted
and wept; for I said, '[b]Who knows, the LORD may be gracious
to me, that the child may live.'
23 "But now he has died; why should I fast? Can I bring
him back again? [a]I shall go to him, but [b]he will not return to
me."
24 Then David comforted his wife Bathsheba, and went in
to her and lay with her; and she gave birth to a son, and [1a]he
named him Solomon. Now the LORD loved him
25 and sent *word* through Nathan the prophet, and he
named him [1]Jedidiah for the LORD's sake.
26 [a]Now Joab fought against Rabbah of the sons of Ammon,
and captured the royal city.
27 And Joab sent messengers to David and said, "I have
fought against Rabbah, I have even captured the city of
waters.
28 "Now therefore gather the rest of the people together
and camp against the city and capture it, lest I capture the city
myself and it be named after me."
29 So David gathered all the people and went to Rabbah,
fought against it, and captured it.
30 Then he took the crown of [1]their king from his head;
and its weight *was* a talent of gold, and *in it* [2]*was* a precious

12 [1]Lit., *before* [a]2 Sam. 11:4-15 [b]2 Sam. 16:22

13 [1]Lit., *caused your sin to pass away* [a]2 Sam. 24:10; 1 Sam. 15:24, 30; Luke 18:13 [b]Prov. 28:13; Lev. 20:10; 24:17; Mic. 7:18

14 [a]Is. 52:5; Rom. 2:24

15 [1]Lit., *wife* [a]1 Sam. 25:38

16 [a]2 Sam. 13:31; Neh. 1:4

17 [a]Gen. 24:2

20 [a]Matt. 6:17

21 [1]Lit., *On account of*

22 [a]Is. 38:1-3 [b]Jonah 3:9

23 [a]Gen. 37:35 [b]Job 7:8-10

24 [1]Some mss. read, *she* [a]1 Chr. 22:9

25 [1]I.e., Beloved of the LORD

26 [a]1 Chr. 20:1-3

30 [1]Or, *Malcam;* Zeph. 1:5 [2]Or, *were precious stones*

31 [1]Cf. 1 Chr. 20:3 [a]Heb. 11:37

1 [a]2 Sam. 3:2, 3; 1 Chr. 3:2 [b]1 Chr. 3:9 [c]2 Sam. 3:2

2 [1]Lit., *hard in Amnon's eyes*

3 [a]1 Sam. 16:9

5 [a]2 Kin. 8:29

6 [a]Gen. 18:6

9 [1]Lit., *poured* [a]Gen. 45:1

10 [1]Or, *inner room*

12 [a]Lev. 20:17 [b]Judg. 19:23; 20:6

13 [1]Lit., *cause to go* [2]Or, *disgraceful ones* [a]Gen. 20:12

14 [1]Lit., *her voice*

stone; and it was *placed* on David's head. And he brought out
the spoil of the city in great amounts.
31 He also brought out the people who were in it, and
[1a]set *them* under saws, sharp iron instruments, and iron axes,
and made them pass through the brickkiln. And thus he did to
all the cities of the sons of Ammon. Then David and all the
people returned *to* Jerusalem.

Chapter 13

NOW it was after this that [a]Absalom the son of David had a
beautiful sister whose name was [b]Tamar, and [c]Amnon the son
of David loved her.
2 And Amnon was so frustrated because of his sister Tamar that he made himself ill, for she was a virgin, and it
seemed [1]hard to Amnon to do anything to her.
3 But Amnon had a friend whose name was Jonadab, the
son of [a]Shimeah, David's brother; and Jonadab was a very
shrewd man.
4 And he said to him, "O son of the king, why are you so
depressed morning after morning? Will you not tell me?"
Then Amnon said to him, "I am in love with Tamar, the sister
of my brother Absalom."
5 Jonadab then said to him, "Lie down on your bed and
pretend to be ill; when your father comes [a]to see you, say to
him, 'Please let my sister Tamar come and give me *some* food
to eat, and let her prepare the food in my sight, that I may see
it and eat from her hand.' "
6 So Amnon lay down and pretended to be ill; when the
king came to see him, Amnon said to the king, "Please let my
sister Tamar come and [a]make me a couple of cakes in my
sight, that I may eat from her hand."
7 Then David sent to the house for Tamar, saying, "Go
now to your brother Amnon's house, and prepare food for
him."
8 So Tamar went to her brother Amnon's house, and he
was lying down. And she took dough, kneaded *it,* made cakes
in his sight, and baked the cakes.
9 And she took the pan and [1]dished *them* out before
him, but he refused to eat. And Amnon said, "[a]Have everyone
go out from me." So everyone went out from him.
10 Then Amnon said to Tamar, "Bring the food into the
[1]bedroom, that I may eat from your hand." So Tamar took the
cakes which she had made and brought them into the bedroom to her brother Amnon.
11 When she brought *them* to him to eat, he took hold of
her and said to her, "Come, lie with me, my sister."
12 But she answered him, "No, my brother, do not violate
me, for [a]such a thing is not done in Israel; do not do this
[b]disgraceful thing!
13 "As for me, where could I [1]get rid of my reproach? And
as for you, you will be like one of the [2]fools in Israel. Now
therefore, please speak to the king, for [a]he will not withhold
me from you."
14 However, he would not listen to [1]her; since he was
stronger than she, he violated her and lay with her.

15 Then Amnon hated her with a very great hatred; for
the hatred with which he hated her was greater than the love
with which he had loved her. And Amnon said to her, "Get up,
go away!"
16 But she said to him, "No, because this wrong in sending me away is greater than the other that you have done to
me!" Yet he would not listen to her.
17 Then he called his young man who attended him and
said, "Now throw this woman out of my *presence,* and lock
the door behind her."
18 Now she had on [a]a [1]long-sleeved garment; for in this
manner the virgin daughters of the king dressed themselves in
robes. Then his attendant took her out and locked the door
behind her.
19 And [a]Tamar put [1]ashes on her head, and [b]tore her
[2]long-sleeved garment which *was* on her; and [c]she put her hand
on her head and went away, crying aloud as she went.
20 Then Absalom her brother said to her, "Has Amnon
your brother been with you? But now keep silent, my sister, he
is your brother; do not take this matter to heart." So Tamar
remained and was desolate [a]in her brother Absalom's house.
21 Now when King David heard of all these matters, he
was very angry.
22 But Absalom did not speak to Amnon [a]either good or
bad; for Absalom hated Amnon because he had violated his
sister Tamar.
23 Now it came about after two full years that Absalom
[a]had sheep-shearers in Baal-hazor, which is near Ephraim, and
Absalom invited all the king's sons.
24 And Absalom came to the king and said, "Behold now,
your servant has sheep-shearers; please let the king and his
servants go with your servant."
25 But the king said to Absalom, "No, my son, we should
not all go, lest we be burdensome to you." Although he [1]urged
him, he would not go, but blessed him.
26 Then [a]Absalom said, "If not, please let my brother
Amnon go with us." And the king said to him, "Why should he
go with you?"
27 But when Absalom [1]urged him, he let Amnon and all
the king's sons go with him.
28 And Absalom commanded his servants, saying, "See
now, [a]when Amnon's heart is merry with wine, and when I say
to you, 'Strike Amnon,' then put him to death. Do not fear;
have not I myself commanded you? Be courageous and be
[1]valiant."
29 And the servants of Absalom did to Amnon just as
Absalom had commanded. Then all the king's sons arose and
each mounted [a]his mule and fled.
30 Now it was while they were on the way that the report
came to David, saying, "Absalom has struck down all the king's
sons, and not one of them is left."
31 Then the king arose, [a]tore his clothes and [b]lay on the
ground; and all his servants were standing by with clothes torn.
32 And [a]Jonadab, the son of Shimeah, David's brother,
[1]responded, "Do not let my lord [2]suppose they have put to
death all the young men, the king's sons, for Amnon alone is

18 [1]Lit., *a varicolored tunic* [a]Gen. 37:3, 23; Judg. 5:30

19 [1]Or, *dust* [2]Lit., *varicolored tunic* [a]1 Sam. 4:12; Esth. 4:1; Jer. 2:37 [b]2 Sam. 1:11; Gen. 37:29 [c]Jer. 2:37

20 [a]2 Sam. 14:24

22 [a]Gen. 31:24

23 [a]1 Sam. 25:7

25 [1]Lit., *broke through*

26 [a]2 Sam. 3:27; 11:13-15

27 [1]Lit., *broke through*

28 [1]Lit., *sons of valor* [a]Judg. 19:6, 9, 22; 1 Sam. 25:36-38

29 [a]2 Sam. 18:9; 1 Kin. 1:33, 38

31 [a]2 Sam. 1:11 [b]2 Sam. 12:16

32 [1]Lit., *answered and said* [2]Lit., *say* [a]2 Sam. 13:3-5

dead; because by the [3]intent of Absalom this has been determined since the day that he violated his sister Tamar.
33 "Now therefore, do not let my lord the king [a]take the
report to [1]heart, namely, 'all the king's sons are dead', for only
Amnon is dead."
34 Now [a]Absalom had fled. And [b]the young man who was
the watchman raised his eyes and looked, and behold, many
people were coming from the road behind him by the side of
the mountain.
35 And Jonadab said to the king, "Behold, the king's sons
have come; according to your servant's word, so it happened."
36 And it came about as soon as he had finished speaking,
that behold, the king's sons came and lifted their voices and
wept; and also the king and all his servants wept [1]very bitterly.
37 Now [a]Absalom fled and went to [b]Talmai the son of
Ammihud, the king of [c]Geshur. And *David* mourned for his
son every day.
38 [a]So Absalom had fled and gone to Geshur, and was
there three years.
39 And *the heart of* King David longed to go out to Absalom; for [a]he was comforted concerning Amnon, since he was
dead.

Chapter 14

NOW Joab the son of Zeruiah perceived that [a]the king's
heart *was* inclined toward Absalom.
2 So Joab sent to [a]Tekoa and [1]brought a wise woman
from there and said to her, "Please [b]pretend to be a mourner,
and put on mourning garments now, and [c]do not anoint yourself with oil, but like a woman who has been mourning for the
dead many days;
3 then go to the king and speak to him in this manner."
So Joab put [a]the words in her mouth.
4 Now when the woman of Tekoa [1]spoke to the king, she
fell on her face to the ground and [a]prostrated herself and said,
"[b]Help, O king."
5 And the king said to her, "What is your trouble?" And
she [1]answered, "[a]Truly I am a widow, for my husband is dead.
6 "And your maidservant had two sons, but the two of
them struggled together in the field, and there was no [1]one to
separate them, so one struck the other and killed him.
7 "Now behold, [a]the whole family has risen against your
maidservant, and they say, 'Hand over the one who struck his
brother, that we may put him to death for the life of his
brother whom he killed, [b]and destroy the heir also.' Thus they
will extinguish my coal which is left, so as to [1]leave my husband neither name nor remnant on the face of the earth."
8 Then the king said to the woman, "Go to your house,
and I will give orders concerning you."
9 And the woman of Tekoa said to the king, "O my lord,
the king, [a]the iniquity is on me and my father's house, but [b]the
king and his throne are guiltless."
10 So the king said, "Whoever speaks to you, bring him to
me, and he will not touch you any more."
11 Then she said, "Please let the king remember the LORD

32 [3]Lit., *mouth*
33 [1]Lit., *his heart* [a]2 Sam. 19:19
34 [a]2 Sam. 13:37, 38 [b]2 Sam. 18:24
36 [1]Lit., *with a very great weeping*
37 [a]2 Sam. 13:34 [b]2 Sam. 3:3 [c]2 Sam. 14:23, 32
38 [a]2 Sam. 13:34
39 [a]2 Sam. 12:19-23
1 [a]2 Sam. 13:39
2 [1]Lit., *took* [a]2 Sam. 23:26; 2 Chr. 11:6; Amos 1:1 [b]1 Kin. 20:35-43 [c]2 Sam. 12:20
3 [a]2 Sam. 14:19
4 [1]Many mss. and ancient versions read, *came* [a]1 Sam. 25:23 [b]2 Kin. 6:26-28
5 [1]Lit., *said* [a]2 Sam. 14:5-21; 2 Sam. 12:1-7
6 [1]Lit., *deliverer between*
7 [1]Lit., *set* [a]Num. 35:19; Deut. 19:12, 13 [b]Matt. 21:38
9 [a]Gen. 43:9; 1 Sam. 25:24 [b]1 Kin. 2:33

your God, [a]*so that* the avenger of blood may not continue to
destroy, lest they destroy my son." And he said, "[b]As the LORD
lives, not one hair of your son shall fall to the ground."
12 Then the woman said, "Please let your maidservant
speak a word to my lord the king." And he said, "Speak."
13 And the woman said, "[a]Why then have you planned
such a thing against the people of God? For in speaking this
word the king is as one who is guilty, *in that* the king does not
bring back [b]his banished one.
14 "For [a]we shall surely die and are [b]like water spilled on
the ground which cannot be gathered up again. Yet God does
not take away life, but plans [1]ways so that [c]the banished one
may not be cast out from him.
15 "Now [1]the reason I have come to speak this word to my
lord the king is because the people have made me afraid; so
your maidservant said, 'Let me now speak to the king, perhaps
the king will perform the [2]request of his maidservant.
16 'For the king will hear [1]and deliver his maidservant from
the [2]hand of the man who would destroy [3]both me and my son
from [a]the inheritance of God.'
17 "Then your maidservant said, 'Please let the word of my
lord the king be [1]comforting, for as [a]the angel of God, so is my
lord the king to discern good and evil. And may the LORD your
God be with you.' "
18 Then the king answered and said to the woman,
"Please do not hide anything from me that I am about to ask
you." And the woman said, "Let my lord the king please
speak."
19 So the king said, "Is the hand of Joab with you in all
this?" And the woman answered and said, "As your soul lives,
my lord the king, no one can turn to the right or to the left
from anything that my lord the king has spoken. Indeed, it was
[a]your servant Joab who commanded me, and it was he who put
all these words in the mouth of your maidservant;
20 in order to change the appearance of things your servant Joab has done this thing. But my lord is wise, [a]like the
wisdom of the angel of God, to know all that is in the earth."
21 Then the king said to Joab, "Behold now, [a]I will surely
do this thing; go therefore, bring back the young man
Absalom."
22 And Joab fell on his face to the ground, prostrated
himself and blessed the king; then Joab said, "Today your
servant knows that I have found favor in your sight, O my lord,
the king, in that the king has performed the [1]request of his
servant."
23 So Joab arose and went to [a]Geshur, and brought Absalom to Jerusalem.
24 However the king said, "Let him turn to [a]his own
house, and let him not see my face." So Absalom turned to his
own house and did not see the king's face.
25 Now in all Israel was no one as handsome as Absalom,
so highly praised; [a]from the sole of his foot to the crown of his
head there was no defect in him.
26 And when he [a]cut the hair of his head (and it was at the
end of every year that he cut *it*, for it was heavy on him so he

11 [a]Num. 35:19, 21; Deut. 19:4-10 [b]1 Sam. 14:45; 1 Kin. 1:52; Matt. 10:30

13 [a]2 Sam. 12:7; 1 Kin. 20:40-42 [b]2 Sam. 13:37, 38

14 [1]Lit., *devices* [a]Job 30:23; 34:15; Heb. 9:27 [b]Ps. 58:7 [c]Num. 35:15, 25, 28

15 [1]Lit., *that* [2]Lit., *word*

16 [1]Lit., *to* [2]Lit., *palm* [3]Lit., *together* [a]Deut. 32:9; 1 Sam. 26:19

17 [1]Lit., *for rest* [a]2 Sam. 14:20; 19:27; 1 Sam. 29:9

19 [a]2 Sam. 14:3

20 [a]2 Sam. 14:17; 19:27

21 [a]2 Sam. 14:11

22 [1]Lit., *word*

23 [a]2 Sam. 13:37, 38

24 [a]2 Sam. 13:20

25 [a]Deut. 28:35; Job. 2:7; Is. 1:6

26 [a]Ezek. 44:20

cut it); he weighed the hair of his head at 200 shekels by the
king's weight.
27 And [a]to Absalom there were born three sons, and one
daughter whose name was [b]Tamar; she was a woman of beautiful appearance.
28 Now Absalom lived two full years in Jerusalem, [a]and
did not see the king's face.
29 Then Absalom sent for Joab, to send him to the king,
but he would not come to him. So he sent again a second time,
but he would not come.
30 Therefore he said to his servants, "See, [a]Joab's [1]field is
next to mine, and he has barley there; go and set it on fire." So
Absalom's servants set the [1]field on fire.
31 Then Joab arose, came to Absalom at his house and
said to him, "Why have your servants set my [1]field on fire?"
32 And Absalom [1]answered Joab, "Behold, I sent for you,
saying, 'Come here, that I may send you to the king, to say,
"Why have I come from Geshur? It would be better for me
still to be there."' Now therefore let me see the king's face;
[a]and if there is iniquity in me, let him put me to death."
33 So when Joab came to the king and told him, he called
for Absalom. Thus he came to the king and prostrated himself
on his face to the ground before the king, and [a]the king kissed
Absalom.

Chapter 15

Now it came about after this that [a]Absalom provided for
himself a chariot and horses, and fifty men as runners before
him.
2 And Absalom used to rise early and [a]stand beside the
way to the gate; and it happened that when any man had a suit
to come to the king for judgment, Absalom would call to him
and say, "From what city are you?" And he would say, "Your
servant is from one of the tribes of Israel."
3 Then Absalom would say to him, "See, your [1]claims are
good and right, but no man listens to you on the part of the
king."
4 Moreover, Absalom would say, "[a]Oh that one would
appoint me judge in the land, then every man who has any suit
or cause could come to me, and I would give him justice."
5 And it happened that when a man came near to prostrate himself before him, he would put out his hand and take
hold of him and [a]kiss him.
6 And in this manner Absalom dealt with all Israel who
came to the king for judgment; so Absalom stole away the
hearts of the men of Israel.
7 Now it came about at the end of [1]forty years that
Absalom said to the king, "Please let me go and pay my vow
which I have vowed to the LORD, in [a]Hebron.
8 "For your servant [a]vowed a vow while I was living at
Geshur in [1]Syria, saying, '[b]If the LORD shall indeed bring me
back to Jerusalem, then I will serve the LORD.'"
9 And the king said to him, "Go in peace." So he arose
and went to Hebron.
10 But Absalom sent spies throughout all the tribes of

27 [a]2 Sam. 18:18 [b]2 Sam. 13:1
28 [a]2 Sam. 14:24
30 [1]Lit., *portion* [a]Judg. 15:3-5
31 [1]Lit., *portion*
32 [1]Lit., *said to* [a]1 Sam. 20:8
33 [a]Gen. 33:4; Luke 15:20
1 [a]1 Kin. 1:5
2 [a]Sam. 19:8; Ruth 4:1
3 [1]Lit., *words*
4 [a]Judg. 9:1-5, 29
5 [a]2 Sam. 14:33; 20:9
7 [1]Some ancient versions render *four* [a]2 Sam. 3:2, 3
8 [1]Heb., *Aram* [a]2 Sam. 13:37, 38 [b]Gen. 28:20, 21

Israel, saying, "As soon as you hear the sound of the trumpet,
then you shall say, '[a]Absalom is king in Hebron.' "
11 Then two hundred men went with Absalom from Jerusalem, [a]who were invited and [b]went [1]innocently, and they did
not know anything.
12 And Absalom sent for [a]Ahithophel the Gilonite, David's counselor, from his city [b]Giloh, while he was offering the
sacrifices. And the conspiracy was strong, for [c]the people increased continually with Absalom.
13 Then a messenger came to David, saying, "[a]The hearts
of the men of Israel are [1]with Absalom."
14 And David said to all his servants who were with him at
Jerusalem, "[a]Arise and let us flee, for *otherwise* none of us
shall escape from Absalom. Go in haste, lest he overtake us
quickly and bring down calamity on us and strike the city with
the edge of the sword."
15 Then the king's servants said to the king, "Behold, your
servants *are ready to do* whatever my lord the king chooses."
16 So the king went out and all his household [1]with him.
But [a]the king left ten concubines to keep the house.
17 And the king went out and all the people [1]with him,
and they stopped at the last house.
18 Now all his servants passed on beside him, [a]all the Cherethites, all the Pelethites, and all the Gittites, [b]six hundred
men who had come [1]with him from Gath, passed on before
the king.
19 Then the king said to [a]Ittai the Gittite, "Why will you
also go with us? Return and remain with the king, for you are a
foreigner and also an exile; *return* to your own place.
20 "You came *only* yesterday, and shall I today make you
wander with us, while [a]I go where I will? Return and take back
your brothers; [b]mercy and [1]truth be with you."
21 But Ittai answered the king and said, "[a]As the LORD
lives, and as my lord the king lives, surely wherever my lord the
king may be, whether for death or for life, there also your
servant will be."
22 Therefore David said to Ittai, "Go and pass over." So
Ittai the Gittite passed over with all his men and all the little
ones who *were* with him.
23 While all the country was weeping with a loud voice,
all the people passed over. The king also passed over [a]the
brook Kidron, and all the people passed over toward [b]the way
of the wilderness.
24 Now behold, [a]Zadok also *came,* and all the Levites
with him [b]carrying the ark of the covenant of God. And they
set down the ark of God, and [c]Abiathar came up until all the
people had finished passing from the city.
25 And the king said to Zadok, "Return the ark of God to
the city. If I find favor in the sight of the LORD, then [a]He will
bring me back again, and show me both it and [b]His habitation.
26 "But if he should say thus, '[a]I have no delight in you,'
behold, here I am, [b]let Him do to me as seems good [1]to Him."
27 The king said also to Zadok the priest, "Are you *not* [a]a
seer? Return to the city in peace and your [b]two sons with you,
your son Ahimaaz and Jonathan the son of Abiathar.

10 [a]1 Kin. 1:34; 2 Kin. 9:13

11 [1]Lit., *in their integrity* [a]1 Sam. 9:13 [b]1 Sam. 22:15

12 [a]2 Sam. 15:31 [b]Josh. 15:51 [c]Ps. 3:1

13 [1]Lit., *after* [a]2 Sam. 15:6; Judg. 9:3

14 [a]2 Sam. 12:11; Ps. 3:title

16 [1]Lit., *at his feet* [a]2 Sam. 16:21, 22

17 [1]Lit., *at his feet*

18 [1]Lit., *at his feet* [a]2 Sam. 8:18 [b]1 Sam. 23:13; 25:13; 30:1, 9

19 [a]2 Sam. 18:2

20 [1]Or, *faithfulness* [a]1 Sam. 23:13 [b]2 Sam. 2:6

21 [a]Ruth 1:16, 17

23 [a]1 Kin. 15:13; 2 Chr. 29:16 [b]2 Sam. 15:28; 16:2

24 [a]2 Sam. 8:17; 20:25 [b]Num. 4:15; 1 Sam. 4:4, 5 [c]1 Sam. 22:20

25 [a]Ps. 43:3 [b]Ex. 15:13; Jer. 25:30

26 [1]Lit., *in His sight* [a]2 Sam. 11:27; 1 Chr. 21:7 [b]1 Sam. 3:18

27 [a]1 Sam. 9:6-9 [b]2 Sam. 17:17

28 "See, I am going to wait [a]at the fords of the wilderness
until word comes from you to inform me."
29 Therefore Zadok and Abiathar returned the ark of
God to Jerusalem and remained there.
30 And David went up the ascent of the *Mount of* Olives,
and wept as he went, and [a]his head was covered and he walked
[b]barefoot. Then all the people who were with him each covered his head and went up weeping as they went.
31 Now someone told David, saying, "[a]Ahithophel is
among the conspirators with Absalom." And David said, "O
LORD, I pray, [b]make the counsel of Ahithophel foolishness."
32 It happened as David was coming to the summit, where
God was worshiped, that behold, Hushai the [a]Archite met him
with his [1]coat torn, and [2]dust on his head.
33 And David said to him, "If you pass over with me, then
you will be [a]a burden to me.
34 "But if you return to the city, and [a]say to Absalom, 'I
will be your servant, O king; as I have been your father's servant in time past, so I will now be your servant.' Then you can
thwart the counsel of Ahithophel for me.
35 "And are not Zadok and Abiathar the priests with you
there? So it shall be that [a]whatever you hear from the king's
house, you shall report to Zadok and Abiathar the priests.
36 "Behold [a]their two sons are with them there, Ahimaaz,
Zadok's son and Jonathan, Abiathar's son; and [b]by them you
shall send me everything that you hear."
37 So Hushai, [a]David's friend, came into the city, and
[b]Absalom came into Jerusalem.

CHAPTER 16

NOW when David had passed [a]a little beyond the summit,
behold, [b]Ziba the servant of Mephibosheth met him [c]with a
couple of saddled donkeys, and on them *were* two hundred
loaves of bread, a hundred clusters of raisins, a hundred summer fruits, and a jug of wine.
2 And the king said to Ziba, "Why do you have these?"
And Ziba said, "[a]The donkeys are for the king's household to
ride, and the bread and summer fruit for the young men to eat,
and the wine, [b]for whoever is faint in the wilderness to drink."
3 Then the king said, "And where is [a]your master's son?"
And [b]Ziba said to the king, "Behold, he is staying in Jerusalem,
for he said, 'Today the house of Israel will restore the kingdom
of my father to me.' "
4 So the king said to Ziba, "Behold, all that belongs to
Mephibosheth is yours." And Ziba said, "I prostrate myself;
let me find favor in your sight, O my lord, the king!"
5 When King David came to [a]Bahurim, behold, there
came out from there a man of the family of the house of Saul
[b]whose name was Shimei, the son of Gera; he came out [c]curs-
ing continually as he came.
6 And he threw stones at David and at all the servants of
King David; and all the people and all the mighty men were at
his right hand and at his left.
7 And thus Shimei said when he cursed, "Get out, get
out, [a]you man of bloodshed, and worthless fellow!

28 [a]2 Sam. 17:16; Josh. 5:10
30 [a]Esth. 6:12; Ezek. 24:17, 23 [b]Is. 20:2-4
31 [a]2 Sam. 15:12 [b]2 Sam. 16:23; 17:14, 23
32 [1]Or., *tunic* [2]Lit., *ground* [a]Josh. 16:2
33 [a]2 Sam. 19:35
34 [a]2 Sam. 16:19
35 [a]2 Sam. 17:15, 16
36 [a]2 Sam. 15:27 [b]2 Sam. 17:17
37 [a]2 Sam. 16:16; 1 Chr. 27:33 [b]2 Sam. 16:15
1 [a]2 Sam. 15:32 [b]2 Sam. 9:2-13 [c]1 Sam. 25:18
2 [a]Judg. 10:4 [b]2 Sam. 17:29
3 [a]2 Sam. 9:9, 10 [b]2 Sam. 19:26, 27
5 [a]2 Sam. 3:16; 17:18 [b]2 Sam. 19:16-23; 1 Kin. 2:8, 9, 44 [c]Ex. 22:28; 1 Sam. 17:43
7 [a]2 Sam. 12:9

8 "[a]The LORD has returned upon you all the bloodshed of
the house of Saul, in whose place you have reigned; and the
LORD has given the kingdom into the hand of your son Absalom. And behold, you are *taken* in your own evil, for you are a
man of bloodshed!"
9 Then [a]Abishai the son of Zeruiah said to the king,
"Why should [b]this dead dog [c]curse my lord the king? Let me
go over now, and [1]cut off his head."
10 But the king said, "[a]What have I to do with you, O
sons of Zeruiah? [b]If he curses, and if the LORD has told him,
'Curse David,' [c]then who shall say, 'Why have you done so?'"
11 Then David said to Abishai and to all his servants,
"Behold, [a]my son who came out from [1]me seeks my life; how
much more now this Benjamite? Let him alone and let him
curse, [b]for the LORD has told him.
12 "Perhaps the LORD will look on my affliction and [1a]re-
turn good to me instead of his cursing this day."
13 So David and his men went on the way; and Shimei
went along on the hillside parallel with him and as he went he
cursed, and cast stones and threw dust at him.
14 And the king and all the people who were with him
arrived weary and he refreshed himself there.
15 [a]Then Absalom and all the people, the men of Israel,
entered Jerusalem, and Ahithophel with him.
16 Now it came about when [a]Hushai the Archite, David's
friend, came to Absalom, that [b]Hushai said to Absalom,
"[c]*Long* live the king! *Long* live the king!"
17 And Absalom said to Hushai, "Is this your [1]loyalty to
your friend? [a]Why did you not go with your friend?"
18 Then Hushai said to Absalom, "No! For whom the
LORD, this people, and all the men of Israel have chosen, his
will I be, and with him I will remain.
19 "And besides, [a]whom should I serve? *Should I* not *serve*
in the presence of his son? As I have served in your father's
presence, so I will be in your presence."
20 Then Absalom said to Ahithophel, "Give your advice.
What shall we do?"
21 And Ahithophel said to Absalom, "[a]Go in to your father's
concubines, whom he has left to keep the house; then all
Israel will hear that you have made yourself odious to your
father. The hands of all who are with you will also be
strengthened."
22 So they pitched a tent for Absalom on the roof, [a]and
Absalom went in to his father's concubines [b]in the sight of all
Israel.
23 And [a]the advice of Ahithophel, which he [1]gave in those
days, *was* as if one inquired of the word of God; [b]so was all the
advice of Ahithophel *regarded* by both David and Absalom.

CHAPTER 17

FURTHERMORE, Ahithophel said to Absalom, "Please let
me choose 12,000 men that I may arise and pursue David
tonight.
2 "And [a]I will come upon him while he is weary and

8 [a]2 Sam. 21:1-9

9 [1]Lit., *take off*
[a]2 Sam. 19:21; 1 Sam. 26:8; Luke 9:54 [b]2 Sam. 9:8 [c]Ex. 22:28

10 [a]2 Sam. 3:39; 19:22 [b]John 18:11 [c]Rom. 9:20

11 [1]Lit., *my body*
[a]2 Sam. 12:11 [b]Gen. 45:5; 1 Sam. 26:19

12 [1]Lit., *the LORD will return*
[a]Deut. 23:5; Rom. 8:28

15 [a]2 Sam. 15:12, 37

16 [a]2 Sam. 15:37 [b]2 Sam. 15:34 [c]1 Sam. 10:24; 2 Kin. 11:12

17 [1]Or, *kindness*
[a]2 Sam. 19:25

19 [a]2 Sam. 15:34

21 [a]2 Sam. 15:16

22 [a]2 Sam. 15:16; 20.3 [b]2 Sam. 12:11, 12

23 [1]Lit., *advised*
[a]2 Sam. 17:14, 23 [b]2 Sam. 15:12

2 [a]2 Sam. 16:14

[1]exhausted and will terrify him so that all the people who are
with him will flee. Then [b]I will strike down the king alone,
3 and I will bring back all the people to you. [1]The return
of everyone depends on the man you seek; *then* all the people
shall be at peace."
4 So the [1]plan pleased Absalom and all the elders of
Israel.
5 Then Absalom said, "[a]Now call [b]Hushai the Archite
also, and let us hear what [1]he has to say."
6 When Hushai had come to Absalom, Absalom said to
[1]him, "Ahithophel has spoken [2]thus. Shall we [3]carry out his
plan? If not, you speak."
7 So Hushai said to Absalom, "[a]This time the advice that
Ahithophel has [1]given is not good."
8 Moreover, Hushai said, "You know your father and his
men, that they are mighty men and they are [1]fierce, [a]like a
bear robbed of her cubs in the field. And your father is an
[2]expert in warfare, and will not spend the night with the
people.
9 "Behold, he has now hidden himself in one of the [1]caves
or in another place; and it will be [2]when he falls on them at the
first attack, that whoever hears *it* will say, 'There has been a
slaughter among the people who follow Absalom.'
10 "And even the one who is valiant, whose heart is like the
heart of a lion, [a]will completely [1]lose heart; for all Israel knows
that your father is a mighty man and those who are with him
are valiant men.
11 "But I counsel that all Israel be surely gathered to you,
[a]from Dan even to Beersheba, [b]as the sand that is by the sea in
abundance, and that [1]you personally go into battle.
12 "So we shall come to him in one of the places where he
can be found, and we will [1]fall on him [a]as the dew falls on the
ground; and of him and of all the men who are with him, not
even one will be left.
13 "And if he withdraws into a city, then all Israel shall
bring ropes to that city, and we will [a]drag it into the [1]valley
until not even a small stone is found there."
14 Then Absalom and all the men of Israel said, "The
counsel of Hushai the Archite is better than the counsel of
Ahithophel." For [a]the LORD had ordained to thwart the good
counsel of Ahithophel, in order that the LORD might bring
calamity on Absalom.
15 Then [a]Hushai said to Zadok and to Abiathar the
priests, "[1]This is what Ahithophel counseled Absalom and the
elders of Israel, and [1]this is what I have counseled.
16 "Now therefore send quickly and tell David, saying,
'[a]Do not spend the night at the fords of the wilderness, but by
all means cross over, lest the king and all the people who are
with him be [1]destroyed."
17 [a]Now Jonathan and Ahimaaz were staying at [b]Enrogel,
and a maidservant would go and tell them, and they would go
and tell King David, for they could not be seen entering the
city.
18 But a lad did see them, and told Absalom; so the two of
them departed quickly and came to the house of a man [a]in

2 [1]Lit., *slack of hands* [b]1 Kin. 22:31

3 [1]Lit., *Like the return of the whole is the man whom you seek*

4 [1]Lit., *word was pleasing in the sight of*

5 [1]Lit., *. . . is in his mouth—even he* [a]2 Sam. 15:32-34 [b]2 Sam. 15:32-34

6 [1]Lit., *him, saying* [2]Lit., *according to this word* [3]Lit., *do his word*

7 [1]Lit., *advised* [a]2 Sam. 16:21

8 [1]Lit., *bitter of soul* [2]Lit., *man of war* [a]Hos. 13:8

9 [1]Lit., *pits* [2]Lit., *according to a falling among them*

10 [1]Lit., *melt* [a]Josh. 2:9-11

11 [1]Lit., *your face go* [a]1 Sam. 3:20 [b]Gen. 22:17; 1 Sam. 13:5

12 [1]Lit., *settle down* [a]Ps. 110:3; Mic. 5:7

13 [1]Or, *wadi* [a]Mic. 1:6

14 [a]2 Sam. 15:31, 34

15 [1]Lit., *Thus and thus* [a]2 Sam. 15:35, 36

16 [1]Lit., *swallowed up* [a]2 Sam. 15:28

17 [a]2 Sam. 15:27, 36 [b]Josh. 15:7; 18:16

18 [a]2 Sam. 3:16 16:5

Bahurim, who had a well in his courtyard, and they went down
[1]into it.
19 And [a]the woman [1]took the covering and spread it over
the well's mouth and scattered grain on it, so that nothing was
known.
20 Then Absalom's servants came to the woman at the
house and said, "Where are Ahimaaz and Jonathan?" And [a]the
woman said to them, "They have crossed the brook of water."
And when they searched and could not find *them,* they returned to Jerusalem.
21 And it came about after they had departed that they
came up out of the well and went and told King David; and
they said to David, "[a]Arise and cross over the water quickly for
thus Ahithophel has counseled against you."
22 Then David and all the people who *were* with him
arose and crossed the Jordan; and by [1]dawn not even one
remained who had not crossed the Jordan.
23 Now when Ahithophel saw that his counsel was not
[1]followed, he [2]saddled *his* donkey and arose and went to his
home, to [a]his city, and [3b]set his house in order, and [c]strangled
himself; thus he died and was buried in the grave of his father.
24 Then David came to [a]Mahanaim. And Absalom
crossed the Jordan, he and all the men of Israel with him.
25 And Absalom set [a]Amasa over the army in place of
Joab. Now Amasa was the son of a man whose name was
[1]Jithra the Israelite, who went in to Abigal the daughter of
[b]Nahash, sister of Zeruiah, Joab's mother.
26 And Israel and Absalom camped in the land of Gilead.
27 Now when David had come to Mahanaim, [a]Shobi the
son of Nahash from [b]Rabbah of the sons of Ammon, [c]Machir
the son of Ammiel from Lo-debar, and [d]Barzillai the Gileadite
from Rogelim,
28 brought beds, basins, pottery, wheat, barley, flour,
parched *grain,* beans, lentils, parched *seeds,*
29 honey, curds, sheep, and cheese of the herd, for David
and for the people who *were* with him, to eat; for they said,
"The people are hungry and weary and thirsty [a]in the
wilderness."

Chapter 18

THEN David [1]numbered the people who were with him and
[a]set over them commanders of thousands and commanders of
hundreds.
2 And David sent the people out, [a]one third under the
[1]command of Joab, one third under the [1]command of Abishai
the son of Zeruiah, Joab's brother, and one third under the
[1]command of [b]Ittai the Gittite. And the king said to the
people, "I myself will surely go out with you also."
3 But the people said, "[a]You should not go out; for if we
indeed flee, they will not care about us, even if half of us die,
they will not care about us. But [1]you are worth ten thousand of
us; therefore now it is better that you *be ready* to help us from
the city."
4 Then the king said to them, "Whatever seems best to

18 [1]Lit., *there*

19 [1]Lit., *took and spread the covering* [a]Josh. 2:4-6

20 [a]Lev. 19:11; Josh. 2:3-5; 1 Sam. 19:12-17

21 [a]2 Sam. 17:15, 16

22 [1]Lit., *the light of the morning*

23 [1]Lit., *done* [2]Lit., *bound* [3]Lit., *gave charge to* [a]2 Sam. 15:12 [b]2 Kin. 20:1 [c]Matt. 27:5

24 [a]2 Sam. 2:8; Gen. 32:2, 10

25 [1]I.e., Jether the Ishmaelite, cf. 1 Chr. 2:17 [a]2 Sam. 19:13; 20:9-12; 1 Kin. 2:5, 32 [b]1 Chr. 2:13, 16

27 [a]2 Sam. 10:1, 2; 1 Sam. 11:1 [b]2 Sam. 12:26, 29 [c]2 Sam. 9:4 [d]2 Sam. 19:31-40; 1 Kin. 2:7

29 [a]2 Sam. 16:2, 14

1 [1]Lit., *mustered* [a]Ex. 18:25; Num. 31:14; 1 Sam. 22:7

2 [1]Lit., *hand* [a]Judg. 7:16; 1 Sam. 11:11 [b]2 Sam. 15:19-22

3 [1]So with some ancient versions; M.T., *for now there are ten thousand like us* [a]2 Sam. 21:17

you I will do." So [a]the king stood beside the gate, and all the
people went out by hundreds and thousands.
5 And the king charged Joab and Abishai and Ittai,
saying, "*Deal* gently for my sake with the young man Absalom." And [a]all the people heard when the king charged all the
commanders concerning Absalom.
6 Then the people went out into the field against Israel,
and the battle took place in [a]the forest of Ephraim.
7 And the people of Israel were [1]defeated there before
the servants of David, and the slaughter there that day was
great, 20,000 men.
8 For the battle there was spread over the whole countryside, and the forest devoured more people that day than the
sword devoured.
9 Now Absalom happened to meet the servants of David.
For Absalom was riding on *his* mule, and the mule went under
the thick branches of a great oak. And [a]his head caught fast in
the oak, so he was [1]left hanging between heaven and earth,
while the mule that was under him kept going.
10 When a certain man saw *it*, he told Joab and said,
"Behold, I saw Absalom hanging in an oak."
11 Then Joab said to the man who had told him, "Now
behold, you saw *him!* Why then did you not strike him there
to the ground? And I would have given you ten *pieces* of silver
and a belt."
12 And the man said to Joab, "Even if I should receive a
thousand *pieces of* silver in my hand, I would not put out my
hand against the king's son; for [a]in our hearing the king
charged you and Abishai and Ittai, saying, '[1]Protect for me the
young man Absalom!'
13 "Otherwise, if I had dealt treacherously against his life
(and [a]there is nothing hidden from the king), then you yourself
would have stood aloof."
14 Then Joab said, "I will not [1]waste time here with you."
[a]So he took three spears in his hand and thrust them through
the heart of Absalom while he was yet alive in the [2]midst of the
oak.
15 And ten young men who carried Joab's armor gathered
around and struck Absalom and killed him.
16 Then [a]Joab blew the trumpet, and the people returned
from pursuing Israel, for Joab restrained the people.
17 And they took Absalom and cast him into [1]a deep pit in
the forest and [a]erected over him a very great heap of stones.
And [b]all Israel fled, each to his tent.
18 Now Absalom in his lifetime had taken and [a]set up for
himself a pillar which is in [b]the King's Valley, for he said, "[c]I
have no son [1]to preserve my name." So he named the pillar
after his own name, and it is called Absalom's monument to
this day.
19 Then [a]Ahimaaz the son of Zadok said, "Please let me
run and bring the king news [b]that the LORD has [1]freed him
from the hand of his enemies."
20 But Joab said to him, "You are not the man to carry
news this day, but you shall carry news another day; however,
you shall carry no news today because the king's son is dead."

4 [a]2 Sam. 18:24

5 [a]2 Sam. 18:12

6 [a]2 Sam. 17:26; Josh. 17:15, 18

7 [1]Lit., *smitten*

9 [1]Lit., *placed* [a]2 Sam. 14:26

12 [1]So with some mss. and the ancient versions; M.T., *Take care whoever* you are *of* [a]2 Sam. 18:5

13 [a]2 Sam. 14:19, 20

14 [1]Lit., *tarry thus* [2]Lit., *heart* [a]2 Sam. 14:30

16 [a]2 Sam. 2:28; 20:22

17 [1]Lit., *the great* [a]Deut. 21:20, 21; Josh. 7:26; 8:29 [b]2 Sam. 19:8; 20:1, 22

18 [1]Lit., *for the sake of remembering* [a]1 Sam. 15:12 [b]Gen. 14:17 [c]2 Sam. 14:27

19 [1]Lit., *vindicated* [a]2 Sam. 15:36 [b]2 Sam. 18:31

21 Then Joab said to the Cushite, "Go, tell the king what
you have seen." So the Cushite bowed to Joab and ran.
22 Now Ahimaaz the son of Zadok said once more to
Joab, "But whatever happens, please let me also run after the
Cushite." And Joab said, "Why would you run, my son, since
[a]you will have no reward for going?"
23 "But whatever happens," *he said*, "I will run." So he said
to him, "Run." Then Ahimaaz ran by way of the plain and
passed up the Cushite.
24 Now [a]David was sitting between the two gates; and
[b]the watchman went up to the roof of the gate by the wall, and
raised his eyes and looked, and behold, a man running by
himself.
25 And the watchman called and told the king. And the
king said, "If he is by himself there is good news in his mouth."
And he came nearer and nearer.
26 Then the watchman saw another man running; and the
watchman called to the gate-keeper and said, "Behold, *another*
man running by himself." And the king said, "This one
also is bringing good news."
27 And the watchman said, "I [1]think the running of the
first one [a]is like the running of Ahimaaz the son of Zadok."
And the king said, "[b]This is a good man and comes with good
news."
28 And Ahimaaz called and said to the king, "[1]All is well."
And [a]he prostrated himself before the king with his face to the
ground. And he said, "[b]Blessed is the LORD your God, who has
delivered up the men who lifted their hands against my lord
the king."
29 And the king said, "[a]Is it well with the young man
Absalom?" And Ahimaaz answered, "When Joab sent the
king's servant, and your servant, I saw a great tumult, but [b]I did
not know what *it was*."
30 Then the king said, "Turn aside and stand here." So he
turned aside and stood still.
31 And behold, the Cushite arrived, and the Cushite said,
"Let my lord the king receive good news, for [a]the LORD has
[1]freed you this day from the hand of all those who rose up
against you."
32 Then the king said to the Cushite, "[a]Is it well with the
young man Absalom?" And the Cushite answered, "[b]Let the
enemies of my lord the king, and all who rise up against you
for evil, be as that young man!"
33 [1]And the king was deeply moved and went up to the
chamber over the gate and wept. And thus he said as he
walked, "[a]O my son Absalom, my son, my son Absalom!
[b]Would I had died instead of you, O Absalom, my son, my
son!"

CHAPTER 19

THEN it was told Joab, "Behold, [a]the king is weeping and
mourns for Absalom."
2 And the [1]victory that day was turned to mourning for
all the people, for the people heard *it* said that day, "The king
is grieved for his son."

22 [a]2 Sam. 18:29
24 [a]2 Sam. 19:8 [b]2 Sam. 13:34; 2 Kin. 9:17
27 [1]Lit., *see* [a]2 Kin. 9:20 [b]1 Kin. 1:42
28 [1]Heb., *"Peace."* [a]2 Sam. 14:4; 1 Sam. 25:23 [b]1 Sam. 17:46
29 [a]2 Sam. 20:9; 2 Kin. 4:26 [b]2 Sam. 18:22
31 [1]Lit., *vindicated* [a]2 Sam. 18:19; Judg. 5:31
32 [a]2 Sam. 18:29 [b]1 Sam. 25:26
33 [1]Ch. 19:1 in Heb. [a]2 Sam. 19:4 [b]Ex. 32:32; Rom. 9:3
1 [a]2 Sam. 18:5, 14
2 [1]Lit., *salvation*

4 [1]Lit., *the king cried* [a]2 Sam. 15:30 [b]2 Sam. 18:33

6 [1]Or, *commanders* [2]Lit., *it would be right in your eyes*

7 [1]Lit., *to the heart*

8 [a]2 Sam. 15:2; 18:24 [b]2 Sam. 18:17

9 [1]Lit., *palm* [a]2 Sam. 8:1-14 [b]2 Sam. 5:20; 8:1 [c]2 Sam. 15:14

11 [a]2 Sam. 15:29

12 [a]2 Sam. 5:1

13 [a]2 Sam. 17:25 [b]1 Kin. 19:2 [c]2 Sam. 8:16 [d]2 Sam. 19:5-7; 3:27-39

14 [a]Judg. 20:1

15 [a]Josh. 5:9; 1 Sam. 11:14, 15

16 [a]2 Sam. 16:5-13; 1 Kin. 2:8

17 [a]2 Sam. 19:26, 27; 16:1-4

3 So the people went by stealth into the city that day, as people who are humiliated steal away when they flee in battle.

4 And the king [a]covered his face and [1]cried out with a loud voice, "[b]O my son Absalom, O Absalom, my son, my son!"

5 Then Joab came into the house to the king and said, "Today you have covered with shame the faces of all your servants, who today have saved your life and the lives of your sons and daughters, the lives of your wives, and the lives of your concubines;

6 by loving those who hate you, and by hating those who love you. For you have shown today that [1]princes and servants are nothing to you; for I know this day that if Absalom were alive and all of us were dead today, then [2]you would be pleased.

7 "Now therefore arise, go out and speak [1]kindly to your servants, for I swear by the LORD, if you do not go out, surely not a man will pass the night with you, and this will be worse for you than all the evil that has come upon you from your youth until now."

8 So the king arose and sat in the gate. When they told all the people, saying, "Behold, the king is [a]sitting in the gate," then all the people came before the king.

Now [b]Israel had fled, each to his tent.

9 And all the people were quarreling throughout all the tribes of Israel, saying, "[a]The king delivered us from the [1]hand of our enemies and [b]saved us from the [1]hand of the Philistines, but now [c]he has fled out of the land from Absalom.

10 "However, Absalom, whom we anointed over us, has died in battle. Now then, why are you silent bringing the king back?"

11 Then [a]King David sent to Zadok and Abiathar the priests, saying, "Speak to the elders of Judah, saying, 'Why are you the last to bring the king back to his house, since the word of all Israel has come to the king, *even* to his house?

12 'You are my brothers; [a]you are my bone and my flesh. Why then should you be the last to bring back the king?'

13 "And [a]say to Amasa, 'Are you not my bone and my flesh? [b]May God do so to me, and more also, if you will not be [c]commander of the army before me continually [d]in place of Joab.'"

14 Thus he turned the hearts of all the men of Judah [a]as one man, so that they sent *word* to the king, *saying*, "Return, you and all your servants."

15 The king then returned and came as far as the Jordan. And Judah came to [a]Gilgal in order to go to meet the king, to bring the king across the Jordan.

16 Then [a]Shimei the son of Gera, the Benjamite who was from Bahurim, hurried and came down with the men of Judah to meet King David.

17 And there were a thousand men of Benjamin with him, with [a]Ziba the servant of the house of Saul, and his fifteen sons and his twenty servants with him; and they rushed to the Jordan before the king.

18 Then they kept crossing the ford to bring over the king's household, and to do what was good in his sight. And

Shimei the son of Gera fell down before the king as he was
about to cross the Jordan.
19 So he said to the king, "[a]Let not my lord consider me
guilty, nor remember what your servant did wrong on the day
when my lord the king came out from Jerusalem, so that the
king should [1]take *it* to heart.
20 "For your servant knows that I have sinned; therefore
behold, I have come today, [a]the first of all the house of Joseph
to go down to meet my lord the king."
21 But Abishai the son of Zeruiah answered and said,
"[a]Should not Shimei be put to death for this, [b]because he cursed
the LORD's anointed?"
22 David then said, "[a]What have I to do with you, O sons
of Zeruiah, that you should this day be an adversary to me?
[b]Should any man be put to death in Israel today? For do I not
know that I am king over Israel today?"
23 And the king said to Shimei, "[a]You shall not die." Thus
the king swore to him.
24 Then [a]Mephibosheth the [1]son of Saul came down to
meet the king; and [b]he had neither [2]cared for his feet, nor
[2]trimmed his mustache, nor [c]washed his clothes, from the day
the king departed until the day he came *home* in peace.
25 And it was when he came from Jerusalem to meet the
king, that the king said to him, "[a]Why did you not go with me,
Mephibosheth?"
26 So he answered, "O my lord, the king, my servant deceived me; for your servant said, 'I will saddle a donkey for
myself that I may ride on it and go with the king,' [a]because
your servant is lame.
27 "Moreover, [a]he has slandered your servant to my lord
the king; but my lord the king is [b]like the angel of God, therefore do what is good in your sight.
28 "For [a]all my father's household was nothing but dead
men before my lord the king; [b]yet you set your servant among
those who ate at your own table. What right do I have yet that
I should [1]complain any more to the king?"
29 So the king said to him, "Why do you still speak of
your affairs? I have [1]decided, 'You and Ziba shall divide the
land.' "
30 And Mephibosheth said to the king, "Let him even
take it all, since my lord the king has come safely to his own
house."
31 Now [a]Barzillai the Gileadite had come down from Rogelim; and he went on to the Jordan with the king to [1]escort
him over the Jordan.
32 Now Barzillai was very old, being eighty years old; and
he had [1]sustained the king while he stayed at Mahanaim, for
he was a very great man.
33 And the king said to Barzillai, "You cross over with me
and I will [1]sustain you in Jerusalem with me."
34 But Barzillai said to the king, "[a]How long [1]have I yet to
live, that I should go up with the king to Jerusalem?
35 "I am [1]now [a]eighty years old. Can I distinguish between
good and bad? Or can your servant taste what I eat or what I
drink? Or can I hear any more [b]the voice of singing men and

19 [1]Lit., *set* [a]2 Sam. 16:6-8; 1 Sam. 22:15
20 [a]2 Sam. 16:5
21 [a]2 Sam. 16:7, 8 [b]Ex. 22:28
22 [a]2 Sam. 3:39; 16:9, 10 [b]1 Sam. 11:13
23 [a]1 Kin. 2:8
24 [1]I.e., grandson [2]Lit., *done* [a]2 Sam. 9:6-10 [b]2 Sam. 12:20 [c]Ex. 19:10
25 [a]2 Sam. 16:17
26 [a]2 Sam. 9:3
27 [a]2 Sam. 16:3, 4 [b]Sam. 14:17, 20
28 [1]Lit., *cry out* [a]2 Sam. 21:6-9 [b]2 Sam. 9:7, 10, 13
29 [1]Lit., *said*
31 [1]Lit., *send* [a]2 Sam. 17:27-29; 1 Kin. 2:7
32 [1]Or, *provided food for*
33 [1]Or, *provide food for*
34 [1]Lit., *are the days of the years of my life* [a]Gen. 47:8
35 [1]Lit., *today* [a]Ps. 90:10 [b]Eccl. 2:8; Is. 5:11, 12

35 [c]2 Sam. 15:33

women? [c]Why then should your servant be an added burden
to my lord the king?
36 "Your servant would merely cross over the Jordan with
the king. Why should the king compensate me *with* this
reward?

37 [a]2 Sam. 19:40; 1 Kin. 2:7; Jer. 41:17

37 "Please let your servant return, that I may die in my own
city near the grave of my father and my mother. However,
here is your servant [a]Chimham, let him cross over with my lord
the king, and do for him what is good in your sight."

38 [1]Lit., *choose*

38 And the king answered, "Chimham shall cross over
with me, and I will do for him what is good in your sight; and
whatever you [1]require of me, I will do for you."

39 [a]2 Sam. 14:33; Gen. 31:55; Ruth 1:14

39 All the people crossed over the Jordan and the king
crossed too. The king then [a]kissed Barzillai and blessed him,
and he returned to his place.

40 [1]Lit., *crossed over with* [a]2 Sam. 19:9, 10

40 Now the king went on to Gilgal, and Chimham went
on with him; and all the people of Judah and also [a]half the
people of Israel [1]accompanied the king.

41 [a]Judg. 8:1; 12:1 [b]2 Sam. 19:11, 12

41 And behold, all the men of Israel came to the king and
said to the king, "[a]Why had our brothers [b]the men of Judah
stolen you away, and brought the king and his household and
all David's men with him over the Jordan?"

42 [1]Lit., *me* [2]Lit., *is it hot to you* [3]Or, *a gift* [a]2 Sam. 19:12

42 Then all the men of Judah answered the men of Israel,
"Because [a]the king is near relative to [1]us. Why then [2]are you
angry about this matter? Have we eaten at all at the king's
expense, or has [3]anything been taken for us?"

43 [1]Singular in Heb. [a]2 Sam. 5:1; 1 Kin. 11:30, 31

43 But the men of Israel answered the men of Judah and
said, "[1a]We have ten parts in the king, therefore [1]we also have
more *claim* on David than you. Why then did you treat us
with contempt? Was it not [1]our advice first to bring back [1]our
king?" Yet the words of the men of Judah were harsher than
the words of the men of Israel.

CHAPTER 20

1 [a]2 Sam. 16:7 [b]Gen. 46:21 [c]2 Sam. 19:43; 1 Kin. 12:16 [d]1 Sam. 22:7-9 [e]2 Sam. 18:17; 1 Sam. 13:2; 2 Chr. 10:16

NOW a worthless fellow happened to be [a]there whose name
was Sheba, the son of [b]Bichri, a Benjamite; and he blew the
trumpet and said,

"[c]We have no portion in David,
Nor do we have inheritance in [d]the son of Jesse;
[e]Every man to his tents, O Israel!"

2 [1]Lit., *went up* [2]Lit., *clung to*

2 So all the men of Israel [1]withdrew from following David, *and* followed Sheba the son of Bichri; but the men of
Judah [2]remained steadfast to their king, from the Jordan even
to Jerusalem.

3 [a]2 Sam. 15:16; 16:21, 22

3 Then David came to his house at Jerusalem, and [a]the
king took the ten women, the concubines whom he had left to
keep the house, and placed them under guard and provided
them with sustenance, but did not go in to them. So they were
shut up until the day of their death, living as widows.

4 [a]2 Sam. 17:25; 19:13

4 Then the king said to [a]Amasa, "Call out the men of
Judah for me within three days, and be present here yourself."

5 [a]1 Sam. 13:8

5 So Amasa went to call out *the men of* Judah, but he
[a]delayed longer than the set time which he had appointed him.

6 [a]2 Sam. 21:17 [b]2 Sam. 11:11; 1 Kin. 1:33

6 And David said to [a]Abishai, "Now Sheba the son of
Bichri will do us more harm than Absalom; [b]take your lord's

servants and pursue him, lest he find for himself fortified cities
and escape from our sight."
7 So Joab's men went out after him, [a]along with the
Cherethites and the Pelethites and [b]all the mighty men; and
they went out from Jerusalem to pursue Sheba the son of
Bichri.
8 When they were at the large stone which is in [a]Gibeon,
Amasa came [1]to meet them. Now Joab was [2]dressed in his
military attire, and over it was a belt with a sword in its sheath
fastened at his waist; and as he went forward, it fell out.
9 And Joab said to Amasa, "Is it well with you, my brother?" And [a]Joab took Amasa by the beard with his right hand
to kiss him.
10 But Amasa was not on guard against the sword which
was in Joab's hand so [a]he struck him in the belly with it and
poured out his inward parts on the ground, and did not *strike*
him again; and he died. Then Joab and Abishai his brother
pursued Sheba the son of Bichri.
11 Now there stood by him one of Joab's young men, and
said, "Whoever favors Joab and whoever is for David, [a]*let him*
follow Joab."
12 But Amasa lay wallowing in *his* blood in the middle of
the highway. And when the man saw that all the people stood
still, he [1]removed Amasa from the highway into the field and
threw a garment over him when he saw that everyone who
came by him stood still.
13 As soon as he was removed from the highway, all the
men passed on after Joab to pursue Sheba the son of Bichri.
14 Now he went through all the tribes of Israel to Abel
even to Beth-maacah and all the [a]Berites; and they were gathered together and also went after him.
15 And they came and besieged him in [a]Abel Beth-maacah,
and [b]they [1]cast up a mound against the city, and it stood
by the rampart; and all the people who were with Joab were
wreaking destruction in order to topple the wall.
16 Then [a]a wise woman called from the city, "Hear, hear!
Please tell Joab, 'Come here that I may speak with you.' "
17 So he approached her, and the woman said, "Are you
Joab?" And he answered, "I am." Then she said to him, "Listen to the words of your maidservant." And he answered, "I
am listening."
18 Then she spoke, saying, "Formerly they used to say,
'They will surely ask *advice* at Abel,' and thus they ended *the
dispute*.
19 "I am of those who are peaceable *and* faithful in Israel.
[a]You are seeking to destroy a city even a mother in Israel. Why
would you swallow up [b]the inheritance of the LORD?"
20 And Joab answered and said, "Far be it, far be it from
me that I should swallow up or destroy!
21 "Such is not the case. But a man from [a]the hill country
of Ephraim, [b]Sheba the son of Bichri by name, has lifted up his
hand against King David. Only hand him over, and I will
depart from the city." And the woman said to Joab, "Behold,
his head will be thrown to you over the wall."
22 Then the woman [a]wisely came to all the people. And
they cut off the head of Sheba the son of Bichri and threw it to

7 [a]2 Sam. 8:18; 1 Kin. 1:38 [b]2 Sam. 15:18

8 [1]Lit., *before* [2]Lit., *girded with military garment as clothing* [a]2 Sam. 2:13; 3:30

9 [a]Matt. 26:49

10 [a]2 Sam. 2:23; 3:27; 1 Kin. 2:5

11 [a]2 Sam. 20:13

12 [1]Lit., *caused to turn*

14 [a]Num. 21:16

15 [1]Lit., *poured out* [a]1 Kin. 15:20; 2 Kin. 15:29 [b]2 Kin. 19:32; Ezek. 4:2

16 [a]2 Sam. 14:2

19 [a]Deut. 20:10 [b]2 Sam. 14:16; 21:3; 1 Sam. 26:19

21 [a]Josh. 24:33 [b]2 Sam. 20:2

22 [a]2 Sam. 21:16; Eccles. 9:13-16

Joab. So [b]he blew the trumpet, and they were dispersed from
the city, each to his tent. Joab also returned to the king at
Jerusalem.
23 [a]Now Joab was over the whole army of Israel, and Benaiah the son of Jehoiada was over the Cherethites and the
Pelethites;
24 and Adoram was over the forced labor, and Jehoshaphat
the son of Ahilud was the recorder;
25 and Sheva was scribe, and Zadok and Abiathar were
priests;
26 and [a]Ira the Jairite was also a priest to David.

Chapter 21

NOW there was [a]a famine in the days of David for three
years, year after year; and [b]David sought the presence of the
LORD. And the LORD said, "It is for Saul and his bloody house,
because he put the Gibeonites to death."
2 So the king called the Gibeonites and spoke to them
(now the Gibeonites were not of the sons of Israel but of the
remnant of the Amorites, and [a]the sons of Israel [1]made a
covenant with them, but Saul had sought to [2]kill them [b]in his
zeal for the sons of Israel and Judah).
3 Thus David said to the Gibeonites, "What should I do
for you? And how can I make atonement [a]that you may bless
the inheritance of the LORD?"
4 Then the Gibeonites said to him, "[a]We have no *concern* of silver or gold with Saul or his house, nor is it for us to
put any man to death in Israel." And he said, "I will do for you
whatever you say."
5 So they said to the king, "[a]The man who consumed us,
and who planned [1]to exterminate us from remaining within
any border of Israel,
6 let seven men from his sons be given to us, and we will
[1]hang them [a]before the LORD in Gibeah of Saul, [b]the chosen of
the LORD." And the king said, "I will give *them.*"
7 But the king spared [a]Mephibosheth, the son of Jonathan
the son of Saul, [b]because of the oath of the LORD which
was between them, between David and Saul's son Jonathan.
8 So the king took the two sons of [a]Rizpah the daughter
of Aiah, Armoni and Mephibosheth whom she had born to
Saul, and the five sons of [1]Merab the daughter of Saul, whom
she had born to Adriel the son of Barzillai the [b]Meholathite.
9 Then he gave them into the hands of the Gibeonites,
and they [1]hanged them in the mountain before the LORD, so
that the seven of them fell together; and they were put to
death in the first days of harvest at [a]the beginning of barley
harvest.
10 [a]And Rizpah the daughter of Aiah took sackcloth and
spread it for herself on the rock, from the beginning of harvest
until [1]it rained on them from the sky; and [b]she [2]allowed neither
the birds of the sky to rest on them by day nor the beasts of
the field by night.
11 When it was told David what Rizpah the daughter of
Aiah, the concubine of Saul, had done,
12 then David went and took [a]the bones of Saul and the

22 [b]2 Sam. 20:1

23 [a]2 Sam. 8:16-18; 1 Kin. 4:3-6

26 [a]2 Sam. 23:38

1 [a]Gen. 12:10; 26:1; 42:5 [b]Num. 27:21

2 [1]Lit., *had sworn to* [2]Lit., *smite* [a]Josh. 9:3, 15-20 [b]Ex. 34:11-16; Deut. 7:2; 1 Sam. 28:3

3 [a]2 Sam. 20:19; 1 Sam. 26:19

4 [a]Num. 35:31, 32

5 [1]Lit., *against us that we should be exterminated* [a]2 Sam. 21:1

6 [1]Lit., *expose them* [a]Num. 25:4 [b]1 Sam. 10:24

7 [a]2 Sam. 4:4; 9:10 [b]1 Sam. 18:3; 20:12-17; 23:18

8 [1]So Gk. and Heb. mss. [a]2 Sam. 3:7 [b]1 Kin. 19:16

9 [1]Lit., *exposed them* [a]Ex. 9:31, 32

10 [1]Lit., *water was poured* [2]Lit., *gave* [a]Deut. 21:23 [b]1 Sam. 17:44, 46

12 [a]1 Sam. 31:11-13

bones of Jonathan his son from the men of Jabesh-gilead, who
had stolen them from the open square of [b]Bethshan, [c]where
the Philistines had hanged them on the day [d]the Philistines
struck down Saul in Gilboa.
13 And he brought up the bones of Saul and the bones of
Jonathan his son from there, and they gathered the bones of
those who had been [1]hanged.
14 And they buried the bones of Saul and Jonathan his
son in the country of Benjamin in [a]Zela, in the grave of Kish
his father; thus they did all that the king commanded, and
after that [b]God was moved by entreaty for the land.
15 Now when [a]the Philistines were at war again with Israel, David went down and his servants with him; and as they
fought against the Philistines, David became weary.
16 Then Ishbi-benob, who was [a]among the descendants of
the [1]giant, the weight of whose spear was three hundred *shekels* of bronze in weight, [2]was girded with a new *sword,* and he
[3]intended to kill David.
17 But [a]Abishai the son of Zeruiah helped him, and struck
the Philistine and killed him. Then the men of David swore to
him, saying, "[b]You shall not go out again with us to battle, that
you may not extinguish [c]the lamp of Israel."
18 [a]Now it came about after this that there was war again
with the Philistines at Gob; then [b]Sibbecai the Hushathite
struck down Saph, who was among the descendants of the
[1]giant.
19 And there was war with the Philistines again at Gob,
and Elhanan the son of Jaare-oregim the Bethlehemite [1]killed
Goliath the Gittite, [a]the shaft of whose spear was like a weaver's beam.
20 And there was war at Gath again, and where there was a
man of *great* stature who had six fingers on each hand and six
toes on each foot, twenty-four in number; and he also had
been born [a]to the [1]giant.
21 And when he defied Israel, Jonathan the son of Shimei,
David's brother, struck him down.
22 [a]These four were born to the [1]giant in Gath, and they
fell by the hand of David and by the hand of his servants.

Chapter 22

[a]And David spoke [b]the words of this song to the Lord in the
day that the Lord delivered him from the [1]hand of all his
enemies and from the [1]hand of Saul.
2 And he said,
"[a]The Lord is my [1]rock and my fortress and my
deliverer;
3 [1a]My God, my rock, in whom I take refuge;
My [b]shield and [c]the horn of my salvation, my stronghold and [d]my refuge:
My savior, Thou dost save me from violence.
4 "I call upon the Lord, [a]who is worthy to be praised;
And I am saved from my enemies.
5 "For [a]the waves of death encompassed me;
[b]The torrents of [1]destruction [2]overwhelmed me;

12 [b]Josh. 17:11 [c]1 Sam. 31:10 [d]1 Sam. 31:4

13 [1]Lit., *exposed*

14 [a]Josh. 18:28 [b]2 Sam. 24:25; Josh. 7:26

15 [a]2 Sam. 5:17-25

16 [1]Heb., *Raphah* [2]Lit., *and he was* [3]Lit., *said* [a]2 Sam. 21:18-22; Num. 13:22, 28; Josh. 15:14

17 [a]2 Sam. 20:6-10 [b]2 Sam. 18:3 [c]2 Sam. 22:29; 1 Kin. 11:36

18 [1]Heb., *Raphah* [a]1 Chr. 20:4-8 [b]1 Chr. 11:29; 27:11

19 [1]Lit., *smote* [a]1 Sam. 17:7

20 [1]Heb., *Raphah* [a]2 Sam. 21:16, 18

22 [1]Heb., *Raphah* [a]1 Chr. 20:8

1 [1]Lit., *palm* [a]Ps. 18:2-50 [b]Ex. 15:1; Deut. 31:30

2 [1]Lit., *crag* [a]1 Sam. 23:25; 24:2; Ps. 31:3; 71:3

3 [1]Lit., *God of my rock* [a]Deut. 32:4, 37; 1 Sam. 2:2 [b]Gen. 15:1; Deut. 33:29 [c]Deut. 33:17; Luke 1:69 [d]Ps. 9:9

4 [a]Ps. 48:1; 96:4

5 [1]Heb., *Belial* [2]Or, *terrified* [a]Ps. 93:4; Jon. 2:3 [b]Ps. 69:14, 15

6 [a]The cords of [1]Sheol surrounded me;
The snares of death confronted me.
7 "[a]In my distress I called upon the LORD,
Yes, I [1]cried to my God;
And from His temple He heard my voice,
And my cry for help *came* into His ears.
8 "Then [a]the earth shook and quaked,
[b]The foundations of heaven were trembling
And were shaken, because He was angry.
9 "[a]Smoke went up [1]out of His nostrils,
And fire from His mouth devoured;
[b]Coals were kindled by it.
10 "He bowed the heavens also, and came down
With [a]thick darkness under His feet.
11 "[a]And He rode on a cherub and flew;
And He [1]appeared on [b]the wings of the wind.
12 "[a]And He made darkness [1]canopies around Him,
A mass of waters, thick clouds of the sky.
13 "From the brightness before Him
[a]Coals of fire were kindled.
14 "[a]The LORD thundered from heaven,
And the Most High uttered His voice.
15 "[a]And He sent out arrows, and scattered them,
Lightning, and [1]routed them.
16 "Then the channels of the sea appeared,
The foundations of the world were [1]laid bare,
By the rebuke of the LORD,
[a]At the blast of the breath of His nostrils.
17 "[a]He sent from on high, He took me;
[b]He drew me out of many waters.
18 "He delivered me from my strong enemy,
From those who hated me, for they were too strong for me.
19 "They confronted me in the day of my calamity,
[a]But the LORD was my support.
20 "[a]He also brought me forth into a broad place;
He rescued me, [b]because He delighted in me.
21 "[a]The LORD has rewarded me according to my righteousness;
[b]According to the cleanness of my hands He has recompensed me.
22 "[a]For I have kept the ways of the LORD,
And have not acted wickedly against my God.
23 "[a]For all His ordinances *were* before me;
And *as for* His statutes, I did not depart from [1]them.
24 "[a]I was also [1]blameless toward Him,
And I kept myself from my iniquity.
25 "[a]Therefore the LORD has recompensed me according to my righteousness,
According to my cleanness before His eyes.
26 "[a]With the [1]kind Thou dost show Thyself [1]kind,
With the [2]blameless Thou dost show Thyself [2]blameless;
27 [a]With the pure Thou dost show Thyself pure,
[b]And with the perverted Thou dost show Thyself [1]astute.

6 [1]I.e., the nether world [a]Ps. 116:3
7 [1]Or, *called* [a]Ps. 116:4; 120:1
8 [a]Judg. 5:4; Ps. 97:4 [b]Job 26:11
9 [1]Or, *in His wrath* [a]Ps. 97:4; Heb. 12:29 [b]2 Sam. 22:13
10 [a]Ex. 19:16; 1 Kin. 8:12; Ps. 97:2; Nah. 1:3
11 [1]Many mss. read, *sped* [a]2 Sam. 6:2 [b]Ps. 104:3
12 [1]Or, *pavilions* [a]Job 36:29
13 [a]2 Sam. 22:9
14 [a]Job 37:2-5; Ps. 29:3
15 [1]Lit., *confused* [a]Deut. 32:23; Josh. 10:10; 1 Sam. 7:10
16 [1]Or, *uncovered* [a]Ex. 15:8; Nah. 1:4
17 [a]Ps. 144:7 [b]Ex. 2:10
19 [a]Ps. 23:4
20 [a]Ps. 31:8; 118:5 [b]2 Sam. 15:26
21 [a]1 Sam. 26:23; 1 Kin. 8:32 [b]Ps. 24:4
22 [a]Gen. 18:19; Ps. 128:1; Prov. 8:32
23 [1]Lit., *it* [a]Deut. 6:6-9; Ps. 119:30, 102
24 [1]Lit., *complete* or *having integrity* [a]Gen. 6:9; 7:1; Eph. 1:4; Col. 1:21, 22
25 [a]2 Sam. 22:21
26 [1]Or, *loyal* [2]Lit., *complete* or *having integrity* [a]Matt. 5:7
27 [1]Lit., *twisted* [a]Matt. 5:8; 1 John 3:3 [b]Lev. 26:23, 24; Rom. 1:28

28 "[a]And Thou dost save an afflicted people;
[b]But Thine eyes are on the haughty *whom* Thou dost abase.
29 "[a]For Thou art my lamp, O LORD;
And the LORD illumines my darkness.
30 "[a]For by Thee I can [1]run upon a troop;
By my God I can leap over a wall.
31 "[a]As for God, His way is [1]blameless;
[b]The word of the LORD is tested;
[c]He is a shield to all who take refuge in Him.
32 "[a]For who is God, besides the LORD?
[b]And who is a rock, besides our God?
33 "[a]God is my strong fortress;
And He [1]sets the [2]blameless in [3]his way.
34 "[a]He makes [1]my feet like hinds' *feet*,
[b]And sets me on my high places.
35 "[a]He trains my hands for battle,
[b]So that my arms can bend a bow of bronze.
36 "Thou hast also given me [a]the shield of Thy salvation,
And Thy [1]help makes me great.
37 "[a]Thou dost enlarge my steps under me,
And my [1]feet have not slipped.
38 "I pursued my enemies and [a]destroyed them,
And I did not turn back until they were consumed.
39 "And I have devoured them and shattered them, so that they did not rise;
And [a]they fell under my feet.
40 "For Thou hast girded me with strength for battle;
Thou hast [1]subdued under me [a]those who rose up against me.
41 "Thou hast also [a]made my enemies turn *their* backs to me,
And I [1]destroyed those who hated me.
42 "[a]They looked, but there was none to save;
[b]*Even* to the LORD, but He did not answer them.
43 "[a]Then I pulverized them as the dust of the earth,
[b]I crushed *and* stamped them as the mire of the streets.
44 "[a]Thou hast also delivered me from the contentions of my people;
[b]Thou hast kept me as head of the nations;
[c]A people whom I have not known serve me.
45 "[a]Foreigners pretend obedience to me;
As soon as they hear, they obey me.
46 "Foreigners [1]lose heart,
[a]And [2]come trembling out of their [3]fortresses.
47 "The LORD lives, and blessed be my rock;
And exalted be [1a]God, the rock of my salvation,
48 [a]The God who executes vengeance for me,
[b]And brings down peoples under me,
49 Who also brings me out from my enemies;
Thou dost even lift me above [a]those who rise up against me;
[b]Thou dost rescue me from the violent man.
50 "[a]Therefore I will give thanks to Thee, O LORD, among the nations,
And I will sing praises to Thy name.

28 [a]Ex. 3:7, 8; Ps. 72:12, 13 [b]Is. 2:11, 12, 17; 5:15

29 [a]2 Sam. 21:17; Ps. 27:1; 1 Kin. 11:36

30 [1]Or, *crush a troop* [a]2 Sam. 5:6-8

31 [1]Lit., *complete* or *having integrity* [a]Deut. 32:4; Matt. 5:48 [b]Ps. 12:6; 119:140; Prov. 30:5 [c]2 Sam. 22:3; Ps. 84:9

32 [a]1 Sam. 2:2 [b]2 Sam. 22:2

33 [1]Or, *sets free* [2]Lit., *complete* or *having integrity* [3]Another reading is, *my* [a]2 Sam. 22:2; Ps. 31:3, 4

34 [1]Another reading is, *His* [a]2 Sam. 2:18; Heb. 3:19 [b]Deut. 32:13

35 [a]Ps. 144:1 [b]Job 20:24

36 [1]Lit., *answering* [a]Eph. 6:16, 17

37 [1]Lit., *ankles* [a]2 Sam. 22:20; Prov. 4:12

38 [a]Ex. 15:9

39 [a]Mal. 4:3

40 [1]Lit., *caused to bow down* [a]Ps. 44:5

41 [1]Or, *silenced* [a]Ex. 23:27; Josh. 10:24

42 [a]Is. 17:7, 8 [b]1 Sam. 28:6; Is. 1:15

43 [a]2 Kin. 13:7 [b]Is. 10:6; Mic. 7:10

44 [a]2 Sam. 3:1; 19:9, 14 [b]2 Sam. 8:1-14 [c]Is. 55:5

45 [a]Ps. 66:3; 81:15

46 [1]Lit., *languish* [2]Lit., *gird themselves* [3]Lit., *fastnesses* [a]1 Sam. 14:11; Mic. 7:17

47 [1]Lit., *the God of the rock* [a]2 Sam. 22:3; Ps. 89:26

48 [a]2 Sam. 4:8; 1 Sam. 24:12; 25:39; Ps. 94:1 [b]Ps. 144:2

49 [a]Ps. 44:5 [b]Ps. 140:1, 4, 11

50 [a]Rom. 15:9

51 [1]I.e., victories; lit., *salvation* [2]Lit., *seed* [a]Ps. 144:10 [b]Ps. 89:24 [c]2 Sam. 7:12-16

1 [a]2 Sam. 7:8, 9; Ps. 78:70, 71 [b]1 Sam. 16:12, 13; Ps. 89:20

2 [a]Matt. 22:43; 2 Pet. 1:21

3 [a]2 Chr. 22:2, 3, 32 [b]Ps. 72:1-3; Is. 11:1-5 [c]2 Chr. 19:7, 9

4 [a]Judg. 5:31; Ps. 72:6

5 [a]2 Sam. 7:12; Ps. 89:29; Is. 55:3

6 [a]Matt. 13:41

7 [1]Lit., *filled* [2]Lit., *sitting* [a]Matt. 3:10; 13:30; Heb. 6:8

8 [1]Or, *three* [a]1 Chr. 11:11-47

9 [1]Lit., *reproached* [2]Lit., *gone up* [a]1 Chr. 27:4 [b]1 Chr. 8:4

10 [1]Lit., *his hand clung* [2]Lit., *salvation* [a]1 Chr. 11:13 [b]1 Sam. 11:13; 19:5

11 [1]Possibly, at Lehi [a]2 Sam. 23:33

12 [1]Lit., *salvation* [a]2 Sam. 23:10

13 [a]1 Sam. 22:1

51 "[a]*He* is a tower of [1]deliverance to His king,
And [b]shows lovingkindness to His anointed,
[c]To David and his [2]descendants forever."

Chapter 23

NOW these are the last words of David.
David the son of Jesse declares,
[a]And the man who was raised on high declares,
[b]The anointed of the God of Jacob,
And the sweet psalmist of Israel,
2 "[a]The Spirit of the LORD spoke by me,
And His word was on my tongue.
3 "The God of Israel said,
[a]The Rock of Israel spoke to me,
'[b]He who rules over men righteously,
[c]Who rules in the fear of God,
4 [a]Is as the light of the morning *when* the sun rises,
A morning without clouds,
When the tender grass *springs* out of the earth,
Through sunshine after rain.'
5 "Truly is not my house so with God?
For [a]He has made an everlasting covenant with me,
Ordered in all things, and secured;
For all my salvation and all *my* desire,
Will He not indeed make *it* grow?
6 "[a]But the worthless, every one of them will be thrust away like thorns,
Because they cannot be taken in hand;
7 But the man who touches them
Must be [1]armed with iron and the shaft of a spear,
And [a]they will be completely burned with fire
in *their* [2]place."

8 [a]These are the names of the mighty men whom David
had: Josheb-basshebeth a Tahchemonite, chief of the [1]cap-
tains, he was called Adino the Eznite, because of eight
hundred slain *by him* at one time;
9 and after him was Eleazar the son of [a]Dodoi the [b]Aho-
hite, one of the three mighty men with David when they
[1]defied the Philistines who were gathered there to battle and
the men of Israel had [2]withdrawn.
10 [a]He arose and struck the Philistines until his hand was
weary and [1]clung to the sword, and [b]the LORD brought about a
great [2]victory that day; and the people returned after him only
to strip *the slain*.
11 Now after him was Shammah the son of Agee a [a]Hara-
rite. And the Philistines were gathered [1]into a troop, where
there was a plot of ground full of lentils, and the people fled
from the Philistines.
12 But he took his stand in the midst of the plot, defended
it and struck the Philistines; and [a]the LORD brought about a
great [1]victory.
13 Then three of the thirty chief men went down and
came to David in the harvest time to the [a]cave of Adullam,

while the troop of the Philistines was camping in [b]the valley of
Rephaim.
14 And David was then [a]in the stronghold, while the garrison of the Philistines was then in Bethlehem.
15 And David had a craving and said, "Oh that someone
would give me water to drink from the well of Bethlehem
which is by the gate!"
16 So the three mighty men broke through the camp of
the Philistines, and drew water from the well of Bethlehem
which was by the gate, and took *it* and brought *it* to David.
Nevertheless he would not drink it, but [a]poured it out to the
LORD;
17 and he said, "Be it far from me, O LORD, that I should
do this. [a]*Shall I drink* the blood of the men who went in
jeopardy of their lives?" Therefore he would not drink it.
These things the three mighty men did.
18 And [a]Abishai, the brother of Joab, the son of Zeruiah,
was [b]chief of the [1]thirty. And he swung his spear against three
hundred [2]and killed *them*, and had a name as well as the three.
19 He was most honored of the thirty, therefore he became their commander; however, he did not attain to the
three.
20 Then [a]Benaiah the son of Jehoiada, the son of a valiant
man of [b]Kabzeel, who had done mighty deeds, [1]killed the [2]two
sons of Ariel of Moab. He also went down and killed a lion in
the middle of a pit on a snowy day.
21 And he [1]killed an Egyptian, [2]an impressive man. Now
the Egyptian *had* a spear in his hand, but he went down to him
with a club and snatched the spear from the Egyptian's hand,
and killed him with his own spear.
22 These *things* [a]Benaiah the son of Jehoiada did, and had
a name as well as the three mighty men.
23 He was honored among the thirty, but he did not attain
to the three. And David appointed him over his guard.
24 [a]Asahel the brother of Joab was among the thirty; Elhanan the son of Dodo of Bethlehem,
25 [a]Shammah the [b]Harodite, Elika the Harodite,
26 Helez the Paltite, Ira the son of Ikkesh the [a]Tekoite,
27 Abiezer the [a]Anathothite, Mebunnai the Hushathite,
28 Zalmon the Ahohite, Maharai the [a]Netophathite,
29 [a]Heleb the son of Baanah the Netophathite, Ittai the
son of Ribai of [b]Gibeah of the sons of Benjamin,
30 Benaiah a [a]Pirathonite, Hiddai of the brooks of
[b]Gaash,
31 Abi-albon the Arbathite, Azmaveth the [a]Barhumite,
32 Eliahba the [a]Shaalbonite, the sons of Jashen, Jonathan,
33 [a]Shammah the Hararite, Ahiam the son of Sharar the
Ararite,
34 Eliphelet the son of Ahasbai, the son of [a]the Maacathite, [b]Eliam the son of [c]Ahithophel the Gilonite,
35 [a]Hezro the [b]Carmelite, Paarai the Arbite,
36 Igal the son of Nathan of [a]Zobah, Bani the Gadite,
37 Zelek the Ammonite, Naharai the [a]Beerothite, armor
bearers of Joab the son of Zeruiah,
38 [a]Ira the [b]Ithrite, Gareb the Ithrite,
39 [a]Uriah the Hittite; thirty-seven in all.

13 [b]2 Sam. 5:18
14 [a]1 Sam. 22:4, 5
16 [a]Gen. 35:14
17 [a]Lev. 17:10
18 [1]So two Heb. mss. and Syriac; M.T. *three* [2]Lit., *slain ones* [a]2 Sam. 10:10, 14; 18:2 [b]1 Chr. 11:20, 21
20 [1]Lit., *smote* [2]Or, *two lion-like heroes* [a]2 Sam. 8:18, 20, 23 [b]Josh. 15:21
21 [1]Lit., *smote* [2]Lit., *a man of appearance*
22 [a]2 Sam. 23:20
24 [a]2 Sam. 2:18; 1 Chr. 27:7
25 [a]1 Chr. 11:27; [b]Judg. 7:1
26 [a]2 Sam. 14:2
27 [a]Josh. 21:18
28 [a]2 Kin. 25:23
29 [a]1 Chr. 11:30 [b]Josh. 18:28
30 [a]Judg. 12:13, 15 [b]Josh. 24:30
31 [a]2 Sam. 3:16
32 [a]Josh. 19:42
33 [a]2 Sam. 23:11
34 [a]2 Sam. 10:6, 8; 20:14 [b]2 Sam. 11:3 [c]2 Sam. 15:12
35 [a]1 Chr. 11:37 [b]Josh. 15:55
36 [a]2 Sam. 8:3
37 [a]2 Sam. 4:2
38 [a]2 Sam. 20:26 [b]1 Chr. 2:53
39 [a]2 Sam. 11:3, 6

1 [a]1 Chr. 21:1
[b]2 Sam. 21:1, 2
[c]1 Chr. 27:23, 24

2 [1]Lit., *muster*
[a]2 Sam. 3:10; Judg. 20:1

3 [a]Deut. 1:11

4 [1]Lit., *muster*

5 [a]Deut. 2:36; Josh. 13:9, 16 [b]Num. 21:32; 32:35

6 [1]Or, *Kadesh in the land of the Hittite*
[a]Josh. 19:28; Judg. 1:31

7 [a]Josh. 19:29 [b]Josh. 11:3; Judg. 3:3 [c]Gen. 21:22-33

9 [1]Lit., *muster*
[a]Num. 1:44-46 [b]1 Chr. 21:5

10 [1]Lit., *smote* [2]Lit., *cause to pass away*
[a]1 Sam. 24:5 [b]2 Sam. 12:13
[c]1 Sam. 13:13; 2 Chr. 16:9

11 [a]1 Sam. 22:5; 1 Chr. 29:29 [b]1 Sam. 9:9

13 [a]1 Chr. 21:12; Ezek. 14:21

14 [a]Ps. 51:1; 130:4, 7

15 [1]Lit., *gave*
[a]1 Chr. 21:14; 27:24
[b]2 Sam. 24:2

Chapter 24

[a]Now [b]again the anger of the Lord burned against Israel,
and it incited David against them to say, "[c]Go, number Israel
and Judah."
2 And the king said to Joab the commander of the army
who was with him, "Go about now through all the tribes of
Israel, [a]from Dan to Beersheba, and [1]register the people, that I
may know the number of the people."
3 But Joab said to the king, "[a]Now may the Lord your
God add to the people a hundred times as many as they are,
while the eyes of my lord the king *still* see; but why does my
lord the king delight in this thing?"
4 Nevertheless, the king's word prevailed against Joab
and against the commanders of the army. So Joab and the
commanders of the army went out from the presence of the
king, to [1]register the people of Israel.
5 And they crossed the Jordan and camped in [a]Aroer, on
the right side of the city that is in the middle of the valley of
Gad, and toward [b]Jazer.
6 Then they came to Gilead and to [1]the land of Tahtim-hodshi,
and they came to Dan-jaan and around to [a]Sidon,
7 and came to the [a]fortress of Tyre and to all the cities of
the [b]Hivites and of the Canaanites, and they went out to the
south of Judah, *to* [c]Beersheba.
8 So when they had gone about through the whole land,
they came to Jerusalem at the end of nine months and twenty
days.
9 And Joab gave [a]the number of the [1]registration of the
people to the king; and there were in Israel [b]eight hundred
thousand valiant men who drew the sword, and the men of
Judah were five hundred thousand men.
10 Now [a]David's heart [1]troubled him after he had numbered
the people. So David said to the Lord, "[b]I have sinned
greatly in what I have done. But now, O Lord, please [2]take
away the iniquity of Thy servant, for [c]I have acted very
foolishly."
11 When David arose in the morning, the word of the
Lord came to [a]the prophet Gad, David's [b]seer, saying,
12 "Go and speak to David, 'Thus the Lord says, "I am
offering you three things; choose for yourself one of them,
which I may do to you." ' "
13 So Gad came to David and told him, and said to him,
"Shall [a]seven years of famine come to you in your land? Or will
you flee three months before your foes while they pursue you?
Or shall there be three days' pestilence in your land? Now
consider and see what answer I shall return to Him who sent
me."
14 Then David said to Gad, "I am in great distress. Let us
now fall into the hand of the Lord [a]for His mercies are great,
but do not let me fall into the hand of man."
15 So [a]the Lord [1]sent a pestilence upon Israel from the
morning until the appointed time; and seventy thousand men
of the people [b]from Dan to Beersheba died.

16 [a]When the angel stretched out his hand toward Jerusalem to destroy it, [b]the LORD relented from the calamity, and
said to the angel who destroyed the people, "It is enough!
Now relax your hand!" And the angel of the LORD was by the
threshing floor of Araunah the Jebusite.
17 Then David spoke to the LORD when he saw the angel
who was striking down the people, and said, "Behold, [a]it is I
who have sinned, and it is I who have done wrong; but [b]these
sheep, what have they done? Please let Thy hand be against
me and against my father's house."
18 So Gad came to David that day and said to him, "Go
up, erect an altar to the LORD on the threshing floor of [a]Arau-
nah the Jebusite."
19 And David went up according to the word of Gad, just
as the LORD had commanded.
20 And Araunah looked down and saw the king and his
servants crossing over toward him; and Araunah went out and
bowed his face to the ground before the king.
21 Then Araunah said, "Why has my lord the king come
to his servant?" And David said, "To buy the threshing floor
from you, in order to build an altar to the LORD, [a]that the
plague may be held back from the people."
22 And Araunah said to David, "Let my lord the king take
and offer up what is good in his sight. Look, [a]the oxen for the
burnt offering, the threshing sledges and the yokes of the oxen
for the wood.
23 "[a]Everything, O king, Araunah gives to the king." And
Araunah said to the king, "May the LORD your God [b]accept
you."
24 However, the king said to Araunah. "No, but I will
surely buy *it* from you for a price, for [a]I will not offer burnt
offerings to the LORD my God [1]which cost me nothing." So
[b]David bought the threshing floor and the oxen for fifty shekels of silver.
25 And David built there an altar to the LORD, and offered
burnt offerings and peace offerings. [a]Thus the LORD was
moved by entreaty for the land, and the plague was held back
from Israel.

16 [a]Ex. 12:23; 2 Kin. 19:35; Acts 12:23 [b]Ex. 32:14; 1 Sam. 15:11

17 [a]2 Sam. 24:10 [b]2 Sam. 7:8; Ps. 74:1

18 [a]2 Chr. 3:1

21 [a]Num. 16:44-50

22 [a]1 Sam. 6:14; 1 Kin. 19:21

23 [a]Gen. 23:8-16 [b]Ezek. 20:40, 41

24 [1]Lit., *gratuitously* [a]Mal. 1:13, 14 [b]1 Chr. 21:24, 25

25 [a]2 Sam. 21:14

THE FIRST BOOK OF THE KINGS

David the Aged.

NOW King David was old, advanced in age; and they covered him with clothes, but he could not keep warm.
2 So his servants said to him, "Let them seek a young
virgin for my lord the king, and let her [1]attend the king and
become his nurse; and let her lie in your bosom, that my lord
the king may keep warm."
3 So they searched for a beautiful girl throughout all the
territory of Israel, and found Abishag the [a]Shunammite, and
brought her to the king.
4 And the girl was very beautiful; and she became the
king's nurse and served him, but the king did not [1]cohabit with
her.
5 Now [a]Adonijah the son of Haggith exalted himself,
saying, "I will be king." So [b]he prepared for himself chariots
and horsemen with fifty men to run before him.
6 And his father had never [1]crossed him at any time by
asking, "Why have you done so?" And he was also a very
handsome man; and [2a]he was born after Absalom.
7 And [1]he had conferred with [a]Joab the son of Zeruiah
and with [b]Abiathar the priest; and following Adonijah they
helped him.
8 But [a]Zadok the priest, [b]Benaiah the son of Jehoiada,
[c]Nathan the prophet, Shimei, Rei, and [d]the mighty men who
belonged to David, were not with Adonijah.
9 And Adonijah sacrificed sheep and oxen and fatlings by
the [1]stone of Zoheleth, which is beside [a]En-rogel; and he invited all his brothers, the king's sons, and all the men of Judah,
the king's servants.
10 But he did not invite Nathan the prophet, Benaiah, the
mighty men, and [a]Solomon his brother.
11 Then Nathan spoke to Bathsheba the mother of Solomon, saying, "Have you not heard that Adonijah the son of
Haggith has become king, and David our lord does not know
it?
12 "So now come, please let me give you counsel and save
your life and the life of your son Solomon.
13 "Go [1]at once to King David and say to him, 'Have you
not, my lord, O king, sworn to your maidservant, saying, "[a]Sure-
ly Solomon your son shall be king after me, and he shall sit
on my throne"? Why then has Adonijah become king?'
14 "Behold, while you are still there speaking with the king,
I will come in after you and confirm your words."
15 So Bathsheba went in to the king in the bedroom. Now
[a]the king was very old, and Abishag the Shunammite was ministering to the king.
16 Then Bathsheba bowed and prostrated herself [1]before
the king. And the king said, "What [2]do you wish?"
17 And she said to him, "My lord, you swore to your

2 [1]Lit., *stand before*

3 [a]Josh. 19:18; 1 Sam. 28:4

4 [1]Lit., *know her*

5 [a]2 Sam. 3:4 [b]2 Sam. 15:1

6 [1]Lit., *pained him* [2]Lit., *she gave him birth* [a]2 Sam. 3:3, 4

7 [1]Lit., *his words were* [a]1 Chr. 11:6 [b]1 Sam. 22:20, 23

8 [a]2 Sam. 20:25; 1 Chr. 16:39 [b]2 Sam. 8:18 [c]2 Sam. 12:1 [d]2 Sam. 23:8-39

9 [1]Or, *Gliding* or *Serpent Stone* [a]Josh. 15:7; 18:16; 2 Sam. 17:17

10 [a]2 Sam. 12:24

13 [1]Lit., *and enter* [a]1 Kin. 1:30; 1 Chr. 22:9-13

15 [a]1 Kin. 1:1

16 [1]Lit., *to* [2]Lit., *to you*

maidservant by the LORD your God, *saying*, '[a]Surely your son
Solomon shall be king after me and he shall sit on my throne.'
18 "And now, behold, Adonijah is king; and now, my lord
the king, you do not know *it*.
19 "And [a]he has sacrificed oxen and fatlings and sheep in
abundance, and has invited all the sons of the king and Abiathar
the priest and Joab the commander of the army; but he has
not invited Solomon your servant.
20 "And as for you now, my lord the king, the eyes of all
Israel are on you, to tell them who shall sit on the throne of my
lord the king after him.
21 "Otherwise it will come about, [a]as soon as my lord the
king sleeps with his fathers, that I and my son Solomon will be
considered [1]offenders."
22 And behold, while she was still speaking with the king,
Nathan the prophet came in.
23 And they told the king, saying, "Here is Nathan the
prophet." And when he came in before the king, he prostrated
himself [1]before the king with his face to the ground.
24 Then Nathan said, "My lord the king, have you said,
'Adonijah shall be king after me, and he shall sit on my
throne'?
25 "[a]For he has gone down today and has sacrificed oxen
and fatlings and sheep in abundance, and has invited all the
king's sons and the commanders of the army and Abiathar the
priest, and behold, they are eating and drinking before him;
and they say, '[b]*Long* live King Adonijah!'
26 "[a]But me, *even* me your servant, and Zadok the priest
and Benaiah the son of Jehoiada and your servant Solomon, he
has not invited.
27 "Has this thing been done by my lord the king, and you
have not shown to your [1]servants who should sit on the throne
of my lord the king after him?"
28 Then King David answered and said, "Call Bathsheba
to me." And she came into the king's presence and stood
before the king.
29 And the king vowed and said, "[a]As the LORD lives, who
has redeemed my life from all distress,
30 surely as [a]I vowed to you by the LORD the God of
Israel, saying, 'Your son Solomon shall be king after me, and
he shall sit on my throne in my place'; I will indeed do so this
day."
31 Then Bathsheba bowed with her face to the ground,
and prostrated herself [1]before the king and said, "[a]May my
lord King David live forever."
32 Then King David said, "Call to me [a]Zadok the priest,
Nathan the prophet, and Benaiah the son of Jehoiada." And
they came into the king's presence.
33 And the king said to them, "Take with you [a]the servants of your lord, and have my son Solomon ride on my own
mule, and bring him down to [b]Gihon.
34 "And let Zadok the priest and Nathan the prophet [a]anoint
him there as king over Israel, and [b]blow the trumpet and
say, '[c]*Long* live King Solomon!'
35 "Then you shall come up after him, and he shall come

17 [a]1 Kin. 1:13
19 [a]1 Kin. 1:9
21 [1]Lit., *sinners* [a]1 Kin. 2:10; Deut. 31:16; 2 Sam. 7:12
23 [1]Lit., *to*
25 [a]1 Kin. 1:9 [b]1 Sam. 10:24
26 [a]1 Kin. 1:8, 10
27 [1]Some mss. read *servant*
29 [a]2 Sam. 4:9
30 [a]1 Kin. 1:13, 17
31 [1]Lit., *to* [a]Dan. 2:4; 3:9
32 [a]1 Kin. 1:8
33 [a]2 Sam. 20:6, 7 [b]2 Chr. 32:30; 33:14
34 [a]1 Sam. 10:1; 16:3, 12 [b]2 Sam. 15:10 [c]1 Kin. 1:25

37 [a]Josh. 1:5, 17; 1 Sam. 20:13 [b]1 Kin. 1:47

38 [a]1 Kin. 1:8 [b]2 Sam. 8:18 [c]1 Kin. 1:33

39 [a]Ex. 30:23-32; 1 Chr. 16:39; Ps. 89:20 [b]1 Chr. 29:22 [c]1 Kin. 1:34

40 [1]Lit., *fluting* [2]Lit., *was split*

41 [1]Lit., *is the sound of the city an uproar*

42 [a]2 Sam. 15:27, 36; 17:17 [b]2 Sam. 18:27

45 [a]1 Kin. 1:40

46 [a]1 Chr. 29:23

47 [a]1 Kin. 1:37 [b]Gen. 47:31

48 [a]1 Kin. 3:6; 2 Sam. 7:12

50 [a]1 Kin. 2:28; Ex. 27:2; 30:10

52 [a]1 Sam. 14:45; 2 Sam. 14:11

and sit on my throne and be king in my place; for I have
appointed him to be ruler over Israel and Judah."
36 And Benaiah the son of Jehoiada answered the king
and said, "Amen! Thus may the LORD, the God of my lord the
king, say.
37 "[a]As the LORD has been with my lord the king, so may
He be with Solomon, and [b]make his throne greater than the
throne of my lord King David!"
38 So [a]Zadok the priest, Nathan the prophet, Benaiah the
son of Jehoiada, [b]the Cherethites, and the Pelethites went
down and had Solomon ride on King David's mule, and
brought him to [c]Gihon.
39 Zadok the priest then [a]took the horn of oil from the
tent and [b]anointed Solomon. Then they [c]blew the trumpet,
and all the people said, "Long live King Solomon!"
40 And all the people went up after him, and the people
[1]were playing on flutes and rejoicing with great joy, so that the
earth [2]shook at their noise.
41 Now Adonijah and all the guests who were with him
heard *it*, as they finished eating. When Joab heard the sound
of the trumpet, he said, "Why [1]is the city making such an
uproar?"
42 While he was still speaking, behold, [a]Jonathan the son
of Abiathar the priest came. Then Adonijah said, "Come in,
for [b]you are a valiant man and bring good news."
43 But Jonathan answered and said to Adonijah, "No!
Our lord King David has made Solomon king.
44 "The king has also sent with him Zadok the priest, Nathan
the prophet, Benaiah the son of Jehoiada, the Cherethites,
and the Pelethites; and they have made him ride on the king's
mule.
45 "And Zadok the priest and Nathan the prophet have
anointed him king in Gihon, and they have come up from
there rejoicing, [a]so that the city is in an uproar. This is the
noise which you have heard.
46 "Besides, [a]Solomon has even taken his seat on the
throne of the kingdom.
47 "And moreover, the king's servants came to bless our
lord King David, saying, 'May [a]your God make the name of
Solomon better than your name and his throne greater than
your throne!' And [b]the king bowed himself on the bed.
48 "The king has also said thus, 'Blessed be the LORD, the
God of Israel, who [a]has granted one to sit on my throne today
while my own eyes see *it*.' "
49 Then all the guests of Adonijah were terrified; and they
arose and each went on his way.
50 And Adonijah was afraid of Solomon, and he arose,
went and [a]took hold of the horns of the altar.
51 Now it was told Solomon, saying, "Behold, Adonijah is
afraid of King Solomon, for behold, he has taken hold of the
horns of the altar, saying, 'Let King Solomon swear to me
today that he will not put his servant to death with the
sword.' "
52 And Solomon said, "If he will be a worthy man, [a]not
one of his hairs will fall to the ground; but if wickedness is
found in him, he will die."

53 So King Solomon sent, and they brought him down
from the altar. And he came and prostrated himself [1]before
King Solomon, and Solomon said to him, "Go to your house."

CHAPTER 2

AS David's [1a]time to die drew near, he charged Solomon his
son, saying,
2 "[a]I am going the way of all the earth. [b]Be strong, therefore, and [1]show yourself a man.
3 "And keep the charge of the LORD your God, to walk in
His ways, to keep His statutes, His commandments, His ordinances, and His testimonies, [a]according to what is written in
the law of Moses, that [b]you may succeed in all that you do and
wherever you turn,
4 so that [a]the LORD may carry out His promise which He
spoke concerning me, saying, [b]'If your sons are careful of their
way, [c]to walk before Me in [1]truth with all their heart and with
all their soul, [2d]you shall not lack a man on the throne of
Israel.'
5 "Now you also know what Joab the [a]son of Zeruiah did
to me, what he did to the two commanders of the armies of
Israel, to [b]Abner the son of Ner, and to [c]Amasa the son of
Jether, whom he killed; he also [1]shed the blood of war in
peace. And he put the blood of war on his belt [2]about his
waist, and on his sandals [3]on his feet.
6 "[a]So act according to your wisdom, and do not let his
gray hair go down to [1]Sheol in peace.
7 "[a]But show kindness to the sons of Barzillai the Gileadite, and [b]let them be among those who eat at your table; [c]for
they [1]assisted me when I fled from Absalom your brother.
8 "And behold, [a]there is with you Shimei the son of Gera
the Benjamite, of Bahurim; now it was he who cursed me with
a [1]violent curse on the day I went to Mahanaim. But when [b]he
came down to me at the Jordan, I swore to him by the LORD,
saying, 'I will not put you to death with the sword.'
9 "Now therefore, do not let him go unpunished, [a]for you
are a wise man; and you will know what you ought to do to
him, and you will bring his gray hair down to [1]Sheol with
blood."
10 Then [a]David slept with his fathers and was buried in
[b]the city of David.
11 And [a]the days that David reigned over Israel *were* forty
years: [b]seven years he reigned in Hebron, and thirty-three years
he reigned in Jerusalem.
12 And [a]Solomon sat on the throne of David his father,
and his kingdom was firmly established.
13 Now Adonijah the son of Haggith came to Bathsheba
the mother of Solomon. And she said, "Do you [a]come peacefully?" And he said, "Peacefully."
14 Then he said, "I have something *to say* to you." And
she said, "Speak."
15 So he said, "You know that [a]the kingdom was mine and
[b]that all Israel [1]expected me to be king; [c]however, the kingdom
has turned about and become my brother's, [d]for it was his
from the LORD.

53 [1]Lit., *to*

1 [1]Lit., *days*
[a]Gen. 47:29; Deut. 31:14

2 [1]Lit., *become a man*
[a]Josh. 23:14 [b]Deut. 31:7, 23; Josh. 1:6, 7

3 [a]Deut. 17:18-20 [b]1 Chr. 22:12, 13

4 [1]Or, *faithfulness* [2]Lit., saying, *there shall not be cast off to you a man from before Me*
[a]2 Sam. 7:25 [b]Ps. 132:12 [c]2 Kin. 20:3 [d]1 Kin. 8:25; 9:5; 2 Sam. 7:12, 13

5 [1]Lit., *made* [2]Lit., *that was about* [3]Lit., *that were on*
[a]2 Sam. 2:13, 18 [b]1 Kin. 2:32; 2 Sam. 3:27 [c]2 Sam. 20:10

6 [1]I.e., the nether world
[a]1 Kin. 2:9

7 [1]Lit., *came near to*
[a]2 Sam. 19:31-38 [b]2 Sam. 9:7, 10 [c]2 Sam. 17:27-29

8 [1]Or, *grievous*
[a]2 Sam. 16:5-8 [b]2 Sam. 19:18-23

9 [1]I.e., the nether world
[a]1 Kin. 2:6

10 [a]Acts 2:29; 13:36 [b]1 Kin. 3:1; 2 Sam. 5:7

11 [a]2 Sam. 5:4, 5; 1 Chr. 29:26, 27 [b]2 Sam. 5:5

12 [a]1 Chr. 29:23; 2 Chr. 1:1

13 [a]1 Sam. 16:4

15 [1]Lit., *set their faces on me*
[a]1 Kin. 2:22; 2 Sam. 3:3, 4 [b]1 Kin. 1:5-25 [c]1 Kin. 1:38-50 [d]1 Chr. 22:9, 10; 28:5-7

16 "And now I am making one request of you; do not
[1]refuse me." And she said to him, "Speak."
17 Then he said, "Please speak to Solomon the king, for
he will not [1]refuse you, that [a]he may give me Abishag the
Shunammite as a wife."
18 And Bathsheba said, "Very well; I will speak to the king
for you."
19 So Bathsheba went to King Solomon to speak to him
for Adonijah. And the king arose to meet her, bowed before
her, and sat on his throne; then he [a]had a throne set for the
king's mother, and [b]she sat on his right.
20 Then she said, "I am making one small request of you;
[a]do not [1]refuse me." And the king said to her, "Ask, my mother, for I will not [2]refuse you."
21 So she said, "[a]Let Abishag the Shunammite be given to
Adonijah your brother as a wife."
22 And King Solomon answered and said to his mother,
"And why are you asking Abishag the Shunammite for Adonijah? [a]Ask for him also the kingdom—[b]for he is my older brother—even for him, for [c]Abiathar the priest, and for Joab the
son of Zeruiah!"
23 Then King Solomon swore by the LORD, saying, "May
God do so to me and more also, if Adonijah has [a]not spoken
this word against his own [1]life.
24 "Now therefore as the LORD lives, who has established
me and set me on the throne of David my father, and [a]who has
made me a house as He promised, surely Adonijah will be put
to death today."
25 So King Solomon [a]sent [1]by Benaiah the son of Jehoiada; and he fell upon him so that he died.
26 Then to Abiathar the priest the king said, "[a]Go to
Anathoth to your own field, [b]for you [1]deserve to die; but I will
not put you to death at this time, because [c]you carried the ark
of the Lord [2]GOD before my father David, and because [d]you
were afflicted in everything with which my father was
afflicted."
27 So Solomon dismissed Abiathar from being priest to
the LORD, in order to fulfill [a]the word of the LORD, which He
had spoken concerning the house of Eli in Shiloh.
28 Now the news came to Joab, [a]for Joab had followed
Adonijah, [b]although he had not followed Absalom. And Joab
fled to the tent of the LORD and [c]took hold of the horns of the
altar.
29 And it was told King Solomon that Joab had fled to the
tent of the LORD, and behold, he is beside the altar. Then
Solomon [a]sent Benaiah the son of Jehoiada, saying, "Go, fall
upon him."
30 So Benaiah came to the tent of the LORD, and said to
him, "Thus the king has said, 'Come out.'" But he said, "No,
for I will die here." And Benaiah brought the king word again,
saying, "Thus spoke Joab, and thus he answered me."
31 And the king said to him, "[a]Do as he has spoken and
fall upon him and bury him, [b]that you may remove from me
and from my father's house the blood which Joab shed without cause.
32 "And [a]the LORD will return his blood on his own head,

16 [1]Lit., *turn away my face*

17 [1]Lit., *turn away your face* [a]1 Kin. 1:3, 4; 2 Sam. 12:8

19 [a]1 Kin. 15:13 [b]Ps. 45:9

20 [1]Lit., *turn away my face* [2]Lit., *turn away your face* [a]1 Kin. 2:16

21 [a]1 Kin. 1:3, 4

22 [a]2 Sam. 12:8 [b]1 Kin. 2:15; 1:6; 1 Chr. 3:2, 5 [c]1 Kin. 1:7

23 [1]Lit., *soul* [a]Ruth 1:17

24 [a]2 Sam. 7:11, 13; 1 Chr. 22:10

25 [1]Lit., *by the hand of* [a]2 Sam. 8:18

26 [1]Lit., *are a man of death* [2]YHWH, usually rendered LORD [a]Josh. 21:18; Jer. 1:1 [b]1 Sam. 26:16 [c]1 Sam. 23:6; 2 Sam. 15:24-29 [d]1 Sam. 22:20-23; 23:8, 9

27 [a]1 Sam. 2:27-36

28 [a]1 Kin. 1:7 [b]2 Sam. 17:25; 18:2 [c]1 Kin. 1:50

29 [a]1 Kin. 2:25

31 [a]Ex. 21:14 [b]Num. 35:33; Deut. 19:13

32 [a]Gen. 9:6; Judg. 9:24, 57

[b]because he fell upon two men more righteous and better than
he and killed them with the sword, while my father David did
not know *it*: [c]Abner the son of Ner, commander of the army of
Israel, and [d]Amasa the son of Jether, commander of the army
of Judah.
33 "[a]So shall their blood return on the head of Joab and on
the head of his [1]descendants forever; but to David and his
[1]descendants and his house and his throne, may there be peace
from the LORD forever."
34 Then [a]Benaiah the son of Jehoiada went up and fell
upon him and put him to death, and he was buried at his own
house in the wilderness.
35 And [a]the king appointed Benaiah the son of Jehoiada
over the army in his place, and the king appointed [b]Zadok the
priest [c]in the place of Abiathar.
36 Now the king sent and called for [a]Shimei and said to
him, "Build for yourself a house in Jerusalem and live there,
and do not go out from there to any place.
37 "For it will happen on the day you go out and [a]cross
over the [1]brook Kidron, you will know for certain that you
shall surely die; [b]your blood shall be on your own head."
38 Shimei then said to the king, "The word is good. As my
lord the king has said, so your servant will do." So Shimei lived
in Jerusalem many days.
39 But it came about at the end of three years, that two of
the servants of Shimei ran away [a]to Achish son of Maacah,
king of Gath. And they told Shimei, saying, "Behold, your
servants are in Gath."
40 Then Shimei arose and saddled his donkey, and went
to Gath to Achish to look for his servants. And Shimei went
and brought his servants from Gath.
41 And it was told Solomon that Shimei had gone from
Jerusalem to Gath, and had returned.
42 So the king sent and called for Shimei and said to him,
"Did I not make you swear by the LORD and solemnly warn
you, saying, 'You will know for certain that on the day you
depart and go anywhere, you shall surely die'? And you said to
me, 'The word which I have heard is good.'
43 "Why then have you not kept the oath of the LORD, and
the command which I [1]have laid on you?"
44 The king also said to Shimei, "[a]You know all the evil
which [1]you acknowledge in your heart, which you did to my
father David; therefore [b]the LORD shall return your evil on
your own head.
45 "But King Solomon shall be blessed, and [a]the throne of
David shall be established before the LORD forever."
46 [a]So the king commanded Benaiah the son of Jehoiada,
and he went out and fell upon him so that he died. [b]Thus the
kingdom was established in the hands of Solomon.

CHAPTER 3

THEN [a]Solomon [1]formed a marriage alliance with Pharaoh
king of Egypt, and took Pharaoh's daughter [b]and brought her
to the city of David, [c]until he had finished building his own

32 [b]2 Chr. 21:13, 14 [c]2 Sam. 3:27 [d]2 Sam. 20:9, 10

33 [1]Lit., *seed* [a]2 Sam. 3:29

34 [a]1 Kin. 2:25

35 [a]1 Kin. 4:4 [b]1 Chr. 29:22 [c]1 Kin. 2:27

36 [a]1 Kin. 2:8

37 [1]Or, *wadi* [a]2 Sam. 15:23 [b]2 Sam. 1:16

39 [a]1 Sam. 27:2

43 [1]Lit., *commanded*

44 [1]Lit., *your heart acknowledges* [a]2 Sam. 16:5-13 [b]1 Sam. 25:39; 2 Kin. 11:1, 12-16

45 [a]2 Sam. 7:13

46 [a]1 Kin. 2:25, 34 [b]1 Kin. 2:12; 2Chr. 1:1

1 [1]Lit., *made himself a son-in-law of Pharaoh* [a]1 Kin. 7:8; 9:16, 24; 2 Chr. 8:11 [b]1 Kin. 9:24 [c]1 Kin. 7:1; 9:10

house and the house of the LORD and [d]the wall around
Jerusalem.
2 [a]The people were still sacrificing on the high places,
because there was no house built for the name of the LORD
until those days.
3 Now [a]Solomon loved the LORD, [b]walking in the statutes
of his father David, except he sacrificed and burned incense on
the high places.
4 [a]And the king went to [b]Gibeon to sacrifice there, [c]for
that was the great high place; Solomon offered a thousand
burnt offerings on that altar.
5 [a]In Gibeon the LORD appeared to Solomon [b]in a dream
at night; and God said, "Ask what *you wish* me to give you."
6 Then Solomon said, "[a]Thou hast shown great lovingkindness to Thy servant David my father, [b]according as he
walked before Thee in [1]truth and righteousness and uprightness of heart toward Thee; and [c]Thou hast [2]reserved for him
this great lovingkindness, that Thou hast given him a son to sit
on his throne, as *it is* this day.
7 "And now, O LORD my God, [a]Thou hast made Thy
servant king in place of my father David; yet [b]I am but a little
child: [c]I do not know how to go out or come in."
8 "And [a]Thy servant is in the midst of Thy people which
Thou hast chosen, [b]a great people who cannot be numbered or
counted for multitude.
9 "So [a]give Thy servant an [1]understanding heart to judge
Thy people [b]to discern between good and evil. For who is able
to judge this [2]great people of Thine?"
10 And [1]it was pleasing in the sight of the Lord that Solomon had asked this thing.
11 And God said to him, "Because you have asked this
thing and have not asked for yourself [1]long life, nor have asked
riches for yourself, nor have you asked for the life of your
enemies, but have asked for yourself [2]discernment to understand justice,
12 behold, [a]I have done according to your words. Behold,
[b]I have given you a wise and discerning heart, so that there has
been no one like you before you, nor shall one like you arise
after you.
13 "[a]And I have also given you what you have not asked,
both riches and honor, so that there will not be any among the
kings like you all your days.
14 "And [a]if you walk in My ways, keeping My statutes and
commandments, as your father David walked, then I will prolong your days."
15 Then [a]Solomon awoke, and behold, it was a dream.
And he came to Jerusalem and stood before the ark of the
covenant of the Lord, and offered burnt offerings and made
peace offerings, and [b]made a feast for all his servants.
16 Then two women who were harlots came to the king
and [a]stood before him.
17 And the one woman said, "Oh, my lord, [1]this woman
and I live in the same house; and I gave birth to a child while
she *was* in the house.
18 "And it happened on the third day after I gave birth,
that this woman also gave birth to a child, and we were togeth-

1 [d]1 Kin. 9:15
2 [a]Lev. 17:3-5; Deut. 12:13, 14
3 [a]Deut. 6:5; Ps. 31:23 [b]1 Kin. 2:3; 9:4; 11:4, 6, 38
4 [a]2 Chr. 1:3 [b]Josh. 18:21-25 [c]1 Chr. 16:39; 21:29
5 [a]1 Kin. 9:2; 11:9 [b]Num. 12:6; Matt. 1:20
6 [1]Or, *faithfulness* [2]Lit., *kept* [a]2 Sam. 7:8-17 [b]1 Kin. 9:4 [c]1 Kin. 1:48
7 [a]1 Chr. 22:9-13 [b]1 Chr. 29:1; Jer. 1:6, 7 [c]Num. 27:17
8 [a]Ex. 19:6; Deut. 7:6 [b]Gen. 15:5; 22:17
9 [1]Lit., *hearing* [2]Lit., *heavy* [a]Prov. 2:3-9; Ps. 72:1, 2; James 1:5 [b]2 Sam. 14:17
10 [1]Lit., *the thing*
11 [1]Lit., *many days* [2]Lit., *hearing*
12 [a]1 John 5:14, 15 [b]1 Kin. 4:29-31; 5:12
13 [a]1 Kin. 4:21-24; 10:23, 27
14 [a]1 Kin. 3:6
15 [a]Gen. 41:7 [b]1 King. 8:65
16 [a]Num. 27:2
17 [1]Lit., *I and this woman*

er. There was no stranger with us in the house, only the two
of us in the house.
19 "And this woman's son died in the night, because she lay
on it.
20 "So she arose in the middle of the night and took my son
from beside me while your maidservant slept, and laid him in
her bosom, and laid her dead son in my bosom.
21 "And when I rose in the morning to nurse my son, behold, he was dead; but when I looked at him carefully in the
morning, behold, he was not my son, whom I had borne."
22 Then the other woman said, "No! For the living one is
my son, and the dead one is your son." But [1]the first woman
said, "No! For the dead one is your son, and the living one is
my son." Thus they spoke before the king.
23 Then the king said, "[1]The one says, 'This is my son
who is living, and your son is the dead one'; and [1]the other
says, 'No! For your son is the dead one, and my son is the
living one.' "
24 And the king said, "Get me a sword." So they brought a
sword before the king.
25 And the king said, "Divide the living child in two, and
give half to the one and half to the other."
26 Then the woman whose child *was* the living one spoke
to the king, for [1a]she was deeply stirred over her son and said,
"Oh, my lord, give her the living child, and by no means kill
him." But the other said, "He shall be neither mine nor yours;
divide *him!*"
27 Then the king answered and said, "Give the first woman the living child, and by no means kill him. She is his
mother."
28 When all Israel heard of the judgment which the king
had [1]handed down, they feared the king; for [a]they saw that the
wisdom of God was in him to [2]administer justice.

Chapter 4

Now king Solomon was king over all Israel.
2 And these were his officials: Azariah the son of Zadok
was [a]the priest;
3 Elihoreph and Ahijah, the sons of Shisha *were* secretaries;
Jehoshaphat the son of Ahilud *was* the recorder;
4 and Benaiah the son of Jehoiada *was* over the army;
and Zadok and Abiathar *were* priests;
5 and Azariah the son of Nathan *was* over [a]the deputies;
and Zabud the son of Nathan, a priest, *was* the king's friend;
6 and Ahishar was over the household; and Adoniram the
son of Abda *was* over the men subject to forced labor.
7 And Solomon had twelve deputies over all Israel, who
[1]provided for the king and his household; each man had to
[2]provide for a month in the year.
8 And these are their names: Ben-hur, in the [a]hill country
of Ephraim;
9 Ben-deker in Makaz and [a]Shaalbim and [b]Beth-shemesh
and Elonbeth-hanan;
10 Ben-hesed, in Arrubboth ([a]Socoh *was* his and all the
land of [b]Hepher);

22 [1]Lit., *this one was saying*

23 [1]Lit., *this one*

26 [1]Lit., *her compassion grew warm* [a]Gen. 43:30; Jer. 31:20

28 [1]Lit., *judged* [2]Lit., *do* [a]1 Kin. 3:9, 11, 12

2 [a]1 Chr. 6:10

5 [a]1 Kin. 4:7

7 [1]Lit., *nourished* [2]Lit., *nourish*

8 [a]Josh. 24:33

9 [a]Judg. 1:35 [b]Josh. 21:16

10 [a]Josh. 15:35 [b]Josh. 12:17

11 Ben-abinadab, *in* all [1]the [a]height of Dor (Taphath the
daughter of Solomon was his wife);
12 Baana the son of Ahilud, *in* [a]Taanach and Megiddo,
and all [b]Beth-shean which is beside [c]Zarethan below Jezreel,
from Beth-shean to [d]Abel-meholah as far as the other side of
[e]Jokmeam;
13 Ben-geber, in [a]Ramoth-gilead ([b]the towns of Jair, the
son of Manasseh, which are in Gilead were his: [c]the region of
Argob, which is in Bashan, sixty great cities with walls and
bronze bars *were* his);
14 Ahinadab the son of Iddo, *in* [a]Mahanaim;
15 [a]Ahimaaz, in Naphtali (he also married Basemath the
daughter of Solomon);
16 Baana the son of [a]Hushai, in Asher and [1]Bealoth;
17 Jehoshaphat the son of Paruah, in Issachar;
18 [a]Shimei the son of Ela, in Benjamin;
19 Geber the son of Uri, in the land of Gilead, [a]the country of Sihon king of the Amorites and of Og king of Bashan;
and *he was* the only deputy who *was* in the land.
20 [a]Judah and Israel *were* as numerous as the sand that is
on the [1]seashore in abundance; *they* were eating and drinking
and rejoicing.
21 [1a]Now Solomon ruled over all the kingdoms [b]from the
[2]River *to* the land of the Philistines and to the border of
Egypt; [c]*they* brought tribute and served Solomon all the days
of his life.
22 And Solomon's [1]provision for one day was thirty [2]kors
of fine flour and sixty [2]kors of meal,
23 ten fat oxen, twenty [1]pasture-fed oxen, a hundred
sheep besides deer, gazelles, roebucks, and fattened fowl.
24 For he had dominion over everything [1]west of the [2]Riv-
er, from Tiphsah even to [a]Gaza, [b]over all the kings [1]west of
the [2]River; and [c]he had peace on all sides around him.
25 [a]So Judah and Israel lived in safety, every man under
his vine and his fig tree, [b]from Dan even to Beersheba, all the
days of Solomon.
26 [a]And Solomon had [1]40,000 stalls of horses for his chariots, and 12,000 horsemen.
27 And those deputies [1]provided for King Solomon and all
who came to King Solomon's table, each in his month; they
left nothing lacking.
28 They also brought barley and straw for the horses and
[a]swift steeds to the place where it should be, each according to
his charge.
29 Now [a]God gave Solomon wisdom and very great discernment and breadth of [1]mind, [b]like the sand that is on the
seashore.
30 And Solomon's wisdom surpassed the wisdom of all
[a]the sons of the east and [b]all the wisdom of Egypt.
31 For [a]he was wiser than all men, than [b]Ethan the Ezrahite, Heman, [c]Calcol and Darda, the sons of Mahol; and his
[1]fame was *known* in all the surrounding nations.
32 [a]He also spoke 3,000 proverbs, and his songs were
1,005.
33 And he spoke of trees, from the cedar that is in

11 [1]Or, *Naphoth-dor* [a]Josh. 11:1, 2

12 [a]Judg. 5:19 [b]Josh. 17:11 [c]Josh. 3:16 [d]1 Kin. 19:16 [e]1 Chr. 6:68

13 [a]1 Kin. 22:3-15 [b]Num. 32:41 [c]Deut. 3:4

14 [a]Josh. 13:26

15 [a]2 Sam. 15:27

16 [1]Or, *in Aloth* [a]2 Sam. 15:32

18 [a]1 Kin. 1:8

19 [a]Deut. 3:8-10

20 [1]Lit., *sea* [a]1 Kin. 3:8; Gen. 32:12

21 [1]Ch. 5, v. 1 in Heb. [2]I.e., Euphrates [a]2 Chr. 9:26 [b]Gen. 15:18 [c]2 Sam. 8:2, 6

22 [1]Lit., *bread* [2]I.e., 1 kor equals approx. 10 bu

23 [1]Lit., *oxen of the pasture*

24 [1]Lit., *beyond* [2]I.e., Euphrates [a]Judg. 1:18 [b]Ps. 72:11 [c]1 Chr. 22:9

25 [a]Jer. 23:6; Mic. 4:4; Zech. 3:10 [b]1 Sam. 3:20

26 [1]One ms. reads *4000*, cf. 2 Chr. 9:25 [a]1 Kin. 10:26

27 [1]Or, *nourished*

28 [a]Esth. 8:10, 14; Mic. 1:13

29 [1]Lit., *heart* [a]1 Kin. 3:12 [b]1 Kin. 4:20

30 [a]Gen. 29:1; Judg. 6:33 [b]Is. 19:11; Acts 7:22

31 [1]Lit., *name* [a]1 Kin. 3:12 [b]1 Chr. 15:19; Ps. 89: title [c]1 Chr. 2:6

32 [a]Prov. 1:1; Eccles. 12:9; Song of Sol. 1:1

Lebanon even to the hyssop that grows on the wall; he spoke
also of animals and birds and creeping things and fish.
34 And [1]men [a]came from all peoples to hear the wisdom
of Solomon, from all the kings of the earth who had heard of
his wisdom.

Chapter 5

1a
NOW Hiram king of Tyre sent his servants to Solomon,
when he heard that they had anointed him king in place of his
father, for [b]Hiram had [2]always been a friend of David.
2 Then Solomon sent *word* to Hiram, saying,
3 "You know that [a]David my father was unable to build a
house for the name of the LORD his God because of the wars
which surrounded him, until the LORD put them under the
soles of his feet.
4 "But now [a]the LORD my God has given me rest on every
side; there is neither adversary nor [1]misfortune.
5 "And behold, [a]I [1]intend to build a house for the name of
the LORD my God, as the LORD spoke to David my father,
saying, 'Your son, whom I will set on your throne in your
place, he will build the house for My name.'
6 "Now therefore, command that they cut for me cedars
from Lebanon, and my servants will be with your servants; and
I will give you wages for your servants according to all that you
say, for you know that there is no one among us who knows
how to cut timber like the Sidonians."
7 And it came about when Hiram heard the words of
Solomon, that he rejoiced greatly and said, "Blessed be the
LORD today, who has given to David a wise son over this great
people."
8 So Hiram sent *word* to Solomon, saying, "I have heard
the message which you have sent me; I will do [1]what you desire
concerning the cedar and cypress timber.
9 "My servants will bring *them* down from Lebanon to the
sea; and I will make them into rafts *to go* by sea [a]to the place
where you [1]direct me, and I will have them broken up there,
and you shall carry *them* away. Then [b]you shall accomplish my
desire by giving food to my household."
10 So [1]Hiram [2]gave Solomon [3]as much as he desired of the
cedar and cypress timber.
11 Solomon then gave Hiram 20,000 kors of wheat as food
for his household, and twenty [1]kors of beaten oil; thus Solomon would give Hiram year by year.
12 And [a]the LORD gave wisdom to Solomon, just as He
[1]promised him; and there was peace between Hiram and Solomon, and the two of them made a covenant.
13 Now [a]King Solomon [1]levied forced laborers from all
Israel; and the forced laborers [2]numbered 30,000 men.
14 And he sent them to Lebanon, 10,000 a month in re-
lays; they were in Lebanon a month *and* two months at home.
And [a]Adoniram *was* over the forced laborers.
15 Now [a]Solomon had 70,000 [1]transporters, and 80,000
hewers *of stone* in the mountains,
16 [a]besides Solomon's 3,300 chief deputies who *were* over

34 [1]Lit., *they* [a]1 Kin. 10:1; 2 Chr. 9:23

1 [1]Ch. 5:15 in Heb. [2]Lit., *all the day* [a]2 Chr. 2:3 [b]2 Sam. 5:11; 1 Chr. 14:1

3 [a]1 Chr. 28:2, 3

4 [1]Lit., *evil occurrence* [a]1 Kin. 4:24; 1 Chr. 22:9

5 [1]Lit., *say* [a]2 Sam. 7:12, 13; 1 Chr. 17:12; 22:10; 28:6

8 [1]Lit., *all your pleasure*

9 [1]Lit., *send* [a]2 Chr. 2:16 [b]Ezra 3:7; Ezek. 27:17

10 [1]Heb., *Hirom* [2]Lit., *was giving* [3]Lit., *all his desire*

11 [1]I.e., 1 kor equals approx. 10 bu.

12 [1]Lit., *spoke to* [a]1 Kin. 3:12

13 [1]Lit., *raised up* [2]Lit., *was* [a]1 Kin. 4:6; 9:15

14 [a]1 Kin. 4:6

15 [1]Or, *burden bearers* [a]1 Kin. 9:20-22; 2 Chr. 2:17, 18

16 [a]1 Kin. 9:23

the [1]project *and* who ruled over the people who were doing
the work.
17 Then [a]the king commanded, and they quarried great
stones, costly stones, to lay the foundation of the house with
cut stones.
18 So Solomon's builders and [1]Hiram's builders and [a]the
Gebalites [2]cut them, and prepared the timbers and the stones
to build the house.

Chapter 6

[a]NOW it came about in the four hundred and eightieth year
after the sons of Israel came out of the land of Egypt, in the
fourth year of Solomon's reign over Israel, in the month of Ziv
which is the second month, that he [1]began to build the house
of the LORD.
2 As for the house which King Solomon built for the
LORD, its length *was* sixty [1]cubits and its width twenty *cubits*
and its height thirty cubits.
3 And the porch in front of the nave of the house *was*
twenty cubits [1]in length, [2]corresponding to the width of the
house, *and* its [3]depth along the front of the house *was* ten
cubits.
4 Also for the house [a]he made windows with *artistic*
frames.
5 And [a]against the wall of the house he built stories en-
compassing the walls of the house around both the nave and
the [b]inner sanctuary; thus he made [c]side chambers all around.
6 The lowest story *was* five cubits wide, and the middle
was six cubits wide, and the third *was* seven cubits wide; for on
the outside he [1]made offsets *in the wall* of the house all
around in order that *the beams* should not [2]be inserted in the
walls of the house.
7 And [a]the house, while it was being built, was built of
stone [1]prepared at the quarry, and there was neither hammer
nor axe nor any iron tool heard in the house while it was being
built.
8 The doorway for the [1]lowest side chamber *was* on the
right side of the house; and they would go up by winding stairs
to the middle *story*, and from the middle to the third.
9 So [a]he built the house and finished it; and he covered
the house with beams and [1]planks of cedar.
10 He also built the stories against the whole house, each
five [1]cubits high; and they [2]were fastened to the house with
timbers of cedar.
11 Now the word of the LORD came to Solomon saying,
12 "*Concerning* this house which you are building, [a]if you
will walk in My statutes and execute My ordinances and keep
all My commandments by walking in them, then I will carry
out My word with you which I spoke to David your father.
13 "And [a]I will dwell among the sons of Israel, and [b]will not
forsake My people Israel."
14 [a]So Solomon built the house and finished it.
15 Then he built the walls of the house on the inside with

16 [1]Lit., *work*

17 [a]1 Kin. 6:7; 1 Chr. 22:2

18 [1]Heb., *Hirom's* [2]Or, *chiseled* [a]Josh. 13:5; Ezek. 27:9

1 [1]Lit., *built* [a]2 Chr. 3:1, 2

2 [1]I.e., 18 inches

3 [1]Lit., *in its length* [2]Lit., *on the face of* [3]Lit., *width*

4 [a]Ezek. 40:16; 41:16

5 [a]Ezek. 41:6 [b]1 Kin. 6:16, 19, 20 [c]Ezek. 41:5, 6

6 [1]Lit., *gave* [2]Lit., *take hold*

7 [1]Lit., *finished* [a]Ex. 20:25; Deut. 27:5, 6

8 [1]So with Gk. & versions; M.T., *middle*

9 [1]Lit., *rows* [a]1 Kin. 6:14, 38

10 [1]Lit., *one cubit equals approx. 18 inches* [2]Lit., *took hold*

12 [a]1 Kin. 9:4; 2 Sam. 7:5-16

13 [a]Ex. 25:8 [b]Deut. 31:6; Josh. 1:5

14 [a]1 Kin. 6:9, 38

boards of cedar; from the floor of the house to the [1]ceiling he
overlaid *the walls* on the inside with wood, and [a]he overlaid
the floor of the house with boards of cypress.
16 [a]And he built twenty cubits on the rear part of the
house with boards of cedar from the floor to the [1]ceiling; he
built *them* for it on the inside as an inner sanctuary, *even* as
[b]the most holy place.
17 And the house, that is, the nave in front of *the inner
sanctuary*, was forty [1]cubits *long*.
18 And there was cedar on the house within, carved *in the
shape* of [a]gourds and open flowers; all was cedar, there was no
stone seen.
19 Then he prepared an inner sanctuary within the house
in order to place there the ark of the covenant of the LORD.
20 And [1]the inner sanctuary *was* twenty cubits in length,
twenty cubits in width, and twenty cubits in height, and he
overlaid it with pure gold. He also overlaid the altar with
cedar.
21 So Solomon overlaid the inside of the house with pure
gold. And he drew chains of gold across the front of the inner
sanctuary; and he overlaid it with gold.
22 And he overlaid the whole house with gold, until all the
house was finished. Also [a]the whole altar which was by the
inner sanctuary he overlaid with gold.
23 [a]Also in the inner sanctuary [b]he made two cherubim of
olive wood, each ten cubits high.
24 And five cubits *was* the one wing of the cherub and five
cubits the other wing of the cherub; from the end of one wing
to the end of the other wing *were* ten cubits.
25 And the other cherub *was* ten cubits; both the cherubim were of the same measure and the same form.
26 The height of the one cherub *was* ten cubits, and so
was the other cherub.
27 And he placed the cherubim in the midst of the inner
house, and [a]the wings of the cherubim were spread out, so that
the wing of the one was touching the *one* wall, and the wing of
the other cherub was touching the other wall. So their wings
were touching each other in the center of the house.
28 He also overlaid the cherubim with gold.
29 Then he carved all the walls of the house round about
with carved engravings of cherubim, palm trees, and open flowers, inner and outer *sanctuaries*.
30 And he overlaid the floor of the house with gold, inner
and outer *sanctuaries*.
31 And for the entrance of the inner sanctuary he made
doors of olive wood, the lintel *and* five-sided doorposts.
32 So *he made* two doors of olive wood, and he carved on
them carvings of cherubim, palm trees, and open flowers, and
overlaid them with gold; and he spread the gold on the cherubim and on the palm trees.
33 So also he made for the entrance of the nave four-sided
doorposts of olive wood
34 and [a]two doors of cypress wood; the two leaves of the
one door turned on pivots, and the two [1]leaves of the other
door turned on pivots.

15 [1]Lit., *walls of ceiling* [a]1 Kin. 7:7

16 [1]Lit., *walls* [a]2 Chr. 3:8 [b]1 Kin. 8:6; Ex. 26:33, 34

17 [1]One cubit equals approx. 18 in.

18 [a]1 Kin. 7:24

20 [1]Lit., *before*

22 [a]Ex. 30:1, 3, 6

23 [a]2 Chr. 3:10-12 [b]Ex. 37:7-9

27 [a]1 Kin. 8:7; Ex. 25:20; 37:9

34 [1]So with Gk.; M.T. *curtains* [a]Ezek. 41:23-25

35 And he carved *on it* cherubim, palm trees, and open
flowers; and he overlaid *them* with gold evenly applied on the
engraved work.
36 And [a]he built the inner court with three rows of cut
stone and a row of cedar beams.
37 [a]In the fourth year the foundation of the house of the
LORD was laid, in the month of Ziv.
38 And in the eleventh year, in the month of Bul, which is
the eighth month, the house was finished throughout all its
parts and according to all its plans. So he was seven years in
building it.

CHAPTER 7

NOW [a]Solomon was building his own house thirteen years,
and he finished all his house.
2 And [a]he built the house of the Forest of Lebanon; its
length was 100 [1]cubits and its width 50 cubits and its height 30
cubits, on four rows of cedar pillars with cedar beams on the
pillars.
3 And it was paneled with cedar above the side-chambers
which were on the 45 pillars, 15 in each row.
4 And *there were artistic window* frames in three rows,
and window was opposite window in three ranks.
5 And all the doorways and doorposts had squared *artistic* frames, and window was opposite window in three ranks.
6 Then he made [a]the hall of pillars; its length was 50
cubits and its width 30 cubits, and a porch *was* in front of them
and pillars and a [b]threshold in front of them.
7 And he made the hall of the throne where he was to
judge, the hall of judgment, and [a]it was paneled with cedar
from floor to floor.
8 And his house where he was to live, the other court
inward from the hall, was of the same workmanship. [a]He also
made a house like this hall for Pharaoh's daughter, [b]whom
Solomon had married.
9 All these were of costly stones, of stone cut according
to measure, sawed with saws, inside and outside; even from the
foundation to the coping, and so on the outside to the great
court.
10 And the foundation was of costly stones, *even* large
stones, stones of ten cubits and stones of eight cubits.
11 And above were costly stones, stone cut according to
measure, and cedar.
12 So [a]the great court all around had three rows of cut
stone and a row of cedar beams even as the inner court of the
house of the LORD, and [b]the porch of the house.
13 Now [a]King Solomon sent and brought Hiram from
Tyre.
14 [a]He was a widow's son from the tribe of Naphtali, and
his father was a man of Tyre, a worker in bronze; and [b]he was
filled with wisdom and understanding and skill, for doing any
work in bronze. So he came to King Solomon and [c]performed
all his work.

36 [a]1 Kin. 7:12; Jer. 36:10
37 [a]1 Kin. 6:1
1 [a]1 Kin. 3:1; 9:10; 2 Chr. 8:1
2 [1]I.e., Approx. 18 inches [a]1 Kin. 10:17, 21; 2 Chr. 9:16
6 [a]1 Kin. 7:12 [b]Ezek. 41:25, 26
7 [a]1 Kin. 6:15, 16
8 [a]1 Kin. 9:24; 2 Chr. 8:11 [b]1 Kin. 3:1
12 [a]1 Kin. 6:36 [b]1 Kin. 7:6
13 [a]2 Chr. 2:13, 14
14 [a]2 Chr. 2:14 [b]Ex. 31:3-5; 35:31 [c]2 Chr. 4:11-16

15 And he fashioned [a]the two pillars of bronze, [b]eighteen
cubits was the height of one pillar, and a line of twelve cubits
[1]measured the circumference of both.
16 He also made two capitals of molten bronze to set on
the tops of the pillars; the height of the one capital was five
[1]cubits and the height of the other capital was five cubits.
17 *There were* nets of network and twisted threads of
chainwork for the capitals which were on the top of the pillars;
seven for the one capital and seven for the other capital.
18 So he made the pillars, and two rows around on the one
network to cover the capitals which were on the top of the
pomegranates; and so he did for the other capital.
19 And the capitals which *were* on the top of the pillars in
the porch were of lily design, four cubits.
20 And *there were* capitals also on the two pillars, close to
the [1]rounded projection which was beside the network; and
[a]the pomegranates *numbered* two hundred in rows around
[2]both capitals.
21 [a]Thus he set up the pillars at the porch of the nave; and
he set up the right pillar and named it [1]Jachin, and he set up
the left pillar and named it [2]Boaz.
22 And on the top of the pillars was lily design. So the
work of the pillars was finished.
23 [a]Now he made the sea of [b]*cast metal* ten cubits from
brim to brim, circular in form, and its height was five cubits,
and [1]thirty cubits in circumference.
24 And under its brim [a]gourds went around encircling it
ten to a cubit, completely surrounding the sea; the gourds were
in two rows, cast [1]with the rest.
25 [a]It stood on twelve oxen, three facing north, three facing west, three facing south, and three facing east; and the sea
was set on top of them, and all their rear parts *turned* inward.
26 And it was a handbreadth thick, and its brim was made
like the brim of a cup, *as* a lily blossom; it could hold two
thousand baths.
27 Then [a]he made the ten stands of bronze; the length of
each stand was four cubits and its width four cubits and its
height three cubits.
28 And this was the design of the stands: they had borders,
even borders between the [1]frames,
29 and on the borders which were between the [1]frames
were lions, oxen and cherubim; and on the [1]frames there *was* a
pedestal above, and beneath the lions and oxen *were* wreaths
of hanging work.
30 Now each stand had four bronze wheels with bronze
axles, and its four feet had supports; beneath the basin *were*
cast supports with wreaths at each side.
31 And its opening inside the crown at the top *was* a cubit,
and its opening *was* round like the design of a pedestal, a cubit
and a half; and also on its opening *there were* engravings, and
their borders were square not round.
32 And the four wheels *were* underneath the borders, and
the axles of the wheels *were* on the stand. And the height of a
wheel *was* a cubit and a half.
33 And the workmanship of the wheels *was* like the

15 [1]Lit., *went around the other pillar* [a]2 Kin. 25:17 [b]1 Kin. 7:41

16 [1]I.e., Approx. 18 inches

20 [1]Lit., *belly* [2]Lit., *on the other capital* [a]1 Kin. 7:42; 2 Chr. 3:16

21 [1]I.e., He shall establish [2]I.e., In it is strength [a]2 Chr. 3:17

23 [1]Lit., *a line of 30 cubits went around it* [a]2 Chr. 4:2 [b]2 Kin. 16:17; 25:13

24 [1]Lit., *in its casting* [a]1 Kin. 6:18

25 [a]Jer. 52:20

27 [a]1 Kin. 7:38; 2 Kin. 25:13; 2 Chr. 4:14

28 [1]Or, *crossbars*

29 [1]Or, *crossbars*

workmanship of a chariot wheel. Their axles, their rims, their
spokes, and their hubs *were* all cast.
34 Now *there were* four supports at the four corners of
each stand; its supports *were* part of the stand itself.
35 And on the top of the stand *there was* a circular form
half a [1]cubit high, and on the top of the stand its [2]stays and its
borders *were* part of it.
36 And he engraved on the plates of its stays and on its
borders, cherubim, lions and palm trees, according to the clear
space on each, with wreaths *all* around.
37 [a]He made the ten stands like this; all of them had one
casting, one measure and one form.
38 [a]And he made ten basins of bronze, one basin held
forty baths; each basin *was* four cubits, *and* on each of the ten
stands *was* one basin.
39 Then he set the stands, five on the right side of the
house and five on the left side of the house; and he set the sea
of cast metal on the right side of the house eastward toward
the south.
40 Now Hiram made the basins and the shovels and the
bowls. So Hiram finished doing all the work which he performed for King Solomon *in* the house of the LORD:
41 the two pillars and the two bowls of the capitals which
were on the top of the [a]two pillars, and the two networks to
cover the two bowls of the capitals which *were* on the top of
the pillars;
42 and the [a]four hundred pomegranates for the two networks, two rows of pomegranates for each network to cover
the two bowls of the capitals which *were* on the tops of the
pillars;
43 and the ten stands with the ten basins on the stands;
44 and [a]the one sea and the twelve oxen under the sea;
45 and the pails and the shovels and the bowls; even all
these utensils which Hiram made for King Solomon *in* the
house of the LORD, *were* of polished bronze.
46 [a]In the plain of the Jordan the king cast them, in the
clay ground between [b]Succoth and [c]Zarethan.
47 And Solomon left all the utensils *unweighed*, because
they were too many; [a]the weight of the bronze could not be
ascertained.
48 And Solomon made all the furniture which *was in* the
house of the LORD: [a]the golden altar and the golden table on
which *was* the Bread of the Presence;
49 and the lampstands, five on the right side and five on
the left, in front of the inner sanctuary, of pure gold; and [a]the
flowers and the lamps and the tongs, of gold;
50 and the cups and the snuffers and the bowls and the
spoons and the [a]firepans, of pure gold; and the hinges both for
the doors of the inner house, the most holy place, *and* for the
doors of the house, *that is,* of the nave, of gold.
51 [a]Thus all the work that King Solomon performed *in*
the house of the LORD was finished. And [b]Solomon brought in
the things dedicated by his father David, the silver and the
gold and the utensils, *and* he *put* them in the treasuries of the
house of the LORD.

35 [1]I.e., Approx. 18 inches [2]Lit., *hands*
37 [a]2 Chr. 4:14
38 [a]2 Chr. 4:6
41 [a]1 Kin. 7:17, 18
42 [a]1 Kin. 7:20
44 [a]1 Kin. 7:23, 25
46 [a]2 Chr. 4:17 [b]Josh. 13:27 [c]Josh. 3:16
47 [a]1 Chr. 22:3, 14
48 [a]Ex. 37:10-29; 2 Chr. 4:8
49 [a]Ex. 25:31-38
50 [a]Ex. 27:3; 2 Kin. 25:15
51 [a]2 Chr. 5:1 [b]2 Sam. 8:11; 2 Chr. 5:1

Chapter 8

a
THEN Solomon assembled the elders of Israel and all [b]the
heads of the tribes, the leaders of the fathers' *households* of
the sons of Israel, to King Solomon in Jerusalem, [c]to bring up
the ark of the covenant of the LORD from [d]the city of David,
which is Zion.
2 And all the men of Israel assembled themselves to King
Solomon at [a]the feast, in the month Ethanim, which is the
seventh month.
3 Then all the elders of Israel came, and [a]the priests took
up the ark.
4 And they brought up the ark of the LORD and [a]the tent
of meeting and all the holy utensils, which were in the tent,
and the priests and the Levites brought them up.
5 And King Solomon and all the congregation of Israel,
who were assembled to him, [a]were with him before the ark,
sacrificing [1]so many sheep and oxen they could not be counted
or numbered.
6 Then [a]the priests brought the ark of the covenant of
the LORD [b]to its place, into the inner sanctuary of the house to
the most holy place, [c]under the wings of the cherubim.
7 For the cherubim spread *their* wings over the place of
the ark, and the cherubim made a covering over the ark and its
poles from above.
8 But [a]the poles were so long that the ends of the poles
could be seen from the holy place before the inner sanctuary,
but they could not be seen outside; they are there to this day.
9 [a]There was nothing in the ark except the two tablets of
stone which Moses put there at Horeb, where [b]the LORD made
a covenant with the sons of Israel, when they came out of the
land of Egypt.
10 And it came about when the priests came from the holy
place, that [a]the cloud filled the house of the LORD,
11 so that the priests could not stand to minister because
of the cloud, for the glory of the LORD filled the house of the
LORD.
12 [a]Then Solomon said, "The LORD has said that [b]He
would dwell in the thick cloud.
13 "[a]I have surely built Thee a lofty house,
[b]A place for Thy dwelling forever."
14 Then the king [1]faced about and [a]blessed all the assembly of Israel, while all the assembly of Israel was standing.
15 And he said, "[a]Blessed be the LORD, the God of Israel,
[b]who spoke with His mouth to My father David and has fulfilled *it* with His hand, saying,
16 '[a]Since the day that I brought My people Israel from
Egypt, I did not choose a city out of all the tribes of Israel *in
which* to build a house that [b]My name might be there, but [c]I
chose David to be over My people Israel.'
17 "[a]Now it was [1]in the heart of my father David to build a
house for the name of the LORD, the God of Israel.
18 "But the LORD said to my father David, 'Because it was
[1]in your heart to build a house for My name, you did well that
it was [1]in your heart.
19 '[a]Nevertheless you shall not build the house, but your

1 [a]2 Chr. 5:2-10 [b]Num. 1:4; 7:2 [c]2 Sam. 6:17 [d]2 Sam. 5:7

2 [a]1 Kin. 8:65; Lev. 23:34; 2 Chr. 7:8-10

3 [a]Num. 7:9

4 [a]1 Kin. 3:4; 2 Chr. 1:3

5 [1]Lit., *sheep, numbered for multitude*
[a]2 Sam. 6:13; 2 Chr. 1:6

6 [a]1 Kin. 8:3 [b]1 Kin. 6:19 [c]1 Kin. 6:27

8 [a]Ex. 25:13-15; 37:4, 5

9 [a]Ex. 25:16, 21; Deut. 10:2-5; Heb. 9:4 [b]Ex. 24:7, 8; Deut. 4:13

10 [a]Ex. 40:34, 35; 2 Chr. 7:1, 2

12 [a]2 Chr. 6:1 [b]Ps. 97:2

13 [a]2 Sam. 7:13 [b]Ex. 15:17

14 [1]Lit., *turned his face about*
[a]1 Kin. 8:55; 2 Sam. 6:18

15 [a]1 Chr. 29:10, 20; Neh. 9:5 [b]2 Sam. 7:12, 13; 1 Chr. 22:10

16 [a]2 Sam. 7:4, 5 [b]Deut. 12:5, 11 [c]1 Sam. 16:1; 2 Sam. 7:8

17 [1]Lit., *with*
[a]2 Sam. 7:2, 3; 1 Chr. 17:1, 2

18 [1]Lit., *with*

19 [a]1 Kin. 5:3, 5; 2 Sam. 7:5, 12, 13; 1 Chr. 22:8-10

son who [1]shall be born to you, he shall build the house for My
name.'
20 "Now the LORD has fulfilled His word which He spoke;
for [a]I have risen in place of my father David and sit on the
throne of Israel, as the LORD [1]promised, and have built the
house for the name of the LORD, the God of Israel.
21 "And there I have set a place for the ark, [a]in which is the
covenant of the LORD, which He made with our fathers when
He brought them from the land of Egypt."
22 Then [a]Solomon stood before the altar of the LORD in
the presence of all the assembly of Israel and [b]spread out his
hands toward heaven.
23 And he said, "O LORD, the God of Israel, [a]there is no
God like Thee in heaven above or on earth beneath, [b]who art
keeping covenant and showing lovingkindness to Thy servants
who walk before Thee with all their heart,
24 who hast kept with Thy servant, my father David, that
which Thou hast [1]promised him; indeed, Thou hast spoken
with Thy mouth and hast fulfilled it with Thy hand as it is this
day.
25 "Now therefore, O LORD, the God of Israel, keep with
Thy servant David my father that which Thou hast [1]promised
him, saying, '[2a]You shall not lack a man to sit on the throne of
Israel, if only your sons take heed to their way to walk before
Me as you have walked.'
26 "Now therefore, O God of Israel, let Thy word, I pray
Thee, be confirmed [a]which Thou hast spoken to Thy servant,
my father David.
27 "But will God indeed dwell on the earth? Behold, [a]heav-
en and the [1]highest heaven cannot contain Thee, how much
less this house which I have built!
28 "Yet have regard to the prayer of Thy servant and to his
supplication, O LORD my God, to listen to the cry and to the
prayer which Thy servant prays before Thee today;
29 [a]that Thine eyes may be open toward this house night
and day, toward the place of which Thou hast said, 'My name
shall be there,' to listen to the prayer which Thy servant shall
pray toward this place.
30 "And listen to the supplication of Thy servant and of
Thy people Israel, [a]when they pray toward this place; hear
Thou in heaven Thy dwelling place; hear and forgive.
31 "[a]If a man sins against his neighbor and is made to take
an oath, and he comes *and* takes an oath before Thine altar in
this house,
32 then hear Thou in heaven and act and judge Thy servants, [a]condemning the wicked by bringing his way on his own
head and justifying the righteous by giving him according to
his righteousness.
33 "[a]When Thy people Israel are [1]defeated before an
enemy, because they have sinned against Thee, [b]if they turn to
Thee again and confess Thy name and pray and make supplication to Thee in this house,
34 then hear Thou in heaven, and forgive the sin of Thy
people Israel, and bring them back to the land which Thou
didst give to their fathers.
35 "[a]When the heavens are shut up and there is no rain,

19 [1]Lit., *is to come forth from your loins*

20 [1]Lit., *spoke* [a]1 Chr. 28:5, 6

21 [a]1 Kin. 8:9

22 [a]1 Kin. 8:54 [b]Ex. 9:33; Ezra 9:5

23 [a]1 Sam. 2:2; 2 Sam. 7:22 [b]Deut. 7:9; Neh. 1:5; 9:32

24 [1]Lit., *spoken to*

25 [1]Lit., *spoken to* [2]Lit., *there shall not be cut off to you a man from before Me.* [a]1 Kin. 2:4

26 [a]2 Sam. 7:25

27 [1]Lit., *heaven of heavens* [a]Ps. 139:7-16; Is. 66:1; Jer. 23:24; Acts 7:49

29 [a]2 Chr. 7:15; Neh. 1:6

30 [a]Dan. 6:10

31 [a]Ex. 22:8-11

32 [a]Deut. 25:1

33 [1]Lit., *smitten* [a]Lev. 26:17, 25; Deut. 28:25, 48 [b]Lev. 26:40-42

35 [a]Lev. 26:19; Deut. 11:16, 17; 2 Sam. 24:10-13

because they have sinned against Thee, and they pray toward
this place and confess Thy name and turn from their sin when
Thou dost afflict them,
36 then hear Thou in heaven and forgive the sin of Thy
servants and of Thy people Israel, [a]indeed, teach them the
good way in which they should walk. And [b]send rain on Thy
land, which Thou hast given Thy people for an inheritance.
37 "[a]If there is famine in the land, if there is pestilence, if
there is blight *or* mildew, locust *or* grasshopper, if their enemy
besieges them in the land of their [1]cities, whatever plague,
whatever sickness there is,
38 whatever prayer or supplication is made by any man *or*
by all Thy people Israel, [1]each knowing the [2]affliction of his
own heart, and spreading his [3]hands toward this house;
39 then hear Thou in heaven Thy dwelling place, and
forgive and act and render to each according to all his ways,
[a]whose heart Thou knowest, for [b]Thou alone dost know the
hearts of all the sons of men,
40 that they may [1]fear Thee all the days that they live [2]in
the land which Thou hast given to our fathers.
41 "Also concerning the foreigner who is not of Thy people
Israel, when he comes from a far country for Thy name's sake
42 (for they will hear of Thy great name [a]and Thy mighty
hand, and of Thine outstretched arm); when he comes and
prays toward this house,
43 hear Thou in heaven Thy dwelling place, and do according
to all for which the foreigner calls to Thee, in order [a]that
all the peoples of the earth may know Thy name, to [1]fear
Thee, as *do* Thy people Israel, and that they may know that
[2]this house which I have built is called by Thy name.
44 "When Thy people go out to battle against [1]their
enemy, by whatever way Thou shalt send them, and [a]they pray
to the LORD [2]toward the city which Thou hast chosen and the
house which I have built for Thy name,
45 then hear in heaven their prayer and their supplication,
and maintain their [1]cause.
46 "When they sin against Thee (for [a]there is no man who
does not sin) and Thou art angry with them and dost deliver
them to an enemy, so that [1]they take them away captive [b]to
the land of the enemy, far off or near,
47 [a]if they [1]take thought in the land where they have been
taken captive, and repent and make supplication to Thee in
the land of those who have taken them captive, saying, '[b]We
have sinned and have committed iniquity, we have acted
wickedly,'
48 [a]if they return to Thee with all their heart and with all
their soul in the land of their enemies who have taken them
captive, and [b]pray to Thee toward their land which Thou hast
given to their fathers, the city which Thou hast chosen, and
the house which I have built for Thy name,
49 then hear their prayer and their supplication in heaven
Thy dwelling place, and maintain their [1]cause,
50 and forgive Thy people who have sinned against Thee
and all their transgressions which they have transgressed
against Thee, and [a]make them *objects of* compassion before

36 [a]1 Sam. 12:23; Ps. 27:11 [b]1 Kin. 18:1, 41-45; Jer. 14:22

37 [1]Lit., *gates* [a]Lev. 26:16, 25, 26; Deut. 28:21-23, 38-42

38 [1]Lit., *who shall know each* [2]Lit., *plague* [3]Lit., *palms*

39 [a]1 Sam. 2:3; 16:7 [b]1 Chr. 28:9; Jer. 17:10; John 2:24, 25

40 [1]Or, *revere* [2]Lit., *on the face of the land*

42 [a]Ex. 13:3; Deut. 3:24

43 [1]Or, *reverence* [2]Lit., *Thy name is called upon this house which I have built* [a]Josh. 4:23; 1 Sam. 17:46

44 [1]Lit., *his* [2]Lit., *in the way of* [a]2 Chr. 14:11, 12

45 [1]Lit., *right* or *justice*

46 [1]Lit., *their captors take them captive* [a]Ps. 130:3, 4; Prov. 20:9; 1 John 1:8-10 [b]Lev. 26:34-39; 2 Kin. 17:6, 18; 25:21

47 [1]Lit., *return to their heart* [a]Lev. 26:40-42; Neh. 9:2 [b]Ezra 9:6, 7; Neh. 1:6

48 [a]Deut. 4:29; 1 Sam. 7:3, 4; Neh. 1:9 [b]Dan. 6:10; Jon. 2:4

49 [1]Lit., *judgment*

50 [a]2 Chr. 30:9; Acts 7:10

those who have taken them captive, that they may have com
passion on them
51 ([a]for they are Thy people and Thine inheritance whic
Thou hast brought forth from Egypt, [b]from the midst of th
iron furnace),
52 [a]that Thine eyes may be open to the supplication o
Thy servant and to the supplication of Thy people Israel, to
listen to them whenever they call to Thee.
53 "For Thou hast separated them from all the peoples o
the earth as Thine inheritance, [a]as Thou didst speak through
Moses Thy servant, when Thou didst bring our fathers forth
from Egypt, O Lord [1]GOD."
54 [a]And it came about that when Solomon had finished
praying this entire prayer and supplication to the LORD, [b]he
arose from before the altar of the LORD, from kneeling on his
knees with his [1]hands spread toward heaven.
55 And he stood and [a]blessed all the assembly of Israel
with a loud voice, saying,
56 "Blessed be the LORD, who has given rest to His people
Israel, according to all that He [1]promised; [a]not one word has
[2]failed of all His good [3]promise, which He [1]promised through
Moses His servant.
57 "May the LORD our God be with us, as He was with our
fathers; [a]may He not leave us or forsake us,
58 that [a]He may incline our hearts to Himself, to walk in
all His ways and to keep His commandments and His statutes
and His ordinances, which He commanded our fathers.
59 "And may these words of mine, with which I have made
supplication before the LORD, be near to the LORD our God
day and night, that He may maintain the [1]cause of His servant
and the [1]cause of His people Israel, [2]as each day requires,
60 so [a]that all the peoples of the earth may know that [b]the
LORD is God; there is no one else.
61 "[a]Let your heart therefore be [1]wholly devoted to the
LORD our God, to walk in His statutes and to keep His commandments, as at this day."
62 [a]Now the king and all Israel with him [b]offered sacrifice
before the LORD.
63 And Solomon offered for the sacrifice of peace offerings, which he offered to the LORD, 22,000 oxen and 120,000
sheep. [a]So the king and all the sons of Israel dedicated the
house of the LORD.
64 On the same day the king consecrated the middle of
the court that *was* before the house of the LORD, because there
he [1]offered the burnt offering and the grain offering and the
fat of the peace offerings; for [a]the bronze altar that *was* before
the LORD *was* too small to hold the burnt offering and the
grain offering and the fat of the peace offerings.
65 So [a]Solomon observed the feast at that time, and all
Israel with him, a great assembly [b]from the entrance of Hamath [c]to the brook of Egypt, before the LORD our God, for
seven days and seven *more* days, *even* fourteen days.
66 On the eighth day he sent the people away and they
blessed the king. Then they went to their tents joyful and glad
of heart for all the goodness that the LORD had [1]shown to
David His servant and to Israel His people.

51 [a]Ex. 32:11, 12; Deut. 9:26-29 [b]Deut. 4:20; Jer. 11:4

52 [a]1 Kin. 8:29

53 [1]YHWH, usually rendered LORD [a]Ex. 19:5, 6; Deut. 9:26-29

54 [1]Lit., *palms* [a]2 Chr. 7:1 [b]2 Chr. 6:13

55 [a]1 Kin. 8:14; Num. 6:23-26

56 [1]Lit., *spoke* [2]Lit., *fallen* [3]Lit., *word* [a]Josh. 21:45; 23:14, 15

57 [a]Josh. 1:5; 1 Sam. 12:22; Rom. 8:31; Heb. 13:5

58 [a]Ps. 119:36; Jer. 31:33

59 [1]Lit., *judgment* [2]Lit., *the thing of a day in its day*

60 [a]1 Kin. 8:43 [b]1 Kin. 18:39; Jer. 10:10-12

61 [1]Lit., *complete with* [a]Deut. 18:13; 2 Kin. 20:3

62 [a]2 Chr. 7:4-10 [b]2 Sam. 6:17-19; Ezra 6:16, 17

63 [a]Ezra 6:15-18; Neh. 12:27

64 [1]Lit., *made* [a]2 Chr. 4:1

65 [a]1 Kin. 8:2; Lev. 23:34-42 [b]Num. 34:8; Josh. 13:5 [c]Gen. 15:18; Ex. 23:31; Josh. 13:3

66 [1]Lit., *done*

CHAPTER 9

NOW it came about when Solomon had finished building
the house of the LORD, and [b]the king's house, and [c]all [1]that
Solomon desired to do,
2 that [a]the LORD appeared to Solomon a second time, as
He had appeared to him at Gibeon.
3 And the LORD said to him, "I have heard your prayer
and your supplication, which you have made before Me; I have
consecrated this house which you have built [a]by putting My
name there forever, and [b]My eyes and My heart will be there
perpetually.
4 "And as for you, [a]if you will walk before Me as your
father David walked, in integrity of heart and uprightness,
doing according to all that I have commanded you *and* will
keep My statutes and My ordinances,
5 then [a]I will establish the throne of your kingdom over
Israel forever, just as I [1]promised to your father David, saying,
'[2]You shall not lack a man on the throne of Israel.'
6 "[a]But if you or your sons shall indeed turn away from
following Me, and shall not keep My commandments and My
statutes which I have set before you and shall go and serve
other gods and worship them,
7 [a]then I will cut off Israel from the land which I have
given them, and [b]the house which I have consecrated for My
name, I will [1]cast out of My sight. So [c]Israel will become a
proverb and a byword among all peoples.
8 "And this house will become [1]a heap of ruins; everyone
who passes by will be astonished and hiss and say, '[a]Why has
the LORD done thus to this land and to this house?'
9 "And they will say, '[a]Because they forsook the LORD
their God, who brought their fathers out of the land of Egypt,
and adopted other gods and worshiped them and served them,
therefore the LORD has brought all this adversity on them.' "
10 [a]And it came about [b]at the end of twenty years in
which Solomon had built the two houses, the house of the
LORD and the king's house,
11 (Hiram king of Tyre had supplied Solomon with cedar
and cypress timber and gold according to all his desire), then
King Solomon gave Hiram twenty cities in the land of Galilee.
12 So Hiram came out from Tyre to see the cities which
Solomon had given him, and they [1]did not please him.
13 And he said, "What are these cities which you have
given me, my brother?" So [1]they were called the land of [2a]Cabul
to this day.
14 [a]And Hiram sent to the king 120 talents of gold.
15 Now this is the account of the forced labor which King
Solomon levied to build the house of the LORD, his own house,
the [1a]Millo, the wall of Jerusalem, [b]Hazor, [c]Meggido, and
Gezer.
16 *For* Pharaoh king of Egypt had gone up and captured
Gezer, and burned it with fire, and killed the [a]Canaanites who
lived in the city, and had [b]given it *as* a dowry to his daughter,
Solomon's wife.
17 So Solomon rebuilt Gezer and the lower [a]Beth-horon

1 [1]Lit., *Solomon's desire which he was pleased to do* [a]2 Chr. 7:11 [b]1 Kin. 7:1, 2 [c]2 Chr. 8:6

2 [a]1 Kin. 3:5; 11:9

3 [a]1 Kin. 8:29 [b]Deut. 11:12; 2 Chr. 6:40

4 [a]1 Kin. 3:14; 11:4, 6, 8

5 [1]Lit., *spoke* [2]Lit., *There shall not be cut off to you a man* [a]1 Kin. 2:4; 6:12; 2 Sam. 7:12, 16

6 [a]2 Sam. 7:14-16; 1 Chr. 28:9

7 [1]Lit., *send* [a]Lev. 18:24-29; Deut. 4:26; 2 Kin. 17:23 [b]Jer. 7:4-14 [c]Deut. 28:37; Jer. 24:9

8 [1]Heb., *high* [a]Deut. 29:24-26; Jer. 22:8, 9, 28

9 [a]Deut. 29:25-28; Jer. 2:10-13

10 [a]2 Chr. 8:1 [b]1 Kin. 9:1; 6:37, 38; 7:1

12 [1]Lit., *were not right in his sight*

13 [1]Lit., *he called them* [2]I.e., As good as nothing [a]Josh. 19:27

14 [a]1 Kin. 9:11

15 [1]I.e., citadel [a]1 Kin. 9:24; 2 Sam. 5:9 [b]Josh. 11:1 [c]Josh. 17:11

16 [a]Josh. 16:10 [b]1 Kin. 3:1; 7:8

17 [a]Josh. 10:10

18 and Baalath and Tamar in the wilderness, in the land of *Judah,*

19 and all the storage cities which Solomon had, even [a]the cities for [1]his chariots and the cities for [1b]his horsemen, and [2c]all that it pleased Solomon to build in Jerusalem, in Lebanon, and in all the land [3]under his rule.

20 *As for* all the people who were left of the Amorites, the Hittites, the Perizzites, the Hivites and the Jebusites, who were not of the sons of Israel,

21 [a]their descendants who were left after them in the land [b]whom the sons of Israel were unable to destroy utterly, [c]from them Solomon levied [d]forced laborers, even to this day.

22 But Solomon did not make slaves [a]of the sons of Israel; for they were men of war, his servants, his princes, his captains, his chariot commanders, and his horsemen.

23 These *were* the [1]chief officers who were over Solomon's work, [a]five-hundred and fifty, [b]who ruled over the people doing the work.

24 As soon as [a]Pharaoh's daughter came up from the city of David to her house which *Solomon* had built for her, [b]then he built the Millo.

25 Now [a]three times in a year Solomon offered burnt offerings and peace offerings on the altar which he built to the LORD, burning incense with them *on the altar* which *was* before the LORD. So he finished the house.

26 [a]King Solomon also built a fleet of ships in [b]Ezion-geber, which is near Eloth on the shore of the [1]Red Sea, in the land of Edom.

27 [a]And Hiram sent his servants with the fleet, sailors who knew the sea, along with the servants of Solomon.

28 And they went to [a]Ophir, and took four hundred and twenty talents of gold from there, and brought *it* to King Solomon.

CHAPTER 10

[a]NOW when the [b]queen of [c]Sheba heard about the fame of Solomon concerning the name of the LORD, she came [d]to test him with difficult questions.

2 So she came to Jerusalem with a very large retinue, with camels [a]carrying spices and very much gold and precious stones. When she came to Solomon, she spoke with him about all that was in her heart.

3 And Solomon [1]answered all her questions; nothing was hidden from the king which he did not [2]explain to her.

4 When the queen of Sheba perceived all the wisdom of Solomon, the house that he had built,

5 the food of his table, the seating of his servants, the attendance of his waiters and their attire, his cup-bearers, and [1a]his stairway by which he went up to the house of the LORD, there was no more spirit in her.

6 Then she said to the king, "It was a true report which I heard in my own land about your words and your wisdom.

7 "Nevertheless I did not believe the [1]reports, until I came and my eyes had seen it. And behold, the half was not told me.

19 [1]Lit., *the* [2]Lit., *the desire of Solomon which he desired to build in Jerusalem* [3]Lit., *of*
[a]1 Kin. 10:26; 2 Chr. 1:14 [b]1 Kin. 4:26 [c]1 Kin. 9:1

21 [a]Judg. 1:21-29; 3:1 [b]Josh. 15:63; 17:12, 13 [c]Judg. 1:28, 35 [d]Gen. 9:25, 26; Ezra 2:55, 58

22 [a]Lev. 25:39

23 [1]Or, *officers of the deputies*
[a]2 Chr. 8:10 [b]1 Kin. 5:16

24 [a]1 Kin. 3:1; 7:8 [b]1 Kin. 9:15; 11:27; 2 Chr. 32:5

25 [a]Ex. 23:14-17; Deut. 16:16

26 [1]Or, *Sea of Reeds*
[a]1 Kin. 22:48 [b]Num. 33:35; Deut. 2:8

27 [a]1 Kin. 5:6, 9; 10:11

28 [a]1 Chr. 29:4

1 [a]2 Chr. 9:1 [b]Matt. 12:42 [c]Gen. 10:7, 28; Ps. 72:10, 15 [d]Judg. 14:12-14; Ps. 49:4

2 [a]1 Kin. 10:10

3 [1]Lit., *told her all her words* [2]Lit., *tell her*

5 [1]Or, *his burnt offering which he offered*
[a]1 Chr. 26:16

7 [1]Lit., *words*

You exceed *in* wisdom and prosperity the report which I
heard.
8 "How blessed are your men, how blessed are these your
servants who stand before you continually *and* hear your
wisdom.
9 "[a]Blessed be the LORD your God who delighted in you to
set you on the throne of Israel; [b]because the LORD loved Israel
forever, therefore He made you king, [c]to do justice and
righteousness."
10 And [a]she gave the king a hundred and twenty talents of
gold, and a very great *amount* of spices and precious stones.
Never again did such abundance of spices come in as that
which the queen of Sheba gave King Solomon.
11 [a]And also the ships of Hiram, which brought gold from
Ophir, brought in from Ophir a very great *number of* almug
trees and precious stones.
12 And the king made of the almug trees supports for the
house of the LORD and for the king's house, also lyres and
harps for the singers; such almug trees have not come in *again*,
nor have they been seen to this day.
13 And King Solomon gave to the queen of Sheba all her
desire which she requested, besides what he gave her according
to [1]his royal bounty. Then she turned and went to her own
land [2]together with her servants.
14 [a]Now the weight of gold which came in to Solomon in
one year *was* 666 talents of gold,
15 besides *that* from the traders and the [1]wares of the
merchants and all the kings of the [2]Arabs and the governors of
the country.
16 And [a]King Solomon made 200 large shields of beaten
gold, [1]using 600 *shekels of* gold on each large shield.
17 And *he made* 300 shields of beaten gold, [1]using three
minas of gold on each shield, and [a]the king put them in the
house of the forest of Lebanon.
18 Moreover, the king made a great throne of [a]ivory and
overlaid it with refined gold.
19 There *were* six steps to the throne and a round top to
the throne at its rear, and [1]arms [2]on each side of the seat, and
two lions standing beside the [1]arms.
20 And twelve lions were standing there on the six steps on
the one side and on the other; nothing like *it* was made for any
other kingdom.
21 And all King Solomon's drinking vessels *were* of gold,
and all the vessels of the house of the forest of Lebanon *were*
of pure gold. None was of silver; it was not considered [1]valu-
able in the days of Solomon.
22 For [a]the king had at sea the ships of Tarshish with the
ships of Hiram; once every three years the ships of Tarshish
came bringing gold and silver, ivory and apes and peacocks.
23 [a]So King Solomon became greater than all the kings of
the earth in riches and in wisdom.
24 And all the earth was seeking the presence of Solomon,
[a]to hear his wisdom which God had put in his heart.
25 And they brought every man his gift, articles of silver
and gold, garments, weapons, spices, horses, and mules, so
much year by year.

9 [a]1 Kin. 5:7 [b]1 Chr. 17:22; 2 Chr. 2:11 [c]2 Sam. 8:15; 23:3

10 [a]1 Kin. 10:2

11 [a]1 Kin. 9:27, 28

13 [1]Lit., *the hand of King Solomon* [2]Lit., *she and*

14 [a]2 Chr. 9:13-28

15 [1]Or, *traffic* [2]Cf. 2 Chr. 9:14

16 [1]Lit., *he brought up* [a]1 Kin. 14:26-28; 2 Chr. 12:9, 10

17 [1]Lit., *he brought up* [a]1 Kin. 7:2

18 [a]1 Kin. 10:22; Ps. 45:8

19 [1]Lit., *hands* [2]Lit., *on this side and on this at the place of the seat*

21 [1]Lit., *anything*

22 [a]1 Kin. 9:26-28; 22:48

23 [a]1 Kin. 3:12, 13; 4:30

24 [a]1 Kin. 3:9, 12, 28

26 [a]Now Solomon gathered chariots and horsemen; and
he had 1,400 chariots and 12,000 horsemen, and he [1]stationed
them in the [b]chariot cities and with the king in Jerusalem.
27 [a]And the king made silver *as common* as stones in Jerusalem, and he made cedars as plentiful as sycamore trees that
are in the [1]lowland.
28 [a]Also Solomon's import of horses was from Egypt and
Kue, and the king's merchants procured *them* from Kue for a
price.
29 And a chariot [1]was imported from Egypt for 600 *shekels* of silver, and a horse for 150; and [2]by the same means they
exported them [a]to all the kings of the Hittites and to the kings
of [3]Syria.

CHAPTER 11

1 NOW [a]King Solomon loved many foreign women along
with the daughter of Pharaoh: Moabite, Ammonite, Edomite,
Sidonian, and Hittite women,
2 from the nations concerning which the LORD had said
to the sons of Israel, "[a]You shall not [1]associate with them,
neither shall they [1]associate with you, for they will surely turn
your heart away after their gods." Solomon held fast to these
in love.
3 [a]And he had seven hundred wives, princesses, and three
hundred concubines, and his wives turned his heart away.
4 For it came about when Solomon was old, his wives
turned his heart away after other gods; and [a]his heart was not
[1]wholly devoted to the LORD his God, as the heart of David his
father *had been*.
5 For Solomon went after [a]Ashtoreth the goddess of the
Sidonians and after [b]Milcom the detestable idol of the
Ammonites.
6 And Solomon did what was evil in the sight of the
LORD, and did not follow the LORD fully, as David his father
had done.
7 Then Solomon built a high place for [a]Chemosh the
detestable idol of Moab, on the mountain which is [1]east of
Jerusalem, and for [b]Molech the detestable idol of the sons of
Ammon.
8 Thus also he did for all his foreign wives, who burned
incense and sacrificed to their gods.
9 Now the LORD was angry with Solomon [a]because his
heart was turned away from the LORD, the God of Israel, [b]who
had appeared to him twice,
10 and [a]had commanded him concerning this thing, that
he should not go after other gods; but he did not observe what
the LORD had commanded.
11 So the LORD said to Solomon, "Because [1]you have
done this, and you have not kept My covenant and My statutes, which I have commanded you, [a]I will surely tear the
kingdom from you, and will give it to your servant.
12 "Nevertheless I will not do it in your days for the sake of
your father David, *but* I will tear it out of the hand of your
son.
13 "However, [a]I will not tear away all the kingdom, but [b]I

26 [1]So with ancient versions, cf. 2 Chr. 9:25; Heb., *led* [a]1 Kin. 4:26; 2 Chr. 1:14-17; 9:25 [b]1 Kin. 9:19

27 [1]Or, *Shephelah* [a]2 Chr. 1:15

28 [a]2 Chr. 1:16; 9:28

29 [1]Lit., *came up and went out from* [2]Lit., *in like manner by their hand* [3]Heb., *Aram* [a]2 Kin. 7:6, 7

1 [a]Deut. 17:17; Neh. 13:23-27

2 [1]Lit., *go among* [a]Ex. 23:31-33; 34:12-16

3 [a]2 Sam. 3:2-5; 5:13-16

4 [1]Lit., *complete with* [a]1 Kin. 9:4

5 [a]Judg. 2:13; 10:6; 1 Sam. 7:3, 4 [b]1 Kin. 10:7

7 [1]Lit., *before* [a]Num. 21:29; Judg. 11:24; 2 Kin. 23:13 [b]Lev. 20:2-5; 2 Kin. 23:10; Acts 7:3

9 [a]1 Kin. 11:2, 4 [b]1 Kin. 3:5; 9:2

10 [a]1 Kin. 6:12; 9:6, 7

11 [1]Lit., *this is with you* [a]1 Kin. 11:29-31; 12:15, 16, 20; 1 Sam. 2:30

13 [a]2 Sam. 7:15; 1 Chr. 17:13 [b]1 Kin. 11:32, 36; 12:20

will give one tribe to your son for the sake of My servant David
and [c]for the sake of Jerusalem which I have chosen."
14 Then the LORD raised up an adversary to Solomon,
Hadad the Edomite; he was of the [1]royal line in Edom.
15 For it came about, [a]when David was in Edom, and
Joab the commander of the army had gone up to bury the
slain, and had struck down every male in Edom
16 (for Joab and all Israel stayed there six months, until he
had cut off every male in Edom)
17 that Hadad fled [1]to Egypt, he and certain Edomites of
his father's servants with him, while Hadad *was* a young boy.
18 And they arose from Midian and came to [a]Paran; and
they took men with them from Paran and came to Egypt, to
Pharaoh king of Egypt, who gave him a house and assigned
him food and gave him land.
19 Now Hadad found great favor [1]before Pharaoh, so that
he gave him in marriage the sister of his own wife, the sister of
Tahpenes the queen.
20 And the sister of Tahpenes bore his son Genubath,
whom Tahpenes weaned in Pharaoh's house; and Genubath
was in Pharaoh's house among the sons of Pharaoh.
21 But [a]when Hadad heard in Egypt that David slept with
his fathers, and that Joab the commander of the army was
dead, Hadad said to Pharaoh, "Send me away, that I may go to
my own country."
22 Then Pharaoh said to him, "But what have you lacked
with me, that behold, you are seeking to go to your own country?" And he answered, "Nothing; nevertheless you must surely [1]let me go."
23 [a]God also raised up *another* adversary to him, Rezon
the son of Eliada, who had fled from his lord [b]Hadadezer king
of Zobah.
24 And he gathered men to himself and became leader of
a marauding band, [a]after David slew them of *Zoba;* and they
went to Damascus and stayed [1]there, and reigned in
Damascus.
25 So he was an adversary to Israel all the days of Solomon, along with the evil that Hadad *did;* and he abhorred
Israel and reigned over [1]Syria.
26 Then [a]Jeroboam the son of Nebat, an Ephraimite of
Zeredah, Solomon's servant, whose mother's name was Ze-
ruah, a widow, [b]also [1]rebelled against the king.
27 Now this was the reason why he [1]rebelled against the
king: [a]Solomon built the [2]Millo, *and* closed up the breach of
the city of his father David.
28 Now the man Jeroboam was a valiant warrior, and
when [a]Solomon saw that the young man was [1]industrious, he
appointed him over all the [2]forced labor of the house of
Joseph.
29 And it came about at that time, when Jeroboam went
out of Jerusalem, that [a]the prophet Ahijah the Shilonite found
him on the road. Now [1]Ahijah had clothed himself with a new
cloak; and both of them were alone in the field.
30 Then [a]Ahijah took hold of the new cloak which was on
him, and tore it into twelve pieces.
31 And he said to Jeroboam, "Take for yourself ten

13 [c]1 Kin. 8:29
14 [1]Lit., *king's seed*
15 [a]2 Sam. 8:14; 1 Chr. 18:12, 13
17 [1]Lit., *to go into*
18 [a]Num. 10:12; Deut. 1:1
19 [1]Lit., *in the sight of*
21 [a]1 Kin. 2:10
22 [1]Lit., *send me away*
23 [a]1 Kin. 11:14 [b]2 Sam. 8:3; 10:16
24 [1]Lit., *in it* [a]2 Sam. 10:8, 18
25 [1]Heb., *Aram*
26 [1]Lit., *lifted up a hand* [a]1 Kin. 11:11, 28; 12:2, 20; 2 Chr. 13:6 [b]2 Sam. 20:21
27 [1]Lit., *lifted up a hand* [2]I.e., citadel [a]1 Kin. 9:15, 24
28 [1]Lit., *a doer of work* [2]Lit., *burden* [a]Prov. 22:29
29 [1]Lit., *he* [a]1 Kin. 12:15; 14:2; 2 Chr. 9:29
30 [a]1 Sam. 15:27, 28

pieces; for thus says the LORD, the God of Israel, 'Behold, [a]I
will tear the kingdom out of the hand of Solomon and give you
ten tribes
32 ([a]but he will have one tribe, for the sake of My servant
David and for the sake of Jerusalem, [b]the city which I have
chosen from all the tribes of Israel),
33 because they have forsaken Me, and [a]have worshiped
Ashtoreth the goddess of the Sidonians, Chemosh the god of
Moab, and Milcom the god of the sons of Ammon; and they
have not walked in My ways, doing what is right in My sight
and *observing* My statutes and My ordinances, as his father
David *did*.
34 'Nevertheless I will not take the whole kingdom out of
his hand, but I will make him [1]ruler all the days of his life, for
the sake of My servant David whom I chose, who observed My
commandments and My statutes;
35 but [a]I will take the kingdom from his son's hand and
give it to you, *even* ten tribes.
36 'But [a]to his son I will give one tribe, [b]that My servant
David may have a lamp always before Me in Jerusalem, [c]the
city where I have chosen for Myself to put My name.
37 'And I will take you, and you shall reign over whatever
[1]you desire, and you shall be king over Israel.
38 'Then it will be, that if you listen to all that I command
you and walk in My ways, and do what is right in My sight by
observing My statutes and My commandments, as My servant
David did, then [a]I will be with you and [b]build you an enduring
house as I built for David, and I will give Israel to you.
39 'Thus I will afflict the [1]descendants of David for this,
but not always.' "
40 Solomon sought therefore to put Jeroboam to death;
but Jeroboam arose and fled to Egypt to [a]Shishak king of
Egypt, and he was in Egypt until the death of Solomon.
41 [a]Now the rest of the acts of Solomon and whatever he
did, and his wisdom, are they not written in the Book of the
Acts of Solomon?
42 Thus the time that Solomon reigned in Jerusalem over
all Israel was forty years.
43 And Solomon [a]slept with his fathers and was buried in
the city of his father David, and his son [b]Rehoboam reigned in
his place.

CHAPTER 12

[a]THEN Rehobaom went to Shechem, for all Israel had come
to [b]Shechem to make him king.
2 Now it came about [a]when Jeroboam the son of Nebat
heard *of it* (for he was yet in Egypt, where he had fled from the
presence of King Solomon while [1]he was living in Egypt,
3 they sent and called him), that Jeroboam and all the
assembly of Israel came and spoke to Rehoboam, saying,
4 "[a]Your father made our yoke hard; therefore lighten the
hard service of your father and his heavy yoke which he put on
us, and we will serve you."
5 Then he said to them, "[a]Depart [1]for three days, then
return to me." So the people departed.

31 [a]1 Kin. 11:11, 12
32 [a]1 Kin. 11:13; 12:21 [b]1 Kin. 11:13; 14:21
33 [a]1 Kin. 11:5-8
34 [1]Or, *prince*
35 [a]1 Kin. 11:12; 12:16, 17
36 [a]1 Kin. 11:13 [b]1 Kin. 15:4; 2 Kin. 8:19 [c]1 Kin. 11:13
37 [1]Lit., *your soul desires*
38 [a]Deut. 31:8; Josh. 1:5 [b]2 Sam. 7:11, 27
39 [1]Lit., *seed*
40 [a]1 Kin. 14:25; 2 Chr. 12:2-9
41 [a]2 Chr. 9:29
43 [a]1 Kin. 2:10 [b]1 Kin. 14:21
1 [a]2 Chr. 10:1 [b]Judg. 9:6
2 [1]Lit., *Jeroboam* [a]1 Kin. 11:26, 40
4 [a]1 Kin. 4:7, 22-25; 9:15; 1 Sam. 8:11-18
5 [1]Lit., *yet three* [a]1 Kin. 12:12

6 And King Rehoboam [a]consulted with the elders who
ad [1]served his father Solomon while he was still alive, saying,
How do you counsel *me* to answer this people?"
7 Then they spoke to him, saying, "If you will be a ser-
ant to this people today, will serve them, [1]grant them their
etition, and speak good words to them, then they will be your
ervants forever."
8 But he forsook the counsel of the elders which they had
iven him, and consulted with the young men who grew up
vith him [1]and served him.
9 So he said to them, "What counsel do you give that we
nay answer this people who have spoken to me, saying, 'Light-
en the yoke which your father put on us'?"
10 And the young men who grew up with him spoke to
im, saying, "Thus you shall say to this people who spoke to
ou, saying, 'Your father made our yoke heavy, now you make
t lighter for us!' But you shall speak to them, 'My little finger
s thicker than my father's loins!
11 'Whereas my father loaded you with a heavy yoke, I will
dd to your yoke; my father disciplined you with whips, but I
vill discipline you with scorpions.'"
12 Then Jeroboam and all the people came to Rehoboam
on the third day as the king had [1]directed, saying, "[a]Return to
me on the third day."
13 And the king answered the people harshly, for he forsook the advice of the elders which they had [1]given him,
14 and he spoke to them according to the advice of the
young men, saying, "[a]My father made your yoke heavy, but I
will add to your yoke; my father disciplined you with whips,
but I will discipline you with scorpions."
15 So the king did not listen to the people; [a]for it was a
turn *of events* from the LORD, [b]that He might establish His
word, which the LORD spoke through Ahijah the Shilonite to
Jeroboam the son of Nebat.
16 When all Israel *saw* that the king did not listen to
them, the people answered the king, saying, "What portion do
we have in David?

We have no inheritance in the son of Jesse;
[a]To your tents, O Israel!
Now look after your own house, David!"

So Israel departed to their tents.
17 But [a]as for the sons of Israel who lived in the cities of
Judah, Rehoboam reigned over them.
18 Then King Rehoboam sent [a]Adoram, who was over the
forced labor, and all Israel stoned him [1]to death. And King
Rehoboam made haste to mount his chariot to flee to
Jerusalem.
19 [a]So Israel has been in rebellion against the house of
David to this day.
20 And it came about when all Israel heard that Jeroboam
had returned, that they sent and called him to the assembly
and made him king over all Israel. [a]None but the tribe of
Judah followed the house of David.
21 [a]Now when Rehoboam had come to Jerusalem, he assembled all the house of Judah and the tribe of Benjamin,
180,000 chosen men who were warriors, to fight against the

6 [1]Lit., *stood before* [a]1 Kin. 4:1-6

7 [1]Lit., *answer them*

8 [1]Lit., *who stood before*

12 [1]Lit., *spoken* [a]1 Kin. 12:5

13 [1]Lit., *advised*

14 [a]Ex. 1:13, 14; 5:5-9, 16-18

15 [a]1 Kin. 12:24; Deut. 2:30; Judg. 14:4 [b]1 Kin. 11:11, 31

16 [a]2 Sam. 20:1

17 [a]1 Kin. 11:13, 36

18 [1]Lit., *with stones that he died* [a]1 Kin. 4:6; 5:14; 2 Sam. 20:24

19 [a]2 Kin. 17:21

20 [a]1 Kin. 11:13, 32, 36

21 [a]2 Chr. 11:1

house of Israel to restore the kingdom to Rehoboam the so
of Solomon.
22 But the word of God came to [a]Shemaiah the man o
God, saying,
23 "Speak to Rehoboam the son of Solomon, king of Ju
dah, and to all the house of Judah and Benjamin and to th
[a]rest of the people, saying,
24 'Thus says the LORD, "You must not go up and figh
against your [1]relatives the sons of Israel; return every man to
his house, [a]for this thing has come from Me." ' " So they lis
tened to the word of the LORD, and returned and went *thei*
way according to the word of the LORD.
25 Then [a]Jeroboam built Shechem in the hill country o
Ephraim, and lived [1]there. And he went out from there and
built [b]Penuel.
26 And Jeroboam said in his heart, "Now the kingdom
will return to the house of David.
27 "[a]If this people go up to offer sacrifices in the house of
the LORD at Jerusalem, then the heart of this people will return
to their lord, *even* to Rehoboam king of Judah; and they will
kill me and return to Rehoboam king of Judah."
28 So the king [1]consulted, and [a]made two golden [b]calves,
and he said to them, "It is too much for you to go up to
Jerusalem; [c]behold your gods, O Israel, that brought you up
from the land of Egypt."
29 And he set [a]one in [b]Bethel, and the other he put in
[c]Dan.
30 Now [a]this thing became a sin, for the people went *to*
worship before the one as far as Dan.
31 And [a]he made houses on high places, and [b]made priests
from among [1]all the people who were not of the sons of Levi.
32 And Jeroboam [1]instituted a feast in the eighth month
on the fifteenth day of the month, [a]like the feast which is in
Judah, and he [2]went up to the altar; thus he did in Bethel,
sacrificing to the calves which he had made. And he stationed
in Bethel [b]the priests of the high places which he had made.
33 Then he [1]went up to the altar which he had made in
Bethel on the fifteenth day in the eighth month, even in the
month which he had [2]devised [3]in his own heart; and he [2]insti-
tuted a feast for the sons of Israel, and [1]went up to the altar [a]to
burn [4]incense.

CHAPTER 13

NOW behold, there came [a]a man of God from Judah to
Bethel by the word of the LORD, while Jeroboam was standing
by the altar [b]to burn incense.
2 And [a]he cried against the altar by the word of the LORD,
and said, "O altar, altar, thus says the LORD, 'Behold, a son
shall be born to the house of David, [b]Josiah by name; and on
you he shall sacrifice the priests of the high places who burn
incense on you, and human bones shall be burned on you.' "
3 Then he gave a [1]sign the same day, saying, "[a]This is the
[1]sign which the LORD has spoken, 'Behold, the altar shall be
split apart and the [2]ashes which are on it shall be poured out.' "
4 Now it came about when the king heard the saying of

22 [a]2 Chr. 12:5-7

23 [a]1 Kin. 12:17

24 [1]Lit., *brothers*
[a]1 Kin. 12:15

25 [1]Lit., *in it*
[a]Judg. 9:45-49 [b]Gen. 32:30, 31; Judg. 8:8, 17

27 [a]Deut. 12:5-7, 14

28 [1]Lit., *took counsel*
[a]2 Kin. 10:29; 17:16; Hos. 8:4-7 [b]Hos. 10:5 [c]Ex. 32:4, 8

29 [a]Hos. 10:5 [b]Gen. 28:19 [c]Judg. 18:26-31

30 [a]1 Kin. 13:34; 2 Kin. 17:21

31 [1]Or, *extremities of*
[a]1 Kin. 13:32 [b]1 Kin. 13:33; 2 Kin. 17:32; 2 Chr. 13:9

32 [1]Lit., *made* [2]Or, *offered upon*
[a]Lev. 23:33, 34; Num. 29:12
[b]Amos 7:10-13

33 [1]Or, *offered upon* [2]Lit., *made* [3]Lit., *from* [4]Or, *sacrifices*
[a]1 Kin. 13:1

1 [a]Kin. 12:22; 2 Kin. 23:17
[b]1 Kin. 12:33

2 [a]1 Kin. 13:32 [b]2 Kin. 23:15, 16

3 [1]Lit., *wonder* [2]Lit., *ashes of fat*
[a]Ex. 4:1-5; Judg. 6:17

he man of God, which he cried against the altar in Bethel,
hat Jeroboam stretched out his hand from the altar, saying,
'Seize him." But his hand which he stretched out against him
lried up, so that he could not draw it back to himself.
5 The altar also was split apart and the [1]ashes were
poured out from the altar, according to the [2]sign which the
nan of God had given by the word of the LORD.
6 And the king answered and said to the man of God,
'Please [1a]entreat the LORD your God, and pray for me, that my
hand may be restored to me." So [b]the man of God [2]entreated
the LORD, and the king's hand was restored to him, and it
became as it was before.
7 Then the king said to the man of God, "Come home
with me and refresh yourself, and [a]I will give you a reward."
8 But the man of God said to the king, "[a]If you were to
give me half your house I would not go with you, nor would I
eat bread or drink water in this place.
9 "For so [1]it was commanded me by the word of the
LORD, saying, 'You shall eat no bread, nor drink water, nor
return by the way which you came.' "
10 So he went another way, and did not return by the way
which he came to Bethel.
11 Now an old prophet [a]was living in Bethel; and his [1]sons
came and told him all the deeds which the man of God had
done that day in Bethel; the words which he had spoken to the
king, these also they related to their father.
12 And their father said to them, "[1]Which way did he
go?" Now his sons [2]had seen the way which the man of God
who came from Judah had gone.
13 Then he said to his sons, "Saddle the donkey for me."
So they saddled the donkey for him and he rode away on it.
14 So he went after the man of God and found him sitting
under [1]an oak; and he said to him, "Are you the man of God
who came from Judah?" And he said, "I am."
15 Then he said to him, "Come home with me and eat
bread."
16 And he said, "[a]I cannot return with you, nor go with
you, nor will I eat bread or drink water with you in this place.
17 "For a command *came* to me [a]by the word of the LORD,
'You shall eat no bread, nor drink water there; do not return by
going the way which you came.' "
18 And he said to him, "I also am a prophet like you, and
an angel spoke to me by the word of the LORD, saying, 'Bring
him back with you to your house, that he may eat bread and
drink water.' " *But* he lied to him.
19 So he went back with him, and ate bread in his house
and drank water.
20 Now it came about, as they were sitting down at the
table, that the word of the LORD came to the prophet who had
brought him back;
21 and he cried to the man of God who came from Judah,
saying, "Thus says the LORD, 'Because you have [1]disobeyed the
[2]command of the LORD, and have not observed the commandment which the LORD your God commanded you,
22 but have returned and eaten bread and drunk water in
the place of which he said to you, "Eat no bread and drink no

5 [1]Lit., *ashes of fat* [2]Lit., *wonder*

6 [1]Lit., *soften the face of* [2]Lit., *softened the face of* [a]Ex. 8:8, 28; 9:28; Acts 8:24 [b]Luke 6:27, 28

7 [a]1 Sam. 9:7, 8; 2 Kin. 5:15

8 [a]1 Kin. 13:16, 17; Num. 22:18; 24:13

9 [1]Lit., *he commanded me*

11 [1]Lit., *son* [a]1 Kin. 13:25; 2 Kin. 23:18

12 [1]Lit., *Where is the way he went* [2]Some ancient versions read *showed him*

14 [1]Or, a *terebinth*

16 [a]1 Kin. 13:8, 9

17 [a]1 Kin. 20:35

21 [1]Lit., *rebelled* against [2]Lit., *mouth*

24 [a]1 Kin. 20:36
25 [a]1 Kin. 13:11
26 [1]Lit., *rebelled* against [2]Lit., *mouth*
31 [a]2 Kin. 23:17, 18
32 [a]1 Kin. 13:2 [b]1 Kin. 12:31 [c]1 Kin. 16:24
33 [1]Or, *extremities of* [a]Judg. 17:5
34 [1]Lit., *by this thing he became* [a]1 Kin. 12:30; 2 Kin. 17:21 [b]1 Kin. 14:10; 15:29, 30
2 [a]1 Sam. 28:8; 2 Sam. 14:2; 2 Chr. 18:29 [b]Josh. 18:1 [c]1 Kin. 11:29-31
3 [a]1 Kin. 13:7; 1 Sam. 9:7, 8; 2 Kin. 4:42

water"; your body shall not come to the grave of you
fathers.' "
23 And it came about after he had eaten bread and afte
he had drunk, that he saddled the donkey for him, for the
prophet whom he had brought back.
24 Now when he had gone, [a]a lion met him on the way
and killed him, and his body was thrown on the road, with the
donkey standing beside it; the lion also was standing beside the
body.
25 And behold, men passed by and saw the body thrown
on the road, and the lion standing beside the body; so they
came and told *it* in the city where [a]the old prophet lived.
26 Now when the prophet who brought him back from
the way heard *it*, he said, "It is the man of God, who [1]disobeyed
the [2]command of the LORD; therefore the LORD has
given him to the lion, which has torn him and killed him,
according to the word of the LORD which He spoke to him."
27 Then he spoke to his sons, saying, "Saddle the donkey
for me." And they saddled *it*.
28 And he went and found his body thrown on the road
with the donkey and the lion standing beside the body; the
lion had not eaten the body nor torn the donkey.
29 So the prophet took up the body of the man of God
and laid it on the donkey, and brought it back and he came to
the city of the old prophet to mourn and to bury him.
30 And he laid his body in his own grave, and they
mourned over him, *saying*, "Alas, my brother!"
31 And it came about after he had buried him, that he
spoke to his sons, saying, "When I die, bury me in the grave in
which the man of God is buried; [a]lay my bones beside his
bones.
32 "[a]For the thing shall surely come to pass which he cried
by the word of the LORD against the altar in Bethel and [b]against
all the houses of the high places which are in the cities of
[c]Samaria."
33 After this event Jeroboam did not return from his evil
way, but again he made priests of the high places from among
[1]all the people; [a]any who would, he ordained, to be priests of
the high places.
34 [a]And [1]this event became sin to the house of Jeroboam,
[b]even to blot *it* out and destroy *it* from off the face of the
earth.

CHAPTER 14

AT that time Abijah the son of Jeroboam became sick.
2 And Jeroboam said to his wife, "Arise now, and [a]dis-
guise yourself so that they may not know that you are the wife
of Jeroboam, and go to [b]Shiloh; behold, Ahijah the prophet is
there, who [c]spoke concerning me *that I would be* king over
this people.
3 "[a]And take ten loaves with you, *some* cakes and a jar of
honey, and go to him. He will tell you what will happen to the
boy."
4 And Jeroboam's wife did so, and arose and went to

Shiloh, and came to the house of [b]Ahijah. Now Ahijah could
not see, [c]for his eyes were [1]dim because of his age.
5 Now the LORD had said to Ahijah, "Behold, the wife of
Jeroboam is coming to [1]inquire of you concerning her son, for
he is sick. You shall say thus and thus to her, for it will be when
she arrives that [a]she will pretend to be another woman."
6 And it came about when Ahijah heard the sound of her
feet coming in the doorway, that he said, "Come in, wife of
Jeroboam, why do you pretend to be another woman? For I
am sent to you *with* a harsh *message*.
7 "Go, say to Jeroboam, 'Thus says the LORD God of
Israel: "[a]Because I exalted you from among the people and
made you leader over My people Israel,
8 and tore the kingdom away from the house of David
and gave it to you—[a]yet you have not been like My servant
David, who kept My commandments and who followed Me
with all his heart, [b]to do only that which was right in My sight;
9 you also have done more evil than all who were before
you, and [a]have gone and made for yourself other gods and
[b]molten images to provoke Me to anger, and [c]have cast Me
behind your back—
10 therefore behold, I am bringing calamity on the house
of Jeroboam, and [a]will cut off from Jeroboam [1]every male
person, [b]both bound and free in Israel, and I [c]will make a clean
sweep of the house of Jeroboam, as one sweeps away dung
until it is all gone.
11 "[a]Anyone belonging to Jeroboam who dies in the city
the dogs will eat. And he who dies in the field the birds of the
heavens will eat; for the LORD has spoken *it*." '
12 "Now you arise, go to your house. [a]When your feet
enter the city the child will die.
13 "And all Israel shall mourn for him and bury him, for
[1]he alone of Jeroboam's *family* shall come to the grave, because in him something good was found toward the LORD God
of Israel in the house of Jeroboam.
14 "Moreover, [a]the LORD will raise up for Himself a king
over Israel who shall cut off the house of Jeroboam this day
[1]and from now on.
15 "For the LORD will strike Israel, as a reed is shaken in the
water; and [a]He will uproot Israel from [b]this good land which
He gave to their fathers, and [c]will scatter them beyond the
Euphrates River, [d]because they have made their [1]Asherim,
provoking the LORD to anger.
16 "And He will give up Israel [a]on account of the sins of
Jeroboam, which he [1]committed and with which he made
Israel to sin."
17 Then Jeroboam's wife arose and departed and came to
[a]Tirzah. [b]As she was entering the threshold of the house, the
child died.
18 [a]And all Israel buried him and mourned for him, according to the word of the LORD which He spoke through His
servant Ahijah the prophet.
19 Now the rest of the acts of Jeroboam, [a]how he made
war and how he reigned, behold, they are written in the Book
of the Chronicles of the Kings of Israel.
20 And the time that Jeroboam reigned *was* twenty-two

4 [1]Lit., *set* [a]1 Kin. 14:2 [b]1 Kin. 11:29 [c]1 Sam. 3:2; 4:5

5 [1]Lit., *seek a word from* [a]2 Sam. 14:2

7 [a]1 Kin. 11:28-31; 16:2

8 [a]1 Kin. 11:33, 38 [b]1 Kin. 15:5

9 [a]1 Kin. 12:28; 2 Chr. 11:15 [b]Ex. 34:17 [c]Ps. 50:17; Ezek. 23:35

10 [1]Lit., *him who urinates against the wall* [a]1 Kin. 21:21; 2 Kin. 9:8 [b]Deut. 32:36; 2 Kin. 14:26 [c]1 Kin. 15:29

11 [a]1 Kin. 16:4; 21:24

12 [a]1 Kin. 14:17

13 [1]Lit., *the one*

14 [1]Lit., *and what even now?* [a]1 Kin. 15:27-29

15 [1]I.e., wooden symbols of a female deity [a]Deut. 29:28; 2 Kin. 17:6 [b]Josh. 23:15, 16 [c]2 Kin. 15:29 [d]Ex. 34:13, 14; Deut. 12:3, 4

16 [1]Lit., *sinned* [a]1 Kin. 12:30; 13:34

17 [a]1 Kin. 15:21, 33; 16:6-9, 15, 23 [b]1 Kin. 14:12

18 [a]1 Kin. 14:13

19 [a]1 Kin. 14:30; 2 Chr. 13:2-20

years; and he slept with his fathers, and Nadab his son reigned in his place.

21 [a]Now Rehoboam the son of Solomon reigned in Judah. Rehoboam was forty-one years old when he became king, and he reigned seventeen years in Jerusalem, [b]the city which the LORD had chosen from all the tribes of Israel to put His name there. And his mother's name was Naamah the Ammonitess.

22 [a]And Judah did evil in the sight of the LORD, and they provoked Him to jealousy more than all that their fathers had done, with [1]the sins which they [2]committed.

23 For they also built for themselves [a]high places and sacred [b]pillars and [1c]Asherim on every high hill and [d]beneath every luxuriant tree.

24 And there were also [a]male cult prostitutes in the land. They did according to all the abominations of the nations which the LORD dispossessed before the sons of Israel.

25 [a]Now it came about in the fifth year of King Rehoboam, that Shishak the king of Egypt came up against Jerusalem.

26 And he took away the treasures of the house of the LORD and the treasures of the king's house, and [a]he took everything, [1b]even taking all the shields of gold which Solomon had made.

27 So King Rehoboam made shields of bronze in their place, and [a]committed them to the [1]care of the commanders of the [2]guard who guarded the doorway of the king's house.

28 Then it happened as often as the king entered the house of the LORD, that the [1]guards would carry them and would bring them back into the [1]guards' room.

29 [a]Now the rest of the acts of Rehoboam and all that he did, are they not written in the Book of the Chronicles of the Kings of Judah?

30 [a]And there was war between Rehoboam and Jeroboam continually.

31 And Rehoboam slept with his fathers, and was buried with his fathers in the city of David; and [a]his mother's name was Naamah the Ammonitess. And Abijam his son became king in his place.

CHAPTER 15

[a]NOW in the eighteenth year of King Jeroboam, the son of Nabat, Abijam became king over Judah.

2 He reigned three years in Jerusalem; and his mother's name was [1]Maacah the daughter of [2]Abishalom.

3 And he walked in all the sins of his father which he had committed before him; and [a]his heart was not [1]wholly devoted to the LORD his God, like the heart of his father David.

4 But for David's sake the LORD his God gave him a [a]lamp in Jerusalem, to raise up his son after him and to establish Jerusalem;

5 [a]because David did what was right in the sight of the LORD, and had not turned aside from any thing that He commanded him all the days of his life, [b]except in the case of Uriah the Hittite.

---

21 [a]2 Chr. 12:13 [b]1 Kin. 11:32, 36

22 [1]Lit., *their* [2]Lit., *sinned* [a]2 Chr. 12:1, 14

23 [1]I.e., wooden symbols of a female deity [a]Deut. 12:2 [b]Deut. 16:22 [c]1 Kin. 14:15 [d]2 Kin. 17:10; Is. 57:5; Jer. 2:20

24 [a]Deut. 23:17

25 [a]2 Chr. 12:2, 9-11

26 [1]Lit., *and he took away* [a]1 Kin. 15:18 [b]1 Kin. 10:17

27 [1]Lit., *hand* [2]Lit., *runner* [a]1 Sam. 8:11; 22:17

28 [1]Lit., *runners*

29 [a]2 Chr. 12:15, 16

30 [a]1 Kin. 12:21-24; 15:6

31 [a]1 Kin. 14:21

1 [a]2 Chr. 13:1

2 [1]Or, *Micaiah, the daughter of Uriel;* cf. 2 Chr. 13:2 [2]Or, *Absalom;* cf. 2 Chr. 11:20

3 [1]Lit., *complete with* [a]1 Kin. 11:4

4 [a]1 Kin. 11:36; 2 Sam. 21:17

5 [a]1 Kin. 9:4; 14:8 [b]2 Sam. 11:4, 15-17; 12:9, 10

6 [a]And there was war between Rehoboam and Jeroboam
ıll the days of his life.
7 Now [a]the rest of the acts of Abijam and all that he did,
ıre they not written in the Book of the Chronicles of the Kings
ɔf Judah? [b]And there was war between Abijam and Jeroboam.
8 [a]And Abijam slept with his fathers and they buried him
.n the city of David; and Asa his son became king in his place.
9 So in the twentieth year of Jeroboam the king of Israel
Asa began to reign as king of Judah.
10 And he reigned forty-one years in Jerusalem; and [a]his
mother's name was Maacah the daughter of Abishalom.
11 And [a]Asa did what was right in the sight of the LORD,
like David his father.
12 [a]He also put away the male cult prostitutes from the
land, and [b]removed all the idols which his fathers had made.
13 [a]And [1]he also removed Maacah his mother from *being*
queen mother, because she had made a horrid image [2]as an
Asherah; and Asa cut down her horrid image and [b]burned *it* at
the brook Kidron.
14 [a]But the high places were not taken away; nevertheless
[b]the heart of Asa was [1]wholly devoted to the LORD all his days.
15 And [a]he brought into the house of the LORD the dedicated things of his father and his own dedicated things: silver
and gold and utensils.
16 [a]Now there was war between Asa and Baasha king of
Israel all their days.
17 [a]And Baasha king of Israel went up against Judah and
[1b]fortified Ramah [c]in order to prevent *anyone* from going out
or coming in to Asa king of Judah.
18 Then [a]Asa took all the silver and the gold which were
left in the treasuries of the house of the LORD and the treasuries of the king's house, and delivered them into the hand of
his servants. And [b]King Asa sent them to Ben-hadad the son of
Tabrimmon, the son of Hezion, king of [1]Syria, who lived in
[c]Damascus, saying,
19 "Let there be a [a]treaty between [1]you and me, *as* between
my father and your father. Behold, I have sent you a present of
silver and gold; go, break your treaty with Baasha king of Israel
so that he will withdraw from me."
20 So Ben-hadad listened to King Asa and sent the commanders of his armies against the cities of Israel, and [1]con-
quered [a]Ijon, [b]Dan, [c]Abel-beth-maacah and all [d]Chinneroth,
besides all the land of Naphtali.
21 And it came about when Baasha heard *of it* that [a]he
ceased [1]fortifying Ramah, and remained in [b]Tirzah.
22 Then King Asa made a proclamation to all Judah—
none was exempt—and they carried away the stones of Ramah
and its timber with which Baasha had built. And King Asa
built with them [a]Geba of Benjamin and Mizpah.
23 [a]Now the rest of all the acts of Asa and all his might
and all that he did and the cities which he built, are they not
written in the Book of the Chronicles of the Kings of Judah?
But in the time of his old age he was diseased in his feet.
24 And Asa slept with his fathers and was buried with his
fathers in the city of David his father; and [a]Jehoshaphat his son
reigned in his place.

6 [a]1 Kin. 14:30

7 [a]2 Chr. 13:2, 21, 22 [b]2 Chr. 13:3-20

8 [a]2 Chr. 14:1

10 [a]1 Kin. 15:2

11 [a]2 Chr. 14:2

12 [a]1 Kin. 14:24; 22:46; Deut. 23:17 [b]1 Kin. 11:7, 8; 14:23; 2 Chr. 14:2-5

13 [1]Lit., *also Maacah his mother and he removed her* [2]Or, *for Asherah* [a]2 Chr. 15:16-18 [b]Ex. 32:20

14 [1]Lit., *complete with* [a]1 Kin. 22:43; 2 Kin. 12:3 [b]1 Kin. 15:3; 8:61

15 [a]1 Kin. 7:51

16 [a]1 Kin. 15:32

17 [1]Lit., *built* [a]2 Chr. 16:1-6 [b]1 Kin. 15:21, 22 [c]1 Kin. 12:26-29

18 [1]Heb., *Aram* [a]1 Kin. 15:15; 14:26 [b]2 Kin. 12:17, 18 [c]1 Kin. 11:23, 24; Gen. 14:15

19 [1]Lit., *me and you* [a]2 Chr. 16:7

20 [1]Lit., *smote* [a]2 Kin. 15:29 [b]1 Kin. 12:29 [c]2 Kin. 15:29 [d]Josh. 11:2; 12:3

21 [1]Lit., *building* [a]1 Kin. 15:17 [b]1 Kin. 14:17; 16:15-18

22 [a]Josh. 18:24; 21:17

23 [a]2 Chr. 16:11-14

24 [a]1 Kin. 22:41-44; 2 Chr. 17:1

25 [a]1 Kin. 14:20

26 [a]1 Kin. 12:28-33; 13:33, 34 [b]1 Kin. 15:30, 34; 14:16

27 [a]1 Kin. 14:14 [b]Josh. 19:44; 21:23

29 [1]Lit., *any breath* [a]1 Kin. 14:9-16

30 [a]1 Kin. 15:26

31 [a]1 Kin. 14:19

32 [a]1 Kin. 15:16

34 [a]1 Kin. 15:26

1 [a]1 Kin. 16:7; 2 Chr. 19:2; 20:34 [b]2 Chr. 16:7-10

2 [a]1 Kin. 14:7 [b]1 Kin. 15:39

3 [a]1 Kin. 14:10; 21:21 [b]1 Kin. 16:11 [c]1 Kin. 15:29

4 [a]1 Kin. 14:11; 21:24

5 [a]1 Kin. 14:19; 15:31

6 [a]1 Kin. 14:17; 15:21

7 [1]Or, *him* [a]1 Kin. 16:1 [b]1 Kin. 14:14; 15:27, 29

25 Now [a]Nadab the son of Jeroboam became king over
Israel in the second year of Asa king of Judah, and he reigned
over Israel two years.
26 And he did evil in the sight of the LORD, and [a]walked in
the way of his father and [b]in his sin which he made Israel sin.
27 Then [a]Baasha the son of Ahijah of the house of Issachar
conspired against him, and Baasha struck him down at
[b]Gibbethon, which belonged to the Philistines, while Nadab
and all Israel were laying siege to Gibbethon.
28 So Baasha killed him in the third year of Asa king of
Judah, and reigned in his place.
29 And it came about, as soon as he was king, he struck
down all the household of Jeroboam. He did not leave to
Jeroboam [1]any persons alive, until he had destroyed them,
[a]according to the word of the LORD, which He spoke by His
servant Ahijah the Shilonite,
30 *and* because of the sins of Jeroboam which he sinned,
and [a]which he made Israel sin, because of his provocation with
which he provoked the LORD, God of Israel, to anger.
31 [a]Now the rest of the acts of Nadab and all that he did,
are they not written in the Book of the Chronicles of the Kings
of Israel?
32 [a]And there was war between Asa and Baasha king of
Israel all their days.
33 In the third year of Asa king of Judah, Baasha the son
of Ahijah became king over all Israel at Tirzah, and reigned
twenty-four years.
34 And he did evil in the sight of the LORD, and [a]walked in
the way of Jeroboam and in his sin which he made Israel sin.

Chapter 16

NOW the word of the LORD came to [a]Jehu the son of [b]Ha-
nani against Baasha, saying,
2 "Inasmuch as I [a]exalted you from the dust and made
you leader over My people Israel, and [b]you have walked in the
way of Jeroboam and have made My people Israel sin, provoking Me to anger with their sins,
3 behold, [a]I will consume [b]Baasha and his house, and [c]I
will make your house like the house of Jeroboam the son of
Nebat.
4 "[a]Anyone of Baasha who dies in the city the dogs shall
eat, and anyone of his who dies in the field the birds of the
heavens will eat."
5 [a]Now the rest of the acts of Baasha and what he did
and his might, are they not written in the Book of the Chronicles of the Kings of Israel?
6 And Baasha slept with his fathers and was buried in
[a]Tirzah, and Elah his son became king in his place.
7 Moreover, the word of the LORD through [a]the prophet
Jehu the son of Hanani also came against Baasha and his
household, both because of all the evil which he did in the
sight of the LORD, provoking Him to anger with the work of his
hands, in being like the house of Jeroboam, and because [b]he
struck [1]it.
8 In the twenty-sixth year of Asa king of Judah Elah the

on of Baasha became king over Israel at Tirzah, *and reigned*
wo years.
9 And his servant [a]Zimri, commander of half his chariots,
:onspired against him. Now he *was* at Tirzah drinking himself
lrunk in the house of Arza, [b]who *was* over the household at
Tirzah.
10 Then Zimri went in and struck him and put him to
leath, in the twenty-seventh year of Asa king of Judah, and
became king in his place.
11 And it came about, when he became king, as soon as he
sat on his throne, that [a]he [1]killed all the household of Baasha;
he did not leave [2]a single male, neither of his [3]relatives nor of
his friends.
12 Thus Zimri destroyed all the household of Baasha, [a]ac-
cording to the word of the LORD, which He spoke against
Baasha through [b]Jehu the prophet,
13 for all the sins of Baasha and the sins of Elah his son,
which they sinned and which they made Israel sin, [a]provoking
the LORD God of Israel to anger with their [1]idols.
14 [a]Now the rest of the acts of Elah and all that he did, are
they not written in the Book of the Chronicles of the Kings of
Israel?
15 In the twenty-seventh year of Asa king of Judah, Zimri
reigned seven days at Tirzah. Now the people were camped
against [a]Gibbethon, which belonged to the Philistines.
16 And the people who were camped heard [1]it said,
"Zimri has conspired and has also struck down the king." Therefore all Israel made Omri, the commander of the army king
over Israel that day in the camp.
17 Then Omri and all Israel with him went up from Gibbethon, and they besieged Tirzah.
18 And it came about, when Zimri saw that the city was
taken, that he went into the citadel of the king's house, and
burned the king's house over him with fire, and [a]died,
19 because of his sins which he sinned, doing evil in the
sight of the LORD, [a]walking in the way of Jeroboam, and in his
sin which he did, making Israel sin.
20 [a]Now the rest of the acts of Zimri and his conspiracy
which he [1]carried out, are they not written in the Book of the
Chronicles of the Kings of Israel?
21 Then the people of Israel were divided into two parts:
half of the people followed Tibni the son of Ginath, to make
him king; the *other* half followed Omri.
22 But the people who followed Omri prevailed over the
people who followed Tibni the son of Ginath. And Tibni died
and Omri became king.
23 In the thirty-first year of Asa king of Judah, Omri became king over Israel, and reigned twelve years; he reigned six
years at [a]Tirzah.
24 And he bought the hill [1]Samaria from Shemer for two
talents of silver; and he built on the hill, and named the city
which he built [1a]Samaria, after the name of Shemer, the owner
of the hill.
25 And [a]Omri did evil in the sight of the LORD, and [b]acted
more wickedly than all who *were* before him.
26 For he [a]walked in all the way of Jeroboam the son of

9 [a]2 Kin. 9:30-33 [b]1 Kin. 18:3; Gen. 24:2; 39:4

11 [1]Lit., *smote* [2]Lit., *him who urinates against the wall* [3]Lit., *redeemers* [a]1 Kin. 16:3; 15:29

12 [a]1 Kin. 16:3 [b]2 Chr. 19:2; 20:34

13 [1]Lit., *vanities* [a]1 Kin. 15:30; Deut. 32:21

14 [a]1 Kin. 16:5

15 [a]1 Kin. 15:27

16 [1]Lit., *saying*

18 [a]1 Sam. 31:4, 5; 2 Sam. 17:23

19 [a]1 Kin. 12:28; 14:16; 15:26

20 [1]Lit., *conspired* [a]1 Kin. 16:5, 14, 27

23 [a]1 Kin. 15:21

24 [1]Heb., *Shomeron* [a]1 Kin. 16:28, 29, 32

25 [a]Mic. 6:16 [b]1 Kin. 16:30-33; 14:9

26 [a]1 Kin. 16:19

Nebat and in his sins which he made Israel sin, provoking the
LORD, God of Israel, with their [1]idols.
27 Now the rest of the acts of Omri which he did and his
might which he [1]showed, are they not written in the Book of
the Chronicles of the Kings of Israel?
28 So Omri slept with his fathers, and was buried in Samaria; and Ahab his son became king in his place.
29 Now Ahab the son of Omri became king over Israel in
the thirty-eight year of Asa king of Judah, and Ahab the son of
Omri reigned over Israel in Samaria twenty-two years.
30 And Ahab the son of Omri did evil in the sight of the
LORD [a]more than all who were before him.
31 And it came about, as though it had been a trivial thing
for him to walk in the sins of Jeroboam the son of Nebat, that
[a]he married Jezebel the daughter of Ethbaal king of the [b]Sidon-
ians, and went to serve Baal and worshiped him.
32 So he erected an altar for Baal in [a]the house of Baal,
which he built in Samaria.
33 And Ahab also made [a]the [1]Asherah. Thus [b]Ahab did
more to provoke the LORD, God of Israel, than all the kings of
Israel who were before him.
34 [a]In his days Hiel the Bethelite built Jericho; he laid its
foundations with the *loss of* Abiram his first-born, and set up
its gates with the *loss of* his youngest son Segub, according to
the word of the LORD, which He spoke by Joshua the son of
Nun.

CHAPTER 17

NOW Elijah the Tishbite, who was of [1a]the settlers of Gilead, said to Ahab, "[b]As the LORD, the God of Israel lives,
before whom I stand, surely [c]there shall be neither dew nor
rain these years, except by my word."
2 And the word of the LORD came to him, saying,
3 "Go away from here and turn eastward, and hide yourself by the brook Cherith, which is [1]east of the Jordan.
4 "And it shall be that you shall drink of the brook, and [a]I
have commanded the ravens to provide for you there."
5 So he went and did according to the word of the LORD,
for he went and lived by the brook Cherith, which is [1]east of
the Jordan.
6 And the ravens brought him bread and meat in the
morning and bread and meat in the evening, and he would
drink from the brook.
7 And it happened after a while, that the brook dried up,
because there was no rain in the land.
8 Then the word of the LORD came to him, saying,
9 "Arise, go to [a]Zarephath, which belongs to Sidon, and
stay there; behold, [b]I have commanded a widow there to provide for you."
10 So he arose and went to Zarephath, and when he came
to the gate of the city, behold, a widow was there gathering
sticks; and [a]he called to her and said, "Please get me a little
water in a [1]jar, that I may drink."
11 And as she was going to get *it*, he called to her and said,
"Please bring me a piece of bread in your hand."

26 [1]Lit., *vanities*

27 [1]Lit., *did*

30 [a]1 Kin. 16:25; 14:9

31 [a]Deut. 7:1-5 [b]1 Kin. 11:1-5; 2 Kin. 10:18; 17:16

32 [a]2 Kin. 10:21, 26, 27

33 [1]I.e., a wooden symbol of a female diety [a]2 Kin. 13:6 [b]1 Kin. 16:29, 30; 14:9

34 [a]Josh. 6:26

1 [1]Or, *Tishbe in Gilead* [a]Judg. 12:4 [b]1 Kin. 18:10; 22:14; 2 Kin. 5:20 [c]1 Kin. 18:1; Luke 4:25; James 5:17

3 [1]Lit., *before*

4 [a]1 Kin. 16:9

5 [1]Lit., *before*

9 [a]Obad. 20; Luke 4:26 [b]1 Kin. 17:4

10 [1]Or, *vessel* [a]Gen. 24:17; John 4:7

12 But she said, "[a]As the LORD your God lives, I have no
[b]bread, only a handful of flour in the [2]bowl and a little oil in
the jar; and behold, I am gathering [3]a few sticks that I may go
in and prepare for me and my son, that we may eat it and die."
13 Then Elijah said to her, "Do not fear; go, do as you
have said, but make me a little bread cake from [1]it first, and
bring *it* out to me, and afterward you may make *one* for
yourself and for your son.
14 "For thus says the LORD God of Israel, 'The [1]bowl of
flour shall not be exhausted, nor shall the jar of oil [2]be empty,
until the day that the LORD sends rain on the face of the
earth.'"
15 So she went and did according to the word of Elijah,
and she and he and her household ate for *many* days.
16 The [1]bowl of flour was not exhausted nor did the jar of
oil [2]become empty, according to the word of the LORD which
He spoke through Elijah.
17 Now it came about after these things, that the son of
the woman, the mistress of the house, became sick; and his
sickness was so severe, that there was no breath left in him.
18 So she said to Elijah, "[a]What do I have to do with you,
O [b]man of God? [1]You have come to me to bring my iniquity
to remembrance, and to put my son to death!"
19 And he said to her, "Give me your son." Then he took
him from her bosom and carried him up to the upper room
where he was living, and laid him on his own bed.
20 And he called to the LORD and said, "O LORD my God,
hast Thou also brought calamity to the widow with whom I
am [1]staying, by causing her son to die?"
21 [a]Then he stretched himself upon the child three times,
and called to the LORD, and said, "O LORD my God, I pray
Thee, let this child's life return [1]to him."
22 And the LORD heard the voice of Elijah, [a]and the life of
the child returned [1]to him and he revived.
23 And Elijah took the child, and brought him down from
the upper room into the house and gave him to his mother;
and Elijah said, "See, your son is alive."
24 Then the woman said to Elijah, "[a]Now I know that you
are a man of God, and that the word of the LORD in your
mouth is truth."

CHAPTER 18

NOW it came about [a]*after* many days, that the word of the
LORD came to Elijah in the third year, saying, "Go, show yourself to Ahab, and I will send rain on the face of the earth."
2 So Elijah went to show himself to Ahab. Now the famine *was* severe in Samaria.
3 And Ahab called Obadiah [a]who *was* over the household. (Now Obadiah [1]feared the LORD greatly;
4 for it came about, [a]when Jezebel [1]destroyed the prophets of the LORD, that Obadiah took a hundred prophets and
hid them by fifties in a cave, and provided them with bread
and water.)
5 Then Ahab said to Obadiah, "Go through the land to
all the springs of water and to all the valleys; perhaps we will

12 [1]Lit., *cake* [2]Lit., *pitcher* [3]Lit., *two* [a]1 Kin. 17:1 [b]2 Kin. 4:2-7

13 [1]Lit., *there*

14 [1]Lit., *pitcher* [2]Lit., *lack*

16 [1]Lit., *pitcher* [2]Lit., *lack*

18 [1]Or, *Have you come . . . death?* [a]2 Sam. 16:10; 2 Kin. 3:13; John 2:4 [b]1 Kin. 12:22

20 [1]Lit., *sojourning*

21 [1]Lit., *upon his inward part* [a]2 Kin. 4:34, 35; Acts 20:10

22 [1]Lit., *upon his inward part* [a]Heb. 11:35

24 [a]John 2:11; 3:2

1 [a]1 Kin. 17:1

3 [1]Or, *revered* [a]1 Kin. 16:9

4 [1]Lit., *cut off* [a]1 Kin. 17:13

5 [1]Lit., *cut off*

6 [1]Lit., *pass through*

7 [1]Lit., *to meet*
[a]2 Kin. 1:6-8

9 [1]Lit., *have I sinned*

10 [a]1 Kin. 17:1

12 [1]Or, *revered*
[a]2 Kin. 2:16; Ezek. 3:12, 14; Acts 8:39

13 [1]Lit., *a hundred men of the prophets*
[a]1 Kin. 18:4

15 [a]1 Kin. 17:1

17 [a]1 Kin. 21:20; Josh. 7:25

18 [a]1 Kin. 9:9; 2 Chr. 15:2
[b]1 Kin. 16:31; 21:25, 26

19 [a]Josh. 19:26 2 Kin. 2:25
[b]1 Kin. 18:22 [c]1 Kin. 16:33

21 [1]Lit., *on the two divided opinions*
[a]2 Kin. 17:41; Matt. 6:24
[b]Josh. 24:15

22 [a]1 Kin. 19:10, 14 [b]1 Kin. 18:19

24 [a] Kin. 18:38

find grass and keep the horses and mules alive, and not [1]have
to kill some of the cattle.
6 So they divided the land between them to [1]survey it;
Ahab went one way by himself and Obadiah went another way
by himself.
7 Now as Obadiah was on the way, behold, Elijah [1]met
him, [a]and he recognized him and fell on his face and said, "Is
this you, Elijah my master?"
8 And he said to him, "It is I. Go, say to your master,
'Behold, Elijah *is here*.'"
9 And he said, "What [1]sin have I committed, that you
are giving your servant into the hand of Ahab, to put me to
death?
10 "[a]As the LORD your God lives, there is no nation or
kingdom where my master has not sent to search for you; and
when they said, 'He is not *here*', he made the kingdom or
nation swear that they could not find you.
11 "And now you are saying, 'Go, say to your master, "Behold, Elijah *is here*."'
12 "And it will come about when I leave you [a]that the
Spirit of the LORD will carry you where I do not know; so when
I come and tell Ahab and he cannot find you, he will kill me,
although *I* your servant have [1]feared the LORD from my youth.
13 "[a]Has it not been told to my master what I did when
Jezebel killed the prophets of the LORD, that I hid [1]a hundred
prophets of the LORD by fifties in a cave, and provided them
with bread and water?
14 "And now you are saying, 'Go, say to your master, "Behold, Elijah *is here*"'; he will then kill me."
15 And Elijah said, "[a]As the LORD of hosts lives, before
whom I stand, I will surely show myself to him today."
16 So Obadiah went to meet Ahab, and told him; and
Ahab went to meet Elijah.
17 And it came about, when Ahab saw Elijah that [a]Ahab
said to him, "Is this you, you troubler of Israel?"
18 And he said, "I have not troubled Israel, but you and
your father's house *have*, because [a]you have forsaken the commandments of the LORD, and [b]you have followed the Baals.
19 "Now then send *and* gather to me all Israel at [a]Mount
Carmel, [b]*together* with 450 prophets of Baal and 400 prophets
of [c]the Asherah, who eat at Jezebel's table."
20 So Ahab sent *a message* among all the sons of Israel,
and brought the prophets together at Mount Carmel.
21 And Elijah came near to all the people and said, "[a]How
long *will* you [1]hesitate between two opinions? [b]If the LORD is
God, follow Him; but if Baal, follow him." But the people did
not answer him a word.
22 Then Elijah said to the people, "I [a]alone am left a
prophet of the LORD, but Baal's prophets are [b]450 men.
23 "Now let them give us two oxen; and let them choose
one ox for themselves and cut it up, and place it on the wood,
but put no fire *under it*; and I will prepare the other ox, and
lay it on the wood, and I will not put a fire *under it*.
24 "Then you call on the name of your god, and I will call
on the name of the LORD, and [a] the God who answers by fire,

He is God." And all the people answered and said, "[1]That is a
good idea."
25 So Elijah said to the prophets of Baal, "Choose one ox
for yourselves and prepare it first for you are many, and call on
the name of your god, but put no fire *under it*."
26 Then they took the ox which [1]was given them and they
prepared it and called on the name of Baal from morning until
noon saying, "O Baal, answer us." But there was no voice and
no one answered. And they [2]leaped about the altar which [3]they
made.
27 And it came about at noon, that Elijah mocked them
and said, "Call out with a loud voice, for he is a god; either he
is occupied or gone aside, or is on a journey, or perhaps he is
asleep and needs to be awakened."
28 So they cried with a loud voice and [a]cut themselves
according to their custom with swords and lances until the
blood gushed out on them.
29 And it came about when midday was past, that they
[1]raved [a]until the time of the offering of the *evening* sacrifice;
but there was no voice, no one answered, and no [2]one paid
attention.
30 Then Elijah said to all the people, "Come near to me."
So all the people came near to him. And [a]he repaired the altar
of the LORD which had been torn down.
31 And Elijah took twelve stones according to the number
of the tribes of the sons of Jacob, to whom the word of the
LORD had come, saying, "[a]Israel shall be your name."
32 So with the stones he built an altar in the name of the
LORD, and he made a trench around the altar, large enough to
hold two [1]measures of seed.
33 [a]Then he arranged the wood and cut the ox in pieces
and laid *it* on the wood. And he said, "Fill four pitchers with
water and pour *it* on the burnt offering and on the wood."
34 And he said, "Do it a second time," and they did it a
second time. And he said, "Do it a third time," and they did it
a third time.
35 And the water flowed around the altar, and he also
filled the trench with water.
36 Then it came about [a]at the time of the offering of the
evening sacrifice, that Elijah the prophet came near and said,
"[b]O LORD, the God of Abraham, Isaac and Israel, today let it
be known that Thou art God in Israel, and that I am Thy
servant, and [c]that I have done all these things at Thy word.
37 "Answer me, O LORD, answer me, that this people may
know that Thou, O LORD, art God, and *that* Thou hast turned
their heart back again."
38 Then [a]fire of the LORD fell, and consumed the burnt
offering and the wood and the stones and the dust, and licked
up the water that was in the trench.
39 And when all the people saw it, they fell on their faces;
and they said, "[a]The LORD, He is God; the LORD, He is God."
40 Then Elijah said to them, "Seize the prophets of Baal;
do not let one of them escape." So they seized them; and
Elijah brought them down to [a]the brook Kishon, [b]and slew
them there.

24 [1]Lit., *The matter is good*

26 [1]Lit., *he gave* [2]Lit., *limped*, i.e., a type of ceremonial dance [3]So some mss. and the ancient versions, M.T., *he*

28 [a]Lev. 19:28; Deut. 14:1; Mic. 6:7

29 [1]Lit., *prophesied* [2]Lit., *attentiveness* [a]Ex. 29:39, 41

30 [a]1 Kin. 19:10, 14; 2 Chr. 33:16

31 [a]Gen. 32:28; 35:10; 2 Kin. 17:34

32 [1]Heb., *seahs;* one seah equals approx. 11 qts.

33 [a]Gen. 22:9; Lev. 1:7, 8

36 [a]1 Kin. 18:29 [b]Ex. 3:6; 4:5 [c]Num. 16:28-32

38 [a]Gen. 15:17; Lev. 10:1, 2; 2 Kin. 1:12; Job 1:16

39 [a]1 Kin. 18:21, 24

40 [a]Judg. 4:7; 5:21 [b]Deut. 13:5; 18:20; 2 Kin. 10:24, 25

41 Now Elijah said to Ahab, "Go up, eat and drink; for there is the sound of the roar of a *heavy* shower."

42 So Ahab went up to eat and drink. But Elijah went up to the top of [a]Carmel; and he crouched down on the earth, and put his face between his knees.

43 And he said to his servant, "Go up now, look toward the sea." So he went up and looked and said, "There is nothing." And he said, "Go back" seven times.

44 And it came about at the seventh *time*, that he said, "Behold, [a]a cloud as small as a man's hand is coming up from the sea." And he said, "Go up, say to Ahab, '[1]Prepare *your chariot* and go down, so that the *heavy* shower does not stop you.' "

45 So it came about in a little while, that the sky grew black with clouds and wind, and there was a heavy shower. And Ahab rode and went to [a]Jezreel.

46 Then [a]the hand of the LORD was on Elijah, and [b]he girded up his loins and [1]outran Ahab to Jezreel.

CHAPTER 19

NOW Ahab told Jezebel all that Elijah had done, and [1a]how he had killed all the prophets with the sword.

2 Then Jezebel sent a messenger to Elijah, saying, "[a]So may the gods do to me and even more, if I do not make your [1]life as the [1]life of one of them by tomorrow about this time."

3 And he [1]was afraid and arose and ran for his [2]life and came to [a]Beersheba, which belongs to Judah, and left his servant there.

4 But he himself went a day's journey into the wilderness, and came and sat down under a [1]juniper tree; and [a]he requested for himself that he might die, and said, "It is enough; now, O LORD, take my [2]life, for I am not better than my fathers."

5 And he lay down and slept under a [1]juniper tree; and behold, there was [a]an angel touching him, and he said to him, "Arise, eat."

6 Then he looked and behold, there was at his head a bread cake *baked on* hot stones, and a jar of water. So he ate and drank and lay down again.

7 And the angel of the LORD came again a second time and touched him and said, "Arise, eat, because the journey is too great for you."

8 So he arose and ate and drank, and went in the strength of that food [a]forty days and forty nights to [b]Horeb, the mountain of God.

9 Then he came there to a cave, and lodged there; and behold, [a]the word of the LORD *came* to him, and he said to him, "What are you doing here, Elijah?"

10 And he said, "[a]I have been very zealous for the LORD, the God of hosts; for the sons of Israel have forsaken Thy covenant, [b]torn down Thine alters and killed Thy prophets with the sword. And I alone am left; and they seek my life, to take it away."

11 So He said, "[a]Go forth, and stand on the mountain before the LORD." And behold, the LORD was passing by! And a

42 [a]1 Kin. 18:19, 20

44 [1]Lit., *tie, harness* [a]Luke 12:54

45 [a]Josh. 17:16; Judg. 6:33

46 [1]Lit., *ran before* [a]2 Kin. 3:15; Is. 8:11 [b]2 Kin. 4:29; Jer. 1:17; 1 Pet. 1:13

1 [1]Lit., *all* about *how* [a]1 Kin. 18:40

2 [1]Lit., *soul* [a]1 Kin. 20:10; 2 Kin. 6:31

3 [1]Reading of many mss.; Heb. text may read, *saw* [2]Lit., *soul* [a]Gen. 21:31

4 [1]Or, *broom-tree* [2]Lit., *soul* [a]Num. 11:15; Jer. 20:14-18; Jon. 4:3, 8

5 [1]Or, *broom-tree* [a]Gen. 28:11-15

8 [a]Ex. 24:18; 34:28; Deut. 9:9-11, 18; Matt. 4:2 [b]Ex. 3:1; 4:27

9 [a]Ex. 33:21, 22

10 [a]Ex. 20:5; 34:14 [b]Rom. 11:4

11 [a]Ex. 19:20; 24:12, 18

great and strong wind was rending the mountains and breaking
in pieces the rocks before the LORD; *but* the LORD *was* not in
the wind. And after the wind an earthquake, *but* the LORD *was*
not in the earthquake.
12 And after the earthquake a fire, *but* the LORD *was* not
in the fire; and after the fire [a]a sound of a gentle blowing.
13 And it came about when Elijah heard *it*, that [a]he
wrapped his face in his mantle, and went out and stood in the
entrance of the cave. And behold, [b]a voice *came* to him and
said, "What are you doing here, Elijah?"
14 Then he said, "[a]I have been very zealous for the LORD,
the God of hosts; for the sons of Israel have forsaken Thy
covenant, torn down Thine altars and killed Thy prophets with
the sword. And I alone am left; and they seek my life, to take it
away."
15 And the LORD said to him, "Go, return on your way to
the wilderness of Damascus, and when you have arrived, [a]you
shall anoint Hazael king over [1]Syria;
16 and [a]Jehu the son of Nimshi you shall anoint king over
Israel; and [b]Elisha the son of Shaphat of Abel-meholah you
shall anoint as prophet in your place.
17 "And it shall come about, the [a]one who escapes from the
sword of Hazael, Jehu [b]shall put to death, and the one who
escapes from the sword of Jehu, Elisha shall put to death.
18 "[a]Yet I will leave 7000 in Israel, all the knees that have
not bowed to Baal and every mouth that has not [b]kissed him."
19 So he departed from there and found Elisha the son of
Shaphat, while he was plowing with twelve pairs *of oxen* before
him, and he with the twelfth. And Elijah passed over to him
and threw [a]his mantle on him.
20 And he left the oxen and ran after Elijah and said,
"Please [a]let me kiss my father and my mother, then I will
follow you." And he said to him, "Go back again, for what
have I done to you?"
21 So he returned from following him, and took the pair
of oxen and sacrificed them and [a]boiled their flesh with the
implements of the oxen, and gave *it* to the people and they
ate. Then he arose and followed Elijah and [b]ministered to
him.

CHAPTER 20

NOW [a]Ben-hadad king of Syria gathered all his army, [b]and
there *were* thirty-two kings with him, and horses and chariots.
And he went up and [c]besieged Samaria, and fought against it.
2 Then he sent messengers to the city to Ahab king of
Israel, and said to him, "Thus says Ben-hadad,
3 'Your silver and your gold are mine; your most beautiful
wives and children are also mine.' "
4 And the king of Israel answered and said, "It is according to your word, my lord, O king; I am yours, and all that I
have."
5 Then the messengers returned and said, "Thus says
[1]Ben-hadad, 'Surely, I sent to you saying, "You shall give me
your silver and your gold and your wives and your children,"
6 but about this time tomorrow I will send my servants to

12 [a]Job 4:16; Zech. 4:6
13 [a]Ex. 3:6 [b]1 Kin. 19:9
14 [a]1 Kin. 19:10
15 [1]Heb., *Aram* [a]2 Kin. 8:8-15
16 [a]2 Kin. 9:1-10 [b]1 Kin. 19:19-21; 2 Kin. 2:9, 15
17 [a]2 Kin. 8:12; 13:3, 22 [b]2 Kin. 9:14-10:25
18 [a]Rom. 11:4 [b]Hos. 13:2
19 [a]2 Kin. 2:8, 13, 14; 1 Sam. 28:14
20 [a]Matt. 8:21, 22; Luke 9:61, 62; Acts 20:37
21 [a]2 Sam. 24:22 [b]1 Kin. 18:43; 2 Kin. 2:3
1 [a]1 Kin. 15:18, 20; 2 Kin. 6:24 [b]1 Kin. 22:31 [c]1 Kin. 16:24; 2 Kin. 6:24-29
5 [1]Lit., *Ben-hadad, saying*

6 [1]Lit., *all the desire of your eyes* [2]Lit., *put*

7 [a]2 Kin. 5:7

10 [1]Lit., *are at my feet* [a]1 Kin. 19:2; 2 Kin. 6:31

11 [a]Prov. 27:1

12 [1]Lit., *he and* [2]Or, *booths* [a]1 Kin. 16:9

13 [a]1 Kin. 20:28 [b]1 Kin. 18:36

14 [1]Lit., *bind* [2]Lit., *said*

16 [1]Or, *booths* [2]Lit., *he and the 32 kings* [a]1 Kin. 20:12

18 [a]2 Kin. 14:8-12

20 [1]Lit., *smote*

21 [1]Lit., *smote*

22 [a]1 Kin. 20:13 [b]1 Kin. 20:26; 2 Sam. 11:1

23 [a]1 Kin. 14:23

you, and they will search your house and the houses of your
servants; and it shall come about, [1]whatever is desirable in your
eyes, they will [2]take in their hand and carry away.' "
7 Then the king of Israel called all the elders of the land
and said, "Please observe and [a]see how this man is looking for
trouble; for he sent to me for my wives and my children and
my silver and my gold, and I did not refuse him."
8 And all the elders and all the people said to him, "Do
not listen or consent."
9 So he said to the messengers of Ben-hadad, "Tell my
lord the king, 'All that you sent for to your servant at the first I
will do, but this thing I cannot do.' " And the messengers
departed and brought him word again.
10 And Ben-hadad sent to him and said, "May [a]the gods
do so to me and more also, if the dust of Samaria shall suffice
for handfuls for all the people who [1]follow me."
11 Then the king of Israel answered and said, "Tell *him*,
'[a]Let not him who girds on *his armor* boast like him who takes
it off.' "
12 And it came about when Ben-hadad heard this message, as [a]he was drinking [1]with the kings in the [2]temporary
shelters, that he said to his servants, "Station *yourselves*." So
they stationed *themselves* against the city.
13 Now behold, a prophet approached Ahab king of Israel
and said, "Thus says the LORD, 'Have you seen all this great
multitude? Behold, [a]I will deliver them into your hand today,
and [b]you shall know that I am the LORD.' "
14 And Ahab said, "By whom?" So he said, "Thus says the
LORD, 'By the young men of the rulers of the provinces.' "
Then he said, "Who shall [1]begin the battle?" And he
[2]answered, "You."
15 Then he mustered the young men of the rulers of the
provinces, and there were 232; and after them he mustered all
the people, *even* all the sons of Israel, 7,000.
16 And they went out at noon, while [a]Ben-hadad was drinking himself drunk in the [1]temporary shelters [2]with the thirty-two kings who helped him.
17 And the young men of the rulers of the provinces went
out first; and Ben-hadad sent out and they told him, saying,
"Men have come out from Samaria."
18 [a]Then he said, "If they have come out for peace, take
them alive; or if they have come out for war, take them alive."
19 So these went out from the city, the young men of the
rulers of the provinces, and the army which followed them.
20 And they [1]killed each his man; and the Syrians fled, and
Israel pursued them, and Ben-hadad king of Syria escaped on a
horse with horsemen.
21 And the king of Israel went out and [1]struck the horses
and chariots, and [1]killed the Syrians with a great slaughter.
22 Then [a]the prophet came near to the king of Israel, and
said to him, "Go, strengthen yourself and observe and see what
you have to do; for [b]at the turn of the year the king of Syria
will come up against you."
23 Now the servants of the king of Syria said to him,
"[a]Their gods are gods of the mountains, therefore they were

stronger than we; but rather let us fight against them in the
plain, *and* surely we shall be stronger than they.
24 "And do this thing: remove the kings, each from his
place, and put captains in their place,
25 and [1]muster an army like the army that you have lost,
horse for horse, and chariot for chariot. Then we will fight
against them in the plain, and surely we shall be stronger than
they." And he listened to their voice and did so.
26 So it came about [a]at the turn of the year, that Ben-
hadad mustered the Syrians and went up to [b]Aphek to fight
against Israel.
27 And the sons of Israel were mustered and were provi-
sioned and went to meet them; and the sons of Israel camped
before them like two little flocks of goats, [a]but the Syrians
filled the country.
28 Then [a]a man of God came near and spoke to the king
of Israel and said, "Thus says the LORD, 'Because the Syrians
have said, "[b]The LORD is a god of *the* mountains, but He is not
a god of *the* valleys"; therefore I [c]will give all this great multitude into your hand, and you shall know that I am the LORD.' "
29 So they camped one over against the other seven days.
And it came about that on the seventh day, the battle was
joined, and the sons of Israel [1]killed *of* the Syrians 100,000 foot
soldiers in one day.
30 But the rest fled to [a]Aphek into the city, and the wall
fell on 27,000 men who were left. And Ben-hadad fled and
came into the city [b]into an inner chamber.
31 And [a]his servants said to him, "Behold now, we have
heard that the kings of the house of Israel are merciful kings,
please let us [b]put sackcloth on our loins and ropes on our
heads, and go out to the king of Israel; perhaps he will save
your [1]life."
32 So [a]they girded sackcloth on their loins and *put* ropes
on their heads, and came to the king of Israel and said, "[b]Your
servant Ben-hadad says, 'Please let me live.' " And he said, "Is
he still alive? He is my brother."
33 Now the men [1]took this as an omen, and quickly [2]catch-
ing his word said, "Your brother Ben-hadad." Then he said,
"Go, bring him." Then Ben-hadad came out to him, and he
[3]took him up into the chariot.
34 And *Ben-hadad* said to him, "[a]The cities which my
father took from your father I will restore, and you shall make
streets for yourself in Damascus, as my father made in Samaria." *Ahab said,* "And I will let you go with this covenant." So
he made a covenant with him and let him go.
35 Now a certain man of [a]the sons of the prophets said to
[1]another [b]by the word of the LORD, "Please strike me." But the
man refused to strike him.
36 Then he said to him, "Because you have not listened to
the voice of the LORD, behold, as soon as you have departed
from me, [a]a lion will [1]kill you." And as soon as he had departed
from him a lion found him, and [2]killed him.
37 Then he found another man and said, "Please [1]strike
me." And the man [2]struck him, [3]wounding him.
38 So the prophet departed and waited for the king by the
way, and [a]disguised himself with a bandage over his eyes.

25 [1]Lit., *number*

26 [a]1 Kin. 20:22 [b]2 Kin. 13:17

27 [a]Judg. 6:3-5; 1 Sam. 13:5-8

28 [a]1 Kin. 17:18 [b]1 Kin. 20:23 [c]1 Kin. 20:13

29 [1]*smote*

30 [a]1 Kin. 20:26 [b]1 Kin. 22:25; 2 Chr. 18:24

31 [1]Lit., *soul* [a]1 Kin. 20:23-26 [b]Gen. 37:34; 2 Sam. 3:31

32 [a]1 Kin. 20:31 [b]1 Kin. 20:3-6

33 [1]Lit., *divined* [2]Lit., *caught from him* [3]Lit., *caused him to come up*

34 [a]1 Kin. 15:20

35 [1]Lit., *his neighbor* [a]2 Kin. 2:3-7 [b]1 Kin. 13:17, 18

36 [1]Lit., *smite* [2]Lit., *smote* [a]1 Kin. 13:24

37 [1]Lit., *smite* [2]Lit., *smote* [3]Lit., *striking and wounding*

38 [a]1 Kin. 14:2

39 [a]2 Kin. 10:24

42 [1]Lit., *soul*
[a]1 Kin. 20:39

43 [a]1 Kin. 21:4

1 [a]1 Kin. 18:45, 46

2 [1]Lit., *it is good in your eyes* [2]Lit., *this*
[a]1 Sam. 8:14

3 [a]Lev. 25:23; Num. 36:7; Ezek. 46:18

4 [1]Lit., *bread*
[a]1 Kin. 20:43

5 [1]Lit., *bread*

7 [1]Lit., *exercises kingship*
[a]1 Sam. 8:14

8 [a]Esth. 3:12; 8:8, 10
[b]1 Kin. 20:7

10 [1]Lit., *so that he dies*

39 And as the king passed by, he cried to the king and said,
"Your servant went out into the midst of the battle; and behold, a man turned aside and brought a man to me and said,
'Guard this man; if for any reason he is missing, [a]then your life
shall be for his life, or else you shall pay a talent of silver.'
40 And while your servant was busy here and there, he was
gone." And the king of Israel said to him, "So shall your judgment be; you yourself have decided *it*."
41 Then he hastily took the bandage away from his eyes,
and the king of Israel recognized him that he was of the
prophets.
42 And he said to him, "Thus says the LORD, 'Because you
have let go out of *your* hand the man whom I had devoted to
destruction, therefore [a]your [1]life shall go for his [1]life, and your
people for his people.' "
43 So [a]the king of Israel went to his house sullen and
vexed, and came to Samaria.

CHAPTER 21

NOW it came about after these things, that Naboth the
Jezreelite had a vineyard which *was* in [a]Jezreel beside the palace of Ahab king of Samaria.
2 And Ahab spoke to Naboth, saying, "[a]Give me your
vineyard, that I may have it for a vegetable garden because it is
close beside my house, and I will give you a better vineyard
than it in its place; if [1]you like, I will give you the price of [2]it in
money."
3 But Naboth said to Ahab, "The LORD forbid me [a]that I
should give you the inheritance of my fathers."
4 [a]So Ahab came into his house sullen and vexed because
of the word which Naboth the Jezreelite had spoken to him;
for he said, "I will not give you the inheritance of my fathers."
And he lay down on his bed and turned away his face and ate
no [1]food.
5 But Jezebel his wife came to him and said to him,
"How is it that your spirit is so sullen that you are not eating
[1]food?"
6 So he said to her, "Because I spoke to Naboth the
Jezreelite, and said to him, 'Give me your vineyard for money;
or else, if it pleases you, I will give you a vineyard in its place.'
But he said, 'I will not give you my vineyard.' "
7 And Jezebel his wife said to him, "[a]Do you now [1]reign
over Israel? Arise, eat bread, and let your heart be joyful; I will
give you the vineyard of Naboth the Jezreelite."
8 [a]So she wrote letters in Ahab's name and sealed them
with his seal, and sent letters to [b]the elders and to the nobles
who were living with Naboth in his city.
9 Now she wrote in the letters, saying, "Proclaim a fast,
and seat Naboth at the head of the people;
10 and seat two worthless men before him, and let them
testify against him, saying, 'You cursed God and the king.'
Then take him out and stone him [1]to death."
11 So the men of his city, the elders and the nobles who
lived in his city, did as Jezebel had sent *word* to them, just as it
was written in the letters which she had sent them.

12 They proclaimed a fast and seated Naboth at the head
f the people.
13 Then the two worthless men came in and sat before
im; and the worthless men testified against him, even against
Naboth, before the people, saying, "Naboth cursed God and
he king." [a]So they took him outside the city and stoned him
to death with stones.
14 Then they sent *word* to Jezebel, saying, "Naboth has
een stoned, and is dead."
15 And it came about when Jezebel heard that Naboth
ad been stoned and was dead, that Jezebel said to Ahab,
Arise, take possession of the vineyard of Naboth, the Jezreel-
te, which he refused to give you for money; for Naboth is not
live, but dead."
16 And it came about when Ahab heard that Naboth was
lead, that Ahab arose to go down to the vineyard of Naboth
he Jezreelite, to take possession of it.
17 Then the word of the LORD came to Elijah the Tishbite, saying,
18 "Arise, go down to meet Ahab king of Israel, [a]who is in
Samaria; behold, he is in the vineyard of Naboth where he has
gone down to take possession of it.
19 "And you shall speak to him, saying, 'Thus says the
LORD, "Have you murdered, and also taken possession?" ' And
ou shall speak to him, saying, 'Thus says the LORD, "[a]In the
place where the dogs licked up the blood of Naboth the dogs
hall lick up your blood, even yours." ' "
20 And Ahab said to Elijah, "[a]Have you found me, O my
enemy?" And he [1]answered, "I have found *you*, [b]because you
ave sold yourself to do evil in the sight of the LORD.
21 "Behold, I will bring evil upon you, and [a]will utterly
weep you away, and will cut off from Ahab every male, both
bond and free in Israel;
22 and [a]I will make your house [b]like the house of Jeroboam the son of Nebat, and like the house of Baasha the son
of Ahijah, because of the provocation with which you have
provoked *Me* to anger, and *because* you [c]have made Israel sin.
23 "And of Jezebel also has the LORD spoken, saying, '[a]The
dogs shall eat Jezebel [b]in the [1]district of Jezreel.'
24 "[a]The one belonging to Ahab, who dies in the city, the
dogs shall eat, and the one who dies in the field the birds of
heaven shall eat."
25 [a]Surely there was no one like Ahab who sold himself to
do evil in the sight of the LORD, [1]because Jezebel his wife
ncited him.
26 And [a]he acted very abominably in following idols, [b]ac-
cording to all that the Amorites had done, whom the LORD
cast out before the sons of Israel.
27 And it came about when Ahab heard these words, that
[a]he tore his clothes and put [1]on sackcloth and fasted, and he
lay in sackcloth and went about [2]despondently.
28 Then the word of the LORD came to Elijah the Tishbite, saying,
29 "Do you see how Ahab has humbled himself before Me?
Because he has humbled himself before Me, I will not bring

13 [1]Lit., *with stones so that he died* [a]2 Kin. 9:26

18 [a]1 Kin. 10:29

19 [a]1 Kin. 22:38; 2 Kin. 9:26

20 [1]Lit., *said* [a]1 Kin. 18:17 [b]1 Kin. 21:25

21 [a]1 Kin. 14:10; 2 Kin. 9:8

22 [a]1 Kin. 15:29 [b]1 Kin. 16:3, 11 [c]1 Kin. 12:30; 13:34; 14:16

23 [1]Lit., *portion;* some mss. read, *rampart* [a]2 Kin. 9:10, 30-37 [b]2 Sam. 20:15

24 [a]1 Kin. 14:11; 16:4

25 [1]Or, *whom Jezebel his wife incited* [a]1 Kin. 21:20; 16:30-33

26 [a]1 Kin. 15:12; 2 Kin. 17:12 [b]Gen. 15:16; Lev. 18:25-30

27 [1]Lit., *sackcloth on his flesh* [2]Or, *softly* [a]2 Sam. 3:31; 2 Kin. 6:30

the evil in his days, *but* I will bring the evil upon his house [a]i
his son's days."

CHAPTER 22

AND [1]three years passed without war between Syria an
Israel.
2 [a]And it came about in the third year, that [b]Jehoshapha
the king of Judah came down to the king of Israel.
3 Now the king of Israel said to his servants, "Do yo
know that [a]Ramoth-gilead belongs to us, and we [1]are sti
doing nothing to take it out of the hand of the king of Syria?
4 And he said to Jehoshaphat, "Will you go with me t
battle at Ramoth-gilead?" And Jehoshaphat said to the king o
Israel, "[a]I am as you are, my people as your people, my horse
as your horses."
5 Moreover, Jehoshaphat said to the king of Israe
"Please inquire [1]first for the word of the LORD."
6 Then [a]the king of Israel gathered the prophets together, about four hundred men, and said to them, "Shall I g
against Ramoth-gilead to battle or shall I refrain?" And the
said, "Go up, for the Lord will give *it* into the hand of th
king."
7 But [a]Jehoshaphat said, "Is there not yet a prophet o
the LORD here, that we may inquire of him?"
8 And the king of Israel said to Jehoshaphat, "There i
yet one man by whom we may inquire of the LORD, but I hat
him, because he does not prophesy good concerning me, bu
evil. *He is* Micaiah son of Imlah." But Jehoshaphat said, "Le
not the king say so."
9 Then the king of Israel called an officer and said
"[1]Bring quickly Micaiah son of Imlah."
10 Now the king of Israel and Jehoshaphat king of Judah
were sitting each on his throne, arrayed in *their* robes, at the
threshing floor at the entrance of the gate of Samaria; and [a]al
the prophets were prophesying before them.
11 Then Zedekiah the son of Chenaanah made [a]horns o
iron for himself and said, "Thus says the LORD, '[b]With these
you shall gore the Syrians until they are consumed.' "
12 And all the prophets were prophesying thus, saying
"Go up to Ramoth-gilead and prosper, for the LORD will give *it*
into the hand of the king."
13 Then the messenger who went to summon Micaiah
spoke to him saying, "Behold now, the words of the prophets
are uniformly favorable to the king. Please let your word be
like the word of one of them, and speak favorably."
14 But Micaiah said, "[a]As the LORD lives, what [b]the LORD
says to me, that I will speak."
15 When he came to the king, the king said to him, "Micaiah, shall we go to Ramoth-gilead to battle, or shall we refrain?" And he [1]answered him, "[a]Go up and succeed, and
the LORD will give *it* into the hand of the king."
16 Then the king said to him, "How many times must I
adjure you to speak to me nothing but the truth in the name of
the LORD?"
17 So he said,

29 [a]2 Kin. 9:25-37

1 [1]Lit., *they sat for three years*

2 [a]2 Chr. 18:2 [b]1 Kin. 15:24

3 [1]Lit., *are silent so as not* [a]1 Kin. 4:13; Deut. 4:43; Josh. 21:38

4 [a]2 Kin. 3:7

5 [1]Lit., *as the day*

6 [a]1 Kin. 18:19

7 [a]2 Kin. 3:11

9 [1]Lit., *Hasten Micaiah*

10 [a]1 Kin. 22:6

11 [a]Zech. 1:18-21 [b]Deut. 33:17

14 [a]1 Kin. 18:10, 15 [b]Num. 22:18; 24:13

15 [1]Lit., *said to* [a]1 Kin. 22:12

"I saw all Israel
Scattered on the mountains,
[a]Like sheep which have no shepherd.
And the LORD said, 'These have no master.
Let each of them return to his house in peace.' "
18 Then the king of Israel said to Jehoshaphat, "[a]Did I
not tell you that he would not prophesy good concerning me,
but evil?"
19 And [1]Micaiah said, "Therefore, hear the word of the
LORD. [a]I saw the LORD sitting on His throne, and [b]all the host
of heaven standing by Him on His right and on His left.
20 "And the LORD said, 'Who will entice Ahab to go up and
fall at Ramoth-gilead?' And one said this while another said
that.
21 "Then a spirit came forward and stood before the LORD
and said, 'I will entice him.'
22 "And the LORD said to him, 'How?' And he said, 'I will
go out and [a]be a deceiving spirit in the mouth of all his prophets.' Then He said, 'You are to entice *him* and also prevail.
Go and do so.'
23 "Now therefore, behold, the LORD has put a deceiving
spirit in the mouth of all these your prophets; and the LORD
has proclaimed disaster against you."
24 Then [a]Zedekiah the son of Chanaanah came near and
struck Micaiah on the cheek and said, "How did the Spirit of
the LORD pass from me to speak to you?"
25 And Micaiah said, "Behold, you shall see on that day
when you [a]enter an inner room to hide yourself."
26 Then the king of Israel said, "Take Micaiah and return
him to Amon the governor of the city and to Joash the king's
son;
27 and say, 'Thus says the king, "[a]Put this man in prison,
and feed him [1]sparingly with bread and water until I return
safely." ' "
28 And Micaiah said, "[a]If you indeed return safely the
LORD has not spoken by me." And he said, "[b]Listen, all you
people."
29 So [a]the king of Israel and Jehoshaphat king of Judah
went up against Ramoth-gilead.
30 And the king of Israel said to Jehoshaphat, "[a]I will
disguise myself and go into the battle, but you put on your
robes." So the king of Israel disguised himself and went into
the battle.
31 Now [a]the king of Syria had commanded the thirty-two
captains of his chariots, saying, "Do not fight with small or
great, but with the king of Israel alone."
32 So it came about, when the captains of the chariots saw
Jehoshaphat, that they said, "Surely it is the king of Israel,"
and they turned aside to fight against him, and Jehoshaphat
cried out.
33 Then it happened, when the captains of the chariots
saw that it was not the king of Israel, that they turned back
from pursuing him.
34 Now a certain man drew his bow at random and struck
the king of Israel [1]in a joint of the armor. So he said to the

17 [a]1 Kin. 22:34-36; Num. 27:17
18 [a]1 Kin. 22:8
19 [1]Lit., *he* [a]Is. 6:1; Ezek. 1:26-28; Dan. 7:9, 10 [b]Job 1:6; 2:1; Dan. 7:10
22 [a]Judg. 9:23; 1 Sam. 16:14; 18:10; 19:9
24 [a]1 Kin. 22:11; Matt. 5:39; Acts 23:2, 3
25 [a]1 Kin. 20:30
27 [1]Lit., *with bread of affliction and water of affliction* [a]2 Chr. 16:10; 18:25-27
28 [a]Deut. 18:22 [b]Mic. 1:2
29 [a]1 Kin. 22:3, 4
30 [a]2 Chr. 35:22
31 [a]1 Kin. 20:1, 16, 24; 2 Chr. 18:30
34 [1]Lit., *between the scale armor and the breastplate*

34 [2]Lit., *your hand* [3]Lit., *camp* [a]2 Chr. 35:23

35 [1]Lit., *went up*

36 [1]Lit., *land* [a]2 Kin. 14:12

38 [a]1 Kin. 21:19

39 [a]Amos 3:15

41 [a]2 Chr. 20:31

43 [a]2 Chr. 17:3 [b]1 Kin. 15:14; 2 Kin. 12:3

44 [a]1 Kin. 22:2; 2 Kin. 8:18; 2 Chr. 19:2

45 [a]2 Chr. 20:34

46 [1]Lit., *consumed* [a]1 Kin. 14:24; 15:12; Gen. 19:5; Deut. 23:17

47 [a]2 Sam. 8:14; 2 Kin. 3:9

48 [a]1 Kin. 10:22 [b]1 Kin. 9:28 [c]1 Kin. 9:26

50 [a]2 Chr. 21:1

51 [a]1 Kin. 22:40

52 [a]1 Kin. 15:26; 21:25

53 [a]1 Kin. 16:30-32

driver of his chariot, "Turn [2]around, and take me out of the
[3]fight; [a]for I am severely wounded."
35 And the battle [1]raged that day, and the king was
propped up in his chariot in front of the Syrians, and died at
evening, and the blood from the wound ran into the bottom of
the chariot.
36 [a]Then a cry passed throughout the army close to sunset, saying, "Every man to his city and every man to his
[1]country."
37 So the king died and was brought to Samaria, and they
buried the king in Samaria.
38 And they washed the chariot by the pool of Samaria,
and the dogs licked up his blood (now the harlots bathed
themselves *there*), [a]according to the word of the LORD which
He spoke.
39 Now the rest of the acts of Ahab and all that he did and
[a]the ivory house which he built and all the cities which he
built, are they not written in the Book of the Chronicles of the
Kings of Israel?
40 So Ahab slept with his fathers, and Ahaziah his son
became king in his place.
41 [a]Now Jehoshaphat the son of Asa became king over
Judah in the fourth year of Ahab king of Israel.
42 Jehoshaphat was thirty-five years old when he became
king, and he reigned twenty-five years in Jerusalem. And his
mother's name was Azubah the daughter of Shilhi.
43 [a]And he walked in all the way of Asa his father; he did
not turn aside from it, doing right in the sight of the LORD.
[b]However, the high places were not taken away; the people still
sacrificed and burnt incense on the high places.
44 [a]Jehoshaphat also made peace with the king of Israel.
45 Now the rest of the acts of Jehoshaphat, and his might
which he showed and how he warred, are they not written [a]in
the Book of the Chronicles of the Kings of Judah?
46 And the remnant of [a]the sodomites who remained in
the days of his father Asa, he [1]expelled from the land.
47 Now [a]there was no king in Edom; a deputy was king.
48 Jehoshaphat made [a]ships of Tarshish to go to [b]Ophir
for gold, but they did not go for the ships were broken at
[c]Ezion-geber.
49 Then Ahaziah the son of Ahab said to Jehoshaphat,
"Let my servants go with your servants in the ships." But
Jehoshaphat was not willing.
50 [a]And Jehoshaphat slept with his fathers and was buried
with his fathers in the city of his father David, and Jehoram his
son became king in his place.
51 Ahaziah the son of Ahab [a]became king over Israel in
Samaria in the seventeenth year of Jehoshaphat king of Judah,
and he reigned two years over Israel.
52 And he did evil in the sight of the LORD and [a]walked in
the way of his father and in the way of his mother and in the
way of Jeroboam the son of Nebat, who caused Israel to sin.
53 [a]So he served Baal and worshiped him and provoked
the LORD God of Israel to anger according to all that his father
had done.

THE SECOND BOOK OF THE KINGS

Ahaziah's Messengers Meet Elijah.

NOW [a]Moab rebelled against Israel after the death of Ahab.
2 And Ahaziah fell through the lattice in his upper chamber which *was* in Samaria, and became ill. So he sent messengers and said to them, "Go, [a]inquire of Baal-zebub, the god of
Ekron, [b]whether I shall recover from this sickness."
3 But the angel of the LORD said to [a]Elijah the Tishbite,
"Arise, go up to meet the messengers of the king of Samaria
and say to them, 'Is it because there is no God in Israel *that*
you are going to inquire of [b]Baal-zebub, the god of Ekron?'
4 "Now therefore thus says the LORD, '[1a]You shall not
come down from the bed where you have gone up, but you
shall surely die.'" Then Elijah departed.
5 When the messengers returned to him he said to them,
"[1]Why have you returned?"
6 And they said to him, "A man came up to meet us and
said to us, 'Go, return to the king who sent you and say to him,
"Thus says the LORD, 'Is it because there is no God in Israel
that you are sending [a]to inquire of Baal-zebub, the god of
Ekron? Therefore [1]you shall not come down from the bed
where you have gone up, but shall surely die.'"'"
7 And he said to them, "What kind of man was he who
came up to meet you and spoke these words to you?"
8 And they [1]answered him, "[a]*He was* a hairy man with a
leather girdle [2]bound about his loins." And he said, "It is
Elijah the Tishbite."
9 Then *the king* sent to him a captain of fifty with his
fifty. And he went up to him, and behold, he was sitting on the
top of the hill. And he said to him, "O man of God, the king
says, 'Come down.'"
10 And Elijah answered and said to the captain of fifty,
"If I am a man of God, [a]let fire come down from heaven and
consume you and your fifty." [b]Then fire came down from
heaven and consumed him and his fifty.
11 So he again sent to him another captain of fifty with his
fifty. And he answered and said to him, "O man of God, thus
says the king, 'Come down quickly.'"
12 And Elijah answered and and said to them, "If I am a
man of God, let fire come down from heaven and consume
you and your fifty." Then the fire of God came down from
heaven and consumed him and his fifty.
13 So he again sent the captain of a third fifty with his
fifty. When the third captain of fifty went up, he came and
bowed down on his knees before Elijah, and begged him and
said to him, "O man of God, please let my life and the lives of
these fifty servants of yours be precious in your sight.
14 "Behold fire came down from heaven, and consumed
the first two captains of fifty with their fifties; but now let my
[1]life be precious in your sight."
15 And [a]the angel of the LORD said to Elijah, "Go down

1 [a]2 Kin. 3:5; 2 Sam. 8:2

2 [a]2 Kin. 1:3, 6, 16; Matt. 10:25; Mark 3:22 [b]2 Kin. 8:7-10

3 [a]1 Kin. 17:1; 21:17 [b]2 Kin. 1:2

4 [1]Lit., *The bed where you went up, you shall not come down from it* [a]2 Kin. 1:6, 16

5 [1]Lit., *What is this that you have returned?*

6 [1]v. 4 [a]2 Kin. 1:2

8 [1]Lit., *said* [2]Or, *girt* [a]Zech. 13:4; Matt. 3:4; Mark 1:6

10 [a]1 Kin. 18:36-38; Luke 9:54 [b]Job 1:16

14 [1]Lit., *soul*

15 [a]2 Kin. 1:3

E46

with him; do not be afraid of him." So he arose and went down
with him to the king.
16 Then he said to him, "Thus says the LORD, 'Because
you have sent messengers [a]to inquire of Baal-zebub, the god of
Ekron—is it because there is no God in Israel to inquire of His
word?—therefore [1]you shall not come down from the bed
where you have gone up, but shall surely die.' "
17 So [1]he died according to the word of the LORD which
Elijah had spoken. And Jehoram became king in his place [a]in
the second year of Jehoram the son of Jehoshaphat, king of
Judah, because he had no son.
18 Now the rest of the acts of Ahaziah which he did, are
they not written in the Book of the Chronicles of the Kings of
Israel?

CHAPTER 2

AND it came about when the LORD was about to [a]take up
Elijah by a [1]whirlwind to heaven, that Elijah went with [b]Elisha
from [c]Gilgal.
2 And Elijah said to Elisha, "[a]Stay here please, for the
LORD has sent me as far as [b]Bethel." But Elisha said, "[c]As the
LORD lives and as you yourself live, I will not leave you." So
they went down to Bethel.
3 Then [a]the sons of the prophets who *were at* Bethel
came out to Elisha and said to him, "Do you know that the
LORD will take away your master from over [1]you today?" And
he said, "Yes, I know; be still."
4 And Elijah said to him, "Elisha, please [a]stay here, for
the LORD has sent me to [b]Jericho." But he said, "[c]As the LORD
lives, and as you yourself live I will not leave you." So they
came to Jericho.
5 And [a]the sons of the prophets who *were* at Jericho
approached Elisha and said to him, "[b]Do you know that the
LORD will take away your master from over [1]you today?" And
he [2]answered, "Yes, I know; be still."
6 Then Elijah said to him, "Please [a]stay here, for the
LORD has sent me to [b]the Jordan." And he said, "As the LORD
lives, and as you yourself live, I will not leave you." So the two
of them went on.
7 Now [a]fifty men of the sons of the prophets went and
stood opposite *them* at a distance, while the two of them stood
by the Jordan.
8 And Elijah [a]took his mantle and folded it together and
[b]struck the waters, and they were divided here and there, so
that the two of them crossed over on dry ground.
9 Now it came about when they had crossed over, that
Elijah said to Elisha, "Ask what I shall do for you before I am
taken from you." And Elisha said, "Please, let a double portion of your spirit be upon me."
10 And he said, "You have asked a hard thing. *Nevertheless,* if you see me when I am taken from you, it shall be so for
you; but if not, it shall not be *so.*"
11 Then it came about as they were going along and talking, that behold, *there appeared* [a]a chariot of fire and horses

16 [1]v. 4 [a]2 Kin. 1:3

17 [1]I.e., Ahaziah [a]2 Kin. 3:1; 8:16

1 [1]Or, *windstorm* [a]Gen. 5:24; Heb. 11:5 [b]1 Kin. 19:16-21 [c]Josh. 4:19

2 [a]Ruth 1:15 [b]1 Kin. 12:28, 29 [c]2 Kin. 4:6; 1 Sam. 1:26

3 [1]Lit., *your head* [a]2 Kin. 4:1, 38; 5:22

4 [a]2 Kin. 2:2 [b]Josh. 6:26 [c]2 Kin. 2:2

5 [1]Lit., *your head* [2]Lit., *said* [a]2 Kin. 2:3 [b]2 Kin. 2:3

6 [a]2 Kin. 2:2 [b]Josh. 3:8, 15-17

7 [a]2 Kin. 2:15, 16

8 [a]1 Kin. 19:13, 19 [b]2 Kin. 2:14; Ex. 14:21, 22

11 [a]2 Kin. 6:17

of fire which separated the two of them. And Elijah went up
by a [1]whirlwind to heaven.
12 And Elisha saw *it* and cried out, "[a]My father, my father,
the [1]chariots of Israel and its horsemen!" And he saw him
no more. Then [b]he took hold of his own clothes and tore them
in two pieces.
13 He also took up the mantle of Elijah that fell from
him, and returned and stood by the bank of the Jordan.
14 And he took the mantle of Elijah that fell from him,
and struck the waters and said, "Where is the LORD, the God
of Elijah?" And when he also had [a]struck the waters, they were
divided here and there; and Elisha crossed over.
15 Now when [a]the sons of the prophets who *were* at Jericho opposite *him* saw him, they said, "The spirit of Elijah
rests on Elisha." And they came to meet him and bowed themselves to the ground before him.
16 And they said to him, "Behold now, there are with your
servants fifty strong men, please let them go and search for
your master; [1]perhaps [a]the Spirit of the LORD has taken him up
and cast him on some mountain or into some valley." And he
said, "You shall not send."
17 But when [a]they urged him until he was ashamed, he
said, "Send." They sent therefore fifty men; and they searched
three days, but did not find him.
18 And they returned to him while he was staying at Jericho; and he said to them, "Did I not say to you, 'Do not
go'?"
19 Then the men of the city said to Elisha, "Behold now,
the situation of this city is pleasant, as my lord sees; but the
water is bad, and the land [1]is unfruitful.
20 And he said, "Bring me a new jar, and put salt [1]in it."
So they brought *it* to him.
21 And he went out to the spring of water, and [a]threw salt
[1]in it and said, "Thus says the LORD, 'I have [2]purified these
waters; there shall not be from there death or [3]unfruitfulness
any longer.' "
22 So the waters have been [1]purified to this day, according
to the word of Elisha which he spoke.
23 Then he went up from there to Bethel; and as he was
going up by the way, young lads came out from the city and
mocked him and said to him, "Go up, you baldhead; go up,
you baldhead!"
24 When he looked behind him and saw them, he [a]cursed
them in the name of the LORD. Then two female bears came
out of the woods and tore up forty-two lads of [1]their number.
25 And he went from there to [a]Mount Carmel, and from
there he returned to Samaria.

CHAPTER 3

NOW Jehoram the son of Ahab became king over Israel at
Samaria [a]in the eighteenth year of Jehoshaphat king of Judah,
and reigned twelve years.
2 And he did evil in the sight of the LORD, though not
like his father and his mother; for [a]he put away the *sacred*
pillar of Baal [b]which his father had made.

11 [1]Or, *windstorm*
12 [1]Lit., *chariot* [a]2 Kin. 13:14 [b]Gen. 37:34; Job 1:20
14 [a]2 Kin. 2:8
15 [a]2 Kin. 2:7
16 [1]Lit., *lest* [a]1 Kin. 18:12; Acts 8:39
17 [a]2 Kin. 8:11
19 [1]Lit., *causes barrenness*
20 [1]Lit., *there*
21 [1]Lit., *there* [2]Lit., *healed* [3]Lit., *barrenness* [a]2 Kin. 4:41; 6:6; Ex. 15:25, 26
22 [1]Lit., *healed*
24 [1]Lit., *them* [a]Neh. 13:25-27
25 [a]2 Kin. 4:25; 1 Kin. 18:19, 20
1 [a]2 Kin. 1:17
2 [a]2 Kin. 10:18; 26-28; Ex. 23:24 [b]1 Kin. 16:31, 32

3 Nevertheless, [a]he clung to the sins of Jeroboam the son
of Nebat, [b]which he made Israel sin; he did not depart from it.
4 Now Mesha king of Moab was a sheep breeder, and
[a]used to pay the king of Israel 100,000 lambs and the wool of
100,000 rams.
5 But it came about, [a]when Ahab died, the king of Moab
rebelled against the king of Israel.
6 And King Jehoram went out of Samaria [1]at that time
and mustered all Israel.
7 The he went and sent *word* to Jehoshaphat the king of
Judah, saying, "The king of Moab has rebelled against me.
Will you go with me to fight against Moab?" And he said, "I
will go up; [a]I am as you are, my people as your people, my
horses as your horses."
8 And he said, "Which way shall we go up?" And he
[1]answered, "The way of the wilderness of Edom."
9 So [a]the king of Israel went with [b]the king of Judah and
[c]the king of Edom; and they made a circuit of seven days'
journey, and there was no water for the army or for the cattle
that followed them.
10 Then the king of Israel said, "Alas! For the LORD has
called these three kings to give them into the hand of Moab."
11 But Jehoshaphat said, "[a]Is there not a prophet of the
LORD here, that we may inquire of the LORD by him?" And one
of the king of Israel's servants answered and said, "[b]Elisha the
son of Shaphat is here, [c]who used to pour water on the hands
of Elijah."
12 And Jehoshaphat said, "The word of the LORD is with
him." So the king of Israel and Jehoshaphat and the king of
Edom went down to him.
13 Now [a]Elisha said to the king of Israel, "What do I have
to do with you? [b]Go to the prophets of your father and to the
prophets of your mother." And the king of Israel said to him,
"No, for the LORD has called these three kings *together* to give
them into the hand of Moab."
14 And Elisha said, "[a]As the LORD of hosts lives, before
whom I stand, were it not that I regard the presence of Jehoshaphat the king of Judah, I would not look at you nor see you.
15 "But now [a]bring me a minstrel." And it came about,
when the minstrel played, that [b]the hand of the LORD came
upon him.
16 And he said, "Thus says the LORD, 'Make this valley
full of trenches.'
17 "For thus says the LORD, 'You shall not see wind nor
shall you see rain; yet that valley shall be filled with water, so
that you shall drink, both you and your cattle and your beasts.
18 'And this is but a slight thing in the sight of the LORD; he
shall also give the Moabites into your hand.
19 '[a]Then you shall strike every fortified city and every
choice city, and fell every good tree and stop all springs of
water, and mar every good piece of land with stones.'"
20 And it happened in the morning [a]about the time of
offering the sacrifice, that behold, water came by the way of
Edom, and the country was filled with water.
21 Now all the Moabites heard that the kings had come

3 [a]1 Kin. 12:28-32 [b]1 Kin. 14:9, 16
4 [a]2 Sam. 8:2; Is. 16:1, 2
5 [a]2 Kin. 1:1
6 [1]Lit., *in that day*
7 [a]1 Kin. 22:4
8 [1]Lit., *said*
9 [a]2 Kin. 3:1 [b]2 Kin. 3:7 [c]1 Kin. 22:47
11 [a]1 Kin. 22:7 [b]2 Kin. 2:25 [c]1 Kin. 19:21; John 13:4, 5, 13, 14
13 [a]Ezek. 14:3-5 [b]1 Kin. 18:19; 22:6-11, 22-25
14 [a]2 Kin. 5:16; 1 Kin. 17:1
15 [a]1 Sam. 16:23; 1 Chr. 25:1 [b]1 Kin. 18:46; Ezek. 1:3
19 [a]2 Kin. 3:25
20 [a]Ex. 29:39, 40

up to fight against them. And all who were able to [1]put on
armor and older were summoned, and stood on the border.
22 And they rose early in the morning, and the sun shone
on the water, and the Moabites saw the water opposite *them* as
red as blood.
23 Then they said, "This is blood; the kings have surely
fought together, and they have slain one another. Now therefore, Moab, to the spoil!"
24 But when they came to the camp of Israel, the Israelites arose and struck the Moabites, so that they fled before
them; and they went forward [1]into the land, [2]slaughtering the
Moabites.
25 [a]Thus they destroyed the cities; and each one threw a
stone on every piece of good land and filled it. So they stopped
all the springs of water and felled all the good trees, until in
[b]Kir-hareseth *only* they left its stones; however, the slingers
went about *it* and struck it.
26 When the king of Moab saw that the battle was too
fierce for him, he took with him 700 men who drew sword, to
break through to the king of Edom; but they could not.
27 Then he took his oldest son who was to reign in his
place, and [a]offered him as a burnt offering on the wall. And
there came great wrath against Israel, and they departed from
him and returned to their own land.

CHAPTER 4

NOW a certain woman of the wives of [a]the sons of the
prophets cried out to [1]Elisha, "Your servant my husband is
dead, and you know that your servant feared the LORD; and
[b]the creditor has come to take my two children to be his
slaves."
2 And Elisha said to her, "What shall I do for you? Tell
me, what do you have in the house?" And she said, "Your
maidservant has nothing in the house except a jar of oil."
3 Then he said, "Go, borrow vessels at large for yourself
from all your neighbors, *even* empty vessels; do not get a few.
4 "And you shall go in and shut the door behind you and
your sons, and pour out into all these vessels; and you shall set
aside what is full."
5 So she went from him and shut the door behind her
and her sons; they were bringing *the vessels* to her and she
poured.
6 And it came about when the vessels were full, that she
said to her son, "Bring me another vessel." And he said to her,
"There is not one vessel more." And the oil stopped.
7 Then she came and told [a]the man of God. And he said,
"Go, sell the oil and pay your debt, and you *and* your sons can
live on the rest."
8 Now there came a day when Elisha passed over to
[a]Shunem, where there was a [1b]prominent woman, and she persuaded him to eat [2]food. And so it was, as often as he passed
by, he turned in there to eat [2]food.
9 And she said to her husband, "Behold now, I perceive
that this is a holy [a]man of God passing by us continually.
10 "Please, let us make a little walled upper chamber and

21 [1]Lit., *gird themselves with a belt*

24 [1]Lit., *into it* [2]Lit., *smiting*

25 [a]2 Kin. 3:19 [b]Is. 16:7; Jer. 48:31, 36

27 [a]Amos 2:1; Mic. 6:7

1 [1]Lit., *Elisha, saying* [a]2 Kin. 2:3 [b]Lev. 25:39-41, 48; 1 Sam. 22:2; Neh. 5:2-5

7 [a]1 Kin. 12:22

8 [1]Lit., *great* [2]Lit., *bread* [a]Josh. 19:18 [b]2 Sam. 19:32

9 [a]2 Kin. 4:7

let us set a bed for him there, and a table and a chair and a
lampstand; and it shall be, when he comes to us, *that* he can
turn in there."
11 [1]One day he came there and turned in to the upper
chamber and [2]rested.
12 Then he said to [a]Gehazi his servant, "Call this Shunammite." And when he had called her, she stood before him.
13 And he said to him, "Say now to her, 'Behold, you have
been [1]careful for us with all this [2]care; what can I do for you?
Would you be spoken for to the king or to the captain of the
army?' " And she [3]answered, "I live among my own people."
14 So he said, "What then is to be done for her?" And
Gehazi [1]answered, "Truly she has no son and her husband is
old."
15 And he said, "Call her." When he had called her, she
stood in the doorway.
16 Then he said, "[a]At this season [1]next year you shall
embrace a son." And she said, "No, my lord, O man of God,
[b]do not lie to your maidservant."
17 And the woman conceived and bore a son at that season [1]the next year, as Elisha had said to her.
18 When the child was grown, the day came that he went
out to his father to the reapers.
19 And he said to his father, "My head, my head." And he
said to his servant, "Carry him to his mother."
20 When he had taken him and brought him to his mother, he sat on her [1]lap until noon, and *then* died.
21 And she went up and [a]laid him on the bed of [b]the man
of God, and shut *the door* behind him, and went out.
22 Then she called to her husband and said, "Please send
me one of the servants and one of the donkeys, that I may run
to the man of God and return."
23 And he said, "Why will you go to him today? It is
neither [a]new moon nor Sabbath." And she said, "*It will be*
well."
24 Then she saddled a donkey and said to her servant,
"Drive and go forward; do not slow down [1]the pace for me
unless I tell you."
25 So she went and came to the man of God to [a]Mount
Carmel. And it came about when the man of God saw her at a
distance, that he said to Gehazi his servant, "Behold, [1]yonder
is the Shunammite.
26 "Please run now to meet her and say to her, 'Is it well
with you? Is it well with your husband? Is it well with the
child?' " And she [1]answered, "It is well."
27 When she came to the man of God [a]to the hill, she
caught hold of his feet. And Gehazi came near to push her
away; but the man of God said, "Let her alone, for her soul is
[1]troubled within her; and the LORD has hid it from me and has
not told me."
28 Then she said, "Did I ask for a son from my lord? Did I
not say, '[a]Do not deceive me'?"
29 Then he said to Gehazi, "[a]Gird up your loins and [b]take
my staff in your hand, and go your way; if you meet any man,
do not [c]salute him, and if anyone salutes you, do not answer
him; and [d]lay my staff on the lad's face."

11 [1]Lit., *Now a day came that* [2]Lit., *lay there*

12 [a]2 Kin. 4:29-31; 5:20-27; 8:4, 5

13 [1]Lit., *fearful* [2]Lit., *fear* [3]Lit., *said*

14 [1]Lit., *said*

16 [1]Lit., *when the time revives* [a]Gen. 18:14 [b]2 Kin. 4:28

17 [1]Lit., *when the time revived*

20 [1]Lit., *knees*

21 [a]2 Kin. 4:32 [b]2 Kin. 4:7

23 [a]Num. 10:10; 28:11; 1 Chr. 23:31

24 [1]Lit., *riding*

25 [1]Lit., *this Shunammite* [a]2 Kin. 2:25

26 [1]Lit., *said*

27 [1]Lit., *bitter* [a]2 Kin. 4:25

28 [a]2 Kin. 4:16

29 [a]2 Kin. 9:1; 1 Kin. 18:46 [b]2 Kin. 2:14; Ex. 4:17 [c]Luke 10:4 [d]Ex. 7:19, 20; 14:16

30 And the mother of the lad said, "[a]As the LORD lives and
as you yourself live, I will not leave you." And he arose and
followed her.
31 Then Gehazi passed on before them and laid the staff
on the lad's face, but there was neither sound nor [1]response. So
he returned to meet him and told [2]him, "The lad has not
awakened."
32 When Elisha came into the house, behold the lad was
dead and laid on his bed.
33 So he entered and [a]shut the door behind them both,
and prayed to the LORD.
34 And [a]he went up and lay on the child, and put his
mouth on his mouth and his eyes on his eyes and his hands on
his hands, and he stretched himself on him; and the flesh of
the child became warm.
35 Then he returned and walked in the house once back
and forth, and went up and stretched himself on him; and the
lad sneezed seven times and the lad opened his eyes.
36 And he called Gehazi and said, "Call this Shunammite." So he called her. And when she came in to him, he said,
"Take up your son."
37 Then she went in and fell at his feet and bowed herself
to the ground, and [a]she took up her son and went out.
38 When Elisha returned to [a]Gilgal, *there was* [b]a famine
in the land. [1]As [c]the sons of the prophets [d]were sitting before
him, he said to his servant, "[e]Put on the large pot and boil stew
for the sons of the prophets."
39 Then one went out into the field to gather herbs, and
found a wild vine and gathered from it his lap full of wild
gourds, and came and sliced them into the pot of stew, for
they did not know *what they were.*
40 So they poured *it* out for the men to eat. And it came
about as they were eating of the stew, that they cried out and
said, "O man of God, there is death in the pot." And they were
unable to eat.
41 But he said, "Now bring meal." [a]And he threw it into
the pot, and he said, "Pour *it* out for the people that they may
eat." Then there was no harm in the pot.
42 Now a man came from Baal-shalishah, and brought the
man of God bread of the first fruits, twenty loaves of barley
and fresh ears of grain in his sack. And he said, "[a]Give *them* to
the people that they may eat."
43 And his attendant said, "What, shall I set this before a
hundred men?" But he said, "Give *them* to the people that
they may eat, for thus says the LORD, 'They shall eat and have
some left over.' "
44 So he set *it* before them, and they ate and had *some*
left over, according to the word of the LORD.

CHAPTER 5

NOW [a]Naaman, captain of the army of the king of Syria,
was a great man [1]with his master, and highly respected, because by him the LORD had given victory to Syria. The man
was also a valiant warrior, *but he was* a leper.
2 Now the Syrians had gone out [a]in bands, and had taken

30 [a]2 Kin. 2:2, 4

31 [1]Lit., *attentiveness* [2]Lit., *him, saying*

33 [a]2 Kin. 4:4; Matt. 6:6; Luke 8:51

34 [a]1 Kin. 17:21-23

37 [a]Heb. 11:35

38 [1]Lit., *And* [a]2 Kin. 2:1 [b]2 Kin. 8:1 [c]2 Kin. 2:3 [d]Luke 10:39; Acts 22:3 [e]Ezek. 11:3, 7, 11; 24:3

41 [a]2 Kin. 2:21; Ex. 15:25

42 [a]Matt. 14:16-21; 15:32-38

1 [1]Lit., *before* [a]Luke 4:27

2 [a]2 Kin. 6:23; 13:20

captive a little girl from the land of Israel; and she [1]waited on
Naaman's wife.
3 And she said to her mistress, "I wish that my master
were [1]with the prophet who is in Samaria! Then he would cure
him of his leprosy."
4 And [1]Naaman went in and told his master, saying,
"Thus and thus spoke the girl who is from the land of Israel."
5 Then the king of Syria said, "Go [1]now, and I will send a
letter to the king of Israel." And he departed and [a]took with
him ten talents of silver and six thousand *shekels* of gold and
ten [b]changes of clothes.
6 And he brought the letter to the king of Israel, saying,
"And now as this letter comes to you, behold, I have sent
Naaman my servant to you, that you may cure him of his
leprosy."
7 And it came about when the king of Israel read the
letter, that [a]he tore his clothes and said, "[b]Am I God, to kill
and to make alive, that this man is sending *word* to me to cure
a man of his leprosy? But [c]consider now, and see how he is
seeking [1]a quarrel against me."
8 And it happened when Elisha [a]the man of God heard
that the king of Israel had torn his clothes, that he sent *word* to
the king, saying, "Why have you torn your clothes? Now let
him come to me, and he shall know that there is a prophet in
Israel."
9 So Naaman came with his horses and his chariots, and
stood at the doorway of the house of Elisha.
10 And Elisha sent a messenger to him, saying, "[a]Go and
wash in the Jordan seven times, and your flesh shall be restored
to you and *you shall* be clean."
11 But Naaman was furious and went away and said, "Behold, I [1]thought, 'He will surely come out to me, and stand
and call on the name of the LORD his God, and wave his hand
over the place, and cure the leper.'
12 "Are not [1]Abanah and Pharpar, the rivers of Damascus,
better than all the waters of Israel? Could I not wash in them
and be clean?" So he turned and went away in a rage.
13 [a]Then his servants came near and spoke to him and
said, "[b]My father, had the prophet told you *to do some* great
thing, would you not have done *it*? How much more *then*,
when he says to you, 'Wash, and be clean'?"
14 So he went down and dipped *himself* seven times in the
Jordan, according to the word of the man of God; and [a]his
flesh was restored like the flesh of a little child, and [b]he was
clean.
15 When he returned to the man of God [1]with all his
company, and came and stood before him, he said, "Behold
now, [a]I know that there is no God in all the earth, but in Israel;
so please [b]take a [2]present from your servant now."
16 But he said, "[a]As the LORD lives, before whom I stand,
[b]I will take nothing." And he urged him to take *it*, but he
refused.
17 And Naaman said, "If not, please let your servant at
least be given two mules' load of [a]earth; for your servant will
no more offer burnt offering nor will he sacrifice to other gods,
but to the LORD.

2 [1]Lit., *was before*

3 [1]Lit., *before*

4 [1]Lit., *he*

5 [1]Lit., *enter*
[a]2 Kin. 4:42; 1 Sam. 9:7
[b]2 Kin. 5:22, 23; Judg. 14:12

7 [1]Lit., *an occasion*
[a]Gen. 37:29 [b]Gen. 30:2; 1 Sam. 2:6 [c]1 Kin. 20:7; Luke 11:54

8 [a]1 Kin. 12:22

10 [a]John 9:7

11 [1]Lit., *said*

12 [1]Another reading is *Amanah*

13 [a]1 Sam. 28:23 [b]2 Kin. 2:12; 6:21; 8:9

14 [a]2 Kin. 5:10; Job 33:25
[b]Luke 4:27; 5:13

15 [1]Lit., *he and* [2]Lit., *blessing*
[a]2 Kin. 5:8; Josh. 2:9-16; 1 Sam. 17:46, 47
[b]1 Sam. 25:27

16 [a]2 Kin. 3:14 [b]2 Kin. 20:26; Gen. 14:22, 23

17 [a]Ex. 20:24

18 "In this matter may the LORD pardon your servant: when
my master goes into the house of [a]Rimmon to worship there,
and [b]he leans on my hand and I bow myself in the house of
Rimmon, when I bow myself in the house of Rimmon the
LORD pardon your servant in this matter."
19 And he said to him, "[a]Go in peace." So he departed
from him some distance.
20 But [a]Gehazi, the servant of Elisha the man of God,
[1]thought, "Behold, my master has spared this Naaman the
Syrian, [2]by not receiving from his hands what he brought. [b]As
the LORD lives, I will run after him and take something from
him."
21 So Gehazi pursued Naaman. When Naaman saw one
running after him, he came down from the chariot to meet
him and said, "Is all well?"
22 And he said, "[a]All is well. My master has sent me,
saying, 'Behold, just now two young men of the sons of the
prophets have come to me from [b]the hill country of Ephraim.
Please give them a talent of silver and [c]two changes of
clothes.'"
23 And Naaman said, "[a]Be pleased to take two talents."
And he urged him, and bound two talents of silver in two bags
with two changes of clothes, and gave them to two of his
servants; and they carried *them* before him.
24 When he came to the [1]hill, he took them from their
hand and [a]deposited them in the house, and he sent the men
away, and they departed.
25 But he went in and stood before his master. And Elisha
said to him, "Where have you been, Gehazi?" And he said,
"[a]Your servant went nowhere."
26 Then he said to him, "Did not my heart go *with you*,
when the man turned from his chariot to meet you? [a]Is it a
time to receive money and to receive clothes and oliveyards
and vineyards and sheep and oxen and male and female
servants?
27 "Therefore, the leprosy of Naaman shall cleave to you
and to your [1]descendants forever." So he went out from his
presence [a]a leper *as white* as snow.

CHAPTER 6

NOW [a]the sons of the prophets said to Elisha, "Behold now,
the place before you where we are living is too limited for us.
2 "Please let us go to the Jordan, and each of us take from
there a beam, and let us make a place there for ourselves where
we may live." So he said, "Go."
3 Then one said, "Please be willing to go with your servants." And he [1]answered, "I shall go."
4 So he went with them; and when they came to the
Jordan, they cut down trees.
5 But as one was felling a beam, [1]the axe head fell into
the water; and he cried out and said, "Alas, my master! For it
was borrowed."
6 Then the man of God said, "Where did it fall?" And
when he showed him the place, [a]he cut off a stick, and threw *it*
in there, and made the iron float.

18 [a]1 Kin. 15:18 [b]2 Kin. 7:2, 17
19 [a]Ex. 4:18; 1 Sam. 1:17; Mark 5:34
20 [1]Lit., *said* [2]Lit., *from* [a]2 Kin. 4:12, 31, 36 [b]2 Kin. 6:31; Ex. 20:7
22 [a]2 Kin. 4:26 [b]Josh. 24:33 [c]2 Kin. 5:5
23 [a]2 Kin. 6:3
24 [1]Lit., *Ophel* [a]Josh. 7:1, 11, 12, 21; 1 Kin. 21:16
25 [a]2 Kin. 5:22
26 [a]2 Kin. 5:16
27 [1]Lit., *seed* [a]Ex. 4:6; Num. 12:10
1 [a]2 Kin. 2:3
3 [1]Lit., *said*
5 [1]Lit., *as for the iron, it fell*
6 [a]2 Kin. 2:21; 4:41; Ex. 15:25

7 And he said, "Take it up for yourself." So he put out
his hand and took it.
8 Now the king of Syria was warring against Israel; and he
[1]counseled with his servants saying, "In such and such a place
shall be my camp."
9 And [a]the man of God sent *word* to the king of Israel
saying, "Beware that you do not pass this place, for the Syrians
are coming down there."
10 And the king of Israel sent to the place about which the
man of God had told him; thus he warned him, so that he
guarded himself there, [1]more than once or twice.
11 Now the heart of the king of Syria was enraged over
this thing; and he called his servants and said to them, "Will
you tell me which of us is for the king of Israel?"
12 And one of his servants said, "No, my lord, O king; but
Elisha, the prophet who is in Israel, tells the king of Israel the
words that you speak in your bedroom."
13 So he said, "Go and see where he is, that I may send
and take him." And it was told him, saying, "Behold, he is in
[a]Dothan."
14 And he sent horses and chariots and a great army there,
and they came by night and surrounded the city.
15 Now when the attendant of the man of God had risen
early and gone out, behold, an army with horses and chariots
was circling the city. And his servant said to him, "Alas, my
master! [1]What shall we do?"
16 So he [1]answered, "[a]Do not fear, for [b]those who are with
us are more than those who are with them."
17 Then Elisha prayed and said, "[a]O LORD, I pray open his
eyes, that he may see." And the LORD opened the servant's
eyes, and he saw; and behold, the mountain was full of [b]horses
and chariots of fire all around Elisha.
18 And when they came down to him, Elisha prayed to
the LORD and said, "Strike this [1]people with blindness, I pray."
So he [a]struck them with blindness according to the word of
Elisha.
19 Then Elisha said to them, "This is not the way, nor is
this the city; follow me and I will bring you to the man whom
you seek." And he brought them to Samaria.
20 And it came about when they had come into Samaria,
that Elisha said, "O [a]Lord, open the eyes of these *men*, that
they may see." So the LORD opened their eyes, and they saw;
and behold, they were in the midst of Samaria.
21 Then the king of Israel when he saw them, said to
Elisha, "[a]My father, shall I [1]kill them? Shall I [1]kill them?"
22 And he [1]answered, "You shall not [2]kill *them*. Would
you [2a]kill those you have taken captive with your sword and
with your bow? [b]Set bread and water before them, that they
may eat and drink and go to their master."
23 So he prepared a great feast for them; and when they
had eaten and drunk he sent them away, and they went to their
master. And [a]the marauding bands of Syria did not come again
into the land of Israel.
24 Now it came about after this, that [a]Ben-hadad king of
Syria gathered all his army and went up and besieged Samaria.
25 And there was a great famine in Samaria; and behold,

8 [1]Lit., *took counsel*

9 [a]2 Kin. 6:12; 4:1, 7

10 [1]Lit., *not once or twice*

13 [a]Gen. 37:17

15 [1]Lit., *How*

16 [1]Lit., *said*
[a]Ex. 14:13 [b]2 Chr. 32:7, 8; Rom. 8:31

17 [a]2 Kin. 6:20 [b]2 Kin. 2:11; Ps. 68:17; Zech. 6:1-7

18 [1]Lit., *nation*
[a]Gen. 19:11

20 [a]2 Kin. 6:17

21 [1]Lit., *smite*
[a]2 Kin. 2:12; 5:13; 8:9

22 [1]Lit., *said* [2]Lit., *smite*
[a]Deut. 20:11-16; 2 Chr. 28:8-15 [b]Rom. 12:20

23 [a]2 Kin. 5:2; 24:2

24 [a]1 Kin. 20:1

they besieged it, until a donkey's head was sold for eighty *shekels* of silver, and a fourth of a [1]kab of dove's dung for five *shekels* of silver.

26 And as the king of Israel was passing by on the wall a woman cried out to him, saying, "Help, my lord, O king!"

27 And he said, "[1]If the LORD does not help you, from where shall I help you? From the threshing floor, or from the winepress?"

28 And the king said to her, "What [1]is the matter with you?" And she [2]answered, "This woman said to me, 'Give your son that we may eat him today, and we will eat my son tomorrow.'

29 "[a]So we boiled my son and ate him; and I said to her on the next day, 'Give your son, that we may eat him'; but she has hidden her son."

30 And it came about when the king heard the words of the woman, that [a]he tore his clothes—now he was passing by on the wall—and the people looked, and behold, he had sackcloth [1]beneath on his [2]body.

31 Then he said, "May [a]God do so to me and more also, if the head of Elisha the son of Shaphat [1]remains on him today."

32 Now Elisha was sitting in his house, and [a]the elders were sitting with him. And *the king* sent a man from his presence; but before the messenger came to him, he said to the elders, "Do you [b]see how this son of a murderer has sent to take away my head? Look, when the messenger comes, shut the door and [1]hold the door shut against him. Is not the sound of his master's feet behind him?"

33 And while he was still talking with them, behold, the messenger came down to him, and he said, "[a]Behold, this evil is from the LORD; why should I wait for the LORD any longer?"

CHAPTER 7

THEN Elisha said, "Listen to the word of the LORD; thus says the LORD, '[a]Tomorrow about this time a [1]measure of fine flour shall be *sold* for a shekel, and two measures of barley for a shekel, in the gate of Samaria.' "

2 And [a]the royal officer on whose hand the king was leaning answered the man of God and said, "Behold, [b]if the LORD should make windows in heaven, could this thing be?" Then he said, "Behold you shall see it with your own eyes, but you shall not eat [1]of it."

3 Now there were four [a]leprous men at the entrance of the gate; and they said to one another, "Why do we sit here until we die?

4 "If we say, 'We will enter the city,' then the famine is in the city and we shall die there; and if we sit here, we die also. Now therefore come, and let us [1]go over to [a] the camp of the Syrians. If they spare us, we shall live; and if they kill us, we shall but die."

5 And they arose at twilight to go the camp of the Syrians; when they came to the outskirts of the camp of the Syrians, behold, there was no one there.

6 For [a]the Lord had caused the army of the Syrians to hear a sound of chariots and a sound of horses, *even* the sound

25 [1]I.e., one kab equals approx. 1 pint

27 [1]Lit., *No, let the LORD help you*

28 [1]Lit., *to you* [2]Lit., *said*

29 [a]Lev. 26:27-29; Deut. 28:52, 53, 57; Lam. 4:10

30 [1]Lit., *within* [2]Lit., *flesh* [a]1 Kin. 21:27

31 [1]Lit., *stands* [a]Ruth 1:17; 1 Kin. 19:2

32 [1]Lit., *press him with the door* [a]Ezek. 8:1; 14:1; 20:1 [b]1 Kin. 18:4, 13, 14; 21:10, 13

33 [a]Is. 8:21; Jer. 2:25

1 [1]Heb., *seah* [a]2 Kin. 7:18

2 [1]Lit., *from there* [a]2 Kin. 7:17, 19; 5:18 [b]Gen. 7:11; Mal. 3:10

3 [a]Lev. 13:45, 46; Num. 5:2-4; 12:10-14

4 [1]Lit., *fall* [a]2 Kin. 6:24

6 [a]2 Sam. 5:24

of a great army, so that they said to one another, "Behold, the
king of Israel has hired against us [b]the kings of the Hittites and
[c]the kings of the Egyptians, to come upon us."
7 Therefore they arose and fled in the twilight, and left
their tents and their horses and their donkeys, even the camp
just as it was, and fled for their life.
8 When these lepers came to the outskirts of the camp,
they entered one tent and ate and drank, and [a]carried from
there silver and gold and clothes, and went and hid *them;* and
they returned and entered another tent and carried from there
also, and went and hid *them.*
9 Then they said to one another, "We are not doing
right. This day is a day of good news, but we are keeping silent;
if we wait until morning light, punishment will [1]overtake us.
Now therefore come, let us go and [a]tell the king's household."
10 So they came and called to the gatekeepers of the city,
and they told them, saying, "We came to the camp of the
Syrians, and behold, there was no one there, nor the voice of
man, only the horses tied and the donkeys tied, and the tents
just as they were."
11 And the gatekeepers called, and told *it* within the king's
household.
12 Then the king arose in the night and said to his servants, "I will now tell you what the Syrians have done to us.
They know that [a]we are hungry; therefore they have gone from
the camp [b]to hide themselves in the field, saying, 'When they
come out of the city, we shall capture them alive and get into
the city.'"
13 And one of his servants answered and said, "Please, let
some *men* take five of the horses which remain, which are left
[1]in the city. Behold, they *will be in any case* like all the multitude of Israel who are left in it; behold, they *will be in any case*
like all the multitude of Israel who have already perished, so
let us send and see."
14 They took therefore two chariots with horses, and the
king sent after the army of the Syrians, saying, "Go and see."
15 And they went after them to the Jordan, and behold,
all the way was full of clothes and equipment, which the Syrians had thrown away in their haste. Then the messengers
returned and told the king.
16 So the people went out and plundered the camp of the
Syrians. Then a [1]measure of fine flour *was sold* for a shekel
and two [1]measures of barley for a shekel, [a]according to the
word of the LORD.
17 Now the king appointed [a]the royal officer on whose
hand he leaned [1]to have charge of the gate; but the people
trampled on him at the gate, and he died just as the man of
God had said, [b]who spoke when the king came down to him.
18 And it came about just as the man of God had spoken
to the king, saying, "Two [1]measures of barley for a shekel and
a [1]measure of fine flour for a shekel, shall be *sold* tomorrow
about this time at the gate of Samaria."
19 Then the royal officer answered the man of God and
said, "Now behold, [a]if the LORD should make windows in heav-
en, could such a thing be?" And he said, "Behold, you shall
see it with your own eyes, but you shall not eat [1]of it."

6 [b]1 Kin. 10:29 [c]2 Chr. 12:2, 3; Is. 31:1; 36:9
8 [a]Josh. 7:21
9 [1]Lit., *find* [a]2 Kin. 6:30
12 [a]2 Kin. 6:25-29 [b]Josh. 8:4-12
13 [1]Lit., *in it*
16 [1]Heb., *seah;* i.e., one seah equals approx. 11 quarts [a]2 Kin. 7:1
17 [1]Lit., *over the gate* [a]2 Kin. 7:2 [b]2 Kin. 6:32
18 [1]Heb., *seah;* i.e., one seah equals approx. 11 quarts
19 [1]Lit., *from there* [a]2 Kin. 7:2

20 And so it happened to him, for the people trampled on
him at the gate, and he died.

CHAPTER 8

NOW [a]Elisha spoke to the woman whose son he had restored
to life, saying, "Arise and go [1]with your household, and
sojourn wherever you can sojourn; for the [b]LORD has called for
a famine, and [c]it shall even come on the land for seven years."
2 So the woman arose and did according to the word of
the man of God, and she went with her household and sojourned in the land of the Philistines seven years.
3 And it came about at the end of seven years, that the
woman returned from the land of the Philistines; and she went
out to [1]appeal to the king for her house and for her field.
4 Now the king was talking with [a]Gehazi, the servant of
the man of God, saying, "Please relate to me all the great
things that Elisha has done."
5 And it came about, as he was relating to the king how
he had restored to life the one who was dead, that behold, the
woman whose son he had restored to life, [1]appealed to the
king for her house and for her field. And Gehazi said, "My
lord, O king, this is the woman and this is her son, whom
Elisha restored to life."
6 When the king asked the woman, she related *it* to him.
So the king appointed for her a certain officer, saying, "Restore
all that was hers and all the produce of the field from the
day that she left the land even until now."
7 Then Elisha came to [a]Damascus. Now [b]Ben-hadad
king of Syria was sick, and it was told him, saying, "[c]The man
of God has come here."
8 And the king said to [a]Hazael, "[b]Take a gift in your
hand and go to meet the man of God, and [c]inquire of the
LORD by him, saying, 'Will I recover from this sickness?' "
9 So Hazael went to meet him and took a gift in his
hand, even every kind of good thing of Damascus, forty camels' loads; and he came and stood before him and said,
"[a]Your son Ben-hadad king of Syria has sent me to you, saying,
'Will I recover from this sickness?' "
10 Then Elisha said to him, "[a]Go, say to him, 'You shall
surely recover,' but the [b]LORD has shown me that he will certainly die."
11 And he [1]fixed his gaze steadily *on him* [a]until he was
ashamed, and the man of God wept.
12 And Hazael said, "Why does my lord weep?" Then he
[1]answered, "Because [a]I know the evil that you will do to the
sons of Israel: their strongholds you will set on fire, and their
young men you will kill with the sword, and their little ones
you [b]will dash in pieces, and their women with child you will
rip up."
13 Then Hazael said, "But what is your servant, [a]*who is
but* a dog, that he should do this great thing?" And Elisha
[1]answered, "[b]The Lord has shown me that you will be king
over Syria."
14 So he departed from Elisha and returned to his master,

1 [1]Lit., *you and your* [a]2 Kin. 4:18, 31-35; [b]Ps. 105:16; Hag. 1:11 [c]Gen. 41:27, 54

3 [1]Lit., *cry out*

4 [a]2 Kin. 4:12; 5:20-27

5 [1]Lit., *cried out*

7 [a]1 Kin. 11:24 [b]2 Kin. 6:24 [c]2 Kin. 5:20

8 [a]1 Kin. 19:15, 17 [b]1 Kin. 14:3 [c]2 Kin. 1:2

9 [a]2 Kin. 5:13

10 [a]2 Kin. 8:14 [b]2 Kin. 8:15

11 [1]Lit., *made his face stand fast and he set* [a]2 Kin. 2:17

12 [1]Lit., *said* [a]2 Kin. 10:32, 33; 12:17; 13:3, 7 [b]2 Kin. 15:16; Nah. 3:10

13 [1]Lit., *said* [a]1 Sam. 17:43; 2 Sam. 9:8 [b]1 Kin. 19:15

who said to him, "What did Elisha say to you?" And he
[1]answered, "He told me that [a]you would surely recover."
15 And it came about on the morrow, that he took the
cover and dipped it in water and spread it on his face, [a]so that
he died. And Hazael became king in his place.
16 Now in the fifth year of [a]Joram the son of Ahab king of
Israel, Jehoshaphat being then the king of Judah, Jehoram the
son of Jehoshaphat king of Judah became king.
17 He was [a]thirty-two years old when he became king, and
he reigned eight years in Jerusalem.
18 And he walked in the way of the kings of Israel, just as
the house of Ahab had done, for [a]the daughter of Ahab became his wife; and he did evil in the sight of the LORD.
19 However, the LORD was not willing to destroy Judah,
for the sake of David His servant, [a]since He had [1]promised him
to give a [2]lamp to him through his sons always.
20 In his days [a]Edom revolted from under the hand of
Judah, and made a king over themselves.
21 Then Joram crossed over to Zair, and all his chariots
with him. And it came about that he arose by night and struck
the Edomites who had surrounded him and the captains of the
chariots; [a]but *his* [1]army fled to their tents.
22 [a]So Edom revolted [1]against Judah to this day. Then
[b]Libnah revolted at the same time.
23 And the rest of the acts of Joram and all that he did,
are they not written in the Book of Chronicles of the Kings of
Judah?
24 So Joram slept with his fathers, and [a]was buried with his
fathers in the city of David; and [b]Ahaziah his son became king
in his place.
25 [a]In the twelfth year of Joram the son of Ahab king of
Israel, Ahaziah the son of Jehoram king of Judah began to
reign.
26 Ahaziah *was* twenty-two years old when he became
king, and he reigned one year in Jersualem. And his mother's
name *was* Athaliah the granddaughter of Omri king of Israel.
27 And he walked in the way of the house of Ahab, and
did evil in the sight of the LORD, like the house of Ahab *had
done,* because he was a son-in-law of the house of Ahab.
28 Then he went with Joram the son of Ahab to war
against [a]Hazael king of Syria at [b]Ramoth-gilead, and the Syrians [1]wounded Joram.
29 So [a]King Joram returned to be healed in Jezreel of the
wounds which the Syrians had [1]inflicted on him at [b]Ramah,
when he fought against Hazael king of Syria. Then [c]Ahaziah
the son of Jehoram king of Judah went down to see Joram the
son of Ahab in Jezreel because he was sick.

CHAPTER 9

NOW Elisha the prophet called one of [a]the sons of the
prophets, and said to him, "[b]Gird up your loins, and [c]take this
flask of oil in your hand, and go to [d]Ramoth-gilead.
2 "When you arrive there, [1]search out [a]Jehu the son of
Jehoshaphat the son of Nimshi, and go in and [2b]bid him arise
from among his brothers, and bring him to an inner room.

14 [1]Lit., *said* [a]2 Kin. 8:10
15 [a]2 Kin. 8:10
16 [a]2 Kin. 1:17; 3:1
17 [a]2 Chr. 21:5-10
18 [a]2 Kin. 8:27
19 [1]Lit., *said* [2]I.e., descendant on the throne [a]2 Sam. 7:12-15; 1 Kin. 11:36
20 [a]2 Kin. 8:22; 3:9, 26, 27; 1 Kin. 22:47
21 [1]Lit., *the people* [a]2 Sam. 18:17; 19:8
22 [1]Lit., *from under the hand of* [a]Gen. 27:40 [b]2 Kin. 19:8; Josh. 21:13
24 [a]2 Chr. 21:20 [b]2 Chr. 21:1, 7
25 [a]2 Chr. 22:1-6
28 [1]Lit., *smote* [a]2 Kin. 8:15 [b]1 Kin. 22:3, 29
29 [1]Lit., *struck* [a]2 Kin. 9:15 [b]2 Kin. 8:28; 2 Chr. 22:5, 6 [c]2 Kin. 9:16
1 [a]2 Kin. 2:3 [b]2 Kin. 4:29 [c]1 Sam. 10:1; 16:1; 1 Kin. 1:39 [d]2 Kin. 8:28, 29
2 [1]Lit., *and look there for* [2]Lit., *cause him to* [a]2 Kin. 9:14, 20; 1 Kin. 19:16, 17 [b]2 Kin. 9:5, 11

3 "Then take the flask of oil and pour it on his head and
say, 'Thus says the LORD, "[a]I have anointed you king over
Israel." ' Then open the door and flee and do not wait."
4 So [a]the young man, the servant of the prophet, went to
Ramoth-gilead.
5 When he came, behold, the captains of the army were
sitting, and he said, "I have a word for you, O captain." And
Jehu said, "[1]For which *one* of us?" And he said, "For you, O
captain."
6 And he arose and went into the house, and he poured
the oil on his head and said to him, "Thus says the LORD, the
God of Israel, '[a]I have anointed you king over the people of
the LORD, *even* over Israel.
7 'And you shall strike the house of Ahab your master,
[a]that I may avenge [b]the blood of My servants the prophets,
and the blood of all the servants of the LORD, [c]at the hand of
Jezebel.
8 'For the whole house of Ahab shall perish, and [a]I will
cut off from Ahab [b]every male person [c]both bound and free in
Israel.
9 'And [a]I will make the house of Ahab like the house of
Jeroboam the son of Nebat, and [b]like the house of Baasha the
son of Ahijah.
10 'And [a]the dogs shall eat Jezebel in the territory of Jezreel, and none shall bury *her.*' " Then he opened the door and
fled.
11 Now Jehu came out to the servants of his master, and
one said to him, "[a]Is all well? Why did this [b]mad fellow come
to you?" And he said to them, "You know very well the man
and his talk."
12 And they said, "It is a lie, tell us now." And he said,
"Thus and thus he said to me, 'Thus says the LORD, "I have
anointed you king over Israel." ' "
13 Then [a]they hurried and each man took his clothes and
placed it under him on the bare steps, and [b]blew the trumpet,
saying, "Jehu is king!"
14 So Jehu the son of Jehoshaphat the son of Nimshi
conspired against Joram. [a]Now Joram [1]with all Israel was [2]de-
fending Ramoth-gilead against Hazael king of Syria,
15 but [a]King [1]Joram had returned to Jezreel to be healed
of the wounds which the Syrians had [2]inflicted on him when he
fought with Hazael king of Syria. So Jehu said, "If this is your
mind, *then* let no one escape *or* [3]leave the city to go tell *it* in
Jezreel."
16 Then Jehu rode in a chariot and went to Jezreel, for
Joram was lying there. [a]And Ahaziah king of Judah had come
down to see Joram.
17 Now the watchman was standing on the tower in Jezreel and he saw the [1]company of Jehu as he came, and said, "I
see a [1]company." And Joram said, "Take a horseman and send
him to meet them and let him say, 'Is it peace?' "
18 So a horseman went to meet him and said, "Thus says
the king, 'Is it peace?' " And Jehu said, "[a]What have you to do
with peace? Turn behind me." And the watchman [1]reported,
"The messenger came to them, but he did not return."
19 Then he sent out a second horseman, who came to

3 [a]2 Chr. 22:7
4 [a]2 Kin. 9:1
5 [1]Lit., *To whom of us all?*
6 [a]2 Kin. 9:3
7 [a]Deut. 32:35, 43 [b]1 Kin. 18:4; 21:15, 21, 25 [c]2 Kin. 9:32-37
8 [a]2 Kin. 10:17; 1 Kin. 21:21 [b]1 Sam. 25:22 [c]2 Kin. 14:26; Deut. 32:36
9 [a]1 Kin. 14:10, 11; 15:29 [b]1 Kin. 16:3-5, 11, 12
10 [a]2 Kin. 9:35, 36; 1 Kin. 21:23
11 [a]2 Kin. 9:17, 19, 22 [b]Jer. 29:26; Hos. 9:7; Mark 3:21
13 [a]Matt. 21:7, 8; Mark 11:7, 8 [b]2 Sam. 15:10; 1 Kin. 1:34, 39
14 [1]Lit., *he and* [2]Lit., *keeping* [a]2 Kin. 8:28; 1 Kin. 22:3
15 [1]Heb., *Jehoram* [2]Lit., *struck* [3]Lit., *go out from* [a]2 Kin. 8:29
16 [a]2 Kin. 8:29
17 [1]Lit., *multitude*
18 [1]Lit., *told, saying* [a]2 Kin. 9:19, 22

them and said, "Thus says the king, 'Is it peace?' " And Jehu
[1]answered, "What have you to do with peace? Turn behind
me."
20 And the watchman [1]reported, "He came even to them,
and he did not return; and [a]the driving is like the driving of
[b]Jehu the son of Nimshi, for he drives furiously."
21 Then [1]Joram said, "[2]Get ready." And they made his
chariot ready. [a]And [1]Joram king of Israel and Ahaziah king of
Judah went out, each in his chariot, and they went out to meet
Jehu and found him in the [3b]property of Naboth the
Jezreelite.
22 And it came about, when [1]Joram saw Jehu, that he said,
"Is it peace, Jehu?" And he [2]answered, "What peace, [a]so long
as the harlotries of your mother Jezebel and her witchcrafts are
so many?"
23 So [1]Joram [2]reined about and fled and said to Ahaziah,
"[a]*There is* treachery, O Ahaziah!"
24 And [a]Jehu [1]drew his bow with his full strength and
[2]shot [3]Joram between his arms; and the arrow went [4]through
his heart, and he sank in his chariot.
25 Then *Jehu* said to Bidkar his officer, "Take *him* up and
[a]cast him into the [1]property of the field of Naboth the Jezreelite, for I remember when [2]you and I were riding together after
Ahab his father, that the [b]LORD laid this [c]oracle against him:
26 'Surely [a]I have seen yesterday the blood of Naboth and
the blood of his sons,' says the LORD, 'and [b]I will repay you in
this [1]property,' says the LORD. Now then, take and cast him
into the [1]property, according to the word of the LORD."
27 [a]When Ahaziah the king of Judah saw *this*, he fled by
the way of the garden house. And Jehu pursued him and said,
"[1]Shoot him too, in the chariot." *So they shot him* at the
ascent of Gur, which is at [b]Ibleam. But he fled to Megiddo
and died there.
28 [a]Then his servants carried him in a chariot to Jerusalem, and buried him in his grave with his fathers in the city of
David.
29 Now in [a]the eleventh year of Joram the son of Ahab
Ahaziah became king over Judah.
30 When Jehu came to Jezreel, Jezebel heard *of it*, and
[a]she painted her eyes and adorned her head, and looked out
the window.
31 And as Jehu entered the gate, she said, "[a]Is it [1]well,
Zimri, [2]your master's murderer?"
32 Then he lifted up his face to the window and said,
"Who is on my side? Who?" And two or three officials looked
down at him.
33 And he said, "Throw her down." So they threw her
down, and some of her blood was sprinkled on the wall and on
the horses, and he trampled her under foot.
34 When he came in, he ate and drank; and he said, "See
now to [a]this cursed woman and bury her, for [b]she is a king's
daughter."
35 And they went to bury her, but they found no more of
her than the skull and the feet and the palms of her hands.
36 Therefore they returned and told him. And he said,
"This is the word of the LORD, which He spoke by His servant

19 [1]Lit., *said*

20 [1]Lit., *told, saying* [a]2 Sam. 18:27 [b]1 Kin. 19:17

21 [1]Heb., *Jehoram* [2]Lit., *Yoke the chariot* [3]Lit., *portion* [a]2 Chr. 22:7 [b]2 Kin. 9:26; 1 Kin. 21:1-7, 15-19

22 [1]Heb., *Jehoram* [2]Lit., *said* [a]1 Kin. 16:30-33; 18:19; 2 Chr. 21:13

23 [1]Heb., *Jehoram* [2]Lit., *turned his hands* [a]2 Kin. 11:14

24 [1]Lit., *filled his hand with the bow* [2]Lit., *smote* [3]Heb., *Jehoram* [4]Lit., *out at* [a]1 Kin. 22:34

25 [1]Lit., *portion* [2]Lit., *I and you* [a]1 Kin. 21:1 [b]1 Kin. 21:19, 24-29 [c]Is. 13:1

26 [1]Lit., *portion* [a]1 Kin. 21:13 [b]2 Kin. 9:21, 25

27 [1]Lit., *smite* [a]2 Chr. 22:7, 9 [b]Josh. 17:11; Judg. 1:27

28 [a]2 Kin. 23:30

29 [a]2 Kin. 8:25

30 [a]Jer. 4:30; Ezek. 23:40

31 [1]Lit., *peace* [2]Lit., *his* [a]2 Kin. 9:18-22; 1 Kin. 16:9-20

34 [a]1 Kin. 21:25 [b]1 Kin. 16:31

Elijah the Tishbite, saying, '[a]In the [1]property of Jezreel the
dogs shall eat the flesh of Jezebel;
37 and [a]the corpse of Jezebel shall be as dung on the face
of the field in the [1]property of Jezreel, so they cannot say,
"This is Jezebel." ' "

Chapter 10

NOW Ahab had seventy sons in [a]Samaria. And Jehu wrote
letters and sent *them* to Samaria, to the rulers of Jezreel, the
elders, and to the guardians of *the children of* Ahab, saying,
2 "And now, when this letter comes to you, since your
master's sons are with you, [1]as well as the chariots and horses
and a fortified city and the weapons,
3 select the best and [1]fittest of your master's sons, and set
him on his father's throne, and fight for your master's house."
4 But they feared greatly and said, "Behold, the two
kings did not stand before him; how then can we stand?"
5 And the one who *was* over the household, and he who
was over the city, the elders, and the guardians of *the children,*
sent *word* to Jehu, saying, "[a]We are your servants, all that you
say to us we will do, we will not make any man king; do what is
good in your sight."
6 Then he wrote a letter to them a second time saying,
"If you are on my side, and you will listen to my voice, take the
heads of the men, your master's sons, and come to me at
Jezreel tomorrow about this time." Now the king's sons, seventy persons, *were* with the great men of the city, *who* were
rearing them.
7 And it came about when the letter came to them, that
they took the king's sons, and [a]slaughtered *them,* seventy persons, and put their heads in baskets, and sent *them* to him at
Jezreel.
8 When the messenger came and told him, saying,
"They have brought the heads of the king's sons," he said,
"Put them in two heaps at the entrance of the gate until
morning."
9 Now it came about in the morning, that he went out
and stood, and said to all the people, "You are [1]innocent;
behold, [a]I conspired against my master and killed him, but
[b]who [2]killed all these?
10 "Know then that [a]there shall fall to the earth nothing of
the word of the LORD, which the LORD spoke concerning the
house of Ahab, for the LORD has done [b]what He spoke
[1]through his servant Elijah."
11 So Jehu [1]killed all who remained of the house of Ahab
in Jezreel, and all his great men and his acquaintances and his
priests, until he left him without a survivor.
12 Then he arose and departed, and went to Samaria. On
the way while he was at [1]Beth-eked of the shepherds,
13 [a]Jehu [1]met the [2]relatives of Ahaziah king of Judah and
said, "Who are you?" And they [3]answered, "We are the [2]rela-
tives of Ahaziah; and we have come down [4]to greet the sons of
the king and the sons of the queen mother."
14 And he said, "Take them alive." So they took them

36 [1]Lit., *portion* [a]1 Kin. 21:23
37 [1]Lit., *portion* [a]Jer. 8:1-3
1 [a]1 Kin. 16:24-29
2 [1]Lit., *and with you the*
3 [1]Lit., *most upright*
5 [a]2 Kin. 18:14; Josh. 9:8, 11; 1 Kin. 20:4, 32
7 [a]2 Kin. 11:1; Judg. 9:5
9 [1]Lit., *just* [2]Lit., *smote* [a]2 Kin. 9:14-24 [b]2 Kin. 10:6
10 [1]Lit., *by the hand of* [a]2 Kin. 9:7-10 [b]1 Kin. 21:19-29
11 [1]Lit., *smote*
12 [1]I.e., house of binding
13 [1]Lit., *found* [2]Lit., *brother* [3]Lit., *said* [4]Lit., *about the welfare of* [a]2 Kin. 8:24, 29; 2 Chr. 21:17; 22:8

15 [1]Lit., *found* [2]Lit., *blessed* [3]Lit., *said* [a]Jer. 35:6-19 [b]1 Chr. 2:55 [c]Ezra 10:19; Ezek. 17:18

16 [1]Lit., *they* [a]1 Kin. 19:10

17 [1]Lit., *smote* [a]2 Kin. 9:8 [b]2 Kin. 10:10

18 [a]1 Kin. 16:31, 32

19 [1]Lit., *insidiousness* [a]1 Kin. 18:19; 22:6

20 [a]Joel 1:14 [b]Ex. 32:4-6

21 [1]Lit., *in all* [a]2 Kin. 11:18; 1 Kin. 16:32

22 [1]Lit., *over the*

24 [1]Lit., *his soul for his soul* [a]1 Kin. 20:30-42

25 [1]Lit., *runners* [2]Lit., *smite* [3]Lit., *smote* [4]Lit., *city* [a]1 Sam. 22:17 [b]1 Kin. 18:40

26 [a]2 Kin. 3:2; 1 Kin. 14:23

27 [a]Ezra 6:11; Dan. 2:5; 3:29

29 [a]1 Kin. 12:28-30; 13:33, 34 [b]1 Kin. 12:29

alive, and killed them at the pit of Beth-eked, forty-two men; and he left none of them.
15 Now when he had departed from there, he [1]met [a]Jehonadab the son of [b]Rechab *coming* to meet him; and he [2]greeted him and said to him, "Is your heart right, as my heart is with your heart?" And Jehonadab [3]answered, "It is." *Jehu said,* "If it is, [c]give *me* your hand." And he gave him his hand, and he took him up to him into the chariot.
16 And he said, "Come with me and [a]see my zeal for the LORD." So [1]he made him ride in his chariot.
17 And when he came to Samaria, [a]he [1]killed all who remained to Ahab in Samaria, until he had destroyed him, [b]according to the word of the LORD, which he spoke to Elijah.
18 Then Jehu gathered all the people and said to them, "[a]Ahab served Baal a little; Jehu will serve him much.
19 "And now, [a]summon all the prophets of Baal, all his worshipers and all his priests; let no one be missing, for I have a great sacrifice for Baal; whoever is missing shall not live." But Jehu did it in [1]cunning, in order that he might destroy the worshipers of Baal.
20 And Jehu said, "[a]Sanctify a solemn assembly for Baal." And [b]they proclaimed *it.*
21 Then Jehu sent [1]throughout Israel and all the worshipers of Baal came, so that there was not a man left who did not come. And when they went into [a]the house of Baal, the house of Baal was filled from one end to the other.
22 And he said to the one who *was* [1]in charge of the wardrobe, "Bring out garments for all the worshipers of Baal." So he brought out garments for them.
23 And Jehu went into the house of Baal with Jehonadab the son of Rechab; and he said to the worshipers of Baal, "Search and see that there may be here with you none of the servants of the LORD, but only the worshipers of Baal."
24 Then they went in to offer sacrifices and burnt offerings. Now Jehu had stationed for himself eighty men outside, and he had said, "[a]The one who permits any of the men whom I bring into your hands to escape, [1]shall give up his life in exchange."
25 Then it came about, as soon as he had finished offering the burnt offering, that Jehu said to the [1a]guard and to the royal officers, "[b]Go in, [2]kill them; let none come out." And they [3]killed them with the edge of the sword; and the [1]guard and the royal officers threw *them* out, and went to the [4]inner room of the house of Baal.
26 And they brought out the *sacred* [a]pillars of the house of Baal, and burned them.
27 They also broke down the *sacred* pillar of Baal and broke down the house of Baal, and [a]made it a latrine to this day.
28 Thus Jehu eradicated Baal out of Israel.
29 However, [a]*as for* the sins of Jeroboam the son of Nebat, which he made Israel sin, from these Jehu did not depart, *even* the [b]golden calves that *were* at Bethel and that *were* at Dan.
30 And the LORD said to Jehu, "Because you have done well in executing what is right in My eyes, *and* have done to

the house of Ahab according to all that *was* in My heart, [a]your
sons of the fourth generation shall sit on the throne of Israel."
31 But Jehu [1]was not careful to walk in the law of the
LORD, the God of Israel, with all his heart; [a]he did not depart
from the sins of Jeroboam, which he made Israel sin.
32 In those days the [a]Lord began to cut off *portions* [1]from
Israel; and [b]Hazael [2]defeated them throughout the territory of
Israel:
33 from the Jordan eastward, all the land of Gilead, the
Gadites and the Reubenites and the Manassites, from [a]Aroer,
which is by the valley of the Arnon, even [b]Gilead and Bashan.
34 Now the rest of the acts of Jehu and all that he did and
all his might, are they not written in the Book of the Chronicles of the Kings of Israel?
35 And Jehu slept with his fathers, and they buried him in
Samaria. And Jehoahaz his son became king in his place.
36 Now the [1]time which Jehu reigned over Israel in Samaria *was* twenty-eight years.

CHAPTER 11

[a]WHEN Athaliah the mother of Ahaziah saw that her son
was dead, she rose and destroyed all the royal [1]offspring.
2 But Jehosheba, the daughter of King Joram, sister of
Ahaziah, [a]took Joash the son of Ahaziah and stole him from
among the king's sons who were being put to death, and placed
him and his nurse in the bedroom. So they hid him from
Athaliah, and he was not put to death.
3 So he was hid with her in the house of the LORD six
years, while Athaliah was reigning over the land.
4 [a]Now in the seventh year Jehoiada sent and brought
the captains of hundreds of [b]the Carites and of the [1]guard, and
brought them to him in the house of the LORD. Then he made
a covenant with them and put them under oath in the house of
the LORD, and showed them to the king's son.
5 And he commanded them, saying, "This is the thing
that you shall do: [a]one third of you, who come in on the
Sabbath and keep watch over the king's house
6 (one third also *shall be* at the gate Sur, and one third at
the gate behind the [1]guards), [2]shall keep watch over the house
for defense.
7 "And two parts of you, *even* all who go out on the
Sabbath, shall also keep watch over the house of the LORD for
the king.
8 "Then you shall surround the king, each with his weapons in his hand; and whoever comes within the ranks shall be
put to death. And [a]be with the king when he goes out and
when he comes in."
9 So the captains of hundreds did according to all that
Jehoiada the priest commanded. And each one of them took
his men who were to come in on the Sabbath, with those who
were to go out on the Sabbath, and came to Jehoiada the
priest.
10 And [a]the priest gave to the captains of hundreds the
spears and shields that had been King David's, which *were* in
the house of the LORD.

30 [a]2 Kin. 15:12

31 [1]Lit., *did not watch* [a]2 Kin. 10:29

32 [1]Lit., *in* [2]Lit., *smote* [a]2 Kin. 13:25; 14:25 [b]2 Kin. 8:12; 13:22; 1 Kin. 19:17

33 [a]Deut. 2:36 [b]Amos 1:3-5

36 [1]Lit., *days*

1 [1]Lit., *seed* [a]2 Chr. 22:10-12

2 [a]2 Kin. 11:21; 12:1

4 [1]Lit., *runners* [a]2 Chr. 23:1-21 [b]2 Kin. 11:19; 2 Sam. 20:23

5 [a]1 Chr. 9:25

6 [1]Lit., *runners* [2]Lit., *and shall*

8 [a]Num. 27:16, 17

10 [a]2 Sam. 8:7; 1 Chr. 18:7

11 [1]Lit., *runners* [2]Lit., *shoulder*

12 [a]2 Sam. 1:10 [b]Ex. 25:16; 31:18 [c]1 Sam. 10:24

14 [1]Lit., *trumpets* [a]2 Kin. 23:3; 2 Chr. 34:31 [b]1 Kin. 1:39, 40 [c]Gen. 37:29; 44:13 [d]2 Kin. 9:23

15 [1]Lit., *from within*

16 [1]Lit., *placed hands to her*

17 [a]Josh. 24:25; 2 Chr. 15:12-14; 34:31 [b]1 Sam. 10:25; 2 Sam. 5:3

18 [1]Lit., *offices* [a]2 Kin. 10:26, 27 [b]Deut. 12:2, 3 [c]1 Kin. 18:40

19 [1]Lit., *runners* [a]2 Kin. 11:4 [b]2 Kin. 11:6

21 [1]Ch. 12:1 in Heb. [a]2 Chr. 24:1-14

3 [a]2 Kin. 14:4; 15:35

4 [1]Lit., *which it comes into . . . to bring* [a]2 Kin. 22:4 [b]Ex. 35:5, 22, 29; 1 Chr. 29:3-9

5 [1]Lit., *breaches* and so through v.12.

11 And the [1]guards stood each with his weapons in his hand, from the right [2]side of the house to the left [2]side of the house, by the altar and by the house, around the king.
12 Then he brought the king's son out and [a]put the crown on him, and *gave him* [b]the testimony; and they made him king and anointed him, and they clapped their hands and said, "[c]Long live the king!"
13 When Athaliah heard the noise of the guard *and of* the people, she came to the people in the house of the LORD.
14 And she looked and behold, the king was standing [a]by the pillar, according to the custom, with the captains and the [1]trumpeters beside the king; and [b]all the people of the land rejoiced and blew trumpets. Then Athaliah [c]tore her clothes and cried, "[d]Treason! Treason!"
15 And Jehoiada the priest commanded the captains of hundreds who were appointed over the army, and said to them, "Bring her out [1]between the ranks, and whoever follows her put to death with the sword." For the priest said, "Let her not be put to death in the house of the LORD."
16 So they [1]seized her, and when she arrived at the horses' entrance of the king's house, she was put to death there.
17 Then [a]Jehoiada made a covenant between the LORD and the king and the people, that they should be the LORD's people, also [b]between the king and the people.
18 And all the people of the land went to [a]the house of Baal, and tore it down; [b]his altars and his images they broke in pieces thoroughly, and [c]killed Mattan the priest of Baal before the altars. And the priest appointed [1]officers over the house of the LORD.
19 And he took the captains of hundreds and the [a]Carites and the [1]guards and all the people of the land; and they brought the king down from the house of the LORD, and came by the way of [b]the gate of the [1]guards to the king's house. And he sat on the throne of the kings.
20 So all the people of the land rejoiced and the city was quiet. For they had put Athaliah to death with the sword at the king's house.
21 [1a]Jehoash was seven years old when he became king.

CHAPTER 12

IN the seventh year of Jehu, Jehoash became king, and he reigned forty years in Jerusalem; and his mother's name was Zibiah of Beersheba.
2 And Jehoash did right in the sight of the LORD all his days in which Jehoiada the priest instructed him.
3 Only [a]the high places were not taken away; the people still sacrificed and burned incense on the high places.
4 Then Jehoash said to the priests, "All the money of the sacred things [a]which is brought into the house of the LORD, in current money *both* [b]the money of each man's assessment *and* all the money [1]which any man's heart prompts him to bring into the house of the LORD,
5 let the priests take it for themselves, each from his acquaintance; and they shall repair the [1]damages of the house wherever any damage may be found.

6 But it came about that in the twenty-third year of King
Jehoash the priests had not repaired the damages of the house.
7 Then King Jehoash called for Jehoiada the priest, and
for the *other* priests and said to them, "Why do you not repair
the damages of the house? Now therefore take no *more* money
from your acquaintances, but pay it for the damages of the
house."
8 So the priests agreed that they should take no *more*
money from the people, or repair the damages of the house.
9 But [a]Jehoiada the priest took a chest and bored a hole
in its lid, and put it beside the altar, on the right side as one
comes into the house of the LORD; and the priests who guarded
the threshold put in it all the money which was brought into
the house of the LORD.
10 And when they saw that there was much money in the
chest, that [a]the king's scribe and the high priest came up and
tied *it* in bags and counted the money which was found in the
house of the LORD.
11 And they gave the money which was weighed out into
the hands of those who did the work, who had the oversight of
the house of the LORD; and they [1]paid it out to the carpenters
and the builders, who worked on the house of the LORD;
12 and [a]to the masons and the stonecutters, and for
buying timber and hewn stone to repair the damages to the
house of the LORD, and for all that was [1]laid out for the house
to repair it.
13 But [a]there were not made for the house of the LORD
[b]silver cups, snuffers, bowls, trumpets, any vessels of gold, or
vessels of silver from the money which was brought into the
house of the LORD;
14 for they gave that to those who did the work, and with
it they repaired the house of the LORD.
15 Moreover, [a]they did not require an accounting from
the men into whose hand they gave the money to pay to those
who did the work, for they dealt faithfully.
16 The [a]money from the guilt offerings and [b]the money
from the sin offerings, was not brought into the house of the
LORD; [c]it was for the priests.
17 Then [a]Hazael king of Syria went up and fought against
Gath and captured it, and [b]Hazael set his face to go up to
Jerusalem.
18 And [a]Jehoash king of Judah took all the sacred things
that Jehoshaphat and Jehoram and Ahaziah, his fathers, kings
of Judah, had dedicated, and [b]his own sacred things and all the
gold that was found among the treasuries of the house of the
LORD and of the king's house, and sent *it* to Hazael king of
Syria. Then he went away from Jerusalem.
19 Now the rest of the acts of Joash and all that he did, are
they not written in the Book of the Chronicles of the Kings of
Judah?
20 [a]And his servants arose and made a conspiracy, and
[b]struck down Joash at [c]the house of Millo *as he was* going
down to Silla.
21 For Jozacar the son of Shimeath, and Jehozabad the
son of [a]Shomer, his servants, struck *him*, and he died; and they

9 [a]Mark 12:41; Luke 21:1

10 [a]2 Kin. 19:2; 22:3, 4, 12; 2 Sam. 8:17

11 [1]Lit., *brought*

12 [1]Lit., *went out* [a]2 Kin. 22:5, 6

13 [a]2 Chr. 24:14 [b]1 Kin. 7:48, 50

15 [a]2 Kin. 22:7

16 [a]Lev. 5:15-18 [b]Lev. 4:24, 29 [c]Lev. 7:7; Num. 18:19

17 [a]2 Kin. 8:12; 10:32, 33; 1 Kin. 19:17 [b]2 Chr. 24:23, 24

18 [a]2 Kin. 16:8; 18:15, 16; 1 Kin. 14:26; 15:18 [b]2 Kin. 12:4

20 [a]2 Chr. 24:25-27 [b]2 Kin. 14:5 [c]Judg. 9:6; 2 Sam. 5:9; 1 Kin. 11:27

21 [a]2 Chr. 24:26

buried him with his fathers in the city of David, and [b]Ahaziah
his son became king in his place.

Chapter 13

IN the twenty-third year of Joash the son of Ahaziah, king of
Judah, Jehoahaz the son of Jehu became king over Israel at
Samaria, *and he reigned* seventeen years.
2 And he did evil in the sight of the LORD, and followed
the sins of Jeroboam the son of Nebat, [a]with which he made
Israel sin; he did not turn from them.
3 [a]So the anger of the LORD was kindled against Israel,
and He gave them continually into the hand of [b]Hazael king
of Syria, and into the hand of [c]Ben-hadad the son of Hazael.
4 Then [a]Jehoahaz entreated the favor of the LORD, and
the LORD listened to him; for [b]He saw the oppression of Israel,
how the king of Syria oppressed them.
5 And the LORD gave Israel a [1a]deliverer, so that they
[2]escaped from under the hand of the Syrians; and the sons of
Israel lived in their tents as formerly.
6 Nevertheless they did not turn away from the sins of
the house of Jeroboam, [a]with which he made Israel sin, but
walked in [1]them; and [b]the Asherah also remained standing in
Samaria.
7 For he left to Jehoahaz of the [1]army not more than
fifty horsemen and ten chariots and 10,000 footmen, for the
king of Syria had destroyed them and [a]made them like the dust
at threshing.
8 Now the rest of the acts of Jehoahaz, and all that he
did and his might, are they not written in the Book of the
Chronicles of the Kings of Israel?
9 And Jehoahaz slept with his fathers, and they buried
him in Samaria; and Joash his son became king in his place.
10 In the thirty-seventh year of Joash king of Judah, Jehoash the son of Jehoahaz, became king over Israel in Samaria,
and reigned sixteen years.
11 And he did evil in the sight of the LORD; he did not turn
away from all the sins of Jeroboam the son of Nebat, with
which he made Israel sin, but he walked in [1]them.
12 [a]Now the rest of the acts of Joash and all that he did
and his might with which he fought against Amaziah king of
Judah, are they not written in the Book of the Chronicles of
the Kings of Israel?
13 So Joash slept with his fathers, and Jeroboam sat on his
throne; and Joash was buried in Samaria with the kings of
Israel.
14 When Elisha [1]became sick with the illness of which he
was to die, Joash the king of Israel came down to him and wept
over [2]him and said, "[a]My father, my father, the chariots of
Israel and its horsemen!"
15 And Elisha said to him, "Take a bow and arrows." So
he [1]took a bow and arrows.
16 Then he said to the king of Israel, "Put your hand on
the bow." And he put his hand *on it,* then Elisha laid his hands
on the king's hands.
17 And he said, "Open the window toward the east," and

21 [b]2 Kin. 14:1

2 [a]1 Kin. 12:26-33

3 [a]Judg. 2:14 [b]2 Kin. 12:17 [c]2 Kin. 13:24, 25

4 [a]Num. 21:7-9 [b]2 Kin. 14:26; Ex. 3:7, 9

5 [1]Or, *savior* [2]Lit., *went out* [a]2 Kin. 13:25; 14:25, 27; Neh. 9:27

6 [1]Lit., *it* [a]2 Kin. 13:2 [b]1 Kin. 16:33

7 [1]Lit., *people* [a]Amos 1:3

11 [1]Lit., *it*

12 [a]2 Kin. 13:14-19; 14:8-15

14 [1]Lit., *was sick with his sickness* [2]Lit., *his face* [a]2 Kin. 2:12

15 [1]Lit., *took to himself*

he opened *it*. Then Elisha said, "Shoot!" And he shot. And he
said, "The LORD's arrow of victory, even the arrow of victory
over Syria; for you shall [1]defeat the Syrians at [a]Aphek until you
have [2]destroyed *them*.
18 Then he said, "Take the arrows," and he took them.
And he said to the king of Israel, "Strike the ground," and he
struck *it* three times and [1]stopped.
19 So [a]the man of God was angry with him and said, "You
should have struck five or six times, then you would have
struck Syria until you would have [1]destroyed *it*. But now you
shall strike Syria [b]*only* three times."
20 And Elisha died, and they buried him. Now [a]the bands
of the Moabites would invade the land in the spring of the
year.
21 And as they were burying a man, behold, they saw a
marauding band; and they cast the man into the grave of
Elisha. And when the man touched the bones of Elisha he
revived and stood up on his feet.
22 Now [a]Hazael king of Syria had oppressed Israel all the
days of Jehoahaz.
23 But the [a]LORD was gracious to them and [b]had compassion on them and turned to them because of [c]His covenant
with Abraham, Isaac, and Jacob, and would not destroy them
or cast them from His presence until now.
24 When Hazael king of Syria died, Ben-hadad his son
became king in his place.
25 Then [a]Jehoash the son of Jehoahaz took again from
the hand of Ben-hadad the son of Hazael the cities which he
had taken in war from the hand of Jehoahaz his father. [b]Three
times Joash [1]defeated him and recovered the cities of Israel.

CHAPTER 14

[a]IN the second year of Joash son of Joahaz king of Israel,
[b]Amaziah the son of Joash king of Judah became king.
2 He was twenty-five years old when he became king, and
he reigned twenty-nine years in Jerusalem. And his mother's
name was Jehoaddin of Jerusalem.
3 And he did right in the sight of the LORD, yet not like
David his father; he did according to all that Joash his father
had done.
4 Only [a]the high places were not taken away; [b]the people
still sacrificed and burned incense on the high places.
5 Now it came about, as soon as the kingdom was firmly
in his hand, that he [1a]killed his servants who had slain the king
his father.
6 But the sons of the [1]slayers he did not put to death,
according to what is written in the Book of the Law of Moses,
as the LORD commanded, saying, "[a]The fathers shall not be
put to death for the sons, nor the sons be put to death for the
fathers; but [b]each shall be put to death for his own sin."
7 [a]He [1]killed *of* Edom in [b]the Valley of Salt 10,000 and
took [c]Sela by war, and named it [d]Joktheel to this day.
8 [a]Then Amaziah sent messengers to Jehoash, the son of
Jehoahaz son of Jehu, king of Israel, saying, "[b]Come, let us
face each other."

17 [1]Lit., *smite* [2]Lit., *made an end of* [a]1 Kin. 20:26

18 [1]Lit., *stood*

19 [1]Lit., *made an end of* [a]2 Kin. 5:20 [b]2 Kin. 13:25

20 [a]2 Kin. 3:7; 24:2

22 [a]2 Kin. 8:12, 13

23 [a]2 Kin. 14:27 [b]1 Kin. 8:28 [c]Gen. 13:16, 17; 17:2-5

25 [1]Lit., *smote* [a]2 Kin. 10:32, 33; 14:25 [b]2 Kin. 13:18, 19

1 [a]2 Chr. 25:1 [b]2 Kin. 13:10

4 [a]2 Kin. 12:3 [b]2 Kin. 16:4

5 [1]Lit., *smote* [a]2 Kin. 12:20

6 [1]Lit., *smiters* [a]Deut. 24:16 [b]Jer. 31:30; Ezek. 18:4, 20

7 [1]Lit., *smote* [a]2 Chr. 25:11 [b]2 Sam. 8:13; 1 Chr. 18:12 [c]Is. 16:1 [d]Josh. 15:38

8 [a]2 Chr. 25:17-24 [b]2 Sam. 2:14-17

9 [a]Judg. 9:8-15
10 [1]Lit., *smitten* [2]Lit., *lifted you up* [a]2 Kin. 14:7 [b]Deut. 8:14; 2 Chr. 26:16
11 [a]2 Kin. 23:29 [b]Josh. 19:38
12 [1]Lit., *before* [a]2 Sam. 18:17
13 [1]One cubit equals approx. 18 in. [a]Neh. 8:16; 12:39 [b]2 Chr. 25:23
14 [a]2 Kin. 12:18; 1 Kin. 14:26
15 [a]2 Kin. 13:12, 13
17 [a]2 Chr. 25:25-28
19 [a]Josh. 10:31; 2 Kin. 18:14, 17
21 [1]In 2 Chr. 26:1, *Uzziah*
22 [a]2 Kin. 16:6; 1 Kin. 9:26; 2 Chr. 8:17
25 [1]Lit., *by* [a]2 Kin. 10:32; 13:25 [b]1 Kin. 8:65 [c]Deut. 3:17 [d]Jon. 1:1; Matt. 12:39, 40 [e]Josh. 19:13
26 [a]2 Kin. 13:4

9 And Jehoash king of Israel sent to Amaziah king of
Judah, saying, "[a]The thorn bush which was in Lebanon sent to
the cedar which was in Lebanon, saying, 'Give your daughter
to my son in marriage.' But there passed by a wild beast that
was in Lebanon, and trampled the thorn bush.
10 "[a]You have indeed [1]defeated Edom, and [b]your heart has
[2]become proud. Enjoy your glory and stay at home; for why
should you provoke trouble so that you, even you, should fall,
and Judah with you?"
11 But Amaziah would not listen. So Jehoash king of Israel went up; [a]and he and Amaziah king of Judah faced each
other at [b]Beth-shemesh, which belongs to Judah.
12 And Judah was defeated [1]by Israel, and [a]they fled each
to his tent.
13 Then Jehoash king of Israel captured Amaziah king of
Judah, the son of Jehoash the son of Ahaziah, at Beth-shemesh, and came to Jerusalem and tore down the wall of Jerusalem from [a]the Gate of Ephraim to [b]the Corner Gate, 400 [1]cubits.
14 And [a]he took all the gold and silver and all the utensils
which were found in the house of the LORD, and in the treasuries of the king's house, the hostages also, and returned to
Samaria.
15 [a]Now the rest of the acts of Jehoash which he did, and
his might and how he fought with Amaziah king of Judah, are
they not written in the Book of the Chronicles of the Kings of
Israel?
16 So Jehoash slept with his fathers and was buried in
Samaria with the kings of Israel; and Jeroboam his son became
king in his place.
17 [a]And Amaziah the son of Joash king of Judah lived
fifteen years after the death of Jehoash son of Jehoahaz king of
Israel.
18 Now the rest of the acts of Amaziah, are they not
written in the Book of the Chronicles of the Kings of Judah?
19 And they conspired against him in Jerusalem, and he
fled to [a]Lachish; but they sent after him to Lachish and killed
him there.
20 Then they brought him on horses and he was buried at
Jerusalem with his fathers in the city of David.
21 And all the people of Judah took [1]Azariah, who *was*
sixteen years old, and made him king in the place of his father
Amaziah.
22 [a]He built Elath and restored it to Judah, after the king
slept with his fathers.
23 In the fifteenth year of Amaziah the son of Joash king
of Judah, Jeroboam the son of Joash king of Israel became
king in Samaria, *and reigned* forty-one years.
24 And he did evil in the sight of the LORD; he did not
depart from all the sins of Jeroboam the son of Nebat, which
he made Israel sin.
25 [a]He restored the border of Israel from [b]the entrance of
Hamath as far as [c]the Sea of the Arabah, according to the word
of the LORD, the God of Israel, which He spoke [1]through His
servant [d]Jonah the son of Amittai, the prophet, who was of
[e]Gath-hepher.
26 For the [a]LORD saw the affliction of Israel, *which was*

very bitter; for [b]there was neither bound nor free, nor was
there any helper for Israel.
27 And the [a]LORD did not say that He would blot out the
name of Israel from under heaven, but He saved them by the
hand of Jeroboam the son of Joash.
28 Now the rest of the acts of Jeroboam and all that he
did and his might, how he fought and how he recovered for
Israel [a]Damascus and [b]Hamath, *which had belonged* to Judah,
are they not written in the Book of the Chronicles of the Kings
of Israel?
29 And Jeroboam slept with his fathers, even with the
kings of Israel, and Zechariah his son became king in his place.

CHAPTER 15

[a]IN the twenty-seventh year of Jeroboam king of Israel, Azariah son of Amaziah king of Judah became king.
2 He was [a]sixteen years old when he became king, and he
reigned fifty-two years in Jerusalem; and his mother's name
was [1]Jecoliah of Jerusalem.
3 And he did right in the sight of the LORD, according to
all that his father Amaziah had done.
4 Only [a]the high places were not taken away; the people
still sacrificed and burned incense on the high places.
5 [a]And the LORD struck the king, so that he was a leper to
the day of his death. And he [b]lived in a separate house, [1]while
Jotham the king's son was over the household, judging the
people of the land.
6 Now the rest of the acts of Azariah and all that he did,
are they not written in the Book of the Chronicles of the Kings
of Judah?
7 And Azariah slept with his fathers, and they buried him
with his fathers in the city of David, and Jotham his son became king in his place.
8 [a]In the thirty-eighth year of Azariah king of Judah,
Zechariah the son of Jeroboam became king over Israel in
Samaria *for* six months.
9 And he did evil in the sight of the LORD, as his fathers
had done; he did not depart from the sins of Jeroboam the son
of Nebat, which he made Israel sin.
10 Then Shallum the son of Jabesh conspired against him
and [a]struck him before the people and [1]killed him, and reigned
in his place.
11 Now the rest of the acts of Zechariah, behold they are
written in the Book of the Chronicles of the Kings of Israel.
12 This is [a]the word of the LORD which He spoke to Jehu,
saying, "Your sons to the fourth generation shall sit on the
throne of Israel." And so it was.
13 Shallum son of Jabesh became king in the [a]thirty-ninth
year of Uzziah king of Judah, and he reigned one month in
[b]Samaria.
14 Then Menahem son of Gadi went up from [a]Tirzah and
came to Samaria, and struck Shallum son of Jabesh in Samaria,
and killed him and became king in his place.
15 Now the rest of the acts of Shallum and his conspiracy

26 [b]Deut. 32:36
27 [a]2 Kin. 13:23
28 [a]1 Kin. 11:24 [b]2 Chr. 8:3
1 [a]2 Kin. 14:17
2 [1]In 2 Chr. 26:3, *Jechiliah* [a]2 Chr. 26:3, 4
4 [a]2 Kin. 12:3
5 [1]Lit., *and* [a]2 Chr. 26:21-23 [b]Lev. 13:46; Num. 12:14
8 [a]2 Kin. 15:1
10 [1]Lit., *smote* [a]Amos 7:9
12 [a]2 Kin. 10:30
13 [a]2 Kin. 15:1, 8 [b]1 Kin. 16:24
14 [a]1 Kin. 14:17

16 [a]2 Kin. 8:12

which he made, behold they are written in the Book of the
Chronicles of the Kings of Israel.
16 Then Menahem struck Tiphsah and all who were in it,
and its borders, from Tirzah, because they did not open *to
him,* therefore he struck *it;* and he ripped up [a]all its women
who were with child.

17 [a]2 Kin. 15:1, 8, 13

17 In the [a]thirty-ninth year of Azariah king of Judah, Menahem son of Gadi became king over Israel *and reigned* ten
years in Samaria.
18 And he did evil in the sight of the LORD; he did not
depart all his days from the sins of Jeroboam the son of Nebat,
which he made Israel sin.
19 [a]Pul king of Assyria came against the land, and Menahem gave Pul a thousand talents of silver so that his hand
might be with him to strengthen the kingdom [1]under his rule.

19 [1]Lit., *in his hand*
[a]1 Chr. 5:25, 26

20 Then Menahem exacted the money from Israel, even
from all the mighty men of wealth, from each man fifty shekels of silver to pay the king of Assyria. So the king of Assyria
returned and did not remain there in the land.
21 Now the rest of the acts of Menahem and all that he
did, are they not written in the Book of the Chronicles of the
Kings of Israel?
22 And Menahem slept with his fathers, and Pekahiah his
son became king in his place.

23 [a]2 Kin. 15:1, 8, 13, 17

23 In [a]the fiftieth year of Azariah king of Judah, Pekahiah
son of Menahem became king over Israel in Samaria, *and
reigned* two years.
24 And he did evil in the sight of the LORD; he did not
depart from the sins of Jeroboam son of Nebat, which he
made Israel sin.
25 Then Pekah son of Remaliah, his officer, conspired

25 [a]1 Kin. 16:18

against him and struck him in Samaria, in [a]the castle of the
king's house with Argob and Arieh; and with him were fifty
men of the Gileadites, and he killed him and became king in
his place.
26 Now the rest of the acts of Pekahiah and all that he
did, behold they are written in the Book of the Chronicles of
the Kings of Israel.
27 In [a]the fifty-second year of Azariah king of Judah, Pe-

27 [a]2 Kin. 15:23

kah son of Remaliah became king over Israel in Samaria, *and
reigned* twenty years.
28 And he did evil in the sight of the LORD; he did not
depart from the sins of Jeroboam son of Nebat, which he
made Israel sin.
29 In the days of Pekah king of Israel, [a]Tiglath-pileser king
of Assyria came and [1]captured Ijon and Abel-beth-maacah and
Janoah and Kedesh and Hazor and Gilead and Galilee, all the
land of Naphtali; and [b]he carried them captive to Assyria.

29 [1]Lit., *took*
[a]2 Kin. 15:19 [b]2 Kin. 17:6

30 And Hoshea the son of Elah made a conspiracy against
Pekah the son of Remaliah, and struck him and put him to
death and became king in his place, in the twentieth year of
Jotham the son of Uzziah.
31 Now the rest of the acts of Pekah and all that he did,
behold, they are written in the Book of the Chronicles of the
Kings of Israel.

32 In the second year of Pekah the son of Remaliah king
of Israel, Jotham the son of Uzziah king of Judah became king.
33 [a]He was twenty-five years old when he became king,
and he reigned sixteen years in Jerusalem; and his mother's
name *was* Jerusha the daughter of Zadok.
34 And [a]he did what was right in the sight of the LORD; he
did according to all that his father Uzziah had done.
35 Only [a]the high places were not taken away; the people
still sacrificed and burned incense on the high places. [b]He built
the upper gate of the house of the LORD.
36 Now the rest of the acts of Jotham and all that he did,
are they not written in the Book of the Chronicles of the Kings
of Judah?
37 In those days [a]the LORD began to send Rezin king of
Syria and Pekah the son of Remaliah against Judah.
38 And Jotham slept with his fathers, and he was buried
with his fathers in the city of David his father; and Ahaz his son
became king in his place.

CHAPTER 16

IN the seventeenth year of Pekah the son of Remaliah, Ahaz
the son of Jotham, king of Judah, became king.
2 [a]Ahaz *was* twenty years old when he became king, and
he reigned sixteen years in Jerusalem; and he did not do what
was right in the sight of the LORD his God, as his father David
had done.
3 But he walked in the way of the kings of Israel, [a]and
even made his son pass through the fire, [b]according to the
abominations of the nations, whom the LORD had [1]driven out
from before the sons of Israel.
4 And he [a]sacrificed and burned incense on the high
places and on the hills and under every green tree.
5 Then [a]Rezin king of Syria and Pekah son of Remaliah,
king of Israel, came up to Jerusalem to *wage* war; and they
besieged Ahaz, [b]but could not [1]overcome him.
6 At that time Rezin king of Syria recovered [a]Elath for
Syria, and cleared the Judeans out of [1]Elath entirely; and the
[2]Syrians came to Elath, and have lived there to this day.
7 [a]So Ahaz sent messengers to [b]Tiglath-pileser king of
Assyria, saying, "I am your servant and your son; come up and
deliver me from the [1]hand of the king of Syria, and from the
[1]hand of the king of Israel, who are rising up against me."
8 And [a]Ahaz took the silver and gold that was found in
the house of the LORD and in the treasuries of the king's house,
and sent a present to the king of Assyria.
9 [a]So the king of Assyria listened to him; and the king of
Assyria went up against Damascus and [b]captured it, and
carried *the people of* it away into exile to [c]Kir, and put Rezin
to death.
10 Now King Ahaz went to Damascus to meet [a]Tiglath-
pileser king of Assyria, and saw the altar which *was* at Damascus; and King Ahaz sent to [b]Urijah the priest the [1]pattern of
the altar and its model, according to all its workmanship.
11 So Urijah the priest built an altar; according to all that

33 [a]2 Chr. 27:1

34 [a]2 Kin. 15:3, 4; 2 Chr. 26:4, 5

35 [a]2 Kin. 12:3 [b]2 Chr. 23:20; 27:3

37 [a]2 Kin. 16:5; Is. 7:1

2 [a]2 Chr. 28:1-4

3 [1]Or, *dispossessed* [a]2 Kin. 17:17; 21:6; Lev. 18:21 [b]2 Kin. 21:2, 11; Deut. 12:31

4 [a]2 Kin. 14:4; Deut. 12:2

5 [1]Lit., *fight* [a]2 Kin. 15:37; Is. 7:1 [b]2 Chr. 28:5, 6

6 [1]Lit., *Eloth* [2]So with some ancient versions; Heb., *Edomites* [a]2 Kin. 14:22; 2 Chr. 26:2

7 [1]Lit., *palm* [a]2 Chr. 28:16 [b]2 Kin. 15:29

8 [a]2 Kin. 12:17, 18; 18:15

9 [a]2 Chr. 28:21 [b]Amos 1:3-5 [c]Is. 22:6; Amos 9:7

10 [1]Lit., *likeness* [a]2 Kin. 15:29 [b]Is. 8:2

King Ahaz had sent from Damascus, thus Urijah the priest made *it* [1]before the coming of King Ahaz from Damascus.

12 And when the king came from Damascus, the king saw the altar; then the king approached the altar and [1]went up to it,

13 and [1]burned his burnt offering and his meal offering, and poured his drink offering and sprinkled the blood of his peace offerings on the altar.

14 And [a]the bronze altar, which *was* before the LORD, [1]he brought from the front of the house, from between [b]*his* altar and the house of the LORD, and he put it on the north side of *his* altar.

15 Then King Ahaz [1]commanded Urijah the priest, saying, "Upon the great altar [2]burn [a]the morning burnt offering and the evening meal offering and the king's burnt offering and his meal offering, with the burnt offering of all the people of the land and their meal offering and their drink offerings; and sprinkle on it all the blood of the burnt offering and all the blood of the sacrifice. But [b]the bronze altar shall be for me to inquire *by*."

16 So Urijah the priest did according to all that King Ahaz commanded.

17 Then King Ahaz [a]cut off the borders of the stands, and removed the laver from them; he also [b]took down the sea from the bronze oxen which were under it, and put it on a pavement of stone.

18 And the covered way for the Sabbath which they had built in the house, and the outer entry of the king, he removed from the house of the LORD because of the king of Assyria.

19 Now the rest of the acts of Ahaz which he did, are they not written [a]in the Book of the Chronicles of the Kings of Judah?

20 So Ahaz slept with his fathers, and [a]was buried with his fathers in the city of David; and his son Hezekiah reigned in his place.

CHAPTER 17

IN the twelfth year of Ahaz king of Judah, [a]Hoshea the son of Elah became king over Israel in Samaria, *and reigned* nine years.

2 And he did evil in the sight of the LORD, only not as the kings of Israel who were before him.

3 [a]Shalmaneser king of Assyria came up [b]against him, and Hoshea became his servant and paid him tribute.

4 But the king of Assyria found conspiracy in Hoshea, who had sent messengers to So king of Egypt and had offered no tribute to the king of Assyria, as *he had done* year by year; so the king of Assyria shut him up and bound him in prison.

5 Then the king of Assyria invaded the whole land and went up to Samaria and [a]besieged it three years.

6 In the ninth year of Hoshea, [a]the king of Assyria captured Samaria and [b]carried Israel away into exile to Assyria, and [c]settled them in Halah and [1]Habor, *on* the river of [d]Gozan, and [e]in the cities of the Medes.

7 Now [a]this came about, because the sons of Israel had

11 [1]Lit., *until*

12 [1]Or, *offered on it*

13 [1]Lit., *offered in smoke*

14 [1]Lit., *he also* [a]Ex. 40:6, 29 [b]2 Kin. 16:11

15 [1]Lit., *commanded him, Urijah* [2]Lit., *offer in smoke* [a]Ex. 29:39-41 [b]2 Kin. 16:14

17 [a]1 Kin. 7:27, 28, 38 [b]1 Kin. 7:23, 25

19 [a]2 Chr. 28:26

20 [a]2 Chr. 28:27

1 [a]2 Kin. 15:30

3 [a]Hos. 10:14 [b]2 Kin. 18:9-12

5 [a]Hos. 13:16

6 [1]cf. 1 Chr. 5:26 [a]Hos. 13:16 [b]Deut. 28:64; 29:27, 28 [c]2 Kin. 18:11; 1 Chr. 5:26 [d]Is. 37:12 [e]Is. 13:17; 21:2

7 [a]Josh. 23:16

sinned against the LORD their God, [b]who had brought them up
from the land of Egypt from under the hand of Pharaoh, king
of Egypt, [c]and they had [1]feared other gods
8 and [a]walked in the [1]customs of the nations whom the
LORD had driven out before the sons of Israel, and *in the*
customs [b]of the kings of Israel which they had [2]introduced.
9 And the sons of Israel [1]did things secretly which were
not right, against the LORD their God. Moreover, they built for
themselves high places in all their towns, from [a]watchtower to
fortified city.
10 And [a]they set for themselves *sacred* pillars and [1b]Asher-
im on every high hill and under every green tree,
11 and there they burned incense on all the high places as
the nations did which the LORD had carried away to exile
before them; and they did evil things provoking the LORD.
12 And they served idols, [a]concerning which the LORD had
said to them, "You shall not do this thing."
13 Yet the [a]LORD warned Israel and Judah, [b]through all
His prophets *and* [c]every seer, saying, "[d]Turn from your evil
ways and keep My commandments, My statutes according to
all the law which I commanded your fathers, and which I sent
to you through My servants the prophets."
14 However, they did not listen, but [a]stiffened their neck
[1]like their fathers, who did not believe in the LORD their God.
15 And [a]they rejected His statutes and [b]His covenant
which He made with their fathers, and His warnings with
which He warned them. And [c]they followed vanity and [d]be-
came vain, and *went* after the nations which surrounded them,
concerning which the [e]LORD had commanded them not to do
like them.
16 And they forsook all the commandments of the LORD
their God and made for themselves molten images, *even* [a]two
calves, and [b]made an [1]Asherah and [c]worshiped all the host of
heaven and [d]served Baal.
17 Then [a]they made their sons and their daughters pass
through the fire, and [b]practiced divination and enchantments,
and [c]sold themselves to do evil in the sight of the LORD, provoking Him.
18 So the LORD was very angry with Israel, and [a]removed
them from His [1]sight; [b]none was left except the tribe of Judah.
19 Also [a]Judah did not keep the commandments of the
LORD their God, but [b]walked in the [1]customs [2]which Israel had
[3]introduced.
20 And the LORD rejected all the [1]descendants of Israel
and afflicted them and [a]gave them into the hand of plunderers, until He had cast them [2]out of His sight.
21 When [a]He had torn Israel from the house of David,
[b]they made Jeroboam the son of Nebat king. Then [c]Jeroboam
drove Israel away from following the LORD, and made them
[1]commit a great sin.
22 And the sons of Israel walked in all the sins of Jeroboam which he did; they did not depart from them,
23 [a]until the LORD removed Israel from His sight, [b]as He
spoke through all His servants the prophets. [c]So Israel was
carried away into exile from their own land to Assyria until this
day.

7 [1]Lit., *revered*, and so throughout the chap. [b]Ex. 14:15-30 [c]Judg. 6:10

8 [1]Lit., *statutes* [2]Lit., *made* [a]Lev. 18:3; Deut. 18:9 [b]2 Kin. 17:19; 16:3

9 [1]Or, *uttered words which* [a]2 Kin. 18:8

10 [1]I.e., wooden symbols of a female deity [a]Ex. 34:12-14 [b]1 Kin. 14:23; Mic. 5:14

12 [a]Ex. 20:4

13 [a]Neh. 9:29, 30 [b]2 Kin. 17:23 [c]1 Sam. 9:9 [d]Jer. 7:3-7; 18:11; Ezek. 18:31

14 [1]Lit., *like the neck of* [a]Ex. 32:9; 33:3; Acts 7:51

15 [a]Jer. 8:9 [b]Ex. 24:6-8; Deut. 29:25 [c]Deut. 32:21 [d]Jer. 2:5; Rom. 1:21-23 [e]Deut. 12:30, 31

16 [1]I.e., a wooden symbol of a female deity [a]1 Kin. 12:28 [b]1 Kin. 14:15, 23 [c]2 Kin. 21:3; Deut. 4:15, 19 [d]1 Kin. 16:31

17 [a]2 Kin. 16:3 [b]Lev. 19:26; Deut. 18:10-12 [c]1 Kin. 21:20

18 [1]Lit., *face* [a]2 Kin. 17:6 [b]1 Kin. 11:13, 32, 36

19 [1]Lit., *statutes* [2]Lit., *of Israel which they* [3]Lit., *made* [a]1 Kin. 14:22, 23 [b]2 Kin. 16:3

20 [1]Lit., *seed* [2]Lit., *from His face* [a]2 Kin. 15:29

21 [1]Lit., *sin* [a]1 Kin. 11:11, 31 [b]1 Kin. 12:20 [c]1 Kin. 12:28-33

23 [a]2 Kin. 17:6 [b]2 Kin. 17:13 [c]2 Kin. 17:6

24 [a]Ezra 4:2, 10 [b]2 Kin. 18:34 [c]1 Kin. 8:65
27 [1]Lit., *exile from there* [2]Lit., *them*
29 [a]1 Kin. 12:31; 13:32
30 [a]2 Kin. 17:24
31 [a]2 Kin. 17:17 [b]2 Kin. 19:37 [c]2 Kin. 17:24
32 [1]Lit., *made for themselves from among* [a]Zeph. 1:5 [b]1 Kin. 12:31
34 [1]Lit., *do according to* [a]Gen. 32:28; 35:10
35 [a]Judg. 6:10 [b]Ex. 20:5
36 [a]Ex. 14:15-30 [b]Ex. 6:6; 9:15 [c]Lev. 19:32; Deut. 6:13
37 [a]Deut. 5:32
38 [a]Deut. 4:23; 6:12

24 [a]And the king of Assyria brought *men* from Babylon
and from Cuthah and from [b]Avva and from [c]Hamath and
Sephar-vaim, and settled *them* in the cities of Samaria in place
of the sons of Israel. So they possessed Samaria and lived in its
cities.
25 And it came about at the beginning of their living
there, that they did not fear the LORD; therefore the LORD sent
lions among them which killed some of them.
26 So they spoke to the king of Assyria, saying, "The nations whom you have carried away into exile in the cities of
Samaria do not know the custom of the god of the land; so He
has sent lions among them, and behold, they kill them because
they do not know the custom of the god of the land."
27 Then the king of Assyria commanded, saying, "Take
there one of the priests whom you carried away into [1]exile, and
let [2]him go and live there; and let him teach them the custom
of the god of the land."
28 So one of the priests whom they had carried away into
exile from Samaria came and lived at Bethel, and taught them
how they should fear the LORD.
29 But every nation still made gods of its own and put
them [a]in the houses of the high places which the people of
Samaria had made, every nation in their cities in which they
lived.
30 And [a]the men of Babylon made Succoth-benoth, the
men of Cuth made Nergal, the men of Hamath made Ashima,
31 and the Avvites made Nibhaz and Tartak; and [a]the
Sepharvites burned their children in the fire to [b]Adram-melech
and Anammelech, the gods of [c]Sepharvaim.
32 [a]They also feared the LORD and [1b]appointed from
among themselves priests of the high places, who acted for
them in the houses of the high places.
33 They feared the LORD and served their own gods according to the custom of the nations from among whom they had
been carried away into exile.
34 To this day they do according to the earlier customs:
they do not fear the LORD, nor do they [1]follow their statutes or
their ordinances or the law, or the commandments which the
LORD commanded the sons of Jacob, [a]whom He named Israel;
35 with whom the LORD made a covenant and commanded them, saying, "[a]You shall not fear other gods, nor
[b]bow down yourselves to them nor serve them nor sacrifice to
them.
36 "But the LORD, [a]who brought you up from the land of
Egypt with great power and with [b]an outstretched arm, [c]Him
you shall fear, and to Him you shall bow yourselves down, and
to Him you shall sacrifice.
37 "And the statutes and the ordinances and the law and
the commandment, which He wrote for you, [a]you shall observe to do forever; and you shall not fear other gods.
38 "And the covenant that I have made with you, [a]you shall
not forget, nor shall you fear other gods.
39 "But the LORD your God you shall fear; and He will
deliver you from the hand of all your enemies."
40 However, they did not listen, but they did according to
their earlier custom.

41 [a]So while these nations feared the LORD, they also
served their [1]idols; their children likewise and their grandchildren, as their fathers did, so they do to this day.

CHAPTER 18

NOW it came about [a]in the third year of Hoshea, the son of
Elah king of Israel, that [b]Hezekiah the son of Ahaz king of
Judah became king.
2 He was [a]twenty-five years old when he became king,
and he reigned twenty-nine years in Jerusalem; and his mother's name was Abi the daughter of Zechariah.
3 [a]And he did right in the sight of the LORD, according to
all that his father David had done.
4 [a]He removed the high places and broke down the
sacred pillars and cut down the [1]Asherah. He also broke in
pieces [b]the bronze serpent that Moses had made, for until
those days the sons of Israel burned incense to it; and it was
called [2]Nehushtan.
5 [a]He trusted in the LORD, the God of Israel; [b]so that
after him there was none like him among all the kings of
Judah, nor *among those* who were before him.
6 For he clung to the LORD; he did not depart from
following Him, but kept His commandments, which the LORD
had commanded Moses.
7 [a]And the LORD was with him; wherever he went he
prospered. And [b]he rebelled against the king of Assyria and did
not serve him.
8 [a]He [1]defeated the Philistines as far as Gaza and its
territory, from [b]watchtower to fortified city.
9 Now it came about in the fourth year of King Hezekiah, which was the seventh year of Hoshea son of Elah king of
Israel, that [a]Shalmaneser king of Assyria came up against Samaria and besieged it.
10 And at the end of three years they captured it; in the
sixth year of Hezekiah, which was the ninth year of Hoshea
king of Israel, Samaria was captured.
11 Then the king of Assyria carried Israel away into exile
to Assyria, and put them in Halah and on the Habor, the river
of Gozan, and in the cities of the Medes,
12 because they did not obey the voice of the LORD their
God, but transgressed His covenant, even all that Moses the
servant of the LORD commanded; they would neither listen,
nor do *it*.
13 [a]Now in the fourteenth year of King Hezekiah, Sennacherib king of Assyria came up against all the fortified cities
of Judah and seized them.
14 Then Hezekiah king of Judah sent to the king of Assyria at Lachish, saying, "[a]I have done wrong. [1]Withdraw from
me; whatever you [2]impose on me I will bear." So the king of
Assyria [3]required of Hezekiah king of Judah three hundred
talents of silver and thirty talents of gold.
15 And [a]Hezekiah gave *him* all the silver which was found
in the house of the LORD, and in the treasuries of the king's
house.
16 At that time Hezekiah cut off *the gold from* the doors

41 [1]Or, *graven images*
[a]Zeph. 1:5; Matt. 6:24

1 [a]2 Kin. 16:2; 17:1 [b]2 Chr. 28:27

2 [a]2 Chr. 29:1, 2

3 [a]2 Kin. 20:3; 2 Chr. 31:20

4 [1]I.e., a wooden symbol of a female deity [2]I.e., a piece of bronze
[a]2 Kin. 18:22; 2 Chr. 31:1
[b]Num. 21:8, 9

5 [a]2 Kin. 19:10 [b]2 Kin. 23:25

7 [a]Gen. 39:2, 3; 1 Sam. 18:14 [b]2 Kin. 16:7

8 [1]Lit., *smote*
[a]2 Chr. 28:18; Is. 14:29
[b]2 Kin. 17:9

9 [a]2 Kin. 17:3-7

13 [a]Is. 36:1-39: 8; 2 Chr. 32:1

14 [1]Lit., *Return* [2]Lit., *give* [3]Lit., *put on*
[a]2 Kin. 18:7

15 [a]2 Kin. 12:18; 16:8; 1 Kin. 15:18, 19

of the temple of the LORD, and *from* the doorposts which
Hezekiah king of Judah had overlaid, and gave it to the king of
Assyria.
17 Then the king of Assyria sent [a]Tartan and Rab-saris
and Rabshakeh from Lachish to king Hezekiah with a large
army to Jerusalem. So they went up and came to Jerusalem.
And when they went up, they came and stood by the [b]conduit
of the upper pool, which is on the highway of the [1]fuller's
field.
18 When they called to the king, [a]Eliakim the son of Hilkiah, who was over the household, and [b]Shebnah the scribe
and Joah the son of Asaph the recorder, came out to them.
19 Then Rabshakeh said to them, "Say now to Hezekiah,
'Thus says the great king, the king of Assyria, "What is this
confidence that you [1]have?
20 "You say (but *they are* [1]only empty words), '*I have*
counsel and strength for the war.' Now on whom do you rely,
[a]that you have rebelled against me?
21 "Now behold, you [1a]rely on the staff of this crushed
reed, *even* on Egypt; on which if a man leans, it will go into his
[2]hand and pierce it. So is Pharaoh king of Egypt to all who rely
on him.
22 "But if you say to me, 'We trust in the LORD our God,' is
it not He whose high places and [a]whose altars Hezekiah has
taken away, and has said to Judah and to Jerusalem, 'You shall
worship before this altar in Jerusalem'?
23 "Now therefore, [1]come, make a bargain with my master
the king of Assyria, and I will give you two thousand horses, if
you are able on your part to set riders on them.
24 "How then can you [1]repulse one [2]official of the least of
my master's servants, and [3]rely on Egypt for chariots and for
horsemen?
25 "Have I now come up [1]without the LORD's approval
against this place to destroy it? The LORD said to me, 'Go up
against this land and destroy it.' " ' "
26 Then Eliakim the son of Hilkiah and Shebnah and
Joah, said to Rabshakeh, "Speak now to your servants in Aramaic, for we [1]understand *it;* and do not speak with us in [2a]Ju-
dean, in the hearing of the people who are on the wall."
27 But Rabshakeh said to them, "Has my master sent me
only to your master and to you to speak these words, *and* not
to the men who sit on the wall, *doomed* to eat their own dung
and drink their own urine with you?"
28 Then Rabshakeh stood and cried with a loud voice in
Judean, [1]saying, "Hear the word of the great king, the king of
Assyria.
29 "Thus says the king, 'Do not let Hezekiah deceive you,
for he will not be able to deliver you from [1]my hand;
30 nor let Hezekiah make you trust in the LORD, saying,
"The LORD will surely deliver us, and this city shall not be
given into the hand of the king of Assyria."
31 'Do not listen to Hezekiah, for thus says the king of
Assyria, "[1]Make your peace with me and come out to me, and
eat [a]each of his vine and each of his fig tree and drink each of
the waters of his own cistern,
32 until I come and take you away [a]to a land like your own

17 [1]I.e., launderer's [a]Is. 20:1 [b]2 Kin. 20:20; Is. 7:3

18 [a]2 Kin. 19:2; Is. 22:20 [b]Is. 22:15

19 [1]Lit., *trust*

20 [1]Lit., *a word of the lips* [a]2 Kin. 18:7

21 [1]Lit., *rely for yourself* [2]Lit., *palm* [a]Is. 30:2, 3, 7; Ezek. 29:6, 7

22 [a]2 Kin. 18:4; 2 Chr. 31:1

23 [1]Lit., *please exchange pledges*

24 [1]Lit., *turn away the face of* [2]Or, *governor* [3]Lit., *rely for yourself*

25 [1]Lit., *without the LORD*

26 [1]Lit., *hear* [2]I.e., Hebrew [a]Ezra 4:7; Dan. 2:4

28 [1]Lit., *and spoke, saying,*

29 [1]Heb., *his*

31 [1]Lit., *Make with me a blessing* [a]1 Kin. 4:20, 25

32 [a]Deut. 8:7-9; 11:12

land, a land of grain and new wine, a land of bread and vineyards, a land of olive trees and honey, that you may live and
not die." But do not listen to Hezekiah, when he misleads you,
saying, "The LORD will deliver us."
33 '[a]Has any one of the gods of the nations delivered his
land from the hand of the king of Assyria?
34 '[a]Where are the gods of Hamath and [b]Arpad? Where
are the gods of Sepharvaim, Hena and [c]Ivvah? Have they delivered Samaria from my hand?
35 'Who among all the gods of the lands [1]have delivered
their land from my hand, that the LORD should deliver Jerusalem from my hand?' "
36 But the people were silent and answered him not a
word, for the king's commandment was, "Do not answer him."
37 Then [a]Eliakim the son of Hilkiah, who was over the
household, and Shebna the scribe and Joah the son of Asaph,
the recorder, came to Hezekiah [b]with their clothes torn and
told him the words of Rabshakeh.

CHAPTER 19

[a]

AND when King Hezekiah heard *it*, he [b]tore his clothes,
[c]covered himself with sackcloth and entered the house of the
LORD.
2 Then he sent Eliakim who was over the household with
Shebna the scribe and the elders of the priests, [a]covered with
sackcloth, to [b]Isaiah the prophet the son of Amoz.
3 And they said to him, "Thus says Hezekiah, 'This day is
a day of distress, rebuke, and rejection; for children have come
to birth, and there is no strength to [1]*deliver*.
4 '[a]Perhaps the LORD your God will hear all the words of
Rabshakeh, whom his master the king of Assyria has sent [b]to
reproach the living God, and will rebuke the words which the
LORD your God has heard. Therefore, offer a prayer for [c]the
remnant that is left.' "
5 So the servants of King Hezekiah came to Isaiah.
6 And Isaiah said to them, "Thus you shall say to your
master, 'Thus says the LORD, "Do not be afraid because of the
words that you have heard, with which the [a]servants of the king
of Assyria [b]have blasphemed Me.
7 "Behold, I will put a spirit in him so that [a]he shall hear a
rumor and return to his own land. And [b]I will make him fall by
the sword in his own land." ' "
8 Then Rabshakeh returned and found the king of Assyria fighting against [a]Libnah, for he had heard that [1]the king
had left [b]Lachish.
9 When he heard *them* say concerning Tirhakah king of
[1]Cush, "Behold, he has come out to fight against you," he sent
messengers again to Hezekiah saying,
10 "Thus you shall say to Hezekiah king of [1]Judah, 'Do not
[a]let your God in whom you trust deceive you saying, "[b]Jerusa-
lem shall not be given into the hand of the king of Assyria."
11 'Behold, you have heard what the kings of Assyria have
done to all the lands, destroying them completely. So will you
be [1]spared?
12 '[a]Did the gods of [1]those nations which my fathers

33 [a]2 Kin. 19:12; Is. 10:10, 11

34 [a]2 Kin. 19:13 [b]Is. 10:9 [c]2 Kin. 17:24

35 [1]Lit., *who have*

37 [a]2 Kin. 18:26 [b]2 Kin. 6:30

1 [a]2 Chr. 32:20-22 Is. 37:1-38 [b]2 Kin. 18:37 [c]1 Kin. 21:27

2 [a]2 Sam. 3:31 [b]Is. 1:1; 2:1

3 [1]Lit., *give birth*

4 [a]Josh. 14:12; 2 Sam. 16:12 [b]2 Kin. 18:35 [c]Is. 1:9

6 [a]2 Kin. 18:17 [b]2 Kin. 18:22-25; 30:35

7 [a]2 Kin. 7:6 [b]2 Kin. 19:37

8 [1]Lit., *he*
[a]Josh. 10:29 [b]2 Kin. 18:14

9 [1]Or, *Ethiopia*

10 [1]Lit., *Judah, saying,*
[a]2 Kin. 18:5 [b]2 Kin. 18:30

11 [1]Lit., *delivered*

12 [1]Lit., *the*
[a]2 Kin. 18:33

destroyed deliver them, *even* [b]Gozan and [c]Haran and Rezeph
and [d]the sons of Eden who *were* in Telassar?
13 '[a]Where is the king of Hamath, the king of Arpad, the
king of the city of Sepharvaim, and *of* Hena and Ivvah?' "
14 Then [a]Hezekiah took the [1]letter from the hand of the
messengers and read it, and he went up to the house of the
LORD and [2]spread it out before the LORD.
15 And Hezekiah prayed before the LORD and said, "O
LORD the God of Israel, [a]who art [1]enthroned *above* the cherubim, [b]Thou art the God, Thou alone, of all the kingdoms of
the earth. Thou hast made heaven and earth.
16 "[a]Incline Thine ear, O LORD, and hear; [b]open Thine
eyes, O LORD, and see; and listen to the words of Sennacherib,
which he has sent [c]to reproach the living God.
17 "Truly, O LORD, the kings of Assyria have devastated the
nations and their lands
18 and have cast their gods into the fire, [a]for they were not
gods but the work of men's hands, wood and stone. So they
have destroyed them.
19 "And now, O LORD our God, I pray deliver us from his
hand [a]that all the kingdoms of the earth may know that Thou
alone, O [b]LORD, art God."
20 Then Isaiah the son of Amoz sent to Hezekiah saying,
"Thus says the LORD, the God of Israel, 'Because you have
prayed to Me about Sennacherib king of Assyria, [a]I have heard
you.'
21 "This is the word that the LORD has spoken against him:
'She has despised you and mocked you,
[a]The virgin daughter of Zion;
She [b]has shaken *her* head behind you,
The daughter of Jerusalem!
22 'Whom have you [a]reproached and [b]blasphemed?
And against whom have you raised *your* voice,
And [1]haughtily lifted up your eyes?
Against the [c]Holy One of Israel!
23 '[a]Through your messengers you have reproached the
Lord,
And you have said, "With my many chariots
I came up to the heights of the mountains,
To the remotest parts of Lebanon;
And I [1]cut down its tall cedars *and* its choice
cypresses.
And I [1]entered its farthest lodging place, its [b]thickest
forest.
24 "I dug *wells* and drank foreign waters,
And with the sole of my feet I [1a]dried up
All the rivers of [2]Egypt."

25 '[a]Have you not heard?
Long ago I did it;
From ancient times I planned it.
[b]Now I have brought it to pass,
That you should turn fortified cities into ruinous
heaps.
26 'Therefore their inhabitants were short of strength,

12 [b]2 Kin. 17:6 [c]Gen. 11:31 [d]Is. 37:12

13 [a]2 Kin. 18:34

14 [1]Lit., *letters. . . .read them* [2]Lit., *Hezekiah spread* [a]Is. 37:14

15 [1]Lit., *seated* [a]Is. 37:14 [b]2 Kin. 5:15

16 [a]Ps. 31:2; Is. 37:17 [b]1 Kin. 8:29; 2 Chr. 6:40 [c]2 Kin. 19:4

18 [a]Is. 44:9-20; Acts 17:29

19 [a]1 Kin. 8:42, 43 [b]2 Kin. 19:15

20 [a]2 Kin. 20:5

21 [a]Jer. 14:17; Lam. 2:13 [b]Ps. 109:25; Matt. 27:39

22 [1]Lit., *on high* [a]2 Kin. 19:4 [b]2 Kin. 19:6 [c]Is. 5:24; 30:11-15

23 [1]So with some ancient versions, M.T., *will cut. . .will enter* [a]2 Kin. 18:17 [b]2 Chr. 26:10; Is. 10:18

24 [1]So with some ancient versions, M.T., *will dry up* [2]Lit., *the besieged place* [a]Is. 19:6

25 [a]Is. 45:7 [b]Is. 10:5

They were dismayed and put to shame;
They were [a]as the vegetation of the field and as the
green herb.
As grass on the housetops is scorched before it is
grown up.
27 'But I know your sitting down,
And your going out and your coming in,
And your raging against Me.
28 'Because of your raging against Me,
And because your [1]arrogance has come up to My
ears.
Therefore I [a]will put My hook in your nose,
And My bridle in your lips,
And [b]I will turn you back by the way which you
came.
29 'Then this shall be [a]the sign for you: [1]you shall eat this
year what grows of itself, in the second year what springs from
the same, and in the third year sow, reap, plant vineyards, and
eat their fruit.
30 '[a]And the surviving remnant of the house of Judah shall
again take root downward and bear fruit upward.
31 'For out of Jerusalem shall go forth a remnant, and [a]out
of Mount Zion [1]survivors. [b]The zeal of [2]the LORD shall perform this.
32 'Therefore thus says the LORD concerning the king of
Assyria, [a]He shall not come to this city or shoot an arrow
there; neither shall he come before it with a shield, nor throw
up a mound against it.
33 '[a]By the way that he came, by the same he shall return,
and he shall not come to this city,' declares the LORD.
34 '[a]For I will defend this city to save it for My own sake
and [b]for My servant David's sake.' "
35 [a]Then it happened that night that [b]the angel of the
LORD went out, and struck 185,000 in the camp of the Assyrians; and when [1]men rose early in the morning, behold, all of
them were dead bodies.
36 So [a]Sennacherib king of Assyria departed and returned
home, and lived at [b]Nineveh.
37 And it came about as he was worshiping in the house of
Nisroch his god, that [1a]Adrammelech and Sharezer killed him
with the sword; and they escaped into [b]the land of Ararat. And
[c]Esarhaddon his son became king in his place.

CHAPTER 20

[a]IN those days Hezekiah became [1]mortally ill. And Isaiah the
prophet the son of Amoz came to him and said to him, "Thus
says the LORD, '[b]Set your house in order, for you shall die and
not live.' "
2 Then he turned his face to the wall, and prayed to the
LORD, saying,
3 "[a]Remember now, O LORD, I beseech Thee, [b]how I have
walked before Thee in truth and with a whole heart, and have
done what is good in Thy sight." And [c]Hezekiah wept
[1]bitterly.
4 And it came about before Isaiah had gone out of the
middle court, that the word of the LORD came to him, saying,

26 [a]Ps. 129:6

28 [1]Lit., *complacency* [a]Ezek. 19:9; 29:4 [b]2 Kin. 19:33, 36

29 [1]Lit., *eating* [a]2 Kin. 20:8, 9; Ex. 3:12

30 [a]2 Kin. 19:4; 2 Chr. 32:22, 23

31 [1]Lit., *those who escape* [2]Some ancient mss. read; *the LORD of hosts* [a]Is. 10:20 [b]Is. 9:7

32 [a]Is. 8:7-10

33 [a]2 Kin. 19:28

34 [a]2 Kin. 20:6; Is. 31:5 [b]1 Kin. 11:12, 13

35 [1]Lit., *they* [a]2 Chr. 32:21 [b]2 Sam. 24:16

36 [a]2 Kin. 19:7, 28, 33 [b]Jon. 1:2

37 [1]Some ancient mss. read, *Adrammelech and Sharezer his sons smote him* [a]2 Kin. 19:17, 31 [b]Gen. 8:4; Jer. 51:27 [c]Ezra 4:2

1 [1]Lit., *sick to the point of death* [a]2 Chr. 32:24; Is. 38:1-22 [b]2 Sam. 17:23

3 [1]Lit., *great weeping* [a]Neh. 5:19; 13:14, 22, 31 [b]2 Kin. 18:3-6 [c]2 Sam. 12:21, 22

5 "Return and say to [a]Hezekiah the leader of My people,
'Thus says the LORD, the God of your father David, "[b]I have
heard your prayer, [c]I have seen your tears; behold, I will heal
you. On the third day you shall go up to the house of the
LORD.
6 "And I will add fifteen years to your [1]life, and I will
deliver you and this city from the hand of the king of Assyria;
and [a]I will defend this city for My own sake and for My servant
David's sake." ' "
7 Then Isaiah said, "Take a cake of figs." And they took
and laid *it* on the boil, and he recovered.
8 Now Hezekiah said to Isaiah, "What will be the sign
that the LORD will heal me, and that I shall go up to the house
of the LORD the third day?"
9 And Isaiah said, "This shall be the sign to you from the
LORD, that the LORD will do the thing that He has spoken: shall
the shadow go forward ten steps or go back ten steps?"
10 So Hezekiah [1]answered, "It is easy for the shadow to
decline ten steps; no, but let the shadow turn backward ten
steps."
11 And Isaiah the prophet cried to the LORD, and [a]He
brought the shadow on the [1]stairway back ten steps by which it
had gone down on the [1]stairway of Ahaz.
12 [a]At that time [1]Berodach-baladan a son of Baladan, king
of Babylon, sent letters and a present to Hezekiah, for he
heard that Hezekiah had been sick.
13 And Hezekiah listened to them, and showed them [a]all
his treasure house, the silver and the gold and the spices and
the precious oil and the house of his armor and all that was
found in his treasuries. There was nothing in his house, nor in
all his dominion, that Hezekiah did not show them.
14 Then Isaiah the prophet came to King Hezekiah and
said to him, "What did these men say, and from where have
they come to you?" And Hezekiah said, "They have come
from a far country, from Babylon."
15 And he said, "What have they seen in your house?" So
Hezekiah [1]answered, "They have seen all that is in my house;
there is nothing among my treasuries that I have not shown
them."
16 Then Isaiah said to Hezekiah, "Hear the word of the
LORD.
17 'Behold, the days are coming when [a]all that is in your
house, and all that your fathers have laid up in store to this day
shall be carried to Babylon; nothing shall be left,' says the
LORD.
18 'And some [a]of your sons who shall issue from you,
whom you shall beget, shall be taken away; and they shall
become [b]officials in the palace of the king of Babylon.' "
19 Then Hezekiah said to Isaiah, "The word of the LORD
which you have spoken is [a]good." For he [1]thought, "Is it not
so, if there shall be peace and truth in my days?"
20 [a]Now the rest of the acts of Hezekiah and all his might,
and how he made the pool and the conduit, and brought water
into the city, are they not written in the Book of the Chronicles of the Kings of Judah?

5 [a]1 Sam. 9:16; 10:1 [b]2 Kin. 19:20 [c]Ps. 39:12
6 [1]Lit., *days* [a]2 Kin. 19:34
10 [1]Lit., *said*
11 [1]Lit., *steps* [a]Josh. 10:12-14
12 [1]Many mss. and ancient versions read, *Merodach-baladan;* cf. Is. 39:1 [a]2 Chr. 32:31; Is. 39:1-8
13 [a]2 Chr. 32:27
15 [1]Lit., *said*
17 [a]2 Kin. 24:13; 25:13-15; Jer. 52:17-19
18 [a]2 Kin. 24:12; 2 Chr. 33:11 [b]Dan. 1:3-7
19 [1]Lit., *said* [a]1 Sam. 3:18
20 [a]2 Chr. 32:32

21 [a]So Hezekiah slept with his fathers, and Manasseh his
son became king in his place.

Chapter 21

[a]MANASSEH was twelve years old when he became king,
and he reigned fifty-five years in Jerusalem; and his mother's
name was Hephzibah.
2 And he did evil in the sight of the LORD, [a]according to
the abominations of the nations whom the LORD dispossessed
before the sons of Israel.
3 For [a]he rebuilt the high places which Hezekiah his father
had destroyed; and [b]he erected altars for Baal and made an
[1]Asherah, as Ahab king of Israel had done, and [c]worshiped all
the host of heaven and served them.
4 And [a]he built altars in the house of the LORD, of which
the LORD had said, "[b]In Jerusalem I will put My name."
5 For he built altars for [a]all the host of heaven in [b]the
two courts of the house of the LORD.
6 And [a]he made his son pass through the fire, [b]practised
witchcraft and used divination, and dealt with mediums and
spiritists. He did much evil in the sight of the LORD provoking
Him to anger.
7 Then [a]he set the carved image of Asherah that he had
made, in the house of which the LORD said to David and to his
son Solomon, "[b]In this house and in Jerusalem, which I have
chosen from all the tribes of Israel, I will put My name forever.
8 "And I [a]will not make the feet of Israel wander any more
from the land which I gave their fathers, if only they will
observe to do according to all that I have commanded them,
and according to all the law that My servant Moses commanded them."
9 But they did not listen, and Manasseh seduced them to
do evil more than the nations whom the LORD destroyed before the sons of Israel.
10 Now the LORD spoke through His servants the prophets, saying,
11 "[a]Because Manasseh king of Judah has done these abominations, [b]having done wickedly more than all the Amorites
did who *were* before him, and [c]has also made Judah sin [d]with
his idols;
12 therefore thus says the LORD, the God of Israel, 'Behold, I am bringing *such* calamity on Jerusalem and Judah,
that whoever hears of it, [a]both his ears shall tingle.
13 '[a]And I will stretch over Jerusalem the line of Samaria
and the plummet of the house of Ahab, and I will wipe Jerusalem as one wipes a dish, wiping it and turning it upside down.
14 'And I will abandon the remnant of My inheritance and
deliver them into the hand of their enemies, and they shall
become as plunder and spoil to all their enemies;
15 because they have done evil in My sight, and have been
provoking Me to anger, since the day their fathers came from
Egypt, even to this day.' "
16 [a]Moreover, Manasseh shed very much innocent blood
until he had filled Jerusalem from one end to another; besides

21 [a]2 Chr. 32:33

1 [a]2 Chr. 33:1-9

2 [a]2 Kin. 16:3

3 [1]I.e., a wooden symbol of a female deity. [a]2 Kin. 18:4 [b]1 Kin. 16:31-33 [c]2 Kin. 17:16; 23:5; Deut. 17:2-5

4 [a]2 Kin. 16:10-16 [b]1 Kin. 8:29

5 [a]2 Kin. 23:4, 5 [b]2 Kin. 23:12; 1 Kin. 7:12

6 [a]2 Kin. 16:3; 17:17; Lev. 18:21 [b]Lev. 19:26, 31; Deut. 18:10-14

7 [a]2 Kin. 23:6; Deut. 16:21 [b]1 Kin. 8:29; 9:3

8 [a]2 Kin. 18:11, 12; 2 Sam. 7:10

11 [a]2 Kin. 21:2; 24: 3, 4 [b]Gen. 15:16; 1 Kin. 21:26 [c]2 Kin. 21:16 [d]2 Kin. 21:21

12 [a]1 Sam. 3:11; Jer. 19:3

13 [a]Is. 34:11; Amos 7:7, 8

16 [a]2 Kin. 24:4

16 [b]2 Kin. 21:11

his sin [b]with which he made Judah sin, in doing evil in the sight of the LORD.

17 [1]Lit., *sinned* [a]2 Chr. 33:11-19

17 [a]Now the rest of the acts of Manasseh and all that he did and his sin which he [1]committed, are they not written in the Book of the Chronicles of the Kings of Judah?

18 [a]2 Chr. 33:20 [b]2 Kin. 21:26

18 [a]And Manasseh slept with his fathers and was buried in the garden of his own house, [b]in the garden of Uzza, and Amon his son became king in his place.

19 Amon was twenty-two years old when he became king, and he reigned two years in Jerusalem; and his mother's name *was* Meshullemeth the daughter of Haruz of Jotbah.

20 [a]2 Kin. 21:2-6, 11, 16

20 And he did evil in the sight of the LORD, [a]as Manasseh his father had done.

21 For he walked in all the way that his father had walked, and served the idols that his father had served and worshiped them.

22 [a]2 Kin. 22:17; 1 Chr. 28:9

22 So [a]he forsook the LORD, the God of his fathers, and did not walk in the way of the LORD.

23 [a]2 Kin. 12:20; 14:19

23 And [a]the servants of Amon conspired against him and killed the king in his own house.

24 [1]Lit., *smote* [a]2 Kin. 14:5

24 Then [a]the people of the land [1]killed all those who had conspired against King Amon, and the people of the land made Josiah his son king in his place.

25 Now the rest of the acts of Amon which he did, are they not written in the Book of the Chronicles of the Kings of Judah?

26 [a]2 Kin. 21:18

26 And he was buried in his grave [a]in the garden of Uzza, and Josiah his son became king in his place.

CHAPTER 22

1 [a]2 Chr. 34:1 [b]Josh. 15:39

[a]JOSIAH was eight years old when he became king, and he reigned thirty-one years in Jerusalem; and his mother's name *was* Jedidah the daughter of Adaiah of [b]Bozkath.

2 [a]Deut. 5:32; Josh. 1:7

2 And he did right in the sight of the LORD and walked in all the way of his father David, nor did he [a]turn aside to the right or to the left.

3 Now it came about in the eighteenth year of King Josiah that the king sent Shaphan, the son of Azaliah the son of Meshullam the scribe, to the house of the LORD saying,

4 [1]Or, *total* [a]2 Kin. 12:4, 9, 10

4 "[a]Go up to Hilkiah the high priest that he may [1]count the money brought in to the house of the LORD which the doorkeepers have gathered from the people.

5 [1]Lit., *breach* [a]2 Kin. 12:11-14

5 "[a]And let them deliver it into the hand of the workmen who have the oversight of the house of the LORD, and let them give it to the workmen who are in the house of the LORD to repair the [1]damages of the house,

6 to the carpenters and the builders and the masons and for buying timber and hewn stone to repair the house.

7 [a]2 Kin. 12:15

7 "Only [a]no accounting shall be made with them for the money delivered into their hands, for they deal faithfully."

8 [a]Deut. 31:24-26; 2 Chr. 34:14, 15

8 Then Hilkiah the high priest said to Shaphan the scribe, "[a]I have found the book of the law in the house of the LORD." And Hilkiah gave the book to Shaphan who read it.

9 And Shaphan the scribe came to the king and brought back word to the king and said, "Your servants have emptied

out the money that was found in the house, and have delivered
it into the hand of the workmen who have the oversight of the
house of the LORD."
10 Moreover, Shaphan the scribe told the king saying,
"Hilkiah the priest has given me a book." And Shaphan read it
in the presence of the king.
11 And it came about when the king heard the words of
the book of the law, that [a]he tore his clothes.
12 Then the king commanded Hilkiah the priest, [a]Ahikam
the son of Shaphan, [1b]Achbor the son of Micaiah, Shaphan the
scribe, and Asaiah the king's servant saying,
13 "Go, inquire of the LORD for me and the people and all
Judah concerning the words of this book that has been found,
for [a]great is the wrath of the LORD that burns against us, because our fathers have not listened to the words of this book,
to do according to all that is written concerning us."
14 So Hilkiah the priest, Ahikam, Achbor, Shaphan, and
Asaiah went to Huldah the prophetess, the wife of Shallum the
son of [1a]Tikvah, the son of Harhas, keeper of the wardrobe
(now she lived in Jerusalem in the [b]Second Quarter); and they
spoke to her.
15 And she said to them, "Thus says the LORD God of
Israel, 'Tell the man who sent you to me,
16 thus says the LORD, "Behold, I bring evil on this place
and on its inhabitants, *even* all the words of the book which
the king of Judah has read.
17 "[a]Because they have forsaken Me and have burned
incense to other gods that they might provoke Me to anger
with all the work of their hands, therefore My wrath burns
against this place, and it shall not be quenched." '
18 "But to the king of Judah who sent you to inquire of the
LORD thus shall you say to him, 'Thus says the LORD God of
Israel, "*Regarding* the words which you have heard,
19 [a]because your heart was tender and [b]you humbled
yourself before the LORD when you heard what I spoke against
this place and against its inhabitants that they should become
[c]a desolation and a [d]curse, and you have [e]torn your clothes and
wept before Me, I truly have heard you," declares the LORD.
20 'Therefore, behold, I will gather you to your fathers,
and [a]you shall be gathered to your grave in peace, neither shall
your eyes see all the evil which I will bring on this place.' " So
they brought back word to the king.

CHAPTER 23

[a]THEN the king sent, and they gathered to him all the elders
of Judah and of Jerusalem.
2 And the king went up to the house of the LORD and all
the men of Judah and all the inhabitants of Jerusalem with
him, and the priests and the prophets and all the people, both
small and great; and [a]he read in their hearing all the words of
the book of the covenant, [b]which was found in the house of
the LORD.
3 And [a]the king stood by the pillar and made a covenant
before the LORD, [b]to walk after the LORD, and to keep His
commandments and His testimonies and His statutes with all

11 [a]Gen. 37:34; Josh. 7:6

12 [1]In 2 Chr. 34:20, *Abdon, son of Micah* [a]2 Kin. 25:22; Jer. 26:24 [b]2 Chr. 34:20

13 [a]Deut. 29:23-28; 31:17, 18

14 [1]In 2 Chr. 34:22, *Tokhath, son of Hasrah* [a]2 Chr. 34:22 [b]Zeph. 1:10

17 [a]2 Kin. 21:22; Deut. 29:25, 26

19 [a]1 Sam. 24:5; Ps. 51:17 [b]Ex. 10:3; 1 Kin. 21:29 [c]Lev. 26:31 [d]Jer. 26:6 [e]2 Kin. 22:11

20 [a]2 Kin. 23:30

1 [a]2 Chr. 34:29-32

2 [a]Deut. 31:10-13 [b]2 Kin. 22:8

3 [a]2 Kin. 11:14, 17 [b]Deut. 13:4

his heart and all *his* soul, to carry out the words of this covenant
that were written in this book. And all the people [1]en-
tered into the covenant.
4 Then the king commanded Hilkiah the high priest and
[a]the priests of the second order and the [1]doorkeepers, [b]to bring
out of the temple of the LORD all the vessels that were made
for Baal, for [2]Asherah, and for all the host of heaven; and [c]he
burned them outside Jerusalem in the fields of the Kidron, and
carried their ashes to Bethel.
5 And he did away with the idolatrous priests whom the
kings of Judah had appointed to burn incense in the high
places in the cities of Judah and in the surrounding area of
Jerusalem, also those who burned incense to Baal, to the sun
and to the moon and to the constellations and to all the host
of heaven.
6 And he brought out the Asherah from the house of the
LORD outside Jerusalem to the brook Kidron, and burned it at
the brook Kidron, and [a]ground *it* to dust, and [b]threw its dust
on the graves of the [1]common people.
7 He also broke down the houses of the [a]*male* cult prostitutes which *were* in the house of the LORD, where [b]the women
were weaving [1]hangings for the Asherah.
8 Then he brought all the priests from the cities of Judah, and defiled the high places where the priests had burned
incense, from [a]Geba to Beersheba; and he broke down the
high places of the gates which *were* at the entrance of the gate
of Joshua the governor of the city, which *were* on one's left at
the city gate.
9 Nevertheless [a]the priests of the high places did not go
up to the altar of the LORD in Jerusalem, but they ate unleavened bread among their brothers.
10 [a]He also defiled [1]Topheth, which is in the valley of the
son of Hinnom, [b]that no man might make his son or his daughter pass through the fire for [c]Molech.
11 And he did away with the horses which the kings of
Judah had given to the sun, at the entrance of the house of the
LORD, by the chamber of Nathan-melech the official, which
was in the precincts; and he burned the chariots of the sun
with fire.
12 And [a]the altars which *were* on the roof, the upper
chamber of Ahaz, which the kings of Judah had made, and
[b]the altars which Manasseh had made in the two courts of the
house of the LORD, the king broke down; and he [1]ran from
there, and [c]threw their dust into the brook Kidron.
13 And the high places which *were* before Jerusalem,
which *were* on the right of [a]the mount of destruction which
Solomon the king of Israel had built for [b]Ashtoreth the abomination of the Sidonians, and for [c]Chemosh the abomination of
Moab, and for Milcom the abomination of the sons of Ammon, the king defiled.
14 And [a]he broke in pieces the *sacred* pillars and cut down
the Asherim and [b]filled their places with human bones.
15 Furthermore, [a]the altar that *was* at Bethel *and* the
[b]high place which Jeroboam the son of Nebat, who made
Israel sin, had made, even that altar and the high place he

3 [1]Lit., *took a stand in*

4 [1]Lit., *keepers of the threshold* [2]I.e., A wooden symbol of a female diety and so throughout the chap. [a]2 Kin. 25:18; Jer. 52:24 [b]2 Kin. 21:3? [c]2 Kin. 23:15

6 [1]Lit., *sons of the people* [a]2 Kin. 23:15 [b]2 Chr. 34:4

7 [1]Or, *tents;* lit., *houses* [a]1 Kin. 14:24; 15:12 [b]Ex. 35:25, 26; Ezek. 16:16

8 [a]Josh. 21:17; 1 Kin. 15:22

9 [a]Ezek. 44:10-14

10 [1]I.e., place of burning [a]Is. 30:33; Jer. 7:31, 32 [b]Lev. 18:21 [c]1 Kin. 11:7

12 [1]Or, *smashed them there* [a]Jer. 19:13; Zeph. 1:5 [b]2 Kin. 21:5 [c]2 Kin. 23:4, 6

13 [a]1 Kin. 11:7 [b]1 Kin. 11:5 [c]Num. 21:29

14 [a]Deut. 7:5, 25 [b]2 Kin. 23:16

15 [a]1 Kin. 13:1 [b]1 Kin. 12:28-33

broke down. Then he [1c]demolished its stones, ground them to
dust, and burned the Asherah.
16 Now when Josiah turned, he saw the graves that *were*
there on the mountain, and he sent and took the bones from
the graves and burned *them* on the altar and defiled it [a]accord-
ing to the word of the LORD which the man of God proclaimed,
who proclaimed these things.
17 Then he said, "What is this monument that I see?"
And the men of the city told him, "[a]It is the grave of the man
of God who came from Judah and proclaimed these things
which you have done against the altar of Bethel."
18 And he said, "Let him alone; let no one disturb his
bones." So they [1]left his bones undisturbed [a]with the bones of
the prophet who came from Samaria.
19 And Josiah also removed all the houses of the high
places which *were* [a]in the cities of Samaria, which the kings of
Israel had made provoking [1]the LORD; and he did to them [2]just
as he had done in Bethel.
20 And all the priests of the high places who *were* there
[a]he slaughtered on the altars and burned human bones on
them; then he returned to Jerusalem.
21 Then the king commanded all the people saying, "[a]Cel-
ebrate the Passover to the LORD your God [b]as it is written in
this book of the covenant."
22 [a]Surely such a Passover had not been celebrated from
the days of the judges who judged Israel, nor in all the days of
the kings of Israel and of the kings of Judah.
23 But in the eighteenth year of King Josiah this Passover
was observed to the LORD in Jerusalem.
24 Moreover, Josiah [1]removed [a]the mediums and the spiritists and the [b]teraphim and [c]the idols and all the abominations
that were seen in the land of Judah and in Jerusalem, [d]that he
might [2]confirm the words of the law which were written [e]in the
book that Hilkiah the priest found in the house of the LORD.
25 And before him there was no king [a]like him who turned
to the LORD with all his heart and with all his soul and with all
his might, according to all the law of Moses; nor did any like
him arise after him.
26 However, the LORD did not turn from the fierceness of
His great wrath with which His anger burned against Judah,
[a]because of all the provocations with which Manasseh had
provoked Him.
27 And the LORD said, "I will remove Judah also from My
sight, [a]as I have removed Israel. And [b]I will cast off Jerusalem,
this city which I have chosen, and the [1]temple of which I said,
'My name shall be there.' "
28 Now the rest of the acts of Josiah and all that he did,
are they not written in the Book of the Chronicles of the Kings
of Judah?
29 [a]In his days [b]Pharaoh Neco king of Egypt went up to
the king of Assyria to the river Euphrates. And King Josiah
went to meet him, and when *Pharaoh Neco* saw him he killed
him at [c]Megiddo.
30 And [a]his servants drove [1]his body in a chariot from
Megiddo, and brought him to Jerusalem and buried him in his
own tomb. [b]Then the people of the land took Jehoahaz the

15 [1]So the Gk.; Heb., *burned the high place* [c]2 Kin. 23:6

16 [a]1 Kin. 13:2

17 [1]1 Kin. 13:1, 30, 31

18 [1]Lit., *let his bones escape with* [a]1 Kin. 13:11, 31

19 [1]So with ancient versions. [2]Lit., *according to all the acts* [a]2 Chr. 34:6, 7

20 [a]2 Kin. 10:25; 11:18

21 [a]2 Chr. 35:1-17 [b]Num. 9:2-4; Deut. 16:2-8

22 [a]2 Chr. 35:18, 19

24 [1]Lit., *consumed* [2]Or, *perform* [a]2 Kin. 21:6; Lev. 19:31 [b]Gen. 31:19 [c]2 Kin. 21:11, 21 [d]Deut. 18:10-22 [e]2 Kin. 22:8

25 [a]2 Kin. 18:5

26 [a]2 Kin. 21:11-13; Jer. 15:4

27 [1]Lit., *house* [a]2 Kin. 18:11 [b]2 Kin. 21:13, 14

29 [a]2 Chr. 35:20-24 [b]Jer. 46:2 [c]Judg. 5:19

30 [1]Lit., *him, dead* [a]2 Kin. 9:28 [b]2 Chr. 36:1-4

son of Josiah and anointed him and made him king in place of
his father.
31 [a]Jehoahaz was twenty-three years old when he became
king, and he reigned three months in Jerusalem; and his mother's name was [b]Hamutal the daughter of Jeremiah of Libnah.
32 And he did evil in the sight of the LORD, [a]according to
all that his fathers had done.
33 And [a]Pharaoh Neco imprisoned him at [b]Riblah in the
land of [c]Hamath, that he might not reign in Jerusalem; and he
imposed on the land a fine of one hundred talents of silver and
a talent of gold.
34 And Pharaoh Neco made [a]Eliakim the son of Josiah
king in the place of Josiah his father, and [b]changed his name to
Jehoiakim. But he took Jehoahaz away and [1c]brought *him* to
Egypt, and he died there.
35 So Jehoiakim [a]gave the silver and gold to Pharaoh, but
he taxed the land in order to give the money at the [1]command
of Pharaoh. He exacted the silver and gold from the people of
the land, each according to his valuation, to give it to Pharaoh
Neco.
36 [a]Jehoiakim was twenty-five years old when he became
king, and he reigned eleven years in Jerusalem; and his mother's name *was* Zebidah the daughter of Pedaiah of Rumah.
37 And he did evil in the sight of the LORD, [a]according to
all that his fathers had done.

CHAPTER 24

[a]IN his days Nebuchadnezzar king of Babylon came up, and
Jehoiakim became his servant *for* three years; then he turned
and rebelled against him.
2 And the LORD sent against him [a]bands of Chaldeans,
[b]bands of Syrians, [c]bands of Moabites, and bands of Ammonites. So He sent them against Judah to destroy it, [d]according
to the word of the LORD, which He had spoken through His
servants the prophets.
3 [a]Surely at the [1]command of the LORD it came upon
Judah, to remove *them* from His sight [b]because of the sins of
Manasseh, according to all that he had done,
4 and [a]also for the innocent blood which he shed, for he
filled Jerusalem with innocent blood; and the LORD would not
forgive.
5 Now the rest of the acts of Jehoiakim and all that he
did, are they not written in the Book of the Chronicles of the
Kings of Judah?
6 So [a]Jehoiakim slept with his fathers, and Jehoiachin his
son became king in his place.
7 And [a]the king of Egypt did not come out of his land
again, [b]for the king of Babylon had taken all that belonged to
the king of Egypt from [c]the brook of Egypt to the river
Euphrates.
8 [a]Jehoiachin was [b]eighteen years old when he became
king, and he reigned three months in Jerusalem; and his mother's name *was* Nehushta the daughter of Elnathan of
Jerusalem.

31 [a]1 Chr. 3:15; Jer. 22:11 [b]2 Kin. 24:18
32 [a]2 Kin. 21:2-7
33 [a]2 Kin. 23:29 [b]2 Kin. 25:6 [c]1 Kin. 8:65
34 [1]So with Gk. Heb., *he came*, cf. 2 Chr. 36:4 [a]1 Chr. 3:15 [b]2 Kin. 24:17 [c]Jer. 22:11, 12; Ezek. 19:3, 4
35 [1]Lit., *mouth* [a]2 Kin. 23:33
36 [a]2 Chr. 36:5
37 [a]2 Kin. 23:32
1 [a]2 Chr. 36:6; Jer. 25:1
2 [a]Jer. 35:11 [b]2 Kin. 6:23 [c]2 Kin. 13:20 [d]2 Kin. 23:27
3 [1]Lit., *mouth* [a]2 Kin. 18:25 [b]2 Kin. 23:26
4 [a]2 Kin. 21:16
6 [a]Jer. 22:18, 19
7 [a]Jer. 37:5-7 [b]Jer. 46:2 [c]Gen. 15:18
8 [a]1 Chr. 3:16 [b]2 Chr. 36:9

9 And he did evil in the sight of the LORD, [a]according to
all that his father had done.
10 At that time the servants of Nebuchadnezzar king of
Babylon went up to Jerusalem, and the city came under siege.
11 And Nebuchadnezzar the king of Babylon came to the
city, while his servants were besieging it.
12 And [a]Jehoiachin the king of Judah went out to the king
of Babylon, he and his mother and his servants and his captains
and his officials. So [b]the king of Babylon took him captive in
the eighth year of his reign.
13 And [a]he carried out from there all the treasures of the
house of the LORD, and the treasures of the king's house, and
[b]cut in pieces all the vessels of gold [c]which Solomon king of
Israel had made in the temple of the LORD, just as the LORD
had said.
14 Then [a]he led away into exile all Jerusalem and all the
captains and all the mighty men of valor, [b]ten thousand captives, and [c]all the craftsmen and the smiths. None remained
[d]except the poorest people of the land.
15 So [a]he led Jehoiachin away into exile to Babylon; also
the king's mother and the king's wives and his officials and the
leading men of the land, he led away into exile from Jerusalem
to Babylon.
16 And all the men of valor, [a]seven thousand, and the
craftsmen and the smiths, one thousand, all strong and fit for
war, and these the king of Babylon brought into exile to
Babylon.
17 [a]Then the king of Babylon made [1]his uncle Mattaniah,
king in his place, and changed his name to Zedekiah.
18 [a]Zedekiah was twenty-one years old when he became
king, and he reigned eleven years in Jerusalem; and his mother's name *was* [b]Hamutal the daughter of Jeremiah of Libnah.
19 And he did evil in the sight of the LORD, [a]according to
all that Jehoiakim had done.
20 For through the anger of the LORD *this* came about in
Jerusalem and Judah until He cast them out from His presence. And [a]Zedekiah rebelled against the king of Babylon.

CHAPTER 25

[a]NOW it came about in the ninth year of his reign, on the
tenth day of the tenth month, that [b]Nebuchadnezzar king of
Babylon came, he and all his army, against Jerusalem, camped
against it, [c]and built a siege wall all around [1]it.
2 So the city was under siege until the eleventh year of
King Zedekiah.
3 On the ninth day of the *fourth* month [a]the famine was
so severe in the city that there was no food for the people of
the land.
4 Then the city was broken into, and all the men of war
fled by night by way of the gate between the two walls which
was by [a]the king's garden, though the Chaldeans were all
around the city. And [1]they went by way of the Arabah.
5 But the army of the Chaldeans pursued the king and
overtook him in the plains of Jericho and all his army was
scattered from him.

9 [a]2 Kin. 21:2-7

12 [a]Jer. 24:1; 29:1, 2 [b]2 Chr. 36:10

13 [a]2 Kin. 20:17; Is. 39:6 [b]2 Kin. 25:13-15 [c]1 Kin. 7:48-50

14 [a]Jer. 24:1 [b]2 Kin. 24:16; Jer. 52:28 [c]Jer. 24:1; 29:2 [d]2 Kin. 25:12

15 [a]2 Chr. 36:10; Jer. 22:24-28

16 [a]2 Kin. 24:14

17 [1]I.e., Jehoiachin's uncle [a]2 Chr. 36:10-13

18 [a]Jer. 52:1 [b]2 Kin. 23:31

19 [a]2 Kin. 23:37

20 [a]2 Chr. 36:13

1 [1]Lit., *against it* [a]2 Chr. 36:17-20; Jer. 39:1-7 [b]Jer. 34:1, 2; Ezek. 24:2 [c]Ezek. 21:22

3 [a]2 Kin. 6:24, 25; Lam. 4:9, 10

4 [1]So some ancient mss. and versions. M.T., *he* [a]Neh. 3:15

6 Then [a]they captured the king and [b]brought him to the
king of Babylon at [c]Riblah, and [1]he passed sentence on him.
7 And [a]they slaughtered the sons of Zedekiah before his
eyes, then [b]put out the eyes of Zedekiah and bound him with
bronze fetters and brought him to Babylon.
8 [a]Now on the seventh day of the [b]fifth month, which
was the nineteenth year of King Nebuchadnezzar, king of Babylon, Nebuzaradan the captain of the guard, a servant of the
king of Babylon, came to Jerusalem.
9 And [a]he burned the house of the LORD, [b]the king's
house, and all the houses of Jerusalem; even every great house
he burned with fire.
10 So all the army of the Chaldeans who *were with* the
captain of the guard [a]broke down the walls around Jerusalem.
11 Then [a]the rest of the people who were left in the city
and the deserters who had deserted to the king of Babylon and
the rest of the multitude, Nebuzaradan the captain of the
guard carried away into exile.
12 But the captain of the guard left some of [a]the poorest
of the land to be vinedressers and plowmen.
13 [a]Now the bronze pillars which were in the house of the
LORD, and the stands and the bronze sea which were in the
house of the LORD, the Chaldeans broke in pieces and carried
the [1]bronze to Babylon.
14 [a]And they took away the pots, the shovels, the snuffers,
the spoons, and all the bronze vessels which were used in
temple service.
15 The captain of the guard also took away the firepans
and the basins, what was fine gold and what was fine silver.
16 The two pillars, the one sea, and the stands which Solomon had made for the house of the LORD—[a]the bronze of all
these vessels was beyond weight.
17 [a]The height of the one pillar was eighteen [1]cubits, and
a bronze capital was on it; the height of the capital was three
[1]cubits, with a network and pomegranates on the capital all
around, all of bronze. And the second pillar was like these with
network.
18 Then the captain of the guard took [a]Seraiah the chief
priest and [b]Zephaniah the second priest, with the three [1]offi-
cers of the temple.
19 And from the city he took one official who was overseer of the men of war, and [a]five [1]of the king's advisors who
were found in the city; and the [2]scribe of the captain of the
army, who mustered the people of the land; and sixty men of
the people of the land who were found in the city.
20 And Nebuzaradan the captain of the guard took them
and brought them to the king of Babylon at [a]Riblah.
21 Then the king of Babylon struck them down and put
them to death at Riblah in the land of Hamath. [a]So Judah was
led away into exile from its land.
22 Now *as for* the people who were left in the land of
Judah, whom Nebuchadnezzar king of Babylon had left, he
appointed [a]Gedaliah the son of Ahikam, the son of Shaphan
over them.
23 [a]When all the captains of the forces, they and *their*
men, heard that the king of Babylon had appointed Gedaliah

6 [1]Lit., *they spoke judgment with him* [a]Jer. 34:21, 22 [b]Jer. 32:4 [c]2 Kin. 23:33

7 [a]Jer. 39:6, 7 [b]Ezek. 12:13

8 [a]Jer. 52:12 [b]Jer. 39:8-12

9 [a]2 Chr. 36:19; Ps. 74:3-7 [b]Amos 2:5

10 [a]2 Kin. 14:13; Neh. 1:3

11 [a]2 Chr. 36:20

12 [a]2 Kin. 24:14; Jer. 40:7

13 [1]Lit., *bronze of them* [a]2 Chr. 36:18

14 [a]1 Kin. 7:47-50

16 [a]1 Kin. 7:47

17 [1]I.e., one cubit equals approx. 18 in. [a]1 Kin. 7:15-22

18 [1]Lit., *keepers of the door* [a]1 Chr. 6:14; Ezra 7:1 [b]Jer. 21:1; 29:25, 29

19 [1]Lit., *men of those seeing the king's face* [2]Or, *scribe, a captain* [a]Esth. 1:14

20 [a]2 Kin. 23:33

21 [a]2 Kin. 23:27; Deut. 28:64

22 [a]Jer. 39:14

23 [a]Jer. 40:7-9

governor, they came to Gedaliah to [b]Mizpah, namely, Ishmael
the son of Nethaniah, and Johanan the son of Kareah, and
Seraiah the son of Tanhumeth the Netophathite, and Jaazaniah the son of the Maacathite, they and their men.
24 And Gedaliah swore to them and their men and said to
them, "Do not be afraid of the servants of the Chaldeans; live
in the land and serve the king of Babylon, and it will be well
with you."
25 [a]But it came about in the seventh month, that Ishmael
the son of Nethaniah, the son of Elishama, of the royal [1]fam-
ily, came [2]with ten men and struck Gedaliah down so that he
died along with the Jews and the Chaldeans who were with
him at Mizpah.
26 [a]Then all the people, both small and great, and the
captains of the forces arose and went to Egypt; for they were
afraid of the Chaldeans.
27 [a]Now it came about in the thirty-seventh year of [b]the
exile of Jehoiachin king of Judah, in the twelfth month, on the
twenty-seventh *day* of the month, that Evil-merodach king of
Babylon, in the year that he became king, [1c]released Jehoiachin
king of Judah from prison;
28 and he spoke kindly to him and set his throne above
the throne of the kings who *were* with him in Babylon.
29 And Jehoiachin changed his prison clothes, and [1a]had
his meals in the king's presence regularly all the days of his life;
30 and for his [a]allowance, a regular allowance was given
him by the king, a portion for each day, all the days of his life.

23 [b]Josh. 18:26

25 [1]Lit., *seed* [2]Lit., *and ten men with him*
[a]Jer. 41:1, 2

26 [a]Jer. 43:4-7

27 [1]Lit., *lifted up the head of*
[a]Jer. 52:31-34 [b]2 Kin. 24:12, 15 [c]Gen. 40:13, 20

29 [1]Lit., *ate bread*
[a]2 Sam. 9:7

30 [a]Neh. 11:23; 12:47

THE FIRST BOOK OF THE CHRONICLES

Descendants of Noah.

[a]ADAM, Seth, Enosh,
2 Kenan, Mahalalel, Jared,
3 Enoch, Methuselah, Lamech,
4 Noah, Shem, Ham and Japheth.
5 [a]The sons of Japheth *were* Gomer, Magog, Madai, Javan, Tubal, Meshech, and Tiras.
6 And the sons of Gomer *were* Ashkenaz, [1]Diphath, and
Togarmah.
7 And the sons of Javan *were* Elishah, Tarshish, Kittim,
and [1]Rodanim.
8 The sons of Ham *were* Cush, Mizraim, Put, and
Canaan.
9 And the sons of Cush *were* Seba, Havilah, Sabta,
Raama, and Sabteca; and the sons of Raamah *were* Sheba and
Dedan.
10 And Cush [1]became the father of Nimrod; he began to
be a mighty one in the earth.

1 [a]Gen. 4:25-5:32

5 [a]Gen. 10:2-4

6 [1]In Gen. 10:3, *Riphath*

7 [1]In Gen. 10:4, *Dodanim*

10 [1]Lit., *begot,* and so throughout the chap.

11 [a]Gen. 10:13-18
12 [1]Or, *people of Pelisht*
17 [1]In Gen. 10:23, *Mash* [a]Gen. 10:22-29
22 [1]In Gen. 10:28, *Obal*
24 [a]Gen. 11:10-26; Luke 3:34-36
29 [a]Gen. 25:13-16
32 [a]Gen. 25:1-4
34 [a]1 Chr. 1:28 [b]Gen. 25:25, 26; 32:28
35 [a]Gen. 36:4-10
36 [1]In Gen. 36:11, *Zepho*
38 [a]Gen. 36:20-28
39 [1]In Gen. 36:22, *Hemam*
40 [1]In Gen. 36:23, *Alvan* [2]In Gen. 36:23, *Shepho*
41 [1]Lit., *sons* [2]In Gen. 36:26, *Hemdan*

11 [a]And Mizraim became the father of the people of Lud,
Anam, Lehab, Naphtuh,
12 Pathrus, Casluh, from which the [1]Philistines came, and
Caphtor.
13 And Canaan became the father of Sidon, his firstborn,
Heth,
14 and the Jebusites, the Amorites, the Girgashites,
15 the Hivites, the Arkites, the Sinites,
16 the Arvadites, the Zemarites, and the Hamathites.
17 [a]The sons of Shem *were* Elam, Asshur, Arpachshad,
Lud, Aram, Uz, Hul, Gether, and [1]Meshech.
18 And Arpachshad became the father of Shelah and Shelah became the father of Eber.
19 And two sons were born to Eber, the name of the one
was Peleg, for in his days the earth was divided, and his brother's name was Joktan.
20 And Joktan became the father of Almodad, Sheleph,
Hazarmaveth, Jerah,
21 Hadoram, Uzal, Diklah,
22 [1]Ebal, Abimael, Sheba,
23 Ophir, Havilah, and Jobab; all these *were* the sons of
Joktan.
24 [a]Shem, Arpachshad, Shelah,
25 Eber, Peleg, Reu,
26 Serug, Nahor, Terah,
27 Abram, that is Abraham.
28 The sons of Abraham *were* Isaac and Ishmael.
29 [a]These are their genealogies: the first-born of Ishmael
was Nebaioth, then Kedar, Adbeel, Mibsam,
30 Mishma, Dumah, Massa, Hadad, Tema,
31 Jetur, Naphish and Kedemah; these *were* the sons of
Ishmael.
32 [a]And the sons of Keturah, Abraham's concubine,
whom she bore, *were* Zimram, Jokshan, Medan, Midian, Ishbak, and Shuah. And the sons of Jokshan *were* Sheba and
Dedan.
33 And the sons of Midian *were* Ephah, Epher, Hanoch,
Abida, and Eldaah. All these were the sons of Keturah.
34 And [a]Abraham became the father of Isaac. The sons of
Isaac *were* [b]Esau and Israel.
35 [a]The sons of Esau *were* Eliphaz, Reuel, Jeush, Jalam,
and Korah.
36 The sons of Eliphaz *were* Teman, Omar, [1]Zephi, Gatam, Kenaz, Timna, and Amalek.
37 The sons of Reuel *were* Nahath, Zerah, Shammah, and
Mizzah.
38 [a]And the sons of Seir *were* Lotan, Shobal, Zibeon,
Anah, Dishon, Ezer, and Dishan.
39 And the sons of Lotan *were* Hori and [1]Homam; and
Lotan's sister *was* Timna.
40 The sons of Shobal *were* [1]Alian, Manahath, Ebal,
[2]Shephi, and Onam. And the sons of Zibeon *were* Aiah and
Anah.
41 The [1]son of Anah *was* Dishon. And the sons of Dishon
were [2]Hamran, Eshban, Ithran, and Cheran.

42 The sons of Ezer *were* Bilhan, and Zaavan, [1]Jaakan.
The sons of Dishan *were* Uz and Aran.
43 [a]Now these are the kings who reigned in the land of
Edom before any king of the sons of Israel reigned. Bela *was*
the son of Beor, and the name of his city was Dinhabah.
44 When Bela died, Jobab the son of Zerah of [a]Bozrah
became king in his place.
45 When Jobab died, Husham of the land of [a]the Teman-
ites became king in his place.
46 When Husham died, Hadad the son of Bedad, who
[1]defeated Midian in the field of Moab, became king in his
place; and the name of his city *was* Avith.
47 When Hadad died, Samlah of Masrekah became king
in his place.
48 When Samlah died, Saul of Rehoboth by the River
became king in his place.
49 When Saul died, Baal-hanan the son of Achbor became king in his place.
50 When Baal-hanan died, [1]Hadad became king in his
place; and the name of his city was [2]Pai, and his wife's name
was Mehetabel, the daughter of Matred, the daughter of Me-
zahab.
51 Then Hadad died. Now the chiefs of Edom were: chief
Timna, chief [1]Aliah, chief Jetheth,
52 chief Oholibamah, chief Elah, chief Pinon,
53 chief Kenaz, chief Teman, chief Mibzar,
54 chief Magdiel, chief Iram. These *were* the chiefs of
Edom.

[a]Chapter 2

THESE are the sons of Israel: Reuben, Simeon, Levi, Judah,
Issachar, Zebulun,
2 Dan, Joseph, Benjamin, Napthali, Gad, and Asher.
3 [a]The sons of Judah *were* Er, Onan, and Shelah; *these*
three were born to him by Bath-shua the Canaanitess. And Er,
Judah's first-born, was wicked in the sight of the LORD, so He
put him to death.
4 And [a]Tamar his daughter-in-law bore him Perez and
Zerah. Judah had five sons in all.
5 The sons of Perez *were* Hezron and Hamul.
6 And the sons of Zerah *were* [1]Zimri, Ethan, Heman,
Calcol, and [2]Dara; five of them in all.
7 And the [1]son of Carmi *was* [2]Achar, the troubler of
Israel, who violated the ban.
8 And the [1]son of Ethan *was* Azariah.
9 Now the sons of Hezron, who were born to him *were*
Jerahmeel, Ram, and Chelubai.
10 And Ram [1]became the father of Nahshon, leader of
the sons of Judah;
11 Nahshon became the father of Salma, Salma became
the father of Boaz,
12 Boaz became the father of Obed, and Obed became
the father of Jesse;
13 and Jesse became the father of Eliab his first-born, then
Abinadab the second, Shimea the third,

42 [1]Or, *and Akan*
43 [a]Gen. 36:31-43
44 [a]Is. 34:6
45 [a]Job 2:11
46 [1]Lit., *smote*
50 [1]In Gen. 36:39, *Hadar* [2]In Gen. 36:39, *Pau*
51 [1]In Gen. 36:40, *Alvah*

1 [a]Gen. 35:22-26; 46:8-25
3 [a]Gen. 38:2-10
4 [a]Gen. 38:13-30
6 [1]In Josh. 7:1, *Zabdi* [2]In 1 Kings 4:31, *Darda*
7 [1]Lit., *sons* [2]In Josh. 7:18, *Achan*
8 [1]Lit., *sons*
10 [1]Lit., *begot*, and so throughout the chap.

16 [1]in 2 Sam. 2:18, *Abishai*

23 [1]Or, *Havvoth-jair*

31 [1]Lit., *sons*

14 Nethanel the fourth, Raddai the fifth,
15 Ozem the sixth, David the seventh;
16 and their sisters *were* Zeruiah and Abigail. And the
three sons of Zeruiah *were* [1]Abshai, Joab, and Asahel.
17 And Abigail bore Amasa, and the father of Amasa was
Jether the Ishmaelite.
18 Now Caleb the son of Hezron had sons by Azubah *his*
wife, and by Jerioth; and these were her sons: Jesher, Shobab,
and Ardon.
19 When Azubah died, Caleb married Ephrath, who bore
him Hur.
20 And Hur became the father of Uri, and Uri became
the father of Bezalel.
21 Afterward Hezron went in to the daughter of Machir
the father of Gilead, whom he married when he was sixty years
old; and she bore him Segub.
22 And Segub became the father of Jair, who had twenty-
three cities in the land of Gilead.
23 But Geshur and Aram took [1]the towns of Jair from
them, with Kenath and its villages, *even* sixty cities. All these
were the sons of Machir, the father of Gilead.
24 And after the death of Hezron in Caleb-ephrathah,
Abijah, Hezron's wife, bore him Ashhur the father of Tekoa.
25 Now the sons of Jerahmeel the first-born of Hezron
were Ram the first-born, then Bunah, Oren, Ozem, *and*
Ahijah.
26 And Jerahmeel had another wife, whose name was Atar-
ah; she was the mother of Onam.
27 And the sons of Ram, the first-born of Jerahmeel, were
Maaz, Jamin, and Eker.
28 And the sons of Onam were Shammai and Jada. And
the sons of Shammai *were* Nadab and Abishur.
29 And the name of Abishur's wife *was* Abihail, and she
bore him Ahban and Molid.
30 And the sons of Nadab *were* Seled and Appaim, and
Seled died without sons.
31 And the [1]son of Appaim *was* Ishi. And the [1]son of Ishi
was Sheshan. And the [1]son of Sheshan *was* Ahlai.
32 And the sons of Jada the brother of Shammai *were*
Jether and Jonathan, and Jether died without sons.
33 And the sons of Jonathan *were* Peleth and Zaza. These
were the sons of Jerahmeel.
34 Now Sheshan had no sons but daughters. And Sheshan
had an Egyptian servant whose name was Jarha.
35 And Sheshan gave his daughter to Jarha his servant in
marriage, and she bore him Attai.
36 And Attai became the father of Nathan, and Nathan
became the father of Zabad,
37 and Zabad became the father of Ephlal, and Ephlal
became the father of Obed,
38 and Obed became the father of Jehu, and Jehu became
the father of Azariah,
39 and Azariah became the father of Helez, and Helez
became the father of Eleasah,
40 and Eleasah became the father of Sismai, and Sismai
became the father of Shallum,

41 and Shallum became the father of Jekamiah, and Jekamiah became the father of Elishama.
42 Now the sons of Caleb, the brother of Jerahmeel, *were*
Mesha his first-born, who was the father of Ziph; and [1]his son
was Mareshah, the father of Hebron.
43 And the sons of Hebron *were* Korah and Tappuah and
Rekem and Shema.
44 And Shema became the father of Raham, the father of
Jorkeam; and Rekem became the father of Shammai.
45 And the son of Shammai was Maon, and Maon *was* the
father of Bethzur.
46 And Ephah, Caleb's concubine, bore Haran, Moza,
and Gazez; and Haran became the father of Gazez.
47 And the sons of Jahdai *were* Regem, Jotham, Geshan,
Pelet, Ephah, and Shaaph.
48 Maacah, Caleb's concubine, bore Sheber and
Tirhanah.
49 She also bore Shaaph the father of Madmannah, Sheva
the father of Machbena and the father of Gibea; and the
daughter of Caleb *was* Achsah.
50 These were the sons of Caleb.
The [1]sons of Hur, the first-born of Ephrathah, *were* Shobal
the father of Kiriath-jearim,
51 Salma the father of Bethlehem *and* Hareph the father
of Beth-gader.
52 And Shobal the father of Kiriath-jearim had sons: Har-
oeh, half of the Manahathites,
53 and the families of Kiriath-jearim: the Ithrites, the Puth-
ites, the Shumathites, and the Mishraites; from these came
the Zorathites and the Eshtaolites.
54 The sons of Salma *were* Bethlehem and the Netophathites, Atroth-beth-joab and half of the Manahathites, the
Zorites.
55 And the families of scribes who lived at Jabez *were* the
Tirathites, the Shimeathites, *and* the Sucathites. Those are the
Kenites who came from Hammath, the father of the house of
Rechab.

Chapter 3

[a]NOW these were the sons of David who were born to him in
Hebron: the first-born *was* Amnon, by Ahinoam the Jezreelitess: the second *was* Daniel, by Abigail the Carmelitess;
2 the third *was* Absalom the son of Maacah, the daughter of Talmai king of Geshur; the fourth *was* Adonijah the
son of Haggith;
3 the fifth *was* Shephatiah, by Abital; the sixth *was* Ithream, by his wife Eglah.
4 Six were born to him in Hebron, and [a]there he reigned
seven years and six months. And in Jerusalem he reigned thirty-
three years.
5 [a]And these were born to him in Jerusalem: Shimea,
Shobab, Nathan, and [b]Solomon, four, by [c]Bath-shua the daughter of Ammiel;
6 and Ibhar, Elishama, Eliphelet,
7 Nogah, Nepheg, and Japhia,

42 [1]Lit., *the sons of*

50 [1]Lit., *son*

1 [a]2 Sam. 3:2-5

4 [a]2 Sam. 2:11; 5:4, 5

5 [a]1 Chr. 14:4-7; 2 Sam. 5:14-16 [b]2 Sam. 12:24, 25 [c]2 Sam. 11:3

9 [a]2 Sam. 13:1

8 Elishama, Eliada, and Eliphelet, nine.
9 All *these were* the sons of David, besides the sons of
the concubines; and [a]Tamar *was* their sister.
10 Now Solomon's son *was* Rehoboam, Abijah *was* his
son, Asa his son, Jehoshaphat his son,

19 [1]Lit., *son*

11 Joram his son, Ahaziah his son, Joash his son,
12 Amaziah his son, Azariah his son, Jotham his son,
13 Ahaz his son, Hezekiah his son, Manasseh his son,
14 Amon his son, Josiah his son.
15 And the sons of Josiah *were* Johanan the first-born, and
the second *was* Jehoiakim, the third Zodekiah, the fourth
Shallum.

21 [1]Lit., *son*

16 And the sons of Jehoiakim *were* Jeconiah his son, Zedekiah his son.
17 And the sons of Jeconiah, the prisoner, *were* Shealtiel
his son,
18 and Malchiram, Pedaiah, Shenazzar, Jekamiah, Hosh-
ama, and Nedabiah.

22 [1]Lit., *sons*

19 And the sons of Pedaiah *were* Zerubbabel and Shimei.
And the [1]sons of Zerubbabel *were* Meshullam and Hananiah,
and Shelomith *was* their sister;
20 and Hashubah, Ohel, Berechiah, Hasadiah, and Jushab-
hesed, five.

23 [1]Lit., *son*

21 And the [1]sons of Hananiah *were* Polatiah and Jeshaiah, the sons of Rephaiah, the sons of Arnan, the sons of
Obadiah, the sons of Shecaniah.
22 And the [1]son of Shecaniah *was* Shemaiah, and the sons
of Shemaiah *were* Hattush, Igal, Bariah, Neariah, and Shaphat,
six.

1 [a]1 Chr. 2:3

23 And the [1]sons of Neariah *were* Elioenai, Hizkiah, and
Azrikam, three.
24 And the sons of Elioenai *were* Hodaviah, Eliashib, Pelaiah, Akkub, Johanan, Delaiah, and Anani, seven.

2 [1]Lit., *begot*, and so throughout the chap.

Chapter 4

[a]THE sons of Judah *were* Perez, Hezron, Carmi, Hur, and
Shobal.
2 And Reaiah the son of Shobal [1]became the father of
Jahath, and Jahath became the father of Ahumai and Lahad.
These *were* the families of the Zorathites.

3 [1]So with some ancient versions, Heb., *father*

3 And these *were* the [1]sons of Etam: Jezreel, Ishma, and
Idbash; and the name of their sister *was* Hazzelelponi.
4 And Penuel *was* the father of Gedor, and Ezer the
father of Hushah. These *were* the sons of Hur, the first-born of
Ephrathah, the father of Bethlehem.
5 And Ashhur, the father of Tekoa, had two wives, Helah
and Naarah.

7 [1]Another reading is *Zohar*

6 And Naarah bore him Ahuzzam, Hepher, Temeni, and
Haahashtari. These were the sons of Naarah.
7 And the sons of Helah *were* Zereth, [1]Izhar and Ethnan.
8 And Koz became the father of Anub and Zobebah, and
the families of Aharhel the son of Harum.
9 And Jabez was more honorable than his brothers, and
his mother named him Jabez saying, "Because I bore *him* with
pain."

10 Now Jabez called on the God of Israel, saying, "Oh
that Thou wouldst bless me indeed, and enlarge my border,
and that Thy hand might be with me, and that Thou wouldst
keep *me* from harm, that *it* may not pain me!" And God
granted him what he requested.
11 And Chelub the brother of Shuhah became the father
of Mehir, who was the father of Eshton.
12 And Eshton became the father of Beth-rapha and Paseah, and Tehinnah the father of [1]Ir-nahash. These are the
men of Recah.
13 Now the sons of Kenaz *were* Othniel and Seraiah. And
the [1]son of Othniel *was* Hathath.
14 And Meonothai became the father of Ophrah, and Seraiah became the father of Joab the father of [1]Ge-harashim,
for they were craftsmen.
15 And the sons of Caleb the son of Jephunneh *were* Iru,
Elah and Naam; and the [1]son of Elah *was* [2]Kenaz.
16 And the sons of Jehallel *were* Ziph and Ziphah, Tiria
and Asarel.
17 And the [1]sons of Ezrah *were* Jether, Mered, Epher, and
Jalon. ([2]And these are the sons of Bithia the daughter of Pharaoh, whom Mered took), and she conceived and *bore* Miriam,
Shammai, and Ishbah the father of Eshtemoa.
18 And his Jewish wife bore Jered the father of Gedor, and
Heber the father of Soco, and Jekuthiel the father of Zanoah.
19 And the sons of the wife of Hodiah, the sister of Na-
ham, *were* the [1]fathers of Keilah the Garmite and Eshtemoa
the Maacathite.
20 And the sons of Shimon *were* Amnon and Rinnah,
Benhanan and Tilon. And the sons of Ishi *were* Zoheth and
Ben-zoheth.
21 The sons of Shelah the son of Judah *were* Er the father
of Lecah and Laadah the father of Mareshah, and the families
of the house of the linen workers at Beth-ashbea;
22 and Jokim, the men of Cozeba, Joash, Saraph, who
ruled in Moab, and Jaashubi-lehem. And the [1]records are
ancient.
23 These were the potters and the inhabitants of Netaim
and Gederah; they lived there with the king for his work.
24 The sons of Simeon *were* [1]Nemuel and Jamin, [2]Jarib,
[3]Zerah, Shaul;
25 Shallum his son, Mibsam his son, Mishma his son.
26 And the sons of Mishma *were* Hammuel his son, Zaccur his son, Shimei his son.
27 Now Shimei had sixteen sons and six daughters; but his
brothers did not have many sons, nor did all their family multiply like the sons of Judah.
28 And they lived at Beersheba, Moladah, and
Hazarshual,
29 at Bilhah, Ezem, Tolad,
30 Bethuel, Hormah, Ziklag,
31 Beth-marcaboth, Hazar-susim, Beth-biri, and Shaaraim.
These *were* their cities until the reign of David.
32 And their villages *were* Etam, Ain, Rimmon, Tochen,
and Ashan, five cities;
33 and all their villages that *were* around the same cities as

12 [1]Or, *the city of Nahash*

13 [1]Lit., *sons*

14 [1]Or, *valley of craftsmen*

15 [1]Lit., *sons* [2]Lit., *and Kenaz*

17 [1]Lit., *son* [2]In the Heb. the words in ( ) are at the end of verse 18

19 [1]Lit., *father*

22 [1]Lit., *words*

24 [1]In Num. 26:12, *Jemuel* [2]In Num. 26:12, *Jachin* [3]In Gen. 46:10; Ex. 6:15, *Zohar*

33 [1]In Josh. 19:8, *Baalath*

40 [a]Judg. 18:7-10

41 [1]Lit., *smote*
[a]1 Chr. 4:33-38

42 [a]Gen. 36:8, 9

43 [1]Lit., *smote*
[a]1 Sam. 15:7, 8; 30:17

1 [a]1 Chr. 2:1; Gen. 29:32
[b]Gen. 35:22; 49:4 [c]Gen. 48:15-22

2 [a]Gen. 49:8-10 [b]Mic. 5:2; Matt. 2:6

3 [a]Num. 26:5-9

4 [a]1 Chr. 5:8

6 [1]In 2 Kin. 15:29, *Tiglath-pileser*

7 [1]Lit., *brothers*
[a]1 Chr. 5:17

8 [a]Num. 32:34; Josh. 12:2

9 [a]Josh. 22:8, 9

10 [1]Lit., *dwelt in* [2]Lit., *all the face of the east*
[a]1 Chr. 5:18-21

11 [a]Deut. 3:10

far as [1]Baal. These *were* their settlements, and they have their
genealogy.
34 And Meshobab and Jamlech and Joshah the son of
Amaziah,
35 and Joel and Jehu the son of Joshibiah, the son of
Seraiah, the son of Asiel,
36 and Elyoenai, Jaakobah, Jeshohaiah, Asaiah, Adiel, Jes-
imiel, Benaiah,
37 Ziza the son of Shiphi, the son of Allon, the son of
Jedaiah, the son of Shimri, the son of Shemaiah;
38 —these mentioned by name *were* leaders in their families; and their fathers' houses increased greatly.
39 And they went to the entrance of Gedor, even to the
east side of the valley, to seek pasture for their flocks.
40 And they found rich and good pasture, and [a]the land
was broad and quiet and peaceful; for those who lived there
formerly *were* Hamites.
41 And [a]these, recorded by name, came in the days of
Hezekiah king of Judah, and [1]attacked their tents, and the
Meunites who were found there, and destroyed them utterly
to this day, and lived in their place; because there was pasture
for their flocks.
42 And from them, from the sons of Simeon, five hundred
men went to [a]Mount Seir, with Pelatiah, Neariah, Rephaiah,
and Uzziel, the sons of Ishi, as their leaders.
43 And [a]they [1]destroyed the remnant of the Amalekites
who escaped, and have lived there to this day.

Chapter 5

NOW the sons of Reuben the first-born of Israel (for [a]he was
the first-born, but because [b]he defiled his father's bed, [c]his
birthright was given to the sons of Joseph the son of Israel; so
that he is not enrolled in the genealogy according to the
birthright.
2 [a]Though Judah prevailed over his brothers, and [b]from
him *came* the leader, yet the birthright belonged to Joseph),
3 [a]the sons of Reuben the first-born of Israel *were* Hanoch and Pallu, Hezron and Carmi.
4 The sons of Joel *were* Shemaiah his son, Gog his son,
[a]Shimei his son,
5 Micah his son, Reaiah his son, Baal his son,
6 Beerah his son, whom [1]Tilgath-pilneser king of Assyria
carried away into exile; he was leader of the Reubenites.
7 And his [1]kinsmen by their families, [a]in the genealogy of
their generations, *were* Jeiel the chief, then Zechariah
8 and Bela the son of Azaz, the son of Shema, the son of
Joel, who lived in [a]Aroer, even to Nebo the Baal-meon.
9 And to the east he settled as far as the entrance of the
wilderness from the river Euphrates, [a]because their cattle had
increased in the land of Gilead.
10 And in the days of Saul [a]they made war with the Hagrites, who fell by their hand, so that they [1]occupied their tents
throughout [2]all the land east of Gilead.
11 Now the sons of Gad lived opposite them in the land
of Bashan as far as [a]Salecah.

12 Joel *was* the chief, and Shapham the second, then Janai
and Shaphat in Bashan.
13 And their [1]kinsmen of their fathers' households *were*
Michael, Meshullam, Sheba, Jorai, Jacan, Zia, and Eber,
seven.
14 These *were* the sons of Abihail, the son of Huri, the
son of Jaroah, the son of Gilead, the son of Michael, the son of
Jeshishai, the son of Jahdo, the son of Buz;
15 Ahi the son of Abdiel, the son of Guni, *was* head of
their fathers' households.
16 And they lived in Gilead, in Bashan and in its towns,
and in all the pasture lands of [a]Sharon, as far as their [1]borders.
17 All of these were enrolled in the genealogies in the days
of [a]Jotham king of Judah and in the days of [b]Jeroboam king of
Israel.
18 The sons of Reuben and the Gadites and the half-tribe
of Manasseh, *consisting* of valiant men, men who bore shield
and sword and shot with bow, and *were* skillful in battle, *were*
44,760, who [a]went to war.
19 And they made war against [a]the Hagrites, [b]Jetur, Naphish, and Nodab.
20 And they were helped against them, and the Hagrites
and all who *were* with them were given into their hand; for
[a]they cried out to God in the battle, and He was entreated for
them, because [b]they trusted in Him.
21 And they took away their cattle: their 50,000 camels,
250,000 sheep, 2,000 donkeys, and 100,000 [1]men.
22 For many fell slain, because [a]the war *was* of God. And
[b]they settled in their place until the [c]exile.
23 Now the sons of the half-tribe of Manasseh lived in the
land; from Bashan to Baal-hermon and [a]Senir and Mount Hermon they were numerous.
24 And these were the heads of their fathers' households,
even Epher, Ishi, Eliel, Azriel, Jeremiah, Hodaviah, and Jah-
diel, mighty men of valor, famous men, heads of their fathers'
households.
25 But they acted treacherously against the God of their
fathers, and [a]played the harlot [b]after the gods of the peoples of
the land, whom God had destroyed before them.
26 So the God of Israel stirred up the spirit of [a]Pul king of
Assyria, even the spirit of [1]Tilgath-pilneser king of Assyria, and
he carried them away into exile, namely the Reubenites, the
Gadites, and the half-tribe of Manasseh, and brought them to
Halah, Habor, Hara, and to the river of Gozan, to this day.

CHAPTER 6

1a
THE sons of Levi *were* [2]Gershon, Kohath and Merari.
2 And the sons of Kohath *were* Amram, Izhar, Hebron,
and Uzziel.
3 And the children of Amram *were* Aaron, Moses, and
Miriam. And the sons of Aaron *were* Nadab, Abihu, Eleazar,
and Ithamar.
4 Eleazar [1]became the father of Phinehas, *and* Phinehas
became the father of Abishua,

13 [1]Lit., *brother*

16 [1]Lit., *goings out* [a]1 Chr. 27:29

17 [a]2 Kin. 15:5, 32 [b]2 Kin. 14:16, 28

18 [a]Num. 1:3

19 [a]1 Chr. 5:10 [b]1 Chr. 1:31

20 [a]2 Chr. 14:11-13 [b]Ps. 9:10; 20:7, 8

21 [1]Lit., *souls of men*

22 [a]Josh. 23:10; 2 Chr. 32:8 [b]1 Chr. 4:41 [c]2 Kin. 15:29; 17:6

23 [a]Deut. 3:9

25 [a]Ex. 34:15 [b]2 Kin. 17:7

26 [1]In 2 Kin. 15:29, *Tiglath-pileser* [a]2 Kin. 15:19, 29; 1 Chr. 5:26

1 [1]Ch. 5:27 in Heb. [2]In vs. 16, *Gershom* [a]Ex. 6:16-25

4 [1]Lit., *begot* and so throughout the chap.

12 [1]In ch. 9:11, *Meshullam*

15 [1]Lit., *by the hand of*

16 [1]Chap. 6:1 in Heb. [2]In vs. 1, *Gershon*

28 [1]Cf. v. 33 and 1 Sam. 8:2

31 [a]1 Chr. 15:16-22, 27; 16:4-6 [b]1 Chr. 15:25- 16:1; 2 Sam. 6:17

32 [1]Lit., *stood over*

5 and Abishua became the father of Bukki, and Bukki
became the father of Uzzi,
6 and Uzzi became the father of Zerahiah, and Zerahiah
became the father of Meraioth,
7 Meraioth became the father of Amariah, and Amariah
became the father of Ahitub,
8 and Ahitub became the father of Zadok, and Zadok
became the father of Ahimaaz,
9 and Ahimaaz became the father of Azariah, and Azariah became the father of Johanan,
10 and Johanan became the father of Azariah (it was he
who served as the priest in the house which Solomon built in
Jerusalem),
11 and Azariah became the father of Amariah, and Amariah became the father of Ahitub,
12 and Ahitub became the father of Zadok, and Zadok
became the father of [1]Shallum,
13 and Shallum became the father of Hilkiah, and Hilkiah
became the father of Azariah,
14 and Azariah became the father of Seraiah, and Seraiah
became the father of Jehozadak;
15 and Jehozadak went *along* when the LORD carried Judah and Jerusalem away into exile [1]by Nebuchadnezzar.
16 [1]The sons of Levi *were* [2]Gershom, Kohath, and Merari.
17 And these are the names of the sons of Gershom: Libni
and Shimei.
18 And the sons of Kohath *were* Amram, Izhar, Hebron,
and Uzziel.
19 The sons of Merari *were* Mahli and Mushi. And these
are the families of the Levites according to their fathers'
households.
20 Of Gershom: Libni his son, Jahath his son, Zimmah his
son,
21 Joah his son, Iddo his son, Zerah his son, Jeatherai his
son.
22 The sons of Kohath *were* Amminadab his son, Korah
his son, Assir his son,
23 Elkanah his son, Ebiasaph his son, and Assir his son,
24 Tahath his son, Uriel his son, Uzziah his son, and Saul
his son.
25 And the sons of Elkanah *were* Amasai and Ahimoth.
26 *As for* Elkanah, the sons of Elkanah *were* Zophai his
son and Nahath his son,
27 Eliab his son, Jeroham his son, Elkanah his son.
28 And the sons of Samuel *were* [1]Joel, the first-born and
Abijah, the second.
29 The sons of Merari *were* Mahli, Libni his son, Shimei
his son, Uzzah his son,
30 Shimea his son, Haggiah his son, Asaiah his son.
31 [a]Now these are those whom David appointed over the
service of song in the house of the LORD, [b]after the ark rested
there.
32 And they ministered with song before the tabernacle of
the tent of meeting, until Solomon had built the house of the
LORD in Jerusalem; and they [1]served in their office according
to their order.

33 And these are those who [1]served with their sons. From
the sons of the Kohathites *were* Heman the singer, the son of
Joel, the son of Samuel,
34 the son of Elkanah, the son of Jeroham, the son of
Eliel, the son of Toah,
35 the son of Zuph, the son of Elkanah, the son of Mahath, the son of Amasai,
36 the son of Elkanah, the son of Joel, the son of Azariah,
the son of Zephaniah,
37 the son of Tahath, the son of Assir, the son of Ebiasaph, the son of Korah,
38 the son of Izhar, the son of Kohath, the son of Levi, the
son of Israel.
39 And his brother Asaph who stood at his right hand,
even Asaph the son of Berechiah, the son of Shimea,
40 the son of Michael, the son of Baaseiah, the son of
Malchijah,
41 the son of Ethni, the son of Zerah, the son of Adaiah,
42 the son of Ethan, the son of Zimmah, the son of
Shimei,
43 the son of Jahath, the son of Gershom, the son of Levi.
44 And on the left hand *were* their [1]kinsmen the sons of
Merari: Ethan the son of Kishi, the son of Abdi, the son of
Malluch,
45 the son of Hashabiah, the son of Amaziah, the son of
Hilkiah,
46 the son of Amzi, the son of Bani, the son of Shemer,
47 the son of Mahli, the son of Mushi, the son of Merari,
the son of Levi.
48 And their [1]kinsmen the Levites were [2]appointed for all
the service of the tabernacle of the house of God.
49 But Aaron and his sons [1a]offered on the altar of burnt
offering and [b]on the altar of incense, for all the work of the
most holy place, and [c]to make atonement for Israel, according
to all that Moses the servant of God had commanded.
50 [a]And these are the sons of Aaron: Eleazar his son, Phinehas his son, Abishua his son,
51 Bukki his son, Uzzi his son, Zerahiah his son,
52 Meraioth his son, Amariah his son, Ahitub his son,
53 Zadok his son, Ahimaaz his son.
54 Now these are their settlements according to their
camps within their borders. To the sons of Aaron of the families
of the Kohathites (for theirs was the [a]*first* lot),
55 to them they gave [a]Hebron in the land of Judah, and its
pasture lands around it;
56 [a]but the fields of the city and its villages, they gave to
Caleb the son of Jephunneh.
57 And [a]to the sons of Aaron they gave the following cities
of refuge: Hebron, Libnah also with its pasture lands, Jatir,
Eshtemoa with its pasture lands,
58 [1]Hilen with its pasture lands, Debir with its pasture
lands,
59 [1]Ashan with its pasture lands, and Bethshemesh with its
pasture lands;
60 and from the tribe of Benjamin: Geba with its pasture
lands, [1]Allemeth with its pasture lands, and Anathoth with its

33 [1]Lit., *stood*

44 [1]Lit., *brothers*

48 [1]Lit., *brothers* [2]Lit., *given*

49 [1]Lit., *offered up in smoke*
[a]Ex. 27:1-8 [b]Ex. 30:1-7 [c]Ex. 30:10-16

50 [a]1 Chr. 6:4-8

54 [a]Josh. 21:4,10

55 [a]Josh. 14:13

56 [a]Josh. 15:13

57 [a]Josh. 21:13, 19

58 [1]In Josh. 21:15, *Holon*

59 [1]In Josh. 21:16, *Ain*

60 [1]In Josh. 21:17, *Almon*

61 [a]1 Chr. 6:66-70; Josh. 21:5
63 [a]Josh. 21:7, 34-40
64 [a]Josh. 21:3, 41, 42
65 [a]1 Chr. 6:57-60
66 [a]Josh. 21:20-26

pasture lands. All their cities throughout their families were
thirteen cities.
61 [a]Then to the rest of the sons of Kohath *were given* by
lot, from the family of the tribe, from the half-tribe, the half of
Manasseh, ten cities.
62 And to the sons of Gershom, according to their families,
were given from the tribe of Issachar and from the tribe of
Asher, the tribe of Naphtali, and the tribe of Manasseh, thirteen cities in Bashan.
63 [a]To the sons of Merari *were given* by lot, according to
their families, from the tribe of Reuben, the tribe of Gad, and
the tribe of Zebulun, twelve cities.
64 [a]So the sons of Israel gave to the Levites the cities with
their pasture lands.
65 And they gave by lot from the tribe of the sons of
Judah, the tribe of the sons of Simeon, and the tribe of the
sons of Benjamin, [a]these cities which are mentioned by name.
66 [a]Now some of the families of the sons of Kohath had
cities of their territory from the tribe of Ephraim.
67 And they gave to them the *following* cities of refuge:
Shechem in the hill country of Ephraim with its pasture lands,
Gezer also with its pasture lands,
68 Jokmeam with its pasture lands, Beth-horon with its
pasture lands,
69 Aijalon with its pasture lands, and Gath-rimmon with
its pasture lands;
70 and from the half-tribe of Manasseh: Aner with its pasture lands and Bileam with its pasture lands, for the rest of the
family of the sons of Kohath.
71 To the sons of Gershom *were given*, from the family of
the half-tribe of Manasseh: Golan in Bashan with its pasture
lands and Ashtaroth with its pasture lands;
72 and from the tribe of Issachar: Kedesh with its pasture
lands, Daberath with its pasture lands,
73 and Ramoth with its pasture lands, Anem with its pasture lands;
74 and from the tribe of Asher: Mashal with its pasture
lands, Abdon with its pasture lands,
75 Hukok with its pasture lands, and Rehob with its pasture lands;
76 and from the tribe of Naphtali: Kedesh in Galilee with
its pasture lands, Hammon with its pasture lands, and Kiriathaim with its pasture lands.
77 To the rest of *the Levites*, the sons of Merari, *were
given*, from the tribe of Zebulun: Rimmono with its pasture
lands, Tabor with its pasture lands;
78 and beyond the Jordan at Jericho, on the east side of
the Jordan, *were given them*, from the tribe of Reuben: Bezer
in the wilderness with its pasture lands, Jahzah with its pasture
lands,
79 Kedemoth with its pasture lands, and Mephaath with
its pasture lands;
80 and from the tribe of Gad: Ramoth in Gilead with its
pasture lands, Mahanaim with its pasture lands,
81 Heshbon with its pasture lands, and Jazer with its pasture lands.

CHAPTER 7

NOW the sons of Issachar *were* four: Tola, [1]Puah, [2]Jashub,
and Shimron.
2 And the sons of Tola *were* Uzzi, Rephaiah, Jeriel, Jah-
mai, Ibsam, and Samuel, heads of their fathers' households.
The sons of Tola *were* mighty men of valor in their generations; [a]their number in the days of David was 22,600.
3 And the [1]son of Uzzi *was* Izrahiah. And the sons of
Izrahiah *were* Michael, Obadiah, Joel, Isshiah; all five of them
were chief men.
4 And with them by their generations according to their
fathers' households were 36,000 [1]troops of the army for war,
for they had many wives and sons.
5 And their [1]relatives among all the families of Issachar
were mighty men of valor, enrolled by genealogy, in all 87,000.
6 [a]*The sons of* Benjamin *were* three: Bela and Becher
and Jediael.
7 And the sons of Bela were five: Ezbon, Uzzi, Uzziel,
Jerimoth, and Iri. They *were* heads of fathers' households,
mighty men of valor, and were 22,034 enrolled by genealogy.
8 And the sons of Becher *were* Zemirah, Joash, Eliezer,
Elioenai, Omri, Jeremoth, Abijah, Anathoth, and Alemeth. All
these *were* the sons of Becher.
9 And they were enrolled by genealogy, according to
their generations, heads of their fathers' households, 20,200
mighty men of valor.
10 And the [1]son of Jediael *was* Bilhan. And the sons of
Bilhan *were* Jeush, Benjamin, Ehud, Chenaanah, Zethan, Tarshish, and Ahishahar.
11 All these *were* sons of Jediael, according to the heads of
their fathers' households, 17,200 mighty men of valor, who
were [1]ready to go out with the army to war.
12 And [1]Shuppim and [2]Huppim *were* the sons of [3]Ir; Hushim *was* the [4]son of [5]Aher.
13 The sons of Naphtali *were* [1]Jahziel, Guni, Jezer, and
[2]Shallum, the sons of Bilhah.
14 The sons of Manasseh *were* Asriel, whom his Ara-
maean concubine bore; she bore Machir the father of Gilead.
15 And Machir took a wife for Huppim and Shuppim,
[1]whose sister's name was Maacah. And the name of the second
was Zelophehad, and Zelophehad had daughters.
16 And Maacah the wife of Machir bore a son, and she
named him Peresh; and the name of his brother *was* Sheresh,
and his sons *were* Ulam and Rakem.
17 And the [1]son of Ulam *was* Bedan. These *were* the sons
of Gilead the son of Machir, the son of Manasseh.
18 And his sister Hammolecheth bore Ishhod and [1]Abie-
zer and Mahlah.
19 And the sons of Shemida were Ahian and Shechem and
Likhi and Aniam.
20 And [a]the sons of Ephraim *were* Shuthelah and Bered
his son, Tahath his son, Eleadah his son, Tahath his son,
21 Zabad his son, Shuthelah his son, and Ezer and Elead
whom the men of Gath who were born in the land killed,
because they came down to take their livestock.

1 [1]In Gen. 46:13, *Puvah* [2]In Gen. 46:13, *Iob*

2 [a]2 Sam. 24:1-9

3 [1]Lit., *sons*

4 [1]Or, *bands*

5 [1]Lit., *brothers*, and so throughout the chap.

6 [a]1 Chr. 8:1-40

10 [1]Lit., *sons*

11 [1]Lit., *going out*

12 [1]In Num. 26:30, *Shephupham* [2]In Num. 26:39, *Hupham* [3]In v. 7, *Iri* [4]Lit., *sons* [5]In Num. 26:38, *Ahiram*

13 [1]In Gen. 46:24, *Jahzeel* [2]In Gen. 46:24; Num. 26:49, *Shillem*

15 [1]Lit., *and his*

17 [1]Lit., *sons*

18 [1]In Num. 26:30, *Iezer*

20 [a]Num. 26:35, 36

22 And their father Ephraim mourned many days, and his
relatives came to comfort him.
23 Then he went in to his wife, and she conceived and
bore a son, and he named him [1]Beriah, because misfortune
had come upon his house.
24 And his daughter was Sheerah, [a]who built lower and
upper Beth-horon, also Uzzen-sheerah.
25 And Rephah was his son *along* with Resheph, Telah his
son, Tahan his son,
26 Ladan his son, Ammihud his son, Elishama his son,
27 [1]Non his son, and [a]Joshua his son.
28 And [a]their possessions and settlements *were* Bethel
with its towns, and to the east [1]Naaran, and to the west Gezer
with its towns, and Shechem with its towns as far as [2]Ayyah
with its towns,
29 and along the borders of the sons of Manasseh, Beth-
shean with its towns, Taanach with its towns, Megiddo with its
towns, Dor with its towns. In these lived the sons of Joseph the
son of Israel.
30 [a]The sons of Asher *were* Imnah, Ishvah, and Ishvi, Beriah, and Serah their sister.
31 And the sons of Beriah *were* Heber and Malchiel, who
was the father of Birzaith.
32 And Heber [1]became the father of Japhlet, [2]Shomer,
and Hotham, and Shua their sister.
33 And the sons of Japhlet *were* Pasach, Bimhal, and Ash-
vath. These were the sons of Japhlet.
34 And the sons of [1]Shemer *were* Ahi and Rohgah, Jehub-
bah and Aram.
35 And the [1]sons of Helem's brother *were* Zophah, Imna,
Shelesh, and Amal.
36 The sons of Zophah *were* Suah, Harnepher, Shual,
Beri, and Imrah,
37 Bezer, Hod, Shamma, Shilshah, Ithran, and Beera.
38 And the sons of Jether *were* Jephunneh, Pispa, and Ara.
39 And the sons of Ulla *were* Arah, Hanniel, and Rizia.
40 All these *were* the sons of Asher, heads of the fathers'
houses, choice and mighty men of valor, heads of the princes.
And the number of them enrolled by genealogy for service in
war was 26,000 men.

Chapter 8

AND [a]Benjamin [1]became the father of Bela his first-born,
Ashbel the second, [b]Aharah the third,
2 Nohah the fourth, and Rapha the fifth.
3 And Bela had sons: [1]Addar, Gera, Abihud,
4 Abishua, Naaman, Ahoah,
5 Gera, Shephuphan, and Huram.
6 And these are the sons of Ehud: these are the heads of
fathers' *households* of the inhabitants of Geba, and they
carried them into exile to Manahath,
7 namely, Naaman, Ahijah, and Gera—he carried them
into exile; and he became the father of Uzza and Ahihud.
8 And Shaharaim became the father of children in the

23 [1]I.e., on misfortune

24 [a]Josh. 16:3, 5

27 [1]In Ex. 33:11, *Nun* [a]Ex. 17:9-14; 24:13

28 [1]In Josh. 16:7, *Naarah* [2]Many mss. read, *Azzah* [a]Josh. 16:2

30 [a]Gen. 46:17; Num. 26:44-46

32 [1]Lit., *begot* [2]In v. 34, *Shemer*

34 [1]In v. 32, *Shomer*

35 [1]Lit., *son*

1 [1]Lit., *begot*, and so throughout the chap. [a]1 Chr. 7:6-12; Gen. 46:21 [b]1 Chr. 7:12

3 [1]In Gen. 46:21; Num. 26:40, *Ard*

[1]country of Moab, after he had [2]sent away Hushim and Baara
his wives.
9 And by Hodesh his wife he became the father of Jobab,
Zibia, Mesha, Malcam,
10 Jeuz, Sachia, Mirmah. These were his sons, heads of
fathers' *households*.
11 And by Hushim he became the father of Abitub and
Elpaal.
12 And the sons of Elpaal *were* Eber, Misham, and
Shemed, who built Ono and Lod, with its towns;
13 and Beriah and Shema, who were heads of fathers' *households* of the inhabitants of Aijalon, who put to flight the
inhabitants of Gath;
14 and [1]Ahio, Shashak, and Jeremoth.
15 And Zebadiah, Arad, Eder,
16 Michael, Ishpah, and Joha *were* the sons of Beriah.
17 And Zebadiah, Meshullam, Hizki, Heber,
18 Ishmerai, Izliah, and Jobab *were* the sons of Elpaal.
19 And Jakim, Zichri, Zabdi,
20 Elienai, Zillethai, Eliel,
21 Adaiah, Beraiah, and Shimrath *were* the sons of
[1]Shimei.
22 And Ishpan, Eber, Eliel,
23 Abdon, Zichri, Hanan,
24 Hananiah, Elam, Anthothijah,
25 Iphdeiah, and Penuel *were* the sons of Shashak.
26 And Shamsherai, Shehariah, Athaliah,
27 Jaareshiah, Elijah, and Zichri *were* the sons of
Jeroham.
28 These were heads of the fathers' *households* according
to their generations, chief men, [1]who lived in Jerusalem.
29 [a]Now in Gibeon, *Jeiel*, the father of Gibeon lived, and
his wife's name was Maacah;
30 and his first-born son *was* Abdon, then Zur, Kish, Baal,
Nadab,
31 Gedor, Ahio, and [1]Zecher.
32 And Mikloth became the father of [1]Shimeah. And they
also lived with their [2]relatives in Jerusalem opposite their *other*
[2]relatives.
33 [a]And Ner became the father of Kish, and Kish became
the father of Saul, and Saul became the father of Jonathan,
Malchi-shua, [1]Abinadab, and [2]Eshbaal.
34 And the son of Jonathan *was* [1]Merib-baal, and Merib-
baal became the father of Micah.
35 And the sons of Micah *were* Pithon, Melech, [1]Tarea,
and Ahaz.
36 And Ahaz became the father of [1]Jehoaddah, and Jeho-
addah became the father of Alemeth, Azmaveth, and Zimri;
and Zimri became the father of Moza.
37 And Moza became the father of Binea; [1]Raphah *was*
his son, Eleasah his son, Azel his son.
38 And Azel had six sons, and these *were* their names:
Azrikam, Bocheru, Ishmael, Sheariah, Obadiah and Hanan.
All these *were* the sons of Azel.
39 And the sons of Eshek his brother *were* Ulam his first-
born, Jeush the second, and Eliphelet the third.

8 [1]Lit., *field* [2]Lit., *sent them away*

14 [1]Or, *his brothers*

21 [1]In v. 13, *Shema*

28 [1]Lit., *these*

29 [a]1 Chr. 9:35-38

31 [1]In v. 9:37, *Zechariah*

32 [1]In v. 9:38, *Shimeam* [2]Lit., *brothers*

33 [1]1 Sam. 14:49, *Ishvi* [2]In 2 Sam. 2:8, *Ishbosheth* [a]1 Chr. 9:39-44

34 [1]In 2 Sam. 4:4, *Mephibosheth*

35 [1]In 9:41, *Tahrea*

36 [1]In 9:42, *Jarah*

37 [1]In 9:43, *Rephaiah*

40 And the sons of Ulam were mighty men of valor, archers, and had many sons and grandsons, 150 *of them.* All these *were* of the sons of Benjamin.

Chapter 9

So all Israel was enrolled by genealogies; and behold, they are written in the Book of the Kings of Israel. And [a]Judah was carried away into exile to Babylon for their unfaithfulness.

2 [a]Now the first who lived in their possessions in their cities *were* Israel, the priests, the Levites and [b]the [1]temple servants.

3 And some of the sons of Judah, of the sons of Benjamin, and of the sons of Ephraim and Manasseh lived in Jerusalem:

4 Uthai the son of Ammihud, the son of Omri, the son of Imri, the son of Bani, from the sons of Perez the son of Judah.

5 And from the Shilonites *were* Asaiah the first-born and his sons.

6 And from the sons of Zerah *were* Jeuel and their [1]relatives, 690 *of them.*

7 And from the sons of Benjamin *were* Sallu the son of Meshullam, the son of Hodaviah, the son of Hassenuah,

8 and Ibneiah the son of Jeroham, and Elah the son of Uzzi, the son of Michri, and Meshullam the son of Shephatiah, the son of Reuel, the son of Ibnijah;

9 and their relatives according to their generations, [a]956. All these *were* heads of fathers' *households* according to their fathers' houses.

10 [a]And from the priests *were* Jedaiah, Jehoiarib, Jachin,

11 and [1]Azariah the son of Hilkiah, the son of Meshullam, the son of Zadok, the son of Meraioth, the son of Ahitub, [a]the chief officer of the house of God;

12 and Adaiah the son of Jeroham, the son of Pashhur, the son of Malchijah, and Maasai the son of Adiel, the son of Jahzerah, the son of Meshullam, the son of Meshillemith, the son of Immer;

13 and their relatives, heads of their fathers' households, 1760 very able men for the work of the service of the house of God.

14 [a]And of the Levites *were* Shemaiah the son of Hasshub, the son of Azrikam, the son of Hashabiah, of the sons of Merari;

15 and Bakbakkar, Heresh and Galal and Mattaniah the son of Mica, the son of [1]Zichri, the son of Asaph,

16 and [1]Obadiah the son of [2]Shemaiah, the son of Galal, the son of Jeduthun, and Berechiah the son of Asa, the son of Elkanah, who lived in the villages of the Netophathites.

17 Now the gatekeepers *were* [1]Shallum and Akkub and Talmon and Ahiman and their relatives, (Shallum the chief

18 *being stationed* until now at [a]the king's gate to the east). These *were* the gatekeepers for the camp of the sons of Levi.

19 And Shallum the son of Kore, the son of Ebiasaph, the son of Korah, and his relatives, of his father's house, the Korahites, *were* over the work of the service, keepers of the thresh-

1 [a]1 Chr. 5:25, 26

2 [1]Heb., *Nethinim* [a]Neh. 11:3-22 [b]Ezra 2:43, 58; 8:20

6 [1]Lit., *brothers,* and so throughout the chap.

9 [a]Neh. 11:8

10 [a]Neh. 11:10-14

11 [1]In Neh. 11:11, *Seraiah* [a]Jer. 20:1

14 [a]Neh. 11:15-19

15 [1]In Neh. 11:17, *Zabdi*

16 [1]In Neh. 11:17, *Abda* [2]In Neh. 11:17, *Shammua*

17 [1]In v. 21, *Meshelemiah; 26:14, Shelemiah;* Neh. 12:25, *Meshullam*

18 [a]Ezek. 46:1, 2

olds of the tent; and their fathers had been over the camp of
the LORD, keepers of the entrance.
20 And [a]Phinehas the son of Eleazar was ruler over them
previously, *and* the LORD was with him.
21 [a]Zechariah the son of Meshelemiah was gatekeeper of
the entrance of the tent of meeting.
22 All these who were chosen to be gatekeepers in the
thresholds were 212. These were enrolled by genealogy in their
villages, [a]whom David and Samuel the seer appointed [b]in their
office of trust.
23 So they and their sons [1]had charge of the gates of the
house of the LORD, *even* the house of the tent, as guards.
24 The gatekeepers were [1]on the four sides, to the east,
west, north, and south.
25 And their relatives [a]in their villages [b]*were* to come in
every seven days from time to time *to be* with [1]them;
26 for the four chief gatekeepers who *were* Levites, were
in an office of trust, and were over the chambers and over the
treasuries in the house of God.
27 And they spent the night around the house of God,
[a]because the watch was [1]committed to them; and they *were* [2]in
charge of opening *it* morning by morning.
28 Now some of them [1]had charge of the utensils of service, for [2]they counted them when they brought them in and
when they took them out.
29 Some of them also were appointed over the furniture
and over all the utensils of the sanctuary and [a]over the fine
flour and the wine and the oil and the frankincense and the
spices.
30 And some of [a]the sons of the priests prepared the mixing of the spices.
31 And Mattithiah, one of the Levites, who was the first-
born of Shallum the Korahite, had [a]the [1]responsibility over the
things which were baked in pans.
32 And some of their relatives of the sons of the Kohathites [a]*were* over the showbread to prepare it every sabbath.
33 Now these are [a]the singers, heads of fathers' *households* of the Levites, *who lived* in the chambers *of the temple*
free *from other service;* for [1]they were engaged [b]in their work
day and night.
34 These were heads of fathers' *households* of the Levites
according to their generations, chief men, [1]who lived in
Jerusalem.
35 [a]And in Gibeon Jeiel the father of Gibeon lived, and
his wife's name was Maacah,
36 and his first-born son *was* Abdon, then Zur, Kish, Baal,
Ner, Nadab,
37 Gedor, Ahio, Zechariah, and Mikloth.
38 And Mikloth became the father of Shimeam. And they
also lived with their relatives in Jersualem opposite their *other*
relatives.
39 [a]And Ner became the father of Kish, and Kish became
the father of Saul, and Saul became the father of Jonathan,
Malchi-shua, Abinadab, and Eshbaal.
40 And the son of Jonathan *was* Merib-baal; and Merib-
baal became the father of Micah.

20 [a]Num. 25:7-13

21 [a]1 Chr. 26:2, 14

22 [a]1 Chr. 26:1 [b]2 Chr. 31:15, 18

23 [1]Lit., were *over the gates*

24 [1]Lit., *to the four winds*

25 [1]Lit., *these*
[a]1 Chr. 10:16 [b]2 Kin. 11:5, 7; 2 Chr. 23:8

27 [1]Lit., *on them* [2]Lit., *over the opening*
[a]1 Chr. 23:30-32

28 [1]Lit., *were over the* [2]Lit., *by count they brought them in and by count they took them out*

29 [a]1 Chr. 23:29

30 [a]Ex. 30:23-25

31 [1]Lit., *office of trust*
[a]1 Chr. 9:22

32 [a]Lev. 24:5-8

33 [1]Lit., *over them in the work*
[a]1 Chr. 6:31-47; 25:1 [b]Ps. 134:1

34 [1]Lit., *these*

35 [a]1 Chr. 8:29-32

39 [a]1 Chr. 8:33-38

41 [a]1 Chr. 8:35-37

41 And the sons of Micah *were* Pithon, Melech, Tahrea,
[a]*and Ahaz.*
42 And Ahaz became the father of Jarah, and Jarah became the father of Alemeth, Azmaveth, and Zimri; and Zimri
became the father of Moza,
43 and Moza became the father of Binea and Rephaiah
his son, Eleasah his son, Azel his son.
44 And Azel had six sons whose names are these: Azrikam,
Bocheru and Ishmael and Sheariah and Obadiah and Hanan.
These were the sons of Azel.

1 [a]1 Sam. 31:1-13

Chapter 10

[a]NOW the Philistines fought against Israel; and the men of
Israel fled before the Philistines, and fell slain on Mount
Gilboa.

2 [1]In 1 Sam. 14:49, *Ishvi*
[a]1 Sam. 31:4

2 And the Philistines closely pursued Saul and his sons,
and the Philistines struck down Jonathan, [1a]Abinadab and
Malchi-shua, the sons of Saul.
3 And the battle became heavy against Saul, and the
archers [1]overtook him; and he was wounded by the archers.

3 [1]Lit., *found him*

4 Then Saul said to his armor bearer, "Draw your sword
and thrust me through with it, lest these uncircumcised come
and abuse me." But his armor bearer would not, for he was
greatly afraid. Therefore Saul took his sword and fell on it.
5 And when his armor bearer saw that Saul was dead, he
likewise fell on his sword and died.
6 Thus Saul died with his three sons, and all *those* of his
house died together.
7 When all the men of Israel who were in the valley saw
that they had fled, and that Saul and his sons were dead, they
forsook their cities and fled; and the Philistines came and lived
in them.
8 And it came about the next day, when the Philistines
came to strip the slain, that they found Saul and his sons fallen
on Mount Gilboa.
9 So they stripped him and took his head and his armor
and sent *messengers* around the land of the Philistines, to carry
the good news to their idols and to the people.
10 And they put his armor in the house of their gods and
fastened his head in the house of Dagon.
11 When all Jabesh-gilead heard all that the Philistines
had done to Saul,
12 all the valiant men arose and took away the body of
Saul and the bodies of his sons, and brought them to Jabesh
and buried their bones under the oak in Jabesh, and fasted
seven days.

13 [a]1 Sam. 13:13, 14; 15:23
[b]1 Sam. 28:7

13 [a]So Saul died for his trespass which he committed
against the LORD, because of the word of the LORD which he
did not keep; and also [b]because he asked counsel of a medium,
making inquiry *of it*,

14 [a]1 Chr. 12:23; 1 Sam. 15:28

14 and did not inquire of the LORD. Therefore He killed
him, and [a]turned the kingdom to David the son of Jesse.

CHAPTER 11

[a]THEN all Israel gathered to David at Hebron [1]and said,
"Behold, we are your bone and your flesh.
2 "In times past, even when Saul was king, you *were* the
one who led out and brought in Israel; and the LORD your God
said to you, '[a]You shall shepherd My people Israel, and you
shall be prince over My people Israel.' "
3 So all the elders of Israel came to the king at Hebron,
and David made a covenant with them in Hebron before the
LORD; and they anointed David king over Israel, [a]according to
the word of the LORD through Samuel.
4 Then David and all Israel went to Jerusalem ([a]that is,
Jebus); and the Jebusites, the inhabitants of the land, *were*
there.
5 And the inhabitants of Jebus said to David, "You shall
not enter here." Nevertheless David captured the stronghold
of Zion (that is, the city of David).
6 Now David had said, "Whoever strikes down a Jebusite
first shall be chief and commander." [a]And Joab the son of
Zeruiah went up first, so he became chief.
7 Then David dwelt in the stronghold; therefore it was
called the city of David.
8 And he [1]built the city all around, from The [2]Millo even
to the surrounding area; and Joab [3]repaired the rest of the city.
9 And [a]David became greater and greater, for the LORD
of hosts *was* with him.
10 [a]Now these are the heads of the mighty men whom
David had, who gave him strong support in his kingdom, together with all Israel, to make him king, [b]according to the word of
the LORD concerning Israel.
11 And these *constitute* the list of the mighty men whom
David had: [a]Jashobeam, the son of a Hachmonite, [b]the chief
of the thirty; he lifted up his spear against three hundred
[1]whom he killed at one time.
12 And after him was Eleazar the son of [a]Dodo, the Ahohite, who *was* [1]one of the three mighty men.
13 He was with David at [1]Pasdammim [a]when the Philistines were gathered together there to battle, and there was a
plot of ground full of barley; and the people fled before the
Philistines.
14 And they took their stand in the midst of the plot, and
defended it, and struck down the Philistines; and the LORD
saved them by a great [1]victory.
15 Now three of the thirty chief men went down to the
rock to David, into the cave of Adullam, while [a]the army of
the Philistines was camping in the valley of Rephaim.
16 And David was then in the stronghold, while [a]the garrison of the Philistines *was* then in Bethlehem.
17 And David had a craving and said, "Oh that someone
would give me water to drink from the well of Bethlehem,
which is by the gate!"
18 So the three broke through the camp of the Philistines,
and drew water from the well of Bethlehem which *was* by the
gate, and took *it* and brought *it* to David; nevertheless David
would not drink it, but poured it out to the LORD;

1 [1]Lit., *saying* [a]2 Sam. 5:1, 3, 6-10
2 [a]2 Sam. 5:2; 7:7
3 [a]1 Sam. 16:1, 3, 12, 13
4 [a]Josh. 15:8, 63; Judg. 1:21
6 [a]2 Sam. 8:16
8 [1]Or, *fortified* [2]I.e., citadel [3]Lit., *revived*
9 [a]2 Sam. 3:1
10 [a]2 Sam. 23:8-39 [b]1 Chr. 11:3
11 [1]Lit., *slain ones* [a]2 Sam. 23:8 [b]1 Chr. 12:18
12 [1]Lit., *among* [a]1 Chr. 27:4
13 [1]In 1 Sam. 17:1, *Ephesdammim* [a]2 Sam. 23:11, 12
14 [1]Or, *salvation*
15 [a]1 Chr. 14:9
16 [a]1 Sam. 10:5

19 and he said, "Be it far from me before my God that I
should do this. Shall I drink the blood of these men *who went*
[1]at the risk of their lives? For at the risk of their lives they
brought it." Therefore he would not drink it. These things the
three mighty men did.
20 As for [1]Abshai the brother of Joab, he was chief of the
[2]thirty, and he swung his spear against three hundred [3]and
killed them; and he had a name as well as the [2]thirty.
21 Of the three in the second *rank* he was the most honored, and became their commander; however, he did not
attain to the *first* three.
22 [a]Benaiah the son of Jehoiada, the son of a valiant man
of Kabzeel, mighty in deeds, struck down the [1]two *sons of* Ariel
of Moab. He also went down and [2]killed a lion inside a pit on a
snowy day.
23 And he [1]killed an Egyptian, a man of *great* stature five
[2]cubits tall. Now in the Egyptian's hand *was* [a]a spear like a
weaver's beam, but he went down to him with a club and
snatched the spear from the Egyptian's hand, and [1]killed him
with his own spear.
24 These *things* Benaiah the son of Johoiada did, and had
a name as well as the three mighty men.
25 Behold, he was honored among the thirty, but he did
not attain to the three; and David appointed him over his
guard.
26 Now the mighty men of the armies *were* Asahel the
brother of Joab, Elhanan the son of Dodo of Bethlehem,
27 [1]Shammoth the Harorite, Helez the [2]Pelonite,
28 Ira the son of Ikkesh the Tekoite, Abiezer the
Anathothite,
29 [1]Sibbecai the Hushathite, [2]Ilai the Ahohite,
30 Maharai the Netophathite, [1]Heled the son of Baanah
the Netophathite,
31 Ithai the son of Ribai of Gibeah of the sons of Benjamin, Benaiah the Pirathonite.
32 [1]Hurai of the brooks of Gaash, [2]Abiel the Arbathite,
33 Azmaveth the Baharumite, Eliahba the Shaalbonite,
34 the sons of [1]Hashem the Gizonite, Jonathan the son of
Shagee the Hararite,
35 Ahiam the son of [1]Sachar the Hararite, [2]Eliphal the son
of Ur,
36 Hepher the Mecherathite, Ahijah the Pelonite,
37 Hezro the Carmelite, [1]Naarai the son of Ezbai,
38 Joel the brother of Nathan, Mibhar the son of Hagri,
39 Zelek the Ammonite, Naharai the Berothite, the armor bearer of Joab the son of Zeruiah,
40 Ira the Ithrite, Gareb the Ithrite,
41 Uriah the Hittite, Zabad the son of Ahlai,
42 Adina the son of Shiza the Reubenite, a chief of the
Reubenites, and thirty with him,
43 Hanan the son of Maacah and Joshaphat the Mithnite.
44 Uzzia the Ashterathite, Shama and Jeiel the sons of
Hotham the Aroerite,
45 Jediael the son of Shimri and Joha his brother, the
Tizite,

19 [1]Lit., *with their souls*

20 [1]In 2 Sam. 23:18, *Abishai* [2]So Syriac; M.T., *three* [3]Lit., *slain ones*

22 [1]Or, *two lion-like heroes of* [2]Lit., *smote*
[a]2 Sam. 8:18

23 [1]Lit., *smote* [2]One cubit equals approx. 18 in.
[a]1 Sam. 17:7

27 [1]In 2 Sam. 23:25, *Shammah the Harodite* [2]In 2 Sam. 23:26, *Paltite*

29 [1]In 2 Sam. 23:27, *Mebunnai* [2]In 2 Sam. 23:28, *Zalmon*

30 [1]In 2 Sam. 23:29, *Heleb*

32 [1]In 2 Sam. 23:30, *Hiddai* [2]In 2 Sam. 23:31, *Abialbon*

34 [1]In 2 Sam. 23:32, *Jashen*

35 [1]In 2 Sam. 23:33, *Sharar* [2]In 2 Sam. 23:34, *Eliphelet the son of Ahasbai*

37 [1]In 2 Sam. 23:35, *Paarai the Arbite*

46 Eliel the Mahavite and Jeribai and Joshaviah, the sons
of Elnaam, and Ithmah the Moabite,
47 Eliel and Obed and Jaasiel the Mezobaite.

Chapter 12

[a]NOW these are the ones who came to David at Ziklag, while
he was still restricted because of Saul the son of Kish; and they
were among the mighty men who helped *him* in war.
2 They were equipped with bows, [a]using both the right
hand and the left *to sling* stones and *to shoot* arrows from the
bow; [b]*they were* Saul's kinsmen from Benjamin.
3 The chief was Ahiezer, then Joash, the sons of Shem-
aah the Gibeathite; and Jeziel and Pelet, the sons of Azmaveth, and Beracah and Jehu the Anathothite,
4 and Ishmaiah the Gibeonite, a mighty man among the
thirty, and over the thirty. [1]Then Jeremiah, Jahaziel, Johanan,
Jozabad the Gederathite,
5 Eluzai, Jerimoth, Bealiah, Shemariah, Shephatiah the
Haruphite,
6 Elkanah, Isshiah, Azarel, Joezer, Jashobeam, the
Korahites,
7 and Joelah and Zebadiah, the sons of Jeroham of
Gedor.
8 And from the Gadites there [1]came over to David in the
stronghold in the wilderness, mighty men of valor, men trained
for war, who could handle shield and spear, and whose faces
were like the faces of lions, and [a]*they were* as swift as the
gazelles on the mountains.
9 Ezer *was* the first, Obadiah the second, Eliab the third,
10 Mishmannah the fourth, Jeremiah the fifth,
11 Attai the sixth, Eliel the seventh,
12 Johanan the eighth, Elzabad the ninth,
13 Jeremiah the tenth, Machbannai the eleventh.
14 These of the sons of Gad were [1]captains of the army;
[a]he who was least was equal to a hundred and the greatest to a
thousand.
15 [a]These are the ones who crossed the Jordan in the first
month when it was overflowing all its banks and they put to
flight all those in the valleys, both to the east and to the west.
16 Then some of the sons of Benjamin and Judah came to
the stronghold to David.
17 And David went out to meet them, and answered and
said to them, "If you come peacefully to me to help me, my
heart shall be united with you; but if to betray me to my
adversaries, since there is no [1]wrong in my hands, may the God
of our fathers look on *it* and decide."
18 Then [a]the Spirit [1]came upon [b]Amasai, who was the
chief of the thirty, *and he said*,

"*We* are yours, O David,
And with you, O son of Jesse!
[c]Peace, peace to you,
And peace to him who helps you;
Indeed, your God helps you!"

Then David received them and made them [2]captains of the
band.

1 [a]1 Sam. 27:2-6

2 [a]Judg. 3:15; 20:16 [b]1 Chr. 12:29

4 [1]In Heb. the beginning of v. 5, making 41 vs. in chap.

8 [1]Lit., *separated themselves* [a]2 Sam. 2:18

14 [1]Or, *chiefs* [a]Deut. 32:30

15 [a]Josh. 3:15; 4:18

17 [1]Lit., *violence*

18 [1]Lit., *clothed* [2]Or, *chiefs* [a]Judg. 3:10; 6:34 [b]1 Chr. 2:17 [c]1 Sam. 25:5, 6

19 [a]From Manasseh also some defected to David, when he
was about to go to battle with the Philistines against Saul. But
they did not help them, for the lords of the Philistines after
consultation sent him away, saying, "At *the cost of* our heads
he may defect to his master Saul."
20 As he went to Ziklag, there defected to him from Manasseh: Adnah, Jozabad, Jediael, Michael, Jozabad, Elihu, and
Zillethai, [1]captains of thousands who belonged to Manasseh.
21 And they helped David against [a]the band of raiders, for
they were all mighty men of valor, and were captains in the
army.
22 For day by day *men* came to David to help him, until
there was a great army [a]like the army of God.
23 Now these are the numbers of the [1]divisions equipped
for war, [a]who came to David at Hebron, [b]to turn the kingdom
of Saul to him, [c]according to the [2]word of the LORD.
24 The sons of Judah who bore shield and spear *were*
6,800, equipped for war.
25 Of the sons of Simeon, mighty men of valor for war,
7,100.
26 Of the sons of Levi 4,600.
27 Now Jehoiada was the leader of *the house of* Aaron,
and with him were 3,700,
28 also [a]Zadok, a young man mighty of valor, and of his
father's house twenty-two captains.
29 And of the sons of Benjamin, [a]Saul's kinsmen, 3,000;
for until now [b]the greatest part of them had kept their allegiance to the house of Saul.
30 And of the sons of Ephraim 20,800, mighty men of
valor, famous men in their fathers' households.
31 And of the half-tribe of Manasseh 18,000, who were
designated by name to come and make David king.
32 And of the sons of Issachar, [a]men who understood the
times, with knowledge of what Israel should do, their chiefs
were two hundred; and all their kinsmen were at their
command.
33 Of Zebulun, there were 50,000 who went out in the
army, who could draw up in battle formation with all kinds of
weapons of war and helped *David* [1]with [a]an undivided heart.
34 And of Naphtali *there were* 1,000 captains, and with
them 37,000 with shield and spear.
35 And of the Danites who could draw up in battle formation, *there were* 28,600.
36 And of Asher *there were* 40,000 who went out in the
army to draw up in battle formation.
37 And from the other side of the Jordan, of the Reubenites and the Gadites and of the half-tribe of Manasseh, *there
were* 120,000 with all *kinds* of weapons of war for the battle.
38 All these, being men of war, who could draw up in
battle formation, came to Hebron with [a]a perfect heart, to
make David king over all Israel; and all the rest also of Israel
were of one mind to make David king.
39 And they were there with David three days, eating and
drinking; for their kinsmen had prepared for them.
40 Moreover those who were near to them, *even* as far as
Issachar and Zebulun and Naphtali, [a]brought food on don-

19 [a]1 Sam. 29:2-9
20 [1]Or, *chiefs*
21 [a]1 Sam. 30:1
22 [a]Gen. 32:2; Josh. 5:13-15
23 [1]Lit., *heads* [2]Lit., *mouth* [a]2 Sam. 2:3, 4 [b]1 Chr. 10:14 [c]1 Chr. 11:10
28 [a]1 Chr. 6:8, 53; 2 Sam. 8:17
29 [a]1 Chr. 12:2 [b]2 Sam. 2:8, 9
32 [a]Esth. 1:13
33 [1]Lit., *not of double heart* [a]Ps. 12:2
38 [a]1 Chr. 13:33; 2 Sam. 5:1-3
40 [a]1 Sam. 25:18

keys, camels, mules, and on oxen, great quantities of flour
cakes, fig cakes and bunches of raisins, wine, oil, oxen and
sheep. There was joy indeed in Israel.

Chapter 13

THEN David consulted with the captains of the thousands
and the hundreds, even with every leader.
2 And David said to all the assembly of Israel, "If it
seems good to you, and if it is from the LORD our God, let us
send everywhere to our kinsmen who remain in all the land of
Israel, also to the priests and Levites who are with them in
their cities with pasture lands, that they may meet with us;
3 and let us bring back the ark of our God to us, [a]for we
did not seek it in the days of Saul."
4 Then all the assembly said that they would do so, for
the thing was right in the eyes of all the people.
5 [a]So David assembled all Israel together, from the Shihor of Egypt even to the entrance of Hamath, [b]to bring the ark
of God from Kiriath-jearim.
6 [a]And David and all Israel went up to [b]Baalah, *that is,* to
Kiriath-jearim, which belongs to Judah, to bring up from there
the ark of God, the LORD [c]who is enthroned *above* the cherubim, where His Name is called.
7 And they [1]carried the ark of God on a new cart from
[a]the house of Abinadab, and Uzza and Ahio drove the cart.
8 And David and all Israel were celebrating before God
with all *their* might, [a]even with songs and with lyres, harps,
tambourines, cymbals, and with trumpets.
9 When they came to [a]the threshing floor of Chidon,
Uzza put out his hand to hold the ark, because the oxen nearly
upset *it.*
10 And the anger of the LORD burned against Uzza, so He
struck him down [a]because he put out his hand to the ark; [b]and
he died there before God.
11 Then David became angry because [1]of the LORD's outburst against Uzza; and he called that place [2]Perez-uzza to this
day.
12 And David was afraid of God that day, saying, "How
can I bring the ark of God *home* to me?"
13 So David did not take the ark with him to the city of
David, but took it aside [a]to the house of Obed-edom the
Gittite.
14 Thus the ark of God remained with the family of
Obed-edom in his house three months; and [a]the LORD blessed
the family of Obed-edom with all that he had.

Chapter 14

[a]NOW Hiram king of Tyre sent messengers to David with
cedar trees, masons, and carpenters, to build a house for him.
2 And David realized that the LORD had established him
as king over Israel, *and* that his kingdom was highly exalted,
for the sake of His people Israel.
3 Then David took more wives at Jerusalem, and David
[1]became the father of more sons and daughters.

3 [a]1 Sam. 7:1, 2
5 [a]1 Chr. 15:3; 2 Sam. 6:1; 1 Kin. 8:65 [b]1 Sam. 6:21; 7:1
6 [a]2 Sam. 6:2-11 [b]Josh. 15:9 [c]2 Kin. 19:15
7 [1]Lit., *caused to ride* [a]1 Sam. 7:1
8 [a]1 Chr. 15:16
9 [a]2 Sam. 6:6
10 [a]1 Chr. 15:13, 15 [b]Lev. 10:2
11 [1]Lit., *the* LORD *had broken through a break-through* [2]I.e., the break-through of Uzza
13 [a]2 Chr. 25
14 [a]1 Chr. 26:4, 5
1 [a]2 Sam. 5:11
3 [1]Lit., *begot*

4 [a]And these are the names of the children [1]born *to him*
in Jerusalem: Shammua, Shobab, Nathan, Solomon,
5 Ibhar, Elishua, Elpelet,
6 Nogah, Nepheg, Japhia,
7 Elishama, Beeliada and Eliphelet.
8 When the Philistines heard that David had been
anointed king over all Israel, all the Philistines went up in
search of David; and David heard of it and went out against
them.
9 Now the Philistines had come and [a]made a raid in the
valley of Rephaim.
10 And David inquired of God, saying, "Shall I go up
against the Philistines? And wilt Thou give them into my
hand?" Then the LORD said to him, "Go up, for I will give
them into your hand."
11 So they came up to Baal-perazim, and David [1]defeated
them there; and David said, "God has broken through my
enemies by my hand, like the break-through of waters." Therefore they named that place [2]Baal-perazim.
12 And they abandoned their gods there; so David gave
the order and they were burned with fire.
13 And the Philistines made [a]yet another raid in the
valley.
14 And David inquired again of God, and God said to
him, "You shall not go up after them; circle around [1]behind
them, and come at them in front of the [2]balsam trees.
15 "And it shall be when you hear the sound of marching in
the tops of the balsam trees, then you shall go out to battle,
for God will have gone out before you to strike the army of the
Philistines."
16 And David did just as God had commanded him, and
they struck down the army of the Philistines from [1]Gibeon
even as far as Gezer.
17 Then the fame of David went out into all the lands;
and [a]the LORD brought the fear of him on all the nations.

CHAPTER 15

NOW *David* built houses for himself in the city of David;
and he prepared a place for the ark of God, and [a]pitched a tent
for it.
2 Then David said, "[a]No one is to carry the ark of God
but the Levites; for the LORD chose them to carry the ark of
God, and to minister to Him forever."
3 And [a]David assembled all Israel at Jerusalem, to bring
up the ark of the LORD [b]to its place, which he had prepared for
it.
4 And David gathered together the sons of Aaron, and
[a]the Levites;
5 of the sons of Kohath, Uriel the chief, and 120 of his
[1]relatives;
6 of the sons of Merari, Asaiah the chief, and 220 of his
relatives;
7 of the sons of Gershom, Joel the chief, and 130 of his
relatives;

14:4 [1]Lit., *were to* [a]1 Chr. 3:5-8

14:9 [a]1 Chr. 15:13; 11:15

14:11 [1]Lit., *smote* [2]I.e., the master of break-through

14:13 [a]1 Chr. 15:9

14:14 [1]Lit., *from upon* [2]Or, *baka shrubs*

14:16 [1]In 2 Sam. 5:25, *Geba*

14:17 [a]Ex. 15:14-16; Deut. 2:25

15:1 [a]1 Chr. 15:3; 16:1; 17:1-5

15:2 [a]Num. 4:15

15:3 [a]1 Chr. 13:5; 1 Kin. 8:1 [b]1 Chr. 15:1, 12; 2 Sam. 6:12, 17

15:4 [a]1 Chr. 6:16-30; 12:26-28

15:5 [1]Lit., *brothers*, i.e., fellow tribesmen, and so throughout the chap.

8 of the sons of Elizaphan, Shemaiah the chief, and 200
of his relatives;
9 of the sons of Hebron, Eliel the chief, and 80 of his
relatives;
10 of the sons of Uzziel, Amminadab the chief, and 112 of
his relatives.
11 Then David called for [a]Zadok and [b]Abiathar the
priests, and for the Levites, for Uriel, Assiah, Joel, Shemaiah,
Eliel, and Amminadab,
12 and said to them, "You are the heads of the fathers'
households of the Levites; [a]consecrate yourselves both you and
your relatives, that you may bring up the ark of the LORD God
of Israel, [b]to *the place* that I have prepared for it.
13 "[a]Because you did not *carry it* at the first, the LORD our
God made an outburst on us, for we did not seek Him according to the ordinance."
14 [a]So the priests and the Levites consecrated themselves
to bring up the ark of the LORD God of Israel.
15 And the sons of [a]the Levites carried the ark of God on
their shoulders, with the poles thereon as Moses had commanded according to the word of the LORD.
16 Then David spoke to the chiefs of the Levites [a]to appoint their relatives the singers, with instruments of music,
harps, lyres, loud-sounding cymbals, to raise sounds of joy.
17 So [a]the Levites appointed Heman the son of Joel, and
from his relatives, Asaph the son of Berechiah; and from the
sons of Merari their relatives, Ethan the son of Kushaiah,
18 and with them their relatives of the second rank, Zechariah, [1]Ben, Jaaziel, Shemiramoth, Jehiel, Unni, Eliab, Benaiah, Maaseiah, Mattithiah, Eliphelehu, Mikneiah, Obed-
edom, and Jeiel, the gatekeepers.
19 So the singers, Heman, Asaph, and Ethan *were appointed* to sound aloud cymbals of bronze;
20 and Zechariah, Aziel, Shemiramoth, Jehiel, Unni,
Eliab, Maaseiah, and Benaiah, with [1]harps *tuned* to [a]alamoth;
21 and Mattithiah, Eliphelehu, Mikneiah, Obed-edom,
Jeiel, and Azaziah, to lead with [1]lyres tuned to [a]the sheminith.
22 And Chenaniah, chief of the Levites, was *in charge of*
the singing; he gave instruction in singing because he was
skillful.
23 And Berechiah and Elkanah were gatekeepers for the
ark.
24 And Shebaniah, Joshaphat, Nethanel, Amasai, Zechariah, Benaiah, and Eliezer, the priests, [a]blew the trumpets before the ark of God. Obed-edom and Jehiah also *were* gatekeepers for the ark.
25 [a]So *it was* David, with the elders of Israel and the
captains over thousands, who went to bring up the ark of the
covenant of the LORD from [b]the house of Obed-edom with joy.
26 And it came about because God was helping the Levites who were carrying the ark of the covenant of the LORD,
that they sacrificed [a]seven bulls and seven rams.
27 Now David was clothed with a robe of fine linen with
all the Levites who were carrying the ark, and the singers and
Chenaniah the leader of the singing *with* the singers. David
also wore an ephod of linen.

11 [a]1 Chr. 12:28 [b]1 Sam. 22:20-23; 1 Kin. 2:26, 35

12 [a]Ex. 19:14, 15; 2 Chr. 35:6 [b]1 Chr. 15:1, 3

13 [a]1 Chr. 13:7; 2 Sam. 6:3

14 [a]1 Chr. 15:12

15 [a]Ex. 25:14; Num. 4:5

16 [a]1 Chr. 13:8; 25:1

17 [a]1 Chr. 25:1

18 [1]Omitted in Gk. and many mss.

20 [1]Or, *harps of maiden-like tone* [a]Ps. 46:title

21 [1]Or, *octave harps* [a]Ps. 6:title

24 [a]1 Chr. 15:28; 16:6

25 [a]2 Sam. 6:12, 15 [b]1 Chr. 13:13

26 [a]Num. 23:1-4, 29

28 Thus all Israel brought up the ark of the covenant of
the LORD with shouting, and with sound of the horn, with
trumpets, with loud-sounding cymbals, with harps and lyres.
29 And it happened when the ark of the covenant of the
LORD came to the city of David, that Michal the daughter of
Saul looked out of the window, and saw King David leaping
and making merry; and she despised him in her heart.

CHAPTER 16

AND they brought in the ark of God and [a]placed it inside the
tent which David had pitched for it, and they offered burnt
offerings and peace offerings before God.
2 When David had finished offering the burnt offering
and the peace offerings, he blessed the people in the name of
the LORD.
3 And he distributed to every one of Israel, both man
and woman, to every one a loaf of bread and a portion *of meat*
and a raisin cake.
4 And he appointed some of the Levites *as* ministers
before the ark of the LORD, even to celebrate and to thank and
praise the LORD God of Israel:
5 Asaph the chief, and second to him Zechariah, *then*
[1]Jeiel, Shemiramoth, Jehiel, Mattithiah, Eliab, Benaiah, Obed-
edom, and Jeiel, with musical instruments, harps, lyres; also
Asaph with loud-sounding cymbals,
6 and Benaiah and Jahaziel the priests *blew* trumpets
continually before the ark of the covenant of God.
7 Then on that day David [a]first assigned [1]Asaph and his
[2]relatives to give thanks to the LORD.

8 [a]Oh give thanks to the LORD, call upon His name;
[b]Make known His deeds among the peoples.
9 Sing to Him, sing praises to Him;
[1]Speak of all His [2]wonders.
10 [1]Glory in His holy name;
Let the heart of those who seek the LORD be glad.
11 [a]Seek the LORD and His strength;
Seek His face continually.
12 [a]Remember His wonderful deeds which He has done,
[b]His marvels and the judgments from His mouth,
13 O seed of Israel His servant,
Sons of Jacob, His chosen ones!
14 He is the LORD our God;
[a]His judgments are in all the earth.
15 Remember His covenant forever,
The word which He commanded to a thousand generations,
16 [a]*The covenant* which He made with Abraham,
And His oath to Isaac.
17 [a]He also confirmed it to Jacob for a statute,
To Israel as an everlasting covenant,
18 Saying, "[a]To you I will give the land of Canaan,
As the portion of your inheritance,
19 [a]When you were only a few in number,
Very few, and strangers in it."
20 And they wandered about from nation to nation,
And from *one* kingdom to another people.

1 [a]1 Chr. 15:1
5 [1]Or, *Jaaziel,* 1 Chr. 15:28
7 [1]Lit., *by the hand of Asaph* [2]Lit., *brothers* [a]2 Sam. 22:1; 23:1
8 [a]Ps. 105:1-15 [b]1 Kin. 8:43; 2 Kin. 19:19
9 [1]Or, *Meditate on* [2]I.e., wonderful acts
10 [1]Or, *Boast*
11 [a]Ps. 24:6
12 [a]Ps. 103:2 [b]Ps. 78:43-68
14 [a]Ps. 48:10
16 [a]Gen. 17:2; 22:16-18; 26:3
17 [a]Gen. 35:11, 12
18 [a]Gen. 13:15
19 [a]Gen. 34:30; Deut. 7:7

21 He permitted no man to oppress them,
And [a]He reproved kings for their sakes, *saying,*
22 "Do not touch My anointed ones,
And [a]do My prophets no harm."
23 [a]Sing to the LORD, all the earth;
Proclaim good tidings of His salvation from day to day.
24 Tell of His glory among the nations,
His wonderful deeds among all the peoples.
25 For [a]great is the LORD, and greatly to be praised;
He also is [b]to be feared above all gods.
26 For all the gods of the peoples are [1a]idols,
[b]But the LORD made the heavens.
27 Splendor and majesty are before Him,
Strength and joy are in His place.
28 Ascribe to the LORD, O families of the peoples,
Ascribe to the LORD glory and strength.
29 Ascribe to the LORD the glory due His name;
Bring an [1]offering, and come before Him;
[a]Worship the LORD in [2]holy array.
30 Tremble before Him, all the earth;
Indeed, the world is firmly established, it will not be moved.
31 [a]Let the heavens be glad, and let the earth rejoice;
And let them say among the nations, "[b]The LORD reigns."
32 [a]Let the sea [1]roar, and [2]all it contains;
Let the field exult, and all that is in it.
33 Then the trees of the forest will sing for joy before the LORD;
For He is coming to judge the earth.
34 [a]O give thanks to the LORD , for *He is* good;
For His lovingkindness is everlasting.
35 [a]Then say, "Save us, O God of our salvation,
And gather us and deliver us from the nations,
To give thanks to Thy holy name,
And [1]glory in Thy praise."
36 [a]Blessed be the LORD, the God of Israel,
From everlasting even to everlasting.
Then all the people [b]said, "Amen," and praised the LORD.
37 So he left Asaph and his [1]relatives there [a]before the ark
of the covenant of the LORD, to minister before the ark continually, [b]as every day's work required;
38 and [a]Obed-edom with [1]his 68 relatives; Obed-edom,
also the son of Jeduthun, and [b]Hosah as gatekeepers.
39 And *he left* [a]Zadok the priest and his [1]relatives the
priests [b]before the [2]tabernacle of the LORD in the high place
which *was* at Gibeon,
40 to offer burnt offerings to the LORD on the altar of
burnt offering continually morning and evening, [a]even according
ing to all that is written in the law of the LORD, which He
commanded Israel.
41 And with them *were* [a]Heman and Jeduthun, and [b]the
rest who were chosen, who were designated by name, to [c]give
thanks to the LORD, because His lovingkindness is everlasting.
42 And with them *were* Heman and Jeduthun *with* trum-

21 [a]Gen. 12:17; 20:3; Ex. 7:15-18
22 [a]Gen. 20:7
23 [a]Ps. 96:1-13
25 [a]Ps. 144:3-6 [b]Ps. 89:7
26 [1]Or, *non-existent things* [a]Lev. 19:4 [b]Ps. 102:25
29 [1]Or, *grain offering* [2]Or, *the splendor of holiness* [a]Ps. 29:2
31 [a]Is. 44:23; 49:13 [b]Ps. 93:1; 96:10
32 [1]Or, *thunder* [2]Lit., *its fulness* [a]Ps. 98:7
34 [a]Ps. 106:1; 136:1
35 [1]Lit., *boast* [a]Ps. 106:47, 48
36 [a]1 Kin. 8:15, 56; Ps. 72:18 [b]Deut. 27:15; Neh. 8:6
37 [1]Lit., *brothers* [a]1 Chr. 16:4, 5 [b]2 Chr. 8:14; Ezra 3:4
38 [1]Lit., *their brothers,* 68 [a]1 Chr. 13:14 [b]1 Chr. 26:10
39 [1]Lit., *brothers* [2]Lit., *dwelling place* [a]1 Chr. 15:11 [b]1 Kin. 3:4
40 [a]Ex. 29:38-42; Num. 28:3, 4
41 [a]1 Chr. 6:33 [b]1 Chr. 25:1-6 [c]2 Chr. 5:13

42 [a]1 Chr. 25:7; 2 Chr. 7:6; 29:27

pets and cymbals for those who should sound aloud, and *with*
instruments *for* [a]the songs of God, and the sons of Jeduthun
for the gate.
43 Then all the people departed each to his house, and
David returned to bless his household.

1 [a]2 Sam. 7:1-29

[a] CHAPTER 17

AND it came about, when David dwelt in his house, that
David said to Nathan the prophet, "Behold, I am dwelling in a
house of cedar, but the ark of the covenant of the LORD is
under curtains."
2 Then Nathan said to David, "Do all that is in your
heart, for God is with you."
3 And it came about the same night, that the word of
God came to Nathan, saying,
4 "Go and tell David My servant, 'Thus says the LORD,
[a]"You shall not build a house for Me to dwell in;
5 for I have not dwelt in a house since the day that I
brought up Israel to this day, [a]but I have [1]gone from tent to
tent and from *one* dwelling place *to another.*
6 "In all places where I have walked with all Israel, have I
spoken a word [a]with any of the judges of Israel, whom I commanded to shepherd My people, saying, 'Why have you not
built for Me a house of cedar?' " '
7 "Now, therefore, thus shall you say to My servant David, 'Thus says the LORD of hosts, "I took you from the pasture, from following the sheep, that you should be leader over
My people Israel.
8 "And I have been with you wherever you have gone, and
have cut off all your enemies from before you; and I will make
you a name like the name of the great ones who are in the
earth.
9 "And I will appoint a place for My people Israel, and
will plant them, that they may dwell in their own place and be
moved no more; neither shall the [1]wicked waste them any
more as formerly,
10 even from the day that I commanded judges *to be* over
My people Israel. And I will subdue all your enemies. Moreover,
I tell you that the LORD will build a house for you.
11 "And it shall come about when your days are fulfilled
that you must go *to be* with your fathers, that I will set up *one*
of your [1]descendants after you, who shall be of your sons; and I
will establish his kingdom.
12 "He shall build for Me a house, and I will establish his
throne forever.
13 "[a]I will be his father, and he shall be My son; and I will
not take My lovingkindness away from him, [b]as I took it from
him who was before you.
14 "But I will settle him in My house and in My kingdom
forever, and his throne shall be established forever." ' "
15 According to all these words and according to all this
vision, so Nathan spoke to David.
16 Then David the king went in and sat before the LORD
and said, "Who am I, O LORD God, and what is my house that
Thou hast brought me thus far?

4 [a]1 Chr. 28:2, 3
5 [1]Lit., *been* [a]Ex. 40:2, 3; 2 Sam. 7:6
6 [a]2 Sam. 7:7
9 [1]Lit., *sons of wickedness*
11 [1]Lit., *seed*
13 [a]Heb. 1:5 [b]1 Chr. 10:14

17 "And this was a small thing in Thine eyes, O God; but
Thou hast spoken of Thy servant's house for a great while to
come, and hast regarded me according to the standard of a
man of high degree, O LORD God.
18 "What more can David still *say* to Thee concerning the
honor *bestowed* on Thy servant? For Thou knowest Thy
servant.
19 "O LORD, [a]for Thy servant's sake, and according to
Thine own heart, Thou hast wrought all this greatness, to
make known all these great things.
20 "O LORD, there is none like Thee, neither is there any
God besides Thee, according to all that we have heard with
our ears.
21 "And what one nation in the earth is like Thy people
Israel, whom God went to redeem for Himself *as* a people, to
make Thee a name by great and terrible things, in driving out
nations from before Thy people, whom Thou didst redeem
out of Egypt?
22 "[a]For Thy people Israel Thou didst make Thine own
people forever, and Thou, O LORD, didst become their God.
23 "And now, O LORD, let the word that Thou hast spoken
concerning Thy servant and concerning his house, be established forever, and do as Thou hast spoken.
24 "And let Thy name be established and magnified forever,
saying, 'The LORD of hosts is the God of Israel, *even* a
God to Israel; and the house of David Thy servant is established before Thee.'
25 "For Thou, O my God, hast revealed to Thy servant
that Thou wilt build for him a house; therefore Thy servant
hath found *courage* to pray before Thee.
26 "And now, O LORD, Thou art God, and hast [1]promised
this good thing to Thy servant.
27 "And now it hath pleased Thee to bless the house of
Thy servant, that it may [1]continue forever before Thee; for
Thou, O LORD, hast blessed, and it is blessed forever."

CHAPTER 18

NOW after this [a]it came about that David [1]defeated the
Philistines and subdued them and took Gath and its towns
from the hand of the Philistines.
2 And he defeated Moab, and the Moabites became servants to David, bringing tribute.
3 David also defeated Hadadezer king of Zobah *as far as*
Hamath, as he went to establish his [1]rule to the Euphrates
River.
4 And David took from him 1,000 chariots and 7,000
horsemen and 20,000 foot soldiers, and David hamstrung all
the chariot horses, but reserved *enough* of them for 100
chariots.
5 When [1]the Syrians of [2]Damascus came to help Hadadezer king [a]of Zobah, David [3]killed 22,000 men of [1]the
Syrians.
6 Then David put *garrisons* in [1]Syria of [2]Damascus; and
[1]the Syrians became servants to David, bringing tribute. And
the LORD helped David wherever he went.

19 [a]2 Sam. 7:21; Is. 37:35

22 [a]Ex. 19:5, 6

26 [1]Lit., *said*

27 [1]Lit., *be*

1 [1]Lit., *smote* and so in v. 1-3 [a]2 Sam. 8:1-18

3 [1]Lit., *hand*

5 [1]Heb., *Aram* [2]Heb., *Darmeseq* [3]Lit., *smote* [a]1 Chr. 19:6

6 [1]Heb., *Aram* [2]Heb., *Darmeseq*

7 And David took the shields of gold which were [1]carried
by the servants of Hadadezer, and brought them to Jerusalem.
8 Also from Tibhath and from Cun, cities of Hadadezer,
David took a very large amount of bronze, with which Solomon made the bronze sea and the pillars and the bronze
utensils.
9 Now when [1]Tou king of Hamath heard that David had
[2]defeated all the army of Hadadezer king of Zobah,
10 he sent [1]Hadoram his son to King David, to [2]greet him
and to bless him, because he had fought against Hadadezer
and had [3]defeated him; for Hadadezer had been at war with
Tou. And *Hadoram brought* all kinds of articles of gold and
silver and bronze.
11 King David also dedicated these to the LORD with the
silver and the gold which he had carried away from all the
nations: from Edom, Moab, the sons of Ammon, the Philistines, and from Amalek.
12 Moreover Abishai the son of Zeruiah [1]defeated 18,000
Edomites in the Valley of Salt.
13 Then he put garrisons in Edom, and all the Edomites
became servants to David. And the LORD helped David wherever
he went.
14 So David reigned over all Israel; and he [1]administered
justice and righteousness for all his people.
15 And [a]Joab the son of Zeruiah *was* over the army, and
Jehoshaphat the son of Ahilud *was* recorder;
16 and Zadok the son of Ahitub and Abimelech the son of
Abiathar *were* priests, and Shavsha *was* secretary;
17 and Benaiah the son of Jehoiada *was* over the Cherethites and the Pelethites, and the sons of David *were* chiefs at
the king's side.

CHAPTER 19

[a]NOW it came about after this, that Nahash the king of the
sons of Ammon died, and his son became king in his place.
2 Then David said, "I will show kindness to Hanun the
son of Nahash, because his father showed kindness to me." So
David sent messengers to console him concerning his father.
And David's servants came into the land of the sons of Amon
to Hanun, to console him.
3 But the princes of the sons of Ammon said to Hanun,
"[1]Do you think that David is honoring your father, in that he
has sent comforters to you? Have not his servants come to you
to search and to overthrow and to spy out the land?"
4 So Hanun took David's servants and shaved them, and
cut off their garments in the middle as far as their hips, and
sent them away.
5 Then *certain persons* went and told David about the
men. And he sent to meet them, for the men were greatly
humiliated. And the king said, "[1]Stay at Jericho until your
beards grow, and *then* return."
6 When the sons of Ammon saw that they had made
themselves odious to David, Hanun and the sons of Ammon
sent 1,000 talents of silver to hire for themselves chariots and

7 [1]Lit., *on*

9 [1]In 2 Sam. 8:10, *Toi*
[2]Lit., *smitten*

10 [1]In 2 Sam. 8:10, *Joram*
[2]Lit., *ask him of his welfare*
[3]Lit., *smitten*

12 [1]Lit., *smote*

14 [1]Lit., *was doing*

15 [a]1 Chr. 11:6

1 [a]2 Sam. 10:1-19

3 [1]Lit., *In your eyes is David honoring your father because*

5 [1]Lit., *Return to*

horsemen from Mesopotamia, from Aram-maacah, and [a]from
Zobah.
7 So they hired for themselves 32,000 chariots, and the
king of Maacah and his people, who came and camped before
[a]Medeba. And the sons of Ammon gathered together from
their cities and came to battle.
8 When David heard *of it,* he sent Joab and all the army,
the mighty men.
9 And the sons of Ammon came out and drew up in
battle array at the entrance of the city, and the kings who had
come were by themselves in the field.
10 Now when Joab saw that the [1]battle was set against him
in front and in the rear, he selected from all the choice men of
Israel and they arrayed themselves against the Syrians.
11 But the remainder of the people he placed in the hand
of [1]Abshai his brother; and they arrayed themselves against the
sons of Ammon.
12 And he said, "If the Syrians are too strong for me, then
you shall help me; but if the sons of Ammon are too strong for
you, then I will help you.
13 "Be strong, and let us show ourselves courageous for the
sake of our people and for the cities of our God; and may the
LORD do what is good in His sight."
14 So Joab and the people who were with him drew near
to the battle against the Syrians, and they fled before him.
15 When the sons of Ammon saw that the Syrians fled,
they also fled before Abshai his brother, and entered the city.
Then Joab came to Jerusalem.
16 When the Syrians saw that they had been [1]defeated by
Israel, they sent messengers, and brought out the Syrians who
were beyond the [2]River, with Shophach the commander of the
army of Hadadezer [3]leading them.
17 When it was told David, he gathered all Israel together
and crossed the Jordan, and came upon them and drew up in
formation against them. And when David drew up in battle
array against the Syrians, they fought against him.
18 And the Syrians fled before Israel, and David killed of
the Syrians 7,000 charioteers and 40,000 foot soldiers, and put
to death Shophach the commander of the army.
19 So when the servants of Hadadezer saw that they were
[1]defeated by Israel, they made peace with David and served
him. Thus the Syrians were not willing to help the sons of
Ammon any more.

CHAPTER 20

[a]THEN it happened [1]in the spring, at the time when kings go
out *to battle,* that Joab led out the army and ravaged the land
of the sons of Ammon, and came and beseiged Rabbah. But
David stayed at Jerusalem. And [b]Joab struck Rabbah and
overthrew it.
2 [a]And David took the crown of [1]their king from his
head, and he found it to weigh a talent of gold, and there was a
precious stone in it; and it was placed on David's head. And he
brought out the spoil of the city, a very great amount.
3 And he brought out the people who *were* in it, [a]and cut

6 [a]1 Chr. 18:5, 9

7 [a]Num. 21:30; Josh. 13:9, 16

10 [1]Lit., *the face of the battle*

11 [1]In 2 Sam. 10:10, *Abishai*

16 [1]Lit., *smitten before* [2]I.e., Euphrates [3]Lit., *before*

19 [1]Lit., *smitten before*

1 [1]Lit., *at the return of the year*
[a]2 Sam. 11:1 [b]2 Sam. 12:26

2 [1]In Zeph. 1:5, *Malcam*
[a]2 Sam. 12:30, 31

3 [a]2 Sam. 12:31

them with saws and with sharp instruments and with axes. And
thus David did to all the cities of the sons of Ammon. Then
David and all the people returned *to* Jerusalem.
4 [a]Now it came about after this, that war [1]broke out at
[2]Gezer with the Philistines; then Sibbecai the Hushathite
[3]killed Sippai, one of the descendants of the [4]giants, and they
were subdued.
5 And there was war with the Philistines again, and Elhanan the son of [a]Jair [1]killed Lahmi the brother of Goliath the
Gittite, the [b]shaft of whose spear *was* like a weaver's beam.
6 And again there was war at Gath, where there was a
man of *great* stature who had twenty-four fingers and toes, six
fingers on each hand and six *toes on each foot;* and he also was
descended from the giants.
7 And when he taunted Israel, Jonathan the son of Shimea, David's brother, [1]killed him.
8 These were descended from the giants in Gath, and
they fell by the hand of David and by the hand of his servants.

[a] Chapter 21

THEN Satan stood up against Israel and moved David to
number Israel.
2 So David said to Joab and to the princes of the people,
"[a]Go, number Israel from Beer-sheba even to Dan, and bring
me *word* that I may know their number."
3 And Joab said, "[a]May the LORD add to His people a
hundred times as many as they are! But, my lord the king, are
they not all my lord's servants? Why does my lord seek this
thing? Why should he be a cause of guilt to Israel?"
4 Nevertheless, the king's word prevailed against Joab.
Therefore, Joab departed and went throughout all Israel, and
came to Jerusalem.
5 And Joab gave the [1]number of the [2]census of all the
people to David. And [a]all Israel *were* 1,100,000 men who drew
the sword; and Judah *was* 470,000 men who drew the sword.
6 [a]But he did not [1]number Levi and Benjamin among
them, for the king's [2]command was abhorrent to Joab.
7 And [1]God was displeased with this thing, so He struck
Israel.
8 And David said to God, "I have sinned greatly, in that I
have done this thing. [a]But now, please take away the iniquity
of Thy servant, for I have done very foolishly."
9 And the LORD spoke to [a]Gad, David's [b]seer, saying,
10 "Go and speak to David, saying, 'Thus says the LORD, "I
[1]offer you three things; choose for yourself one of them, that I
may do *it* to you." ' "
11 So Gad came to David and said to him, "Thus says the
LORD, 'Take for yourself
12 [a]either three years of famine, or three months to be
swept away before your foes, while the sword of your enemies
overtakes *you,* or else three days of the sword of the LORD,
even pestilence in the land, and the angel of the LORD destroying throughout all the territory of Israel.' Now, therefore,
consider what answer I shall return to Him who sent me."
13 And David said to Gad, "I am in great distress; please

20:4 [1]Lit., *stood up* [2]In 2 Sam. 21:18, *Gob* [3]Lit., *smote* [4]Heb., *Raphah,* and so in vs. 6, 8 [a]2 Sam. 21:18-22
20:5 [1]Lit., *smote* [a]2 Sam. 21:19 [b]1 Chr. 11:23; 1 Sam. 17:7
20:7 [1]Lit., *smote*
21:1 [a]2 Sam. 24:1-25
21:2 [a]1 Chr. 27:23, 24
21:3 [a]Deut. 1:11
21:5 [1]Lit., *muster* [2]Lit., *numbering* [a]2 Sam. 24:9
21:6 [1]Lit., *muster* [2]Lit., *word* [a]1 Chr. 27:24
21:7 [1]Lit., *it was evil in the sight of God*
21:8 [a]2 Sam. 12:13
21:9 [a]1 Chr. 29:29; 2 Sam. 24:11 [b]1 Sam. 9:9
21:10 [1]Lit., *stretch out to*
21:12 [a]2 Sam. 24:13

let me fall into the hand of the LORD, [a]for His mercies are very
great. But do not let me fall into the hand of man."
14 [a]So the LORD [1]sent a pestilence on Israel; 70,000 men of
Israel fell.
15 And God sent an angel to Jerusalem to destroy it; but
as he was about to destroy *it*, the LORD saw and [a]was sorry over
the calamity, and said to the destroying angel, "It is enough;
now relax your hand." And the angel of the LORD was standing
by the threshing floor of [1]Ornan the Jebusite.
16 Then David lifted up his eyes and saw the angel of the
LORD standing between earth and heaven, with his drawn
sword in his hand stretched out over Jerusalem. Then David
and the elders, [a]covered with sackcloth, fell on their faces.
17 And David said to God, "Is it not I who [1]commanded
to count the people? Indeed, I am the one who has sinned and
done very wickedly, [a]but these sheep, what have they done? O
LORD my God, please let Thy hand be against me and my
father's household, but not against Thy people that they
should be plagued."
18 [a]Then the angel of the LORD [1]commanded Gad to say
to David, that David should go up and build an altar to the
LORD on the threshing floor of Ornan the Jebusite.
19 So David went up at the word of Gad, which he spoke
in the name of the LORD.
20 Now Ornan turned back and saw the angel, and his
four sons *who were* with him hid themselves. And Ornan was
threshing wheat.
21 And as David came to Ornan, Ornan looked and saw
David, and went out from the threshing floor, and prostrated
himself [1]before David with his face to the ground.
22 Then David said to Ornan, "Give me the [1]site of *this*
threshing floor, that I may build on it an altar to the LORD; for
the full price you shall give it to me, that the plague may be
restrained from the people."
23 And Ornan said to David, "Take *it* for yourself; and let
my lord the king do what is good in his sight. See, I will give
the oxen for burnt offerings and the threshing sledges for wood
and the wheat for the grain offering; I will give *it* all."
24 But King David said to Ornan, "No, but I will surely
buy *it* for the full price; for I will not take what is yours for the
LORD, or offer a burnt offering [1]which costs me nothing."
25 So [a]David gave Ornan 600 shekels of gold by weight for
the [1]site.
26 Then David built an altar to the LORD there, and offered burnt offerings and peace offerings. And he called to the
LORD and [a]He answered him with fire from heaven on the altar
of burnt offering.
27 And the LORD commanded the angel, and he put his
sword back in its sheath.
28 At that time, when David saw that the LORD had answered him on the threshing floor of Ornan the Jebusite, he
offered sacrifice there.
29 [a]For the tabernacle of the LORD, which Moses had
made in the wilderness, and the altar of burnt offering *were* in
the high place at Gibeon at that time.

13 [a]Ps. 51:1; 130:4, 7

14 [1]Lit., *gave*
[a]1 Chr. 27:24

15 [1]In 2 Sam. 24:16, *Araunah*
[a]Ex. 32:14; 1 Sam. 15:11; Jon. 3:10

16 [a]1 Kin. 21:27

17 [1]Lit., *said*
[a]2 Sam. 7:8; Ps. 74:1

18 [1]Lit., *said*
[a]2 Chr. 3:1

21 [1]Lit., *to*

22 [1]Lit., *place*

24 [1]Lit., *gratuitously*

25 [1]Lit., *place*
[a]2 Sam. 24:24

26 [a]Lev. 9:24; Judg. 6:21

29 [a]1 Chr. 16:39; 1 Kin. 3:4

30 But David could not go before it to inquire of God, for
he was terrified by the sword of the angel of the LORD.

CHAPTER 22

THEN David said, "[a]This is the house of the LORD God, and
this is the altar of burnt offering for Israel."
2 So David [1]gave orders to gather [a]the foreigners who
were in the land of Israel, and [b]he set stonecutters to hew out
stones to build the house of God.
3 And David [a]prepared large quantities of iron [1]to make
the nails for the doors of the gates and for the clamps, and
more [b]bronze than could be weighed;
4 and timbers of cedar logs beyond number, for [a]the Sidonians and Tyrians brought large quantities of cedar timber
to David.
5 And David said, "My son [a]Solomon is young and inexperienced, and the house that is to be built for the LORD shall
be exceedingly magnificent, famous and glorious throughout
all lands. Therefore I will make preparation for it." So David
made ample preparations before his death.
6 Then he called for his son Solomon, and charged him
to build a house for the LORD God of Israel.
7 And David said to Solomon, "[a]My son, [1]I had intended
to build a house to the name of the LORD my God.
8 "But the word of the LORD came to me, saying, '[a]You
have shed much blood, and have [1]waged great wars; you shall
not build a house to My name, because you have shed *so* much
blood on the earth before Me.
9 'Behold, a son shall be born to you, who shall be a man
of rest; and [a]I will give him rest from all his enemies on every
side; for [b]his name shall be [1]Solomon, and I will give peace and
quiet to Israel in his days.
10 '[a]He shall build a house for My name, and he shall be
My son, and I will be his father; and I will establish the throne
of his kingdom over Israel forever.'
11 "Now, my son, [a]the LORD be with you that you may be
successful, and build the house of the LORD your God just as
He has spoken concerning you.
12 "[a]Only the LORD give you discretion and understanding,
and give you charge over Israel, so that you may keep the law
of the LORD your God.
13 "[a]Then you shall prosper, if you are careful to observe
the statutes and the ordinances which the LORD commanded
Moses concerning Israel. [b]Be strong and courageous, do not
fear nor be dismayed.
14 "Now behold, [1]with great pains, I have prepared for the
house of the LORD [a]100,000 talents of gold and 1,000,000 talents of silver, and [b]bronze and iron beyond weight, for [2]they
are in great quantity; also timber and stone I have prepared,
and you may add to them.
15 "Moreover, there are many workmen with you, stonecutters and masons of stone and carpenters, and all men who
are skillful in every kind of work.

1 [a]1 Chr. 21:18-28; 2 Chr. 3:1
2 [1]Lit., *said to* [a]1 Kin. 9:20, 21; 2 Chr. 2:17 [b]1 Kin. 5:17, 18
3 [1]Lit., *for* [a]1 Chr. 29:27 [b]1 Chr. 22:14
4 [a]1 Kin. 5:6-10
5 [a]1 Chr. 29:1; 1 Kin. 3:7
7 [1]Lit., *as for me, it was in my heart* [a]1 Chr. 17:1; 2 Sam. 7:2, 3
8 [1]Lit., *made* [a]1 Chr. 28:3
9 [1]I.e., Peaceful [a]1 Kin. 4:20, 25 [b]2 Sam. 12:24, 25
10 [a]1 Chr. 17:12; 2 Sam. 7:13, 14
11 [a]1 Chr. 22:16
12 [a]1 Kin. 3:9-12; 2 Chr. 1:10
13 [a]1 Chr. 28:7 [b]Josh. 1:6-9
14 [1]Lit., *in my affliction* [2]Lit., *it is* [a]1 Chr. 29:4 [b]1 Chr. 22:3

16 "Of the gold, the silver and the bronze and the iron,
there is no limit. Arise and work, and may [a]the LORD be
with you."
17 [a]David also commanded all the leaders of Israel to help
his son Solomon, *saying*,
18 "Is not the LORD your God with you? And [a]has He not
given you rest on every side? For He has given the inhabitants
of the land into my hand, and the land is subdued before the
LORD and before His people.
19 "Now [a]set your heart and your soul to seek the LORD
your God; arise, therefore, and build the sanctuary of the
LORD God, [b]so that you may bring the ark of the covenant of
the LORD, and the holy vessels of God into the house that is to
be built [c]for the name of the LORD."

CHAPTER 23

[a]NOW when David [1]reached old age, [b]he made his son Solomon king over Israel.
2 And he gathered together all the leaders of Israel with
the priests and the Levites.
3 And [a]the Levites were numbered from thirty years old
and upward, and [b]their number by [1]census of men was 38,000.
4 Of these, 24,000 were [a]to oversee the work of the house
of the LORD; and 6,000 *were* [b]officers and judges,
5 and 4,000 *were* gatekeepers, and [a]4,000 *were* praising
the LORD with the instruments which [1]David made for giving
praise.
6 And David divided them into divisions [a]according to
the sons of Levi: Gershon, Kohath, and Merari.
7 Of the Gershonites *were* [1]Ladan and Shimei.
8 The sons of Ladan *were* Jehiel the first and Zethan and
Joel, three.
9 The sons of Shimei *were* Shelemoth and Haziel and
Haran, three. These were the heads of the fathers' *households*
of Ladan.
10 And the sons of Shimei *were* Jahath, [1]Zina, Jeush, and
Beriah. These four *were* the sons of Shimei.
11 And Jahath was the first, and Zizah the second; but
Jeush and Beriah did not have many sons, so they became a
father's household, one [1]class.
12 The sons of Kohath were four: Amram, Izhar, Hebron
and Uzziel.
13 [a]The sons of Amram were Aaron and Moses. And [b]Aa-
ron was set apart to sanctify him as most holy, he and his sons
forever, [c]to burn incense before the LORD, to minister to Him
and to bless in His name forever.
14 But *as for* [a]Moses the man of God, his sons were
named among the tribe of Levi.
15 The sons of Moses *were* Gershom and Eliezer.
16 The [1]son of Gershom *was* [2]Shebuel the chief.
17 And the [1]son of Eliezer was Rehabiah the chief; and
Eliezer had no other sons, but the sons of Rehabiah were very
many.
18 The [1]son of Izhar was [2]Shelomith the chief.

16 [a]1 Chr. 22:11
17 [a]1 Chr. 28:1-6
18 [a]1 Chr. 22:9; 23:25
19 [a]1 Chr. 28:9 [b]1 Kin. 8:6, 21; 2 Chr. 5:7 [c]1 Chr. 22:7

1 [1]Lit., *became old and sated with days* [a]1 Chr. 29:28 [b]1 Chr. 28:5; 29:22
3 [1]Lit., *their heads* [a]Num. 4:3-49 [b]1 Chr. 23:24; Num. 4:48
4 [a]Ezra 3:8, 9 [b]1 Chr. 26:29
5 [1]Lit., *I made* [a]1 Chr. 15:16
6 [a]1 Chr. 6:1
7 [1]In Ex. 6:17, *Libni*
10 [1]In v. 11, *Zizah*
11 [1]Lit., *mustering*
13 [a]Ex. 6:20 [b]Ex. 28:1 [c]Ex. 30:6-10
14 [a]Deut. 33:1; Ps. 90: title
16 [1]Lit., *sons* [2]In Ch. 24:20, *Shubael*
17 [1]Lit., *sons. . . .were*
18 [1]Lit., *sons* [2]In ch. 24:22, *Shelomoth*

19 The sons of Hebron *were* Jeriah the first, Amariah the second, Jehaziel the third and Jekameam the fourth.

20 The sons of Uzziel *were* Micah the first and Isshiah the second.

21 The sons of Merari were Mahli and Mushi. The sons of Mahli *were* Eleazar and Kish.

22 And Eleazar died and had no sons, but daughters only, so their brothers the sons of Kish took them *as wives*.

23 The sons of Mushi *were* three: Mahli, Eder, and Jeremoth.

24 [a]These were the sons of Levi according to their fathers' households, *even* the heads of the fathers' *households* of those of them who were [1]counted, in the number of names by their [2]census, doing the work for the service of the house of the LORD, [b]from twenty years old and upward.

25 For David said, "The LORD God of Israel [a]has given rest to His people, and He dwells in Jerusalem forever.

26 "And also, [a]the Levites will no longer need to carry the tabernacle and all its utensils for its service."

27 For by the last words of David the sons of Levi *were* numbered, from twenty years old and upward.

28 For their office is [1]to assist the sons of Aaron with the service of the house of the LORD, in the courts and in the chambers and in the purifying of all holy things, even the work of the service of the house of God,

29 [a]and with the show bread, and [b]the fine flour for a grain offering, and unleavened wafers, or [c]what is baked in the pan, or [d]what is well-mixed, and [e]all measures of volume and size.

30 And they are to stand every morning to thank and to praise the LORD, and likewise at evening,

31 and to offer all burnt offerings to the LORD, [a]on the sabbaths, the new moons and [b]the fixed festivals in the number *set* by the ordinance concerning them, continually before the LORD.

32 Thus [a]they are to keep charge of the tent of meeting, and charge of the holy place, and [b]charge of the sons of Aaron their [1]relatives, for the service of the house of the LORD.

CHAPTER 24

NOW the divisions of the [1]descendants of Aaron *were these*. [a]The sons of Aaron *were* Nadab, Abihu, Eleazar, and Ithamar.

2 [a]But Nadab and Abihu died before their father and had no [1]sons. So Eleazar and Ithamar served as priests.

3 And David, with [a]Zadok of the sons of Eleazar and Ahimelech of the sons of Ithamar, divided them according to their offices [1]for their ministry.

4 Since more chief men were found from the [1]descendants of Eleazar than the [1]descendants of Ithamar, they divided them thus: *there were* sixteen heads of fathers' households of the [1]descendants of Eleazar, and eight of the [1]descendants of Ithamar according to their fathers' households.

5 [a]Thus they were divided by lot, the one as the other; for they were officers of the sanctuary and officers of God,

24 [1]Lit., *mustered* [2]Lit., *heads* [a]Num. 10:17, 21 [b]1 Chr. 23:3

25 [a]1 Chr. 22:18

26 [a]Num. 4:5, 15; 7:9

28 [1]Lit., *at the hand of*

29 [a]Lev. 24:5-9 [b]Lev. 6:20 [c]1 Chr. 9:31 [d]Lev. 6:21 [e]Lev. 19:35, 36

31 [a]Is. 1:13, 14 [b]Lev. 23:2-4

32 [1]Lit., *brothers* [a]1 Chr. 9:27; Num. 1:53 [b]Num. 3:6-9, 38

1 [1]Lit., *sons* [a]Ex. 6:23

2 [1]Or, *children* [a]Lev. 10:2

3 [1]Lit., *in their service* [a]1 Chr. 3:31; 6:8

4 [1]Lit., *sons*

5 [a]1 Chr. 24:31

both from the [1]descendants of Eleazar and the [1]descendants of
Ithamar.
6 And Shemaiah, the son of Nethanel the scribe, from
the Levites, recorded them in the presence of the king, the
princes, Zadok the priest, [a]Ahimelech the son of Abiathar, and
the heads of the fathers' *households* of the priests and of the
Levites; one fathers' household taken for Eleazar and one tak-
en for Ithamar.
7 Now the first lot came out for Jehoiarib, the second for
Jedaiah,
8 the third for Harim, the fourth for Seorim,
9 the fifth for Malchijah, the sixth for Mijamin,
10 the seventh for Hakkoz, the eighth for [a]Abijah,
11 the ninth for Jeshua, the tenth for Shecaniah,
12 the eleventh for Eliashib, the twelfth for Jakim,
13 the thirteenth for Huppah, the fourteenth for
Jeshebeab,
14 the fifteenth for Bilgah, the sixteenth for Immer,
15 the seventeenth for Hezir, the eighteenth for
Happizzez,
16 the nineteenth for Pethahiah, the twentieth for
Jehezkel,
17 the twenty-first for Jachin, the twenty-second for
Gamul,
18 the twenty-third for Delaiah, the twenty-fourth for
Maaziah.
19 [a]These were their offices for their ministry, when *they*
came in to the house of the LORD according to the ordinance
given to them through Aaron their father, just as the LORD
God of Israel had commanded him.
20 Now for the rest of the sons of Levi: of the sons of
Amram, [1]Shubael; of the sons of Shubael, Jehdeiah.
21 Of Rehabiah: of the sons of Rehabiah, Isshiah the first.
22 Of the Izharites, [1]Shelomoth; of the sons of Shelomoth, Jahath.
23 And the sons [a]*of Hebron:* Jeriah *the first,* Amariah the
second, Jahaziel the third, Jekameam the fourth.
24 *Of* the sons of Uzziel, Micah; of the sons of Micah,
Shamir.
25 The brother of Micah, Isshiah; of the sons of Isshiah,
Zechariah.
26 The sons of Merari, Mahli and Mushi; the sons of
Jaaziah, Beno.
27 The sons of Merari: by Jaaziah *were* Beno, Shoham,
Zaccur, and Ibri.
28 By Mahli: Eleazar, who had no sons.
29 By Kish: the sons of Kish, Jerahmeel.
30 And the sons of Mushi: Mahli, Eder, and Jerimoth.
These *were* the sons of the Levites according to their fathers'
households.
31 [a]These also cast lots just as their [1]relatives the sons of
Aaron in the presence of David the king, [b]Zadok, Ahimelech,
and the heads of the fathers' *households* of the priests and of
the Levites—the head of fathers' *households* as well as those of
his younger brother.

5 [1]Lit., *sons*
6 [a]1 Chr. 18:16
10 [a]Neh. 12:4; Luke 1:5
19 [a]1 Chr. 9:25
20 [1]In 23:16, *Shebuel*
22 [1]In 23:18, *Shelomith*
23 [a]1 Chr. 23:19
31 [1]Lit., *brothers*
[a]1 Chr. 24:5, 6 [b]1 Chr. 24:6

CHAPTER 25

MOREOVER, David and the commanders of the army set apart for the service *some* of the sons of [a]Asaph and of Heman and of Jeduthun, who *were* to [b]prophesy with lyres, [c]harps, and cymbals; and the number of [1]those who performed their service was:

2 of the sons of Asaph: Zaccur, Joseph, Nethaniah, and [1]Asharelah; the sons of Asaph *were* under the [2]direction of Asaph, who prophesied under the [2]direction of the king.

3 [a]Of Jeduthun, the sons of Jeduthun: Gedaliah, [1]Zeri, Jeshaiah, [2]Shimei, Hashabiah, and Mattithiah, six, under the [3]direction of their father Jeduthun with the harp, who prophesied in giving thanks and praising the LORD.

4 Of Heman, the sons of Heman: Bukkiah, Mattaniah, [1]Uzziel, [2]Shebuel and Jerimoth, Hananiah, Hanani, Eliathah, Giddalti and Romamti-ezer, Joshbekashah, Mallothi, Hothir, Mahazioth.

5 All these *were* the sons of Heman [a]the king's seer to [1]exalt him according to the words of God, for God gave fourteen sons and three daughters to Heman.

6 All these were under the [1]direction of their father to sing in the house of the LORD, [a]with cymbals, harps and lyres, for the service of the house of God. [b]Asaph, Jeduthun and Heman *were* under the [1]direction of the king.

7 And their number who were trained in singing to the LORD, with their [1]relatives, all who were skillful, *was* [a]288.

8 And [a]they cast lots for their duties, all alike, the small as well as the great, the teacher *as well* as the pupil.

9 Now the first lot came out for Asaph to Joseph, the second for Gedaliah, he with his relatives and sons *were* twelve;

10 the third to Zaccur, his sons and his relatives, twelve;

11 the fourth to Izri, his sons and his relatives, twelve;

12 the fifth to Nethaniah, his sons and his relatives, twelve;

13 the sixth to Bukkiah, his sons and his relatives, twelve;

14 the seventh to Jesharelah, his sons and his relatives, twelve;

15 the eighth to Jeshaiah, his sons and his relatives, twelve;

16 the ninth to Mattaniah, his sons and his relatives, twelve;

17 the tenth to Shimei, his sons and his relatives, twelve;

18 the eleventh to Azarel, his sons and his relatives, twelve;

19 the twelfth to Hashabiah, his sons and his relatives, twelve;

20 for the thirteenth, Shubael, his sons and his relatives, twelve;

21 for the fourteenth, Mattithiah, his sons and his relatives, twelve;

22 for the fifteenth to Jeremoth, his sons and his relatives, twelve;

23 for the sixteenth to Hananiah, his sons and his relatives, twelve;

24 for the seventeenth to Joshbekashah, his sons and his relatives, twelve;

1 [1]Lit., *workmen according to their service* [a]1 Chr. 6:33, 39 [b]2 Kin. 3:15 [c]1 Chr. 15:16

2 [1]In v. 14, *Jesharelah* [2]Lit., *hand*(s)

3 [1]In v. 11, *Izri* [2]So with mss. and ancient versions, cf. v. 17 [3]Lit., *hands* [a]1 Chr. 16:41, 42

4 [1]In v. 18, *Azarel* [2]In v. 20, *Shubael*

5 [1]Lit., *lift up the horn* [a]1 Chr. 21:9; 2 Sam. 24:11

6 [1]Lit., *hands* [a]1 Chr. 15:16 [b]1 Chr. 15:19

7 [1]Lit., *brothers,* and so throughout the chap. [a]1 Chr. 23:5

8 [a]1 Chr. 26:13

25 for the eighteenth to Hanani, his sons and his relatives,
twelve;
26 for the nineteenth to Mallothi, his sons and his relatives, twelve;
27 for the twentieth to Eliathah, his sons and his relatives,
twelve;
28 for the twenty-first to Hothir, his sons and his relatives,
twelve;
29 for the twenty-second to Giddalti, his sons and his relatives, twelve;
30 for the twenty-third to Mahazioth, his sons and his
relatives, twelve;
31 for the twenty-fourth to Romamti-ezer, his sons and his
relatives, twelve.

Chapter 26

FOR the divisions of the gatekeepers *there were* of the Korahites, [1]Meshelemiah the son of Kore, of the sons of [2]Asaph.
2 And Meshelemiah had sons: Zechariah the first-born,
Jediael the second, Zebadiah the third, Jathniel the fourth,
3 Elam the fifth, Johanan the sixth, Eliehoenai the
seventh.
4 And Obed-edom had sons: Shemaiah the first-born, Jehozabad the second, Joah the third, Sacar the fourth, Nethanel the fifth,
5 Ammiel the sixth, Issachar the seventh, *and* Peullethai
the eighth; God had indeed blessed him.
6 Also to his son Shemaiah sons were born who ruled
over the house of their father, for they were mighty men of
valor.
7 The sons of Shemaiah *were* Othni, Rephael, Obed, and
Elzabad, whose brothers, Elihu and Semachiah, were valiant
men.
8 All these *were* of the sons of Obed-edom; they and
their sons and their [1]relatives *were* able men with strength for
the service, 62 from Obed-edom.
9 And Meshelemiah had sons and relatives, 18 valiant
men.
10 Also [a]Hosah, *one* of the sons of Merari had sons:
Shimri the first (although he was not the first-born, his father
made him first),
11 Hilkiah the second, Tebaliah the third, Zechariah the
fourth; all the sons and relatives of Hosah *were* 13.
12 To these divisions of the gatekeepers, the chief men,
were given duties like their relatives to minister in the house of
the LORD.
13 [a]And they cast lots, the small and the great alike, according to their fathers' households, for every gate.
14 And the lot to the east fell to Shelemiah. Then they
cast lots *for* his son Zechariah, a counsellor with insight, and
his lot came out to the north.
15 For Obed-edom *it fell* to the south, and to his sons
went the storehouse.
16 For Shuppim and Hosah *it was* to the west, by the gate

1 [1]In vs. 14, *Shelemiah* [2]In 9:19, *Ebiasaph*

8 [1]Lit., *brothers*, and so throughout the chap.

10 [a]1 Chr. 16:38

13 [a]1 Chr. 24:5, 31; 25:8

18 [1]Possibly *court* or *colonnade* [a]2 Kin. 23:11

20 [1]So Gk.; Heb., *As for the Levites, Ahijah had* [2]Lit., *were over* [a]1 Chr. 26:22, 24, 26; 28:12; Ezra 2:69

22 [1]Lit., *were over*

26 [1]Lit., *were over* [a]2 Sam. 8:11

27 [1]Heb., *from the battles and from the spoil*

28 [1]Lit., *under the hand* [2]Heb., *Shelomith*

29 [a]Neh. 11:16 [b]1 Chr. 23:4

30 [1]Lit., *beyond the Jordan westward* [a]1 Chr. 27:17

31 [1]Heb., *according to the Hebronites. . .father's households* [a]1 Chr. 23:19 [b]1 Chr. 6:81

32 [1]Lit., *every matter of God and matter of the king.* [a]2 Chr. 19:11

of Shallecheth, on the ascending highway. Guard corresponded
to guard.
17 On the east there were six Levites, on the north four
daily, on the south four daily, and at the storehouse two by
two.
18 At the [1a]Parbar on the west *there were* four at the
highway and two at the Parbar.
19 These were the divisions of the gatekeepers of the sons
of Korah and of the sons of Merari.
20 [1]And the Levites, their relatives, [2]had [a]charge of the
treasures of the house of God, and of the treasures of the
dedicated gifts.
21 The sons of Ladan the sons of the Gershonites belonging to Ladan, *namely,* the Jehielites, *were* the heads of the
fathers' *households,* belonging to Ladan the Gershonite,
22 The sons of Jehieli, Zetham and Joel his brother, [1]had
charge of the treasures of the house of the LORD.
23 As for the Amramites, the Izharites, the Hebronites,
and the Uzzielites,
24 Shebuel the son of Gershom, the son of Moses, was
officer over the treasures.
25 And his relatives by Eliezer *were* Rehabiah his son,
Jeshaiah his son, Joram his son, Zichri his son, and Shelomoth
his son.
26 This Shelomoth and his relatives [1]had charge of all the
treasures of the dedicated gifts, [a]which King David and the
heads of the fathers' *households,* the commanders of thousands and hundreds, and commanders of the army, had
dedicated.
27 They dedicated [1]part of the spoil won in battles to
repair the house of the LORD.
28 And all that Samuel the seer had dedicated and Saul
the son of Kish, Abner the son of Ner and Joab the son of
Zeruiah, every one who had dedicated *any thing, all of this*
was [1]in the care of [2]Shelomoth and his relatives.
29 As for the Izharites, Chenaniah and his sons [a]were *assigned* to outside duties for Israel, as [b]officers and judges.
30 As for the Hebronites, [a]Hashabiah and his relatives,
1,700 capable men, had charge of the affairs of Israel [1]west of
the Jordan, for all the work of the LORD and the service of the
king.
31 As for the Hebronites, [a]Jerijah the chief [1](these Hebronites were investigated according to their genealogies and fathers' *households,* in the fortieth year of David's reign, and
men of outstanding capability were found among them at
[b]Jazer of Gilead)
32 and his relatives, capable men, *were* 2,700 in number,
heads of fathers' *households.* And King David made them
overseers over the Reubenites, the Gadites and the half-tribe
of the Manassites [a]concerning [1]all the affairs of God and of
the king.

CHAPTER 27

NOW *this is* the enumeration of the sons of Israel, the heads
of fathers' *households,* the commanders of thousands and of

hundreds, and their officers who served the king in all the
affairs of the divisions which came in and went out month by
month throughout all the months of the year, each division
numbering 24,000.
2 Jashobeam the son of Zabdiel [1a]had charge of the first
division for the first month; and in his division *were* 24,000.
3 *He was* from the sons of Perez, *and was* chief of all the
commanders of the army for the first month.
4 Dodai the Ahohite and his division had charge of the
division for the second month, Mikloth *being* the chief officer;
and in his division *were* 24,000.
5 The third commander of the army for the third month
was Benaiah, the son of Jehoiada the priest, *as* chief; and in his
division *were* 24,000.
6 This Benaiah *was* the mighty man of the thirty, and
had charge of thirty; and over his division was Ammizabad his
son.
7 The fourth for the fourth month *was* Asahel the brother of Joab, and Zebadiah his son after him; and in his division
were 24,000.
8 The fifth for the fifth month *was* the commander
Shamhuth the Izrahite; and in his division *were* 24,000.
9 The sixth for the sixth month *was* Ira the son of Ikkesh
the Tekoite; and in his division *were* 24,000.
10 The seventh for the seventh month *was* Helez the Pelonite of the sons of Ephraim; and in his division *were* 24,000.
11 The eighth for the eighth month *was* Sibbecai the Hushathite of the Zerahites; and in his division *were* 24,000.
12 The ninth for the ninth month *was* Abiezer the Anathothite of the Benjamites; and in his division *were* 24,000.
13 The tenth for the tenth month *was* Maharai the Netophathite of the Zerahites; and in his division *were* 24,000.
14 The eleventh for the eleventh month *was* Benaiah the
Pirathonite of the sons of Ephraim; and in his division *were*
24,000.
15 The twelfth for the twelfth month *was* Heldai the Netophathite of Othniel; and in his division *were* 24,000.
16 Now in charge of the tribes of Israel; chief officer for
the Reubenites was Eliezer the son of Zichri; that for the
Simeonites, Shephatiah the son of Maacah;
17 for Levi, Hashabiah the son of Kemuel; for Aaron,
Zadok;
18 for Judah, Elihu, *one* of David's brothers; for Issachar,
Omri the son of Michael;
19 for Zebulun, Ishmaiah the son of Obadiah; for Naphtali, Jeremoth the son of Azriel;
20 for the sons of Ephraim, Hoshea the son of Azaziah;
for the half-tribe of Manasseh, Joel the son of Pedaiah;
21 for the half-tribe of Manasseh in Gilead, Iddo the son
of Zechariah; for Benjamin, Jaasiel the son of Abner;
22 for Dan, Azarel the son of Jeroham. [a]These *were* the
princes of the tribes of Israel.
23 But David did not [1]count those twenty years of age and
under, [a]because the LORD had said he would multiply Israel [b]as
the stars of heaven.

2 [1]Lit., *was over*, and so throughout the chap. [a]1 Chr. 11:11-31; 2 Sam. 23:8-30

22 [a]1 Chr. 28:1

23 [1]Lit., *take their number from* [a]1 Chr. 21:2-5 [b]Gen. 15:5

24 Joab the son of Zeruiah had begun to count *them*, but did not finish; and because of [a]this wrath came upon Israel, and the number was not included in the account of the chronicles of King David.

25 Now Azmaveth the son of Adiel had charge of the king's storehouses. And Jonathan the son of Uzziah had charge of the storehouses in the country, in the cities, in the villages, and in the towers.

26 And Ezri the son of Chelub had charge of the [1]agricultural workers who tilled the soil.

27 And Shimei the Ramathite had charge of the vineyards; and Zabdi the Shiphmite had charge of the [1]produce of the vineyards *stored* in the wine-cellars.

28 And Baalhanan the Gederite had charge of the olive and [a]sycamore trees in the [1]Shephelah; and Joash had charge of the stores of oil.

29 And Shitrai the Sharonite had charge of the cattle which were grazing in [a]Sharon; and Shaphat the son of Adlai had charge of the cattle in the valleys.

30 And Obil the Ishmaelite had charge of the camels; and Jehdeiah the Meronothite had charge of the donkeys.

31 And Jaziz the [a]Hagrite had charge of the flocks. All these were [1]overseers of the property which belonged to King David.

32 Also Jonathan, David's uncle, *was* a counselor, a man of understanding, and a scribe; and Jehiel the son of Hachmoni [1]tutored the king's sons.

33 And [a]Ahithophel was counselor to the king; and [b]Hushai the Archite was the king's friend.

34 And Jehoiada the son of [a]Benaiah, and [b]Abaiathar [1]succeeded Ahithophel; and Joab was the [c]commander of the king's army.

Chapter 28

NOW [a]David assembled at Jerusalem all the officials of Israel, the princes of the tribes, and the commanders of the divisions that served the king, and the commanders of thousands, and the commanders of hundreds, and the overseers of all the property and livestock belonging to the king and his sons, with the officials and [b]the mighty men, even all the valiant men.

2 Then King David rose to his feet and said, "Listen to me, my brethren and my people; I [a]*had* [1]intended to build a [2]permanent home for the ark of the covenant of the LORD and for [b]the footstool of our God. So I had made preparations to build *it*.

3 "But God said to me, '[a]You shall not build a house for My name because you are a man of war and have shed blood.'

4 "Yet, the LORD, the God of Israel, [a]chose me from all the house of my father to be king over Israel [b]forever. For [c]He has chosen Judah to be a leader; and [d]in the house of Judah, my father's house, and among the sons of my father He took pleasure in me to make *me* king over all Israel.

24 [a]1 Chr. 21:1-7; 2 Sam. 24:12-15

26 [1]Lit., *doers of the work of the field for the tilling of...*

27 [1]Lit., *what was in the vineyards of the storehouses of wine*

28 [1]Or, *lowlands* [a]1 Kin. 10:27; 2 Chr. 1:15

29 [a]1 Chr. 5:16

31 [1]Or, *rulers* [a]1 Chr. 5:10

32 [1]Lit., was *with*

33 [a]2 Sam. 15:12 [b]2 Sam. 15:32, 37

34 [1]Lit., *after* [a]1 Chr. 27:5 [b]1 Kin. 1:7 [c]1 Chr. 11:6

1 [a]1 Chr. 23:2; 27:1-31 [b]1 Chr. 11:10-47

2 [1]Lit., *in my heart* [2]Lit., *house of rest* [a]1 Chr. 17:1, 2 [b]Ps. 132:7; Is. 66:1

3 [a]1 Chr. 22:8

4 [a]1 Sam. 16:6-13 [b]1 Chr. 17:23, 27 [c]1 Chr. 5:2; Gen. 49:8-10 [d]1 Sam. 16:1

5 "And [a]of all my sons (for the LORD has given me many
sons), [b]He has chosen my son Solomon to sit on the throne of
the kingdom of the LORD over Israel.
6 "And He said to me, 'Your son [a]Solomon is the one who
shall build My house and My courts; for I have chosen him to
be a son to Me, and I will be a father to him.
7 'And I will establish his kingdom forever, [a]if he resolutely performs My commandments and My ordinances, as [1]is
done now.'
8 "So now, in the sight of all Israel, the assembly of the
LORD, and in the hearing of our God, observe and seek after all
the commandments of the LORD your God in order that you
may possess the good land and bequeath *it* to your sons after
you forever.
9 "As for you, my son Solomon, know the God of your
father, and [a]serve Him with [1]a whole heart and a willing [2]mind;
[b]for the LORD searches all hearts, and understands every intent
of the thoughts. [c]If you seek Him, He will let you find Him;
but if you forsake Him, He will reject you forever.
10 "Consider now, for the LORD has chosen you to build a
house for the sanctuary; [a]be courageous and act."
11 Then David gave to his son Solomon [a]the plan of [b]the
porch *of the temple,* its buildings, its storehouses, its upper
rooms, its inner rooms, and [c]the room for the mercy-seat;
12 and the plan of all that he had in [1]mind, for the courts
of the house of the LORD, and for all the surrounding rooms,
for [a]the storehouses of the house of God, and for the storehouses of the dedicated things;
13 also for [a]the divisions of the priests and [b]the Levites
and for all the work of the service of the house of the LORD
and for all the utensils of service in the house of the LORD;
14 for the golden *utensils,* the weight of gold for all utensils for every kind of service; for the silver utensils, the weight
of silver for all utensils for every kind of service;
15 and the weight *of gold* for the [a]golden lampstands and
their golden lamps, with the weight of each lampstand and its
lamps; and *the weight of silver* for the silver lampstands, with
the weight of each lampstand and its lamps according to the
use of each lampstand;
16 and the gold by weight for the tables of showbread, for
each table; and silver for the silver tables;
17 and the forks, the basins, and the pitchers of pure gold;
and for the golden bowls with the weight for each bowl; and
for the silver bowls with the weight for each bowl;
18 and for [a]the altar of incense refined gold by weight; and
gold for the model of the chariot, *even* [b]the cherubim, that
spread out *their wings,* and covered the ark of the covenant of
the LORD.
19 "All *this,*" *said David,* "the LORD made me understand
in writing by His hand upon me, [a]all the [1]details of this
pattern."
20 Then David said to his son Solomon, "[a]Be strong and
courageous, and act; do not fear nor be dismayed, for the
LORD God, my God, is with you. [b]He will not fail you nor
forsake you until all the work for the service of the house of
the LORD is finished.

5 [a]1 Chr. 3:1-9; 14:3-7 [b]1 Chr. 22:9, 10
6 [a]2 Sam. 7:13, 14
7 [1]Lit., *at this day* [a]1 Chr. 22:13
9 [1]Or, *the same* [2]Lit., *soul* [a]1 Chr. 29:17-19; 1 Kin. 8:61 [b]1 Sam. 16:7 [c]2 Chr. 15:2; Jer. 29:13
10 [a]1 Chr. 22:13
11 [a]1 Chr. 28:12, 19; Ex. 25:40 [b]1 Kin. 6:3 [c]Ex. 25:17-22
12 [1]Lit., *the spirit with him* [a]1 Chr. 26:20, 28
13 [a]1 Chr. 24:1 [b]1 Chr. 23:6
15 [a]Ex. 25:31-39
18 [a]Ex. 30:1-10 [b]Ex. 25:18-22
19 [1]Lit., *works* [a]1 Chr. 28:11, 12
20 [a]1 Chr. 22:13 [b]Josh. 1:5; Heb. 13:5

21 "Now behold, [a]*there are* the divisions of the priests and
the Levites for all the service of the house of God, and [b]every
willing man of any skill will be with you in all the work for all
kinds of service. The officials also and all the people will be
entirely at your command."

Chapter 29

THEN King David said to the entire assembly, "My son
Solomon, whom alone God has chosen [a]is still young and
inexperienced, and the work is great; for [b]the [1]temple is not for
man, but for the LORD God.
2 "Now [a]with all my ability I have provided for the house
of my God the gold for the *things of* gold, and the silver for
the *things of* silver, and the bronze for the *things of* bronze, the
iron for the *things of* iron, and wood for the *things of* wood,
onyx stones and inlaid *stones*, stones of antimonys, and stones
of various colors, and all kinds of precious stones, and alabaster in abundance.
3 "And moreover, in my delight in the house of my God,
the treasure I have of gold and silver, I give to the house of my
God, over and above all that I have already provided for the
holy [1]temple,
4 *namely*, [a]3,000 talents of gold, of [b]the gold of Ophir,
and 7,000 talents of refined silver, to overlay the walls of the
[1]buildings;
5 of gold for the *things of* gold, and of silver for the
things of silver, that is, for all the work [1]done by the craftsmen.
Who then is willing to [b]consecrate himself this day to the
LORD?"
6 Then [a]the rulers of the fathers' *households*, and the
princes of the tribes of Israel, and the commanders of thousands and of hundreds, with [b]the overseers over the king's
work, offered willingly;
7 and for the service for the house of God they gave
5,000 talents and 10,000 [a]darics of gold, and 10,000 talents of
silver, and 18,000 talents of brass, and 100,000 talents of iron.
8 And [1]whoever possessed *precious* stones gave them to
the treasury of the house of the LORD, [2]in care of [a]Jehiel the
Gershonite.
9 Then the people rejoiced because they had offered so
willingly, for they made their offering to the LORD [a]with a
whole heart, and King David also rejoiced greatly.
10 So David blessed the LORD in the sight of all the assembly; and David said, "Blessed art Thou, O LORD God of Israel
our father, forever and ever.
11 "[a]Thine, O LORD, is the greatness and the power and the
glory and the victory and the majesty, indeed everything that is
in the heavens and the earth; Thine is the dominion, O LORD,
and Thou dost exalt Thyself as head over all.
12 "[a]Both riches and honor *come* from Thee, and Thou
dost rule over all, and [b]in Thy hand is power and might; and it
lies in Thy hand to make great, and to strengthen everyone.
13 "Now therefore, our God, we thank Thee, and praise
Thy glorious name.

21 [a]1 Chr. 28:13 [b]Ex. 35:25-35; 36:1, 2

1 [1]Lit., *palace*
[a]1 Chr. 22:5 [b]1 Chr. 29:19

2 [a]1 Chr. 22:3-5

3 [1]Lit., *house*

4 [1]Lit., *houses*
[a]1 Chr. 22:14 [b]1 Kin. 9:28

5 [1]Lit., *by the hand of the craftsmen* [2]Lit., *to fill his hand*

6 [a]1 Chr. 27:1; 28:1
[b]1 Chr. 27:25-31

7 [a]Ezra 2:69; Neh. 7:70

8 [1]Lit., *those with whom were found* [2]Lit., *under the hand of*
[a]1 Chr. 23:8

9 [a]1 Kin. 8:61; 2 Cor. 9:7

11 [a]Rev. 5:13

12 [a]2 Chr. 1:12 [b]2 Chr. 20:6

14 "But who am I and who are my people that we should
[1]be able to offer as generously as this? For all things come
from Thee, and from Thy hand we have given Thee.
15 "For [a]we are sojourners before Thee, and tenants, as all
our fathers were; [b]our days on the earth are like a shadow, and
there is no hope.
16 "O LORD our God, all this abundance that we have provided to build Thee a house for Thy holy name, it is from Thy
hand, and all is Thine.
17 "Since I know, O my God, that [a]Thou triest the heart
and [b]delightest in uprightness, I, in the integrity of my heart,
have willingly offered all these *things;* so now with joy I have
seen Thy people, who are present here, make *their* offerings
willingly to Thee.
18 "O LORD, the God of Abraham, Isaac, and Israel, our
fathers, preserve this forever in the [1]intentions of the heart of
Thy people, and direct their heart to Thee;
19 "and [a]give to my son Solomon a perfect heart to keep
Thy commandments, Thy testimonies, and Thy statutes, and
to do *them* all, and [b]to build the [1]temple, for which I have
made provision."
20 Then David said to all the assembly, "Now bless the
LORD your God." And [a]all the assembly blessed the LORD, the
God of their fathers, and [b]bowed low and did homage to the
LORD and to the king.
21 And on the next day [a]they [1]made sacrifices to the LORD
and offered burnt offerings to the LORD, 1,000 bulls, 1,000
rams *and* 1,000 lambs, with their drink offerings and sacrifices
in abundance for all Israel.
22 So they ate and drank that day before the LORD with
great gladness.
And they made Solomon the son of David king [a]a second
time, and they [b]anointed *him* as ruler for the LORD and Zadok
as priest.
23 Then Solomon sat on the throne of the LORD as king
instead of David his father; and he prospered, and all Israel
obeyed him.
24 And all the officials, the mighty men, and also all the
sons of King David [1]pledged allegiance to King Solomon.
25 And [a]the LORD highly exalted Solomon in the sight of
all Israel, and [b]bestowed on him royal majesty which had not
been on any king before him in Israel.
26 Now [a]David the son of Jesse reigned over all Israel.
27 [a]And the period which he reigned over Israel *was* forty
years; he reigned in Hebron seven years and [1]in Jerusalem
thirty-three *years.*
28 Then he died in [a]a [1]ripe old age, [b]full of days, riches
and honor; and his son Solomon reigned in his place.
29 Now the acts of King David, from first to last, are
written in the Chronicles of [a]Samuel the seer, in the Chronicles of [b]Nathan the prophet, and in the Chronicles of [c]Gad
the seer,
30 with all his reign, his power, and [a]the circumstances
which came on him, on Israel, and on all the kingdoms of the
lands.

14 [1]Lit., *retain strength*

15 [a]Lev. 25:23 [b]Job 14:2, 10-12

17 [a]1 Chr. 28:9 [b]Ps. 15:2

18 [1]Lit., *intent of the thoughts of the heart*

19 [1]Lit., *palace*
[a]1 Chr. 28:9; Ps. 72:1 [b]1 Chr. 29:1, 2

20 [a]Josh. 22:33 [b]Ex. 4:31

21 [1]Lit., *sacrificed*
[a]1 Kin. 8:62, 63

22 [a]1 Chr. 23:1 [b]1 Kin. 1:33-39

24 [1]Lit., *put a hand under Solomon*

25 [a]2 Chr. 1:1 [b]1 Kin. 3:13; 2 Chr. 1:12

26 [a]1 Chr. 18:14

27 [1]Lit., *he reigned in*
[a]2 Sam. 5:4, 5; 1 Kin. 2:11

28 [1]Lit., *good*
[a]Gen. 15:15; Acts 13:36
[b]1 Chr. 23:1

29 [a]1 Sam. 9:9 [b]2 Sam. 7:2-4; 12:1-7 [c]1 Sam. 22:5

30 [a]Dan. 4:23, 25

THE SECOND BOOK OF CHRONICLES

Solomon Worships at Gibeon. His Prayer for Wisdom. His Wealth.

NOW [a]Solomon the son of David established himself securely over his kingdom, and the LORD his God *was* with him and
[b]exalted him greatly.
2 And Solomon spoke to all Israel, [a]to the commanders
of thousands and of hundreds and to the judges and to every
leader in all Israel, the heads of the fathers' *households.*
3 Then Solomon, and all the assembly with him, went to
[a]the high place which was at Gibeon; [b]for God's tent of meeting was there, which Moses the servant of the LORD had made
in the wilderness.
4 However, David had brought up [a]the ark of God from
Kiriath-jearim [1]to the place he had prepared for it; for he had
pitched a tent for it in Jerusalem.
5 Now [a]the bronze altar, which Bezalel the son of Uri,
the son of Hur, had made, [1]was there before the tabernacle of
the LORD, and Solomon and the assembly sought it out.
6 And Solomon went up there before the LORD to the
bronze altar which *was* at the tent of meeting, and [a]offered a
thousand burnt offerings on it.
7 [a]In that night God appeared to Solomon and said to
him, "Ask what I shall give you."
8 And Solomon said to God, "Thou hast dealt with my
father David with great lovingkindness, and [a]hast made me
king in his place.
9 "Now, O LORD God, [a]Thy [1]promise to my father David
is fulfilled; for Thou hast made me king over [b]a people as
numerous as the dust of the earth.
10 "Give me now wisdom and knowledge, [a]that I may go
out and come in before this people; for who can rule this great
people of Thine?"
11 And God said to Solomon, "Because [1]you had this in
mind, and did not ask for riches, wealth, or honor, or the life of
those who hate you, nor have you even asked for long life, but
you have asked for yourself wisdom and knowledge, that you
may rule My people, over whom I have made you king,
12 wisdom and knowledge have been granted to you. And
[a]I will give you riches and wealth and honor, [1]such as none of
the kings who were before you has possessed, nor those who
will [2]come after you."
13 [a]So Solomon went [1]from the high place which was at
Gibeon, from the tent of meeting, to Jerusalem, and he
reigned over Israel.
14 [a]And Solomon amassed chariots and horsemen. [b]He
had 1,400 chariots, and 12,000 horsemen, and he stationed
them in [c]the chariot cities and with the king at Jerusalem.
15 And the king made silver and gold as plentiful in Jerusalem as stones, and he made cedars as plentiful as sycamores
in the [1]lowland.

1 [a]1 Kin. 2:12, 46 [b]1 Chr. 29:25
2 [a]1 Chr. 28:1
3 [a]1 Kin. 3:4 [b]Ex. 36:8
4 [1]Lit., *where David had prepared for it* [a]1 Chr. 15:25-28
5 [1]Lit., *he put* [a]Ex. 31:9; 38:1-7
6 [a]1 Kin. 3:4
7 [a]1 Kin. 3:5-14
8 [a]1 Chr. 28:5
9 [1]Lit., *word* [a]2 Sam. 7:12-16 [b]Gen. 13:16; 22:17
10 [a]2 Sam. 5:2
11 [1]Lit., *this was in your heart*
12 [1]Lit., *which was not so to the kings who were before you* [2]Lit., *be* [a]2 Chr. 9:22; 1 Chr. 29:25
13 [1]Lit., *to* [a]2 Chr. 1:3
14 [a]1 Kin. 10:26-29 [b]1 Kin. 4:26 [c]1 Kin. 9:19
15 [1]Or, *Shephelah*

16 And Solomon's horses were imported from Egypt and from Kue; the king's traders procured them from Kue for a price.

17 And they [1]imported chariots from Egypt for 600 *shekels* of silver apiece, and horses for 150 apiece, and [2]by the same means they [3]exported them to all the kings of the Hittites and the kings of Aram.

Chapter 2

1a

Now Solomon [2]decided to build a house for the name of the Lord, and a [3]royal palace for himself.

2 [1]So [a]Solomon [2]assigned 70,000 men to carry loads, and 80,000 men to quarry *stone* in the mountains, and 3,600 to supervise them.

3 [a]Then Solomon sent *word* to [1]Huram the king of Tyre, saying, "[b]As you dealt with David my father, and sent him cedars to build him a house to dwell in, so do for me.

4 "Behold, I am about to build a house for the name of the Lord my God, dedicating it to Him, [a]to burn fragrant incense before Him, and *to set out* [b]the showbread continually, and to offer [c]burnt offerings morning and evening, [d]on sabbaths and on new moons and on the appointed feasts of the Lord our God, this *being required* forever in Israel.

5 "And the house which I am about to build *will be* great; for [a]greater is our God than all the gods.

6 "But [a]who is able to build a house for Him, for the heavens and the highest heavens cannot contain Him? So who am I, that I should build a house for Him, except to [1]burn *incense* before Him?

7 "And now [a]send me a skilled man to work in gold, silver, brass and iron, and in purple, crimson and violet *fabrics*, and who knows how to make engravings, to *work* with the skilled men [1b]whom I have in Judah and Jersualem, whom David my father provided.

8 "Send me also cedar, cypress and algum timber from Lebanon, for I know that your servants know how to cut timber of Lebanon; and indeed, [a]my servants *will work* with your servants,

9 to prepare timber in abundance for me, for the house which I am about to build *will be* great and wonderful.

10 "Now behold, I will give to your servants, the woodsmen who cut the timber, 20,000 [1]kors of crushed wheat, and 20,000 [1]kors of barley, and 20,000 baths of wine, and 20,000 baths of oil."

11 Then Huram, king of Tyre, [1]answered in a letter sent to Solomon: "[a]Because the Lord loves His people, He has made you king over them."

12 Then Huram [1]continued, "Blessed be [a]the Lord, the God of Israel, who has made heaven and earth, who has given King David a wise son, [2]endowed with discretion and understanding, [b]who will build a house for the Lord and a [3]royal palace for himself.

17 [1]Lit., *brought up and brought out* [2]Lit., *and in like manner by their hand* [3]Lit., *brought out*

1 [1]Ch. 1:18 in Heb. [2]Lit., *said* [3]Lit., *house for his royalty* [a]1 Kin. 5:5

2 [1]Ch. 2:1 in Heb. [2]Lit., *numbered* [a]2 Chr. 2:18; 1 Kin. 5:15, 16

3 [1]In 1 Kin. 5:18, *Hiram* [a]1 Kin. 5:2-11 [b]1 Chr. 14:1

4 [a]Ex. 30:7 [b]Ex. 25:30 [c]Ex. 29:38-42 [d]Num. 28:9, 10

5 [a]Ex. 15:11; 1 Chr. 16:25

6 [1]Lit., *offer up in smoke* [a]2 Chr. 6:18; 1 Kin. 8:27

7 [1]Lit., *who are with me* [a]2 Chr. 2:13, 14; Ex. 31:3-5 [b]1 Chr. 22:15

8 [a]2 Chr. 9:10,11

10 [1]A kor equals approx. 10 bu.

11 [1]Lit., *said. . . . and he sent* [a]2 Chr. 9:8; 1 Kin. 10:9

12 [1]Lit., *said* [2]Lit., *knowing discretion* [3]Lit., *house for his royalty* [a]Ps. 33:6; 102:25 [b]2 Chr. 2:1

13 "And now I am sending a skilled man, [1]endowed with
understanding, Huram-abi,
14 [a]the son of a [1]Danite woman and [2]a Tyrian father, who
knows how to work in gold, silver, bronze, iron, stone and
wood, *and* in purple, violet, linen and crimson fabrics, and *who*
knows how to make all kinds of engravings and to [3]execute any
design which may be assigned to him, *to work* with your skilled
men, and with [4]those of my lord David your father.
15 "Now then, let my lord send to his servants wheat and
barley, oil and wine, of [a]which he has spoken.
16 "And [a]we will cut whatever timber you need from Lebanon, and bring it to you on rafts by sea to Joppa, so that you
may carry it up to Jerusalem."
17 And Solomon numbered all the aliens who *were* in the
land of Israel, [a]following the [1]census which his father David
had [2]taken; and 153,600 were found.
18 [a]And he appointed 70,000 of them to carry loads, and
80,000 to quarry *stones* in the mountains, and 3,600 supervisors to make the people work.

CHAPTER 3

[a]THEN Solomon began to build the house of the LORD in
Jerusalem on Mount Moriah, where *the* LORD had appeared to
his father David, at the place that David had prepared, [b]on the
threshing floor of Ornan the Jebusite.
2 And he began to build on the second *day* in the second
month [1]of the fourth year of his reign.
3 Now these are the [1]foundations which Solomon laid
for building the house of God. The length in [2]cubits, according to the old standard *was* sixty cubits, and the width twenty
cubits.
4 And the porch which was in front of the house [1]was as
long as the width of the house, twenty cubits, and the height
120; and inside he overlaid it with pure gold.
5 And he overlaid [a]the [1]main room with cypress wood
and overlaid it with fine gold, and [2]ornamented it with palm
trees and chains.
6 Further, he [1]adorned the house with precious stones;
and the gold was gold from [2]Parvaim.
7 [a]He also overlaid the house with gold—the beams, the
thresholds, and its walls, and its doors; and he [b]carved cherubim on the walls.
8 Now he made [a]the [1]room of the holy of holies: its
length, across the width of the house, *was* twenty cubits, and
its width *was* twenty cubits; and he overlaid it with fine gold,
amounting to 600 talents.
9 And the weight of the nails was fifty shekels of gold. He
also overlaid [a]the upper rooms with gold.
10 [a]Then he made two [1]sculptured cherubim in the room
of the holy of holies and overlaid them with gold.
11 And the wingspan of the cherubim *was* twenty cubits;
the wing of one, of five cubits, touched the wall of the house,
and *its* other wing, of five cubits, touched the wing of the other
cherub.

13 [1]Lit., *knowing understanding*

14 [1]Lit., *a woman of the daughters of Dan* [2]Lit., *whose father is a Tyrean man* [3]Lit., *devise any device* [4]Lit., *skilled men* [a]1 Kin. 7:14

15 [a]2 Chr. 2:10

16 [a]1 Kin. 5:8, 9

17 [1]Lit., *numbering* [2]Lit., *numbered of them* [a]1 Chr. 22:2

18 [a]2 Chr. 2:2

1 [a]1 Kin. 6:1 [b]1 Chr. 21:18

2 [1]Lit., *in*

3 [1]Lit., *founding of Solomon to build* [2]I.e., approx. 18 inches

4 [1]1 Kin. 6:3

5 [1]Lit., *great house* [2]Lit., *put on it palm trees* [a]1 Kin. 6:17

6 [1]Lit., *overlaid. . . . for beauty* [2]Or, *country of gold*

7 [a]1 Kin. 6:20-22 [b]1 Kin. 6:29-35

8 [1]Lit., *house* [a]Ex. 26:33; 1 Kin. 6:16

9 [a]1 Chr. 28:11

10 [1]Lit., *cherubim of sculptured work* [a]1 Kin. 6:23-28

12 And the wing of the other cherub, of five cubits,
touched the wall of the house; and *its* other wing of five cubits,
was attached to the wing of the [1]first cherub.
13 The wings of these cherubim extended twenty cubits,
and they stood on their feet [1]facing the *main* room.
14 [a]And he made the veil of violet, purple, crimson and
fine linen, and he worked cherubim on it.
15 [a]He also made two pillars for the front of the house,
thirty-five cubits [1]high, and the capital on the top of each *was*
five cubits.
16 And he made chains in the inner sanctuary, and placed
them on the tops of the pillars; and he made one hundred
pomegranates and placed *them* on the chains.
17 [a]And he erected the pillars in front of the temple, one
on the right and the other on the left, and named the one on
the right Jachin and the one on the left Boaz.

Chapter 4

THEN [a]he made a bronze altar, twenty cubits in length and
twenty cubits in width and ten cubits in height.
2 [a]Also he made the cast-metal sea, ten cubits from brim
to brim, circular in form, and its height *was* five cubits and [1]its
circumference thirty cubits.
3 Now figures like oxen *were* under it *and* all around it,
ten cubits, entirely encircling the sea. The oxen *were* in two
rows, cast [1]in one piece.
4 It stood on twelve oxen, three facing the north, three
facing west, three facing south, and three facing east; and the
sea *was set* on top of them, and all their hindquarters turned
inwards.
5 And it was a handbreadth thick, and its brim was made
like the brim of a cup, *like* a lily blossom; it [a]could hold 3,000
baths.
6 [a]He also made ten basins in which to wash, and he set
five on the right side and five on the left, [1]to rinse things for
the burnt offering; but the sea *was* for the priests to wash in.
7 Then [a]he made the ten golden lampstands in the way
prescribed for them, and he set them in the temple, five on the
right side and five on the left.
8 He also made [a]ten tables and placed them in the
temple, five on the right side and five on the left. And he made
one hundred golden bowls.
9 Then he made [a]the court of the priests and [b]the great
court and doors for the court, and overlaid their doors with
bronze.
10 And [a]he set the sea on the right [1]side *of the house*
toward the southeast.
11 [a]Huram also made the pails, the shovels, and the bowls.
So Huram finished doing the work which he performed for
King Solomon in the house of God:
12 the two pillars, the bowls and the two capitals on top of
the pillars, and the two networks to cover the two bowls of the
capitals which were on top of the pillars,

12 [1]Lit., *other*
13 [1]Lit., *and their faces to*
14 [a]Ex. 26:31
15 [1]Lit., *long* [a]1 Kin. 7:15-20
17 [a]1 Kin. 7:21
1 [a]Ex. 27:1, 2; 2 Kin. 16:14
2 [1]Lit., *a line of 30 cubits encircling it round about* [a]1 Kin. 7:23-26
3 [1]Lit., *in its casting*
5 [a]1 Kin. 7:26
6 [1]Lit., *in which to* [a]1 Kin. 7:38, 40
7 [a]1 Kin. 7:49
8 [a]1 Kin. 7:48
9 [a]1 Kin. 6:36 [b]2 Kin. 21:5
10 [1]Lit., *shoulder* [a]1 Kin. 7:39
11 [a]1 Kin. 7:40-51

13 [a]1 Kin. 7:20

14 [a]1 Kin. 7:27-43

16 [a]2 Chr. 2:13; 1 Kin. 7:14

18 [a]1 Kin. 7:47

19 [a]2 Chr. 5:8

20 [a]2 Chr. 5:7; Ex. 25:31-37

1 [1]Lit., *dedicated things of David,*

2 [a]1 Kin. 8:1-9 [b]2 Chr. 1:4

4 [a]2 Chr. 5:7

6 [1]Lit., *sheep.... numbered for multitude*

8 [1]Lit., *poles above*

9 [1]Lit., *it is*
[a]1 Kin. 8:8, 9

13 and [a]the four hundred pomegranates for the two networks, two rows of pomegranates for each network to cover
the two bowls of the capitals which were on the pillars.
14 [a]He also made the stands and he made the basins on
the stands,
15 *and* the one sea with the twelve oxen under it.
16 And the pails, the shovels, the forks, and all its utensils,
[a]Huram-abi made of polished bronze for King Solomon for
the house of the LORD.
17 On the plain of the Jordan the king cast them, in the
clay ground between Succoth and Zeredah.
18 [a]Thus Solomon made all these utensils in great quantities, for the weight of the bronze could not be found out.
19 Solomon also made all the things that *were* in the
house of God: even the golden altar, [a]the tables with the bread
of the Presence on them,
20 the lampstands with their lamps of pure gold, [a]to burn
in front of the inner sanctuary in the way prescribed;
21 the flowers, the lamps, and the tongs of gold, of purest
gold;
22 and the snuffers, the bowls, the spoons, and the firepans of pure gold; and the entrance of the house, its inner
doors for the holy of holies, and the doors of the house, *that is,*
of the nave, of gold.

CHAPTER 5

THUS all the work that Solomon performed for the house of
the LORD was finished. And Solomon brought in the [1]things
that David his father had dedicated, even the silver and the
gold and all the utensils, *and* put *them* in the treasuries of the
house of God.
2 [a]Then Solomon assembled to Jerusalem the elders of
Israel and all the heads of the tribes, the leaders of the fathers'
households of the sons of Israel, to bring up the ark of the
covenant of the LORD out [b]of the city of David, which is Zion.
3 And all the men of Israel assembled themselves to the
king at the feast, that is *in* the seventh month.
4 Then all the elders of Israel came, and [a]the Levites
took up the ark.
5 And they brought up the ark and the tent of meeting
and all the holy utensils which *were* in the tent; the Levitical
priests brought them up.
6 And King Solomon and all the congregation of Israel
who were assembled with him before the ark were sacrificing
[1]so many sheep and oxen, that they could not be counted or
numbered.
7 Then the priests brought the ark of the covenant of the
LORD to its place, into the inner sanctuary of the house, to the
holy of holies, under the wings of the cherubim.
8 For the cherubim spread their wings over the place of
the ark, so that the cherubim made a covering over the ark and
its [1]poles.
9 And the poles were so long that [a]the ends of the poles
of the ark could be seen in front of the inner sanctuary, but
they could not be seen outside; and [1]they are there to this day.

10 [a]There was nothing in the ark except the two tablets
which Moses put *there* at Horeb, where the LORD made a
covenant with the sons of Israel, when they came out of Egypt.
11 And when the priests came forth from the holy place
(for all the priests who were present had sanctified themselves,
without regard [a]to divisions),
12 and all the Levitical singers, [a]Asaph, Heman, Jeduthun,
and their sons and kinsmen, clothed in fine linen, [b]with cymbals, harps, and lyres, standing east of the altar, and with them
one hundred and twenty priests [c]blowing trumpets,
13 in unison when the trumpeters and the singers were to
make themselves heard with one voice to praise and to glorify
the LORD, and when they lifted up their voice [a]accompanied by
trumpets and cymbals and instruments of music, and when
they praised the LORD *saying*, "[b]*He* indeed is good for His
lovingkindness is everlasting," then the house, the house of the
LORD, was filled with a cloud,
14 so that the priests could not stand to minister because
of the cloud, for [a]the glory of the LORD filled the house of
God.

CHAPTER 6

[a]THEN Solomon said,
"The LORD has said that He would dwell in the thick
cloud.
2 "I have built Thee a lofty house,
And a place for Thy dwelling forever."
3 Then the king [1]faced about and blessed all the assembly of Israel, while all the assembly of Israel was standing.
4 And he said, "Blessed be the LORD, the God of Israel,
who spoke with His mouth to my father David and has fulfilled *it* with His hands, saying,
5 'Since the day that I brought My people from the land
of Egypt, I did not choose a city out of all the tribes of Israel
in which to build a house that My name might be there, nor
did I choose any man for a leader over My people Israel;
6 but [a]I have chosen Jerusalem that My name might be
there, and I [b]have chosen David to be over My people Israel.'
7 "[a]Now it was [1]in the heart of my father David to build a
house for the name of the LORD, the God of Israel.
8 "But the LORD said to my father David, 'Because it was
[1]in your heart to build a house for My name, you did well that
it was [1]in your heart.
9 'Nevertheless you shall not build the house, but your
son who [1]shall be born to you, he shall build the house for My
name.'
10 "Now the LORD has fulfilled His word which He spoke;
for I have risen in the place of my father David and sit on the
throne of Israel, as the LORD [1]promised, and have built the
house for the name of the LORD, the God of Israel.
11 "And there I have set the ark, [a]in which is the covenant
of the LORD, which He made with the sons of Israel."
12 Then he stood before the altar of the LORD in the
presence of all the assembly of Israel and spread out his hands.

5:10 [a]Deut. 10:2-5; Heb. 9:4
5:11 [a]1 Chr. 24:1-5
5:12 [a]1 Chr. 25:1-4 [b]1 Chr. 13:8; 15:16, 24 [c]2 Chr. 7:6
5:13 [a]1 Chr. 16:42 [b]2 Chr. 7:3; 1 Chr. 16:34
5:14 [a]1 Kin. 8:11
6:1 [a]1 Kin. 8:12-50
6:3 [1]Lit., *turned his face about*
6:6 [a]2 Chr. 12:13 [b]1 Chr. 28:4
6:7 [1]Lit., *with* [a]1 Kin. 5:3
6:8 [1]Lit., *with*
6:9 [1]Lit., *is to come forth from your loins*
6:10 [1]Lit., *spoke*
6:11 [a]2 Chr. 5:7, 10

13 [a]Neh. 8:4 [b]1 Kin. 8:54

13 [a]Now Solomon had made a bronze platform, five cubits long, five cubits wide, and three cubits high, and had set it
in the midst of the court; and he stood on it, [b]knelt on his
knees in the presence of all the assembly of Israel, and spread
out his hands toward heaven.
14 And he said, "O LORD, the God of Israel, [a]there is no
God like Thee in heaven or on earth, [b]keeping covenant and
showing lovingkindness to thy servants who walk before Thee
with all their heart;

14 [a]Ex. 15:11; Deut. 3:24 [b]Deut. 7:9

15 [a]who has kept with Thy servant David my father that
which Thou hast [1]promised him; indeed, Thou hast spoken
with Thy mouth, and hast fulfilled it with Thy hand, as it is
this day.

15 [1]Lit., *spoken to* [a]1 Chr. 22:9, 10

16 "Now therefore, O LORD, the God of Israel, keep with
Thy servant David my father that which Thou hast [1]promised
him, saying, '[2a]You shall not lack a man to sit on the throne of
Israel, if only your sons take heed to their way, to walk in My
law as you have walked before Me.'
17 "Now therefore, O LORD, the God of Israel, let Thy
word be confirmed which Thou hast spoken to Thy servant
David.

16 [1]Lit., *spoken to* [2]Lit., *there shall not be cut off to you a man from before Me* [a]2 Chr. 7:18; 1 Kin. 2:4

18 "But will God indeed dwell with mankind on the earth?
Behold, [a]heaven and the [1]highest heaven cannot contain Thee;
how much less this house which I have built.
19 "Yet have regard to the prayer of Thy servant and to his
supplication, O LORD my God, to listen to the cry and to the
prayer which Thy servant prays before Thee;
20 that Thine eyes may be open toward this house day
and night, toward the place of which Thou hast said that *Thou
wouldst* put Thy name there, to listen to the prayer which Thy
servant shall pray toward this place.

18 [1]Lit., *heaven of heavens* [a]2 Chr. 2:6

21 "And listen to the supplications of Thy servant and of
Thy people Israel, when they pray toward this place; hear
Thou from Thy dwelling-place, from heaven; [a]hear Thou and
forgive.

21 [a]Mic. 7:18

22 "If a man sins against his neighbor, and is made to take
an oath, and he comes *and* takes an oath before Thine altar in
this house;
23 then hear Thou from heaven and act and judge Thy
servants, [1]punishing the wicked by bringing his way on his own
head and justifying the righteous by giving him according to
his righteousness.

23 [1]Lit., *returning*

24 "And if Thy people Israel [1]are defeated before an
enemy, because they have sinned against Thee, and they return *to Thee* and confess Thy name, and pray and make supplication before Thee in this house;
25 then hear Thou from heaven and forgive the sin of Thy
people Israel, and bring them back to the land which Thou
hast given to them and to their fathers.

24 [1]Lit., *smitten*

26 "When the heavens are shut up and there is no rain
because they have sinned against Thee, and they pray toward
this place and confess Thy name, and turn from their sin when
Thou dost afflict them;
27 then hear Thou in heaven and forgive the sin of Thy
servants and Thy people Israel, indeed, teach them the good

way in which they should walk. And send rain on Thy land,
which Thou hast given to Thy people for an inheritance.
28 "If there is famine in the land, if there is pestilence, if
there is blight or mildew, if there is locust or grasshopper, if
their enemies besiege them in the land of their [1]cities, whatever
plague or whatever sickness *there is*,
29 whatever prayer or supplication is made by any man or
by all Thy people Israel, [1]each knowing his own affliction and
his own pain, and spreading his hands toward this house,
30 then hear Thou from heaven Thy dwelling-place, and
forgive, and render to each according to all his ways, whose
heart Thou knowest [a]for Thou alone dost know the hearts of
the sons of men,
31 that they may [1]fear Thee, to walk in Thy ways [2]as long
as they live in the land which Thou hast given to our fathers.
32 "Also concerning the foreigner who is not from Thy
people Israel, when he comes from a far country for Thy great
name's sake and Thy mighty hand and Thine outstretched
arm, when they come and pray toward this house,
33 then hear Thou from heaven, from Thy dwelling place,
and do according to all for which the foreigner calls to Thee,
in order that all the peoples of the earth may know Thy name,
and [1]fear Thee, as *do* Thy people Israel, and that they may
know that [2]this house which I have built is [a]called by Thy
name.
34 "When Thy people go out to battle against their enemies,
by whatever way Thou shalt send them, and they pray to
Thee toward this city which Thou hast chosen, and the house
which I have built for Thy name,
35 then hear Thou from heaven their prayer and their
supplication, and maintain their cause.
36 "When they sin against Thee ([a]for there is no man who
does not sin) and Thou art angry with them and dost deliver
them to an enemy, so that [1]they take them away captive to a
land far off or near,
37 if they [1]take thought in the land where they are taken
captive, and repent and make supplication to Thee in the land
of their captivity, saying, 'We have sinned, we have committed
iniquity, and have acted wickedly';
38 if they return to Thee with all their heart and with all
their soul in the land of their captivity, where they have been
taken captive, and pray toward their land which Thou hast
given to their fathers, and the city which Thou hast chosen,
and toward the house which I have built for Thy name,
39 then hear from heaven, from Thy dwelling place, their
prayer and supplications, and maintain their cause, and forgive
Thy people who have sinned against Thee.
40 "Now, O my God, I pray Thee, [a]let Thine eyes be open,
and [b]Thine ears attentive to the prayer *offered* in this place.
41 "[a]Now therefore arise, O LORD God, to Thy resting
place, Thou and the ark of Thy might; let Thy priests, O LORD
God, be clothed with salvation, and let Thy godly ones rejoice
in what is good.
42 "O LORD God, do not turn away the face of Thine
anointed; remember *Thy* lovingkindness to Thy servant
David."

28 [1]Lit., *gates*

29 [1]Lit., *whoever shall know*

30 [a]1 Sam. 16:7; 1 Chr. 28:9

31 [1]Or, *reverence* [2]Lit., *all the days that they live on the face of the land*

33 [1]Or, *reverence* [2]Lit., *Thy name is called upon this house* [a]2 Chr. 7:14

36 [1]Lit., *their captors take them captive* [a]Job 15:14-16; James 3:2; 1 John 1:8-10

37 [1]Lit., *return to their heart*

40 [a]2 Chr. 7:15; Neh. 1:6, 11 [b]Ps. 17:1

41 [a]Ps. 132:8, 9

Chapter 7

[a]NOW when Solomon had finished praying, [b]fire came down from heaven and consumed the burnt offering and the sacrifices; and the glory of the LORD filled the house.

2 And the priests could not enter into the house of the LORD, because the glory of the LORD filled the LORD's house.

3 And all the sons of Israel, seeing the fire come down and the glory of the LORD upon the house, bowed down on the pavement with their faces to the ground, and they worshiped and gave praise to the LORD, *saying,* "[a]Truly He is good, truly His lovingkindness is everlasting."

4 [a]Then the king and all the people offered sacrifice before the LORD.

5 And King Solomon offered a sacrifice of 22,000 oxen, and 120,000 sheep. Thus the king and all the people dedicated the house of God.

6 And the priests stood at their posts and [a]the Levites, with the instruments of music to the LORD, which King David had made for giving praise to the LORD—"for His lovingkindness is everlasting"—whenever [1]he gave praise by their [2]means, while [b]the priests on the other side blew trumpets; and all Israel was standing.

7 [a]Then Solomon consecrated the middle of the court that *was* before the house of the LORD, for there he offered the burnt offerings and the fat of the peace offerings, because the bronze altar which Solomon had made was not able to contain the burnt offering, the grain offering, and the fat.

8 So Solomon observed the feast at that time for seven days, and all Israel with him, a very great assembly, *who came* [a]from the entrance of Hamath to the brook of Egypt.

9 And on the eighth day they held [a]a solemn assembly, for the dedication of the altar they observed seven days, and the feast seven days.

10 Then on the twenty-third day of the seventh month he sent the people to their tents, rejoicing and happy of heart because of the goodness that the LORD had shown to David and to Solomon and to His people Israel.

11 [a]Thus Solomon finished the house of the LORD and the king's palace, and successfully completed all that [1]he had planned on doing in the house of the LORD and in his palace.

12 Then the LORD appeared to Solomon at night and said to him, "I have heard your prayer, and [a]have chosen this place for Myself as a house of sacrifice.

13 "[a]If I shut up the heavens so that there is no rain, or if I command the locust to devour the land, or if I send pestilence among My people,

14 [a]and My people [1]who are called by My name humble themselves and pray, and seek My face and turn from their wicked ways, then I will hear from heaven, will forgive their sin, and will heal their land.

15 "[a]Now My eyes shall be open and My ears attentive to the [1]prayer *offered* in this place.

16 "For [a]now I have chosen and consecrated this house that My name may be there forever, and My eyes and My heart will be there perpetually.

1 [a]1 Kin. 8:54 [b]1 Kin. 18:24, 38
3 [a]2 Chr. 5:13; 20:21
4 [a]1 Kin. 8:62, 63
6 [1]Lit., *David* [2]Lit., *hand* [a]1 Chr. 15:16-21 [b]2 Chr. 5:12
7 [a]1 Kin. 8:64-66
8 [a]1 Kin. 8:65
9 [a]Lev. 23:36
11 [1]Lit., *came upon the heart of Solomon to do* [a]1 Kin. 9:1-9
12 [a]Deut. 12:5, 11
13 [a]2 Chr. 6:26-28
14 [1]Lit., *over whom My name is called* [a]2 Chr. 6:37-39
15 [1]Lit., *prayer of this place* [a]2 Chr. 6:20, 40
16 [a]2 Chr. 7:12

17 "And as for you, if you walk before Me as your father
David walked even to do according to all that I have commanded you and will keep My statutes and My ordinances,
18 then I will establish your royal throne as I covenanted
with your father David, saying, '[1a]You shall not lack a man *to*
be ruler in Israel.'
19 "[a]But if you turn away and forsake My statutes and My
commandments which I have set before you and shall go and
serve other gods and worship them,
20 [a]then I will uproot you from My land which I have
given [1]you, and this house which I have consecrated for My
name I will cast out of My sight, and I will make it [b]a proverb
and a byword among all peoples.
21 "As for this house, which was exalted, every one who
passes by it will be astonished and say, '[a]Why has the LORD
done thus to this land and to this house?'
22 "And they will say, 'Because they forsook the LORD, the
God of their fathers, who brought them from the land of
Egypt, and they adopted other gods and worshiped them and
served them, therefore He has brought all this adversity on
them.' "

CHAPTER 8

[a]NOW it came about at the end of the twenty years in which
Solomon had built the house of the LORD and his own house
2 that he built the cities which Huram had given to [1]him,
and settled the sons of Israel there.
3 Then Solomon went to Hamath-zobah and captured it.
4 And he built Tadmor in the wilderness and all the
storage cities which he had built in Hamath.
5 He also built upper [a]Beth-horon and lower Beth-horon,
[b]fortified cities *with* walls, gates, and bars;
6 and Baalath and all the storage cities that Solomon
had, and all the cities for [1]his chariots and cities for [1]his horsemen, and all that it pleased Solomon to build in Jerusalem, in
Lebanon, and in all the land [2]under his rule.
7 [a]All of the people who were left of the Hittites, the
Amorites, the Perizzites, the Hivites, and the Jebusites, who
were not of Israel,
8 namely, from their descendants who were left after
them in the land whom the sons of Israel had not destroyed,
[a]them Solomon raised as forced laborers to this day.
9 But Solomon did not make slaves for his work from the
sons of Israel; they were men of war, his chief captains, and
commanders of his chariots and his horsemen.
10 And these were the chief [1]officers of King Solomon,
two hundred and fifty who ruled over the people.
11 [a]Then Solomon brought Pharaoh's daughter up from
the city of David to the house which he had built for her; for
he said, "My wife shall not dwell in the house of David king of
Israel, because [1]the places are holy where the ark of the LORD
has entered."
12 Then Solomon offered burnt offerings to the LORD on
[a]the altar of the LORD which he had built before the porch;
13 and [a]*did so* according to the daily rule, offering *them*

18 [1]Lit., *there shall not be cut off to you a man* [a]2 Chr. 6:16

19 [a]Lev. 26:14, 33; Deut. 28:15

20 [1]Ancient versions, Heb. read, *them* [a]Deut. 29:28; 1 Kin. 14:15 [b]Deut. 28:37

21 [a]Deut. 29:24, 25

1 [a]1 Kin. 9:1-28

2 [1]Lit., *Solomon*

5 [a]1 Chr. 7:24 [b]2 Chr. 14:7

6 [1]Lit., *the* [2]Lit., *of*

7 [a]Gen. 15:18-21

8 [a]1 Kin. 4:6; 9:21

10 [1]Or, *deputies*

11 [1]Lit., *they are* [a]1 Kin. 3:1; 7:8

12 [a]2 Chr. 4:1

13 [a]Ex. 29:38-42

13 [b]Num. 28:3 [c]Ex. 23:14-17

up [b]according to the commandment of Moses, for the sabbaths, the new moons, and the [c]three annual feasts—the feast
of unleavened bread, the feast of weeks, and the feast of
tabernacles.

14 [a]1 Chr. 24:1 [b]1 Chr. 25:1 [c]1 Chr. 26:1 [d]Neh. 12:24, 36

14 Now according to the ordinance of his father David, he
appointed [a]the divisions of the priests for their service, and
[b]the Levites for their duties of praise and ministering before
the priests according to the daily rule, and [c]the gatekeepers by
their divisions at every gate; for [d]David the man of God had so
commanded.

15 And they did not depart from the commandment of
the king to the priests and Levites in any manner or concerning
the storehouses.

16 [1]So ancient versions; M.T., *as far as*

16 Thus all the work of Solomon was carried out [1]from
the day of the foundation of the house of the LORD, and until
it was finished. So the house of the LORD was completed.

17 [a]1 Kin. 9:26 [b]2 Kin. 14:22

17 Then Solomon went to [a]Ezion-geber and to [b]Eloth on
the seashore in the land of Edom.

18 [a]2 Chr. 9:10, 13

18 And Huram by his servants sent him ships and servants
who knew the sea; and they went with Solomon's servants to
Ophir, and [a]took from there four hundred and fifty talents of
gold, and brought them to King Solomon.

CHAPTER 9

1 [a]1 Kin. 10:1-13; Matt. 12:42; Luke 11:31

[a]NOW when the queen of Sheba heard of the fame of Solomon, she came to Jerusalem to test Solomon with difficult
questions. She had a very large retinue, with camels carrying
spices, and a large amount of gold and precious stones; and
when she came to Solomon, she spoke with him about all that
was on her heart.

2 [1]Lit., *told her all her words* [2]Lit., *tell*

2 And Solomon [1]answered all her questions; nothing was
hidden from Solomon which he did not [2]explain to her.

3 And when the queen of Sheba had seen the wisdom of
Solomon, the house which he had built,

4 [1]Or, *his burnt offering which he offered*

4 the food at his table, the seating of his servants, the
attendance of his ministers and their attire, his cupbearers and
their attire, and [1]his stairway by which he went up to the house
of the LORD, she was breathless.

5 Then she said to the king, "It was a true report which I
heard in my own land about your words and your wisdom.

6 "Nevertheless I did not believe their reports until I came
and my eyes had seen it. And behold, the half of the greatness
of your wisdom was not told me. You surpass the report that I
heard.

7 [1]Or, *happy*

7 "How [1]blessed are your men, how [1]blessed are these
your servants who stand before you continually and hear your
wisdom.

8 [a]1 Chr. 28:5; 29:23 [b]2 Chr. 2:11; Deut. 7:8

8 "Blessed be the LORD your God who delighted in you,
[a]setting you on His throne as king for the LORD your God;
[b]because your God loved Israel establishing them forever,
therefore He made you king over them, to do justice
and righteousness."

9 Then she gave the king one hundred and twenty talents
of gold, and a very great *amount of* spices and precious stones;

there had never been spice like that which the queen of Sheba
gave to King Solomon.
10 And the servants of Huram and the servants of Solomon [a]who brought gold from Ophir, also brought algum trees
and precious stones.
11 And from the algum the king made steps for the house
of the LORD and for the king's palace, and lyres and harps for
the singers; and none like that was seen before in the land of
Judah.
12 And King Solomon gave to the queen of Sheba all her
desire which she requested besides *a return for* what she had
brought to the king. Then she turned and went to her own
land with her servants.
13 [a]Now the weight of gold which came to Solomon in
one year was 666 talents of gold,
14 besides that which the traders and merchants brought;
and all the kings of Arabia and the governors of the country
brought gold and silver to Solomon.
15 And King Solomon made 200 large shields of beaten
gold, [1]using 600 *shekels of* beaten gold on each large shield.
16 And *he made* 300 shields of beaten gold, [1]using three
hundred shekels of gold on each shield, and the king put them
in the house of the forest of Lebanon.
17 Moreover, the king made a great throne of ivory and
overlaid it with pure gold.
18 And *there were* six steps to the throne and a footstool
in gold attached to the throne, and [1]arms [2]on each side of the
seat, and two lions standing beside the [1]arms.
19 And twelve lions were standing there on the six steps on
the one side and on the other; nothing like *it* was made for any
other kingdom.
20 And all King Solomon's drinking vessels *were* of gold,
and all the vessels of the house of the forest of Lebanon *were*
of pure gold; silver was not considered [1]valuable in the days of
Solomon.
21 [a]For the king had ships which went to Tarshish with the
servants of Huram; once every three years the ships of Tarshish
came bringing gold and silver, ivory and apes and peacocks.
22 [a]So King Solomon became greater than all the kings of
the earth in riches and wisdom.
23 And all the kings of the earth were seeking the presence
of Solomon, to hear his wisdom which God had put in his
heart.
24 And they brought every man his gift, articles of silver
and gold, garments, weapons, spices, horses, and mules, so
much year by year.
25 Now Solomon had [a]4,000 stalls for horses and chariots
and 12,000 horsemen, and he stationed them in the chariot
cities and with the king in Jerusalem.
26 [a]And he was the ruler over all the kings from the Euphrates River even to the land of the Philistines, and as far as
the border of Egypt.
27 [a]And the king made silver *as common* as stones in Jerusalem, and he made cedars as plentiful as sycamore trees that
are in the [1]lowland.

10 [a]2 Chr. 8:18

13 [a]1 Kin. 10:14-28

15 [1]Lit., *he brought up*

16 [1]Lit., *he brought up*

18 [1]Lit., *hands* [2]Lit., *on this side and on this at the place of the seat*

20 [1]Lit., *anything*

21 [a]2 Chr. 20:36, 37

22 [a]2 Chr. 1:12; 1 Kin. 3:13

25 [a]2 Chr. 1:14; 1 Kin. 4:26; 10:26; Deut. 17:16

26 [a]1 Kin. 4:21, 24

27 [1]Or, *shephelah* [a]2 Chr. 1:15-17

28 [a]2 Chr. 1:16

28 [a]And they were bringing horses for Solomon from
Egypt and from all countries.
29 [a]Now the rest of the acts of Solomon, from first to last,
[b]are they not written in the [1]records of Nathan the prophet,
and in the prophecy of Ahijah the Shilonite, and in the visions
of [2]Iddo the seer concerning Jeroboam the son of Nebat?

29 [1]Lit., *words* [2]Heb., *Jedo* [a]1 Kin. 11:41-43 [b]1 Chr. 29:29

30 And Solomon reigned forty years in Jerusalem over all
Israel.
31 And Solomon slept with his fathers and was buried in
[a]the city of his father David; and his son Rehoboam reigned in
his place.

31 [a]1 Kin. 2:10

Chapter 10

[a]THEN Rehoboam went to Shechem, for all Israel had come
to Shechem to make him king.
2 And it came about when Jeroboam the son of Nebat
heard *of it* (for [a]he was in Egypt where he had fled from the
presence of King Solomon), that Jeroboam returned from
Egypt.

1 [a]1 Kin. 12:1-20

3 So they sent and summoned him. When Jeroboam and
all Israel came, they spoke to Rehoboam, saying,
4 "Your father made our yoke hard; now therefore lighten
the hard service of your father and his heavy yoke which he put
on us, and we will serve you."

2 [a]1 Kin. 11:40

5 And he said to them, "Return to me again in three
days." So the people departed.
6 Then King Rehoboam consulted with the elders who
had [1]served his father Solomon while he was still alive, saying,
"How do you counsel *me* to answer this people?"

6 [1]Lit., *stood before*

7 And they spoke to him, saying, "If you will be kind to
this people and please them and speak good words to them,
then they will be your servants forever."
8 But he forsook the counsel of the elders which they had
given him, and consulted with the young men who grew up
with him [1]and served him.

8 [1]Lit., *who stood before*

9 So he said to them, "What counsel do you give that we
may answer this people, who have spoken to me, saying, 'Light-
en the yoke which your father put on us'?"
10 And the young men who grew up with him spoke to
him, saying, "Thus you shall say to the people who spoke to
you, saying, 'Your father made our yoke heavy, but you make
it lighter for us.' Thus you shall say to them, 'My little finger is
thicker than my father's loins!

12 [1]Lit., *spoke*

11 'Whereas my father loaded you with a heavy yoke, I will
add to your yoke; my father disciplined you with whips, but I
will discipline you with scorpions.' "
12 So Jeroboam and all the people came to Rehoboam on
the third day as the king had [1]directed, saying, "Return to me
on the third day."

14 [1]Many mss. read, *I have made*

13 And the king answered them harshly, and King Rehoboam forsook the counsel of the elders.
14 And he spoke to them according to the advice of the
young men, saying, "[1]My father made your yoke heavy, but I
will add to it; my father disciplined you with whips, but I *will*
discipline you with scorpions."

15 So the king did not listen to the people, [a]for it was a
turn *of events* from God [b]that the LORD might establish His
word, which He spoke through Ahijah the Shilonite to Jeroboam the son of Nebat.
16 And when all Israel *saw* that the king did not listen to
them the people answered the king, saying, "[a]What portion do
we have in David? *We have* no inheritance in the son of Jesse.
Every man to your tents, O Israel;
Now look after your own house, David."
[b]So all Israel departed to their tents.
17 But as for the sons of Israel who lived in the cities of
Judah, Rehoboam reigned over them.
18 Then King Rehoboam sent [a]Hadoram, who was over
the forced labor, and the sons of Israel stoned him [1]to death.
And King Rehoboam made haste to mount his chariot to flee
to Jerusalem.
19 So Israel has been in rebellion against the house of
David to this day.

CHAPTER 11

[a]NOW when Rehoboam had come to Jerusalem, he assembled the house of Judah and Benjamin, 180,000 chosen
men who were warriors, to fight against Israel to restore the
kingdom to Rehoboam.
2 But the word of the LORD came to [a]Shemaiah the man
of God, saying,
3 "Speak to Rehoboam the son of Solomon, king of Judah, and to all Israel in Judah and Benjamin, saying,
4 'Thus says the LORD, "You shall not go up or fight
against [a]your [1]relatives; return every man to his house, [b]for this
thing is from Me." ' " So they listened to the words of the
LORD and returned from going against Jeroboam.
5 Rehoboam lived in Jerusalem and [a]built cities for defense in Judah.
6 Thus he built Bethlehem, Etam, Tekoa,
7 Beth-zur, Soco, Adullam,
8 Gath, Mareshah, Ziph,
9 Adoraim, Lachish, Azekah,
10 Zorah, Aijalon, and Hebron, which are fortified cities
in Judah and in Benjamin.
11 He also strengthened the fortresses and put officers in
them and stores of food, oil and wine.
12 And *he put* shields and spears in every city and strengthened them greatly. So he held Judah and Benjamin.
13 Moreover, the priests and the Levites who were in all
Israel stood with him from all their districts.
14 For [a]the Levites left their pasture lands and their property and came to Judah and Jerusalem, for [b]Jeroboam and his
sons had excluded them from serving as priests to the LORD.
15 And [a]he set up priests of his own for the high places, for
the satyrs, and for the calves which he had made.
16 And [a]those from all the tribes of Israel who set their
hearts on seeking the LORD God of Israel, [1]followed them to
Jerusalem to sacrifice to the LORD God of their fathers.
17 [a]And they strengthened the kingdom of Judah and sup-

15 [a]2 Chr. 25:16-20 [b]1 Kin. 11:29-39

16 [a]2 Sam. 20:1 [b]2 Chr. 10:19

18 [1]Lit., *with stones that he died*
[a]1 Kin. 4:6; 5:14

1 [a]1 Kin. 12:21-24

2 [a]2 Chr. 12:5-7, 15

4 [1]Lit., *brothers*
[a]2 Chr. 28:8-11 [b]2 Chr. 10:15

5 [a]2 Chr. 11:23; 8:2-6

14 [a]Num. 35:2-5 [b]2 Chr. 13:9; 1 Kin. 12:28-33

15 [a]1 Kin. 12:31; 13:33

16 [1]Lit., *came after*
[a]2 Chr. 15:9

17 [a]2 Chr. 12:1

ported Rehoboam the son of Solomon for three years, for they
walked in the way of David and Solomon for three years.
18 Then Rehoboam took as a wife Mahalath the daughter
of Jerimoth the son of David *and of* Abihail the daughter of
[a]Eliab the son of Jesse,
19 and she bore him sons: Jeush, Shemariah, and Zaham.
20 And after her he took Maacah the daughter of Absalom, and she bore him Abijah, Attai, Ziza, and Shelomith.
21 And Rehoboam loved Maacah the daughter of Absalom more than all his *other* wives and concubines. For [a]he had
taken eighteen wives and sixty concubines and fathered
twenty-eight sons and sixty daughters.
22 And [a]Rehoboam appointed Abijah the son of Maacah
as head and leader among his brothers, for he *intended* to
make him king.
23 And he acted wisely and distributed [1]some of his sons
through all the territories of Judah and Benjamin to all the
fortified cities, and he gave them food in abundance. And he
sought many wives *for them.*

Chapter 12

IT took place [a]when the kingdom of Rehoboam was established and strong that [b]he and all Israel with him forsook the
law of the LORD.
2 [a]And it came about in King Rehoboam's fifth year,
because they had been unfaithful to the LORD, that [b]Shishak
king of Egypt came up against Jerusalem
3 with 1200 chariots and 60,000 horsemen. And the
people who came with him from Egypt were without number:
[a]the Lubim, the Sukkiim, and the Ethiopians.
4 And he captured [a]the fortified cities of Judah and came
as far as Jerusalem.
5 Then [a]Shemaiah the prophet came to Rehoboam and
the princes of Judah who had gathered at Jerusalem because of
Shishak, and he said to them, "Thus says the LORD, '[b]You have
forsaken Me, so I also have forsaken you [1]to Shishak.' "
6 So the princes of Israel and the king humbled themselves and said, "The [a]LORD is righteous."
7 And when the LORD saw that they humbled themselves,
the word of the LORD came to Shemaiah, saying, "[a]They have
humbled themselves so I will not destroy them, but I will grant
them some *measure* of deliverance, and [b]My wrath shall not
be poured out on Jerusalem by means of Shishak.
8 "But they will become his slaves so [a]that they may learn
the difference between My service and the service of the kingdoms of the countries."
9 [a]So Shishak king of Egypt came up against Jerusalem,
and took the treasures of the house of the LORD and the treasures of the king's palace. He took everything; [b]he even took
the golden shields which Solomon had made.
10 Then King Rehoboam made shields of bronze in their
place, and committed them to the [1]care of the commanders of
the [2]guard who guarded the door of the king's house.
11 And it happened as often as the king entered the house

18 [a]1 Sam. 16:6
21 [a]Deut. 17:17
22 [a]Deut. 21:15-17
23 [1]Lit., *from all*
1 [a]2 Chr. 12:13; 11:17 [b]2 Chr. 26:13-16
2 [a]1 Kin. 14:25 [b]1 Kin. 11:40
3 [a]2 Chr. 16:8; Nah. 3:9
4 [a]2 Chr. 11:5-12
5 [1]Lit., *in the hand of* [a]2 Chr. 11:2 [b]2 Chr. 15:2; Deut. 28:15
6 [a]Ex. 9:27; Dan. 9:14
7 [a]1 Kin. 21:29 [b]2 Chr. 34:25-27; Ps. 78:38
8 [a]Deut. 28:47, 48
9 [a]1 Kin. 14:26-28 [b]2 Chr. 9:15, 16
10 [1]Lit., *hands* [2]Lit., *runners*

of the LORD, the [1]guards came and carried them and *then*
brought them back into the [1]guards' room.
12 And [a]when he humbled himself, the anger of the LORD
turned away from him, so as not to destroy *him* completely;
and also conditions [b]were good in Judah.
13 [a]So King Rehoboam strengthened himself in Jerusalem, and reigned. Now Rehoboam was forty-one years old
when he began to reign, and he reigned seventeen years in
Jerusalem, the city which the LORD had chosen from all the
tribes of Israel, to put His name there. And his mother's name
was Naamah the Ammonitess.
14 And he did evil [a]because he did not set his heart to seek
the LORD.
15 [a]Now the acts of Rehoboam, from first to last, are they
not written in the [1]records of [b]Shemaiah the prophet and of
[c]Iddo the seer, according to genealogical enrollment? And
there were wars between Rehoboam and Jeroboam
continually.
16 And Rehoboam slept with his fathers, and was buried
in the city of David; and his son [a]Abijah became king in his
place.

CHAPTER 13

[a]IN the eighteenth year of King Jeroboam Abijah became king
over Judah.
2 He reigned three years in Jerusalem; and his mother's
name was [a]Micaiah the daughter of Uriel of Gibeah. [b]And
there was war between Abijah and Jeroboam.
3 And Abijah began the battle with an army of valiant
warriors, 400,000 chosen men, while Jeroboam drew up in
battle formation against him with 800,000 chosen men *who
were* valiant warriors.
4 Then Abijah stood on Mount [a]Zemaraim, which is in
the hill country of Ephraim, and said, "Listen to me, Jeroboam and all Israel:
5 "Do you not know that [a]the LORD God of Israel gave
the rule over Israel forever to David [1]and his sons by [b]a covenant
of salt?
6 "Yet [a]Jeroboam the son of Nebat, the servant of Solomon the son of David, rose up and rebelled against his [1]master,
7 and worthless men gathered about him, scoundrels,
who proved too strong for Rehoboam, the son of Solomon,
when [1a]he was young and timid and could not hold his own
against them.
8 "So now you intend to resist the kingdom of the LORD
[1]through the sons of David, [2]being a great multitude and *having* with you [a]the golden calves which Jeroboam made for
gods for you.
9 "[a]Have you not driven out the priests of the LORD, the
sons of Aaron and the Levites, and made for yourselves priests
like the peoples of other lands? Whoever comes [b]to consecrate
himself with a young bull and seven rams, even he may become a priest of *what are* [c]no gods.
10 "But as for us, the LORD is our God, and we have not

11 [1]Lit., run

12 ...r. 12:6, 7 [b]2 C...
19:3

13 [a]1

14 [a]2 C

15 [1]Lit.,
[a]1 Kin. 14
[c]2 Chr. 9:

16 [a]2 Chr.

1 [a]1 Kin. 1

2 [a]2 Chr. 11:20 [b]1 Kin.
15:7

4 [a]Josh. 18:22

5 [1]Lit., *to him and to his sons*
[a]2 Sam. 7:12-16 [b]Lev. 2:13;
Num. 18:19

6 [1]Or, *lord*
[a]1 Kin. 11:26

7 [1]Lit., *Rehoboam*
[a]2 Chr. 12:13

8 [1]Lit., *in the hands of*
[2]Lit., *and you are a*
[a]2 Chr. 11:15; 1 Kin. 12:28

9 [a]2 Chr. 11:14 [b]Ex. 29:29-
33 [c]Jer. 2:11; 5:7

forsaken Him; and the sons of Aaron are ministering to the
LORD as priests, and the Levites [1]attend to their work.
11 "And every morning [a]they [1]burn to the LORD burnt offerings and fragrant incense, and [b]the showbread is *set* on the
clean table, and the golden lampstand with its lamps is *ready*
to light every evening; for we keep the charge of the LORD our
God, but you have forsaken Him.
12 "Now behold, God is with us at *our* head and [a]His
priests with the signal trumpets to sound the alarm against
you. O sons of Israel, do not fight against the LORD God of
your fathers, for you will not succeed."
13 But Jeroboam [a]had set an ambush to come from the
rear, so that *Israel* was in front of Judah, and the ambush was
behind them.
14 When Judah turned around, behold, [1]they were attacked both front and rear; so [a]they cried to the LORD, and the
priests blew the trumpets.
15 Then the men of Judah raised a war cry, and when the
men of Judah raised the war cry, then it was that God [1a]routed
Jeroboam and all Israel before Abijah and Judah.
16 And when the sons of Israel fled before Judah, [a]God
gave them into their hand.
17 And Abijah and his people defeated them with a great
slaughter, so that 500,000 chosen men of Israel fell slain.
18 Thus the sons of Israel were subdued at that time, and
the sons of Judah [1]conquered [a]because they trusted in the
LORD, the God of their fathers.
19 And Abijah pursued Jeroboam, and captured from him
several cities, Beth-el with its villages, Jeshanah with its villages, and [1]Ephron with its villages.
20 And Jeroboam did not again recover strength in the
days of Abijah; and the [a]LORD struck him and [b]he died.
21 But Abijah became powerful, and took fourteen wives
to himself; and became the father of twenty-two sons and
sixteen daughters.
22 Now the rest of the acts of Abijah, and his ways and his
words are written in [a]the [1]treatise of [b]the prophet Iddo.

CHAPTER 14

1a So Abijah slept with his fathers, and they buried him in the
city of David, and his son Asa became king in his place. The
land was undisturbed for ten years during his days.
2 [1]And Asa did good and right in the sight of the LORD
his God,
3 for he removed [a]the foreign altars and [b]high places,
tore down the sacred pillars, cut down the [1c]Asherim,
4 and commanded Judah to seek the LORD God of their
fathers and to observe the law and the commandment.
5 He also removed the high places and the [a]incense altars
from all the cities of Judah. And the kingdom was undisturbed
under him.
6 And [a]he built fortified cities in Judah, since the land
was undisturbed, and [1]there was no one at war with him during
those years, [b]because the LORD had given him rest.
7 For he said to Judah, "[a]Let us build these cities and

…e battle was *behind them*
…:11

…it., *smote*
…. 14:12

…6 [a]2 Chr. 16:8

18 … *were strong*
[a]2 Chr. 14:11

19 [1]Another reading is, *Ephrain*

20 [a]1 Sam. 25:38 [b]1 Kin. 14:20

22 [1]Heb., *midrash*
[a]2 Chr. 24:27 [b]2 Chr. 9:29

1 [1]Heb. 13:23
[a]1 Kin. 15:8

2 [1]Heb. 14:1

3 [1]I.e., wooden symbols of a female deity
[a]Deut. 7:5 [b]1 Kin. 15:12-14
[c]Ex. 34:13

5 [a]2 Chr. 34:4, 7

6 [1]Lit., *there was not with him war*
[a]2 Chr. 11:5 [b]2 Chr. 15:15

7 [a]2 Chr. 8:5

of the LORD, the [1]guards came and carried them and *then*
brought them back into the [1]guards' room.
12 And [a]when he humbled himself, the anger of the LORD
turned away from him, so as not to destroy *him* completely;
and also conditions [b]were good in Judah.
13 [a]So King Rehoboam strengthened himself in Jerusalem, and reigned. Now Rehoboam was forty-one years old
when he began to reign, and he reigned seventeen years in
Jerusalem, the city which the LORD had chosen from all the
tribes of Israel, to put His name there. And his mother's name
was Naamah the Ammonitess.
14 And he did evil [a]because he did not set his heart to seek
the LORD.
15 [a]Now the acts of Rehoboam, from first to last, are they
not written in the [1]records of [b]Shemaiah the prophet and of
[c]Iddo the seer, according to genealogical enrollment? And
there were wars between Rehoboam and Jeroboam
continually.
16 And Rehoboam slept with his fathers, and was buried
in the city of David; and his son [a]Abijah became king in his
place.

CHAPTER 13

[a]IN the eighteenth year of King Jeroboam Abijah became king
over Judah.
2 He reigned three years in Jerusalem; and his mother's
name was [a]Micaiah the daughter of Uriel of Gibeah. [b]And
there was war between Abijah and Jeroboam.
3 And Abijah began the battle with an army of valiant
warriors, 400,000 chosen men, while Jeroboam drew up in
battle formation against him with 800,000 chosen men *who*
were valiant warriors.
4 Then Abijah stood on Mount [a]Zemaraim, which is in
the hill country of Ephraim, and said, "Listen to me, Jeroboam and all Israel:
5 "Do you not know that [a]the LORD God of Israel gave
the rule over Israel forever to David [1]and his sons by [b]a covenant
of salt?
6 "Yet [a]Jeroboam the son of Nebat, the servant of Solomon the son of David, rose up and rebelled against his [1]master,
7 and worthless men gathered about him, scoundrels,
who proved too strong for Rehoboam, the son of Solomon,
when [1a]he was young and timid and could not hold his own
against them.
8 "So now you intend to resist the kingdom of the LORD
[1]through the sons of David, [2]being a great multitude and *hav-*
ing with you [a]the golden calves which Jeroboam made for
gods for you.
9 "[a]Have you not driven out the priests of the LORD, the
sons of Aaron and the Levites, and made for yourselves priests
like the peoples of *other* lands? Whoever comes [b]to consecrate
himself with a young bull and seven rams, even he may become a priest of *what are* [c]no gods.
10 "But as for us, the LORD is our God, and we have not

11 [1]Lit., *runners*

12 [a]2 Chr. 12:6, 7 [b]2 Chr. 19:3

13 [a]1 Kin. 14:21

14 [a]2 Chr. 19:3

15 [1]Lit., *words* [a]1 Kin. 14:29 [b]2 Chr. 12:5 [c]2 Chr. 9:29

16 [a]2 Chr. 11:20

1 [a]1 Kin. 15:1, 2

2 [a]2 Chr. 11:20 [b]1 Kin. 15:7

4 [a]Josh. 18:22

5 [1]Lit., *to him and to his sons* [a]2 Sam. 7:12-16 [b]Lev. 2:13; Num. 18:19

6 [1]Or, *lord* [a]1 Kin. 11:26

7 [1]Lit., *Rehoboam* [a]2 Chr. 12:13

8 [1]Lit., *in the hands of* [2]Lit., *and you are a* [a]2 Chr. 11:15; 1 Kin. 12:28

9 [a]2 Chr. 11:14 [b]Ex. 29:29-33 [c]Jer. 2:11; 5:7

forsaken Him; and the sons of Aaron are ministering to the
LORD as priests, and the Levites [1]attend to their work.
11 "And every morning [a]they [1]burn to the LORD burnt offerings and fragrant incense, and [b]the showbread is *set* on the
clean table, and the golden lampstand with its lamps is *ready*
to light every evening; for we keep the charge of the LORD our
God, but you have forsaken Him.
12 "Now behold, God is with us at *our* head and [a]His
priests with the signal trumpets to sound the alarm against
you. O sons of Israel, do not fight against the LORD God of
your fathers, for you will not succeed."
13 But Jeroboam [a]had set an ambush to come from the
rear, so that *Israel* was in front of Judah, and the ambush was
behind them.
14 When Judah turned around, behold, [1]they were attacked both front and rear; so [a]they cried to the LORD, and the
priests blew the trumpets.
15 Then the men of Judah raised a war cry, and when the
men of Judah raised the war cry, then it was that God [1a]routed
Jeroboam and all Israel before Abijah and Judah.
16 And when the sons of Israel fled before Judah, [a]God
gave them into their hand.
17 And Abijah and his people defeated them with a great
slaughter, so that 500,000 chosen men of Israel fell slain.
18 Thus the sons of Israel were subdued at that time, and
the sons of Judah [1]conquered [a]because they trusted in the
LORD, the God of their fathers.
19 And Abijah pursued Jeroboam, and captured from him
several cities, Beth-el with its villages, Jeshanah with its villages, and [1]Ephron with its villages.
20 And Jeroboam did not again recover strength in the
days of Abijah; and the [a]LORD struck him and [b]he died.
21 But Abijah became powerful, and took fourteen wives
to himself; and became the father of twenty-two sons and
sixteen daughters.
22 Now the rest of the acts of Abijah, and his ways and his
words are written in [a]the [1]treatise of [b]the prophet Iddo.

CHAPTER 14

1a
SO Abijah slept with his fathers, and they buried him in the
city of David, and his son Asa became king in his place. The
land was undisturbed for ten years during his days.
2 [1]And Asa did good and right in the sight of the LORD
his God,
3 for he removed [a]the foreign altars and [b]high places,
tore down the sacred pillars, cut down the [1c]Asherim,
4 and commanded Judah to seek the LORD God of their
fathers and to observe the law and the commandment.
5 He also removed the high places and the [a]incense altars
from all the cities of Judah. And the kingdom was undisturbed
under him.
6 And [a]he built fortified cities in Judah, since the land
was undisturbed, and [1]there was no one at war with him during
those years, [b]because the LORD had given him rest.
7 For he said to Judah, "[a]Let us build these cities and

10 [1]Lit., *in the work*

11 [1]Lit., *offer up in smoke* [a]2 Chr. 2:4; Ex. 29:38 [b]Ex. 25:30-39; Lev. 24:5-9

12 [a]Num. 10:8, 9

13 [a]Josh. 8:4-9

14 [1]Lit., *the battle was before and behind them* [a]2 Chr. 14:11

15 [1]Lit., *smote* [a]2 Chr. 14:12

16 [a]2 Chr. 16:8

18 [1]Lit., *were strong* [a]2 Chr. 14:11

19 [1]Another reading is, *Ephrain*

20 [a]1 Sam. 25:38 [b]1 Kin. 14:20

22 [1]Heb., *midrash* [a]2 Chr. 24:27 [b]2 Chr. 9:29

1 [1]Heb. 13:23 [a]1 Kin. 15:8

2 [1]Heb. 14:1

3 [1]I.e., wooden symbols of a female deity [a]Deut. 7:5 [b]1 Kin. 15:12-14 [c]Ex. 34:13

5 [a]2 Chr. 34:4, 7

6 [1]Lit., *there was not with him war* [a]2 Chr. 11:5 [b]2 Chr. 15:15

7 [a]2 Chr. 8:5

surround *them* with walls and towers, gates and bars. The land
is still [1]ours, because we have sought the LORD our God; we
have sought Him, and He has given us rest on every side." So
they built and prospered.
8 Now Asa had an army of [a]300,000 from Judah, bearing
large shields and spears, and 280,000 from Benjamin, bearing
shields and wielding bows; all of them were valiant warriors.
9 Now Zerah the Ethiopian [a]came out against them with
an army of a million men and 300 chariots, and he came to
[b]Mareshah.
10 So Asa went out [1]to meet him, and they drew up in
battle formation in the valley of Zephathah at Mareshah.
11 Then Asa [a]called to the LORD his God, and said, "Lord,
there is no one besides Thee to help *in the battle* between the
powerful and those who have no strength; so help us, O LORD
our God, [b]for we trust in Thee, and in Thy name have come
against this multitude. O LORD, Thou art our God; let not man
prevail against Thee."
12 So [a]the LORD [1]routed the Ethiopians before Asa and
before Judah, and the Ethiopians fled.
13 And Asa and the people who *were* with him pursued
them as far as [a]Gerar; and so many Ethiopians fell that [1]they
could not recover, for they were shattered before the LORD,
and before his army. And they carried away very much
plunder.
14 And they [1]destroyed all the cities around Gerar, [a]for
the dread of the LORD had fallen on them; and they despoiled
all the cities, for there was much plunder in them.
15 They also struck down [1]those who owned livestock, and
they carried away large numbers of sheep and camels. Then
they returned to Jerusalem.

CHAPTER 15

NOW [a]the Spirit of God came on Azariah the son of Oded,
2 and he went out [1]to meet Asa and said to him, "Listen
to me, Asa, and all Judah and Benjamin: [a]the LORD is with you
when you are with Him. And [b]if you seek Him, He will let you
find Him; but if you forsake Him, He will forsake you.
3 "And [a]for many days Israel was without the true God
and without [b]a teaching priest and without law.
4 "But [a]in their distress they turned to the LORD God of
Israel, and they sought Him, and He let them find Him.
5 "[a]And in those times there was no peace to him who
went out or to him who came in, for many disturbances [1]af-
flicted all the inhabitants of the lands.
6 "And nation was crushed by nation, and city by city, for
God troubled them with every kind of distress.
7 "But you, [a]be strong and do not [1]lose courage, for there
is reward for your work."
8 Now when Asa heard these words and the [1]prophecy
which Azariah the son of Oded the prophet spoke, he took
courage and removed the abominable idols from all the land
of Judah and Benjamin and from [a]the cities which he had
captured in the hill country of Ephraim. [b]He then restored the
altar of the LORD which was in front of the porch of the LORD.

7 [1]Lit., *before us*

8 [a]2 Chr. 13:3

9 [a]2 Chr. 12:2, 3; 16:8 [b]2 Chr. 11:8

10 [1]Lit., *before him*

11 [a]2 Chr. 13:14 [b]2 Chr. 13:18

12 [1]Lit., *struck* [a]2 Chr. 13:15

13 [1]Or, *there was none left alive* [a]Gen. 10:19

14 [1]Lit., *smote* [a]2 Chr. 17:10

15 [1]Lit., *tents of livestock*

1 [a]2 Chr. 20:14; 24:20

2 [1]Lit., *before Asa* [a]2 Chr. 20:17 [b]2 Chr. 15:4, 15

3 [a]1 Kin. 12:28-33 [b]2 Chr. 17:9; Lev. 10:8-11

4 [a]Deut. 4:29

5 [1]Lit., *were on* [a]Judg. 5:6

7 [1]Lit., *let your hands drop* [a]Josh. 1:7, 9

8 [1]With several ancient versions; Heb., *the prophecy, Oded the prophet* [a]2 Chr. 13:19 [b]2 Chr. 4:1; 8:12

9 [a]2 Chr. 11:16

9 And he gathered all Judah and Benjamin and those
from Ephraim, Manasseh, and Simeon [a]who resided with
them, for many defected to him from Israel when they saw
that the LORD his God was with him.

11 [a]2 Chr. 14:13-15

10 So they assembled at Jerusalem in the third month of
the fifteenth year of Asa's reign.
11 And [a]they sacrificed to the LORD that day 700 oxen and
7,000 sheep from the spoil they had brought.

12 [a]2 Chr. 23:16

12 And [a]they entered into the covenant to seek the LORD
God of their fathers with all their heart and soul;

13 [a]Ex. 22:20; Deut. 13:6-9

13 and whoever would not seek the LORD God of Israel
[a]should be put to death, whether small or great, man or
woman.
14 Moreover, they made an oath to the LORD with a loud
voice, with shouting, with trumpets, and with horns.

15 [1]Lit., *with their whole desire*
[a]2 Chr. 14:7

15 And all Judah rejoiced concerning the oath, for they
had sworn with their whole heart and had sought Him [1]earnest-
ly, and He let them find Him. So [a]the LORD gave them rest on
every side.

16 [1]Or, for *Asherah*
[a]1 Kin. 15:13-15 [b]Ex. 34:13
[c]2 Chr. 14:2-5

16 [a]And he also removed Maacah, the mother of King
Asa, from the *position of* queen mother, because she had made
a horrid image [1]as [b]an Asherah, and [c]Asa cut down her horrid
image, crushed *it* and burned *it* at the brook Kidron.
17 But the high places were not removed from Israel; nevertheless Asa's heart was blameless all his days.
18 And he brought into the house of God the dedicated
things of his father and his own dedicated things: silver and
gold and utensils.
19 And there was no more war until the thirty-fifth year of
Asa's reign.

1 [1]Lit., *built*
[a]1 Kin. 15:17-22

2 [1]Heb., *Aram*

3 [1]Lit., *me and you*

[a] CHAPTER 16

IN the thirty-sixth year of Asa's reign Baasha king of Israel
came up against Judah and [1]fortified Ramah in order to prevent *anyone* from going out or coming in to Asa king of Judah.
2 Then Asa brought out silver and gold from the treasuries of the house of the LORD and the king's house, and sent
them to Ben-hadad king of [1]Syria, who lived in Damascus,
saying,
3 "*Let there be* a treaty between [1]you and me, *as* between
my father and your father. Behold, I have sent you silver and
gold; go, break your treaty with Baasha king of Israel so that he
will withdraw from me."

4 [1]Lit., *smote* [2]Lit., *storage places of the cities*
[a]Ex. 1:11

5 [1]Lit., *building*

6 [1]Lit., *built*

4 So Ben-hadad listened to King Asa and sent the commanders of his armies against the cities of Israel, and they
[1]conquered Ijon, Dan, Abel-maim, and all [a]the [2]store cities of
Naphtali.
5 And it came about when Baasha heard *of it* that he
ceased [1]fortifying Ramah and stopped his work.
6 Then King Asa brought all Judah, and they carried
away the stones of Ramah and its timber with which Baasha
had been building, and with them he [1]fortified Geba and
Mizpah.

7 [a]2 Chr. 19:2; 1 Kin. 16:1
[b]2 Chr. 14:11; 32:7, 8

7 At that time [a]Hanani the seer came to Asa king of
Judah and said to him, "[b]Because you have relied on the king

of [1]Syria and have not relied on the LORD your God, therefore
the army of the king of [1]Syria has escaped out of your hand.
8 "Were not [a]the Ethiopians and the Lubim [b]an immense
army with very many chariots and horsemen? Yet, [c]because
you relied on the LORD, He delivered them into your hand.
9 "For [a]the eyes of the LORD move to and fro throughout
the earth that He may strongly support those [b]whose heart is
completely His. You have acted foolishly in this. Indeed, from
now on you will surely have wars."
10 Then Asa was angry with the seer and put him in [1]pris-
on, for he was enraged at him for this. And Asa oppressed
some of the people at the same time.
11 [a]And now, the acts of Asa from first to last, behold,
they are written in the book of the kings of Judah and Israel.
12 And in the thirty-ninth year of his reign Asa became
diseased in his feet. His disease was severe, yet even in his
disease he did not seek the LORD but the physicians.
13 So Asa slept with his fathers, [1]having died in the forty-
first year of his reign.
14 And they buried him in his own tomb which he had cut
out for himself in the city of David, and they laid him in the
resting place which he had filled [a]with spices of various kinds
blended by the perfumers art; and [b]they made a very great fire
for him.

CHAPTER 17

[a]JEHOSHAPHAT his son then became king in his place, and
made his position over Israel firm.
2 He placed troops in all [a]the fortified cities of Judah,
and set garrisons in the land of Judah, and in the cities of
Ephraim [b]which Asa his father had captured.
3 And the LORD was with Jehoshaphat because he [1]fol-
lowed the example of his father David's earlier days and did
not seek the Baals,
4 but sought the God of his father, [1]followed His commandments, [a]and did not act as Israel did.
5 So the LORD established the kingdom in his [1]control,
and all Judah brought tribute to Jehoshaphat, and [a]he had
great riches and honor.
6 And [1]he took great pride in the ways of the LORD and
again [a]removed the high places and the Asherim from Judah.
7 Then in the third year of his reign he sent his officials,
Ben-hail, Obadiah, Zechariah, Nethanel, and Micaiah, [a]to
teach in the cities of Judah;
8 and with them [a]the Levites, Shemaiah, Nethaniah, Zebadiah, Asahel, Shemiramoth, Jehonathan, Adonijah, Tobijah,
and Tobadonijah, the Levites; and with them Elishama and
Jehoram, the priests.
9 And they taught in Judah, *having* [a]the book of the law
of the LORD with them; and they went throughout all the cities
of Judah and taught among the people.
10 Now [a]the dread of the LORD was on all the kingdoms of
the lands which *were* around Judah, so that they did not make
war against Jehoshaphat.
11 And [a]some of the Philistines brought gifts and silver as

7 [1]Heb., *Aram*

8 [a]2 Chr. 14:9 [b]2 Chr. 12:3 [c]2 Chr. 13:16, 18

9 [a]Prov. 15:3; Zech. 4:10 [b]2 Chr. 15:17

10 [1]Lit., *house of the stocks*

11 [a]1 Kin. 15:23, 24

13 [1]Lit., *and*

14 [a]Gen. 50:2; John 12:7; 19:39, 40 [b]2 Chr. 21:19

1 [a]1 Kin. 15:24

2 [a]2 Chr. 11:5 [b]2 Chr. 15:8

3 [1]Lit., *walked in the earlier ways of his father*

4 [1]Lit., *walked in* [a]1 Kin. 12:28

5 [1]Lit., *hand* [a]2 Chr. 18:1

6 [1]Lit., *his heart was high* [a]2 Chr. 15:17

7 [a]2 Chr. 15:3; 35:3

8 [a]2 Chr. 19:8

9 [a]Deut. 6:4-9

10 [a]2 Chr. 14:14

11 [a]2 Chr. 9:14; 26:8

16 [a]Judg. 5:2, 9; 1 Chr. 29:9
tribute to Jehoshaphat; the Arabians also brought him flocks,
7,700 rams and 7,700 male goats.
12 So Jehoshaphat grew greater and greater, and he built
fortresses and store cities in Judah.
13 And he had large supplies in the cities of Judah, and
warriors, valiant men, in Jerusalem.
14 And this was their muster according to their fathers'
19 [a]2 Chr. 17:2
households: of Judah, commanders of thousands, Adnah *was*
the commander, and with him 300,000 valiant warriors;
15 and next to him *was* Johanan the commander, and with
him 280,000;
16 and next to him Amasiah the son of Zichri, [a]who volunteered for the LORD, and with him 200,000 valiant warriors;
17 and of Benjamin, Eliada a valiant warrior, and with
him 200,000 armed with bow and shield;
1 [a]2 Chr. 17:5
18 and next to him Jehozabad, and with him 180,000
equipped for war.
19 These are they who served the king, apart from [a]those
whom the king put in the fortified cities through all Judah.

CHAPTER 18

NOW [a]Jehoshaphat had great riches and honor; and he
2 [a]1 Kin. 22:2-35
allied himself by marriage with Ahab.
2 [a]And some years later he went down to *visit* Ahab at
Samaria. And Ahab slaughtered many sheep and oxen for him
and the people who were with him, and induced him to go up
against Ramoth-gilead.
3 And Ahab king of Israel said to Jehoshaphat king of
Judah, "Will you go with me *against* Ramoth-gilead?" And he
said to him, "I am as you are, and my people as your people,
4 [1]Lit., *as the day*
and *we will be* with you in the battle."
4 Moreover, Jehoshaphat said to the king of Israel,
"Please inquire [1]first for the word of the LORD.
5 Then the king of Israel assembled the prophets, four
hundred men, and said to them, "Shall we go against Ramoth-
gilead to battle, or shall I refrain?" And they said, "Go up, for
God will give *it* into the hand of the king."
6 But Jehoshaphat said, "Is there not yet a prophet of
8 [1]Lit., *hasten*
the LORD here that we may inquire of him?"
7 And the king of Israel said to Jehoshaphat, "There is
yet one man by whom we may inquire of the LORD, but I hate
him, for he never prophesies good concerning me but always
evil. He is Micaiah, son of Imla." But Jehoshaphat said, "Let
not the king say so."
8 Then the king of Israel called an officer and said,
9 [a]Ruth 4:1
"[1]Bring quickly Micaiah, son."
9 Now the king of Israel and Jehoshaphat the king of
Judah were sitting each on his throne, arrayed in *their* robes,
and *they* were sitting [a]at the threshing floor at the entrance of
the gate of Samaria; and all the prophets were prophesying
before them.
10 And Zedekiah the son of Chenaanah made horns of
iron for himself and said, "Thus says the LORD, 'With these
you shall gore the Syrians, until they are consumed.' "
11 And all the prophets were prophesying thus, saying,

"Go up to Ramoth-gilead and succeed, for the LORD will give
it into the hand of the king."
12 Then the messenger who went to summon Micaiah
spoke to him saying, "Behold, the words of the prophets are
uniformly favorable to the king. So please let your word be like
one of them and speak favorably."
13 But Micaiah said, "As the LORD lives, [a]what my God
says, that I will speak."
14 And when he came to the king, the king said to him,
"Micaiah, shall we go to Ramoth-gilead to battle, or shall I
refrain?" He said, "Go up and succeed, for they will be given
into your hand."
15 Then the king said to him, "How many times must I
adjure you to speak to me nothing but the truth in the name of
the LORD?"
16 So he said,

"I saw all Israel
Scattered on the mountains,
[a]Like sheep which have no shepherd;
And the LORD said,
'These have no master.
Let each of them return to his house in peace.' "

17 Then the king of Israel said to Jehoshaphat, "Did I not
tell you that he would not prophesy good concerning me, but
evil?"
18 And Micaiah said, "Therefore, hear the word of the
LORD. [a]I saw the LORD sitting on His throne, and all the host of
heaven standing on His right and on His left.
19 "And the LORD said, 'Who will entice Ahab king of
Israel to go up and fall at Ramoth-gilead?' And one said this
while another said that.
20 "Then a spirit came forward and stood before the LORD
and said, 'I will entice him.' And the LORD said to him, 'How?'
21 "And he said, 'I will go and be a deceiving spirit in the
mouth of all his prophets.' Then He said, 'You are to entice
him and prevail also. Go and do so.'
22 "Now therefore, the LORD has put a deceiving spirit in
the mouth of these your prophets; for the LORD has proclaimed
disaster against you."
23 Then Zedekiah the son of Chenaanah came near and
struck Micaiah on the cheek and said, "[1]How did the Spirit of
the LORD pass from me to speak to you?"
24 And Micaiah said, "Behold, you shall see on that day,
when you enter an inner room to hide yourself."
25 Then the king of Israel said, "[a]Take Micaiah and return him to Amon [b]the governor of the city, and to Joash the
king's son;
26 and say, 'Thus says the king, "[a]Put this *man* in prison,
and feed him [1]sparingly with bread and water until I return
safely." ' "
27 And Micaiah said, "If you indeed return safely, the
LORD has not spoken by me." And he said, "[a]Listen, all you
people."
28 So the king of Israel and Jehoshaphat king of Judah
went up against Ramoth-gilead.
29 And the king of Israel said to Jehoshaphat, "I will dis-

13 [a]Num. 22:18-20, 35

16 [a]Num. 27:17; Ezek. 35:5-8; Matt. 9:36

18 [a]Is. 6:1-5; Dan. 7:9, 10

23 [1]Lit., *Which way*

25 [a]2 Chr. 18:8 [b]2 Chr. 34:8

26 [1]Lit., *with bread of affliction and water of affliction*
[a]2 Chr. 16:10

27 [a]Mic. 1:2

guise myself and go into battle, but you put on your robes." So
the king of Israel disguised himself, and they went into battle.
30 Now the king of Syria had commanded the captains of
his chariots, saying, "Do not fight with small or great, but with
the king of Israel alone."
31 So it came about when the captains of the chariots saw
Jehoshaphat, that they said, "It is the king of Israel," and they
turned aside to fight against him. But Jehoshaphat [a]cried out,
and the LORD helped him, and God diverted them from him.
32 Then it happened when the captains of the chariots
saw that it was not the king of Israel, that they turned back
from pursuing him.
33 And a certain man drew his bow at random and struck
the king of Israel [1]in a joint of the armor. So he said to the
driver of the chariot, "Turn [2]around, and take me out of the
[3]fight; for I am severely wounded."
34 And the battle raged that day, and the king of Israel
propped himself up in his chariot in front of the Syrians until
the evening; and at sunset he died.

CHAPTER 19

THEN Jehoshaphat the king of Judah returned in safety to
his house in Jerusalem.
2 And [a]Jehu the son of Hanani the seer went out to meet
him and said to King Jehoshaphat, "[b]Should you help the
wicked and love those who hate the LORD and [1c]so *bring* wrath
on yourself from the LORD?
3 "But [1a]there is *some* good in you, for [b]you have removed
the [2]Asheroth from the land and you [c]have set your heart to
seek God."
4 So Jehoshaphat lived in Jerusalem and went out again
among the people from Beer-sheba to the hill country of
Ephraim and [a]brought them back to the LORD, the God of
their fathers.
5 And he appointed [a]judges in the land in all the fortified
cities of Judah, city by city.
6 And he said to the judges, "Consider what you are
doing, for [a]you do not judge for man but for the LORD who is
with you [1]when you render judgment.
7 "Now then let the fear of the LORD be upon you; [1]be
very careful what you do, for [2]the LORD our God will [a]have no
part in unrighteousness, [b]or partiality, or the taking of a bribe."
8 And in Jerusalem also Jehoshaphat appointed some [a]of
the Levites and priests, and some of the heads of the fathers'
households of Israel, for the judgment of the LORD and to
judge [1]disputes among the inhabitants of Jerusalem.
9 Then he charged them saying, "Thus you shall do in
the fear of the LORD, faithfully and wholeheartedly.
10 "[a]And whenever any dispute comes to you from your
brethren who live in their cities, between blood and blood,
between law and commandment, statutes and ordinances, you
shall warn them that they may not be guilty before the LORD,
and [b]wrath may *not* come on you and your brethren. Thus you
shall do and you will not be guilty.
11 "And behold, Amariah the chief priest will be over you

31 [a]2 Chr. 13:14, 15

33 [1]Lit., *between the scale armor and the breastplate* [2]Lit., *your hand* [3]Lit., *camp*

2 [1]Lit., *by this* [a]2 Chr. 20:34; 1 Kin. 16:1 [b]2 Chr. 18:1, 3 [c]2 Chr. 24:18

3 [1]Lit., *good things are found* [2]I.e., wooden pillars [a]2 Chr. 12:12 [b]2 Chr. 17:6 [c]2 Chr. 12:14

4 [a]2 Chr. 15:8-13

5 [a]Deut. 16:18-20

6 [1]Lit., *in the word of judgment* [a]Lev. 19:15; Deut. 1:17

7 [1]Lit., *be careful and do* [2]Lit., *there is not with the LORD God* [a]Gen. 18:25; Deut. 32:4 [b]Deut. 10:17, 18

8 [1]So the versions. Heb. reads *disputes. And they returned to Jerusalem.* Or, *And they lived in Jerusalem* [a]2 Chr. 17:8, 9

10 [a]Deut. 17:8 [b]2 Chr. 19:2

in [1a]all that pertains to the LORD; and Zebadiah the son of
Ishmael, the ruler of the house of Judah, in [1]all that pertains to
the king. Also the Levites shall be officers before you. [2b]Act
resolutely, and the LORD be with the upright."

11 [1]Lit., *every matter of* [2]Lit., *Be strong and do* [a]2 Chr. 19:8 [b]1 Chr. 28:20

CHAPTER 20

NOW it came about after this that the sons of Moab and the
sons of Ammon, together with some of the [1]Meunites, came to
make war against Jehoshaphat.
2 Then some came and reported to Jehoshaphat, saying,
"A great multitude is coming against you from beyond the sea,
out of [1]Syria and behold, they are in [a]Hazazontamar (that is
En-ged)."
3 And Jehoshaphat was afraid and [1a]turned his attention
to seek the LORD; and [b]proclaimed a fast throughout all Judah.
4 So Judah gathered together to seek help from the
LORD; they even came from all the cities of Judah to seek the
LORD.
5 Then Jehoshaphat stood in the assembly of Judah and
Jerusalem, in the house of the LORD before the new court,
6 and he said, "O LORD, the God of our fathers, [a]art
Thou not God in the heavens? And [b]art Thou not ruler over
all the kingdoms of the nations? Power and might are in Thy
hand so that no one can stand against Thee.
7 "Didst Thou not, O our God, drive out the inhabitants
of this land before Thy people Israel, and [a]give it to the descendants of Abraham Thy friend forever?
8 "And they lived in it, and have built Thee a sanctuary
there for Thy name, saying,
9 '[a]Should evil come upon us, the sword, *or* judgment, or
pestilence, or famine, we will stand before this house and before Thee (for [b]Thy name is in this house) and cry to Thee in
our distress, and Thou wilt hear and deliver *us.*'
10 "And now behold, [a]the sons of Ammon and Moab and
Mount Seir, [b]whom Thou didst not let Israel invade, when
they came out of the land of Egypt (they turned aside from
them and did not destroy them),
11 behold *how* they are rewarding us, by coming to drive
us out from Thy possession which Thou hast given us as an
inheritance.
12 "O our God, [a]wilt Thou not judge them? For we are
powerless before this great multitude who are coming against
us; nor do we know what to do, but [b]our eyes are on Thee."
13 And all Judah was standing before the LORD, with their
infants, their wives, and their children.
14 Then in the midst of the assembly the Spirit of the
LORD [a]came upon Jahaziel the son of Zechariah, the son of
Benaiah, the son of Jeiel, the son of Mattaniah, the Levite of
the sons of Asaph;
15 and he said, "Listen, all Judah and the inhabitants of
Jerusalem and King Jehoshaphat: thus says the LORD to you,
'[a]Do not fear or be dismayed because of this great multitude,
for [b]the battle is not yours but God's.
16 'Tomorrow go down against them. Behold, they will

1 [1]So with Gk., Heb., *Ammonites,* 1 Chr. 4:41; 2 Chr. 26:7

2 [1]Another reading is *Edom* [a]Gen. 14:7

3 [1]Lit., *set his face* [a]2 Chr. 19:3 [b]1 Sam. 7:6; Ezra 8:21

6 [a]Deut. 4:39 [b]1 Chr. 29:11

7 [a]Is. 41:8

9 [a]2 Chr. 6:28-30 [b]2 Chr. 6:20

10 [a]2 Chr. 20:1, 22 [b]Num. 20:17-21

12 [a]Judg. 11:27 [b]Ps. 25:15; 121:1, 2

14 [a]2 Chr. 15:1; 24:20

15 [a]2 Chr. 32:7, 8; Ex. 14:13 [b]1 Sam. 17:47

come up by the ascent of Ziz, and you will find them at the
end of the valley in front of the wilderness of Jeruel.
17 'You *need* not fight in this *battle;* station yourselves,
[a]stand and see the salvation of the LORD on your behalf, O
Judah and Jerusalem.' Do not fear or be dismayed; tomorrow
go out to face them, [b]for the LORD is with you."
18 And Jehoshaphat bowed his head with *his* face to the
ground, and all Judah and the inhabitants of Jerusalem fell
down before the LORD, worshiping the LORD.
19 And the Levites, from the sons [a]of the Kohathites and
of the sons of the Korahites, stood up to praise the LORD God
of Israel, with a very loud voice.
20 And they rose early in the morning and went out to the
wilderness of Tekoa; and when they went out, Jehoshaphat
stood and said, "Listen to me, O Judah and inhabitants of
Jerusalem, [a]put your trust in the LORD your God, and you will
be established. Put your trust in His prophets and succeed."
21 And when he had consulted with the people, he
appointed those who sang to the LORD and those who [a]praised
Him in holy attire, as they went out before the army and said,
"[b]Give thanks to the LORD, for His lovingkindness is
everlasting."
22 And when they began singing and praising, the LORD
[a]set ambushes against the sons of [b]Ammon, Moab, and Mount
Seir, who had come against Judah; so they were [1]routed.
23 For the sons of Ammon and Moab rose up against the
inhabitants of Mount Seir destroying *them* completely, and
when they had finished with the inhabitants of Seir, [a]they
helped to destroy one another.
24 When Judah came to the lookout of the wilderness,
they looked toward the multitude; and behold, they *were*
corpses lying on the ground, and no one had escaped.
25 And when Jehoshaphat and his people came to take
their spoil, they found much among them, *including* goods,
[1]garments, and valuable things which they took for themselves,
more than they could carry. And they were three days taking
the spoil because there was so much.
26 Then on the fourth day they assembled in the valley of
Beracah, for there they blessed the LORD. Therefore they have
named that place "The Valley of [1]Beracah" until today.
27 And every man of Judah and Jerusalem returned with
Jehoshaphat at their head, returning to Jerusalem with joy, for
the LORD had made them to rejoice over their enemies.
28 And they came to Jerusalem with harps, lyres, and
trumpets to the house of the LORD.
29 And [a]the dread of God was on all the kingdoms of the
lands when they heard that the LORD had fought against the
enemies of Israel.
30 So the kingdom of Jehoshaphat was at peace, [a]for his
God gave him rest on all sides.
31 [a]Now Jehoshaphat reigned over Judah. He *was* thirty-
five years old when he became king, and he reigned in Jerusalem twenty-five years. And his mother's name *was* Azubah the
daughter of Shilhi.
32 And he walked in the way of his father Asa and did not
depart from it, doing right in the sight of the LORD.

17 [a]Ex. 14:13 [b]2 Chr. 15:2
19 [a]2 Chr. 7:3
20 [a]Is. 7:9
21 [a]1 Chr. 16:29; Ps. 29:2 [b]1 Chr. 16:34
22 [1]Lit., *struck down* [a]2 Chr. 13:13 [b]2 Chr. 20:10
23 [a]Judg. 7:22; 1 Sam. 14:20
25 [1]So several ancient mss.; others read, *corpses*
26 [1]I.e., Blessing
29 [a]2 Chr. 14:6, 7; 15:15
30 [a]1 Kin. 22:41-43
31 [a]2 Chr. 17:6

33 [a]The high places, however, were not removed; [b]the
people had not yet directed their hearts to the God of their
fathers.
34 Now the rest of the acts of Jehoshaphat, first [1]to last,
behold, they are written in the annals of [a]Jehu the son of
Hanani, [b]which is [2]recorded in the Book of the Kings of Israel.
35 [a]And after this Jehoshaphat king of Judah allied himself with Ahaziah king of Israel. He acted wickedly [1]in so
doing.
36 So he allied himself with him to make ships to go [a]to
Tarshish, and they made the ships in Ezion-geber.
37 Then Eliezer the son of Dodavahu of Mareshah prophesied against Jehoshaphat saying, "Because you have allied
yourself with Ahaziah, the LORD has destroyed your works." So
the ships were broken and could not go to Tarshish.

CHAPTER 21

[a]THEN Jehoshaphat slept with his fathers and was buried
with his fathers in the city of David, and Jehoram his son
became king in his place.
2 And he had brothers, the sons of Jehoshaphat: Azariah,
Jehiel, Zechariah, Michael, and Shephatiah. All these *were* the
sons of Jehoshaphat king [a]of Israel.
3 And their father gave them many gifts of silver, gold
and precious things, [a]with fortified cities in Judah, but he gave
the kingdom to Jehoram because he was the first-born.
4 Now when Jehoram had [1]taken over the kingdom of his
father and made himself [2]secure, he killed all his brothers with
the sword, and some of the rulers of Israel also.
5 [a]Jehoram *was* thirty-two years old when he became
king, and he reigned eight years in Jerusalem.
6 [a]And he walked in the way of the kings of Israel, just as
the house of Ahab did ([b]for Ahab's daughter was his wife), and
he did evil in the sight of the LORD.
7 Yet the LORD was not willing to destroy the house of
David because of the covenant which he had made with David,
[a]and since He had promised to give a lamp to him and his sons
forever.
8 In his days [a]Edom revolted [1]against the rule of Judah,
and set up a king over themselves.
9 Then Jehoram crossed over with his commanders and
all his chariots with him. And it came about that he arose by
night and struck down the Edomites who were surrounding
him and the commanders of the chariots.
10 So Edom revolted [1]against Judah to this day. Then
Libnah revolted at the same time [2]against his rule, because he
had forsaken the LORD God of his fathers.
11 Moreover, [a]he made high places in the mountains of
Judah, and caused the inhabitants of Jerusalem [b]to play the
harlot and led Judah astray.
12 Then a letter came to him from Elijah the prophet
saying, "Thus says the LORD God of your father David, 'Because [a]you have not walked in the ways of Jehoshaphat your
father [b]and the ways of Asa king of Judah,
13 but [a]have walked in the way of the kings of Israel, and

33 [a]2 Chr. 17:6 [b]2 Chr. 19:3
34 [1]Lit., *and* [2]Lit., *taken up* [a]2 Chr. 19:2 [b]1 Kin. 16:1, 7
35 [1]Lit., *to do* [a]1 Kin. 22:48, 49
36 [a]2 Chr. 9:21
1 [a]1 Kin. 22:50
2 [a]2 Chr. 12:6; 23:2
3 [a]2 Chr. 11:5
4 [1]Lit., *risen up* [2]Lit., *strong*
5 [a]2 Kin. 8:17-22
6 [a]1 Kin. 12:28-30 [b]2 Chr. 18:1
7 [a]2 Sam. 7:12-17; 1 Kin. 11:13
8 [1]Lit., *from under the hand of* [a]2 Chr. 21:10; 20:22, 23
10 [1]Lit., *from under the hand of* [2]Lit., *from under his hand*
11 [a]1 Kin. 11:7 [b]Lev. 20:5
12 [a]2 Chr. 17:3, 4 [b]2 Chr. 14:2-5
13 [a]2 Chr. 21:6

have caused Judah and the inhabitants of Israel to play the
harlot [b]as the house of Ahab played the harlot, and you [c]have
also killed your brothers, [1]your own family, who were better
than you,
14 behold, the LORD is going to strike your people, your
sons, your wives, and all your possessions with a great
[1]calamity;
15 and [a]you [1]will suffer severe sickness, a disease of your
bowels, until your bowels come out because of the sickness,
day by day.' "
16 Then [a]the LORD stirred up against Jehoram the spirit of
the Philistines and [b]the Arabs who [1]bordered the Ethiopians;
17 and they came against Judah and invaded it, and
carried away all the possessions found in the king's house together with his sons and his wives, so that no son was left to
him except [1a]Jehoahaz, the youngest of his sons.
18 So after all this the LORD smote him [a]in his bowels with
an incurable sickness.
19 Now it came about in the course of time, at the end of
two years, that his bowels came out because of his sickness and
he died in great pain. And his people made no fire for him like
[a]the fire for his fathers.
20 He was thirty-two years old when he became king, and
he reigned in Jerusalem eight years; and he departed [1a]with no
one's regret, and they buried him in the city of David, [b]but not
in the tombs of the kings.

[a] CHAPTER 22

THEN the inhabitants of Jerusalem made [1]Ahaziah his
youngest son, king in his place, for the band of men who came
with [b]the Arabs to the camp had slain all the older *sons*. So
Ahaziah the son of Jehoram king of Judah began to reign.
2 Ahaziah *was* [1]twenty-two years old when he became
king, and he reigned one year in Jerusalem. And his mother's
name was [a]Athaliah, the [2]granddaughter of Omri.
3 He also walked in the ways of the house of Ahab, for
his mother was his counsellor to do wickedly.
4 And he did evil in the sight of the LORD like the house
of Ahab, for they were his counselors after the death of his
father, to his destruction.
5 He also walked according to their counsel, and went
with Jehoram the son of Ahab king of Israel to wage war
against Hazael king of Syria at Ramoth-gilead. But the [1]Syri-
ans [2]wounded Joram.
6 So he returned to be healed in Jezreel of the wounds
[1]which they had inflicted on him at Ramah, when he fought
against Hazael king of Syria. And [2]Ahaziah the son of Jehoram, king of Judah went down to see Jehoram the son of Ahab
in Jezreel, because he was sick.
7 Now [a]the destruction of Ahaziah was from God, in that
[1]he went to [2]Joram. For when he came, [b]he went out with
Jehoram against Jehu the son of Nimshi, [c]whom the LORD had
anointed to cut off the house of Ahab.
8 [a]And it came about when Jehu was executing judgment
on the house of Ahab, he found the princes of Judah and the

13 [1]Lit., *your father's house* [b]1 Kin. 16:31-33 [c]2 Chr. 21:4

14 [1]Lit., *blow*

15 [1]Lit., *in many sicknesses* [a]2 Chr. 21:18, 19

16 [1]Lit., *were at the hand of* [a]2 Chr. 33:11 [b]2 Chr. 17:11; 22:1

17 [1]In 2 Chr. 22:19, *Ahaziah* [a]2 Chr. 25:23

18 [a]2 Chr. 21:15

19 [a]2 Chr. 16:14

20 [1]Lit., *without desire* [a]Jer. 22:18, 28 [b]2 Chr. 24:25; 28:27

1 [1]In 2 Chr. 21:17, *Jehoahaz* [a]2 Kin. 8:24-29 [b]2 Chr. 21:16

2 [1]So some versions and 2 Kin. 8:26; Heb., *42 years* [2]Lit., *daughter* [a]2 Chr. 21:6

5 [1]So with 2 Kin. 8:28; Heb., *archers* [2]Lit., *smote*

6 [1]Lit., *with which. . . . smitten* [2]So with 2 Kin. 8:29; Heb., *Azariah*

7 [1]Lit., *to go* [2]I.e., Jehoram [a]2 Chr. 10:15 [b]2 Kin. 9:21 [c]2 Kin. 9:6, 7

8 [a]2 Kin. 10:11-14

sons of Ahaziah's brothers, ministering to Ahaziah, and slew
them.
9 [a]He also sought Ahaziah, and they caught him while he
was hiding in Samaria; they brought him to Jehu, put him to
death, [b]and buried him. For they said, "He is the son of Jehoshaphat, [c]who sought the LORD with all his heart." So there was
no one of the house of Ahaziah to retain the power of the
kingdom.
10 [a]Now when Athaliah the mother of Ahaziah saw that
her son was dead, she rose and [1]destroyed all the royal [2]off-
spring of the house of Judah.
11 But Jehoshabeath the king's daughter took Joash the
son of Ahaziah, and stole him from among the king's sons who
were being put to death, and placed him and his nurse in the
bedroom. So Jehoshabeath, the daughter of King Jehoram, the
wife of Jehoiada the priest (for she was the sister of Ahaziah),
hid him from Athaliah so that she would not put him to death.
12 And he was hidden with them in the house of God six
years while Athaliah reigned over the land.

CHAPTER 23

[a]NOW in the seventh year Jehoiada strengthened himself,
and took captains of hundreds: Azariah the son of Jeroham,
Ishmael the son of Johanan, Azariah the son of Obed, Maaseiah
the son of Adaiah, and Elishaphat the son of Zichri, *and
they entered* into a covenant with him.
2 And they went throughout Judah and gathered the Levites from all the cities of Judah, and the heads of the fathers'
households of [a]Israel, and they came to Jerusalem.
3 Then all the assembly made a covenant with the king in
the house of God. And [1]Jehoiada said to them, "Behold, the
king's son shall reign, [a]as the LORD has spoken concerning the
sons of David.
4 "This is the thing which you shall do: one third of you,
of the priests and Levites [a]who come in on the sabbath, *shall
be* gatekeepers,
5 and one third *shall be* at the king's house, and a third at
the Gate of the Foundation; and all the people *shall be* in the
courts of the house of the LORD.
6 "But let no one enter the house of the LORD except the
priests and [a]the ministering Levites; they may enter, for they
are holy. And let all the people keep the charge of the LORD.
7 "And the Levites will surround the king, each man with
his weapons in his hand; and whoever enters the house, let him
be killed. Thus be with the king when he comes in and when
he goes out."
8 So the Levites and all Judah did according to all that
Jehoiada the priest commanded. And each one of them took
his men who were to come in on the Sabbath, with those who
were to go out on the Sabbath, for Jehoiada the priest did not
dismiss *any of* [a]the divisions.
9 Then Jehoiada the priest gave to the captains of hundreds the spears and the large and small shields which had
been King David's, which *were* in the house of God.
10 And he stationed all the people, each man with his

9 [a]2 Kin. 9:27 [b]2 Kin. 9:28 [c]2 Chr. 17:4

10 [1]So with 2 Kin. 11:1; Heb., *said* [2]Lit., *seed* [a]2 Kin. 11:1-3

1 [a]2 Kin. 11:4-20

2 [a]2 Chr. 21:2; 11:13-17

3 [1]Lit., *he* [a]2 Chr. 21:7

4 [a]1 Chr. 9:25

6 [a]1 Chr. 23:28-32

8 [a]1 Chr. 24:1

weapon in his hand, from the right [1]side of the house to the
left [1]side of the house, by the altar and by the house, around
the king.
11 Then they brought out the king's son and put the
crown on him, and *gave him* [a]the testimony, and made him
king. And Jehoiada and his sons anointed him and said,
"[b]*Long* live the king!"
12 When Athaliah heard the noise of the people running
and praising the king, she came into the house of the LORD to
the people.
13 And she looked, and behold, the king was standing by
his pillar at the entrance, and the captains and the [1]trumpeters
were beside the king. And all the people of the land rejoiced
and blew trumpets, the singers with *their* musical instruments
[2]leading the praise. Then Athaliah tore her clothes and said,
"Treason! Treason!"
14 And Jehoiada the priest brought out the captains of
hundreds who were appointed over the army, and said to
them, "Bring her out [1]between the ranks; and whoever follows
her, put to death with the sword." For the priest said, "Let her
not be put to death in the house of the LORD."
15 So they [1]seized her, and when she arrived at [a]the entrance of the Horse Gate of the king's house, they [b]put her
to death there.
16 Then Jehoiada made a covenant between himself and
all the people and the king, that they should be the LORD's
people.
17 And all the people went to the house of Baal, and tore
it down, and they broke in pieces his altars and his images, and
[a]killed Mattan the priest of Baal before the altars.
18 Moreover, Jehoiada placed the offices of the house of
the LORD under the [1]authority of [a]the Levitical priests, [b]whom
David had assigned over the house of the LORD, to offer the
burnt offerings of the LORD, as it is written in the law of
Moses—[c]with rejoicing and singing according to the [2]order of
David.
19 And he stationed [a]the gatekeepers of the house of the
LORD, so that no one should enter *who was* in any way
unclean.
20 And he took the captains of hundreds, the nobles, the
rulers of the people, and all the people of the land, and
brought the king down from the house of the LORD, and came
through the Upper Gate to the king's house. And they placed
the king upon the royal throne.
21 So all of the people of the land rejoiced and the city
was quiet. For they had put Athaliah to death with the sword.

CHAPTER 24

[a]JOASH *was* seven years old when he became king, and he
reigned forty years in Jerusalem; his mother's name *was* Zibiah
from Beersheba.
2 And [a]Joash did what was right in the sight of the LORD
all the days of Jehoiada the priest.
3 And Jehoiada took two wives for him, and he became
the father of sons and daughters.

10 [1]Lit., *shoulder*
11 [a]Ex. 25:16, 21 [b]1 Sam. 10:24
13 [1]Lit., *trumpets* [2]Lit., *and leading for praising*
14 [1]Lit., *from within*
15 [1]Lit., *placed hands to her* [a]Neh. 3:28; Jer. 31:40 [b]2 Chr. 22:10
17 [a]Deut. 13:6-9; 1 Kin. 18:40
18 [1]Lit., *hand* [2]Lit., *hands of* [a]2 Chr. 5:5; 1 Chr. 23:6, 25-31 [b]1 Chr. 9:22 [c]2 Kin. 11:21; 12:1-15
19 [a]2 Chr. 26:4, 5
1 [a]2 Kin. 11:21; 12:1-15
2 [a]2 Chr. 26:4, 5

4 Now it came about after this that Joash [1]decided [a]to
restore the house of the LORD.
5 And he gathered the priests and Levites, and said to
them, "Go out to the cities of Judah, and collect money from
all [a]Israel to [1]repair the house of your God [2]annually, and you
shall do the matter quickly." But the Levites did not act
quickly.
6 So the king summoned Jehoiada the chief *priest* and
said to him, "Why have you not required the Levites to bring
in from Judah and from Jerusalem [a]the levy *fixed by* Moses the
servant of the LORD on the congregation of Israel [b]for the tent
of the testimony?"
7 For [a]the sons of the wicked Athaliah had broken into
the house of God and even [1]used the holy things of the house
of the LORD for the Baals.
8 So the king commanded, and they made a chest and set
it outside by the gate of the house of the LORD.
9 And [a]they made a proclamation in Judah and Jerusalem to bring to the LORD [b]the levy *fixed by* Moses the servant
of God on Israel in the wilderness.
10 And all the officers and all the people rejoiced and
brought in their levies and [1]dropped *it* into the chest until they
had finished.
11 And it came about whenever the chest was brought in
to the king's officer by the Levites, and when they saw that
there was much money, then the king's scribe and the chief
priest's officer would come, empty the chest, take it, and return it to its place. Thus they did daily and collected much
money.
12 And the king and Jehoiada gave it to those who did the
work of the service of the house of the LORD; and they hired
masons and carpenters to restore the house of the LORD, and
also workers in iron and bronze to [1]repair the house of the
LORD.
13 So the workmen labored, and the repair work progressed
in their hands, and they [1]restored the house of God
[2]according to its specifications, and strengthened it.
14 And when they had finished, they brought the rest of
the money before the king and Jehoiada; and it was made into
utensils for the house of the LORD, utensils for the service and
the burnt offering, and pans and utensils of gold and silver.
And they offered burnt offerings in the house of the LORD
continually all the days of Jehoiada.
15 Now when Jehoiada [1]reached a ripe old age he died; he
was one hundred and thirty years old at his death.
16 And they buried him [a]in the city of David among the
kings, because he had done well in [b]Israel and [1]to God and His
house.
17 But after the death of Jehoiada the officials of Judah
came and bowed down to the king, and the king listened to
them.
18 And [a]they abandoned the house of the LORD the God
of their fathers, and [b]served the [1]Asherim and the idols; so
[c]wrath came upon Judah and Jerusalem for this their guilt.
19 Yet [a]He sent prophets to them to bring them back to

4 [1]Lit., *was with a heart*
[a]2 Chr. 24:7

5 [1]Lit., *to strengthen* [2]Lit., *from year to year*
[a]2 Chr. 21:2

6 [a]Ex. 30:12-16 [b]Num. 1:50

7 [1]Lit., *made*
[a]2 Chr. 21:17

9 [a]2 Chr. 36:22 [b]2 Chr. 24:6

10 [1]Lit., *threw*

12 [1]Lit., *to strengthen*

13 [1]Lit., *set up* [2]Lit., *upon its proportion*

15 [1]Lit., *became old and satisfied with days*

16 [1]Lit., *with*
[a]2 Chr. 21:20 [b]2 Chr. 21:2

18 [1]I.e., wooden symbols of a female deity
[a]2 Chr. 24:4 [b]Ex. 34:12-14 [c]Josh. 22:20

19 [a]Jer. 7:25

the LORD; though they testified against them, they would not
listen.
20 [a]Then the Spirit of God [1]came on Zechariah the son of
Jehoiada the priest; and he stood above the people and said to
them, "Thus God has said, 'Why do you transgress the commandments of the LORD and do not prosper? [b]Because you
have forsaken the LORD, He has also forsaken you.' "
21 So [a]they conspired against him and at the command of
the king they stoned him [1]to death in the court of the house of
the LORD.
22 Thus Joash the king did not remember the kindness
which his father Jehoiada had shown him, but he murdered his
son. And as he died he said, "May [a]the LORD see and [1]avenge!"
23 Now it came about at the turn of the year that [a]the
army of the Syrians came up against him; and they came to
Judah and Jerusalem, destroyed all the officials of the people
from among the people, and sent all their spoil to the king of
Damascus.
24 Indeed the army of the Syrians came with a small number of men; yet [a]the LORD delivered a very great army into
their hands, [b]because they had forsaken the LORD, the God of
their fathers. Thus they executed judgment on Joash.
25 [a]And when they had departed from him (for they left
him very sick), his own servants conspired against him because
of the blood of the [1]son of Jehoiada the priest, and murdered
him on his bed. So he died, and they buried him in the city of
David, but they did not bury him in the tombs of the kings.
26 Now these are those who conspired against him: Zabad
the son of Shimeath the Ammonitess, and Jehozabad the son
of Shimrith the Moabitess.
27 As to his sons and the many [1]oracles against him and
[a]the [2]rebuilding of the house of God, behold, they are written
in the [3b]treatise of the Book of the Kings. Then Amaziah his
son became king in his place.

[a] CHAPTER 25

AMAZIAH was twenty-five years old when he became king,
and he reigned twenty-nine years in Jerusalem. And his mother's name was Jehoaddan of Jerusalem.
2 And he did right in the sight of the LORD, [a]yet not with
a whole heart.
3 Now it came about as soon as the kingdom was [1]firmly
in his grasp, that he killed his servants who had slain his father
the king.
4 However, he did not put their children to death, but
did as it is written in the law in the book of Moses, which the
LORD commanded, saying, "[a]Fathers shall not be put to death
for sons, nor sons be put to death for fathers, but each shall be
put to death for his own sin."
5 Moreover, Amaziah assembled Judah and appointed
them according to *their* fathers' households under commanders of thousands and commanders of hundreds throughout
Judah and Benjamin; and he [1]took a census of those [a]from
twenty years old and upward, and found them to be [b]300,000
choice men, *able* to go to war *and* handle spear and shield.

20 [1]Lit., *clothed* [a]2 Chr. 20:14 [b]Num. 14:41
21 [1]Lit., *with stones* [a]2 Chr. 15:2
22 [1]Lit., *seek*, or *require* [a]Neh. 9:26; Matt. 23:34, 35
23 [a]Gen. 9:5
24 [a]2 Kin. 12:17 [b]2 Chr. 16:7, 8
25 [1]So some ancient versions; Heb., *sons* [a]2 Kin. 12:20, 21
27 [1]Or, *burdens upon* [2]Lit., *founding* [3]Heb., *midrash* [a]2 Chr. 24:12 [b]2 Chr. 13:22
1 [a]2 Kin. 14:1-6
2 [a]2 Chr. 25:14
3 [1]Lit., *firm upon him*
4 [a]Deut. 24:16
5 [1]Lit., *mustered* [a]Num. 1:3 [b]2 Chr. 26:13

6 He hired also 100,000 valiant warriors out of Israel for
one hundred talents of silver.
7 But [a]a man of God came to him saying, "O king, do
not let the army of Israel go with you, for the LORD is not with
Israel *nor with* any of the sons of Ephraim.
8 "But if you do go, do *it*, be strong for the battle; *yet*
God will [1]bring you down before the enemy, [a]for God has
power to help and to [1]bring down."
9 And Amaziah said to the man of God, "But what *shall*
we do for the hundred talents which I have given to the troops
of Israel?" And the man of God answered, "The LORD has
much more to give you than this."
10 Then Amaziah [1]dismissed them, the troops which
came to him from Ephraim, to go home; so their anger burned
against Judah and they returned [2]home in fierce anger.
11 Now Amaziah strengthened himself, and led his people
forth, and went to [a]the Valley of Salt, and struck down 10,000
of the sons of Seir.
12 The sons of Judah also captured 10,000 alive and
brought them to the top of the cliff, and threw them down
from the top of the cliff so that they were all dashed to pieces.
13 But the [1]troops whom Amaziah sent back from going
with him to battle, raided the cities of Judah, [a]from Samaria to
Beth-horon, and struck down 3,000 of them, and plundered
much spoil.
14 Now it came about after Amaziah came from slaughtering the Edomites that [a]he brought the gods of the sons of
Seir, set them up as his gods, bowed down before them, and
burned incense to them.
15 Then the anger of the LORD burned against Amaziah,
and he sent him a prophet who said to him, "Why have you
sought the gods of the people [a]who have not delivered their
own people from your hand?"
16 And it came about as he was talking with him that [1]the
king said to him, "Have we appointed you a royal counsellor?
Stop! Why should you be struck down?" Then the prophet
stopped and said, "I know that God has planned to destroy
you, because you have done this, and have not listened to my
counsel."
17 [a]Then Amaziah king of Judah took counsel and sent to
Joash the son of Jehoahaz the son of Jehu, the king of Israel,
saying, "Come, let us face each other."
18 And Joash the king of Israel sent to Amaziah king of
Judah, saying, "[a]The thornbush which was in Lebanon sent to
the cedar which was in Lebanon, saying, 'Give your daughter
to my son in marriage.' But there passed by a wild beast that
was in Lebanon, and trampled the thornbush.
19 "You said, 'Behold, you have [1]defeated Edom.' And
[a]your heart has [2]become proud in boasting. Now stay at home;
for why should you provoke trouble that you, even you, should
fall and Judah with you?"
20 But Amaziah would not listen, for it was from God,
that he might deliver them into the hand *of Joash* because they
had sought the gods of Edom.
21 So Joash king of Israel went up, and he and Amaziah

7 [a]2 Kin. 4:9

8 [1]Lit., *cause to stumble* [a]2 Chr. 14:11; 20:6

10 [1]Lit., *separated* [2]Lit., *to their own place*

11 [a]2 Kin. 14:7

13 [1]Lit., *sons of the troops* [a]2 Chr. 19:4

14 [a]2 Chr. 28:23

15 [a]2 Chr. 25:11, 12

16 [1]Lit., *he*

17 [a]2 Kin. 14:8-14

18 [a]Judg. 9:8-15

19 [1]Lit., *smitten* [2]Lit., *lifted you up to boast* [a]2 Chr. 26:16; 32:25

king of Judah faced each other at Beth-shemesh, which belonged to Judah.
22 And Judah was defeated [1]by Israel, and they fled each
to his tent.
23 Then Joash king of Israel captured Amaziah king of
Judah, the son of Joash the son of [a]Jehoahaz, at Beth-shemesh,
and brought him to Jerusalem, and tore down the wall of
Jerusalem from the Gate of Ephraim to the Corner Gate,
400 [1]cubits.
24 And *he took* all the gold and silver, and all the utensils
which were found in the house of God with [a]Obed-edom, and
the treasures of the king's house, the hostages also, and returned to Samaria.
25 [a]And Amaziah the son of Joash king of Judah lived
fifteen years after the death of Joash son of Jehoahaz king of
Israel.
26 Now the rest of the acts of Amaziah, from first to last,
behold, are they not written in the Book of the Kings of Judah
and Israel?
27 And from the time that Amaziah turned away from
following the LORD they conspired against him in Jerusalem,
and he fled to Lachish; but they sent after him to Lachish and
killed him there.
28 Then they brought him on horses and buried him with
his fathers in the city of Judah.

CHAPTER 26

AND all the people of Judah took [1]Uzziah, who *was* sixteen
years old, and made him king in the place of his father
Amaziah.
2 He built Eloth and restored it to Judah after the king
slept with his fathers.
3 Uzziah was [a]sixteen years old when he became king,
and he reigned fifty-two years in Jerusalem; and his mother's
name was [1]Jechiliah of Jerusalem.
4 And he did right in the sight of the LORD according to
all that his father Amaziah had done.
5 And [a]he continued to seek God in the days of Zechariah, [b]who had understanding [1]through the vision of God; and
[2c]as long as he sought the LORD, God prospered him.
6 Now he went out and [a]warred against the Philistines,
and broke down the wall of Gath and the wall of Jabneh and
the wall of Ashdod; and he built cities in *the area of* Ashdod
and among the Philistines.
7 And [a]God helped him against the Philistines, and
against the Arabians who lived in Gur-baal, and the Meunites.
8 [a]The Ammonites also gave tribute to Uzziah, and his
[1]fame extended to the border of Egypt, for he became very
strong.
9 Moreover, Uzziah built towers in Jerusalem at [a]the
Corner Gate and at the Valley Gate and at [b]the corner-
buttress and fortified them.
10 And he built towers in the wilderness and [a]hewed many
cisterns, for he had much livestock, both in the [1]lowland and in

22 [1]Lit., *before*

23 [1]One cubit equals approximately 18 inches [a]2 Chr. 21:17; 22:1

24 [a]1 Chr. 26:15

25 [a]2 Kin. 14:17-22

1 [1]In 2 Kin. 14:20, *Azariah*

3 [1]In 2 Kin. 15:2, *Jecoliah* [a]2 Kin. 15:2, 3

5 [1]Many mss. read *in the fear of God* [2]Lit., *in the days of his seeking* [a]2 Chr. 24:2 [b]Dan. 1:17 [c]2 Chr. 15:2

6 [a]Is. 14:29

7 [a]2 Chr. 21:16

8 [1]Lit., *name went to the entering of Egypt* [a]2 Chr. 17:11

9 [a]2 Chr. 25:23 [b]Neh. 2:13, 15; 3:13

10 [1]Or, *Shephelah* [a]Gen. 26:18-21

the plain. *He also had* plowmen and vinedressers in the hill
country and the fertile fields, for he loved the soil.
11 Moreover, Uzziah had an army ready for battle, which
[1]entered combat by divisions, according to the number of their
muster, [2]prepared by Jeiel the scribe and Maaseiah the official,
under the direction of Hananiah, one of the king's officers.
12 The total number of the heads of the [1]*households*, of
valiant warriors, was 2,600.
13 And under their direction was an [1]elite army of
[a]307,500, who could wage war with great power, to help the
king against the enemy.
14 Moreover, Uzziah prepared [1]for all the army shields,
spears, helmets, body armor, bows and sling stones.
15 And in Jerusalem he made engines *of war* invented by
skillful men to be on the towers and on the corners, for the
purpose of shooting arrows and great stones. Hence his [1]fame
spread afar, for he was marvelously helped until he *was* strong.
16 But [a]when he became strong, his heart was so [1]proud
that he acted corruptly, and he was unfaithful to the LORD his
God, for [b]he entered the temple of the LORD to burn incense
on the altar of incense.
17 Then [a]Azariah the priest entered after him and with
him eighty priests of the LORD, valiant men.
18 And [a]they opposed Uzziah the king and said to him,
"[b]It is not for you, Uzziah, to burn incense to the LORD, [c]but
for the priests, the sons of Aaron who are consecrated to burn
incense. Get out of the sanctuary, for you have been unfaithful, and will have no honor from the LORD God."
19 But Uzziah, with a censer in his hand for burning incense, was enraged; and while he was enraged with the priests,
[a]the leprosy broke out on his forehead before the priests in the
house of the LORD, beside the altar of incense.
20 And Azariah the chief priest and all the priests looked
at him, and behold, he *was* leprous on his forehead; and they
hurried him out of there, and he himself also hastened to get
out because the LORD had smitten him.
21 [a]And King Uzziah was a leper to the day of his death;
and he lived in [b]a separate house, being a leper, for he was cut
off from the house of the LORD. And Jotham his son *was* over
the king's house judging the people of the land.
22 Now the rest of the acts of Uzziah, first to last, the
prophet [a]Isaiah, the son of Amoz, has written.
23 So Uzziah slept with his fathers, and they buried him
with his fathers [a]in the field of the grave which belonged to the
kings, for they said, "He is a leper." And Jotham his son became king in his place.

CHAPTER 27

[a]JOTHAM was twenty-five years old when he became king,
and he reigned sixteen years in Jerusalem. And his mother's
name was Jerushah the daughter of Zadok.
2 And he did right in the sight of the LORD, according to
all that his father Uzziah had done; [a]however he did not enter
the temple of the LORD. But the people continued acting
corruptly.

11 [1]Lit., *goes out to* [2]Lit., *by the hand of*

12 [1]Lit., *fathers' houses;* i.e., clans

13 [1]Lit., *powerful* [a]2 Chr. 25:5

14 [1]Lit., *for them, for all*

15 [1]Lit., *name*

16 [1]Lit., *lifted up* [a]Chr. 25:19; Deut. 32:15 [b]1 Kin. 13:1-4

17 [a]1 Chr. 6:10

18 [a]2 Chr. 19:2 [b]Num. 16:39, 40 [c]Ex. 30:7, 8

19 [a]2 Kin. 5:25-27

21 [a]2 Kin. 15:5-7 [b]Lev. 13:46

22 [a]Is. 1:1

23 [a]2 Chr. 21:20; 28:27

1 [a]2 Kin. 15:33-35

2 [a]2 Chr. 26:16

3 He built the upper gate of the house of the LORD, and he built extensively the wall of [a]Ophel.

4 Moreover, he built [a]cities in the hill country of Judah, and he built fortresses and towers on the wooded *hills*.

5 He fought also with the king of the Ammonites and prevailed over them so that the Ammonites gave him during that year one hundred talents of silver, ten thousand [1]kors of wheat and ten thousand of barley. The Ammonites also paid him this *amount* in the second and in the third year.

6 [a]So Jotham became mighty because he ordered his ways before the LORD his God.

7 [a]Now the rest of the acts of Jotham, even all his wars and his acts, behold, they are written in the Book of the Kings of Israel and Judah.

8 He was [a]twenty-five years old when he became king, and he reigned sixteen years in Jerusalem.

9 And Jotham slept with his fathers, and they buried him in the city of David; and Ahaz his son became king in his place.

CHAPTER 28

[a]AHAZ *was* twenty years old when he became king, and he reigned sixteen years in Jerusalem; and [b]he did not do right in the sight of the LORD as David his father *had done*.

2 [a]But he walked in the ways of the kings of Israel; he also [b]made molten images for the Baals.

3 Moreover, [a]he burned incense in the valley of Ben-Hinnom, and [b]burned his sons in fire, [c]according to the abominations of the nations whom the LORD had driven out before the sons of Israel.

4 And he sacrificed and [a]burned incense on the high places, on the hills, and under every green tree.

5 Wherefore, [a]the LORD his God delivered him into the hand of the king of Syria; and they [1]defeated him and carried away from him a great number of captives, and brought *them* to Damascus. And he was also delivered into the hand of the king of Israel, who [2]inflicted him with heavy casualties.

6 For [a]Pekah the son of Remaliah slew in Judah 120,000 in one day, all valiant men, because they had forsaken the LORD God of their fathers.

7 And Zichri, a mighty man of Ephraim, slew Maaseiah the king's son, and Azrikam the ruler of the house and Elkanah the second to the king.

8 And [a]the sons of Israel carried away captive of [b]their brethren 200,000 women, sons, and daughters; and [1]took also a great deal of spoil from them, and they brought the spoil to Samaria.

9 But a prophet of the LORD was there, whose name *was* Oded; and [a]he went out to meet the army which came to Samaria and said to them, "Behold, because the LORD, the God of your fathers, [b]was angry with Judah, He has delivered them into your hand, and you have slain them in a rage [c]*which* has even reached heaven.

10 "And now you are proposing to subjugate for yourselves the people of Judah and Jerusalem for male and female slaves.

---

3 [a]2 Chr. 33:14; Neh. 3:26

4 [a]2 Chr. 11:5

5 [1]A kor equals approx. 10 bu.

6 [a]2 Chr. 26:5

7 [a]2 Kin. 15:36

8 [a]2 Chr. 27:1

1 [a]2 Kin. 16:2-4 [b]2 Chr. 27:2

2 [a]2 Chr. 22:3 [b]Ex. 34:17

3 [a]Josh. 15:8 [b]2 Chr. 33:6; Lev. 18:21 [c]2 Chr. 33:2

4 [a]2 Chr. 28:25

5 [1]Lit., *smote* [2]Lit., *smote him with a great smiting* [a]2 Chr. 24:24

6 [a]2 Kin. 16:5

8 [1]Lit., *plundered* [a]Deut. 28:25, 41 [b]2 Chr. 11:4

9 [a]2 Chr. 25:15 [b]Is. 47:6 [c]Ezra 9:6; Rev. 18:5

Surely, *do* you not *have* transgressions of your own against the
LORD your God?
11 "Now therefore, listen to me and return the captives
[a]whom you captured from your brothers, for the burning anger
of the LORD is against you."
12 Then some of the heads of the sons of Ephraim—Azariah the son of Johanan, Berechiah the son of Meshillemoth,
Jehizkiah the son of Shallum, and Amasa the son of Hadlai—
arose against those who were coming from the battle,
13 and said to them, "You must not bring the captives in
here, for you are proposing *to bring* upon us guilt against the
LORD adding to our sins and our guilt; for our guilt is great so
that *His* burning anger is against Israel."
14 So the armed men left the captives and the spoil before
the officers and all the assembly.
15 Then [a]the men who were designated by name arose,
took the captives, and they clothed all their naked ones from
the spoil; and they gave them clothes and sandals, fed them
and [b]gave them drink, anointed them *with oil*, led all their
feeble ones on donkeys, and brought them to Jericho, [c]the city
of palm trees, to their brothers; then they returned to Samaria.
16 [a]At that time King Ahaz sent to the [1]kings of Assyria
for help.
17 [a]For again the Edomites had come and attacked Judah,
and carried away captives.
18 [a]The Philistines also had invaded the cities of the [1]low-
land and of the Negev of Judah, and had taken Bethshemesh,
Aijalon, Gederoth, and Soco with its villages, Timnah with its
villages, and Gimzo with its villages, and they settled there.
19 For the LORD humbled Judah because of Ahaz king of
[a]Israel, for he had brought about a lack of restraint in Judah
and was very unfaithful to the LORD.
20 So [a]Tilgath-pilneser king of Assyria came against him
and afflicted him instead of strengthening him.
21 [a]And Ahaz took a portion out of the house of the LORD
and out of the palace of the king and of the princes, and gave
it to the king of Assyria; but it did not help him.
22 Now in the time of his distress this same King Ahaz
became yet more unfaithful to the LORD.
23 [a]For he sacrificed to the gods of Damascus which had
[1]defeated him, and said, "[b]Because the gods of the kings of
Syria helped them, I will sacrifice to them that they may help
me." But they became the [2]downfall of him and all Israel.
24 Moreover, when Ahaz gathered together the utensils of
the house of God, he [a]cut the utensils of the house of God in
pieces; and he [b]closed the doors of the house of the LORD, and
[c]made altars for himself in every corner of Jerusalem.
25 And in every city of Judah he made high places to burn
incense to other gods, and provoked the LORD, the God of his
fathers, to anger.
26 [a]Now the rest of his acts and all his ways, from first to
last, behold, they are written in the Book of the Kings of Judah
and Israel.
27 So Ahaz slept with his fathers, and they buried him in
the city, in Jerusalem, [a]for they did not bring him into the

11 [a]2 Chr. 28:8

15 [a]2 Chr. 28:12 [b]2 Kin. 6:22; Prov. 25:21, 22 [c]Deut. 34:3

16 [1]Ancient versions read *King*
[a]2 Kin. 16:7

17 [a]Obad. 10:14

18 [1]Or, *Shephelah*
[a]Ezek. 16:57

19 [a]2 Chr. 21:2

20 [a]1 Chr. 5:26

21 [a]2 Kin. 16:8, 9

23 [1]Lit., *smitten* [2]Lit., *stumbling*
[a]2 Chr. 25:14 [b]Jer. 44:17, 18

24 [a]2 Kin. 16:17 [b]2 Chr. 29:7 [c]2 Chr. 30:14; 33:3-5

26 [a]2 Kin. 16:19, 20

27 [a]2 Chr. 24:25

27 [b]2 Chr. 21:2

tombs of the kings of [b]Israel; and Hezekiah his son reigned in his place.

1 [a]2 Kin. 18:1-3

[a] Chapter 29

HEZEKIAH became king *when he was* twenty-five years old; and he reigned twenty-nine years in Jerusalem. And his mother's name *was* Abijah, the daughter of Zechariah.

2 [a]2 Chr. 28:1; 34:2

2 And [a]he did right in the sight of the LORD, according to all that his father David had done.

3 [a]2 Chr. 29:7; 28:24

3 In the first year of his reign, in the first month, he [a]opened the doors of the house of the LORD and repaired them.

4 And he brought in the priests and the Levites, and gathered them into the square on the east.

5 [a]2 Chr. 15:34; 35:6

5 Then he said to them, "Listen to me, O Levites. [a]Consecrate yourselves now, and consecrate the house of the LORD, the God of your fathers, and carry the uncleanness out from the holy place.

6 [1]Lit., *given* [a]Ezek. 8:16

6 "For our fathers have been unfaithful and have done evil in the sight of the LORD our God, and have forsaken Him and [a]turned their faces away from the dwelling place of the LORD, and have [1]turned *their* backs.

7 "They have also shut the doors of the porch and put out the lamps, and have not burned incense or offered burnt offerings in the holy place to the God of Israel.

8 [a]2 Chr. 24:15 [b]2 Chr. 28:5 [c]Deut. 28:25 [d]Jer. 25:9, 18

8 "Therefore [a]the wrath of the LORD was against Judah and Jerusalem, and [b]He has made them an [c]object of terror, of horror, and of [d]hissing, as you see with your own eyes.

9 [a]2 Chr. 28:5-8, 17

9 "For behold, [a]our fathers have fallen by the sword, and our sons and our daughters and our wives are in captivity for this.

10 [a]2 Chr. 23:16

10 "Now it is in my heart [a]to make a covenant with the LORD God of Israel, that His burning anger may turn away from us.

11 [a]Num. 3:6; 8:6

11 "My sons, do not be negligent now, for [a]the LORD has chosen you to stand before Him, to minister to Him, and to be His ministers and burn incense."

12 [a]2 Chr. 31:13 [b]Num. 3:19, 20

12 Then the Levites arose: [a]Mahath, the son of Amasai and Joel the son of Azariah, from the sons of [b]the Kohathites; and from the sons of Merari, Kish the son of Abdi and Azariah the son of Jehallelel; and from the Gershonites, Joah the son of Zimmah and Eden the son of Joah;

13 [1]Or, *Jeuel*

13 and from the sons of Elizaphan, Shimri and [1]Jeiel; and from the sons of Asaph, Zechariah and Mattaniah;

14 [1]Or, *Jehuel*, 1 Chr. 15:18, 20

14 and from the sons of Heman, [1]Jehiel and Shimei; and from the sons of Jeduthun, Shemaiah and Uzziel.

15 [a]2 Chr. 29:5 [b]1 Chr. 23:28 [c]2 Chr. 30:12

15 And they assembled their brothers, [a]consecrated themselves, and went in [b]to cleanse the house of the LORD, according to the commandment of the king [c]by the words of the LORD.

16 [1]Or, *wadi* [a]2 Chr. 15:16

16 So the priests went in to the inner part of the house of the LORD to cleanse *it*, and every unclean thing which they found in the temple of the LORD they brought out to the court of the house of the LORD. Then the Levites received *it* to carry out to [a]the Kidron [1]valley.

17 Now they began [1]the consecration [a]on the first *day* of
the first month, and on the eighth day of the month they
entered the porch of the LORD. Then they consecrated the
house of the LORD in eight days, and finished on the sixteenth
day of the first month.
18 Then they went in to King Hezekiah and said, "We
have cleansed the whole house of the LORD, the altar of burnt
offering with all of its utensils, and the table of showbread with
all of its utensils.
19 "Moreover, [a]all the utensils which King Ahaz had dis-
carded during his reign in his unfaithfulness, we have prepared
and consecrated; and behold, they are before the altar of the
LORD."
20 Then King Hezekiah arose early and assembled the
princes of the city and went up to the house of the LORD.
21 And they brought seven bulls, seven rams, seven lambs,
and seven male goats [a]for a sin offering for the kingdom, the
sanctuary, and Judah. And he ordered the priests, the sons of
Aaron, to offer *them* on the altar of the LORD.
22 So they slaughtered the bulls, and the priests took the
blood and sprinkled it on the altar. They also slaughtered the
rams and sprinkled the blood on the altar; they slaughtered the
lambs also and [a]sprinkled the blood on the altar.
23 Then they brought the male goats of the sin offering
before the king and the assembly, and [a]they laid their hands on
them.
24 And the priests slaughtered them and purged the altar
with their blood [a]to atone for all Israel, for the king ordered
the burnt offering and the sin offering for all Israel.
25 [a]He then stationed the Levites in the house of the
LORD with cymbals, with harps, and with lyres, [b]according to
the command of David and of [c]Gad the king's seer, and of
[d]Nathan the prophet; for the command was from the LORD
through His prophets.
26 And the Levites stood with [a]the *musical* instruments of
David, and [b]the priests with the trumpets.
27 Then Hezekiah gave the order to offer the burnt offering on the altar. When the burnt offering began, [a]the song to
the LORD also began with the trumpets, [1]*accompanied* by the
instruments of David, king of Israel.
28 While the whole assembly worshiped, the singers also
sang and the trumpets sounded; all this *continued* until the
burnt offering was finished.
29 Now at the completion of the burnt offerings [a]the king
and all who were present with him bowed down and
worshiped.
30 Moreover, King Hezekiah and the officials ordered the
Levites to sing praises to the LORD with the words of David and
Asaph the seer. So they sang praises with joy, and bowed down
and worshiped.
31 Then Hezekiah answered and said, "[a]Now *that* you
have [1]consecrated yourselves to the LORD, come near and bring
sacrifices and thank offerings to the house of the LORD." And
the assembly brought sacrifices and thank offerings, and [b]all
those who [2]were willing *brought* burnt offerings.
32 And the number of the burnt offerings which the as-

17 [1]Lit., *to consecrate* [a]2 Chr. 29:3

19 [a]2 Chr. 28:24

21 [a]Lev. 4:3-14

22 [a]Lev. 4:18

23 [a]Lev. 4:15

24 [a]Lev. 4:26

25 [a]1 Chr. 25:6 [b]2 Chr. 8:14 [c]2 Sam. 24:11 [d]2 Sam. 7:2

26 [a]1 Chr. 23:5 [b]2 Chr. 5:12

27 [1]Lit., *and according to the authority of the instruments* [a]2 Chr. 23:18

29 [a]2 Chr. 20:18

31 [1]Lit., *filled your hands* [2]Lit., *willing of heart* [a]2 Chr. 13:9 [b]Ex. 35:5, 22

sembly brought was 70 bulls, 100 rams, and 200 lambs: all these
were for a burnt offering to the LORD.
33 And the consecrated things were 600 bulls and 3,000
sheep.
34 But the priests were too few, so that they were unable
to skin all the burnt offerings; [a]therefore their brothers the
Levites helped them until the work was completed, and until
the *other* priests had consecrated themselves. For [b]the Levites
were [1]more conscientious to consecrate themselves than the
priests.
35 And there *were* also [1a]many burnt offerings with [b]the
fat of the peace offerings and with [c]the libations for the burnt
offerings. Thus the service of the house of the LORD was established *again*.
36 Then Hezekiah and all the people rejoiced over what
God had prepared for the people, because the thing came
about suddenly.

Chapter 30

NOW Hezekiah sent to all Israel and Judah and wrote letters also to Ephraim and Manasseh, that they should come to
the house of the LORD at Jerusalem, to [1]celebrate the Passover
to the LORD God of Israel.
2 For the king and his princes and all the assembly in
Jerusalem, had decided [a]to celebrate the Passover in the second month,
3 since they could not celebrate it [a]at that time, because
the priests had not consecrated themselves in sufficient numbers, nor had the people been gathered to Jerusalem.
4 Thus the thing was right in the sight of the king and [1]all
the assembly.
5 So they established a decree to circulate a [1]proclama-
tion throughout all Israel [a]from Beer-sheba even to Dan, that
they should come to celebrate the Passover to the LORD God
of Israel at Jerusalem. For they had not celebrated *it* in great
numbers as it was [2]prescribed.
6 And [a]the [1]couriers went throughout all Israel and Judah with the letters from the hand of the king and his princes,
even according to the command of the king, saying, "O sons of
Israel, return to the LORD God of Abraham, Isaac, and Israel,
that He may return to those of you who escaped *and* are left
from [b]the [2]hand of the kings of Assyria.
7 "[a]And do not be like your fathers and your brothers,
who were unfaithful to the LORD God of their fathers, so that
[b]He made them a horror, as you see.
8 "Now do not [a]stiffen your neck like your fathers, but
[1]yield to the LORD and enter His sanctuary which He has
consecrated forever, and serve the LORD your God, [b]that His
burning anger may turn away from you.
9 "For [a]if you return to the LORD, your brothers and your
sons *will find* compassion before those who led them captive,
and will return to this land. [b]For the LORD your God is gracious and compassionate, and will not turn *His* face away from
you if you return to Him."
10 So the [1]couriers passed from city to city through the

34 [1]Lit., *upright of heart* [a]2 Chr. 35:11 [b]2 Chr. 30:3

35 [1]Lit., *the burnt offerings to an abundance* [a]2 Chr. 29:32 [b]Lev. 3:16 [c]Num. 15:5-10

1 [1]Lit., *do*, so in v. 2, 3, 5, 13, 21, 23

2 [a]2 Chr. 30:13, 15; Num. 9:10, 11

3 [a]2 Chr. 29:17, 34

4 [1]Lit., *in the sight of all*

5 [1]Lit., *voice* [2]Lit., *written* [a]Judg. 20:1

6 [1]Lit., *runners* [2]Lit., *palm* [a]Esth. 8:14; Job. 9:25; Jer. 51:31 [b]2 Chr. 28:20

7 [a]Ezek. 20:13 [b]2 Chr. 29:8

8 [1]Lit., *give a hand* [a]Ex. 32:9 [b]2 Chr. 29:10

9 [a]Deut. 30:2 [b]Ex. 34:6, 7; Mic. 7:18

10 [1]Lit., *runners*

country of Ephraim and Manasseh, and as far as Zebulun, but
[a]they laughed them to scorn, and mocked them.
11 Nevertheless [a]some men of Asher, Manasseh, and Zebulun humbled themselves and came to Jerusalem.
12 The hand of God was also on Judah to give them one
heart to do what the king and the princes commanded by the
word of the LORD.
13 Now many people were gathered at Jerusalem to celebrate the feast of unleavened bread [a]in the second month, a very
large assembly.
14 And they arose and removed the altars which *were* in
Jerusalem; they also [a]removed all the incense altars and [b]cast
them into the brook Kidron.
15 Then [a]they slaughtered the Passover *lambs* on the fourteenth of the second month. And [b]the priests and Levites were
ashamed of themselves and consecrated themselves, and
brought burnt offerings to the house of the LORD.
16 And [a]they stood at their stations after their custom,
according to the law of Moses the man of God; the priests
sprinkled the blood *which they received* from the hand of the
Levites.
17 For *there were* many in the assembly who had not
consecrated themselves; therefore, [a]the Levites *were* over the
slaughter of the Passover *lambs* for every one who *was* unclean, in order to consecrate *them* to the LORD.
18 For a multitude of the people, [a]*even* many from Ephraim and Manasseh, Issachar and Zebulun, had not purified
themselves, [b]yet they ate the Passover [c]otherwise than [1]pre-
scribed. For Hezekiah prayed for them, saying, "May the good
LORD pardon
19 [a]everyone who prepares his heart to seek God, the
LORD God of his fathers, though not according to the purification *rules* of the sanctuary."
20 So the LORD heard Hezekiah and healed the people.
21 And the sons of Israel present in Jerusalem [a]celebrated
the Feast of Unleavened Bread *for* seven days with great joy,
and the Levites and the priests praised the LORD day after day
with loud instruments to the LORD.
22 Then Hezekiah [a]spoke [1]encouragingly to all the Levites
who showed good insight *in the things* of the LORD. So they
ate for the appointed seven days, sacrificing peace offerings
and [b]giving thanks to the LORD God of their fathers.
23 Then the whole assembly [a]decided to celebrate *the*
feast another seven days, so they celebrated the seven days
with joy.
24 For [a]Hezekiah king of Judah had contributed to the
assembly 1000 bulls and 7000 sheep, and the princes had contributed to the assembly 1000 bulls and 10,000 sheep; and [b]a
large number of priests consecrated themselves.
25 And all the assembly of Judah rejoiced, with the priests
and the Levites, and [a]all the assembly that came from Israel,
both the sojourners who came from the land of Israel and
those living in Judah.
26 So there was great joy in Jerusalem, because there was
nothing like this in Jerusalem [a]since the days of Solomon the
son of David, king of Israel.

10 [a]Chr. 36:16
11 [a]2 Chr. 30:18, 21, 25
13 [a]2 Chr. 30:2
14 [a]2 Chr. 28:24 [b]2 Chr. 29:16
15 [a]2 Chr. 30:2, 3 [b]2 Chr. 29:34
16 [a]2 Chr. 35:10, 15
17 [a]2 Chr. 29:34
18 [1]Lit., *written* [a]2 Chr. 30:11, 25 [b]Num. 9:10 [c]Ex. 12:43-49
19 [a]2 Chr. 19:3
21 [a]Ex. 12:15; 13:6
22 [1]Lit., *to the heart of* [a]2 Chr. 32:6 [b]Ezra 10:11
23 [a]1 Kin. 8:65
24 [a]2 Chr. 35:7, 8 [b]2 Chr. 30:3; 29:34
25 [a]2 Chr. 30:11, 18
26 [a]2 Chr. 7:8-10

E 54-1

27 Then [a]the Levitical priests arose and [b]blessed the
people; and their voice was heard and their prayer came to
[c]His holy dwelling place, to heaven.

CHAPTER 31

NOW when all this was finished, all Israel who were present
went out to the cities of Judah, [a]broke the pillars in pieces, cut
down the [1]Asherim, and pulled down the high places and the
altars throughout all Judah and Benjamin, as well as in
Ephraim and Manasseh, [2]until they had destroyed them all.
Then all the sons of Israel returned to their cities, each to his
possession.
2 And Hezekiah appointed [a]the divisions of the priests
and the Levites by their divisions, each according to his service,
both the priests and the Levites, [b]for burnt offerings and for
peace offerings, to minister and to give thanks and to praise in
the gates of the camp of the LORD.
3 *He* also *appointed* [a]the king's portion of his goods for
the burnt offerings, *namely,* for the morning and evening
burnt offerings, and the burnt offerings for the sabbaths and
for the new moons and for the fixed festivals, [b]as it is written in
the law of the LORD.
4 Also he [1]commanded the people who lived in Jerusalem to give [a]the portion due to the priests and the Levites, that
they might devote themselves to the law of the LORD.
5 And as soon as the [1]order spread, the sons of Israel
provided in abundance the first fruits of grain, new wine, oil,
honey, and of all the produce of the field; and they brought in
abundantly [a]the tithe of all.
6 And the sons of Israel and Judah who lived in the cities
of Judah, also brought in the tithe of oxen and sheep, and [a]the
tithe of [1]sacred gifts which were consecrated to the LORD their
God, and placed *them* in heaps.
7 In the third month they began to [1]make the heaps, and
finished *them* by the seventh month.
8 And when Hezekiah and the rulers came and saw the
heaps, they blessed the LORD and His people Israel.
9 Then Hezekiah questioned the priests and the Levites
concerning the heaps.
10 And Azariah the chief priest [a]of the house of Zadok
said to [1]him, "[b]Since the contributions began to be brought
into the house of the LORD, we have had enough to eat with
plenty left over, for the LORD has blessed His people, and this
great quantity is left over."
11 Then Hezekiah commanded *them* to prepare [a]rooms
in the house of the LORD, and they prepared *them.*
12 And they faithfully brought in the contributions and
the tithes and the consecrated things; and Conaniah the Levite
was the officer in charge [a]of them and his brother Shimei *was*
second.
13 And Jehiel, Azaziah, Nahath, Asahel, Jerimoth, Jozabad,
Eliel, Ismachiah, Mahath, and Benaiah *were* overseers
[1]under the authority of Conaniah and Shimei his brother by
the appointment of King Hezekiah, and [a]Azariah *was* the *chief*
officer of the house of God.

27 [a]2 Chr. 23:18 [b]Num. 6:23 [c]Deut. 26:15; Ps. 68:5

1 [1]I.e., wooden symbols of a female deity [2]Lit., *even to completion* [a]2 Kin. 18:4

2 [a]1 Chr. 24:1 [b]1 Chr. 23:28-31

3 [a]2 Chr. 35:7 [b]Num. 28:1-29, 40

4 [1]Lit., *said to* [a]Num. 18:8

5 [1]Lit., *word* [a]Neh. 13:12

6 [1]Lit., *consecrated things* [a]Lev. 27:30; Deut. 14:28

7 [1]Lit., *found*

10 [1]Lit., *him, and he said* [a]1 Chr. 6:8, 9 [b]Mal. 3:10

11 [a]1 Kin. 6:5, 8

12 [a]2 Chr. 35:9

13 [1]Lit., *from the hand of* [a]2 Chr. 31:10

14 And Kore the son of Imnah the Levite, the keeper of
the eastern *gate, was* over the freewill offerings of God, to
apportion the contributions for the LORD and the most holy
things.
15 And [1]under his authority *were* [a]Eden, Miniamin, Jeshua, Shemaiah, Amariah, and Shecaniah in [b]the cities of the
priests, to distribute [c]faithfully *their portions* to their brothers
by divisions, whether great or small,
16 without regard to their genealogical enrollment, to the
males from [1]thirty years old and upward—everyone who
entered the house of the LORD [a]for his daily obligations—for
their work in their duties according to their divisions;
17 as well as the priests who were enrolled genealogically
according to their fathers' households, and the Levites [a]from
twenty years old and upwards, by their duties *and* their
divisions.
18 And the genealogical enrollment *included* [1]all their
little children, their wives, their sons, and their daughters, for
the whole assembly, for they consecrated themselves [2]faith-
fully in holiness.
19 Also for the sons of Aaron the priests *who were* in [a]the
pasture lands of their cities, or in each and every city, [b]*there
were* men who were designated by name to distribute portions
to every male among the priests and to everyone genealogically enrolled among the Levites.
20 And thus Hezekiah did throughout all Judah; and [a]he
did what *was* good, right, and true before the LORD his God.
21 And every work which he began in the service of the
house of God in law and in commandment, seeking his God,
he did with all his heart and prospered.

CHAPTER 32

[a]AFTER these [1]acts of faithfulness Sennacherib king of Assyria came and invaded Judah and besieged the fortified cities,
and [2]thought to break into them for himself.
2 Now when Hezekiah saw that Sennacherib had come,
and that [1]he intended to make war on Jerusalem,
3 he decided with his officers and his warriors to cut off
the *supply of* water from the springs which *were* outside the
city, and they helped him.
4 So many people assembled [a]and stopped up all the
springs and [b]the stream which flowed [1]through the region,
saying, "Why should the kings of Assyria come and find abundant water?"
5 And he took courage and [a]rebuilt all the wall that had
been broken down, and [1]erected towers on it, and *built* [b]another
outside wall, and strengthened [c]Millo *in* the city of David,
and made weapons and shields in great number.
6 And he appointed military officers over the people,
and gathered them to him in the square at the city gate, and
[a]spoke [1]encouragingly to them, saying,
7 "[a]Be strong and courageous, do not fear or be dismayed
because of the king of Assyria, nor because of all the multitude
which is with him; [b]for the one with us is greater than the one
with him.

15 [1]Lit., *over his hand* [a]2 Chr. 29:12 [b]Josh. 21:9-19 [c]1 Chr. 9:22

16 [1]Heb., *three;* cf. 1 Chr. 23:3 [a]Ezra 3:4

17 [a]1 Chr. 23:24

18 [1]Lit., *with all* [2]Lit., *in their faithfulness*

19 [a]Lev. 25:34; Num. 35:2-5 [b]2 Chr. 31:12-15

20 [a]2 Kin. 20:3; 22:2

1 [1]Lit., *things and this faithfulness* [2]Lit., *said* [a]2 Kin. 18:13-19, 37; Is. 36:1-37:38

2 [1]Lit., *his face for war against*

4 [1]Lit., *in the midst of the land* [a]2 Kin. 20:20 [b]2 Chr. 32:30

5 [1]Lit., *raised on the towers* [a]2 Chr. 25:23 [b]2 Kin. 25:4 [c]1 Kin. 9:24

6 [1]Lit., *upon their hearts* [a]2 Chr. 30:22

7 [a]1 Chr. 22:13 [b]2 Kin. 6:16

8 [a]Jer. 17:5 [b]2 Chr. 20:17
9 [1]Lit., *against*
11 [1]Lit., *palm*
12 [1]Lit., *Jerusalem, saying,* [2]Lit., *offer up in smoke* [a]2 Chr. 31:1
14 [a]Is. 10:9-11
17 [1]Lit., *who have* [a]2 Chr. 32:14
19 [1]Lit., *to*
21 [1]Lit., *in shame of face*
22 [1]Another reading is *gave them rest*
23 [a]2 Sam. 8:10
24 [1]Lit., *sick to the point of death* [a]2 Kin. 20:1-11; Is. 38:1-8

8 "With him is *only* [a]an arm of flesh, but [b]with us is the
LORD our God to help us and to fight our battles." And the
people relied on the words of Hezekiah king of Judah.
9 After this Sennacherib king of Assyria sent his servants
to Jerusalem while he *was* [1]besieging Lachish with all his forces
with him, against Hezekiah king of Judah and against all Judah
who *were* at Jerusalem, saying,
10 "Thus says Sennacherib king of Assyria, 'On what are
you trusting that you are remaining in Jerusalem under siege?
11 'Is not Hezekiah misleading you to give yourselves over
to die by hunger and by thirst, saying, "The LORD our God will
deliver us from the [1]hand of the king of Assyria"?
12 '[a]Has not the same Hezekiah taken away His high
places and His altars, and said to Judah and [1]Jerusalem, "You
shall worship before one altar, and on it you shall [2]burn
incense"?
13 'Do you not know what I and my fathers have done to
all the peoples of the lands? Were the gods of the nations of
the lands able at all to deliver their land from my hand?
14 '[a]Who *was there* among all the gods of those nations
which my fathers utterly destroyed who could deliver his
people out of my hand, that your God should be able to
deliver you from my hand?
15 'Now therefore, do not let Hezekiah deceive you or
mislead you like this, and do not believe him, for no god of any
nation or kingdom was able to deliver his people from my
hand or from the hand of my fathers. How much less shall
your God deliver you from my hand?' "
16 And his servants spoke further against the LORD God
and against His servant Hezekiah.
17 He also wrote letters to insult the LORD God of Israel,
and to speak against Him, saying, "[a]As the gods of the nations
of the lands [1]have not delivered their people from my hand, so
the God of Hezekiah shall not deliver His people from my
hand."
18 And they called this out with a loud voice in the language of Judah to the people of Jerusalem who were on the
wall, to frighten and terrify them, so that they might take the
city.
19 And they spoke [1]of the God of Jerusalem as of the gods
of the peoples of the earth, the work of men's hands.
20 But King Hezekiah and Isaiah the prophet, the son of
Amoz, prayed about this and cried out to heaven.
21 And the LORD sent an angel who destroyed every mighty
warrior, commander and officer in the camp of the king of
Assyria. So he returned [1]in shame to his own land. And when
he had entered the temple of his god, some of his own children
killed him there with the sword.
22 So the LORD saved Hezekiah and the inhabitants of
Jerusalem from the hand of Sennacherib the king of Assyria,
and from the hand of all *others,* and [1]guided them on every
side.
23 And [a]many were bringing gifts to the LORD at Jerusalem and choice presents to Hezekiah king of Judah, so that he
was exalted in the sight of all nations thereafter.
24 [a]In those days Hezekiah became [1]mortally ill; and he

prayed to the LORD, and [2]the LORD spoke to him and gave him
a sign.
25 But Hezekiah gave no return for the benefit [1]he received, [a]because his heart was [2]proud; [b]therefore wrath came
on him and on Judah and Jerusalem.
26 However, [a]Hezekiah [1]humbled the pride of his heart,
both he and the inhabitants of Jerusalem, so that the wrath of
the LORD did not come on them in the days of Hezekiah.
27 Now Hezekiah had immense riches and honor; and he
made for himself treasuries for silver, gold, precious stones,
spices, shields and all kinds of valuable articles,
28 storehouses also for the produce of grain, wine and oil,
pens for all kinds of cattle and [1]sheepfolds for the flocks.
29 And he made cities for himself, and acquired flocks and
herds in abundance; for God had given him very great [1]wealth.
30 It was Hezekiah who [a]stopped the upper outlet of the
waters of [b]Gihon and directed them to the west side of the city
of David. And Hezekiah prospered in all that he did.
31 And even *in the matter of* [a]the envoys of the rulers of
Babylon, who sent to him to inquire of [b]the wonder that had
happened in the land, God left him *alone only* [c]to test him,
that He might know all that was in his heart.
32 Now the rest of the acts of Hezekiah and his deeds of
devotion, behold, they are written in the vision of Isaiah the
prophet, the son of Amoz, in the Book of the Kings of Judah
and Israel.
33 So Hezekiah slept with his fathers, and they buried him
in the [1]upper section of the tombs of the sons of David; and all
Judah and the inhabitants of Jerusalem honored him at his
death. And his son Manasseh became king in his place.

CHAPTER 33

[a]MANASSEH was twelve years old when he became king,
and he reigned fifty-five years in Jerusalem.
2 And he did evil in the sight of the LORD [a]according to
the abominations of the nations whom the LORD dispossessed
before the sons of Israel.
3 For [a]he rebuilt the high places which Hezekiah his father
had broken down; [b]he also erected altars for the Baals and
made [1]Asherim, and worshiped all the host of heaven and
served them.
4 And [a]he built altars in the house of the LORD of which
the LORD had said, "My name shall be [b]in Jerusalem forever."
5 For he built altars for all the host of heaven in [a]the two
courts of the house of the LORD.
6 And [a]he made his sons pass through the fire in the
valley of Ben-hinnom; and he practiced witchcraft, used divination, practiced sorcery, and [b]dealt with mediums and spiritists. He did much evil in the sight of the LORD, provoking
Him *to anger.*
7 Then he put [a]the carved image of the idol which he had
made in the house of God, of which God had said to David
and to Solomon his son, "[b]In this house and in Jerusalem,
which I have chosen from all the tribes of Israel, I will put My
name forever;

24 [2]Lit., *He*

25 [1]Lit., *to him* [2]Lit., *high*
[a]2 Chr. 32:31; 26:16 [b]2 Chr. 24:18

26 [1]Lit., *humbled himself in*
[a]Jer. 26:18, 19

28 [1]So ancient versions; Heb., *flocks for the sheepfolds*

29 [1]Lit., *possessions, property*

30 [a]2 Kin. 20:20 [b]1 Kin. 1:33

31 [a]2 Kin. 20:12; Is. 39:1
[b]2 Chr. 32:24; Is. 38:7, 8
[c]Deut. 8:16

33 [1]Or, *ascent to*

1 [a]2 Kin. 21:1-9

2 [a]2 Chr. 28:3

3 [1]I.e., wooden symbols of a female deity
[a]2 Chr. 31:1 [b]Deut. 16:21; 2 Kin. 23:5, 6

4 [a]2 Chr. 28:24 [b]2 Chr. 7:16

5 [a]2 Chr. 4:9

6 [a]2 Chr. 28:3 [b]Lev. 19:31; 20:27

7 [a]2 Chr. 33:15 [b]2 Chr. 33:4

8 [a]2 Sam. 7:10

11 [1]I.e., Thong put through the nose [a]Deut. 28:36 [b]2 Chr. 36:6

12 [a]2 Chr. 32:26

13 [a]1 Chr. 20; Ezra 8:23 [b]Dan. 4:32

14 [a]1 Kin. 1:33 [b]Neh. 3:3 [c]2 Chr. 27:3

15 [a]2 Chr. 33:3-7

17 [a]2 Chr. 32:12

18 [a]2 Chr. 33:12, 13 [b]2 Chr. 33:10 [c]2 Chr. 21:2

19 [1]Gk. reads *seers* [a]2 Chr. 33:13 [b]2 Chr. 33:3

21 [a]2 Kin. 21:19-24

22 [a]2 Chr. 33:2-7 [b]2 Chr. 34:3, 4

23 [1]Lit., *humbled himself* [a]2 Chr. 33:12, 19

8 and I will not again remove the foot of Israel from the
land [a]which I have appointed for your fathers, if only they will
observe to do all that I have commanded them according to all
the law, the statutes, and the ordinances *given* through
Moses."
9 Thus Manasseh misled Judah and the inhabitants of
Jerusalem to do more evil than the nations whom the LORD
destroyed before the sons of Israel.
10 And the LORD spoke to Manasseh and his people, but
they paid no attention.
11 [a]Therefore the LORD brought the commanders of the
army of the king of Assyria against them, and they captured
Manasseh with [1]hooks, [b]bound him with bronze *chains*, and
took him to Babylon.
12 And when he was in distress, he entreated the LORD his
God and [a]humbled himself greatly before the God of his
fathers.
13 When he prayed to Him, [a]He was moved by his entreaty and heard his supplication, and brought him again to
Jerusalem to his kingdom. Then Manasseh [b]knew that the
LORD *was* God.
14 Now after this he built the outer wall of the city of
David on the west side of [a]Gihon, in the valley, even to the
entrance of the [b]Fish Gate; and he encircled the [c]Ophel *with it*
and made it very high. Then he put army commanders in all
the fortified cities of Judah.
15 He also [a]removed the foreign gods and the idol from
the house of the LORD, as well as all the altars which he had
built on the mountain of the house of the LORD and in Jerusalem, and he threw *them* outside the city.
16 And he set up the altar of the LORD and sacrificed
peace offerings and thank offerings on it; and he ordered Judah to serve the LORD God of Israel.
17 Nevertheless [a]the people still sacrificed in the high
places, *although* only to the LORD their God.
18 Now the rest of the acts of Manasseh even [a]his prayer
to his God, and the words of [b]the seers who spoke to him in
the name of the LORD God of Israel, behold, they are among
the records of the kings of [c]Israel.
19 His prayer also and [a]*how God* was entreated by him,
and all his sin, his unfaithfulness, and [b]the sites on which he
built high places and erected the Asherim and the carved
images, before he humbled himself, behold, they are written in
the records of the [1]Hozai.
20 So Manasseh slept with his fathers, and they buried
him in his own house. And Amon his son became king in his
place.
21 [a]Amon *was* twenty-two years old when he became king,
and he reigned two years in Jerusalem.
22 And he did evil in the sight of the LORD as Manasseh
his father [a]had done, and Amon sacrificed to all [b]the carved
images which his father Manasseh had made, and he served
them.
23 Moreover, he did not humble himself before the LORD
[a]as his father Manasseh had [1]done, but Amon multiplied guilt.

24 Finally [a]his servants conspired against him and put him to death in his own house.

25 But the people of the land [1]killed all the conspirators against King Amon, and the people of the land made Josiah his son king in his place.

CHAPTER 34

[a]JOSIAH *was* eight years old when he became king, and he reigned thirty-one years in Jerusalem.

2 And [a]he did right in the sight of the LORD, and walked in the ways of his father David and did not turn aside to the right or to the left.

3 For in the eighth year of his reign while he was still a youth, he began to seek the God of his father David; and in the twelfth year he began [a]to purge Judah and Jerusalem of the high places, the Asherim, the carved images, and the molten images.

4 And they tore down the altars of the Baals in his presence, and [a]the incense altars that were high above them he chopped down; also the Asherim, the carved images, and the molten images he broke in pieces and [b]ground to powder and scattered *it* on the graves of those who had sacrificed to them.

5 Then [a]he burned the bones of the priests on their altars, and purged Judah and Jerusalem.

6 And [a]in the cities of Manasseh, Ephraim, Simeon even as far as Naphtali, in their surrounding ruins,

7 he also tore down the altars and [a]beat the Asherim and the carved images into powder, and chopped down all the incense altars throughout the land of Israel. Then he returned to Jerusalem.

8 [a]Now in the eighteenth year of his reign, when he had purged the land and the house, he sent Shaphan the son of Azaliah, and Maaseiah [b]an official of the city, and Joah the son of Joahaz the recorder, to repair the house of the LORD his God.

9 And they came to [a]Hilkiah the high priest and delivered the money that was brought into the house of God, which the Levites, the [1]doorkeepers had collected [2]from [b]Manasseh and Ephraim, and from all the remnant of Israel, and from all Judah and Benjamin and the inhabitants of Jerusalem.

10 Then they gave *it* into the hands of the workmen who had the oversight of the house of the LORD, and the workmen who were working in the house of the LORD [1]used it to restore and repair the house.

11 They in turn gave *it* to the carpenters and to the builders to buy quarried stone and timber for couplings and to make beams for the houses [a]which the kings of Judah had let go to ruin.

12 And the men did the work faithfully with foremen over them to supervise: Jahath and Obadiah, the Levites of the sons of Merari, Zechariah and Meshullam of the sons of the Kohathites, and [a]the Levites, all who were skillful with musical instruments.

13 *They were* also over [a]the burden bearers, and super-

24 [a]2 Chr. 25:27
25 [1]Lit., *smote*
1 [a]2 Kin. 22:1, 2
2 [a]2 Chr. 29:2
3 [a]2 Chr. 33:22
4 [a]2 Kin. 23:4, 5, 11 [b]Ex. 32:20
5 [a]2 Kin. 23:20
6 [a]2 Kin. 23:15, 19
7 [a]2 Chr. 31:1
8 [a]2 Kin. 22:3-20 [b]2 Chr. 18:25
9 [1]Lit., *guardians of the threshold* [2]Lit., *from the hand of* [a]2 Chr. 35:8 [b]2 Chr. 30:10, 18
10 [1]Lit., *gave*
11 [a]2 Chr. 33:4-7
12 [a]1 Chr. 25:1
13 [a]2 Chr. 8:10; Neh. 4:10

14 [a]2 Chr. 34:9

vised all the workmen from job to job; and *some* of the Levites
were scribes and officials and gatekeepers.
14 When they were bringing out the money which had
been brought into the house of the LORD, [a]Hilkiah the priest
found the book of the law of the LORD *given* by Moses.
15 And Hilkiah responded and said to Shaphan the scribe,
"I have found the book of the law in the house of the LORD."

16 [1]Lit., *returned* [2]Lit., *given into the hand of*

And Hilkiah gave the book to Shaphan.
16 Then Shaphan brought the book to the king and [1]re-
ported further word to the king, saying, "Everything that was
[2]entrusted to your servants they are doing.
17 "They have also emptied out the money which was

19 [a]Josh. 7:6

found in the house of the LORD, and have delivered it into the
hands of the supervisors and the workmen."
18 Moreover, Shaphan the scribe told the king saying,
"Hilkiah the priest gave me a book." And Shaphan read from
it in the presence of the king.
19 And it came about when the king heard the words of

20 [1]In 2 Kin. 22:12, *Achbor, son of Micaiah*

the law that [a]he tore his clothes.
20 Then the king commanded Hilkiah, Ahikam the son of
Shaphan, [1]Abdon the son of Micah, Shaphan the scribe, and
Asaiah the king's servant, saying,
21 "Go, inquire of the LORD for me and for those who are
left in Israel and in Judah, concerning the words of the book

21 [a]2 Chr. 29:8

which has been found; for [a]great is the wrath of the LORD
which is poured out on us because our fathers have not observed the word of the LORD, to do according to all that is
written in this book."
22 So Hilkiah and *those* whom the king [1]had told went to

22 [1]So with Gk. [2]In 2 Kin. 22:14 *Tikvah, son of Harhas*

Huldah the prophetess, the wife of Shallum the son of [2]Tok-
hath, the son of Hasrah, the keeper of the wardrobe (now she
lived in Jerusalem in the Second Quarter); and they spoke to
her regarding this.
23 And she said to them, "Thus says the LORD, the God of
Israel, 'Tell the man who sent you to Me,'

24 [a]2 Chr. 36:14-20 [b]Deut. 28:15-68

24 thus says the LORD, 'Behold, [a]I am bringing evil on this
place and on its inhabitants, *even* all [b]the curses written in the
book which they have read in the presence of the king of
Judah.
25 '[a]Because they have forsaken Me and have burned incense to other gods, that they might provoke Me to anger with
all the works of their hands, therefore My wrath will be poured

25 [a]2 Chr. 33:3

out on this place, and it shall not be quenched.'
26 "But to the king of Judah who sent you to inquire of the
LORD, thus you will say to him, 'Thus says the LORD God of
Israel *regarding* the words which you have heard,
27 "[a]Because your heart was tender and you humbled

27 [1]Cf. 2 Kin. 22:19 [a]2 Chr. 12:7; 32:26

yourself before God, when you heard [1]His words against this
place and against its inhabitants, and *because* you humbled
yourself before Me, tore your clothes, and wept before Me, I
truly have heard you," declares the LORD.
28 "Behold, I will gather you to your fathers and you shall
be gathered to your grave in peace, so your eyes shall not see
all the evil which I will bring on this place and on its inhabitants." ' " And they brought back word to the king.

29 [a]Then the king sent and gathered all the elders of Judah and Jerusalem.
30 And the king went up to the house of the LORD and [a]all
the men of Judah, the inhabitants of Jerusalem, the priests, the
Levites, and all the people, from the greatest to the least; and
he read in their hearing all the words of the book of the
covenant which was found in the house of the LORD.
31 Then the king [a]stood in his [1]place and [b]made a covenant
before the LORD to walk after the LORD, and to keep His
commandments and His testimonies and His statutes with all
his heart and with all his soul, to perform the words of the
covenant written in this book.
32 Moreover, he made all who were present in Jerusalem
and Benjamin to stand *with him*. So the inhabitants of Jerusalem did according to the covenant of God, the God of their
fathers.
33 And Josiah [a]removed all the abominations from all the
lands belonging to the sons of Israel, and made all who were
present in Israel to serve the LORD their God. Throughout his
[1]lifetime they did not turn from following the LORD God of
their fathers.

CHAPTER 35

THEN Josiah [a]celebrated the Passover to the LORD in Jerusalem, and [b]they slaughtered the Passover *animals* on the fourteenth *day* of the first month.
2 And he set the priests in their offices and [a]encouraged
them in the service of the house of the LORD.
3 He also said to [a]the Levites who taught all Israel *and*
who were holy to the LORD, "Put the holy ark in the house
which Solomon the son of David king of Israel built; [b]it will be
a burden on *your* shoulders no longer. Now serve the LORD
your God and His people Israel.
4 "And [a]prepare *yourselves* by your fathers' households in
your divisions, according to the writing of David king of Israel
and [b]according to the writing of his son Solomon.
5 "Moreover, [a]stand in the holy place according to the
sections of the fathers' households of your brethren the [1]lay
people, and according to the Levites, by division of a father's
household.
6 "Now [a]slaughter the Passover *animals*, [b]sanctify yourselves, and prepare for your brethren to do according to the
word of the LORD by Moses."
7 And Josiah contributed to the lay people, to all who
were present, flocks of lambs and kids, all for the Passover
offerings, numbering 30,000 plus 3000 bulls; these were from
the king's possessions.
8 His officers also contributed a freewill offering to the
people, the priests, and the Levites. Hilkiah and Zechariah and
Jehiel, [a]the officials of the house of God, gave to the priests for
the Passover offerings 2,600 *from the flocks* and 300 bulls.
9 [a]Conaniah also, and Shemaiah and Nethanel, his brothers, and Hashabiah and Jeiel and Jozabad, the officers of the
Levites, contributed to the Levites for the Passover offerings
5,000 *from the flocks* and 500 bulls.

29 [a]2 Kin. 23:1-3

30 [a]Neh. 8:1-3

31 [1]So with some versions, cf. 2 Kin. 23:3
[a]2 Chr. 30:16; 2 Kin. 11:14
[b]2 Chr. 23:16; 29:10

33 [1]Lit., *days*
[a]2 Chr. 34:3-7

1 [a]2 Kin. 23:21 [b]Ex. 12:6; Num. 9:3

2 [a]2 Chr. 29:11

3 [a]2 Chr. 17:8, 9; Neh. 8:7
[b]1 Chr. 23:26

4 [a]1 Chr. 9:10-13 [b]2 Chr. 8:14

5 [1]Lit., *sons of the people*, and so throughout the chap.
[a]Ezra 6:18

6 [a]2 Chr. 35:1 [b]2 Chr. 29:5

8 [a]2 Chr. 31:13

9 [a]2 Chr. 31:12

10 So the service was prepared, and [a]the priests stood at
their stations and the Levites by their divisions according to
the king's command.
11 And [1a]they slaughtered the Passover *animals,* and while
[b]the priests sprinkled [2]the blood *received* from their hand, [c]the
Levites skinned them.
12 Then they removed the burnt offerings that *they* might
give them to the sections of the fathers' households of the lay
people to present to the LORD, as it is written in the Book of
Moses. They did this also with the bulls.
13 So [a]they roasted the Passover *animals* on the fire according to the ordinance, and they boiled [b]the holy things in pots,
in kettles, in pans, and carried *them* speedily to all the lay
people.
14 And afterwards they prepared for themselves and for
the priests, because the priests, the sons of Aaron, *were* offering the burnt offerings and the fat until night; therefore the
Levites prepared for themselves and for the priests, the sons of
Aaron.
15 The singers, the sons of Asaph, *were* also at their stations [a]according to the command of David, Asaph, Hemen,
and Jeduthun the king's seer; and [b]the gate keepers at each
gate did not have to depart from their service, because the
Levites their brethren prepared for them.
16 So all the service of the LORD was prepared on that day
to celebrate the Passover, and to offer burnt offerings on the
altar of the LORD according to the command of King Josiah.
17 Thus the sons of Israel who were present celebrated the
Passover at that time, and [a]the Feast of Unleavened Bread
seven days.
18 And [a]there had not been celebrated a Passover like it in
Israel since the days of Samuel the prophet; nor had any of the
kings of Israel celebrated such a Passover as Josiah did with the
priests, the Levites, all Judah and Israel who were present, and
the inhabitants of Jerusalem.
19 In the eighteenth year of Josiah's reign this Passover
was celebrated.
20 [a]After all this, when Josiah had set the [1]temple in order,
Neco king of Egypt came up to make war at [b]Carchemish on
the Euphrates, and Josiah went out to engage him.
21 But [1]Neco sent messengers to him, saying, "[a]What
have we to do with each other, O King of Judah? *I am* not
coming against you today but against the house with which I
am at war, and God has ordered me to hurry. Stop for your
own sake *from interfering with* God who is with me, that He
may not destroy you."
22 However, Josiah would not turn [1]away from him, but
[a]disguised himself in order to make war with him; nor did he
listen to the words of Neco [b]from the mouth of God, but
came to make war on the Plain of [c]Megiddo.
23 And the archers shot King Josiah, and the king said to
his servants, "Take me away, for I am badly wounded."
24 So his servants took him out of the chariot and carried
him in the second chariot which he had, and brought him to
Jerusalem [1]where he died and was buried in the tombs of his
fathers. [a]And all Judah and Jerusalem mourned for Josiah.

10 [a]2 Chr. 35:5

11 [1]I.e., the Levites [2]So with the Gk. [a]2 Chr. 35:1, 6 [b]2 Chr. 29:22 [c]2 Chr. 29:34

13 [a]Ex. 12:8, 9 [b]Lev. 6:25

15 [a]1 Chr. 25:1 [b]1 Chr. 26:12-19

17 [a]2 Chr. 30:21

18 [a]2 Chr. 30:5; 2 Kin. 23:21

20 [1]Lit., *house* [a]2 Kin. 23:29, 30 [b]Is. 10:9; Jer. 46:2

21 [1]Lit., *he* [a]2 Chr. 25:19

22 [1]Lit., *his face* [a]2 Chr. 18:29 [b]2 Chr. 35:21 [c]Judg. 5:19

24 [1]Lit., *and* [a]Zech. 12:11; Lam. 4:20

25 Then [a]Jeremiah chanted a lament for Josiah. And all
the male and female singers speak about Josiah in their lamentations to this day. And they made them an ordinance in Israel; behold, they are also written in the Lamentations.
26 Now the rest of the acts of Josiah and his deeds of
devotion as written in the law of the LORD,
27 and his acts, first to last, behold, they are written in the
Book of the Kings of Israel and Judah.

CHAPTER 36

[a]THEN the people of the land took [1b]Joahaz the son of Josiah, and made him king in place of his father in Jerusalem.
2 Joahaz was twenty-three years old when he became
king, and he reigned three months in Jerusalem.
3 Then the king of Egypt deposed him at Jerusalem, and
imposed on the land a fine of one hundred talents of silver and
one talent of gold.
4 And the king of Egypt made Eliakim his brother king
over Judah and Jerusalem, and changed his name to Jehoiakim. But [a]Neco took Joahaz his brother and brought him to
Egypt.
5 [a]Jehoiakim was twenty-five years old when he became
king, and he reigned eleven years in Jerusalem; and he did evil
in the sight of the LORD his God.
6 Nebuchadnezzar king of Babylon came up [a]against him
and [b]bound him with bronze *chains* [c]to take him to Babylon.
7 [a]Nebuchadnezzar also brought *some* of the articles of
the house of the LORD to Babylon and put them in his temple
at Babylon.
8 [a]Now the rest of the acts of Jehoiakim and [1]the abominations which he did, and what was found against him, behold,
they are written in the Book of the Kings of Israel and Judah.
And Jehoiachin his son became king in his place.
9 [a]Jehoiachin was eight years old when he became king,
and he reigned three months and ten days in Jerusalem, and he
did evil in the sight of the LORD.
10 And [a]at the turn of the year King Nebuchadnezzar sent
and brought him to Babylon with the valuable articles of the
house of the LORD, and he made his kinsman [b]Zedekiah king
over Judah and Jerusalem.
11 [a]Zedekiah was twenty-one years old when he became
king, and he reigned eleven years in Jerusalem.
12 And he did evil in the sight of the LORD his God; [a]he
did not humble himself [b]before Jeremiah the prophet [1]who
spoke for the LORD.
13 And [a]he also rebelled against King Nebuchadnezzar
who had made him swear *allegiance* by God. But [b]he stiffened
his neck and hardened his heart against turning to the LORD
God of Israel.
14 Furthermore, all the officials of the priests and the
people were very unfaithful *following* all the abominations of
the nations; and they defiled the house of the LORD which He
had sanctified in Jerusalem.
15 And the LORD, the God of their fathers, [a]sent *word* to

25 [a]Jer. 22:10

1 [1]I.e., short form of Jehoahaz [a]2 Kin. 23:30-34 [b]Jer. 22:11

4 [a]Jer. 22:10-12

5 [a]2 Kin. 23:36, 37; Jer. 22:13-19

6 [a]2 Kin. 24:1 [b]2 Chr. 33:11 [c]Jer. 22:19, 20

7 [a]2 Kin. 24:13

8 [1]Lit., *his* [a]2 Kin. 24:5

9 [a]2 Kin. 24:8-17

10 [a]2 Sam. 11:1 [b]Jer. 37:1

11 [a]2 Kin. 24:18-20; Jer. 52:1

12 [1]Lit., *from the mouth of the* LORD [a]2 Chr. 33:23 [b]Jer. 21:3-7

13 [a]Jer. 52:3; Ezek. 17:15 [b]2 Chr. 30:8

15 [a]Jer. 7:13; 25:3

them again and again by His messengers, because He had
compassion on His people and on His dwelling place;
16 but they *continually* [a]mocked the messengers of God,
[b]despised His words and scoffed at His prophets, [c]until the
wrath of the LORD arose against His people, until there was no
remedy.
17 [a]Therefore He brought up against them the king of the
Chaldeans who slew their young men with the sword in the
house of their sanctuary, and had no compassion on young
man or virgin, old man or infirm; He gave *them* all into his
hand.
18 And [a]all the articles of the house of God, great and
small, and the treasures of the house of the LORD, and the
treasures of the king and of his officers, he brought *them* all to
Babylon.
19 Then [a]they burned the house of God, and broke down
the wall of Jerusalem and burned all its fortified buildings with
fire, and destroyed all its valuable articles.
20 And those who had escaped from the sword he [a]carried
away to Babylon; and [b]they were servants to him and to his
sons until the rule of the kingdom of Persia,
21 [a]to fulfill the word of the LORD by the mouth of Jeremiah, until [b]the land had enjoyed its sabbaths. [c]All the days of
its desolation it kept sabbath [1]until seventy years were
complete.
22 [a]Now in the first year of Cyrus king of Persia—in order
to fulfill the word of the LORD [b]by the mouth of Jeremiah—
the LORD [c]stirred up the spirit of Cyrus king of Persia, so that
he sent a proclamation throughout his kingdom, and also *put*
it in writing, saying,
23 "Thus says Cyrus king of Persia, 'The LORD, the God of
heaven, has given me all the kingdoms of the earth, and He has
appointed me to build Him a house in Jerusalem, which is in
Judah. Whoever there is among you of all His people, may the
LORD his God be with him, and let him go up!' "

THE BOOK OF EZRA

Cyrus' Proclamation.

[a]NOW in the first year of Cyrus king of Persia, in order to
fulfill the word of the LORD by the mouth of Jeremiah, the
LORD stirred up the spirit of Cyrus king of Persia, so that he
[b]sent a proclamation throughout all his kingdom, and also *put
it* in writing, saying,
2 "Thus says Cyrus king of Persia, 'The LORD, the God of
heaven, has given me all the kingdoms of the earth, and [a]He
has appointed me to build Him a house in Jerusalem, which is
in Judah.
3 'Whoever there is among you of all His people, may his
God be with him! Let him go up to Jerusalem which is in
Judah, and rebuild the house of the LORD, the God of Israel,
[a]He is the God who is in Jerusalem.

16 [a]2 Chr. 30:10; Jer. 5:12, 13 [b]Prov. 1:24-32 [c]Ezra 5:12
17 [a]2 Kin. 25:1-7
18 [a]2 Chr. 36:7, 10
19 [a]2 Kin. 25:9; Jer. 52:13
20 [a]2 Kin. 25:11 [b]Jer. 27:7
21 [1]Lit., *to fulfill seventy years* [a]Jer. 29:10 [b]Lev. 26:33 [c]Lev. 25:4
22 [a]Ezra 1:1-3 [b]Jer. 25:12; 29:10 [c]Is. 44:28
1 [a]2 Chr. 36:22 [b]Ezra 5:13
2 [a]Is. 44:28; 45:1, 12, 13
3 [a]Dan. 6:26

4 'And every survivor, at whatever place he may [1]live, let
the men of [2]that place support him with silver and gold, with
goods and cattle, together with a freewill offering for the
house of God which is in Jerusalem.' "
5 Then the heads of fathers' *households* of Judah and
Benjamin and the priests and the Levites arose, [a]even everyone
whose spirit God had stirred to go up and rebuild the house of
the LORD which is in Jerusalem.
6 And all those about them [1a]encouraged them with
articles of silver, with gold, with goods, with cattle, and with
valuables, aside from all that was given as a freewill offering.
7 [a]Also King Cyrus brought out the articles of the house
of the LORD, [b]which Nebuchadnezzar had carried away from
Jerusalem and put in the house of his gods;
8 and Cyrus, king of Persia, had them brought out by the
hand of Mithredath the treasurer, and he counted them out to
[a]Sheshbazzar, the prince of Judah.
9 Now this *was* their number: [a]30 gold dishes, 1,000 silver
dishes, 29 [1]duplicates;
10 30 gold bowls, 410 silver bowls of a second *kind, and*
1,000 other articles.
11 All the articles of gold and silver *numbered* 5,400. Sheshbazzar brought them all up with the exiles who went up from
Babylon to Jerusalem.

CHAPTER 2

[a]NOW these are the [1]people of the province who came up
out of the captivity of the exiles whom Nebuchadnezzar the
king of Babylon had carried away to Babylon, and returned to
Jerusalem and Judah, each to his city.
2 [1]These came with Zerubbabel, Jeshua, Nehemiah, [2]Se-
raiah, [3]Reelaiah, Mordecai, Bilshan, [4]Mispar, Bigvai, [5]Rehum,
and Baanah.
The number of the men of the people of Israel:
3 the sons of Parosh, 2,172;
4 the sons of Shephatiah, 372;
5 the sons of Arah, 775;
6 the sons of Pahath-moab of the sons of Jeshua *and*
Joab, 2,812;
7 the sons of Elam, 1,254;
8 the sons of Zattu, 945;
9 the sons of Zaccai, 760;
10 the sons of [1]Bani, 642;
11 the sons of Bebai, 623;
12 the sons of Azgad, 1,222;
13 the sons of Adonikam, 666;
14 the sons of Bigvai, 2,056;
15 the sons of Adin, 454;
16 the sons of Ater of Hezekiah, 98;
17 the sons of Bezai, 323;
18 the sons of [1]Jorah, 112;
19 the sons of Hashum, 223;
20 the sons of [1]Gibbar, 95;
21 the [1]men of Bethlehem, 123;
22 the men of Netophah, 56;

4 [1]Or, *reside as an alien* [2]Lit., *his*

5 [a]Ezra 1:1

6 [1]Lit., *strengthened their hands* [a]Neh. 6:22; Is. 35:3

7 [a]Ezra 5:14; 6:5 [b]2 Chr. 36:7

8 [a]Ezra 5:14

9 [1]Heb. obscure, other possible meanings are *knives, censors* [a]Ezra 8:27

1 [1]Lit., *sons* [a]Neh. 7:6-73

2 [1]Lit., *Who* [2]In Neh. 7:7, *Azariah* [3]In Neh. 7:7, *Raamiah* [4]In Neh. 7:7, *Mispereth* [5]In Neh. 7:7, *Nehum*

10 [1]In Neh. 7:1, *Binnui*

18 [1]In Neh. 7:24, *Hariph*

20 [1]In Neh. 7:25, *Gibeon*

21 [1]Lit., *sons*

24 [1]In Neh. 7:28, *Beth-azmaveth*

25 [1]In Neh. 7:29, *Kiriath-jearim*

34 [1]Lit., *sons*

36 [a]1 Chr. 24:7-18

38 [a]1 Chr. 9:12

40 [1]In Neh. 7:43, *Judah* [2]In Neh. 7:43, *Hodevah*

44 [1]In Neh. 7:47, *Sia*

50 [1]In Neh. 7:52, *Nephushesim*

52 [1]In Neh. 7:54, *Bazlith*

55 [1]In Neh. 7:57, *Sophereth* [2]In Neh. 7:57 *Perida*

57 [1]In Neh. 7:59, *Amon*

59 [1]In Neh. 7:61, *Addon*

23 the men of Anathoth, 128;
24 the sons of [1]Azmaveth, 42;
25 the sons of [1]Kiriath-arim, Chephirah, and Beeroth, 743;
26 the sons of Raman and Geba, 621;
27 the men of Michmas, 122;
28 the men of Bethel and Ai, 223;
29 the sons of Nebo, 52;
30 the sons of Magbish, 156;
31 the sons of the other Elam, 1,254;
32 the sons of Harim, 320;
33 the sons of Lod, Hadid, and Ono, 725;
34 the [1]men of Jericho, 345;
35 the sons of Senaah, 3,630.
36 [a]The priests: the sons of Jedaiah of the house of Jeshua,
973;
37 the sons of Immer, 1,052;
38 [a]the sons of Pashhur, 1,247;
39 the sons of Harim, 1,017.
40 The Levites: the sons of [1]Jeshua and Kadmiel, of the
sons of [2]Hodaviah, 74.
41 The singers: the sons of Asaph, 128.
42 The sons of the gatekeepers: the sons of Shallum, the
sons of Ater, the sons of Talmon, the sons of Akkub, the sons
of Hatita, the sons of Shobai, in all 139.
43 The temple servants: the sons of Ziha, the sons of Hasu-
pha, the sons of Tabbaoth,
44 the sons of Keros, the sons of [1]Siaha, the sons of
Padon,
45 the sons of Lebanah, the sons of Hagabah, the sons of
Akkub,
46 the sons of Hagab, the sons of Shalmai, the sons of
Hanan,
47 the sons of Giddel, the sons of Gahar, the sons of
Reaiah,
48 the sons of Rezin, the sons of Nekoda, the sons of
Gazzam,
49 the sons of Uzza, the sons of Paseah, the sons of Besai,
50 the sons of Asnah, the sons of Meunim, the sons of
[1]Nephisim,
51 the sons of Bakbuk, the sons of Hakupha, the sons of
Harhur,
52 the sons of [1]Bazluth, the sons of Mehida, the sons of
Harsha,
53 the sons of Barkos, the sons of Sisera, the sons of
Temah,
54 the sons of Neziah, the sons of Hatipha.
55 The sons of Solomon's servants: the sons of Sotai, the
sons of [1]Hassophereth, the sons of [2]Peruda,
56 the sons of Jaalah, the sons of Darkon, the sons of
Giddel,
57 the sons of Shephatiah, the sons of Hattil, the sons of
Pochereth-hazzebaim, the sons of [1]Ami.
58 All the temple servants, and the sons of Solomon's servants, were 392.
59 Now these are those who came up from Tel-melah,
Tel-harsha, Cherub, [1]Addan, *and* Immer, but they were not

able to [2]give evidence of their fathers' households, and their
[3]descendants, whether they were of Israel:
60 the sons of Delaiah, the sons of Tobiah, the sons of
Nekoda, 652.
61 And of the sons of the priests: the sons of [1]Habaiah, the
sons of Hakkoz, the sons of [a]Barzillai, who took a wife from
the daughters of Barzillai the Gileadite, and he was called by
their name.
62 These searched *among* their ancestral registration, but
they could not be located; [a]therefore they were considered
unclean and *were excluded* from the priesthood.
63 And the [1]governor said to them [a]that they should not
eat from the most holy things until a priest stood up with
[b]Urim and Thummin.
64 The whole assembly [1]numbered 42,360,
65 besides their male and female servants, [1]who numbered
7,337; and they had 200 [a]singing men and women.
66 Their horses were 736; their mules, 245;
67 their camels, 435; *their* donkeys, 6,720.
68 And some of the heads of fathers' *households*, when
they arrived at the house of the LORD which is in Jerusalem,
offered willingly for the house of God to [1]restore it on its
foundation.
69 According to their ability they gave [a]to the treasury for
the work 61,000 gold drachmas, and 5,000 silver minas, and
100 priestly [1]garments.
70 Now the priests and the Levites, some of the people,
the singers, the gatekeepers, and the temple servants lived in
their cities, and all Israel in their cities.

CHAPTER 3

[a]NOW when the seventh month came, and the sons of Israel
were in the cities, the people gathered together as one man to
Jerusalem.
2 Then [a]Jeshua the son of Jozadak and his brothers the
priests, and [b]Zerubbabel the son [c]of Shealtiel, and his brothers
arose and built the altar of the God of Israel, to offer burnt
offerings on it, [d]as it is written in the law of Moses, the man of
God.
3 So they set up the altar on its foundation, for [1a]they
were terrified because of the peoples of the lands; and they
[b]offered burnt offerings on it to the LORD, burnt offerings
morning and evening.
4 [a]And they celebrated the Feast of [1]Booths, [b]as it is
written, and *offered* [2]the fixed number of burnt offerings daily,
[c]according to the ordinance, as each day required;
5 and afterward *there was* a continual burnt offering,
also [a]for the new moons and [b]for all the fixed festivals of the
LORD that were consecrated, and from every one who offered a
freewill offering to the LORD.
6 From the first day of the seventh month they began to
offer burnt offerings to the LORD, but the foundation of the
temple of the LORD had not been laid.
7 Then they gave money to the masons and carpenters,
and [a]food, drink, and oil to the Sidonians and to the Tyrians,

59 [2]Lit., *tell* [3]Lit., *seed*

61 [1]In Neh. 7:63, *Hobaiah* [a]2 Sam. 17:27

62 [a]Num. 16:39, 40

63 [1]Heb., *Tirshatha*, a Persian title. [a]Lev. 2:3, 10 [b]Ex. 28:30

64 [1]Lit., *together was*

65 [1]Lit., *they were* [a]2 Chr. 35:25

68 [1]Lit., *establish*

69 [1]Or, *tunics* [a]Ezra 8:25-34

1 [a]Neh. 7:73; 8:1

2 [a]Neh. 12:1, 8 [b]Ezra 2:2 [c]1 Chr. 3:17 [d]Deut. 12:5, 6

3 [1]Lit., *terror* was *upon them* [a]Ezra 4:4 [b]Num. 28:2

4 [1]Or, *Tabernacles* [2]Lit., *by number* [a]Neh. 8:14 [b]Ex. 23:16 [c]Num. 29:12

5 [a]Num. 28:11 [b]Num. 29:39

7 [a]2 Chr. 2:10

[b]to bring cedar wood from Lebanon to the sea at Joppa, [c]ac-
cording to the permission they had [1]from Cyrus king of Persia.
8 Now in the second year of their coming to the house of
God at Jerusalem in the second month, [a]Zerubbabel the son
of Shealtiel and Jeshua the son of Jozadak and the rest of their
brothers the priests and the Levites, and all who came from the
captivity to Jerusalem, began *the work* and [b]appointed the
Levites from twenty years and older to oversee the work of the
house of the LORD.
9 Then Jeshua *with* his sons and brothers stood united
with Kadmiel and his sons, the sons of [1]Judah *and* the sons of
Henadad *with* their sons and brothers the Levites, to oversee
the workmen in the temple of God.
10 Now when the builders had laid the foundation of the
temple of the LORD, [1]the priests stood in their apparel with
trumpets, and the Levites the sons of Asaph with cymbals, to
praise the LORD [a]according to the [2]directions of King David of
Israel.
11 And [a]they sang praising and giving thanks to the LORD,
saying, "[b]For He is good, for His lovingkindness is upon Israel
forever." And all the people shouted with a great shout when
they praised the LORD because the foundation of the house of
the LORD was laid.
12 Yet many of the priests and Levites and heads of fathers'
households, [a]the old men who had seen the first [1]temple,
wept with a loud voice when the foundation of this house was
laid before their eyes, while many shouted aloud for joy;
13 so that the people could not distinguish the sound of
the shout of joy from the sound of the weeping of the people,
for the people shouted with a loud shout, and the sound was
heard far away.

CHAPTER 4

NOW when [a]the enemies of Judah and Benjamin heard that
[b]the people of the exile were building a temple to the LORD
God of Israel,
2 they approached Zerubbabel and the heads of fathers'
households, and said to them, "Let us build with you, for we
like you seek your God; [a]and we have been sacrificing to Him
since the days of [b]Esar-haddon king of Assyria, who brought us
up here."
3 But Zerubbabel and Jeshua and the rest of the heads of
fathers' *households* of Israel said to them, "[a]You have nothing
in common with us in building a house to our God; but we
ourselves will together build to the LORD God of Israel, [b]as
King Cyrus, the king of Persia has commanded us."
4 Then [a]the people of the land [1]discouraged the people
of Judah, and frightened them from building,
5 and hired counselors against them to frustrate their
counsel all the days of Cyrus king of Persia, even until the
reign of Darius king of Persia.
6 Now in the reign of [1a]Ahasuerus, in the beginning of his
reign, they wrote an accusation against the inhabitants of Judah and Jerusalem.
7 And in the days of [1]Artaxerxes, Bishlam, Mithredath,

7 [1]Lit., *of* [b]2 Chr. 2:16 [c]Ezra 1:2; 6:3

8 [a]Ezra 3:2; 4:3 [b]1 Chr. 23:4, 24

9 [1]In Ezra 2:40, *Hodaviah*

10 [1]So with the Gk. and some mss., M.T., *they set the priests* [2]Lit., *hands* [a]1 Chr. 6:31; 25:1

11 [a]Neh. 12:24, 40 [b]1 Chr. 16:34

12 [1]Lit., *house* [a]Hag. 2:3

1 [a]Ezra 4:7-10 [b]Ezra 1:11

2 [a]2 Kin. 17:32 [b]2 Kin. 19:37

3 [a]Neh. 2:20 [b]Ezra 1:1, 2

4 [1]Lit., *weakened the hands of* [a]Ezra 3:3

6 [1]Or, *Xerxes,* Heb., *Ahash-verosh* [a]Esth. 1:1; Dan. 9:1

7 [1]Heb., *Artah-shashta*

Tabeel, and the rest of his colleagues, wrote to Artaxerxes king
of Persia; and the [2]text of the letter was written in Aramaic and
translated [a]*from* Aramaic.
8 [1]Rehum the commander and Shimshai the scribe wrote
a letter against Jerusalem to King Artaxerxes, as follows—
9 then *wrote* Rehum the commander and Shimshai the
scribe and [a]the rest of their colleagues, the judges and [b]the
lesser governors, the officials, the secretaries, the men of
Erech, the Babylonians, the men of Shusha, that is, the
Elamites,
10 and the rest of the nations which the great and honorable [1]Osnappar deported and settled in the city of Samaria,
and in the rest of the region beyond the [2]River; [a]and now
11 this is the copy of the letter which they sent to him:
"To King Artaxerxes: Your servants, the men in the region
beyond the River, and now
12 let it be known to the king, that the Jews who came up
from you have come to us at Jerusalem; they are rebuilding
[a]the rebellious and evil city, and [b]are finishing the walls and
repairing the foundations.
13 "Now let it be known to the king, that if that city is
rebuilt and the walls are finished, [a]they will not pay tribute,
custom, or toll, and it will damage the revenue of the kings.
14 "Now because we [1]are in the service of the palace, and it
is not fitting for us to see the king's dishonor, therefore we
have sent and informed the king,
15 so that a search may be made in the record books of
your fathers. And you will discover in the record books, and
learn that that city is a rebellious city and damaging to kings
and provinces, and that they have incited revolt within it in
past days; therefore that city was laid waste.
16 "We inform the king that, if that city is rebuilt and the
walls finished, as a result you will have no possession in *the*
province beyond the River."
17 *Then* the king sent an answer to Rehum the commander, to Shimshai the scribe, and to the rest of their colleagues
who live in Samaria and in the rest of *the provinces* beyond the
River: "Peace. And now
18 the document which you sent to us has been [1a]trans-
lated and read before me.
19 "And a decree has been [1]issued by me, and a search has
been made and it has been discovered that that city has risen
up against the kings in past days, that rebellion and revolt have
been perpetrated in it,
20 [a]that mighty kings have [1]ruled over Jerusalem, governing all *the provinces* beyond the River, and that [b]tribute,
custom, and toll were paid to them.
21 "So, now issue a decree to make these men stop *work*,
that the city may not be rebuilt until a decree is issued by me.
22 "And beware of being negligent in carrying out this *mat-*
ter; why should damage increase to the detriment of the
kings?"
23 Then as soon as the copy of King Artaxerxes' document was read before Rehum and Shimshai the scribe and
their colleagues, they went in haste to Jerusalem to the Jews
and stopped them by force of arms.

7 [2]Lit., *written*
[a]2 Kin. 18:26; Dan. 2:4

8 [1]Ch. 4:8-6:18 is in Aramaic

9 [a]2 Kin. 17:24 [b]Ezra 5:6; 6:6

10 [1]I.e., probably Ashurbanipal [2]I.e., Euphrates River and so throughout the chap.
[a]Ezra 4:11, 17; 7:12

12 [a]2 Chr. 36:13 [b]Ezra 5:3, 9

13 [a]Ezra 4:20

14 [1]Lit., *eat the salt*

18 [1]Lit., *plainly read before*
[a]Neh. 8:8

19 [1]Lit., *put* forth

20 [1]Lit., *been*
[a]1 Kin. 4:21; 1 Chr. 18:3
[b]Ezra 4:13; 7:24

24 Then work on the house of God in Jerusalem ceased,
and it was stopped until the second year of the reign of Darius
king of Persia.

Chapter 5

WHEN the prophets, [a]Haggai the prophet and [b]Zechariah
the son of Iddo, prophesied to the Jews who were in Judah and
Jerusalem, in the name of the God of Israel, who was over
them,
2 then [a]Zerubbabel the son of Shealtiel and Jeshua the
son of Jozadak arose and began to rebuild the house of God
which is in Jerusalem; and [b]the prophets of God were with
them supporting them.
3 At that time [a]Tattenai, the governor of *the province*
beyond the [1]River, and Shethar-bozenai, and their colleagues
came to them and spoke to them thus, "[b]Who issued you a
decree to rebuild this [2]temple and to finish this structure?"
4 [a]Then we told them accordingly what the names of the
men were who were reconstructing this building.
5 But [a]the eye of their God was on the elders of the Jews,
and they did not stop them until a report should come to
Darius, and then a written reply be returned concerning it.
6 *This is* the copy of the letter which [a]Tattenai, the governor of *the province* beyond the River, and Shethar-bozenai
and his colleagues [b]the officials, who were beyond the River,
sent to Darius the king.
7 They sent a report to him in which it was written thus:
"To Darius the king, all peace.
8 "Let it be known to the king, that we have gone to the
province of Judah, to the house of the great God, which is
being built with huge stones, and [1]beams are being laid in the
walls; and this work is going on with great care and is succeeding in their hands.
9 "Then we asked those elders and said to them thus,
'Who issued you a decree to rebuild this temple and to finish
this structure?'
10 "We also asked them their names so as to inform you,
and that we might write down the names of the men who were
at their head.
11 "And thus they [1]answered us, saying, 'We are the servants of the God of heaven and earth and are rebuilding the
temple that was built many years ago, [a]which a great king of
Israel built and finished.
12 'But [a]because our fathers had provoked the God of
heaven to wrath, He gave them into the hand of Nebuchadnezzar king of Babylon, the Chaldean, *who* destroyed this
temple and deported the people to Babylon.
13 'However, [a]in the first year of Cyrus king of Babylon,
King Cyrus issued a decree to rebuild this house of God.
14 'And also [a]the gold and silver utensils of the house of
God which Nebuchadnezzar had taken from the temple [1]in
Jerusalem, and brought them to the temple of Babylon, these
King Cyrus took from the temple of Babylon, and they were
given to one [b]whose name was Sheshbazzar, whom he had
appointed governor.

1 [a]Hag. 1:1 [b]Zech. 1:1

2 [a]Ezra 3:2 [b]Ezra 6:14; Hag. 2:4; Zech. 3:1

3 [1]I.e., Euphrates River, and so throughout the chap. [2]Lit., *house*, and so throughout the chap. [a]Ezra 6:6, 13 [b]Ezra 5:9; 1:3

4 [a]Ezra 5:10

5 [a]Ezra 7:6, 28

6 [a]Ezra 5:3 [b]Ezra 4:9

8 [1]Lit., *timber is*

11 [1]Lit., *returned us the word* [a]1 Kin. 6:1, 38

12 [a]2 Chr. 36:16, 17

13 [a]Ezra 1:1

14 [1]Lit., *that was in* [a]Ezra 1:7; 6:5; Dan. 5:2 [b]Ezra 5:16; 1:8

15 'And he said to him, "Take these utensils, go *and* deposit them in the temple [1]in Jerusalem, and let the house of God
be rebuilt in its place."
16 'Then that Sheshbazzar came *and* [a]laid the foundations
of the house of God [1]in Jerusalem; and from then until now it
has been under construction, and it is [b]not *yet* completed.'
17 "And now, if it pleases the king [a]let a search be conducted in the king's treasure house, which is there in Babylon,
if it be that a decree was issued by King Cyrus to rebuild this
house of God at Jerusalem; and let the king send to us his
decision concerning this *matter*."

Chapter 6

THEN King Darius issued a decree, and [a]search was made in
the [1]archives, where the treasures were stored in Babylon.
2 And in [1]Ecbatana in the fortress, which is [a]in the province of Media, a scroll was found and there was written in it as
follows: "Memorandum—
3 "[a]In the first year of King Cyrus, Cyrus the king issued a
decree: '*Concerning* the house of God at Jerusalem, let the
temple, the place where sacrifices are offered, be rebuilt and
let its foundations be [1]retained, its height being 60 cubits and
its width 60 cubits;
4 [a]with three layers of huge stones, and [1]one layer of
timbers. And let the cost be paid from the [2]royal treasury.
5 'And also let [a]the gold and silver utensils of the temple
of God, which Nebuchadnezzar took from the temple in Jerusalem and brought to Babylon, be returned and [1]brought to
their places in the temple in Jerusalem; and you shall put *them*
in the house of God.'
6 "Now therefore, [a]Tattenai, governor of *the province*
beyond the [1]River, Shethar-bozenai, and [2]your colleagues, the
officials of *the provinces* beyond the [1]River, [3]keep away from
there.
7 "Leave this work on the house of God alone; let the
governor of the Jews and the elders of the Jews rebuild this
house of God on its site.
8 "Moreover, [a]I issue a decree concerning what you are to
do for these elders of Judah in the rebuilding of this house of
God: the full cost is to be paid to these people from the royal
treasury out of the taxes of *the provinces* beyond the River,
and that without delay.
9 "And whatever is needed, both young bulls, rams, and
lambs for a burnt offering to the God of heaven, and wheat,
salt, wine, and anointing oil, as the priests in Jerusalem request, *it* is to be given to them daily without fail,
10 that they may offer [1]acceptable sacrifices to the God of
heaven and [a]pray for the life of the king and his sons.
11 "And I issued a decree that [a]any man who violates this
edict, a timber shall be drawn from his house and he shall be
impaled on it and [b]his house shall be made a refuse heap on
account of this.
12 "And may the God who [a]has caused His name to dwell
there overthrow any king or people who [1]attempts to change

15 [1]Lit., *that is in*

16 [1]Lit., *that is in*
[a]Ezra 3:8, 10 [b]Ezra 6:15

17 [a]Ezra 6:1, 2

1 [1]Lit., *house of the books*
[a]Ezra 5:17

2 [1]Aramaic, *Achmetha*
[a]2 Kin. 17:6

3 [1]Or, *fixed, laid*
[a]Ezra 1:1; 5:13

4 [1]So Gk.; Aramaic, *a layer of new timber* [2]Lit., *king's house*
[a]1 Kin. 6:36

5 [1]Lit., *go*
[a]Ezra 1:7; 5:14

6 [1]I.e., Euphrates River, and so throughout the chap. [2]Aram., *their* [3]Lit., *be distant*
[a]Ezra 6:13

8 [a]Ezra 6:4; 7:14-22

10 [1]Lit., *pleasing* or *sweet-smelling sacrifices*
[a]Ezra 7:23

11 [a]Ezra 7:26 [b]Dan. 2:5; 3:29

12 [1]Lit., *sends his hand*
[a]Deut. 12:5, 11

it, so as to destroy this house of God in Jerusalem. I, Darius,
have issued *this* decree, let *it* be carried out with all diligence!"
13 Then [a]Tattenai, the governor of *the province* beyond
the River, Shethar-bozenai, and their colleagues carried out
the decree with all diligence, just as King Darius had sent.
14 And [a]the elders of the Jews [1]were successful in building
through the prophesying of Haggai the prophet and Zechariah
the son of Iddo. And [2]they finished building according to the
command of the God of Israel and the decree [b]of Cyrus,
[c]Darius, and [d]Artaxerxes king of Persia.
15 And this temple was completed [1]on the third day of the
[a]month Adar; it was the sixth year of the reign of King Darius.
16 And the sons of Israel, the priests, the Levites, and the
rest of the [1]exiles, [a]celebrated the dedication of this house of
God with joy.
17 And they offered for the dedication of this temple of
God 100 bulls, 200 rams, 400 lambs, and as a sin offering for all
Israel [a]12 male goats, corresponding to the number of the
tribes of Israel.
18 Then they appointed the priests to [a]their divisions and
the Levites in [b]their orders for the service of God [1]in Jerusalem, [c]as it is written in the book of Moses.
19 And [a]the exiles observed the Passover on [b]the fourteenth of the first month.
20 [a]For the priests and the Levites had purified themselves
together; all of them were pure. Then [b]they slaughtered the
Passover *lamb* for all the exiles, both for their brothers the
priests and for themselves.
21 And the sons of Israel who returned from exile and [a]all
those who had separated themselves from [b]the impurity of the
nations of the land to *join* them, to seek the LORD God of
Israel, ate *the Passover.*
22 And [a]they observed the Feast of Unleavened Bread
seven days with joy, for the LORD had caused them to rejoice,
and [b]had turned the heart of [c]the king of Assyria toward them
to [1]encourage them in the work of the house of God, the God
of Israel.

CHAPTER 7

[a]NOW after these things, in the reign of [b]Artaxerxes king of
Persia, *there went up* Ezra son of Seraiah, son of Azariah, son
of Hilkiah,
2 son of Shallum, son of Zadok, son of Ahitub,
3 son of Amariah, son of Azariah, son of Meraioth,
4 son of Zerahiah, son of Uzzi, son of Bukki,
5 son of Abishua, son of Phinehas, son of Eleazar, son of
Aaron the chief priest.
6 This Ezra went up from Babylon, and he was a [a]scribe
skilled in the law of Moses, which the LORD God of Israel had
given; and the king granted him all [1]he requested [b]because the
hand of the LORD his God *was* upon him.
7 And [a]some of the sons of Israel and some of the priests,
the Levites, the singers, the gatekeepers, and the temple servants went up to Jerusalem in the seventh year of King
Artaxerxes.

---

13 [a]Ezra 6:6

14 [1]Lit., *were building and succeeding* [2]Lit., *built and finished* [a]Ezra 5:1, 2 [b]Ezra 1:1 [c]Ezra 6:12 [d]Ezra 7:1

15 [1]Lit., *until* [a]Esth. 3:7

16 [1]Lit., *sons of the captivity* [a]2 Chr. 7:5

17 [a]Ezra 8:35

18 [1]Lit., *which is in* [a]2 Chr. 35:5 [b]1 Chr. 23:6 [c]Num. 3:6; 8:9

19 [a]Ezra 1:11 [b]Ex. 12:6

20 [a]2 Chr. 29:34; 30:15 [b]2 Chr. 35:11

21 [a]Neh. 9:2; 10:28 [b]Ezra 9:11

22 [1]Lit., *strengthen their hands* [a]Ex. 12:15 [b]Ezra 7:27 [c]Ezra 1:1; 6:1

1 [a]Chr. 6:4-14 [b]Ezra 7:12, 21; Neh. 2:1

6 [1]Lit., *his request* [a]Ezra 7:11, 12, 21 [b]Ezra 7:9, 28

7 [a]Ezra 8:1-20

8 And he came to Jerusalem in the fifth month, which
was in the seventh year of the king.
9 For on the first of the first month [1]he began to go up
from Babylon; and on the first of the fifth month he came to
Jerusalem, [a]because the good hand of his God *was* upon him.
10 For Ezra had set his heart to [1]study the law of the
LORD, and to practice *it*, and [a]to teach *His* statutes and ordinances in Israel.
11 Now this is the copy of the decree which King Artaxerxes gave to Ezra the priest, the scribe, [1]learned in the words
of the commandments of the LORD and His statutes to Israel:
12 "[1]Artaxerxes, [a]king of kings, to Ezra the priest, the scribe
of the law of the God of heaven, perfect *peace*. And now
13 [a]I have issued a decree that any of the people of Israel
and their priests and the Levites in my kingdom who are willing to go to Jerusalem, may go with you.
14 "Forasmuch as you are sent [1]by the king and his [a]seven
counselors to inquire concerning Judah and Jerusalem according to the law of your God which is in your hand,
15 and to bring the silver and gold, which the king and his
counselors have freely offered to the God of Israel, [a]whose
dwelling is in Jerusalem,
16 with [a]all the silver and gold which you shall find in the
whole province of Babylon, along [b]with the freewill offering of
the people and of the priests, who offered willingly for the
house of their God which is in Jerusalem;
17 with this money, therefore, you shall diligently buy
bulls, rams, and lambs, [a]with their grain offerings and their
libations and [b]offer them on the altar of the house of your
God which is in Jerusalem.
18 "And whatever seems good to you and to your brothers
to do with the rest of the silver and gold, you may do according
to the will of your God.
19 "Also the utensils which are given to you for the service
of the house of your God, deliver in full before the God of
Jerusalem.
20 "And the rest of the needs for the house of your God,
for which you may have occasion to provide, [a]provide *for it*
from the royal treasury.
21 "And I, even I King Artaxerxes, issue a decree to all the
treasurers who are *in the provinces* beyond the [1]River, that
whatever Ezra the priest, [a]the scribe of the law of the God of
heaven, may require of you, it shall be done diligently,
22 *even* up to 100 talents of silver, 100 [1]kors of wheat, 100
baths of wine, 100 baths of oil, and salt [2]as needed.
23 "Whatever is [1]commanded by the God of heaven, let it
be done with zeal for the house of the God of heaven, [a]lest
there be wrath against the kingdom of the king and his sons.
24 "We also inform you that [a]it is not allowed to [1]impose
tax, tribute or toll [b]*on* any of the priests, Levites, singers, doorkeepers, Nethinim, or servants of this house of God.
25 "And you, Ezra, according to the wisdom of your God
which is in your hand, [a]appoint magistrates and judges that
they may judge all the people who are in *the province* beyond
the River, *even* all those who know the laws of your God; and
you may [b]teach anyone who is ignorant *of them*.

9 [1]Lit., *was the foundation* [a]Ezra 7:6

10 [1]Lit., *seek* [a]Ezra 7:25; Neh. 8:1

11 [1]Lit., *the scribe of*

12 [1]Ch. 7:12-26 is in Aramaic [a]Ezek. 26:7; Dan. 2:37

13 [a]Ezra 6:1

14 [1]Lit., *from before* [a]Ezra 7:15, 28; 8:25

15 [a]Ezra 6:12

16 [a]Ezra 8:25 [b]Ezra 1:4, 6

17 [a]Num. 15:4-13 [b]Deut. 12:5-11

20 [a]Ezra 6:4

21 [1]Euphrates River and so throughout the chap. [a]Ezra 7:6

22 [1]One kor equals approx. ten bushels [2]Lit., *without prescription*

23 [1]Lit., *from the decree of* [a]Ezra 6:10

24 [1]Lit., *throw on them* [a]Ezra 4:13, 20 [b]Ezra 7:7

25 [a]Ex. 18:21; Deut. 16:18 [b]Ezra 7:10

26 "And [a]whoever will not observe the law of your God and
the law of the king, let judgment be executed upon him strictly, whether for death or for [1]banishment or for confiscation of
goods or for imprisonment."
27 Blessed be the LORD, the God of our fathers, [a]who has
put *such a thing* as this in the king's heart, to adorn the house
of the LORD which is in Jerusalem,
28 and [a]has extended lovingkindness to me before the king
and his counselors and before all the king's mighty princes.
Thus I was strengthened according to the hand of the LORD
my God upon me, and I gathered [1]leading men from Israel to
go up with me.

CHAPTER 8

NOW these are the heads of their fathers' *households* and
the genealogical enrollment of those who went up with me
from Babylon in the reign of King Artaxerxes:
2 Of the sons of Phinehas, Gershom; of the sons of Ithamar, Daniel; of the sons of David, Hattush.
3 Of the sons of Shecaniah *who was* of the sons of Parosh, Zechariah and with him 150 males *who were in* the
genealogical list.
4 Of the sons of Pahath-moab, Eliehoenai the son of
Zerahiah and 200 males with him.
5 Of the sons of Shecaniah, the son of Jahaziel and 300
males with him;
6 and of the sons of Adin, Ebed the son of Jonathan and
50 males with him;
7 and of the sons of Elam, Jeshaiah the son of Athaliah
and 70 males with him;
8 and of the sons of Shephatiah, Zebadiah the son of
Michael and 80 males with him.
9 Of the sons of Joab, Obadiah the son of Jehiel and 218
males with him;
10 and of the sons of Shelomith, the son of Josiphiah and
160 males with him;
11 and of the sons of Bebai, Zechariah the son of Bebai
and 28 males with him;
12 and of the sons of Azgad, Johanan the son of Hakkatan
and 110 males with him;
13 and of the sons of Adonikam, the last ones, these being
their names, Eliphelet, Jeuel, and Shemaiah and 60 males with
them;
14 and of the sons of Bigvai, Uthai and [1]Zabbud and 70
males with [2]them.
15 Now I assembled them at [a]the river that runs to Ahava,
where we camped for three days; and when I observed the
people and the priests, I [b]did not find any Levites there.
16 So I sent for Eliezer, Ariel, Shemaiah, Elnathan, Jarib,
Elnathan, Nathan, Zechariah, and Meshullam, [1]leading men,
and for Joiarib and Elnathan, teachers.
17 And I sent them to Iddo the [1]leading man at the place
Casiphia; and I [2]told them what to say to [3]Iddo *and* his brothers, [a]the temple servants at the place Casiphia, *that is,* to
bring ministers to us for the house of our God.

26 [1]Lit., *rooting out* [a]Ezra 6:11, 12

27 [a]Ezra 6:22

28 [1]Lit., *heads* [a]Ezra 9:9

14 [1]Or, *Zakkur* [2]Or, *him*

15 [a]Ezra 8:21, 31 [b]Ezra 8:2; 7:7

16 [1]Lit., *heads*

17 [1]Lit., *head* [2]Lit., *put words in their mouth to say* [3]So Gk.; Heb., *Iddo his brother* [a]Ezra 2:43

Prayer for Safe Journey.
Gifts for the Temple.

18 And [a]according to the good hand of our God upon us
they brought us a man of insight of the sons of Mahli, the son
of Levi, the son of Israel, namely Sherebiah, and his sons and
brothers, 18 men;
19 and Hashabiah and [1]Jeshaiah of the sons of Morari,
with his brothers and their sons, 20 men;
20 and 220 of [a]the temple servants, whom David and the
princes had given for the service of the Levites, all of them
designated by name.
21 Then I proclaimed [a]a fast there at [b]the river of Ahava,
that we might humble ourselves before our God to seek from
Him a [1]safe journey for us, our little ones, and all our
possessions.
22 For I was ashamed to request from the king troops and
horsemen to [1]protect us from the enemy on the way, because
we had said to the king, "[a]The hand of our God is [2]favorably
disposed to all those who seek Him, but [b]His power and His
anger are against all those who forsake Him."
23 So we fasted and sought our God concerning this *mat-*
ter, and He [1]listened to our entreaty.
24 Then I set apart twelve of the leading priests besides
[a]Sherebiah, Hashabiah, and with them ten of their brothers;
25 and I [a]weighed out to them [b]the silver, the gold, and
the utensils, the offering for the house of our God which the
king and [c]his counselors and his princes, and all Israel present
there, had offered.
26 [a]Thus I weighed into their hands 650 talents of silver,
and silver utensils *worth* 100 talents, *and* gold talents,
27 and 20 gold bowls, *worth* 1,000 darics; and two utensils
of fine shiny bronze, precious as gold.
28 Then I said to them, "[a]You are holy to the LORD, and
the [b]utensils are holy; and the silver and the gold are a freewill
offering to the LORD God of your fathers.
29 "Watch and keep *them* [a]until you weigh *them* before
the leading priests, the Levites, and the heads of the fathers'
households of Israel at Jerusalem, *in* the chambers of the
house of the LORD."
30 So the priests and the Levites [a]accepted the weighed
out silver and gold and the utensils, to bring *them* to Jerusalem
to the house of our God.
31 Then we journeyed from [a]the river Ahava on [b]the
twelfth of the first month to go to Jerusalem; and [c]the hand of
our God was over us, and He delivered us from the hand of the
enemy and the ambushes by the way.
32 [a]Thus we came to Jerusalem and remained there three
days.
33 And on the fourth day the silver and the gold and the
utensils [a]were weighed out in the house of our God into the
hand of [b]Meremoth the son of Uriah the priest, and with him
was Eleazar the son of Phinehas; and with them *were* the
Levites, Jozabad the son of Jeshua and Noadiah the son of
Binnui.
34 Everything *was* numbered and weighed, and all the
weight was recorded at that time.
35 [a]The exiles who had come from the captivity offered
burnt offerings to the God of Israel: [b]12 bulls for all Israel, 96

18 [a]Ezra 7:6

19 [1]So Gk.; Heb., *with him Jeshaiah*

20 [a]Ezra 2:43; 7:7

21 [1]Lit., *straight way* [a]1 Sam. 7:6; 2 Chr. 20:3 [b]Ezra 8:15, 31

22 [1]Lit., *help* [2]Lit., *upon all . . . for good* [a]Ezra 7:6, 9, 28 [b]Josh. 22:16

23 [1]Lit., *was entreated by us*

24 [a]Ezra 8:18, 19

25 [a]Ezra 8:33 [b]Ezra 7:15, 16 [c]Ezra 7:14

26 [a]Ezra 1:9-11

28 [a]Lev. 21:6-8 [b]Lev. 22:2, 3

29 [a]Ezra 8:33, 34

30 [a]Ezra 1:9

31 [a]Ezra 8:15, 21 [b]Ezra 7:9 [c]Ezra 8:22

32 [a]Neh. 2:11

33 [a]Ezra 8:30 [b]Neh. 3:4, 21

35 [a]Ezra 2:1 [b]Ezra 6:17

rams, 77 lambs, 12 male goats for a sin offering, all as a burnt
offering to the LORD.
36 Then [a]they delivered the king's edicts to [b]the king's
satraps, and to the governors *in the provinces* beyond the
[1]River, and they supported the people and the house of God.

CHAPTER 9

NOW when these things had been completed, the princes
approached me, saying, "The people of Israel and the priests
and the Levites have not [a]separated themselves from the
peoples of the lands, [b]according to their abominations, *those*
of the Canaanites, the Hittites, the Perizzites, the Jebusites,
the Ammonites, the Moabites, the Egyptians, and the
Amorites.
2 "For [a]they have taken some of their daughters *as wives*
for themselves and for their sons, so that [b]the holy [1]race has
[c]intermingled with the peoples of the lands; indeed, the hands
of the princes and the rulers have been foremost in this
unfaithfulness."
3 And when I heard about this matter, I [a]tore my garment and my robe, and pulled some of the hair from my head
and my beard, and [b]sat down appalled.
4 Then [a]everyone who trembled at the words of the God
of Israel on account of the unfaithfulness of the exiles gathered to me, and I sat appalled until [b]the evening offering.
5 But at the evening offering I arose from my [1]humiliation,
even with my garment and my robe torn, and I fell on my
knees and [a]stretched out my [2]hands to the LORD my God;
6 and I said, "O my God, I am ashamed and embarrassed
to lift up my face to Thee, my God, for our iniquities have
[1]risen above our heads, and our [a]guilt has grown even to the
heavens.
7 "[a]Since the days of our fathers to this day we *have been*
in great guilt, and on account of our iniquities we, our kings
and our priests have been given into the hand of the kings of
the lands, to the sword, to captivity, and to plunder and to
[1b]open shame, as *it is* this day.
8 "But now for a brief moment grace has been *shown*
from the LORD our God, [a]to leave us an escaped remnant and
to give us a [b]peg in His holy place, that our God may enlighten
our eyes and grant us a little reviving in our bondage.
9 "[a]For we are slaves; yet in our bondage, our God has not
forsaken us, but [b]has extended lovingkindness to us in the sight
of the kings of Persia, to give us reviving to raise up the house
of our God, to restore its ruins, and to give us a wall in Judah
and Jerusalem.
10 "And now, our God, what shall we say after this? For we
have forsaken Thy commandments,
11 which Thou hast commanded by Thy servants the
prophets, saying, 'The land which you are entering to take
possession of it is an unclean land with the uncleanness of the
peoples of the lands, with their abominations which have filled
it from end to end and [a]with their impurity.
12 'So now do not [a]give your daughters to their sons nor
take their daughters to your sons, and never seek their peace or

36 [1]I.e. Euphrates River [a]Ezra 7:21-24 [b]Ezra 4:7; 5:6

1 [a]Ezra 6:21; Neh. 9:2 [b]Lev. 18:24-30

2 [1]Lit., *seed* [a]Ezra 10:2, 18 [b]Ex. 22:31 [c]Neh. 13:3

3 [a]2 Kin. 18:37 [b]Neh. 1:4

4 [a]Ezra 10:3 [b]Ex. 29:39

5 [1]Or, *fasting* [2]Lit., *palms* [a]Ex. 9:29

6 [1]Lit., *multiplied over the head* [a]Ezra 9:13, 15; 2 Chr. 28:9; Rev. 18:5

7 [1]Lit., *shame of faces* [a]2 Chr. 29:6 [b]Dan. 9:7

8 [a]Ezra 9:13-15 [b]Is. 22:23

9 [a]Neh. 9:36 [b]Ezra 7:28

11 [a]Ezra 6:21

12 [a]Ezra 9:2

their prosperity, that you may be strong and eat the good
things of the land and [b]leave *it* as an inheritance to your sons
forever.'
13 "And after all that has come upon us for our evil deeds
and [a]our great guilt, since Thou our God hast requited *us* less
than our iniquities *deserve*, and hast given us [b]an escaped remnant as this,
14 [a]shall we again break Thy commandments and intermarry with the peoples who commit these abominations?
[b]Wouldst Thou not be angry with us [1]to the point of destruction, until there is no remnant nor any who escape?
15 "O LORD God of Israel, [a]Thou art righteous, for we have
been left an escaped remnant, as *it is* this day; behold, we are
before Thee in [b]our guilt, for [c]no one can stand before Thee
because of this."

CHAPTER 10

NOW [a]while Ezra was praying and making confession, weeping and prostrating himself [b]before the house of God, a very
large assembly, men, women, and children, gathered to him
from Israel; for the people wept bitterly.
2 And Shecaniah the son of Jehiel, one of the sons of
Elam, answered and said to Ezra, "[a]We have been unfaithful
to our God, and have [1]married foreign women from the
peoples of the land; yet now there is hope for Israel in spite of
this.
3 "So now [a]let us make a covenant with our God to put
away all the wives and [1b]their children, according to the counsel of [2]my lord and of [c]those who tremble at the commandment of our God; and let it be done [d]according to the law.
4 "Arise! For *this* matter is [1]your responsibility, but we will
be with you; [a]be courageous and act."
5 Then Ezra rose and [a]made the leading priests, the Levites, and all Israel, take oath that they would do according to
this [1]proposal; so they took the oath.
6 Then Ezra [a]rose from before the house of God and
went into the chamber of Jehohanan the son of Eliashib. Although he went there, [b]he did not eat bread, nor drink water,
for he was mourning over the unfaithfulness of the exiles.
7 And they made a proclamation throughout Judah and
Jerusalem to all the exiles, that they should assemble at
Jerusalem,
8 and that whoever would not come within three days,
according to the counsel of the leaders and the elders, all his
possessions should be forfeited and he himself excluded from
the assembly of the exiles.
9 So all the men of Judah and Benjamin assembled at
Jerusalem within the three days. It was the ninth month on the
twentieth of the month, and all the people sat in the open
square *before* the house of God, [a]trembling because of this
matter and the heavy rain.
10 Then Ezra the priest stood up and said to them, "You
have been unfaithful and have married foreign wives adding to
the guilt of Israel.
11 "Now, therefore, [a]make confession to the LORD God of

12 [b]Prov. 13:22

13 [a]Ezra 9:6, 7 [b]Ezra 9:8

14 [1]Lit., *to destroy* [a]Ezra 9:2 [b]Deut. 9:8, 14

15 [a]Neh. 9:33; Dan. 9:7 [b]Ezra 9:6 [c]Job 9:2

1 [a]Dan. 9:4, 20 [b]2 Chr. 20:9

2 [1]Lit., *given dwelling to* [a]Ezra 9:2

3 [1]Lit., *that which is born of them* [2]Or, *the Lord* [a]2 Chr. 34:31 [b]Ezra 10:44 [c]Ezra 9:4 [d]Deut. 7:2, 3

4 [1]Lit., *upon you* [a]1 Chr. 28:10

5 [1]Lit., *word, thing* [a]Neh. 5:12; 13:25

6 [a]Ezra 10:1 [b]Deut. 9:18

9 [a]Ezra 10:3; 9:4

11 [a]Lev. 26:40

11 [b]Ezra 10:3

12 [1]Lit., *upon us*

14 [1]Lit., *stand for* [a]2 Chr. 29:10; 30:8

15 [1]Lit., *stood against*

16 [1]Heb. reads, *there were set apart Ezra the priest, men. . .* [2]Lit., *sat*

19 [1]Lit., *gave their hand* [a]2 Kin. 10:15 [b]Lev. 5:15; 6:6

your fathers, and do His will; and [b]separate yourselves from
the peoples of the land and from the foreign wives."
12 Then all the assembly answered and said with a loud
voice, "That's right! As you have said, so it is [1]our duty to *do*.
13 "But there are many people, it is the rainy season, and
we are not able to stand in the open. Nor can the task be done
in one or two days, for we have transgressed greatly in this
matter.
14 "Let our leaders [1]represent the whole assembly and let
all those in our cities who have married foreign wives come at
appointed times, together with the elders and judges of each
city, until the [a]fierce anger of our God on account of this
matter is turned away from us."
15 Only Jonathan the son of Asahel and Jahzeiah the son
of Tikvah [1]opposed this, with Meshullam and Shabbethai the
Levite supporting them.
16 But the exiles did so. And Ezra the priest [1]selected men
who were heads of fathers' *households* for each of their father's
households, all of them by name. So they [2]convened on
the first day of the tenth month to investigate the matter.
17 And they finished *investigating* all the men who had
married foreign wives by the first of the first month.
18 And among the sons of the priests who had married
foreign wives were found of the sons of Jeshua the son of
Jozadak, and his brothers: Maaseiah, Eliezer, Jarib, and
Gedaliah.
19 And they [1a]pledged to put away their wives, and being
guilty, [b]*they offered* a ram of the flock for their offense.
20 And of the sons of Immer *there were* Hanani and
Zebadiah;
21 and of the sons of Harim: Maaseiah, Elijah, Shemaiah,
Jehiel, and Uzziah;
22 and of the sons of Pashhur: Elioenai, Maaseiah, Ishmael,
Nethanel, Jozabad, and Elasah.
23 And of Levites *there were* Jozabad, Shimei, Kelaiah
(that is, Kelita), Pethahiah, Judah, and Eliezer.
24 And of the singers *there was* Eliashib; and of the gatekeepers:
Shallum, Telem, and Uri.
25 And of Israel, of the sons of Parosh *there were* Ramiah,
Izziah, Malchijah, Mijamin, Eleazar, Malchijah, and Benaiah;
26 and of the sons of Elam: Mattaniah, Zechariah, Jehiel,
Abdi, Jeremoth, and Elijah;
27 and of the sons of Zattu: Elioenai, Eliashib, Mattaniah,
Jeremoth, Zabad, and Aziza;
28 and of the sons of Bebai: Jehohanan, Hananiah, Zabbai,
and Athlai;
29 and of the sons of Bani: Meshullam, Malluch, and
Adaiah, Jashub, Sheal, *and* Jeramoth;
30 and of the sons of Pahath-moab: Adna, Chelal, Benaiah,
Maaseiah, Mattaniah, Bezalel, Binnui, and Manasseh;
31 and *of* the sons of Harim: Eliezer, Isshijah, Malchijah,
Shemaiah, Shimeon,
32 Benjamin, Malluch, *and* Shemariah;
33 of the sons of Hashum: Mattenai, Mattattah, Zabad,
Eliphelet, Jeremai, Manasseh, *and* Shimei;
34 of the sons of Bani: Maadai, Amram, Uel,

35 Benaiah, Bedeiah, Cheluhi,
36 Vaniah, Meremoth, Eliashib,
37 Mattaniah, Mattenai, Jaasu,
38 Bani, Binnui, Shimei,
39 Shelemiah, Nathan, Adaiah,
40 Machnadebai, Shashai, Sharai,
41 Azarel, Shelemiah, Shemariah,
42 Shallum, Amariah, *and* Joseph.
43 Of the sons of Nebo *there were* Jeiel, Mattithiah, Zabad, Zebina, Jaddai, Joel, *and* Benaiah.
44 All these had married foreign wives, and [a]some of them
had wives *by whom* they had children.

THE BOOK OF NEHEMIAH

Nehemiah's Grief for Exiles.

THE words of [a]Nehemiah the son of Hacaliah.
Now it happened in [b]the month Chislev, [c]*in* the twentieth
year, while I was in [d]Susa the [1]capitol,
2 that [a]Hanani, one of my brothers, and [1]some men from
Judah came; and I asked them concerning the Jews who had
escaped *and* had survived the captivity, and about Jerusalem.
3 And they said to me, "The remnant there in the [a]prov-
ince who survived the captivity are in great distress and [b]re-
proach, and [c]the wall of Jerusalem is broken down and [d]its
gates are burned with fire."
4 Now it came about when I heard these words, [a]I sat
down and wept and mourned for days; and I was fasting and
praying before [b]the God of heaven.
5 And I said, "I beseech Thee, O LORD God of heaven,
[a]the great and awesome God, who preserves the covenant and
lovingkindness for those who love Him and keep His
commandments,
6 [a]let Thine ear now be attentive and Thine eyes open to
hear the prayer of Thy servant which I am praying before
Thee now, day and night, on behalf of the sons of Israel Thy
servants, [b]confessing the sins of the sons of Israel which we
have sinned against Thee; [c]I and my father's house have
sinned.
7 "[a]We have acted very corruptly against Thee and have
not kept the commandments, nor the statutes, nor the ordinances [b]which Thou didst command Thy servant Moses.
8 "Remember the word which Thou didst command Thy
servant Moses, saying, '[a]If you are unfaithful I will scatter you
among the peoples;
9 [a]but if you return to Me and keep My commandments
and do them, though those of you who have been scattered
were in the most remote part of the heavens, I [b]will gather
them from there and will bring them [c]to the place where I
have chosen to cause My name to dwell.'
10 "And [a]they are Thy servants and Thy people whom

44 [a]Ezra 10:3

1 [1]Or, *palace or citadel* [a]Neh. 10:1 [b]Zech. 7:1 [c]Neh. 2:1 [d]Esth. 1:2; Dan. 8:2

2 [1]Lit., *he and some* [a]Neh. 7:2

3 [a]Neh. 7:6 [b]Neh. 2:17 [c]Neh. 2:17 [d]Neh. 2:3

4 [a]Ezra 9:3; 10:1 [b]Neh. 2:4

5 [a]Neh. 4:14; 9:32

6 [a]Dan. 9:17 [b]Ezra 10:1; Dan. 9:20 [c]2 Chr. 29:6

7 [a]Dan. 9:5 [b]Deut. 28:14

8 [a]Lev. 26:33

9 [a]Deut. 30:2, 3 [b]Deut. 30:4 [c]Deut. 12:5

10 [a]Ex. 32:11; Deut. 9:29

Thou didst redeem by Thy great power and by Thy strong
hand.
11 "O Lord, I beseech Thee, [a]may Thine ear be attentive
to the prayer of Thy servant and the prayer of Thy servants
who delight to [1]revere Thy name, and make Thy servant successful today, and grant him compassion before this man."
Now I was the [b]cupbearer to the king.

Chapter 2

AND it came about in the month Nisan, [a]in the twentieth
year of King [b]Artaxerxes, that wine *was* before him, and [c]I
took up the wine and gave it to the king. Now I had not been
sad in his presence.
2 So the king said to me, "Why is your face sad though
you are not sick? [a]This is nothing but sadness of heart." Then I
was very much afraid.
3 And I said to the king, "[a]Let the king live forever. Why
should my face not be sad [b]when the city, the place of my
fathers' tombs, lies desolate and its gates have been consumed
by fire?"
4 Then the king said to me, "What would you request?"
[a]So I prayed to the God of heaven.
5 And I said to the king, "If it please the king, and if your
servant has found favor before you, send me to Judah, to the
city of my fathers' tombs, that I may rebuild it."
6 Then the king said to me, the queen sitting beside him,
"How long will your journey be, and when will you return?" So
it pleased the king to send me, and [a]I gave him a definite time.
7 And I said to the king, "If it please the king, let letters
be given me [a]for the governors *of the provinces* beyond the
River, that they may allow me to pass through until I come to
Judah,
8 and a letter to Asaph the keeper of the king's [a]forest,
that he may give me timber to make beams for the gates of
[b]the fortress which is by the [1]temple, for the wall of the city,
and for the house to which I will go." And the king granted
them to me because [c]the good hand of my God *was* on me.
9 Then I came to [a]the governors *of the provinces* beyond
the River and gave them the king's letters. Now [b]the king had
sent with me officers of the army and horsemen.
10 And when [a]Sanballat the Horonite and Tobiah the
Ammonite [1]official heard *about it*, it was very displeasing to
them that someone had come to seek the welfare of the sons
of Israel.
11 So I came to Jerusalem and was there three days.
12 And I arose in the night, I and a few men with me. I did
not tell any one what my God was putting into my [1]mind to do
for Jerusalem and there was no animal with me except the
animal on which I was riding.
13 So I went out at night by [a]the Valley Gate in the
direction of the Dragon's Well and *on* to the [1]Refuse Gate,
inspecting the walls of Jerusalem [b]which were broken down
and its [c]gates which were consumed by fire.
14 Then I passed on to [a]the Fountain Gate and [b]the
King's Pool, but there was no place for [1]my mount to pass.

11 [1]Or, *fear* [a]Neh. 1:6 [b]Neh. 2:1; Gen. 40:21

1 [a]Neh. 1:1 [b]Ezra 7:1 [c]Neh. 1:11

2 [a]Prov. 15:13

3 [a]Dan. 2:4 [b]Neh. 1:3

4 [a]Neh. 1:4

6 [a]Neh. 5:14; 13:6

7 [a]Ezra 7:21; 8:36

8 [1]Lit., *house* [a]Eccles. 2:5, 6 [b]Neh. 7:2 [c]Neh. 2:18; Ezra 7:6

9 [a]Neh. 2:7 [b]Ezra 8:22

10 [1]Lit., *servant* [a]Neh. 2:19; 4:1

12 [1]Lit., *heart*

13 [1]Lit., *Gate of Ash-heaps* [a]Neh. 3:13 [b]Neh. 1:3 [c]Neh. 2:3, 17

14 [1]Lit., *the animal under me* [a]Neh. 3:15 [b]2 Kin. 20:20

15 So I went up at night by the ravine and inspected the
wall. Then I entered the Valley Gate again and returned.
16 And the officials did not know where I had gone or
what I had done; nor had I as yet told the Jews, the priests, the
nobles, the officials, or the rest who did the work.
17 Then I said to them, "You see the bad situation we are
in, that [a]Jerusalem is desolate and its gates burned by fire.
Come, let us rebuild the wall of Jerusalem that we may no
longer be a reproach."
18 And I told them how the hand of my God had been
favorable to me, and also about the king's words which he had
spoken to me. Then they said, "Let us arise and build." [a]So
they put their hands to the good *work.*
19 But when Sanballat the Horonite, and Tobiah the Ammonite [1]official, and [a]Geshem the Arab heard *it,* [b]they
mocked us and despised us and said, "What is this thing you
are doing? [c]Are you rebelling against the king?"
20 So I answered them and said to them, "[a]The God of
heaven will give us success; therefore we His servants will arise
and build, but you have no portion, right, or memorial in
Jerusalem."

Chapter 3

THEN [a]Eliashib the high priest arose with his brothers the
priests and built [b]the Sheep Gate; they consecrated it and
[c]hung its doors. They consecrated [1]the wall to [d]the Tower of
the Hundred *and* [e]the Tower of Hananel.
2 And next to him [a]the men of Jericho built, and next to
[1]them Zaccur the son of Imri built.
3 Now the sons of Hassenaah built [a]the Fish Gate; they
laid its beams and hung its doors with its bolts and bars.
4 And next to them Meremoth the son of Uriah, the son
of Hakkoz made repairs. And next to him Meshullam the son
of Berechiah the son of Meshezabel made repairs. And next to
[1]him Zadok the son of Baana also made repairs.
5 Moreover, next to [1]him the Tekoites made repairs, but
their nobles did not [2]support the work of their masters.
6 And Joiada the son of Paseah and Meshullam the son
of Besodeiah repaired [a]the Old Gate; they laid its beams and
hung its doors, with its bolts and its bars.
7 Next to them Melatiah the Gibeonite and Jadon the
Meronothite, the men of Gibeon and of Mizpah, [1]also [a]made
repairs for the official seat of the governor *of the province*
beyond the River.
8 Next to him Uzziel the son of Harhaiah of the [a]gold-
smiths made repairs. And next to him Hananiah, one of the
perfumers, made repairs, and they restored Jerusalem as far as
[b]the Broad Wall.
9 And next to them Rephaiah the son of Hur, [a]the official of half the district of Jerusalem, made repairs.
10 Next to them Jedaiah the son of Harumaph made repairs opposite his house. And next to him Hattush the son of
Hashabneiah made repairs.
11 Malchijah the son of Harim and Hasshub the son of

17 [a]Neh. 1:3

18 [a]2 Sam. 2:7

19 [1]Lit., *servant* [a]Neh. 6:6 [b]Neh. 4:1 [c]Neh. 6:6

20 [a]Neh. 2:4

1 [1]Lit., *it* [a]Neh. 3:20; 13:28 [b]Neh. 3:32; 12:39 [c]Neh. 6:1; 7:1 [d]Neh. 12:39 [e]Jer. 31:38

2 [1]Lit., *him* [a]Neh. 7:36

3 [a]Neh. 12:39

4 [1]Lit., *them*

5 [1]Lit., *them* [2]Lit., *bring their neck to*

6 [a]Neh. 12:39

7 [1]Or, *which was under the jurisdiction of the governor* of the province *beyond the River, also made repairs* [a]Neh. 2:7

8 [a]Neh. 31:32 [b]Neh. 12:38

9 [a]Neh. 3:12, 17

Pahath-moab repaired another section and [a]the Furnace
Tower.
12 And next to him Shallum the son of Hallohesh, [a]the
official of half the district of Jerusalem, made repairs, he and
his daughters.
13 Hanun and the inhabitants of Zanoah repaired [a]the
Valley Gate. They built it and hung its doors with its bolts and
its bars, and a thousand cubits of the wall to the [1]Refuse Gate.
14 And Malchijah the son of Rechab, the official of the
district of [a]Beth-haccherem repaired the [1b]Refuse Gate. He
built it and hung its doors with its bolts and its bars.
15 Shallum the son of Col-hozeh, the official of the district of Mizpah, repaired [a]the Fountain Gate. He built it,
covered it, and hung its doors with its bolts and its bars, and
the wall of the Pool of Shelah at [b]the King's Garden as far as
[c]the steps that descend from the city of David.
16 After him Nehemiah the son of Azbuk, [a]official of half
the district of Beth-zur, made repairs as far as *a point* opposite
the tombs of David, and as far as [b]the Artificial Pool and the
House of the Mighty Men.
17 After him the Levites carried out repairs *under* Rehum
the son of Bani. Next to him Hashabiah, the official of half
the district of Keilah, carried out repairs for his district.
18 After him their brothers carried out repairs *under* Bav-
vai the son of Henadad, official of *the other* half of the district
of Keilah.
19 And next to him Ezer the son of Jeshua, [a]the official of
Mizpah, repaired [1]another section, in front of the ascent of the
armory [b]at the Angle.
20 After him Baruch the son of Zabbai zealously repaired
another section, from the Angle to the doorway of the house
of [a]Eliashib the high priest.
21 After him Meremoth the son of Uriah, the son of Hakkoz repaired another section, from the doorway of Eliashib's
house even as far as the end of [1]his house.
22 And after him the priests, [a]the men of the [1]valley,
carried out repairs.
23 After [1]them Benjamin and Hasshub carried out repairs
in front of their house. After [1]them Azariah the son of Maaseiah, son of Ananiah carried out repairs beside his house.
24 After him Binnui the son of Henadad repaired another
section, from the house of Azariah as far as [a]the Angle and as
far as the corner.
25 Palal the son of Uzai *made repairs* in front of the
Angle and the tower projecting from the upper house of the
king, which is by [a]the court of the guard. After him Pedaiah
the son of Parosh *made repairs.*
26 And [a]the temple servants living in [b]Ophel *made repairs*
as far as the front of [c]the Water Gate toward the east and the
projecting tower.
27 After him [a]the Tekoites repaired another section in
front of the great projecting tower and as far as the wall of
Ophel.
28 Above [a]the Horse Gate the priests carried out repairs,
each in front of his house.
29 After [1]them Zadok the son of Immer carried out

11 [a]Neh. 12:38
12 [a]Neh. 3:9
13 [1]Lit., *Gate of Ash-heaps* [a]Neh. 2:13
14 [1]Lit., *Gate of Ash-heaps* [a]Jer. 6:1 [b]Neh. 2:13
15 [a]Neh. 2:17 [b]2 Kin. 25:4 [c]Neh. 12:37
16 [a]Neh. 3:9, 12, 17 [b]2 Kin. 20:20; Is. 7:3
19 [1]Lit., *a second measure,* so in v. 20, 21, 24, 30. [a]Neh. 3:15 [b]2 Chr. 26:9
20 [a]Neh. 3:1
21 [1]Lit., *Eliashib's*
22 [1]Lit., *circle;* i.e., lower Jordan valley [a]Neh. 12:28
23 [1]Lit., *him*
24 [a]Neh. 3:19
25 [a]Jer. 32:2
26 [a]Neh. 7:46 [b]Neh. 11:21 [c]Neh. 8:1
27 [a]Neh. 3:5
28 [a]2 Kin. 11:16; 2 Chr. 23:15; Jer. 31:40
29 [1]Lit., *him*

repairs in front of his house. And after him Shemaiah the son
of Shecaniah, the keeper of the East Gate, carried out repairs.
30 After him Hananiah the son of Shelemiah, and Hanun
the sixth son of Zalaph, repaired another section. After him
Meshullam the son of Berechiah carried out repairs in front of
[a]his own [1]quarters.
31 After him Malchijah [1]one of [a]the goldsmiths, carried
out repairs as far as the house of the temple servants and of the
merchants, in front of the [2]Inspection Gate and as far as the
upper room of the corner.
32 And between the upper room of the corner and [a]the
Sheep Gate the goldsmiths and the merchants carried out
repairs.

Chapter 4

1 NOW it came about that when [a]Sanballat heard that we
were rebuilding the wall, he became furious and very angry and
mocked the Jews.
2 And he spoke in the presence of his brothers and [a]the
[1]wealthy *men* of Samaria and said, "What are these feeble
Jews doing? Are they going to restore *it* for themselves? Can
they offer sacrifices? Can they finish in a day? Can they revive
the stones from the [2b]dusty rubble even the burned ones?"
3 Now Tobiah the Ammonite *was* near him and he said,
"Even what they are building—[a]if a fox should [1]jump on *it*, he
would break their stone wall down!"
4 [a]Hear, O our God, how we are despised! [b]Return their
reproach on their own heads and give them up for plunder in a
land of captivity.
5 Do not [1a]forgive their iniquity and let not their sin be
blotted out before Thee, for they have [2]demoralized the
builders.
6 So we built the wall and the whole wall was joined
together to half its *height*, for the people had a [1]mind to work.
7 [1]Now it came about when Sanballat, Tobiah, the
Arabs, the Ammonites, and the Ashdodites heard that the [2]re-
pair of the walls of Jerusalem went on, *and* that the breaches
began to be closed, they were very angry.
8 And all of them conspired together to come *and* fight
against Jerusalem and to cause a disturbance in it.
9 But we prayed to our God, and because of them we [a]set
up a guard against them day and night.
10 Thus [1]in Judah it was said,
"The strength of the burden bearers is failing,
Yet there is much [2]rubbish;
And we ourselves are unable
To rebuild the wall."
11 And our enemies said, "They will not know or see until
we come among them, kill them, and put a stop to the work."
12 And it came about when the Jews who lived near them
came and told us ten times, "[1]They will come up against us
from every place where you may turn,"
13 then I stationed *men* in the lowest parts of the space
behind the wall, the [1]exposed places, and I [a]stationed the
people in families with their swords, spears, and bows.

30 [1]Or, *cell* [a]Neh. 13:7

31 [1]Lit., *son of* [2]Or, *Mustering* [a]Neh. 3:8, 32

32 [a]Neh. 3:1

1 [1]Ch. 3:33 in Heb. [a]Neh. 2:10

2 [1]Or, *army* [2]Lit., *heaps of dust* [a]Ezra 4:9, 10 [b]Neh. 4:10

3 [1]Lit., *go up* [a]Lam. 5:18

4 [a]Ps. 123:3, 4 [b]Ps. 79:12

5 [1]Lit., *cover* [2]Lit., *offended against* [a]Ps. 69:27, 28; Jer. 18:23

6 [1]Lit., *heart*

7 [1]Ch. 4:1 in Heb. [2]Lit., *healing*

9 [a]Neh. 4:11

10 [1]Lit., *Judah said* [2]Lit., *dust*

12 [1]Gk., Heb. omits *they . . . up*

13 [1]Lit., *bare* [a]Neh. 4:17, 18

14 [a]Num. 14:9; Deut. 1:29, 30 [b]2 Sam. 10:12

14 When I *saw their fear*, I rose and spoke to the nobles,
the officials, and the rest of the people: "[a]Do not be afraid of
them; remember the Lord who is great and awesome, and
[b]fight for your brothers, your sons, your daughters, your wives,
and your houses."

15 [a]2 Sam. 17:14

15 And it happened when our enemies heard that it was
known to us, and that [a]God had frustrated their plan, then all
of us returned to the wall, each one to his work.
16 And it came about from that day on, that half of my
servants carried on the work while half of them held the spears,
the shields, the bows, and the breastplates; and the captains
were behind the whole house of Judah.
17 Those who were rebuilding the wall and those who
carried burdens took *their* load with one hand doing the work
and the other holding a weapon.

18 [1]Lit., *he who sounded the trumpet*

18 As for the builders, each *wore* his sword girded at his
side as he built, while [1]the trumpeter *stood* near me.
19 And I said to the nobles, the officials, and the rest of
the people, "The work is great and extensive, and we are separated on the wall far from one another.

20 [1]Lit., *assemble yourselves* [a]Ex. 14:14; Deut. 1:30

20 "At whatever place you hear the sound of the trumpet,
[1]rally to us there. [a]Our God will fight for us."

21 [1]Lit., *rising of the dawn* [2]Lit., *came out*

21 So we carried on the work with half of them holding
spears from [1]dawn until the stars [2]appeared.
22 At that time I also said to the people, "Let each man
with his servant spend the night within Jerusalem so that they
may be a guard for us by night and a laborer by day."
23 So neither I, my brothers, my servants, nor the men of
the guard who followed me, none of us removed our clothes,
each *took* his weapon *even to* the water.

Chapter 5

1 [a]Lev. 25:35; Deut. 15:7

NOW [a]there was a great outcry of the people and of their
wives against their Jewish brothers.
2 For there were those who said, "We, our sons and our
daughters, are many; therefore let us get grain that we may eat
and live."
3 And there were others who said, "We are mortgaging
our fields, our vineyards, and our houses that we might get
grain because of the famine."

4 [a]Ezra 4:13; 7:24

4 Also there were those who said, "We have borrowed
money [a]for the king's tax *on* our fields and our vineyards.

5 [1]Lit., *there is not to the power in our hands* [a]Gen. 37:27 [b]Lev. 25:39

5 "And now [a]our flesh is like the flesh of our brothers, our
children like their children. Yet behold, [b]we are forcing our
sons and our daughters to be slaves, and some of our daughters
are forced into bondage *already*, and [1]we are helpless because
our fields and vineyards belong to others."
6 Then I was very angry when I had heard their outcry
and these words.

7 [a]Ex. 22:25; Lev. 25:36

7 And I consulted with myself, and contended with the
nobles and the rulers and said to them, "[a]You are exacting
usury, each from his brother!" Therefore, I held a great assembly against them.

8 [1]Lit., *bought* [a]Lev. 25:48

8 And I said to them, "We according to our ability [a]have
[1]redeemed our Jewish brothers who were sold to the nations;

now would you even sell your brothers that they may be sold
to us?" Then they were silent and could not find a word *to say.*
9 Again I said, "The thing which you are doing is not
good; should you not walk in the fear of our God because of
[a]the reproach of the nations, our enemies?
10 "And likewise I, my brothers and my servants, are lend-
ing them money and grain. Please, let us leave off this usury.
11 "Please, give back to them this very day their fields, their
vineyards, their olive groves, and their houses, also the hundredth *part* of the money and of the grain, the new wine, and
the oil that you are exacting from them."
12 Then they said, "We [a]will give *it* back and [b]will require
nothing from them; we will do exactly as you say." So I called
the priests and [c]took an oath from them that they would do
according to this [1]promise.
13 I [a]also shook out the [1]front of my garment and said,
"Thus may God shake out every man from his house and from
his possessions who does not fulfill this [2]promise; even thus
may he be shaken out and emptied." And [b]all the assembly
said, "Amen!" And they praised the LORD. Then the people
did according to this [2]promise.
14 Moreover, from the day that I was appointed to be
their governor in the land of Judah, from [a]the twentieth year
to the [b]thirty-second year of King Artaxerxes, *for* twelve years,
neither [c]I nor my [1]kinsmen have eaten the governor's food
allowance.
15 But the former governors who were before me [1]laid
burdens on the people and took from them bread and wine
besides forty shekels of silver; even their servants domineered
the people. But I did not do so [a]because of the fear of God.
16 And I also [1]applied myself to the work on this wall; we
did not buy any land, and all my servants were gathered there
for the work.
17 Moreover, [a]*there were* at my table one hundred and
fifty Jews and officials, besides those who came to us from the
nations that were around us.
18 Now [a]that which was prepared for each day was one ox
and six choice sheep, also birds were prepared for me; and
once in ten days all sorts of wine *were furnished* in abundance.
Yet for all this [b]I did not demand the governor's food *allowance,* because the servitude was heavy on this people.
19 [a]Remember me, O my God, for good, *according to* all
that I have done for this people.

CHAPTER 6

NOW it came about when it was reported to Sanballat,
Tobiah, to Geshem the Arab, and to the rest of our enemies
that I had rebuilt the wall, and *that* no breach remained in it
[a]although at that time I had not set up the doors in the gates,
2 that Sanballat and Geshem sent *a message* to me,
saying, "Come, let us meet together at [1]Chephirim in the plain
of [a]Ono." But they were planning to [2]harm me.
3 So I sent messengers to them, saying, "I am doing a
great work and I cannot come down. Why should the work
stop while I leave it and come down to you?"

9 [a]Neh. 4:4

12 [1]Lit., *word* [a]2 Chr. 28:15 [b]Neh. 10:31 [c]Ezra 10:5

13 [1]Lit., *bosom* [2]Lit., *word* [a]Acts 18:6 [b]Neh. 8:6

14 [1]Lit., *brothers* [a]Neh. 1:1 [b]Neh. 13:6 [c]Ezra 4:13, 14

15 [1]Lit., *made heavy* [a]Neh. 5:9

16 [1]Or, *held fast*

17 [a]1 Kin. 18:19

18 [a]1 Kin. 4:22, 23 [b]2 Thess. 3:8

19 [a]Neh. 13:14, 22, 31

1 [a]Neh. 3:1, 3

2 [1]Another reading is, one of *the villages* [2]Lit., *do evil to me* [a]1 Chr. 8:12

4 And they sent *messages* to me four times in this manner, and I answered them in the same way.
5 Then Sanballat sent his servant to me in the same manner a fifth time with an open letter in his hand.
6 In it was written, "It is reported among the nations,
and [1]Gashmu says, that [a]you and the Jews are planning to
rebel; therefore you are rebuilding the wall. And you are to be
their king, according to these reports.
7 "And you have also appointed prophets to proclaim in
Jerusalem concerning [1]you, 'A king is in Judah!' And now it
will be reported to the king according to these reports. So
come now, let us take counsel together."
8 Then I sent *a message* to him saying, "Such things as
you are saying have not been done, but you are inventing them
[1]in your own mind."
9 For all of them were *trying* to frighten us, [1]thinking,
"[2]They will become discouraged with the work and it will not
be done." But now, *O God,* strengthen my hands.
10 And when I entered the house of Shemaiah the son of
Delaiah, son of Mehetabel, [a]who was [1]confined at home, he
said, "Let us meet together in the house of God, within the
temple, and let us close the doors of the temple, for they are
coming to kill you, and they are coming to kill you at night."
11 But I said, "Should a man like me flee? And could one
such as I go into the temple [1]to save his life? I will not go in."
12 Then I perceived [1]that surely God had not sent him,
but he uttered *his* prophecy against me because Tobiah and
Sanballat had hired him.
13 He was hired for this reason, [a]that I might become
frightened and act accordingly and sin, so that they might have
an evil report in order that they could reproach me.
14 [a]Remember, O my God, Tobiah and Sanballat according to these works of theirs, and also Noadiah [b]the prophetess
and the rest of the prophets who were *trying* to frighten me.
15 So [a]the wall was completed on the twenty-fifth of *the
month* Elul, in fifty-two days.
16 And it came about [a]when all our enemies heard *of it,*
and all the nations surrounding us saw *it,* they [1]lost their confidence; for [b]they recognized that this work had been accomplished [2]with the help of our God.
17 Also in those days many letters went from the nobles of
Judah to Tobiah, and Tobiah's *letters* came to them.
18 For many in Judah were bound by oath to him because
he was the son-in-law of Shecaniah the son of Arah, and his son
Jehohanan had married the daughter of Meshullam the son of
Berechiah.
19 Moreover, they were speaking about his good deeds in
my presence and reported my words to him. Then Tobiah sent
letters to frighten me.

Chapter 7

NOW it came about when [a]the wall was rebuilt and I had set
up the doors, and the gatekeepers and the singers and the
Levites were appointed,
2 that I put [a]Hanani my brother, and [b]Hanaiah the

6 [1]In v. 1 and elsewhere *Geshem* [a]Neh. 2:19

7 [1]Lit., *you, saying*

8 [1]Lit., *from your heart*

9 [1]Lit., *saying,* [2]Lit., *Their hands will drop from*

10 [1]Lit., *shut up* [a]Jer. 36:5

11 [1]Lit., *and live*

12 [1]Lit., *and behold God*

13 [a]Neh. 6:6

14 [a]Neh. 13:29 [b]Ezek. 13:17

15 [a]Neh. 4:1, 2

16 [1]Lit., *fell exceedingly in their own eyes* [2]Lit., *from our God* [a]Neh. 2:10; 4:1, 7 [b]Ex. 14:25

1 [a]Neh. 6:1, 15

2 [a]Neh. 1:2 [b]Neh. 10:23

commander of [c]the fortress, in charge of Jerusalem, for he was
[d]a faithful man and feared God more than many.
3 Then I said to them, "Do not let the gates of Jerusalem
be opened until the sun is hot, and while they are standing
guard, let them shut and bolt the doors. Also appoint guards
from the inhabitants of Jerusalem, each at his post, and each in
front of his own house."
4 Now the city was large and spacious but the people in it
were few and the houses were not built.
5 Then my God put it into my heart to assemble the
nobles, the officials, and the people to be enrolled by genealogies. Then I found the book of the genealogy of those who
came up first [1]in which I found the following record:
6 [a]These are the people of the province who came up
from the captivity of the exiles whom Nebuchadnezzar the
king of Babylon had carried away, and who returned to Jerusalem and Judah, each to his city,
7 who came with Zerubbabel, Jeshua, Nehemiah, [1]Aza-
riah, [2]Raamiah, Nahamani, Mordecai, Bilshan, [3]Mispereth,
Bigvai, [4]Nehum, Baanah.
The number of men of the people of Israel:
8 The sons of Parosh, 2,172;
9 the sons of Shephatiah, 372;
10 the sons of Arah, 652;
11 the sons of Pahath-moab of the sons of Jeshua and
Joab, 2,818;
12 the sons of Elam, 1,254;
13 the sons of Zattu, 845;
14 the sons of Zaccai, 760;
15 the sons of [1]Binnui, 648;
16 the sons of Bebai, 628;
17 the sons of Azgad, 2,322;
18 the sons of Adonikam, 667;
19 the sons of Bigvai, 2,067;
20 the sons of Adin, 655;
21 the sons of Ater, of Hezekiah, 98;
22 the sons of Hashum, 328;
23 the sons of Bezai, 324;
24 the sons of [1]Hariph, 112;
25 the sons of [1]Gibeon, 95;
26 the men of Bethlehem and Netophah, 188;
27 the men of Anathoth, 128;
28 the men of [1]Beth-azmaveth, 42;
29 the men of [1]Kiriath-jearim, Chephirah, and Beeroth,
743;
30 the men of Ramah and Geba, 621;
31 the men of Michmas, 122;
32 the men of Bethel and Ai, 123;
33 the men of the other Nebo, 52;
34 the sons of the other Elam, 1,254;
35 the sons of Harim, 320;
36 the [1]men of Jericho, 345;
37 the sons of Lod, Hadid, and Ono, 721;
38 the sons of Senaah, 3,930.
39 The priests: The sons of Jedaiah of the house of Jeshua, 973;

2 [c]Neh. 2:8 [d]Neh. 13:13

5 [1]Lit., *and I found written in it*

6 [a]Ezra 2:1-70

7 [1]In Ezra 2:2, *Seraiah* [2]In Ezra 2:2, *Reelaiah* [3]In Ezra 2:2, *Mispar* [4]In Ezra 2:2, *Rehum*

15 [1]In Ezra 2:10, *Bani*

24 [1]In Ezra 2:18, *Jorah*

25 [1]In Ezra 2:20, *Gibbar*

28 [1]In Ezra 2:24, *Azmareth*

29 [1]In Ezra 2:25, *Kiriath-arim*

36 [1]Lit., *sons*

43 [1]In Ezra 2:40, *Hodariah*
47 [1]In Ezra 2:44, *Siaha*
52 [1]In Ezra 2:50, *Nephisim*
54 [1]In Ezra 2:52, *Bazluth*
57 [1]In Ezra 2:55, *Hassophereth* [2]In Ezra 2:55, *Peruda*
59 [1]In Ezra 2:57, *Ami*
61 [1]Lit., *seed*
65 [1]Heb. *Tirshathah,* a Persian title [a]Neh. 8:9; 10:1
67 [1]Lit., *these*
68 [1]So with some ancient mss. and Gk.; Ezra 2:66

40 the sons of Immer, 1,052;
41 the sons of Pashhur, 1,247;
42 the sons of Harim, 1,017.
43 The Levites: the sons of Jeshua, of Kadmiel, of the sons
of [1]Hodevah, 74.
44 The singers: the sons of Asaph, 148.
45 The gatekeepers: the sons of Shallum, the sons of Ater,
the sons of Talmon, the sons of Akkub, the sons of Hatita, the
sons of Shobai, 138.
46 The temple servants: the sons of Ziha, the sons of Hasu-
pha, the sons of Tabbaoth,
47 the sons of Keros, the sons of [1]Sia, the sons of Padon,
48 the sons of Lebana, the sons of Hagaba, the sons of
Shalmai,
49 the sons of Hanan, the sons of Giddel, the sons of
Gahar,
50 the sons of Reaiah, the sons of Rezin, the sons of
Nekoda,
51 the sons of Gazzam, the sons of Uzza, the sons of
Paseah,
52 the sons of Besai, the sons of Meunim, the sons of
[1]Nephushesim,
53 the sons of Bakbuk, the sons of Hakupha, the sons of
Harhur,
54 the sons of [1]Bazlith, the sons of Mehida, the sons of
Harsha,
55 the sons of Barkos, the sons of Sisera, the sons of
Temah,
56 the sons of Neziah, the sons of Hatipha.
57 The sons of Solomon's servants: the sons of Sotai, the
sons of [1]Sophereth, the sons of [2]Perida,
58 the sons of Jaala, the sons of Darkon, the sons of
Giddel,
59 the sons of Shephatiah, the sons of Hattil, the sons of
Pochereth-hazzebaim, the sons of [1]Amon.
60 All the temple servants and the sons of Solomon's servants, *were* 392.
61 And these *were* they who came up from Tel-melah,
Tel-harsha, Cherub, Addon, and Immer; but they could not
show their fathers' houses or their [1]descendants, whether they
were of Israel:
62 The sons of Delaiah, the sons of Tobiah, the sons of
Nekoda, 642.
63 And of the priests: the sons of Hobaiah, the sons of
Hakkoz, the sons of Barzillai, who took a wife of the daughters
of Barzillai, the Gileadite, and was named after them.
64 These searched *among* their ancestral registration, but
it could not be located; therefore they were considered unclean *and excluded* from the priesthood.
65 And [a]the [1]governor said to them that they should not
eat from the most holy things until a priest arose with Urim
and Thummin.
66 The whole assembly together *was* 42,360,
67 besides their male and their female servants, [1]of whom
there were 7,337; and they had 245 male and female singers.
68 [1]Their horses were 736; their mules, 245;

69 *their* camels, 435; *their* donkeys, 6,720.
70 And some from among the heads of fathers' *house-*
holds gave to the work. The [1a]governor gave to the treasury
1,000 gold drachmas, 50 basins, 530 priests' garments.
71 And some of the heads of fathers' *households* gave into
the treasury of the work 20,000 gold drachmas, and 2,200 silver
minas.
72 And that which the rest of the people gave was 20,000
gold drachmas and 2,000 silver minas, and 67 priests' garments.
73 Now the priests, the Levites, the gatekeepers, the singers, some of the people, the temple servants, and all Israel,
lived in their cities.
[a]And when the seventh month came, the sons of Israel
were in their cities.

Chapter 8

AND all the people gathered as one man at the square which
was in front of [a]the Water Gate, and they [1]asked [b]Ezra the
scribe to bring [c]the book of the law of Moses which the LORD
had [2]given to Israel.
2 Then [a]Ezra the priest brought the law before the assembly of men, women, and all who *could* listen with understanding, on [b]the first day of the seventh month.
3 And he read from it before the square which was in
front of [a]the Water Gate from [1]early morning until midday, in
the presence of men and women, those who could understand;
and all the people were attentive to the book of the law.
4 And Ezra the scribe stood at a wooden podium which
they had made for the purpose. And beside him stood Mattithiah, Shema, Anaiah, Uriah, Hilkiah, and Maaseiah on his
right hand; and Pedaiah, Mishael, Malchijah, Hashum, Hash-
baddanah, Zechariah, *and* Meshullam on his left hand.
5 And Ezra opened [a]the book in the sight of all the
people for he was standing above all the people; and when he
opened it, all the people stood up.
6 Then Ezra blessed the LORD the great God. And all the
people answered, "[a]Amen, Amen!" [b]while lifting up their
hands; then [c]they bowed low and worshiped the LORD with
their faces to the ground.
7 Also Jeshua, Bani, Sherebiah, Jamin, Akkub, Shabbethai,
Hodiah, Maaseiah, Kelita, Azariah, Jozabad, Hanan, Pelaiah, and the Levites, explained the law to the people while
the people *remained* in their place.
8 And they read from the book, from the law of God,
[1]translating to give the sense so that they understood the
reading.
9 Then Nehemiah, who was the [1a]governor, and Ezra
[b]the priest *and* scribe, and the Levites who taught the people
said to all the people, "[c]This day is holy to the LORD your God;
do not [d]mourn or weep." For all the people were weeping
when they heard the words of the law.
10 Then he said to them, "Go, eat of the fat, drink of the
sweet, and [a]send portions to him who has nothing prepared;
for this day is holy to our Lord. Do not be grieved, for the joy
of the LORD is your strength."

70 [1]Heb. *Tirshathah*, a Persian title [a]Neh. 7:65; 8:9

73 [a]Ezra 3:1

1 [1]Lit., *said to* [2]Lit., *commanded* [a]Neh. 3:26 [b]Ezra 7:6 [c]2 Chr. 34:15

2 [a]Neh. 8:9; Deut. 31:9-11 [b]Lev. 23:24

3 [1]Lit., *from the light* [a]Neh. 8:1

5 [a]Neh. 8:3

6 [a]Neh. 5:13 [b]Gen. 14:22 [c]Ex. 4:31

8 [1]Or, *explaining*

9 [1]Heb., *Tirshatha*, a Persian title [a]Neh. 7:65, 70 [b]Neh. 12:26 [c]Neh. 8:2 [d]Deut. 12:7, 12

10 [a]Deut. 26:11-13

11 So the Levites calmed all the people, saying, "Be still,
for the day is holy, do not be grieved."
12 And all the people went away to eat, to drink, [a]to send
portions and to [1]celebrate a great festival, [b]because they understood the words which had been made known to them.
13 Then on the second day the heads of fathers' *house-*
holds of all the people, the priests, and the Levites were gathered to Ezra the scribe that they might gain insight into the
words of the law.
14 And they found written in the law how the LORD had
commanded through Moses that the sons of Israel [a]should live
in booths during the feast of the seventh month.
15 [1a]So they proclaimed and circulated a proclamation in
all their cities and [b]in Jerusalem, saying, "[c]Go out to the hills,
and bring olive branches, and [2]wild olive branches, myrtle
branches, palm branches, and branches of *other* leafy trees, to
make booths, as it is written."
16 So the people went out and brought *them* and made
booths for themselves, each [a]on his roof, and in their courts,
and in the courts of the house of God, and in the square at
[b]the Water Gate, and in the square at [c]the Gate of Ephraim.
17 And the entire assembly of those who had returned
from the captivity made booths and lived in [1]them. The sons
of Israel [a]had indeed not done so from the days of Joshua the
son of Nun to that day. And [b]there was great rejoicing.
18 And [a]he read from the book of the law of God daily,
from the first day to the last day. And they [b]celebrated the
feast seven days, and on [c]the eighth day *there was* a solemn
assembly according to the ordinance.

CHAPTER 9

NOW on the twenty-fourth day of [a]this month the sons of
Israel assembled [b]with fasting, in sackcloth, and with [c]dirt
upon them.
2 And the [1]descendants of Israel separated themselves
from all foreigners, and stood and confessed their sins and the
iniquities of their fathers.
3 While [a]they stood in their place, they read from the
book of the law of the LORD their God for a fourth of the day;
and for *another* fourth they confessed and worshiped the
LORD their God.
4 [a]Now on the Levites' platform stood Jeshua, Bani,
Kadmiel, Shebaniah, Bunni, Sherebiah, Bani, *and* Chenani,
and cried with a loud voice to the LORD their God.
5 Then the Levites, Jeshua, and Kadmiel, Bani, Hashabneiah, Sherebiah, Hodiah, Shebaniah, *and* Pethahiah, said,
"Arise, bless the LORD your God forever and ever!"
"O may Thy glorious name be blessed
And exalted above all blessing and praise!
6 "[a]Thou alone art the LORD.
[b]Thou hast made the heavens,
The heaven of heavens with all their host,
The earth and all that is on it,
The seas and all that is in them.
[c]Thou dost give life to all of them
And the heavenly host bows down before Thee.

12 [1]Lit., *make a great rejoicing* [a]Neh. 8:10 [b]Neh. 8:7, 8

14 [a]Lev. 23:34, 40, 42

15 [1]Lit., *and that they will cause to be heard* [2]Heb., *oil tree*, species unknown [a]Lev. 23:4 [b]Deut. 16:16 [c]Lev. 23:40

16 [a]Jer. 32:29 [b]Neh. 8:1 [c]Neh. 12:39; 2 Kin. 14:13

17 [1]Lit., *the booths* [a]2 Chr. 7:8; 8:13 [b]2 Chr. 30:21

18 [a]Deut. 31:11 [b]Lev. 23:36 [c]Num. 29:35

1 [a]Neh. 8:2 [b]Ezra 8:23 [c]1 Sam. 4:12

2 [1]Lit., *seed*

3 [a]Neh. 8:4

4 [a]Neh. 8:7

6 [a]Deut. 6:4; 2 Kin. 19:15 [b]Gen. 1:1 [c]Col. 1:17

7 "Thou art the LORD God,
[a]Who chose Abram
And brought him out from [b]Ur of the Chaldees.
And [c]gave him the name Abraham.
8 "And Thou didst find [a]his heart faithful before Thee,
And didst make a covenant with him
To give *him* the land of the Canaanite,
Of the Hittite and the Amorite,
Of the Perizzite, the Jebusite, and the Girgashite—
To give *it* to his [1]descendants.
And Thou [b]hast fulfilled Thy promise,
For Thou art righteous.

9 "[a]Thou didst see the affliction of our fathers in Egypt,
And didst [b]hear their cry by the [1]Red Sea.
10 "Then Thou didst perform signs and wonders against Pharaoh,
Against all his servants and all the people of his land;
For Thou didst know that [a]they acted arrogantly toward them,
And [b]didst make a name for Thyself as *it is* this day.
11 "And [a]Thou didst divide the sea before them,
So they passed through the midst of the sea on dry ground;
And [b]their pursuers Thou didst hurl into the depths,
Like a stone into [1]raging waters.
12 "And with a pillar of cloud [a]Thou didst lead them by day,
And with a pillar of fire by night
To light for them the way
In which they were to go.
13 "Then [a]Thou didst come down on Mount Sinai,
And didst [b]speak with them from heaven;
Thou didst give to them [c]just ordinances and true laws,
Good statutes and commandments.
14 "So Thou didst make known to them [a]Thy holy sabbath,
And didst lay down for them commandments, statutes, and law,
Through Thy servant Moses.
15 "Thou didst [a]provide bread from heaven for them for their hunger,
Thou didst [b]bring forth water from a rock for them for their thirst,
And Thou didst [c]tell them to enter in order to possess
The land which Thou didst [1]swear to give them.

16 "But they, our fathers, [a]acted arrogantly;
They [1b]became stubborn and would not listen to Thy commandments.
17 "And they refused to listen,
And [a]did not remember Thy wondrous deeds which Thou hadst performed among them;
So they became stubborn and [b]appointed a leader to return to their slavery [1]in Egypt.

7 [a]Gen. 12:1 [b]Gen. 11:31 [c]Gen. 17:5

8 [1]Lit., *seed*
[a]Gen. 15:6, 18-21 [b]Josh. 21:43-45

9 [1]Or, *Sea of Reeds*
[a]Ex. 3:7 [b]Ex. 14:10-12; 7:8-14, 31

10 [a]Ex. 5:2 [b]Ex. 9:16

11 [1]Lit., *strong, mighty*
[a]Ex. 14:21 [b]Ex. 15:1, 5, 10

12 [a]Ex. 13:21, 22

13 [a]Ex. 19:11, 18-20 [b]Ex. 20:1 [c]Ps. 19:7-9

14 [a]Ex. 16:23; 20:8

15 [1]Lit., *lift up Thy hand*
[a]Ex. 16:4, 14, 15 [b]Ex. 17:6; Num. 20:7-13 [c]Deut. 1:8

16 [1]Lit., *stiffened their neck*; so also v. 17.
[a]Neh. 9:10 [b]Neh. 9:29; Deut. 31:27

17 [1]So Gk. and some Heb. mss.; Heb. reads, *in their rebellion*
[a]Ps. 78:11, 42-55 [b]Num. 14:4

17 [c]Ex. 34:6, 7

18 [1]Lit., *acts of contempt* [a]Ex. 32:4-8, 31

19 [a]Neh. 9:27, 31 [b]Neh. 9:12

20 [a]Neh. 9:30; Num. 11:17; Is. 63:11-14

21 [a]Deut. 2:7

22 [1]Lit., *side, corner* [2]So the Gk. and the Latin. Heb. reads, *and the land of the king of Heshbon* [a]Num. 21:21-35

23 [a]Gen. 15:5

24 [1]Lit., *according to their desire* [a]Josh. 21:43 [b]Josh. 18:1

25 [1]Lit., *fat* [a]Deut. 3:5 [b]Num. 13:20 [c]Deut. 6:11 [d]Deut. 32:15 [e]1 Kin. 8:66

26 [1]Lit., *acts of contempt* [a]Judg. 2:11 [b]1 Kin. 14:9 [c]2 Chr. 36:16 [d]Neh. 9:30 [e]Neh. 9:18

27 [a]Judg. 2:14 [b]Deut. 4:29

But Thou art a God [c]of forgiveness,
Gracious and compassionate,
Slow to anger, and abounding in lovingkindness;
And Thou didst not forsake them.
18 "Even when they [a]made for themselves
A calf of molten metal
And said, 'This is your God
Who brought you up from Egypt,'
And committed great [1]blasphemies,
19 "[a]Thou, in Thy great compassion,
Didst not forsake them in the wilderness;
[b]The pillar of cloud did not leave them by day,
To guide them on their way,
Nor the pillar of fire by night, to light for them the way in which they were to go.
20 "And [a]Thou didst give Thy good Spirit to instruct them,
Thy manna Thou didst not withhold from their mouth,
And Thou didst give them water for their thirst.
21 "Indeed, [a]forty years Thou didst provide for them in the wilderness *and* they were not in want,
Their clothes did not wear out, nor did their feet swell.
22 "Thou didst also give them kingdoms and peoples,
And Thou didst allot *them* to them as a [1]boundary.
[a]And they took possession of the land of Sihon [2]the king of Heshbon,
And the land of Og the king of Bashan.
23 "And Thou didst make their sons numerous as [a]the stars of heaven,
And Thou didst bring them into the land
Which Thou hadst told their fathers to enter and possess.
24 "[a]So their sons entered and possessed the land.
And [b]Thou didst subdue before them the inhabitants of the land, the Canaanites,
And Thou didst give them into their hand, with their kings, and the peoples of the land,
To do with them [1]as they desire.
25 "And [a]they captured fortified cities and a [1b]fertile land.
They took possession of [c]houses full of every good thing,
Hewn cisterns, vineyards, olive groves,
Fruit trees in abundance.
So they ate, were filled, and [d]grew fat,
And [e]reveled in Thy great goodness.

26 "[a]But they became disobedient and rebelled against Thee,
And [b]cast Thy law behind their backs
And [c]killed Thy prophets who had [d]admonished them
So that they might return to Thee,
And [e]they committed great [1]blasphemies.
27 "Therefore Thou didst [a]deliver them into the hand of their oppressors who oppressed them,
But when they cried to Thee [b]in the time of their distress,

Thou didst hear from heaven, and according to Thy
great compassion
Thou didst [c]give them deliverers who delivered them
from the hand of their oppressors.
28 "But [a]as soon as they had rest, they did evil again before
Thee;
Therefore Thou didst abandon them to the hand of
their enemies, so that they ruled over them.
When they cried again to Thee, Thou didst hear from
heaven,
And [b]many times Thou didst rescue them according to
Thy compassion,
29 "And [a]admonished them in order to turn them back to
Thy law.
Yet [b]they acted arrogantly and did not listen to Thy
commandments but sinned against Thy
ordinances,
By [c]which if a man observes them he shall live.
And they [1d]turned a stubborn shoulder and stiffened
their neck, and would not listen.
30 "[a]However, Thou didst bear with them for many years,
And [b]admonished them by [c]Thy Spirit through Thy
prophets,
Yet they would not give ear.
Therefore Thou didst give them into the hand of the
peoples of the lands.
31 "Nevertheless in Thy great compassion Thou [a]didst not
make an end of them or forsake them,
For Thou art [b]a gracious and compassionate God.

32 "Now therefore, our God, [a]the great, the mighty, and
the awesome God, who dost keep covenant and
lovingkindness,
Do not let all the hardship seem insignificant before
Thee,
Which has come upon us, our kings, our princes, our
priests, our prophets, our fathers, and on all Thy
people,
[b]From the days of the kings of Assyria to this day.
33 "However, [a]Thou art just in all that hast come upon us;
For Thou hast dealt faithfully, but we have acted
wickedly.
34 "For our kings, our leaders, our priests, and our fathers
have not kept Thy law
Or paid attention to Thy commandments and Thy
[1]admonitions with which Thou hast [2]admonished
them.
35 "But [a]they, in their own kingdom,
[b]With Thy great goodness which Thou didst give
them,
With the broad and rich land which Thou didst set
before them,
Did not serve Thee or turn from their evil deeds.
36 "Behold [a]we are slaves today,

27 [c]Judg. 2:16

28 [a]Judg. 3:11 [b]Ps. 106:43

29 [1]Lit., *gave* [a]Neh. 9:26, 30 [b]Neh. 9:10, 16 [c]Lev. 18:5 [d]Zech. 7:11

30 [a]Ps. 95:10; Acts 13:18 [b]Neh. 9:26, 29 [c]Neh. 9:20

31 [a]Jer. 4:27 [b]Neh. 9:17

32 [a]Neh. 1:5 [b]2 Kin. 15:19

33 [a]Gen. 18:25; Jer. 12:1

34 [1]Lit., *testimonies* [2]Or, *witnessed*

35 [a]Deut. 28:47 [b]Neh. 9:25

36 [a]Deut. 28:48

37 [a]Deut. 28:33

And as to the land which Thou didst give to our fathers
to eat of its fruit and its bounty,
Behold, we are slaves on it.
37 "And [a]its abundant produce is for the kings
Whom Thou hast set over us because of our sins;
They also rule over our bodies
And over our cattle as they please,
So we are in great distress.
38 "[1]Now because of all this
[a]We are making an agreement in writing;
And on the [b]sealed document *are the names of* our
leaders, our Levites *and* our priests."

38 [1]Ch. 10:1 in Heb. [a]Neh. 10:29 [b]Neh. 10:1

Chapter 10

1 NOW on the [a]sealed document *were the names of:* Nehemiah the [2]governor, the son of Hacaliah, and Zedekiah,
2 Seraiah, Azariah, Jeremiah,
3 Pashhur, Amariah, Malchijah,
4 Hattush, Shebaniah, Malluch,
5 Harim, Meremoth, Obadiah,
6 Daniel, Ginnethon, Baruch,
7 Meshullam, Abijah, Mijamin,
8 Maaziah, Bilgai, Shemaiah. These *were* the priests.
9 And the Levites: Jeshua the son of Azaniah, Binnui of
the sons of Henadad, Kadmiel;
10 also their brothers Shebaniah, Hodiah, Kelita, Pelaiah,
Hanan,
11 Mica, Rehob, Hashabiah,
12 Zaccur, Sherebiah, Shebaniah,
13 Hodiah, Bani, Beninu.
14 The leaders of the people: Parosh, Pahath-moab,
Elam, Zattu, Bani,
15 Bunni, Azgad, Bebai,
16 Adonijah, Bigvai, Adin,
17 Ater, Hezekiah, Azzur,
18 Hodiah, Hashum, Bezai,
19 Hariph, Anathoth, Nebai,
20 Magpiash, Meshullam, Hezir,
21 Meshezabel, Zadok, Jaddua,
22 Pelatiah, Hanan, Anaiah,
23 Hoshea, Hananiah, Hasshub,
24 Hallohesh, Pilha, Shobek,
25 Rehum, Hashabnah, Maaseiah,
26 Ahiah, Hanan, Anan,
27 Malluch, Harim, Baanah.
28 Now [a]the rest of the people, the priests, the Levites, the
gatekeepers, the singers, the temple servants, and [b]all those
who had separated themselves from the peoples of the lands to
the law of God, their wives, their sons and their daughters, all
those who had knowledge and understanding,
29 are joining with their [1]kinsmen, their nobles, and are
[2a]taking on themselves a curse and an oath to walk in God's
law, which was given through Moses, God's servant, and to
keep and to observe all the commandments of [3]GOD our Lord,
and His ordinances and His statutes;

1 [1]Ch. 10:2 in Heb. [2]Heb., *Tirshatha,* a Persian title [a]Neh. 9:38

28 [a]Ezra 2:36-58 [b]Neh. 9:2

29 [1]Lit., *brothers* [2]Lit., *entering into a* [3]YHWH, usually renderd LORD [a]Neh. 5:12

30 and [a]that we will not give our daughters to the peoples
of the land or take their daughters for our sons.
31 As [a]for the peoples of the land who bring wares or any
grain on the sabbath day to sell, we will not buy from them on
the sabbath or a holy day; and we will forego *the crops* the
[b]seventh year and the [c]exaction of every debt.
32 We also [1]placed ourselves under obligation to contrib-
ute yearly [a]one third of a shekel for the service of the house
of our God:
33 for the showbread, for the continual grain offering, for
the continual burnt offering, the sabbaths, the new moon, for
the appointed times, for the holy things and for the sin offerings to make atonement for Israel, and all the work of the
house of our God.
34 Likewise [a]we cast lots [b]for the supply of wood *among*
the priests, the Levites, and the people in order that they
might bring it to the house of our God, according to our
fathers' households, at fixed times annually, to burn on the
altar of the LORD our God as it is written in the law;
35 and in order that they might bring the first fruits of our
ground and [a]the first fruits of all the fruit of every tree to the
house of the LORD annually,
36 and bring to the house of our God the first-born of our
sons and of our cattle, and the first-born of our herds and our
flocks [a]as it is written in the law, for the priests who are ministering in the house of our God.
37 [a]We will also bring the first of our [1]dough, our contributions, the fruit of every tree, the new wine and the oil [b]to the
priests at the chambers of the house of our God, and the [c]tithe
of our ground to the Levites for the Levites are they who
receive the tithes in all the rural towns.
38 And [a]the priest the son of Aaron shall be with the
Levites when the Levites receive tithes, and the Levites shall
bring up the tenth of the tithes to the house of our God, to the
chambers of [b]the storehouse.
39 For the sons of Israel and the sons of Levi shall bring
the [a]contribution of the grain, the new wine and the oil, to the
chambers; there are the utensils of the sanctuary, the priests
who are ministering, the gatekeepers, and the singers. Thus
[b]we will not [1]neglect the house of our God.

CHAPTER 11

NOW [a]the leaders of the people lived in Jerusalem, but the
rest of the people [b]cast lots to bring one out of ten to live in
Jerusalem, [c]the holy city, while nine-tenths *remained* in the
other cities.
2 And the people blessed all the men who volunteered to
live in Jerusalem.
3 [a]Now these are the heads of the provinces who lived in
Jerusalem, but in the cities of Judah [b]each lived on his own
property in their cities—the [1]Israelites, the priests, the Levites,
the [2c]temple servants and the [3d]descendants of Solomon's
servants.
4 And some of the sons of Judah and some of the sons of
Benjamin lived in Jerusalem. From the sons of Judah: Athaiah
the son of Uzziah, the son of Zechariah, the son of Amariah,

30 [a]Ex. 34:16; Deut. 7:3

31 [a]Neh. 13:15-22 [b]Ex. 23:10, 11 [c]Deut. 15:1, 2

32 [1]Lit., *imposed commandments on us* [a]Ex. 30:11-16; Matt. 17:24

34 [a]Neh. 11:1 [b]Neh. 13:31

35 [a]Ex. 23:19

36 [a]Ex. 13:2

37 [1]Or, *coarse meal* [a]Lev. 23:17 [b]Neh. 13:5, 9 [c]Lev. 27:30

38 [a]Num. 18:26 [b]Neh. 13:12, 13

39 [1]Lit., *forsake* [a]Deut. 12:6 [b]Neh. 13:10, 11

1 [a]Neh. 7:4 [b]Neh. 10:34 [c]Neh. 11:18; Is. 48:2

3 [1]Lit., *Israel* [2]Heb., *Nethinim* [3]Lit., *sons* [a]1 Chr. 9:2-34 [b]Neh. 11:20 [c]Ezra 2:43 [d]Neh. 7:57

the son of Shephatiah, the son of Mahalalel, of the sons of
Perez;
5 and Maaseiah the son of Baruch, the son of Col-hozeh,
the son of Hazaiah, the son of Adaiah, the son of Joiarib, the
son of Zechariah, the son of the Shilonite.
6 All the sons of Perez who lived in Jerusalem were 468
able men.
7 Now these are the sons of Benjamin: Sallu the son of
Meshullam, the son of Joed, the son of Pedaiah, the son of
Kolaiah, the son of Maaseiah, the son of Ithiel, the son of
Jeshaiah;
8 and after him Gabbai *and* Sallai, 928.
9 And Joel the son of Zichri was their overseer, and Judah the son of Hassenuah was second [1]in command of the city.
10 From the priests: Jedaiah the son of Joiarib, Jachin,
11 Seraiah the son of Hilkiah, the son of Meshullam, the
son of Zadok, the son of Meraieth, the son of Ahitub, the
leader of the house of God,
12 and their [1]kinsmen who performed the work of the
[2]temple, 822; and Adaiah the son of Jeroham, the son of Pela-
liah, the son of Amzi, the son of Zechariah, the son of Pashhur, the son of Malchijah,
13 and his kinsmen, heads of fathers' *households,* 242; and
Amashsai the son of Azarel, the son of Ahzai, the son of Meshillemoth, the son of Immer,
14 and their brothers, valiant warriors, 128. And their overseer was Zabdiel, the son of [1]Haggedolim.
15 Now from the Levites: Shemaiah the son of Hasshub,
the son of Azrikam, the son of Hashabiah, the son of Bunni;
16 and Shabbethai and Jozabad, from the [1]leaders of the
Levites, who [2]were in charge of [a]the outside work of the house
of God;
17 and Mattaniah the son of Mica, the son of [1]Zabdi, the
son of Asaph, who was the [2]leader in beginning the thanksgiving at prayer, and Bakbukiah, the second among his brethren;
and [3]Abda the son of [4]Shammua, the son of Galal, the son of
Jeduthun.
18 All the Levites in [a]the holy city *were* 284.
19 Also the gatekeepers, Akkub, Talmon, and their brethren, who kept watch at the gates, *were* 172.
20 And the rest of Israel, of the priests, *and* of the Levites,
were in all the cities of Judah, each [a]on his own inheritance.
21 But [a]the temple servants were living in Ophel, and Ziha
and Gishpa were [1]in charge of the temple servants.
22 Now [a]the overseer of the Levites in Jerusalem was Uzzi
the son of Bani, the son of Hashabiah, the son of Mattaniah,
the son of Mica, from the sons of Asaph, who were the singers
for the [1]service of the house of God.
23 [a]For *there was* a commandment from the king concerning them and a firm regulation for the song leaders [b]day by
day.
24 And Pethahiah the son of Meshezabel, of the sons of
Zerah the son of Judah, was the king's [1]representative in all
matters concerning the people.
25 Now as for the villages with their fields, some of the

9 [1]Lit., *over*
12 [1]Lit., *brothers,* and so through the chap. [2]Lit., *house*
14 [1]Or, *the great ones*
16 [1]Lit., *heads* [2]Lit., *over* [a]1 Chr. 26:29
17 [1]In 1 Chr. 9:15, *Zichri* [2]Lit., *head* [3]In 1 Chr. 9:16, *Obadiah* [4]In 1 Chr. 9:16, *Shemaiah*
18 [a]Neh. 11:1
20 [a]Neh. 11:3
21 [1]Lit., *over* [a]Neh. 3:26; 2 Chr. 27:3
22 [1]Or, *work* [a]Neh. 11:9, 14
23 [a]Ezra 6:8; 7:20 [b]Neh. 12:47
24 [1]Lit., *hand*

sons of Judah lived in [a]Kiriath-arba and its [1]towns, in [b]Dibon
and its [1]towns, and in Jekabzeel and its villages,
26 and in Jeshua, in Moladah and Beth-pelet,
27 and in Hazar-shual, in Beersheba and its towns
28 and in Ziklag, in Meconah and in its towns
29 and in En-rimmon, in Zorah and in Jarmuth,
30 Zanoah, Adullam, and their villages, Lachish and its
fields, Azekah and its towns. So they encamped from Beersheba as far as the valley of Hinnom.
31 The sons of Benjamin also *lived* from Geba *onward*, at
Michmash and Aija, at Bethel and its towns,
32 at Anathoth, Nob, Ananiah,
33 Hazor, Ramah, Gittaim,
34 Hadid, Zeboim, Neballat,
35 Lod and Ono, the valley of craftsmen.
36 And from the Levites, *some* divisions in Judah belonged to Benjamin.

Chapter 12

NOW these are [a]the priests and the Levites who came up
with Zerubbabel the son of Shealtiel, and Jeshua: Seraiah,
Jeremiah, Ezra,
2 Amariah, Malluch, Hattush,
3 Shecaniah, Rehum, Meremoth,
4 Iddo, Ginnethoi, Abijah,
5 Mijamin, Maadiah, Bilgah,
6 Shemaiah and Joiarib, Jedaiah,
7 Sallu, Amok, Hilkiah, and Jedaiah. These were the
heads of the priests and their [1]kinsmen in the days of Jeshua.
8 And the Levites *were* Jeshua, Binnui, Kadmiel, Sherebiah, Judah, *and* Mattaniah *who was* [1]in charge of the songs of
thanksgiving, he and his brothers.
9 Also Bakbukiah and Unni, their brothers, stood opposite them [a]in *their* service divisions.
10 And Jeshua [1]became the father of Joiakim, and Joiakim
[1]became the father of Eliashib, and Eliashib [1]became the
father of Joiada,
11 and Joiada became the father of Jonathan, and Jonathan
became the father of Jaddua.
12 Now in the days of Joiakim the priests, the heads of
fathers' *households* were: of Seraiah, Meraiah; of Jeremiah,
Hananiah;
13 of Ezra, Meshullam; of Amariah, Jehohanan;
14 of [1]Malluchi, Jonathan; of Shebaniah, Joseph;
15 of Harim, Adna; of Meraioth, Helkai;
16 of Iddo, Zechariah; of Ginnethon, Meshullam;
17 of Abijah, Zichri; of Miniamin, of Moadiah, Piltai;
18 of Bilgah, Shammua; of Shemaiah, Jehonathan;
19 of Joiarib, Mattenai; of Jedaiah, Uzzi;
20 of Sallai, Kallai; of Amok, Eber;
21 of Hilkiah, Hashabiah; of Jedaiah, Nethanel.
22 As for the Levites, the heads of fathers' *households*
were registered in the days of Eliashib, Joiada, and Johanan,
and Jaddua; so *were* the priests in the reign of Darius the
Persian.

25 [1]Lit., *daughters*, and so throughout the chap. [a]Josh. 14:15 [b]Josh. 13:9, 17

1 [a]Ezra 2:1; 7:7

7 [1]Lit., *brothers*

8 [1]Lit., *over*

9 [a]Neh. 12:24

10 [1]Lit., *begot* and so in v. 11, 12

14 [1]In Neh. 12:2, *Malluch*

23 The sons of Levi, the heads of fathers' *households*, were registered in the Book of the Chronicles up to the days of Johanan the son of Eliashib.

24 And the heads of the Levites *were* Hashabiah, Sherebiah, and Jeshua the son of Kadmiel, with their brothers opposite them, [a]to praise *and* give thanks, [1]as prescribed by David the man of God, [b]division corresponding to division.

25 Mattaniah, and Bakbukiah, Obadiah, Meshullam, Talmon, *and* Akkub were gatekeepers keeping watch at [a]the storehouses of the gates.

26 These *served* in the days of Joiakim the son of Jeshua, the son of Jozadak, and in the days of [a]Nehemiah the governor and of Ezra the priest *and* scribe.

27 Now at the dedication of the wall of Jerusalem they sought out the Levites from all their places, to bring them to Jerusalem so that they might celebrate the dedication with gladness, with hymns of thanksgiving and with songs [a]*to the accompaniment* of cymbals, harps, and lyres.

28 So the sons of the singers were assembled from the district around Jerusalem, and from [a]the villages of the Nethophathites,

29 from Beth-gilgal, and from *their* fields in Geba and Azmaveth, for the singers had built themselves villages around Jerusalem.

30 And the priests and the Levites [a]purified themselves; they also purified the people, the gates, and the wall.

31 Then I had the leaders of Judah come up on top of the wall, and I appointed two great [1]choirs, [2a]the first proceeding to the right on top of the wall toward [b]the Refuse Gate.

32 Hoshaiah and half of the leaders of Judah followed them,

33 with Azariah, Ezra, Meshullam,

34 Judah, Benjamin, Shemaiah, Jeremiah,

35 and some of the sons of the priests with trumpets; *and* Zechariah the son of Jonathan, the son of Shemaiah, the son of Mattaniah, the son of Micaiah, the son of Zaccur, the son of Asaph,

36 and his [1]kinsmen, Shemaiah, Azarel, Milalai, Gilalai, Maai, Nethanel, Judah *and* Hanani, [a]with the musical instruments of David the man of God. And Ezra the scribe went before them.

37 And at [a]the Fountain Gate they went directly up [b]the steps of the city of David by the stairway of the wall above the house of David to [c]the Water Gate on the east.

38 [a]The second [1]choir proceeded to the [2]left, while I followed them with half of the people on the wall, [b]above the Towers of the Furnaces, to [c]the broad wall,

39 and above [a]the Gate of Ephraim, by [b]the Old Gate, by the [c]Fish Gate, [d]the Tower of Hananel, and the Tower of the Hundred, as far as the Sheep Gate, and they stopped at [e]the Gate of the Guard.

40 Then the two choirs took their stand in the house of God. So did I and half of the officials with me;

41 and the priests, Eliakim, Maaseiah, Miniamin, Micaiah, Elioenai, Zechariah, and Hananiah, with the trumpets;

42 and Maaseiah, Shemaiah, Eleazar, Uzzi, Jehohanan,

24 [1]Lit., *in the commandment of* [a]Neh. 11:17 [b]Neh. 12:9

25 [a]1 Chr. 26:15

26 [a]Neh. 8:9

27 [a]1 Chr. 15:16, 28

28 [a]1 Chr. 9:16

30 [a]Neh. 13:22, 30

31 [1]Lit., *thanksgiving choirs* [2]Heb. reads *and processions to the right* . . . cf. v. 38 [a]Neh. 12:38 [b]Neh. 2:13

36 [1]Lit., *brothers* [a]Neh. 12:24

37 [a]Neh. 2:14 [b]Neh. 3:15 [c]Neh. 3:26

38 [1]Lit., *thanksgiving choir* [2]Lit., *front* [a]Neh. 12:31 [b]Neh. 3:11 [c]Neh. 3:8

39 [a]Neh. 8:16 [b]Neh. 3:6 [c]Neh. 3:3 [d]Neh. 3:1 [e]Neh. 3:25

Malchijah, Elam, and Ezer. And the singers [1]sang, with Jezra-
hiah *their* leader,
43 and on that day they offered great sacrifices and rejoiced because God had given them great joy, even the women
and children rejoiced, so that the joy of Jerusalem was heard
from afar.
44 On that day [a]men were also appointed over the chambers for the stores, the contributions, the first fruits, and the
tithes, to gather into them from the fields of the cities the
portions required by the law for the priests and Levites; for
Judah rejoiced over the priests and Levites who [1]served.
45 For they performed the [1]worship of their God and the
service of purification, together with the singers and the gatekeepers [a]in accordance with the command of David *and* of his
son Solomon.
46 For in the days of David and [a]Asaph, in ancient times,
there were [1]leaders of the singers, songs of praise and hymns of
thanksgiving to God.
47 And so all Israel in the days of Zerubbabel and Nehemiah gave the portions due the singers and the gatekeepers [a]as
each day required, and [b]set apart the consecrated *portion* for
the Levites, and the Levites set apart the consecrated *portion*
for the sons of Aaron.

Chapter 13

ON that day [a]they read aloud from the book of Moses in the
hearing of people; and there was found written in it that [b]no
Ammonite or Moabite should ever enter the assembly of God,
2 because they did not meet the sons of Israel with bread
and water, but [a]hired Balaam against them to curse them.
However, our God turned the curse into a blessing.
3 So it came about, that when they heard the law, [a]they
excluded all foreigners from Israel.
4 Now prior to this, Eliashib the priest, [a]who was appointed over the chambers of the house of our God, being
[1]related to [b]Tobiah,
5 had prepared a large [1]room for him, where formerly
they put the grain offerings, the frankincense, the utensils, and
the tithes of grain, wine and oil [a]prescribed for the Levites, the
singers and the gatekeepers, and the [2]contributions for the
priests.
6 But during all this *time* I was not in Jerusalem, for in
[a]the thirty-second year of [b]Artaxerxes king of Babylon I had
gone to the king. After some time, however, I asked leave from
the king,
7 and I came to Jerusalem and [1]learned about the evil
that Eliashib had done for Tobiah, [a]by preparing a [2]room for
him in the courts of the house of God.
8 And it was very displeasing to me, so I threw all of
Tobiah's household goods out of the room.
9 Then I gave an order and [a]they cleansed the rooms;
and I returned there the utensils of the house of God with the
grain offerings and the frankincense.
10 I also [1]discovered that [a]the portions of the Levites had

42 [1]Lit., *caused their voices to be heard*

44 [1]Lit., *stood* cf. 2 Chr. 29:11
[a]Neh. 13:5, 12, 13

45 [1]Lit., *service*
[a]1 Chr. 25:1; 26:1

46 [1]Lit., *heads,* cf. 1 Chr. 9:33
[a]2 Chr. 29:30

47 [a]Neh. 11:23 [b]Num. 18:21

1 [a]Neh. 9:3 [b]Neh. 13:23; Deut. 23:3-5

2 [a]Num. 22:3-11

3 [a]Neh. 9:2

4 [1]Lit., *close to*
[a]Ex. 12:38 [b]Neh. 12:44

5 [1]Or, *chamber* [2]Lit., *heave offerings*
[a]Neh. 2:10; 6:1, 17, 18

6 [a]Neh. 5:14 [b]Ezra 6:22

7 [1]Or, *understood* [2]Or, *chamber,* and so in v. 8, 9
[a]Neh. 13:5

9 [a]2 Chr. 29:5, 15, 16

10 [1]Or, *knew*
[a]Neh. 10:37

not been given *them,* so that the Levites and the singers who
performed the service had [2]gone away, [b]each to his own field.
11 So I [1a]reprimanded the officials and said, "[b]Why is the
house of God forsaken?" Then I gathered them together and
restored them to their posts.
12 All Judah then brought [a]the tithe of the grain, wine,
and oil into the storehouses.
13 And in charge of the storehouses I appointed Shelemiah the priest, Zadok the scribe, and Pedaiah of the Levites,
and in addition to them was Hanan the son of Zaccur, the son
of Mattaniah; for [a]they were considered reliable, and it was
[1]their task to distribute to their [2]kinsmen.
14 [a]Remember me for this, O my God, and do not blot
out my loyal deeds which I have performed for the house of
my God and its services.
15 In those days I saw in Judah some who were treading
wine presses [a]on the sabbath, and bringing in sacks of grain and
loading *them* on donkeys, as well as wine, grapes, figs, and all
kinds of loads, [b]and they brought *them* into Jerusalem on the
sabbath day. So [c]I admonished *them* on the day they sold
food.
16 Also men of Tyre were living [1]there *who* imported fish
and all kinds of merchandise, and sold *them* to the sons of
Judah on the sabbath, even in Jerusalem.
17 Then [a]I [1]reprimanded the nobles of Judah and said to
them, "What is this evil thing you are doing, [2]by profaning the
sabbath day?
18 "[a]Did not your fathers do the same so that our God
brought on us, and on this city, all this trouble? Yet you are
adding to the wrath on Israel by profaning the sabbath."
19 [a]And it came about that just as it grew dark at the gates
of Jerusalem before the sabbath, I commanded that the doors
should be shut [1]and that they should not open them until after
the sabbath. Then I stationed some of my servants at the gates
that no load should enter on the sabbath day.
20 Once or twice the traders and merchants of every kind
of merchandise spent the night outside Jerusalem.
21 Then [a]I [1]warned them and said to them, "Why do you
spend the night in front of the wall? If you do so again, I will
[2]use force against you." From that time on they did not come
on the sabbath.
22 And I commanded the Levites that [a]they should purify
themselves and come as gatekeepers to sanctify the sabbath
day. *For* this also [b]remember me, O my God, and have compassion on me according to the greatness of Thy
lovingkindness.
23 In those days I also saw that the Jews had [1a]married
women from [b]Ashdod, [c]Ammon, *and* Moab.
24 As for their children, half spoke in the language of
Ashdod, and none of them was able to speak the language of
Judah, but [1]the language of his own people.
25 So [a]I contended with them and cursed them and
[b]struck some of them and pulled out their hair, and [c]made
them swear by God, "You shall not give your daughters to
their sons, nor take of their daughters for your sons or for
yourselves.

10 [2]Lit., *fled* [b]Neh. 12:28, 29

11 [1]Or, *contended with* [a]Neh. 13:17, 25 [b]Neh. 10:39

12 [a]Neh. 10:37; 12:44

13 [1]Lit., *on them to* [2]Lit., *brothers* [a]Neh. 7:2

14 [a]Neh. 13:22, 31; Neh. 5:19

15 [a]Ex. 20:8; 34:21 [b]Neh. 10:31 [c]Neh. 13:21; 9:29

16 [1]Lit., *in it*

17 [1]Or, *contended with* [2]Lit., *and* [a]Neh. 13:11, 25

18 [a]Ezra 9:13; Jer. 17:21

19 [1]Lit., *and commanded* [a]Lev. 23:32

21 [1]Lit., *witnessed against* [2]Lit., *send a hand against* [a]Neh. 13:15

22 [a]Neh. 12:30; 1 Chr. 15:12 [b]Neh. 13:14, 31

23 [1]Lit., *given dwelling to* [a]Neh. 10:30; Ezra 9:2 [b]Neh. 4:7 [c]Neh. 13:1; Ezra 9:1

24 [1]Lit., *according to the tongue of people and people*

25 [a]Neh. 13:11, 17 [b]Deut. 25:2 [c]Neh. 10:29, 30

26 "[a]Did not Solomon king of Israel sin regarding these
things? [b]Yet among the many nations there was no king like
him, and he was loved by his God, and God made him king
over all Israel; nevertheless the foreign woman caused even
him to sin.
27 "[1]Do we then hear about you that you have committed
all this great evil [a]by acting unfaithfully against our God by
[2]marrying foreign women?"
28 Even one of the sons of Joiada, the son Eliashib the
high priest, was a son-in-law of [a]Sanballat the Horonite, so I
drove him away from me.
29 [a]Remember them, O my God, [1]because they have defiled the priesthood and the [b]covenant of the priesthood and
the Levites.
30 [a]Thus I purified them from everything foreign and appointed duties for the priests and the Levites, each in his task,
31 and *I arranged* [a]for the supply of wood at appointed
times and for the first fruits. [b]Remember me, O my God, for
good.

26 [a]1 Kin. 11:1 [b]1 Kin. 3:13; 2 Chr. 1:12

27 [1]Or, *Is it reported* [2]Lit., *giving dwelling to* [a]Neh. 13:23; Ezra 10:2

28 [a]Neh. 2:10, 19

29 [1]Lit., *for the defilings of* [a]Neh. 6:14 [b]Num. 25:13

30 [a]Neh. 10:30

31 [a]Neh. 10:34 [b]Neh. 13:14, 22

THE BOOK OF ESTHER

The Banquets of Ahasuerus.

NOW it took place in the days of [a]Ahasuerus, the Ahasuerus
who reigned [b]from India to [1]Ethiopia over [c]127 provinces,
2 in those days as King Ahasuerus sat on his royal throne
which *was* in [a]Susa the capital,
3 in the third year of his reign, [a]he gave a banquet for all
his princes and attendants, the army *officers* of Persia and
Media, the nobles, and the princes of his provinces being in his
presence,
4 when he displayed the riches of his royal glory and the
splendor of his great majesty for many days, 180 days.
5 And when these days were completed, the king gave a
banquet lasting seven days for all the people who were present
in Susa the capital, from the greatest to the least, in the court
of [a]the garden of the king's palace.
6 *There were hangings of* fine white and violet linen held
by cords of fine purple linen on silver rings and marble columns, [a]*and* couches of gold and silver on a mosaic pavement
of prophyry, marble, mother-of-pearl, and precious stones.
7 Drinks were served in golden vessels of various kinds,
and the royal wine was plentiful [a]according to the king's
[1]bounty.
8 And the drinking was *done* according to the law, there
was no compulsion, for so the king had given orders to each
official of his household that he should do according to the
desires of each person.

1 [1]Lit., *Cush* [a]Ezra 4:6; Dan. 9:1 [b]Esth. 8:9 [c]Esth. 9:30

2 [a]Neh. 1:1

3 [a]Esth. 2:8

5 [a]Esth. 7:7-8

6 [a]Ezek. 23:41; Amos 6:4

7 [1]Lit., *hand* [a]Esth. 2:18

9 Queen Vashti also gave a banquet for the women in
the [1]palace which belonged to King Ahasuerus.
10 On the seventh day, when the heart of the king was
[a]merry with wine, he commanded Mehuman, Biztha, Har-
bona, Bigtha, Abagtha, Zethar, and Carkas, the seven eunuchs
who served in the presence of King Ahasuerus,
11 to bring Queen Vashti before the king with *her* royal
[a]crown in order to display her beauty to the people and the
princes, for she was beautiful.
12 But Queen Vashti refused to come at the king's command delivered by the eunuchs. Then the king became very
angry and his wrath burned within him.
13 Then the king said to [a]the wise men [b]who understood
the times—for it was the custom of the king so *to speak* before
all who knew law and justice,
14 and were close to him: Carshena, Shethar, Admatha,
Tarshish, Meres, Marsena, and Memucan, the seven princes of
Persia and Media [a]who [1]had access to the king's presence and
sat in the first place in the kingdom—
15 "According to law, what is to be done with Queen Vashti, because she did not [1]obey the command of King Ahasuerus *delivered* by the eunuchs?"
16 And in the presence of the king and the princes Memucan said, "Queen Vashti has wronged not only the king but
also all the princes and all the peoples who are in all the
provinces of King Ahasuerus.
17 "For the queen's conduct will [1]become known to all the
women causing them [2]to look with contempt on their husbands by saying, 'King Ahasuerus commanded Queen Vashti
to be brought in to his presence, but she did not come.'
18 "And this day the ladies of Persia and Media who have
heard of the queen's conduct will speak in *the same way* to all
the king's princes, and there will be plenty of contempt and
anger.
19 "If it pleases the king, let a royal [1]edict be issued by him
and let it be written in the laws of Persia and Media so [a]that it
cannot [2]be repealed, that Vashti should come no more into
the presence of King Ahasuerus, and let the king give her royal
position to [3]another who is more worthy than she.
20 "And when the king's edict which he shall make is heard
throughout all his kingdom, [1]great as it is, then [a]all women will
give honor to their husbands, great and small."
21 And *this* word pleased the king and the princes, and the
king did [1]as Memucan proposed.
22 So he sent letters to all the king's provinces, [a]to each
province according to its script and to every people according
to their language, that every man should be the master in his
own house and the one who speaks in the language of his own
people.

CHAPTER 2

AFTER these things [a]when the anger of King Ahasuerus had
subsided, he remembered Vashti and what she had done and
[b]what had been decreed against her.

9 [1]Lit., *royal house*

10 [a]Judg. 16:25

11 [a]Esth. 2:17; 6:8

13 [a]Jer. 10:7; Dan. 2:2 [b]1 Chr. 12:32

14 [1]Lit., *saw the face of the king* [a]2 Kin. 25:19; Matt. 18:10

15 [1]Lit., *do*

17 [1]Lit., *go forth* [2]Lit., *to despise . . . in their eyes*

19 [1]Lit., *word go forth from* [2]Lit., *pass away* [3]Lit., *her neighbor* [a]Esth. 8:8; Dan. 6:8

20 [1]Lit., *for great is it* [a]Eph. 5:22; Col. 3:18

21 [1]Lit., *according to the word of*

22 [a]Esth. 3:12; 8:9

1 [a]Esth. 7:10 [b]Esth. 1:19, 20

**A Replacement for Vashti Is Sought.
Esther Finds Favor.**

2 Then the king's attendants, who served him, said, "Let
beautiful young virgins be sought for the king.
3 "And let the king appoint overseers in [a]all the provinces
of his kingdom that they may gather every beautiful young
virgin to Susa the capital, to the harem, into the custody of
[b]Hegai, the king's eunuch, who was in charge of the women;
and [c]let their cosmetics be given *them.*
4 "Then let the young lady who pleases the king be queen
in place of Vashti." And the matter pleased the king, and he
did accordingly.
5 *Now* there was a Jew in Susa the capital whose name
was [a]Mordecai, the son of Jair, the son of Shimei, the son of
Kish, a Benjaminite,
6 [a]who had been taken into exile from Jerusalem with
the captives who had been exiled with Jeconiah king of Judah,
whom Nebuchadnezzar the king of Babylon had exiled.
7 And he was bringing up Hadassah, that is [a]Esther, his
uncle's daughter, for she had neither father nor mother. Now
the young lady was beautiful of form and [1]face, and when her
father and her mother died, Mordecai took her as his own
daughter.
8 So it came about when the command and decree of the
king were heard and [a]many young ladies were gathered to Susa
the capital into the custody of [b]Hegai, that Esther was taken to
the king's [1]palace into the custody of Hegai, who was in charge
of the women.
9 Now the young lady pleased him and found favor with
him. So he quickly provided her with her [a]cosmetics and [1]food,
gave her seven choice maids from the king's palace, and transferred her and her maids to the best place in the harem.
10 [a]Esther did not make known her people or her kindred,
for Mordecai had instructed her that she should not make
them known.
11 And every day Mordecai walked back and forth in front
of the court of the harem to learn how Esther was and how she
fared.
12 Now when the turn of each young lady came to go in
to King Ahasuerus, after the end of her twelve months under
the regulations for the women—for the days of their beautifi-
cation were completed as follows: six months with oil of myrrh
and six months with spices and the cosmetics for women—
13 the young lady would go in to the king in this way:
anything that she [1]desired was given her to take with her from
the harem to the king's palace.
14 In the evening she would go in and in the morning she
would return to the second harem, to the [1]custody of Shaash-
gaz, the king's eunuch who was in charge of the concubines.
She would not again go in to the king unless the king delighted
in her and she was summoned by name.
15 Now when the turn of Esther, [a]the daughter of Abihail
the uncle of Mordecai who had taken her as his daughter,
came to go in to the king, she did not request anything except
what [b]Hegai, the king's eunuch who was in charge of the wom-
en, [1]advised. And Esther found favor in the eyes of all who
saw her.
16 So Esther was taken to King Ahasuerus to his royal

3 [a]Esth. 1:1, 2 [b]Esth. 2:8, 15 [c]Esth. 2:9, 12
5 [a]Esth. 3:2
6 [a]2 Kin. 24:14, 15
7 [1]Lit., *good of appearance* [a]Esth. 2:15
8 [1]Lit., *house* [a]Esth. 2:3 [b]Esth. 2:3, 15
9 [1]Lit., *portions* [a]Esth. 2:3, 12
10 [a]Esth. 2:20
13 [1]Lit., *said*
14 [1]Lit., *hand*
15 [1]Lit., *said* [a]Esth. 2:7; 9:29 [b]Esth. 2:3, 8

palace in the tenth month which is the month Tebeth, in the
seventh year of his reign.
17 And the king loved Esther more than all the women,
and she found favor and kindness with him more than all the
virgins, so that [a]he set the royal crown on her head and made
her queen instead of Vashti.
18 Then [a]the king gave a great banquet, Esther's banquet,
for all his princes and his servants; he also made a holiday for
the provinces and gave gifts [b]according to the king's bounty.
19 And [a]when the virgins were gathered together the second time, then Mordecai [b]was sitting at the king's gate.
20 [a]Esther had not yet made known her kindred or her
people, even as Mordecai had commmanded her, for Esther
did [1]what Mordecai told her as she had done [b]when under his
care.
21 In those days, while Mordecai was sitting at the king's
gate, [a]Bigthan and Teresh, two of the king's officials from
those who guarded the door, became angry and sought to [1]lay
hands on king Ahasuerus.
22 But the [1]plot became known to Mordecai, and [a]he told
Queen Esther, and Esther [2]informed the king in Mordecai's
name.
23 Now when the plot was investigated and found *to be
so,* they were both hanged on a [1]gallows; and it was written in
[a]the Book of the Chronicles in the king's presence.

Chapter 3

AFTER these events King Ahasuerus [a]promoted Haman, the
son of Hammedatha [b]the Agagite, and [c]advanced him and
[1]established his authority over all the princes who *were* with
him.
2 And all the king's servants who were at the king's gate
bowed down [1]and paid homage to Haman; for so the king had
commanded concerning him. But [a]Mordecai neither bowed
down nor paid homage.
3 Then the king's servants who were at [a]the king's gate
said to Mordecai, "[b]Why are you transgressing the king's
command?"
4 Now it was when they had spoken daily to him and he
would not listen to them, that they told Haman to see whether
Mordecai's reason would stand; for he had told them that he
was a Jew.
5 When Haman saw that Mordecai neither bowed down
nor paid homage to him, Haman was filled with rage.
6 But he [1]disdained to [2]lay hands on Mordecai alone, for
they had told him *who* the people of Mordecai *were;* therefore
Haman sought to destroy all the Jews, the people of Mordecai,
who *were* throughout the whole kingdom of Ahasuerus.
7 In the first month, which is the month Nisan, in the
twelfth year of King Ahasuerus, [1]Pur, that is the lot, was [a]cast
before Haman from day to day and from month *to month,*
[2]until the twelfth month, that is [b]the month Adar.
8 Then Haman said to King Ahasuerus, "There is a certain people scattered and dispersed among the peoples in all
the provinces of your kingdom; [a]their laws are different from

17 [a]Esth. 1:11
18 [a]Esth. 1:3 [b]Esth. 1:7
19 [a]Esth. 2:3, 4 [b]Esth. 2:21; 3:2
20 [1]Lit., *the word of Mordecai* [a]Esth. 2:10 [b]Esth. 2:7
21 [1]Lit., *send a hand against* [a]Esth. 6:2
22 [1]Lit., *matter,* so also v. 23 [2]Lit., *told* [a]Esth. 6:1, 2
23 [1]Lit., *tree* [a]Esth. 10:2
1 [1]Lit., *set his seat* [a]Esth. 5:11 [b]Esth. 3:10; 8:3 [c]Esth. 5:11
2 [1]Lit., *and prostrated themselves before* [a]Esth. 5:9
3 [a]Esth. 2:19 [b]Esth. 3:2
6 [1]Lit., *despised in his eyes* [2]Lit., *send a hand aganist*
7 [1]Lit., *he cast Pur . . . before* [2]Gk., *and the lot fell on the thriteenth day of* [a]Esth. 9:24-26 [b]Ezra 6:15
8 [a]Ezra 4:12-15; Acts 16:20, 21

those of all *other* people, and they do not observe the king's
laws, so it is not in the king's interest to let them remain.
9 "If it is pleasing to the king, let it be [1]decreed that they
be destroyed, and I will pay ten thousand talents of silver into
the hands of those who carry on the king's business, to put into
the king's treasuries."
10 Then [a]the king took his signet ring from his hand and
gave it to Haman, the son of Hammedatha [b]the Agagite, the
enemy of [c]the Jews.
11 And the king said to Haman, "The silver is [1]yours, and
the people *also*, to do with them as you please."
12 [a]Then the king's scribes were summoned on the thirteenth day of the first month, and it was written just as Haman
commanded to [b]the king's satraps, to the governors who were
over each province, and to the princes of each people, each
province according to its script, each people according to its
language, being written [c]in the name of King Ahasuerus and
sealed with the king's signet ring.
13 And letters were sent by [a]couriers to all the king's provinces [b]to destroy, to kill, and to annihilate all the Jews, both
young and old, women and children, [c]in one day, the thirteenth *day* of the twelfth month, which is the month Adar,
and to [d]seize their possessions as plunder.
14 [a]A copy of the edict to be [1]issued as law in every province was published to all the peoples so that they should be
ready for this day.
15 The couriers went out impelled by the king's command
while the decree was [1]issued in Susa the capital, and while the
king and Haman sat down to drink, [a]the city of Susa was in
confusion.

Chapter 4

WHEN Mordecai learned [a]all that had been done, [1]he tore
his clothes, put on sackcloth and ashes, and went out into the
midst of the city and wailed loudly and bitterly.
2 And he went as far as the king's gate, for no one was to
enter the king's gate clothed in sackcloth.
3 And in each and every province where the command
and decree of the king came, there was great mourning among
the Jews, with [a]fasting, weeping, and wailing; and many lay on
sackcloth and ashes.
4 Then Esther's maidens and her eunuchs came and told
her, and the queen writhed in great anguish. And she sent
garments to clothe Mordecai that he might remove his sackcloth from him, but he did not accept *them*.
5 Then Esther summoned Hathach from the king's eunuchs whom [1]the king had appointed to attend her and ordered him *to go* to Mordecai to learn what this *was* and why it
was.
6 So Hathach went out to Mordecai to the city square in
front of the king's gate.
7 And Mordecai told him all that had happened to him,
and [a]the exact amount of money that Haman had promised to
pay to the king's treasuries for the destruction of the Jews.
8 He also gave him [a]a copy of the text of the edict which

9 [1]Lit., *written*

10 [a]Esth. 8:2; Gen. 41:42 [b]Esth. 3:1 [c]Esth. 7:6

11 [1]Lit., *given to you*

12 [a]Esth. 8:9 [b]Ezra 8:36 [c]Esth. 8:8, 10; 1 Kin. 21:8

13 [a]Esth. 8:10, 14; 2 Chr. 30:6 [b]Esth. 7:4 [c]Esth. 8:12 [d]Esth. 8:11; 9:10

14 [1]Lit., *given* [a]Esth. 8:13, 14

15 [1]Lit., *given* [a]Esth. 8:15

1 [1]Lit., *Mordecai* [a]Esth. 3:8-10; 2 Sam. 1:11; Jon. 3:5,6

3 [a]Esth. 4:16

5 [1]Lit., *he*

7 [a]Esth. 3:9

8 [a]Esth. 3:14

had been issued in Susa for their destruction that he might
show Esther and inform her, and to order her to go in to the
king to implore his favor and to plead with him for her people.
9 And Hathach came back and related Mordecai's words
to Esther.
10 Then Esther spoke to Hathach and ordered him *to
reply* to Mordecai:
11 "All the king's servants and the people of the king's
provinces know that for any man or woman who [a]comes to the
king to the inner court who is not summoned, [b]he has but one
law, that he be put to death; unless the king holds out [c]to him
the golden scepter so that he may live. And I have not been
summoned to come to the king for these thirty days."
12 And they related Esther's words to Mordecai.
13 Then Mordecai told *them* to reply to Esther, "Do not
imagine that you in the king's palace can escape any more than
all the Jews.
14 "For if you remain silent at this time, relief and deliverance will arise for the Jews from another place and you and
your father's house will perish. And who knows whether you
have not attained royalty for such a time as this?"
15 Then Esther told *them* to reply to Mordecai,
16 "Go, assemble all the Jews who are found in Susa, and
fast for me; do not eat or drink for [a]three days, night or day. I
and my maidens also will fast in the same way. And thus I will
go in to the king, which is not according to the law; and if I
perish, I perish."
17 So Mordecai went away and did just as Esther had
commanded him.

Chapter 5

NOW it came about [a]on the third day that Esther put on her
royal robes and stood [b]in the inner court of the king's palace in
front of the king's [1]rooms, and the king was sitting on his royal
throne in the [2]throne room, opposite the entrance to the
palace.
2 And it happened when the king saw Esther the queen
standing in the court, [a]she obtained favor in his sight; and [b]the
king extended to Esther the golden scepter which was in his
hand. So Esther came near and touched the top of the scepter.
3 Then the king said to her, "What is *troubling* you,
Queen Esther? And what is your request? [a]Even to half of the
kingdom it will be given to you."
4 And Esther said, "If it please the king, may the king
and Haman come this day to the banquet that I have prepared
for him."
5 Then the king said, "[a]Bring Haman quickly that we
may do [1]as Esther desires." So the king and Haman came to
the banquet which Esther had prepared.
6 And, [1]as they drank their wine at the banquet, [a]the king
said to Esther, "[b]What is your petition, for it shall be granted
to you. And what is your request? Even to half of the kingdom
it shall be done."
7 So Esther answered and said, "My petition and my
request is:

11 [a]Esth. 5:1; 6:4 [b]Dan. 2:9 [c]Esth. 5:2; 8:4

16 [a]Esth. 5:1

1 [1]Lit., *house* [2]Lit., *royal house* [a]Esth. 4:16 [b]Esth. 4:11; 6:4

2 [a]Esth. 2:9 [b]Esth. 4:11; 8:4

3 [a]Esth. 7:2; Mark 6:23

5 [1]Lit., *the word of Esther* [a]Esth. 6:14

6 [1]Lit., *at the banquet of wine* [a]Esth. 7:2 [b]Esth. 5:3

8 [a]If I have found favor in the sight of the king, and if it
please the king to grant my petition and do [1]what I request,
may the king and Haman come to [b]the banquet which I shall
prepare for them, and tomorrow I will do [2]as the king says."
9 Then Haman went out that day glad and pleased of
heart; but when Haman saw Mordecai [a]in the king's gate, and
[b]that he did not stand up or [1]tremble before him, Haman was
filled with anger against Mordecai.
10 Haman controlled himself, however, went to his house,
and [1]sent for his friends and his wife [a]Zeresh.
11 Then Haman recounted to them the glory of his riches,
and the [1a]number of his sons, and every *instance* where the
king had magnified him, and how he had [2b]promoted him
above the princes and servants of the king.
12 Haman also said, "Even Esther the queen let no one
but me come with the king to the banquet which she had
prepared; and [a]tomorrow also I am [1]invited by her with the
king.
13 "Yet all of this [1]does not satisfy me every time I see
Mordecai the Jew sitting at [a]the king's gate."
14 Then Zeresh his wife and all his friends said to him,
"[a]Have a [1]gallows fifty cubits high made and in the morning
ask the king to have Mordecai hanged on it, then go joyfully
with the king to the banquet." And the [2]advice pleased Haman, so he had the gallows made.

Chapter 6

[a]DURING that night [1]the king [b]could not sleep so he gave an
order to bring [c]the book of records, the chronicles, and they
were read before the king.
2 And it was found written what [a]Mordecai had reported
concerning Bigthana and Teresh, two of the king's eunuchs
who were doorkeepers, that they had sought to lay hands on
King Ahasuerus.
3 And the king said, "What honor or dignity has been
bestowed on Mordecai for this?" Then the king's servants who
attended him said, "Nothing has been done for him."
4 So the king said, "Who is in the court?" Now Haman
had just [a]entered the outer court of the king's palace in order
to speak to the king about [b]hanging Mordecai on the gallows
which he had prepared for him.
5 And the king's servants said to him, "Behold, Haman is
standing in the court." And the king said, "Let him come in."
6 So Haman came in and the king said to him, "What is
to be done for the man [a]whom the king desires to honor?" And
Haman said [1]to himself, "Whom would the king desire to
honor more than me?"
7 Then Haman said to the king, "For the man whom the
king desires to honor,
8 let them bring a royal robe which the king has worn,
and [a]the horse on which the king has ridden, and on whose
head [b]a royal crown has been placed;
9 and let the robe and the horse be handed over to one of
the king's most noble princes and let them array the man
whom the king desires to honor and lead him on horseback

8 [1]Lit., *my request* [2]Lit., *according to the word of the king*
[a]Esth. 7:3; 8:5 [b]Esth. 6:14

9 [1]Or, *move for*
[a]Esth. 2:19 [b]Esth. 3:5

10 [1]Lit., *sent and brought*
[a]Esth. 6:13

11 [1]Lit., *multitude* [2]Lit., *lifted*
[a]Esth. 9:7-10 [b]Esth. 3:1

12 [1]Lit., *summoned to her*
[a]Esth. 5:8

13 [1]Lit., *is not suitable to me*
[a]Esth. 5:9

14 [1]Lit., *tree* [2]Lit., *thing*
[a]Esth. 6:4; 7:9, 10

1 [1]Lit., *the king's sleep fled*
[a]Esth. 5:8 [b]Dan. 6:18 [c]Esth. 2:23; 10:2

2 [a]Esth. 2:21, 22

4 [a]Esth. 4:11; 5:1 [b]Esth. 5:14

6 [1]Lit., *in his heart*
[a]Esth. 6:7, 9, 11

8 [a]1 Kin. 1:33 [b]Esth. 1:11; 2:17

through the city square, [a]and proclaim before him, 'Thus it
shall be done to the man whom the king desires to honor.' "
10 Then the king said to Haman, "[a]Take quickly the robes
and the horse as you have said, and do so for Mordecai the
Jew, who is sitting at the king's gate; do not fall short in anything
of all that you have said."
11 So Haman took the robe and the horse, and arrayed
Mordecai, and led him *on horseback* through the city square,
and proclaimed before him, "Thus it shall be done to the man
whom the king desires to honor."
12 Then Mordecai returned to the king's gate. But Haman hurried home, mourning, [a]with *his* head covered.
13 And Haman recounted [a]to Zeresh his wife and all his
friends everything that had happened to him. Then his wise
men and Zeresh his wife said to him, "If Mordecai, before
whom you have begun to fall, is [1]of Jewish origin, you will not
overcome him, but will surely fall before him."
14 While they were still talking with him, the king's eunuchs arrived and hastily [a]brought Haman to the banquet
which Esther had prepared.

Chapter 7

NOW the king and Haman came to drink *wine* with Esther
the queen.
2 And the king said to Esther on the second day also [1]as
they drank their wine at the banquet, "[a]What is your petition,
Queen Esther? It shall be granted you. And what is your request? [b]Even to half of the kingdom it shall be done."
3 Then Queen Esther answered and said, "[a]If I have
found favor in your sight, O king, and if it please the king, let
my life be given me as my petition, and my people as my
request;
4 for [a]we have been sold, I and my people, to be
destroyed, [b]to be killed and to be annihilated. Now if we had
only been sold as slaves, men and women, I would have remained silent, for the [1]trouble would not be commensurate
with the [2]annoyance to the king."
5 Then King Ahasuerus [1]asked Queen Esther, "Who is
he, and where is he, [2]who would presume to do thus?"
6 And Esther said, "[a]A foe and an enemy, is this wicked
Haman!" Then Haman became terrified before the king and
queen.
7 And the king arose [a]in his anger from [1]drinking wine
and went into [b]the palace garden; but Haman stayed to beg
for his life from Queen Esther, for he saw that harm had been
determined against him by the king.
8 Now when the king returned from the palace garden
into the [1]place where they were drinking wine, Haman was
falling on [a]the couch where Esther was. Then the king said,
"Will he even assault the queen with me in the house?" As the
word went out of the king's mouth, they covered Haman's
face.
9 Then Harbonah, one of the eunuchs who *were* before
the king said, "Behold indeed, [a]the gallows standing at Haman's house fifty cubits high, which Haman made for

9 [a]Gen. 41:43

10 [a]Esth. 5:5

12 [a]2 Sam. 15:30

13 [1]Lit., *from the seed of the Jews* [a]Esth. 5:10

14 [a]Esth. 5:8

2 [1]Lit., *at the banquet of wine* [a]Esth. 5:6; 9:12 [b]Esth. 5:3

3 [a]Esth. 5:8; 8:5

4 [1]Or, *enemy could not compensate for the loss* [2]Or, *damage* [a]Esth. 3:19 [b]Esth. 3:13

5 [1]Lit., *said and said to* [2]Lit., *whose heart has been filled*

6 [a]Esth. 3:10

7 [1]Lit., *the banquet of wine* [a]Esth. 1:12 [b]Esth. 1:5

8 [1]Lit., *house of the banquet of wine* [a]Esth. 1:6

9 [a]Esth. 5:14

Mordecai [b]who spoke good on behalf of the king!" And the
king said, "Hang him on it."
10 [a]So they hanged Haman on the [1]gallows which he had
prepared for Mordecai, [b]and the king's anger subsided.

9 [b]Esth. 2:22

10 [1]Lit., *tree*
[a]Ps. 7:16; 94:23 [b]Esth. 7:7, 8

CHAPTER 8

ON that day King Ahasuerus gave the house of Haman, the
enemy of [a]the Jews, to Queen Esther; and Mordecai came
before the king, for Esther had disclosed [b]what he was to her.
2 [a]And the king took off his signet ring which he had
taken away from Haman, and gave it to Mordecai. And Esther
set Mordecai over the house of Haman.
3 Then Esther spoke again to the king, fell at his feet,
wept, and implored him to avert the evil *scheme* of Haman the
Agagite and his plot which he had devised against the Jews.
4 [a]And the king extended the golden scepter to Esther.
So Esther arose and stood before the king.
5 Then she said, "[a]If it pleases the king and if I have
found favor before him and the matter *seems* proper to the
king and I am pleasing in his sight, let it be written to revoke
the [b]letters devised by Haman, the son of Hammedatha the
Agagite, which he wrote to destroy the Jews who are in all the
king's provinces.
6 "For [a]how can I endure to see the calamity which shall
befall my people, and how can I endure to see the destruction
of my kindred?"
7 So King Ahasuerus said to Queen Esther and to Mordecai the Jew, "Behold, [a]I have given the house of Haman to
Esther, and him they have hanged on the gallows because he
had stretched out his hands against the Jews.
8 "Now you write to the Jews [1]as you see fit, in the king's
name, and [a]seal *it* with the king's signet ring; for a decree
which is written in the name of the king and sealed with the
king's signet ring [b]may not be revoked."
9 [a]So the king's scribes were called at that time in the
third month (that is, the month Sivan), on the twenty-third
[1]day; and it was written according to all that Mordecai commanded to the Jews, the satraps, the governors, and the princes
of the provinces which *extended* [b]from India to [2]Ethiopia, 127
provinces, to [c]every province according to its script, and to
every people according to their language, as well as to the Jews
according to their script and their language.
10 And he wrote in the name of King Ahasuerus, and
sealed it with the king's signet ring, and sent letters by couriers
on [a]horses, riding on steeds sired by the royal stud.
11 [1]In them the king granted the Jews who were in each
and every city *the right* [a]to assemble and to defend their lives,
[b]to destroy, to kill, and to annihilate the entire army of any
people or province which might attack them, including children and women, and [c]to plunder their spoil,
12 on one day in all the provinces of King Ahasuerus, the
thirteenth *day* of the twelfth month (that is, the month Adar).
13 [a]A copy of the edict to be [1]issued as law in each and
every province, was published to all the peoples, so that the

1 [a]Esth. 7:6 [b]Esth. 2:7, 15

2 [a]Esth. 3:10

4 [a]Esth. 4:11; 5:2

5 [a]Esth. 5:8; 7:3 [b]Esth. 3:13

6 [a]Esth. 7:4; 9:1

7 [a]Esth. 8:1

8 [1]Lit., *according to the good in your eyes*
[a]Esth. 8:10; 3:12 [b]Esth. 1:19

9 [1]Lit., *in it* [2]Lit., *Cush*
[a]Esth. 3:12 [b]Esth. 1:1 [c]Esth. 1:22; 3:12

10 [a]1 Kin. 4:28

11 [1]Lit., *Which*
[a]Esth. 9:2 [b]Esth. 3:13 [c]Esth. 9:10

13 [1]Lit., *given*
[a]Esth. 3:14

Jews should be ready for this day to avenge themselves on their
enemies.
14 The couriers, hastened and impelled by the king's command, went out, riding on the royal steeds; and the decree was
given out in Susa the capital.
15 Then Mordecai went out from the presence of the king
[a]in royal robes of [1]blue and white, with a large crown of gold
and [b]a garment of fine linen and purple; and the city of Susa
shouted and rejoiced.
16 For the Jews there was light and gladness and joy and
honor.
17 And in each and every province, and in each and every
city, wherever the king's commandment and his decree arrived
there was gladness and joy for the Jews, a feast and a [1a]holiday.
And [b]many among the peoples of the land became Jews, for
the dread of the Jews had fallen on them.

Chapter 9

NOW [a]in the twelfth month (that is, the month Adar), on
[b]the thirteenth [1]day [c]when the king's command and edict
[2]were about to be executed, on the day when the enemies of
the Jews hoped to gain the mastery over them, it was turned to
the contrary so that the Jews themselves gained the mastery
over those who hated them.
2 [a]The Jews assembled in their cities throughout all the
provinces of King Ahasuerus to lay hands on those who sought
their harm; and no one could stand before them, [b]for the
dread of them had fallen on all the peoples.
3 Even all the princes of the provinces, [a]the satraps, the
governors, and those who were doing the king's business
[1]assisted the Jews, because the dread of Mordecai had fallen
on them.
4 Indeed, Mordecai was great in the king's house, and his
fame spread throughout all the provinces; for the man Mordecai [a]became greater and greater.
5 Thus [a]the Jews struck all their enemies with [1]the sword,
killing and destroying; and they did what they pleased to those
who hated them.
6 And in Susa the capital the Jews killed and destroyed
five hundred men,
7 and Parshandatha, Dalphon, Aspatha,
8 Poratha, Adalia, Aridatha,
9 Parmashta, Arisai, Aridai, and Vaizatha,
10 [a]the ten sons of Haman the son of Hammedatha, the
Jews' enemy; but they did not lay their hands [b]on the plunder.
11 On that day the number of those who were killed in
Susa the capital [1]was reported to the king.
12 And the king said to Queen Esther, "The Jews have
killed and destroyed five hundred men and the ten sons of
Haman in Susa the capital. What then have they done in the
rest of the king's provinces! [a]Now what is your petition? It shall
even be granted you. And what is your further request? It shall
also be done."
13 Then said Esther, "If it pleases the king, [a]let tomorrow
also be granted to the Jews who are in Susa to do according to

15 [1]Or, *violet* [a]Esth. 5:11; Gen. 41:42 [b]Esth. 3:15

17 [1]Lit., *good day* [a]Esth. 9:19 [b]Esth. 9:27

1 [1]Lit., *day in it* [2]Lit., *drew near* [a]Esth. 8:12 [b]Esth. 9:17 [c]Esth. 3:13

2 [a]Esth. 9:15-18; 8:11 [b]Esth. 8:17

3 [1]Lit., *lifted up* [a]Ezra 8:36

4 [a]2 Sam. 3:1

5 [1]Lit., *the stroke of* [a]Esth. 3:13

10 [a]Esth. 5:11 [b]Esth. 8:11

11 [1]Lit., *came*

12 [a]Esth. 7:2

13 [a]Esth. 9:15; 8:11

the edict of today; and let Haman's ten sons be hanged on the
gallows."
14 So the king commanded that it should be done so; and
an edict was issued in Susa, and Haman's ten sons were
hanged.
15 And the Jews who were in Susa assembled also on the
fourteenth day of the month Adar and killed [a]three hundred
men in Susa, but they did not lay their hands [b]on the plunder.
16 Now [a]the rest of the Jews who *were* in the king's provinces assembled, to defend their lives and [1]rid themselves of
their enemies, and kill 75,000 of those who hated them; but
they did not lay their hands on the plunder.
17 *This was done* on [a]the thirteenth day of the month
Adar, and [b]on the fourteenth [1]day they rested and made it a
day of feasting and rejoicing.
18 But the Jews who were in Susa [a]assembled on the thirteenth and [b]the fourteenth [1]of the same month, and they
rested on the fifteenth [1]day and made it a day of feasting and
rejoicing.
19 Therefore the Jews of the rural areas, who live in [a]the
rural towns, make the fourteenth day of the month Adar *a*
[1b]*holiday* for rejoicing and feasting and [c]sending portions *of*
food to one another.
20 Then Mordecai recorded these events, and he sent letters to all the Jews who were in all the provinces of King
Ahasuerus, both near and far,
21 obliging them to celebrate the fourteenth day of the
month Adar, and the fifteenth day [1]of the same month,
annually,
22 because on those days the Jews [1]rid themselves of their
enemies, and *it was a* month which was turned for them from
sorrow into gladness and from mourning into a [2]holiday; that
they should make them days of feasting and rejoicing and
sending portions *of food* to one another and gifts to the poor.
23 Thus the Jews undertook what they had started to do,
and what Mordecai had written to them.
24 For Haman the son of Hammedatha, the Agagite, the
adversary of all the Jews, had schemed against the Jews to
destroy them, and [a]had cast Pur, that is the lot, to disturb them
and destroy them.
25 But [a]when it came [1]to the king's attention, he commanded by letter [b]that his wicked scheme which he had [2]de-
vised against the Jews, [c]should return on his own head, and
that he and his sons should be hanged on the [3]gallows.
26 Therefore they called these days Purim after the name
of Pur. [1]And [a]because of the instructions in this letter, both
what they had seen in this regard and what had happened to
them,
27 the Jews established and [1]made a custom for themselves, and for their [2]descendants, and for [a]all those who allied
themselves with them, so that [3]they should not fail [b]to celebrate
these two days according to their [4]regulation, and according to their appointed time annually.
28 So these days were to be remembered and celebrated
throughout every generation, every family, every province, and
every city; and these days of Purim were not to [1]fail from

15 [a]Esth. 9:12 [b]Esth. 9:10

16 [1]Lit., *have rest from* [a]Esth. 9:2

17 [1]Lit., *in it* [a]Esth. 9:1 [b]Esth. 9:21

18 [1]Lit., *in it* [a]Esth. 9:2; 8:11 [b]Esth. 9:21

19 [1]Lit., *good day* [a]Deut. 3:5; Zech. 2:4 [b]Esth. 9:22 [c]Neh. 8:10

21 [1]Lit., *in it*

22 [1]Lit., *had rest from* [2]Lit., *good day*

24 [a]Esth. 3:7

25 [1]Lit., *before the king, he* [2]Lit., *schemed* [3]Lit., *tree* [a]Esth. 7:4-10 [b]Esth. 3:6-15 [c]Ps. 7:16

26 [1]Lit., *Therefore because of all the words* [a]Esth. 9:20

27 [1]Lit., *received* [2]Lit., *seed* [3]Lit., *it should not pass away* [4]Lit., *writing* [a]Esth. 8:17 [b]Esth. 9:20, 21

28 [1]Lit., *pass away*

28 [2]Lit., *end* [3]Lit., *seed*

among the Jews, or their memory [2]fade from their [3]descendants.

29 [a]Esth. 2:15 [b]Esth. 9:20, 21

29 Then Queen Esther, [a]daughter of Abihail, with Mordecai the Jew, wrote with full authority to confirm [b]this second letter about Purim.

30 [a]Esth. 1:1

30 And he sent letters to all the Jews, [a]to the 127 provinces of the kingdom of Ahasuerus, namely, words of peace and truth,

31 [1]Lit., *seed* [2]Lit., *words* [a]Esth. 4:3

31 to establish these days of Purim at their appointed times, just as Mordecai the Jew and Queen Esther had established for them, and just as they had established for themselves and for their [1]descendants with [2]instructions [a]for their times of fasting and their lamentations.

32 [1]Lit., *words* [a]Esth. 9:26

32 And the command of Esther established these [1]customs for [a]Purim, and it was written in the book.

CHAPTER 10

1 [a]Is. 11:11; 24:15

NOW King Ahasuerus laid a tribute on the land and on the [a]coastlands of the sea.

2 [1]Lit., *doings* [2]Lit., *made him great* [a]Esth. 8:15; 9:4 [b]Esth. 2:23

2 And all the [1]accomplishments of his authority and strength, and the full account of the greatness of Mordecai, [a]to which the king [2]advanced him, are they not written in [b]the Book of the Chronicles of the kings of Media and Persia?

3 [a]Gen. 41:43, 44 [b]Neh. 2:10

3 For Mordecai the Jew was [a]second *only* to King Ahasuerus and great among the Jews, and in favor with the multitude of his kinsmen, [b]one who sought the good of his people and one who spoke for the welfare of his whole nation.

THE BOOK OF JOB

Job's Character and Wealth.

1 [a]Jer. 25:20; Lam. 4:21 [b]Ezek. 14:14, 20; James 5:11 [c]Gen. 6:9; 17:1; Deut. 18:13 [d]Gen. 22:12; 42:18; Ex. 18:21 [e]Job 28:28

THERE was a man in the land of [a]Uz, whose name was [b]Job, and that man was [c]blameless, upright, [d]fearing God, and [e]turning away from evil.

2 [a]Job 42:13

2 [a]And seven sons and three daughters were born to him.

3 [1]Lit., *sons* [a]Job 42:12 [b]Job 29:25; 31:37

3 [a]His possessions also were 7,000 sheep, 3,000 camels, 500 yoke of oxen, 500 female donkeys, and very many servants; and that man was [b]the greatest of all the [1]men of the east.

4 And his sons used to go and hold a feast in the house of each one on his day, and they would send and invite their three sisters to eat and drink with them.

5 [a]Job 42:8 [b]Job 8:4

5 And it came about, when the days of feasting had completed their cycle, that Job would send and consecrate them, rising up early in the morning and offering [a]burnt offerings *according to* the number of them all; for Job said, "[b]Perhaps my sons have sinned and cursed God in their hearts." Thus Job did continually.

6 [1]I.e., the adversary; so through chaps. 1 & 2

6 Now there was a day when the sons of God came to present themselves before the LORD, [1]Satan also came among them.

7 And the LORD said to Satan, "From where do you
come?" Then Satan answered the LORD and said, "[a]From roam-
ing about on the earth and walking around on it."
8 And the LORD said to Satan, "Have you [1]considered
[a]My servant Job? For there is no one like him on the earth, [b]a
blameless and upright man, [2]fearing God and turning away
from evil."
9 Then Satan answered the [1]LORD, "Does Job fear God
for nothing?
10 "[a]Hast Thou not made a hedge about him and his house
and all that he has, on every side? [b]Thou hast blessed the work
of his hands, and his [c]possessions have increased in the land.
11 "[a]But put forth Thy hand now and [b]touch all that he
has; he will surely curse Thee to Thy face."
12 Then the LORD said to Satan, "Behold, all that he has is
in your [1]power, only do not put forth your hand on him." So
Satan departed from the presence of the LORD.
13 Now it happened on the day when his sons and his
daughters were eating and drinking wine in their oldest brother's house,
14 that a messenger came to Job and said, "The oxen were
plowing and the [1]donkeys feeding beside them,
15 and [1]the [a]Sabeans [2]attacked and took them. They also
[3]slew the servants with the edge of the sword, and [4]I alone have
escaped to tell you."
16 While he was still speaking, another also came and
said, "[a]The fire of God fell from heaven and burned up the
sheep and the servants and consumed them; and I alone have
escaped to tell you."
17 While he was still speaking, another also came and
said, "The [a]Chaldeans formed three bands and made a raid on
the camels and took them and [1]slew the servants with the edge
of the sword; and I alone have escaped to tell you."
18 While he was still speaking, another also came and
said, "Your sons and your daughters were eating and drinking
wine in their oldest brother's house,
19 and behold, a great wind came from across the wilderness and struck the four corners of the house, and it fell on the
young people and they died; and I alone have escaped to tell
you."
20 Then Job arose and [a]tore his robe and shaved his head,
and he fell to the ground and worshiped.
21 And he said,
"[a]Naked I came from my mother's womb,
And naked I shall return there.
The [b]LORD gave and the LORD has taken away.
Blessed be the name of the LORD."
22 [a]Through all this Job did not sin nor did he [1]blame
God.

CHAPTER 2

[a]AGAIN there was a day when the sons of God came to
present themselves before the LORD, and Satan also came
among them to present himself before the LORD.
2 And the LORD said to Satan, "Where have you come

7 [a]1 Pet. 5:8

8 [1]Lit., *set your heart to* [2]Or, *revering* [a]Num. 12:7; Josh. 1:2, 7; Job 7:8 [b]Job 1:1

9 [1]Lit., *LORD and said*

10 [a]Job 29:2-6 [b]Job 31:25 [c]Job 1:3; 31:25

11 [a]Job 2:5 [b]Job 19:21

12 [1]Lit., *hand*

14 [1]Lit., *female donkeys*

15 [1]Lit., *Sheba* [2]Lit., *fell upon* [3]Lit., *smote* [4]Lit., *only I alone* so also v. 16, 17, 19 [a]Job 6:19

16 [a]Gen. 19:24; Lev. 10:2; Num. 11:1-3

17 [1]Lit., *smote* [a]Gen. 11:28, 31

20 [a]Gen. 37:29, 34; Josh. 7:6

21 [a]Eccles. 5:15 [b]Job 2:10; 1 Sam. 2:7, 8

22 [1]Lit., *ascribe unseemliness to* [a]Job 2:10

1 [a]Job 1:6-8

3 [1]Lit., *set your heart to* [2]Or, *revering* [3]Lit., *swallow him up*

5 [a]Job 1:11

6 [1]Lit., *hand*

7 [a]Job 7:5; 13:28; 30:17, 18, 30; Deut. 28:35

8 [a]Job 42:6; Jer. 6:26; Jon. 3:6

10 [a]Job 1:21 [b]Job 1:22

11 [a]Job 6:19

12 [a]Job 1:20 [b]Josh. 7:6; Lam. 2:10

13 [a]Ezek. 3:15

1 [1]Lit., *his day*

2 [1]Lit., *answered and said*

3 [1]Lit., *man-child* [a]Jer. 20:14-18

8 [1]Or, *skillful* [a]Job 41:25

from?" Then Satan answered the LORD and said, "From roam-
ing about on the earth, and walking around on it."
3 And the LORD said to Satan, "Have you [1]considered
My servant Job? For there is no one like him on the earth, a
blameless and upright man [2]fearing God and turning away
from evil. And he still holds fast his integrity, although you
incited Me against him, to [3]ruin him without cause."
4 And Satan answered the LORD and said, "Skin for skin!
Yes, all that a man has he will give for his life.
5 "[a]However, put forth Thy hand, now, and touch his
bone and his flesh; he will curse Thee to Thy face."
6 So the LORD said to Satan, "Behold, he is in your [1]pow-
er only spare his life."
7 Then Satan went out from the presence of the LORD,
and smote Job with [a]sore boils from the sole of his foot to the
crown of his head.
8 And he took a potsherd to scrape himself while [a]he was
sitting among the ashes.
9 Then his wife said to him, "Do you still hold fast your
integrity? Curse God and die!"
10 But he said to her, "You speak as one of the foolish
women speaks. [a]Shall we indeed accept good from God and
not accept adversity?" [b]In all this Job did not sin with his lips.
11 Now when Job's three friends heard of all this adversity
that had come upon him, they came each one from his own
place, Eliphaz the [a]Temanite, Bildad the Shuhite, and Zophar
the Naamathite; and they made an appointment together to
come to sympathize with him and comfort him.
12 And when they lifted up their eyes at a distance, and
did not recognize him, they raised their voices and wept. And
each of them [a]tore his robe, and they [b]threw dust over their
heads toward the sky.
13 [a]Then they sat down on the ground with him for seven
days and seven nights with no one speaking a word to him, for
they saw that *his* pain was very great.

CHAPTER 3

AFTERWARD Job opened his mouth and cursed [1]the day
of his *birth*.
2 And Job [1]said:
3 "[a]Let the day perish on which I was to be born,
And the night *which* said, 'A [1]boy is conceived.'
4 "May that day be darkness;
Let not God above care for it,
Nor light shine on it.
5 "Let darkness and black gloom claim it;
Let a cloud settle on it;
Let the blackness of the day terrify it.
6 "*As for* that night, let darkness seize it;
Let it not rejoice among the days of the year;
Let it not come into the number of the months.
7 "Behold, let that night be barren;
Let no joyful shout enter it.
8 "Let those curse it who curse the day,
Who are [1]prepared to [a]rouse Leviathan.

9 "Let the stars of its twilight be darkened;
Let it wait for light but have none,
Neither let it see the [1a]breaking dawn;
10 "Because it did not shut the opening of my *mother's* womb,
Or hide trouble from my eyes.

11 "[a]Why did I not die [1]at birth,
Come forth from the womb and expire?
12 "Why did the knees receive me,
And why the breasts, that I should suck?
13 "For now I [a]would have lain down and been quiet;
I would have slept then, I would have been at rest,
14 With [a]kings and *with* [b]counselors of the earth,
Who rebuilt [c]ruins for themselves;
15 Or with [a]princes [b]who had gold,
Who were filling their houses *with* silver.
16 "Or like a miscarriage which is [1]discarded, I would not be,
As infants that never saw light.
17 "There the wicked cease from raging,
And there the [1]weary are at [a]rest.
18 "The prisoners are at ease together;
They do not hear the voice of the taskmaster.
19 "The small and the great are there,
And the slave is free from his master.

20 "Why is light given to him who suffers,
And life to the bitter of soul;
21 Who [1]long for death, but there is none,
And dig for it more than for hidden treasures;
22 Who rejoice greatly,
They exult when they find the grave?
23 "*Why is light given* to a man [a]whose way is hidden,
And whom [b]God has hedged in?
24 "For [a]my groaning comes at the sight of my food,
And [b]my cries pour out like water.
25 "For [1a]what I fear comes upon me,
And what I dread befalls me.
26 "I [a]am not at ease, nor am I quiet,
And I am not at rest, but turmoil comes."

Chapter 4

THEN Eliphaz the Temanite [1]answered,
2 "If one ventures a word with you, will you become impatient?
But [a]who can refrain [1]from speaking?
3 "Behold, [a]you have admonished many,
And you have strengthened weak hands.
4 "Your words have [1]helped the tottering to stand,
And you have strengthened [2]feeble knees.
5 "But now it has come to you, and you [a]are impatient;
It [b]touches you, and you are dismayed.
6 "Is not your [1a]fear *of God* your confidence,
And the integrity of your ways your hope?

9 [1]Lit., *eyelids* [a]Job 41:18

11 [1]Lit., *from the womb* [a]Job 10:18, 19

13 [a]Job 3:13-19; 7:8-10, 21; 10:21, 22; 14:10-15, 20-22; 16:22; 17:13-16; 19:25-27; 21:13, 23-26; 24:19, 20; 26:5, 6; 34:22

14 [a]Job 12:18 [b]Job 12:17 [c]Job 15:28; Is. 58:12

15 [a]Job 12:21 [b]Job 27:16, 17

16 [1]Lit., *hidden*

17 [1]Lit., *weary of strength* [a]Job 17:16

21 [1]Lit., *wait*

23 [a]Job 19:6, 8, 12 [b]Job 19:8; Ps. 88:8

24 [a]Job 6:7; 33:20 [b]Job 30:16; Ps. 42:4

25 [1]Lit., *the fear I fear and* [a]Job 9:28; 30:15

26 [a]Job 7:13, 14

1 [1]Lit., *answered and said*

2 [1]Lit., *in words* [a]Job 32:18-20

3 [a]Job 4:3, 4; 29:15, 16, 21, 25

4 [1]Lit., *caused* [2]Lit., *bowing*

5 [a]Job 6:14 [b]Job 19:21

6 [1]Or, *reverence* [a]Job 1:1

7 "Remember now, [a]who *ever* perished being innocent?
Or where were the upright destroyed?
8 "According to what I have seen, [a]those who plow iniquity
And those who sow trouble harvest it.
9 "By [a]the breath of God they perish,
And [b]by the [1]blast of His anger they come to an end.
10 "The [a]roaring of the lion and the voice of the *fierce* lion,
And the teeth of the young lions are broken.
11 "The [a]lion perishes for lack of prey,
And the [b]whelps of the lioness are scattered.

12 "Now a word [a]was brought to me stealthily,
And my ear received a [b]whisper of it.
13 "Amid disquieting thoughts from the visions of the night,
When deep sleep falls on men,
14 Dread came upon me, and trembling,
And made [1]all my bones shake.
15 "Then a [1]spirit passed by my face;
The hair of my flesh bristled up.
16 "It stood still, but I could not discern its appearance;
A form *was* before my eyes;
There was silence, then I heard a voice:
17 'Can [a]mankind be just [1]before God?
Can a man be pure [1]before his [b]Maker?
18 '[a]He puts no trust even in His servants;
And against His angels He charges error.
19 'How much more those who dwell in [a]houses of clay,
Whose [b]foundation is in the dust,
Who are crushed before the moth!
20 '[a]Between morning and evening they are broken in pieces;
Unobserved, they [b]perish forever.
21 'Is not their [a]tent-cord plucked up within them?
They die, yet [b]without wisdom.'

Chapter 5

"CALL now, is there anyone who will answer you?
And to which of the [a]holy ones will you turn?
2 "For [a]vexation slays the foolish man,
And anger kills the simple.
3 "I have seen the [a]foolish taking root,
And I [b]cursed his abode immediately.
4 "His [a]sons are far from safety,
They are even [1]oppressed in the gate,
Neither is there a deliverer.
5 "[1]His harvest the hungry devour,
And take it to a *place of* thorns
And the [2a]schemer is eager for their wealth.
6 "For [a]affliction does not come from the dust,
Neither does trouble sprout from the ground,
7 For [a]man is born for trouble,
As sparks fly upward.

7 [a]Job 8:20; 36:6, 7; Ps. 37:25

8 [a]Job 15:31, 35; Prov. 22:8; Hos. 10:13; Gal. 6:7

9 [1]Lit., *wind*
[a]Job 15:30; Is. 11:4; 30:33; 2 Thess. 2:8 [b]Job 40:11-13

10 [a]Job 5:15; Ps. 58:6

11 [a]Job 29:17 [b]Job 5:4; 20:10; 27:14

12 [a]Job 4:12-17; 33:15-18 [b]Job 26:14

14 [1]Lit., *the multitude of*

15 [1]Or, *breath passed over*

17 [1]Lit., *from*
[a]Job 9:2; 25:4 [b]Job 31:15; 32:22; 35:10; 36:3

18 [a]Job 15:15

19 [a]Job 10:9; 33:6 [b]Job 22:16; Gen. 2:7; 3:19

20 [a]Job 14:2 [b]Job 14:20; 20:7

21 [a]Job 8:22 [b]Job 18:21; 36:12

1 [a]Job 15:15

2 [a]Prov. 12:16; 27:3

3 [a]Jer. 12:2 [b]Job 24:18; 31:30

4 [1]Lit., *crushed*
[a]Job 4:11

5 [1]Lit., *Whose* [2]Ancient versions read, *thirsty*
[a]Job 18:8-10; 22:10

6 [a]Job 15:35

7 [a]Job 14:1

8 "But as for me, I would [a]seek God,
And I would place my cause before God;
9 Who [a]does great and unsearchable things,
[1]Wonders without number.
10 "He [a]gives rain on the earth,
And sends water on the fields,
11 So that [a]He sets on high those who are lowly,
And those who mourn are lifted to safety.
12 "He [a]frustrates the plotting of the shrewd,
So that their hands cannot attain success.
13 "He [a]captures the wise by their own shrewdness
And the advice of the cunning is quickly thwarted.
14 "By day they [a]meet with darkness,
And grope at noon as in the night.
15 "But He saves from [a]the sword of their mouth,
And [b]the poor from the hand of the mighty.
16 "So the helpless has hope,
And [a]unrighteousness must shut its mouth.

17 "Behold, how [a]happy is the man whom God reproves,
So do not despise the [b]discipline of [1]the Almighty.
18 "For [a]He inflicts pain, and [1]gives relief;
He wounds, and His hands *also* heal.
19 "[1]From six troubles He will deliver you,
Even in seven evil will not touch you.
20 "In [a]famine He will redeem you from death,
And [b]in war from the power of the sword.
21 "You will be [a]hidden from the scourge of the tongue,
[b]Neither will you be afraid of violence when it comes.
22 "You will [a]laugh at violence and famine,
[b]Neither will you be afraid of [1]wild beasts.
23 "For you will be in league with the stones of the field;
And [a]the beasts of the field will be at peace with you.
24 "And you will know that your [a]tent is secure,
For you will visit your abode and fear no loss.
25 "You will know also that your [1a]descendants will be many,
And [b]your offspring as the grass of the earth.
26 "You will [a]come to the grave in full vigor,
Like the stacking of grain in its season.
27 "Behold this, we have investigated it, thus it is;
Hear it, and know for yourself."

Chapter 6

THEN Job [1]answered,
2 "[a]Oh that my vexation were actually weighed,
And laid in the balances together with my iniquity!
3 "For then it would be [a]heavier than the sand of the seas,
Therefore my words have been rash.
4 "For the [a]arrows of the Almighty are within me;
[1]Their [b]poison my spirit drinks;
The [c]terrors of God are arrayed against me.
5 "Does the [a]wild donkey bray over *his* grass,
Or does the ox low over his fodder?

8 [a]Job 13:2, 3
9 [1]Or, *miracles* [a]Job 9:10; 37:14, 16; 42:3
10 [a]Job 36:27-29; 37:6-11; 38:26
11 [a]Job 22:29; 36:7
12 [a]Ps. 33:10
13 [a]Job 37:24; 1 Cor. 3:19
14 [a]Job 12:25; 15:30; 18:18; 20:26; 24:13
15 [a]Job 4:10, 11; Ps. 35:10 [b]Job 29:17; 34:28; 36:6, 15; 38:15
16 [a]Ps. 107:42
17 [1]Heb., *Shaddai*, and so throughout the chap. [a]Ps. 94:12 [b]Job 36:15, 16; Prov. 3:11; Heb. 12:5-11
18 [1]Lit., *binds* [a]Deut. 32:39; 1 Sam. 2:6; Is. 30:26; Hos. 6:1
19 [1]Lit., *in*
20 [a]Ps. 33:19; 37:19 [b]Ps. 144:10
21 [a]Job 5:15; Ps. 31:20 [b]Ps. 91:5, 6
22 [1]Lit., *beasts of the earth* [a]Job 8:21 [b]Ps. 91:13; Ezek. 34:25; Hos. 2:18
23 [a]Is. 11:6-9; 65:25
24 [a]Job 8:6
25 [1]Lit., *seed* [a]Ps. 112:2 [b]Is. 44:3, 4; 48:19
26 [a]Job 42:17
1 [1]Lit., *answered and said*
2 [a]Job 31:6
3 [a]Job 23:2
4 [1]Lit., *Whose* [a]Job 16:13; Ps. 38:2 [b]Job 20:16; 21:20 [c]Job 30:15
5 [a]Job 39:5-8

6 "Can something tasteless be eaten without salt,
Or is there any taste in the [1]white of an egg?
7 "My soul [a]refuses to touch *them;*
They are like loathsome food to me.

8 "Oh that my request might come to pass,
And that God would grant my longing!
9 "Would that God were [a]willing to crush me;
That He would loose His hand and cut me off!
10 "But it is still my consolation,
And I rejoice in unsparing pain,
That I [a]have not [1]denied the words of the Holy One.
11 "What is my strength, that I should wait?
And what is my end, that I should [1a]endure?
12 "Is my strength the strength of stones,
Or is my flesh bronze?
13 "Is it that my [a]help is not within me,
And that [1b]deliverance is driven from me?

14 "For the [a]despairing man *there should be* kindness from his friend;
Lest he [b]forsake the [1]fear of the Almighty.
15 "My brothers have acted [a]deceitfully like a [1]wadi,
Like the torrents of [1]wadis which vanish,
16 Which are turbid because of ice,
And into which the snow [1]melts.
17 "When [a]they become waterless, they [1]are silent,
When it is hot, they vanish from their place.
18 "The [1]paths of their course wind along,
They go up into nothing and perish.
19 "The caravans of [a]Tema looked,
The travelers of [b]Sheba hoped for them.
20 "They [a]were [1]disappointed for they had trusted,
They came there and were confounded.
21 "Indeed, you have now become such,
You see a terror and are afraid.
22 "Have I said, 'Give me *something*',
Or, 'Offer a bribe for me from your wealth'?
23 "Or, 'Deliver me from the hand of the adversary'?
Or, 'Redeem me from the hand of the tyrants'?

24 "Teach me, and I will be silent;
And show me how I have erred.
25 "Honest words are [1]not painful,
But what does your argument prove?
26 "Do you intend to reprove *my* words,
When the [a]words of one in despair belong to the wind?
27 "You would even [a]cast *lots* for [b]the orphans,
And [c]barter over your friend.
28 "And now please look at me,
And *see* if I [a]lie to your face.
29 "Desist now, let there be no injustice;
Even desist, [a]my righteousness is yet in it.
30 "Is there injustice on my tongue?
Cannot [a]my palate discern [1]calamities?

6 [1]Heb., *hallamuth,* meaning uncertain. Perhaps the juice of a plant.

7 [a]Job 3:24; 33:20

9 [a]Job 7:16; 9:21; 10:1; Num. 11:15; 1 Kin. 19:4

10 [1]Lit., *hidden* [a]Job 22:22; 23:11, 12

11 [1]Lit., *prolong my soul* [a]Job 21:4

13 [1]So ancient versions [a]Job 26:2 [b]Job 26:3

14 [1]Or, *reverence* [a]Job 4:5 [b]Job 1:5; 15:4

15 [1]Or, *brook* [a]Jer. 15:18

16 [1]Lit., *hides itself*

17 [1]Or, *cease* [a]Job 24:19

18 [1]Or, *caravans turn from their course, they go up into the waste and perish.*

19 [a]Gen. 25:15; Is. 21:14; Jer. 25:23 [b]Job 1:15

20 [1]Lit., *ashamed* [a]Jer. 14:3

25 [1]Or, *in what way . . . .?*

26 [a]Job 8:2; 15:2; 16:3

27 [a]Joel 3:3; Nah. 3:10 [b]Job 22:9; 24:3, 9 [c]2 Pet. 2:3

28 [a]Job 27:4; 33:3; 36:4

29 [a]Job 13:18; 19:6; 23:10; 27:5, 6; 34:5; 42:1-6

30 [1]Or, *words* [a]Job 12:11

Chapter 7

"[1]Is not man [a]forced to labor on earth,
And *are not* his days like the days of [b]a hired man?
2 "As a slave who pants for the shade,
And as a hired man who eagerly waits for his wages,
3 So am I allotted months of vanity,
And [a]nights of trouble are appointed me.
4 "When I [a]lie down I say,
'When shall I arise?'
But the night continues,
And I am [1]continually tossing until dawn.
5 "My [a]flesh is clothed with worms and a crust of dirt;
My skin hardens and runs.
6 "My days are [a]swifter than a weaver's shuttle,
And come to an end [b]without hope.

7 "Remember that my life [a]is *but* breath,
My eye will [b]not again see good.
8 "The [a]eye of him who sees me will behold me no more;
Thine eyes *will be* on me, but [b]I will not be.
9 "When a [a]cloud vanishes, it is gone,
So [b]he who goes down to [c]Sheol does not come up.
10 "He will not return again to his house,
Nor will [a]his place know him any more.

11 "Therefore, [a]I will not restrain my mouth;
I will speak in the anguish of my spirit,
I will complain in the bitterness of my soul.
12 "Am I the sea, or [a]the sea monster,
That Thou dost set a guard over me?
13 "If I say, '[a]My bed will comfort me,
My couch will [1]ease my complaint,'
14 Then Thou dost frighten me with dreams
And terrify me by visions;
15 So that my soul would choose suffocation,
Death rather than my [1]pains.
16 "I [1a]waste away; I will not live forever.
Leave me alone, [b]for my days are *but* a breath.
17 "[a]What is man that Thou dost magnify him,
And that Thou [1]art concerned about him,
18 That [a]Thou dost examine him every morning,
And try him every moment?
19 "[1a]Wilt Thou never turn Thy gaze away from me,
Nor let me alone until I swallow my spittle?
20 "[a]Have I sinned? What have I done to Thee,
O watcher of men?
Why hast Thou set me as Thy target,
So that I am a burden to myself?
21 "Why then [a]dost Thou not pardon my transgression
And take away my iniquity?
For now I will [b]lie down in the dust;
And Thou wilt seek me, [c]but I will not be."

1 [1]Lit., *Has not man compulsory labor* [a]Job 5:7; 10:17; 14:1, 14 [b]Job 14:6

3 [a]Job 16:7

4 [1]Lit., *sated with* [a]Job 7:13, 14; Deut. 28:67

5 [a]Job 2:7

6 [a]Job 9:25 [b]Job 13:15; 14:19; 17:15, 16; 19:10

7 [a]Job 7:16 [b]Job 9:25

8 [a]Job 8:18; 20:9 [b]Job 7:21

9 [a]Job 30:15 [b]Job 3:13-19 [c]Job 11:8; 14:13; 17:13, 16

10 [a]Job 8:18; 20:9; 27:21, 23

11 [a]Job 10:1; 21:4; 23:2

12 [a]Ezek. 32:2, 3

13 [1]Lit., *bear* [a]Job 7:4; Ps. 6:6

15 [1]Lit., *bones*

16 [1]Or, *loathe* my life [a]Job 6:9; 9:21; 10:1 [b]Job 7:7

17 [1]Lit., *shouldst set Thy heart on* [a]Job 22:2; Ps. 8:4; 144:3; Heb. 2:6

18 [a]Job 14:3

19 [1]Lit., *How long wilt Thou not* [a]Job 9:18; 10:20; 14:6

20 [a]Job 35:3, 6

21 [a]Job 9:28; 10:14 [b]Job 10:9 [c]Job 7:8

Chapter 8

THEN Bildad the Shuhite [1]answered,
2 "How long will you say these *things*,
And the [a]words of your mouth be a mighty wind?
3 "Does [a]God pervert justice
Or does [1]the Almighty pervert what is right?
4 "[a]If your sons sinned against Him,
Then He delivered them into the [1]power of their transgression.
5 "If you would [a]seek God
And implore the compassion of [1]the Almighty,
6 "If you are pure and upright,
Surely now [a]He would rouse Himself for you
And restore your righteous [1b]estate.
7 "Though your beginning was insignificant,
Yet your [a]end will increase greatly.

8 "Please [a]inquire of past generations,
And consider the things searched out by their fathers.
9 "For we are *only* of yesterday and know nothing,
Because [a]our days on earth are as a shadow.
10 "Will they not teach you *and* tell you,
And bring forth words from their minds?

11 "Can the papyrus grow up without marsh?
Can the rushes grow without water?
12 "While it is still green *and* not cut down,
Yet it withers before any *other* [1]plant.
13 "So are the paths of [a]all who forget God,
And the [b]hope of the godless will perish,
14 Whose confidence is fragile,
And whose trust a [a]spider's [1]web.
15 "He [1]trusts in his [a]house, but it does not stand;
He holds fast to it, but it does not endure.
16 "He [1a]thrives before the sun,
And his [b]shoots spread out over his garden.
17 "His roots wrap around a rock pile,
He [1]grasps a house of stones.
18 "If he is [1]removed from [a]his place,
Then it will deny him, *saying,* '[b]I never saw you.'
19 "Behold, [a]this is the joy of His way;
And out of the dust others will spring.
20 "Lo, [a]God will not reject *a man of* integrity,
Nor [b]will He [1]support the evildoers.
21 "He will yet fill [a]your mouth with laughter,
And your lips with [b]shouting.
22 "Those who hate you will be [a]clothed with shame;
And the [b]tent of the wicked will be no more."

Chapter 9

THEN Job [1]answered,
2 "In truth I know that this is so,
But how can a [a]man be in the right [1]before God?
3 "If one wished to [a]dispute with Him,
He could not [b]answer Him once in a thousand *times.*

1 [1]Lit., *answered and said*
2 [a]Job 6:26
3 [1]Heb., *Shaddai* [a]Job 34:10, 12; 36:23; 37:23; Gen. 18:25; Deut. 32:4; 2 Chr. 19:7; Rom. 3:5
4 [1]Lit., *hand* [a]Job 1:5, 18, 19
5 [1]Heb., *Shaddai* [a]Job 5:17-27
6 [1]Lit., *place* [a]Job 22:27; 34:28; Ps. 7:6 [b]Job 5:24
7 [a]Job 42:12
8 [a]Job 15:18; 20:4; Deut. 4:32; 32:7
9 [a]Job 14:2
12 [1]Lit., *reed*
13 [a]Ps. 9:17 [b]Job 11:20; 13:16; 15:34; 20:5; 27:8
14 [1]Lit., *house* [a]Is. 59:5, 6
15 [1]Lit., *leans on* [a]Job 8:22; 27:18; Ps. 49:11
16 [1]Lit., *is lush* [a]Ps. 37:35; Jer. 11:16 [b]Ps. 80:11
17 [1]Heb., *sees*
18 [1]Lit., *swallowed up* [a]Job 7:10 [b]Job 7:8
19 [a]Job 20:5
20 [1]Lit., *strengthen the hand of* [a]Job 4:7 [b]Job 21:30
21 [a]Job 5:22; Ps. 126:1, 2 [b]Ps. 132:16
22 [a]Ps. 132:18 [b]Job 8:15; 15:34; 18:14; 21:28

1 [1]Lit., *answered and said*
2 [1]Lit., *with* [a]Job 4:17; 25:4
3 [a]Job 10:2; 13:19; 23:6; 40:2 [b]Job 15:32

4 "[a]Wise in heart and [b]mighty in strength,
Who has [1c]defied Him [2]without harm?
5 "[a]Who removes the mountains, they know not *how*,
When He overturns them in His anger;
6 Who [a]shakes the earth out of its place,
And its [b]pillars tremble;
7 Who commands the [a]sun [1]not to shine,
And sets a seal upon the stars;
8 Who alone [a]stretches out the heavens,
And [1b]tramples down the waves of the sea;
9 Who makes the [a]Bear, Orion, and the Pleiades,
And the [b]chambers of the south;
10 Who [a]does great things, [1]unfathomable,
And wondrous works without number.
11 "Were He to pass by me, [a]I would not see Him;
Were He to move past *me*, I would not perceive Him.
12 "Were He to snatch away, who could [a]restrain Him?
Who could say to Him, '[b]What art Thou doing?'

13 "God will not turn back His anger;
Beneath Him crouch the helpers of [a]Rahab.
14 "How then can [a]I [1]answer Him,
And choose my words [2]before Him?
15 "For [a]though I were right, I could not [1]answer;
I would have to [b]implore the mercy of my Judge.
16 "If I called and He answered me,
I could not believe that He was listening to my voice.
17 "For He [a]bruises me with a tempest,
And mulitplies my wounds without cause.
18 "He will [a]not allow me to get my breath,
But saturates me with [b]bitterness.
19 "If *it is a matter* of power, [a]behold, *He is* the strong one!
And if *it is a matter* of justice, who can summon [1]Him?
20 "[a]Though I am righteous, my mouth will [b]condemn me;
Though I am guiltless, He will declare me guilty.
21 "I am [a]guiltless;
I do not take notice of myself;
I [b]despise my life.
22 "It is *all* one; therefore I say,
'He [a]destroys the guiltless and the wicked.'
23 "If the scourge kills suddenly,
He [a]mocks the despair of the innocent.
24 "The earth [a]is given into the hand of the wicked;
He [b]covers the faces of its judges.
If *it is* not *He*, then who is it?

25 "Now [a]my days are swifter than a runner;
They flee away, [b]they see no good.
26 "They slip by like [a]reed boats,
Like an [b]eagle that swoops on [1]its prey.
27 "Though I say, 'I will forget [a]my complaint,
I will leave off my *sad* countenance and be cheerful,'
28 "I am [a]afraid of all my pains,
I know that [b]Thou wilt not acquit me.
29 "I am accounted [a]wicked,
Why then should I toil in vain?

4 [1]Lit., *stiffened his neck against* [2]Lit., *and remained safe*
[a]Job 11:6; 12:13; 28:23; 38:36, 37 [b]Job 9:19; 23:6 [c]2 Chr. 13:12; Prov. 29:1

5 [a]Job 9:5-10; 26:6-14; 41:11

6 [a]Is. 2:19, 21; 13:13; Hag. 2:6 [b]Ps. 75:3

7 [1]Lit., *and it does not shine*
[a]Is. 13:10; Ezek. 32:7, 8

8 [1]Lit., *treads upon the heights of*
[a]Job 37:18; Gen. 1:1; Ps. 104:2; Is. 40:22 [b]Job 38:16; Ps. 77:19

9 [a]Job 38:31, 32; Amos 5:8 [b]Job 37:9

10 [1]Lit., *until there is no searching out*
[a]Job 5:9

11 [a]Job 23:8, 9; 35:14

12 [a]Job 10:7; 11:10 [b]Is. 45:9

13 [a]Job 26:12; Ps. 89:10; Is. 30:7; 51:9

14 [1]Or, *plead my case* [2]Lit., *with*
[a]Job 9:3, 32

15 [1]Or, *plead my case*
[a]Job 9:20, 21; 10:15 [b]Job 8:5

17 [a]Job 16:12, 14; 30:22

18 [a]Job 7:19; 10:20 [b]Job 13:26; 27:2

19 [1]So with Gk. Heb., *me*
[a]Job 9:4

20 [a]Job 9:15 [b]Job 9:29; 15:6

21 [a]Job 1:1; 12:4; 13:18 [b]Job 7:16

22 [a]Job 10:7, 8

23 [a]Job 24:12

24 [a]Job 10:3; 12:6; 16:11 [b]Job 12:17

25 [a]Job 7:6 [b]Job 7:7

26 [1]Lit., *food*
[a]Is. 18:2 [b]Job 39:29; Hab. 1:8

27 [a]Job 7:11

28 [a]Job 3:25 [b]Job 7:21; 10:14

29 [a]Job 10:2; Ps. 37:33

30 "If I should [a]wash myself with snow
And cleanse [b]my hands with lye,
31 Yet Thou wouldst plunge me into the pit,
And [a]my own clothes would abhor me.
32 "For *He is* not a man as I am that [a]I may answer Him,
That we may go to [1]court together.
33 "There is no [a]umpire between us,
Who may lay his hand upon us both.
34 "Let Him [a]remove his rod from me,
And let not dread of Him terrify me.
35 "*Then* I [a]would speak and not fear Him;
But I am not like that in myself.

Chapter 10

"[1a]I LOATHE my own life;
I will give full vent to [b]my complaint;
I will speak in the bitterness of my soul.
2 "I will say to God, '[a]Do not condemn me;
Let me know why Thou dost contend with me.
3 'Is it [1]right for Thee indeed to [a]oppress,
To reject [b]the labor of Thy hands,
And [2]to look favorably on [c]the schemes of the wicked?
4 'Hast Thou eyes of flesh?
Or dost Thou [a]see as a man sees?
5 'Are Thy days as the days of a mortal,
Or [a]Thy years as man's years,
6 That [a]Thou shouldst seek for my guilt,
And search after my sin?
7 'According to Thy knowledge [a]I am indeed not guilty;
Yet there is [b]no deliverance from Thy hand.

8 '[a]Thy hands fashioned and made me [1]altogether,
[b]And wouldst Thou destroy me?
9 'Remember now, that Thou hast made me as [a]clay;
And wouldst Thou [b]turn me into dust again?
10 'Didst Thou not pour me out like milk,
And curdle me like cheese;
11 'Clothe me with skin and flesh,
And knit me together with bones and sinews?
12 'Thou hast [a]granted me life and lovingkindness;
And Thy care has preserved my spirit.
13 'Yet [a]these things Thou hast concealed in Thy heart;
I know that this is within Thee:
14 'If I sin, then Thou wouldst [a]take note of me,
And [b]wouldst not acquit me of my guilt.
15 'If [a]I am wicked, woe to me!
And [b]if I am righteous, I dare not lift up my head.
I am sated with disgrace and [1]conscious of my misery.
16 'And should *my head* be lifted up, [a]Thou wouldst hunt me like a lion;
And again Thou wouldst show Thy [b]power against me.
17 'Thou dost renew [a]Thy witnesses against me,
And increase Thine anger toward me,
[b]Hardship after hardship is with me.

---

30 [a]Jer. 2:22 [b]Job 31:7
31 [a]Job 7:17
32 [1]Lit., *judgment* [a]Job 9:3
33 [a]Job 9:19; 1 Sam. 2:25; Is. 1:18
34 [a]Job 13:21
35 [a]Job 13:22
1 [1]Lit., *My soul* [a]Job 7:16 [b]Job 7:11
2 [a]Job 9:29
3 [1]Lit., *good* [2]Lit., *you shine forth* [a]Job 9:22-24; 16:11; 19:6; 27:2 [b]Job 10:8; 14:15; Ps. 138:8; Is. 64:8 [c]Job 21:16; 22:18
4 [a]Job 28:24; 34:21; 1 Sam. 16:7
5 [a]Job 36:26
6 [a]Job 14:16
7 [a]Job 9:21; 13:18 [b]Job 9:12; 23:13; 27:22
8 [1]Lit., *together round about* [a]Job 10:3 Ps. 119:73 [b]Job 9:22
9 [a]Job 4:19; 33:6 [b]Job 7:21
12 [a]Job 33:4
13 [a]Job 23:13
14 [a]Job 7:20 [b]Job 7:21; 9:28
15 [1]Lit., *see* [a]Job 10:7 [b]Job 6:29
16 [a]Is. 38:13; Lam. 3:10; Hos. 13:7 [b]Job 5:9
17 [a]Job 16:8; Ruth 1:21 [b]Job 7:1

18 ‘[a]Why then hast Thou brought me out of the womb?
Would that I had died and no eye had seen me!
19 ‘I should have been as though I had not been,
Carried from womb to tomb.’
20 “Would He not let [a]my few days alone?
[1b]Withdraw from me that I may have a little cheer
21 Before I go—[a]and I shall not return—
To the land of darkness and [b]deep shadow;
22 The land of utter gloom as darkness *itself*,
Of deep shadow without order,
And which shines as the darkness.”

CHAPTER 11

THEN Zophar the Naamathite [1]answered,
2 “Shall a multitude of words go unanswered,
And a [a]talkative man be acquitted?
3 “Shall your boasts silence men?
And shall you [a]scoff and none rebuke?
4 “For [a]you have said, ‘My teaching is pure,
And [b]I am innocent in your eyes.’
5 “But would that God might speak,
And open His lips against you,
6 And show you the secrets of wisdom!
For sound wisdom [1a]has two sides.
Know then that God [2]forgets a part of [b]your iniquity.

7 “[a]Can you discover the depths of God?
Can you discover the limits of the Almighty?
8 “*It is* [a]high as [1]the heavens, what can you do?
Deeper than [2b]Sheol, what can you know?
9 “Its measure is longer than the earth,
And broader than the sea.
10 “If He passes by or shuts up,
Or calls an assembly, [a]who can restrain Him?
11 “For [a]He knows false men,
And He [b]sees iniquity [1]without investigating.
12 “And [1a]an idiot will become intelligent
When the [2]foal of a [b]wild donkey is born a man.

13 “[a]If you would [b]direct your heart right,
And [c]spread out your hand to Him;
14 If iniquity is in your hand, [a]put it far away,
And do not let wickedness dwell in your tents.
15 “Then, indeed, you could [a]lift up your face without *moral* defect,
And you would be steadfast and [b]not fear.
16 “For you would [a]forget *your* trouble,
As [b]waters that have passed by, you would remember *it*.
17 “And your [1]life would be [2a]brighter than noonday;
Darkness would be like the morning.
18 “Then you would trust, because there is hope;
And you would look around and rest securely.
19 “You would [a]lie down and none would disturb *you*,
And many would [b]entreat your [1]favor.
20 “But the [a]eyes of the wicked will fail,

18 [a]Job 3:11-13

20 [1]Lit., *Put* [a]Job 14:1 [b]Job 7:19

21 [a]Job 3:13-19; 16:22; 2 Sam. 12:23 [b]Job 10:22; 34:22; 38:17

1 [1]Lit., *answered and said*

2 [a]Job 8:2; 15:2; 18:2

3 [a]Job 17:2; 21:3

4 [a]Job 6:10 [b]Job 10:7

6 [1]Lit., *is double* [2]Lit., *causes to be forgotten for you* [a]Job 9:4 [b]Job 15:5; 22:5

7 [a]Job 33:12, 13; 36:26; 37:5, 23

8 [1]Lit., *the heights of heaven* [2]I.e., the nether world [a]Job 22:12; 35:5 [b]Job 26:6; 38:17

10 [a]Job 9:12

11 [1]Or, *even He does not consider* [a]Job 34:21-23 [b]Job 24:23; 28:24; 31:4

12 [1]Lit., *a hollow man* [2]Lit., *donkey* [a]Ps. 39:5, 11; 62:9; 144:4; Eccles. 1:2; 10:11 [b]Job 39:5

13 [a]Job 11:13-20; 5:17-27 [b]Ps. 78:8 [c]Job 22:27; Ps. 88:9; 143:6

14 [a]Job 22:23

15 [a]Job 22:26 [b]Ps. 27:3; 46:2

16 [a]Is. 65:16 [b]Job 22:11

17 [1]Lit., *duration of life* [2]Lit., *above noonday* [a]Job 22:26

19 [1]Lit., *face* [a]Lev. 26:6; Is. 17:2; Zeph. 3:13; Mic. 4:4 [b]Is. 45:14

20 [a]Job 17:5; Deut. 28:65

And [1]there will [b]be no escape for them;
And their [c]hope is [2d]to breathe their last."

CHAPTER 12

THEN Job [1]responded,
2 "Truly then [a]you are the people,
And with you wisdom will die.
3 "But [a]I have intelligence as well as you;
I am not inferior to you.
And [1]who does not know such things as these?
4 "I am a [a]joke to [1]my friends.
The one who called on God, and He answered him;
The just *and* [b]blameless *man* is a joke.
5 "[1]He who is at ease holds calamity in contempt,
As prepared for those whose feet slip.
6 "The [a]tents of the destroyers prosper,
And those who provoke God [b]are secure,
[1]Whom God brings [c]into his power.

7 "But now ask the beasts, and let them teach you;
And the birds of the heavens, and let them tell you.
8 "Or speak to the earth, and let it teach you;
And let the fish of the sea declare to you.
9 "Who among all these does not know
That [a]the hand of the LORD has done this,
10 [a]In whose hand is the life of every living thing,
And [b]the breath of all mankind?
11 "Does not [a]the ear test words,
As the palate [1]tastes its food?
12 "Wisdom is with [a]aged men,
With [1]long life is understanding.

13 "With Him are [a]wisdom and [b]might;
To Him belong counsel and [c]understanding.
14 "Behold, He [a]tears down, and it cannot be rebuilt;
He [1b]imprisons a man, and [2]there can be no release.
15 "Behold, He [a]restrains the waters, and they dry up;
And He [b]sends them out, and they [1]inundate the earth.
16 "With Him are strength and sound wisdom,
The [a]misled and the misleader belong to Him.
17 "He makes [a]counselors walk [1b]barefoot,
And makes fools of [c]judges.
18 "He [a]loosens the [1]bond of kings,
And binds their loins with a girdle.
19 "He makes priests walk [1]barefoot,
And overthrows [a]the secure ones.
20 "He deprives the trusted ones of speech,
And [a]takes away the discernment of the elders.
21 "He [a]pours contempt on nobles,
And [b]loosens the belt of the strong.
22 "He [a]reveals mysteries from the darkness,
And brings the deep darkness into light.
23 "He [a]makes the nations great, then destroys them;
He [1]enlarges the nations, then leads them away.

20 [1]Lit., *escape has perished from them* [2]Lit., *the expiring of the soul* [b]Job 27:22; 34:22 [c]Job 8:13 [d]Job 6:9

1 [1]Lit., *answered and said*

2 [a]Job 2:3; 16:1, 2; 17:10

3 [1]Lit., *with whom is there not like these?* [a]Job 13:2

4 [1]Lit., *his* [a]Job 17:6; 30:1, 9, 10; 34:7 [b]Job 6:29

5 [1]Lit., *Contempt for calamity is the thought of him who is at ease*

6 [1]Or, *He who brings God into his hand* [a]Job 9:24; 21:9 [b]Job 24:23 [c]Job 22:18

9 [a]Is. 41:20

10 [a]Acts 17:28 [b]Job 27:3; 33:4

11 [1]Lit., *tastes food for itself* [a]Job 34:3

12 [1]Lit., *length of days* [a]Job 15:10; 32:7

13 [a]Job 9:4 [b]Job 9:4 [c]Job 11:6; 26:12; 32:8; 36:5; 38:36

14 [1]Lit., *shuts against* [2]Lit., *it is not opened* [a]Job 19:10; Is. 25:2 [b]Job 37:7

15 [1]Lit., *overturn* [a]Deut. 11:17; 1 Kin. 8:35; 17:1 [b]Gen. 7:11-24

16 [a]Job 13:7, 9

17 [1]Or, *stripped* [a]Job 3:14 [b]Job 19:9 [c]Job 9:24

18 [1]Or, *discipline* [a]Ps. 116:16

19 [1]Or, *stripped* [a]Job 21:7; 22:8; 24:22; 34:24-28; 35:9

20 [a]Job 17:4; 32:9

21 [a]Job 34:19; Ps. 107:40 [b]Job 12:18

22 [a]Dan. 2:22; 1 Cor. 4:5

23 [1]Or, *spreads out* [a]Is. 9:3; 26:15

24 "He [a]deprives of intelligence the chiefs of the earth's people,
And makes them wander in a pathless waste.
25 "They [a]grope in darkness with no light,
And He makes them [b]stagger like a drunken man.

Chapter 13

"[a]Behold, my eye has seen all *this*,
My ear has heard and understood it.
2 "[a]What you know I also know.
I am not inferior to you.

3 "But [a]I would speak to the [1]Almighty,
And I desire to [b]argue with God.
4 "But you [a]smear with lies;
You are all [b]worthless physicians.
5 "O that you would [a]be completely silent,
And that it would become your wisdom!
6 "Please hear my argument,
And listen to the contentions of my lips.
7 "Will you [a]speak what is unjust for God,
And speak what is deceitful for Him?
8 "Will you [a]show partiality for Him?
Will you contend for God?
9 "Will it be well when He examines you?
Or [a]will you deceive Him as one deceives a man?
10 "He will surely reprove you,
If you secretly [a]show partiality.
11 "Will not [a]His [1]majesty terrify you,
And the dread of Him fall on you?
12 "Your memorable sayings are [a]proverbs of ashes,
Your defenses are defenses of clay.

13 "[a]Be silent before me so that I may speak;
Then let what may come on me.
14 "Why should I take my flesh in my teeth,
And put my life in my [1]hands.
15 "[a]Though He slay me,
I [b]will hope in Him.
Nevertheless I will argue my ways [1]before Him.
16 "This also will be my [a]salvation,
For [b]a godless man may not come before His presence.
17 "Listen carefully to my speech,
And let my declaration *fill* your ears.
18 "Behold now, I have [a]prepared my case;
I know that [b]I will be vindicated.
19 "Who will contend with me?
For then I would be silent and [a]die.

20 "Only two things do not do to me,
Then I will not hide from Thy face:
21 [a]Remove Thy [1]hand from me,
And let not the dread of Thee terrify me.
22 "Then call, and [a]I will answer;
Or let me speak, then reply to me.

24 [a]Job 12:20
25 [a]Job 5:14 [b]Is. 24:20
1 [a]Job 12:9
2 [a]Job 12:3
3 [1]Heb., *Shaddai* [a]Job 13:22; 23:4 [b]Job 13:15
4 [a]Ps. 119:69 [b]Jer. 23:32
5 [a]Job 13:13; 21:5
7 [a]Job 27:4
8 [a]Lev. 19:15
9 [a]Job 12:16
10 [a]Job 13:8; 32:21; 34:19
11 [1]Lit., *exaltation* [a]Job 31:23
12 [a]Job 27:1; 29:1
13 [a]Job 13:5
14 [1]Lit., *palm*
15 [1]Lit., *to His face* [a]Job 7:6 [b]Job 27:5
16 [a]Job 23:7 [b]Job 34:21-23
18 [a]Job 6:29; 23:4 [b]Job 9:21; 10:7; 12:4
19 [a]Job 7:21; 10:8
21 [1]Lit., *palm* [a]Job 9:34; Ps. 39:10
22 [a]Job 9:16; 14:15

23 "[a]How many are my iniquities and sins?
Make known to me my [1]rebellion and my sin.
24 "Why dost Thou [a]hide Thy face,
And consider me [b]Thine enemy?
25 "Wilt Thou cause a [a]driven leaf to tremble?
Or wilt Thou pursue the dry [b]chaff?
26 "For Thou dost write [a]bitter things against me,
And dost make me to inherit the iniquities of my youth.
27 "Thou [a]dost put my feet in the stocks,
And dost watch all my paths;
Thou dost [1]set a limit for the soles of my feet,
28 While [1]I am decaying like a [a]rotten thing,
Like a garment that is moth-eaten.

CHAPTER 14

"[a]MAN, who is born of woman,
Is [1]short-lived and full of turmoil.
2 "[a]Like a flower he comes forth and withers.
He also flees like [b]a shadow and does not remain.
3 "Thou also dost [a]open Thine eyes on him,
And bring [1]him into judgment with Thyself.
4 "[a]Who can make the clean out of the unclean?
No one!
5 "Since his days are determined,
The [a]number of his months is with Thee,
And his limits Thou hast [1]set so that he cannot pass.
6 "[a]Turn your gaze from him that he may [1]rest,
Until he [2]fulfills his day like a hired man.

7 "For there is hope for a tree,
When it is cut down, that it will sprout again,
And its shoots will not [1]fail.
8 "Though its roots grow old in the ground,
And its stump dies in the dry soil,
9 At the scent of water it will flourish
And put forth sprigs like a plant.
10 "But [a]man [b]dies and lies prostrate.
Man expires, and where is he?
11 "*As* [a]water [1]evaporates from the sea,
And a river becomes parched and dried up,
12 So [a]man lies down and does not rise.
Until the heavens be no more,
[1]He will not awake nor be aroused out of [2]his sleep.

13 "Oh that Thou wouldst [a]hide me in [1]Sheol,
That Thou wouldst conceal me [b]until Thy wrath returns *to Thee,*
That Thou wouldst set a limit for me and remember me!
14 "If a man dies, will he live *again?*
All the days of my struggle I will wait,
Until my change comes.
15 "Thou wilt call, and I will answer Thee;
Thou wilt long for [a]the work of Thy hands.

23 [1]Or, *transgression* [a]Job 7:21

24 [a]Ps. 13:1; 44:24; 88:14 [b]Job 19:11; 33:10

25 [a]Lev. 26:36 [b]Job 21:18

26 [a]Job 9:18

27 [1]Lit., *carve for* [a]Job 33:11

28 [1]Lit., *he* [a]Job 2:7

1 [1]Lit., *short of days* [a]Job 5:7

2 [a]Ps. 90:5, 6; 103:15; Is. 40:6, 7 [b]Job 8:9

3 [1]So with some ancient versions; M.T., *me* [a]Ps. 8:4; 144:3

4 [a]Job 15:14; 25:4

5 [1]Lit., *made* [a]Job 21:21

6 [1]Lit., *cease* [2]Lit., *makes acceptable* [a]Job 7:19

7 [1]Or, *cease*

10 [a]Job 14:10-15; 3:13 [b]Job 13:9

11 [1]Lit., *disappears* [a]Is. 19:5

12 [1]Lit., *they* [2]Lit., *their.* [a]Job 3:13

13 [1]I.e., the nether world [a]Job 3:13 [b]Is. 26:20

15 [a]Job 10:3

16 "For now Thou dost [a]number my steps,
Thou dost not [b]observe my sin.
17 "My transgression is [a]sealed up in a bag,
And Thou dost [1]wrap up my iniquity.

18 "But the falling mountain [1]crumbles away,
And the rock moves from its place;
19 Water wears away stones,
Its torrents wash away the dust of the earth;
So Thou dost [a]destroy man's hope.
20 "Thou dost forever overpower him and he [a]departs;
Thou dost change his appearance and send him away.
21 "His sons achieve honor, but he does not know *it;*
Or they become insignificant, but he does not perceive it.
22 "But his [1]body pains him,
And he mourns only for himself."

Chapter 15

THEN Eliphaz the Temanite [1]responded,
2 "Should a wise man answer with windy knowledge,
[a]And fill [1]himself with the east wind?
3 "Should he argue with useless talk,
Or with words which are not profitable?
4 "Indeed, you do away with [1]reverence,
And hinder meditation before God.
5 "For [a]your guilt teaches your mouth,
And you choose the language of [b]the crafty.
6 "Your [a]own mouth condemns you, and not I;
And your own lips testify against you.

7 "Were you the first man to be born,
Or [a]were you brought forth before the hills?
8 "Do you hear the [a]secret counsel of God,
And limit wisdom to yourself?
9 "[a]What do you know that we do not know?
What do you understand that [1]we do not?
10 "Both the [a]gray-haired and the aged are among us,
Older than your father.
11 "Are [a]the consolations of God too small for you,
Even the [b]word *spoken* gently with you?
12 "Why does your [a]heart carry you away?
And why do your eyes flash,
13 That you should turn your spirit against God,
And allow *such* words to go out of your mouth?
14 "What is man, that [a]he should be pure,
Or [b]he who is born of a woman, that he should be righteous?
15 "Behold, He puts no trust in His [a]holy ones,
And the [b]heavens are not pure in His sight;
16 How much less one who is [a]detestable and corrupt,
Man, who [b]drinks iniquity like water!

17 "I will tell you, listen to me;
And what I have seen I will also declare;

16 [a]Job 31:4; 34:21 [b]Job 10:6
17 [1]Lit., *plaster or glue together* [a]Deut. 32:32-34
18 [1]Lit., *withers*
19 [a]Job 7:6
20 [a]Job 4:20; 20:7
22 [1]Lit., *flesh*
1 [1]Lit., *answered and said*
2 [1]Lit., *his belly* [a]Job 6:26
4 [1]Lit., *fear*
5 [a]Job 22:5 [b]Job 5:12, 13
6 [a]Job 18:7
7 [a]Job 38:4, 21
8 [a]Job 29:4; Rom. 11:34
9 [1]Lit., *is not within us?* [a]Job 12:3; 13:2
10 [a]Job 12:12; 32:6, 7
11 [a]Job 5:17-19; 36:15, 16 [b]Job 6:10; 23:12
12 [a]Job 11:13; 36:13
14 [a]Job 14:4 [b]Job 25:4
15 [a]Job 5:1 [b]Job 25:5
16 [a]Ps. 14:1 [b]Job 34:7

18 What wise men have told,
And have not concealed from [a]their fathers,
19 To whom alone the land was given,
And no alien passed among them.
20 "The wicked man writhes [a]in pain all *his* days,
And [1]numbered are the years [b]stored up for the ruthless.
21 "[1]Sounds of [a]terror are in his ears,
[b]While at peace the destroyer comes upon him.
22 "He does not believe that he will [a]return from darkness,
And he is destined for [b]the sword.
23 "He wanders about for food, saying, 'Where is it?'
He knows that a day of [a]darkness is [1]at hand.
24 "Distress and anguish terrify him,
They overpower him like a king ready for the attack,
25 Because he has stretched out his hand against God,
And conducts himself [a]arrogantly against [1]the Almighty.
26 "He rushes [1]headlong at Him
With [2]his massive shield.
27 "For he has [a]covered his face with his fat,
And made his thighs heavy with flesh.
28 "And he has [a]lived in desolate cities,
In houses no one would inhabit,
Which are destined to become [1]ruins.
29 "He [a]will not become rich, nor will his wealth endure;
And his grain will not bend down to the ground.
30 "He will [a]not [1]escape from darkness;
The [b]flame will wither his shoots,
And by [c]the breath of His mouth he will go away.
31 "Let him not [a]trust in emptiness, deceiving himself;
For emptiness will be his [1]reward.
32 "It will be accomplished [a]before his time,
And his palm [b]branch will not be green.
33 "He will drop off his unripe grape like the vine,
And will [a]cast off his flower like the olive tree.
34 "For the company of [a]the godless is barren,
And fire consumes [b]the tents of [1]the corrupt.
35 "They [a]conceive [1]mischief and bring forth iniquity,
And their [2]mind prepares deception."

Chapter 16

THEN Job [1]answered,
2 "I have heard many such things;
[1a]Sorry comforters are you all.
3 "Is there *no* limit to [a]windy words?
Or what plagues you that you answer?
4 "I too could speak like you,
If [1]I were in your place.
I could compose words against you,
And [a]shake my head at you.
5 "I could strengthen you with my mouth,
And the solace of my lips could lessen *your pain.*

6 "If I speak, [a]my pain is not lessened,
And if I hold back, what has left me?

18 [a]Job 8:8; 20:4

20 [1]Lit., *the number of years are* [a]Job 15:24 [b]Job 24:1; 27:13

21 [1]Lit., *A sound of terrors* [a]Job 15:24; 18:11; 20:25; 24:17; 27:20 [b]Job 20:21; 1 Thess. 5:3

22 [a]Job 15:30 [b]Job 19:29; 27:14; 33:18; 36:12

23 [1]Lit., *ready at his hand* [a]Job 15:22, 30

25 [1]Heb., *Shaddai* [a]Job 36:9

26 [1]Lit., *with a stiff neck* [2]Lit., *the thick-bossed shields*

27 [a]Ps. 17:10; 73:7; 119:70

28 [1]Or, *heaps* [a]Job 3:14; Is. 5:8, 9

29 [a]Job 27:16, 17

30 [1]Lit., *turn aside* [a]Job 15:22; 5:14 [b]Job 15:34; 20:26; 22:20; 31:12 [c]Job 4:9

31 [1]Lit., *exchange* [a]Job 35:13; Is. 59:4

32 [a]Job 22:16; Eccles. 7:17 [b]Job 18:16

33 [a]Job 14:2

34 [1]Lit., *bribe* [a]Job 8:13 [b]Job 8:22

35 [1]Or, *pain* [2]Lit., *belly* [a]Ps. 7:14; Is. 59:4

1 [1]Lit., *answered and said*

2 [1]Lit., *Comforters of trouble* [a]Job 13:4; 21:34

3 [a]Job 6:26

4 [1]Lit., *your soul were in place of my soul* [a]Ps. 22:7; 109:25; Zeph. 2:15; Matt. 27:39

6 [a]Job 9:27, 28

7 "But now He has [a]exhausted me;
Thou hast laid [b]waste all my company.
8 "And Thou hast shriveled me up,
[a]It has become a witness;
And my [b]leanness rises up against me,
It testifies to my face.
9 "His anger has [a]torn me and [1]hunted me down,
He has [b]gnashed at me with His teeth;
My [c]adversary [2]glares at me.
10 "They have [a]gaped at me with their mouth,
They have [1b]slapped me on the cheek with contempt;
They have [c]massed themselves against me.
11 "God hands me over to ruffians,
And tosses me into the hands of the wicked.
12 "I was at ease, but [a]He shattered me,
And He has grasped me by the neck and shaken me to pieces;
He has also set me up as His [b]target.
13 "His [a]arrows surround me.
Without mercy He splits my kidneys open;
He pours out [b]my gall on the ground.
14 "He [a]breaks through me with breach after breach;
He [b]runs at me like a warrior.
15 "I have sewed [a]sackcloth over my skin,
And thrust my [b]horn in the dust.
16 "My face is flushed from [a]weeping,
[b]And deep darkness is on my eyelids,
17 Although there is no [a]violence in my hands,
And [b]my prayer is pure.

18 "O earth, do not cover my blood,
And let there be no place for my cry.
19 "Even now, behold, [a]my witness is in heaven,
And my [1]advocate is [b]on high.
20 "My [a]friends are my scoffers;
[b]My eye [1]weeps to God.
21 "O that a man might plead with God
As a man with his neighbor!
22 "For when a few years are past,
I shall go the way [a]of no return.

Chapter 17

"MY spirit is broken, my days are extinguished,
The [1a]grave is *ready* for me.
2 "[a]Surely mockers are with me,
And my eye [1]gazes on their provocation.

3 "Lay down, now, a pledge [a]for me with Thyself;
Who is there that will [1]be my guarantor?
4 "For Thou hast [1a]kept their heart from understanding;
Therefore Thou wilt not exalt *them*.
5 "He who [a]informs against friends for a share *of the spoil*,
The [b]eyes of his children also shall languish.

7 [a]Job 7:3 [b]Job 16:20; 19:13-15

8 [a]Job 10:17 [b]Job 19:20; Ps. 109:24

9 [1]Lit., *borne a grudge against me* [2]Lit., *sharpens his eyes*
[a]Job 19:11; Hos. 6:1 [b]Ps. 35:16; Lam. 2:16; Acts 7:54 [c]Job 13:24; 33:10

10 [1]Lit., *struck*
[a]Ps. 22:13 [b]Is. 50:6; Lam. 3:30; Acts 23:2 [c]Job 30:12; Ps. 35:15

12 [a]Job 9:17 [b]Job 7:20; Lam. 3:12

13 [a]Job 6:4; 19:12; 25:3 [b]Job 20:25

14 [a]Job 9:17 [b]Joel 2:7

15 [a]Job 2:8; Gen. 37:34; Ps. 69:11 [b]Job 19:9; Lam. 2:3

16 [a]Job 16:20 [b]Job 24:17

17 [a]Is. 59:6; Jon. 3:8 [b]Job 27:4

19 [1]Or, *witness*
[a]Job 19:25-27; Gen. 31:50; Phil. 1:8 [b]Job 31:2

20 [1]Or, *drips*
[a]Job 16:7 [b]Job 17:7

22 [a]Job 3:13

1 [1]Lit., *graves*
[a]Ps. 88:3, 4

2 [1]Lit., *lodges*
[a]Job 17:6; 12:4

3 [1]Lit., *strike hands with me*
[a]Ps. 119:122; Is. 38:14

4 [1]Lit., *hidden*
[a]Job 12:20

5 [a]Lev. 19:13, 16 [b]Job 11:20

6 "But He has made me a [a]byword of the people,
And I am [1]one at whom men [b]spit.
7 "My eye has also grown [a]dim because of grief,
And all my [b]members are as a shadow.
8 "The upright shall be appalled at this,
And the [a]innocent shall stir up himself against the godless.
9 "Nevertheless [a]the righteous shall hold to his way,
And [b]he who has clean hands shall grow stronger and stronger.
10 "But come again all of [1]you now,
For I [a]do not find a wise man among you.
11 "My [a]days are past, my plans are torn apart,
Even the wishes of my heart.
12 "They make night into day, *saying*,
'The light is near,' in the presence of darkness.
13 "If I look for [a]Sheol as my home,
I [1]make my bed in the darkness;
14 If I call to the [a]pit, 'You are my father';
To the [b]worm, 'my mother and my sister';
15 Where now is [a]my hope?
And who regards my hope?
16 "[1]Will it go down with me to Sheol?
Shall we together [a]go down into the dust?"

Chapter 18

THEN Bildad the Shuhite [1]responded,
2 "How long will you hunt for words?
Show understanding and then we can talk.
3 "Why are we [a]regarded as beasts,
As stupid in your eyes?
4 "O [1]you who tear yourself in your anger—
For your sake is the earth to be abandoned,
Or the rock to be moved from its place?

5 "Indeed, the [a]light of the wicked goes out,
And the [1]flame of his fire gives no light.
6 "The light in his tent is [a]darkened,
And his lamp goes out above him.
7 "His [1]vigorous stride is shortened,
And his [a]own scheme brings him down.
8 "For he is [a]thrown into the net by his own feet,
And he steps on the webbing.
9 "A snare seizes *him* by the heel,
And a trap snaps shut on him.
10 "A noose for him is hid in the ground,
And a trap for him on the path.
11 "All around [a]terrors frighten him,
And [b]harry him at every step.
12 "His strength is [a]famished,
And calamity is ready at his side.
13 "[1]His skin is devoured by disease,
The first-born of death [a]devours his [2]limbs.
14 "He is [a]torn from [1]the security of his tent,
And [2]they march him before the king of [b]terrors.

17:6 [1]Lit., *a spitting to the faces* [a]Job 17:2 [b]Job 30:10
7 [a]Job 16:16 [b]Job 16:8
8 [a]Job 22:19
9 [a]Prov. 4:18 [b]Job 22:30; 31:7
10 [1]With some ancient mss. and versions; M.T., *them* [a]Job 12:2
11 [a]Job 7:6
13 [1]Lit., *spread out* [a]Job 3:13
14 [a]Job 7:5 13:28; 30:18, 30 [b]Job 21:26; 25:6
15 [a]Job 7:6
16 [1]So the Gk. Heb. possibly, *let my* limbs *sink down to Sheol, since there is rest in the dust for all.* [a]Job 3:17; 21:33

18:1 [1]Lit., *answered and said*
3 [a]Ps. 73:22
4 [1]Lit., *he . . . tears himself . . . his*
5 [1]Lit., *spark* [a]Job 21:17; Prov. 13:9; 20:20; 24:20
6 [a]Job 12:25
7 [1]Lit., *steps of his strength* [a]Job 15:6
8 [a]Job 22:10; Ps. 9:15; 35:8; Is. 24:17, 18
11 [a]Job 15:21 [b]Job 18:18; 20:8
12 [a]Is. 8:21
13 [1]Heb., *it eats parts of his skin* [2]Or, *parts* [a]Zech. 14:12
14 [1]Lit., *his tent his trust* [2]Or, *you or she shall march* [a]Job 18:6; 8:22; 27:18 [b]Job 15:21

15 "[1]There dwells in his tent nothing of his;
[a]Brimstone is scattered on his habitation.
16 "His [a]roots are dried below,
And his [b]branch is cut off above.
17 "[a]Memory of him perishes from the earth,
And he has no name abroad.
18 "[1]He is driven from light [a]into darkness,
And [b]chased from the inhabited world.
19 "He has no [a]offspring or posterity among his people,
Nor any survivor where he sojourned.
20 "Those [1]in the west are appalled at [a]his [2]fate,
And those [3]in the east are seized with horror.
21 "Surely such are the [a]dwellings of the wicked,
And this is the place of him who does not know God."

Chapter 19

THEN Job [1]responded,
2 "How long will you torment [1]me,
And crush me with words?
3 "These ten times you have insulted me,
You are not ashamed to wrong me.
4 "Even if I have truly erred,
My error lodges with me.
5 "If indeed you [a]vaunt yourselves against me,
And prove my disgrace to me,
6 Know then that [a]God has wronged me,
And has closed [b]His net around me.

7 "Behold, [a]I cry, 'Violence!' but I get no answer;
I shout for help, but there is no justice.
8 "He has [a]walled up my way so that I cannot pass;
And He has put [b]darkness on my paths.
9 "He has [a]stripped my honor from me,
And removed the [b]crown from my head.
10 "He [a]breaks me down on every side, and I am gone;
And He has uprooted my [b]hope [c]like a tree.
11 "He has also [a]kindled His anger against me,
And [b]considered me as His enemy.
12 "His [a]troops come together,
And [b]build up their [1]way against me,
And camp around my tent.

13 "He has [a]removed my brothers far from me,
And my [b]acquaintances are completely estranged from me.
14 "My relatives have failed,
And my [a]intimate friends have forgotten me.
15 "Those who live in my house and my maids consider me a stranger.
I am a foreigner in their sight.
16 "I call to my servant, but he does not answer,
I have to implore him with my mouth.
17 "My breath is [1]offensive to my wife,
And I am loathsome to my own brothers.

15 [1]A suggested reading is, *fire dwells in his tent* [a]Ps. 11:6

16 [a]Is. 5:24; Hos. 9:16; Amos 2:9; Mal. 4:1 [b]Job 15:30, 32

17 [a]Job 24:20; Ps. 34:16; Prov. 10:7

18 [1]Lit., *They drive him . . .And chase him* [a]Job 5:14, Is. 8:21; 15:30; 20:8 [b]Job 27:21-23

19 [a]Job 27:14, 15; Is. 14:22

20 [1]Lit., *who come after* [2]Lit., *day* [3]Lit., *who have gone before* [a]Ps. 37:13; Jer. 50:27; Obad. 12

21 [a]Job 21:28

1 [1]Lit., *answered and said*

2 [1]Lit., *my soul*

5 [a]Ps. 35:26; 38:16; 55:12

6 [a]Job 16:11; 27:2 [b]Job 18:8-10; Ps. 66:11; Lam. 1:13

7 [a]Job 9:24; 30:20, 24; Hab. 1:2

8 [a]Job 3:23; Lam. 3:7, 9 [b]Job 30:26

9 [a]Job 12:17, 19; Ps. 89:44 [b]Job 16:15; Ps. 89:39; Lam. 5:16

10 [a]Job 12:14 [b]Job 7:6 [c]Job 24:20

11 [a]Job 16:9 [b]Job 13:24; 33:10

12 [1]I.e., siegework [a]Job 16:13 [b]Job 30:12

13 [a]Job 16:7; Ps. 69:8 [b]Job 16:20; Ps. 88:8, 18

14 [a]Job 19:19

17 [1]Lit., *strange*

18 "Even young children [a]despise me;
I rise up and they speak against me.
19 "All [1]my [a]associates abhor me,
And those I love have turned against me.
20 "My [a]bone clings to my skin and my flesh,
And I have escaped *only* by the skin of my teeth.
21 "Pity me, pity me, O you my friends,
For the [a]hand of God has struck me.
22 "Why do you [a]persecute me as God *does,*
And are not satisfied with my flesh?

23 "Oh that my words were written!
Oh that they were [a]inscribed in a book!
24 "That with an iron stylus and lead
They were engraved in the rock forever!
25 "And as for me, I know that [a]my [1]Redeemer lives,
And [2]at the last He will take His stand on the [3]earth.
26 "Even after my skin [1]is flayed,
Yet without my flesh I shall [a]see God;
27 "Whom I [1]myself shall behold,
And whom my eyes shall see and not another.
My [2]heart [a]faints [3]within me.
28 "If you say, 'How shall we [a]persecute him?'
And '[1]what pretext for a case against him can we find?'
29 "*Then* be afraid of [a]the sword for yourselves,
For wrath *brings* the punishment of the sword,
So that you may know [b]there is judgment."

Chapter 20

THEN Zophar the Naamathite [1]answered,
2 "Therefore my disquieting thoughts make me [1]respond,
Even because of my [2]inward agitation.
3 "I listened to [a]the reproof which insults me,
And the spirit of my understanding makes me answer.
4 "Do you know this from [a]of old,
From the establishment of man on earth,
5 That the [a]triumphing of the wicked is short,
And [b]the joy of the godless momentary?
6 "Though his loftiness [1a]reaches the heavens,
And his head touches the clouds;
7 He [a]perishes forever like his refuse;
Those who have seen him [b]will say, 'Where is he?'
8 "He flies away like a [a]dream, and they cannot find him;
Even like a vision of the night he is [b]chased away.
9 "The [a]eye which saw him sees him no more,
And [b]his place no longer beholds him.
10 "His [a]sons [1]favor the poor,
And his hands [b]give back his wealth.
11 "His [a]bones are full of his youthful vigor,
But it lies down with him [1]in the dust.

12 "Though [a]evil is sweet in his mouth,
And he hides it under his tongue,
13 *Though* he [1]desires it and will not let it go,
But holds it [a]in his [2]mouth,

18 [a]Job 12:4

19 [1]Lit., *the men of my council* [a]Ps. 38:11; 55:13

20 [a]Job 16:8; 33:21; Ps. 102:5; Lam. 4:8

21 [a]Job 1:11; Ps. 38:2

22 [a]Job 19:6; 13:24, 25; Ps. 69:26; 16:11

23 [a]Is. 30:8; Jer. 36:2

25 [1]Or, *Vindicator, defender;* lit., *kinsman* [2]Or, *as the Last* [3]Lit., *dust* [a]Job 16:19; Ps. 78:35; Prov. 23:11; Is. 43; 14; Jer. 50:34

26 [1]Lit., *they are flayed thus* [a]Ps. 17:15; Matt. 5:8; 1 Cor. 13:12; 1 John 3:2

27 [1]Or, *on my side* [2]Lit., *kidneys* [3]Lit., *in my loins* [a]Ps. 73:26

28 [1]Or, *the root of the matter is found in him* [a]Job 19:22

29 [a]Job 15:22 [b]Job 22:4; Ps. 1:5; 9:7; Eccles. 12:14

1 [1]Lit., *answered and said*

2 [1]Lit., *return* [2]Lit., *haste within me*

3 [a]Job 19:3

4 [a]Job 8:8

5 [a]Job 8:12, 13; Ps. 37:35, 36 [b]Job 8:13

6 [1]Lit., *goes up to* [a]Is. 14:13, 14; Obad. 3:4

7 [a]Job 4:20; 14:20 [b]Job 7:10; 8:18

8 [a]Ps. 73:20; 90:5 [b]Job 18:18; 27:21-23

9 [a]Job 7:8; 8:18 [b]Job 7:10

10 [1]Or, *seek the favor of* [a]Job 5:4; 27:14 [b]Job 20:18; 27:16, 17

11 [1]Lit., *on* [a]Job 21:23, 24

12 [a]Job 15:16

13 [1]Lit., *has compassion on* [2]Lit., *palate* [a]Job 20:23; Num. 11:20, 33

14 *Yet* his food in his stomach is changed
To the [1]venom of cobras within him.
15 "He swallows riches,
But will [a]vomit them up;
God will expel them out of his belly.
16 "He sucks [a]the poison of cobras;
The viper's tongue slays him.
17 "He does not look at [a]the streams,
The rivers flowing with honey and curds.
18 "He [a]returns what he has attained
And cannot swallow *it;*
As to the riches of his trading,
He cannot even enjoy *them.*
19 "For he has [a]oppressed *and* forsaken the poor;
He has seized a house which he has not built.

20 "Because he knew no quiet [1]within him
He does [a]not retain anything he desires.
21 "Nothing remains [1]for him to devour,
Therefore [a]his prosperity does not endure.
22 "In [a]the fulness of his plenty he will be cramped;
The [b]hand of everyone who suffers will come *against* him.
23 "When he [a]fills his belly,
God will send His fierce anger on him
And will [b]rain *it* on him [1]while he is eating.
24 "He may flee from the iron weapon,
But the bronze bow will pierce him.
25 "It is drawn forth and comes out of his back,
Even the glittering point from [a]his gall.
[b]Terrors come upon him,
26 Complete [a]darkness is held in reserve for his treasures.
And unfanned [b]fire will devour him;
It will consume the survivor in his tent.
27 "The [a]heavens will reveal his iniquity,
And the earth will rise up against him.
28 "The [a]increase of his house will depart;
His possessions will flow away [b]in the day of His anger.
29 "This is the wicked man's [a]portion from God,
Even the heritage decreed to him by God."

CHAPTER 21

THEN Job [1]answered,
2 "Listen carefully to my speech,
And let this be your *way of* consolation.
3 "Bear with me that I may speak.
Then after I have spoken, you may [a]mock.
4 "As for me, is [a]my complaint [1]to man?
And [b]why should [2]I not be impatient?
5 "Look at me, and be astonished,
And [a]put *your* hand over *your* mouth.
6 "Even when I remember I am disturbed,
And [a]horror takes hold of my flesh.
7 "Why [a]do the wicked *still* live,
Continue on, also become very [b]powerful?

14 [1]Lit., *gall*

15 [a]Job 20:10; 20:20, 21

16 [a]Deut. 32:24, 33

17 [a]Job 29:6; Deut. 32:13, 14

18 [a]Job 20:10, 15

19 [a]Job 24:2-4; 35:9

20 [1]Lit., *in his belly* [a]Eccles. 5:13-15

21 [1]Or, *of what he devours* [a]Job 15:29

22 [a]Job 15:21 [b]Job 5:5

23 [1]Or, *as his food* [a]Job 20:13, 14 [b]Num. 11:20, 33; Ps. 78:30, 31

25 [a]Job 16:13 [b]Job 18:11, 14

26 [a]Job 18:18 [b]Job 15:30

27 [a]Deut. 31:28

28 [a]Deut. 28:31 [b]Job 20:15, 21:30

29 [a]Job 27:13; 31:2, 3

1 [1]Lit., *answered and said*

3 [a]Job 11:3; 17:2

4 [1]Or, *against* [2]Lit., *my spirit* [a]Job 7:11 [b]Job 6:11

5 [a]Job 13:5; 29:9; 40:4; Judg. 18:19

6 [a]Ps. 55:5

7 [a]Job 9:24 Ps. 73:3; Jer. 12:1; Hab. 1:13 [b]Job 12:19

8 "Their [1a]descendants are established with them in their
sight,
And their offspring before their eyes,
9 Their houses [a]are safe from fear,
Neither is the rod of God on them.
10 "His ox mates [1]without fail;
His cow calves and does not abort.
11 "They send forth their little ones like the flock,
And their children skip about.
12 "They [1]sing to the timbrel and harp
And rejoice at the sound of the flute.
13 "They [a]spend their days in prosperity,
And [1]suddenly they go down to [2]Sheol.
14 "And they say to God, '[a]Depart from us!
We do not even desire the knowledge of Thy ways.
15 '[1]Who is [2]the Almighty, that we should serve Him,
And [a]what would we gain if we entreat Him?'
16 "Behold, their prosperity is not in their hand;
The [a]counsel of the wicked is far from me.

17 "How often is [a]the lamp of the wicked put out,
Or their [b]calamity fall on them?
Does [1]God apportion destruction in His anger?
18 "Are they as [a]straw before the wind,
And like [b]chaff which the storm carries away?
19 "*You say,* '[a]God stores away [1]a man's iniquity for his
sons.'
Let [2]God repay him so that he may know *it.*
20 "Let his [a]own eyes see his decay,
And let him [b]drink of the wrath of [1]the Almighty.
21 "For what does he care for his household [1]after him,
When the number of his months is cut off?
22 "Can anyone [a]teach God knowledge,
In that He [b]judges those on high?
23 "One [a]dies in his full strength,
Being wholly at ease and [1]satisfied;
24 "His [1]sides are filled out with fat,
And the [a]marrow of his bones is moist,
25 While another dies with a bitter soul,
Never even [1]tasting *anything* good.
26 "Together they [a]lie down in the dust,
And [b]worms cover them.

27 "Behold, I know your thoughts,
And the plans by which you would wrong me.
28 "For you say, 'Where is the house of [a]the nobleman,
And where is the [b]tent, the dwelling places of the
wicked?'
29 "Have you not asked wayfaring men,
And do you not recognize their [1]witness?
30 "For the [a]wicked is reserved for the day of calamity;
They will be led forth at [b]the day of fury.
31 "Who will [1]confront him with his actions,
And who will repay him for what he has done?
32 "While he is carried to the grave,
Men will keep watch over *his* tomb.

8 [1]Lit., *seed*
[a]Ps. 17:14

9 [a]Job 12:6

10 [1]Lit., *and does not fail*

12 [1]Lit., *lifted up the voice*

13 [1]So with most versions. M.T., *are shattered by Sheol.* [2]I.e., the nether world
[a]Job 21:23; 36:11

14 [a]Job 22:17

15 [1]Lit., *What* [2]Heb., *Shaddai*
[a]Job 22:17; 34:9

16 [a]Job 22:18

17 [1]Lit., *He*
[a]Job 18:5, 6 [b]Job 31:2, 3

18 [a]Job 13:25; Ps. 83:13 [b]Ps. 1:4; 35:5; Is. 17:13; Hos. 13:3

19 [1]Lit., *his* [2]Lit., *Him*
[a]Ex. 20:5; Jer. 31:29; Ezek. 18:2

20 [1]Heb., *Shaddai*
[a]Num. 14:28-32; Jer. 31:30; Ezek. 18:4 [b]Ps. 60:3; Is. 51:17; Jer. 25:15; Rev. 14:10

21 [1]I.e., after he dies

22 [a]Job 35:11; 36:22; Is. 40:14; Rom. 11:34 [b]Job 4:18; 15:15; Ps. 82:1

23 [1]Or, *quiet*
[a]Job 21:13; 20:11

24 [1]So with Syr.; Heb. uncertain. Some render as, *his pails are full of milk*
[a]Prov. 3:8

25 [1]Lit., *eating*

26 [a]Job 3:13; 20:11; Eccles. 9:2 [b]Job 24:20; Is. 14:11

28 [a]Job 1:3; 31:37 [b]Job 8:22; 18:21

29 [1]Lit., *signs*

30 [a]Job 20:29; Prov. 16:4; 2 Pet. 2:9 [b]Job 17:20; 40:11

31 [1]Lit., *declare his way to his face*

33 "The [a]clods of the valley will [1]gently cover him;
Moreover, [b]all men will [2]follow after him,
While countless ones *go* before him.
34 "How then will you vainly [a]comfort me,
For your answers remain *full of* [1]falsehood?"

CHAPTER 22

THEN Eliphaz the Temanite [1]responded,
2 "Can a vigorous [a]man be of use to God,
Or a wise man be useful to himself?
3 "Is there any pleasure to [1]the Almighty if you are righteous,
Or profit if you make your ways perfect?
4 "Is it because of your [1]reverence that He reproves you,
That He [a]enters into judgment against you?
5 "Is not [a]your wickedness great,
And your iniquities without end?
6 "For you have [a]taken pledges of your brothers without cause,
And [b]stripped [1]men naked.
7 "To the weary you have [a]given no water to drink,
And from the hungry you have [b]withheld bread.
8 "But the earth [a]belongs to the [1b]mighty man,
And [c]the honorable man dwells in it.
9 "You have sent [a]widows away empty,
And the [1]strength of the [b]orphans has been crushed.
10 "Therefore [a]snares surround you,
And sudden [b]dread terrifies you,
11 Or [a]darkness, so that you can not see,
And an [b]abundance of water covers you.

12 "Is not God [a]*in* the height of heaven?
Look also at the [1]distant stars, how high they are!
13 "And you say, '[a]What does God know?
Can He judge through the thick darkness?
14 '[a]Clouds are a hiding place for Him, so that He cannot see;
And He walks on the [1]vault of heaven.'
15 "Will you keep to the ancient path
Which [a]wicked men have trod,
16 Who were snatched away [a]before their time,
Whose [b]foundations were [1]washed away by a river?
17 "They [a]said to God, 'Depart from us!'
And 'What can [1]the Almighty do to them?'
18 "Yet He [a]filled their houses with good *things;*
But [b]the counsel of the wicked is far from me.
19 "The [a]righteous see and are glad,
And the innocent mock them,
20 *Saying,* 'Truly our adversaries are cut off,
And their [1]abundance [a]the fire has consumed.'

21 "[1a]Yield now and be at peace with Him;
Thereby good will come to you.
22 "Please receive [1a]instruction from His mouth,
And establish His words in your heart.

33 [1]Lit., *be sweet to him* [2]Lit., *draw* [a]Job 3:22; 17:16 [b]Job 3:19; 24:24

34 [1]Or, *faithlessness* [a]Job 16:2

1 [1]Lit., *answered and said*

2 [a]Job 35:7; Luke 17:10

3 [1]Heb., *Shaddai*

4 [1]Or, *fear* [a]Job 14:3; 19:29

5 [a]Job 11:6; 15:5

6 [1]Lit., *clothing of the naked* [a]Job 24:3, 9; Ex. 22:26; Deut. 24:6, 17; Ezek. 18:16 [b]Job 31:19, 20

7 [a]Job 31:16, 17 [b]Job 31:31

8 [1]Lit., *man of arm* [a]Job 9:24 [b]Job 12:19 [c]Is. 3:3; 9:15

9 [1]Lit., *arms* [a]Job 24:3, 21; 29:13; 31:16, 18 [b]Job 6:27

10 [a]Job 18:8 [b]Job 15:21

11 [a]Job 5:14 [b]Job 38:34; Ps. 69:2; 124:5; Lam. 3:54

12 [1]Lit., *head, top-most* [a]Job 11:7-9

13 [a]Ps. 10:11; 59:7; 64:5; 94:7; Is. 29:15; Ezek. 8:12

14 [1]Lit., *circle* [a]Job 26:9

15 [a]Job 34:36

16 [1]Lit., *poured out* [a]Job 15:32; 21:13, 18 [b]Job 14:19; Ps. 90:5; Is. 28:2; Matt. 7:26, 27

17 [1]Heb., *Shaddai* [a]Job 21:14, 15

18 [a]Job 12:6 [b]Job 21:16

19 [a]Ps. 52:6; 58:10; 107:42

20 [1]Or, *excess* [a]Job 15:30

21 [1]Or, *Know intimately* [a]Ps. 34:10

22 [1]Or, *law* [a]Job 6:10; 23:12; Prov. 2:6

23 "If you [a]return to [1]the Almighty, you will be [2]restored;
If you [b]remove unrighteousness far from your tent,
24 And [a]place *your* [1]gold in the dust,
And *the gold of* Ophir among the stones of the brooks,
25 Then [1]the Almighty will be your [2]gold
And choice silver to you.
26 "For then you will [a]delight in [1]the Almighty,
And lift up your face to God.
27 "You will [a]pray to Him, and [b]He will hear you;
And you will pay your vows.
28 "You will also decree a thing, and it will be established for you;
And [a]light will shine on your ways.
29 "When [1]you are cast down, you will speak with [2]confidence
And the [3][a]humble person He will save.
30 "He will deliver one who is not innocent,
And he will be [a]delivered through the cleanness of your hands."

Chapter 23

THEN Job [1]replied,
2 "Even today my [a]complaint is rebellion;
[1]His hand is [b]heavy despite my groaning.
3 "Oh that I knew where I might find Him,
That I might come to His seat!
4 "I would [a]present *my* case before Him
And fill my mouth with arguments.
5 "I would learn the words *which* He would [1]answer,
And perceive what He would say to me.
6 "Would He contend with me by [a]the greatness of *His* power?
No, surely He would pay attention to me.
7 "There the upright would [a]reason with Him;
And I [1]would be [b]delivered forever from my Judge.

8 "Behold, I go forward but He is not *there*,
And backward, but I [a]cannot perceive Him;
9 When He acts on the left, I cannot behold *Him;*
He turns on the right, I cannot see Him.
10 "But He knows the [1]way I take;
When He has [a]tried me, I shall come forth as gold.
11 "My foot has [a]held fast to His path;
I have kept His way and not turned aside.
12 "I have not departed from the command of His lips;
I have treasured the [a]words of His mouth [1]more than my [2]necessary food.
13 "But He is unique and who can turn Him?
And *what* His soul desires, that He does.
14 "For He performs what is appointed for me,
And many such *decrees* are with Him.
15 "Therefore, I would be dismayed at His presence;
When I consider, I am terrified of Him.
16 "*It is* God *who* has made my [a]heart faint,
And the Almighty *who* has dismayed me,

23 [1]Heb. *Shaddai* [2]Lit., *built up* [a]Job 8:5; 11:13; Is. 19:22; 31:6; Zech. 1:3 [b]Job 11:14

24 [1]Lit., *ore* [a]Job 31:24, 25

25 [1]I.e., Shaddai [2]Lit., *ore*

26 [1]I.e., Shaddai [a]Job 27:10; Ps. 37:4; Is. 58:14

27 [a]Job 11:13; 33:26; Is. 58:9 [b]Job 34:28

28 [a]Job 11:17; Ps. 112:4

29 [1]Lit., *they cast* you *down* [2]Lit., *pride* [3]Lit., *lowly of eyes* [a]Job 5:11; 36:7; Matt. 23:12; James 4:6; 1 Pet. 5:5

30 [a]Job 42:7, 8; Ps. 18:20; 24:3, 4

1 [1]Lit., *answered and said*

2 [1]So with Gr. and Syr. M.T., *My* [a]Job 7:11 [b]Job 6:2, 3; Ps. 32:4

4 [a]Job 13:18

5 [1]Lit., *answer me*

6 [a]Job 9:4

7 [1]Or, *bring forth my justice forever* [a]Job 13:3 [b]Job 23:10; 13:16

8 [a]Job 9:11; 35:14

10 [1]Lit., *way with me* [a]Job 7:18; Ps. 7:9; 11:5; 66:10; Zech. 13:9; 1 Pet. 1:7

11 [a]Job 31:7; Ps. 17:5; 44:18

12 [1]Or, with some versions, *in my breast* [2]Lit., *prescribed portion* [a]Job 6:10; 22:22

16 [a]Job 27:2; Deut. 20:3; Jer. 51:46

17 "But I [a]am not silenced by the darkness,
Nor [b]deep gloom *which* covers *me*.

CHAPTER 24

"WHY are [1]times not stored up by the Almighty,
And why do those who know Him not see [a]His days?
2 "[1]Some [a]remove the landmarks;
They seize and [2]devour flocks.
3 "They drive away the donkeys of the [a]orphans;
They take the [b]widow's ox for a pledge.
4 "They push [a]the needy aside from the road;
The [b]poor of the land are made to hide themselves altogether.
5 "Behold as [a]wild donkeys in the wilderness
They [b]go forth seeking food in their activity,
As [1]bread for *their* children in the desert.
6 "They harvest their fodder in the field,
And they glean the vineyard of the wicked.
7 "They spend the night naked, without clothing,
And have no covering against the cold.
8 "They are wet with the mountain rains,
And they [a]hug the rock for want of a shelter.
9 "[1]Others snatch the [a]orphan from the breast,
And against the poor they take a pledge.
10 "They cause *the poor* to go about naked without clothing,
And they take away the sheaves from the hungry.
11 "Within the walls they produce oil;
They tread wine presses but thirst.
12 "From the city men groan,
And the souls of the wounded cry out;
Yet God [a]does not pay attention to folly.

13 "[1]Others have been with those who rebel against the light;
They do not want to know its ways,
Nor abide in its paths.
14 "The murderer [a]arises at dawn;
He [b]kills the poor and the needy,
And at night he is as a thief.
15 And the eye of the [a]adulterer waits for the twilight,
Saying, 'No eye will see me.'
And he [1]disguises his face.
16 "In the dark they [a]dig into houses,
They shut themselves up by day;
They do not know the light.
17 "For the morning is the same to him as thick darkness,
For he is familiar with the [a]terrors of thick darkness.

18 "They are [1a]insignificant on the surface of the water;
Their portion is [b]cursed on the earth.
They do not turn [2]toward the [c]vineyards.
19 "Drought and heat [1a]consume the snow waters,
So does [2b]Sheol *those who* have sinned.
20 "A [1a]mother will forget him;

17 [a]Job 10:18, 19 [b]Job 19:8

1 [1]I.e., times of judgment [a]Is. 2:12; Jer. 46:10; Obad. 15; Zeph. 1:7

2 [1]Lit., *They* [2]Or, *pasture* [a]Deut. 19:14; 27:17

3 [a]Job 6:27 [b]Job 22:9

4 [a]Job 24:14; 29:16; 30:25; 31:19 [b]Job 29:12; Ps. 41:1; Prov. 14:31; Amos 8:4

5 [1]Lit., *his bread* [a]Job 39:5-8 [b]Ps. 104:23

8 [a]Lam. 4:5

9 [1]Lit., *they* [a]Job 6:27

12 [a]Job 9:23, 24

13 [1]Lit., *they*

14 [a]Mic. 2:1 [b]Ps. 10:8

15 [1]Or, *puts a covering on his face* [a]Prov. 7:9

16 [a]Ex. 22:2; Matt. 6:19

17 [a]Job 15:21

18 [1]Or, *light* or *swift* [2]Lit., *to the path of* [a]Job 22:11, 16; 27:20 [b]Job 5:3 [c]Job 24:6, 11

19 [1]Lit., *seize* [2]I.e., nether world [a]Job 6:16, 17 [b]Job 21:13

20 [1]Lit., *womb* [a]Is. 49:15

The [b]worm feeds sweetly till he is remembered [c]no more.
And wickedness will be broken [d]like a tree.
21 "He wrongs the [1]barren woman,
And does no good for [a]the widow.
22 "But He drags off the valiant by [a]His power;
He rises, but [b]no one has assurance of life.
23 "He provides them [a]with security, and they are supported;
And His [b]eyes are on their ways.
24 "They are exalted a [a]little while, then they are gone;
Moreover, they are [b]brought low and like everything gathered up;
Even like the heads of grain they are cut off.
25 "Now if it is not so, [a]who can prove me a liar,
And make my speech worthless?"

Chapter 25

THEN Bildad the Shuhite [1]answered,
2 "[a]Dominion and awe [1]belong to Him
Who establishes peace in [b]His heights.
3 "Is there any number to [a]His troops?
And upon whom does His light not rise?
4 "How then can a man be [a]just with God?
Or how can he be [b]clean who is born of woman?
5 "If even [a]the moon has no brightness
And the [b]stars are not pure in His sight,
6 How much less [a]man, *that* [b]maggot,
And the son of man, *that* worm!"

Chapter 26

THEN Job [1]responded,
2 "What a help you are to [1a]the weak!
How you have saved the arm [b]without strength!
3 "What counsel you have given to *one* without wisdom!
What helpful insight you have abundantly [1]provided!
4 "To whom have you uttered words?
And whose [1]spirit was expressed through you?

5 "The [1a]departed spirits tremble
Under the waters and their inhabitants.
6 "Naked is [1a]Sheol before Him
And [2b]Abaddon has no covering.
7 "He [a]stretches out the north over empty space,
And hangs the earth on nothing.
8 "He [a]wraps up the waters in His clouds;
And the cloud does not burst under them.
9 "He [1a]obscures the face of the [2]full moon,
And spreads His cloud over it.
10 "He has inscribed a [a]circle on the surface of the waters,
At the [b]boundary of light and darkness.
11 "The pillars of heaven tremble,
And are amazed at His rebuke.
12 "He [a]quieted the sea with His power,
And by His [b]understanding He shattered [c]Rahab.

---

20 [b]Job 21:26 [c]Job 18:17; Ps. 34:16; Prov. 10:7 [d]Job 19:10; Dan. 4:14

21 [1]Lit., *barren who does not bear* [a]Job 22:9

22 [a]Job 9:4 [b]Job 18:20

23 [a]Job 12:6 [b]Job 10:4; 11:11

24 [a]Ps. 37:10 [b]Job 14:21

25 [a]Job 6:28; 27:4

1 [1]Lit., *answered and said*

2 [1]Lit., *are with Him* [a]Job 9:4; 36:5, 22; 37:23; 42:2 [b]Job 16:19; 31:2

3 [a]Job 16:13

4 [a]Job 4:17; 9:2 [b]Job 14:4

5 [a]Job 31:26 [b]Job 15:15

6 [a]Job 7:17 [b]Job 17:14

1 [1]Lit., *responded and said*

2 [1]Lit., *no power* [a]Job 6:11, 12 [b]Ps. 71:9

3 [1]Lit., *made known*

4 [1]Lit., *breath has gone forth*

5 [1]Or, *shades;* Heb., *Rephaim* [a]Job 3:13, Ps. 88:10

6 [1]I.e., the nether world [2]I.e., place of destruction [a]Job 26:6-14; 9:5-10; 38:17; 41:11 [b]Job 28:22; 31:12

7 [a]Job 9:8

8 [a]Job 37:11; Prov. 30:4

9 [1]Lit., *covers* [2]Or, *throne* [a]Job 22:14; Ps. 97:2; 105:39

10 [a]Job 38:1-11; Prov. 8:29 [b]Job 38:19, 20, 24

12 [a]Is. 51:15; Jer. 31:35 [b]Job 12:13 [c]Job 9:13

13 "By His breath the [a]heavens are [1]cleared;
His hand has pierced [b]the fleeing serpent.
14 "Behold, these are the fringes of His ways;
And how faint [a]a word we hear of Him!
But His mighty [b]thunder, who can understand?"

Chapter 27

THEN Job [1]continued his [a]discourse and said,
2 "As God lives, [a]who has taken away my right,
And the Almighty, [b]who has embittered my soul,
3 For as long as [1]life is in me,
And the [2a]breath of God is in my nostrils,
4 My lips certainly will not speak unjustly,
Nor will [a]my tongue mutter deceit.
5 "Far be it from me that I should declare you right;
Till I die [a]I will not put away my integrity from me.
6 "I [a]hold fast my righteousness and will not let it go.
My heart does not reproach any of my days.

7 "May my enemy be as the wicked,
And [1]my opponent as the unjust.
8 "For what is [a]the hope of the godless [1]when he is cut off,
When God requires [b]his [2]life?
9 "Will God [a]hear his cry,
When [b]distress comes upon him?
10 "Will he take [a]delight in the Almighty,
Will he call on God at all times?
11 "I will instruct you in the [1a]power of God;
What is with the Almighty I will not conceal.
12 "Behold, all of you have seen *it*;
Why then do you [1]act foolishly?

13 "This is [a]the portion of a wicked man from God,
And the inheritance *which* [b]tyrants receive from the Almighty.
14 "Though his sons are many, [1]they are destined [a]for the sword;
And his [b]descendants will not be satisfied with bread.
15 "His survivors will be buried because of the plague,
And [1]their [a]widows will not be able to weep.
16 "Though he piles up silver like dust,
And prepares garments as *plentiful as* the clay;
17 He may prepare *it*, [a]but the just will wear *it*,
And the innocent will divide the silver.
18 "He has built his [a]house like the [1]spider's web,
Or as a hut *which* the watchman has made.
19 "He lies down rich, but never [1]again;
He opens his eyes, and [a]it is no more.
20 "[a]Terrors overtake him like a flood;
A tempest steals him away [b]in the night.
21 "The east [a]wind carries him away, and he is gone,
For it whirls him [b]away from his place.
22 "For it will hurl at him [a]without sparing;
He will surely try to [b]flee from its [1]power.

13 [1]Lit., *made beautiful* [a]Job 9:8 [b]Is. 27:1
14 [a]Job 4:12 [b]Job 36:29; 37:4, 5
1 [1]Or, *again took up* [a]Job 13:12; 29:1
2 [a]Job 16:11; 34:5 [b]Job 9:18
3 [1]Lit., *breath* [2]Or, *spirit* [a]Job 32:8; 33:4
4 [a]Job 6:28; 33:3
5 [a]Job 6:29
6 [a]Job 2:3; 13:18
7 [1]Lit., *he who rises up against me*
8 [1]Or, *though he gains* [2]Lit., *soul* [a]Job 8:13; 11:20 [b]Job 12:10
9 [a]Job 35:12, 13; Ps. 18:41; Prov. 1:28; Is. 1:15; Jer. 14:12; Mic. 3:4 [b]Prov. 1:27
10 [a]Job 22:26, 27; Ps. 37:4; Is. 58:14
11 [1]Lit., *hand* [a]Job 27:13
12 [1]Or, *speak vanity*
13 [a]Job 20:29 [b]Job 15:20
14 [1]Lit., *the sword is for them* [a]Job 15:22; 18:19 [b]Job 20:10
15 [1]So ancient versions; Heb., *his* [a]Ps. 78:64
17 [a]Job 20:18-21
18 [1]So ancient versions; Heb., *moth* [a]Job 8:15; 18:14
19 [1]So ancient versions; Heb., *will be gathered* [a]Job 7:8, 21; 20:7
20 [a]Job 15:21 [b]Job 20:8; 34:20
21 [a]Job 21:18 [b]Job 7:10
22 [1]Lit., *hand* [a]Jer. 13:14; Ezek. 5:11; 24:14 [b]Job 11:20

23 "*Men* will clap their hands at him,
And will [a]hiss him from his place.

Chapter 28

"SURELY there is a [1]mine for silver,
And a place [2]where they refine gold.
2 "Iron is taken from the dust,
And from rock copper is smelted.
3 "*Man* puts an end to darkness
And to the farthest limit he searches out
The rock in gloom and deep shadow.
4 "He [1]sinks a shaft far from [2]habitation,
Forgotten by the foot;
They hang and swing to and fro far from men.
5 "The earth, from it comes food,
And underneath it is turned up as fire.
6 "Its rocks are the [1]source of sapphires,
And its dust *contains* gold.
7 "The path no bird of prey knows,
Nor has the falcon's eye caught sight of it.
8 "The [1]proud beasts have not trodden it,
Nor has the *fierce* lion passed over it.
9 "He puts his hand on the flint;
He overturns the mountains at the [1]base.
10 "He hews out channels through the rocks;
And his eye sees anything precious.
11 "He dams up the streams from [1]flowing;
And what is hidden he brings out to the light.

12 "But [a]where can wisdom be found?
And where is the place of understanding?
13 "Man does not know its value,
Nor is it found in the land of the living.
14 "The deep says, 'It is not in me';
And the sea says, 'It is not with me.'
15 "Pure gold cannot be given in exchange for it,
Nor can silver be weighed as its price.
16 "It cannot be valued in the gold of Ophir,
In precious onyx, or sapphire.
17 "[a]Gold or glass cannot equal it,
Nor can it be exchanged for articles of fine gold.
18 "Coral and crystal are not to be mentioned;
And the acquisition of [a]wisdom is above *that of* pearls.
19 "The topaz of Ethiopia cannot equal it,
Nor can it be valued in [a]pure gold.
20 "[a]Where then does wisdom come from?
And where is the place of understanding?
21 "Thus it is hidden from the eyes of all living,
And concealed from the birds of the sky.
22 "[1a]Abaddon and Death say,
'With our ears we have heard a report of it.'

23 "[a]God understands its way;
And He knows its place.

23 [a]Job 18:18; 20:8
1 [1]Or, *source* [2]Lit., *for gold they refine*
4 [1]Lit., *breaks open* [2]Lit., *sojourning*
6 [1]Or, *place*
8 [1]Lit., *sons of pride*
9 [1]Lit., *roots*
11 [1]Lit., *weeping*
12 [a]Job 28:23, 28
17 [a]Prov. 8:10; 16:16
18 [a]Prov. 8:11
19 [a]Prov. 8:19
20 [a]Job 28:23, 28
22 [1]I.e., Destruction [a]Job 26:6; Prov. 8:22-36
23 [a]Job 9:4; Prov. 8:22-36

24 "For He [a]looks to the ends of the earth,
And sees everything under the heavens.
25 When He imparted [a]weight to the wind,
And [b]meted out the waters by measure,
26 "When He set a [a]limit for the rain,
And a course for the [b]thunderbolt,
27 Then He saw it and declared it;
He established it and also searched it out.
28 "And to man He said, 'Behold, the [a]fear of the Lord, that is wisdom;
And to depart from evil is understanding.' "

CHAPTER 29

AND Job again took up his [a]discourse and said,
2 "Oh that I were as in months gone by,
As in the days when God [a]watched over me;
3 When His lamp shone over my head,
And [a]by His light I walked through darkness;
4 "As I was in [1]the prime of my days,
When the [2a]friendship of God *was* over my tent;
5 When [1]the Almighty was yet with me,
And my children were around me;
6 When my steps were bathed in [a]butter,
And the [b]rock poured out for me streams of oil!
7 "When I went out to [a]the gate of the city,
When I [1]took my seat in the square;
8 The young men saw me and hid themselves,
And the old men arose *and* stood.
9 "The princes [a]stopped talking,
And [b]put *their* hands on their mouths;
10 The voice of the nobles was [1a]hushed,
And their tongue stuck to their palate.
11 "For when [a]the ear heard, it called me blessed;
And when the eye saw, it gave witness of me,
12 Because I delivered [a]the poor who cried for help,
And the [b]orphan who had no helper.
13 "The blessing of the one [a]ready to perish came upon me,
And I made the [b]widow's heart sing for joy.
14 "I [a]put on righteousness, and it clothed me;
My justice was like a robe and a turban.
15 "I was eyes to the blind,
And feet to the lame.
16 "I was a father to [a]the needy,
And I investigated the case which I did not know.
17 "And I [a]broke the jaws of the wicked,
And snatched the prey from his teeth.
18 "Then I [1]thought, 'I shall die [2]in my nest,
And I shall multiply *my* days as the sand.
19 'My [a]root is spread out to the waters,
And [b]dew lies all night on my branch.
20 'My glory is *ever* new with me,
And my [a]bow is renewed in my hand.'

21 "To me [a]they listened and waited,
And kept silent for my counsel.

24 [a]Ps. 11:4; 33:13, 14; 66:7; Prov. 15:3
25 [a]Ps. 135:7 [b]Job 12:15; 38:8-11
26 [a]Job 37:6, 11, 12; 38:26-28 [b]Job 37:3; 38:25
28 [a]Ps. 111:10; Prov. 1:7; 9:10
1 [a]Job 13:12; 27:1; Num. 23:7; 24:3
2 [a]Jer. 31:28
3 [a]Job 11:17
4 [1]Lit., *the days of my autumn* [2]Lit., *counsel* [a]Job 15:8; Ps. 25:14; Prov. 3:32
5 [1]Heb., *Shaddai*
6 [a]Job 20:17; Deut. 32:14 [b]Deut. 32:13
7 [1]Lit., *sat up* [a]Job 31:21
9 [a]Job 29:21 [b]Job 21:5
10 [1]Lit., *hidden* [a]Job 29:22
11 [a]Job 4:3, 4
12 [a]Job 24:4, 9; 34:28 [b]Job 31:17, 21
13 [a]Job 31:19 [b]Job 22:9
14 [a]Job 27:5, 6; Ps. 132:9; Is. 59:17; 61:10; Eph. 6:14
16 [a]Job 24:4
17 [a]Ps. 3:7
18 [1]Lit., *said* [2]Lit., *with*
19 [a]Jer. 17:8 [b]Hos. 14:5
20 [a]Gen. 49:24; Ps. 18:34
21 [a]Job 29:9; 4:3

22 "After my words they did not [a]speak again,
And [b]my speech dropped on them.
23 "And they waited for me as for the rain,
And opened their mouth as for the spring rain.
24 "I smiled on them when they did not believe,
And the light of my face they did not cast down.
25 "I chose a way for them and sat as [a]chief,
And dwelt as a king among the troops,
As one who [b]comforted the mourners.

Chapter 30

"BUT now those younger than I [a]mock me,
Whose fathers I disdained to put with the dogs of my flock.
2 "Indeed, what *good was* the strength of their hands to me?
Vigor had perished from them.
3 "From want and famine they are gaunt
Who gnaw the dry ground by night in waste and desolation,
4 Who pluck [1]mallow by the bushes,
And whose food is the root of the broom shrub.
5 "They are driven from the community;
They shout against them as *against* a thief,
6 So that they dwell in dreadful [1]valleys,
In holes of the earth and of the rocks.
7 "Among the bushes they [1]cry out;
Under the nettles they are gathered together.
8 "[1]Fools, even [2]those without a name,
They were scourged from the land.

9 "And now I have become their [1a]taunt,
I have even become a byword to them.
10 "They abhor me *and* stand aloof from me,
And they do not [1]refrain from [a]spitting at my face.
11 "Because [1]He has loosed [2]His [3]bowstring and [a]afflicted me,
They have cast off [b]the bridle before me.
12 "On the right hand their [1]brood arises;
They [a]thrust aside my feet [b]and build up against me their ways of destruction.
13 "They [a]break up my path,
They profit [1]from my destruction,
No one restrains them.
14 "As *through* a wide breach they come,
[1]Amid the tempest they roll on.
15 "[a]Terrors are turned against me,
They pursue my [1]honor as the wind,
And my [2]prosperity has passed away [b]like a cloud.

16 "And now [a]my soul is poured out [1]within me;
Days of affliction have seized me.
17 "At night it pierces [a]my bones [1]within me,
And my gnawing *pains* take no rest.
18 "By a great force my garment is [a]distorted;
It binds me about as the collar of my coat.

22 [a]Job 29:10 [b]Deut. 32:2

25 [a]Job 1:3; 31:37 [b]Job 4:4; 16:5

1 [a]Job 12:4

4 [1]I.e., plant of the salt marshes (Job 24:24) cf. Job 30:4

6 [1]Or, *wadis*

7 [1]Or, *bray*

8 [1]Lit., *sons of fools* [2]Lit., *sons*

9 [1]Lit., *song*
[a]Job 12:4

10 [1]Lit., *withhold spit from my face*
[a]Job 17:6; Num. 12:14; Deut. 25:9; Is. 50:6; Matt. 26:67

11 [1]Or, *they* [2]Some mss. read, *my* [3]Or, *cord*
[a]Ruth 1:21; Ps. 88:7 [b]Ps. 32:9

12 [1]Possibly *sprout* or *offspring*
[a]Ps. 140:4, 5 [b]Job 19:12

13 [1]Lit., *for*
[a]Is. 3:12

14 [1]Lit., *under*

15 [1]Or, *nobility* [2]Or, *welfare*
[a]Job 3:25; 31:23; Ps. 55:3-5
[b]Job 7:9; Hos. 13:3

16 [1]Lit., *upon*
[a]Job 3:24; Ps. 22:14; 42:4; Is. 53:12

17 [1]Lit., *from upon*
[a]Job 30:30

18 [a]Job 2:7

19 "He has cast me into the [a]mire,
And I have become like dust and ashes.
20 "I [a]cry out to Thee for help, but Thou dost not answer me;
I stand up, and Thou dost turn Thy attention against me.
21 "Thou hast [1]become cruel to me;
With the might of Thy hand Thou dost [a]persecute me.
22 "Thou dost [a]lift me up to the wind *and* cause me to ride;
And Thou dost dissolve me in a storm.
23 "For I know that Thou [a]wilt bring me to death
And to the [b]house of meeting for all living.

24 "Yet does not one in a heap of ruins stretch out *his* hand,
Or in his disaster therefore [a]cry out for help?
25 "Have I not [a]wept for the [1]one whose life is hard?
Was not my soul grieved for [b]the needy?
26 "When I [a]expected good, then evil came,
When I waited for light, [b]then darkness came.
27 "[1]I am seething [a]within, and cannot relax;
Days of affliction confront me.
28 "I go about [1a]mourning without comfort;
I stand up in the assembly *and* [b]cry out for help.
29 "I have become a brother to [a]jackals,
And a companion of ostriches.
30 "My [a]skin turns black [1]on me,
And my [b]bones burn with [2]fever.
31 "Therefore my [a]harp [1]is turned to mourning,
And my flute to the sound of those who weep.

Chapter 31

"I HAVE made a covenant with my [a]eyes;
How then could I gaze at a virgin?
2 "And what is [a]the portion of God from above
Or the heritage of the Almighty from on high?
3 "Is it not [a]calamity to the unjust,
And disaster to [b]those who work iniquity?
4 "Does He not [a]see my ways,
And [b]number all my steps?

5 "If I have [a]walked with falsehood,
And my foot has hastened after deceit,
6 Let Him [a]weigh me with [1]accurate scales,
And let God know [b]my integrity.
7 "If my step has [a]turned from the way,
Or my heart [1]followed my eyes,
Or if any [b]spot has stuck to my hands,
8 Let me [a]sow and another eat,
And let my [1b]crops be uprooted.

9 "If my heart has been [a]enticed by a woman,
Or I have lurked at my neighbor's doorway,
10 May my wife [a]grind for another,
And let [b]others [1]kneel down over her.

19 [a]Ps. 69:2, 14

20 [a]Job 19:7

21 [1]Lit., *turned to be* [a]Job 10:3; 16:9, 14; 19:6, 22

22 [a]Job 9:17; 27:21

23 [a]Job 9:22; 10:8 [b]Job 3:19; Eccles. 12:5

24 [a]Job 19:7

25 [1]Lit., *hard of day* [a]Ps. 35:13, 14; Rom. 12:15 [b]Job 24:4

26 [a]Job 3:25, 26; Jer. 8:15 [b]Job 19:8

27 [1]Lit., *My inward parts are boiling* [a]Lam. 2:11

28 [1]Or, *blackened, but not by the heat of the sun* [a]Job 30:30; Ps. 38:6; 42:9; 43:2 [b]Job 19:7

29 [a]Ps. 44:19; Mic. 1:8

30 [1]Lit., *from upon* [2]Lit., *heat* [a]Job 2:7 [b]Ps. 102:3

31 [1]Lit., *become* [a]Is. 24:8

1 [a]Matt. 5:28

2 [a]Job. 20:29

3 [a]Job 18:12; 21:30 [b]34:22

4 [a]Job 24:23; 28:24; 34:21; 36:7; 2 Chr. 16:9; Prov. 5:21; 15:3 [b]Job 31:37; 14:16

5 [a]Job 15:31; Mic. 2:11

6 [1]Lit., *just* [a]Job 6:2,3 [b]Job 23:10; 27:5, 6

7 [1]Lit., *walked after* [a]Job 23:11 [b]Job 9:30

8 [1]Or, *offspring* [a]Job 20:18; Lev. 26:16; Mic. 6:15 [b]Job 31:12

9 [a]Job 31:1; 24:15

10 [1]I.e. sexual relations [a]Judg. 16:21; Is. 47:2 [b]Deut. 28:30; Jer. 8:10

11 [a]Lev. 20:10; Deut. 22:24 [b]Job 31:28

12 [1]I.e., place of destruction [2]Or, *yield* [a]Job 15:30 [b]Job 26:6 [c]Job 31:8; 20:28

13 [a]Deut. 24:14, 15

15 [a]Job 10:3

16 [a]Job 5:16; 20:19 [b]Job 22:9; Ex. 22:22-24

17 [1]Lit., *eaten from it* [a]Job 22:7 [b]Job 29:12

18 [1]Lit., *my mother's womb* [2]Cf. v. 16

19 [a]Job 22:6; 29:13 [b]Job 24:4

20 [1]Lit., *blessed*

21 [1]Lit., *my help* [a]Job 31:17; 29:12 [b]Job 29:7

22 [1]Lit., *shoulder or back* [2]Lit., *from the bone of the upper arm* [a]Job 38:15

23 [1]Lit., *exaltation* [a]Job 31:3 [b]Job 13:11

24 [a]Job 22:24; Mark 10:24

25 [a]Job 1:3, 10; Ps. 62:10

26 [1]Lit., *light* [a]Deut. 4:19; 17:3; Ezek. 8:16

27 [1]Lit., *kissed my mouth*

28 [1]Lit., *judges* [a]Job 31:11; Deut. 17:2-7 [b]Josh. 24:27; Is. 59:13

29 [1]Lit., *lifted myself up* [a]Prov. 17:5; 24:17; Obad. 12

30 [1]Lit., *And* [2]Lit., *given my palate* [a]Ps. 7:4 [b]Job 5:3

31 [1]Lit., *give* [a]Job 22:7

32 [1]M.T., *way*

33 [1]Or, *mankind* [a]Gen. 3:10; Prov. 28:13

11 "For that would be a [a]lustful crime;
Moreover, it would be [b]an iniquity *punishable by* judges.
12 "For it would be [a]fire that consumes to [1b]Abaddon,
And would [c]uproot all my [2]increase.

13 "If I have [a]despised the claim of my male or female slaves
When they filed a complaint against me,
14 What then could I do when God arises,
And when He calls me to account, what will I answer Him?
15 "Did not [a]He who made me in the womb make him,
And the same one fashion us in the womb?

16 "If I have kept [a]the poor from *their* desire,
Or have caused the eyes of [b]the widow to fail,
17 Or have [a]eaten my morsel alone,
And [b]the orphan has not [1]shared it
18 (But from my youth he grew up with me as with a father,
And from [1]infancy I guided [2]her);
19 If I have seen anyone perish [a]for lack of clothing,
Or that [b]the needy had no covering,
20 If his loins have not [1]thanked me,
And if he has not been warmed with the fleece of my sheep;
21 If I have lifted up my hand against [a]the orphan,
Because I saw [1]I had support [b]in the gate,
22 Let my shoulder fall from the [1]socket,
And my [a]arm be broken off [2]at the elbow.
23 "For [a]calamity from God is a terror to me,
And because of [b]His [1]majesty I can do nothing.

24 "If I have put my confidence *in* [a]gold,
And called fine gold my trust,
25 If I have [a]gloated because my wealth was great,
And because my hand had secured *so* much;
26 If I have [a]looked at the [1]sun when it shone,
Or the moon going in splendor,
27 And my heart became secretly enticed,
And my hand [1]threw a kiss from my mouth,
28 That too would have been [a]an iniquity *calling for* [1]judgment,
For I would have [b]denied God above.

29 "Have I [a]rejoiced at the extinction of my enemy,
Or [1]exulted when evil befell him?
30 "[1]No, [a]I have not [2]allowed my mouth to sin
By asking for his life in [b]a curse.
31 "Have the men of my tent not said,
'Who can [1]find one who has not been [a]satisfied with his meat'?
32 "The alien has not lodged outside,
For I have opened my doors to the [1]traveler.
33 "Have I [a]covered my transgressions like [1]Adam,
By hiding my iniquity in my bosom,

34 Because I [a]feared the great multitude,
And the contempt of families terrified me,
And kept silent and did not go out of doors?
35 "Oh that I had one to hear me!
Behold, here is my [1]signature;
[a]Let the Almighty answer me!
And the indictment which my [b]adversary has written,
36 Surely I would carry it on my shoulder;
I would bind it to myself like a crown.
37 "I would declare to Him [a]the number of my steps;
Like [b]a prince I would approach Him.

38 "If my [a]land cries out against me,
And its furrows weep together;
39 If I have [a]eaten its [1]fruit without money,
Or have [b]caused [2]its owners to lose their lives,
40 Let [a]briars [1]grow instead of wheat,
And stinkweed instead of barley."
The words of Job are ended.

Chapter 32

THEN these three men ceased answering Job, because he
was [a]righteous in his own eyes.
2 But the anger of Elihu the son of Barachel the Buzite,
of the family of Ram burned; against Job his anger burned,
[a]because he justified himself [1b]before God.
3 And his anger burned against his three friends because
they had found no answer, and yet had condemned Job.
4 Now Elihu had waited [1]to speak to Job because they
were years older than he.
5 And when Elihu saw that there was no answer in the
mouth of the three men his anger burned.
6 So Elihu the son of Barachel the Buzite [1]spoke out and
said,
"I am young in years and you are [a]old;
Therefore I was shy and afraid to tell you [2]what I think.
7 "I [1]thought [2]age should speak,
And [3]increased years should teach wisdom.
8 "But it is a spirit in man,
And the [a]breath of the Almighty gives them [b]understanding.
9 "The [1]abundant *in years* may not be wise,
Nor may [a]elders understand justice.
10 "So I [1]say, 'Listen to me,
I too will tell [2]what I think.'

11 "Behold, I waited for your words,
I listened to your reasonings,
While you [1]pondered what to say.
12 "I even paid close attention to you,
[1]Indeed, there was no one who refuted Job,
Not one of you who answered his words.
13 "[1]Do not say,
'We have found wisdom;
God will [2]rout him, not man.'

34 [a]Ex. 23:2

35 [1]Lit., *mark* [a]Job. 19:7; 30:20, 24, 28; 35:14 [b]Job 27:7

37 [a]Job 31:4 [b]Job 1:3; 29:25

38 [a]Job 24:2

39 [1]Lit., *strength* [2]Lit., *the soul of its owners to expire* [a]Job 24:6, 10-12; James 5:4 [b]1 Kin. 21:19

40 [1]Lit., *come forth* [a]Is. 5:6; Job 32:13

1 [a]Job 10:7; 13:18; 27:2; 31:6

2 [1]Or, *more than* [a]Job 27:5, 6 [b]Job 30:21

4 [1]Lit., *for Job with words,* or possibly, *while they were speaking with Job*

6 [1]Lit., *answered* [2]Lit., *my knowledge* [a]Job 15:10

7 [1]Lit., *said* [2]Lit., *days* [3]Lit., *many*

8 [a]Job 33:4 [b]Job 38:36

9 [1]Or, *nobles* [a]Job 32:7

10 [1]Or, *said* [2]Lit., *my knowledge*

11 [1]Lit., *searched out words*

12 [1]Lit., *Behold*

13 [1]Lit., *Lest you say* [2]Lit., *drive away*

14 "For he has not arranged *his* words against me;
Nor will I reply to him with your [1]arguments.

15 "They are dismayed, they answer no more;
Words have [1]failed them.
16 "And shall I wait, because they do not speak,
Because they [1]stop *and* answer no more?
17 "I too will answer my share,
I also will tell my opinion.
18 "For I am full of words;
The spirit within me constrains me.
19 "Behold, my belly is like unvented wine,
Like new wineskins it is about to burst.
20 "Let me speak that I may get relief;
Let me open my lips and answer.
21 "Let me now [a]be partial to no one;
Nor flatter *any* man.
22 "For I do not know how to flatter,
Else my Maker would soon take me away.

Chapter 33

"HOWEVER now, Job, please hear my speech,
And listen to all my words.
2 "Behold now, I open my mouth:
My tongue in my [1]mouth speaks.
3 "My words are *from* the uprightness of my heart;
And my lips speak [a]knowledge sincerely.
4 "The [a]Spirit of God has made me,
And the [b]breath of [1]the Almighty gives me life.
5 "[a]Refute me if you can;
Array yourselves before me, take your stand.
6 "Behold, I belong to God like you;
I too have been [1]formed out of the [a]clay.
7 "Behold, no fear of me should terrify you,
Nor should my pressure weigh heavily on you.

8 "Surely you have spoken in my hearing,
And I have heard the sound of *your* words:
9 'I am [a]pure, [b]without transgression;
I am innocent and there [c]is no guilt in me.
10 'Behold, He [1]invents pretexts against me;
He [a]counts me as His enemy.
11 'He [a]puts my feet in the stocks;
He watches all my paths.'
12 "Behold, let me [1]tell you, you are not right in this,
For God is greater than man.

13 "Why do you [a]complain against Him,
That He does not give an account of all His doings?
14 "Indeed [a]God speaks once,
Or twice, *yet* no one notices it.
15 "In a [a]dream, a vision of the night,
When sound sleep falls on men,
While they slumber in their beds,

14 [1]Lit., *words*
15 [1]Lit., *moved away from*
16 [1]Lit., *stand*
21 [a]Job 13:8, 10; 34:19; Lev. 19:15
2 [1]Lit., *palate*
3 [a]Job 6:28; 27:4; 36:4
4 [1]Heb., *Shaddai* [a]Job 10:3; 32:8 [b]Job 27:3
5 [a]Job 33:32
6 [1]Lit., *cut out of* [a]Job 4:19
9 [a]Job 6:10; 9:21; 10:7; 13:18; 16:17 [b]Job 7:21; 13:23; 14:17 [c]Job 10:14
10 [1]Lit., *finds* [a]Job 13:24
11 [a]Job 13:27
12 [1]Lit., *answer*
13 [a]Job 40:2; Is. 45:9
14 [a]Job 33:29; 40:5; Ps. 62:11
15 [a]Job 33:15-18; 4:12-17

16 Then [a]He opens the ears of men,
And seals their instruction,
17 That He may turn man aside *from his* conduct,
And [1]keep man from pride;
18 He [a]keeps back his soul from the pit,
And his life from [1]passing over [b]into Sheol.

19 "[1]Man is also chastened with [a]pain on his bed,
And with unceasing complaint in his bones;
20 So that his life [a]loathes bread,
And his soul favorite food.
21 "His [a]flesh wastes away from sight,
And his [b]bones which were not seen stick out.
22 "Then [a]his soul draws near to the pit,
And his life to those who bring death.

23 "If there is an angel *as* [a]mediator for him,
One out of a thousand,
To remind a man what is [1]right for him,
24 Then let him be gracious to him, and say,
'Deliver him from [a]going down to the pit,
I have found a [b]ransom;'
25 Let his flesh become fresher than in youth,
Let him return to the days of his youthful vigor;
26 Then he will [a]pray to God, and He will accept him,
That [b]he may see His face with joy,
And He may restore His righteousness to man.
27 "He will [a]sing to men and say,
'I [b]have sinned and perverted what is right,
And it is not [c]proper for me.
28 'He has redeemed my soul from going to the pit,
And my life shall [a]see the light.'

29 "Behold, God does [a]all these [1]oftentimes with men,
30 To [a]bring back his soul from the pit,
That he may be enlightened with the light of life.
31 "Pay attention, O Job, listen to me;
Keep silent and let me speak.
32 "*Then* if [1]you have anything to say, answer me;
Speak, for I desire to justify you.
33 "If not, listen to me;
Keep silent, and I will teach you wisdom."

CHAPTER 34

THEN Elihu answered and said,
2 "Hear my words, you wise men,
And listen to me, you who know.
3 "For [a]the ear tests words,
As the palate tastes food.
4 "Let us choose for ourselves what is right;
Let us know among ourselves what is good.
5 "For Job has said, '[a]I am righteous,
But God has taken away my right;
6 [1]Should I lie concerning my right?

16 [a]Job 36:10, 15
17 [1]Lit., *hide*
18 [1]M.T., *perishing by the sword*
[a]Job 33:22, 24, 28, 30 [b]Job 15:22
19 [1]Lit., *He*
[a]Job 30:17
20 [a]Job 3:24; 6:7; Ps. 107:18
21 [a]Job 16:8 [b]Job 19:20; Ps. 22:17
22 [a]Job 33:18, 28
23 [1]Lit., *his uprightness*
[a]Gen. 40:8
24 [a]Job 33:18, 28; Is. 38:17
[b]Job 36:18; Ps. 49:7
26 [a]Job 22:27; 34:28 [b]Job 22:26
27 [a]Job 8:21 [b]2 Sam. 12:13; Luke 15:21 [c]Rom. 6:21
28 [a]Job 22:28
29 [1]Lit., *twice, three times*
[a]Eph. 1:11; Phil. 2:13
30 [a]Job 33:18
32 [1]Lit., *there are words*
3 [a]Job 12:11
5 [a]Job 13:18 [b]Job 27:2
6 [1]Or, *Although I am right I am accounted a liar*

My [2a]wound is incurable, *though I am* without transgression.'
7 "What man is like Job,
Who [a]drinks up derision like water,
8 Who goes [a]in company with the workers of iniquity,
And walks with wicked men?
9 "For he has said, '[a]It profits a man nothing
When he [1]is pleased with God.'

10 "Therefore, listen to me, you men of understanding.
Far be it from God to [a]do wickedness,
And from the Almighty to do wrong.
11 "For He pays a man according to [a]his work,
And makes [1]him find it according to his way.
12 "Surely, [a]God will not act wickedly,
And the Almighty will not pervert justice.
13 "Who [a]gave Him authority over the earth?
And who [b]has laid *on Him* the whole world?
14 "If He should [1]determine to do so,
If He should [a]gather to Himself His spirit and His breath,
15 All [a]flesh would perish together,
And man would [b]return to dust.

16 "But if *you have* understanding, hear this;
Listen to the sound of my words.
17 "Shall [a]one who hates justice rule?
And [b]will you condemn a righteous mighty one,
18 Who says to a king, 'Worthless one,'
To nobles, 'Wicked ones';
19 Who shows no [a]partiality to princes,
Nor regards the rich above the poor,
For they all are the [b]work of His hands?
20 "In a moment they die, and [a]at midnight
People are shaken and pass away,
And [b]the mighty are taken away without a hand.

21 "For [a]His eyes are upon the ways of a man,
And He sees all his steps.
22 "There is [a]no darkness or deep shadow,
Where the workers of iniquity may hide themselves.
23 "For He does not [a]*need to* consider a man further,
That he should go before God in judgment.
24 "He breaks in pieces [a]mighty men without inquiry,
And sets others in their place.
25 "Therefore He [a]knows their works,
And [b]He overthrows *them* in the night,
And they are crushed.
26 "He [a]strikes them like the wicked
[1]In a public place,
27 Because they [a]turned aside from following Him,
And [b]had no regard for any of His ways;
28 So that they caused [a]the cry of the poor to come to Him,
And that He might [b]hear—the cry of the afflicted—
29 "When He keeps quiet, who then can condemn?

6 [2]Lit., *arrow*
[a]Job 6:4

7 [a]Job 15:16

8 [a]Job 22:15

9 [1]Or, *takes delight in God*
[a]Job 21:15; 35:3; Ps. 50:18

10 [a]Job 34:12; 8:3

11 [1]Lit., *a man*
[a]Job 34:25; Ps. 62:12; Prov. 24:12; Jer. 32:19; Ezek. 33:20; Matt. 16:27; Rom. 2:6; 2 Cor. 5:10; Rev. 22:12

12 [a]Job 34:10

13 [a]Job 38:4 [b]Job 38:5

14 [1]Lit., *set His mind on Himself*
[a]Job 12:10; Ps. 104:29

15 [a]Job 9:22; Gen. 7:21 [b]Job 10:9; Gen. 3:19

17 [a]Job 34:30; 2 Sam. 23:3 [b]Job 40:8

19 [a]Lev. 19:15; Deut. 10:17; 2 Chr. 19:7; Acts 10:34; Rom. 2:11; Gal. 2:6; Eph. 6:9; Col. 3:25; 1 Pet. 1:17 [b]Job 10:3

20 [a]Job 34:25; Job 36:20; Ex. 12:29 [b]Job 12:19

21 [a]Job 29:23; 31:4; Prov. 5:21; 15:3; Jer. 16:17

22 [a]Ps. 139:11, 12; Amos 9:2, 3

23 [a]Job 11:11

24 [a]Job 12:19

25 [a]Job 34:11 [b]Job 34:20

26 [1]Lit., *in the place of the ones seeing*
[a]Ps. 9:5; 11:5

27 [a]1 Sam. 15:11 [b]Job 21:14

28 [a]Job 35:9 [b]Job 22:27; Ex. 22:23

And when He hides His face, who then can behold Him
That is, in regard to both nation and man?—
30 So that [a]godless men should not rule,
Nor be snares of the people.

31 "For has any one said to God,
'I have [a]borne *chastisement;*
I will not offend *any more;*
32 Teach Thou me what I do not see;
I will do it no more'?
If I have [a]done iniquity,
33 "Shall He [a]recompense on your terms, because you have rejected *it?*
For you must choose, and not I;
Therefore declare what you know.
34 "Men of understanding will say to me,
And a wise man who hears me,
35 'Job [a]speaks without knowledge,
And his words are without wisdom.
36 'Job ought to be tried [1]to the limit,
Because he answers [a]like wicked men.
37 'For he adds [a]rebellion to his sin;
He [b]claps his hands among us,
And multiplies his words against God.' "

Chapter 35

THEN Elihu answered and said,
2 "Do you think this is according to [a]justice?
Do you say, 'My righteousness is more than God's'?
3 "For you say, '[a]What advantage will it be to [1]You?
[b]What profit shall I have, more than if I had sinned?'
4 "I will answer you,
And your friends with you.
5 "[a]Look at the heavens and see;
And behold [b]the clouds—they are higher than you.
6 "If you have sinned, [a]what do you accomplish against Him?
And if your transgressions are many, what do you do to Him?
7 "If you are righteous, [a]what do you give to Him?
Or what does He receive from your hand?
8 "Your wickedness is for a man like yourself,
And your righteousness is for a son of man.

9 "Because of the multitude of oppressions they cry out;
They cry for help because of the arm [a]of the mighty.
10 "But [a]no one says, 'Where is God my Maker,
Who [b]gives songs in the night,
11 Who [a]teaches us more than the beasts of the earth,
And makes us wiser than the birds of the heavens?'
12 "There they cry out, but He does not answer
Because of the pride of evil men.
13 "Surely [a]God will not listen to [1]an empty *cry,*
Nor will the Almighty regard it.

30 [a]Job 34:17; 5:15; 20:5
31 [a]Job 33:27
32 [a]Job 33:27
33 [a]Job 41:11
35 [a]Job 35:16
36 [1]Or, *to the end* [a]Job 22:15
37 [a]Job 23:2 [b]Job 27:23

2 [a]Job 27:2
3 [1]Or, *you* [a]Job 34:9 [b]Job 9:30, 31
5 [a]Gen. 15:5; Ps. 8:3 [b]Job 22:12
6 [a]Job 7:20; Prov. 8:36; Jer. 7:19
7 [a]Job 22:2, 3; Prov. 9:12; Luke 17:10
9 [a]Job 12:19
10 [a]Job 24:14; 27:10; 36:13 [b]Job 8:21; Ps. 42:8; 77:6; 149:5; Acts 16:25
11 [a]Job 36:22; Ps. 94:12; Jer. 32:33
13 [1]Or, *falsehood* [a]Job 27:9; Prov. 15:29; Is. 1:15; Jer. 11:11; Mic. 3:4

14 "How much less when [a]you say you do not behold Him,
The [b]case is before Him, and you must wait for Him!
15 "And now, because He has not visited *in* His anger,
Nor has He acknowledged [1]transgression well,
16 So Job opens his mouth [1]emptily;
He multiplies words [a]without knowledge."

CHAPTER 36

THEN Elihu continued and said,
2 "Wait for me a little, and I will show you
That there [1]is yet more to be said in God's behalf.
3 "I will fetch my knowledge from afar,
And I will ascribe [a]righteousness to my Maker.
4 "For truly [a]my words are not false;
One who is [b]perfect in knowledge is with you.
5 "Behold, God is mighty but does not [a]despise *any;*
He is [b]mighty in strength of understanding.
6 "He does not [a]keep the wicked alive,
But gives justice to [b]the afflicted.
7 "He does not [a]withdraw His eyes from the righteous;
But [b]with kings on the throne
He has seated them forever, and they are exalted.
8 "And if they are bound in fetters,
And are caught in the cords of [a]affliction,
9 Then he declares to them their work
And their transgressions, that they have [a]magnified themselves.
10 "And [a]He opens their ear to instruction,
And [b]commands that they return from evil.
11 "If they hear and serve *Him,*
They shall end their days in prosperity,
And their years in pleasures.
12 "But if they do not hear, they shall [1]perish [a]by the sword,
And they shall [b]die without knowledge.
13 "But the godless in heart lay up anger;
They do not cry for help when He binds them.
14 "[1]They die in youth,
And their life *perishes* among the [a]cult prostitutes.
15 "He delivers the afflicted in [1]their [a]affliction,
And [b]opens their ear [2]in *time of* oppression.
16 "Then indeed, He [a]enticed you from the mouth of distress,
Instead of it, a broad place with no constraint;
And that which was set on your table was full of [1]fatness.

17 "But you were full of [a]judgment on the wicked;
Judgment and justice take hold *of you.*
18 "*Beware* lest [a]wrath entice you to scoffing;
And do not let the greatness of the [b]ransom turn you aside.
19 "Will your [1]riches keep *you* from distress,
Or all the forces of *your* strength?
20 "Do not long for [a]the night,
When people [1]vanish in their place.

35:14 [a]Job 9:11; 23:8, 9 [b]Job 31:35

15 [1]Or, *arrogance*

16 [1]Lit., *vainly* [a]Job 34:35

36:2 [1]Lit., *are yet words for God*

3 [a]Job 8:3; 37:23

4 [a]Job 33:3 [b]Job 37:16

5 [a]Ps. 22:24; 69:33; 102:17 [b]Job 12:13

6 [a]Job 8:22; 34:26 [b]Job 5:15

7 [a]Ps. 33:18; 34:15 [b]Job 5:11; Ps. 113:8

8 [a]Job 36:15, 21

9 [a]Job 15:25

10 [a]Job 36:15; 33:16 [b]Job 36:21; 2 Kin. 17:13; Jon. 3:8

12 [1]Lit., *pass away* [a]Job 15:22 [b]Job 4:21

14 [1]Or, *Their soul dies* [a]Deut. 23:17

15 [1]Lit., *his* [2]Or, *in adversity* [a]Job 36:8, 21 [b]Job 36:10

16 [1]Or, *rich food* [a]Hos. 2:14

17 [a]Job 22:5, 10, 11

18 [a]Job 34:33; Jon. 4:4, 9 [b]Job 33:24

19 [1]Or, *cry*

20 [1]Lit., *go up* [a]Job 34:20, 25

21 "Be careful, do [a]not turn to evil;
For you have preferred this to [b]affliction.
22 "Behold, God is exalted in His power;
Who is a [a]teacher like Him?
23 "Who has appointed Him His way,
And who has said, '[a]Thou hast done wrong'?

24 "Remember that you should exalt His work,
Of which men have [a]sung.
25 "All men have seen it;
Man beholds from afar.
26 "Behold, God is [a]exalted, and we do not know *Him*;
The [b]number of His years is unsearchable.
27 "For [a]He draws up the drops of water,
They distill rain from [1]the [2]mist,
28 Which the clouds pour down,
They drip upon man abundantly.
29 "Can anyone understand the [a]spreading of the clouds,
The [b]thundering of His [1]pavilion?
30 "Behold, He spreads His [1]lightning about Him,
And He covers the depths of the sea.
31 "For by these He [a]judges peoples;
He [b]gives food in abundance.
32 "He covers *His* hands with the [1]lightning,
And [a]commands it to strike the mark.
33 "Its [a]noise declares [1]His presence;
The cattle also, concerning what is coming up.

CHAPTER 37

"AT this also my heart trembles,
And leaps from its place.
2 "Listen closely to the [a]thunder of His voice,
And the rumbling that goes out from His mouth.
3 "Under the whole heaven He lets it loose,
And His [1]lightning to the [a]ends of the earth.
4 "After it, a voice roars;
He thunders with His majestic voice;
And He does not restrain [1]*the lightnings* when His voice is heard.
5 "God [a]thunders with His voice wondrously,
Doing [b]great things which we cannot comprehend.
6 "For to [a]the snow He says, 'Fall on the earth,'
And to the [1b]downpour and the rain, 'Be strong.'
7 "He [a]seals the hand of every man,
That all men may know His work.
8 "Then the beast goes into its [a]lair,
And remains in its [1]den.
9 "Out of the [1a]south comes the storm,
And out of the [2]north the cold.
10 "From the breath of God [a]ice is made,
And the expanse of the waters is frozen.
11 "Also with moisture He [a]loads the thick cloud;
He [b]disperses [c]the cloud of His [1]lightning.
12 "And it changes direction, turning around by His guidance,

21 [a]Job 36:10; Ps. 31:6; 66:18 [b]Job 36:8, 15
22 [a]Job 35:11
23 [a]Job 8:3
24 [a]Ex. 15:1; Judg. 5:1; 1 Chr. 16:9; Ps. 59:16; 138:5
26 [a]Job 11:7-9; 37:23 [b]Job 10:5; Ps. 90:2; 102:24; 27
27 [1]Lit., *its* [2]Or, *flood* [a]Job 36:26-29; 5:10; 37:6, 11; 38:28; Ps. 147:8
29 [1]Lit., *booth* [a]Job 37:11, 16 [b]Job 26:14
30 [1]Lit., *light*
31 [a]Job 37:13 [b]Ps. 104:27; 136:25; Acts 14:17
32 [1]Lit., *light* [a]Job 37:11, 12, 15
33 [1]Lit., *concerning Him* [a]Job 37:2
2 [a]Job 36:33; 37:4, 5; Ps. 29:3-9
3 [1]Lit., *light* [a]Job 37:12; 28:24; 38:13
4 [1]Lit., *them*
5 [a]Job 26:14 [b]Job 37:14, 16, 23; 5:9
6 [1]Lit., *shower of rain and shower of rains* [a]Job 38:22 [b]Job 36:27
7 [a]Job 12:14
8 [1]Lit., *dens* [a]Job 38:40; Ps. 104:22
9 [1]Lit., *chamber* [2]Lit., *scattering winds* [a]Job 9:9
10 [a]Job 38:29; Ps. 147:17
11 [1]Lit., *light* [a]Job 36:27 [b]Job 36:29 [c]Job 37:15

That [1]it may do whatever He [a]commands [2]it
On the [b]face of the inhabited earth.
13 "Whether for [1a]correction, or for [b]His world,
Or for [c]lovingkindness, He causes it to [2]happen.

14 "Listen to this, O Job,
Stand and consider the wonders of God.
15 "Do you know how God establishes them,
And makes the [1]lightning of His cloud to shine?
16 "Do you know about the layers of the thick clouds,
The [a]wonders of one [b]perfect in knowledge,
17 You whose garments are hot,
When the land is still because of the south wind?
18 "Can you, with Him, [a]spread out the skies,
Strong as a molten mirror?
19 "Teach us what we shall say to Him;
We [a]cannot arrange *our case* because of darkness.
20 "Shall it be told Him that I would speak?
[1]Or should a man say that he would be swallowed up?

21 "And now [1]men do not see the light which is bright in the skies;
But the wind has passed and cleared them.
22 "Out of the north comes golden *splendor;*
Around God is awesome majesty.
23 "The Almighty—[a]we cannot find Him;
He is [b]exalted in power;
And [c]He will not do violence [d]to justice and abundant righteousness.
24 "Therefore men fear Him;
He does not [a]regard any who are wise of heart."

Chapter 38

THEN the LORD [a]answered Job out of the whirlwind and said,
2 "Who is this that [a]darkens counsel
By words without knowledge?
3 "Now [a]gird up your loins like a man,
And [b]I will ask you, and you instruct Me!
4 "Where were you [a]when I laid the foundation of the earth!
Tell *Me,* if you [1]have understanding,
5 "Who set its [a]measurements, since you know?
Or who stretched the line on it?
6 "On what [a]were its bases sunk?
Or who laid its cornerstone,
7 When the morning stars sang together,
And all the [a]sons of God shouted for joy?

8 "Or *who* enclosed the sea with doors,
When, bursting forth, it went out from the womb;
9 When I made a cloud its garment,
And thick darkness its swaddling band,
10 And I [1a]placed boundaries on it,
And I set a bolt and doors,

12 [1]Lit., *they* [2]Lit., *them* [a]Job 36:32; Ps. 148:8 [b]Is. 14:21; 27:6

13 [1]Lit., *rod* [2]Lit., *be found* [a]Ex. 9:18, 23; 1 Sam. 12:18, 19 [b]Job 38:26, 27 [c]1 Kin. 18:45

15 [1]Lit., *light*

16 [a]Job 37:5, 14, 23 [b]Job 36:4

18 [a]Job 9:8; Ps. 104:2; Is. 45:12; Jer. 10:12; Zech. 12:1

19 [a]Job 9:14; Rom. 8:26

20 [1]Or, *If a man speak, surely he shall be swallowed up*

21 [1]Lit., *they*

23 [a]Job 11:7, 8; Rom. 11:13; 1 Tim. 8:16 [b]Job 9:4; 36:5 [c]Is. 63:9; Nah. 1:12; Lam. 3:33 [d]Job 8:3

24 [a]Job 5:13; 1 Cor. 1:26

1 [a]Job 40:6

2 [a]Job 35:16; 42:3

3 [a]Job 40:7 [b]Job 42:4

4 [1]Lit., *know understanding* [a]Job 15:7; Ps. 104:5; Prov. 30:4

5 [a]Prov. 8:29; Is. 40:12

6 [a]Job. 26:7

7 [a]Job 1:6

10 [1]Lit., *broke My decree on it* [a]Gen. 1:9; Ps. 33:7; 104:9; Prov. 8:29; Jer. 5:22

God Speaks of Job's Ignorance of Creation.

11 And I said, 'Thus far you shall come, but no farther;
And here shall your proud waves stop'?

12 "Have you [1]ever in your life commanded the morning,
And caused the dawn to know its place;
13 That it might take hold of [a]the ends of the earth,
And [b]the wicked be shaken out of it?
14 "It is changed like clay *under* the seal;
And they stand forth like a garment.
15 "And [a]from the wicked their light is withheld,
And the [b]uplifted arm is broken.

16 "Have you entered into [a]the springs of the sea?
Or have you walked [1]in the recesses of the deep?
17 "Have the gates of death been revealed to you?
Or have you seen the gates of [a]deep darkness?
18 "Have you understood the [1]expanse of [a]the earth?
Tell *Me*, if you know all this.

19 "Where is the way to the dwelling of light?
And darkness, where is its place,
20 That you may take it to [a]its territory,
And that you may discern the paths to its [1]home?
21 "You know, for [a]you were born then,
And the number of your days is great!
22 "Have you entered the storehouses [a]of the snow,
Or have you seen the storehouses of the [b]hail,
23 Which I have reserved for the time of distress,
For the day of war and battle?
24 "Where is the way that [a]the light is divided,
Or the east wind scattered on the earth?

25 "Who has cleft a channel for the flood,
Or a way for the thunderbolt;
26 To bring [a]rain on a land without [1]people,
On a desert without a man in it,
27 To [a]satisfy the waste and desolate land,
And to make the [1]seeds of grass to sprout?
28 "Has [a]the rain a father?
Or who has begotten the drops of dew?
29 "From whose womb has come the [a]ice?
And the frost of heaven, who has given it birth?
30 "Water [1]becomes hard like stone,
And the surface of the deep is imprisoned.

31 "Can you bind the chains of the [a]Pleiades,
Or loose the cords of Orion?
32 "Can you lead forth a [1]constellation in its season,
And guide the Bear with her [2]satellites?
33 "Do you know the [a]ordinances of the heavens,
Or fix their rule over the earth?

34 "Can you lift up your voice to the clouds,
So that an [a]abundance of water may cover you?
35 "Can you [a]send forth lightnings that they may go,
And say to you, 'Here we are'?

12 [1]Lit., *from your days*

13 [a]Job 28:24; 37:3 [b]Job 34:25, 26; 36:6

15 [a]Job 5:14 [b]Num. 15:30; Ps. 10:15; 37:17

16 [1]Or, *in search of* [a]Gen. 7:11; 8:2; Prov. 8:24, 28

17 [a]Job 10:21; 26:6; 34:22

18 [1]Or, *width* [a]Job 28:24

20 [1]Lit., *house* [a]Job 26:10

21 [a]Job 15:7

22 [a]Job 37:6 [b]Ex. 9:18; Josh. 10:11; Is. 30:30; Ezek. 13:11, 13; Rev. 16:21

24 [a]Job 26:10

26 [1]Lit., *man* [a]Job 36:27

27 [1]Or, *growth* [a]Ps. 104:13, 14

28 [a]Job 36:27, 28; Ps. 147:8; Jer. 14:22

29 [a]Job 37:10; Ps. 147:17

30 [1]Lit., *hides itself*

31 [a]Job 9:9; Amos 5:8

32 [1]Lit., *Mazzaroth* [2]Lit., *sons*

33 [a]Ps. 148:6; Jer. 31:35, 36

34 [a]Job 38:37; 22:11; 36:27, 28

35 [a]Job 36:32; 37:3

36 "Who has [a]put wisdom in the innermost being,
Or has given [b]understanding to the [1]mind?
37 "Who can count the clouds by wisdom,
Or [a]tip the water jars of the heavens,
38 When the dust hardens into a mass,
And the clods stick together?

39 "Can you hunt the [a]prey for the lion,
Or satisfy the appetite of the young lions,
40 When they [a]crouch in *their* dens,
And lie in wait in *their* lair?
41 "Who prepares for [a]the raven its nourishment,
When its young cry to God,
And wander about without food?

Chapter 39

1 "Do you know the time the [1a]mountain goats give birth?
Do you observe the calving of the [b]deer?
2 "Can you count the months they fulfill,
Or do you know the time they give birth?
3 "They kneel down, they bring forth their young,
They get rid of their labor pains.
4 "Their offspring become strong, they grow up in the open field;
They leave and do not return to them.

5 "Who sent out the [a]wild donkey free?
And who loosed the bonds of the swift donkey,
6 To whom I gave [a]the wilderness for a home,
And the salt land for his dwelling place?
7 "He scorns the tumult of the city,
The shoutings of the driver he does not hear.
8 "He explores the mountains for his pasture,
And he searches after every green thing.
9 "Will the [a]wild ox consent to serve you?
Or will he spend the night at your manger?
10 "Can you bind the wild ox in a furrow with [1]ropes?
Or will he harrow the valleys after you?
11 "Will you trust him because his strength is great
And leave your labor to him?
12 "Will you have faith in him that he will return your [1]grain,
And gather *it from* your threshing floor?

13 "The ostriches' wings flap joyously
With the pinion and plumage of [1]love?
14 "For she abandons her eggs to the earth,
And warms them in the dust,
15 And she forgets that a foot may crush [1]them,
Or that a wild beast may trample [1]them.
16 "She treats her young [a]cruelly, as if *they* were not hers;
Though her labor be in vain, *she* is [1]unconcerned;
17 Because God has made her forget wisdom,
And has not given her a share of understanding.

36 [1]Or, *cock* [a]Job 9:4; Ps. 51:6; Eccles. 2:26 [b]Job 32:8

37 [a]Job 38:34

39 [a]Ps. 104:21

40 [a]Job 37:8

41 [a]Ps. 147:9; Matt 6:26; Luke 12:24

1 [1]Lit., *goats of the rock* [a]Deut. 14:5; 1 Sam. 24:2; Ps. 104:18 [b]Ps. 29:9

5 [a]Job 6:5; 11:12; 24:5; Ps. 104:11

6 [a]Job 24:5; Jer. 2:24; Hos. 8:9

9 [a]Num. 23:22; Deut. 33:17; Ps. 22:21; 29:6; 92:10; Is. 34:7

10 [1]Lit., *his rope*

12 [1]Lit., *seed*

13 [1]Or, *a stork*

15 [1]Lit., *it*

16 [1]Lit., *without fear* [a]Lam. 4:3

18 "When she lifts herself [1]on high,
She laughs at the horse and his rider.

19 "Do you give the horse *his* might?
Do you clothe his neck with a mane?
20 "Do you make him [a]leap like the locust?
His majestic [b]snorting is terrible.
21 "[1]He paws in the valley, and rejoices in *his* strength;
He [a]goes out to meet the weapons.
22 "He laughs at fear and is not dismayed;
And he does not turn back from the sword.
23 "The quiver rattles against him,
The flashing spear and javelin.
24 "With shaking and rage he [1]races over the ground;
And he does not stand still at the voice of the trumpet.
25 "As often as the trumpet *sounds* he says, 'Ha!'
And he scents the battle from afar,
And thunder of the captains, and the war cry.

26 "Is it by your understanding that the hawk soars,
Stretching his wings toward the south?
27 "Is it at your [1]command that the eagle mounts up,
And makes [a]his nest on high?
28 "On the cliff he dwells and lodges,
Upon the rocky crag, an inaccessible place.
29 "From there he [a]spies out food;
His eyes see *it* from afar.
30 "His young ones also suck up blood;
And [a]where the slain are, there is he."

CHAPTER 40

THEN the LORD answered Job and said,
2 "Will the faultfinder [a]contend with the Almighty?
Let him who [b]reproves God answer it."

3 Then Job answered the LORD and said,
4 "Behold, I am insignificant; what can I reply to Thee?
I [a]lay my hand on my mouth.
5 "Once I have spoken, and [a]I will not answer;
Even twice, and I will add no more."

6 Then the [a]LORD answered Job out of the storm, and said,
7 "Now [a]gird up your loins like a man;
I will [b]ask you, and you instruct Me.
8 "Will you really annul My judgment?
Will you [a]condemn Me [b]that you may be justified?
9 "Or do you have an arm like God,
And can you [a]thunder with a voice like His?

10 "Adorn yourself with eminence and dignity;
And clothe yourself with honor and majesty.
11 "Pour out [a]the overflowings of your anger;
And look on everyone who is [b]proud, and make him low.

18 [1]Or, *to flee*

20 [a]Joel 2:5 [b]Jer. 8:16

21 [1]Lit., *they paw* [a]Jer. 8:6

24 [1]Or, *swallows up*

27 [1]Lit., *mouth* [a]Jer. 49:16; Obad. 4

29 [a]Job 9:26

30 [a]Matt. 24:28; Luke 17:37

2 [a]Job 9:3; 10:2; 33:13 [b]Job 13:3; 23:4; 31:35

4 [a]Job 21:5; 29:9

5 [a]Job 9:3, 15

6 [a]Job 38:1

7 [a]Job 38:3 [b]Job 38:3; 42:4

8 [a]Job 10:3, 7; 16:11; 19:6; 27:2 [b]Job 13:18; 27:6

9 [a]Job 37:5

11 [a]Is. 42:25; Nah. 1:6, 8 [b]Is. 2:12; Dan. 4:37

12 "Look on everyone who is proud, *and* [a]humble him;
And [b]tread down the wicked [1]where they stand.
13 "[a]Hide them in the dust together;
Bind [1]them in the hidden *place.*
14 "Then I will also [1]confess to you,
That your own right hand can save you.

15 "Behold now, [1]Behemoth, which [a]I made [2]as well as you;
He eats grass like an ox.
16 "Behold now, his strength in his loins,
And his power in the muscles of his belly.
17 "He bends his tail like a cedar;
The sinews of his thighs are knit together.
18 "His bones are tubes of bronze;
His [1]limbs are like bars of iron.

19 "He is the [a]first of the ways of God;
Let his [b]maker bring near his sword.
20 "Surely the mountains bring him food,
And all the beasts of the field [a]play there.
21 "Under the lotus plants he lies down,
In the covert of the reeds and the marsh.
22 "The lotus plants cover him with [1]shade;
The willows of the brook surround him.
23 "If a river [1]rages, he is not alarmed;
He is confident, though the Jordan rushes to his mouth.
24 "Can anyone capture him [1]when he is on watch,
With [2]barbs can anyone pierce *his* nose?

Chapter 41

"[1]Can you draw out [2][a]Leviathan with a fishhook?
Or press down his tongue with a cord?
2 "Can you [a]put a [1]rope in his nose?
Or pierce his jaw with a [2]hook?
3 "Will he make many supplications to you?
Or will he speak to you soft words?
4 "Will he make a covenant with you?
Will you take him for a servant forever?
5 "Will you play with him as with a bird?
Or will you bind him for your maidens?
6 "Will the [1]traders bargain over him?
Will they divide him among the merchants?
7 "Can you fill his skin with harpoons,
Or his head with fishing spears?
8 "Lay your hand on him;
Remember the battle; [1]you will not do it again!
9 "Behold, [1]your expectation is false;
Will [2]you be laid low even at the sight of him?
10 "No one is so fierce that he dares to [a]arouse him;
Who then is he that can stand before Me?
11 "Who has [1]given to Me that I should repay *him?*
Whatever is [a]under the whole heaven is Mine.

12 "I will not keep silence concerning his limbs,
Or his mighty strength, or his [1]orderly frame.

---

12 [1]Lit., *under them* [a]1 Sam. 2:7; Is. 13:11 [b]Is. 63:3

13 [1]Or, *their faces* [a]Is. 2:10-12

14 [1]Or, *praise you*

15 [1]Or, the *hippopotamus* [2]Lit., *with* [a]Job 40:19

18 [1]Lit., *bones*

19 [a]Job 41:33 [b]Job 40:15

20 [a]Ps. 104:26

22 [1]Lit., *his shade*

23 [1]Or, *oppresses*

24 [1]Lit., *in his eyes* [2]Lit., *snares*

1 [1]Ch. 40:25 in Heb. [2]Or, *the crocodile* [a]Job 3:8; Ps. 74:14; 104:26; Is. 27:1

2 [1]Lit., *a rope of rushes* [2]Or, *thorn, or ring* [a]2 Kin. 19:28 Is. 37:29

6 [1]Lit., *partners*

8 [1]Lit., *do not add*

9 [1]Lit., *his* [2]Lit., *he*

10 [a]Job 3:8

11 [1]Lit., *anticipated* [a]Job 9:5-10; 26:6-14; 28:24; Ex. 19:5; Deut. 10:14; Ps. 24:1; 50:12; 1 Cor. 10:26

12 [1]Or, *graceful*

13 "Who can [1]strip off his outer armor?
Who can come within his double [2]mail?
14 "Who can open the doors of his face?
Around his teeth there is terror.
15 "*His* [1]strong scales are *his* pride,
Shut up *as with* a tight seal,
16 "One is so near to another,
That no air can come between them.
17 "They are joined one to another;
They clasp each other and cannot be separated.
18 "His sneezes flash forth light,
And his eyes are like the [a]eyelids of the morning.
19 "Out of his mouth go burning torches;
Sparks of fire leap forth.
20 "Out of his nostrils smoke goes forth,
As *from* a boiling pot and *burning* rushes.
21 "His breath kindles coals,
And a flame goes forth from his mouth.
22 "In his neck lodges strength,
And dismay leaps before him.
23 "The folds of his flesh are joined together,
Firm on him and immovable.
24 "His heart is as hard as a stone;
Even as hard as a lower millstone.
25 "When he raises himself up, the [1]mighty fear;
Because of the crashing they are bewildered.
26 "The sword that reaches him cannot avail;
Nor the spear, the dart, or the javelin.
27 "He regards iron as straw,
Bronze as rotten wood.
28 "The [1]arrow cannot make him flee;
Slingstones are turned into stubble for him.
29 "Clubs are regarded as stubble;
He laughs at the rattling of the javelin.
30 "His underparts are *like* sharp potsherds;
He [1]spreads out *like* a threshing sledge on the mire.
31 "He makes the depths boil like a pot;
He makes the sea like a jar of ointment.
32 "Behind him he makes a wake to shine;
One would think the deep to be gray-haired.
33 "[a]Nothing on [1]earth is like him,
One made without fear.
34 "[1]He looks on everything that is high;
He is king over all the [a]sons of pride."

Chapter 42

THEN Job answered the LORD, and said,
2 "I know that Thou canst do all things,
And that no purpose of Thine can be thwarted.
3 'Who is this that [a]hides counsel without knowledge?'
"Therefore I have declared that which I did not understand,
Things [b]too wonderful for me, which I did not know.
4 'Hear, now, and I will speak;
I will [a]ask you, and you instruct Me.'

13 [1]Lit., *uncover the face of his garment* [2]So Gk.; Heb., *bridle*
15 [1]Lit., *rows of shields*
18 [a]Job 3:9
25 [1]or, *gods*
28 [1]Lit., *son of the bow*
30 [1]Or, *moves across*
33 [1]Lit., *dust* [a]Job 40:19
34 [1]Job 41:26 in Heb. [a]Job 28:8
3 [a]Job 38:2 [b]Ps. 40:5; 131:1; 139:6
4 [a]Job 38:3; 40:7

5 "I have [a]heard of Thee by the hearing of the ear;
But now my [b]eye sees Thee;
6 Therefore I retract,
And I repent in dust and ashes."
7 And it came about after the LORD had spoken these
words to Job, then the LORD said to Eliphaz the Temanite,
"My wrath is kindled against you and against your two friends,
because you have not spoken of Me what is right [a]as My
servant Job has.
8 "Now therefore, take for yourselves seven bulls and sev-
en rams, and go to My servant Job, and offer up a [a]burnt
offering for yourselves, and My servant Job will pray for you.
[b]For I will [1]accept him so that I may not do with you *according to your* folly, because you have not spoken of Me what is
right, as My servant Job has."
9 So Eliphaz the Temanite and Bildad the Shuhite *and*
Zophar the Naamathite went and did as the LORD told them;
and the LORD [1]accepted Job.
10 And the LORD [a]restored the fortunes of Job when he
prayed for his friends, and the LORD increased all that Job had
twofold.
11 Then all his [a]brothers, and all his sisters, and all who
had known him before, came to him, and they ate bread with
him in his house; and they [b]consoled him and comforted him
for all the evil that the LORD had brought on him. And each
one gave him one [1]piece of money, and each a ring of gold.
12 [a]And the LORD blessed the latter *days* of Job more than
his beginning, [b]and he had 14,000 sheep, and 6,000 camels, and
1,000 yoke of oxen, and 1,000 female donkeys.
13 And [a]he had seven sons and three daughters.
14 And he named the first Jemimah, and the second Ke-
ziah, and the third Keren-happuch.
15 And in all the land no women were found so fair as
Job's daughters; and their father gave them inheritance among
their brothers.
16 And after this Job lived 140 years, and saw his sons, and
his grandsons, four generations.
17 [a]And Job died, an old man and full of days.

5 [a]Job 26:14 [b]Is. 6:5
7 [a]Job 42:1-6; 40:3-5
8 [1]Lit., *lift up his face* [a]Job 1:5 [b]Job 22:30
9 [1]Lit., *lifted up the face of*
10 [a]Deut. 30:3; Ps. 14:7; 85:1-3; 126:1-6
11 [1]Lit., *Qesitah* [a]Job 19:13 [b]Job 2:11
12 [a]Job 1:10 [b]Job 1:3
13 [a]Job 1:2
17 [a]Job 5:26; Gen. 15:15; 25:8; 38:29

THE PSALMS

Book 1

PSALM 1

The Righteous and the Wicked Contrasted.

HOW blessed is the man who [a]does not walk in the [b]counsel
of the wicked,
Nor stand in the [1c]path of sinners,
Nor [d]sit in the seat of scoffers!
2 But his [a]delight is in the law of the LORD,
And in His law he meditates [b]day and [c]night.
3 And he will be like [a]a tree firmly planted by [1]streams of
water,
Which yields its fruit in its season,
And its [2]leaf does not wither;
And [3]in whatever he does, [b]he prospers.

4 The wicked are not so,
But they are like [a]chaff which the wind drives away.
5 Therefore [a]the wicked will not stand in the [b]judgment,
Nor sinners in [c]the assembly of the righteous.
6 For the LORD [1a]knows the way of the righteous,
But the way of [b]the wicked will perish.

PSALM 2

The Reign of the LORD'S Anointed.

WHY are [a]the [1]nations in an uproar,
And the peoples [b]devising a vain thing?
2 The [a]kings of the earth take their stand,
And the rulers take counsel together
[b]Against the LORD and against His [1]Anointed:
3 "Let us [a]tear their fetters apart,
And cast away their cords from us!"

4 He who [1]sits in the heavens [a]laughs,
The Lord [b]scoffs at them.
5 Then He will speak to them in His [a]anger
And [b]terrify them in His fury:
6 "But as for Me, I have [1]installed [a]My King
Upon Zion, [b]My holy mountain."

7 "I will surely tell of the [1]decree of the LORD:
He said to Me, 'Thou art [a]My Son,
Today I have begotten Thee.
8 'Ask of Me, and [a]I will surely give [b]the [1]nations as Thy
inheritance,
And the *very* [c]ends of the earth as Thy possession.
9 'Thou shalt [1a]break them with a [2]rod of iron,
Thou shalt [b]shatter them like [3]earthenware.' "

10 Now therefore, O kings, [a]show discernment;
Take [b]warning, O [1]judges of the earth.

---

1 [1]Or, *way*
[a]Prov. 4:14 [b]Ps. 5:9, 10; 10:2-11; 36:1-4 [c]Ps. 17:4; 119:104 [d]Ps. 26:5; Jer. 15:17

2 [a]Ps. 119:14, 16 [b]Ps. 25:5 [c]Ps. 63:5, 6

3 [1]Or, *canals* [2]Or, *foliage* [3]Or, *all that he does prospers*
[a]Ps. 92:12-14; Jer. 17:8; Ezek. 19:10 [b]Gen. 39:2, 3, 23; Ps. 128:2

4 [a]Ps. 35:5; Is. 17:13; Job 21:18

5 [a]Ps. 5:5 [b]Ps. 9:7, 8, 16 [c]Ps. 89:5, 7

6 [1]Or, *approves;* or, *has regard to*
[a]Nah. 1:7; John 10:14; 2 Tim. 2:19 [b]Ps. 9:5, 6; 11:6

1 [1]Or, *Gentiles*
[a]Ps. 46:6; 83:2-5; Acts 4:25, 26 [b]Ps. 21:11

2 [1]Or, *Messiah*
[a]Ps. 48:4-6 [b]Ps. 74:18, 23

3 [a]Jer. 5:5

4 [1]Or, *is enthroned*
[a]Ps. 37:13 [b]Ps. 59:8

5 [a]Ps. 21:8, 9; 76:7 [b]Ps. 78:49, 50

6 [1]Or, *consecrated*
[a]Ps. 45:6 [b]Ps. 48:1, 2

7 [1]Or, . . . *decree: The* LORD *said* . . .
[a]Acts 13:33; Heb. 1:5; 5:5

8 [1]Or, *Gentiles*
[a]Ps. 21:1, 2 [b]Ps. 22:27 [c]Ps. 65:2; 67:7

9 [1]Another reading is: *rule* [2]Or, *scepter;* or, *staff* [3]Lit., *potter's ware*
[a]Ps. 110:5, 6; Rev. 2:37; 12:5; 19:15 [b]Ps. 28:5; 52:5; 72:4

10 [1]Or, *leaders*
[a]Prov. 8:15; 27:11 [b]Ps. 32:8

11 [1]Or, *Serve* [2]Or, *fear* [a]Ps. 5:7 [b]Ps. 119:119, 120

12 [1]Lit., *Kiss;* some ancient versions read, *Do homage purely*, or, *Lay hold of instruction* [2]Or, *quickly, suddenly, easily* [a]Ps. 2:7 [b]Ps. 5:11; 34:22

£ 2 Sam. 15:13-17, 29

1 [a]Ps. 69:4; 2 Sam. 15:12

2 [1]Or, *to* [2]Or, *salvation* [3]*Selah* may mean: *Pause, Crescendo* or *Musical interlude* [a]Ps. 22:7, 8; 71:11

3 [a]Ps. 5:12 [b]Ps. 62:7 [c]Ps. 9:13; 27:6

4 [1]Or, *hill* [a]Ps. 4:3 [b]Ps. 2:6; 15:1; 43:3

5 [1]Or, *As for me, I* [a]Ps. 4:8; Prov. 3:24

6 [a]Ps. 23:4; 27:3 [b]Ps. 118:10-13

7 [1]Or, *dost smite* [2]Or, *jaw* [3]Or, *dost shatter* [a]Ps. 7:6 [b]Ps. 6:4; 22:21 [c]Job 16:10 [d]Ps. 57:4; 58:6

8 [1]Or, *deliverance* [2]Or, *is* [a]Ps. 28:8; 35:3 [b]Ps. 29:11

£ I.e., Belonging to the choir director's anthology

1 [1]I.e., *who maintainest my right* [2]Lit., *made room for* [a]Ps. 3:4; 17:6 [b]Ps. 18:6 [c]Ps. 18:18, 19 [d]Ps. 25:16 [e]Ps. 17:6; 39:12

2 [1]Or, *glory* [2]*Selah* may mean: *Pause, Crescendo* or *Musical interlude* [a]Ps. 3:3 [b]Ps. 69:7-10, 19, 20 [c]Ps. 12:2; 31:6 [d]Ps. 31:18

3 [1]Another reading is, *dealt wonderfully with* [a]Ps. 135:4 [b]Ps. 31:23; 50:5; 79:2 [c]Ps. 6:8, 9; 17:6

4 [1]I.e., with anger or fear [2]Or, *but* [3]Lit., *speak* [a]Ps. 99:1 [b]Ps. 119:11; Eph. 4:26 [c]Ps. 77:6

11 [1]Worship the LORD with [2a]reverence,
And rejoice with [b]trembling.
12 [1]Do homage to [a]the Son, lest He become angry, and you perish *in* the way,
For His wrath may [2]soon be kindled.
How blessed are all who [b]take refuge in Him!

PSALM 3

Morning Prayer of Trust in God.

A Psalm of David, when [£]he fled from Absalom his son.

O LORD, how [a]my adversaries have increased!
Many are rising up against me.
2 Many are saying [1]of my soul,
"There is no [2a]deliverance for him in God." [[3]Selah.

3 But Thou, O LORD, art [a]a shield about me,
My [b]glory, and the One who [c]lifts my head.
4 I was crying to the LORD with my voice,
And He [a]answered me from [b]His holy [1]mountain. [Selah.
5 [1]I [a]lay down and slept;
I awoke, for the LORD sustains me.
6 I will [a]not be afraid of ten thousands of people
Who have [b]set themselves against me round about.

7 [a]Arise, O LORD; [b]save me, O my God!
For Thou [1]hast [c]smitten all my enemies on the [2]cheek;
Thou [3]hast [d]shattered the teeth of the wicked.
8 [1a]Salvation belongs to the LORD;
Thy [b]blessing [2]*be* upon Thy people! [Selah.

PSALM 4

Evening Prayer of Trust in God.

[£]For the choir director; on stringed instruments. A Psalm of David.

[a]ANSWER me when [b]I call, O God [1]of my righteousness!
Thou hast [2c]relieved me in my distress;
Be [d]gracious to me and [e]hear my prayer.

2 O sons of men, how long will [a]my [1]honor become [b]a reproach?
How long will you love [c]what is worthless and aim at [d]deception? [[2]Selah.
3 But know that the LORD has [1a]set apart the [b]godly man for Himself;
The LORD [c]hears when I call to Him.

4 [1a]Tremble, [2b]and do not sin;
[3c]Meditate in your heart upon your bed, and be still. [Selah.

5 Offer [1]the [a]sacrifices of righteousness,
And [b]trust in the LORD.

6 Many are saying, "[a]Who will show us *any* good?"
[b]Lift up the light of Thy countenance upon us, O LORD!
7 Thou hast put [a]gladness in my heart,
More than [b]when their grain and new wine abound.
8 In peace I will [1]both [a]lie down and sleep,
For Thou alone, O LORD, dost make me to [b]dwell in safety.

PSALM 5

Prayer for Protection from the Wicked.

For the choir director; for [£]flute accompaniment. A Psalm of David.

[a]GIVE ear to my words, O LORD,
Consider my [1b]groaning.
2 Heed [a]the sound of my cry for help, [b]my King and my God,
For to Thee do I pray.
3 In the morning, O LORD, [1]Thou wilt hear my voice;
In the [a]morning I will order *my* [2]*prayer* to Thee and *eagerly* [b]watch.

4 For Thou art not a God [a]who takes pleasure in wickedness;
[b]No evil [1]dwells with thee.
5 The [a]boastful shall not [b]stand before Thine eyes;
Thou [c]dost hate all who do iniquity.
6 Thou [a]dost destroy those who speak falsehood;
The LORD abhors [b]the man of bloodshed and deceit.
7 But as for me, [a]by Thine abundant lovingkindness I will enter Thy house,
[1]At Thy holy temple I will [b]bow in [c]reverence for Thee.

8 O LORD, [a]lead me [b]in Thy righteousness [c]because of [1]my foes;
Make Thy way [2]straight before me.
9 There is [a]nothing [1]reliable in [2]what they say;
Their [b]inward part is destruction *itself*;
Their [c]throat is an open grave;
They [3]flatter with their tongue.
10 Hold them guilty, O God;
[a]By their own devices let them fall!
In the multitude of their transgressions [b]thrust them out,
For they are [c]rebellious against Thee.

11 But let all who [a]take refuge in Thee [b]be glad,
Let them ever sing for joy;
And [1]mayest Thou [c]shelter them,
That those who [d]love Thy name may exult in Thee.

---

5 [1]Or, *righteous sacrifices* [a]Ps. 51:19; Deut. 33:19 [b]Ps. 37:3, 5; 62:8

6 [a]Job 7:7; 9:25 [b]Num. 6:26; Ps. 80:3, 7, 19

7 [a]Ps. 97:11, 12 [b]Ps. 119:14, 72

8 [1]Or, *at the same time* [a]Job 11:19; Ps. 3:5 [b]Deut. 12:10; Ps. 16:9

[£]Heb., *Nehiloth*

1 [1]Or, *meditation* [a]Ps. 54:2 [b]Ps. 104:34

2 [a]Ps. 140:6 [b]Ps. 84:3

3 [1]Or, *mayest Thou hear* [2]Or, *sacrifice* [a]Ps. 88:13 [b]Ps. 130:5

4 [1]Lit., *sojourns* [a]Ps. 11:5; 34:16 [b]Ps. 92:15

5 [a]Ps. 73:3; 75:4 [b]Ps. 1:5 [c]Ps. 11:5; 45:7

6 [a]Ps. 52:4, 5 [b]Ps. 55:23

7 [1]Or, *Toward* [a]Ps. 69:13 [b]Ps. 138:2 [c]Ps. 115:11, 13

8 [1]Or, *those who lie in wait for me* [2]Or, *smooth* [a]Ps. 31:3 [b]Ps. 31:1 [c]Ps. 27:11

9 [1]Or, *true* [2]Lit., *his mouth* [3]Or, *make their tongue smooth* [a]Ps. 52:3 [b]Ps. 7:14 [c]Rom. 3:13

10 [a]Ps. 9:16 [b]Ps. 36:12 [c]Ps. 107:10, 11

11 [1]Or, *Thou dost shelter* [a]Ps. 2:12 [b]Ps. 33:1; 64:10 [c]Ps. 12:7 [d]Ps. 69:36

12 For it is Thou who dost [a]bless the righteous man, O Lord,
Thou dost [b]surround him with favor as with a shield.

Psalm 6

Prayer for Mercy in Time of Trouble.

For the choir director; with stringed instruments, [£]upon an eight-stringed *lyre.* A Psalm of David.

O LORD, [a]do not rebuke me in Thine anger,
Nor chasten me in Thy wrath.
2 Be gracious to me, O Lord, for I *am* [a]pining away;
[b]Heal me, O Lord, for [c]my bones are dismayed.
3 And my [a]soul is greatly dismayed;
But Thou, O Lord—[b]how long?

4 Return, O Lord, [a]rescue my [1]soul;
Save me because of Thy lovingkindness.
5 For [a]there is no [1]mention of Thee in death;
In [2]Sheol who will give Thee thanks?

6 I am [a]weary with my sighing;
Every night I make my bed swim,
I dissolve my couch with [b]my tears.
7 My [a]eye has wasted away with grief;
It has become old because of all my adversaries.

8 [a]Depart from me, all you who do iniquity,
For the Lord [b]has heard the voice of my weeping.
9 The Lord [a]has heard my supplication,
The Lord [b]receives my prayer.
10 All my enemies shall [a]be ashamed and greatly dismayed;
They shall [1]turn back, they shall [b]suddenly be ashamed.

Psalm 7

The Lord Implored to Defend the Psalmist against the Wicked.

A [£]Shiggaion of David, which he sang to the Lord [•]concerning Cush, a Benjamite.

O LORD my God, [a]in Thee have I taken refuge;
Save me from all those who pursue me, and [b]deliver me,
2 Lest he tear [1]my soul [a]like a lion,
[2]Dragging me away, while there is none to deliver.

3 O Lord my God, if I have done this,
If there is [a]injustice in my hands,
4 If I have [a]rewarded evil to [1]my friend,
Or have [b]plundered [2]him who without cause was my adversary,
5 Let the enemy pursue [1]my soul and overtake [2]*it;*

12 [a]Ps. 29:11 [b]Ps. 32:7, 10

[£]Or, *according to a* lower *octave* (Heb., *Sheminith)*

1 [a]Ps. 38:1; Ps. 118:18

2 [a]Ps. 102:4, 11 [b]Ps. 41:4; 147:3 [c]Ps. 22:14; 31:10

3 [a]Ps. 88:3; John 12:27 [b]Ps. 90:13

4 [1]Or, *life* [a]Ps. 17:13

5 [1]Or, *remembrance* [2]I.e., the nether world [a]Ps. 30:9; 88:10-12; 115:17; Eccles. 9:10; Is. 38:18

6 [a]Ps. 69:3 [b]Ps. 42:3

7 [a]Ps. 31:9; 38:10

8 [a]Ps. 119:115 [b]Ps. 28:6

9 [a]Ps. 116:1 [b]Ps. 66:19, 20

10 [1]Or, *again be ashamed suddenly* [a]Ps. 71:24 [b]Ps. 73:19

[£]I.e., Dithyrambic rhythm, or, wild passionate song [•]Or, *concerning the words of*

1 [a]Ps. 31:1; 71:1 [b]Ps. 31:15

2 [1]Or, *me* [2]Or, *Rending it in pieces, while* [a]Ps. 57:4

3 [a]1 Sam. 24:11

4 [1]Lit., *him who was at peace with me* [2]Or, *my adversary without cause* [a]Ps. 109:4, 5 [b]1 Sam. 24:7; 26:9

5 [1]Or, *me* [2]Or, *me*

And let him trample my life down to the ground,
And lay my glory in the dust. [[3]Selah.

6 [a]Arise, O LORD, in Thine anger;
[b]Lift up Thyself against [c]the rage of my adversaries,
And [d]arouse Thyself [1]for me; Thou hast appointed
judgment.
7 And let the assembly of the [a]peoples encompass Thee;
And over [1]them return Thou on high.
8 The LORD [a]judges the peoples;
[1b]Vindicate me, O LORD, according to my righteousness and my integrity that is in me.
9 O let [a]the evil of the wicked come to an end, but
[b]establish the righteous;
For the righteous God [c]tries the hearts and [1]minds.
10 My [a]shield is [1]with God,
Who [b]saves the upright in heart.
11 God is a [a]righteous judge,
And a God who has [b]indignation every day.

12 If [1]a man [a]does not repent, He will [b]sharpen His sword;
He has [c]bent His bow and [2]made it ready.
13 He has also prepared [1]for Himself deadly weapons;
He makes His [a]arrows fiery shafts.
14 Behold, he travails with wickedness,
And he [a]conceives mischief, and brings forth falsehood.
15 He has dug a pit and hollowed it out,
And has [a]fallen into the hole which he made.
16 His [a]mischief will return upon his own head,
And his [b]violence will descend upon [1]his own pate.

17 I will give thanks to the LORD [a]according to His
righteousness,
And will [b]sing praise to the name of the LORD Most
High.

PSALM 8

The LORD'S Glory and Man's Dignity.

For the choir director; on the Gittith.
A Psalm of David.

O LORD, our Lord,
How majestic is Thy name in all the earth,
Who hast [1a]displayed Thy splendor above the heavens!
2 [a]From the mouth of infants and nursing babes Thou
hast established [1b]strength,
Because of Thine adversaries,
To make [c]the enemy and the revengeful cease.

3 When I [1]consider [a]Thy heavens, the work of Thy
fingers,
The [b]moon and the stars, which Thou hast [2]ordained;
4 [a]What is man, that Thou [1]dost take thought of him?
And the son of man, that Thou dost care for him?
5 Yet Thou hast made him a [a]little lower than [1]God,
And [b]dost crown him with [c]glory and majesty!

---

5 [3]*Selah* may mean: *Pause, Crescendo* or *Musical interlude*

6 [1]One ancient version reads, *O my God*
[a]Ps. 3:7 [b]Ps. 94:2 [c]Ps. 138:7 [d]Ps. 35:23

7 [1]Lit., *it*
[a]Ps. 22:27

8 [1]Lit., *Judge*
[a]Ps. 96:13; 98:9 [b]Ps. 26:1; 35:24; 43:1

9 [1]Lit., *kidneys*, figurative for inner man
[a]Ps. 34:21; 94:23 [b]Ps. 37:23; 40:2 [c]Ps. 11:4, 5; Jer. 11:20

10 [1]Lit., *upon*
[a]Ps. 18:2, 30 [b]Ps. 97:10, 11

11 [a]Ps. 50:6 [b]Ps. 90:9

12 [1]Lit., *he* [2]Lit., *fixed it*
[a]Ps. 58:4, 5 [b]Deut. 32:41 [c]Ps. 64:7

13 [1]Or, *His deadly weapons*
[a]Ps. 18:14; 45:5

14 [a]Job 15:35; Is. 59:4; James 1:15

15 [a]Ps. 57:6

16 [1]I.e., the crown of his own head
[a]Ps. 140:9 [b]Ps. 140:11

17 [a]Ps 71:15, 16 [b]Ps. 9:2; 66:1, 2, 4

1 [1]Or, *set*
[a]Ps. 57:5, 11; 148:13

2 [1]Or, *a bulwark*
[a]Matt. 21:16 [b]Ps. 29:1; 118:14 [c]Ps. 44:16

3 [1]Or, *see* [2]Or, *appointed, fixed*
[a]Ps. 89:11; 144:5 [b]Ps. 136:9

4 [1]Or, *dost remember him*
[a]Job 7:17; Ps. 144:3; Heb. 2:6-8

5 [1]Or, *the angels*; Heb., *Elohim*
[a]Ps. 82:6; Gen. 1:26 [b]Ps. 103:4 [c]Ps. 21:5

6 Thou dost make him to [a]rule over the works of Thy hands;
Thou hast [b]put all things under his feet,
7 All sheep and oxen,
And also the [1]beasts of the field,
8 The birds of the heavens, and the fish of the sea,
Whatever passes through the paths of the seas.

9 O LORD, our Lord,
How majestic is Thy name in all the earth!

PSALM 9

A Psalm of Thanksgiving for God's Justice.

For the choir director; on [£]Muth-labben.
A Psalm of David.

I WILL give thanks to the LORD with all [a]my heart;
I will [b]tell of all Thy [1]wonders.
2 I will be glad and [a]exult in Thee;
I will [b]sing praise to Thy name, O [c]Most High.

3 When my enemies turn back,
They stumble and [a]perish before Thee.
4 For Thou hast [a]maintained [1]my just cause;
Thou dost sit on the throne [2b]judging righteously.
5 Thou hast [a]rebuked the nations, Thou hast destroyed the wicked;
Thou hast [b]blotted out their name forever and ever.
6 [1]The enemy has come to an end in [a]perpetual ruins,
And Thou hast uprooted the cities;
The very [b]memory of them has perished.

7 But the [a]LORD [1]abides forever;
He has established His [b]throne for judgment,
8 And He will [a]judge the world in righteousness;
He will execute judgment for the peoples with equity.
9 [1]The LORD also will be a [a]stronghold for the oppressed,
A stronghold in times of trouble,
10 And [1]those who [a]know Thy name will put their trust in Thee;
For Thou, O LORD, hast not [b]forsaken those who seek Thee.

11 Sing praises to the LORD, who [a]dwells in Zion;
[b]Declare among the peoples His deeds.
12 For [a]He who [1]requires blood remembers them;
He does not forget [b]the cry of the afflicted.
13 Be gracious to me, O LORD;
Behold my affliction from those [a]who hate me,
Thou who [b]dost lift me up from the gates of death;
14 That I may tell of [a]all Thy praises,
That in the gates of the daughter of Zion
I may [b]rejoice in Thy [1]salvation.
15 The nations have sunk down [a]in the pit which they have made;

---

6 [a]Gen. 1:26, 28 [b]1 Cor. 15:27

7 [1]Or, *animals*

[£]I.e., *"Death to the Son"*

1 [1]Or, *miracles* [a]Ps. 86:12 [b]Ps. 26:7

2 [a]Ps. 104:34 [b]Ps. 66:2, 4 [c]Ps. 92:1

3 [a]Ps. 27:2

4 [1]Lit., *my right and my cause* [2]Or, *a righteous Judge* [a]Ps. 140:12 [b]Ps. 50:6

5 [a]Ps. 119:21 [b]Ps. 69:28

6 [1]Or, *O enemy, desolations are finished forever; And their cities Thou hast plucked up.* [a]Ps. 40:15 [b]Ps. 34:16

7 [1]Or, *sits* as king [a]Ps. 10:16 [b]Ps. 89:14

8 [a]Ps. 96:13; 98:9

9 [1]Or, *Let the LORD also be* [a]Ps. 59:9, 16, 17

10 [1]Or, *let those . . . name put* [a]Ps. 91:14 [b]Ps. 37:28; 94:14

11 [a]Ps. 76:2 [b]Ps. 105:1

12 [1]I.e., *avenges bloodshed* [a]Ps. 72:14; Gen. 9:5 [b]Ps. 9:18

13 [a]Ps. 38:19 [b]Ps. 30:3; 86:13

14 [1]Or, *deliverance* [a]Ps. 106:2 [b]Ps. 13:5; 20:5; 35:9; 51:12

15 [a]Ps. 7:15

In the [b]net which they hid, their own foot has been caught.
16 The LORD has made Himself known;
He has [a]executed judgment.
In the work of his own hands the wicked is snared. [[1]Higgaion [2]Selah.

17 The wicked will [1a]return to [2]Sheol,
Even all the nations who [b]forget God.
18 For the [a]needy will not always be forgotten,
Nor the [b]hope of the afflicted perish forever.
19 [a]Arise, O LORD, do not let man prevail;
Let the nations be [b]judged before Thee.
20 Put them [a]in fear, O LORD;
Let the nations know that they are [b]but men. [Selah.

PSALM 10

A Prayer for the Overthrow of the Wicked.

WHY [a]dost Thou stand afar off, O LORD?
Why [b]dost Thou hide [1]*Thyself* in times of trouble?
2 In [a]pride the wicked [1]hotly pursues the afflicted;
[2]Let them be [b]caught in the plots which they have devised.

3 For the wicked [a]boasts of his [b]heart's desire,
And [1]the greedy man curses *and* [c]spurns the LORD.
4 The wicked, in the haughtiness of his countenance, [a]does not seek *Him*.
All his [1]thoughts are, "[b]There is no God."

5 His ways [1a]prosper at all times;
Thy judgments are on high, [b]out of his sight;
As for all his adversaries, he snorts at them.
6 He says to himself, "[a]I shall not be moved;
[1]Throughout all generations I shall not be in adversity."
7 His [a]mouth is full of curses and deceit and [b]oppression;
[c]Under his tongue is mischief and wickedness.
8 He sits in the [a]lurking places of the villages;
In the hiding places he [b]kills the innocent;
His eyes [1]stealthily watch for the [2c]unfortunate.
9 He lurks in a hiding place as [a]a lion in his [1]lair;
He [b]lurks to catch [c]the afflicted;
He catches the afflicted when he draws him into his [d]net.
10 He [1]crouches, he [2]bows down,
And the [3]unfortunate fall [4]by his mighty ones.
11 He [a]says to himself, "God has forgotten;
He has hidden His face; He will never see it."

12 Arise, O LORD; O God, [a]lift up Thy hand.
[b]Do not forget the afflicted.
13 Why has the wicked [a]spurned God?
He has said to himself, "Thou wilt not require *it*."

15 [b]Ps. 57:6

16 [1]Perhaps, resounding music, or meditation [2]*Selah* may mean: *Pause, Crescendo* or *Musical interlude*
[a]Ps. 9:4

17 [1]Or, *turn* [2]I.e., the nether world
[a]Ps. 49:14 [b]Ps. 50:22

18 [a]Ps. 9:12 [b]Ps. 62:5; 71:5

19 [a]Num. 10:35 [b]Ps. 9:5

20 [a]Ps. 14:5 [b]Ps. 62:9

1 [1]Or, Thine eyes
[a]Ps. 22:1 [b]Ps. 13:1; 55:1

2 [1]Lit., *burns* [2]Or, *They will be caught*
[a]Ps. 73:6, 8 [b]Ps. 9:16

3 [1]Or, *blesses the greedy man*
[a]Ps. 49:6; 94:3, 4 [b]Ps. 112:10
[c]Ps. 10:13

4 [1]Or, *plots*
[a]Ps. 10:13; Ps. 36:2 [b]Ps. 14:1; 36:1

5 [1]Lit., *are strong*
[a]Ps. 52:7 [b]Ps. 28:5

6 [1]Lit., To
[a]Ps. 49:11

7 [a]Rom. 3:14 [b]Ps. 73:8 [c]Ps. 140:3; Job 20:12

8 [1]Lit., *lie in wait* [2]Or, *poor*
[a]Ps. 11:2 [b]Ps. 94:6 [c]Ps. 72:12

9 [1]Or, *thicket*
[a]Ps. 17:12 [b]Ps. 59:3; Mic. 7:2
[c]Ps. 10:2 [d]Ps. 140:5

10 [1]Or, *is crushed* [2]Or, *is bowed down* [3]Or, *poor* [4]Or, *into his claws*

11 [a]Ps. 10:4

12 [a]Ps. 17:7; Mic. 5:9 [b]Ps. 9:12

13 [a]Ps. 10:3

14 Thou hast seen *it*, for Thou hast beheld [a]mischief and
vexation to [1]take it into Thy hand.
The [2b]unfortunate commits *himself* to Thee;
Thou hast been the [c]helper of the orphan.
15 [a]Break the arm of the wicked and the evildoer,
[1b]Seek out his wickedness until Thou dost find none.

16 The LORD is [a]King forever and ever;
[b]Nations have perished from His land.
17 O LORD, Thou hast heard the [a]desire of the [1]humble;
Thou wilt [b]strengthen their heart, [c]Thou wilt incline
Thine ear
18 To [1]vindicate the [a]orphan and the [b]oppressed,
That man who is of the earth may cause [c]terror no
more.

PSALM 11

The LORD a Refuge and Defense.

For the choir director. A *Psalm* of David.

IN the LORD I [a]take refuge;
How can you say to my soul, "Flee *as* a bird to your
[b]mountain;
2 For, behold, the wicked [a]bend the bow,
They [1b]make ready their arrow upon the string,
To [c]shoot in darkness at the upright in heart;
3 If the [a]foundations are destroyed,
What can the righteous do?"

4 The LORD is in His [a]holy temple, the [1]LORD's [b]throne is
in heaven;
His [c]eyes behold, His eyelids test the sons of men.
5 The LORD [a]tests the righteous and [b]the wicked,
And the one who loves violence His soul hates.
6 Upon the wicked He will [a]rain [1]snares;
[b]Fire and brimstone and [c]burning wind will be the portion of [d]their cup.
7 For the LORD is [a]righteous; [b]He loves [1]righteousness;
The upright will [c]behold His face.

PSALM 12

God a Helper against the Treacherous.

For the choir director; [£]upon an eight-stringed
lyre. A Psalm of David.

HELP, LORD, for [a]the godly man ceases to be,
For the faithful disappear from among the sons of
men.
2 They [a]speak [1]falsehood to one another;
With [b]flattering [2]lips and with a double heart they
speak.
3 May the LORD cut off all flattering lips,
The tongue that [a]speaks great things;

14 [1]Lit., *put, give* [2]Or, *poor* [a]Ps. 10:7 [b]Ps. 22:11 [c]Ps. 68:5

15 [1]Or, *Mayest Thou seek* [a]Ps. 37:17 [b]Ps. 140:11

16 [a]Ps. 29:10 [b]Deut. 8:20

17 [1]Or, *afflicted* [a]Ps. 9:18 [b]1 Chr. 29:18 [c]Ps. 34:15

18 [1]Lit., *judge* [a]Ps. 146:9 [b]Ps. 9:9; 74:21 [c]Is. 29:20

1 [a]Ps. 2:12 [b]Ps. 121:1

2 [1]Or, *fixed* [a]Ps. 7:12; 37:14 [b]Ps. 64:3 [c]Ps. 64:4

3 [a]Ps. 87:1; 119:152

4 [1]Lit., LORD, *His throne* [a]Ps. 18:6; Mic. 1:2; Hab. 2:20 [b]Ps. 103:19; Is. 66:1; Matt. 5:34; Rev. 4:2 [c]Ps. 34:15, 16

5 [a]Ps. 34:19; Gen. 22:1; James 1:12 [b]Ps. 5:5

6 [1]Or, *coals of fire* [a]Ps. 18:13, 14 [b]Gen. 19:24; Ezek. 38:22 [c]Jer. 4:11, 12 [d]Ps. 75:8

7 [1]Or, *righteous deeds* [a]Ps. 7:9, 11 [b]Ps. 33:5 [c]Ps. 16:11; 17:15

[£]Or, *according to a lower octave* (Heb., *Sheminith*)

1 [a]Is. 57:1; Mic. 7:2

2 [1]Or, *emptiness* [2]Lit., *lip* [a]Ps. 41:6 [b]Ps. 28:3; 55:21; Jer. 9:8; Rom. 16:18

3 [a]Dan. 7:8; Rev. 13:5

4 Who [a]have said, "With our tongue we will prevail;
Our lips are [1]our own; who is lord over us?"
5 "Because of the [a]devastation of the afflicted, because of the groaning of the needy,
Now [b]I will arise," says the LORD; "I will [c]set him in the safety for which he longs."

6 The [a]words of the LORD are pure words;
As silver [b]tried in a furnace on the earth, refined seven times.
7 Thou, O LORD, wilt keep them;
Thou wilt [a]preserve him from this generation forever.
8 The [a]wicked strut about on every side,
When [1b]vileness is exalted among the sons of men.

PSALM 13

Prayer for Help in Trouble.

For the choir director. A Psalm of David.

HOW long, O LORD? Wilt Thou [a]forget me forever?
How long [b]wilt Thou hide Thy face from me?
2 How long shall I [a]take counsel in my soul,
Having [b]sorrow in my heart all the day?
How long will my enemy be exalted over me?

3 [a]Consider *and* answer me, O LORD, my God;
[b]Enlighten my eyes, lest I sleep the *sleep of* death,
4 Lest my enemy [a]say, "I have overcome him,"
Lest [b]my adversaries rejoice when I am shaken.

5 But I have [a]trusted in Thy lovingkindness;
My heart shall [b]rejoice in Thy salvation.
6 I will [a]sing to the LORD,
Because He has [b]dealt bountifully with me.

PSALM 14

Folly and Wickedness of Men.

For the choir director. *A Psalm* of David.

THE fool has [a]said in his heart, "There is no God."
They are corrupt, they have committed abominable [1]deeds;
There is [b]no one who does good.
2 The LORD has [a]looked down from heaven upon the sons of men,
To see if there are any who [1b]understand,
Who [c]seek after God.
3 They have all [a]turned aside; together they have become corrupt;
There is [b]no one who does good, not even one.

4 Do all the workers of wickedness [a]not know,
Who [b]eat up My people *as* they eat bread,
And [c]do not call upon the Lord?

4 [1]Lit., *with us*
[a]Ps. 73:8, 9

5 [a]Ps. 9:9; 10:18 [b]Is. 33:10 [c]Ps. 34:6; 35:10

6 [a]Ps. 119:140; 19:8, 10 [b]Prov. 30:5

7 [a]Ps. 37:28; 97:10

8 [1]Or, *worthlessness*
[a]Ps. 55:10, 11 [b]Is. 32:5

1 [a]Ps. 44:24 [b]Ps. 89:46

2 [a]Ps. 42:4 [b]Ps. 42:9

3 [a]Ps. 5:1 [b]Ps. 18:28; 1 Sam. 14:29; Ezra 9:8; Job 33:30

4 [a]Ps. 12:4 [b]Ps. 25:2; 38:16

5 [a]Ps. 52:8 [b]Ps. 9:14

6 [a]Ps. 96:1, 2 [b]Ps. 116:7; 119:17; 142:7

1 [1]Lit., *doing*
[a]Ps. 10:4; 53:1 [b]Ps. 14:1-3; Rom. 3:10-12; Ps. 130:3

2 [1]Or, *act wisely*
[a]Ps. 33:13, 14; 102:19 [b]Ps. 92:6 [c]1 Chr. 22:19

3 [a]Ps. 58:3 [b]Ps. 143:2

4 [a]Ps. 82:5 [b]Ps. 27:2; Jer. 10:25; Amos 8:4; Mic. 3:3 [c]Ps. 79:6; Is. 64:7

5 There they are in great dread,
For God is with the [a]righteous generation.
6 You would [a]put to shame the counsel of the afflicted,
But the LORD is his [b]refuge.

7 O that [a]the salvation of Israel would come out of Zion!
When the LORD [1b]restores His captive people,
Jacob will rejoice, Israel will be glad.

PSALM 15

Description of a Citizen of Zion.

A Psalm of David.

O LORD, who may [1]abide [a]in Thy tent?
Who may dwell on Thy [b]holy hill?
2 He who [a]walks with integrity, and works righteousness,
And [b]speaks truth in his heart.
3 He [a]does not slander [1]with his tongue,
Nor [b]does evil to his neighbor,
Nor [c]takes up a reproach against his friend;
4 In [1]whose eyes a [a]reprobate is despised,
But [2]who [b]honors those who fear the LORD;
He [c]swears to his own hurt, and does not change;
5 He [a]does not put out his money [1]at interest,
Nor [b]does he take a bribe against the innocent.
He who does these things will never be shaken.

PSALM 16

The LORD the Psalmist's Portion in Life and Deliverer in Death.

[a] [£]Mikhtam of David.

PRESERVE me, O God, for [b]I take refuge in Thee.
2 [1]I said to the LORD, "Thou art [2]my LORD;
I [a]have no good besides Thee."
3 As for the [1a]saints who are in the earth,
[2]They are the majestic ones [b]in whom is all my delight.
4 The [1a]sorrows of those who have [2]bartered for another
god will be multiplied;
I shall not pour out their drink offerings of [b]blood,
Nor shall I [c]take their names upon my lips.

5 The LORD is the [a]portion of my inheritance and my
[b]cup;
Thou dost support my [c]lot.
6 The [a]lines have fallen to me in pleasant places;
Indeed, my heritage is [b]beautiful to me.

7 I will bless the LORD who has [a]counseled me;
Indeed, my [1b]mind instructs me in the night.
8 [a]I have [b]set the LORD continually before me;
Because He is [c]at my right hand, [d]I will not be shaken.
9 Therefore [a]my heart is glad, and [b]my glory rejoices;
My flesh also will [c]dwell securely.

---

5 [a]Ps. 73:15; 112:2

6 [a]Ps. 42:3, 10 [b]Ps. 40:17; 46:1; 142:5

7 [1]Or, *restores the fortunes of his people* [a]Ps. 53:6 [b]Ps. 85:1, 2

1 [1]Lit., *sojourn* [a]Ps. 27:5, 6; 61:4 [b]Ps. 24:3

2 [a]Ps. 24:4; Is. 33:15 [b]Zech. 8:16; Eph. 4:25

3 [1]Lit., *according to* [a]Ps. 50:20 [b]Ps. 28:3 [c]Ex. 23:1

4 [1]Lit., *his* [2]Lit., *he* [a]Ps. 53:5; Ps. 73:20 [b]Acts 28:10 [c]Judg. 11:35

5 [1]I.e., to a fellow Israelite. Ex. 22:25, Deut. 23:20 [a]Ex. 22:25; Lev. 25:36; Ezek. 18:8 [b]Ex. 23:8; Deut. 16:19

[£] Possibly, *Epigrammatic Poem*, or *Atonement Psalm*

1 [a]Ps. 17:8 [b]Ps. 7:1

2 [1]Or, O my soul, *you said* [2]Or, *the Lord* [a]Ps. 73:25

3 [1]Lit., *holy ones*; *i.e.*, the godly [2]Lit., *And the majestic ones . . . delight* [a]Ps. 101:6 [b]Ps. 119:63

4 [1]I.e., sorrows due to idolatry [2]Or, *hastened to* [a]Ps. 32:10 [b]Ps. 106:37, 38 [c]Ex. 23:13; Josh. 23:7

5 [a]Ps. 73:26; 119:57; 142:5; Lam. 3:24 [b]Ps. 23:5 [c]Ps. 125:3

6 [a]Ps. 78:55 [b]Jer. 3:19

7 [1]Lit., *kidneys*, figurative for inner man [a]Ps. 73:24 [b]Ps. 77:6

8 [a]Ps. 16:8-11; Acts 2:25-28 [b]Ps. 27:8; 123:1, 2 [c]Ps. 73:23; 110:5; 121:5 [d]Ps. 112:6

9 [a]Ps. 4:7; 13:5 [b]Ps. 30:12; 57:8; 108:1 [c]Ps. 4:8

10 For Thou [a]wilt not abandon my soul to [1]Sheol;
Neither wilt Thou [2b]allow Thy [3]Holy One to [4]see the pit.
11 Thou wilt make known to me [a]the path of life;
In [b]Thy presence is fulness of joy;
In Thy right hand there are [c]pleasures forever.

Psalm 17

Prayer for Protection against Oppressors.

A Prayer of David.

HEAR a [a]just cause, O LORD, [b]give heed to my cry;
[c]Give ear to my prayer, which is not from [d]deceitful lips.
2 Let [a]my [1]judgment come forth from Thy presence;
Let Thine eyes look with [b]equity.
3 Thou hast [a]tried my heart;
Thou hast visited *me* by night;
Thou hast [b]tested me and [c]dost find [1]nothing;
I have [d]purposed that my mouth will not transgress.
4 As for the deeds of men, [a]by the word of Thy lips
I have kept from the [b]paths of the violent.
5 My [a]steps have held fast to Thy [1]paths.
My [b]feet have not slipped.

6 I have [a]called upon Thee, for Thou wilt answer me, O God;
[b]Incline Thine ear to me, hear my speech.
7 [a]Wondrously show Thy lovingkindness,
O [b]Savior of those who take refuge [1]at Thy right hand
From those who rise up *against them.*
8 Keep me as [1]the [a]apple of the eye;
Hide me [b]in the shadow of Thy wings,
9 From the [a]wicked who despoil me,
My [b]deadly enemies, who surround me.
10 They have [a]closed their [1]unfeeling *heart*;
With their mouth they [b]speak proudly.
11 They have now [a]surrounded us in our steps;
They set their eyes [b]to cast *us* down to the ground.
12 He is [a]like a lion that is eager to tear,
And as a young lion [b]lurking in hiding places.

13 [a]Arise, O LORD, confront him, [b]bring him low;
[c]Deliver my soul from the wicked with [d]Thy sword,
14 From men with [a]Thy hand, O LORD,
From men [1]of the world, [b]whose portion is in *this* life;
And whose belly Thou [c]dost fill with Thy treasure;
They are satisfied with children,
And leave their abundance to their babes.
15 As for me, I shall [a]behold Thy face in righteousness;
I will be satisfied [1]with Thy [b]likeness when I awake.

16:10 [1]I.e., the nether world [2]Lit., *give* [3]Or, *godly one* [4]Or, *undergo decay* [a]Ps. 49:15; 86:13 [b]Acts 13:35

11 [a]Ps. 139:24; Matt. 7:14 [b]Ps. 21:6; 43:4 [c]Ps. 36:7, 8; 46:4

17:1 [a]Ps. 9:4 [b]Ps. 61:1; 142:6 [c]Ps. 88:2 [d]Is. 29:13

2 [1]I.e., vindication [a]Ps. 103:6 [b]Ps. 98:9; 99:4

3 [1]Or, *no evil device in me; My mouth* [a]Ps. 26:1, 2 [b]Ps. 66:10; Zech. 13:9; 1 Pet. 1:7 [c]Jer. 50:20 [d]Ps. 39:1

4 [a]Ps. 119:9, 101 [b]Ps. 10:5-11

5 [1]Lit., *tracks* [a]Job 23:11; Ps. 44:18 [b]Ps. 18:36; 37:31

6 [a]Ps. 86:7 [b]Ps. 88:2

7 [1]Or, *from those who rise up . . . at Thy right hand* [a]Ps. 31:21 [b]Ps. 20:6

8 [1]Lit., *the pupil, the daughter of the eye* [a]Deut. 32:10; Zech. 2:8 [b]Ruth 2:12; Ps. 36:7; 57:1; 61:4; 63:7; 91:1, 4

9 [a]Ps. 31:20 [b]Ps. 27:12

10 [1]Lit., *fat* [a]Ps. 73:7; Job 15:27 [b]1 Sam. 2:3; Ps. 31:18; 73:8

11 [a]Ps. 88:17 [b]Ps. 37:14

12 [a]Ps. 7:2 [b]Ps. 10:9

13 [a]Ps. 3:7 [b]Ps. 55:23 [c]Ps. 22:20 [d]Ps. 7:12

14 [1]Or, *whose portion in life is of the world* [a]Ps. 17:7 [b]Ps. 73:3-7; Luke 16:25 [c]Ps. 49:6

15 [1]Or, *with* beholding [a]Ps. 11:7, 16:11; 140:13 [b]Num. 12:8

PSALM 18

The LORD Praised for Giving Deliverance.

For the choir director. *A Psalm* of David the
servant of the LORD, [£]who spoke to the LORD
the words of this song in the day that the LORD
delivered him from the hand of all his enemies
and from the hand of Saul. And he said,

I LOVE Thee, O LORD,
[a]my strength."
2 The LORD is [a]my [1]rock and [b]my fortress and my [c]deliverer,
My God, my rock, in whom I take refuge;
My [d]shield and the [e]horn of my salvation, my [f]stronghold.
3 I call upon the LORD, who is [a]worthy to be praised,
And I am [b]saved from my enemies.

4 The [a]cords of death encompassed me,
And the [b]torrents of [1]ungodliness [2]terrified me.
5 The [a]cords of [1]Sheol surrounded me;
The snares of death confronted me.
6 In my [a]distress I called upon the LORD,
And cried to my God for help;
He heard my voice [b]out of His temple,
And my [c]cry for help before Him came into His ears.

7 Then the [a]earth shook and quaked;
And the [b]foundations of the mountains were trembling
And were shaken, because He was angry.
8 Smoke went up [1]out of His nostrils,
And [a]fire from His mouth devoured;
Coals were kindled by it.
9 He [a]bowed the heavens also, and came down
With thick [b]darkness under His feet.
10 And He rode upon a [a]cherub and flew;
And He sped upon the [b]wings of the wind.
11 He made [a]darkness His hiding place, His [1]canopy around Him,
Darkness of waters, thick clouds of the skies.
12 From the [a]brightness before Him passed His thick clouds,
Hailstones and [b]coals of fire.
13 The LORD also [a]thundered in the heavens,
And the Most High uttered His voice,
Hailstones and coals of fire.
14 And He [a]sent out His arrows, and scattered them,
And lightning flashes in abundance, and [1]routed them.
15 Then the [a]channels of water appeared,
And the foundations of the world were [1]laid bare,
At Thy [b]rebuke, O LORD,
At the blast of the [c]breath of Thy nostrils.

16 He [a]sent from on high, He took me;
He drew me out of [b]many waters.

[£] 2 Sam. 22:1-51

1 [a]Ps. 59:17

2 [1]Lit., *crag*
[a]Ps. 18:31, 46; Deut. 32:18; 1 Sam. 2:2; Ps. 28:1; 31:3; 42:9; 71:3; 78:15 [b]Ps. 144:2 [c]Ps. 19:14 [d]Ps. 28:7; 33:20; 59:11; 84:9, 11; Prov. 30:5 [e]Ps. 75:10 [f]Ps. 59:9

3 [a]Ps. 48:1; 96:4; 145:3 [b]Ps. 34:6

4 [1]Or, *destruction;* Heb., *Belial* [2]Or, *were assailing,* or *terrifying*
[a]Ps. 116:3 [b]Ps. 69:2; 124:3, 4

5 [1]I.e., the nether world
[a]Ps. 116:3

6 [a]Ps. 50:15; 120:1 [b]Ps. 3:4 [c]Ps. 34:15

7 [a]Ps. 68:7, 8; Judg. 5:4; Is. 13:13; Hag. 2:6 [b]Ps. 114:4, 6

8 [1]Or, *in His wrath*
[a]Ps. 50:3

9 [a]Ps. 144:5 [b]Ps. 97:2

10 [a]Ps. 80:1; 99:1 [b]Ps. 104:3

11 [1]Or, *pavilion*
[a]Deut. 4:11

12 [a]Ps. 104:2 [b]Ps. 140:10; Hab. 3:5

13 [a]Ps. 29:3; 104:7

14 [1]Lit., *confused*
[a]Ps. 144:6; Hab. 3:11

15 [1]Or, *uncovered*
[a]Ps. 106:9 [b]Ps. 76:6 [c]Ps. 18:8

16 [a]Ps. 144:7 [b]Ps. 32:6

17 He [a]delivered me from my strong enemy,
And from those who hated me, for they were [b]too mighty for me.
18 They confronted me in [a]the day of my calamity,
But [b]the LORD was my stay.
19 He brought me forth also into a [a]broad place;
He rescued me, because [b]He delighted in me.

20 The LORD has [a]rewarded me according to my righteousness;
According to the [b]cleanness of my hands He has recompensed me.
21 For I have [a]kept the ways of the LORD,
And have [b]not wickedly departed from my God.
22 For all [a]His ordinances were before me,
And I did not put away His [b]statutes from me.
23 I was also [1a]blameless with Him,
And I [b]kept myself from my iniquity.
24 Therefore the LORD has [a]recompensed me according to my righteousness;
According to the cleanness of my hands in His eyes.

25 With [a]the kind Thou dost show Thyself kind;
With the [1]blameless [b]Thou dost show Thyself blameless;
26 With the pure thou dost show Thyself [a]pure;
And with the crooked [b]Thou dost show Thyself [1]astute.
27 For Thou dost [a]save an afflicted people;
But [b]haughty eyes Thou dost abase.
28 For Thou dost [a]light my lamp;
The LORD my God [b]illumines my darkness.
29 For by Thee I can [1a]run upon a troop;
And by my God I can [b]leap over a wall.

30 As for God, His way is [1a]blameless;
The [b]word of the LORD is tried;
He is a [c]shield to all who take refuge in Him.
31 For [a]who is God, but the LORD?
And who is a [b]rock, except our God,
32 The God who [a]girds me with strength,
And [1]makes my way [2b]blameless?
33 He [a]makes my feet like hinds' *feet*,
And sets me upon my high places.
34 He [a]trains my hands for battle,
So that my arms can [b]bend a bow of bronze.
35 Thou hast also given me [a]the shield of Thy salvation,
And Thy [b]right hand upholds me;
And [c]Thy [1]gentleness makes me great.
36 Thou dost [a]enlarge my steps under me,
And my [1b]feet have not slipped.

37 I [a]pursued my enemies and overtook them,
And I did not turn back [b]until they were consumed.
38 I shattered them, so that they were [a]not able to rise;
They fell [b]under my feet.

17 [a]Ps. 59:1 [b]Ps. 35:10; 142:6
18 [a]Ps. 59:16 [b]Ps. 16:8
19 [a]Ps. 4:1; 31:8; 118:5 [b]Ps. 37:23; 41:11
20 [a]Ps. 7:8; Job 33:26 [b]Ps. 24:4; Job 22:30
21 [a]Ps. 37:34; 119:33; Prov. 8:32 [b]2 Chr. 34:33; Ps. 119:102
22 [a]Ps. 119:30 [b]Ps. 119:83
23 [1]Lit., *complete*; or, *having integrity*; or, *perfect* [a]Ps. 18:32 [b]Ps. 19:12, 13; 25:11; 66:18
24 [a]Ps. 18:20
25 [1]Note v. 23 [a]Ps. 62:12; Matt. 5:7 [b]Ps. 18:30
26 [1]Lit., *twisted* [a]Job 25:5; Hab. 1:13 [b]Lev. 26:23, 24; Prov. 3:34
27 [a]Ps. 72:12 [b]Ps. 101:5; Prov. 6:17
28 [a]1 Kin. 15:4; Job 18:6; Ps. 132:17 [b]Ps. 27:1
29 [1]Or, *crush a troop* [a]Ps. 118:10-12 [b]Ps. 18:33; Ps. 40:2
30 [1]Note v. 23 [a]Ps. 19:7; 145:17 [b]Ps. 12:6 [c]Ps. 91:4
31 [a]Ps. 86:8-10; Is. 45:5 [b]Ps. 18:2; 62:2; Deut. 32:31
32 [1]Or, *has made* [2]Lit., *complete*; or, *having integrity* [a]Ps. 18:39; Is. 45:5 [b]Ps. 18:23
33 [a]Hab. 3:19
34 [a]Ps. 144:1 [b]Job 29:20
35 [1]Or, *condescension* [a]Ps. 33:20 [b]Ps. 63:8; 119:117 [c]Ps. 138:6
36 [1]Lit., *ankles* [a]Ps. 18:33 [b]Ps. 66:9
37 [a]Ps. 44:5 [b]Ps. 37:20
38 [a]Ps. 36:12 [b]Ps. 47:3

39 For Thou hast [a]girded me with strength for battle;
Thou hast [1b]subdued under me those who rose up against me.
40 Thou hast also made my enemies [a]turn their backs to me,
And I [1b]destroyed those who hated me.
41 They cried for help, but there was [a]none to save,
Even to the LORD, but [b]He did not answer them.
42 Then I beat them fine as the [a]dust before the wind;
I emptied them out as the mire of the streets.

43 Thou hast delivered me from the [a]contentions of the people;
Thou hast placed me as [b]head of the nations;
A [c]people whom I have not known serve me.
44 As soon as they hear, they obey me;
Foreigners [1a]submit to me.
45 Foreigners [a]fade away,
And [b]come trembling out of their [1]fortresses.

46 The LORD [a]lives, and blessed be [b]my rock;
And exalted be [c]the God of my salvation,
47 The God who [a]executes vengeance for me,
And [b]subdues peoples under me.
48 He [a]delivers me from my enemies;
Surely Thou [b]dost lift me above those who rise up against me;
Thou dost rescue me from the [c]violent man.
49 Therefore I will [a]give thanks to Thee among the nations, O LORD,
And I will [b]sing praises to Thy name.
50 He gives great [1a]deliverance to His king,
And shows lovingkindness to [b]His anointed,
To David and [c]his [2]descendants forever.

PSALM 19

The Works and the Word of God.

For the choir director. A Psalm of David.

THE [a]heavens are telling of the glory of God;
And the [b]firmament is declaring the work of His hands.
2 Day to [a]day pours forth speech,
And [b]night to night reveals knowledge.
3 There is no speech, nor are there words;
Their voice is not heard.
4 Their [1a]line has gone out through all the earth,
And their utterances to the end of the world.
In them He has [b]placed a tent for the sun,
5 Which is as a bridegroom coming out of his chamber;
It rejoices as a strong man to run his course.
6 Its [a]rising is from [1]one end of the heavens,
And its circuit to the [2]other end of them;
And there is nothing hid from its heat.

7 The law of the LORD is [1a]perfect, [b]restoring the soul;

39 [1]Lit., *caused to bow down* [a]Ps. 18:32 [b]Ps. 18:47

40 [1]Or, *silenced* [a]Ps. 21:12 [b]Ps. 94:23

41 [a]Ps. 50:22 [b]Job 27:9; Prov. 1:28

42 [a]Ps. 83:13

43 [a]Ps. 35:1; 2 Sam. 3:1; 19:9 [b]Ps. 89:27 [c]Is. 55:5

44 [1]Lit., *deceive me;* i.e., give feigned obedience [a]Ps. 66:3

45 [1]Lit., *fastnesses* [a]Ps. 37:2 [b]Mic. 7:17

46 [a]Job 19:25 [b]Ps. 18:2 [c]Ps. 51:14

47 [a]Ps. 94:1 [b]Ps. 18:43; 47:3; 144:2

48 [a]Ps. 3:7 [b]Ps. 27:6 [c]Ps. 11:5

49 [a]Rom. 15:9 [b]Ps 108:1

50 [1]I.e., victories; lit., *salvations* [2]Lit., *seed* [a]Ps. 21:1 [b]Ps. 28:8 [c]Ps. 89:4

1 [a]Ps. 8:1; 50:6; Rom. 1:19, 20 [b]Gen. 1:6, 7

2 [a]Ps. 74:16 [b]Ps. 139:12

4 [1]Another reading is, *sound* [a]Rom. 10:18 [b]Ps. 104:2

6 [1]Lit., *the* [2]Lit., *the ends* [a]Ps. 113:3

7 [1]I.e., blameless [a]Ps. 119:160 [b]Ps. 23:3

The testimony of the LORD is [c]sure, making [d]wise the simple.
8 The precepts of the LORD are [a]right, [b]rejoicing the heart;
The commandment of the LORD is [c]pure, [d]enlightening the eyes.
9 The fear of the LORD is clean, enduring forever;
The judgments of the LORD are [a]true; they are [b]righteous altogether.
10 They are more desirable than [a]gold, yes, than much fine gold;
[b]Sweeter also than honey and the drippings of the honeycomb.
11 Moreover, by them [a]Thy servant is warned;
In keeping them there is great [b]reward.
12 Who can [a]discern *his* errors? [b]Acquit me of [c]hidden *faults.*
13 Also keep back thy servant [a]from presumptuous *sins;*
Let them not [b]rule over me;
Then I shall be [1c]blameless,
And I shall be acquitted of [d]great transgression.
14 Let the words of my mouth and [a]the meditation of my heart
Be acceptable in Thy sight,
O LORD, [b]my rock and my [c]redeemer.

PSALM 20

Prayer for Victory over Enemies.

For the choir director. A Psalm of David.

MAY the LORD answer you [a]in the day of trouble!
May the [b]name of the [c]God of Jacob set you *securely* on high!
2 May He send you help [a]from the sanctuary,
And [b]support you from Zion!
3 May He [a]remember all your meal offerings,
And [b]find your burnt offering [1]acceptable! [[2]Selah.

4 May He grant you your [a]heart's desire,
And [b]fulfill all your [1]counsel!
5 [1]We will [a]sing for joy over your [2]victory,
And in the name of our God we will [b]set up our banners.
May the LORD [c]fulfill all your petitions.

6 Now [a]I know that the LORD saves His anointed;
He will [b]answer him from His holy heaven,
With the [1c]saving strength of His right hand.
7 Some [1]*boast* in chariots, and some in [a]horses;
But [b]we [2]will boast in the name of the LORD, our God.
8 They have [a]bowed down and fallen;
But we have [b]risen and stood upright.
9 [1a]Save, O LORD;
May the [b]King answer us in the day we call.

7 [c]Ps. 93:5 [d]Ps. 119:98-100

8 [a]Ps. 119:128 [b]Ps. 119:14 [c]Ps. 12:6 [d]Ps. 36:9

9 [a]Ps. 119:142 [b]Ps. 119:138

10 [a]Ps. 119:72, 127 [b]Ps. 119:103

11 [a]Ps. 17:4 [b]Ps. 24:5, 6; Prov. 29:18

12 [a]Ps. 40:12; 139:6 [b]Ps. 51:1, 2 [c]Ps. 90:8; 139:23, 24

13 [1]Lit., *complete* [a]Num. 15:30 [b]Ps. 119:133 [c]Ps. 18:32 [d]Ps. 25:11

14 [a]Ps. 104:34 [b]Ps. 18:2 [c]Ps. 31:5

1 [a]Ps. 50:15 [b]Ps. 91:14 [c]Ps. 46:7, 11

2 [a]Ps. 3:4 [b]Ps. 110:2

3 [1]Lit., *fat* [2]*Selah* may mean: *Pause, Crescendo* or *Musical interlude* [a]Acts 10:4 [b]Ps. 51:19

4 [1]Or, *purpose* [a]Ps. 21:2 [b]Ps. 145:19

5 [1]Or, *Let us sing* [2]Or, *salvation* [a]Ps. 9:14 [b]Ps. 60:4 [c]1 Sam. 1:17

6 [1]Or, *mighty deeds of the victory of His right hand* [a]Ps. 41:11 [b]Is. 58:9 [c]Ps. 28:8

7 [1]Or, praise *chariots,* or, trust, or, are strong *through* [2]Lit., *make mention of;* or, *praise the name* [a]Ps. 33:17 [b]2 Chr. 32:8

8 [a]Is. 2:11, 17 [b]Ps. 37:24; Mic. 7:8

9 [1]Or, *O LORD, save the king; answer us . . .* [a]Ps. 3:7 [b]Ps. 17:6

Psalm 21

Praise for Deliverance.

For the choir director. A Psalm of David.

O LORD, in Thy strength the king will [a]be glad,
And in Thy [1]salvation how greatly he will rejoice!
2 Thou hast [a]given him his heart's desire,
And Thou hast not withheld the request of his lips. [[1]Selah.
3 For Thou [a]dost meet him with the blessings of good things;
Thou dost set a [b]crown of fine gold on his head.
4 He asked life of Thee,
Thou [a]didst give it to him,
[b]Length of days forever and ever.
5 His [a]glory is great through Thy [1]salvation,
[b]Splendor and majesty Thou dost place upon him.
6 For Thou dost make him [1]most [a]blessed forever;
Thou dost make him joyful [b]with gladness in Thy presence.

7 For the king [a]trusts in the LORD,
And through the lovingkindness of the Most High [b]he will not be shaken.
8 Your hand will [a]find out all your enemies;
Your right hand will find out those who hate you.
9 You will make them [a]as a fiery oven in the time [1]of your anger;
The LORD will [b]swallow them up in His wrath,
And [c]fire will devour them.
10 Their [1]offspring Thou wilt destroy from the earth,
And their [2a]descendants from among the sons of men.
11 Though they [1a]intended evil against Thee,
And [b]devised a plot,
They will not succeed.
12 For Thou wilt [a]make them turn their back;
Thou wilt [1]aim [b]with Thy bowstrings at their faces.
13 Be Thou exalted, O LORD, in Thy strength;
We will [a]sing and praise Thy power.

Psalm 22

A Cry of Anguish and a Song of Praise.

For the choir director; upon £aijeleth hashshahar. A Psalm of David.

[a]My God, my God, why hast Thou forsaken me?
[1b]Far from my deliverance are the words of my [2c]groaning.
2 O my God, I [a]cry by day, but Thou dost not answer;
And by night, but [1]I have no rest.
3 Yet [a]Thou art holy,
O Thou who [1]art enthroned upon [b]the praises of Israel.
4 In Thee our fathers [a]trusted;
They trusted, and Thou didst [b]deliver them.

1 [1]Or, *victory* [a]Ps. 59:16, 17

2 [1]*Selah* may mean: *Pause, Crescendo* or *Musical interlude* [a]Ps. 20:4; 37:4

3 [a]Ps. 59:10 [b]2 Sam. 12:30

4 [a]Ps. 61:6; 133:3 [b]Ps. 91:16

5 [1]Or, *victory* [a]Ps. 9:14; 20:5 [b]Ps. 8:5; 96:6

6 [1]Lit., *blessings* [a]1 Chr. 17:27 [b]Ps. 43:4

7 [a]Ps. 125:1 [b]Ps. 112:6

8 [a]Is. 10:10

9 [1]Or, *of your presence* [a]Mal. 4:1 [b]Lam. 2:2 [c]Ps. 50:3

10 [1]Lit., *fruit* [2]Lit., *seed* [a]Ps. 37:28

11 [1]Lit., *stretched out* [a]Ps. 2:1-3 [b]Ps. 10:2

12 [1]Lit., *make ready* [a]Ps. 18:40 [b]Ps. 7:12, 13

13 [a]Ps. 59:16; 81:1

£ Lit., *the hind of the morning*

1 [1]Or, Why art Thou so *far from helping me*, and from *the words of my groaning?* [2]Lit., *roaring* [a]Matt. 27:46; Mark 15:34 [b]Ps. 10:1 [c]Ps. 6:6; 32:3; 38:8; Job 3:24

2 [1]Lit., *there is no silence for me* [a]Ps. 42:3; 88:1

3 [1]Or, *dost inhabit the praises* [a]Ps. 99:9 [b]Ps. 148:14

4 [a]Ps. 78:53 [b]Ps. 107:6

5 To Thee they cried out, and were delivered;
In Thee they trusted, and were not [1]disappointed.

6 But I am a [a]worm, and not a man,
A [b]reproach of men, and [c]despised by the people.
7 All who see me [1a]sneer at me;
They [2]separate with the lip, they [b]wag the head, *saying,*
8 "[1]Commit *thyself* to the LORD; [a]let Him deliver him;
Let Him rescue him, because He delights in him."

9 Yet Thou art He who [a]didst bring me forth from the womb;
Thou didst make me trust *when* upon my mother's breasts.
10 Upon Thee I was cast [a]from [1]birth;
Thou hast been my God from my mother's womb.

11 [a]Be not far from me, for [1]trouble is near;
For there is [b]none to help.
12 Many [a]bulls have surrounded me;
Strong *bulls* of [b]Bashan have encircled me.
13 They [a]open wide their mouth at me,
As a ravening and a roaring [b]lion.
14 I am [a]poured out like water,
And all my [b]bones are out of joint;
My [c]heart is like wax;
It is melted within [1]me.
15 My [a]strength is dried up like a potsherd,
And my tongue cleaves to my jaws;
And Thou dost [b]lay me [1]in the dust of death.
16 For [a]dogs have surrounded me;
A [1]band of evildoers has encompassed me;
[2]They [b]pierced my hands and my feet.
17 I can count all my bones.
They look, they stare at me;
18 They [a]divide my garments among them,
And for my clothing they cast lots.

19 But Thou, O LORD, [a]be not far off;
O Thou my help, [b]hasten to my assistance.
20 Deliver my [1]soul from [a]the sword,
My [b]only *life* from the [2]power of the dog.
21 Save me from the [a]lion's mouth;
And from the horns of the [b]wild oxen Thou dost [c]answer me.

22 I will [a]tell of Thy name to my brethren;
In the midst of the assembly I will praise Thee.
23 [a]You who fear the LORD, praise Him;
All you [1]descendants of Jacob, [b]glorify Him,
And [c]stand in awe of Him, all you [1]descendants of Israel.
24 For He has [a]not despised nor abhorred the affliction of the afflicted;
Neither has He [b]hid His face from him;
But [c]when he cried to Him for help, He heard.

5 [1]Or, *ashamed*

6 [a]Job 25:6; Is. 41:14 [b]Ps. 31:11 [c]Is. 49:7

7 [1]Or, *mock me* [2]I.e., make mouths at me [a]Ps. 79:4; Is. 53:3 [b]Matt. 27:39; Mark 15:29

8 [1]Lit., *Roll;* another reading is, *He committed himself* [a]Matt. 27:43

9 [a]Ps. 71:5, 6

10 [1]Lit., a *womb* [a]Is. 46:3; 49:1

11 [1]Or, *distress* [a]Ps. 71:12 [b]2 Kin. 14:26; Ps. 72:12; Is. 63:5

12 [a]Ps. 22:21; 68:30 [b]Deut. 32:14; Amos 4:1

13 [a]Ps. 35:21; Job 16:10; Lam. 2:16; 3:46 [b]Ps. 10:9; 17:12

14 [1]Lit., *my inward parts* [a]Job 30:16 [b]Ps. 31:10; Dan. 5:6 [c]Ps. 73:26; Josh. 7:5; Job 23:16; Nah. 2:10

15 [1]Lit., *to* [a]Ps. 38:10 [b]Ps. 104:29

16 [1]Or, *assembly* [2]Another reading is, *Like a lion, my . . .* [a]Ps. 59:6, 7 [b]Matt. 27:35; John 20:25

18 [a]Matt. 27:35; Luke 23:34; John 19:24

19 [a]Ps. 22:11 [b]Ps. 70:5

20 [1]Or, *life* [2]Lit., *paw* [a]Ps. 37:14 [b]Ps. 35:17

21 [a]Ps. 22:13 [b]Ps. 22:12 [c]Ps. 34:4; 118:5; 120:1

22 [a]Ps. 40:10; Heb. 2:12

23 [1]Lit., *seed* [a]Ps. 135:20 [b]Ps. 86:12 [c]Ps. 33:8

24 [a]Ps. 69:33 [b]Ps. 27:9; 69:17; 102:2 [c]Ps. 31:22; Heb. 5:7

25 [a]Ps. 35:18; 40:9, 10 [b]Ps. 61:8

26 [1]Or, *poor* [a]Ps. 107:9 [b]Ps. 40:16 [c]Ps. 69:32

27 [1]Some versions read, *Him* [a]Ps. 2:8; 82:8 [b]Ps. 86:9

28 [a]Ps. 47:7; Obad. 21; Zech. 14:9 [b]Ps. 47:8

29 [1]Lit., *fat ones* [2]Or, *did not* [a]Ps. 17:10; Is. 10:16; Hab. 1:16 [b]Ps. 28:1 [c]Ps 89:48

30 [1]Lit., *A seed* [a]Ps. 102:28 [b]Ps. 102:18

31 [a]Ps. 40:9; 71:18 [b]Ps. 78:6

1 [1]Or, *do* [a]Ps. 78:52; 80:1; Is. 40:11; Jer. 31:10; Ezek. 34:11-13; John 10:11; 1 Pet. 2:25 [b]Ps. 34:9, 10

2 [1]Lit., *waters of rest* [a]Ps. 65:11-13; Ezek. 34:14 [b]Ps. 36:8; 46:4

3 [1]Lit., *tracks* [a]Ps. 19:7 [b]Ps. 5:8; 31:3 [c]Ps. 85:13; Prov. 4:11; 8:20

4 [1]Or, *valley of deep darkness* [2]Or, *harm* [a]Ps. 107:14 [b]Ps. 27:1 [c]Ps. 16:8; Is. 43:2 [d]Mic. 7:14

5 [1]Or, *dost anoint* [a]Ps. 78:19 [b]Ps. 92:10; Luke 7:46 [c]Ps. 16:5

6 [1]Or, *Only* [2]Another reading is, *return* [3]Lit., *for length of days* [a]Ps. 25:7, 10 [b]Ps. 27:4-6

1 [1]Lit., *its fulness* [a]1 Cor. 10:26 [b]Ps. 89:11

2 [a]Ps. 104:3, 5; 136:6

25 From Thee *comes* [a]my praise in the great assembly;
I shall [b]pay my vows before those who fear Him.
26 The [1]afflicted shall eat and [a]be satisfied;
Those who seek Him will [b]praise the LORD.
Let your [c]heart live forever!
27 All the [a]ends of the earth will remember and turn to the LORD,
And all the [b]families of the nations will worship before [1]Thee.
28 For the [a]kingdom is the LORD's,
And He [b]rules over the nations.
29 All the [1a]prosperous of the earth will eat and worship,
All those who [b]go down to the dust will bow before Him,
Even he who [2c]cannot keep his soul alive.
30 [1a]Posterity will serve Him;
It will be told of the Lord to [b]the *coming* generation.
31 They will come and [a]will declare His righteousness
To a people [b]who will be born, that He has performed *it*.

PSALM 23

The LORD, the Psalmist's Shepherd.

A Psalm of David.

THE LORD is my [a]shepherd,
I [1]shall [b]not want.
2 He makes me lie down in [a]green pastures;
He leads me beside [1b]quiet waters.
3 He [a]restores my soul;
He [b]guides me in the [1c]paths of righteousness
For His name's sake.

4 Even though I [a]walk through the [1]valley of the shadow of death,
I [b]fear no [2]evil; for [c]Thou art with me;
Thy [d]rod and Thy staff, they comfort me.
5 Thou dost [a]prepare a table before me in the presence of my enemies;
Thou [1]hast [b]anointed my head with oil;
My [c]cup overflows.
6 [1]Surely [a]goodness and lovingkindness will follow me all the days of my life,
And I will [2b]dwell in the house of the LORD [3]forever.

PSALM 24

The King of Glory Entering Zion.

A Psalm of David.

THE [a]earth is the LORD's, and [1]all it contains,
The [b]world, and those who dwell in it.
2 For He has [a]founded it upon the seas,
And established it upon the rivers.

3 Who may [a]ascend into the [b]hill of the LORD?
And who may stand in His holy [c]place?
4 He who has [a]clean hands and a [b]pure heart,
Who has not [c]lifted up his soul [1]to falsehood,
And has not [d]sworn deceitfully.
5 He shall receive a [a]blessing from the LORD
And [1b]righteousness from the God of his salvation.
6 [1]This is the generation of those who [a]seek Him,
Who seek Thy face—*even* Jacob. [[2]Selah.

7 [a]Lift up your heads, O gates,
And be lifted up, O [1]ancient doors,
That the King of [b]glory may come in!
8 Who is the King of glory?
The LORD [a]strong and mighty,
The LORD [b]mighty in battle.
9 Lift up your heads, O gates,
And lift them up, O [1]ancient doors,
That the King of [a]glory may come in!
10 Who is this King of glory?
The LORD of [a]hosts,
He is the King of glory. [Selah.

PSALM 25

Prayer for Protection, Guidance and Pardon.

A Psalm of David.

TO Thee, O LORD, I [a]lift up my soul.
2 O my God, in Thee [a]I trust,
Do not let me [b]be ashamed;
Do not let my [c]enemies exult over me.
3 Indeed, [a]none of those who wait for Thee will be ashamed;
[1]Those who [b]deal treacherously without cause will be ashamed.

4 [a]Make me know Thy ways, O LORD;
Teach me Thy paths.
5 Lead me in [a]Thy truth and teach me,
For Thou art the [b]God of my salvation;
For Thee I [c]wait all the day.
6 [a]Remember, O LORD, Thy compassion and Thy lovingkindnesses,
For they have been [1b]from of old.
7 Do not remember the [a]sins of my youth or my transgressions;
[b]According to Thy lovingkindness remember Thou me,
For Thy [c]goodness' sake, O LORD.

8 [a]Good and [b]upright is the LORD;
Therefore He [c]instructs sinners in the way.
9 He [a]leads the [1]humble in justice,
And He [b]teaches the [1]humble His way.
10 All the paths of the LORD are [a]lovingkindness and truth
To [b]those who keep His covenant and His testimonies.

3 [a]Ps. 15:1 [b]Ps. 2:6 [c]Ps. 65:4; Deut. 12:5

4 [1]Or, *in vain*
[a]Ps. 26:6; Job 17:9; 22:30 [b]Ps. 51:10; 73:1; Matt. 5:8 [c]Ezek. 18:15 [d]Ps. 15:4

5 [1]I.e., as vindicated
[a]Ps. 115:13 [b]Ps. 36:10

6 [1]Or, *Such* [2]*Selah* may mean: *Pause, Crescendo* or *Musical interlude*
[a]Ps. 27:4, 8

7 [1]Lit., *everlasting*
[a]Ps. 118:20; Is. 26:2 [b]Ps. 29:2, 9; 97:6; Acts 7:2; 1 Cor. 2:8

8 [a]Ps. 96:7; Deut. 4:34 [b]Ps. 76:3-6; Ex. 15:3, 6

9 [1]Lit., *everlasting*
[a]Ps. 26:8; 57:11

10 [a]Gen. 32:2; Josh. 5:14; 2 Sam. 5:10; Neh. 9:6

1 [a]Ps. 86:4; 143:8

2 [a]Ps. 31:1 [b]Ps. 25:20; 31:1 [c]Ps. 41:11

3 [1]Or, *Let those . . . be ashamed*
[a]Ps. 37:9; 40:1; Is. 49:23 [b]Ps. 119:158; Is. 21:2; Hab. 1:13

4 [a]Ps. 27:11; 86:11

5 [a]Ps. 25:10; 43:3 [b]Ps. 79:9 [c]Ps. 40:1

6 [1]Or, *everlasting*
[a]Ps. 98:3 [b]Ps. 103:17

7 [a]Job 13:26; 20:11 [b]Ps. 51:1 [c]Ps. 31:19

8 [a]Ps. 86:5 [b]Ps. 92:15 [c]Ps. 32:8

9 [1]Or, *afflicted*
[a]Ps. 23:3 [b]Ps. 27:11

10 [a]Ps. 40:11 [b]Ps. 103:18

11 For [a]Thy name's sake, O LORD,
[b]Pardon my iniquity, for it is great.

12 Who is the man who [a]fears the LORD?
He will [b]instruct him in the way he should choose.
13 His soul will [a]abide in [1]prosperity,
And his [2]descendants will [b]inherit the [3]land.
14 The [1a]secret of the LORD is for those who fear Him,
[2]And He will [b]make them know His covenant.
15 My [a]eyes are continually toward the LORD,
For He will [1b]pluck my feet out of the net.

16 [a]Turn to me and be gracious to me,
For I am [b]lonely and afflicted.
17 [1]The [a]troubles of my heart are enlarged;
Bring me [b]out of my distresses.
18 Look upon my [a]affliction and my [1]trouble,
And [b]forgive all my sins.
19 Look upon my enemies, for they [a]are many;
And they [b]hate me with violent hatred.
20 [a]Guard my soul and deliver me;
Do not let me [b]be ashamed, for I take refuge in Thee.
21 Let [a]integrity and uprightness preserve me,
For [b]I wait for Thee.
22 [a]Redeem Israel, O God,
Out of all his troubles.

PSALM 26

Protestation of Integrity and Prayer for Protection.

A Psalm of David.

1 [a]VINDICATE me, O LORD, for I have [b]walked in my integrity;
And I have [c]trusted in the LORD [2d]without wavering.
2 [a]Examine me, O LORD, and try me;
[b]Test my [1]mind and my heart.
3 For Thy [a]lovingkindness is before my eyes,
And I have [b]walked in Thy [1]truth.
4 I do not [a]sit with [1]deceitful men,
Nor will I go with [2b]pretenders.
5 I [a]hate the assembly of evildoers,
And I will not sit with the wicked.
6 I shall [a]wash my hands in innocence,
And I will go about [b]Thine altar, O LORD,
7 That I may proclaim with the voice of [a]thanksgiving,
And declare all Thy [1]wonders.

8 O LORD, I [a]love the habitation of Thy house,
And the place [1]where Thy [b]glory dwells.
9 Do not [1]take my soul away *along* with sinners,
Nor my life with [a]men of bloodshed,
10 In whose hands is a [a]wicked scheme,
And whose right hand is full of [b]bribes.
11 But as for me, I shall [a]walk in my integrity;
[b]Redeem me, and be gracious to me.

---

11 [a]Ps. 79:9 [b]Ex. 34:9

12 [a]Ps. 31:19 [b]Ps. 25:8

13 [1]Lit., *good* [2]Lit., *seed* [3]Or, *earth* [a]Prov. 1:33; Jer. 23:6 [b]Ps. 37:11; 69:36

14 [1]Or, *counsel,* or, *intimacy* [2]Or, *And His covenant, to make them know it.* [a]Job 29:4; Prov. 3:32 [b]Gen. 17:1, 2

15 [1]Lit., *bring out* [a]Ps. 123:2 [b]Ps. 31:4; 124:7

16 [a]Ps. 69:16 [b]Ps. 143:4

17 [1]Some commentators read, *Relieve the troubles of my heart* [a]Ps. 40:12 [b]Ps. 107:6

18 [1]Lit., *toil* [a]Ps. 31:7 [b]Ps. 103:3

19 [a]Ps. 3:1 [b]Ps. 9:13

20 [a]Ps. 86:2 [b]Ps. 25:2

21 [a]Ps. 41:12 [b]Ps. 25:3

22 [a]Ps. 130:8

1 [1]Lit., *Judge* [2]Lit., *I do not slide* [a]Ps. 7:8 [b]Prov. 20:7 [c]Ps. 13:5 [d]Heb. 10:23

2 [1]Lit., *kidneys,* figurative for inner man [a]Ps. 139:23 [b]Ps. 7:9

3 [a]Or, *faithfulness* [a]Ps. 48:9 [b]Ps. 86:11

4 [1]Or, *worthless men;* lit., *men of falsehood* [2]Or, *dissemblers, hypocrites* [a]Ps. 1:1 [b]Ps. 28:3

5 [a]Ps. 31:6; 139:21

6 [a]Ps. 73:13 [b]Ps. 43:3, 4

7 [1]Or, *miracles* [a]Ps. 9:1

8 [1]Lit., *of the tabernacle of Thy glory* [a]Ps. 27:4 [b]Ps. 24:7

9 [1]Lit., *gather* [a]Ps. 139:19

10 [a]Ps. 37:7 [b]Ps. 15:5

11 [a]Ps. 26:1 [b]Ps. 44:26; 69:18

12 My foot stands on a [a]level place;
In the [b]congregations I shall bless the LORD.

PSALM 27

A Psalm of Fearless Trust in God.

A Psalm of David.

THE LORD is my [a]light and my [b]salvation;
Whom shall I fear?
The LORD is the [1c]defense of my life;
[d]Whom shall I dread?
2 When evildoers came upon me to [a]devour my flesh,
My adversaries and my enemies, they [b]stumbled and fell.
3 Though a [a]host encamp against me,
My heart will not fear;
Though war arise against me,
In *spite of* this I [1]shall be [b]confident.

4 One thing I have asked from the LORD, that I shall seek;
That I may [a]dwell in the house of the LORD all the days of my life,
To behold [b]the [1]beauty of the LORD,
And to [2c]meditate in His temple.
5 For in the [a]day of trouble He will [b]conceal me in His [1]tabernacle;
In the secret place of His tent He will [c]hide me;
He will [d]lift me up on a rock.
6 And now [a]my head will be lifted up above my enemies around me;
And I will offer in His tent [b]sacrifices [1]with shouts of joy;
I will [c]sing, yes, I will sing praises to the LORD.

7 [a]Hear, O LORD, when I cry with my voice,
And be gracious to me and [b]answer me.
8 *When Thou didst say*, "[a]Seek My face," my heart said to Thee,
"Thy face, O LORD, [b]I shall seek."
9 [a]Do not hide Thy face from me,
Do not turn Thy servant away in [b]anger;
Thou hast been [c]my help;
[d]Do not abandon me nor [e]forsake me,
O God of my salvation!
10 [1]For my father and [a]my mother have forsaken me,
But [b]the LORD will take me up.

11 [a]Teach me Thy way, O LORD,
And lead me in a [b]level path,
Because of [1]my foes.
12 Do not deliver me over to the [1a]desire of my adversaries;
For [b]false witnesses have risen against me,
And such as [c]breathe out violence.

12 [a]Ps. 27:11 [b]Ps. 22:22

1 [1]Or, *refuge* [a]Ps. 18:28; Is. 60:20; Mic. 7:8 [b]Ps. 62:7; 118:14; Ex. 15:2; Is. 33:2; Jonah 2:9 [c]Ps. 28:8 [d]Ps. 118:6

2 [a]Ps. 14:4 [b]Ps. 9:3

3 [1]Lit., *am confident* [a]Ps. 3:6 [b]Job 4:6

4 [1]Lit., *delightfulness* [2]Lit., *inquire* [a]Ps. 23:6 [b]Ps. 90:17 [c]Ps. 18:6

5 [1]Or, *shelter* [a]Ps. 50:15 [b]Ps. 31:20 [c]Ps. 17:8 [d]Ps. 40:2

6 [1]Lit., *of shouts* [a]Ps. 3:3 [b]Ps. 107:22 [c]Ps. 13:6

7 [a]Ps. 4:3; 61:1 [b]Ps. 13:3

8 [a]Ps. 105:4; Amos 5:6 [b]Ps. 34:4

9 [a]Ps. 69:17 [b]Ps. 6:1 [c]Ps. 40:17 [d]Ps. 94:14 [e]Ps. 37:28

10 [1]Or, *If my father . . . forsake me, Then the* LORD [a]Is. 49:15 [b]Is. 40:11

11 [1]Or, *those who lie in wait for me* [a]Ps. 25:4; 86:11 [b]Ps. 5:8; 26:12

12 [1]Lit., *soul* [a]Ps. 41:2 [b]Ps. 35:11; Deut. 19:18; Matt. 26:60 [c]Acts 9:1

13 [1]*I would have despaired* unless I had believed that I
would see the [a]goodness of the LORD
In the [b]land of the living.
14 [a]Wait for the LORD;
Be [b]strong, and let your heart take courage;
Yes, wait for the LORD.

PSALM 28

A Prayer for Help, and Praise for Its Answer.

A Psalm of David.

TO Thee, O LORD, I call;
My [a]rock, do not be deaf to me,
Lest, if Thou [b]be silent to me,
I become like those who [c]go down to the pit.
2 Hear the [a]voice of my supplications when I cry to Thee
for help,
When I [b]lift up my hands [c]toward [1]Thy holy [d]sanctuary.
3 [a]Do not drag me away with the wicked
And with those who work iniquity;
Who [b]speak peace with their neighbors,
While evil is in their hearts.
4 Requite them [a]according to their work and according
to the evil of their practices;
Requite them according to the deeds of their hands;
Repay them their [1]recompense.
5 Because they [a]do not regard the works of the LORD
Nor the deeds of His hands,
He will tear them down and not build them up.

6 Blessed be the LORD,
Because He [a]has heard the voice of my supplication.
7 The LORD is my [a]strength and my [b]shield;
My heart [c]trusts in Him, and I am helped;
Therefore [d]my heart exults,
And with [e]my song I shall thank Him.
8 The LORD is [1]their [a]strength,
And He is a [2b]saving defense to His anointed.
9 [a]Save Thy people, and bless [b]Thine inheritance;
Be their [c]shepherd also, and [d]carry them forever.

PSALM 29

The Voice of the LORD in the Storm.

[a] A Psalm of David.

ASCRIBE to the LORD, O [1]sons of the mighty,
Ascribe to the LORD glory and strength.
2 Ascribe to the LORD the glory [1]due to His name;
Worship the LORD [a]in [2]holy array.

3 The [a]voice of the LORD is upon the waters;
The God of glory [b]thunders,
The LORD upon [1c]many waters.

---

13 [1]Or, *Surely I believed* [a]Ps. 31:19 [b]Ps. 52:5; 116:9; 142:5; Job 28:13; Is. 38:11; Jer. 11:19

14 [a]Ps. 25:3; 37:34; 40:1; 62:5; 130:5; Prov. 20:22; Is. 25:9 [b]Ps. 31:24

1 [a]Ps. 18:2 [b]Ps. 35:22; 39:12; 83:1 [c]Ps. 88:4; 143:7; Prov. 1:12

2 [1]Lit., *the innermost place of Thy sanctuary* [a]Ps. 140:6 [b]Ps. 134:2; 141:2; Lam. 2:19; 1 Tim. 2:8 [c]Ps. 5:7; 138:2 [d]1 Kin. 6:5

3 [a]Ps. 26:9 [b]Ps. 12:2; 55:21; 62:4; Jer. 9:8

4 [1]Or, *dealings* [a]Ps. 62:12; 2 Tim. 4:14

5 [a]Is. 5:12

6 [a]Ps. 28:2

7 [a]Ps. 59:17 [b]Ps. 3:3 [c]Ps. 13:5; 112:7 [d]Ps. 16:9 [e]Ps. 40:3; 69:30

8 [1]A few mss. and ancient versions read, *the strength of His people* [2]Or, *refuge of salvation* [a]Ps. 89:17 [b]Ps. 27:1; 140:7

9 [a]Ps. 106:47 [b]Ps. 33:12; 106:40; Deut. 9:29; 32:9; 1 Kin. 8:51 [c]Ps. 80:1 [d]Deut. 1:31; Is. 40:11; 46:3; 63:9

1 [1]Or, *sons of gods* [a]1 Chr. 16:28, 29; Ps. 96:7-9

2 [1]Lit., *of His name* [2]Or, *the majesty of holiness* [a]2 Chr. 20:21; Ps. 110:3

3 [1]Or, *great* [a]Ps. 104:7 [b]Job 37:4, 5; Ps. 18:13 [c]Ps. 18:16; 107:23

4 The voice of the LORD is [a]powerful,
The voice of the LORD is majestic.
5 The voice of the LORD breaks the cedars;
Yes, the LORD breaks in pieces [a]the cedars of Lebanon.
6 And He makes them [a]skip like a calf,
Lebanon and [b]Sirion like a young wild ox.
7 The voice of the LORD hews out [1]flames of fire.
8 The voice of the LORD [1]shakes the wilderness;
The LORD shakes the wilderness of [a]Kadesh.
9 The voice of the LORD makes [a]the deer to calve,
And strips the forests bare,
And [b]in His temple everything says, "Glory!"

10 The LORD sat *as King* at the [a]flood;
Yes, the LORD sits as [b]King forever.
11 [1]The LORD will give [a]strength to His people;
[2]The LORD will bless His people with [b]peace.

PSALM 30

Thanksgiving for Deliverance from Death.

A Psalm; a Song at the Dedication of the House. *A Psalm* of David.

I WILL [a]extol Thee, O LORD, for Thou hast [b]lifted me up,
And hast not let my [c]enemies rejoice over me.
2 O LORD my God,
I [a]cried to Thee for help, and Thou didst [b]heal me.
3 O LORD, Thou hast [a]brought up my soul from [1]Sheol;
Thou hast kept me alive, [2]that I should not [b]go down to the pit.
4 [a]Sing praise to the LORD, you [b]His godly ones,
And [c]give thanks to His holy [1d]name.
5 For [a]His anger is but for a moment,
His [b]favor is for a lifetime;
Weeping may [c]last for the night,
But a shout of joy *comes* in the morning.

6 Now as for me, [a]I said in my prosperity,
"I will [b]never be moved."
7 O LORD, by Thy favor Thou hast made my mountain to stand strong;
Thou didst [a]hide Thy face, I was dismayed.
8 To Thee, O LORD, I called,
And to the LORD I made supplication:
9 "What profit is there in my blood, if I [a]go down to the pit?
Will the [b]dust praise Thee? Will it declare Thy faithfulness?

10 "[a]Hear, O LORD, and be gracious to me;
O LORD, be Thou my [b]helper."
11 Thou hast turned for me [a]my mourning into dancing;
Thou hast [b]loosed my sackcloth and girded me with [c]gladness;

4 [a]Ps. 68:33

5 [a]Ps. 104:16; Judg. 9:15; 1 Kin. 5:6; Is. 2:13; 14:8

6 [a]Ps. 114:4, 6 [b]Deut. 3:9

7 [1]I.e., lightning

8 [1]Or, *causes . . . to whirl* [a]Num. 13:26

9 [a]Job 39:1 [b]Ps. 26:8

10 [a]Gen. 6:17 [b]Ps. 10:16

11 [1]Or, *May the LORD give . . .* [2]Or, *May the LORD bless . . .* [a]Ps. 28:8; 68:35; Is. 40:29 [b]Ps. 37:11

1 [a]Ps. 118:28; 145:1 [b]Ps. 3:3 [c]Ps. 25:2; 35:19, 24

2 [a]Ps. 88:13 [b]Ps. 6:2; 103:3

3 [1]I.e., the nether world [2]Some mss. read, *from among those who go down* [a]Ps. 86:13 [b]Ps. 28:1

4 [1]Lit., *memorial* [a]Ps. 149:1 [b]Ps. 50:5 [c]Ps. 97:12 [d]Ex. 3:15; Ps. 135:13; Hos. 12:5

5 [a]Ps. 103:9; Is. 26:20; 54:7, 8 [b]Ps. 118:1 [c]Ps. 126:5; 2 Cor. 4:17

6 [a]Job 29:18 [b]Ps. 10:6; 62:2, 6

7 [a]Ps. 104:29; 143:7; Deut. 31:17

9 [a]Ps. 28:1 [b]Ps. 6:5

10 [a]Ps. 4:1; 27:7 [b]Ps. 27:9; 54:4

11 [a]Ps. 6:8; Eccles. 3:4; Jer. 31:4, 13 [b]Is. 20:2 [c]Ps. 4:7

12 [1]Lit., *glory*
[a]Ps. 16:9; 57:8; 108:1 [b]Ps. 44:8

1 [a]Ps. 31:1-3; 71:1-3 [b]Ps. 25:2 [c]Ps. 143:1

2 [1]Or, *refuge, protection*
[a]Ps. 17:6; 86:1; 102:2 [b]Ps. 18:2; 71:3

3 [1]Or, *crag*
[a]Ps. 18:2 [b]Ps. 25:11

4 [a]Ps. 25:15 [b]Ps. 46:1

5 [1]Or, *faithfulness*
[a]Luke 23:46; Acts 7:59 [b]Ps. 55:18; 71:23 [c]Ps. 71:22; Deut. 32:4

6 [1]Lit., *empty vanities*
[a]Ps. 144:11; Jonah 2:8 [b]Ps. 52:8

7 [a]Ps. 90:14 [b]Ps. 10:14

8 [a]Deut. 32:30; Ps. 37:33 [b]Ps. 4:1

9 [a]Ps. 66:14; 69:17 [b]Ps. 6:7 [c]Ps. 63:1

10 [1]Or, *bones, substance*
[a]Ps. 13:2 [b]Ps. 39:11 [c]Ps. 32:3; 38:3; 102:3

11 [a]Ps. 69:19 [b]Ps. 38:11; 88:8, 18; Job 19:13

12 [a]Ps. 88:5

13 [1]Lit., *whispering*
[a]Ps. 50:20; Jer. 20:10 [b]Ps. 62:4; Matt. 27:1 [c]Ps. 41:7

14 [a]Ps. 140:6

15 [a]Job 14:5; 24:1 [b]Ps. 143:9

12 That *my* [1a]soul may sing praise to Thee, and not be silent.
O LORD my God, I will [b]give thanks to Thee forever.

PSALM 31

A Psalm of Complaint and of Praise.

For the choir director. A Psalm of David.

[a]IN Thee, O LORD, I have taken refuge;
Let me never [b]be ashamed;
[c]In Thy righteousness deliver me.
2 [a]Incline Thine ear to me, rescue me quickly;
Be Thou to me a [b]rock of [1]strength,
A stronghold to save me.
3 For Thou art my [1]rock and [a]my fortress;
For [b]Thy name's sake Thou wilt lead me and guide me.
4 Thou wilt [a]pull me out of the net which they have secretly laid for me;
For Thou art my [b]strength.
5 [a]Into Thy hand I commit my spirit;
Thou hast [b]ransomed me, O LORD, [c]God of [1]truth.

6 I hate those who [a]regard [1]vain idols;
But I [b]trust in the LORD.
7 I will [a]rejoice and be glad in Thy lovingkindness,
Because Thou hast [b]seen my affliction;
Thou hast known the troubles of my soul,
8 And Thou hast not [a]given me over into the hand of the enemy;
Thou hast set my feet [b]in a large place.

9 Be gracious to me, O LORD, for [a]I am in distress;
My [b]eye is wasted away from grief, [c]my soul and my body *also*.
10 For my life is spent with [a]sorrow,
And my years with sighing;
My [b]strength has failed because of my iniquity,
And [c]my [1]body has wasted away.
11 Because of all my adversaries, I have become a [a]reproach,
Especially to my [b]neighbors,
And an object of dread to my acquaintances;
Those who see me in the street flee from me.
12 I am [a]forgotten as a dead man, out of mind,
I am like a broken vessel.
13 For I have heard the [1a]slander of many,
Terror is on every side,
While they [b]took counsel together against me,
They [c]schemed to take away my life.

14 But as for me, I trust in Thee, O LORD,
I say, "[a]Thou art my God."
15 My [a]times are in Thy hand;
[b]Deliver me from the hand of my enemies, and from those who persecute me.

16 Make Thy [a]face to shine upon Thy servant;
[b]Save me in Thy lovingkindness.
17 Let me not be [a]put to shame, O LORD, for I call upon Thee;
Let the [b]wicked be put to shame, let them [c]be silent in [1]Sheol.
18 Let the [a]lying lips be dumb,
Which [b]speak arrogantly against the righteous,
With [c]pride and contempt.

19 How great is Thy [a]goodness,
Which Thou hast stored up for those who fear Thee,
Which Thou hast wrought for those who [b]take refuge in Thee,
[c]Before the sons of men!
20 Thou dost hide them in the [a]secret place of Thy presence from the [b]conspiracies of man;
Thou dost keep them secretly in a [1]shelter from the [c]strife of tongues.
21 [a]Blessed be the LORD,
For He has made [b]marvelous His lovingkindness to me in a [c]besieged city.
22 As for me, [a]I said in my alarm,
I am [b]cut off from before Thine eyes;
Nevertheless Thou didst [c]hear the voice of my supplications
When I cried to Thee.

23 O love the LORD, all you [a]His godly ones!
The LORD [b]preserves the faithful,
And fully [c]recompenses the proud doer.
24 [a]Be strong, and let your heart take courage,
All you who [1]hope in the LORD.

PSALM 32

Blessedness of Forgiveness and of Trust in God.

A Psalm of David. A [£]Maskil.

[a]HOW blessed is he whose transgression is forgiven,
Whose sin is covered!
2 How blessed is the man to whom the LORD [a]does not impute iniquity,
And in whose spirit there is [b]no deceit!

3 When [a]I kept silent *about my sin,* [b]my [1]body wasted away
Through my [2c]groaning all day long.
4 For day and night [a]Thy hand was heavy upon me;
My [1b]vitality was drained away *as* with the fever-heat of summer. [[2]Selah.
5 I [a]acknowledged my sin to Thee,
And my iniquity I [b]did not hide;
I said, "[c]I will confess my transgressions to the LORD";
And Thou [d]didst forgive the [1]guilt of my sin. [Selah.

16 [a]Ps. 4:6; 80:3; Num. 6:25 [b]Ps. 6:4

17 [1]I.e., the nether world [a]Ps. 25:20 [b]Ps. 25:3 [c]Ps. 94:17; 115:17; 1 Sam. 2:9

18 [a]Ps. 109:2; 120:2 [b]1 Sam. 2:3; Jude 15 [c]Ps. 94:4

19 [a]Ps. 65:4; 145:7; Rom. 2:4; 11:22 [b]Ps. 5:11 [c]Ps. 23:5

20 [1]Or, *pavilion* [a]Ps. 27:5 [b]Ps. 37:12 [c]Ps. 31:13; Job 5:21

21 [a]Ps. 28:6 [b]Ps. 17:7 [c]Ps. 87:5; 1 Sam. 23:7

22 [a]Ps. 116:11 [b]Ps. 88:5; Is. 38:11, 12; Lam. 3:54 [c]Ps. 18:6; 66:19; 145:19

23 [a]Ps. 30:4; 37:28; 50:5 [b]Ps. 145:20; Rev. 2:10 [c]Ps. 94:2; Deut. 32:41

24 [1]Or, *wait for* [a]Ps. 27:14

[£] Possibly, *Contemplative,* or *Didactic,* or *Skillful Psalm*

1 [a]Ps. 85:2; 103:3; Rom. 4:7, 8

2 [a]2 Cor. 5:19 [b]John 1:47

3 [1]Or, *bones, substance* [2]Lit., *roaring* [a]Ps. 39:2, 3 [b]Ps. 31:10 [c]Ps. 38:8

4 [1]Lit., *life juices were turned into the drought of summer* [2]*Selah* may mean: *Pause, Crescendo* or *Musical interlude* [a]Ps. 38:2; 39:10; 1 Sam. 5:6; Job 23:2; 33:7 [b]Ps. 22:15

5 [1]Or, *iniquity* [a]Lev. 26:40 [b]Job 31:33 [c]Ps. 38:18; Prov. 28:13; 1 John 1:9 [d]Ps. 103:12

6 [1]Lit., *in a time of finding out*
[a]Ps. 69:13 [b]Ps. 46:1-3; 69:1; 124:5; 144:7; Is. 43:2

7 [1]Or, *shouts*
[a]Ps. 31:20; 91:1; 119:114 [b]Ps. 121:7 [c]Ps. 40:3; Ex. 15:1; Judg. 5:1

8 [a]Ps. 25:8 [b]Ps. 33:18

9 [a]Prov. 26:3

10 [a]Ps. 16:4; Prov. 13:21; Rom. 2:9 [b]Ps. 5:11, 12

11 [a]Ps. 64:10; 68:3; 97:12 [b]Ps. 7:10; 64:10

1 [a]Ps. 32:11; Phil. 3:1; 4:4 [b]Ps. 92:1; 147:1

2 [a]Ps. 71:22; 147:7 [b]Ps. 144:9

3 [a]Ps. 40:3; 96:1; 98:1; 144:9; Is. 42:10; Rev. 5:9 [b]Ps. 98:4

4 [a]Ps. 19:8 [b]Ps. 119:90

5 [a]Ps. 11:7; 37:28 [b]Ps. 119:64

6 [a]Ps. 148:5; Gen. 1:6; Heb. 11:3 [b]Ps. 104:30 [c]Gen. 2:1

7 [1]Some versions read, *in a water skin;* I.e., container
[a]Ps. 78:13; Ex. 15:8; Josh. 3:16

8 [a]Ps. 67:7 [b]Ps. 96:9

9 [1]Or, *stood forth*
[a]Gen. 1:3; Ps. 148:5

10 [a]Ps. 2:1-3; Is. 8:10; 19:3

11 [a]Job 23:13; Prov. 19:21 [b]Ps. 40:5; 92:5; 139:17; Is. 55:8

12 [a]Ps. 144:15 [b]Ps. 28:9; Deut. 7:6

13 [a]Ps. 14:2; Job 28:24 [b]Ps. 11:4

6 Therefore, let everyone who is godly pray to Thee [1a]in
a time when Thou mayest be found;
Surely [b]in a flood of great waters they shall not reach
him.
7 Thou art [a]my hiding place; Thou [b]dost preserve me
from trouble;
Thou dost surround me with [1c]songs of deliverance.
[Selah.

8 I will [a]instruct you and teach you in the way which you
should go;
I will counsel you [b]with My eye upon you.
9 Do not be [a]as the horse or as the mule which have no
understanding;
Whose trappings include bit and bridle to hold them in
check,
Otherwise they will not come near to you.
10 Many are the [a]sorrows of the wicked;
But [b]he who trusts in the LORD, lovingkindness shall
surround him.
11 Be [a]glad in the LORD and rejoice you righteous ones,
And shout for joy all you who are [b]upright in heart.

PSALM 33

Praise to the Creator and Preserver.

[a]SING for joy in the LORD, O you righteous ones;
Praise is [b]becoming to the upright.
2 Give thanks to the LORD with the [a]lyre;
Sing praises to Him with a [b]harp of ten strings.
3 Sing to Him a [a]new song;
Play skillfully with [b]a shout of joy.
4 For the word of the LORD [a]is upright;
And all His work is *done* [b]in faithfulness.
5 He [a]loves righteousness and justice;
The [b]earth is full of the lovingkindness of the LORD.

6 By the [a]word of the LORD the heavens were made,
And [b]by the breath of His mouth [c]all their host.
7 He gathers the [a]waters of the sea together [1]as a heap;
He lays up the deeps in storehouses.
8 Let [a]all the earth fear the LORD;
Let all the inhabitants of the world [b]stand in awe of
Him.
9 For [a]He spoke, and it was done;
He commanded, and it [1]stood fast.
10 The LORD [a]nullifies the counsel of the nations;
He frustrates the plans of the peoples.
11 The [a]counsel of the LORD stands forever,
The [b]plans of His heart from generation to generation.
12 Blessed is the [a]nation whose God is the LORD,
The people whom He has [b]chosen for His own inheritance.

13 The LORD [a]looks from heaven;
He [b]sees all the sons of men;

14 From [a]His dwelling-place He looks out
On all the inhabitants of the earth,
15 He who [a]fashions [1]the hearts of them all,
He who [b]understands all their works.
16 [a]The king is not saved by a mighty army;
A warrior is not delivered by great strength.
17 A [a]horse is a false hope for victory;
Nor does it deliver anyone by its great strength.

18 Behold, [a]the eye of the LORD is on those who fear Him,
On those who [1b]hope for His lovingkindness;
19 To [a]deliver their soul from death,
And to keep them alive [b]in famine.
20 Our soul [a]waits for the LORD;
He is our [b]help and our shield.
21 For our [a]heart rejoices in Him,
Because we trust in His holy name.
22 Let Thy lovingkindness, O LORD, be upon us,
According as we have [1]hoped in Thee.

PSALM 34

The LORD a Provider and Deliverer.

A Psalm of David; when he [£]feigned madness before •Abimelech, who drove him away and he departed.

I WILL [a]bless the LORD at all times;
His [b]praise shall continually be in my mouth.
2 My soul shall [a]make its boast in the LORD;
The [b]humble shall hear it and rejoice.
3 O [a]magnify the LORD with me,
And let us [b]exalt His name together.

4 I [a]sought the LORD, and He answered me,
And [b]delivered me from all my fears.
5 They [a]looked to Him and were radiant,
And their faces shall [b]never be ashamed.
6 This [1]poor man cried and [a]the LORD heard him;
And saved him out of all his troubles.
7 The [a]angel of the LORD encamps around those who fear Him,
And rescues them.

8 O [a]taste and see that the LORD is good;
How [b]blessed is the man who takes refuge in Him!
9 O fear the LORD, you [a]His saints;
For to those who fear Him, there is [b]no want.
10 The young lions do lack and suffer hunger;
But they who seek the LORD shall [a]not be in want of any good thing.
11 [a]Come, you children, listen to me;
I will teach you [b]the fear of the LORD.
12 [a]Who is the man who desires life,
And loves *length of* days that he may [b]see good?

14 [a]Ps. 102:19; 1 Kin. 8:39, 43

15 [1]Or, *their heart together* [a]Ps. 119:73; Job 10:8 [b]2 Chr. 16:9; Job 34:21

16 [a]Ps. 44:6; 60:11

17 [a]Ps. 20:7; 147:10; Prov. 21:31

18 [1]Or, *wait* [a]Ps. 32:8; 34:15; Job 36:7; 1 Pet. 3:12 [b]Ps. 32:10; 147:11

19 [a]Ps. 56:13; Acts 12:11 [b]Ps. 37:19; Job 5:20

20 [a]Ps. 62:1; 130:6; Is. 8:17 [b]Ps. 115:9

21 [a]Ps. 13:5; 28:7; Zech. 10:7; John 16:22

22 [1]Or, *waited for*

[£] Or, *changed his behavior*
• Possibly a title of King Achish of Gath. See 1 Sam. 21:10-15

1 [a]Eph. 5:20; 1 Thess. 5:18 [b]Ps. 71:6

2 [a]Ps. 44:8; Jer. 9:24; 1 Cor. 1:31 [b]Ps. 69:32

3 [a]Ps. 35:27; 69:30; Luke 1:46 [b]Ps. 18:46

4 [a]Ps. 9:10; 2 Chr. 15:2; Matt. 7:7 [b]Ps. 34:6, 17, 19

5 [a]Ps. 36:9; Is. 60:5 [b]Ps. 25:3

6 [1]Or, *afflicted* [a]Ps. 34:4

7 [a]Ps. 91:11; Dan. 6:22

8 [a]Ps. 119:103; Heb. 6:5; 1 Pet. 2:3 [b]Ps. 2:12

9 [a]Ps. 31:23 [b]Ps. 23:1

10 [a]Ps. 84:11

11 [a]Ps. 66:16 [b]Ps. 111:10

12 [a]Ps. 34:12, 16; 1 Pet. 3:10-12 [b]Eccles. 3:13

13 [a]Ps. 141:3; Prov. 13:3; James 1:26 [b]1 Pet. 2:22

14 [a]Ps. 37:27; Is. 1:16, 17 [b]Rom. 14:19; Heb. 12:14

15 [a]Ps. 33:18

16 [a]Jer. 44:11; Amos 9:4 [b]Ps. 9:6; Ps. 109:15; Job 18:17

17 [a]Ps. 34:6

18 [1]Or, *contrite* [a]Ps. 145:18 [b]Ps. 147:3; Is. 61:1 [c]Ps. 51:17; Is. 57:15

19 [a]Ps. 71:20; 2 Tim. 3:11, 12 [b]Ps. 34:4, 6, 17

21 [1]Or, *held guilty* [a]Ps. 94:23; 140:11; Prov. 24:16

22 [1]Note, v. 21 [a]Ps. 71:23 [b]Ps. 37:40

1 [a]Ps. 18:43; Is. 49:25 [b]Ps. 56:2

2 [1]I.e., small shield [a]Ps. 91:4 [b]Ps. 44:26

3 [1]Or, *close up the path against those* [a]Ps. 62:2

4 [1]Or, *soul* [a]Ps. 70:2 [b]Ps. 40:14; 129:5

5 [a]Ps. 83:13; Job 21:18; Is. 29:5

6 [a]Ps. 73:18; Jer. 23:12

7 [1]*Pit* has been transposed from line above [a]Ps. 69:4; 109:3; 140:5

8 [a]Ps. 55:23; Is. 47:11; 1 Thess. 5:3 [b]Ps. 9:15 [c]Ps. 73:18

9 [a]Is. 61:10 [b]Ps. 9:14; 13:5; Luke 1:47

10 [a]Ps. 51:8 [b]Ex. 15:11; Ps. 86:8; Mic. 7:18 [c]Ps. 18:17

13 Keep [a]your tongue from evil,
And your lips from speaking [b]deceit.
14 [a]Depart from evil, and do good;
Seek peace, and [b]pursue it.

15 The [a]eyes of the LORD are toward the righteous,
And His ears are *open* to their cry.
16 The [a]face of the LORD is against evildoers,
To [b]cut off the memory of them from the earth.
17 *The righteous* [a]cry and the LORD hears,
And delivers them out of all their troubles.
18 The LORD [a]is near to the [b]brokenhearted,
And saves those who are [1c]crushed in spirit.

19 Many are the [a]afflictions of the righteous;
But the LORD [b]delivers him out of them all.
20 He keeps all his bones;
Not one of them is broken.
21 [a]Evil shall slay the wicked;
And those who hate the righteous will be [1]condemned.
22 The LORD [a]redeems the soul of His servants;
And none of those who [b]take refuge in Him will be [1]condemned.

PSALM 35

Prayer for Rescue from Enemies.

A Psalm of David.

CONTEND, O LORD, with those who [a]contend with me;
Fight against those who [b]fight against me.
2 Take hold of [1a]buckler and shield,
And rise up for [b]my help.
3 Draw also the spear and [1]the battle-axe to meet those who pursue me;
Say to my soul, "I am [a]your salvation."
4 Let those be [a]ashamed and dishonored who seek my [1]life;
Let those be [b]turned back and humiliated who devise evil against me.
5 Let them be [a]like chaff before the wind,
With the angel of the LORD driving *them* on.
6 Let their way be dark and [a]slippery,
With the angel of the LORD pursuing them.
7 For [a]without cause they hid their net for me;
Without cause they dug a [1]pit for my soul.
8 Let [a]destruction come upon him unawares;
And [b]let the net which he hid catch himself;
Into that very [c]destruction let him fall.

9 And my soul shall [a]rejoice in the LORD;
It shall [b]exult in His salvation.
10 All my [a]bones will say, "LORD, [b]who is like Thee,
Who delivers the afflicted from him [c]who is too strong for him,

And [d]the afflicted and the needy from him who robs him?"
11 [a]Malicious witnesses rise up;
They ask me of things that I do not know.
12 They [a]repay me evil for good,
To the bereavement of my soul.
13 But as for me, [a]when they were sick, my [b]clothing was sackcloth;
I [c]humbled my soul with fasting;
And my [d]prayer kept returning to my bosom.
14 I went about as though it were my friend or brother;
I [a]bowed down [1]mourning, as one who sorrows for a mother.
15 But [a]at my [1]stumbling they rejoiced, and gathered themselves together;
The [2b]smiters whom I did not know gathered together against me,
They [3c]slandered me without ceasing.
16 Like godless jesters at a feast,
They [a]gnashed at me with their teeth.

17 Lord, [a]how long wilt Thou look on?
Rescue my soul [b]from their ravages,
My [c]only *life* from the lions.
18 I will [a]give Thee thanks in the great congregation;
I will [b]praise Thee among a mighty throng.
19 [a]Do not let those who are wrongfully [b]my enemies rejoice over me;
Neither let those [c]who hate me without cause [1d]wink maliciously.
20 For they do not speak peace,
But they devise [a]deceitful words against those who are quiet in the land.
21 And they [a]opened their mouth wide against me;
They said, "[b]Aha, aha, our eyes have seen it."

22 [a]Thou hast seen it, O LORD, [b]do not keep silent;
O Lord, [c]do not be far from me.
23 [a]Stir up Thyself, and awake to my right,
And to my cause, my God and my Lord.
24 [a]Judge me, O LORD my God, according to Thy righteousness;
And [b]do not let them rejoice over me.
25 Do not let them say in their heart, "[a]Aha, our desire!"
Do not let them say, "We have [b]swallowed him up!"
26 Let [a]those be ashamed and humiliated altogether who rejoice at my distress;
Let those be clothed with shame and dishonor who [b]magnify themselves over me.

27 Let them [a]shout for joy and rejoice, who favor [b]my vindication;
And [c]let them say continually, "The LORD be magnified,
Who [d]delights in the prosperity of His servant."

10 [d]Ps. 37:14; 109:16
11 [a]Ps. 27:12
12 [a]Ps. 38:20; 109:5; Jer. 18:20; John 10:32
13 [a]Job 30:25 [b]Ps. 69:11 [c]Ps. 69:10 [d]Matt. 10:13; Luke 10:6
14 [1]Or, *dressed in black* [a]Ps. 38:6
15 [1]Or, *limping* [2]Or, *smitten ones* [3]Lit., *tore* [a]Obad. 12 [b]Job 30:1, 8, 12 [c]Ps. 7:2
16 [a]Job 16:9; Ps. 37:12; Lam. 2:16
17 [a]Ps. 13:1; Hab. 1:13 [b]Ps. 35:7 [c]Ps. 22:20, 21
18 [a]Ps. 22:22 [b]Ps. 22:25
19 [1]Or, *wink the eye* [a]Ps. 13:4; 30:1; 38:16 [b]Ps. 38:19; 69:4; 119:78 [c]John 15:25 [d]Prov. 6:13; 10:10
20 [a]Ps. 55:21; Jer. 9:8; Mic. 6:12
21 [a]Ps. 22:13; Job 16:10 [b]Ps. 40:15; 70:3
22 [a]Ps. 10:14; Ex. 3:7 [b]Ps. 28:1 [c]Ps. 10:1; 22:11; 38:21; 71:12
23 [a]Ps. 7:6; 44:23; 59:4; 80:2
24 [a]Ps. 9:4; 26:1; 43:1 [b]Ps. 35:19
25 [a]Ps. 35:21 [b]Ps. 56:1; 124:3; Prov. 1:12; Lam. 2:16
26 [a]Ps. 40:14 [b]Ps. 38:16; Job 19:5
27 [a]Ps. 32:11 [b]Ps. 9:4 [c]Ps. 40:16; 70:4 [d]Ps. 147:11; 149:4

28 And [a]my tongue shall declare Thy righteousness
And Thy praise all day long.

Psalm 36

Wickedness of Men and Lovingkindness of God.

For the choir Director. A *Psalm* of David
the servant of the Lord.

TRANSGRESSION speaks to the ungodly within [1]his heart;
There is [a]no fear of God before his eyes.
2 For [1]it [a]flatters him in his *own* eyes,
Concerning the discovery of his iniquity *and* the hatred
of it.
3 The [a]words of his mouth are wickedness and deceit;
He has [b]ceased to [1]be wise *and* to do good.
4 He [a]plans wickedness upon his bed;
He sets himself on a [b]path that is not good;
He [c]does not despise evil.

5 Thy [a]lovingkindness, O Lord, [1]extends to the heavens,
Thy faithfulness *reaches* to the skies.
6 Thy [a]righteousness is like the [1]mountains of God;
Thy [b]judgments are *like* a great deep.
O Lord, Thou [c]preservest man and beast.
7 How [a]precious is Thy lovingkindness, O God!
And the children of men [b]take refuge in the shadow of
Thy wings.
8 They [a]drink their fill of the [1]abundance of Thy house;
And Thou dost give them to drink of the [b]river of Thy
delights.
9 For with Thee is the [a]fountain of life;
In Thy light we see light.

10 O continue Thy lovingkindness to [a]those who know
Thee,
And Thy [b]righteousness to the upright in heart.
11 Let not the foot of pride come upon me,
And let not the hand of the wicked drive me away.
12 There the doers of iniquity have fallen;
They have been thrust down and [a]cannot rise.

Psalm 37

Security of Those Who Trust in the Lord, and Insecurity of the Wicked.

[a] A *Psalm* of David.

FRET not yourself because of evildoers,
Be not [b]envious toward wrongdoers.
2 For they will [a]wither quickly like the grass,
And [b]fade like the green herb.
3 [a]Trust in the Lord, and do good;
[b]Dwell in the land and [1c]cultivate faithfulness.
4 [a]Delight yourself in the Lord;
And He will [b]give you the desires of your heart.
5 [a]Commit your way to the Lord,
Trust also in Him, and He will do it.

28 [a]Ps. 51:14; 71:15, 24

1 [1]Another reading is, *my heart* [a]Rom. 3:18

2 [1]Or, *he flatters himself* [a]Deut. 29:19; Ps. 10:11; 49:18

3 [1]Or, *understand to do good* [a]Ps. 10:7; 12:2 [b]Ps. 94:8; Jer. 4:22

4 [a]Prov. 4:16; Mic. 2:1 [b]Is. 65:2 [c]Ps. 52:3; Rom. 12:9

5 [1]Lit., *is in* [a]Ps. 57:10; 103:11; 108:4

6 [1]Or, *mighty mountains* [a]Ps. 71:19 [b]Ps. 77:19; Job 11:8; Rom 11:33 [c]Ps. 104:14, 15; 145:16; Neh. 9:6

7 [a]Ps. 40:5; 139:17 [b]Ps. 57:1; 91:4; Ruth 2:12

8 [1]Lit., *fatness* [a]Ps. 63:5; Is. 25:6; Jer. 31:12-14 [b]Ps. 46:4; Job 20:17; Rev. 22:1

9 [a]Jer. 2:13

10 [a]Jer 22:16 [b]Ps. 24:5

12 [a]Ps. 140:10; Is. 26:14

1 [a]Prov. 23:17; 24:19 [b]Ps. 73:3; Prov. 3:31

2 [a]Job 14:2; Ps. 90:6; 92:7 [b]Ps. 129:6

3 [1]Or, *feed securely;* or, *feed on His faithfulness* [a]Ps. 62:8 [b]Deut. 30:20 [c]Is. 40:11; Ezek. 34:13, 14

4 [a]Ps. 94:19; Job 22:26; Is. 58:14 [b]Ps. 21:2; 145:19; Matt. 7:7, 8

5 [a]Ps. 55:22; Prov. 16:3; 1 Pet. 5:7

6 And He will bring forth [a]your righteousness as the light,
And your judgment [b]as the noonday.

7 [1][a]Rest in the LORD and [b]wait [2]patiently for Him;
[c]Fret not yourself because of him who [d]prospers in his way,
Because of the man who carries out wicked schemes.
8 Cease from anger, and [a]forsake wrath;
Fret not yourself, *it leads* only to evildoing.
9 For [a]evildoers will be cut off,
But those who wait for the LORD, they will [b]inherit the land.
10 Yet [a]a little while and the wicked man will be no more;
And you will look carefully for [b]his place, and he will not be *there*.
11 But [a]the humble will inherit the land,
And will delight themselves in [b]abundant prosperity.

12 The wicked [a]plots against the righteous,
And [b]gnashes at him with his teeth.
13 The LORD [a]laughs at him;
For He sees [b]his day is coming.
14 The wicked have drawn the sword and [a]bent their bow,
To cast down the [b]afflicted and the needy,
To [c]slay those who are upright in conduct.
15 Their sword will enter their own heart,
And their [a]bows will be broken.

16 [a]Better is the little of the righteous
Than the abundance of many wicked.
17 For the [a]arms of the wicked will be broken;
But the LORD [b]sustains the righteous.
18 The LORD [a]knows the days of the [1]blameless;
And their [b]inheritance will be forever.
19 They will not be ashamed in the time of evil;
And [a]in the days of famine they will have abundance.
20 But the [a]wicked will perish;
And the enemies of the LORD will be [b]like the [1]glory of the pastures,
They vanish—[c]like smoke they vanish away.
21 The wicked borrows and does not pay back,
But the righteous [a]is gracious and gives.
22 For those blessed by Him will [a]inherit the land;
But those [b]cursed by Him will be cut off.

23 [a]The steps of a man are established by the LORD;
And He [b]delights in his way.
24 When [a]he falls, he shall not be hurled headlong;
Because [b]the LORD is the One [1]who holds his hand.
25 I have been young, and now I am old;
Yet [a]I have not seen the righteous forsaken,
Or [b]his [1]descendants begging bread.
26 All day long [a]he is gracious and lends;
And [b]his [1]descendants are a blessing.

27 [a]Depart from evil, and do good,
[1]So you will abide [b]forever.

6 [a]Ps. 97:11; Is. 58:8, 10; Mic. 7:9 [b]Job 11:17

7 [1]Or, *Be still* [2]Or, *longingly*
[a]Ps. 62:5 [b]Ps. 40:1 [c]Ps. 37:1, 8 [d]Jer. 12:1

8 [a]Eph. 4:31; Col. 3:8

9 [a]Ps. 37:2, 22 [b]Ps. 25:13; Prov. 2:21; Is. 60:21

10 [a]Job 24:24 [b]Ps. 37:35, 36; Job 7:10

11 [a]Matt. 5:5 [b]Ps. 72:7

12 [a]Ps. 31:13, 20 [b]Ps. 35:16

13 [a]Ps. 2:4 [b]1 Sam. 26:10; Job 18:20

14 [a]Ps. 11:2; Lam. 2:4 [b]Ps. 35:10; 86:1 [c]Ps. 11:2

15 [a]Ps. 46:9; 1 Sam. 2:4

16 [a]Ps. 4:7; Prov. 15:16; 16:8

17 [a]Ps. 10:15; Job 38:15; Ezek. 30:21 [b]Ps. 71:6; 145:14

18 [1]Lit., *complete*; or, *perfect*
[a]Ps. 1:6; 31:7 [b]Ps. 37:27, 29

19 [a]Ps. 33:19; Job 5:20

20 [1]I.e., flowers
[a]Ps. 73:27 [b]Lev. 3:11 [c]Ps. 68:2; 102:3

21 [a]Ps. 112:5

22 [a]Ps. 37:9 [b]Job 5:3

23 [a]Ps. 40:2; 66:9; 119:5; 1 Sam. 2:9 [b]Ps. 147:11

24 [1]Or, *who sustains him with His hand*
[a]Ps. 145:14; Prov. 24:16; Mic. 7:8 [b]Ps. 147:6

25 [1]Lit., *seed*
[a]Ps. 37:28; Is. 41:17; Heb. 13:5 [b]Ps. 109:10

26 [1]Lit., *seed*
[a]Ps. 37:21 [b]Ps. 147:13

27 [1]Or, *And dwell forever*
[a]Ps. 34:14 [b]Ps. 37:18; 102:28

28 [1]Lit., *judgment* [a]Ps. 11:7; 33:5 [b]Ps. 37:25 [c]Ps. 31:23 [d]Ps. 37:9; Ps. 21:10; Prov. 2:22; Is. 14:20

29 [a]Ps. 37:9 [b]Ps. 37:18

30 [a]Ps. 49:3; Prov. 10:13 [b]Ps. 101:1; 119:13

31 [a]Ps. 40:8; 119:11; Deut. 6:6; Is. 51:7; Jer. 31:33 [b]Ps. 37:23; 26:1

32 [a]Ps. 10:8; 17:11 [b]Ps. 37:14

33 [a]Ps. 31:8; 2 Pet. 2:9 [b]Ps. 34:22; 109:31

34 [a]Ps. 37:9; 27:14 [b]Ps. 52:5, 6; 91:8

35 [1]Lit., *native,* Heb., *obscure* [a]Job 5:3; Jer. 12:2 [b]Job 8:16

36 [1]Ancient versions read, *I passed by* [a]Ps. 37:10; Job 20:5

37 [1]Lit., *complete;* or, *perfect* [2]Lit., *end* [a]Ps. 37:18 [b]Ps. 7:10 [c]Is. 57:1, 2

38 [1]Lit., *end* [a]Ps. 37:20, 28 [b]Ps. 37:9; 73:17

39 [a]Ps. 3:8; 62:1 [b]Ps. 37:19; 9:9

40 [a]Ps. 54:4 [b]Ps. 22:4; Dan. 3:17; 6:23 [c]Ps. 34:22

1 [a]Ps. 6:1

2 [a]Job 6:4 [b]Ps. 32:4

3 [a]Is. 1:6 [b]Ps. 102:10 [c]Ps. 6:2; 31:10; Job 33:19

4 [a]Ps. 40:12; Ezra 9:6

5 [1]Or, *stripes* [a]Ps. 69:5

6 [a]Ps. 35:14 [b]Ps. 42:9; 43:2; Job 30:28

7 [a]Ps. 102:3 [b]Ps. 38:3

8 [1]Or, *greatly* [2]Lit., *roar* [3]Lit., *growling* [a]Lam. 1:13; 5:17 [b]Ps. 22:1; 32:3; Job 3:24

28 For the LORD [a]loves [1]justice,
And [b]does not forsake His godly ones;
They are [c]preserved forever;
But the [d]seed of the wicked will be cut off.
29 The righteous will [a]inherit the land,
And [b]dwell in it forever.
30 The mouth of the righteous [a]utters wisdom,
And his tongue [b]speaks justice.
31 The [a]Law of his God is in his heart;
His [b]steps do not slip.
32 The [a]wicked spies upon the righteous,
And [b]seeks to kill him.
33 The LORD will [a]not leave him in his hand,
Or [b]let him be condemned when he is judged.
34 [a]Wait for the LORD, and keep His way,
And He will exalt you to inherit the land;
When the [b]wicked are cut off, you will see it.

35 I have [a]seen a violent, wicked man
Spreading himself like a [b]luxuriant [1]tree in its native soil.
36 Then [1]he passed away, and lo, he [a]was no more;
I sought for him, but he could not be found.
37 Mark the [1a]blameless man, and behold the [b]upright;
For the man of peace will have a [2c]posterity.
38 But transgressors will be altogether [a]destroyed;
The [1]posterity of the wicked will be [b]cut off.
39 But the [a]salvation of the righteous is from the LORD;
He is their strength [b]in time of trouble.
40 And [a]the LORD helps them, and delivers them;
He [b]delivers them from the wicked, and saves them,
Because they [c]take refuge in Him.

PSALM 38

Prayer of a Suffering Penitent.

A Psalm of David, for a memorial.

O LORD, [a]rebuke me not in Thy wrath;
And chasten me not in Thy burning anger.
2 For Thine [a]arrows have sunk deep into me,
And [b]Thy hand has pressed down on me.
3 There is [a]no soundness in my flesh [b]because of Thine indignation;
There is no health [c]in my bones because of my sin.
4 For my [a]iniquities are gone over my head;
As a heavy burden they weigh too much for me.
5 My [1]wounds grow foul *and* fester.
Because of [a]my folly,
6 I am bent over and [a]greatly bowed down;
I [b]go mourning all day long.
7 For my loins are filled with [a]burning;
And there is [b]no soundness in my flesh.
8 I am [a]benumbed and [1]badly crushed;
I [2b]groan because of the [3]agitation of my heart.

9 Lord, all [a]my desire is [1]before Thee;
And my [b]sighing is not hidden from Thee.
10 My heart throbs, [a]my strength fails me;
And the [b]light of my eyes, even [1]that [2]has gone from me.
11 My [1a]loved ones and my friends stand aloof from my plague;
And my kinsmen [b]stand afar off.
12 Those who [a]seek my life [b]lay snares *for me;*
And those who [c]seek to injure me have [1d]threatened destruction,
And they [e]devise treachery all day long.

13 But I, like a deaf man, do not hear;
And I am like a [a]dumb man who does not open his mouth.
14 Yes, I am like a man who does not hear,
And in whose mouth are no arguments.
15 For [a]I [1]hope in Thee, O LORD;
Thou [b]wilt answer, O Lord my God.
16 For I said, "May they not rejoice over me,
Who, when my foot slips, [a]would magnify themselves against me."
17 For I am [a]ready to fall,
And [b]my [1]sorrow is continually before me.
18 For I [1a]confess my iniquity;
I am full of [b]anxiety because of my sin.
19 But my [a]enemies are vigorous *and* [1]strong;
And many are those who [b]hate me wrongfully.
20 And those who [a]repay evil for good,
They [b]oppose me, because I follow what is good.
21 Do not forsake me, O LORD;
O my God, [a]do not be far from me!
22 Make [a]haste to help me,
O Lord, [b]my salvation!

PSALM 39

The Vanity of Life.

For the choir director, for [£]Jeduthun.
A Psalm of David.

I SAID, "I will [a]guard my ways,
That I [b]may not sin with my tongue;
I will guard [c]my mouth as with a muzzle,
While the wicked are in my presence."
2 I was [a]dumb [1]*and* silent,
I [2]refrained *even* from good;
And my [3]sorrow grew worse.
3 My [a]heart was hot within me;
While I was musing the fire burned;
Then I spoke with my tongue:
4 "LORD, make me to know [a]my end,
And what is the extent of my days,
Let me know how [b]transient I am.
5 "Behold, Thou hast made [a]my days *as* handbreadths,

9 [1]Or, known *to Thee*
[a]Ps. 10:17 [b]Ps. 6:6; 102:5

10 [1]Lit., *they* [2]Lit., *is not with me*
[a]Ps. 31:10 [b]Ps. 6:7; 69:3; 88:9

11 [1]Or, *lovers*
[a]Ps. 31:11; 88:18 [b]Luke 23:49

12 [1]Lit., *spoken*
[a]Ps. 54:3 [b]Ps. 140:5 [c]Ps. 35:4 [d]Eccles. 10:13; Mic. 7:3 [e]Ps. 35:20

13 [a]Ps. 39:2, 9

15 [1]Or, *wait for*
[a]Ps. 39:7 [b]Ps. 17:6

16 [a]Ps. 35:26

17 [1]Lit., *pain*
[a]Ps. 35:15 [b]Ps. 13:2

18 [1]Or, *declare*
[a]Ps. 32:5 [b]2 Cor. 7:9, 10

19 [1]Or, *numerous*
[a]Ps. 18:17 [b]Ps. 35:19

20 [a]Ps. 35:12 [b]Ps. 109:4; 1 John 3:12

21 [a]Ps. 22:19; 35:22

22 [a]Ps. 40:13, 17 [b]Ps. 27:1

[£]1 Chr. 16:41

1 [a]Ps. 119:9; 1 Kin. 2:4; 2 Kin. 10:31 [b]Ps. 34:13; Job 2:10; James 3:5-12 [c]Ps. 141:3; James 3:2

2 [1]Lit., *with silence* [2]Lit., *kept silence* [3]Lit., *pain*
[a]Ps. 38:13

3 [a]Ps. 32:4; Jer. 20:9; Luke 24:32

4 [a]Ps. 90:12; 119:84; Job 6:11 [b]Ps. 78:39; 103:14

5 [a]Ps. 89:47

And my [b]lifetime as nothing in Thy sight,
Surely every man [1]at his best is [2]a mere [c]breath. [[3]Selah.
6 "Surely every man [a]walks about as a [1]phantom;
Surely they make an [b]uproar for nothing;
He [c]amasses *riches,* and does not know who will gather them.

7 "And now, Lord, for what do I wait?
My [a]hope is in Thee.
8 "[a]Deliver me from all my transgressions;
Make me not the [b]reproach of the foolish.
9 "I have become [a]dumb, I do not open my mouth,
Because it is [b]Thou who hast done *it.*
10 "[a]Remove Thy plague from me;
Because of [b]the opposition of Thy hand, I am [1]perishing.
11 "With [a]reproofs Thou dost chasten a man for iniquity;
Thou dost [b]consume as a moth what is precious to him;
Surely [c]every man is a mere breath. [Selah.

12 "[a]Hear my prayer, O LORD, and give ear to my cry;
Do not be silent [b]at my tears;
For I am [c]a stranger with Thee,
A sojourner like all my fathers.
13 "[a]Turn Thy gaze away from me, that I may [1]smile *again,*
Before I depart and am no more."

PSALM 40

God Sustains His Servant.

For the choir director. A Psalm of David.

I [a]WAITED [1]patiently for the LORD;
And He inclined to me, and [b]heard my cry.
2 He brought me up out of the [a]pit of destruction, out of the [1]miry clay;
And [b]He set my feet upon a rock [c]making my footsteps firm.
3 And He put a [a]new song in my mouth, a song of praise to our God;
Many will [b]see and fear,
And will trust in the LORD.

4 How [a]blessed is the man who has made the LORD his trust,
And [b]has not [1]turned to the proud, nor to those who [c]lapse into falsehood.
5 Many, O LORD my God, are [a]the wonders which Thou hast done,
And Thy [b]thoughts toward us;
There is none to compare with Thee;
If I would declare and speak of them,
They [c]would be too numerous to count.

6 [1a]Sacrifice and meal offering Thou hast not desired;
My ears Thou hast [2]opened;
Burnt offering and sin offering Thou hast not required.

---

5 [1]Lit., *standing firm* [2]Or, *altogether vanity* [3]*Selah* may mean: *Pause, Crescendo* or *Musical interlude*
[b]Ps. 144:4 [c]Ps. 62:9; Job 14:2; Eccles. 6:12

6 [1]Lit., *image*
[a]1 Cor. 7:31; James 1:10, 11; 1 Pet. 1:24 [b]Ps. 127:2; Eccles. 5:17 [c]Ps. 49:10; Eccles. 2:26; 5:14; Luke 12:20

7 [a]Ps. 38:15

8 [a]Ps. 51:9, 14; 79:9 [b]Ps. 44:13; 79:4; 119:22

9 [a]Ps. 39:2 [b]2 Sam. 16:10; Job 2:10

10 [1]Or, *wasting away*
[a]Job 9:34; 13:21 [b]Ps. 32:4

11 [a]Ezek. 5:15; 2 Pet. 2:16 [b]Ps. 90:7; Job 13:28; Is. 50:9 [c]Ps. 39:5

12 [a]Ps. 102:1; 143:1 [b]Ps. 56:8; 2 Kin. 20:5 [c]Lev. 25:23; 1 Chr. 29:15; Ps. 119:19; Heb. 11:13; 1 Pet. 2:11

13 [1]Or, *become cheerful*
[a]Ps. 102:24; Job 7:19; 14:6

1 [1]Or, *intently*
[a]Ps. 25:5; 27:14; 37:7 [b]Ps. 34:15

2 [1]Lit., *mud of the mire*
[a]Ps. 69:2; Jer. 38:6 [b]Ps. 27:5 [c]Ps. 37:23

3 [a]Ps. 32:7; 33:3 [b]Ps. 52:6; 64:9

4 [1]Lit., *regard*
[a]Ps. 84:12 [b]Job 37:24 [c]Ps. 125:5

5 [a]Ps. 136:4; Job 5:9 [b]Ps. 139:17; Is. 55:8 [c]Ps. 71:15; 139:18

6 [1]I.e., Blood sacrifice [2]Lit., *dug,* or possibly, *pierced*
[a]Ps. 51:16; 1 Sam. 15:22; Is. 1:11; Jer. 6:20; 7:22, 23; Amos 5:22; Mic. 6:6-8; Heb. 10:5-7

7 Then I said, "Behold, I come;
In the scroll of the book it is [1]written of me;
8 I delight to do Thy will, O my God;
[a]Thy Law is within my heart."

9 I have [a]proclaimed glad tidings of righteousness in the great congregation;
Behold, I will [b]not restrain my lips,
O LORD, [c]Thou knowest.
10 I have [a]not hidden Thy righteousness within my heart;
I have [b]spoken of Thy faithfulness and Thy salvation;
I have not concealed Thy lovingkindness and Thy truth from the great congregation.

11 Thou, O LORD, wilt not withhold Thy compassion from me;
[1]Thy [a]lovingkindness and Thy truth will continually preserve me.
12 For evils beyond number have [a]surrounded me;
My [b]iniquities have overtaken me, so that I am not able to see;
They are [c]more numerous than the hairs of my head;
And my [d]heart has [1]failed me.

13 Be pleased, O LORD, to deliver me;
Make [a]haste, O LORD, to help me.
14 Let those be [a]ashamed and humiliated together
Who [b]seek my [1]life to destroy it;
Let those be turned back and dishonored
Who delight [2]in my hurt.
15 Let those [a]be [1]appalled because of their shame
Who [b]say to me, "Aha, aha."
16 Let all who seek Thee rejoice and be glad in Thee;
Let those who love Thy salvation [a]say continually,
"The LORD be magnified!"
17 Since [a]I am afflicted and needy,
[1b]Let the Lord be mindful of me;
Thou art my help and my deliverer;
Do not delay, O my God.

PSALM 41

The Psalmist in Sickness Complains of Enemies and False Friends.

For the choir director. A Psalm of David.

HOW blessed is he who [a]considers the [1]helpless;
The LORD will deliver him [b]in a day of [2]trouble.
2 The LORD will [a]protect him, and keep him alive,
And he shall [1]be called [b]blessed upon the earth;
And [c]do not give him over to the desire of his enemies.
3 The LORD will sustain him upon his [a]sickbed;
In his illness, Thou dost [1]restore him to health.

4 As for me, I said, "O LORD, be gracious to me;
[a]Heal my soul, for [b]I have sinned against Thee."

7 [1]Or, *prescribed for*

8 [a]Ps. 37:31; 2 Cor. 3:3

9 [a]Ps. 22:25 [b]Ps. 119:13 [c]Ps. 139:4; Josh. 22:22

10 [a]Acts 20:20, 27 [b]Ps. 89:1

11 [1]Or, *May . . . preserve* [a]Ps. 43:3; 57:3; 61:7; Prov. 20:28

12 [1]Lit., *forsaken* [a]Ps. 18:5; 116:3 [b]Ps. 38:4; 65:3 [c]Ps. 69:4 [d]Ps. 73:26

13 [a]Ps. 22:19; 71:12

14 [1]Or, *soul* [2]Or, *to injure me* [a]Ps. 35:4, 26; 70:2; 71:13 [b]Ps. 63:9

15 [1]Or, *desolated* [a]Ps. 70:3 [b]Ps. 35:21; 70:3

16 [a]Ps. 35:27

17 [1]Or, *The Lord is mindful* [a]Ps. 70:5; 86:1; 109:22 [b]Ps. 40:5; 1 Pet. 5:7

1 [1]Or, *poor* [2]Or, *evil* [a]Ps. 82:3, 4; Prov. 14:21 [b]Ps. 27:5; 37:19

2 [1]Or, *be blessed* [a]Ps. 37:28 [b]Ps. 37:22 [c]Ps. 27:12

3 [1]Lit., *dost turn all his bed* [a]Ps. 6:6

4 [a]Ps. 6:2; 103:3; 147:3 [b]Ps. 51:4

5 My enemies [a]speak evil against me,
"When will he die, and his name perish?"
6 And [1]when he comes to see *me*, he [a]speaks [2]falsehood;
His heart gathers wickedness to itself;
When he goes outside, he tells it.
7 All who hate me whisper together against me;
Against me they [a]devise my hurt, *saying*
8 "A wicked thing is poured out [1]upon him,
That when he lies down, he will [a]not rise up again."
9 Even my [a]close friend, in whom I trusted,
Who ate my bread,
Has lifted up his heel against me.

10 But Thou, O LORD, be gracious to me, and [a]raise me up,
That I may repay them.
11 By this I know that [a]Thou art pleased with me,
Because [b]my enemy does not shout in triumph over me.
12 As for me, [a]Thou dost uphold me in my integrity,
And Thou dost set me [b]in Thy presence forever.

13 [a]Blessed be the LORD, the God of Israel,
From everlasting to everlasting.
Amen, and Amen.

BOOK 2

PSALM 42

Thirsting for God in Trouble and Exile.

For the choir director. A [£]Maskil of the sons of Korah.

As the deer [1]pants for the water brooks,
So my soul [1a]pants for Thee, O God.
2 My soul [a]thirsts for God, for the [b]living God;
When shall I come and [1c]appear before God?
3 My [a]tears have been my food day and night,
While *they* [b]say to me all day long, "Where is your God?"
4 These things I remember, and I [a]pour out my soul within me.
For I [b]used to go along with the throng *and* [1]lead them in procession to the house of God,
With the voice of [c]joy and thanksgiving, a multitude keeping festival.

5 Why are you [1a]in despair, O my soul?
And *why* have you become [b]disturbed within me?
[2c]Hope in God, for I shall [3]again praise [4]Him
For the [5d]help of His presence.
6 O my God, my soul is [1]in despair within me;
Therefore I [a]remember Thee from [b]the land of the Jordan,
And the [2]peaks of [c]Hermon, from Mount Mizar.

---

5 [a]Ps. 38:12

6 [1]Or, *if he* [2]Or, *emptiness* [a]Ps. 12:2; 62:4; Prov. 26:24-26

7 [a]Ps. 56:5

8 [1]Or, *within* [a]Ps. 71:10, 11

9 [a]Job 19:13, 19; Ps. 55:12, 13, 20; Jer. 20:10; Mic. 7:5; John 13:18

10 [a]Ps. 3:3

11 [a]Ps. 37:23; 147:11 [b]Ps. 25:2

12 [a]Ps. 18:32; 37:17; 63:8 [b]Ps. 21:6; Job 36:7

13 [a]Ps. 72:18, 19; 89:52; 106:48; 150:6

[£] Possibly, *Contemplative*, or *Didactic*, or *Skillful Psalm*

1 [1]Lit., *longs for* [a]Ps. 119:131

2 [1]Some mss. read, *see the face of God* [a]Ps. 63:1; 84:2; 143:6 [b]Ps. 84:2; Josh. 3:10; Jer. 10:10; Dan. 6:26; Matt. 26:63; Rom. 9:26; 1 Thess. 1:9 [c]Ps. 43:4; 84:7; Ex. 23:17

3 [a]Ps. 80:5; 102:9 [b]Ps. 79:10; 115:2; Joel 2:17; Mic. 7:10

4 [1]Or, *move slowly with them* [a]Ps. 62:8; 1 Sam. 1:15; Job 30:16; Lam. 2:19 [b]Ps. 55:14; 122:1; Is. 30:29 [c]Ps. 100:4

5 [1]Or, *sunk down* [2]Or, *Wait for* [3]Or, *still* [4]Some ancient versions read, *Him, the help of my countenance and my God* [5]Or, *saving acts of* [a]Ps. 38:6; Matt. 26:38 [b]Ps. 77:3 [c]Ps. 71:14; Lam. 3:24 [d]Ps. 44:3

6 [1]Or, *sunk down* [2]Lit., *Hermons* [a]Ps. 61:2 [b]2 Sam. 17:22 [c]Deut. 3:8

7 Deep calls to deep at the sound of Thy waterfalls;
All Thy [a]breakers and Thy waves have rolled over me.
8 The LORD will [a]command His lovingkindness in the daytime;
And His song will be with me [b]in the night,
A prayer to [c]the God of my life.

9 I will say to God [a]my rock, "Why hast Thou forgotten me?
Why do I go [b]mourning [1]because of the [c]oppression of the enemy?"
10 As a shattering of my bones, my adversaries revile me,
While they [a]say to me all day long, "Where is your God?"
11 Why are you [1a]in despair, O my soul?
And why have you become disturbed within me?
[2]Hope in God, for I shall yet praise Him,
The [3]help of my countenance, and my God.

PSALM 43

Prayer for Deliverance.

[a]VINDICATE me, O God, and [b]plead my case against an ungodly nation;
[1]O deliver me from [c]the deceitful and unjust man!
2 For Thou art the [a]God of my strength; why hast Thou [b]rejected me?
Why do I go [c]mourning [1]because of the oppression of the enemy?

3 O send out Thy [a]light and Thy truth, let them lead me;
Let them bring me to Thy [b]holy hill,
And to Thy [c]dwelling places.
4 Then I will go to [a]the altar of God,
To God [1]my exceeding [b]joy;
And upon the [c]lyre I shall praise Thee, O God, my God.

5 Why are you [1a]in despair, O my soul?
And why are you disturbed within me?
[2]Hope in God, for I shall [3]again praise Him,
The [4]help of my countenance, and my God.

PSALM 44

Former Deliverances and Present Troubles.

For the choir director. A [£]Maskil of the sons of Korah.

O GOD, we have heard with our ears,
Our [a]fathers have told us,
The [b]work that Thou didst in their days,
In the [c]days of old.

7 [a]Ps. 69:1, 2; 88:7; Jonah 2:3

8 [a]Ps. 57:3; 133:3 [b]Ps. 16:7; 63:6; 77:6; 149:5; Job 35:10 [c]Eccles. 5:18; 8:15

9 [1]Or, *while the enemy oppresses* [a]Ps. 18:2 [b]Ps. 38:6 [c]Ps. 17:9

10 [a]Ps. 42:3

11 [1]Or, *sunk down* [2]Or, *Wait for* [3]Or, *saving acts of* [a]Ps. 42:5

1 [1]Or, *Mayest Thou* [a]Ps. 26:1; 35:24 [b]1 Sam. 24:15 [c]Ps. 5:6; 38:12

2 [1]Or, *while the enemy oppresses* [a]Ps. 18:1; 28:7; 31:4 [b]Ps. 44:9; 88:14 [c]Ps. 42:9

3 [a]Ps. 36:9 [b]Ps. 2:6; 42:4; 46:4 [c]Ps. 84:1

4 [1]Lit., *the gladness of my joy* [a]Ps. 26:6 [b]Ps. 21:6 [c]Ps. 33:2; 49:4; 57:8; 71:22

5 [1]Or, *sunk down* [2]Or, *Wait for* [3]Or, *still* [4]Or, *saving acts of* [a]Ps. 42:11

[£]Possibly, *Contemplative*, or *Didactic*, or *Skillful Psalm*

1 [a]Ps. 78:3; Ex. 12:26, 27; Deut. 6:20; Judg. 6:13 [b]Ps. 78:12 [c]Ps. 77:5; Deut. 32:7; Is. 51:9; 63:9

2 [a]Ps. 78:55; 80:8; Josh. 3:10; Neh. 9:24 [b]Ex. 15:17; 2 Sam. 7:10; Jer. 24:6; Amos 9:15 [c]Ps. 135:10-12 [d]Ps. 80:9-11; Zech. 2:6

3 [a]Josh. 24:12 [b]Ps. 77:15 [c]Ps. 4:6; 89:15 [d]Ps. 106:4; Deut. 4:37; 7:7, 8; 10:15

4 [1]Lit., *salvation* [a]Ps. 74:12 [b]Ps. 42:8

5 [a]Ps. 60:12; Deut. 33:17; Dan. 8:4 [b]Ps. 108:13; Zech. 10:5

6 [a]Ps. 33:16; 1 Sam. 17:47; Hos. 1:7

7 [a]Ps. 136:24 [b]Ps. 53:5

8 [1]*Selah* may mean: *Pause, Crescendo* or *Musical interlude* [a]Ps. 34:2 [b]Ps. 30:12

9 [a]Ps. 43:2; 60:1, 10; 74:1; 89:38; 108:11 [b]Ps. 69:19 [c]Ps. 60:10; 108:11

10 [a]Ps. 89:43; Lev. 26:17; Josh. 7:8, 12 [b]Ps. 89:41

11 [1]Lit., *for food* [a]Ps. 44:22 [b]Ps. 106:27; Lev. 26:33; Deut. 4:27; 28:64; Ezek. 20:23

12 [1]Lit., *for no wealth* [2]Or, *set a high price on them* [a]Deut. 32:30; Judg. 2:14; 3:8; Jer. 15:13

13 [a]Ps. 79:4; 89:41 [b]Ps. 80:6; Ezek. 23:32

14 [1]Lit., *shaking of the head* [a]Ps. 69:11; Job 17:6; Jer. 24:9 [b]Ps. 109:25; 2 Kin. 19:21

15 [1]Lit., *the shame of my face has covered me* [a]Ps. 69:7; 2 Chr. 32:21

16 [a]Ps. 74:10 [b]Ps. 8:2

17 [a]Ps. 78:7; 119:61, 83, 109, 141, 153, 176 [b]Ps. 78:57

18 [a]Ps. 78:57 [b]Ps. 119:51, 157; Job 23:11

19 [a]Ps. 51:8; 94:5 [b]Job 30:29; Is. 13:22; Jer. 9:11 [c]Job 3:5

20 [1]Lit., *palms* [a]Ps. 78:11 [b]Ps. 81:9

21 [a]Ps. 139:1, 2; Jer. 17:10

2 Thou with Thine own hand didst [a]drive out the nations;
Then Thou didst [b]plant them;
Thou didst [c]afflict the peoples,
Then Thou didst [d]spread them abroad.
3 For by their own sword they [a]did not possess the land;
And their own arm did not save them;
But Thy right hand, and Thine [b]arm, and the [c]light of Thy presence,
For Thou didst [d]favor them.

4 Thou art [a]my King, O God;
[b]Command [1]victories for Jacob.
5 Through Thee we will [a]push back our adversaries;
Through Thy name we will [b]trample down those who rise up against us.
6 For I will [a]not trust in my bow,
Nor will my sword save me.
7 But Thou [a]hast saved us from our adversaries,
And Thou hast [b]put to shame those who hate us.
8 In God we have [a]boasted all day long,
And we will [b]give thanks to Thy name forever. [[1]Selah.

9 Yet Thou [a]hast rejected *us* and brought us to [b]dishonor,
And [c]dost not go out with our armies.
10 Thou dost cause us to [a]turn back from the adversary;
And those who hate us [b]have taken spoil for themselves.
11 Thou dost give us as [a]sheep [1]to be eaten,
And hast [b]scattered us among the nations.
12 Thou dost [a]sell Thy people [1]cheaply,
And hast not [2]profited by their sale.
13 Thou dost make us a [a]reproach to our neighbors,
A scoffing and a [b]derision to those around us.
14 Thou dost make us [a]a byword among the nations,
A [1b]laughingstock among the peoples.
15 All day long my dishonor is before me,
And [1]my [a]humiliation has overwhelmed me,
16 Because of the voice of him who [a]reproaches and reviles,
Because of the presence of the [b]enemy and the avenger.

17 All this has come upon us, but we have [a]not forgotten Thee,
And we have not [b]dealt falsely with Thy covenant.
18 Our heart has not [a]turned back,
And our steps [b]have not deviated from Thy way,
19 Yet Thou hast [a]crushed us in a place of [b]jackals,
And covered us with [c]the shadow of death.

20 If we had [a]forgotten the name of our God,
Or extended our [1]hands to [b]a strange god;
21 Would not God [a]find this out?
For He knows the secrets of the heart.

22 But [a]for Thy sake we are killed all day long;
We are considered as [b]sheep to be slaughtered.
23 [a]Arouse Thyself, why [b]dost Thou sleep, O Lord?
Awake, [c]do not reject us forever.
24 Why dost Thou [a]hide Thy face,
And [b]forget our affliction and our oppression?
25 For our [a]soul has sunk down into the dust;
Our body cleaves to the earth.
26 [a]Rise up, be our help,
And [b]redeem us for the sake of Thy lovingkindness.

Psalm 45

A Song Celebrating the King's Marriage.

For the choir director; according to the [£]Shoshannim. A •Maskil of the sons of Korah. A Song of Love.

My heart [1]overflows with a good theme;
I [2]address my [3]verses to the [4]King;
My tongue is the pen of [a]a ready writer.
2 Thou art fairer than the sons of men;
Grace is poured [1]upon Thy lips;
Therefore God has [a]blessed Thee forever.

3 Gird Thy sword on *Thy* thigh, O [1a]Mighty One,
In Thy splendor and Thy majesty!
4 And in Thy majesty ride on victoriously,
For the cause of truth and [a]meekness *and* righteousness;
Let Thy [b]right hand teach Thee [1]awesome things.
5 Thy [a]arrows are sharp;
The [b]peoples fall under Thee;
Thy arrows are [c]in the heart of the King's enemies.

6 [a]Thy throne, O God, is forever and ever;
A scepter of [b]uprightness is the scepter of Thy kingdom.
7 Thou hast [a]loved righteousness, and hated wickedness;
Therefore God, Thy God, has [b]anointed Thee
With the oil of joy above Thy fellows.
8 All Thy garments are fragrant with [a]myrrh and aloes *and* cassia;
Out of ivory palaces [b]stringed instruments have made Thee glad.
9 Kings' daughters are among [a]Thy noble ladies;
At Thy [b]right hand stands the queen in [c]gold from Ophir.

10 Listen, O daughter, give attention and incline your ear;
[a]Forget your people and your father's house;
11 Then the King will desire your beauty;
Because He is your [a]Lord, [b]bow down to Him.
12 And the daughter of [a]Tyre *will come* with a gift;
The [b]rich among the people will entreat your favor.

22 [a]Rom. 8:36 [b]Is. 53:7; Jer. 12:3

23 [a]Ps. 7:6 [b]Ps. 78:65 [c]Ps. 77:7

24 [a]Ps. 88:14; Job 13:24 [b]Ps. 42:9; Lam. 5:20

25 [a]Ps. 119:25

26 [a]Ps. 35:2 [b]Ps. 6:4; 25:22

[£] Or possibly, *Lilies*
• Possibly, *Contemplative*, or *Didactic*, or *Skillful Psalm*

1 [1]Lit., *is astir* [2]Lit., *am saying* [3]Lit., *works* [4]Probably refers to Solomon as a type of Christ.
[a]Ezra 7:6

2 [1]Or, *through*
[a]Ps. 21:6

3 [1]Or, *warrior*
[a]Is. 9:6

4 [1]Or, *fearful*
[a]Zeph. 2:3 [b]Ps. 21:8

5 [a]Ps. 18:14; 120:4; Is. 5:28; 7:13 [b]Ps. 92:9 [c]2 Sam. 18:14

6 [a]Ps. 93:2; Heb. 1:8, 9 [b]Ps. 98:9

7 [a]Ps. 11:7; 33:5 [b]Ps. 2:2

8 [a]Song of Sol. 4:14; John 19:39 [b]Ps. 150:4

9 [a]Song of Sol. 6:8 [b]1 Kin. 2:19 [c]1 Kin. 9:28; Is. 13:12

10 [a]Deut. 21:13; Ruth 1:16, 17

11 [a]Gen. 18:12; 1 Pet. 3:6 [b]Eph. 5:33

12 [a]Ps. 87:4 [b]Ps. 22:29; 68:29; 72:10, 11

13 [a]Ex. 39:2, 3

14 [a]Song of Sol. 1:4 [b]Judg. 5:30; Ezek. 16:10 [c]Ps. 45:9

17 [a]Mal. 1:11 [b]Ps. 138:4

£ Possibly, *for soprano voices*

1 [1]Or, *Abundantly available for help* [2]Or, *tight places*
[a]Ps. 14:6; 62:7, 8 [b]Ps. 145:18; Deut. 4:7 [c]Ps. 9:9

2 [1]Lit., *seas*
[a]Ps. 23:4; 27:1 [b]Ps. 82:5 [c]Ps. 18:7

3 [1]*Selah may mean: Pause, Crescendo* or *Musical interlude*
[a]Ps. 93:3, 4; Jer. 5:22

4 [a]Ps. 36:8; 65:9; Is. 8:6; Rev. 22:1 [b]Ps. 48:1; 87:3; 101:8; Is. 60:14; Rev. 3:12 [c]Ps. 43:3

5 [1]Lit., *at the turning of the morning*
[a]Deut. 23:14; Is. 12:6; Ezek. 43:7, 9; Hos. 11:9; Joel 2:27; Zech. 2:5 [b]Ps. 37:40; Is. 41:14; Luke 1:54

6 [1]Or, *Gentiles* [2]Lit., *gave forth*
[a]Ps. 2:1, 2 [b]Ps. 18:13; 68:33; Jer. 25:30; Joel 2:11; Amos 1:2 [c]Amos 9:5; Mic. 1:4; Nah. 1:5

7 [a]Num. 14:9; 2 Chr. 13:12 [b]Ps. 9:9; 48:3

8 [1]Or, *Which He has wrought as desolations*
[a]Ps. 66:5 [b]Is. 61:4; Jer. 51:43

9 [a]Is. 2:4; Mic. 4:3 [b]Ps. 76:3; 1 Sam. 2:4 [c]Is. 9:5; Ezek. 39:9

10 [1]Or, *Let go, relax* [2]Or, *Gentiles*
[a]Ps. 100:3 [b]Is. 2:11, 17

13 The King's daughter is all glorious within;
Her clothing is [a]interwoven with gold.
14 She will be [a]led to the King [b]in embroidered work;
The [c]virgins, her companions who follow her,
Will be brought to Thee.
15 They will be led forth with gladness and rejoicing;
They will enter into the King's palace.

16 In place of Thy fathers will be Thy sons;
Thou shalt make them princes in all the earth.
17 I will cause [a]Thy name to be remembered in all generations;
Therefore the peoples [b]will give Thee thanks forever and ever.

Psalm 46

God the Refuge of His People.

For the choir director. *A Psalm* of the sons of Korah, £set to Alamoth. A Song.

GOD is our [a]refuge and strength,
[1]A very [b]present help [c]in [2]trouble.
2 Therefore we will [a]not fear, though [b]the earth should change,
And though [c]the mountains slip into the heart of the [1]sea;
3 Though its [a]waters roar *and* foam,
Though the mountains quake at its swelling pride. [[1]Selah.

4 There is a [a]river whose streams make glad the [b]city of God,
The holy [c]dwelling places of the Most High.
5 God is [a]in the midst of her, she will not be moved;
God will [b]help her [1]when morning dawns.
6 The [1]nations [a]made an uproar, the kingdoms tottered;
He [2b]raised His voice, the earth [c]melted.
7 The LORD of hosts [a]is with us;
The God of Jacob is [b]our stronghold. [Selah.

8 Come, [a]behold the works of the LORD,
[1]Who has wrought [b]desolations in the earth.
9 He [a]makes wars to cease to the end of the earth;
He [b]breaks the bow and cuts the spear in two;
He [c]burns the chariots with fire.
10 "[1]Cease *striving* and [a]know that I am God;
I will be [b]exalted among the [2]nations, I will be exalted in the earth."
11 The LORD of hosts is with us;
The God of Jacob is our stronghold. [Selah.

Psalm 47

God the King of the Earth.

For the choir director. A Psalm of the sons of Korah.

O [a]CLAP your hands, all peoples;
Shout to God with the voice of [1b]joy.
2 For the LORD Most High is to be [a]feared,
A [b]great King over all the earth.
3 He [a]subdues peoples under us,
And nations under our feet.
4 He chooses our [a]inheritance for us,
The [b]glory of Jacob whom He loves. [[1]Selah.

5 God has [a]ascended [1]with a shout,
The LORD, [1]with the [b]sound of a trumpet.
6 [a]Sing praises to God, sing praises;
Sing praises to [b]our King, sing praises.
7 For God is the [a]King of all the earth;
Sing praises [b]with a [1]skillful psalm.
8 God [a] reigns over the nations,
God [1]sits on [b]His holy throne.
9 The [1a]princes of the people have assembled themselves *as* the [b]people of the God of Abraham;
For the [c]shields of the earth belong to God;
He [2]is [d]highly exalted.

Psalm 48

The Beauty and Glory of Zion.

A Song; a Psalm of the sons of Korah.

[a]GREAT is the LORD, and greatly to be praised,
In the [b]city of our God, His [c]holy mountain.
2 [a]Beautiful in elevation, [b]the joy of the whole earth,
Is Mount Zion *in* the far north,
The [c]city of the great King.
3 God, in her palaces,
Has made Himself known as a [a]stronghold.

4 For, lo, the [a]kings assembled themselves,
They passed by together.
5 They saw *it*, then they were amazed;
They were [a]terrified, they [1]fled in alarm.
6 [1]Panic seized them there,
Anguish, as of [a]a woman in childbirth.
7 With the [a]east wind
Thou [b]dost break the [c]ships of Tarshish.
8 As we have heard, so have we seen
In the city of the LORD of hosts, in the city of our God;
God will [a]establish her forever. [[1]Selah.

9 We have thought on [a]Thy lovingkindness, O God,
In the midst of Thy temple.
10 As is Thy [a]name, O God,

Psalm 47
1 [1]Or, *a ringing cry* [a]Ps. 98:8 [b]Ps. 106:47
2 [a]Ps. 66:3, 5; 68:35; Deut. 7:21; Neh. 1:5 [b]Mal. 1:14
3 [a]Ps. 18:47
4 [1]*Selah* may mean: *Pause, Crescendo* or *Musical interlude* [a]1 Pet. 1:4 [b]Amos 6:8; 8:7; Nah. 2:2
5 [1]Or, *amid* [a]Ps. 68:18, 25 [b]Ps. 98:6
6 [a]Ps. 68:4 [b]Ps. 89:18
7 [1]Heb., *Maskil* [a]Zech. 14:9 [b]1 Cor. 14:15
8 [1]Or, *has taken His seat* [a]Ps. 22:28; 1 Chr. 16:31 [b]Ps. 97:2
9 [1]Or, *nobles* [2]Lit., *has greatly exalted Himself* [a]Ps. 72:11; 102:22; Is. 49:7, 23 [b]Rom. 4:11, 12 [c]Ps. 89:18 [d]Ps. 97:9

Psalm 48
1 [a]Ps. 96:4; 145:3; 1 Chr. 16:25 [b]Ps. 46:4 [c]Ps. 2:6; 87:1; Is. 2:3; Mic. 4:1; Zech. 8:3
2 [a]Ps. 50:2 [b]Lam. 2:15 [c]Matt. 5:35
3 [a]Ps. 46:7
4 [a]2 Sam. 10:6-19
5 [1]Lit., *were hurried away* [a]Ex. 15:15
6 [1]Lit., *Trembling* [a]Is. 13:8
7 [a]Jer. 18:17 [b]1 Kin. 22:48 [c]1 Kin. 10:22; Ezek. 27:25
8 [1]*Selah* may mean: *Pause, Crescendo* or *Musical interlude* [a]Ps. 87:5
9 [a]Ps. 26:3; 40:10
10 [a]Deut. 28:58; Josh. 7:9; Mal. 1:11

So is Thy [b]praise to the ends of the earth;
Thy [c]right hand is full of righteousness.
11 Let Mount [a]Zion be glad,
Let the [a]daughters of Judah rejoice,
Because of Thy judgments.
12 Walk about Zion, and go around her;
Count her [a]towers;
13 Consider her [a]ramparts;
Go through her palaces;
That you may [b]tell *it* to the next generation.
14 For [1]such is God,
Our God forever and ever;
He will [a]guide us [2]until death.

Psalm 49

The Folly of Trusting in Riches.

For the choir director. A Psalm of the sons of Korah.

[a]HEAR this, all peoples;
Give ear, all [b]inhabitants of the world.
2 Both [a]low and high,
Rich and poor together.
3 My mouth will [a]speak wisdom;
And the meditation of my heart *will be* [b]understanding.
4 I will incline my ear to [a]a proverb;
[b]I will [1]express my [c]riddle on the harp.

5 Why should I [a]fear in days of adversity,
When the iniquity of my [1]foes surrounds me,
6 Even those who [a]trust in their wealth,
And boast in the abundance of their riches?
7 No man can by any means [a]redeem *his* brother,
Or give to God a [b]ransom for him—
8 For the redemption of [1]his soul is costly,
And he should cease *trying* forever—
9 That he should [a]live on eternally;
That he should not [1b]see the pit.

10 For he sees *that even* [a]wise men die;
The [b]stupid and the senseless alike perish,
And [c]leave their wealth to others.
11 Their [1a]inner thought is, *that* their houses [b]are forever,
And their dwelling places to all generations;
They have [c]called their lands after their own names.
12 But [a]man in *his* [1]pomp will not endure;
He is like the [2]beasts that [3]perish.

13 This is the [a]way of those who are foolish,
And of those after them who [b]approve their words. [[1]Selah.
14 As sheep they are appointed [a]for [1]Sheol;
Death shall be their shepherd;
And the [b]upright shall rule over them in the morning;

10 [b]Ps. 65:1, 2; 100:1 [c]Is. 41:10

11 [a]Ps. 97:8

12 [a]Neh. 3:1, 11, 25-27

13 [a]Ps. 122:7 [b]Ps. 78:5-7

14 [1]Lit., *this* [2]Lit., *upon.* Some mss. and the Greek version read, *forever.* [a]Ps. 23:4; Is. 58:11

1 [a]Ps. 78:1; Is. 1:2; Mic. 1:2 [b]Ps. 33:8

2 [a]Ps. 62:9

3 [a]Ps. 37:30 [b]Ps. 119:130

4 [1]Lit., *open up* [a]Ps. 78:2 [b]2 Kin. 3:15 [c]Num. 12:8

5 [1]Lit., *supplanters* [a]Ps. 23:4; 27:1

6 [a]Ps. 52:7; Job 31:24; Prov. 11:28; Mark 10:24

7 [a]Matt. 25:8, 9 [b]Job 36:18, 19

8 [1]Lit., *their*

9 [1]Or, *undergo decay* [a]Ps. 22:29 [b]Ps. 16:10; 89:48

10 [a]Eccles. 2:16 [b]Ps. 92.6; 94:8 [c]Ps. 39:6; Eccles. 2:18, 21; Luke 12:20

11 [1]Some versions read, *graves are their houses* [a]Ps. 64:6 [b]Ps. 10:6 [c]Deut. 3:14

12 [1]Lit., *honor* [2]Or, *animals* [3]Lit., *are destroyed* [a]Ps. 49:20

13 [1]*Selah* may mean: *Pause, Crescendo* or *Musical interlude* [a]Jer. 17:11 [b]Ps. 49:18

14 [1]I.e., the nether world [a]Ps. 9:17 [b]Dan. 7:18; Mal. 4:3; 1 Cor. 6:2; Rev. 2:26

And their form shall be for [1]Sheol [c]to consume,
[2]So that they have no habitation.
15 But God will [a]redeem my soul from the [1]power of [2]Sheol;
For [b]He will receive me. [Selah.

16 Do not be afraid [a]when a man becomes rich,
When the [1]glory of his house is increased;
17 For when he dies he will [a]carry nothing away;
His [1]glory will not descend after him.
18 Though while he lives he [a]congratulates [1]himself—
And though *men* praise you when you do well for yourself—
19 [1]He shall [a]go to the generation of his fathers;
They shall never see [b]the light.
20 [a]Man in *his* [1]pomp, yet without understanding,
Is like the [2]beasts that [3]perish.

Psalm 50

God the Judge of the Righteous and the Wicked.

A Psalm of Asaph.

[a]THE Mighty One, God, the LORD, has spoken,
And summoned the earth [b]from the rising of the sun to its setting.
2 Out of Zion, [a]the perfection of beauty.
God [b]has shone forth.
3 May our God [a]come and not keep silence;
[b]Fire devours before Him,
And it is very [c]tempestuous around Him.
4 He [a]summons the heavens above,
And the earth, to judge His people:
5 "Gather My [a]godly ones to Me,
Those who have made a [b]covenant with Me by [c]sacrifice."
6 And the [a]heavens declare His righteousness,
For [b]God Himself is judge. [[1]Selah.

7 "[a]Hear, O My people, and I will speak;
O Israel, and I will testify [1]against you,
I am God, [b]your God.
8 "I do [a]not reprove you for your sacrifices,
And your burnt offerings are continually before Me.
9 "I shall take no [a]young bull out of your house,
Nor male goats out of your folds.
10 "For [a]every beast of the forest is Mine,
The cattle on a thousand hills.
11 "I know every [a]bird of the mountains,
And everything that moves in the field is [1]Mine.
12 "If I were hungry, I would not tell you;
For the [a]world is Mine, and [1]all it contains.
13 "Shall I eat the flesh of [1a]bulls,
Or drink the blood of male goats?
14 "Offer to God [a]a sacrifice of thanksgiving,
And [b]pay your vows to the Most High;

14 [1]I.e., the nether world [2]Lit., *Away from his habitation* [c]Job 24:19

15 [1]Lit., *hand* [2]I.e., the nether world [a]Ps. 16:10; 56:13; Hos. 13:14 [b]Ps. 16:11; 73:24; Gen. 5:24

16 [1]Or, *wealth* [a]Ps. 37:7

17 [1]Or, *wealth* [a]Ps. 17:14; 1 Tim. 6:7

18 [1]Lit., *his soul* [a]Ps. 10:3, 6; Deut. 29:19; Luke 12:19

19 [1]Lit., *You*, or, *It* [a]Gen. 15:15 [b]Ps. 56:13; Job 33:30

20 [1]Lit., *honor* [2]Or, *animals* [3]Lit., *are destroyed* [a]Ps. 49:12

1 [a]Josh. 22:22 [b]Ps. 113:3

2 [a]Ps. 48:2; Lam. 2:15 [b]Ps. 80:1; 94:1; Deut. 33:2

3 [a]Ps. 96:13 [b]Ps. 97:3; Lev. 10:2; Num. 16:35; Dan. 7:10 [c]Ps. 18:12, 13

4 [a]Deut. 4:26; 31:28; 32:1; Is. 1:2

5 [a]Ps. 30:4; 37:28; 52:9, [b]Ps. 25:10; Ex. 24:7; 2 Chr. 6:11 [c]Ps. 50:8

6 [1]*Selah* may mean: *Pause, Crescendo* or *Musical interlude* [a]Ps. 89:5; 97:6 [b]Ps. 96:13

7 [1]Or, *to* [a]Ps. 49:1; 81:8 [b]Ps. 48:14; Ex. 20:2

8 [a]Ps. 40:6; 51:16; Is. 1:11; Hos. 6:6

9 [a]Ps. 69:31

10 [a]Ps. 104:24

11 [1]Or, *in My mind*, lit., *with Me* [a]Matt. 6:26

12 [1]Lit., its fulness [a]Ps. 24:1; Ex. 19:5; Deut. 10:14

13 [1]Lit., *strong ones* [a]Ps. 50:9

14 [a]Ps. 27:6; 69:30; 107:22; 116:17; Hos. 14:2; Rom. 12:1; Heb. 13:15 [b]Ps. 22:25; 56:12; 61:8; 65:1; 76:11; Num. 30:2; Deut. 23:21

15 "And [a]call upon Me in the day of trouble;
I shall [b]rescue you, and you will [c]honor Me."

16 But to the wicked God says,
"What right have you to tell of My statutes,
And to take [a]My covenant in your mouth?
17 "For you [a]hate discipline,
And you [b]cast My words behind you.
18 "When you see a thief, you [1a]are pleased with him,
And [2]you [b]associate with adulterers.
19 "You [1a]let your mouth loose in evil,
And your [b]tongue frames deceit.
20 "You sit and [a]speak against your brother;
You slander your own mother's son.
21 "These things you have done, and [a]I kept silence;
You thought that I was just like you;
I will [b]reprove you, and state *the case* in order before your eyes.

22 "Now consider this, you who [a]forget God,
Lest I [b]tear *you* in pieces, and there be none to deliver.
23 "He who [a]offers a sacrifice of thanksgiving honors Me;
And to him who [1b]orders *his* way *aright*
I shall [c]show the salvation of God."

Psalm 51

A Contrite Sinner's Prayer for Pardon.

For the choir director. A Psalm of David, when [£]Nathan the prophet came to him, after he had gone in to Bathsheba.

[a]BE gracious to me, O God, according to Thy lovingkindness;
According to the greatness of [b]Thy compassion [c]blot out my transgressions.
2 [a]Wash me thoroughly from my iniquity,
And [b]cleanse me from my sin.
3 For [1]I [a]know my transgressions,
And my sin is ever before me.
4 [a]Against Thee, Thee only, I have sinned,
And done what is [b]evil in Thy sight,
So that [c]Thou [1]art justified [2]when Thou dost speak,
And [3]blameless when Thou dost judge.

5 Behold, I was [a]brought forth in iniquity,
And in sin my mother conceived me.
6 Behold, Thou dost desire [a]truth in the [1]innermost being,
And in the hidden part Thou wilt [b]make me know wisdom.
7 [1]Purify me [a]with hyssop, and I shall be clean;
[2]Wash me, and I shall be [b]whiter than snow.
8 [1]Make me to hear [a]joy and gladness,
Let the [b]bones which Thou hast broken rejoice.
9 [a]Hide Thy face from my sins,
And blot out all my iniquities.

15 [a]Ps. 91:15; 107:6, 13; Zech. 13:9 [b]Ps. 81:7 [c]Ps. 22:23

16 [a]Is. 29:13

17 [a]Prov. 5:12; 12:1; Rom. 2:21, 22 [b]1 Kin. 14:9; Neh. 9:26

18 [1]Some ancient versions read, *run together* [2]Lit., *your part is with* [a]Rom. 1:32 [b]1 Tim. 5:22

19 [1]Lit., *send* [a]Ps. 10:7 [b]Ps. 36:3; 52:2

20 [a]Job 19:18; Matt. 10:21

21 [a]Eccles. 8:11; Is. 42:14; 57:11 [b]Ps. 90:8

22 [a]Job 8:13; Ps. 9:17 [b]Ps. 7:2

23 [1]Lit., *sets* [a]Ps. 50:14 [b]Ps. 85:13 [c]Ps. 91:16

[£]2 Sam. 12:1

1 [a]Ps. 4:1; 109:26 [b]Ps. 69:16; 106:45 [c]Ps. 51:9; Is. 43:25; 44:22; Acts 3:19; Col. 2:14

2 [a]Ps. 51:7; Is. 1:16; 4:4; Jer. 4:14; Acts 22:16; Rev. 1:5 [b]Jer. 33:8; Ezek. 36:33; Heb. 9:14; 1 John 1:7,9

3 [1]Or, *I myself know* [a]Is. 59:12

4 [1]Or, *mayest be in the right* [2]Many mss. read, *in Thy words* [3]Lit., *pure* [a]Ps. 41:4; Gen. 20:6; 39:9; 2 Sam. 12:13 [b]Luke 15:21 [c]Rom. 3:4

5 [a]Ps. 58:3; Job 14:4; 15:14; Eph. 2:3

6 [1]Or, *inward parts* [a]Ps. 15:2; Job 38:36 [b]Prov. 2:6; Eccles. 2:26; James 1:5

7 [1]Or, *Mayest Thou purify . . . that I may be clean* [2]Or, *Mayest Thou wash* [a]Ex. 12:22; Lev. 14:4; Num. 19:18; Heb. 9:19 [b]Is. 1:18

8 [1]Or, *Mayest Thou make* [a]Is. 35:10; Joel 1:16 [b]Ps. 35:10

9 [a]Jer. 16:17

10 [a]Create [1]in me a [b]clean heart, O God,
And renew [2]a [c]steadfast spirit within me.
11 [a]Do not cast me away from Thy presence,
And do not take Thy [b]Holy Spirit from me.
12 Restore to me the [a]joy of Thy salvation,
And sustain me with a [b]willing spirit.
13 *Then* I will [a]teach transgressors Thy ways,
And sinners will [1]be [b]converted to Thee.

14 Deliver me from [a]bloodguiltiness, O God, Thou [b]God of my salvation;
Then my [c]tongue will joyfully sing of Thy righteousness.
15 O LORD, [1a]open my lips,
That my mouth may [b]declare Thy praise.
16 For Thou [a]dost not delight in sacrifice, otherwise I would give it;
Thou art not pleased with burnt offering.
17 The sacrifices of God are a [a]broken spirit;
A broken and a contrite heart, O God, Thou wilt not despise.

18 [a]By Thy favor do good to Zion;
[1b]Build the walls of Jerusalem.
19 Then Thou wilt delight in [1a]righteous sacrifices,
In [b]burnt offering and whole burnt offering;
Then [2]young bulls will be offered on Thine altar.

PSALM 52

Futility of Boastful Wickedness.

For the choir director. A [£]Maskil of David, •when Doeg the Edomite came and told Saul, and said to him, "David has come to the house of Ahimelech."

WHY do you [a]boast in evil, O mighty man?
The [b]lovingkindness of God *endures* all day long.
2 Your tongue devises [a]destruction,
Like a [b]sharp razor, [c]O worker of deceit.
3 You [a]love evil more than good,
[b]Falsehood more than speaking what is right. [[1]Selah.
4 You love all words that devour,
O [a]deceitful tongue.

5 [1]But God will break you down forever;
He will snatch you up, and [a]tear you away from *your* tent,
And [b]uproot you from the [c]land of the living. [Selah.
6 And the righteous will [a]see and fear,
And will [b]laugh at him, *saying*,
7 "Behold, the man who would not make God his refuge,
But [a]trusted in the abundance of his riches,
And [b]was strong in [1]his *evil* desire."

10 [1]Lit., *for* [2]Or, *an upright* [a]Eph. 2:10 [b]Ps. 24:4; Matt. 5:8; Acts 15:9 [c]Ps. 78:37

11 [a]2 Kin. 13:23; 24:20; Jer. 7:15 [b]Is. 63:10, 11

12 [a]Ps. 13:5 [b]Ps. 110:3

13 [1]Or, *turn back* [a]Acts 9:21, 22 [b]Ps. 22:27

14 [a]Ps. 26:9; 2 Sam. 12:9 [b]Ps. 25:5 [c]Ps. 35:28; 71:15

15 [1]Or, *mayest Thou open* [a]Ex. 4:15 [b]Ps. 9:14

16 [a]Ps. 40:6

17 [a]Ps. 34:18

18 [1]Or, *Mayest Thou build* [a]Ps. 69:35; Is. 51:3 [b]Ps. 102:16; 147:2

19 [1]Or, *sacrifices of righteousness* [2]Lit., *they will offer young bulls* [a]Ps. 4:5 [b]Ps. 66:13, 15

£ Possibly, *Contemplative*, or *Didactic*, or *Skillful Psalm* • 1 Sam. 22:9

1 [a]Ps. 94:4 [b]Ps. 52:8

2 [a]Ps. 5:9 [b]Ps. 57:4; 59:7 [c]Ps. 101:7

3 [1]*Selah* may mean: *Pause, Crescendo* or *Musical interlude* [a]Ps. 36:4 [b]Ps. 58:3; Jer. 9:5

4 [a]Ps. 120:3

5 [1]Or, *Also* [a]Is. 22:18, 19 [b]Prov. 2:22 [c]Ps. 27:13

6 [a]Ps. 37:34; 40:3 [b]Job 22:19

7 [1]Or, *his destruction* [a]Ps. 49:6 [b]Ps. 10:6

8 [a]Ps. 92:12; 128:3; Jer. 11:16 [b]Ps. 13:5

9 [a]Ps. 30:12 [b]Ps. 54:6

[£]I.e., sickness, a sad tone • Possibly, *Contemplative*, or *Didactic*, or *Skillful Psalm*

1 [a]Ps. 53:1-6; Ps. 14:1-7

2 [1]Or, *acts wisely*

5 [1]Or, *dread* [2]Or possibly, *those* [a]Lev. 26:17, 36; Prov. 28:1 [b]Ps. 141:7; Jer. 8:1, 2; Ezek. 6:5 [c]Ps. 44:7 [d]2 Kin. 17:20; Jer. 6:30; Lam. 5:22

6 [1]Or, *restores the fortunes of His people* [2]Or, *Jacob will rejoice, Israel will be glad*

[£]Possibly, *Contemplative*, or *Didactic*, or *Skillful Psalm* • 1 Sam. 23:19

1 [1]Lit., *judge* [a]Ps. 20:1 [b]2 Chr. 20:6

2 [a]Ps. 17:6; 55:1 [b]Ps. 5:1

3 [1]Or, *soul* [2]*Selah* may mean: *Pause, Crescendo* or *Musical interlude* [a]Ps. 86:14 [b]Ps. 18:48; 86:14; 140:1, 4, 11 [c]1 Sam. 20:1; 25:29; Ps. 40:14; 63:9; 70:2 [d]Ps. 36:1

4 [1]Lit., *as those who sustain* [a]Ps. 30:10; 37:40; 118:7 [b]Ps. 37:17, 24; 41:12; 51:12; 145:14; Is. 41:10

8 But as for me, I am like a [a]green olive tree in the house of God;
I [b]trust in the lovingkindness of God forever and ever.
9 I will [a]give Thee thanks forever, because Thou hast done *it*,
And I will wait on Thy name, [b]for *it is* good, in the presence of Thy godly ones.

Psalm 53

Folly and Wickedness of Men.

For the choir director; according to [£]mahalath.
A •Maskil of David.

[a]THE fool has said in his heart, "There is no God,"
They are corrupt, and have committed abominable injustice;
There is no one who does good.
2 God has looked down from heaven upon the sons of men,
To see if there is anyone who [1]understands,
Who seeks after God.
3 Every one of them has turned aside; together they have become corrupt;
There is no one who does good, not even one.

4 Have the workers of wickedness no knowledge,
Who eat up My people *as though* they ate bread,
And have not called upon God?
5 There they were in great [1]fear [a]*where* no [1]fear had been;
For God [b]scattered the bones of [2]him who encamped against you;
You [c]put *them* to shame, because [d]God had rejected them.
6 O that the salvation of Israel would come out of Zion!
When God [1]restores His captive people,
[2]Let Jacob rejoice, let Israel be glad.

Psalm 54

Prayer for Defense against Enemies.

For the choir director; on stringed instruments.
A [£]Maskil of David, •when the Ziphites came and said to Saul, "Is not David hiding himself among us?"

SAVE me, O God, by [a]Thy name,
And [1]vindicate me by [b]Thy power.
2 [a]Hear my prayer, O God;
[b]Give ear to the words of my mouth.
3 For strangers have [a]risen against me,
And [b]violent men have [c]sought my [1]life;
They have [d]not set God before them. [[2]Selah.

4 Behold, [a]God is my helper;
The Lord is [1]the [b]sustainer of my soul.

5 [1]He will [a]recompense the evil to [2]my foes;
[3b]Destroy them [c]in Thy [4]faithfulness.

6 [1a]Willingly I will sacrifice to Thee;
I will give [b]thanks to Thy name, O LORD, for it is good.
7 For [1]He has [a]delivered me from all [2]trouble;
And my eye has [b]looked *with satisfaction* upon my enemies.

PSALM 55

Prayer for the Destruction of the Treacherous.

For the choir director; on stringed instruments.
A [£]Maskil of David.

[a]GIVE ear to my prayer, O God;
And [b]do not hide Thyself from my supplication.
2 Give [a]heed to me, and answer me;
I am restless in my [b]complaint and [1c]am surely distracted,
3 Because of the voice of the enemy,
Because of the [a]pressure of the wicked;
For they [b]bring down [1]trouble upon me,
And in anger they [c]bear a grudge against me.

4 My [a]heart is in anguish within me,
And the terrors of [b]death have fallen upon me.
5 Fear and [a]trembling come upon me;
And [1b]horror has overwhelmed me.
6 And I said, "O that I had wings like a dove!
I would fly away and [1a]be at rest.
7 "Behold, I would wander far away,
I would [a]lodge in the wilderness. [[1]Selah.
8 "I would hasten to my place of refuge
From the [a]stormy wind *and* tempest."

9 [1]Confuse, O Lord, [a]divide their tongues,
For I have seen [b]violence and strife in the city.
10 Day and night they go around her upon her walls;
And iniquity and mischief are in her midst.
11 [a]Destruction is in her midst;
[b]Oppression and deceit do not depart from her [1]streets.

12 For it is not an enemy who reproaches me,
Then I could bear *it;*
Nor is it one who hates me who [a]has exalted himself against me,
Then I could hide myself from him.
13 But it is you, a man [1]my equal,
My companion and my [2a]familiar friend.
14 We who had sweet [1]fellowship together,
[a]Walked in the house of God in the throng.
15 Let [1]death come [a]deceitfully upon them;
Let them [b]go down alive to [2]Sheol,
For evil is in their dwelling, in their midst.

5 [1]Lit., *The evil will return* [2]Or, *those who lie in wait for me* [3]Or, *Put to silence* [4]Or, *truth*
[a]Ps. 94:23 [b]Ps. 143:12 [c]Ps. 89:49; 96:13; Is. 42:3

6 [1]Or, *With a freewill offering*
[a]Num. 15:3; Ps. 116:17 [b]Ps. 50:14

7 [1]Or, *it*, i.e., His name [2]Or, *distress*
[a]Ps. 34:6 [b]Ps. 59:10; 92:11; 112:8; 118:7

[£] Possibly, *Contemplative*, or *Didactic*, or *Skillful Psalm*

1 [a]Ps. 54:2; 61:1; 86:6 [b]Ps. 27:9

2 [1]Or, *I must moan*
[a]Ps. 66:19; 86:6, 7 [b]Ps. 64:1; 77:3; 142:2; 1 Sam. 1:16; Job 9:27 [c]Is. 38:14; 59:11; Ezek. 7:16

3 [1]Or, *wickedness*
[a]Ps. 17:9 [b]2 Sam. 16:7, 8 [c]Ps. 71:11; 143:3

4 [a]Ps. 38:8 [b]Ps. 18:4, 5; 116:3

5 [1]Lit., *shuddering*
[a]Ps. 119:120 [b]Job 21:6; Is. 21:4; Ezek. 7:18

6 [1]Lit., *settle down*
[a]Job 3:13

7 [1]*Selah* may mean: *Pause, Crescendo* or *Musical interlude*
[a]1 Sam. 23:14

8 [a]Is. 4:6; 25:4; 29:6

9 [1]Lit., *Swallow up*
[a]Gen. 11:9 [b]Ps. 11:5; Jer. 6:7

11 [1]Or, *plaza*
[a]Ps. 5:9 [b]Ps. 10:7; 17:9

12 [a]Ps. 35:26

13 [1]Lit., *according to my valuation* [2]Or, *acquaintance*
[a]Ps. 41:9; Job 19:14

14 [1]Lit., *counsel*, or, *intimacy*
[a]Ps. 42:4

15 [1]Another reading is, *desolations be upon them* [2]I.e., the nether world
[a]Ps. 64:7; Prov. 6:15; Is. 47:11; 1 Thess. 5:3 [b]Num. 16:30, 33

16 [a]Ps. 57:2, 3

17 [a]Ps. 141:2; Dan. 6:10; Acts 3:1; 10:3, 30 [b]Ps. 5:3; 88:13; 92:2 [c]Acts 10:9

18 [1]Or, *so that none may approach me* [a]Ps. 103:4 [b]Ps. 56:2

19 [1]Or, *afflict* [2]Or, *abides from* [3]Lit., *are no changes* [a]Ps. 78:59 [b]Ps. 90:2; 93:2; Deut. 33:27 [c]Job 10:17 [d]Ps. 36:1

20 [1]Lit., *profaned* [a]Ps. 7:4; 120:7 [b]Ps. 89:34; Num. 30:2

21 [1]Lit., *mouth* [a]Ps. 12:2; 28:3; Prov. 5:3, 4 [b]Ps. 57:4; 59:7

22 [1]Or, *what He has given you* [2]Or, *totter* [a]Ps. 37:5; 1 Pet. 5:7 [b]Ps. 15:5; 112:6

23 [1]Or, *lowest pit* [a]Ps. 73:18; Is. 38:17; Ezek. 28:8 [b]Ps. 5:6 [c]Job 15:32; Prov. 10:27 [d]Ps. 25:2; 56:3

£ Or, *The silent dove of those who are far off*, or, *The dove of the distant terebinths.*

•Possibly, *Epigrammatic Poem*, or Atonement Psalm

Δ1 Sam. 21:10, 11

1 [1]Or, *snapped at* [2]Or, *A fighting man* [a]Ps. 57:3 [b]Ps. 17:9

2 [1]Or, *snapped at* [2]Or, *many are fighting* [a]Ps. 35:25; 57:3; 124:3 [b]Ps. 35:1

3 [1]Lit., *In the day* [2]Or, *I am one who puts* [a]Ps. 55:4, 5 [b]Ps. 11:1

4 [1]Lit., *flesh* [a]Ps. 56:10, 11 [b]Ps. 118:6; Heb. 13:6

5 [1]Or, *trouble my affairs* [2]Or, *purposes* [a]2 Pet. 3:16 [b]Ps. 41:7

6 [1]Or, *stir up strife* [2]Lit., *heels* [3]Lit., *soul* [a]Ps. 59:3; 140:2; Is. 54:15 [b]Ps. 17:11 [c]Ps. 71:10

7 [1]Or, *will they have escape?* [a]Ps. 36:12; Prov. 19:5; Ezek. 17:15; Rom. 2:3 [b]Ps. 55:23

8 [a]Ps. 139:3

16 As for me, I shall [a]call upon God,
And the LORD will save me.
17 [a]Evening and [b]morning and at [c]noon, I will complain and murmur,
And He will hear my voice.
18 He will [a]redeem my soul in peace [1]from the battle *which is* against me,
For they are [b]many *who strive* with me.
19 God will [a]hear and [1]answer them—
Even the one [b]who [2]sits enthroned from of old— [Selah.
With whom there [3]is no [c]change,
And who [d]do not fear God.
20 He has put forth his hands against [a]those who were at peace with him;
He has [1b]violated his covenant.
21 His [1]speech was [a]smoother than butter,
But his heart was war;
His words were [a]softer than oil,
Yet they were drawn [b]swords.

22 [a]Cast [1]your burden upon the LORD, and He will sustain you;
He will never allow the righteous to [2b]be shaken.
23 But Thou, O God, wilt bring them down to the [1a]pit of destruction;
[b]Men of bloodshed and deceit will [c]not live out half their days.
But I will [d]trust in Thee.

PSALM 56

Supplication for Deliverance, and Grateful Trust in God.

For the choir director; according to £Jonath elem rehokim. A •Mikhtam of David, Δwhen the Philistines seized him in Gath.

BE gracious, O God, for man has [1a]trampled upon me;
[2]Fighting all day long he [b]oppresses me.
2 My foes have [1a]trampled upon me all day long,
For [2]they are many who [b]fight proudly against me.
3 [1]When I am [a]afraid,
[2]I will [b]put my trust in Thee.
4 [a]In God, whose word I praise,
In God I have put my trust;
I shall not be afraid.
[b]What can *mere* [1]man do to me?
5 All day long they [1a]distort my words;
All their [2b]thoughts are against me for evil.
6 They [1a]attack, they lurk,
They [b]watch my [2]steps,
As they have [c]waited *to take* my [3]life.
7 Because of wickedness, [1a]cast them forth,
In anger [b]put down the peoples, O God!

8 Thou [a]hast taken account of my wanderings;

Put my [b]tears in Thy bottle;
Are *they* not in [c]Thy book?
9 Then my enemies will [a]turn back [b]in the day when I call;
This I know, [1]that [c]God is for me.
10 In God, *whose* word I praise,
In the LORD, *whose* word I praise,
11 In God I have put my [1]trust, I shall not be afraid.
What can man do to me?
12 Thy [a]vows are *binding* upon me, O God;
I will render thank offerings to Thee.
13 For Thou hast [a]delivered my soul from death.
[1]Indeed [b]my feet from stumbling,
So that I may [c]walk before God
In the [d]light of the [2]living.

PSALM 57

Prayer for Rescue from Persecutors.

For the choir director; *set to* [£]Al-tashheth. A •Mikhtam of David, [Δ]when he fled from Saul, in the cave.

BE gracious to me, O God, be gracious to me,
For my soul [a]takes refuge in Thee;
And in the [b]shadow of Thy wings I will take refuge,
Until destruction [c]passes by.
2 I will cry to God Most High,
To God who [a]accomplishes *all things* for me.
3 He will [a]send from heaven and save me;
He reproaches him who [1b]tramples upon me. [[2]Selah.
God will send forth His [c]lovingkindness and His [3]truth.

4 My soul is among [a]lions;
I must lie among those who breathe forth fire,
Even the sons of men, whose [b]teeth are spears and arrows,
And their [c]tongue a sharp sword.
5 [a]Be exalted above the heavens, O God;
Let Thy glory *be* above all the earth.
6 They have [1]prepared a [a]net for my steps;
My soul is [b]bowed down;
They [c]dug a pit before me;
They *themselves* have [d]fallen into the midst of it. [Selah.

7 [a]My [b]heart is steadfast, O God, my heart is steadfast;
I will sing, yes, I will sing praises!
8 Awake, [a]my glory;
Awake, [b]harp and lyre,
I will awaken the dawn!
9 I will give thanks to Thee, O Lord, among the peoples;
I will sing praises to Thee among the [1]nations.
10 For Thy [a]lovingkindness is great to the heavens,
And Thy [1]truth to the clouds.
11 Be exalted above the heavens, O God;
Let Thy glory *be* above all the earth.

---

8 [b]Ps. 39:12; 2 Kin. 20:5 [c]Mal. 3:16

9 [1]Or, *because* [a]Ps. 9:3 [b]Ps. 102:2 [c]Ps. 41:11; 118:6; Rom. 8:31

11 [1]Or, *trust without fear*

12 [a]Ps. 50:14

13 [1]Or, Hast Thou *not* delivered [2]Or, *life* [a]Ps. 33:19; 49:15; 86:13 [b]Ps. 116:8 [c]Ps. 116:9 [d]Job 33:30

[£] Lit., *Do Not Destroy*

• Possibly, *Epigrammatic Poem*, or *Atonement Psalm*

[Δ] 1 Sam. 22:1; 24:3

1 [a]Ps. 2:12; 34:22 [b]Ps. 17:8; 36:7; 63:7; 91:4; Ruth 2:12 [c]Is. 26:20

2 [a]Ps. 138:8

3 [1]Or, *snaps at* [2]*Selah* may mean: *Pause, Crescendo* or *Musical interlude* [3]Or, *faithfulness* [a]Ps. 18:16; 144:5, 7 [b]Ps. 56:2 [c]Ps. 25:10; 40:11

4 [a]Ps. 35:17; 58:6 [b]Prov. 30:14 [c]Ps. 55:21; 59:7; 64:3; Prov. 12:18

5 [a]Ps. 57:11; Ps. 108:5

6 [1]Or, *spread* [a]Ps. 10:9; 31:4; 35:7; 140:5 [b]Ps. 145:14 [c]Ps. 7:15 [d]Prov. 26:27; 28:10; Eccles. 10:8

7 [a]Ps. 57:7-11; Ps. 108:1-5 [b]Ps. 112;7

8 [a]Ps. 16:9; 30:12 [b]Ps. 150:3

9 [1]Lit., *peoples*

10 [1]Or, *faithfulness* [a]Ps. 36:5

£ Lit., *Do Not Destroy*

• Possibly, *Epigrammatic Poem,* or *Atonement Psalm*

1 [1]Another reading is, *speak righteousness in silence* [2]Or, *mighty ones,* or, *judges* [3]Or, *uprightly the sons of men*
[a]Ps. 82:2

2 [a]Mal. 3:15 [b]Ps. 94:20; Is. 10:1

3 [1]Lit., the *womb*
[a]Ps. 51:5; Is. 48:8 [b]Ps. 53:3

4 [a]Ps. 140:3; Deut. 32:33

5 [1]Or, *whisperers*
[a]Ps. 81:11; Jer. 8:17 [b]Eccles. 10:11

6 [a]Ps. 3:7; Job 4:10

7 [1]Lit., *bends* [2]Lit., *though they were cut off*
[a]Ps. 112:10; Josh. 2:11; 7:5; Is. 13:7; Ezek. 21:7 [b]Ps. 64:3

8 [1]I.e., secretes slime
[a]Job 3:16; Eccles. 6:3

9 [1]Lit., *living*
[a]Ps. 118:12; Eccles. 7:6 [b]Ps. 83:15; Job 27:21; Prov. 10:25

10 [a]Ps. 32:11; 64:10; 107:42; Job 22:19 [b]Ps. 91:8; Deut. 32:43; Jer. 11:20; 20:12 [c]Ps. 68:23

11 [1]Lit., *fruit* [2]Or, *in*
[a]Ps. 18:20; 19:11; Is. 3:10; Luke 6:23, 35 [b]Ps. 9:8; 67:4; 75:7; 94:2

£ Lit., *Do Not Destroy*

•Possibly, *Epigrammatic Poem,* or *Atonement Psalm*

Δ 1 Sam. 19:11

1 [1]Or, *Mayest Thou put me in an inaccessibly high place*
[a]Ps. 143:9 [b]Ps. 20:1; 69:29

2 [a]Ps. 14:4; 28:3; 36:12; 53:4; 92:7; 94:16; [b]Ps. 26:9; 139:19; Prov. 29:10

3 [1]Or, *lain in wait* [2]Lit., *soul* [3]Or, *strong* [4]Or, *stir up strife*
[a]Ps. 56:6 [b]Ps. 7:3, 4; 69:4; 1 Sam. 24:11

4 [1]Lit., *Without guilt* [2]Lit., *meet*
[a]Ps. 35:19 [b]Ps. 7:6; 35:23

Psalm 58

Prayer for the Punishment of the Wicked.

For the choir director; *set to* £Al-tashheth.
A •Mikhtam of David.

DO you indeed [1]speak righteousness, O [2]gods?
Do you [a]judge [3]uprightly, O sons of men?
2 No, in heart you [a]work unrighteousness;
On earth you [b]weigh out the violence of your hands.
3 The wicked are estranged [a]from the womb;
These who speak lies [b]go astray from [1]birth.
4 They have venom like the [a]venom of a serpent;
Like a deaf cobra that stops up its ear,
5 So that it [a]does not hear the voice of [1b]charmers,
Or a skillful caster of spells.

6 O God, [a]shatter their teeth in their mouth;
Break out the fangs of the young lions, O LORD.
7 Let them [a]flow away like water that runs off;
When he [1b]aims his arrows, let them be as [2]headless shafts.
8 *Let them be* as a snail which [1]melts away as it goes along,
Like the [a]miscarriages of a woman which never see the sun.
9 Before your [a]pots can feel *the fire of* thorns,
He will [b]sweep them away with a whirlwind, the [1]green and the burning alike.

10 The [a]righteous will rejoice when he [b]sees the vengeance;
He will [c]wash his feet in the blood of the wicked.
11 And men will say, "Surely there is a [1a]reward for the righteous;
Surely there is a God who [b]judges [2]on earth!"

Psalm 59

Prayer for Deliverance from Enemies.

For the choir director; *set to* £Al-tashheth. A •Mikhtam of David, Δwhen Saul sent *men,* and
a they watched the house in order to kill him.

DELIVER me from my enemies, O my God;
[1b]Set me *securely* on high away from those who rise up against me.
2 Deliver me from [a]those who do iniquity,
And save me from [b]men of bloodshed.
3 For behold, they [1a]have set an ambush for my [2]life;
[3]Fierce men [4a]launch an attack against me,
[b]Not for my transgression, nor for my sin, O LORD,
4 [1a]For no guilt of *mine,* they run and set themselves against me.
[b]Arouse Thyself to [2]help me, and see!

5 And Thou, [a]O LORD God of hosts, the God of Israel,
Awake to [1b]punish all the nations;
[c]Do not be gracious to any *who are* treacherous in iniquity. [[2]Selah.
6 They return at evening, they howl like a [a]dog,
And go around the city.
7 Behold, they [1a]belch forth with their mouth;
[b]Swords are in their lips,
For, *they say*, "[c]Who hears?"
8 But Thou, O LORD, dost [a]laugh at them;
Thou dost [b]scoff at all the nations.

9 [1]*Because of* his [a]strength I will watch for Thee,
For God is my [b]stronghold.
10 [1]My God [a]in His lovingkindness will meet me;
God will let me [b]look *triumphantly* upon [2]my foes,
11 Do not slay them, [a]lest my people forget;
[1b]Scatter them by Thy power, and bring them down,
O Lord, [c]our shield.
12 [1]*On account of* the [a]sin of their mouth *and* the words of their lips,
Let them even be [b]caught in their pride,
And on account of [c]curses and [2]lies which they utter.
13 [1a]Destroy *them* in wrath, [1]destroy *them*, that they may be no more;
That *men* may [b]know that God [2]rules in Jacob,
To the ends of the earth. [Selah.
14 And they [a]return at evening, they howl like a dog,
And go around the city.
15 They wander about [1]for food,
And [2]growl if they are not satisfied.

16 But as for me, I shall [a]sing of Thy strength;
Yes, I shall [b]joyfully sing of Thy lovingkindness in the [c]morning,
For Thou hast been my [d]stronghold,
And a [e]refuge in the day of my distress.
17 [a]O my strength, I will sing praises to Thee;
For God is my [b]stronghold, the [1]God who shows me lovingkindness.

PSALM 60

Lament over Defeat in Battle, and Prayer for Help.

For the choir director; according to [£]Shushan Eduth. [•]Mikhtam of David, to teach; [Δ]when he struggled with Aram-naharaim and with Aram-zobah, and Joab returned, and smote twelve thousand of Edom in the Valley of Salt.

O GOD, [a]Thou hast rejected us. Thou hast [1b]broken us;
Thou hast been [c]angry; O, [d]restore us.
2 Thou hast made the [1a]land quake, Thou hast split it open;
[b]Heal its breaches, for it totters.

---

5 [1]Lit., *visit* [2]*Selah* may mean: *Pause, Crescendo* or *Musical interlude* [a]Ps. 69:6; 80:4; 84:8 [b]Ps. 9:5; Is. 26:14 [c]Is. 2:9; Jer. 18:23

6 [a]Ps. 22:16

7 [1]Or, *your* [a]Ps. 94:4; Prov. 15:2, 28 [b]Ps. 57:4 [c]Ps. 10:11; 73:11; 94:7; Job 22:13

8 [a]Ps. 37:13 [b]Ps. 2:4

9 [1]Many mss. and the ancient versions read, *My strength* [a]Ps. 18:17 [b]Ps. 9:9

10 [1]Many mss. and some ancient versions read, *The God of my lovingkindness* [2]Lit., *those who lie in wait for me* [a]Ps. 21:3 [b]Ps. 54:7

11 [1]Or, *Make them wander* [a]Deut. 4:9; 6:12 [b]Ps. 106:27; 144:6; Is. 33:3 [c]Ps. 84:9

12 [1]Or, *The sin of their mouth is the word of their lips*, [2]Lit., *lying* [a]Prov. 12:13 [b]Zeph. 3:11 [c]Ps. 10:7

13 [1]Lit., *Bring to an end* [2]Or, *is Ruler* [a]Ps. 104:35 [b]Ps. 83:18

14 [a]Ps. 59:6

15 [1]Or, *to devour* [2]Another reading is, *tarry all night*

16 [a]Ps. 21:13 [b]Ps. 101:1, [c]Ps. 5:3; 88:13 [d]Ps. 59:9 [e]Ps. 46:1; 2 Sam. 22:3

17 [1]Lit., *God of my lovingkindness* [a]Ps. 59:9 [b]Ps. 59:10

[£] Lit., *The lily of testimony.*

[•] Possibly, *Epigrammatic Poem*, or *Atonement Psalm*

[Δ] 2 Sam. 8:3, 13; 1 Chr. 18:12

1 [1]Or, *broken out upon us* [a]Ps. 44:9 [b]2 Sam. 5:20 [c]Ps. 79:5 [d]Ps. 80:3

2 [1]Or, *earth* [a]Ps. 18:7 [b]2 Chr. 7:14; Is. 30:26

3 Thou hast [1a]made Thy people experience hardship;
Thou hast given us [2]wine to [b]drink that makes us stagger.
4 Thou hast given a [a]banner to those who fear Thee,
That it may be displayed because of the truth. [[1]Selah.
5 [a]That Thy [b]beloved may be delivered,
[c]Save with Thy right hand, and answer [1]us!

6 God has spoken in His [1a]holiness:
"I will exult, I will portion out [b]Shechem and measure out the valley of [c]Succoth.
7 "[a]Gilead is Mine, and Manasseh is Mine;
[b]Ephraim also is the [1]helmet of My head;
Judah is My [2c]scepter.
8 "[a]Moab is My washbowl;
Over [b]Edom I shall throw My shoe;
Shout loud, O [c]Philistia, because of Me!"

9 Who will bring me into the beseiged city?
Who [1]will lead me to Edom?
10 Hast not Thou Thyself, O God, [a]rejected us?
And [b]wilt Thou not go forth with our armies, O God?
11 O give us help against the adversary,
For [a]deliverance [1]by man is in vain.
12 [1]Through God we shall [a]do valiantly,
And it is He who will [b]tread down our adversaries.

Psalm 61

Confidence in God's Protection.

For the choir director; on a stringed instrument. *A Psalm* of David.

[a]HEAR my cry, O God;
[b]Give heed to my prayer.
2 From the [a]end of the earth I call to Thee, when my heart is [b]faint;
Lead me to [c]the rock that is higher than I.
3 For Thou hast been a [a]refuge for me,
A [b]tower of strength [1]against the enemy.
4 Let me [1a]dwell in Thy tent forever;
Let me [b]take refuge in the shelter of Thy wings. [[2]Selah.

5 For Thou hast heard my [a]vows, O God;
Thou hast given *me* the inheritance of those who [b]fear Thy name.
6 Thou wilt [1a]prolong the king's [2]life;
His years will be as many generations.
7 He will [1]abide [a]before God forever;
Appoint [b]lovingkindness and truth, that they may preserve him.
8 So I will [a]sing praise to Thy name forever,
That I may [b]pay my vows day by day.

---

3 [1]Lit., *caused Thy people to see* [2]Lit., *wine of staggering*
[a]Ps. 66:12; 71:20 [b]Ps. 75:8; Is. 51:17, 22; Jer. 25:15

4 [1]*Selah* may mean: *Pause, Crescendo* or *Musical interlude*
[a]Ps. 20:5; Is. 5:26; 11:12; 13:2

5 [1]Some authorities read, *me*
[a]Ps. 60:5-12; Ps. 108:6-13 [b]Ps. 127:2; Deut. 33:12; Is. 5:1; Jer. 11:15 [c]Ps. 17:7

6 [1]Or, *sanctuary*
[a]Ps. 89:35 [b]Gen. 12:6; 33:18; Josh. 17:7 [c]Gen. 33:17; Josh. 13:27

7 [1]Lit., *protection* [2]Or, *lawgiver*
[a]Josh. 13:31 [b]Deut. 33:17 [c]Gen. 49:10

8 [a]2 Sam. 8:2 [b]2 Sam. 8:14 [c]2 Sam. 8:1

9 [1]Or, *has led*

10 [a]Ps. 60:1 [b]Ps. 44:9

11 [1]Lit., *of*
[a]Ps. 146:3

12 [1]Or, *In*, or, *With*
[a]Ps. 118:16; Num. 24:18 [b]Ps. 44:5; Is. 63:3

1 [a]Ps. 64:1 [b]Ps. 86:6

2 [a]Ps. 42:6 [b]Ps. 77:3 [c]Ps. 18:2; 94:22

3 [1]Lit., *from*
[a]Ps. 62:7 [b]Ps. 59:9; Prov. 18:10

4 [1]Or, *sojourn* [2]*Selah* may mean: *Pause, Crescendo* or *Musical interlude*
[a]Ps. 23:6; 27:4 [b]Ps. 17:8; 91:4

5 [a]Ps. 56:12; Job 22:27 [b]Ps. 86:11; 102:15; Deut. 28:58; Neh. 1:11; Is. 59:19; Mal. 2:5; 4:2

6 [1]Lit., *add days to* [2]Lit., *days*
[a]Ps. 21:4

7 [1]Or, *sit enthroned*
[a]Ps. 41:12 [b]Ps. 40:11

8 [a]Ps. 30:4; 33:2; 71:22; Judg. 5:3 [b]Ps. 65:1; Is. 19:21

Psalm 62

God Alone a Refuge from Treachery and Oppression.

For the choir director; [£]according to Jeduthun.
A Psalm of David.

MY soul *waits* in silence for God only;
From Him [a]is my salvation.
2 He only is my [a]rock and my salvation,
My [b]stronghold; I shall not be greatly shaken.

3 How long will you assail a man,
That you may murder *him*, all of you,
Like a [a]leaning wall, like a tottering fence?
4 They have counseled only to thrust him down from his high position;
They [a]delight in falsehood;
They [b]bless with [1]their mouth,
But inwardly they curse. [[2]Selah.

5 My soul, [a]wait in silence for God only,
For my hope is from Him.
6 He only is [a]my rock and my salvation,
My stronghold; I shall not be shaken.
7 On God my [a]salvation and my glory *rest;*
The rock of my strength, my [b]refuge is in God.
8 [a]Trust in Him at all times, O people;
[b]Pour out your heart before Him;
God is a refuge for us. [Selah.

9 Men of [a]low degree are only [b]vanity, and men of rank are a [c]lie;
In the [d]balances they go up;
They are together lighter than breath.
10 [a]Do not trust in oppression,
And do not [1]vainly hope in [b]robbery;
If riches increase, [c]do not set *your* heart *upon them.*

11 [1]Once God has [a]spoken;
[2]Twice I have heard this:
That [b]power belongs to God;
12 And lovingkindness [a]is Thine, O Lord,
For Thou [b]dost recompense a man according to his work.

Psalm 63

The Thirsting Soul Satisfied in God.

A Psalm of David, [£]when he was in the wilderness of Judah.

O GOD, [a]Thou art my God; I shall seek Thee [1]earnestly;
My soul [b]thirsts for Thee, my flesh [2]yearns for Thee,
In a [c]dry and weary land where there is no water.
2 Thus I have [a]beheld Thee in the sanctuary,
To see Thy power and Thy glory.

[£] Cf. Ps. 39 and 77 titles; 1 Chr. 16:41

1 [a]Ps. 37:39

2 [a]Ps. 89:26 [b]Ps. 59:17; 62:6

3 [a]Is. 30:13

4 [1]Lit., *his* [2]*Selah* may mean: *Pause, Crescendo* or *Musical interlude* [a]Ps. 4:2 [b]Ps. 28:3; 55:21

5 [a]Ps. 62:1

6 [a]Ps. 62:2

7 [a]Ps. 85:9 [b]Ps. 46:1

8 [a]Ps. 37:3, 5; 52:8; Is. 26:4 [b]Ps. 42:4; 1 Sam. 1:15; Lam. 2:19

9 [a]Ps. 49:2 [b]Ps. 39:5; Job 7:16; Is. 40:17 [c]Ps. 116:11 [d]Is. 40:15

10 [1]Lit., *become vain in robbery* [a]Is. 30:12 [b]Is. 61:8; Ezek. 22:29; Nah. 3:1 [c]Ps. 49:6; 52:7; Job 31:25; Mark 10:24; Luke 12:15; 1 Tim. 6:10

11 [1]Or, *One thing* [2]Or, *These two things I have heard* [a]Job 33:14; 40:5 [b]Ps. 59:17; Rev. 19:1

12 [a]Ps. 86:5; 103:8; 130:7 [b]Ps. 28:4; Job 34:11; 1 Cor. 3:8

[£] 1 Sam. 23:14

1 [1]Lit., *early* [2]Lit., *faints* [a]Ps. 118:28 [b]Ps. 42:2; 84:2; Matt. 5:6 [c]Ps. 143:6

2 [a]Ps. 27:4

3 [a]Ps. 69:16

4 [a]Ps. 104:33; 146:2 [b]Ps. 28:2; 143:6

5 [1]Lit., *fat* [a]Ps. 36:8 [b]Ps. 71:23

6 [a]Ps. 4:4 [b]Ps. 16:7; 42:8; 119:55

7 [a]Ps. 27:9 [b]Ps. 17:8

8 [1]Lit., *after* [a]Num. 32:12; Deut. 1:36; Hos. 6:3 [b]Ps. 18:35; 41:12

9 [1]Lit., *soul* [2]Lit., *lowest places* [a]Ps. 40:14 [b]Ps. 55:15

10 [1]Lit., *They will pour him out* [2]Lit., *poured out by* [3]Lit., *portion* [a]Jer. 18:21; Ezek. 35:5 [b]Lam. 5:18

11 [a]Ps. 21:1 [b]Deut. 6:13; Is. 45:23; 65:16 [c]Job 5:16; Ps. 107:42; Rom. 3:19

1 [1]Or, *concern* [a]Ps. 55:2 [b]Ps. 140:1

2 [a]Ps. 56:6 [b]Ps. 59:2

3 [a]Ps. 140:3 [b]Ps. 58:7

4 [1]Lit., *in* [a]Ps. 10:8; 11:2 [b]Ps. 55:19

5 [1]Lit., *make firm* [2]Lit., *tell of* [a]Ps. 140:5 [b]Job 22:13

6 [1]Or, *search out* [2]Lit., *complete* [3]Or, *inward part* [4]Or, *unsearchable* [a]Ps. 49:11

7 [1]Or, *shot* [2]Or, *they were wounded;* lit., *their wounds occurred* [a]Ps. 7:12, 13

8 [1]Or, *they make their tongue a stumbling for themselves* [2]Or, *made* [a]Ps. 9:3 [b]Prov. 12:13; 18:7 [c]Ps. 22:7; 44:14; Jer. 18:16; 48:27; Lam. 2:15

9 [1]Or, *feared* [2]Or, *declared* [3]Or, *considered* [4]Lit., *His work* [a]Ps. 40:3

10 [a]Ps. 32:11; Job 22:19 [b]Ps. 11:1; 25:20

3 Because Thy [a]lovingkindness is better than life,
My lips will praise Thee.
4 So I will bless Thee [a]as long as I live;
I will [b]lift up my hands in Thy name.
5 My soul is [a]satisfied as with [1]marrow and fatness.
And my mouth offers [b]praises with joyful lips;

6 When I remember Thee [a]on my bed.
I meditate on Thee in the [b]night watches.
7 For [a]Thou hast been my help,
And in the [b]shadow of Thy wings I sing for joy.
8 My soul [a]clings [1]to Thee;
Thy [b]right hand upholds me.

9 But those who [a]seek my [1]life, to destroy it,
Will go into the [2b]depths of the earth.
10 [1]They will be [2a]delivered over to the power of the sword;
They will be a [3b]prey for foxes.
11 But the [a]king will rejoice in God;
Everyone who [b]swears by Him will glory,
For the [c]mouths of those who speak lies will be stopped.

Psalm 64

Prayer for Deliverance from Secret Enemies.

For the choir director. A Psalm of David.

HEAR my voice, O God, in [a]my [1]complaint;
[b]Preserve my life from dread of the enemy.
2 Hide me from the [a]secret counsel of evildoers,
From the tumult of [b]those who do iniquity,
3 Who [a]have sharpened their tongue like a sword;
They [b]aimed bitter speech *as* their arrow,
4 To [a]shoot [1]from concealment at the blameless;
Suddenly they shoot at him, and [b]do not fear.
5 They [1]hold fast to themselves an evil purpose;
They [2]talk of [a]laying snares secretly;
They say, "[b]Who can see them?"
6 They [1]devise injustices, *saying,*
"We are [2]ready with a well-conceived plot";
For the [3a]inward thought and the heart of a man are [4]deep.

7 But [a]God [1]will shoot at them with an arrow;
Suddenly [2]they will be wounded.
8 So [1]they [2]will [a]make him stumble;
[b]Their own tongue is against them;
All who see them will [c]shake the head.
9 Then all men [1]will [a]fear,
And [2]will declare the work of God,
And [3]will consider [4]what He has done.
10 The righteous man will be [a]glad in the LORD, and will [b]take refuge in Him;
And all the upright in heart will glory.

Psalm 65

God's Abundant Favor to Earth and Man.

For the choir director. A Psalm of David.
A Song.

THERE will be silence [1]before Thee, *and* praise in Zion, O God;
And to Thee the [a]vow will be performed.
2 O Thou who dost hear prayer,
To Thee [a]all [1]men come.
3 [1a]Iniquities prevail against me;
As for our transgressions, Thou dost [2b]forgive them.
4 How [a]blessed is the one whom Thou dost choose, and bring near *to Thee,*
To dwell in Thy courts.
We will be [b]satisfied with the goodness of Thy house,
Thy holy temple.

5 By [a]awesome *deeds* Thou dost answer us in righteousness, O [b]God of our salvation,
Thou who art the trust of all the [c]ends of the earth and of the farthest [1d]sea;
6 Who dost [a]establish the mountains by His strength,
Being [b]girded with might;
7 Who dost [a]still the roaring of the seas,
The roaring of their waves,
And the [b]tumult of the peoples.
8 And they who dwell in the [a]ends *of the earth* stand in awe of Thy signs;
Thou dost make the [1]dawn and the sunset shout for joy.

9 Thou dost visit the earth, and [a]cause it to overflow;
Thou dost greatly [b]enrich it;
The [1c]stream of God is full of water;
Thou dost prepare their [d]grain, for thus Thou dost prepare [2]the earth.
10 Thou dost water its furrows abundantly;
Thou dost [1]settle its ridges;
Thou dost soften it [a]with showers;
Thou dost bless its growth.
11 Thou hast crowned the year [1]with Thy [2a]bounty,
And Thy [3]paths [b]drip *with* fatness.
12 [a]The pastures of the wilderness drip,
And the [b]hills gird themselves with rejoicing.
13 The meadows are [a]clothed with flocks,
And the valleys are [b]covered with grain;
They [c]shout for joy, yes, they sing.

1 [1]Lit., *to* [a]Ps. 116:18

2 [1]Lit., *flesh* [a]Ps. 86:9; 145:21; Is. 66:23

3 [1]Lit., *Words of iniquities* [2]Or, *cover over, atone for* [a]Ps. 38:4; 40:12 [b]Ps. 79:9

4 [a]Ps. 33:12; 84:4 [b]Ps. 36:8

5 [1]Or, *seas* [a]Ps. 45:4; 66:3 [b]Ps. 85:4 [c]Ps. 22:27; 48:10 [d]Ps. 107:23

6 [a]Ps. 95:4 [b]Ps. 93:1

7 [a]Ps. 89:9; 93:3, 4; 107:29; Matt. 8:26 [b]Ps. 2:1; 74:23; Is. 17:12, 13

8 [1]Lit., *the outgoings of the morning and evening* [a]Ps. 2:8; 139:9; Is. 24:16

9 [1]Or, *channel* [2]Lit., *it* [a]Ps. 68:9; 104:13; 147:8; Lev. 26:4; Job 5:10 [b]Ps. 104:24 [c]Ps. 46:4 [d]Ps. 104:14; 147:14

10 [1]Or, *smooth* [a]Ps. 72:6; 147:8; Deut. 32:2

11 [1]Lit., *of* [2]Or, *goodness* [3]I.e., wagon tracks [a]Ps. 104:28 [b]Ps. 147:14; Job 36:28

12 [a]Job 38:26, 27; Joel 2:22 [b]Ps. 98:8; Is. 55:12

13 [a]Ps. 144:13; Is. 30:23 [b]Ps. 72:16 [c]Ps. 98:8; Is. 44:23

1 [a]Ps. 81:1; 95:1; 98:4; 100:1

2 [a]Ps. 79:9; Is. 42:8 [b]Is. 42:12

3 [1]Lit., *deceive* [a]Ps. 47:2; 65:5; 145:6 [b]Ps. 18:44; 81:15

4 [1]*Selah* may mean: *Pause, Crescendo* or *Musical interlude* [a]Ps. 22:27; 67:7; 86:9; Zech. 14:16 [b]Ps. 67:4

5 [a]Ps. 46:8 [b]Ps. 106:22

6 [a]Ps. 106:9; Ex. 14:21 [b]Ps. 114:3; Josh. 3:16 [c]Ps. 105:43

7 [a]Ps. 145:13 [b]Ps. 11:4 [c]Ps. 140:8

8 [1]Lit., *cause to hear the sound of His praise* [a]Ps. 98:4

9 [1]Lit., *puts our soul in life* [2]Or, *dodder, stumble* [a]Ps. 30:3 [b]Ps. 121:3

10 [a]Ps. 7:9; 17:3; 26:2; Job 23:10 [b]Is. 48:10; Zech. 13:9; Mal. 3:3; 1 Pet. 1:7

11 [a]Lam. 1:13; Ezek. 12:13

12 [a]Is. 51:23 [b]Ps. 78:21; Is. 43:2 [c]Ps. 18:19

13 [a]Ps. 96:8; Jer. 17:26 [b]Ps. 22:25; 116:14

14 [a]Ps. 18:6

15 [1]Or, *cattle* [a]Ps. 51:19 [b]Num. 6:14

16 [1]Or, *revere* [a]Ps. 34:11 [b]Ps. 71:15, 24

17 [1]Or, *praise was under my tongue* [a]Ps. 30:1

18 [1]Or, *had regarded* [2]Or, *would* [3]Or, *have heard* [a]Job 36:21 [b]Ps. 18:41; Job 27:9; Prov. 1:28; 28:9; Is. 1:15; James 4:3

19 [a]Ps. 18:6; 116:1, 2

20 [a]Ps. 68:35 [b]Ps. 22:24

Psalm 66

Praise for God's Mighty Deeds and for His Answer to Prayer.

[a]For the choir director. A Song. A Psalm.

SHOUT joyfully to God, all the earth;
2 Sing the [a]glory of His name;
Make His [b]praise glorious.
3 Say to God, "How [a]awesome are Thy works!
Because of the greatness of Thy power Thine enemies will [1b]give feigned obedience to Thee.
4 "[a]All the earth will worship Thee,
And will [b]sing praises to Thee;
They will sing praises to Thy name." [[1]Selah.

5 [a]Come and see the works of God,
Who is [b]awesome in *His* deeds toward the sons of men.
6 He [a]turned the sea into dry land;
They passed through [b]the river on foot;
There let us [c]rejoice in Him!
7 He [a]rules by His might forever;
His [b]eyes keep watch on the nations;
Let not the rebellious [c]exalt themselves. [Selah.

8 Bless our God, O peoples,
And [1a]sound His praise abroad,
9 Who [1a]keeps us in life,
And [b]does not allow our feet to [2]slip.
10 For Thou hast [a]tried us, O God;
Thou hast [b]refined us as silver is refined.
11 Thou [a]didst bring us into the net;
Thou didst lay an oppressive burden upon our loins.
12 Thou didst make men [a]ride over our heads;
We went through [b]fire and through water;
Yet Thou [c]didst bring us out into *a place of* abundance.
13 I shall [a]come into Thy house with burnt offerings;
I shall [b]pay Thee my vows,
14 Which my lips uttered
And my mouth spoke when I was [a]in distress.
15 I shall [a]offer to Thee burnt offerings of fat beasts,
With the smoke of [b]rams;
I shall make *an offering of* [1]bulls with male goats. [Selah.

16 [a]Come *and* hear, all who [1]fear God,
And I will [b]tell of what He has done for my soul.
17 I cried to Him with my mouth,
And [1]He was [a]extolled with my tongue.
18 If I [1a]regard wickedness in my heart,
The [b]Lord [2]will not [3]hear;
19 But certainly [a]God has heard;
He has given heed to the voice of my prayer.
20 [a]Blessed be God,
Who [b]has not turned away my prayer,
Nor His lovingkindness from me.

Psalm 67

The Nations Exhorted to Praise God.

For the choir director; with stringed instruments. A Psalm. A Song.

1 God be gracious to us and [a]bless us,
And [b]cause His face to shine [1]upon us— [[2]Selah.
2 That [a]Thy way may be known on the earth,
Thy salvation among all nations.
3 Let the [a]peoples praise Thee, O God;
Let all the peoples praise Thee.
4 Let the [a]nations be glad and sing for joy;
For Thou wilt [b]judge the peoples with uprightness,
And [c]guide the nations on the earth. [Selah.
5 Let the [a]peoples praise Thee, O God;
Let all the peoples praise Thee.
6 The [a]earth has yielded its produce;
God, our God, [b]blesses us.
7 God blesses us,
[1]That [a]all the ends of the earth may fear Him.

Psalm 68

The God of Sinai and of the Sanctuary.

For the choir director. A Psalm of David. A Song.

1 Let [a]God arise, [2]let His enemies be scattered;
And [3]let those who hate Him flee before Him.
2 As [a]smoke is driven away, *so* drive *them* away;
As [b]wax melts before the fire,
So let the [c]wicked perish before God.
3 But let the [a]righteous be glad; let them exult before God;
Yes, let them rejoice with gladness.
4 Sing to God, [a]sing praises to His name;
[b]Cast up a highway for Him who [c]rides through the deserts,
Whose [d]name is [1]the Lord, and exult before Him.

5 A [a]father of the fatherless and a [b]judge [1]for the widows,
Is God in His [c]holy habitation.
6 God [1a]makes a home for the lonely;
He [b]leads out the prisoners into prosperity,
Only [c]the rebellious dwell in a parched land.

7 O God, when Thou [a]didst go forth before Thy people,
When Thou didst [b]march through the wilderness, [[1]Selah.
8 The [a]earth quaked;
The [b]heavens also dropped *rain* at the presence of God;
[1c]Sinai itself *quaked* at the presence of God, the God of Israel.

---

1 [1]Lit., *with* [2]*Selah* may mean: *Pause, Crescendo* or *Musical interlude*
[a]Num. 6:25 [b]Ps. 4:6; 31:16; 80:3, 7, 19; 119:135

2 [a]Ps. 98:2; Acts 18:25; Titus 2:11

3 [a]Ps. 66:4

4 [a]Ps. 100:1, 2 [b]Ps. 9:8; 96:10, 13; 98:9 [c]Ps. 47:8

5 [a]Ps. 67:3

6 [a]Ps. 85:12; Lev. 26:4; Ezek. 34:27; Zech. 8:12 [b]Ps. 29:11; 115:12

7 [1]Or, *And let . . . earth fear Him*
[a]Ps. 22:27; 33:8

1 [1]Or, *God shall* [2]Or, *His enemies shall* [3]Or, *those who hate Him shall*
[a]Ps. 12:5; 132:8; Num. 10:35

2 [a]Ps. 37:20; Is. 9:18; Hos. 13:3 [b]Ps. 22:14; 97:5; Mic. 1:4 [c]Ps. 9:3; 37:20; 80:16

3 [a]Ps. 32:11; 64:10; 97:12

4 [1]Heb., *Yah*
[a]Ps. 66:2 [b]Is. 57:14; 62:10 [c]Ps. 68:33; Ps. 18:10; Is. 40:3 [d]Ps. 83:18

5 [1]Lit., *of*
[a]Ps. 10:14; 146:9 [b]Deut. 10:18 [c]Deut. 26:15

6 [1]Lit., *makes the solitary to dwell in a house*
[a]Ps. 113:9 [b]Ps. 69:33; 102:20; 107:10, 14; 146:7; Acts 12:7; 16:26 [c]Ps. 78:17; 107:34, 40

7 [1]*Selah* may mean: *Pause, Crescendo* or *Musical interlude*
[a]Ps. 78:14; Ex. 13:21; Hab. 3:13 [b]Ps. 78:52; Judg. 5:4

8 [1]Lit., *This is Sinai* which
[a]Ps. 77:18; Ex. 19:18; Judg. 5:4; 2 Sam. 22:8; Jer. 10:10 [b]Ps. 18:9; Judg. 5:4; Is. 45:8 [c]Ex. 19:18; Judg. 5:5

9 [1]Lit., *weary*
[a]Ps. 78:24; Lev. 26:4; Job 5:10; Ezek. 34:26

10 [a]Ps. 65:9; 74:19; 78:20; 107:9

11 [1]Lit., *word*
[a]Ex. 15:20; 1 Sam. 18:6

12 [a]Ps. 135:11; Judg. 5:19 [b]Judg. 5:30; 1 Sam. 30:24

13 [1]Lit., *If* [2]Or, *cookingstones*, or, *saddle bags*
[a]Gen. 49:14; Judg. 5:16

14 [1]Lit., *in it*
[a]Josh. 10:10 [b]Judg. 9:48

15 [1]Or, *mighty mountain is*
[a]Ps. 36:6

16 [a]Ps. 87:1, 2; 132:13; Deut. 12:5 [b]Ps. 132:14

17 [1]Lit., *twice ten thousand* [2]Another reading, *The Lord came from Sinai into the sanctuary*
[a]2 Kin. 6:17; Hab. 3:8 [b]Deut. 33:2; Dan. 7:10

18 [1]Heb., *YAH*
[a]Ps. 7:7; 47:5; Eph. 4:8 [b]Judg. 5:12

19 [a]Ps. 55:22; Is. 46:4 [b]Ps. 65:5

20 [1]*YHWH, usually rendered LORD* [2]I.e., in view of; lit., *for*
[a]Ps. 106:43 [b]Ps. 49:15; 56:13

21 [a]Ps. 110:6; Heb. 3:13

22 [1]Or, *says*
[a]Amos 9:1-3

23 [1]Some versions render, you may *bathe your foot in blood*
[a]Ps. 58:10 [b]1 Kin. 21:19; Jer. 15:3

24 [1]Lit., *goings* [2]Lit., *in the sanctuary*; or, *in holiness*
[a]Ps. 77:13 [b]Ps. 63:2

25 [1]Or, *The maidens in the midst*
[a]Ps. 47:5; 1 Chr. 13:8; 15:6 [b]Ex. 15:20; Judg. 11:34

26 [a]Ps. 22:22, 23; 26:12 [b]Deut. 33:28; Is. 48:1

27 [1]Or, *smallest* [2]Or, *their ruler*
[a]Judg. 5:14; 1 Sam. 9:21 [b]Judg. 5:18

9 Thou didst [a]shed abroad a plentiful rain, O God;
Thou didst confirm Thine inheritance, when it was [1]parched.
10 Thy creatures settled in it;
Thou didst [a]provide in Thy goodness for the poor, O God.

11 The Lord gives the [1]command;
The [a]women who proclaim the *good* tidings are a great host:
12 "[a]Kings of armies flee, they flee,
And she who remains at home will [b]divide the spoil!"
13 [1]When you lie down [a]among the [2]sheepfolds,
You are like the wings of a dove covered with silver,
And its pinions with glistening gold.
14 When the Almighty [a]scattered the kings [1]there,
It was snowing in [b]Zalmon.

15 A [1a]mountain of God is the mountain of Bashan;
A mountain *of many* peaks is the mountain of Bashan.
16 Why do you look with envy, O mountains with *many* peaks,
At the mountain which God has [a]desired for His abode?
Surely, [b]the LORD will dwell *there* forever.
17 The [a]chariots of God are [1]myriads, [b]thousands upon thousands;
[2]The Lord is among them *as at* Sinai, in holiness.
18 Thou hast [a]ascended on high, Thou hast [b]led captive *Thy* captives;
Thou hast received gifts among men,
Even *among* the rebellious also, that [1]the LORD God may dwell *there*.

19 Blessed be the Lord, who daily [a]bears our burden,
[b]The God *who* is our salvation. [Selah.
20 God is to us a [a]God of deliverances;
And [b]to [1]GOD the Lord belong escapes [2]from death.
21 Surely God will [a]shatter the head of His enemies,
The hairy crown of him who goes on in his guilty deeds.
22 The Lord [1]said, "[a]I will bring *them* back from Bashan.
I will bring *them* back from the depths of the sea;
23 That [1a]your foot may shatter *them* in blood,
The tongue of your [b]dogs *may have* its portion from *your* enemies."

24 They have seen [a]Thy [1]procession, O God,
The [1]procession of my God, my King, [2b]into the sanctuary.
25 The [a]singers went on, the musicians after *them*,
[1]In the midst of the [b]maidens beating tambourines.
26 [a]Bless God in the congregations,
Even the LORD, *you who are* of the [b]fountain of Israel.
27 There is [a]Benjamin, the [1]youngest, [2]ruling them,
The princes of Judah *in* their throng,
The princes of [b]Zebulun, the princes of Naphtali.

28 [1]Your God has [a]commanded your strength;
Show Thyself strong, O God, [b]who hast acted [2]on our behalf.
29 [1]Because of Thy temple at Jerusalem
[a]Kings will bring gifts to Thee.
30 Rebuke the [a]beasts [1]in the reeds,
The herd of [b]bulls with the calves of the peoples,
Trampling under foot the pieces of silver;
He has [c]scattered the peoples who delight in war.
31 Envoys will come out of [a]Egypt;
[1b]Ethiopia will quickly stretch out her hands to God.

32 Sing to God, O [a]kingdoms of the earth;
[b]Sing praises to the Lord, [Selah.
33 To Him who [a]rides upon the [1b]highest heavens, which are from ancient times;
Behold, [c]He [2]speaks forth with His voice, a [d]mighty voice.
34 [a]Ascribe strength to God;
His majesty is over Israel,
And [b]His strength is in the [1]skies.
35 [1]O God, *Thou art* [a]awesome from Thy [2]sanctuary.
The God of Israel Himself [b]gives strength and power to the people.
[c]Blessed be God!

PSALM 69

A Cry of Distress, and Imprecation on Adversaries.

For the choir director; according to [£]Shoshannim. *A Psalm* of David.

SAVE me, O God,
For [a]the waters have come up to my soul.
2 I have sunk in deep [a]mire, and there is no foothold;
I have come into deep waters, and a [1b]flood overflows me.
3 I am [a]weary with my crying; my throat is parched;
My [b]eyes fail while I wait for my God.
4 Those [a]who hate me without a cause are more than the hairs of my head;
Those who would [1]destroy me [b]are powerful,
[c]What I did not steal, I then have to restore.

5 O God, it is Thou who dost know [a]my folly,
And [b]my wrongs are not hidden from Thee.
6 May those who wait for Thee not [a]be ashamed through me, O Lord [1]GOD of hosts;
May those who seek Thee not be dishonored through me, O God of Israel,
7 Because [a]for Thy sake I have borne reproach;
[b]Dishonor has covered my face.
8 I have become [a]estranged [1]from my brothers,
And an alien to my mother's sons.
9 For [a]zeal for Thy house has consumed me,

28 [1]Some mss. read, *Command God* [2]Lit., *for us* [a]Ps. 29:11; 44:4 [b]Is. 26:12

29 [1]Or, *From Thy temple* [a]Ps. 45:12; 72:10; 1 Kin. 10:10, 25; 2 Chr. 32:23; Is. 18:7

30 [1]Lit., *of* [a]Job 40:21; Ezek. 29:3 [b]Ps. 22:12 [c]Ps. 18:14; 89:10

31 [1]Lit., *Cush* [a]Is. 19:19, 21 [b]Is. 45:14; Zeph. 3:10

32 [a]Ps. 102:22 [b]Ps. 67:4

33 [1]Lit., *heaven of heavens of old* [2]Lit., *gives forth* [a]Ps. 18:10; 104:3; Deut. 33:26 [b]Deut. 10:14; 1 Kin. 8:27 [c]Ps. 46:6 [d]Ps. 29:4

34 [1]Lit., *clouds* [a]Ps. 29:1 [b]Ps. 150:1

35 [1]Or, *Awesome is God from your sanctuary* [2]Lit., *holy places* [a]Ps. 47:2; 66:5; Deut. 7:21; 10:17 [b]Ps. 29:11; Is. 40:29 [c]Ps. 66:20; 2 Cor. 1:3

[£] Or possibly, *Lilies*

1 [a]Ps. 69:14, 15; Ps. 32:6; 42:7; Job 22:11

2 [1]Lit., *flowing stream* [a]Ps. 40:2 [b]Jon. 2:3

3 [a]Ps. 6:6 [b]Ps. 38:10; 119:82, 123; Deut. 28:32; Is. 38:14

4 [1]Or, *silence* [a]Ps. 35:19; John 15:25 [b]Ps. 35:19; 38:19; 59:3 [c]Ps. 35:11; Jer. 15:10

5 [a]Ps. 38:5 [b]Ps. 44:21

6 [1]*YHWH, usually rendered* LORD [a]2 Sam. 12:14

7 [a]Jer. 15:15 [b]Ps. 44:15; Is. 50:6; Jer. 51:51

8 [1]Lit., *to* [a]Ps. 31:11; 38:11; Job 19:13-15

9 [a]Ps. 119:139; John 2:17

9 [b]Ps. 89:41, 50; Rom. 15:3

10 [a]Ps. 35:13

11 [a]Ps. 35:13; 1 Kin. 20:31 [b]Ps. 44:14; 1 Kin. 9:7; Job 17:6; Jer. 24:9

12 [1]Lit., *sons* [a]Gen. 19:1; Ruth 4:1 [b]Job 30:9

13 [1]Or, *the faithfulness of Thy salvation* [a]Ps. 32:6; Is. 49:8; 2 Cor. 6:2 [b]Ps. 51:1

14 [1]Lit., *those who hate me* [2]Lit., *deep places of water* [a]Ps. 69:2 [b]Ps. 144:7; [c]Ps. 69:2

15 [1]Lit., *stream* [a]Ps. 124:4, 5 [b]Ps. 28:1; 141:7; Num. 16:33

16 [a]Ps. 63:3; 109:21 [b]Ps. 51:1; 106:45 [c]Ps. 25:16; 86:16

17 [a]Ps. 27:9; 102:2; 143:7 [b]Ps. 31:9; 66:14

18 [a]Ps. 26:11; 49:15; 2 Sam. 4:9 [b]Ps. 119:134

19 [1]Or, known *to Thee* [a]Ps. 22:6; 31:11

20 [a]Jer. 23:9 [b]Ps. 142:4 [c]Job 16:2

21 [1]Or, *poison* [2]Or, *in* [a]Deut. 29:18 [b]Matt. 27:34, 48; Mark 15:23; Luke 23:36; John 19:28-30

22 [1]Lit., *for those who are secure* [a]Rom. 11:9, 10 [b]1 Thess. 5:3

23 [a]Is. 6:10 [b]Dan. 5:6

24 [a]Ps. 79:6; Jer. 10:25; Ezek. 20:8; Hos. 5:10

25 [1]Lit., *encampment* [a]Matt. 23:38; Luke 13:35; Acts 1:20

26 [1]Lit., *pierced* [a]2 Chr. 28:9; Zech. 1:15 [b]Is. 53:4 [c]Ps. 109:22

27 [a]Ps. 109:14; Neh. 4:5; Rom. 1:28 [b]Ps. 103:17

28 [1]Lit., *written* [a]Ex. 32:33; Rev. 3:5 [b]Phil. 4:3; Rev. 13:8; 20:15 [c]Ps. 87:6; Ezek. 13:9; Luke 10:20; Heb. 12:23

29 [1]Or, *Thy salvation, O God, will set . . .* [a]Ps. 70:5 [b]Ps. 20:1; 59:1

And [b]the reproaches of those who reproach Thee have fallen on me.
10 When I wept [a]in my soul with fasting,
It became my reproach.
11 When I made [a]sackcloth my clothing,
I became [b]a byword to them.
12 Those who [a]sit in the gate talk about me,
And I *am* the [1b]song of the drunkards.

13 But as for me, my prayer is to Thee, O LORD, [a]at an acceptable time;
O God, in the [b]greatness of Thy lovingkindness,
Answer me with [1]Thy saving truth.
14 Deliver me from the [a]mire, and do not let me sink;
May I be [b]delivered from [1]my foes, and from the [2c]deep waters.
15 May the [1a]flood of water not overflow me,
And may the deep not swallow me up,
And may the [b]pit not shut its mouth on me.

16 Answer me, O LORD, for [a]Thy lovingkindness is good;
[b]According to the greatness of Thy compassion, [c]turn to me,
17 And [a]do not hide Thy face from Thy servant,
For I am [b]in distress; answer me quickly.
18 Oh draw near to my soul *and* [a]redeem it;
[b]Ransom me because of my enemies!
19 Thou dost know my [a]reproach and my shame and my dishonor;
All my adversaries are [1]before Thee.

20 Reproach has [a]broken my heart, and I am so sick.
And [b]I looked for sympathy, but there was none;
And for [c]comforters, but I found none.
21 They also gave me [1a]gall [2]for my food,
And for my thirst they [b]gave me vinegar to drink.

22 May [a]their table before them become a snare;
And [1b]when they are in peace, *may it become* a trap.
23 May their [a]eyes grow dim so that they cannot see,
And make their [b]loins shake continually.
24 [a]Pour out Thine indignation on them,
And may Thy burning anger overtake them.
25 May their [1a]camp be desolate;
May none dwell in their tents.
26 For they have [a]persecuted him whom [b]Thou Thyself hast smitten,
And they tell of the pain of those whom [c]Thou hast [1]wounded.
27 Do Thou add [a]iniquity to their iniquity,
And may they not come into [b]Thy righteousness.
28 May they be [a]blotted out of the [b]book of life,
And may they not be [1c]recorded with the righteous.

29 But I am [a]afflicted and in pain;
[1]May Thy salvation, O God, [b]set me *securely* on high.

30 I will [a]praise the name of God with song,
And shall [b]magnify Him with [c]thanksgiving.
31 And it will [a]please the LORD better than an ox
Or a young bull with horns and hoofs.
32 The [a]humble [1]have seen *it and* are glad;
You who seek God, [b]let your heart [2]revive.
33 For [a]the LORD hears the needy,
And [b]does not despise His *who are* prisoners.

34 Let [a]heaven and earth praise Him,
The seas and everything that moves in them.
35 For God will [a]save Zion and [b]build the cities of Judah,
That they may dwell there and [c]possess it.
36 And the [1a]descendants of His servants will inherit it,
And those who love His name [b]will dwell in it.

PSALM 70

Prayer for Help against Persecutors.

For the choir director. *A Psalm* of David; for a memorial.

[a]O GOD, *hasten* to deliver me;
O LORD, hasten to my help!
2 Let those be ashamed and humiliated
Who seek my [1]life;
Let those be turned back and dishonored
Who delight [2]in my hurt.
3 Let those be [1]turned back because of their shame
Who say, "Aha, aha."

4 Let all who seek Thee rejoice and be glad in Thee;
And let those who love Thy salvation say continually,
"Let God be magnified."
5 But I am afflicted and needy;
[a]Hasten to me, O God!
Thou art my help and my deliverer;
O LORD, do not delay.

PSALM 71

Prayer of an Old Man for Deliverance.

[a]IN Thee, O LORD, I have taken refuge;
Let me never be ashamed.
2 In Thy righteousness deliver me, and rescue me;
Incline Thine ear to me, and save me.
3 Be Thou to me a rock of [a]habitation, to which I may continually come;
Thou hast given [b]commandment to save me,
For Thou art [c]my [1]rock and my fortress.
4 [a]Rescue me, O my God, out of the hand of the wicked,
Out of the [1]grasp of the wrongdoer and ruthless man,
5 For Thou art my [a]hope;
O Lord [1]GOD, *Thou art* my [b]confidence from my youth.

30 [a]Ps. 28:7 [b]Ps. 34:3 [c]Ps. 50:14

31 [a]Ps. 50:13, 14; 51:16

32 [1]Some mss. and ancient versions read, *will see* [2]Or, *live*
[a]Ps. 34:2 [b]Ps. 22:26

33 [a]Ps. 12:5 [b]Ps. 68:6

34 [a]Ps. 96:11; 98:7; 148:1-13; Is. 44:23; 49:13

35 [a]Ps. 46:5; 51:18 [b]Ps. 147:2; Is. 44:26 [c]Obad. 17

36 [1]Lit., *seed*
[a]Ps. 25:13; 102:28 [b]Ps. 37:29

1 [a]Ps. 70:1-5; 40:13-17

2 [1]Or, *soul* [2]Or, *to injure me*

3 [1]Some mss. read *appalled;* cf. Ps. 40:15

5 [a]Ps. 141:1

1 [a]Ps. 71:1-3; 31:1-3

3 [1]Or, *crag*
[a]Ps. 90:1; 91:9; Deut. 33:27 [b]Ps. 7:6; 42:8 [c]Ps. 18:2

4 [1]Lit., *palm*
[a]Ps. 140:1, 4

5 [1]*YHWH, usually rendered* LORD
[a]Ps. 39:7; Jer. 14:8; 17:7, 13, 17; 50:7 [b]Ps. 22:9

6 [1]Lit., *Upon Thee I have been supported* [2]Lit., *in* [a]Ps. 22:10; Is. 46:3 [b]Ps. 22:9; Job 10:18 [c]Ps. 34:1

7 [a]Is. 8:18; 1 Cor. 4:9 [b]Ps. 61:3

8 [a]Ps. 63:5 [b]Ps. 96:6; 104:1

9 [a]Ps. 71:18; 92:14; Is. 46:4

10 [1]Lit., *with reference to* [2]Lit., *soul* [a]Ps. 56:6 [b]Ps. 31:13; 83:3; Matt. 27:1

11 [a]Ps. 3:2 [b]Ps. 7:2

12 [a]Ps. 10:1; 22:11; 35:22; 38:21 [b]Ps. 38:22; 40:13; 70:5

13 [1]Lit., *my injury* [a]Ps. 35:4, 26; 40:14 [b]Ps. 109:29 [c]Ps. 71:24; Esth. 9:2

14 [1]Lit., *add upon all Thy praise* [a]Ps. 130:7 [b]Ps. 71:8

15 [1]Lit., *numbers* [a]Ps. 35:28 [b]Ps. 96:2 [c]Ps. 40:5

16 [1]*YHWH, usually rendered* LORD [a]Ps. 106:2 [b]Ps. 51:14

17 [a]Deut. 4:5; 6:7 [b]Ps. 26:7; 40:5; 119:27

18 [1]Lit., *arm* [a]Ps. 71:9 [b]Ps. 22:31; 78:4, 6

19 [1]Or, *And* [2]Lit., *height* [a]Ps. 36:6; 57:10 [b]Ps. 126:2; Luke 1:49 [c]Ps. 35:10; Deut. 3:24

20 [1]Another reading is, *us* [a]Ps. 60:3 [b]Ps. 80:18; 85:6; 119:25; 138:7; Hos. 6:2 [c]Ps. 86:13

21 [a]Ps. 18:35 [b]Ps. 23:4; 86:17; Is. 12:1; 49:13

22 [1]Lit., *an instrument of a harp* [2]Or, *faithfulness* [a]Ps. 33:2; 81:2; 144:9 [b]Ps. 33:2; 147:7 [c]Ps. 78:41; 89:18; Is. 1:4

23 [a]Ps. 5:11; 32:11; 132:9, 16 [b]Ps. 34:22; 55:18; 103:4

6 [1]By Thee I have been [a]sustained from *my* birth;
Thou art He who [b]took me from my mother's womb;
My [c]praise is continually [2]of Thee.

7 I have become a [a]marvel to many;
For Thou art [b]my strong refuge.
8 My [a]mouth is filled with Thy praise,
And with [b]Thy glory all day long.
9 Do not cast me off in the [a]time of old age;
Do not forsake me when my strength fails.
10 For my enemies have spoken [1]against me;
And those who [a]watch for my [2]life [b]have consulted together,
11 Saying, "[a]God has forsaken him;
Pursue and seize him, for there is [b]no one to deliver."

12 O God, [a]do not be far from me;
O my God, [b]hasten to my help!
13 Let those who are adversaries of my soul be [a]ashamed *and* consumed;
Let them be [b]covered with reproach and dishonor, who [c]seek [1]to injure me.
14 But as for me, I will [a]hope continually,
And will [1b]praise Thee yet more and more.
15 My [a]mouth shall tell of Thy righteousness,
And of [b]Thy salvation all day long;
For I [c]do not know the [1]sum *of them.*
16 I will come [a]with the mighty deeds of the Lord [1]GOD;
I will [b]make mention of Thy righteousness, Thine alone.

17 O God, Thou [a]hast taught me from my youth;
And I still [b]declare Thy wondrous deeds.
18 And even when *I am* [a]old and gray, O God, do not forsake me,
Until I [b]declare Thy [1]strength to *this* generation,
Thy power to all who are to come.
19 [1]For Thy [a]righteousness, O God, *reaches* to the [2]heavens,
Thou who hast [b]done great things;
O God, [c]who is like Thee?
20 Thou, who hast [a]showed [1]me many troubles and distresses,
Wilt [b]revive [1]me again,
And wilt bring [1]me up again [c]from the depths of the earth.
21 Mayest Thou increase my [a]greatness,
And turn *to* [b]comfort me.

22 I will also praise Thee with [1a]a harp,
Even Thy [2]truth, O my God;
To Thee I will sing praises with the [b]lyre,
O Thou [c]Holy One of Israel.
23 My lips will [a]shout for joy when I sing praises to Thee;
And my [b]soul, which Thou hast redeemed.

24 My [a]tongue also will utter Thy righteousness all day long;
For they are [b]ashamed, for they are humiliated who seek [1]my hurt

Psalm 72

The Reign of the Righteous King.

A Psalm of Solomon.

GIVE the king [a]Thy judgments, O God,
And [b]Thy righteousness to the king's son.
2 [1]May [2]he [a]judge Thy people with righteousness,
And [3b]Thine afflicted with justice.
3 [1]Let the mountains bring [2a]peace to the people,
And the hills in righteousness.
4 [1]May he [a]vindicate the [2]afflicted of the people,
Save the children of the needy,
And crush the oppressor.

5 [1]Let them fear Thee [a]while the sun endures,
And [2]as long as the moon, throughout all generations.
6 [1]May he come down [a]like rain upon the mown grass,
Like [b]showers that water the earth.
7 In his days [1]may the [a]righteous flourish,
And abundance of peace till the moon is no more.

8 May he also rule [a]from sea to sea,
And from the river to the ends of the earth.
9 [1]Let [a]the nomads of the desert [b]bow before him;
And his enemies [c]lick the dust.
10 [1]Let the kings of [a]Tarshish and of the [2b]islands bring presents;
The kings of [c]Sheba and [d]Seba [e]offer [3]gifts.
11 [1]And let all [a]kings bow down before him,
All [b]nations serve him.

12 For he will [a]deliver the needy when he cries for help,
The [1]afflicted also, and him who has no helper.
13 He will have [a]compassion on the poor and needy,
And the [1]lives of the needy he will save.
14 He will [1a]rescue their [2]life from oppression and violence;
And their blood will be [b]precious in his sight;
15 So may he live; and may the [a]gold of Sheba be given to him;
And let [1]them pray for him continually;
Let [1]them bless him all day long.

16 May there be abundance of grain in the earth on top of the mountains;
Its fruit will wave like *the cedars of* [a]Lebanon;
And may those from the city flourish like [b]vegetation of the earth.
17 May his [a]name endure forever;
May his name [1]increase [2b]as long as the sun *shines;*

24 [1]Or, *to injure me*
[a]Ps. 35:28 [b]Ps. 71:13

1 [a]1 Chr. 22:13; 1 Kin. 3:9
[b]Ps. 24:5

2 [1]Or, *He will judge*
[2]Many of the pronouns in this Psalm may be rendered *He* since the typical reference is to the Messiah.
[3]Or, *Thy humble*
[a]Is. 9:7; 11:2-5; 32:1 [b]Ps. 82:3

3 [1]Or, *The mountains will bring* [2]Or, *prosperity*
[a]Is. 2:4; 9:5, 6; Mic. 4:3, 4; Zech. 9:10

4 [1]Or, *He will vindicate*
[2]Or, *humble*
[a]Is. 11:4

5 [1]Or, *They will fear* [2]Lit., *before the moon*
[a]Ps. 89:36, 37

6 [1]Or, *He will come down*
[a]Deut. 32:2; 2 Sam. 23:4; Hos. 6:3 [b]Ps. 65:10

7 [1]Or, *The righteous will flourish*
[a]Ps. 92:12

8 [a]Ex. 23:31; Zech. 9:10

9 [1]Or, *The nomads . . . will bow*
[a]Ps. 74:14; Is. 23:13 [b]Ps. 22:29 [c]Is. 49:23; Mic. 7:17

10 [1]Or, *The kings . . . will bring* [2]Or, *coastlands* [3]Or, *tribute*
[a]2 Chr. 9:21; Ps. 48:7 [b]Ps. 97:1; Is. 42:4, 10; Zeph 2:11 [c]1 Kin. 10:1; Job 6:19; Is. 60:6 [d]Gen. 10:7; Is. 43:3 [e]Ps. 45:12; 68:29

11 [1]Or, *All kings will bow down*
[a]Ps. 138:4; Is. 49:23 [b]Ps. 86:9

12 [1]Or, *humble*
[a]Ps. 72:4; Job 29:12

13 [1]Lit., *souls*
[a]Prov. 19:17; 28:8

14 [1]Lit., *redeem* [2]Lit., *soul*
[a]Ps. 69:18 [b]Ps. 116:15; 1 Sam. 26:21

15 [1]Lit., *him*
[a]Is. 60:6

16 [a]Ps. 104:16 [b]Job 5:25

17 [1]Or, *sprout forth* [2]Lit., *before the sun*
[a]Ps. 135:13; Ex. 3:15 [b]Ps. 89:36

And let *men* [c]bless themselves by him;
[d]Let all nations call him blessed.

18 [a]Blessed be the LORD God, the God of Israel,
Who alone [b]works wonders.
19 And blessed be His [a]glorious name forever;
And may the whole [b]earth be filled with His glory.
[c]Amen, and Amen.

20 The prayers of David the son of Jesse are ended.

BOOK 3

PSALM 73

The End of the Wicked Contrasted with That of the Righteous.

A Psalm of Asaph.

SURELY God is [a]good to Israel,
To those who are [b]pure in heart!
2 But as for me, [a]my feet came close to stumbling;
My steps [1]had almost slipped.
3 For I was [a]envious of the [1]arrogant,
As I saw the [b]prosperity of the wicked.
4 For there are no pains in their death;
And their [1]body is [a]fat.
5 They are [a]not [1]in trouble *as other* [2]men;
Nor are they [b]plagued [3]like mankind.
6 Therefore pride is [a]their necklace;
The [b]garment of violence covers them.
7 Their eye [1]bulges from [a]fatness;
The imaginations of *their* heart [2]run riot.
8 They [a]mock, and [1]wickedly speak of oppression;
They [b]speak from on high.
9 They have set their mouth [1]against the heavens,
And their tongue [2]parades through the earth.

10 Therefore [1]his people return to this place;
And waters of [a]abundance are [2]drunk by them.
11 And they say, "[a]How does God know?
And is there knowledge [1]with the Most High?"
12 Behold, [a]these are the wicked;
And always [b]at ease, they have increased *in* wealth.
13 Surely [a]in vain I have [1]kept my heart pure,
And [b]washed my hands in innocence;
14 For I have been stricken [a]all day long,
And [1b]chastened every morning.

15 If I had said, "I will speak thus";
Behold, I should have betrayed the [a]generation of Thy children.
16 When I [a]pondered to understand this,
It was [1]troublesome in my sight,
17 Until I came into the [1a]sanctuary of God;
Then I perceived their [b]end.

17 [c]Gen. 12:3; 22:18 [d]Luke 1:48

18 [a]Ps. 41:13; 89:52; 106:48 [b]Ps. 77:14; 86:10; 136:4; Ex. 15:11; Job 5:9

19 [a]Ps. 96:8; Neh. 9:5 [b]Num. 14:21 [c]Ps. 41:13

1 [a]Ps. 86:5 [b]Ps. 24:4; 51:10; Matt. 5:8

2 [1]Lit., *were caused to slip* [a]Ps. 94:18

3 [1]Or, *boasters* [a]Ps. 37:1; Prov. 23:17 [b]Ps. 37:7; Jer. 12:1

4 [1]Or, *belly* [a]Ps. 10:5

5 [1]Lit., *in the trouble of men* [2]Or, *mortals* [3]Lit., *with* [a]Ps. 73:12; Job 21:9 [b]Ps. 73:14

6 [a]Gen. 41:42; Prov. 1:9 [b]Ps. 109:18

7 [1]Lit., *goes forth* [2]Lit., *overflow* [a]Ps. 17:10; Job 15:27

8 [1]Or, *they speak in wickedness; From on high they speak of oppression.* [a]Ps. 1:1 [b]Ps. 17:10; 2 Pet. 2:18; Jude 16

9 [1]Or, *in* [2]Lit., *walks*

10 [1]Or, *His* [2]Lit., *drained out* [a]Ps. 23:5

11 [1]Lit., *in* [a]Job 22:13

12 [a]Ps. 49:6; 52:7 [b]Jer. 49:31; Ezek. 23:42

13 [1]Or, *cleansed my heart* [a]Job 21:15; 34:9; 35:3 [b]Ps. 26:6

14 [1]Lit., *my chastening* [a]Ps. 38:6 [b]Ps. 118:18; Job 33:19

15 [a]Ps. 14:5

16 [1]Lit., *labor, trouble* [a]Eccles. 8:17

17 [1]Lit., *sanctuaries* [a]Ps. 27:4; 77:13 [b]Ps. 37:38

18 Surely Thou dost set them in [a]slippery places;
Thou dost cast them down to [1b]destruction.
19 How they are [1a]destroyed in a moment!
They are utterly swept away by [b]sudden terrors!
20 Like a [a]dream when one awakes,
O Lord, when [b]aroused, Thou wilt [c]despise their [1]form.

21 When my [a]heart was embittered,
And I was [b]pierced [1]within,
22 Then I was [a]senseless and ignorant;
I was *like* a [1b]beast [2]before Thee.
23 Nevertheless [a]I am continually with Thee;
Thou hast taken hold of my right hand.
24 With Thy counsel Thou wilt [a]guide me,
And afterward [b]receive me [1]to glory.

25 [a]Whom have I in heaven *but thee?*
And [1]besides Thee, I desire nothing on earth.
26 My [a]flesh and my heart may fail;
But God is the [1]strength of my heart and my [b]portion
forever.
27 For, behold, those who are far from Thee will [a]perish;
Thou hast [1]destroyed all those who [2b]are unfaithful to
Thee.
28 But as for me, [a]the nearness of God is my good;
I have made the Lord [1]God my [b]refuge.
That I may [c]tell of all Thy works.

Psalm 74

An Appeal against the Devastation of the Land by the Enemy.

A [£]Maskil of Asaph.

O GOD, why hast Thou [a]rejected *us* forever?
Why does Thine anger [b]smoke against the [c]sheep of
Thy [1]pasture?
2 Remember Thy congregation, which Thou hast [a]pur-
chased of old,
Which Thou hast [b]redeemed to be the [c]tribe of Thine
inheritance;
And Mount [d]Zion, where Thou hast dwelt.
3 [1]Turn Thy footsteps toward the [a]perpetual ruins,
The enemy [b]has damaged everything within the
sanctuary.
4 Thine adversaries have [a]roared in the midst of Thy
meeting place;
They have set up their [b]own [1]standards [c]for signs.
5 It seems as if one had lifted up
His [1a]axe in a [2]forest of trees.
6 And now [1]all its [a]carved work
They smash with hatchet and [2]hammers.
7 They have [1a]burned Thy sanctuary [2]to the ground;
They have [b]defiled the dwelling place of Thy name.
8 They [a]said in their heart, "Let us [1]completely [2]subdue
them."

18 [1]Lit., *ruins*
[a]Ps. 35:6 [b]Ps. 35:8; 36:12

19 [1]Lit., *become a desolation*
[a]Num. 16:21; Is. 47:11 [b]Job 18:11

20 [1]Or, *image*
[a]Job 20:8 [b]Ps. 78:65 [c]1 Sam. 2:30

21 [1]Lit., *in my kidneys*
[a]Judg. 10:16 [b]Acts 2:37

22 [1]Or, *animal* [2]Lit., *with Thee*
[a]Ps. 49:10; 92:6 [b]Ps. 49:20; Job 18:3; Eccles. 3:18

23 [a]Ps. 16:8

24 [1]Or, *with honor*
[a]Ps. 32:8; 48:14; Is. 58:11 [b]Ps. 49:15; Gen. 5:24

25 [1]Or, *with*
[a]Ps. 16:2

26 [1]Lit., *rock*
[a]Ps. 38:10; 40:12; 84:2; 119:81 [b]Ps. 16:5

27 [1]Or, *silenced* [2]Lit., *go to a whoring from*
[a]Ps. 37:20 [b]Ps. 106:39; Ex. 34:15; Num. 15:39; Hos. 4:12; 9:1

28 [1]*YHWH, usually rendered* Lord
[a]Ps. 65:4; Heb. 10:22; James 4:8 [b]Ps. 14:6; 71:7 [c]Ps. 40:5; 107:22; 118:17

[£] Possibly, *Contemplative*, or *Didactic*, or *Skillful Psalm*

1 [1]Or, *pasturing*
[a]Ps. 44:9; 77:7 [b]Ps. 18:8; 89:46; Deut. 29:20 [c]Ps. 79:13; 95:7; 100:3

2 [a]Ex. 15:16; Deut. 32:6 [b]Ps. 77:15; 106:10; Ex. 15:13; Is. 63:9 [c]Deut. 32:9; Is. 63:17; Jer. 10:16; 51:19 [d]Ps. 9:11; 68:16

3 [1]Lit., *Lift up*
[a]Is. 61:4 [b]Ps. 79:1

4 [1]Lit., *signs*
[a]Lam. 2:7 [b]Num. 2:2 [c]Ps. 74:9

5 [1]Lit., *axes* [2]Lit., *thicket*
[a]Jer. 46:22

6 [1]Lit., *altogether* [2]Or, *axes*
[a]1 Kin. 6:18, 29, 32, 35

7 [1]Lit., *set on fire* [2]Or, *To the ground they . . .*
[a]2 Kin. 25:9 [b]Ps. 89:39; Lam. 2:2

8 [1]Lit., *altogether* [2]Or, *oppress*
[a]Ps. 83:4

They have burned all the meeting places of God in the land.
9 We do not see our [a]signs,
There is [b]no longer any prophet,
Nor is there any among us who knows [c]how long.
10 How long, O God, will the adversary [a]revile,
And the enemy [b]spurn Thy name forever?
11 Why [a]dost Thou withdraw Thy hand, even Thy right hand?
From within Thy bosom, [b]destroy *them!*

12 Yet God is [a]my king from of old,
Who works deeds of deliverance in the midst of the earth.
13 [1]Thou didst [a]divide the sea by Thy strength;
[1]Thou [b]didst break the heads of the [c]sea-monsters [2]in the waters.
14 [1]Thou didst crush the heads of [2a]Leviathan;
[1]Thou didst give him as food for the [3]creatures [b]of the wilderness.
15 [1]Thou didst [a]break open springs and torrents;
[1]Thou didst [b]dry up ever-flowing streams.
16 Thine is the day, Thine is the night;
[1]Thou hast [a]prepared the [2]light and the sun.
17 [1]Thou hast [a]established all the boundaries of the earth;
[1]Thou hast [2]made [b]summer and winter.

18 Remember this, [1]O LORD, that the enemy has [a]reviled;
And a [b]foolish people has spurned Thy name.
19 Do not deliver the soul of Thy [a]turtle-dove to the wild beast;
[b]Do not forget the life of Thine afflicted forever.
20 Consider the [a]covenant;
For the [b]dark places of the land are full of the habitations of violence.
21 Let not the [a]oppressed return dishonored;
Let the [b]afflicted and needy praise Thy name.

22 Do arise, O God, *and* [a]plead Thine own cause;
Remember [1]how the [b]foolish man reproaches Thee all day long.
23 Do not forget the voice of Thine [a]adversaries,
The [b]uproar of those who rise against Thee which ascends continually.

PSALM 75

God Abases the Proud, but Exalts the Righteous.

For the choir director; *set to* [£]Al-tashheth.
A Psalm of Asaph, a Song.

WE [a]give thanks to Thee, O God, we give thanks,
For Thy name is [b]near;
Men declare [c]Thy wondrous works.
2 "When I select an [a]appointed time;
It is I who [b]judge with equity.

9 [a]Ps. 78:43 [b]1 Sam. 3:1; Lam. 2:9; Ezek. 7:26; Amos 8:11 [c]Ps. 6:3; 79:5; 80:4

10 [a]Ps. 44:16; 79:12; 89:51 [b]Lev. 24:16

11 [a]Lam. 2:3 [b]Ps. 59:13

12 [a]Ps. 44:4

13 [1]Or, *Thou Thyself* [2]Lit., *on*
[a]Ps. 78:13; Ex. 14:21 [b]Is. 51:9 [c]Ps. 148:7; Jer. 51:34

14 [1]Or, *Thou Thyself* [2]Or, *sea-monster* [3]Lit., *people*
[a]Ps. 104:26; Job 41:1 [b]Ps. 72:9

15 [1]Or, *Thou Thyself*
[a]Ps. 78:15; 105:41; 114:8; Ex. 17:5, 6; Num. 20:11; Is. 48:21 [b]Ps. 114:3; Ex. 14:21, 22; Josh. 2:10; 3:13

16 [1]Or, *Thou Thyself* [2]Or, *luminary*
[a]Ps. 104:19; 136:7, 8; Gen. 1:14-18

17 [1]Or, *Thou Thyself* [2]Or, *formed*
[a]Deut. 32:8; Acts 17:26 [b]Ps. 147:16-18

18 [1]Or, *that the enemy has reviled the LORD*
[a]Ps. 74:10 [b]Ps. 39:8; Deut. 32:6; Ps. 14:1; 53:1

19 [a]Song of Sol. 2:14 [b]Ps. 9:18

20 [a]Ps. 106:45; Gen. 17:7 [b]Ps. 88:6; 143:3

21 [a]Ps. 103:6 [b]Ps. 35:10; Is. 41:17

22 [1]Lit., *Thy reproach from the foolish man*
[a]Ps. 43:1; Is. 3:13; 43:26; Ezek. 20:35 [b]Ps. 14:1; 53:1; 74:18

23 [a]Ps. 74:10 [b]Ps. 65:7

[£] Lit., *Do Not Destroy*

1 [a]Ps. 79:13 [b]Ps. 145:18 [c]Ps. 26:7; 44:1; 71:17

2 [a]Ps. 102:13 [b]Ps. 9:8; 67:4; Is. 11:4

3 "The [a]earth and all who dwell in it [1]melt;
It is I who have firmly set its [b]pillars. [[2]Selah.
4 "I said to the boastful, 'Do not boast,'
And to the wicked, '[a]Do not lift up the horn;
5 Do not lift up your horn on high,
[a]Do not speak with insolent [1]pride.' "

6 For not from the east, nor from the west,
Nor from the [1a]desert *comes* exaltation;
7 But [a]God is the Judge;
He [b]puts down one, and exalts another.
8 For a [a]cup is in the hand of the LORD, and the wine foams;
It is [1b]well mixed, and He pours out of this;
Surely all the wicked of the earth must drain *and* [c]drink down its dregs.

9 But as for me, I will [a]declare *it* forever,
I will sing praises to the God of Jacob.
10 And all the [a]horns of the wicked I will cut off,
But [b]the horns of the righteous will be lifted up.

PSALM 76

The Victorious Power of the God of Jacob.

For the choir director; on stringed instruments.
A Psalm of Asaph, a Song.

GOD is [a]known in Judah;
His name is [b]great in Israel.
2 And His [1a]tabernacle is in [b]Salem,
His [c]dwelling place also is in Zion.
3 There He [a]broke the [1]flaming arrows,
The shield, and the sword, and the [2]weapons of war. [[3]Selah.

4 Thou art resplendent,
[1]More majestic than the mountains of prey.
5 The [a]stouthearted were plundered;
[1]They sank into sleep;
And none of the [2]warriors could use his hands.
6 At Thy [a]rebuke, O God of Jacob,
Both [1b]rider and horse were cast into a dead sleep.
7 Thou, even Thou, art [a]to be feared;
And [b]who may stand in Thy presence when once [1]Thou art angry?

8 Thou didst cause judgment to be heard from heaven;
The earth [a]feared, and was still,
9 When God [a]arose to judgment,
To save all the humble of the earth. [Selah.
10 For the [1a]wrath of man shall praise Thee;
With a remnant of wrath Thou shalt gird Thyself.

11 Make vows to the LORD your God and [a]fulfill *them*;

---

3 [1]Or, *totter* [2]*Selah* may mean: *Pause, Crescendo* or *Musical interlude*
[a]Ps. 46:6; Is. 24:19 [b]1 Sam. 2:8

4 [a]Zech. 1:21

5 [1]Lit., *neck*
[a]Ps. 94:4; 1 Sam. 2:3

6 [1]Or, *mountainous desert*
[a]Ps. 3:3; 113:7

7 [a]Ps. 50:6 [b]Ps. 147:6; 1 Sam. 2:7; Dan. 2:21

8 [1]Lit., *full of mixture*
[a]Ps. 11:6; 60:3; Job 21:20; Jer. 25:15 [b]Prov. 23:30 [c]Obad. 16

9 [a]Ps. 22:22; 40:10

10 [a]Jer. 48:25 [b]Ps. 89:17; 92:10; 148:14; 1 Sam. 2:1

1 [a]Ps. 48:3 [b]Ps. 99:3

2 [1]Lit., *shelter*
[a]Ps. 27:5; Lam. 2:6 [b]Gen. 14:18 [c]Ps. 9:11; 132:13; 135:21

3 [1]Lit., *fiery shafts of the bow* [2]Lit., *battle* [3]*Selah* may mean: *Pause, Crescendo* or *Musical interlude*
[a]Ps. 46:9

4 [1]Or, *Majestic from the mountains*

5 [1]Lit., *they slumbered their sleep* [2]Lit., *men of might have found their hands*
[a]Is. 10:12; 46:12

6 [1]Lit., *chariot*
[a]Ps. 80:16 [b]Ps. 78:53; Ex. 15:1, 21

7 [1]Lit., *Thine anger is*
[a]Ps. 89:7; 96:4; 1 Chr. 16:25 [b]Ps. 130:3; Ezra 9:15; Nah. 1:6; Mal. 3:2; Rev. 6:17

8 [a]Ps. 33:8; 1 Chr. 16:30

9 [a]Ps. 74:22; 82:8

10 [1]Lit., *wraths*
[a]Ex. 9:16; Rom. 9:17

11 [a]Ps. 50:14

11 [b]Ps. 68:29

12 [1]Lit., *awesome* [a]Ps. 47:2

1 [a]Ps. 3:4; 142:1

2 [1]Lit., *and did not grow numb* [a]Ps. 50:15; 86:7 [b]Ps. 63:6; Is. 26:9 [c]Ps. 88:9; Job 11:13 [d]Gen. 37:35

3 [1]*Selah* may mean: *Pause, Crescendo* or *Musical interlude* [a]Ps. 42:5, 11; 43:5 [b]Ps. 55:2; 142:2 [c]Ps. 61:2; 143:4

4 [1]Lit., *watching* [a]Ps. 39:9

5 [a]Ps. 44:1; 143:5; Deut. 32:7; Is. 51:9

6 [1]Lit., *searched* [a]Ps. 42:8 [b]Ps. 4:4

7 [a]Ps. 44:9 [b]Ps. 85:1, 5

8 [1]Lit., *word* [2]Lit., *from generation to generation* [a]Ps. 89:49 [b]2 Pet. 3:9

9 [1]Lit., *shut up* [a]Is. 49:15 [b]Ps. 25:6; 40:11; 51:1

10 [1]Or, *infirmity, the years of the right hand of the Most High* [a]Ps. 31:22; 73:15 [b]Ps. 44:2, 3

11 [1]Heb., YAH [a]Ps. 105:5; 143:5

12 [a]Ps. 145:5

13 [a]Ps. 63:2; 73:17 [b]Ps. 71:19; 86:8; Ex. 15:11

14 [a]Ps. 72:18 [b]Ps. 106:8

15 [1]Lit., *arm* [a]Ps. 74:2; 78:42; Ex. 6:6; Deut. 9:29 [b]Ps. 80:1

16 [a]Ps. 114:3; Ex. 14:21; Hab. 3:8, 10

17 [1]Lit., *went* [a]Judg. 5:4 [b]Ps. 68:33 [c]Ps. 18:14

18 [a]Ps. 18:13; 104:7

Let all who are around Him [b]bring gifts to Him who is
to be feared.
12 He will cut off the spirit of princes;
He is [1a]feared by the kings of the earth.

Psalm 77

Comfort in Trouble from Recalling God's Mighty Deeds.

For the choir director; according to Jeduthun.
A Psalm of Asaph.

MY voice *rises* to God, and I will [a]cry aloud;
My voice *rises* to God, and He will hear me.
2 In the [a]day of my trouble I sought the Lord;
[b]In the night my [c]hand was stretched out [1]without
weariness;
My soul [d]refused to be comforted.
3 *When* I remember God, then I am [a]disturbed;
When I [b]sigh, then [c]my spirit grows faint. [[1]Selah.
4 Thou hast held my eyelids [1]*open;*
I am so troubled that I [a]cannot speak.
5 I have considered the [a]days of old,
The years of long ago.
6 I will remember my [a]song in the night;
I [b]will meditate with my heart;
And my spirit [1]ponders.

7 Will the Lord [a]reject forever?
And will He [b]never be favorable again?
8 Has His [a]lovingkindness ceased forever?
Has *His* [1b]promise come to an end [2]forever?
9 Has God [a]forgotten to be gracious?
Or has He in anger [1]withdrawn His [b]compassion?
[Selah.
10 Then I said, "[a]It is my [1]grief,
That the [b]right hand of the Most High has changed."

11 I shall remember the [a]deeds of [1]the LORD;
Surely I will [a]remember Thy wonders of old.
12 I will [a]meditate on all Thy work,
And muse on Thy deeds.
13 Thy way, O God, is [a]holy;
[b]What god is great like our God?
14 Thou art the [a]God who workest wonders;
Thou hast [b]made known Thy strength among the
peoples.
15 Thou hast by Thy [1]power [a]redeemed Thy people,
The sons of Jacob and [b]Joseph. [Selah.

16 The [a]waters saw Thee, O God;
The waters saw Thee, they were in anguish;
The deeps also trembled.
17 The [a]clouds poured out water;
The skies [b]gave forth a sound;
Thy [c]arrows [1]flashed here and there.
18 The [a]sound of Thy thunder was in the whirlwind;

The [b]lightnings lit up the world;
The [c]earth trembled and shook,
19 Thy [a]way was in the sea,
And Thy paths in the mighty waters,
And Thy footprints may not be known.
20 Thou [a]didst lead Thy people like a flock,
By the hand of [b]Moses and Aaron.

PSALM 78

God's Guidance of His People in Spite of Their Unfaithfulness.

[£]Maskil of Asaph.

[a]LISTEN, O my people, to my [1]instruction;
[b]Incline your ears to the words of my mouth.
2 I will [a]open my mouth in a parable;
I will utter [b]dark sayings of old,
3 Which we have heard and known,
And [a]our fathers have told us.
4 We will [a]not conceal them from their children,
But tell to the [b]generation to come the praises of the LORD,
And His strength and His [c]wondrous works that He has done.

5 For He established a [a]testimony in Jacob,
And appointed a [b]law in Israel,
Which He [c]commanded our fathers,
That they should [1d]teach them to their children;
6 That the generation to come might know, *even* [a]the children *yet* to be born,
That they may arise and [b]tell *them* to their children,
7 That they should put their confidence in God,
And [a]not forget the works of God,
But [b]keep His commandments,
8 And [a]not be like their fathers,
A [b]stubborn and rebellious generation,
A generation that [c]did not [1]prepare its heart,
And whose spirit was not [d]faithful to God.

9 The sons of Ephraim [1]were [a]archers equipped with bows,
Yet [b]they turned back in the day of battle.
10 They [a]did not keep the covenant of God,
And refused to [b]walk in His Law;
11 And they [a]forgot His deeds,
And His [1]miracles that He had shown them.
12 [a]He wrought wonders before their fathers,
In the land of Egypt, in the [b]field of Zoan.
13 He [a]divided the sea, and caused them to pass through;
And He made the waters stand [b]up like a heap.
14 Then He led them with the cloud by [a]day,
And all the night with a [b]light of fire.
15 He [a]split the rocks in the wilderness,
And gave *them* abundant drink like the ocean depths.

18 [b]Ps. 97:4 [c]Ps. 18:7; Judg. 5:4

19 [a]Is. 51:10; Hab. 3:15

20 [a]Ps. 78:52; 80:1; Ex. 13:21; 14:19; Is. 63:11-13 [b]Ps. 105:26; Ex. 6:26

[£] Possibly, *Contemplative*, or *Didactic*, or *Skillful Psalm*

1 [1]Or, *law, teaching* [a]Is. 51:4 [b]Is. 55:3

2 [a]Ps. 49:4; Matt. 13:35 [b]Prov. 1:6

3 [a]Ps. 44:1

4 [a]Ps. 145:4; Ex. 12:26; Deut. 11:19; Job 15:18; Is. 38:19; Joel 1:3 [b]Ps. 22:30 [c]Ps. 26:7; 71:17; Job 37:16

5 [1]Lit., *make them known* [a]Ps. 19:7; 81:5; Is. 8:20 [b]Ps. 147:19 [c]Deut. 6:4-9 [d]Deut. 4:9

6 [a]Ps. 22:31 [b]Deut. 11:19

7 [a]Deut. 4:9; 6:12; 8:14 [b]Deut. 4:2; 5:1, 29; 27:1; Josh. 22:5

8 [1]Or, *put right* [a]2 Chr. 30:7; Ezek. 20:18 [b]Deut. 9:7, 24; 31:27; Judg. 2:19; Is. 30:9 [c]Ps. 78:37; Job 11:13 [d]Ps. 51:10

9 [1]Or, *being* [a]1 Chr. 12:2 [b]Ps. 78:57; Judg. 20:39

10 [a]Judg. 2:20; 1 Kin. 11:11; 2 Kin. 18:12 [b]Ps. 119:1; Jer. 32:23; 44:10, 23

11 [1]Or, *wonderful works* [a]Ps. 106:13

12 [a]Ps. 106:22; Ex. 7:12 [b]Ps. 78:43; Num. 13:22; Is. 19:11; 30:4; Ezek. 30:14

13 [a]Ps. 74:13; 136:13; Ex. 14:21 [b]Ps. 33:7; Ex. 15:8

14 [a]Ps. 105:39; Ex. 13:21 [b]Ex. 14:24

15 [a]Ps. 105:41; 114:8; Ex. 17:6; Is. 48:21; 1 Cor. 10:4

16 [a]Num. 20:8, 10, 11

17 [a]Deut. 9:22; Is. 63:10

18 [a]Ps. 78:41, 56; 95:9; 106:14; Ex. 17:6; Deut. 6:16; 1 Cor. 10:9 [b]Num. 11:4

19 [a]Ex. 16:3; Num. 11:4; 20:3; 21:5

20 [1]Lit., *flesh* [a]Ps. 78:15, 16 [b]Num. 11:18

21 [1]Or, *became infuriated* [a]Num. 11:1

22 [a]Deut. 1:32; 9:23; Heb. 3:18

23 [a]Gen. 7:11; Mal. 3:10

24 [1]Lit., *grain* [a]Ex. 16:4 [b]Ps. 105:40; John 6:31

25 [1]Lit., *mighty ones* [2]Or, *provision* [3]Lit., *to satiation* [a]Ex. 16:3

26 [1]Or, *strength* [a]Num. 11:31

27 [1]Lit., *flesh* [a]Ps. 105:40; Ex. 16:13

28 [1]Lit., *His*

29 [a]Num. 11:19, 20

30 [1]Lit., *They were not estranged from*

31 [1]Lit., *among their fat ones* [2]Lit., *caused to bow down* [a]Num. 11:33, 34; Job 20:23 [b]Is. 10:16

32 [a]Num. 14:16, 17 [b]Num. 14:11; Ps. 78:11

33 [1]Lit., *vanity, a mere breath* [a]Num. 14:29, 35

34 [a]Num. 21:7; Hos. 5:15 [b]Ps. 63:1

35 [a]Deut. 32:4 [b]Ps. 74:2; Ex. 15:13; Deut. 9:26

36 [a]Ex. 24:7, 8; Ezek. 33:31 [b]Ex. 32:7, 8; Is. 57:11

37 [a]Ps. 78:8; 51:10

38 [1]Lit., *covered over, atoned for* [2]Lit., *turned away* [a]Ex. 34:6 [b]Num. 14:20

16 He [a]brought forth streams also from the rock,
And caused waters to run down like rivers.

17 Yet they still continued to sin against Him,
To [a]rebel against the Most High in the desert.
18 And in their heart they [a]put God to the test
By asking [b]food according to their desire.
19 Then they spoke against God;
They said, "[a]Can God prepare a table in the wilderness?
20 "Behold, He [a]struck the rock, so that waters gushed out,
And streams were overflowing;
Can He give bread also?
Will He provide [1b]meat for His people?"

21 Therefore the LORD heard and [1]was [a]full of wrath,
And a fire was kindled against Jacob,
And anger also mounted against Israel;
22 Because they [a]did not believe in God,
And did not trust in His salvation.
23 Yet He commanded the clouds above,
And [a]opened the doors of heaven;
24 And He [a]rained down manna upon them to eat,
And gave them [1b]food from heaven.
25 Man did eat the bread of [1]angels;
He sent them [2]food [3a]in abundance.
26 He [a]caused the east wind to blow in the heavens;
And by His [1]power He directed the south wind.
27 When He rained [1]meat upon them like the dust,
Even [a]winged fowl like the sand of the seas;
28 Then He let *them* fall in the midst of [1]their camp,
Round about their dwellings.
29 So they [a]ate and were well filled;
And their desire He gave to them.
30 [1]Before they had satisfied their desire,
While their food was in their mouths,
31 The [a]anger of God rose against them,
And killed [1]some of their [b]stoutest ones,
And [2]subdued the choice men of Israel.
32 In spite of all this they [a]still sinned,
And [b]did not believe in His wonderful works.
33 So He brought [a]their days to an end in [1]futility,
And their years in sudden terror.

34 When He killed them, then they [a]sought Him,
And returned and searched [b]diligently for God;
35 And they remembered that God was their [a]rock,
And the Most High God their [b]redeemer.
36 But they [a]deceived Him with their mouth,
And [b]lied to Him with their tongue.
37 For their heart was not [a]steadfast toward Him,
Nor were they faithful in His covenant.
38 But He, being [a]compassionate, [1b]forgave *their* iniquity, and did not destroy *them;*
And often He [2]restrained His anger,
And did not arouse all His wrath.

39 Thus [a]He remembered that they were but [b]flesh,
A [1c]wind that passes and does not return.

40 How often they [a]rebelled against Him in the wilderness,
And [b]grieved Him in the [c]desert!
41 And again and again they [1a]tempted God,
And pained the [b]Holy One of Israel.
42 They [a]did not remember [b]His [1]power,
The day when He [c]redeemed them from the adversary,
43 When He performed His [a]signs in Egypt,
And His [b]marvels in the field of Zoan,
44 And [a]turned their rivers to blood,
And their streams, they could not drink.
45 He sent among them swarms of [a]flies, which devoured them,
And [b]frogs which destroyed them.
46 He gave also their crops to the [a]grasshopper,
And the product of their labor to the [b]locust.
47 He [1]destroyed their vines with [a]hailstones,
And their sycamore trees with frost.
48 He gave over their [a]cattle also to the hailstones,
And their herds to bolts of lightning.
49 He [a]sent upon them His burning anger,
Fury, and indignation, and trouble,
[1]A band of destroying angels.
50 He leveled a path for His anger;
He [a]did not spare their soul from death,
But [b]gave over their life to the plague,
51 And [a]smote all the first-born in Egypt,
The [b]first *issue* of their virility in the tents of [c]Ham.
52 But He [a]led forth His own people like sheep,
And guided them in the wilderness [b]like a flock;
53 And He led them [a]safely, so that they did not fear;
But [b]the sea engulfed their enemies.

54 So [a]He brought them to His holy [1]land,
To this [2b]hill country which His right hand had gained.
55 He also [a]drove out the nations before them,
And He [b]apportioned them for an inheritance by measurement,
And made the tribes of Israel dwell in their tents.
56 Yet they [1a]tempted and [b]rebelled against the Most High God,
And did not keep His testimonies,
57 But turned back and [a]acted treacherously like their fathers;
They turned aside like a treacherous bow.
58 For they [a]provoked Him with their [b]high places,
And [c]aroused His jealousy with their [d]graven images.
59 When God heard, He [1]was filled with [a]wrath,
And greatly [b]abhorred Israel;
60 So that He [a]abandoned the dwelling place at Shiloh,
The tent [1]which He had pitched among men;
61 And gave up His [a]strength to captivity,
And His glory [b]into the hand of the adversary.

39 [1]Or, *breath* [a]Ps. 103:14; Job 10:9 [b]Gen. 6:3 [c]Job 7:7; Ps. 103:14; James 4:14

40 [a]Ps. 106:43; 107:11 [b]Ps. 95:10; Is. 63:10; Eph. 4:30 [c]Ps. 106:14

41 [1]Or, *put God to the test* [a]Num. 14:22 [b]Ps. 89:18; 2 Kin. 19:22

42 [1]Lit., *hand* [a]Judg. 8:34 [b]Ps. 44:3 [c]Ps. 106:10

43 [a]Ps. 105:27 [b]Ex. 4:21; 7:3

44 [a]Ps. 105:29

45 [a]Ps. 105:31; Ex. 8:24 [b]Ps. 105:30; Ex. 8:6

46 [a]Ps. 105:34; 1 Kin. 8:37 [b]Ex. 10:14

47 [1]Lit., *was killing* [a]Ps. 105:32; Ex. 9:23

48 [a]Ex. 9:19

49 [1]Lit., *A deputation of angels of evil* [a]Ex. 15:7

50 [a]Job 27:22 [b]Ex. 12:29, 30

51 [a]Ps. 105:36; 135:8; 136:10 [b]Gen. 49:3 [c]Ps. 105:23, 27; 106:22

52 [a]Ex. 15:22 [b]Ps. 77:20

53 [a]Ex. 14:19, 20 [b]Ps. 106:11; Ex. 14:27, 28

54 [1]Lit., *border, territory* [2]Or, *mountain* [a]Ex. 15:17 [b]Ps. 68:16; Is. 11:9

55 [a]Ps. 44:2 [b]Ps. 105:11; 135:12; Josh. 23:4

56 [1]Or, *put to the test* [a]Ps. 78:18 [b]Ps. 78:40

57 [a]Ezek. 20:28

58 [a]Deut. 4:25; 1 Kin. 14:9; Is. 65:3 [b]Lev. 26:30; 1 Kin. 3:2; 2 Kin. 16:4; Jer. 17:3 [c]Deut. 32:16, 21; 1 Kin. 14:22 [d]Ex. 20:4; Lev. 26:1; Deut. 4:25

59 [1]Or, *became infuriated* [a]Ps. 106:40; Deut. 1:34; 9:19 [b]Lev. 26:30; Deut. 32:19; Amos 6:8

60 [1]Some ancient versions read, *where He dwelt* [a]Ps. 78:67; 1 Sam. 4:11; Jer. 7:12, 14; 26:6

61 [a]Ps. 63:2; 132:8 [b]1 Sam. 4:17

62 He also [a]delivered His people to the sword,
And [1]was filled with wrath at His inheritance.
63 [a]Fire devoured [1]His young men;
And [1]His [b]virgins had no wedding songs.
64 [1]His [a]priests fell by the sword;
And [1]His [b]widows could not weep.

65 Then the Lord [a]awoke as *if from* sleep,
Like a [b]warrior [1]overcome by wine.
66 And He [1a]drove His adversaries backward;
He put on them an everlasting reproach.
67 He also [a]rejected the tent of Joseph,
And did not choose the tribe of Ephraim,
68 But chose the tribe of Judah,
Mount [a]Zion which He loved.
69 And He [a]built His sanctuary like the heights,
Like the earth which He has founded forever.
70 He also [a]chose David His servant,
And took him from the sheepfolds;
71 From [1a]the care of the [2]ewes [b]with suckling lambs He brought him,
To [c]shepherd Jacob His people,
And Israel [d]His inheritance.
72 So he shepherded them according to the [a]integrity of his heart,
And guided them with his skillful hands.

Psalm 79

A Lament over the Destruction of Jerusalem, and Prayer for Help.

A Psalm of Asaph.

O GOD, the [a]nations have [1]invaded [b]Thine inheritance;
They have defiled Thy [c]holy temple;
They have [d]laid Jerusalem in ruins.
2 They have given the [a]dead bodies of Thy servants for food to the birds of the heavens,
The flesh of Thy godly ones to the beasts of the earth.
3 They have poured out their blood like water round about Jerusalem;
And there was [a]no one to bury them.
4 We have become a [a]reproach to our neighbors,
A scoffing and derision to those around us.
5 [a]How long, O LORD? Wilt Thou be angry forever?
Will Thy [b]jealousy [c]burn like fire?
6 [a]Pour out Thy wrath upon the nations which [b]do not know Thee,
And upon the kingdoms which [c]do not call upon Thy name.
7 For they have [a]devoured Jacob,
And [b]laid waste his [1]habitation.

8 [a]Do not remember [1]the iniquities of *our* forefathers against us;
Let Thy compassion come quickly to [b]meet us;
For we are [c]brought very low.

62 [1]Or, *became infuriated* [a]Judg. 20:21; 1 Sam. 4:10

63 [1]Or, *their* [a]Num. 11:1; 21:28; Is. 26:11; Jer. 48:45 [b]Jer. 7:34; 16:9; Lam. 2:21

64 [1]Or, *their* [a]1 Sam. 4:17; 22:18 [b]Job 27:15; Ezek. 24:23

65 [1]Or, *sobered up from* [a]Ps. 44:23; 73:20 [b]Is. 42:13

66 [1]Lit., *smote* [a]1 Sam. 5:6

67 [a]Ps. 78:60

68 [a]Ps. 87:2; 132:13

69 [a]1 Kin. 6:1-38

70 [a]1 Sam. 16:12

71 [1]Lit., *following* [2]Lit., *ewes which gave suck, He . . .* [a]2 Sam. 7:8 [b]Gen. 33:13 [c]2 Sam. 5:2; 1 Chr. 11:2; Ps. 28:9 [d]1 Sam. 10:1

72 [a]1 Kin. 9:4

1 [1]Lit., *come into* [a]Lam. 1:10 [b]Ps. 74:2 [c]Ps. 74:3, 7 [d]2 Kin. 25:9, 10; Jer. 26:18; Mic. 3:12

2 [a]Deut. 28:26; Jer. 7:33; 16:4; 19:7; 34:20

3 [a]Jer. 14:16; 16:4

4 [a]Ps. 44:13; 80:6; Dan. 9:16

5 [a]Ps. 13:1; 74:1, 10; 85:5; 89:46 [b]Deut. 29:20; Ezek. 36:5; 38:19 [c]Ps. 89:46

6 [a]Ps. 69:24; Ezek. 21:31; Zeph. 3:8 [b]1 Thess. 4:5; 2 Thess. 1:8 [c]Ps. 14:4; 53:4

7 [1]Lit., *pasture* [a]Ps. 53:4 [b]2 Chr. 36:19; Jer. 39:8

8 [1]Or, our *former iniquities* [a]Ps. 106:6; Is. 64:9 [b]Ps. 21:3 [c]Ps. 116:6; 142:6; Deut. 28:43; Is. 26:5

9 [a]Help us, O God of our salvation, for the glory of [b]Thy name;
And deliver us, and [1c]forgive our sins, for Thy name's sake.
10 [a]Why should the nations say, "Where is their God?"
Let there be known among the nations in our sight,
[b]Vengeance for the blood of Thy servants, which has been shed.
11 Let [a]the groaning of the prisoner come before Thee;
According to the greatness of Thy [1]power preserve [2]those who are [a]doomed to die.
12 And return to our neighbors [a]sevenfold [b]into their bosom
[1]The [c]reproach with which they have reproached Thee, O Lord.
13 So we Thy people and the [a]sheep of Thy [1]pasture
Will [b]give thanks to Thee forever;
To all generations we will [c]tell of Thy praise.

Psalm 80

God Implored to Rescue His People from Their Calamities.

For the choir director; *set to* [£]El Shoshannim; [•]Eduth.
A Psalm of Asaph.

Oh give ear, [a]Shepherd of Israel,
Thou who dost lead [b]Joseph like a flock;
Thou who [c]art enthroned *above* the cherubim, shine forth!
2 Before [a]Ephraim and Benjamin and Manasseh, [b]stir up Thy power,
And come to save us!
3 O God, [a]restore us,
And [b]cause Thy face to shine *upon us,* [1]and we will be saved.

4 O [a]Lord God *of* hosts,
[b]How long wilt Thou [1]be angry with the prayer of Thy people?
5 Thou hast fed them with the [a]bread of tears,
And Thou hast made them to drink tears in [1]large measure.
6 Thou dost make us [1]an object of contention [a]to our neighbors;
And our enemies laugh among themselves.
7 O God *of* hosts, restore us,
And cause Thy face to shine *upon us,* [1]and we will be saved.

8 Thou didst remove a [a]vine from Egypt;
Thou didst [b]drive out the [1]nations, and didst [c]plant it.
9 Thou didst [a]clear *the ground* before it,
And it [b]took deep root and filled the land.
10 The mountains were covered with its shadow;
And [1]the cedars of God with its [a]boughs.

9 [1]Lit., *cover over, atone for*
[a]2 Chr. 14:11 [b]Ps. 31:3 [c]Ps. 25:11; 65:3

10 [a]Ps. 115:2 [b]Ps. 94:1, 2

11 [1]Lit., *arm* [2]Lit., *the children of death*
[a]Ps. 102:20

12 [1]Lit., *Their*
[a]Gen. 4:15; Lev. 26:21, 28; Ps. 12:6; 119:164; Prov. 6:31; 24:16; Is. 30:26 [b]Ps. 35:13; Is. 65:6, 7; Jer. 32:18; Luke 6:38 [c]Ps. 74:10, 22

13 [1]Or, *pasturing*
[a]Ps. 74:1; 95:7; 100:3 [b]Ps. 44:8 [c]Ps. 89:1; Is. 43:21

[£] Possibly, *to the Lilies*

[•] Lit., *A testimony*

1 [a]Ps. 23:1 [b]Ps. 77:15; 78:67; Amos 5:15 [c]Ps. 99:1; Ex. 25:22; 1 Sam. 4:4; 2 Sam. 6:2

2 [a]Num. 2:18-24 [b]Ps. 35:23

3 [1]Or, *that we may*
[a]Ps. 80:7, 19; 60:1; 85:4; 126:1; Lam. 5:21 [b]Ps. 31:16; Num. 6:25

4 [1]Lit., *smoke against*
[a]Ps. 59:5; 84:8 [b]Ps. 79:5; 85:5

5 [1]Lit., *a third part of a*
[a]Ps. 42:3; 102:9

6 [1]Lit., *a strife to*
[a]Ps. 44:13; 79:4

7 [1]Or, *that we may*

8 [1]Or, *Gentiles*
[a]Ps. 80:15; Is. 5:2, 7; Jer. 2:21; 12:10; Ezek. 17:6; 19:10 [b]Ps. 44:2; Josh. 13:6; 2 Chr. 20:7; Acts 7:45 [c]Jer. 11:17; 32:41; Ezek. 17:23; Amos 9:15

9 [a]Ex. 23:28; Josh. 24:12; Is. 5:2 [b]Hos. 14:5

10 [1]Or, *its boughs are like the cedars of God*
[a]Gen. 49:22

11 [a]Ps. 72:8

12 [1]Or, *walls, fences* [a]Ps. 89:40; Is. 5:5 [b]Deut. 28:63

13 [a]Jer. 5:6

14 [a]Ps. 90:13 [b]Ps. 102:19; Is. 63:15

15 [1]Or, *root* [2]Or figuratively: *branch* [3]Or, *secured* [a]Ps. 80:8

16 [a]Ps. 74:8; 2 Chr. 36:19; Jer. 52:13 [b]Ps. 39:11; 76:6

17 [a]Ps. 89:21 [b]Ps. 80:15

18 [a]Is. 50:5 [b]Ps. 71:20

19 [1]Or, *that we may* [a]Ps. 80:3

[£] Or, *according to*

1 [a]Ps. 51:14; 59:16; 95:1 [b]Ps. 46:1 [c]Ps. 66:1; 95:2; 98:4 [d]Ps. 84:8

2 [a]Ps. 149:3; Ex. 15:20 [b]Ps. 92:3; 98:5; 147:7 [c]Ps. 108:2; 144:9

3 [a]Num. 10:10 [b]Lev. 23:24

5 [1]Lit., *went out over* [a]Ex. 11:4 [b]Ps. 114:1 Deut. 28:49; Jer. 5:15

6 [1]Lit., *removed his shoulder from* [2]Or, *brick load* [a]Is. 9:4; 10:27

7 [1]*Selah* may mean: *Pause, Crescendo* or *Musical interlude* [a]Ps. 50:15; Ex. 2:23; 14:10 [b]Ex. 19:19; 20:18 [c]Ps. 95:8; Ex. 17:6, 7

8 [1]Or, *bear witness against* [a]Ps. 50:7 [b]Ps. 95:7

9 [a]Ps. 44:20; Ex. 20:3; Deut. 32:12; Is. 43:12

10 [a]Ex. 20:2 [b]Job 29:23 [c]Ps. 37:4; 78:25; 107:9

11 [1]Lit., *yield to* [a]Ps. 106:25

11 It was sending out its branches [a]to the sea,
And its shoots to the River.
12 Why hast Thou [a]broken down its [1]hedges,
So that all who pass *that* way [b]pick its *fruit?*
13 A boar from the forest [a]eats it away,
And whatever moves in the field feeds on it.

14 O God *of* hosts, [a]turn again now, we beseech Thee;
[b]Look down from heaven and see, and take care of this vine,
15 Even the [1a]shoot which Thy right hand has planted,
And on the [2]son whom Thou hast [3]strengthened for Thyself.
16 It is [a]burned with fire, it is cut down;
They perish at the [b]rebuke of Thy countenance.
17 Let [a]Thy hand be upon the man of Thy right hand,
Upon the son of man whom Thou [b]didst make strong for Thyself.
18 Then we shall not [a]turn back from Thee;
[b]Revive us, and we will call upon Thy name.
19 O LORD God *of* hosts, [a]restore us;
Cause Thy face to shine *upon us,* [1]and we will be saved.

PSALM 81

God's Goodness and Israel's Waywardness.

For the choir director; [£]on the Gittith.
A Psalm of Asaph.

[a]SING for joy to God our [b]strength;
Shout [c]joyfully to the [d]God of Jacob.
2 Raise a song, strike [a]the timbrel,
The sweet sounding [b]lyre with the [c]harp.
3 Blow the trumpet at the [a]new moon,
At the full moon, on our [b]feast day.
4 For it is a statute for Israel,
An ordinance of the God of Jacob.
5 He established it for a testimony in Joseph,
When he [1a]went throughout the land of Egypt.
I heard a [b]language that I did not know:

6 "I [1a]relieved his shoulder of the burden,
His hands were freed from the [2]basket.
7 "You [a]called in trouble, and I rescued you;
I [b]answered you in the hiding place of thunder;
I proved you at the [c]waters of Meribah. [[1]Selah.
8 "[a]Hear, O My people, and I will [1]admonish you;
O Israel, if you [b]would listen to Me!
9 "Let there be no [a]strange god among you;
Nor shall you worship any foreign god.
10 "[a]I, the LORD, am your God,
Who brought you up from the land of Egypt;
[b]Open your mouth wide and I will [c]fill it.

11 "But My people [a]did not listen to My voice;
And Israel did not [1]obey Me.

12 "So I [a]gave [1]them over to the stubbornness of their
heart,
To walk in their own devices.
13 "Oh that My people [a]would listen to Me,
That Israel would [b]walk in My ways!
14 "I would quickly [a]subdue their enemies,
And [b]turn My hand against their adversaries.
15 "Those who hate the LORD would [a]pretend obedience to
Him;
And their time *of punishment* would be forever.
16 "[1]But I would feed you with the [2a]finest of the wheat;
And with [b]honey from the rock I would satisfy you."

PSALM 82

Unjust Judgments Rebuked.

A Psalm of Asaph.

GOD takes His [a]stand in [1]His own congregation;
He [b]judges in the midst of the [2c]rulers.
2 How long will you [a]judge unjustly,
And [b]show partiality to the wicked? [[1]Selah.
3 [a]Vindicate the weak and fatherless;
Do justice to the afflicted and destitute.
4 [a]Rescue the weak and needy;
Deliver *them* out of the hand of the wicked.

5 They [a]do not know nor do they understand;
They [b]walk about in darkness;
All the [c]foundations of the earth are shaken.
6 [1]I [a]said, "You are gods,
And all of you are [b]sons of the Most High.
7 "Nevertheless [a]you will die like men,
And fall like *any* [b]one of the princes."
8 [a]Arise, O God, [b]judge the earth!
For it is Thou who dost [c]possess all the nations.

PSALM 83

God Implored to Confound His Enemies.

A Song, a Psalm of Asaph.

O GOD, [a]do not remain quiet;
[b]Do not be silent, and, O God, do not be still.
2 For, behold, Thine enemies [a]make an uproar;
And those who hate Thee have [1b]exalted themselves.
3 They [a]make shrewd plans against Thy people,
And [1]conspire together against [b]Thy [2]treasured ones.
4 They have said, "Come, and [a]let us wipe them out [1]as a
nation;
That the [b]name of Israel be remembered no more."
5 For they have [1a]conspired together with one mind;
Against Thee do they make a covenant:
6 The tents of [a]Edom and the [b]Ishmaelites;
[c]Moab, and the [d]Hagarites;

12 [1]Lit., *him*
[a]Job 8:4; Acts 7:42; Rom. 1:24, 26

13 [a]Ps. 81:8; Deut. 5:29; Is. 48:18 [b]Ps. 128:1; Is. 42:24; Jer. 7:23

14 [a]Ps. 18:47; 47:3 [b]Amos 1:8

15 [a]Ps. 18:44; 66:3

16 [1]Lit., *He would feed him* [2]Lit., *fat*
[a]Ps. 147:14; Deut. 32:14 [b]Deut. 32:13

1 [1]Lit., *the congregation of God* [2]Lit., *gods*
[a]Is. 3:13 [b]Ps. 58:11 [c]Ex. 21:6; 22:8, 28

2 [1]*Selah* may mean: *Pause, Crescendo* or *Musical interlude*
[a]Ps. 58:1 [b]Deut. 1:17; Prov. 18:5

3 [a]Ps. 10:18; Deut. 24:17; Is. 11:4; Jer. 22:16

4 [a]Job 29:12

5 [a]Ps. 14:4; Jer. 4:22; Mic. 3:1 [b]Prov. 2:13; Is. 59:9; Jer. 23:12 [c]Ps. 11:3

6 [1]Lit., *I, on my part*
[a]Ps. 82:1; John 10:34 [b]Ps. 89:26

7 [a]Ps. 49:12; Job 21:32; Ezek. 31:14 [b]Ps. 83:11

8 [a]Ps. 12:5 [b]Ps. 58:11; 96:13 [c]Ps. 2:8; Rev. 11:15

1 [a]Ps. 28:1; 35:22 [b]Ps. 109:1

2 [1]Lit., *lifted up the head*
[a]Ps. 2:1; Is. 17:12 [b]Judg. 8:28; Zech. 1:21

3 [1]Or, *consult* [2]Or, *hidden ones*
[a]Ps. 64:2; Is. 29:15 [b]Ps. 27:5; 31:20

4 [1]Lit., *from*
[a]Ps. 74:8; Esth. 3:6; Jer. 48:2 [b]Ps. 41:5

5 [1]Or, *consulted*
[a]Ps. 2:2; Dan. 6:7

6 [a]2 Chr. 20:10; Ps. 137:7 [b]Gen. 25:12-16 [c]2 Chr. 20:10 [d]1 Chr. 5:10

7 [a]Josh. 13:5; Ezek. 27:9 [b]2 Chr. 20:10 [c]1 Sam. 15:2 [d]1 Sam. 4:1; 29:1 [e]Ezek. 27:3; Amos 1:9

8 [1]Lit., *an arm* [2]*Selah* may mean: *Pause, Crescendo* or *Musical interlude* [a]2 Kin. 15:19 [b]Deut. 2:9

9 [a]Judg. 7:22 [b]Judg. 4:22, 23

11 [a]Judg. 7:25 [b]Judg. 8:21

12 [a]2 Chr. 20:11 [b]Ps. 132:13

13 [1]Or, *tumbleweed* [a]Is. 17:13 [b]Job 21:18; Is. 40:24; Jer. 13:24

14 [a]Is. 9:18 [b]Ex. 19:18; Deut. 32:22

15 [a]Ps. 58:9; Job 9:17

16 [a]Ps. 109:29; 132:18; Job 10:15

17 [a]Ps. 35:4; 70:2

18 [a]Ps. 86:10; Is. 45:21 [b]Ps. 9:2; 18:13; 97:9

[£] Or, *according to*

1 [a]Ps. 43:3; 132:5

2 [a]Ps. 42:2; 63:1 [b]Ps. 42:2

3 [a]Ps. 43:4 [b]Ps. 5:2

4 [1]*Selah* may mean: *Pause, Crescendo* or *Musical interlude* [a]Ps. 65:4 [b]Ps. 42:5, 11

5 [1]Lit., *their* [a]Ps. 81:1 [b]Ps. 86:11; 122:1; Jer. 31:6

6 [1]Probably, *Weeping*, or *balsam trees* [2]Or, *place of springs* [a]Ps. 107:35; Joel 2:23

7 [1]Some ancient versions read, *The God of gods will be seen in Zion.* [a]Prov. 4:18; Is. 40:31; John 1:16; 2 Cor. 3:18 [b]Ps. 42:2; Ex. 34:23; Deut. 16:16

7 [a]Gebal, and [b]Ammon, and [c]Amalek;
[d]Philistia with the inhabitants of [e]Tyre;
8 [a]Assyria also has joined with them;
They have become [1]a help to the [b]children of Lot. [[2]Selah.

9 Deal with them [a]as with Midian,
As [b]with Sisera *and* Jabin, at the torrent of Kishon,
10 Who were destroyed at En-dor,
Who became as dung for the ground.
11 Make their nobles like [a]Oreb and Zeeb,
And all their princes like [b]Zebah and Zalmunna,
12 Who said, "[a]Let us possess for ourselves
The [b]pastures of God."

13 O my God, make them like the [1a]whirling dust;
Like [b]chaff before the wind.
14 Like [a]fire that burns the forest,
And like a flame that [b]sets the mountains on fire,
15 So pursue them [a]with Thy tempest,
And terrify them with Thy storm.
16 [a]Fill their faces with dishonor,
That they may seek Thy name, O LORD.
17 Let them be [a]ashamed and dismayed forever;
And let them be humiliated and perish,
18 That they may know that [a]Thou alone, whose name is the LORD,
Art the [b]Most High over all the earth.

PSALM 84

Longing for the Temple Worship.

For the choir director; [£]on the Gittith.
A Psalm of the sons of Korah.

HOW lovely are Thy [a]dwelling places,
O LORD of hosts!
2 My [a]soul longed and even yearned for the courts of the LORD;
My heart and my flesh sing for joy to the [b]living God.
3 The bird also has found a house,
And the swallow a nest for herself, where she may lay her young,
Even Thine [a]altars, O LORD of hosts,
[b]My King and my God.
4 How [a]blessed are those who dwell in Thy house!
They are [b]ever praising Thee. [[1]Selah.

5 How blessed is the man whose [a]strength is in Thee;
In [1]whose heart are the [b]highways *to Zion!*
6 Passing through the valley of [1]Baca, they make it a [2]spring,
The [a]early rain also covers it with blessings.
7 They [a]go from strength to strength,
[1]*Every one of them* [b]appears before God in Zion.

8 O [a]LORD God of hosts, hear my prayer;
Give ear, O [b]God of Jacob!
9 Behold our [a]shield, O God,
And look upon the face of [b]Thine anointed.
10 For [a]a day in Thy courts is better than a thousand *outside*.
I would rather stand at the [b]threshold of the house of my God,
Than dwell in the tents of wickedness.
11 For LORD God is [a]a sun and shield;
The LORD gives grace and [b]glory;
No [c]good thing does He withhold [1]from those who walk [2]uprightly.
12 O LORD of hosts,
How [a]blessed is the man who trusts in Thee!

PSALM 85

Prayer for God's Mercy upon the Nation.

For the choir director. A Psalm of the sons of Korah.

O LORD, Thou didst show [a]favor to Thy land;
Thou didst [1b]restore the captivity of Jacob.
2 Thou didst [a]forgive the iniquity of Thy people;
Thou didst [b]cover all their sin. [[1]Selah.
3 Thou didst [a]withdraw all Thy fury;
Thou didst [b]turn away from Thy burning anger.

4 [a]Restore us, O God of our salvation,
And [b]cause Thine indignation toward us to cease.
5 Wilt [a]Thou be angry with us forever?
Wilt Thou prolong Thine anger to [1]all generations?
6 Wilt Thou not Thyself [1a]revive us again,
That Thy people may [b]rejoice in Thee?
7 Show us Thy lovingkindness, O LORD,
And [a]grant us Thy salvation.

8 [1]I will hear what God the LORD will say;
For He will [a]speak peace to His people, [2]to His godly ones;
But let them not [b]turn back to [3]folly.
9 Surely [a]His salvation is near to those who [1]fear Him,
That [b]glory may dwell in our land.
10 [a]Lovingkindness and [1]truth have met together;
[b]Righteousness and peace have kissed each other.
11 [1]Truth [a]springs from the earth;
And righteousness looks down from heaven.
12 Indeed, [a]the LORD will give what is good;
And our [b]land will yield its produce.
13 [a]Righteousness will go before Him,
And will make His footsteps into a way.

8 [a]Ps. 84:1; 59:5; 80:4 [b]Ps. 81:1

9 [a]Ps. 3:3; 28:7; 59:11; 115:9-11; Gen. 15:1 [b]Ps. 2:2; 132:17; 1 Sam. 16:6; 2 Sam. 19:21

10 [a]Ps. 27:4 [b]1 Chr. 23:5

11 [1]Lit., *with regard to* [2]Lit., *with integrity* [a]Is. 60:19, 20; Mal. 4:2; Rev. 21:23 [b]Ps. 85:9 [c]Ps. 34:10

12 [a]Ps. 2:12; 40:4

1 [1]Or, *restore the fortunes* [a]Ps. 77:7; 106:4 [b]Ps. 14:7; 126:1; Ezra 1:11; Jer. 30:18; Ezek. 39:25; Hos. 6:11; Joel 3:1

2 [1]*Selah* may mean: *Pause, Crescendo* or *Musical interlude* [a]Ps. 78:38; 103:3; Num. 14:19; 1 Kin. 8:34; Jer. 31:34 [b]Ps. 32:1

3 [a]Ps. 78:38; 106:23 [b]Ps. 106:23; Ex. 32:12; Deut. 13:17; Jon. 3:9

4 [a]Ps. 80:3 [b]Dan. 9:16

5 [1]Lit., *generation and generation* [a]Ps. 74:1; 79:5; 80:4

6 [1]Or, *bring to life* [a]Ps. 71:20; 80:18 [b]Ps. 33:1; 90:14; 149:2

7 [a]Ps. 106:4

8 [1]Or, *Let me hear* [2]Lit., *even to* [3]Or, *stupidity* [a]Ps. 29:11; Hag. 2:9; Zech. 9:10 [b]Ps. 78:57; 2 Pet. 2:21

9 [1]Or, *reverence* [a]Ps. 34:18; Is. 46:13 [b]Ps. 84:11; Hag. 2:7; Zech. 2:5; John 1:14

10 [1]Or, *faithfulness* [a]Ps. 25:10; 89:14; Prov. 3:3 [b]Ps. 72:3; Is. 32:17

11 [1]Or, *Faithfulness* [a]Is. 45:8

12 [a]Ps. 84:11; James 1:17 [b]Ps. 67:6; Lev. 26:4; Ezek. 34:27; Zech. 8:12

13 [a]Ps. 89:14

Psalm 86

A Psalm of Supplication and Trust.

A Prayer of David.

[a]INCLINE Thine ear, O LORD, *and* answer me;
For I am [b]afflicted and needy.
2 [a]Do preserve my [1]soul, for I am a [b]godly man;
O Thou my God, save Thy servant who [c]trusts in Thee.
3 Be [a]gracious to me, O LORD,
For [b]to Thee I cry all day long.
4 Make glad the soul of Thy servant,
For to Thee, O Lord, [a]I lift up my soul.
5 For Thou, Lord, art [a]good, and [b]ready to forgive,
And [c]abundant in lovingkindness to all who call upon Thee.
6 [a]Give ear, O LORD, to my prayer;
And give heed to the voice of my supplications!
7 In [a]the day of my trouble I shall call upon Thee,
For [b]Thou wilt answer me.
8 There is [a]no one like Thee among the gods, O Lord;
Nor are there any works [b]like Thine.
9 [a]All nations whom Thou hast made shall come and worship before Thee, O Lord;
And they shall glorify Thy name.
10 For Thou art [a]great and [b]doest [1]wondrous deeds;
Thou alone [c]art God.

11 [a]Teach me Thy way, O LORD;
I will walk in Thy truth;
[b]Unite my heart to fear Thy name.
12 I will [a]give thanks to Thee, O Lord my God, with all my heart,
And will glorify Thy name forever.
13 For Thy lovingkindness toward me is great,
And Thou hast [a]delivered my soul from the [1]depths of [2]Sheol.

14 O God, arrogant men have [a]risen up against me,
And a [1]band of violent men have sought my [2]life,
And they have not set Thee before them.
15 But Thou, O Lord, art a God [a]merciful and gracious,
Slow to anger and abundant in lovingkindness and [1]truth.
16 [a]Turn to me, and be gracious to me;
Oh [b]grant Thy strength to Thy servant,
And save the [c]son of Thy handmaid.
17 [a]Show me a sign for good,
That those who hate me may [b]see *it*, and be ashamed,
Because Thou, O LORD, [c]hast helped me and comforted me.

1 [a]Ps. 17:6; 31:2; 71:2 [b]Ps. 40:17; 70:5

2 [1]Or, *life* [a]Ps. 25:20 [b]Ps. 4:3; 50:5 [c]Ps. 25:2; 31:14; 56:4

3 [a]Ps. 4:1; 57:1 [b]Ps. 25:5; 88:9

4 [a]Ps. 25:1; 143:8

5 [a]Ps. 25:8 [b]Ps. 130:4 [c]Ps. 103:8; 145:8; Ex. 34:6; Neh. 9:17; Joel 2:13; Jon. 4:2

6 [a]Ps. 55:1

7 [a]Ps. 50:15; 77:2 [b]Ps. 17:6

8 [a]Ps. 89:6; Ex. 15:11; 2 Sam. 7:22; 1 Kin. 8:23; Jer. 10:6 [b]Deut. 3:24

9 [a]Ps. 22:27; 66:4; Is. 66:23; Rev. 15:4

10 [1]Or, *miracles* [a]Ps. 77:13 [b]Ps. 72:18; 77:14; 136:4; Ex. 15:11 [c]Ps. 83:18; Deut. 6:4; 32:39; Is. 37:16; 44:6, 8; Mark 12:29; 1 Cor. 8:4

11 [a]Ps. 25:5 [b]Jer. 32:39

12 [a]Ps. 111:1

13 [1]Lit., *lowest Sheol* [2]I.e., the nether world [a]Ps. 30:3

14 [1]Or, *assembly* [2]Lit., *soul* [a]Ps. 54:3

15 [1]Or, *faithfulness* [a]Ps. 86:5

16 [a]Ps. 25:16 [b]Ps. 68:35 [c]Ps. 116:16

17 [a]Ps. 119:122; Judg. 6:17 [b]Ps. 112:10 [c]Ps. 118:13

Psalm 87

The Privileges of Citizenship in Zion.

A Psalm of the sons of Korah. A Song.

His [a]foundation is in the holy mountains.
2 The LORD [a]loves the gates of Zion
More than all the *other* dwelling places of Jacob.
3 [a]Glorious things are spoken of you,
O [b]city of God. [[1]Selah.
4 "I shall mention [1a]Rahab and Babylon [2]among those who know Me;
Behold, Philistia and [b]Tyre with [3c]Ethiopia:
'This one was born there.' "
5 But of Zion it shall be said, "This one and that one were born in her";
And the Most High Himself will [a]establish her.
6 The LORD shall count when He [a]registers the peoples,
"This one was born there." [Selah.
7 Then those who [a]sing as well as those who [1b]play the flutes *shall say*,
"All my [c]springs *of joy* are in you."

Psalm 88

A Petition to be Saved from Death.

A Song. A Psalm of the sons of Korah. For the choir director; according to Mahalath Leannoth. •Maskil of Heman £the Ezrahite.

O LORD, the [a]God of my salvation,
I have [b]cried out by day and in the night before Thee.
2 Let my prayer [a]come before Thee;
[b]Incline Thine ear to my cry!
3 For my [a]soul has [1]had enough troubles,
And [b]my life has drawn near to [2]Sheol.
4 I am reckoned among those who [a]go down to the pit;
I have become like a man [b]without strength,
5 [1]Forsaken [a]among the dead,
Like the slain who lie in the grave,
Whom Thou dost remember no more,
And they are [b]cut off from Thy hand.
6 Thou hast put me in [a]the lowest pit,
In [b]dark places, in the [c]depths.
7 Thy wrath [a]has rested upon me,
And Thou hast afflicted me with [b]all Thy waves. [[1]Selah.
8 Thou hast removed [a]my acquaintances far from me;
Thou hast made me an [1b]object of loathing to them;
I am [c]shut up and cannot go out.
9 My [a]eye has wasted away because of affliction;
I have [b]called upon Thee every day, O LORD;
I have [c]spread out my [1]hands to Thee.

10 Wilt Thou perform wonders for the dead?
Will [a]the [1]departed spirits rise *and* praise Thee? [Selah.

---

1 [a]Ps. 78:69; Is. 28:16

2 [a]Ps. 78:67, 68

3 *Selah* may mean: *Pause, Crescendo* or *Musical interlude*
[a]Is. 60:1 [b]Ps. 46:4; 48:8

4 [1]I.e., Egypt [2]Or, *as* [3]Lit., *Cush*
[a]Ps. 89:10; Job 9:13; Is. 19:23-25 [b]Ps. 45:12 [c]Ps. 68:31

5 [a]Ps. 48:8

6 [a]Ps. 69:28; Is. 4:3

7 [1]Or, *dance*
[a]Ps. 68:25; 149:3 [b]Ps. 30:11; 2 Sam. 6:14 [c]Ps. 36:9

• Possibly, *Contemplative*, or *Didactic*, or *Skillful Psalm* £ Ps. 89:title; 1 Chr. 2:6; 1 Kin. 4:31

1 [a]Ps. 24:5; 27:9 [b]Ps. 22:2; 86:3; Luke 18:7

2 [a]Ps. 18:6 [b]Ps. 31:2; 86:1

3 [1]Or, *been satisfied with* [2]I.e., the nether world
[a]Ps. 107:26 [b]Ps. 107:18; 116:3

4 [a]Ps. 28:1; 143:7 [b]Ps. 22:11; Job 29:12

5 [1]Lit., *A freed one among the dead*
[a]Ps. 31:12 [b]Ps. 31:22; Is.53:8

6 [a]Ps. 86:13; Lam. 3:55
[b]Ps. 143:3 [c]Ps. 69:15

7 [1]*Selah* may mean: *Pause, Crescendo* or *Musical interlude*
[a]Ps. 32:4; 39:10 [b]Ps. 42:7

8 [1]Lit., *abomination to them*
[a]Ps. 31:11; 142:4; Job 19:13, 19 [b]Job 30:10 [c]Ps. 142:7; Jer. 32:2; 36:5

9 [1]Lit., *palms*
[a]Ps. 6:7; 31:9 [b]Ps. 22:2; 86:3
[c]Ps. 143:6; Job 11:13

10 [1]Or, *ghosts, shades*
[a]Ps. 6:5; 30:9

11 [1]Lit., *Abaddon*

12 [1]I.e., faithfulness to His gracious promises [a]Ps. 88:6; Job 10:21

13 [a]Ps. 30:2 [b]Ps. 5:3; 119:147

14 [a]Ps. 43:2; 44:9 [b]Ps. 13:1; 44:24; Job 13:24

15 [1]Or, *embarrassed* [a]Prov. 24:11 [b]Job 6:4; 31:23

16 [1]Or, *silenced* [a]2 Chr. 28:11; Is. 13:13; Lam. 1:12 [b]Lam. 3:54; Ezek. 37:11

17 [a]Ps. 118:10-12 [b]Ps. 124:4 [c]Ps. 17:11; 22:12, 16

18 [a]Ps. 88:8; 31:11; 38:11; Job 19:13

• Possibly, *Contemplative*, or *Didactic*, or *Skillful Psalm* £ Ps. 88:title

1 [a]Ps. 59:16; 101:1 [b]Ps. 40:10 [c]Ps. 89:5, 8, 24, 33, 49; Ps. 36:5; 88:11; 92:2; 119:90; Is. 25:1; Lam. 3:23

2 [a]Ps. 103:17 [b]Ps. 36:5

3 [a]1 Kin. 8:16 [b]Ps. 132:11

4 [1]*Selah* may mean: *Pause, Crescendo* or *Musical interlude* [a]2 Sam. 7:16 [b]Is. 9:7; Luke 1:33

5 [a]Ps. 19:1; 97:6 [b]Ps. 149:1 [c]Job 5:1

6 [1]Or, *sons of gods* [a]Ps. 86:8; 113:5 [b]Ps. 29:1; 82:1

7 [a]Ps. 47:2; 68:35 [b]Ps. 89:5 [c]Ps. 96:4

8 [1]*YHWH, usually rendered* LORD [2]Heb., YAH [a]Ps. 35:10; 71:19

9 [a]Ps. 65:7; 107:29

10 [1]I.e., Egypt [2]Lit., *an arm of might* [a]Ps. 87:4; Is. 30:7; 51:9 [b]Ps. 18:14; 68:1; 144:6

11 [1]Lit., *its fullness* [a]Ps. 96:5; Gen. 1:1; 1 Chr. 29:11 [b]Ps. 24:1

12 [a]Job 26:7 [b]Josh. 19:22; Judg. 4:6; Jer. 46:18 [c]Ps. 133:3; Deut. 3:8; Josh. 11:17; Song of Sol. 4:8 [d]Ps. 98:8

13 [1]Lit., *an arm with strength* [a]Ps. 98:1; 118:16

11 Will Thy lovingkindness be declared in the grave,
Thy faithfulness in [1]the place of destruction?
12 Will Thy wonders be made known in the [a]darkness?
And Thy [1]righteousness in the land of forgetfulness?

13 But I, O LORD, have cried out [a]to Thee for help,
And [b]in the morning my prayer comes before Thee.
14 O LORD, why [a]dost Thou reject my soul?
Why dost Thou [b]hide Thy face from me?
15 I was afflicted and [a]about to die from my youth on;
I suffer [b]Thy terrors; I am [1]overcome.
16 Thy [a]burning anger has passed over me;
Thy terrors have [1b]destroyed me.
17 They have [a]surrounded me [b]like water all day long;
They have [c]encompassed me altogether.
18 Thou hast removed [a]lover and friend far from me;
My acquaintances are *in* darkness.

PSALM 89

The LORD'S Covenant with David, and Israel's Afflictions.

A •Maskil of Ethan £the Ezrahite.

I WILL [a]sing of the lovingkindness of the LORD forever;
To all generations I will [b]make known Thy [c]faithfulness with my mouth.
2 For I have said, "[a]Lovingkindness will be built up forever;
In the heavens Thou wilt establish Thy [b]faithfulness.
3 "I have made a covenant with [a]My chosen;
I have [b]sworn to David My servant,
4 I will establish your [a]seed forever,
And build up your [b]throne to all generations." [[1]Selah.

5 And the [a]heavens will praise Thy wonders, O LORD;
Thy faithfulness also [b]in the assembly of the [c]holy ones.
6 For [a]who in the skies is comparable to the LORD?
Who among the [1b]sons of the mighty is like the LORD,
7 A God [a]greatly feared in the council of the [b]holy ones,
And [c]awesome above all those who are around Him?
8 O Lord [1]GOD of hosts, [a]who is like Thee, O mighty [2]LORD?
Thy faithfulness also surrounds Thee.
9 Thou dost rule the swelling of the sea;
When its waves rise, Thou [a]dost still them.
10 Thou Thyself didst crush [1a]Rahab like one who is slain;
Thou didst [b]scatter Thine enemies with [2]Thy mighty arm.

11 The [a]heavens are Thine, the earth also is Thine;
The [b]world and [1]all it contains, Thou hast founded them.
12 The [a]north and the south, Thou hast created them;
[b]Tabor and [c]Hermon [d]shout for joy at Thy name.
13 Thou hast [1]a strong arm;
Thy hand is mighty, Thy [a]right hand is exalted.

14 [a]Righteousness and justice are the foundation of Thy throne;
[b]Lovingkindness and [1]truth go before Thee.
15 How blessed are the people who know the [1a]joyful sound!
O LORD, they walk in the [b]light of Thy countenance.
16 In [a]Thy name they rejoice all the day,
And by Thy righteousness they are exalted.
17 For Thou art the glory of [a]their strength,
And by Thy favor [1]our [b]horn is exalted.
18 For our [a]shield belongs to the LORD,
[1]And [2]our king to the [b]Holy One of Israel.

19 [1]Once Thou didst speak in vision to Thy godly [2]ones,
And didst say, "I have [3]given help to one who is [a]mighty;
I have exalted one [b]chosen from the people.
20 "I have [a]found David My servant;
With My holy [b]oil I have anointed him,
21 With whom [a]My hand will be established;
My arm also will [b]strengthen him.
22 "The enemy will not [1]deceive him,
Nor the [2a]son of wickedness afflict him.
23 "But I shall [a]crush his adversaries before him,
And strike those who hate him.
24 "And My [a]faithfulness and My lovingkindness will be with him,
And in My name his [b]horn will be exalted.
25 "I shall also set his hand [a]on the sea,
And his right hand on the rivers.
26 "He will cry to Me, 'Thou art [a]my Father,
My God, and the [b]rock of my salvation.'
27 "I also shall make him *My* [a]first-born,
The [b]highest of the kings of the earth.
28 "My [a]lovingkindness I will keep for him forever,
And My [b]covenant shall be confirmed to him.
29 "So I will establish his [1a]descendants forever,
And his [b]throne as the days of heaven.

30 "If his sons [a]forsake My law,
And do not walk in My judgments,
31 If they [1]violate My statutes,
And do not keep My commandments,
32 Then I will visit their transgression with the [a]rod,
And their iniquity with stripes.
33 "But I will not break off [a]My lovingkindness from him,
Nor deal falsely in My faithfulness.
34 "My [a]covenant I will not [1]violate,
Nor will I [b]alter [2]the utterance of My lips.
35 "[1]Once I have [a]sworn by My holiness;
I will not lie to David.
36 "His [1a]descendants shall endure forever,
And his [b]throne as the sun before Me.
37 "It shall be established forever [a]like the moon,
And the [b]witness in the sky is faithful." [[1]Selah.

14 [1]Or, *faithfulness* [a]Ps. 97:2 [b]Ps.85:13

15 [1]Or, *blast of the trumpet, shout of joy* [a]Ps. 98:6; Lev. 23:24; Num. 10:10 [b]Ps. 4:6; 44:3; 67:1; 80:3; 90:8

16 [a]Ps. 105:3

17 [1]Another reading is, *Thou dost exalt our horn* [a]Ps. 28:8 [b]Ps. 75:10; 92:10; 148:14

18 [1]Or, *Even* [2]Or, *to the Holy One of Israel our King* [a]Ps. 47:9 [b]Ps. 71:22; 78:41

19 [1]Or, *At that time* [2]Some mss. read, *one* [3]Lit., *placed help upon* [a]2 Sam. 17:10 [b]Ps. 78:70; 1 Kin. 11:34

20 [a]Acts 13:22 [b]1 Sam. 16:13

21 [a]Ps. 18:35; 80:17 [b]Ps. 18:32

22 [1]Or, *exact usury from him* [2]Or, *wicked man* [a]Ps. 125:3; 2 Sam. 7:10

23 [a]Ps. 18:40; 2 Sam. 7:9

24 [a]Ps. 89:1 [b]Ps. 132:17

25 [a]Ps. 72:8

26 [a]2 Sam. 7:14; 1 Chr. 22:10; Jer. 3:19 [b]Ps. 95:1; 2 Sam. 22:47

27 [a]Ps. 2:7; Ex.4:22; Jer. 31:9; Col. 1:15, 18 [b]Ps. 72:11; Num. 24:7; Rev. 19:16

28 [a]Ps. 89:33 [b]Ps. 89:3, 34

29 [1]Lit., *seed* [a]Ps. 89:4, 36; 18:50 [b]Ps. 89:4; 132:12; 1 Kin. 2:4; Is. 9:7; Jer. 33:17

30 [a]2 Sam. 7:14

31 [1]Lit., *profane*

32 [a]Job 9:34; 21:9

33 [a]2 Sam. 7:15

34 [1]Lit., *profane* [2]Lit., *that which goes forth* [a]Deut. 7:9; Jer. 33:20, 21 [b]Num. 23:19

35 [1]Or, *One thing* [a]Ps. 60:6; Amos 4:2

36 [1]Lit., *seed* [a]Ps. 89:29 [b]Ps. 72:5

37 [1]*Selah* may mean: *Pause, Crescendo* or *Musical interlude* [a]Ps. 72:5 [b]Job 16:19

38 [1]Lit., *with*
[a]Ps. 44:9 [b]Ps. 89:20, 51; Ps. 20:6

39 [1]Lit., *to the ground*
[a]Ps. 78:59; Lam. 2:7 [b]Ps. 74:7 [c]Lam. 5:16

40 [a]Ps. 80:12 [b]Lam. 2:2, 5

41 [a]Ps. 80:12 [b]Ps. 44:13; 69:9, 19; 79:4

42 [a]Ps. 13:2 [b]Ps. 80:6

43 [a]Ps. 44:10

44 [1]Lit., *clearness, luster*
[a]Ezek. 28:7

45 [a]Ps. 102:23 [b]Ps. 44:15; 71:13; 109:29

46 [a]Ps. 13:1; 44:24 [b]Ps. 79:5; 80:4

47 [1]Lit., *of what duration I am* [2]Or, *hast Thou . . . men?*
[a]Job 7:7; 10:9; 14:1 [b]Ps. 39:5; 62:9; Eccles. 1:2; 2:11

48 [1]Lit., *hand* [2]I.e., the nether world
[a]Ps. 22:29; 49:9 [b]Ps. 49:15

49 [a]Jer. 30:9; Ezek. 34:23

50 [1]Lit., *My bearing in my bosom*
[a]Ps. 69:9; 74:18, 22

51 [a]Ps. 74:10 [b]Ps. 89:38

52 [a]Ps. 41:13; 72:19; 106:48

[£]Deut. 33:1

1 [1]Or, *hiding place;* some ancient mss. read, *place of refuge*
[a]Ps. 71:3; 91:1; Deut. 33:27; Ezek. 11:16

2 [1]Or, *and*
[a]Job 15:7; Prov. 8:25 [b]Ps. 102:25; 104:5; Gen. 1:1 [c]Ps. 93:2; 102:24, 27; Jer. 10:10

3 [a]Ps. 104:29; Gen. 3:19; Job 34:14, 15

4 [a]2 Pet. 3:8

38 But Thou hast [a]cast off and rejected,
Thou hast been full of wrath [1]against Thine [b]anointed.
39 Thou hast [a]spurned the covenant of Thy servant;
Thou hast [b]profaned [c]his crown [1]in the dust.
40 Thou hast [a]broken down all his walls;
Thou hast [b]brought his strongholds to ruin.
41 [a]All who pass along the way plunder him;
He has become a [b]reproach to his neighbors.
42 Thou hast [a]exalted the right hand of his adversaries;
Thou hast [b]made all his enemies rejoice.
43 Thou dost also turn back the edge of his sword,
And hast [a]not made him stand in battle.
44 Thou hast made his [1a]splendor to cease,
And cast his throne to the ground.
45 Thou hast [a]shortened the days of his youth;
Thou hast [b]covered him with shame. [Selah.

46 [a]How long, O LORD?
Wilt Thou hide Thyself forever?
Will Thy [b]wrath burn like fire?
47 [a]Remember [1]what my span of life is;
For what [b]vanity [2]Thou hast created all the sons of men!
48 What man can live and not [a]see death?
Can he [b]deliver his soul from the [1]power of [2]Sheol? [Selah.

49 Where are Thy former lovingkindnesses, O Lord,
Which Thou didst [a]swear to David in Thy faithfulness?
50 Remember, O Lord, the [a]reproach of Thy servants;
[1]How I do bear in my bosom *the reproach of* all the many peoples,
51 With which [a]Thine enemies have reproached, O LORD,
With which they have reproached the footsteps of [b]Thine anointed.

52 [a]Blessed be the LORD forever!
Amen and Amen.

BOOK 4

PSALM 90

God's Eternity and Man's Transitoriness.

A Prayer of [£]Moses the man of God.

LORD, Thou hast been our [1a]dwelling place in all generations.
2 Before [a]the mountains were born,
[1]Or Thou [b]didst give birth to the earth and the world,
Even [c]from everlasting to everlasting, Thou art God.

3 Thou dost [a]turn man back into dust,
And dost say, "Return, O children of men."
4 For [a]a thousand years in Thy sight

Are like [b]yesterday when it passes by,
[1]Or *as* a [c]watch in the night.
5 Thou [a]hast [1]swept them away like a flood, they [2b]fall asleep;
In the morning they are like [c]grass which [3]sprouts anew.
6 In the morning it [a]flourishes, and [1]sprouts anew;
Towards evening it [b]fades, and [c]withers away.

7 For we have been [a]consumed by Thine anger,
And by Thy wrath we have been [1]dismayed.
8 Thou hast [a]placed our iniquities before Thee,
Our [b]secret *sins* in the light of Thy presence.
9 For [a]all our days have declined in Thy fury;
We have finished our years like a [1]sigh.
10 As for the days of our [1]life, [2]they contain seventy years,
Or if due to strength, [a]eighty years,
Yet their pride is *but* [b]labor and sorrow;
For soon it is gone and we [c]fly away.
11 Who [1]understands the [a]power of Thine anger,
And Thy fury, according to the [b]fear [2]that is due Thee?
12 So [a]teach us to number our days,
That we may [1b]present to Thee a heart of wisdom.

13 Do [a]return, O LORD; [b]how long *will it be?*
And [1]be [c]sorry for Thy servants.
14 O [a]satisfy us in the morning with Thy lovingkindness,
That we may [b]sing for joy and be glad all our days.
15 [a]Make us glad [1]according to the days Thou hast afflicted us,
And the [b]years we have seen [2]evil.
16 Let Thy [a]work appear to Thy servants,
And Thy [b]majesty [1]to their children.
17 And let the [a]favor of the Lord our God be upon us;
And do [1b]confirm for us the work of our hands;
Yes, [1]confirm the work of our hands.

Psalm 91

Security of the One Who Trusts in the LORD.

HE who dwells in the [a]shelter of the Most High
Will abide in the [b]shadow of the Almighty.
2 I will say to the LORD, "My [a]refuge and my [b]fortress,
My God, in whom I [c]trust!"
3 For it is He who delivers you from the [a]snare of the trapper,
And from the deadly [b]pestilence.
4 He will [a]cover you with His pinions,
And [b]under His wings you may seek refuge;
His [c]faithfulness is a [d]shield and bulwark.

5 You [a]will not be afraid of the [b]terror by night,
Or of the [c]arrow that flies by day;
6 Of the [a]pestilence that [1]stalks in darkness,
Or of the [b]destruction that lays waste at noon.
7 A thousand may fall at your side,

---

4 [1]Or, *and*
[b]Ps. 39:5 [c]Ex. 14:24; Judg. 7:19

5 [1]Or, *flooded* [2]Lit., *become asleep* [3]Or, *passes away*
[a]Job 22:16; 27:20 [b]Job 14:12; 20:8; Ps. 76:5 [c]Ps. 103:15; Is. 40:6

6 [1]Or, *passes away*
[a]Job 14:2 [b]Ps. 92:7; Matt. 6:30 [c]James 1:11

7 [1]Or, *terrified*
[a]Ps. 39:11

8 [a]Ps. 50:21; Jer. 16:17 [b]Ps.19:12; Eccles. 12:14

9 [1]Or, *whisper*
[a]Ps. 78:33

10 [1]Lit., *years* [2]Lit., *in them are*
[a]2 Kin. 19:35 [b]Eccles. 12:2-7; Jer. 20:18 [c]Ps. 78:39; Job 20:8

11 [1]Or, *knows* [2]Lit., *of Thee*
[a]Ps. 76:7 [b]Neh. 5:9

12 [1]Or, *gain, bring in*
[a]Ps. 39:4; Deut. 32:29 [b]Prov.2:1-6

13 [1]Or, *repent in regard to*
[a]Ps. 6:4; 80:14 [b]Ps. 6:3; 74:10 [c]Ps. 106:45; 135:14; Ex. 32:12; Deut. 32:36; Amos 7:3, 6; Jon. 3:9

14 [a]Ps. 36:8; 65:4; 103:5; Jer. 31:14 [b]Ps. 31:7; 85:6

15 [1]Or, *as many days as* [2]Or, *trouble*
[a]Ps. 86:4; [b]Ps. 31:10; Deut. 2:14-16

16 [1]Or, *upon*
[a]Ps. 44:1; 77:12; 92:4; Deut. 32:4; Hab. 3:2 [b]1 Kin. 8:11; Is. 6:3

17 [1]Or, *give permanence to*
[a]Ps. 27:4 [b]Ps. 37:23; Is.26:12; 1 Cor. 3:7

1 [a]Ps. 27:5; 31:20; 32:7 [b]Ps. 17:8; 121:5; Is. 25:4; 32:2

2 [a]Ps. 91:9; 14:6; 94:22 [b]Ps. 18:2; 31:3; Jer. 16:19 [c]Ps. 25:2; 56:4

3 [a]Ps. 124:7; Prov. 6:5 [b]Ps. 91:6; 1 Kin. 8:37; 2 Chr. 20:9

4 [a]Is. 51:16 [b]Ps. 36:7; 57:1; 63:7 [c]Ps. 40:11 [d]Ps. 35:2

5 [a]Ps. 23:4; 27:1; Job 5:19-23 [b]Song of Sol. 3:8 [c]Ps. 64:4

6 [1]Or, *walks*
[a]Ps. 91:10; 2 Kin. 19:35 [b]Job 5:22

And ten thousand at your right hand;
But [a]it shall not approach you.
8 You will only look on with your eyes,
And [a]see the recompense of the wicked.
9 [1]For you have made the LORD, my refuge,
Even the Most High, your dwelling place.
10 [a]No evil will befall you,
Nor will any plague come near your [1]tent.

11 For He will give [a]His angels charge concerning you,
To guard you in all your ways.
12 They will bear you up in their hands,
Lest you strike your foot against a stone.
13 You will [a]tread upon the lion and cobra,
The young lion and the [1]serpent you will trample down.

14 [a]Because he has loved Me, therefore I will deliver him;
I will [b]set him *securely* on high, because he has [c]known My name.
15 He will [a]call upon Me, and I will answer him;
I will be with him in [1]trouble;
I will rescue him, and [b]honor him.
16 With [1]a [a]long life I will satisfy him,
And [2][b]let him behold My salvation.

PSALM 92

Praise for the LORD'S Goodness.

A Psalm, a Song for the Sabbath day.

It is [a]good to give thanks to the LORD,
And to [b]sing praises to Thy name, O Most High;
2 To [a]declare Thy lovingkindness in the morning,
And Thy [b]faithfulness [1]by night.
3 [1]With the [a]ten-stringed lute, and [1]with the [a]harp;
[1]With resounding music [2]upon the [a]lyre.
4 For Thou, O LORD, hast made me glad by [1]what Thou [a]hast done,
I will [b]sing for joy at the [c]works of Thy hands.

5 How [a]great are Thy works, O LORD!
Thy [1][b]thoughts are very [c]deep.
6 A [a]senseless man has no knowledge;
Nor does a [a]stupid man understand this:
7 That when the wicked [a]sprouted up like grass,
And all [b]who did iniquity flourished,
It *was only* that they might be [c]destroyed for evermore.
8 But Thou, O LORD, art [a]on high forever.
9 For, behold, Thine enemies, O LORD,
For, behold, [a]Thine enemies will perish;
All who do iniquity will be [b]scattered.

10 But Thou hast exalted my [a]horn like *that of* the wild ox;
I have [1]been [b]anointed with fresh oil.

---

7 [a]Gen. 7:23; Josh. 14:10

8 [a]Ps. 37:34; 58:10

9 [1]Or, *For Thou O Lord art my Refuge; You have made the Most High your dwelling place.*

10 [1]Or, *dwelling* [a]Prov. 12:21

11 [a]Ps. 34:7; Matt. 4:6; Luke 4:10, 11

13 [1]Or, *dragon* [a]Judg. 14:6; Dan. 6:22; Luke 10:19

14 [a]Ps. 145:20 [b]Ps. 59:1 [c]Ps. 9:10

15 [1]Or, *distress* [a]Ps. 50:15; Job 12:4 [b]1 Sam. 2:30; John 12:26

16 [1]Lit., *length of days* [2]Or, *cause him to feast his eyes on* [a]Ps. 21:4; Deut. 6:2 [b]Ps. 50:23

1 [a]Ps. 147:1 [b]Ps. 135:3

2 [1]Lit., *nights* [a]Ps. 59:16 [b]Ps. 89:1

3 [1]Lit, *upon* [2]Lit., *by means of* [a]Ps. 33:2; 1 Sam. 10:5; 1 Chr. 13:8; Neh. 12:27

4 [1]Lit., *Thy working* [a]Ps. 40:5; 90:16 [b]Ps. 106:47 [c]Ps. 8:6; 111:7; 143:5

5 [1]Or, *purposes* [a]Ps. 40:5; 111:2; Rev. 15:3 [b]Ps. 33:11; 40:5; 139:17 [c]Ps. 36:6; Rom. 11:33

6 [a]Ps. 49:10; 94:8

7 [a]Ps. 90:5 [b]Ps. 94:4 [c]Ps. 37:38

8 [a]Ps. 93:4; 113:5

9 [a]Ps. 37:20 [b]Ps. 68:1; 89:10

10 [1]Or, *become moist* [a]Ps. 75:10; 89:17; 112:9 [b]Ps. 23:5; 45:7

11 And my eye has [a]looked *exultantly* upon [1]my foes,
My ears hear of the evildoers who rise up against me.
12 The [a]righteous man will [1]flourish like the palm tree,
He will grow a [b]cedar in Lebanon.
13 [a]Planted in the house of the LORD,
They will flourish [b]in the courts of our God.
14 They will still [1a]yield fruit in old age;
They shall be [2]full of sap and very green,
15 To [1]declare that [a]the LORD is upright;
He is my [b]rock, and there is [c]no unrighteousness in Him.

PSALM 93

The Majesty of the LORD.

[a]THE LORD [1]reigns, He is [b]clothed with majesty;
The LORD has [c]clothed and girded Himself with strength;
Indeed, the [d]world is firmly established, it will not be moved.
2 Thy [a]throne is established from of old;
Thou [b]art from everlasting.

3 The [a]floods have lifted up, O LORD,
The floods have lifted up their voice;
The floods lift up their pounding waves.
4 More than the sounds of many waters,
Than the mighty breakers of the sea,
The LORD [a]on high is mighty.
5 Thy [a]testimonies are fully confirmed;
[b]Holiness befits Thy house,
O LORD, for [1]evermore.

PSALM 94

The LORD Implored to Avenge His People.

O LORD, God of [1a]vengeance;
God of [1]vengeance, [2b]shine forth!
2 [a]Rise up, O [b]Judge of the earth;
Render recompense [c]to the proud.
3 How long shall the wicked, O LORD,
How long shall the [a]wicked exult?
4 They pour forth *words,* they [a]speak arrogantly;
All who do wickedness [b]vaunt themselves.
5 They [a]crush Thy people, O LORD,
And [b]afflict Thy heritage.
6 They [a]slay the widow and the [1]stranger,
And murder the orphans.
7 And [a]they have said, "[1]The LORD does not see,
Nor does the God of Jacob pay heed."

8 Pay heed, you [a]senseless among the people;
And when will you understand, [a]stupid ones?
9 He who [a]planted the ear, [1]does He not hear?
He who formed the eye, [1]does He not see?

11 [1]Or, *those who lie in wait for me* [a]Ps. 54:7; 91:8

12 [1]Lit., *sprout* [a]Ps. 1:3; 52:8; 72:7; Num. 24:6; Jer. 17:8; Hos. 14:5, 6 [b]Ps. 104:16; Ezek. 31:3

13 [a]Ps. 80:15; Is. 60:21 [b]Ps. 100:4; 116:19

14 [1]Or, *thrive in* [2]Lit., *fat and* [a]Prov. 11:30; Is. 37:31; John 15:2; James 3:18

15 [1]Or, *show forth* [a]Ps. 25:8; Job 34:10 [b]Ps. 18:2; 94:22 [c]Rom. 9:14

1 [1]Or, *has assumed kingship* [a]Ps. 96:10; 97:1; 99:1 [b]Ps. 104:1 [c]Ps. 65:6; Is. 51:9 [d]Ps. 96:10

2 [a]Ps. 45:6; Lam. 5:19 [b]Ps. 90:2

3 [a]Ps. 96:11; 98:7, 8

4 [a]Ps. 65:7; 89:6, 9; 92:8

5 [1]Lit., *length of days* [a]Ps. 19:7 [b]Ps. 29:2; 96:9; 1 Cor. 3:17

1 [1]Or, *avenging acts* [2]Or, *has shone forth* [a]Deut. 32:35; Is. 35:4; Nah. 1:2; Rom. 12:19 [b]Ps. 50:2; 80:1

2 [a]Ps. 7:6 [b]Gen. 18:25 [c]Ps. 31:23

3 [a]Job 20:5

4 [a]Ps. 31:18; 75:5 [b]Ps. 10:3; 52:1

5 [a]Is. 3:15 [b]Ps. 79:1

6 [1]Or, *sojourner* [a]Is. 10:2

7 [1]Heb., *YAH* [a]Job 22:13

8 [a]Ps. 92:6

9 [1]Or, *can* [a]Ex. 4:11; Prov. 20:12

10 [1]Or, *instructs*
[a]Ps. 44:2 [b]Job 35:11; Is. 28:26

11 [1]Or, *For*
[a]Job 11:11; 1 Cor. 3:20

12 [1]Heb. *YAH*
[a]Ps. 119:71; Deut. 8:5; Job 5:17; Prov. 3:11, 12; Heb.12:5, 6 [b]Ps.119:171

13 [a]Job 34:29; Hab. 3:16 [b]Ps. 49:5 [c]Ps. 9:15; 55:23

14 [a]1 Sam. 12:22; Lam. 3:31; Rom. 11:2 [b]Ps. 37:28

15 [1]I.e., administration of justice [2]Lit., *will return to righteousness* [3]Lit., *will be after it*
[a]Ps. 97:2; Is. 42:3; Mic. 7:9

16 [a]Num. 10:35. Is. 28:21; 33:10 [b]Ps. 17:13; 59:2

17 [a]Ps. 124:1, 2

18 [a]Ps. 38:16; 73:2

19 [1]Or, *are many*
[a]Is. 57:18; 66:13

20 [1]Or, *tribunal* [2]Or, *trouble, misfortune*
[a]Amos 6:3 [b]Ps. 50:16; 58:2

21 [1]Or, *soul* [2]Lit., *innocent blood*
[a]Ps. 56:6; 59:3 [b]Ps. 106:38; Ex. 23:7; Prov. 17:15; Matt. 27:4

22 [a]Ps. 9:9; 59:9 [b]Ps. 18:2; 71:7

23 [1]Or, *silence*
[a]Ps. 7:16; 140:9, 11 [b]Gen. 19:15

1 [a]Ps. 66:1; 81:1 [b]Ps. 89:26

2 [1]Or, *a song of thanksgiving* [2]Or, *songs* (with instrumental accompaniment)
[a]Mic. 6:6 [b]Ps. 100:4; 147:7; Jon. 2:9 [c]Ps. 81:2; Eph. 5:19; James 5:13

3 [a]Ps. 48:1; 135:5; 145:3 [b]Ps. 96:4; 97:9

4 [a]Ps. 135:6

5 [1]Lit., *Who has the sea*
[a]Ps. 146:6; Gen. 1:9, 10; Jon. 1:9

6 [a]Ps. 96:9; 99:5, 9 [b]2 Chr. 6:13; Dan. 6:10 [c]Ps. 100:3; 149:2; Is. 17:7; Hos. 8:14

7 [1]Lit., *pasturing* [2]Or, *O that you would obey*
[a]Ps. 74:1 [b]Heb. 3:7-11, 15; 4:7

10 He who [1a]chastens the nations, will He not rebuke,
Even He who [b]teaches man knowledge?
11 The LORD [a]knows the thoughts of man,
[1]That they are a *mere* breath.

12 Blessed is the man whom [a]Thou dost chasten, O [1]LORD,
And [b]dost teach out of Thy law;
13 That Thou mayest grant him [a]relief from the [b]days of adversity,
Until [c]a pit is dug for the wicked.
14 For [a]the LORD will not abandon His people,
Nor will He [b]forsake His inheritance.
15 For [1a]judgment [2]will again be righteous;
And all the upright in heart [3]will follow it.
16 Who will [a]stand up for me against evildoers?
Who will take his stand for me [b]against those who do wickedness?

17 If [a]the LORD had not been my help,
My soul would soon have dwelt in *the abode of* silence.
18 If I should say, "[a]My foot has slipped,"
Thy lovingkindness, O LORD, will hold me up.
19 When my anxious thoughts [1]multiply within me,
Thy [a]consolations delight my soul.
20 Can a [1a]throne of destruction be allied with Thee,
One [b]which devises [2]mischief by decree?
21 They [a]band themselves together against the [1]life of the righteous,
And [b]condemn [2]the innocent to death.
22 But the LORD has been my [a]stronghold,
And my God the [b]rock of my refuge.
23 And He has [a]brought back their wickedness upon them,
And will [1b]destroy them in their evil;
The LORD our God will [1]destroy them.

PSALM 95

Praise to the LORD and Warning against Unbelief.

O COME, let us [a]sing for joy to the LORD;
Let us shout joyfully to [b]the rock of our salvation.
2 Let us [a]come before His presence [b]with [1]thanksgiving;
Let us shout joyfully to Him [c]with [2]psalms.
3 For the LORD is a [a]great God,
And a great King [b]above all gods,
4 In whose hand are the [a]depths of the earth;
The peaks of the mountains are His also.
5 [1]The sea is His, for it was He [a]who made it;
And His hands formed the dry land.

6 Come, let us [a]worship and bow down;
Let us [b]kneel before the LORD our [c]Maker.
7 For He is our God,
And we are the people of His [1a]pasture, and the sheep of His hand.
[b]Today, [2]if you would hear His voice,

8 Do not harden your hearts, as at [1a]Meribah,
As in the day of [2b]Massah in the wilderness;
9 "When your fathers [a]tested Me,
They tried Me, though they had seen My work.
10 "For [a]forty years I loathed *that* generation,
And said, they are a people who err in their heart.
And they do not know My ways.
11 "Therefore I [a]swore in My anger,
Truly they shall not enter into my [b]rest."

Psalm 96

A Call to Worship the Lord the Righteous Judge.

SING to the Lord a [a]new song;
Sing to the Lord, all the earth.
2 Sing to the Lord, bless His name;
[a]Proclaim good tidings of His salvation from day to day.
3 Tell of [a]His glory among the nations,
His wonderful deeds among all the peoples.
4 For [a]great is the Lord, and greatly to be praised;
He is to be [b]feared above all gods.
5 For [a]all the gods of the peoples are [1]idols,
But [b]the Lord made the heavens.
6 [a]Splendor and majesty are before Him,
Strength and beauty are in His sanctuary.

7 [1]Ascribe to the Lord, O [a]families of the peoples,
[1b]Ascribe to the Lord glory and strength.
8 [1]Ascribe to the Lord the [a]glory of His name;
Bring an [2b]offering, and come into His courts.
9 [a]Worship the Lord in [1]holy attire;
[b]Tremble before Him, all the earth.
10 Say among the nations, "[a]The Lord reigns;
Indeed, the [a]world is firmly established, it will not be moved;
He will [b]judge the peoples with [1]equity."

11 Let the [a]heavens be glad, and let the [b]earth rejoice;
Let [c]the sea [1]roar, and [2]all it contains;
12 Let the [a]field exult, and all that is in it.
Then all the [b]trees of the forest will sing for joy
13 Before the Lord, [a]for He is coming;
For He is coming to judge the earth.
He will judge the world in righteousness,
And the peoples in His faithfulness.

Psalm 97

[a] The Lord's Power and Dominion.

THE Lord [1]reigns; let the [b]earth rejoice;
Let the many [2c]islands be glad.
2 [a]Clouds and thick darkness surround Him;

8 [1]Or, *place of strife* [2]Or, *temptation* [a]Ex. 17:7; Num. 20:13 [b]Ex. 17:7; Deut. 6:16

9 [a]Num. 14:22; 1 Cor. 10:9

10 [a]Acts. 7:36; 13:18; Heb. 3:17

11 [a]Num. 14:23; 28-30; Deut. 1:35; Heb. 4:3, 5 [b]Deut. 12:9

1 [a]Ps. 40:3

2 [a]Ps. 71:15

3 [a]Ps. 145:12

4 [a]Ps. 48:1 [b]Ps. 89:7

5 [1]Or, *non-existent things* [a]1 Chr. 16:26 [b]Ps. 115:15; Is. 42:5

6 [a]Ps. 104:1

7 [1]Lit., *Give* [a]Ps. 22:27 [b]Ps. 29:1, 2; 1 Chr. 16:28, 29

8 [1]Lit., *Give* [2]Or, *meal offering* [a]Ps. 79:9; 115:1 [b]Ps. 45:12; 72:10

9 [1]Or, *the splendor of holiness* [a]Ps. 29:2; 110:3; 1 Chr 16:29; 2 Chr. 20:21 [b]Ps. 33:8; 114:7

10 [1]Or, *uprightness* [a]Ps. 93:1 [b]Ps. 9:8; 58:11; 67:4; 98:9

11 [1]Or, *thunder* [2]Lit., *its fullness* [a]Is. 49:13 [b]Ps. 97:1 [c]Ps. 98:7

12 [a]Ps. 65:13; Is. 35:1; 55:12, 13 [b]Is. 44:23

13 [a]Ps. 98:9

1 [1]Or, *has assumed Kingship* [2]Or, *coast lands* [a]Ps. 96:10 [b]Ps. 96:11 [c]Is. 42:10, 12

2 [a]Ps. 18:11; Ex. 19:9; Deut. 4:11; 1 Kin. 8:12

[b]Righteousness and justice are the foundation of His throne.
3 [a]Fire goes before Him,
And [b]burns up His adversaries round about.
4 His [a]lightnings lit up the world;
The earth saw and [b]trembled.
5 The mountains [a]melted like wax at the presence of the LORD,
At the presence of the [b]Lord of the whole earth.
6 The [a]heavens declare His righteousness,
And [b]all the peoples have seen His glory.

7 Let all those be ashamed who serve [a]graven images,
Who boast themselves of [b]idols;
[1c]Worship Him, all you [2]gods.
8 Zion [1]heard *this* and [a]was glad,
And the daughters of Judah have rejoiced
Because of Thy judgments, O LORD.
9 For Thou are the LORD [a]Most High over all the earth;
Thou art exalted far [b]above all [1]gods.

10 [a]Hate evil, you who love the LORD,
Who [b]preserves the souls of His godly ones,
He [c]delivers them from the hand of the wicked.
11 [a]Light is sown *like seed* for the righteous,
And [b]gladness for the upright in heart.
12 Be [a]glad in the LORD, you righteous ones;
And [b]give thanks [1]to His holy name.

PSALM 98

A Call to Praise the LORD for His Righteousness.

A Psalm.

O SING to the LORD a [a]new song,
For He has done [b]wonderful things,
His [c]right hand and His [d]holy arm have [1]gained the victory for Him.
2 The LORD has made known His salvation;
He has revealed His [1a]righteousness in the sight of the nations.
3 He has [a]remembered His lovingkindness and His faithfulness to the house of Israel;
[b]All the ends of the earth have seen the salvation of our God.

4 [a]Shout joyfully to the LORD, all the earth;
[b]Break forth and sing for joy and sing praises.
5 Sing praises to the LORD with the [a]lyre;
With the lyre and the [1b]sound of melody.
6 With [a]trumpets and the sound of the horn
[b]Shout joyfully before [c]the King, the LORD.

7 Let the [a]sea roar and [1]all it contains,
The [b]world and those who dwell in it.

2 [b]Ps. 89:14

3 [a]Ps. 18:8; 50:3; Dan. 7:10; Hab.3:5 [b]Mal. 4:1; Heb. 12:29

4 [a]Ps. 77:18 [b]Ps. 96:9; 104:32

5 [a]Ps. 46:6; Amos 9:5; Mic. 1:4; Nah. 1:5 [b]Josh. 3:11

6 [a]Ps. 50:6 [b]Ps. 98:2; Is. 6:3; 40:5; 66:18

7 [1]Or, *All the gods have worshiped Him* [2]Or, *supernatural powers* [a]Ps. 78:58; Is. 42:17; 44:9, 11; Jer. 10:14 [b]Ps. 106:36; Jer. 50:2; Hab. 2:18 [c]Heb. 1:6

8 [1]Or possibly, *hears and is glad* [a]Ps. 48:11; Zeph. 3:14

9 [1]Or, *supernatural powers* [a]Ps. 83:18 [b]Ps. 95:3; 96:4; 135:5; Ex. 18:11

10 [a]Prov. 8:13; Amos 5:15; Rom. 12:9 [b]Ps. 31:23; 145:20; Prov. 2:8 [c]Ps. 37:40; Jer. 15:21; Dan. 3:28

11 [a]Ps. 112:4; Job 22:28; Prov. 4:18 [b]Ps. 64:10

12 [1]Lit., *for the memory of His holiness* [a]Ps. 32:11 [b]Ps. 30:4

1 [1]Or, *accomplished salvation* [a]Ps. 33:3 [b]Ps. 40:5; 96:3 [c]Ex. 15:6 [d]Is. 52:10

2 [1]I.e., faithfulness to His gracious promises [a]Rom. 3:25

3 [a]Luke 1:54, 72 [b]Ps. 22:27

4 [a]Ps. 100:1 [b]Is. 44:23

5 [1]Or, *voice of song* (accompanied by music) [a]Ps. 92:3 [b]Is. 51:3

6 [a]Num. 10:10; 2 Chr. 15:14 [b]Ps. 66:1 [c]Ps. 47:7

7 [1]Lit., *its fulness* [a]Ps. 96:11 [b]Ps.24:1

8 Let the [a]rivers clap their hands;
Let the [b]mountains sing together for joy
9 Before the LORD; for He is coming to [a]judge the earth;
He will judge the world with righteousness,
And [b]the peoples with [1]equity.

PSALM 99

Praise to the LORD for His Fidelity to Israel.

[a] THE LORD reigns, let the peoples tremble;
He [1b]is enthroned *above* the cherubim, let the earth shake!
2 The LORD [1]is [a]great in Zion,
And He is [b]exalted above all the peoples.
3 Let them praise Thy [a]great and awesome name;
[b]Holy is [1]He.
4 And the [1]strength of the King [a]loves [2]justice;
Thou hast established [3b]equity;
Thou hast [c]executed [2]justice and righteousness in Jacob.
5 [1a]Exalt the LORD our God,
And [b]worship at His footstool;
[c]Holy is He.

6 [a]Moses and Aaron were among His [b]priests,
And [c]Samuel was among those who [d]called on His name;
They [e]called upon the LORD, and He answered them.
7 He [a]spoke to them in the pillar of cloud;
They [b]kept His testimonies,
And the statute that He gave them.
8 O LORD our God, Thou didst [a]answer them;
Thou wast a [b]forgiving God to them,
And *yet* an [c]avenger of their *evil* deeds.
9 Exalt the LORD our God,
And worship at His holy hill;
For holy is the LORD our God.

PSALM 100

All Men Exhorted to Praise God.

A Psalm for [£]thanksgiving.

[a] SHOUT joyfully to the LORD, all the earth.
2 [a]Serve the LORD with gladness;
[b]Come before Him with joyful singing.
3 Know that [a]the LORD [1]Himself is God;
It is He who has [b]made us, and [2]not we ourselves;
We are [c]His people and the sheep of His pasture.

4 Enter His gates [a]with [1]thanksgiving,
And His courts with praise.
Give thanks to Him; [b]bless His name.
5 For [a]the LORD is good;
His lovingkindness is everlasting,
And His [b]faithfulness to all generations.

8 [a]Ps. 93:3; Is. 55:12 [b]Ps. 65:12, 89:12

9 [1]Or, *uprightness* [a]Ps. 96:13 [b]Ps. 96:10

1 [1]Lit., *sits* [a]Ps. 97:1 [b]Ps. 80:1; Ex. 25:22; 1 Sam. 4:4

2 [1]Or, *in Zion is great* [a]Ps. 48:1; Is. 12:6 [b]Ps. 97:9; 113:4

3 [1]Or, *it* [a]Ps. 76:1; Deut. 28:58 [b]Ps. 22:3; Lev. 19:2; Josh. 24:19; 1 Sam. 2:2; Is. 6:3

4 [1]Or, *Thou hast established in equity the strength of the King who loves justice* [2]Or, *judgment* [3]Or, *uprightness* [a]Ps. 11:7; 33:5 [b]Ps. 17:2; 98:9 [c]Ps. 103:6; 146:7; Jer. 23:5

5 [1]The verb is plural. [a]Ps.34:3; 107:32; 118:28 [b]Ps. 132:7 [c]Ps. 99:3

6 [a]Jer. 15:1 [b]Ex. 24:6-8; 29:26; 40:23-27; Lev. 8:1-30 [c]Jer. 15:1 [d]Ps. 22:4, 5; 1 Sam. 7:9; 12:18 [e]Ex. 15:25; 32:30-34

7 [a]Ex. 33:9; Num. 12:5 [b]Ps. 105:28

8 [a]Ps. 106:44 [b]Ps. 78:38; Num. 14:20 [c]Ps. 95:11; 107:12; Ex. 32:28; Num. 20:12

[£] Or, *thank offering*

1 [a]Ps. 98:4, 6

2 [a]Deut. 12:11, 12; 28:47 [b]Ps. 95:2

3 [1]Or, *He* [2]Some mss. read, *His we are* [a]Ps. 46:10; Deut.4:35; 1 Kin. 18:39 [b]Ps. 95:6; 119:73; Job 10:3, 8 [c]Ps. 74:1, 2; 95:7; Is. 40:11; Ezek. 34:30, 31

4 [1]Or, *a thank offering* [a]Ps. 95:2 [b]Ps. 96:2

5 [a]Ps. 25:8; 86:5; 106:1; Jer. 33:11; Nah. 1:7 [b]Ps. 119:90

1 [1]Or, *judgment*
[a]Ps. 51:14; 89:1; 145:7

2 [1]Or, *behave prudently in* [2]Or, *way of integrity* [3]Or, *blamelessness*
[a]1 Sam. 18:5, 14 [b]1 Kin. 9:4

3 [1]Or, *practice of apostasy*
[a]Deut. 15:9 [b]Ps. 40:4

4 [a]Prov. 11:20

5 [1]Or, *silence*
[a]Ps. 50:20; Jer. 9:4 [b]Ps. 10:4; 18:27; Prov. 6:17

6 [1]Or, *way of integrity*
[a]Ps. 119:1

7 [1]Lit., *be established before my eyes*
[a]Ps. 43:1; 52:2 [b]Ps. 52:4, 5

8 [1]Or, *silence*
[a]Ps. 75:10 [b]Ps. 118:10-12 [c]Ps. 46:4

[£]Ps. 142:2

1 [a]Ps. 39:12; 61:1 [b]Ex. 2:23; 1 Sam. 9:16

2 [a]Ps. 69:17 [b]Ps. 31:2 [c]Ps. 69:17

3 [1]Or, *finished*
[a]Ps. 37:20; James 4:14 [b]Job 30:30; Lam. 1:13

4 [1]Lit., *herbage*
[a]Ps. 90:5, 6 [b]Ps. 37:2; Is. 40:7 [c]1 Sam. 1:7; 2 Sam. 12:17; Ezra 10:6; Job 33:20

5 [1]Lit., *voice* [2]Lit., *have cleaved*
[a]Job 19:20; Lam. 4:8

PSALM 101

The Psalmist's Profession of Uprightness.

A Psalm of David.

I WILL [a]sing of lovingkindness and [1]justice,
To Thee, O LORD, I will sing praises.
2 I will [1a]give heed to the [2]blameless way.
When wilt Thou come to me?
I will walk within my house in the [3b]integrity of my heart.
3 I will set no [a]worthless thing before my eyes;
I hate the [1]work of those who [b]fall away;
It shall not fasten its grip on me.
4 A [a]perverse heart shall depart from me;
I will know no evil.
5 Whoever secretly [a]slanders his neighbor, him I will [1]destroy;
No one who has a [b]haughty look and an arrogant heart will I endure.

6 My eyes shall be upon the faithful of the land, that they may dwell with me;
He who walks in a [1a]blameless way is the one who will minister to me.
7 He who [a]practices deceit shall not dwell within my house;
He who speaks falsehood [b]shall not [1]maintain his position before me.
8 Every morning I will [1a]destroy all the wicked of the land,
So as to [b]cut off from the [c]city of the LORD all those who do iniquity.

PSALM 102

Prayer of an Afflicted Man for Mercy on Himself and on Zion.

A Prayer of the Afflicted, when he is faint, and [£]pours out his complaint before the Lord.

[a]HEAR my prayer, O LORD!
And let my cry for help [b]come to Thee.
2 [a]Do not hide Thy face from me in the day of my distress;
[b]Incline Thine ear to me;
In the day when I call [c]answer me quickly.
3 For my days [a]have been [1]consumed in smoke,
And my [b]bones have been scorched like a hearth.
4 My heart [a]has been smitten like [1]grass and [b]withered away,
Indeed, I [c]forget to eat my bread.
5 Because of the [1]loudness of my groaning
My [a]bones [2]cling to my flesh.

6 I [1]resemble a [a]pelican of the wilderness;
I have become like an owl of the waste places.
7 I [a]lie awake,
I have become like a lonely bird on a housetop.

8 My enemies [a]have reproached me all day long;
Those who [1b]deride me [2]have used my *name* as a [c]curse.
9 For I have eaten ashes like bread,
And [a]mingled my drink with weeping,
10 [a]Because of Thine indignation and Thy wrath;
For Thou hast [b]lifted me up and cast me away.
11 My days are like a [1a]lengthened shadow;
And [2]I [b]wither away like [3]grass.

12 But Thou, O LORD, dost [1a]abide forever;
And Thy [2b]name to all generations.
13 Thou wilt [a]arise *and* have [b]compassion on Zion;
For [c]it is time to be gracious to her,
For the [d]appointed time has come.
14 Surely Thy servants [1]find pleasure in her stones,
And feel pity for her dust.
15 [1]So the [2a]nations will fear the name of the LORD,
And [b]all the kings of the earth Thy glory.
16 For the LORD has [a]built up Zion;
He has [b]appeared in His glory.
17 He has [a]regarded the prayer of the [1]destitute,
Nor has He despised their prayer.

18 [1]This will be [a]written for the [b]generation to come;
[2]That [c]a people yet to be created [3]may praise [4]the LORD.
19 For He [a]looked down from His holy height;
[b]From heaven the LORD gazed [1]upon the earth,
20 To hear the [a]groaning of the prisoner;
To [b]set free [1]those who were doomed to death;
21 That *men* may [a]tell of the name of the LORD in Zion,
And His praise in Jerusalem;
22 When [a]the peoples are gathered together,
And the kingdoms, to serve the LORD.

23 He has weakened my strength in the way;
He has [a]shortened my days.
24 I say, "O my God, [a]do not take me away in the [1]midst of my days,
Thy [b]years are throughout all generations.
25 "Of old Thou didst [a]found the earth;
And the [b]heavens are the work of Thy hands.
26 "[1]Even they will [a]perish, but Thou dost endure;
And all of them will wear out like a garment;
Like clothing Thou wilt change them, and they will be changed.
27 "But Thou art [1a]the same,
And Thy years will not come to an end.

6 [1]Lit., *have become similar to*
[a]Is. 34:11; Zeph. 2:14

7 [a]Ps. 77:4

8 [1]Or, *made a fool of* [2]Lit., *have sworn by me*
[a]Ps. 31:11 [b]Acts 26:11 [c]Is. 65:15; Jer. 29:22; 2 Sam. 16:5

9 [a]Ps. 42:3; 80:5

10 [a]Ps. 38:3 [b]Job 27:21; 30:22

11 [1]Lit., *stretched out* [2]Or, *as for me, I* [3]Lit., *herbage*
[a]Ps. 109:23; Job 14:2 [b]Ps. 102:4

12 [1]Or, *sit enthroned* [2]Lit., *memorial*
[a]Ps. 9:7; 10:16; Lam. 5:19 [b]Ps. 135:13; Ex. 3:15

13 [a]Ps. 12:5; 44:26 [b]Is. 60:10; Zech. 1:12; [c]Ps. 119:126 [d]Ps. 75:2; Dan. 8:19

14 [1]Or, *have found*

15 [1]Or, *And* [2]Or, *Gentiles, heathen*
[a]Ps. 67:7; 1 Kin. 8:43 [b]Ps. 138:4

16 [a]Ps. 147:2 [b]Is. 60:1, 2

17 [1]Or, *naked*
[a]Ps. 22:24; Neh. 1:6

18 [1]Or, *Let this be written* [2]Or, *And* [3]Or, *will* [4]Heb., *YAH*
[a]Deut. 31:19; 1 Cor. 10:11 [b]Ps. 22:30; 48:13 [c]Ps. 22:31

19 [1]Lit., *toward*
[a]Ps. 14:2; 53:2; Deut. 26:15 [b]Ps. 33:13

20 [1]Lit., *the sons of death*
[a]Ps. 79:11 [b]Ps. 146:7

21 [a]Ps. 22:22

22 [a]Ps. 22:27; 86:9; Is. 49:22, 23; 60:3; Zech. 8:20-23

23 [a]Ps. 39:5

24 [1]Lit., *half*
[a]Ps. 39:13; Is. 38:10 [b]Ps. 102:12; 90:2; Job 36:26; Hab. 1:12

25 [a]Gen. 1:1; Neh. 9:6; Heb. 1:10-12 [b]Ps. 96:5

26 [1]Lit., *They themselves*
[a]Is. 34:4; 51:6; Matt. 24:35; 2 Pet. 3:10; Rev. 20:11

27 [1]Lit., *He*
[a]Is. 41:4; 43:10; Mal. 3:6; James 1:17

28 [1]Lit., *seed*
[a]Ps. 69:36 [b]Ps. 89:4

1 [a]Ps. 104:1, 35 [b]Ps. 33:21; 105:3; 145:21; Ezek. 36:21; 39:7

2 [a]Deut. 6:12; 8:11

3 [a]Ps. 86:5; 130:8; Ex. 34:7; Is. 43:25 [b]Ps. 30:2; Ex. 15:26; Jer. 30:17

4 [a]Ps. 49:15 [b]Ps. 5:12

5 [1]Or, *desire*
[a]Ps. 107:9; 145:16 [b]Is. 40:31

6 [1]Or, *deeds of vindication*
[a]Ps. 99:4; 146:7 [b]Ps. 12:5

7 [a]Ps. 99:7; 147:19; Ex. 33:13 [b]Ps. 78:11; 106:22

8 [a]Ps. 86:15; Ex. 34:6; Num. 14:18; Neh. 9:17; Jonah 4:2 [b]Ps. 145:8; Joel 2:13; Nah. 1:3

9 [a]Ps. 30:5; Is. 57:16 [b]Jer. 3:5, 12; Mic. 7:18

10 [a]Ezra 9:13; Lam. 3:22

11 [1]Or, *revere*
[a]Ps. 36:5; 57:10

12 [a]2 Sam. 12:13; Is. 38:17; Zech. 3:9; Heb. 9:26

13 [1]Or, *revere*
[a]Mal. 3:17

14 [1]I.e., what we are made of
[a]Is. 29:16 [b]Ps. 78:39 [c]Gen. 3:19; Eccles. 12:7

15 [a]Ps. 90:5; Is. 40:6; 1 Pet. 1:24 [b]Job 14:2; James 1:10, 11

16 [a]Is. 40:7 [b]Job 7:10; 8:18; 20:9

17 [1]Or, *revere* [2]I.e., faithfulness to His gracious promises
[a]Ps. 25:6 [b]Ps. 105:8; Ex. 20:6; Deut. 5:10

18 [a]Ps. 25:10; Deut. 7:9

19 [1]Or, *kingdom* [2]I.e., the universe
[a]Ps. 11:4 [b]Ps. 47:2, 8; Dan. 4:17

20 [a]Ps. 148:2 [b]Ps. 29:1; 78:25 [c]Matt. 6:10 [d]Ps. 91:11; Heb. 1:14

28 "The [a]children of Thy servants will continue,
And their [1b]descendants will be established before Thee."

Psalm 103

Praise for the LORD'S Mercies.

[a] *A Psalm* of David.

BLESS the LORD, O my soul;
And all that is within me, *bless* His [b]holy name.
2 Bless the LORD, O my soul,
And [a]forget none of His benefits;
3 Who [a]pardons all your iniquities;
Who [b]heals all your diseases;
4 Who [a]redeems your life from the pit;
Who [b]crowns you with lovingkindness and compassion;
5 Who [a]satisfies your [1]years with good things,
So that your youth is [b]renewed like the eagle.

6 The LORD [a]performs [1]righteous deeds,
And judgments for all who are [b]oppressed.
7 He [a]made known His ways to Moses,
His [b]acts to the sons of Israel.
8 The LORD is [a]compassionate and gracious,
[b]Slow to anger and abounding in lovingkindness.
9 He [a]will not always strive *with us;*
Nor will He [b]keep *His anger* forever.
10 He has [a]not dealt with us according to our sins,
Nor rewarded us according to our iniquities.
11 For high [a]as the heavens are above the earth,
So great is His lovingkindness toward those who [1]fear Him.
12 As far as the east is from the west,
So far has He [a]removed our transgressions from us.
13 Just [a]as a father has compassion on *his* children,
So the LORD has compassion on those who [1]fear Him.
14 For [a]He Himself knows [1]our frame;
He [b]is mindful that we are *but* [c]dust.

15 As for man, his days are [a]like grass;
As a [b]flower of the field, so he flourishes.
16 When the [a]wind has passed over it, it is no more;
And its [b]place acknowledges it no longer.
17 But the [a]lovingkindness of the LORD is from everlasting to everlasting on those who [1]fear Him,
And His [2b]righteousness [b]to children's children,
18 To [a]those who keep His covenant,
And who remember His precepts to do them.

19 The LORD has established His [a]throne in the heavens;
And His [1b]sovereignty rules over [2]all.
20 Bless the LORD, you [a]His angels,
[b]Mighty in strength, who [c]perform His word,
[d]Obeying the voice of His word!

21 Bless the LORD, all you [a]His hosts,
You [b]who serve Him, doing His will.
22 Bless the LORD, [a]all you works of His,
In all places of His dominion;
Bless the LORD, O my soul!

PSALM 104

The LORD'S Care over All His Works.

BLESS the LORD, O my soul!
O LORD my God, Thou art very great;
Thou art [b]clothed with splendor and majesty,
2 Covering Thyself with [a]light as with a cloak,
[b]Stretching out heaven like a *tent* curtain.
3 [1]He [a]lays the beams of His upper chambers in the waters;
[1]He makes the [b]clouds His chariot;
[1]He walks upon the [c]wings of the wind;
4 [1]He makes [2a]the winds His messengers,
[3]Flaming [b]fire His ministers.

5 He [a]established the earth upon its foundations,
So that it will not [1]totter forever and ever.
6 Thou [a]didst cover it with the deep as with a garment;
The waters were standing above the mountains.
7 At Thy [a]rebuke they fled;
At the [b]sound of Thy thunder they hurried away.
8 The mountains rose; the valleys sank down
To the [a]place which Thou didst establish for them.
9 Thou didst set a [a]boundary that they may not pass over;
That they may not return to cover the earth.

10 [1]He sends forth [a]springs in the valleys;
They flow between the mountains;
11 They [a]give drink to every beast of the field;
The [b]wild donkeys quench their thirst.
12 [1]Beside them the birds of the heavens [a]dwell;
They [2]lift up *their* voice among the branches.
13 [1]He [a]waters the mountains from His upper chambers;
The earth is satisfied with the fruit of His works.

14 [1]He causes the [a]grass to grow for the [2]cattle,
And [b]vegetation for the [3]labor of man,
So that [4]he may bring forth [5]food [c]from the earth,
15 And [a]wine which makes man's heart glad,
[b]So that he may make *his* face glisten with oil,
And [1]food which [c]sustains man's heart.
16 The trees of the LORD [1]drink their fill,
The cedars of Lebanon which He planted,
17 Where the [a]birds build their nests,
And the [b]stork, *whose home* is the [1]fir trees.

18 The high mountains are for the [a]wild goats;
The [b]cliffs are a refuge for the [c]rock badgers.

21 [a]Ps. 148:2; 1 Kin. 22:19; Neh. 9:6; Luke 2:13 [b]Ps. 104:4
22 [a]Ps. 145:10
1 [a]Ps. 103:22 [b]Ps. 93:1
2 [a]Dan. 7:9 [b]Is. 40:22
3 [1]Lit., *the one who* [a]Amos 9:6 [b]Is. 19:1 [c]Ps. 18:10
4 [1]Lit., *Who* [2]Or, *His angels, spirits* [3]Or, *His ministers flames of fire* [a]Ps. 148:8; Heb. 1:7 [b]2 Kin. 2:11; 6:17
5 [1]Or, *move out of place* [a]Ps. 24:2; Job 38:4
6 [a]Gen. 1:2
7 [a]Ps. 18:15; 106:9; Is. 50:2 [b]Ps. 29:3; 77:18
8 [a]Ps. 33:7
9 [a]Job 38:10, 11; Jer. 5:22
10 [1]Lit., *The one who sends* [a]Ps. 107:35; Is. 41:18
11 [a]Ps. 104:13 [b]Job 39:5
12 [1]Or, *Over, Above* [2]Lit., *give forth* [a]Matt. 8:20
13 [1]Lit., *Who* [a]Ps. 65:9; 147:8
14 [1]Lit., *Who* [2]Or, *beasts* [3]Or, *cultivation by; or, service of* [4]Or, *He* [5]Lit., *bread* [a]Ps. 147:8; Job 38:27 [b]Gen. 1:29 [c]Job 28:5
15 [1]Lit., *bread* [a]Judg. 9:13; Prov. 31:6; Eccles. 10:19 [b]Ps. 23:5; 92:10; 141:5; Luke 7:46 [c]Gen. 18:5; Judg. 19:5, 8
16 [1]Lit., *are satisfied*
17 [1]Or, *cypress* [a]Ps. 104:12 [b]Lev. 11:19
18 [a]Job 39:1 [b]Prov. 30:26 [c]Lev. 11:5

19 [a]Gen. 1:14 [b]Ps. 19:6

20 [1]Lit., *creep* [a]Ps. 74:16; Is. 45:7 [b]Ps. 50:10; Is. 56:9; Mic. 5:8

21 [1]Lit., *And to seek* [a]Job 38:39 [b]Ps. 145:15; Joel 1:20

22 [a]Job 37:8

23 [a]Gen. 3:19

24 [1]Or, *With* [2]Or possibly, *creatures* [a]Ps. 40:5 [b]Ps. 136:5; Prov. 3:19; Jer. 10:12; 51:15 [c]Ps. 65:9

25 [1]Or, *This* [2]Or, *broad of dimensions* (lit., hands) [a]Ps. 8:8; 69:34

26 [1]Or, *a sea-monster* [a]Ps. 107:23; Ezek. 27:9 [b]Ps. 74:14; Job 41:1

27 [1]Lit., *its appointed time* [a]Ps. 145:15 [b]Ps. 136:25; 147:9; Job 36:31; 38:41

28 [a]Ps. 145:16

29 [1]Or, *breath* [a]Ps. 30:7; Deut. 31:17 [b]Ps. 146:4; Job 34:14; Eccles. 12:7 [c]Ps. 90:3; Gen. 3:19; Job 10:9

30 [1]Or, *breath* [a]Job 33:4; Ezek. 37:9

31 [a]Ps. 86:12; 111:10 [b]Gen. 1:31

32 [1]Lit., *The one who* [a]Ps. 97:4, 5; 114:7; Judg. 5:5 [b]Ps. 144:5; Ex. 19:18

33 [1]Or, *Let me sing* [2]Lit., *in my lifetime* [3]Lit., *while I still am* [a]Ps. 63:4 [b]Ps. 146:2

34 [a]Ps. 19:14 [b]Ps. 9:2

35 [1]Or, *Hallelujah!* [2]Heb., *YAH* [a]Ps. 59:13 [b]Ps. 37:10 [c]Ps. 104:1 [d]Ps. 105:45; 106:48

1 [a]Ps. 106:1; 1 Chr. 16:8-22, 34; Is. 12:4 [b]Ps. 99:6 [c]Ps. 145:12

2 [1]Or, *Meditate on* [2]I.e., wonderful acts [a]Ps. 96:1; 98:5 [b]Ps. 77:12; 119:27; 145:5

3 [1]Or, *Boast* [a]Ps. 33:21

19 He made the moon [a]for the seasons;
The [b]sun knows the place of its setting.
20 Thou [a]dost appoint darkness and it becomes night,
In which all the [b]beasts of the forest [1]prowl about.
21 The [a]young lions roar after their prey,
[1]And [b]seek their food from God.
22 *When* the sun rises they withdraw,
And lie down in their [a]dens.
23 Man goes forth to [a]his work
And to his labor until evening.

24 O LORD, how [a]many are Thy works!
[1]In [b]wisdom Thou hast made them all;
The [c]earth is full of Thy [2]possessions.
25 [1]There is the [a]sea, great and [2]broad,
In which are swarms without number,
Animals both small and great.
26 There the [a]ships move along,
And [1b]leviathan, which Thou hast formed to sport in it.

27 They all [a]wait for Thee,
To [b]give them their food in [1]due season.
28 Thou dost give to them, they gather *it* up;
Thou [a]dost open Thy hand, they are satisfied with good.
29 Thou [a]dost hide Thy face, they are dismayed;
Thou [b]dost take away their [1]spirit, they expire,
And [c]return to their dust.
30 Thou dost send forth Thy [1a]Spirit, they are created;
And Thou dost renew the face of the ground.

31 Let the [a]glory of the LORD endure forever;
Let the LORD [b]be glad in His works;
32 [1]He [a]looks at the earth, and it trembles;
He [b]touches the mountains, and they smoke.
33 [1]I will sing to the LORD [2a]as long as I live;
[1]I will [b]sing praise to my God [3]while I have my being.
34 Let my [a]meditation be pleasing to Him;
As for me, I shall [b]be glad in the LORD.
35 Let sinners be [a]consumed from the earth,
And let the [b]wicked be no more.
[c]Bless the LORD, O my soul.
[1d]Praise [2]the LORD!

PSALM 105

The LORD'S Wonderful Works in Behalf of Israel.

OH [a]give thanks to the LORD, [b]call upon His name;
[c]Make known His deeds among the peoples.
2 Sing to Him, [a]sing praises to Him;
[1b]Speak of all His [2]wonders.
3 [1]Glory in His holy name;
Let the [a]heart of those who seek the LORD be glad.

4 Seek the LORD and [a]His strength;
[b]Seek His face continually.
5 Remember His [1a]wonders which He has done,
His marvels, and the [b]judgments [2]uttered by His mouth,
6 O seed of [a]Abraham His servant,
O sons of [b]Jacob, His [c]chosen ones!
7 He is the LORD our God;
His [a]judgments are in all the earth.

8 He has [a]remembered His covenant forever,
The word which He commanded to a [b]thousand generations,
9 *The* [a]*covenant* which He made with Abraham,
And His [b]oath to Isaac.
10 Then He [a]confirmed it to Jacob for a statute,
To Israel as an everlasting covenant,
11 Saying, "[a]To you I will give the land of Canaan
As the [1b]portion of your inheritance,"
12 When they were only a [a]few men in number,
Very few, and [b]strangers in it.
13 And they wandered about from nation to nation,
From *one* kingdom to another people.
14 He [a]permitted no man to oppress them,
And He [b]reproved kings for their sakes:
15 "[a]Do not touch My anointed ones,
And do My prophets no harm."

16 And He [a]called for a famine upon the land;
He [b]broke the whole staff of bread.
17 He [a]sent a man before them:
Joseph was [b]sold as a slave.
18 They afflicted his [a]feet with fetters;
[1]He himself was laid in irons,
19 Until the time that his [a]word came to pass,
The word of the LORD [1b]tested him.
20 The [a]king sent and released him,
The ruler of peoples, and set him free.
21 He [a]made him lord of his house,
And ruler over all his possessions,
22 To [1]imprison his princes [2a]at will,
That he might teach his elders wisdom.
23 [a]Israel also came into Egypt;
Thus Jacob [b]sojourned in the land of Ham.
24 And He [a]caused His people to be very fruitful,
And made them stronger than their adversaries.

25 He [a]turned their heart to hate His people,
To [b]deal craftily with His servants.
26 He [a]sent Moses His servant,
And [b]Aaron whom He had chosen.
27 They [1a]performed His wondrous acts among them,
And miracles in the land of Ham.

4 [a]Ps. 63:2 [b]Ps. 27:8

5 [1]I.e., wonderful acts [2]Lit., *of His mouth* [a]Ps. 40:5; 77:11 [b]Ps.119:13

6 [a]Ps. 105:42 [b]Ps. 135:4 [c]Ps. 106:5; 135:4; 1 Chr. 16:13

7 [a]Is. 26:9

8 [a]Ps. 105:42; 106:45; Luke 1:72 [b]Deut. 7:9

9 [a]Gen. 17:2; 22:16-18; Gal. 3:17 [b]Gen. 26:3

10 [a]Gen. 28:13-15

11 [1]Lit., *measuring line* [a]Gen. 13:15; 15:18 [b]Ps. 78:55; Josh 23:4

12 [a]Gen. 34:30; Deut. 7:7 [b]Gen. 23:4; Heb. 11:9

14 [a]Gen. 20:7; 35:5 [b]Gen. 12:17; 20:3, 7

15 [a]Gen. 26:11

16 [a]Gen. 41:54 [b]Lev. 26:26; Is. 3:1; Ezek. 4:16

17 [a]Gen. 45:5 [b]Gen. 37:28, 36; Acts 7:9

18 [1]Lit., *His soul came into* [a]Gen. 39:20

19 [1]Or, *refined* [a]Gen. 40:20, 21 [b]Ps. 66:10

20 [a]Gen. 41:14

21 [a]Gen. 41:40-44

22 [1]Lit., *bind* [2]Lit., *at his* [a]Gen. 41:44

23 [a]Gen. 46:6; Acts 7:15 [b]Acts 13:17

24 [a]Ex. 1:7, 9

25 [a]Ex. 1:8; 4:21 [b]Ex. 1:10; Acts 7:19

26 [a]Ex. 3:10; 4:12 [b]Ex. 4:14; Num. 16:5; 17:5-8

27 [1]Lit., *set the words of His signs* [a]Ps. 105:27-36; 78:43-51

28 He [a]sent darkness and made *it* dark;
And they did not [b]rebel against His words.
29 He [a]turned their waters into blood,
And caused their fish to die.
30 Their land swarmed with [a]frogs
Even in the [b]chambers of their kings.
31 He spoke, and there came a [a]swarm of flies,
And [b]gnats in all their territory.
32 He [1]gave them [a]hail for rain,
And flaming fire in their land.
33 He struck down their vines also and their fig trees,
And shattered the trees of their territory.
34 He spoke, and [a]locusts came,
And young locusts, even without number,
35 And ate up all vegetation in their land,
And ate up the fruit of their ground.
36 He also [a]struck down all the first-born in their land,
The first fruits of all their vigor.

37 Then He brought them out with [a]silver and gold;
And among His tribes there was not one who stumbled.
38 Egypt was [a]glad when they departed;
For the [b]dread of them had fallen upon them.
39 He spread a [a]cloud for a [1]covering,
And [b]fire to illumine by night.
40 [1]They [a]asked, and He brought [b]quail,
And satisfied them with the [2c]bread of heaven.
41 He opened the [1]rock, and [a]water flowed out;
[2]It ran in the dry places *like* a river.
42 For He [a]remembered His holy word
With Abraham His servant;
43 And He brought forth His people with joy,
His chosen ones with a joyful [a]shout.
44 He [a]gave them also the lands of the [1]nations,
That they [b]might take possession of *the fruit of* the peoples' labor,
45 So that they might [a]keep His statutes,
And observe His laws,
[1]Praise [2]the LORD!

PSALM 106

Israel's Rebelliousness and the LORD's Deliverances.

1 PRAISE [2]the LORD!
Oh [a]give thanks to the LORD, for He [b]is good;
For [c]His lovingkindness is everlasting.
2 Who can speak of the [a]mighty deeds of the LORD,
Or can show forth all His praise?
3 How blessed are those who keep [1]justice,
[2]Who [a]practice righteousness at all times!

4 Remember me, O LORD, in *Thy* [a]favor [1]toward Thy people;
Visit me with Thy salvation,

---

28 [a]Ex. 10:21, 22 [b]Ps. 99:7

29 [a]Ex. 7:20, 21

30 [a]Ex. 8:6 [b]Ex. 8:3

31 [a]Ex. 8:21 [b]Ex. 8:16

32 [1]Or, *made their rain hail* [a]Ex. 9:23-25

34 [a]Ex. 10:12-15

36 [a]Ps. 135:8; 136:10; Ex. 12:29; 13:15

37 [a]Ex. 12:35, 36

38 [a]Ex. 12:33 [b]Ex. 15:16

39 [1]Or, *curtain* [a]Ps. 78:14; Ex. 13:21; Neh. 9:12; Is. 4:5 [b]Ex. 40:38

40 [1]Or, *One* [2]Or, *food* [a]Ps. 78:18 [b]Ps. 78:27; Ex. 16:13; Num. 11:31 [c]Ps. 78:24; Ex. 16:15; Neh. 9:15; John 6:31

41 [1]Or, *boulder* [2]Lit., *They went* [a]Ps. 78:15; 114:8; Ex. 17:6; Num. 20:11; Is. 48:21; 1 Cor. 10:4

42 [a]Ps. 105:8

43 [a]Ps. 106:12; Ex. 15:1

44 [1]Or, *Gentiles* [a]Ps. 78:55; Josh. 13:7 [b]Deut. 6:10, 11

45 [1]Or, *Hallelujah!* [2]Heb., *YAH* [a]Deut. 4:40

1 [1]Or, *Hallelujah!* [2]Heb., *YAH* [a]Ps. 105:1; 107:1 [b]Ps. 100:5 [c]1 Chr. 16:34, 41

2 [a]Ps. 145:4, 12; 150:2

3 [1]Or, *judgment* [2]Many Heb. mss. read, *The one who performs* [a]Ps. 15:2

4 [1]Lit., *of* [a]Ps. 44:3; 119:132

5 That I may see the [a]prosperity of Thy chosen ones,
That I may [b]rejoice in the gladness of Thy nation,
That I may [c]glory with Thine [1]inheritance.

6 [a]We have sinned [1b]like our fathers,
We have committed iniquity, we have behaved wickedly.
7 Our fathers in Egypt did not understand Thy [1]wonders;
They [a]did not remember [2]Thine abundant kindnesses,
But [b]rebelled by the sea, at the [3]Red Sea.
8 Nevertheless He saved them [a]for the sake of His name,
That He might [b]make His power known.
9 Thus He [a]rebuked the [1]Red Sea and it [b]dried up;
And He [c]led them through the deeps, as through the wilderness.
10 So He [a]saved them from the [1]hand of the one who hated *them*,
And [b]redeemed them from the [1]hand of the enemy.
11 And [a]the waters covered their adversaries;
Not one of them was left.
12 Then they [a]believed His words;
They [b]sang His praise.

13 They quickly [a]forgot His works;
They [b]did not wait for His counsel,
14 But [a]craved intensely in the wilderness,
And [1b]tempted God in the desert.
15 So He [a]gave them their request,
But [b]sent a [1]wasting disease among them.

16 When they became [a]envious of Moses in the camp,
Of Aaron, the holy one of the LORD,
17 The [a]earth opened and swallowed up Dathan,
And engulfed the [1]company of Abiram.
18 And a [a]fire blazed up in their [1]company;
The flame consumed the wicked.

19 They [a]made a calf in Horeb,
And worshiped a molten image.
20 Thus they [a]exchanged their glory
For the image of an ox that eats grass.
21 They [a]forgot God their Savior,
Who had done [b]great things in Egypt,
22 [1a]Wonders in the land of Ham,
And awesome things by the [2]Red Sea.
23 Therefore [a]He said that He would destroy them,
Had not [b]Moses His chosen one stood in the breach before Him,
To turn away His wrath from destroying *them*.
24 Then they [a]despised the [b]pleasant land;
They [c]did not believe in His word,
25 But [a]grumbled in their tents;
They did not listen to the voice of the LORD.

5 [1]I.e., people
[a]Ps. 1:3 [b]Ps. 118:15 [c]Ps. 105:3

6 [1]Lit., *with*
[a]1 Kin. 8:47; Ezra 9:7; Neh. 1:7; Jer. 3:25; Dan. 9:5 [b]Ps. 78:8, 57; 2 Chr. 30:7; Neh. 9:2; Zech. 1:4

7 [1]I.e., wonderful acts
[2]Lit., *the multitude of Thy lovingkindnesses* [3]Or, *Sea of Reeds*
[a]Ps. 78:11, 42; Judg. 3:7 [b]Ps. 78:17; Ex. 14:11, 12

8 [a]Ezek. 20:9 [b]Ex. 9:16

9 [1]Or, *Sea of Reeds*
[a]Ps. 18:15; 78:13; Is. 50:2; Nah. 1:4 [b]Ex. 14:21; Is. 51:10 [c]Is. 63:11-13

10 [1]Or, *power*
[a]Ex. 14:30 [b]Ps. 78:42; 107:2

11 [a]Ps. 78:53; Ex. 14:28; 15:5

12 [a]Ex. 14:31 [b]Ps. 105:43; Ex. 15:1-21

13 [a]Ex. 15:24; 16:2; 17:2
[b]Ps. 107:11

14 [1]Or, *put God to the test*
[a]Ps. 78:18; Num 11:4; 1 Cor. 10:6 [b]Ex. 17:2; 1 Cor. 10:9

15 [1]Or, *leanness into their soul*
[a]Ps. 78:29; Num. 11:31 [b]Is. 10:16

16 [a]Num. 16:3

17 [1]Or, *assembly, band*
[a]Num. 16:32

18 [1]Or, *assembly, band*
[a]Num. 16:35

19 [a]Ex. 32:4; Deut. 9:8; Acts 7:41

20 [a]Jer. 2:11; Rom. 1:23

21 [a]Ps. 106:7, 13; 78:11
[b]Deut. 10:21

22 [1]I.e., Wonderful acts
[2]Or, *Sea of Reeds*
[a]Ps. 105:27

23 [a]Ex. 32:10; Deut. 9:14; Ezek. 20:8, 13 [b]Ex. 32:11-14; Deut. 9:25-29

24 [a]Num. 14:31 [b]Deut. 8:7; Jer. 3:19; Ezek. 20:6 [c]Deut. 1:32; 9:23

25 [a]Num. 14:2; Deut. 1:27

26 [1]Lit., *lifted up his hand* [a]Ps. 95:11; Num. 14:28-35; Ezek. 20:15; Heb. 3:11

27 [a]Deut. 4:27 [b]Ps. 44:11

28 [1]Or, *Baal of peor* [a]Num. 25:3; Deut. 4:3; Hos. 9:10 [b]Num. 25:2

29 [a]Num. 25:4

30 [a]Num. 25:7 [b]Num. 25:8

31 [a]Gen. 15:6; Num. 25:11-13

32 [1]Lit., *strife* [a]Ps. 81:7; 95:9; Num. 20:2-13 [b]Num. 20:12

33 [1]Or, *his spirit* [a]Ps. 78:40; 107:11; Num. 20:3, 10

34 [a]Judg. 1:21, 27-36 [b]Deut. 7:2, 16

35 [1]Lit., *works* [a]Judg. 3:5, 6

36 [a]Judg. 2:12

37 [a]Deut. 12:31; 32:17; 2 Kin. 17:17; Ezek. 16:20, 21; 1 Cor. 10:20

38 [a]Ps. 94:21 [b]Deut. 18:10 [c]Num. 35:33; Is. 24:5; Jer. 3:1, 2

39 [1]Lit., *works* [a]Lev. 18:24; Ezek. 20:18 [b]Lev. 17:7; Num. 15:39; Judg. 2:17; Hos. 4:12

40 [1]I.e., people [a]Ps. 78:59; Judg. 2:14 [b]Lev. 26:30; Deut. 32:19

41 [1]Or, *Gentiles* [a]Judg. 2:14; Neh. 9:27

42 [1]Lit., *hand* [a]Judg. 4:3; 10:12

43 [a]Judg. 2:16-18 [b]Ps. 81:12 [c]Judg. 6:6

44 [a]Judg. 3:9; 6:7; 10:10

45 [1]Lit., *was sorry* [a]Ps. 105:8; Lev. 26:42 [b]Judg. 2:18

26 Therefore He [1a]swore to them,
That He would cast them down in the wilderness,
27 And that He would [a]cast their seed among the nations,
And [b]scatter them in the lands.

28 They [a]joined themselves also to [1]Baal-peor,
And ate [b]sacrifices offered to the dead.
29 Thus they [a]provoked *Him* to anger with their deeds;
And the plague broke out among them.
30 Then Phinehas [a]stood up and interposed;
And so the [b]plague was stayed.
31 And it was [a]reckoned to him for righteousness,
To all generations forever.

32 They also [a]provoked *Him* to wrath at the waters of [1]Meribah,
So that it [b]went hard with Moses on their account;
33 Because they [a]were rebellious against [1]His Spirit,
He spoke rashly with his lips.

34 They [a]did not destroy the peoples,
As [b]the LORD commanded them,
35 But [a]they mingled with the nations,
And learned their [1]practices,
36 And [a]served their idols,
Which became a snare to them.
37 They even [a]sacrificed their sons and their daughters to the demons,
38 And shed [a]innocent blood,
The blood of their [b]sons and their daughters,
Whom they sacrificed to the idols of Canaan;
And the land was [c]polluted with the blood.
39 Thus they became [a]unclean in their [1]practices,
And [b]played the harlot in their deeds.

40 Therefore the [a]anger of the LORD was kindled against His people,
And He [b]abhorred His [1]inheritance.
41 Then [a]He gave them into the hand of the [1]nations;
And those who hated them ruled over them.
42 Their enemies also [a]oppressed them,
And they were subdued under their [1]power.
43 Many times He would [a]deliver them;
They, however, were rebellious in their [b]counsel,
And *so* [c]sank down in their iniquity.

44 Nevertheless He looked upon their distress,
When He [a]heard their cry;
45 And He [a]remembered His covenant for their sake,
And [1b]relented according to the greatness of His lovingkindness.

46 He also made them [a]*objects* of compassion
In the presence of all their captives.

47 [a]Save us, O LORD our God,
And [b]gather us from among the nations,
To give thanks to Thy holy name,
And [1c]glory in Thy praise.
48 [a]Blessed be the LORD, the God of Israel,
From everlasting even to everlasting.
And let all the people say, "Amen."
[1]Praise [2]the LORD!

BOOK 5

PSALM 107

The LORD Delivers Men from Manifold Troubles.

OH [a]give thanks to the LORD, for He is good;
For His lovingkindness is everlasting.
2 Let [a]the redeemed of the LORD say *so,*
Whom He has [b]redeemed from the hand of the adversary,
3 And [a]gathered from the lands,
From the east and from the west,
From the north and from the [1]south.

4 They [a]wandered in the wilderness in a [1]desert region;
They did not find a way to [2]an inhabited [b]city.
5 *They were* hungry [1]and thirsty;
Their [a]soul fainted within them.
6 Then they [a]cried out to the LORD in their trouble;
He delivered them out of their distresses.
7 He led them also by a [1a]straight way,
To go to [2b]an inhabited city.
8 [a]Let them give thanks to the LORD for His lovingkindness,
And for His [1]wonders to the sons of men!
9 For He has [a]satisfied the [1]thirsty soul,
And the [b]hungry soul He has filled with what is good.

10 There were those who [a]dwelt in darkness and in the shadow of death,
[b]Prisoners in [1]misery and [2]chains,
11 Because they had [a]rebelled against the words of God,
And [b]spurned the counsel of the Most High.
12 Therefore He humbled their heart with labor;
They stumbled and there was [a]none to help.
13 Then they [a]cried out to the LORD in their trouble;
He saved them out of their distresses.
14 He [a]brought them out of darkness and the shadow of death,
And [b]broke their bands apart.
15 Let them give thanks to the LORD for His lovingkindness,
And for His [1]wonders to the sons of men!

46 [1]1 Kin. 8:50; 2 Chr. 30:9; Ezra 9:9; Neh. 1:11; Jer. 42:12

47 [1]Lit., *boast*
[a]1 Chr. 16:35, 36 [b]Ps. 147:2 [c]Ps. 47:1

48 [1]Or, *Hallelujah!* [2]Heb., YAH
[a]Ps. 41:13; 72:18; 89:52

1 [a]Ps. 106:1

2 [a]Is. 35:9, 10; 62:12; 63:4 [b]Ps. 78:42; 106:10

3 [1]Lit., *sea*
[a]Ps. 106:47; Deut. 30:3; Neh. 1:9; Is. 11:12; 43:5; 56:8; Ezek. 11:17; 20:34

4 [1]Lit., *waste* [2]Or, *a habitable city;* lit., *a city of habitation*
[a]Num. 14:33; 32:13; Deut. 2:7; Josh. 5:6; 14:10 [b]Ps. 107:7, 36

5 [1]Lit., *also*
[a]Ps. 77:3

6 [a]Ps. 107:13, 19, 28; 50:15

7 [1]Or, *level* [2]Or, *a habitable city;* lit., *a city of habitation*
[a]Ps. 5:8; Ezra 8:21; Jer. 31:9 [b]Ps. 107:4, 36

8 [1]I.e., wonderful acts
[a]Ps. 107:15, 21, 31

9 [1]Or, *parched*
[a]Ps. 22:26; 63:5; 103:5 [b]Ps. 146:7; Matt. 5:6; Luke 1:53

10 [1]Lit., *affliction* [2]Lit., *irons*
[a]Ps. 143:3; Is. 42:7; Mic. 7:8; Luke 1:79 [b]Ps. 102:20; Job 36:8

11 [a]Ps. 78:40; 106:7 [b]Num. 15:31; 2 Chr. 36:16; Prov. 1:25; Is. 5:24

12 [a]Ps. 22:11; 72:12

13 [a]Ps. 107:6

14 [a]Ps. 107:10; 86:13 [b]Ps. 116:16; Jer. 2:20; 30:8; Nah. 1:13; Luke 13:16; Acts 12:7

15 [1]I.e., wonderful acts

16 [a]Is. 45:1, 2

17 [1]Lit., *the way of their transgression* [a]Is. 65:6, 7; Jer. 30:14, 15; Ezek. 24:23

18 [a]Ps. 102:4; Job 33:20 [b]Ps. 88:3; Job 33:22 [c]Ps. 9:13; Job 38:17

20 [1]Or, *pits* [a]Ps. 147:15, 18; Matt. 8:8 [b]Ps. 30:2; 103:3; 147:3; 2 Kin. 20:5 [c]Ps. 30:3; 49:15; 56:13; 103:4; Job 33:28, 30

21 [1]I.e., wonderful acts

22 [a]Ps. 50:14; 116:17; Lev. 7:12 [b]Ps. 9:11; 73:28; 118:17

23 [a]Is. 42:10; Jonah 1:3

24 [1]I.e., wonderful acts

25 [1]Lit., *of it* [a]Ps. 105:31, 34 [b]Ps. 148:8; Jonah 1:4 [c]Ps. 93:3, 4

26 [a]Ps. 22:14; 119:28

27 [1]Lit., *all their wisdom was swallowed up* [a]Job 12:25; Is. 24:20

29 [1]Lit., *of it* [a]Ps. 65:7; 89:9; Matt. 8:26; Luke 8:24

31 [1]I.e., wonderful acts [a]Ps. 78:4; 111:4

32 [a]Ps. 34:3; 99:5; Is. 25:1 [b]Ps. 22:22, 25 [c]Ps. 35:18

33 [1]Or, *turns* [2]Or, *desert* [a]Ps. 74:15; Is. 42:15; 50:2

34 [a]Gen. 13:10; 14:3; 19:24, 25; Deut. 29:23 [b]Job 39:6; Jer. 17:6

35 [1]Or, *turns* [2]Or, *desert* [a]Ps. 105:41; 114:8; Is. 35:6, 7; 41:18

36 [1]Or, *a habitable city;* lit., *a city of habitation* [a]Ps. 107:4, 7

37 [1]Lit., *acquire fruits of yield* [a]2 Kin. 19:29; Is. 65:21; Amos 9:14

38 [a]Gen. 12:2; 17:20; Ex. 1:7; Deut. 1:10 [b]Deut. 7:14

16 For He has [a]shattered gates of bronze,
And cut bars of iron asunder.

17 Fools, because of [1]their rebellious way,
And [a]because of their iniquities, were afflicted.
18 Their [a]soul abhorred all kinds of food;
And they [b]drew near to the [c]gates of death.
19 Then they cried out to the LORD in their trouble;
He saved them out of their distresses.
20 He [a]sent His word and [b]healed them,
And [c]delivered *them* from their [1]destructions.
21 Let them give thanks to the LORD for His lovingkindness,
And for His [1]wonders to the sons of men!
22 Let them also offer [a]sacrifices of thanksgiving,
And [b]tell of His works with joyful singing.

23 Those who [a]go down to the sea in ships,
Who do business on great waters;
24 They have seen the works of the LORD,
And His [1]wonders in the deep.
25 For He [a]spoke and raised up a [b]stormy wind,
Which [c]lifted up the waves [1]of the sea.
26 They rose up to the heavens, they went down to the depths;
Their soul [a]melted away in *their* misery.
27 They reeled and [a]staggered like a drunken man,
And [1]were at their wits' end.
28 Then they cried to the LORD in their trouble,
And He brought them out of their distresses.
29 He [a]caused the storm to be still,
So that the waves [1]of the sea were hushed.
30 Then they were glad because they were quiet;
So He guided them to their desired haven.
31 Let them give thanks to the LORD for His lovingkindness,
And for His [1a]wonders to the sons of men!
32 Let them [a]extol Him also [b]in the congregation of the people,
And [c]praise Him at the seat of the elders.

33 He [1a]changes rivers into a [2]wilderness,
And springs of water into a thirsty ground;
34 A [a]fruitful land into a [b]salt waste,
Because of the wickedness of those who dwell in it.
35 He [1a]changes a [2]wilderness into a pool of water,
And a dry land into springs of water;
36 And there He makes the hungry to dwell,
So that they may establish [1a]an inhabited city,
37 And sow fields, and [a]plant vineyards,
And [1]gather a fruitful harvest.
38 Also He blesses them and they [a]multiply greatly;
And He [b]does not let their cattle decrease,

39 When they are [a]diminished and [b]bowed down
Through oppression, misery, and sorrow,
40 He [a]pours contempt upon [1]princes,
And [b]makes them wander [c]in a pathless waste.
41 But He [1a]sets the needy securely on high away from affliction,
And [b]makes *his* families like a flock.
42 The [a]upright see it, and are glad;
But all [b]unrighteousness shuts its mouth.
43 Who is [a]wise? Let him give heed to these things;
And consider the [b]lovingkindnesses of the LORD.

PSALM 108

God Praised and Supplicated to Give Victory.

A Song, a Psalm of David.

[a]MY heart is steadfast, O God;
I will sing, I will sing praises, even with my [1]soul.
2 Awake, harp and lyre;
I will awaken the dawn!
3 I will give thanks to Thee, O LORD, among the peoples;
And I will sing praises to Thee among the nations.
4 For Thy lovingkindness is great [a]above the heavens;
And Thy truth *reaches* to the skies.
5 Be exalted, O God, above the heavens,
And Thy glory above all the earth.
6 [a]That Thy beloved may be delivered,
Save with Thy right hand, and answer me!

7 God has spoken in His [1]holiness:
"I will exult, I will portion out Shechem,
And measure out the valley of Succoth.
8 "Gilead is Mine, Manasseh is Mine;
Ephraim also is the [1]helmet of My head;
Judah is My [2]scepter.
9 "Moab is My washbowl;
Over Edom I shall throw My shoe;
Over Philistia I will shout aloud."

10 Who will bring me into the beseiged city?
Who [1]will lead me to Edom?
11 Hast not Thou Thyself, O God, [a]rejected us?
And wilt Thou not go forth with our armies, O God?
12 Oh give us help against the adversary,
For deliverance [1]by man is in vain.
13 [1]Through God we shall do valiantly;
And it is He who will tread down our adversaries.

39 [a]Ezek. 5:11; 29:15 [b]Ps. 38:6; 44:25; 57:6

40 [1]Or, *nobles*
[a]Job 12:21 [b]Job 12:24 [c]Deut. 32:10

41 [1]Lit., *puts in an inaccessibly high place*
[a]Ps. 59:1; 113:7, 8; 1 Sam. 2:8
[b]Ps. 113:9; Job 21:11

42 [a]Ps. 52:6; Job 22:19
[b]Ps. 63:11; Job 5:16; Rom. 3:19

43 [a]Ps. 64:9; Jer. 9:12; Hos. 14:9 [b]Ps. 107:1

1 [1]Lit., *glory*
[a]Ps. 108:1-5; 57:7-11

4 [a]Ps. 113:4

6 [a]Ps. 108:6-13; 60:5-12

7 [1]Or, *sanctuary*

8 [1]Lit., *protection* [2]Or, *law-giver*

10 [1]Or, *has led*

11 [a]Ps. 44:9

12 [1]Lit., *of*

13 [1]Or, *In*, or, *With*

1 [a]Deut. 10:21 [b]Ps. 28:1; 83:1

2 [1]Lit., *wicked mouth and the deceitful* [2]Lit., *with* [a]Ps. 10:7; 52:4 [b]Ps. 120:2

3 [a]Ps. 69:4

4 [a]Ps. 38:20 [b]Ps. 69:13; 141:5

5 [1]Lit., *laid upon me* [a]Ps. 35:12; 38:20 [b]John 7:7; 10:32

6 [1]Or, *adversary, Satan* [a]Zech. 3:1

7 [a]Ps. 1:5 [b]Prov. 28:9

8 [a]Ps. 55:23 [b]Acts 1:20

9 [a]Ex. 22:24 [b]Jer. 18:21

10 [1]Or, *out of their desolate places* [a]Ps.59:15; Gen. 4:12; Job 30:5-8 [b]Ps. 37:25

11 [1]Lit., *ensnare, strike at* [a]Job 20:15; Neh. 5:7 [b]Is. 1:7; Lam. 5:2; Ezek. 7:21

12 [1]Lit., *continue* [a]Ezra 7:28; 9:9 [b]Job 5:4; Is. 9:17

13 [1]Lit., *for cutting off* [a]Ps. 21:10; 37:28 [b]Ps. 9:5; Prov. 10:7

14 [1]Lit., *to* [a]Ex. 20:5; Num. 14:18; Is. 65:6, 7; Jer. 32:18 [b]Neh. 4:5; Jer. 18:23

15 [a]Ps. 90:8; Jer. 16:17 [b]Ps. 34:16

16 [a]Ps. 37:14 [b]Ps. 37:32; 94:6

17 [a]Prov. 14:14; Ezek. 35:9; Matt. 7:2

18 [1]Lit., *his inward parts* [a]Ps. 109:29; 73:6; Ezek. 7:27 [b]Num. 5:22

19 [a]Ps. 109:29; 73:6; Ezek. 7:27 [b]Ps. 30:11; 2 Sam. 22:40; Is. 11:5

20 [1]Lit., *This is* [a]Ps. 54:5; 94:23; Is. 3:11; 2 Tim. 4:14 [b]Ps. 41:5; 71:10

PSALM 109

Vengeance Invoked upon Adversaries.

For the choir director. A Psalm of David.

O [a]GOD of my praise,
[b]Do not be silent!
2 For they have opened the [1]wicked and [a]deceitful mouth against me;
They have spoken [2]against me with a [b]lying tongue.
3 They have also surrounded me with words of hatred,
And fought against me [a]without cause.
4 In return [a]for my love they act as my accusers;
But [b]I am *in* prayer.
5 Thus they have [1a]repaid me evil for good,
And [b]hatred for my love.

6 Appoint a wicked man over him;
And let an [1a]accuser stand at his right hand.
7 When he is judged, let him [a]come forth guilty;
And let his [b]prayer become sin.
8 Let [a]his days be few;
Let [b]another take his office.
9 Let his [a]children be fatherless,
And his [b]wife a widow.
10 Let his [a]children wander about and beg;
And let them [b]seek *sustenance* [1]far from their ruined homes.
11 Let [a]the creditor [1]seize all that he has;
And let [b]strangers plunder the product of his labor.
12 Let there be none to [1a]extend lovingkindness to him,
Nor [b]any to be gracious to his fatherless children.
13 Let his [a]posterity be [1]cut off;
In a following generation let their [b]name be blotted out.

14 Let [a]the iniquity of his fathers be remembered [1]before the LORD,
And do not let the sin of his mother be [b]blotted out.
15 Let [a]them be before the LORD continually,
That He may [b]cut off their memory from the earth;
16 Because he did not remember to show lovingkindness,
But persecuted the [a]afflicted and needy man,
And the despondent in heart, to [b]put *them* to death.
17 He also loved cursing, so [a]it came to him;
And he did not delight in blessing, so it was far from him.
18 But he [a]clothed himself with cursing as with his garment,
And it [b]entered into [1]his body like water,
And like oil into his bones.
19 Let it be to him as [a]a garment with which he covers himself,
And for a belt with which he constantly [b]girds himself.
20 [1]Let this be the [a]reward of my accusers from the LORD,
And of those who [b]speak evil against my soul.

21 But Thou, O [1]God, the Lord, deal *kindly* with me [a]for
Thy name's sake;
Because [b]Thy lovingkindness is good, deliver me;
22 For [a]I am afflicted and needy,
And [1]my heart is [b]wounded within me.
23 I am passing [a]like a shadow when it lengthens;
I am shaken off [b]like the locust.
24 My [a]knees [1]are weak from [b]fasting;
And my flesh has grown lean, without fatness.
25 I also have become a [a]reproach to them;
When they see me, they [b]wag their head.

26 [a]Help me, O Lord my God;
Save me according to Thy lovingkindness.
27 [1]And let them [a]know that this is Thy hand;
Thou, Lord, hast done it.
28 [a]Let them curse, but do Thou bless;
When they arise, they shall be ashamed,
But Thy [b]servant shall be glad.
29 [1]Let [a]my accusers be clothed with dishonor,
And [2]let them [b]cover themselves with their own shame
as with a robe.

30 With my mouth I will give thanks abundantly to the
Lord;
And in the midst of many [a]I will praise Him.
31 For He stands [a]at the right hand of the needy,
To save him from those who [b]judge his soul.

Psalm 110

The Lord Gives Dominion to the King.

A Psalm of David.

[a]The Lord says to my Lord:
"[b]Sit at My right hand,
Until I make [c]Thine enemies a footstool for Thy feet."
2 The Lord will stretch forth Thy strong [a]scepter from
Zion, *saying,*
"[b]Rule in the midst of Thine enemies."
3 Thy [a]people [1]will volunteer freely in the day of Thy
[2]power;
[b]In [3]holy array, from the womb of the dawn,
[4]Thy youth are to Thee *as* the [c]dew.

4 [a]The Lord has sworn and will [b]not [1]change His mind,
"Thou art a [c]priest forever
According to the order of Melchizedek."
5 The Lord is [a]at Thy right hand;
He [1]will [b]shatter kings in the [c]day of His wrath.
6 He will [a]judge among the nations,
He [1]will fill *them* with [b]corpses,
He [2]will [c]shatter the [3]chief men over a broad country.
7 He will [a]drink from the brook by the wayside;
Therefore He will [b]lift up *His* head.

21 [1]*YHWH, usually rendered* Lord [a]Ps. 23:3; 25:11; 79:9; 106:8; Ezek. 36:22 [b]Ps. 69:16

22 [1]Lit., *one has pierced my heart within me* [a]Ps. 40:17; 86:1 [b]Ps. 143:4; Job 24:12; Prov. 18:14

23 [a]Ps. 102:11 [b]Ex. 10:19; Job 39:20

24 [1]Or, *totter* [a]Heb. 12:12 [b]Ps. 35:13

25 [a]Ps. 22:6 [b]Ps. 22:7; Jer. 18:16; Lam. 2:15

26 [a]Ps. 119:86

27 [1]Or, *That they may know* [a]Job 37:7

28 [a]2 Sam. 16:11, 12 [b]Is. 65:14

29 [1]Or, *My accusers will be* [2]Or, *they will cover* [a]Ps. 132:18; Job 8:22 [b]Ps. 35:26; Job 8:22

30 [a]Ps. 22:22

31 [a]Ps. 16:8; 73:23; 110:5; 121:5 [b]Ps. 37:33

1 [a]Matt. 22:44; Mark 12:36; Luke 20:42, 43; Acts 2:34, 35; Heb. 1:13 [b]Matt. 26:64; Eph. 1:20; Col. 3:1; Heb. 1:3; 8:1; 10:12; 12:2 [c]1 Cor. 15:25; Eph 1:22

2 [a]Ps. 45:6; Jer. 48:17; Ezek. 19:14 [b]Ps. 2:9; 72:8; Dan. 7:13, 14

3 [1]Lit., *will be freewill offerings* [2]Or, *army* [3]Or, *the splendor of holiness* [4]Or, *The dew of Thy youth is Thine.* [a]Judg. 5:2; Neh. 11:2 [b]Ps. 96:9; 1 Chr. 16:29 [c]2 Sam. 17:12; Mic. 5:7

4 [1]Lit., *be sorry* [a]Heb. 7:21 [b]Num. 23:19 [c]Heb. 5:6, 10; 6:20; 7:17; Zech 6:13

5 [1]Or, *has shattered* [a]Ps. 109:31 [b]Ps. 68:14; 76:12 [c]Ps. 2:5, 12; Rom. 2:5; Rev. 6:17

6 [1]Or, *has filled* [2]Or, *has shattered* [3]Lit., *head over* [a]Is. 2:4; Joel 3:12; Mic. 4:3 [b]Is. 66:24 [c]Ps. 68:21

7 [a]Judg. 7:5, 6 [b]Ps. 27:6

PSALM 111

The LORD Praised for His Goodness.

1 PRAISE [2]the LORD!
I [a]will give thanks to the LORD with all *my* heart,
In the [b]company of the upright and in the assembly.
2 Great are the [a]works of the LORD;
They are [1]studied by all who delight in them.
3 [1a]Splendid and majestic is His work;
And [b]His righteousness endures forever.
4 He has made His [1]wonders [2]to be remembered;
The LORD is [a]gracious and compassionate.
5 He has [a]given [1]food to those who [2]fear Him;
He will [b]remember His covenant forever.
6 He has made known to His people the power of His works,
In giving them the heritage of the nations.

7 The works of His hands are [1a]truth and justice;
All His precepts [b]are [2]sure.
8 They are [a]upheld forever and ever;
They are performed in [1b]truth and uprightness.
9 He has sent [a]redemption to His people;
He has [1]ordained His covenant forever;
[b]Holy and [2]awesome is His name.
10 The [1a]fear of the LORD is the beginning of wisdom;
A [b]good understanding have all those who [2]do *His commandments;*
His [c]praise endures forever.

PSALM 112

Prosperity of the One Who Fears the LORD.

1 PRAISE [2]the LORD!
How [a]blessed is the man who [3]fears the LORD,
Who greatly [b]delights in His commandments.
2 His [1a]descendants will be mighty [2]on earth;
The generation of the [b]upright will be blessed.
3 [a]Wealth and riches are in his house,
And his righteousness endures forever.
4 Light arises in the darkness [a]for the upright;
He is [b]gracious and compassionate and righteous.
5 It is well with the man who [a]is gracious and lends;
He will [1]maintain his cause in judgment.
6 For he will [a]never be shaken;
The [b]righteous will be [1]remembered forever.

7 He will not fear [a]evil tidings;
His [b]heart is steadfast, [c]trusting in the LORD.
8 His [a]heart is upheld, he [b]will not fear,
Until he [c]looks *with satisfaction* on his adversaries.
9 [1]He [a]has given freely to the poor;
His righteousness endures forever;
His [b]horn will be exalted in honor.

---

1 [1]Or, *Hallelujah! I will...* [2]Heb., *YAH* [a]Ps. 138:1 [b]Ps. 89:7; 149:1

2 [1]Lit., *sought out* [a]Ps. 92:5

3 [1]Lit., *Splendor and majesty* [a]Ps. 96:6; 145:5 [b]Ps. 112:3, 9; 119:142

4 [1]I.e., wonderful acts [2]Lit., *a memorial* [a]Ps. 86:15; 103:8; 145:8

5 [1]Lit., *prey* [2]Or, *revere* [a]Matt. 6:31-33 [b]Ps. 105:8

7 [1]Or, *faithfulness* [2]Or, *trustworthy* [a]Rev. 15:3 [b]Ps. 19:7; 93:5

8 [1]Or, *faithfulness* [a]Ps. 119:160; Is. 40:8; Matt. 5:18 [b]Ps. 19:9

9 [1]Lit., *commanded* [2]I.e., inspiring reverence [a]Luke 1:68 [b]Ps. 99:3

10 [1]Or, *reverence for* [2]Lit., *do them* [a]Prov. 1:7; 9:10 [b]Ps. 119:98; Prov. 3:4 [c]Ps. 145:2

1 [1]Or, *Hallelujah! Blessed...* [2]Heb., *YAH* [3]Or, *reveres* [a]Ps. 128:1 [b]Ps. 1:2; 119:14

2 [1]Lit., *seed* [2]Or, *in the land* [a]Ps. 127:4 [b]Ps. 128:4

3 [a]Prov. 3:16; 8:18

4 [a]Ps. 97:11; Job 11:17 [b]Ps. 37:26

5 [1]Or, *conduct his affairs with justice* [a]Ps. 37:21

6 [1]Lit., *for an eternal remembrance* [a]Ps. 15:5; 55:22 [b]Prov. 10:7

7 [a]Prov. 1:33 [b]Ps. 57:7; 108:1 [c]Ps. 56:4

8 [a]Heb. 13:9 [b]Ps. 27:1; 56:11; Prov. 3:24; Is. 12:2 [c]Ps. 54:7

9 [1]Lit., *He has scattered, he has given to...* [a]2 Cor. 9:9 [b]Ps. 75:10; 89:17; 92:10; 148:14

10 The [a]wicked will see it and be [1]vexed;
He will [b]gnash his teeth and [c]melt away;
The [d]desire of the wicked will perish.

Psalm 113

The Lord Exalts the Humble.

1 PRAISE [2]the LORD!
[a]Praise, O [b]servants of the LORD.
Praise the name of the LORD.
2 [a]Blessed be the name of the LORD
From this time forth and forever.
3 [a]From the rising of the sun to its setting
The [b]name of the LORD is to be praised.
4 The LORD is [a]high above all nations;
His [b]glory is above the heavens.

5 [a]Who is like the LORD our God,
Who [b]is enthroned on high,
6 Who [1a]humbles Himself to behold
The things that are in heaven and in the earth?
7 He [a]raises the poor from the dust,
And lifts the needy from the ash heap,
8 To make *them* [a]sit with [1]princes,
With the [1]princes of His people.
9 He [a]makes the barren woman abide in the house
As a joyful mother of children.
[1]Praise [2]the LORD!

Psalm 114

God's Deliverance of Israel from Egypt.

WHEN Israel went forth [a]from Egypt,
The house of Jacob from a people of [b]strange language,
2 Judah became [a]His sanctuary,
Israel [b]His dominion.

3 The [a]sea looked and fled;
The [b]Jordan turned back.
4 The mountains [a]skipped like rams,
The hills like lambs.
5 What [a]ails you, O sea, that you flee?
O Jordan, that you turn back?
6 O mountains, that you skip like rams?
O hills, like lambs?

7 [a]Tremble, O earth, before the Lord,
Before the God of Jacob,
8 Who [a]turned the rock into a [b]pool of water,
The [c]flint into a fountain of water.

---

10 [1]Or, *angry* [a]Ps. 86:17 [b]Ps. 35:16; 37:12; Matt. 8:12; 25:30; Luke 13:28 [c]Ps. 58:7 [d]Job 8:13; Prov. 10:28; 11:7

1 [1]Or, *Hallelujah! Praise. . .* [2]Heb., YAH [a]Ps. 135:1 [b]Ps. 34:22; 69:36; 79:10; 90:13

2 [a]Ps. 145:21; Dan. 2:20

3 [a]Ps. 50:1 [b]Ps. 18:3; 48:1, 10

4 [a]Ps. 97:9; 99:2 [b]Ps. 8:1; 57:11; 148:13

5 [a]Ps. 35:10; 89:6; Ex. 15:11 [b]Ps. 103:19

6 [1]Or, *looks far below in the heavens and on the earth?* [a]Ps. 11:4; 138:6; Is. 57:15

7 [a]Ps. 107:41; 1 Sam. 2:8

8 [1]Or, *nobles* [a]Job 36:7

9 [1]Or, *Hallelujah!* [2]Heb., YAH [a]Ps. 68:6; 1 Sam. 2:5; Is. 54:1

1 [a]Ex. 13:3 [b]Ps. 81:5

2 [a]Ps. 78:68, 69; Ex. 15:17; 29:45, 46 [b]Ex. 19:6

3 [a]Ps. 77:16 [b]Josh. 3:13, 16

4 [a]Ps. 18:7; 29:6; Ex. 19:18; Judg. 5:5; Hab. 3:6

5 [a]Hab. 3:8

7 [a]Ps. 96:9

8 [a]Ps. 78:15; 105:41; Ex. 17:6; Num. 20:11 [b]Ps. 107:35 [c]Deut. 8:15

Psalm 115

[a]

Heathen Idols Contrasted with the Lord.

NOT to us, O LORD, not to us,
But [b]to Thy name give glory
Because of Thy lovingkindness, because of Thy [1]truth.
2 [a]Why should the nations say,
"[b]Where, now, is their God?"
3 But our [a]God is in the heavens;
He [b]does whatever He pleases.
4 Their [a]idols are silver and gold,
The [b]work of man's hands.
5 They have mouths, but they [a]cannot speak;
They have eyes, but they cannot see;
6 They have ears, but they cannot hear;
They have noses, but they cannot smell;
7 [1]They have hands, but they cannot feel;
[2]They have feet, but they cannot walk;
They cannot make a sound with their throat.
8 Those who make them [1]will become like them,
Everyone who trusts in them.

9 O [a]Israel, [b]trust in the LORD;
He is their [c]help and their shield.
10 O house of [a]Aaron, trust in the LORD;
He is their help and their shield.
11 You who [1a]fear the LORD, trust in the LORD;
He is their help and their shield.
12 The LORD [a]has been mindful of us; He will bless *us;*
He will bless the house of Israel;
He will bless the house of Aaron.
13 He will [a]bless those who [1]fear the LORD,
The small together with the great.
14 May the LORD [a]give you increase,
You and your children.
15 May you be blessed of the LORD,
[a]Maker of heaven and earth.

16 The heavens are [a]the heavens of the LORD;
But [b]the earth He has given to the sons of men.
17 The [a]dead do not praise [1]the LORD,
Nor *do* any who go down into [b]silence;
18 But as for us, we will [a]bless [1]the LORD
From this time forth and forever.
[2]Praise [1]the LORD!

Psalm 116

[a]

Thanksgiving for Deliverance from Death.

I LOVE the LORD, because He [b]hears
My voice *and* my supplications.
2 Because He has [a]inclined His ear to me,
Therefore I shall call *upon Him* as long as I live.
3 The [a]cords of death encompassed me,
And the [1]terrors of [2]Sheol [3]came upon me;
I found distress and sorrow.

1 [1]Or, *faithfulness* [a]Is. 48:11; Ezek. 36:22 [b]Ps. 29:2; 96:8
2 [a]Ps. 79:10 [b]Ps. 42:3
3 [a]Ps. 103:19 [b]Ps. 135:6; Dan. 4:35
4 [a]Ps. 115:4-8; 135:15-18 [b]Deut. 4:28; 2 Kin. 19:18; Is. 37:19; 44:10, 20
5 [a]Jer. 10:5
7 [1]Lit., *Their hands* [2]Lit., *Their feet*
8 [1]Or, *are like them*
9 [a]Ps. 118:2; 135:19 [b]Ps. 37:3; 62:8 [c]Ps. 33:20
10 [a]Ps. 118:2; 135:19
11 [1]Or, *revere* [a]Ps. 22:23; 103:11; 135:20
12 [a]Ps. 98:3
13 [1]Or, *revere* [a]Ps. 103:11; 112:1; 128:1
14 [a]Deut. 1:11
15 [a]Ps. 102:25; 121:2; 124:8; 134:3; 146:6; Gen. 1:1; Neh. 9:6; Acts 14:15; Rev. 14:7
16 [a]Ps. 89:11 [b]Ps. 8:6
17 [1]Heb., *YAH* [a]Ps. 6:5 [b]Ps. 31:17
18 [1]Heb., *YAH* [2]Or, *Hallelujah!* [a]Ps. 113:2

1 [a]Ps. 18:1 [b]Ps. 6:8; 66:19; Is. 37:17; Dan. 9:18
2 [a]Ps. 17:6; 31:2; 40:1
3 [1]Lit., *straits* [2]Ie., the nether world [3]Lit., *found me* [a]Ps. 18:4, 5

4 Then [a]I called upon the name of the LORD:
"O LORD, I beseech Thee, [1b]save my life!"

5 [a]Gracious is the LORD, and [b]righteous;
Yes, our God is [c]compassionate.
6 The LORD preserves [a]the simple;
I was [b]brought low, and He saved me.
7 Return to your [a]rest, O my soul,
For the LORD has [b]dealt bountifully with you.
8 For Thou hast [a]rescued my soul from death,
My eyes from tears,
My feet from stumbling.
9 I shall walk before the LORD
In the [1a]land of the living.
10 I [a]believed when I said,
"I am [b]greatly afflicted."
11 I [a]said in my alarm,
"[b]All men are liars."

12 What shall I [a]render to the LORD
For all His [b]benefits [1]toward me?
13 I shall lift up the [a]cup of salvation,
And [b]call upon the name of the LORD.
14 I shall [a]pay my vows to the LORD,
Oh *may it be* [b]in the presence of all His people.
15 [a]Precious in the sight of the LORD
Is the death of His godly ones.
16 O LORD, [1]surely I am [a]Thy servant,
I am Thy servant, the [b]son of Thy handmaid,
Thou hast [c]loosed my bonds.
17 To Thee I shall offer [a]a sacrifice of thanksgiving,
And [b]call upon the name of the LORD.
18 I shall [a]pay my vows to the LORD,
Oh *may it be* in the presence of all His people,
19 In the [a]courts of the LORD's house,
In the midst of you, O [b]Jerusalem.
[1]Praise [2]the LORD!

PSALM 117

A Psalm of Praise.

[a]PRAISE the LORD, all nations;
Laud Him, all peoples!
2 For His [a]lovingkindness [1]is great toward us,
And the [2b]truth of the LORD is everlasting.
[3]Praise [4]the LORD!

PSALM 118

Thanksgiving for the LORD's Saving Goodness.

[a]GIVE thanks to the LORD, for He is good;
[b]For His lovingkindness is everlasting.
2 Oh let [a]Israel say,
"His lovingkindness is everlasting."

4 [1]Or, *deliver my soul* [a]Ps. 18:6; 118:5 [b]Ps. 17:13; 22:20

5 [a]Ps. 86:15; 103:8 [b]Ps. 119:137; 145:17; Ezra 9:15; Neh. 9:8; Jer. 12:1; Dan. 9:14 [c]Ex. 34:6

6 [a]Ps. 19:7; Prov. 1:4 [b]Ps. 79:18; 142:6

7 [a]Jer. 6:16; Matt. 11:29 [b]Ps. 13:6; 142:7

8 [a]Ps. 49:15; 56:13; 86:13

9 [1]Lit., *lands* [a]Ps. 27:13

10 [a]2 Cor. 4:13 [b]Ps. 88:7

11 [a]Ps. 31:22 [b]Ps. 62:9; Rom. 3:4

12 [1]Lit., *upon* [a]2 Chr. 32:25; 1 Thess. 3:9 [b]Ps. 103:2

13 [a]Ps. 16:5 [b]Ps. 80:18; 105:1

14 [a]Ps. 50:14 [b]Ps. 22:25

15 [a]Ps. 72:14

16 [1]Or, *because* [a]Ps. 86:16; 119:125; 143:12 [b]Ps. 86:16 [c]Ps. 107:14

17 [a]Ps. 50:14 [b]Ps. 116:13

18 [a]Ps. 116:14

19 [1]Or, *Hallelujah!* [2]Heb., YAH [a]Ps. 92:13; 96:8; 135:2 [b]Ps. 102:21

1 [a]Rom. 15:11

2 [1]Lit., *prevails over us* [2]Or, *faithfulness* [3]Or, *Hallelujah!* [4]Heb., YAH [a]Ps. 103:11 [b]Ps. 100:5; 146:6

1 [a]Ps. 106:1 [b]Ps. 136:1-26

2 [a]Ps. 115:9

3 [a]Ps. 115:10

4 [1]Or, *revere*
[a]Ps. 115:11

5 [1]Heb., *YAH*
[a]Ps. 18:6; 86:7; 120:1 [b]Ps. 18:19

6 [a]Ps. 56:9; Job 19:27; Heb. 13:6 [b]Ps. 23:4; 27:1 [c]Ps. 56:4, 11

7 [a]Ps. 54:4 [b]Ps. 54:7

8 [a]Ps. 108:12; 2 Chr. 32:7, 8; Is. 31:1, 3; 57:13; Jer. 17:5

9 [a]Ps. 146:3

10 [a]Ps. 3:6; 88:17 [b]Ps. 18:40

12 [a]Deut. 1:44 [b]Ps. 58:9

13 [1]Or, *fell*
[a]Ps. 140:4 [b]Ps. 86:17

14 [1]Heb., *YAH*
[a]Ex. 15:2; Is. 12:2 [b]Ps. 27:1

15 [a]Ps. 68:3 [b]Ps. 89:13; Ex. 15:6; Luke 1:51

16 [a]Ps. 89:13

17 [1]Heb., *YAH*
[a]Ps. 116:8, 9; Hab. 1:12 [b]Ps. 73:28; 107:22

18 [1]Heb., *YAH*
[a]Ps. 73:14; Jer. 31:18; 1 Cor. 11:32; 2 Cor. 6:9 [b]Ps. 86:13

19 [1]Heb., *YAH*
[a]Is. 26:2

20 [a]Ps. 15:1, 2; 24:3-6; 140:13

21 [a]Ps. 118:5; 116:1 [b]Ps. 118:14

22 [a]Matt. 21:42; Mark 12:10, 11; Luke 20:17; Acts 4:11; Eph. 2:20; 1 Pet. 2:7

23 [1]Lit., *from the LORD*

24 [a]Ps. 31:7

25 [a]Ps. 106:47 [b]Ps. 122:6, 7

3 Oh let the [a]house of Aaron say,
"His lovingkindness is everlasting."
4 Oh let those [a]who [1]fear the LORD say,
"His lovingkindness is everlasting."

5 From *my* [a]distress I called upon [1]the LORD;
[1]The LORD answered me *and* [b]*set me* in a large place.
6 The LORD is [a]for me; I will [b]not fear;
[c]What can man do to me?
7 The LORD is for me [a]among those who help me;
Therefore I shall [b]look *with satisfaction* on those who hate me.
8 It is [a]better to take refuge in the LORD
Than to trust in man.
9 It is [a]better to take refuge in the LORD
Than to trust in princes.

10 All nations [a]surrounded me;
In the name of the LORD I will surely [b]cut them off.
11 They surrounded me, yes, they surrounded me;
In the name of the LORD I will surely cut them off.
12 They surrounded me [a]like bees;
They were extinguished as a [b]fire of thorns;
In the name of the LORD I will surely cut them off.
13 You [a]pushed me violently so that I [1]was falling,
But the LORD [b]helped me.
14 [1a]The LORD is my strength and song,
And He has become [b]my salvation.

15 The sound of [a]joyful shouting and salvation is in the tents of the righteous;
The [b]right hand of the LORD does valiantly.
16 The [a]right hand of the LORD is exalted;
The right hand of the LORD does valiantly.
17 I [a]shall not die, but live,
And [b]tell of the works of [1]the LORD.
18 [1]The LORD has [a]disciplined me severely,
But He has [b]not given me over to death.

19 [a]Open to me the gates of righteousness;
I shall enter through them, I shall give thanks to [1]the LORD.
20 This is the gate of the LORD;
The [a]righteous will enter through it.
21 I shall give thanks to Thee, for Thou hast [a]answered me;
And Thou hast [b]become my salvation.

22 The [a]stone which the builders rejected
Has become the chief corner *stone*.
23 This is [1]the LORD's doing;
It is marvelous in our eyes.
24 This is the day which the LORD has made;
Let us [a]rejoice and be glad in it.
25 O LORD, [a]do save, we beseech Thee;
O LORD, we beseech Thee, do send [b]prosperity!

26 [a]Blessed is the one who comes in the name of the LORD;
We have [b]blessed you from the house of the LORD.
27 [a]The LORD is God, and He has given us [b]light;
Bind the festival sacrifice with cords [1]to the [c]horns of the altar.
28 [a]Thou art my God, and I give thanks to Thee;
Thou art my God, [b]I extol Thee.
29 [a]Give thanks to the LORD, for He is good;
For His lovingkindness is everlasting.

26 [a]Matt. 21:9; 23:39; Mark 11:9; Luke 13:35; 19:38; John 12:13 [b]Ps. 129:8

27 [1]Lit., *unto*
[a]1 Kin. 18:39 [b]Ps. 18:28; 27:1; Esther 8:16; 1 Pet. 2:9 [c]Ex. 27:2

28 [a]Ps. 63:1; 140:6 [b]Ex. 15:2; Is. 25:1

29 [a]Ps.118:1

PSALM 119

Meditations and Prayers Relating to the Law of God.

Aleph.

HOW blessed are those whose way is [1a]blameless,
Who [b]walk in the law of the LORD.
2 How blessed are those who [a]observe His testimonies,
Who [b]seek Him [c]with all *their* heart.
3 They also [a]do no unrighteousness;
They walk in His ways.
4 Thou hast [1a]ordained Thy precepts,
[2]That we should keep *them* diligently.
5 Oh that my [a]ways may be established
To [b]keep Thy statutes!
6 Then I [a]shall not be ashamed,
When I look [1]upon all Thy commandments.
7 I shall [a]give thanks to Thee with uprightness of heart,
When I learn Thy righteous judgments.
8 I shall keep Thy statutes;
Do not [a]forsake me utterly!

Beth.

9 How can a young man keep his way pure?
By [a]keeping *it* according to Thy word.
10 With all my [a]heart I have sought Thee;
Do not let me [b]wander from Thy commandments.
11 Thy word I have [a]treasured in my heart,
That I may not sin against Thee.
12 Blessed art Thou, O LORD;
[a]Teach me Thy statutes.
13 With my lips I have [a]told of
All the [b]ordinances of Thy mouth.
14 I have [a]rejoiced in the way of Thy testimonies,
[1]As much as in all riches.
15 I will [a]meditate on Thy precepts,
And [1]regard [b]Thy ways.
16 I shall [1a]delight in Thy statutes;
I shall [b]not forget Thy word.

Gimel.

17 [a]Deal bountifully with Thy servant,
That I may live and keep Thy word.
18 Open my eyes, that I may behold
Wonderful things from Thy law.

1 [1]Lit., *complete*, or, *having integrity*
[a]Ps. 101:2, 6; Prov. 11:20; 13:6 [b]Ps. 128:1; Ezek. 11:20; 18:17; Mic. 4:2

2 [a]Ps. 119:22, 168; 25:10; 99:7 [b]Ps. 119:10; Deut. 4:29 [c]Deut. 6:5; 10:12; 11:13; 13:3; 30:2

3 [a]1 John 3:9; 5:18

4 [1]Lit., *commanded* [2]Lit., *To keep*
[a]Deut. 4:13; Neh. 9:13

5 [a]Ps. 40:2; Prov. 4:26 [b]Deut. 12:1; 2 Chr. 7:17

6 [1]Lit., *to*
[a]Ps. 119:80

7 [a]Ps. 119:62

8 [a]Ps. 38:21; 71:9, 18

9 [a]1 Kin. 2:4; 8:25; 2 Chr. 6:16

10 [a]Ps. 119:2, 145 [b]Ps. 119:21, 118

11 [a]Ps. 37:31; 40:8; Luke 2:19, 51

12 [a]Ps. 119:26, 64, 108, 124, 135, 171

13 [a]Ps. 40:9 [b]Ps. 119:72

14 [1]Lit., *As over all*
[a]Ps. 119:111, 162

15 [1]Or, *look upon*
[a]Ps. 119:23, 48, 78, 97, 148; 1:2 [b]Ps. 25:4; 27:11; Is. 58:2

16 [1]Lit., *delight myself*
[a]Ps. 119:24, 35, 47, 70, 77, 92, 143, 174 [b]Ps. 119:93

17 [a]Ps. 13:6

19 [a]Ps. 119:54; 39:12; Gen. 47:9; Lev. 25:23; 1 Chr. 29:15; Heb. 11:13

20 [1]Lit., *for* [a]Ps. 119:40, 131

21 [1]Or, *Cursed are those who wander . . .* [a]Ps. 68:30 [b]Ps. 37:22; Deut. 27:26 [c]Ps. 119:10, 118

22 [a]Ps. 119:39 [b]Ps. 119:2

23 [a]Ps. 119:161 [b]Ps. 119:15

24 [1]Lit., *the men of my counsel* [a]Ps. 119:16

25 [a]Ps. 44:25 [b]Ps. 119:37, 40, 88, 93, 107, 149, 154, 156, 159 [c]Ps. 119:65

26 [a]Ps. 119:12

27 [a]Ps. 105:2

28 [1]Lit., *drops* [a]Ps. 22:14; 107:26 [b]Ps. 20:2; 1 Pet. 5:10

30 [1]Or, *accounted Thine ordinances worthy*

31 [a]Deut. 11:22

32 [a]1 Kin. 4:29; Is. 60:5; 2 Cor. 6:11, 13

33 [a]Ps. 119:5, 12

34 [a]Ps. 119:27 73, 125, 144, 169 [b]1 Chr. 22:12; Ezek. 44:24 [c]Ps. 119:2, 69

35 [a]Ps. 25:4; Is. 40:14 [b]Ps. 119:16; 112:1

36 [a]1 Kin. 8:58 [b]Luke 12:15; Heb. 13:5

37 [a]Is. 33:15 [b]Ps. 119:25; 71:20

38 [1]Or, *promise* [2]Lit., *Which is for the fear of Thee* [a]2 Sam. 7:25

39 [a]Ps. 119:22

40 [a]Ps. 119:20

41 [1]Or, *promise* [a]Ps. 119:77 [b]Ps. 119:58, 76, 116, 170

42 [a]Prov. 27:11 [b]Ps. 119:39; 102:8

43 [1]Or, *hope in* [a]Ps. 119:49, 74, 81, 114, 147

19 I am a [a]stranger in the earth;
Do not hide Thy commandments from me.
20 My soul is crushed [1a]with longing
After Thine ordinances at all times.
21 Thou dost [a]rebuke the arrogant, [1]the [b]cursed,
Who [c]wander from Thy commandments.
22 [a]Take away reproach and contempt from me,
For I [b]observe Thy testimonies.
23 Even though [a]princes sit and talk against me,
Thy servant [b]meditates on Thy statutes.
24 Thy testimonies also are my [a]delight;
They are [1]my counselors.

Daleth.

25 My [a]soul cleaves to the dust;
[b]Revive me [c]according to Thy word.
26 I have told of my ways, and Thou hast answered me;
[a]Teach me Thy statutes.
27 Make me understand the way of Thy precepts,
So I will [a]meditate on Thy wonders.
28 My [a]soul [1]weeps because of grief;
[b]Strengthen me according to Thy word.
29 Remove the false way from me,
And graciously grant me Thy law.
30 I have chosen the faithful way;
I have [1]placed Thine ordinances *before me.*
31 I [a]cleave to Thy testimonies;
O LORD, do not put me to shame!
32 I shall run the way of Thy commandments,
For Thou wilt [a]enlarge my heart.

He.

33 [a]Teach me, O LORD, the way of Thy statutes,
And I shall observe it to the end.
34 [a]Give me understanding, that I may [b]observe Thy law,
And keep it [c]with all *my* heart.
35 Make me walk in the [a]path of Thy commandments,
For I [b]delight in it.
36 [a]Incline my heart to Thy testimonies,
And not to [b]*dishonest* gain.
37 Turn away my [a]eyes from looking at vanity,
And [b]revive me in Thy ways.
38 [a]Establish Thy [1]word to Thy servant,
[2]As that which produces reverence for Thee.
39 [a]Turn away my reproach which I dread,
For Thine ordinances are good.
40 Behold, I [a]long for Thy precepts;
Revive me through Thy righteousness.

Vav.

41 May Thy [a]lovingkindnesses also come to me, O LORD,
Thy salvation [b]according to Thy [1]word;
42 So I shall have an [a]answer for him who [b]reproaches me,
For I trust in Thy word.
43 And do not take the word of truth utterly out of my mouth,
For I [1a]wait for Thine ordinances.

44 So I will [a]keep Thy law continually,
Forever and ever.
45 And I will [a]walk [1]at liberty,
For I [b]seek Thy precepts.
46 I will also speak of Thy testimonies [a]before kings,
And shall not be ashamed.
47 And I shall [1a]delight in Thy commandments,
Which I [b]love.
48 And I shall lift up my hands to Thy commandments, which I [a]love;
And I will [b]meditate on Thy statutes.

Zayin.

49 Remember the word to Thy servant,
[1]In which Thou has made me hope.
50 This is my [a]comfort in my affliction,
That Thy word has [1]revived me.
51 The arrogant [a]utterly deride me,
Yet I do not [b]turn aside from Thy law.
52 I have [a]remembered Thine ordinances from [1]of old, O Lord,
And comfort myself.
53 Burning [a]indignation has seized me because of the wicked,
Who [b]forsake Thy law.
54 Thy statutes are my songs
In the house of my [a]pilgrimage.
55 O Lord, I [a]remember Thy name [b]in the night,
And keep Thy law.
56 This has become mine,
[1]That I [a]observe Thy precepts.

Heth.

57 The Lord is my [a]portion;
I have [1]promised to [b]keep Thy words.
58 I [a]entreated Thy favor [b]with all *my* heart;
[c]Be gracious to me [d]according to Thy [1]word.
59 I [a]considered my ways,
And turned my feet to Thy testimonies.
60 I hastened and did not delay,
To keep Thy commandments.
61 The [a]cords of the wicked have encircled me,
But I have [b]not forgotten Thy law.
62 At [a]midnight I shall rise to give thanks to Thee
Because of Thy [b]righteous ordinances.
63 I am a [a]companion of all those who [1]fear Thee,
And of those who keep Thy precepts.
64 [a]The earth is full of Thy lovingkindness, O Lord;
[b]Teach me Thy statutes.

Teth.

65 Thou hast dealt well with Thy servant,
O Lord, according to Thy word.
66 Teach me good [1a]discernment and knowledge,
For I believe in Thy commandments.

44 [a]Ps. 119:33

45 [1]Lit., *in a wide place* [a]Prov. 4:12 [b]Ps. 119:94, 155

46 [a]Matt. 10:18; Acts 26:1, 2

47 [1]Lit., *delight myself* [a]Ps. 119:16 [b]Ps. 119:97, 127, 159

48 [a]Ps. 119:97, 127, 159 [b]Ps. 119:15

49 [1]Lit., *On*

50 [1]Or, *preserved me alive* [a]Job 6:10; Rom. 15:4

51 [a]Job 30:1; Jer. 20:7 [b]Ps. 119:157; 44:18; Job 23:11

52 [1]Or, *everlasting* [a]Ps. 103:18

53 [a]Ps. 119:158; Ex. 32:19; Ezra 9:3; Neh. 13:25 [b]Ps. 89:30

54 [a]Ps. 119:19; Gen. 47:9

55 [a]Ps. 63:6 [b]Ps. 119:62; 42:8; 92:2; Is. 26:9; Acts 16:25

56 [1]Or, *Because* [a]Ps. 119:22, 69, 100

57 [1]Lit., *said that I would keep* [a]Ps. 16:5 [b]Deut. 33:9

58 [1]Or, *promise* [a]1 Kin. 13:6 [b]Ps. 119:2 [c]Ps. 41:4; 56:1; 57:1 [d]Ps. 119:41

59 [a]Mark 14:72; Luke 15:17

61 [a]Ps. 140:5; Job 36:8 [b]Ps. 119:83, 141, 153, 176

62 [a]Ps. 119:55 [b]Ps. 119:7

63 [1]Or, *revere* [a]Ps. 101:6

64 [a]Ps. 33:5 [b]Ps. 119:12

66 [1]Or, *judgment* [a]Phil. 1:9

67 [a]Ps. 119:71, 75; Jer. 31:18, 19; Heb. 12:5-11

68 [a]Ps. 86:5; 100:5; 106:1 [b]Ps. 125:4; Deut. 8:16; 28:63; 30:5 [c]Ps. 119:12

69 [1]Lit., *besmear me with lies* [a]Job 13:4 [b]Ps. 119:56

70 [1]Lit., *gross like fat* [a]Ps. 17:10; Deut. 32:15; Job 15:27; Is. 6:10; Jer. 5:28 [b]Ps. 119:16

71 [a]Ps. 119:67, 75

72 [a]Ps. 119:127; 19:10; Prov. 8:10, 11, 19

73 [1]Lit., *established* [a]Ps. 138:8; 139:15, 16; Job 10:8; 31:15 [b]Ps. 119:34

74 [1]Or, *revere* [2]Or, *hope in* [a]Ps. 34:2; 35:27; 107:42 [b]Ps. 119:43

75 [a]Ps. 119:138 [b]Heb. 12:10

76 [1]Lit., *be for my comfort* [2]Or, *promise*

77 [a]Ps. 119:41 [b]Ps. 119:16

78 [a]Jer. 50:32 [b]Ps. 119:86 [c]Ps. 119:15

79 [1]Or, *revere*

80 [1]Lit., *complete;* or, *having integrity* [a]Ps. 119:1 [b]Ps. 119:46

81 [1]Or, *hope in* [a]Ps. 84:2 [b]Ps. 119:43

82 [1]Or, *promise* [2]Lit., *Saying* [a]Ps. 119:123; 69:3; Is. 38:14; Lam. 2:11

83 [a]Job 30:30 [b]Ps. 119:61

84 [a]Ps. 39:4 [b]Rev. 6:10

85 [1]Lit., *according to Thy law* [a]Ps. 7:15; 57:6; Jer. 18:22

86 [a]Ps. 119:138 [b]Ps. 119:78, 161; 35:19 [c]Ps. 109:26

87 [1]Lit., *in the earth* [a]Is. 58:2

89 [1]Lit., *stands firm* [a]Ps. 119:160; Is. 40:8; Matt. 24:35; 1 Pet. 1:25

67 [a]Before I was afflicted I went astray,
But now I keep Thy word.
68 Thou art [a]good and [b]doest good;
[c]Teach me Thy statutes.
69 The arrogant [1]have [a]forged a lie against me;
With all *my* heart I will [b]observe Thy precepts.
70 Their heart is [1a]covered with fat,
But I [b]delight in Thy law.
71 It is [a]good for me that I was afflicted,
That I may learn Thy statutes.
72 The [a]law of Thy mouth is better to me
Than thousands of gold and silver *pieces.*

Yodh.

73 [a]Thy hands made me and [1]fashioned me;
[b]Give me understanding, that I may learn Thy commandments.
74 May those who [1]fear Thee [a]see me and be glad,
Because I [2b]wait for Thy word.
75 I know, O LORD, that Thy judgments are [a]righteous,
And that [b]in faithfulness Thou hast afflicted me.
76 O may thy lovingkindness [1]comfort me,
According to Thy [2]word to Thy servant.
77 May [a]Thy compassion come to me that I may live,
For Thy law is my [b]delight.
78 May [a]the arrogant be ashamed, for they subvert me [b]with a lie;
But I shall [c]meditate on Thy precepts.
79 May those who [1]fear Thee turn to me,
Even those who know Thy testimonies.
80 May my heart be [1a]blameless in Thy statutes,
That I may not [b]be ashamed.

Kaph.

81 My [a]soul languishes for Thy salvation;
I [1b]wait for Thy word.
82 My [a]eyes fail *with longing* for Thy [1]word,
[2]While I say, "When wilt Thou comfort Me?"
83 Though I have [a]become like a wineskin in the smoke,
I do [b]not forget Thy statutes.
84 How many are the [a]days of Thy servant?
When wilt Thou [b]execute judgment on those who persecute me?
85 The arrogant have [a]dug pits for me,
Men who are not [1]in accord with Thy law.
86 All Thy commandments are [a]faithful;
They have [b]persecuted me with a lie; [c]help me!
87 They almost destroyed me [1]on earth,
But as for me, I [a]did not forsake Thy precepts.
88 Revive me according to Thy lovingkindness,
So that I may keep the testimony of Thy mouth.

Lamedh.

89 [a]Forever, O LORD,
Thy word [1]is settled in heaven.

90 Thy [a]faithfulness *continues* [1]throughout all generations;
Thou didst [b]establish the earth, and it [c]stands.
91 They stand this day according to Thine [a]ordinances,
For [b]all things are Thy servants.
92 If Thy law had not been my [a]delight,
Then I would have perished [b]in my affliction.
93 I will [a]never forget Thy precepts,
For by them Thou hast [1b]revived me.
94 I am Thine, [a]save me;
For I have [b]sought Thy precepts.
95 The wicked [a]wait for me to destroy me;
I shall diligently consider Thy testimonies.
96 I have seen [1]a limit to all perfection;
Thy commandment is exceedingly broad.

Mem.

97 O how I [a]love Thy law!
It is my [b]meditation all the day.
98 Thy [a]commandments make me wiser than my enemies,
For they are ever [1]mine.
99 I have more insight than all my teachers,
For Thy testimonies are my [a]meditation.
100 I understand [a]more than the aged,
Because I have [b]observed Thy precepts.
101 I have [a]restrained my feet from every evil way,
That I may keep Thy word.
102 I have not [a]turned aside from Thine ordinances,
For Thou Thyself hast taught me.
103 How [a]sweet are Thy [1]words to my [2]taste!
Yes, sweeter than honey to my mouth!
104 From Thy precepts I [a]get understanding;
Therefore I [b]hate every false way.

Nun.

105 Thy word is a [a]lamp to my feet,
And a light to my path.
106 I have [a]sworn, and I will confirm it,
That I will keep Thy righteous ordinances.
107 I am exceedingly [a]afflicted;
[1b]Revive me, O LORD, according to Thy word.
108 O accept the [a]freewill offerings of my mouth, O LORD,
And [b]teach me Thine ordinances.
109 My [1a]life is continually [2]in my hand,
Yet I do not [b]forget Thy law.
110 The wicked have [a]laid a snare for me,
Yet I have not [b]gone astray from Thy precepts.
111 I have [a]inherited Thy testimonies forever,
For they are the [b]joy of my heart.
112 I have [a]inclined my heart to perform Thy statutes
Forever, *even* [b]to the end.

Samekh.

113 I hate those who are [a]double-minded,
But I love Thy [b]law.

90 [1]Lit., *to* [a]Ps. 36:5; 89:1, 2 [b]Ps. 148:6 [c]Eccles. 1:4
91 [a]Jer. 31:35 [b]Ps. 104:2-4
92 [a]Ps. 119:16 [b]Ps. 119:50
93 [1]Or, *kept me alive* [a]Ps. 119:16, 83 [b]Ps. 119:25
94 [a]Ps. 119:146 [b]Ps. 119:45
95 [a]Ps. 40:14; Is. 32:7
96 [1]Lit., *an end of*
97 [a]Ps. 119:47, 48, 127, 163, 165 [b]Ps. 119:15
98 [1]Or, *with me* [a]Ps. 119:130; Deut. 4:6
99 [a]Ps. 119:15
100 [a]Job 32:7-9 [b]Ps. 119:22, 56
101 [a]Prov. 1:15
102 [a]Deut. 17:20; Josh. 23:6; 1 Kin. 15:5
103 [1]Or, *promises* [2]Lit., *palate* [a]Ps. 19:10; Prov. 24:13, 14
104 [a]Ps. 119:130 [b]Ps. 119:128
105 [a]Prov. 6:23
106 [a]Neh. 10:29
107 [1]Or, *Keep me alive* [a]Ps. 119:25, 50 [b]Ps. 119:25
108 [a]Hos. 14:2; Heb. 13:15 [b]Ps. 119:12
109 [1]Lit., *soul* [2]I.e., in danger [a]Judg. 12:3; Job 13:14 [b]Ps. 119:16
110 [a]Ps. 91:3; 140:5; 141:9 [b]Ps. 119:10
111 [a]Deut. 33:4 [b]Ps. 119:14, 162
112 [a]Ps. 119:36 [b]Ps. 119:33
113 [a]1 Kin. 18:21; James 1:8; 4:8 [b]Ps. 119:47

114 [1]Or, *hope in* [a]Ps. 31:20; 32:7; 61:4; 91:1 [b]Ps. 84:9 [c]Ps. 119:74

115 [a]Ps. 6:8; 139:19; Matt. 7:23 [b]Ps. 119:22

116 [1]Or, *promise* [2]Lit., *put to shame because of* [a]Ps. 37:17, 24; 54:4 [b]Ps. 25:2, 20; 31:1, 17; Rom. 5:5; 9:33; Phil. 1:20

117 [a]Ps. 12:5; Prov. 29:25 [b]Ps. 119:6, 15

118 [1]Lit., *made light of* [2]Lit., *falsehood* [a]Ps. 119:10, 21

119 [1]Lit., *caused to cease* [a]Is. 1:22, 25; Ezek. 22:18, 19 [b]Ps. 119:47

120 [1]Lit., *bristles up from* [a]Job 4:14; Hab. 3:16 [b]Ps. 119:161

121 [a]2 Sam. 8:15; Job 29:14

122 [a]Job 17:3 [b]Ps. 119:134

123 [1]Or, *promise* [a]Ps. 119:82

124 [a]Ps. 119:88, 149, 159; 51:1; 106:45; 109:26 [b]Ps. 119:12

125 [a]Ps. 116:16 [b]Ps. 119:27

126 [a]Jer. 18:23; Ezek. 31:11

127 [a]Ps. 119:47

128 [a]Ps. 19:8 [b]Ps. 119:104

129 [a]Ps. 119:18 [b]Ps. 119:22

130 [a]Prov. 6:23 [b]Ps. 19:7

131 [a]Ps. 81:10; Job 29:23 [b]Ps. 42:1 [c]Ps. 119:20

132 [1]Lit., *to* [a]Ps. 25:16

133 [1]Or, *promise* [a]Ps. 17:5 [b]Ps. 19:13

134 [a]Ps. 119:84; 142:6

135 [a]Ps. 4:6; 31:16; 67:1; 80:3, 7, 19; Num. 6:25 [b]Ps. 119:12

136 [1]Lit., *run down* [a]Jer. 9:1, 18; 14:17; Lam. 3:48 [b]Ps. 119:158

114 Thou art my [a]hiding place and my [b]shield;
I [1c]wait for Thy word.
115 [a]Depart from me, evildoers,
That I may [b]observe the commandments of my God.
116 [a]Sustain me according to Thy [1]word, that I may live;
And [b]do not let me be [2]ashamed of my hope.
117 Uphold me that I may be [a]safe,
That I may [b]have regard for Thy statutes continually.
118 Thou hast [1]rejected all those [a]who wander from Thy statutes,
For their deceitfulness is [2]useless.
119 Thou hast [1]removed all the wicked of the earth *like* [a]dross;
Therefore I [b]love Thy testimonies.
120 My flesh [1a]trembles for fear of Thee,
And I am [b]afraid of Thy judgments.

Ayin.

121 I have [a]done justice and righteousness;
Do not leave me to my oppressors.
122 Be [a]surety for Thy servant for good;
Do not let the arrogant [b]oppress me.
123 My [a]eyes fail *with longing* for Thy salvation,
And for Thy righteous [1]word.
124 Deal with Thy servant [a]according to Thy lovingkindness,
And [b]teach me Thy statutes.
125 I [a]am Thy servant; [b]give me understanding,
That I may know Thy testimonies.
126 It is time for the LORD to [a]act,
For they have broken Thy law.
127 Therefore I [a]love Thy commandments
Above gold, yes, above fine gold.
128 Therefore I esteem right all *Thy* [a]precepts concerning everything,
I [b]hate every false way.

Pe.

129 Thy testimonies are [a]wonderful;
Therefore my soul [b]observes them.
130 The [a]unfolding of Thy words gives light;
It gives [b]understanding to the simple.
131 I [a]opened my mouth wide and [b]panted,
For I [c]longed for Thy commandments.
132 [a]Turn to me and be gracious to me,
After Thy manner [1]with those who love Thy name.
133 Establish my [a]footsteps in Thy [1]word,
And do not let any iniquity [b]have dominion over me.
134 [a]Redeem me from the oppression of man,
That I may keep Thy precepts.
135 [a]Make Thy face shine upon Thy servant,
And [b]teach me Thy statutes.
136 My eyes [1]shed [a]streams of water,
Because they [b]do not keep Thy law.

Tsadhe.

137 [a]Righteous art Thou, O LORD,
And upright are Thy judgments.
138 Thou hast commanded Thy testimonies in [a]righteousness
And exceeding [b]faithfulness.
139 My [a]zeal has [1]consumed me,
Because my adversaries have forgotten Thy words.
140 Thy [1a]word is very [2]pure,
Therefore Thy servant [b]loves it.
141 I am small and [a]despised,
Yet I do not [b]forget Thy precepts.
142 Thy righteousness is an everlasting righteousness,
And [a]Thy law is truth.
143 Trouble and anguish have [1]come upon me;
Yet Thy commandments are my [a]delight.
144 Thy [a]testimonies are righteous forever;
[b]Give me understanding that I may live.

Qoph.

145 I cried [a]with all my heart; answer me, O LORD!
I will [b]observe Thy statutes.
146 I cried to Thee; [a]save me,
And I shall keep Thy testimonies.
147 I [1a]rise before dawn and cry for help;
I [2]wait for Thy words.
148 My eyes anticipate the night watches,
That I may [a]meditate on Thy [1]word.
149 Hear my voice [a]according to Thy lovingkindness;
[b]Revive me, O LORD, according to Thine ordinances.
150 Those who follow after wickedness draw near;
They are far from Thy law.
151 Thou art [a]near, O LORD,
And all Thy commandments are [b]truth.
152 Of old I have [a]known from Thy testimonies,
That Thou hast founded them [b]forever.

Resh.

153 Look upon my [a]affliction and rescue me,
For I do not [b]forget Thy law.
154 [a]Plead my cause and [b]redeem me;
Revive me according to Thy [1]word.
155 Salvation is [a]far from the wicked,
For they [b]do not seek Thy statutes.
156 [1a]Great are Thy mercies, O LORD;
Revive me according to Thine ordinances.
157 Many are my [a]persecutors and my adversaries,
Yet I do not [b]turn aside from Thy testimonies.
158 I behold the [a]treacherous and [b]loathe *them*,
Because they do not keep Thy [1]word.
159 Consider how I [a]love Thy precepts;
[b]Revive me, O LORD, according to Thy lovingkindness.
160 The [a]sum of Thy word is [b]truth,
And every one of Thy righteous ordinances [c]is everlasting.

137 [a]Ps. 116:5; 129:4; 145:17; Ezra 9:15; Jer. 12:1; Lam. 1:18; Dan. 9:7, 14
138 [a]Ps. 119:144, 172 [b]Ps. 119:86, 90
139 [1]Lit., *put an end to* [a]Ps. 69:9
140 [1]Or, *promise* [2]Lit., *refined* [a]Ps. 12:6; 19:8 [b]Ps. 119:47
141 [a]Ps. 22:6 [b]Ps. 119:61
142 [a]Ps. 119:151, 160
143 [1]Lit., *found me* [a]Ps. 119:24
144 [a]Ps. 19:9 [b]Ps. 119:27
145 [a]Ps. 119:10 [b]Ps. 119:22, 55
146 [a]Ps. 3:7
147 [1]Lit., *anticipate the dawn* [2]Or, *hope in* [a]Ps. 57:8; 108:2
148 [1]Or, *promise* [a]Ps. 119:15
149 [a]Ps. 119:124 [b]Ps. 119:25
151 [a]Ps. 34:18; 145:18; Is. 50:8 [b]Ps. 119:142
152 [a]Ps. 119:125 [b]Ps. 119:89; Luke 21:33
153 [a]Ps. 119:50 [b]Ps. 119:16; Prov. 3:1; Hos. 4:6
154 [1]Or, *promise* [a]Ps. 35:1; 1 Sam. 24:15; Mic. 7:9 [b]Ps. 119:134
155 [a]Job 5:4 [b]Ps. 119:45, 94
156 [1]Or, *Many* [a]2 Sam. 24:14
157 [a]Ps. 119:86, 161; 7:1 [b]Ps. 119:51
158 [1]Or, *promise* [a]Is. 21:2; 24:16 [b]Ps. 139:21
159 [a]Ps. 119:47 [b]Ps. 119:25
160 [a]Ps. 139:17 [b]Ps. 119:142 [c]Ps. 119:89, 152

Shin.

161 [a]Princes persecute me without cause,
But my heart [b]stands in awe of Thy words.
162 I [a]rejoice at Thy [1]word,
As one who [b]finds great spoil.
163 I [a]hate and despise falsehood,
But I [b]love Thy law.
164 Seven times a day I praise Thee,
Because of Thy [a]righteous ordinances.
165 Those who love Thy law have [a]great peace,
And [1b]nothing causes them to stumble.
166 I [a]hope for Thy salvation, O LORD,
And do Thy commandments.
167 My [a]soul keeps Thy testimonies,
And I [b]love them exceedingly.
168 I [a]keep Thy precepts and Thy testimonies,
For all my [b]ways are before Thee.

Tav.

169 Let my [a]cry [1]come before Thee, O LORD;
[b]Give me understanding [c]according to Thy word.
170 Let my [a]supplication come before Thee;
[b]Deliver me according to Thy [1]word.
171 Let my [a]lips utter praise,
For Thou [b]dost teach me Thy statutes.
172 Let my [a]tongue sing of Thy [1]word,
For all Thy [b]commandments are righteousness.
173 Let Thy [a]hand be [1]ready to help me,
For I have [b]chosen Thy precepts.
174 I [a]long for Thy salvation, O LORD,
And Thy law is my [b]delight.
175 Let my [a]soul live that it may praise Thee,
And let Thine ordinances help me.
176 I have [a]gone astray like a lost sheep; seek Thy servant:
For I do [b]not forget Thy commandments.

PSALM 120

Prayer for Deliverance from the Treacherous.

A Song of [£]Ascents.

[a]IN my trouble I cried to the LORD,
And He answered me.
2 Deliver my soul, O LORD, from [a]lying lips,
From a [b]deceitful tongue.
3 What shall be given to you, and what more shall be done to you,
You [a]deceitful tongue?
4 [a]Sharp arrows of the warrior,
With the *burning* [b]coals of the broom tree.

5 Woe is me, for I sojourn in [a]Meshech,
For I dwell among the [b]tents of [c]Kedar!
6 Too long has my soul had its dwelling
With those who [a]hate peace.

161 [a]Ps. 119:23; 1 Sam. 24:11; 26:18 [b]Ps. 119:120

162 [1]Or, *promise* [a]Ps. 119:14, 111 [b]1 Sam. 30:16; Is. 9:3

163 [a]Ps. 119:104, 128; Ps. 31:6; Prov. 13:5 [b]Ps. 119:47

164 [a]Ps. 119:7, 160

165 [1]Lit., *they have no stumbling block* [a]Ps. 37:11; Prov. 3:2; Is. 26:3 [b]Prov. 3:23; Is. 63:13; 1 John 2:10

166 [a]Ps. 119:81, 174; Gen. 49:18

167 [a]Ps. 119:129 [b]Ps. 119:47

168 [a]Ps. 119:22 [b]Ps. 139:3; Job 24:23; Prov. 5:21

169 [1]Lit., *come near before* [a]Ps. 18:6; 102:1; Job 16:18 [b]Ps. 119:27 [c]Ps. 119:65, 154

170 [1]Or, *promise* [a]Ps. 28:2; 130:2; 140:6; 143:1 [b]Ps. 22:20; 31:2; 59:1

171 [a]Ps. 51:15; 63:3 [b]Ps. 119:12; 94:12; Is. 2:3; Mic. 4:2

172 [1]Or, *promise* [a]Ps. 51:14 [b]Ps. 119:138

173 [1]Lit., *to help me* [a]Ps. 37:24; 73:23 [b]Josh. 24:22; Luke 10:42

174 [a]Ps. 119:166 [b]Ps. 119:24

175 [a]Is. 55:3

176 [a]Is. 53:6; Jer. 50:6; Matt. 18:12; Luke 15:4 [b]Ps. 119:16

[£]Ex. 34:24; 1 Kin. 12:27

1 [a]Ps. 18:6; 66:14; 102:2

2 [a]Ps. 109:2; Prov. 12:22 [b]Ps. 52:4; Zeph. 3:13

3 [a]Ps. 52:4; Zeph. 3:13

4 [a]Ps. 45:5; Prov. 25:18; Is. 5:28 [b]Ps. 140:10

5 [a]Gen. 10:2; 1 Chr. 1:5; Ezek. 27:13; 38:2, 3; 39:1 [b]Song of Sol. 1:5 [c]Gen. 25:13; Is. 21:16; 60:7; Jer. 2:10; 49:28; Ezek. 27:21

6 [a]Ps. 35:20

7 I [a]am *for* peace, but when I speak,
They are [b]for war.

Psalm 121

The Lord the Keeper of Israel.

A Song of Ascents.

I WILL [a]lift up my eyes to [b]the mountains;
From whence shall my help come?
2 My [a]help *comes* from the Lord,
Who [b]made heaven and earth.
3 He will not [a]allow your foot to slip;
He who [b]keeps you will not slumber.
4 Behold, He who keeps Israel
Will neither slumber nor sleep.

5 The Lord is your [a]keeper;
The Lord is your [b]shade on your right hand.
6 The [a]sun will not smite you by day,
Nor the moon by night.
7 The Lord will [1a]protect you from all evil;
He will keep your soul.
8 The Lord will [1]guard your going out and your coming in
[a]From this time forth and forever.

Psalm 122

Prayer for the Peace of Jerusalem.

A Song of Ascents, of David.

I WAS glad when they said to me,
"Let us [a]go to the house of the Lord."
2 Our feet are standing
Within your [a]gates, O Jerusalem,
3 Jerusalem, that is [a]built
As a city that is [b]compact together;
4 To which the tribes [a]go up, even the tribes of [1]the Lord—
An [2]ordinance for Israel—
To give thanks to the name of the Lord.
5 For there [a]thrones were set for judgment,
The thrones of the house of David.

6 Pray for the [a]peace of Jerusalem:
"May they prosper who [b]love you.
7 "May peace be within your [a]walls,
And prosperity within your [b]palaces."
8 For the sake of my [a]brothers and my friends,
I will now say, "[b]May peace be within you."
9 For the sake of the house of the Lord our God
I will [a]seek your good.

---

7 [a]Ps. 109:4 [b]Ps. 55:21

1 [a]Ps. 123:1; Is. 40:26 [b]Ps. 87:1

2 [a]Ps. 124:8 [b]Ps. 115:15

3 [a]Ps. 66:9 [b]Ps. 41:2; 127:1

5 [a]Ps. 91:4 [b]Ps. 91:1

6 [a]Is. 49:10; Jon. 4:8; Rev. 7:16

7 [1]Or, *keep* [a]Ps. 91:10-12

8 [1]Or, *keep* [a]Ps. 113:2; 115:18

1 [a]Ps. 42:4; Is. 2:3; Mic. 4:2; Zech. 8:21

2 [a]Ps. 9:14; 87:2; 116:19; Jer. 7:2

3 [a]Ps. 48:13; 147:2 [b]Neh. 4:6

4 [1]Heb., *Yah* [2]Or, *testimony* [a]Ps. 84:5; Deut. 16:16

5 [a]Ps. 89:29; Deut. 17:8; 2 Chr. 19:8

6 [a]Ps. 29:11; Jer. 29:7 [b]Ps. 102:14

7 [a]Ps. 51:18; Is. 62:6 [b]Ps. 48:3, 13; Jer. 17:27

8 [a]Ps. 133:1 [b]1 Sam. 25:6; John 20:19

9 [a]Neh. 2:10; Esth. 10:3

1 [a]Ps. 121:1; 141:8 [b]Ps. 2:4; 11:4

2 [a]Prov. 27:18; Mal. 1:6; [b]Ps. 25:15

3 [a]Ps. 4:1; 51:1 [b]Ps. 119:22; Neh. 4:4

4 [a]Ps. 79:4; Neh. 2:19 [b]Job 12:5; Is. 32:9, 11; Amos 6:1 [c]Ps. 119:22; Neh. 4:4

1 [a]Ps. 94:17 [b]Ps. 129:1

3 [a]Ps. 35:25; 56:1; 57:3; Num. 16:30; Prov. 1:12 [b]Ps. 138:7; Gen. 39:19

4 [1]Or, *passed over* [a]Ps. 18:16; 32:6; 69:2; 144:7; Job. 22:11

5 [1]Or, *passed over* [a]Job 38:11

6 [1]Lit., *as a prey to* [a]Ps. 27:2; Prov. 30:14

7 [a]Ps. 141:10; 2 Cor. 11:33; Heb. 11:34 [b]Prov. 6:5 [c]Ps. 91:3; Hos. 9:8

8 [a]Ps. 121:2

1 [a]Ps. 46:5 [b]Ps. 61:7; Eccles. 1:4

2 [a]Zech. 2:5 [b]Ps. 121:8

3 [1]Lit., *lot* [a]Ps. 89:22; Prov. 22:8; Is. 14:5

Psalm 123

Prayer for the Lord's Help.

A Song of Ascents.

TO Thee I [a]lift up my eyes,
O Thou who [b]art enthroned in the heavens!
2 Behold, as the eyes of [a]servants *look* to the hand of their master,
As the eyes of a maid to the hand of her mistress;
So our [b]eyes *look* to the Lord our God,
Until He shall be gracious to us.

3 [a]Be gracious to us, O Lord, be gracious to us;
For we are greatly filled [b]with contempt.
4 Our soul is greatly filled
With the [a]scoffing of [b]those who are at ease,
And with the [c]contempt of the proud.

Psalm 124

Praise for Rescue from Enemies.

A Song of Ascents, of David.

"[a]HAD it not been the Lord who was on our side,"
[b]Let Israel now say,
2 "Had it not been the Lord who was on our side,
When men rose up against us;
3 Then they would have [a]swallowed us alive,
When their [b]anger was kindled against us;
4 Then the [a]waters would have engulfed us,
The stream would have [1]swept over our soul;
5 Then the [a]raging waters would have [1]swept over our soul."

6 Blessed be the Lord,
Who has not given us [1]to be [a]torn by their teeth.
7 Our soul has [a]escaped [b]as a bird out of the [c]snare of the trapper;
The snare is broken and we have escaped.
8 Our [a]help is in the name of the Lord,
Who made heaven and earth.

Psalm 125

The Lord Surrounds His People.

A Song of Ascents.

THOSE who trust in the Lord
Are as Mount Zion, which [a]cannot be moved, but [b]abides forever.
2 As the mountains surround Jerusalem,
So [a]the Lord surrounds His people
[b]From this time forth and forever.
3 For the [a]scepter of wickedness shall not rest upon the [1]land of the righteous;

That the righteous [b]may not put forth their hands to
do wrong.

4 [a]Do good, O LORD, to those who are good,
And to those who are [b]upright in their hearts.
5 But as for those who [a]turn aside to their [b]crooked ways,
The LORD will lead them away with the [c]doers of
iniquity.
[d]Peace be upon Israel.

PSALM 126

Thanksgiving for Return from Captivity.

A Song of Ascents.

WHEN the LORD [a]brought back [1]the captive ones of Zion,
We were [b]like those who dream.
2 Then our [a]mouth was filled with laughter,
And our [b]tongue with joyful shouting;
Then they said among the nations,
"The LORD has [c]done great things for them."
3 The LORD has done great things for us;
We are [a]glad.

4 Restore our captivity, O LORD,
As the [1a]streams in the [2]South.
5 Those who sow in [a]tears shall reap with [b]joyful
shouting.
6 He who goes to and fro weeping, carrying *his* bag of
seed,
Shall indeed come again with a shout of joy, bringing
his sheaves *with him.*

PSALM 127

Prosperity Comes from the LORD.

A Song of Ascents, of Solomon.

UNLESS the LORD [a]builds the house,
They labor in vain who build it;
Unless the LORD [b]guards the city,
The watchman keeps awake in vain.
2 It is vain for you to rise up early,
To [1]retire late,
To [a]eat the bread of [2]painful labors;
For He gives to His [b]beloved [c]*even in his* sleep.

3 Behold, [a]children are a [1]gift of the LORD;
The [b]fruit of the womb is a reward.
4 Like arrows in the hand of a [a]warrior,
So are the children of one's youth.
5 How [a]blessed is the man whose quiver is full of them;
They shall not be ashamed,
When they [b]speak with their enemies [c]in the gate.

3 [b]Ps. 55:20; 1 Sam. 24:10; Acts 12:1

4 [a]Ps. 119:68 [b]Ps. 7:10; 11:2; 32:11; 36:10; 94:15

5 [a]Ps. 40:4; 101:3; Job 23:11 [b]Prov. 2:15; Is. 59:8 [c]Ps. 92:7; 94:4 [d]Ps. 128:6; Gal. 6:16

1 [1]Or, *those who returned to* [a]Ps. 85:1; Jer. 29:14; Hos. 6:11 [b]Acts 12:9

2 [a]Job 8:21 [b]Ps. 51:14; Is. 35:6 [c]Ps. 71:19; 1 Sam. 12:24; Luke 1:49

3 [a]Is. 25:9; Zeph. 3:14

4 [1]Lit., *stream-beds* [2]Heb., *Negev* [a]Is. 35:6; 43:19

5 [a]Ps. 80:5; Jer. 31:16; Lam. 1:2 [b]Is. 35:10; 51:11; 61:7; Gal 6:9

1 [a]Ps. 78:69 [b]Ps. 121:4

2 [1]Lit., *delay sitting* [2]Lit., *toils* [a]Gen. 3:17 [b]Ps. 60:5 [c]Job 11:18, 19; Prov. 3:24; Eccles. 5:12

3 [1]Or, *heritage* [a]Ps. 113:9; Gen. 33:5 [b]Deut. 7:13; 28:4; Is. 13:18

4 [a]Ps. 112:2; 120:4

5 [a]Ps. 128:2, 3 [b]Is. 29:21; Amos 5:12 [c]Gen. 34:20

Psalm 128

Blessedness of the Fear of the Lord.

[a]A Song of Ascents.

HOW blessed is everyone who fears the LORD,
Who [b]walks in His ways.
2 When you shall [a]eat of the [1b]fruit of your hands,
You will be happy and [c]it will be well with you.
3 Your wife shall be like a [a]fruitful vine,
[1]Within your house,
Your children like [b]olive plants
Around your table.
4 Behold, for thus shall the man be blessed
Who fears the LORD.

5 [a]The LORD bless you [b]from Zion,
And may you see the [c]prosperity of Jerusalem all the days of your life.
6 Indeed, may you see your [a]children's children.
[b]Peace be upon Israel!

Psalm 129

Prayer for the Overthrow of Zion's Enemies.

A Song of Ascents.

"[1]MANY times they have [2a]persecuted me from my [b]youth up,"
Let Israel now say,
2 "[1]Many times they have [2]persecuted me from my youth up;
Yet they have [a]not prevailed against me.
3 "The plowers plowed upon my back;
They lengthened their furrows."
4 The LORD [a]is righteous;
He has cut in two the [b]cords of the wicked.

5 May all who [a]hate Zion,
Be [b]put to shame and turned backward,
6 Let them be like [a]grass upon the housetops,
Which withers before it [1]grows up;
7 With which the reaper does not fill his [1]hand,
Or the binder of sheaves his [a]bosom;
8 Nor do those who pass by say,
"The [a]blessing of the LORD be upon you;
We bless you in the name of the LORD."

Psalm 130

Hope in the Lord's Forgiving Love.

A Song of Ascents.

OUT of the [a]depths I have cried to Thee, O LORD.
2 Lord, [a]hear my voice!

---

1 [a]Ps. 112:1 [b]Ps. 119:3

2 [1]Lit., *labor* [a]Is. 3:10 [b]Ps. 109:11; Ezek. 23:29; Hag. 2:17 [c]Eccles. 8:12; Eph. 6:3

3 [1]Lit., *In the innermost parts of* [a]Ezek. 19:10 [b]Ps. 52:8; 144:12

5 [a]Ps. 134:3 [b]Ps. 20:2; 135:21 [c]Ps. 122:9

6 [a]Ps. 103:17; Gen. 48:11; Prov. 17:6 [b]Ps. 125:5

1 [1]Lit., *Much* [2]Lit., *showed hostility toward* [a]Ps. 88:15; Ex. 1:11; Judg. 3:8 [b]Is. 47:12; Jer. 2:2; 22:21; Ezek. 16:22; Hos. 2:15; 11:1

2 [1]Lit., *Much* [2]Lit., *showed hostility toward* [a]Jer. 1:19; 15:20; 20:11; Matt. 16:18; 2 Cor. 4:8, 9

4 [a]Ps. 119:137 [b]Ps. 140:5

5 [a]Mic. 4:11 [b]Ps. 70:3; 71:13

6 [1]Lit., *draws out* [a]Ps. 37:2; 2 Kin. 19:26; Is. 37:27

7 [1]Lit., *palm* [a]Ps. 79:12

8 [a]Ps. 118:26; Ruth 2:4

1 [a]Ps. 42:7; 69:2

2 [a]Ps. 64:1; 119:149

Let [b]Thine ears be attentive
To the [c]voice of my supplications.
3 If Thou, [1]LORD, shouldst mark iniquities,
O Lord, who could [a]stand?
4 But there is [a]forgiveness with Thee,
That Thou mayest be [b]feared.

5 I wait for the LORD, my [a]soul does wait,
And [1b]in His word do I hope.
6 My soul *waits* for the Lord
More than the watchmen [a]for the morning;
Indeed, more than the watchmen for the morning.
7 O Israel, [a]hope in the LORD;
For with the LORD there is [b]lovingkindness,
And with Him is [c]abundant redemption.
8 And He will [a]redeem Israel
From all his iniquities.

PSALM 131

Childlike Trust in the LORD.

A Song of Ascents, of David.

O LORD, my heart is not [a]proud, or my eyes [1b]haughty;
Nor do I [2]involve myself in [c]great matters,
Or in things [d]too [3]difficult for me.
2 Surely I have [a]composed and quieted my soul;
Like a weaned [b]child *rests* [1]against his mother,
My soul is like a weaned child [1]within me.
3 O Israel, [a]hope in the LORD
[b]From this time forth and forever.

PSALM 132

Prayer for the LORD's Blessing upon the Sanctuary.

A Song of Ascents.

REMEMBER, O LORD, on David's behalf,
All [a]his affliction;
2 How he swore to the LORD,
And vowed to [a]the Mighty One of Jacob;
3 "Surely I will not [1]enter [a]my house,
Nor [2]lie on my bed;
4 I will not [a]give sleep to my eyes,
Or slumber to my eyelids;
5 Until I find a [a]place for the LORD,
[1]A dwelling place for [b]the Mighty One of Jacob."

6 Behold, we heard of it in [a]Ephrathah;
We found it in the [b]field of [1]Jaar.
7 Let us go into His [1a]dwelling place;
Let us [b]worship at His [c]footstool.
8 [a]Arise, O LORD, to Thy [b]resting place;
Thou and the ark of Thy [c]strength.
9 Let Thy priests be [a]clothed with righteousness;
And let Thy [b]godly ones sing for joy.

2 [b]2 Chr. 6:40; Neh. 1:6, 11 [c]Ps. 28:2; 140:6

3 [1]Heb., *YAH* [a]Ps. 76:7; 143:2; Nah. 1:6; Mal. 3:2; Rev. 6:17

4 [a]Ps. 86:5; Ex. 34:7; Neh. 9:17; Is. 55:7; Dan. 9:9 [b]1 Kin. 8:39, 40; Jer. 33:8, 9

5 [1]Lit., *for* [a]Ps. 33:20; 40:1; 62:1, 5; Is. 8:17; 26:8 [b]Ps. 119:74, 81

6 [a]Ps. 63:6; 119:147

7 [a]Ps. 131:3 [b]Ps. 103:4 [c]Ps. 111:9; Rom. 3:24; Eph. 1:7

8 [a]Luke 1:68; Titus 2:14

1 [1]Or, *lofty* [2]Lit., *go after, walk* [3]Or, *marvelous* [a]Ps. 101:5; 2 Sam. 22:28; Is. 2:12; Zeph. 3:11 [b]Prov. 30:13; Is. 5:15 [c]Jer. 45:5; Rom. 12:16 [d]Ps. 139:6; Job 42:3

2 [1]Or, *upon* [a]Ps. 62:1 [b]Matt. 18:3; 1 Cor. 14:20

3 [a]Ps. 130:7 [b]Ps. 113:2

1 [a]2 Sam. 16:12; 1 Chr. 22:14

2 [a]Gen. 49:24; Is. 49:26; 60:16

3 [1]Lit., *come into the tabernacle of* [2]Lit., *go up into the couch of* [a]Job 21:28

4 [a]Prov. 6:4

5 [1]Lit., *Dwelling places* [a]Ps. 26:8; 1 Kin. 8:17; 1 Chr. 22:7; Acts 7:46 [b]Ps. 132:2

6 [1]Or, *the wood* [a]Gen. 35:19; 1 Sam. 17:12 [b]1 Sam. 7:1

7 [1]Lit., *Dwelling places* [a]Ps. 43:3 [b]Ps. 5:7; 99:5 [c]1 Chr. 28:2

8 [a]Ps. 68:1; Num. 10:35; 2 Chr. 6:41 [b]Ps. 132:14 [c]Ps. 78:61

9 [a]Job 29:14 [b]Ps. 132:16; 30:4; 149:5

10 For the sake of David Thy servant,
Do not turn away the face of Thine [a]anointed.
11 The LORD has [a]sworn to David,
A truth from which He will not turn back;
"[b]Of the fruit of your body I will set upon your throne.
12 "If your sons will keep My covenant,
And My testimony which I will teach them,
Their sons also shall [a]sit upon your throne forever."

13 For the LORD has [a]chosen Zion;
He has [b]desired it for His habitation.
14 "This is My [a]resting place forever;
Here I will [b]dwell, for I have desired it.
15 "I will abundantly [a]bless her provision;
I will [b]satisfy her needy with bread.
16 "Her [a]priests also I will clothe with salvation;
And her [a]godly ones will sing aloud for joy.
17 "There I will cause the [a]horn of David to spring forth;
I have prepared a [b]lamp for Mine anointed.
18 "His enemies I will [a]clothe with shame;
But upon himself his [b]crown shall shine."

PSALM 133

The Excellency of Brotherly Unity.

A Song of Ascents, of David.

BEHOLD, how good and how pleasant it is
For [a]brothers to dwell together in unity!
2 It is like the precious [a]oil upon the head,
Coming down upon the beard,
Even Aaron's beard,
Coming down upon the [b]edge of his robes.
3 It is like the [a]dew of [b]Hermon,
Coming down upon the [c]mountains of Zion;
For there the LORD [d]commanded the blessing—[e]life forever.

PSALM 134

Greetings of Night Watchers.

A Song of Ascents.

BEHOLD, [a]bless the LORD, all [b]servants of the LORD,
Who [1][c]serve [d]by night in the house of the LORD!
2 [a]Lift up your hands to the [b]sanctuary,
And bless the LORD.
3 May the LORD [a]bless you from Zion,
He who [b]made heaven and earth.

PSALM 135

Praise the LORD's Wonderful Works. Vanity of Idols.

[1][a]PRAISE [2]the LORD!
Praise the name of the LORD;
Praise *Him*, O [b]servants of the LORD,

---

10 [a]Ps. 132:17; 2:2

11 [a]Ps. 89:3, 35 [b]2 Sam. 7:12-16; 2 Chr. 6:16

12 [a]Luke 1:32; Acts 2:30

13 [a]Ps. 78:68 [b]Ps. 68:16

14 [a]Ps. 132:8 [b]Matt. 23:21

15 [a]Ps. 147:14 [b]Ps. 107:9

16 [a]Ps. 132:9

17 [a]Ezek. 29:21; Luke 1:69 [b]Ps. 18:28; 1 Kin. 11:36; 15:4; 2 Kin. 8:19; 2 Chr. 21:7

18 [a]Ps. 35:26; 109:29; Job 8:22 [b]Ps. 21:3

1 [a]Gen. 13:8; Heb. 13:1

2 [a]Ex. 29:7; 30:25, 30; Lev. 8:12 [b]Ex. 28:33; 39:24

3 [a]Prov. 19:12; Hos. 14:5; Mic. 5:7 [b]Deut. 3:9; 4:48 [c]Ps. 48:2; 74:2; 78:68 [d]Ps. 42:8; Lev. 25:21; Deut. 28:8 [e]Ps. 21:4

1 [1]Lit., *stand* [a]Ps. 103:21 [b]Ps. 135:1, 2 [c]Deut. 10:8; 1 Chr. 23:30; 2 Chr. 29:11 [d]1 Chr. 9:33

2 [a]Ps. 28:2 [b]Ps. 63:2

3 [a]Ps. 128:5 [b]Ps. 124:8

1 [1]Or, *Hallelujah!* [2]Heb., YAH [a]Ps. 113:1 [b]Ps. 134:1

2 You who stand in the house of the LORD,
In the [a]courts of the house of our God!
3 [1]Praise [2]the LORD, for [a]the LORD is good;
[b]Sing praises to His name, [c]for it is lovely.
4 For [1]the LORD has [a]chosen Jacob for Himself,
Israel for His [2b]own possession.

5 For I know that [a]the LORD is great,
And that our Lord is [b]above all gods.
6 [a]Whatever the LORD pleases, He does,
In heaven and in earth, in the seas and in all deeps.
7 [1]He [a]causes the [2]vapors to ascend from the ends of the earth;
Who [b]makes lightnings for the rain;
Who [c]brings forth the wind from His treasuries.

8 [1]He [a]smote the first-born of Egypt,
[2]Both of man and beast.
9 [1]He sent [a]signs and wonders into your midst, O Egypt,
Upon [b]Pharaoh and all his servants.
10 [1a]He [b]smote many nations,
And slew mighty kings,
11 [a]Sihon, king of the Amorites,
And [b]Og, king of Bashan,
And [c]all the kingdoms of Canaan;
12 And He [a]gave their land as a heritage,
A heritage to Israel His people.
13 Thy [a]name, O LORD, is everlasting,
Thy [1]remembrance, O LORD, [2]throughout all generations.
14 For the LORD will [a]judge His people,
And [b]will have compassion on His servants.
15 The [a]idols of the nations are *but* silver and gold,
The work of man's hands.
16 They have mouths, but they do not speak;
They have eyes, but they do not see;
17 They have ears, but they do not hear;
Nor is there any breath at all in their mouth.
18 Those who make them will be like them,
Yes, everyone who trusts in them.

19 O house of [a]Israel, bless the LORD;
O house of Aaron, bless the LORD;
20 O house of Levi, bless the LORD;
You [a]who [1]revere the LORD, bless the LORD.
21 Blessed be the LORD [a]from Zion,
Who [b]dwells in Jerusalem.
[1]Praise [2]the LORD!

PSALM 136

Thanks for the LORD's Goodness to Israel.

[a]GIVE thanks to the LORD, for He is good;
For [b]His lovingkindness is everlasting.

2 [a]Ps. 92:13; 116:19

3 [1]Or, *Hallelujah!* [2]Heb., YAH
[a]Ps. 100:5; 119:68 [b]Ps. 68:4 [c]Ps. 147:1

4 [1]Heb., YAH [2]Or, *special treasure*
[a]Ps. 105:6; Deut. 7:6; 10:15 [b]Ex. 19:5; Mal. 3:17; Titus 2:14; 1 Pet. 2:9

5 [a]Ps. 48:1; 145:3 [b]Ps. 97:9

6 [a]Ps. 115:3

7 [1]Lit., *The one who* [2]I.e., clouds
[a]Jer. 10:13; 51:16 [b]Job 28:25, 26; 38:25, 26; Zech. 10:1 [c]Jer. 10:13; 51:16

8 [1]Lit., *The one who* [2]Lit., *From man to beast*
[a]Ps. 78:51; 105:36

9 [1]Lit., *The one who*
[a]Ps. 78:43; Deut. 6:22 [b]Ps. 136:15

10 [1]Lit., *The one who*
[a]Ps. 135:10-12; 136:17-21 [b]Ps. 44:2

11 [a]Num. 21:21-26; Deut. 29:7 [b]Num. 21:33-35 [c]Josh. 12:7-24

12 [a]Ps. 78:55; Deut. 29:8

13 [1]Or, *memorial* [2]Lit., *to*
[a]Ps. 102:12; Ex. 3:15

14 [a]Ps. 50:4; Deut. 32:36 [b]Ps. 90:13; 106:45

15 [a]Ps. 135:15-18; 115:4-8

19 [a]Ps. 115:9

20 [1]Lit., *fear*
[a]Ps. 118:4

21 [1]Or, *Hallelujah!* [2]Heb., YAH
[a]Ps. 128:5; 134:3 [b]Ps. 132:14

1 [a]Ps. 106:1; 118:1 [b]Ps. 107:1; 118:1-4; 1 Chr. 16:41; 2 Chr. 20:21

2 [a]Deut. 10:17

3 [a]Deut. 10:17

4 [1]I.e., wonderful acts [a]Ps. 72:18; Deut. 6:22; Job. 9:10

5 [1]Lit., *with understanding* [a]Ps. 104:24; Prov. 3:19; Jer. 10:12; 51:15

6 [a]Ps. 24:2; Is. 42:5; 44:24

7 [a]Ps. 74:16; Gen. 1:16

8 [1]Or, *over the* [a]Gen. 1:16

9 [1]Or, *over the* [a]Gen. 1:16

10 [1]Lit., *Egypt* [a]Ps. 78:51; 135:8; Ex. 12:29

11 [a]Ps. 105:43; Ex. 12:51; 13:3

12 [a]Ps. 44:3; Ex. 6:1; 13:9; 1 Kin. 8:42; Neh. 1:10; Jer. 32:21 [b]Ex. 6:6; Deut. 4:34; 5:15; 7:19; 9:29; 11:2; 2 Kin. 17:36; 2 Chr. 6:32; Jer. 32:17

13 [1]Or, *Sea of Reeds* [2]Lit., *in parts* [a]Ps. 66:6; 78:13; Ex. 14:21

14 [a]Ps. 106:9; Ex. 14:22

15 [1]Lit., *shook off* [2]Or, *Sea of Reeds* [a]Ps. 78:53; 106:11; Ex. 14:27

16 [a]Ps. 78:52; Ex. 13:18; 15:22; Deut. 8:15

17 [a]Ps. 136:17-22; 135:10-12

18 [1]Lit., *majestic*

22 [a]Ps. 105:6; Is. 41:8; 44:1; 45:4

23 [a]Ps. 9:12; 103:14; 106:45

24 [a]Ps. 107:2; Judg. 6:9; Neh. 9:28

25 [a]Ps. 104:27; 145:15

26 [a]Gen. 24:3, 7; 2 Chr. 36:23; Ezra. 1:2; 5:11; Neh. 1:4

2 Give thanks to the [a]God of gods,
For His lovingkindness is everlasting.
3 Give thanks to the [a]Lord of lords,
For His lovingkindness is everlasting.
4 To Him who [a]alone does great [1]wonders,
For His lovingkindness is everlasting;
5 To Him who made the heavens [1a]with skill,
For His lovingkindness is everlasting;
6 To Him who [a]spread out the earth above the waters,
For His lovingkindness is everlasting;
7 To Him who [a]made *the* great lights,
For His lovingkindness is everlasting:
8 The [a]sun to rule [1]by day,
For His lovingkindness is everlasting,
9 The [a]moon and stars to rule [1]by night,
For His lovingkindness is everlasting;

10 To Him who [a]smote [1]the Egyptians in their first-born,
For His lovingkindness is everlasting,
11 And [a]brought Israel out from their midst,
For His lovingkindness is everlasting,
12 With a [a]strong hand and an [b]outstretched arm,
For His lovingkindness is everlasting;
13 To Him who [a]divided the [1]Red Sea [2]asunder,
For His lovingkindness is everlasting,
14 And [a]made Israel pass through the midst of it,
For His lovingkindness is everlasting;
15 But [1a]He overthrew Pharaoh and his army in the [2]Red Sea,
For His lovingkindness is everlasting;
16 To Him who [a]led His people through the wilderness,
For His lovingkindness is everlasting;
17 To Him who [a]smote great kings,
For His lovingkindness is everlasting,
18 And slew [1]mighty kings,
For His lovingkindness is everlasting:
19 Sihon, king of the Amorites,
For His lovingkindness is everlasting,
20 And Og, king of Bashan,
For His lovingkindness is everlasting,
21 And gave their land as a heritage,
For His lovingkindness is everlasting,
22 Even a heritage to Israel His [a]servant,
For His lovingkindness is everlasting;

23 Who [a]remembered us in our low estate,
For His lovingkindness is everlasting,
24 And has [a]rescued us from our adversaries,
For His lovingkindness is everlasting;
25 Who [a]gives food to all flesh,
For His lovingkindness is everlasting.
26 Give thanks to the [a]God of heaven,
For His lovingkindness is everlasting.

Psalm 137

An Experience of the Captivity.

BY the [a]rivers of Babylon,
There we sat down and [b]wept,
When we remembered Zion.
2 Upon the [1a]willows in the midst of it
We [b]hung our [2]harps.
3 For there our captors [1a]demanded of us [2]songs,
And [b]our tormentors mirth, *saying*,
"Sing us one of the songs of Zion."

4 How can we sing [a]the LORD's song
In a foreign land?
5 If I [a]forget you, O Jerusalem,
May my right hand [1]forget *her skill.*
6 May my [a]tongue cleave to the roof of my mouth,
If I do not remember you,
If I do not [1b]exalt Jerusalem
Above my chief joy.

7 Remember, O LORD, against the sons of [a]Edom
The day of Jerusalem,
Who said, "Raze it, raze it,
[b]To its very foundation."
8 O daughter of Babylon, you [1a]devastated one,
How blessed will be the one who [b]repays you
With [2]the recompense with which you have repaid us.
9 How blessed will be the one who seizes and [a]dashes your little ones
Against the rock.

Psalm 138

Thanksgiving for the LORD's Favor.

A Psalm of David.

[a]I WILL give Thee thanks with all my heart;
I will sing praises to Thee before the [b]gods.
2 I will bow down [a]toward Thy holy temple,
And [b]give thanks to Thy name for Thy lovingkindness and Thy [1]truth;
For Thou hast [c]magnified Thy [2]word [3]according to all Thy name.
3 On the day I [a]called Thou didst answer me;
Thou didst make me bold with [b]strength in my soul.

4 [a]All the kings of the earth will give thanks to Thee, O LORD,
When they have heard the words of Thy mouth.
5 And they will [a]sing of the ways of the LORD.
For [b]great is the glory of the LORD.
6 For [a]though the LORD is exalted,
Yet He [b]regards the lowly;
But the [c]haughty He knows from afar.

1 [a]Ezek. 1:1, 3 [b]Neh. 1:4

2 [1]Or, *poplars* [2]Lit., *lyres* [a]Lev. 23:40; Is. 44:4 [b]Job 30:31; Is. 24:8; Ezek. 26:13

3 [1]Lit., *asked* [2]Lit., *words of song* [a]Ps. 80:6 [b]Ps. 79:7; Is. 49:17; 64:11

4 [a]2 Chr. 29:27; Neh. 12:46

5 [1]I.e., become lame [a]Is. 65:11

6 [1]Lit., *cause to ascend* [a]Ps. 22:15; Job 29:10; Ezek. 3:26 [b]Neh. 2:3

7 [a]Ps. 83:4-8; Is. 34:5, 6; Jer. 49:7-22; Lam. 4:21; Ezek. 25:12-14; 35:2; Amos 1:11; Obad, 10-14 [b]Ps. 74:7; Hab. 3:13

8 [1]Or, *devastator* [2]Lit., *your recompense* [a]Is. 13:1-22; 47:1-15; Jer. 25:12; 50:1-46; 51:1-64 [b]Jer. 50:15; 51:24, 35, 36, 49

9 [a]2 Kin. 8:12; Is. 13:16; Hos. 13:16; Nah. 3:10

1 [a]Ps. 111:1 [b]Ps. 95:3; 96:4; 97:7

2 [1]Or, *faithfulness* [2]Or, *promise* [3]Or, *together with* [a]Ps. 5:7; 28:2; 1 Kin. 8:29 [b]Ps. 140:13 [c]Is. 42:21

3 [a]Ps. 118:5 [b]Ps. 28:7; 46:1

4 [a]Ps. 72:11; 102:15

5 [a]Ps. 145:7 [b]Ps. 21:5

6 [a]Ps. 113:4-7 [b]Prov. 3:34; Is. 57:15; Luke 1:48; James 4:6 [c]Ps. 40:4; 101:5

7 Though I [a]walk in the midst of trouble, Thou wilt
[1b]revive me;
Thou wilt [c]stretch forth Thy hand against the wrath of
my enemies,
And Thy right hand will [d]save me.
8 The LORD will [a]accomplish what concerns me;
Thy [b]lovingkindness, O LORD, is everlasting;
[c]Do not forsake the [d]works of Thy hands.

PSALM 139

God's Omnipresence and Omniscience.

For the choir director. A Psalm of David.

O LORD, Thou hast [a]searched me and known *me.*
2 Thou [a]dost know [1]when I sit down and [2]when I rise up;
Thou [b]dost understand my thought from afar.
3 Thou [a]dost [1]scrutinize my [2]path and my lying down,
And art intimately acquainted with all my ways.
4 [1]Even before there is a word on my tongue,
Behold, O LORD, Thou [a]dost know it all.
5 Thou hast [a]enclosed me behind and before,
And [b]laid Thy hand upon me.
6 *Such* [a]knowledge is [b]too wonderful for me;
It is *too* high, I cannot attain to it.

7 [a]Where can I go from Thy Spirit?
Or where can I flee from Thy presence?
8 [a]If I ascend to heaven, Thou art there;
If I make my bed in [1]Sheol, behold, [b]Thou art there.
9 If I take the wings of the dawn,
If I dwell in the remotest part of the sea,
10 Even there Thy hand will [a]lead me,
And Thy right hand will lay hold of me.
11 If I say, "Surely the [a]darkness will [1]overwhelm me,
And the light around me will be night,"
12 Even the [a]darkness is not dark [1]to Thee,
And the night is as bright as the day.
[b]Darkness and light are alike *to Thee.*

13 For Thou didst [a]form my [1]inward parts;
Thou didst [b]weave me in my mother's womb.
14 I will give thanks to Thee, for [1]I am fearfully and won-
derfully made;
[a]Wonderful are Thy works,
And my soul knows it very well.
15 My [1a]frame was not hidden from Thee,
When I was made in secret,
And skillfully wrought in the [b]depths of the earth.
16 Thine [a]eyes have seen my unformed substance;
And in [b]Thy book they were all written,
The [c]days that were ordained *for me,*
When as yet there was not one of them.

17 How precious also are Thy [a]thoughts to me, O God!
How vast is the sum of them!

7 [1]Or, *keep me alive* [a]Ps. 23:4; 143:11 [b]Ps. 71:20; Ezra 9:8, 9; Is. 57:15 [c]Ex. 7:5; 15:12; Is. 5:25; Jer. 51:25; Ezek. 6:14; 25:13 [d]Ps. 20:6; 60:5

8 [a]Ps. 57:2; Phil. 1:6 [b]Ps. 136:1 [c]Ps. 27:9; 71:9; 119:8 [d]Ps. 100:3; Job 10:3; 14:15

1 [a]Ps. 17:3; 44:21; Jer. 12:3

2 [1]Lit., *my sitting* [2]Lit., *my rising* [a]2 Kin. 19:27 [b]Ps. 94:11; Is. 66:18

3 [1]Lit., *winnow* [2]Or, *journeying* [a]Job 14:16; 31:4

4 [1]Lit., *For there is not* [a]Heb. 4:13

5 [a]Ps. 34:7; 125:2 [b]Job 9:33

6 [a]Rom. 11:33 [b]Job 42:3

7 [a]Jer. 23:24

8 [1]I.e., the nether world [a]Amos 9:2-4 [b]Job 26:6; Prov. 15:11

10 [a]Ps. 23:2, 3

11 [1]Lit., *bruise;* some commentators read, *cover* [a]Job 22:13

12 [1]Lit., *from* [a]Job 34:22; Dan. 2:22 [b]1 John 1:5

13 [1]Lit., *kidneys* [a]Ps. 119:73; Is. 44:24 [b]Job 10:11

14 [1]Some ancient versions read, *Thou art fearfully wonderful* [a]Ps. 40:5

15 [1]Lit., *bones* [a]Job 10:8-10; Eccles. 11:5 [b]Ps. 63:9

16 [a]Job 10:8-10; Eccles. 11:5 [b]Ps. 56:8 [c]Job 14:5

17 [a]Ps. 92:5

18 If I should count them, they would [a]outnumber the sand.
When [b]I awake, I am still with Thee.

19 O that Thou wouldst [a]slay the wicked, O God;
[b]Depart from me, therefore, [c]men of bloodshed.
20 For they [a]speak [1]against Thee wickedly,
And Thine enemies [2b]take *Thy name* in vain.
21 Do I not [a]hate those who hate Thee, O LORD?
And do I not [b]loathe those who rise up against Thee?
22 I hate them with the utmost hatred;
They have become my enemies.

23 [a]Search me, O God, and know my heart;
[b]Try me and know my anxious thoughts;
24 And see if there be any [1a]hurtful way in me,
And [b]lead me in the [c]everlasting way.

PSALM 140

Prayer for Protection against the Wicked.

For the choir director. A Psalm of David.

[a]RESCUE me, O LORD, from evil men;
Preserve me from [b]violent men,
2 Who [a]devise evil things in *their* hearts;
They [b]continually stir up wars.
3 They [a]sharpen their tongues as a serpent;
[b]Poison of a viper is under their lips. [[1]Selah.

4 Keep me, O LORD, from the hands of the wicked;
[a]Preserve me from violent men,
Who have [1]purposed to [2b]trip up my feet.
5 The proud have [a]hidden a trap for me, and cords;
They have spread a [b]net by the [1]wayside;
They have set [c]snares for me. [Selah.

6 I [a]said to the LORD, "Thou art my God;
[b]Give ear, O LORD, to the [c]voice of my supplications.
7 "O [1]GOD the Lord, [a]the strength of my salvation,
Thou hast [b]covered my head in the day of [2]battle.
8 "Do not grant, O LORD, the [a]desires of the wicked;
Do not promote [b]his *evil* device, *lest* they be exalted. [Selah.

9 "As for the head of those who surround me,
May the [a]mischief of their lips cover them.
10 "May [a]burning coals fall upon them;
May they be [b]cast into the fire,
Into [1]deep pits from which they [c]cannot rise.
11 "May a [1]slanderer not be established in the earth;
[a]May evil hunt the violent man [2]speedily."

12 I know that the LORD will [a]maintain the cause of the afflicted,
And [b]justice for the poor.

18 [a]Ps. 40:5 [b]Ps. 3:5

19 [a]Is. 11:4 [b]Ps. 6:8; 119:115 [c]Ps. 5:6

20 [1]Or *of* [2]Some mss. read, *lift themselves up* against Thee
[a]Jude 15 [b]Ex. 20:7; Deut. 5:11

21 [a]Ps. 26:5; 31:6 [b]Ps. 119:158

23 [a]Ps. 26:2 [b]Ps. 7:9; Prov. 17:3; Jer. 11:20; 1 Thess. 2:4

24 [1]Lit., *way of pain*
[a]Ps. 146:9; Prov. 15:9; 28:10; Jer. 25:5; 36:3 [b]Ps. 5:8; 143:10 [c]Ps. 16:11

1 [a]Ps. 17:13; 59:2; 71:4 [b]Ps. 140:11; 18:48; 86:14

2 [a]Ps. 7:14; 36:4; 52:2; Prov. 6:14; Is. 59:4; Hos. 7:15 [b]Ps. 56:6

3 [1]*Selah* may mean: *Pause, Crescendo* or *Musical interlude*
[a]Ps. 57:4; 64:3 [b]Ps. 58:4; Rom. 3:13; James 3:8

4 [1]Or, *devised* [2]Lit., *push violently*
[a]Ps. 140:1 [b]Ps. 36:11

5 [1]Lit., *track*
[a]Ps. 35:7; 141:9; 142:3; Job 18:9 [b]Ps. 31:4; 57:6; Lam. 1:13 [c]Ps. 141:9; Is. 8:14; Amos 3:5

6 [a]Ps. 16:2; 31:14 [b]Ps. 143:1 [c]Ps. 116:1; 130:2

7 [1]*YHWH, usually rendered* LORD [2]Lit., *weapons*
[a]Ps. 28:8; 118:14 [b]Ps. 144:10

8 [a]Ps. 112:10 [b]Ps. 10:2, 3; Esth. 9:25

9 [a]Ps. 7:16; Prov. 18:7

10 [1]Lit., *watery*
[a]Ps. 11:6 [b]Ps. 21:9; Matt. 3:10 [c]Ps. 36:12

11 [1]Lit., *man of tongue* [2]Lit., *thrust upon thrust*
[a]Ps. 34:21

12 [a]Ps. 9:4; 18:27; 82:3; 1 Kin. 8:45, 49 [b]Ps. 12:5; 35:10

13 Surely the [a]righteous will give thanks to Thy name;
The [b]upright will dwell in Thy presence.

Psalm 141

An Evening Prayer for Sanctification and Protection.

A Psalm of David.

O LORD, I call upon Thee; [a]hasten to me!
[b]Give ear to my voice when I call to Thee!
2 May my prayer be [1]counted as [a]incense before Thee;
The lifting up of my hands as the [b]evening offering.
3 Set a [a]guard, O LORD, [1]over my mouth;
Keep watch over the [b]door of my lips.
4 [a]Do not incline my heart to any evil thing,
To practice deeds [1]of wickedness
With men who [b]do iniquity;
And [c]do not let me eat of their delicacies.

5 Let the [a]righteous smite me [1]in kindness and reprove me;
It is [b]oil upon the head;
Do not let my head refuse it,
[2]For still my prayer [c]is [3]against their wicked deeds.
6 Their judges are [a]thrown down by the sides of the rock,
And they hear my words, for they are pleasant.
7 As when one [a]plows and breaks open the earth,
Our [b]bones have been scattered at the [c]mouth of [1]Sheol.

8 For my [a]eyes are toward Thee, O [1]GOD, the Lord;
In Thee I [b]take refuge; [c]do not [2]leave me defenseless.
9 Keep me from the [1a]jaws of the trap which they have set for me,
And from the [b]snares of those who do iniquity.
10 Let the wicked [a]fall into their own nets,
While I pass by [1b]safely.

Psalm 142

Prayer for Help in Trouble.

[£]Maskil of David, when he was [•]in the cave.
A Prayer.

I [a]CRY aloud with my voice to the LORD;
I [b]make supplication with my voice to the LORD.
2 I [a]pour out my complaint before Him;
I declare my [b]trouble before Him.
3 When [a]my spirit [1]was overwhelmed within me;
Thou didst know my path.
In the way where I walk
They have [b]hidden a trap for me.
4 Look to the right and see;
For there is [a]no one who regards me;
[1]There is no [b]escape for me;
[c]No one cares for my soul.

---

13 [a]Ps. 97:12 [b]Ps. 11:7; 16:11; 17:15

1 [a]Ps. 22:19; 38:22; 70:5 [b]Ps. 5:1; 143:1

2 [1]Lit., *fixed* [a]Ex. 30:8; Luke 1:10; Rev. 5:8; 8:3, 4 [b]Ex. 29:41; 1 Kin. 18:29, 36; Dan. 9:21

3 [1]Lit., *to* [a]Ps. 34:13; 39:1; Prov. 13:3; 21:23 [b]Mic. 7:5

4 [1]Lit., *in* [a]Ps. 119:36 [b]Is. 32:6; Hos. 6:8; Mal. 3:15 [c]Prov. 23:6

5 [1]Or, *lovingly* [2]Lit., *And my prayer* [3]Or, *in spite of their calamities* [a]Prov. 9:8; 19:25; 25:12; 27:6; Eccles. 7:5; Gal. 6:1 [b]Ps. 23:5; 133:2 [c]Ps. 35:14

6 [a]2 Chr. 25:12

7 [1]I.e., the nether world [a]Ps. 129:3 [b]Ps. 53:5 [c]Ps. 88:3-5; Num. 16:32, 33

8 [1]*YHWH, usually rendered* LORD [2]Lit., *pour out my soul* [a]Ps. 25:15; 123:2 [b]Ps. 2:12; 11:1 [c]Ps. 27:9

9 [1]Lit., *hands of the trap* [a]Ps. 38:12; 64:5; 91:3 [b]Ps. 140:5

10 [1]Lit., *altogether* [a]Ps. 7:15; 57:6 [b]Ps. 124:7

[£] Possibly, *Contemplative*, or, *Didactic*, or *Skillful Psalm*

[•] 1 Sam. 22:1; 24:3

1 [a]Ps. 77:1 [b]Ps. 30:8

2 [a]Ps. 102:title [b]Ps. 77:2

3 [1]Lit., *fainted* [a]Ps. 77:3; 143:4 [b]Ps. 140:5

4 [1]Lit., *Escape has perished from me* [a]Ps. 31:11; 88:8, 18 [b]Job 11:20; Jer. 25:35 [c]Jer. 30:17

5 I cried out to Thee, O LORD;
I said, "Thou art [a]my refuge,
My [b]portion in the [c]land of the living.
6 "[a]Give heed to my cry,
For I am [b]brought very low;
Deliver me from my persecutors,
For they are too [c]strong for me.
7 "[a]Bring my soul out of prison,
So that I may give thanks to Thy name;
The righteous will surround me,
For Thou wilt [b]deal bountifully with me."

PSALM 143

Prayer for Deliverance and Guidance.

A Psalm of David.

HEAR my prayer, O LORD,
[a]Give ear to my supplications!
Answer me in Thy [b]faithfulness, in Thy [c]righteousness!
2 And [a]do not enter into judgment with Thy servant,
For in Thy sight [b]no man living is righteous.
3 For the enemy has persecuted my soul;
He has crushed my life [a]to the ground;
He [b]has made me dwell in dark places, like those who have long been dead.
4 Therefore [a]my spirit [1]is overwhelmed within me;
My heart is [2b]appalled within me.

5 I [a]remember the days of old;
I [b]meditate on all Thy doings;
I [c]muse on the work of Thy hands.
6 I [a]stretch out my hands to Thee;
My [b]soul *longs* for Thee, as a [1]parched land. [[2]Selah.

7 [a]Answer me quickly, O LORD, my [b]spirit fails;
[c]Do not hide Thy face from me,
Lest I become like [d]those who go down to the pit.
8 Let me hear Thy [a]lovingkindness in the morning;
For I trust [b]in Thee;
Teach me the [c]way in which I should walk;
For to Thee I [d]lift up my soul.
9 [a]Deliver me, O LORD, from my enemies;
[1]I take refuge in Thee.

10 [a]Teach me to do Thy will,
For Thou art my God;
Let [b]Thy good Spirit [c]lead me on level [1]ground.
11 [a]For the sake of Thy name, O LORD, revive me.
[b]In Thy righteousness bring my soul out of trouble.
12 And in Thy lovingkindness [1a]cut off my enemies,
And [b]destroy all those who afflict my soul;
For [c]I am Thy servant.

5 [a]Ps. 91:2, 9 [b]Ps. 16:5; 73:26 [c]Ps. 27:13

6 [a]Ps. 17:1 [b]Ps. 79:8; 116:6 [c]Ps. 18:17

7 [a]Ps. 143:11; 146:7 [b]Ps. 13:6

1 [a]Ps. 140:6 [b]Ps. 89:1, 2 [c]Ps. 71:2

2 [a]Job 14:3; 22:4 [b]Ps. 130:3; 1 Kin. 8:46; Job 4:17; 9:2; 25:4; Eccles. 7:20

3 [a]Ps. 44:25 [b]Ps. 88:6; Lam. 3:6

4 [1]Lit., *faints* [2]Or *desolate* [a]Ps. 142:3 [b]Lam. 3:11

5 [a]Ps. 77:5, 10, 11 [b]Ps. 77:12 [c]Ps. 105:2

6 [1]Lit., *weary* [2]*Selah* may mean: *Pause, Crescendo* or *Musical interlude* [a]Ps. 88:9; Job 11:13 [b]Ps. 42:2; 63:1

7 [a]Ps. 69:17 [b]Ps. 73:26; 84:2; Jer. 8:18; Lam. 1:22 [c]Ps. 27:9; 69:17; 102:2 [d]Ps. 28:1; 88:4

8 [a]Ps. 90:14 [b]Ps. 25:2 [c]Ps. 27:11; 32:8; 86:11 [d]Ps. 25:1; 86:4

9 [1]Lit., *To Thee have I hidden* [a]Ps. 31:15; 59:1

10 [1]Lit., *land* [a]Ps. 25:4, 5; 119:12 [b]Neh. 9:20 [c]Ps. 23:3

11 [a]Ps. 25:11 [b]Ps. 31:1; 71:2

12 [1]Or, *silence* [a]Ps. 54:5 [b]Ps. 52:5 [c]Ps. 116:16

1 [a]Ps. 18:2 [b]Ps. 18:34

2 [1]Another reading is, *peoples*
[a]Ps. 18:2; 91:2 [b]Ps. 59:9 [c]Ps. 3:3; 28:7; 84:9 [d]Ps. 18:39

3 [a]Ps. 8:4

4 [a]Ps. 39:11 [b]Ps. 102:11; 109:23; Job 8:9; 14:2

5 [a]Ps. 18:9 [b]Is. 64:1 [c]Ps. 104:32

6 [a]Ps. 18:14 [b]Ps. 7:13; 58:7; Hab. 3:11; Zech. 9:14

7 [a]Ps. 18:16 [b]Ps. 69:1, 14 [c]Ps. 18:44; 54:3

8 [a]Ps. 12:2; 41:6 [b]Ps. 106:26; Gen. 14:22; Deut. 32:40; Is. 44:20

9 [a]Ps. 40:3 [b]Ps. 33:2

10 [a]Ps. 18:50 [b]Ps. 140:7; 2 Sam. 18:7

11 [a]Ps. 18:44; 54:3 [b]Ps. 12:2; 41:6 [c]Ps. 106:26; Gen. 14:22; Deut. 32:40; Is. 44:20

12 [1]Lit., *cut after the pattern of*
[a]Ps. 92:12-14; 128:3 [b]Song of Sol. 4:4; 7:4

13 [1]Lit., *outside*
[a]Prov. 3:9, 10

14 [1]Lit., *be laden* [2]Lit., *bursting forth* [3]Lit., *going out*
[a]Prov. 14:4 [b]Ps. 60:2; 2 Kin. 25:10, 11 [c]Amos 5:3 [d]Is. 24:11; Jer. 14:2

15 [a]Ps. 33:12

Psalm 144

Prayer for Rescue and Prosperity.

A Psalm of David.

BLESSED be the LORD, [a]my rock,
Who [b]trains my hands for war,
And my fingers for battle;
2 My lovingkindness and [a]my fortress,
My [b]stronghold and my deliverer;
My [c]shield and He in whom I take refuge;
Who [d]subdues [1]my people under me.
3 O LORD, [a]what is man, that Thou dost take knowledge of him?
Or the son of man, that Thou dost think of him?
4 [a]Man is like a mere breath;
His [b]days are like a passing shadow.

5 [a]Bow Thy heavens, O LORD, and [b]come down;
[c]Touch the mountains, that they may smoke.
6 Flash forth [a]lightning and scatter them;
Send out Thy [b]arrows and confuse them.
7 Stretch forth Thy hand [a]from on high;
Rescue me and [b]deliver me out of great waters,
Out of the hand of [c]aliens;
8 Whose mouth [a]speaks deceit,
And whose [b]right hand is a right hand of falsehood.

9 I will sing a [a]new song to Thee, O God;
Upon a [b]harp of ten strings I will sing praises to Thee,
10 Who dost [a]give salvation to kings;
Who [b]dost rescue David His servant from the evil sword.
11 Rescue me, and deliver me out of the hand of [a]aliens,
Whose mouth [b]speaks deceit,
And whose [c]right hand is a right hand of falsehood.

12 Let our sons in their youth be as [a]grown-up plants,
And our daughters as [b]corner pillars [1]fashioned as for a palace;
13 *Let* our [a]garners be full, furnishing every kind of produce,
And our flocks bring forth thousands and ten thousands in our [1]fields;
14 *Let* our [a]cattle [1]bear,
Without [2b]mishap and without [3c]loss,
Let there be no [d]outcry in our streets;
15 How blessed are the people who are so situated;
How [a]blessed are the people whose God is the LORD!

Psalm 145

The Lord Extolled for His Goodness.

A Psalm of Praise, of David.

I WILL [a]extol Thee, [b]my God, O King;
And I will [c]bless Thy name forever and ever.
2 Every day I will bless Thee,
And I will [a]praise Thy name forever and ever.
3 [a]Great is the Lord, and highly to be praised;
And His [b]greatness is unsearchable.
4 One [a]generation shall praise Thy works to another,
And shall declare Thy mighty acts.
5 On the [a]glorious [1]splendor of Thy majesty,
And [b]on Thy wonderful works, I will meditate.
6 And men shall speak of the [1]power of Thy [a]awesome acts;
And I will [b]tell of Thy greatness.
7 They shall [1]eagerly utter the memory of Thine [a]abundant goodness,
And shall [b]shout joyfully of Thy righteousness.

8 The Lord is [a]gracious and merciful;
Slow to anger and great in lovingkindness.
9 The Lord is [a]good to all,
And His [b]mercies are over all His works.
10 [a]All Thy works shall give thanks to Thee, O Lord,
And Thy [b]godly ones shall bless Thee.
11 They shall speak of the [a]glory of Thy kingdom,
And talk of Thy power;
12 To [a]make known to the sons of men [1]Thy mighty acts,
And the [b]glory of the majesty of [1]Thy kingdom.
13 Thy kingdom is [1]an [a]everlasting kingdom,
And Thy dominion *endures* throughout all generations.

14 The Lord [a]sustains all who fall,
And [b]raises up all who are bowed down.
15 The eyes of all [1a]look to Thee,
And Thou [a]dost give them their food in due time.
16 Thou [a]dost open Thy hand,
And dost satisfy the desire of every living thing.

17 The Lord is [a]righteous in all His ways,
And kind in all His deeds.
18 The Lord is [a]near to all who call upon Him,
To all who call upon Him [b]in truth.
19 He will [a]fulfill the desire of those who fear Him;
He will also [b]hear their cry and will save them.
20 The Lord [a]keeps all who love Him;
But all the [b]wicked, He will destroy.
21 My [a]mouth will speak the praise of the Lord;
And [b]all flesh will [c]bless His holy name forever and ever.

1 [a]Ps. 30:1; 66:17 [b]Ps. 5:2 [c]Ps. 34:1
2 [a]Ps. 71:6
3 [a]Ps. 48:1; 86:10; 147:5 [b]Job 5:9; 9:10; 11:7; Is. 40:28; Rom. 11:33
4 [a]Ps. 22:30, 31; Is. 38:19
5 [1]Or, *majesty of Thy splendor* [a]Ps. 145:12 [b]Ps. 119:27
6 [1]Or, *strength* [a]Ps. 66:3; 106:22; Deut. 10:21 [b]Deut. 32:3
7 [1]Or, *bubble over with* [a]Ps. 31:19; Is. 63:7 [b]Ps. 51:14
8 [a]Ps. 86:5, 15; 103:8; Ex. 34:6
9 [a]Ps. 100:5; 136:1; Jer. 33:11; Nah. 1:7; Matt. 19:17; Mark 10:18 [b]Ps. 145:15
10 [a]Ps. 19:1; 103:22 [b]Ps. 68:26
11 [a]Jer. 14:21
12 [1]Lit., *His* [a]Ps. 105:1 [b]Ps. 145:5; Is. 2:10, 19, 21
13 [1]Lit., *a kingdom of all ages* [a]Ps. 10:16; 29:10; 2 Pet. 1:11
14 [a]Ps. 37:24 [b]Ps. 146:8
15 [1]Lit., *wait;* or, *hope for* [a]Ps. 104:27
16 [a]Ps. 104:28
17 [a]Ps. 116:5
18 [a]Ps. 34:18; 119:151; Deut. 4:7 [b]John 4:24
19 [a]Ps. 21:2; 37:4 [b]Ps. 10:17; Prov. 15:29; 1 John 5:14
20 [a]Ps. 31:23; 91:14; 97:10 [b]Ps. 9:5; 37:38
21 [a]Ps. 71:8 [b]Ps. 65:2; 150:6 [c]Ps. 145:1, 2

PSALM 146

The LORD an Abundant Helper.

1 PRAISE [2]the LORD!
[a]Praise the LORD, O my soul!
2 I will praise the LORD [a]while I live;
I will [b]sing praises to my God while I have my being.
3 [a]Do not trust in princes,
In [1]mortal [b]man, in whom there is [c]no salvation.
4 His [a]spirit departs, he [b]returns to [1]the earth;
In that very day his [c]thoughts perish.
5 How [a]blessed is he whose help is the God of Jacob,
Whose [b]hope is in the LORD his God;
6 Who [a]made heaven and earth,
The [b]sea and all that is in them;
Who [c]keeps [1]faith forever;
7 Who [a]executes justice for the oppressed;
Who [b]gives food to the hungry.
The LORD [c]sets the prisoners free;

8 The LORD [a]opens *the eyes* of the blind;
The LORD [b]raises up those who are bowed down;
The LORD [c]loves the righteous;
9 The LORD [1a]protects the [2]strangers;
He [3b]supports the fatherless and the widow;
But He [4]thwarts [c]the way of the wicked.
10 The LORD will [a]reign forever,
Thy God, O Zion, to all generations.
[1]Praise [2]the LORD!

1 [1]Or, *Hallelujah!* [2]Heb., *YAH* [a]Ps. 103:1
2 [a]Ps. 63:4 [b]Ps. 104:33
3 [1]Lit., *a son of a man* [a]Ps. 118:9 [b]Ps. 118:8; Is. 2:22 [c]Ps. 60:11; 108:12
4 [1]Lit., *his earth* [a]Ps. 104:29 [b]Eccles. 12:7 [c]Ps. 33:10
5 [a]Ps. 144:15 [b]Ps. 71:5
6 [1]Or, *truth* [a]Ps. 115:15 [b]Acts 14:15 [c]Ps. 117:2
7 [a]Ps. 103:6 [b]Ps. 107:9; 145:15 [c]Ps. 68:6; Is. 61:1
8 [a]Matt. 9:30; John 9:7 [b]Ps. 145:14 [c]Ps. 11:7
9 [1]Or, *keeps* [2]Or, *sojourners* [3]Or, *relieves* [4]Lit., *makes crooked* [a]Ex. 22:21; Lev. 19:34 [b]Ps. 68:5; Deut. 10:18 [c]Ps. 147:6
10 [1]Or, *Hallelujah!* [2]Heb., *YAH* [a]Ps. 10:16; Ex. 15:18

PSALM 147

Praise for Jerusalem's Restoration and Prosperity.

1 PRAISE [2]the LORD!
For [a]it is good to sing praises to our God;
For [3]it is pleasant *and* praise is [b]becoming.
2 The LORD [a]builds up Jerusalem;
He [b]gathers the outcasts of Israel.
3 He heals the [a]broken-hearted,
And [b]binds up their [1]wounds.
4 He [a]counts the number of the stars;
He [1b]gives names to all of them.
5 [a]Great is our Lord, and abundant in strength;
His [b]understanding is [1]infinite.
6 The LORD [1a]supports the afflicted;
He brings down the wicked to the ground.

7 [a]Sing to the LORD with thanksgiving;
Sing praises to our God on the lyre,
8 Who [a]covers the heavens with clouds,
Who [b]provides rain for the earth,
Who [c]makes grass to [1]grow on the mountains.
9 He [a]gives to the beast its food,
And to the [b]young ravens which cry.

1 [1]Or, *Hallelujah!* [2]Heb., *YAH* [3]Or, *He is gracious* [a]Ps. 135:3 [b]Ps. 33:1
2 [a]Ps. 51:18; 102:16 [b]Ps. 106:47; Deut. 30:3; Is. 11:12; 56:8; Ezek. 39:28
3 [1]Lit., *sorrows* [a]Ps. 34:18; Is. 61:1 [b]Job 5:18; Is. 30:26; Ezek. 34:16
4 [1]Or, *calls them all by their names* [a]Gen. 15:5 [b]Is. 40:26
5 [1]Lit., *innumerable* [a]Ps. 48:1; 145:3 [b]Is. 40:28
6 [1]Or, *relieves* [a]Ps. 37:24; 146:9
7 [a]Ps. 33:2; 95:1, 2
8 [1]Lit., *spring forth* [a]Job 26:8 [b]Ps. 104:13; Job 5:10; 38:26 [c]Ps. 104:14; Job 38:27
9 [a]Ps. 104:27, 28; 145:15 [b]Job 38:41

10 He does not delight in the strength of the [a]horse;
He [b]does not take pleasure in the legs of a man.
11 The LORD [a]favors those who fear Him,
[b]Those who wait for His lovingkindness.

12 Praise the LORD, O Jerusalem!
Praise your God, O Zion!
13 For He has strengthened the [a]bars of your gates;
He has [b]blessed your sons within you.
14 He [a]makes [1]peace in your borders;
He satisfies you with [b]the [2]finest of the wheat.
15 He sends forth His [a]command to the earth;
His [b]word runs very swiftly.
16 He gives [a]snow like wool;
He scatters the [b]hoarfrost like ashes.
17 He casts forth His [a]ice as fragments;
Who can stand before His [b]cold?
18 He [a]sends forth His word and melts them;
He [b]causes His wind to blow and the waters to flow.
19 He [a]declares His words to Jacob,
His [b]statutes and His ordinances to Israel.
20 He [a]has not dealt thus with any nation;
And as for His ordinances, they have [b]not known them.
[1]Praise [2]the LORD!

PSALM 148

The Whole Creation Invoked to Praise the LORD.

1 PRAISE [2]the LORD!
Praise the LORD [a]from the heavens;
Praise Him [b]in the heights!
2 Praise Him, [a]all His angels;
Praise Him, [b]all His hosts!
3 Praise Him, sun and moon;
Praise Him, all stars of light!
4 Praise Him, [1a]highest heavens,
And the [b]waters that are above the heavens!
5 Let them praise the name of the LORD,
For [a]He commanded and they were created.
6 He has also [a]established them forever and ever;
He has made a [b]decree which will not pass away.

7 Praise the LORD from the earth,
[a]Sea-monsters and all [b]deeps;
8 [a]Fire and hail, [b]snow and [c]clouds;
[d]Stormy wind, [e]fulfilling His word;
9 [a]Mountains and all hills;
Fruit [b]trees and all cedars;
10 [a]Beasts and all cattle;
[b]Creeping things and winged fowl;
11 [a]Kings of the earth and all peoples;
Princes and all judges of the earth;
12 Both young men and virgins;
Old men and children.

13 Let them praise the name of the LORD,

10 [a]Ps. 33:17 [b]1 Sam. 16:7

11 [a]Ps. 149:4 [b]Ps. 33:18

13 [a]Neh. 3:3; 7:3 [b]Ps. 37:26

14 [1]Lit., *your borders peace* [2]Lit., *fat* [a]Ps. 29:11; Is. 54:13; 60:17, 18 [b]Ps. 81:16; Deut. 32:14

15 [a]Ps. 148:5; Job 37:12 [b]Ps. 104:4

16 [a]Ps. 148:8; Job 37:6 [b]Job 38:29

17 [a]Job 37:10 [b]Job 37:9

18 [a]Ps. 147:15; 33:9; 107:20 [b]Ps. 107:25

19 [a]Deut. 33:3, 4 [b]Mal. 4:4

20 [1]Or, *Hallelujah!* [2]Heb., *YAH* [a]Deut. 4:7, 8, 32-34 [b]Ps. 79:6; Jer. 10:25

1 [1]Or, *Hallelujah!* [2]Heb., *YAH* [a]Ps. 69:34 [b]Ps. 102:19; Job 16:19; Matt. 21:9

2 [a]Ps. 103:20 [b]Ps. 103:21

4 [1]Lit., *heavens of heavens* [a]Ps. 68:33; Deut. 10:14; 1 Kin. 8:27; Neh. 9:6 [b]Gen. 1:7

5 [a]Ps. 33:6, 9; Gen. 1:1

6 [a]Jer. 31:35, 36; 33:20, 25 [b]Job 38:33

7 [a]Ps. 74:13; Gen. 1:21 [b]Gen. 1:2; Deut. 33:13; Hab. 3:10

8 [a]Ps. 18:12 [b]Ps. 147:16 [c]Ps. 135:7 [d]Ps. 107:25 [e]Ps. 103:20; Job 37:12

9 [a]Is. 44:23; 49:13 [b]Is. 55:12

10 [a]Is. 43:20 [b]Hos. 2:18

11 [a]Ps. 102:15

13 [a]Is. 12:4 [b]Ps. 8:1; 113:4

14 [1]Or, *Hallelujah!* [2]Heb., YAH
[a]Ps. 75:10; 1 Sam. 2:1 [b]Ps. 109:1; Deut. 10:21; Jer. 17:14 [c]Lev. 10:3; Eph. 2:17

For His [a]name alone is exalted;
His [b]glory is above earth and heaven.
14 And He has [a]lifted up a horn for His people,
[b]Praise for all His godly ones;
Even for the sons of Israel, a people [c]near to Him.
[1]Praise [2]the LORD!

PSALM 149

Israel Invoked to Praise the LORD.

1 [1]Or, *Hallelujah!* [2]Heb., YAH
[a]Ps. 33:3 [b]Ps. 35:18; 89:5

2 [a]Ps. 95:6 [b]Ps. 47:6; Judg. 8:23

3 [a]Ps. 150:4; 2 Sam. 6:14 [b]Ps. 81:2; Ex. 15:20

4 [a]Ps. 35:27; 147:11 [b]Ps. 132:16; Is. 61:3

5 [a]Ps. 132:16 [b]Ps. 42:8; Job 35:10

6 [1]Lit., *throat*
[a]Ps. 66:17 [b]Neh. 4:17

7 [a]Ezek. 25:17; Mic. 5:15

8 [a]Job 36:8 [b]Nah. 3:10

9 [1]Or, *Hallelujah!* [2]Heb., YAH
[a]Ezek. 28:26 [b]Ps. 112:9

1 [1]PRAISE [2]the LORD!
Sing to the LORD a [a]new song,
And His praise [b]in the congregation of the godly ones.
2 Let Israel be glad in [a]his Maker;
Let the sons of Zion rejoice in their [b]King.
3 Let them praise His name with [a]dancing;
Let them sing praises to Him with [b]timbrel and lyre.
4 For the LORD [a]takes pleasure in His people;
He will [b]beautify the afflicted ones with salvation.

5 Let the [a]godly ones exult in glory;
Let them [b]sing for joy on their beds.
6 *Let* the [a]high praises of God *be* in their [1]mouth.
And a two-edged [b]sword in their hand,
7 To [a]execute vengeance on the nations,
And punishment on the peoples;
8 To bind their kings [a]with chains,
And their [b]nobles with fetters of iron;
9 To [a]execute on them the judgment written;
This is an [b]honor for all His godly ones.
[1]Praise [2]the LORD!

PSALM 150

A Psalm of Praise.

1 [1]Or, *Hallelujah!* [2]Heb., YAH [3]Or, *firmament*
[a]Ps. 73:17; 102:19 [b]Ps. 19:1

2 [a]Ps. 145:12 [b]Ps. 145:3; Deut. 3:24

3 [a]Ps. 98:6 [b]Ps. 33:2

4 [a]Ps. 149:3 [b]Ps. 45:8; Is. 38:20 [c]Gen. 4:21; Job 21:12

5 [a]2 Sam. 6:5; 1 Chr. 13:8; 15:16; Ezra 3:10; Neh. 12:27

6 [1]Heb., YAH [2]Or, *Hallelujah!*
[a]Ps. 103:22; 145:21

1 [1]PRAISE [2]the LORD!
Praise God in His [a]sanctuary;
Praise Him in His mighty [3b]expanse.
2 Praise Him for His [a]mighty deeds;
Praise Him according to His excellent [b]greatness.

3 Praise Him with [a]trumpet sound;
Praise Him with [b]harp and lyre.
4 Praise Him with [a]timbrel and dancing;
Praise Him with [b]stringed instruments and [c]pipe.
5 Praise Him with loud [a]cymbals;
Praise Him with resounding cymbals.
6 Let [a]everything that has breath praise [1]the LORD.
[2]Praise [1]the LORD!

THE PROVERBS

Use of the Proverbs. Enticement by Sinners.

THE [a]proverbs of Solomon [b]the son of David, king of Israel:
2 To know [a]wisdom and instruction,
To discern the sayings of [b]understanding,
3 To [a]receive instruction in wise behavior,
[b]Righteousness, justice and equity;
4 To give [a]prudence to the [1]naive,
To the youth [b]knowledge and discretion,
5 A wise man will hear and [a]increase in learning,
And a [b]man of understanding will acquire wise counsel,
6 To understand a proverb and a figure,
The words of the wise and their [a]riddles.

7 [a]The fear of the LORD is the beginning of knowledge;
Fools despise wisdom and instruction.

8 [a]Hear, my son, your father's instruction,
And [b]do not forsake your mother's teaching;
9 Indeed, they are a [a]graceful wreath to your head,
And [1b]ornaments about your neck.
10 My son, if sinners [a]entice you,
[b]Do not consent.
11 If they say, "Come with us,
Let us [a]lie in wait for blood,
Let us [b]ambush the innocent without cause;
12 Let us [a]swallow them alive like Sheol,
Even whole, as those who [b]go down to the pit;
13 We shall find all *kinds* of precious wealth,
We shall fill our houses with spoil;
14 Throw in your lot [1]with us,
We shall all have one purse";
15 My son, [a]do not walk in the way with them,
[b]Keep your feet from their path;
16 For [a]their feet run to evil,
And they hasten to shed blood.
17 Indeed, it is [1]useless to spread the net
In the eyes of any [2]bird;
18 But they [a]lie in wait for their own blood;
They ambush their own lives.
19 So are the ways of everyone who [a]gains by violence,
It takes away the life of its possessors.

20 [a]Wisdom shouts in the street,
She [1]lifts her voice in the square;
21 At the head of the noisy *streets* she cries out;
At the entrance of the gates in the city, she utters her sayings:
22 "How long, O [1a]naive ones, will you love [2]simplicity?
And [b]scoffers delight themselves in scoffing,
And fools [c]hate knowledge?
23 "Turn to my reproof,

1 [a]Prov. 10:1; 25:1; 1 Kin. 4:32; Eccles. 12:9 [b]Eccles. 1:1

2 [a]Prov. 15:33 [b]Prov. 4:1

3 [a]Prov. 19:20 [b]Prov. 2:9

4 [1]Lit., *simple ones* [a]Prov. 8:5, 12 [b]Prov. 2:10, 11; 3:21

5 [a]Prov. 9:9 [b]Prov. 14:6; Eccles. 9:11

6 [a]Num. 12:8; Ps. 49:4; 78:2; Dan. 8:23

7 [a]Prov. 9:10; 15:33; Job 28:28; Ps. 111:10; Eccles. 12:13

8 [a]Prov. 4:1 [b]Prov. 6:20

9 [1]Lit., *necklaces* [a]Prov. 4:9 [b]Gen. 41:42; Dan. 5:29

10 [a]Prov. 16:29 [b]Deut. 13:8; Ps. 50:18

11 [a]Prov. 12:6 [b]Prov. 1:18; Ps. 10:8

12 [a]Ps. 124:3 [b]Ps. 28:1

14 [1]Lit., *in the midst of us*

15 [a]Prov. 4:14; Ps. 1:1 [b]Ps. 119:101

16 [a]Prov. 6:17, 18; Is. 59:7

17 [1]Lit., *in vain* [2]Lit., *possessor of wing*

18 [a]Prov. 11:19

19 [a]Prov. 15:27

20 [1]Lit., *gives* [a]Prov. 8:1-3; 9:3

22 [1]Lit., *simple ones* [2]Or, *naivete* [a]Prov. 4:32; 8:5; 9:4; 22:3 [b]Ps. 1:1 [c]Prov. 1:29; 5:12

Behold, I will [a]pour out my spirit on you;
I will make my words known to you,
24 Because [a]I called, and you [b]refused;
I [c]stretched out my hand, and no one paid attention;
25 And you [a]neglected all my counsel,
And did not [b]want my reproof;
26 I will even [a]laugh at your [b]calamity;
I will mock when your [c]dread comes,
27 When your dread comes like a storm,
And your calamity comes on like a [a]whirlwind,
When distress *and* anguish come on you.
28 "Then they will [a]call on me, but I will not answer;
They will [b]seek me diligently, but they shall not find me,
29 Because they [a]hated knowledge,
And did not choose the fear of the LORD.
30 "They [a]would not accept my counsel,
They spurned all my reproof.
31 "So they shall [a]eat of the fruit of their own way,
And be [b]satiated with their own devices.
32 "For the [a]waywardness of the [1]naive shall kill them,
And the complacency of fools shall destroy them.
33 "But [a]he who listens to me shall [1]live securely,
And shall be at ease from the dread of evil."

CHAPTER 2

MY son, if you will [a]receive my sayings,
And [b]treasure my commandments within you,
2 [a]Make your ear attentive to wisdom,
Incline your heart to understanding;
3 For if you cry for discernment,
[1]Lift your voice for understanding;
4 If you seek her as [a]silver,
And search for her as for [b]hidden treasures;
5 Then you will discern the [a]fear of the LORD,
And discover the knowledge of God.
6 For [a]the LORD gives wisdom;
From His mouth *come* knowledge and understanding.
7 He stores up sound wisdom for the upright;
He is a [a]shield to those who walk in integrity,
8 Guarding the paths of justice,
And He [a]preserves the way of His godly ones.
9 Then you will discern [a]righteousness and justice
And equity *and* every [b]good course.
10 For [a]wisdom will enter your heart,
And [b]knowledge will be pleasant to your soul;
11 Discretion will [a]guard you,
Understanding will watch over you,
12 To [a]deliver you from the way of evil,
From the man who speaks [b]perverse things;
13 From those who [a]leave the paths of uprightness,
To walk in the [b]ways of darkness;
14 Who [a]delight in doing evil,
And rejoice in the perversity of evil;
15 Whose paths are [a]crooked,

23 [a]Is. 32:15; Joel 2:28
24 [a]Is. 65:12; 66:4; Jer. 7:13 [b]Prov. 15:32; Zech. 7:11 [c]Is. 65:2; Rom. 10:21
25 [a]Ps. 107:11; Luke 7:30 [b]Prov. 15:10
26 [a]Ps. 2:4 [b]Prov. 6:15 [c]Prov. 10:24
27 [a]Prov. 10:25
28 [a]1 Sam. 8:18; Job 27:9; 35:12; Ps. 18:41; Is. 1:15; Jer. 11:11; 14:12; Ezek. 8:18; Mic. 3:4; Zech. 7:13 [b]Prov. 8:17
29 [a]Prov. 1:22; Job 21:14
30 [a]Prov. 1:25; Ps. 81:11
31 [a]Prov. 5:22, 23; 22:8; Job 4:8; Jer. 6:19 [b]Prov. 14:14
32 [1]Lit., *simple ones* [a]Jer. 2:19
33 [1]Lit., *dwell* [a]Prov. 3:24-26; Ps. 25:12, 13
1 [a]Prov. 4:10 [b]Prov. 3:1
2 [a]Prov. 22:17
3 [1]Lit., *give*
4 [a]Prov. 3:14 [b]Job 3:21; Matt. 13:44
5 [a]Prov. 1:7
6 [a]1 Kin. 3:12; Job 32:8; James 1:5
7 [a]Prov. 30:5; Ps. 84:11
8 [a]1 Sam. 2:9; Ps. 66:9
9 [a]Prov. 8:20 [b]Prov. 4:18
10 [a]Prov. 14:33 [b]Prov. 22:18
11 [a]Prov. 4:6; 6:22
12 [a]Prov. 28:26 [b]Prov. 6:12
13 [a]Prov. 21:16 [b]Prov. 4:19; Ps. 82:5; John 3:19, 20
14 [a]Prov. 10:23; Jer. 11:15
15 [a]Prov. 21:8; Ps. 125:5

And who are devious in their ways;
16 To [a]deliver you from the strange woman,
From the [1b]adulteress who flatters with her words;
17 That leaves the [a]companion of her youth,
And forgets the covenant of her God;
18 For [a]her house [1]sinks down to death,
And her tracks *lead* to the [2]dead;
19 None who go to her return again,
Nor do they reach the [a]paths of life.
20 So that you will walk in the way of good men,
And keep to the [a]paths of the righteous.
21 For [a]the upright will [1]live in the land,
And [b]the blameless will remain in it;
22 But [a]the wicked will be cut off from the land,
And [b]the treacherous will be [c]uprooted from it.

Chapter 3

My son, [a]do not forget my [1]teaching,
But let your heart [b]keep my commandments;
2 For [a]length of days and years of life,
And peace they will add to you.
3 Do not let [a]kindness and truth leave you;
[b]Bind them around your neck,
[c]Write them on the tablet of your heart.
4 So you will [a]find favor and [b]good [1]repute
In the sight of God and man.
5 [a]Trust in the Lord with all your heart,
And [b]do not lean on your own understanding.
6 In all your ways [a]acknowledge Him,
And He will [b]make your paths straight.
7 [a]Do not be wise in your own eyes;
[b]Fear the Lord and turn away from evil.
8 It will be [a]healing to your [1]body,
And [b]refreshment to your bones.
9 [a]Honor the Lord from your wealth,
And from the [b]first of all your produce;
10 So your [a]barns will be filled with plenty,
And your [b]vats will overflow with new wine.
11 [a]My son, do not reject the [1]discipline of the Lord;
Or loathe His reproof,
12 For whom the Lord loves He reproves,
Even [a]as a father the son in whom he delights.

13 [a]How blessed is the man who finds wisdom,
And the man who gains understanding.
14 For its [a]profit is better than the profit of silver,
And its gain than fine gold.
15 She is [a]more precious than [1]jewels;
And [b]nothing you desire compares with her.
16 [1a]Long life is in her right hand;
In her left hand are [b]riches and honor.
17 Her ways are pleasant ways,
And all her paths are [a]peace.
18 She is a [a]tree of life to those who take hold of her,
And happy are all who hold her fast.

16 [1]Lit., *foreign woman* [a]Prov. 6:24; 7:5 [b]Prov. 23:27
17 [a]Mal. 3:14, 15
18 [1]Lit., *bows down* [2]Lit., *departed spirits* [a]Prov. 7:27
19 [a]Prov. 5:6; Ps. 16:11
20 [a]Prov. 4:18
21 [1]Or, *dwell* [a]Prov. 10:30; Ps. 37:9, 29 [b]Prov. 28:10
22 [a]Prov. 10:30; Ps. 37:38 [b]Prov. 11:3 [c]Deut. 28:63; Ps. 52:5
1 [1]Or, *law* [a]Prov. 4:5; Ps. 119:61 [b]Ex. 20:6; Deut. 30:16
2 [a]Prov. 3:16; 4:10; 9:11; 10:27; Ps. 91:16
3 [a]Prov. 14:22; 2 Sam. 15:20 [b]Prov. 1:9; 6:21; Deut. 6:8; 11:18 [c]Prov. 7:3; Jer. 17:1; 2 Cor. 3:3
4 [1]Lit., *understanding* [a]Prov. 8:35; 1 Sam. 2:26; Luke 2:52 [b]Ps. 111:10
5 [a]Prov. 22:19; Ps. 37:3, 5 [b]Prov. 23:4; Jer. 9:23
6 [a]Prov. 16:3; 1 Chr. 28:9 [b]Is. 45:13
7 [a]Rom. 12:16 [b]Prov. 8:13; 16:6; Job 1:1; 28:28
8 [1]Lit., *navel* [a]Prov. 4:22 [b]Job 21:24
9 [a]Is. 43:23 [b]Ex. 23:19; Deut. 26:2; Mal. 3:10
10 [a]Deut. 28:8 [b]Joel 2:24
11 [1]Or, *instruction* [a]Job 5:17; Heb. 12:5, 6
12 [a]Prov. 13:24; Deut. 8:5
13 [a]Prov. 8:32, 34
14 [a]Prov. 8:10, 19; 16:16; Job 28:15-19
15 [1]Lit., *corals* [a]Prov. 8:11; Job 28:18 [b]Prov. 3:8, 11
16 [1]Lit., *Length of days* [a]Prov. 3:2 [b]Prov. 8:18; 22:4
17 [a]Prov. 16:7; Ps. 119:165
18 [a]Prov. 11:30; 13:12; 15:4; Gen. 2:9; Rev. 2:7

19 The LORD [a]by wisdom founded the earth;
By understanding He [b]established the heavens.
20 By His knowledge the [a]deeps were broken up,
And the [b]skies drip with dew.
21 My son, [a]let them not depart from your sight;
Keep sound wisdom and discretion,
22 So they will be [a]life to your soul,
And [b]adornment to your neck.
23 Then you will [a]walk in your way securely,
And your foot will not [b]stumble.
24 When you [a]lie down, you will not be afraid;
When you lie down, your sleep will be sweet.
25 [a]Do not be afraid of sudden fear,
Nor of the [1b]onslaught of the wicked when it comes;
26 For the LORD will be [1]your confidence,
And will [a]keep your foot from being caught.

27 [a]Do not withhold good from [1]those to whom it is due,
When it is in your power to do *it*.
28 [a]Do not say to your neighbor, "Go, and come back,
And tomorrow I will give *it*,"
When you have it with you.
29 [a]Do not devise harm against your neighbor,
While he lives in security beside you.
30 [a]Do not contend with a man without cause,
If he has done you no harm.
31 [a]Do not envy a man of violence,
And do not choose any of his ways.
32 For the [a]crooked *man* is an abomination to the LORD;
But [1]He is [b]intimate with the upright.
33 The [a]curse of the LORD is on the house of the wicked,
But He [b]blesses the dwelling of the righteous.
34 Though [a]He scoffs at the scoffers,
Yet [b]He gives grace to the afflicted.
35 The wise will inherit honor,
But fools [1]display dishonor.

CHAPTER 4

HEAR, O sons, the [a]instruction of a father,
And [b]give attention that you may [1]gain understanding,
2 For I give you [1]sound [a]teaching;
[b]Do not abandon my [2]instruction.
3 When I was a son to my father,
[a]Tender and [b]the only son in the sight of my mother,
4 Then he taught me and said to me,
"Let your heart [a]hold fast my words;
[b]Keep my commandments and live;
5 [a]Acquire wisdom! [b]Acquire understanding!
Do not forget, nor turn away from the words of my mouth.
6 "Do not forsake her, and she will guard you;
[a]Love her, and she will watch over you.
7 "[a]The [1]beginning of wisdom *is:* [b]Acquire wisdom;
And with all your acquiring, get understanding.
8 "Prize her, and she will exalt you;
She will honor you if you embrace her.

19 [a]Prov. 8:27; Ps. 104:24 [b]Prov. 8:27, 28

20 [a]Gen. 7:11 [b]Deut. 33:28; Job 36:28

21 [a]Prov. 4:21

22 [a]Prov. 4:22; 8:35; 16:22; 21:21; Deut. 32:47 [b]Prov. 1:9

23 [a]Prov. 4:12; 10:9 [b]Ps. 91:12; Is. 5:27; 63:13

24 [a]Prov. 1:33; 6:22; Job 11:19; Ps. 3:5

25 [1]Lit., *storm* [a]Ps. 91:5; 1 Pet. 3:14 [b]Job 5:21

26 [1]Or, *at your side* [a]1 Sam. 2:9

27 [1]Lit., *its owners* [a]Rom. 13:7; Gal. 6:10

28 [a]Lev. 19:13; Deut. 24:15

29 [a]Prov. 6:14; 14:22

30 [a]Prov. 26:17; Rom. 12:18

31 [a]Prov. 24:1; Ps. 37:1

32 [1]Lit., *His private counsel is* [a]Prov. 11:20 [b]Job 29:4; Ps. 25:14

33 [a]Deut. 11:28; Mal. 2:2 [b]Job 8:6

34 [a]James 4:6 [b]1 Pet. 5:5

35 [1]Lit., *raise high*

1 [1]Lit., *know* [a]Prov. 1:8 [b]Prov. 1:2; 2:2

2 [1]Lit., *good* [2]Or, *law* [a]Deut. 32:2; Job 11:4 [b]Prov. 3:1; Ps. 89:30; 119:87

3 [a]1 Chr. 22:5 [b]Zech. 12:10

4 [a]Ps. 119:168 [b]Prov. 7:2

5 [a]Prov. 4:7 [b]Prov. 16:16

6 [a]2 Thess. 2:10

7 [1]Or, *the primary thing is wisdom* [a]Prov. 8:23 [b]Prov. 23:23

9 "She will place [a]on your head a garland of grace;
She will present you with a crown of beauty."

10 Hear, my son, and [a]accept my sayings,
And the [b]years of your life will be many.
11 I have [a]directed you in the way of wisdom;
I have led you in upright paths.
12 When you walk, your [a]steps will not be impeded;
And if you run, you [b]will not stumble.
13 [a]Take hold of instruction; do not let go.
Guard her, for she is your [b]life.
14 [a]Do not enter the path of the wicked,
And do not proceed in the way of evil men.
15 Avoid it, do not pass by it;
Turn away from it and pass on.
16 For they [a]cannot sleep unless they do evil;
And [1]they are robbed of sleep unless they make *someone* stumble.
17 For they [a]eat the bread of wickedness,
And drink the wine of violence.
18 But the [a]path of the righteous is like the [b]light of dawn,
That [c]shines brighter and brighter until the [d]full day.
19 The [a]way of the wicked is like darkness;
They do not know over what they [1b]stumble.

20 My son, [a]give attention to my words;
[b]Incline your ear to my sayings.
21 [a]Do not let them depart from your sight;
[b]Keep them in the midst of your heart.
22 For they are [a]life to those who find them,
And [b]health to all [1]their whole body.
23 Watch over your heart with all diligence,
For [a]from it *flow* the springs of life.
24 Put away from you a [a]deceitful mouth,
And [b]put devious lips far from you.
25 Let your eyes look directly ahead,
And let your [1]gaze be fixed straight in front of you.
26 [a]Watch the path of your feet,
And all your [b]ways will be established.
27 [a]Do not turn to the right nor to the left;
[b]Turn your foot from evil.

Chapter 5

My son, [a]give attention to my wisdom,
[b]Incline your ear to my understanding;
2 That you may [a]observe discretion,
And your [b]lips may reserve knowledge.
3 For the lips of an [1a]adulteress [b]drip honey,
And [c]smoother than oil is her [2]speech;
4 But in the end she is [a]bitter as wormwood,
[b]Sharp as a two-edged sword.
5 Her feet [a]go down to death,
Her steps lay hold of Sheol.
6 [1]She does not ponder the [a]path of life;
Her ways are [b]unstable, she [c]does not know *it*.

9 [a]Prov. 1:9
10 [a]Prov. 2:1 [b]Prov. 3:2
11 [a]1 Sam. 12:23
12 [a]Job 18:7; Ps. 18:36 [b]Prov. 3:23
13 [a]Prov. 3:18 [b]Prov. 3:22; John 6:63
14 [a]Prov. 1:15; Ps. 1:1
16 [1]Lit., *their sleep is robbed* [a]Ps. 36:4; Mic. 2:1
17 [a]Prov. 13:2
18 [a]Is. 26:7 [b]2 Sam. 23:4 [c]Dan. 12:3 [d]Job 11:17
19 [1]Or, *may stumble* [a]Prov. 2:13; Job 18:5, 6; Is. 59:9, 10; Jer. 23:12; John 12:35 [b]John 11:10
20 [a]Prov. 5:1 [b]Prov. 2:2
21 [a]Prov. 3:21 [b]Prov. 7:1, 2
22 [1]Lit., *his* [a]Prov. 3:22 [b]Prov. 3:8; 12:18
23 [a]Matt. 12:34; 15:18, 19; Mark 7:21; Luke 6:45
24 [a]Prov. 6:12; 10:32 [b]Prov. 19:1
25 [1]Or, *eyelids*
26 [a]Prov. 5:21; Heb. 12:13 [b]Ps. 119:5
27 [a]Deut. 5:32; 28:14 [b]Prov. 1:15
1 [a]Prov. 4:20 [b]Prov. 22:17
2 [a]Prov. 3:21 [b]Mal. 2:7
3 [1]Lit., *strange woman* [2]Lit., *palate* [a]Prov. 5:20; 2:16; 7:5; 22:14 [b]Song of Sol. 4:11 [c]Ps. 55:21
4 [a]Eccles. 7:26 [b]Ps. 57:4
5 [a]Prov. 7:27
6 [1]Lit., *Lest she watch* [a]Prov. 5:21; 4:26 [b]2 Pet. 2:14 [c]Prov. 30:20

7 [a]Now then, *my* sons, listen to me,
And [b]do not depart from the words of my mouth.
8 [a]Keep your way far from her,
And do not go near the [b]door of her house,
9 Lest you give your vigor to others,
And your years to the cruel one;
10 Lest strangers be filled with your strength,
And your hard-earned goods *go* to the house of an alien;
11 And you groan at your latter end,
When your flesh and your body are consumed;
12 And you say, "How I have [a]hated instruction!
And my heart [b]spurned reproof!
13 "And I have not listened to the voice of my [a]teachers,
Nor inclined my ear to my instructors!
14 "I was almost in utter ruin
In the midst of the assembly and congregation."

15 Drink water from your own cistern,
And [1]fresh water from your own well.
16 Should your [a]springs be dispersed abroad,
Streams of water in the streets?
17 Let them be yours alone,
And not for strangers with you.
18 Let your [a]fountain be blessed,
And [b]rejoice in the [c]wife of your youth.
19 *As* a loving [a]hind and a graceful doe,
Let her breasts satisfy you at all times;
Be [1]exhilarated always with her love.
20 For why should you, my son, be exhilarated with an [1a]adulteress,
And embrace the bosom of a [b]foreigner?
21 For the [a]ways of a man are before the eyes of the LORD,
And He [b]watches all his paths.
22 His [a]own iniquities will capture the wicked,
And he will be held with the cords of his sin.
23 He will [a]die for lack of instruction,
And in the greatness of his folly he will go astray.

Chapter 6

My son, if you have become [a]surety for your neighbor,
Have [1]given a pledge for a stranger,
2 *If* you have been snared with the words of your mouth,
Have been caught with the words of your mouth,
3 Do this then, my son, and deliver yourself;
Since you have come into the [1]hand of your neighbor,
Go, humble yourself, and importune your neighbor.
4 Do not give [a]sleep to your eyes,
Nor slumber to your eyelids;
5 Deliver yourself like a gazelle from *the hunter's* hand,
And like a [a]bird from the hand of the fowler.

6 Go to the [a]ant, O [b]sluggard,
Observe her ways and be wise,

7 [a]Prov. 7:24 [b]Ps. 119:102
8 [a]Prov. 7:25 [b]Prov. 9:14
12 [a]Prov. 1:7, 22, 29 [b]Prov. 1:25; 12:1
13 [a]Prov. 1:8
15 [1]Lit., *flowing*
16 [a]Prov. 5:18; 9:17; Song of Sol. 4:12, 15
18 [a]Prov. 5:18; 9:17; Song of Sol. 4:12, 15 [b]Eccles. 9:9 [c]Mal. 2:14
19 [1]Lit., *intoxicated* [a]Song of Sol. 2:9, 17; 4:5; 7:3
20 [1]Lit., *strange woman* [a]Prov. 5:3 [b]Prov. 2:16; 6:24; 7:5; 23:27
21 [a]Prov. 15:3; Job 14:16; 31:4; 34:21; Ps. 119:168; Jer. 16:17; 32:19; Hos. 7:2; Heb. 4:13 [b]Prov. 4:26
22 [a]Prov. 1:31, 32; Num. 32:23; Ps. 7:15; 9:15; 40:12
23 [a]Job 4:21; 36:12
1 [1]Lit., *clapped your palms* [a]Prov. 11:15; 17:18; 20:16; 22:26; 27:13
3 [1]Lit., *palm*
4 [a]Ps. 132:4
5 [a]Ps. 91:3; 124:7
6 [a]Prov. 30:24, 25 [b]Prov. 6:9; 10:26; 13:4; 20:4; 26:16

7 Which, having [a]no chief,
Officer or ruler,
8 Prepares her food [a]in the summer,
And gathers her provision in the harvest.
9 How long will you lie down, O sluggard?
When will you arise from your sleep?
10 "[a]A little sleep, a little slumber,
A little folding of the hands to [1]rest"—
11 And your poverty will come in like a [1]vagabond,
And your need like [2]an armed man.

12 A [a]worthless person, a wicked man,
Is the one who walks with a [b]false mouth,
13 Who [a]winks with his eyes, who [1]signals with his feet,
Who [2]points with his fingers;
14 Who *with* [a]perversity in his heart [b]devises evil continually,
Who [1c]spreads strife.
15 Therefore [a]his calamity will come suddenly;
[b]Instantly he will be broken, and there will be [c]no healing.

16 There are six things which the LORD hates,
Yes, seven which are an abomination [1]to Him:
17 [a]Haughty eyes, a [b]lying tongue,
And hands that [c]shed innocent blood,
18 A heart that devises [a]wicked plans,
[b]Feet that run rapidly to evil,
19 A [a]false witness *who* utters lies,
And one who [1b]spreads strife among brothers.

20 My son, observe the commandment of your father,
And do not forsake the [1]teaching of your mother;
21 [a]Bind them continually on your heart;
Tie them around your neck.
22 When you [a]walk about, [1]they will guide you;
When you sleep, [1]they will watch over you;
And when you awake, [1]they will talk to you.
23 For [a]the commandment is a lamp, and the [1]teaching is light;
And reproofs for discipline are the way of life,
24 To [a]keep you from the evil woman,
From the smooth tongue of the [1]adulteress.
25 [a]Do not desire her beauty in your heart,
Nor let her catch you with her [b]eyelids.
26 For [a]on account of a harlot *one is reduced* to a loaf of bread,
And [1]an adulteress [b]hunts for the precious life.
27 Can a man [1]take fire in his bosom,
And his clothes not be burned?
28 Or can a man walk on hot coals,
And his feet not be scorched?
29 So is the one who [a]goes in to his neighbor's wife;
Whoever touches her [b]will not [1]go unpunished.
30 [1]Men do not despise a thief if he steals
To [a]satisfy [2]himself when he is hungry;

7 [a]Prov. 30:27

8 [a]Prov. 10:5

10 [1]Lit., *lie down* [a]Prov. 24:33, 34

11 [1]Lit., *one who walks* [2]Lit., *a man of a shield*

12 [a]Prov. 16:27 [b]Prov. 4:24; 10:32

13 [1]Lit., *scrapes* [2]Lit., *instructs with* [a]Prov. 10:10; Ps. 35:19

14 [1]Lit., *sends out* [a]Prov. 17:20 [b]Prov. 3:29; Mic. 2:1 [c]Prov. 6:19; 16:28

15 [a]Prov. 24:22 [b]Is. 30:13, 14; Jer. 19:11 [c]2 Cor. 36:16

16 [1]Lit., *of His soul*

17 [a]Prov. 21:4; 30:13; Ps. 18:27; 101:5 [b]Prov. 12:22; 17:7; Ps. 31:18; 120:2 [c]Prov. 28:17; Deut. 19:10; Is. 1:15; 59:7

18 [a]Prov. 24:2; Gen. 6:5 [b]Prov. 1:16

19 [1]Lit., *sends out* [a]Prov. 12:17; 19:5, 9; 21:28; Ps. 27:12 [b]Prov. 6:14

20 [1]Or, *law*

21 [a]Prov. 3:3

22 [1]Lit., *she* [a]Prov. 3:23

23 [1]Or, *law* [a]Ps. 119:105

24 [1]Lit., *foreign woman* [a]Prov. 7:5; 5:3; 7:21

25 [a]Matt. 5:28 [b]2 Kin. 9:30; Jer. 4:30; Ezek. 23:40

26 [1]Lit., *a man's wife* [a]Prov. 5:9, 10; 29:3 [b]Prov. 7:23; Ezek. 13:18

27 [1]Lit., *snatch up*

29 [1]Lit., *be innocent* [a]Ezek. 18:6; 33:26 [b]Prov. 16:5

30 [1]Lit., *They do not;* or, *Do not men. . . ?* [2]Lit., *his soul* [a]Job 38:39

31 But when he is found, he must [a]repay sevenfold;
He must give all the [1]substance of his house.
32 The one who commits adultery with a woman is [a]lacking [1]sense;
He who would [b]destroy [2]himself does it.
33 Wounds and disgrace he will find,
And his reproach will not be blotted out.
34 For [a]jealousy [1]enrages a man,
And he will not spare in the [b]day of vengeance.
35 He will not [1]accept any ransom,
Nor will he be [2]content though you give many [3]gifts.

Chapter 7

My son, [a]keep my words,
And treasure my commandments within you.
2 [a]Keep my commandments and live,
And my [1]teaching [b]as the [2]apple of your eye.
3 Bind them on your fingers;
[a]Write them on the tablet of your heart.
4 Say to wisdom, "You are my sister,"
And call understanding *your* intimate friend;
5 That they may keep you from an [1]adulteress,
From the foreigner who [2]flatters with her words.

6 For [a]at the window of my house
I looked out [b]through my lattice,
7 And I saw among the [1a]naive,
I discerned among the [2]youths,
A young man [b]lacking [3]sense,
8 Passing through the street near [a]her corner;
And he [1]takes the way to [b]her house,
9 In the [a]twilight, in the [1]evening,
In the [2]middle of the night and *in* the darkness.
10 And behold, a woman *comes* to meet him,
[a]Dressed as a harlot and cunning of heart.
11 She is [a]boisterous and rebellious;
Her feet do not remain at home;
12 *She is* now in the streets, now [a]in the squares,
And [b]lurks by every corner.
13 So she seizes him and kisses him,
[1]And with a [a]brazen face she says to him:
14 "[1]I was due to offer [a]peace offerings;
Today I have [b]paid my vows.
15 "Therefore I have come out to meet you,
To seek your presence earnestly, and I have found you.
16 "I have spread my couch with [a]coverings,
With colored [b]linens of Egypt.
17 "I have sprinkled my bed
With [a]myrrh, aloes and [b]cinnamon.
18 "Come, let us drink our fill of love until morning;
Let us delight ourselves with caresses.
19 "For [1]the man is not at home,
He has gone on a long journey;
20 He has taken a [a]bag of money [1]with him
At full moon he will come home."

31 [1]Or, *wealth* [a]Ex. 22:1-4

32 [1]Lit., *heart* [2]Lit., *his soul* [a]Prov. 7:7; 9:4, 16; 10:13, 21; 11:12; 12:11 [b]Prov. 7:22, 23

34 [1]Lit., *is the rage of* [a]Prov. 27:4; Song of Sol. 8:6 [b]Prov. 11:4; Lev. 20:10

35 [1]Lit., *lift up the face of any* [2]Lit., *willing* [3]Or, *bribes*

1 [a]Prov. 2:1; 6:20

2 [1]Or, *law* [2]Lit., *pupil* [a]Prov. 4:4 [b]Deut. 32:10; Ps. 17:8; Zech. 2:8

3 [a]Prov. 3:3

5 [1]Lit., *strange woman* [2]Lit., *is smooth*

6 [a]Judg. 5:28 [b]Song of Sol. 2:9

7 [1]Lit., *simple ones* [2]Lit., *sons* [3]Lit., *heart* [a]Prov. 1:22 [b]Prov. 6:32

8 [1]Lit., *steps* [a]Prov. 7:12 [b]Prov. 7:27

9 [1]Lit., *evening of the day* [2]Lit., *pupil* (of the eye) [a]Job 24:15

10 [a]Gen. 38:14, 15

11 [a]Prov. 9:13

12 [a]Prov. 9:14 [b]Prov. 23:28

13 [1]Lit., *She makes bold her face and says* [a]Prov. 21:29

14 [1]Lit., *"Sacrifices of peace offerings are with me* [a]Lev. 7:11 [b]Lev. 7:16

16 [a]Prov. 31:22 [b]Is. 19:9; Ezek. 27:7

17 [a]Ps. 45:8 [b]Ex. 30:23

19 [1]I.e., my husband

20 [1]Lit., *in his hand* [a]Gen. 42:35

21 With her many persuasions she entices him;
With her [1a]flattering lips she seduces him.
22 Suddenly he follows her,
As an ox goes to the slaughter,
Or as [1]*one in* fetters to the discipline of a fool,
23 Until an arrow pierces through his liver,
As a [a]bird hastens to the snare,
So he does not know that it *will cost him* his life.

24 Now therefore, *my* sons, [a]listen to me,
And pay attention to the words of my mouth.
25 Do not let your heart [a]turn aside to her ways,
Do not stray into her paths.
26 For many are the [1]victims she has cast down,
And [a]numerous are all her slain.
27 Her [a]house is the way to Sheol,
Descending to the chambers of death.

Chapter 8

DOES not [a]wisdom call,
And understanding [1]lift up her voice?
2 On top of [a]the heights beside the way,
Where the paths meet, she takes her stand;
3 Beside the [a]gates, at the opening to the city,
At the entrance of the doors, she cries out:
4 "To you, O men, I call,
And my voice is to the sons of men.
5 "O [1a]naive ones, discern prudence;
And, O [b]fools, discern [2]wisdom.
6 "Listen, for I shall speak [a]noble things;
And the opening of my lips *will produce* [b]right things.
7 "For my [a]mouth will utter truth;
And wickedness is an abomination to my lips.
8 "All the utterances of my mouth are in righteousness;
There is nothing [a]crooked or perverted in them.
9 "They are all [a]straightforward to him who understands,
And right to those who [b]find knowledge.
10 "Take my [a]instruction, and not silver,
And knowledge rather than choicest gold.
11 "For wisdom is [a]better than [1]jewels;
And [b]all desirable things can not compare with her.

12 "I, wisdom, [a]dwell with prudence,
And I find [b]knowledge *and* discretion.
13 "The [a]fear of the LORD is to hate evil;
[b]Pride and arrogance and [c]the evil way,
And the [d]perverted mouth, I hate.
14 "[a]Counsel is mine and [b]sound wisdom;
I am understanding, [c]power is mine.
15 "By me [a]kings reign,
And rulers decree justice.
16 "By me princes rule, and nobles,
All who judge rightly.
17 "I [a]love those who love me;
And [b]those who diligently seek me will find me.

21 [1]Lit., *smooth* [a]Prov. 5:3; 6:24

22 [1]Or, *as a stag goes into a trap;* so some ancient versions.

23 [a]Eccles. 9:12

24 [a]Prov. 5:7

25 [a]Prov. 5:8

26 [1]Lit., *mortally wounded* [a]Prov. 9:18

27 [a]Prov. 2:18; 5:5; 9:18

1 [1]Lit., *give* [a]Prov. 8:1-3; 1:20, 21

2 [a]Prov. 9:3, 14

3 [a]Job 29:7

5 [1]Lit., *simple* [2]Lit., *heart* [a]Prov. 1:4 [b]Prov. 1:22, 32; 3:35

6 [a]Prov. 22:20 [b]Prov. 23:16

7 [a]Ps. 37:30

8 [a]Prov. 2:15; Deut. 32:5; Phil. 2:15

9 [a]Prov. 14:6 [b]Prov. 3:13

10 [a]Prov. 8:19; 3:14, 15

11 [1]Lit., *corals* [a]Job 28:18 [b]Prov. 3:15

12 [a]Prov. 8:5 [b]Prov. 1:4

13 [a]Prov. 3:7; 16:6 [b]Prov. 16:18; 1 Sam. 2:3; Is. 13:11 [c]Prov. 15:9 [d]Prov. 6:12

14 [a]Prov. 1:25; 19:20; Is. 28:29; Jer. 32:19 [b]Prov. 2:7; 3:21; 18:1 [c]Eccles. 7:19; 9:16

15 [a]Prov. 29:4; 2 Chr. 1:10

17 [a]Prov. 4:6; 1 Sam. 2:30; John 14:21 [b]Prov. 2:4, 5; James 1:5

18 "[a]Riches and honor are with me,
Enduring [b]wealth and righteousness.
19 "My fruit is [a]better than gold, even pure gold,
And my yield than [b]choicest silver.
20 "I walk in the way of righteousness,
In the midst of the paths of justice,
21 To endow those who love me with wealth,
That I may [a]fill their treasuries.

22 "The LORD possessed me [a]at the beginning of His way,
Before His works [1]of old.
23 "From everlasting I was [1]established
From the beginning, [a]from the earliest times of the earth.
24 "When there were no [a]depths I was [1]brought forth,
When there were no springs abounding with water.
25 "[a]Before the mountains were settled,
Before the hills I was [1]brought forth;
26 While He had not yet made the earth and the [1]fields,
Nor the first dust of the world.
27 "When He [a]established the heavens, I was there,
When [b]He inscribed a circle on the face of the deep,
28 When He made firm the skies above,
When the springs of the deep became [1]fixed,
29 When [a]He set for the sea its boundary,
So that the water should not transgress His [1]command,
When He marked out [b]the foundations of the earth;
30 Then [a]I was beside Him, *as* a master workman;
And I was daily *His* delight,
[1]Rejoicing always before Him,
31 [1]Rejoicing in the world, His earth,
And *having* my delight in the sons of men.

32 "Now therefore, O sons, [a]listen to me,
For [b]blessed are they who keep my ways.
33 "[a]Heed instruction and be wise,
And do not neglect *it*.
34 "[a]Blessed is the man who listens to me,
Watching daily at my gates,
Waiting at my doorposts.
35 "For [a]he who finds me finds life,
And [b]obtains favor from the LORD.
36 "But he who [1]sins against me [a]injures himself;
All those who [b]hate me [c]love death."

CHAPTER 9

WISDOM has [a]built her house,
She has hewn out her seven pillars;
2 She has [1a]prepared her food, she has [b]mixed her wine;
She has also [c]set her table;
3 She has [a]sent out her maidens, she [b]calls
From the [c]tops of the heights of the city:
4 "[a]Whoever is [1]naive, let him turn in here!"
To him who [b]lacks [2]understanding she says,
5 "Come, [a]eat of my food,
And drink of the wine I have mixed.

---

18 [a]Prov. 3:16 [b]Ps. 112:3; Matt. 6:33

19 [a]Prov. 3:14 [b]Prov. 10:20

21 [a]Prov. 24:4

22 [1]Lit., *from then* [a]Prov. 3:19; Job 28:26-28; Ps. 104:24

23 [1]Or, *consecrated* [a]John 17:5

24 [1]Or, *born* [a]Prov. 3:20; Gen. 1:2; Ex. 15:5; Job 38:16

25 [1]Or, *born* [a]Ps. 90:2

26 [1]Lit., *outside places*

27 [a]Prov. 3:19 [b]Job 26:10

28 [1]Lit., *strong*

29 [1]Lit., *mouth* [a]Job 38:10; Ps. 104:9 [b]Job 38:6; Ps. 104:5

30 [1]Or, *Playing* [a]John 1:2, 3

31 [1]Or, *Playing*

32 [a]Prov. 5:7; 7:24 [b]Prov. 29:18; Ps. 119:1, 2; 128:1; Luke 11:28

33 [a]Prov. 4:1

34 [a]Prov. 3:13, 18

35 [a]Prov. 4:22; John 17:3 [b]Prov. 3:4; 12:2

36 [1]Or, *misses me* [a]Prov. 1:31, 32; 15:32 [b]Prov. 5:12; 12:1 [c]Prov. 21:6

1 [a]1 Cor. 3:9, 10; Eph. 2:20-22; 1 Pet. 2:5

2 [1]Lit., *slaughtered her slaughter* [a]Matt. 22:4 [b]Song of Sol. 8:2 [c]Luke 14:16, 17

3 [a]Ps. 68:11; Matt. 22:3 [b]Prov. 8:1, 2 [c]Prov. 9:14

4 [1]Lit., *simple* [2]Lit., *heart* [a]Prov. 9:16; 8:5 [b]Prov. 6:32

5 [a]Song of Sol. 5:1; Is. 55:1; John 6:27

6 "Forsake [1]*your* folly and [a]live,
And [b]proceed in the way of understanding."

7 He who [a]corrects a scoffer gets dishonor for himself,
And he who reproves a wicked man *gets* [1]insults for himself.
8 [a]Do not reprove a scoffer, lest he hate you,
[b]Reprove a wise man, and he will love you.
9 Give *instruction* to a wise man, and he will be still wiser,
Teach a righteous man, and he will [a]increase *his* learning.
10 The fear of the LORD is the beginning of wisdom,
And the knowledge of the Holy One is understanding.
11 For [a]by me your days will be multiplied,
And years of life will be added to you.
12 If you are wise, you are wise [a]for yourself,
And if you [b]scoff, you alone will bear it.

13 The [1]woman of folly is [a]boisterous,
She is [2]naive, and [b]knows nothing.
14 And she sits at the doorway of her house,
On a seat by [a]the high places of the city,
15 Calling to those who pass by,
Who are making their paths straight:
16 "[a]Whoever is [1]naive, let him turn in here,"
And to him who lacks [2]understanding she says,
17 "Stolen [a]water is sweet;
And [b]bread *eaten* in secret is pleasant."
18 But he does not know that the [1]dead are there,
That her guests are in the [a]depths of Sheol.

CHAPTER 10

THE [a]proverbs of Solomon.
[b]A wise son makes a father glad,
But [c]a foolish son is a grief to his mother.
2 [1a]Ill-gotten gains do not profit,
But righteousness delivers from death.
3 The LORD [a]will not allow the [1]righteous to hunger,
But He [b]will thrust *aside* the craving of the wicked.
4 Poor is he who works with a negligent hand,
But the hand of the diligent makes rich.
5 He who gathers in summer is a son who acts wisely,
But he who sleeps in harvest is a son who acts shamefully.
6 [a]Blessings are on the head of the righteous,
But [b]the mouth of the wicked conceals violence.
7 The [a]memory of the righteous is blessed,
But [b]the name of the wicked will rot.
8 The [a]wise of heart will receive commands,
But [1]a babbling fool will be thrown down.
9 He [a]who walks in integrity walks securely,
But [b]he who perverts his ways will be found out.
10 He [a]who winks the eye causes trouble,
And [1b]a babbling fool will be thrown down.

6 [1]Or, *the simple ones* [a]Prov. 9:11; 8:35 [b]Ezek. 11:20; 37:24

7 [1]Lit., *a blemish* [a]Prov. 23:9

8 [a]Prov. 15:12; Matt. 7:6 [b]Prov. 10:8; Ps. 141:5

9 [a]Prov. 1:5

11 [a]Prov. 3:16; 10:27

12 [a]Prov. 14:14; Job 22:2 [b]Prov. 19:29

13 [1]Or, *foolish woman* [2]Lit., *simple* [a]Prov. 7:11 [b]Prov. 5:6

14 [a]Prov. 9:3

16 [1]Lit., *simple* [2]Lit., *heart* [a]Prov. 9:4

17 [a]Prov. 5:15 [b]Prov. 20:17

18 [1]Lit., *departed spirits* [a]Prov. 7:27

1 [a]Prov. 1:1 [b]Prov. 15:20; 29:3 [c]Prov. 17:25; 29:15

2 [1]Lit., *Treasures of wickedness* [a]Prov. 11:4; 21:6; Ps. 49:6, 7; Ezek. 7:19; Luke 12:19, 20

3 [1]Lit., *soul of the righteous* [a]Prov. 28:25; Ps. 34:9, 10; 37:25; Matt. 6:33 [b]Prov. 28:9; Ps. 112:10

6 [a]Prov. 28:20 [b]Prov. 10:11; Obad. 10

7 [a]Ps. 112:6 [b]Ps. 9:5, 6; 109:13; Eccles. 8:10

8 [1]Lit., *the foolish of lips* [a]Prov. 9:8; Matt. 7:24

9 [a]Prov. 3:23; 28:18; Ps. 23:4; Is. 33:15, 16 [b]Prov. 26:26; Matt. 10:26; 1 Tim. 5:25

10 [1]Lit., *the foolish of lips* [a]Prov. 6:13; Ps. 35:19 [b]Prov. 10:8

11 The [a]mouth of the righteous is a fountain of life,
But [b]the mouth of the wicked conceals violence.
12 Hatred stirs up strife,
But [a]love covers all transgressions.
13 On [a]the lips of the discerning, wisdom is found,
But [b]a rod is for the back of him who lacks [1]understanding.
14 Wise men [a]store up knowledge,
But with [b]the mouth of the foolish ruin is at hand.
15 The [a]rich man's wealth is his [1]fortress,
The [b]ruin of the poor is their poverty.
16 The [1a]wages of the righteous is life,
The income of the wicked, punishment.
17 He [a]is *on* the path of life who heeds instruction,
But he who forsakes reproof goes astray.
18 He [a]who conceals hatred *has* lying lips,
And he who spreads slander is a fool.
19 When there are [a]many words, transgression is unavoidable,
But [b]he who restrains his lips is wise.
20 The tongue of the righteous is *as* [a]choice silver,
The heart of the wicked is *worth* little.
21 The [a]lips of the righteous feed many,
But the fools [b]die for lack of [1]understanding.
22 It is the [a]blessing of the LORD that makes rich,
And he adds no sorrow to it.
23 Doing wickedness is like [a]sport to a fool;
And *so is* wisdom to a man of understanding.
24 What [a]the wicked fears will come upon him,
And the [b]desire of the righteous will be granted.
25 When the [a]whirlwind passes, the wicked is no more,
But the [b]righteous *has* an everlasting foundation.
26 Like vinegar to the teeth and smoke to the eyes,
So is the [a]lazy one to those who send him.
27 The [a]fear of the LORD prolongs [1]life,
But the [b]years of the wicked will be shortened.
28 The [a]hope of the righteous is gladness,
But the [b]expectation of the wicked perishes.
29 The [a]way of the LORD is a stronghold to the upright,
But [b]ruin to the workers of iniquity.
30 The [a]righteous will never be shaken,
But [b]the wicked will not dwell in the land.
31 The [a]mouth of the righteous flows with wisdom,
But the [b]perverted tongue will be cut out.
32 The lips of the righteous bring forth [a]what is acceptable,
But the [b]mouth of the wicked, what is perverted.

CHAPTER 11

A [a]FALSE balance is an abomination to the LORD,
But a [b]just weight is His delight.
2 When [a]pride comes, then comes dishonor,
But with the humble is wisdom.
3 The [a]integrity of the upright will guide them,
But the [b]falseness of the treacherous will destroy them.

11 [a]Prov. 13:14; 18:4; Ps. 37:30 [b]Prov. 10:6

12 [a]Prov. 17:9; 1 Cor. 13:4-7; James 5:20; 1 Pet. 4:8

13 [1]Lit., *heart* [a]Prov. 10:31 [b]Prov. 19:29; 26:3

14 [a]Prov. 9:9 [b]Prov. 10:8, 10; 13:3; 18:7; 21:15

15 [1]Lit., *strong city* [a]Prov. 18:11; Job 31:24; Ps. 52:7 [b]Prov. 19:7

16 [1]Or, *work* [a]Prov. 11:18, 19

17 [a]Prov. 6:23

18 [a]Prov. 26:24

19 [a]Prov. 18:21; Job 11:2; Eccles. 5:3 [b]Prov. 17:27; James 1:19; 3:2

20 [a]Prov. 8:19

21 [1]Lit., *heart* [a]Prov. 10:11 [b]Prov. 5:23; Hos. 4:6

22 [a]Prov. 8:21; Gen. 24:35; 26:12; Deut. 8:18

23 [a]Prov. 2:14; 15:21

24 [a]Prov. 1:27; Job 15:21; Is. 66:4 [b]Prov. 15:8; Ps. 145:19; Matt. 5:6; 1 John 5:14, 15

25 [a]Prov. 12:7; Job 21:18; Ps. 58:9 [b]Prov. 12:3; Ps. 15:5; Matt. 7:24, 25

26 [a]Prov. 26:6

27 [1]Lit., *days* [a]Prov. 3:2; 9:11; 14:27 [b]Job 15:32, 33; 22:16; Ps. 55:23

28 [a]Prov. 11:23 [b]Prov. 11:7; Job 8:13; 11:20

29 [a]Prov. 13:6 [b]Prov. 21:15

30 [a]Prov. 2:21; Ps. 37:29; 125:1 [b]Prov. 2:22

31 [a]Prov. 10:13; Ps. 37:30 [b]Prov. 17:20

32 [a]Eccles. 12:10 [b]Prov. 2:12; 6:12

1 [a]Prov. 20:10, 23; Lev. 19:35, 36; Deut. 25:13-16; Mic. 6:11 [b]Prov. 16:11

2 [a]Prov. 16:18; 18:12; 29:23

3 [a]Prov. 13:6 [b]Prov. 19:3; 22:12

4 [a]Riches do not profit in the day of wrath,
But [b]righteousness delivers from death.
5 The [a]righteousness of the blameless will smooth his way,
But [b]the wicked will fall by his own wickedness.
6 The righteousness of the upright will deliver them,
But the treacherous will [a]be caught by *their own* greed.
7 When a wicked man dies, *his* [a]expectation will perish,
And the [b]hope of strong men perishes.
8 The righteous is delivered from trouble,
But the wicked [1]takes his place.
9 With *his* [a]mouth the godless man destroys his neighbor,
But through knowledge the [b]righteous will be delivered.
10 When it [a]goes well with the righteous, the city rejoices,
And when the wicked perish, there is glad shouting.
11 By the blessing of the upright a city is exalted,
But by the mouth of the wicked it is torn down.
12 He who despises his neighbor lacks [1]sense,
But a man of understanding keeps silent.
13 He [a]who goes about as a talebearer reveals secrets,
But he who is [1]trustworthy [b]conceals a matter.
14 Where there is no [a]guidance, the people fall,
But in abundance of counselors there is [1]victory.
15 He who is [a]surety for a stranger will surely suffer for it,
But he who hates [1]going surety is safe.
16 A [a]gracious woman attains honor,
And violent men attain riches.
17 The [a]merciful man does [1]himself good,
But the cruel man [2]does himself harm.
18 The wicked earns deceptive wages,
But he who [a]sows righteousness *gets* a true reward.
19 He who is steadfast in [a]righteousness *will attain* to life,
And [b]he who pursues evil *will bring about* his own death.
20 The perverse in heart are an abomination to the LORD,
But the [a]blameless in *their* [1]walk are His [b]delight.
21 [1]Assuredly, the evil man will not go unpunished,
But the [2]descendants of the righteous will be delivered.
22 *As* a [a]ring of gold in a swine's snout,
So is a beautiful woman who lacks [1]discretion.
23 The desire of the righteous is only good,
But the [a]expectation of the wicked is wrath.
24 There is one who scatters, yet increases all the more,
And there is one who withholds what is justly due, but *it results* only in want.
25 The [1a]generous man will be [2]prosperous,
And he who [b]waters will himself be watered.
26 He who withholds grain, the [a]people will curse him,
But [b]blessing will be on the head of him who [c]sells *it*.
27 He who diligently seeks good seeks favor,
But [a]he who searches after evil, it will come to him.
28 He who [a]trusts in his riches will fall,
But [b]the righteous will flourish like the *green* leaf.

4 [a]Prov. 10:2; Ezek. 7:19; Zeph. 1:18 [b]Gen. 7:1
5 [a]Prov. 3:6 [b]Prov. 5:22
6 [a]Ps. 7:15, 16; 9:15; Eccles. 10:8
7 [a]Prov. 10:28 [b]Job 8:13, 14
8 [1]Lit., *enters*
9 [a]Prov. 16:29 [b]Prov. 11:6
10 [a]Prov. 28:12
12 [1]Lit., *heart*
13 [1]Lit., *faithful of spirit* [a]Prov. 20:19; Lev. 19:16; 1 Tim. 5:13 [b]Prov. 19:11
14 [1]Lit., *deliverance* [a]Prov. 15:22; 20:18; 24:6
15 [1]Lit., *those who strike hands* [a]Prov. 6:1; 27:13
16 [a]Prov. 31:28, 30
17 [1]Lit., *good to his own soul* [2]Lit., *troubles his flesh* [a]Matt. 5:7; 25:34-36
18 [a]Hos. 10:12; Gal. 6:8, 9; James 3:18
19 [a]Prov. 10:16; 12:28; 19:23 [b]Prov. 21:16; Rom. 6:23; James 1:15
20 [1]Lit., *way* [a]Prov. 13:6; Ps. 119:1 [b]1 Chr. 29:17
21 [1]Lit., *Hand to hand* [2]Lit., *seed*
22 [1]Lit., *taste* [a]Gen. 27:47
23 [a]Prov. 10:28; Rom. 2:8, 9
25 [1]Lit., *soul of blessing* [2]Lit., *made fat* [a]Prov. 3:9, 10; 2 Cor. 9:6, 7 [b]Matt. 5:7
26 [a]Prov. 24:24 [b]Job 29:13 [c]Gen. 42:6
27 [a]Esth. 7:10; Ps. 7:15, 16; 57:6
28 [a]Ps. 49:6; Mark 10:24; 1 Tim. 6:17 [b]Ps. 1:3; 92:12; Jer. 17:8

29 [a]Prov. 15:27 [b]Eccles. 5:16 [c]Prov. 14:19

30 [1]Lit., *takes* [a]Prov. 3:18 [b]Prov. 14:25; Dan. 12:3; 1 Cor. 9:19-22; James 5:20

31 [a]Prov. 13:21; 2 Sam. 22:21, 25

1 [1]Or, *instruction*

2 [1]Lit., of *evil devices* [a]Prov. 3:4; 8:35

3 [a]Prov. 11:5 [b]Prov. 10:25

4 [1]Or, *virtuous* [a]Prov. 31:11; 1 Cor. 11:7 [b]Prov. 14:30; Hab. 3:16

6 [a]Prov. 1:11, 16 [b]Prov. 14:3

7 [a]Prov. 10:25; Job 34:25 [b]Matt. 7:24-27

8 [1]Lit., *heart*

10 [a]Deut. 25:4

11 [1]Lit., *heart*

12 [1]Lit., *net* [a]Prov. 21:10 [b]Prov. 11:30

13 [1]Lit., *In the transgression of the lips is an evil snare* [a]Prov. 11:8; 21:23; 2 Pet. 2:9

14 [1]Lit., *mouth* [a]Prov. 13:2; 15:23; 18:20 [b]Prov. 1:31; 24:12; Job 34:11; Is. 3:10, 11; Hos. 4:9

15 [a]Prov. 14:12; 16:2; 21:2

16 [a]Prov. 14:33; 27:3; 29:11

17 [1]Lit., *breathes*

18 [a]Ps. 57:4 [b]Prov. 4:22; 15:4

19 [a]Prov. 19:9; Ps. 52:4, 5

21 [a]Prov. 1:33; Ps. 91:10; 121:7; 1 Pet. 3:13

23 [a]Prov. 10:14; 11:13; 13:16; 15:2; 29:11

29 He who [a]troubles his own house will [b]inherit wind,
And [c]the foolish will be servant to the wisehearted.
30 The fruit of the righteous is [a]a tree of life,
And [b]he who is wise [1]wins souls.
31 If [a]the righteous will be rewarded in the earth,
How much more the wicked and the sinner!

Chapter 12

WHOEVER loves [1]discipline loves knowledge,
But he who hates reproof is stupid.
2 A [a]good man will obtain favor from the LORD,
But He will condemn a man [1]who devises evil.
3 A man will [a]not be established by wickedness,
But the root of the [b]righteous will not be moved.
4 An [1a]excellent wife is the crown of her husband,
But she who shames *him* is as [b]rottenness in his bones.
5 The thoughts of the righteous are just,
But the counsels of the wicked are deceitful.
6 The [a]words of the wicked lie in wait for blood,
But the [b]mouth of the upright will deliver them.
7 The [a]wicked are overthrown and are no more,
But the [b]house of the righteous will stand.
8 A man will be praised according to his insight,
But one of perverse [1]mind will be despised.
9 Better is he who is lightly esteemed and has a servant,
Than he who honors himself and lacks bread.
10 A [a]righteous man has regard for the life of his beast,
But the compassion of the wicked is cruel.
11 He who tills his land will have plenty of bread,
But he who pursues vain *things* lacks [1]sense.
12 The [a]wicked desires the [1]booty of evil men,
But the root of the righteous [b]yields *fruit*.
13 [1]An evil man is ensnared by the transgression of his lips,
But the [a]righteous will escape from trouble.
14 A man will be [a]satisfied with good by the fruit of his [1]words,
And the [b]deeds of a man's hands will return to him.
15 The [a]way of a fool is right in his own eyes,
But a wise man is he who listens to counsel.
16 A [a]fool's vexation is known at once,
But a prudent man conceals dishonor.
17 He who [1]speaks truth tells what is right,
But a false witness, deceit.
18 There is one who [a]speaks rashly like the thrusts of a sword,
But the [b]tongue of the wise brings healing.
19 Truthful lips will be established forever,
But a [a]lying tongue is only for a moment.
20 Deceit is in the heart of those who devise evil,
But counselors of peace have joy.
21 [a]No harm befalls the righteous,
But the wicked are filled with trouble.
22 Lying lips are an abomination to the LORD,
But those who deal faithfully are His delight.
23 A [a]prudent man conceals knowledge,
But the heart of fools proclaims folly.

24 The hand of the diligent will rule,
But the [1]slack *hand* will be [a]put to forced labor.
25 [a]Anxiety in the heart of a man weighs it down,
But a [b]good word makes it glad.
26 The righteous is a guide to his neighbor,
But the way of the wicked leads them astray.
27 A [1]slothful man does not [2]roast his prey,
But the [a]precious possession of a man *is* diligence.
28 In the way of righteousness is life,
And in *its* pathway there is no death.

CHAPTER 13

A [a]WISE son *accepts his* father's discipline,
But a [b]scoffer does not listen to rebuke.
2 From the fruit of a man's mouth he [1a]enjoys good,
But the [2]desire of the treacherous is [b]violence.
3 The one who [a]guards his mouth preserves his life;
The one who [b]opens wide his lips [1]comes to ruin.
4 The soul of the sluggard craves and *gets* nothing,
But the soul of the diligent is made fat.
5 A righteous man hates falsehood,
But a wicked man [1a]acts disgustingly and shamefully.
6 Righteousness guards the [1]one whose way is blameless,
But wickedness subverts the [2]sinner.
7 There is one who [a]pretends to be rich, but has nothing;
Another [1]pretends to be [b]poor, but has great wealth.
8 The ransom of a man's life is his riches,
But the poor hears no rebuke.
9 The [a]light of the righteous [1]rejoices,
But the [b]lamp of the wicked goes out.
10 Through presumption [1]comes nothing but strife,
But with those who receive counsel is wisdom.
11 Wealth *obtained* by [1]fraud dwindles,
But the one who gathers [2]by labor increases *it*.
12 Hope deferred *makes* the heart sick,
But desire [1]fulfilled is a tree of life.
13 The one who [a]despises the word will be [1]in debt to it,
But the one who fears the commandment will be [b]rewarded.
14 The [1]teaching of the wise is a [a]fountain of life,
To turn aside from the [b]snares of death.
15 [a]Good understanding produces favor,
But the way of the treacherous is hard.
16 Every prudent man acts with knowledge,
But a fool [1]displays folly.
17 A wicked messenger falls into adversity,
But [a]a faithful envoy *brings* healing.
18 Poverty and shame *will come* to him who [a]neglects [1]discipline,
But he who regards reproof will be honored.
19 Desire realized is sweet to the soul,
But it is an abomination to fools to depart from evil.
20 [a]He who walks with wise men will be wise,
But the [b]companion of fools will suffer harm.

24 [1]Lit., *slackness* [a]Gen. 49:15; Judg. 1:28; 1 Kin. 9:21
25 [a]Prov. 15:13 [b]Is. 50:4
27 [1]Lit., *slackness* [2]Or, *catch* [a]Prov. 10:4; 13:4
1 [a]Prov. 10:1; 15:20 [b]Prov. 9:7, 8; 15:12
2 [1]Lit., *eats* [2]Lit., *soul* [a]Prov. 12:14 [b]Prov. 1:31; Hos. 10:13
3 [1]Lit., *ruin is his* [a]Prov. 18:21; 21:23; James 3:2 [b]Prov. 18:7; 20:19
5 [1]Lit., *causes a bad odor and causes shame* [a]Prov. 3:35
6 [1]Lit., *blamelessness of way* [2]Lit., *sin*
7 [1]Lit., *impoverishes himself* [a]Prov. 11:24; Luke 12:20, 21 [b]Luke 12:33; 2 Cor. 6:10; James 2:5
9 [1]I.e., shines brightly [a]Prov. 4:18; Job 29:3 [b]Prov. 24:20; Job 18:5
10 [1]Lit., *gives*
11 [1]Lit., *vanity* [2]Or, *gradually;* lit., *on the hand*
12 [1]Lit., *coming*
13 [1]Lit., *pledged to it* [a]Num. 15:31; 2 Chr. 36:16 [b]Prov. 13:21
14 [1]Or, *law* [a]Prov. 10:11; 14:27 [b]Ps. 18:5
15 [a]Prov. 3:4; Ps. 111:10
16 [1]Lit., *spreads out*
17 [a]Prov. 25:13
18 [1]Or, *instruction* [a]Prov. 15:5, 32
20 [a]Prov. 2:20; 15:31 [b]Prov. 28:19

21 [a]Adversity pursues sinners,
But the [b]righteous will be rewarded with prosperity.
22 A good man [a]leaves an inheritance to his [1]children's children,
And the [b]wealth of the sinner is stored up for the righteous.
23 Abundant food *is in* the fallow ground of the poor,
But [1]it is swept away by injustice.
24 He who [a]spares his rod hates his son,
But he who loves him [1b]disciplines him diligently.
25 The [a]righteous [1]has enough to satisfy his appetite,
But the stomach of the [b]wicked is in want.

Chapter 14

THE wise woman builds her house,
But the foolish tears it down with her own hands.
2 He who [a]walks in his uprightness fears the LORD,
But he who is [b]crooked in his ways despises Him.
3 In the mouth of the foolish is a rod [1]for *his* back,
But the lips of the wise will preserve them.
4 Where no oxen are, the manger is clean,
But much increase comes by the strength of the ox.
5 A [a]faithful witness will not lie,
But a [b]false witness [1c]speaks lies.
6 A scoffer seeks wisdom, and *finds* none,
But knowledge is easy to him who has understanding.
7 Leave the [a]presence of a fool,
Or you will not [1]discern [2]words of knowledge.
8 The wisdom of the prudent is to understand his way,
But the folly of fools is deceit.
9 [a]Fools mock at [1]sin,
But [b]among the upright there is [2]good will.
10 The heart knows its own [a]bitterness,
And a stranger does not share its joy.
11 The house of the wicked will be destroyed,
But the tent of the upright will flourish.
12 There [a]is a way *which seems* right to a man,
But its [b]end is the way of death.
13 Even in laughter the heart may be in pain,
And the [a]end of joy may be grief.
14 The backslider in heart will have his [a]fill of his own ways,
But a good man will [b]*be satisfied* [1]with his.
15 The [1]naive believes everything,
But the prudent man considers his steps.
16 A wise man [1]is cautious and [a]turns away from evil,
But a fool is arrogant and careless.
17 A quick-tempered man acts foolishly,
And a man of evil devices is hated.
18 The [1]naive inherit folly,
But the prudent are crowned with knowledge.
19 The [a]evil will bow down before the good,
And the wicked at the gates of the righteous.
20 The poor is hated even by his neighbor,
But those who love the rich are many.

21 [a]Ps. 32:10; 54:5; Is. 47:11 [b]Prov. 13:13; 11:31; Is. 3:10

22 [1]Lit., *sons' sons* [a]Ezra 9:12; Ps. 37:25 [b]Prov. 28:8; Job 27:16, 17; Eccles. 2:26

23 [1]Lit., *there is what is swept*

24 [1]Lit., *seeks him diligently with discipline* [a]Prov. 19:18; 22:15; 23:13, 14; 29:15, 17 [b]Prov. 3:12; Deut. 8:5; Heb. 12:7

25 [1]Lit., *eats to the satisfaction of his soul* [a]Prov. 10:3; Ps. 34:10; 103:5; 132:15 [b]Prov. 13:18; Luke 15:14

2 [a]Prov. 19:1; 28:6 [b]Prov. 2:15

3 [1]Lit., *of pride*

5 [1]Lit., *breathes out* [a]Rev. 1:5; 3:14 [b]Prov. 6:19; 12:17; Ex. 23:1; Deut. 19:16 [c]Prov. 19:5

7 [1]Lit., *know* [2]Lit., *lips* [a]Prov. 23:9

9 [1]Lit., *guilt* [2]Or, the *favor* of God [a]Is. 1:11; Hos. 4:19 [b]Prov. 3:34; 11:20

10 [a]1 Sam. 1:10; Job 21:25

12 [a]Prov. 12:15; 16:25 [b]Rom. 6:21

13 [a]Eccles. 2:1, 2

14 [1]Lit., *from himself* [a]Prov. 1:31; 12:21 [b]Prov. 12:14; 18:20

15 [1]Lit., *simple*

16 [1]Lit., *fears* [a]Prov. 3:7; 22:3; Job 28:28; Ps. 34:14

18 [1]Lit., *simple*

19 [a]Prov. 11:29; 1 Sam. 2:36

21 He who [a]despises his neighbor sins,
But [b]happy is he who is gracious to the [1]poor.
22 Will they not go astray who [a]devise evil?
But kindness and truth *will be to* those who devise good.
23 In all labor there is profit,
But [1]mere talk *leads* only to poverty.
24 The [a]crown of the wise is their riches,
But the folly of fools is foolishness.
25 A truthful witness saves lives,
But he who [1a]speaks lies is [2]treacherous.
26 In the [1a]fear of the LORD there is strong confidence,
And his children will have refuge.
27 The [1]fear of the LORD is a fountain of life,
That one may avoid the snares of death.
28 In a [a]multitude of people is a king's glory,
But in the dearth of people is a prince's ruin.
29 He who is [a]slow to anger has great understanding,
But he who is [1]quick-tempered exalts folly.
30 A [a]tranquil heart is life to the body,
But passion is [b]rottenness to the bones.
31 He who oppresses the poor reproaches his Maker,
But he who is gracious to the needy honors Him.
32 The wicked is [a]thrust down by his [1]wrong-doing,
But the [b]righteous has a refuge when he dies.
33 Wisdom rests in the heart of one who has understanding,
But in the [1]bosom of fools it is made known.
34 Righteousness exalts a nation,
But sin is a disgrace to *any* people.
35 The king's favor is toward a servant who acts wisely,
But his anger is toward him who acts shamefully.

CHAPTER 15

A [a]GENTLE answer turns away wrath,
But a [1b]harsh word stirs up anger.
2 The [a]tongue of the wise makes knowledge [1]acceptable,
But the [b]mouth of fools spouts folly.
3 The [a]eyes of the LORD are in every place,
Watching the evil and the good.
4 A [1]soothing tongue is a tree of life,
But perversion in it [2]crushes the spirit.
5 A fool [1]rejects his father's discipline,
But he who regards reproof is prudent.
6 Much wealth is *in* the house of the [a]righteous,
But trouble is in the income of the wicked.
7 The lips of the wise spread knowledge,
But the hearts of fools are not so.
8 The [a]sacrifice of the wicked is an abomination to the LORD,
But [b]the prayer of the upright is His delight.
9 The way of the wicked is an abomination to the LORD,
But He loves him who pursues righteousness.
10 Stern discipline is for him who forsakes the way;
He who hates reproof will die.

21 [1]Or, *afflicted* [a]Prov. 11:12 [b]Prov. 19:17; 28:8; Ps. 41:1
22 [a]Prov. 3:29; 12:2; Ps. 36:4; Mic. 2:1
23 [1]Lit., *word of lips*
24 [a]Prov. 10:22; 13:8; 21:20
25 [1]Lit., *breathes out* [2]Lit., *treachery* [a]Prov. 14:5
26 [1]Or, *reverence* [a]Prov. 18:10; 19:23; Is. 33:6
27 [1]Or, *reverence*
28 [a]1 Kin. 4:20
29 [1]Lit., *short of spirit* [a]Prov. 16:32; 19:11; Eccles. 7:9; James 1:19
30 [a]Prov. 15:13 [b]Prov. 12:4; Hab. 3:16
32 [1]Or, *calamity* [a]Prov. 6:15; 24:16 [b]Gen. 49:18; Ps. 16:11; 17:15; 37:37; 73:24; 2 Cor. 1:9; 5:8; 2 Tim. 4:18
33 [1]Lit., *midst*
1 [1]Lit., *painful* [a]Prov. 15:18; 25:15; Judg. 8:1-3 [b]1 Sam. 25:10-13
2 [1]Lit., *good* [a]Prov. 15:7 [b]Prov. 15:28; 12:23; 13:16
3 [a]Job 31:4; Heb. 4:13
4 [1]Lit., *healing* [2]Lit., *is the crushing of the spirit.*
5 [1]Or, *despises*
6 [a]Prov. 8:21
8 [a]Prov. 21:27; Eccles. 5:1; Is. 1:11; Jer. 6:20; Mic. 6:7 [b]Prov. 15:29

11 [1a]Sheol and [2]Abaddon *lie open* before the LORD,
How much more the [b]hearts of [3]men!
12 A [a]scoffer does not love one who reproves him,
He will not go to the wise.
13 A [a]joyful heart makes a [1]cheerful face,
But [2]when the heart is [b]sad, the [c]spirit is broken.
14 The [a]mind of the intelligent seeks knowledge,
But the mouth of fools feeds on folly.
15 All the days of the afflicted are bad,
But a [1]cheerful heart *has* a continual feast.
16 [a]Better is a little with the [1]fear of the LORD,
Than great treasure and turmoil with it.
17 [a]Better is a [1]dish of [2]vegetables where love is,
Than a [b]fattened ox and hatred with it.
18 A [a]hot-tempered man stirs up strife,
But the [b]slow to anger [c]pacifies contention.
19 The way of the sluggard is as a hedge of thorns,
But the path of the upright is a highway.
20 A [a]wise son makes a father glad,
But a foolish man [b]despises his mother.
21 Folly is joy to him who lacks [1]sense,
But a man of understanding [a]walks straight.
22 Without consultation, plans are frustrated,
But with many counselors they [1]succeed.
23 A [a]man has joy in an [1]apt answer,
And how delightful is a timely [b]word!
24 The [a]path of life *leads* upward for the wise,
That he may keep away from [1]Sheol below.
25 The LORD will [a]tear down the house of the proud,
But He will [b]establish the boundary of the [c]widow.
26 Evil plans are an abomination to the LORD,
But pleasant words are pure.
27 He who [a]profits illicitly troubles his own house,
But he who [b]hates bribes will live.
28 The heart of the righteous [a]ponders how to answer,
But the [b]mouth of the wicked pours out evil things.
29 The LORD is [a]far from the wicked,
But He [b]hears the prayer of the righteous.
30 [1]Bright eyes gladden the heart;
Good news puts fat on the bones.
31 He whose ear listens to the life-giving reproof
Will dwell among the wise.
32 He who [a]neglects discipline [b]despises himself,
But he who [c]listens to reproof acquires [1]understanding.
33 The [1]fear of the LORD is the instruction for wisdom,
And before honor *comes* humility.

CHAPTER 16

THE [a]plans of the heart belong to man,
But the answer of the tongue is from the LORD.
2 All the ways of a man are clean in his own sight,
But the LORD weighs the [1]motives.
3 [1a]Commit your works to the LORD,
And your plans will be established.
4 The LORD [a]has made everything for [1]its own purpose,
Even the [b]wicked for the day of evil.

11 [1]I.e., the nether world [2]I.e., destruction [3]Lit., *sons of Adam* [a]Job 26:6; Ps. 139:8 [b]1 Sam. 16:7; 2 Chr. 6:30; Ps. 44:21; Acts 1:24

12 [a]Prov. 13:1; Amos 5:10

13 [1]Lit., *good* [2]Lit., *in sadness of heart* [a]Prov. 17:22 [b]Prov. 12:25 [c]Prov. 17:22; 18:14

14 [a]Prov. 18:15

15 [1]Lit., *good*

16 [1]Or, *reverence* [a]Prov. 16:8; Ps. 37:16; Eccles. 4:6; 1 Tim. 6:6

17 [1]Or, *portion* [2]Or, *herbs* [a]Prov. 17:1 [b]Matt. 22:4; Luke 15:23

18 [a]Prov. 16:28; 26:21; 29:22 [b]Prov. 14:29 [c]Prov. 16:14; Gen. 13:8; Eccles. 10:4

20 [a]Prov. 10:1; 29:3 [b]Prov. 30:17

21 [1]Lit., *heart* [a]Prov. 14:8; Eph. 5:15

22 [1]Or, *are established*

23 [1]Lit., *answer of his mouth* [a]Prov. 12:14 [b]Prov. 25:11; Is. 50:4

24 [1]I.e., the nether world [a]Is. 4:18

25 [a]Prov. 12:7; 14:11 [b]Prov. 23:10; Deut. 19:14 [c]Ps. 68:5; 146:9

27 [a]Prov. 1:19; 28:25; 1 Tim. 6:10 [b]Ex. 23:8; Deut. 16:19; 1 Sam. 12:3; Is. 33:15

28 [a]1 Pet. 3:15 [b]Prov. 15:2; 10:32

29 [a]Prov. 1:28; Ps. 18:41 [b]Ps. 145:18, 19

30 [1]Lit., *the light of the eyes*

32 [1]Lit., *heart* [a]Prov. 1:7; 8:33 [b]Prov. 8:36 [c]Prov. 15:5

33 [1]Or, *reverence*

1 [a]Prov. 16:9; 19:21

2 [1]Lit., *spirits*

3 [1]Lit., *Roll* [a]Prov. 3:6; Ps. 37:5; 55:22; 1 Pet. 5:7

4 [1]Or, *His* [a]Gen. 1:31; Eccles. 3:11 [b]Job 31:30; Rom. 9:22

5 Everyone who is proud in heart is an abomination to the LORD;
Assuredly, he will not be unpunished.
6 By [a]lovingkindness and truth iniquity is atoned for,
And by the [1b]fear of the LORD one keeps away from evil.
7 When a man's ways are pleasing to the LORD,
He [a]makes even his enemies to be at peace with him.
8 Better is a little with righteousness
Than great income with injustice.
9 The mind of [a]man plans his way,
But [b]the LORD directs his steps.
10 A divine [a]decision is in the lips of the king;
His mouth should not [1]err in judgment.
11 A [a]just balance and scales belong to the LORD;
All the [1]weights of the bag are His [2]concern.
12 It is an abomination for kings to commit wickedness,
For a [a]throne is established on righteousness.
13 Righteous lips are the delight of kings,
And he who speaks right is loved.
14 The wrath of a king is *as* messengers of death,
But a wise man will appease it.
15 In the light of a king's face is life,
And his favor is like a cloud with the [1a]spring rain.
16 How much [a]better it is to get wisdom than gold!
And to get understanding is to be chosen above silver.
17 The highway of the upright is to depart from evil;
He who watches his way preserves his [1]life.
18 [a]Pride *goes* before destruction,
And a haughty spirit before stumbling.
19 It is better to be of a [a]humble spirit with the lowly,
Than to [b]divide the spoil with the proud.
20 He who gives attention to the word shall [a]find good,
And [b]blessed is he who trusts in the LORD.
21 The [a]wise in heart will be called discerning,
And sweetness of [1]speech [b]increases [2]persuasiveness.
22 Understanding is a fountain of life to him who has it,
But the discipline of fools is folly.
23 The [a]heart of the wise teaches his mouth,
And adds [1]persuasiveness to his lips.
24 [a]Pleasant words are a honeycomb,
Sweet to the soul and [b]healing to the bones.
25 There is a way *which seems* right to a man,
But its end is the way of death.
26 A worker's appetite works for him,
For his [1]hunger urges him *on*.
27 A [a]worthless man digs up evil,
While [1]his words are as a [b]scorching fire.
28 A perverse man spreads strife,
And a slanderer separates intimate friends.
29 A man of violence [a]entices his neighbor,
And leads him in a way that is not good.
30 He who winks his eyes *does so* to devise perverse things;
He who compresses his lips brings evil to pass.
31 A [a]gray head is a crown of glory;
It [b]is found in the way of righteousness.

6 [1]Or, *reverence* [a]Dan. 4:27; Luke 11:41 [b]Prov. 8:13; 14:16

7 [a]Gen. 33:4; 2 Chr. 17:10

9 [a]Prov. 16:1; 19:21 [b]Prov. 20:24; Ps. 37:23; Jer. 10:23

10 [1]Lit., *be unfaithful* [a]1 Kin. 3:28

11 [1]Lit., *stones* [2]Lit., *work* [a]Prov. 11:1

12 [a]Prov. 25:5

15 [1]Lit., *latter* [a]Job 29:23

16 [a]Prov. 8:10, 19

17 [1]Lit., *soul*

18 [a]Prov. 11:2; 18:12; Jer. 49:16; Obad. 3, 4

19 [a]Prov. 3:34; 29:23; Is. 57:15 [b]Prov. 1:13, 14; Ex. 15:9; Judg. 5:30

20 [a]Prov. 19:8 [b]Ps. 2:12; 34:8; Jer. 17:7

21 [1]Lit., *lips* [2]Or, *learning* [a]Hos. 14:9 [b]Prov. 16:23

23 [1]Or, *learning* [a]Prov. 15:28; Ps. 37:30; Matt. 12:34

24 [a]Prov. 15:26; 24:13, 14; Ps. 19:10 [b]Prov. 4:22; 17:22

26 [1]Lit., *mouth*

27 [1]Lit., *on his lips* [a]Prov. 6:12, 14, 18 [b]James 3:6

29 [a]Prov. 1:10; 12:26

31 [a]Prov. 20:29 [b]Prov. 3:1, 2

32 He who is slow to anger is better than the mighty,
And he who rules his spirit, than he who captures a city.
33 The [a]lot is cast into the lap,
But its every [b]decision is from the LORD.

CHAPTER 17

[a]BETTER is a dry morsel and quietness with it
Than a house full of [1]feasting with strife.
2 A servant who acts wisely will rule over a son who acts shamefully,
And will share in the inheritance among brothers.
3 The [a]refining pot is for silver and the furnace for gold,
But [b]the LORD tests hearts.
4 An [a]evildoer listens to wicked lips,
A [1]liar pays attention to a destructive tongue.
5 He who mocks the [a]poor reproaches his Maker;
He who [b]rejoices at calamity will not go unpunished.
6 [a]Grandchildren are the crown of old men,
And the [b]glory of sons is their fathers.
7 [1a]Excellent speech is not fitting for a fool;
Much less are [b]lying lips to a prince.
8 A [a]bribe is a [1]charm in the sight of its owner;
Wherever he turns, he prospers.
9 He who [a]covers a transgression seeks love,
But he who repeats a matter [b]separates intimate friends.
10 A rebuke goes deeper into one who has understanding
Than a hundred blows into a fool.
11 A rebellious man seeks only evil,
So a cruel messenger will be sent against him.
12 Let a [a]man meet a [b]bear robbed of her cubs,
Rather than a fool in his folly.
13 He who [a]returns evil for good,
[b]Evil will not depart from his house.
14 The beginning of strife is *like* letting out water,
So [a]abandon the quarrel before it breaks out.
15 He who [a]justifies the wicked, and he who condemns the righteous,
Both of them alike are an abomination to the LORD.
16 Why is there a price in the hand of a fool to [a]buy wisdom,
When [1]he has no sense?
17 A [a]friend loves at all times,
And a brother is born for adversity.
18 A man lacking in [1]sense [2a]pledges,
And becomes surety in the presence of his neighbor.
19 He who [a]loves transgression loves strife;
He who [b]raises his door seeks destruction.
20 He who has a crooked [1]mind [a]finds no good,
And he who is [b]perverted in his language falls into evil.
21 He who [a]begets a fool *does so* to his sorrow,
And the father of a fool has no joy.
22 A [a]joyful heart [1]is good medicine,
But a broken spirit [b]dries up the bones.

16:33 [a]Prov. 18:18 [b]Prov. 29:26

17:1 [1]Lit., *sacrifices of strife* [a]Prov. 15:17

3 [a]Prov. 27:21 [b]Prov. 15:11; 1 Chr. 29:17; Ps. 26:2; Jer. 17:10; Mal. 3:3

4 [1]Lit., *falsehood* [a]Prov. 14:15

5 [a]Prov. 14:31 [b]Prov. 24:17; Job 31:29; Obad. 12

6 [a]Prov. 13:22; Gen. 48:11 [b]Ex. 20:12; Mal. 1:6

7 [1]Lit., *a lip of abundance* [a]Prov. 24:7 [b]Prov. 12:22; Ps. 31:18

8 [1]Lit., *stone of favor* [a]Prov. 21:14; Is. 1:23; Amos 5:12

9 [a]Prov. 10:12; James 5:20; 1 Pet. 4:8 [b]Prov. 16:28

12 [a]2 Sam. 17:8; Hos. 13:8 [b]Prov. 29:9

13 [a]Ps. 35:12; 109:5; Jer. 18:20 [b]Prov. 13:21; 2 Sam. 12:10; 1 Kin. 21:22

14 [a]Prov. 20:3; 25:8

15 [a]Prov. 18:5; 24:24; Ex. 23:7; Is. 5:23

16 [1]Lit., *there is no heart* [a]Prov. 23:23

17 [a]Prov. 18:24; Ruth 1:16

18 [1]Lit., *heart* [2]Lit., *shakes hands* [a]Prov. 6:1; 11:15; 22:26

19 [a]Prov. 29:22 [b]Prov. 11:2; 16:18; 29:23

20 [1]Lit., *heart* [a]Prov. 24:20 [b]James 3:8

21 [a]Prov. 17:25; 10:1; 19:13

22 [1]Lit., *causes good healing* [a]Prov. 15:13 [b]Ps. 22:15

23 A wicked man receives a [a]bribe from the bosom
To [b]pervert the ways of justice.
24 Wisdom is in the presence of the one who has understanding,
But the [a]eyes of a fool are on the ends of the earth.
25 A foolish son is a grief to his father,
And bitterness to her who bore him.
26 It is also not good to fine the righteous,
Nor to strike the noble for *their* uprightness.
27 He who [a]restrains his words [1]has knowledge,
And he who has a [b]cool spirit is a man of understanding.
28 Even a fool, when he [a]keeps silent, is considered wise;
When he closes his lips, he is *counted* prudent.

Chapter 18

HE who separates himself seeks *his own* desire,
He [1]quarrels against all sound wisdom.
2 A fool does not delight in understanding,
But only [a]in revealing his own [1]mind.
3 When a wicked man comes, contempt also comes,
And with dishonor *comes* reproach.
4 The words of a man's mouth are [a]deep waters;
[1]The fountain of wisdom is a bubbling brook.
5 To [a]show partiality to the wicked is not good,
Nor to [b]thrust aside the righteous in judgment.
6 A fool's lips [1]bring strife,
And his mouth calls for blows.
7 A [a]fool's mouth is his ruin,
And his lips are the snare of his soul.
8 The words of a whisperer are like dainty morsels,
And they go down into the [1]innermost parts of the body.
9 He also who is [a]slack in his work
Is brother to him who destroys.
10 The [a]name of the LORD is a [b]strong tower;
The righteous runs into it and [c]is [1]safe.
11 A rich man's wealth is his strong city,
And like a high wall in his own imagination.
12 Before destruction the heart of man is haughty,
But humility *goes* before honor.
13 He who [a]gives an answer before he hears,
It is folly and shame to him.
14 The spirit of a man can endure his sickness,
But a [a]broken spirit who can bear?
15 The [1]mind of the prudent acquires knowledge,
And the ear of the wise seeks knowledge.
16 A man's [a]gift makes room for him,
And brings him before great men.
17 The first [1]to plead his case *seems* just,
Until [2]another comes and examines him.
18 The [a]lot puts an end to contentions,
And [1]decides between the mighty.
19 A brother offended *is harder to be won* than a strong city,
And contentions are like the bars of a castle.

23 [a]Prov. 17:8 [b]Ex. 23:8; Mic. 3:11; 7:3
24 [a]Eccles. 2:14
27 [1]Lit., *knows* [a]Prov. 10:19; James 1:19 [b]Prov. 14:29
28 [a]Job 13:5
1 [1]Lit., *breaks out*
2 [1]Lit., *heart* [a]Prov. 12:23; 13:16; Eccles. 10:3
4 [1]Or, *A bubbling brook, a fountain of wisdom* [a]Prov. 20:5
5 [a]Prov. 17:15; 24:23; 28:21; Lev. 19:15; Deut. 1:17; 16:19; Ps. 82:2 [b]Prov. 17:26; 31:5; Ex. 23:2, 6; Mic. 3:9
6 [1]Lit., *come with*
7 [a]Prov. 10:14; 12:13; 13:3; Ps. 64:8; 140:9 Eccles. 10:12
8 [1]Lit., *chambers of the belly*
9 [a]Prov. 10:4
10 [1]Lit., *set on high* [a]Ex. 3:15 [b]2 Sam. 22:2, 3, 33; Ps. 18:2; 61:3; 91:2; 144:2 [c]Prov. 29:25
13 [a]Prov. 20:25; John 7:51
14 [a]Prov. 15:13
15 [1]Lit., *heart*
16 [a]Gen. 32:20; 1 Sam. 25:27
17 [1]Lit., *in his plea* [2]Lit., *his neighbor*
18 [1]Lit., *makes a division* [a]Prov. 16:33

20 With the [1]fruit of a man's mouth his stomach will be
satisfied;
He will be satisfied *with* the product of his lips.
21 [a]Death and life are in the [1]power of the tongue,
And those who love it will eat its [b]fruit.
22 He who finds a [a]wife finds a good thing,
And obtains favor from the LORD.
23 The [a]poor man utters supplications,
But the [b]rich man [c]answers roughly.
24 A man of *many* friends *comes* to [1]ruin,
But there is a [2]friend who sticks closer than a brother.

CHAPTER 19

BETTER is a poor man who [a]walks in his integrity
Than he who is perverse in [1]speech and is a fool.
2 Also it is not good for a person to be without
knowledge,
And he who makes haste with his feet [1]errs.
3 The [a]foolishness of man subverts his way,
And his heart [b]rages against the LORD.
4 [a]Wealth adds many friends,
But a poor man is separated from his friend.
5 A [a]false witness will not go unpunished,
And he who [1]tells lies will not escape.
6 [a]Many will entreat the favor of a [1]generous man,
And every man is a friend to him who [b]gives gifts.
7 All the brothers of a poor man hate him;
How much more do his [a]friends go far from him!
He [b]pursues *them with* words, *but* they are [1]gone.
8 He who gets [1]wisdom loves his own soul;
He who keeps understanding will [a]find good.
9 A [a]false witness will not go unpunished,
And he who [1]tells lies will perish.
10 Luxury is [a]not fitting for a fool;
Much less for a [b]slave to rule over princes.
11 A man's [a]discretion makes him slow to anger,
And it is his glory [b]to overlook a transgression.
12 The king's wrath is like the roaring of a lion,
But his favor is like [a]dew on the grass.
13 A foolish son is destruction to his father,
And the [a]contentions of a wife are a constant dripping.
14 House and wealth are an [a]inheritance from fathers,
But a prudent wife is from the LORD.
15 [a]Laziness casts into a deep sleep,
And an idle [1]man will suffer hunger.
16 He who [a]keeps the commandment keeps his soul,
But he who [1]is careless of his ways will die.
17 He who [a]is gracious to a poor man lends to the LORD,
And He will repay him for his [1b]good deed.
18 Discipline your son while there is hope,
And do not desire [1]his death.
19 *A man of* great anger shall bear the penalty,
For if you rescue *him*, you will only have to do it again.
20 [a]Listen to counsel and accept discipline,
That you may be wise [1]the rest of your days.

---

20 [1]I.e., speech

21 [1]Lit., *hand*
[a]Prov. 12:13; 13:3; Matt. 12:37 [b]Prov. 13:2; Is. 3:10; Hos. 10:13

22 [a]Prov. 12:4; 19:14; 31:10-31; Gen. 2:18

23 [a]Prov. 19:7 [b]James 2:3, 6 [c]1 Kin. 12:13; 2 Chr. 10:13

24 [1]Lit., *be broken in pieces* [2]Or, *lover*

1 [1]Lit., *his lips*
[a]Prov. 14:2; 20:7; Ps. 26:11

2 [1]Lit., *sins*

3 [a]Prov. 11:3 [b]Ps. 37:7; Is. 8:21

4 [a]Prov. 14:20

5 [1]Lit., *breathes*
[a]Prov. 19:9; 21:28; Ex. 23:1; Deut. 19:16-19

6 [1]Or, *noble*
[a]Prov. 29:26 [b]Prov. 18:16; 21:14

7 [1]Lit., *not*
[a]Ps. 38:11 [b]Prov. 18:23

8 [1]Lit., *heart*
[a]Prov. 16:20

9 [1]Lit., *breathes*
[a]Prov. 19:5

10 [a]Prov. 17:7; 26:1; Eccles. 10:6, 7 [b]Prov. 30:22

11 [a]Prov. 14:29; 16:32 [b]Matt. 5:44; Eph. 4:32; Col. 3:13

12 [a]Gen. 27:28; Deut. 33:28; Ps. 133:3; Hos. 14:5; Mic. 5:7

13 [a]Prov. 21:9, 19; 27:15

14 [a]2 Cor. 12:14

15 [1]Lit., *soul*
[a]Prov. 6:9, 10; 24:33

16 [1]Lit., *despises*
[a]Prov. 16:17; Luke 10:28; 11:28

17 [1]Or, *benefits*
[a]Prov. 14:31; 28:27; Deut. 15:7, 8; Eccles. 11:1, 2; Matt. 10:42; 25:40; 2 Cor. 9:6-8; Heb. 6:10 [b]Prov. 12:14; Luke 6:38

18 [1]Lit., *causing him to die*

20 [1]Lit., *in your latter end*
[a]Prov. 4:1; 8:33; 12:15

21 Many are the plans in a man's heart,
But the [a]counsel of the LORD, it will stand.
22 What is desirable in a man is his [1]kindness,
And *it is* better to be a poor man than a liar.
23 The [1a]fear of the LORD *leads* to life,
So that one may sleep [b]satisfied, [2c]untouched by evil.
24 The sluggard buries his hand [a]in the dish,
And will not even bring it back to his mouth.
25 Strike a scoffer and the [1]naive may become shrewd,
But reprove one who has understanding and he will [2]gain knowledge.
26 He who assaults *his* father *and* drives *his* mother away
Is a shameful and disgraceful son.
27 Cease listening, my son, to discipline,
And you will stray from the words of knowledge.
28 A rascally witness makes a mockery of justice,
And the mouth of the wicked [1a]spreads iniquity.
29 [1]Judgments are prepared for [a]scoffers,
And [b]blows for the back of fools.

CHAPTER 20

[a]WINE is a mocker, [b]strong drink a brawler,
And whoever [1]is intoxicated by it is not wise.
2 The terror of a king is like the growling of a lion;
He who provokes him to anger [1a]forfeits his own life.
3 [1]Keeping away from strife is an honor for a man,
But any fool will [2]quarrel.
4 The sluggard does not plow after the autumn,
So he [1]begs during the harvest and has nothing.
5 A plan in the heart of a man is *like* deep water,
But a man of understanding draws it out.
6 Many a man [a]proclaims his own loyalty,
But who can find a [b]trustworthy man?
7 A righteous man who [a]walks in his integrity—
[b]How blessed are his sons after him.
8 A king who sits on the throne of justice
[1]Disperses all evil with his eyes.
9 [a]Who can say, "I have cleansed my heart,
I am pure from my sin"?
10 [1]Differing weights and differing measures,—
Both of them are abominable to the LORD.
11 It is by his deeds that a lad [1a]distinguishes himself
If his conduct is pure and right.
12 The hearing [a]ear and the seeing eye,
The LORD has made both of them.
13 [a]Do not love sleep, lest you become poor;
Open your eyes, *and* you will be satisfied with [1]food.
14 "Bad, bad," says the buyer;
But when he goes his way, then he boasts.
15 There is gold, and an abundance of [1]jewels;
But the lips of knowledge are a more precious thing.
16 Take his garment when he becomes surety for a stranger;
And for foreigners, hold him in pledge.

21 [a]Ps. 33:10, 11; Is. 14:26, 27

22 [1]Or, *loyalty*

23 [1]Or, *reverence* [2]Lit., *not visited*
[a]Prov. 14:27; 1 Tim. 4:8 [b]Ps. 25:13 [c]Prov. 12:21; Ps. 91:10

24 [a]Matt. 26:23; Mark 14:20

25 [1]Lit., *simple* [2]Lit., *discern*

28 [1]Or, *swallows*
[a]Job 15:16; 20:12, 13; 34:7

29 [1]Gk., *Rods*
[a]Prov. 9:12; Ps. 1:1 [b]Prov. 10:13; 18:6; 26:3

1 [1]Lit., *errs*
[a]Prov. 23:29, 30; Gen. 9:21; Is. 28:7; Hos. 4:11 [b]Prov. 31:4; Is. 5:22; 56:12

2 [1]Lit., *sins against*
[a]Prov. 8:36; Num. 16:38; 1 Kin. 2:23; Hab. 2:10

3 [1]Lit., *ceasing* [2]Lit., *burst out*

4 [1]Lit., *asks*

6 [a]Prov. 25:14; Matt. 6:2; Luke 18:11 [b]Ps. 12:1; Luke 18:8

7 [a]Prov. 19:1 [b]Ps. 37:26; 112:2

8 [1]Or, *Sifts*

9 [a]1 Kin. 8:46; 2 Chr. 6:36; Job 14:4; Eccles. 7:20; Rom. 3:9; 1 John 1:8

10 [1]Lit., *A stone and a stone, an ephah and an ephah*

11 [1]Or, *makes himself known*
[a]Matt. 7:16

12 [a]Ex. 4:11; Ps. 94:9

13 [1]Lit., *bread*
[a]Prov. 6:9, 10; 19:15; 24:33

15 [1]Or, *corals*

17 [a]Bread obtained by falsehood is sweet to a man,
But afterward his mouth will be filled with gravel.
18 Prepare [a]plans by consultation,
And [b]make war by wise guidance.
19 He who goes about as a slanderer reveals secrets,
Therefore do not associate with [1]a gossip.
20 He who [a]curses his father or his mother,
His [b]lamp will go out in time of darkness.
21 An inheritance gained hurriedly at the beginning,
Will not be blessed in the end.
22 [a]Do not say, "I will repay evil";
[b]Wait for the LORD, and He will save you.
23 [1]Differing weights are an abomination to the LORD,
And a [2]false scale is not good.
24 Man's steps are *ordained* by the LORD,
How then can man understand his way?
25 It is a snare for a man to say rashly, "It is holy!"
And [a]after the vows to make inquiry.
26 A [a]wise king winnows the wicked,
And [1]drives the [b]*threshing*-wheel over them.
27 The [1a]spirit of man is the lamp of the LORD,
Searching all the [2]innermost parts of his being.
28 [1]Loyalty and [a]truth preserve the king,
And he upholds his throne by [1]righteousness.
29 The glory of young men is their strength,
And the [1]honor of old men is their gray hair.
30 Stripes that wound scour away evil,
And strokes *reach* the [1]innermost parts.

CHAPTER 21

THE king's heart is *like* channels of water in the hand of the LORD;
He [a]turns it wherever He wishes.
2 Every man's way is right in his own eyes,
But the LORD [a]weighs the hearts.
3 To do [a]righteousness and justice
Is desired by the LORD rather than sacrifice.
4 Haughty eyes and a proud heart,
The [a]lamp of the wicked, is sin.
5 The plans of the diligent *lead* surely to advantage,
But everyone who is hasty *comes* surely to poverty.
6 The [a]getting of treasures by a lying tongue
Is a fleeting vapor, the [1]pursuit of [b]death.
7 The violence of the wicked will drag them away,
Because they [a]refuse to act with justice.
8 The way of a guilty man is [a]crooked,
But as for the pure, his conduct is upright.
9 It is better to live in a corner of a roof,
Than [1]in a house shared with a contentious woman.
10 The soul of the wicked desires evil;
His [a]neighbor finds no favor in his eyes.
11 When the [a]scoffer is punished, the [1]naive becomes wise;
But when the wise is instructed, he receives knowledge.
12 The Righteous One considers the house of the wicked,
Turning the [a]wicked to ruin.

17 [a]Prov. 9:17

18 [a]Prov. 11:14; 15:22 [b]Luke 14:31

19 [1]Lit., *one who opens his lips*

20 [a]Prov. 30:11; Ex. 21:17; Lev. 20:9; Matt. 15:4 [b]Prov. 13:9; 24:20; Job 18:5

22 [a]Prov. 24:29; Matt. 5:39; Rom. 12:17, 19; 1 Thess. 5:15; 1 Pet. 3:9 [b]Ps. 27:14

23 [1]Lit., *A stone and a stone* [2]Lit., *balance of deceit*

25 [a]Eccles. 5:4, 5

26 [1]Lit., *turns* [a]Prov. 20:8 [b]Is. 28:27

27 [1]Lit., *breath* [2]Lit., *chambers of the body* [a]1 Cor. 2:11

28 [1]Lit., *Covenant loyalty* [a]Prov. 29:14

29 [1]Or, *splendor*

30 [1]Lit., *chambers of the body*

1 [a]Ezra 6:22

2 [a]Prov. 16:2; 24:12; Luke 16:15

3 [a]Prov. 11:14; 15:22

4 [a]Luke 14:31

6 [1]Lit., *seekers* [a]Prov. 30:11; Ex. 21:17; Lev. 20:9; Matt. 15:4 [b]Prov. 13:9; 24:20; Job 18:5

7 [a]Prov. 24:29; Matt. 5:39; Rom. 12:17, 19; 1 Thess. 5:15; 1 Pet. 3:9

8 [a]Ps. 27:14

9 [1]Lit., *a woman of contentions and a house of association*

10 [a]Jer. 10:23

11 [1]Lit., *simple* [a]Eccles. 5:4, 5

12 [a]Prov. 21:8

13 He who [a]shuts his ear to the cry of the poor
Will also cry himself and not be [b]answered.
14 A [a]gift in secret subdues anger,
And a bribe in the bosom, strong wrath.
15 The execution of justice is joy for the righteous,
But is [a]terror to the workers of iniquity.
16 A man who wanders from the way of understanding
Will [a]rest in the assembly of the [1]dead.
17 He who [a]loves pleasure *will become* a poor man;
He who loves wine and oil will not become rich.
18 The wicked is a [a]ransom for the righteous,
And the treacherous is in the place of the upright.
19 It is better to live in a desert land,
Than with a contentious and vexing woman.
20 There is precious [a]treasure and oil in the dwelling of the wise,
But a foolish man [b]swallows it up.
21 He who [a]pursues righteousness and loyalty
Finds life, righteousness and honor.
22 A [a]wise man scales the city of the mighty,
And brings down the [1]stronghold in which they trust.
23 He who [a]guards his mouth and his tongue
Guards his soul from troubles.
24 "Proud," "Haughty," "[a]Scoffer," are his names,
Who acts with [b]insolent pride.
25 The desire of the sluggard puts him to death,
For his hands refuse to work;
26 All day long he [1]is craving,
While the righteous [a]gives and does not hold back.
27 The [a]sacrifice of the wicked is an abomination,
How much more when he brings it with evil intent!
28 A false witness will perish,
But the man who listens *to the truth* will speak forever.
29 A wicked man [1][a]shows a bold face,
But as for the [b]upright, he makes his way sure.
30 There is [a]no wisdom and no understanding
And no counsel against the LORD.
31 The [a]horse is prepared for the day of battle,
But [b]victory belongs to the LORD.

CHAPTER 22

A *GOOD* name is to be more desired than great riches,
Favor is better than silver and gold.
2 The rich and the poor [1]have a common bond,
The LORD is the [a]maker of them all.
3 The prudent sees the evil and hides himself,
But the [1]naive go on, and are punished for it.
4 The reward of humility *and* the [1]fear of the LORD
Are riches, honor and life.
5 Thorns *and* snares are in the way of the perverse;
He who guards himself will be far from them.
6 [a]Train up a child [1]in the way he should go,
Even when he is old he will not depart from it.
7 The [a]rich rules over the poor,
And the borrower *becomes* the lender's slave.

13 [a]Matt. 18:30-34; 1 John 3:17 [b]James 2:13
14 [a]Prov. 18:16; 19:6
15 [a]Prov. 10:29
16 [1]Lit., *departed spirits* [a]Ps. 49:14
17 [a]Prov. 23:21
18 [a]Is. 43:3
20 [a]Prov. 8:21; 22:4; Ps. 112:3 [b]Job 20:15, 18
21 [a]Prov. 15:9; Matt. 5:6
22 [1]Lit., *strength of trust* [a]Prov. 24:5; 2 Sam. 5:6-9; Eccles. 7:19; 9:15, 16
23 [a]Prov. 12:13; 13:3; 18:21; James 3:2
24 [a]Prov. 1:22; 3:34; 24:9; Ps. 1:1; Is. 29:20 [b]Is. 16:6; Jer. 48:29
26 [1]Lit., *desires desire* [a]Ps. 37:26; 112:5, 9; Matt. 5:42; Eph. 4:28
27 [a]Prov. 15:8; Ps. 50:9; Is. 66:3; Jer. 6:20; Amos 5:22
29 [1]Lit., *makes firm with his face* [a]Eccles. 8:1 [b]Prov. 11:5; Ps. 119:5
30 [a]Is. 8:9, 10; Jer. 9:23; Acts 5:38, 39; 1 Cor. 3:19, 20
31 [a]Ps. 20:7; 33:17; Is. 31:1 [b]Ps. 3:8; Jer. 3:23; 1 Cor. 15:57
2 [1]Lit., *meet together* [a]Prov. 14:31; Job 31:15
3 [1]Lit., *simple*
4 [1]Or, *reverence*
6 [1]Lit., *according to his way* [a]Eph. 6:4
7 [a]Prov. 18:23; James 2:6

8 He who [a]sows iniquity will reap vanity,
And the [b]rod of his fury will perish.
9 He who [1]is [a]generous will be blessed,
For he [b]gives some of his food to the poor.
10 [a]Drive out the scoffer, and contention will go out,
Even strife and dishonor will cease.
11 He who loves [a]purity of heart
And [1]whose speech is gracious, the king is his friend.
12 The eyes of the LORD preserve knowledge,
But He overthrows the words of the treacherous man.
13 The [a]sluggard says, "There is a lion outside;
I shall be slain in the streets!"
14 The mouth of [1a]an adulteress is a deep pit;
He who is [b]cursed of the LORD will fall [2]into it.
15 Foolishness is bound up in the heart of a child;
The [a]rod of discipline will remove it far from him.
16 He who oppresses the poor to make much for himself
Or who gives to the rich, *will* only *come to* poverty.

17 Incline your ear and hear the words of the wise,
And apply your mind to my knowledge;
18 For it will be pleasant if you keep them within you,
[1]That they may be ready on your lips.
19 So that your trust may be in the LORD,
I have [1]taught you today, even you.
20 Have I not written to you [1]excellent things
Of counsels and knowledge,
21 To make you [a]know the [1]certainty of the words of truth
That you may [2b]correctly answer to him who sent you?

22 [a]Do not rob the poor because he is poor,
Or [b]crush the afflicted at the gate;
23 For the LORD will [a]plead their case,
And [1]take the life of those who rob them.

24 Do not associate with a man *given* to anger;
Or go with a [a]hot-tempered man,
25 Lest you [a]learn his ways,
And [1]find a snare for yourself.

26 Do not be among those who give [1]pledges,
Among those who become sureties for debts.
27 If you have nothing with which to pay,
Why should he [a]take your bed from under you?

28 [a]Do not move the ancient boundary
Which your fathers have set.

29 Do you see a man [a]skilled in his work?
He will [b]stand before kings;
He will not stand before obscure men.

8 [a]Prov. 24:16; Job 4:8 [b]Ps. 125:3
9 [1]Lit., *has a good eye* [a]Prov. 19:17; 2 Cor. 9:6 [b]Luke 14:13
10 [a]Prov. 18:6; Gen. 21:9, 10
11 [1]Lit., *has grace on his lips* [a]Ps. 24:4; Matt. 5:8
13 [a]Prov. 26:13
14 [1]Lit., *strange woman* [2]Lit., *there* [a]Prov. 5:3 [b]Eccles. 7:26
15 [a]Prov. 13:24; 23:14
18 [1]Lit., *They together*
19 [1]Lit., *made you know*
20 [1]Or, *previous*
21 [1]Lit., *truth* [2]Lit., *return words of truth* [a]Luke 1:3, 4 [b]Prov. 25:13
22 [a]Prov. 23:10; Ex. 23:6; Job 31:16 [b]Zech. 7:10; Mal. 3:5
23 [1]Lit., *rob the soul* [a]Prov. 23:11; 1 Sam. 25:39; Ps. 12:5; 35:10; 140:12; Jer. 51:36
24 [a]Prov. 29:22
25 [1]Lit., *take* [a]1 Cor. 15:33
26 [1]Lit., *strike hands*
27 [a]Prov. 20:16; Ex. 22:26
28 [a]Prov. 23:10; Deut. 19:14; 27:17; Job 24:2
29 [a]Rom. 12:11 [b]Gen. 41:46; 1 Kin. 10:8

CHAPTER 23

WHEN you sit down to dine with a ruler,
Consider carefully [1]what is before you;
2 And put a knife to your throat,
If you are a man of *great* appetite.
3 Do not desire his [a]delicacies,
For it is deceptive food.

4 [a]Do not weary yourself to gain riches,
[b]Cease from your [1]consideration *of it.*
5 [1]When you set your eyes on it, it is gone.
For [a]*wealth* certainly makes itself wings,
Like an eagle that flies *toward* the heavens.

6 [a]Do not eat the bread of a [1b]selfish man,
Or desire his delicacies;
7 For as he [1]thinks within himself, so he is.
He says to you, "Eat and drink!"
But his heart is not with you.
8 You will vomit up [1]the morsel you have eaten,
And waste your [2]compliments.

9 Do not speak in the [1]hearing of a fool,
For he will despise the wisdom of your words.

10 Do not move the ancient boundary,
Or [a]go into the fields of the fatherless;
11 For their [a]Redeemer is strong;
He will plead their case against you.
12 Apply your heart to discipline,
And your ears to words of knowledge.

13 Do not hold back discipline from the child,
Although you [1]beat him with the rod, he will not die.
14 You shall [1]beat him with the rod,
And [a]deliver his soul from Sheol.

15 My son, if your heart is wise,
My own heart also will be glad;
16 And my [1]inmost being will rejoice,
When your lips speak what is right.

17 [a]Do not let your heart envy sinners,
But *live* in the [1]fear of the LORD [2]always.
18 Surely there is a [1a]future,
And your [b]hope will not be cut off.
19 Listen, my son, and [a]be wise,
And [b]direct your heart in the way.
20 Do not be with [a]heavy drinkers of wine,
Or with [b]gluttonous eaters of meat;
21 For the heavy drinker and the glutton will come to poverty,
And drowsiness will clothe *a man* with rags.

22 Listen to your father who begot you,
And do not despise your mother when she is old.

1 [1]Or, *who*
3 [a]Ps. 141:4; Dan. 1:5, 8, 13, 15, 16
4 [1]Or, *understanding* [a]Prov. 15:27; 28:20; Matt. 6:19; 1 Tim. 6:9; Heb. 13:5 [b]Prov. 3:5, 7; Rom. 12:16
5 [1]Lit., *Will your eyes fly upon it and it is not?* [a]Prov. 27:24; 1 Tim. 6:17
6 [1]Lit., *evil eye* [a]Ps. 141:4 [b]Prov. 28:22
7 [1]Lit., *reckons in his soul*
8 [1]Lit., *your* [2]Lit., *pleasant words*
9 [1]Lit., *ears*
10 [a]Jer. 22:3; Zech. 7:10
11 [a]Job 19:25
13 [1]Lit., *smite*
14 [1]Lit., *smite* [a]1 Cor. 5:5
16 [1]Lit., *kidneys*
17 [1]Or, *reverence* [2]Lit., *all the day* [a]Prov. 24:1, 19; Ps. 37:1
18 [1]Lit., *latter end* [a]Prov. 24:14; Ps. 19:11; 58:11 [b]Ps. 9:18
19 [a]Prov. 6:6 [b]Prov. 4:23; 9:6
20 [a]Prov. 23:29, 30; 20:1; Is. 5:22; Matt. 24:49; Luke 21:34; Rom. 13:13; Eph. 5:18 [b]Prov. 28:7; Deut. 21:20

23 [a]Prov. 4:7; 18:15; Matt. 13:44

24 [a]Prov. 10:1; 15:20; 29:3

26 [1]Another reading is, *observe* [a]Ps. 1:2; 119:24

27 [1]Lit., *strange*

28 [1]Lit., *treacherous* [a]Prov. 6:26; 7:12; Eccles. 7:26

29 [a]Is. 5:11, 22

30 [1]Or, *search out* [a]Prov. 20:1; 1 Sam. 25:36; Is. 5:11; 28:7; Eph. 5:18 [b]Ps. 75:8

31 [1]Lit., *gives its eye* [a]Song of Sol. 7:9

32 [a]Job 20:16 [b]Ps. 91:13; Is. 11:8

33 [1]Lit., *heart*

34 [1]Lit., *heart* [2]Or, *lookout*

35 [1]Lit., *it yet again* [a]Jer. 5:3 [b]Prov. 26:11; Is. 56:12

1 [a]Prov. 24:19; 3:31; 23:17; Ps. 37:1 [b]Prov. 1:15; Ps. 1:1

2 [1]Lit., *hearts* [a]Is. 30:12; Jer. 22:17 [b]Job 15:35; Ps. 10:7; 38:12

5 [1]Lit., *in strength* [2]Lit., *strengthens power*

6 [1]Lit., *make battle for yourself*

7 [a]Prov. 14:6; 17:16; Ps. 10:5 [b]Job 5:4; Ps. 127:5

23 [a]Buy truth, and do not sell *it*,
Get wisdom and instruction and understanding.

24 The father of the righteous will greatly rejoice,
And [a]he who begets a wise son will be glad in him.
25 Let your father and your mother be glad,
And let her rejoice who gave birth to you.

26 Give me your heart, my son,
And let your eyes [1a]delight in my ways.
27 For a harlot is a deep pit,
And an [1]adulterous woman is a narrow well.
28 Surely she [a]lurks as a robber,
And increases the [1]faithless among men.

29 Who has [a]woe? Who has sorrow?
Who has contentions? Who has complaining?
Who has wounds without cause?
Who has redness of eyes?
30 Those who [a]linger long over wine,
Those who go to [1]taste [b]mixed wine.
31 Do not look on the wine when it is red,
When it [1]sparkles in the cup,
When it [a]goes down smoothly;
32 At the last it [a]bites like a serpent,
And stings like a [b]viper.
33 Your eyes will see strange things,
And your [1]mind will utter perverse things.
34 And you will be like one who lies down in the [1]middle of the sea,
Or like one who lies down on the top of a [2]mast.
35 "They [a]struck me, *but* I did not become ill;
They beat me, *but* I did not know *it*.
When shall I awake?
I will [b]seek [1]another drink."

Chapter 24

Do not be [a]envious of evil men,
Nor desire to [b]be with them;
2 For their [1]minds devise [a]violence,
And their lips [b]talk of trouble.

3 By wisdom a house is built,
And by understanding it is established;
4 And by knowledge the rooms are filled
With all precious and pleasant riches.

5 A wise man is [1]strong,
And a man of knowledge [2]increases power.
6 For by wise guidance you will [1]wage war,
And in abundance of counselors there is victory.

7 Wisdom is [a]too high for a fool,
He does not open his mouth [b]in the gate.

8 He who [a]plans to do evil,
Men will call him a [1]schemer.
9 The [a]devising of folly is sin,
And the scoffer is an abomination to men.

10 If you [a]are slack in the day of distress,
Your strength is limited.

11 [a]Deliver those who are being taken away to death,
And those who are staggering to slaughter, O hold *them* back.
12 If you say, "See, we did not know this,"
Does He not [a]consider *it* [b]who weighs the hearts?
And [c]does He not know *it* who [d]keeps your soul?
And will He not [1e]render to man according to his work?

13 My son, eat [a]honey, for it is good,
Yes, the [b]honey from the comb is sweet to your taste;
14 Know *that* wisdom is thus for your soul;
If you find *it*, then there will be a [1]future,
And your hope will not be cut off.

15 [a]Do not lie in wait, O wicked man, against the dwelling of the righteous;
Do not destroy his resting place;
16 For a [a]righteous man falls seven times, and rises again,
But the [b]wicked stumble in *time of* calamity.

17 [a]Do not rejoice when your enemy falls,
And do not let your heart be glad when he stumbles;
18 Lest the LORD see *it* and [1]be displeased,
And He turn away His anger from him.

19 [a]Do not fret yourself because of evildoers,
Or be [b]envious of the wicked;
20 For [a]there will be no [1b]future for the evil man;
The [c]lamp of the wicked will be put out.

21 My son, [1a]fear the LORD and the king;
Do not associate with those who are given to change;
22 For their [a]calamity will rise suddenly,
And who knows the ruin *that comes* from both of them?

23 These also are [a]sayings of the wise.
To [1b]show partiality in judgment is not good.
24 He who says to the wicked, "You are righteous,"
Peoples will curse him, nations will abhor him;
25 But to those who rebuke the *wicked* will be delight,
And a good blessing will come upon them.
26 He kisses the lips
Who gives a [1]right answer.

27 Prepare your work outside,
And make it ready for yourself in the field;
Afterwards, then, build your house.

8 [1]Or, *deviser of evil* [a]Prov. 6:14; 14:22; Rom. 1:30

9 [a]Is. 59:7

10 [a]Deut. 20:8; Job 4:5; Jer. 51:46; Heb. 12:3

11 [a]Ps. 82:4; Is. 58:6, 7

12 [1]Lit., *bring back* [a]Prov. 21:2; 1 Sam. 16:7 [b]Eccles. 5:8 [c]Ps. 121:3-8 [d]Ps. 94:9-11 [e]Prov. 12:14; Job 34:11

13 [a]Prov. 25:16; Ps. 19:10; 119:103; Song of Sol. 5:1 [b]Prov. 16:24; 27:7; Song of Sol. 4:11

14 [1]Lit., *latter end*

15 [a]Ps. 10:9, 10

16 [a]Job 5:19; Ps. 37:24; Mic. 7:8 [b]Prov. 24:22; 6:15; 14:32; Jer. 18:17

17 [a]Prov. 17:5; Job 31:29; Ps. 35:15, 19; Obad. 12

18 [1]Lit., it *is evil in His eyes*

19 [a]Ps. 37:1 [b]Prov. 24:1; 23:17

20 [1]Lit., *latter end* [a]Job 15:31 [b]Prov. 23:18 [c]Prov. 13:9; 20:20; Job 18:5, 6; 21:17

21 [1]Or, *reverence* [a]Rom. 13:1-7; 1 Pet. 2:17

22 [a]Prov. 24:16

23 [1]Lit., *regard the face* [a]Prov. 1:6; 22:17 [b]Prov. 18:5; 28:21

26 [1]Or, *honest*

28 Do not be a [a]witness against your neighbor without
cause,
And [b]do not deceive with your lips.
29 [a]Do not say, "Thus I shall do to him as he has done to
me;
I will [1]render to the man according to his work."

30 I passed by the field of the sluggard,
And by the vineyard of the man [a]lacking [1]sense;
31 And behold, it was completely overgrown with thistles,
Its surface was covered with [1a]nettles,
And its stone [b]wall was broken down.
32 When I saw, I [1]reflected upon it;
I looked, *and* received instruction.
33 "A little sleep, a little slumber,
A little folding of the hands to rest,"
34 Then your poverty will come *as* [1]a robber,
And your want like [2]an armed man.

CHAPTER 25

THESE also are [a]proverbs of Solomon which the men of
Hezekiah king of Judah transcribed.
2 It is the glory of God to [a]conceal a matter,
But the glory of [b]kings is to search out a matter.
3 *As* the heavens for height and the earth for depth,
So the heart of kings is unsearchable.
4 Take away the [a]dross from the silver,
And there comes out a vessel for the [b]smith;
5 Take away the [a]wicked *from* before the king,
And his throne will be established in righteousness.
6 Do not claim honor in the presence of the king,
And do not stand in the place of great men;
7 For [a]it is better that it be said to you, "Come up here,"
Than that you should be put lower in the presence of
the prince,
Whom your eyes have seen.

8 Do not go out [a]hastily to [1]argue *your case;*
[2]Otherwise, what will you do in [3]the end,
When your neighbor puts you to shame?
9 [1a]Argue your case with your neighbor,
And [b]do not reveal the secret of another,
10 Lest he who hears *it* reproach you,
And the evil report about you not [1]pass away.

11 *Like* apples of gold in settings of silver
Is a [a]word spoken in [1]right circumstances.
12 *Like* [1]an [a]earring of gold and an [b]ornament of [c]fine
gold
Is a wise reprover to a [d]listening ear.
13 Like the cold of snow in the [1]time of harvest
Is a faithful messenger to those who send him,
For he refreshes the soul of his masters.
14 *Like* [a]clouds and [b]wind without rain
Is a man who boasts [1]of his gifts falsely.

28 [a]Prov. 25:18 [b]Lev. 6:2, 3; 19:11; Eph. 4:25

29 [1]Lit., *bring back* [a]Prov. 20:22; Matt. 5:39; Rom. 12:17

30 [1]Lit., *heart* [a]Prov. 6:32

31 [1]I.e., a kind of weed [a]Job 30:7 [b]Is. 5:5

32 [1]Lit., *set my heart*

34 [1]Or, *a vagabond;* lit., *one who walks* [2]Lit., *a man of a shield*

1 [a]Prov. 1:1

2 [a]Deut. 29:29; Rom. 11:33 [b]Ezra 6:1

4 [a]Prov. 26:23; Ezek. 22:18 [b]Mal. 3:2, 3

5 [a]Prov. 20:8

7 [a]Luke 14:7-11

8 [1]Lit., *contend* [2]Lit., *Lest* [3]Lit., *its* [a]Prov. 17:14; Matt. 5:25

9 [1]Lit., *Contend* [a]Matt. 18:15 [b]Prov. 11:13

10 [1]Lit., *return*

11 [1]Lit., *its* [a]Prov. 15:23

12 [1]Or, *a nose ring* [a]Ex. 32:2; 35:22; Ezek. 16:12 [b]2 Sam. 1:24 [c]Job 28:17 [d]Prov. 15:31; 20:12

13 [1]Lit., *day*

14 [1]Lit., *in a gift of falsehood* [a]Jude 1:12 [b]Jer. 5:13; Mic. 2:11

15 By [1][a]forbearance a ruler may be persuaded,
And a soft tongue breaks the bone.
16 Have you [a]found honey? Eat *only* [1]what you need,
Lest you have it in excess and vomit it.
17 Let your foot rarely be in your neighbor's house,
Lest he become [1]weary of you and hate you.
18 *Like* a club and a [a]sword and a sharp [b]arrow
Is a man who bears [c]false witness against his neighbor.
19 *Like* a bad tooth and [1]an unsteady foot
Is confidence in a [a]faithless man in time of trouble.
20 *Like* one who takes off a garment on a cold day, *or like* vinegar on [1]soda,
Is he who sings songs to a [2]troubled heart.
21 [a]If [1]your enemy is hungry, give him food to eat;
And if he is thirsty, give him water to drink;
22 For you will [1]heap burning coals on his head,
And [a]the LORD will reward you.
23 The north wind brings forth rain,
And a [1][a]backbiting tongue, an angry countenance.
24 It is better to live in a corner of the roof
Than [1]in a house shared with a contentious woman.
25 *Like* cold water to a weary soul,
So is good news from a distant land.
26 *Like* a [a]trampled spring and a [1]polluted well
Is a righteous man who gives way before the wicked.
27 It is not good to eat much honey,
Nor is it glory to search out [1]one's own glory.
28 *Like* a [a]city that is broken into *and* without walls
Is a man [b]who has no control over his spirit.

CHAPTER 26

LIKE snow in summer and like [a]rain in harvest,
So honor is not [b]fitting for a fool.
2 Like a [a]sparrow in *its* [1]flitting, like a swallow in *its* flying,
So a [b]curse without cause does not [2]alight.
3 A [a]whip is for the horse, a bridle for the donkey,
And a [b]rod for the back of fools.
4 [a]Do not answer a fool according to his folly,
Lest you also be like him.
5 [a]Answer a fool as his folly *deserves*,
Lest he be [b]wise in his own eyes.
6 He cuts off *his own* feet, *and* drinks violence
Who sends a message by the hand of a fool.
7 *Like* the legs *which* hang down from the lame,
So is a proverb in the mouth of fools.
8 Like [1]one who binds a stone in a sling,
So is he who gives honor to a fool.
9 *Like* a thorn *which* [1]falls into the hand of a drunkard,
So is a proverb in the mouth of fools.
10 [1]*Like* an archer who wounds everyone,
So is he who hires a fool or who hires those who pass by.
11 Like [a]a dog that returns to its vomit
Is a fool who [b]repeats [1]his folly.

15 [1]Lit., *length of anger* [a]Gen. 32:4; 1 Sam. 25:24; Eccles. 10:4

16 [1]Lit., *your sufficiency* [a]Judg. 14:8; 1 Sam. 14:25

17 [1]Lit., *surfeited with*

18 [a]Prov. 12:18; Ps. 57:4 [b]Jer. 9:8 [c]Prov. 24:28; Ex. 20:16

19 [1]Lit., *a slipping foot* [a]Job 6:15

20 [1]I.e., natron [2]Lit., *evil*

21 [1]Lit., *one who hates you* [a]Ex. 23:4, 5; 2 Kin. 6:22; 2 Chr. 28:15; Matt. 5:44; Rom. 12:20

22 [1]Lit., *snatch up* [a]Matt. 6:4, 6

23 [1]Lit., *tongue of secrecy* [a]Ps. 101:5

24 [1]Lit., *a woman of contentions and a house of association*

26 [1]Lit., *ruined* [a]Ezek. 32:2; 34:18, 19

27 [1]Lit., *their*

28 [a]Prov. 16:32 [b]2 Chr. 32:5; Neh. 1:3

1 [a]1 Sam. 12:17 [b]Prov. 17:7

2 [1]Lit., *wandering* [2]Lit., *come* [a]Prov. 27:8; Is. 16:2 [b]Num. 23:8; Deut. 23:5; 2 Sam. 16:12

3 [a]Ps. 32:9 [b]Prov. 10:13; 19:29

4 [a]Prov. 23:9; 29:9

5 [a]Matt. 16:1-4; 21:24-27 [b]Prov. 3:7; 28:11; Rom. 12:16

8 [1]Lit., *the binding of*

9 [1]Lit., *goes up*

10 [1]Or, *A master* workman *produces all things, But he who hires a fool is* like *one who hires those who pass by.*

11 [1]Lit., *with his* [a]2 Pet. 2:22 [b]Ex. 8:15

12 Do you see a man [a]wise in his own eyes?
There is more hope for a fool than for him.
13 The sluggard says, "There is a lion in the road!
A lion is [1]in the open square!"
14 *Like* the door turns on its hinges,
So *does* the sluggard on his bed.
15 The sluggard buries his hand in the dish;
He is weary of bringing it to his mouth again.
16 The sluggard is [a]wiser in his own eyes
Than seven men who can [1]give a discreet answer.
17 *Like* one who takes a dog by the ears
Is he who passes by *and* [1]meddles with [a]strife not belonging to him.
18 Like a madman who throws
[a]Firebrands, arrows and death,
19 So is the man who [a]deceives his neighbor,
And says, "Was I not joking?"
20 For lack of wood the fire goes out,
And where there is no [a]whisperer, contention quiets down.
21 *Like* charcoal to hot embers and wood to fire,
So is a contentious man to kindle strife.
22 The words of a whisperer are like dainty morsels,
And they go down into the [1]innermost parts of the body.
23 *Like* an earthen [a]vessel overlaid with silver dross
Are burning lips and a wicked heart.
24 He who [a]hates disguises *it* with his lips,
But he lays up [b]deceit in his [1]heart.
25 When [1]he [a]speaks graciously, do not believe him,
For there are seven abominations in his heart.
26 *Though his* hatred [a]covers itself with guile,
His wickedness will be [b]revealed before the assembly.
27 He who digs a pit will fall into it,
And he who rolls a stone, it will come back on him.
28 A lying tongue hates [1]those it crushes,
And a flattering mouth works ruin.

CHAPTER 27

Do not boast about tomorrow,
For you [a]do not know what a day may bring forth.
2 Let [a]another praise you, and not your own mouth;
A stranger, and not your own lips.
3 A stone is heavy and the sand weighty,
But the provocation of a fool is heavier than both of them.
4 Wrath is fierce and anger is a flood,
But who can stand before jealousy?
5 Better is [a]open rebuke
Than love that is concealed.
6 Faithful are the [a]wounds of a friend,
But [1]deceitful are the [b]kisses of an enemy.
7 A sated [1]man [2]loathes honey,
But to a famished [1]man any bitter thing is sweet.

26:12 [a]Prov. 3:7; 26:5
13 [1]Lit., *within*
16 [1]Lit., *return discreetly* [a]Prov. 27:11; 1 Pet. 3:15
17 [1]Lit., *infuriates himself* [a]Prov. 3:30
18 [a]Is. 50:11
19 [a]Prov. 24:28
20 [a]Prov. 16:28
22 [1]Lit., *chambers of the belly*
23 [a]Matt. 23:27; Luke 11:39
24 [1]Lit., *inward part* [a]Prov. 10:18; Ps. 41:6 [b]Prov. 12:20
25 [1]Lit., *his voice is gracious* [a]Prov. 26:23; Ps. 28:3; Jer. 9:8
26 [a]Matt. 23:28 [b]Luke 8:17
28 [1]Lit., *its crushed ones*
27:1 [a]Luke 12:19, 20; James 4:14
2 [a]Prov. 25:27; 2 Cor. 10:12, 18; 12:11
5 [a]Prov. 28:23; Gal. 2:14
6 [1]Or, *excessive* [a]Prov. 20:30; Ps. 141:5 [b]Matt. 26:49
7 [1]Lit., *soul* [2]Lit., *tramples on*

8 Like a [a]bird that wanders from her nest,
So is a man who [b]wanders from his [1]home.
9 [a]Oil and perfume make the heart glad,
So a [1]man's counsel is sweet to his friend.
10 Do not forsake your own friend or [a]your father's friend,
And do not go to your brother's house in the day of your calamity;
Better is a neighbor who is near than a brother far away.
11 [a]Be wise, my son, and make my heart glad,
That I may [b]reply to him who reproaches me.
12 A prudent man sees evil *and* hides himself,
The [1]naive proceed *and* pay the penalty.
13 Take his garment when he becomes surety for a stranger;
And for an [1]adulterous woman hold him in pledge.
14 He who blesses his friend with a loud voice early in the morning,
It will be reckoned a curse to him.
15 A constant dripping on a day of steady rain
And a contentious woman are alike;
16 He who would [1]restrain her [1]restrains the wind,
And [2]grasps oil with his right hand.
17 Iron sharpens iron,
So one man sharpens another.
18 He who tends the [a]fig tree will eat its fruit;
And he who [b]cares for his master will be honored.
19 As in water face *reflects* face,
So the heart of man *reflects* man.
20 [1a]Sheol and [2]Abaddon are [b]never satisfied,
Nor are the [c]eyes of man ever satisfied.
21 The crucible is for silver and the furnace for gold,
And a man [a]*is tested* by the praise accorded him.
22 Though you [a]pound a fool in a mortar with a pestle along with crushed grain,
Yet his folly will not depart from him.

23 [a]Know well the [1]condition of your flocks,
And pay attention to your herds;
24 For riches are not forever,
Nor does a [a]crown *endure* to all generations.
25 *When* the grass disappears, the new growth is seen,
And the herbs of the mountains are [a]gathered in,
26 The lambs *will be* for your clothing,
And the goats *will bring* the price of a field,
27 And *there will be* goats' milk enough for your food,
For the food of your household,
And sustenance for your maidens.

Chapter 28

THE wicked [a]flee when no one is pursuing,
But the righteous are [1]bold as a lion.
2 By the transgression of a land [a]many are its princes,
But by a man of understanding *and* knowledge, so it endures.

8 [1]Lit., *place* [a]Prov. 26:2; Is. 16:2 [b]Gen. 21:14

9 [1]Lit., *soul's* [a]Ps. 23:5; 141:5

10 [a]1 Kin. 12:6-8; 2 Chr. 10:6-8

11 [a]Prov. 10:1; 23:15; 29:3 [b]Ps. 119:42

12 [1]Lit., *simple*

13 [1]Lit., *strange*

16 [1]Lit., *hide(s)* [2]Lit., *encounters*

18 [a]2 Kin. 18:31; Song of Sol. 8:12; Is. 36:16; 1 Cor. 3:8; 9:7; 2 Tim. 2:6 [b]Luke 12:42-44; 19:17

20 [1]I.e., The nether world [2]I.e., the place of perishing [a]Prov. 15:11; Job 26:6 [b]Prov. 30:15, 16; Hab. 2:5 [c]Eccl. 1:8; 4:8

21 [a]Luke 6:26

22 [a]Prov. 23:35; 26:11; Jer. 5:3

23 [1]Lit., *face* [a]Jer. 31:10; Ezek. 34:12; John 10:3

24 [a]Job 19:9; Ps. 89:39; Jer. 13:18; Lam. 5:16; Ezek. 21:26

25 [a]Is. 17:5; Jer. 40:10, 12

1 [1]Lit., *confident* [a]Lev. 26:17, 36; Ps. 53:5

2 [a]1 Kin. 16:8-28; 2 Kin. 15:8-15

3 [1]Lit., *and there is no bread*
[a]Matt. 18:28

4 [a]Ps. 49:18; Rom. 1:32 [b]1 Kin. 18:18; Neh. 13:11, 15; Matt. 3:7; 14:4; Eph. 5:11

5 [a]Ps. 92:6; Is. 6:9; 44:18 [b]Prov. 2:9; Ps. 119:100; John 7:17; 1 Cor. 2:15; 1 John 2:20, 27

6 [1]Lit., *perverse of two ways*

8 [a]Ex. 22:25; Lev. 25:36 [b]Prov. 13:22; Job 27:17

9 [a]Prov. 15:8; 21:27; Ps. 66:18; 109:7

10 [a]Prov. 26:27; Ps. 7:15 [b]Matt. 6:33; Heb. 6:12; 1 Pet. 3:9

11 [1]Lit., *examine him*

12 [1]Lit., *will be searched for*
[a]Prov. 28:28; Eccles. 10:5, 6

13 [a]Job 31:33; Ps. 32:3 [b]Ps. 32:5; 1 John 1:9

14 [a]Prov. 23:17 [b]Ps. 95:8; Rom. 2:5

15 [a]Prov. 19:12; 1 Pet. 5:8 [b]Prov. 29:2; Ex. 1:14; Matt. 2:16

16 [a]Eccles. 10:16; Is. 3:12

17 [1]Lit., *flee to the pit*
[a]Gen. 9:6; Ex. 21:14

18 [1]Lit., *perverse of two ways*

20 [a]Prov. 10:6; Matt. 24:45; 25:21 [b]Prov. 28:22; 20:21; 1 Tim. 6:9

21 [1]Lit., *regard the face*
[a]Prov. 24:23 [b]Ezek. 13:19

22 [a]Prov. 23:6

25 [1]Lit., *broad soul* [2]Lit., *be made fat*

26 [a]Prov. 3:5

27 [1]Lit., *hides*
[a]Prov. 11:24; 19:17

3 A [a]poor man who oppresses the lowly
Is *like* a driving rain [1]which leaves no food.
4 Those who forsake the law [a]praise the wicked,
But those who keep the law [b]strive with them.
5 Evil men [a]do not understand justice,
But those who seek the LORD [b]understand all things.
6 Better is the poor who walks in his integrity,
Than he who is [1]crooked though he be rich.
7 He who keeps the law is a discerning son,
But he who is a companion of gluttons humiliates his father.
8 He who increases his wealth by [a]interest and usury,
Gathers it [b]for him who is gracious to the poor.
9 He who turns away his ear from listening to the law,
Even his [a]prayer is an abomination.
10 He who leads the upright astray in an evil way
Will [a]himself fall into his own pit,
But the [b]blameless will inherit good.
11 The rich man is wise in his own eyes,
But the poor who has understanding [1]sees through him.
12 When the righteous triumph, there is great glory,
But [a]when the wicked rise, men [1]hide themselves.
13 He who [a]conceals his transgressions will not prosper,
But he who [b]confesses and forsakes *them* will find compassion.
14 How blessed is the man who [a]fears always,
But he who [b]hardens his heart will fall into calamity.
15 *Like* a [a]roaring lion and a rushing bear
Is a [b]wicked ruler over a poor people.
16 A [a]leader who is a great oppressor lacks understanding,
But he who hates unjust gain will prolong *his* days.
17 A man who is [a]laden with the guilt of human blood
Will [1]be a fugitive until death; let no one support him.
18 He who walks blamelessly will be delivered,
But he who is [1]crooked will fall all at once.
19 He who tills his land will have plenty of food,
But he who follows empty *pursuits* will have poverty in plenty.
20 A [a]faithful man will abound with blessings,
But he who [b]makes haste to be rich will not go unpunished.
21 To [1a]show partiality is not good,
[b]Because for a piece of bread a man will transgress.
22 A man with an [a]evil eye hastens after wealth,
And does not know that want will come upon him.
23 He who rebukes a man will afterward find *more* favor
Than he who flatters with the tongue.
24 He who robs his father or his mother,
And says, "It is not a transgression,"
Is the companion of a man who destroys.
25 An [1]arrogant man stirs up strife,
But he who trusts in the LORD will [2]prosper.
26 He who [a]trusts in his own heart is a fool,
But he who walks wisely, will be delivered.
27 He who [a]gives to the poor will never want,
But he who [1]shuts his eyes will have many curses.

28 When the wicked rise, men hide themselves;
But when they perish, the righteous increase.

CHAPTER 29

A MAN who hardens *his* neck after [a]much reproof
Will suddenly be broken [1]beyond remedy.
2 When the [a]righteous [1]increase, the people rejoice,
But when a wicked man rules, people groan.
3 A man who [a]loves wisdom makes his father glad,
But he who [b]keeps company with harlots wastes *his* wealth.
4 The [a]king gives stability to the land by justice,
But a man who takes bribes overthrows it.
5 A man who [a]flatters his neighbor
Is spreading a net for his steps.
6 By transgression an evil man is [a]ensnared,
But the righteous [b]sings and rejoices.
7 The [a]righteous [1]is concerned for the rights of the poor,
The wicked does not understand *such* [2]concern.
8 Scorners set a city aflame,
But wise men turn away anger.
9 When a wise man has a controversy with a foolish man,
[1]The foolish man either rages or laughs, and there is no rest.
10 Men of [a]bloodshed hate the blameless,
But the upright [1]are concerned for his life.
11 A fool [1]always loses his temper,
But a [a]wise man holds it back.
12 If a [a]ruler pays attention to falsehood,
All his ministers *become* wicked.
13 The poor man and the oppressor [1]have this in common:
The LORD gives [a]light to the eyes of both.
14 If a [a]king judges the poor with truth,
His throne will be established forever.
15 The [a]rod and reproof give wisdom,
But a child [1]who gets his own way brings shame to his mother.
16 When the wicked [1]increase, transgression increases;
But the [a]righteous will see their fall.
17 [a]Correct your son, and he will give you comfort;
He will also [1]delight your soul.
18 Where there is [a]no [1]vision, the people [b]are unrestrained,
But [c]happy is he who keeps the law.
19 A slave will not be instructed by words *alone;*
For though he understands, there will be no response.
20 Do you see a man who is [a]hasty in his words?
There is more hope for a fool than for him.
21 He who pampers his slave from childhood
Will in the end find him to be a son.
22 An angry man stirs up strife,
And a hot-tempered man abounds in transgression.
23 A man's [a]pride will bring him low,
But a [b]humble spirit will obtain honor.

1 [1]Lit., *and there is no remedy* [a]Prov. 1:24-31; 1 Sam. 2:25; 2 Chr. 36:16

2 [1]Or, *become great* [a]Prov. 11:10; 28:12; Esth. 8:15

3 [a]Prov. 10:1; 15:20; 27:11; 28:7 [b]Prov. 5:10; 6:26; Luke 15:30

4 [a]Prov. 28:14; 8:15; 2 Chr. 9:8

5 [a]Ps. 5:9

6 [a]Prov. 22:5; Eccles. 9:12 [b]Ex. 15:1

7 [1]Lit., *knows the cause* [2]Lit., *knowledge* [a]Prov. 31:8, 9; Job 29:16; Ps. 41:1

9 [1]Lit., *He*

10 [1]Lit., *seek his soul* [a]Gen. 4:5-8; 1 John 3:12

11 [1]Lit., *sends forth all his spirit* [a]Prov. 19:11

12 [a]1 Kin. 12:14

13 [1]Lit., *meet together* [a]Ezra 9:8; Ps. 13:3

14 [a]Ps. 72:4; Is. 11:4

15 [1]Lit., *left to himself* [a]Prov. 13:24; 22:15

16 [1]Or, *become great* [a]Prov. 21:12; Ps.37:34, 36; 58:10; 91:8; 92:11

17 [1]Lit., *give delight to* [a]Prov. 29:15

18 [1]Or, *revelation* [a]1 Sam. 3:1; Ps. 74:9; Amos 8:11, 12 [b]Ex. 32:25 [c]Prov. 8:32; Ps. 1:1, 2; 106:3; 119:2; John 13:17

20 [a]James 1:19

23 [a]Prov. 11:2; 16:18; 2 Sam. 22:28; Dan. 4:30, 31; Matt. 23:12; James 4:6 [b]Prov. 15:33; 18:12; 22:4; Is. 66:2; Luke 14:11; 18:14; James 4:10

24 He who is a partner with a thief hates his own life;
He [a]hears the oath but tells nothing.
25 The [a]fear of man [1]brings a snare,
But he who [b]trusts in the LORD will be exalted.
26 Many seek the ruler's [1]favor,
But [a]justice for man *comes* from the LORD.
27 An [a]unjust man is abominable to the righteous,
And he who is [b]upright in the way is abominable to the wicked.

CHAPTER 30

THE words of Agur the son of Jakeh, the [1]oracle.
The man declares to Ithiel, to Ithiel and Ucal:
2 Surely I am more [a]stupid than any man,
And I do not have the understanding of a man.
3 And I have not learned wisdom,
But I have knowledge of the Holy One.
4 Who has [a]ascended into heaven and descended?
Who has gathered the [b]wind in His fists?
Who has [c]wrapped the waters in [1]His garment?
Who has [d]established all the ends of the earth?
What is His [e]name or His son's name?
Surely you know!

5 Every [a]word of God is tested;
He is a [b]shield to those who take refuge in Him.
6 [a]Do not add to His words
Lest He reprove you, and you be proved a liar.

7 Two things I asked of Thee,
Do not refuse me before I die:
8 Keep deception and [1]lies far from me,
Give me neither poverty nor riches,
Feed me with the [a]food that is my portion,
9 Lest I be [a]full and deny [b]*Thee* and say, "Who is the LORD?"
Or lest I be in want and steal,
And [c]profane the name of my God.

10 Do not slander a slave to his master,
Lest he [a]curse you and you be found guilty.

11 There is a [1]kind of *man* who [a]curses his father,
And does not bless his mother.
12 There is a [1]kind who is [a]pure in his own eyes,
Yet is not washed from his filthiness.
13 There is a [1]kind—oh how [a]lofty are his eyes!
And his eyelids are raised *in arrogance.*
14 There is a [1]kind of *man* whose [a]teeth are *like* swords,
And his [b]jaw teeth *like* knives,
To [c]devour the afflicted from the earth,
And the needy from among men.

15 The leech has two daughters,
"Give," "Give."

24 [a]Lev. 5:1

25 [1]Lit., *gives* [a]Gen. 12:12; 20:2; Luke 12:4; John 12:42, 43 [b]Prov. 18:10; 28:25; Ps. 91:1-16

26 [1]Lit., *face* [a]Is. 49:4; 1 Cor. 4:4

27 [a]Prov. 12:8; Ps. 6:8; 139:21, 22 [b]Prov. 29:10; Ps. 69:4; Matt. 10:22; 24:9; John 15:18; 17:14; 1 John 3:13

1 [1]Or, *burden*

2 [a]Prov. 12:1; Ps. 49:10

4 [1]Lit., *the* [a]Ps. 68:18; John 3:13; Eph. 4:8 [b]Ex. 15:10; Ps. 135:7 [c]Job 26:8; 38:8, 9 [d]Ps. 24:2; Is. 45:18 [e]Rev. 19:12

5 [a]Ps. 12:6; 18:30 [b]Prov. 2:7; Ps. 3:3; 84:11

6 [a]Deut. 4:2; 12:32; Rev. 22:18

8 [1]Lit., *words of falsehood* [a]Job 23:12; Matt. 6:11

9 [a]Deut. 8:12; 31:20; Neh. 9:25; Hos. 13:6 [b]Josh. 24:27; Job 31:28 [c]Ex. 20:7

10 [a]Eccles. 7:21

11 [1]Or, *generation* [a]Prov. 20:20; Ex. 21:17

12 [1]Or, *generation* [a]Prov. 16:2; Luke 18:11

13 [1]Or, *generation* [a]Prov. 6:17; Is. 2:11; 5:15

14 [1]Or, *generation* [a]Ps. 57:4 [b]Job 29:17 [c]Ps. 14:4; Amos 8:4

There are three things that will not be satisfied,
Four that will not say, "Enough":
16 [1a]Sheol, and the [b]barren womb,
Earth that is never satisfied with water,
And fire that never says, "Enough."
17 The eye that [a]mocks a father,
And [1]scorns a mother,
The [b]ravens of the valley will pick it out,
And the young [b]eagles will eat it.

18 There are three things which are too wonderful for me,
Four which I do not understand:
19 The way of an [a]eagle in the sky,
The way of a serpent on a rock,
The way of a ship in the middle of the sea,
And the way of a man with a maid.
20 This is the way of an adulterous woman:
She eats and wipes her mouth,
And says, "I have done no wrong."

21 Under three things the earth quakes,
And under four, it cannot bear up:
22 Under a slave when he becomes king,
And a fool when he is satisfied with food,
23 Under an unloved woman when she gets a husband,
And a maidservant when she supplants her mistress.

24 Four things are small on the earth,
But they are exceedingly wise:
25 The ants are not a strong folk,
But they prepare their food in the summer;
26 The [a]badgers are not mighty folk,
Yet they make their houses in the rocks;
27 The locusts have no king,
Yet all of them go out in [a]ranks;
28 The lizard you may grasp with the hands,
Yet it is in kings' palaces.

29 There are three things which are stately in *their* march,
Even four which are stately when they walk:
30 The lion *which* is [a]mighty among beasts
And does not [1b]retreat before any,
31 The [1]strutting cock, the male goat also,
And a king *when his* army is with him.

32 If you have been foolish in exalting yourself
Or if you have plotted *evil*, [a]*put your* hand on your mouth.
33 For the [1]churning of milk produces butter,
And pressing the nose brings forth blood;
So the [1]churning of anger produces strife.

Chapter 31

THE words of King Lemuel, the [1]oracle which his mother taught him.

16 [1]I.e., The nether world [a]Prov. 27:20 [b]Gen. 30:1

17 [1]Lit., *despises to obey* [a]Gen. 9:22 [b]Deut. 28:26

19 [a]Deut. 28:49; Jer. 48:40; 49:22

26 [a]Lev. 11:5; Ps. 104:18

27 [a]Joel 2:7

30 [1]Lit., *turn back* [a]Judg. 14:18; 2 Sam. 1:23 [b]Mic. 5:8

31 [1]Heb., *girt in the loins*

32 [a]Job 21:5; 40:4; Mic. 7:16

33 [1]Lit., *pressing*

1 [1]Or, *burden*

2 What, O my son?
And what, O [a]son of my womb?
And what, O son of my [b]vows?
3 Do not give your strength to women,
Or your ways to that which [a]destroys kings.
4 It is not for [a]kings, O Lemuel,
It is not for kings to [b]drink wine,
Or for rulers to desire strong drink.
5 Lest they drink and forget what is decreed,
And [a]pervert the [1]rights of all the [2]afflicted.
6 Give strong drink to him who is [a]perishing,
And wine to him [1b]whose life is bitter.
7 Let him drink and forget his poverty,
And remember his trouble no more.
8 [a]Open your mouth for the dumb,
For the [1]rights of all the [2]unfortunate.
9 Open your mouth, [a]judge righteously,
And [1]defend the [b]rights of the afflicted and needy.

10 An [a]excellent wife, who can find?
For her worth is far [b]above jewels.
11 The heart of her husband trusts in her,
And he will have no lack of gain.
12 She does him good and not evil
All the days of her life.
13 She looks for wool and flax,
And works with her [1]hands [2]in delight.
14 She is like [a]merchant ships;
She brings her food from afar.
15 She [a]rises also while it is still night,
And [b]gives food to her household,
And [1]portions to her maidens.
16 She considers a field and buys it;
From [1]her earnings she plants a vineyard.
17 She [a]girds [1]herself with strength,
And makes her arms strong.
18 She senses that her gain is good;
Her lamp does not go out at night.
19 She stretches out her hands to the distaff,
And her [1]hands grasp the spindle.
20 She [1a]extends her hand to the poor;
And she stretches out her hands to the needy.
21 She is not afraid of the snow for her household,
For all her household are [a]clothed with scarlet.
22 She makes [a]coverings for herself;
Her clothing is [b]fine linen and [c]purple.
23 Her husband is known [a]in the gates,
When he sits among the elders of the land.
24 She makes [a]linen garments and sells *them*,
And [1]supplies belts to the [2]tradesmen.
25 Strength and dignity are her clothing,
And she smiles at the [1]future.
26 She opens her mouth in wisdom,
And the [1]teaching of kindness is on her tongue.
27 She looks well to the ways of her household,
And does not eat the bread of idleness.

2 [a]Is. 49:15 [b]1 Sam. 1:11

3 [a]Deut. 17:17; 1 Kin. 11:1; Neh. 13:26

4 [a]Eccles. 10:17 [b]Prov. 20:1; Is. 5:22; Hos. 4:11

5 [1]Lit., *judgment* [2]Lit., *sons of affliction* [a]Prov. 17:15; Ex. 23:6; Deut. 16:19

6 [1]Lit., *bitter of soul* [a]Job 29:13 [b]Job 3:20; Is. 38:15

8 [1]Lit., *judgment* [2]Lit., *sons of passing away* [a]Prov. 24:11; Job 29:12-17; Ps. 82

9 [1]Lit., *judge the afflicted* [a]Lev. 19:15; Deut. 1:16 [b]Is. 1:17; Jer. 22:16

10 [a]Prov. 12:4; 19:14; Ruth 3:11 [b]Prov. 8:11; Job 28:18

13 [1]Lit., *palms* [2]Or, *willingly*

14 [a]Ezek. 27:25

15 [1]Or, *prescribed tasks* [a]Prov. 20:13; Rom. 12:11 [b]Luke 12:42

16 [1]Lit., *the fruit of her palms*

17 [1]Lit., *her loins* [a]1 Kin. 18:46; 2 Kin. 4:29; Job 38:3

19 [1]Lit., *palms*

20 [1]Lit., *spreads out her palm* [a]Prov. 22:9; Deut. 15:11; Job 31:16-20; Rom. 12:13; Eph. 4:28

21 [a]2 Sam. 1:24

22 [a]Prov. 7:16 [b]Gen. 41:42; Rev. 19:8, 14 [c]Judg. 8:26; Luke 16:19

23 [a]Ruth 4:1, 11

24 [1]Lit., *gives* [2]Lit., *Canaanite* [a]Judg. 14:12

25 [1]Lit., *latter days*

26 [1]Or, *law*

28 Her children rise up and bless her;
Her husband *also*, and he praises her, *saying*:
29 "Many daughters have done nobly,
But you excel them all."
30 Charm is deceitful and beauty is vain,
But a woman who [1]fears the LORD, she shall be praised.
31 Give her the [1]product of her hands,
And let her works praise her in the gates.

THE BOOK OF ECCLESIASTES

The Futility of All Endeavor.

THE words of the [a]Preacher, the son of David, king in
Jerusalem.
2 "[1a]Vanity of vanities," says the Preacher,
"[1]Vanity of vanities! All is [2]vanity."

3 [a]What advantage does man have in all his work
Which he does under the sun?
4 A generation goes and a generation comes,
But the [a]earth [1]remains forever.
5 Also, [a]the sun rises and the sun sets;
And [1]hastening to its place it rises there *again*.
6 [1a]Blowing toward the south,
Then turning toward the north,
The wind continues [2]swirling along;
And on its circular courses the wind returns.
7 All the rivers [1]flow into the sea,
Yet the sea is not full.
To the place where the rivers [1]flow,
There they [1]flow again.
8 All things are wearisome;
Man is not able to tell *it*.
[a]The eye is not satisfied with seeing,
Nor is the ear filled with hearing.
9 [a]That which has been is that which will be,
And that which has been done is that which will be done.
So, there is nothing new under the sun.
10 Is there anything of which one might say,
"See this, it is new?"
Already it has existed for ages
Which were before us.
11 There is [a]no remembrance of [1]earlier things;
And also of the [2]later things which will occur,
There will be for them no remembrance
Among those who will come [2]later *still*.
12 I, the [a]Preacher, have been king over Israel in
Jerusalem.
13 And I [a]set my [1]mind to seek and [b]explore by wisdom

30 [1]Or, *reverences*

31 [1]Lit., *fruit*

1 [a]Eccles. 1:12; 7:27; 12:8-10

2 [1]Or, *Futility of futilities* [2]Or, *futile* [a]Eccles. 12:8; Ps. 39:5, 6; 62:9; 144:4; Rom. 8:20

3 [a]Eccles. 2:11; 3:9; 5:16

4 [1]Lit., *stands* [a]Ps. 104:5; 119:90

5 [1]Lit., *panting* [a]Ps. 19:4-6

6 [1]Lit., *Going* [2]Lit., *turning* [a]Eccles. 11:5

7 [1]Lit., *go*

8 [a]Eccles. 4:8; Prov. 27:20

9 [a]Eccles. 2:12; 3:15; 6:10

11 [1]Lit., *first* or *former* [2]Lit., *latter* or *after* [a]Eccles. 2:16; 9:5

12 [a]Eccles. 1:12; 7:27; 12:8-10

13 [1]Lit., *heart* [a]Eccles. 1:17 [b]Eccles. 3:10, 11; 7:25; 8:17

concerning all that has been done under heaven. *It* is a [2]griev-
ous [c]task *which* God has given to the sons of men to be
afflicted with.
14 I have seen all the works which have been done under
the sun, and behold, all is [1a]vanity and striving after wind.
15 What is [a]crooked cannot be straightened, and what is
lacking cannot be counted.
16 I [1]said to myself, "Behold, I have magnified and increased [a]wisdom more than all who were over Jerusalem before me; and my [2]mind has observed a [3]wealth of wisdom and
knowledge."
17 And I [a]set my [1]mind to know wisdom and to [b]know
madness and folly; I realized that this also is striving after
wind.
18 Because [a]in much wisdom there is much grief, and increasing knowledge *results in* increasing pain.

CHAPTER 2

I SAID [1]to myself, "Come now, I will test you with [a]pleasure.
So [2]enjoy yourself." And behold, it too was futility.
2 [a]I said of laughter, "It is madness," and of pleasure,
"What does it accomplish?"
3 I explored with my [1]mind *how* to [a]stimulate my body
with wine while my [1]mind was guiding *me* wisely, and how to
take hold of [b]folly, until I could see [c]what good there is for the
sons of men [2]to do under heaven the [3]few years of their lives.
4 I enlarged my works: I [a]built houses for myself, I
planted [b]vineyards for myself;
5 I made [a]gardens and [b]parks for myself, and I planted in
them all kinds of fruit trees;
6 I made [a]ponds of water for myself from which to irri-
gate a forest of growing trees.
7 I bought male and female slaves, and I had [1a]homeborn
slaves. Also I possessed flocks and [b]herds larger than all who
preceded me in Jerusalem.
8 Also, I collected for myself silver and [a]gold, and the
treasure of [b]kings and provinces. I provided for myself [c]male
and female singers and the pleasures of men—many
concubines.
9 Then I became [a]great and increased more than all who
preceded me in Jerusalem. My wisdom also stood by me.
10 And [a]all that my eyes desired I did not refuse them. I
did not withhold my heart from any pleasure, for my heart was
pleased because of all my labor and this was my [b]reward for all
my labor.
11 Thus I considered all my activities which my hands had
done and the labor which I had [1]exerted, and behold all was
[2a]vanity and striving after wind and there was [b]no profit under
the sun.
12 So I turned to [a]consider wisdom, madness and folly, for
what *will* the man *do* who will come after the king *except*
[b]what has already been done?
13 And I saw that [a]wisdom excels folly as light excels
darkness.

13 [2]Lit., *evil* [c]Eccles. 2:23, 26; 3:10

14 [1]Or, *futility* [a]Eccles. 2:11, 17; 4:4; 6:9

15 [a]Eccles. 7:13

16 [1]Lit., *spoke with my heart, saying* [2]Lit., *heart* [3]Lit., *abundance* [a]Eccles. 2:9; 1 Kin. 3:12; 4:30; 10:23

17 [1]Lit., *heart* [a]Eccles. 1:13 [b]Eccles. 2:12; 7:25

18 [a]Eccles. 2:23; 12:12

1 [1]Lit., *in my heart* [2]Lit., *consider with goodness* [a]Eccles. 7:4; 8:15

2 [a]Eccles. 7:3, 6; Prov. 14:13

3 [1]Lit., *heart* [2]Lit., *which they do* [3]Lit., *days* [a]Eccles. 10:19; Judg. 9:13; Ps. 104:15 [b]Eccles. 7:25 [c]Eccles. 1:24; 3:12, 13; 5:18; 6:12; 8:15; 12:13

4 [a]1 Kin. 7:1-12 [b]Song of Sol. 8:10, 11

5 [a]Song of Sol. 4:16; 5:1 [b]Neh. 2:8

6 [a]Neh. 2:14; 3:15, 16

7 [1]Lit., *sons of the house* [a]Gen. 14:14; 15:3 [b]1 Kin. 4:23

8 [a]1 Kin. 9:28; 10:10, 14, 21 [b]1 Kin. 20:14; Lam. 1:1 [c]2 Sam. 19:35

9 [a]Eccles. 1:16; 1 Chr. 29:25

10 [a]Eccles. 6:2 [b]Eccles. 3:22; 5:18; 9:9

11 [1]Lit., *labored to do* [2]Or, *futility*, and so throughout the chap. [a]Eccles. 2:22, 23; 1:14 [b]Eccles. 1:3; 3:9; 5:16

12 [a]Eccles. 1:17 [b]Eccles. 1:9, 10

13 [a]Eccles. 7:11, 12, 19; 9:18; 10:10

14 The wise man's eyes are in his head, but the [a]fool walks
in darkness. And yet I know that [b]one fate befalls them both.
15 Then I said [1]to myself, "[a]As is the fate of the fool, it
will also befall me. [b]Why then have I been extremely wise?"
So [2]I said to myself, "This too is vanity."
16 For there is [a]no [1]lasting remembrance of the wise man
as with the fool, inasmuch as *in* the coming days all will be
forgotten. And [b]how the wise man and the fool alike die!
17 So I [a]hated life, for the work which had been done
under the sun was [1]grievous to me; because everything is futility and striving after wind.
18 Thus I hated [a]all the fruit of my labor for which I had
labored under the sun, for I must [b]leave it to the man who will
come after me.
19 And who knows whether he will be a wise man or a
fool? Yet he will have [1]control over all the fruit of my labor for
which I have labored by acting wisely under the sun. This too
is vanity.
20 Therefore I [1]completely despaired of all the fruit of my
labor for which I had labored under the sun.
21 When there is a man who has labored with wisdom,
knowledge and [a]skill, then he [b]gives his [1]legacy to one who has
not labored with them. This too is vanity and a great evil.
22 For what does a man get in [a]all his labor and in [1]his
striving with which he labors under the sun?
23 Because all his days his task is painful and [a]grievous;
even at night his [1]mind [b]does not rest. This too is vanity.
24 There is [a]nothing better for a man *than* to eat and
drink and [1]tell himself that his labor is good. This also I have
seen, that it is [b]from the hand of God.
25 For who can eat and who can have enjoyment without
[1]Him?
26 For to a person who is good in His sight [a]He has given
wisdom and knowledge and joy, while [b]to the sinner He has
given the task of gathering and collecting so that He may [c]give
to one who is good in God's sight. This too is [d]vanity and
striving after wind.

Chapter 3

THERE is an appointed time for everything. And there is a
[a]time for every [1]event under heaven—
2 A time to give birth, and a [a]time to die;
A time to plant, and a time to uproot what is planted.
3 A time to kill, and a time to heal;
A time to tear down, and a time to build up.
4 A time to [a]weep, and a time to [b]laugh;
A time to mourn, and a time to [c]dance.
5 A time to throw stones, and a time to gather stones;
A time to embrace, and a time to shun embracing.
6 A time to search, and a time to give up as lost;
A time to keep, and a time to throw away.
7 A time to tear apart, and a time to sew together;
A time to [a]be silent, and a time to speak.
8 A time to love, and a time to [a]hate;
A time for war, and a time for peace.

14 [a]Prov. 17:24; 1 John 2:11 [b]Eccles. 3:19; 6:6; 7:2; 9:2, 3; Ps. 49:10

15 [1]Lit., *in my heart* [2]Lit., *I spoke in heart* [a]Eccles. 2:16 [b]Eccles. 6:8, 11

16 [1]Lit., *forever* [a]Eccles. 1:11; 4:16; 9:5 [b]Eccles. 2:14

17 [1]Lit., *evil* [a]Eccles. 4:2

18 [a]Eccles. 2:11; 1:3 [b]Ps. 39:6; 49:10

19 [1]Lit., *dominion*

20 [1]Lit., *turned aside my heart to despair*

21 [1]Lit., *share* [a]Eccles. 4:4 [b]Eccles. 2:18

22 [1]Lit., *the striving of his heart* [a]Eccles. 2:11; 1:3

23 [1]Lit., *heart* [a]Eccles. 1:18; 5:17; Job 5:7; 14:1 [b]Ps. 127:2

24 [1]Lit., *causes his soul to see good in his labor* [a]Eccles. 2:3; 3:12, 13, 22; 5:18; 6:12; 8:15; 9:7; 1 Tim. 6:17 [b]Eccles. 3:13

25 [1]So Gk.; Heb., *me*

26 [a]Job 32:8; Prov. 2:6 [b]Job 15:20 [c]Job 27:16, 17; Prov. 13:22 [d]Eccles. 1:14

1 [1]Lit., *delight* [a]Eccles. 3:17; 8:6

2 [a]Job 14:5; Heb. 9:27

4 [a]Rom. 12:15 [b]Ps. 126:2 [c]Ex. 15:20

7 [a]Amos 5:13

8 [a]Ps. 101:3; Prov. 13:5

9 [a]What profit is there to the worker from that in which
he toils?
10 I have seen the [a]task which God has given the sons of
men with which to occupy themselves.
11 He has [a]made everything [1]appropriate in its time. He
has also set eternity in their heart, [2]yet so that man [b]will not
find out the work which God has done from the beginning
even to the end.
12 I know that there is [a]nothing better for them than to
rejoice and to do good in one's lifetime,
13 moreover, that every man who eats and drinks sees
good in all his labor—it is the [a]gift of God.
14 I know that everything God does will remain forever;
there is nothing to add to it and there is nothing to take from
it, for God has *so* worked that men should [1a]fear Him.
15 That [a]which is has been already, and that which will be
has already been, for God seeks what has passed by.
16 Furthermore, I have seen under the sun *that* in the
place of justice there is [a]wickedness, and in the place of righteousness there is wickedness.
17 I said [1]to myself, "[a]God will judge both the righteous
man and the wicked man," for a [b]time for every [2]matter and
for every deed is there.
18 I said [1]to myself concerning the sons of men, "God has
surely tested them in order for them to see that they are but
[a]beasts."
19 [a]For the fate of the sons of men and the fate of beasts
[1]is the same. As one dies so dies the other; indeed, they all have
the same breath and there is no advantage for man over beast,
for all is [2]vanity.
20 All go to the same place. All came from the [a]dust and
all return to the dust.
21 Who knows that the [a]breath of man ascends upward
and the breath of the beast descends downward to the earth?
22 And I have seen that [a]nothing is better than that man
should be happy in his activities, for that is his *lot*. For who will
bring him to see [b]what will occur after him?

Chapter 4

THEN I looked again at all the acts of [a]oppression which
were being done under the sun. And behold *I saw* the tears of
the oppressed and *that* they had [b]no one to comfort *them;* and
on the side of their oppressors was power, but they had no one
to comfort *them.*
2 So [a]I congratulated the dead who are already dead
more than the living who are still living.
3 But [a]better *off* than both of them is the one who has
never existed, who has never seen the evil activity that is done
under the sun.
4 And I have seen that every labor and every [a]skill which
is done is *the result of* rivalry between a man and his neighbor.
This too is [1b]vanity and striving after wind.
5 The fool [a]folds his hands and [b]consumes his own flesh.
6 One hand full of rest is [a]better than two fists full of
labor and striving after wind.

9 [a]Eccles. 1:3; 2:11; 5:16

10 [a]Eccles. 1:13; 2:26

11 [1]Lit., *beautiful* [2]Or, *without which men* [a]Gen. 1:31 [b]Eccles. 7:23; 8:17; Job 5:9; Rom. 11:33

12 [a]Eccles. 2:24

13 [a]Eccles. 2:24; 5:19

14 [1]Or, *be in awe before Him* [a]Eccles. 5:7; 7:18; 8:12, 13; 12:13

15 [a]Eccles. 1:9; 6:10

16 [a]Eccles. 4:1; 5:8; 8:9

17 [1]Lit., *in my heart* [2]Or, *delight* [a]Eccles. 11:9; Gen. 18:25; Ps. 96:13; 98:9; Matt. 16:27; Rom. 2:6-10; 2 Thess. 1:6-9 [b]Eccles. 3:1; 8:6

18 [1]Lit., *in my heart* [a]Ps. 49:12, 20; 73:22

19 [1]Lit., *and they have one fate* [2]Or, *futility* [a]Eccles. 9:12

20 [a]Eccles. 12:7; Gen. 3:19; Ps. 103:14

21 [a]Eccles. 12:7

22 [a]Eccles. 2:24 [b]Eccles. 2:18; 6:12; 8:7; 10:14

1 [a]Eccles. 3:16; 5:8; Job 35:9; Ps. 12:5; Is. 5:7 [b]Lam. 1:9

2 [a]Eccles. 2:17; Job 3:11-26

3 [a]Eccles. 6:3

4 [1]Or, *futility,* and so throughout the chap. [a]Eccles. 2:21 [b]Eccles. 1:14

5 [a]Prov. 6:10; 24:33 [b]Is. 9:20

6 [a]Prov. 15:16, 17; 16:8

7 Then I looked again at vanity under the sun.
8 There was a certain man without a [1]dependent, having
neither a son nor a brother, yet there was no end to all his
labor. Indeed, [a]his eyes were not satisfied with riches *and he
never asked*, "And [b]for whom am I laboring and depriving
myself of pleasure?" This too is vanity and it is a [c]grievous task.
9 Two are better than one because they have a good
return for their labor.
10 For if [1]either of them falls, the one will lift up his
companion. But woe to the one who falls when there is not
[2]another to lift him up.
11 Furthermore, if two lie down together they [1]keep
warm, but [a]how can one be warm *alone?*
12 And if [1]one can overpower him who is alone, two can
resist him. A cord of three *strands* is not quickly torn apart.
13 A [a]poor, yet wise lad is better than an old and foolish
king who no longer knows *how* to receive [1]instruction.
14 For he has come [a]out of prison to become king, even
though he was born poor in his kingdom.
15 I have seen all the living under the sun throng to the
side of the second lad who [1]replaces him.
16 There is no end to all the people, to all who were
before them, and even the ones who will come later will not be
happy with him, for this too is [a]vanity and striving after wind.

Chapter 5

1a
GUARD your steps as you go to the house of God, and draw
near to listen rather than to offer the [b]sacrifice of fools; for
they do not know they are doing evil.
2 [1]Do not be [a]hasty [2]in word or [3]impulsive in thought to
bring up a matter in the presence of God. For God is in heaven
and you are on the earth; therefore let your [b]words be few.
3 For the dream comes through much [1]effort, and the
voice of a [a]fool through many words.
4 When you [a]make a vow to God, do not be late in
paying it, for He takes no delight in fools. [b]Pay what you vow!
5 It is [a]better that you should not vow than that you
should vow and not pay.
6 Do not let your [1]speech cause [2]you to sin and do not
say in the presence of the messenger *of God* that it was a
[a]mistake. Why should God be angry on account of your voice
and destroy the work of your hands?
7 For in many dreams and in many words there is [1]empti-
ness. Rather [2]fear [a]God.
8 If you see [a]oppression of the poor and [b]denial of justice
and righteousness in the province, do not be [c]shocked at the
[1]sight, for one [2]official watches over another [2]official, and
there are [d]higher [3]officials over them.
9 After all, a king who cultivates the field is an advantage
to the land.
10 [a]He who loves money will not be satisfied with money,
nor he who loves abundance *with its* income. This too is
[1]vanity.
11 [a]When good things increase, those who consume them

8 [1]Lit., *second*
[a]Eccles. 1:8; 5:10; Prov. 27:20
[b]Eccles. 2:21 [c]Eccles. 1:13

10 [1]Lit., *they fall* [2]Lit., *a second*

11 [1]Lit., *have warmth*
[a]1 Kin. 1:1

12 [1]Lit., *he*

13 [1]Or, *warning*
[a]Eccles. 7:19; 9:15

14 [a]Gen. 41:14, 41-43

15 [1]Lit., *stands in his stead*

16 [a]Eccles. 1:14

1 [1]4:17 in Heb.
[a]Ex. 3:5; 30:18-20; Is. 1:12
[b]1 Sam. 15:22; Prov. 15:8; 21:27

2 [1]5:1 in Heb. [2]Lit., *with your mouth* [3]Lit., *hurry your heart*
[a]Prov. 20:25 [b]Prov. 10:19; Matt. 6:7

3 [1]Lit., *task*
[a]Eccles. 10:14; Job 11:2

4 [a]Num. 30:2; Ps. 50:14; 76:11 [b]Ps. 66:13, 14

5 [a]Prov. 20:25; Acts 5:4

6 [1]Lit., *mouth* [2]Lit., *your body*
[a]Lev. 4:2, 22; Num. 15:25

7 [1]Lit., *vanity* [2]Or, *revere*
[a]Eccles. 3:14; 7:18; 8:12, 13; 12:13

8 [1]Lit., *delight* [2]Lit., *high one* [3]Lit., *ones*
[a]Eccles. 4:1 [b]Ezek. 18:18
[c]1 Pet. 4:12 [d]Ex. 2:25; Ps. 12:5

10 [1]Or, *futility*
[a]Eccles. 2:10, 11

11 [a]Eccles. 2:9

increase. So what is the advantage to their owners except to
[1]look on?
12 The sleep of the working man is [a]pleasant, whether he
eats little or much. But the [1]full stomach of the rich man does
not allow him to sleep.
13 There is a grievous evil *which* I have seen under the
sun: [a]riches being [1]hoarded by their owner to his hurt.
14 When those riches were lost through a [1]bad investment
and he had fathered a son, then there was nothing [2]to support
him.
15 [a]As he had come naked from his mother's womb, so
will he return as he came. He will take [b]nothing from the fruit
of his labor that he can carry in his hand.
16 And this also is a grievous evil—exactly as a man [1]is
born, thus will he [2]die. So, [a]what is the advantage to him who
[b]toils for the wind?
17 Throughout his life *he* also eats in darkness with [a]great
vexation, sickness and anger.
18 Here is what I have seen to be [a]good and [1]fitting: to
eat, to drink and [2]enjoy oneself in all one's labor in which he
toils under the sun *during* the few [3]years of his life which God
has given him; for this is his [4b]reward.
19 Furthermore, as for every man to whom [a]God has giv-
en riches and wealth, He has also [b]empowered him to eat
from them and to receive his [1]reward and rejoice in his labor;
this is the [c]gift of God.
20 For he will not often [1]consider the [2]years of his life,
because God keeps [3]him occupied with the gladness of his
heart.

Chapter 6

THERE is an [a]evil which I have seen under the sun and it is
prevalent [1]among men—
2 a man to whom God has [a]given riches and wealth and
honor so that his soul [b]lacks nothing of all that he desires, but
God has not empowered him to eat from them, for a foreigner
[1]enjoys them. This is [2]vanity and a sore affliction.
3 If a man fathers a hundred *children* and lives many
years, however many [1]they be, but his soul is not satisfied with
good things, and he does not even have a *proper* [a]burial, *then* I
say, "Better [b]the miscarriage than he,
4 for it comes in futility and goes into obscurity; and its
name is covered in obscurity.
5 "It never sees the sun and it never knows *anything;* [1]it is
better off than he.
6 "Even if the *other* man lives a thousand years twice and
does not [1]enjoy good things—[a]do not all go to one place?"
7 [a]All a man's labor is for his mouth and yet the [1]appetite
is not [2]satisfied.
8 For [a]what advantage does the wise man have over the
fool? What *advantage* does the poor man have, knowing *how*
to walk before the living?
9 What the eyes [a]see is better than what the soul [1]desires.
This too is [b]futility and a striving after wind.
10 Whatever [a]exists has already been named, and it is

11 [1]Lit., *see with their eyes*

12 [1]Lit., *satiety* [a]Prov. 3:24

13 [1]Lit., *guarded* [a]Eccles. 6:2

14 [1]Lit., *evil task* [2]Lit., *in his hand*

15 [a]Job 1:21 [b]Ps. 49:17; 1 Tim. 6:7

16 [1]Lit., *comes* [2]Lit., *go* [a]Eccles. 1:3; 2:11; 3:9 [b]Prov. 11:29

17 [a]Eccles. 2:23

18 [1]Lit., *beautiful* [2]Lit., *see good* [3]Or, *days* [4]Or, *share* [a]Eccles. 2:24 [b]Eccles. 2:10

19 [1]Or, *share* [a]Eccles. 6:2; 2 Chr. 1:12 [b]Eccles. 6:2 [c]Eccles. 3:13

20 [1]Lit., *remember* [2]Or, *days* [3]So with Gk.

1 [1]Lit., *upon* [a]Eccles. 5:13

2 [1]Lit., *eats from them* [2]Or, *futility* [a]1 Kin. 3:13 [b]Ps. 17:14; 73:7

3 [1]Lit., *the days of his years* [a]Is. 14:20; Jer. 8:2; 22:19 [b]Eccles. 4:3; Job 3:16

5 [1]Lit., *more rest has this one than that*

6 [1]Lit., *see* [a]Eccles. 2:14

7 [1]Lit., *soul* [2]Lit., *filled* [a]Prov. 16:26

8 [a]Eccles. 2:15

9 [1]Lit., *goes after* [a]Eccles. 11:9 [b]Eccles. 1:14

10 [a]Eccles. 1:9; 3:15

known what man is; for he [b]cannot dispute with him who is
stronger than he is.
11 For there are many words which increase futility. What
then is the advantage to a man?
12 For who knows what is good for a man during *his* lifetime, *during* the few [1]years of his futile life? He will [2]spend
them like a shadow. For who can tell a man [a]what will be after
him under the sun?

CHAPTER 7

A [a]GOOD name is better than a good ointment,
And the [b]day of *one's* death is better than the day of one's birth.
2 It is better to go to a house of mourning
Than to go to a house of feasting,
Because [1]that is the [a]end of every man,
And the living [2b]takes *it* to [3]heart.
3 [a]Sorrow is better than laughter,
For [b]when a face is sad a heart may be happy.
4 The [1]mind of the wise is in the house of mourning,
While the [1]mind of fools is in the house of pleasure.
5 It is better to [a]listen to the rebuke of a wise man
Than for one to listen to the song of fools.
6 For as the [1]crackling of [a]thorn bushes under a pot,
So is the [b]laughter of the fool,
And this too is futility.
7 For [a]oppression makes a wise man mad,
And a [b]bribe [1]corrupts the heart.
8 The [a]end of a matter is better than its beginning;
[b]Patience of spirit is better than haughtiness of spirit.
9 Do not be [1a]eager in your heart to be angry,
For anger resides in the bosom of fools.
10 Do not say, "Why is it that the former days were better than these?"
For it is not from wisdom that you ask about this.
11 Wisdom along with an inheritance is good
And an [a]advantage to those who see the sun.
12 For [a]wisdom is [1]protection *just as* money is [1]protection.
But the advantage of knowledge is that [b]wisdom preserves the lives of its possessors.
13 Consider the [a]work of God,
For who is [b]able to straighten what He has bent?
14 [a]In the day of prosperity be happy,
But [b]in the day of adversity consider—
God has made the one as well as the other
So that man may [c]not discover anything *that will be* after him.
15 I have seen everything during my [1a]lifetime of futility;
there is [b]a righteous man who perishes in his righteousness, and
there is [c]a wicked man who prolongs *his life* in his wickedness.
16 Do not be excessively righteous, and do not [a]be overly
wise. Why should you ruin yourself?
17 Do not be excessively wicked, and do not be a fool.
Why should you [a]die before your time?

10 [b]Prov. 21:30; Job 9:32; 40:2; Is. 45:9

12 [1]Lit., *days* [2]Lit., *do* [a]Eccles. 3:22

1 [a]Prov. 22:1 [b]Eccles. 7:8; 4:2

2 [1]I.e., death [2]Lit., *gives* [3]Lit., *his heart* [a]Eccles. 2:16; 3:19, 20; 6:6; 9:2, 3 [b]Ps. 90:12

3 [a]Eccles. 2:2 [b]2 Cor. 7:10

4 [1]Lit., *heart*

5 [a]Eccles. 9:17; Ps.141:5; Prov. 6:23; 13:18; 15:31, 32; 25:12

6 [1]Lit., *voice* [a]Ps. 58:9; 118:12 [b]Eccles. 2:2

7 [1]Lit., *destroys* [a]Eccles. 4:1; 5:8 [b]Ex. 23:8; Deut. 16:19; Prov. 17:8, 23

8 [a]Eccles. 7:1 [b]Prov. 14:29; 16:32; Gal. 5:22; Eph.4:2

9 [1]Lit., *hasty in your spirit* [a]Prov. 14:17; James 1:19

11 [a]Prov. 8:10, 11

12 [1]Lit., *in a shadow* [a]Eccles. 7:19; 9:18 [b]Prov. 3:18; 8:35

13 [a]Eccles. 3:11; 8:17 [b]Eccles. 1:15

14 [a]Eccles. 3:22; 9:7; 11:9; Deut. 26:11 [b]Deut. 8:5 [c]Eccles. 3:22

15 [1]Lit., *days* [a]Eccles. 6:12; 9:9 [b]Eccles. 8:14 [c]Eccles. 8:12, 13

16 [a]Rom. 12:3

17 [a]Job 22:16; Ps. 55:23; Prov. 10:27

18 It is good that you grasp [a]one thing, and also not [1b]let go of the other, for the one who [c]fears God comes forth with [2]both of them.

19 [a]Wisdom strengthens a wise man more than ten rulers who are in a city.

20 Indeed, [a]there is not a righteous man on earth who *continually* does good and who never sins.

21 Also, do not [1]take seriously all words which are spoken, lest you hear your servant [a]cursing you.

22 For [1]you also have realized that you likewise have many times cursed others.

23 I tested all this with wisdom, *and* I said, "I will be wise," [a]but it was far from me.

24 What has been is remote and [a]exceedingly [1]mysterious. [b]Who can discover it?

25 I [1]directed my [2]mind to know, to investigate, and to seek wisdom and an explanation, and to know the evil of folly and the [a]foolishness of madness.

26 And I discovered more [a]bitter than death the woman whose heart is [b]snares and nets, whose hands are chains. [c]One who is pleasing to God will escape from her, but [d]the sinner will be captured by her.

27 "Behold, I have discovered this," says the Preacher, "*adding* one thing to another to find an explanation,

28 which [1]I am still seeking but have not found. I have found one man among a thousand, but I have not found a [a]woman among all these.

29 "Behold, I have found only this, that [a]God made men upright, but they have sought out many devices."

Chapter 8

WHO is like the wise man and who knows the interpretation of a matter? A man's wisdom illumines [1a]him and causes his [b]stern face to [2]beam.

2 I say, "Keep the [1]command of the king because of the [a]oath [2]before God.

3 Do not be in a hurry [1a]to leave him. Do not join in an evil matter, for he will do whatever he pleases.

4 Since the word of the king is authoritative, [a]who will say to him, "What are you doing?"

5 He who [a]keeps a *royal* command [b]experiences no [1]trouble, for a wise heart knows the proper time and procedure.

6 For there is a proper time and procedure [a]for every delight, when a man's trouble is heavy upon him.

7 If no one [a]knows what will happen, who can tell him when it will happen?

8 [a]No man has authority to restrain the wind with the wind, or authority over the day of death; and there is no [b]discharge in the time of war, and evil [c]will not deliver [1]those who practice it.

9 All this I have seen and applied my [1]mind to every deed that has been done under the sun wherein a man has exercised [a]authority over *another* man to his hurt.

18 [1]Lit., *rest your hand* [2]Lit., *all* [a]Eccles. 7:16 [b]Eccles. 7:17 [c]Eccles. 3:14; 5:7; 8:12, 13; 12:13

19 [a]Eccles. 7:12; 9:13-18

20 [a]1 Kin. 8:46; 2 Chr. 6:36; Ps. 143:2; Prov. 20:9; Rom. 3:23

21 [1]Lit., *give your heart to* [a]Prov. 30:1

22 [1]Lit., *your heart knows also*

23 [a]Eccles. 3:11; 8:17

24 [1]Lit., *deep* [a]Rom. 11:33 [b]Job 11:7; 37:23

25 [1]Lit., *turned about* [2]Lit., *heart* [a]Eccles. 1:17; 10:13

26 [a]Prov. 5:4 [b]Prov. 7:23 [c]Prov. 6:23, 24 [d]Prov. 22:14

28 [1]Lit., *my soul* [a]1 Kin. 11:3

29 [a]Gen. 1:27

1 [1]Lit., *his face* [2]Or, *change* [a]Ex. 34:29, 30 [b]Deut. 28:50

2 [1]Lit., *mouth* [2]Lit., *of* [a]Ex. 22:11; 2 Sam. 21:7; Ezek. 17:18

3 [1]Lit., *to go out from his presence* [a]Eccles. 10:4

4 [a]Job 9:12; Dan. 4:35

5 [1]Lit., *evil thing* [a]Eccles. 12:13 [b]Prov. 12:21

6 [a]Eccles. 3:1, 17

7 [a]Eccles. 3:22; 6:12; 7:14; 9:12

8 [1]Lit., *its possessors* [a]Ps. 49:7-9 [b]Deut. 20:5-8 [c]Eccles. 8:13

9 [1]Lit., *heart* [a]Eccles. 4:1; 5:8; 7:7

10 So then, I have seen the wicked buried, those who used
to go in and out from the holy place, and they are [a]*soon*
forgotten in the city where they did thus. This too is futility.
11 Because the [a]sentence against an evil deed is not executed quickly, therefore [b]the hearts of the sons of men among
them are given fully to do evil.
12 Although a sinner does evil a hundred *times* and may
[a]lengthen his *life*, still I know that it will be [b]well for those who
fear God, who fear [1]Him openly.
13 But it will [a]not be well for the evil man and he will not
lengthen his days like a [b]shadow, because he does not fear
God.
14 There is futility which is done on the earth, that is,
there are [a]righteous men to whom it [1]happens according to the
deeds of the wicked. On the other hand, there are [b]evil men to
whom it [1]happens according to the deeds of the righteous. I
say that this too is futility.
15 So I commended pleasure, for there is nothing good for
[a]a man under the sun except to eat and to drink and to be
merry, and this will stand by him in his [1]toils *throughout* the
days of his life which God has given him under the sun.
16 When I [a]gave my heart to know wisdom and to see the
task which has been done on the earth (even though one
should [1b]never sleep day or night),
17 and I saw every work of God, *I concluded* that [a]man
cannot discover the work which has been done under the sun.
Even though man should seek laboriously, he will not discover;
and [b]though the wise man should say, "I know," he cannot
discover.

Chapter 9

FOR I have taken all this to my heart and explain [1]it that
righteous men, wise men, and their deeds are [a]in the hand of
God. [b]Man does not know whether *it will be* [c]love or hatred;
anything [2]awaits him.
2 [a]It is the same for all. There is [b]one fate for the righteous and for the wicked; for the good, for the clean, and for
the unclean; for the man who offers a sacrifice and for the one
who does not sacrifice. As the good man is, so is the sinner; as
the swearer is, so is the one who [1]is afraid to swear.
3 This is an evil in all that is done under the sun, that
there is [a]one fate for all men. Furthermore, [b]the hearts of the
sons of men are full of evil, and [c]insanity is in their hearts
throughout their lives. Afterwards they *go* to the dead.
4 For whoever is joined with the living, there is hope;
surely a live dog is better than a dead lion.
5 For the living know they will die; but the dead do not
[a]know anything, nor have they any longer a reward, for their
[b]memory is forgotten.
6 Indeed their love, their hate, and their zeal have already perished, and they will no longer have a [a]share in all that
is done under the sun.
7 Go *then*, [a]eat your bread in happiness, and drink your
wine with a cheerful heart; for God has already approved your
works.

10 [a]Eccles. 1:11; 2:16; 4:16; 9:5, 15

11 [a]Ex. 34:6; Ps. 86:15; Rom. 2:4; 2 Pet. 3:9 [b]Eccles. 9:3

12 [1]Lit., *before Him* [a]Eccles. 7:15; Is. 65:20 [b]Deut. 4:40; 12:25; Ps. 37:11; Prov. 1:33; Is. 3:10

13 [a]Eccles. 8:8; Is. 3:11 [b]Eccles. 6:12; Job 14:2

14 [1]Lit., *strikes* [a]Eccles. 7:15; Ps. 73:14 [b]Job 21:7; Ps. 73:3, 12; Jer. 12:1; Mal. 3:15

15 [1]Lit., *labor* [a]Eccles. 2:24; 3:12, 13; 5:18; 9:7

16 [1]Lit., *see no sleep in his eyes* [a]Eccles. 1:13, 14 [b]Eccles. 2:23

17 [a]Eccles. 3:11 [b]Eccles. 7:23; Ps. 73:16; Rom. 11:33

1 [1]Lit., *all this* [2]Lit., *is before them* [a]Deut. 33:3; Job 12:10; Ps. 110:109 [b]Eccles. 10:14 [c]Eccles. 9:6

2 [1]Lit., *fears an oath* [a]Eccles. 9:11 Job 9:22 [b]Eccles. 2:14; 3:19; 6:6; 7:2

3 [a]Eccles. 9:2 [b]Eccles. 8:11 [c]Eccles. 1:7

5 [a]Job 14:21 [b]Eccles. 1:11; 2:16; 8:10; Ps. 88:12; Is. 26:14

6 [a]Eccles. 2:10; 3:22

7 [a]Eccles. 2:24

8 Let your [a]clothes be white all the time, and let not oil
be lacking on your [b]head.
9 Enjoy life with the woman whom you love all the days
of your [1]fleeting [a]life which He has given to you under the sun;
for this is your reward in life, and in your toil in which you
have labored under the sun.
10 Whatever your hand finds to do, verily, [a]do *it* with all
your might; for there is no [b]activity or planning or wisdom in
[c]Sheol where you are going.
11 I again saw under the sun that the [a]race is not to the
swift, and the [b]battle is not to the warriors, and neither is bread
to the wise, nor [c]wealth to the discerning, nor favor to men of
ability; for time and [d]chance overtake them all.
12 Moreover, man does not [a]know his time: like fish
caught in a treacherous net, and [b]birds trapped in a snare, so
the sons of men are [c]ensnared at an evil time when it [d]suddenly
falls on them.
13 Also this I came to see as wisdom under the sun, and it
[1]impressed me.
14 There was a small city with few men in it and a great
king came to it, surrounded it, and constructed large siege-
works against it.
15 But there was found in it a [a]poor wise man and he
[1]delivered the city [b]by his wisdom. Yet [c]no one remembered
that poor man.
16 So I said, "[a]Wisdom is better than strength." But the
wisdom of the poor man is despised and his words are not
heeded.
17 The [a]words of the wise heard in quietness are *better*
than the shouting of a ruler among fools.
18 [a]Wisdom is better than weapons of war, but [b]one sinner destroys much good.

Chapter 10

DEAD flies make a [a]perfumer's oil stink, so a little foolishness is weightier than wisdom *and* honor.
2 A wise man's heart *directs him* toward the right, but
the foolish man's heart *directs him* toward the left.
3 Even when the fool walks along the road his [1]sense is
lacking, and he [2a]demonstrates to everyone *that* he is a fool.
4 If the ruler's [1]temper rises against you, [a]do not abandon
your position, because [b]composure allays great offenses.
5 There is an evil I have seen under the sun, like an [a]error
which goes forth from the ruler—
6 [a]folly is set in many exalted places while rich men sit in
humble places.
7 I have seen [a]slaves *riding* [b]on horses and princes walking like slaves on the land.
8 [a]He who digs a pit may fall into it, and a [b]serpent may
bite him who breaks through a wall.
9 He who quarries stones may be hurt by them, and he
who splits logs may be endangered by them.
10 If the [1]axe is dull and he does not sharpen *its* edge, then
he must [2]exert more strength. Wisdom has the advantage of
giving success.

8 [a]Rev. 3:4 [b]Ps. 23:5
9 [1]Lit., *life of vanity* [a]Eccles. 6:12; 7:15
10 [a]Eccles. 11:6; Rom. 12:11; Col. 3:23 [b]Eccles. 9:5 [c]Gen. 37:35; Job 21:13; Is. 38:10
11 [a]Amos 2:14, 15 [b]2 Chr. 20:15; Ps. 76:5; Is. 40:29; Zech. 4:6 [c]Deut. 8:17, 18 [d]1 Sam. 6:9
12 [a]Eccles. 8:7 [b]Prov. 7:23 [c]Prov. 29:6; Is. 24:18; Hos. 9:8 [d]Luke 21:34, 35
13 [1]Lit., *great it was to me*
15 [1]Or, *might have delivered* [a]Eccles. 4:13 [b]2 Sam. 20:22 [c]Eccles. 2:16; 8:10
16 [a]Eccles. 7:12, 19
17 [a]Eccles. 7:5; 10:12
18 [a]Eccles. 9:16 [b]Josh. 7:1-26; 2 Kin. 21:2-17
1 [a]Ex. 30:25
3 [1]Lit., *heart* [2]Lit., *says* [a]Prov. 13:16; 18:2
4 [1]Lit., *spirit* [a]Eccles. 8:3 [b]1 Sam. 25:24-33; Prov. 25:15
5 [a]Eccles. 5:6
6 [a]Esth. 3:1; Prov. 28:12; 29:2
7 [a]Prov. 19:10 [b]Esth. 6:8
8 [a]Ps. 7:15; Prov. 26:27 [b]Amos 5:19
10 [1]Lit., *iron* [2]Lit., *strengthen*

11 If the serpent bites [a]before [1]being charmed, there is no
profit for the charmer.
12 [a]Words from the mouth of a wise man are gracious,
while the lips of a [b]fool consume him;
13 the beginning of [1]his talking is folly, and the end of [2]it
is wicked [a]madness.
14 Yet the [a]fool multiplies words. No man knows what
will happen, and who can tell him [b]what will come after him?
15 The toil of a [1]fool *so* wearies him that he does not *even*
know how to go to a city.
16 Woe to you, O land, whose [a]king is a lad and whose
princes [1]feast in the morning.
17 Blessed are you, O land, whose king is of nobility and
whose princes eat at the appropriate time—for strength, and
not for [a]drunkenness.
18 Through [a]indolence the rafters sag, and through slackness the house leaks.
19 *Men* prepare a meal for enjoyment, and [a]wine makes
life merry, and [b]money [1]is the answer to everything.
20 Furthermore, [a]in your bedchamber do not [b]curse a
king, and in your sleeping rooms do not curse a rich man, for a
bird of the heavens will carry the sound, and the winged creature will make the matter known.

Chapter 11

[a]CAST your bread on the surface of the waters, for you [b]will
find it [1]after many days.
2 [a]Divide your portion to seven, or even to eight, for you
do not know what [b]misfortune may occur on the earth.
3 If the clouds are full, they pour out rain upon the earth;
and whether a tree falls toward the south or toward the north,
wherever the tree falls, there it [1]lies.
4 He who watches the wind will not sow and he who
looks at the clouds will not reap.
5 Just as you do not [a]know [1]the path of the wind and
[b]how bones *are formed* in the womb of the [2]pregnant woman,
so you do not [c]know the activity of God who makes all things.
6 Sow your seed [a]in the morning, and do not [1]be idle in
the evening, for you do not know whether [2]morning or evening
sowing will succeed, or whether both of them alike will be
good.
7 The light is pleasant, and *it is* good for the eyes to [a]see
the sun.
8 Indeed, if a man should live many years, let him [a]re-
joice in them all, and let him remember the [b]days of darkness,
for they shall be many. Everything that is to come *will be*
futility.
9 [a]Rejoice, young man, during your childhood, and let
your heart be pleasant during the days of young manhood.
And [b]follow the [1]impulses of your heart and the [2]desires of
your eyes. Yet know that [c]God will bring you to judgment for
all these things.
10 So, remove vexation from your heart and put away
[1a]pain from your body, because childhood and the prime of
life are fleeting.

11 [1]Lit., *without enchantment* [a]Ps. 58:4, 5; Jer. 8:17

12 [a]Prov. 10:32; 22:11; Luke 4:22 [b]Eccles. 4:5; Prov. 10:14; 18:7

13 [1]Lit., *the words of his mouth* [2]Lit., *his mouth* [a]Eccles. 7:25

14 [a]Eccles. 5:3; Prov. 15:2 [b]Eccles. 3:22; 6:12; 7:14; 8:7

15 [1]Lit., *fools*

16 [1]Lit., *eat* [a]Is. 3:4, 12

17 [a]Prov. 31:4; Is. 5:11

18 [a]Prov. 24:30-34

19 [1]Lit., *answers all* [a]Eccles. 2:3; Judg. 9:13; Ps. 104:15 [b]Eccles. 7:12

20 [a]2 Kin. 6:12; Luke 12:3 [b]Ex. 22:28; Acts 23:5

1 [1]Lit., *in, within* [a]Is. 32:20 [b]Deut. 15:10; Prov. 19:17; Matt. 10:42; 2 Cor. 9:8; Gal. 6:9; Heb. 6:10

2 [a]Ps. 112:9; Matt. 5:42; Luke 6:30; 1 Tim. 6:18, 19 [b]Eccles. 11:8; 12:1

3 [1]Lit., *is*

5 [1]Or, with many mss., *how the spirit enters the bones in the womb* [2]Lit., *full* [a]John 3:8 [b]Ps. 139:13-16 [c]Eccles. 1:13; 3:10, 11; 8:17

6 [1]Lit., *let down your hand* [2]Lit., *this or that* [a]Eccles. 9:10

7 [a]Eccles. 6:5; 7:11

8 [a]Eccles. 9:7 [b]Eccles. 12:1

9 [1]Lit., *ways* [2]Lit., *sights* [a]Eccles. 2:10 [b]Num. 15:39; Job 31:7 [c]Eccles. 3:17; 12:4; Rom. 14:10

10 [1]Lit., *evil* [a]2 Cor. 7:1; 2 Tim. 2:22

1 [a]Deut. 8:18; Neh. 4:14; Ps. 63:6; 119:55 [b]Eccles. 11:8 [c]2 Sam. 19:35

2 [a]Is. 5:30; 13:10; Ezek. 32:7, 8; Joel 3:5; Matt. 24:29

3 [1]Or, *holes* [a]Ps. 35:14; 38:6 [b]Gen. 27:1; 48:10; 1 Sam. 3:2

4 [1]Lit., *be brought low* [a]Ps. 141:3 [b]Jer. 25:10; Rev. 18:22 [c]2 Sam. 19:35

5 [1]Lit., *they* [a]Job 17:13; 30:32 [b]Gen. 50:10; Jer. 9:7

6 [1]So with Gk.; Heb., *removed* [a]Zech. 4:2, 3

7 [1]Or, *breath* [a]Eccles. 3:20; Gen. 3:19; Job 34:15; Ps. 104:29 [b]Eccles. 3:21; Job 34:14; Luke 23:46; Acts 7:59 [c]Num. 16:22; 27:16; Is. 57:16; Zech. 12:1

8 [a]Eccles. 1:2

9 [a]1 Kin. 4:32

10 [a]Prov. 10:32 [b]Prov. 22:20, 21

11 [1]Lit., *planted* [a]Eccles. 7:5; 10:12; Prov. 1:6; 22:17 [b]Acts 2:37 [c]Ezra 9:8; Is. 22:23

12 [1]Lit., *making* [a]1 Kin. 4:32, 33 [b]Eccles. 1:18

13 [a]Eccles. 3:14; 5:7; 7:18; 8:12 [b]Eccles. 8:5; Deut. 4:2 [c]Deut. 10:12; Mic. 6:8

14 [a]Eccles. 3:17; 11:9; Matt. 10:26; Rom. 2:16; 1 Cor. 4:5

Chapter 12

[a]REMEMBER also your Creator in the days of your youth,
before the [b]evil days come and the years draw near when you
will say, "[c]I have no delight in them";
2 before the [a]sun, the light, the moon, and the stars are
darkened, and clouds return after the rain;
3 in the day that the watchmen of the house tremble,
and mighty men [a]stoop, the grinding ones stand idle because
they are few, and [b]those who look through [1]windows grow dim;
4 and the [a]doors on the street are shut as the [b]sound of
the grinding mill is low, and one will arise at the sound of the
bird, and all the [c]daughters of song will [1]sing softly.
5 Furthermore, [1]men are afraid of a high place and of
terrors on the road; the almond tree blossoms, the grasshopper
drags himself along, and the caperberry is ineffective. For
man goes to his eternal [a]home while [b]mourners go about in the
street.
6 *Remember Him* before the silver cord is [1]broken and
the [a]golden bowl is crushed, the pitcher by the well is shattered
and the wheel at the cistern is crushed;
7 then the [a]dust will return to the earth as it was, and the
[1b]spirit will return to [c]God who gave it.
8 "[a]Vanity of vanities," says the Preacher, "all is vanity!"
9 In addition to being a wise man, the Preacher also
taught the people knowledge; and he pondered, searched out
and arranged [a]many proverbs.
10 The Preacher sought to find [a]delightful words and to
write [b]words of truth correctly.
11 The [a]words of wise men are like [b]goads, and masters of
these collections are like [1]well-driven [c]nails; they are given by
one Shepherd.
12 But beyond this, my son, be warned: the [1]writing of
[a]many books is endless, and excessive [b]devotion *to books* is
wearying to the body.
13 The conclusion, when all has been heard, *is:* [a]fear God
and [b]keep His commandments, because this *applies to* [c]every
person.
14 Because [a]God will bring every act to judgment, everything which is hidden, whether it is good or evil.

THE SONG OF SOLOMON

The Bride Speaks to Jerusalem's Daughters.

THE [1]Song of [a]Songs, which is Solomon's.
2 "[1]May he kiss me with the kisses of his mouth!
For your [a]love is better than wine.
3 "Your [a]oils have a pleasing fragrance,
Your [b]name is *like* [1]purified oil;
Therefore the [2c]maidens love you.
4 "Draw me after you *and* let us run *together!*
The [a]king has brought me into his chambers.

[1]**W**e will rejoice in you and be glad;
We will [2]extol your [b]love more than wine.
Rightly do they love you.

5 "[1]I am black but [a]lovely,
O [b]daughters of Jerusalem,
Like the [c]tents of [d]Kedar,
Like the curtains of Solomon.
6 "Do not stare at me because I am [1]swarthy,
For the sun has burned me.
My [a]mother's sons were angry with me;
They made me [b]caretaker of the vineyards,
But I have not taken care of my own vineyard.
7 "Tell me, O you [a]whom my soul loves,
Where do you [b]pasture *your flock*,
Where do you make *it* [c]lie down at noon?
For why should I be like one who [1]veils herself
Beside the flocks of [d]your companions?"

8 "[1]If you yourself do not know,
[a]Most beautiful among women,
Go forth on the trail of the flock,
And pasture your young goats
By the tents of the shepherds."

9 "[1]To me, [a]my darling, you are like
My [b]mare among the chariots of Pharaoh.
10 "Your [a]cheeks are lovely with ornaments,
Your neck with strings of [b]beads.

11 "[1]We will make for you ornaments of gold
With beads of silver."

12 "[1]While the king was at his [2]table,
My [3a]perfume gave forth its fragrance.
13 "My beloved is to me a pouch of [a]myrrh
Which lies all night between my breasts.
14 "My beloved is to me a cluster of [a]henna blossoms
In the vineyards of [b]En-gedi."

15 "[1,2]How beautiful [a]you are, my darling,

---

1 [1]Or, *Best of the Songs*
[a]1 Kin. 4:32

2 [1]BRIDE
[a]Song of Sol. 1:4; 4:10

3 [1]Lit., *which is emptied* (from one vessel to another) [2]Or, *virgins*
[a]Song of Sol. 4:10; John 12:3 [b]Eccles. 7:1 [c]Ps. 45:14

4 [1]CHORUS [2]Lit., *mention with praise*
[a]Ps. 45:14, 15 [b]Song of Sol. 1:4; 4:10

5 [1]BRIDE
[a]Song of Sol. 2:14; 4:3; 6:4 [b]Song of Sol. 2:7; 3:5, 10; 5:8, 16; 8:4 [c]Ps. 120:5 [d]Is. 60:7

6 [1]Or, *black*
[a]Ps. 69:8 [b]Song of Sol. 8:11; Job 27:18

7 [1]Some versions read: *wanders*
[a]Song of Sol. 3:1-4 [b]Song of Sol. 2:16; 6:3 [c]Is. 13:20; Jer. 33:12 [d]Song of Sol. 8:13

8 [1]BRIDEGROOM
[a]Song of Sol. 5:9; 6:1

9 [1]Lit., *I have compared you to*
[a]Song of Sol. 1:15; 2:2, 10, 13 [b]2 Chr. 1:16, 17

10 [a]Song of Sol. 5:13 [b]Gen. 24:53; Is. 61:10

11 [1]CHORUS

12 [1]BRIDE [2]Or, *couch* [3]Lit., *nard*
[a]Song of Sol. 4:13, 14; Mark 14:3; John 12:3

13 [a]Ps. 45:8; John 19:39

14 [a]Song of Sol. 4:13
[b]1 Sam. 23:29

15 [1]BRIDEGROOM [2]Lit., *Behold*
[a]Song of Sol. 1:16; 2:10, 13; 4:1, 7; 6:4, 10

[2]How beautiful you are!
Your [b]eyes are *like* doves."

16 "[1,2]How handsome you are, [a]my beloved,
And so pleasant!
Indeed, our couch is luxuriant!
17 "The beams of our houses are [a]cedars,
Our rafters, [1b]cypresses.

Chapter 2

"[1]I AM the [2a]rose of [b]Sharon,
The [c]lily of the valleys."

2 "[1]Like a lily among the thorns,
So is [a]my darling among the [2]maidens."

3 "[1]Like an [2a]apple tree among the trees of the forest,
So is my beloved among the [3]young men.
In his shade I took great delight and sat down,
And his [b]fruit was sweet to my [4]taste.
4 "He has [a]brought me to *his* [1]banquet hall,
And his [b]banner over me is love.
5 "Sustain me with [a]raisin cakes,
Refresh me with [1b]apples,
Because [c]I am lovesick.
6 "*Let* [a]his left hand be under my head
And [a]his right hand [b]embrace me."

7 "[1]I [a]adjure you, O [b]daughters of Jerusalem,
By the [c]gazelles or by the [d]hinds of the field,
[a]That you will not arouse or awaken *my* love,
Until [2]she pleases."

8 "[1]Listen, my beloved!
Behold, he is coming,
Climbing [a]on the mountains,
Leaping on the hills!
9 "My beloved is like a [a]gazelle or a [b]young [1]stag.
Behold, he is standing behind our wall,
He is looking through the windows,
He is peering [c]through the lattice.

10 "My beloved responded and said to me,
'[a]Arise, my darling, my beautiful one,
And come along.'
11 'For behold, the winter is past,
The rain is over *and* gone.
12 'The flowers have *already* appeared in the land;
The time has arrived for [1]pruning *the vines*,
And the voice of the [a]turtledove has been heard in our land.
13 'The [a]fig tree has ripened its figs,
And the [b]vines in blossom have given forth *their* fragrance.
Arise, my darling, my beautiful one,
And come along!

15 [2]Lit., *Behold*
[b]Song of Sol. 4:1; 5:12

16 [1]BRIDE [2]Lit., *Behold*
[a]Song of Sol. 2:3, 9, 17; 5:2, 5, 6, 8

17 [1]Or, *junipers*
[a]1 Kin. 6:9, 10; Jer. 22:14
[b]2 Chr. 3:5

1 [1]BRIDE [2]Lit., *crocus*
[a]Is. 35:1 [b]Is. 33:9; 35:2 [c]Song of Sol. 5:13; 7:2; Hos. 14:5

2 [1]BRIDEGROOM [2]Lit., *daughters*
[a]Song of Sol. 1:9

3 [1]BRIDE [2]Or, *apricot*
[3]Lit., *sons* [4]Lit., *palate*
[a]Song of Sol. 8:5 [b]Song of Sol. 4:13, 16; 8:11, 12

4 [1]Lit., *house of wine*
[a]Song of Sol. 1:4 [b]Ps. 20:5

5 [1]Or, *apricots*
[a]2 Sam. 6:19; 1 Chr. 16:3; Hos. 3:1 [b]Song of Sol. 7:8
[c]Song of Sol. 5:8

6 [a]Song of Sol. 8:3 [b]Prov. 4:8

7 [1]BRIDEGROOM [2]Or, *it*
[a]Song of Sol. 3:5; 5:8, 9; 8:4
[b]Song of Sol. 1:5 [c]Song of Sol. 2:9, 17; 3:5; 8:14; Prov. 6:5 [d]Gen. 49:21; Ps. 18:33; Hab. 3:19

8 [1]BRIDE
[a]Song of Sol. 2:17; Is. 52:7

9 [1]Lit., *of the stags*
[a]Song of Sol. 2:9, 17; 3:5; 8:14; Prov. 6:5 [b]Song of Sol. 2:17; 8:14 [c]Judg. 5:28

10 [a]Song of Sol. 2:13

12 [1]Or, *singing*
[a]Gen. 15:9; Ps. 74:19; Jer. 8:7

13 [a]Matt. 24:32 [b]Song of Sol. 7:12

14 'O [a]my dove, [b]in the clefts of the [1]rock,
In the secret place of the steep [2]pathway,
Let me see your [3]form,
[c]Let me hear your voice;
For your voice is sweet,
And your [3]form is [d]lovely.'

15 "Catch the foxes for us,
The [1]little foxes that are ruining the vineyards,
While our [a]vineyards are in blossom.
16 "[a]My beloved is mine, and I am his;
He [b]pastures *his flock* among the lilies.
17 "[a]Until [1]the cool of the day when the shadows flee away,
Turn, my beloved, and be like a [b]gazelle
Or a young stag [c]on the mountains of [2]Bether."

Chapter 3

"[1]On my bed night after night I sought him
[a]Whom my soul loves;
I [b]sought him but did not find him.
2 '[1]I must arise now and [1]go about the city;
In the [a]streets and in the squares
[1]I must seek him whom my soul loves.'
I sought him but did not find him.
3 "[a]The watchmen who make the rounds in the city found me,
And I said, 'Have you seen him whom my soul loves?'
4 "Scarcely had I [1]left them
When I found him whom my soul loves;
I held on to him and would not let him go,
Until I had [a]brought him to my mother's house,
And into the room of her who conceived me."

5 "[1]I [a]adjure you, O daughters of Jerusalem,
By the [b]gazelles or by the hinds of the field,
That you will not arouse or awaken *my* love,
Until [2]she pleases."

6 [1,2a]What is this coming up from the wilderness
Like [b]columns of smoke,
Perfumed with [c]myrrh and [d]frankincense,
With all scented powders of the merchant?
7 Behold, it is the *traveling* couch of Solomon;
Sixty mighty men around it,
Of the mighty men of Israel.
8 All of them are wielders of the sword,
[a]Expert in war;
Each man has his [b]sword at his side,
Guarding against the [1c]terrors of the night.
9 King Solomon has made for himself a sedan chair
From the timber of Lebanon.
10 He made its posts of silver,
Its [1]back of gold
And its seat of purple fabric,

14 [1]Or, *crag* [2]Or, *cliff* [3]Lit., *appearance* [a]Song of Sol. 5:2; 6:9 [b]Jer. 48:28 [c]Song of Sol. 8:13 [d]Song of Sol. 1:5

15 [1]Or, *young* [a]Song of Sol. 2:13

16 [a]Song of Sol. 6:3; 7:10 [b]Song of Sol. 4:5; 6:2, 3

17 [1]Lit., *the day blows* [2]Or, *cleavage;* or *a kind of spice* [a]Song of Sol. 4:6 [b]Song of Sol. 2:9 [c]Song of Sol. 2:8

1 [1]BRIDE [a]Song of Sol. 1:7 [b]Song of Sol. 5:6

2 [1]Or, *Let me arise . . . go. . . search* [a]Jer. 5:1

3 [a]Song of Sol. 5:7

4 [1]Lit., *passed* [a]Song of Sol. 8:2

5 [1]BRIDEGROOM [2]Or, *it* [a]Song of Sol. 2:7; 8:4 [b]Song of Sol. 2:7

6 [1]CHORUS [2]Lit., *Who* [a]Song of Sol. 8:5 [b]Ex. 13:21; Joel 2:30 [c]Song of Sol. 1:13; 4:6, 14; Matt. 2:11 [d]Ex. 30:34; Rev. 18:13

8 [1]Lit., *terror in the nights* [a]Jer. 50:9 [b]Ps. 45:3 [c]Ps. 91:5

10 [1]Or, *support*

10 [a]Song of Sol. 1:5

11 [1]Or, *wreath*
[a]Is. 3:16, 17; 4:4 [b]Is. 62:5

1 [1]BRIDEGROOM [2]Lit., *Behold*
[a]Song of Sol. 1:15 [b]Song of Sol. 1:15; 5:12 [c]Song of Sol. 6:7 [d]Song of Sol. 6:5 [e]Mic. 7:14

2 [1]Or, *miscarried*
[a]Song of Sol. 6:6

3 [a]Josh. 2:18 [b]Song of Sol. 5:16 [c]Song of Sol. 6:7

4 [1]Or, *for an arsenal*
[a]Song of Sol. 7:4 [b]Neh. 3:19 [c]Ezek. 27:10, 11 [d]2 Sam. 1:21

5 [a]Song of Sol. 7:3 [b]Song of Sol. 2:16; 6:2, 3

6 [1]Lit., *the day blows*
[a]Song of Sol. 2:17 [b]Song of Sol. 4:14

7 [a]Song of Sol. 1:15

8 [1]Or, *Look*
[a]1 Kin. 4:33; Ps. 72:16 [b]Song of Sol. 5:1; Is. 62:5 [c]2 Kin. 5:12 [d]Deut. 3:9; 1 Chr. 5:23; Ezek. 27:5

9 [a]Song of Sol. 4:10, 12; 5:1, 2 [b]Gen. 41:42; Prov. 1:9; Ezek. 16:11; Dan. 5:7

10 [1]Or, *balsam odors*
[a]Song of Sol. 7:6 [b]Song of Sol. 1:2, 4 [c]Song of Sol. 1:3

11 [a]Prov. 5:3 [b]Ps. 19:10; Prov. 24:13 [c]Gen. 27:27; Hos. 14:6

With its interior lovingly fitted out
By the [a]daughters of Jerusalem.
11 Go forth, O [a]daughters of Zion,
And gaze on King Solomon with the [1]crown
With which his mother has crowned him
On the [b]day of his wedding,
And on the day of his gladness of heart.

Chapter 4

"[1,2]How beautiful [a]you are, my darling,
[2]How beautiful you are!
Your [b]eyes are *like* doves [c]behind your veil;
Your [d]hair is like a flock of goats
That have descended from Mount [e]Gilead.
2 "Your [a]teeth are like a flock of *newly* shorn ewes
Which have come up from *their* washing,
All of which bear twins,
And not one among them has [1]lost her young.
3 "Your lips are like a scarlet [a]thread,
And your [b]mouth is lovely.
Your [c]temples are like a slice of a pomegranate
Behind your veil.
4 "Your [a]neck is like the tower of David
Built [1]with [b]rows of stones,
On which are [c]hung a thousand shields,
All the round [d]shields of the mighty men.
5 "Your [a]two breasts are like two fawns,
Twins of a gazelle,
Which [b]feed among the lilies.
6 "[a]Until [1]the cool of the day
When the shadows flee away,
I will go my way to the mountain of [b]myrrh
And to the hill of [b]frankincense.

7 "[a]You are altogether beautiful, my darling,
And there is no blemish in you.
8 "*Come* with me from [a]Lebanon, *my* [b]bride,
May you come with me from Lebanon.
[1]Journey down from the summit of [c]Amana,
From the summit of [d]Senir and Hermon,
From the dens of lions,
From the mountains of leopards.
9 "You have made my heart beat faster, [a]my sister, *my* bride;
You have made my heart beat faster with a single *glance* of your eyes,
With a single [b]strand of your necklace.
10 "[a]How beautiful is your love, my sister, *my* bride!
How much [b]better is your love than wine,
And the [c]fragrance of your oils
Than all *kinds* of [1]spices!
11 "Your lips, *my* bride, [a]drip [b]honey;
Honey and milk are under your tongue,
And the fragrance of your garments is like the [c]fragrance of Lebanon.

12 "A garden locked is my sister, *my* bride,
A [1]rock-garden locked, a [a]spring [b]sealed up.
13 "Your shoots are an [1a]orchard of [b]pomegranates
With [c]choice fruits, [d]henna with nard plants,
14 "[a]Nard and saffron, [b]calainus and cinnamon,
With all the trees of [c]frankincense,
[d]Myrrh and aloes, along with all the finest [1]spices.
15 "*You are* a garden spring,
A well of [1a]fresh water,
And streams *flowing* from Lebanon."

16 "[1]Awake, O north *wind*,
And come, *wind of* the south;
Make my [a]garden breathe out *fragrance*,
Let its [2]spices [3]be wafted abroad.
May [b]my beloved come into his garden
And eat its [c]choice fruits!"

Chapter 5

"[1]I HAVE [a]come into my garden, [b]my sister, *my* bride;
I have gathered my [c]myrrh along with my balsam.
I have eaten my [d]honeycomb [2]and my honey;
I have [e]drunk my wine [2]and my milk.
Eat, [f]friends;
Drink and [3]imbibe deeply, O lovers."

2 "[1]I was asleep, but my heart was awake.
A voice! My beloved was knocking:
'Open to me, [a]my sister, my darling,
[b]My dove, my perfect one!
For my head is [2]drenched with dew,
My [c]locks with the [3]damp of the night.'
3 "I have [a]taken off my dress,
How can I put it on *again?*
I have [b]washed my feet,
How can I dirty them *again?*
4 "My beloved extended his hand through the opening,
And my [1a]feelings were aroused for him.
5 "I arose to open to my beloved;
And my hands [a]dripped with myrrh,
And my fingers with [1]liquid myrrh,
On the handles of the bolt.
6 "I opened to my beloved,
But my beloved had [a]turned away *and* had gone!
My [1]heart went out *to him* as he [b]spoke.
I [c]searched for him, but I did not find him;
I [d]called him, but he did not answer me.
7 "The [a]watchmen who make the rounds in the city found
me,
They struck me *and* wounded me;
The guardsmen of the walls took away my shawl from
me.
8 "I [a]adjure you, O daughters of Jerusalem,
If you find my beloved,

12 [1]Lit., *stone heap* [a]Prov. 5:15-18 [b]Gen. 29:3

13 [1]Or, *park;* or *paradise* [a]Neh. 2:8; Eccles. 2:5 [b]Song of Sol. 6:11; 7:12 [c]Song of Sol. 4:16; 2:3; 7:13 [d]Song of Sol. 1:14

14 [1]Or, *balsam odors* [a]Song of Sol. 1:12 [b]Ex. 30:23 [c]Song of Sol. 4:6 [d]Song of Sol. 3:6; Ps. 45:8; John 19:39

15 [1]Lit., *living* [a]Zech. 14:8

16 [1]BRIDE [2]Or, *balsam odors* [3]Lit., *flow forth* [a]Song of Sol. 5:1; 6:2 [b]Song of Sol. 1:13; 2:3, 8; 6:2 [c]Song of Sol. 4:13

1 [1]BRIDEGROOM [2]Lit., *with* [3]Or, *become drunk* [a]Song of Sol. 6:2 [b]Song of Sol. 4:9 [c]Song of Sol. 1:13; 4:14 [d]Song of Sol. 4:11 [e]Prov. 9:5; Is. 55:1 [f]Judg. 14:11, 20; John 3:29

2 [1]BRIDE [2]Lit., *filled* [3]Lit., *drops* [a]Song of Sol. 4:9 [b]Song of Sol. 2:14; 6:9 [c]Song of Sol. 5:11

3 [a]Luke 11:7 [b]Gen. 19:2

4 [1]Lit., *bowels* [a]Jer. 31:20

5 [1]Lit., *passing* [a]Song of Sol. 5:13

6 [1]Lit., *soul* [a]Song of Sol. 6:1 [b]Song of Sol. 5:2 [c]Song of Sol. 3:1 [d]Prov. 1:28

7 [a]Song of Sol. 3:3

8 [a]Song of Sol. 2:7; 3:5

As to what you will tell him:
For [b]I am lovesick."

9 "[1,2]What kind of beloved is your beloved,
O [a]most beautiful among women?
[2]What kind of beloved is your beloved,
Thus you adjure us?"

10 "[1]My beloved is dazzling and [a]ruddy,
[2b]Outstanding among ten thousand.
11 "His hand is *like* gold, pure gold;
His [a]locks are *like* clusters of dates,
And black as a raven.
12 "His [a]eyes are like doves,
Beside streams of water,
Bathed in milk,
And [1]reposed in *their* [b]setting.
13 "His cheeks are like a [a]bed of balsam,
Banks of sweet-scented herbs;
His lips are [b]lilies,
[c]Dripping with liquid myrrh.
14 "His hands are rods of gold
Set with [a]beryl;
His abdomen is carved ivory
Inlaid with [1b]sapphires.
15 "His legs are pillars of alabaster
Set on pedestals of pure gold;
His appearance is like [a]Lebanon,
Choice as the [b]cedars.
16 "His [1a]mouth is *full of* sweetness.
And he is wholly [b]desirable.
This is my beloved and this my friend,
O daughters of Jerusalem."

Chapter 6

"[1a]WHERE has your beloved gone,
O [b]most beautiful among women?
Where has your beloved turned,
That we may seek him with you?"

2 "[1]My beloved has gone down to his [a]garden,
To the [b]beds of balsam,
To [c]pasture *his flock* in the gardens
And gather [d]lilies.
3 "[a]I am my beloved's and my beloved is mine,
He who [b]pastures *his flock* among the lilies."

4 "[1a]You are as beautiful as [b]Tirzah, my darling,
As [c]lovely as [d]Jerusalem,
As [e]awesome as [2]an army with banners.
5 "Turn your eyes away from me,
For they have confused me;
[a]Your hair is like a flock of goats
That have descended from Gilead.
6 "[a]Your teeth are like a flock of ewes
Which have come up from *their* washing,

---

8 [b]Song of Sol. 2:5

9 [1]CHORUS [2]Or, *What is your beloved more than another beloved* [a]Song of Sol. 1:8; 6:1

10 [1]BRIDE [2]Lit., *Lifted up banner* [a]1 Sam. 16:12 [b]Ps. 45:2

11 [a]Song of Sol. 5:2

12 [1]Lit., *sitting upon* [a]Song of Sol. 1:15; 4:1 [b]Ex. 25:7

13 [a]Song of Sol. 6:2 [b]Song of Sol. 2:1 [c]Song of Sol. 5:5

14 [1]Lit., *lapis lazuli* [a]Ex. 28:20; 39:13; Ezek. 1:16; Dan. 10:6 [b]Ex. 24:10; 28:18; Job 28:16; Is. 54:11

15 [a]Song of Sol. 7:4 [b]1 Kin. 4:33; Ps. 80:10; Ezek. 17:23; 31:8

16 [1]Lit., *palate* [a]Song of Sol. 7:9 [b]2 Sam. 1:23

1 [1]CHORUS [a]Song of Sol. 5:6 [b]Song of Sol. 1:8

2 [1]BRIDE [a]Song of Sol. 4:16; 5:1 [b]Song of Sol. 5:13 [c]Song of Sol. 1:7 [d]Song of Sol. 2:1; 5:13

3 [a]Song of Sol. 2:16; 7:10 [b]Song of Sol. 2:16; 4:5

4 [1]BRIDEGROOM [2]Lit., *bannered ones* [a]Song of Sol. 1:15 [b]1 Kin. 14:17 [c]Song of Sol. 1:5 [d]Ps. 48:2; 50:2 [e]Song of Sol. 6:10

5 [a]Song of Sol. 4:1

6 [a]Song of Sol. 4:2

All of which bear twins,
And not one among them has [1]lost her young.
7 "[a]Your temples are like a slice of a pomegranate
Behind your veil.
8 "There are sixty [a]queens and eighty concubines,
And [1b]maidens without number;
9 "*But* [a]my dove, my perfect one, is [1]unique:
She is her mother's [1]only *daughter;*
She is the pure *child* of the one who bore her.
The [2b]maidens saw her and called her blessed,
The [c]queens and the concubines *also,* and they praised her, *saying,*

10 'Who is this that [1]grows like the dawn,
As beautiful as the full [a]moon,
As pure [b]as the sun,
As [c]awesome as [2]an army with banners?' "
11 "I went down to the orchard of nut trees
To see the blossoms of the valley,
To see whether [a]the vine had budded
Or the [b]pomegranates had bloomed.
12 "Before I was aware, my soul set me
Over the chariots of [1]my noble people."

13 "[1,2]Come back, come back, O Shulammite;
Come back, come back, that we may gaze at you!"

"[3]**W**hy should you gaze at the Shulammite,
As at the [a]dance of [4b]the two companies?"

Chapter 7

"[1]How beautiful are your [2]feet in sandals,
O [3a]prince's daughter!
The curves of your hips are like [4]jewels,
The work of the hands of an artist.
2 "Your navel is *like* a round goblet
Which never lacks mixed wine;
Your belly is like a heap of wheat
Fenced about with lilies.
3 "Your [a]two breasts are like two fawns,
Twins of a gazelle.
4 "Your [a]neck is *like* a tower of ivory,
Your eyes *like* the pools in [b]Heshbon
By the gate of Bath-rabbim;
Your nose is like the tower of Lebanon,
Which faces toward Damascus.
5 "Your head [1]crowns you like [a]Carmel,
And the flowing locks of your head are like purple threads;
The king is captivated by *your* tresses.
6 "How [a]beautiful and how delightful you are,
[1]*My* love, with *all* your charms!
7 "[1]Your stature is like a palm tree,
And your breasts are *like its* clusters.
8 "I said, 'I will climb the palm tree,

6 [1]Or, *miscarried*

7 [a]Song of Sol. 4:3

8 [1]Or, *virgins*
[a]1 Kin. 11:3 [b]Song of Sol. 1:3

9 [1]Lit., *one* [2]Lit., *daughters*
[a]Song of Sol. 2:14; 5:2 [b]Gen. 30:13 [c]1 Kin. 11:3

10 [1]Lit., *looks down* [2]Lit., *bannered ones*
[a]Job 31:26 [b]Matt. 17:2; Rev. 1:16 [c]Song of Sol. 6:4

11 [a]Song of Sol. 7:12 [b]Song of Sol. 4:13

12 [1]Another reading is *Ammi-nadib*

13 [1]CHORUS [2]Chap. 7:1 in Heb. [3]BRIDEGROOM [4]Or, *Mahanaim*
[a]Judg. 21:21 [b]Gen. 32:2; 2 Sam. 17:24

1 [1]Chap. 7:2 in Heb. [2]Lit., *footsteps* [3]Or, *nobleman's* [4]Or, *ornaments*
[a]Ps. 45:13

3 [a]Song of Sol. 4:5

4 [a]Song of Sol. 4:4 [b]Num. 21:26

5 [1]Lit., *is upon*
[a]Is. 35:2

6 [1]Or, With *love among your delights*
[a]Song of Sol. 1:15, 16; 4:10

7 [1]Lit., *This stature of yours*

I will take hold of its fruit stalks.'
Oh, may your breasts be like clusters of the vine,
And the fragrance of your [1]breath like [2a]apples,
9 And your [1a]mouth like the best wine!"

"[2]**I**t [b]goes *down* smoothly for my beloved,
Flowing gently *through* the lips of those who fall asleep.

10 "[a]I am my beloved's,
And his [b]desire is for me.
11 "Come, my beloved, let us go out into the [1]country,
Let us spend the night in the villages.
12 "Let us rise early *and go* to the vineyards;
Let us [a]see whether the vine has budded
And its blossoms have opened,
And whether the pomegranates have bloomed.
There I will give you my love.
13 "The [a]mandrakes have given forth fragrance;
And over our doors are all [b]choice *fruits*,
Both new and old,
Which I have saved up for you, my beloved.

Chapter 8

"Oh that you were like a brother to me
Who nursed at my mother's breasts.
If I found you outdoors, I would kiss you;
No one would despise me, either.
2 "I would lead you *and* [a]bring you
Into the house of my mother, who used to instruct me;
I would give you spiced wine to drink from the juice of my pomegranates.
3 "Let [a]his left hand be under my head,
And his right hand embrace me."

4 "[1a]I want you to swear, O daughters of Jerusalem,
[2]Do not arouse or awaken *my* love,
Until [3]she pleases."

5 "[1a]Who is this coming up from the wilderness,
Leaning on her beloved?"

"[2]**B**eneath the [3b]apple tree I awakened you;
There your mother was in labor with you,
There she was in labor *and* gave you birth.
6 "Put me like a [1]seal over your heart,
Like a [a]seal on your arm.
For love is as strong as death,
[2b]Jealousy is as severe as Sheol;
Its flashes are flashes of fire,
[3]The *very* flame of the LORD.
7 "Many waters cannot quench love,
Nor will rivers overflow it;
If a man were to give all the riches of his house for love,
It would be utterly despised."

7:8 [1]Lit., *nose* [2]Or, *apricots*
[a]Song of Sol. 2:5

7:9 [1]Lit., *palate* [2]BRIDE
[a]Song of Sol. 5:16 [b]Prov. 23:31

7:10 [a]Song of Sol. 2:16; 6:3 [b]Ps. 45:11

7:11 [1]Lit., *field*

7:12 [a]Song of Sol. 6:11

7:13 [a]Gen. 30:14 [b]Song of Sol. 2:3; 4:13, 16

8:2 [a]Song of Sol. 3:4

8:3 [a]Song of Sol. 2:6

8:4 [1]BRIDEGROOM [2]Or, *Why should you arouse* [3]Or, *it*
[a]Song of Sol. 2:7; 3:5

8:5 [1]CHORUS [2]BRIDEGROOM [3]Or, *apricot*
[a]Song of Sol. 3:6 [b]Song of Sol. 2:3

8:6 [1]Or, *signet* [2]Or, *Its ardor is as inflexible* [3]Another reading is: *a vehement flame.*
[a]Is. 49:16; Jer. 22:24; Hag. 2:23 [b]Prov. 6:34

8 "[1]We have a little sister,
And she [a]has no breasts;
What shall we do for our sister
On the day when she is spoken for?
9 "If she is a wall,
We shall build on her a battlement of silver;
But if she is a door,
We shall barricade her with [a]planks of cedar."

10 "[1]I was a wall, and my breasts were like towers;
Then I became in his eyes as one who finds peace.
11 "Solomon had a [a]vineyard at Baal-hamon;
He [b]entrusted the vineyard to [c]caretakers;
Each one was to bring a [d]thousand *shekels* of silver for
its [e]fruit.
12 "My very own vineyard is [1]at my disposal;
The thousand *shekels* are for you, Solomon,
And two hundred are for those who take care of its
fruit."
13 "[1]O you who sit in the gardens,
My [a]companions are listening for your voice—
Let me hear it!"
14 "[1,2]Hurry, my beloved,
And be [a]like a gazelle or a young [3]stag
On the [b]mountains of spices."

8 [1]CHORUS [a]Ezek. 16:7

9 [a]1 Kin. 6:15

10 [1]BRIDE

11 [a]Eccles. 2:4 [b]Matt. 21:33 [c]Song of Sol. 1:6 [d]Is. 7:23 [e]Song of Sol. 8:12; 2:3

12 [1]Lit., *before me*

13 [1]BRIDEGROOM [a]Song of Sol. 1:7

14 [1]BRIDE [2]Lit., *Flee* [3]Lit., *of the stags* [a]Song of Sol. 2:7, 9, 17 [b]Song of Sol. 4:6

THE BOOK OF ISAIAH

Rebellion of God's People.

THE vision of Isaiah the son of Amoz, concerning [a]Judah
and Jerusalem which he saw during the [1]reigns of [b]Uzziah,
Jotham, Ahaz, *and* [c]Hezekiah, kings of Judah.
2 [a]Listen, O heavens, and hear, O [b]earth;
For the LORD speaks:
"[c]Sons I have reared and brought up,
But they have [d]revolted against Me.
3 "An ox knows its owner,
And a donkey its master's manger,
But Israel does not know,
My people do not understand."

4 Alas, sinful nation,
People weighed down with iniquity,
[1]Offspring of evildoers,
Sons who act corruptly!
They have [a]abandoned the LORD,
They have [b]despised the Holy One of Israel,
They have turned away [2]from Him.

5 Where will you be stricken again,
As you [a]continue in *your* rebellion?

1 [1]Lit., *days* [a]Is. 2:1; 40:9 [b]2 Kin. 15:1, 13 [c]2 Kin. 18:1

2 [a]Deut. 32:1 [b]Mic. 1:2 [c]Jer. 3:22 [d]Is. 30:1, 9; 65:2

4 [1]Lit., *Seed* [2]Lit., *backward* [a]Is. 1:28 [b]Is. 5:24

5 [a]Is. 31:6

5 [b]Is. 33:24; Ezek. 34:4, 16

6 [a]Ps. 38:3

7 [1]Lit., *And*
[a]Rev. 26:33; Jer. 44:6

9 [a]Rom. 9:29 [b]Is. 10:20-22; 11:11, 16; 37:4, 31, 32; 46:3

11 [1]Or, *am sated with*
[a]Jer. 6:20; Mal. 1:10

12 [1]Lit., *of your hand*
[a]Ex. 23:17

13 [a]1 Chr. 23:31 [b]Ex. 12:16
[c]Jer. 7:9, 10

15 [a]1 Kin. 8:22; Lam. 1:17
[b]Mic. 3:4

16 [a]Ps. 26:6 [b]Is. 52:11 [c]Jer. 25:5

17 [1]Or, *vindicate the fatherless*
[a]Jer. 22:3; Zeph. 2:3 [b]Ps. 82:3

The whole head is [b]sick,
And the whole heart is faint.
6 From the sole of the foot even to the head
There is [a]nothing sound in it.
Only bruises, welts, and raw wounds,
Not pressed out or bandaged,
Nor softened with oil.

7 Your [a]land is desolate,
Your cities are burned with fire,
Your fields—strangers are devouring them in your presence,
[1]It is desolation, as overthrown by strangers.
8 And the daughter of Zion is left like a shelter in a vineyard,
Like a watchman's hut in a cucumber field, like a besieged city.
9 [a]Unless the LORD of hosts
Had left us a few [b]survivors,
We would be like Sodom,
We would be like Gomorrah.

10 Hear the word of the LORD,
You rulers of Sodom;
Give ear to the instruction of our God,
You people of Gomorrah.
11 "[a]What are your multiplied sacrifices to Me?"
Says the LORD.
"I [1]have had enough of burnt offerings of rams,
And the fat of fed cattle.
And I take no pleasure in the blood of bulls, lambs, or goats.
12 "When you come [a]to appear before Me,
Who requires [1]of you this trampling of My courts?
13 "Bring your worthless offerings no longer,
Their incense is an abomination to Me.
[a]New moon and sabbath, the [b]calling of assemblies—
I cannot [c]endure iniquity and the solemn assembly.
14 "I hate your new moon *festivals* and your appointed feasts,
They have become a burden to Me.
I am weary of bearing *them.*
15 "So when you [a]spread out your hands *in prayer,*
I will hide my eyes from you,
Yes, even though you [b]multiply prayers,
I will not listen.
Your hands are full of bloodshed.

16 "[a]Wash yourselves, [b]make yourselves clean;
Remove the evil of your deeds from My sight.
[c]Cease to do evil,
17 "Learn to do good;
[a]Seek justice,
[b]Reprove the ruthless;
[1]Defend the orphan,
Plead for the widow.

18 "Come now, and [a]let us reason together,"
Says the LORD,
"[b]Though your sins are as scarlet,
They will be as white as snow;
Though they are red like crimson,
They will be like wool.
19 "[a]If you consent and obey,
You will eat the best of the land:
20 "But if you refuse and rebel,
You will be devoured by the sword."
Truly, the mouth of the LORD has spoken.

21 How the faithful city has become a harlot,
She *who* was full of justice!
Righteousness once lodged in her,
But now murderers.
22 Your silver has become dross,
Your drink diluted with water.
23 Your [a]rulers are rebels,
And companions of thieves;
Every one [b]loves a bribe,
And chases after rewards.
They [c]do not [1]defend the [2]orphan,
Nor does the widow's plea come before them.

24 Therefore the Lord [1]GOD of hosts,
The Mighty One of Israel declares,
"Ah, I will be relieved of My adversaries,
And [a]avenge Myself on My foes.
25 "I will also turn My hand against you,
And will [a]smelt away your dross as with lye,
And will remove all your alloy.
26 "Then I will restore your [a]judges as at the first,
And your counselors as at the beginning;
After that you will be called the [b]city of righteousness,
A faithful city."

27 Zion will be [a]redeemed with justice,
And her [1]repentant ones with righteousness.
28 But [1]transgressors and sinners will be [a]crushed together,
And those who forsake the LORD shall come to an end.
29 Surely, [1]you will be ashamed of the [2a]oaks which you
have desired,
And you will be embarrassed at the [b]gardens which you
have chosen.
30 For you will be like an [1]oak whose [a]leaf fades away,
Or as a garden that has no water.
31 And the strong man will become tinder,
His work also a spark.
Thus they shall both [a]burn together,
And there will be none to quench *them*.

18 [a]Is. 41:1, 21; 43:26; Mic. 6:2 [b]Is. 44:22; 43:25; Ps. 51:7; Rev. 7:14

19 [a]Deut. 30:15, 16

23 [1]Or, *vindicate* [2]Or, *fatherless* [a]Hos. 5:10; Mic. 7:3 [b]Ex. 23:8; Mic. 7:3 [c]Jer. 5:28; Ezek. 22:7; Zech. 7:10

24 [1]YHWH, usually rendered LORD [a]Is. 35:4; 59:18

25 [a]Ezek. 22:19-22; Mal. 3:3

26 [a]Is. 60:17; Jer. 33:7, 11 [b]Is. 33:5; 60:14; 62:1, 2; Zech. 8:3

27 [1]Or, *returnees* [a]Is. 35:9; 62:12; 63:4

28 [1]Lit., the *crushing of transgressors and sinners shall be together* [a]Is. 66:24; Ps. 9:5; 2 Thess. 1:8, 9

29 [1]So with some mss.; M.T. *they* [2]Or, *terebinths* [a]Is. 57:5 [b]Is. 65:3; 66:17

30 [1]Or, *terebinth* [a]Is. 64:6

31 [a]Is. 5:24; 9:19; 26:11; 33:11-14

Chapter 2

THE word which [a]Isaiah the son of Amoz saw concerning
Judah and Jerusalem. Now it will come about that
2 [a]In the last days,
The [b]mountain of the house of the LORD
Will be established [1]as the chief of the mountains,
And will be raised above the hills;
And [c]all the nations will stream to it.
3 And many peoples will come and say,
"Come, let us go up to the mountain of the LORD,
To the house of the God of Jacob;
That He may teach us [1]concerning His ways,
And that we may walk in His paths,
For the [2]law will go forth [a]from Zion,
And the word of the LORD from Jerusalem."
4 And He will judge between the nations,
And will [1]render decisions for many peoples;
And [a]they will hammer their swords into plowshares,
and their spears into pruning hooks.
[b]Nation will not lift up sword against nation,
And never again will they learn war.

5 Come, [a]house of Jacob, and let us walk in the [b]light of
the LORD.
6 For Thou hast [a]abandoned Thy people, the house of
Jacob,
Because they are filled with influences from the East,
And *they are* soothsayers [b]like the Philistines,
And they [c]strike *bargains* with the children of
foreigners.
7 Their land has also been filled with silver and gold,
And there is no end to their treasures,
Their land has also been filled with horses,
And there is no end to their chariots.
8 Their land has also been [a]filled with idols;
They worship the [b]work of their hands,
That which their fingers have made.
9 So the [a]*common* man has been humbled,
And the man *of* [a]*importance* has been abased,
But do not forgive them.
10 [a]Enter the rock and hide in the dust
[b]From the terror of the LORD and from the splendor of
His majesty.
11 The [1a]proud look of man will be abased,
And the [b]loftiness of man will be humbled,
And the LORD alone will be exalted in that day.

12 For the LORD of hosts will have a day of reckoning,
Against [a]everyone who is proud and lofty,
And against everyone who is lifted up,
That he may be abased.
13 And *it will be* against all the cedars of Lebanon that are
lofty and lifted up,
Against all the oaks of Bashan,

1 [a]Is. 1:1

2 [1]Lit., *on*
[a]Mic. 4:1-3 [b]Is. 27:13; 66:20
[c]Is. 56:7

3 [1]Or, *some of* [2]Or, *instruction*
[a]Is. 51:4, 5; Luke 24:47

4 [1]Or, *reprove many*
[a]Is. 32:17, 18; Joel 3:10 [b]Is. 9:5, 7; 11:6-9; Hos. 2:18; Zech. 9:10

5 [a]Is. 58:1 [b]Is. 60:1, 2, 19, 20; 1 John 1:5

6 [a]Deut. 31:17 [b]2 Kin. 1:2
[c]2 Kin. 16:7, 8; Prov. 6:1

8 [a]Is. 10:11 [b]Is. 17:8; 37:19; 40:19; 44:17; Ps. 115:4-8

9 [a]Is. 5:15; Ps. 49:2; 62:9

10 [a]Is. 2:19, 21; Rev. 6:15, 16 [b]2 Thess. 1:9

11 [1]Lit., *eyes of the loftiness of men*
[a]Is. 5:15; 37:23 [b]Is. 13:11; 23:9; Ps. 18:27; 2 Cor. 10:5

12 [a]Is. 24:4, 21; Job 40:11, 12; Mal. 4:1

14 Against all the [a]lofty mountains,
Against all the hills that are lifted up,
15 Against every [a]high tower,
Against every fortified wall,
16 Against all the [a]ships of Tarshish,
And against all the beautiful craft.
17 And the pride of man will be humbled,
And the loftiness of men will be abased,
And the LORD alone will be exalted in that day.
18 But the [a]idols will completely vanish.
19 And *men* will go into caves of the rocks,
And into holes of the [1]ground
Before the terror of the LORD,
And before the splendor of His majesty,
When He arises [a]to make the earth tremble.
20 In that day men will [a]cast away to the moles and the bats
Their idols of silver and their idols of gold,
Which they made for themselves to worship,
21 In order to [a]go into the caverns of the rocks and the clefts of the cliffs,
Before the terror of the LORD and the splendor of His majesty,
When He arises to make the earth tremble.
22 [1a]Stop regarding man, whose breath *of life* is in his nostrils;
For [2b]why should he be esteemed?

CHAPTER 3

FOR behold, the Lord [1]GOD of hosts, [a]is going to remove
from Jerusalem and Judah
Both [2]supply and support, the whole [2]supply of bread,
And the whole [2]supply of water;
2 [a]The mighty man and the warrior,
The judge and the prophet,
The diviner and the elder,
3 The captain of fifty and the honorable man,
The counselor and the expert artisan,
And the skillful enchanter.
4 And I will make mere [a]lads their princes
And [1]capricious children will rule over them,
5 And the people will be [a]oppressed,
Each one by another, and each one by his [b]neighbor;
The youth will storm against the elder,
And the inferior against the honorable.
6 When a man [a]lays hold of his brother in his father's house, *saying*,
"You have a cloak, you shall be our ruler,
And these ruins will be under your [1]charge,"
7 On that day will he [1]protest, saying,
"I will not be *your* [2a]healer,
For in my house there is neither bread nor cloak;
You should not appoint me ruler of the people."

14 [a]Is. 40:4
15 [a]Is. 25:12
16 [a]Is. 23:1, 14; 60:9; 1 Kin. 10:22
18 [a]Is. 21:9; Mic. 1:7
19 [1]Lit., *dust* [a]Is. 13:13; 24:1, 19, 20; Ps. 18:7; Hag. 2:6, 7; Heb. 12:26
20 [a]Is. 30:22; 31:7
21 [a]Is. 3:19
22 [1]Lit., *Cease from man* [2]Lit., *in what* [a]Ps. 146:3; Jer. 17:5 [b]Is. 40:15, 17; Ps. 8:4; 144:3, 4; James 4:14
1 [1]YHWH, usually rendered LORD [2]Lit., *staff* [a]Is. 5:13; 9:20; Lev. 26:26; Ezek. 4:16
2 [a]Is. 9:14, 15; 2 Kin. 24:14; Ezek. 17:12, 13
4 [1]Lit., *arbitrary power will rule* [a]Eccles. 10:16
5 [a]Mic. 7:3-6 [b]Is. 9:19; Jer. 9:3-8
6 [1]Lit., *hand* [a]Is. 4:1
7 [1]Lit., *lift up his voice* [2]Lit., *binder of wounds* [a]Ezek. 34:4; Hos. 5:13

8 For [a]Jerusalem has stumbled, and Judah has fallen,
Because their [1b]speech and their actions are against the LORD,
To rebel against [2]His glorious presence.
9 [1]The expression of their faces bears witness against them.
And they display their sin like [a]Sodom;
They do not *even* conceal *it.*
Woe to [2]them!
For they have [b]brought evil on themselves.
10 Say to the [a]righteous that *it will go* well *with them,*
For they will eat the fruit of their actions.
11 Woe to the wicked! *It will go* badly *with him,*
For [1a]what he deserves will be done to him.
12 O My people! Their oppressors [1]are [a]children,
And women rule over them.
O My people! [b]Those who guide you lead *you* astray,
And confuse the direction of your paths.

13 [a]The LORD arises to contend,
And stands to judge the people.
14 The LORD [a]enters into judgment with the elders and princes of His people:
"It is you who have [b]devoured the vineyard;
The [c]plunder of the poor is in your houses.
15 "What do you mean by [a]crushing My people,
And grinding the face of the poor?"
Declares the Lord [1]GOD of hosts.

16 Moreover, the LORD said, "Because the daughters of Zion are proud,
And walk with [1]heads held high and seductive eyes,
And go along with mincing steps,
And tinkle the bangles on their feet,
17 Therefore the Lord will afflict the scalp of the daughters of Zion with scabs,
And the LORD will make their foreheads bare.
18 In that day the Lord will take away the beauty of *their*
anklets, headbands, [a]crescent ornaments,
19 dangling earrings, bracelets, veils,
20 [a]headdresses, ankle chains, sashes, perfume boxes,
amulets,
21 [1]finger rings, [a]nose rings,
22 festal robes, outer tunics, cloaks, money purses,
23 hand mirrors, undergarments, turbans, and veils.
24 Now it will come about that instead of [1]sweet [a]perfume there will be putrefaction;
Instead of a belt, a rope;
Instead of [b]well-set hair, a [c]plucked-out scalp;
Instead of fine clothes, a [d]donning of sackcloth;
And branding instead of beauty.
25 Your men will [a]fall by the sword,
And your [1]mighty ones in battle.
26 And her [1a]gates will lament and mourn;
And deserted she will [b]sit on the ground.

8 [1]Lit., *tongue* [2]Lit., *the eyes of His glory* [a]Is. 1:7; 6:11 [b]Is. 9:17; 59:3; Ps. 73:9-11

9 [1]Or, *Their partiality bears* [2]Lit., *their soul* [a]Is. 1:10; Gen. 13:13 [b]Prov. 8:36; 15:32; Rom. 6:23

10 [a]Is. 54:17; Deut. 28:1-14; Eccles. 8:12

11 [1]Lit., *the dealing of his hands* [a]Is. 65:6, 7; Deut. 28:15-68

12 [1]Or, *deal severely* [a]Is. 3:4 [b]Is. 9:16; 28:14, 15

13 [a]Is. 66:16; Hos. 4:1; Mic. 6:2

14 [a]Ezek. 20:35, 36; Job 22:4; Ps. 143:2 [b]Mic. 3:3; Ps. 14:4 [c]Is. 10:1, 2; Job 24:9, 14; Ps. 10:9; Prov. 30:14; Ezek. 18:12; James 2:6

15 [1]YHWH, usually rendered LORD [a]Ps. 94:5

16 [1]Lit., *outstretched necks*

18 [a]Judg. 8:21, 26

20 [a]Ex. 39:28

21 [1]Or, *signet rings* [a]Gen. 24:47; Ezek. 16:12

24 [1]Or, *balsam oil* [a]Esth. 2:12 [b]1 Pet. 3:3 [c]Is. 22:12; Ezek. 27:31; Amos 8:10 [d]Is. 15:3; Lam. 2:10

25 [1]Lit., *strength* [a]Is. 1:20; 65:12

26 [1]Lit., *entrances* [a]Jer. 14:2; Lam. 1:4 [b]Lam. 2:10

Chapter 4

FOR seven women will take hold of [a]one man in that day,
saying, "We will eat our own bread and wear our own clothes,
only let us be called by your name; [b]take away our reproach!"
2 In that day the [a]Branch of the LORD will be beautiful
and glorious, and the [b]fruit of the earth *will* be the pride and
the adornment of the [c]survivors of Israel.
3 And it will come about that he who is [a]left in Zion and
remains in Jerusalem will be called [b]holy—everyone who is
[c]recorded for life in Jerusalem.
4 When the LORD has washed away the filth of the daughters of Zion, and [1]purged the [a]bloodshed of Jerusalem from
her midst, by the [b]spirit of judgment and the [c]spirit of burning,
5 then the LORD will create over the whole area of Mount
Zion and over her assemblies [a]a cloud by day, even smoke, and
the brightness of a flaming fire by night; for over all the glory
will be a canopy.
6 And there will be a [a]shelter to *give* shade from the heat
by day, and refuge and [1]protection from the storm and the
rain.

Chapter 5

LET me sing now for my well-beloved a song of my beloved
concerning his vineyard.
My well-beloved had a [a]vineyard on a [1]fertile hill.
2 And he dug it all around, removed its stones,
And planted it with [1]the [a]choicest vine.
And he built a tower in the middle of it,
And hewed out a [2]wine vat in it;
Then he [b]expected *it* to produce *good* grapes,
But it produced *only* [3]worthless ones.

3 "And now, O inhabitants of Jerusalem and men of Judah,
[a]Judge between Me and My vineyard.
4 "[a]What more was there to do for My vineyard [1]that I have not done in it?
Why, when I expected *it* to produce *good* grapes did it produce [2]worthless ones?
5 "So now let Me tell you what I am going to do to My vineyard:
I will [a]remove its hedge and it will be consumed;
I will [b]break down its wall and it will become [c]trampled ground.
6 "And I will [a]lay it waste;
It will not be pruned or hoed,
But briars and thorns will come up.
I will also charge the clouds to [b]rain no rain on it."

7 For the vineyard of the LORD of hosts is the house of Israel,
And the men of Judah His delightful plant.
Thus He looked for justice, but behold, [a]bloodshed;
For righteousness, but behold, a cry of distress.

4:1 [a]Is. 13:12 [b]Is. 54:4; Gen. 30:23

4:2 [a]Is. 11:1; 53:2; Jer. 23:5; 33:15; Zech. 3:8; 6:12 [b]Ps. 72:16 [c]Is. 10:20; 37:31, 32; Joel 2:32; Obad. 17

4:3 [a]Is. 28:5; 46:3; Rom. 11:4, 5 [b]Is. 52:1; 62:12 [c]Ex. 32:32; Ps. 69:28; Luke 10:20

4:4 [1]Lit., *rinsed away* [a]Is. 1:15 [b]Is. 28:6 [c]Is. 1:31; 9:19

4:5 [a]Ex. 13:21, 22; Num. 9:15-23

4:6 [1]Lit., *a hiding place* [a]Is. 25:4; 32:1, 2; Ps. 27:5

5:1 [1]Lit., *a horn, the son of fatness* [a]Ps. 80:8; Jer. 12:10; Matt. 21:33; Mark 12:1; Luke 20:9

5:2 [1]Lit., *a bright red grape* [2]Or, *winepress* [3]Or, *wild grapes* [a]Jer. 2:21 [b]Matt. 21:19; Mark 11:13; Luke 13:6

5:3 [a]Matt. 21:40

5:4 [1]Lit., *and I have not done* [2]Or, *wild grapes* [a]2 Chr. 36:15; Jer. 2:5; 7:25, 26; Mic. 6:3; Matt. 23:37

5:5 [a]Ps. 89:40 [b]Ps. 80:12 [c]Is. 10:6; 28:18; Lam. 1:15; Luke 21:24; Rev. 11:2

5:6 [a]2 Chr. 36:19-21; Jer. 25:11 [b]1 Kin. 8:35; 17:1; Jer. 14:1-22

5:7 [a]Is. 3:14, 15; 30:12; 59:13

8 Woe to those who [a]add house to house *and* join field
to field,
Until there is no more room,
So that you have to live alone in the midst of the land!
9 In my ears the LORD of hosts *has sworn,* "Surely, [a]many
houses shall become [b]desolate,
Even great and fine ones, without occupants.
10 "For [a]ten acres of vineyard will yield *only* one [1]bath *of
wine,*
And a homer of seed will yield *but* an [2]ephah of grain."
11 Woe to those who rise early in the morning that they
may pursue [a]strong drink;
Who stay up late in the evening that wine may inflame
them!
12 And their banquets are *accompanied* by lyre and [a]harp,
by tambourine and flute, and by wine;
But they [b]do not pay attention to the deeds of the
LORD,
Nor do they consider the work of His hands.

13 Therefore My people go into exile for their [a]lack of
knowledge;
And [1]their honorable men are famished,
And their multitude is parched with thirst.
14 Therefore Sheol has enlarged its [1]throat and opened its
mouth without measure;
And [2]Jerusalem's splendor, her multitude, her din *of
revelry,* and the jubilant within her, descend *into
it.*
15 So the *common* man will be humbled, and the man of
importance abased,
[a]The eyes of the proud also will be abased.
16 But the [a]LORD of hosts will be [b]exalted in judgment,
And the holy God will show Himself [c]holy in
righteousness.
17 [a]Then the lambs will graze as in their pasture,
And strangers will eat in the waste places of the
[1]wealthy.

18 Woe to those who drag [a]iniquity with the cords of
[1]falsehood,
And sin as if with cart ropes;
19 [a]Who say, "Let Him make speed, let Him hasten His
work, that we may see *it;*
And let the purpose of the Holy One of Israel draw
near
And come to pass, that we may know *it!*"
20 Woe to those who [a]call evil good, and good evil;
Who [1b]substitute darkness for light and light for
darkness;
Who [1]substitute bitter for sweet, and sweet for bitter!
21 Woe to those who are [a]wise in their own eyes,
And clever in their own sight!
22 [a]Woe to those who are heroes in drinking wine,
And valiant men in mixing strong drink;
23 [a]Who justify the wicked for a bribe,

8 [a]Jer. 22:13-17; Mic. 2:2; Hab. 2:9-12

9 [a]Is. 6:11, 12 [b]Matt. 23:38

10 [1]I.e., about 10½ gal. [2]I.e., 1/10 of a homer [a]Is. 7:23; Lev. 26:26; Hag. 1:6; 2:16

11 [a]Is. 22:13; 28:1, 3, 7, 8; Prov. 23:29, 30; Eccles. 10:16, 17

12 [a]Amos 6:5, 6 [b]Job 34:27; Ps. 28:5

13 [1]Lit., *their glory are men of famine* [a]Is. 1:3; 27:11; Hos. 4:6

14 [1]Or, *appetite* [2]Lit., *her*

15 [a]Is. 2:11; 10:33

16 [a]Is. 8:13; 29:23; 1 Pet. 3:15 [b]Is. 2:11, 17; 33:5, 10 [c]Is. 8:13; 29:23; 1 Pet. 3:15

17 [1]Lit., *the fat* [a]Is. 7:25; Mic. 2:12; Zeph. 2:6

18 [1]Or, *worthlessness* [a]Is. 59:4-8; Jer. 23:10-14

19 [a]Ezek. 12:22; 2 Pet. 3:4

20 [1]Lit., *set* [a]Prov. 17:15; Amos 5:7 [b]Job 17:12; Matt. 6:22, 23; Luke 11:34, 35

21 [a]Prov. 3:7; Rom. 12:16; 1 Cor. 3:18-20

22 [a]Is. 6:11; Is. 56:12; Prov. 23:20; Hab. 2:15

23 [a]Is. 1:23; 10:1, 2; Ex. 23:8; Mic. 3:11; 7:3

And [b]take away the [1]rights of the ones who are in the
right!

24 Therefore, [a]as a tongue of fire consumes stubble,
And dry grass collapses into the flame,
So their [b]root will become [c]like rot and their blossom
[1]blow away as dust;
For they have [d]rejected the law of the LORD of hosts,
And despised the word of the Holy One of Israel.
25 On this account the [a]anger of the LORD has burned
against His people,
And He has stretched out His hand against them and
struck them down,
And the mountains quaked; and their [b]corpses [1]lay like
refuse in the middle of the streets.
[c]For all this His anger [2]is not spent,
But His [d]hand is still stretched out.

26 He will also lift up a [a]standard to the nations afar off,
And will [b]whistle for [1]it [c]from the ends of the earth;
And behold, it will [d]come with speed swiftly.
27 [a]No one in it is weary or stumbles,
None slumbers or sleeps;
Nor is the [b]belt at its waist undone,
Nor its sandal strap broken.
28 [1a]Its arrows are sharp, and all its bows are bent;
The hoofs of its horses [2]seem like flint, and its *chariot*
[b]wheels like a whirlwind.
29 Its [a]roaring is like a lioness, and it roars like young lions;
It growls as it [b]seizes the prey,
And carries *it* off with [c]no one to deliver *it*.
30 And it shall [a]growl over it in that day like the roaring of
the sea.
If one [b]looks to the land, behold, there is darkness *and*
distress;
Even the light is darkened by its clouds.

CHAPTER 6

IN the year of King Uzziah's death, [a]I saw the Lord sitting on
a throne, lofty and exalted, with the train of His robe filling
the temple.
2 Seraphim stood above Him, [a]each having six wings;
with two he covered his face, and with two he covered his feet,
and with two he flew.
3 And one called out to another and said, "Holy, Holy,
Holy, is the LORD of hosts, the [1a]whole earth is full of His
glory."
4 And the [1]foundations of the thresholds trembled at the
voice of Him who called out, while the [2]temple was filling with
smoke.
5 Then I said, "[a]Woe is me, for I am ruined!
Because I am a man of [b]unclean lips,
And I live among a [c]people of unclean lips;
For my eyes have seen the [d]King, the LORD of hosts."

23 [1]Lit., *righteousness* [b]Ps. 94:21; James 5:6

24 [1]Lit., *ascend* [a]Is. 9:18, 19; Joel 2:5 [b]Job 18:16 [c]Hos. 5:12 [d]Is. 8:6; 30:9, 12; Acts 13:41

25 [1]Lit., *were* [2]Lit., *has not turned away* [a]Is. 66:15; 2 Kin. 22:13, 17 [b]2 Kin. 9:37; Jer. 16:4 [c]Is. 9:12, 17, 21; 10:4; Jer. 4:8; Dan. 9:16 [d]Is. 23:11; Ex. 7:19

26 [1]Probably Assyria [a]Is. 13:2, 3 [b]Is. 7:18; Zech. 10:8 [c]Deut. 28:49 [d]Is. 13:4, 5

27 [a]Joel 2:7, 8 [b]Job 12:18; Dan. 5:6

28 [1]Lit., *Which, its arrows* [2]Lit., *are regarded as* [a]Is. 13:18; Ps. 7:12, 13; 45:5 [b]Is. 21:1; Jer. 4:13

29 [a]Jer. 51:38; Zeph. 3:3; Zech. 11:3 [b]Is. 10:6; 49:24, 25; Mic. 5:8 [c]Is. 42:22

30 [a]Is. 17:12; Jer. 6:23; Luke 21:25 [b]Is. 8:22; Jer. 4:23-28; Joel 2:10; Luke 21:25, 26

1 [a]John 12:41; Rev. 4:2, 3; 20:11

2 [a]Rev. 4:8

3 [1]Lit., *fulness of the whole earth is His glory* [a]Num. 14:21; Ps. 72:19

4 [1]Lit., *door sockets* [2]Lit., *house*

5 [a]Ex. 33:20; Luke 5:8 [b]Ex. 6:12, 30 [c]Is. 59:3; Jer. 9:3-8 [d]Jer. 51:57

6 Then one of the seraphim flew to me, with a burning
coal in his hand which he had taken from the altar with tongs.
7 And he [a]touched my mouth *with it* and said, "Behold,
this has touched your lips; and [b]your iniquity is taken away,
and your sin is [1]forgiven."
8 Then I heard the [a]voice of the Lord, saying, "Whom
shall I send, and who will go for us?" Then [b]I said, "Here am I.
Send me!"
9 And He said, "Go, and tell this people:
'Keep on listening, but do not perceive;
Keep on looking, but do not understand.'
10 "Render the hearts of this people [1]insensitive,
Their ears [2]dull,
And their eyes [3]dim,
[a]Lest they see with their eyes,
Hear with their ears,
Understand with their hearts,
And repent and be healed."
11 Then I said, "Lord, [a]how long?" And He answered,
"Until [b]cities are devastated *and* without inhabitant,
Houses are without people,
And the land is utterly desolate,
12 "The LORD has removed men far away,
And the [1a]forsaken places are many in the midst of the
land.
13 "Yet there will be a tenth portion in it,
And it will again be *subject* to burning,
Like a terebinth or an [a]oak
Whose stump remains when it is felled.
The [b]holy seed is its stump."

CHAPTER 7

NOW it came about in the days of Ahaz, the son of Jotham,
the son of Uzziah, king of Judah, that Rezin the king of Syria
and Pekah the son of Remaliah, king of Israel, went up to
Jerusalem to *wage* war against it, but [a]could not [1]conquer it.
2 When it was reported to the [a]house of David saying,
"Syria [1b]has camped in [c]Ephraim," his heart and the hearts of
his people shook as the trees of the forest shake [2]with the wind.
3 Then the LORD said to Isaiah, "Go out now to meet
Ahaz, you and your son [1]Shearjashub, at the end of the [a]con-
duit of the upper pool, on the highway to the [2]fuller's field,
4 and say to him, 'Take care, and be [a]calm, have no [b]fear
and [c]do not be fainthearted because of these two stubs of
smoldering [d]firebrands, on account of the fierce anger of Rezin and Syria, and the [e]son of Remaliah.
5 'Because [a]Syria, *with* Ephraim and the son of Remaliah,
has planned evil against you, saying,
6 "Let us go up against Judah and [1]terrorize it, and make
for ourselves a breach in [2]its walls, and set up the son of Tabeel
as king in the midst of it,"
7 thus says the Lord [1]GOD, "[a]It shall not stand nor shall it
come to pass.
8 "For the head of Syria is Damascus and the head of

7 [1]Lit., *atoned for* [a]Jer. 1:9; Dan. 10:16 [b]Is. 40:2; 53:5, 6, 11; John 1:7

8 [a]Ezek. 10:5; Acts 9:4 [b]Acts 26:19

10 [1]Lit., *fat* [2]Lit., *heavy* [3]Lit., *besmeared* [a]Jer. 5:21

11 [a]Ps. 79:5 [b]Lev. 26:31; Is. 1:7; 3:8, 26

12 [1]Or, *forsakenness will be great* [a]Jer. 4:29

13 [a]Job 14:7 [b]Deut. 7:6; Ezra 9:2

1 [1]Lit., *fight against* [a]Is. 7:6, 7

2 [1]Lit., *has settled down on* [2]Lit., *from before* [a]Is. 7:13; 22:22 [b]Is. 8:12 [c]Is. 9:9

3 [1]I.e., a remnant shall return [2]I.e., laundryman's [a]Is. 36:2; 2 Kin. 18:17

4 [a]Is. 30:15; Ex. 14:13; Lam. 3:26 [b]Is. 10:24; Matt. 24:6 [c]Is. 35:4; Deut. 20:3; 1 Sam. 17:32 [d]Amos 4:11; Zech. 3:2 [e]Is. 7:1, 9

5 [a]Is. 7:2

6 [1]Lit., *cause it a sickening dread* [2]Lit., *it*

7 [1]YHWH, usually rendered LORD [a]Is. 8:10; 28:18; Ps. 2:4-6; Acts 4:25, 26

[a]Damascus is Rezin (now within another 65 years Ephraim will
be shattered, *so that it is* no longer a people),
9 and the head of Ephraim is Samaria and the head of
Samaria is the son of Remaliah. [a]If you will not believe, you
surely shall not [1]last.'"'"
10 Then the LORD spoke again to Ahaz, saying,
11 "Ask a [a]sign for yourself from the LORD your God;
[1]make *it* deep as Sheol or high as [2]heaven."
12 But Ahaz said, "I will not ask, nor will I test the LORD!"
13 Then he said, "Listen now, O [a]house of David! Is it too
slight a thing for you to try the patience of men, that you will
[b]try the patience of [c]my God as well?"
14 Therefore the Lord Himself will give you a sign: Behold, [a]a [1]virgin will be with child and bear a son, and she will
call His name [2b]Immanuel.
15 He will eat [a]curds and honey [1]at the time He knows
enough to refuse evil and choose good.
16 [a]For before the boy will know *enough* to refuse evil and
choose good, [b]the land whose two kings you dread will be
forsaken.
17 The LORD will bring on you, on your people, and on
your father's house such days as have never come since the day
that [a]Ephraim separated from Judah—the [b]king of Assyria.
18 And it will come about in that day, that the LORD will
[a]whistle for the fly that is in the [1b]remotest part of the rivers of
Egypt, and for the bee that is in the land of Assyria.
19 And they will all come and settle on the steep [1]ravines,
on the [a]ledges of the cliffs, [b]on all the thorn bushes, and on all
the [2]watering places.
20 In that day the Lord will [a]shave with a [b]razor, [c]hired
from regions beyond [d]the [1]Euphrates (*that is,* with the king of
Assyria), the head and the hair of the legs; and it will also
remove the beard.
21 Now it will come about in that day that a man may
keep alive a [a]heifer and a pair of sheep;
22 and it will happen that because of the abundance of
the milk produced he will eat curds, for every one that is left
within the land will eat [a]curds and honey.
23 And it will come about in that day, [a]that every place
where there used to be a thousand vines, *valued* at a thousand
shekels of silver, will become [b]briars and thorns.
24 *People* will come there with bows and arrows because
all the land will be briars and thorns.
25 And as for all the hills which used to be cultivated with
the hoe, you will not go there for fear of briars and thorns; but
they will become a place for [1a]pasturing oxen and for sheep to
trample.

CHAPTER 8

THEN the LORD said to me, "Take for yourself a large tablet
and [a]write on it [1]in ordinary letters: [2]Swift is the booty, speedy
is the prey.
2 "And [1]I will take to Myself faithful witnesses for testimony, [a]Uriah the priest and Zechariah the son of
Jeberechiah."

8 [a]Is. 17:1-3; Gen. 14:15

9 [1]Or, *be established*
[a]Is. 5:24; 8:6-8; 30:12-14; 2 Chr. 20:20

11 [1]So with the versions; M.T. *make the request deep or high . . .* [2]Lit., *heights*
[a]Is. 37:30; 38:7, 8; 55:13; 2 Kin. 19:29

13 [a]Is. 7:2 [b]Is. 1:14; 43:24 [c]Is. 25:1

14 [1]Or, *maiden* [2]I.e., God is with us
[a]Matt. 1:23 [b]Is. 8:8, 10

15 [1]Lit., *with respect to his knowing*
[a]Is. 7:22

16 [a]Is. 8:4 [b]Is. 8:14; 17:3; Jer. 7:15; Hos. 5:3, 9, 14; Amos 1:3-5

17 [a]1 Kin. 12:16 [b]Is. 8:7, 8; 10:5, 6; 2 Chr. 28:20

18 [1]Or, *mouth of the rivers,* i.e., the Nile Delta
[a]Is. 5:26 [b]Is. 13:5

19 [1]Or, *wadis* [2]Or, *pastures*
[a]Is. 2:19; Jer. 16:16 [b]Is. 24:25

20 [1]Lit., *River*
[a]Is. 24:1; 2 Kin. 18:13-16 [b]Ezek. 5:1-4 [c]Is. 10:5, 15 [d]Is. 8:7; 11:15; Jer. 2:18

21 [a]Is. 14:30; 27:10; Jer. 39:10

22 [a]Is. 8:15

23 [a]Is. 5:10; 32:13, 14 [b]Is. 5:6

25 [1]Lit., *sending*
[a]Is. 5:17

1 [1]Lit., *with the stylus of man* [2]Heb., *Maher-shalal-hash-baz;* cf. v. 3
[a]Is. 30:8; Hab. 2:2

2 [1]Another reading, *take for me*
[a]2 Kin. 16:10, 11, 15, 16

3 So I approached the prophetess, and she conceived and
gave birth to a son. Then the LORD said to me, "Name him
[1]Maher-shalal-hash-baz;
4 for [a]before the boy knows how to cry out 'My father' or
'My mother,' the wealth of Damascus and the spoil of Samaria
will be carried away before the king of Assyria."
5 And again the LORD spoke to me further, saying,
6 "Inasmuch as these people have [a]rejected the gently flowing waters of Shiloah,
And rejoice in Rezin and the son of Remaliah;
7 "Now therefore, behold, the Lord is about to bring on them the strong and abundant [a]waters of the [1]Euphrates,
Even the king of Assyria and all his glory;
And it will [b]rise up over all its channels and go over all its banks.
8 "Then [a]it will sweep on into Judah, it will overflow and pass through,
It will [b]reach even to the neck;
And the spread of its wings will [1]fill the breadth of [2]your land, O [c]Immanuel.

9 "[a]Be broken, O peoples, and be [1b]shattered;
And give ear all remote places of the earth.
Gird yourselves, yet be [1]shattered;
Gird yourselves, yet be [1]shattered.
10 "[a]Devise a plan but it will be thwarted;
State a [1]proposal, but [b]it will not stand,
For [2c]God is with us."
11 For thus the LORD spoke to me [1]with [a]mighty power
and instructed me [b]not to walk in the way of this people,
saying,
12 "You are not to say, '*It is* a [a]conspiracy!'
In regard to all that this people call a conspiracy,
And [b]you are not to fear [1]what they fear or be in dread of *it*.
13 "It is the [a]LORD of hosts [b]whom you should regard as holy.
And He shall be your fear,
And He shall be your dread.
14 "Then He shall become a [a]sanctuary;
But to both the houses of Israel, a [b]stone to strike and a rock to stumble over,
And a snare and a [c]trap for the inhabitants of Jerusalem.
15 "And many will stumble over them,
Then they will fall and be broken;
They will even be snared and caught."
16 [a]Bind up the testimony, [b]seal the [1]law among [c]my
disciples.
17 And I will [a]wait for the LORD [b]who is hiding His face
from the house of Jacob; I will even look eagerly for Him.
18 [a]Behold, I and the children whom the LORD has given
me are for [b]signs and wonders in Israel from the LORD of hosts,
who [c]dwells on Mount Zion.
19 And when they say to you, "[a]Consult the mediums and

3 [1]I.e., Swift is the booty, speedy is the prey; cf. v. 1
4 [a]Is. 1:20; 5:24; 7:9; 30:12
6 [a]Is. 1:20; 5:24; 7:9; 30:12
7 [1]Lit., *River* [a]Is. 17:12, 13 [b]Amos 8:8; 9:5
8 [1]Lit., *be the fulness of* [2]Or, *Your* [a]Is. 10:6 [b]Is. 30:28 [c]Is. 7:14
9 [1]Or, *dismayed* [a]Is. 17:12-14 [b]Dan. 2:34, 35
10 [1]Lit., *word* [2]Heb., *Immanu-el* [a]Is. 28:18; Job 5:12 [b]Is. 7:7 [c]Is. 8:8; Rom. 8:31
11 [1]Lit., *with strength of the hand* [a]Ezek. 3:14 [b]Ezek. 2:8
12 [1]Lit., *their fear* [a]Is. 7:2; 30:1 [b]1 Pet. 3:14, 15
13 [a]Is. 5:16; 29:23 [b]Num. 20:12
14 [a]Is. 4:6; 25:4; Ezek. 11:16 [b]Luke 2:34; Rom. 9:33; 1 Pet. 2:8 [c]Is. 24:17, 18
16 [1]Or, *teaching* [a]Is. 8:1, 2; 29:11, 12 [b]Dan. 12:4 [c]Is. 50:4
17 [a]Is. 25:9; 30:18; Hab. 2:3 [b]Is. 1:15; 45:15; 54:8; Deut. 31:17
18 [a]Heb. 2:13 [b]Luke 2:34 [c]Ps. 9:11; Zech. 8:3
19 [a]Is. 19:3; 29:4; 47:12, 13; Lev. 20:6; 2 Kin. 21:6; 23:24

the wizards who whisper and mutter," should not a people
[b]consult their God? *Should they consult* the dead on behalf of
the living?
20 To the [1a]law and to the testimony! If they do not speak
according to this word, it is because they have no dawn.
21 And they will pass through [1]the land [a]hard pressed and
famished, and it will turn out that when they are hungry, they
will be enraged and curse [2]their king and their God as they face
upward.
22 Then they will [a]look to the earth, and behold, distress
and darkness, the gloom of anguish; and *they will be* driven
away into darkness.

1
Chapter 9

BUT there will be no *more* [a]gloom for her who was in anguish; in earlier times He [b]treated the land of [c]Zebulun and
the land of Naphthali with contempt, but later on He shall
make *it* glorious, by the way of the sea, on the other side of
Jordan, Galilee of the [2]Gentiles.

2 [1]The people who walk in darkness
Will see a great light;
Those who live in a dark land,
The light will shine on them.
3 [a]Thou shalt multiply the nation,
Thou [b]shalt [1]increase [2]their gladness;
They will be glad in Thy presence
As with the gladness [3]of harvest,
As [4]men rejoice when they divide the spoil.
4 For thou shalt break the yoke of their burden and the staff on their shoulders,
The rod of their [a]oppressor, as [1]at the battle of Midian.
5 For every boot of the booted warrior in the *battle* tumult,
And cloak rolled in blood, will be for burning, fuel for the fire.
6 For a [a]child will be born to us, a [b]son will be given to us;
And the [c]government will [1]rest [d]on His shoulders;
And His name will be called [e]Wonderful Counselor, [f]Mighty God,
Eternal [g]Father, Prince of [h]Peace.
7 There will be [a]no end to the increase of *His* government or of peace,
On the [b]throne of David and over his kingdom,
To establish it and to uphold it with [c]justice and righteousness
From then on and forevermore.
[d]The zeal of the LORD of hosts will accomplish this.

8 The Lord sends a [1]message against Jacob,
And it falls on Israel.
9 And all the people know *it*,
That is, Ephraim and the inhabitants of Samaria,
Asserting in pride and in [a]arrogance of heart:
10 "The bricks have fallen down,
But we will [a]rebuild with smooth stones;

19 [b]Is. 30:2; 45:11

20 [1]Or, *teaching*
[a]Is. 8:16; 1:10; Luke 16:29

21 [1]Lit., *it* [2]Or, *by their King*
[a]Is. 9:20, 21

22 [a]Jer. 13:16; Amos 5:18, 20; Zeph. 1:14, 15

1 [1]Ch. 8:23 in Heb. [2]Or, *nations*
[a]Is. 8:22 [b]2 Kin. 15:29; 2 Chr. 16:4 [c]Matt. 4:15, 16

2 [1]Ch. 9:1 in Heb. text

3 [1]Another reading: *not increase* [2]Lit., *the* [3]Lit., *in* [4]Lit., *they*
[a]Is. 26:15 [b]Is. 35:10; 65:14, 18, 19; 66:10

4 [1]Lit., *in the day of Midian*
[a]Is. 14:4; 49:26; 51:13; 54:14

6 [1]Lit., *be*
[a]Is. 7:14; 11:1, 2; 53:2; Luke 2:11 [b]John 3:16 [c]Matt. 28:18; 1 Cor. 15:25 [d]Is. 22:22 [e]Is. 28:29 [f]Is. 10:21; Deut. 10:17; Neh. 9:32 [g]Is. 63:16; 64:8 [h]Is. 26:3, 12; 53:5; 54:10; 66:12

7 [a]Dan. 2:44; Luke 1:32, 33 [b]Is. 16:5 [c]Is. 11:4, 5; 32:1; 42:3, 4; 63:1 [d]Is. 37:32; 59:17

8 [1]Lit., *word*

9 [a]Is. 46:12

10 [a]Mal. 1:4

The sycamores have been cut down,
But we will replace *them* with cedars."
11 Therefore the LORD raises against them adversaries from Rezin,
And spurs their enemies on,
12 The Syrians on the east and the [a]Philistines on the west;
And they [b]devour Israel with [1]gaping jaws.
[c]In *spite of* all this His anger does not turn away,
And His hand is still stretched out.

13 Yet the people [a]do not turn back to Him who struck them,
Nor do they [b]seek the LORD of hosts.
14 So the LORD cuts off [a]head and tail from Israel,
Both palm branch and bulrush [b]in a single day.
15 The head is [a]the elder and honorable man,
And the prophet who teaches falsehood is the tail.
16 [a]For those who guide this people are leading *them* astray;
And those who are guided by them are [1]brought to confusion.
17 Therefore the Lord does [a]not take pleasure in their young men,
[b]Nor does He have pity on their [1]orphans or their widows;
For every one of them is [c]godless and an evildoer,
And every [d]mouth is speaking foolishness.
In *spite of* all this His anger does not turn away,
And His hand is still stretched out.

18 [a]For wickedness burns like a fire;
It consumes briars and thorns;
It even sets the thickets of the forest aflame,
And they roll upward in a column of smoke.
19 By the [a]fury of the LORD of hosts the [b]land is burned up,
And the [c]people are like fuel for the fire
No [d]man spares his brother.
20 And [1]they slice off *what is* on the right hand but *still* are [a]hungry,
And [1]they eat *what is* on the left hand but they are not satisfied;
Each of them eats the [b]flesh of his own arm.
21 Manasseh *devours* Ephraim, and Ephraim Manasseh,
[a]*And* together they are against Judah.
In *spite of* all this His anger does not turn away,
And His hand is still stretched out.

CHAPTER 10

WOE to those who [a]enact evil statutes,
And to those who constantly record [1]unjust decisions,
2 So as [a]to [1]deprive the needy of justice,
And rob the poor of My people of *their* rights,
In order [b]that widows may be their spoil,
And that they may plunder the [2]orphans.

12 [1]Lit., *the whole mouth* [a]2 Chr. 28:18 [b]Ps. 79:7; Jer. 10:25 [c]Is. 5:25

13 [a]Jer. 5:3; Hos. 7:10 [b]Is. 31:1; Hos. 3:5

14 [a]Is. 19:15 [b]Rev. 18:8

15 [a]Is. 3:2, 3

16 [1]Or, *swallowed up* [a]Is. 3:12; Matt. 15:14; 23:16, 24

17 [1]Or, *fatherless* [a]Jer. 18:21; Amos 4:10; 8:13 [b]Is. 27:11 [c]Is. 10:6; 32:6 [d]Matt. 12:34

18 [a]Is. 1:7; Ps. 83:14; Nah. 1:10; Mal. 4:1

19 [a]Is. 10:6; 13:9, 13; 42:25 [b]Joel 2:3 [c]Is. 1:31; 24:6 [d]Mic. 7:2, 6

20 [1]Lit., *he* [a]Is. 8:21, 22 [b]Is. 49:26

21 [a]Is. 11:13; 2 Chr. 28:6, 8

1 [1]Lit., *mischief* or *misfortune* [a]Is. 29:21; 59:4, 13; Ps. 94:20

2 [1]Lit., *turn aside from* [2]Or, *fatherless* [a]Is. 5:23 [b]Is. 1:23; 3:14, 15

3 Now [a]what will you do in the [b]day of punishment,
And in the devastation which will come [c]from afar?
[d]To whom will you flee for help?
And where will you leave your [1]wealth?
4 Nothing *remains* but to crouch [1]among the [a]captives
Or fall [1]among the [b]slain.
In *spite of* all this His anger does not turn away,
And His hand is still stretched out.

5 Woe to [a]Assyria, the [b]rod of My anger
And the staff in whose hands is [c]My indignation,
6 I send it against a [a]godless nation
And commission it against the [b]people of My fury
[c]To capture booty and [d]to seize plunder,
And to [1]trample them down like [e]mud in the streets.
7 Yet it [a]does not so intend
Nor does [1]it plan so in its heart,
But rather it is [2]its purpose to destroy,
And to cut off [3]many nations.
8 For it says, "Are not my princes [1]all kings?
9 "Is not Calno like Carchemish,
Or Hamath like Arpad,
Or Samaria like Damascus?
10 "As my hand has reached to the [a]kingdoms of the idols,
Whose graven images *were* greater than those of Jerusalem and Samaria,
11 Shall I not [1]do to Jerusalem and her images
Just as I have done to Samaria and [a]her idols?"
12 So it will be that when the Lord has completed all His
[a]work on Mount Zion and on Jerusalem, *He will say,* "I will
[1]punish the fruit of the arrogant heart of the king of Assyria
and [b]the pomp of [2]his haughtiness."
13 For [a]he has said,
"By the power of my hand and by my wisdom I did *this,*
For I have understanding;
And I [b]removed the boundaries of the peoples,
And plundered their treasures,
And like a mighty man I brought down [1]*their* inhabitants,
14 "And my hand reached to the riches of the peoples like a [a]nest,
And as one gathers abandoned eggs, I gathered all the earth;
And there was not one that flapped its wing or opened *its* beak or chirped."

15 Is the [a]axe to [b]boast itself over the one who chops with it?
Is the saw to exalt itself over the one who wields it?
That would be like [c]a [1]club wielding those who lift it,
Or like [d]a rod lifting *him who* is not wood.
16 Therefore the Lord, the [1]GOD of hosts, will send a [a]wasting disease among his [b]stout warriors;
And under his [c]glory a fire will be kindled like a burning flame.

3 [1]Lit., *glory*
[a]Job 31:14 [b]Is. 13:6; 26:14, 21; 29:6; Jer. 9:9; Hos. 9:7; Luke 19:44 [c]Is. 5:26 [d]Is. 20:6; 30:57; 31:3

4 [1]Lit., *under*
[a]Is. 24:22 [b]Is. 22:2; 34:3; 66:16

5 [a]Is. 7:17; 8:7 [b]Jer. 51:20 [c]Is. 13:5; 30:30; 34:2; 66:14

6 [1]Lit., *make them a trampled place*
[a]Is. 9:17 [b]Is. 9:19 [c]Is. 37:26, 27 [d]Is. 59:29 [e]Is. 5:25

7 [1]Lit., *its heart so plan* [2]Lit., *in its heart* [3]Lit., *not a few*
[a]Gen. 50:20; Micah 4:11, 12; Acts 2:23, 24

8 [1]Lit., *altogether*

10 [a]2 Kin. 19:17, 18

11 [1]Lit., *do thus*
[a]Is. 2:8

12 [1]Lit., *visit* [2]Lit., *haughtiness of his eyes*
[a]Is. 28:21, 22; 29:14; 65:7; 2 Kin. 19:31 [b]Is. 37:23

13 [1]Or, *those who sit on thrones*
[a]Is. 37:24-27; 2 Kin. 19:22-24; Ezek. 28:4; Dan. 4:30 [b]Hab. 2:6-11

14 [a]Jer. 49:16; Obad. 4

15 [1]Lit., *staff*
[a]Jer. 51:20 [b]Is. 29:16; 45:9; Rom. 9:20, 21 [c]Is. 10:5 [d]Is. 10:5

16 [1]YHWH, usually rendered LORD
[a]Ps. 106:15 [b]Is. 17:4 [c]Is. 10:18; 8:7

17 And the [a]light of Israel will become a fire and his [b]Holy One a flame,
And it will [c]burn and devour his thorns and his briars in a single day.
18 And He will [a]destroy the glory of his forest and of his fruitful garden, both soul and body;
And it will be as when a sick man wastes away.
19 And the [a]rest of the trees of his forest will be so small in number
That a child could write them down.
20 Now it will come about in that day that the remnant of
Israel, and those of the house of Jacob who have escaped, will
never again rely on the one who struck them, but will truly
[a]rely on the LORD, the Holy One of Israel.
21 A [a]remnant will return, the remnant of Jacob, to the mighty God.
22 For [a]though your people, O Israel, may be like the sand of the sea,
Only a remnant within them will return;
A [b]destruction is determined, overflowing with righteousness.
23 For a complete destruction, one that is decreed, the
Lord [1]GOD of hosts will execute in the midst of the whole land.
24 Therefore thus says the Lord [1]GOD of hosts, "O My
people who dwell in [a]Zion, do not fear the Assyrian [2]who
[b]strikes you with the rod and lifts up his staff against you, the
way Egypt *did.*
25 "For in a very [a]little while My indignation *against you*
will be spent, and My anger *will be directed* to their
destruction."
26 And the LORD of hosts will [a]arouse a scourge against
him like the slaughter of Midian at the rock of Oreb; and His
[b]staff will be over the sea, and He will lift it up [c]the way *He did*
in Egypt.
27 So it will be in that day, that [1]his [a]burden will be removed from your shoulders and his yoke from your neck, and
the yoke will be broken because [b]of fatness.
28 He has come against Aiath,
He has passed through Migron;
At Michmash he deposited his [a]baggage,
29 They have gone through the pass, saying,
"They have made a lodging place in Geba."
Ramah is terrified, and Gibeah of Saul has fled away.
30 Cry aloud with your voice, O daughter of Gallim!
Pay attention, Laishah and [1]wretched Anathoth!
31 Madmenah has fled.
The inhabitants of Gebim have sought refuge.
32 Yet today he will halt at Nob;
He [a]shakes his fist at the mountain of the [1b]daughter of Zion, the hill of Jerusalem.

33 Behold, the Lord, the [1]GOD of hosts, will lop off the boughs with a terrible crash;
Those also who are [a]tall in stature will be cut down,
And those who are lofty will be abased.

17 [a]Is. 30:33; 31:9 [b]Is. 37:23 [c]Is. 27:4; 33:12; Num. 11:1-3; Jer. 4:4; 7:20
18 [a]Is. 10:33, 34
19 [a]Is. 21:17
20 [a]Is. 17:7, 8; 50:10; 2 Chr. 14:11
21 [a]Is. 7:3
22 [a]Rom. 9:27, 28 [b]Is. 28:22; Dan. 9:27; Rom. 9:28
23 [1]YHWH, usually rendered LORD
24 [1]YHWH, usually rendered LORD [2]Lit., *he* [a]Ps. 8:5, 6 [b]Ex. 5:14-16
25 [a]Is. 17:14; Hag. 2:6
26 [a]Is. 37:36-38 [b]Ex. 14:16 [c]Ex. 14:27
27 [1]I.e., The Assyrian [a]Is. 9:4; 14:25 [b]Is. 30:23; 55:2
28 [a]Judg. 18:21; 1 Sam. 17:22
30 [1]An ancient version reads, *Answer her, O Anathoth*
32 [1]Another reading is, *house of* [a]Is. 19:16; Zech. 2:9 [b]Is. 1:8; Jer. 6:23
33 [1]YHWH, usually rendered LORD [a]Is. 37:24, 36-38; Ezek. 31:3; Amos 2:9

34 And He will cut down the thickets of the forest with an
iron *axe*,
And Lebanon will fall [1]by the Mighty One.

Chapter 11

THEN a [a]shoot will spring from the [b]stem of Jesse,
And a [c]branch from his roots will bear fruit.
2 And the [a]Spirit of the LORD will rest on Him,
The spirit of [b]wisdom and understanding,
The spirit of counsel and [c]strength,
The spirit of knowledge and the fear of the LORD.
3 And He will delight in the fear of the LORD,
And He will not judge by what His eyes [a]see,
Nor make a decision by what His ears hear;
4 But with [a]righteousness He will judge the [b]poor,
And decide with fairness for the afflicted of the earth;
And He will strike the earth with the [c]rod of His
mouth,
And with the [d]breath of His lips He will slay the
wicked.
5 Also [a]righteousness will be the belt about His loins,
And [b]faithfulness the belt about His waist.

6 And the [a]wolf will dwell with the lamb,
And the leopard will lie down with the kid,
And the calf and the young lion [1]and the fatling
together;
And a little boy will lead them.
7 Also the cow and the bear will graze;
Their young will lie down together;
And the [a]lion will eat straw like the ox.
8 And the nursing child will play by the hole of the cobra,
And the weaned child will put his hand on the viper's
den.
9 They will [a]not hurt or destroy in all My holy mountain,
For the [b]earth will be full of the knowledge of the LORD
As the waters cover the sea.

10 Then it will come about in that day
That the [a]nations will resort to the [b]root of Jesse,
Who will stand as a [1c]signal for the peoples;
And His resting place will be [2]glorious.

11 Then it will happen on that day that the Lord
Will again recover the second time with His hand
The remnant of His people, who will remain,
From Assyria, Egypt, Pathros, Cush, Elam, Shinar,
Hamath,
And from the [1a]islands of the sea.
12 And He will lift up a standard for the nations,
And will [a]assemble the banished ones of Israel,
And will gather the dispersed of Judah
From the four corners of the earth.
13 Then the [a]jealousy of Ephraim will depart,
And those who harass Judah will be cut off;

34 [1]Or, *as a mighty one*

1 [a]Is. 4:2; 53:2 [b]Is. 11:10; 9:7; Acts 13:23 [c]Is. 6:13; Jer. 23:5; Zech. 3:8

2 [a]Is. 42:1; 48:16; 61:1; Matt. 3:16; John 1:32 [b]John 16:13; 1 Cor. 1:30; Eph. 1:17, 18 [c]2 Tim. 1:7

3 [a]John 2:25; 7:24

4 [a]Is. 9:7; 16:5; 32:1 [b]Is. 3:14; Ps. 72:2, 14 [c]Is. 49:2; Ps. 2:9; Mal. 4:6 [d]Is. 30:28, 33; Job 4:9; 2 Tim. 2:8

5 [a]Eph. 6:14 [b]Is. 25:1

6 [1]Some versions read, *will feed together*
[a]Is. 65:25

7 [a]Is. 65:25

9 [a]Is. 65:25; Job 5:23; Ezek. 34:25; Hos. 2:18 [b]Is. 45:6; 52:10; 66:18-23; Ps. 98:2, 3; Hab. 2:14

10 [1]Or, *standard* [2]Lit., *glory*
[a]Luke 2:32; Acts 11:18 [b]Is. 11:1; Rom. 15:12 [c]Is. 11:12; 49:22; 62:10; John 3:14, 15; 12:32

11 [1]Or, *coastlands*
[a]Is. 24:15; 42:4, 10, 12; 49:1; 51:5; 60:9; 66:19

12 [a]Is. 56:8; Zeph. 3:10; Zech. 10:6

13 [a]Is. 9:21; Jer. 3:18; Ezek. 37:16, 17, 22; Hos. 1:11

Ephraim will not be jealous of Judah,
And Judah will not harass Ephraim.
14 And they will [a]swoop down on the slopes of the Philistines on the west;
Together they will [b]plunder the sons of the east;
[1]They will possess Edom and Moab;
And the sons of Ammon will be [2]subject to them.
15 And the LORD will [1a]utterly destroy
The tongue of the [2]Sea of Egypt;
And He will wave His hand over the [3b]River
With His scorching wind;
And He will strike it into seven streams,
And make *men* walk over [4]dry-shod.
16 And there will be a [a]highway from Assyria
For the remnant of His people who will be left,
Just as there was for Israel
In [b]the day that they came up out of the land of Egypt.

CHAPTER 12

THEN you will say on that day,
"[a]I will give thanks to Thee, O LORD;
For [b]although Thou wast angry with me,
Thine anger is turned away,
And Thou dost comfort me.
2 "Behold, [a]God is my salvation,
I will [b]trust and not be afraid;
For [c]the LORD GOD is my strength and song,
And He has become my salvation."
3 Therefore you will joyously [a]draw water
From the [b]springs of salvation.
4 And in that day you will [a]say,
"[b]Give thanks to the LORD, call on His name.
[c]Make known His deeds among the peoples;
[1]Make *them* remember that His name is exalted."
5 [a]Praise the LORD in song, for He has done [1]excellent things;
Let this be known throughout the earth.
6 [a]Cry aloud and shout for joy, O inhabitant of Zion,
For [b]great in your midst is the Holy One of Israel.

CHAPTER 13

THE [1]oracle concerning Babylon which Isaiah the son of Amoz saw.
2 [a]Lift up a standard on the [1b]bare hill,
Raise your voice to them,
[c]Wave the hand that they may [d]enter the doors of the nobles.
3 I have commanded My consecrated ones,
I have even called My [a]mighty warriors,
My proudly exulting ones,
To *execute* My anger.
4 A [a]sound of tumult on the mountains,
Like that of many people!
A sound of the uproar of kingdoms,

14 [1]Lit., *Edom and Moab will be the outstretching of their hand* [2]Lit., *their obedience*
[a]Jer. 48:40; 49:22; Hab. 1:8 [b]Jer. 49:28

15 [1]Another reading is, *dry up the tongue* [2]Perhaps the Red Sea [3]I.e., the Euphrates [4]Lit., *in sandals*
[a]Is. 43:16; 44:27; 50:2; 51:10, 11 [b]Is. 7:20; 8:7

16 [a]Is. 19:23; 35:8; 40:3; 62:10 [b]Ex. 14:26-29

1 [a]Is. 25:1; Ps. 9:1 [b]Is. 40:1, 2; 54:7-10; Ps. 30:5

2 [a]Is. 32:2; 45:17; 62:11 [b]Is. 26:3 [c]Ex. 15:2; Ps. 118:14

3 [a]John 4:10; 7:37, 38 [b]Is. 41:18; Jer. 2:13

4 [1]Or, *Proclaim* to them *that*
[a]Is. 24:15; 42:12; 48:20 [b]Ps. 105:1 [c]Ps. 145:4

5 [1]Or, *gloriously*
[a]Is. 24:14; 42:10, 11; 44:23; Ex. 15:1; Ps. 98:1

6 [a]Is. 52:9; 54:1; Zeph. 3:14 [b]Is. 1:24; 49:26; 60:16; Zeph. 3:15-17; Zech. 2:5, 10, 11

1 [1]Lit., *burden of*

2 [1]Or, *wind-swept mountain*
[a]Is. 5:26; Jer. 50:2 [b]Jer. 51:25 [c]Is. 10:32; 19:16 [d]Is. 45:1-3; Jer. 51:58

3 [a]Joel 3:11

4 [a]Is. 5:30; 17:12; Joel 3:14

Of nations gathered together!
The LORD of hosts is mustering the army for battle.
5 They are coming from a far country
From the [1a]farthest horizons,
The LORD and His instruments of indignation,
To destroy the whole land.
6 Wail, for the [a]day of the LORD is near!
It will come as destruction from [1]the Almighty.
7 Therefore all hands will fall limp,
And every man's [a]heart will melt.
8 And they will be [a]terrified,
Pains and anguish will take hold of *them*;
They will [b]writhe like a woman in labor,
They will look at one another in astonishment,
Their faces aflame.
9 Behold, the day of the LORD is coming,
Cruel, with fury and burning anger,
To make the land a desolation;
And He will exterminate its sinners from it.
10 For the [a]stars of heaven and their constellations
Will not flash forth their light;
The [b]sun will be dark when it rises,
And the moon will not shed its light.
11 Thus I will punish the world for its evil,
And the wicked for their iniquity;
I will also put an end to the [a]arrogance of the proud,
And abase the [b]haughtiness of the [1]ruthless.
12 I will make mortal man [1a]scarcer than pure gold,
And mankind than the gold of Ophir.
13 Therefore I shall make the [a]heavens tremble,
And the earth will be shaken from its place
At the fury of the LORD of hosts
In the day of His burning anger.
14 And it will be that like a hunted gazelle,
Or like [a]sheep with none to gather *them*,
They will each turn to his own people,
And each one flee to his own land.
15 Anyone who is found will be [a]thrust through,
And anyone who is captured will fall by the sword.
16 Their [a]little ones also will be dashed to pieces
Before their eyes;
Their houses will be plundered
And their wives ravished.

17 Behold, I am going to stir up the Medes against them,
Who will not value silver or [a]take pleasure in gold,
18 And *their* bows will [1]mow down the [a]young men,
They will not even have compassion on the fruit of the womb,
Nor will their [b]eye pity [2]children.
19 And Babylon, the [a]beauty of kingdoms, the glory of the Chaldeans' pride,
Will be as when God [b]overthrew Sodom and Gomorrah.
20 It will [a]never be inhabited or lived in from generation to generation;

5 [1]Lit., *end of heaven* [a]Is. 5:26; 7:18

6 [1]Heb., *Shaddai* [a]Is. 13:9; 2:12; 10:3; 34:2, 8; 61:2; Ezek. 30:3; Amos 5:18; Zeph. 1:7

7 [a]Is. 19:1; Ezek. 21:7; Nah. 2:10

8 [a]Is. 21:3; 2 Kin. 19:26; Jer. 46:5 [b]Is. 26:17; Jer. 4:31; John 16:21

10 [a]Is. 5:30; Joel 2:10; Matt. 24:29; Mark 13:24; Luke 21:25 [b]Is. 24:23; 50:3; Acts 2:20

11 [1]Or, *tyrants, despots* [a]Is. 2:11; 23:9; Dan. 5:22, 23 [b]Jer. 48:29

12 [1]Lit., *more precious* [a]Is. 4:1; 6:11, 12

13 [a]Is. 34:4; 51:6

14 [a]1 Kin. 22:17; Matt. 9:36; Mark 6:34; 1 Pet. 2:25

15 [a]Is. 14:19; Jer. 50:25; 51:3, 4

16 [a]Is. 13:18; 14:21; Ps. 137:8, 9; Hos. 10:14; Nah. 3:10

17 [a]Prov. 6:34, 35

18 [1]Lit., *dash in pieces* [2]Lit., *sons* [a]2 Kin. 8:12; 2 Chr. 36:17 [b]Ezek. 9:5, 10

19 [a]Dan. 4:30; Rev. 18:11-16, 19 [b]Gen. 19:24; Deut. 29:23; Jer. 49:18; Amos 4:11

20 [a]Is. 14:23; 34:10-15; Jer. 51:37-43

20 [b]2 Chr. 17:11

21 [1]Or, *howling creatures* [2]Or, *goat demons* [a]Is. 34:11-15; Zeph. 2:14

22 [1]Or, *howling creatures* [2]Lit., *is near to come* [a]Is. 25:2; 32:14; 34:13

1 [a]Is. 49:13, 15; 54:7, 8; Ps. 102:13 [b]Is. 41:8, 9; 44:1; 49:7; Zech. 1:17; 2:12

2 [a]Is. 45:14; 49:23; 54:3 [b]Is. 60:10; 61:5; Dan. 7:18, 27

3 [a]Is. 11:10; 40:2; Ezra 9:8, 9; Jer. 30:10; 46:27

4 [1]Or, *proverb* [2]Amended from the meaningless *medhebah* to *marshebah*

6 [1]Or, *ruled* [a]Is. 10:14; 47:6

7 [a]Ps. 47:1-3; 98:1-9; 126:1-3

9 [1]Or, *shades* (Heb., *Repha'im*) [2]Lit., *male goats*

10 [a]Ezek. 32:21

11 [a]Is. 5:14; Ezek. 28:13

12 [1]Lit., *Helel;* i.e., shining one [a]Is. 34:4; Luke 10:18; Rev. 9:1

Nor will the [b]Arab pitch *his* tent there,
Nor will shepherds make *their flocks* lie down there.
21 But [a]desert creatures will lie down there,
And their houses will be full of [1]owls,
Ostriches also will live there, and [2]shaggy goats will frolic there.
22 And [1]hyenas will howl in their fortified towers
And jackals in their luxurious [a]palaces.
Her *fateful* time also [2]will soon come
And her days will not be prolonged.

Chapter 14

WHEN the LORD will [a]have compassion on Jacob, and
again [b]choose Israel, and settle them in their own land, then
strangers will join them and attach themselves to the house of
Jacob.
2 And the peoples will take them along and bring them
to their place, and the [a]house of Israel will possess them as an
inheritance in the land of the LORD [b]as male and female servants; and they will take them as their captors, and will rule
over their oppressors.
3 And it will be in the day when the LORD gives you [a]rest
from your pain and turmoil and harsh service in which you
have been enslaved,
4 that you will take up this [1]taunt against the king of
Babylon, and say:
"How the oppressor has ceased,
And how [2]fury has ceased!
5 "The LORD has broken the staff of the wicked,
The scepter of rulers
6 [a]Which used to strike the peoples in fury with unceasing strokes,
Which [1]subdued the nations in anger with unrestrained persecution.
7 "The whole earth is at rest *and* is quiet;
They [a]break forth into shouts of joy.
8 "Even the cypress trees rejoice over you, *and* the cedars of Lebanon, *saying,*
'Since you were laid low, no *tree* cutter comes up against us.'
9 "Sheol from beneath is excited over you to meet you when you come;
It arouses for you the [1]spirits of the dead, all the [2]leaders of the earth;
It raises all the kings of the nations from their thrones.
10 "[a]They will all respond and say to you,
'Even you have been made weak as we,
You have become like *us.*
11 'Your [a]pomp *and* the music of your harps
Have been brought down to Sheol;
Maggots are spread out *as your bed* beneath you,
And worms are your covering.'
12 "How you have [a]fallen from heaven,
O [1]star of the morning, son of the dawn!

You have been cut down to the earth,
You who have weakened the nations!
13 "But you said in your heart,
'I will [a]ascend to heaven;
I will [b]raise my throne above the stars of God,
And I will sit on the mount of assembly
In the recesses of the north.
14 'I will ascend above the heights of the clouds;
I will make myself like the Most High.'
15 "Nevertheless you will be thrust down to Sheol,
To the recesses of the pit.
16 "Those who see you will gaze at you,
They will [1]ponder over you, *saying,*
'Is this the man who made the earth tremble,
Who shook kingdoms,
17 Who made the world like a wilderness
And overthrew its cities,
Who did not [1]allow his prisoners to *go* home?'
18 "All the kings of the nations lie in glory,
Each in his own [1]tomb.
19 "But you have been cast out of your tomb
Like [1]a rejected branch,
[2]Clothed with the slain who are pierced with a sword,
Who go down to the stones of the pit,
Like a [a]trampled corpse.
20 "You will not be united with them in burial,
Because you have ruined your country,
You have slain your people.
May the [a]offspring of evildoers not be mentioned forever.
21 "Prepare for his sons a place of slaughter
Because of the [a]iniquity of their fathers.
They must not arise and take possession of the earth
And fill the face of the world with cities.
22 "And I will rise up against them," declares the LORD of
hosts, "and will cut off from Babylon [a]name and survivors,
[b]offspring and posterity," declares the LORD.
23 "I will also make it a possession for the hedgehog, and
swamps of water, and I will sweep it with the broom of [a]destruc-
tion," declares the LORD of hosts.
24 The LORD of hosts has sworn saying, "Surely, [a]just as I
have intended so it has happened, and just as I have planned so
it will stand,
25 to break Assyria in My land, and I will trample him on
My mountains. Then his [a]yoke will be removed from them,
and his burden removed from their shoulder.
26 "This is the [a]plan [1]devised against the whole earth; and
this is the [b]hand that is stretched out against all the nations.
27 "For [a]the LORD of hosts has planned, and who can frustrate *it?* And as for His stretched-out hand, who can turn it
back?"
28 In the [a]year that King Ahaz died this [1]oracle came:
29 "Do not rejoice, O Philistia, all of you,
Because the rod that [a]struck you is broken;
For from the serpent's root a viper will come out,
And its fruit will be a flying serpent.

13 [a]Ezek. 28:2 [b]Dan. 5:22; 8:10; 2 Thess. 2:4

16 [1]Lit., *show themselves attentive to*

17 [1]Lit., *open*

18 [1]Lit., *house*

19 [1]Lit., *an abhorred branch* [2]Or, *As the clothing of those who are slain* [a]Is. 5:25

20 [a]Is. 1:4; 31:2; Job 18:16, 19; Ps. 21:10; 37:28

21 [a]Is. 13:16; Ex. 20:5; Lev. 26:39; Matt. 23:35

22 [a]Prov. 10:7 [b]Is. 47:9; Job 18:19

23 [a]Is. 13:6; 1 Kin. 14:10

24 [a]Is. 46:11; 55:8, 9; Job 23:13; Acts 4:28

25 [a]Is. 9:4; 10:27; Nah. 1:13

26 [1]Lit., *planned* [a]Is. 23:9; Zeph. 3:6, 8 [b]Ex. 15:12

27 [a]Is. 43:13; 2 Chr. 20:6; Dan. 4:31, 35

28 [1]Or, *burden* [a]2 Kin. 16:20; 2 Chr. 28:27

29 [a]2 Chr. 26:6

30 [1]Lit., *the first-born of the helpless* [2]Lit., *put to death*
[a]Is. 3:14, 15; 7:21, 22; 11:4 [b]Is. 8:21; 9:20; 51:19

31 [1]Or, Become *demoralized*
[a]Is. 3:26; 24:12; 45:2 [b]Jer. 1:14 [c]Is. 34:16

32 [a]Is. 37:9 [b]Is. 4:6; 25:4; 57:13; Zeph. 3:12; Heb. 11:10; James 2:5

1 [1]Or, *burden of*

2 [1]Lit., *house*
[a]Lev. 21:5; Jer. 48:37

3 [1]Lit., *going down in weeping*
[a]Jon. 3:6-8 [b]Jer. 48:38 [c]Is. 22:4

4 [1]Another reading is, *the loins of*

5 [a]Is. 59:7; Jer. 4:20

6 [1]Lit., *desolations* [2]Lit., *come to an end*
[a]Is. 19:5-7; Jer. 48:34 [b]Joel 1:10-12; 2:3

7 [1]Or, *the poplars*
[a]Is. 30:6; Jer. 48:36

9 [1]Heb., *dam* (a word-play)
[a]2 Kin. 17:25; Jer. 50:17

1 [1]I.e., Petra in Edom
[a]2 Kin. 3:4; Ezra 7:17 [b]Is. 42:11; 2 Kin. 14:7 [c]Is. 10:32

2 [1]Or, *fluttering* [2]Lit., *nest*
[a]Prov. 27:8

30 "And [1]those who are most [a]helpless will eat,
And the needy will lie down in security;
I will [2]destroy your root with [b]famine,
And it will kill off your survivors.
31 "Wail, O [a]gate; cry, O city;
[1]Melt away, O Philistia, all of you;
For smoke comes from the [b]north,
And [c]there is no straggler in his ranks.
32 "How then will one answer the [a]messengers of the nation?
That the LORD has founded Zion,
And [b]the afflicted of His people will seek refuge in it."

CHAPTER 15

THE [1]oracle concerning Moab.
Surely in a night Ar of Moab is devastated *and* ruined,
Surely in a night Kir of Moab is devastated *and* ruined.
2 They have gone up to the [1]temple and *to* Dibon, *even* to the high places to weep.
Moab wails over Nebo and Medeba;
Everyone's head is [a]bald and every beard is cut off.
3 In their streets they have girded themselves with [a]sackcloth;
[b]On their housetops and in their squares
Everyone is wailing, [1c]dissolved in tears.
4 Heshbon and Elealeh also cry out,
Their voice is heard all the way to Jahaz;
Therefore the [1]armed men of Moab cry aloud;
His soul trembles within him.
5 My heart cries out for Moab;
His fugitives are as far as Zoar *and* Eglath-shelishiyah,
For they go up the ascent of Luhith weeping;
Surely on the road to Horonaim they raise a cry of distress [a]over *their* ruin.
6 For the [a]waters of Nimrim are [1]desolate.
Surely the grass is withered, the tender grass [2]died out,
There is [b]no green thing.
7 Therefore the [a]abundance *which* they have acquired and stored up
They carry off over the brook of [1]Arabim.
8 For the cry of distress has gone around the territory of Moab,
Its wail *goes* as far as Eglaim and its wailing even to Beer-elim.
9 For the waters of Dimon are full of [1]blood;
Surely I will bring added *woes* upon Dimon,
A [a]lion upon the fugitives of Moab and upon the remnant of the land.

CHAPTER 16

[a]SEND the *tribute* lamb to the ruler of the land,
From [1b]Sela by way of the wilderness to the [c]mountain of the daughter of Zion.
2 Then, like [1a]fleeing birds *or* scattered [2]nestlings,

The daughters of Moab will be at the fords of the
Arnon.
3 "[1]Give *us* advice, make a decision;
[2]Cast your [a]shadow like night [3]at high noon;
Hide the outcasts, do not betray the fugitive.
4 "Let the [1]outcasts of Moab stay with you;
Be a hiding place to them from the destroyer."
For the extortioner has come to an end, destruction
has ceased,
[a]Oppressors have completely *disappeared* from the
land.
5 A [a]throne will even be established in lovingkindness,
And a judge will sit on it in faithfulness in the tent of
[b]David;
Moreover, he will seek justice
And be prompt in righteousness.

6 [a]We have heard of the pride of Moab, an excessive
pride;
Even of his arrogance, pride, and fury;
[b]His idle boasts are [1]false.
7 Therefore Moab shall wail; everyone of Moab shall
wail.
You shall moan for the [a]raisin cakes of [b]Kir-hareseth
As those who are utterly stricken.
8 For the fields of Heshbon have [1]withered, the vines of
Sibmah *as well*;
The lords of the nations have trampled down its choice
clusters
Which reached as far as Jazer *and* wandered to the
deserts;
[a]Its tendrils spread themselves out *and* passed over the
sea.
9 Therefore I will [a]weep bitterly for Jazer for the vine of
Sibmah;
I will drench you with my tears, O Heshbon and
Elealeh;
For the shouting over your [b]summer fruits and your
harvest has fallen away.
10 And [a]gladness and joy are taken away from the fruitful
field;
In the [b]vineyards also there will be no cries of joy or
jubilant shouting,
No [c]treader treads out wine in the presses,
For I have made the shouting to cease.
11 Therefore my [1a]heart intones like a harp for Moab,
And my inward [2]feelings for Kir-hareseth.
12 So it will come about when Moab [a]presents himself,
When he [b]wearies himself upon *his* [c]high place,
And comes to his sanctuary to pray,
That he will not prevail.
13 This is the word which the LORD spoke earlier concerning Moab.
14 But now the LORD speaks, saying, "Within three years,
as [1a]a hired man would count them, the glory of [b]Moab will be

3 [1]Lit., *bring* [2]Lit., *set* [3]Lit., *in the midst of the noon* [a]Is. 25:4; 32:2; 1 Kin. 18:4

4 [1]So the Versions; M.T., *My outcasts, as for Moab . . .* [a]Is. 9:4; 14:4; 49:26; 51:13; 54:14

5 [a]Is. 9:6, 7; 32:1; 55:4; Dan. 7:14; Mic. 4:7; Luke 1:33 [b]Is. 9:7

6 [1]Lit., *not so* [a]Jer. 48:29; Amos 2:1; Obad. 3, 4; Zeph. 2:8, 10 [b]Jer. 48:30

7 [a]1 Chr. 16:3 [b]2 Kin. 3:25; Jer. 48:31

8 [1]Or, *languished* [a]Jer. 48:32

9 [a]Jer. 48:32 [b]Jer. 40:10, 12; 48:32

10 [a]Is. 24:8; Jer. 48:33 [b]Is. 24:7; Judg. 9:27; Amos 11:17 [c]Job 24:11; Amos 9:13

11 [1]Lit., *entrails murmur* [2]Lit., *inward part* [a]Is. 15:5; 63:15; Jer. 48:36; Hos. 11:8; Phil. 2:1

12 [a]Num. 22:39-41; Jer. 48:35 [b]1 Kin. 18:29 [c]Is. 15:2

14 [1]Lit., *the years of a hireling* [a]Is. 21:16; Job 7:1; 16:6 [b]Is. 25:10; Jer. 48:42

14 [2]Lit., *not mighty*

1 [1]Or, *burden of* [a]Is. 7:16; 8:4; 10:9 [b]Is. 25:2; Jer. 49:2; Mic. 1:6

2 [1]Gk. reads, *forever and ever* [2]Lit., *and they will lie down* [a]Is. 7:21, 22; Ezek. 25:5; Zeph. 2:6 [b]Mic. 4:4

3 [1]Or, *fortification* [2]Or, *royal power, kingdom* [a]Is. 7:8, 16; 8:4 [b]Is. 17:4; Hos. 9:11

4 [1]Lit., *become thin* [a]Is. 10:3

5 [1]Lit., *gathering of the harvest, the standing grain* [a]Is. 17:11; Jer. 51:33; Joel 3:13; Matt. 13:30

6 [1]Lit., *striking* [a]Is. 24:13; 27:12; Deut. 4:27; Obad. 5

7 [a]Is. 10:20; Hos. 3:5; 6:1; Mic. 7:7

8 [1]I.e., wooden symbols of a female deity [2]Or, *Sun pillars* [a]Is. 27:9; 2 Chr. 34:7 [b]Is. 2:8, 20; 30:22; 31:7 [c]Ex. 34:13; Deut. 7:5; Mic. 5:14

9 [1]I.e., man's [2]Gk. reads, *the deserted places of the Amorites and the Hivites which they abandoned . . .* [3]Or, *the tree-top* [4]Lit., *it*

10 [a]Is. 51:13 [b]Is. 12:2; 33:2; 61:10; 62:11; Ps. 68:19 [c]Is. 26:4; 30:29; 44:8; Deut. 32:4, 18, 31

11 [a]Matt. 21:23 [b]Ps. 90:6 [c]Job 4:8; Hos. 8:7; 10:13

12 [a]Jer. 6:23; Ezek. 43:2; Luke 21:25 [b]Ps. 18:4

degraded along with all *his* great population, and *his* remnant will be very small *and* [2]impotent."

Chapter 17

THE [1]oracle concerning Damascus.
Behold, Damascus is about to be [a]removed from being a city,
And it will become a [b]fallen ruin.
2 The cities [1]of Aroer are forsaken;
They will be for [a]flocks [2]to lie down in,
And there will be [b]no one to frighten *them.*
3 The [1a]fortified city will disappear from Ephraim,
And [2]sovereignty from Damascus
And the remnant of Syria;
They will be like the [b]glory of the sons of Israel,
Declares the LORD of hosts.

4 Now it will come about in that day that the [a]glory of Jacob will [1]fade,
And the fatness of his flesh will become lean.
5 It will be [a]even like the [1]reaper gathering the standing grain,
As his arm harvests the ears,
Or it will be like one gleaning ears of grain
In the valley of Rephaim.
6 Yet [a]gleanings will be left in it like the [1]shaking of an olive tree,
Two *or* three olives on the topmost bough,
Four *or* five on the branches of a fruitful tree,
Declares the LORD, the God of Israel.
7 In that day man will [a]have regard for his Maker,
And his eyes will look to the Holy One of Israel.
8 And he will not have regard for the [a]altars, the work of his hands,
Nor will he look to that which his [b]fingers have made,
Even the [1c]Asherim and [2]incense stands.
9 In that day [1]their strong cities will be like [2]forsaken places in the forest,
Or like [3]branches which they abandoned before the sons of Israel;
And [4]the land will be a desolation.
10 For [a]you have forgotten the [b]God of your salvation
And have not remembered the [c]rock of your refuge.
Therefore you plant delightful plants
And set them with vine slips of a strange *god.*
11 In the day that you plant *it* you carefully [a]fence *it* in,
And in the [b]morning you bring your seed to blossom;
But the harvest will [c]be a heap
In a day of sickliness and incurable pain.

12 Alas, the uproar of many peoples
[a]Who roar like the roaring of the seas,
And the rumbling of nations
Who rush on like the [b]rumbling of mighty waters!

13 The [a]nations rumble on like the rumbling of many waters,
But He will [b]rebuke them and they will flee far away,
And be chased [c]like chaff in the mountains before the wind,
Or like whirling dust before a gale.
14 At evening time, behold, *there is* terror!
Before morning [a]they are no more.
[1]Such *will be* the portion of those who plunder us,
And the lot of those who pillage us.

Chapter 18

ALAS, oh land of whirring wings
Which lies beyond the rivers of [1]Cush,
2 Which sends envoys by the sea,
Even in [a]papyrus vessels on the surface of the waters.
Go, swift messengers, to a nation [1b]tall and smooth,
To a people feared [2]far and wide,
A powerful and oppressive nation
Whose land the rivers divide.
3 [a]All you inhabitants of the world and dwellers on earth,
As soon as a standard is raised on the mountains, you will see *it*,
And as soon as the trumpet is blown, you will hear *it*.
4 For thus the LORD has told me:
"I will look [1]from My [a]dwelling place quietly
Like dazzling heat in the [2b]sunshine,
Like a cloud of dew in the heat of harvest."
5 For [a]before the harvest, as soon as the bud [1]blossoms
And the flower becomes a ripening grape,
Then He will cut off the sprigs with pruning knives
And remove *and* cut away the spreading branches.
6 They will be left together for mountain birds [a]of prey,
And for the beasts of the earth;
And the birds of prey will spend the summer *feeding* on them,
And all the beasts of the earth will spend harvest time on them.
7 At that time a gift of homage will be brought to the LORD of hosts
[1]From a [a]people [2]tall and smooth,
Even from a people feared [3]far and wide,
A powerful and oppressive nation,
Whose land the rivers divide—
To the [b]place of the name of the LORD of hosts, *even* Mount Zion.

Chapter 19

THE [1]oracle concerning Egypt.
Behold, the LORD is [a]riding on a swift cloud, and is about to come to Egypt;
The [b]idols of Egypt will tremble at His presence,
And the [c]heart of the Egyptians will melt within them.

13 [a]Is. 33:3 [b]Is. 41:11; Ps. 9:5 [c]Is. 29:5; 41:15, 16; Job 21:18; Ps. 1:4; 83:13

14 [1]Lit., *this* [a]Is. 41:12; 2 Kin. 19:35

1 [1]Or, *Ethiopia*

2 [1]Lit., *drawn out* [2]Lit., *from it and beyond* [a]Is. 18:7 [b]Gen. 10:8, 9; 2 Chr. 12:2-4; 14:9; 16:8

3 [a]Ps. 49:1; Mic. 1:2

4 [1]Lit., *in* [2]Lit., *light* [a]Is. 26:21; Hos. 5:15 [b]2 Sam. 23:4

5 [1]Lit., *is finished* [a]Is. 17:10, 11; Ezek. 17:6-10

6 [a]Is. 46:11; 56:9; Jer. 7:33; Ezek. 32:4-6; 39:17-20

7 [1]So with some ancient versions and DSS; M.T. implies: *Consisting of a people* . . . [2]Lit., *drawn out* [3]Lit., *from it and beyond* [a]Is. 45:14; Ps. 68:31; Zeph. 3:10; Acts 8:27-38 [b]Zech. 14:16, 17

1 [1]Or, *burden of* [a]Ps. 18:9, 10; 104:3; Matt. 26:64; Rev. 1:7 [b]Ex. 12:12; Jer. 43:12; 44:8 [c]Is. 13:7; Josh. 2:11

2 "So I will incite Egyptians against Egyptians;
And they will [a]each fight against his brother, and each against his neighbor,
City against city, *and* kingdom against kingdom.
3 "Then the spirit of the Egyptians will be demoralized within them;
And I will confound their strategy,
So that [a]they will resort to idols and ghosts of the dead,
And to [1]mediums and spiritists.
4 "Moreover, I will deliver the Egyptians into the hand of a [a]cruel master,
And a [1]mighty king will rule over them," declares the Lord [2]GOD of hosts.

5 [a]And the waters from the sea will dry up,
And the river will be parched and dry.
6 And the [1a]canals will emit a stench,
The [2b]streams of Egypt will thin out and dry up;
[c]The reeds and rushes will rot away.
7 The bulrushes by the [a]Nile, by the [1]edge of the Nile
And all the sown fields by the Nile
Will become dry, be driven away, and be no more.
8 And the [a]fishermen will lament,
And all those who cast a [1]line into the Nile will mourn,
And those who spread nets on the waters will [2]pine away.
9 Moreover, the manufacturers of linen made from combed flax
And the weavers of white [a]cloth will be [1]utterly dejected.
10 And [1]the [a]pillars of *Egypt* will be crushed;
All the hired laborers will be grieved in soul.

11 The princes of [1]Zoan are mere fools;
The advice of Pharaoh's wisest advisors has become [2]stupid.
How can you *men* say to Pharaoh,
"I am a son of the [a]wise, a son of ancient kings"?
12 Well then, where are your wise men?
Please let them tell you,
And let them [1]understand what the LORD of hosts
Has [a]purposed against Egypt.
13 The princes of [1]Zoan have acted foolishly,
The princes of [a]Memphis are deluded;
Those who are the [b]cornerstone of her tribes
Have [2]led Egypt astray.
14 The LORD has mixed within her a spirit of [a]distortion;
[b]They have led Egypt astray in all [1]that it does,
As a drunken man [2]staggers in his vomit.
15 And there will be no work for Egypt
[a]Which its head or tail, *its* palm branch or bulrush, may do.
16 In that day the Egyptians will become like women, and
they will tremble and be in [a]dread because of the waving of the

2 [a]Judg. 7:22; 1 Sam. 14:20; 2 Chr. 20:23; Matt. 10:21, 36

3 [1]Or, *ghosts and spirits* [a]Is. 8:19; 1 Chr. 10:13; Dan. 2:2

4 [1]Or, *fierce* [2]YHWH, usually rendered LORD [a]Is. 20:4; Jer. 46:26; Ezek. 29:19

5 [a]Is. 50:2; Jer. 51:36; Ezek. 30:12

6 [1]Lit., *rivers* [2]Or, *Nile branches;* i.e., the delta [a]Ex. 7:18 [b]Is. 37:25 [c]Is. 15:6; Ex. 2:3; Job 8:11

7 [1]Or, *mouth* [a]Is. 23:3, 10

8 [1]Lit., *hook* [2]Or, *languish* [a]Ezek. 47:10; Hab. 1:15

9 [1]Lit., *ashamed* [a]Prov. 7:16; Ezek. 27:7

10 [1]Lit., *her pillars* or, *her weavers* [a]Ps. 11:13

11 [1]Or, *Tanis* [2]Or, *brutish* [a]Gen. 41:38, 39; 1 Kin. 4:30; Acts 7:22

12 [1]Or, *know* [a]Is. 14:24; Rom. 9:17

13 [1]Or, *Tanis* [2]Or, *have caused Egypt to stagger* [a]Jer. 2:16; 46:14, 19; Ezek. 30:13 [b]Zech. 10:4

14 [1]Lit., *its work* [2]Or, *goes astray* [a]Prov. 12:8; Matt. 17:17 [b]Is. 3:12; 9:16

15 [a]Is. 9:14, 15

16 [a]2 Cor. 5:11; Heb. 10:31

hand of the LORD of hosts, which He is going to wave over
them.
17 And the land of Judah will become a [1]terror to Egypt;
everyone [2]to whom it is mentioned will be in dread of it,
because of the [a]purpose of the LORD of hosts which He is
purposing against them.
18 In that day five cities in the land of Egypt will be
speaking the language of Canaan and [a]swearing *allegiance* to
the LORD of hosts; one will be called the City of [1]Destruction.
19 In that day there will be an [a]altar to the LORD in the
midst of the land of Egypt, and a [b]pillar to the LORD near its
border.
20 And it will become a sign and a witness to the LORD of
hosts in the land of Egypt; for they will cry to the LORD because of oppressors, and He will send them a [a]Savior and a
[1b]Champion, and He will deliver them.
21 Thus the LORD will make Himself known to Egypt, and
the Egyptians will know the LORD in that day. They will even
worship with [a]sacrifice and offering, and will make a vow to the
LORD and perform it.
22 And the LORD will strike Egypt, striking but [a]healing; so
they will [b]return to the LORD, and He will respond to them and
will heal them.
23 In that day there will be a [a]highway from Egypt to
Assyria, and the Assyrians will come into Egypt and the Egyptians into Assyria, and the Egyptians will [b]worship with the
Assyrians.
24 In that day Israel will be the third *party* with Egypt and
Assyria, a blessing in the midst of the earth,
25 whom the LORD of hosts has blessed, saying, "Blessed is
[a]Egypt My people, and Assyria the work of My hands, and
Israel My inheritance."

CHAPTER 20

IN the year that the [1]commander came to Ashdod, when
Sargon the king of Assyria sent him and he fought against
Ashdod and captured it,
2 at that time the LORD spoke through Isaiah the son of
Amoz, saying, "Go and loosen the [a]sackcloth from your hips,
and take your [b]shoes off your feet." And he did so, going
[c]naked and barefoot.
3 And the LORD said, "Even as My servant Isaiah has
gone naked and barefoot three years as a [1a]sign and token
against Egypt and [2b]Cush,
4 so the [a]king of Assyria will lead away the captives of
Egypt and the exiles of Cush, [b]young and old, naked and
barefoot with buttocks uncovered, to the [1]shame of Egypt.
5 "Then they shall be [a]dismayed and ashamed because of
Cush their hope and Egypt their [b]boast.
6 "So the inhabitants of this coastland will say in that day,
'Behold, such is our hope, where we fled [a]for help to be delivered from the king of Assyria; and we, [b]how shall we
escape?' "

17 [1]Or, *cause of shame* [2]Lit., *who mentions it will be in dread to it* [a]Is. 14:24; Dan. 4:35

18 [1]Some ancient mss. and versions read, *the Sun* [a]Is. 45:23; 65:16

19 [a]Is. 56:7; 60:7 [b]Gen. 28:18; Ex. 24:4; Josh. 22:10, 26, 27

20 [1]Lit., *Mighty One* [a]Is. 43:3, 11; 45:15, 21; 49:26; 60:16; 63:8 [b]Is. 49:25

21 [a]Is. 56:7; 60:7; Zech. 14:16-18

22 [a]Is. 30:26; 57:18; Deut. 32:39; Heb. 12:11 [b]Is. 27:13; 45:14; Hos. 14:1

23 [a]Is. 11:16; 35:8; 49:11; 62:10 [b]Is. 27:13

25 [a]Is. 45:14

1 [1]Heb., *Tartan*

2 [a]Zech. 13:4; Matt. 3:4 [b]Ezek. 24:17, 23 [c]1 Sam. 19:24; Mic. 1:8

3 [1]Or, *wonder* [2]Or, *Ethiopia*, so in v. 4, 5 [a]Is. 8:18 [b]Is. 37:9; 43:3

4 [1]Lit., *nakedness* [a]Is. 19:4 [b]Is. 47:2, 3

5 [a]Is. 30:3-5; 31:1; 2 Kin. 18:21; Ezek. 29:6, 7 [b]Jer. 9:23, 24; 17:5; 1 Cor. 3:21

6 [a]Is. 10:3; 30:7; 31:3; Jer. 30:1, 7, 15-17; 31:1-3 [b]Matt. 23:33; 1 Thess. 5:3; Heb. 2:3

1 [1]Or, *burden of* [2]Or, *sandy wastes, sea country* [3]I.e., South country [a]Is. 13:20-22; 14:23; Jer. 51:42 [b]Dan. 11:40; Zech. 9:14

2 [1]Lit., *her groaning* [a]Ps. 60:3 [b]Is. 24:16; 33:1

3 [a]Is. 13:8; 16:11 [b]Is. 13:8; 26:17; Ps. 48:6; 1 Thess. 5:3

4 [1]Lit., *heart has wandered* [2]Lit., *shuddering* [a]Deut. 28:67

5 [1]Or, *spread out the rugs;* or possibly, *they arranged the seating* [a]Jer. 51:39, 57; Dan. 5:1-4

6 [a]2 Kin. 9:17-20

7 [a]Is. 21:9

8 [1]Lit., *he;* i.e., the sentry, cf. v. 6 [a]Hab. 2:1

9 [1]Lit., *he has shattered to the earth* [a]Is. 13:19; 47:5, 9; 48:14; Jer. 51:8; Rev. 14:8 [b]Is. 46:1; Jer. 50:2; 51:44

10 [1]Lit., *son* [a]Jer. 51:33; Mic. 4:13

11 [1]Lit., *burden* [2]So the Gk.; Heb., *Dumah, silence* [3]Lit., *what* is the time *of the night?* [a]Gen. 25:14 [b]Gen. 32:3

13 [1]Or, *burden* [2]Or, *will spend* [a]Jer. 25:23, 24; 49:28 [b]Gen. 10:7; Ezek. 27:15

14 [1]Lit., *to meet* [a]Gen. 25:15; Job 6:19

15 [a]Is. 13:14, 15; 17:13

Chapter 21

THE [1]oracle concerning the [2a]wilderness of the sea.
As [b]windstorms in the [3]Negev sweep on,
It comes from the wilderness, from a terrifying land.
2 A [a]harsh vision has been shown to me;
The [b]treacherous one still deals treacherously, *and* the destroyer still destroys.
Go up, Elam, lay siege, Media;
I have made an end of all [1]the groaning she has caused.
3 For this reason my [a]loins are full of anguish;
Pains have seized me like the pains of a [b]woman in labor.
I am so bewildered I cannot hear, so terrified I cannot see.
4 My [1]mind reels, [2]horror overwhelms me;
The twilight I longed for has been [a]turned for me into trembling.
5 They [a]set the table, they [1]spread out the cloth, they eat, they drink;
"Rise up, captains, oil the shields,"
6 For thus the Lord says to me,
"Go, station the sentry, let him [a]report what he sees.
7 "When he sees [a]riders, horsemen in pairs,
A train of donkeys, a train of camels,
Let him pay close attention, very close attention."
8 Then [1]the sentry called *like* a lion,
"[a]O Lord, I stand continually by day on the watchtower,
And I am stationed every night at my guard post.
9 "Now behold, here comes a troop of riders, horsemen in pairs."
And one answered and said, "[a]Fallen, fallen is Babylon;
And all the [b]images of her gods [1]are shattered on the ground."
10 O my [a]threshed *people,* and my [1]afflicted of the threshing floor!
What I have heard from the LORD of hosts,
The God of Israel, I make known to you.

11 The [1]oracle concerning [2a]Edom.
One keeps calling to me from [b]Seir,
"Watchman, [3]how far gone is the night?
Watchman, [3]how far gone is the night?"
12 The watchman says,
"Morning comes but also night.
If you would inquire, inquire;
Come back again."

13 The [1]oracle about [a]Arabia.
In the thickets of Arabia you [2]must spend the night,
O caravans of [b]Dedanites.
14 Bring water [1]for the thirsty,
O inhabitants of the land of [a]Tema,
Meet the fugitive with bread.
15 For they have [a]fled from the swords,
From the drawn sword, and from the bent bow,
And from the press of battle.

16 For thus the Lord said to me, "In a [a]year, as [1]a hired
man would count it, all the splendor of Kedar will terminate;
17 and the [a]remainder of the number of bowmen, the
mighty men of the sons of Kedar, will be few; for the LORD
God of Israel [b]has spoken."

CHAPTER 22

THE [1]oracle concerning the [a]valley of vision.
What is the matter with you now, that you have all
gone up to the [b]housetops?
2 You who were full of noise,
You boisterous town, you [a]exultant city;
Your slain were [b]not slain with the sword,
Nor [1]did they die in battle.
3 All your rulers have fled together,
And have been captured [1]without the bow;
All of you who were found were taken captive together,
[2]Though they had fled far away.
4 Therefore I say, "Turn your eyes away from me,
Let me weep bitterly,
Do not [1]try to comfort me concerning the destruction
of the daughter of my people."
5 [a]For the Lord [1]GOD of hosts has a [b]day of panic, [c]subjugation, and confusion
[d]In the valley of vision,
A breaking down of walls
And a crying [2]to the mountain.
6 And [a]Elam took up the quiver
With the chariots, [1]infantry, *and* horsemen;
And Kir uncovered the shield.
7 Then your choicest valleys were [a]full of chariots,
And the horsemen took up fixed positions at the gate.
8 And He removed the [1]defense of Judah.
In that day you [2]depended on the weapons of the
[a]house of the forest,
9 And you saw that the breaches
In the *wall* of the city of David were many;
And you [a]collected the waters of the lower pool.
10 Then you counted the houses of Jerusalem,
And you tore down houses to fortify the wall.
11 And you made a reservoir [a]between the two walls
For the waters of the [b]old pool.
But you did not [1]depend on Him who made it,
Nor did you [2]take into consideration Him who planned
it long ago.

12 Therefore in that day the Lord [1]GOD of hosts, called
you to [a]weeping, to wailing,
To shaving the head, and to wearing sackcloth.
13 Instead, there is [a]gaiety and gladness,
Killing of cattle and slaughtering of sheep,
Eating of meat and drinking of wine:
"[b]Let us eat and drink, for tomorrow we may die."
14 But the LORD of hosts revealed Himself [1]to me,

16 [1]Lit., *the years of a hireling* [a]Is. 16:14

17 [a]Is. 10:19 [b]Num. 23:19; Zech. 1:6

1 [1]Or, *burden of* [a]Ps. 125:2; Jer. 21:13; Joel 3:12, 14 [b]Is. 15:3

2 [1]Lit., *dead in battle* [a]Is. 23:7; 32:13 [b]Jer. 14:18; Lam. 2:20

3 [1]Lit., *from a bow* [2]So with ancient versions; Heb., *They fled far away*

4 [1]Lit., *insist*

5 [1]YHWH, usually rendered LORD [2]Or, *against* [a]Lam. 1:5; 2:2 [b]Is. 37:3 [c]Is. 10:6; 63:3 [d]Is. 22:1

6 [1]Lit., *man* [a]Is. 21:2; Jer. 49:35

7 [a]2 Chr. 32:1

8 [1]Lit., *screen, covering* [2]Or, *looked to, considered* [a]1 Kin. 7:2; 10:17

9 [a]Neh. 3:16

11 [1]Or, *look to, consider* [2]Lit., *see . . . Him* [a]2 Kin. 25:4; Jer. 39:4 [b]2 Kin. 20:20; 2 Chr. 32:3, 4

12 [1]YHWH, usually rendered LORD [a]Is. 32:11; Joel 1:13; 2:17

13 [a]Is. 5:11, 22; 28:7, 8; Luke 17:26-29 [b]Is. 56:12; 1 Cor. 15:32

14 [1]Lit., *in my ears*

"Surely this iniquity shall not be [2]forgiven you
[a]Until you die," says the Lord [3]GOD of hosts.
15 Thus says the Lord [1]GOD of hosts,
"Come, go to this steward,
To Shebna, who is in charge of the *royal* household:
16 'What right do you have here,
And whom do you have here,
That you have [a]hewn a tomb for yourself here,
You who hew a tomb on the height,
You who carve a resting place for [1]yourself in the rock?
17 'Behold, the LORD is about to hurl you headlong, O man.
And He is about to grasp you firmly,
18 *And* roll you tightly like a ball,
To be [a]*cast* into a vast country;
There you will die,
And there your splendid chariots will be,
You shame of your master's house.'
19 "And I will [a]depose you from your office,
And [1]I will pull you down from your station.
20 "Then it will come about in that day,
That I will summon My servant [a]Eliakim the son of Hilkiah
21 "And I will clothe him with your tunic,
And tie your sash securely about him,
I will entrust him with your [1]authority,
And he will become a [a]father to the inhabitants of Jerusalem and to the house of Judah.
22 "Then I will set [a]the key of the [b]house of David on his shoulder,
When he opens no one will shut,
When he shuts no one will [c]open.
23 "And I will drive him *like* a [a]peg in a firm place,
And he will become a [b]throne of glory to his father's house.
24 "So they will hang on him all the glory of his father's
house, offspring and [1]issue, all the least of vessels, from bowls
to all the jars.
25 "In that day," declares the LORD of hosts, "the [a]peg
driven in a firm place will give way; it will even [b]break off and
fall, and the load hanging on it will be cut off, for the [c]LORD
has spoken."

CHAPTER 23

THE [1]oracle concerning [a]Tyre.
Wail, O [b]ships of [c]Tarshish,
For *Tyre* is destroyed, without house *or* [2d]harbor;
It is reported to them from the land of [3e]Cyprus.
2 [a]Be silent, you inhabitants of the coastland,
You merchants of Sidon;
[1]Your messengers crossed the sea
3 And *were* on many waters.
[a]The grain of the [1b]Nile, the harvest of the River was her revenue;
And she was the [c]market of nations.

---

14 [2]Lit., *atoned for* [3]YHWH, usually rendered LORD [a]Is. 65:20

15 [1]YHWH, usually rendered LORD

16 [1]Lit., *himself* [a]2 Sam. 18:18; 2 Chr. 16:14; Matt. 27:60

18 [a]Is. 17:13; Job 18:18

19 [1]So with many ancient versions; Heb., *He* [a]Job 40:11, 12; Ezek. 17:24

20 [a]Is. 36:3, 22; 37:2; 2 Kin. 18:18

21 [1]Lit., *rule* [a]Gen. 45:8

22 [a]Rev. 3:7 [b]Is. 7:2, 13 [c]Job 12:14

23 [a]Ezra 9:8; Zech. 10:4 [b]1 Sam. 2:8; Job 36:7

24 [1]Or perhaps, *leaf*

25 [a]Is. 22:23 [b]Esth. 9:24, 25 [c]Is. 46:11; Mic. 4:4

1 [1]Or, *burden of* [2]Lit., *entering* [3]Heb., *Kittim* [a]Josh. 19:29; 1 Kin. 5:1; Jer. 25:22; 47:4; Ezek. 26:1-28; Amos 1:9; Zech. 9:2-4 [b]Is. 2:16 [c]Gen. 10:4; 1 Kin. 10:22 [d]Is. 24:10 [e]Is. 23:12; Gen. 10:4; Ezek. 27:6

2 [1]So DSS; M.T., *who passed over the sea, they replenished you.* [a]Is. 47:5

3 [1]Heb., *Shihor* [a]Is. 19:7-9 [b]Josh. 13:3; 1 Chr. 13:5; Jer. 2:18 [c]Ezek 27:3-23

4 Be ashamed, O [a]Sidon;
For the sea speaks, the stronghold of the sea, saying,
"I have neither travailed nor given birth,
I have neither brought up young men *nor* reared virgins."
5 When the report *reaches* Egypt,
They will be in [a]anguish at the report of Tyre.
6 Pass over to Tarshish;
Wail, O inhabitants of the coastland.
7 Is this your [a]jubilant *city*,
Whose origin is from antiquity,
Whose feet used to carry her to [1]colonize distant places?

8 Who has planned this against Tyre, the bestower of crowns,
Whose merchants were princes, whose traders were the honored of the earth?
9 [a]The LORD of hosts has planned it to [b]defile the pride of all beauty,
To despise all the [c]honored of the earth.
10 [1]Overflow your land like the Nile, O daughter of Tarshish,
There is no more [2]restraint.
11 He has [a]stretched His hand out [b]over the sea,
He has made the kingdoms tremble;
The LORD has given a command concerning Canaan to [c]demolish its strongholds.
12 And He has said, "You shall exult no more, O crushed virgin daughter of Sidon.
Arise, pass over to [1]Cyprus; even there you will find no rest."
13 Behold, the land of the Chaldeans—this is the people
which was not; [a]Assyria appointed it for [b]desert creatures—
they erected their siege towers, they stripped its palaces, [c]they
made it a ruin.
14 Wail, O ships of Tarshish,
For your stronghold is destroyed.
15 Now it will come about in that day that Tyre will be
forgotten for [a]seventy years like the days of one king. At the
end of seventy years it will happen to Tyre as *in* the song of the
harlot:
16 Take *your* harp, walk about the city,
O forgotten harlot;
Pluck the strings skillfully, sing many songs,
That you may be remembered.
17 And it will come about at the end of seventy years that
the LORD will visit Tyre. Then she will go back to her harlot's
wages, and will [a]play the harlot with all the kingdoms [1]on the
face of the earth.
18 And her [a]gain and her harlot's wages will be [b]set apart
to the LORD; it will not be stored up or hoarded, but her gain
will become sufficient food and choice attire for those who
dwell in the presence of the LORD.

4 [a]Gen. 10:15, 19; Josh. 11:8; Judg. 10:6; Jer. 25:22; 27:3; 47:4; Ezek. 28:21, 22

5 [a]Ex. 15:14-16; Josh. 2:9-11

7 [1]Lit., *sojourn afar off* [a]Is. 22:2; 32:13

9 [a]Is. 2:11; 13:11 [b]Job 40:11, 12; Dan. 4:37 [c]Is. 5:13; 9:15

10 [1]Lit., *Pass over* [2]Perhaps *girdle* or *shipyard*

11 [a]Is. 14:26; Ex. 14:21 [b]Is. 19:5; 50:2 [c]Is. 25:2; Zech. 9:3, 4

12 [1]Heb., *Kittim*

13 [a]Is. 10:5 [b]Is. 13:21; 18:6 [c]Is. 10:7

15 [a]Jer. 25:11, 22

17 [1]Lit., *of the earth on the face of the land* [a]Ezek. 16:25-29; Nah. 3:4

18 [a]Is. 60:5-9; Ps. 72:10, 11; Mic. 4:13 [b]Ex. 28:36; Zech. 14:20

Chapter 24

BEHOLD, the LORD [a]lays the earth waste, devastates it, distorts its surface, and scatters its inhabitants.
2 And the people will be like the priest, the servant like
his master, the maid like her mistress, the buyer like the seller,
the lender like the borrower, the [a]creditor like the debtor.
3 The earth will be completely laid waste and completely
despoiled, for the LORD has spoken this word.
4 The earth mourns *and* withers, the world fades *and*
withers, the [a]exalted of the people of the earth fade away.
5 The earth is also [a]polluted [1]by its inhabitants, for they
transgressed laws, violated statutes, [b]broke the everlasting
covenant.
6 Therefore, a [a]curse devours the earth, and those who
live in it are held guilty. Therefore, the inhabitants of the earth
are burned, and few men are left.

7 The [a]new wine mourns,
The vine decays,
All the merry-hearted sigh.
8 The gaiety of tambourines ceases,
The noise of revelers stops,
The gaiety of the harp ceases.
9 They do not drink wine with song;
[a]Strong drink is [b]bitter to those who drink it.
10 The [a]city of chaos is broken down;
[b]Every house is shut up so that none may enter.
11 There is an [a]outcry in the streets concerning the wine;
[b]All joy [1]turns to gloom.
The gaiety of the earth is banished.
12 Desolation is left in the city,
And the [a]gate is battered to ruins.
13 For [a]thus it will be in the midst of the earth among the peoples,
As the [1]shaking of an olive tree,
As the gleanings when the grape harvest is over.
14 [a]They raise their voices, they shout for joy.
They cry out from the [1]west concerning the majesty of the LORD.
15 Therefore [a]glorify the LORD in the [1]east,
The [b]name of the LORD, the God of Israel
In the [2c]coastlands of the sea.
16 From the [a]ends of the earth we hear songs, "[b]Glory to the Righteous One,"
But I say, "[1c]Woe to me! [1]Woe to me! Alas for me!
The [d]treacherous deal treacherously,
And the treacherous deal very treacherously."
17 Terror and pit and snare
[1]Confront you, O inhabitant of the earth.
18 Then it will be that he who flees the [1]report of disaster will fall into the pit,
And he who [2]climbs out of the pit will be caught in the snare;
For the [a]windows [3]above are opened, and the [b]foundations of the earth shake.
19 The earth is broken asunder,

1 [a]Is. 24:19, 20; 2:19; 13:13; 30:32; 32:9

2 [a]Lev. 25:36, 37; Deut. 23:19, 20

4 [a]Is. 24:21; 2:12

5 [1]Lit., *under* [a]Is. 9:17; 10:6; Gen. 3:17; Num. 35:33 [b]Is. 33:8

6 [a]Is. 34:5; 43:28; Josh. 23:15; Zech. 5:3, 4

7 [a]Is. 16:10; Joel 1:10, 12

9 [a]Is. 5:11, 22 [b]Is. 5:20

10 [a]Is. 34:11; Gen. 1:2 [b]Is. 23:1

11 [1]Lit., is *darkened* [a]Jer. 14:2; 46:12 [b]Is. 10:10; 32:13

12 [a]Is. 14:31; 45:2

13 [1]Lit., *striking* [a]Is. 17:6; 27:12

14 [1]Lit., *sea* [a]Is. 12:6; 48:20; 52:8; 54:1

15 [1]Lit., *region of light* [2]Or, *islands* [a]Is. 25:3 [b]Mal. 1:1 [c]Is. 11:11; 42:4, 10, 12; 49:1; 51:5; 60:9; 66:19

16 [1]Lit., *Wasting to me!* [a]Is. 11:12; 42:10 [b]Is. 28:5; 60:21 [c]Lev. 26:39 [d]Is. 21:2; 33:1; Jer. 3:20; 5:1

17 [1]Lit., *Are upon you*

18 [1]Lit., *sound of terror* [2]Lit., *goes up from the midst of* [3]Lit., *from the height;* i.e., heaven [a]Gen. 7:11 [b]Is. 2:19, 21; 13:13; Ps. 18:7; 46:2

The earth is [a]split through,
The earth is shaken violently.
20 The earth [a]reels to and fro like a drunkard,
And it totters like a [1]shack,
For its [b]transgression is heavy upon it,
And it will fall, [c]never to rise again.
21 So it will happen in that day,
That the LORD will [a]punish the host of [1]heaven, on high,
And the [b]kings of the earth, on earth.
22 And they will be gathered together
Like [a]prisoners in the [1]dungeon,
And will be confined in prison;
And after many days they will [b]be punished.
23 Then the moon will be abashed and the sun ashamed,
For the [a]LORD of hosts will reign on [b]Mount Zion and in Jerusalem,
And *His* glory will be before His elders.

CHAPTER 25

O LORD, Thou art [a]my God;
I will exalt Thee, I will give thanks to Thy name;
For Thou hast [b]worked wonders,
[c]Plans formed long ago, with perfect faithfulness.
2 For Thou hast made a city into a [a]heap,
A fortified city into a ruin;
A [b]palace of strangers is a city no more,
It will never be rebuilt.
3 Therefore a strong people will [a]glorify Thee;
[b]Cities of ruthless nations will revere Thee.
4 For Thou hast been a [a]defense for the helpless.
A defense for the needy in his distress,
A [b]refuge from the storm, a shade from the heat,
For the breath of the [c]ruthless
Is like a *rain* storm *against* a wall.
5 Like heat in drought, Thou dost subdue the [a]uproar of aliens;
Like heat by the shadow of a cloud, the song of the ruthless is [1]silenced.

6 And the LORD of hosts will prepare a [1]lavish banquet for all peoples on this mountain;
A banquet of [2]aged wine, [3]choice pieces with marrow,
And [4]refined, aged wine.
7 And on this mountain He will swallow up the [1a]covering which is over all peoples,
Even the veil which is [2]stretched over all nations.
8 He will [a]swallow up death for all time,
And the Lord [1]GOD will [b]wipe tears away from all faces,
And He will remove the [c]reproach of His people from all the earth;
For the LORD has spoken.
9 And it will be said in that day,
"Behold, [a]this is our God for whom we have [b]waited that [c]He might save us.

19 [a]Num. 16:31, 32; Deut. 11:6

20 [1]Or, *hut* [a]Is. 24:1; 19:14; 28:7 [b]Is. 1:28; 43:27; 66:24 [c]Dan. 11:19; Amos 8:14

21 [1]Lit., *the height in the height* [a]Is. 10:12; 13:11 [b]Ps. 76:12

22 [1]Lit., *pit* [a]Is. 10:4; 42:22 [b]Ezek. 38:8; Zech. 9:11, 12

23 [a]Is. 60:19, 20; Zech. 14:6, 7; Rev. 21:23; 22:5 [b]Mic. 4:7; Heb. 12:22

1 [a]Is. 7:13; 49:4, 5; 61:10; Ex. 15:2; Ps. 118:28 [b]Ps. 40:5; 98:1 [c]Eph. 1:11

2 [a]Is. 17:1; 26:5; 27:10; 32:19 [b]Is. 13:22; 32:14; 34:13

3 [a]Is. 24:15 [b]Is. 13:11

4 [a]Is. 14:32; 17:10; 27:5; 33:16 [b]Is. 4:6; 32:2 [c]Is. 29:5, 20; 49:25

5 [1]Lit., *humbled* [a]Jer. 51:54-56

6 [1]Lit., *feast of fat things;* i.e., abundance [2]Lit., *wine on the lees* [3]Lit., *fat pieces* [4]Lit., *wine refined on the lees.*

7 [1]Lit., *face of the covering* [2]Lit., *woven* [a]2 Cor. 3:15, 16; Eph. 4:18

8 [1]YHWH, usually rendered LORD [a]Hos. 13:14; 1 Cor. 15:54 [b]Is. 30:19; 35:10; 51:11; 65:19; Rev. 7:17; 21:4 [c]Is. 51:7; 54:4; Ps. 69:9; 89:50, 51; Matt. 5:11; 1 Pet. 4:14

9 [a]Is. 35:2; 40:9; 52:10 [b]Is. 8:17; 30:18; 33:2 [c]Is. 33:32; 35:4; 49:25, 26; 60:16

This is the LORD for whom we have waited;
[d]Let us rejoice and be glad in His salvation."
10 For the hand of the LORD will rest on this mountain,
And Moab will be trodden down in his place
As straw is trodden down in the water of a manure pile.
11 And he will spread out his hands in the middle of it
As a swimmer spreads out *his hands* to swim,
But *the Lord* will [a]lay low his pride together with the trickery of his hands.
12 And the [a]unassailable fortifications of your walls He will bring down,
Lay low, *and* cast to the ground, even to the dust.

[a] CHAPTER 26

IN that day this song will be sung in the land of Judah:
"We have a [b]strong city;
He sets up walls and ramparts for [1c]security.
2 "Open the [a]gates, that the [b]righteous nation may enter,
The one that [1]remains faithful.
3 "Thou wilt [1]keep *the nation of* steadfast purpose in perfect [2a]peace,
Because [3]it trusts in Thee.
4 "[a]Trust in the LORD forever,
For in [1]GOD the LORD, *we have* an everlasting [b]Rock.
5 "For He has brought low those who dwell on high, the unassailable city;
[a]He lays it low, He lays it low to the ground, He casts it to the dust.
6 "The foot will trample it,
The feet of the [a]afflicted, the steps of the helpless."

7 The [a]way of the righteous is smooth;
O Upright One, [b]make the path of the righteous level.
8 Indeed, *while following* the way of Thy judgments, O LORD,
We have waited for Thee eagerly;
[a]Thy name, even Thy [b]memory, is the desire of *our* souls.
9 [a]At night [1]my soul longs for Thee,
Indeed, [2]my spirit within me [b]seeks Thee diligently;
For when the earth [3]experiences Thy judgments
The inhabitants of the world [c]learn righteousness.
10 *Though* the wicked is shown favor,
He does not [a]learn righteousness;
He [b]deals unjustly in the land of uprightness,
And does not perceive the majesty of the LORD.

11 O LORD, Thy hand is lifted up *yet* they do not see it.
[1]They see [a]*Thy* zeal for the people and are put to shame;
Indeed, [2]fire will devour Thine enemies.
12 LORD, Thou wilt establish peace for us,
Since Thou hast also performed for us all our works.
13 O LORD our God, [a]other masters than Thou have ruled us;
But through Thee alone we [1b]confess Thy name.

9 [d]Is. 35:1, 2, 10; 65:18; 66:10; Ps. 20:5

11 [a]Is. 16:6, 14

12 [a]Is. 25:2; 15:1; 26:5

1 [1]Or, *salvation* [a]Is. 4:2; 12:1 [b]Is. 14:31; 31:5, 9; 33:5, 6, 20-24 [c]Is. 60:18

2 [1]Lit., *keeps faithfulness* [a]Is. 60:11, 18; 62:10 [b]Is. 45:25; 54:14, 17; 58:8; 60:21; 61:3; 62:1, 2

3 [1]Or, *keep* the man of [2]Or, *safety* [3]Or, *he* [a]Is. 26:12; 27:5; 57:19; 66:12

4 [1]YAH, usually rendered LORD [a]Is. 12:2; 50:10; 51:5 [b]Is. 17:10; 30:29; 44:8

5 [a]Job 40:11-13

6 [a]Is. 3:14, 15; 11:4; 29:19

7 [a]Is. 57:2 [b]Is. 42:16; 52:12; Ps. 25:4, 5; 27:11

8 [a]Is. 26:13; 12:4; 24:15; 25:1 [b]Ex. 3:15

9 [1]Lit., with *my soul I long* [2]Lit., with *my spirit . . . I seek* [3]Lit., *has* [a]Is. 50:10; Ps. 63:5, 6; 77:2; 119:62; Luke 6:12 [b]Is. 55:6; Ps. 63:1; 78:34; Matt. 6:33 [c]Hos. 5:15

10 [a]Is. 22:12, 13; 32:6, 7 [b]Hos. 11:7; John 5:37, 38

11 [1]Or, *Let them see . . . and be* [2]Or, *let the fire for Thine adversaries devour them* [a]Is. 9:7; 37:32; 59:17

13 [1]Or, *cause to be remembered* [a]Is. 2:8; 10:11 [b]Is. 63:7

14 [a]The dead will not live, the [1]departed spirits will not
rise;
Therefore Thou hast [b]punished and destroyed them,
And Thou hast wiped out all remembrance of them.
15 [a]Thou hast increased the nation, O LORD,
Thou hast increased the nation, Thou art glorified;
Thou hast [b]extended all the borders of the land.
16 O LORD, they sought Thee [a]in distress;
They [1]could only whisper a prayer,
Your chastening was upon them.
17 [a]As the pregnant woman approaches *the time* to give
birth,
She writhes *and* cries out in her labor pains,
Thus were we before Thee, O LORD.
18 We were pregnant, we writhed in *labor*,
We [a]gave birth, as it were, *only* to wind.
We could not accomplish deliverance for the earth
Nor were inhabitants of the world [1]born.
19 Your [a]dead will live;
[1]Their corpses will rise.
You who lie in the dust, [b]awake and shout for joy,
For your dew is as the dew of the [2]dawn,
And the earth will [3]give birth to the [4]departed spirits.

20 *Come*, my people, [a]enter into your rooms,
And close your doors behind you;
Hide for a little [1b]while,
Until indignation [2]runs *its* course.
21 For behold, the LORD is about to [a]come out from His
place
To punish the inhabitants of the earth for their
iniquity;
And the earth will [b]reveal her bloodshed,
And will no longer cover her slain.

CHAPTER 27

IN that day the LORD will punish [1a]Leviathan the fleeing
serpent,
With His fierce and great and mighty sword,
Even [1]Leviathan the twisted serpent;
And He will kill the dragon who *lives* in the sea.

2 In that day,
"A [1a]vineyard of wine, sing of it!
3 "I the LORD am its keeper;
I water it every moment.
Lest any one [1]damage it,
I [a]guard it night and day.
4 "I have no wrath.
Should [1]someone give me [a]briars *and* thorns in battle,
Then I would step on them, [b]I would burn them
[2]completely.
5 "Or let him [1]rely on My protection,
Let him make peace with Me,
Let him [a]make peace with Me."

14 [1]Or, *shades*
[a]Is. 8:19; Deut. 4:28; Ps. 135:17; Hab. 2:19 [b]Is. 10:3

15 [a]Is. 9:3 [b]Is. 33:17; 54:2, 3

16 [1]Lit., *sound forth a whisper*
[a]Is. 37:3; Hos. 5:15

17 [a]Is. 13:8; 21:3; John 16:21

18 [1]Lit., *fallen*
[a]Is. 33:11; 59:4

19 [1]So with some ancient versions; Heb., *My* [2]Lit., *lights* [3]Lit., *cause to fall* [4]Or, *shades*
[a]Is. 25:8; Ezek. 37:1-14; Dan. 12:2; Hos. 13:14 [b]Eph. 5:14

20 [1]Lit., *moment* [2]Lit., *passes over*
[a]Ex. 12:22, 23; Ps. 91:1, 4 [b]Is. 54:7, 8; Ps. 30:5; 2 Cor. 4:17

21 [a]Mic. 1:3; Jude 14 [b]Job 16:18; Luke 11:50

1 [1]Or, *sea monster*
[a]Job 3:8; 41:1; Ps. 74:14; 104:26

2 [1]Some mss. read, *a vineyard of delight*
[a]Is. 5:7; Ps. 80:8; Jer. 2:21

3 [1]Lit., *punish*
[a]Is. 31:5; 1 Sam. 2:9; John 10:28

4 [1]Lit., *who* [2]Lit., *altogether*
[a]Is. 10:17; 2 Sam. 23:6 [b]Is. 33:12; Matt. 3:12; Heb. 6:8

5 [1]Lit., *take hold of*
[a]Is. 26:3, 12; Job 22:21; Rom. 5:1; 2 Cor. 5:20

6 [1]In the days to come Jacob will take root,
Israel will [a]blossom and sprout;
And they will fill the [2]whole world with fruit.

7 Like the striking of Him who has struck them, has [a]He struck them?
Or like the slaughter of His slain, [1]have they been slain?
8 Thou didst contend with them [1]by banishing them, by [a]driving them away.
With His fierce wind He has expelled *them* on the day of the [b]east wind.
9 Therefore through this Jacob's iniquity will be [a]forgiven;
And this will be [1]the full price of the [2b]pardoning of his sin:
When he makes all the [c]altar stones like pulverized chalk stones;
When [3]Asherim and incense altars will not stand.
10 For the fortified city is isolated,
A [1]homestead forlorn and forsaken like the desert;
There the calf will graze,
And there it will lie down and [2]feed on its branches.
11 When its limbs are dry, they are broken off;
Women come *and* make a fire with them.
For they are not a people of [a]discernment.
Therefore [b]their Maker will not have compassion on them.
And their Creator will not be gracious to them.
12 And it will come about in that day, that the LORD [a]will
start *His* threshing from the flowing stream of the Euphrates
to the brook of Egypt; and you will be [b]gathered up one by
one, O sons of Israel.
13 It will come about also in that day that a great [a]trum-
pet will be blown; and those who were perishing in the land of
Assyria and who were scattered in the land of Egypt will come
and [b]worship the LORD in the holy mountain at Jerusalem.

CHAPTER 28

WOE to the proud crown of the drunkards of Ephraim,
And to the fading flower of its glorious beauty,
Which is at the head of the [1]fertile valley
Of those who are [2]overcome with wine!
2 Behold, the Lord has a strong and [a]mighty *agent;*
As a storm of hail, a tempest of destruction,
Like a storm of [b]mighty overflowing waters,
He has cast *it* down to the earth with *His* hand.
3 The proud crown of the drunkards of Ephraim are trodden under foot.
4 And the fading flower of its glorious beauty,
Which is at the head of the [1]fertile valley,
Will be like the [a]first-ripe fig prior to summer;
Which [2]one sees,
And [3]as soon as it is in his [4]hand,
He swallows it.

6 [1]Lit., *those coming* [2]Lit., *face of*
[a]Is. 35:1, 2; Hos. 14:5, 6

7 [1]Lit., *he was slain*
[a]Is. 10:12, 17; 30:31-33; 31:8, 9; 37:36-38

8 [1]Some ancient versions read, *by exact measure*
[a]Is. 50:1; 54:7 [b]Jer. 4:11; Ezek. 19:12; Hos. 13:15

9 [1]Lit., *all the fruit* [2]Lit., *removing* [3]I.e., wooden symbols of female deities
[a]Is. 1:25; 48:10; Dan. 11:35 [b]Rom. 11:27 [c]Is. 17:8; Ex. 34:13; Deut. 12:3; 2 Kin. 10:26

10 [1]Lit., *pasture* [2]Lit., *consume*

11 [a]Is. 1:3; 5:13; Deut. 32:28; Jer. 8:7 [b]Is. 43:1, 7; 44:2, 21, 24; Deut. 32:18

12 [a]Is. 11:11; 17:6; 24:13; 56:8 [b]Deut. 30:3, 4; Neh. 1:9

13 [a]Lev. 25:9; 1 Chr. 15:24; Matt. 24:31; Rev. 11:15 [b]Is. 19:21, 23; 49:7; 66:23; Zech. 14:16; Heb. 12:22

1 [1]Lit., *valley of fatness* [2]Lit., *smitten*

2 [a]Is. 8:7; 40:10 [b]Is. 8:6, 7; 30:28; Nah. 1:8

4 [1]Lit., *valley of fatness* [2]Lit., *the one seeing sees* [3]Lit., *while it is yet* [4]Lit., *palm*
[a]Hos. 9:10; Mic. 7:1; Nah. 3:12

5 In that day the [a]LORD of hosts will become a beautiful
[b]crown
And a glorious diadem to the remnant of His people,
6 A [a]spirit of justice for him who sits in judgment,
A [b]strength to those who repel the [1]onslaught at the
gate.
7 And these also reel with wine and stagger from strong
drink:
[a]The priest and [b]the prophet reel with strong drink,
They are confused by wine, they stagger from [c]strong
drink;
They reel while [1]having visions,
They totter *when rendering* judgment.
8 For all the tables are full of filthy [a]vomit, without a
single clean place.

9 "To [a]whom would he teach knowledge?
And to whom would he interpret the message?
Those *just* weaned from milk?
Those *just* taken from the breast?
10 "For *he says,*
'[1a]Order on order, order on order,
Line on line, line on line,
A little here, a little there.' "
11 Indeed, He will speak to this people
Through [a]stammering lips and a foreign tongue,
12 He who said to them, "Here is [a]rest, give rest to the
weary,"
And, "Here is repose," but they would not listen.
13 So the word of the LORD to them will be,
"[1]Order on order, order on order,
Line on line, line on line,
A little here, a little there,"
That they may go and [a]stumble backward, be broken,
snared, and taken captive.
14 Therefore, hear the word of the LORD, O [a]scoffers,
Who rule this people who are in Jerusalem,
15 Because you have said, "We have made a [a]covenant
with death,
And with [1]Sheol we have made a [2]pact.
[b]The overwhelming [3]scourge will not reach us when it
passes by,
For we have made [c]falsehood our refuge and we have
concealed ourselves with deception."
16 Therefore thus says the Lord [1]GOD,
"[a]Behold, I am laying in Zion a stone, a tested [b]stone,
A costly cornerstone *for* the foundation, [2]firmly placed.
He who believes *in it* will not be [3]disturbed.
17 "And I will make [a]justice the measuring-line,
And righteousness the level;
Then hail shall sweep away the refuge of lies,
And the waters shall overflow the secret place.
18 "And your covenant with death shall be [1]canceled,
And your pact with Sheol shall not stand;

5 [a]Is. 41:16; 45:25; 60:1, 19 [b]Is. 62:3

6 [1]Lit., *battle*
[a]Is. 11:2; 32:15, 16; 1 Kin. 3:28; John 5:30 [b]Is. 25:4; 2 Chr. 32:6-8

7 [1]Lit., *seeing*
[a]Is. 24:2 [b]Is. 9:15 [c]Hab. 2:15, 16

8 [a]Jer. 48:26

9 [a]Is. 28:26; 2:3; 30:20; 48:17; 50:4; 54:13

10 [1]Heb., *Sav lasav sav lasav, Kav lakav Kav lakav Ze'er sham ze'er sham.* These Hebrew monosyllables, imitating the babbling of a child, mock the prophet's preaching.
[a]2 Chr. 36:15; Neh. 9:30

11 [a]Is. 33:19; 1 Cor. 14:21

12 [a]Is. 11:10; 30:15; 32:17, 18; Jer. 6:16; Matt. 11:28, 29

13 [1]Heb., same as note, v. 10. The Lord responds to their scoffing by imitating their mockery, to represent the unintelligible language of a conqueror.
[a]Is. 8:15; Matt. 21:44

14 [a]Is. 29:20

15 [1]I.e., the nether world [2]So some ancient versions; Heb., *seer* [3]Or, *flood*
[a]Is. 28:18 [b]Is. 28:2; 8:8; 30:28; Dan. 11:22 [c]Is. 9:15; 30:9; 44:20; 59:3, 4; Ezek. 13:22

16 [1]YHWH, usually rendered LORD [2]Lit., *well-laid* [3]Lit., *in a hurry*
[a]Rom. 9:33; 10:11; 1 Pet. 2:6 [b]Is. 8:14, 15; Ps. 118:22; Matt. 21:42; Mark 12:10; Luke 20:17; Acts 4:11; Eph. 2:20

17 [a]Is. 5:16; 30:18; 61:8; 2 Kin. 21:13; Amos 7:7-9

18 [1]Lit., *covered over*

When the overwhelming scourge passes through,
Then you become its [a]trampling *place*.
19 As [a]often as it passes through, it will [1]seize you.
For [b]morning after morning it will pass through, *any-time* during the day or night.
And it will be [2]sheer terror to understand [3]what it means."
20 The bed is too short on which to stretch out,
And the [a]blanket is too [1]small to wrap oneself in.
21 For the LORD will rise up as *at* Mount [a]Perazim,
He will be stirred up as in the valley of Gibeon;
To do His [b]task, His [1c]unusual task,
And to work His work, His [2]extraordinary work.
22 And now do not carry on as scoffers,
Lest your fetters be made stronger;
For I have heard from the Lord [1]GOD of hosts,
Of decisive destruction on all the earth.

23 Give ear and hear my voice,
Listen and hear my words.
24 Does the [1]farmer plow [2]continually to plant seed?
Does he *continually* [3]turn and harrow the ground?
25 Does he not level its surface,
And sow dill and scatter [a]cummin,
And [1]plant [b]wheat in rows,
Barley in its place, and [c]rye within its [2]area?
26 For his God instructs and teaches him properly.
27 For dill is not threshed with a [a]threshing sledge,
Nor is the cartwheel [1]driven over cummin;
But dill is beaten out with a rod, and cummin with a club.
28 *Grain for* bread is crushed,
Indeed, he does not continue to thresh it forever.
Because the wheel of *his* cart and his horses *eventually* [1]damage *it*,
He does not thresh it longer.
29 This also comes from the LORD of hosts,
Who has made *His* counsel [a]wonderful and *His* wisdom [b]great.

CHAPTER 29

WOE, O [1]Ariel, [1]Ariel the city *where* David *once* [a]camped!
Add year to year, [2b]observe *your* feasts on schedule.
2 And I will bring distress to Ariel,
And she shall be *a city of* lamenting and [a]mourning;
And she shall be like an Ariel to me.
3 And I will [a]camp against you [1]encircling *you*,
And I will set siege-works against you,
And I will raise up battle towers against you.
4 Then you shall [a]be brought low;
From the earth you shall speak.
And from the dust *where* you are prostrate,
Your words *shall come*.
Your voice shall also be like that of a [1]spirit from the ground,
And your speech shall whisper from the dust.

18 [a]Is. 28:3; Dan. 8:13

19 [1]Lit., *take* [2]Lit., *only* [3]Lit., *the report*, or message [a]2 Kin. 24:2 [b]Is. 50:4

20 [1]Lit., *narrow* [a]Is. 59:6

21 [1]Lit., *His task is strange* [2]Lit., *His work is alien* [a]2 Sam. 5:20; 1 Chr. 14:11 [b]Is. 10:12; 29:14; 65:7 [c]Lam. 2:15; 3:33; Luke 19:41-44

22 [1]YHWH, usually rendered LORD

24 [1]Lit., *plowman* [2]Lit., *all day* [3]Lit., *open*

25 [1]Lit., *put* [2]Lit., *region* [a]Matt. 23:23 [b]Ex. 9:32 [c]Amos 1:3

27 [1]Lit., *rolled* [a]Amos 1:3

28 [1]Lit., *discomfit*

29 [a]Is. 9:6 [b]Is. 31:2; Rom. 11:33

1 [1]I.e., Lion of God, or, *Jerusalem* [2]Lit., *let your feasts run their round* [a]2 Sam. 5:9 [b]Is. 9:13; 1:14; 5:12; 22:12, 13

2 [a]Is. 3:26; Lam. 2:5

3 [1]Lit., *like a circle* [a]Luke 19:43, 44

4 [1]Or, *ghost* [a]Is. 8:19

5 But the multitude of your [1]enemies shall become like
fine [a]dust,
And the multitude of the ruthless ones like the chaff
which [2]blows away;
And it shall happen [b]instantly, suddenly.
6 From the LORD of hosts you will be punished with
[a]thunder and earthquake and loud noise,
With whirlwind and tempest and the flame of a consuming fire.
7 And the [a]multitude of all the nations who wage war
against [1]Ariel,
Even all who wage war against her and her stronghold,
and who distress her,
Shall be like a dream, a [b]vision of the night.
8 And it will be as when a hungry man dreams—
And behold, he is eating;
But when he awakens, his [1]hunger is not satisfied,
Or as when a thirsty man dreams—
And behold, he is drinking,
But when he awakens, behold, he is faint,
And his [1]thirst is not quenched.
[a]Thus the multitude of all the nations shall be,
Who wage war against Mount Zion.

9 Be delayed and wait.
Blind yourselves and be blind.
They become drunk, but not with wine;
They stagger, but not with strong drink.
10 For the LORD has poured over you a spirit of deep
[a]sleep,
He has [b]shut your eyes, the prophets;
And He has covered your heads, the seers.
11 And the entire vision shall be to you like the words of a
sealed [1a]book, which when they give it to the one who [2]is
literate, saying, "Please read this," he will say, "I cannot, for it
is sealed."
12 Then the [1]book will be given to the one who [2]is illiter-
ate, saying, "Please read this." And he will say, "I [3]cannot
read."
13 Then the Lord said,
"Because [a]this people draw near with their [1]words
And honor Me with their [2]lipservice,
But they remove their hearts far from Me,
And their [3]reverence for Me [4]consists of [5]tradition
learned *by rote*,
14 Therefore behold, I will once again deal [a]marvelously
with this people, wondrously marvelous;
And [b]the wisdom of their wise men shall perish,
And the discernment of their discerning men shall be
concealed.

15 Woe to those who deeply [a]hide their [1]plans from the
LORD,
And whose deeds are *done* in a dark place,
And they say, "[b]Who sees us?" or "Who knows us?"
16 You turn *things* around!

5 [1]Lit., *strangers* [2]Lit., *passes away*
[a]Is. 17:13; 41:15, 16 [b]Is. 17:14; 30:13; 47:11; 1 Thess. 5:3

6 [a]1 Sam. 2:10; Matt. 24:7; Mark 13:8; Luke 21:11; Rev. 11:13, 19; 16:18

7 [1]See note, v. 1
[a]Mic. 4:11, 12; Zech. 12:9
[b]Is. 17:14; Job 20:8; Ps. 73:20

8 [1]Lit., *soul*
[a]Is. 54:17

10 [a]Is. 6:9, 10; Ps. 69:23; Mic. 3:6; Rom. 11:8 [b]Is. 44:18; 2 Thess. 2:9-12

11 [1]Or, *scroll* [2]Lit., *knows books*
[a]Is. 8:16; Dan. 12:4, 9; Matt. 13:11

12 [1]Or, *scroll* [2]Lit., *does not know books* [3]Lit., *do not know books*

13 [1]Lit., *mouth* [2]Lit., *lips* [3]Lit., *fear of Me* [4]Lit., *is* [5]Lit., *commandment of rulers*
[a]Ezek. 33:31; Matt. 15:8, 9; Mark 7:6, 7

14 [a]Is. 6:9, 10; 28:21; 65:7; Hab. 1:5 [b]Is. 44:25; Jer. 8:9; 49:7; 1 Cor. 1:19

15 [1]Lit., *counsel*
[a]Is. 28:15; 30:1; Ps. 10:11, 13 [b]Is. 47:10; Ps. 94:7; Mal. 2:17

Shall the potter be considered [1]as equal with the clay,
That [a]what is made should say to its maker, "He did not make me";
Or what is formed say to him who formed it, "He has no understanding"?

17 Is it not yet just a little while
[1]Before Lebanon will be turned into a [a]fertile field,
And the fertile field will be considered as a forest?
18 And on that day the deaf shall hear words of a book,
And out of *their* gloom and darkness the [a]eyes of the blind shall see.
19 The [a]afflicted also shall increase their gladness in the LORD,
And the [b]needy of mankind shall rejoice in the Holy One of Israel.
20 For the ruthless will come to an end, and the scorner will be finished,
Indeed [a]all who [1]are intent on doing evil will be cut off;
21 Who [1]cause a person to be indicted by a word,
And [a]ensnare him who adjudicates at the gate,
And [2b]defraud the one in the right with [3]meaningless arguments.
22 Therefore thus says the LORD, who redeemed [a]Abra-
ham, concerning the house of Jacob:
"Jacob shall not now be ashamed, nor shall his face now turn pale;
23 But when [1]he sees his children, the [a]work of My hands, in his midst,
They will sanctify My name;
Indeed, they will [b]sanctify the Holy One of Jacob,
And will stand in awe of the God of Israel.
24 "And those who [a]err in [1]mind will [b]know [2]the truth,
And those who [3]criticize will [4c]accept instruction.

CHAPTER 30

"WOE to the rebellious children," declares the LORD,
"Who [a]execute a plan but not Mine,
And [1b]make an alliance but not of My Spirit,
In order to add sin to sin;
2 Who [a]proceed down to Egypt,
Without [b]consulting [1]Me,
[c]To take refuge in the safety of Pharaoh,
And to seek shelter in the shadow of Egypt!
3 "Therefore the safety of Pharaoh will be [a]your shame,
And the shelter in the shadow of Egypt, your humiliation.
4 "For [a]their princes are at Zoan,
And their ambassadors arrive at Hanes.
5 "Everyone will be [a]ashamed because of a people who cannot profit them,
Who are [b]not for help or profit, but for shame and also for reproach."

6 The [1]oracle concerning the [a]beasts of the [b]Negev.

16 [1]Lit., *like* [a]Is. 45:9; 64:8; Jer. 18:1-6; Rom. 9:19-21

17 [1]Lit., *and* [a]Is. 32:15; Ps. 84:6; 107:33, 35

18 [a]Is. 32:3; Ps. 119:18; Prov. 20:12

19 [a]Is. 11:4; 61:1; Ps. 25:9; 37:11; Matt. 5:5; 11:29 [b]Is. 3:14, 15; 11:4; 14:30, 32; 25:4; 26:6; Matt. 11:5; James 1:9; 2:5

20 [1]Lit., *watch evil* [a]Is. 59:4

21 [1]Lit., *bring a person under condemnation* [2]Lit., *turn aside* [3]Lit., *confusion* [a]Amos 5:10 [b]Is. 32:7; Amos 5:12

22 [a]Is. 41:8; 51:2; 63:16

23 [1]Or, *his children see* [a]Is. 26:12; 45:11; Eph. 2:10 [b]Is. 5:16; 8:13

24 [1]Lit., *spirit* [2]Lit., *understanding* [3]Lit., *murmur* [4]Lit., *learn* [a]Is. 30:21; Heb. 5:2 [b]Is. 41:20; 60:16 [c]Is. 54:13

1 [1]Lit., *pour out a drink offering* [a]Is. 29:15 [b]Is. 8:11, 12

2 [1]Lit., *My mouth* [a]Is. 31:1; Jer. 43:7 [b]Is. 8:19 [c]Is. 36:9

3 [a]Is. 20:5, 6; 36:6; Jer. 42:18, 22

4 [a]Is. 19:11

5 [a]Jer. 2:36 [b]Is. 30:7; 10:3; 31:3

6 [1]Lit., *burden* [a]Is. 46:1, 2; 1 Kin. 10:2 [b]Gen. 12:9

Through a land of [c]distress and anguish,
From [2]where *come* lioness and lion, viper and [d]flying
serpent,
They [e]carry their riches on the [3]backs of young donkeys
And their treasures on camels' humps,
To a people who cannot profit *them;*
7 Even Egypt, whose help is vain and empty.
Therefore, I have called [1]her
[2a]Rahab who has been exterminated.
8 Now go, [a]write it on a tablet before them
And inscribe it on a scroll,
That it may [1]serve in the time to come
[2]As a witness forever.
9 For this is a rebellious people, [a]false sons,
Sons who [1]refuse to [b]listen
To the [2]instruction of the LORD;
10 Who say to the seers, "You must not see *visions*";
And to the prophets, "You must not [a]prophesy to us
what is right,
[b]Speak to us [1]pleasant words,
Prophesy illusions.
11 "Get out of the way, turn aside from the path,
[1]Let us hear no more about the Holy One of Israel."
12 Therefore thus says the Holy One of Israel,
"[a]Since you have rejected this word,
And have put your trust in [b]oppression and guile, and
have relied on them,
13 Therefore this iniquity will be to you
Like a [a]breach about to fall,
A bulge in a high wall,
Whose collapse comes suddenly in an instant.
14 And whose collapse is like the smashing of a [a]potter's
jar;
[1]So ruthlessly shattered
That a sherd will not be found among its pieces
To [2]take fire from a hearth,
Or to scoop water from a cistern."
15 For thus the Lord [1]GOD, the Holy One of Israel, has
said:
"In [2a]repentance and [b]rest you shall be saved,
In [c]quietness and trust is your strength."
But you were not willing,
16 And you said, "No, for we will flee on [a]horses,"
Therefore you shall flee!
"And we will ride on swift *horses*."
Therefore those who pursue you shall be swift.
17 [a]One thousand *shall flee* at the threat of one *man*,
You shall flee at the threat of five;
Until you [b]are left as a [1]flag on a mountain top,
And as a signal on a hill.

18 Therefore the LORD [1a]longs to be gracious to you,
And therefore He [2]waits on [b]high to have compassion
on you.
For the LORD is a [c]God of justice;
How blessed are all those who [3d]long for Him.

6 [2]Lit., *them* [3]Lit., *shoulders* [c]Is. 5:30; 8:22; Ex. 5:10, 21; Deut. 4:20; 8:15; Jer. 11:4 [d]Is. 14:29; Deut. 8:15 [e]Is. 15:17; 46:1, 2

7 [1]Lit., *this* one [2]M.T. reads; *They are Rahab* (or *arrogance*), *to remain* [a]Is. 51:9; Job 9:13; Ps. 87:4; 89:10

8 [1]Lit., *be* [2]So the versions; Heb., *Forever and ever* [a]Is. 8:1

9 [1]Lit., *are not willing* [2]Or, *law* [a]Is. 28:15; 59:3, 4 [b]Is. 1:10; 5:24; 24:5

10 [1]Lit., *smooth things* [a]Is. 5:20; Jer. 11:21; Amos 2:12; 7:13 [b]1 Kin. 22:8, 13; Jer. 6:14; 23:17, 26; Ezek. 13:7; Rom. 16:18; 2 Tim. 4:3, 4

11 [1]Lit., *Cause to cease from our presence* the . . .

12 [a]Is. 5:24; 7:9; 8:6 [b]Is. 3:14, 15; 5:7; 59:13

13 [a]Is. 58:12; 1 Kin. 20:30; Ps. 62:4

14 [1]Lit., *Crushed, it will not be spared* [2]Lit., *snatch up* [a]Ps. 2:9; Jer. 19:10, 11

15 [1]YHWH, usually rendered LORD [2]Lit., *returning* [a]Is. 7:4; Ps. 116:7 [b]Is. 28:12 [c]Is. 32:17

16 [a]Is. 2:7; 31:1, 3

17 [1]Lit., *pole* [a]Lev. 26:36; Deut. 28:25; 32:30; Josh. 23:10; Prov. 28:1 [b]Is. 6:13; 27:11

18 [1]Lit., *waits* [2]Lit., *is on high* [3]Lit., *wait* [a]Is. 42:14, 16; 48:9; Jon. 3:4, 10; 2 Pet. 3:9, 15 [b]Is. 2:11, 17; 33:5 [c]Is. 5:16; 28:17; 61:8 [d]Is. 8:17; 25:9; 26:8; 33:2

19 [1]O people in Zion, [a]inhabitant in Jerusalem, you will
[b]weep no longer. He will surely be gracious to you at the sound
of your cry; when He hears it, He will [c]answer you.
20 Although the Lord has given you [a]bread of privation
and water of oppression, *He,* your Teacher will no longer [b]hide
Himself, but your eyes will behold your Teacher.
21 And your ears will hear a word behind you, [1]"This is
the [a]way, walk in it," whenever you [b]turn to the right or to the
left.
22 And you will defile your graven [a]images, overlaid with
silver, and your molten [a]images plated with gold. You will
scatter them as an impure thing; *and* say to [1]them, "Be gone!"
23 Then He will give *you* rain for [1]the seed which you will
sow in the ground, and bread *from* the yield of the ground, and
it will be [2]rich and [3]plenteous; on that day [a]your livestock will
graze in a roomy pasture.
24 Also the oxen and the donkeys which work the ground
will eat salted fodder, which [1]has been [a]winnowed with shovel
and fork.
25 And on every lofty mountain and on [a]every high hill
there will be [1]streams running with water on the day of the
great slaughter, when the towers fall.
26 And [a]the light of the moon will be as the light of the
sun, and the light of the sun will be seven times *brighter,* like
the light of seven days, on that day that [b]the LORD binds up the
[c]fracture of His people and [d]heals the bruise [1]He has inflicted.

27 Behold, [a]the name of the LORD comes from a [1]remote
place;
Burning is His anger, and [2]dense is *His* [3]smoke;
His lips are filled with [b]indignation,
And His tongue is like a [c]consuming fire;
28 And His [a]breath is like an overflowing torrent,
Which [b]reaches to the neck,
To [c]shake the nations back and forth in a [1]sieve,
And to *put* in the jaws of the peoples [d]the bridle which
[2]leads to ruin.
29 You will have [1]songs as in the night when you keep the
festival;
And gladness of heart as when one marches to *the
sound of* the flute,
To go to the mountain of the LORD, to the Rock of
Israel.
30 And the LORD will cause [1]His voice of authority to be
heard.
And the [2]descending of His arm to be seen,
And *in* the flame of a consuming fire,
In cloudburst, downpour, and hailstones.
31 For [a]at the voice of the LORD Assyria will be terrified,
When He strikes with the [b]rod.
32 And every [1]blow of the [2a]rod of punishment,
Which the LORD will lay on him,
Will be with *the music of* [b]tambourines and lyres;
And in battles, [c]brandishing weapons, He will fight
them.
33 For [1]Topheth has long been ready,
Indeed, it has been prepared for the king.

19 [1]M.T. reads: *A people will inhabit Zion, Jerusalem.* [a]Is. 65:9; Ezek. 37:25, 28 [b]Is. 25:8; 60:20; 61:1-3 [c]Is. 58:9; 65:24; Ps. 50:15; Matt. 7:7-11

20 [a]1 Kin. 22:27; Ps. 80:5 [b]Ps. 74:9; Amos 8:11

21 [1]Lit., *saying, This* [a]Is. 35:8, 9; 42:16; Ps. 25:8, 9; Prov. 3:6 [b]Is. 29:24

22 [1]Lit., *it "Go out"* [a]Is. 46:6; Ex. 32:2, 4; Judg. 17:3, 4

23 [1]Lit., *your* [2]Lit., *fatness* [3]Lit., *fat* [a]Is. 32:20; Ps. 144:13; Hos. 4:16

24 [1]Lit., *one winnows* [a]Matt. 3:12; Luke 3:17

25 [1]Lit., *canals, streams of water* [a]Is. 35:6, 7; 41:18; 43:19, 20

26 [1]Lit., *of His blow* [a]Is. 24:23; 60:19, 20; Rev. 21:23; 22:5 [b]Is. 61:1 [c]Is. 13:14; 1:6 [d]Is. 33:24; Deut. 32:39; Job 5:18; Jer. 33:6; Hos. 6:1, 2

27 [1]Lit., *distance* [2]Lit., *heaviness* [3]Lit., *uplifting* [a]Is. 59:19 [b]Is. 10:5; 13:5; 66:14 [c]Is. 66:15

28 [1]Lit., *sifting of the worthless* [2]Lit., *misleads* [a]Is. 30:33; 11:4; 2 Thess. 2:8 [b]Is. 8:8 [c]Amos 9:9 [d]Is. 37:29; 2 Kin. 19:28

29 [1]Lit., *the song*

30 [1]Lit., *the majesty of His voice* [2]Lit., *descent*

31 [a]Is. 11:4 [b]Is. 10:26; 11:4

32 [1]Lit., *passing* [2]Lit., *staff of foundation* [a]Is. 10:24 [b]1 Sam. 18:6; Jer. 31:4 [c]Ezek. 32:10

33 [1]I.e., the place of human sacrifice to Molech.

He has made it deep and large,
[2]A pyre of fire with plenty of wood;
The breath of the LORD, like a torrent of [a]brimstone,
sets it afire.

CHAPTER 31

WOE to those who go down to Egypt for help,
And [a]rely on horses,
And trust in chariots because they are many,
And in horsemen because they are very strong,
But they do not [b]look to the [c]Holy One of Israel, nor
seek the LORD!
2 Yet He also is [a]wise and will bring disaster,
And does [b]not retract His words,
But will arise against the house of evildoers,
And against the help of the [c]workers of iniquity.
3 Now the Egyptians are [a]men, and not God,
And their [b]horses are flesh and not spirit;
So the LORD will [c]stretch out His hand,
And he who helps will stumble
And he who is helped will fall,
And all of them will come to an end together.

4 For thus says the LORD to me,
"As the [a]lion or the young lion growls over his prey,
Against which a band of shepherds is called out,
Will not be terrified at their voice, nor disturbed at
their noise,
So will the LORD of hosts come down to wage [b]war on
Mount Zion and on its hill."
5 Like [1]flying [a]birds so the LORD of hosts will protect
Jerusalem.
He will protect and deliver *it;*
He will pass over and rescue *it.*
6 [a]Return to Him from whom [1]you have deeply de-
fected, O sons of Israel.
7 For in that day every man will [a]cast away his silver idols
and his gold idols, which your hands have made as a sin.
8 And the [a]Assyrian will fall by a sword not of man,
And a sword not of man will devour him.
So he will [1b]not escape the sword,
And his young men will become [c]forced laborers.
9 "And his [a]rock will pass away because of panic,
And his princes will be terrified at the [b]standard,"
Declares the LORD, whose fire is in Zion and whose
furnace is in Jerusalem.

CHAPTER 32

BEHOLD, a [a]king will reign righteously,
And princes will rule justly.
2 And each will be like a [a]refuge from the wind,
And a shelter from the storm,
Like [1b]streams of water in a dry country,
Like the [a]shade of a [2]huge rock in a [3]parched land.

33 [2]Lit., *its pile*
[a]Is. 34:9; Gen. 19:24

1 [a]Is. 2:7; 30:16; Deut. 17:16; Ps. 20:7; 33:17 [b]Is. 9:13; Dan. 9:13; Amos 5:4-8 [c]Is. 10:17; 43:15; Hos. 11:9; Hab. 1:12; 3:3

2 [a]Is. 28:29; Rom. 16:27 [b]Num. 23:19; Jer. 44:29 [c]Is. 22:14; 32:6

3 [a]Ezek. 28:9; 2 Thess. 2:4 [b]Is. 36:9 [c]Is. 9:17; Jer. 15:6; Ezek. 20:33, 34

4 [a]Num. 24:9; Hos. 11:10; Amos 3:8 [b]Is. 42:13; Zech. 12:8

5 [1]Or, *hovering*
[a]Deut. 32:11; Ps. 91:4

6 [1]Heb., *they*
[a]Is. 44:22; 55:7; Jer. 3:10, 14, 22; Ezek. 18:31, 32

7 [a]Is. 2:20; 30:22

8 [1]Lit., *flee*
[a]Is. 10:12; 14:25; 30:31-33; 37:7, 36-38 [b]Is. 21:15 [c]Is. 14:2; Gen. 49:15

9 [a]Deut. 32:31, 37 [b]Is. 5:26; 13:2; 18:3

1 [a]Is. 9:6, 7; 11:4, 5; Ps. 72:1-4; Jer. 23:5; 33:15; Ezek. 37:24; Zech. 9:9

2 [1]Lit., *canals* [2]Lit., *heavy* [3]Lit., *exhausted*
[a]Is. 4:6; 25:4 [b]Is. 35:6; 41:18; 43:19, 20

3 Then the eyes of those who see will not be [1]blinded,
And ears of those who hear will listen.
4 And the [1]mind of the [a]hasty will discern the [2]truth,
And the tongue of the stammerers will hasten to speak clearly.
5 No longer will the [a]fool be called noble,
Or the rogue be spoken of *as* generous.
6 For a fool speaks nonsense,
And his heart [1a]inclines toward wickedness,
To practice [b]ungodliness and to speak error against the LORD,
To [2c]keep the hungry person unsatisfied
And to [3]withhold drink from the thirsty.
7 As for a rogue, his weapons are evil;
He [a]devises wicked schemes,
To destroy *the* afflicted with [1]slander,
[b]Even though *the* needy one speaks [2]what is right.
8 But the noble man devises noble plans;
And by noble plans he stands.

9 Rise up you [a]women who are at ease,
And hear my voice;
Give ear to my word
You complacent daughters.
10 Within a year and *a few* days,
You will be troubled O complacent daughters;
[a]For the vintage is ended,
And the *fruit* gathering will not come.
11 Tremble, you *women* who are at ease;
[a]Be troubled, you complacent *daughters;*
Strip, undress, and put on *sackcloth* on *your* waist,
12 Beat your breasts for the pleasant fields, for the fruitful vine,
13 [a]For the land of my people *in which* thorns *and* briars shall come up;
Yea, for all the joyful houses, *and for* the [b]jubilant city.
14 Because [a]the palace has been abandoned, the [1]populated [b]city forsaken.
[2]Hill and watch-tower have become [c]caves forever,
A delight for wild donkeys, a pasture for flocks;
15 Until the [a]Spirit is poured out upon us from on high,
And the wilderness becomes a [b]fertile field
And the fertile field is considered as a forest.
16 Then [a]justice will dwell in the wilderness,
And righteousness will abide in the fertile field.
17 And the [a]work of righteousness will be peace,
And the service of righteousness, quietness and [1]confidence forever.
18 Then my people will live in a [a]peaceful habitation,
And in secure dwellings and in undisturbed [b]resting places;
19 And it will hail when the forest comes down.
And [a]the city will be utterly laid low.
20 How [a]blessed will you be, you who sow beside all waters,
Who [1]let out freely the ox and the donkey.

3 [1]Or, *turned away*

4 [1]Lit., *heart* [2]Lit., *knowledge* [a]Is. 29:24

5 [a]1 Sam. 25:25

6 [1]Or, *does* [2]Lit., *make empty the hungry soul* [3]Lit., *he causes to lack* [a]Is. 59:7, 13; Prov. 19:3; 24:7-9 [b]Is. 9:17; 10:6 [c]Is. 3:15; 10:2

7 [1]Lit., *words of falsehood* [2]Lit., *justly* [a]Jer. 5:26-28; Mic. 7:3 [b]Is. 5:23

9 [a]Is. 47:8; Zeph. 2:15

10 [a]Is. 5:5, 6; 7:23; 24:7

11 [a]Is. 22:12

13 [a]Is. 5:6, 10, 17; 27:10 [b]Is. 22:2; 23:9

14 [1]Lit., *multitude of* [2]Or, *Ophel* [a]Is. 13:22; 25:2; 34:13 [b]Is. 6:11; 22:2; 24:10, 12 [c]Is. 13:21; 34:13

15 [a]Is. 11:2; 44:3; 59:21; Ezek. 39:29; Joel 2:28 [b]Is. 29:17; 35:1, 2; Ps. 107:35

16 [a]Is. 33:5

17 [1]Or, *security* [a]Is. 2:4; Ps. 72:2, 3; 85:8; 119:165; Rom. 14:17; James 3:18

18 [a]Is. 26:3, 12 [b]Is. 11:10; 14:3; 30:15; Hos. 2:18-23; Zech. 2:5; 3:10

19 [a]Is. 24:10, 12; 26:5; 27:10; 29:4

20 [1]Lit., *send out the foot of the ox* [a]Is. 30:23, 24; Eccles. 11:1

CHAPTER 33

WOE [a]to you, O destroyer,
While you were not destroyed;
And he [b]who is treacherous, while *others* did not deal treacherously with him.
As soon as you shall finish destroying, [c]you shall be destroyed;
As soon as you shall cease to deal treacherously, *others* shall [d]deal treacherously with you.
2 O LORD, [a]be gracious to us; we have [b]waited for Thee.
Be Thou [1]their [2c]strength every morning,
Our salvation also in the [d]time of distress.
3 At the sound of the tumult peoples flee;
At the [a]lifting up of Thyself nations disperse.
4 And your spoil is gathered *as* the caterpillar gathers;
As locusts rushing about, men rush about on it.
5 The LORD is [a]exalted, for He dwells on high;
He has [b]filled Zion with justice and righteousness.
6 And He shall be the [1a]stability of your times,
A [b]wealth of salvation, wisdom, and [c]knowledge;
The [d]fear of the LORD is his treasure.
7 Behold, their brave men cry in [1]the streets,
The [2a]ambassadors of peace weep bitterly.
8 The highways are desolate, the [1a]traveler has ceased,
He has [b]broken the covenant, he has despised the cities,
He has no regard for man.
9 [a]The land mourns and pines away,
[b]Lebanon is shamed and withers;
[c]Sharon is like a desert plain,
And Bashan and Carmel [1]lose *their foliage.*
10 "Now [a]I will arise," says the LORD,
Now I will be exalted, now I will be lifted up.
11 "You have [a]conceived [1]chaff, you will give birth to stubble;
[2]My [b]breath will consume you like a fire.
12 "And the peoples will be burned to lime,
[a]Like cut thorns which are burned in the fire.

13 "You who are far away, [a]hear what I have done;
And you who are near, [1]acknowledge My might."
14 [a]Sinners in Zion are terrified;
[b]Trembling has seized the godless.
"Who among us can live with [c]the consuming fire?
"Who among us can live with [1]continual [d]burning?"
15 He who [a]walks righteously, and speaks with sincerity,
He who rejects [1]unjust gain,
And shakes his hands so that they hold no bribe;
He who stops his ears from hearing about bloodshed,
And [b]shuts his eyes from looking upon evil;
16 He will dwell on the heights;
His refuge will be the [1]impregnable rock;
[a]His bread will be given *him;*
His water will be sure.

1 [a]Is. 10:6; 21:2 [b]Is. 24:16; 48:8 [c]Is. 10:12; 14:25; 13:8; Hab. 2:8 [d]Jer. 25:12-14; Matt. 7:2

2 [1]Some versions read, *our* [2]Lit., *arm* [a]Is. 30:18, 19 [b]Is. 25:9 [c]Is. 40:10; 51:5; 59:16 [d]Is. 37:3

3 [a]Is. 10:33; 17:13; 59:16-18; Jer. 25:30, 31

5 [a]Ps. 97:9 [b]Is. 1:26; 28:6; 32:16

6 [1]Or, *faithfulness* [a]Is. 33:20 [b]Is. 45:17; 51:6 [c]Is. 11:9 [d]Is. 11:3; 2 Kin. 18:7; Ps. 112:1-3; Matt. 6:33

7 [1]Lit., *the outside* [2]Lit., *messengers* [a]2 Kin. 18:18, 37

8 [1]Lit., *He who passes along the way* [a]Is. 35:8 [b]Is. 24:5

9 [1]Lit., *shake off* [a]Is. 3:26; 24:4; 29:2 [b]Is. 2:13; 10:34 [c]Is. 35:2; 65:10

10 [a]Is. 2:19, 21; Ps. 12:5

11 [1]Lit., *dry grass* [2]So one ancient version; M.T. reads: *Your breath will* [a]Is. 26:18; 59:4; Ps. 7:14; James 1:15 [b]Is. 1:31

12 [a]Is. 10:17; 27:4; 2 Sam. 23:6, 7

13 [1]Lit., *know* [a]Is. 49:1; Ps. 48:10

14 [1]Lit., *everlasting* [a]Is. 1:28 [b]Is. 32:11 [c]Is. 30:27, 30; Heb. 12:29 [d]Is. 9:18, 19; 10:16; 47:14

15 [1]Lit., *gain of extortioners* [a]Is. 58:6-11; Ps. 15:2; 24:4 [b]Ps. 119:37

16 [1]Lit., *stronghold of rock* [a]Is. 49:10

17 Your eyes will see [a]the king in his beauty;
They will behold [b]a far-distant land.
18 Your heart will meditate on terror;
"Where is [a]he who counts?
Where is he who weighs?
Where is he who counts the towers?"
19 You will no longer see a fierce people,
A people of [1a]unintelligible speech [2]which no one comprehends,
Of a stammering tongue [3]which no one understands.
20 [a]Look upon Zion, the city of our appointed feasts;
Your eyes shall see Jerusalem an [b]undisturbed habitation,
[c]A tent which shall not be folded,
Its stakes shall never be pulled up
Nor any of its cords be torn apart.
21 But there the majestic *One*, the LORD, shall be for us;
A place of [a]rivers and wide canals,
On which no boat with oars shall go,
And on which no mighty ship shall pass—
22 For the LORD is our [a]judge,
The LORD is [b]our lawgiver,
The LORD is [c]our king;
[d]He will save us—
23 Your tackle hangs slack;
It cannot hold the base of its mast firmly,
Nor spread out the sail.
Then the [a]prey of an abundant spoil will be divided;
[b]The lame will take the plunder.
24 And no resident will say, "I am sick";
The people who dwell [1]there will be [a]forgiven *their* iniquity.

CHAPTER 34

DRAW near, [a]O nations, to hear; and listen, O peoples!
[b]Let the earth and [1]all it contains hear, and the world and all that springs from it.
2 For the LORD's indignation is against all the nations,
And *His* wrath against all their armies;
He has [1]utterly destroyed them,
He has given them over to slaughter.
3 So their slain will be thrown out,
And their corpses [1]will give off their stench,
And the mountains will [2]be drenched with their [a]blood.
4 And [a]all the host of heaven will [1]wear away,
And the [b]sky will be rolled up like a scroll;
All their hosts will also wither away
As a leaf withers from the vine,
Or as *one* withers from the fig tree.
5 For My sword is satiated in heaven,
Behold it shall descend for judgment upon Edom,
And upon the people whom I have [a]devoted to destruction.
6 The sword of the LORD is filled with blood,
It is [1]sated with fat, with the blood of lambs and goats,

17 [a]Is. 33:21, 22; 6:5; 24:23 [b]Is. 26:15

18 [a]1 Cor. 1:20

19 [1]Lit., *deepness of lip* [2]Lit., *from hearing* [3]Lit., *there is no understanding* [a]Is. 28:11; Deut. 28:49, 50; Jer. 5:15

20 [a]Ps. 48:12 [b]Is. 32:18; Ps. 46:5; 125:1, 2 [c]Is. 54:2

21 [a]Is. 41:18; 43:19, 20; 48:18; 66:12

22 [a]Is. 2:4; 11:4; 16:5; 51:5 [b]Is. 1:10; 51:4, 7; James 4:12 [c]Is. 33:17; Ps. 89:18; Zech. 9:9 [d]Is. 25:9; 35:4; 49:25, 26; 60:16

23 [a]2 Kin. 7:16 [b]Is. 35:6; 2 Kin. 7:8

24 [1]Lit., *in it* [a]Is. 40:2; 44:22; Jer. 50:20; Mic. 7:18, 19; 1 John 1:7-9

1 [1]Lit., *its fullness* [a]Is. 41:1; 43:9; Ps. 49:1 [b]Is. 1:2; Deut. 32:1

2 [1]Lit., *put under the ban*

3 [1]Lit., *their stench will go up* [2]Lit., *dissolve* [a]Ezek. 14:19; 35:6; 38:22

4 [1]Lit., *rot* [a]Is. 13:13; 51:6; Ezek. 32:7, 8; Joel 2:31; Matt. 24:29; 2 Pet. 3:10 [b]Rev. 6:12-14

5 [a]Is. 24:6; 43:28

6 [1]Lit., *made fat*

With the fat of the kidneys of rams.
For the LORD has a sacrifice in [a]Bozrah,
And a great slaughter in the land of Edom.
7 [a]Wild oxen shall also [1]fall with them,
And [b]young bulls with strong ones;
Thus their land shall be soaked with blood,
And their dust [2]become greasy with fat.
8 For the LORD has a day of [a]vengeance,
A year of recompense for the [1]cause of Zion.
9 And [1]its streams shall be turned into pitch,
And its loose earth into brimstone,
And its land shall become burning pitch.
10 It shall [a]not be quenched night or day;
Its [b]smoke shall go up forever;
From [c]generation to generation it shall be desolate;
[d]None shall pass through it forever and ever.
11 But [1]pelican and hedgehog shall possess it,
And [2]owl and raven shall dwell in it;
And He shall stretch over it the [a]line of [3]desolation
And the [4]plumb line of emptiness.
12 Its nobles—there is [a]no one there
Whom they may proclaim King—
And all its princes shall be nothing.
13 And thorns shall come up in its [a]fortified towers,
Nettles and thistles in its fortified cities;
It shall also be a haunt of [b]jackals
And an abode of ostriches.
14 And the desert [a]creatures shall meet with the [1]wolves,
The [2b]hairy goat also shall cry to its kind;
Yes, the [3]night-monster shall settle there
And shall find herself a resting place.
15 The snake shall make its nest and lay *eggs* there,
And it will hatch *them* and gather *its brood* under its shade;
Yes, the [1]hawks shall be gathered there,
Every one with its kind.

16 Seek from the [a]book of the LORD, and read:
Not one of these will be missing;
None will lack its mate.
For [1b]His mouth has commanded,
And His Spirit has gathered them.
17 And He has cast the [a]lot for them,
And His hand has divided it to them by line.
They shall possess it forever;
From generation to generation they shall dwell in it.

CHAPTER 35

THE [a]wilderness and the desert will be glad,
And the [1b]Arabah will rejoice and blossom;
Like the crocus
2 It will [a]blossom profusely
And [b]rejoice with rejoicing and shout of joy.
The [c]glory of Lebanon will be given to it,
The majesty of Carmel and Sharon.

6 [a]Is. 63:1; Jer. 49:13

7 [1]Lit., *go down* [2]Lit., *made fat*
[a]Num. 23:22; Ps. 22:21 [b]Ps. 68:30; Jer. 50:27

8 [1]Or, *controversy*
[a]Is. 13:6; 35:4; 47:3; 61:2; 63:4

9 [1]I.e., Edom's

10 [a]Is. 1:31; 66:24 [b]Rev. 14:11; 19:3 [c]Is. 34:10-15; 13:20-22; 24:1; Mal. 1:3, 4 [d]Ezek. 29:11

11 [1]Or, *owl;* or, *jackdaw* [2]Or, *great horned owl* [3]Or, *formlessness* [4]Lit., *the stones of void*
[a]Is. 24:10; 2 Kin. 21:13; Lam. 2:8

12 [a]Jer. 27:20; 39:6

13 [a]Is. 13:22; 25:2; 32:13 [b]Ps. 44:19; Jer. 9:11; 10:22

14 [1]Or, *howling creatures* [2]Or, *demon* [3]Heb., *Lilith*
[a]Is. 13:21 [b]Is. 30:8

15 [1]Or, *kites*

16 [1]So DSS; M.T., *My*
[a]Is. 30:8 [b]Is. 1:20; 40:5; 58:14

17 [a]Is. 17:13, 14; Jer. 13:25

1 [1]Or, *desert*
[a]Is. 6:11; 7:21-25; 27:10; 41:18; 55:12, 13 [b]Is. 41:19; 51:3

2 [a]Is. 27:6; 32:15 [b]Is. 35:10; 25:9; 55:12, 13; 66:10, 14 [c]Is. 60:13

They will see the [d]glory of the LORD,
The majesty of our God.
3 [a]Encourage the [1]exhausted, and strengthen the [2]feeble.
4 Say to those with [a]palpitating heart,
"Take courage, fear not.
Behold, your God will come *with* [b]vengeance;
The [c]recompense of God will come,
But He will [d]save you."
5 Then the [a]eyes of the blind will be opened,
And the ears of the deaf will be unstopped.
6 Then the [a]lame will leap like a deer,
And the [b]tongue of the dumb will shout for joy.
For waters will break forth in the [c]wilderness
And streams in the [1]Arabah.
7 And the [1]scorched land will become a pool,
And the thirsty ground [a]springs of water;
In the [b]haunt of jackals, its resting place,
Grass *becomes* reeds and rushes.
8 And [a]a highway will be there, [b]a roadway,
And it will be called "the highway of [c]holiness."
The unclean will not travel on it,
But it *will* be for him who walks *that* way,
And [d]fools will not wander *on it*.
9 No lion will be there,
Nor will any vicious beast go up on it;
[1]These will not be found there.
But [a]the redeemed will walk *there*,
10 And [a]the ransomed of the LORD will return,
And come with joyful shouting to Zion,
With everlasting joy upon their heads.
They will [1]find gladness and joy,
And [b]sorrow and sighing will flee away.

CHAPTER 36

NOW it came about in the fourteenth year of King Hezekiah, Sennacherib king of Assyria came up against all the fortified cities of Judah and seized them.
2 And the [a]king of Assyria sent Rabshakeh from Lachish
to Jerusalem to King Hezekiah with a large army. And he
stood by the conduit of the upper pool on the highway of the
[1]fuller's field.
3 Then Eliakim the son of Hilkiah, who was over the
household, and Shebna the scribe, and Joah the son of Asaph,
the recorder, came out to him.
4 Then [a]Rabshakeh said to them, "Say now to Hezekiah,
'Thus says the great king, the king of Assyria, "What is this
confidence that you [1]have?
5 "I say, 'your counsel and strength for the war are only
[1]empty words.' Now on whom do you rely, that [a]you have
rebelled against me?
6 "Behold, you rely on the [a]staff of this crushed reed, *even*
on Egypt; on which if a man leans, it will go into his [1]hand and
pierce it. [b]So is Pharaoh king of Egypt to all who rely on him.
7 "But if you say to me, 'We trust in the LORD our God,' is
it not He [a]whose high places and whose altars Hezekiah has

2 [d]Is. 25:9

3 [1]Lit., *slack hands* [2]Lit., *tottering knees* [a]Job 4:3, 4; Heb. 12:12

4 [a]Is. 32:4 [b]Is. 1:24; 47:3; 61:2; 63:4 [c]Is. 34:8; 59:18 [d]Is. 33:22; 35:4; Ps. 145:19

5 [a]Is. 29:18; 32:3, 4; 42:7, 16; 50:4; Matt. 11:5; John 9:6, 7

6 [1]Or, *desert* [a]Matt. 15:30; John 5:8, 9; Acts 3:8 [b]Matt. 9:32; Luke 11:14 [c]Is. 35:1; 41:18; 43:19; 49:10; 51:3; John 7:38

7 [1]Or, *mirage* [a]Is. 49:10 [b]Is. 13:22; 34:13

8 [a]Is. 11:16; 19:23; 40:3; 49:11; 62:10 [b]Is. 30:21; 51:10 [c]Is. 4:3; 52:1; Matt. 7:13, 14; 1 Pet. 1:15, 16 [d]Is. 33:8; Jer. 14:8

9 [1]Lit., *It* [a]Is. 51:10; 62:12; 63:4

10 [1]Lit., *overtake* [a]Is. 1:27; 51:11 [b]Is. 25:8; 30:19; 65:19; Rev. 7:17; 21:4

2 [1]I.e., launderer's [a]Is. 36:2-38:8; 2 Kin. 18:17-20:11; 2 Chr. 32:9-24

4 [1]Lit., *trust* [a]2 Kin. 18:19

5 [1]Lit., *words of lips* [a]2 Kin. 18:7

6 [1]Lit., *palm* [a]Ezek. 29:6, 7 [b]Is. 30:3, 5, 7; Ps. 146:3

7 [a]Deut. 12:2-5; 2 Kin. 18:4, 5

taken away, and has said to Judah and to Jerusalem, 'You shall
worship before this altar'?
8 "Now therefore, [1]come make a bargain with my master
the king of Assyria, and I will give you two thousand horses, if
you are able on your part to set riders on them.
9 "How then can you [1]repulse one [2]official of the least of
my master's servants, and [3a]rely on Egypt for chariots and for
horsemen?
10 "And have I now come up [1]without the LORD's approval
against this land to destroy it? [a]The LORD said to me, 'Go up
against this land, and destroy it.' " ' "
11 Then Eliakim and Shebna and Joah said to Rabshakeh,
"Speak now to your servants in [a]Aramaic, for we [1]understand
it; and do not speak with us in [2]Judean, in the hearing of the
people who are on the wall."
12 But Rabshakeh said, "Has my master sent me only to
your master and to you to speak these words, *and* not to the
men who sit on the wall, *doomed* to eat their own dung and
drink their own urine with you?"
13 Then Rabshakeh stood and [a]cried with a loud voice in
Judean, and said, "Hear the words of the great king, the king
of Assyria.
14 "Thus says the king, 'Do not let Hezekiah [a]deceive you,
for he will not be able to deliver you;
15 nor let Hezekiah make you [a]trust in the LORD, saying,
"The LORD will surely deliver us, this city shall not be given
into the hand of the king of Assyria."
16 'Do not listen to Hezekiah,' for thus says the king of
Assyria, '[1]Make your peace with me and come out to me, and
eat each of his [a]vine and each of his fig tree and drink each of
the [b]waters of his own cistern,
17 until I come and take you away to a land like your own
land, a land of grain and new wine, a land of bread and
vineyards.
18 '*Beware* lest Hezekiah misleads you, saying, "[a]The
LORD will deliver us." Has anyone of the gods of the nations
delivered his land from the hand of the king of Assyria?
19 'Where are the gods of [a]Hamath and Arpad? Where are
the gods of [a]Sepharvaim? And when have they [b]delivered Samaria from my hand?
20 'Who among all the [a]gods of these lands have delivered
their land from my hand, that the [b]LORD should deliver Jerusalem from my hand?' "
21 But they were silent and answered him not a word; for
the king's commandment was, "Do not answer him."
22 Then [a]Eliakim the son of Hilkiah, who was over the
household, and [b]Shebna the scribe and Joah the son of Asaph,
the recorder, came to Hezekiah with their clothes torn and
told him the words of Rabshakeh.

CHAPTER 37

AND [a]when King Hezekiah heard *it,* he tore his clothes,
covered himself with sackcloth and entered the house of the
LORD.
2 Then he sent [a]Eliakim who was over the household

8 [1]Lit., *please exchange pledges*
9 [1]Lit., *turn away the face of* [2]Or, *governor* [3]Lit., *rely on for yourself* [a]Is. 20:5; 30:2-5, 7; 31:3
10 [1]Lit., *without the LORD* [a]1 Kin. 13:18; 22:6, 12
11 [1]Lit., *hear* [2]I.e., Hebrew [a]Ezra 4:7; Dan. 2:4
13 [a]2 Chr. 32:18
14 [a]Is. 37:10
15 [a]Is. 36:18, 20; 37:10, 11
16 [1]Lit., *Make with me a blessing* [a]1 Kin. 4:25; Mic. 4:4; Zech. 3:10 [b]Prov. 5:15
18 [a]Is. 36:15
19 [a]Is. 10:9-11; 37:11-13; Jer. 49:23 [b]2 Kin. 17:6
20 [a]1 Kin. 20:23, 28 [b]Is. 36:15
22 [a]Is. 36:3; 22:20 [b]Is. 22:15
1 [a]Is. 37:1-38; 2 Kin. 19:1-37
2 [a]Is. 22:20

2 [b]Is. 22:15 [c]Is. 1:1; 20:2

3 [1]Lit., *give birth* [a]Is. 22:5; 26:16; 33:2 [b]Is. 26:17, 18; 66:9; Hos. 13:13

4 [a]Is. 36:15, 18, 20 [b]Is. 37:31, 32; 1:9; 10:20-22; 46:3

6 [a]Is. 7:4; 35:4

7 [a]Is. 37:9 [b]Is. 37:37, 38

8 [1]Lit., *he* [a]Num. 33:20; Josh. 10:29 [b]Josh. 10:31, 32

9 [1]Or, *Ethiopia* [a]Is. 37:7 [b]Is. 18:1; 20:5

10 [1]Lit., *Judah, saying* [a]Is. 36:15

11 [1]Lit., *delivered* [a]Is. 10:9-11; 36:18-20

12 [1]Lit., *the* [a]2 Kin. 17:6; 18:11 [b]Gen. 11:31; 12:1-4; Acts 7:2

14 [1]Lit., *letters* [2]Lit., *Hezekiah spread*

16 [a]Ex. 25:22; 1 Sam. 4:4; Ps. 80:1; 99:1 [b]Deut. 10:17; Ps. 86:10; 136:2, 3 [c]Is. 42:5; 45:12; Jer. 10:12

17 [a]2 Chr. 6:40; Ps. 17:6; Dan. 9:18 [b]Ps. 74:22 [c]Is. 37:4

19 [a]Is. 2:8; 17:8; 41:24, 29 [b]Is. 26:14

20 [1]So DSS and 2 Kin. 19:19; M.T. omits *God* [a]Is. 25:9; 33:22; 35:4 [b]Is. 37:16; 1 Kin. 18:36, 37; Ps. 46:10; Ezek. 36:23

with [b]Shebna the scribe and the elders of the priests, covered with sackcloth, to [c]Isaiah the prophet, the son of Amoz.

3 And they said to him, "Thus says Hezekiah, 'This day is a [a]day of distress, rebuke, and rejection; for [b]children have come to birth, and there is no strength to [1]deliver.

4 'Perhaps the LORD your God will hear the words of Rabshakeh, whom his master the king of Assyria has sent to [a]reproach the living God, and will rebuke the words which the LORD your God has heard. Therefore, offer a prayer for [b]the remnant that is left.' "

5 So the servants of King Hezekiah came to Isaiah.

6 And Isaiah said to them, "Thus you shall say to your master, 'Thus says the LORD, "[a]Do not be afraid because of the words that you have heard, with which the servants of the king of Assyria have blasphemed Me.

7 "Behold, I will put a spirit in him so that he shall [a]hear a rumor and [b]return to his own land. And I will make him fall by the sword in his own land." ' "

8 Then Rabshakeh returned and found the king of Assyria fighting against [a]Libnah, for he had heard that [1]the king had left [b]Lachish.

9 When he [a]heard *them* say concerning Tirhakah king of [1b]Cush, "He has come out to fight against you," and when he heard *it* he sent messengers to Hezekiah, saying,

10 "Thus you shall say to Hezekiah king of [1]Judah. '[a]Do not let your God in whom you trust deceive you, saying, "Jerusalem shall not be given into the hand of the king of Assyria."

11 '[a]Behold, you have heard what the kings of Assyria have done to all the lands, destroying them completely. So will you be [1]spared?

12 'Did the gods of [1]those nations which my fathers have destroyed deliver them, *even* [a]Gozan and [b]Haran and Rezeph and the sons of Eden who *were* in Telassar?

13 'Where is the king of Hamath, the king of Arpad, the king of the city of Sepharvaim, *and of* Hena and Ivvah?' "

14 Then Hezekiah took the [1]letter from the hand of the messengers and read it, and he went up to the house of the LORD and [2]spread it out before the LORD.

15 And Hezekiah prayed to the LORD saying,

16 "O LORD of hosts the God of Israel, [a]who art enthroned *above* the cherubim, Thou art the [b]God, Thou alone, of all the kingdoms of the earth. [c]Thou hast made heaven and earth.

17 "[a]Incline Thine ear, O LORD, and hear; open Thine eyes, O LORD, and see; and [b]listen to all the words of Sennacherib, who sent to [c]reproach the living God.

18 "Truly, O LORD, the kings of Assyria have devastated all the countries and their lands,

19 and have cast their gods into the fire, for they were not gods but the [a]work of men's hands, wood and stone. So they have [b]destroyed them.

20 "And now, O LORD our God, [a]deliver us from his hand that [b]all the kingdoms of the earth may know that Thou alone, LORD, [1]art God."

21 Then Isaiah the son of Amoz sent word to Hezekiah, saying, "Thus says the LORD, the God of Israel, 'Because you have prayed to Me about Sennacherib king of Assyria,

22 this is the word that the LORD has spoken against him:
"She has despised you and mocked you,
The [a]virgin [b]daughter of Zion;
She has [c]shaken *her* head behind you,
The daughter of Jerusalem!
23 "Whom have you reproached and blasphemed?
And against whom have you raised *your* voice,
And [1]haughtily [a]lifted up your eyes?
Against the [b]Holy One of Israel!
24 Through your servants you have reproached the Lord,
And you have said, 'With my many chariots I came up
to the heights of the mountains,
To the remotest parts of [a]Lebanon;
And I cut down its tall [b]cedars *and* its choice cypresses.
And I will go to its [1]highest peak, its thickest forest.
25 'I dug *wells* and drank waters,
And [a]with the sole of my feet I dried up
All the rivers of [1]Egypt.'
26 "[a]Have you not heard?
Long ago I did it,
From ancient times I [b]planned it.
Now I have brought it to pass,
That [c]you should turn fortified cities into [d]ruinous
heaps.
27 "Therefore their inhabitants were short of strength,
They were dismayed and put to shame;
They were *as* the [a]vegetation of the field and *as* the
green herb,
As [b]grass on the housetops [1]is scorched before it is
grown up.
28 "But I [a]know your sitting down,
And your going out and your coming in,
And your raging against Me.
29 "Because of your raging against Me,
And because your [1a]arrogance has come up to my ears,
Therefore I will put My [b]hook in your nose,
And My [c]bridle in your lips,
And I will turn you back [d]by the way which you came.
30 "Then this shall be the sign for you: [1]you shall eat this
year what [a]grows of itself, in the second year what springs from
the same, and in the third year sow, reap, plant vineyards, and
eat their fruit.
31 "And the [a]surviving [b]remnant of the house of Judah
shall again [c]take root downward and bear fruit upward.
32 "For out of Jerusalem shall go forth a [a]remnant, and out
of Mount Zion [1]survivors. The [b]zeal of the LORD of hosts shall
perform this." ' "
33 "Therefore, thus says the LORD concerning the king of
Assyria, 'He shall not come to this city, or shoot an arrow
there; neither shall he come before it with a shield, nor throw
up a [a]mound against it.
34 '[a]By the way that he came, by the same he shall return,
and he shall not come to this city,' declares the LORD.
35 'For I will [a]defend this city to save it [b]for My own sake
and for My servant David's sake.' "

22 [a]Jer. 14:17; Lam. 2:13 [b]Ps. 9:14; Zeph. 3:14; Zech. 2:10 [c]Job 16:4

23 [1]Lit., *on high* [a]Is. 2:11; 5:15, 21 [b]Ezek. 39:7; Hab. 1:12

24 [1]Lit., *farthest height* [a]Is. 10:33, 34 [b]Is. 14:8

25 [1]Or, *the besieged place* [a]Deut. 11:10; 1 Kin. 20:10

26 [a]Is. 40:21, 28 [b]Acts 2:23; 4:27, 28; 1 Pet. 2:8 [c]Is. 10:6 [d]Is. 17:1; 25:2

27 [1]So DSS and 2 Kin. 19:26; M.T. as *a plowed field* [a]Is. 40:7 [b]Ps. 129:6

28 [a]Ps. 139:1

29 [1]Lit., *complacency* [a]Is. 10:12 [b]Ezek. 29:4; 38:4 [c]Is. 30:28 [d]Is. 37:34

30 [1]*eating* [a]Lev. 25:5, 11

31 [a]Is. 4:2; 10:20 [b]Is. 37:4 [c]Is. 27:6

32 [1]Lit., *those who escape* [a]Is. 37:4 [b]Is. 9:7; 59:17; 2 Kin. 19:31; Joel 2:18; Zech. 1:14

33 [a]Jer. 6:6; 32:24

34 [a]Is. 37:29

35 [a]Is. 31:5; 38:6; 2 Kin. 20:6 [b]Is. 43:25; 48:9, 11

36 Then the [a]angel of the LORD went out, and struck
185,000 in the camp of the Assyrians; and when [1]men arose
early in the morning, behold, all of them were dead bodies.
37 So Sennacherib, king of Assyria, departed and [1]re-
turned *home*, and lived at [a]Nineveh.
38 And it came about as he was worshiping in the house of
Nisroch his god, that Adrammelech and Sharezer his sons
killed him with the sword; and they escaped into the land of
[a]Ararat. And [b]Esarhaddon his son became king in his place.

Chapter 38

[a]IN those days Hezekiah became [1]mortally ill. And [b]Isaiah the
prophet the son of Amoz came to him and said to him, "Thus
says the LORD, '[c]Set your house in order, for you shall die and
not live.' "
2 Then Hezekiah turned his face to the wall, and prayed
to the LORD,
3 and said, "[a]Remember now, O LORD, I beseech Thee,
how I have [b]walked before Thee in truth and with a [c]whole
heart, and [d]have done what is good in Thy sight." And Hezekiah [e]wept [1]bitterly.
4 Then the word of the LORD came to Isaiah, saying,
5 "Go and say to Hezekiah, 'Thus says the LORD, the God
of your father David, "I have heard your prayer, I have seen
your tears; behold, I will add [a]fifteen years to your [1]life.
6 "And I will [a]deliver you and this city from the hand of
the king of Assyria; and I will defend this city." '
7 "And this shall be the [a]sign to you from the LORD, that
the LORD will do this thing that He has spoken:
8 "Behold, I will [a]cause the shadow on the stairway, which
has gone down with the sun on the stairway of Ahaz, to go
back ten steps." So the [b]sun's *shadow* went back ten steps on
the stairway on which it had gone down.
9 A writing of Hezekiah king of Judah, after his illness
and [1]recovery:

10 I said, "[a]In the middle of my [1]life
I am to enter the [b]gates of Sheol;
I am to be [c]deprived of the rest of my years."
11 I said, "I shall not see the LORD,
The LORD [a]in the land of the living;
I shall look on man no more among the inhabitants of
the world.
12 "Like a shepherd's [a]tent my dwelling is pulled up and
removed from me;
As a [b]weaver I [c]rolled up my life.
He [d]cuts me off from the loom;
From [e]day until night Thou dost make an end of me.
13 "I composed *my soul* until morning.
[a]Like a lion—so He [b]breaks all my bones,
From [c]day until night Thou dost make an end of me.
14 "[a]Like a swallow, *like* a crane, so I twitter;
I [b]moan like a dove;
My [c]eyes look wistfully to the heights;
O Lord, I am oppressed, be my [d]security.

36 [1]Lit., *they*
[a]Is. 10:12, 33, 34; 2 Kin. 19:35

37 [1]Lit., *went and returned*
[a]Gen. 10:11; Jon. 1:2; 3:3; 4:11; Zeph. 2:13

38 [a]Gen. 8:4; Jer. 51:27 [b]Ezra 4:2

1 [1]Lit., *sick to the point of death*
[a]Is. 38:1-8; 2 Kin. 20:1-6, 9-11; 2 Chr. 32:24 [b]Is. 1:1; 37:2 [c]2 Sam. 17:23

3 [1]Lit., *great weeping*
[a]Neh. 13:14 [b]2 Kin. 18:5, 6; Ps. 26:3 [c]1 Chr. 28:9; 29:19 [d]Deut. 6:18 [e]Ps. 6:6-8

5 [1]Lit., *days*
[a]2 Kin. 18:2, 13

6 [a]Is. 31:5; 37:35

7 [a]Is. 7:11, 14; 37:30; Judg. 6:17, 21, 36-40

8 [a]2 Kin. 20:9-11 [b]Josh. 10:12-14

9 [1]Lit., *he lived after his illness*

10 [1]Lit., *days*
[a]Ps. 102:24 [b]Ps. 107:18 [c]Job 17:11, 15; 2 Cor. 1:9

11 [a]Ps. 27:13; 116:9

12 [a]2 Cor. 5:1, 4; 2 Pet. 1:13, 14 [b]Job 7:6 [c]Heb. 1:12 [d]Job 6:9 [e]Job 4:20; Ps. 73:14

13 [a]Job 10:16; 16:12 [b]Ps. 51:8; Dan. 6:24 [c]Ps. 32:4

14 [a]Job 30:29; Ps. 102:6 [b]Is. 59:11; Ezek. 7:16; Nah. 2:7 [c]Ps. 119:123 [d]Job 17:3; Ps. 119:122

15 "[a]What shall I say?
[1]For He has spoken to me, and He Himself has done it;
I shall [b]wander about all my years because of the [c]bitterness of my soul.
16 "O Lord, [a]by *these* things *men* live;
And in all these is the life of my spirit;
[1][b]O restore me to health, and [c]let me live!
17 "Lo, for *my own* welfare I had great bitterness;
It is Thou who hast [1][a]kept my soul from the pit of [2]nothingness,
For Thou hast [b]cast all my sins behind Thy back.
18 "For Sheol cannot thank Thee,
Death cannot praise Thee;
Those who go down [a]to the pit cannot hope for Thy faithfulness.
19 "It is the [a]living who give thanks to Thee, as I do today;
A [b]father tells his sons about Thy faithfulness.
20 "The LORD will surely save me;
So we will [a]play my songs on stringed instruments
[b]All *the* days of our life [c]at the house of the LORD."
21 Now Isaiah had said, "Let them take a cake of figs, and
apply it to the boil, that he may recover."
22 Then Hezekiah had said, "What is the sign that I shall
go up to the house of the LORD?"

CHAPTER 39

[a]AT that time Merodach-baladan son of Baladan, king of
Babylon, sent letters and a present to Hezekiah, for he heard
that he had been sick and had recovered.
2 And Hezekiah [1]was [a]pleased, and showed them all his
treasure house, the [b]silver and the gold and the spices and the
precious oil and his whole armory and all that was found in his
treasuries. There was nothing in his house, nor in all his dominion, that Hezekiah did not show them.
3 Then Isaiah the [a]prophet came to King Hezekiah and
said to him, "What did these men say, and from where have
they come to you?" And Hezekiah said, "They have come to
me from a far [b]country, from Babylon."
4 And he said, "What have they seen in your house?" So
Hezekiah [1]answered, "They have seen all that is in my house;
there is nothing among my treasuries that I have not shown
them."
5 Then Isaiah said to Hezekiah, "Hear the [a]word of the
LORD of hosts:
6 'Behold, the days are coming when [a]all that is in your
house, and all that your fathers have laid up in store to this day
shall be carried to Babylon; nothing shall be left,' says the
LORD.
7 'And *some* of your sons who shall issue from you, whom
you shall beget, shall be taken away; and they shall become
officials in the palace of the king of Babylon.' "
8 [a]Then Hezekiah said to Isaiah, "The word of the LORD
which you have spoken is good." For he [1]thought, "For there
will be peace and truth [b]in my days."

15 [1]Targum and DSS read, *And what shall I say for He . . .* [a]Ps. 39:9 [b]1 Kin. 21:27 [c]Is. 38:17; Job 7:11; 10:1

16 [1]Lit., *Thou wilt* [a]Ps. 119:71, 75 [b]Ps. 39:13 [c]Ps. 119:25

17 [1]So some versions; Heb., *loved* [2]Or, *destruction* [a]Ps. 30:3; 86:13; Jon. 2:6 [b]Is. 43:25; Jer. 31:34; Mic. 7:19

18 [a]Num. 16:33; Ps. 28:1

19 [a]Ps. 118:17; 119:175 [b]Deut. 6:7; 11:19; Ps. 78:5-7

20 [a]Ps. 33:1-3; 68:24-26 [b]Ps. 104:33; 116:2; 146:2 [c]Ps. 116:17-19

1 [a]Is. 39:1-8; 2 Kin. 20:12-19; 2 Chr. 32:31

2 [1]Lit., *rejoiced over them* [a]2 Chr. 32:25, 31; Job 31:25 [b]2 Kin. 18:15, 16

3 [a]2 Sam. 12:1; 2 Chr. 16:7 [b]Deut. 28:49; Jer. 5:15

4 [1]Lit., *said*

5 [a]1 Sam. 13:13, 14; 15:16

6 [a]2 Kin. 24:13; 25:13-15; Jer. 20:5

8 [1]Lit., *said* [a]2 Chr. 32:26 [b]2 Chr. 34:28

1 [a]Is. 12:1; 49:13; 51:3, 12; 52:9; 61:2; 66:13; Jer. 31:10-14; Zeph. 3:14-17; 2 Cor. 1:4

2 [1]Lit., *to the heart of* [2]Or, *hard service* [3]Or, *penalty of iniquity accepted as paid off* [a]Is. 35:4; Zech. 1:13 [b]Is. 41:11-13; 49:25; 54:15, 17 [c]Is. 33:24; 53:5, 6, 11 [d]Jer. 16:18; Zech. 9:12; Rev. 18:6

3 [1]Or, *of one calling out* [a]Matt. 3:3; Mark 1:3; Luke 3:4-6; John 1:25 [b]Mal. 3:1; 4:5, 6

4 [a]Ezek. 17:24

5 [1]Or, *In order that the . .* [a]Is. 6:3; Hab. 2:14 [b]Is. 52:10; Joel 2:28

6 [1]Another reading is, *I said* [2]Or, *constancy* [a]Job 14:2; Ps. 102:11; 103:15; 1 Pet. 1:24, 25

7 [1]Or, *Because* [a]Ps. 90:5, 6; James 1:10, 11

8 [a]Is. 55:11; 59:21; Matt. 5:18

9 [a]Is. 52:7 [b]Is. 61:1 [c]Is. 25:9; 35:2

10 [1]YHWH, usually rendered LORD [a]Is. 9:6, 7 [b]Is. 59:16, 18 [c]Is. 62:11; Rev. 22:12

11 [a]Jer. 31:10; Ezek. 34:12-14, 23, 31; Mic. 5:4; John 10:11, 14-16

12 [1]DSS reads, *waters of the sea* [2]Or, *half cubit;* i.e., 9 inches [3]Lit., *contained, or comprehended* [a]Is. 48:13; Job 38:8-11; Ps. 102:25, 26; Heb. 1:10-12

13 [1]Or, *measured, marked off* [a]Rom. 11:34; 1 Cor. 2:16 [b]Is. 41:28

14 [a]Job 38:4 [b]Job 21:22; Col. 2:3

CHAPTER 40

"[a]COMFORT, O comfort My people," says your God.
2 "[a]Speak [1]kindly to Jerusalem;
And call out to her, that her [2b]warfare has ended,
That her [3c]iniquity has been removed,
That she has received of the LORD's hand
[d]Double for all her sins."

3 [a]A voice [1]is calling,
"[b]Clear the way for the LORD in the wilderness;
Make smooth in the desert a highway for our God.
4 "Let every valley be [a]lifted up,
And every mountain and hill be made low;
And let the rough ground become a plain,
And the rugged terrain a broad valley;
5 "[1]Then the [a]glory of the LORD will be revealed,
And [b]all flesh will see *it* together;
For the mouth of the LORD has spoken."
6 A voice says, "Call out."
Then [1]He answered, "What shall I call out?"
[a]All flesh is grass, and all its [2]loveliness is like the flower of the field.
7 The [a]grass withers, the flower fades,
[1]When the breath of the LORD blows upon it;
Surely the people are grass.
8 The grass withers, the flower fades,
But [a]the word of our God stands forever.

9 Get yourself up on a [a]high mountain,
O Zion, bearer of [b]good news,
Lift up your voice mightily,
O Jerusalem, bearer of good news;
Lift *it* up, do not fear.
Say to the cities of Judah,
"[c]Here is your God!"
10 Behold, the Lord [1]GOD will come [a]with might,
With His [b]arm ruling for Him.
Behold, His [c]reward is with Him,
And His recompense before Him.
11 Like a shepherd He will [a]tend His flock,
In His arm He will gather the lambs,
And carry *them* in His bosom;
He will gently lead the nursing *ewes.*

12 Who has [a]measured the [1]waters in the hollow of His hand,
And marked off the heavens by the [2]span,
And [3]calculated the dust of the earth by the measure,
And weighed the mountains in a balance,
And the hills in a pair of scales?
13 [a]Who has [1]directed the Spirit of the LORD,
Or as His [b]counselor has informed Him?
14 [a]With whom did He consult and *who* [b]gave Him understanding?

And *who* taught Him in the path of justice and taught
Him knowledge,
And informed Him of the way of understanding?
15 Behold, the [a]nations are like a drop from a bucket,
And are regarded as a speck of [b]dust on the scales;
Behold, He lifts up the [1]islands like fine dust.
16 Even Lebanon is not enough to burn,
Nor its beasts enough for a burnt offering.
17 [a]All the nations are as nothing before Him,
They are regarded by Him as less than nothing and
[1]meaningless.

18 [a]To whom then will you liken God?
Or what likeness will you compare with Him?
19 *As for* the [a]idol, a craftsman casts it,
A goldsmith plates it with gold,
And a silversmith *fashions* chains of silver.
20 He who is too impoverished for *such* an offering
Selects a tree that does not rot;
He seeks out for himself a skillful craftsman
To [1]prepare an idol that [a]will not totter.

21 [a]Do you not know? Have you not heard?
Has it not been declared to you from the beginning?
Have you not understood [b]from the foundations of the
earth?
22 It is He who [1]sits above the [2a]vault of the earth,
And its inhabitants are like [b]grasshoppers,
Who [c]stretches out the heavens like a [d]curtain
And spreads them out like a [e]tent to dwell in.
23 He *it is* who reduces [a]rulers to nothing,
Who [b]makes the judges of the earth [1]meaningless.
24 [1]Scarcely have they been planted,
[1]Scarcely have they been sown,
[1]Scarcely has their stock taken root in the earth,
But He merely blows on them, and they wither,
And the [a]storm carries them away like stubble.
25 "[a]To whom then will you liken Me
That I should be *his* equal?" says the Holy One.
26 [a]Lift up your eyes on high
And see [b]who has created these *stars*,
The [c]One who leads forth their host by number
He calls them all by name;
Because of the [d]greatness of His might and the
[1]strength of *His* power
[e]Not one *of them* is missing.

27 [a]Why do you say, O Jacob, and assert, O Israel,
"My way is [b]hidden from the LORD
And the [c]justice due me [1]escapes the notice of [d]my
God?"
28 [a]Do you not know? Have you not heard?
The [b]everlasting God, the LORD, the creator of the
ends of the earth
Does not become weary or tired.
His understanding is [c]inscrutable.

15 [1]Or, *coastlands*
[a]Jer. 10:10 [b]Is. 17:13; 29:5

17 [1]Or, *void*
[a]Is. 29:7

18 [a]Is. 40:25; 46:5; Ex. 8:10; 15:11; 1 Sam. 2:2; Mic. 7:18

19 [a]Is. 41:7; 44:10; Ps. 115:4-8; Hab. 2:18, 19

20 [1]Or, *set up*
[a]Is. 41:7; 46:7; 1 Sam. 5:3, 4

21 [a]Is. 37:26; Ps. 19:1; 50:6; Acts 14:17; Rom. 1:19 [b]Is. 48:13; 51:13

22 [1]Or, *is enthroned* [2]Or, *circle*
[a]Job 22:14; Prov. 8:27 [b]Num. 13:33 [c]Is. 37:16; 42:5; 44:24; Job 9:8 [d]Ps. 104:2 [e]Job 36:29; Ps. 18:11; 19:4

23 [1]Or, *void*
[a]Is. 34:12; Job 12:21; Ps. 107:40 [b]Is. 5:21; Jer. 25:18-27

24 [1]Or, *Not even*
[a]Is. 17:13; 41:16

25 [a]Is. 40:18

26 [1]So DSS and ancient versions. M.T., *strong*
[a]Is. 51:6 [b]Is. 42:5; 48:12, 13 [c]Ps. 147:4 [d]Ps. 89:11-13 [e]Is. 34:16; 48:13

27 [1]Lit., *passes by my God*
[a]Is. 49:4, 14 [b]Is. 54:8 [c]Job 27:2; 34:5; Luke 18:7, 8 [d]Is. 25:1

28 [a]Is. 40:21 [b]Gen. 21:33; Ps. 90:2 [c]Ps. 147:5; Rom. 11:33

29 He gives strength to the [a]weary,
And to *him who* lacks might He [b]increases power.
30 Though [a]youths grow weary and tired,
And vigorous [b]young men stumble badly,
31 Yet those who [1]wait for the LORD
Will [a]gain new strength;
They will [2b]mount up *with* [3]wings like eagles,
They will run and not get tired,
They will walk and not become weary.

CHAPTER 41

"COASTLANDS, listen to Me [a]in silence,
And let the peoples [b]gain new strength;
[c]Let them come forward, then let them speak;
[d]Let us come together for judgment.
2 "[a]Who has aroused one from the east
Whom He [b]calls in righteousness to His [1]feet?
He [c]delivers up nations before him,
And subdues kings.
He makes them like dust with his sword,
As the wind-driven [d]chaff with his bow.
3 "He pursues them, passing on in safety,
By a way he had not been [1]traversing with his feet.
4 "[a]Who has performed and accomplished *it*,
Calling forth the generations from the beginning?
'[b]I, the LORD, am the first, and with the last. [c]I am He.' "

5 The [a]coastlands have seen and are afraid;
The [b]ends of the earth tremble;
They have drawn near and have come.
6 Each one [a]helps his neighbor,
And says to his brother, "Be strong!"
7 So the craftsman encourages the smelter,
And he who smooths *metal* with the hammer *encourages* him who beats the anvil,
Saying of the soldering, "It is good";
And he fastens it with nails,
[a]*That* it should not totter.
8 "But you, Israel, My servant,
Jacob whom I have chosen,
Descendant of [a]Abraham My [b]friend.
9 "You whom I have [1a]taken from the ends of the earth,
And called from its remotest parts,
And said to you, 'You are My servant,
I have [b]chosen you and not rejected you.
10 'Do not [a]fear, for I am with you;
Do not anxiously look about you, for I am your God.
I will strengthen you, surely [b]I will help you,
Surely, I will uphold you with My righteous [c]right hand.'
11 "Behold, all those who are angered at you will be shamed and dishonored;
[a]Those who contend with you will be as nothing, and will perish.

29 [a]Is. 50:4; Jer. 31:25 [b]Is. 41:10

30 [a]Jer. 6:11; 9:21 [b]Is. 9:17

31 [1]Or, *hope in* [2]Or, *sprout wings* [3]Or, *pinions* [a]Job 17:9; Ps. 103:5; 2 Cor. 4:8-10, 16 [b]Ex. 19:4; Deut. 32:11; Luke 18:1; 2 Cor. 4:1, 16; Gal. 6:9; Heb. 12:3

1 [a]Hab. 2:20; Zech. 2:13 [b]Is. 40:31 [c]Is. 34:1; 48:16 [d]Is. 1:18; 43:26; 50:8

2 [1]Lit., *foot* [a]Is. 41:25; 45:1-3; 46:11 [b]Is. 42:6 [c]2 Chr. 36:23; Ezra 1:2 [d]Is. 40:24

3 [1]Lit., *going*

4 [a]Is. 41:26; 44:7; 46:10 [b]Is. 43:10; 44:6; Rev. 1:8, 17; 22:13 [c]Is. 43:13; 46:4; 48:12

5 [a]Is. 41:1; Ezek. 26:15, 16 [b]Josh. 5:1; Ps. 67:7

6 [a]Joel 3:9-11

7 [a]Is. 40:20; 46:7

8 [a]Is. 29:22; 51:2; 63:16 [b]2 Chr. 20:7; James 2:23

9 [1]Or, *taken hold of* [a]Is. 11:11 [b]Deut. 7:6; 14:2; Ps. 135:4

10 [a]Is. 41:13, 14; 43:2, 5; Deut. 20:1; 31:6; Josh. 1:9; Ps. 27:1; Rom. 8:31 [b]Is. 41:14; 44:2; 49:8 [c]Ps. 89:13, 14

11 [a]Is. 17:13; 29:5, 7, 8

12 "[a]You will seek those who quarrel with you, but will not find them,
Those who war with you will be as nothing, and non-existent.
13 "For I am the LORD your God, [a]who upholds your right hand,
Who says to you, 'Do not fear, I will help you.'
14 "Do not fear, you worm Jacob, you men of Israel;
I will help you," declares the LORD, "[1]and [a]your Redeemer is the Holy One of Israel.
15 "Behold, I have made you a new, sharp threshing sledge with double edges;
[a]You will thresh the mountains, and pulverize *them*,
And will make the hills like chaff.
16 "You will winnow them, and the wind will carry them away,
And the storm will scatter them;
But you will [a]rejoice in the LORD,
You will glory in the Holy One of Israel.

17 "The [1]afflicted and needy are seeking [a]water, but there is none,
And their tongue is parched with thirst;
I the LORD [b]will answer them Myself,
As the God of Israel I [c]will not forsake them.
18 "I will open [a]rivers on the bare heights,
And springs in the midst of the valleys;
I will make [b]the wilderness a pool of water,
And the dry land fountains of water.
19 "I will put the cedar in the wilderness,
The acacia, and the [a]myrtle, and the [1]olive tree;
I will place the [a]juniper in the desert,
Together with the box tree and the cypress,
20 That they may see and recognize,
And consider and gain insight as well,
That the [a]hand of the LORD has done this,
And the Holy One of Israel has created it.

21 "[1]Present your case," the LORD says.
"Bring forward your strong *arguments*,"
The King of Jacob says.
22 [a]Let them bring forth and declare to us what is going to take place;
As for the [b]former *events*, declare what they *were*,
That we may consider them, and know their outcome;
Or announce to us what is coming.
23 [a]Declare the things that are going to come afterward,
That we may know that you are gods;
Indeed, [b]do good or evil, that we may anxiously look about us and fear together.
24 Behold, [a]you are of [1]no account,
And your work amounts to nothing;
He who chooses you is an abomination.

25 "I have aroused [a]one from the north, and he has come;
From the rising of the sun he will call on My name;

12 [a]Is. 17:14; Job 20:7-9; Ps. 37:35, 36
13 [a]Is. 42:6; 45:1
14 [1]Or, *even your Redeemer, the Holy One* [a]Is. 35:10; 43:14; 46:6, 22-24
15 [a]Mic. 4:13; Hab. 3:12
16 [a]Is. 25:9; 35:10; 51:3; 61:10
17 [1]Or, *poor* [a]Is. 43:20; 44:3; 49:10; 55:1 [b]Is. 30:19; 65:24 [c]Is. 42:16; 62:12
18 [a]Is. 30:25; 43:19 [b]Is. 35:6, 7; Ps. 107:35
19 [1]Or, *oleaster* [a]Is. 35:1; 55:13; 60:13
20 [a]Is. 66:14; Job 12:9
21 [1]Lit., *Bring near*
22 [a]Is. 44:7; 45:21; 46:10 [b]Is. 43:9
23 [a]Is. 42:9; 44:7, 8; 45:3; John 13:19 [b]Jer. 10:5
24 [1]Lit., *nothing* [a]Is. 44:9; Ps. 115:8; 1 Cor. 8:4
25 [a]Is. 41:2; Jer. 50:3

25 [b]Is. 10:6; 2 Sam. 22:43; Mic. 7:10; Zech. 10:5

26 [a]Is. 41:22; 44:7; 45:21 [b]Hab. 2:18, 19

27 [a]Is. 48:3-8 [b]Is. 40:9; 44:28; 52:7; Nah. 1:15

28 [1]Lit., *out of those* [a]Is. 50:2; 59:16; 63:5 [b]Is. 40:13, 14

29 [1]Another reading is, *nothing* [a]Is. 41:24; 2:8; 17:8 [b]Jer. 5:13

1 [1]Or, *hold fast* [2]Or, *Gentiles* [a]Matt. 12:18-21 [b]Is. 41:8; 43:10; 49:3-6; 52:13; 53:11; Matt. 12:18-21; Phil. 2:7 [c]1 Pet. 2:4, 6 [d]Matt. 3:17; 17:5 [e]Is. 11:2; 59:21; 61:1; Matt. 3:16; Luke 4:18, 19, 21

3 [a]Is. 57:15 [b]Ps. 72:2, 4; 96:13

4 [1]Or, *instruction* [a]Is. 40:28 [b]Is. 42:10, 12; 11:11; 24:15; 49:1; 51:5; 60:9; 66:19

5 [1]Or, *vegetation* [a]Is. 45:18; Ps. 102:25, 26 [b]Is. 40:22; Ps. 104:2 [c]Ps. 24:1, 2; 136:6 [d]Is. 57:16; Job 12:10; 33:4; Dan. 5:23; Acts 17:25

6 [a]Is. 41:2; Jer. 23:5, 6 [b]Is. 26:3; 27:3 [c]Is. 49:6, 8 [d]Is. 51:4; 60:1, 3; Luke 2:32

7 [a]Is. 29:18; 35:5 [b]Is. 49:9; 61:1

8 [1]Or, *idols* [a]Ex. 3:15; Ps. 83:18 [b]Is. 48:11; Ex. 20:3-5

9 [a]Is. 43:19; 48:6

10 [a]Ps. 33:3; 40:3; 98:1 [b]Is. 49:6; 62:11 [c]Ps. 65:5; 107:23 [d]Ex. 20:11; 1 Chr. 16:32; Ps. 96:11

And he will come upon rulers as *upon* [b]mortar,
Even as the potter treads clay."
26 Who has [a]declared *this* from the beginning, that we might know?
Or from former times, that we may say, "*He is* right!"?
Surely there was [b]no one who declared,
Surely there was no one who proclaimed,
Surely there was no one who heard your words.
27 "[a]Formerly *I said* to Zion, 'Behold, here they are.'
And to Jerusalem, 'I will give a [b]messenger of good news.'
28 "But [a]when I look, there is no one,
And there is no [b]counselor [1]among them
Who, if I ask, can give an answer.
29 "Behold, all of them are [1]false;
Their [a]works are worthless,
Their molten images are [b]wind and emptiness.

Chapter 42

"[a]BEHOLD, My [b]Servant, whom I [1]uphold;
My [c]chosen one *in whom* My [d]soul delights.
I have put My [e]Spirit upon him;
He will bring forth justice to the [2]nations.
2 "He will not cry out or raise *His voice,*
Nor make His voice heard in the street.
3 "A [a]bruised reed He will not break,
And a dimly burning wick He will not extinguish;
He will faithfully bring forth [b]justice.
4 "He will not be [a]disheartened or crushed,
Until He has established justice in the earth;
And the [b]coastlands will wait expectantly for His [1]law."

5 Thus says God the LORD,
Who [a]created the heavens and [b]stretched them out,
Who spread out the [c]earth and its [1]offspring,
Who [d]gives breath to the people on it,
And spirit to those who walk in it,
6 "I am the LORD, I have [a]called you in righteousness,
I will also hold you by the hand and [b]watch over you,
And I will appoint you as a [c]covenant to the people,
As a [d]light to the nations,
7 To [a]open blind eyes,
To [b]bring out prisoners from the dungeon,
And those who dwell in darkness from the prison.
8 "I am the LORD, that is [a]My name;
I will not give My [b]glory to another,
Nor My praise to [1]graven images.
9 "Behold, the former things have come to pass,
Now I declare [a]new things;
Before they spring forth I proclaim *them* to you."

10 Sing to the LORD a [a]new song,
Sing His praise from the [b]end of the earth!
[c]You who go down to the sea, and [d]all that is in it.
You islands and those who dwell on them.

11 Let the [a]wilderness and its cities lift up *their voice,*
The settlements where [b]Kedar inhabits.
Let the inhabitants of [c]Sela sing aloud,
Let them shout for joy from the tops of the [d]mountains.
12 Let them give glory to the LORD,
And declare His praise in the coastlands.
13 The LORD will go forth like a warrior,
He will arouse *His* [a]zeal like a man of war.
He will utter a shout, yes, He will raise a war cry.
He will [b]prevail against His enemies.

14 "I have kept silent for a long time,
I have kept still and restrained myself.
Now like a woman in labor I will groan,
I will both gasp and pant.
15 "I will [a]lay waste the mountains and hills,
And wither all their vegetation;
I will [b]make the rivers into coastlands,
And dry up the ponds.
16 "And I will [a]lead the blind by a way they do not know,
In paths they do not know I will guide them.
I will [b]make darkness into light before them
And [c]rugged places into plains.
These are the things I will do,
And I will [d]not leave them undone."
17 They shall be turned back and be [a]utterly put to shame,
Who trust in [1]idols,
Who say to molten images,
"You are our gods."

18 [a]Hear, you deaf!
And look, you blind, that you may see.
19 Who is blind but My servant,
Or so deaf as My [a]messenger whom I send?
Who is so blind as he that is [1b]at peace *with Me,*
Or so blind as the servant of the LORD?
20 You have seen many things, but you do not observe *them;*
Your ears are open, but none hears.
21 The LORD was pleased [a]for His righteousness' sake
To make the law [b]great and glorious.
22 But this is a people plundered and despoiled;
All of them are [a]trapped in [1]caves,
Or are hidden away in prisons;
They have become a prey with none to deliver *them,*
And a spoil, with none to say, "Give *them* back!"

23 Who among you will give ear to this?
Who will give heed and listen hereafter?
24 [a]Who gave Jacob up for spoil, and Israel to plunderers?
Was it not the LORD, against whom we have sinned,
And in whose ways they [b]were not willing to walk,
And whose law they did not [c]obey?
25 So He poured out on him the heat of His anger
And the [a]fierceness of battle;

11 [a]Is. 32:16; 35:1, 6 [b]Is. 21:16; 60:7 [c]Is. 16:1 [d]Is. 52:7; Nah. 1:15
13 [a]Is. 9:7; 26:11; 37:32; 59:17 [b]Is. 66:14-16
15 [a]Is. 2:12-16; Ezek. 38:19, 20 [b]Is. 44:27; 50:2; Nah. 1:4-6
16 [a]Is. 29:18; 30:21; 32:3; Jer. 31:8, 9; Luke 1:78, 79 [b]Is. 29:18; Eph. 5:8 [c]Is. 40:4; Luke 3:5 [d]Is. 41:17; Josh. 1:5; Ps. 94:14; Heb. 13:5
17 [1]Or, *graven images* [a]Is. 1:29; 44:9, 11; 45:16; Ps. 97:7
18 [a]Is. 29:18; 35:5
19 [1]Or, *the devoted one* [a]Is. 44:26 [b]Is. 26:3; 27:5
21 [a]Is. 43:25 [b]Is. 42:4; 51:4
22 [1]Or, *holes* [a]Is. 24:18
24 [a]Is. 10:5 [b]Is. 30:15 [c]Is. 48:18; 57:17
25 [a]Is. 5:25; 9:19

And it set him aflame all around,
Yet he did not recognize *it;*
And it burned him, but he [1b]paid no attention.

25 [1]Lit., *did not lay* it to *heart*
[b]Is. 29:13; 47:7; 57:1; Hos. 7:9

CHAPTER 43

BUT now thus says the LORD your [a]creator, O Jacob,
And He who [b]formed you, O Israel:
"Do not [c]fear, for I have [d]redeemed you;
I have [e]called you by name; you are [f]Mine!
2 "When you [a]pass through the waters, [b]I will be with you;
And through the rivers, they will not overflow you.
When you [c]walk through the fire, you will not be scorched,
Nor will the flame burn you.
3 "For I am the LORD your God,
The Holy One of Israel, your [a]Saviour;
I have given Egypt as your ransom,
[1]Cush and Seba in your place.
4 "Since you are precious in My sight,
Since you are honored and I [a]love you,
I will give *other* men in your place and *other* peoples in exchange for your life.
5 "Do not fear, for [a]I am with you;
I will bring [b]your offspring from the east,
And [c]gather you from the west.
6 "I will say to the [a]north, 'Give *them* up!'
And to the south, 'Do not hold *them* back.'
Bring My [b]sons from afar,
And My daughters from the [c]ends of the earth,
7 Every one who is [a]called by My name,
And whom I have [b]created for My [c]glory,
Whom I have formed even whom I have made."

8 Bring out the people who are blind, even though they have eyes,
And the deaf, even though they have ears.
9 All the nations have [a]gathered together
In order that the peoples may be assembled.
Who among them can declare this
And proclaim to us the former things?
Let them present [b]their witnesses that they may be justified,
Or let them hear and say, "It is true."
10 "You are My witnesses," declares the LORD,
"And My servant whom I have chosen,
In order that you may know and believe Me,
And understand that I am He.
Before Me there was no God formed,
And there will be none after Me.
11 "I, even I, am the LORD;
And there is no [a]saviour [b]besides Me.
12 "It is I who have declared and saved and proclaimed,
And there was no [a]strange *god* among you;
So you are My witnesses," declares the LORD,
"And I am God.

1 [a]Is. 43:15 [b]Is. 43:7, 21; 44:2, 21, 24 [c]Is. 43:5 [d]Is. 44:22, 23; 48:20 [e]Is. 43:7; 45:3, 4; Gen. 32:28 [f]Is. 43:21
2 [a]Is. 8:7, 8; Ps. 66:12 [b]Deut. 31:6, 8 [c]Is. 29:6; 30:27-29; Dan. 3:25, 27
3 [1]Or, *Ethiopia* [a]Is. 43:11; 19:20; 45:15, 21; 49:26; 60:16; 63:8
4 [a]Is. 63:9
5 [a]Is. 43:2; 8:10 [b]Is. 41:8; 49:12; 61:9 [c]Is. 49:12
6 [a]Ps. 107:3 [b]2 Cor. 6:18 [c]Is. 45:22
7 [a]Is. 56:5; 62:2; James 2:7 [b]Is. 29:23; Ps. 100:3; Eph. 2:10 [c]Is. 44:23; 46:13
9 [a]Is. 34:1; 41:1 [b]Is. 44:9
11 [a]Is. 43:3; 45:21; Hos. 13:4 [b]Is. 44:6, 8
12 [a]Deut. 32:16; Ps. 81:9

13 "Even [a]from [1]eternity I am He;
And there is [b]none who can deliver out of My hand;
[c]I act and who can reverse it?"

14 Thus says the LORD your [a]Redeemer, the Holy One of Israel:
"For your sake I have sent to Babylon,
And will bring them all down as fugitives,
[1]Even the [b]Chaldeans, into the [c]ships [2]in which they rejoice.
15 "I am the LORD, your Holy One,
The Creator of Israel, your [a]King."
16 Thus says the LORD,
Who [a]makes a way through the sea
And a [b]path through the mighty waters,
17 Who brings forth the [a]chariot and the horse,
The army and the mighty man
(They will lie down together *and* not rise again;
They have been [b]quenched *and* [c]extinguished like a wick):
18 "[a]Do not call to mind the former things,
Or ponder things of the past.
19 "Behold, I will do something [a]new,
Now it will spring forth;
Will you not be aware of it?
I will even [b]make a roadway in the wilderness,
Rivers in the desert.
20 "The beasts of the field will glorify Me;
The jackals and the ostriches;
Because I have [a]given waters in the wilderness
And rivers in the desert,
To give drink to My chosen people.
21 "The people whom I formed for Myself,
[a]Will declare My praise.

22 "Yet you have not called on Me, O Jacob;
But you have become [a]weary of Me, O Israel.
23 "You have [a]not brought to Me the sheep of your burnt offerings;
Nor have you [b]honored Me with your sacrifices.
I have not [c]burdened you with [1]offerings,
Nor wearied you with [d]incense.
24 "You have bought Me no [1a]sweet cane with money,
Neither have you [2]filled Me with the fat of your sacrifices;
Rather you have burdened Me with your sins,
You have [b]wearied Me with your iniquities.

25 "I, even I, am the one who [a]wipes out your transgressions [b]for My own sake;
And I will [c]not remember your sins.
26 "[1]Put Me in remembrance; let us argue our case together,
State your *cause,* that you may be proved right.
27 "Your [a]first [1]forefather sinned,
And your [2b]spokesmen have [3]transgressed against Me.

13 [1]So with Gk.; Heb., *from the day*
[a]Is. 48:16; Ps. 90:2 [b]Ps. 50:22 [c]Is. 14:27; Job 9:12

14 [1]Another reading is: *As for the Chaldeans, their rejoicing* is turned *into lamentations* [2]Lit., *of their rejoicing*
[a]Is. 41:14 [b]Is. 23:13 [c]Jer. 51:13

15 [a]Is. 41:21; 44:6

16 [a]Is. 11:15; 44:27; 50:2; 51:10; 63:11, 12; Ex. 14:21, 22; Ps. 77:19 [b]Josh. 3:15, 16

17 [a]Ex. 15:19 [b]Is. 1:31; Ps. 118:12 [c]Ps. 76:5, 6

18 [a]Is. 65:17; Jer. 16:14; 23:7

19 [a]Is. 42:9; 48:6; 2 Cor. 5:17 [b]Is. 35:1, 6; 41:18, 19; 49:10; 51:3; Ex. 17:6; Num. 20:11; Deut. 8:15; Ps. 78:16

20 [a]Is. 41:17, 18; 48:21

21 [a]Is. 42:12; Ps. 102:18; Luke 1:74, 75; 1 Pet. 2:9

22 [a]Mic. 6:3; Mal. 1:13; 3:14

23 [1]Or, *a meal offering*
[a]Amos 5:25 [b]Zech. 7:5, 6; Mal. 1:6-8 [c]Jer. 7:21-26 [d]Ex. 30:34; Lev. 2:1; 24:7

24 [1]Or, *calamus* [2]Or, *saturated*
[a]Ex. 30:23; Jer. 6:20 [b]Is. 1:14; 7:13; Ps. 95:10; Ezek. 6:9; Mal. 2:17

25 [a]Is. 44:22; 55:7; Jer. 50:20 [b]Is. 37:35; 48:9, 11; Ezek. 36:22 [c]Is. 38:17; Jer. 31:34

26 [1]Or, *Report to Me*

27 [1]Lit., *father* [2]Or, *interpreters* [3]Or, *rebelled*
[a]Is. 51:2; Ezek. 16:3 [b]Is. 9:15; 28:7; 29:10; Jer. 5:31

28 [1]Or, *pierce through* [2]Or, *holy princes*
[a]Is. 24:6; 34:5; Jer. 24:9; Dan. 9:11; Zech. 8:13 [b]Ps. 79:4; Ezek. 5:15

28 "So I will [1]pollute the [2]princes of the sanctuary;
And I will consign Jacob to the [a]ban, and Israel to [b]revilement.

CHAPTER 44

1 [a]Is. 41:8; Jer. 30:10; 46:27, 28

"BUT now listen, O Jacob My [a]servant;
And Israel, whom I have chosen:

2 [a]Deut. 32:15; 33:5, 26

2 Thus says the LORD who made you
And formed you from the womb, who will help you:
'Do not fear, O Jacob My servant;
And you [a]Jeshurun whom I have chosen.

3 [1]Or, *him who is thirsty*
[a]Is. 32:15; Joel 2:28 [b]Is. 61:9; 65:23

3 'For I will pour out water on [1]the thirsty *land*
And streams on the dry ground;
I will [a]pour out My Spirit on your [b]offspring,
And My blessing on your descendants;

4 [1]Another reading is, *like grass among the waters*
[a]Lev. 23:40; Job 40:22

4 And they will spring up [1]among the grass
Like [a]poplars by streams of water.'

5 [1]Another reading is, *will be called by the name of Jacob* [2]Or, *with*

5 "This one will say, 'I am the LORD's';
And that one [1]will call on the name of Jacob;
And another will write [2]*on* his hand, 'Belonging to the LORD,'
And will name Israel's name with honor.

6 [a]Is. 41:21; 43:15 [b]Is. 41:4; 43:10; 48:12; Rev. 1:8, 17; 22:13 [c]Is. 44:8; 43:11; 45:5, 6, 21

6 "Thus says the LORD, the [a]King of Israel
And his Redeemer, the LORD of hosts:
'I am the [b]first and I am the last,
And there is no God [c]besides Me.

7 [1]Or, *people*

7 'And who is like Me? Let him proclaim and declare it;
Yes, let him recount it to Me in order,
From the time that I established the ancient [1]nation.
And let them declare to them the things that are coming
And the events that are going to take place.

8 [a]Is. 45:5; Deut. 4:35, 39; 1 Sam. 2:2; Joel 2:27 [b]Is. 17:10; 26:4; 30:29

8 'Do not tremble and do not be afraid;
Have I not long since announced it to you and declared it?
And you are My witnesses.
Is there any God [a]besides Me,
Or is there any *other* [b]Rock?
I know of none.' "

9 [1]Or, *idol*
[a]Is. 44:11; 42:17; 45:16; Ps. 97:7

9 Those who fashion a [1]graven image are all of them
futile, and their precious things are of no profit; even their own
witnesses fail to see or know, so that they will be [a]put to shame.

10 [1]Or, *graven image*
[a]Is. 41:29; Jer. 10:5; Hab. 2:18; Acts 19:26

10 Who has fashioned a god or cast an [1]idol to [a]no profit?
11 Behold, all his companions will be put to shame, for
the craftsmen themselves are mere men. Let them all assemble
themselves, let them stand up, let them tremble, let them
together be put to shame.

12 [1]Lit., *and fashions* [2]Lit., *there is no strength*
[a]Is. 40:19, 20; 41:6, 7; 46:6, 7; Jer. 10:3-5; Hab. 2:18

12 The [a]man shapes iron into a cutting tool, and does his
work over the coals, [1]fashioning it with hammers, and working
it with his strong arm. He also gets hungry and [2]his strength
fails; he drinks no water and becomes weary.

13 [a]Is. 41:7

13 [a]*Another* shapes wood, he extends a measuring line; he
outlines it with red chalk. He works it with planes, and outlines

it with a compass, and makes it like the form of a man, like the
beauty of [b]man, so that it may sit in a [c]house.
14 Surely he cuts cedars for himself, and takes a [1]cypress
or an oak, and [2]raises *it* for himself among the trees of the
forest. He plants a fir, and the rain makes it grow.
15 Then it becomes *something* for a man to burn, so he
takes one of them and warms himself; he also makes a fire to
bake bread. He also makes a god and worships it; he makes it a
graven image, and [a]falls down before it.
16 Half of it he burns in the fire; over the half he eats
meat as he roasts a roast, and is satisfied. He also warms himself and says, "Ah, I am warm, I have seen the fire."
17 But the rest of it he makes into a god, his graven image.
He falls down before it and worships; he also [a]prays to it and
says, "Deliver me, for thou art my god."
18 They do not [a]know, nor do they understand, for He has
[b]smeared over their eyes so that they cannot see and their
hearts so that they cannot comprehend.
19 And no one [1]recalls, nor is there knowledge or understanding to say, "I have burned half of it in the fire, and also
have baked bread over its coals. I roast meat and eat *it*. Then
[2]I make the rest of it into an [a]abomination, [3]I fall down before
a block of wood!"
20 He [1a]feeds on ashes; a [b]deceived heart has turned him
aside. And he cannot deliver [2]himself, nor say, "Is there not a
lie in my right hand?"

21 "Remember these things, O Jacob,
And Israel, for you are My servant;
I have formed you, you are My servant,
O Israel, you will not be forgotten by Me.
22 I have [a]wiped out your transgressions like a thick cloud,
And your sins like a [1]heavy mist.
[b]Return to Me, for I have [c]redeemed you."
23 [a]Shout for joy, O heavens, for the LORD has done *it!*
Shout joyfully, you lower parts of the earth;
[b]Break forth into a shout of joy, you mountains,
O forest, and every tree in it;
For the LORD has redeemed Jacob
And in Israel He shows forth His glory.

24 Thus says the LORD, your Redeemer, and the one who
formed you from the womb:
"I, the LORD, am the maker of all things,
[a]Stretching out the heavens by Myself,
And spreading out the earth [1]all alone,
25 Causing the [1]omens of boasters to fail,
[2]Making fools out of diviners,
[a]Causing wise men to draw back,
And [3]turning their knowledge into foolishness,
26 Confirming the word of His servant,
And [1]performing the purpose of His messengers.
It is I who says of Jerusalem, 'She shall be inhabited!'
And of the cities of Judah, '[a]They shall be built.'
And I will raise up her ruins *again*.
27 "*It is I* who says to the depth of the sea, 'Be dried up!'
And I will make your rivers [a]dry.

13 [b]Ps. 115:5-7 [c]Judg. 17:4, 5; Ezek. 8:10, 11

14 [1]Or, *holm-oak* [2]Lit., *make strong*

15 [a]2 Chr. 25:14

17 [a]Is. 45:20; 1 Kin. 18:26, 28

18 [a]Is. 1:3; Jer. 10:8, 14 [b]Is. 6:9, 10; 29:10; Ps. 81:12

19 [1]Lit., *returns to his heart* [2]Or, *shall I make . . . . . .?* [3]Or, *shall I fall . . . .?* [a]Deut. 27:15; 1 Kin. 11:5, 7; 2 Kin. 23:14

20 [1]Or, *is a companion of ashes* [2]Lit., *his soul* [a]Ps. 102:9 [b]Job 15:31; Hos. 4:12; Rom. 1:21, 22; 2 Thess. 2:11; 2 Tim. 3:13

22 [1]Or, *cloud* [a]Is. 43:25; Ps. 51:1, 9; Acts 3:19 [b]Is. 31:6; 55:7 [c]Is. 43:1; 48:20; 1 Cor. 6:20; 1 Pet. 1:18, 19

23 [a]Is. 42:10; 49:13; Ps. 69:34; 96:11, 12 [b]Is. 55:12; Ps. 98:7, 8; 148:7, 9

24 [1]Or, *who was with Me?* [a]Is. 40:22; 42:5; 45:12, 18; 51:13

25 [1]Lit., *signs* [2]Lit., *He makes* [3]Lit., *He turns* [a]Is. 29:14; 2 Sam. 15:31; Job 5:12-14; Ps. 33:10; Jer. 51:57; 1 Cor. 1:20, 27

26 [1]Lit., *He performs* [a]Jer. 32:15, 44

27 [a]Is. 42:15; 50:2; Jer. 50:38; 51:36

28 "*It is I* who says of Cyrus, '*He is* My Shepherd!
And He will perform all My desire.'
And [1]he declares of Jerusalem, '[a]She will be built,'
And of the temple, '[2]Your foundation will be laid.' "

CHAPTER 45

THUS says the LORD to Cyrus His anointed,
Whom I have taken by the right [a]hand,
To [b]subdue nations before him,
And [1]to [c]loose the loins of kings;
To open doors before him so that gates will not be shut:
2 "I will go before you and [a]make the [1]rough places smooth;
I will [b]shatter the doors of bronze, and cut through their iron [c]bars.
3 "And I will give you the [1a]treasures of darkness,
And hidden wealth of secret places,
In order that you may know that it is I,
The LORD, the God of Israel, who [b]calls you by your name.
4 "For the sake of [a]Jacob My servant,
And Israel My chosen *one*,
I have also [b]called you by your name;
I have given you a title of honor
Though you have [c]not known Me.
5 "I am the LORD, and [a]there is no other;
[b]Besides Me there is no God.
I will [1c]gird you, though you have not known Me;
6 That [1a]men may know from the rising to the setting of the sun
That there is no one besides Me.
I am the LORD, and there is no other,
7 The One [a]forming light and [b]creating darkness,
Causing [1]well-being and [c]creating calamity;
I am the LORD who does all these.

8 "[a]Drip down, O heavens, from above,
And let the clouds pour down righteousness;
Let the [b]earth open up and salvation bear fruit,
[c]And righteousness spring up with it.
I the LORD have created it.

9 "Woe to *the one* who [a]quarrels with his [1]Maker—
An earthenware vessel [2]among the vessels of earth!
Will the [b]clay say to the [1]potter, 'What are you doing?'
Or the thing you are making *say*, 'He has no hands'?
10 "Woe to him who says to a father, 'What are you begetting?'
Or to a woman, 'To what are you [1]giving birth?' "

11 Thus says the [a]LORD, the Holy One of Israel, and his [1b]Maker:
"[2c]Ask me about the things to come [3]concerning my [d]sons,
And you shall commit to Me the work of My hands.

28 [1]Lit., *to say* [2]Lit., *You will be founded*
[a]Is. 14:32; 45:13; 54:11; 2 Chr. 36:22, 23; Ezra 1:1

1 [1]Lit., *I will loose*
[a]Is. 41:13; 42:6; Ps. 73:23 [b]Is. 41:2, 25; Jer. 50:3, 35; 51:11, 20, 24 [c]Is. 45:5; Job 12:21

2 [1]Another reading is, *mountains*
[a]Is. 40:4 [b]Ps. 107:16 [c]Jer. 51:30

3 [1]Or, *hoarded treasures*
[a]Jer. 41:8; 50:37 [b]Is. 43:1; 49:1; Ex. 33:12, 17

4 [a]Is. 41:8, 9; 44:1 [b]Is. 43:1 [c]Acts 17:23

5 [1]Or, *arm*
[a]Is. 45:6, 14, 18, 21; 46:9 [b]Is. 44:6, 8 [c]Ps. 18:39

6 [1]Lit., *they*
[a]Ps. 102:15; Mal. 1:11

7 [1]Or, *peace*
[a]Is. 42:16 [b]Ps. 104:20; 105:28 [c]Is. 31:2; 47:11; Amos 3:6

8 [a]Ps. 72:6; Hos. 10:12; 14:5; Joel 3:18 [b]Ps. 85:11 [c]Is. 60:21; 61:11

9 [1]Lit., *Fashioner* [2]Lit., *with*
[a]Job 15:25; 40:8, 9; Ps. 2:2, 3; Prov. 21:30; Jer. 50:24 [b]Is. 29:16; 64:8; Jer. 18:6; Rom. 9:20, 21

10 [1]Lit., *in labor pains with*

11 [1]Lit., *Fashioner* [2]Or, *Will you ask . . .* [3]Or, *upon*
[a]Is. 43:15; 48:17; Ezek. 39:7 [b]Is. 44:2; 54:5 [c]Is. 8:19 [d]Jer. 31:9

12 "It is I who [a]made the earth, and created man upon it.
I [b]stretched out the heavens with My hands,
And I [1]ordained [c]all their host.
13 "I have aroused him in righteousness,
And I will make all his ways smooth;
He will [a]build My city, and will let My exiles go [b]free,
Without any payment or reward," says the LORD of hosts.

14 Thus says the LORD,
"The [1]products of [a]Egypt and the merchandise of [2b]Cush
And the Sabeans, men of stature,
Will [c]come over to you and will be yours;
They will walk behind you, they will come over in [d]chains
And will [e]bow down to you;
They will make supplication to you:
'[3]Surely, [f]God is [4]with you, and there is none else,
No other God.' "
15 Truly, Thou art a God who [a]hides Himself,
O God of Israel, Savior!
16 They will be put to shame and even humiliated, all of them,
The [a]manufacturers of idols will go away together in humiliation.
17 Israel has been saved by the LORD
With an [a]everlasting salvation;
You will not be put to shame or humiliated
To all eternity.

18 For thus says the LORD, who [a]created the heavens,
(He is the God who [b]formed the earth and made it,
He established it and did not create it a [1c]waste place,
But formed it to be [d]inhabited):
"I am the LORD, and [e]there is none else.
19 "I have not spoken in secret,
In [1]some dark land;
I did not say to the [2]offspring of Jacob,
'[a]Seek me in [3]a waste place':
I, the LORD, [b]speak righteousness
[c]Declaring things that are upright.

20 "[a]Gather yourselves and come;
Draw near together, you fugitives of the nations;
[b]They have no knowledge,
Who [c]carry about [1]their wooden idol,
And [d]pray to a god who cannot save.
21 "[a]Declare and set forth *your case;*
Indeed, let them consult together.
[b]Who has announced this from of old?
Who has long since declared it?
Is it not I, the LORD?
And there is no other God besides Me,
A righteous God and a [c]Savior;
There is none except Me.

12 [1]Or, *commanded*
[a]Is. 45:18; 42:5; Jer. 27:5 [b]Is. 42:5; 44:24; Ps. 104:2 [c]Gen. 2:1; Neh. 9:6

13 [a]Is. 44:28; 2 Chr. 36:22, 23 [b]Is. 52:3

14 [1]Lit., *labor* [2]Or, *Ethiopia* [3]Or, *God is with you alone* [4]Or, *in*
[a]Is. 19:21; Ps. 68:31 [b]Is. 18:1; 43:3 [c]Is. 14:1, 2; 49:23; 54:3 [d]Ps. 149:8 [e]Is. 49:23; 60:14 [f]Jer. 16:19; Zech. 8:20-23; 1 Cor. 14:25

15 [a]Is. 1:15; 8:17; 57:17; Ps. 44:24

16 [a]Is. 44:11

17 [a]Is. 26:4; 51:6; Rom. 11:26

18 [1]Or, *in vain*
[a]Is. 42:5 [b]Is. 45:12 [c]Gen. 1:2 [d]Gen. 1:26; Ps. 115:16 [e]Is. 45:5

19 [1]Lit., *a place of a land of darkness* [2]Lit., *seed* [3]Or, *vain*
[a]2 Chr. 15:2; Ps. 78:34; Jer. 29:13, 14; Hos. 3:5 [b]Is. 45:23; 63:1; Ps. 19:8 [c]Is. 43:12; 44:8

20 [1]Lit., *the wood of their graven image*
[a]Is. 43:9 [b]Is. 44:18, 19; 48:5-7 [c]Is. 46:1, 7; Jer. 10:5 [d]Is. 44:17; 46:6, 7

21 [a]Is. 41:23; 43:9 [b]Is. 41:26; 44:7; 48:14 [c]Is. 43:3, 11

22 [a]Num. 21:8, 9; 2 Chr. 20:12; Mic. 7:7; Zech. 12:10 [b]Is. 30:15; 49:6, 12; 52:10

23 [a]Rom. 14:11; Phil. 2:10

25 [a]Is. 53:11; 1 Kin. 8:32

1 [1]Lit., *carried by you* [a]Is. 2:18; 21:9; Jer. 50:2-4; 51:44

2 [1]Or, *their soul has* [a]Judg. 18:17, 18, 24; 2 Sam. 5:21; Jer. 43:12, 13; 48:7; Hos. 10:5, 6

3 [1]Lit., *the belly* [a]Is. 10:21, 22

4 [1]Lit., *I am He* [2]Lit., *gray hairs* [3]Or, *made* you [a]Is. 41:4; 43:13; 48:12

5 [a]Is. 40:18, 25

6 [a]Is. 40:19; 41:7; 44:12-17; Jer. 10:4 [b]Is. 44:15, 17

7 [a]Is. 46:1; 45:20; Jer. 10:5 [b]Is. 40:20; 41:7 [c]Is. 45:20

8 [1]Lit., *firm* [2]Lit., *heart* [a]Is. 44:21

9 [a]Is. 42:9; 65:17; Deut. 32:7 [b]Is. 45:5, 21 [c]Is. 41:26, 27

22 "[a]Turn to Me, and [b]be saved, all the ends of the earth;
For I am God, and there is no other.
23 "I have sworn by Myself,
The word has gone forth from My mouth in righteousness
And will not turn back,
That to Me [a]every knee will bow, every tongue will swear *allegiance*.
24 "They will say of Me, 'Only in the LORD are righteousness and strength.'
Men will come to Him,
And all who were angry at Him shall be put to shame.
25 "In the LORD all the offspring of Israel
Will be [a]justified, and will glory."

Chapter 46

[a]BEL has bowed down, Nebo stoops over;
Their images are *consigned* to the beasts and the cattle.
The things [1]that you carry are burdensome,
A load for the weary *beast*.
2 They stooped over, they have bowed down together;
They could not rescue the burden,
But [1]have themselves [a]gone into captivity.

3 "Listen to Me, O house of Jacob,
And all [a]the remnant of the house of Israel,
You who have been borne by Me from [1]birth,
And have been carried from the womb;
4 Even to your old age, [a]I [1]shall be the same,
And even to your [2]graying years I shall bear *you!*
I have [3]done *it*, and I shall carry *you;*
And I shall bear *you*, and I shall deliver *you*.

5 "[a]To whom would you liken Me,
And make Me equal and compare Me,
That we should be alike?
6 "Those who [a]lavish gold from the purse
And weigh silver on the scale
Hire a goldsmith, and he makes it *into* a god;
They [b]bow down, indeed they worship it.
7 "They [a]lift it upon the shoulder and carry it;
They set it in its place and it stands *there*.
[b]It does not move from its place.
Though one may cry to it, it cannot answer;
It cannot [c]deliver him from his distress.

8 "[a]Remember this, and be [1]assured;
Recall it to [2]mind, you transgressors.
9 "Remember the [a]former things long past,
For I am God, and there is [b]no other;
I am God, and there is [c]no one like Me,
10 Declaring the end from the beginning
And from ancient times things which have not been done,

Saying, '[a]My purpose will be established,
And I will accomplish all My good pleasure';
11 Calling a bird of prey from the east,
The man of [1]My purpose from a far country.
Truly I have [a]spoken; truly I will bring it to pass.
I have planned *it, surely* I will do it.

12 "Listen to Me, you [a]stubborn-minded,
Who are far from righteousness.
13 "I [a]bring near My righteousness, it is not far off;
And My salvation will not delay.
And I will grant [b]salvation in Zion,
And My glory for Israel.

Chapter 47

"[a]COME down and sit in the dust,
O virgin daughter of Babylon;
Sit on the ground without a throne,
O daughter of the Chaldeans.
For you shall no longer be called [b]tender and delicate.
2 "Take the [a]millstones and grind meal.
Remove your [b]veil, strip off the skirt,
Uncover the leg, cross the rivers.
3 "Your nakedness will be uncovered,
Your shame also will be exposed;
I will [a]take vengeance and will not [1]spare a man."
4 Our Redeemer, the LORD of hosts is His name,
The Holy One of Israel.
5 "[a]Sit silently, and go into darkness,
O daughter of the Chaldeans;
For you will no more be called
The [b]queen of kingdoms.
6 "I was angry with My people,
I profaned My heritage,
And gave them into your hand.
You did not show mercy to them,
On the [a]aged you made your yoke very heavy.
7 "Yet you said, 'I shall be a queen forever.'
These things you did not [a]consider,
Nor remember the [b]outcome of [1]them.

8 "Now, then, hear this, you [a]sensual one,
Who [b]dwells securely,
Who says in [1]your heart,
'[c]I am, and there is no one besides me.
I shall [d]not sit as a widow,
Nor shall I know loss of children.'
9 "But these [a]two things shall come on you [b]suddenly in one day:
Loss of children and widowhood.
They shall come on you in full measure
In spite of your many [c]sorceries,
In spite of the great power of your spells.
10 "And you felt [a]secure in your wickedness and said,
'[b]No one sees me,'

10 [a]Is. 14:24; 25:1; 40:8; Ps. 33:11; Prov. 19:21; Acts 5:39

11 [1]Lit., *His*
[a]Is. 14:24; 37:26; Num. 23:19

12 [a]Is. 48:4; Ps. 76:5; Zech. 7:11, 12; Mal. 3:13

13 [a]Is. 51:5; 61:11; Rom. 3:21 [b]Is. 61:3; 62:11; Joel 3:17; 1 Pet. 2:6

1 [a]Is. 3:26; Jer. 48:18 [b]Deut. 28:56

2 [a]Ex. 11:5; Jer. 25:10 [b]Is. 3:23; Gen. 24:65; 1 Cor. 11:5

3 [1]Lit., *meet*
[a]Is. 34:8; 63:4

5 [a]Is. 23:2; Jer. 8:14; Lam. 2:10 [b]Is. 47:7; Gen. 16:4, 8, 9; Prov. 30:23

6 [a]Deut. 28:50

7 [1]Lit., *it*
[a]Is. 42:25; 57:11 [b]Deut. 32:29; Jer. 5:31; Ezek. 7:2, 3

8 [1]Lit., *her*
[a]Is. 22:13; 32:9; Jer. 50:11 [b]Is. 32:9, 11; Zeph. 2:15 [c]Is. 47:10; 45:5, 6, 18; Zeph. 2:15 [d]Rev. 18:7

9 [a]Is. 13:16, 18; 14:22 [b]Ps. 73:19; 1 Thess. 5:3; Rev. 18:8, 10 [c]Is. 47:13; Nah. 3:4; Rev. 18:23

10 [a]Is. 59:4; Ps. 52:7; 62:10 [b]Is. 29:15; Ezek. 8:12; 9:9

Your [c]wisdom and your knowledge, [1]they have deluded
you;
For you have said in your heart,
'I am, and there is no one besides me.'
11 "But evil will come on you
Which you will not know how to charm away;
And disaster will fall on you
For which you cannot atone,
And [a]destruction about which you do not know
Will come on you suddenly.

12 "Stand *fast* now in your spells
And in your many sorceries
With which you have labored from your youth;
Perhaps you will be able to profit,
Perhaps you may cause trembling.
13 "You are [a]wearied with your many counsels,
Let now the [b]astrologers,
Those who prophesy by the stars,
Those who predict by the new moons,
Stand up and [c]save you from what will come upon you.
14 "Behold, they have become [a]like stubble,
[b]Fire burns them;
They cannot deliver themselves from the power of the
flame;
There will be no coal to warm by,
Nor a fire to sit before!
15 "So have those become to you with whom you have
labored,
Who have [a]trafficked with you from your youth;
Each has wandered in his own [1]way.
There is none to save you.

Chapter 48

"[a]HEAR this, O house of Jacob, who are named Israel
And who came forth from the [1b]loins of Judah,
Who [c]swear by the name of the LORD
And invoke the God of Israel,
But not in truth nor in righteousness.
2 "For they call themselves after the [a]holy city,
And [b]lean on the God of Israel;
The LORD of hosts is His name.
3 "I [a]declared the former things long ago
And they went forth from My mouth, and I proclaimed
them.
Suddenly I acted, and they came to pass.
4 "Because I know that you are [1a]obstinate,
And your neck is an iron sinew,
And your forehead bronze,
5 Therefore I declared *them* to you long ago,
Before [1]they took place I proclaimed *them* to you,
Lest you should say, 'My [a]idol has done them,
And my graven image and my molten image have commanded them.'

10 [1]Lit., *it*
[c]Is. 5:21; 44:20

11 [a]Jer. 51:8, 43

13 [a]Jer. 51:58, 64 [b]Is. 47:9; 8:19; 44:25; Dan. 2:2, 10 [c]Is. 47:15

14 [a]Is. 5:24; Nah. 1:10; Mal. 4:1 [b]Is. 10:17; Jer. 51:30, 32, 58

15 [1]Lit., *side, region*
[a]Rev. 18:11

1 [1]Lit., *waters*
[a]Is. 46:12 [b]Num. 24:7; Deut. 33:28; Ps. 68:26 [c]Is. 45:23; 65:16; Deut. 6:13

2 [a]Is. 52:1; 64:10 [b]Is. 10:20; Jer. 7:4; 21:2; Mic. 3:11; Rom. 2:17

3 [a]Is. 41:22; 42:9; 43:9; 44:7, 8; 45:21; 46:10

4 [1]Or, *harsh*
[a]Ezek. 2:4; 3:7

5 [1]Lit., *it*
[a]Jer. 44:15-18

6 "You have heard; look at all this.
And you, will you not declare it?
I proclaim to you [a]new things from this time,
Even hidden things which you have not known.
7 "They are created now and not long ago;
And before today you have not heard them,
Lest you should say, 'Behold, I knew them.'
8 "You have not [a]heard, you have not known.
Even from long ago your ear has not been open,
Because I knew that you would deal very treacherously;
And you have been called a [1b]rebel from [2]birth.
9 "For the sake of My name I [a]delay My wrath,
And *for* My praise I restrain *it* for you,
In order not to cut you off.
10 "Behold, I have refined you, but [a]not as silver;
I have tested you in the [b]furnace of affliction.
11 "[a]For My own sake, for My own sake, I will act;
For how can *My name* be profaned?
And My [b]glory I will not give to another.

12 "Listen to me, O Jacob, even Israel [1]whom I called;
[a]I am He, I am the first, I am also the last.
13 "Surely My hand [a]founded the earth,
And My right hand spread out the heavens;
When I call to them, they stand together.
14 "Assemble, all of you, and listen!
Who among them has declared these things?
The LORD loves him; he shall carry out his good pleasure on Babylon,
And his arm *shall be against* the Chaldeans.
15 "I, even I, have spoken; indeed I have [a]called him,
I have brought him, and he will make his ways successful.
16 "[a]Come near to Me, listen to this:
From the first I have [b]not spoken in secret,
[c]From the time it took place, I was there.
And now the Lord [1]GOD has sent Me, and His Spirit."

17 Thus says the LORD, your [a]Redeemer, the Holy One of Israel;
"I am the LORD your God, who teaches you to profit,
Who [b]leads you in the way you should go.
18 "If only you had [a]paid attention to My commandments!
Then your [1b]well-being would have been like a river,
And your [c]righteousness like the waves of the sea.
19 "Your [1a]descendants would have been like the sand,
And [2]your offspring like its grains;
Their name would never be cut off or destroyed from My presence."

20 Go forth from Babylon! Flee from the Chaldeans!
Declare with the sound of [a]joyful shouting, proclaim this,
[b]Send it out to the end of the earth;
Say, "The LORD has redeemed His servant Jacob."

6 [a]Is. 42:9; 43:19

8 [1]Or, *transgressor* [2]Lit., *the belly*
[a]Is. 42:25; 47:11; Hos. 7:9 [b]Is. 46:8; Deut. 9:7, 24; Ps. 58:3

9 [a]Is. 30:18; 65:8; Neh. 9:30, 31; Ps. 78:38; 103:8-10

10 [a]Jer. 9:7; Ezek. 22:18-22 [b]Deut. 4:20; 1 Kin. 8:51; Jer. 11:4

11 [a]1 Sam. 12:22; Ps. 25:11; 106:8; Jer. 14:7; Ezek. 20:9, 14, 22, 44; Dan. 9:17-19 [b]Is. 42:8; Deut. 32:26, 27

12 [1]Lit., *my called one*
[a]Is. 41:4; 43:10, 13; 46:4

13 [a]Is. 42:5; 45:12, 18; Ex. 20:11; Ps. 102:25; Heb. 1:10-12

15 [a]Is. 41:2; 45:1, 2

16 [1]YHWH, usually rendered LORD
[a]Is. 34:1; 41:1; 57:3 [b]Is. 45:19 [c]Is. 43:13

17 [a]Is. 41:14; 43:14; 49:7, 26; 54:5, 8 [b]Is. 30:21; 49:9, 10; Ps. 32:8

18 [1]Or, *peace*
[a]Deut. 5:29; 32:29; Ps. 81:13-16 [b]Is. 32:16-18; 66:12; Ps. 119:165 [c]Is. 45:8; 61:10, 11; 62:1; Hos. 10:12; Amos 5:24

19 [1]Lit., *seed* [2]Lit., *the offspring of your inward parts*
[a]Is. 10:22; 44:4; 54:3; Gen. 22:17; Jer. 33:22

20 [a]Is. 42:10; 49:13; 52:9 [b]Is. 62:11; Jer. 31:10; 50:2

21 And they did not [a]thirst when He led them through the
deserts.
He [b]made the water flow out of the rock for them;
He split the rock, and [c]the water gushed forth.
22 "[a]There is no peace for the wicked," says the LORD.

CHAPTER 49

LISTEN to Me, O islands,
And pay attention, you peoples from afar.
The LORD called Me from the womb;
From the [1]body of My mother He named Me.
2 And He has made My [a]mouth like a sharp sword;
In the [b]shadow of His hand He has concealed Me,
And He has also made Me a [1]select [c]arrow;
He has hidden Me in His quiver.
3 And He said to Me, "You are My Servant, Israel,
In Whom I will [1]show My glory."
4 But I said, "I have toiled in vain,
I have spent My strength for nothing and vanity;
Yet surely the justice *due* to Me is with the LORD,
And My [a]reward with My God."

5 And now says the LORD, who formed Me from the
womb to be His Servant,
To bring Jacob back to Him, in order that Israel might
be gathered to Him
(For I am [a]honored in the sight of the LORD,
And My God is My [b]strength).
6 He says, "It is too [1]small a thing that You should be
My Servant
To raise up the tribes of Jacob, and to restore the
[a]preserved ones of Israel;
I will also make You a [b]light [2]of the nations
So that My salvation may [3]reach to the end of the
earth."
7 Thus says the LORD, the [a]Redeemer of Israel, *and* its
Holy One,
To the [b]despised One,
To the One abhorred by the nation,
To the Servant of rulers,
"[c]Kings shall see and arise,
Princes shall also [d]bow down;
Because of the LORD who is faithful, the Holy One of
Israel who has chosen You."

8 Thus says the LORD, "In a [a]favorable time I have answered You,
And in a day of salvation I have helped You;
And I will [b]keep You and give You for a covenant of
the people,
To [1][c]restore the land, to make *them* inherit the desolate heritages;
9 Saying to those who are [a]bound, 'Go forth,'
To those who are in darkness, 'Show yourselves.'

21 [a]Is. 30:25; 35:6, 7; 41:17, 18; 43:19, 20; 49:10 [b]Ex. 17:6; Ps. 78:15, 16 [c]Ps. 78:20; 105:41

22 [a]Is. 57:21

1 [1]Lit., *inward parts*

2 [1]Or, *sharpened* [a]Is. 11:4; Heb. 4:12; Rev. 1:16; 2:12, 16 [b]Is. 51:16 [c]Hab. 3:11

3 [1]Or, *glorify Myself*

4 [a]Is. 35:4; 59:18

5 [a]Is. 43:4 [b]Is. 12:2

6 [1]Lit., *light* [2]Or, *to* [3]Lit., *be* [a]Ps. 37:28; 97:10 [b]Is. 42:6; 51:4; Acts 13:47

7 [a]Is. 48:17 [b]Is. 53:3; Ps. 22:6-8; 69:7-9 [c]Is. 52:15 [d]Is. 19:21, 23; 27:13; 66:23

8 [1]Lit., *establish* [a]Ps. 69:13; 2 Cor. 6:2 [b]Is. 26:3; 27:3; 42:6 [c]Is. 44:26

9 [a]Is. 42:7; 61:1; Luke 4:18

Along the roads they will feed,
And their pasture will be on all bare heights.
10 "They will [a]not hunger or thirst,
Neither will the scorching [b]heat or sun strike them down;
For He who has compassion on them will [c]lead them,
And will guide them to [d]springs of water.
11 "And I will make all My mountains a road,
And My [a]highways will be raised up.
12 "Behold, these shall come from afar;
And lo, these *will come* from the [a]north and from the west,
And these from the land of Sinim."
13 [a]Shout for joy, O heavens! And rejoice, O earth!
Break forth into joyful shouting, O mountains!
For the [b]LORD has comforted His people,
And will [c]have compassion on His afflicted.

14 But Zion said, "The LORD has forsaken me,
And the Lord has forgotten me."
15 "Can a woman forget her nursing child,
And have no compassion on the son of her womb?
Even these may forget, but I will not forget you.
16 "Behold, I have [a]inscribed you on the palms *of My hands;*
Your [b]walls are continually before Me.
17 "Your [1]builders hurry;
Your [a]destroyers and devastators
Will depart from you.
18 "[a]Lift up your eyes and look around;
All of them gather together, they come to you.
[b]As I live," declares the LORD,
"You shall surely put on all of them as [1]jewels, and bind them on as a bride.
19 "For [a]your waste and desolate places, and your destroyed land—
Surely now you will be [b]too cramped for the inhabitants,
And those who [c]swallowed you will be far away.
20 "The [a]children of [1]whom you were bereaved will yet say in your ears,
'The place is too cramped for me;
Make room for me that I may live *here.*'
21 "Then you will [a]say in your heart,
'Who has begotten these for me,
Since I have been bereaved of my children,
And am [b]barren, an [c]exile and a wanderer?
And who has reared these?
Behold, I was [d]left alone;
From where did these come?' "

22 Thus says the Lord [1]GOD,
"Behold I will lift up My hand to the nations,
And set up My [a]standard to the peoples;
And they will [b]bring your sons in *their* bosom,
And your daughters will be carried on *their* shoulders.

10 [a]Is. 33:16; 48:21; Rev. 7:16 [b]Ps. 121:6 [c]Is. 40:11; Ps. 23:2 [d]Is. 35:7; 41:17

11 [a]Is. 11:16; 19:23; 35:8; 62:10

12 [a]Is. 43:5, 6

13 [a]Is. 44:23 [b]Is. 40:1; 51:3, 12 [c]Is. 54:7, 8, 10

16 [a]Song of Sol. 8:6; Hag. 2:23 [b]Is. 62:6, 7; Ps. 48:12, 13

17 [1]So ancient versions and DSS; M.T. reads, *sons* [a]Is. 10:6; 37:18

18 [1]Lit., *an ornament* [a]Is. 60:4; John 4:35 [b]Is. 45:23; 54:9

19 [a]Is. 1:7; 3:8; 5:6; 51:3 [b]Is. 54:1, 2; Zech. 10:10 [c]Ps. 56:1, 2

20 [1]Lit., *your bereavement* [a]Is. 54:1-3

21 [a]Is. 29:23; 54:6, 7 [b]Is. 27:10; Lam. 1:1 [c]Is. 5:13 [d]Is. 1:8

22 [1]YHWH, usually rendered LORD [a]Is. 11:10, 12; 18:3; 62:10 [b]Is. 14:2; 43:6; 60:4

23 [a]Is. 14:1, 2; 60:3, 10, 11 [b]Is. 45:14; 60:14 [c]Ps. 72:9; Mic. 7:17 [d]Is. 41:20; 43:10; 60:16 [e]Is. 25:9; 26:8; Ps. 37:9 [f]Is. 45:17; Ps. 25:3; Joel 2:27

24 [1]So ancient versions and DSS; M.T. reads, *the righteous*, cf. v. 25

25 [a]Is. 10:6; 14:1, 2; Jer. 50:33, 34

26 [a]Is. 9:4; 14:4; 16:4; 51:13; 54:14 [b]Is. 45:6; Ezek. 39:7

1 [a]Deut. 24:1, 3; Jer. 3:8 [b]Is. 54:6, 7 [c]Deut. 32:30; 2 Kin. 4:1; Neh. 5:5 [d]Is. 52:3; 59:2 [e]Jer. 3:8

2 [a]Is. 59:1; Gen. 18:14; Num. 11:23 [b]Is. 19:5; 43:16; 44:27; Ex. 14:21 [c]Is. 42:15; Josh. 3:16

3 [a]Is. 13:10; Rev. 6:12

4 [1]YHWH, usually rendered LORD, and so throughout the chap. [a]Is. 57:19; Jer. 31:25 [b]Ps. 5:3; 88:13; 119:147; 143:8

5 [a]Matt. 26:39; John 8:29; 14:31; 15:10; Acts 26:19; Phil. 2:8; Heb. 5:8; 10:7

6 [a]Matt. 26:67; 27:30; Mark 15:19; Luke 22:63

7 [a]Is. 42:1; 49:8 [b]Is. 45:17; 54:4

23 "And [a]kings will be your guardians,
And their princesses your nurses.
They will [b]bow down to you with their faces to the earth,
And [c]lick the dust of your feet;
And *you* will [d]know that I am the LORD;
Those who hopefully [e]wait for Me will [f]not be put to shame.

24 "Can the prey be taken from the mighty man,
Or the captives of [1]a tyrant be rescued?"
25 Surely thus says the LORD,
"Even the [a]captives of the mighty man will be taken away,
And the prey of the tyrant will be rescued;
For I will contend with the one who contends with you,
And I will save your sons.
26 "And I will feed your [a]oppressors with their own flesh,
And they will become drunk with their own blood as with sweet wine;
And [b]all flesh will know that I, the LORD, am your Savior,
And your Redeemer, the Mighty One of Jacob."

CHAPTER 50

THUS says the LORD,
"Where is the [a]certificate of divorce,
By which I have [b]sent your mother away?
Or to whom of My creditors did I [c]sell you?
Behold, you were sold for your [d]iniquities,
And for your transgressions your mother [e]was sent away.
2 "Why was there no man when I came?
When I called, *why* was there none to answer?
Is My [a]hand so short that it cannot ransom?
Or have I no power to deliver?
Behold, I [b]dry up the sea with My rebuke,
I [c]make the rivers a wilderness;
Their fish stink for lack of water,
And die of thirst.
3 "I [a]clothe the heavens with blackness,
And I make sackcloth their covering."

4 The Lord [1]GOD has given Me the tongue of disciples,
That I may know how to [a]sustain the weary one with a word.
He awakens *Me* [b]morning by morning,
He awakens My ear to listen as a disciple.
5 The Lord GOD has opened My ear;
And I was [a]not disobedient,
Nor did I turn back.
6 I [a]gave My back to those who strike *Me*,
And My cheeks to those who pluck out the beard;
I did not cover My face from humiliation and spitting.
7 For the Lord GOD [a]helps Me,
Therefore, I am [b]not disgraced;

Therefore, I have set My face like [c]flint,
And I know that I shall not be ashamed.
8 He who [a]vindicates Me is near;
Who will contend with Me?
Let us [b]stand up to each other;
Who has a case against Me?
Let him draw near to Me.
9 Behold, the Lord GOD helps Me;
[a]Who is he who condemns Me?
Behold, they will all wear out like a garment;
The moth will eat them.
10 Who is among you that fears the LORD,
That obeys the voice of his [a]Servant,
That [b]walks in darkness and has no light?
Let him trust in the name of the LORD and rely on his God.
11 Behold, all you who [a]kindle a fire,
Who [1]encircle yourselves with firebrands,
Walk in the light of your fire
And among the brands you have set ablaze.
This you will have from My hand;
And you will [b]lie down in torment.

CHAPTER 51

"[a]LISTEN to me, you who [b]pursue righteousness,
Who seek the LORD:
Look to the [c]rock from which you were hewn,
And to the [1]quarry from which you were dug.
2 "Look to Abraham your father,
And to Sarah who gave birth to you in pain;
When *he* [a]*was* one I called him,
Then I blessed him and multiplied him."
3 Indeed, the LORD will comfort Zion;
He will comfort all her waste places.
And her [a]wilderness He will make like [b]Eden,
And her desert like the garden of the LORD;
[c]Joy and gladness will be found in her,
Thanksgiving and sound of a melody.

4 "[a]Pay attention to Me, O My people;
And give ear to Me, O My [1]nation;
For a [b]law will go forth from Me,
And I will [2]set My [c]justice for a [d]light of the peoples.
5 "My [a]righteousness is near, My salvation has gone forth,
And My arms will judge the peoples;
The [b]coastland will wait for Me,
And for My [c]arm they will wait expectantly.
6 "[a]Lift up your eyes to the sky,
Then look to the earth beneath;
For the [b]sky will vanish like smoke,
And the [b]earth will wear out like a garment,
And its inhabitants will die [1]in like manner,
But My salvation shall be forever,
And My righteousness shall not [2]wane.
7 "Listen to Me, you who know righteousness,

7 [c]Ezek. 3:8, 9

8 [a]Is. 45:25; Rom. 8:33, 34 [b]Is. 1:18; 41:1; 43:26

9 [a]Is. 54:17

10 [a]Is. 50:4; 49:2, 3 [b]Is. 9:2; 26:9; Eph. 5:8

11 [1]Lit., *gird* [a]Is. 9:18; Prov. 26:18; James 3:6 [b]Is. 8:22; 65:13-15; Amos 4:9, 10

1 [1]Lit., *the excavation of a pit* [a]Is. 51:7; 46:3; 48:12 [b]Ps. 94:15; Prov. 15:9 [c]Gen. 17:15-17

2 [a]Gen. 12:1; 15:5; Deut. 1:10; Ezek. 33:24

3 [a]Is. 35:1; 41:19 [b]Gen. 2:8; Joel 2:3 [c]Is. 25:9; 41:16; 65:18; 66:10

4 [1]Or, *people* [2]Lit., *cause to rest* [a]Ps. 50:7; 78:1 [b]Is. 2:3; Deut. 18:18; Mic. 4:2 [c]Is. 1:27; 42:4 [d]Is. 42:6; 49:6

5 [a]Is. 46:13; 54:17 [b]Is. 42:4; 60:9 [c]Is. 59:16; 63:5

6 [1]Or, *like gnats* [2]Lit., *be broken* [a]Is. 40:26 [b]Is. 13:13; 34:4; Ps. 102:25, 26; Matt. 24:35; Heb. 1:10-12; 2 Pet. 3:10

A people in whose [a]heart is My law;
Do not fear the [b]reproach of man,
Neither be dismayed at their revilings.
8 "For the moth will eat them like a garment,
And the [a]grub will eat them like wool.
But My righteousness shall be forever,
And My salvation to all generations."

9 Awake, awake, put on strength, O arm of the LORD;
Awake as in the [a]days of old, the generations of long ago.
Was it not Thou who cut Rahab in pieces,
Who pierced the dragon?
10 Was it not Thou who [a]dried up the sea,
The waters of the great deep;
Who made the depths of the sea a pathway
For the [b]redeemed to cross over?
11 So the ransomed of the LORD will return,
And come with joyful shouting to Zion;
And [a]everlasting joy *will be* on their heads.
They will obtain gladness and joy,
And sorrow and sighing will [b]flee away.

12 "I, even I, am He who comforts you.
Who are you that you are afraid of [a]man who dies,
And of the son of man who is made [b]like grass;
13 That you have [a]forgotten the LORD your Maker,
Who [b]stretched out the heavens,
And laid the foundations of the earth;
That you fear continually all day long because of the fury of the oppressor,
As he makes ready to destroy?
But where is the fury of the oppressor?
14 "The [1a]exile will soon be set free, and will not die in the
dungeon, [b]nor will his bread be lacking.
15 "For I am the LORD your God, who [a]stirs up the sea and
its waves roar (the LORD of hosts is His name).
16 "And I have [a]put My words in your mouth, and have
[b]covered you with the shadow of My hand, to [1c]establish the
heavens, to found the earth, and to say to Zion, 'You are My
people.' "
17 Rouse yourself! Rouse yourself! Arise, O Jerusalem,
You who have [a]drunk from the LORD's hand the cup of His anger;
The [1]chalice of reeling you have [2]drained to the dregs.
18 There is [a]none to guide her among all the sons she has borne;
Nor is there one to take her by the hand among all the sons she has reared.
19 These two things have befallen you;
Who will mourn for you?—
The [a]devastation and destruction, famine and sword;
How shall I comfort you?
20 Your sons have fainted,
They [a]lie *helpless* at the head of every street,
Like an antelope in a net,

7 [a]Ps. 37:31 [b]Is. 25:8; 54:4; Matt. 5:11; Acts 5:41

8 [a]Is. 14:11; 66:24

9 [a]Ex. 6:6; Deut. 4:34

10 [a]Is. 11:15, 16; 50:2; 63:11, 12 [b]Is. 63:9, 16; Ex. 15:13; Ps. 106:10

11 [a]Is. 60:19; 61:7 [b]Is. 25:8; 60:20; 65:19; Rev. 7:17; 21:1, 4; 22:3

12 [a]Is. 2:22; Ps. 118:6 [b]Is. 40:6, 7; 1 Pet. 1:24

13 [a]Is. 17:10; Deut. 6:12; 8:11 [b]Is. 40:22; 45:12, 18; 48:13; Job 9:8; Ps. 104:2

14 [1]Lit., *one in chains* [a]Is. 48:20; 52:2 [b]Is. 33:6; 49:10

15 [a]Ps. 107:25; Jer. 31:35

16 [1]Lit., *plant* [a]Is. 59:21; Deut. 18:18 [b]Is. 49:2; Ex. 33:22 [c]Is. 66:17, 22

17 [1]Lit., *bowl of the cup of reeling* [2]Lit., *drunk* [a]Is. 29:9; 63:6; Job 21:20; Jer. 25:15

18 [a]Is. 49:21; Ps. 88:18; 142:4

19 [a]Is. 8:21; 9:20; 14:30

20 [a]Is. 5:25; Jer. 14:16

Full of the wrath of the LORD,
The [b]rebuke of your God.

21 Therefore, please hear this, you afflicted,
Who are drunk, but not with wine:
22 Thus says your Lord, the LORD, even your God
Who [a]contends for His people,
"Behold, I have taken out of your hand the cup of reeling;
The [1]chalice of My anger,
You will never drink it again.
23 "And I will [a]put it into the hand of your tormentors,
Who have said to [1]you, '[b]Lie down that we may walk over you.'
You have even made your back like the ground,
And like the street for those who walk over *it*."

CHAPTER 52

AWAKE, awake,
Clothe yourself in your strength, O Zion;
Clothe yourself in your [a]beautiful garments,
O Jerusalem, the [b]holy city.
For the uncircumcised and the unclean
Will no more come into you.
2 Shake yourself from the dust, [a]rise up,
O captive Jerusalem;
Loose yourself from the chains around your neck,
O captive daughter of Zion.
3 For thus says the LORD, "You were [a]sold for nothing
and you will be [b]redeemed without money."
4 For thus says the Lord [1]GOD, "My people [a]went down
at the first into Egypt to reside there, then the Assyrian oppressed them without cause.
5 "Now therefore, what do I have here," declares the
LORD, "seeing that My people have been taken away without
cause?" *Again* the LORD declares, "Those who rule over them
howl, and My [a]name is continually blasphemed all day long.
6 "Therefore My people shall know My name; therefore
in that day I am the one who is speaking, 'Here I am.' "
7 How lovely on the mountains
Are the feet of him who brings [a]good news,
Who announces [1]peace
And brings good news of [2]happiness,
Who announces salvation,
And says to Zion, "Your [b]God [3]reigns!"
8 Listen! Your watchmen lift up *their* [a]voices,
They shout joyfully together;
For they will see [1]with their own eyes
When the LORD restores Zion.
9 [a]Break forth, shout joyfully together,
You [b]waste places of Jerusalem;
For the LORD has comforted His people,
He has [c]redeemed Jerusalem.
10 The LORD has bared His holy [a]arm
In the sight of all the nations;

20 [b]Is. 66:15

22 [1]Lit., *bowl of the cup of* [a]Is. 3:12, 13; 49:25; Jer. 50:34

23 [1]Lit., *your soul* [a]Is. 49:26; Jer. 25:15-17, 26, 28; Zech. 12:2 [b]Josh. 10:24

1 [a]Is. 49:18; 61:3, 10; Ex. 28:2, 40; 1 Chr. 16:29; Ps. 110:3; Zech. 3:4 [b]Is. 48:2; 64:10; Neh. 11:1; Zech. 14:20, 21; Matt. 4:5

2 [a]Is. 60:1

3 [a]Ps. 44:12; Jer. 15:13 [b]Is. 1:27; 62:12; 63:4

4 [1]YHWH, usually rendered LORD [a]Gen. 46:6

5 [a]Ezek. 36:20, 23; Rom. 2:24

7 [1]Or, *well-being* [2]Lit., *good* [3]Or, *is King* [a]Is. 40:9; 61:1; Nah. 1:15; Rom. 10:15 [b]Is. 24:23; Ps. 93:1

8 [1]Lit., *eye to eye* [a]Is. 62:6

9 [a]Is. 44:23; Ps. 98:4 [b]Is. 44:26; 51:3; 61:4 [c]Is. 43:1; 48:20

10 [a]Is. 51:9; 66:18, 19; Ps. 98:1-3

[1]That [b]all the ends of the earth may see
The salvation of our God.

11 Depart, depart, go out from there,
[a]Touch nothing unclean;
Go out of the midst of her, [b]purify yourselves,
You who carry the vessels of the LORD.
12 But you will not go out in [a]haste,
Nor will you go [1]as fugitives;
For the [b]LORD will go before you,
And [c]the God of Israel *will be* your rear guard.

13 Behold, My servant will prosper,
He will be high and lifted up, and [1]greatly [a]exalted.
14 Just as many were astonished at you, my people,
So His [a]appearance was marred more than any man,
And His form more than the sons of men,
15 Thus He will sprinkle many nations,
Kings will [a]shut their mouths on account of Him;
For [b]what had not been told them they will see,
And what they had not heard they will understand.

CHAPTER 53

[a]WHO has believed our message?
And to whom has the arm of the LORD been revealed?
2 For He grew up before Him like a [a]tender [1]shoot,
And like a root out of parched ground;
He has [b]no *stately* form or majesty
That we should look upon Him.
Nor appearance that we should [2]be attracted to Him.
3 He was [a]despised and forsaken of men,
A man of [1]sorrows, and [b]acquainted with [2]grief;
And like one from whom men hide their face.
He was [c]despised, and we did not [d]esteem Him.

4 Surely our [1]griefs He Himself [a]bore,
And our [2]sorrows He carried;
Yet we ourselves esteemed Him stricken,
[3]Smitten of [b]God, and afflicted.
5 But He was [1]pierced through for [a]our transgressions,
He was crushed for [b]our iniquities;
The [c]chastening for our [2]well-being *fell* upon Him,
And by [d]His scourging we are healed.
6 All of us like sheep have gone astray,
Each of us has turned to his own way;
But the LORD has caused the iniquity of us all
To [1]fall on Him.

7 He was oppressed and He was afflicted,
Yet He did not [a]open His mouth;
[b]Like a lamb that is led to slaughter,
And like a sheep that is silent before its shearers,
So He did not open His mouth.
8 By oppression and judgment He was taken away;
And as for His generation, who considered

10 [1]Lit., *and . . . earth will see* [b]Is. 45:22; 48:20

11 [a]Num. 19:11, 16 [b]Is. 1:16; Lev. 22:2

12 [1]Lit., *in flight* [a]Ex. 12:11, 33; Deut. 16:3 [b]Is. 26:7; 42:16; 49:10, 11 [c]Is. 58:8; Ex. 14:19, 20

13 [1]Or, *very high* [a]Is. 57:15

14 [a]Is. 53:2, 3

15 [a]Job 21:5 [b]Rom. 15:21

1 [a]John 12:38; Rom. 10:16

2 [1]Lit., *suckling* [2]Lit., *desire* [a]Is. 11:1 [b]Is. 52:14

3 [1]Or, *pains* [2]Or, *sickness* [a]Is. 49:7; Ps. 22:6; Luke 18:31-33 [b]Is. 53:10 [c]Mark 10:33, 34 [d]John 1:10, 11

4 [1]Or, *sickness* [2]Or, *pains* [3]Or, *Struck down by* [a]Matt. 8:17 [b]John 19:7

5 [1]Or, *wounded* [2]Or, *peace* [a]Is. 53:8; Heb. 9:28 [b]Is. 53:10; Rom. 4:25; 1 Cor. 15:3 [c]Deut. 11:2; Heb. 5:8 [d]1 Pet. 2:24, 25

6 [1]Lit., *encounter Him*

7 [a]Matt. 26:63; 27:12-14; Mark 14:61; 15:5; Luke 23:9; John 19:9 [b]Acts 8:32, 33

That He was cut off out of the land of the [1]living,
[a]For the transgression of my people to whom the stroke
was due?
9 His grave was assigned to be with wicked men,
Yet with a [a]rich man in His death;
[b]Although He had [c]done no violence,
Nor was there any deceit in His mouth.

10 But the LORD was pleased
To crush Him, [1]putting *Him* to grief;
If [2]He would render Himself *as* a guilt [a]offering,
He will see [b]*His* [3]offspring,
He will prolong *His* days,
And the [4]good [c]pleasure of the LORD will prosper in his
hand.
11 As a result of the [1]anguish of His soul,
He will [a]see [2]*it* and be satisfied;
By His [b]knowledge the Righteous One,
My Servant, will justify the many,
As He will bear their iniquities.
12 Therefore, I will allot Him a [a]portion with the great,
And He will divide the booty with the strong;
Because He poured out [1b]Himself to death,
And was [c]numbered with the transgressors;
Yet He Himself [d]bore the sin of many,
And interceded for the transgressors.

CHAPTER 54

"[a]SHOUT for joy, O barren one, you who have borne no
child;
Break forth into joyful shouting and cry aloud, you
who have not travailed;
For the sons of the [b]desolate one *will be* [c]more numerous
Than the sons of the married woman," says the LORD.
2 "[a]Enlarge the place of your tent;
[1]Stretch out the curtains of your dwellings, spare not;
Lengthen your [b]cords,
And strengthen your [b]pegs.
3 "For you will [a]spread abroad to the right and to the left.
And your [1]descendants will [b]possess nations,
And they will [c]resettle the desolate cities.

4 "Fear not for you will not be put to shame;
Neither feel humiliated, for you will not be disgraced;
But you will forget the shame of your youth,
And the [a]reproach of your widowhood you will remember no more.
5 "For your [a]husband is your Maker,
Whose name is the LORD of hosts;
And your [b]Redeemer is the Holy One of Israel,
Who is called the [c]God of all the earth.
6 "For the LORD has called you,
Like a wife [a]forsaken and grieved in spirit,
Even like a wife of *one's* youth when she is rejected,"
Says your God.

8 [1]Or, *life*
[a]Is. 53:5, 12

9 [a]Matt. 27:57-60 [b]Is. 42:1-3 [c]1 Pet. 2:22

10 [1]Lit., *He made Him sick* [2]Lit., *His soul* [3]Lit., *seed* [4]Or, *will of*
[a]Is. 53:6-12; John 1:29 [b]Is. 54:3; 61:9; 66:22; Ps. 22:30 [c]Is. 46:10

11 [1]Or, *toilsome labor* [2]Another reading is, *light*
[a]John 10:14-18 [b]Is. 45:25; Rom. 5:18, 19

12 [1]Lit., *His soul*
[a]Is. 52:13; Phil. 2:9-11 [b]Matt. 26:38, 39, 42 [c]Luke 22:37 [d]Is. 53:6, 11; 2 Cor. 5:21

1 [a]Gal. 4:27 [b]Is. 62:4 [c]Is. 49:20; 1 Sam. 2:5

2 [1]Lit., *Let them stretch out*
[a]Is. 33:20; 49:19, 20 [b]Ex. 35:18; 39:40

3 [1]Lit., *seed*
[a]Is. 43:5, 6; 60:3-11; Gen. 28:14 [b]Is. 14:1, 2; 43:14; 49:23 [c]Is. 49:19

4 [a]Is. 4:1; 25:8; 51:7

5 [a]Jer. 3:14; Hos. 2:19 [b]Is. 43:14; 48:17 [c]Is. 6:3; 11:9; 65:16

6 [a]Is. 49:14-21; 50:1, 2; 62:4

7 [1]Lit., *in*
[a]Is. 26:20 [b]Is. 11:12; 43:5; 49:18

8 [1]Lit., *overflowing*
[a]Is. 60:10 [b]Is. 49:10, 13

9 [1]Some mss. read, *the waters of Noah this is to me* [2]Lit., *cross over*
[a]Gen. 9:11 [b]Is. 12:1; Ezek. 39:29

10 [a]Is. 51:6; Ps. 102:26 [b]Is. 55:3; 59:21; 61:8; 2 Sam. 23:5; Ps. 89:34

11 [1]Or, *lapis lazuli*
[a]Is. 14:32; 28:16; 44:28

12 [1]I.e., bright red [2]Or, *carbuncles* [3]Lit., *border, boundary*

13 [1]Or, *disciples*
[a]John 6:45 [b]Is. 48:18; 66:12

14 [a]Is. 1:26, 27; 9:7; 62:1 [b]Is. 9:4; 14:4

15 [a]Is. 41:11-16

17 [1]Lit., *rises against*
[a]Is. 17:12-14; 29:8 [b]Is. 50:8, 9 [c]Is. 45:24; 46:13

1 [1]Lit., *silver*
[a]Is. 41:17; 44:3; Ps. 42:1, 2; 63:1; 143:6; John 4:14; 7:37 [b]Lam. 5:4 [c]Hos. 14:4; Matt. 10:8

2 [1]Lit., *weigh out silver*
[a]Eccles. 6:2; Hos. 8:7 [b]Is. 1:19; 62:8, 9; Ps. 22:26

3 [1]Lit., *your soul* [2]Lit., *of David*
[a]Is. 51:4 [b]Lev. 18:5; Rom. 10:5 [c]Is. 61:8 [d]Acts 13:34

7 "[1]For a [a]brief moment I forsook you,
But with great compassion I will [b]gather you.
8 "In an [1a]outburst of anger
I hid My face from you for a moment;
But with everlasting lovingkindness I will [b]have compassion on you,"
Says the LORD your Redeemer.

9 "For [1]this is like the days of Noah to me:
When I swore that the waters of Noah
Should [a]not [2]flood the earth again,
So I have sworn that I will [b]not be angry with you,
Nor will I rebuke you.
10 "For the [a]mountains may be removed and the hills may shake,
But my lovingkindness will not be removed from you,
And My [b]covenant of peace will not be shaken,"
Says the LORD who has compassion on you.

11 "O afflicted one, storm-tossed, and not comforted,
Behold, I will set your stones in antimony,
And your foundations I will [a]lay in [1]sapphires.
12 "Moreover, I will make your battlements of [1]rubies,
And your gates of [2]crystal,
And your entire [3]wall of precious stones.
13 "And [a]all your sons will be [1]taught of the LORD;
And the well-being of your sons will be [b]great.
14 "In [a]righteousness you will be established;
You will be far from [b]oppression, for you will not fear;
And from terror, for it will not come near you.
15 "If anyone fiercely assails *you* it will not be from Me.
[a]Whoever assails you will fall because of you.
16 "Behold, I Myself have created the smith who blows the fire of coals,
And brings out a weapon for its work;
And I have created the destroyer to ruin.
17 "[a]No weapon that is formed against you shall prosper;
And [b]every tongue that [1]accuses you in judgment you will condemn.
This is the heritage of the servants of the LORD,
And their [c]vindication is from Me," declares the LORD.

CHAPTER 55

"HO! Every one who [a]thirsts, come to the waters;
And you who have [b]no [1]money come, buy and eat.
Come, buy wine and milk
[c]Without money and without cost.
2 "Why do you [1]spend money for what is [a]not bread,
And your wages for what does not satisfy?
Listen carefully to Me, and [b]eat what is good,
And delight yourself in abundance.
3 "[a]Incline your ear and come to Me.
Listen, that [1]you may [b]live;
And I will make [c]an everlasting covenant with you,
According to the [d]faithful mercies [2]shown to David.

4 "Behold, I have made [a]him a witness to the peoples,
A [b]leader and commander for the peoples.
5 "Behold, you will call a [a]nation you do not know,
And a nation which knows you not will [b]run to you,
Because of the LORD your God, even the Holy One of Israel;
For He has [c]glorified you."

6 [a]Seek the LORD while He may be found;
[b]Call upon Him while He is near.
7 [a]Let the wicked forsake his way,
And the unrighteous man his [b]thoughts;
And let him [c]return to the LORD,
And He will have [d]compassion on him;
And to our God,
For He will [e]abundantly pardon.
8 "For My thoughts are not [a]your thoughts,
Neither are [b]your ways My ways," declares the LORD.
9 "For [a]*as* the heavens are higher than the earth,
So are My ways higher than your ways,
And My thoughts than your thoughts.
10 "For as the [a]rain and the snow come down from heaven,
And do not return there without watering the earth,
And making it bear and sprout,
And furnishing [b]seed to the sower and bread to the eater;
11 So shall My [a]word be which goes forth from My mouth;
It shall [b]not return to Me empty,
Without [c]accomplishing what I desire,
And without succeeding *in the matter* for which I sent it.
12 "For you will go out with [a]joy,
And be led forth with [b]peace;
The [c]mountains and the hills will break forth into shouts of joy before you,
And all the [d]trees of the field will clap *their* hands,
13 "Instead of the thornbush the cypress will come up;
And instead of the nettle the myrtle will come up;
And [1]it will be a [2a]memorial to the LORD,
For an everlasting sign which [b]will not be cut off."

CHAPTER 56

THUS says the LORD,
"[a]Preserve justice, and do righteousness,
For My [b]salvation is about to come
And My righteousness to be revealed.
2 "How [a]blessed is the man who does this,
And the son of man who takes hold of it;
Who [b]keeps from profaning the sabbath,
And keeps his hand from doing any evil."
3 Let not the foreigner who has joined himself to the LORD say,
"The LORD will surely separate me from His people."
Neither let the eunuch say, "Behold, I am a dry tree."

4 [a]Ps. 18:43; Jer. 30:9; Hos. 3:5 [b]Ezek. 34:24; 37:24, 25; Dan. 9:25; Mic. 5:2

5 [a]Is. 45:14, 22-24; 49:6, 12, 23 [b]Zech. 8:22 [c]Is. 60:9

6 [a]Is. 45:19, 22; 49:8; Ps. 32:6; Amos 5:6 [b]Is. 58:9; 65:24

7 [a]Is. 1:16, 19; 58:6 [b]Is. 32:7; 59:7 [c]Is. 31:6; 44:22 [d]Is. 14:1; 54:8, 10 [e]Is. 1:18; 40:2; 43:25; 44:22

8 [a]Is. 65:2; 66:18 [b]Is. 53:6

9 [a]Ps. 103:11

10 [a]Is. 30:23 [b]2 Cor. 9:10

11 [a]Is. 45:23; Matt. 24:35 [b]Is. 44:26; 59:21 [c]Is. 46:10; 53:10

12 [a]Is. 51:11; 52:9; Ps. 105:43 [b]Is. 54:10, 13; Jer. 29:11 [c]Is. 44:23; 49:13 [d]1 Chr. 16:33

13 [1]I.e., the transformation of the desert [2]Lit., *name* [a]Is. 63:12, 14; Jer. 33:9 [b]Is. 56:5

1 [a]Is. 1:17; 33:5; 61:8 [b]Is. 46:13; 51:5; Ps. 85:9

2 [a]Ps. 112:1; 119:1, 2 [b]Ex. 20:8-11; 31:13-17; Jer. 17:21, 22; Ezek. 20:12, 20

4 For thus says the LORD,
"To the eunuchs who keep My sabbaths,
And choose what pleases Me,
And hold fast My covenant,
5 To them I will give in My [a]house and within My [b]walls a memorial,
And a name better than that of sons and daughters;
I will give [1]them an everlasting [c]name which will not be cut off.

6 "Also the foreigners who join themselves to the LORD,
To minister to Him, and to love the name of the LORD,
To be His servants, every one who [a]keeps from profaning the sabbath,
And holds fast My covenant;
7 Even [a]those I will bring to My [b]holy mountain,
And [c]make them joyful in My house of prayer.
Their burnt offerings and their sacrifices will be acceptable on My altar;
For [d]My house will be called a house of prayer for all the peoples."
8 The Lord [1]GOD, who gathers the dispersed of Israel, declares,
"Yet [a]*others* I will gather to [2]them, to those *already* gathered."

9 All you [a]beasts of the field,
All you beasts in the forest,
Come to eat.
10 His [a]watchmen are [b]blind,
All of them know nothing.
All of them are dumb dogs unable to bark,
[1]Dreamers lying down, who love to slumber;
11 And the dogs are [1a]greedy, they [2]are not satisfied.
And they are shepherds who have no understanding;
They have all [b]turned to their own way,
Each one to his unjust gain, to the last one.
12 "Come," *they say*, "let [1]us get wine, and let us drink heavily of strong drink;
And [a]tomorrow will be like today, only more so."

CHAPTER 57

THE righteous man perishes, and no man [a]takes it to heart;
And devout men are taken away, while no one understands.
For the righteous man is taken away from [b]evil,
2 He enters into peace;
They rest in their [1]beds,
Each one who [a]walked in his upright way.
3 "But come here, you sons of a sorceress,
Offspring of an adulterer and [1]a prostitute.
4 "Against whom do you jest?
Against whom do you open wide your mouth
And stick out your tongue?

5 [1]So DSS; M.T. reads, *him* [a]Is. 56:7; 2:2, 3; 66:20 [b]Is. 26:1; 60:18 [c]Is. 62:2

6 [a]Is. 56:2, 4

7 [a]Is. 2:2, 3; 60:11; Mic. 4:1, 2 [b]Is. 11:9; 65:25 [c]Is. 61:10 [d]Matt. 21:13; Mark 11:17; Luke 19:46

8 [1]YHWH, usually rendered LORD. [2]Lit., *him* [a]Is. 60:3-11; 66:18-21; John 10:16

9 [a]Is. 18:6; 46:11

10 [1]So DSS; M. T., *Ravers* [a]Ezek. 3:17 [b]Is. 29:9-14; Jer. 14:13, 14

11 [1]Lit., *strong of soul/appetite* [2]Lit., *do not know satisfaction* [a]Is. 28:7; Ezek. 13:19; Mic. 3:5, 11 [b]Is. 57:17; Jer. 22:17

12 [1]So DSS and many versions; M. T., *me* [a]Ps. 10:6; Luke 12:19, 20

1 [a]Is. 42:25; 47:7 [b]Is. 47:11; 2 Kin. 22:20; Jer. 18:11

2 [1]I.e., graves [a]Is. 26:7

3 [1]Reading with the versions; Heb., *she prostitutes herself*

Are you not children of [a]rebellion,
Offspring of deceit,
5 *Who* inflame yourselves among the [1]oaks,
[a]Under every luxuriant tree,
Who [b]slaughter the children in the [2]ravines,
Under the clefts of the crags?
6 "Among the [1a]smooth *stones* of the [2]ravine
Is your portion, [3]they are your lot;
Even to them you have [b]poured out a libation,
You have made a grain offering.
Shall I [4c]relent concerning these things?
7 "Upon a [a]high and lofty mountain
You have made your bed.
You also went up there to offer sacrifice.
8 "And behind the door and the doorpost
You have set up your sign;
Indeed, far removed from Me, you have uncovered yourself;
And have gone up and made your bed wide.
And you have made an agreement for yourselves with them,
You have loved their [1]bed,
You have looked on *their* [2]manhood.
9 "And you have journeyed to the King with oil
And increased your perfumes;
You have [a]sent your envoys a great distance,
And made *them* go down to [1]Sheol.
10 "You were tired out by the length of your road,
Yet you did not say, '[a]It is hopeless.'
You found [1]renewed strength,
Therefore you did not [2]faint.

11 "Of [a]whom were you worried and fearful,
When you lied, and did [b]not remember Me,
[1]Nor [c]give *Me* a thought.
Was I not silent even for a long time
So you do not fear Me?
12 "I will declare your righteousness and your [a]deeds,
But they will not profit you.
13 "When you cry out, [a]let your collection *of idols* deliver you.
But the wind will carry all of them up,
And a breath will take *them away*.
But he who [b]takes refuge in Me shall [c]inherit the land,
And shall [d]possess My holy mountain."

14 And it shall be said,
"[a]Build up, build up, prepare the way,
Remove *every* obstacle out of the way of My people."
15 For thus says the [a]high and exalted One
Who [1b]lives forever, whose name is Holy,
"I [c]dwell *on* a high and holy place,
And *also* with the [d]contrite and lowly of spirit
In order to [e]revive the spirit of the lowly
And to revive the heart of the contrite.
16 "For I will [a]not contend forever,

4 [a]Is. 48:8

5 [1]Or, *terebinths* [2]Or, *wadis*
[a]2 Kin. 16:4; Jer. 2:20; 3:13 [b]2 Kin. 23:10; Ps. 106:37, 38; Jer. 7:31

6 [1]I.e., symbols of fertility gods [2]Or, *wadi* [3]Lit., *they, they* [4]Or, *repent*
[a]Jer. 3:9; Hab. 2:19 [b]Jer. 7:18 [c]Jer. 5:9, 29; 9:9

7 [a]Jer. 3:16; Ezek. 16:16

8 [1]Or, *lying down* [2]Lit., *hand*

9 [1]Or, *the nether world*
[a]Ezek. 23:16, 40

10 [1]Lit., *the life of your hand* [2]Or, *become sick*
[a]Jer. 2:25; 18:12

11 [1]Lit., *You did not set it upon your heart*
[a]Is. 51:12, 13; Prov. 29:25 [b]Jer. 2:32; 3:21 [c]Is. 42:14; Ps. 50:21

12 [a]Is. 29:15; 59:6; 65:7; 66:18; Mic. 3:2-4

13 [a]Jer. 22:20; 30:14 [b]Is. 25:4; Ps. 37:3, 9 [c]Is. 49:8; 60:21 [d]Is. 65:9

14 [a]Is. 62:10; Jer. 18:15

15 [1]Or, *dwell in eternity*
[a]Is. 52:13 [b]Is. 40:28; Deut. 33:27 [c]Is. 33:5; 66:1 [d]Is. 66:2; Ps. 34:18; 51:17 [e]Is. 61:1-3; Ps. 147:3

16 [a]Gen. 6:3

[b]Neither will I always be angry;
For the spirit would grow faint before Me,
And the breath *of those whom* I have made.
17 "Because of the iniquity of his [a]unjust gain I was angry and struck him;
I hid *My face* and was angry,
And he went on [b]turning away, in the way of his heart.
18 "I have seen his ways, but I will [a]heal him;
I will lead him and [b]restore comfort to him and to his mourners,
19 Creating the [1a]praise of the lips.
[b]Peace, peace to him who is [c]far and to him who is near,"
Says the LORD, "and I will heal him."
20 But the [a]wicked are like the tossing sea,
For it cannot be quiet,
And its waters toss up refuse and mud.
21 "[a]There is no peace," says my God, "for the wicked."

CHAPTER 58

"[a]CRY loudly, do not hold back;
Raise your voice like a trumpet,
And declare to My people their transgression,
And to the house of Jacob their sins.
2 "Yet they [a]seek Me day by day, and delight to know My ways;
As a nation that has done [b]righteousness,
And has not forsaken the ordinance of their God.
They ask Me *for* just decisions,
They delight [c]in the nearness of God.
3 'Why have we [a]fasted and Thou dost not see?
Why have we humbled ourselves and Thou dost not [1]notice?'
Behold, on the [b]day of your fast you find *your* desire,
And drive hard all your workers.
4 "Behold, you fast for contention and [a]strife and to strike with a wicked fist.
You do not fast like *you do* today to [b]make your voice heard on high.
5 "Is it a fast like this which I choose, a day for a man to humble himself?
Is it for bowing [1]one's head like a reed,
And for spreading out [a]sackcloth and ashes as a bed?
Will you call this a fast, even an [b]acceptable day to the LORD?
6 "Is this not the fast which I chose,
To [a]loosen the bonds of wickedness,
To undo the bands of the yoke,
And to [b]let the oppressed go free,
And break every yoke?
7 "Is it not to [a]divide your bread [1]with the hungry,
And [b]bring the homeless poor into the house;
When you see the [c]naked, to cover him;
And not to [d]hide yourself from your own flesh?
8 "Then your light will break out like the dawn,

16 [b]Ps. 85:5; 103:9; Mic. 7:18

17 [a]Is. 2:7; 56:11; Jer. 6:13 [b]Is. 1:4; Jer. 3:14, 22

18 [a]Is. 19:22; 30:26; 53:5 [b]Is. 61:1-3

19 [1]Lit., *fruit of the lips* [a]Is. 6:7; 51:16; 59:21; Heb. 13:15 [b]Is. 26:12; 32:17 [c]Acts 2:39; Eph. 2:17

20 [a]Is. 3:9, 11; Job 18:5-14

21 [a]Is. 48:22; 59:8

1 [a]Is. 40:6, 8

2 [a]Is. 1:11; Titus 1:16 [b]Is. 48:1; Jer. 7:9, 10 [c]Is. 29:13; 57:3; Ps. 119:150; James 4:8

3 [1]Lit., *know* [a]Mal. 3:14; Luke 18:12 [b]Is. 22:12, 13; Zech. 7:5, 6

4 [a]Is. 3:14, 15; 59:6 [b]Is. 1:15; 59:2; Joel 2:12-14

5 [1]Lit., *his* [a]1 Kin. 21:27 [b]Is. 49:8; 61:2

6 [a]Neh. 5:10-12; Jer. 34:8 [b]Is. 1:17

7 [1]Lit., *for* [a]Is. 58:10; Job 31:19, 20; Ezek. 18:7, 16 [b]Is. 16:3, 4; Heb. 13:2 [c]Matt. 25:35; Luke 3:11 [d]Deut. 22:1-4; Luke 10:31, 32

And your [a]recovery will speedily spring forth;
And your [b]righteousness will go before you;
The glory of the [c]LORD will be your rear guard.
9 "Then you will [a]call, and the LORD will answer;
You will cry, and He will say, 'Here I am.'
If you remove the yoke from your midst
The [1]pointing of the finger, and speaking wickedness,
10 And if you [1a]give yourself to the hungry,
And satisfy the [2]desire of the afflicted,
Then your [b]light will rise in darkness,
And your gloom *will become* like midday.
11 "And the [a]LORD will continually guide you,
And [b]satisfy your [1]desire in scorched places,
And [c]give strength to your bones;
And you will be like a [d]watered garden,
And like a [e]spring of water whose waters do not [2]fail.
12 "And those from among you will [a]rebuild the ancient ruins;
You will [b]raise up the age-old foundations;
And you will be called the repairer of the [c]breach,
The restorer of the [1]streets in which to dwell.

13 "If because of the sabbath, you [a]turn your foot,
From doing your *own* pleasure on My holy day,
And call the sabbath a [b]delight, the holy of the LORD honorable,
And shall honor it, desisting from your [c]*own* ways,
From seeking your *own* pleasure,
And speaking *your own* word,
14 Then you will take [a]delight in the LORD,
And I will make you ride on the heights of the earth;
And I will feed you *with* the heritage of Jacob your father,
For the mouth of the LORD has spoken."

CHAPTER 59

BEHOLD, [a]the LORD's hand is not so short
That it cannot save;
[b]Neither is His ear so dull
That it cannot hear.
2 But your [a]iniquities have made a separation between you and your God,
And your sins have hid [1]His face from you, so that *He* does [b]not hear.
3 For your [a]hands are defiled with blood,
And your fingers with iniquity;
Your lips have spoken [b]falsehood,
Your tongue mutters wickedness.
4 [a]No one sues righteously and [b]no one pleads [1]honestly.
They trust in confusion, and speak lies;
They [c]conceive mischief, and bring forth iniquity.
5 They hatch adders' eggs and [a]weave the spider's web;
He who eats of their eggs dies,
And *from* that which is crushed a snake breaks forth.
6 Their webs will not become clothing,

8 [a]Is. 30:26; 33:24; Jer. 30:17; 33:6 [b]Is. 62:1; Ps. 85:13 [c]Is. 52:12; Ex. 14:19

9 [1]Lit., *sending out*
[a]Is. 55:6; 65:24; Ps. 50:15

10 [1]Lit., *furnish* [2]Or, *soul*
[a]Is. 58:7; Deut. 15:7 [b]Is. 58:8; 42:16; Job 11:17; Ps. 37:6

11 [1]Or, *soul* [2]Or, *deceive*
[a]Is. 49:10; 57:18 [b]Is. 41:17; Ps. 107:9 [c]Is. 66:14 [d]Is. 27:3; Song of Sol. 4:15; Jer. 31:12 [e]John 4:14; 7:38

12 [1]Lit., *paths*
[a]Is. 49:8; 61:4; Ezek. 36:10 [b]Is. 44:28 [c]Is. 30:13; Amos 9:11

13 [a]Is. 56:2, 4, 6; Ex. 31:16, 17; 35:2, 3; Jer. 17:21-27 [b]Ps. 27:4; 42:4; 84:2, 10 [c]Is. 55:8

14 [a]Is. 61:10

1 [a]Is. 50:2; Num. 11:23; Jer. 32:17 [b]Is. 58:9; 65:24; Ezek. 8:18

2 [1]So versions; M. T., *faces*
[a]Is. 1:15; 50:1 [b]Is. 58:4

3 [a]Is. 1:15, 21; Jer. 2:30, 34; Ezek. 7:23; Hos. 4:2 [b]Is. 59:13; 28:15; 30:9

4 [1]Lit., *in truth*
[a]Is. 59:14; 5:7 [b]Is. 59:14, 15 [c]Is. 33:11; Job 15:35; Ps. 7:14

5 [a]Job 8:14

Nor will they [a]cover themselves with their works;
Their [b]works are works of iniquity,
And an [c]act of violence is in their [1]hands.
7 [a]Their feet run to evil,
And they hasten to shed innocent blood;
[b]Their thoughts are thoughts of iniquity,
Devastation and destruction are in their highways.
8 They do not know the [a]way of peace,
And there is [b]no justice in their tracks;
They have made their paths crooked;
[c]Whoever treads on [1]them does not know peace.

9 Therefore, [a]justice is far from us,
And righteousness does not overtake us;
We [b]hope for light, but behold, darkness;
For brightness, but we walk in gloom.
10 We grope along the wall like blind men,
We grope like those who have no eyes;
We [a]stumble at midday as in the twilight,
Among those who are vigorous we are [b]like dead men.
11 All of us growl like bears,
And [a]moan sadly like doves;
We hope for justice, but there is none,
For salvation, *but* it is far from us.
12 For our [a]transgressions are multiplied before Thee,
And our [b]sins [1]testify against us;
For our transgressions are with us,
And [2]we know our iniquities:
13 Transgressing and [a]denying the LORD,
And turning away from our God,
Speaking [b]oppression and revolt,
Conceiving *in* and [c]uttering from the heart lying words.
14 And [a]justice is turned back,
And [b]righteousness stands far away;
For truth has stumbled in the street,
And uprightness cannot enter.
15 Yes, truth is lacking;
And he who turns aside from evil [a]makes himself a prey.

Now the LORD saw,
And it was [1]displeasing in His sight [b]that there was no justice.
16 And He saw that there was no man,
And was astonished that there was no one to intercede;
Then His [a]own arm brought salvation to Him;
And His righteousness upheld Him.
17 And He put on [a]righteousness like a breastplate,
And a helmet of salvation on His head;
And He put on garments of vengeance for clothing,
And wrapped Himself with [b]zeal as a mantle.
18 [a]According to *their* [1]deeds, [2]so He will repay,
Wrath to His adversaries, recompense to His enemies;
To the coastlands He will [3]make recompense.
19 So they will fear the name of the LORD from the west
And His glory from the rising of the sun,

6 [1]Lit., *palms*
[a]Is. 28:20 [b]Is. 57:12; Jer. 6:7 [c]Is. 58:4; Ezek. 7:11

7 [a]Prov. 1:16; 6:17; Rom. 3:15-17 [b]Is. 65:2; 66:18; Mark 7:21, 22

8 [1]Lit., *it*
[a]Luke 1:79 [b]Is. 59:9, 11; Hos. 4:1 [c]Is. 57:20, 21

9 [a]Is. 59:14 [b]Is. 5:30; 8:21, 22

10 [a]Is. 8:14, 15; 28:13 [b]Lam. 3:6

11 [a]Is. 38:14; Ezek. 7:16

12 [1]Lit., *answer* [2]Lit., *our iniquities we know them*
[a]Is. 58:1; Ezra 9:6 [b]Is. 3:9; Jer. 14:7; Hos. 5:5

13 [a]Josh. 24:27; Prov. 30:9; Matt. 10:33; Titus 1:16 [b]Is. 5:7; 30:12; Jer. 9:3, 4 [c]Is. 59:3, 4; Mark 7:21, 22

14 [a]Is. 1:21; 5:7 [b]Is. 46:12; Hab. 1:4

15 [1]Or, *evil*
[a]Is. 5:23; 10:2; 29:21; 32:7 [b]Is. 1:21-23

16 [a]Is. 52:10; 63:5; Ps. 98:1

17 [a]Eph. 6:14 [b]Is. 9:7; 37:32; Zech. 1:4

18 [1]Lit., *recompense* [2]Lit., *accordingly* [3]Lit., *repay*
[a]Is. 65:6, 7; 66:6; Job 34:11; Jer. 17:10

For He will [a]come like a [1]rushing stream,
Which the wind of the LORD drives.
20 "And a [a]Redeemer will come to Zion,
And to those who [b]turn from transgression in Jacob,"
declares the LORD.
21 "And as for me, this is My [a]covenant with them," says
the LORD: "My [b]Spirit which is upon you, and My words which
I have put in your mouth, shall not depart from your mouth,
nor from the mouth of your [1]offspring, nor from the mouth of
your [1]offspring's offspring," says the LORD, "from now and
forever."

CHAPTER 60

"ARISE, shine; for your [a]light has come,
And the [b]glory of the LORD has risen upon you.
2 "For behold, [a]darkness will cover the earth,
And deep darkness the peoples;
But the LORD will rise upon you,
And His [b]glory will appear upon you.
3 "And [a]nations will come to your light,
And kings to the brightness of your rising.

4 "[a]Lift up your eyes round about, and see;
They all gather together, they come to you.
Your sons will come from afar,
And your daughters will be [1]carried in the arms.
5 "Then you will see and be [a]radiant,
And your heart will [1]thrill and rejoice;
Because the [b]abundance of the sea will be turned to you,
The [c]wealth of the nations will come to you.
6 "A multitude of camels will cover you,
The young camels of Midian and Ephah;
All those from Sheba will come;
They will bring gold and frankincense,
And will [a]bear good news of the praises of the LORD.
7 "All the flocks of [a]Kedar will be gathered together to you,
The rams of Nebaioth will minister to you;
They will go up with acceptance on My [b]altar,
And I shall [1]glorify My [2]glorious house.
8 "[a]Who are these who fly like a cloud,
And like the doves to their [1]lattices?
9 "Surely the coastlands will wait for Me;
And the [a]ships of Tarshish *will come* first,
To [b]bring your sons from afar,
Their silver and their gold with them,
For the name of the LORD your God,
And for the Holy One of Israel because He has [1]glorified you.

10 "And foreigners will build up your walls,
And their [a]kings will minister to you;

19 [1]Lit., *narrow* [a]Is. 30:28; 66:12

20 [a]Rom. 11:26, 27 [b]Ezek. 18:30, 31; Acts 2:38, 39

21 [1]Lit., *seed* [a]Jer. 31:31-44 [b]Is. 11:2; 32:15; 44:3

1 [a]Is. 60:19, 20 [b]Is. 24:23; 35:2; 58:8

2 [a]Is. 58:10; Jer. 13:16; Col. 1:13 [b]Is. 4:5

3 [a]Is. 2:3; 45:14, 22-25; 49:23

4 [1]Lit., *nursed upon the side* [a]Is. 11:12; 49:18

5 [1]Lit., *tremble and be enlarged* [a]Ps. 34:5 [b]Is. 23:18; 24:14 [c]Is. 61:6

6 [a]Is. 42:10

7 [1]Or, *beautify* [2]Or, *beautiful* [a]Gen. 25:13 [b]Is. 19:19; 56:7

8 [1]Or, *dovecotes, windows* [a]Is. 49:21

9 [1]Lit., *beautified* [a]Is. 2:16; Ps. 48:7 [b]Is. 14:2; 43:6; 49:22; Gal. 3:26

10 [a]Is. 49:23

For in My wrath I struck you,
And in My favor I have had compassion on you.
11 "And your [a]gates will be open continually;
They will not be closed day or night,
So that *men* may bring to you the wealth of the nations,
With [b]their kings led in procession.
12 "For the [a]nation and the kingdom which will not serve you will perish,
And the nations will be utterly ruined.
13 "The glory of Lebanon will come to you,
The juniper, the box tree, and the cypress together,
To beautify the place of My sanctuary;
And I shall make the [a]place of My feet glorious.
14 "And the [a]sons of those who afflicted you will come bowing to you,
And all those who despised you will bow themselves at the soles of your feet;
And they will call you the [b]city of the LORD,
The [c]Zion of the Holy One of Israel.

15 "Whereas you have been [a]forsaken and hated
With no one passing through,
I will make you an everlasting [b]pride,
A joy from generation to generation.
16 "You will also suck the milk of nations,
And will suck the breast of kings;
Then you will know that I, the LORD, am your [a]Saviour,
And your [b]Redeemer, the Mighty One of Jacob.
17 "Instead of bronze I will bring gold,
And instead of iron I will bring silver,
And instead of wood, bronze,
And instead of stones, iron.
And I will make peace your administrators,
And righteousness your overseers.
18 "[a]Violence will not be heard again in your land,
Nor [b]devastation or destruction within your borders;
But you will call your [c]walls salvation, and your [d]gates praise.
19 "No longer will you have the [a]sun for light by day,
Nor for brightness will the moon give you light;
But you will have the [b]LORD for an everlasting light,
And your [c]God for your [1]glory.
20 "Your [a]sun will set no more,
Neither will your moon wane;
For you will have the LORD for an everlasting light,
And the days of your [b]mourning will be finished.
21 "Then all your [a]people *will be* righteous;
They will [b]possess the land forever,
The branch of [1]My planting,
The work of My hands,
That I may be glorified.
22 "The [a]smallest one will become a [1]clan,
And the least one a mighty nation.
I, the LORD, will hasten it in its time."

11 [a]Is. 60:18; 26:2; 62:10 [b]Is. 24:21; Ps. 149:8

12 [a]Is. 14:2; Zech. 14:17

13 [a]1 Chr. 28:2; Ps. 99:5; 132:7

14 [a]Is. 14:1, 2; 45:14, 23; 49:23 [b]Is. 1:26 [c]Heb. 12:22

15 [a]Is. 1:7-9; 6:11-13; Jer. 30:17 [b]Is. 4:2; 65:18

16 [a]Is. 19:2; 43:3, 11; 45:15, 21; 63:8 [b]Is. 59:20; 63:16

18 [a]Is. 54:14 [b]Is. 51:19 [c]Is. 26:1 [d]Is. 60:11

19 [1]Or, *beauty* [a]Rev. 21:23; 22:5 [b]Is. 2:5; 9:2 [c]Is. 41:16; 45:25; Zech. 2:5

20 [a]Is. 30:26 [b]Is. 35:10; 65:19; Rev. 21:4

21 [1]Lit., *His* [a]Is. 45:24, 25; 52:1 [b]Is. 57:13; 61:7; Ps. 37:11, 22

22 [1]Or, *thousand* [a]Is. 6:13; 10:22; 51:2

Chapter 61

THE [a]Spirit of the Lord [1]God is upon me,
Because the Lord has anointed me—
To bring good news to the [2b]afflicted;
He has sent me to [c]bind up the brokenhearted,
To [d]proclaim liberty to captives,
And [3]freedom to prisoners;
2 To [a]proclaim the favorable year of the Lord,
And the [b]day of vengeance of our God;
To [c]comfort all who mourn,
3 To [a]grant those who mourn *in* Zion,
Giving them a garland instead of ashes,
The [b]oil of gladness instead of mourning,
The mantle of praise instead of a spirit of fainting.
So they will be called [1c]oaks of righteousness,
The planting of the Lord, that He may be glorified.

4 Then they will [a]rebuild the ancient ruins,
They will raise up the former devastations,
And they will repair the ruined cities,
The desolations of many generations.
5 And [a]strangers will stand and pasture your flocks,
And [1]foreigners will be your farmers and your vinedressers.
6 But you will be called the [a]priests of the Lord;
You will be spoken of *as* [b]ministers of our God.
You will eat the [c]wealth of nations,
And in their [1]riches you will boast.
7 Instead of your shame *you will have a* double *portion*,
And *instead of* humiliation they will shout for joy over their portion.
Therefore they will possess a double *portion* in their land,
[a]Everlasting joy will be theirs.
8 For I, the Lord, [a]love justice,
I hate robbery [1]in the burnt offering;
And I will faithfully give them their recompense,
And I will make an [b]everlasting covenant with them.
9 Then their offspring will be known among the nations,
And their descendants in the midst of the peoples.
All who see them will recognize them
Because they are the offspring *whom* the Lord has blessed.

10 I will [a]rejoice greatly in the Lord,
My soul will exult in [b]my God;
For He has [c]clothed me with garments of salvation,
He has wrapped me with a robe of righteousness,
As a bridegroom decks himself with a garland,
And as a bride adorns herself with her jewels.
11 For as the earth brings forth its sprouts,
And as a garden causes the things sown in it to spring up,
So the Lord [1]God will [a]cause [b]righteousness and praise
To spring up before all the nations.

1 [1]YHWH, usually rendered Lord [2]Or, *humble* [3]Lit., *opening to those who are bound*
[a]Is. 11:2; 48:16; Luke 4:18, 19 [b]Is. 11:4; 28:19; 32:7 [c]Is. 57:15 [d]Is. 42:7; 49:9

2 [a]Is. 49:8; 60:10 [b]Is. 2:12; 13:6; 34:2, 8 [c]Is. 57:18; Jer. 31:13; Matt. 5:4

3 [1]Or, *terebinths*
[a]Is. 60:20 [b]Ps. 23:5; 45:7; 104:15 [c]Is. 60:21; Jer. 17:7, 8

4 [a]Is. 49:8; 58:12; Ezek. 36:33; Amos 9:14

5 [1]Lit., *sons of the foreigner*
[a]Is. 14:2; 60:10

6 [1]Or, *glory*
[a]Is. 66:21 [b]Is. 56:6 [c]Is. 60:5, 11

7 [a]Ps. 16:11

8 [1]Or, *with iniquity*
[a]Is. 5:16; 28:17; 30:18 [b]Is. 55:3; Gen. 17:7; Ps. 105:10; Jer. 32:40

10 [a]Is. 12:1, 2; 25:9; 4:16; 51:3 [b]Is. 49:4 [c]Is. 49:18; 52:1

11 [1]YHWH, usually rendered Lord
[a]Is. 45:23, 24; 60:18, 21 [b]Ps. 72:3; 85:11

E 78-1

CHAPTER 62

FOR Zion's sake I will not keep silent,
And for Jerusalem's sake I will not keep quiet,
Until her righteousness goes forth like brightness,
And her [a]salvation like a torch that is burning.
2 And the [a]nations will see your righteousness,
And all kings your glory;
And you will be called by a new [b]name,
Which the mouth of the LORD will designate.
3 You will also be a [a]crown of beauty in the hand of the LORD,
And a royal [1]diadem in the hand of your God.
4 It will no longer be said to you, "[1a]Forsaken,"
Nor to your land will it any longer be said, "[2]Desolate";
But you will be called, "[3]My delight is in her,"
And your land, "[4]Married";
For the [b]LORD delights in you,
And *to Him* your land will be married.
5 For *as* a young man marries a virgin,
So your sons will marry you;
And *as* the [1]bridegroom rejoices over the bride,
So your [a]God will rejoice over you.

6 On your walls, O Jerusalem, I have appointed [a]watchmen;
All day and all night they will never keep silent.
You who [b]remind the LORD, take no rest for yourselves;
7 And [a]give Him no rest until He establishes
And makes [b]Jerusalem a praise in the earth.
8 The LORD has sworn by His right hand and by His strong arm,
"I will [a]never again give your grain *as* food for your enemies;
Nor will [1]foreigners drink your new wine, for which you have labored."
9 But those who [a]garner it will eat it, and praise the LORD;
And those who gather it will drink it in the courts of My sanctuary.

10 Go through, [a]go through the gates;
Clear the way [1]for the people;
[b]Build up, build up the [c]highway;
Remove the stones, lift up a standard over the peoples.
11 Behold, the LORD has proclaimed to the [a]end of the earth,
[b]Say to the daughter of Zion, "Lo, your salvation comes;
[c]Behold His reward is with Him, and His recompense before Him."
12 And they will call them, "[a]The holy people,
The redeemed of the LORD";
And you will be called, "Sought out, a city [b]not forsaken."

1 [a]Is. 46:13; 52:10

2 [a]Is. 60:3 [b]Is. 62:4, 12; 56:5; 65:15

3 [1]Lit., *turban* [a]Is. 28:5; Zech. 9:16; 1 Thess. 2:19

4 [1]I.e., Azubah [2]I.e., Shemamah [3]I.e., Hephzibah [4]I.e., Beulah [a]Is. 54:6, 7; 16:15, 18 [b]Jer. 32:41; Zeph. 3:17

5 [1]Lit., *exultation of the bridegroom* [a]Is. 65:19

6 [a]Is. 52:8; Jer. 6:17; Ezek. 3:17; 33:7 [b]Ps. 74:2; Jer. 14:21; Lam. 5:1, 20

7 [a]Matt. 15:21-28; Luke 18:1-8 [b]Is. 60:18; Jer. 33:9; Zeph. 3:19, 20

8 [1]Lit., *sons of foreigners* [a]Is. 1:7; Lev. 26:16; Deut. 28:31, 33; Judg. 6:3-6; Jer. 5:17

9 [a]Is. 65:13, 21-23

10 [1]Lit., *of* [a]Is. 26:1; 60:11, 18 [b]Is. 57:14 [c]Is. 11:16; 19:23; 35:8; 49:11

11 [a]Is. 42:10; 49:6 [b]Matt. 21:5; Zech. 9:9 [c]Is. 40:10

12 [a]Is. 4:3; Deut. 7:6; 1 Pet. 2:9 [b]Is. 62:4; 41:17; 42:16

CHAPTER 63

WHO is this who comes from Edom,
With garments of [1]glowing colors from [a]Bozrah,
This one who is majestic in His apparel,
[2]Marching in the greatness of His strength?
"It is I who speak in righteousness, [b]mighty to save."
2 Why is Your apparel red,
And Your garments like the one who [a]treads in the wine press?
3 "I have trodden the wine trough alone,
And from the peoples there was no man with Me.
I also [a]trod them in My anger,
And [b]trampled them in My wrath;
And their [1]life blood is sprinkled on My garments,
And I [2]stained all My raiment.
4 "For the [a]day of vengeance was in My heart,
And My year of redemption has come.
5 "And I looked, and there was [a]no one to help,
And I was astonished and there was no one to uphold;
So My own arm brought salvation to Me;
And My wrath upheld Me.
6 "And I [a]trod down the peoples in My anger,
And made them drunk in My wrath,
And I [1]poured out their lifeblood on the earth."

7 I shall make mention of the [a]lovingkindnesses of the LORD, the praises of the LORD,
According to all that the LORD has granted us,
And the great [b]goodness toward the house of Israel,
Which He has granted them according to His [c]compassion,
And according to the multitude of His lovingkindnesses.
8 For he said, "Surely, they are [a]My people,
Sons who will not deal falsely."
So He became their Savior.
9 In all their affliction [1a]He was afflicted,
And the [b]angel of His presence saved them;
In His [c]love and in His mercy He [d]redeemed them;
And He [e]lifted them and carried them all the days of old.
10 But they [a]rebelled
And grieved His [b]Holy Spirit;
Therefore, He turned Himself to become their enemy,
He fought against them.
11 Then [a]His people remembered the days of old, of Moses.
Where is [b]He who brought them up out of the sea with the [1]shepherds of His flock?
Where is He who [c]put His Holy Spirit in the midst of [2]them,
12 Who caused His [a]glorious arm to go at the right hand of Moses,
Who [b]divided the waters before them to make for Himself an everlasting name,

1 [1]Or, *crimson* [2]Lit., *Inclining* [a]Is. 34:6; Jer. 49:13; Amos 1:12 [b]Zeph. 3:7
2 [a]Rev. 19:13, 15
3 [1]Lit., *juice* [2]Lit., *defiled* [a]Is. 22:5; 28:3 [b]Mic. 7:10
4 [a]Is. 34:8; 35:4; 61:2; Jer. 51:6
5 [a]Is. 59:16
6 [1]Lit., *brought down their juice to the earth* [a]Is. 22:5; 34:2; 65:12
7 [a]Is. 54:8, 10; Ps. 25:6; 92:2 [b]1 Kin. 8:66; Neh. 9:25, 35 [c]Is. 54:7, 8; Ps. 51:1; 86:5, 15; Eph. 2:4
8 [a]Is. 3:15; 51:4; Ex. 6:7
9 [1]Another reading is, *He was not an adversary.* [a]Judg. 10:16 [b]Ex. 23:20-23; 33:14, 15 [c]Deut. 7:7, 8 [d]Is. 43:1; 52:9 [e]Is. 46:3; Deut. 1:31; 32:10-12
10 [a]Ps. 78:40; 106:33; Acts 7:51; Eph. 4:30 [b]Is. 63:11; Ps. 51:11
11 [1]Some mss. read, *shepherd* [2]Lit., *him* [a]Ps. 106:44, 45 [b]Is. 51:9, 10 [c]Num. 11:17, 25, 29; Hag. 2:5
12 [a]Ex. 6:6; 15:16 [b]Is. 11:15; 51:10, 11; Ex. 14:21, 22

13 Who led them through the depths?
Like the horse in the wilderness, they did not [a]stumble;
14 As the cattle which go down into the valley,
The Spirit of the [a]LORD gave [1]them rest.
So didst Thou [b]lead Thy people,
To make for Thyself a glorious name.

15 [a]Look down from heaven, and see from Thy holy and glorious [b]habitation;
Where are Thy [c]zeal and Thy mighty deeds?
The [d]stirrings of Thy heart and Thy compassion are restrained toward me.
16 For Thou art our [a]Father, though [b]Abraham does not know us,
And Israel does not recognize us.
Thou, O LORD, art our Father,
Our [c]Redeemer from of old is Thy name.
17 Why, O LORD, dost Thou [a]cause us to stray from Thy ways,
And [b]harden our heart from fearing Thee?
Return for the sake of Thy servants, the tribes of Thy heritage.
18 Thy holy people possessed Thy sanctuary for a little while,
Our adversaries have [a]trodden *it* down.
19 We have become *like* those over whom Thou hast never ruled,
Like those who were not called by Thy name.

CHAPTER 64

1 O THAT Thou wouldst rend the heavens *and* [a]come down,
That the mountains might [b]quake at Thy presence—
2 [1]As fire kindles the brushwood, *as* fire causes water to boil—
To make Thy name known to Thine adversaries,
That the [a]nations may tremble at Thy presence!
3 When Thou didst [a]awesome things which we did not expect,
Thou didst come down, the mountains quaked at Thy presence.
4 For from of old [a]they have not heard nor perceived by ear,
Neither has the eye seen a God besides Thee,
Who acts in behalf of the one who [b]waits for Him.
5 Thou dost [a]meet him who rejoices in [b]doing righteousness,
Who [c]remembers Thee in Thy ways.
Behold, Thou wast angry, for we sinned,
We continued in them a long time;
And shall we be saved?
6 For all of us have become like one who is unclean,
And all our [a]righteous deeds are like a filthy garment;
And all of us [b]wither like a leaf,
And our iniquities, like the wind, take us away.
7 And there is [a]no one who calls on Thy name,

13 [a]Jer. 31:9
14 [1]Lit., *him* [a]Josh. 21:44; 23:1 [b]Deut. 32:12
15 [a]Deut. 26:15; Ps. 80:14 [b]Ps. 68:5; 123:1 [c]Is. 9:17; 26:11; 37:32; 42:13; 59:17 [d]Jer. 31:20; Hos. 11:8
16 [a]Is. 1:2; 64:8 [b]Is. 29:22; 41:8; 51:2 [c]Is. 41:14; 44:6; 60:16
17 [a]Is. 30:28; Ezek. 14:7-9 [b]Is. 29:13, 14
18 [a]Is. 64:11; Ps. 74:3-7
1 [1]63:19b in Heb. [a]Ex. 19:18; Ps. 18:9; 144:5; Mic. 1:3, 4; Hab. 3:13 [b]Judg. 5:5; Ps. 68:8; Nah. 1:5
2 [1]V. 1 in Heb. [a]Ps. 99:1; Jer. 5:22; 33:9
3 [a]Ps. 65:5; 66:3, 5; 106:22
4 [a]1 Cor. 2:9 [b]Is. 25:9; 30:18; 40:31
5 [a]Ex. 20:24 [b]Is. 56:1 [c]Is. 26:13; 63:7
6 [a]Is. 46:12; 48:1 [b]Is. 1:30; Ps. 90:5, 6
7 [a]Is. 59:4; Ezek. 22:40

Who arouses himself to take hold of Thee;
For Thou hast [b]hidden Thy face from us,
And hast [1]delivered us into the power of our iniquities.

8 But now, O LORD, [a]Thou art our Father,
We are the [b]clay, and Thou our potter;
And all of us are the [c]work of Thy hand.
9 Do not be [a]angry beyond measure, O LORD,
[b]Neither remember iniquity forever;
Behold, look now, all of us are [c]Thy people.
10 Thy [a]holy cities have become a wilderness,
Zion has become a wilderness,
Jerusalem a desolation.
11 Our holy and beautiful [a]house,
Where our fathers praised Thee,
Has been burned *by* fire;
And all our precious things have become a ruin.
12 Wilt Thou restrain Thyself at these things, O LORD?
Wilt Thou keep silent and afflict us beyond measure?

CHAPTER 65

"I PERMITTED Myself to be sought by those who did not ask *for Me;*
I permitted Myself to be found by those who did not seek Me.
I said, 'Here am I, here am I,'
To a nation which did [a]not call on My name.
2 "[a]I have spread out My hands all day long to a [b]rebellious people,
Who walk *in* the way which is not good, [1]following their own [c]thoughts,
3 A people who continually [a]provoke Me to My face,
Offering sacrifices in gardens and burning incense on bricks;
4 Who sit among graves, and spend the night in secret places;
Who [a]eat swine's flesh,
And the broth of unclean meat is *in* their pots.
5 "Who say, '[a]Keep to yourself, do not come near Me,
For I am holier than you!'
These are smoke in My [1]nostrils,
A fire that burns all the day.
6 "Behold, it is written before Me,
I will [a]not keep silent, but I will repay;
I will even repay into their bosom,
7 Both [1]their own [a]iniquities and the iniquities of their father together," says the LORD.
"Because they have [b]burned incense on the mountains,
And [c]scorned Me on the hills,
Therefore I will [d]measure their former work into their bosom."

8 Thus says the LORD, "As the new wine is found in the cluster,

7 [1]Reading with the DSS and versions; M.T., *melted* [b]Is. 1:15; 54:8; Deut. 31:18

8 [a]Is. 63:16 [b]Is. 20:16; 45:9 [c]Is. 60:21; Ps. 100:3

9 [a]Is. 57:17; 60:10 [b]Is. 43:25; Mic. 7:18 [c]Is. 63:8; Ps. 79:13

10 [a]Is. 48:2; 52:1

11 [a]Is. 63:18; 2 Kin. 25:9; Ps. 74:5-7

1 [a]Hos. 1:10

2 [1]Lit., *after* [a]Rom. 10:21 [b]Is. 1:2, 23; 30:1, 9 [c]Is. 59:7; 66:18; Ps. 81:11, 12

3 [a]Is. 3:8; Job 1:11; 2:5

4 [a]Is. 66:3, 17; Lev. 11:7

5 [1]Lit., *nose* [a]Matt. 9:11; Luke 7:39; 18:9-12

6 [a]Is. 42:14; 64:12; Ps. 50:3, 21

7 [1]Lit., *your* [a]Is. 13:11; 22:14; 26:21; 30:13, 14 [b]Is. 57:7; Hos. 2:13 [c]Ezek. 20:27, 28 [d]Jer. 5:29; 13:25

8 [1]Lit., *blessing* [2]Lit., *the whole*

9 [a]Is. 49:8; 60:21; Amos 9:11-15 [b]Is. 32:18

10 [a]Is. 33:9; 35:2

11 [1]Heb., *Gad* [2]Heb., *Meni* [a]Is. 1:4, 28; Deut. 29:24, 25 [b]Is. 2:2, 3; 66:20

12 [a]Is. 41:28; 50:2; 66:4; 2 Chr. 36:15, 16; Prov. 1:24; Jer. 7:13

13 [1]YHWH, usually rendered LORD [a]Is. 5:13

14 [1]Lit., *pain of* [a]Is. 51:11; Ps. 66:4; James 5:13 [b]Is. 13:6; Matt. 8:12

15 [1]YHWH, usually rendered LORD [2]So with Gk.; Heb., *He will call His servants* [a]Jer. 24:9; 25:18; Zech. 8:13

16 [1]Or, *bless(es) himself* [a]Ex. 34:6; Ps. 31:5 [b]Is. 19:18; 45:23

17 [1]Lit., *heart* [a]Is. 66:22; 2 Pet. 3:13 [b]Is. 43:18; Jer. 3:16

18 [a]Is. 12:1, 2; 25:9; 35:10; 41:16; 51:3; 61:10; Ps. 98

19 [a]Is. 62:4, 5; Jer. 32:41

20 [1]Lit., *fill out* [a]Deut. 4:40; Job 5:26; Ps. 34:12

And one says, 'Do not destroy it, for there is [1]benefit in it',
So I will act on behalf of My servants
In order not to destroy [2]all of them.
9 "And I will bring forth offspring from Jacob,
And an [a]heir of My mountains from Judah;
Even My chosen ones shall inherit it,
And [b]My servants shall dwell there.
10 "And [a]Sharon shall be a pasture land for flocks,
And the valley of Achor a resting place for herds,
For My people who seek Me.
11 "But you who [a]forsake the LORD,
Who forget My [b]holy mountain,
Who set a table for [1]Fortune,
And who fill *cups* with mixed wine for [2]Destiny,
12 I will destine you for the sword,
And all of you shall bow down to the slaughter.
Because I called, but you did [a]not answer;
I spoke, but you did not hear.
And you did evil in My sight,
And chose that in which I did not delight."

13 Therefore, thus says the Lord [1]GOD,
"Behold, My servants shall eat, but you shall be hungry.
Behold, My servants shall drink, but you shall be [a]thirsty.
Behold, My servants shall rejoice, but you shall be put to shame.
14 "Behold, My servants shall [a]shout joyfully with a glad heart,
But you shall [b]cry out with a [1]heavy heart,
And you shall wail with a broken spirit.
15 "And you will leave your name for a [a]curse to my chosen ones,
And the Lord [1]GOD will slay you.
But [2]My servants will be called by another name.
16 "Because he who [1]is blessed in the earth
Shall [1]be blessed by the [a]God of truth;
And he who swears in the earth
Shall [b]swear by the God of truth;
Because the former troubles are forgotten,
And because they are hid from My sight!

17 "For behold, I create [a]new heavens and a new earth;
And the [b]former things shall not be remembered or come to [1]mind.
18 "But be [a]glad and rejoice forever in what I create;
For behold, I create Jerusalem *for* rejoicing,
And her people *for* gladness.
19 "I will also [a]rejoice in Jerusalem, and be glad in My people;
And there will no longer be heard in her
The voice of weeping and the sound of crying.
20 "No longer will there be *in it* an infant *who lives but a few* days,
Or an old man who does [a]not [1]live out his days;

For the youth will die at the age of one hundred
And the [2b]one who does not reach the age of one hundred
Shall be *thought* accursed.
21 "And they shall [a]build houses and inhabit *them;*
They shall also [b]plant vineyards and eat their fruit.
22 "They shall not build, and [a]another inhabit,
They shall not plant, and another eat;
For [b]as the [1]lifetime of a tree, *so shall be* the days of My people,
And My chosen ones shall [c]wear out the work of their hands.
23 "They shall [a]not labor in vain,
Or bear *children* for calamity;
For they are the [1b]offspring of those blessed by the LORD,
And their descendants with them.
24 "It will also come to pass that before they call, I will
[a]answer; and while they are still speaking, I will hear.
25 "The [a]wolf and the lamb shall graze together, and the
lion shall eat straw like the ox; and [b]dust shall be the serpent's
food. They shall [c]do no evil or harm in all My holy mountain,"
says the LORD.

CHAPTER 66

THUS says the LORD,
"[a]Heaven is My throne, and the earth is My footstool.
Where then is a [b]house you could build for Me?
And where is a place that [1]I may rest?
2 "For [a]My hand made all these things,
Thus all these things came into being," declares the LORD.
"But to this one I will look,
To him who is humble and [b]contrite of spirit, and who trembles at My word.

3 "*But* he who kills an ox is *like* one who slays a man;
He who sacrifices a lamb is *like* the one who breaks a dog's neck;
He who offers a grain offering *is like one who offers* swine's blood;
He who [1a]burns incense is *like* the one who blesses an idol.
As they have chosen their [b]*own* ways,
And their soul delights in their abominations,
4 So I will [a]choose their [1]punishments,
And I will [b]bring on them what they dread.
Because I called, but [c]no one answered;
I spoke, but they did not listen.
And they did [d]evil in My sight,
And chose that in which I did not delight."
5 Hear the word of the LORD, you who tremble at His word:
"Your brothers who [a]hate you, who [b]exclude you for My name's sake,

20 [2]Lit., *one who misses the mark* [b]Is. 3:11; 22:14; Eccles. 8:12, 13

21 [a]Is. 32:18; Amos 9:14 [b]Is. 30:23; 37:30; Jer. 31:5

22 [1]Lit., *days* [a]Is. 62:8, 9 [b]Ps. 92:12-14 [c]Deut. 32:46, 47; Ps. 21:4; 91:16

23 [1]Lit., *seed* [a]Is. 55:2; Deut. 28:3-12 [b]Is. 61:9; Jer. 32:38, 39; Acts 2:39

24 [a]Is. 55:6; 58:9; Ps. 91:15; Dan. 9:20-23; 10:12

25 [a]Is. 11:6 [b]Gen. 3:14; Mic. 7:17 [c]Is. 11:9; Mic. 4:3

1 [1]Lit., *is My resting place?* [a]1 Kin. 8:27; Ps. 11:4; Matt. 5:34, 35 [b]2 Sam. 7:5-7; Jer. 7:4; John 4:20, 21; Acts 7:48-50

2 [a]Is. 40:26 [b]Is. 57:15; 34:18; Matt. 5:3, 4; Luke 18:13, 14

3 [1]Lit., *offers a memorial of incense* [a]Is. 1:13; Lev. 2:2 [b]Is. 57:17; 65:2

4 [1]Lit., *ill treatments* [a]Is. 65:7; Prov. 1:31, 32 [b]Prov. 10:24 [c]Is. 65:12; Prov. 1:24; Jer. 7:13 [d]Is. 59:7; 65:12; 2 Kin. 21:2, 6; Jer. 7:30

5 [a]Is. 60:15; Ps. 38:20 [b]Matt. 5:10-12; 10:22; John 9:34; 15:18-20

Have said, 'Let the LORD be glorified, that we may see your joy.'
But [c]they will be put to shame.
6 "A voice of uproar from the city, a voice from the temple,
The voice of the LORD who is [a]rendering recompense to His enemies.

7 "Before she travailed, she brought forth;
Before her pain came, she gave birth to a boy.
8 "Who has heard such a thing? Who has seen such things?
Can a land be [1]born in one day?
Can a nation be brought forth all at once?
As soon as Zion travailed, she also brought forth her sons.
9 "Shall I bring to the point of birth, and [a]not give delivery?" says the LORD.
"Or shall I who gives delivery shut *the womb?*" says your God.
10 "Be [a]joyful with Jerusalem and rejoice for her, all you who [b]love her;
Be exceedingly [c]glad with her, all you who mourn over her;
11 That you may nurse and [a]be satisfied with her comforting breasts;
That you may suck and be delighted with her [b]bountiful bosom."
12 For thus says the LORD, "Behold I extend [a]peace to her like a river,
And the [b]glory of the nations like an overflowing stream;
And you shall [1]be nursed, you shall be [c]carried on the [2]hip and fondled on the knees.
13 "As one whom his mother comforts, so I will comfort you;
And you shall be comforted in Jerusalem."
14 Then you shall [a]see *this,* and your [b]heart shall be glad,
And your [c]bones shall flourish like the new grass;
And the [d]hand of the LORD shall be made known to His servants,
But He shall be indignant toward His enemies.
15 For behold, the LORD will come in fire
And His chariots like the whirlwind,
To render His anger with fury,
And His rebuke with flames of fire.
16 For the LORD will execute judgment by [a]fire
And by His [b]sword on all flesh,
And those slain by the LORD will be many.
17 "Those who sanctify and purify themselves *to go* to the [a]gardens,
[1]Following one in the center,
Who eat [b]swine's flesh, detestable things, and mice,
Shall come to an end altogether," declares the LORD.
18 "For I [1]know their works and their thoughts; [2]the time is

5 [c]Luke 13:17
6 [a]Is. 59:18; 65:6; Joel 3:7
8 [1]Lit., *travailed with*
9 [a]Is. 37:3
10 [a]Is. 65:18; Deut. 32:43; Rom. 15:10 [b]Ps. 26:8; 122:6 [c]Ps. 137:6
11 [a]Is. 49:23; 60:16; Joel 3:18 [b]Is. 60:1, 2; 62:2
12 [1]Lit., *nurse* [2]Lit., *side* [a]Is. 48:18; Ps. 72:3, 7 [b]Is. 60:5; 61:6 [c]Is. 60:4
14 [a]Is. 33:20 [b]Zech. 10:7 [c]Is. 58:11; Prov. 3:8 [d]Ezra 7:9; 8:31
16 [a]Is. 30:30; Ezek. 38:22 [b]Is. 65:12; Ezek. 38:21
17 [1]Lit., *After* [a]Is. 1:29; 65:3 [b]Is. 65:4; Lev. 11:7
18 [1]So with Gk.; Heb. omits [2]Lit., *it is coming*

coming to [a]gather all nations and tongues. And they shall
come and see My glory.
19 "And I will set a [a]sign among them and will send survivors from them to the nations: Tarshish, [1]Put, Lud, [2]Mashech,
Rosh, Tubal, and [3]Javan, to the distant coastlands that have
neither heard My fame nor seen My glory. And they will [b]de-
clare My glory among the nations.
20 "Then they shall [a]bring all your brethren from all the
nations as a grain offering to the LORD, on horses, in chariots,
in litters, on mules, and on camels, to My [b]holy mountain
Jerusalem," says the LORD, "just as the sons of Israel bring
their grain offering in a [c]clean vessel to the house of the LORD.
21 "I will also take some of them for [a]priests *and* for Levites," says the LORD.
22 "For just as the [a]new heavens and the new earth
Which I make will endure before Me," declares the LORD,
"So your [b]offspring and your name will endure.
23 "And it shall be from new moon to new moon
And from sabbath to sabbath,
All [1]mankind will come to [a]bow down before Me," says the LORD.
24 "Then they shall go forth and look
On the corpses of the men
Who have [1]transgressed against Me.
For their worm shall not die,
[a]And their fire shall not be quenched;
And they shall be an [b]abhorrence to all [2]mankind."

18 [a]Is. 45:22-25; Jer. 3:17

19 [1]So with Gk.; Heb., *Pul* [2]So with Gk.; Heb., *those who draw the bow* [3]I.e., Greece [a]Is. 11:10, 12; 49:22; 62:10 [b]Is. 42:12; 1 Chr. 16:24

20 [a]Is. 43:6; 49:22; 60:4 [b]Is. 2:2, 3; 11:9; 56:7; 65:11, 25 [c]Is. 52:11

21 [a]Is. 61:6; 1 Pet. 2:5, 9

22 [a]Is. 65:17; Heb. 12:26, 27; 2 Pet. 3:13; Rev. 21:1 [b]Is. 61:8, 9; 65:22, 23; John 10:27-29; 1 Pet. 1:4, 5

23 [1]Lit., *flesh* [a]Is. 19:21, 23; 27:13; 49:7

24 [1]Or, *rebelled* [2]Lit., *flesh* [a]Is. 1:31; Matt. 3:12 [b]Dan. 12:2

THE BOOK OF JEREMIAH

Jeremiah's Call and Commission.

THE words of [a]Jeremiah, the son of Hilkiah, of the priests
who were in Anathoth in the land of Benjamin,
2 to whom the word of the LORD came in the days of
[a]Josiah, the son of Amon, king of Judah, in the thirteenth year
of his reign.
3 It came also in the days of [a]Jehoiakim, the son of Josiah, king of Judah, until the end of the eleventh year of [b]Zede-
kiah, the son of Josiah, king of Judah, until the exile of
Jerusalem in the fifth month.
4 Now the word of the LORD came to me saying,
5 "Before I [a]formed you in the womb I knew you,
And [b]before you were born I consecrated you;
I have [c]appointed you a prophet to the nations."
6 Then [a]I said, "Alas, Lord [1]GOD!
Behold, I do not know how to speak,
Because [b]I am a youth."

1 [a]2 Chr. 35:25; 36:12, 21, 22; Ezra 1:1; Dan. 9:2; Matt. 2:17; 16:14; 27:9

2 [a]Jer. 3:6; 36:2; 1 Kin. 13:2; 2 Kin. 21:24

3 [a]Jer. 25:1; 2 Kin. 23:34; 1 Chr. 3:15 [b]Jer. 39:2; 2 Kin. 24:17; 1 Chr. 3:15

5 [a]Ps. 139:15, 16 [b]Is. 49:1, 5 [c]Jer. 1:10; 25:15-26

6 [1]YHWH, usually rendered LORD [a]Ex. 4:10 [b]1 Kin. 3:17

7 But the LORD said to me,
"Do not say, 'I am a youth,'
[a]Because everywhere I send you, you shall go,
And all that I command you, you shall speak.
8 [a]Do not be afraid of them,
For I am with you to deliver you," declares the LORD.
9 Then the LORD stretched out His hand and [a]touched
my mouth, and the LORD said to me,
"Behold, I have [b]put My words in your mouth.
10 See, I have appointed you this day over the nations and
over the kingdoms,
[a]To pluck up and to break down,
To destroy and to overthrow,
[b]To build and to plant."
11 And the word of the LORD came to me saying, "What
do you see, [a]Jeremiah?" And I said, "I see a rod of an [1]almond
tree."
12 Then the LORD said to me, "You have seen well, for [a]I
am [1]watching over My word to perform it."
13 And the word of the LORD came to me a second time
saying, "[a]What do you see?" And I said, "I see a boiling [b]pot,
facing away from the north."
14 Then the LORD said to me, "[a]Out of the north the evil
[1]will break forth on all the inhabitants of the land.
15 "For, behold, I am calling [a]all the families of the kingdoms of the north," declares the LORD; "and they will come,
and they will [b]set each one his throne at the entrance of the
gates of Jerusalem, and against all its walls round about, and
against all the cities of Judah.
16 "And I will [1]pronounce My judgments on them concerning all their wickedness, whereby they have forsaken Me and
have [2a]offered sacrifices to other gods, and worshiped the
[b]works of their own hands.
17 "Now, [a]gird up your loins, and arise, and speak to them
all which I command you. [b]Do not be dismayed before them,
lest I dismay you before them.
18 "Now behold, I have made you today as a fortified city,
and as a pillar of iron and as walls of bronze against the whole
land, to the kings of Judah, to its princes, to its priests and to
the people of the land.
19 "And they will fight against you, but they will not overcome you, for [a]I am with you to deliver you," declares the
LORD.

CHAPTER 2

NOW the word of the LORD came to me saying,
2 "Go and [a]proclaim in the ears of Jerusalem, saying,
'Thus says the LORD,
"I remember concerning you the [1b]devotion of your youth,
The love of your betrothals,
Your following after Me in the wilderness,
Through a land not sown.
3 "Israel was [a]holy to the LORD,
The first of His harvest;

7 [a]Ezek. 2:3, 4
8 [a]Ezek. 2:6
9 [a]Mark 7:33-35 [b]Ex. 4:11-16; Deut. 18:18
10 [a]Jer. 18:7-10; Ezek. 32:18 [b]Jer. 24:6; 31:28, 40; Is. 44:26-28
11 [1]Heb., *shaked* [a]Jer. 24:3; Amos 7:8
12 [1]Heb., *shoked* [a]Jer. 31:28; Deut. 32:35
13 [a]Zech. 4:2 [b]Ezek. 11:3, 7
14 [1]Lit., *will be opened* [a]Jer. 4:6; 10:22; Is. 41:25
15 [a]Jer. 25:9 [b]Jer. 39:3; Is. 22:7
16 [1]Lit., *speak* [2]Or, *burned incense* [a]Jer. 7:9; 19:4; 44:17 [b]Jer. 10:3-5; Is. 2:8; 37:19
17 [a]1 Kin. 18:46; Job 38:3 [b]Ezek. 2:6; 3:16-18
19 [a]Jer. 1:8; 20:11
2 [1]Or, *lovingkindness* [a]Jer. 7:2; 11:6; Is. 58:1 [b]Ezek. 16:8
3 [a]Ex. 19:5, 6; Deut. 7:6; 14:2

[b]All who ate of it became guilty;
Evil came upon them," declares the LORD.' "
4 Hear the word of the LORD, O house of Jacob, and all
the families of the house of Israel.
5 Thus says the LORD,
"[a]What injustice did your fathers find in Me,
That they went far from Me
And walked after [b]emptiness and became empty?
6 "And they did not say, 'Where is the LORD
Who brought us up out of the land of Egypt,
Who [a]led us through the wilderness,
Through a land of deserts and of pits,
Through a land of drought and of [1]deep darkness,
Through a land that no one crossed
And where no man dwelt?'
7 "And I brought you into the [a]fruitful land,
To eat its fruit and its good things.
But you came and [b]defiled My land,
And My inheritance you made an abomination.
8 "The [a]priests did not say, 'Where is the LORD?'
And those who handle the law [b]did not know Me;
The [1]rulers also transgressed against Me,
And the [c]prophets prophesied by Baal
And walked after things that [d]did not profit.

9 "Therefore I will yet [a]contend with you," declares the LORD,
"And with your sons' sons I will contend.
10 "For [a]cross to the coastlands of [1]Kittim and see,
And send to [b]Kedar and observe closely,
And see if there has been such *a thing* as this!
11 "Has a nation changed gods,
[a]When they were not gods?
But My people have [b]changed their glory
For that which does not profit.
12 "Be appalled, O [a]heavens, at this,
And shudder, be very desolate," declares the LORD.
13 "For My people have committed two evils:
They have forsaken Me,
The [a]fountain of living waters,
To hew for themselves cisterns,
Broken cisterns,
That can hold no water.

14 "Is Israel a slave? Or is he a homeborn servant?
Why has he become a prey?
15 "The young [a]lions have roared at him,
They have [1]roared loudly.
And they have [b]made his land a waste;
His cities have been destroyed, without inhabitant.
16 "Also the [1]men of [a]Memphis and Tahpanhes
Have [2]shaved the [b]crown of your head.
17 "Have you not [a]done this to yourself,
By your forsaking the LORD your God,
When He [a]led you in the way?
18 "But now what are you doing on the road to Egypt,

3 [b]Jer. 30:16; 50:7; Is. 41:11

5 [a]Is. 5:4; Mic. 6:3 [b]Jer. 8:19; 2 Kin. 17:15

6 [1]Or, *shadow of death* [a]Deut. 8:15; 32:10

7 [a]Deut. 8:7-9; 11:10-12 [b]Jer. 3:2; 16:18; Ps. 106:38

8 [1]Lit., *shepherds* [a]Jer. 10:21 [b]Jer. 4:22; Mal. 2:6, 7 [c]Jer. 23:13 [d]Jer. 16:19; Hab. 2:18

9 [a]Jer. 2:35; Ezek. 20:35, 36

10 [1]I.e., Cyprus and other islands [a]Is. 23:12 [b]Jer. 49:28; Ps. 120:5; Is. 21:16

11 [a]Jer. 5:7; 16:20; Is. 37:19 [b]Ps. 106:20; Rom. 1:23

12 [a]Jer. 4:23; Is. 1:2

13 [a]Jer. 17:13; Ps. 36:9

15 [1]Lit., *given their voice* [a]Jer. 50:17 [b]Jer. 4:7

16 [1]Or, *sons* [2]Lit., *grazed* [a]Jer. 44:1; Is. 19:13; Hos. 9:6 [b]Jer. 48:45; Deut. 33:20

17 [a]Deut. 32:10

To drink the waters of the [1]Nile?
Or what are you doing on the road to Assyria,
To drink the waters of the [2]Euphrates?
19 "[a]Your own wickedness will correct you,
And your [b]apostasies will reprove you;
Know therefore and see that it is evil and [c]bitter
For you to forsake the LORD your God,
And [d]the dread of Me is not in you," declares the Lord
[1]GOD of hosts.

20 "For long ago [1a]I broke your yoke
And tore off your bonds;
But you said, 'I will not serve!'
For on every [b]high hill
And under every green tree
You have lain down as a harlot.
21 "Yet I [a]planted you a choice vine,
A completely faithful seed.
How then have you turned yourself before Me
Into the [b]degenerate shoots of a foreign vine?
22 "Although you [a]wash yourself with lye
And [1]use much soap,
The stain of your iniquity is before Me," declares the
Lord [2]GOD.
23 "[a]How can you say, 'I am not defiled,
I have not gone after the [b]Baals'?
Look at your way in the [c]valley!
Know what you have done!
You are a swift young camel [d]entangling her ways,
24 "A [a]wild donkey accustomed to the wilderness,
That sniffs the wind in her passion.
In *the time of* her [1]heat who can turn her away?
All who seek her will not become weary;
In her month they will find her.
25 "Keep your feet from being unshod
And your throat from thirst;
But you said, '[a]It is [1]hopeless!
No! For I have [b]loved strangers,
And after them I will walk.'

26 "As the [a]thief is shamed when he is discovered,
So the house of Israel is shamed;
They, their kings, their princes,
And their priests, and their prophets,
27 Who say to a tree, 'You are my father,'
And to a stone, 'You gave me birth.'
For they have turned *their* [a]back to Me,
And not *their* face;
But in the [b]time of their [1]trouble they will say,
'Arise and save us.'
28 "But where are your [a]gods
Which you made for yourself?
Let them arise, if they can [b]save you
In the time of your [1]trouble;
For [c]*according to* the number of your cities
Are your gods, O Judah.

18 [1]Heb., *Shihor* [2]Lit., *the River*

19 [1]YHWH, usually rendered LORD
[a]Jer. 4:18; Is. 3:9; Hos. 5:5
[b]Jer. 3:6, 8, 11, 14; Hos. 11:7
[c]Job 20:11-16; Amos 8:10
[d]Jer. 5:24; Ps. 36:1

20 [1]Or, *you*
[a]Lev. 26:13 [b]Jer. 3:2, 6; 17:2; Deut. 12:2; Is. 57:5, 7

21 [a]Ex. 15:17; Ps. 44:2; 80:8; Is. 5:2 [b]Is. 5:4

22 [1]Lit., *cause to be great to you* [2]YHWH, usually rendered LORD
[a]Jer. 4:14

23 [a]Prov. 30:12 [b]Jer. 9:14
[c]Jer. 7:31 [d]Jer. 2:33, 36; 31:22

24 [1]Lit., *occasion*
[a]Jer. 14:6

25 [1]Or, *desperate*
[a]Jer. 18:12 [b]Jer. 14:10; Deut. 32:16

26 [a]Jer. 48:27

27 [1]Or, *evil*
[a]Jer. 18:17; 32:33 [b]Jer. 22:23; Is. 26:16

28 [1]Or, *evil*
[a]Jer. 1:16; Deut. 32:37; Is. 45:20 [b]Jer. 11:12, 13 [c]Jer. 11:13; 2 Kin. 17:30, 31

29 "Why do you contend with Me?
You have [a]all transgressed against Me," declares the LORD.
30 "[a]In vain I have struck your sons;
They accepted no chastening.
Your [b]sword has devoured your prophets
Like a destroying lion.
31 "O generation, heed the word of the LORD.
Have I been a wilderness to Israel?
Or a land of thick [a]darkness?
Why do My people say, '[b]We *are free to* roam;
We will come no more to Thee'?
32 "Can a virgin forget her ornaments,
Or a bride her attire?
Yet My people have [a]forgotten Me
Days without number.
33 "How well you prepare your way
To seek love!
Therefore even [1]the wicked women
You have taught your ways.
34 "Also on your skirts is found
The [a]lifeblood of the innocent poor;
You did not find them [b]breaking in.
But in spite of all these things,
35 Yet you said, 'I am innocent;
Surely His anger is turned away from me.'
Behold, I will [a]enter into judgment with you
Because you [b]say, 'I have not sinned.'
36 "Why do you [a]go around so much
Changing your way?
Also, you shall be put to shame by Egypt
As you were put to shame by [b]Assyria.
37 "From this *place* also you shall go out
With [a]your hands on your head;
For the LORD has rejected those in whom you trust,
And you shall not prosper with them."

CHAPTER 3

GOD [1]says, "[a]If a husband divorces his wife,
And she goes from him,
And belongs to another man,
Will he still return to her?
Will not that land be completely [2]polluted?
But you [b]are a harlot *with* many [3]lovers;
Yet you [c]turn to Me," declares the LORD.
2 "Lift up your eyes to the [a]bare heights and see;
Where have you not been violated?
By the roads you have [b]sat for them
Like an Arab in the desert,
And you have [c]polluted a land
With your harlotry and with your wickedness.
3 "Therefore the [a]showers have been withheld,
And there has been no spring rain.
Yet you had a harlot's forehead;
You refused to be ashamed.

29 [a]Jer. 5:1; 6:13; Dan. 9:11

30 [a]Jer. 5:3; 7:28; Is. 1:5 [b]Jer. 26:20-24; Neh. 9:26

31 [a]Is. 45:19 [b]Jer. 2:20, 25; Deut. 32:15

32 [a]Jer. 3:21; 13:25; Is. 17:10; Hos. 8:14

33 [1]Or, *in wickedness*

34 [a]Jer. 7:6; 19:4; 2 Kin. 21:16; 24:4 [b]Ex. 22:2

35 [a]Jer. 25:31 [b]Prov. 28:13; 1 John 1:8, 10

36 [a]Jer. 2:23; Hos. 12:1 [b]2 Chr. 28:16, 20, 21

37 [a]Jer. 14:3, 4; 2 Sam. 13:19

1 [1]Heb., *saying* [2]Or, *alienated* [3]Lit., *companions* [a]Deut. 24:1-4 [b]Jer. 2:20; Ezek. 16:26, 28, 29 [c]Jer. 4:1; Zech. 1:3

2 [a]Jer. 2:20; Deut. 12:2 [b]Ezek. 16:25 [c]Jer. 2:7

3 [a]Jer. 14:3-6; Lev. 26:19

4 "Have you not just now called to Me,
'[a]My Father, Thou art the [1b]friend of my youth?
5 '[a]Will He be angry forever?
Will He [1]be indignant to the end?'
Behold, you have spoken
And have done evil things,
And you have [2]had your way."
6 Then the LORD said to me in the days of Josiah the
king, "Have you seen what faithless Israel did? She [a]went up
on every high hill and under every green tree, and she was a
harlot there.
7 "And I [1]thought, 'After she has done all these things, she
will return to me'; but she did not return, and her [a]treacherous
sister Judah saw it.
8 "And I saw that for all the adulteries of faithless Israel, I
had sent her away and [a]given her a writ of divorce, yet her
[b]treacherous sister Judah did not fear; but she went and was a
harlot also.
9 "And it came about because of the lightness of her harlotry, that she polluted the [a]land and committed adultery with
[b]stones and trees.
10 "And yet in spite of all this her treacherous sister Judah
did not return to Me with all her heart, but rather in [a]decep-
tion," declares the LORD.
11 And the LORD said to me, "[a]Faithless Israel has proved
herself more righteous than treacherous Judah.
12 "Go, and proclaim these words toward the north and
say,
'[a]Return, faithless Israel,' declares the LORD;
'[b]I will not [1]look upon you in anger.
For I am [c]gracious,' declares the LORD;
'I will not be angry forever.
13 'Only [1a]acknowledge your iniquity,
That you have transgressed against the LORD your God
And have [b]scattered your [2]favors to the strangers [c]un-
der every green tree,
And you have not obeyed My voice,' declares the
LORD.
14 'Return, O faithless sons,' declares the LORD;
'For I am a [a]master to you,
And I will take you one from a city and two from a
family,
And I will bring you to Zion.'
15 "Then I will give you [a]shepherds after My own heart,
who will [b]feed you on knowledge and understanding.
16 "And it shall be in those days when you are multiplied
and increased in the land," declares the LORD, "they shall [a]say
no more, 'The ark of the covenant of the LORD.' And it shall
not come to mind, nor shall they remember it, nor shall they
miss *it*, nor shall it be made again.
17 "At that time they shall call Jerusalem 'The [a]throne of
the LORD,' and [b]all the nations will be gathered to it, for the
[c]name of the LORD in Jerusalem; [d]nor shall they walk any more
after the stubbornness of their evil heart.
18 "[a]In those days the house of Judah will walk with the
house of Israel, and they will come together [b]from the land of

4 [1]Lit., *leader* [a]Jer. 3:19; 31:9 [b]Ps. 71:17

5 [1]Lit., *keep it* [2]Lit., *been able* [a]Jer. 3:12; Ps. 103:9; Is. 57:16

6 [a]Jer. 17:2; Ezek. 23:4-10

7 [1]Lit., *said* [a]Jer. 3:11; Ezek. 16:47

8 [a]Deut. 24:1, 3; Is. 50:1 [b]Ezek. 16:46, 47

9 [a]Jer. 3:2; 2:7 [b]Jer. 2:27; 10:8; Is. 57:6

10 [a]Jer. 12:2; Hos. 7:14

11 [a]Ezek. 16:51, 52; 23:11

12 [1]Heb., *cause My countenance to fall* [a]Jer. 3:14, 22 [b]Jer. 3:5 [c]Jer. 12:15; 31:20; 33:26; Ps. 86:15

13 [1]Lit., *know* [2]Lit., *ways* [a]Jer. 3:25; 14:20; Deut. 30:1-3 [b]Jer. 3:2, 6; 2:20, 25 [c]Deut. 12:2

14 [a]Jer. 31:32; Hos. 2:19

15 [a]Jer. 23:4; 31:10; 50:19; Ezek. 34:23 [b]Acts 20:28

16 [a]Is. 65:17

17 [a]Jer. 17:12; Ezek. 43:7 [b]Jer. 3:19; 4:2; 12:15, 16; 16:19 [c]Is. 60:9 [d]Jer. 11:8

18 [a]Jer. 50:4, 5; Hos. 1:11 [b]Jer. 16:15; 31:8

the north to the land that I [c]gave your fathers as an
inheritance.

19 "Then I said,
'How I would set you among [1]My sons,
And give you a pleasant land,
The most [a]beautiful inheritance of the nations!'
And I said, 'You shall call Me, [b]My Father,
And not turn away from following Me.'
20 "Surely, as a woman treacherously departs from her
[1]lover,
So you have [a]dealt treacherously with Me,
O house of Israel," declares the LORD.

21 A voice is heard on the [a]bare heights,
The weeping *and* the supplications of the sons of
Israel;
Because they have perverted their way,
They have [b]forgotten the LORD their God.
22 "Return, O faithless sons,
[a]I will heal your faithlessness."
"Behold, we come to Thee;
For Thou art the LORD our God.
23 "Surely, [a]the hills are a deception,
A tumult *on* the mountains.
Surely, in the [b]LORD our God
Is the salvation of Israel."
24 "But the shameful thing has consumed the labor of our
fathers since our youth, their flocks and their herds, their sons
and their daughters.
25 "Let us lie down in our shame, and let our humiliation
cover us; for we have [a]sinned against the LORD our God, we
and our fathers, [b]since our youth even to this day. And we have
not obeyed the voice of the LORD our God."

CHAPTER 4

"[a]IF you will return, O Israel," declares the LORD,
"*Then* you should return to Me.
And [b]if you will put away your detested things from My
presence,
And will not waver,
2 And you will [a]swear, 'As the LORD lives,'
In truth, in justice, and in righteousness;
Then the [b]nations will bless themselves in Him,
And [c]in Him they will glory."

3 For thus says the LORD to the men of Judah and to
Jerusalem,
"[1a]Break up your fallow ground,
And do not sow among thorns.
4 "[a]Circumcise yourselves to the LORD
And remove the foreskins of your heart,
Men of Judah and inhabitants of Jerusalem,
Lest My [b]wrath go out like fire
And burn with [c]none to quench it
Because of the evil of your deeds."

18 [c]Amos 9:15

19 [1]Lit., *the*
[a]Ps. 16:6 [b]Jer. 3:4; Is. 63:16

20 [1]Or, *companion*
[a]Is. 48:8

21 [a]Jer. 3:2; 7:29; Is. 15:2
[b]Jer. 2:32; 13:25; Is. 17:10

22 [a]Jer. 30:17; 33:6; Hos. 6:1; 14:4

23 [a]Jer. 17:2 [b]Jer. 17:14; 31:7; Ps. 3:8

25 [a]Ezra 9:7 [b]Jer. 22:21

1 [a]Jer. 3:22; Joel 2:12 [b]Jer. 7:3, 7; 15:19; 35:15

2 [a]Jer. 12:16; Deut. 10:20; Is. 65:16 [b]Jer. 3:17; 12:15, 16; Gen. 22:18 [c]Jer. 9:24; Is. 45:25

3 [1]Lit., *Plow for yourselves plowed ground*
[a]Hos. 10:12

4 [a]Jer. 9:25, 26; Deut. 10:16; 30:6; Rom. 2:28, 29
[b]Jer. 21:12; Is. 30:27, 33
[c]Amos 5:6; Mark 9:43, 48

5 [a]Jer. 6:1; Hos. 8:1 [b]Jer. 8:14; Josh. 10:20

6 [a]Jer. 4:21; 50:2; Is. 62:10 [b]Jer. 1:14, 15; 6:1, 22

7 [a]Jer. 5:6; 25:38; 50:17 [b]Jer. 25:9; Ezek. 26:7-10 [c]Jer. 2:15; Is. 1:7; 6:11

8 [a]Jer. 6:26; Is. 22:12 [b]Jer. 30:24; Is. 5:25; 10:4

9 [a]Jer. 48:41; Is. 22:3-5 [b]Is. 29:9, 10; Ezek. 13:9-16

10 [1]YHWH, usually rendered LORD [2]Or, *life* [a]Ezek. 14:9; 2 Thess. 2:11 [b]Jer. 5:12; 14:13

12 [1]Lit., *these* [2]Lit., *for Me*

13 [a]Is. 19:1; Nah. 1:3 [b]Is. 5:28; 66:15 [c]Lam. 4:19 [d]Is. 3:8

14 [a]Jer. 6:19; 13:27; Prov. 1:22

16 [a]Jer. 5:15; Is. 39:3 [b]Ezek. 21:22

17 [a]2 Kin. 25:1, 4 [b]Jer. 5:23; Is. 1:20, 23

18 [1]Lit., *done* [a]Jer. 2:17, 19; Ps. 107:17; Is. 50:1

5 "Declare in Judah and proclaim in Jerusalem, and say,
'[a]Blow the trumpet in the land';
Cry aloud and say,
'[b]Assemble yourselves, and let us go
Into the fortified cities.'
6 "Lift up a [a]standard toward Zion!
Seek refuge, do not stand *still*,
For I am bringing [b]evil from the north,
And great destruction.
7 "A [a]lion has gone up from his thicket,
And a [b]destroyer of nations has set out;
He has gone out from his place
To [c]make your land a waste.
Your cities will be ruins
Without inhabitant.
8 "For this [a]put on sackcloth,
Lament and wail;
For the [b]fierce anger of the LORD
Has not turned back from us."
9 "And it shall come about in that day," declares the
LORD, "that the [a]heart of the king and the heart of the princes
will fail; and the priests will be appalled, and the [b]prophets will
be astounded."
10 Then I said, "Ah, Lord [1]GOD! Surely Thou hast utterly
[a]deceived this people and Jerusalem, saying, '[b]You will have
peace'; whereas a sword touches the [2]throat."
11 In that time it will be said to this people and to Jerusalem, "A scorching wind from the bare heights in the wilderness
in the direction of the daughter of My people—not to winnow, and not to cleanse!
12 "A wind too strong for [1]this—will come [2]at My command; now I will also pronounce judgments against them."
13 "Behold, he [a]goes up like clouds,
And his [b]chariots like the whirlwind;
His horses are [c]swifter than eagles.
Woe to us, for [d]we are ruined!"

14 Wash your heart from evil, O Jerusalem,
That you may be saved.
How long will your [a]wicked thoughts
Lodge within you?
15 For a voice declares from Dan,
And proclaims wickedness from Mount Ephraim.
16 "Report *it* to the nations, now!
Proclaim over Jerusalem,
'Besiegers come from a [a]far country,
And [b]lift their voice against the cities of Judah.
17 'Like watchmen of a field they are [a]against her round about,
Because she has [b]rebelled against Me,' declares the LORD.
18 "Your [a]ways and your deeds
Have [1]brought these things to you.
This is your evil. How bitter!
How it has touched your heart!"

19 [a]My [1]soul, my [1]soul! I am in anguish! [2]Oh my heart!
My [b]heart is pounding in me;
I cannot be silent,
Because [3]you have heard, O my soul,
The [c]sound of the trumpet,
The alarm of war.
20 [a]Disaster on disaster is proclaimed,
For the whole land is devastated;
Suddenly my tents are devastated,
My curtains in an instant.
21 How long must I see the standard,
And hear the sound of the trumpet?
22 "[a]For My people are foolish,
They know Me not;
They are stupid children,
And they have no understanding.
They are shrewd to [b]do evil,
But to do good they do not know."

23 I looked on the earth, and behold, *it was* [1a]formless and void;
And to the heavens, and they had no light.
24 I looked on the mountains, and behold, they were [a]quaking,
And all the hills [1]moved to and fro.
25 I looked, and behold, there was no man,
And all the [a]birds of the heavens had fled.
26 I looked, and behold, the [1a]fruitful land was a wilderness,
And all its cities were pulled down
Before the LORD, before His fierce anger.

27 For thus says the LORD,
"The [a]whole land shall be a desolation,
Yet I will [b]not execute a complete destruction.
28 "For this the [a]earth shall mourn,
And the [b]heavens above be dark,
Because I have [c]spoken, I have purposed,
And I will not [1]change My mind, nor will I turn from it."
29 At the sound of the horseman and bowman every city flees;
They [a]go into the thickets and climb among the rocks;
Every city is forsaken,
And no man dwells in them.
30 And you, O desolate one, [a]what will you do?
Although you dress in scarlet,
Although you decorate *yourself with* ornaments of gold,
Although you [b]enlarge your eyes with paint,
In vain you make yourself beautiful;
Your [1c]lovers despise you;
They seek your life.
31 For I heard a [1]cry as of a woman in labor,
The anguish as of one giving birth to her first child,

19 [1]Lit., *inward parts* [2]Lit., *the walls of my heart* [3]Or, *I, my soul, heard*
[a]Jer. 9:1, 10; 20:9; Is. 15:5; 16:11; 21:3; 22:4 [b]Hab. 3:16 [c]Num. 10:9

20 [a]Ps. 42:7; Ezek. 7:26

22 [a]Jer. 5:4, 21; 10:8 [b]Jer. 9:3; 13:23; Rom. 16:19

23 [1]Or, *a waste and emptiness*
[a]Gen. 1:2; Is. 24:19

24 [1]Lit., *moved lightly*
[a]Jer. 10:10; Is. 5:25; Ezek. 38:20

25 [a]Jer. 9:10; 12:4; Zeph. 1:3

26 [1]Or, *Carmel*
[a]Jer. 9:10

27 [a]Jer. 12:11, 12; 25:11
[b]Jer. 5:10, 18; 30:11; 46:28

28 [1]Lit., *be sorry*
[a]Jer. 12:4, 11; 14:2; Hos. 4:3
[b]Is. 5:30; 50:3; Joel 2:30, 31
[c]Jer. 23:20; 30:24; Num. 23:19

29 [a]Jer. 16:16; Is. 2:19-21

30 [1]Lit., *paramours*
[a]Jer. 13:21; Is. 10:3; 20:6
[b]2 Kin. 9:30; Ezek. 23:40
[c]Jer. 22:20, 22; Ezek. 23:9, 10, 22

31 [1]Lit., *sound*

31 [1]Lit., *sound* [2]Lit., *palms* [3]Lit., *my soul faints* [a]Is. 42:14 [b]Is. 1:15; Lam. 1:17

The [1]cry of the daughter of Zion [a]gasping for breath,
[b]Stretching out her [2]hands, *saying*,
"Ah, woe is me, for [3]I faint before murderers."

CHAPTER 5

1 [1]Lit., *faithfulness* [a]2 Chr. 16:9; Dan. 12:4 [b]Ezek. 22:30 [c]Gen. 18:26, 32

"[a]ROAM to and fro through the streets of Jerusalem,
And look now, and take note.
And seek in her open squares,
If you can find a [b]man,
If there is one who does justice, who seeks [1]truth,
Then I will [c]pardon her.
2 "And although they say, 'As the LORD lives,'
Surely they swear falsely."
3 O LORD, do not [a]Thine eyes look for [1]truth?
Thou hast smitten them,
But they did not [2]weaken;
Thou hast consumed them,
But they [b]refused to take correction.
They have made their faces [c]harder than rock;
They have refused to repent.

3 [1]Lit., *faithfulness* [2]Or, *become sick* [a]2 Chr. 16:9 [b]Jer. 7:28; 8:5; Zeph. 3:2 [c]Jer. 7:26; 19:15; Ezek. 3:8

4 Then I said, "They are only the poor,
They are foolish;
For they do not [a]know the way of the LORD
Or the ordinance of their God.
5 "I will go to the great
And will speak to them,
For they know the way of the LORD,
And the ordinance of their God."
But they too, with one accord, have [a]broken the yoke
And burst the bonds.
6 Therefore a lion from the forest shall slay them,
A [a]wolf of the deserts shall destroy them,
A [b]leopard is watching their cities.
Every one who goes out of them shall be torn in pieces,
Because their transgressions are many,
Their apostasies are numerous.

4 [a]Jer. 8:7; Is. 27:11; Hos. 4:6

5 [a]Jer. 2:20; Ex. 32:25; Ps. 2:3

6 [a]Ezek. 22:27; Hab. 1:8; Zeph. 3:3 [b]Hos. 13:7

7 "Why should I pardon you?
Your sons have forsaken Me
And [a]sworn by those who are [b]not gods.
When I had fed them to the full,
They committed adultery
And trooped to the harlot's house.
8 "They were well-fed lusty horses,
Each one neighing after his [a]neighbor's wife.
9 "Shall I not punish [1]these *people*," declares the LORD,
"And on a nation such as this
Shall I not avenge Myself?

7 [a]Jer. 12:16; Josh. 23:7; Zeph. 1:5 [b]Jer. 2:11; Deut. 32:21; Gal. 4:8

8 [a]Jer. 29:23; Ezek. 22:11

9 [1]Or, *for these things*

10 "Go up through her [a]vine rows and destroy,
But do not execute a complete destruction;
Strip away her branches,
For they are not the LORD's.

10 [a]Jer. 39:8

11 "For the [a]house of Israel and the house of Judah
Have dealt very treacherously with Me," declares the
LORD.
12 They have lied about the LORD
And said, "[1a]Not He;
Misfortune will [b]not come on us;
And we will [c]not see sword or famine.
13 "And the [a]prophets are *as* wind,
And the word is not in them.
Thus it will be done to them!"

14 Therefore, thus says the LORD, the God of hosts,
"Because you have spoken this word,
Behold, I am making My words in your mouth [a]fire
And this people wood, and it will consume them.
15 "Behold, I am [a]bringing a nation against you from afar,
O house of Israel," declares the LORD.
"It is an enduring nation,
It is an ancient nation,
A nation whose [b]language you do not know,
Nor can you understand what they say.
16 "Their quiver is like an [a]open grave,
All of them are mighty men.
17 "And they will [a]devour your harvest and your food;
They will devour your sons and your daughters;
They will devour your flocks and your herds;
They will devour your [b]vines and your fig trees;
They will demolish with the sword your [c]fortified cities
in which you trust.

18 "Yet even in those days," declares the LORD, "I will not
make you a complete destruction.
19 "And it shall come about [a]when [1]they say, 'Why has the
LORD our God done all these things to us?' then you shall say
to them, 'As you have forsaken Me and served foreign gods in
your land, so you shall [b]serve strangers in a land that is not
yours.'
20 "Declare this in the house of Jacob
And proclaim it in Judah, saying,
21 'Hear this, O foolish and [1]senseless people,
Who have [a]eyes, but see not;
Who have ears, but hear not.
22 'Do you not [a]fear Me?' declares the LORD.
'Do you not tremble in My presence?
For I have [b]placed the sand as a boundary for the sea,
An eternal decree, so it cannot cross over it.
Though the waves toss, yet they cannot prevail;
Though they roar, yet they cannot cross over it.
23 'But this people has a [a]stubborn and rebellious heart;
They have turned aside and departed.
24 'They do not say in their heart,
"Let us now fear the LORD our God,
Who [a]gives rain in its season,
Both the autumn rain and the [b]spring rain,
Who keeps for us
The [c]appointed weeks of the harvest."

11 [a]Jer. 3:6, 7, 20

12 [1]Lit., *He is not*
[a]Jer. 14:22; 43:1-4; Prov. 30:9
[b]Jer. 23:17 [c]Jer. 14:13

13 [a]Jer. 14:13, 15; 22:22; Job 8:2

14 [a]Jer. 23:29; Is. 24:6; Zech. 1:6

15 [a]Jer. 4:16; Deut. 28:49; Is. 5:26 [b]Is. 28:11

16 [a]Ps. 5:9; Is. 5:28; 13:18

17 [a]Jer. 8:16; 50:7, 17; Lev. 26:16; Deut. 28:31, 33 [b]Jer. 8:13 [c]Hos. 8:14

19 [1]Or, *you*
[a]Jer. 16:10-13; Deut. 29:24-26; 1 Kin. 9:8, 9 [b]Jer. 16:13; Deut. 28:48

21 [1]Lit., *without heart*
[a]Is. 6:9; 43:8; Ezek. 12:2; Matt. 13:14

22 [a]Jer. 2:19; 10:7; Deut. 28:58; Ps. 119:120 [b]Job 38:8-11; Ps. 104:9

23 [a]Jer. 4:17; 6:28; Deut. 21:18; Ps. 78:8

24 [a]Jer. 3:3; Ps. 147:8; Matt. 5:45 [b]Joel 2:23 [c]Gen. 8:22

25 [a]Jer. 2:17; 4:18

26 [1]Perhaps, *crouching down* [a]Jer. 18:22; Ps. 10:9; Prov. 1:11; Hab. 1:15

28 [1]Lit., *pass over*, or, *overlook deeds . . .* [2]Or, *fatherless* [3]Lit., *judge* [a]Deut. 32:15 [b]Jer. 7:6; 22:3; Is. 1:23; Zech. 7:10

29 [1]Or, *for these things*

30 [a]Jer. 23:14; Hos. 6:10

31 [1]Lit., *over their own hands* [a]Mic. 2:11

1 [1]I.e., House of the vineyard [a]Jer. 6:22; 1:14; 4:6

2 [a]Deut. 28:56

3 [1]Lit., *against her round about* [2]Lit., *hand* [a]Jer. 12:10 [b]Jer. 4:17; 2 Kin. 25:1; Luke 19:43

4 [1]Lit., *Sanctify* [2]Lit., *go up* [a]Jer. 6:23; Joel 3:9 [b]Jer. 15:8; Zeph. 2:4

5 [1]Lit., *go up* [2]Or, *fortified towers* [a]Jer. 52:13; Is. 32:14

6 [a]Deut. 20:19, 20 [b]Jer. 22:17

7 [1]Lit., *keeps cold* [a]James 3:10-12 [b]Jer. 20:8; Ps. 59:9-11; Ezek. 7:11, 23 [c]Jer. 30:12, 13

8 [1]Lit., *my soul* [a]Jer. 7:28; 17:23 [b]Ezek. 23:18; Hos. 9:12

25 'Your [a]iniquities have turned these away,
And your sins have withheld good from you.
26 'For wicked men are found among My people,
They [a]watch like fowlers [1]lying in wait;
They set a trap,
They catch men.
27 'Like a cage full of birds,
So their houses are full of deceit;
Therefore they have become great and rich.
28 'They are [a]fat, they are sleek,
They also [1]excel in deeds of wickedness;
They do not plead the cause,
The cause of the [2b]orphan, that they may prosper;
And they do not [3]defend the rights of the poor.
29 'Shall I not punish [1]these *people?*' declares the LORD,
'On a nation such as this
Shall I not avenge Myself?' "

30 An appalling and [a]horrible thing
Has happened in the land:
31 The prophets prophesy falsely,
And the priests rule [1]on their *own* authority;
And My people [a]love it so!
But what will you do at the end of it?

CHAPTER 6

"FLEE for safety, O sons of Benjamin,
From the midst of Jerusalem!
Now blow a trumpet in Tekoa,
And raise a signal over [1]Beth-hakkerem;
For evil looks down from the [a]north,
And a great destruction.
2 "The comely and [a]dainty one, the daughter of Zion, I will cut off.
3 "[a]Shepherds and their flocks will come to her,
They will [b]pitch *their* tents [1]around her,
They will pasture each in his [2]place.
4 "[1a]Prepare war against her;
Arise, and let us [2]attack at [b]noon.
Woe to us, for the day declines,
For the shadows of the evening lengthen!
5 "Arise, and let us [1]attack by night
And [a]destroy her [2]palaces!"
6 For thus says the LORD of hosts,
"[a]Cut down her trees,
And cast up a siege against Jerusalem.
This is the city to be punished,
In whose midst there is only [b]oppression.
7 "[a]As a well [1]keeps its waters fresh,
So she [1]keeps fresh her wickedness.
[b]Violence and destruction are heard in her;
[c]Sickness and wounds are ever before Me.
8 "[a]Be warned, O Jerusalem,
Lest [1b]I be alienated from you;

Lest I make you a desolation,
A land not inhabited."

9 Thus says the LORD of hosts,
"They will [a]thoroughly glean as the vine the [b]remnant of Israel;
Pass your hand again like a grape gatherer
Over the branches."
10 To whom shall I speak and give warning,
That they may hear?
Behold, their ears are [1]closed,
And they cannot listen.
Behold, the word of the LORD has become a reproach to them;
They have no delight in it.
11 But I am [a]full of the wrath of the LORD:
I am [b]weary with holding *it* in.
"[c]Pour *it* out on the children in the street,
And on the [1]gathering of young men together;
For both husband and wife shall be taken,
The aged and the [2]very old.
12 "And their [a]houses shall be turned over to others,
Their fields and their wives together;
For I will [b]stretch out My hand
Against the inhabitants of the land," declares the LORD.
13 "For [a]from the least of them even to the greatest of them,
Every one is [b]greedy for gain,
And from the prophet even to the priest
Every one [1]deals falsely.
14 "And they have [a]healed the wound of My people slightly,
Saying, 'Peace, peace,'
But there is no peace.
15 "Were they [a]ashamed because of the abomination they have done?
They were not even ashamed at all;
They did not even know how to blush.
Therefore they shall fall among those who fall;
At the time that I punish them,
They shall be cast down," says the LORD.

16 Thus says the LORD,
"Stand by the ways and see and ask for the [a]ancient paths,
Where the good way is, and walk in it;
And [b]you shall find rest for your souls.
But they said, 'We will not walk *in it*.'
17 "And I set [a]watchmen over you, *saying*,
'Listen to the sound of the trumpet!'
But they said, 'We will not listen.'
18 "Therefore hear, O nations,
And know, O congregation, what is among them.
19 "[a]Hear, O earth: behold, I am bringing disaster on this people,

9 [a]Jer. 16:16; 49:9; Obad. 5, 6 [b]Jer. 8:3; 11:23

10 [1]Lit., *uncircumcised*

11 [1]Lit., *council* [2]Lit., *with fulness of days*
[a]Job 32:18, 19; Mic. 3:8 [b]Jer. 15:6; 20:9 [c]Jer. 7:20; 9:21

12 [a]Jer. 8:10; 38:22; Deut. 28:30 [b]Jer. 15:6

13 [1]Or, *makes lies*
[a]Jer. 8:10; 22:17 [b]Jer. 8:10; 22:17; Is. 56:11; 57:17

14 [a]Jer. 8:11, 12; Ezek. 13:10

15 [a]Jer. 3:3; 8:12

16 [a]Jer. 12:16; 18:15; 31:21; Is. 8:20; Mal. 4:4; Luke 16:29
[b]Matt. 11:29

17 [a]Jer. 25:4; Is. 21:11; 58:1; Ezek. 3:17; Hab. 2:1

19 [a]Jer. 22:29; Is. 1:2

19 [1]Or, *devices* [b]Prov. 1:31 [c]Jer. 8:9

20 [1]Lit., *good* [a]Ps. 40:6; 50:7-9; Is. 1:11; 66:3; Amos 5:21; Mic. 6:6 [b]Is. 60:6 [c]Ex. 30:23

21 [1]Lit., *giving* [2]Lit., *his friend* [a]Jer. 13:16; Is. 8:14 [b]Jer. 9:21, 22; Is. 9:14-17

22 [a]Neh. 1:9

23 [a]Jer. 4:29; Is. 13:18 [b]Jer. 50:42 [c]Is. 5:30

24 [a]Jer. 4:19-21; Is. 28:19

25 [a]Jer. 14:18

26 [1]Lit., *Make for yourself mourning* [a]Jer. 4:8 [b]Jer. 25:34; Mic. 1:10 [c]Amos 8:10; Zech. 12:10

27 [a]Jer. 1:18; 15:20

28 [a]Jer. 9:4 [b]Ezek. 22:18

29 [1]Or, *drawn off* [a]Jer. 15:19

30 [a]Ps. 119:119; Is. 1:22

The [b]fruit of their [1]plans,
Because they have not listened to My words,
And as for My law, they have [c]rejected it also.
20 "[a]For what purpose does [b]frankincense come to Me from Sheba,
And the [1c]sweet cane from a distant land?
Your burnt offerings are not acceptable,
And your sacrifices are not pleasing to Me."
21 Therefore, thus says the LORD,
"Behold, [a]I am [1]laying stumbling blocks before this people.
And they will stumble against them,
[b]Fathers and sons together;
Neighbor and [2]friend will perish."

22 Thus says the LORD,
"Behold, a people is coming from the north land,
And a great nation will be aroused from the [a]remote parts of the earth.
23 "They seize [a]bow and spear;
They are [b]cruel and have no mercy;
Their voice [c]roars like the sea,
And they ride on horses,
Arrayed as a man for the battle
Against you, O daughter of Zion!"
24 We have [a]heard the report of it;
Our hands are limp.
Anguish has seized us,
Pain as of a woman in childbirth.
25 [a]Do not go out into the field,
And do not walk on the road,
For the enemy has a sword,
Terror is on every side.
26 O daughter of my people, [a]put on sackcloth
And [b]roll in ashes;
[1c]Mourn as for an only son,
A lamentation most bitter.
For suddenly the destroyer
Will come upon us.

27 "I have [a]made you an assayer *and* a tester among My people,
That you may know and assay their way."
28 All of them are stubbornly rebellious,
[a]Going about as a talebearer.
They are [b]bronze and iron;
They, all of them, are corrupt.
29 The bellows blow fiercely,
The lead is consumed by the fire;
In vain the refining goes on,
But the [a]wicked are not [1]separated.
30 [a]They call them rejected silver,
Because the LORD has rejected them.

CHAPTER 7

THE word that came to Jeremiah from the LORD, saying,
2 "[a]Stand in the gate of the LORD's house and proclaim
there this word, and say, 'Hear the word of the LORD, all you of
Judah, who enter by these gates to worship the LORD!' "
3 Thus says the LORD of hosts, the God of Israel,
"[a]Amend your ways and your deeds, and I will let you dwell in
this place.
4 "[a]Do not trust in deceptive words, saying, '[1]This is the
temple of the LORD, the temple of the LORD, the temple of the
LORD.'
5 "For [a]if you truly amend your ways and your deeds, if
you truly [b]practice justice between a man and his neighbor,
6 *if* you do not oppress the alien, the [1a]orphan, or the
widow, and do not shed innocent blood in this place, nor [b]walk
after other gods to your own ruin,
7 then I will let you [a]dwell in this place, in the land that I
gave to your fathers forever and ever.
8 "Behold, you are trusting in deceptive words to no avail.
9 "Will you steal, murder, and commit adultery, and
swear falsely, and [1a]offer sacrifices to Baal, and walk after
[b]other gods that you have not known,
10 then [a]come and stand before Me in [b]this house, which
is called by My name, and say, 'We are delivered!'—that you
may do all these abominations?
11 "Has [a]this house, which is called by My name, become a
[b]den of robbers in your sight? Behold, [c]I, even I, have seen *it*,"
declares the LORD.
12 "But go now to My place which was in [a]Shiloh, where I
[b]made My name dwell at the first, and [c]see what I did to it
because of the wickedness of My people Israel.
13 "And now, because you have done all these things,"
declares the LORD, "and I spoke to you, rising up early and
[a]speaking, but you did not hear, and I [b]called you but you did
not answer,
14 therefore, I will do to the house which is called by My
name, [a]in which you trust, and to the place which I gave you
and your fathers, as I [b]did to Shiloh.
15 "And I will [a]cast you out of My sight, as I have cast out
all your brothers, all the [1]offspring of [b]Ephraim.
16 "As for you, do not [a]pray for this people, and do not lift
up cry or prayer for them, and do not intercede with Me; for I
do not hear you.
17 "Do you not see what they are doing in the cities of
Judah and in the streets of Jerusalem?
18 "The [1]children gather wood, and the fathers kindle the
fire, and the women knead dough to make cakes for the queen
of heaven; and *they* [a]pour out drink offerings to other gods in
order to [b]spite Me.
19 "[a]Do they spite Me?" declares the LORD. "Is it not themselves *they spite*, to [1]their own [b]shame?"
20 Therefore thus says the Lord [1]GOD, "Behold, My anger
and My wrath will be poured out on this place, on man and on
beast and on the [a]trees of the field and on the fruit of the
ground; and it will burn and not be quenched."

2 [a]Jer. 17:19

3 [a]Jer. 7:5; 4:1; 18:11; 26:13

4 [1]Lit., *They are* [a]Jer. 7:8; Mic. 3:11

5 [a]Jer. 4:1, 2; Is. 1:19 [b]Jer. 21:12; 22:3; 1 Kin. 6:12, 13

6 [1]Or, *fatherless* [a]Jer. 5:28; Ex. 22:21-24 [b]Jer. 13:10; Deut. 6:14, 15; 8:19; 11:28

7 [a]Jer. 4:1; Deut. 4:40

9 [1]Or, *burn incense* [a]Jer. 11:13, 17 [b]Jer. 7:6; 19:4

10 [a]Ezek. 23:39 [b]Jer. 7:11, 14, 30; 32:34

11 [a]Is. 56:7 [b]Matt. 21:13; Mark 11:17; Luke 19:46 [c]Jer. 29:23

12 [a]Jer. 26:6; Judg. 18:31 [b]Josh. 18:1, 10 [c]Jer. 17:19

13 [a]Jer. 7:5; 4:1; 18:11; 26:13 [b]Jer. 7:8; Mic. 3:11

14 [a]Jer. 4:1, 2; Is. 1:19 [b]Jer. 21:12; 22:3; 1 Kin. 6:12, 13

15 [1]Lit., *seed* [a]Jer. 5:28; Ex. 22:21-24 [b]Jer. 13:10; Deut. 6:14, 15; 8:19; 11:28

16 [a]Jer. 4:1; Deut. 4:40

18 [1]Lit., *sons* [a]Jer. 19:13 [b]Jer. 11:17; Deut. 32:16, 21; 1 Kin. 14:9; 16:2; Ezek. 8:7

19 [1]Lit., *their faces'* [a]Job 35:6 [b]Jer. 9:19; 15:9; 22:22

20 [1]YHWH, usually rendered LORD [a]Jer. 8:13; 11:16

21 Thus says the LORD of hosts, the God of Israel, "[a]Add
your burnt offerings to your sacrifices and [b]eat flesh.
22 "For I did not [a]speak to your fathers, or command them
in the day that I brought them out of the land of Egypt,
concerning burnt offerings and sacrifices.
23 "But this is [1]what I commanded them, saying, '[a]Obey
My voice, and [b]I will be your God, and you will be My people;
and you will walk in all the way which I command you, that it
may [c]be well with you.'
24 "Yet they did not [a]obey or incline their ear, but walked
in *their own* counsels *and* in the stubbornness of their evil
heart, and [1]went backward and not forward.
25 "Since the day that your fathers came out of the land of
Egypt until this day, I have sent you all My servants the prophets, daily rising early and sending *them*.
26 "Yet they did not listen to Me or incline their ear, but
[a]stiffened their neck; they [b]did evil more than their fathers.
27 "And you shall [a]speak all these words to them, but they
will not listen to you; and you shall call to them, but they will
[b]not answer you.
28 "And you shall say to them, 'This is the nation that did
[a]not obey the voice of the LORD their God [b]or accept correction; [1]truth has perished and has been cut off from their
mouth.
29 '[a]Cut off [1]your hair and cast *it* away,
And take up a lamentation on the bare heights;
For the LORD has [b]rejected and forsaken
The generation of His wrath.'
30 "For the sons of Judah have done that which is evil in
My sight," declares the LORD, "they have [a]set their detestable
things in the house which is called by My name, to defile it.
31 "And they have [a]built the high places of Topheth, which
is in the valley of the son of Hinnom, to [b]burn their sons and
their daughters in the fire; which I [c]did not command, and it
did not come into My [1]mind.
32 "[a]Therefore, behold, days are coming," declares the
LORD, "when it will no more be called Topheth, or the valley
of the son of Hinnom, but the valley of the Slaughter; for they
will bury in Topheth [1]because there is no *other* place.
33 "And the [a]dead bodies of this people will be food for the
birds of the sky, and for the beasts of the earth; and no one will
frighten *them away*.
34 "Then I will make to [a]cease from the cities of Judah and
from the streets of Jerusalem the voice of joy and the voice of
gladness, the voice of the bridegroom and the voice of the
bride; for the [b]land will become a ruin.

CHAPTER 8

"AT that time," declares the LORD, "they will [a]bring out the
bones of the kings of Judah, and the bones of its princes, and
the bones of the priests, and the bones of the prophets, and the
bones of the inhabitants of Jerusalem from their graves.
2 "And they will spread them out to the sun, the moon,
and to all the [a]host of heaven, which they have loved, and
which they have served, and which they have gone after, and

21 [a]Jer. 6:20; 14:12; Is. 1:11; Amos 5:21 [b]Ezek. 33:25; Hos. 8:13

22 [a]1 Sam. 15:22; Ps. 51:16; Hos. 6:6

23 [1]Lit., *the word which*, cf. Ex. 16:32 [a]Ex. 15:26; Deut. 6:3 [b]Jer. 11:4; 13:11; Ex. 19:5, 6; Lev. 26:12 [c]Jer. 38:20; 42:6; Is. 3:10

24 [1]Lit., *they were* [a]Jer. 11:8; Ps. 81:11; Ezek. 20:8, 13, 16, 21

26 [a]Jer. 17:23; 19:15; Neh. 9:17 [b]Jer. 16:12; Matt. 23:32

27 [a]Jer. 1:8; 26:2; Ezek. 2:7 [b]Is. 50:2; 65:12; Zech. 7:13

28 [1]Lit., *faithfulness* [a]Jer. 6:17; 11:10 [b]Jer. 9:5; Is. 59:14, 15

29 [1]Lit., *your crown* [a]Jer. 16:6; Job 1:20; Is. 15:2; 22:12; Mic. 1:16 [b]Jer. 6:30; 14:19

30 [a]Jer. 32:34, 35; 2 Kin. 21:4; 2 Chr. 33:4, 5, 7; Ezek. 7:20; Dan. 9:27; 11:31

31 [1]Lit., *heart* [a]Jer. 19:5; 2 Kin. 23:10 [b]2 Kin. 17:17; Ps. 106:38 [c]Deut. 17:3

32 [1]Or, *until there is no place left* [a]Jer. 19:6, 7

33 [a]Jer. 12:9; Deut. 28:26; Ps. 79:2

34 [a]Jer. 16:9; Is. 24:7, 8; Ezek. 26:13; Hos. 2:11 [b]Jer. 4:27; Is. 1:7

1 [a]Ezek. 6:5

2 [a]Jer. 19:13; 2 Kin. 23:5; Zeph. 1:5; Acts 7:42

which they have sought, and which they have worshiped. They
will not be gathered [b]or buried; they will be as dung on the
face of the ground.
3 "And [a]death will be chosen rather than life by all the
remnant that remains of this evil family, that remains in all the
[b]places to which I have driven them," declares the LORD of
hosts.

4 "And you shall say to them, 'Thus says the LORD,
"Do *men* fall and [a]not get up again?
Does one turn away and not [1]repent?
5 "Why then has this people [a]turned away,
Jerusalem, in continual apostasy?
They [b]hold fast to deceit,
They refuse to return.
6 "I [a]have listened and heard,
They have spoken what is not right;
No man repented of his wickedness,
Saying, 'What have I done?'
Every one turned to his course,
Like a [b]horse charging into the battle.
7 "Even the [a]stork in the sky
Knows her seasons;
And the [b]turtledove and the swift and the thrush
Observe the time of their [1]migration;
But My people do not know
The ordinance of the LORD.

8 "How can you say, '[a]We are wise,
And the law of the LORD is with us'?
But behold, the lying pen of the scribes
Has made *it* into a lie.
9 "The wise men are [a]put to shame,
They are dismayed and caught;
Behold, they have rejected the word of the LORD,
And what kind of wisdom do they have?
10 "Therefore I will [a]give their wives to others,
Their fields to [1]new owners;
Because from the least even to the greatest
Every one is [b]greedy for gain;
From the prophet even to the priest
Every one practices deceit.
11 "And they [a]heal the brokenness of the daughter of My
people superficially
By saying, '[1]All is well, all is well';
But there is no peace.
12 "Were they [a]ashamed because of the abomination they
had done?
They certainly were not ashamed,
And they did not know how to blush;
Therefore they shall [b]fall among those who fall;
At the [c]time of their punishment they shall be brought
down,"
Declares the LORD.

13 "I will [a]surely snatch them away," declares the LORD;
"There will be no grapes on the vine,

2 [b]Jer. 22:19; 36:30

3 [a]Job 3:21, 22; 7:15, 16; Jon. 4:3; Rev. 9:6 [b]Jer. 23:3, 8; 29:14; Deut. 30:1, 4

4 [1]Lit., *turn back*
[a]Prov. 24:16; Amos 5:2; Mic. 7:8

5 [a]Jer. 5:6; 7:24 [b]Jer. 5:27; 9:6

6 [a]Ps. 74:2; Mal. 3:16 [b]Job 39:21-25

7 [1]Lit., *coming*
[a]Prov. 6:6-8; Is. 1:3 [b]Song of Sol. 2:12

8 [a]Jer. 4:22; Job 5:12, 13; Rom. 1:22; 2:17

9 [a]Jer. 6:15; Is. 19:11; 1 Cor. 1:27

10 [1]Lit., *possessing ones*
[a]Jer. 6:12, 13; 38:22; Deut. 28:30 [b]Jer. 6:13; Is. 56:11; 57:17

11 [1]Lit., *Peace, peace*
[a]Jer. 6:14; 14:13, 14; Lam. 2:14; Ezek. 13:10

12 [a]Jer. 3:3; 6:15; Ps. 52:1, 7; Is. 3:9; Zeph. 3:5 [b]Jer. 6:21; Is. 9:14; Hos. 4:5 [c]Jer. 10:15; Deut. 32:35

13 [a]Jer. 14:12; Ezek. 22:20, 21

13 [b]Matt. 21:19

14 [a]Jer. 4:5 [b]Jer. 35:11; 2 Sam. 20:6 [c]Jer. 9:15; Deut. 29:18; Ps. 69:21; Lam. 3:19; Matt. 27:34 [d]Jer. 3:25; 14:20

15 [a]Jer. 8:11; 14:19

16 [a]Jer. 4:15; Judg. 18:29 [b]Judg. 5:22

17 [a]Num. 21:6; Deut. 32:24 [b]Ps. 58:4, 5

18 [1]So Gk. and versions [a]Is. 22:4; Lam. 1:16, 17

19 [1]Lit., *vanities* [a]Jer. 4:16; 9:16; Is. 13:5; 39:3 [b]Jer. 7:19; Deut. 32:21 [c]Ps. 31:6

21 [a]Jer. 4:19; 9:1; 14:17 [b]Jer. 14:2; Nah. 2:10

22 [1]Or, *healing* [2]Lit., *gone up* [a]Jer. 46:11; Gen. 37:25 [b]Jer. 14:19; 30:13

1 [1]8:23 in Heb. [a]Jer. 8:18; 13:17; Is. 22:4; Lam. 2:18 [b]Jer. 6:26; 9:21, 22

2 [1]9:1 in Heb. [a]Ps. 55:6, 7; 120:5, 6

3 [a]Jer. 9:8; Ps. 64:3; Is. 59:4 [b]Jer. 5:4, 5; 1 Sam. 2:12; Hos. 4:1

4 [a]Jer. 12:6

And [b]no figs on the fig tree,
And the leaf shall wither;
And what I have given them shall pass away." ' "
14 Why are we sitting still?
[a]Assemble yourselves, and let us [b]go into the fortified cities,
And let us perish there,
Because the LORD our God has doomed us
And given us [c]poisoned water to drink,
For [d]we have sinned against the LORD.
15 *We* [a]waited for peace, but no good *came;*
For a time of healing, but behold, terror!
16 From [a]Dan is heard the snorting of his horses;
At the sound of the neighing of his [b]steeds
The whole land quakes;
For they come and devour the land and its fullness,
The city and its inhabitants.
17 "For behold, I am [a]sending serpents against you,
Adders, for which there is [b]no charm,
And they will bite you," declares the LORD.

18 [1]My sorrow is [a]beyond healing,
My heart is faint *within me!*
19 Behold, listen! The cry of the daughter of my people from a [a]distant land:
"Is the LORD not in Zion? Is her King not within her?
Why have they [b]provoked Me with their graven images, with foreign [1c]idols?"
20 "Harvest is past, summer is ended,
And we are not saved."
21 For the [a]brokenness of the daughter of my people I am broken;
I [b]mourn, dismay has taken hold of me.
22 Is there no [a]balm in Gilead?
Is there no physician there?
[b]Why then has not the [1]health of the daughter of my people [2]been restored?

CHAPTER 9

1a O THAT my head were waters,
And my eyes a fountain of tears,
That I might weep day and night
For the slain of the [b]daughter of my people!
2 [1a]O that I had in the desert
A wayfarers' lodging place;
That I might leave my people,
And go from them!
For all of them are adulterers,
An assembly of treacherous men.
3 "And they [a]bend their tongue *like* their bow;
Lies and not truth prevail in the land;
For they proceed from evil to evil,
And they do not [b]know Me," declares the LORD.
4 "Let every one be on guard against his neighbor,
And do not [a]trust any brother;

Because every [b]brother deals [1]craftily,
And every neighbor [c]goes about as a slanderer.
5 "And everyone [a]deceives his neighbor,
And does not speak the truth,
They have taught their tongue to speak lies;
They [b]weary themselves committing iniquity.
6 "Your [a]dwelling is in the midst of deceit;
Through deceit they [b]refuse to know Me," declares
the LORD.

7 Therefore thus says the LORD of hosts,
"Behold, I will refine them and [a]assay them;
For [b]what *else* can I do, because of the daughter of My
people?
8 "Their [a]tongue is a deadly arrow;
It speaks deceit;
With his mouth one [b]speaks peace to his neighbor,
But inwardly he [c]sets an ambush for him.
9 "[a]Shall I not punish them for these things?" declares the
LORD.
"On a nation such as this
Shall I not avenge Myself?

10 "For the [a]mountains I will take up a weeping and
wailing,
And for the pastures of the [b]wilderness a dirge,
Because they are [c]laid waste, so that no one passes
through,
And the lowing of the cattle is not heard;
Both the [d]birds of the sky and the beasts have fled; they
are gone.
11 "And I will make Jerusalem a [a]heap of ruins,
A haunt of [b]jackals;
And I will make the cities of Judah a [c]desolation, without inhabitant."
12 Who is the [a]wise man that may understand this? And
who is he to whom [b]the mouth of the LORD has spoken, that he
may declare it? [c]Why is the land ruined, laid waste like a
desert, so that no one passes through?
13 And the LORD said, "Because they have [a]forsaken My
law which I set before them, and have not obeyed My voice
nor walked according to it,
14 but have [a]walked after the stubbornness of their heart
and after the [b]Baals, as their [c]fathers taught them,"
15 therefore thus says the LORD of hosts, the God of Israel, "behold, I will feed them, this people, with wormwood
and give them [a]poisoned water to drink.
16 "And I will [a]scatter them among the nations, whom neither they nor their fathers have known; and I will send the
[b]sword after them until I have annihilated them."
17 Thus says the LORD of hosts,
"Consider and call for the [a]mourning women, that they
may come;
And send for the [1b]wailing women, that they may
come!
18 "And let them make haste, and take up a wailing for us,

4 [1]I.e., like Jacob (a play on words) [b]Gen. 27:35 [c]Jer. 6:28; Ps. 15:3; Prov. 10:18

5 [a]Mic. 6:12 [b]Jer. 12:13; 51:58, 64

6 [a]Jer. 5:27; 8:5; Ps. 120:5, 6 [b]Jer. 11:10; 13:10; Job 21:14, 15; John 3:14, 20

7 [a]Jer. 6:27; Is. 1:25; Mal. 3:3 [b]Hos. 11:8

8 [a]Jer. 9:3 [b]Ps. 28:3 [c]Jer. 5:26

9 [a]Jer. 5:9, 29; Is. 1:24

10 [a]Jer. 4:24; 7:29 [b]Jer. 4:26; Hos. 4:3 [c]Jer. 12:4, 10; Ezek. 14:15; 29:11; 33:28 [d]Jer. 4:25; 12:4; Hos. 4:3

11 [a]Jer. 51:37; Is. 25:2 [b]Is. 13:22; 34:13 [c]Jer. 4:27; 26:9

12 [a]Ps. 107:43; Hos. 14:9 [b]Jer. 9:20; 23:16 [c]Jer. 23:10; Ps. 107:34

13 [a]Jer. 5:19; 22:9; 2 Chr. 7:19; Ps. 89:30

14 [a]Jer. 7:24; 11:8; Rom. 1:21-24 [b]Jer. 2:8, 23; 23:27 [c]Gal. 1:14; 1 Pet. 1:18

15 [a]Jer. 8:14; 23:15; Deut. 29:18

16 [a]Jer. 13:24; Lev. 26:33; Deut. 28:64 [b]Jer. 44:27; Ezek. 5:2, 12

17 [1]Lit., *skilled in mourning for the dead* [a]2 Chr. 35:25; Eccles. 12:5 [b]Amos 5:16

That our [a]eyes may shed tears,
And our eyelids flow with water.
19 "For a voice of [a]wailing is heard from Zion,
'[b]How are we ruined!
We are put to great shame,
For we have [c]left the land,
Because they have cast down our dwellings.' "
20 Now hear the word of the LORD, O you [a]women,
And let your ear receive the word of His mouth;
Teach your daughters wailing,
And every one her neighbor a dirge.
21 For [a]death has come up through our windows;
It has entered our palaces
To cut off the [b]children from the streets,
The young men from the town squares.
22 Speak, "Thus declares the LORD,
'The corpses of men will fall like [a]dung on the open field,
And like the sheaf after the reaper,
But no one will gather *them.*' "

23 Thus says the LORD, "[a]Let not a wise man boast of his
wisdom, and let not the [b]mighty man boast of his might, let
not a [c]rich man boast of his riches;
24 but let him who boasts [a]boast of this, that he understands and knows Me, that I am the LORD who [b]exercises
lovingkindness, justice, and righteousness on earth; for I [c]de-
light in these things," declares the LORD.
25 "Behold, the days are coming," declares the LORD, "that
I will punish all who are circumcised and yet [a]uncircumcised—
26 Egypt, and Judah, and Edom, and the sons of Ammon,
and Moab, and [a]all those inhabiting the desert who clip the
hair on their temples; for all the nations are uncircumcised,
and all the house of Israel are [b]uncircumcised of heart."

CHAPTER 10

HEAR the word which the LORD speaks to you,
O house of Israel.
2 Thus says the LORD, "Do not [a]learn the way of the
nations, and do not be terrified by the signs of the heavens
although the [b]nations are terrified by them;
3 "For the customs of the peoples are [1][a]delusion;
Because [b]it is wood cut from the forest,
The work of the hands of a craftsman with a cutting tool.
4 "They [a]decorate *it* with silver and with gold;
They [b]fasten it with nails and with hammers
So that it will not totter.
5 "Like a scarecrow in a cucumber field are they,
And they cannot speak;
They [a]must be carried,
Because they cannot walk!
Do not fear them,
For they [b]can do no harm,
Nor can they do any good."

18 [a]Jer. 9:1; 14:17; Is. 22:4

19 [a]Jer. 7:29; Ezek. 7:16-18 [b]Jer. 4:13; Deut. 28:29 [c]Jer. 7:15; 15:1

20 [a]Is. 32:9

21 [a]Jer. 15:7; 18:21; 2 Chr. 36:17; Ezek. 9:5, 6; Amos 6:9, 10 [b]Jer. 6:11

22 [a]Jer. 8:2; 16:4; 26:33; Ps. 83:10; Is. 5:25

23 [a]Eccles. 9:11; Is. 47:10; Ezek. 28:3-7 [b]1 Kin. 20:10, 11; Is. 10:8-12 [c]Job 31:24, 25; Ps. 49:6-9

24 [a]Jer. 4:2; Ps. 44:8; Is. 41:16; 1 Cor. 1:31; 2 Cor. 10:17; Gal. 6:14 [b]Ex. 34:6, 7; Ps. 36:5, 7; 51:1 [c]Is. 61:8; Mic. 7:18

25 [a]Jer. 4:4; Rom. 2:8, 9

26 [a]Jer. 25:23 [b]Jer. 4:4; 6:10; Lev. 26:41; Ezek. 44:7; Rom. 2:28

2 [a]Lev. 18:3; Deut. 12:30 [b]Is. 47:12-14

3 [1]Lit., *vanity* [a]Jer. 14:22 [b]Is. 44:9-20

4 [a]Jer. 10:14; Is. 40:19 [b]Is. 40:20; 41:7

5 [a]Is. 46:1, 7 [b]Is. 41:23, 24

6 [a]There is none like Thee, O LORD;
Thou art [b]great, and great is Thy name in might.
7 Who would not fear Thee, O [a]King of the nations?
Indeed it is thy due!
For among all the [b]wise men of the nations,
And in all their kingdoms,
There is none like Thee.
8 But they are altogether stupid and foolish
In their discipline of [1]delusion—[2]their idol is wood!
9 Beaten [a]silver is brought from [b]Tarshish,
And [c]gold from Uphaz,
The work of a craftsman and of the hands of a goldsmith;
Violet and purple are their clothing;
They are all the work of skilled [d]men.
10 But the LORD is the [a]true God;
He is the [b]living God and the [c]everlasting King.
At His wrath the earth quakes,
And the nations cannot [d]endure His indignation.
11 [1]Thus you shall say to them, "The [a]gods that did not
make the heavens and the earth shall [b]perish from the earth
and from under the [2]heavens."
12 *It is* [a]He who made the earth by His power,
Who [b]established the world by His wisdom;
And by His understanding He has [c]stretched out the heavens.
13 When He utters His [a]voice, *there is* a tumult of waters in the heavens,
And He causes the [b]clouds to ascend from the end of the earth;
He makes lightning for the rain,
And brings out the [c]wind from His storehouses.
14 Every man is stupid, devoid of knowledge;
Every goldsmith is put to shame by his [1]idols;
For his molten images are deceitful,
And there is no breath in them.
15 They are [a]worthless, a work of mockery;
In the [b]time of their punishment they will perish.
16 The [a]Portion of Jacob is not like these;
For the [1b]Maker of all is He,
And [c]Israel is the tribe of His inheritance;
The [d]LORD of hosts is His name.

17 [a]Pick up your bundle from the ground,
You who dwell under siege!
18 For thus says the LORD,
"Behold, I am [a]slinging out the inhabitants of the land
At this time,
And will cause them distress,
That they may [1]be found."

19 [a]Woe is me, because of my [1]injury!
My [b]wound is incurable.
But I said, "Truly this is a sickness,
And I [c]must bear it."
20 My [a]tent is destroyed,

6 [a]Jer. 10:16; Deut. 33:26 [b]Jer. 32:18; Ps. 48:1; 96:4; Is. 12:6

7 [a]Ps. 22:28 [b]Dan. 2:27, 28; 1 Cor. 1:19, 20

8 [1]Lit., *vanities*, or *idols* [2]Lit., *it is*

9 [a]Is. 40:19 [b]Ps. 72:10; Is. 23:6 [c]Dan. 10:5 [d]Ps. 115:4

10 [a]Is. 65:16 [b]Jer. 4:2 [c]Ps. 10:16; 29:10 [d]Ps. 76:7

11 [1]This verse is in Aramaic [2]Or, *these heavens* [a]Ps. 96:5 [b]Is. 2:18; Zeph. 2:11

12 [a]Jer. 51:15-19; Job 38:4-7; Ps. 148:4, 5 [b]Ps. 78:69; Is. 45:18 [c]Job 9:8; Is. 40:22

13 [a]Ps. 29:3-9 [b]Job 36:27-29 [c]Ps. 135:7

14 [1]Or, *graven image*

15 [a]Jer. 8:19; 14:22; Is. 41:24 [b]Jer. 8:12; 51:8

16 [1]Lit., *Fashioner* [a]Jer. 51:19; Ps. 73:26 [b]Jer. 10:12; Is. 45:7 [c]Deut. 32:9 [d]Jer. 31:35; 32:18

17 [a]Ezek. 12:3-12

18 [1]Lit., *find* [a]1 Sam. 25:29

19 [1]Lit., *breaking* [a]Jer. 4:31 [b]Jer. 14:17 [c]Ps. 39:9; Mic. 7:9

20 [a]Jer. 4:20; Lam. 2:4

And all my ropes are broken;
My [b]sons have gone from me and are no more.
There is [c]no one to stretch out my tent again
Or to set up my curtains.
21 For the shepherds have become stupid
And have not sought the LORD;
Therefore they have not prospered,
And [a]all their flock is scattered.
22 The sound of a [a]report! Behold, it comes—
A great commotion out of the land of the north—
To [b]make the cities of Judah
A desolation, a haunt of jackals.

23 I know, O LORD, that a man's [a]way is not in himself;
[b]Nor is it in a man who walks to direct his steps.
24 [a]Correct me, O LORD, but with justice;
Not with Thy anger, lest Thou [1]bring me to nothing.
25 [a]Pour out Thy wrath on the nations that do not know Thee,
And on the families that do not [b]call Thy name;
For they have devoured Jacob;
They have [c]devoured him and consumed him,
And have laid waste his [1]habitation.

CHAPTER 11

THE word which came to Jeremiah from the LORD, saying,
2 "[a]Hear the words of this [b]covenant, and speak to the
men of Judah and to the inhabitants of Jerusalem;
3 and say to them, 'Thus says the LORD, the God of
Israel, "[a]Cursed is the man who does not heed the words of
this covenant
4 which I commanded your forefathers in the [a]day that I
brought them out of the land of Egypt, from the [b]iron furnace,
saying, 'Listen to My voice, and [1]do according to all which I
command you; so you shall be [c]My people, and I will be your
God;
5 in order to confirm the [a]oath which I swore to your
forefathers, to give them a land flowing with milk and honey,
as *it is* this day.' " ' " Then I answered and said, "[b]Amen, O
LORD."
6 And the LORD said to me, "[a]Proclaim all these words in
the cities of Judah and in the streets of Jerusalem, saying,
'Hear the words of this covenant and do them.
7 'For I solemnly [a]warned your fathers in the [b]day that I
brought them up from the land of Egypt, even to this day,
[1c]warning persistently, saying, "Listen to My voice."
8 'Yet they did not [a]obey or incline their ear, but walked,
every one, in the stubbornness of their evil heart; therefore I
brought on them all the [b]words of this covenant, which I commanded
them to do, but they did not.' "
9 Then the LORD said to me, "A [a]conspiracy has been
found among the men of Judah and among the inhabitants of
Jerusalem.
10 "They have [a]turned back to the iniquities of their [1]ancestors
who [b]refused to hear My words, and they [c]have gone

20 [b]Jer. 31:15; Lam. 1:5 [c]Is. 51:18
21 [a]Jer. 23:2
22 [a]Jer. 4:15 [b]Jer. 9:11; 49:33
23 [a]Prov. 20:24 [b]Is. 26:7
24 [1]Lit., *diminish me* [a]Ps. 6:1
25 [1]Or, *pasture* [a]Ps. 79:6, 7; Zeph. 3:8 [b]Zeph. 1:6 [c]Jer. 8:16; 50:7, 17
2 [a]Jer. 10:6 [b]Ex. 19:5
3 [a]Jer. 17:5; Deut. 27:26; Gal. 3:10
4 [1]Lit., *do them* [a]Jer. 31:32; Ex. 24:3-8 [b]Deut. 4:20; 1 Kin. 8:51 [c]Jer. 24:7; Zech. 8:8
5 [a]Jer. 32:22; Ex. 13:5; Deut. 7:12 [b]Jer. 28:6
6 [a]Jer. 3:12; 7:2
7 [1]Lit., *rising early and warning* [a]1 Sam. 8:9 [b]Jer. 11:4; Ex. 15:26 [c]Jer. 7:25; 2 Chr. 36:15
8 [a]Jer. 7:24; 9:14; 35:15; Ezek. 20:8 [b]Lev. 26:14-43
9 [a]Ezek. 22:25; Hos. 6:9
10 [1]Lit., *the former fathers* [a]Jer. 3:10, 11; 1 Sam. 15:11 [b]Jer. 13:10; Deut. 9:7; Ps. 78:8-10 [c]Judg. 2:11-13

after other gods to serve them; the house of Israel and the
house of Judah have [d]broken My covenant which I made with
their fathers."
11 Therefore thus says the LORD, "Behold I am [a]bringing
disaster on them which they will [b]not be able to escape; though
they will cry to Me, yet I will not listen to them.
12 "Then the cities of Judah and the inhabitants of Jerusalem will [a]go and cry to the gods to whom they burn incense,
but they surely will not save them in the time of their disaster.
13 "For your gods are [1a]as many as your cities, O Judah;
and [1]as many as the streets of Jerusalem are the altars you have
set up to the shameful thing, altars to [b]burn incense to Baal.
14 "Therefore do not [a]pray for this people, nor lift up a cry
or prayer for them; for I will [b]not listen when they call to Me
because of their disaster.

15 "What right has My beloved in My house
When she has done many vile deeds?
Can the sacrificial flesh take away from you your disaster,
[1]So *that* you can rejoice?"
16 The LORD called your name,
"A [a]green olive tree, beautiful in fruit and form";
With the noise of a great [b]tumult
He has [c]kindled fire on it,
And its branches are worthless.

17 And the LORD of hosts, who [a]planted you, has pronounced evil against you because of the evil of the house of
Israel and of the house of Judah, which they have [1]done to
provoke Me by [2b]offering up sacrifices to Baal.

18 Moreover, the LORD [a]made it known to me and I knew it;
Then Thou didst show me their deeds.
19 But I was like a gentle [a]lamb led to the slaughter;
And I did not know that they had devised plots against me, *saying*,
"Let us destroy the tree with its [1]fruit,
And [b]let us cut him off from the [c]land of the living,
That his [d]name be remembered no more."
20 But, O LORD of hosts, who [a]judges righteously,
Who [b]tries the [1]feelings and the heart,
Let me see Thy vengeance on them,
For to Thee have I [2]committed my cause.

21 Therefore thus says the LORD concerning the men of
[a]Anathoth, who [b]seek your life, saying, "Do not prophesy in
the name of the LORD, that you might not [c]die at our hand";
22 therefore, thus says the LORD of hosts, "Behold, I am
about to punish them! The [a]young men will die by the sword,
their sons and daughters will die by famine;
23 and a remnant will [a]not be left to them, for I will [b]bring
disaster on the men of Anathoth—the year of their
punishment."

CHAPTER 12

[a]RIGHTEOUS art Thou, O LORD, that I would plead *my* case with Thee;

10 [d]Jer. 3:6-11; Ezek.16:59

11 [a]Jer. 11:17; 6:19; 2 Kin. 22:16 [b]Jer. 25:35; Is. 24:17

12 [a]Jer. 44:17; Deut. 32:37

13 [1]Lit., *the number of* [a]Jer. 2:28; 2 Kin. 23:13 [b]Jer. 7:9

14 [a]Jer. 7:16; 14:11; Ex. 32:10 [b]Jer. 11:11; Ps. 66:18; Hos. 5:6

15 [1]Lit., *then*

16 [a]Ps. 52:8 [b]Ps. 83:2 [c]Jer. 21:14; Ps. 80:16; Is. 27:11

17 [1]Or, *done for themselves* [2]Or, *burning incense* [a]Jer. 2:21; 12:2 [b]Jer. 11:13; 7:9; 32:29

18 [a]1 Sam. 23:11, 12; 2 Kin. 6:9, 10; Ezek. 8:6

19 [1]Lit., *bread* [a]Is. 53:7 [b]Ps. 83:4; Is. 53:8 [c]Job 28:13; Ps. 52:5 [d]Ps. 109:13

20 [1]Lit., *reins* [2]Lit., *revealed* [a]Jer. 20:12; Gen. 18:25 [b]Jer. 17:10; Ps. 7:9

21 [a]Jer. 1:1 [b]Jer. 12:5, 6; 20:10 [c]Jer. 26:8; 38:4

22 [a]Jer. 18:21; 2 Chr. 36:17

23 [a]Jer. 6:9 [b]Jer. 23:12; Hos. 9:7; Mic. 7:4

1 [a]Jer. 11:20; Ezra 9:15; Ps. 129:4

Indeed I would [b]discuss matters of justice with Thee:
Why has the [c]way of the wicked prospered?
Why are all those who deal in treachery at ease?
2 Thou hast [a]planted them, they have also taken root;
They grow, they have even produced fruit.
Thou art [b]near [1]to their lips
But far from their [2]mind.
3 But Thou [a]knowest me, O LORD;
Thou seest me;
And Thou dost [b]examine my heart's *attitude* toward Thee.
Drag them off like sheep for the slaughter
And [1]set them apart for a day of carnage!
4 How long is the land to mourn
And the [a]vegetation of the countryside to wither?
For the wickedness of those who dwell in it,
[b]Animals and birds have been snatched away,
Because *men* have said, "He will not see our latter [c]ending."

5 "If you have run with footmen and they have tired you out,
Then how can you compete with horses?
If you fall down in a land of peace,
How will you do in the [1]thicket of the Jordan?
6 "For even your [a]brothers and the household of your father,
Even they have dealt treacherously with you,
Even they have cried aloud after you.
Do not believe them, although they may say [b]nice things to you."

7 "I have [a]forsaken My house,
I have abandoned My inheritance;
I have given the [b]beloved of My soul
Into the hand of her enemies.
8 "My inheritance has become to Me
Like a lion in the forest;
She has [1a]roared against Me;
Therefore I have come to [b]hate her.
9 "Is My inheritance like a speckled bird of prey to Me?
Are the [a]birds of prey against her on every side?
Go, gather all the [b]beasts of the field,
Bring them to devour!
10 "Many shepherds have [a]ruined My [b]vineyard,
They have [c]trampled down My field;
They have made My [d]pleasant field
A desolate wilderness.
11 "[1]It has been made a desolation,
Desolate, it mourns [2]before Me;
The [a]whole land has been made desolate,
Because no man [b]lays it to heart.
12 "On all the [1]bare heights in the wilderness
Destroyers have come,
For a [a]sword of the LORD is devouring

1 [b]Job 13:3 [c]Jer. 5:27, 28; Hab. 1:4; Mal. 3:15

2 [1]Lit., *near in their mouth* [2]Lit., *kidneys* [a]Jer. 11:17; 45:4; Ezek. 17:5-10 [b]Jer. 3:10; Is. 29:13; Ezek. 33:31; Titus 1:16

3 [1]Lit., *sanctify them* [a]Ps. 139:1-4 [b]Jer. 11:20; Ps. 7:9; 11:5

4 [a]Joel 1:10-17 [b]Hos. 4:3; Hab. 3:17 [c]Jer. 5:31; Ezek. 7:2

5 [1]Lit., *pride*

6 [a]Jer. 9:4, 5; Gen. 37:4-11; Job 6:15; Ps. 69:8 [b]Ps. 12:9; Prov. 26:25

7 [a]Jer. 7:29; 23:39; Is. 2:6 [b]Jer. 11:15; Lam. 2:1; Hos. 11:1-8

8 [1]Lit., *raised her voice* [a]Is. 59:13 [b]Hos. 9:15; Amos 6:8

9 [a]2 Kin. 24:2; Ezek. 23:22-25 [b]Jer. 7:33; 15:3; 34:20; Is. 56:9

10 [a]Jer. 23:1 [b]Ps. 80:8-16; Is. 5:1-7 [c]Is. 63:18 [d]Jer. 3:19; Lam. 1:10

11 [1]Lit., *One has made it* [2]Or, *upon* [a]Jer. 4:20, 27; 25:11 [b]Is. 42:25

12 [1]Or, *caravan trails* [a]Jer. 47:6; Is. 34:6; Amos 9:4

From one end of the land even to the [2]other;
There is no [b]peace for [3]anyone.
13 "They have sown wheat and have reaped thorns,
They have [a]strained themselves [1]to no profit.
But be ashamed of your [2b]harvest
Because of the [c]fierce anger of the LORD."
14 Thus says the LORD concerning all My [a]wicked neighbors who [b]strike at the inheritance with which I have endowed My people Israel, "Behold I am about to uproot them
from their land and will [c]uproot the house of Judah from
among them.
15 "And it will come about that after I have uprooted
them, I will [a]again have compassion on them; and I will bring
them back, each one to his inheritance and each one to his
land.
16 "Then it will come about that if they will really [a]learn
the ways of My people, to [b]swear by My name, 'As the Lord
lives,' even as they taught My people to [c]swear by Baal, then
they will be [d]built up in the midst of My people.
17 "But if they will not listen, then I will [a]uproot that nation, uproot and destroy it," declares the LORD.

CHAPTER 13

THUS the LORD said to me, "Go and [a]buy yourself a linen
waistband, and put it around your waist, but you do not put it
in water."
2 So I bought the waistband in accordance with the
[a]word of the LORD and put it around my waist.
3 Then the word of the LORD came to me a second time,
saying,
4 "Take the waistband that you have bought, which is
around your waist, and arise, go to [1]the [a]Euphrates and hide it
there in a crevice of the rock."
5 So I went and hid it by the Euphrates, [a]as the LORD had
commanded me.
6 And it came about after many days that the LORD said
to me, "Arise, go to the Euphrates and take from there the
waistband which I commanded you to hide there."
7 Then I went to the Euphrates and dug, and I took the
waistband from the place where I had hidden it; and lo, the
waistband was ruined, it was totally worthless.
8 Then the word of the LORD came to me, saying,
9 "Thus says the LORD, 'Just so will I destroy the [a]pride of
Judah and the great pride of Jerusalem.
10 'This wicked people, who refuse to listen to My words,
who walk in the stubbornness of their hearts and have gone
after other gods to serve them and to bow down to them, let
them be just like this waistband, which is totally worthless.
11 'For as the waistband clings to the waist of a man, so I
made the whole household of Israel and the whole household
of Judah [a]cling to Me', declares the LORD, 'that they might be
for Me a people, for [1b]renown, for [c]praise, and for glory; but
they [d]did not listen.'
12 "Therefore you are to speak this word to them, 'Thus
says the LORD, the God of Israel, "Every jug is to be filled with

12 [2]Lit., *other end of the land* [3]Lit., *all flesh* [b]Jer. 16:5; 30:5

13 [1]Lit., *they do not profit* [2]Lit., *products* [a]Jer. 9:5; Is. 55:2 [b]Jer. 17:10 [c]Jer. 4:26; 25:37, 38

14 [a]Jer. 49:1, 7; Zeph. 2:8-10 [b]Jer. 2:3; 50:11, 12; Zech. 2:8 [c]Deut. 30:3; Ps. 106:47; Is. 11:11-16

15 [a]Jer. 48:7; 49:6, 39

16 [a]Is. 42:6; 49:6 [b]Jer. 4:2 [c]Jer. 5:7; Josh. 23:7 [d]Jer. 3:17; 4:2; 16:19

17 [a]Ps. 2:8-12; Is. 60:12

1 [a]Jer. 13:11; 19:1; 27:2; Ezek. 4:1

2 [a]Is. 20:2; Ezek. 2:8

4 [1]Or, *Parah*, cf. Josh. 18:23; so through v. 7 [a]Jer. 51:63

5 [a]Ex. 39:42, 43; 40:16

9 [a]Jer. 15:17; Lev. 26:19; Is. 2:10-17; 23:9; Zeph. 3:11

11 [1]Lit., *a name* [a]Ex. 19:5, 6; Deut. 32:10, 11 [b]Jer. 32:20 [c]Jer. 33:9; Is. 43:21 [d]Jer. 7:13, 24, 26; Ps. 81:11

wine; and when they say to you, 'Do we not very well know
that every jug is to be filled with wine?'
13 "then say to them, 'Thus says the LORD, "Behold I am
about to fill all the inhabitants of this land—the kings that sit
for David on his throne, the priests, the prophets and all the
inhabitants of Jerusalem—with [a]drunkenness!
14 "And I will [a]dash them against each other, both the
[b]fathers and the sons together," declares the LORD. "I will [c]not
show pity nor be sorry nor have compassion that I should not
destroy them." ' "

15 Listen and give heed, do not be [a]haughty,
For the LORD has spoken.
16 [a]Give glory to the LORD your God,
Before He [b]brings darkness
And before your feet stumble
On the dusky mountains,
And while you are hoping for light
He makes it into deep darkness,
And turns *it* into [c]gloom.
17 But [a]if you will not listen to it,
My soul will [b]sob in secret for *such* pride;
And my eyes will bitterly weep
And flow down with tears,
Because the flock of the [c]LORD has been taken captive.
18 Say to the [a]king and the queen mother,
"[b]Take a lowly seat,
For your beautiful [c]crown
Has come down from your heads."
19 The cities of the Negev have been locked up,
And there is no one to open *them*;
All Judah has been carried into exile,
Wholly carried into exile.

20 "Lift up your eyes and see
Those coming [a]from the north.
Where is the [b]flock that was given you,
Your beautiful sheep?
21 "What will you say when He appoints over you—
And you yourself had taught them—
Former [1a]companions to be head over you?
Will not [b]pangs take hold of you,
Like a woman in childbirth?
22 "And if you [a]say in your heart,
'Why have these things happened to me?'
Because of the [b]magnitude of your iniquity
Your skirts have been removed,
And your heels have [1]been exposed.
23 "[a]Can the Ethiopian change his skin
Or the leopard his spots?
Then you also can [b]do good
Who are accustomed to do evil.
24 "Therefore I will [a]scatter them like drifting straw
To the desert [b]wind.
25 "This is your [a]lot, the portion measured to you
From Me," declares the LORD,

13 [a]Jer. 25:27; 51:57; Ps. 60:3; 75:8

14 [a]Jer. 19:9-11; Is. 9:20, 21 [b]Jer. 6:21; Ezek. 5:10 [c]Jer. 16:5; 21:7; Deut. 29:20; Is. 27:11

15 [a]Prov. 16:5; Is. 28:14-22

16 [a]Ps. 96:8 [b]Is. 5:30; 59:9; Amos 5:18 [c]Jer. 2:6; Ps. 107:10, 14

17 [a]Mal. 2:2 [b]Jer. 9:1; 14:17; Ps. 119:136; Luke 19:41, 42 [c]Jer. 23:1, 2; Ps. 80:1

18 [a]Jer. 22:26; 2 Kin. 24:12, 15 [b]2 Chr. 33:12, 19 [c]Ex. 39:28; Is. 3:20; Ezek. 24:17, 23; 44:18

20 [a]Jer. 1:15; 6:22; Hab. 1:6 [b]Jer. 13:17; 23:2

21 [1]Or, *chieftains* [a]Jer. 2:25; 38:22 [b]Jer. 4:31; Is. 13:8

22 [1]Or, *suffered violence* [a]Deut. 7:17 [b]Jer. 2:17-19; 9:2-9

23 [a]Prov. 27:22; Is. 1:5; Matt. 19:24 [b]Jer. 4:22; 9:5

24 [a]Jer. 9:16; Lev. 26:33; Ezek. 5:2, 12 [b]Jer. 4:11; 18:17

25 [a]Ps. 11:6; Matt. 24:51

"Because you have [b]forgotten Me
And trusted in falsehood.
26 "So I Myself have also [a]stripped your skirts off over your face,
That your shame may be seen.
27 "As for your [a]adulteries and your *lustful* neighings,
The [b]lewdness of your prostitution
On the [c]hills in the field,
I have seen your abominations.
Woe to you, O Jerusalem!
How [d]long will you remain unclean?"

Chapter 14

THAT which came as the word of the LORD to Jeremiah in regard to the drought:
2 "Judah mourns,
And her gates languish
They sit on the ground [a]in mourning,
And the [b]cry of Jerusalem has ascended.
3 "And their nobles have [a]sent their [1]servants for water;
They have come to the cisterns and found no water.
They have returned with their vessels empty;
They have been [b]put to shame and humiliated,
And they [c]cover their heads.
4 "Because the [a]ground is [1]cracked,
For there has been no rain on the land;
The [b]farmers have been put to shame,
They have covered their heads.
5 "For even the doe in the field has given birth only to abandon *her young*,
Because there is [a]no grass.
6 "And the [a]wild donkeys stand on the bare heights;
They pant for air like jackals,
Their eyes fail
For there is [b]no vegetation."
7 "Although our [a]iniquities testify against us,
O LORD, act for Thy name's sake!
Truly our [b]apostasies have been many,
We have sinned against Thee.
8 "Thou [a]Hope of Israel,
Its [b]Savior in [c]time of distress,
Why art Thou like a stranger in the land
Or like a traveler who has pitched his *tent* for the night?
9 "Why art Thou like a man dismayed,
Like a mighty man who [a]cannot save?
Yet [b]Thou art in our midst, O LORD,
And we are [c]called by Thy name;
Do not forsake us!"

10 Thus says the LORD to this people, "Even so they have
[a]loved to wander; they have not [b]kept their feet in check.
Therefore the LORD does [c]not accept them; now He will [d]re-
member their iniquity and call their sins to account."
11 So the LORD said to me, "Do not [a]pray for the welfare
of this people.

25 [b]Jer. 2:32; 3:21; Ps. 9:17; 106:21, 22

26 [a]Lam. 1:8

27 [a]Jer. 5:7, 8 [b]Jer. 11:15 [c]Jer. 2:20 [d]Prov. 1:22; Hos. 8:5

2 [a]Jer. 8:21 [b]Jer. 11:11; 46:12; Zech. 7:13

3 [1]Lit., *little ones* [a]1 Kin. 18:5 [b]Job 6:20; Ps. 40:14 [c]2 Sam. 15:30

4 [1]Lit., *shattered* [a]Joel 1:19, 20 [b]Joel 1:11

5 [a]Is. 15:6

6 [a]Jer. 2:24; Job 39:5, 6 [b]Joel 1:18

7 [a]59:12; Hos. 5:5 [b]Jer. 5:6; 8:5

8 [a]Jer. 17:13 [b]Is. 43:3; 63:8 [c]Ps. 9:9; 50:15

9 [a]Num. 11:23; Is. 50:2 [b]Jer. 8:19; Ps. 46:5 [c]Jer. 15:16; Is. 63:19

10 [a]Jer. 2:25; 3:13 [b]Ps. 119:101 [c]Jer. 6:20; Amos 5:22 [d]Jer. 44:21-23; Hos. 8:13

11 [a]Jer. 7:16; 11:14; Ex. 32:10

12 [a]Jer. 11:11; Is. 1:15 [b]Jer. 8:13 [c]Jer. 21:9

13 [1]YHWH, usually rendered LORD [2]Lit., *peace of truth* [a]Jer. 5:12; 23:17 [b]Jer. 6:14; 8:11

14 [1]Lit., *hearts* [a]Jer. 5:31; 23:25 [b]Jer. 23:16, 26; 27:9, 10; Ezek. 12:24

15 [1]Lit., *be finished* [a]Ezek. 14:10

16 [a]Jer. 7:33; 15:2, 3; Ps. 79:2,3 [b]Jer. 13:22-25; Prov. 1:31

17 [a]Jer. 9:1; 13:17 [b]Jer. 8:21; Is. 37:22; Lam. 1:15; 2:13

18 [1]Lit., *pierced* [2]Or, *gone around trading* [a]Jer. 6:25; Lam. 1:20; Ezek. 7:15

19 [1]Lit., *Thy soul* [a]Jer. 30:13 [b]Jer. 8:15; Job 30:26; 1 Thess. 5:3

20 [a]Jer. 3:25; Neh. 9:2; Ps. 32:5

21 [a]Jer. 14:7; Ps. 25:11 [b]Jer. 3:17; 17:12

22 [1]Lit., *vanities* [2]Or, *wait for* [a]Jer. 10:3; Is. 41:29 [b]Jer. 5:24; 1 Kin. 17:1 [c]Lam. 3:26

12 "When they fast, I am [a]not going to listen to their cry;
and when they offer burnt offering and grain offering, I am
not going to accept them. Rather I am going to [b]make an end
of them by the [c]sword, famine and pestilence."
13 But, "Ah, Lord [1]God!" I said, "Look, the prophets are
telling them, 'You [a]will not see the sword nor will you have
famine, but I will give you [2]lasting [b]peace in this place.' "
14 Then the LORD said to me, "The [a]prophets are prophesying falsehood in My name. I have neither sent them nor
commanded them nor spoken to them; they are prophesying
to you a [b]false vision, divination, futility and the deception of
their own [1]minds.
15 "Therefore thus says the LORD concerning the prophets
who are prophesying in My name, although it was not I who
sent them—yet they keep saying, 'There shall be no sword or
famine in this land'—by [a]sword and famine those prophets
shall [1]meet their end!
16 "The people also to whom they are prophesying will be
[a]thrown out into the streets of Jerusalem because of the famine and the sword; and there will be no one to bury them—
neither them, *nor* their wives, nor their sons, nor their daughters—for I shall [b]pour out their *own* wickedness on them.

17 "And you will say this word to them:
'[a]Let my eyes flow down with tears night and day,
And let them not cease;
For the virgin [b]daughter of my people has been crushed
with a mighty blow,
With a sorely infected wound.
18 'If I [a]go out to the country,
Behold, those [1]slain with the sword!
Or if I enter the city,
Behold, diseases of famine!
For both prophet and priest
Have [2]gone roving about in the land that they do not
know.' "

19 Hast Thou completely rejected Judah?
Or hast [1]Thou loathed Zion?
Why hast Thou stricken us so that we [a]are beyond
healing?
[b]*We* waited for peace, but nothing good *came;*
And for a time of healing, but behold, terror!
20 We [a]know our wickedness, O LORD,
The iniquity of our fathers, for we have sinned against
Thee.
21 Do not despise *us,* [a]for Thine own name's sake;
Do not disgrace the [b]throne of Thy glory;
Remember *and* do not annul Thy covenant with us.
22 Are there any among the [1a]idols of the nations who
[b]give rain?
Or can the heavens grant showers?
Is it not Thou, O LORD our God?
Therefore we [2c]hope in Thee,
For Thou art the one who hast done all these things.

CHAPTER 15

THEN the LORD said to me, "Even [a]though [b]Moses and [c]Samuel were to stand before Me, My [1]heart would not be [2]with this people; [d]send them away from My presence and let them go!

2 "And it shall be that when they say to you, 'Where should we go?' then you are to tell them, 'Thus says the LORD:
"Those destined [a]for death, to death;
And those destined for the sword, to the sword;
And those *destined* for famine, to famine;
And those *destined* for captivity, to captivity." '

3 "And I shall [a]appoint over them four kinds *of doom*," declares the LORD: "the sword to slay, the [b]dogs to drag off, and the [c]birds of the sky and the beasts of the earth to devour and destroy.

4 "And I shall [a]make them an object of horror among all the kingdoms of the earth because of [b]Manasseh, the son of Hezekiah, the king of Judah, for what he did in Jerusalem.

5 "Indeed, who will have [a]pity on you, O Jerusalem,
Or who will mourn for you,
Or who will turn aside to ask about your welfare?
6 "You who have forsaken Me," declares the LORD,
"You keep [a]going backward.
So I will [b]stretch out My hand against you and destroy you;
I am [c]tired of relenting!
7 "And I will [a]winnow them with a winnowing fork
At the gates of the land;
I will [b]bereave *them* of children, I will destroy My people;
They did not [1]repent of their ways.
8 "Their [a]widows will be more numerous before Me
Than the sand of the seas;
I will bring against them, against the mother of a young man,
A destroyer at noonday;
I will suddenly bring down on her
Anguish and dismay.
9 "She who [a]bore seven *sons* pines away;
[1]Her breathing is labored.
Her [b]sun has set while it was yet day;
She has been shamed and humiliated.
So I shall give over their [c]survivors to the sword
Before their enemies," declares the LORD.

10 [a]Woe to me, my mother, that you have born me
As a [b]man of strife and a man of contention to all the land!
I have neither [c]lent, nor have men lent money to me,
Yet every one curses me.
11 The LORD said, "Surely I will [a]set you free for *purposes of* good;
Surely I will cause the enemy to make supplication to you
In a time of disaster and a time of distress."

1 [1]Lit., *soul* [2]Lit., *toward* [a]Ps. 99:6; Ezek. 14:14, 20 [b]Ex. 32:11-14; Num. 14:13-20; Ps. 106:23 [c]1 Sam. 7:9; 12:23 [d]Jer. 7:15; 10:18; 52:3; 2 Kin. 17:20

2 [a]Jer. 14:12; 24:10; 43:11; Ezek. 5:2, 12

3 [a]Lev. 26:16, 22, 25; Ezek. 14:21 [b]1 Kin. 21:23, 24 [c]Jer. 7:33; Deut. 28:26; Is. 18:6

4 [a]Jer. 24:9; 29:18; Lev. 26:33 [b]2 Kin. 21:1-18; 23:26, 27; 24:3, 4

5 [a]Jer. 13:14; 21:7; Ps. 69:20

6 [a]Jer. 7:24; Is. 1:4 [b]Jer. 6:12; Zeph. 1:4 [c]Jer. 6:11; 7:16

7 [1]Lit., *turn back from* [a]Jer. 51:2; Ps. 1:4 [b]Jer. 18:21; Hos. 9:12-16

8 [a]Is. 3:25, 26; 4:1

9 [1]Or, *She has breathed out her soul* [a]1 Sam. 2:5; Is. 47:9 [b]Jer. 6:4; Amos 8:9 [c]Jer. 21:7

10 [a]Jer. 20:14; Job 3:3 [b]Jer. 15:20; 1:18, 19; 20:7, 8 [c]Ex. 22:25; Lev. 25:36, 37; Deut. 23:19

11 [a]Ps. 138:3; Is. 41:10

13 [a]Jer. 17:3; 20:5 [b]Is. 52:3, 5

14 [1]I. e., your possessions [a]Jer. 16:13; Deut. 28:36, 64 [b]Jer. 17:4; Ps. 21:9

15 [a]Jer. 20:8; Ps. 44:22; 69:7-9

16 [a]Ezek. 3:3 [b]Job 23:12; Ps. 119:103 [c]Jer. 14:9

17 [a]Jer. 16:8; 2 Cor. 6:17 [b]Jer. 13:17; Ps. 102:7; Lam. 3:28; Ezek. 3:24, 25

18 [a]Jer. 30:12, 15; Job 34:6; Mic. 1:9 [b]Jer. 14:3; Job 6:15, 20

19 [1]Lit., *as My mouth* [a]Jer. 15:1; 35:19; 1 Kin. 17:1 [b]Jer. 6:29; Ezek. 22:26; 44:23

20 [a]Jer. 1:18, 19; 6:27; Ezek. 3:9 [b]Jer. 15:15; Jer. 1:8, 19; Ps. 46:7; Is. 41:10

21 [1]Lit., *palm* [a]Jer. 20:13; 39:11, 12; Gen. 48:16; Ps. 37:40 [b]Jer. 31:11; 50:34; Is. 49:26; 60:16

3 [a]Jer. 6:21

4 [a]Jer. 15:2

12 "Can anyone smash iron,
Iron from the north, or bronze?
13 "Your [a]wealth and your treasures
I will give for booty [b]without cost,
Even for all your sins
And within all your borders.
14 "Then I will cause your enemies to bring [1]*it*
Into a [a]land you do not know;
For a [b]fire has been kindled in My anger,
It will burn upon you."

15 Thou who knowest, O LORD;
Remember me, take notice of me,
And take vengeance for me on my persecutors.
Do *not*, in view of Thy patience, take me away;
Know that [a]for Thy sake I endure reproach.
16 Thy words were found and I [a]ate them,
And Thy [b]words became for me a joy and the delight of my heart;
For I have been [c]called by Thy name,
O LORD God of hosts.
17 I did not [a]sit in the circle of merrymakers,
Nor did I exult.
Because of Thy hand *upon me* I sat [b]alone,
For Thou didst fill me with indignation.
18 Why has my pain been perpetual
And my [a]wound incurable, refusing to be healed?
Wilt Thou indeed be to me [b]like a deceptive *stream*
With water that is unreliable?

19 Therefore, thus says the LORD,
"If you return, then I will restore you—
Before Me [a]you will stand;
And [b]if you extract the precious from the worthless,
You will become [1]My spokesman.
They for their part may turn to you,
But as for you, you must not turn to them.
20 "Then I will [a]make you to this people
A fortified wall of bronze;
And though they fight against you,
They will not prevail over you;
For [b]I am with you to save you
And deliver you," declares the LORD.
21 "So I will [a]deliver you from the hand of the wicked,
And I will [b]redeem you from the [1]grasp of the violent."

CHAPTER 16

THE word of the LORD also came to me saying,
2 "You shall not take a wife for yourself nor have sons or
daughters in this place."
3 For thus says the LORD concerning the sons and daughters born in this place, and concerning their mothers who
bear them, and their [a]fathers who beget them in this land:
4 "They will [a]die of deadly diseases, they will not be lamented or buried; they will be as dung on the surface of the

ground and come to an end by sword and famine, and their
carcasses will become food for the [b]birds of the sky and for the
beasts of the earth."
5 For thus says the LORD, "Do not enter a house of
[1a]mourning, or go to lament or to console them; for I have
withdrawn My [b]peace from this people," declares the LORD,
"*My* [c]lovingkindness and compassion.
6 "Both [a]great men and small will die in this land; they
will not be buried, they will not be lamented, nor will anyone
[b]gash himself or shave his head for them.
7 "Neither will men [a]break *bread* in mourning for them,
to comfort anyone for the dead, nor give them a cup of consolation to drink for anyone's father or mother.
8 "Moreover you shall [a]not go into a house of feasting to
sit with them to eat and drink."
9 For thus says the LORD of hosts, the God of Israel:
"Behold, I am going to [1a]eliminate from this place, before
your eyes and in your time, the voice of rejoicing and the voice
of gladness, the voice of the groom and the voice of the bride.
10 "Now it will come about when you tell this people all
these words that they will say to you, '[a]For what reason has the
LORD declared all this great calamity against us? And what is
our iniquity, or what is our sin which we have committed
against the LORD our God?'
11 "Then you are to say to them, '*It is* [a]because your forefathers have forsaken Me,' declares the LORD, 'and have followed [b]other gods and served them and bowed down to them;
but Me they have forsaken and have not kept My law.
12 'You too have done evil, *even* more than your forefathers;
for behold, you are each one walking according to the
[a]stubbornness of his own [b]evil heart, without listening to Me.
13 'So I will [a]hurl you out of this land into the [b]land which
you have not known, neither you nor your fathers; and there
you will [c]serve other gods day and night, for I shall grant you
no favor.
14 "[a]Therefore behold, days are coming," declares the
LORD, "when it will no longer be said, 'As the LORD lives, who
[b]brought up the sons of Israel out of the land of Egypt,'
15 but, 'As the LORD lives, who brought up the sons of
Israel from the [a]land of the north and from all the countries
where He had banished them.' For I will restore them to their
own land which I gave to their fathers.
16 "Behold, I am going to send for many [a]fishermen," declares the LORD, "and they will fish for them; and afterwards I
shall send for many hunters, and they will [b]hunt them [c]from
every mountain and every hill, and from the clefts of the rocks.
17 "[a]For My eyes are on all their ways; they are not hidden
from My face, nor is their iniquity concealed from My eyes.
18 "And I will first doubly [a]repay their iniquity and their
sin, because they have [b]polluted My land; they have filled My
inheritance with the carcasses of their detestable idols and with
their abominations."
19 O LORD, my [a]strength and my stronghold,
And my [b]refuge in the day of distress,
To Thee the [c]nations will come
From the ends of the earth and say,

4 [b]Jer. 15:3; 34:20; Ps. 79:2; Is. 18:6

5 [1]Or, *banqueting* [a]Ezek. 24:16-23 [b]Jer. 12:12; 15:1-4 [c]Jer. 13:14; Is. 27:11; Ps. 25:6

6 [a]2 Chr. 36:17; Ezek. 9:6 [b]Jer. 41:5; 47:5; Deut. 14:1

7 [a]Deut. 26:14; Ezek. 24:17; Hos. 9:4

8 [a]Jer. 15:17; Eccles. 7:2-4; Is. 22:12-14; Amos 6:4-6

9 [1]Lit., *cause to cease* [a]Jer. 7:34; 25:10; Hos. 2:11

10 [a]Jer. 5:19; 13:22; Deut. 29:24, 25; 1 Kin. 9:8, 9

11 [a]Jer. 5:7-9; Neh. 9:26-29; Ps. 106:35-41 [b]Jer. 8:2; Ezek. 11:21; 1 Pet. 4:3

12 [a]Jer. 7:24; 9:14; 13:10; 1 Sam. 15:23 [b]Eccles. 9:3; Mark 7:21

13 [a]Jer. 15:1; Deut. 4:26, 27; 2 Chr. 7:20 [b]Jer. 15:14; 17:4 [c]Jer. 5:19; Deut. 4:28; 28:36

14 [a]Jer. 23:7, 8; Is. 43:18, 19; Hos. 3:4, 5 [b]Ex. 20:2; Deut. 15:15

15 [a]Jer. 3:18; 24:6; Ps. 106:47; Is. 11:11-16; 14:1

16 [a]Amos 4:2; Hab. 1:14, 15 [b]1 Sam. 26:20; Mic. 7:2 [c]Is. 2:21; Amos 9:1-3

17 [a]Jer. 23:24; 32:19; Ps. 90:8; Luke 12:2; 1 Cor. 4:5; Heb. 4:13

18 [a]Jer. 17:18; Rev. 18:6 [b]Jer. 2:7; 3:9; Num. 35:33, 34

19 [a]Jer. 15:11; Ps. 18:1, 2; Is. 25:4 [b]Nah. 1:7 [c]Jer. 3:17; 4:2

19 [1]Lit., *there is nothing profitable in them*

20 [a]Jer. 2:11; 5:7; Ps. 115:4-8; Is. 37:19; Hos. 8:4-6

21 [1]Lit., *hand*
[a]Ps. 9:16 [b]Jer. 33:2; Ps. 83:18; Is. 43:3; Amos 5:8

1 [1]So ancient versions; M.T., *your*
[a]Job 19:24 [b]Prov. 3:3; 7:3; Is. 49:16; 2 Cor. 3:3

2 [1]I.e., wooden symbols of a female deity
[a]Jer. 7:18 [b]Ex. 34:13 [c]Jer. 3:6

3 [a]Jer. 26:18; Mic. 3:12 [b]Jer. 15:13; 20:5; 2 Kin. 24:13; Is. 39:4-6

4 [a]Jer. 12:7; Lam. 5:2 [b]Jer. 15:14; 27:12, 13; Deut. 28:48; Is. 14:3 [c]Jer. 7:20; 15:14; Is. 5:25

5 [1]Lit., *arm*
[a]Ps. 146:3; Is. 2:22; 30:1; Ezek. 29:6, 7 [b]2 Chr. 32:8; Is. 31:3

6 [1]Lit., *and is not inhabited*
[a]Jer. 48:6 [b]Deut. 29:23; Job 39:6

7 [a]Ps. 34:8; 84:12 [b]Ps. 40:4

8 [a]Ps. 1:3; 92:12-14; Ezek. 31:3-9

9 [a]Mark 7:21, 22; Rom. 7:11; Eph. 4:22 [b]Eccles. 9:3; Is. 1:6; 6:10; Matt. 13:15; Mark 2:17; Rom. 1:21

10 [1]Lit., *kidneys* [2]Lit., *fruit*
[a]Jer. 11:20; 20:12; 1 Sam. 16:7; Rom. 8:27

"Our fathers have inherited nothing but falsehood,
Futility and [1]things of no profit."
20 Can man make gods for himself?
Yet they are [a]not gods!

21 "Therefore behold, I am going to make them know—
This time I will [a]make them know
My [1]power and My might;
And they shall [b]know that My name is the LORD."

CHAPTER 17

THE sin of Judah is written down with an iron [a]stylus;
With a diamond point it is [b]engraved upon the tablet of their heart,
And on the horns of [1]their altars,
2 As they remember their [a]children,
So they *remember* their altars and their [1b]Asherim
By [c]green trees on the high hills.
3 O [a]mountain of Mine in the countryside,
I will [b]give over your wealth and all your treasures for booty,
Your high places for sin throughout your borders.
4 And you will, even of yourself, [a]let go of your inheritance
That I gave you;
And I will make you serve your [b]enemies
In the land which you do not know;
For you have [c]kindled a fire in My anger
Which will burn forever.

5 Thus says the LORD,
"[a]Cursed is the man who trusts in mankind
And makes [b]flesh his [1]strength,
And whose heart turns away from the LORD.
6 "For he will be like a [a]bush in the desert
And will not see when prosperity comes,
But will live in stony wastes in the wilderness,
A land of [b]salt [1]without inhabitant.
7 "[a]Blessed is the man who trusts in the LORD
And whose [b]trust is the LORD.
8 "For he will be like a [a]tree planted by the water,
That extends its roots by a stream
And will not fear when the heat comes;
But its leaves will be green,
And it will not be anxious in a year of drought
Nor cease to yield fruit.

9 "The heart is more [a]deceitful than all else
And is desperately [b]sick;
Who can understand it?
10 "I the LORD [a]search the heart,
I test the [1]mind,
Even to give to each man according to his ways,
According to the [2]results of his deeds.
11 "As a partridge that hatches eggs which it has not laid,

So is he who makes a fortune, but unjustly;
In the midst of his days it will forsake him,
And in [1]the end he will be a fool."

12 [a]A glorious throne on high from the beginning
Is the place of our sanctuary.
13 O LORD, the [a]hope of Israel,
All who forsake Thee will be put to shame.
Those who turn [1]away on earth will be written down,
Because they have forsaken the fountain of living water, even the LORD.
14 [a]Heal me, O LORD, and I will be healed;
[b]Save me and I will be saved,
For Thou art my [c]praise.
15 Look, they keep [a]saying to me,
"Where is the word of the LORD?
Let it come now!"
16 But as for me, I have not hurried away from *being* a shepherd after Thee,
Nor have I longed for the woeful day;
Thou Thyself knowest the utterance of my lips
Was in Thy presence.
17 Do not be a [a]terror to me;
Thou art my [b]refuge in the day of disaster.
18 Let those who persecute me be [a]put to shame, but as for me let me not be put to shame;
Let them be dismayed, but let me not be dismayed.
[b]Bring on them a day of disaster,
And crush them with twofold destruction!

19 Thus the LORD said to me, "Go and stand in the [1]pub-
lic gate, through which the kings of Judah come in and go out,
as well as in all the gates of Jerusalem;
20 and say to them, 'Listen to the word of the LORD, [a]kings
of Judah, and all Judah, and all inhabitants of Jerusalem, who
come in through these gates:
21 'Thus says the LORD, "[a]Take heed for yourselves, and
do not [b]carry any load on the sabbath day or bring anything in
through the gates of Jerusalem.
22 "And you shall not bring a load out of your houses on
the sabbath day nor do any [a]work, but keep the sabbath day
holy, as I [b]commanded your [1]forefathers.
23 "Yet they did not listen or incline their ears, but [a]stif-
fened their necks in order not to listen or take correction.
24 "But it will come about, if you listen [a]attentively to
Me," declares the LORD, "to bring no load in through the gates
of this city on the sabbath day, [b]but to keep the sabbath day
holy by doing no work on it,
25 [a]then there will come in through the gates of this city
kings and princes [b]sitting on the throne of David, riding in
chariots and on horses, they and their princes, the men of
Judah, and the inhabitants of Jerusalem; and this city will [c]be
inhabited forever.
26 "They will come in from the cities of Judah and from
the environs of Jerusalem, from the land of Benjamin, from
the [a]lowland, from the hill country, and from the [a]Negev,
bringing burnt offerings, sacrifices, grain offerings and incense,

11 [1]Lit., *his*

12 [a]Jer. 3:17; 14:21

13 [1]Heb., *away from Me* [a]Jer. 14:8; 50:7

14 [a]Jer. 30:17; 33:6 [b]Ps. 54:1; 60:5 [c]Deut. 10:21; Ps. 109:1

15 [a]Is. 5:19; Amos 5:18

17 [a]Ps. 88:15 [b]Jer. 16:19; Nah. 1:7

18 [a]Jer. 17:13; 20:11; Ps. 35:4, 26 [b]Ps. 35:8

19 [1]Lit., *gate of the sons of the people*

20 [a]Jer. 19:3, 4; Ps. 49:1,2; Hos. 5:3; Amos 4:1

21 [a]Deut. 4:9; 16:23; Mark 4:24 [b]Num. 15:32-36; Neh. 13:15-21; John 5:9-12

22 [1]Lit., *fathers* [a]Ex. 16:23-29; 20:8-10; Deut. 5:12-14; Is. 56:2-6; 58:13[b]Ex.31:13-17; Ezek. 20:12; Zech. 1:4

23 [a]Jer. 7:26; 19:15; Prov. 29:1

24 [a]Ex. 15:26; Deut. 11:13; Is. 21:7; 55:2 [b]Ex. 20:8-11; Ezek. 20:20

25 [a]Jer. 22:4 [b]Jer. 13:15, 17, 21; 2 Sam. 7:16; 9:7; Luke 1:32 [c]Ps. 132:13, 14; Heb. 12:22

26 [a]Zech. 7:7

and [b]bringing sacrifices of thanksgiving to the house of the
LORD.
27 "But if you do not listen to Me to keep the sabbath day
holy by not carrying a load and coming in through the gates of
Jerusalem on the sabbath day, then I shall kindle a fire in its
gates, and it will [a]devour the palaces of Jerusalem and [b]not be
quenched." ' "

CHAPTER 18

THE word which came to Jeremiah from the LORD saying,
2 "Arise and [a]go down to the potter's house, and there I
shall announce My words to you."
3 Then I went down to the potter's house, and there he
was, making something on the [1]wheel.
4 But the vessel that he was making of clay was spoiled in
the hand of the potter; so he remade it into another vessel, as it
pleased the potter to make.
5 Then the word of the LORD came to me saying,
6 "Can I not, O house of Israel, deal with you as this
potter *does*?" declares the LORD. "Behold, like the [a]clay in the
potter's hand, so are you in My hand, O house of Israel.
7 "At one moment I might speak concerning a nation or
concerning a kingdom to [a]uproot, to pull down, or to destroy
it;
8 [a]if that nation against which I have spoken turns from
its evil, I will [1]relent concerning the calamity I planned to
bring on it.
9 "Or at another moment I might speak concerning a
nation or concerning a kingdom to [a]build up or to plant *it*;
10 if it does [a]evil in My sight by not obeying My voice,
then I will [1b]think better of the good with which I had promised to [2]bless it.
11 "So now then, speak to the men of Judah and against
the inhabitants of Jerusalem saying, 'Thus says the LORD: "Behold, I am [a]fashioning calamity against you and devising a plan
against you. Oh [b]turn back, each of you from his evil way, and
[1]reform your ways and your deeds." '
12 "But [a]they will say, 'It's hopeless! For we are going to
follow our own plans, and each of us will act [b]according to the
stubbornness of his evil heart.'

13 "Therefore thus says the LORD,
'[a]Ask now among the nations,
Who ever heard the like of [1]this?
The virgin of Israel
Has done a most [b]appalling thing.
14 'Does the snow of Lebanon forsake the rock of the
open country?
Or is the cold flowing water *from* a foreign *land* ever
snatched away?
15 'For [a]My people have forgotten Me,
[b]They burn incense [1]to worthless gods
And they [2]have stumbled [3]from their ways,
[3]From the [c]ancient paths,
To walk in bypaths,
Not on a [d]highway,

26 [b]Jer. 33:11; Ps. 107:22

27 [a]Jer. 39:8; Amos 2:5 [b]Jer. 7:20; Ezek. 20:47

2 [a]Jer. 19:1, 2

3 [1]Lit., *pair of stone discs*

6 [a]Is. 45:9; 64:8; Matt. 20:15; Rom. 9:21

7 [a]Jer. 1:10

8 [1]Lit., *repent of* [a]Jer. 7:3-7; 12:16; Ezek. 18:21

9 [a]Jer. 1:10; 31:28; Amos 9:11-15

10 [1]Lit., *repent* [2]Lit., *do it good* [a]Jer. 7:24-28; Ps. 125:5; Ezek. 33:18 [b]1 Sam. 2:30; 13:13

11 [1]Lit., *make good* [a]Jer. 4:6; 11:11; Is. 5:5 [b]Jer. 4:1; 2 Kin 17:13; Is. 1:16-19; Acts 26:20

12 [a]Jer. 2:25; Is. 57:10 [b]Jer. 7:24; 16:12; Deut. 29:19

13 [1]Lit., *these* [a]Jer. 2:10, 11; Is. 66:8 [b]Jer. 5:30; 23:14; Hos. 6:10

15 [1]Lit., *to worthlessness* [2]So ancient versions; Heb., *caused them to* [3]Or, *in* [a]Jer. 2:32; 3:21 [b]Jer. 7:9; 44:17; Is. 65:7 [c]Jer. 6:16 [d]Is. 57:14; 62:10

16 To make their land a [a]desolation,
An object of perpetual hissing;
Everyone who passes by it will be astonished
And [b]shake his head.
17 'Like an east wind I will [a]scatter them
Before the enemy;
I will [1]show them My back and not *My* face
In the day of their calamity.' "
18 Then they said, "Come and let us [a]devise plans against
Jeremiah. Surely the [b]law is not going to be lost to the priest,
nor [c]counsel to the sage, nor the *divine* [d]word to the prophet!
[e]Come on and let us strike at him with *our* tongue, and let us
give [f]no heed to any of his words."
19 Do give heed to me, O LORD,
And listen to [1]what my opponents are saying!
20 Should good be repaid with evil?
For they have [a]dug a pit for [1]me.
Remember how I [b]stood before Thee
To speak good on their behalf,
So as to turn away Thy wrath from them.
21 Therefore, [a]give their children over to famine,
And deliver them up to the [1]power of the sword;
And let their wives become [b]childless and [c]widowed.
Let their men also be smitten to death,
Their [d]young men struck down by the sword in battle.
22 May an [a]outcry be heard from their houses,
When Thou suddenly bringest raiders upon them;
[b]For they have dug a pit to capture me
And [c]hidden snares for my feet.
23 Yet Thou, O LORD, knowest
All their [1]deadly designs against me;
Do not [2a]forgive their iniquity
Or blot out their sin from Thy sight.
But may they be [3b]overthrown before Thee;
Deal with them in the [c]time of Thine anger!

CHAPTER 19

THUS says the LORD, "Go and buy a [a]potter's earthenware
[b]jar, and *take* some of the [c]elders of the people and some of
the [1d]senior priests.
2 "Then go out to the [a]valley of Ben-Hinnom, which is by
the entrance of the Potsherd Gate; and proclaim there the
words that I shall tell you,
3 and say, 'Hear the word of the LORD, O kings of Judah
and inhabitants of Jerusalem: Thus says the LORD of hosts, the
God of Israel, "Behold I am about to bring a calamity upon
this place, at which the [a]ears of everyone that hears of it will
tingle.
4 "Because they have [a]forsaken Me and have made this an
[b]alien place and have burned [1]sacrifices in it to [c]other gods
that neither they nor their forefathers nor the kings of Judah
had *ever* known, and *because* they have filled this place with
the [d]blood of the innocent
5 and have built the [a]high places of Baal to burn their

16 [a]Jer. 25:9; 50:13; Ezek. 33:28, 29 [b]Jer. 48:27; Ps. 22:7; Is. 37:22

17 [1]So ancient versions; M.T. reads: *look them in the back and not in the face* [a]Jer. 13:24; Job 27:21

18 [a]Jer. 18:11; 11:19 [b]Jer. 2:8; Mal. 2:7 [c]Jer. 8:8; Job 5:13 [d]Jer. 5:13 [e]Jer. 20:10; Ps. 52:2 [f]Jer. 43:2

19 [1]Lit., *the voice of my opponents*

20 [1]Lit., *my soul* [a]Jer. 18:22; 5:26; Ps. 35:7; 57:6 [b]Ps. 106:23

21 [1]Lit., *hands of* [a]Jer. 11:22; 14:16; Ps. 109:9-20 [b]1 Sam. 15:33; Is. 13:18 [c]Jer. 15:8; Ezek. 22:25 [d]Jer. 9:21; 11:22

22 [a]Jer. 6:26; 25:34, 36 [b]Jer. 18:20 [c]Ps. 140:5

23 [1]Lit., *unto death* [2]Or, *atone for* [3]Lit., *ones made to stumble* [a]Ps. 109:14; Is. 2:9 [b]Jer. 6:15, 21 [c]Jer. 7:20; 17:4

1 [1]Or, *elders of* [a]Jer. 18:2 [b]Jer. 19:10 [c]Num. 11:16 [d]2 Kin. 19:2

2 [a]Jer. 7:31, 32; Josh. 15:8

3 [a]1 Sam. 3:11; 4:18

4 [1]Or, *incense* [a]Jer. 17:13; Is. 65:11 [b]Ezek. 7:22; Dan. 11:31 [c]Jer. 7:9; 11:13 [d]Jer. 2:34; 7:6; 2 Kin. 21:6, 16

5 [a]Jer. 32:35; Num. 22:41

[b]sons in the fire as burnt offerings to Baal, a thing which I
never commanded or spoke of, nor did it *ever* enter My [1]mind;
6 therefore, behold, days are coming," declares the LORD,
"when this place will no longer be called [a]Topheth or the
valley of Ben-Hinnom, but rather the valley of Slaughter.
7 "And I shall [a]make void the counsel of Judah and Jerusalem in this place, and I shall cause them to fall by the sword
before their enemies and by the hand of those who seek their
life; and I shall give over their [b]carcasses as food for the birds
of the sky and the beasts of the earth.
8 "I shall also make this city a [a]desolation and an *object of*
hissing; [b]everyone who passes by it will be astonished and hiss
because of all its [1]disasters.
9 "And I shall make them [a]eat the flesh of their sons and
the flesh of their daughters, and they will eat one another's
flesh in the siege and in the distress with which their enemies
and those who seek their life will distress them." '
10 "Then you are to break the jar in the sight of the men
who accompany you
11 and say to them, 'Thus says the LORD of hosts: "Just so
shall I [a]break this people and this city, even as one breaks a
potter's vessel, which cannot again be repaired; and they will
[b]bury in Topheth [1]because there is no *other* place for burial.
12 "This is how I shall treat this place and its inhabitants,"
declares the LORD, "so as to make this city like Topheth.
13 "And the [a]houses of Jerusalem and the houses of the
kings of Judah will be defiled [b]like the place Topheth, because
of all the [c]houses on whose rooftops they burned [1]sacrifice to
[d]all the heavenly host and [e]poured out libations to other
gods." ' "
14 Then Jeremiah came from Topheth, where the LORD
had sent him to prophesy; and he stood in the [a]court of the
LORD's house and said to all the people:
15 "Thus says the LORD of hosts, the God of Israel, 'Behold, I am about to bring on this city and all its towns the
entire calamity that I have declared against it; because they
have [a]stiffened their necks so [b]as not to heed My words.' "

CHAPTER 20

WHEN Pashhur the Priest, the son of [a]Immer, who was
[b]chief officer in the house of the LORD, heard Jeremiah prophesying these things,
2 Pashhur had Jeremiah the prophet [a]beaten, and put
him in the [b]stocks that were at the upper Benjamin [c]gate,
which was by the house of the LORD.
3 Then it came about on the next day, when Pashhur
released Jeremiah from the stocks, that Jeremiah said to him,
"Pashhur is not the name the LORD has [a]called you, but rather
[1]Magomassabib.
4 "For thus says the LORD, 'Behold, I am going to make
you a [a]terror to yourself and to all your friends; and while
[b]your eyes look on, they will fall by the sword of their enemies.
So I shall give over all Judah to the hand of the king of Babylon, and he will carry them away as exiles to Babylon and will
slay them with the sword.

5 [1]Lit., *heart* [b]2 Kin. 106:37, 38

6 [a]Is. 30:33

7 [a]Jer. 8:8, 9; Ps. 33:10, 11; Is. 28:17, 18 [b]Jer. 16:4; Ps. 79:2, 3

8 [1]Lit., *blows* [a]Jer. 18:16 [b]1 Kin. 9:8; 2 Chr. 7:21

9 [a]Deut. 28:53, 55; Lam. 4:10; Ezek. 5:10

11 [1]Or, *until there is no place left to bury* [a]Ps. 2:9; Is. 30:14; Rev. 2:27 [b]Jer. 7:32

13 [1]Or, *incense* [a]Jer. 52:13 [b]Ps. 74:7; 79:1; Ezek. 7:21, 22 [c]Jer. 32:29; Zeph. 1:5 [d]Jer. 8:2; Deut. 4:19; 2 Kin. 17:16 [e]Jer. 7:18; 44:18; Ezek. 20:28

14 [a]Jer. 26:2

15 [a]Jer. 7:26; 17:23; Neh. 9:17, 29 [b]Ps. 58:4

1 [a]1 Chr. 24:14; Ezra 2:37, 38 [b]2 Kin. 25:18

2 [a]Jer. 1:19; 1 Kin. 22:27; 2 Chr. 16:10; 24:21; Amos 7:10-13 [b]Job 13:27; 33:11 [c]Jer. 37:13; 38:7; Zech. 14:10

3 [1]I. e., Terror on every side [a]Is. 8:3; Hos. 1:4, 9

4 [a]Job 18:11-21; Ezek. 26:21 [b]Jer. 29:21; 39:6, 7

5 'I shall also give over all the [a]wealth of this city, all its
produce, and all its costly things; even all the treasures of the
kings of Judah I shall give over to the [b]hand of their enemies,
and they will plunder them, take them away, and bring them
to Babylon.
6 'And you, Pashhur, and all who live in your house will
go into captivity; and you will enter Babylon, and there you
will die, and there you will be buried, you and all your [a]friends
to whom you have falsely prophesied.' "

7 O LORD, Thou hast deceived me and I was deceived;
Thou hast [a]overcome me and prevailed.
I have become a [b]laughingstock all day long;
Everyone [c]mocks me.
8 For each time I speak, I cry aloud;
I proclaim violence and destruction,
Because for me the [a]word of the LORD has [1]resulted
In reproach and derision all day long.
9 But if I say, "I will not [a]remember Him
Or speak any more in His name,"
Then in my heart it becomes like a burning fire
Shut up [b]in my bones;
And I am weary of holding *it* in,
And I cannot endure *it*.
10 For I have heard the whispering of many,
"Terror on every side!
[a]Denounce *him*; yes, let us denounce him!"
[1]All my [b]trusted friends,
Watching for my fall, say:
"Perhaps he will be [2]deceived, so that we may [c]prevail against him
And take our revenge on him."
11 But the [a]LORD is with me like a dread champion;
Therefore my [b]persecutors will stumble and not prevail.
They will be utterly ashamed, because they have [1]failed,
With an everlasting disgrace that will not be forgotten.
12 Yet, O LORD of hosts, Thou who dost [a]test the righteous,
Who seest the [1]mind and the heart;
Let me [b]see Thy vengeance on them;
For [c]to Thee I have set forth my cause.
13 Sing to the LORD, praise the LORD!
For He has [a]delivered the soul of the needy one
From the hand of evildoers.

14 Cursed be the [a]day when I was born;
Let the day not be blessed when my mother bore me!
15 Cursed be the man who brought the news
To my father, saying,
"A [1a]baby boy has been born to you!"
And made him very happy.
16 But let that man be like the cities
Which the LORD overthrew without [1]relenting,
And let him hear an [a]outcry in the morning
And a [2]shout of alarm at noon;

5 [a]Jer. 15:13; 17:3 [b]Jer. 27:21, 22; 2 Kin. 20:17, 18; 2 Chr. 36:10

6 [a]Jer. 19:4; 14:14, 15; Lam. 2:14

7 [a]Ezek. 3:14; Mic. 3:8 [b]Lam. 3:14 [c]Jer. 38:19; Ps. 22:7

8 [1]Lit., *become* [a]Jer. 6:10; 2 Chr. 36:16

9 [a]1 Kin. 19:3, 4; Jon. 1:2, 3 [b]Jer. 4:19; 23:19; Job 38:18-20; Ps. 39:3; Ezek. 3:14; Acts 4:20

10 [1]Lit., *Every man of my peace* [2]Or, *persuaded* [a]Jer. 18:18; Neh. 6:6-13; Is. 29:21 [b]Ps. 41:9 [c]1 Kin. 19:2; 22:27

11 [1]Lit., *not succeeded*, or, *not acted wisely* [a]Jer. 1:8; 15:20 [b]Jer. 15:15; Deut. 32:35, 36

12 [1]Lit., *kidneys* [a]Jer. 11:20; 17:10; Ps. 7:9; 11:5; 17:3; 139:23 [b]Jer. 11:20; Ps. 59:10 [c]Ps. 62:8

13 [a]Jer. 15:21; Ps. 34:6; 69:33

14 [a]Job 3:3-6

15 [1]Lit., *male child* [a]Gen. 21:6, 7

16 [1]Lit., *being sorry* [2]Or, *trumpet blast* [a]Jer. 48:3, 4

17 Because he did not [a]kill me [1]before birth,
So that my mother would have been my grave,
And her womb ever pregnant.
18 Why did I ever come forth from the womb
To [a]look on trouble and sorrow,
So that my [b]days have been spent in [c]shame?

17 [1]Lit., *from the womb* [a]Job 3:10, 11, 16; 10:18, 19

18 [a]Jer. 15:10; Job 3:20; 5:7; 14:1 [b]Ps. 90:9; 102:3 [c]Jer. 3:25; Ps. 69:19; 1 Cor. 4:9-13

Chapter 21

THE word which came to Jeremiah from the LORD when
King Zedekiah sent to him [a]Pashhur the son of Malchijah, and
[b]Zephaniah the priest, the son of Maaseiah, saying,
2 "Please inquire of the LORD on our behalf, for [a]Nebuchad-
nezzar king of Babylon is warring against us; perhaps the
LORD will deal with us [b]according to all His [1]wonderful acts,
that *the enemy* may withdraw from us."
3 Then Jeremiah said to them, "You shall say to Zedekiah as follows:
4 'Thus says the LORD God of Israel, "Behold, I am about
to [a]turn back the weapons of war which are in your hands, with
which you are warring against the king of Babylon and the
Chaldeans who are besieging you outside the wall; and I shall
[b]gather them into the center of this city.
5 "And I [a]Myself shall war against you with an [b]outstretched
hand and a mighty arm, even in [c]anger and wrath and
great indignation.
6 "I shall also strike down the inhabitants of this city, both
man and beast; they will die of a great [a]pestilence.
7 "Then afterwards," declares the LORD, "I shall give over
Zedekiah king of Judah and his servants and the people, even
those who survive in this city from the pestilence, the sword,
and the famine, into the hand of Nebuchadnezzar king of
Babylon, and into the hand of their foes, and into the hand of
those who seek their lives; and he will strike them down with
the edge of the sword. He will not [a]spare them nor have pity
nor compassion." '
8 "You shall also say to this people, 'Thus says the LORD,
"Behold, I set before you the [a]way of life and the way of death.
9 "He who [a]dwells in this city will die by the sword and by
famine and by pestilence; but he who goes out and falls away
to the Chaldeans who are besieging you will live, and he will
have his own life as booty.
10 "For I have [a]set My face against this city for [1]harm and
not for good," declares the LORD, "It will be [b]given into the
hand of the king of Babylon, and he will [c]burn it with fire.
11 "Then *say* to the household of the king of Judah, 'Hear
the word of the LORD,
12 O [a]house of David, thus says the LORD:
"[b]Administer justice [1]every [c]morning;
And deliver the *person* who has been robbed from the
[2]power of his oppressor,
[d]That My wrath may not go forth like fire
And burn with [e]none to extinguish *it*,
Because of the evil of their deeds.

13 "Behold, I am against you, O [a]valley dweller,

1 [a]Jer. 38:1; 1 Chr. 9:12 [b]Jer. 29:25, 29; 37:3; 52:24; 2 Kin. 25:18-21

2 [1]Or, *miracles* [a]2 Kin. 25:1, 2 [b]Jer. 32:17; Ps. 44:1-4

4 [a]Jer. 32:5; 33:5; 37:8-10; 38:2, 3, 17, 18 [b]Jer. 39:3; Is. 5:5; Lam. 2:5, 7; Zech. 14:2

5 [a]Is. 63:10 [b]Jer. 6:12; Deut. 4:34 [c]Jer. 32:37; Is. 5:25

6 [a]Jer. 14:12; 32:24

7 [a]Jer. 13:14; 2 Chr. 36:17; Ezek. 7:9; Hab. 1:6-10

8 [a]Deut. 30:15, 19; Is. 1:19, 20

9 [a]Jer. 38:2; 39:18; 45:5

10 [1]Lit., *evil* [a]Jer. 44:11, 27; Amos 9:4 [b]Jer. 32:28, 29 [c]Jer. 39:8; 52:13; 2 Chr. 36:19

12 [1]Or, *in the* [2]Lit., *hand* [a]Is. 7:2, 13 [b]Jer. 7:5; 22:3; Ps. 72:1; Is. 1:17; Zech. 7:9, 10 [c]Zeph. 3:5 [d]Jer. 4:4; 17:4; Ezek. 20:47, 48; Nah. 1:6 [e]Jer. 7:20; Is. 1:31

13 [a]Ps. 125:2; Is. 22:1

O [1]rocky plain," declares the LORD,
"You men who say, '[b]Who will come down against us?
Or who will enter into our habitations?'
14 "But I shall punish you according to the [1]results of your deeds," declares the LORD,
"And I shall kindle a fire in its forest
That it may [a]devour all its environs." ' "

13 [1]Lit., *rock of the level place* [b]2 Sam. 5:6, 7; Lam. 4:12; Obad. 3, 4

14 [1]Lit., *fruit* [a]Jer. 52:13; 2 Chr. 36:19

CHAPTER 22

THUS says the LORD, "Go down to the house of the king of
Judah, and there [a]speak this word,
2 and say, 'Hear the word of the LORD, O king of Judah,
who [a]sits on David's throne, you and your servants and your
people who enter these gates.
3 'Thus says the LORD, "[a]Do justice and righteousness,
and deliver the one who has been robbed from the power of
his [b]oppressor. Also [c]do not mistreat *or* do violence to the
stranger, the orphan, or the widow; and do not [d]shed innocent
blood in this place.
4 "For if you men will indeed perform this thing, then
kings will enter the gates of this house, sitting [1]in David's place
on his throne, riding in chariots and on horses, *even the king*
himself and his servants and his people.
5 "But if you will not obey these words, I [a]swear by Myself," declares the LORD, "that this house will become a
desolation." ' "
6 For thus says the LORD concerning the house of the
king of Judah:
"You are *like* [a]Gilead to Me,
Like the summit of Lebanon;
Yet most assuredly I shall make you like a [b]wilderness,
Like cities which are not inhabited.
7 "For I shall set apart [a]destroyers against you,
Each with his weapons;
And they will cut down your choicest [b]cedars
And throw *them* on the fire.
8 "And many nations will pass by this city; and they will
[a]say to one another, 'Why has the LORD done thus to this great
city?'
9 "Then they will [1]answer, 'Because they [a]forsook the covenant of the LORD their God and bowed down to other gods
and served them.' "
10 Do not weep for the dead or mourn for him,
But weep continually for the one who goes away;
For he will never return
Or see his native land.
11 For thus says the LORD in regard to [1]Shallum the son of
Josiah, king of Judah, who became king in the place of Josiah
his father, who went forth from this place: "He will never
return there;
12 but in the place where they led him captive, there he
will [a]die and not see this land again."
13 "Woe to him who builds his house without [a]righteousness
And his [1]upper rooms without justice,

1 [a]2 Chr. 25:15, 16

2 [a]Jer. 22:4, 30; 17:25; Is. 9:7; Luke 1:32

3 [a]Jer. 7:5; 21:12 [b]Ps. 72:4 [c]Ex. 22:21-24 [d]Jer. 22:17; 7:6; 19:4

4 [1]Lit., *for David*

5 [a]Gen. 22:16; Amos 6:8; Heb. 6:13

6 [a]Gen. 37:25; Num. 32:1; Song of Sol. 4:1 [b]Jer. 7:34; Ps. 107:34; Is. 6:11

7 [a]Jer. 4:6, 7; Is. 10:3-6 [b]Is. 10:33, 34

8 [a]Jer. 16:10; Deut. 29:24-26; 1 Kin. 9:8, 9; 2 Chr. 7:20-22

9 [1]Lit., *say* [a]Jer. 11:3; 2 Chr. 34:25

11 [1]I. e., Jehoahaz

12 [a]Jer. 22:18; 2 Kin. 23:34

13 [1]Or, *roof chambers* [a]Jer. 17:11; Mic. 3:10; Hab. 2:9

Who uses his neighbor's services without pay
And does not give him his wages,
14 Who says, 'I will [a]build myself a roomy house
With spacious [1]upper rooms,
And cut out its windows,
[2]Paneling *it* with [b]cedar and painting *it* [3]bright red.'
15 "Do you become a king because you are competing in cedar?
Did not your father eat and drink,
And [a]do justice and righteousness?
Then it was [b]well with him.
16 "He pled the cause of the [a]afflicted and needy;
Then it was well.
[b]Is not that what it means to know Me?"
Declares the LORD.
17 "But your eyes and your heart
Are *intent* only upon your own [a]dishonest gain,
And on shedding innocent blood
And on practicing oppression and extortion."
18 Therefore thus says the LORD in regard to Jehoiakim
the son of Josiah, king of Judah,
"They will not lament for him:
'Alas, my brother!' or, 'Alas, sister!'
They will not lament for him:
'Alas for the master!' or, 'Alas for his splendor!'
19 "He will be [a]buried with a donkey's burial,
Dragged off and thrown out beyond the gates of Jerusalem.
20 "Go up to Lebanon and cry out,
And lift up your voice in Bashan;
Cry out also from [a]Abarim,
For all your [b]lovers have been crushed.
21 "I spoke to you in your prosperity;
But you said, 'I will not listen!'
This has been your practice from your youth,
That you have not obeyed My voice.
22 "The wind will sweep away all your shepherds,
And your [a]lovers will go into captivity;
Then you will surely be ashamed and humiliated
Because of all your wickedness.
23 "You who dwell in Lebanon,
Nested in the cedars,
How you will groan when pangs come upon you,
Pain like a woman in childbirth!"
24 "As I live," declares the LORD, "even though [1]Coniah
the son of Jehoiakim king of Judah were a [a]signet *ring* on My
right hand, yet I would pull [1]you [2]off;
25 and I shall [a]give you over into the hand of those who
are seeking your life, yes, into the hand of those whom you
dread, even into the hand of Nebuchadnezzar king of Babylon,
and into the hand of the Chaldeans.
26 "I shall hurl you and your [a]mother who bore you into
another country where you were not born, and there you will
die.
27 "But as for the land to which they desire to return, they
will not return to it.

14 [1]Or, *roof chambers* [2]Or, *paneled* [3]Or, *vermilion* [a]Is. 5:8, 9 [b]2 Sam. 7:2; Hag. 1:4
15 [a]Jer. 7:5; 21:12; 2 Kin. 23:25 [b]Jer. 42:6
16 [a]Ps. 72:1-4, 12, 13 [b]Jer. 9:24; 1 Chr. 28:9
17 [a]Jer. 6:13; 8:10; Luke 12:15-20
19 [a]Jer. 36:30; 1 Kin. 21:23, 24
20 [a]Num. 27:12; Deut. 32:49 [b]Jer. 2:25; 3:1
22 [a]Jer. 30:14
24 [1]I.e., Jehoiachin [2]Lit., *off from there* [a]Song of Sol. 8:6; Is. 49:16; Hag 2:23
25 [a]Jer. 21:7; 34:20, 21; 2 Kin. 24:15, 16
26 [a]2 Kin. 24:8

28 "Is this man Coniah a despised, shattered jar?
Or is he an undesirable [a]vessel?
Why have he and his descendants been [b]hurled out
And cast into a land that they had not known?
29 "[a]O land, land, land,
Hear the word of the LORD!
30 "Thus says the LORD,
'Write this man down [a]childless,
A man who will not [b]prosper in his days;
For no man of his [c]descendants will prosper
Sitting on the throne of David
Or ruling again in Judah.' "

CHAPTER 23

"[a]WOE to the shepherds who are [b]destroying and scattering the [c]sheep of My pasture!" declares the LORD.
2 Therefore thus says the LORD God of Israel concerning
the shepherds who are [1]tending My people: "You have scattered My flock and driven them away, and have not attended
to them; behold, I am about to [a]attend to you for the [b]evil of
your deeds," declares the LORD.
3 "Then I myself shall gather the [a]remnant of My flock
out of all the countries where I have driven them and shall
bring them back to their pasture; and they will be fruitful and
multiply.
4 "I shall also raise up [a]shepherds over them and they will
[1]tend them; and they will not be afraid any longer, nor be
terrified, nor will [b]any be missing," declares the LORD.
5 "Behold, *the* days are coming," declares the LORD,
"When I shall raise up for David a righteous [1a]Branch;
And He will [b]reign as king and [2]act wisely
And [c]do justice and righteousness in the land.
6 "In His days Judah will be saved,
And [a]Israel will dwell securely;
And this is His [b]name by which He will be called,
'The [c]LORD our righteousness.'
7 "[a]Therefore behold, *the* days are coming," declares the
LORD, "when they will no longer say, 'As the LORD lives, who
brought up the sons of Israel from the land of Egypt,'
8 but, 'As the LORD lives, who brought up and led back
the descendants of the household of Israel from *the* north
land and from all the countries where I had driven them.'
Then they will live on their own soil."
9 As for the prophets:
My [a]heart is broken within me,
All my bones tremble;
I have become like a drunken man,
Even like a man overcome with wine,
Because of the LORD
And because of His holy words.
10 For the land is full of [a]adulterers;
For the land mourns because of the curse.
The [b]pastures of the wilderness have dried up.
Their course also is evil,
And their might is not right.

28 [a]Hos. 8:8 [b]Jer. 15:1
29 [a]Jer. 6:19; Deut. 4:26; Mic. 1:2
30 [a]1 Chr. 3:17; Matt. 1:12 [b]Jer. 2:37; 10:21 [c]Jer. 36:30; Ps. 94:20
1 [a]Ezek. 13:3; 34:2; Zech. 11:17 [b]Jer. 10:21; 50:6; Is. 56:9-12 [c]Ezek. 34:31
2 [1]Lit., *shepherding* [a]Ex. 32:34 [b]Jer. 21:12; 44:22
3 [a]Jer. 31:7, 8; 32:37; Is. 11:11-16
4 [1]Or, *shepherd* [a]Jer. 3:15; 31:10; Ezek. 34:23 [b]John 6:39; 10:28; 1 Pet. 1:5
5 [1]Lit., *sprout* [2]Or, *succeed* [a]Jer. 30:9; 33:15, 16; Is. 4:2; 11:1-5; 53:2; Zech. 3:8; 6:12, 13 [b]Is. 9:7; 52:13; Luke 1:32, 33 [c]Ps. 72:2
6 [a]Jer. 30:10; Deut. 33:28; Zech. 14:11 [b]Is. 7:14; 9:6; Matt. 1:21-23 [c]Jer. 33:16; Is. 45:24, 25; 54:17; Dan. 9:24; Rom. 3:22
7 [a]Jer. 16:14, 15; Is. 43:18, 19
9 [a]Jer. 8:18; Hab. 3:16
10 [a]Jer. 9:2; Hos. 4:2, 3; Mal. 3:5 [b]Jer. 9:10; Ps. 107:34

12 [a]Jer. 13:16; Ps. 35:6 [b]Is. 8:22; John 12:35 [c]Jer. 11:23

13 [a]Hos. 9:7, 8 [b]Jer. 2:8; 1 Kin. 18:18-21

14 [a]Jer. 23:22; Ezek. 13:22, 23 [b]Jer. 20:16; 49:18; Is. 1:9, 10; Matt. 11:24

15 [a]Jer. 8:14; 9:15; Deut. 29:18

16 [1]Lit., *heart* [a]Jer. 27:9, 10, 14-17; 1 John 4:1 [b]Matt. 7:15; 2 Cor. 11:13-15; Gal. 1:8, 9 [c]Jer. 14:14; Ezek. 13:3, 6

17 [a]Mic. 2:11 [b]Jer. 8:11 [c]Jer. 5:12; Amos 9:10; Mic. 3:11

18 [1]Another reading is, *My* [a]Jer. 23:22; Job 15:8, 9 [b]Job 33:31

19 [a]Jer. 30:23; Amos 1:14

20 [a]Jer. 30:24; Is. 55:11; Zech. 1:6

22 [a]Jer. 35:15; Zech. 1:4; 1 Thess. 1:9, 10

11 "For both prophet and priest are polluted;
Even in My house I have found their wickedness," declares the LORD.
12 "Therefore their way will be like [a]slippery paths to them,
They will be driven away into the [b]gloom and fall down in it;
For I shall bring [c]calamity upon them,
The year of their punishment," declares the LORD.

13 "Moreover, among the prophets of Samaria I saw an [a]offensive thing:
They [b]prophesied by Baal and led My people Israel astray.
14 "Also among the prophets of Jerusalem I have seen a horrible thing:
The committing of adultery and walking in falsehood;
And they strengthen the hands of [a]evildoers,
So that no one has turned back from his wickedness.
All of them have become to Me like [b]Sodom,
And her inhabitants like Gomorrah.
15 "Therefore thus says the LORD of hosts concerning the prophets,
'Behold, I am going to [a]feed them wormwood
And make them drink poisonous water,
For from the prophets of Jerusalem
Pollution has gone forth into all the land.' "

16 Thus says the LORD of hosts,
"[a]Do not listen to the words of the prophets who are prophesying to you.
They are [b]leading you into futility;
They speak a [c]vision of their own [1]imagination,
Not from the mouth of the LORD.
17 "They keep saying to those who [a]despise Me,
'The LORD has said, "[b]You will have peace" ';
And as for every one who walks in the stubbornness of his own heart,
They say, '[c]Calamity will not come upon you.'
18 "But [a]who has stood in the council of the LORD,
That he should see and hear His word?
Who has given [b]heed to [1]His word and listened?
19 "Behold, the [a]storm of the LORD has gone forth in wrath,
Even a whirling tempest;
It will swirl down on the head of the wicked.
20 "The [a]anger of the LORD will not turn back
Until He has performed and carried out the purposes of His heart;
In the last days you will clearly understand it.
21 "I did not send *these* prophets,
But they ran.
I did not speak to them,
But they prophesied.
22 "But if they had stood in My council,
Then they would have [a]announced My words to My people,

And would have turned them back from their evil way
And from the evil of their deeds."

23 "Am I a God who is [a]near," declares the LORD,
"And not a God [b]far off?
24 "Can a man [a]hide himself in hiding places,
So I do not see him?" declares the LORD.
"[b]Do I not fill the heavens and the earth?" declares the LORD.
25 "I have [a]heard what the prophets have said who prophesy falsely in My name, saying, 'I had a [b]dream, I had a dream!'
26 "How long? Is there *anything* in the hearts of the prophets who prophesy falsehood, even *these* prophets of the [a]deception of their own heart,
27 who intend to [a]make My people forget My name by their dreams which they relate to one another, just as their fathers [b]forgot My name because of Baal?
28 "The prophet who has a dream may relate *his* dream, but let him who has My word speak My word in truth. [a]What does straw have *in common* with grain?" declares the LORD.
29 "Is not My word like [a]fire?" declares the LORD, "and like a [b]hammer which shatters a rock?
30 "Therefore behold, I am against the prophets," declares the LORD, "who steal My words from each other.
31 "Behold, I am against the prophets," declares the LORD, "who use their tongues and declare, '*The Lord declares.*'
32 "Behold, I am against those who have prophesied [a]false dreams," declares the LORD, "and related them, and led My people astray by their falsehoods and reckless boasting; yet [b]I did not send them or command them, nor do they [c]furnish this people the slightest benefit," declares the LORD.
33 "Now when this people or the prophet or a priest asks you saying, 'What is the [1a]oracle of the LORD?' then you shall say to them, 'What [1]oracle?' The LORD declares, 'I shall [b]abandon you.'
34 "Then as for the prophet or the priest or the people who say, 'The [a]oracle of the LORD,' I shall bring punishment upon that man and his household.
35 "Thus shall each of you say to his neighbor and to his brother, 'What has the LORD answered?' or, '[a]What has the LORD spoken?'
36 "For you will no longer remember the oracle of the LORD, because every man's own word will become the oracle, and you have [a]perverted the words of the [b]living God, the LORD of hosts, our God.
37 "Thus you will say to *that* prophet, 'What has the LORD answered you?' and, 'What has the LORD spoken?'
38 "For if you say, 'The oracle of the LORD!' surely thus says the LORD, 'Because you said this word, "The oracle of the LORD!" I have also sent to you, saying, "You shall not say, 'The oracle of the LORD!' " '
39 "Therefore behold, [a]I shall surely forget you and cast you away from My presence, along with the city which I gave you and your fathers.

23 [a]Ps. 139:1-10 [b]Jer. 51:50; Ps. 113:5; Jon. 1:3, 4

24 [a]Jer. 49:10; Job 22:13, 14; Ps. 139:7-12; Is. 29:15 [b]1 Kin. 8:27; Is. 66:1

25 [a]Jer. 8:6; 1 Cor. 4:5 [b]Jer. 23:28, 32; 29:8; Num. 12:6; Joel 2:28

26 [a]1 Tim. 4:1, 2

27 [a]Jer. 29:8; Deut. 13:1-3 [b]Judg. 3:7; 8:33, 34

28 [a]1 Cor. 3:12, 13

29 [a]Jer. 5:14; 20:9 [b]2 Cor. 10:4, 5

32 [a]Jer. 23:25; Deut. 13:1, 2 [b]Jer. 23:21; Lam. 3:37 [c]Jer. 7:8; Lam. 2:14

33 [1]Or, *burden*, and so throughout the chap. [a]Is. 13:1; Nah. 1:1; Hab. 1:1; Zech. 9:1 [b]Jer. 23:39; 12:7

34 [a]Lam. 2:14; Zech. 13:3

35 [a]Jer. 33:3; 42:4

36 [a]2 Pet. 3:16 [b]Jer. 10:10; 2 Kin. 19:4

39 [a]Jer. 23:33; 7:14, 15; Ezek. 8:18

40 "And I will put an everlasting [a]reproach on you and an
everlasting humiliation which will not be forgotten."

Chapter 24

AFTER [a]Nebuchadnezzar king of Babylon had carried away
captive Jaconiah the son of Jehoiakim, king of Judah, and the
officials of Judah with the craftsmen and smiths from Jerusalem and had brought them to Babylon, the LORD showed me:
behold, two baskets of [b]figs set before the temple of the LORD!
2 One basket had very good figs, like [a]first-ripe figs; and
the other basket had [b]very bad figs, which could not be eaten
due to rottenness.
3 Then the LORD said to me, "[a]What do you see, Jeremiah?" And I said, "Figs, the good figs, very good; and the bad
figs, very bad, which cannot be eaten due to rottenness."
4 Then the word of the LORD came to me, saying,
5 "Thus says the LORD God of Israel, 'Like these good
figs, so I will regard [a]as good the captives of Judah, whom I
have sent out of this place *into* the land of the Chaldeans.
6 'For I will set My eyes on them for good, and I will
[a]bring them again to this land; and I will [b]build them up and
not overthrow them, and I will [c]plant them and not pluck
them up.
7 'And I will give them a [a]heart to know Me, for I am the
LORD; and they will be [b]My people, and I will be their God, for
they will [c]return to Me with their whole heart.
8 'But like the [a]bad figs which cannot be eaten due to
rottenness—for thus says the LORD,—so I will [1]abandon [b]Zede-
kiah king of Judah and his officials, and the [c]remnant of
Jerusalem who remain in this land, and the ones who dwell in
the land of [d]Egypt.
9 'And I will [a]make them a terror *and* evil for all the
kingdoms of the earth, as a [b]reproach and a proverb, a taunt
and a [c]curse in all places where I shall scatter them.
10 'And I will send the [a]sword, the famine, and the pestilence upon them until they are destroyed from the land which
I gave to them and their forefathers.' "

Chapter 25

THE word that came to Jeremiah concerning all the people
of Judah, in the [a]fourth year of [b]Jehoiakim the son of Josiah,
king of Judah (that was the [c]first year of Nebuchadnezzar king
of Babylon),
2 which Jeremiah the prophet spoke to all the [a]people of
Judah and to all the inhabitants of Jerusalem, saying,
3 "From the [a]thirteenth year of [b]Josiah the son of Amon,
king of Judah, even to this day, [1]these [c]twenty-three years the
word of the LORD has come to me, and I have spoken to you
[2d]again and again, but you have not listened.
4 "And the LORD has sent to you all his [a]servants the

40 [a]Jer. 20:11; 42:18; Ezek. 5:14, 15

1 [a]Jer. 27:20; 29:1, 2; 2 Kin. 24:10-16; 2 Chr. 36:10 [b]Amos 8:1

2 [a]Mic. 7:1; Nah. 3:12 [b]Jer. 29:17; Is. 5:4, 7

3 [a]Jer. 1:11, 13; Amos 8:2; Zech. 4:2

5 [a]Nah. 1:7; Zech. 13:9

6 [a]Jer. 29:10; 32:37; Ezek. 11:17 [b]Jer. 31:4; 33:7 [c]Jer. 32:41; 42:10

7 [a]Jer. 31:33; 32:40 [b]Zech. 8:8; Heb. 8:10 [c]Jer. 29:13; 1 Sam. 7:3

8 [1]Lit., *give up* [a]Jer. 29:17 [b]Jer. 39:5; Ezek. 12:13 [c]Jer. 39:9 [d]Jer. 44:26-30

9 [a]Jer. 15:4; 29:18; 34:17 [b]1 Kin. 9:7; Ps. 44:13, 14 [c]Is. 65:15

10 [a]Jer. 21:9; 27:8; Is. 51:19; Ezek. 5:12-17

1 [a]Jer. 36:1; 46:2 [b]2 Kin. 24:1, 2; 2 Chr. 36:4-6 [c]Jer. 32:1

2 [a]Jer. 18:11

3 [1]Lit., *this* [2]Lit., *rising early and speaking* [a]Jer. 1:2 [b]2 Chr. 34:1-3, 8 [c]Jer. 36:2 [d]Jer. 7:25; 11:7; 26:5

4 [a]Jer. 26:5

prophets [1]again and again, but you have not listened nor inclined your ear to hear,
5 saying, '[a]Turn now every one from his evil way and
from the evil of your deeds, and dwell on the land which the
LORD has given to you and your forefathers [b]forever and ever;
6 and do not [a]go after other gods to [1]serve them and to
[2]worship them, and do not provoke Me to anger with the work
of your hands, and I will do you no harm.'
7 "Yet you have not listened to Me," declares the LORD,
"in order that you might [a]provoke Me to anger with the work
of your hands to your own harm.
8 "Therefore thus says the LORD of hosts, 'Because you
have not obeyed My words,
9 behold, I will send and take all the families of the
north,' declares the LORD, 'and *I will send* to Nebuchadnezzar
king of Babylon, [a]My servant, and will bring them against this
land, and against its inhabitants, and against all these nations
round about; and I will [1]utterly destroy them, and make them
a horror, and a hissing, and an everlasting desolation.
10 'Moreover, I will [1]take from them the voice of joy and
the [a]voice of gladness, the voice of the bridegroom and the
voice of the bride, the [b]sound of the millstones and the light of
the lamp.
11 'And this whole land shall be a desolation and a horror,
and these nations shall serve the king of Babylon [a]seventy
years.
12 'Then it will be [a]when seventy years are completed I will
[b]punish the king of Babylon and that nation,' declares the
LORD, 'for their iniquity, and the land of the Chaldeans; and I
will make it an everlasting desolation.
13 'And I will bring upon that land all My words which I
have pronounced against it, all that is written in [a]this book,
which Jeremiah has prophesied against all the nations.
14 '([1]For [a]many nations and great kings shall make slaves
of them, even them; and I will [b]recompense them according to
their deeds, and according to the work of their hands.)' "
15 For thus the LORD, the God of Israel, says to me,
"Take this [a]cup of the wine of wrath from My hand, and cause
all the nations, to whom I send you, to drink it.
16 "And they shall drink and stagger and go mad because of
the sword that I will send among them."
17 Then I took the cup from the LORD's hand, and [a]made
all the nations drink, to whom the LORD sent me:
18 Jerusalem and the cities of Judah, and its kings *and* its
princes, to make them a ruin, a horror, a hissing, and a curse, as
it is this day;
19 [a]Pharaoh king of Egypt, his servants, his princes, and all
his people;
20 and all the [1a]foreign people, all the kings of the [b]land of
Uz, all the kings of the land of the Philistines (even Ashkelon,
Gaza, Ekron, and the remnant of [c]Ashdod);
21 [a]Edom, [b]Moab, and the sons of [c]Ammon;
22 and all the kings of [a]Tyre, all the kings of Sidon, and
the kings of [b]the coastlands which are beyond the sea;
23 and [a]Dedan, Tema, [b]Buz, and all who cut the [c]corners
of their hair;

4 [1]Lit., *rising early and sending*

5 [a]Jer. 4:1; 35:15; Is. 55:6, 7; Ezek. 18:30; Jon. 3:8-10 [b]Jer. 7:7; 17:25; Gen. 17:8

6 [1]Or, *worship* [2]Or, *bow down to* [a]Jer. 35:15; Deut. 6:14; 8:19; 2 Kin. 17:35

7 [a]Jer. 7:19; 32:30-33; 2 Kin. 17:17; 21:15

9 [1]Or, *put them under the ban* [a]Jer. 27:6; 43:10; Is. 13:3

10 [1]Lit., *cause to perish* [a]Jer. 16:9; Is. 24:8-11; Ezek. 26:13 [b]Eccles. 12:4; Is. 47:2

11 [a]Dan. 9:2; Zech. 7:5

12 [a]Jer. 29:10; Ezra 1:1 [b]Jer. chaps. 50, 51; Is. 13:14

13 [a]Jer. 36:4, 29, 32

14 [1]Or, *For they have served many nations and great kings* [a]Jer. 27:7; 50:9; 51:27, 28 [b]Jer. 51:6, 24, 56

15 [a]Jer. 51:7; Ps. 75:8; Is. 51:17, 22

17 [a]Jer. 25:28; 1:10; 27:3; Ezek. 43:3

19 [a]Jer. 46:2-28; Nah. 3:8-10

20 [1]Or, *mixed multitude* [a]Jer. 25:24; 50:37; Ezek. 30:5 [b]Job 1:1; Lam. 4:21 [c]Is. 20:1

21 [a]Jer. 49:7-22; Ps. 137:7 [b]Jer. 48:1-47; Amos 2:1-3 [c]Jer. 49:1-6; Amos 1:13-15

22 [a]Jer. 47:4; Zech. 9:2-4 [b]Jer. 31:10

23 [a]Jer. 49:7, 8; Is. 21:13 [b]Gen. 22:21 [c]Jer. 9:26; 49:32

24 and all the kings of [a]Arabia and all the kings of the
[1]foreign people who dwell in the desert;
25 and all the kings of Zimri, all the kings of [a]Elam, and
all the kings of Media;
26 and all the kings of the north, near and far, one with
another; and [a]all the kingdoms of the earth which are upon the
face of the ground, and the king of [1]Sheshach shall drink after
them.
27 "And you shall say to them, 'Thus says the LORD of
hosts, the God of Israel, "Drink, be drunk, vomit, fall, and rise
no more because of the [a]sword which I will send among you." '
28 "And it will be, if they [a]refuse to take the cup from your
hand to drink, then you will say to them, 'Thus says the LORD
of hosts: "You shall surely drink!
29 "For behold, I am [a]beginning to work calamity in *this*
city which is [b]called by My name, and shall you be completely
free from punishment? You will not be free from punishment;
for I am summoning a sword against all the inhabitants of the
earth," declares the LORD of hosts.'
30 "Therefore you shall prophesy against them all these
words, and you shall say to them,

'The [a]LORD will [b]roar from on high,
And utter His voice from His holy habitation;
He will roar mightily against his [1]fold.
He will shout like those who tread *the grapes*,
Against all the inhabitants of the earth.
31 'A clamor has come to the end of the earth,
Because the LORD has a controversy with the nations.
He is entering into [a]judgment with all flesh;
As for the wicked, He has given them to the sword,' "
declares the LORD.

32 Thus says the LORD of hosts,
"Behold, evil is going forth
From [a]nation to nation,
And a great [b]storm is being stirred up
From the remotest parts of the earth.
33 "And those [a]slain by the LORD on that day shall be from
one end of the earth to the [1]other. They shall [b]not be la-
mented, gathered, or buried; they shall be like [c]dung on the
face of the ground.
34 "Wail, you shepherds, and cry;
And [a]wallow *in ashes*, you masters of the flock;
For the days of your [b]slaughter and your dispersions
[1]have come,
And you shall fall like a choice vessel.
35 "Flight shall [a]perish from the shepherds,
And escape from the masters of the flock.
36 "The sound of the cry of the shepherds,
And the wailing of the masters of the flock!
For the LORD is destroying their pasture.
37 "And the peaceful [1a]folds are made silent
Because of the fierce anger of the LORD.
38 "He has [a]left His hiding place like the lion;
For their land has become a horror

24 [1]Or, *mixed multitude* [a]2 Chr. 9:14

25 [a]Jer. 49:34; Gen. 10:22; Is. 11:11

26 [1]*Possibly a cipher for Babylon* [a]Jer. 25:9; 50:9

27 [a]Ezek. 21:4, 5

28 [a]Job 34:33

29 [a]Jer. 13:13; Prov. 11:31; Is. 10:12; Ezek. 9:6; 1 Pet. 4:17 [b]1 Kin. 8:43

30 [1]Or, *pasture* [a]Jer. 25:38; Is. 42:13 [b]Joel 2:11; Amos 1:2

31 [a]Is. 66:16; Ezek. 20:35, 36

32 [a]2 Chr. 15:6; Is. 34:2 [b]Jer. 23:19; Is. 30:30

33 [1]Lit., *other end of the earth* [a]Is. 34:2, 3; 66:16 [b]Jer. 16:4; Ps. 79:3; Ezek. 39:4, 17 [c]Is. 5:25

34 [1]Lit., *are full* [a]Jer. 6:26; Ezek. 27:30 [b]Jer. 50:27; Is. 34:7

35 [a]Jer. 11:11; Job 11:20; Amos 2:14

37 [1]Or, *pastures* [a]Jer. 5:17; 13:20; Is. 27:10, 11

38 [a]Jer. 4:7; 5:6; Hos. 5:14; 13:7, 8

Because of the fierceness of the [1]oppressing *sword*,
And because of His fierce anger."

38 [1]Or., *oppressor*

CHAPTER 26

IN the beginning of the reign of [a]Jehoiakim the son of Josiah,
king of Judah, this word came from the LORD, saying,
2 "Thus says the LORD, 'Stand in the [a]court of the LORD's
house, and speak to all the cities of Judah, who have come to
worship *in* the LORD's house, [b]all the words that I have commanded you to speak to them. [c]Do not omit a word!
3 '[a]Perhaps they will listen and everyone will turn from his
evil way, that I may repent of the calamity which I am planning to do to them because of the evil of their deeds.'
4 "And you will say to them, 'Thus says the LORD, "[a]If you
will not listen to Me, to [b]walk in My law, which I have set
before you,
5 to listen to the words of [a]My servants the prophets
whom I have been sending to you [1]again and again, but you
have not listened;
6 then I will make this house like [a]Shiloh, and this city I
will make a [b]curse to all the nations of the earth." ' "
7 And the [a]priests and the prophets and all the people
heard Jeremiah speaking these words in the house of the LORD.
8 And when Jeremiah finished speaking all that the LORD
had commanded *him* to speak to all the people, the priests and
the prophets and all the people seized him, saying, "[a]You must
die!"
9 "Why have you prophesied in the name of the LORD
saying, 'This house will be like Shiloh, and this city will be
desolate, without inhabitant'?" And [a]all the people gathered
about Jeremiah in the house of the LORD.
10 And when the princes of Judah heard these things, they
[a]came up from the king's house *to* the house of the LORD and
sat in the [b]entrance of the New Gate of the LORD's *house*.
11 Then the priests and the prophets [a]spoke to the officials and to all the people, saying, "A [b]death sentence for this
man! For he has prophesied [c]against this city as you have heard
in your hearing."
12 Then Jeremiah spoke to all the officials and to all the
people, saying, "The LORD sent me to prophesy against this
house and against this city all the words that you have heard.
13 "Now therefore [a]amend your ways and your deeds, and
obey the voice of the LORD your God; and the LORD will
[1]change His mind about the misfortune which He has pronounced against you.
14 "But as for me, behold, I am in your hands; do with me
as is good and right in your sight.
15 "Only know for certain that if you put me to death, you
will bring [a]innocent blood on yourselves, and on this city, and
on its inhabitants; for truly the LORD has sent me to you to
speak all these words in your hearing."
16 Then the officials and all the people [a]said to the priests
and to the prophets, "No [b]death sentence for this man! For he
has spoken to us in the name of the LORD our God."

1 [a]2 Kin. 23:36; 2 Chr. 36:4, 5

2 [a]Jer. 7:2; 19:14; 2 Chr. 24:20, 21; Luke 19:47, 48 [b]Jer. 1:17; 42:4; Acts 20:20, 27 [c]Deut. 4:2

3 [a]Jer. 36:3-7; Is. 1:16-19

4 [a]Jer. 17:27; 22:5; Lev. 26:14; 1 Kin. 9:6; Is. 1:20 [b]Jer. 32:23; 44:10, 23

5 [1]Lit., *rising early and sending* [a]Jer. 25:4; 2 Kin. 9:7; Ezra 9:11

6 [a]Jer. 7:12, 14; 1 Sam. 4:10-12, 22; Ps. 78:60, 61 [b]Jer. 24:9; 25:18; 2 Kin. 22:19

7 [a]Jer. 5:31; Mic. 3:11

8 [a]Jer. 11:19; 18:23; Lam. 4:13, 14; Matt. 21:35, 36; 23:34, 35

9 [a]Acts 3:11; 5:12

10 [a]Acts 21:31, 32 [b]Jer. 36:10

11 [a]Jer. 18:23 [b]Deut. 18:20; Matt. 26:66 [c]Jer. 38:4; Acts 6:11-14

13 [1]Lit., *be sorry for* [a]Jer. 7:3, 5; 18:11; 35:15

15 [a]Jer. 7:6; Num. 35:33; Prov. 6:16, 17

16 [a]Jer. 26:11; 36:19, 25; 38:7, 13 [b]Acts 5:34-39; 23:9, 29; 25:25; 26:31

17 Then some of the elders of the land rose up and spoke
to all the assembly of the people, saying,
18 "[1][a]Micah of Moresheth prophesied in the days of Hezekiah king of Judah; and he spoke to all the people of Judah,
saying, 'Thus the LORD of hosts has said:

> [b]Zion will be plowed *as* a field,
> And Jerusalem will become ruins,
> And the [c]mountain of the house as the [2]high places of a forest.'

19 "Did Hezekiah king of Judah and all Judah put him to
death? Did he not [a]fear the LORD and entreat the favor of the
LORD, and the LORD [1]changed His mind about the misfortune
which He had pronounced against them? But we are [b]commit-
ting a great evil against ourselves."
20 Indeed there was also a man who prophesied in the
name of the LORD, Uriah the son of Shemaiah from Kiriath-
jearim; and he prophesied against this city and against this land
words similar to all those of Jeremiah.
21 When King Jehoiakim and all his mighty men and all
the officials heard his words, then the [a]king sought to put him
to death; but Uriah heard *it*, and he was afraid and [b]fled, and
went to Egypt.
22 Then King Jehoiakim sent men to Egypt: [a]Elnathan
the son of Achbor and *certain* men with him into Egypt.
23 And they brought Uriah from Egypt and led him to
King Jehoiakim, who [a]slew him with a sword, and cast his dead
body into the [1]burial place of the [2]common people.
24 But the hand of [a]Ahikam the son of Shaphan was with
Jeremiah, so that he was [b]not given into the hands of the
people to put him to death.

CHAPTER 27

IN the beginning of the reign of [1]Zedekiah the son of Josiah,
king of Judah, this word came to Jeremiah from the LORD,
saying—
2 thus says the LORD to me—"Make for yourself [a]bonds
and [b]yokes and put them on your neck,
3 and send [1]word to the king of [a]Edom, to the king of
[a]Moab, to the king of the sons of [a]Ammon, to the king of
[a]Tyre, and to the king of [a]Sidon [2]by the messengers who come
to Jerusalem to Zedekiah king of Judah.
4 "And command them *to go* to their masters, saying,
'Thus says the LORD of hosts, the God of Israel, thus you shall
say to your masters:
5 "[a]I have made the earth, the men and the beasts which
are on the face of the earth [b]by My great power and by My
outstretched arm, and I will [c]give it to the one who is [1]pleasing
in My sight.
6 "And now I [a]have given all these lands into the hand of
Nebuchadnezzar king of Babylon, [b]My servant, and I have
given him also the [c]wild animals of the field to serve him.
7 "And [a]all the nations shall serve him, and his son, and his

18 [1]Lit., *Micaiah the Morashtite* [2]Or, *a wooded height*
[a]Mic. 1:1 [b]Jer. 9:11; Neh. 4:2; Ps. 79:1; Mic. 3:12 [c]Jer. 17:3; Is. 2:2, 3; Mic. 4:1; Zech. 8:3

19 [1]Lit., *was sorry for*
[a]2 Chr. 29:6-11; 32:26; Is. 37:1, 4, 15-20 [b]Jer. 44:7; Hab. 2:10

21 [a]Jer. 36:26; 2 Chr. 16:10; Matt. 14:5 [b]1 Kin. 19:2-4; Matt. 10:23, 28

22 [a]Jer. 36:12

23 [1]Lit., *graves* [2]Lit., *sons of the people*
[a]Jer. 2:30

24 [a]Jer. 39:14; 40:5-7; 2 Kin. 22:12-14 [b]Jer. 1:18, 19; 1 Kin. 18:4

1 [1]Many mss. read, *Jehoiakim*

2 [a]Jer. 30:8 [b]Jer. 28:10, 13

3 [1]Lit., *them* [2]Lit., *by the hand of*
[a]Jer. 25:21, 22

5 [1]Or, *upright*
[a]Jer. 10:12; 51:15; Ps. 146:5, 6 [b]Jer. 32:17; Deut. 9:29 [c]Ps. 115:15, 16; Acts 17:26

6 [a]Jer. 21:7; 22:25; Ezek. 29:18-20 [b]Jer. 25:9; 43:10; Is. 44:28 [c]Jer. 28:14

7 [a]Jer. 44:30; 46:13

grandson, [b]until the time of his own land comes; then [c]many
nations and great kings will [1]make him their servant.
8 "And it will be, *that* the nation or the kingdom which
[a]will not serve him, Nebuchadnezzar king of Babylon, and
which will not put its neck under the yoke of the king of
Babylon, I will punish that nation with the [b]sword, with famine, and with pestilence," declares the LORD, "until I have
destroyed [1]it by his hand.
9 "But as for you, do not [a]listen to your prophets, your
diviners, your [1]dreamers, your soothsayers, or to your sorcerers,
who speak to you, saying, 'You shall not serve the king of
Babylon.'
10 "For they prophesy a [a]lie to you, in order to [b]remove
you far from your land; and I will drive you out, and you will
perish.
11 "But the nation which will bring its neck under the yoke
of the king of Babylon and serve him, I will [a]let remain on its
land," declares the LORD, "and they will till it and dwell in
it." ' "
12 And I spoke words like all these to [a]Zedekiah king of
Judah, saying, "Bring your necks under the yoke of the king of
Babylon, and serve him and his people, and live!
13 "Why will you [a]die, you and your people, by the sword,
famine, and pestilence, as the LORD has spoken to that nation
which will not serve the king of Babylon?
14 "So do not [a]listen to the words of the prophets who
speak to you, saying, 'You shall not serve the king of Babylon,'
for they prophesy a [b]lie to you;
15 for [a]I have not sent them," declares the LORD, "but
they prophesy [b]falsely in My name, in order that I may [c]drive
you out, and that you may perish, you and the prophets who
prophesy to you."
16 *Then* I spoke to the priests and to all this people,
saying, "Thus says the LORD: Do not listen to the words of
your prophets who prophesy to you, saying, 'Behold, the [a]ves-
sels of the LORD's house will now shortly be brought again
from Babylon'; for they are prophesying a lie to you.
17 "Do not listen to them; serve the king of Babylon, and
live! Why should this city become a ruin?
18 "But [a]if they are prophets, and if the word of the LORD is
with them, let them now [b]entreat the LORD of hosts, that the
vessels which are left in the house of the LORD, in the house of
the king of Judah, and in Jerusalem, may not go to Babylon.
19 "For thus says the LORD of hosts concerning the [a]pillars,
concerning the sea, concerning the stands, and concerning the
rest of the vessels that are left in this city,
20 which Nebuchadnezzar king of Babylon did not take
when he [a]carried into exile Jeconiah the son of Jehoiakim, king
of Judah, from Jerusalem to Babylon, and all the nobles of
Judah and Jerusalem.
21 "Yes, thus says the LORD of hosts, the God of Israel,
concerning the vessels that are left in the house of the LORD,
and in the house of the king of Judah, and in Jerusalem,
22 'They shall be [a]carried to Babylon, and they shall be
there until the [b]day I visit them,' declares the LORD. 'Then I
will [c]bring them [1]back and restore them to this place.' "

7 [1]Or, *enslave him* [b]Zech. 2:8, 9 [c]Jer. 25:12; Is. 14:4-6

8 [1]Lit., *them* [a]Jer. 38:17-19; 42:15, 16; Ezek. 17:19-21 [b]Jer. 27:13; 24:10; 29:17, 18; Ezek. 14:21

9 [1]Lit., *dreams* [a]Ex. 22:18; Deut. 18:10; Is. 8:19; Mal. 3:5

10 [a]Jer. 23:25 [b]Jer. 8:19; 32:31

11 [a]Jer. 21:9; 38:2; 40:9-12; 42:10, 11

12 [a]Jer. 27:3; 28:1

13 [a]Jer. 27:8; 38:23; Prov. 8:36; Ezek. 18:31

14 [a]Jer. 27:9; 2 Chr. 11:13-15 [b]Jer. 27:10; Ezek. 13:22

15 [a]Jer. 23:21; 29:9 [b]Jer. 23:25 [c]Jer. 27:10; 2 Chr. 25:16

16 [a]Jer. 28:3; 2 Kin. 24:13; 2 Chr. 36:7, 10

18 [a]1 Kin. 18:24 [b]Jer. 18:20; 1 Sam. 7:8; 12:19, 23

19 [a]Jer. 52:17-23; 1 Kin. 7:15; 2 Kin. 25:13, 17

20 [a]Jer. 22:28; 24:1; 2 Kin. 24:12, 14-16; 2 Chr. 36:10, 18

22 [1]Lit., *up* [a]Jer. 29:10; 34:2, 3 [b]Jer. 27:7; 25:11, 12; 29:10; 32:5 [c]Ezra 1:7-11; 5:13-15; 7:9, 19

CHAPTER 28

1 [a]Jer. 49:34 [b]Jer. 27:3, 12 [c]Jer. 28:17 [d]Josh. 9:3; 10:12; 1 Kin. 3:4

NOW it came about in the same year, [a]in the beginning of
the reign of [b]Zedekiah king of Judah, in the fourth year, in the
fifth month, that [c]Hananiah the son of Azzur, the prophet,
who was from [d]Gibeon, spoke to me in the house of the LORD
in the presence of the priests and all the people, saying,

2 [a]Jer. 28:11

2 "[a]Thus says the LORD of hosts, the God of Israel, 'I have
broken the yoke of the king of Babylon.

3 [a]Jer. 27:16; 2 Kin. 24:13; 2Chr. 36:10; Dan. 1:2

3 'Within two years I am going to bring back to this place
[a]all the vessels of the LORD's house, which Nebuchadnezzar
king of Babylon took away from this place and carried to
Babylon.

4 [a]Jer. 22:26, 27 [b]Jer. 22:24; 24:1; 2 Kin. 25:27 [c]Jer. 22:10 [d]Jer. 27:8

4 'I am [a]also going to bring back to this place [b]Jeconiah
the son of Jehoiakim, king of Judah, and all the [c]exiles of
Judah who went to Babylon,' declares the LORD, 'for I will
break the [d]yoke of the king of Babylon.' "

5 [a]Jer. 28:1

5 Then the prophet Jeremiah spoke to the prophet Hananiah in the presence of the priests and in the presence of all
the people who were standing in the [a]house of the LORD,

6 [1]Or, *fulfill* [a]Jer. 11:5; 1 Kin. 1:36; Ps. 41:13 [b]Jer. 17:16

6 and the prophet Jeremiah said, "[a]Amen! May the LORD
do so; may the LORD [1b]confirm your words which you have
prophesied to bring back the vessels of the LORD's house and
all the exiles, from Babylon to this place.

7 [a]1 Kin. 22:28

7 "Yet [a]hear now this word which I am about to speak in
your hearing and in the hearing of all the people!

8 [a]Lev. 26:14; 1 Kin. 14:15; 17:1; 22:17; Is. 5:5-7; Joel 1:20; Amos 1:2; Nah. 1:2

8 "The prophets who were before me and before you
from ancient times [a]prophesied against many lands and against
great kingdoms, of war and of calamity and of pestilence.

9 [a]Deut. 18:22

9 "The prophet who prophesies of peace, [a]when the word
of the prophet shall come to pass, then that prophet will be
known *as* one whom the LORD has truly sent."

10 [a]Jer. 27:2 [b]Jer. 36:23; 1 Kin. 22:11, 24

10 Then Hananiah the prophet took the [a]yoke from the
neck of Jeremiah the prophet and [b]broke it.

11 [a]Jer. 28:15; 14:14; 27:10

11 And Hananiah spoke in the presence of all the people,
saying, "[a]Thus says the LORD, 'Even so will I break within two
full years, the yoke of Nebuchadnezzar king of Babylon from
the neck of all the nations.' " Then the prophet Jeremiah went
his way.

12 [a]Jer. 1:2

12 And the [a]word of the LORD came to Jeremiah, after
Hananiah the prophet had broken the yoke from off the neck
of the prophet Jeremiah, saying,

13 [a]Ps. 107:16; Is. 45:2

13 "Go and speak to Hananiah, saying, 'Thus says the
LORD, "You have broken the yokes of wood, but you have
made instead of them [a]yokes of iron."

14 [a]Jer. 27:8; Deut. 28:48 [b]Jer. 25:11 [c]Jer. 27:6

14 'For thus says the LORD of hosts, the God of Israel, "I
have put a [a]yoke of iron on the neck of all these nations, that
they may serve Nebuchadnezzar king of Babylon; and they
shall [b]serve him. And [c]I have also given him the beasts of the
field." ' "

15 [a]Jer. 29:31; Ezek. 13:2, 3, 22; 22:28; Lam. 2:14; Zech. 13:3

15 Then Jeremiah the prophet said to Hananiah the prophet, "Listen now, Hananiah, the LORD has not sent you, and
[a]you have made this people trust in a lie.

16 [1]Lit., *send you away* [a]Gen. 7:4; Ex. 32:12; Deut. 6:15; 1 Kin. 13:34

16 "Therefore thus says the LORD, '[a]Behold, I am about to
[1]remove you from the face of the earth. This year you are

going to [b]die, because you have [2c]counseled rebellion against
the LORD.' "
17 So Hananiah the prophet died in the same year in the
seventh month.

CHAPTER 29

NOW these are the words of the [a]letter which Jeremiah the
prophet sent from Jerusalem to the rest of the elders of the
exile, the priests, the prophets, and all the people whom Nebuchadnezzar had taken into exile from Jerusalem to Babylon.
2 (This was after King [a]Jeconiah and the [b]queen mother,
the court officials, the princes of Judah and Jerusalem, the
craftsmen and the smiths had departed from Jerusalem.)
3 *The letter was sent* by the hand of Elasah the son of
Shaphan, and Gemariah the son of [a]Hilkiah, whom Zedekiah
king of Judah sent to Babylon to Nebuchadnezzar king of
Babylon, saying,
4 "Thus says the LORD of hosts, the God of Israel, to all
the exiles whom I have [a]sent into exile from Jerusalem to
Babylon,
5 '[a]Build houses and live *in them;* and plant gardens, and
eat their [1]produce.
6 'Take [a]wives and [1]become the fathers of sons and daughters, and take wives for your sons and give your daughters to
husbands, that they may bear sons and daughters; and multiply
there and do not decrease.
7 'And [a]seek the [1]welfare of the city where I have sent you
into exile, and [b]pray to the LORD on its behalf; for in its [1]wel-
fare you will have [1]welfare.'
8 "For thus says the LORD of hosts, the God of Israel, 'Do
not let your [a]prophets who are in your midst and your diviners
[b]deceive you, and do not listen to [1c]the dreams which [2]they
dream.
9 'For they [a]prophesy falsely to you in My name; [b]I have
not sent them,' declares the LORD.
10 "For thus says the LORD, 'When [a]seventy years have
been completed for Babylon, I will visit you and fulfill My
[b]good word to you, to bring you back to this place.
11 'For I know the [a]plans that I [1]have for you,' declares the
LORD, 'plans for [b]welfare and not for calamity to give you a
future and a [c]hope.
12 'Then you will [a]call upon Me and come and pray to Me,
and I will [b]listen to you.
13 'And you will [a]seek Me and find *Me,* when you [b]search
for Me with all your heart.
14 'And I will be [a]found by you,' declares the LORD, 'and I
will [b]restore your [1]fortunes and will [c]gather you from all the
nations and from all the places where I have driven you,' declares
the LORD, 'and I will [d]bring you back to the place from
where I sent you into exile.'
15 "Because you have said, 'The LORD has raised up prophets for us in [a]Babylon'—
16 for thus says the LORD concerning the king who sits on
the throne of David, and concerning all the people who dwell
in this city, your brothers who did [a]not go with you into exile—
17 thus says the LORD of hosts, 'Behold, I am sending

16 [2]Lit., *spoken* [b]Jer. 20:6 [c]Jer. 29:32; Deut. 13:5

1 [a]Jer. 29:25, 29; 2 Chr. 30:1, 6; Esth. 9:20

2 [a]Jer. 22:24-28; 24:1; 27:20; 2 Kin. 24:12-16; 2 Chr. 36:9, 10 [b]Jer. 13:18

3 [a]1 Chr. 6:13

4 [a]Jer. 24:5; Is. 10:5, 6

5 [1]Lit., *fruit* [a]Jer. 29:10, 28

6 [1]Lit., *beget* [a]Jer. 16:2-4

7 [1]Or, *peace* [a]Dan. 4:27; 6:4, 5 [b]Ezra 6:10; 7:23; Dan. 4:19; 1 Tim. 2:1, 2

8 [1]Lit., *your* [2]Lit., *you* [a]Jer. 29:1; 27:9 [b]Jer. 14:14; 23:21; 28:15 [c]Jer. 23:25, 27

9 [a]Jer. 29:21; 27:15 [b]Jer. 29:31

10 [a]Jer. 25:12; 2 Chr. 36:21-23; Dan. 9:2; Zech. 7:5 [b]Jer. 24:6, 7; Zeph. 2:7

11 [1]Lit., *am planning* [a]Jer. 23:5, 6; 30:9, 10; Ps. 40:5 [b]Jer. 30:18-22; Is. 40:9-11 [c]Jer. 31:17; Hos. 2:15

12 [a]Jer. 33:3; Ps. 50:15 [b]Ps. 145:19

13 [a]Deut. 4:29 [b]Jer. 24:7; 1 Chr. 22:19; 2 Chr. 22:9

14 [1]Or, *captivity* [a]Deut. 30:1-10 [b]Jer. 30:3; 32:37-41 [c]Jer. 28:8; Is. 43:5, 6 [d]Jer. 3:14; 12:15; 16:15

15 [a]Jer. 29:21, 24

16 [a]Jer. 38:2, 3, 17-23

upon them the [a]sword, famine, and pestilence, and I will make
them like [b]split-open figs that cannot be eaten due to
rottenness.
18 'And I will pursue them with the sword, with famine
and with pestilence; and I will [a]make them a terror to all the
kingdoms of the earth, to be a [b]curse, and a horror, and a
[c]hissing, and a reproach among all the nations where I have
driven them,
19 because they have [a]not listened to My words,' declares
the LORD, 'which I sent to them again and again by [b]My servants the prophets; but you did not listen,' declares the LORD.
20 "You, therefore, hear the word of the LORD, all you
exiles, whom I have [a]sent away from Jerusalem to Babylon.
21 "Thus says the LORD of hosts, the God of Israel, concerning Ahab the son of Kolaiah and concerning Zedekiah the
son of Maaseiah, who are [a]prophesying to you falsely in My
name: 'Behold, I will deliver them into the hand of Nebuchadnezzar king of Babylon, and he shall slay them before your
eyes.
22 'And because of them a [a]curse shall be [1]used by all the
exiles from Judah who are in Babylon, saying, "May the LORD
make you like Zedekiah and like Ahab, whom the king of
Babylon [b]roasted in the fire,
23 because they have [a]acted foolishly in Israel, and [b]have
committed adultery with their neighbors' wives, and have spoken words in My name [c]falsely, which I did not command
them; and I am He who [d]knows, and am a witness," declares
the LORD.' "
24 And to [a]Shemaiah the Nehelamite you shall speak,
saying,
25 "Thus says the LORD of hosts, the God of Israel, 'Because you have sent [a]letters in your own name to all the people
who are in Jerusalem, and to [b]Zephaniah the son of Maaseiah,
the priest, and to all the priests, saying,
26 "The LORD has made you priest instead of Jehoiada the
priest, to be the [1a]overseer in the house of the LORD over every
[b]mad man who [c]prophesies to [d]put him in the stocks and in the
iron collar.
27 "Now then, why have you not rebuked Jeremiah of [a]Ana-
thoth who prophesies to you?
28 "For he has [a]sent to us in Babylon, saying, '*The exile* will
be [b]long; [c]build houses and live *in them* and plant gardens and
eat their [1]produce.' " ' "
29 And [a]Zephaniah the priest read this letter [1]to Jeremiah
the prophet.
30 Then came the word of the LORD to Jeremiah, saying,
31 "Send to [a]all the exiles, saying, 'Thus says the LORD
concerning [b]Shemaiah the Nehelamite: Because Shemaiah has
[c]prophesied to you, although I did not send him, and he has
[d]made you trust in a lie;'
32 therefore thus says the LORD, 'Behold, I am about to
[a]punish Shemaiah the Nehelamite and his [1]descendants; he
shall [b]not have anyone living among this people, [c]and he shall
not see the good that I am about to do to My people,' declares
the LORD, 'because he has [2d]preached rebellion against the
LORD.' "

17 [a]Jer. 29:18; 27:8; 32:24 [b]Jer. 24:3, 8-10

18 [a]Jer. 24:9; 34:17; Ezek. 12:15 [b]Jer. 42:18; Is. 65:15 [c]Jer. 25:9; Lam. 2:15, 16

19 [a]Jer. 6:19 [b]Jer. 26:5; 35:15

20 [a]Jer. 24:5; Ezek. 11:9

21 [a]Jer. 29:8, 9; 14:14, 15; Lam. 2:14

22 [1]Lit., *taken* [a]Is. 65:15 [b]Dan. 3:6, 21

23 [a]Gen. 34:7; 2 Sam. 13:12 [b]Jer. 5:8; 23:14 [c]Jer. 29:8, 9, 21 [d]Jer. 7:11; 16:17; Prov. 5:21; Mal. 3:5

24 [a]Jer. 29:31, 32

25 [a]Jer. 29:1 [b]Jer. 29:29; 21:1; 37:3; 52:24; 2 Kin. 25:18

26 [1]Lit., *overseers* [a]Jer. 20:1 [b]2 Kin. 9:11; Hos. 9:7; Mark 3:21; John 10:20; Acts 26:24, 25; 2 Cor. 5:13 [c]Deut. 13:1-5; Zech. 13:1-5 [d]Jer. 20:1, 2; Acts 16:24

27 [a]Jer. 1:1

28 [1]Lit., *fruit* [a]Jer. 29:1 [b]Jer. 29:10 [c]Jer. 29:5

29 [1]Lit., *in the ears of* [a]Jer. 29:25

31 [a]Jer. 29:20 [b]Jer. 29:24 [c]Jer. 29:9, 23; 14:14, 15; Ezek. 13:8-16, 22, 23 [d]Jer. 28:15

32 [1]Lit., *seed* [2]Lit., *spoken* [a]Jer. 36:31 [b]Jer. 22:30; 1 Sam. 2:30-34 [c]Jer. 29:10; 17:6; 2 Kin. 7:2, 19, 20 [d]Jer. 28:16; Deut. 13:5

Chapter 30

THE word which came to Jeremiah from the LORD, saying,
2 "Thus says the LORD, the God of Israel, '[a]Write all the
words which I have spoken to you in a book.
3 'For, behold, [a]days are coming,' declares the LORD,
'when I will [b]restore the [1]fortunes of My people [c]Israel and
Judah.' The LORD says, 'I will also [d]bring them back to the land
that I gave to their forefathers, and they shall possess it.' "
4 Now these are the words which the LORD spoke concerning Israel and concerning Judah,
5 "For thus says the LORD,
'[1]I have heard a sound of [a]terror,
Of dread, and there is no peace.
6 'Ask now, and see,
If a male can give birth.
Why do I see every man
With his [a]hands on his loins, as a [b]woman in childbirth?
And *why* have all faces turned pale?
7 'Alas! for that [a]day is great,
There is [b]none like it;
And it is the time of Jacob's [c]distress,
But he will be [d]saved from it.
8 'And it shall come about on that day,' declares the LORD
of hosts, 'that I will [a]break his yoke from off [1]their neck, and
will tear off [1]their bonds; and strangers shall no longer [b]make
[2]them their slaves.
9 'But they shall serve the LORD their God, and [a]David
their king, whom I will raise up for them.
10 '[a]And fear not, O Jacob My servant,' declares the LORD,
'And do not be dismayed, O Israel;
For behold, I will save you from [b]afar,
And your [1]offspring from the land of their captivity.
And Jacob shall return, and shall be [c]quiet and at ease,
And [d]no one shall make him afraid.
11 'For [a]I am with you,' declares the LORD, 'to save you;
For I will [b]destroy completely all the nations where I
have scattered you,
Only I will [c]not destroy you completely.
But I will [d]chasten you justly,
And will by no means leave you unpunished.'

12 "For thus says the LORD,
'Your wound is incurable,
And your [a]injury is serious.
13 'There is no one to plead your cause;
No healing for *your* sore,
[a]No recovery for you.
14 'All your [a]lovers have forgotten you,
They do not seek you;
For I have [b]wounded you with the wound of an enemy,
With the punishment of a cruel one,
Because your iniquity is great
And your sins are numerous.
15 'Why do you cry out over your injury?
Your pain is incurable.

2 [a]Jer. 25:13; 36:4, 28, 32; Hab. 2:2

3 [1]Or, *captivity* [a]Jer. 29:10 [b]Jer. 30:18; 29:14; Ps. 53:6; Zeph. 3:20 [c]Jer. 3:18 [d]Jer. 16:15; 23:7, 8; Ezek. 20:42; 36:24

5 [1]Lit., *We* [a]Jer. 6:25; 8:16; Is. 5:30; Amos 5:16-18

6 [a]Jer. 6:24; 22:23 [b]Jer. 4:31

7 [a]Is. 2:12; Hos. 1:11; Joel 2:11 [b]Lam. 1:12; Dan. 9:12 [c]Jer. 2:27, 28; 14:8 [d]Jer. 30:10; 50:19

8 [1]So Gk.; Heb., *your* [2]Lit., *him* [a]Jer. 2:20; Is. 9:4; Ezek. 34:27 [b]Ezek. 34:27

9 [a]Is. 55:3-5; Ezek. 34:23, 24; 37:24, 25; Hos. 3:5; Luke 1:69; Acts 2:30; 13:23, 34, 38

10 [1]Lit., *seed* [a]Jer. 46:27, 28; Is. 43:5; 44:2 [b]Jer. 23:3, 8; 29:14; Is. 60:4 [c]Jer. 33:16; Is. 35:9; Hos 2:18 [d]Mic. 4:4

11 [a]Jer. 1:8, 19 [b]Jer. 46:28 [c]Jer. 4:27; 5:10, 18 [d]Jer. 10:24

12 [a]Jer. 30:15; 15:18

13 [a]Jer. 14:19; 46:11

14 [a]Jer. 22:20, 22 [b]Lam. 2:4, 5

Because your iniquity is great
And your sins are numerous,
I have done these things to you.
16 'Therefore all who [a]devour you shall be devoured;
And all your adversaries, every one of them, [b]shall go into captivity;
And those who plunder you shall be for plunder,
And all who prey upon you I will give for prey.
17 'For I will [1]restore you to [2a]health
And I will heal you of your wounds,' declares the LORD,
'Because they have called you an [b]outcast, saying:
"It is Zion; no one [3]cares for her." '

18 "Thus says the LORD,
'Behold, I will restore the [1]fortunes of the tents of Jacob
And have compassion on his dwelling places;
And the [a]city shall be rebuilt on its ruin,
And the [b]palace shall stand on its rightful place.
19 'And from them shall proceed [a]thanksgiving
And the voice of those who [1b]make merry;
And I will multiply them, and they shall not be diminished;
I will also [c]honor them, and they shall not be insignificant.
20 '[1]Their children also shall be as formerly,
And [1]their congregation shall be [a]established before Me;
And I will punish all [1]their oppressors.
21 'And [1]their leader shall be one of them,
And [1]their ruler shall come forth from [1]their midst;
And I will [a]bring him near, and he shall approach Me;
For [2]who would dare to risk his life to [b]approach Me?' declares the LORD.
22 'And you shall be [a]My people,
And I will be your God.' "

23 Behold, the [a]tempest of the LORD!
Wrath has gone forth,
A [1]sweeping tempest;
It will burst on the head of the wicked.
24 The fierce anger of the LORD will not turn back,
Until He has performed, and until He has accomplished
The intent of His heart;
In the [a]latter days you will understand this.

CHAPTER 31

"AT that time," declares the LORD, "I will be the [a]God of all the [b]families of Israel, and they shall be My people."
2 Thus says the LORD,
"The people who survived the sword
[a]Found grace in the wilderness—
Israel, when it went to [b]find its rest."
3 The LORD appeared to [1]him from afar, *saying*,
"I have [a]loved you with an everlasting love;
Therefore I have drawn you with [b]lovingkindness.

16 [a]Jer. 2:3; 8:16; 10:25 [b]Is. 14:2; Joel 3:8

17 [1]Lit., *cause to go up* [2]Or, *healing* [3]Lit., *is seeking* [a]Jer. 8:22; 33:6; Ps. 107:20 [b]Jer. 33:24; Is. 11:12; 56:8

18 [1]Or, *captivity* [a]Jer. 31:4, 38-40 [b]1 Chr. 29:1, 19; Ps. 48:3, 13; 122:7

19 [1]Or, *dance* [a]Jer. 17:26; 33:11; Is. 12:1; 51:3 [b]Jer. 31:4; Ps. 126:1, 2; Is. 51:11; Zeph. 3:14 [c]Is. 55:5; 60:9

20 [1]Lit., *His* [a]Is. 54:14

21 [1]Lit., *his* [2]Lit., *who is he that gives his heart in pledge* [a]Num. 16:5; Ps. 65:4 [b]Jer. 50:44; Ex. 3:5

22 [a]Jer. 32:38; Ex. 6:7; Hos. 2:23; Zech. 13:9

23 [1]Or, *raging* [a]Jer. 23:19, 20

24 [a]Jer. 23:20

1 [a]Jer. 30:22 [b]Gen. 17:7, 8; Is. 41:10; Rom. 11:26-28

2 [a]Num. 14:20 [b]Ex. 33:14; Josh. 1:13

3 [1]Lit., *me* [a]Deut. 4:37; 7:8 [b]Ps. 25:6

4 "[a]Again I will build you, and you shall be rebuilt,
O virgin of Israel!
Again you shall [1]take up your [b]tambourines,
And go forth to the dances of the [c]merrymakers.
5 "Again you shall [a]plant vineyards
On the [1]hills of Samaria;
The planters shall plant
And shall [2]enjoy *them*.
6 "For there shall be a day when watchmen
On the hills of Ephraim shall call out,
'Arise, and let us go up *to* Zion,
To the LORD our God.' "

7 For thus says the LORD,
"[a]Sing aloud with gladness for Jacob,
And shout among the [1b]chiefs of the nations;
Proclaim, give praise, and say,
'O LORD, [c]save Thy people,
The [d]remnant of Israel.'
8 "Behold, I am bringing them from the north country,
And I will [a]gather them from the remote parts of the earth,
Among them the [b]blind and the [c]lame,
The woman with child and she who is in labor with child, together;
A great [1]company, they shall return here.
9 "With weeping they shall come,
And by supplication I will lead them;
I will make them walk by [a]streams of waters,
On a straight path in which they shall [b]not stumble;
For I am a father to Israel,
And Ephraim is My first-born."

10 Hear the word of the LORD, O nations,
And declare in the [a]coastlands afar off,
And say, "He who scattered Israel will gather him,
And keep him as a [b]shepherd keeps his flock."
11 For the LORD has ransomed Jacob,
And redeemed him from the hand of him who was [a]stronger than he.
12 "And they shall come and shout for joy on the [a]height of Zion,
And they shall be [b]radiant over the [1]bounty of the LORD—
Over the [c]grain, and the new wine, and the oil,
And over the young of the flock and the herd;
And their life shall be like a [d]watered garden,
And they shall never [e]languish again.
13 "Then the virgin shall rejoice in the [a]dance,
And the young men and the old, together;
For I will [b]turn their mourning into joy,
And will comfort them, and give them [c]joy for their sorrow.
14 "And I will [1]fill the soul of the priests with abundance,

4 [1]Or, *be adorned with* [a]Jer. 24:6; 33:7 [b]Is. 30:32 [c]Jer. 30:19

5 [1]Or, *mountains* [2]Lit., *defile* [a]Ps. 107:37; Is. 65:21; Ezek. 28:26

7 [1]Lit., *head* [a]Jer. 20:13; Ps. 14:7 [b]Deut. 28:13; Is. 61:9 [c]Ps. 28:9 [d]Jer. 23:3; Is. 37:31

8 [1]Or, *assembly* [a]Deut. 30:4; Is. 43:6 [b]Is. 42:16 [c]Is. 40:11; Ezek. 34:16; Mic. 4:6

9 [a]Is. 43:20; 49:10 [b]Is. 63:13

10 [a]Jer. 25:22; Is. 66:19 [b]Is. 40:11

11 [a]Ps. 142:9

12 [1]Lit., *goodness* [a]Ezek. 17:23 [b]Is. 2:2; Mic. 4:1 [c]Hos. 2:22; Joel 3:18 [d]Is. 58:11 [e]Is. 35:10; 60:20; 65:19; John 16:22

13 [a]Judg. 21:21; Ps. 30:11; Zech. 8:4, 5 [b]Is. 61:3 [c]Is. 51:11

14 [1]Lit., *saturate* [2]Lit., *fatness*

And My people shall be [a]satisfied with My goodness,"
declares the LORD.

15 Thus says the LORD,
"A voice is heard in Ramah,
Lamentation *and* bitter weeping.
Rachel is weeping for her children;
She [a]refuses to be comforted for her children,
Because [b]they are no more."
16 Thus says the LORD,
"[a]Restrain your voice from weeping,
And your eyes from tears;
For your work shall be [b]rewarded," declares the LORD,
"And they shall [c]return from the land of the enemy.
17 "And there is [a]hope for your future," declares the LORD,
"And *your* children shall return to their own territory.
18 "I have surely heard Ephraim grieving,
'Thou hast [a]chastised me, and I was chastised,
Like an untrained [b]calf;
[c]Bring me back that I may be restored,
For Thou art the LORD my God.
19 'For after I turned back, I [a]repented;
And after I was instructed, I [b]smote on *my* thigh;
I was ashamed, and also humiliated,
Because I bore the reproach of my youth.'
20 "Is [a]Ephraim My dear son?
Is he a delightful child?
Indeed, as often as I have spoken against him,
I *certainly still* remember him;
Therefore My [1b]heart yearns for him;
I will surely [c]have mercy on him," declares the LORD.

21 "Set up for yourself roadmarks,
Place for yourself guide posts;
Direct your [1]mind to the highway,
The way by which you went.
[a]Return, O virgin of Israel,
Return to these your cities.
22 "How long will you go here and there,
O [a]faithless daughter?
For the LORD has created a new thing in the earth—
A woman will encompass a man."
23 Thus says the LORD of hosts, the God of Israel, "Once
again they will speak this word in the land of Judah and in its
cities, when I restore their [1]fortunes,
'The LORD bless you, O [a]abode of righteousness,
[b]O holy hill!'
24 "And Judah and all its cities will [a]dwell together in it, the
farmer and they who go about with flocks.
25 "[a]For I satisfy the weary ones and [1]refresh every one who
languishes."
26 At this I [a]awoke and looked, and my [b]sleep was pleasant to me.
27 "Behold, days are coming," declares the LORD, "when I
will [a]sow the house of Israel and the house of Judah with the
seed of man and with the seed of beast.

14 [a]Jer. 50:19

15 [a]Gen. 37:35; Ps. 77:2 [b]Jer. 10:20; Gen. 5:24; 42:13, 36

16 [a]Is. 25:8; 30:19 [b]Ruth 2:12; Heb. 6:10 [c]Jer. 30:3; Ezek. 11:17

17 [a]Jer. 29:11

18 [a]Job 5:17; Ps. 94:12 [b]Hos. 4:16 [c]Jer. 17:14; Ps. 80:3, 7, 19; Acts 3:26

19 [a]Ezek. 36:31; Zech. 12:10 [b]Ezek. 21:12; Luke 18:13

20 [1]Lit., *inward parts* [a]Hos. 11:8 [b]Gen. 43:30; Judg. 10:16 [c]Is. 55:7; Hos. 14:4

21 [1]Lit., *heart* [a]Is. 48:20; 52:11

22 [a]Jer. 49:4

23 [1]Or, *captivity* [a]Jer. 50:7; Is. 1:26 [b]Ps. 48:1; 87:1

24 [a]Jer. 31:12; Ezek. 36:10; Zech. 8:4-8

25 [1]Lit., *fill* [a]Jer. 31:12, 14; Ps. 107:9; Matt. 5:6; John 4:14

26 [a]Zech. 4:1 [b]Prov. 3:24

27 [a]Ezek. 36:9, 11; Hos. 2:23

28 "And it will come about that as I have [a]watched over
them to pluck up, to break down, to overthrow, to destroy, and
to bring disaster, so I will watch over them to build and to
plant," declares the LORD.
29 "In those days they will not say again,
'[a]The fathers have eaten sour grapes,
And the children's teeth are [1]set on edge.'
30 "But [a]every one will die for his own iniquity; each man
who eats the sour grapes, his teeth will be [1]set on edge.
31 "[a]Behold, days are coming," declares the LORD, "when I
will make a [b]new covenant with the house of Israel and with
the house of Judah,
32 not like the [a]covenant which I made with their fathers
in the day I [b]took them by the hand to bring them out of the
land of Egypt, My covenant which they broke, although I was
a husband to them," declares the LORD.
33 "But [a]this is the covenant which I will make with the
house of Israel after those days," declares the LORD, "I will put
My law within them, and on their heart I will write it; and I
will be their God, and they shall be My people.
34 "And they shall not [a]teach again, each man his neighbor
and each man his brother, saying, 'Know the LORD,' for they
shall all [b]know Me, from the least of them to the greatest of
them," declares the LORD, "for I will [c]forgive their iniquity,
and their [d]sin I will remember no more."
35 Thus says the LORD,
Who [a]gives the sun for light by day,
And the [1]fixed order of the moon and the stars for light
by night,
Who stirs up the sea so that its waves roar;
The LORD of hosts is His name:
36 "[a]If [1]this fixed order departs
From before Me," declares the LORD,
"Then the offspring of Israel also shall [b]cease
From being a nation before Me [2]for ever."
37 Thus says the LORD,
"[a]If the heavens above can be measured,
And the foundations of the earth searched out below,
Then I will also [b]cast off all the offspring of Israel
For all that they have done," declares the LORD.
38 "Behold, days are coming," declares the LORD, "when
the city shall be rebuilt for the LORD from the [a]tower of Hananel *to* the [b]Corner Gate.
39 "And the measuring line shall go out farther straight
ahead to the hill Gareb; then it will turn to Goah.
40 "And the whole valley of the dead bodies and of the
ashes, and all the fields as far as the brook [a]Kidron, to the
corner of the [b]Horse Gate toward the east, shall be [c]holy to the
LORD; it shall not be plucked up, or overthrown any more
forever."

CHAPTER 32

THE word that came to Jeremiah from the LORD in the
[a]tenth year of Zedekiah king of Judah, which was the eighteenth year of Nebuchadnezzar.

28 [a]Jer. 44:27; Dan. 9:14

29 [1]Or, *dull*
[a]Ezek. 18:2; Lam. 5:7

30 [1]Or, *dull*
[a]Deut. 24:16; Is. 3:11; Ezek. 18:4, 20

31 [a]Jer. 31:31-34; Heb. 8:8-12 [b]Jer. 32:40; Ezek. 37:26; Luke 22:20; 1 Cor. 11:25; 2 Cor. 3:6; Heb. 8:8-12

32 [a]Ex. 19:5; 24:6-8; Deut. 5:2, 3 [b]Deut. 1:31; Is. 63:12

33 [a]Heb. 10:16, 17

34 [a]1 Thess. 4:9; 1 John 2:27 [b]Jer. 24:7; Is. 11:9; 54:13; Heb. 2:14 [c]Jer. 50:20; Mic. 7:18 [d]Is. 43:25

35 [1]Lit., *statutes*
[a]Gen. 1:14-18; Deut. 4:19; Ps. 19:1-6; 136:7-9

36 [1]Lit., *these statutes*
[2]Lit., *all the days*
[a]Jer. 33:20-26; Ps. 89:36, 37; Is. 54:9, 10 [b]Amos 9:8, 9

37 [a]Jer. 33:22; Is. 40:12 [b]Jer. 33:24-26; Rom. 11:2-5, 26, 27

38 [a]Neh. 3:1; 12:39; Zech. 14:10 [b]2 Kin. 14:13; 2 Chr. 26:9

40 [a]2 Sam. 15:23; 2 Kin. 23:6, 12; John 18:1 [b]2 Kin. 11:16; 2 Chr. 23:15; Neh. 3:28 [c]Joel 3:17; Zech 14:20

1 [a]Jer. 39:1, 2; 2 Kin. 25:1, 2

E 82-1

2 Now at that time the army of the king of Babylon was
besieging Jerusalem, and Jeremiah the prophet was shut up in
the court of the guard, which was *in* the house of the [a]king of
Judah,
3 because Zedekiah king of Judah had [a]shut him up,
saying, "Why do you [b]prophesy, saying, 'Thus says the LORD,
"Behold, I am about to [c]give this city into the hand of the king
of Babylon, and he will take it;
4 and Zedekiah king of Judah shall [a]not escape out of the
hand of the Chaldeans, but he shall surely be given into the
hand of the king of Babylon, and he shall [b]speak with him
[1]face to face, and see him eye to eye;
5 and he shall [a]take Zedekiah to Babylon, and he shall be
there until I visit him," declares the LORD. "If you fight against
the Chaldeans, you shall [b]not succeed" ' ? "
6 And Jeremiah said, "The word of the LORD came to
me, saying:
7 'Behold, Hanamel the son of Shallum your uncle is
coming to you, saying: Buy for yourself my field which is at
Anathoth, for you have the [a]right of redemption to buy *it*.'
8 "Then Hanamel my uncle's son came to me in the court
of the guard according to the word of the LORD, and said to
me, 'Buy my field, please, that is at Anathoth, which is in the
land of Benjamin; for you have the right of possession and the
redemption is yours; buy *it* for yourself.' Then I knew that this
was the [a]word of the LORD.
9 "And I bought the field which was at Anathoth from
Hanamel my uncle's son, and I [a]weighed out the silver for him,
seventeen [b]shekels of silver.
10 "And I [1a]signed and [b]sealed the deed, and [c]called in
witnesses, and weighed out the silver on the scales.
11 "Then I took the deeds of purchase, both the sealed
copy containing the [a]terms and conditions, and the open *copy*;
12 and I gave the deed of purchase to Baruch the son of
Neriah, the son of Mahseiah, in the sight of Hanamel my
uncle's *son*, and in the sight of the witnesses who signed the
deed of purchase, before all the Jews who were sitting in the
court of the guard.
13 "And I commanded Baruch in their presence, saying,
14 'Thus says the LORD of hosts, the God of Israel, "Take
these deeds, this sealed deed of purchase, and this open deed,
and put them in an earthenware jar, that they may [1]last a long
time."
15 'For thus says the LORD of hosts, the God of Israel,
"[a]Houses and fields and vineyards shall again be bought in this
land." '
16 "After I had given the deed of purchase to Baruch the
son of Neriah, then I [a]prayed to the LORD, saying,
17 'Ah Lord [1]GOD! Behold, Thou hast [a]made the heavens
and the earth by Thy great power and by Thine outstretched
arm! [b]Nothing is too difficult for Thee,
18 who [a]showest lovingkindness to thousands, but repayest
the iniquity of [b]fathers into the bosom of their children after
them, O [c]great and [d]mighty God, the [e]LORD of hosts is His
name;
19 [a]great in counsel and mighty in deed, whose [b]eyes are

2 [a]Neh. 3:25

3 [a]2 Kin. 6:31, 32 [b]Jer. 26:8, 9; Amos 7:13 [c]Jer. 32:28, 29; 21:4-7; 34:2, 3

4 [1]Lit., *mouth to mouth* [a]Jer. 37:17; 38:18, 23; 39:4-7; 2 Kin. 25:4-7 [b]Jer. 39:5

5 [a]Jer. 39:7; Ezek. 12:12, 13 [b]Ezek. 17:9, 10, 15

7 [a]Lev. 25:25; Ruth 4:3, 4

8 [a]Jer. 32:25; 1 Sam. 9:16, 17; 10:3-7; 1 Kin. 22:25

9 [a]Gen. 23:16 [b]Gen. 24:22; Ex. 21:32; Neh. 5:15; Ezek. 4:10

10 [1]Or, *I wrote . . . on the document* [a]Jer. 32:44; Is. 44:5 [b]Deut. 32:34; Job 14:17 [c]Ruth 4:1, 9; Is. 8:1, 2

11 [a]Luke 2:27

14 [1]Lit., *stand many days*

15 [a]Jer. 32:37, 43, 44; 30:18; 31:5, 12, 24; 33:12, 13; Amos 9:14, 15; Zech. 3:10

16 [a]Jer. 12:1; Gen. 32:9-12; Phil. 4:6, 7

17 [1]YHWH, usually rendered LORD [a]Jer. 27:5; 2 Kin. 19:15; Ps. 102:25; Is. 40:26-29 [b]Jer. 32:27; Gen. 18:14

18 [a]Ex. 34:6, 7; Deut. 7:9, 10 [b]1 Kin. 14:9, 10; 16:1-3; Matt. 23:32-36 [c]Ps. 145:3 [d]Jer. 20:11; Ps. 50:1 [e]Jer 10:16; 31:35

19 [a]Is. 9:6; 28:29 [b]Jer. 23:24; Job 34:21

open to all the ways of the sons of men, [c]giving to every one
according to his ways and according to the fruit of his deeds;
20 who hast [a]set signs and wonders in the land of Egypt,
and even to this day both in Israel and among mankind; and
Thou hast [b]made a name for Thyself, as at this day.
21 'And didst [a]bring Thy people Israel out of the land of
Egypt with signs and with wonders, and with a strong hand and
with an outstretched arm, and with great terror;
22 and gavest them this land, which Thou didst [a]swear to
their forefathers to give them, a land flowing with milk and
honey.
23 'And they [a]came in and took possession of it, but they
did not obey Thy voice or [b]walk in Thy law; they have done
nothing of all that Thou commandedst them to do; therefore
Thou hast made [c]all this calamity come upon them.
24 'Behold, the siege mounds have reached the city to take
it; and the city is given into the hand of the Chaldeans who
fight against it, because of the [a]sword, the famine, and the
pestilence; and what Thou hast spoken has [b]come to pass; and,
behold, Thou seest *it*.
25 'And Thou hast said to me, O Lord [1]GOD, "Buy for
yourself the field with money, and call in witnesses"—although the city is given into the hand of the Chaldeans." ' "
26 Then the word of the LORD came to Jeremiah, saying,
27 "Behold, I am the LORD, the [a]God of all flesh; is anything
[b]too difficult for Me?
28 "Therefore thus says the LORD, 'Behold, I am about to
[a]give this city into the hand of the Chaldeans and into the
hand of Nebuchadnezzar king of Babylon, and he shall take it.
29 "And the Chaldeans who are fighting against this city
shall enter and [a]set this city on fire and burn it, with the
[b]houses where *people* have offered incense to Baal on their
roofs and poured out drink offerings to other gods to provoke
Me to anger.
30 "Indeed the sons of Israel and the sons of Judah have
been only doing evil in My sight from their youth; for the sons
of Israel have been only provoking Me to anger by the work of
their hands," declares the LORD.
31 "Indeed this city has been to Me *a* [a]*provocation of* My
anger and My wrath from the day that they built it, even to
this day; that it should be [b]removed from before My face,
32 because of all the evil of the sons of Israel and the sons
of Judah, which they have done to provoke Me to anger—
they, their [a]kings, their leaders, their priests, their prophets, the
men of Judah, and the inhabitants of Jerusalem.
33 "And they have turned *their* back to Me, and not *their*
face; though *I* taught them, [1a]teaching again and again, they
would not listen [2]and receive instruction.
34 "But they put their detestable things in the house which
is called by My name to defile it.
35 "And they built the [a]high places of Baal that are in the
valley of Ben-Hinnom to cause their sons and their daughters
to pass through *the fire* to [b]Molech, which I had not commanded them nor had it [1]entered My mind that they should
do this abomination, to cause Judah to sin.
36 "Now therefore thus says the LORD God of Israel con-

19 [c]Jer. 17:10; 21:14; Ps. 62:12; Matt. 16:27; John 5:29

20 [a]Ps. 78:43; 105:27 [b]Is. 63:12, 14; Dan. 9:15

21 [a]Deut. 4:34; 7:19; 26:8; 1 Chr. 17:21

22 [a]Jer. 11:5; Ex. 13:5; Deut. 1:8; Ps. 105:9-11

23 [a]Jer. 2:7; Ps. 44:2, 3; 78:54, 55 [b]Jer. 26:4; 44:10; Ezra 9:7 [c]Lam. 1:18; Dan. 9:11, 12

24 [a]Jer. 32:36; 29:17, 18; 34:17; Ezek. 14:21 [b]Deut. 4:26; Josh. 23:15, 16; Zech. 1:6

25 [1]YHWH, usually rendered LORD

27 [a]Num. 16:22; 27:16 [b]Jer. 32:17; Matt. 19:26

28 [a]Jer. 32:3, 24, 36; 19:7-12; 34:2, 3

29 [a]Jer. 21:10; 39:8; 2 Chr. 36:19 [b]Jer. 19:13; 44:17-19, 25; 52:13

31 [a]Jer. 5:9-11; 6:6, 7; 1 Kin. 11:7, 8; 2 Kin. 21:4-7, 16; Matt. 23:37 [b]Jer. 27:10; 2 Kin. 23:27; 24:3, 4

32 [a]Jer. 2:26; 44:17, 21; Ezra 9:7; Is. 1:4-6, 23

33 [1]Lit., *rising up early and teaching* [2]Lit., *to* [a]Jer. 25:3; 26:5; 35:15; 2 Chr. 36:15, 16; John 8:2

35 [1]Lit., *come up into My heart* [a]Jer. 7:31; 19:5; 2 Chr. 28:2, 3; 33:6 [b]Lev. 18:21; 20:2-5; 1 Kin. 11:7; 2 Kin. 33:10; Acts 7:43

cerning this city of which you say, 'It is given into the hand of
the king of Babylon by sword, by famine, and by pestilence.'
37 "Behold, I will [a]gather them out of all the lands to which
I have driven them in My anger, in My wrath, and in great
indignation; and I will bring them back to this place and [b]make
them dwell in safety.
38 "And they shall be My people, and I will be their God;
39 and I will [a]give them one heart and one way, that they
may fear Me always, for their own [b]good, and for *the good of*
their children after them.
40 "And I will make an [a]everlasting covenant with them
that I will not turn away from them—to do them good; and I
will put the fear of Me in their hearts so that they will not turn
away from Me.
41 "And I will [a]rejoice over them to do them good, and I
will [1]faithfully [b]plant them in this land with [c]all My heart and
with all My soul.
42 "For thus says the LORD, '[a]Just as I brought all this calamity on this people, so I am going to bring on them all the
good that I am promising them.
43 'And [a]fields shall be bought in this land of which you
say, "It is a desolation, without man or beast; it is given into
the hand of the Chaldeans."
44 'Men shall buy fields for money, [1]sign and seal deeds,
and call in witnesses in the land of Benjamin, in the environs of
Jerusalem, in the cities of Judah, in the cities of the hill country, in the cities of the lowland, and in the cities of the [2]Negev;
for I will restore their [3]fortunes,' declares the LORD."

CHAPTER 33

THEN the word of the LORD came to Jeremiah the second
time, while he was still [1]confined in the court of the guard,
saying,
2 "Thus says the LORD who made [1]*the earth*, the LORD
who formed it to establish it—the [a]LORD is His name,
3 '[a]Call to Me, and I will answer you, and I will tell you
[b]great and mighty things, which you do not [c]know.'
4 "For thus says the LORD God of Israel concerning the
[a]houses of this city, and concerning the houses of the kings of
Judah, which are broken down to *make a defense* against the
siege mounds and against the sword—
5 while *they* are coming to [a]fight with the Chaldeans,
and to fill them with the corpses of men whom I have slain in
My anger and in My wrath, and I have [b]hidden My face from
this city because of all their wickedness:
6 "Behold, I will bring to it [a]health and healing, and I will
heal them; and I will reveal to them an [b]abundance of peace
and truth.
7 "And I will [a]restore the [1]fortunes of Judah and the fortunes of Israel, and I will [b]rebuild them as they were at first.
8 "And I will [a]cleanse them from all their iniquity by
which they have sinned against Me, and I will pardon all their
iniquities by which they have sinned against Me, and by which
they have transgressed against Me.
9 "And [1]it shall be to Me a [a]name of joy, praise, and glory

37 [a]Deut. 30:3; Ps. 106:47; Is. 11:11-16; Ezek. 11:17; Hos. 1:11; Amos 9:14, 15 [b]Jer. 23:6; Ezek. 34:25, 28; Zech. 14:11

39 [a]Jer. 31:33; 2 Chr. 30:12; John 17:21; Acts 4:32 [b]Deut. 11:18-21; Ezek. 37:25

40 [a]Jer. 31:33; 50:5; Is. 55:3

41 [1]Or, *truly* [a]Deut. 30:9; Is. 62:5; 65:19 [b]Jer. 31:28; Amos 9:15 [c]Hos. 2:19, 20

42 [a]Jer. 31:28; Zech. 8:14, 15

43 [a]Jer. 32:15, 25; Ezek. 37:11-14

44 [1]Or, *write . . . on the document* [2]I.e., South country [3]Or, *captivity*

1 [1]Lit., *shut up*

2 [1]Lit., *it* [a]Ex. 3:15; 6:3; 15:3

3 [a]Jer. 29:12; Ps. 50:15; Is. 55:6, 7 [b]Jer. 32:17, 27 [c]Is. 48:6

4 [a]Is. 32:13, 14

5 [a]Jer. 21:4-7; 32:5 [b]Jer. 21:10; Is. 8:17; Mic. 3:4

6 [a]Jer. 17:14; 30:17; Hos. 6:1 [b]Is. 66:12; Gal. 5:22, 23

7 [1]Or, *captivity* [a]Jer. 33:26; 32:44; Ps. 85:1 [b]Jer. 30:18; 31:4, 38; Amos 9:14, 15

8 [a]Jer. 50:20; Ps. 51:2; Is. 44:22; Ezek. 36:25, 33; Mic. 7:18, 19; Zech. 13:1; Heb. 9:11-14

9 [1]I.e., this city [a]Jer. 13:11; Is. 62:2, 4

before [b]all the nations of the earth, which shall hear of all the
[c]good that I do for them, and they shall [d]fear and tremble
because of all the good and all the peace that I make for it."
10 "Thus says the LORD, 'Yet again there shall be heard in
this place, of which you say, "It is a waste, without man and
without beast," *that is,* in the cities of Judah and in the streets
of Jerusalem that are desolate, without man and without inhabitant and without beast,
11 the voice of [a]joy and the voice of gladness, the voice of
the bridegroom and the voice of the bride, the voice of those
who say,

"Give thanks to the LORD of hosts,
For the LORD is good,
For His lovingkindness is everlasting";

and of those who bring a thank offering into the house of the
LORD. For I will restore the [1]fortunes of the land as they were
at first,' says the LORD.
12 "Thus says the LORD of hosts, 'There shall again be in
this place which is waste, without man or beast, and in all its
cities, a [1]habitation of shepherds who rest their [a]flocks.
13 'In the cities of the hill country, in the cities of the
lowland, in the cities of the Negev, in the land of Benjamin, in
the environs of Jerusalem, and in the cities of Judah, the flocks
shall again [a]pass under the hands of the one who numbers
them,' says the LORD.
14 'Behold, days are coming,' declares the LORD, 'when I
will [a]fulfill the good word which I have spoken concerning the
house of Israel and the house of Judah.
15 'In those days and at that time I will cause a [a]righteous
Branch of David to spring forth; and he shall execute [b]justice
and righteousness on the earth.
16 'In those days [a]Judah shall be saved, and Jerusalem shall
dwell in safety; and this is *the name* by which she shall be
called: the [b]LORD is our righteousness.'
17 "For thus says the LORD, '[1]David shall [a]never lack a man
to sit on the throne of the house of Israel;
18 [1]and the Levitical [a]priests shall never lack a man before
Me to offer burnt offerings, to burn grain offerings, and to
[b]prepare sacrifices [2]continually.' "
19 And the word of the LORD came to Jeremiah, saying,
20 "Thus says the LORD, 'If you can [a]break My covenant for
the day, and My covenant for the night, so that day and night
will not be at their appointed time,
21 then [a]My covenant may also be broken with David My
servant that he shall not have a son to reign on his throne, and
with the Levitical priests, My ministers.
22 As the [a]host of heaven cannot be counted, and the
[b]sand of the sea cannot be measured, so I will multiply the
[1]descendants of David My servant and the Levites who minister to Me.' "
23 And the word of the LORD came to Jeremiah, saying,
24 "Have you not observed what this people have spoken,
saying, 'The [a]two families which the LORD chose, He has rejected them'? Thus they [b]despise My people, no longer are
they as a nation [1]in their sight.

9 [b]Jer. 3:17, 19; 4:2; 16:19 [c]Jer. 24:6; 32:42 [d]Neh. 6:16; Ps. 40:3; Hos. 3:5

11 [1]Or, *captivity* [a]Is. 35:10; 51:3, 11

12 [1]Or, *pasture* [a]Jer. 31:12; Is. 65:10; Ezek. 34:12-14; Zeph. 2:6, 7

13 [a]Lev. 27:32; Luke 15:4

14 [a]Jer. 33:9; 32:42; Is. 32:1, 2; Ezek. 34:23-25; Hag. 2:6-9

15 [a]Jer. 23:5, 6; 30:9; Is. 4:2; 11:1-5; Zech. 3:8; 6:12, 13 [b]Ps. 72:1-5

16 [a]Jer. 23:6; Is. 45:17, 22 [b]Jer. 23:6; Is. 45:24, 25; 1 Cor. 1:30; 2 Cor. 5:21; Phil. 3:9

17 [1]Lit., *There shall not be cut off for David* [a]2 Sam. 7:16; 1 Kin. 2:4; 8:25; Ps. 89:29-37

18 [1]Lit., *there shall not be cut off for the Levitical priests* [2]Lit., *all the days* [a]Deut. 18:1; 24:8; Josh. 3:3; Ezek. 44:15 [b]Ex. 29:4; Ezra 3:5; Heb. 13:15

20 [a]Jer. 33:25; 31:35-37; Ps. 89:37; 104:19-23; Is. 54:9, 10

21 [a]2 Sam. 23:5; 2 Chr. 7:18; 21:7

22 [1]Lit., *seed* [a]Gen. 15:5 [b]Gen. 22:17

24 [1]Lit., *to their faces* [a]Jer. 33:26; 3:7, 8, 10, 18; Is. 7:17; 11:13; Ezek. 37:22 [b]Neh. 4:2-4; Esth. 3:6-8; Ps. 44:13, 14; 83:4; Ezek. 36:2

25 [1]Lit., *statutes* (cf. 31:35) [a]Jer. 33:20; 31:35, 36 [b]Ps. 74:16, 17

25 "Thus says the LORD, 'If My [a]covenant *for* day and night
stand not, *and* the [1]fixed patterns of heaven and earth I have
[b]not established,

26 [1]Lit., *seed* [2]Lit., *from taking* [3]Or, *captivity* [a]Gen. 49:10 [b]Jer. 31:20; Is. 14:1; 54:8; Ezek. 39:25; Hos. 1:7; 2:23

26 then I would reject the [1]descendants of Jacob and David My servant, [2]not taking from His [1]descendants [a]rulers over
the [1]descendants of Abraham, Isaac, and Jacob. But I will
restore their [3]fortunes and will have [b]mercy on them.'"

CHAPTER 34

1 [a]Jer. 1:15; 27:7; Dan. 2:37, 38

THE word which came to Jeremiah from the LORD, when
Nebuchadnezzar king of Babylon and all his army, with [a]all the
kingdoms of the earth that were under his dominion and all
the peoples, were fighting against Jerusalem and against all its
cities, saying,

2 [a]Jer. 22:1, 2; 37:1-4; 2 Chr. 36:11, 12

2 "Thus says the LORD God of Israel, '[a]Go and speak to
Zedekiah king of Judah and say to him: "Thus says the LORD,
'Behold, I am giving this city into the hand of the king of
Babylon, and he will burn it with fire.

3 [1]Lit., *mouth to mouth* [a]Jer. 34:21; 21:7; 2 Kin. 25:4, 5 [b]Jer. 39:6, 7; 2 Kin. 25:6, 7

3 'And [a]you will not escape from his hand, for you will
surely be captured and delivered into his hand; and you will
[b]see the king of Babylon eye to eye, and he will speak with you
[1]face to face, and you will go to Babylon.'"'

4 "Yet hear the word of the LORD, O Zedekiah king of
Judah! Thus says the LORD concerning you, 'You will not die
by the sword.

5 [a]2 Chr. 16:14; 21:19

5 'You will die in peace; and as spices were burned for
your fathers, the former kings who were before you, so they
will [a]burn spices for you; and they will lament for you: "Alas,
lord!"' For I have spoken the word," declares the LORD.

6 [a]1 Sam. 3:18; 15:16-24; 1 Kin. 21:18

6 Then Jeremiah the prophet spoke [a]all these words to
Zedekiah king of Judah in Jerusalem

7 [a]Josh. 10:3, 5; 2 Kin. 14:19; 18:14; Is. 36:2 [b]Josh. 10:10; 2 Chr. 11:9 [c]2 Chr. 11:5-10

7 when the army of the king of Babylon was fighting
against Jerusalem and against all the remaining cities of Judah,
that is, [a]Lachish and [b]Azekah, for they *alone* remained as
[c]fortified cities among the cities of Judah.

8 [1]Or, *liberty* [a]2 Kin. 11:17; 23:2, 3 [b]Jer. 34:14, 17; Lev. 25:10, 39-46; Neh. 5:1-13

8 The word which came to Jeremiah from the LORD,
after King Zedekiah had [a]made a covenant with all the people
who were in Jerusalem to [b]proclaim [1]release to them,

9 [a]Gen. 14:13; Ex. 2:6

9 that each man should set free his male servant and each
man his female servant, a [a]Hebrew man or a Hebrew woman;
so that no one should keep them, a Jew his brother, in
bondage.

10 And all the officials and all the people obeyed, who
had entered into the covenant that each man should set free
his male servant and each man his female servant, so that no
one should keep them any longer in bondage; they obeyed,
and set *them free.*

11 [a]Jer. 34:21; 37:5; Ps. 78:34-36; Hos. 6:4

11 But [a]afterward they turned around and took back the
male servants and the female servants, whom they had set free,
and brought them into subjection for male servants and for
female servants.

12 Then the word of the LORD came to Jeremiah from the
LORD, saying,

13 "Thus says the LORD God of Israel, 'I [a]made a covenant
with your forefathers in the day that I [b]brought them out of
the land of Egypt, from the house of bondage, saying,
14 "[a]At the end of seven years each of you shall set free his
Hebrew brother, who [1]has been sold to you and has served you
six years, you shall send him out free from you; but your
forefathers did not [b]obey Me, or incline their ear to Me.
15 "Although recently you *had* turned and done what is
right in My sight, each man proclaiming [1]release to his neighbor, and you had [a]made a covenant before Me in the house
which is called by My name.
16 "Yet you [a]turned and [b]profaned My name, and each
man [1]took back his male servant and each man his female
servant, whom you had set free according to their desire, and
you brought them into subjection to be your male servants and
female servants." '
17 "Therefore thus says the LORD, 'You have not obeyed
Me in proclaiming [1]release each man to his brother, and each
man to his neighbor. Behold, I am [a]proclaiming a [1]release to
you,' declares the LORD, 'to the [b]sword, to the pestilence, and
to the famine; and I will make you a [c]terror to all the kingdoms
of the earth.
18 'And I will give the men who have [a]transgressed My
covenant, who have not fulfilled the words of the covenant
which they made before Me, *when* they [b]cut the calf in two
and passed between its parts—
19 the [a]officials of Judah, and the officials of Jerusalem,
the court officers, and the priests, and all the people of the
land, who passed between the parts of the calf—
20 and I will give them into the hand of their enemies and
into the hand of those who seek their life. And their [a]dead
bodies shall be food for the birds of the sky and the beasts of
the earth.
21 'And [a]Zedekiah king of Judah and his officials I will give
into the hand of their enemies, and into the hand of those who
seek their life, and into the hand of the army of the king of
Babylon which has gone away from you.
22 'Behold, I am going to command,' declares the LORD,
'and I will bring them back to this city; and they shall fight
against it and take it and burn it with fire; and I will make the
cities of Judah a [a]desolation [b]without inhabitant.' "

CHAPTER 35

THE word which came to Jeremiah from the LORD in the
days of [a]Jehoiakim the son of Josiah, king of Judah, saying,
2 "Go to the house of the [a]Rechabites, and speak to them,
and bring them into the house of the LORD, into one of the
[b]chambers, and give them wine to drink."
3 Then I took Jaazaniah the son of Jeremiah, son of
Habazziniah, and his brothers, and all his sons, and the whole
house of the Rechabites.
4 And I brought them into the house of the LORD, into
the chamber of the sons of Hanan the son of Igdaliah, the
[a]man of God, which was near the chamber of the officials,

13 [a]Jer. 31:32; Ex. 24:3, 7, 8; Deut. 5:2, 3, 27 [b]Ex. 20:2

14 [1]Or, *has sold himself* [a]Ex. 21:2; Deut. 15:12; 1 Kin. 9:22 [b]1 Sam. 8:7, 8; 2 Kin. 17:13, 14

15 [1]Or, *liberty* [a]2 Kin. 23:3; Neh. 10:29

16 [1]Lit., *caused them to return* [a]Jer. 34:11; 1 Sam. 15:11; Ezek. 3:20; 18:24 [b]Ex. 20:7

17 [1]Or, *liberty* [a]Lev. 26:34, 35; Esth. 7:10; Dan. 6:24; Matt. 7:2 [b]Jer. 32:24; 38:2 [c]Jer. 29:18; Deut. 28:25, 64

18 [a]Deut. 17:2; Hos. 6:7; 8:1 [b]Gen. 15:10

19 [a]Jer. 34:10; Ezek. 22:27; Mic. 7:1-5; Zeph. 3:3, 4

20 [a]Jer. 19:7; 1 Sam. 17:44, 46; 1 Kin. 14:11; 16:4

21 [a]Jer. 32:3, 4; 39:6; 52:10, 24-27; 2 Kin. 25:18-21; Ezek. 17:16

22 [a]Jer. 4:7 [b]Jer. 33:10; 44:22

1 [a]Jer. 1:3; 27:20; 2 Kin. 23:34-36; 24:1; Dan. 1:1

2 [a]1 Chr. 2:55 [b]1 Kin. 6:5, 6, 8; 1 Chr. 9:26, 33

4 [a]Deut. 33:1; Josh. 14:6; 1 Kin. 12:22; 2 Kin. 1:9-13

which was above the chamber of Maaseiah the son of Shallum,
the doorkeeper.
5 Then I set before the [1]men of the house of the Rechabites pitchers full of wine, and cups; and I said to them, "[a]Drink
wine!"
6 But they said, "We will not drink wine, for [a]Jonadab
the son of [b]Rechab, our father, commanded us, saying, 'You
shall [c]not drink wine, you or your sons, forever.
7 'And you shall not build a house, and you shall not sow
seed, and you shall not plant a vineyard or own one; but in
[a]tents you shall dwell all your days, that you may live [b]many
days in the land where you [c]sojourn.'
8 "And we have [a]obeyed the voice of Jonadab the son of
Rechab, our father, in all that he commanded us, not to drink
wine all our days, we, our wives, our sons, or our daughters,
9 nor to build ourselves houses to dwell in; and we do not
[a]have vineyard or field or seed.
10 "We have only dwelt in tents, and have obeyed, and
have done according to all that Jonadab our father commanded us.
11 "But it came about, when [a]Nebuchadnezzar king of Babylon came up against the land, that we said, 'Come and let us
go to Jerusalem before the army of the Chaldeans and before
the army of the Syrians.' So we have dwelt in Jerusalem."
12 Then the word of the LORD came to Jeremiah, saying,
13 "Thus says the LORD of hosts, the God of Israel, 'Go and
say to the men of Judah and the inhabitants of Jerusalem:
"[a]Will you not receive instruction by listening to My words?"
declares the LORD.
14 "The words of Jonadab the son of Rechab, which he
commanded his sons not to drink wine, are observed. So they
do not drink *wine* to this day, for they have obeyed their
father's command. But I have spoken to you [1a]again and again;
yet you have [b]not listened to Me.
15 "Also I have sent to you all My [a]servants the prophets,
sending *them* [1]again and again, saying: '[b]Turn now every man
from his evil way, and amend your deeds, and do not [c]go after
other gods to worship them, then you shall dwell in the land
which I have given to you and to your forefathers; but you
have not inclined your ear or listened to Me.
16 'Indeed, the sons of Jonadab the son of Rechab have
[a]observed the command of their father which he commanded
them, but this people has not listened to Me.' " '
17 "Therefore thus says the LORD, the God of hosts, the
God of Israel, 'Behold, [a]I am bringing on Judah and on all the
inhabitants of Jerusalem all the disaster that I have pronounced against them; because I [b]spoke to them but they did
not listen, and I have called them but they did not answer.' "
18 Then Jeremiah said to the house of the Rechabites,
"Thus says the LORD of hosts, the God of Israel, 'Because you
have [a]obeyed the command of Jonadab your father, kept all
his commands, and done according to all that he commanded
you;
19 therefore thus says the LORD of hosts, the God of Israel, "Jonadab the son of Rechab [a]shall not lack a man to
[b]stand before Me [1]always." ' "

5 [1]Lit., *sons*
[a]Amos 2:12; 2 Cor. 2:9

6 [a]2 Kin. 10:15, 23 [b]1 Chr. 2:55 [c]Lev. 10:9; Num. 6:2-4; Judg. 13:7, 14; Luke 1:15

7 [a]Gen. 25:27; Heb. 11:9 [b]Ex. 20:12; Eph. 6:2, 3 [c]Gen. 36:7; 1 Chr. 16:19

8 [a]Prov. 1:8, 9; 4:1, 2, 10; 6:20; Eph. 6:1; Col. 3:20

9 [a]Jer. 35:7; Ps. 37:16; 1 Tim. 6:6

11 [a]2 Kin. 24:1, 2; Dan. 1:1, 2

13 [a]Jer. 5:3; 6:8-10; 32:33; Is. 28:9-12

14 [1]Lit., *rising early and speaking*
[a]Jer. 7:13, 25; 11:7; 25:3, 4; 2 Chr. 36:15 [b]Is. 30:9; 50:2

15 [1]Lit., *rising early and speaking*
[a]Jer. 26:5; 29:19; 32:33 [b]Jer. 4:1; 18:11; Is. 1:16, 17; Ezek. 18:30-32; Acts 26:20 [c]Jer. 7:6; 13:10; 25:6; Deut. 6:14

16 [a]Jer. 35:14; Mal. 1:6

17 [a]Jer. 19:3, 15; 21:4-10; Mic. 3:12 [b]Jer. 7:13, 26, 27; 26:5; Prov. 1:24, 25; Is. 65:12; 66:4; Luke 13:34, 35; Rom. 10:21

18 [a]Ex. 20:12; Eph. 6:1-3

19 [1]Lit., *all the days*
[a]Jer. 33:17; 1 Chr. 2:55 [b]Jer. 15:19; Luke 21:36

Chapter 36

AND it came about in the [a]fourth year of Jehoiakim the son
of Josiah, king of Judah, that this word came to Jeremiah from
the LORD, saying,
2 "Take a [1a]scroll and write on it all the [b]words which I
have spoken to you concerning [c]Israel, and concerning [c]Judah,
and concerning all the [d]nations, from the [e]day I *first* spoke to
you, from the days of Josiah, even to this day.
3 "[a]Perhaps the house of Judah will hear all the calamity
which I plan to bring on them, in order that every man will
[b]turn from his evil way; then I will [c]forgive their iniquity and
their sin."
4 Then Jeremiah called [a]Baruch the son of Neriah, and
Baruch wrote [1]at the dictation of Jeremiah all the words of the
LORD, which He had spoken to him, on a [2b]scroll.
5 And Jeremiah commanded Baruch, saying, "I am [1a]re-
stricted; I cannot go into the house of the LORD.
6 So you go and [a]read from the scroll which you have
[b]written [1]at my dictation the words of the LORD [2]to the people
in the LORD's house on a [c]fast day. And also you shall read
them [2]to all *the people of* Judah who come from their cities.
7 "[a]Perhaps their supplication will [1]come before the LORD,
and everyone will turn from his evil way, for [b]great is the anger
and the wrath that the LORD has pronounced against this
people."
8 And Baruch the son of Neriah did according to all that
Jeremiah the prophet commanded him, [a]reading from the
book the words of the LORD in the LORD's house.
9 Now it came about in the [a]fifth year of Jehoiakim the
son of Josiah, king of Judah, in the [b]ninth month, that all the
people in Jerusalem and all the people who [c]came from the
cities of Judah to Jerusalem proclaimed a [d]fast before the
LORD.
10 Then Baruch read from the book the words of Jeremiah in the house of the LORD in the [a]chamber of [b]Gemariah
the son of Shaphan the [c]scribe, in the upper court, at the
[d]entry of the New Gate of the LORD's house, to all the people.
11 Now when [a]Micaiah the son of Gemariah, the son of
Shaphan, had heard all the words of the LORD from the book,
12 he went down to the king's house, into the scribe's
chamber. And, behold, all the officials were sitting there—[a]Eli-
shama the scribe, and [b]Delaiah the son of Shemaiah, and
[c]Elnathan the son of Achbor, and Gemariah the son of Shaphan,
and Zedekiah the son of Hananiah, and all the *other*
officials.
13 And Micaiah [a]declared to them all the words that he
had heard, when Baruch read from the book to the people.
14 Then all the officials sent [a]Jehudi the son of Nethaniah, the son of Shelemiah, the son of Cushi, to Baruch,
saying, "Take in your hand the scroll from which you have
read [1]to the people and come." So Baruch the son of Neriah
[b]took the scroll in his hand and went to them.
15 And they said to him, "Sit down please, and read it to
us." So Baruch [a]read it to them.
16 Now it came about when they had heard all the words,

1 [a]Jer. 25:1, 3; 45:1; 46:2; 2 Kin. 24:1

2 [1]Lit., *scroll of a book* [a]Jer. 36:6, 23, 28; Ex. 17:14; Zech. 5:1, 2 [b]Jer. 1:9, 10 [c]Jer. 3:3-10; 23:13, 14; 32:30-32 [d]Jer. 1:5, 10; 25:9-29; chaps. 47-51 [e]Jer. 1:2, 3; 25:3

3 [a]Jer. 36:7; 26:3; Ezek. 12:3 [b]Jer. 18:8, 11; 35:15; Deut. 30:2, 8; 1 Sam. 7:3; Is. 55:7 [c]John 3:10; Mark 4:12; Acts 3:19

4 [1]Lit., *from the mouth of* [2]Lit., *scroll of a book* [a]Jer. 36:18; 32:12; 43:3 [b]Jer. 36:14; Ezek. 2:9

5 [1]Lit., *shut up* [a]Jer. 32:2; 33:1; 2 Cor. 11:23

6 [1]Lit., *from my mouth* [2]Lit., *in the ears of*, and so throughout this context [a]Jer. 36:8 [b]Jer. 36:4 [c]Jer. 36:9; Zech. 8:19

7 [1]Lit., *fall* [a]Jer. 36:3; 26:3; 1 Kin. 8:33; 2 Chr. 33:12, 13 [b]Jer. 4:4; 21:5; 2 Kin. 22:13, 17; Lam. 4:11

8 [a]Jer. 36:6; 1:17

9 [a]Jer. 36:1 [b]Jer. 36:22 [c]Jer. 36:6 [d]2 Chr. 20:3; Esth. 4:16; Joel 1:14; 2:15; Jon. 3:5

10 [a]Jer. 35:4 [b]Jer. 36:11, 25 [c]Jer. 52:25; 2 Sam. 8:17 [d]Jer. 26:10

11 [a]Jer. 36:13

12 [a]Jer. 36:20 [b]Jer. 36:25 [c]Jer. 26:22

13 [a]2 Kin. 22:10

14 [1]Lit., *in the ears of* [a]Jer. 36:21 [b]Jer. 36:2; Ezek. 2:6, 7

15 [a]Jer. 36:21

they turned in [a]fear one to another and said to Baruch, "We
will surely [b]report all these words to the king."
17 And they asked Baruch, saying, "Tell us please, [a]how
did you write all these words? [1]*Was it* at his dictation?"
18 Then Baruch said to them, "He [a]dictated all these
words to me, and I wrote them with ink on the book."
19 Then the officials said to Baruch, "Go, [a]hide yourself,
you and Jeremiah, and do not let anyone know where you
are."
20 So they went to the [a]king in the court, but they had
deposited the scroll in the chamber of [a]Elishama the scribe,
and they reported all the words to the king.
21 Then the king sent Jehudi to get the scroll, and he took
it out of the chamber of Elishama the scribe. And [a]Jehudi read
it [1]to the king as well as [1]to all the officials who stood beside
the king.
22 Now the king was sitting in the [a]winter house in the
ninth month, with *a fire* burning in the brazier before him.
23 And it came about, when Jehudi had read three or four
columns, *the king* cut it with a scribe's knife and [a]threw *it* into
the fire that was in the brazier, until all the scroll was consumed in the fire that was in the brazier.
24 Yet the king and all his servants who heard all these
words were [a]not afraid, nor did they [b]rend their garments.
25 Even though Elnathan and Delaiah and Gemariah [a]en-
treated the king not to burn the scroll, he would not listen to
them.
26 And the king commanded Jerahmeel the king's son,
Seraiah the son of Azriel, and Shelemiah the son of Abdeel to
[a]seize Baruch the scribe and Jeremiah the prophet, but the
LORD hid them.
27 Then the word of the LORD came to Jeremiah after the
king had burned the scroll and the words which Baruch had
written at the dictation of Jeremiah, saying,
28 "[a]Take again another scroll and write on it all the former words that were on the first scroll which Jehoiakim the
king of Judah burned.
29 "And concerning Jehoiakim king of Judah you shall say,
'Thus says the LORD: "You have [a]burned this scroll, saying,
'[b]Why have you written on it [1]that the [c]king of Babylon shall
certainly come and destroy this land, and shall make man and
beast to cease from it?' "
30 'Therefore thus says the LORD concerning Jehoiakim
king of Judah: "He shall have [a]no one to sit on the throne of
David, and his dead body shall be cast out to the heat of the
day and the frost of the night.
31 "I shall also punish him and his [1]descendants and his
servants for their iniquity, and I shall [a]bring on them and the
inhabitants of Jerusalem and the men of Judah all the calamity
that I have declared to them—but they did not listen." ' "
32 Then Jeremiah took another scroll and gave it to Baruch the son of Neraiah, the scribe, and he [a]wrote on it at the
dictation of Jeremiah all the words of the book which Jehoiakim king of Judah had burned in the fire; and many [1]similar
words were added to them.

16 [a]Jer. 36:24; Acts 24:25 [b]Jer. 13:18; Amos 7:10, 11

17 [1]Lit., *from his mouth,* and so throughout this context [a]John 9:10, 15, 26

18 [a]Jer. 36:4; 43:2, 3

19 [a]Jer. 36:26; 26:20-24; 1 Kin. 17:3; 18:4, 10

20 [a]Jer. 36:12

21 [a]2 Kin. 22:10; 2 Chr. 34:18; Ezek. 2:4, 5

22 [a]Amos 3:15

23 [a]Jer. 36:29; 1 Kin. 22:8, 27; Prov. 1:30; Is. 5:18, 19; 28:14, 22

24 [a]Jer. 36:16; Ps. 36:1; 64:5; Is. 26:11 [b]1 Kin. 21:27; 2 Kin. 19:1, 2; 22:11, 19; Is. 36:22; 37:1; Jon. 3:6

25 [a]Gen. 37:22, 26, 27; Acts 5:34-39

26 [a]1 Kin. 19:1-3, 10, 14

28 [a]Jer. 28:13, 14; 44:28; Zech. 1:5, 6

29 [1]Lit., *saying* . [a]Deut. 29:19; Job 15:24, 25; Is. 45:9 [b]Jer. 26:9; 32:3; Is. 29:21; 30:10 [c]Jer. 25:9-11

30 [a]Jer. 22:30; 2 Kin. 24:12-15

31 [1]Lit., *seed* [a]Jer. 19:15; 35:17; Deut. 28:15; Prov. 29:1

32 [1]Lit., *like those* [a]Jer. 36:4, 23; Ex. 4:15, 16; 34:1

CHAPTER 37

NOW [a]Zedekiah the son of Josiah whom Nebuchadnezzar
king of Babylon had [b]made king in the land of Judah, reigned
as king in place of [c]Coniah the son of Jehoiakim.
2 But [a]neither he nor his servants nor the people of the
land listened to the words of the LORD which He spoke
through Jeremiah the prophet.
3 Yet King Zedekiah sent Jehucal the son of Shelemiah,
and [a]Zephaniah the son of Maaseiah, the priest, to Jeremiah
the prophet, saying, "[b]Please pray to the LORD our God on our
behalf."
4 Now Jeremiah was *still* coming in and going out among
the people, for they had not *yet* put him in the prison.
5 Meanwhile, [a]Pharaoh's army had set out from Egypt;
and when the Chaldeans who had been besieging Jerusalem
heard the report about them, they lifted the *siege* from
Jerusalem.
6 Then the word of the LORD came to Jeremiah the prophet, saying,
7 "Thus says the LORD God of Israel, '[a]Thus you are to say
to the king of Judah, who sent you to Me to inquire of Me:
"Behold, [b]Pharaoh's army which has come out for your assistance is going to return to its own land of Egypt.
8 "The Chaldeans will also [a]return and fight against this
city, and they will capture it and burn it with fire." '
9 "Thus says the LORD, 'Do not [a]deceive yourselves,
saying, "The Chaldeans will surely go away from us," for they
will not go.
10 'For [a]even if you had defeated the entire army of Chaldeans who were fighting against you, and there were *only*
wounded men left among them, each man in his tent, they
would [b]rise up and burn this city with fire.' "
11 Now it happened, when the army of the Chaldeans had
lifted *the siege* from Jerusalem because of Pharaoh's army,
12 that Jeremiah went out from Jerusalem to go to the
land of Benjamin in order to take [1]possession of *some* [a]prop-
erty there among the people.
13 While he was at the [a]Gate of Benjamin, a captain of
the guard whose name was Irijah, the son of Shelemiah the son
of Hananiah was there; and he arrested Jeremiah the prophet,
saying, "You are [1b]going over to the Chaldeans!"
14 But Jeremiah said, "[a]A lie! I am not [1]going over to the
Chaldeans"; yet he would not listen to him. So Irijah arrested
Jeremiah and brought him to the officials.
15 Then the officials were [a]angry at Jeremiah and beat
him, and they [b]put him in jail in the house of Jonathan the
scribe, which they had made into the prison.
16 For Jeremiah had come into the [1]dungeon, that is, the
vaulted cell; and Jeremiah stayed there many days.
17 Now King Zedekiah sent and took him *out;* and in his
palace the king secretly [a]asked him and said, "Is there a [b]word
from the LORD?" And Jeremiah said, "There is!" Then he said,
"You will be [c]given into the hand of the king of Babylon!"
18 Moreover Jeremiah said to King Zedekiah, "[a]*In* what

1 [a]2 Kin. 24:17; 1 Chr. 3:15; 2 Chr. 36:10 [b]Ezek. 17:12-21 [c]Jer. 22:24, 28; 24:1; 52:31; 2 Kin. 24:12; 1 Chr. 3:16; 2 Chr. 36:9, 10

2 [a]2 Kin. 24:19, 20; 2 Chr. 36:12-16; Prov. 29:12

3 [a]Jer. 29:25; 52:24 [b]Jer. 2:27; 15:11; 21:1, 2; 42:1-4, 20; 1 Kin. 13:6; Acts 8:24

5 [a]Jer. 37:7; 2 Kin. 24:7; Ezek. 17:15

7 [a]Jer. 37:3; 21:1, 2; 2 Kin. 22:18 [b]Jer. 2:18, 36; Is. 30:1-3; 31:1-3; Lam. 4:17; Ezek. 17:17

8 [a]Jer. 34:22; 38:23; 39:2-8

9 [a]Jer. 29:8; Obad. 3; Matt. 24:4, 5; Eph. 5:6

10 [a]Lev. 26:36-38; Is. 30:17 [b]Joel 2:11

12 [1]Or, *part in a dividing* [a]Jer. 32:8; 1 Kin. 19:3, 9; Matt. 10:23; Acts 17:10, 14

13 [1]Lit., *falling* [a]Jer. 38:7; Zech. 14:10 [b]Jer. 18:18; 20:10; Amos 7:10; Luke 23:2; Acts 6:11; 24:5-9, 13

14 [1]Lit., *falling* [a]Jer. 40:4-6; Ps. 27:12; 52:1, 2; Matt. 5:11, 12

15 [a]Jer. 18:23; 20:1-3; 26:16; Matt. 21:35 [b]Gen. 39:20; 2 Chr. 16:10; 18:26; Acts 5:18

16 [1]Lit., *house of the cistern-pit*

17 [a]Jer. 38:5, 14-16, 24-27; 1 Kin. 14:1-4 [b]Jer. 37:3; 15:11; 21:1, 2; 1 Kin. 22:15, 16; 2 Kin. 3:11-13 [c]Jer. 21:7; 24:8; Ezek. 12:12, 13; 17:19-21

18 [a]1 Sam. 24:9; 26:18; Dan. 6:22; John 10:32; Acts 25:8, 11, 25

way have I sinned against you, or against your servants, or
against this people, that you have put me in prison?
19 “[a]Where then are your prophets who prophesied to you,
saying, ‘The king of Babylon will not come against you or
against this land?’
20 “But now, please listen, O my lord the king; please let
my [a]petition [1]come before you, and do not make me return to
the house of Jonathan the scribe, that I may not die there.”
21 Then King Zedekiah gave commandment, and they
committed Jeremiah to the court of the guardhouse and gave
him a loaf of [a]bread daily from the bakers’ street, until all the
bread in the city was [b]gone. So Jeremiah remained in the court
of the guardhouse.

Chapter 38

NOW Shaphatiah the son of Mattan, and Gedaliah the son
of Pashhur, and Jucal the son of Shelemiah, and Pashhur the
son of Malchijah heard the words that Jeremiah was speaking
to all the people, saying,
2 “Thus says the LORD, ‘He who stays in this city will die
by the sword and by famine and by pestilence, but he who goes
out to the Chaldeans will live and have his *own* [a]life as booty
and stay alive.’
3 “Thus says the LORD, ‘This city will certainly be [a]given
into the hand of the army of the king of Babylon, and he will
capture it.’ ”
4 Then the [a]officials said to the king, “Now let this man
be put to death, inasmuch as he is [1b]discouraging the men of
war who are left in this city and [2]all the people, by speaking
such words to them; for this man is not seeking the well-being
of this people, but rather their harm.”
5 So King Zedekiah said, “Behold, he is in your [1]hands;
for the king [a]can *do* nothing against you.”
6 Then they took Jeremiah and cast him into the [a]cistern
of Malchijah the king’s son, which was in the court of the
guardhouse; and they let Jeremiah down with ropes. Now in
the cistern there was no water but only [b]mud, and Jeremiah
sank into the mud.
7 But Ebed-melech the Ethiopian, a [1a]eunuch, while he
was in the king’s palace, heard that they had put Jeremiah into
the cistern. Now the king was sitting in the [b]Gate of Benjamin;
8 and Ebed-melech went out from the king’s palace and
spoke to the king, saying,
9 “My lord the king, these men have acted wickedly in all
that they have done to Jeremiah the prophet whom they have
cast into the cistern; and he [1]will die right where he is because
of the famine, for there is [a]no more bread in the city.
10 Then the king commanded Ebed-melech the Ethiopian,
saying, “Take thirty men from here [1]under your authority,
and bring up Jeremiah the prophet from the cistern before
he dies.”
11 So Ebed-melech took the men under his [1]authority and
went into the king’s palace to *a place* beneath the storeroom
and took from there worn-out clothes and worn-out rags and
let them down by ropes into the cistern to Jeremiah.

19 [a]Jer. 2:28; Deut. 32:37, 38; 2 Kin. 3:13

20 [1]Lit., *fall* [a]Jer. 36:7; 38:26

21 [a]Job 5:20; Ps. 33:18, 19; Is. 33:16 [b]Jer. 38:9; 52:6; 2 Kin. 25:3

2 [a]Jer. 21:9; 39:18; 45:5

3 [a]Jer. 21:10; 32:3-5

4 [1]Lit., *weakening the hands of* [2]Lit., *the hands of all* [a]Jer. 18:23; 26:11, 21; 36:12 [b]Ex. 5:4; 1 Kin. 18:17, 18; 21:20; Ezra 4:12; Neh. 6:9; Amos 7:10; Acts 16:20

5 [1]Lit., *hand* [a]1 Sam. 15:24; 29:9; 2 Sam. 3:39

6 [a]Jer. 37:16, 21; Acts 16:24 [b]Jer. 38:22; Ps. 40:2; 69:2, 14, 15; Zech. 9:11

7 [1]Or, *official* [a]Jer. 29:2; Acts 8:27 [b]Jer. 37:13; Deut. 21:19; Job 29:7; Amos 5:10

9 [1]M.T. reads: *has died* [a]Jer. 37:21; 52:6

10 [1]Lit., *in your hand*

11 [1]Lit., *hand*

12 Then Ebed-melech the Ethiopian said to Jeremiah,
"Now put these worn-out clothes and rags under your armpits
under the ropes"; and Jeremiah did so.
13 So they pulled Jeremiah up with the ropes and lifted
him out of the cistern, and Jeremiah stayed in the [a]court of the
guardhouse.
14 Then King Zedekiah [a]sent and [1]had Jeremiah the prophet brought to him at the third entrance that is in the house of
the LORD; and the king said to Jeremiah, "I am going to [b]ask
you something; do not hide anything from me."
15 Then Jeremiah said to Zedekiah, "[a]If I tell you, will
you not certainly put me to death? Besides, if I give you advice, you will not listen to me."
16 But King Zedekiah swore to Jeremiah in [a]secret, saying
"As the LORD lives, who made this [1b]life for us, surely I will not
put you to death nor will I give you over to the hand of [c]these
men who are seeking your [1]life."
17 Then Jeremiah said to Zedekiah, "Thus says the LORD
[a]God of hosts, the [b]God of Israel, 'If you will indeed [c]go out to
the officers of the king of Babylon, then [1]you will live, this city
will not be burned with fire, and you and your household will
[2]survive.
18 'But if you will [a]not go out to the officers of the king of
Babylon, then this city [b]will be given over to the hand of the
Chaldeans; and they will burn it with fire, and [c]you yourself
will not escape from their hand.' "
19 Then King Zedekiah said to Jeremiah, "I [a]dread the
Jews who have [1b]gone over to the Chaldeans, lest they give me
over into their hand and they [c]abuse me."
20 But Jeremiah said, "They will not give you over. Please
[1a]obey the LORD in what I am saying to you, that it may go
[b]well with you and [2c]you may live.
21 "But if you keep refusing to go out, this is the word
which the LORD has shown me:
22 'Then behold, all of the [a]women who have been left in
the palace of the king of Judah are going to be brought out to
the [1]officers of the king of Babylon; and those women will say,

> "[2]Your close friends
> Have misled and overpowered you;
> While your feet were sunk in the mire,
> They turned back."

23 'They will also bring out all your wives and your [a]sons to
the Chaldeans, and [b]you yourself will not escape from their
hand, but will be seized by the hand of the king of Babylon,
and [b]this city will be burned with fire.' "
24 Then Zedekiah said to Jeremiah, "Let no man know
about these words and you will not die.
25 "But if the [a]officials hear that I have talked with you and
come to you and say to you, 'Tell us now what you said to the
king, and what the king said to you; do not hide *it* from us, and
we will not put you to death;'
26 then you are to say to them, 'I was [a]presenting my
petition before the king, not to make me return to the house
of Jonathan to die there.' "
27 Then all the officials came to Jeremiah and questioned
him. So he [a]reported to them in accordance with all these

13 [a]Jer. 38:6; 37:21; 39:14, 15; Acts 23:35; 24:27; 28:16, 30

14 [1]Lit., *took Jeremiah to him*
[a]Jer. 21:1, 2; 37:17 [b]Jer. 15:11; 42:2-5, 20; 1 Sam. 3:17, 18; 1 Kin. 22:16

15 [a]Luke 22:67, 68

16 [1]Lit., *soul*
[a]Jer. 37:17; John 3:2 [b]Num. 16:22; 27:16; Is. 57:16; Zech. 12:1 [c]Jer. 38:4-6; 34:20

17 [1]Lit., *your soul* [2]Lit., *live*
[a]Ps. 80:7, 14; Amos 5:27 [b]1 Chr. 17:24; Ezek. 8:4 [c]Jer. 38:2; 21:8-10; 27:12, 17; 2 Kin. 24:12; 25:27-30

18 [a]Jer. 27:8 [b]Jer. 38:3; 24:8-10; 32:3-5; 37:8; 2 Kin. 25:4-10 [c]Jer. 32:4; 34:3

19 [1]Lit., *fallen*
[a]Is. 51:12, 13; 57:11; John 12:42; 19:12, 13 [b]Jer. 39:9 [c]Jer. 38:22; 2 Chr. 30:10; Neh. 4:1

20 [1]Lit., *listen to the voice of* [2]Lit., *your soul*
[a]Jer. 11:4, 8; 26:13; 2 Chr. 20:20; Dan. 4:27; Acts 26:29 [b]Jer. 7:23 [c]Gen. 19:20; Is. 55:3

22 [1]Or, *princes* [2]Lit., *the men of your peace*
[a]Jer. 6:12; 8:10; 43:6

23 [a]Jer. 39:6; 41:10; 2 Kin. 25:7 [b]Jer. 38:18

25 [a]Jer. 38:4-6, 27

26 [a]Jer. 37:15, 20

27 [a]1 Sam. 10:15, 16; 16:2-5

words which the king had commanded; and they ceased speaking with him, since the [1]conversation had not been overheard.

28 So Jeremiah [a]stayed in the court of the guardhouse until the day that Jerusalem was captured.

Chapter 39

1 NOW it came about when Jerusalem was captured [2a]in the ninth year of Zedekiah king of Judah, in the tenth month, Nebuchadnezzar king of Babylon and all his army came to Jerusalem and laid siege to it;

2 in the eleventh year of Zedekiah, in the fourth month, in the ninth *day* of the month, the city *wall* was [a]breached,

3 then all the officials of the king of Babylon came in and sat down at the [a]Middle Gate: Nergal-sar-ezer, Samgar-nebu, Sar-sekim, the [1]Rab-saris, Nergal-sar-ezer *the* [2]Rab-mag, and all the rest of the officials of the king of Babylon.

4 And it came about, when Zedekiah the king of Judah and all the men of war saw them, that they [a]fled and went out of the city at night by way of the king's garden through the gate [b]between the two walls; and he went out toward the [1]Arabah.

5 But the army of the [a]Chaldeans pursued after them and overtook Zedekiah in the [b]plains of Jericho; and they seized him and brought him up to Nebuchadnezzar king of Babylon at [c]Riblah in the land of Hamath, and he passed sentence on him.

6 Then the [a]king of Babylon slew the sons of Zedekiah [b]before his eyes at Riblah; the king of Babylon also slew all the [c]nobles of Judah.

7 He then [a]blinded Zedekiah's eyes and bound him in [b]fetters of bronze to bring him to Babylon.

8 The Chaldeans also [a]burned with fire the king's palace and the houses of the people, and they [b]broke down the walls of Jerusalem.

9 And as for the rest of the people who were left in the city, the [1a]deserters who had gone over to him, and the rest of the people who remained [b]Nebuzaradan the [c]captain of the bodyguard carried *them* into exile in Babylon.

10 But some of the [a]poorest people who had nothing, [a]Nebuzaradan the captain of the bodyguard left behind in the land of Judah, and gave them vineyards and fields [1]at that time.

11 Now Nebuchadnezzar king of Babylon gave orders about [a]Jeremiah through Nebuzaradan the captain of the bodyguard, saying,

12 "Take him and [1]look after him, and [a]do nothing harmful to him; but rather deal with him just as he tells you."

13 So Nebuzaradan the captain of the bodyguard sent *word,* along with Nebushazban the [1]Rab-saris, and Nergal-sar-ezer the [2]Rab-mag, and all the leading officers of the king of Babylon;

14 they even sent and [a]took Jeremiah out of the court of the guardhouse and entrusted him to Gedaliah, the son of [b]Ahikam, the son of Shaphan, to take him home. So he stayed among the people.

---

27 [1]Lit., *word*

28 [a]Jer. 38:13; 15:20, 21; 37:20, 21; 39:13, 14; Ps. 23:4

1 [1]38:28-b in Heb. [2]39:1 in Heb.
[a]Jer. 52:4; 2 Kin. 25:1-12; Ezek. 24:1, 2

2 [a]Jer. 52:7; 2 Kin. 25:4

3 [1]I.e., chief official [2]title of a high official
[a]Jer. 21:4

4 [1]I.e., Jordan valley
[a]Jer. 52:7; 2 Kin. 25:4; Is. 30:15, 16; Amos 2:14 [b]2 Chr. 32:5

5 [a]Jer. 32:4, 5; 38:18, 23; 52:8; Lam. 4:20 [b]Josh. 4:13; 5:10 [c]Jer. 52:9, 26, 27

6 [a]Jer. 52:10; 2 Kin. 25:7 [b]Deut. 28:34 [c]Jer. 21:7; 24:8-10; 34:19-21

7 [a]Jer. 52:11; 2 Kin. 25:7; Ezek. 12:13 [b]Judg. 16:21

8 [a]Jer. 21:10; 52:13 [b]Jer. 52:14; 2 Kin. 25:10; Neh. 1:3

9 [1]Lit., *fallers who had fallen*
[a]Jer. 38:19; 52:15 [b]Jer. 39:13; 40:1; 52:12-16, 26; 2 Kin. 25:11, 20 [c]Gen. 37:36

10 [1]Lit., *on that day*
[a]Jer. 52:16; 2 Kin. 25:12

11 [a]Jer. 1:8; 15:20, 21; Job 5:15, 16; Acts 24:23

12 [1]Lit., *set your eyes on*
[a]Ps. 105:14, 15; Prov. 16:7; 21:1; 1 Pet. 3:13

13 [1]I.e., chief official (Akkad) [2]title of a high officer

14 [a]Jer. 38:28; 40:1-6 [b]Jer. 26:24; 2 Kin. 22:12, 14; 2 Chr. 34:20

15 Now the word of the LORD had come to Jeremiah while
he was confined in the court of the guardhouse, saying,
16 "Go and speak to Ebed-melech the Ethiopian, saying,
'Thus says the LORD of hosts, the God of Israel, "Behold, I am
about to bring My words on this city [a]for disaster and not for
[1]prosperity; and they will take place [b]before you on that day.
17 "But I will [a]deliver you on that day," declares the LORD,
"and you shall not be given into the hand of the men whom
you dread.
18 "For I will certainly rescue you, and you will not fall by
the sword; but you will have your *own* [a]life as booty, because
you have [b]trusted in Me," ' " declares the LORD.

CHAPTER 40

THE word which came to Jeremiah from the LORD after
Nebuzaradan captain of the bodyguard had released him from
[a]Ramah, when he had taken him bound in [b]chains, among all
the exiles of Jerusalem and Judah, who were being exiled to
Babylon.
2 Now the captain of the bodyguard had taken Jeremiah
and said to him, "The [a]LORD your God promised this calamity
against this place;
3 and the LORD has brought *it* on and done just as He
promised. Because you *people* [a]sinned against the LORD and
did not listen to His voice, therefore this thing has happened
to you.
4 "But now, behold, I am [a]freeing you today from the
chains which are on your hands. If [1]you would prefer to come
with me to Babylon, come *along,* and I will [2]look after you;
but if [3]you would prefer not to come with me to Babylon,
[4]never mind. Look, the [b]whole land is before you; go wherever
it seems good and right for you to go."
5 As [1]Jeremiah was still not going back, [2]*he said,* "Go on
back then to Gedaliah the son of Ahikam, the son of Shaphan,
whom the king of Babylon has [a]appointed over the cities of
Judah, and stay with him among the people; or else go anywhere
it seems right for you to go." So the captain of the bodyguard gave him a [b]ration and a [c]gift and let him go.
6 Then Jeremiah went to [a]Mizpah to Gedaliah the son of
Ahikam and stayed with him among the people who were left
in the land.
7 [a]Now all the [1]commanders of the forces that were in
the field, they and their men, heard that the king of Babylon
had appointed Gedaliah the son of Ahikam over the land and
that he had put him in charge of the men, women and [2]chil-
dren, those of the [b]poorest of the land who had not been
exiled to Babylon.
8 So they came to Gedaliah at Mizpah, along with [a]Ish-
mael the son of Nethaniah, and [b]Johanan and Jonathan the
sons of Kareah, and Seraiah the son of Tanhumeth, and the
sons of Ephai the [c]Netophathite, and Jezaniah the son of the
[d]Maacathite, *both* they and their men.
9 Then Gedaliah the son of Ahikam, the son of Shaphan,
[a]swore to them and to their men, saying, "Do not be [b]afraid of

16 [1]Lit., *good* [a]Jer. 21:10; Dan. 9:12; Zech. 1:6 [b]Ps. 91:8, 9

17 [a]Ps. 41:1, 2; 50:15

18 [a]Jer. 21:9; 38:2; 45:5 [b]Jer. 17:7, 8; Ps. 34:22

1 [a]Jer. 31:15 [b]Acts. 12:6, 7; 21:13; 28:20; Eph. 6:20

2 [a]Jer. 22:8, 9; Deut. 29:24-28

3 [a]Jer. 50:7; Rom. 2:5

4 [1]Lit., *it is good in your eyes* [2]Lit., *set my eyes on* [3]Lit., *it is evil in your eyes* [4]Lit., *refrain!* [a]Jer. 39:11, 12 [b]Gen. 13:9; 20:15; 47:6

5 [1]Lit., *he* [2]I.e., Nebuzaradan [a]2 Kin. 25:23 [b]Jer. 52:34 [c]2 Kin. 8:7-9

6 [a]Judg. 20:1; 21:1; 1 Sam. 7:5; 2 Chr. 16:6

7 [1]Or, *princes* [2]Lit., *infants* [a]2 Kin. 25:23, 24 [b]Jer. 39:10; 52:16

8 [a]Jer. 40:14; 41:2 [b]Jer. 40:13, 15; 42:1; 43:2 [c]2 Sam. 23:28, 29; Ezra 2:22; Neh. 7:26 [d]Deut. 3:14; Josh. 12:5; 2 Sam. 10:6, 8

9 [a]1 Sam. 20:16, 17; 2 Kin. 25:24 [b]Jer. 27:11; 38:17-20

serving the Chaldeans; stay in the land and serve the king of
Babylon, that it may go well with you.
10 "Now as for me, behold, I am going to stay at Mizpah to
[a]stand *for you* before the Chaldeans who come to us; but as for
you, [b]gather in wine and [c]summer fruit and oil, and put *them*
in your *storage* vessels, and live in your cities that you have
taken over."
11 Likewise also all the Jews who were in [a]Moab and
among the sons of [b]Ammon and in [c]Edom, and who were in all
the *other* countries, heard that the king of Babylon had left a
remnant for Judah and that he had appointed over them Gedaliah the son of Ahikam, the son of Shaphan.
12 Then all the Jews returned from all the places to which
they had been driven away and came to the land of Judah, to
Gedaliah at Mizpah, and gathered in wine and summer fruit in
great abundance.
13 Now Johanan the son of Kareah and all the commanders of the forces that were in the field came to Gedaliah at
Mizpah,
14 and said to him, "Are you well aware that Baalis the
king of the sons of [a]Ammon has sent Ishmael the son of Nethaniah to take your life?" But Gedaliah the son of Ahikam did
not believe them.
15 Then Johanan the son of Kareah spoke secretly to Gedaliah in Mizpah, saying, "[a]Let me go and kill Ishmael the son
of Nethaniah, and not a man will know! Why should he [b]take
your life, so that all the Jews who are gathered to you should
be scattered and the [c]remnant of Judah perish?"
16 But Gedaliah the son of Ahikam said to Johanan the
son of Kareah, "[a]Do not do this thing, for you are telling a lie
about Ishmael."

CHAPTER 41

NOW it [a]came about in the seventh month that [b]Ishmael
the son of Nethaniah, the son of Elishama, of the royal [1]family
and *one* of the chief officers of the king, along with ten men,
came to Mizpah to [c]Gedaliah the son of Ahikam. While they
[d]were eating bread together there in Mizpah,
2 Ishmael the son of Nethaniah and the ten men who
were with him arose and [a]struck down Gedaliah the son of
Ahikam, the son of Shaphan, with the sword and put to [b]death
the one [c]whom the king of Babylon had appointed over the
land.
3 Ishmael also struck down all the Jews who were with
him, *that is* with Gedaliah at Mizpah, and the Chaldeans who
were found there, the men of war.
4 Now it happened on the [1]next day after the killing of
Gedaliah, when no one knew about *it*,
5 that eighty men [a]came from [b]Shechem, from [c]Shiloh,
and from [d]Samaria with their beards shaved off and their
clothes torn and [1]their bodies [e]gashed, having grain offerings
and incense in their hands to bring to the [f]house of the LORD.
6 Then Ishmael the son of Nethaniah went out from
Mizpah to meet them, [a]weeping as he went; and it came about

10 [a]Jer. 35:19; Deut. 1:38; 1 Kin. 10:8 [b]Jer. 39:10 [c]Jer. 40:12; 48:32; Is. 16:9

11 [a]Jer. 9:26; Num. 22:1; 25:1, 2; Is. 16:4 [b]1 Sam. 11:1; 12:12 [c]Gen. 36:8; Is. 11:14

14 [a]Jer. 25:21; 41:10; 1 Sam. 11:1-3; 2 Sam. 10:1-6

15 [a]1 Sam. 26:8 [b]2 Sam. 21:17 [c]Jer. 42:2

16 [a]Matt. 10:16

1 [1]Lit., *seed*
[a]2 Kin. 25:25 [b]Jer. 40:8, 14 [c]Jer. 39:14; 40:5, 6 [d]Jer. 40:13, 14

2 [a]2 Sam. 3:27; 20:9, 10; Ps. 41:9; 109:5; John 13:18 [b]2 Kin. 25:25 [c]Jer. 40:5

4 [1]Or, *second*

5 [1]Lit., *having cut themselves*
[a]2 Kin. 10:13, 14 [b]Gen. 33:18; 37:12; 1 Kin. 12:1 [c]Josh. 18:1; Judg. 18:31; 1 Sam. 3:21; Ps. 78:60 [d]1 Kin. 16:24, 29 [e]Jer. 16:6; Deut. 14:1 [f]2 Kin. 25:9; Ps. 102:14

6 [a]Jer. 50:4; 2 Sam. 3:16

as he met them that he said to them, "Come to Gedaliah the
son of Ahikam!"
7 Yet it turned out that as soon as they came inside the
city Ishmael the son of Nethania and the men that were with
him [a]slaughtered them, *and cast them* into the cistern.
8 But ten men who were found among them said to Ishmael,
"Do not put us to death; for we have [a]stores of wheat,
barley, oil and honey hidden in the field." So he refrained and
did not put them to death along with their companions.
9 Now as for the cistern where Ishmael had cast all the
corpses of the men whom he had struck down [1]because of
Gedaliah, it was the [a]one that King Asa had made on [b]account
of Baasha, king of Israel; Ishmael the son of Nethaniah filled it
with the slain.
10 Then Ishmael took captive all the remnant of the
people who were in Mizpah, the [a]king's daughters and all the
people who were left in Mizpah, whom Nebuzaradan the captain
of the bodyguard had put under the charge of Gedaliah
the son of Ahikam; thus Ishmael the son of Nethaniah took
them captive and proceeded to cross over to the sons of
[b]Ammon.
11 But Johanan the son of Kareah and all the [a]commanders
of the forces that were with him heard of all the evil that
Ishmael the son of Nethaniah had done.
12 So they took all the men and went to [a]fight with Ishmael
the son of Nethaniah and they found him by the [b]great
[1]pool that is in Gibeon.
13 Now it came about, as soon as all the people who were
with Ishmael saw Johanan the son of Kareah and the commanders
of the forces that were with him, they were glad.
14 So all the people whom Ishmael had taken captive
from Mizpah turned around and came back, and went to Johanan
the son of Kareah.
15 But Ishmael the son of Nethaniah [a]escaped from Johanan
with eight men and went to the sons of Ammon.
16 Then Johanan the son of Kareah and all the commanders
of the forces that were with him took from Mizpah [a]all
the remnant of the people whom he had [1]recovered from
Ishmael the son of Nethaniah, after he had struck down Gedaliah
the son of Ahikam, *that is,* the men who were [2]soldiers,
the women, *the* [3]children, and *the* eunuchs, whom he had
brought back from Gibeon.
17 And they went and stayed in [1a]Geruth-Chimham,
which is beside Bethlehem, in order to proceed into Egypt
18 because of the Chaldeans; for they were [a]afraid of
them, since Ishmael the son of Nethaniah had struck down
Gedaliah the son of Ahikam, whom the king of Babylon had
appointed over the land.

CHAPTER 42

THEN all the [1]commanders of the forces, Johanan the son
of Kareah, Jezaniah the son of Hoshaiah, and all the people
[a]both small and great approached
2 and said to Jeremiah the prophet, "Please let our [a]petition
[1]come before you, and [b]pray for us to the LORD your God,

7 [a]Ps. 55:23; Is. 59:7; Ezek. 22:27; 33:24, 26

8 [a]Is. 45:3

9 [1]Or, *by the side of* [a]1 Kin. 15:17-22; 2 Chr. 16:1-6 [b]Judg. 6:2; 1 Sam. 13:6; 2 Sam. 17:9; Heb. 11:38

10 [a]Jer. 43:6 [b]Jer. 40:14; Neh. 2:10, 19; 4:7, 8; 6:17, 18

11 [a]Jer. 40:7, 8, 14-16

12 [1]Lit., *waters* [a]Gen. 14:14-16; 1 Sam. 30:1-8, 18, 20 [b]2 Sam. 2:13

15 [a]1 Sam. 30:17; 1 Kin. 20:20; Job 21:30; Prov. 28:17

16 [1]Lit., *brought back* [2]Lit., *men of war* [3]Lit., *infants* [a]Jer. 42:8; 43:4-7

17 [1]Or., *the lodging place of Chimham* [a]2 Sam. 19:37, 38, 40

18 [a]Jer. 42:11, 16; 43:2, 3; Is. 51:12, 13; 57:11; Luke 12:4, 5

1 [1]Or, *princes* [a]Jer. 42:8; 6:13; 8:10; 44:12; Acts 8:10

2 [1]Lit., *fall* [a]Jer. 36:7; 37:20 [b]Jer. 42:20; 37:3; Ex. 8:28; 1 Kin. 13:6; Acts 8:24

that is for all this remnant; because we are left *but* a [c]few out
of many, as your own eyes *now* see us,
3 that the LORD your God may tell us the [a]way in which
we should walk and the thing that we should do."
4 Then Jeremiah the prophet said to them, "I have heard
you. Behold, I am going to [a]pray to the LORD your God in
accordance with your words; and it will come about that the
whole [1]message which the [b]LORD will answer you I will tell you.
I will [c]not keep back a word from you."
5 Then they said to Jeremiah, "May the [a]LORD be a true
and faithful witness against us, if we do not act in accordance
with the whole [1]message with which the LORD your God will
send you to us.
6 "Whether *it* is [1]pleasant or [2]unpleasant, we will [a]listen to
the voice of the LORD our God to whom we are sending you, in
order that it may go [b]well with us when we listen to the voice
of the LORD our God."
7 Now it came about at the [a]end of ten days that the
word of the LORD came to Jeremiah.
8 Then he called for Johanan the son of Kareah, and all
the [1]commanders of the forces that were with him, and for all
the people both small and great,
9 and said to them, "Thus [a]says the LORD the God of
Israel, to whom you sent me to present your petition before
Him:
10 'If you will indeed stay in this land, then I will [a]build
you up and not tear you down, and I will plant you and not
uproot you; for I [1]shall [b]relent concerning the calamity that I
have inflicted on you.
11 '[a]Do not be afraid of the king of Babylon, whom you
are *now* fearing; do not be afraid of him,' declares the LORD,
'for [b]I am with you to save you and deliver you from his hand.
12 'I will also show you compassion, so that [a]he will have
compassion on you and restore you to your own soil.
13 'But if you are going to say, "We will [a]not stay in this
land," so as not to listen to the voice of the LORD your God,
14 saying, "No, but we will [a]go to the land of Egypt, where
we shall not see war or [b]hear the sound of a trumpet or hunger
for bread, and we will stay there";
15 then [1]in that case listen to the word of the LORD, O
remnant of Judah: Thus says the LORD of hosts, the God of
Israel, 'If you really set your [2]mind to enter [a]Egypt, and go in
to reside there,
16 then it will come about that the [a]sword, which you are
afraid of will overtake you there in the land of Egypt; and the
famine, about which you are anxious, will follow closely after
you there *in* Egypt; and you will die there.
17 'So all the men who set their [1]mind to go to Egypt to
reside there will die by the [a]sword, by famine, and by pestilence; and they will have no survivors or refugees from the
calamity that I am going to bring on them.' "
18 For thus says the LORD of hosts, the God of Israel, "As
My [a]anger and wrath have been poured out on the inhabitants
of Jerusalem, so My wrath will be poured out on you when you
enter Egypt; and you will become a [b]curse, an object of horror,

2 [c]Deut. 28:62; Is. 1:9; Lam. 1:1

3 [a]Jer. 6:16; Ps. 86:11; Prov. 3:6; Mic. 4:2

4 [1]Lit., *word* [a]Ex. 8:29; 1 Sam. 12:23 [b]Jer. 23:28; 1 Kin. 22:14 [c]1 Sam. 3:17, 18; Ps. 40:10

5 [1]Lit., *word* [a]Jer. 43:2; Gen. 31:50; Judg. 11:10; Mic. 1:2; Mal. 2:14; 3:5

6 [1]Lit., *good* [2]Lit., *evil* [a]Ex. 24:7; Deut. 5:27; Josh. 24:24 [b]Jer. 7:23; Deut. 5:29, 33

7 [a]Ps. 27:14; Is. 30:18

8 [1]Or, *princes*

9 [a]2 Kin. 19:4, 6, 20; 22:15

10 [1]Or, *shall have changed my mind about* [a]Jer. 24:6; 31:28; Ezek. 36:36 [b]Jer. 18:7, 8; Hos. 11:8; Joel 2:13; Amos 7:3, 6; Jon. 3:10; 4:2

11 [a]Jer. 1:8; 27:12, 17; 41:18 [b]Jer. 1:19; 15:20; 2 Chr. 32:7, 8; Ps. 46:7, 11; Is. 8:9, 10; 43:2, 5; Rom. 8:31

12 [a]Neh. 1:11; Ps. 106:46; Prov. 16:7

13 [a]Jer. 44:16; Ex. 5:2

14 [a]Jer. 41:17; Is. 31:1 [b]Jer. 4:19, 21; Ex. 16:3; Num. 11:4

15 [1]Lit., *now therefore* [2]Lit., *face* [a]Jer. 42:17; 44:12-14; Deut. 17:16

16 [a]Jer. 44:13, 27; Ezek. 11:8; Amos 9:1-4

17 [1]Lit., *face* [a]Jer. 42:22; 38:2; 44:13

18 [a]Jer. 7:20; 33:5; 39:1-9; 2 Chr. 36:16-19 [b]Jer. 29:18; Deut. 29:21; Is. 65:15

an imprecation, and a reproach; and you will see this place no
more."
19 The LORD has spoken to you, O remnant of Judah,
"Do not [a]go into Egypt!" You should clearly [b]understand that
today I have [c]testified against you.
20 For you have *only* [1a]deceived yourselves; for it is you
who sent me to the LORD your God, saying, "Pray for us to the
LORD our God; and whatever the LORD our God says, tell us so,
and we will do it."
21 So, I have [a]told you today, but you have not [1]obeyed
the LORD your God, even in whatever He has sent me to *tell*
you.
22 Therefore you should now clearly understand that you
will die by the sword, by famine, and by pestilence, in the
[a]place where you wish to go to reside.

CHAPTER 43

BUT it came about, as soon as Jeremiah whom the LORD
their God had sent, had [a]finished telling all the people all the
words of the LORD their God—that is, all these words—
2 that Azariah the son of Hoshaiah, and Johanan the son
of Kareah, and all the arrogant men said to Jeremiah, "You are
[a]telling a lie! The LORD our God has not sent you to say, 'You
are not to enter Egypt to reside there';
3 but [a]Baruch the son of Neriah is inciting you against us
to give us over into the hand of the Chaldeans, so they may
put us to death or exile us to Babylon."
4 So [a]Johanan the son of Kareah and all the [1]command-
ers of the forces, and all the people, did not [b]obey the voice
of the LORD, so as to [c]stay in the land of Judah.
5 But Johanan the son of Kareah and all the [1]command-
ers of the forces took the [a]entire remnant of Judah who had
returned from all the nations to which they had been driven
away, in order to reside in the land of Judah—
6 the men, the women, the [1]children, the king's daughters and [a]every person that Nebuzaradan the captain of the
bodyguard had left with Gedaliah the son of Ahikam [2]and
grandson of Shaphan, together with [b]Jeremiah the prophet
and Baruch the son of Neriah—
7 and they entered the land of Egypt (for they did not
obey the voice of the LORD) and went in as far as Tahpanhes.
8 Then the word of the LORD came to [a]Jeremiah in [b]Tah-
panhes, saying,
9 "Take *some* large stones in your [1]hands and hide them
in the mortar in the [2]brick *terrace* which is at the entrance of
Pharaoh's [3]palace in Tahpanhes, in the sight of [4]some *of the*
Jews;
10 and say to them, 'Thus says the LORD of hosts, the God
of Israel: "Behold, I am going to send and get Nebuchadnezzar the king of Babylon, [a]My servant, and I am going to set his
throne *right* over these stones that I have hidden; and he will
spread his [b]canopy over them.
11 "He will also come and strike the land of Egypt: those
who are *meant* for death *will be given over* to death, and those
for captivity to captivity, and those for the sword to the sword.

19 [a]Is. 30:1-7 [b]Ezek. 2:5 [c]Neh. 9:26, 29, 30

20 [1]Or, *acted errantly in your souls* [a]Jer. 41:17; 43:2; Ezek. 14:3

21 [1]Lit., *listened to the voice of* [a]Jer. 43:1; Deut. 11:26; Ezek. 2:7; Acts 20:26, 27

22 [a]Hos. 9:6

1 [a]Jer. 26:8; 51:63

2 [a]Jer. 5:12, 13; 42:5; 2 Chr. 36:13; Is. 7:9

3 [a]Jer. 43:6; 36:4, 10, 26, 32; 45:1-3

4 [1]Or, *princes* [a]Jer. 42:6 [b]Jer. 42:5, 6; 44:5; 2 Chr. 25:16 [c]Jer. 42:10-12; Ps. 37:3

5 [1]Or, *princes* [a]Jer. 40:11

6 [1]Lit., *infants* [2]Lit., *the son* [a]Jer. 39:10; 40:7 [b]Eccles. 9:1, 2; Lam. 3:1

8 [a]Ps. 139:7; 2 Tim. 2:9 [b]Jer. 2:16; 44:1; 46:14; Ezek. 30:18

9 [1]Lit., *hand* [2]Or, *brickwork* [3]Lit., *house* [4]Lit., *men*

10 [a]Jer. 25:9; 27:6; Is. 44:28; 45:1 [b]Ps. 18:11; 27:5; 31:20

12 "And [1]I shall set fire to the temples of the [a]gods of
Egypt, and he will burn them and take them captive. So he will
[b]wrap himself with the land of Egypt as a shepherd wraps
himself with his garment, and he will depart from there safely.
13 "He will also shatter the [1]obelisks of [2]Heliopolis, which
is in the land of Egypt; and the temples of the gods of Egypt
he will burn with fire." ' "

CHAPTER 44

THE word that came to Jeremiah for all the Jews living in
the land of Egypt, those who were living in Migdol, Tahpanhes, Memphis, and the land of Pathros, saying,
2 "Thus says the LORD of hosts, the God of Israel: 'You
yourselves have seen all the calamity that I have brought on
Jerusalem and all the cities of Judah; and behold, this day they
are in [a]ruins and no one lives in them,
3 [a]because of their wickedness which they committed so
as to [b]provoke Me to anger by continuing to burn [1]sacrifices
and to [c]serve other gods whom they had not known, *neither*
they, you, nor your fathers.
4 'Yet I [a]sent you all My servants the prophets, [1]again and
again, saying, "Oh, do not do this [b]abominable thing which I
hate."
5 'But they did not listen or incline their ears to turn from
their wickedness, so as not to burn [1]sacrifices to other gods.
6 'Therefore My [a]wrath and My anger were poured out
and burned in the [b]cities of Judah and in the streets of Jerusalem, so they have become a ruin and a desolation as it is this
day.
7 'Now then thus says the LORD God of hosts, the God of
Israel: "Why are you [a]doing great harm to yourselves, so as to
[b]cut off from you man and woman, child and infant, from
among Judah, leaving yourselves without remnant,
8 [a]provoking Me to anger with the works of your hands,
[b]burning [1]sacrifices to other gods in the land of Egypt, where
you are entering to reside, so that you might be cut off and
become a [c]curse and a reproach among all the nations of the
earth?
9 "Have you forgotten the [a]wickedness of your fathers,
the wickedness of the kings of Judah, and the wickedness of
their wives, your own wickedness, and the wickedness of your
wives, which they committed in the land of Judah and in the
streets of Jerusalem?
10 "But they have not become [1a]contrite even to this day,
nor have they feared nor [b]walked in My law or My statutes,
which I have set before you and before your fathers." '
11 "Therefore thus says the LORD of hosts, the God of
Israel: 'Behold, I am going to [a]set My face against you for
[1]woe, even to cut off all Judah.
12 'And I will [a]take away the remnant of Judah who have
set their [1]mind on entering the land of Egypt to reside there,
and they will all [2b]meet their end in the land of Egypt; they
will fall by the sword *and* meet their end by famine. Both
small and great will die by the sword and famine; and they will

12 [1]Some ancient versions read, *he will set* [a]Jer. 46:25; Ex. 12:12; Is. 19:1; Ezek. 30:13 [b]Ps. 104:2; 109:18, 19; Is. 49:18

13 [1]Or, *stone pillars* [2]Heb., *Beth-shemesh;* i.e., the House of the Sun-god

2 [a]Jer. 4:7; 9:11; 34:22; Is. 6:11; Mic. 3:12

3 [1]Or, *incense* [a]Jer. 44:23; 2:17-19; Neh. 9:33; Ezek. 8:17, 18; Dan. 9:5 [b]Jer. 44:8; 7:19; 32:30-32; Is. 3:8 [c]Deut. 13:6; 29:26; 32:17

4 [1]Lit., *rising early and sending* [a]Jer. 7:13, 25; 25:4; 26:5; 35:15; Zech. 7:7 [b]Jer. 16:18; 32:34, 35; Ezek. 8:10

5 [1]Or, *incense*

6 [a]Jer. 42:18; Is. 51:17-20; Ezek. 8:18 [b]Jer. 7:17, 34

7 [a]Jer. 26:19; Ezek. 33:11; Hab. 2:10 [b]Jer. 3:24; 9:21; 51:22

8 [1]Or, *incense* [a]Jer. 44:3; 2 Kin. 17:15-17; 1 Cor. 10:21, 22 [b]Jer. 44:3; 7:9; 11:12, 17; Hos. 4:13; Hab. 1:16 [c]Jer. 42:18; 1 Kin. 9:7, 8; 2 Chr. 7:20

9 [a]Jer. 44:17, 21; 7:9, 10, 17, 18

10 [1]Lit., *crushed* [a]Jer. 6:15; 8:12 [b]Jer. 44:23; 26:4; 32:23

11 [1]Lit., *evil* [a]Jer. 21:10; Lev. 26:17; Amos 9:4

12 [1]Lit., *face* [2]Lit., *be finished* [a]Jer. 42:15-18, 22 [b]Jer. 44:7; 16:4; Is. 1:28

become a [c]curse, an object of horror, an imprecation and a
reproach.
13 'And I will [a]punish those who live in the land of Egypt,
as I have punished Jerusalem, with the sword, with famine, and
with pestilence.
14 'So there will be [a]no refugees or survivors for the remnant of Judah who have entered the land of Egypt to reside
there and then to return to the land of Judah, to which they
are [1b]longing to return and live; for none will [c]return except *a*
few refugees.' "
15 Then [a]all the men who were aware that their wives were
burning [1]sacrifices to other gods, along with all the women
who were standing by, *as* a large assembly, [2]including all the
people who were living in Pathros in the land of Egypt, responded to Jeremiah, saying,
16 "As for the [1]message that you have spoken to us in the
name of the LORD, we are not going to listen to you!
17 "But rather we will certainly carry out every word that
has proceeded from our mouths, [1]by burning [2]sacrifices to the
[a]queen of heaven and pouring out libations to her, just as [b]we
ourselves, our forefathers, our kings and our princes did in the
cities of Judah and in the streets of Jerusalem; for *then* we had
[c]plenty of [3]food, and were well off, and saw no [4]misfortune.
18 "But since we stopped burning [1]sacrifices to the queen
of heaven and pouring out libations to her, we have [a]lacked
everything and have [2]met our end by the sword and by
famine."
19 "And," *said the women,* "when we were burning [1]sacri-
fices to the queen of heaven, and [2]were pouring out libations
to her, was it [a]without our husbands that we made for her
sacrificial cakes [3]in her image and poured out libations to
her?"
20 Then Jeremiah said to all the people, to the men and
women—even to all the people who were giving him *such* an
answer—saying,
21 "As for the [1a]smoking sacrifices that you burned in the
cities of Judah and in the [b]streets of Jerusalem, you and your
forefathers, your kings and your princes, and the people of the
land, did not the LORD [c]remember them, and did not *all this*
come into His [2]mind?
22 "So the LORD was [a]no longer able to endure *it,* because
of the evil of your deeds, [b]because of the abominations which
you have committed; thus your land has become a [c]ruin, an
object of horror and a curse, without an inhabitant, as *it is* this
day.
23 "Because you have burned [1]sacrifices and have sinned
against the LORD and [a]not obeyed the voice of the LORD or
[b]walked in His law, His statutes or His testimonies, therefore
this [c]calamity has befallen you, as *it has* this day."
24 Then Jeremiah said to all the people, including all the
women, "[a]Hear the word of the LORD, all Judah who are [b]in
the land of Egypt,
25 thus says the LORD of hosts, the God of Israel, as follows: 'As for you and your wives, you have spoken with your
mouths and fulfilled *it* with your hands, saying, "We will [a]cer-

12 [c]Jer. 29:18; 42:18; Is. 65:15

13 [a]Jer. 44:27, 28; 11:22

14 [1]Lit., *lifting up their soul* [a]Jer. 44:27; 22:10 [b]Jer. 22:26, 27 [c]Jer. 44:28; Is. 4:2; 10:20; Rom. 9:27

15 [1]Or, *incense* [2]Lit., *and* [a]Jer. 5:1-5; Prov. 11:21; Is. 1:5

16 [1]Lit., *word*

17 [1]Or, *so as to burn* [2]Or, *incense* [3]Lit., *bread* [4]Lit., *evil* [a]Jer. 7:18; 2 Kin. 17:16 [b]Jer. 44:21; 32:32; Neh. 9:34 [c]Ex. 16:3; Is. 48:5; Hos. 2:5-9; Phil. 3:19

18 [1]Or, *incense* [2]Lit., *been finished* [a]Jer. 40:12; Num. 11:5, 6; Mal. 3:13-15

19 [1]Or, *incense* [2]Lit., *to pour* [3]Lit., *to make an image of her* [a]Jer. 44:15; Num. 30:6, 7

21 [1]Or, *incense* [2]Lit., *heart* [a]Ezek. 8:10, 11 [b]Jer. 44:9, 17; 11:13; Ezek. 16:24 [c]Jer. 14:10; Ps. 79:8; Is. 64:9; Hos. 7:2; Amos 8:7

22 [a]Is. 7:13; Mal. 2:17 [b]Jer. 4:4; 21:12; 30:14 [c]Jer. 44:13; 25:11, 18, 38; 29:18; 42:18

23 [1]Or, *incense* [a]Jer. 7:13-15; 40:3 [b]Jer. 44:10; Ps. 119:136, 150 [c]Jer. 44:2; 1 Kin. 9:9; Neh. 13:18

24 [a]Jer. 44:16; 42:15 [b]Jer. 44:15, 26; 43:7

25 [a]Jer. 44:17; Matt. 14:9; Acts 23:12

tainly perform our vows that we have vowed, to burn [1]sacri-
fices to the queen of heaven and pour out libations to her."
[2]Go ahead and [b]confirm your vows, and certainly perform
your vows!'
26 "[1]Nevertheless hear the word of the LORD, all Judah who
are living in the land of Egypt: 'Behold, I have [a]sworn by My
great name,' says the LORD, '[b]never shall My name be invoked
again by the mouth of any man of Judah in all the land of
Egypt, saying, "[c]As the Lord [2]GOD lives . . ."
27 'Behold, I am watching over them [a]for harm and not for
good, and [b]all the men of Judah who are in the land of Egypt
will [1]meet their end by the sword and by famine until they [2]are
completely gone.
28 '[a]And those who escape the sword will return out of the
land of Egypt to the land of Judah [1b]few in number. Then all
the remnant of Judah who have gone to the land of Egypt to
reside there will know whose word will stand, [c]Mine or theirs.
29 'And this will be the [a]sign to you,' declares the LORD,
'that I am going to punish you in this place, so that you may
know that [b]My words will surely stand against you for harm.'
30 "Thus says the LORD, 'Behold, I am going to give over
[a]Pharaoh Hophra king of Egypt to the hand of his enemies, to
the hand of those who seek his life, just as I gave over [b]Zede-
kiah king of Judah to the hand of Nebuchadnezzar king of
Babylon, *who was* his enemy and was seeking his life.' "

CHAPTER 45

THIS *is* the message which Jeremiah the prophet spoke to
[a]Baruch the son of Neriah, when he had [b]written down these
words in a book [1]at Jeremiah's dictation, in the [c]fourth year of
Jehoiakim the son of Josiah, king of Judah, saying:
2 "Thus says the LORD the God of Israel to you, O
Baruch:
3 'You said, "Ah, woe is me! For the LORD has added
sorrow to my pain; I am [a]weary with my groaning and have
found no rest." ' "
4 "Thus you are to say to him, 'Thus says the LORD, "Behold, what I have built I am about to tear down, and what I
have planted I am about to uproot, that is, the whole land."
5 'But you, are you [a]seeking great things for yourself? Do
not seek *them;* for behold, I am going to [b]bring disaster on all
flesh,' declares the LORD, 'but I will give your life to you as
booty in all the places where you may go.' "

CHAPTER 46

THAT which came as the word of the LORD to Jeremiah the
prophet [a]concerning the nations.
2 To [a]Egypt concerning the army of [b]Pharaoh Necho
king of Egypt, which was by the Euphrates River at [c]Carchem-
ish, which Nebuchadnezzar king of Babylon defeated in the
fourth year of Jehoiakim the son of Josiah, king of Judah:
3 "[a]Line up the shield and [1]buckler,
And draw near for the battle!

25 [1]Or, *incense* [2]Lit., *surely cause to stand* [b]Ezek. 20:39; James 1:14, 15

26 [1]Lit., *Therefore* [2]YHWH, usually rendered LORD [a]Jer. 22:5; Gen. 22:16; Deut. 32:40, 41; Amos 6:8; Heb. 6:13, 18 [b]Ps. 50:16; Ezek. 20:39 [c]Jer. 5:2; Is. 48:1, 2

27 [1]Lit., *be finished* [2]Lit., *come to an end* [a]Jer. 39:16 [b]Jer. 44:14; 2 Kin. 21:14

28 [1]Lit., *men of number* [a]Jer. 44:14 [b]Is. 10:19; 27:12, 13 [c]Ps. 33:11; Is. 14:27; 46:10, 11; Zech. 1:6

29 [a]Jer. 44:30; Is. 7:11, 14; 8:18; Matt. 24:15, 16, 32 [b]Prov. 19:21; Is. 40:8

30 [a]Jer. 43:9-13; 46:25; Ezek. 29:3 [b]Jer. 34:21; 39:5-7; 2 Kin. 25:4-7

1 [1]Lit., *from the mouth of Jeremiah* [a]Jer. 32:12, 16; 43:3, 6 [b]Jer. 36:4, 18, 32 [c]Jer. 25:1; 36:1; 46:1

3 [a]Ps. 6:6; 69:3; 2 Cor. 4:1, 16; Gal. 6:9

5 [a]1 Kin. 3:9, 11; 2 Kin. 5:26; Matt. 6:25, 32; Rom. 12:16 [b]Jer. 25:31; Is. 66:16

1 [a]Jer. 1:10; 25:15-38

2 [a]Jer. 46:14; 25:19; Ezek. chaps. 29-32 [b]2 Kin. 18:21; 23:29, 33-35 [c]2 Chr. 35:20; Is. 10:9

3 [1]I.e., small shield [a]Jer. 51:11; Is. 21:5; Joel 3:9; Nah. 2:1; 3:14

4 "Harness the horses,
And [1]mount the steeds,
And take your stand with helmets *on;*
[a]Polish the spears,
Put on the [b]scale-armor.
5 "Why have I seen *it?*
They are terrified,
They are [a]drawing back,
And their [b]mighty men are defeated
And have taken refuge in flight,
Without facing back:
[1]Terror is on every side,"
Declares the LORD.
6 Let not the [a]swift man flee,
Nor the mighty man escape;
In the north beside the River Euphrates
They have [b]stumbled and fallen.
7 Who is this that rises like the Nile,
Like the rivers whose waters surge about?
8 Egypt rises like the Nile,
Even like the rivers whose waters surge about;
And He has said, "I will [a]rise and cover *that* land;
I will surely [b]destroy the city and its inhabitants."
9 Go up, you horses, and [1a]drive madly, you chariots,
That the mighty men may [2]march forward:
Ethiopia and [3b]Put, that handle the shield,
And the [4c]Lydians, that handle *and* bend the bow.
10 For that day belongs to the Lord [1]GOD of hosts,
A day of vengeance, so as to avenge Himself on His foes;
And the [a]sword will devour and be satiated
And [2]drink its fill of their blood;
For there will be a [b]slaughter for the Lord [1]GOD of hosts,
In the land of the north by the River Euphrates.
11 Go up to Gilead and obtain balm,
O virgin daughter of Egypt!
In vain have you multiplied [1]remedies;
There is [a]no healing for you.
12 The nations have heard of your [a]shame,
And the earth is full of your cry *of distress;*
For one warrior has stumbled over [1]another,
And both of them have fallen down together.

13 *This is* the [1]message which the LORD spoke to Jeremiah
the prophet about the coming of Nebuchadnezzar king of
Babylon to smite the land of Egypt:

14 "Declare in Egypt and proclaim in Migdol,
Proclaim also in Memphis and Tahpanhes;
Say, 'Take your stand and get yourself ready,
For the sword has [a]devoured those around you.'
15 "Why have your [a]mighty ones become prostrate?
They do not stand because the LORD has [b]thrust them down.
16 "They have repeatedly [a]stumbled;
Indeed, they have fallen one against another.
Then they said, 'Get up! And let us go back

4 [1]Or, *go up, you horsemen* [a]Ezek. 21:9-11 [b]Jer. 51:3; 1 Sam. 17:5, 38; 2 Chr. 26:14; Neh. 4:16

5 [1]Heb., *magor missabib,* cf. 20:3 [a]Jer. 46:21; Is. 42:17 [b]Is. 5:25; Ezek. 39:18

6 [a]Is. 30:16 [b]Jer. 46:12, 16; Dan. 11:19

8 [a]Is. 37:24 [b]Is. 10:13

9 [1]Lit., *act like madmen* [2]Lit., *go forth* [3]I.e., Libya (or Somaliland) [4]Heb., *Ludim* [a]Jer. 47:3; Nah. 2:4 [b]Nah. 3:9 [c]Is. 66:19

10 [1]YHWH, usually rendered LORD [2]Lit., *be saturated with* [a]Jer. 12:12; Is. 31:8 [b]Is. 34:6; Zeph. 1:7

11 [1]Lit., *healings* [a]Jer. 30:13; Mic. 1:9; Nah. 3:19

12 [1]Lit., *warrior* [a]Jer. 2:36; Nah. 3:8-10

13 [1]Lit., *word*

14 [a]Jer. 46:10; 2:30; Is. 1:20; Nah. 2:13

15 [a]Jer. 46:5; Is. 66:15, 16 [b]Ps. 18:14, 39; 68:1, 2

16 [a]Jer. 46:6; Lev. 26:36, 37

To our own people and our native land
Away from the [1]sword of the oppressor.'
17 "[1]They cried there, 'Pharaoh king of Egypt *is* [a]*but* a big noise;
He has let the appointed time pass by!'
18 "As I live," declares the [a]King
Whose name is the LORD of hosts,
"Surely one shall come *who looms up* like [b]Tabor among the mountains,
Or like [c]Carmel by the sea.
19 "Make your baggage [a]ready for exile,
O daughter dwelling in Egypt,
For [b]Memphis will become a desolation;
It will even be burned down *and* [1]bereft of inhabitants.
20 "Egypt is a pretty heifer,
But a [1]horsefly is coming from the north—it is coming!
21 "Also her [a]mercenaries in her midst
Are like [1]fattened [b]calves,
For even they too have turned back *and* have fled away together;
They did not stand *their ground.*
For the day of their calamity has come upon them,
The time of their [c]punishment.
22 "Its sound moves along like a serpent;
For they move on [1]like an army
And come to her as woodcutters with axes.
23 "They have cut down her forest," declares the LORD;
"Surely it will no *more* be found,
Even though [1]they are *now* more numerous than [a]locusts
And are without number.
24 "The daughter of Egypt has been put to shame,
Given over to the [1]power of the people of the north."
25 The LORD of hosts, the God of Israel, says, "Behold, I
am going to punish Amon of [a]Thebes, and Pharaoh, and
Egypt along with her [b]gods and her kings, even Pharaoh and
those who [c]trust in him.
26 "And I shall give them over to the [1]power of those who
are [a]seeking their lives, even into the hand of Nebuchadnezzar
king of Babylon and into the hand of his [2]officers. [b]Afterwards,
however, it will be inhabited as in the days of old," declares the
LORD.
27 "But as for you, O Jacob My servant, do not [a]fear,
Nor be dismayed, O Israel!
For, see, I am going to [b]save you from afar,
And your descendants from the land of their captivity;
And Jacob shall return and be undisturbed
And secure, with no one making *him* tremble.
28 "O Jacob My servant, do not fear," declares the LORD,
"For [a]I am with you.
For I shall make a full end of all the nations
Where I have driven you,
Yet I shall [b]not make a full end of you;
But I shall [c]correct you properly
And by no means leave you unpunished."

16 [1]Lit., *oppressing sword*

17 [1]Some ancient versions read: *Call the name of Pharaoh a big noise* [a]Ex. 15:9, 10; 1 Kin. 20:10, 11; Is. 19:11-16

18 [a]Jer. 48:15; Mal. 1:14 [b]Josh. 19:22; Judg. 4:6; Ps. 89:12 [c]Josh. 12:22; 1 Kin. 18:42

19 [1]Lit., *without* [a]Is. 20:4 [b]Jer. 46:14; Ezek. 30:13

20 [1]Or, possibly, *mosquito*

21 [1]Lit., *of the stall* [a]Jer. 46:5; 2 Sam. 10:6; 2 Kin. 7:6 [b]Is. 34:7 [c]Jer. 48:44; Hos. 9:7; Obad. 13; Mic. 7:4

22 [1]Or, *in force*

23 [1]I.e., trees of the forest, the Egyptians [a]Judg. 6:5; 7:12; 2:25

24 [1]Lit., *hand*

25 [a]Ezek. 30:14, 15, 16; Nah. 3:8 [b]Jer. 43:12, 13; Ex. 12:12; Ezek. 30:13; Zeph. 2:11 [c]Is. 20:5

26 [1]Lit., *hand* [2]Lit., *servants* [a]Jer. 44:30; Ezek. 32:11 [b]Ezek. 29:8-14

27 [a]Jer. 30:10, 11; Is. 41:13, 14 [b]Jer. 23:3, 4; 29:14; Is. 11:11; Mic. 7:12

28 [a]Jer. 1:19; Ps. 46:7, 11; Is. 8:9, 10; 43:2 [b]Jer. 4:27; Amos 9:8, 9 [c]Jer. 10:24; Hab. 3:2

CHAPTER 47

THAT which came as the word of the LORD to Jeremiah the prophet concerning the Philistines, before Pharaoh [1]conquered [a]Gaza.

2 Thus says the LORD:
"Behold, waters are going to rise from [a]the north
And become an overflowing torrent,
And [b]overflow the land and all its fulness,
The city and those who live in it;
And the men will [c]cry out,
And every inhabitant of the land will wail.
3 "Because of the noise of the [1a]galloping hoofs of his [2]stallions,
The tumult of his chariots, *and* the rumbling of his wheels,
The fathers have not turned back for *their* children,
Because of the limpness of *their* hands;
4 On account of the day that is coming
To [a]destroy all the Philistines,
To cut off from Tyre and Sidon
Every ally that is left;
For the LORD is going to destroy the Philistines,
The remnant of the coastland of [b]Caphtor.
5 "[a]Baldness has come upon Gaza;
[b]Ashkelon has been ruined.
O remnant of their valley,
How long will you gash yourself?
6 "Ah, [a]sword of the LORD,
How long will you not be quiet?
Withdraw into your sheath;
Be at rest and stay still.
7 "How can [1]it be quiet,
When the LORD has [a]given it an order?
Against Ashkelon and against the seacoast—
There He has [b]assigned it."

CHAPTER 48

CONCERNING Moab.
Thus says the LORD of hosts, the God of Israel,
"Woe to [a]Nebo, for it has been destroyed;
[b]Kiriathaim has been put to shame, it has been captured;
The lofty stronghold has been put to shame and [1]shattered.
2 "There is praise for Moab no longer;
In [a]Heshbon they have devised calamity against her:
'Come and let us cut her off from *being* a nation!'
You too, [1]Madmen, will be silenced;
The sword will follow after you.
3 "The sound of an outcry from [a]Horonaim,
'Devastation and great destruction!'
4 "Moab is broken,
Her little ones have sounded out a cry *of distress*.
5 "For by the ascent of [a]Luhith

47:1 [1]Lit., *smote* [a]Jer. 25:20; Gen. 10:19; 1 Kin. 4:24
2 [a]Jer. 1:14; 6:22; 46:20, 24; Is. 14:31 [b]Is. 8:7, 8 [c]Jer. 46:12; Is. 15:2-5
3 [1]Lit., *stamping of the* [2]Lit., *mighty ones* [a]Jer. 8:16; Judg. 5:22
4 [a]Is. 14:31 [b]Gen. 10:14; Deut. 2:23; Amos 9:7
5 [a]Jer. 48:37; Mic. 1:16 [b]Jer. 25:20; Judg. 1:18; Amos 1:7, 8; Zeph. 2:4, 7; Zech. 9:5
6 [a]Jer. 12:12; Judg. 7:20; Ezek. 21:3-5
7 [1]Lit., *you* [a]Is. 10:6; Ezek. 14:17 [b]Mic. 6:9

48:1 [1]Or, *dismayed* [a]Jer. 48:22; Num. 32:3, 37 [b]Jer. 48:23; Num. 32:37; Ezek. 25:9
2 [1]I.e., a city of Moab [a]Jer. 48:34, 45; 49:3; Num. 21:25
3 [a]Jer. 48:5, 34; Is. 15:5
5 [a]Is. 15:5

They will ascend with continual weeping;
For at the descent of Horonaim
They have heard the [1]anguished cry of destruction.
6 "[a]Flee, save your lives,
That you may be like a juniper in the wilderness.
7 "For because of your trust in your own achievements and treasures,
Even you yourself will be captured;
And [a]Chemosh will go off into exile
Together with his priests and his princes.
8 "And a destroyer will come to every city,
So that no city will escape;
The valley also will be ruined,
And the [a]plateau will be destroyed,
As the LORD has said.
9 "Give [1a]wings to Moab,
For she will [2]flee away;
And her cities will become a desolation,
Without inhabitants in them.
10 "Cursed be the one who does the LORD's work with [a]deceit,
And cursed be the one who restrains his [b]sword from blood.

11 "Moab has been [a]at ease since his youth;
He has also been [b]undisturbed on his lees,
Neither has he been [c]emptied from vessel to vessel,
Nor has he gone into exile.
Therefore [1]he retains his [d]flavor,
And his aroma has not changed.
12 "Therefore behold, the days are coming," declares the
LORD, "when I shall send to him those who [a]tip *vessels*, and
they will tip him over, and they will empty his vessels and
shatter [1]his jars.
13 "And Moab will be ashamed of Chemosh, as the house
of Israel was [a]ashamed of [b]Bethel, their confidence.
14 "How can you say, 'We are [a]mighty warriors,
And men valiant for battle'?
15 "Moab has been destroyed, and [1]men have gone up to [2]his cities;
His choicest [3a]young men have also gone down to the slaughter,"
Declares the [b]King, whose name is the LORD of hosts.
16 "The disaster of Moab will soon [a]come,
And his calamity has swiftly hastened.
17 "Mourn for him, all you who *live* around him,
Even all of you who know his name;
Say, 'How has the mighty [1a]scepter been broken,
A staff of spendor!'
18 "[a]Come down from your glory
And sit [1]on the parched ground,
O [b]inhabitant in [c]Dibon
For the destroyer of Moab has come up against you,
He has ruined your strongholds.
19 "Stand by the road and keep watch,
O inhabitant of [a]Aroer;

5 [1]Lit., *distresses of outcry*

6 [a]Jer. 51:6

7 [a]Jer. 48:13, 46; Num. 21:29; 1 Kin. 11:33

8 [a]Josh. 13:9, 17, 21

9 [1]Or, *salt* [2]Or, *fall in ruins* [a]Jer. 48:28; Ps. 11:1; Is. 16:2

10 [a]1 Sam. 15:39; 1 Kin. 20:42; 2 Kin. 13:19 [b]Jer. 47:6, 7

11 [1]Lit., *his flavor has stayed in him* [a]Jer. 22:21; Zech. 1:15 [b]Zeph. 1:12 [c]Nah. 2:2 [d]Ezek. 16:49, 50

12 [1]Lit., *their* [a]Nah. 2:2

13 [a]Jer. 48:39; Is. 45:16 [b]1 Kin. 12:29; Hos. 8:5, 6

14 [a]Ps. 33:16; Is. 10:13-16

15 [1]Lit., *one has* [2]Lit., *her* [3]I.e., warriors [a]Is. 40:30, 31 [b]Jer. 46:18

16 [a]Is. 13:22

17 [1]Or, *rod* [a]Is. 14:5

18 [1]Lit., *in thirst* [a]Jer. 46:19 [b]Jer. 48:22; Josh. 13:9, 17 [c]Is. 47:1

19 [a]Deut. 2:36; Josh. 12:2

[b]Ask him who flees and her who escapes
And say, 'What has happened?'
20 "Moab has been put to shame, for it has been
[1]shattered.
Wail and cry out;
Declare by the Arnon
That Moab has been destroyed.
21 "Judgment has also come upon the plain, upon Holon,
[a]Jahzah, and against [b]Mephaath,
22 against Dibon, Nebo, and Beth-diblathaim,
23 against Kiriathaim, Beth-gamul, and [a]Beth-meon,
24 against [a]Kerioth, Bozrah, and all the cities of the land
of Moab, far and near.
25 "The [a]horn of Moab has been cut off, and his [b]arm
broken," declares the LORD.
26 "Make him drunk, for he has [1]become [a]arrogant toward
the LORD; so Moab will [2]wallow in his vomit, and he also will
become a laughingstock.
27 "Now was not Israel a [a]laughingstock to you? Or was he
[1]caught among thieves? For each time you speak about him
you [b]shake *your head in scorn.*
28 "Leave the cities and dwell among the [a]crags,
O inhabitants of Moab,
And be like a [b]dove that nests
Beyond the mouth of the chasm.
29 "[a]We have heard of the pride of Moab—he *is* very
proud—
Of his haughtiness, his [b]pride, his arrogance and [1]his
self-exaltation.
30 "I know his [a]fury," declares the LORD,
"But it is [1]futile;
His idle boasts have accomplished [1]nothing.
31 "Therefore I shall [a]wail for Moab,
Even for all Moab shall I cry out;
[1]I will moan for the men of [b]Kir-heres.
32 "More than the [a]weeping for [b]Jazer
I shall weep for you, O vine of Sibmah!
Your tendrils stretched across the sea,
They reached to the sea of Jazer;
Upon your summer fruits and your grape harvest
The destroyer has fallen.
33 "So [a]gladness and joy are taken away
From the fruitful field, even from the land of Moab
And I have made the wine to [b]cease from the wine
presses;
No one will tread *them* with shouting,
The shouting will not be shouts *of joy.*
34 "[a]From the outcry at Heshbon even to [b]Elealeh, even to
Jahaz they have [1]raised their voice, from [c]Zoar even to Horonaim *and to* Eglath-shelishiyah; for even the waters of Nimrim
will become desolate.
35 "And I shall make an end of Moab," declares the LORD,
"the one who offers *sacrifice* on the [a]high place and the one
who [1b]burns incense to his gods.
36 "Therefore My [a]heart [1]wails for Moab like flutes; My

19 [b]1 Sam. 4:13, 14, 16

20 [1]Or, *dismayed*

21 [a]Jer. 48:34; Num. 21:23; Is. 15:4 [b]Josh. 13:18

23 [a]Josh. 13:17

24 [a]Jer. 48:41; Amos 2:2

25 [a]Ps. 75:10; Zech. 1:19-21 [b]Job 22:9; Ps. 10:15

26 [1]Or, *magnified himself against* [2]Or, *splash into* [a]Jer. 48:42; Ex. 5:2; Dan. 5:23

27 [1]Or, *found* [a]Lam. 2:15-17; Mic. 7:8-10 [b]Jer. 18:16; Job 16:4

28 [a]Jer. 49:16; Judg. 6:2; Is. 2:19; Obad. 3 [b]Ps. 55:6; Song of Sol. 2:14

29 [1]Lit., *elevation of his heart* [a]Is. 16:6; Zeph. 2:8 [b]Job 40:11, 12; Ps. 138:6

30 [1]Lit., *not so* [a]Is. 37:28

31 [1]Another reading is, *He* [a]Is. 15:5; 16:7, 11 [b]Jer. 48:36; 2 Kin. 3:25; Is. 16:7, 11

32 [a]Is. 16:8, 9 [b]Num. 21:32

33 [a]Jer. 25:10; Is. 16:10; Joel 1:12 [b]Is. 5:10; Hag. 2:16

34 [1]Lit., *given forth* [a]Is. 15:4-6 [b]Num. 32:3, 37 [c]Gen. 13:10; 14:2

35 [1]Or, *offers up in smoke* [a]Is. 16:12 [b]Jer. 7:9; 11:13

36 [1]Lit., *sounds* [a]Is. 16:11

heart also [1]wails like flutes for the men of Kir-heres. Therefore
they have lost the [b]abundance it produced.
37 "For [a]every head is bald and every beard cut short; there
are gashes on all the hands and sackcloth on the [b]loins.
38 "On all the [a]housetops of Moab and in its streets [1]there
is lamentation everywhere; for I have broken Moab like an
undesirable vessel," declares the LORD.
39 "How [1]shattered it is! *How* they have wailed! How
Moab has turned his back—he is ashamed! So Moab will become a laughingstock and an object of [a]terror to all around
him."

40 For thus says the LORD,
"Behold, one will [a]fly swiftly like an eagle,
And [b]spread out his wings against Moab.
41 "Kerieth has been captured
And the strongholds have been seized,
So the [a]hearts of the mighty men of Moab in that day
Will be like the heart of a [b]woman in labor.
42 "And Moab will be [a]destroyed from *being* a people
Because he has [1]become [b]arrogant toward the LORD.
43 "[a]Terror, pit, and snare are *coming* upon you,
O inhabitant of Moab," declares the LORD.
44 "The one who [a]flees from the terror
Will fall into the pit,
And the one who climbs up out of the pit
Will be caught in the snare;
For I shall bring upon her, *even* upon Moab,
The year of their [b]punishment," declares the LORD.

45 "In the shadow of Heshbon
The fugitives stand without strength;
For a fire has gone forth from Heshbon,
And a [a]flame from the midst of [b]Sihon,
And it has devoured the [c]forehead of Moab
And the scalps of the [1]riotous revelers.
46 "Woe to you, Moab!
The people of [a]Chemosh have perished;
For your sons have been taken away captive,
And your daughters into captivity.
47 "Yet I will [a]restore the [1]fortunes of Moab
In the [2]latter days," declares the LORD.
Thus for the judgment on Moab.

CHAPTER 49

CONCERNING the sons of Ammon.
Thus says the LORD:
"Does Israel have no sons?
Or has he no heirs?
Why then has [1a]Malcam taken possession of Gad
And his people settled in its cities?
2 "Therefore behold, the days are coming," declares the
LORD,
"That I shall cause a [1]trumpet [a]blast of war to be heard
Against [b]Rabbah of the sons of Ammon;
And it will become a desolate heap,

36 [1]Lit., *sounds* [b]Is. 15:7

37 [a]Jer. 16:6; Is. 15:2 [b]Is. 15:3; 20:2

38 [1]Lit., *all of it is lamentation* [a]Is. 22:1

39 [1]Or, *dismayed* [a]Ezek. 26:16

40 [a]Jer. 49:22; Hos. 8:1 [b]Is. 8:8

41 [a]Jer. 49:22 [b]Jer. 30:6; Mic. 4:9, 10

42 [1]Or, *magnified himself against* [a]Jer. 48:2; Ps. 83:4 [b]Jer. 48:26; Is. 37:23

43 [a]Is. 24:17, 18; Lam. 3:47

44 [a]1 Kin. 19:17; Amos 5:19 [b]Jer. 46:21

45 [1]Lit., *sons of tumult* [a]Num. 21:28, 29 [b]Num. 21:21, 26; Ps. 135:11 [c]Num. 24:17

46 [a]Jer. 48:7; Judg. 11:24; 1 Kin. 11:7

47 [1]Or, *captivity* [2]Lit., *end of the days* [a]Jer. 12:14-17; 49:6, 39

1 [1]Or, *Milcom*; cf. 1 Kin. 11:5 [a]1 Kin. 11:5, 33; Zeph. 1:5

2 [1]Or, *shout of* [a]Jer. 4:19; Num. 10:9 [b]Deut. 3:11; 2 Sam. 11:1; Ezek. 21:20

And her [c]towns will be set on fire.
Then Israel will take [d]possession of his possessors,"
Says the LORD.
3 "Wail, O [a]Heshbon, for [b]Ai has been destroyed!
Cry out, O daughters of Rabbah,
[c]Gird yourselves with sackcloth and lament,
And rush back and forth inside the walls;
For [1]Malcam will [d]go into exile
Together with his priests and his princes.
4 "How boastful you are about the valleys!
Your valley is flowing *away*,
O backsliding daughter
Who trusts in her [a]treasures, *saying*,
'Who will come against me?'
5 "Behold, I am going to bring terror upon you,"
Declares the Lord [1]GOD of hosts,
"From all *directions* around you;
And each of you will be [a]driven out [2]headlong,
With no one to gather the [b]fugitives together.
6 "But afterward I will [a]restore
The [1]fortunes of the sons of Ammon,"
Declares the LORD.

7 Concerning Edom.
Thus says the LORD of hosts,
"Is there no longer any [a]wisdom in [b]Teman?
Has good counsel been lost to the prudent?
Has their wisdom decayed?
8 "Flee away, turn back, dwell in the depths,
O inhabitants of [a]Dedan,
For I [1]will bring the [b]disaster of Esau upon him
At the time I [2]punish him.
9 "[a]If grape gatherers came to you,
Would they not leave gleanings?
If thieves *came* by night,
They would destroy *only* [1]until they had enough.
10 "But I have [a]stripped Esau bare,
I have uncovered his hiding places
So that he will not be able to conceal himself;
His [1]offspring has been destroyed along with his [2]relatives
And his neighbors, and he is no more.
11 "Leave your [1a]orphans behind, I will keep *them* alive;
And let your [b]widows trust in Me."
12 For thus says the LORD, "Behold, those [1]who were not
sentenced to drink the [a]cup will certainly drink *it*, and are you
the one who will be [b]completely acquitted? You will not be
acquitted, but you will certainly drink *it*.
13 "For I have [a]sworn by Myself," declares the LORD, "that
Bozrah will become an [b]object of horror, a reproach, a ruin
and a curse; and all its cities will become perpetual ruins."
14 I have [a]heard a message from the LORD,
And an [b]envoy is sent among the nations, *saying*,
"Gather yourselves together and come against her,
And rise up for battle!"

2 [c]Josh. 17:11, 16 [d]Is. 14:2

3 [1]Cf. v. 1
[a]Jer. 48:2 [b]Josh. 7:2-5; 8:1-29; Ezra 2:28 [c]Jer. 48:37 [d]Jer. 46:25; 48:7

4 [a]Ps. 62:10; Ezek. 28:4, 5; 1 Tim. 6:17

5 [1]YHWH, usually rendered LORD [2]Lit., *before him*
[a]Jer. 16:16; 46:5 [b]Lam. 4:15

6 [1]Or, *captivity*
[a]Jer. 49:39; 48:47

7 [a]Jer. 8:9; Job 2:11; [b]Jer. 49:20; Gen. 36:11, 15, 34

8 [1]Or, *brought* [2]Or, *punished*
[a]Jer. 25:23; Is. 21:13 [b]Jer. 46:21

9 [1]Lit., *their sufficiency*
[a]Obad. 5

10 [1]Lit., *seed* [2]Lit., *brothers*
[a]Jer. 13:26

11 [1]Or, *fatherless*
[a]Ps. 68:5 [b]Ps. 68:5; Zech. 7:10

12 [1]Lit., *whose judgment was not to*
[a]Jer. 25:15 [b]Jer. 25:28, 29; 1 Pet. 4:17

13 [a]Jer. 44:26; Gen. 22:16; Is. 45:23 [b]Jer. 18:16; Is. 34:9-15

14 [a]Obad. 1-4 [b]Is. 18:2; 30:4

15 "For behold, I have made you [a]small among the nations,
Despised among men.
16 "As for the [a]terror of you,
The arrogance of your heart has deceived you,
O you who live in the clefts of [1]the [b]rock,
Who occupy the height of the hill.
Though you make your nest as [c]high as an eagle's,
I will [d]bring you down from there," declares the LORD.
17 "And Edom will become an [a]object of horror; everyone
who passes by it will be horrified and will [b]hiss at all its
wounds.
18 "Like the overthrow of Sodom and Gomorrah with its
neighbors," says the LORD, "[a]no one will live there, nor will a
son of man reside in it.
19 "Behold, one will come up like a lion from the [1]thickets
of the Jordan against a [2a]perennially watered pasture; for in an
instant I shall make him run away from it, and whoever is
[b]chosen I shall appoint over it. For who is [c]like Me, and who
will summon Me *into court?* And who then is the shepherd
who can stand against Me?"
20 Therefore hear the [a]plan of the LORD which He has
planned against Edom, and His purposes which He has purposed against the inhabitants of Teman: surely they will drag
them off, *even* the little ones of the flock; surely He will make
their [1]pasture [b]desolate because of them.
21 The [a]earth has quaked at the noise of their downfall.
There is an outcry! The noise of it has been heard at the [1]Red
Sea.
22 Behold, [1]He will mount up and [a]swoop like an eagle,
and spread out His wings [2]against Bozrah; and the [b]hearts of
the mighty men of Edom in that day will be like the heart of a
woman in labor.
23 Concerning Damascus.
"[a]Hamath and [b]Arpad are put to shame,
For they have heard bad news;
They are [c]disheartened.
There is anxiety by the sea,
It [d]cannot be calmed.
24 "Damascus has become helpless;
She has turned away to flee,
And panic has gripped her;
Distress and pangs have taken hold of her
Like a woman in childbirth.
25 "How [1]the [a]city of praise has not been deserted,
The town of My joy!
26 "Therefore, her [a]young men will fall in her streets,
And all the men of war will be [1]silenced in that day,"
declares the LORD of hosts.
27 "And I shall [a]set fire to the wall of Damascus,
And it will devour the [1]fortified towers of [b]Ben-hadad."

28 Concerning [a]Kedar and the kingdoms of Hazor, which
Nebuchadnezzar king of Babylon defeated.
Thus says the LORD,
"Arise, go up to Kedar
And devastate the [1b]men of the east.

15 [a]Luke 1:51

16 [1]Or, *Sela*
[a]Is. 25:5 [b]Jer. 48:28; 2 Kin. 14:7 [c]Job 39:27; Is. 14:13-15 [d]Amos 9:2

17 [a]Jer. 49:13; Ezek. 35:7 [b]Jer. 51:37; 1 Kin. 9:8

18 [a]Jer. 49:33; Job 18:15-18

19 [1]Lit., *pride* [2]Or, *enduring habitation*
[a]Jer. 12:5; Josh. 3:15 [b]Num. 16:5 [c]Is. 46:9

20 [1]Or, *habitation*
[a]Jer. 50:45; Is. 14:24, 27 [b]Mal. 1:3, 4

21 [1]Lit., *Sea of Reeds*
[a]Jer. 50:46; Ezek. 26:15, 18

22 [1]Or, *one* [2]Or, *over*
[a]Jer. 4:13; 48:40, 41; Hos. 8:1 [b]Jer. 30:6; 48:41; Is. 13:8

23 [a]Jer. 39:5; Num. 13:21; Is. 10:9; Amos 6:2 [b]2 Kin. 18:34; 19:13; Is. 10:9 [c]Ex. 15:15; Nah. 2:10 [d]Is. 57:20

25 [1]Or, *deserted is the city of praise*
[a]Jer. 33:9; 51:41

26 [1]Or, *destroyed*
[a]Jer. 11:22; 50:30; Amos 4:10

27 [1]Or, *palaces*
[a]Jer. 43:12; Amos 1:3-5 [b]1 Kin. 15:18-20

28 [1]Lit., *sons*
[a]Jer. 2:10; Gen. 25:13; Is. 21:16, 17; Ezek. 27:21 [b]Is. 11:14

29 "They will take away their tents and their flocks;
They will carry off for themselves
Their tent [a]curtains, all their goods, and their [b]camels,
And they will call out to one another, 'Terror on every side!'
30 "Run away, flee! Dwell in the depths,
O inhabitants of Hazor," declares the LORD;
"For [a]Nebuchadnezzar king of Babylon has formed a plan against you
And devised a scheme against you.
31 "Arise, go up against a nation which is [a]at ease,
Which lives securely," declares the LORD.
"It has [b]no gates or bars;
They dwell alone.
32 "And their camels will become plunder,
And the multitude of their cattle for booty,
And I shall scatter to all the winds those who cut the [a]corners *of their hair;*
And I shall bring their disaster from every side," declares the LORD.
33 "And Hazor will become a haunt of [a]jackals,
A desolation forever;
No one will live there,
Nor will a son of man reside in it.
34 That which came as the word of the LORD to Jeremiah
the prophet concerning [a]Elam, [b]at the beginning of the reign
of Zedekiah king of Judah, saying,
35 "Thus says the LORD of hosts,
'Behold, I am going to [a]break the bow of Elam,
The [1]finest of their might.
36 'And I shall bring upon Elam the [a]four winds
From the four ends of heaven,
And shall [b]scatter them to all these winds;
And there will be no nation
To which the outcasts of Elam will not go.
37 'So I shall [1]shatter Elam before their enemies
And before those who seek their lives;
And I shall [a]bring calamity upon them,
Even My [b]fierce anger,' declares the LORD,
'And I shall send out the sword after them
Until I have consumed them.
38 'Then I shall set My throne in Elam,
And I shall destroy [1]out of it king and princes,'
Declares the LORD.
39 'But it will come about in the last days
That I shall restore the [1]fortunes of Elam,'"
Declares the LORD.

CHAPTER 50

THE word which the LORD spoke concerning Babylon, the
land of the Chaldeans, through Jeremiah the prophet:
2 "[a]Declare and proclaim among the nations.
Proclaim it and [b]lift up a standard.
Do not conceal *it but* say,
'[c]Babylon has been captured,

29 [a]Hab. 3:7 [b]1 Chr. 5:21
30 [a]Jer. 25:9, 24; 27:6
31 [a]Judg. 18:7; Is. 47:8 [b]Is. 42:11
32 [a]Jer. 9:26; 25:23
33 [a]Jer. 10:22; 51:37; Is. 13:20-22; Zeph. 2:9, 13-15
34 [a]Jer. 25:25; Gen. 10:22; 14:1, 9; Is. 11:11; Ezek. 32:24; Dan. 8:2 [b]Jer. 28:1; 2 Kin. 24:17, 18
35 [1]Lit., *first* [a]Jer. 51:56; Ps. 46:9; Is. 22:6
36 [a]Dan. 7:2; 8:8; Rev. 7:1 [b]Jer. 50:32; Ezek. 5:10; Amos 9:9
37 [1]Or, *dismay* [a]Jer. 6:19 [b]Jer. 30:24
38 [1]Or, *from there*
39 [1]Or, *captivity*
2 [a]Jer. 4:16 [b]Jer. 51:27 [c]Jer. 51:31

2 [1]Heb., *Merodach* [2]Or, *dismayed* [d]Is. 46:1 [e]Jer. 6:19

3 [a]Jer. 50:13; Is. 14:22, 23 [b]Jer. 9:10; Zeph. 1:3

4 [a]Jer. 3:18; 31:31; 33:7; Is. 11:12, 13; Hos. 1:11 [b]Jer. 31:9; Ezra 3:12, 13

5 [1]Lit., *hither* [2]M.T. reads, *come ye!* [3]Or, *will have come* [a]Jer. 6:16; Is. 35:8 [b]Jer. 32:40; Is. 55:3; Heb. 8:6-10

6 [a]Ezek. 34:15, 16; Is. 53:6; Matt. 9:36; 10:6 [b]Jer. 23:11-14 [c]Jer. 13:16; Ezek. 34:6 [d]Jer. 50:19; 33:12

7 [a]Jer. 31:23 [b]Jer. 14:8; 17:13

8 [1]Another reading is: *"Let them go forth"* [2]Or, *in front of*

9 [1]So M.T. reads, *a warrior who makes childless*

10 [1]Or, *the Chaldeans* [a]Jer. 51:24, 35; Ezek. 11:24

11 [1]Another reading is, *in the grass* [2]Lit., *mighty ones* [a]Jer. 12:14

12 [1]Or, *has become* [a]Jer. 15:9 [b]Jer. 22:6; 51:43

13 [a]Jer. 18:16; 49:17

14 [1]Lit., *tread* (in order to string)

[d]Bel has been put to shame, [1]Marduk has been [2]shattered;
Her [e]images have been put to shame, her idols have been shattered.'

3 For a nation has come up against her out of the north;
it will make her land [a]an object of horror, and there will be [b]no
inhabitant in it. Both man and beast have wandered off, they
have gone away!
4 "In those days and at that time," declares the LORD,
"the sons of Israel will come, *both* they and the sons of Judah
[a]as well; they will go along [b]weeping as they go, and it will be
the LORD their God they will seek.
5 "They will [a]ask for the way to Zion, *turning* their faces
[1]in its direction; [2]they [3]will come that they may join themselves to the LORD *in* an [b]everlasting covenant that will not be
forgotten.

6 "My people have become [a]lost sheep;
[b]Their shepherds have led them astray.
They have made them turn aside *on* the [c]mountains;
They have gone along from mountain to hill
And have forgotten their [d]resting place.
7 "All who came upon them have devoured them;
And their adversaries have said, 'We are not guilty,
Inasmuch as they have sinned against the LORD *who is* the [a]habitation of righteousness,
Even the LORD, the [b]hope of their fathers.'
8 "Wander away from the midst of Babylon,
And [1]go forth from the land of the Chaldeans;
Be also like male goats [2]at the head of the flock.
9 "For behold, I am going to arouse and bring up against Babylon
A horde of great nations from the land of the north,
And they will draw up *their* battle lines against her;
From there she will be taken captive.
Their arrows will be like [1]an expert warrior
Who does not return empty-handed.
10 "And [1a]Chaldea will become plunder;
All who plunder her will have enough," declares the LORD.

11 "Because you are glad, because you are jubilant,
O you who [a]pillage My heritage,
Because you skip about like a [1]threshing heifer
And neigh like [2]stallions,
12 Your [a]mother [1]will be greatly ashamed,
She who gave you birth [1]will be humiliated.
Behold, *she will be* the least of the nations,
A [b]wilderness, a parched land, and a desert.
13 "Because of the indignation of the LORD she will not be inhabited,
But she will be completely desolate;
Everyone who passes by Babylon [a]will be horrified
And will hiss because of all her wounds.
14 "Draw up your battle lines against Babylon on every side,
All you who [1]bend the bow;

Shoot at her, do not be sparing with *your* arrows,
For she has [a]sinned against the LORD.
15 "Raise your battle cry against her on every side!
She has [a]given [1]herself up, her pillars have fallen,
Her [b]walls have been torn down.
For this is the vengeance of the LORD:
Take vengeance on her;
As she has done *to others,* so do to her.
16 "Cut off the [a]sower from Babylon,
And the one who wields the sickle at the time of harvest;
From before [1]the sword of the [b]oppressor
They will each turn back to his own people,
And they will each flee to his own land.
17 "Israel is a scattered [1]flock, the [a]lions have driven *them*
away. The first one *who* devoured him was the [b]king of Assyria, and this last one *who* has broken his bones is [c]Nebuchad-
nezzar king of Babylon.
18 "Therefore thus says the LORD of hosts, the God of
Israel: 'Behold, I am going to punish the king of Babylon and
his land, just as I [a]punished the king of Assyria.
19 'And I shall [a]bring Israel back to his pasture, and he will
graze on Carmel and Bashan, and his [1]desire will be satisfied in
the hill country of Ephraim and Gilead.
20 'In those days and at that time,' declares the LORD,
'search will be made for the iniquity of Israel, but [a]there will be
none; and for the sins of Judah, but they will not be found; for
I shall pardon those whom I leave as a remnant.
21 "Against the land of [1]Merathaim, go up against it,
And against the inhabitants of [2a]Pekod.
Slay and [3]utterly destroy them," declares the LORD,
"And do according to all that I have commanded you.
22 "The [a]noise of battle is in the land,
And great destruction.
23 "How the [a]hammer of the whole earth
Has been cut off and broken!
How Babylon has become
An object of horror among the nations!
24 "I [a]set a snare for you, and you were also [b]caught, O Babylon,
While you yourself were not aware;
You have been found and also seized
Because you have engaged in [c]conflict with the LORD."
25 The LORD has opened His armory
And has brought forth the [a]weapons of His indignation,
For it is a [b]work of the Lord [1]GOD of hosts
In the land of the Chaldeans.
26 Come to her from the [1]farthest border;
[a]Open up her barns,
Pile her up like heaps
And [2]utterly [b]destroy her,
Let nothing be left to her.
27 Put all her young bulls to the [a]sword;
Let them go down to the slaughter!

14 [a]Hab. 2:8, 17

15 [1]Lit., *her hand* [a]1 Chr. 29:24 [b]Jer. 50:29; Ps. 137:8

16 [1]Or, *the oppressing sword* [a]Joel 1:11 [b]Jer. 25:38; 46:16

17 [1]Lit., *sheep* [a]Jer. 2:15; 4:7 [b]2 Kin. 15:19; 17:6; 18:9-13 [c]2 Kin. 24:1, 10-12; 25:1-7

18 [a]Is. 10:12; Ezek. 31:3, 11, 12; Nah. 1:1; 3:7, 18, 19

19 [1]Lit., *soul* [a]Jer. 31:10; 33:12

20 [a]Jer. 31:34; Is. 43:25; Mic. 7:19

21 [1]Or, *Double Rebellion* [2]Or, *Punishment* [3]Lit., *put under the ban* [a]Ezek. 23:23

22 [a]Jer. 4:19-21; 51:54-56

23 [a]Jer. 51:20-24

24 [a]Jer. 48:43, 44; 51:31 [b]Dan. 5:30, 31 [c]Job 9:4; 40:2, 9

25 [1]YHWH, usually rendered LORD [a]Is. 13:5 [b]Jer. 50:16; 51:12, 25, 55

26 [1]Lit., *end* [2]Lit., *put under the ban* [a]Jer. 50:10; Is. 45:3 [b]Is. 14:23

27 [a]Is. 34:7

Woe be upon them, for their [b]day has come,
The time of their punishment.
28 There is a [a]sound of fugitives and refugees from the land of Babylon,
To declare in Zion the [b]vengeance of the LORD our God,
Vengeance for His [c]temple.

29 "Summon [1]many against Babylon,
All those who [2]bend the bow:
Encamp against her on every side,
Let there be no escape[3].
Repay her according to her work;
[a]According to all that she has done, *so* do to her;
For she has become [b]arrogant against the LORD,
Against the Holy One of Israel.
30 "Therefore her young [a]men will fall in her streets,
And all her men of war will be [1]silenced in that day," declares the LORD.
31 "Behold, [a]I am against you, O [1]arrogant one,"
Declares the Lord [2]GOD of hosts,
"For your day has come,
The time [3]when I shall punish you.
32 "And the [1a]arrogant one will stumble and fall
With no one to raise him up;
And I shall [b]set fire to his cities,
And it will devour all his environs."

33 Thus says the LORD of hosts:
"The sons of Israel are oppressed,
And the sons of Judah as well;
And [a]all who took them captive have held them fast,
They have refused to let them go.
34 "Their [a]Redeemer is strong, the Lord of hosts is His name;
He will vigorously [b]plead their case,
So that He may [c]bring rest to [1]the earth,
But turmoil to the inhabitants of Babylon.
35 "A [a]sword against the Chaldeans," declares the LORD,
"And against the inhabitants of Babylon,
And against her officials and her [b]wise men!
36 "A sword against the [a]oracle priests, and they will become fools!
A sword against her [b]mighty men, and they will be [1c]shattered!
37 "A sword against [1]their [a]horses and against [1]their chariots,
And against all the [2b]foreigners who are in the midst of her,
And they will become [c]women!
A sword against her treasures, and they will be plundered!
38 "A [1]drought on her waters, and they will be dried up!
For it is a land of idols,
And they are mad over fearsome idols.
39 "Therefore the desert creatures will live *there* along with the jackals;

27 [b]Jer. 46:21; Ps. 37:13; Ezek. 7:7

28 [a]Is. 48:20 [b]Jer. 50:15; 51:10; Ps. 149:6-9 [c]Lam. 1:10; 2:6, 7

29 [1]Another reading is, *archers* [2]Lit., *tread* (in order to string) [3]Some mss. add: *to her*
[a]Jer. 50:15; 51:56; Ps. 137:8 [b]Jer. 49:16; Ex. 10:3; Dan. 4:37

30 [1]Or, *made lifeless;* or, *destroyed*
[a]Jer. 9:21; 18:21; 49:26; Is. 13:17, 18

31 [1]Lit., *arrogance* [2]YHWH, usually rendered LORD [3]Another reading is, *of your punishment*
[a]Jer. 21:13; Nah. 2:13

32 [1]Lit., *arrogance*
[a]Is. 10:12-15 [b]Jer. 21:14; 49:27

33 [a]Is. 14:17; 58:6

34 [1]Or, their *land*
[a]Jer. 15:21; 31:11; Is. 43:14 [b]Jer. 51:36; Mic. 7:9 [c]Is. 14:3-7

35 [a]Jer. 47:6; Hos. 11:6 [b]Dan. 5:7, 8

36 [1]Or, *dismayed*
[a]Is. 44:25 [b]Jer. 49:42 [c]Nah. 3:13

37 [1]Lit., *his* [2]Lit., *mixed multitude*
[a]Jer. 51:21, 22; Ps. 20:7, 8 [b]Jer. 25:20; Ezek. 30:5 [c]Jer. 48:41; 51:30

38 [1]Another reading is, *sword*

The ostriches also will live in it,
And it will [a]never again be inhabited
Or dwelt in from generation to generation.
40 "As when God overthrew [a]Sodom,
And Gomorrah with its neighbors," declares the LORD,
"No man will live there,
Nor will *any* son of man reside in it.

41 "Behold, a people is coming [a]from the north,
And a great nation and many kings
Will be aroused from the remote parts of the earth.
42 "They seize *their* bow and javelin;
They are [a]cruel and have no mercy.
Their voice roars like the sea,
And they ride on [b]horses,
Marshalled like a man [c]for the battle
Against you, O daughter of Babylon.
43 "The king of Babylon has heard the report about them,
And his hands hang limp;
[a]Distress has gripped him,
Agony like a woman in childbirth.
44 "[a]Behold, one will come up like a lion from the [1]thicket
of the Jordan to a [2]perennially watered pasture; for in an instant I shall make them run away from it, and whoever is
[b]chosen I shall appoint over it. For who is [c]like Me, and who
will summon Me *into court*? And who then is the shepherd
who can [d]stand before Me?"
45 Therefore hear the [a]plan of the LORD which He has
planned against Babylon, and His purposes which He has purposed against the land of the Chaldeans: surely they will drag
them off, *even* the little ones of the flock; surely He will make
their [1]pasture desolate because of them.
46 At the [1]shout, "Babylon has been seized!" the [a]earth is
shaken, and an [b]outcry is heard among the nations.

CHAPTER 51

THUS says the LORD:
"Behold, I am going to arouse against Babylon
And against the inhabitants of [1]Leb-kamai
[2]The spirit of a [a]destroyer.
2 "And I shall dispatch [1]foreigners to Babylon that they
may [a]winnow her
And may devastate her land;
For on every side they will be opposed to her
In the day of *her* calamity.
3 "[1]Let not [2]him who [3]bends his bow [3]bend *it*,
[1]Nor let him rise up in his scale armor;
So do not spare her young men;
Devote all her army to destruction.
4 "And they will fall down [1]slain in the land of the
Chaldeans,
And [a]pierced through in their streets."

5 For [a]neither Israel nor Judah has been [1]forsaken
By his God, the LORD of hosts,

---

39 [a]Is. 13:20

40 [a]Jer. 49:18; Luke 17:28-30; 2 Pet. 2:6; Jude 7

41 [a]Jer. 50:3, 9; 51:27, 28; Is. 13:2-5

42 [a]Is. 13:17, 18; 47:6 [b]Jer. 8:16; 47:3; Hab. 1:8 [c]Jer. 50:9, 14; Joel 2:5

43 [a]Jer. 30:6

44 [1]Lit., *pride* [2]Or, *enduring habitation* [a]Jer. 49:19-21 [b]Num. 16:5 [c]Is. 46:9 [d]Jer. 30:21; Job 41:10

45 [1]Or, *habitation* [a]Jer. 51:10, 11; Is. 14:24

46 [1]Lit., *voice* [a]Jer. 10:10; 49:21; Ezek. 26:18; 31:16 [b]Jer. 46:12; 51:54; Is. 5:7; 15:5; Ezek. 27:28

1 [1]Code name for Chaldea; or else, *the heart of those who rise up against Me* [2]Or, *a destroying wind* [a]Jer. 4:11, 12; 23:19; Hos. 13:15

2 [1]Some versions read, *winnowers* [a]Jer. 15:7; Is. 41:16; Matt. 3:12

3 [1]M.T. reads: *Against him who . . .* [2]I.e., the Chaldean defender [3]Lit., *tread(s)* (in order to string)

4 [1]Or, *wounded* [a]Jer. 13:15; 14:19

5 [1]Lit., *widowed* [a]Jer. 33:24-26; Is. 54:7, 8

Although their land is [b]full of guilt
[2]Before the Holy One of Israel.
6 Flee from the midst of Babylon,
And each of you save his life!
Do not be [1a]destroyed in her [2]punishment,
For this is the LORD's time of vengeance;
He is going to render recompense to her.
7 Babylon has been a golden [a]cup in the hand of the LORD,
Intoxicating all the earth.
The [b]nations have drunk of her wine;
Therefore the nations are going mad.
8 Suddenly Babylon has fallen and been broken;
[a]Wail over her!
Bring [1]balm for her pain;
Perhaps she may be healed.
9 We applied healing to Babylon, but she was not healed;
Forsake her and [a]let us each go to his own country,
For her judgment has reached to [b]heaven
And [1]towers up to the very skies.
10 The LORD has [a]brought [1]about our vindication;
Come and let us [b]recount in Zion
The work of the LORD our God.

11 [a]Sharpen the arrows, fill the quivers!
The LORD has aroused the spirit of the kings of the Medes,
Because His purpose is against Babylon to destroy it;
For it is the vengeance of the LORD, vengeance for His temple.
12 [a]Lift up a [1]signal against the walls of Babylon;
Post a strong guard,
Station [2]sentries,
Place men in ambush!
For the LORD has both [b]purposed and performed
What He spoke concerning the inhabitants of Babylon.
13 O you who dwell by many waters,
Abundant in [a]treasures,
Your end has come,
The [1]measure of your [2b]end.
14 The LORD of hosts has sworn by Himself:
"Surely I will fill you with a [1]population like [a]locusts,
And they will cry out with [2]shouts of victory over you."

15 *It is* [a]He who made the earth by His power,
Who established the world by His wisdom,
And by His understanding He [b]stretched out the heavens.
16 When He utters His [a]voice, *there is* a tumult of waters in the heavens,
And He causes the [b]clouds to ascend from the end of the earth;
He makes lightning for the rain,
And brings forth the [c]wind from His storehouses.

5 [2]Lit., *From* [b]Hos. 4:1, 2

6 [1]Or, *silenced;* or, *made lifeless* [2]Or, *penalty for iniquity* [a]Num. 16:26

7 [a]Jer. 25:15; Hab. 2:16; Rev. 14:8 [b]Rev. 18:3

8 [1]Or, *balsam resin* [a]Is. 13:6

9 [1]Lit., *is lifted* [a]Jer. 46:16; 50:16; Is. 13:14 [b]Ezra 9:6

10 [1]Lit., *forth* [a]Ps. 37:6; Mic. 7:9 [b]Jer. 50:28; Is. 40:2

11 [a]Jer. 46:4, 9; Joel 3:9, 10

12 [1]Or, *standard* [2]Or, *watchmen* [a]Jer. 51:27; 50:2; Is. 13:2 [b]Jer. 51:29; 4:28; 23:20

13 [1]Lit., *cubit* [2]Lit., *being cut off* [a]Is. 45:3 [b]Is. 57:17; Hab. 2:9-11

14 [1]Or, *mankind* [2]I.e., like the song of grape treaders [a]Jer. 51:27; Nah. 3:15

15 [a]Jer. 51:15, 19; 10:12-16 [b]Jer. 32:17; Ps. 146:5, 6; Acts 14:15; Rom. 1:20

16 [a]Job 37:2-6; Ps. 18:13 [b]Jer. 10:13; Ps. 135:7 [c]Jon. 1:4

17 [a]All mankind is stupid, devoid of knowledge,
Every goldsmith is put to shame by his idols;
For his molten images are [b]deceitful,
And there is no breath in them.
18 They are worthless, a work of mockery;
In the time of their punishment they will perish.
19 The [a]portion of Jacob is not like these;
For the [1]Maker of all is He,
And of the [2]tribe of His inheritance;
The LORD of hosts is His name.
20 *He says,* "You are My [1a]war-club, *My* weapon of war;
And with you I [b]shatter nations,
And with you I destroy kingdoms.
21 "And with you I [a]shatter the horse and his rider,
22 And with you I shatter the [a]chariot and its rider,
And with you I shatter [b]man and woman,
And with you I shatter old man and [c]youth,
And with you I shatter young man and virgin,
23 And with you I shatter the shepherd and his flock,
And with you I shatter the farmer and his team,
And with you I shatter governors and prefects."
24 "But I will repay Babylon and all the inhabitants of
Chaldea for all their evil that they have done in Zion before
your eyes," declares the LORD.
25 "Behold, I am against you, O destroying mountain,
Who destroy the whole earth," declares the LORD,
"And I will stretch out My hand against you,
And roll you down from the crags
And I will make you a [a]burnt out mountain.
26 "And they will not take from you *even* a stone for a corner
Nor a stone for foundations,
But you will be [a]desolate forever," declares the LORD.

27 [a]Lift up a [1]signal in the land,
Blow a trumpet among the nations!
Consecrate the nations against her,
Summon against her the kingdoms of [b]Ararat, Minni and [c]Ashkenaz;
Appoint a marshal against her,
Bring up the [d]horses like bristly locusts.
28 Consecrate the nations against her,
The kings of the Medes,
[1]Their governors and all [1]their [2]prefects,
And every land of [3]their dominion.
29 So the [a]land quakes and writhes,
For the purposes of the LORD against Babylon stand,
To make the land of Babylon
A [1b]desolation without inhabitants.
30 The [a]mighty men of Babylon have ceased fighting,
They stay in the strongholds;
[b]Their strength is [1]exhausted,
They are becoming [b]*like* women;
Their dwelling places are set on fire,
The [c]bars of her *gates* are broken.
31 One [1a]courier runs to meet [1]another,

17 [a]Jer. 10:14; Is. 44:18-20 [b]Hab. 2:18, 19

19 [1]Lit., *Fashioner* [2]Or, *Scepter;* cf. Num. 24:17 [a]Jer. 10:16; Ps. 73:26

20 [1]Lit., *shatterer* [a]Jer. 50:23; Is. 41:15, 16 [b]Is. 8:9; 41:15, 16; Mic. 4:12, 13

21 [a]Ex. 15:1

22 [a]Ex. 15:4; Is. 43:17 [b]2 Chr. 36:17 [c]Is. 13:15, 16, 18

25 [a]Rev. 8:8

26 [a]Jer. 51:29; Is. 50:13; Is. 13:19-22

27 [1]Or, *standard* [a]Jer. 51:12; 50:2; Is. 13:2-5; 18:3 [b]Gen. 8:4; 2 Kin. 19:37; Is. 37:38 [c]Gen. 10:3 [d]Jer. 50:42

28 [1]Lit., *her* [2]I.e., lieutenant governors [3]Lit., *his*

29 [1]Or, *object of horror* [a]Jer. 8:16; 10:10; 50:46; Amos 8:8 [b]Jer. 51:26, 43; Is. 13:19, 20; 47:11

30 [1]Lit., *dried up* [a]Jer. 50:15, 36, 37; Ps. 76:5 [b]Is. 13:7, 8; Nah. 3:13 [c]Is. 45:1, 2; Lam. 2:9; Amos 1:5; Nah. 3:13

31 [1]Lit., *runner* [a]2 Chr. 30:6

31 [2]Lit., *announcer* [b]2 Sam. 18:19-31

33 [1]Lit., *of treading it* [a]Is. 21:10; 41:15, 16 [b]Hos. 6:11; Joel 3:13

34 [a]Is. 24:1-3 [b]Jer. 51:44; Job 20:15; Amos 8:4

35 [1]Lit., *inhabitress* [a]Ps. 137:8

36 [1]Or, *broad river* [a]Ps. 140:12 [b]Jer. 51:6, 11; Rom. 12:19

38 [a]Jer. 2:15

39 [a]Jer. 51:57; 25:27; 48:26 [b]Ps. 76:5

40 [1]Or, *young rams* [a]Jer. 48:15; 50:27

41 [1]Code name for Babylon

42 [1]Or, *broad river* [a]Jer. 51:55; Is. 8:7, 8; Dan. 9:26

43 [a]Jer. 2:6; Is. 13:20

44 [a]Ezra 1:7, 8

And one [2b]messenger to meet [2]another,
To tell the king of Babylon
That his city has been captured from end *to end;*
32 The fords also have been seized,
And they have burned the marshes with fire,
And the men of war are terrified.

33 For thus says the LORD of hosts, the God of Israel:
"The daughter of Babylon is like a [a]threshing floor
At the time [1]it is stamped firm;
Yet in a little while the time of [b]harvest will come for her.

34 "Nebuchadnezzar king of Babylon has devoured me *and* crushed me,
He has set me down *like* an [a]empty vessel;
He has swallowed me [b]like a monster,
He has filled his stomach with my delicacies;
He has washed me away.
35 "May the [a]violence *done* to me and to my flesh be upon Babylon,"
The [1]inhabitant of Zion will say;
And, "May my blood be upon the inhabitants of Chaldea,"
Jerusalem will say.
36 Therefore thus says the LORD,
"Behold, I am going to [a]plead your case
And [b]exact full vengeance for you;
And I shall dry up her [1]sea
And make her fountain dry.
37 "And Babylon will become a heap *of ruins,* a haunt of jackals,
An object of horror and hissing, without inhabitants.
38 "They will roar together like [a]young lions,
They will growl like lions' cubs.
39 "When they become heated up, I shall serve *them* their banquet
And [a]make them drunk, that they may become jubilant
And may [b]sleep a perpetual sleep
And not wake up," declares the LORD.
40 "I shall bring them down like [1]lambs [a]to the slaughter,
Like rams together with male goats.

41 "How [1]Sheshak has been captured,
And the praise of the whole earth been seized!
How Babylon has become an object of horror among the nations!
42 "The [1a]sea has come up over Babylon;
She has been engulfed with its tumultuous waves.
43 "Her cities have become an object of horror,
A parched land and a desert,
A land in which no man [a]lives,
And through which no son of man passes.
44 "And I shall punish Bel in Babylon,
And I shall make what he has swallowed [a]come out of his mouth;

And the nations will no longer [b]stream to him.
Even the [c]wall of Babylon has fallen down!

45 "[a]Come forth from her midst, My people,
And each of you [b]save yourselves
From the fierce anger of the LORD.
46 "Now [a]lest your heart grow faint,
And you be afraid at the [b]report that *will be* heard in the land—
For the report will come [1]one year,
And after that [2]another report in [2]another year,
And violence *will be* in the land
With [c]ruler against ruler—
47 "Therefore behold, days are coming
When I shall punish the [a]idols of Babylon;
And her whole land will be [b]put to shame,
And all her slain will fall in her midst.
48 "Then [a]heaven and earth and all that is in them
Will shout for joy over Babylon,
For the destroyers will come to her from the north,"
Declares the LORD.

49 [a]Indeed Babylon is to fall *for* the slain of Israel,
As also for Babylon the slain of all the earth have fallen.
50 You who have escaped the sword,
Depart! Do not stay!
[a]Remember the LORD from afar,
And let Jerusalem [1]come to your mind.
51 We are ashamed because we have heard reproach;
Disgrace has covered our faces,
For [a]aliens have entered
The holy places of the LORD's house.

52 "Therefore behold, the days are coming," declares the LORD,
"When I shall punish her idols,
And the mortally wounded will groan throughout her land.
53 "Though Babylon should [a]ascend to the heavens,
And though she should fortify [1]her lofty stronghold,
From [b]Me destroyers will come to her," declares the LORD.

54 The sound of an outcry from Babylon,
And of great destruction from the land of the Chaldeans!
55 For the LORD is going to destroy Babylon,
And He will make *her* loud [1]noise vanish from her.
And their [a]waves will roar like many waters;
The tumult of their voices [2] sounds forth.
56 For the [a]destroyer is coming against her, against Babylon,
And her mighty men will be captured,
Their [b]bows are shattered;
For the LORD is a God of [c]recompense,
He will fully repay.

44 [b]Is. 2:2 [c]Jer. 51:58; 50:15

45 [a]Jer. 51:6; 50:8, 28; Is. 48:20 [b]Gen. 19:12-16; Acts 2:40

46 [1]Lit., *in the* [2]Lit., *the* [a]Jer. 46:27, 28; Is. 43:5 [b]2 Kin. 19:7; Is. 13:3-5 [c]Is. 19:2

47 [a]Jer. 51:52; 50:2; Is. 21:9; 46:1, 2 [b]Jer. 50:12, 35-37

48 [a]Is. 44:23; 48:20; 49:13

49 [a]Jer. 50:29; Ps. 137:8

50 [1]Lit., *come up on your heart* [a]Deut. 4:29-31; Ps. 137:6

51 [a]Ps. 74:3-8; Lam. 1:10

53 [1]Lit., *the height of her strength* [a]Jer. 49:16; Job 20:6; Ps. 139:8-10; Is. 14:12, 13 [b]Is. 13:3

55 [1]Or, *voice* [2]Lit., *is given* [a]Jer. 51:42; Ps. 18:4; 69:2; 124:2, 4, 5

56 [a]Jer. 51:48; Hab. 2:8 [b]Ps. 46:9; 76:3 [c]Jer. 51:6, 24; Ps. 94:1, 2

57 "And I shall make her princes and her wise men drunk,
Her governors, her prefects, and her mighty men,
That they may sleep a [a]perpetual sleep and not wake
up,"
Declares the [b]King, whose name is the LORD of hosts.
58 Thus says the LORD of hosts,
"The broad wall of Babylon will be completely razed,
And her high [a]gates will be set on fire;
So the peoples will [b]toil for nothing,
And the nations become [c]exhausted *only* for fire."
59 The [1]message which Jeremiah the prophet commanded Seraiah the son of [a]Neriah, the grandson of Mahseiah,
when he went with [b]Zedekiah the king of Judah to Babylon in
the fourth year of his reign. (Now Seraiah was quartermaster.)
60 So Jeremiah [a]wrote in a single [1]scroll all the calamity
which would come upon Babylon, *that is,* all these words
which have been written concerning Babylon.
61 Then Jeremiah said to Seraiah, "As soon as you come
to Babylon, then see that you read all these words aloud,
62 and say, 'Thou, O LORD, hast [1]promised concerning
this place to [a]cut if off, so that there will be [b]nothing dwelling
in it, [2]whether man or beast, but it will be a perpetual
desolation.'
63 "And it will come about as soon as you finish reading
this [1]scroll, you will tie a stone to it and [a]throw it into the
middle of the Euphrates,
64 and say, 'Just so shall Babylon sink down and [a]not rise
again, because of the calamity that I am going to bring upon
her; and they will become [b]exhausted.' " [c]Thus far are the
words of Jeremiah.

[a] CHAPTER 52

ZEDEKIAH was twenty-one years old when he became king,
and he reigned eleven years in Jerusalem; and his mother's
name was [1]Hamutal the daughter of Jeremiah of [b]Libnah.
2 And he did [a]evil in the sight of the LORD like all that
[b]Jehoiakim had done.
3 For through the [a]anger of the LORD *this* came about in
Jerusalem and Judah until He cast them out from His presence. And Zedekiah [b]rebelled against the king of Babylon.
4 [a]Now it came about in the ninth year of his reign, on
the tenth day of the tenth month, that Nebuchadnezzar king
of Babylon came, he and all his army, against Jerusalem,
camped against it, and built a [b]siege wall all around [1]it.
5 So the city was under siege until the eleventh year of
King Zedekiah.
6 On the ninth day of the [a]fourth month the [b]famine was
so severe in the city that there was no food for the people of
the land.
7 Then the city was [a]broken into, and all the [b]men of war
fled and went forth from the city at night by way of the gate
between the two walls which *was* by the king's garden, though

57 [a]Ps. 76:5, 6 [b]Jer. 46:18; 48:15

58 [a]Is. 45:1, 2 [b]Hab. 2:13 [c]Jer. 51:64; 9:5; Lam. 5:5

59 [1]Lit., *word* [a]Jer. 32:12; 36:4; 45:1 [b]Jer. 28:1; 52:1

60 [1]Or, *book* [a]Jer. 30:2, 3; 36:2, 4, 32; Is. 30:8

62 [1]Lit., *spoken* [2]Lit., *from man even to beast* [a]Jer. 50:3, 13, 39, 40; Is. 13:19-22; 14:22, 23 [b]Jer. 51:43; Ezek. 35:9

63 [1]Or, *book* [a]Jer. 19:10, 11; Rev. 18:21

64 [a]Nah. 1:8, 9 [b]Jer. 51:58 [c]Job 31:40; Ps. 72:20

1 [1]Another reading is: *Hamital* [a]2 Kin. 24:18-20; 2 Chr. 36:11-36 [b]Josh. 10:29; 2 Kin. 8:22; Is. 37:8

2 [a]1 Kin. 14:22 [b]Jer. 36:30, 31

3 [a]Is. 3:1, 4, 5 [b]2 Chr. 36:13

4 [1]Lit., *against it* [a]Jer. 39:1; 2 Kin. 25:1-7; Ezek. 24:1, 2 [b]Jer. 32:24

6 [a]Jer. 39:2 [b]Jer. 38:9; 2 Kin. 25:3

7 [a]Jer. 39:2 [b]Jer. 39:4-7; 51:32

the Chaldeans were [1]all around the city. And they went by way
of the Arabah.
8 But the army of the Chaldeans pursued the king and
[a]overtook Zedekiah in the [1]plains of Jericho, and all his army
was scattered from him.
9 Then they captured the king and [a]brought him up to
the king of Babylon at [b]Riblah in the land of [c]Hamath; and he
[1]passed sentence on him.
10 And the king of Babylon [a]slaughtered the sons of Zedekiah before his eyes, and he also slaughtered all the [1]princes of
Judah in Riblah.
11 Then he [a]blinded the eyes of Zedekiah; and the king of
Babylon bound him with bronze fetters and brought him to
Babylon, and put him in prison until the day of his death.
12 [a]Now on the tenth day of the fifth month, which was
the [b]nineteenth year of King Nebuchadnezzar, king of Babylon, Nebuzaradan the captain of the bodyguard, [1]who was in
the service of the king of Babylon, came to Jerusalem.
13 And he [a]burned the house of the LORD, the [b]king's
house, and all the houses of Jerusalem; even every large house
he burned with fire.
14 So all the army of the Chaldeans who *were* with the
captain of the guard [a]broke down all the walls around
Jerusalem.
15 Then Nebuzaradan the captain of the guard [a]carried
away into exile some of the poorest of the people, the rest of
the people who were left in the city, the [1b]deserters who had
deserted to the king of Babylon, and the rest of the artisans.
16 But [a]Nebuzaradan the captain of the guard left some
of the poorest of the land to be vinedressers and [1]plowmen.
17 Now the bronze [a]pillars which belonged to the house of
the LORD and the [b]stands and the bronze [c]sea, which were in
the house of the LORD, the Chaldeans broke in pieces and
carried all their bronze to Babylon.
18 And they also took away the [a]pots, the shovels, the
snuffers, the basins, the [1]pans, and all the bronze vessels which
were used in *temple* service.
19 The captain of the guard also took away the [a]bowls, the
firepans, the basins, the pots, the lampstands, the [1]pans and
the libation bowls, what was fine gold and what was fine silver.
20 The two pillars, the one sea, and the twelve bronze
bulls that were under [1]the sea, *and* the stands, which King
Solomon had made for the house of the LORD—the bronze of
all these vessels was [a]beyond weight.
21 As for the pillars, the [a]height of each pillar was eighteen
[1]cubits, and it [2]was twelve cubits in [a]circumference and four
fingers in thickness, *and* hollow.
22 Now a [a]capital of bronze was on it; and the height of
each capital was five cubits, with network and [b]pomegranates
upon the capital all around, all of bronze. And the second
pillar was like these, including pomegranates.
23 And there were ninety-six [1]exposed pomegranates; all
the pomegranates *numbered* a hundred on the network all
around.
24 Then the captain of the guard took [a]Seraiah the chief

7 [1]Lit., *against the city on every side*

8 [1]Lit., *Arabah*
[a]Jer. 21:7; 32:4; 34:21; 37:17; 38:23

9 [1]Lit., *spoke judgments with*
[a]Jer. 39:5; 2 Kin. 25:6 [b]Jer. 39:5; Num. 34:11 [c]Num. 13:21; Josh. 13:5

10 [1]Or, *commanders*
[a]Jer. 22:30; 39:6

11 [a]Jer. 39:7; Ezek. 12:13

12 [1]Lit., *stood before the king*
[a]2 Kin. 25:8-21 [b]Jer. 52:29; 2 Kin. 24:12; 25:8

13 [a]2 Chr. 36:19; Ps. 74:6-8; 79:1; Is. 64:10, 11; Lam. 2:7; Mic. 3:12 [b]Jer. 39:8

14 [a]2 Kin. 25:10; Neh. 1:3

15 [1]Lit., *fallers who had fallen*
[a]2 Kin. 25:11 [b]Jer. 39:9

16 [1]Or, *unpaid laborers*
[a]Jer. 39:10; 40:2-6; 2 Kin. 25:12

17 [a]Jer. 52:21-23; 27:19-22; 1 Kin. 7:15-22 [b]1 Kin. 7:27-36 [c]1 Kin. 7:23-26

18 [1]Or, *spoons* for incense
[a]1 Kin. 7:40, 45

19 [1]Or, *spoons* for incense
[a]1 Kin. 7:49, 50

20 [1]So Gk. and Syriac; Heb. omits *the sea*
[a]1 Kin. 7:47

21 [1]A cubit equals approx. 18 inches. [2]Lit., *a line of 12 cubits would encircle it*
[a]1 Kin. 7:15

22 [a]1 Kin. 7:16 [b]1 Kin. 7:20, 42

23 [1]Lit., *windward*

24 [a]2 Kin. 25:18; 1 Chr. 6:14; Ezra 7:1

priest and Zephaniah the second priest, with the three [1b]officers of the temple.
25 He also took from the city one official who was overseer of the men of war, and seven [1a]of the king's advisors who were found in the city; and the scribe of the commander of the army who mustered the people of the land, and sixty men of the people of the land who were found in the midst of the city.
26 And Nebuzaradan the captain of the guard took them and [a]brought them to the king of Babylon at Riblah.
27 Then the king of Babylon [a]struck them down and put them to death at Riblah in the land of Hamath. So Judah was [b]led away into exile from its land.
28 These are the people whom [a]Nebuchadnezzar carried away into exile: in the [1]seventh year 3,023 Jews;
29 in the eighteenth year of Nebuchadnezzar 832 persons from Jerusalem;
30 in the twenty-third year of Nebuchadnezzar, Nebuzaradan the captain of the guard carried into exile 745 Jewish people; there were 4,600 persons in all.
31 [a]Now it came about in the thirty-seventh year of the exile of Jehoiachin king of Judah, in the twelfth month, on the twenty-fifth of the month, that [1]Evilmerodach king of Babylon, in the *first* year of his reign, [2b]showed favor to Jehoiachin king of Judah and brought him out of prison.
32 Then he spoke kindly to him and set his throne above the thrones of the kings who *were* with him in Babylon.
33 So [1]Jehoiachin [a]changed his prison clothes, and [2b]had his meals in [3]the king's presence regularly all the days of his life.
34 And for his allowance, a [a]regular allowance was given him by the king of Babylon, a daily portion all the days of his life until the day of his death.

24 [1]Lit., *keepers of the door* [b]Jer. 35:4; 1 Chr. 9:19; Ps. 84:10

25 [1]Lit., *men of those seeing the king's face* [a]Esth. 1:14; Matt. 18:10

26 [a]2 Kin. 25:20, 21

27 [a]Ezek. 8:11-18 [b]Jer. 13:19; 20:4; 25:9-11; 39:9; Is. 6:11, 12; 27:10; 32:13, 14; Ezek. 33:28; Mic. 4:10

28 [1]Or possibly, *seventeenth* [a]2 Kin. 24:2, 3, 12-16; 2 Chr. 36:20; Ezra 2:1; Neh. 7:6; Dan. 1:1-3

31 [1]Or, *Awil-Marduk* ("Man of Marduk") [2]Lit., *lifted up the head of* [a]2 Kin. 25:27-30 [b]Gen. 40:13, 20; Ps. 3:3; 27:6

33 [1]Lit., *he* [2]Lit., *ate* [3]Lit., *his presence* [a]Gen. 41:14, 42 [b]2 Sam. 9:7, 13; 1 Kin. 2:7

34 [a]2 Sam. 9:10

THE LAMENTATIONS OF JEREMIAH

Sorrows of Zion.

HOW lonely sits the city
That was [a]full of people!
She has become like a [b]widow
Who was once [c]great among the nations!
She who was a princess among the [1]provinces
Has become a [d]forced laborer!
2 She [a]weeps bitterly in the night,
And her tears are on her cheeks;
She has none to comfort her
Among all her [b]lovers.
All her friends have [c]dealt treacherously with her;
They have become her enemies.
3 Judah has gone into exile [1]under affliction,

1 [1]Or, *districts* [a]Is. 22:2 [b]Is. 54:4 [c]1 Kin. 4:21; Ezra 4:20; Jer. 31:7 [d]2 Kin. 23:35; Jer. 40:9

2 [a]Lam. 1:16; Ps. 6:6; 77:2-6 [b]Jer. 2:25; 3:1; 22:20-22 [c]Job 19:13, 14; Ps. 31:11; Mic. 7:5

3 [1]Or, *by reason of*

And [1]under [2]harsh servitude;
She dwells [a]among the nations,
But she has found no rest;
All [b]her pursuers have overtaken her
In the midst of [3]distress.
4 The roads [1]of Zion are in mourning
Because [a]no one comes to the appointed feasts.
All her gates are [b]desolate;
Her priests are groaning,
Her virgins are afflicted,
And she herself [2]is bitter.
5 Her adversaries have become [1]her masters,
Her enemies [2]prosper;
For the LORD has [a]caused her grief
Because of the multitude of her transgressions;
Her little ones have gone away
As captives before the adversary.
6 And all her [a]majesty
Has departed from the daughter of Zion;
Her princes have become like bucks
That have found no pasture;
And they have [1b]fled without strength
Before the pursuer.
7 In the days of her affliction and homelessness
Jerusalem remembers all her precious things
That were from the days of old
When her people fell into the hand of the adversary,
And [a]no one helped her.
The adversaries saw her,
They [b]mocked at her [1]ruin.
8 Jerusalem sinned [a]greatly,
Therefore she has become an unclean thing;
All who honored her despise her
Because they have seen her nakedness;
Even she herself groans and turns away.
9 Her [a]uncleanness was in her skirts;
She [1]did not consider her future;
Therefore she has [2b]fallen astonishingly;
[c]She has no comforter.
"See, O LORD, my affliction,
For the enemy has [d]magnified himself!"
10 The adversary has stretched out his hand
Over all her precious things,
For she has seen the [a]nations enter her sanctuary,
The ones whom Thou commanded
That they should not enter into Thy congregation.
11 All her people groan [a]seeking bread;
They have given their precious things for food
To [b]restore their [1]lives themselves.
"See, O LORD, and look,
For I am [c]despised."
12 "Is [a]it nothing to all you who pass this way?
Look and see if there is any [1]pain like my [1]pain
Which was severely dealt out to me,
Which the LORD inflicted on the day of His [b]fierce anger.

3 [1]Or, *by reason of* [2]Lit., *great* [3]Or, *narrow places*
[a]Lev. 26:39; Deut. 28:64-67 [b]2 Kin. 25:4, 5

4 [1]Or, *to* [2]Or, *suffers bitterly*
[a]Lam. 2:6, 7; Is. 24:4-6 [b]Jer. 9:11; 10:22

5 [1]Lit., *head* [2]Or, *are at ease*
[a]Ps. 90:7, 8; Ezek. 8:17, 18; 9:9, 10

6 [1]Lit., *gone*
[a]Ps. 132:13; Jer. 13:18 [b]2 Kin. 25:4, 5

7 [1]Lit., *cessation*
[a]Lam. 4:17; Jer. 37:7 [b]Ps. 79:4; Jer. 48:27

8 [a]Lam. 1:5, 20; Is. 59:2-13

9 [1]Lit., *did not remember her latter end* [2]Lit., *come down*
[a]Jer. 2:34; Ezek. 24:13 [b]Is. 3:8; Jer. 13:17, 18 [c]Eccles. 4:1; Jer. 16:7 [d]Ps. 74:23; Zeph. 2:10

10 [a]Ps. 74:4-8; Is. 64:10, 11; Jer. 51:51

11 [1]Lit., *soul*
[a]Jer. 38:9; 52:6 [b]1 Sam. 30:12 [c]Jer. 15:19

12 [1]Or, *sorrow*
[a]Jer. 18:16; 48:27 [b]Is. 13:13; Jer. 4:8

13 "From on high He sent fire into my [a]bones,
And it [1]prevailed *over them;*
He has spread a [b]net for my feet;
He has turned me back;
He has made me [c]desolate,
[2]Faint all day long.
14 "The [a]yoke of my transgressions is bound;
By His hand they are knit together;
They have [b]come upon my neck;
He has made my strength [1]fail;
The Lord [c]has given me into the hands
Of *those against whom* I am not able to stand.
15 "The [a]Lord has rejected all my strong men
In my midst;
He has called an appointed [1]time against me
To crush my [b]young men;
The Lord has trodden *as in* a winepress
The virgin daughter of Judah.
16 "For these things I weep;
[1]My eyes run down with water;
Because far from me is a [a]comforter,
One who restores my soul;
My children are desolate
Because the enemy has prevailed."
17 Zion [a]stretches out her hands;
There is no one to comfort her;
The LORD has [b]commanded concerning Jacob
That the ones round about him should be his adversaries;
Jerusalem has become an unclean thing among them.
18 "The LORD is [a]righteous;
For I have [b]rebelled against His [1]command;
Hear now, all peoples,
And behold my [2]pain;
My virgins and my young men
Have gone into captivity.
19 "I [a]called to my lovers, *but* they deceived me;
My [b]priests and my elders perished in the city,
While they sought food to restore [1]their strength themselves.
20 "See, O LORD, for I am in distress;
My [1a]spirit is greatly troubled;
My heart is overturned within me,
For I have been very rebellious.
In the street the sword [2]slays;
In the house it is like death.
21 "They have heard that I groan;
There is no one to comfort me;
All my enemies have heard of my [1]calamity;
They are [a]glad that Thou hast done *it.*
O that Thou wouldst bring the day which Thou hast proclaimed,
That they may become [b]like me.
22 "Let all their wickedness come before Thee;
And [a]deal with them as Thou hast dealt with me

13 [1]Or, *descended, overthrew* [2]Or, *Sick* [a]Job 30:30; Ps. 22:14; Hab. 3:16 [b]Job 19:6; Ps. 66:11 [c]Jer. 44:6

14 [1]Lit., *stumble* [a]Prov. 5:22; Is. 47:6 [b]Jer. 28:13, 14 [c]Jer. 32:3, 5; Ezek. 25:4, 7

15 [1]Or, *feast* [a]Is. 41:2; Jer. 13:24; 37:10 [b]Jer. 6:11; 18:21

16 [1]Lit., *My eye, my eye* [a]Lam. 1:2; Ps. 69:20; Eccles. 4:1

17 [a]Is. 1:15; Jer. 4:31 [b]2 Kin. 24:2-4; Jer. 12:9

18 [1]Lit., *mouth* [2]Or, *sorrow* [a]Ps. 119:75; Jer. 12:1 [b]1 Sam. 12:14, 15; Jer. 4:17

19 [1]Lit., *their soul* [a]Lam. 1:2; Job 19:13-19 [b]Lam. 2:20; Jer. 14:15

20 [1]Lit., *inward parts are in ferment* [2]Lit., *bereaves* [a]Lam. 2:11; Is. 16:11

21 [1]Lit., *evil* [a]Lam. 2:15; Ps. 35:15; Jer. 50:11 [b]Is. 14:5, 6; 47:6, 11; Jer. 30:16

22 [a]Neh. 4:4, 5; Ps. 137:7, 8

For all my transgressions;
For my groans are many, and my heart is faint."

Chapter 2

How the Lord has covered the daughter of Zion
With a cloud in His anger!
He has [a]cast from heaven to earth
The [b]glory of Israel,
And has not remembered His [c]footstool
In the day of His anger.
2 The Lord has [a]swallowed up; He has not spared
All the habitations of Jacob.
In His wrath He has thrown down
The strongholds of the daughter of Judah;
He has [b]brought *them* down to the ground;
He has [c]profaned the kingdom and its princes.
3 In fierce anger he has cut off
[1]All the [a]strength of Israel;
He has [b]drawn back His right hand
From before the enemy.
And He has [c]burned in Jacob like a flaming fire
Consuming round about.
4 He has bent His [a]bow like an enemy,
He has set His right hand like an adversary
And slain all that were [b]pleasant to the eye;
In the tent of the daughter of Zion
He has [c]poured out His wrath like fire.
5 The Lord has become like an [a]enemy.
He has swallowed up Israel;
He has swallowed up all its [b]palaces;
He has destroyed its strongholds
And multiplied in the daughter of Judah
Mourning and moaning.
6 And He has violently treated His [1]tabernacle like a garden *booth;*
He has [a]destroyed His appointed [2]meeting place;
The Lord has [b]caused to be forgotten
The appointed feast and sabbath in Zion,
And He has despised king and priest
In the indignation of His anger.
7 The Lord has [a]rejected His altar,
He has abandoned His sanctuary;
He [b]has delivered into the hand of the enemy
The walls of her palaces.
They have made a [c]noise in the house of the Lord
As in the day of an appointed feast.
8 The Lord [1]determined to destroy
The wall of the daughter of Zion.
He has [a]stretched out a line,
He has not restrained His hand from [2]destroying;
And He has caused rampart and wall to lament;
They have languished together.
9 Her [a]gates have sunk into the ground,
He has destroyed and broken her bars.
Her king and her princes are among the nations;

1 [a]Is. 14:12-15; Ezek. 28:14-16 [b]Is. 64:11 [c]Ps. 99:5; 132:7

2 [a]Lam. 3:43; Ps. 21:9 [b]Is. 25:12; 26:5 [c]Ps. 89:39, 40; Is. 43:28

3 [1]Lit., *Every horn* [a]Ps. 75:5, 10; Jer. 48:25 [b]Ps. 74:11; Jer. 21:4, 5 [c]Is. 42:25; Jer. 21:14

4 [a]Lam. 3:12, 13; Job 6:4; 16:13 [b]Ezek. 24:25 [c]Is. 42:25; Jer. 7:20

5 [a]Jer. 30:14 [b]Lam. 2:2; Jer. 52:13

6 [1]Lit., *booth* [2]Or, *feast* [a]Jer. 52:13 [b]Lam. 1:4; Jer. 17:27; Zeph. 3:18

7 [a]Ps. 78:59-61; Is. 64:11; Ezek. 7:20-22 [b]Jer. 33:4, 5; 52:13 [c]Ps. 74:3-8

8 [1]Lit., *thought* [2]Lit., *swallowing up* [a]2 Kin. 21:13; Is. 34:11; Amos 7:7-9

9 [a]Neh. 1:3

The law is no more;
Also, her prophets find
[b]No vision from the LORD.
10 The elders of the daughter of Zion
[a]Sit on the ground, they [b]are silent.
They have thrown [c]dust on their heads;
They have girded themselves with [d]sackcloth.
The virgins of Jerusalem
Have bowed their heads to the ground.
11 My eyes fail because of tears,
My [1a]spirit is greatly troubled;
My [2b]heart is poured out on the earth,
Because of the [3]destruction of the daughter of my people,
When [c]little ones and infants faint
In the streets of the city.
12 They say to their mothers,
"[a]Where is grain and wine?"
As they faint like a wounded man
In the streets of the city,
As their [b]life is poured out
On their mothers' bosom.
13 How shall I admonish you?
To what [a]shall I compare you,
O daughter of Jerusalem?
To what shall I liken you as I comfort you,
O virgin daughter of Zion?
For your [1]ruin is as vast as the sea;
Who can [b]heal you?
14 Your [a]prophets have seen for you
False and foolish visions;
And they have not [b]exposed your iniquity
So as to restore you from captivity,
But they have [c]seen for you false and misleading [1]oracles.
15 All who pass along the way
[a]Clap their hands *in derision* at you;
They hiss and [b]shake their heads
At the daughter of Jerusalem:
"Is this the city of which they said,
'[c]The perfection of beauty,
[d]A joy to all the earth'?"
16 All [a]your enemies
Have opened their mouths wide against you;
They hiss and gnash *their* teeth.
They say, "We have [b]swallowed *her* up!
Surely this is the [c]day for which we waited;
We have reached *it*, we have seen *it*."
17 The LORD has done what He purposed;
He has accomplished His word
Which He commanded from days of old.
He has thrown down without sparing,
And He has caused the enemy to [a]rejoice over you;
He has [b]exalted the [1]might of your adversaries.
18 Their [a]heart cried out to the Lord,
"O [b]wall of the daughter of Zion,

9 [b]Jer. 14:14; 23:16; Ezek. 7:26

10 [a]Job 2:13; Is. 3:26; 47:1 [b]Amos 8:3 [c]Job 2:12; Ezek. 27:30 [d]Is. 15:3; Jon. 3:6-8

11 [1]Lit., *inward parts are in ferment* [2]Lit., *liver* [3]Lit., *breaking* [a]Jer. 4:19 [b]Job 16:13 [c]Lam. 2:19; Jer. 44:7

12 [a]Jer. 1:11; 5:17 [b]Job 30:16; Ps. 42:4; 62:8

13 [1]Lit., *breaking* [a]Lam. 1:12 [b]Jer. 8:22; 30:12-15

14 [1]Lit., *burdens* [a]Jer. 23:25-29; 29:8, 9 [b]Is. 58:1; Mic. 3:8; Ezek. 23:36 [c]Jer. 23:36; Ezek. 22:25, 28

15 [a]Job 27:23; Ezek. 25:6 [b]Ps. 22:7; Is. 37:22; Jer. 18:16 [c]Ps. 50:2 [d]Ps. 48:2

16 [a]Lam. 3:46; Job 16:10; Ps. 22:13 [b]Ps. 56:2; 124:3; Jer. 51:34 [c]Obad. 12-15

17 [1]Lit., *horn* [a]Ps. 35:24, 26; 89:42; Is. 14:29 [b]Lam. 1:5; Deut. 28:43, 44

18 [a]Ps. 119:145; Hos. 7:14 [b]Lam. 2:8; Hab. 2:11

Let *your* tears run down like a river day and night;
Give yourself no relief;
Let your [1]eyes have no rest.
19 "Arise, cry aloud in the [a]night
At the beginning of the night watches;
Pour [b]out your heart like water
Before the presence of the Lord;
Lift up your hands to Him
For the life of your little ones
Who are [c]faint because of hunger
At the head of every street."
20 See, O LORD, and look!
With [a]whom hast Thou dealt thus?
Should women eat their [1]offspring,
The little ones who were [2]born healthy?
Should [b]priest and prophet be slain
In the sanctuary of the Lord?
21 On the ground in the streets
Lie [a]young and old,
My virgins and my young men
Have fallen by the sword.
Thou hast slain *them* in the day of Thine anger,
Thou hast slaughtered, not sparing.
22 Thou didst call as in the day of an appointed feast
My [a]terrors on every side;
And there was [b]no one who escaped or survived
In the day of the LORD's anger,
Those [c]whom I [1]bore and reared,
My enemy annihilated them.

CHAPTER 3

I AM the man who has seen affliction
Because of the rod of His wrath.
2 He has driven me and made me walk
In [a]darkness and not in light.
3 Surely against me He has [a]turned His hand
Repeatedly all the day.
4 He has caused my [a]flesh and my skin to waste away,
He has broken my bones.
5 He has [a]besieged and encompassed me with [b]bitterness
and hardship.
6 In [a]dark places He has made me dwell,
Like those who have long been dead.
7 He has [a]walled *me* in so that I cannot go out;
He has made my [1b]chain heavy.
8 Even when I cry out and call for help,
He [a]shuts out my prayer.
9 He has [a]blocked my ways with hewn stone;
He has made my paths crooked.
10 He is to me like a bear lying in wait,
Like a lion in secret places.
11 He has turned aside my ways and [a]torn me to pieces;
He has made me desolate.
12 He bent His bow
And set me as a target for the arrow.

18 [1]Lit., *the daughter of your eye*

19 [a]Ps. 42:3; Is. 26:9 [b]1 Sam. 1:15; Ps. 42:4; 62:8 [c]Is. 51:20

20 [1]Lit., *fruit* [2]Or, *tenderly cared for*
[a]Ex. 32:11; Deut. 9:26 [b]Ps. 78:64; Jer. 14:15; 23:11, 12

21 [a]Jer. 6:11

22 [1]Lit., *bore healthy* or, *tenderly cared for*
[a]Ps. 31:13; Is. 24:17, 18; Jer. 6:25 [b]Jer. 11:11 [c]Jer. 16:2-4; 44:7

2 [a]Job 30:26; Is. 59:9; Jer. 4:23

3 [a]Ps. 38:2; Is. 5:25

4 [a]Ps. 31:9, 10; 38:2-8; 102:3-5

5 [a]Job 19:8 [b]Lam. 3:19; Ps. 69:21; Jer. 23:15

6 [a]Ps. 88:5, 6; 143:3

7 [1]Lit., *bronze piece*
[a]Job 3:23; 19:8 [b]Jer. 40:4

8 [a]Job 30:20; Ps. 22:2

9 [a]Is. 63:17

11 [a]Job 16:12, 13; Jer. 15:3

13 He made the [1]arrows of His [a]quiver
To enter into my [2]inward parts.
14 I have become a [a]laughingstock to all my people,
Their *mocking* [b]song all the day.
15 He has filled me with bitterness,
He has made me drunk with wormwood.
16 And He has [a]broken my teeth with [b]gravel;
He has made me cower in the [c]dust.
17 And my soul has been rejected [a]from peace;
I have forgotten [1]happiness.
18 So I say, "My strength has perished,
And *so has* my [a]hope from the LORD."

19 Remember my affliction and my [1]wandering, the [a]wormwood and bitterness.
20 Surely my soul remembers
And is [a]bowed down within me.
21 This I recall to my mind,
Therefore I have [a]hope.
22 The LORD's [a]lovingkindnesses [1]indeed never cease,
[b]For His compassions never fail.
23 *They* are new [a]every morning;
Great is Thy faithfulness.
24 "The LORD is my [a]portion," says my soul,
"Therefore I [b]have hope in Him."
25 The LORD is good to those who [a]wait for Him,
To the [1]person who [b]seeks Him.
26 *It is* good that he waits silently
For the salvation of the LORD.
27 *It is* good for a man that he should bear
The yoke in his youth.
28 Let him sit alone and be silent
Since He has laid *it* on him.
29 Let him [1]put his mouth in the [a]dust,
Perhaps there is [b]hope.
30 Let him give his [a]cheek to [1]the smiter;
Let him be filled with reproach.
31 For the Lord will [a]not reject forever,
32 For if He causes grief,
Then He will have [a]compassion
According to His abundant lovingkindness.
33 For He does not afflict [1]willingly,
Or grieve the sons of men.
34 To crush under His feet
All the prisoners of the [1]land,
35 To [1]deprive a man of [a]justice
In the presence of the Most High,
36 To [1a]defraud a man in his lawsuit—
Of these things the Lord does not [2]approve.
37 Who is [1]there who speaks and it comes to pass,
Unless the Lord has commanded *it*?
38 *Is it* not from the mouth of the Most High
That [1]both good and ill [a]go forth?

39 Why should *any* living [1]mortal, or *any* man,
Offer [a]complaint [2]in view of his sins?

13 [1]Lit., *sons* [2]Lit., *kidneys*
[a]Jer. 5:16

14 [a]Ps. 22:6, 7; 123:3, 4; Jer. 20:7 [b]Lam. 3:63; Job 30:9

16 [a]Ps. 3:7; 58:6 [b]Prov. 20:17 [c]Jer. 6:26

17 [1]Lit., *good*
[a]Is. 59:11; Jer. 12:12

18 [a]Job 17:15; Ezek. 37:11

19 [1]Or, *bitterness*
[a]Lam. 3:5, 15; Jer. 9:15

20 [a]Ps. 42:5, 6, 11; 43:5; 44:25

21 [a]Ps. 130:7

22 [1]Or, *that we are not consumed*
[a]Ps. 78:38; Jer. 3:12; 30:11 [b]Mal. 3:6

23 [a]Zeph. 3:5

24 [a]Ps. 16:5; 73:26 [b]Ps. 23:18

25 [1]Lit., *soul*
[a]Ps. 27:14; Is. 25:9 [b]Is. 26:9

29 [1]Lit., *give*
[a]Job 16:15; 40:4 [b]Jer. 31:17

30 [1]Lit., *his*
[a]Job 16:10; Is. 50:6

31 [a]Ps. 77:7, 10; 54:7-10

32 [a]Ps. 78:38; 106:43-45; Hos. 11:8

33 [1]Lit., *from His heart*

34 [1]Or, *earth*

35 [1]Or, *turn aside a man's case*
[a]Ps. 140:12; Prov. 17:15

36 [1]Lit., *make crooked* [2]Lit., *see*
[a]Jer. 22:3; Hab. 1:13

37 [1]Lit., *this*

38 [1]Lit., *the evil* things *and the good*
[a]Job 2:10; Is. 45:7; Jer. 32:42

39 [1]Or, *human being* [2]Or, *on the basis of*
[a]Jer. 30:15; Mic. 7:9; Heb. 12:5, 6

40 Let us [a]examine and probe our ways,
And let us return to the LORD.
41 We [a]lift up our heart [1]and hands
Toward God in heaven:
42 We have [a]transgressed and rebelled;
Thou hast not pardoned.
43 Thou hast covered *Thyself* with anger
And pursued us;
Thou hast slain *and* hast not spared.
44 Thou hast covered Thyself with a cloud
So that [a]no prayer can pass through.
45 *Mere* offscouring and refuse Thou hast made us
In the midst of the peoples.
46 All our enemies have [a]opened their mouth against us.
47 [a]Panic and pitfall have befallen us,
Devastation and destruction;
48 My eyes run down with streams of water
Because of the destruction of the daughter of my people.
49 My eyes pour down [a]unceasingly,
Without stopping,
50 Until the LORD [a]looks down
And sees from heaven.
51 My [1]eyes bring pain to my soul
Because of all the daughters of my city.
52 My enemies [a]without cause
Hunted me down [b]like a bird;
53 They have silenced [1]me in the pit
And have [2]placed a stone on me.
54 Waters flowed [a]over my head;
I said, "I am cut off!"
55 I called on Thy name, O LORD,
Out of the lowest pit.
56 Thou hast [a]heard my voice,
"Do not [b]hide Thine ear from my *prayer for* relief,
From my cry for help."
57 Thou didst [a]draw near when I called on Thee;
Thou didst say, "Do not [b]fear!"
58 O Lord, Thou didst [a]plead my soul's cause;
Thou hast [b]redeemed my life.
59 O LORD, Thou hast [a]seen my oppression;
[b]Judge my case.
60 Thou hast seen all their vengeance,
All their schemes against me.
61 Thou hast heard their [a]reproach, O LORD,
All their schemes against me.
62 The [a]lips of my assailants and their whispering
Are against me all day long.
63 Look on their sitting and their rising;
[a]I am their mocking song.
64 Thou wilt [a]recompense them, O LORD,
According to the work of their hands.
65 Thou wilt give them [1a]hardness of heart,
Thy curse will be on them.
66 Thou wilt pursue them in anger and destroy them
From under the heavens of the LORD!

40 [a]Ps. 119:59; 139:23, 24; 2 Cor. 13:5
41 [1]Lit., *to* [a]Ps. 25:1; 28:2; 141:2
42 [a]Neh. 9:26; Jer. 14:20; Dan. 9:5
44 [a]Lam. 3:8; Zech. 7:13
46 [a]Lam. 2:16; Job 30:9, 10; Ps. 22:6-8
47 [a]Is. 24:17, 18; Jer. 48:43, 44
49 [a]Ps. 77:2; Jer. 14:17
50 [a]Lam. 5:1; Ps. 80:14; Is. 63:15
51 [1]Lit., *eye*
52 [a]Ps. 35:7, 19 [b]1 Sam. 26:20; Ps. 11:1; 124:7
53 [1]Lit., *my life* [2]Or, *cast stones*
54 [a]Ps. 69:2; Jon. 2:3-5
56 [a]Job 34:28; Ps. 116:12 [b]Ps. 55:1
57 [a]Ps. 145:18 [b]Is. 41:10, 14
58 [a]Jer. 50:34 [b]Ps. 34:22
59 [a]Jer. 18:19, 20 [b]Ps. 26:1; 43:1
61 [a]Lam. 5:1; Ps. 74:18; 89:50; Zeph. 2:8
62 [a]Ps. 59:7, 12; 140:3; Ezek. 36:3
63 [a]Lam. 3:14; Job 30:9
64 [a]Ps. 28:4; Jer. 51:6, 24, 56
65 [1]Or, *insolence* [a]Ex. 14:8; Deut. 2:30; Is. 6:10

1 [1]Lit., *head* [a]2 Kin. 25:9, 10; Ezek. 7:19-22

2 [a]Is. 30:14; Jer. 19:1, 11

3 [a]Is. 13:22; 34:13 [b]Is. 49:15; Ezek. 5:10

4 [a]Jer. 14:3

5 [1]Lit., *established in crimson*

6 [1]Or, *punishment for iniquity* [2]Or, *punishment for sin* [3]Or, *wrung over her* [a]Gen. 19:25; Jer. 20:16

7 [1]Or, *Nazirites* [2]Lit., *bones* [3]Heb., *sappir* [a]Ps. 51:7

8 [a]Lam. 5:10, 14; Job 30:30

9 [1]Lit., *pierced* [2]Lit., *flow away* [3]Lit., *my fields* [a]Lev. 26:39; Ezek. 24:23

10 [a]Lam. 2:20; 2 Kin. 6:29; Jer. 19:9 [b]Deut. 28:53-55

12 [a]Jer. 21:13

13 [a]Jer. 2:30; 26:8, 9

14 [a]Deut. 28:28, 29; Is. 29:10; 56:10; 59:9, 10

Chapter 4

How [a]dark the gold has become,
How the pure gold has changed!
The sacred stones are poured out
At the [1]corner of every street.
2 The precious sons of Zion,
Weighed against fine gold,
How they are regarded as [a]earthen jars,
The work of a potter's hands!
3 Even [a]jackals offer the breast,
They nurse their young;
But the daughter of my people has become [b]cruel
Like ostriches in the wilderness.
4 The tongue of the infant cleaves
To the roof of its mouth because of [a]thirst;
The little ones ask for bread;
But no one breaks *it* for them.
5 Those who ate delicacies
Are desolate in the streets;
Those [1]reared in purple
Embrace ash pits.
6 For the [1]iniquity of the daughter of my people
Is greater than the [2]sin of Sodom,
Which was [a]overthrown as in a moment,
And no hands were [3]turned toward her.
7 Her [1]consecrated ones were [a]purer than snow,
They were whiter than milk;
They were more ruddy *in* [2]body than corals,
Their polishing *was* like [3]lapis lazuli.
8 Their appearance is [a]blacker than soot,
They are not recognized in the streets;
Their skin is shriveled on their bones,
It is withered, it has become like wood.
9 Better are those [1]slain with the sword
Than those [1]slain with hunger;
For they [2a]pine away, being stricken
For lack of the fruits of [3]the field.
10 The hands of compassionate women
[a]Boiled their own children;
They became [b]food for them
Because of the destruction of the daughter of my people.
11 The LORD has accomplished His wrath,
He has poured out His fierce anger;
And He has kindled a fire in Zion
Which has consumed its foundations.
12 The kings of the earth did not believe,
Nor *did* any of the inhabitants of the world,
That the adversary and the enemy
Could [a]enter the gates of Jerusalem.
13 Because of the sins of her prophets
And the iniquities of her priests,
Who have shed in her midst
The [a]blood of the righteous,
14 They wandered, [a]blind, in the streets;

They were defiled with blood
So that no one could touch their garments.
15 "Depart! [a]Unclean!" [1]they cried of themselves.
"Depart, depart, do not touch!"
So they fled and wandered;
Men among the nations said,
"They shall not continue to dwell *with us*."
16 The presence of the LORD has scattered them;
He will not continue to regard them.
They did not [1a]honor the priests,
They did not favor the elders.
17 Yet our eyes failed;
Looking for [1]help was [a]useless.
In our watching we have watched
For a [b]nation that could not save.
18 They [a]hunted our steps
So that we could not walk in our streets;
Our [b]end drew near,
Our days were [1]finished
For our end had come.
19 Our pursuers were [a]swifter
Than the eagles of the sky.
They chased us on the mountains;
They waited in ambush for us in the [b]wilderness.
20 The breath of our nostrils, the LORD's anointed,
Was [a]captured in their pits,
Of whom we had said, "Under his [b]shadow
We shall live among the nations."
21 Rejoice and be glad, O daughter of Edom,
Who dwells in the land of Uz;
But the cup will come around to you as well,
You will become drunk and make yourself naked.
22 *The punishment* of your iniquity has been [a]completed,
O daughter of Zion;
He [b]will exile you no longer.
But He will punish your iniquity, O daughter of Edom;
He will expose your sins!

CHAPTER 5

REMEMBER, O LORD, what has befallen us;
Look, and see our [a]reproach!
2 Our inheritance has been turned over to [a]strangers,
Our houses to aliens.
3 We have become orphans [a]without a father,
Our mothers are like widows.
4 [1]We have to pay for our drinking [a]water,
Our wood comes *to us* at a price.
5 [1]Our pursuers are at our necks;
We are worn out, there is [a]no rest for us.
6 We have [1]submitted to Egypt *and* Assyria [2]to get enough bread.
7 Our [a]fathers sinned, *and* are no more;
It is we who have borne their iniquities.
8 [a]Slaves rule over us;
There is [b]no one to deliver us from their hand.

15 [1]Or, *they* (men) *cried to them*
[a]Lev. 13:45, 46

16 [1]Lit., *lift up the faces of*
[a]Is. 9:14-16; Jer. 52:24-27

17 [1]Lit., *our help*
[a]Lam. 1:7; Jer. 37:7 [b]Ezek. 29:6, 7, 16

18 [1]Lit., *full*
[a]Jer. 16:16 [b]Jer. 5:31; Ezek. 7:2-12; Amos 8:2

19 [a]Is. 5:26-28; 30:16, 17; Jer. 4:13; Hab. 1:8 [b]1 Sam. 13:6

20 [a]Jer. 39:5 [b]Dan. 4:12

22 [a]Is. 40:2; Jer. 33:7, 8 [b]Jer. 49:10; Mal. 1:3, 4

1 [a]Ps. 44:13-16

2 [a]Is. 1:7; Hos. 8:7, 8

3 [a]Ex. 22:24; Jer. 15:8; 18:21

4 [1]Lit., *We drink our water for silver*
[a]Is. 3:1

5 [1]Lit., *We have been pursued upon*
[a]Neh. 9:36, 37

6 [1]Lit., *given the hand to*
[2]Lit., *to be satisfied with*

7 [a]Jer. 14:20; 16:12

8 [a]Neh. 5:15 [b]Ps. 7:2; Zech. 11:6

9 We get our bread [1]at the [a]risk of our lives
[2]Because of the sword in the wilderness.
10 Our skin has become as [a]hot as an oven,
Because of [1]the burning heat of famine.
11 They ravished the [a]women in Zion,
The virgins in the cities of Judah.
12 Princes were hung by their hands;
[1a]Elders were not respected.
13 Young men [1]worked at the grinding mill;
And youths stumbled under *loads* of wood.
14 Elders [1]are gone from the gate,
Young men from their [a]music.
15 The joy of our hearts has [a]ceased;
Our dancing has been turned into mourning.
16 The [a]crown has fallen from our head;
Woe to us, for we have sinned!
17 Because of this our [a]heart is faint;
Because of these things our [b]eyes are dim;
18 Because of Mount Zion which lies desolate,
Foxes prowl in it.

19 Thou, O LORD, dost [1]rule forever;
Thy [a]throne is from generation to generation.
20 Why dost Thou [a]forget us forever;
Why dost Thou forsake us [1]so long?
21 [a]Restore us to Thee, O LORD, that we may be restored;
Renew [b]our days as of old,
22 Unless [a]Thou hast utterly rejected us,
And art exceedingly [b]angry with us.

9 [1]Lit., *with our soul* [2]Or, *in the face of* [a]Jer. 40:9-12

10 [1]Or, *the ravages of hunger* [a]Lam. 4:8; Job 30:30

11 [a]Is. 13:16; Zech. 14:2

12 [1]Lit., *The faces of elders* [a]Lam. 4:16; Is. 47:6

13 [1]Lit., *carry*

14 [1]Lit., *have ceased* [a]Is. 24:8; Jer. 7:34

15 [a]Jer. 25:10; Amos 8:10

16 [a]Job 19:9; Ps. 89:39; Jer. 13:18

17 [a]Is. 1:5 [b]Lam. 2:11; Job 17:7

19 [1]Lit., *sit* [a]Ps. 45:6

20 [1]Lit., *to length of days* [a]Ps. 13:1; 44:24

21 [a]Ps. 80:3; Jer. 31:18 [b]Is. 60:20-22

22 [a]Ps. 60:1, 2; Jer. 7:29 [b]Is. 64:9

THE BOOK OF EZEKIEL

The Appearance of Four Figures.

NOW it came about in the thirtieth year, on the fifth *day* of
the fourth month, while I was by the river Chebar among the
exiles, the [a]heavens were opened and I saw [1b]visions of God.
2 (On the fifth of the month [1]in the [a]fifth year of King
Jehoiachin's exile,
3 the word of the LORD came expressly to Ezekiel the
priest, son of Buzi, in the land of the Chaldeans by the river
Chebar; and there the hand of the LORD came upon him.)
4 And as I looked, behold, a [a]storm wind was coming
from the north, a great cloud with fire flashing forth continually and a bright light around it, and in its midst something
like glowing metal in the midst of the fire.
5 And within it there were figures resembling [a]four living
beings. And this was their appearance: they had human [b]form.
6 Each of them had [a]four faces and [b]four wings.
7 And their legs were straight and [1]their feet were like a
calf's hoof, and they gleamed like [a]burnished bronze.

1 [1]Some ancient mss. and versions read, *a vision* [a]Matt. 3:16; Mark 1:10; Luke 3:21; John 1:15; Acts 7:56; 10:11; Rev. 4:1; 19:11 [b]Ezek. 8:3; 11:24; 40:2; Ex. 24:10; Num. 12:6; Is. 1:1; 6:1; Dan. 8:1, 2

2 [1]Lit., *it was* [a]Ezek. 8:1; 20:1; 2 Kin. 24:12-15

4 [a]Ezek. 13:11, 13; Is. 21:1; Jer. 23:19

5 [a]Ezek. 10:15, 17, 20; Rev. 4:6-8 [b]Ezek. 1:26

6 [a]Ezek 1:10; 10:14, 21 [b]Ezek. 1:23

7 [1]Lit., *the soles of their feet* [a]Rev. 1:15; 2:13

8 Under their wings on their [a]four sides *were* human
[b]hands. As for the faces and wings of the four of them,
9 their wings touched one another; their *faces* did not
turn when they moved, each [a]went straight forward.
10 As for the [a]form of their faces, *each* had the [b]face of a
man, [1]all four had the face of a lion on the right and the face
of a bull on the left, and [1]all four had the face of an eagle.
11 Such were their faces. Their wings were spread out
above; each had two touching another *being,* and [a]two covering their bodies.
12 And each went straight forward; [a]wherever the spirit
was about to go, they would go, without turning as they went.
13 [1]In the midst of the living beings there was something
that looked like burning coals of [a]fire, [2]like torches darting
back and forth among the living beings. The fire was bright,
and lightning was [3]flashing from the fire.
14 And the living beings [a]ran to and fro like bolts of
[b]lightning.
15 Now as I looked at the living beings, behold, there was
one [a]wheel on the earth beside the living beings, [1]for *each of*
the four of them.
16 The [a]appearance of the wheels and their workmanship
was like [1]sparkling [b]beryl, and all four of them had the same
form, their appearance and workmanship *being* as if [2]one
wheel were within another.
17 Whenever they [1]moved, they [1]moved in any of their
four [2]directions, without [a]turning as they [1]moved.
18 As for their rims they were lofty and awesome, and the
rims of all four of them were [a]full of eyes round about.
19 And [a]whenever the living beings [1]moved, the wheels
[1]moved with them. And whenever the living beings [b]rose from
the earth, the wheels rose *also.*
20 [a]Wherever the spirit was about to go, they would go in
that direction[1]. And the wheels rose close beside them; for the
spirit of the living [2]beings *was* in the wheels.
21 [a]Whenever those went, these went; and whenever those
stood still, these stood still. And whenever those rose from the
earth, the wheels rose close beside them; for the spirit of the
living [1]beings *was* in the wheels.
22 Now [a]over the heads of the living [1]beings *there was*
something like an expanse, like the awesome gleam of [2]crystal,
extended over their heads.
23 And under the expanse their wings *were stretched out*
straight, one toward the other; each one also had [a]two wings
covering their bodies on the one side and on the other.
24 I also heard the sound of their wings like the [a]sound of
abundant waters as they went, like the [b]voice of [1]the Almighty,
a sound of tumult like the [c]sound of an army camp; whenever
they stood still, they dropped their wings.
25 And there came a voice from above the [a]expanse that
was over their heads; whenever they stood still, they dropped
their wings.
26 Now [a]above the expanse that was over their heads there
was something [b]resembling a throne, like [1c]lapis lazuli in appearance; and on that which resembled a throne, high up, *was*
a figure with the appearance of a [d]man.

8 [a]Ezek. 1:17; 10:11 [b]Ezek. 10:8, 21

9 [a]Ezek. 1:12; 10:22

10 [1]Lit., *the four of them* [a]Rev. 4:7 [b]Ezek. 10:14

11 [a]Ezek. 1:23; Is. 6:2

12 [a]Ezek. 1:20

13 [1]So with some ancient versions; Heb., *As the likeness of the living beings.* [2]Lit., *like the appearance of* [3]Lit., *coming out* [a]Ps. 104:4

14 [a]Zech. 4:10 [b]Matt. 24:27; Luke 17:24

15 [1]Lit., *for his four faces* [a]Ezek. 1:19-21

16 [1]Lit., *the look of beryl* [2]Lit., *the wheel in the midst of the wheel* [a]Ezek. 10:9-11 [b]Ezek. 10:9; Dan. 10:6

17 [1]Lit., *went* [2]Lit., *sides* [a]Ezek. 1:9, 12; 10:11

18 [a]Ezek. 10:12; Rev. 4:6, 8

19 [1]Lit., *went* [a]Ezek. 10:16 [b]Ezek. 10:19

20 [1]M.T. adds: *the spirit to go* [2]M.T. reads: *being* [a]Ezek. 1:12

21 [1]M.T. reads: *being* [a]Ezek. 10:17

22 [1]So some ancient mss. and versions; M.T. reads: *being* [2]Or, *ice* [a]Ezek. 10:1

23 [a]Ezek. 1:6, 11

24 [1]Heb., *Shaddai* [a]Ezek. 43:2; Rev. 1:15; 19:6 [b]Ezek. 10:5 [c]2 Kin. 7:6; Dan. 10:6

25 [a]Ezek. 1:22; 10:1

26 [1]Heb., *eben-sappir* [a]Ezek. 1:22; 10:1 [b]Ezek. 10:1; Is. 6:1; Dan. 7:9 [c]Ex. 24:10; Is. 54:11 [d]Ezek. 43:6, 7; Rev. 1:13

27 Then I [1]noticed from the appearance of his loins and upward something [a]like [2]glowing metal that looked like fire all around within it, and from the appearance of his loins and downward I saw something like fire; and *there was* a radiance around him.

28 As the appearance of the [a]rainbow [1]in the clouds on a rainy day, so *was* the appearance of the surrounding radiance. Such *was* the appearance of the likeness of the glory of the LORD. And when I saw *it*, I [b]fell on my face and heard a voice speaking.

CHAPTER 2

THEN He said to me, "Son of man, [a]stand on your feet that I may speak with you!"

2 And as He spoke to me the [a]Spirit entered me and set me on my feet; and I heard *Him* speaking to me.

3 Then He said to me, "Son of man, I am sending you to the sons of Israel, to a rebellious people who have [a]rebelled against Me; [b]they and their fathers have transgressed against Me to this very day.

4 "And I am sending you to them who are [1a]stubborn and obstinate children; and you shall say to them, 'Thus says the Lord [2]GOD.'

5 "As for them, [a]whether they listen or [1]not—for they are a rebellious house—they will [b]know that a prophet has been among them.

6 "And you, son of man, [a]neither fear them nor fear their words, though [b]thistles and thorns are with you and you sit on scorpions; neither fear their words nor be dismayed at their presence, for they are a rebellious house.

7 "But you shall [a]speak My words to them whether they listen or [1]not, for they are rebellious.

8 "Now you, son of man, listen to what I am speaking to you; do not be rebellious like that rebellious house. Open your mouth and [a]eat what I am giving you."

9 Then I looked, behold, a hand was extended to me; and lo, a [1a]scroll *was* in it.

10 When He spread it out before me, it was written on the front and back; and written on it were lamentations, mourning and [a]woe.

CHAPTER 3

THEN He said to me, "Son of man, eat what you find; eat this scroll, and go, speak to the house of Israel."

2 So I [a]opened my mouth, and He fed me this scroll.

3 And He said to me, "Son of man, feed your stomach, and [a]fill your [1]body with this scroll which I am giving you." Then I [b]ate it, and it was sweet as [c]honey in my mouth.

4 Then He said to me, "Son of man, [1]go to the house of Israel and speak with My words to them.

5 "For [a]you are not being sent to a people of [1b]unintelligible speech or difficult language, *but* to the house of Israel,

6 nor to many peoples of [1]unintelligible speech or diffi-

---

27 [1]Lit., *saw* [2]Or, *electrum* [a]Ezek. 1:4; 8:2

28 [1]Lit., *which occurs in* [a]Gen. 9:13; Rev. 4:3; 10:1 [b]Ezek. 3:23; Gen. 17:3; Dan. 8:17; Rev. 1:17

1 [a]Dan. 10:11; Acts 9:6

2 [a]Ezek. 3:24; Dan. 8:18

3 [a]1 Sam. 8:7, 8; Jer. 3:25 [b]Ezek. 20:18, 30

4 [1]Lit., *the sons, stiff-faced and hard-hearted* [2]Heb., YHWH, usually rendered LORD [a]Ezek. 3:7; Ps. 95:8; Is. 48:4; Jer. 5:3; 6:15

5 [1]Lit., *forbear* [a]Ezek. 2:7; 3:11, 27; Matt. 10:12-15; Acts 13:46 [b]Ezek. 33:33; Luke 10:10, 11; John 15:22

6 [a]Ezek. 3:9; Is. 51:12; Jer. 1:8, 17 [b]Ezek. 28:24; 2 Sam. 23:6, 7; Mic. 7:4

7 [1]Lit., *forbear* [a]Ezek. 3:10, 17; Jer. 1:7, 17

8 [a]Ezek. 3:3; Jer. 15:16

9 [1]Lit., *scroll of a book* [a]Ezek. 3:1; Jer. 36:2; Rev. 5:1-5; 10:8-11

10 [a]Rev. 8:13

2 [a]Jer. 25:17

3 [1]Lit., *inward parts* [a]Jer. 6:11; 20:9 [b]Jer. 15:16 [c]Ps. 19:10; 119:103; Rev. 10:9, 10

4 [1]Lit., *go, come*

5 [1]Lit., *deepness of lip and heaviness of tongue* [a]Jon. 1:2; Acts 14:11; 26:17 [b]Is. 28:11; 33:19

6 [1]Lit., *deepness of lip and heaviness of tongue*

cult language, whose words you cannot understand. [2]But I
have sent you to them [3]who should listen to you;
7 "Yet the house of Israel will not be willing to listen to
you, since they are not willing to listen to Me. Surely the whole
house of Israel is [1]stubborn and obstinate.
8 "Behold, I have made your face as hard as their faces,
and your forehead as hard as their foreheads.
9 "Like [1]emery harder than flint I have made your forehead. Do not be afraid of them or be dismayed before them,
though they are a rebellious house."
10 Moreover, He said to me, "Son of man, take into your
heart all My [a]words which I shall speak to you, and listen
[1]closely.
11 "And [1]go to the exiles, to the sons of your people, and
speak to them and tell them, whether they listen or [2]not: 'Thus
says the Lord [3]GOD.' "
12 Then the [a]Spirit lifted me up, and I heard a great [b]rum-
bling sound behind me: "Blessed be the glory of the LORD [1]in
His place."
13 And I *heard* the sound of the wings of the living beings
touching one another, and the sound of the [a]wheels beside
them, even a great rumbling sound.
14 So the Spirit lifted me up and took me away; and I
went embittered in the rage of my spirit, and the hand of the
LORD was strong on me.
15 Then I came to the exiles who lived beside the river
Chebar at Tel-abib, and I sat there [a]seven days where they
were living, causing consternation among them.
16 Now it came about [a]at the end of seven days that the
word of the LORD came to me, saying,
17 "Son of man, I have appointed you a [a]watchman to the
house of Israel; whenever you hear a word from My mouth,
[b]warn them from Me.
18 "When I say to the wicked, 'You shall surely die'; and
you do not warn him or speak out to warn the wicked from his
wicked way that he may live, that wicked man shall die in his
iniquity, but his [a]blood I will require at your hand.
19 "Yet if you have [a]warned the wicked, and he does not
turn from his wickedness or from his wicked way, he shall die
in his iniquity; but [b]you have delivered yourself.
20 "Again, [a]when a righteous man turns away from his righteousness and commits iniquity, and I place an [b]obstacle
before him, he shall die; since you have not warned him, he
shall die in his sin, and his righteous deeds which he has done
shall not be remembered; but his blood I will require at your
hand.
21 "However, if you have [a]warned [1]the righteous man that
the righteous should not sin, and he does not sin, he shall
surely live because he took warning; and you have delivered
yourself."
22 And the hand of the LORD was on me there, and He
said to me, "Get up, go out to the plain, and there I will [a]speak
to you."
23 So I got up and went out to the plain; and behold, the
[a]glory of the LORD was standing there, like the glory which I
saw by the river Chebar, and I fell on my face.

6 [2]Or, *If I had sent you to them, they would listen to you.* [3]Lit., *they*

7 [1]Lit., *of a hard forehead and a stiff heart*

9 [1]Lit., *corundum*

10 [1]Lit., *with your ears* [a]Ezek. 3:1-3; 2:8; Job 22:22

11 [1]Lit., *go, come* [2]Lit., *forbear* [3]YHWH, usually rendered LORD

12 [1]Or, *from* [a]Ezek. 3:14; 8:3; Acts 8:39 [b]Acts 2:2

13 [a]Ezek. 1:15; 10:16, 17

15 [a]Job 2:13

16 [a]Jer. 42:7

17 [a]Ezek. 33:7-9; Is. 52:8; 56:10; 62:6; Jer. 6:17 [b]2 Chr. 19:10; Is. 58:1; Hab. 2:1

18 [a]Ezek. 3:20; 33:6, 8

19 [a]Ezek. 33:3, 9; 2 Kin. 17:13, 14 [b]Ezek. 14:14, 20; Acts 18:6; 1 Tim. 4:16

20 [a]Ezek. 18:24; 33:18; Ps. 125:5; Zeph. 1:6 [b]Ezek. 14:3, 7-9; Is. 8:14; Jer. 6:21

21 [1]Lit., *him, the righteous* [a]Acts 20:31

22 [a]Acts 9:6

23 [a]Ezek. 1:28; Acts 7:55

24 The [a]Spirit then entered me and made me stand on my
feet, and He spoke with me and said to me, "Go, shut yourself
up in your house.
25 "As for you, son of man, they will [a]put ropes on you and
bind you with them, so that you cannot go out among them.
26 "Moreover, I will make your tongue stick to [1]the roof of
your mouth so that you will be dumb, and cannot be a man
who [a]rebukes them, for they are a rebellious house.
27 "But when I speak to you, I will open your mouth, and
you will say to them, 'Thus says the Lord [1]GOD.' He who hears,
let him hear; and he who refuses, let him refuse; for they are a
rebellious house."

CHAPTER 4

"NOW you son of man, [a]get yourself a brick, place it before
you, and inscribe a city on it, Jerusalem.
2 "Then [a]lay siege against it, build a siege wall, [1]raise up a
ramp, pitch camps, and place battering rams against it all
around.
3 "Then get yourself an iron plate and set it up as an iron
wall between you and the city, and set your face toward it so
that [a]it is under siege, and besiege it. This is a [b]sign to the
house of Israel.
4 "As for you, lie down on your left side, and lay the
iniquity of the house of Israel on it; you shall [a]bear their
iniquity for the number of days that you lie on it.
5 "For I have assigned you a number of days corresponding to the years of their iniquity, three hundred and ninety
days; thus you shall bear the iniquity of the house of Israel.
6 "When you have completed these, you shall lie down a
second time, *but* on your right side, and bear the iniquity of
the house of Judah; I have assigned it to you for forty days, a
day for [a]each year.
7 "Then you shall set your face toward the siege of Jerusalem with your arm bared, and [a]prophesy against it.
8 "Now behold, I will [a]put ropes on you so that you cannot turn from one side to the other, until you have completed
the days of your siege.
9 "But as for you, take wheat, barley, beans, lentils, millet
and [a]spelt, put them in one vessel and make them into bread
for yourself; you shall eat it according to the number of the
days that you lie on your side, three hundred and ninety days.
10 "And your food which you eat *shall be* [a]twenty shekels a
day by weight; you shall eat it from time to time.
11 "And the water you drink will be the sixth part of a hin
by measure; you shall drink it from time to time.
12 "And you shall eat it as a barley cake, having baked *it* in
their sight over human [a]dung."
13 Then the LORD said, "Thus shall the sons of Israel eat
their bread [a]unclean among the nations where I shall banish
them."
14 But I said, "[a]Ah, Lord [1]GOD! Behold, I have [b]never
been defiled; for from my youth until now I have never eaten
what [c]died of itself or was torn by beasts, nor has any [d]unclean
meat ever entered my mouth."

24 [a]Ezek. 2:2

25 [a]Ezek. 4:8

26 [1]Lit., *your palate* [a]Hos. 4:17; Amos 8:11, 12

27 [1]YHWH, usually rendered LORD

1 [a]Ex. 5:1; 12:3; Is. 20:2; Jer. 13:1; 18:2; 19:1

2 [1]Lit., *cast* [a]Ezek. 21:22; Jer. 6:6

3 [a]Ezek. 5:2; Jer. 39:1, 2 [b]Ezek. 12:6, 11; 24:24-27; Is. 8:18; 20:3

4 [a]Lev. 10:17; 16:22; Num. 18:1

6 [a]Num. 14:34; Dan. 9:24-26; 12:11, 12; Rev. 11:2, 3

7 [a]Ezek. 21:2

8 [a]Ezek. 3:25

9 [a]Ex. 9:32; Is. 28:25

10 [a]Ezek. 45:12

12 [a]Is. 36:12

13 [a]Dan. 1:8; Hos. 9:3

14 [1]YHWH, usually rendered LORD [a]Ezek. 9:8; 20:49; Jer. 1:6 [b]Acts 10:14 [c]Ezek. 44:31; Lev. 17:15; 22:8 [d]Deut. 14:3; Is. 65:4; 66:17

15 Then He said to me, "See, I shall give you cow's dung
in place of human dung over which you will prepare your
bread."
16 Moreover, He said to me, "Son of man, behold, I am
going to [a]break the staff of bread in Jerusalem, and they will
eat bread by [b]weight and with anxiety, and drink water by
[c]measure and in horror,
17 because bread and water will be scarce; and they will be
appalled with one another and [a]waste away in their iniquity.

Chapter 5

"As for you, son of man, take a [a]sharp sword; take and [1]use
it *as* a barber's razor on your head and beard. Then take [b]scales
for weighing and divide [2]the hair.
2 "One third you shall burn in the fire at the center of the
city, when the [a]days of the siege are completed. Then you shall
take one third and strike *it* with the sword all around [1]the city,
and one third you shall scatter to the wind; and I will [b]un-
sheathe a sword behind them.
3 "Take also a [a]few in number from [1]them and bind them
in the edge of your *robes.*
4 "And take again some of them and throw them into the
fire, and [a]burn them in the fire; from it a fire will [1]spread to all
the house of Israel.
5 "Thus says the Lord [1]God, 'This is [a]Jerusalem; I have set
her at the [b]center of the nations, with lands around her.
6 'But she has rebelled against My ordinances more wickedly than the nations and against My statutes [a]more than the
lands which surround her; for they have [b]rejected My ordinances and have not walked [1]in My statutes.'
7 "Therefore, thus says the Lord God, 'Because you have
[a]more turmoil than the nations which surround you, and have
not walked in My statutes, nor observed My ordinances, nor
observed the ordinances of the nations which surround you,'
8 therefore, thus says the Lord God, 'Behold, I, even I,
am [a]against you, and I will [b]execute judgments among you in
the sight of the nations.
9 'And because of all your abominations, I will do among
you what I have [a]not done, and the like of which I will never
do again.
10 'Therefore, [a]fathers will eat *their* sons among you, and
sons will eat their fathers; for I will execute judgments on you,
and [b]scatter all your remnant to every wind.
11 'So as I live,' [1]declares the Lord God, 'surely, because
you have [a]defiled My sanctuary with all your [b]detestable idols
and with all your abominations, therefore I will also [c] withdraw, and My eye shall have no pity and I will not spare.
12 'One third of you will die by [a]plague or be consumed by
famine among you, one third will fall by the sword around
you, and one third I will [b]scatter to every wind, and I will
[c]unsheathe a sword behind them.
13 'Thus My anger will be spent, and I will [1]satisfy My
wrath on them, and I shall be [2][a]appeased; then they will know

16 [a]Ezek. 5:16; 14:13; Lev. 26:26; Is. 3:1 [b]Ezek. 4:10, 11; 12:19 [c]Ezek. 12:18, 19; Lam. 5:4

17 [a]Ezek. 24:23; 33:10

1 [1]Lit., *make it pass over your head* [2]Lit., *them* [a]Ezek. 44:20; Lev. 21:5; Is. 7:20 [b]Dan. 5:27

2 [1]Lit., *it* [a]Ezek. 4:2-8; Jer. 39:1, 2 [b]Lev. 26:33

3 [1]Lit., *there* [a]2 Kin. 25:12; Jer. 39:10

4 [1]Lit., *go out* [a]Jer. 42:16, 17, 22

5 [1]YHWH, usually rendered Lord, and so throughout the chap. [a]Ezek. 4:1; Jer. 6:6 [b]Ezek. 16:14; Deut. 4:6; Lam. 1:1

6 [1]Lit., *in them, My statutes* [a]Ezek. 16:47, 48, 51; 2 Kin. 17:8-20 [b]Neh. 9:16, 17; Ps. 78:10; Jer. 11:10; Zech. 7:11

7 [a]2 Kin. 21:9-11; 2 Chr. 33:9; Jer. 2:10, 11

8 [a]Ezek. 15:7; 21:3; Jer. 21:5, 13; Zech. 14:2 [b]Ezek. 5:15; 11:9; Jer. 24:9

9 [a]Dan. 9:12; Matt. 24:21

10 [a]Lev. 26:29; Jer. 19:9 [b]Ezek. 5:2, 12; 6:8; 12:14; Ps. 44:11; Amos 9:9; Zech. 2:6; 7:14

11 [1]Lit., *utterance of,* and so throughout the chap. [a]Ezek. 8:5, 6, 16; Jer. 7:9-11 [b]Ezek. 7:20; Jer. 16:18 [c]Ps. 107:39

12 [a]Ezek. 5:17; 6:11, 12; Jer. 15:2; 21:9 [b]Ezek. 5:2, 10; Amos 9:9; Zech. 2:6 [c]Ezek. 5:2; 12:14; Jer. 43:10, 11; 44:27

13 [1]Lit., *cause to rest* [2]Lit., *comforted* [a]Is. 1:24

that I, the LORD, have [b]spoken in My zeal when I have spent
My wrath upon them.
14 'Moreover, I will make you a desolation and a [a]reproach
among the nations which surround you, in the sight of all who
pass by.
15 'So [1]it will be a reproach, a reviling, a [a]warning and an
object of horror to the nations who surround you, when I
[b]execute judgments against you in anger, wrath, and raging
rebukes. I, the LORD, have spoken.
16 'When I send against them the [1]deadly arrows of famine which [2]were for the destruction of those whom I shall
send to destroy you, then I shall also intensify the famine upon
you, and break the staff of bread.
17 'Moreover, I will send on you famine and wild beasts,
and they will bereave you of children; plague and bloodshed
also will pass through you, and I will bring the sword on you.
I, the LORD, have spoken.' "

CHAPTER 6

AND the word of the LORD came to me saying,
2 "Son of man, set your face toward the mountains of
Israel, and prophesy against them,
3 and say, 'Mountains of Israel, listen to the word of the
Lord [1]GOD! Thus says the Lord [1]GOD to the mountains, the
hills, the ravines and the valleys: "Behold, I Myself am going
to bring a sword on you, and I will destroy your high places.
4 "So your [a]altars will become desolate, and your incense
altars will be smashed; and I shall make your slain fall in front
of your idols.
5 "I shall also lay the dead bodies of the sons of Israel in
front of their idols; and I shall scatter your [a]bones around your
altars.
6 "In all your dwellings, [a]cities will become waste and the
high places will be desolate, that your altars may become waste
and [1]desolate, your [b]idols may be broken and brought to an
end, your incense altars may be cut down, and your works may
be blotted out.
7 "And the slain will fall among you, and you will know
that I am the LORD.
8 "However, I shall leave a [a]remnant, for you will have
those who [b]escaped the sword among the nations when you are
scattered among the countries.
9 "Then those of you who escape will [a]remember Me
among the nations to which they will be carried captive, how I
have [1b]been hurt by their adulterous hearts which turned away
from Me, and by their eyes, which played the harlot after their
idols; and they will [c]loathe themselves in their own sight for
the evils which they have committed, for all their
abominations.
10 "Then they will know that I am the LORD; I have not
said in vain [1]that I would inflict this disaster on them." '
11 "Thus says the Lord [1]GOD, 'Clap your hand, [a]stamp your
foot, and say, "[b]Alas, because of all the evil abominations of

13 [b]Ezek. 36:5, 6; 38:19; Is. 59:17

14 [a]Ezek. 22:4; Ps. 74:3-10; 79:1-4

15 [1]Ancient versions: *you* [a]Is. 26:9; Jer. 22:8, 9; 1 Cor. 10:11 [b]Ezek. 5:8; 25:17; Is. 66:15, 16

16 [1]Lit., *evil* [2]Or, *are for destruction, which I will send . . .*

3 [1]YHWH, usually rendered LORD.

4 [a]Ezek. 6:6; Lev. 26:30; 2 Chr. 14:5; Is. 27:9

5 [a]2 Kin. 23:14, 16, 20; Jer. 8:1, 2

6 [1]So some ancient versions; Heb., *bear their guilt* [a]Ezek. 5:14; Lev. 26:31; Is. 6:11 [b]Ezek. 6:4; Mic. 1:7; Zech. 13:2

8 [a]Is. 6:13; Jer. 30:11 [b]Ezek. 7:16; 14:22; Jer. 44:14, 28

9 [1]Lit., *been broken,* or, *broken for Myself their* [a]Deut. 4:29; 30:2; Jer. 51:50 [b]Ps. 78:40; Is. 7:13; 43:24; Hos. 11:8 [c]Ezek. 20:43; 36:31; Job 42:6

10 [1]Lit., *to do this evil to*

11 [1]YHWH, usually rendered LORD [a]Ezek. 25:6 [b]Ezek. 9:4

the house of Israel, which will fall by [c]sword, famine, and
plague!
12 "He who is [a]far off will die by the plague, and he who is
near will fall by the sword, and he who remains and is besieged
will die by the famine. Thus shall I [b]spend My wrath on them.
13 "Then you will know that I am the LORD, when their
[a]slain are among their idols around their altars, on [b]every high
hill on all the tops of the mountains, under every green tree,
and under every leafy oak—the places where they offered soothing aroma to all their idols.
14 "So throughout all their habitations I shall [a]stretch out
My hand against them and make the land more desolate and
waste than the wilderness toward Diblah; thus they will know
that I am the LORD." ' "

CHAPTER 7

MOREOVER, the word of the LORD came to me saying,
2 "And you, son of man, thus says the Lord [1]GOD to the
land of Israel, 'An [a]end! The end is coming on the four corners
of the land.
3 'Now the end is upon you, and I shall send My anger
against you, I shall judge you according to your ways, and I
shall bring all your abominations upon you.
4 'For My eye will have no pity on you, nor shall I spare
you, but I shall [a]bring your ways upon you, and your abominations will be among you; then you will [b]know that I am the
LORD!'
5 "Thus says the Lord [1]GOD, 'A [a]disaster, unique disaster,
behold it is coming!
6 'An end is coming; the end has come! It has [a]awakened
against you; behold, it has come!
7 'Your doom has come to you, O inhabitant of the land.
The [a]time has come, the [b]day is near—tumult rather than
joyful shouting on the mountains.
8 'Now I will shortly [a]pour out My wrath on you, and
spend My anger against you, [b]judge you according to your
ways, and bring on you all your abominations.
9 'And My eye will show no pity, nor will I spare. I will
[1]repay you according to your ways, while your abominations
are in your midst; then you will know that I, the LORD, do the
smiting.
10 'Behold, the day! Behold, it is coming! *Your* doom has
gone forth; the [a]rod has budded, arrogance has blossomed.
11 'Violence [1]has grown into a rod of [a]wickedness. None of
them *shall remain*, none of their multitude, none of their
[b]wealth, nor anything eminent among them.
12 'The [a]time has come, the day has arrived. Let not the
[b]buyer rejoice nor the seller mourn; for [c]wrath is against all
their multitude.
13 'Indeed, the seller will not [1a]regain [2]what he sold as long
as [3]they *both* live, for the vision regarding all their multitude
will not [4]be averted; nor will any of them maintain his life by
his iniquity.

11 [c]Ezek. 5:12; 7:15

12 [a]Dan. 9:7 [b]Ezek. 5:13; Lam. 4:11, 22

13 [a]Ezek. 6:4-7 [b]Ezek. 20:28; 1 Kin. 14:23; 2 Kin. 16:4; Is. 57:5-7; Hos. 4:13

14 [a]Ezek. 14:13; 20:33, 34; Is. 5:25; 9:12

2 [1]YHWH, usually rendered LORD [a]Ezek. 7:3, 5, 6; 11:13; Amos 8:2, 10

4 [a]Ezek. 11:21; 22:31; Hos. 9:7 [b]Ezek. 7:27; 6:7, 14

5 [1]YHWH, usually rendered LORD [a]2 Kin. 21:12, 13; Nah. 1:9

6 [a]Zech. 13:7

7 [a]Ezek. 7:12; 12:23-25, 28 [b]Is. 22:5

8 [a]Ezek. 9:8; 14:19; Is. 42:25; Nah. 1:6 [b]Ezek. 7:3; 33:20; 36:19

9 [1]Lit., *give*

10 [a]Is. 10:5; Ps. 89:32

11 [1]Lit., *has risen* [a]Ps. 73:8; 125:3; Is. 59:6-8 [b]Zeph. 1:18

12 [a]Ezek. 7:5-7, 10; 1 Cor. 7:29-31; James 5:8, 9 [b]Prov. 20:14; 1 Cor. 7:30 [c]Ezek. 7:14; 6:11, 12; Is. 5:13, 14

13 [1]Lit., *return to* [2]Lit., *thing sold*, i.e., his inherited land [3]Lit., *their life among the living ones* [4]Lit., *return* [a]Lev. 25:24-28, 31

14 ‘They have [a]blown the trumpet and made everything
ready, but no one is going to the battle; for My wrath is against
all [1]their multitude.
15 ‘The [a]sword is outside, and the plague and the famine
are within; he who is in the field will die by the sword, famine
and the plague will also consume those in the city.
16 ‘Even when their survivors [a]escape, they will be on the
mountains like [b]doves of the valleys, all of them [1c]mourning,
each over his own iniquity.
17 ‘All [a]hands will hang limp, and all knees will [1]become
like water.
18 ‘And they will [a]gird themselves with sackcloth, and
[b]shuddering will overwhelm them; and shame *will be* on all
faces, and [c]baldness on all their heads.
19 ‘They shall [a]fling their silver into the streets, and their
gold shall become an abhorrent thing; their [b]silver and their
gold shall not be able to deliver them in the day of the wrath
of the LORD. They cannot satisfy their [1]appetite, nor can they
fill their stomachs, for their iniquity has become an occasion
of stumbling.
20 ‘And they transformed the beauty of His ornaments
into pride, and they made the images of their abominations
and their detestable things with it; therefore I will make it an
abhorrent thing to them.
21 ‘And I shall give it into the hands of the [a]foreigners as
plunder and to the wicked of the earth as spoil, and they will
profane it.
22 ‘I shall also turn my [a]face from them, and they will
profane My secret place; then robbers will enter and profane
it.
23 ‘[a]Make the chain, for the land is full of [1b]bloody crimes,
and the city is [c]full of violence.
24 ‘Therefore, I shall bring the worst of the [a]nations, and
they will possess their houses. I shall also make the [b]pride of
the strong ones cease, and their [c]holy places will be profaned.
25 ‘When anguish comes, they will seek [a]peace, but there
will be none.
26 ‘[a]Disaster will come upon disaster, and [b]rumor will be
added to rumor; then they will seek a [c]vision from a prophet,
but the [d]law will be lost from the priest and [e]counsel from the
elders.
27 ‘The king will mourn, the prince will be [a]clothed with
horror, and the hands of the people of the land will [1]tremble.
According to their conduct I shall deal with them, and by their
judgments I shall judge them. And they will know that I am
the LORD.’ ”

CHAPTER 8

AND it came about in the sixth year, on the fifth *day* of the
sixth month, as I was sitting in my house with the elders of
Judah sitting before me, that the hand of the Lord [1]GOD fell
on me there.
2 Then I looked, and behold, a likeness as the appearance of [1]a man; from His loins and downward *there was* the

14 [1]Lit., *her* [a]Num. 10:9; Jer. 4:5

15 [a]Ezek. 5:12; 6:11, 12; 12:16; Jer. 14:18

16 [1]Lit., *moaning* [a]Ezek. 6:8; 14:22; Ezra 9:15; Is. 37:31 [b]Is. 38:14 [c]Is. 59:11; Nah. 2:7

17 [1]Lit., *run with water* [a]Ezek. 21:7; 22:14; Is. 13:7; Heb. 12:12

18 [a]Ezek. 27:31; Is. 15:3; Amos 8:10 [b]Job 21:6; Ps. 55:5 [c]Ezek. 27:31

19 [1]Lit., *soul* [a]Is. 2:20; 30:22 [b]Prov. 11:4; Zeph. 1:18

21 [a]2 Kin. 24:13; Ps. 74:2-8; Jer. 52:13

22 [a]Ezek. 39:23, 24; Jer. 18:17

23 [1]Lit., *judgment of blood* [a]Jer. 27:2 [b]Ezek. 9:9; Hos. 4:2 [c]Ezek. 8:17

24 [a]Ezek. 21:31; 28:7 [b]Ezek. 33:28 [c]Ezek. 24:21; 2 Chr. 7:20

25 [a]Ezek. 13:10, 16

26 [a]Is. 47:11; Jer. 4:20 [b]Ezek. 21:7 [c]Jer. 21:2; 37:17 [d]Ezek. 22:26; Ps. 74:9; Mic. 3:6 [e]Ezek. 11:2; Jer. 18:18

27 [1]Lit., *be terrified* [a]Ezek. 26:16; Job 8:22; Ps. 35:26; 109:18, 29

1 [1]YHWH, usually rendered LORD

2 [1]Heb., *fire*

[a]appearance of fire, and from His loins and upward the appearance of brightness, like the appearance [b]of [2]glowing metal.
3 And He stretched out the form of a hand and caught
me by a lock of my head; and the [a]Spirit lifted me up between
earth and heaven and brought me in the visions of God to
Jerusalem, to the entrance of the [1]north gate of the inner
court, where the seat of the idol of jealousy, which provokes to
jealousy, was *located.*
4 And behold, the [a]glory of the God of Israel *was* there,
like the appearance which I saw in the plain.
5 Then He said to me, "Son of man, [a]raise your eyes,
now, toward the north." So I raised my eyes toward the north,
and behold, to the north of the altar gate *was* this [b]idol of
jealousy at the entrance.
6 And He said to me, "Son of man, do you see what they
are doing, the great [a]abominations which the house of Israel
are committing here, that I should be far from My sanctuary?
But yet you will see still greater abominations."
7 Then He brought me to the entrance of the court, and
when I looked, behold, a hole in the wall.
8 And He said to me, "Son of man, now [a]dig through the
wall." So I dug through the wall, and behold, an entrance.
9 And He said to me, "Go in and see the wicked abominations that they are committing here."
10 So I entered and looked, and behold, every form of
creeping things and beasts *and* detestable things, with all the
idols of the house of Israel, were carved on the wall all around.
11 And standing in front of them were [a]seventy [b]elders of
the house of Israel, with Jaazaniah the son of Shaphan standing among them, each man with his [c]censer in his hand, and
the fragrance of the cloud of incense rising.
12 Then He said to me, "Son of man, do you see what the
elders of the house of Israel are committing in the dark, each
man in the room of his carved images? For they say, 'The
LORD does not see us; the LORD has forsaken the land.' "
13 And He said to me, "Yet you will see still greater abominations which they are committing."
14 Then he brought me to the entrance of the [a]gate of the
LORD's house which *was* toward the north; and behold, women
were sitting there weeping for Tammuz.
15 And He said to me, "Do you see *this,* son of man? Yet
you will see still greater abominations than these."
16 Then He brought me into the inner court of the LORD's
house. And behold, at the entrance to the temple of the LORD,
between the porch and the altar, *were* about twenty-five men
with their [a]backs to the temple of the LORD and their faces
toward the east; and [b]they were [1]prostrating themselves eastward toward the sun.
17 And he said to me, "Do you see *this,* son of man? Is it
too light a thing for the house of Judah to commit the abominations which they have committed here, that they have [a]filled
the land with violence and [b]provoked Me repeatedly? For behold, they are putting the twig to their nose.
18 "Therefore, I indeed shall deal in wrath. My eye will
have no pity nor shall I spare; and [a]though they cry in My ears
with a loud voice, yet I shall not listen to them."

2 [2]Or, *electrum* [a]Ezek. 1:27 [b]Ezek. 1:4, 27

3 [1]Lit., *facing north* [a]Ezek. 3:12; 11:1

4 [a]Ezek. 1:28

5 [a]Jer. 3:2; Zech. 5:5 [b]Ezek. 8:3; Ps. 78:58; Jer. 7:30; Jer. 32:34

6 [a]Ezek. 8:9, 17; 5:11; 2 Kin. 23:4, 5

8 [a]Job 34:22; Is. 29:15

11 [a]Ezek. 24:1, 9; Num. 11:16, 25; Luke 10:1 [b]Jer. 19:1 [c]Num. 16:17, 35

14 [a]Ezek. 44:4; 46:9

16 [1]I.e., worshiping [a]Ezek. 23:39; 2 Kin. 8:30; 2 Chr. 29:6; Jer. 2:27 [b]Deut. 4:19; 17:3; Job 31:26-28; Jer. 44:17

17 [a]Ezek. 7:11, 23; 9:9; Amos 3:10; Mic. 2:2 [b]Ezek. 16:26; Jer. 7:18, 19

18 [a]Is. 1:15; Jer. 11:11; Mic. 3:4; Zech. 7:13

CHAPTER 9

THEN He cried out in my hearing with a loud [a]voice saying,
"Draw near, [1]O executioners of the city, each with his destroying weapon in his hand."
2 And behold, six men came from the direction of the
upper gate which faces north, each with his shattering weapon
in his hand; and among them was a certain man clothed in
linen with a [1]writing case at his loins. And they went in and
stood beside the bronze altar.
3 Then the [a]glory of the God of Israel went up from the
cherub on which it had been, to the threshold of the [1]temple.
And He called to the man clothed in linen at whose loins was
the writing case.
4 And the LORD said to him, "Go through the midst of
the city, *even* through the midst of Jerusalem, and put a [a]mark
on the foreheads of the men who [b]sigh and groan over all the
abominations which are being committed in its midst."
5 But to the others He said in my hearing, "Go through
the city after him and strike; do not let your eye have pity, and
do not spare.
6 "[1]Utterly [a]slay old men, young men, maidens, little children, and women, but do not [b]touch any man on whom is the
mark; and you shall [c]start from My sanctuary." So they started
with the [2]elders who *were* before the [3]temple.
7 And He said to them, "[a]Defile the [1]temple and fill the
courts with the slain. Go out!" Thus they went out and struck
down *the people* in the city.
8 Then it came about as they were striking and I *alone*
was left, that I [a]fell on my face and cried out [1]saying, "[b]Alas,
Lord [2]GOD! Art Thou destroying the whole remnant of Israel
[3]by pouring out Thy wrath on Jerusalem?"
9 Then He said to me, "The iniquity of the house of
Israel and Judah is very, very great, and the land is [a]filled with
blood, and the city is [b]full of perversion; for [c]they say, 'The
LORD has forsaken the land, and the LORD does not see!'
10 "But as for Me, [a]My eye will have no pity nor shall I
spare, but [b]I shall bring their conduct upon their heads."
11 Then behold, the man clothed in linen at whose loins
was the [1]writing case [2]reported, saying, "I have done just as
Thou hast commanded me."

CHAPTER 10

THEN I looked, and behold, in the [1a]expanse that was over
the heads of the cherubim something like a [b]sapphire stone, in
appearance resembling a [c]throne, appeared above them.
2 And He spoke to the man clothed in linen and said,
"Enter between the [a]whirling wheels under the [1]cherubim, and
fill your hands with [b]coals of fire from between the cherubim,
and scatter *them* over the city." And he entered in my sight.
3 Now the cherubim were standing on the right side of
the [1]temple when the man entered, and the cloud filled the
[a]inner court.
4 Then the [a]glory of the LORD went up from the cherub
to the threshold of the temple, and the [b]temple was filled with

1 [1]Lit., *you who punish* [a]Is. 6:8

2 [1]Or, *scribal inkhorn*

3 [1]Lit., *house* [a]Ezek. 10:4; 11:22, 23

4 [a]Ezek. 9:6; Ex. 12:7, 13; 2 Cor. 1:22; 2 Tim. 2:19; Rev. 7:2, 3 [b]Ezek. 6:11; 21:6; Ps. 119:53, 136; Jer. 13:17

6 [1]Lit., To *destruction* [2]Or, *old men* [3]Lit., *house* [a]2 Chr. 36:17 [b]Ex. 12:23; Rev. 9:4 [c]Jer. 25:29; Amos 3:2; Luke 12:47

7 [1]Lit., *house* [a]Ezek. 7:20-22; 2 Chr. 36:17

8 [1]Lit., *and said* [2]YHWH, usually rendered LORD [3]Lit., *by Thy pouring* [a]1 Chr. 21:16 [b]Ezek. 11:13; Amos 7:2-6

9 [a]Ezek. 7:23; 22:2, 3; 2 Kin. 21:16; Jer. 2:34 [b]Ezek. 22:29; Mic. 3:1-3; 7:3 [c]Ezek. 8:12; Job 22:13; Ps. 10:11; 94:7; Is. 29:15

10 [a]Ezek. 8:18; 24:14; Is. 65:6 [b]Ezek. 7:4; 11:21; Hos. 9:7

11 [1]Or, *scribal inkhorn* [2]Lit., *brought back word*

1 [1]Or, *firmament* [a]Ezek. 1:22, 26 [b]Ex. 24:10 [c]Rev. 4:2, 3

2 [1]So with Gk.; Heb., *cherub* [a]Ezek. 10:13; 1:15-21 [b]Ezek. 1:13; Ps. 18:10-13; Is. 6:6; Rev. 8:5

3 [1]Lit., *house*, and so throughout the chap. [a]Ezek. 8:3, 16

4 [a]Ezek. 9:3; 11:22, 23 [b]Ex. 40:34, 35; Is. 6:1-4

the cloud, and the court was filled with the [c]brightness of the
glory of the LORD.
5 Moreover, the sound of the wings of the cherubim was
heard as far as the outer court, like the [a]voice of [1]God Almighty
when He speaks.
6 And it came about when He commanded the man
clothed in linen, saying, "Take fire from between the whirling
wheels, from between the cherubim," he entered and stood
beside a wheel.
7 Then the cherub stretched out his hand from between
the cherubim to the fire which *was* between the cherubim,
took some and put it into the hands of the one clothed in
linen, who took *it* and went out.
8 And the cherubim appeared to have the form of a
man's hand under their wings.
9 Then I looked, and behold, [a]four wheels beside the
cherubim, one wheel beside each cherub; and the appearance
of the wheels *was* like the gleam of a [1b]Tarshish stone.
10 And as for their appearance, all four of them had the
same likeness, as if one wheel were within another wheel.
11 When they moved, they went [a]in *any of* their four
[1]directions without turning as they went; but they followed in
the direction which [2]they faced, without turning as they went.
12 And their [a]whole body, their backs, their hands, their
wings, and the [b]wheels were full of eyes all around, the wheels
belonging to all four of them.
13 The wheels were called in my hearing, the whirling
wheels.
14 And [a]each one had four faces. The first face *was* the
face of a cherub, the second face *was* the face of a man, the
third the face of a lion, and the fourth the face of an eagle.
15 Then the cherubim rose up. They are the [a]living beings
that I saw by the river Chebar.
16 Now when the cherubim moved, the wheels would go
beside them; also when the cherubim lifted up their wings to
rise from the ground, the wheels would not turn from beside
them.
17 When [1]the cherubim [a]stood still, the [1]wheels would
stand still; and when they rose up, the [1]wheels would rise with
them; for the spirit of the living beings *was* in them.
18 Then the glory of the LORD departed from the threshold of the temple and stood [a]over the cherubim.
19 When the cherubim departed, they lifted their wings
and rose up from the earth in my sight with the wheels beside
them; and they stood still at the entrance of the east gate of
the LORD's house. And the glory of the God of Israel [1]hovered
over them.
20 These are the [a]living beings that I saw beneath the God
of Israel by the river Chebar; so I knew that they *were*
cherubim.
21 [a]Each one had four faces and each one four wings, and
beneath their wings *was* the form of human hands.
22 As for the likeness of their faces, they were the same
faces whose appearance I had seen by the river Chebar. Each
one went straight ahead.

4 [c]Ezek. 1:28

5 [1]Heb. *El Shaddai*
[a]Ezek. 1:24; Job 40:9; Rev. 10:3

9 [1]Perhaps, *beryl*
[a]Ezek. 1:15-17 [b]Dan. 10:6; Rev. 21:20

11 [1]Lit., *sides* [2]Lit., *the head*
[a]Ezek. 1:17

12 [a]Rev. 4:6, 8 [b]Ezek. 1:18

14 [a]Ezek. 10:21; 1:6, 10; 1 Kin. 7:29, 36; Rev. 4:7

15 [a]Ezek. 1:3, 5

17 [1]Lit., *they*
[a]Ezek. 1:21

18 [a]Ps. 18:10

19 [1]Lit., *over them from above*

20 [a]Ezek. 10:15; 1:5, 26

21 [a]Ezek. 10:14; 1:6, 8; 41:18, 19

CHAPTER 11

MOREOVER, the Spirit [a]lifted me up and brought me to
the east gate of the LORD's house which faced eastward. And
behold, *there were* twenty-five men at the entrance of the gate,
and among them I saw Jaazaniah son of Azzur and [b]Pelatiah
son of Benaiah, leaders of the people.
2 And He said to me, "Son of man, these are the men
who devise iniquity and [a]give evil advice in this city,
3 who say, '[1]Is not *the time* near to build houses? [2]This
[a]*city* is the pot and we are the flesh.'
4 "Therefore, [a]prophesy against them, son of man,
prophesy!"
5 Then the Spirit of the LORD fell upon me, and He said
to me, "Say, 'Thus says the LORD, "So you think, house of
Israel, for [a]I know [1]your [b]thoughts.
6 "You have [a]multiplied your slain in this city, filling its
streets with [1]them."
7 'Therefore, thus says the Lord [1]GOD, "Your [a]slain
whom you have laid in the midst of [2]the city are the flesh, and
this *city* is the pot; but [3]I shall [b]bring you out of it.
8 "You have feared a sword; so I will [a]bring a sword upon
you," the Lord GOD declares.
9 "And I shall bring you out of the midst of [1]the city, and
I shall deliver you into the hands of [a]strangers and [b]execute
judgments against you.
10 "You will [a]fall by the sword. I shall judge you to the
[b]border of Israel; so you shall know that I am the LORD.
11 "This *city* will [a]not be a pot for you, nor will you be flesh
in the midst of it, *but* I shall judge you to the border of Israel.
12 "Thus you will know that I am the LORD; for you have
not walked in my statutes nor have you [a]executed My ordinances, but have acted according to the ordinances of the
[b]nations around you." ' "
13 Now it came about as I prophesied, that [a]Pelatiah son
of Benaiah died. Then I fell on my face and cried out with a
loud voice and said, "[b]Alas, Lord GOD! Wilt Thou bring the
remnant of Israel to a complete end?"
14 Then the word of the LORD came to me, saying,
15 "Son of man, your brothers, your [1]relatives, [2]your fellow
exiles, and the whole house of Israel, all of them, *are those* to
whom the inhabitants of Jerusalem have said, 'Go far from the
LORD; this land has been given [a]us as a possession.'
16 "Therefore say, 'Thus says the Lord GOD, "Though I
had removed them far away among the nations, and though I
had scattered them among the countries, yet I was a [a]sanctuary
for them a little while in the countries where they had gone." '
17 "Therefore say, 'Thus says the Lord GOD, "I shall [a]gath-
er you from the peoples and assemble you out of the
countries among which you have been scattered, and I shall
give you the land of Israel." '
18 "When they come there, they will [a]remove all its [b]detest-
able things and all its abominations from it.
19 "And I shall [a]give them one heart, and shall put a new
spirit within [1]them. And I shall take the heart of [b]stone out of
their flesh and give them a [c]heart of flesh,

1 [a]Ezek. 11:24; 3:12, 14; 8:3; 43:5 [b]Ezek. 11:13

2 [a]Ps. 2:1, 2; 52:2; Is. 30:1; Jer. 5:5; Mic. 2:1

3 [1]Or, *The* time *is not near . . .* [2]Or, *This is . . .* [a]Ezek. 11:7, 11; 24:3, 6; Jer. 1:13

4 [a]Ezek. 3:4, 17

5 [1]Lit., *what comes up in your spirit* [a]Jer. 11:20; 17:10 [b]Ezek. 38:10

6 [1]Lit., *the slain* [a]Ezek. 7:23; 22:2-6, 9, 12, 27; Is. 1:15; Jer. 7:9

7 [1]YHWH, usually rendered LORD, and so throughout the chap. [2]Lit., *it* [3]So with Gk.; Heb., *he will bring you out* [a]Ezek. 24:3-13; Mic. 3:2, 3 [b]Ezek. 11:9; 2 Kin. 25:18-22; Jer. 52:24-27

8 [a]Job 3:25; Is. 24:17, 18

9 [1]Lit., *it* [a]Deut. 28:36, 49, 50; Ps. 106:41 [b]Ezek. 5:8; 16:41

10 [a]Jer. 52:9, 10 [b]2 Kin. 14:25

11 [a]Ezek. 11:3, 7; 24:3, 6

12 [a]Ezek. 18:8, 9 [b]Ezek. 8:10, 14, 16

13 [a]Ezek. 11:1 [b]Ezek. 9:8

15 [1]Lit., *brothers* [2]So with Gk. and some ancient versions; Heb., *the men of your redemption* [a]Ezek. 33:24

16 [a]Is. 8:14; Jer. 29:7, 11

17 [a]Ezek. 20:41, 42; 28:25; Is. 11:11-16; Jer. 3:12, 18; 24:5

18 [a]Ezek. 37:23 [b]Ezek. 5:11; 7:20

19 [1]So with Gk. and many mss.; Heb., *you* [a]Ezek. 18:31; 36:26; Jer. 24:7; 32:39 [b]Zech. 7:12; Rom. 2:4, 5 [c]2 Cor. 3:3

20 that they may [a]walk in My statutes and keep My ordinances, and do them. Then they will be [b]My people, and I
shall be their God.
21 "[1]But as for those whose hearts go after their [a]detestable
things and abominations, I shall [b]bring their conduct down on
their heads," declares the Lord GOD.
22 Then the cherubim [a]lifted up their wings with the
wheels beside them, and the glory of the God of Israel [1]hov-
ered over them.
23 And the [a]glory of the LORD went up from the midst of
the city, and [b]stood over the mountain which is east of the city.
24 And the [a]Spirit lifted me up and brought me in a vision
by the Spirit of God to the exiles [1]in Chaldea. So the vision
that I had seen [2b]left me.
25 Then I [a]told the exiles all the things that the LORD had
shown me.

CHAPTER 12

THEN the word of the LORD came to me saying,
2 "Son of man, you live in the [a]midst of the [b]rebellious
house, who [c]have eyes to see but do not see, ears to hear but do
not hear; for they are a rebellious house.
3 "Therefore, son of man, prepare for yourself baggage
for exile and go into exile by day in their sight; even go into
exile from your place to another place in their sight. [a]Perhaps
they will [1]understand though they are a rebellious house.
4 "And bring your baggage out by day in their sight, as
baggage for exile. Then you will go out [a]at evening in their
sight, as those going into exile.
5 "Dig a hole through the wall in their sight and [1]go out
through it.
6 "Load *the baggage* on *your* shoulder in their sight, *and*
carry *it* out in the dark. You shall [a]cover your face so that you
can not see the land, for I have set you as a [b]sign to the house
of Israel."
7 And I [a]did so, as I had been commanded. By day I
[b]brought out my baggage like the baggage of an exile. Then in
the evening I dug through the wall with my hands; I went out
in the dark *and* carried *the baggage* on *my* shoulder in their
sight.
8 And in the morning the word of the LORD came to me,
saying,
9 "Son of man, has not the house of Israel, the [a]rebellious
house, said to you, '[b]What are you doing?'
10 "Say to them, 'Thus says the Lord [1]GOD, "This [2a]burden
concerns the prince in Jerusalem, as well as all the house of
Israel who are [3]in it." '
11 "Say, 'I am a [a]sign [1]to you. As I have done, so it will be
done to them; they will [b]go into exile, into captivity'.
12 "And the [a]prince who is among them will load *his baggage* on *his* shoulder in the dark and go out. [1]They will dig a
hole through the wall to bring *it* out. He will cover his face so
that he can not see the land with *his* eyes.
13 "I shall also spread My [a]net over him, and he will be
caught in My snare. And I shall bring him to Babylon in the

20 [a]Ezek. 36:27; Ps. 105:45 [b]Ezek. 14:11

21 [1]Lit., *And to the heart of their detestable things and their abomination their heart goes.* [a]Ezek. 11:18; Jer. 16:18 [b]Ezek. 9:10; 16:43

22 [1]Lit., *over them from above* [a]Ezek. 10:19

23 [a]Ezek. 8:4 [b]Zech. 14:4

24 [1]I.e., Babylonia [2]Lit., *went up from* [a]Ezek. 11:1; 8:3; 37:1; 2 Cor. 12:2-4 [b]Acts 10:16

25 [a]Ezek. 2:7; 3:4, 17, 27

2 [a]Is. 6:5 [b]Ezek. 2:7, 8; Ps. 78:40; Is. 1:23 [c]Jer. 5:21; Matt. 13:13, 14; John 9:39-41

3 [1]Or, *see that they are* [a]Jer. 26:3; 36:3, 7; Luke 20:13; 2 Tim. 2:25

4 [a]Ezek. 12:12; 2 Kin. 25:4; Jer. 39:4

5 [1]Lit., *bring it out*

6 [a]Ezek. 12:12, 13; 1 Sam. 28:8 [b]Ezek. 12:11; 4:3; 24:24; Is. 8:18; 20:3

7 [a]Ezek. 24:18; 37:7, 10 [b]Ezek. 12:3-6

9 [a]Ezek. 12:1-3; 2:5-8 [b]Ezek. 17:12; 20:49; 24:19

10 [1]YHWH, usually rendered LORD, and so throughout the chap. [2]Or, *oracle* [3]Lit., *in their midst* [a]Ezek. 12:3-8; 2 Kin. 9:25; Is. 13:1

11 [1]Lit., *your sign* [a]Ezek. 12:6 [b]Ezek. 12:3; Jer. 15:2; 52:15, 28-30

12 [1]I.e., the king's attendants [a]Ezek. 12:6; 2 Kin. 25:4; Jer. 39:4; 52:7

13 [a]Ezek. 17:20; 19:8; Is. 24:17, 18; Hos. 7:12

land of the Chaldeans; yet he will [b]not see it, though he will
die there.
14 "And I shall [a]scatter to every wind all who are around
him, his helpers and all his troops; and I shall draw out a sword
after them.
15 "So they will [a]know that I am the LORD when I scatter
them among the nations, and spread them among the
countries.
16 "But I shall [1]spare a few of them from the [a]sword, the
famine, and the pestilence that they may tell all their abominations among the nations where they go, and [2]may [b]know that I
am the LORD."
17 Moreover, the word of the LORD came to me saying,
18 "Son of man, eat your bread with trembling, and drink
your water with quivering and anxiety.
19 "Then say to the people of the land, 'Thus says the Lord
GOD concerning the inhabitants of Jerusalem in the land of
Israel, "They will eat their bread with anxiety and drink their
water with horror, because [1]their land will be [2a]stripped of its
fullness on account of the violence of all who live in it.
20 "And the inhabited [a]cities will be laid waste, and the
[b]land will be a desolation. So you will know that I am the
LORD." ' "
21 Then the word of the LORD came to me saying,
22 "Son of man, what is this [a]proverb you *people* have
concerning the land of Israel, saying, 'The [b]days are long and
every [c]vision fails'?
23 "Therefore say to them, 'Thus says the Lord GOD, "I
will make this proverb cease so that they will no longer use it as
a proverb in Israel." But tell them, "The days draw near as well
as the [1]fulfillment of every vision.
24 "For there will no longer be any [1a]false vision or flattering divination within the house of Israel.
25 "For I the LORD shall speak, and whatever [a]word I speak
will be performed. It will no longer be delayed, for in [b]your
days, O [c]rebellious house, I shall speak the word and perform
it," declares the Lord GOD.' "
26 Furthermore, the word of the LORD came to me saying,
27 "Son of man, behold, the house of Israel is saying, 'The
vision that he sees is for [a]many [1]years *from now*, and he prophesies of times far off.'
28 "Therefore say to them, 'Thus says the Lord GOD,
"None of My words will be delayed any longer. Whatever
word I speak will be performed," ' declares the Lord GOD."

CHAPTER 13

THEN the word of the LORD came to me saying,
2 "Son of man, prophesy against the [a]prophets of Israel
who prophesy, and say to those who prophesy from their own
[1]inspiration, '[b]Listen to the word of the LORD!
3 'Thus says the Lord [1]GOD, "Woe to the [a]foolish prophets who are following their own spirit and have [b]seen nothing.
4 "O Israel, your prophets have been like foxes among
ruins.
5 "You have not [a]gone up into the [b]breaches, nor did you

13 [b]Jer. 39:7; 52:11

14 [a]Ezek. 5:2; 17:21; 2 Kin. 25:4, 5

15 [a]Ezek. 12:16, 20; 6:7, 14

16 [1]Lit., *leave over* [2]Or, *they will know* [a]Ezek. 7:15; 14:21 [b]Jer. 22:8, 9

19 [1]Lit., *her* [2]Lit., *desolate* [a]Ezek. 6:6, 7, 14; Jer. 10:22; Mic. 7:13; Zech. 7:14

20 [a]Ezek. 5:14; Is. 3:26; Jer. 4:7 [b]Ezek. 36:3; Is. 7:23, 24; Jer. 25:9

22 [a]Ezek. 16:44; 18:2, 3 [b]Ezek. 12:27; 11:3; Jer. 5:12; Amos 6:3; 2 Pet. 3:4 [c]Ezek. 7:26

23 [1]Lit., *word*

24 [1]Lit., *vain* [a]Ezek. 13:6, 23; Jer. 14:13-16; Zech. 13:2-4

25 [a]Ezek. 12:28; 6:10; Num. 14:28-34; Is. 14:24 [b]Jer. 16:9; Hab. 1:5 [c]Ezek. 12:2

27 [1]Lit., *days* [a]Ezek. 12:22; Dan. 10:14

2 [1]Lit., *heart* [a]Ezek. 22:25, 28; Is. 9:15; Jer. 37:19 [b]Is. 1:10; Amos 7:16

3 [1]YHWH, usually rendered LORD, and so throughout the chap. [a]Lam. 2:14; Hos. 9:7; Zech. 11:15 [b]Jer. 23:28-32

5 [a]Ezek. 22:30; Ps. 106:23; Jer. 23:22 [b]Is. 58:12

build the wall around the house of Israel to stand in the battle
on the [c]day of the LORD.
6 "They see [1a]falsehood and lying divination who are
saying, 'The LORD declares,' when the LORD has not sent them;
[b]yet they hope for the fulfillment of *their* word.
7 "[a]Did you not see a false vision and speak a lying divination when you said, 'the LORD declares,' but it is not I who
have spoken?" ' "
8 Therefore, thus says the Lord GOD, "Because you have
spoken [1]falsehood and seen a lie, therefore behold, I am [a]against
you," declares the Lord GOD.
9 "So My hand will be against the [a]prophets who see false
visions and utter lying divinations. They will [1]have no place in
the council of My people, [b]nor will they be written down in
the register of the house of Israel, nor will they enter the land
of Israel, [2]that you may know that I am the Lord GOD.
10 "It is definitely because they have [a]misled My people by
saying, '[b]Peace!' when there is [c]no peace. And when anyone
builds a wall, behold, they plaster it over with whitewash;
11 *so* tell those who plaster it over with whitewash, that it
will fall. A [a]flooding rain will come, and you, O hailstones, will
fall; and a violent wind will break out.
12 "Behold, when the wall has fallen, will you not be asked,
'Where is the plaster with which you plastered *it*?' "
13 Therefore, thus says the Lord GOD, "I will make a
violent wind break out in my wrath. There will also be in My
anger a flooding rain and [a]hailstones to consume *it* in wrath.
14 "So I shall tear down the wall which you plastered over
with whitewash and bring it down to the ground, so that its
[a]foundation is laid bare; and when it falls, you will be [b]con-
sumed in its midst. And you will [c]know that I am the LORD.
15 "Thus I shall spend My wrath on the wall and on those
who have plastered it over with whitewash; and I shall say to
you, 'The wall [1]is gone and its plasterers are gone,
16 *along with* the prophets of Israel who prophesy to Jerusalem, and who [a]see visions of peace for her when there is [b]no
peace,' declares the Lord GOD.
17 "Now you, son of man, set your face against the daughters of your people who are [a]prophesying [b]from their own
[1]inspiration. Prophesy against them,
18 and say, 'Thus says the Lord GOD, "Woe to the women
who sew *magic* bands on [1]all wrists, and make veils for the
heads of *persons* of every stature to hunt down [2]lives! Will you
hunt down the [2]lives of My people, but preserve the [2]lives *of
others* for yourselves?
19 "And for handfuls of barley and fragments of bread, you
have profaned Me to My people to put to death [1]some who
should not die and to [a]keep [1]others alive who should not live,
by your lying to My people who listen to lies." ' "
20 Therefore, thus says the Lord GOD, "Behold, I am
against your *magic* bands by which you hunt [1]lives there as
[2]birds, and I will tear them off your arms; and I will let [1]them
go, even those [1]lives whom you hunt as [2]birds.
21 "I will also tear off your veils and [a]deliver My people
from your hands, and they will no longer be in your hands to
be hunted; and you will know that I am the LORD.

5 [c]Ezek. 7:19; Is. 13:6, 9

6 [1]Lit., *vanity*
[a]Ezek. 22:28; Jer. 29:8 [b]Jer. 28:15; 37:19

7 [a]Ezek. 22:28

8 [1]Lit., *vanity*
[a]Ezek. 5:8; 21:3; Nah. 2:13

9 [1]Lit., *not be in* [2]Or, *and you will know*
[a]Jer. 20:3-6; 28:15-17 [b]Ps. 69:28; 87:6; Jer. 17:13; Dan. 12:1

10 [a]Jer. 23:32; 50:6 [b]Jer. 8:11; 14:13 [c]Ezek. 13:16; 7:25

11 [a]Ezek. 38:22

13 [a]Ex. 9:24, 25; Ps. 18:12, 13; Is. 30:30; Rev. 11:19; 16:21

14 [a]Mic. 1:6; Hab. 3:13 [b]Jer. 6:15; 14:15 [c]Ezek. 13:9

15 [1]Lit., *is not . . . . are not*

16 [a]Ezek. 13:10; Jer. 6:14; 8:11 [b]Is. 57:21

17 [1]Lit., *heart*
[a]Judg. 4:4; 2 Kin. 22:14; Luke 2:36; Acts 21:9 [b]Ezek. 13:2; Rev. 2:20

18 [1]Lit., *all joints of the hand;* M.T. reads, *of my hands* [2]Or, *souls*

19 [1]Or, *souls*
[a]Jer. 23:14, 17

20 [1]Lit., *souls* [2]Or, *flying ones*

21 [a]Ps. 91:3; 124:7

22 "Because you [a]disheartened the righteous with falsehood when I did not cause him grief, but have [1b]encouraged
the wicked not to [c]turn from his wicked way *and* preserve his
life,
23 therefore, you women will no longer see [1a]false visions
or practice divination, and I will [b]deliver My people out of
your hand. Thus you will [c]know that I am the LORD."

CHAPTER 14

THEN some [a]elders of Israel came to me and [b]sat down
before me.
2 And the word of the LORD came to me saying,
3 "Son of man, these men have [a]set up their idols in their
hearts, and have [b]put right before their faces the stumbling
block of their iniquity. Should I be [c]consulted by them at all?
4 "Therefore speak to them and tell them, 'Thus says the
Lord [1]GOD, "Any man of the house of Israel who sets up his
idols in his heart, puts right before his face the stumbling block
of his iniquity, and *then* comes to the prophet, I the LORD will
be brought to give him an answer in the [2]matter in view of the
[a]multitude of his idols,
5 in order to lay hold of [1a]the hearts of the house of
Israel who are [2b]estranged from Me through all their idols." '
6 "Therefore say to the house of Israel, 'Thus says the
Lord GOD, "[a]Repent and turn away from your idols, and turn
your faces away from all your [b]abominations.
7 "For anyone of the house of Israel or of the [a]immigrants
who stay in Israel who separates himself from Me, sets up his
idols in his heart, puts right before his face the stumbling block
of his iniquity, and *then* comes to the prophet to inquire of
Me for himself, [b]I the LORD will be brought to answer him in
My own person.
8 "And I shall [a]set My face against that man and make
him a [b]sign and [1]a proverb, and I shall cut him off from among
My people. So you will know that I am the LORD.
9 "But if the prophet is [1]prevailed upon to speak a word, it
is I, the LORD, who have [1]prevailed upon that prophet, and I
will stretch out My hand against him and [a]destroy him from
among My people Israel.
10 "And they will bear *the punishment of* their iniquity; as
the iniquity of the inquirer is, so the iniquity of the prophet
will be,
11 in order that the house of Israel may no longer [a]stray
from Me and no longer [b]defile themselves with all their transgressions. Thus they will be [c]My people, and I shall be their
God," ' declares the Lord GOD."
12 Then the word of the LORD came to me saying,
13 "Son of man, if a country sins against Me by [a]commit-
ting unfaithfulness, and I stretch out My hand against it, [1]destroy
its supply of bread, send famine against it, and cut off
from it both man and beast,
14 even [a]*though* these three men, [b]Noah, [c]Daniel, and
[d]Job were in its midst, by their *own* righteousness they could
only deliver [e]themselves," declares the Lord GOD.
15 "If I were to cause [a]wild beasts to pass through the land,

22 [1]Lit., *strengthen the hands of* [a]Amos 5:12 [b]Jer. 23:14; 34:16, 22 [c]Ezek. 18:21, 27, 30-32; 33:14-16

23 [1]Lit., *vanity* [a]Ezek. 13:6; 12:24; Mic. 3:6; Zech. 13:3 [b]Ezek. 13:21; 34:10 [c]Ezek. 13:9, 21

1 [a]Ezek. 8:1; 20:1; 2 Kin. 6:32 [b]Ezek. 33:31, 32; Is. 29:13

3 [a]Ezek. 20:16 [b]Ezek. 14:4, 7; 7:19; Zeph. 1:3 [c]Ezek. 20:3, 31; Is. 1:15; Jer. 11:11

4 [1]YHWH, usually rendered LORD, and so throughout the chap. [2]Lit., *it* [a]1 Kin. 21:20-24; 2 Kin. 1:16; Is. 66:4

5 [1]Lit., *their* [2]Or, *all estranged from Me through their idols* [a]Jer. 17:10; Zech. 7:12 [b]Is. 1:4; Jer. 2:11; Zech. 11:8

6 [a]Ezek. 18:30; 1 Sam. 7:3; Neh. 1:9; Is. 2:20; 30:22; 55:6,7 [b]Ezek. 14:4; 8:6

7 [a]Ex. 12:48; 20:10 [b]Ezek. 14:4

8 [1]Lit., *proverbs* [a]Ezek. 15:7; Jer. 44:11 [b]Ezek. 5:15; Is. 65:15

9 [1]Or, *enticed* [a]Jer. 6:14, 15; 14:15

11 [a]Ezek. 44:10, 15; 48:11 [b]Ezek. 11:18; 37:23 [c]Ezek. 11:20; 34:30; 36:28

13 [1]Lit., *break the staff* [a]Ezek. 15:8; 20:27

14 [a]Jer. 15:1 [b]Gen. 6:8; 7:1; Heb. 11:7 [c]Ezek. 28:3; Dan. 1:6; 9:21; 10:11 [d]Job. 1:1, 5; 42:8, 9 [e]Ezek. 16:18, 20; 18:20

15 [a]Ezek. 14:21; 5:17

and they [1]depopulated it, and it became desolate so that no
one would pass through it because of the beasts,
16 *though* these three men were in its midst, as I live,"
declares the Lord GOD, "they could not deliver either *their*
sons or *their* daughters. [a]They alone would be delivered, but
the country would be desolate.
17 "Or *if* I should bring a sword on that country and say,
'Let the sword pass through the country and cut off man and
beast from it,'
18 even *though* these three men were in its midst, as I
live," declares the Lord GOD, "they could not deliver either
their sons or *their* daughters, but they alone would be
delivered.
19 "Or *if* I should send a [a]plague against that country and
pour out My wrath in blood on it, to cut off man and beast
from it,
20 even *though* Noah, Daniel, and Job were in its midst,
as I live," declares the Lord GOD, "they could not deliver
either *their* son or *their* daughter. They would deliver only
themselves by their righteousness.
21 "For thus says the Lord GOD, 'How much more when I
send my four [1]severe judgments against Jerusalem: sword, famine, wild beasts, and [a]plague to cut off man and beast from
it!
22 'Yet, behold, [1]survivors will be left in it who will be
brought out, *both* sons and daughters. Behold, they are going
to come forth to you and you will [a]see their conduct and
actions; then you will be [b]comforted for the calamity which I
have brought against Jerusalem for everything which I have
brought upon it.
23 'Then they will comfort you when you see their conduct
and actions, for you will know that I have not done in vain
whatever I did [1]to it,' declares the Lord GOD."

CHAPTER 15

THEN the word of the LORD came to me saying,
2 "Son of man, how is the wood of the [a]vine *better* than
any wood of a branch which is among the trees of the forest?
3 "Can wood be taken from it to make [1]anything, or can
men take a peg from it on which to hang any vessel?
4 "[1]If it has been put into the [a]fire for fuel, *and* the fire
has consumed both of its ends, and its middle part has been
charred, is it *then* useful for [2]anything?
5 "Behold, while it is intact, it is not made into [1]anything.
How much less, when the fire has consumed it and it is
charred, can it still be made into [1]anything!
6 "Therefore, thus says the Lord [1]GOD, 'As the wood of
the vine among the trees of the forest, which I have given to
the fire for fuel, so have I given up the inhabitants of
Jerusalem;
7 and I [a]set My face against them. *Though* they have
[b]come out of the fire, yet the fire will consume them. Then
you will know that I am the LORD, when I set My face against
them.

15 [1]Lit., *bereave of children*

16 [a]Ezek. 18:20; Gen. 19:29

19 [a]Ezek. 14:21; 5:12; Jer. 14:12

21 [1]Lit., *evil* [a]Amos 4:6-10

22 [1]Lit., *escaped ones* [a]Ezek. 12:16; 36:20 [b]Ezek. 16:54; 31:16; 32:31

23 [1]Or, *in*

2 [a]Ps. 80:8-16; Is. 5:1-7; Hos. 10:1

3 [1]Lit., *a work*

4 [1]Or, *Behold* [2]Lit., *a work* [a]Ezek. 15:6; 19:14; Is. 27:11

5 [1]Lit., *a work*

6 [1]YHWH, usually rendered LORD, and so throughout the chap.

7 [a]Ezek. 14:8; Lev. 26:17; Ps. 34:16; Jer. 21:10 [b]1 Kin. 19:17; Is. 24:18; Amos 9:1-4

8 [a]Ezek. 14:13; 17:20

2 [a]Ezek. 20:4; 22:2; Is. 58:1

3 [1]YHWH, usually rendered LORD, and so throughout the chap.

5 [1]Lit., *surface* [2]Lit., *in the loathing of your soul* [a]Deut. 32:10

6 [a]Ex. 19:4; Ps. 105:10-15

7 [1]Lit., *a myriad* [a]Ex. 1:7; Deut. 1:10

8 [1]Lit., *your time was* [a]Ruth 3:9; Jer. 2:2 [b]Gen. 22:16-18 [c]Ex. 24:7, 8 [d]Ezek. 20:5; Ex. 19:5; Hos. 2:19, 20

9 [a]Ruth 3:3

10 [1]Or, *dolphin* [a]Ezek. 16:13, 18; 26:16; 27:7, 16; Ex. 26:36

11 [a]Ezek. 23:42; Gen. 24:22, 47; Is. 3:19 [b]Gen. 41:42; Prov. 1:9

12 [a]Gen. 24:47; Is. 3:21 [b]Ezek. 16:14; Is. 28:5; Jer. 13:18

13 [a]Ezek. 16:17; Ps. 45:13, 14 [b]1 Sam. 10:1; 1 Kin. 4:21

14 [a]1 Kin. 10:1, 24 [b]Ps. 50:2; Lam. 2:15

15 [1]Lit., *to whom it might be* [a]Ezek. 16:25; 27:3

16 [1]Lit., *things which had not happened nor will it be*

17 [1]Lit., *articles of beauty* [a]Ezek. 16:11, 12

8 'Thus I will make the land desolate, because they have
[a]acted unfaithfully,' " declares the Lord GOD.

CHAPTER 16

THEN the word of the LORD came to me saying,
2 "Son of man, [a]make known to Jerusalem her
abominations,
3 and say, 'Thus says the Lord [1]GOD to Jerusalem, "Your
origin and your birth are from the land of the Canaanite, your
father was an Amorite and your mother a Hittite.
4 "As for your birth, on the day you were born your navel
cord was not cut, nor were you washed with water for cleansing; you were not rubbed with salt or even wrapped in cloths.
5 "No eye looked with pity on you to do any of these
things for you, to have compassion on you. Rather you were
thrown out into the [1a]open field, [2]for you were abhorred on
the day you were born.
6 "When I passed by you and saw you squirming in your
blood, I said to you *while you were* in your blood, '[a]Live!'
I said to you while you were in your blood, 'Live!'
7 "I [a]made you [1]numerous like plants of the field. Then
you grew up, became tall, and reached the age for fine ornaments; *your* breasts were formed and your hair had grown. Yet
you were naked and bare.
8 "Then I passed by you and saw you, and behold, [1]you
were at the time for love; so I [a]spread my skirt over you and
covered your nakedness. I also [b]swore to you and [c]entered into
a covenant with you so that you [d]became mine," declares the
Lord GOD.
9 "Then I bathed you with water, washed off your blood
from you, and [a]anointed you with oil.
10 "I also clothed you with [a]embroidered cloth, and put
sandals of [1]porpoise skin on your feet; and I wrapped you with
fine linen and covered you with silk.
11 "And I adorned you with ornaments, put [a]bracelets on
your hands, and a [b]necklace around your neck.
12 "I also put a [a]ring in your nostril, earrings in your ears,
and a [b]beautiful crown on your head.
13 "Thus you were adorned with [a]gold and silver, and your
dress was of fine linen, silk, and embroidered cloth. You ate
fine flour, honey, and oil; so you were exceedingly beautiful
and advanced to [b]royalty.
14 "Then your [a]fame went forth among the nations on
account of your beauty, for it was [b]perfect because of My
splendor which I bestowed on you," declares the Lord GOD.
15 "But you [a]trusted in your beauty and played the harlot
because of your fame, and you poured out your harlotries on
every passer-by [1]who might be *willing*.
16 "And you took some of your clothes, made for yourself
high places of various colors, and played the harlot on them,
[1]which should never come about nor happen.
17 "You also took your beautiful [1a]jewels *made* of My gold
and of My silver, which I had given you, and made for yourself
male images that you might play the harlot with them.

18 "Then you took your embroidered cloth and covered
them, and offered My oil and My incense before them.
19 "Also my bread which I gave you, fine flour, oil, and
honey with which I fed you, [1]you would offer before them for
a soothing aroma; so it happened," declares the Lord GOD.
20 "Moreover, you took your sons and daughters whom
you had borne to [a]Me, and you [b]sacrificed them to [1]idols to be
devoured. Were your harlotries so small a matter?
21 "You slaughtered My children, and offered them up to
[1]idols by [a]causing them to pass through *the fire.*
22 "And besides all your abominations and harlotries you
did not remember the days of your youth, when you were
naked and bare and squirming in your blood.
23 "Then it came about after all your wickedness ('Woe,
woe to you!' declares the Lord GOD),
24 that you built yourself a [a]shrine and made yourself a
[b]high place in every square.
25 "You built yourself a high place at the top of every
street, and made your beauty abominable; and you spread
your legs to every passer-by to multiply your harlotry.
26 "You also played the harlot with the Egyptians, your
[1]lustful neighbors, and multiplied your harlotry to [a]make Me
angry.
27 "Behold now, I have stretched out My hand against you
and diminished your rations. And I delivered you up to the
desire of those who hate you, the [a]daughters of the Philistines,
who are ashamed of your lewd conduct.
28 "Moreover, you played the harlot with the [a]Assyrians
because you were not satisfied; you even played the harlot with
them and still were not satisfied.
29 "You also multiplied your harlotry with the land of merchants, Chaldea, yet even with this you were not satisfied." ' "
30 "How [a]languishing is your heart," declares the Lord
GOD, "while you do all these things, the actions of a [1b]bold-
faced harlot.
31 "When you built your shrine at the beginning of every
street and made your high place in every square, in [a]disdaining
money, you were not like a harlot.
32 "You adulteress wife, who takes strangers instead of her
husband!
33 "[1]Men give gifts to all harlots, but you [a]give your gifts to
all your lovers to bribe them to come to you from every direction for your harlotries.
34 "Thus you are different from those women in your harlotries, in that no one plays the harlot [1]as you do, because you
give money and no money is given you; thus you are
different."
35 Therefore, O harlot, hear the word of the LORD.
36 Thus says the Lord GOD, "Because your lewdness was
poured out and your nakedness uncovered through your harlotries with your lovers and with all your detestable [a]idols, and
because of the blood of your sons which you gave to [1]idols,
37 therefore, behold, I shall [a]gather all your lovers with
whom you took pleasure, even all those whom you loved *and*
all those whom you [b]hated. So I shall gather them against you

19 [1]Lit., *and you . . . offer it*

20 [1]Lit., *them*
[a]Ex. 13:2, 12; Deut. 29:11, 12 [b]Ezek. 20:31; 23:37; Ps. 106:37, 38; Jer. 7:31

21 [1]Lit., *them*
[a]2 Kin. 17:17; Jer. 19:5

24 [a]Ezek. 16:31, 39; 20:28, 29; Jer. 11:30 [b]Ps. 78:58; Is. 57:5,7

26 [1]Lit., *great of flesh*
[a]Ezek. 8:17; Jer. 7:18, 19

27 [a]Ezek. 16:57; Is. 9:12

28 [a]Ezek. 23:12; 2 Kin. 16:7, 10-18; 2 Chr. 28:16, 20-23; Jer. 2:18, 36; Hos. 10:6

30 [1]Lit., *domineering*
[a]Prov. 9:13; Is. 1:3; Jer. 4:22 [b]Is. 3:9; Jer. 3:3

31 [a]Is. 52:3

33 [1]Lit., *they*
[a]Ezek. 16:41; Is. 57:9; Hos. 8:9, 10

34 [1]Lit., *after you*

36 [1]Lit., *them*
[a]Ezek. 20:31; 23:37; Jer. 19:5

37 [a]Ezek. 23:9, 22; Jer. 13:22, 26; Hos. 2:3, 10; Nah. 3:5,6 [b]Ezek. 23:17, 18

from every direction and [c]expose your nakedness to them that
they may see all your nakedness.
38 "Thus I shall [a]judge you, like women who commit adultery or shed blood are judged; and I shall bring on you the
blood of [b]wrath and jealousy.
39 "I shall also give you into [1]the hands of your lovers, and
they will tear down your shrines, demolish your high places,
strip you of your clothing, take away your [2]jewels, and will
leave you naked and bare.
40 "They will [1]incite a [a]crowd against you, and they will
stone you and cut you to pieces with their swords.
41 "And they will [a]burn your houses with fire and execute
judgments on you in the sight of many women. Then I shall
[b]stop you from playing the harlot, and you will also no longer
pay [1]your lovers.
42 "So I [a]shall calm My fury against you, and My jealousy
will depart from you, and I shall be pacified and angry [b]no
more.
43 "Because you have [a]not remembered the days of your
youth but [1]have [b]enraged Me by all these things, behold, I in
turn will [c]bring your conduct down on your own head," declares
the Lord GOD, "so that you will not commit this lewdness
on top of all your *other* abominations.
44 "Behold, every one who quotes [a]proverbs will quote *this*
proverb concerning you, saying, '[1]Like mother, [1]like daughter.'
45 "You are the daughter of your mother, who loathed her
husband and children. You are also the [a]sister of your sisters,
who [b]loathed their husbands and children. Your mother was a
Hittite and your father an Amorite.
46 "Now your [a]older sister is Samaria, who lives [1]north of
you with her [2]daughters; and your younger sister, who lives
[3]south of you, is [b]Sodom with her [2]daughters.
47 "Yet you have not merely walked in their ways or done
according to their abominations; but, as if that were [a]too little,
you acted [b]more corruptly in all your conduct than they.
48 "As I live," declares the Lord GOD, "Sodom, your sister,
and her daughters, have [a]not done as you and your daughters
have done.
49 "Behold, this was the guilt of your sister Sodom: she and
her daughters had [a]arrogance, [b]abundant food, and careless
[c]ease, but she did not [1]help the [d]poor and needy.
50 "Thus they were haughty and committed abominations
before Me. Therefore I [a]removed them [1]when I saw *it*.
51 "Furthermore, Samaria did not commit half of your
sins, for you have multiplied your abominations more than
they. Thus you have made your sisters appear [a]righteous by all
your abominations which you have committed.
52 "Also bear your disgrace in that you have [1]made judgment favorable for your sisters. Because of your sins in which
you acted [a]more abominably than they, they are more in the
right than you. Yes, be also ashamed and bear your disgrace, in
that you made your sisters appear righteous.
53 "Nevertheless, I will restore their captivity, the captivity
of Sodom and her daughters, the captivity of Samaria and her
daughters, and [1]along with them [2a]your own captivity,

37 [c]Is. 47:3

38 [a]Ezek. 23:45 [b]Ezek. 23:25; Ps. 79:3, 5; Jer. 18:21; Zeph. 1:17

39 [1]Lit., *their hands, and they* [2]Lit., *articles of beauty*

40 [1]Lit., *bring up an assembly* [a]Ezek. 23:47; Hab. 1:6-10

41 [1]Lit., *a harlot's hire* [a]2 Kin. 25:9; Jer. 39:8; 52:13 [b]Ezek. 23:48

42 [a]Ezek. 5:13; 21:17; 2 Sam. 24:25; Zech. 6:8 [b]Ezek. 39:29; Is. 40:1, 2; 54:9, 10

43 [1]So with ancient versions; Heb., *are angry against* [a]Ezek. 16:22; Ps. 78:42; 106:13 [b]Ezek. 6:9; Is. 63:10 [c]Ezek. 11:21; 22:31

44 [1]Lit., *Her* [a]Ezek. 12:22, 23; 18:2, 3; 1 Sam. 24:13

45 [a]Ezek. 23:2 [b]Ezek. 23:37-39; Gen. 18:20; Is. 1:4; Zech. 11:8

46 [1]Lit., *on your left* [2]I.e., environs; so through v.55 [3]Lit., *from your right* [a]Ezek. 23:4; Jer. 3:8-11 [b]Ezek. 16:48, 49, 53-56, 61; Gen. 13:11-13; 18:20

47 [a]1 Kin. 16:31 [b]Ezek. 16:48, 51; 5:6; 2 Kin. 21:9

48 [a]Matt. 11:23, 24

49 [1]Lit., *grasp the hand of* [a]Ezek. 28:2, 9, 17; Gen. 19:9; Ps. 138:6; Is. 3:9 [b]Gen. 13:10; Is. 22:13; Amos 6:4-6 [c]Luke 12:16-20; 16:19 [d]Ezek. 18:7, 12, 16

50 [1]Many ancient mss. and versions read: *as you have seen* [a]Gen. 19:24, 25

51 [a]Jer. 3:8-11; Matt. 12:41, 42

52 [1]Lit., *mediated for* [a]Ezek. 16:47, 48, 51

53 [1]Lit., *in their midst* [2]Lit., *the captivity of your captivity* [a]Is. 19:24, 25

54 in order that you may bear your humiliation, and feel
[a]ashamed for all that you have done when you become a consolation to them.
55 "And your sisters, Sodom with her daughters and Samaria with her daughters, [1]will return to their former state, and
you with your daughters will *also* return to your former state.
56 "As *the name of* your sister Sodom was [a]not heard from
your lips in your day of pride,
57 before your [a]wickedness was uncovered, [1]so now you
have become the [b]reproach of the daughters of [2]Edom, and of
all who are around her, of the daughters of the Philistines—
those surrounding *you* who despise you.
58 "You have [a]borne *the penalty of* your lewdness and
abominations," the LORD declares.
59 For thus says the Lord GOD, "I will also do with you as
you have done, you who have [a]despised the oath by breaking
the covenant.
60 "Nevertheless, I will remember My covenant with you
in the days of your youth, and I will establish an [a]everlasting
covenant with you.
61 "Then you will [a]remember your ways and be ashamed
when you receive your sisters, *both* your older and your younger; and I will give them to you as daughters, but not because
of your covenant.
62 "Thus I will [a]establish My covenant with you, and you
shall [b]know that I am the LORD,
63 in order that you may [a]remember and be ashamed, and
[b]never open your mouth any more because of your humiliation,
when I have [c]forgiven you for all that you have done,"
the Lord GOD declares.

CHAPTER 17

NOW the word of the LORD came to me saying,
2 "Son of man, [a]propound a riddle, and speak a parable to
the house of Israel,
3 [1]saying, 'Thus says the Lord [2]GOD, "A great [a]eagle with
[b]great wings, long pinions and a full plumage of many colors,
came to [c]Lebanon and took away the top of the cedar.
4 "He plucked off the topmost of its young twigs and
brought it to a land of merchants; he set it in a city of traders.
5 "He also took some of the seed of the land and planted
it in [1a]fertile soil. He [2]placed *it* beside abundant waters; he set
it *like* a [b]willow.
6 "Then it sprouted and became a low, spreading vine
with its branches turned toward him, but its roots remained
under it. So it became a vine, and yielded shoots and sent out
branches.
7 "But there was [1]another great eagle with great wings and
much plumage; and behold, this vine bent its roots toward him
and sent out its branches toward him from the beds where it
was [a]planted, that he might water it.
8 "It was planted in good [1]soil beside abundant waters,

54 [a]Jer. 2:26

55 [1]Heb. includes *will return . . . state* after Sodom also

56 [a]Is. 65:5; Luke 15:28-30

57 [1]Heb., *as at the time of* [2]So with many mss. and one version; M.T., *Syria* [a]Ezek. 16:36, 37 [b]Ezek. 5:14, 15; 22:4; 2 Kin. 16:5-7; 2 Chr. 28:5,6, 18-23

58 [a]Ezek. 23:49

59 [a]Ezek. 17:19; Is. 24:5

60 [a]Ezek. 37:26; Is. 55:3; Jer. 32:38-41

61 [a]Ezek. 6:9; Jer. 50:4, 5

62 [a]Ezek. 20:37; 34:25; 37:26 [b]Ezek. 20:43, 44; Jer. 24:7

63 [a]Ezek. 36:31, 32; Dan. 9:7, 8 [b]Ps. 39:9; Rom. 3:19 [c]Ps. 65:3; 78:38; 79:9

2 [a]Ezek. 20:49; 24:3

3 [1]Lit., *and you shall say* [2]YHWH, usually rendered LORD, and so throughout the chap. [a]Ezek. 17:12; Jer. 48:40; Hos. 8:1 [b]Dan. 4:22 [c]Jer. 22:23

5 [1]Lit., *a field of seed* [2]Lit., *took* [a]Deut. 8:7-9 [b]Is. 44:4

7 [1]So with several ancient versions; M.T., *one* [a]Ezek. 31:4

8 [1]Lit., *field*

that it might yield branches and bear fruit, *and* become a
splendid vine.
9 "Say, 'Thus says the Lord GOD, "Will it thrive? Will he
not pull up its roots and cut off its fruit, so that it withers—so
that all its sprouting leaves wither? And neither by great
[1]strength nor by many people can it be raised from its roots
again.
10 "Behold, though it is planted, will it thrive? Will it not
[a]completely wither as soon as the east wind strikes it—wither
on the beds where it grew?" ' "
11 Moreover, the word of the LORD came to me saying,
12 "Say now to the [a]rebellious house, 'Do you not [b]know
what these things *mean?*' Say, 'Behold, the [c]king of Babylon
came to Jerusalem, took its king and princes, and brought
them to him in Babylon.
13 'And he took one of the royal [1a]family and made a
covenant with him, [2]putting him under [b]oath. He also took
away the [c]mighty of the land,
14 that the kingdom might be [1]in subjection, not exalting
itself, *but* keeping his covenant, that it might continue.
15 'But he [a]rebelled against him by sending his envoys to
Egypt that they might give him horses and many [1]troops. Will
he succeed? Will he who does such things [b]escape? Can he
indeed break the covenant and escape?
16 'As I live,' declares the Lord GOD, 'Surely in the [1]coun-
try of the king who [2]put him on the throne, whose oath he
[a]despised, and whose covenant he broke, [3b]in Babylon he shall
die.
17 'And [a]Pharaoh with *his* mighty army and great company
will not [1]help him in the war, when they cast up mounds and
build siege walls to cut off many lives.
18 'Now he despised the oath by breaking the covenant,
and behold, he [1]pledged his allegiance, yet did all these things;
he shall not escape.' "
19 Therefore, thus says the Lord GOD, "As I live, surely
My oath which he despised and My covenant which he broke,
I will [1]inflict on his head.
20 "And I will spread My [a]net over him, and he will be
[b]caught in My snare. Then I will bring him to Babylon and
[c]enter into judgment with him there *regarding* the unfaithful
act which he has committed against Me.
21 "And all the [1a]choice men in all his troops will fall by the
sword, and the survivors will be scattered to every wind; and
you will know that I, the LORD, have spoken."
22 Thus says the Lord GOD, "I shall also take *a sprig* from
the lofty top of the cedar and set *it* out; I shall pluck from the
topmost of its young twigs a tender one, and I shall plant *it* on
a [a]high and lofty mountain.
23 "On the high mountain of Israel I shall plant it, that it
may bring forth boughs and bear fruit, and become a stately
[a]cedar. And birds of every [1]kind will [2]nest under it; they will
[2]nest in the shade of its branches.
24 "And all the [a]trees of the field will know that I am the
LORD; I bring down the high tree, exalt the low tree, dry up the
green tree, and make the dry tree [b]flourish. I am the LORD; I
have spoken, and I will perform *it.*"

9 [1]Lit., *arm*

10 [a]Ezek. 19:14; Hos. 13:15

12 [a]Ezek. 2:3-5 [b]Ezek. 12:9-11; 24:19 [c]Ezek. 17:3; 1:2; 2 Kin. 24:11, 12, 15

13 [1]Lit., *seed* [2]Lit., *and caused him to enter into an oath* [a]Ezek. 17:5; 2 Kin. 24:17 [b]2 Chr. 36:13 [c]2 Kin. 24:15, 16

14 [1]Lit., *low*

15 [1]Lit., *people* [a]Ezek. 17:7; 2 Kin. 24:20; 2 Chr. 36:13; Jer. 52:3 [b]Ezek. 17:18; Jer. 34:3; 38:18, 23

16 [1]Lit., *place* [2]Lit., *made him king* [3]Lit., *with him in Babylon* [a]Ezek. 17:13, 18, 19; 16:59; 2 Kin. 24:17, 20 [b]Ezek. 12:13; Jer. 52:11

17 [1]Lit., *act with* [a]Ezek. 29:6, 7; Is. 36:6; Jer. 37:5, 7

18 [1]Lit., *gave his hand*

19 [1]Lit., *give it*

20 [a]Ezek. 12:13; 32:3 [b]Jer. 39:5-7 [c]Jer. 20:35, 36; Jer. 2:35

21 [1]So many ancient mss. and versions; M.T., *fugitives* [a]Ezek. 5:2, 10, 12-14; 2 Kin. 25:5, 11

22 [a]Ezek. 20:40; 37:22; Ps. 72:16

23 [1]Lit., *wing* [2]Lit., *dwell* [a]Ps. 92:12; Is. 27:6

24 [a]Ps. 96:12; Is. 55:12 [b]Is. 37:3, 13; Amos 9:11

CHAPTER 18

THEN the word of the LORD came to me saying,
2 "[a]What do you mean by using this proverb concerning
the land of Israel saying,
'[b]The fathers eat the sour grapes,
But the children's teeth [1]are set on edge'?
3 "As I live," declares the Lord [1]GOD, "you are surely not
going to use this proverb in Israel any more.
4 "Behold, [a]all [1]souls are Mine; the [2]soul of the father as
well as the [2]soul of the son is Mine. The [2]soul who [b]sins will
die.
5 "But if a man is righteous, and practices justice and
righteousness,
6 and does not [a]eat at the mountain *shrines* or [b]lift up his
eyes to the idols of the house of Israel, or [c]defile his neighbor's
wife, or approach a woman during her menstrual period—
7 if a man does not oppress any one, but [a]restores to the
debtor his pledge, [b]does not commit robbery, *but* [c]gives his
bread to the hungry, and covers the naked with clothing,
8 if he does not lend *money* on [a]interest or take [b]in-
crease, *if* he keeps his hand from iniquity, *and* [c]executes true
justice between man and man,
9 *if* he walks in My statutes and My ordinances so as to
deal faithfully—he is righteous *and* will surely [a]live," declares
the Lord GOD.
10 "Then he may [1]have a violent son who sheds blood, and
who does any of these things to a brother
11 (though he himself did not do any of these things), that
is, he even eats at the mountain *shrines*, and defiles his neighbor's wife,
12 oppresses the [a]poor and needy, [b]commits robbery, does
not restore a pledge, but lifts up his eyes to the idols, *and*
[c]commits abomination,
13 he lends *money* on interest and takes increase; will he
live? He will not live! He has committed all these abominations, he will surely be put to death; his [a]blood will be [1]on his
own head.
14 "Now behold, he [1]has a son who has observed all his
father's sins which he committed, and [a]observing does not do
likewise.
15 "He does not eat at the mountain *shrines* or lift up his
eyes to the idols of the house of Israel, or defile his neighbor's
wife,
16 or oppress anyone, or retain a pledge, or commit robbery, *but* he [a]gives his bread to the hungry, and covers the
naked with clothing,
17 he keeps his hand from [1]the poor, does not take interest or increase, *but* executes My ordinances, and walks in My
statutes; he will not die for his father's iniquity, he will surely
live.
18 "As for his father, because he practiced extortion,
robbed *his* brother, and did what was not good among his
people, behold, he will die for his iniquity.

2 [1]Lit., *become dull* [a]Is. 3:15 [b]Jer. 31:29; Lam. 5:7; Matt. 23:36

3 [1]YHWH, usually rendered LORD, and so throughout the chap.

4 [1]Or, *lives* [2]Or, *life* [3]Or, *person* [a]Num. 16:22; 27:16; Is. 42:5; 57:16 [b]Ezek. 18:20; Rom. 6:23

6 [a]Ezek. 18:15; 6:13; 22:9 [b]Ezek. 18:12, 15; 20:24; 33:25; Deut. 4:19 [c]Ezek. 18:15; 22:11

7 [a]Ezek. 33:15; Deut. 24:13; Amos 2:8 [b]Lev. 19:13; Amos 3:10 [c]Ezek. 18:16; Deut. 15:11; Matt. 25:35-40; Luke 3:11

8 [a]Ex. 22:25; Deut. 23:19, 20 [b]Lev. 25:36 [c]Zech. 7:9; 8:16

9 [a]Hab. 2:4; Rom. 1:17

10 [1]Lit., *beget*

12 [a]Amos 4:1; Zech. 7:10 [b]Ezek. 18:7, 16, 18; 7:23; Is. 59:6, 7; Jer. 22:3, 17 [c]Ezek. 8:6, 17; 2 Kin. 21:11

13 [1]Lit., *on him* [a]Ezek. 33:4, 5

14 [1]Lit., *begets* [a]2 Chr. 29:6-10; 34:21

16 [a]Ezek. 18:7; Job 31:16, 20; Ps. 41:1; Is. 58:7, 10

17 [1]So M.T.; Gk. reads: *iniquity* as in v. 8

19 "Yet you say, '[a]Why should the son not bear the punishment for the father's iniquity?' When the son has practiced
[b]justice and righteousness, and has observed all My statutes
and done them, he shall surely live.
20 "The person who [a]sins will die. The [b]son will not bear
the punishment for the father's iniquity, nor will the father
bear the punishment for the son's iniquity; the [c]righteousness
of the righteous will be upon himself, and the wickedness of
the wicked will be upon himself.
21 "But if the [a]wicked man turns from all his sins which he
has committed and observes all My statutes and practices justice and righteousness, he shall surely live; he shall not die.
22 "[a]All his transgressions which he has committed will not
be remembered against him; because of his [b]righteousness
which he has practiced, he will live.
23 "[a]Do I have any pleasure in the death of the wicked,"
declares the Lord God, "[1]rather than that he should [b]turn
from his ways and live?
24 "But when a righteous man [a]turns away from his righteousness, commits iniquity, and does according to all the
abominations that a wicked man does, will he live? [b]All his
righteous deeds which he has done will not be remembered for
his [c]treachery which he has committed and his sin which he has
committed; for them he will die.
25 "Yet you say, '[a]The way of the Lord is not right.' Hear
now, O house of Israel! Is [b]My way not right? Is it not your
ways that are not right?
26 "When a righteous man turns away from his righteousness, commits iniquity, and dies because of [1]it, for his iniquity
which he has committed he will die.
27 "Again, when a wicked man turns away from his wickedness which he has committed and practices justice and righteousness, he will save his life.
28 "Because he considered and turned away from all his
transgressions which he had committed, he shall surely live; he
shall not die.
29 "But the house of Israel says, 'The way of the Lord is
not right.' Are My ways not right, O house of Israel? Is it not
your ways that are not right?
30 "Therefore I will judge you, O house of Israel, each
according to his conduct," declares the Lord God. "[a]Repent
and turn away from all your transgressions, so that iniquity
may not become a stumbling block to you.
31 "[a]Cast away from you all your transgressions which you
have committed, and make yourselves a [b]new heart and a new
spirit! For why will you die, O house of Israel?
32 "For I have [a]no pleasure in the death of anyone who
dies," declares the Lord God. "Therefore, repent and live."

Chapter 19

"As for you, take up a [a]lamentation for the [b]princes of
Israel,
2 and say:

19 [a]Ezek. 18:2; Ex. 20:5; Jer. 15:4 [b]Ezek. 18:9; 20:18-20; Zech. 1:3-6

20 [a]Ezek. 18:4; 2 Kin. 14:6; 22:18-20 [b]Deut. 24:16; Jer. 31:30 [c]1 Kin. 8:32; Is. 3:10, 11; Matt. 16:27; Rom. 2:6-9

21 [a]Ezek. 18:27, 28; 33:12, 19

22 [a]Ezek. 18:24; 33:16; Is. 43:25; Jer. 50:20; Mic. 7:19 [b]Ps. 18:20-24

23 [1]Lit., *is it not* [a]Ezek. 18:32; 33:11; Lam. 3:33; Hos. 11:8 [b]Ps. 147:11; Mic. 7:18

24 [a]Ezek. 18:26; 3:20; 33:18; 1 Sam. 15:11; 2 Chr. 24:2, 17-22 [b]Ezek. 18:22; Gal. 3:3, 4 [c]Ezek. 17:20; 20:27; Prov. 21:16

25 [a]Ezek. 18:29; 33:17, 20; Mal. 2:17; 3:13-15 [b]Gen. 18:25; Jer. 12:1; Zeph. 3:5

26 [1]Lit., *then*

30 [a]Ezek. 14:6; 33:11; Hos. 12:6

31 [a]Is. 1:16, 17; 55:7 [b]Ezek. 11:19; 36:26; Ps. 51:10

32 [a]Ezek. 18:23; 33:11

1 [a]Ezek. 19:14; 2:10 [b]2 Kin. 23:29, 30, 34; 24:6, 12; 25:5-7

'[1]What was your mother?
A lioness among lions!
She lay down among young lions,
She reared her cubs.
3 'When she brought up one of her cubs,
He became a lion,
And he learned to tear *his* prey;
He devoured men.
4 'Then nations heard about him;
He was [a]captured in their pit,
And they brought him with hooks
To the land of Egypt.
5 'When she saw, as she waited,
That her hope was lost,
She took [1]another of her cubs
And made him a young lion.
6 'And he [a]walked about among the lions;
He became a young lion,
He learned to tear *his* prey;
He devoured men.
7 'And he [1]destroyed their [2]fortified towers
And laid waste their cities;
And the land and its fulness were appalled
Because of the sound of his roaring.
8 'Then [a]nations set against him
On every side from *their* provinces,
And they spread their net over him;
He was captured in their pit.
9 'And they put him in a cage with hooks
And [a]brought him to the king of Babylon;
They brought him in hunting nets
So that his voice should be heard no more
On the mountains of Israel.
10 'Your mother was [a]like a vine in your [1]vineyard,
Planted by the waters;
It was fruitful and full of branches
Because of abundant waters.
11 'And it had [1a]strong branches *fit* for scepters of rulers,
And its [b]height was raised above the clouds
So that it was seen in its height with the mass of its branches.
12 'But it was [a]plucked up in fury;
It was [b]cast down to the ground;
And the [c]east wind dried up its fruit.
Its [1d]strong branch [2]was torn off
So that [3]it withered;
The fire consumed it.
13 'And now it is planted in the [a]wilderness,
In a dry and thirsty land.
14 'And [a]fire has gone out from *its* branch;
It has consumed its shoots *and* fruit,
So that there is not in it a [1]strong branch,
A scepter to rule.
This is a lamentation, and has become a lamentation.' "

2 [1]Or, *Why did your mother, a lioness, lie down among lions; among young lions rear her cubs?*

4 [a]2 Kin. 23:34; 2 Chr. 36:4, 6

5 [1]Lit., *one*

6 [a]2 Kin. 24:9; 2 Chr. 36:9

7 [1]So Targum; M.T., *knew* [2]Or, *widows*

8 [a]2 Kin. 24:11

9 [a]2 Kin. 24:15

10 [1]So with some ancient mss.; M.T., *blood* [a]Ps. 80:8-11

11 [1]Lit., *rods of strength* [a]Ps. 80:15 [b]Ezek. 31:3

12 [1]Lit., *rods of her strength* [2]So Gk.; M.T., *they were* [3]So Gk.; M.T., *they* [a]Jer. 31:28 [b]Ezek. 28:17; Lam. 2:1 [c]Ezek. 17:10; Hos. 13:15 [d]Ezek. 19:11; Is. 27:11

13 [a]Ezek. 19:10; 20:35; 2 Kin. 24:12-16; Hos. 2:3

14 [1]Lit., *rod of strength* [a]Ezek. 15:4; 20:47, 48

Chapter 20

NOW it came about in the seventh year, in the fifth *month*, on the tenth of the month, that [1]certain of the [a]elders of Israel came to inquire of the LORD, and sat before me.

2 And the word of the LORD came to me saying,

3 "Son of man, speak to the elders of Israel, and say to them, 'Thus says the Lord [1]GOD, "Do you come to inquire of Me? As I live," declares the Lord GOD, "I will not be inquired of by you." '

4 "Will you judge them, will you judge them, son of man? [a]Make them know the abominations of their fathers;

5 and say to them, 'Thus says the Lord GOD, "On the day when I [a]chose Israel and [1]swore to the [2]descendants of the house of Jacob and made Myself known to them in the land of Egypt, when I [1]swore to them, saying, [b]I am the LORD your God,

6 on that day I swore to them, to bring them out from the land of Egypt into a land that I had [1]selected for them, [a]flowing with milk and honey, which is the glory of all lands.

7 "And I said to them, '[a]Cast away, each of you, the detestable things of his eyes, and [b]do not defile yourselves with the idols of Egypt; [c]I am the LORD your God.'

8 "But they [a]rebelled against Me and were not willing to listen to Me; [1]they did not cast away the detestable things of their eyes, nor did they forsake the [b]idols of Egypt.

Then I [2]resolved to [c]pour out My wrath on them, to accomplish My anger against them in the midst of the land of Egypt.

9 "But I acted [a]for the sake of My name, that it should [b]not be profaned in the sight of the nations among whom they *lived*, in whose sight I made Myself known to them by bringing them out of the land of Egypt.

10 "So I took them out of the land of Egypt and brought them into the [a]wilderness.

11 "And I gave them My [a]statutes and informed them of My ordinances, by [b]which, if a man [1]observes them, he will live.

12 "And also I gave them My sabbaths to be a [a]sign between Me and them, that they might know that I am the LORD who sanctifies them.

13 "But the house of Israel [a]rebelled against Me in the wilderness. They did not walk in My statutes, and they rejected My ordinances, by which, if a man [1]observes them, he will live; and My [b]sabbaths they greatly profaned. Then I [2]resolved to [c]pour out My wrath on them in the wilderness, to annihilate them.

14 "But I acted for the sake of My name, that it should not be profaned in the sight of the nations, before whose sight I had brought them out.

15 "And also I swore to them in the wilderness that I would not bring them into the land which I had given them, flowing with milk and honey, which is the glory of all lands,

16 because they rejected My ordinances, and as for My

---

1 [1]Lit., *men*
[a]Ezek. 8:1, 11, 12

3 [1]YHWH, usually rendered LORD, and so throughout the chap.

4 [a]Ezek. 16:2; 22:2

5 [1]Lit., *lifted up My hand*, and so throughout the chap. [2]Lit., *seed*
[a]Ex. 6:6-8 [b]Ex. 6:2, 3

6 [1]Lit., *spied out*
[a]Ex. 13:5; 33:3

7 [a]Ex. 20:4, 5; 22:20 [b]Lev. 18:3; Deut. 29:16, 18 [c]Ex. 20:2

8 [1]Lit., *each one* [2]Lit., *said*
[a]Deut. 9:7; Is. 63:10 [b]Ex. 32:1-9 [c]Ezek. 20:13, 21; 5:13; 7:8

9 [a]Ezek. 20:14, 22; 36:21, 22; Ex. 32:11-14 [b]Ezek. 39:7

10 [a]Ex. 19:1

11 [1]Lit., *does*
[a]Ex. 20:1-23, 33 [b]Ezek. 20:13; Lev. 18:5

12 [a]Ezek. 20:20; Ex. 31:13, 17

13 [1]Lit., *does* [2]Lit., *said*
[a]Ezek. 20:8; Num. 14:11, 12, 22 [b]Ezek. 20:21; Is. 56:6
[c]Ezek. 20:8, 21; Ex. 32:10; Deut. 9:8

statutes, they did not walk in them; they even profaned My
sabbaths, for their [a]heart continually went after their idols.
17 "Yet My eye spared them rather than destroying them,
and I did not cause their [a]annihilation in the wilderness.
18 "And I said to their [1a]children in the wilderness, '[b]Do
not walk in the statutes of your fathers, or keep their ordinances, or defile yourselves with their idols.
19 '[a]I am the LORD your God; walk in My statutes, and
keep My ordinances, and [1]observe them.
20 'And sanctify My sabbaths; and they shall be a sign
between Me and you, that you may know that I am the LORD
your God.'
21 "But the [a]children rebelled against Me; they did not
walk in My statutes, nor were they careful to observe My
ordinances, by which, *if* a man observes them, he will live; they
profaned My sabbaths. So I [1]resolved to pour out My wrath on
them, to accomplish My anger against them in the wilderness.
22 "But I [a]withdrew My hand and acted [b]for the sake of
My name, that it should not be profaned in the sight of the
nations in whose sight I had brought them out.
23 "Also I swore to them in the wilderness that I would
[a]scatter them among the nations and disperse them among the
lands,
24 because they had not observed My ordinances, but had
rejected My statutes, and had profaned My sabbaths, and their
eyes were [1]on the idols of their fathers.
25 "And I also gave them statutes that were [a]not good and
ordinances by which they could not live;
26 and I pronounced them [a]unclean because of their gifts,
in that they [b]caused all [1]their first-born to pass through *the fire*
so that I might make them desolate, in order that they might
[c]know that I am the LORD." '
27 "Therefore, son of man, [a]speak to the house of Israel,
and say to them, 'Thus says the Lord GOD, "Yet in this your
fathers have [b]blasphemed Me by [c]acting treacherously against
Me.
28 "When I had [a]brought them into the land which I swore
to give to them, then they saw every [b]high hill and every leafy
tree, and they offered there their sacrifices, and there they
presented the provocation of their offering. There also they
made their soothing aroma, and there they poured out their
libations.
29 "Then I said to them, 'What is the high place to which
you go?' So its name is called [1]Bamah to this day." '
30 "Therefore, say to the house of Israel, 'Thus says the
Lord GOD, "Will you defile yourselves [1]after the manner of
your [a]fathers and play the harlot after their detestable things?
31 "And [1]when you offer your gifts, when you cause your
sons to [a]pass through the fire, you are defiling yourselves with
all your idols to this day. And shall I be inquired of by you, O
house of Israel? As I live," declares the Lord GOD, "I will not
be inquired of by you.
32 "And what comes [1]into your mind will not come about,
when you say: 'We will be like the nations, like the tribes of
the lands, [a]serving wood and stone.'
33 "As I live," declares the Lord GOD, "surely with a mighty

16 [a]Ezek. 20:8; 11:21; 14:3-7

17 [a]Ezek. 11:13; Jer. 4:27; 5:18

18 [1]Lit., *sons* [a]Num. 14:31; Deut. 4:3-6 [b]Zech. 1:4

19 [1]Lit., *do* [a]Ex. 6:7; 20:2

21 [1]Lit., *said* [a]Num. 21:5; 25:1-3

22 [a]Ezek. 20:17; Job 13:21; Ps. 78:38 [b]Ezek. 20:9, 14; Is. 48:9-11; Jer. 14:7, 21

23 [a]Lev. 26:33; Deut. 4:27; 28:64

24 [1]Lit., *after*

25 [a]Ps. 81:12; Is. 66:4; Rom. 1:21-25, 28

26 [1]Lit., *that which opens the womb* [a]Ezek. 20:30; Lev. 18:21; 20:2-5; Is. 63:17; Rom. 11:8 [b]Jer. 7:31; 19:4-9 [c]Ezek. 20:12, 20; 6:7

27 [a]Ezek. 20:2, 7; 3:4, 11, 27 [b]Num. 15:30; Rom. 2:24 [c]Ezek. 18:24; 39:23, 26

28 [a]Josh. 23:3, 14; Neh. 9:22-26; Ps. 78:55 [b]Ezek. 6:13; 1 Kin. 14:23; Ps. 78:58; Is. 57:5-7; Jer. 2:7; 3:6

29 [1]Or, *High Place*

30 [1]Lit., *in the way of* [a]Judg. 2:19; Jer. 7:26; 16:12

31 [1]Lit., *in your lifting up* [a]Ezek. 20:26; 16:20; Ps. 106:37-39; Jer. 7:31

32 [1]Lit., *upon your spirit* [a]Jer. 2:25; 44:17

hand and with an outstretched arm and with wrath poured out, I shall be [a]king over you.

34 "And I shall [a]bring you out from the peoples and gather you from the lands where you are scattered, with a mighty hand and with an outstretched arm and with [b]wrath poured out;

35 and I shall bring you into the [a]wilderness of the peoples, and there I shall enter into judgment with you face to face.

36 "As I [a]entered into judgment with your fathers in the [b]wilderness of the land of Egypt, so I will enter into judgment with you," declares the Lord GOD.

37 "And I shall make you [a]pass under the rod, and I shall bring you into the bond of the covenant;

38 and I shall [a]purge from you the rebels and those who transgress against Me; I shall bring them out of the land where they sojourn, but they will [b]not enter the [1]land of Israel. Thus you will know that I am the LORD.

39 "As for you, O house of Israel," thus says the Lord GOD, "[a]Go, serve every one his idols; [1]but later, you will surely listen to Me, and My holy name you will [b]profane no longer with your gifts and with your idols.

40 "For on My holy mountain, on the high mountain of Israel," declares the Lord GOD, "there the whole house of Israel, [a]all of them, will serve Me in the land; there I shall [b]accept them, and there I shall [1]seek your contributions and the choicest of your gifts, with all your holy things.

41 "[1]As a soothing aroma I shall accept you, when I [a]bring you out from the peoples and gather you from the lands where you are scattered; and I shall prove Myself [b]holy among you in the sight of the nations.

42 "And you will know that I am the LORD, when I bring you into the land of Israel, into the [a]land which I swore to give to your forefathers.

43 "And there you will [a]remember your ways and all your deeds, with which you have defiled yourselves; and you will [b]loathe yourselves in your own [1]sight for all the evil things that you have done.

44 "Then you will know that I am the LORD when I have dealt with you for My name's sake, not according to your evil ways or according to your corrupt deeds, O house of Israel," declares the Lord GOD.' "

45 [1]Now the word of the LORD came to me saying,

46 "Son of man, set your face toward [1]Teman, and speak out against the [a]south, and [b]prophesy against the [c]forest [2]land of the Negev,

47 and say to the forest of the Negev, 'Hear the word of the LORD: Thus says the Lord GOD, "Behold, I am about to [a]kindle a fire in you, and it shall consume every [1]green tree in you, as well as every dry tree; the blazing flame will not be quenched, and [2b]the whole surface from south to north will be burned by it.

48 "And all flesh will see that I, the LORD, have kindled it; it shall [a]not be quenched." ' "

49 Then I said, "Ah Lord GOD! They are saying of me, 'Is he not *just* speaking [a]parables?' "

33 [a]Jer. 51:57

34 [a]Ezek. 20:38; 34:16; Is. 27:12, 13 [b]Jer. 42:18; 44:6; Lam. 2:4

35 [a]Ezek. 20:36; 19:13; Hos. 2:14

36 [a]Ezek. 20:13, 21; Num. 11:1-35; Ps. 106:15; 1 Cor. 10:5-10 [b]Deut. 32:10

37 [a]Lev. 27:32; Jer. 33:13

38 [1]Lit., *ground* or *soil* [a]Ezek. 34:17-22; Amos 9:9, 10; Zech. 13:8, 9; Mal. 3:3; 4:1-3 [b]Ezek. 20:15, 16; 13:9; Num. 14:29, 30; Ps. 95:11; Heb. 4:3

39 [1]Or, *and afterwards, if you will not listen to Me, but* [a]Jer. 44:25, 26 [b]Ezek. 23:38, 39; 43:7; Is. 1:13-15

40 [1]Or, *require* [a]Ezek. 37:22, 24; Is. 66:23 [b]Ezek. 43:12, 27; Is. 56:7; 60:7

41 [1]Lit., *With* [a]Ezek. 11:17; 28:25; Is. 27:12, 13 [b]Ezek. 28:25; 36:23; Is. 5:16

42 [a]Ezek. 20:6, 15

43 [1]Lit., *faces* [a]Ezek. 6:9; 16:61, 63; Hos. 5:15 [b]Ezek. 36:31; Jer. 31:18; Zech. 12:10

45 [1]Chap. 21:1 in Heb.

46 [1]Or, *the South* [2]Lit., *of the field* [a]Ezek. 21:4; Jer. 13:19 [b]Ezek. 21:2; Amos 7:16 [c]Is. 30:6-11

47 [1]Lit., *moist* [2]Or, *all the faces* [a]Is. 9:18, 19; Jer. 21:14 [b]Is. 13:8

48 [a]Jer. 7:20; 17:27

49 [a]Ezek. 17:2; Matt. 13:13, 14; John 16:25

CHAPTER 21

1
AND the word of the LORD came to me saying,
2 "Son of man, [a]set your face toward Jerusalem, and
[1b]speak against the sanctuaries, and prophesy against the land
of Israel;
3 and say to the land of Israel, 'Thus says the LORD,
"Behold, [a]I am against you; and I shall draw My sword out of
its sheath and cut off from you the [b]righteous and the wicked.
4 "Because I shall cut off from you the righteous and the
wicked, therefore My sword shall go forth from its sheath
against [a]all flesh from south *to* north.
5 "Thus all flesh will know that I, the LORD, have drawn
My sword out of its sheath. It will [a]not return *to its sheath*
again." '
6 "As for you, son of man, groan with breaking [1]heart and
bitter grief, groan in their sight.
7 'And it will come about when they say to you, 'Why do
you groan?' that you will say, 'Because of the [a]news that is
coming; and [b]every heart will melt, all hands will be feeble,
every spirit will [1]faint, and all knees will [2]be weak as water.
Behold, it comes and it will happen,' declares the Lord [3]GOD."
8 Again the word of the LORD came to me saying,
9 "Son of man, prophesy and say, 'Thus says the LORD.'
Say,

'A sword, a sword sharpened
And also polished!
10 'Sharpened to make a [a]slaughter,
Polished [1]to flash like lightning!'

Or shall we rejoice, the [2]rod of my son [b]despising every tree?
11 "And it is given to be polished, that it may be handled;
the sword is sharpened and polished, to give it into the hand of
the slayer.
12 "[a]Cry out and wail, son of man; for it is against My
people, it is against all the [b]officials of Israel. They are delivered over to the sword with My people, therefore strike *your*
thigh.
13 "For *there is* a testing; and what if even the [1]rod which
despises will be no more?" declares the Lord GOD.
14 'You therefore, son of man, prophesy, and clap *your*
hands together; and let the sword be [a]doubled the third time,
the sword for the slain. It is the sword for the great one slain,
which [b]surrounds them,
15 that *their* [a]hearts may melt, and [b]many fall at all their
[c]gates. I have given the glittering sword. Ah! It is made *for*
striking like lightning, it is wrapped up *in readiness* for
slaughter.
16 "[1]Show yourself sharp, go to the right; set yourself; go to
the left, wherever your [2]edge is appointed.
17 "I shall also clap My hands together, and I shall [1a]ap-
pease My wrath; I, the LORD, have spoken."
18 And the word of the LORD came to me saying,
19 "As for you, son of man, [1a]make two ways for the sword
of the king of Babylon to come; both of them will go out of
one land. And [2]make a signpost; [3]make it at the head of the
way to the city.

1 [1]Chap. 21:6 in *Heb.*

2 [1]Lit., *drip*
[a]Ezek. 20:46; 25:2; 28:21
[b]Ezek. 20:46; Job 29:22

3 [a]Ezek. 5:8; Jer. 21:13; Nah. 2:13; 3:5 [b]Is. 57:1

4 [a]Ezek. 7:2; 20:47; Jer. 12:12

5 [a]Ezek. 21:30; 1 Sam. 3:12; Jer. 23:20; Nah. 1:9

6 [1]Lit., *loins*

7 [1]Lit., *be dim* [2]Lit., *flow* [3]YHWH, usually rendered LORD, and so throughout the chap.
[a]Ezek. 7:26 [b]Is. 13:7; Nah. 2:10

10 [1]Lit., *lightning to be to her* [2]Or, *scepter*
[a]Is. 34:5, 6 [b]Ezek. 20:47; Ps. 110:5, 6

12 [a]Ezek. 21:6; Joel 1:13
[b]Ezek. 21:25; 22:6

13 [1]Or, *scepter*

14 [a]Lev. 26:21, 24; 2 Kin. 24:1, 10-16; 25:1 [b]1 Kin. 22:25

15 [a]Ezek. 21:7; Josh. 2:11; 2 Sam. 17:10; Ps. 22:2 [b]Is. 59:10; Jer. 13:16; 18:15
[c]Ezek. 21:19; Jer. 17:27

16 [1]Or, *Unite yourself* [2]Lit., *face*

17 [1]Lit., *cause to rest*
[a]Ezek. 5:13

19 [1]Or, *set for yourself* [2]Lit., *cut out a hand* [3]Lit., *cut it*
[a]Ezek. 4:1-3; Jer. 1:10

20 "You shall [1]mark a way for the word to come to [a]Rab-
bah of the sons of Ammon, and to Judah into [b]fortified
Jerusalem.
21 "For the king of Babylon stands at the [1]parting of the
way, at the head of the two ways, to use [a]divination; he [b]shakes
the arrows, he consults the [2c]household idols, he looks at the
liver.
22 "Into his right hand came the divination, 'Jerusalem,' [a]to
set battering rams, to open the mouth [1]for slaughter, to lift up
the voice with a battle cry, [b]to set battering rams against the
gates, to cast up mounds, to build a siege wall.
23 "And it will be to them like a false divination in their
eyes; [a]they have *sworn* solemn oaths. But He brings iniquity to
[b]remembrance, that they may be seized.
24 "Therefore, thus says the Lord GOD, 'Because you have
made your iniquity to be remembered, in that your transgressions are uncovered, so that in all your deeds your sins appear—because you have come to remembrance, you will be
seized with the hand.
25 'And you, O slain, wicked one, the prince of Israel,
whose [a]day has come, in the time of the [1]punishment of the
end,'
26 thus says the Lord GOD, 'Remove the turban, and take
off the [a]crown; this will *be* [1]no more the same. [b]Exalt that
which is low, and abase that which is high.
27 'A ruin, a ruin, a ruin, I shall [a]make it. This also will be
no more, until he comes whose [b]right it is; and I shall give it *to
him.*'
28 "And you, son of man, prophesy and say, 'Thus says the
Lord GOD concerning the sons of Ammon and concerning
their [a]reproach,' and say: 'A sword, a sword is drawn, polished
for the slaughter, to cause it [1]to [b]consume, that it may be like
lightning—
29 while they see for you [a]false visions, while they divine
lies for you—to place you on the necks of the wicked who are
slain, whose day has come in the [b]time of the [1]punishment of
the end.
30 '[a]Return *it* to its sheath. In the [b]place where you were
created, in the land of your origin, I shall judge you.
31 'And I shall [a]pour out My indignation on you; I shall
[b]blow on you with the fire of My wrath, and I shall give you
into the hand of brutal men, [1c]skilled in destruction.
32 'You will be [1a]fuel for the fire; your blood will be in the
midst of the land. You will [b]not be remembered, for I, the
LORD, have spoken.' "

CHAPTER 22

THEN the word of the LORD came to me saying,
2 "And you, son of man, will you judge, will you judge the
bloody city; Then cause her to know all her abominations.
3 "And you shall say, 'Thus says the Lord [1]GOD, "A city
[a]shedding blood in her midst, so that her time will come, and
that makes idols, contrary to her *interest,* for defilement!
4 "You have become [a]guilty by [1]the blood which you have
shed, and defiled by your idols which you have made. Thus

20 [1]Lit., *set* [a]Ezek. 25:5; Deut. 3:11; Jer. 49:2; Amos 1:14 [b]Ps. 48:12, 13; 125:1, 2

21 [1]Lit., *mother* [2]Heb., *teraphim;* cf. Gen. 31:19; Judg. 18:17, 20 [a]Num. 22:7; 23:23 [b]Prov. 16:33; 21:1 [c]Gen. 31:19, 30; Judg. 17:5

22 [1]Lit., *in* [a]Ezek. 4:2 [b]Ezek. 26:9

23 [a]Ezek. 17:16, 18 [b]Ezek. 21:24; 29:16; Num. 5:15

25 [1]Or, *iniquity* [a]Ezek. 7:2, 3, 7; Ps. 37:13

26 [1]Lit., *not this* [a]Ezek. 16:12; Jer. 13:18 [b]Ezek. 17:24; Ps. 75:7

27 [a]Hag. 2:21, 22 [b]Ezek. 34:24; 37:24; Ps. 2:6; 72:7, 10; Jer. 23:5, 6

28 [1]Lit., *to finish* [a]Ezek. 36:15; Zeph. 2:8-10 [b]Is. 31:8; Jer. 12:12; 46:10, 14

29 [1]Or, *iniquity* [a]Ezek. 13:6-9; 22:28; Jer. 27:9 [b]Ezek. 21:25; 35:5

30 [a]Jer. 47:6, 7 [b]Ezek. 25:5

31 [1]Or, *artisans of* [a]Ezek. 14:19; 25:7; Nah. 1:6 [b]Ezek. 22:20, 21; Ps. 18:15; Is. 30:33; Hag. 1:9 [c]Jer. 4:7; 6:22, 23; 51:20, 21; Hab. 1:6, 10

32 [1]Lit., *food* [a]Ezek. 20:47, 48; Mal. 4:1 [b]Ezek. 25:10

3 [1]YHWH, usually rendered LORD, and so throughout the chap. [a]Ezek. 22:6, 27; 23:37, 45; Zeph. 3:3

4 [1]Lit., *your* [a]Ezek. 24:7, 8; 2 Kin. 21:16

you have brought your [2]day near and have come to your years;
therefore I have made you a [b]reproach to the nations, and a
mocking to all the lands.
5 "Those who are near and those who are far from you
will mock you, you of ill repute, full of [a]turmoil.
6 "Behold, the [a]rulers of Israel, each according to his [1]pow-
er, have been in you for the purpose of shedding blood.
7 "They have [a]treated father and mother lightly within
you. The alien they have [b]oppressed in your midst; the [c]father-
less and the widow they have wronged in you.
8 "You have despised My [a]holy things and profaned My
[b]sabbaths.
9 "Slanderous men have been in you for the purpose of
shedding blood, and in you they have eaten at the mountain
shrines. In your midst they have [a]committed acts of lewdness.
10 "In you [1]they have [a]uncovered *their* fathers' nakedness;
in you they have humbled her who was [b]unclean in her menstrual impurity.
11 "And one has committed abomination with his [a]neigh-
bor's wife, and another has lewdly defiled his [b]daughter-in-
law. And another in you has [c]humbled his sister, his father's
daughter.
12 "In you they have [a]taken bribes to shed blood; you have
taken [b]interest and profits, and you have injured your neighbors for gain by [c]oppression, and you have [d]forgotten Me,"
declares the Lord GOD.
13 "Behold, then, I smite My hand at your [a]dishonest gain
which you have acquired and at [1]the bloodshed which is
among you.
14 "Can your heart endure, or can your hands be strong, in
the days that I shall deal with you? I, the LORD, have spoken
and shall act.
15 "And I shall [a]scatter you among the nations, and I shall
disperse you through the lands, and I shall [b]consume your
uncleanness from you.
16 "And you will profane yourself in the sight of the nations, and you will [a]know that I am the LORD."'"
17 And the word of the LORD came to me saying,
18 "Son of man, the house of Israel has become [a]dross to
Me; all of them are [b]bronze and tin and iron and lead in the
[c]furnace; they are the dross of silver.
19 "Therefore, thus says the Lord GOD, 'Because all of you
have become dross, therefore, behold, I am going to gather
you into the midst of Jerusalem.
20 'As they gather silver and bronze and iron and lead and
tin into the [a]furnace to blow fire on it in order to melt *it*, so I
shall gather *you* in My anger and in My wrath, and I shall lay
you *there* and melt you.
21 'And I shall gather you and blow on you with the fire of
My wrath, and you will be melted in the midst of it.
22 'As silver is melted in the furnace, so you will be melted
in the midst of it; and you will know that I, the LORD, have
[a]poured out My wrath on you.'"
23 And the word of the LORD came to me saying,
24 "Son of man, say to her, 'You are a land that is [a]not
cleansed or rained on in the day of indignation.'

4 [2]Lit., *days* [b]Ezek. 5:14, 15; 16:57; Ps. 44:13, 14

5 [a]Is. 22:2

6 [1]Lit., *arm* [a]Ezek. 22:27; Is. 1:23

7 [a]Lev. 20:9; Deut. 27:16 [b]Ex. 23:9; Jer. 7:6; Zech. 7:10 [c]Ezek. 22:25; Ex. 22:22; Mal. 3:5

8 [a]Ezek. 22:26 [b]Ezek. 20:13, 21, 24; 23:38, 39

9 [a]Ezek. 23:29; Hos. 4:2, 10, 14

10 [1]Lit., *he has* [a]Lev. 18:8 [b]Ezek. 18:6; Lev. 18:19

11 [a]Ezek. 18:11; 33:26 [b]Lev. 18:15 [c]2 Sam. 13:14

12 [a]Deut. 27:25; Mic. 7: 2, 3 [b]Lev. 25:36 [c]Lev. 19:13 [d]Ezek. 23:35; Ps. 106:21

13 [1]Lit., *your* [a]Is. 33:15; Amos 2:6-8; Mic. 2:2

15 [a]Ezek. 20:23; Deut. 4:27; Neh. 1:8; Zech. 7:14 [b]Ezek. 23:27, 48

16 [a]Ezek. 6:7; Ps. 83:18

18 [a]Ps. 119:119; Is. 1:22; Lam. 4:1 [b]Jer. 6:28-30 [c]Prov. 17:3; Is. 48:10

20 [a]Is. 1:25

22 [a]Ezek. 20:8, 33; Hos. 5:10

24 [a]Ezek. 24:13; 2 Chr. 28:22; Is. 9:13; Jer. 2:30; Zeph. 3:2

25 "There is a [a]conspiracy of her prophets in her midst, like a roaring lion tearing the prey. They have [b]devoured lives; they have taken treasure and precious things; they have made many [c]widows in the midst of her.

26 "Her [a]priests have done violence to My law and have [b]profaned My holy things; they have made no [c]distinction between the holy and the profane, and they have not taught the difference between the [d]unclean and the clean; and they hide their eyes from My sabbaths, and I am profaned among them.

27 "Her princes within her are like wolves tearing the prey, by shedding blood *and* [a]destroying lives in order to get [b]dishonest gain.

28 "And her prophets have smeared whitewash for them, seeing [a]false visions and divining lies for them, saying, 'Thus says the Lord GOD,' when the LORD has not spoken.

29 "The people of the land have practiced [a]oppression and committed robbery, and they have wronged the poor and needy and have [b]oppressed the sojourner without justice.

30 "And I [a]searched for a man among them who should [b]build up the wall and [c]stand in the gap before Me for the land, that I should not destroy it; but I found [1]no one.

31 "Thus I have poured out My [a]indignation on them; I have consumed them with the fire of My wrath; [b]their way I have brought upon their heads," declares the Lord GOD.

CHAPTER 23

THE word of the LORD came to me again saying,

2 "Son of man, there were two women, the daughters of one mother;

3 and they played the harlot in Egypt. They [a]played the harlot in their youth; there their breasts were pressed, and there their virgin bosom was handled.

4 "And their names were Oholah the elder and Oholibah her sister. And they became Mine, and they bore sons and daughters. And *as for* their names, Samaria is Oholah, and Jerusalem is Oholibah.

5 "And Oholah played the harlot [1]while she was Mine; and she lusted after her lovers, after the [a]Assyrians, *her* neighbors,

6 who were clothed in purple, [a]governors and officials, all of them desirable young men, horsemen riding on horses.

7 "And she bestowed her harlotries on them, all of whom *were* the choicest [1]men of Assyria; and with all whom she lusted after, with all their idols she [a]defiled herself.

8 "And she did not forsake her harlotries [a]from the time in Egypt; for in her youth [1]men had lain with her, and they handled her virgin bosom and poured out their [2]lust on her.

9 "Therefore, I gave her into the hand of her [a]lovers, into the hand of the [1]Assyrians, after whom she lusted.

10 "They uncovered her nakedness; they took her sons and her daughters, but they slew her with the sword. Thus she became a [1]byword among women, and they executed judgments on her.

11 "Now her sister Oholibah saw *this,* yet she was [a]more

---

25 [a]Jer. 11:9; Hos. 6:9 [b]Ezek. 22:27; 13:19; Jer. 2:34 [c]Ezek. 22:7; Jer. 15:8

26 [a]Ezek. 7:26; Jer. 2:8, 26 [b]Ezek. 22:8; 1 Sam. 2:12-17, 22 [c]Ezek. 44:23; Lev. 10:10 [d]Hag. 2:11-14

27 [a]Ezek. 22:25 [b]Ezek. 22:13

28 [a]Ezek. 13:6; Jer. 23:25-32

29 [a]Ezek. 22:7; 9:9; Is. 5:7; Amos 3:10 [b]Ex. 23:9

30 [1]Lit., *not* [a]Is. 59:16; 63:5; Jer. 5:1 [b]Ezek. 13:5 [c]Ps. 106:23; Jer. 15:1

31 [a]Ezek. 22:20; Is. 10:5; 13:5; 30:27 [b]Ezek. 7:3, 8, 9; 9:10; 16:43; Rom. 2:8, 9

3 [a]Jer. 3:9

5 [1]Lit., *under Me* [a]Ezek. 16:28; 2 Kin. 15:19; 16:7; 17:3; Hos. 5:13; 8:9, 10

6 [a]Ezek. 23:12, 13

7 [1]Lit., *sons of Asshur* [a]Ezek. 20:7; 22:3, 4; Hos. 5:3; 6:10

8 [1]Lit., *they* [2]Lit., *harlotry* [a]Ezek. 23:3, 19; Ex. 32:4; 1 Kin. 12:28; 2 Kin. 10:29; 17:16

9 [1]Lit., *sons of Asshur* [a]Ezek. 23:22; 16:37

10 [1]Lit., *a name*

11 [a]Ezek. 16:51; Jer. 3:8-11

corrupt in her lust than she, and her harlotries were more than
the harlotries of her sister.
12 "She lusted after the [1]Assyrians, governors and officials,
the ones near, magnificently dressed, horsemen riding on
horses, all of them desirable young men.
13 "And I saw that she had defiled herself; they both took
[1]the same way.
14 "So she increased her harlotries. And she saw men [a]portrayed on the wall, images of the [b]Chaldeans portrayed with
vermilion,
15 girded with belts on their loins, with flowing turbans on
their heads, all of them looking like officers, [1]like the [2]Babylonians *in* Chaldea, the land of their birth.
16 "And [1]when she saw them she [a]lusted after them and
sent messengers to them in Chaldea.
17 "And the [1a]Babylonians came to her to the bed of love,
and they defiled her with their harlotry. And when she had
been defiled by them, [2]she became disgusted with them.
18 "And she uncovered her harlotries and [a]uncovered her
nakedness; then [1]I became [b]disgusted with her, as [1]I had become disgusted with her [c]sister.
19 "Yet she multiplied her harlotries, remembering the
days of her youth, when she played the harlot in the land of
Egypt.
20 "And she [a]lusted after their paramours, whose flesh is
like the flesh of donkeys and whose issue is *like* the issue of
horses.
21 "Thus you longed for the [a]lewdness of your youth, when
[1]the Egyptians handled your bosom because of the breasts of
your youth.
22 "Therefore, O Oholibah, thus says the Lord [1]God, 'Behold I will arouse your lovers against you, from whom [2]you
were alienated, and I will bring them against you from every
side:
23 the [1a]Babylonians and all the [b]Chaldeans, [c]Pekod and
Shoa and Koa, *and* all the [2d]Assyrians with them; desirable
young men, governors and officials all of them, officers and
[3]men of renown, all of them riding on horses.
24 'And they will come against you with weapons, [a]chariots, and [1]wagons, and with a company of peoples. They will
set themselves against you on every side with buckler and
shield and helmet; and I shall commit the [b]judgment to them,
and they will judge you according to their customs.
25 'And I will set My [a]jealousy against you, that they may
deal with you in wrath. They will remove your nose and your
ears; and your [1]survivors will fall by the sword. They will take
your [b]sons and your daughters; and your [1]survivors will be
consumed by the fire.
26 'They will also [a]strip you of your clothes and take away
your [b]beautiful jewels.
27 'Thus I shall make your lewdness and your harlotry
brought from the land of Egypt to cease from you, so that you
will not lift up your eyes to them or remember Egypt any
more.'
28 "For thus says the Lord God, 'Behold, I will give you

12 [1]Lit., *sons of Asshur*

13 [1]Lit., *one*

14 [a]Ezek. 8:10 [b]Ezek. 16:29

15 [1]Lit., *the likeness of* [2]Lit., *sons of Babel*

16 [1]Lit., *at the sight of her eyes* [a]Ezek. 23:20; Matt. 5:28

17 [1]Lit., *sons of Babel* [2]Lit., *her soul* [a]2 Kin. 24:17

18 [1]Lit., *My soul* [a]Ezek. 23:10; 21:24; Jer. 8:12 [b]Ps. 78:59; 106:40; Jer. 12:8 [c]Ezek. 23:9; Amos 5:21

20 [a]Ezek. 16:26; 17:15

21 [1]So two mss. M.T., *from Egypt* [a]Ezek. 23:3; Jer. 3:9

22 [1]YHWH, usually rendered Lord, and so throughout the chap. [2]Lit., *your soul was alienated*

23 [1]Lit., *sons of Babylon* [2]Lit., *sons of Assyria* [3]Lit., *the called ones* [a]Ezek. 23:14-17; 21:19; 2 Kin. 20:14-17 [b]2 Kin. 24:2; Job 1:17; Is. 23:13 [c]Jer. 50:21 [d]Gen. 2:14; 25:18; Ezra 6:22

24 [1]Lit., *wheel* [a]Ezek. 26:10; Jer. 47:3; Nah. 2:3, 4 [b]Ezek. 23:45; 16:38; Jer. 39:5, 6

25 [1]Lit., *remainder* [a]Ezek. 5:13; 8:17, 18; Ezek. 34:14; Zeph. 1:8 [b]Ezek. 23:47; Hos. 2:4

26 [a]Ezek. 23:29; 16:39; Jer. 13:22 [b]Is. 3:18-23

into the hand of those whom you [a]hate, into the hand of those
from whom [1]you were alienated.
29 'And they will [a]deal with you in hatred, take all your
property, and leave you naked and bare. And the nakedness of
your harlotries shall be uncovered, both your lewdness and
your harlotries.
30 'These things will be done to you because you have
played the harlot with the nations, because you have defiled
yourself with their idols.
31 'You have walked in the way of your sister; therefore I
will give [a]her cup into your hand.'
32 "Thus says the Lord GOD,
'You will [a]drink your sister's cup,
Which is deep and *wide*.
[1]You will be [b]laughed at and held in derision;
It contains much.
33 'You will be filled with [a]drunkenness and sorrow,
The cup of horror and desolation,
The cup of your sister Samaria.
34 'And you will [a]drink it and drain it.
Then you will gnaw its fragments
And tear your breasts;
for I have spoken,' declares the Lord GOD.
35 "Therefore, thus says the Lord GOD, 'Because you have
[a]forgotten Me and [b]cast Me behind your back, bear now the
punishment of your lewdness and your harlotries.' "
36 Moreover, the LORD said to me, "Son of man, will you
[a]judge Oholah and Oholibah? Then [b]declare to them their
abominations.
37 "For they have committed adultery, and blood is on
their hands. Thus they have committed adultery with their
idols and even caused their sons, whom they bore to Me, to
pass through *the fire* to [1]them as food.
38 "Again, they have done this to Me: they have [a]defiled
My sanctuary on the same day and have profaned My
[b]sabbaths.
39 "For when they had slaughtered their children for their
idols, they entered My [a]sanctuary on the same day to profane
it; and lo, thus they did within My house.
40 "Furthermore, [1]they have even sent for men who come
from afar, to whom a messenger was sent; and lo, they came—
for whom you bathed, [a]painted your eyes, and [b]decorated
yourselves with ornaments;
41 and you sat on a splendid [a]couch with a [b]table arranged
before it, on which you had set My [c]incense and My [c]oil.
42 "And the sound of a [1a]carefree multitude was with her;
and [b]drunkards were brought from the wilderness with men of
the [2]common sort. And they put [c]bracelets on [3]the hands of
the women and beautiful crowns on their heads.
43 "Then I said concerning her who was [a]worn out by adulteries, '[1]Will they now commit adultery with her when she is
thus?'
44 "[1]But they went in to her as they would go in to a harlot.
Thus they went in to Oholah and to Oholibah, the lewd
women.

28 [1]Lit., *your soul was alienated* [a]Ezek. 23:17, 22; 16:37; Jer. 21:7-10; 34:20

29 [a]Ezek. 23:25, 26, 45-47; Deut. 28:48

31 [a]Ezek. 23:33; 2 Kin. 21:13; Jer. 7:14, 15

32 [1]Or, *It will be for jesting and deriding because of its great size* [a]Ps. 60:3; Is. 51:17; Jer. 25:15 [b]Ezek. 5:14, 15; 16:57; 22:4, 5

33 [a]Jer. 25:15, 16, 27; Hab. 2:16

34 [a]Ps. 75:8; Is. 51:17

35 [a]Ezek. 22:12; Is. 17:10; Jer. 3:21; Hos. 8:14; 13:6 [b]1 Kin. 14:9; Jer. 2:27; 32:33

36 [a]Ezek. 20:4; 22:2; Jer. 1:10 [b]Ezek. 16:2; Is. 58:1; Mic. 3:8

37 [1]I.e., idols

38 [a]Ezek. 5:11; 7:20; 2 Kin. 21:4, 7 [b]Ezek. 20:13, 24; Jer. 17:27

39 [a]Jer. 7:9-11

40 [1]Or, *you* (women) [a]2 Kin. 9:30; Jer. 4:30 [b]Ezek. 16:13-16; Is. 3:18-23

41 [a]Esth. 1:6; Is. 57:7; Amos 6:4 [b]Ezek. 44:16; Is. 65:11 [c]Jer. 44:17; Hos. 2:8

42 [1]Lit., *at ease* [2]Lit., *multitude of mankind* [3]Lit., *their hands* [a]Ezek. 16:49; Amos 6:3-6 [b]Jer. 51:7 [c]Ezek. 16:11, 12; Gen. 24:30

43 [1]Or, *Now they will commit adultery with her, and she with them.* [a]Ezek. 23:3; Ezra 9:7; Ps. 106:6

44 [1]Or, *And*

45 "But they, righteous men, will judge them with the judgment of adulteresses, and with the judgment of women who
shed blood, because they are adulteresses and blood is on their
hands.
46 "For thus says the Lord GOD, 'Bring up a company
against them, and give them over to [a]terror and plunder.
47 'And the company will [a]stone them with stones and cut
them down with their swords; they will slay their sons and their
daughters and [b]burn their houses with fire.
48 'Thus I shall make lewdness cease from the land, that
all women may be admonished and not commit [1]lewdness as
you have done.
49 'And your lewdness [1]will be [a]requited upon you, and
you will bear *the penalty of worshiping* your idols; thus you
will know that I am the Lord GOD.' "

CHAPTER 24

AND the word of the LORD came to me in the ninth year, in
the tenth month, on the tenth of the month, saying,
2 "Son of man, write the name of the day, this very day.
The king of Babylon [1]has [a]laid siege to Jerusalem this very day.
3 "And speak a [a]parable to the [b]rebellious house, and say
to them, 'Thus says the Lord [1]GOD,

"Put on the [c]pot, put *it* on, and also pour water in it;
4 "[1a]Put in it the pieces,
Every good piece, the thigh, and the shoulder;
Fill *it* with choice bones.
5 "Take the [a]choicest of the flock,
And also pile [1]wood under [2]the pot.
Make it boil vigorously.
Also seethe its bones in it."

6 'Therefore, thus says the Lord GOD,
"Woe to the [a]bloody city,
To the pot in which there is rust
And whose rust has not gone out of it!
Take out of it piece after piece,
[1]Without making a choice.
7 "For her blood is in her midst;
She placed it on the bare rock;
She did not [a]pour it on the ground
To cover it with dust.
8 "That it may [a]cause wrath to come up to take vengeance,
I have put her blood on the bare rock,
That it may [b]not be covered."
9 'Therefore, thus says the Lord GOD,
"[a]Woe to the bloody city!
I also shall make the pile great.
10 "Heap on the wood, kindle the fire,
[1]Boil the flesh well,
And mix in the spices,
And let the bones be burned.

46 [a]Jer. 15:4; 24:9; 29:18

47 [a]Ezek. 16:40; Lev. 20:10 [b]Jer. 39:8

48 [1]Lit., *according to your lewdness*

49 [1]Lit., *they will give* [a]Ezek. 23:35; 7:4, 9; 9:10; Is. 59:18

2 [1]Lit., *leaned on* [a]2 Kin. 25:1; Jer. 39:1; 52:4

3 [1]YHWH, usually rendered LORD, and so throughout the chap. [a]Ezek. 17:2; 20:49; Ps. 78:2 [b]Ezek. 2:3, 6, 8; Is. 1:2; 30:1, 9 [c]Ezek. 24:6; 11:3, 7, 11; Jer. 1:13, 14

4 [1]Lit., *Gather her pieces* [a]Ezek. 22:19-22; Mic. 3:2,3

5 [1]Lit., *bones* [2]Lit., *it* [a]Jer. 39:6; 52:10, 24-27

6 [1]Lit., *no lot has fallen on it* [a]Ezek. 22:2, 3, 27; 2 Kin. 24:3, 4; Mic. 7:2; Nah. 3:1

7 [a]Lev. 17:13; Deut. 12:16

8 [a]Is. 26:21 [b]Jer. 22:8, 9

9 [a]Ezek. 24:6; Hab. 2:12

10 [1]Lit., *complete*

11 "Then [a]set it empty on its coals,
So that it may be hot,
And its bronze may [1]glow,
And its [b]filthiness may be melted in it,
Its rust consumed.
12 "She has [a]wearied *Me* with toil,
Yet her great rust has not gone from her;
Let her rust *be* in the fire!
13 "In your filthiness is lewdness.
Because I have cleansed you,
Yet you are [a]not clean,
You will not be cleansed from your filthiness again,
Until I have [1b]spent My wrath on you.
14 "I, the LORD, have spoken; it is [a]coming and I shall act. I
shall not relent, and I shall not [b]pity, and I shall not be sorry;
[c]according to your ways and according to your deeds [1]I shall
judge you," declares the Lord GOD.' "
15 And the word of the LORD came to me saying,
16 "Son of man, behold, I am about to take from you the
[a]desire of your eyes with a [b]blow; but you shall not [c]mourn,
and you shall not weep, and your [d]tears shall not come.
17 "Groan silently; make [a]no mourning for the dead. Bind
on your turban, and put your shoes on your feet, and do not
cover *your* mustache, and do not [b]eat the bread of men."
18 So I spoke to the people in the morning, and in the
evening my wife died. And in the morning I did as I was
commanded.
19 And the people said to me, "Will you not tell us what
these things that you are doing mean for us?"
20 Then I said to them, "The word of the LORD came to
me saying,
21 'Speak to the house of Israel, "Thus says the Lord GOD,
'Behold, I am about to profane My sanctuary, the pride of
your power, the [a]desire of your eyes, and the delight of your
soul; and your [b]sons and your daughters whom you have left
behind will fall by the sword.
22 'And you will do as I have done; you will not cover *your*
mustache, and you will not eat the bread of men.
23 'And your turbans will be on your heads and your shoes
on your feet. You will not mourn, and you will not weep; but
you will rot away in your iniquities, and you will groan [1]to one
another.
24 'Thus Ezekiel will be a [a]sign to you; according to all that
he has done you will do; when it comes, then you will know
that I am the Lord GOD.' "
25 'As for you, son of man, will *it* not be on the day when I
take from them their [a]stronghold, the joy of their [1]pride, the
desire of their eyes, and [2]their heart's delight, their sons and
their daughters,
26 that on that day he who [a]escapes will come to you with
information for *your* ears?
27 'On that day your [a]mouth will be opened to him who
escaped, and you will speak and be dumb no longer. Thus you
will be a sign to them, and they will know that I am the
LORD.' "

11 [1]Lit., *become hot* [a]Jer. 21:10; Mal. 4:1 [b]Ezek. 22:15; 23:27

12 [a]Jer. 9:5

13 [1]Lit., *caused to rest* [a]Ezek. 22:24; Is. 5:4; 9:13; Jer. 6:28-30 [b]Ezek. 5:13; 8:18

14 [1]So with several ancient mss. and versions; M.T., *they* [a]Ps. 33:9; Is. 55:11 [b]Ezek. 9:10; Jer. 13:14 [c]Ezek. 18:30; 36:19; Is. 3:11

16 [a]Ezek. 24:18; Song of Sol. 7:10 [b]Job 23:2 [c]Jer. 16:5; 22:10 [d]Jer. 13:17

17 [a]Lev. 21:10-12 [b]Jer. 16:7; Hos. 9:4

21 [a]Ezek. 24:16; Ps. 27:4; 84:1 [b]Ezek. 23:25, 47; Jer. 6:11; 16:3, 4

23 [1]Lit., *a man to his brother*

24 [a]Ezek. 4:3; Hos. 1:2; 3:1; Luke 11:29, 30

25 [1]Or, *beauty* [2]Lit., *the lifting up of their soul* [a]Ezek. 24:21; Ps. 48:2; 50:2

26 [a]1 Sam. 4:12; Job 1:15-19

27 [a]Ezek. 3:26; 33:22

CHAPTER 25

AND the word of the LORD came to me saying,
2 "Son of man, set your face toward the sons of Ammon,
and prophesy against them,
3 and say to the sons of Ammon, 'Hear the word of the
Lord [1]GOD! Thus says the Lord GOD, "Because you said,
'[a]Aha!' against My sanctuary when it was profaned, and against
the land of Israel when it was made desolate, and against the
house of Judah when they went into exile,
4 therefore, behold, I am going to give you to the [a]sons
of the east for a possession, and they will set their encamp-
ments among you and make their dwellings among you; they
will [b]eat your fruit and drink your milk.
5 "And I shall make [a]Rabbah a pasture for camels and the
sons of Ammon a resting place for flocks. Thus you will know
that I am the LORD."
6 'For thus says the Lord GOD, "Because you have [a]clapped
your hands and stamped your feet and [b]rejoiced with
all the scorn of your soul against the land of Israel,
7 therefore, behold, I have [a]stretched out My hand
against you, and I shall give you for [b]spoil to the nations. And I
shall [c]cut you off from the peoples and [d]make you perish from
the lands; I shall destroy you. Thus you will [e]know that I am
the LORD."
8 'Thus says the Lord GOD, "Because Moab and Seir say,
'Behold, the house of Judah is like all the nations,'
9 therefore, behold, I am going to [1]deprive the slopes of
Moab of *its* cities, of its cities which are on its [2]frontiers, the
glory of the land, [a]Beth-jeshimoth, [b]Baal-meon, and
[c]Kiriathaim,
10 and I will give it for a possession, along with the sons of
Ammon, to the [a]sons of the east, that the sons of Ammon may
not be remembered among the nations.
11 "Thus I will execute judgments on Moab, and they will
know that I am the LORD."
12 'Thus says the Lord GOD, "Because Edom has acted
against the house of Judah by taking vengeance, and has in-
curred grievous guilt, and avenged themselves upon them,"
13 therefore, thus says the Lord GOD, "I will also stretch
out My [a]hand against Edom and [b]cut off man and beast from
it. And I will lay it waste; from [c]Teman even to [d]Dedan they
will fall by the sword.
14 "And I will lay My vengeance on Edom by the hand of
My people Israel. Therefore, they will act in Edom according
to My [a]anger and according to My wrath; thus they will know
My vengeance," declares the Lord GOD.
15 'Thus says the Lord GOD, "Because the Philistines have
acted in [a]revenge and have taken vengeance with scorn of soul
to destroy with everlasting enmity,"
16 therefore, thus says the Lord GOD, "Behold, I will [a]stretch
out My hand against the Philistines, even cut off the
[b]Cherethites and destroy the remnant of the seacoast.
17 "And I will execute great vengeance on them with wrathful rebukes; and they will know that I am the LORD when I lay
My vengeance on them." ' "

3 [1]YHWH, usually rendered LORD, and so throughout the chap. [a]Ezek. 25:6; 21:28; 26:2; 36:2; Ps. 70:2, 3

4 [a]Judg. 6:3, 33; 1 Kin. 4:30 [b]Deut. 28:33, 51; Is. 1:7

5 [a]Ezek. 21:20; Deut. 3:11; 2 Sam. 12:26; Jer. 49:2

6 [a]Job 27:23; Nah. 3:19 [b]Zeph. 2:8, 10; Obad. 12

7 [a]Ezek. 24:13, 16; Zeph. 1:4 [b]Ezek. 26:5; Is. 33:4 [c]Ezek. 21:32 [d]Amos 1:14, 15 [e]Ezek. 6:14

9 [1]Lit., *open* [2]Lit., *end* [a]Num. 33:49; Josh. 12:3; 13:20 [b]Num. 32:3, 38; Josh. 13:17; 1 Chr. 5:8; Jer. 48:23 [c]Num. 32:37; Josh. 13:19; Jer. 48:1, 23

10 [a]Ezek. 24:4

13 [a]Jer. 49:8, 13 [b]Ezek. 29:8; Mal. 1:3, 4 [c]Gen. 36:34; Jer. 49:7; Amos 1:12 [d]Jer. 25:23; 49:8

14 [a]Ezek. 35:11

15 [a]Ezek. 25:6, 12; Is. 14:29-31; Joel 3:4

16 [a]Jer. 25:20; 47:1-7 [b]1 Sam. 30:14; Zeph. 2:5

CHAPTER 26

NOW it came about in the eleventh year, on the first of the
month, that the word of the LORD came to me saying,
2 "Son of man, because [a]Tyre has said concerning Jerusalem, 'Aha, the [b]gateway of the peoples is broken; it has [1c]opened
to me. I shall be filled, *now that* she is laid waste,'
3 therefore, thus says the Lord [1]GOD, 'Behold, I am
against you, O Tyre, and I will bring up [a]many nations against
you, as the [b]sea brings up its waves.
4 'And they will destroy the [a]walls of Tyre and break
down her towers; and I will scrape her debris from her and
make her a bare rock.
5 'She will be a place for the spreading of nets in the
midst of the sea, for I have spoken,' declares the Lord GOD,
'and she will become [a]spoil for the nations.
6 'Also her [a]daughters who are [1]on the mainland will be
slain by the sword, and they will know that I am the LORD.' "
7 For thus says the Lord GOD, "Behold, I will bring upon
Tyre from the north Nebuchadnezzar king of Babylon, [a]king
of kings, with horses, [b]chariots, cavalry, and a [1]great army.
8 "He will slay your daughters [1]on the mainland with the
sword; and he will make [a]siege walls against you, cast up a
[b]mound against you, and raise up a large shield against you.
9 "And the blow of his battering rams he will direct
against your walls, and with his [1]axes he will break down your
towers.
10 "Because of the multitude of his [a]horses the dust *raised
by* them will cover you; your walls will [b]shake at the noise of
cavalry and [1]wagons and chariots, when he [c]enters your gates as
men enter a city that is breached.
11 "With the hoofs of his [a]horses he will trample all your
streets. He will slay your people with the sword; and your
strong pillars will [b]come down to the ground.
12 "Also they will make a spoil of your riches and a prey of
your [a]merchandise, [b]break down your walls and destroy your
[c]pleasant houses, and [1]throw your stones and your timbers and
your debris [d]into the water.
13 "So I will [1]silence the sound of your [a]songs, and the
sound of your [b]harps will be heard no more.
14 "And I will make you a bare rock; you will be a place for
the spreading of nets. You will be built [a]no more, for I the
[b]LORD have spoken," declares the Lord GOD.
15 Thus says the Lord GOD to Tyre, "Shall not the [a]coast-
lands [b]shake at the sound of your fall when the wounded
groan, when the slaughter occurs in your midst?
16 "Then all the princes of the sea will [a]go down from their
thrones, remove their robes, and strip off their embroidered
garments. They will [b]clothe themselves with [1]trembling; they
will sit on the ground, [c]tremble every moment, and be appalled at you.
17 "And they will take up a [a]lamentation over you and say
to you,

> '[b]How you have perished, O inhabited One,
> From the seas, O renowned city,
> Which was [c]mighty on the sea,

2 [1]Lit., *turned*
[a]2 Sam. 5:11; Is. 23:1; Jer. 25:22 [b]Is. 62:10 [c]Ezek. 25:8; 35:10

3 [1]YHWH, usually rendered LORD, and so throughout the chap.
[a]Mic. 4:11 [b]Is. 5:30; Jer. 50:42; 51:42

4 [a]Ezek. 26:9; Is. 23:11; Amos 1:10

5 [a]Ezek. 25:7; 29:19

6 [1]Lit., *in the field*
[a]Ezek. 26:8; 16:46, 53; Jer. 47:4; 49:2

7 [1]Lit., *an assembly, even many people*
[a]Ezra 7:12; Is. 10:8; Jer. 52:32; Dan. 2:37, 47 [b]Ezek. 23:24; Nah. 2:3, 4

8 [1]Lit., *in the field*
[a]Ezek. 21:22; Jer. 52:4 [b]Jer. 6:6; 32:24

9 [1]Lit., *swords*

10 [1]Lit., *wheels*
[a]Jer. 4:13; 47:3 [b]Ezek. 26:15; 27:28 [c]Jer. 39:3

11 [a]Is. 5:28; Hab. 1:8 [b]Is. 26:5; Jer. 43:13

12 [1]Lit., *put*
[a]Ezek. 27:3-27; Is. 23:8, 18; Zech. 9:3 [b]Jer. 52:14 [c]2 Chr. 32:27; Amos 5:11 [d]Ezek. 27:27, 32, 34; 28:8

13 [1]Lit., *cause to cease*
[a]Is. 23:16; 24:8, 9; Amos 6:5 [b]Is. 5:12

14 [a]Deut. 13:16; Job 12:14; Mal. 1:4 [b]Is. 14:27

15 [a]Ezek. 26:18; 27:35 [b]Ezek. 31:16; Jer. 49:21

16 [1]Lit., *tremblings*
[a]Jon. 3:6 [b]Ezek. 7:27; Job 8:22; Ps. 35:26; 1 Pet. 3:4; 5:5 [c]Ezek. 32:10; Hos. 11:10

17 [a]Ezek. 19:1, 14; 27:2, 32; 32:2, 16 [b]Is. 14:12; Jer. 48:39; 50:23 [c]Ezek. 27:3, 10, 11; 28:2

She and her inhabitants,
Who [1]imposed [2]her terror
On all her inhabitants!
18 'Now the [a]coastlands will tremble
On the day of your fall;
Yes, the coastlands which are by the sea
Will be terrified at your [b]passing.'"
19 For thus says the Lord GOD, "When I shall make you a
desolate city, like the cities which are not inhabited, when I
shall [a]bring up the deep over you, and the great waters will
cover you,
20 then I shall bring you down with those who [a]go down to
the pit, to the people of old, and I shall make you dwell in the
[b]lower parts of the earth, like the ancient waste places, with
those who go down to the pit, so that you will not [1]be inhabited; but I shall set [c]glory in the land of the living.
21 "I shall [1]bring [a]terrors on you, and you will be no more;
though you will be sought, you will never be found again,"
declares the Lord GOD.

CHAPTER 27

MOREOVER, the word of the LORD came to me saying,
2 "And you, son of man, [a]take up a lamentation over
Tyre;
3 and say to Tyre, who dwells at the [1]entrance to the sea,
merchant of the peoples to many coastlands, 'Thus says the
Lord [2]GOD,
"O Tyre, you have said, 'I am perfect in beauty.'
4 "Your borders are in the heart of the seas;
Your builders have perfected your beauty.
5 "They have [1]made all *your* planks of fir trees from
[a]Senir;
They have taken a cedar from Lebanon to make a mast
for you.
6 "Of [a]oaks from [b]Bashan they have made your oars;
With ivory they have [1]inlaid your deck of boxwood
from the coastlands of [c]Cyprus.
7 "Your sail was of fine embroidered linen from Egypt
So that it became your [1]distinguishing mark;
Your [2]awning was [3a]blue and purple from the coastlands of [b]Elishah.
8 "The inhabitants of Sidon and [a]Arvad were your rowers;
Your [b]wise men, O Tyre, were [1]aboard; they were your
pilots.
9 "The elders of Gebal and her wise men were with you
repairing your seams;
All the ships of the sea and their sailors were with you
in order to deal in your merchandise.
10 "[a]Persia and [a]Lud and [a]Put were in your army, your men
of war. They hung shield and helmet in you; they set forth
your splendor.
11 "The sons of Arvad and your army were on your walls,
all around, and the [1]Gammadim were in your towers. They
hung their shields on your walls, *all* around; they perfected
your beauty.

17 [1]Lit., *put* [2]Lit., *their*

18 [a]Ezek. 26:15; 27:35; Is. 41:5 [b]Is. 23:5-7, 10, 11, 15

19 [a]Ezek. 26:3; Is. 8:7, 8

20 [1]Or, *return* [a]Ezek. 32:30; Is. 14:9, 10 [b]Ps. 88:6; Amos 9:2; Jon. 2:2, 6 [c]Jer. 33:9; Zech. 2:8

21 [1]Lit., *give you terrors* [a]Ezek. 26:15, 16; 27:36

2 [a]Ezek. 28:12; Jer. 9:10, 17-20

3 [1]Lit., *entrances* [2]YHWH, usually rendered LORD, and so throughout the chap.

5 [1]Lit., *built* [a]Deut. 3:9; 1 Chr. 5:23; Song of Sol. 4:8

6 [1]Lit., *made* [a]Is. 2:13; Zech. 11:2 [b]Num. 21:33; Is. 2:13; Jer. 22:20 [c]Gen. 10:4; Is. 23:1, 12; Jer. 2:10

7 [1]Or, *standard* [2]Lit., *covering* [3]Or, *violet* [a]Ex. 25:4; Jer. 10:9 [b]Gen. 10:4

8 [1]Lit., *in you* [a]Ezek. 27:11; Gen. 10:18; 1 Chr. 1:16 [b]1 Kin. 9:27

10 [a]Ezek. 30:5; 38:5

11 [1]Or, *valorous ones*

12 "Tarshish was your customer because of the abundance
of all *kinds* of wealth; with silver, iron, tin, and lead, they paid
for your wares.
13 "[a]Javan, [a]Tubal, and [b]Meshech, they were your traders;
with the [c]lives of men and vessels of bronze they paid for your
merchandise.
14 "Those from [a]Beth-togarmah gave horses and war horses
and mules for your wares.
15 "The sons of [a]Dedan were your traders. Many coastlands were [1]your market; [b]ivory tusks and ebony they brought
as your payment.
16 "[1][a]Syria was your customer because of the abundance of
your [2]goods; they paid for your wares with [b]emeralds, purple,
[c]embroidered work, fine linen, coral, and rubies.
17 "Judah and the land of Israel, they were your traders;
with the wheat of [a]Minnith, [1]cakes, honey, oil, and balm they
paid for your merchandise.
18 "[a]Damascus was your customer because of the abundance of your [1]goods, because of the abundance of all *kinds* of
wealth, because of the wine of Helbon and white wool.
19 "Vedan and Javan paid for your wares [1]from Uzal;
wrought iron, cassia, and [2]sweet cane were among your
merchandise.
20 "Dedan traded with you in saddlecloths for riding.
21 "[a]Arabia and all the princes of Kedar, they were [1]your
customers for [b]lambs, rams, and goats; for these they were your
customers.
22 "The traders of [a]Sheba and Raamah, they traded with
you; they paid for your wares with the best of all *kinds* of
[b]spices, and with all *kinds* of precious stones, and gold.
23 "Haran, Canneh, [a]Eden, the traders of Sheba, Asshur,
and Chilmad traded with you.
24 "They traded with you in choice garments, in clothes of
[1]blue and embroidered work, and in carpets of many colors,
and tightly wound cords, *which were* among your
merchandise.
25 "The ships of Tarshish were [1]the carriers for your
merchandise.

And you were filled and were very [2]glorious
In the heart of the seas.

26 "Your rowers have brought you
Into [a]great waters;
The [b]east wind has broken you
In the heart of the seas.
27 "Your wealth, your wares, your merchandise,
Your sailors, and your pilots,
Your repairers of seams, your dealers in merchandise,
And all your men of war who are in you,
With all your company that is in your midst,
Will fall into the heart of the seas
On the day of your overthrow.
28 "At the sound of the cry of your pilots
The pasture lands will [a]shake.
29 "And all who handle the oar,
The [a]sailors, *and* all the pilots of the sea

13 [a]Ezek. 27:19; Gen. 10:2; Is. 66:19 [b]Ezek. 38:2; 39:1; Gen. 10:2, 3 [c]Joel 3:3; Rev. 18:13

14 [a]Ezek. 39:6; Gen. 10:3

15 [1]Lit., *the market of your hand* [a]Ezek. 27:20; 25:13; Jer. 25:23 [b]1 Kin. 10:22; Rev. 18:12

16 [1]Lit., *Aram* [2]Lit., *works* [a]Ezek. 16:57; Judg. 10:6; Is. 7:1-8 [b]Ezek. 28:13; Ex. 28:18; 39:11 [c]Ezek. 16:13, 18

17 [1]Lit., *pannag* [a]Judg. 11:33

18 [1]Lit., *works* [a]Ezek. 47:16-18; Gen. 14:15; Is. 7:8; Jer. 49:23

19 [1]Or, *with yarn* [2]Or, *calamus*

21 [1]Lit., *customers of your hand* [a]Is. 21:13 [b]Is. 60:7

22 [a]Ezek. 38:13; Gen. 10:7; Is. 60:6 [b]Gen. 43:11; 1 Kin. 10:2

23 [a]2 Kin. 19:12; Is. 37:12; Amos 1:5

24 [1]Or, *violet*

25 [1]Lit., *your travelers* [2]Lit., *honored*

26 [a]Ezek. 26:19 [b]Ps. 48:7; Jer. 18:17; Acts 27:14

28 [a]Ezek. 26:10, 15, 18

29 [a]Rev. 18:17-19

Will come down from their ships;
They will stand on the land,
30 And they will [a]make their voice heard over you
And will cry bitterly.
They will [b]cast dust on their heads,
They will [c]wallow in ashes.
31 "Also they will make themselves [a]bald for you
And [b]gird themselves with sackcloth;
And they will [c]weep for you in bitterness of soul
With bitter mourning.
32 "Moreover, in their wailing they will take up a [a]lamentation for you
And lament over you:
Who is [b]like Tyre,
Like her who is silent in the midst of the sea?
33 'When your wares went out from the seas,
You satisfied many peoples;
With the [a]abundance of your wealth and your merchandise
You enriched the kings of earth.
34 '[1]Now that you are [a]broken by the seas
In the depths of the waters,
Your [b]merchandise and all your company
Have fallen in the midst of you.
35 'All the [a]inhabitants of the coastlands
Are appalled at you,
And their kings are horribly afraid;
They are troubled in countenance.
36 'The merchants among the peoples [a]hiss at you;
You have become [1]terrified,
And you [b]will be no more.' "

Chapter 28

THE word of the LORD came again to me saying,
2 "Son of man, say to the [1]leader of Tyre, 'Thus says the
Lord [2]GOD,
"Because your heart is lifted up
And you have said, '[a]I am a god,
I sit in the seat of [3]gods,
In the heart of the seas';
Yet you are a [b]man and not God,
Although you make your heart like the heart of God—
3 "Behold, you are wiser than [a]Daniel;
There is no secret that is a match for you.
4 "By your wisdom and understanding
You have acquired [a]riches for yourself,
And have acquired gold and silver for your treasuries.
5 "By your great wisdom, by your [a]trade
You have increased your riches,
And your [b]heart is lifted up because of your riches—
6 "Therefore, thus says the Lord GOD,
'Because you have [a]made your heart
Like the heart of God,
7 'Therefore, behold, I will bring [a]strangers upon you,
The most [b]ruthless of the nations.

30 [a]Ezek. 26:17; Is. 23:1-6 [b]1 Sam. 4:12; 2 Sam. 1:2; Lam. 2:10; Rev. 18:19 [c]Jer. 6:26; Jon. 3:6

31 [a]Ezek. 29:18; Is. 15:2 [b]Ezek. 7:18; Is. 22:12 [c]Is. 16:9; 22:4

32 [a]Ezek. 27:2; 26:17; 28:12 [b]Lam. 2:13

33 [a]Ezek. 27:12, 18; 28:4, 5

34 [1]Lit., *The time* [a]Ezek. 27:26, 27; 26:12 [b]Zech. 9:3, 4

35 [a]Ezek. 26:16; Is. 23:6

36 [1]Lit., *terrors* [a]Jer. 18:16; 19:8; 49:17; 50:13; Zeph. 2:15 [b]Ps. 37:10, 36

2 [1]Or, *ruler, prince* [2]YHWH, usually rendered LORD, and so throughout the chap. [3]Or, *God* [a]Ezek. 28:9; Is. 14:14; 47:8; 2 Thess. 2:4 [b]Ezek. 28:9; Ps. 9:20; 82:6, 7; Is. 31:3

3 [a]Dan. 1:20; 2:20-23, 28; 5:11, 12

4 [a]Ezek. 27:33; Zech. 9:2, 3

5 [a]Ezek. 27:12; Hos. 12:7, 8 [b]Ezek. 28:2; Job. 31:24, 25; Ps. 52:7; Hos. 13:6

6 [a]Ezek. 28:2; Ex. 9:17

7 [a]Ezek. 26:7 [b]Ezek. 30:11; 31:12; 32:12; Hab. 1:6-8

8 [a]Ezek. 27:26, 27, 34

And they will draw their swords
Against the beauty of your wisdom
And defile your splendor.
8 'They will bring you down to the pit.
And you will [a]die the death of those who are slain
In the heart of the seas.
9 'Will you still say, "I am a god,"
In the presence of your slayer,
Although you are a man and not God,
In the hands of those who wound you?

10 [a]Ezek. 31:18; 32:30; 1 Sam. 17:26, 36

10 'You will die the death of the [a]uncircumcised
By the hand of strangers,
For I have spoken!' declares the Lord GOD!" ' "

11 Again the word of the LORD came to me saying,

12 [1]Lit., were *the one sealing a pattern* [a]Ezek. 19:1; 26:17; 27:2

12 "Son of man, [a]take up a lamentation over the king of
Tyre, and say to him, 'Thus says the Lord GOD,
"You [1]had the seal of perfection,
Full of wisdom and perfect in beauty.

13 [1]Or, *tambourines* [2]Or, *flutes* [a]Ezek. 31:8, 9, 16; 36:35; Gen. 2:8; Is. 51:3 [b]Ezek. 27:16, 22 [c]Ex. 28:17-20 [d]Is. 24:8; 30:32

13 "You were in [a]Eden, the garden of God;
[b]Every precious stone was your covering:
The [c]ruby, the topaz, and the diamond;
The beryl, the onyx, and the jasper;
The lapis lazuli, the turquoise, and the emerald;
And the [c]gold, the workmanship of your [1d]settings and [2]sockets,
Was in you.
On the day that you were created
They were prepared.

14 [1]Or, *guards* [a]Ezek. 28:16; Ex. 25:17-20; 30:26; 40:9 [b]Ezek. 28:16; 20:40 [c]Ezek. 28:13, 16; Rev. 18:16

14 "You were the [a]anointed cherub who [1]covers;
And I placed you *there*.
You were on the holy [b]mountain of God;
You walked in the midst of the [c]stones of fire.

15 [a]Ezek. 28:3-6, 12; 27:3, 4 [b]Ezek. 28:17, 18; Is. 14:12

15 "You were [a]blameless in your ways
From the day you were created,
Until [b]unrighteousness was found in you.

16 [1]Lit., *They filled your midst* [2]Or, *guardian* [a]Ezek. 26:17; 27:12 [b]Ezek. 8:17; Hab. 2:8, 17

16 "By the [a]abundance of your trade
[1]You were internally [b]filled with violence,
And you sinned;
Therefore I have cast you as profane
From the mountain of God.
And I have destroyed you, O [2]covering cherub,
From the midst of the stones of fire.

17 [a]Ezek. 28:7; 27:3, 4 [b]Is. 19:11 [c]Ezek. 26:16

17 "Your heart was lifted up because of your [a]beauty;
You [b]corrupted your wisdom by reason of your splendor.
I cast you to the ground;
I put you before [c]kings,
That they may see you.

18 [a]Amos 1:9, 10 [b]Mal. 4:3

18 "By the multitude of your iniquities,
In the unrighteousness of your trade,
You profaned your sanctuaries.
Therefore I have brought [a]fire from the midst of you;
It has consumed you,
And I have turned you to [b]ashes on the earth
In the eyes of all who see you.

19 "All who know you among the peoples
Are appalled at you;
You have become [1a]terrified,
And you will be [b]no more." ' "

20 And the word of the LORD came to me saying,
21 "Son of man, [a]set your face toward [b]Sidon, prophesy
against her,
22 and say, 'Thus says the Lord GOD,
"Behold, I am against you, O Sidon,
And I shall [1]be glorified in your midst." '
"Then they will know that I am the LORD, when I [a]execute judgments in her,
And I shall manifest My holiness in her.
23 "For I shall send pestilence to her
And blood to her streets,
And the [a]wounded will [1]fall in her midst
By the sword upon her on every side;
Then they will know that I am the LORD.
24 "And there will be no more for the house of Israel a
[a]prickling brier or a painful thorn from any round about them
who scorned them; then they will know that I am the Lord
GOD."
25 'Thus says the Lord GOD, "When I [a]gather the house of
Israel from the peoples among whom they are scattered, and
shall manifest My holiness in them in the sight of the nations,
then they will [b]live in their [1]land which I gave to My servant
Jacob.
26 "And they will [a]live in it securely; and they will [b]build
houses, plant vineyards, and live securely, when I [c]execute judgments upon all who scorn them round about them. Then
they will know that I am the LORD their God." ' "

CHAPTER 29

IN the [a]tenth year, in the tenth *month,* on the twelfth of the
month, the word of the LORD came to me saying,
2 "Son of man, set your face against [a]Pharaoh king of
Egypt, and prophesy against him and against all [b]Egypt.
3 "Speak and say, 'Thus says the Lord [1]GOD,
"Behold, I am against you, Pharaoh king of Egypt,
The great [2a]monster that lies in the midst of his [3]rivers,
That [b]has said, 'My Nile is mine, and I myself have made it.'
4 "And I shall put [a]hooks in your jaws,
And I shall make the fish of your [1]rivers cling to your scales.
And I shall bring you up out of the midst of your [1]rivers,
And all the fish of your [1]rivers will cling to your scales.
5 "And I shall [a]abandon you to the wilderness, you and all the fish of your [1]rivers;
You will fall on the [2]open field; you will not be brought together or [3]gathered.
I have given you for [b]food to the beasts of the earth and to the birds of the sky.

19 [1]Lit., *terrors* [a]Ezek. 26:21; 27:36 [b]Jer. 51:64

21 [a]Ezek. 6:2; 25:2 [b]Ezek. 27:8; Gen. 10:15, 19; Is. 23:2, 4

22 [1]Or, *glorify Myself* [a]Ezek. 28:26; 30:19

23 [1]Or, *be judged* [a]Jer. 51:52

24 [a]Ezek. 2:6; Num. 33:55; Josh. 23:13; Is. 55:13

25 [1]Lit., *ground* [a]Ezek. 20:41; 34:13, 27; Ps. 106:47; Is. 11:12, 13; Jer. 32:37 [b]Jer. 23:8; 27:11

26 [a]Ezek. 34:25-28; 38:8; Jer. 23:6 [b]Jer. 32:15, 43, 44; Amos 9:13, 14 [c]Ezek. 28:22; 25:11

1 [a]Ezek. 29:17; 26:1; 30:20

2 [a]Jer. 44:30 [b]Ezek. 30:1-32; Is. 19:1-17; Jer. 46:2-26

3 [1]YHWH, usually rendered LORD, and so throughout the chap. [2]Lit., *tannim* [3]Or, *Nile* [a]Ezek. 32:2; Is. 27:1 [b]Ezek. 29:9; 30:12; Is. 10:13

4 [1]Or, *Nile* [a]Ezek. 38:4; 2 Kin. 19:28

5 [1]Or, *Nile* [2]Lit., *faces of the field* [3]Or, with several mss. and Targum, *buried;* cf. Jer. 8:2; 25:33 [a]Ezek. 32:4-6 [b]Ezek. 39:4; Jer. 7:33; 34:20

6 "Then all the inhabitants of Egypt will know that I am
the LORD,
Because they have been *only* a [a]staff *made* of reed to
the house of Israel.
7 "When they took hold of you with the hand,
You [a]broke and tore all their [1]hands;
And when they leaned on you,
You broke and made all their loins [2]quake."
8 'Therefore, thus says the Lord GOD, "Behold, I shall
[a]bring upon you a sword, and I shall cut off from you man and
beast.
9 "And the [a]land of Egypt will become a desolation and
waste. Then they will know that I am the LORD.
Because [1]you [b]said, 'The Nile is mine, and I have made
it,'
10 therefore, behold, I am [a]against you and against your
[1]rivers, and I will make the land of Egypt an utter waste and
desolation, from Migdol *to* Syene and even to the border of
[2]Ethiopia.
11 "A man's foot will [a]not pass through it, and the foot of a
beast will not pass through it, and it will not be inhabited forty
years.
12 "So I shall make the land of Egypt a desolation in the
[a]midst of desolated lands. And her cities, in the midst of cities
that are laid waste, will be desolate forty years; and I shall
[b]scatter the Egyptians among the nations and disperse them
among the lands."
13 'For thus says the Lord GOD, "At the end of forty years
I shall [a]gather the Egyptians from the peoples [1]among whom
they were scattered.
14 "And I shall turn the fortunes of Egypt and shall make
them return to the land of [a]Pathros, to the land of their origin;
and there they will be a lowly kingdom.
15 "It will be the [a]lowest of the kingdoms; and it will never
again lift itself up above the nations. And I shall make them so
small that they will not [b]rule over the nations.
16 "And it will never again be the [a]confidence of the house
of Israel, [1b]bringing to mind the iniquity of their having turned
[2]to Egypt. Then they will know that I am the Lord GOD." ' "
17 Now in the [a]twenty-seventh year, in the first *month,* on
the first of the month, the word of the LORD came to me
saying,
18 "Son of man, [a]Nebuchadnezzar king of Babylon made
his army labor [1]hard against Tyre; every head was made [b]bald,
and every shoulder was rubbed bare. But he and his army had
no wages from Tyre for the labor that he had [2]performed
against it."
19 'Therefore, thus says the Lord GOD, "Behold, I shall
give the land of [a]Egypt to Nebuchadnezzar king of Babylon.
And he will carry off her [1b]wealth, and capture her spoil and
seize her plunder; and it will be wages for his army.
20 "I have given him the land of Egypt *for* his labor which
he [1a]performed, because they acted for Me," declares the Lord
GOD.
21 "On that day I shall make a [a]horn sprout for the house

6 [a]Is. 36:6

7 [1]So with some ancient versions; M.T., *shoulders;* cf. 2 Kin. 18:21; Is. 36:6 [2]Lit., *stand* [a]Ezek. 17:15-17; Jer. 37:5-11

8 [a]Ezek. 14:17; Jer. 46:13

9 [1]Lit., *he* [a]Ezek. 29:10-12; 30:7, 8, 13-18 [b]Ezek. 29:3; Prov. 16:18; 18:12

10 [1]Or, *Nile* [2]Lit., *Cush* [a]Ezek. 29:3; 13:8; 21:3; 26:3

11 [a]Ezek. 32:13; Jer. 43:11, 12; 46:19

12 [a]Ezek. 30:7; Jer. 25:15-19; 27:6-11 [b]Ezek. 30:23, 26; Jer. 46:19

13 [1]Lit., *where* [a]Is. 19:22; Jer. 46:26

14 [a]Is. 30:14; Is. 11:11; Jer. 44:1, 15

15 [a]Ezek. 17:6, 14; 30:13; Zech. 10:11 [b]Ezek. 31:2; 32:2; Nah. 3:8-10

16 [1]Lit., *causing to remember* [2]Lit., *after them* [a]Ezek. 29:6, 7; 17:15; Is. 20:5; 30:1-3; 31:1; 36:6 [b]Ezek. 21:23; Is. 64:9; Jer. 14:10; Hos. 8:13

17 [a]Ezek. 29:1; 24:1; 26:1; 30:20; 40:1

18 [1]Lit., *a great labor* [2]Lit., *labored* [a]Ezek. 26:7-12; Jer. 25:9; 27:6 [b]Ezek. 27:31; Jer. 48:37

19 [1]Or, *multitude* [a]Ezek. 30:10, 24, 25; 32:11 [b]Ezek. 30:14; Jer. 43:10-13

20 [1]Lit., *labored* [a]Is. 10:6, 7; 45:1-3; Jer. 25:9

21 [a]1 Sam. 2:10; Ps. 92:10; Ps. 132:17

of Israel, and I shall [1b]open your mouth in their midst. Then
they will know that I am the LORD." ' "

CHAPTER 30

THE word of the LORD came again to me saying,
2 "Son of man, prophesy and say, 'Thus says the Lord
[1]GOD,
"[a]Wail, 'Alas for the day!'
3 "For the day is near,
Even [a]the day of the LORD is near;
It will be a day of [b]clouds,
A time *of doom* for the nations.
4 "And a sword will come upon Egypt,
And anguish will be in [1]Ethiopia
When the slain fall in Egypt,
They take away her [2]wealth,
And her foundations are torn down.
5 "[1]Ethiopia, Put, Lud, all [2a]Arabia, [3]Libya, and the
[4]people of the land [5]that is in league will fall with them by the
sword."

6 'Thus says the LORD,
"Indeed, those who support [a]Egypt will fall,
And the pride of her power will come down;
From Migdol *to* Syene
They will fall within her by the sword,"
Declares the Lord GOD.
7 "And they will be desolate
In the [a]midst of the desolated lands;
And her cities will be
In the midst of the devastated cities.
8 "And they will [a]know that I am the LORD,
When I set a [b]fire in Egypt
And all her helpers are broken.
9 "On that day [a]messengers will go forth from Me in ships
to frighten [b]secure [1]Ethiopia; and [c]anguish will be on them as
on the day of Egypt; for, behold, it comes!"
10 'Thus says the Lord GOD,
"I will also make the [1]multitude of Egypt cease
By the hand of Nebuchadnezzar king of Babylon.
11 "He and his people with him,
The most ruthless of the nations,
Will be brought in to destroy the land;
And they will draw their swords against Egypt
And fill the land with the slain.
12 "Moreover, I will make the [a]Nile canals dry
And sell the land into the hands of evil men.
And I will make the land desolate,
And [1]all that is in it,
By the hand of strangers; I, the LORD, have spoken."

13 'Thus says the Lord GOD,
"I will also [a]destroy the idols
And make the [1]images cease from [2b]Memphis.

21 [1]Lit., *give you an opening of the mouth* [b]Ezek. 3:27; 24:27; 33:22; Amos 3:7, 8; Luke 21:15

2 [1]YHWH, usually rendered LORD, and so throughout the chap. [a]Ezek. 21:12; Is. 13:6; 15:2; Joel 1:5, 11, 13

3 [a]Ezek. 7:19; 13:5; Joel 1:15; 2:1; Obad. 15 [b]Ezek. 30:18; 32:7; 34:12

4 [1]Or, *Cush* [2]Or, *multitude*

5 [1]Or, *Cush* [2]Or, *the mixed people* [3]Or, *Cub* [4]Lit., *sons* [5]Lit., *of the covenant* [a]Jer. 25:20, 24

6 [a]Is. 20:3-6

7 [a]Ezek. 29:12; Jer. 25:18-26

8 [a]Ezek. 29:6, 9, 16; Ps. 58:11 [b]Ezek. 30:14, 16; 22:31; Amos 1:4, 7, 10, 12, 14

9 [1]Or, *Cush* [a]Is. 18:1, 2 [b]Ezek. 38:11; 39:6; Is. 47:8 [c]Ezek. 32:9, 10; Is. 19:17; 23:5

10 [1]Or, *wealth*

12 [1]Lit., *her fullness* [a]Ezek. 29:3, 9

13 [1]Or, *futile ones* [2]Or, *Noph* [a]Is. 2:18 [b]Ezek. 30:16; Is. 19:13; Jer. 2:16; 44:1; 46:14

And there will no longer be a prince in the land of
Egypt;
And I will put fear in the land of Egypt.
14 "And I will make [a]Pathros desolate,
Set a fire in [b]Zoan,
And execute judgments on [1c]Thebes.
15 "And I will pour out My wrath on [1]Sin,
The stronghold of Egypt;
I will also cut off the multitude of [2]Thebes.
16 "And I will set a fire in Egypt;
[1]Sin will writhe in anguish,
[2]Thebes will be breached,
And [3]Memphis *will have* [4]distresses daily.
17 "The young men of [1a]On and of Pi-beseth
Will fall by the sword,
And the [2]women will go into captivity.
18 "And in [a]Tehaphnehes the day will [1]be [b]dark
When I [c]break there the yoke bars of Egypt.
Then the pride of her power will cease in her;
A cloud will cover her,
And her daughters will go into captivity.
19 "Thus I will [a]execute judgments on Egypt,
And they will know that I am the LORD." ' "
20 And it came about in the [a]eleventh year, in the first
month, on the seventh of the month, that the word of the
LORD came to me saying,
21 "Son of man, I have [a]broken the arm of Pharaoh king of
Egypt; and, behold, it has not been [b]bound up [1]for healing [2]or
wrapped with a bandage, that it may be strong to hold the
sword.
22 "Therefore, thus says the Lord GOD, 'Behold, I am
[a]against Pharaoh king of Egypt and will break his arms, both
the strong and the [b]broken; and I will make the sword [c]fall
from his hand.
23 'And I will [a]scatter the Egyptians among the nations
and disperse them among the lands.
24 'For I will [a]strengthen the arms of the king of Babylon
and put [b]My sword in his hand; and I will break the arms of
Pharaoh, so that he will groan before him with the groanings
of a wounded man.
25 'Thus I will strengthen the arms of the king of Babylon,
but the arms of Pharaoh will fall. Then they will know that I
am the LORD, when I put My sword into the hand of the king
of Babylon and he [a]stretches it out against the land of Egypt.
26 'When I scatter the Egyptians among the nations and
disperse them among the lands, then they will know that I am
the LORD.' "

CHAPTER 31

AND it came about in the [a]eleventh year, in the third *month,*
on the first of the month, that the word of the LORD came to
me saying,
2 "Son of man, say to Pharaoh king of Egypt, and to his
[a]multitude:
'Whom are you like in your greatness?

14 [1]Or, *No* [a]Ezek. 29:14; Is. 11:11; Jer. 44:1, 15 [b]Ps. 78:12, 43; Is. 19:11, 13 [c]Ezek. 30:15, 16; Jer. 46:25; Nah. 3:8

15 [1]Or, *Pelusium* [2]Or, *No*

16 [1]Or, *Pelusium* [2]Or, *No* [3]Or, *Noph* [4]Or, *adversaries*

17 [1]Or, *Aven* [2]Lit., *they* [a]Gen. 41:45; 46:20

18 [1]So with many mss. and ancient versions; M.T., *restrain* [a]Jer. 43:8-13 [b]Ezek. 30:3 [c]Ezek. 34:27; Lev. 26:13; Is. 10:27; Jer. 27:2; 28:10, 13; 30:8

19 [a]Ezek. 30:14; 5:8, 15; 25:11; Ps. 9:16

20 [a]Ezek. 26:1; 29:1, 17; 31:1

21 [1]Lit., *to give healing* [2]Lit., *to put a bandage, to wrap it* [a]Ezek. 30:24; Ps. 10:15; 37:17 [b]Jer. 30:13; 46:11

22 [a]Ezek. 29:3; Jer. 46:25 [b]2 Kin. 24:7; Jer. 37:7 [c]Jer. 46:21

23 [a]Ezek. 30:17, 18, 26; 29:12

24 [a]Ezek. 30:10, 25; Neh. 6:9; Is. 45:1, 5; Zech. 10:12 [b]Ezek. 30:11, 25; Is. 10:5, 6, 15; Zeph. 2:12

25 [a]Josh. 8:18; 1 Chr. 21:16; Is. 5:25

1 [a]Ezek. 30:20; 32:1; Jer. 52:5, 6

2 [a]Ezek. 29:19; 30:10; Nah. 3:8, 9

3 'Behold, Assyria *was* a [a]cedar in Lebanon
With beautiful branches and forest shade,
And [1]very [b]high;
And its top was among the [2]clouds.
4 'The [a]waters made it grow, the [1]deep made it high.
With its rivers it continually [2]extended all around its planting place, and it sent out its channels to all the trees of the field.
5 'Therefore its height was loftier than all the trees of the field
And its boughs became many and its branches long
Because of [a]many waters [1]as it spread them out.
6 'All the [a]birds of the heavens nested in its boughs,
And under its branches all the beasts of the field gave birth,
And all great nations lived under its shade.
7 'So it was beautiful in its greatness, in the length of its branches;
For its [1]roots extended to many waters.
8 'The [a]cedars in God's [b]garden [1]could not match it;
The [2]cypresses [1]could not compare with its boughs,
And the plane trees [3]could not match its branches.
No tree in God's [b]garden [1]could compare with it in its beauty.
9 'I made it beautiful with the multitude of its branches,
And all the trees of [a]Eden, which were in the [a]garden of God, were jealous of it.

10 'Therefore, thus says the Lord [1]GOD, "Because [2]it is high in stature, and it has set its top among the [3]clouds, and its [a]heart is haughty in its loftiness,

11 therefore, I will give it into the hand of a [1a]despot of the nations; he will thoroughly deal with it. According to its wickedness I have [b]driven it away.

12 "And [a]alien [b]tyrants of the nations have cut it down and left it; on the [c]mountains and in all the valleys its branches have fallen, and its boughs have been broken in all the ravines of the land. And all the peoples of the earth have [d]gone down from its shade and left it.

13 "On its ruin all the [a]birds of the heavens will dwell. And all the beasts of the field will be on its *fallen* branches

14 in order that all the trees by the waters may not be exalted in their stature, nor set their top among the [1]clouds, nor their [2]well-watered mighty ones stand *erect* in their height. For they have all been given over to death, to the earth [a]beneath, among the sons of men, with those who go down to the pit."

15 'Thus says the Lord GOD, "On the day when it went down to Sheol I [a]caused lamentations; I closed the [1]deep over it and held back its rivers. And *its* many waters were stopped up, and I made Lebanon [2]mourn for it, and all the trees of the field wilted away on account of it.

16 "I made the nations [a]quake at the sound of its fall when I made it [b]go down to Sheol with those who go down to the pit; and all the [1]well-watered trees of Eden, the choicest and best of [c]Lebanon, were [d]comforted in the earth beneath.

17 "They also [a]went down with it to Sheol to those who

3 [1]Lit., *high of stature* [2]So Gk.; M.T., *thick boughs* [a]Ezek. 31:16; 17:3, 4, 22; Is. 10:33, 34; Dan. 4:10, 20-23 [b]Ezek. 31:5, 10; Is. 10:33

4 [1]I.e., subterranean waters [2]Lit., *was going* [a]Ezek. 17:5, 8; Rev. 17:1, 15

5 [1]Lit., *in its sending forth* [a]Ezek. 17:5; Ps. 1:3

6 [a]Ezek. 31:12, 13; 17:23; Dan. 4:12, 21; Matt. 13:32

7 [1]Lit., *root was*

8 [1]Lit., *did* [2]Or, *Phoenician junipers* [3]Lit., *were not like* [a]Ezek. 31:3; Ps. 80:10 [b]Ezek. 31:16, 18; 28:13; Gen. 2:8, 9; 13:10; Is. 51:3

9 [a]Ezek. 31:16, 18; 28:13; Gen. 2:8, 9; 13:10; Is. 51:3

10 [1]YHWH, usually rendered LORD, and so throughout the chap. [2]Lit., *you are* [3]Or, *thick boughs* [a]Ezek. 28:17; 2 Chr. 32:25; Is. 10:12; 14:13, 14; Dan. 5:20

11 [1]Or, *mighty one* [a]Ezek. 30:10, 11; 32:11, 12; Dan. 5:18, 19 [b]Deut. 18:12; Nah. 3:18

12 [a]Ezek. 7:21; 28:7; 30:12; Hab. 1:6 [b]Ezek. 28:7; 30:11; 32:12 [c]Ezek. 32:5; 35:8 [d]Ezek. 31:17; Dan. 4:14; Nah. 3:17, 18

13 [a]Ezek. 31:6; 29:5; 32:4; Is. 18:6

14 [1]Or, *thick boughs* [2]Lit., *drinkers of water* [a]Ezek. 31:18; 26:20; 32:24; Num. 16:30, 33; Ps. 63:9; Amos 9:2; Jon. 2:2, 6; Eph. 4:9

15 [1]I.e., subterranean waters [2]Lit., *be darkened* [a]Ezek. 32:7; Nah. 2:10

16 [1]Lit., *drinkers of water* [a]Ezek. 26:15; 27:28; Hag. 2:7 [b]Ezek. 32:18; Is. 14:15 [c]Is. 14:8; Hab. 2:17 [d]Ezek. 14:22, 23; 32:31

17 [a]Ps. 9:17

were [b]slain by the sword; and those who were its [1]strength lived
[c]under its shade among the nations.
18 "To which among the trees of Eden are you thus [1]equal
in glory and greatness? Yet you will be brought down with the
trees of Eden to the earth beneath; you will lie in the midst of
the [a]uncircumcised, with those who were slain by the sword.
[b]So is Pharaoh and all his multitude!"' declares the Lord
GOD."

CHAPTER 32

AND it came about in the [a]twelfth year, in the twelfth
month, on the first of the month, that the word of the LORD
came to me saying,
2 "Son of man, take up a [a]lamentation over Pharaoh king
of Egypt, and say to him,
'You [1]compared yourself to a young [b]lion of the
nations,
Yet you are like the [c]monster in the seas;
And you [d]burst forth in your rivers,
And muddied the waters with your feet,
And [2]fouled their rivers.'"
3 Thus says the Lord [1]GOD,
"Now I will spread My net over you
With a company of many peoples,
And they shall lift you up in My net.
4 "And I will leave you on the [a]land;
I will cast you on the [1]open field.
And I will cause all the [b]birds of the heavens to dwell
on you,
And I will satisfy the beasts of the whole earth [2]with
you.
5 "And I will lay your flesh on the mountains,
And fill the valleys with your refuse.
6 "I will also make the land drink the discharge of your
[a]blood,
As far as the mountains,
And the ravines shall be full of you.
7 "And when *I* [a]extinguish you,
I will [b]cover the heavens, and darken their [c]stars;
I will cover the [d]sun with a cloud,
And the moon shall not give its light.
8 "All the shining [a]lights in the heavens
I will darken over you
And will set darkness on your land,"
Declares the Lord GOD.
9 "I will also [a]trouble the hearts of many peoples, when I
[b]bring your destruction among the nations, into lands which
you have not known.
10 "And I will make many peoples appalled at you, and
their kings shall be horribly afraid for you when I brandish My
sword before them; and they shall tremble every moment,
every man for his own life, on the day of your fall."
11 For thus says the Lord GOD, "The sword of the king of
Babylon shall come upon you.

17 [1]Lit., *arm* [b]Ezek. 32:18-20; Is. 14:9; Nah. 3:17, 18 [c]Ezek. 31:3, 6; Dan. 4:12

18 [1]Lit., *like* [a]Ezek. 28:10; 32:19, 21; Jer. 9:25, 26 [b]Ps. 52:7; Matt. 13:19

1 [a]Ezek. 32:17; 30:20; 31:1; 33:21

2 [1]Or, *were like* [2]Lit., *fouled by stamping* [a]Ezek. 32:16; 19:1; 27:2; 28:12 [b]Ezek. 19:2-6; 38:13; Jer. 4:7; Nah. 2:11-13 [c]Ezek. 29:3; Is. 27:1 [d]Jer. 46:7,8

3 [1]YHWH, usually rendered LORD, and so throughout the chap.

4 [1]Lit., *surface of the field* [2]Lit., *from* [a]Ezek. 29:5; 31:12, 13; 39:4, 5, 17-20; Jer. 8:2 [b]Is. 18:6

6 [a]Ezek. 35:6; Ex. 7:17; Is. 34:3, 7; Rev. 14:20

7 [a]Job 18:5, 6; Prov. 13:9 [b]Ezek. 30:3, 18; 34:12; Ex. 10:21-23; Is. 34:4 [c]Is. 13:10 [d]Joel 2:2, 31; 3:15; Amos 8:9

8 [a]Gen. 1:14

9 [a]Ezek. 27:29-32; 28:19; Rev. 18:10-15 [b]Ex. 15:14-16

12 "By the swords of the mighty ones I will cause your
multitude to fall; all of them are tyrants of the nations,
And they shall devastate the pride of Egypt,
And all its multitude shall be destroyed.
13 "I will also destroy all its cattle from beside many
waters;
And the foot of man shall not muddy them any more,
And the hoofs of beasts shall not muddy them.
14 "Then I will make their waters settle,
And will cause their rivers to run like oil,"
Declares the Lord GOD.
15 "When I make the land of Egypt a [a]desolation,
And the land is destitute of that which filled it,
When I smite all those who live in it,
Then they shall [b]know that I am the LORD.
16 "This is a [a]lamentation and they shall [1]chant it. The
daughters of the nations shall [1]chant it. Over Egypt and over
all her multitude they shall [1]chant it," declares the Lord GOD.
17 And it came about in the [a]twelfth year, on the [a]fif-
teenth of the month, that the word of the LORD came to me
saying,
18 "Son of man, [a]wail for the multitude of Egypt, and
[b]bring it down, her and the daughters of the powerful nations,
to the [c]nether world, with those who go down to the pit;
19 'Whom do you surpass in beauty?
Go down and make your bed with the [a]uncircumcised.'
20 "They shall fall in the midst of those who are slain by
the sword. [1]She is given over to the sword; they have [a]drawn
her and all her multitudes away.
21 "The [a]strong among the mighty ones shall speak of him
and his helpers from the midst of Sheol, 'They have gone
down, they lie still, the uncircumcised, slain by the sword.'
22 "[a]Assyria is there and all her company; [1]her graves are
round about [2]her. All of them are slain, fallen by the sword,
23 whose graves are set in the remotest parts of the pit,
and her company is round about her grave. All of them are
slain, fallen by the sword, who [1]spread terror in the land of the
living.
24 "[a]Elam is there and all her multitude around her grave;
all of them slain, fallen by the sword, who went down uncircumcised to the [b]lower parts of the earth, who instilled their
terror in the [c]land of the living, and [d]bore their disgrace with
those who went down to the pit.
25 "They have made a [a]bed for her among the slain with all
her multitude. Her graves are around it, they are all uncircumcised, slain by the sword (although their terror was [1]instilled in
the land of the living) and they bore their disgrace with those
who go down to the pit; [2]they were put in the midst of the
slain.
26 "[a]Meshech-[b]Tubal and all its multitude are there; its
graves [1]surround them. All of them were slain by the sword
[c]uncircumcised, though they instilled their terror in the land of
the living.
27 "[a]Nor do they lie beside the fallen [1b]heroes of the uncircumcised, who went down to Sheol with their weapons of war,
and whose swords were laid under their heads; but the punish-

15 [a]Ezek. 29:12, 19, 20; Ps. 107:34 [b]Ezek. 6:7; 30:19, 26; Ex. 7:5; 14:4, 18; Ps. 9:16; 83:17, 18

16 [1]Or, *lament* [a]Ezek. 32:2; 26:17; 2 Sam. 1:17; 3:33, 34; 2 Chr. 35:25; Jer. 9:17

17 [a]Ezek. 32:1; 31:1; 33:21

18 [a]Ezek. 32:2, 16; 21:6; Is. 16:9; Mic. 1:8 [b]Ezek. 43:3; Jer. 1:10; Hos. 6:5 [c]Ezek. 32:24; 31:14, 16, 18

19 [a]Ezek. 32:21, 24, 29, 30; 31:18; Jer. 9:25, 26

20 [1]Or, *The sword is given* [a]Ps. 28:3

21 [a]Ezek. 32:27; Is. 14:9-12

22 [1]Lit., *his* [2]Lit., *him* [a]Ezek. 27:23; 31:3, 16

23 [1]Lit., *gave*, and so throughout the chap.

24 [a]Gen. 10:22; 14:1; Is. 11:11; Jer. 25:25; 49:34-39 [b]Ezek. 32:18; 26:20; 31:14, 18 [c]Job 28:13; Ps. 27:13; 52:5; 142:5; Is. 38:11; Jer. 11:19 [d]Ezek. 32:25, 30; 16:52, 54

25 [1]Lit., *given* [2]So with ancient versions; M.T. reads: *he was* [a]Ps. 139:8

26 [1]Lit., *are around him* [a]Ezek. 27:13; 38:2, 3; 39:1; Gen. 10:2 [b]Ezek. 27:13; 38:2, 3; 39:1; Gen. 10:2; Is. 66:19 [c]Ezek. 32:19

27 [1]Or, *mighty ones* [a]Is. 14:18, 19 [b]Ezek. 32:21; Job 3:13-15

ment for their [c]iniquity rested on their bones, though the
terror of *these* [1]heroes *was* once on the land of the living.
28 "But in the midst of the uncircumcised you will be broken
and lie with those slain by the sword.
29 "There also is [a]Edom, its kings, and all its [1]princes, who
[2]for *all* their might are laid with those slain by the sword; they
will lie with the uncircumcised, and with those who go down to
the pit.
30 "There also are the [1]chiefs of the [a]north, all of them,
and all the [b]Sidonians, who in spite of the terror resulting from
their might in shame went down with the slain. So they lay
down uncircumcised with those slain by the sword, and bore
their disgrace with those who go down to the pit.
31 "These Pharaoh will see, and he will be [a]comforted for
all his multitude slain by the sword, *even* Pharaoh and all his
army," declares the Lord God.
32 "Though I instilled a terror of him in the land of the
living, yet he will be made to lie down among *the* uncircumcised *along* with those slain by the sword, *even* Pharaoh and all
his multitude," declares the Lord God.

Chapter 33

AND the word of the LORD came to me saying,
2 "Son of man, speak to the [a]sons of your people, and say
to them, 'If I bring a sword upon a land, and the people of the
land take one man from among them and make him their
watchman;
3 and he sees the sword coming upon the land, and he
[a]blows on the trumpet and warns the people,
4 then he who hears the sound of the trumpet and does
not [a]take warning, and a sword comes and takes him away, his
blood will be on his [b]*own* head.
5 'He heard the sound of the trumpet, but did not take
warning; his blood will be on himself. But had he taken warning, he would have [a]delivered his life.
6 'But if the watchman sees the sword coming and does
not blow the trumpet, and the people are not warned, and a
sword comes and takes a person from them, he is [a]taken away
[1]in his iniquity; but his [b]blood I will require from the watchman's hand.'
7 "Now as for you, son of man, I have [1a]appointed you a
watchman for the house of Israel; so you will hear a [2]message
from My mouth, and give them [b]warning from Me.
8 "When I say to the wicked, 'O wicked man, you shall
[a]surely die,' and you do not speak to warn the wicked from his
way, that wicked man shall die in his iniquity, but his blood I
will require from your hand.
9 "But if you on your part warn a wicked man to turn
from his way, and he does not [a]turn from his way, he will die in
his iniquity; but you have [b]delivered your life.
10 "Now as for you, son of man, say to the house of Israel,
'Thus you have spoken, saying, "Surely our transgressions and
our sins are upon us, and we are [a]rotting away in them; [b]how
then can we [1]survive?"'
11 "Say to them, '[a]As I live!' declares the Lord [1]God, 'I take

27 [1]Or, *mighty ones* [c]Job 20:11; Ps. 109:18

29 [1]Or, *leaders* [2]Or, *in* [a]Ezek. 25:13; 35:9, 15; Is. 34:5-15; Jer. 49:7-22

30 [1]Or, *princes* [a]Ezek. 38:6, 15; 39:2; Jer. 1:15; 25:26 [b]Ezek. 28:21-23; Jer. 25:22

31 [a]Ezek. 14:22; 31:16

2 [a]Ezek. 33:12, 17, 30; 3:11; 37:18

3 [a]Ezek. 33:9; Neh. 4:18-20; Is. 58:1; Hos. 8:1; Joel 2:1

4 [a]2 Chr. 25:16; Jer. 6:17; Zech. 1:4 [b]Ezek. 33:5, 9; 18:13; Acts 18:6

5 [a]Ex. 9:19-21; Heb. 11:7

6 [1]Or, *for,* and so throughout the chap. [a]Ezek. 33:8, 9; 18:20, 24 [b]Ezek. 3:18, 20

7 [1]Or, *given* [2]Lit., *word* [a]Ezek. 3:17-21; Is. 62:6 [b]Ezek. 2:7, 8; Jer. 1:17; 26:2; Acts 5:20

8 [a]Ezek. 33:14; 18:4, 13, 18, 20; Is. 3:11

9 [a]Acts 13:40, 41, 46 [b]Ezek. 3:19, 21; Acts 20:26

10 [1]Lit., *live* [a]Ezek. 4:17; 24:23; Lev. 26:39 [b]Ezek. 37:11; Is. 49:14

11 [1]YHWH, usually rendered LORD, and so throughout the chap. [a]Ezek. 5:11; Is. 49:18

[b]no pleasure in the death of the wicked, but rather that the
wicked [c]turn from his way and live. [d]Turn back, turn back from
your evil ways! Why then will you die, O house of Israel?'
12 "And you, son of man, say to [1]your fellow-citizens, 'The
[a]righteousness of a righteous man will not deliver him in the
day of his transgression, and as for the wickedness of the
wicked, he will [b]not stumble because of it in the day when he
turns from his wickedness; whereas a righteous man will not be
able to live [2]by his righteousness on the day when he commits
sin.'
13 "When I say to the righteous he will surely live, and he
so trusts in his righteousness that he [a]commits iniquity, none of
his righteous deeds will be remembered; but in that same iniquity of his which he has committed he will die.
14 "But when I say to the wicked, 'You will surely die,' and
he [a]turns from his sin and practices [b]justice and righteousness,
15 *if a* wicked man restores a pledge, [a]pays back what he
has taken by robbery, walks by the [b]statutes [1]which ensure life
without committing iniquity, he will surely live; he shall not
die.
16 "[a]None of his sins that he has committed will be remembered against him. He has practiced justice and righteousness;
he will surely live.
17 "Yet [1]your fellow citizens say, 'The way of the Lord is
not right', when it is their own way that is not right.
18 "When the righteous turns from his righteousness and
[a]commits iniquity, then he shall die in [1]it.
19 "But when the wicked turns from his wickedness and
practices justice and righteousness, he will live by them.
20 "Yet you say, 'The way of the Lord is not right.' O house
of Israel, I will judge each of you according to his ways."
21 Now it [a]came about in the [b]twelfth year of our exile, on
the fifth of the tenth month, that the [1]refugees from Jerusalem
came to me, saying, "The city has been [2]taken."
22 Now the [a]hand of the LORD had been upon me in the
evening, before the [1]refugees came. And he [b]opened my
mouth [2]at the time *they* came to me in the morning; so my
mouth was [c]opened, and I was no longer [3]speechless.
23 Then the word of the LORD came to me saying,
24 "Son of man, they who [a]live in these waste places in the
land of Israel are saying, '[b]Abraham was *only* one, yet he possessed the land; so to [c]us who are many the land has been given
as a possession.'
25 "Therefore, say to them, 'Thus says the Lord GOD,
"You eat *meat* with the [a]blood *in it*, lift up your eyes to your
idols as you shed blood. [b]Should you then possess the land?
26 "You [1a]rely on your sword, you commit abominations,
and each of you defiles his neighbor's wife. Should you then
possess the land?" '
27 "Thus you shall say to them, 'Thus says the Lord GOD,
"As I live, surely those who are in the waste places will [a]fall by
the sword, and whoever is in the [1]open field I will give to the
beasts to be devoured, and those who are in the strongholds
and in the [b]caves will die of pestilence.
28 "And I shall make the land a desolation and a [a]waste,

11 [b]Ezek. 18:23, 32; Hos. 11:8 [c]1 Tim. 2:4; 2 Pet. 3:9 [d]Ezek. 18:30, 31; Is. 55:6, 7; Jer. 3:22; 31:20; Hos. 14:1; Acts 3:19

12 [1]Lit., *the sons of your people* [2]Lit., *by it* [a]Ezek. 33:18; 3:18; 18:24 [b]Ezek. 33:19; 18:21; 2 Chr. 7:14

13 [a]Ezek. 18:26; Heb. 10:38; 2 Pet. 2:20, 21

14 [a]Ezek. 33:8; 18:27; Is. 55:7; Jer. 18:7, 8; Hos. 14:1, 4 [b]Mic. 6:8

15 [1]Lit., *of life* [a]Ex. 22:1-4; Lev. 6:4, 5; Luke 19:8 [b]Ezek. 20:11; Ps. 119:59; 143:8

16 [a]Ezek. 18:22; Is. 1:18; 43:25

17 [1]Lit., *the sons of your people*

18 [1]Lit., *them* [a]Ezek. 33:12, 13; 3:20; 18:24

21 [1]Or, *refugee* [2]Lit., *smitten* [a]Ezek. 31:1; 32:1, 17; 40:1 [b]Ezek. 24:1, 2; Jer. 39:1, 2; 52:4-7

22 [1]Lit., *refugee* [2]Lit., *until he came* [3]Or, *dumb* [a]Ezek. 1:3; 8:1; 37:1 [b]Ezek. 3:26, 27; 24:27 [c]Luke 1:64

24 [a]Ezek. 33:27; Jer. 39:10; 40:7 [b]Is. 51:2; Acts 7:5 [c]Ezek. 11:15; Luke 3:8; Rom. 4:12

25 [a]Lev. 17:10, 12, 14; Deut. 12:16, 23; 15:23 [b]Jer. 7:9, 10

26 [1]Lit., *stand* [a]Mic. 2:1, 2; Zeph. 3:3

27 [1]Lit., *surface of the field* [a]Ezek. 33:24; 5:12-14; Jer. 15:2-4; 42:22 [b]1 Sam. 13:6; Is. 2:19

28 [a]Ezek. 5:15; 6:14; Jer. 42:22; Mic. 7:13

and the [b]pride of her power will cease; and the mountains of
Israel will be desolate, so that no one will pass through.
29 "Then they will know that I am the LORD, when I make
the land a desolation and a waste because of all their abominations which they have committed." '
30 "But as for you, son of man, [1]your fellow citizens who
talk about you by the walls and in the doorways of the houses,
speak to one another, each to his brother, saying, '[a]Come now,
and hear what the [2]message is which comes forth from the
LORD.'
31 "And they come to you as people come, and they sit
before you *as* My people, but they do the lustful desires
expressed by their [a]mouth, *and* their heart [b]goes after their
gain.
32 "And behold, you are to them like a sensual song by one
who has a [a]beautiful voice and plays well on an instrument; for
they hear your words, but they do not practice them.
33 "So when it [a]comes to pass—[1]as surely it will—then they
will know that a prophet has been in their midst."

CHAPTER 34

THEN the word of the LORD came to me saying,
2 "Son of man, prophesy against the [a]shepherds of Israel.
Prophesy and say to [1]those shepherds, 'Thus says the Lord
[2]GOD, "Woe, shepherds of Israel who have been [3]feeding
[b]themselves! Should not the shepherds [3]feed the [c]flock?
3 "You [a]eat the fat and clothe yourselves with the wool,
you [b]slaughter the fat *sheep* without [1]feeding the flock.
4 "Those who are sickly you have not strengthened, the
[1]diseased you have not healed, the broken you have not
[a]bound up, the scattered you have not brought back, nor have
you [b]sought for the lost; but with force and with severity you
have dominated them.
5 "And they were [a]scattered for lack of a shepherd, and
they became [b]food for every beast of the field and were
scattered.
6 "My flock [a]wandered through all the mountains and on
every high hill, and [b]My flock was scattered over all the surface
of the earth; and there was [c]no one to seek *for them*." ' "
7 Therefore, you shepherds, hear the word of the LORD:
8 "As I live," declares the Lord GOD, "surely because My
flock has become a [a]prey, My flock has even become food for
all the beasts of the field for lack of a shepherd, and My
shepherds did not search for My flock, but *rather* the shepherds fed themselves and did not feed My flock;
9 therefore, you shepherds, hear the word of the LORD:
10 'Thus says the Lord GOD, "Behold, I am [a]against the
shepherds, and I shall demand My [1]sheep [2]from them and
make them [b]cease from feeding [1]sheep. So the shepherds will
not [3]feed themselves any more, but I shall [c]deliver My flock
from their mouth, that they may not be food for them." ' "
11 For thus says the Lord GOD, "Behold, [a]I Myself will
search for My sheep and seek them out.
12 "[a]As a shepherd [1]cares for his herd in the day when he is
among his scattered [2]sheep, so I will [1b]care for My [2]sheep and

28 [b]Ezek. 7:24; 24:21; 30:6, 7

30 [1]Lit., *the sons of your people* [2]Lit., *word* [a]Ezek. 14:3; 20:3, 31; Is. 29:13; 58:2

31 [a]Ps. 78:36, 37; Is. 29:13; 1 John 3:18 [b]Ezek. 22:13, 27; Luke 12:15

32 [a]Mark 6:20; John 5:35

33 [1]Lit., *behold, it is coming* [a]Ezek. 33:29; Jer. 28:9

2 [1]Lit., *them, the shepherds* [2]YHWH, usually rendered LORD, and so throughout the chap. [3]Lit., *pasturing, pasture* [a]Jer. 2:8; 3:15; 10:21; 12:10 [b]Ezek. 34:8-10; 22:25; Jer. 23:1; Mic. 3:1-3, 11 [c]Ezek. 34:14, 15; Ps. 78:71, 72; Is. 40:11; John 10:11; 21:15-17

3 [1]Lit., *pasturing* [a]Zech. 11:5, 16 [b]Ezek. 22:25, 27

4 [1]Lit., *sick* [a]Zech. 11:15, 16 [b]Matt. 9:36; 10:6; 18:12, 13; Luke 15:4

5 [a]Jer. 10:21; 50:6, 7 [b]Ezek. 34:8, 28; Jer. 23:2

6 [a]Ezek. 7:16; Jer. 40:11, 12; 1 Pet. 2:25 [b]John 10:16 [c]Ps. 142:4

8 [a]Acts 20:29

10 [1]Or, (a) *flock* [2]Lit., *from their hand* [3]Lit., *pasture*, and so throughout the chap. [a]Ezek. 34:2; 5:8; 13:8; Jer. 21:13; Zech. 10:3 [b]1 Sam. 2:29, 30; Jer. 52:24-27 [c]Ezek. 13:23; Ps. 72:12-14

11 [a]Ezek. 11:17; 20:41; Is. 51:12

12 [1]Or, *seek(s) out* [2]Or, *flock* [a]Jer. 31:10 [b]Is. 40:11; 56:8; Jer. 23:3; 31:8; Luke 19:10; John 10:16

will deliver them from all the places to which they were scattered on a [c]cloudy and gloomy day.
13 "And I will bring them out from the peoples and gather
them from the countries and bring them to their own land;
and I will [a]feed them on the mountains of Israel, by the
[b]streams, and in all the inhabited places of the land.
14 "I will feed them in a [a] good pasture, and their grazing
ground will be on the mountain heights of Israel. There they
will lie down in good grazing ground, and they will feed in
[1b]rich pasture on the mountains of Israel.
15 "[a]I will feed My flock and I will [1]lead them to rest,"
declares the Lord GOD.
16 "I will seek the lost, bring back the scattered, bind up
the broken, and strengthen the sick; but the [a]fat and the strong
I will destroy. I will feed them with [b]judgment.
17 "And as for you, My flock, thus says the Lord GOD,
'Behold, I will [a]judge between one [1]sheep and another, between
the rams and the male goats.
18 'Is it too [a]slight a thing for you that you should feed in
the good pasture, that you must [b]tread down with your feet
the rest of your pastures? Or that you should drink of the clear
waters, that you must [1]foul the rest with your feet?
19 'And as for My flock, they must eat what you tread
down with your feet, and they must drink what you [1]foul with
your feet!' "
20 Therefore, thus says the Lord GOD to them, "Behold, I,
even I, will judge between the fat sheep and the lean sheep.
21 "Because you [a]push with side and with shoulder, and
thrust at all the [1]weak with your horns, until you have scattered
them [2]abroad,
22 therefore, I will [a]deliver My flock, and they will no
longer be a prey; and I will judge between one sheep and
another.
23 "Then I will set over them one shepherd, My servant
David, and he will feed them; he will feed them himself and be
their shepherd.
24 "And I, the LORD, will be their God, and My servant
[a]David will be prince among them; I, the LORD, have spoken.
25 "And I will make a [a]covenant of peace with them and
[b]eliminate harmful beasts from the land, so that they may [c]live
securely in the wilderness and sleep in the woods.
26 "And I will make them and the places around My hill a
[a]blessing. And I will cause [b]showers to come down in their
season; they will be showers of [c]blessing.
27 "Also the tree of the field will yield its fruit, and the
earth will yield its increase, and they will be [a]secure on their
land. Then they will know that I am the LORD, when I have
[b]broken the bars of their yoke and have delivered them from
the hand of those who enslaved them.
28 "And they will no longer be a prey to the nations, and
the beasts of the earth will not devour them; but they will live
[a]securely, and no one will make *them* afraid.
29 "And I will establish for them a renowned [a]planting
place, and they will not again be [1]victims of [b]famine in the
land, and they will not [c]endure the insults of the nations any
more.

12 [c]Ezek. 30:3; Jer. 13:16; Joel 2:2

13 [a]Ezek. 34:23; 36:29, 30; Mic. 7:14 [b]Is. 30:25

14 [1]Lit., *fat* [a]Ps. 23:1, 2; Jer. 31:12-14, 25; John 10:9 [b]Ezek. 28:25, 26; 36:29, 30

15 [1]Lit., *cause them to lie down* [a]Ezek. 34:23; Ps. 23:1, 2

16 [a]Is. 10:16 [b]Is. 49:26

17 [1]Or, *lamb* [a]Ezek. 34:20-22; 20:38; Mal. 4:1; Matt. 25:32

18 [1]Lit., *foul by trampling* [a]Num. 16:9, 13; 2 Sam. 7:19; Is. 7:13 [b]Matt. 23:13; Luke 11:52

19 [1]Lit., *foul by trampling*

21 [1]Or, *sick* [2]Lit., *to the outside* [a]Deut. 33:17; Dan. 8:4; Luke 13:14-16

22 [a]Ezek. 34:10; Ps. 72:12-14; Jer. 23:2, 3

24 [a]Ezek. 37:24, 25; Is. 55:3-5; Jer. 30:9; Hos. 3:5

25 [a]Ezek. 16:60; 20:37; 37:26 [b]Job 5:22; Is. 11:6-9 [c]Ezek. 34:27, 28; 28:26; Jer. 33:16

26 [a]Ezek. 34:14; Gen. 12:2 [b]Deut. 11:13-15; 28:12 [c]Lev. 25:21; Is. 44:3

27 [a]Ezek. 38:8, 11 [b]Lev. 26:13; Is. 52:2, 3; Jer. 30:8

28 [a]Ezek. 39:26; Jer. 30:10

29 [1]Lit., *those gathered* [a]Is. 4:2; 60:21; 61:3 [b]Ezek. 34:26, 27; 36:29 [c]Ezek. 36:6, 15

30 "Then they will know that [a]I, the LORD their God, am
with them, and that they, the house of Israel, are My people,"
declares the Lord GOD.
31 "As for you, [a]My sheep, the sheep of [b]My pasture, you
are men, and I am your God," declares the Lord GOD.

CHAPTER 35

MOREOVER, the word of the LORD came to me saying,
2 "Son of man, set your face against [a]Mount Seir, and
prophesy against it,
3 and say to it, 'Thus says the Lord [1]GOD,
"Behold, I am against you, Mount Seir,
And I will [a]stretch out My hand against you,
And I will make you a [b]desolation and a waste.
4 "I will [a]lay waste your cities,
And you will become a desolation.
Then you will know that I am the LORD.
5 "Because you have had everlasting [a]enmity and have
[1]delivered the sons of Israel to the power of the sword at the
time of their calamity, at the time of the [2b]punishment of the
end,
6 therefore, as I live," declares the Lord GOD, "I will
[1]give you over to [a]bloodshed, and bloodshed will pursue you;
since you have not hated bloodshed, therefore bloodshed will
pursue you.
7 "And I will make Mount Seir a waste and a desolation,
and I will cut off from it the one who passes through and
returns.
8 "And I will [a]fill its mountains with its slain; on your hills
and in your valleys and in all your ravines those slain by the
sword will [1]fall.
9 "I will make you an everlasting [a]desolation, and your
cities will not be inhabited. Then you will know that I am the
LORD.
10 "Because you have [a]said, 'These two nations and these
two lands will be mine, and we will possess [1]them,' although
the [b]LORD was there,
11 therefore, as I live," declares the Lord GOD, "I will deal
with you [a]according to your anger and according to your envy
which you showed because of your hatred against them; so I
will [b]make Myself known among them when I judge you.
12 "Then you will know [1]that I, the LORD, have heard all
your revilings which you have spoken against the mountains of
Israel saying, 'They are laid desolate; they are [a]given to us for
food.'
13 "And you have [1a]spoken arrogantly against Me and have
multiplied your words against Me; [b]I have heard."
14 'Thus says the Lord GOD, "As all the earth [a]rejoices, I
will make you a desolation.
15 "As you [a]rejoiced over the inheritance of the house of
Israel because it was desolate, [b]so I will do to you. You will be
a [c]desolation, O Mount Seir, and all Edom, all of it. Then they
will know that I am the LORD." '

30 [a]Ezek. 14:11; 36:28; Ps. 46:7, 11

31 [a]Ezek. 36:38; Ps. 78:52; 80:1 [b]Ps. 100:3; Jer. 23:1

2 [a]Ezek. 25:12; 36:5; Gen. 36:8

3 [1]YHWH, usually rendered LORD, and so throughout the chap. [a]Ezek. 25:13; Jer. 6:12; 15:6 [b]Ezek. 35:7; Jer. 49:13, 17, 18

4 [a]Ezek. 35:9; 6:6; Mal. 1:3, 4

5 [1]Lit., *poured* [2]Or, *iniquity* [a]Ezek. 25:12, 15; 36:5; Ps. 137:7; Amos 1:11; Obad. 10 [b]Ezek. 7:2; 21:25, 29

6 [1]Lit., *prepare you for* [a]Ezek. 16:38; 32:6; Is. 63:2-6

8 [1]Lit., *fall in them* [a]Ezek. 31:12; 32:4, 5; 39:4, 5; Is. 34:5, 6

9 [a]Ezek. 25:13; Jer. 49:13

10 [1]Lit., *it* [a]Ezek. 36:2, 5; Ps. 83:4-12 [b]Ezek. 48:35; Ps. 48:1-3; 132:13, 14; Is. 12:6; Zeph. 3:15

11 [a]Ezek. 25:14; Ps. 137:7; Amos 1:11 [b]Ps. 9:16; 73:17, 18

12 [1]Or, *that I am the LORD: I have heard* [a]Ezek. 36:2; Jer. 50:7

13 [1]Lit., *made great with your mouth* [a]Is. 10:13, 14; 36:20; Jer. 48:26, 42; Dan. 11:36 [b]Jer. 7:11; 29:23

14 [a]Is. 44:23; 49:13; Jer. 51:48

15 [a]Jer. 50:11; Lam. 4:21 [b]Obad. 12, 15 [c]Ezek. 35:3, 4; Is. 34:5, 6

Chapter 36

"And you, son of man, prophesy to the mountains of Israel
and say, 'O mountains of Israel, hear the word of the Lord.
2 'Thus says the Lord [1]God, "Because the enemy has
spoken against you, 'Aha!' and, 'The everlasting [2a]heights have
become our possession,'
3 therefore, prophesy and say, 'Thus says the Lord God,
"[1]For good cause they have made you [a]desolate and [b]crushed
you from every side, that you should become a possession of
the rest of the nations, and you have been taken up in the
[2c]talk and the whispering of the people."' "
4 'Therefore, O [a]mountains of Israel, hear the word of
the Lord God. Thus says the Lord God to the mountains and
to the hills, to the ravines and to the valleys, to the desolate
wastes and to the forsaken cities, which have become a [b]prey
and a derision to the rest of the nations which are round about,
5 therefore, thus says the Lord God, "Surely in the fire of
My [a]jealousy I have spoken against the [b]rest of the nations,
and against all Edom, who [1]appropriated My land for themselves as a possession with wholehearted [c]joy *and* with scorn of
soul, to drive it out for a prey."
6 'Therefore, prophesy concerning the land of Israel, and
say to the mountains and to the hills, to the ravines and to the
valleys, "Thus says the Lord God, 'Behold, I have spoken in
My jealousy and in My wrath because you have [a]endured the
insults of the nations.'
7 "Therefore, thus says the Lord God, 'I have [1]sworn that
surely the nations which are around you will themselves endure their insults.
8 'But you, O mountains of Israel, you will [a]put forth
your branches and bear your fruit for My people Israel; for
they will soon come.
9 'For, behold, I am for you, and I will [a]turn to you, and
you shall be [b]cultivated and sown.
10 'And I will multiply men on you, [a]all the house of Israel,
all of it; and the [b]cities will be inhabited, and the waste places
will be rebuilt.
11 'And I will multiply on you man and beast; and they will
increase and be fruitful; and I will cause you to be inhabited as
you were [a]formerly and will [1]treat you [b]better than at the first.
Thus you will know that I am the Lord.
12 'Yes, I will cause [a]men—My people Israel—to walk on
you and possess you, so that you will become their [b]inheritance
and never again [c]bereave them of children.'
13 "Thus says the Lord God, 'Because they say to you,
"You are a devourer of men and have bereaved your [1]nation of
children,"
14 therefore, you will no longer devour men, and no longer bereave your nation of children,' declares the Lord God.
15 "And I will not let you hear [a]insults from the nations any
more, nor will you bear [b]disgrace from the peoples any longer,
nor will you cause your nation to [c]stumble any longer," declares
the Lord God.' "
16 Then the word of the Lord came to me saying,
17 "Son of man, when the house of Israel was living in their

2 [1]YHWH, usually rendered Lord, and so throughout the chap. [2]Lit., *Bamoth* [a]Deut. 32:13; Ps. 78:69; Is. 58:14; Hab. 3:19

3 [1]Lit., *because, by the cause* [2]Lit., *lip of the tongue* [a]Jer. 2:15 [b]Ps. 35:25; Jer. 51:34; Lam. 2:2, 5, 16 [c]Ezek. 35:13; Ps. 44:13, 14; Jer. 18:16

4 [a]Ezek. 36:1, 6, 8; Deut. 11:11 [b]Ezek. 34:8, 28

5 [1]Lit., *gave* [a]Ezek. 36:6; 5:13; 38:19; Is. 66:15, 16 [b]Ezek. 36:3; Jer. 25:9, 15-29 [c]Ezek. 35:15; Jer. 50:11; Mic. 7:8

6 [a]Ezek. 34:29; Ps. 74:10; 123:3, 4

7 [1]Lit., *lifted up My hand*

8 [a]Ezek. 17:23; 34:26-29; Is. 4:2; 27:6

9 [a]Lev. 26:9 [b]Ezek. 36:34; 28:26; 34:14

10 [a]Ezek. 37:21, 22; Is. 27:6; 49:17-23 [b]Ezek. 36:33; Jer. 31:27, 28; 33:12

11 [1]Lit., *cause good* [a]Ezek. 16:55; Jer. 30:18; Mic. 7:14 [b]Job 42:12; Is. 51:3

12 [a]Ezek. 34:13, 14 [b]Ezek. 47:14 [c]Num. 13:32

13 [1]Or, *nations*, and so throughout the chap.

15 [a]Ezek. 36:7; 34:29; Is. 54:4; 60:14 [b]Ezek. 22:4; Ps. 89:50 [c]Is. 63:13; Jer. 13:16; 18:15

own land, they defiled it by their ways and their deeds; their
way before Me was like the uncleanness of a woman in her
impurity.
18 "Therefore, I [a]poured out My wrath on them for the
blood which they had shed on the land, because they had
defiled it with their idols.
19 "Also I [a]scattered them among the nations, and they
were dispersed throughout the lands. [b]According to their ways
and their deeds I judged them.
20 "When they came to the nations where they went, they
[a]profaned My holy name, because it was said of them, 'These
are the [b]people of the LORD; yet they have come out of His
land.'
21 "But I had [1]concern for My [a]holy name, which the
house of Israel had profaned among the nations where they
went.
22 "Therefore, say to the house of Israel, 'Thus says the
Lord GOD, "It is not for your sake, O house of Israel, that I am
about to [a]act, but for My holy name, which you have profaned
among the nations where you went.
23 "And I will [a]vindicate the holiness of My great name
which has been profaned among the nations, which you have
profaned in their midst. Then the [b]nations will know that I am
the LORD," declares the Lord GOD, "when I prove Myself holy
among you in their sight.
24 "For I will [a]take you from the nations, gather you from
all the lands, and bring you into your own land.
25 "Then I will [a]sprinkle clean water on you, and you will
be clean; I will cleanse you from all your [b]filthiness and from
all your [c]idols.
26 "Moreover, I will give you a [a]new heart and put a new
spirit within you; and I will remove the heart of [b]stone from
your flesh and give you a heart of flesh.
27 "And I will [a]put My Spirit within you and cause you to
walk in My statutes, and you will be careful to observe My
ordinances.
28 "And you will live in the land that I gave to your forefathers; so you will be [a]My people, and I will be your God.
29 "Moreover, I will save you from all your uncleanness;
and I will call for the grain and multiply it, and I will not
[1a]bring a famine on you.
30 "And I will [a]multiply the fruit of the tree and the produce of the field, that you may not receive again the disgrace
of famine among the nations.
31 "Then you will [a]remember your evil ways and your
deeds that were not good, and you will loathe yourselves in
your own sight for your iniquities and your abominations.
32 "I am not doing *this* for your sake," declares the Lord
GOD, "let it be known to you. Be ashamed and confounded for
your ways, O house of Israel!"
33 'Thus says the Lord GOD, "On the day that I cleanse
you from all your iniquities, I will cause the [a]cities to be inhabited, and the [b]waste places will be rebuilt.
34 "And the desolate land will be cultivated instead of
being a desolation in the sight of everyone who passed by.
35 "And they will say, 'This desolate land has become like

18 [a]Ezek. 22:20; 2 Chr. 34:21, 25; Lam. 2:4; 4:11

19 [a]Ezek. 5:12; 22:15; Deut. 28:64; Amos 9:9 [b]Ezek. 24:14; 39:24; Rom. 2:6

20 [a]Ezek. 12:16; 14:22; Is. 52:5; Rom. 2:24 [b]Jer. 33:24

21 [1]Lit., *compassion* [a]Ezek. 20:44; Ps. 74:18; Is. 37:35; 48:9

22 [a]Ezek. 36:32; Deut. 7:7, 8; 9:5-7; Ps. 108:6

23 [a]Ezek. 20:41; 38:23; 39:7, 25; Is. 5:16; 1 Pet. 3:15 [b]Ps. 102:13, 15; 126:2

24 [a]Ezek. 34:13; 37:21; Is. 43:5, 6

25 [a]Num. 19:17-19; Ps. 51:7; Titus 3:5, 6; Heb. 9:13, 19; 10:22 [b]Is. 4:4; Zech. 13:1 [c]Is. 2:18, 20; Hos. 14:3, 8

26 [a]Ezek. 11:19; 18:31; Ps. 51:10; John 3:3, 5; 2 Cor. 5:17 [b]Ezek. 11:19; Zech. 7:12

27 [a]Ezek. 37:14; 39:29; Is. 44:3; 59:21; Joel 2:28, 29

28 [a]Ezek. 14:11; 37:23, 27

29 [1]Lit., *put* [a]Ezek. 34:27, 29; Hos. 2:21-23

30 [a]Lev. 26:4

31 [a]Ezek. 16:61-63; 20:43

33 [a]Ezek. 36:10; Zech. 8:7, 8 [b]Is. 58:12

the [a]garden of Eden; and the waste, desolate, and ruined cities
are fortified *and* inhabited.'
36 "Then the nations that are left round about you will
know that I, the LORD, have rebuilt the ruined places *and*
planted that which was desolate; I, the LORD, have spoken and
[a]will do it."
37 'Thus says the Lord GOD, "This also I will let the house
of Israel ask Me to do for them: I will increase their men like a
flock.
38 "Like the [a]flock [1]for sacrifices, like the flock at Jerusalem during her appointed feasts, so will the waste cities be
filled with [b]flocks of men. Then they will know that I am the
LORD." ' "

CHAPTER 37

THE [a]hand of the LORD was upon me, and He [b]brought me
out [1]by the Spirit of the LORD and set me down in the middle
of the [c]valley; and it was full of bones.
2 And He caused me to pass among them round about,
and behold, *there were* very many on the surface of the valley;
and lo, *they were* very dry.
3 And He said to me, "Son of man, [a]can these bones
live?" And I answered, "O Lord [1]GOD, [b]Thou knowest."
4 Again He said to me, "[a]Prophesy over these bones, and
say to them, 'O dry bones, [b]hear the word of the LORD.'
5 "Thus says the Lord GOD to these bones, 'Behold, I will
cause [1a]breath to enter you that you may come to life.
6 'And I will put sinews on you, make flesh grow back on
you, cover you with skin, and put breath in you that you may
come alive; and you will [a]know that I am the LORD.' "
7 So I prophesied [a]as I was commanded; and as I prophesied, there was a [1]noise, and behold, a rattling; and the bones
came together, bone to its bone.
8 And I looked, and behold, sinews were on them, and
flesh grew, and skin covered them; but there was no breath in
them.
9 Then He said to me, "Prophesy to the breath, prophesy, son of man, and say to the breath, 'Thus says the Lord
GOD, "Come from the four winds, O breath, and breathe on
these slain, that they [a]come to life." ' "
10 So I prophesied as He commanded me, and the breath
came into them, and they came to life, and stood on their feet,
an [a]exceedingly great army.
11 Then He said to me, "Son of man, these bones are the
[a]whole house of Israel; behold, they say, '[b]Our bones are dried
up, and our hope has perished. We are [1]completely [c]cut off.'
12 "Therefore prophesy, and say to them, 'Thus says the
Lord GOD, "Behold, I will open your graves and [a]cause you to
come up out of your graves, My people; and I will bring you
into the land of Israel.
13 "Then you will know that I am the LORD, when I have
opened your graves and caused you to come up out of your
graves, My people.
14 "And I will [a]put My [1]Spirit within you, and you will
come to life, and I will place you on your own land. Then you

35 [a]Ezek. 31:9; Is. 51:3; Joel 2:3

36 [a]Hos. 14:4-9

38 [1]Lit., *of holy things* [a]1 Kin. 8:63; 2 Chr. 35:7-9; John 2:14 [b]Ps. 74:1; 100:3; Jer. 23:1; Zech. 11:17; John 10:7, 9, 16

1 [1]Or, *in* [a]Ezek. 1:3; 33:22; 40:1 [b]Ezek. 8:3; 11:24; 43:5; Acts 8:39 [c]Jer. 7:32-8:2

3 [1]YHWH, usually rendered LORD, and so throughout the chap. [a]Ezek. 26:19 [b]Deut. 32:39; 1 Sam. 2:6

4 [a]Ezek. 37:9, 12; Num. 20:8; 1 Kin. 13:2 [b]Ezek. 36:1; Is. 42:18; Jer. 22:29

5 [1]Or, *spirit*, and so throughout the chap. [a]Ezek. 37:9, 10, 14; Gen. 2:7; Ps. 104:29, 30

6 [a]Ezek. 35:9; 38:23; 39:6; Is. 49:23; Joel 2:27; 3:17

7 [1]Lit., *voice;* or *thunder* [a]Jer. 13:5-7

9 [a]Hos. 13:14

10 [a]Jer. 30:19; 33:22

11 [1]Lit., *cut off to ourselves* [a]Ezek. 36:10; 39:25; Jer. 33:24 [b]Ps. 141:7; Is. 40:27 [c]Ps. 88:5; Lam. 3:54

12 [a]Deut. 32:39; 1 Sam. 2:6; Is. 26:19; 66:14; Hos. 13:14

14 [1]Or, *breath* [a]Ezek. 37:9; 11:19; 36:27; 39:29; Is. 32:15; Joel 2:28, 29; Zech. 12:10

16 [a]Num. 17:2, 3 [b]2 Chr. 10:17; 11:11-17; 15:9 [c]1 Kin. 12:16-20; 2 Chr. 10:19

17 [a]Ezek. 37:22-24; Is. 11:13; Jer. 50:4; Hos. 1:11; Zeph. 3:9

18 [a]Ezek. 12:9; 17:12; 20:49; 24:19

21 [a]Ezek. 36:24; 39:27; Is. 43:5, 6; Jer. 29:14; Amos 9:14, 15

22 [a]Ezek. 36:10; Jer. 3:18; 50:4, 5 [b]Ezek. 37:24; 34:23, 24

23 [1]Another reading is, *backslidings.*

24 [a]Ezek. 37:25; 34:24; Jer. 30:9; Hos. 3:5 [b]Ezek. 34:23; Ps. 78:71; Is. 40:11

25 [a]Ezek. 37:24; Is. 11:1; Zech. 6:12

26 [1]Lit., *give* [a]Ezek. 16:62; 20:37; 34:25 [b]Ezek. 16:60; Ps. 89:3, 4; Is. 55:3; 59:21 [c]Ezek. 36:10, 11, 37; Jer. 30:19 [d]Ezek. 20:40; 43:7

27 [a]John 1:14 [b]Ezek. 37:23; 2 Cor. 6:16

28 [a]Ezek. 20:12; Ex. 31:13

2 [1]Or, *chief prince of Meshech* [a]Ezek. 38:3, 14, 16, 18; 39:1, 11; Rev. 20:8 [b]Ezek. 39:6; Gen. 10:2; Rev. 20:8 [c]Ezek. 38:3; 39:1 [d]Ezek. 38:3; 27:13; 39:1

will know that I, the LORD, have spoken and done it," declares
the LORD.' "
15 The word of the LORD came again to me saying,
16 "And you, son of man, take for yourself [a]one stick and
write on it, '[b]For Judah and for the sons of Israel, his companions';
then take another stick and write on it, 'For [c]Joseph,
the stick of Ephraim and all the house of Israel, his
companions.'
17 "Then [a]join them for yourself one to another into one
stick, that they may become one in your hand.
18 "And when the sons of your people speak to you saying,
'Will you not declare to us [a]what you mean by these?'
19 say to them, 'Thus says the Lord GOD, "Behold, I will
take the stick of Joseph, which is in the hand of Ephraim, and
the tribes of Israel, his companions; and I will put them with it,
with the stick of Judah, and make them one stick, and they will
be one in My hand." '
20 "And the sticks on which you write will be in your hand
before their eyes.
21 "And say to them, 'Thus says the Lord GOD, "Behold, I
will [a]take the sons of Israel from among the nations where they
have gone, and I will gather them from every side and bring
them into their own land;
22 and I will make them [a]one nation in the land, on the
mountains of Israel; and [b]one king will be king for all of them;
and they will no longer be two nations, and they will no longer
be divided into two kingdoms.
23 "And they will no longer defile themselves with their
idols, or with their detestable things, or with any of their transgressions;
but I will deliver them from all their [1]dwelling places
in which they have sinned, and will cleanse them. And they will
be My people, and I will be their God.
24 "And My servant [a]David will be king over them, and
they will all have [b]one shepherd; and they will walk in My
ordinances, and keep My statutes, and observe them.
25 "And they shall live on the land that I gave to Jacob My
servant, in which your fathers lived; and they will live on it,
they, and their sons, and their sons' sons, forever; and [a]David
My servant shall be their prince forever.
26 "And I will make a [a]covenant of peace with them; it will
be an [b]everlasting covenant with them. And I will [1]place them
and [c]multiply them, and will set My [d]sanctuary in their midst
forever.
27 "My [a]dwelling place also will be with them; and [b]I will
be their God, and they will be My people.
28 "And the nations will know that I am the LORD [a]who
sanctifies Israel, when My sanctuary is in their midst
forever." ' "

CHAPTER 38

AND the word of the LORD came to me saying,
2 "Son of man, set your face toward [a]Gog of the land of
[b]Magog, the [1]prince of [c]Rosh, [d]Meshech, and [d]Tubal, and
prophesy against him,

3 and say, 'Thus says the Lord [1]GOD, "Behold, I am
against you, O Gog, [2]prince of Rosh, Meshech, and Tubal.
4 "And I will turn you about, and put hooks into your
jaws, and I will [a]bring you out, and all your army, [b]horses and
horsemen, all of them [1]splendidly attired, a great company
with buckler and shield, all of them wielding swords;
5 [a]Persia, [1b]Ethiopia, and [c]Put with them, all of them
with shield and helmet;
6 [a]Gomer with all its troops; Beth-[b]togarmah *from* the
remote parts of the north with all its troops—many peoples
with you.
7 "Be prepared, and prepare yourself, you and all your
companies that are assembled about you, and be a guard for
them.
8 "[a]After many days you will be summoned; in the latter
years you will come into the land that is restored from the
sword, *whose inhabitants* have been [b]gathered from many [1]na-
tions to the [c]mountains of Israel which had been a continual
waste; but [2]its people were brought out from the [1]nations, and
they are [d]living securely, all of them.
9 "And you will go up, you will come [a]like a storm; you
will be like a [b]cloud covering the land, you and all your troops,
and many peoples with you."
10 'Thus says the Lord GOD, "It will come about on that
day, that [1]thoughts will come into your mind, and you will
[a]devise an evil plan,
11 and you will say, 'I will go up against the land of [1a]un-
walled villages. I will go against those who are [b]at rest, that live
securely, all of them living without walls, and having no bars or
gates;
12 to [a]capture spoil and to seize plunder, to turn your
hand against the waste places which are *now* inhabited, and
against the people who are gathered from the nations, who
have acquired cattle and goods, who live at the [1]center of the
world.
13 "[a]Sheba, and [b]Dedan, and the merchants of [c]Tarshish,
with all its [1d]villages, will say to you, 'Have you come to capture spoil? Have you assembled your company to seize plunder, to carry away silver and gold, to take away cattle and
goods, to capture great [e]spoil?' " '
14 "Therefore, prophesy, son of man, and say to Gog,
'Thus says the Lord GOD, "On that day when My people Israel
are [a]living securely, will you not know *it*?
15 "And you will come from your place out of the remote
parts of the north, you and many peoples with you, all of them
riding on horses, a great assembly and a mighty army;
16 and you will come up against My people Israel like a
cloud to cover the land. It will come about in the last days that
I shall bring you against My land, in order that the nations
may [a]know Me when I shall be [b]sanctified through you before
their eyes, O Gog."
17 'Thus says the Lord GOD, "Are you the one of whom I
spoke in former days through My servants the prophets of
Israel, who [a]prophesied in those days for *many* years that I
would bring you against them?
18 "And it will come about on that day, when Gog comes

3 [1]YHWH, usually rendered LORD, and so throughout the chap. [2]Or, *chief prince of Meshech*

4 [1]Or, *clothed in full armor*
[a]Is. 43:17 [b]Ezek. 38:15; Dan. 11:40

5 [1]Lit., *Cush*
[a]Ezek. 27:10; 2 Chr. 36:20; Ezra 1:1; Dan. 8:20 [b]Ezek. 30:4, 5; Gen. 10:6-8 [c]Ezek. 27:10; 30:5

6 [a]Gen. 10:2, 3 [b]Ezek. 27:14; Gen. 10:3

8 [1]Lit., *peoples* [2]Lit., *it was*
[a]Is. 24:22 [b]Ezek. 38:12; 36:24; 37:21; 39:27, 28; Is. 11:11 [c]Ezek. 34:13; 36:1-8 [d]Ezek. 38:11, 14; 39:26

9 [a]Is. 5:28; 21:1; 25:4; 28:2; Jer. 4:13 [b]Ezek. 39:16; 30:18; Joel 2:2

10 [1]Lit., *words*
[a]Ps. 36:4; Mic. 2:1

11 [1]Or, *open country*
[a]Zech. 2:4 [b]Jer. 49:31

12 [1]Lit., *navel*
[a]Ezek. 29:19; Is. 10:6

13 [1]Or, *young lions*
[a]Ezek. 27:22, 23 [b]Ezek. 25:13; 27:15, 20 [c]Ezek. 27:12 [d]Ezek. 32:2; Nah. 2:11-13 [e]Is. 10:6; 33:23; Jer. 15:13

14 [a]Ezek. 38:8, 11; Jer. 23:6; Zech. 2:5, 8

16 [a]Ezek. 38:23; 36:23; Ps. 83:18 [b]Ezek. 28:22; Is. 5:16; 8:13; 29:23

17 [a]Is. 5:26-29; 34:1-6; 63:1-6; 66:15, 16; Joel 3:9-14

against the land of Israel," declares the Lord GOD, "that My fury will mount up in My [a]anger.

18 [a]Ps. 18:8, 15

19 "And in My [a]zeal and in My blazing wrath I declare *that* on that day there will surely be a great [1b]earthquake in the land of Israel.

19 [1]Or, *shaking* [a]Ezek. 5:13; 36:5, 6; Deut. 32:22; Ps. 18:7, 8; Nah. 1:2; Heb. 12:29 [b]Ezek. 37:7; Joel 3:16; Hag. 2:6, 7, 21, 22

20 "[a]And the fish of the sea, the birds of the heavens, the beasts of the field, all the creeping things that creep on the earth, and all the men who are on the face of the earth will shake at My presence; the [b]mountains also will be thrown down, the steep pathways will [1]collapse, and every wall will fall to the ground.

20 [1]Lit., *fall* [a]Jer. 4:24, 25; Hos. 4:3; Nah. 1:4-6 [b]Zech. 14:4

21 "And I shall call for a [a]sword against [1]him on all My mountains," declares the Lord GOD. "[b]Every man's sword will be against his brother.

21 [1]I.e. Gog [a]Ezek. 14:17 [b]Judg. 7:22; 1 Sam. 14:20; 2 Chr. 20:23; Hag. 2:22

22 "And with pestilence and with blood I shall enter into [a]judgment with him; and I shall rain on him, and on his troops, and on the many peoples who are with him, a [1]torrential rain, with [b]hailstones, fire, and brimstone.

22 [1]Lit., *overflowing* [a]Is. 66:16; Jer. 25:31 [b]Ps. 11:6; 18:12-14; Is. 28:17

23 "And I shall magnify Myself, sanctify Myself, and make [a]Myself known in the sight of many nations; and they will know that I am the LORD."

23 [a]Ezek. 38:16; 37:28; Ps. 9:16

CHAPTER 39

1 "AND you, son of man, prophesy against Gog, and say, 'Thus says the Lord [1]GOD, "Behold, I am against you, O Gog, [2]prince of Rosh, Meshech, and Tubal;

1 [1]YHWH, usually rendered LORD, and so throughout the chap. [2]Or, *chief prince of Meshech*

2 and I shall turn you around, drive you on, take you up from the remotest parts of the north, and bring you against the mountains of Israel.

3 "And I shall [a]strike your bow from your left hand, and dash down your arrows from your right hand.

3 [a]Ezek. 30:21-24; Ps. 76:3; Jer. 21:4, 5; Hos. 1:5

4 "You shall [a]fall on the mountains of Israel, you and all your troops, and the peoples who are with you; I shall give you as food to every [1]kind of [b]predatory bird and beast of the field.

4 [1]Lit., *wing* [a]Ezek. 39:17-20; Is. 14:24, 25 [b]Ezek. 29:5; 32:4, 5; 33:27

5 "You will fall on the [1]open field; for it is I who have spoken," declares the Lord GOD.

5 [1]Lit., *face of the*

6 "And I shall send [a]fire upon Magog and those who inhabit the [b]coastlands in safety; and they will know that I am the LORD.

6 [a]Ezek. 30:8, 16; 38:19, 22; Amos 1:4, 7, 10; Nah. 1:6 [b]Ps. 72:10; Is. 66:19; Jer. 25:22

7 "And My [a]holy name I shall make known in the midst of My people Israel; and I shall not let My holy name be [b]profaned any more. And the [c]nations will know that I am the LORD, the [d]Holy One in Israel.

7 [a]Ezek. 39:25; 36:20-22 [b]Ezek. 20:9, 14, 39; Ez. 20:7 [c]Ezek. 38:16, 23 [d]Is. 12:6; 43:3, 14; 55:5; 60:9, 14

8 "Behold, it is coming and it shall be done," declares the Lord GOD. "That is the day of which I have spoken.

9 "Then those who inhabit the cities of Israel will [a]go out, and make [b]fires with the weapons and burn *them*, both shields and bucklers, bows and arrows, war clubs and spears and for seven years they will make fires of them.

9 [a]Is. 66:24; Mal. 1:5 [b]Josh. 11:6; Ps. 46:9

10 "And they will not take wood from the field or gather firewood from the forests, for they will make fires with the weapons; and they will take the spoil of those who despoiled them, and seize the [a]plunder of those who plundered them," declares the Lord GOD.

10 [a]Is. 14:2; 33:1; Mic. 5:8; Hab. 2:8

11 "And it will come about on that day that I shall give
Gog a burial ground there in Israel, the valley of those who
pass by east of the sea, and it will block off the passers-by. So
they will bury Gog there with all his multitude, and they will
call *it* The Valley of [1]Hamon-Gog.
12 "For seven months the house of Israel will be burying
them in order to [a]cleanse the land.
13 "Even all the people of the land will bury *them;* and it
will be [1]to their [a]renown *on* the day that I [b]glorify Myself,"
declares the Lord GOD.
14 "And they will set apart men who will constantly pass
through the land, [a]burying those who were passing through,
even those left on the surface of the ground, in order to
cleanse it. At the end of seven months they will make a search.
15 "And as those who pass through the land pass through
and anyone sees a man's bone, then he will [1]set up a marker by
it until the buriers have buried it in the valley of [2]Hamon-Gog.
16 "And even *the* name of *the* city will be Hamonah. So
they will cleanse the land."' "
17 "And as for you, son of man, thus says the Lord GOD,
'Speak to every [1]kind of a [a]bird and to every [a]beast of the field,
"Assemble and come, gather from every side to My sacrifice
which I am going to [b]sacrifice for you, as a great sacrifice on
the mountains of Israel, that you may eat flesh and drink
blood.
18 "You shall eat the [a]flesh of mighty men, and drink the
blood of the princes of the earth, as *though they were* [b]rams,
lambs, goats, and [c]bulls, all of them fatlings of [d]Bashan.
19 "So you will eat fat until you are glutted, and drink
blood until you are drunk, from My sacrifice which I have
sacrificed for you.
20 "And you will be glutted at My table with [a]horses and
charioteers, with mighty men and all the men of war," declares
the Lord GOD.
21 "And I shall set My [a]glory among the nations; and all the
nations will see My judgment which I have executed, and My
hand which I have laid on them.
22 "And the house of Israel will [a]know that I am the LORD
their God from that day onward.
23 "And the nations will know that the house of Israel went
into exile for their [a]iniquity because they acted treacherously
against Me, and I [b]hid My face from them; so I gave them into
the hand of their adversaries, and all of them fell by the sword.
24 "According to their [a]uncleanness and according to their
transgressions I dealt with them, and I hid My face from
them."' "
25 Therefore thus says the Lord GOD, "Now I shall [1a]restore
the fortunes of Jacob, and have mercy on the whole
[b]house of Israel; and I shall be [c]jealous for My holy name.
26 "And they shall [1a]forget their disgrace and all their treachery which they [2]perpetrated against Me, when they [b]live securely on their *own* land with [c]no one to make them afraid.
27 "When I [a]bring them back from the peoples and gather
them from the lands of their enemies, then I shall be [b]sanctified
[1]through them in the sight of the many nations.

11 [1]Or, *the multitude of Gog*

12 [a]Ezek. 39:14, 16; Deut. 21:23

13 [1]Or, *a memorial for them*
[a]Jer. 33:9; Zeph. 3:19, 20 [b]Ezek. 28:22

14 [a]Jer. 14:16

15 [1]Lit., *build* [2]Or, *the multitude of Gog*

17 [1]Lit., *wing*
[a]Ezek. 39:4; Is. 56:9; Jer. 12:9; Zeph. 1:7; Rev. 19:17, 18 [b]Is. 34:6, 7; Jer. 46:10; Zeph. 1:7

18 [a]Ezek. 29:5; Rev. 19:18 [b]Jer. 51:40 [c]Jer. 50:27 [d]Ps. 22:12; Amos 4:1

20 [a]Ezek. 38:4; Ps. 76:5, 6; Hag. 2:22; Rev. 19:18

21 [a]Ezek. 39:13; 36:23; 38:16, 23; Ex. 9:16; Is. 37:20

22 [a]Jer. 24:7

23 [a]Ezek. 36:18, 19; Jer. 22:8, 9; 44:22 [b]Ezek. 39:29; Is. 1:15; 59:2

24 [a]Ezek. 36:19; 2 Kin. 17:7; Jer. 2:17, 19; 4:18

25 [1]Or, *return the captivity*
[a]Ezek. 34:13; Is. 27:12, 13; Jer. 33:7 [b]Ezek. 36:10; 37:21, 22; Jer. 31:1; Hos. 1:11 [c]Ex. 20:5; Nah. 1:2

26 [1]Another reading is, *bear* [2]Lit., *did treacherously*
[a]Ezek. 16:63; 20:43; 36:31 [b]Ezek. 34:25-28; 1 Kin. 4:25 [c]Is. 17:2; Mic. 4:4

27 [1]Lit., *in*
[a]Ezek. 36:24; 37:21 [b]Ezek. 36:23; 38:16, 23

28 "Then they will know that I am the LORD their God
because I made them go into exile among the nations, and
then gathered them *again* to their own land; and I will leave
none of them there any longer.
29 "And I will not hide My face from them any longer, for
I shall have [a]poured out My Spirit on the house of Israel,"
declares the Lord GOD.

CHAPTER 40

IN the [a]twenty-fifth year of our exile, at the beginning of the
year, on the tenth of the month, in the fourteenth year after
the city was [1b]taken, on that same day the [c]hand of the LORD
was upon me and He brought me there.
2 In the [a]visions of God He brought me into the land of
Israel, and set me on a very [b]high mountain; and on it to the
[c]south *there was* a [d]structure like a city.
3 So He brought me there; and behold, there was a man
whose appearance was like the appearance of [a]bronze, with a
[b]line of flax and a measuring [1c]rod in his hand; and he was
standing in the gateway.
4 And the man said to me, "[a]Son of man, [b]see with your
eyes, hear with your ears, and give attention to all that I am
going to show you; for you have been brought here in order to
show *it* to you. [c]Declare to the house of Israel all that you
see."
5 And behold, there was a [a]wall on the outside of the
[1]temple all around, and in the man's hand was a measuring rod
of six cubits, *each of which was* a cubit and a [2]handbreadth. So
he measured the thickness of the [3]wall, one rod; and the
height, one rod.
6 Then he went to the gate which faced [a]east, went up its
steps, and measured the threshold of the gate, one rod [1]in
width; and the other threshold *was* one rod [1]in width.
7 And the [a]guardroom *was* one rod long and one rod
wide; and *there were* five cubits between the guardrooms. And
the threshold of the gate by the porch of the gate [1]facing
inward *was* one rod.
8 Then he measured the porch of the gate [1]facing inward, one rod.
9 And he measured the porch of the gate, eight cubits;
and its side pillars, two cubits. And the porch of the gate was
[1]faced inward.
10 And the guardrooms of the gate towards the east *numbered* three on each side; the three of them had the same
measurement. The side pillars also had the same measurement
on each side.
11 And he measured the width of the [1]gateway, ten cubits,
and the length of the gate, thirteen cubits.
12 And *there was* a [1]barrier *wall* one cubit *wide* in front of
the guardrooms on each side; and the guardrooms *were* six
cubits *square* on each side.
13 And he measured the gate from the roof of the one
guardroom to the roof of the other, a width of twenty-five
cubits from *one* door to *the* door opposite.

29 [a]Ezek. 36:27; 37:14; Is. 32:15; Joel 2:28

1 [1]Lit., *struck* [a]Ezek. 32:1, 17; 33:21 [b]Ezek. 33:21; 2 Kin. 25:1-7; Jer. 39:1-9; 52:4-11 [c]Ezek. 1:3; 3:14, 22; 37:1

2 [a]Ezek. 1:1; 8:3; Dan. 7:1, 7 [b]Ezek. 17:23; 20:40; 37:22; Is. 2:2, 3; Mic. 4:1; Rev. 21:10 [c]1 Chr. 28:12, 19 [d]Ps. 48:2; Is. 14:13

3 [1]Lit., *reed*, and so throughout the chap. [a]Ezek. 1:7; Dan. 10:5, 6; Rev. 1:15 [b]Ezek. 47:3; Zech. 2:1, 2 [c]Rev. 11:1; 21:15

4 [a]Ezek. 2:1, 3, 6, 8; 44:5 [b]Ezek. 2:7, 8; 43:10; 44:5 [c]Is. 21:10; Jer. 26:2; Acts 20:27

5 [1]Lit., *house* [2]I.e., 20.4 inches [3]Lit., *building* [a]Ezek. 42:20

6 [1]Or, *in depth* [a]Ezek. 40:20; 8:16; 11:1; 43:1

7 [1]Lit., *from the house* [a]Ezek. 40:10-16, 21, 29, 33, 36

8 [1]Lit., *from the house*

9 [1]Lit., *from the house*

11 [1]Lit., *entrance of the gate*

12 [1]Lit., *border*

14 And he made the side pillars sixty cubits *high;* the gate
extended round about to the side pillar of the [a]courtyard.
15 And *from* the front of the entrance gate to the front of
the inner porch of the gate *was* fifty cubits.
16 And *there were* [1a]shuttered windows *looking* toward
the guardrooms, and toward their side pillars within the gate
all around, and likewise for the porches. And *there were* windows all around inside; and on *each* side pillar *were* [b]palm tree
ornaments.
17 Then he brought me into the [a]outer court, and behold,
there were [b]chambers and a pavement, made for the court all
around; thirty chambers [1]faced the pavement.
18 And the pavement(*that is,* the lower [a]pavement) *was*
by the [1]side of the gates, corresponding to the length of the
gates.
19 Then he measured the width from the front of the
lower gate to the front of the exterior of the inner court, a
[a]hundred cubits on the east and on the north.
20 And *as for* the [a]gate of the outer court which faced the
north, he measured its length and its width.
21 And [1]it had three [a]guardrooms on each side; and its
[b]side pillars and its porches [2]had the same measurement as the
first gate. Its length *was* [c]fifty cubits, and the width [d]twenty-
five cubits.
22 And its [a]windows, and its porches, and its palm tree
ornaments *had* the same measurements as the [b]gate which
faced toward the east; and [1]it was reached by seven [c]steps, and
its [2]porch *was* in front of them.
23 And the inner court had a gate opposite the gate on the
north as well as *the gate* on the east; and he measured a
[a]hundred cubits from gate to gate.
24 Then he led me toward the [a]south, and behold, there
was a gate toward the south; and he measured its [b]side pillars
and its porches according to [1]those same measurements.
25 And [1]the gate and its porches had [a]windows all around
like [2]those other windows; the length *was* [b]fifty cubits and the
width twenty-five cubits.
26 And *there were* seven [a]steps going up to it, and its
porches *were* in front of them; and it had [b]palm tree ornaments on its side pillars, one on each side.
27 And the inner court had a gate toward the [a]south; and
he measured from gate to gate toward the south, a [b]hundred
cubits.
28 Then he brought me to the inner court by the south
gate; and he measured the south gate [a]according to those same
measurements.
29 Its [a]guardrooms also, its side pillars, and its [b]porches
were according to those same measurements. And [1]the gate
and its porches had [b]windows all around; it *was* [c]fifty cubits
long and twenty-five cubits wide.
30 And *there were* [a]porches all around, twenty-five cubits
long and five cubits wide.
31 And its porches *were* toward the outer court; and [a]palm
tree ornaments *were* on its side pillars, and its stairway had
eight [b]steps.

14 [a]Ezek. 8:7; 42:1; Ex. 27:9; 1 Chr. 28:6; Ps. 100:4; Is. 62:9

16 [1]Or, *beveled inwards* [a]Ezek. 41:16, 26; 1 Kin. 6:4 [b]Ezek. 40:22, 26, 31, 34, 37; 41:18-20, 25, 26; 1 Kin. 6:29, 32, 35; 2 Chr. 3:5

17 [1]Lit., *to* [a]Ezek. 10:5; 42:1; 46:21; Rev. 11:2 [b]Ezek. 40:38; 2 Kin. 23:11; 1 Chr. 9:26; 23:28; 2 Chr. 31:11

18 [1]Lit., *shoulder* [a]Ezek. 40:23, 27; 46:1, 2

19 [a]Ezek. 40:23, 27

20 [a]Ezek. 40:6

21 [1]Lit., *its guardrooms were three* [2]Lit., *was* [a]Ezek. 40:7 [b]Ezek. 40:16, 30 [c]Ezek. 40:15 [d]Ezek. 40:13

22 [1]Lit., *they were going up into it* [2]Or, *porches* [a]Ezek. 40:16 [b]Ezek. 40:6 [c]Ezek. 40:6, 26, 31, 34, 37, 49

23 [a]Ezek. 40:19, 27

24 [1]Lit., *these measurements,* and so throughout the chap. [a]Ezek. 40:6, 20, 35; 46:9 [b]Ezek. 40:21

25 [1]Lit., *it* [2]Lit., *these windows* [a]Ezek. 40:16, 22, 29 [b]Ezek. 40:21, 33

26 [a]Ezek. 40:6, 22 [b]Ezek. 40:16

27 [a]Ezek. 40:23, 32 [b]Ezek. 40:19, 23

28 [a]Ezek. 40:32, 35

29 [1]Lit., *it* [a]Ezek. 40:7, 10, 21 [b]Ezek. 40:16, 22, 25 [c]Ezek. 40:21

30 [a]Ezek. 40:16, 21

31 [a]Ezek. 40:16 [b]Ezek. 40:22, 26, 34, 37

32 And he brought me into the [a]inner court toward the
east. And he measured the gate [b]according to those same
measurements.
33 Its [a]guardrooms also, its side pillars, and its porches
were according to those same measurements. And [1]the gate
and its porches had [b]windows all around; it *was* [c]fifty cubits
long and twenty-five cubits wide.
34 And its [a]porches *were* toward the outer court; and
[a]palm tree ornaments *were* on its side pillars, on each side, and
its stairway had eight [b]steps.
35 Then he brought me to the [a]north gate; and he measured *it* according to those same measurements,
36 *with* its [a]guardrooms, its side pillars, and its [b]porches.
And [1]the gate had [b]windows all around; the length *was* [c]fifty
cubits and the width twenty-five cubits.
37 And its side pillars *were* toward the outer court; and
[a]palm tree ornaments *were* on its side pillars on each side, and
its stairway had eight [b]steps.
38 And a [a]chamber with its doorway was by the side pillars
at the gates; there they [b]rinse the burnt offering.
39 And in the porch of the gate *were* two [a]tables on each
side, on which to slaughter the [b]burnt offering, the sin offering,
and the guilt offering.
40 And on the outer [1]side, [2]as one went up to the [3]gateway
toward the north, were two tables; and on the other [1]side of
the porch of the gate *were* two tables.
41 Four [a]tables *were* on each side [1]next to the gate; *or,*
eight tables on which they slaughter *sacrifices.*
42 And for the burnt offering *there were* [a]four tables of
[b]hewn stone, a cubit and a half long, a cubit and a half wide,
and one cubit high, on which they lay the instruments with
which they slaughter the [c]burnt offering and the sacrifice.
43 And the double [1]hooks, one handbreadth in length,
were installed [2]in the house all around; and on the tables *was*
the flesh of the offering.
44 And from the outside to the [a]inner gate were [1b]cham-
bers for the [c]singers in the inner court, *one of* which was at the
[2]side of the north gate, with [3]its front toward the south, and
one at the [2]side of the [4]east gate facing toward the north.
45 And he said to me, "This is the [a]chamber which faces
toward the south, *intended* for the priests who [b]keep charge of
the [1]temple;
46 but the [a]chamber which faces toward the north is for
the priests who [b]keep charge of the altar. These are the [c]sons
of Zadok, who from the sons of Levi [d]come near to the LORD
to minister to Him."
47 And he measured the court, a *perfect* square, a
[a]hundred cubits long and a hundred cubits wide; and the altar
was in front of the [1]temple.
48 Then he brought me to the [a]porch of the [1]temple and
measured *each* side pillar of the porch, five cubits on each
side; and the width of the gate was three cubits on each side.
49 The length of the porch was twenty cubits, and the
width eleven cubits; and at the [a]stairway by which it was ascended *were* [b]columns belonging to the side pillars, one on
each side.

32 [a]Ezek. 40:28-31, 35 [b]Ezek. 40:28

33 [1]Lit., *it* [a]Ezek. 40:29 [b]Ezek. 40:16 [c]Ezek. 40:21

34 [a]Ezek. 40:16 [b]Ezek. 40:22, 37

35 [a]Ezek. 40:27, 32; 44:4; 47:2

36 [1]Lit., *it* [a]Ezek. 40:7, 29 [b]Ezek. 40:16 [c]Ezek. 40:21

37 [a]Ezek. 40:16 [b]Ezek. 40:35

38 [a]Ezek. 40:17; 41:10; 42:13; 1 Chr. 28:12; Neh. 13:5, 9; Jer. 35:4; 36:10 [b]2 Chr. 4:6

39 [a]Ezek. 40:42 [b]Ezek. 46:2; Lev. 1:3-17

40 [1]Lit., *shoulder* [2]Lit., *to the one going up* [3]Lit., *entrance of the gate*

41 [1]Lit., *by the shoulder of* [a]Ezek. 40:39, 40

42 [a]Ezek. 40:39 [b]Ex. 20:25 [c]Ezek. 40:39

43 [1]Or, *ledges* [2]Or, *inside*

44 [1]Gk. reads: *in two chambers* [2]Lit., *shoulder* [3]Lit., *their* [4]Gk. reads: *south* [a]Ezek. 40:23, 27 [b]Ezek. 40:17, 38 [c]1 Chr. 6:31, 32; 16:41-43; 25:1-7

45 [1]Or, *house* [a]Ezek. 40:17, 38 [b]1 Chr. 9:23; Ps. 134:1

46 [a]Ezek. 40:17, 38 [b]Ezek. 44:15; Lev. 6:12, 13 [c]Ezek. 43:19; 44:15; 48:11; 1 Kin. 2:35 [d]Ezek. 42:13; 45:4; Lev. 10:3; Num. 16:5, 40

47 [1]Lit., *house* [a]Ezek. 40:19, 23, 27

48 [1]Lit., *house* [a]1 Kin. 6:3; 2 Chr. 3:4

49 [a]Ezek. 40:31, 34, 37 [b]1 Kin. 7:15-21; 2 Chr. 3:17; Jer. 52:17-23; Rev. 3:12

CHAPTER 41

THEN he [a]brought me to the [1b]nave and measured the [c]side
pillars; six cubits wide on each side *was* the width of the [2]side
pillar.
2 And the width of the entrance *was* ten cubits, and the
[1]sides of the entrance were five cubits on each side. And he
measured [2]the length of the nave, [a]forty cubits, and the width,
[a]twenty cubits.
3 Then he went [1a]inside and measured each [b]side pillar of
the doorway, two cubits, and the doorway, six cubits *high;* and
the width of the doorway, seven cubits.
4 And he measured its length, twenty cubits, and the
width, [a]twenty cubits, before the [b]nave; and he said to me,
"This is the [c]most holy *place.*"
5 Then he measured the wall of the [1]temple, six cubits;
and the width of the [a]side chambers, four cubits, all around
about the house on every side.
6 And the side chambers were in three stories, [1]one above
another, and [2]thirty in each story; and [3]the side chambers
[a]extended to the wall which *stood* on [4]their inward side all
around, that they might be fastened, and not be fastened into
the wall of the temple *itself.*
7 And the side chambers surrounding the temple were
wider at each successive story. Because the structure [a]surround-
ing the temple went upward by stages on all sides of the
temple, therefore the width of the temple increased as it went
higher; and thus one went up from the lowest *story* to the
highest by way of the [1]second *story.*
8 I saw also that the house had a raised [1]platform all
around; the foundations of the side chambers were a full rod
of [a]six [2]long cubits *in height.*
9 The [1]thickness of the outer wall of the side chambers
was five cubits. But the [a]free space between the side chambers
belonging to the temple
10 and the [1]*outer* [a]chambers *was* twenty cubits in width all
around the temple on every side.
11 And the [1]doorways of the [2]side chambers toward the
[a]free space *consisted of* one doorway toward the north and
another doorway toward the south; and the width of the [a]free
space was five cubits all around.
12 And the [a]building that *was* in front of the [b]separate
area at the side toward the west *was* seventy cubits wide; and
the wall of the building was five cubits [1]thick all around, and
its length *was* ninety cubits.
13 Then he measured the temple, a [a]hundred cubits long;
the [b]separate area with the [c]building and its walls *were* also a
[a]hundred cubits long.
14 Also the width of the front of the temple and *that of*
the separate [1]areas along the east *side totaled* a hundred
cubits.
15 And he measured the length of the [a]building [1]along the
front of the [b]separate area behind it, with a [2c]gallery on each
side, a hundred cubits; *he* also *measured* the inner nave and
the porches of the court.
16 The [a]thresholds, the [1b]latticed windows, and the [2c]galler-

1 [1]I.e., the main inner hall [2]Heb., *tent* [a]Ezek. 40:2, 3, 17 [b]Ezek. 41:21, 23; 42:8 [c]Ezek. 41:3; 40:9

2 [1]Lit., *shoulders* [2]Lit., *its length,* [a]1 Kin. 6:2, 17; 2 Chr. 3:3

3 [1]I.e., of the inner sanctuary [a]Ezek. 40:16 [b]Ezek. 41:1

4 [a]1 Kin. 6:20 [b]1 Kin. 6:5 [c]Ex. 26:33, 34; Heb. 9:3-8; 1 Kin. 6:16; 7:50; 8:6; 2 Chr. 5:7

5 [1]Lit., *house,* and so throughout the chap. [a]Ezek. 41:6-11; 1 Kin. 6:5

6 [1]Lit., *chamber upon chamber* [2]Lit., *thirty times;* [3]Lit., they were *coming* [4]Lit., *to the inside of the side chambers* [a]1 Kin. 6:6, 10

7 [1]Lit., *middle* [a]1 Kin. 6:8

8 [1]Lit., *height* [2]Or, *to the joint* [a]Ezek. 40:5

9 [1]Lit., *width* [a]Ezek. 41:11

10 [1]cf. 42:1 [a]Ezek. 40:17

11 [1]Lit., *doorway* [2]Lit., *side chamber* [a]Ezek. 41:9

12 [1]Lit., *wide* [a]Ezek. 41:13, 15; 42:1 [b]Ezek. 41:13-15; 42:1, 10, 13

13 [a]Ezek. 40:47 [b]Ezek. 41:13-15; 42:1, 10, 13 [c]Ezek. 41:13, 15; 42:1

14 [1]Lit., *area*

15 [1]Lit., *to* [2]Or, *passageway* [a]Ezek. 41:13, 15; 42:1 [b]Ezek. 41:13-15; 42:1, 10, 13 [c]Ezek. 41:16; 42:3, 5

16 [1]Or, *framed* [2]Or, *passageways* [a]Ezek. 41:25; 10:18; 40:6; Is. 6:4 [b]Ezek. 41:26; 40:16, 25; 1 Kin. 6:4 [c]Ezek. 41:15

16 [d]Ezek. 42:3 [e]1 Kin. 6:15

18 [1]Lit., *made* [a]Ezek. 41:20, 25; 1 Kin. 6:29, 32, 35; 7:36 [b]Ezek. 40:16; 2 Chr. 3:5

19 [1]Lit., *made* [a]Ezek. 1:10; 10:14

20 [1]Lit., *made* [a]Ezek. 41:18

21 [a]Ezek. 41:1; 40:9, 14, 16; 1 Kin. 6:33 [b]Ezek. 41:1

22 [1]Lit., *length* [2]Lit., *walls* [a]Ex. 30:1-3; 1 Kin. 6:20; Rev. 8:3 [b]Ezek. 23:41; 44:16; Ex. 25:23, 30; Lev. 24:6; Mal. 1:7, 12

23 [a]Ezek. 41:1 [b]Ezek. 41:4 [c]1 Kin. 6:31-35

24 [1]Or, *turning* [a]1 Kin. 6:34

25 [1]Lit., *made* [2]Or, *canopy of wood over* [a]Ezek. 41:18 [b]Ezek. 41:16

26 [1]Or, *framed* [2]Or, *canopies* [a]Ezek. 41:16 [b]Ezek. 40:16 [c]Ezek. 40:9, 48 [d]Ezek. 41:5

1 [a]Ezek. 40:17, 28, 48; 41:1 [b]Ezek. 40:17, 20 [c]Ezek. 40:20 [d]Ezek. 42:4; 40:17 [e]Ezek. 42:10, 13; 41:12 [f]Ezek. 41:12

2 [a]Ezek. 41:13

3 [1]Or, *passageway* [a]Ezek. 41:10 [b]Ezek. 40:17 [c]Ezek. 42:5; 41:15, 16

4 [a]Ezek. 46:19

5 [1]Lit., *shorter* [2]Or, *passageways* [a]Ezek. 42:3

6 [1]Or, *reduced* [a]Ezek. 41:6

7 [a]Ezek. 42:10, 12

ies round about their [d]three stories, opposite the threshold,
were [e]paneled with wood all around, and *from* the ground to
the windows (but the windows were covered),
17 over the entrance, and to the inner house, and on the
outside, and on all the wall all around inside and outside, by
measurement.
18 And it was [1]carved with [a]cherubim and [b]palm trees; and
a palm tree was between cherub and cherub, and every cherub
had two faces,
19 a [a]man's face toward the palm tree on one side, and a
young [a]lion's face toward the palm tree on the other side; [1]they
were carved on all the house all around.
20 From the ground to above the entrance [a]cherubim and
[a]palm trees were [1]carved, as well as *on* the wall of the nave.
21 The [a]doorposts of the [b]nave were square; as for the
front of the sanctuary, the appearance of one doorpost was
like that of the other.
22 The [a]altar *was* of wood, three cubits high, and its
length two cubits; its corners, its [1]base, and its [2]sides *were* of
wood. And he said to me, "This is the [b]table that is before the
LORD."
23 And the [a]nave and the [b]sanctuary each had a double
[c]door.
24 And each of the doors had two leaves, two [1a]swinging
leaves; two *leaves* for one door and two leaves for the other.
25 Also there were [1]carved on them, on the doors of the
nave, [a]cherubim and [a]palm trees like those [1]carved on the
walls; and *there was* a [2b]threshold of wood on the front of the
porch outside.
26 And *there were* [1a]latticed windows and [b]palm trees on
one side and on the other, on the sides of the [c]porch; thus *were*
the [d]side chambers of the house and the [2]thresholds.

Chapter 42

THEN he [a]brought me out into the [b]outer court, the way
[c]toward the north; and he brought me to the [d]chamber which
was opposite the [e]separate area and opposite the [f]building
toward the north.
2 Along the length, *which was* a [a]hundred cubits, *was* the
north door; the width *was* fifty cubits.
3 Opposite the [a]twenty *cubits* which belonged to the inner court, and opposite the [b]pavement which belonged to the
outer court, *was* [1c]gallery corresponding to [1]gallery in three
stories.
4 And before the [a]chambers *was* an inner walk ten cubits
wide, a way of one *hundred* cubits; and their openings *were* on
the north.
5 Now the upper chambers *were* [1]smaller because the
[2a]galleries took more *space* away from them than from the
lower and middle ones in the building.
6 For they *were* in [a]three stories and had no pillars like
the pillars of the courts; therefore *the upper chambers* were
[1]set back from the ground upward, more than the lower and
middle ones.
7 As for the outer [a]wall by the side of the chambers,

toward the outer court facing the chambers, its length *was* fifty
cubits.
8 For the length of the chambers which *were* in the outer
court *was* fifty cubits; and behold, the length of those facing
the temple *was* a [a]hundred cubits.
9 And below these chambers *was* the [a]entrance on the
east side, as one enters them from the outer court.
10 In the [1]thickness of the [a]wall of the court toward the
east, facing the [b]separate area and facing the building, *there
were* [c]chambers.
11 And the [a]way in front of them *was* like the appearance
of the chambers which *were* on the north, according to their
length so was their width; and all their exits *were* both according to their arrangements and openings.
12 And corresponding to the openings of the chambers
which were toward the south was an opening at the head of the
way, the way in front of the [a]wall toward the east, as one enters
them.
13 Then he said to me, "The north chambers *and* the
south chambers, which are opposite the [a]separate area, they
are the [b]holy chambers where the priests who are [c]near to the
LORD shall eat the [d]most holy things. There they shall lay the
most holy things, the grain offering, the sin offering, and the
guilt offering; for the place is holy.
14 "When the priests enter, then they shall not go out into
the outer court from the sanctuary [1]without [a]laying there their
[b]garments in which they minister, for they are holy. They shall
put on other garments; then they shall approach that which is
for the people."
15 Now when he had finished measuring the inner house,
he brought me out by the way of the [a]gate which faced toward
the east, and measured it all around.
16 He measured on the east side with the measuring reed
five hundred reeds, by the measuring [a]reed.
17 He measured on the north side five hundred reeds by
the measuring reed.
18 On the south side he measured five hundred reeds with
the measuring reed.
19 He turned to the west side, *and* measured five hundred
reeds with the measuring reed.
20 He measured it [1]on the four sides; it had a [a]wall all
around, the [b]length five hundred and the [b]width five hundred,
to [c]divide between the holy and the profane.

CHAPTER 43

THEN he led me to the [a]gate, the gate facing toward the
east;
2 and behold, the [a]glory of the God of Israel was coming
from the way of the [b]east. And His [c]voice was like the sound of
many waters; and the earth [d]shone with His glory.
3 And *it was* like the appearance of the vision which I
saw, like the [a]vision which I saw when [1]He came to [b]destroy
the city. And the visions *were* like the vision which I saw by the
[c]river Chebar; and I [d]fell on my face.

8 [a]Ezek. 41:13, 14

9 [a]Ezek. 44:5; 46:19

10 [1]Lit., *width*
[a]Ezek. 42:7 [b]Ezek. 42:1, 13
[c]Ezek. 40:17

11 [a]Ezek. 42:4

12 [a]Ezek. 42:7

13 [a]Ezek. 42:1, 10 [b]Ex. 29:31; Lev. 7:6; 10:13, 14, 17 [c]Ezek. 40:46; Lev. 10:3; Deut. 21:5 [d]Lev. 6:25, 29; 14:13; Num. 18:9, 10

14 [1]Lit., *but there they shall lay*
[a]Ezek. 44:19 [b]Ex. 29:4-9; Lev. 8:7, 13; Is. 61:10; Zech. 3:4, 5

15 [a]Ezek. 40:6; 43:1

16 [a]Ezek. 40:3

20 [1]Lit., *toward the four winds*
[a]Ezek. 40:5; Is. 60:18; Zech. 2:5 [b]Ezek. 45:2; Rev. 21:16 [c]Ezek. 22:26; 44:23; 48:15

1 [a]Ezek. 43:4; 10:19; 40:6; 42:15; 44:1; 46:1

2 [a]Ezek. 1:28; 3:23; 10:18, 19; Is. 6:3 [b]Ezek. 11:23 [c]Ezek. 1:24; Rev. 1:15; 14:2 [d]Ezek. 1:28; 10:4; Rev. 18:1

3 [1]So with some mss. and some ancient versions; M.T., *I*
[a]Ezek. 1:4-28 [b]Ezek. 9:1, 5; 32:18; Jer. 1:10 [c]Ezek. 1:3; 10:20 [d]Ezek. 1:28; 3:23

4 And the glory of the LORD came into the house by the
way of the gate facing toward the [a]east.
5 And the [a]Spirit lifted me up and brought me into the
inner court; and behold, the [b]glory of the LORD filled the
house.
6 Then I heard one speaking to me from the house, while
a [a]man was standing beside me.
7 And He said to me, "Son of man, *this is* the place of
My [a]throne and the place of the soles of My feet, where I will
[b]dwell among the sons of Israel forever. And the house of
Israel will not again defile My holy name, neither they nor
their kings, by their harlotry and by the [1c]corpses of their kings
[2]when they [d]die,
8 by setting their threshold by My threshold, and their
door post beside My door post, with *only* the wall between Me
and them. And they have [a]defiled My holy name by their
abominations which they have committed. So I have consumed them in My anger.
9 "Now let them [a]put away their harlotry and the [1]corpses
of their kings far from Me; and I will [b]dwell among them
forever.
10 "As for you, son of man, [1a]describe the [2]temple to the
house of Israel, that they may be [b]ashamed of their iniquities;
and let them measure the [3]plan.
11 "And if they are ashamed of all that they have done,
make known to them the [1]design of the house, its structure, its
[a]exits, its entrances, all its [2]designs, all its [3]statutes, and all its
laws. And write *it* [b]in their sight, so that they may observe its
whole [1]design and all its statutes, and [c]do them.
12 "This is the [1]law of the house: its entire [2]area on the top
of the [a]mountain all around *shall be* most holy. Behold, this is
the [1]law of the house.
13 "And these are the measurements of the [a]altar by cubits
(the [b]cubit being a cubit and a handbreadth): the [1]base *shall be*
a cubit, and the width a cubit, and its border on its edge round
about one span; and this *shall be* the *height of the* [2]base of the
altar.
14 "And from the base on the ground to the lower [a]ledge
shall be two cubits, and the width one cubit; and from the
smaller ledge to the larger ledge *shall be* four cubits, and the
width [1]one cubit.
15 "And the [1]altar hearth *shall be* four cubits; and from the
[1]altar hearth shall extend upwards four [a]horns.
16 "Now the [1]altar hearth *shall be* twelve *cubits* long by
twelve wide, [a]square in its four sides.
17 "And the ledge *shall be* fourteen *cubits* long by fourteen
wide in its four sides, the border around it *shall be* half a cubit,
and its base *shall be* a cubit round about; and its [a]steps shall
[1b]face the east."
18 And He said to me, "[a]Son of man, thus says the Lord
[1]GOD, 'These are the statutes for the altar on the day it is built,
to offer [b]burnt offerings on it and to [c]sprinkle blood on it.
19 'And you shall give to the Levitical priests who are from
the offspring of [a]Zadok, who draw [b]near to Me to minister to
Me,' declares the Lord GOD, 'a [c]young bull for a [d]sin offering.
20 'And you shall take some of its blood, and put it on its

4 [a]Ezek. 43:2; 10:19; 11:23

5 [a]Ezek. 3:14; 8:3; 11:1, 24; 2 Cor. 12:2-4 [b]Ezek. 10:4

6 [a]Ezek. 1:26

7 [1]Or, *monuments* as in Ugaritic; cf. Lev. 26:30 [2]Or, *in their high places* [a]Ezek. 1:26; Ps. 47:8 [b]Ezek. 37:26, 28 [c]Ezek. 6:5, 13 [d]Ezek. 20:29, 30

8 [a]Ezek. 8:3, 16

9 [1]Or, *monuments* as in Ugaritic [a]Ezek. 18:30, 31 [b]Ezek. 43:7; 37:26-28

10 [1]Lit., *declare* [2]Lit., *house* [3]Lit., *perfection* or *pattern;* cf. 28:12 [a]Ezek. 40:4 [b]Ezek. 43:11; 16:61, 63

11 [1]Or, *form* [2]Or, *forms* [3]M.T. adds, *and all its designs* after *statutes* [a]Ezek. 44:5 [b]Ezek. 12:3 [c]Ezek. 11:20; 36:27

12 [1]Or, *instruction for* [2]Lit., *border* [a]Ezek. 40:2; 42:20

13 [1]Lit., *lap* [2]Or, *back* [a]Ex. 27:1-8, 2 Chr. 4:1 [b]Ezek. 40:5; 41:8

14 [1]Lit., *the* [a]Ezek. 43:17, 20; 45:19

15 [1]Or, *ariel* shall [a]Ex. 27:2; Lev. 9:9; 1 Kin. 1:50; Ps. 118:27

16 [1]Or, *ariel* shall [a]Ex. 27:1

17 [1]Or, *be on the east side* [a]Ex. 20:26 [b]Ezek. 40:6

18 [1]YHWH, usually rendered LORD, and so throughout the chap. [a]Ezek. 2:1 [b]Ex. 40:29 [c]Lev. 1:5, 11; Heb. 9:21, 22

19 [a]Ezek. 40:46; 44:15; 1 Kin. 2:35 [b]Num. 16:5, 40 [c]Ezek. 43:23; 45:18, 19; Lev. 4:3 [d]Heb. 7:27

four [a]horns, and on the four corners of the [b]ledge, and on the
border round about; thus you shall [c]cleanse it and make atonement for it.
21 'You shall also take the bull for the sin offering; and it
shall be [a]burned in the appointed place of the house, outside
the sanctuary.
22 'And on the second day you shall offer a [a]male goat
without blemish for a sin offering; and they shall [b]cleanse the
altar, as they cleansed *it* with the bull.
23 'When you have finished cleansing *it*, you shall present
a young [a]bull without blemish and a [b]ram from the flock without blemish.
24 'And you shall present them before the LORD, and the
priests shall throw [a]salt on them, and they shall offer them up
as a burnt offering to the LORD.
25 '[a]For seven days you shall prepare daily a goat for a sin
offering; also a young bull and a ram from the flock, without
blemish, shall be prepared.
26 'For seven days they shall make atonement for the altar
and purify it; so shall they [1]consecrate it.
27 'And when they have completed the days, it shall be
that on the [a]eighth day and onward, the priests shall [1]offer
your burnt offerings on the altar, and your [b]peace offerings;
and I will [c]accept you,' declares the Lord GOD."

CHAPTER 44

THEN he brought me back by the way of the [a]outer gate of
the sanctuary, which faces the east; and it was shut.
2 And the LORD said to me, "This gate shall be shut; it
shall not be opened, and no one shall enter by it, for the [a]LORD
God of Israel has entered by it; therefore it shall be shut.
3 "As for the [a]prince, he shall sit in it as prince to [b]eat
bread before the LORD; he shall [c]enter by way of the [d]porch of
the gate, and shall go out [1]by the same way."
4 Then he brought me by way of the [a]north gate to the
front of the house; and I looked, and behold, the [b]glory of the
LORD filled the house of the LORD, and I [c]fell on my face.
5 And the LORD said to me, "[a]Son of man, [1a]mark well,
see with your eyes, and hear with your ears all that I say to you
concerning all the [b]statutes of the house of the LORD and
concerning all its laws; and [1]mark well the entrance of the
house, with all exits of the sanctuary.
6 "And you shall say to the [1a]rebellious ones, to the house
of Israel, 'Thus says the Lord [2]GOD, "[b]Enough of all your
abominations, O house of Israel,
7 when you brought in [a]foreigners, uncircumcised in
[b]heart and uncircumcised in flesh, to be in My sanctuary to
profane it, *even* My house, when you [c]offered My food, the fat
and the blood; for they made My covenant [d]void—*this* in
addition to all your abominations.
8 "And you have not [a]kept charge of My holy things yourselves, but you have set *foreigners* [1]to keep charge of My
sanctuary."
9 'Thus says the Lord GOD, "[a]No foreigner, uncircum-

20 [a]Ezek. 43:15; Lev. 8:15; 9:9 [b]Ezek. 43:14, 16, 17 [c]Ezek. 43:22, 26; Lev. 16:19

21 [a]Ex. 29:14; Lev. 4:12; Heb. 13:11

22 [a]Ezek. 43:25 [b]Ezek. 43:20, 26

23 [a]Ezek. 45:18; Ex. 29:1, 10 [b]Ex. 29:1

24 [a]Lev. 2:13; Num. 18:19; Mark 9:49, 50; Col. 4:6

25 [a]Ex. 29:35-37; Lev. 8:33, 35

26 [1]Lit., *fill its hands*

27 [1]Lit., *make* [a]Lev. 9:1 [b]Lev. 3:1; 17:5 [c]Ezek. 20:40

1 [a]Ezek. 40:6, 17; 42:14

2 [a]Ezek. 43:2-4

3 [1]Lit., *by his way* [a]Ezek. 34:24; 37:25 [b]Gen. 31:54; Ex. 24:9-11 [c]Ezek. 46:2, 8-10 [d]Ezek. 40:9

4 [a]Ezek. 40:20, 40 [b]Ezek. 1:28; 3:23; 43:4, 5; Is. 6:3, 4; Hag. 2:7 [c]Ezek. 1:28; 43:3

5 [1]Lit., *set your heart on* [a]Ezek. 40:4; Deut. 32:46 [b]Ezek. 43:10, 11; Deut. 12:32

6 [1]Lit., *rebellion* [2]YHWH, usually rendered LORD, and so throughout the chap. [a]Ezek. 2:5-7; 3:9 [b]Ezek. 45:9; 1 Pet. 4:3

7 [a]Ex. 12:43-49 [b]Lev. 26:41; Deut. 10:16; Jer. 4:4; 9:26 [c]Lev. 22:25 [d]Gen. 17:14

8 [1]Lit., *as keepers of My charge in My* [a]Num. 18:7

9 [a]Ezek. 44:7; Joel 3:17; Zech. 14:21

cised in heart and uncircumcised in flesh, of all the foreigners who are among the sons of Israel, shall enter My sanctuary.

10 "But the Levites who [a]went far from Me, when Israel went astray, who went astray from Me after their idols, shall [b]bear the punishment for their iniquity.

11 "Yet they shall be [a]ministers in My sanctuary, having oversight at the [b]gates of the house and [c]ministering in the house; they shall [d]slaughter the burnt offering and the sacrifice for the people, and they shall [e]stand before them to minister to them.

12 "Because they ministered to them [a]before their idols and became a stumbling block of iniquity to the house of Israel, therefore I have [1]sworn against them," declares the Lord GOD, "that they shall bear the punishment for their iniquity.

13 "And they shall [a]not come near to Me to serve as a priest to Me, nor come near to any of My holy things, to the things that are most holy; but they shall [b]bear their shame and their abominations which they have committed.

14 "Yet I will [1]appoint them [2]to [a]keep charge of the house, of all its service, and of all that shall be done in it.

15 "But the Levitical [a]priests, the sons of Zadok, who [b]kept charge of My sanctuary when the sons of Israel [c]went astray from Me, shall come near to Me to minister to Me; and they shall [d]stand before Me to offer Me the [e]fat and the blood," declares the Lord GOD.

16 "They shall [a]enter My sanctuary; they shall come near to My [b]table to minister to Me and keep My charge.

17 "And it shall be that when they enter at the gates of the inner court, they shall be clothed with [a]linen garments; and wool shall not [1]be on them while they are ministering in the gates of the inner court and in the house.

18 "Linen [a]turbans shall be on their heads, and linen [b]undergarments shall be on their loins; they shall not gird themselves with *anything which makes them* sweat.

19 "And when they go out into the outer court, into the outer court to the people, they shall [a]put off their garments in which they have been ministering and lay them in the holy chambers; then they shall put on other garments that they may not transmit [b]holiness to the people with their garments.

20 "Also they shall not [a]shave their heads, yet they shall not [b]let their locks [1]grow long; they shall only trim *the hair of* their heads.

21 "Nor shall any of the priests drink wine when they enter the inner court.

22 "And they shall not [1]marry a widow or a divorced woman but shall take virgins from the offspring of the house of Israel, or a widow who is the widow of a priest.

23 "Moreover, they shall teach My people *the* [a]*difference* between the holy and the profane, and cause them to discern between the unclean and the clean.

24 "And in a dispute [a]they shall take their stand to judge; they shall judge it according to My ordinances. They shall also keep My laws and My statutes in all My [b]appointed feasts, and sanctify My sabbaths.

10 [a]Ezek. 44:12; 22:26; 2 Kin. 23:8, 9 [b]Num. 18:23

11 [a]Num. 3:5-37; 4:1-33; 18:2-6 [b]1 Chr. 26:1-19 [c]Ezek. 44:14; 40:45 [d]2 Chr. 29:34; 30:17 [e]Num. 16:9

12 [1]Lit., *lifted up My hand* [a]2 Kin. 16:10-16; Hos. 4:6; 5:1

13 [a]Num. 18:3 [b]Ezek. 16:61, 63; 39:26

14 [1]Lit., *give* [2]Lit., *keepers of the charge* [a]Ezek. 44:11; Num. 18:4; 1 Chr. 23:28-32

15 [a]Jer. 33:18-22 [b]Ezek. 40:45; Num. 18:7 [c]Ezek. 44:10; 48:11 [d]Zech. 3:1, 7 [e]Ezek. 44:7; Lev. 3:16, 17

16 [a]Num. 18:5, 7, 8 [b]Ezek. 41:22; Mal. 1:7, 12

17 [1]Lit., *come upon* [a]Ex. 28:42, 43; 39:27-29; Rev. 19:8

18 [a]Ezek. 24:17, 23; Ex. 28:40; Is. 3:20 [b]Ex. 28:42

19 [a]Ezek. 42:14; Lev. 6:10; 16:4, 23, 24 [b]Ezek. 46:20; Lev. 6:27

20 [1]Or, *hang loose* [a]Lev. 21:5 [b]Num. 6:5

22 [1]Lit., *take as wives for themselves*

23 [a]Ezek. 22:26; Lev. 10:10, 11; Hos. 4:6; Mic. 3:9-11; Zeph. 3:4; Hag. 2:11-13; Mal. 2:6-8

24 [a]Deut. 17:8, 9; 19:17; 21:5; 1 Chr. 23:4; 2 Chr. 19:8-10 [b]Lev. 23:2, 4, 44

25 "And [1]they shall not go to a dead person to defile *them-*
selves; however, for father, for mother, for son, for daughter,
for brother, or for a sister who has not had a husband, they
may defile themselves.
26 "And after he is [a]cleansed, seven days shall [1]elapse for
him.
27 "And on the day that he goes into the sanctuary, into
the inner court to minister in the sanctuary, he shall offer his
[a]sin offering," declares the Lord GOD.
28 "And it shall be with regard to an inheritance for them,
that [a]I am their inheritance; and you shall give them no possession in Israel—I am their possession.
29 "They shall [a]eat the grain offering, the sin offering, and
the guilt offering; and every [1b]devoted thing in Israel shall be
theirs.
30 "And the first of all the [a]first fruits of every kind and
every [1]contribution of every kind, from all your [1]contributions,
shall be for the priests; you shall also give to the priest the [b]first
of your [2]dough to cause a [c]blessing to rest on your house.
31 "The priests shall not eat any bird or beast that [1]has
[a]died a natural death or has been torn to pieces.

CHAPTER 45

1 "AND when you shall [a]divide by lot the land for inheritance, you shall offer an [1b]allotment to the LORD, a [c]holy
portion of the land; the length shall be the length of 25,000
[d]*cubits,* and the width shall be [2]10,000. It shall be holy within
all its boundary round about.
2 "Out of this there shall be for the holy place a square
round about five hundred by five hundred *cubits,* and fifty
cubits for its [1]open space round about.
3 "And from this [1]area you shall measure a length of
25,000 *cubits,* and a width of 10,000 *cubits;* and in it shall be
the sanctuary, the most holy place.
4 "It shall be the holy portion of the land; it shall be for
the [a]priests, the ministers of the sanctuary, who [b]come near to
minister to the LORD, and it shall be a place for their houses
and a holy place for the sanctuary.
5 "And *an area* 25,000 *cubits* in length and 10,000 in
width shall be for the Levites, the ministers of the house, *and*
for their possession [1]cities to dwell in.
6 "And you shall give the [a]city possession of *an area* 5,000
cubits wide and 25,000 *cubits* long, alongside the [1]allotment of
the holy portion; it shall be for the whole house of Israel.
7 "And the [a]prince shall have *land* on either side of the
holy [1]allotment and the [2]property of the city, adjacent to the
holy [1]allotment and the [2]property of the city, on the west side
toward the west and on the east side toward the east, and in
length comparable to one of the portions, from the west border to the east border.
8 "This shall be his land for a possession in Israel; so My
princes shall no longer [a]oppress My people, but they shall give
the rest of the land to the house of Israel [b]according to their
tribes."

25 [1]Lit., *he*

26 [1]Lit., *be counted* [a]Num. 19:13-19

27 [a]Lev. 5:3, 6; Num. 6:9-11

28 [a]Num. 18:20; Deut. 10:9; 18:1, 2; Josh. 13:33

29 [1]Or, *dedicated;* cf. Num. 18:14 [a]Num. 18:9, 14; Josh. 13:14 [b]Lev. 27:21, 28

30 [1]Or, *heave offering* [2]Or, *coarse meal* [a]Num. 18:12; 2 Chr. 31:4-6, 10; Neh. 10:35-37 [b]Num. 15:20, 21 [c]Mal. 3:10

31 [1]Lit., *a corpse* [a]Ezek. 4:14; Lev. 22:8; Deut. 14:21

1 [1]Or, *contribution* [2]Or, with Gk., *20,000* [a]Ezek. 47:21; 48:29; Num. 34:13; Josh. 13:7; 14:3 [b]Ezek. 48:8, 9 [c]Zech. 14:20, 21 [d]Ezek. 45:2; 42:16

2 [1]Or, *pasture land;* cf. 27:28

3 [1]Lit., *measure*

4 [a]Ezek. 48:10, 11 [b]Ezek. 40:45; 43:19; Num. 16:5

5 [1]So with Gk.; M.T., *twenty chambers*

6 [1]Or, *contribution* [a]Ezek. 48:15-18, 30-35

7 [1]Or, *contribution* [2]Lit., *possession* [a]Ezek. 34:24; 37:24; 46:16-18; 48:21

8 [a]Ezek. 19:7; 22:27; 46:18; Is. 11:3-5; Jer. 23:5 [b]Josh. 11:23

9 'Thus says the Lord [1]GOD, "Enough, you princes of Israel; put away [a]violence and destruction, and [b]practice justice and righteousness. Stop your [c]expropriations from My people," declares the Lord GOD.

10 "You shall have [a]just balances, a just [b]ephah, and a just [b]bath.

11 "The ephah and the bath shall be [1]the same quantity, so that the bath may contain a tenth of a [a]homer, and the ephah a tenth of a homer; [2]their standard shall be according to the homer.

12 "And the [a]shekel shall be twenty [a]gerahs; twenty shekels, twenty-five shekels, *and* fifteen shekels shall be your [1]maneh.

13 "This is the offering that you shall offer: a sixth of an ephah from a homer of wheat; a sixth of an ephah from a homer of barley;

14 and the prescribed portion of oil (*namely,* the bath of oil), a tenth of a bath from *each* cor (*which is* ten baths *or* a homer, for ten baths are a homer);

15 and one sheep from *each* flock of two hundred from the watering places of Israel—for a grain offering, for a burnt offering, and for peace offerings, to [a]make atonement for them," declares the Lord GOD.

16 "[a]All the people of the land shall [1]give to this offering for the [b]prince in Israel.

17 "And it shall be the prince's part *to provide* the [a]burnt offerings, the grain offerings, and the drink offerings, at the [b]feasts, on the [c]new moons, and on the sabbaths, at all the appointed feasts of the house of Israel; he shall provide the sin offering, the grain offering, the burnt offering, and the [d]peace offerings, to make atonement for the house of Israel."

18 'Thus says the Lord GOD, "In the [a]first *month,* on the first of the month, you shall take a young bull [b]without blemish and [c]cleanse the sanctuary.

19 "And the priest shall take some of the blood from the sin offering and put *it* on the door posts of the house, on the [a]four corners of the [b]ledge of the altar, and on the posts of the gate of the inner court.

20 "And thus you shall do on the seventh *day* of the month for every one who goes [a]astray or is [1]naive; so you shall make [b]atonement for the house.

21 "In the first *month,* on the fourteenth day of the month, you shall have the [a]Passover, a feast of seven days; unleavened bread shall be eaten.

22 And on that day the prince shall provide for himself and all the people of the land a [a]bull for a sin offering.

23 "And *during* the [a]seven days of the feast he shall provide as a [b]burnt offering to the LORD [c]seven bulls and seven rams without blemish on every day of the seven days, and a male goat daily for a sin offering.

24 "And he shall provide as a [a]grain offering an ephah [1]with a bull, an ephah [1]with a ram, and a hin of oil [1]with an ephah.

25 "In the [a]seventh *month,* on the fifteenth day of the month, at the feast, he shall provide like this seven days [1]for the sin offering, the burnt offering, the grain offering, and the oil."

9 [1]YHWH, usually rendered LORD, and so throughout the chap. [a]Ezek. 7:11, 23; 8:17; Jer. 6:7 [b]Jer. 22:3; Zech. 8:16 [c]Neh. 5:1-5

10 [a]Lev. 19:36; Deut. 25:15; Prov. 16:11; Amos 8:4-6; Mic. 6:10, 11 [b]Is. 5:10

11 [1]Lit., *one* [2]Lit., *its measure* [a]Is. 5:10

12 [1]Or, *mina* [a]Ex. 30:13; Lev. 27:25; Num. 3:47

15 [a]Lev. 1:4; 6:30

16 [1]Lit., *be* [a]Ex. 30:14, 15 [b]Is. 16:1

17 [a]1 Kin. 8:64; 1 Chr. 16:2; 2 Chr. 31:3 [b]Lev. 23:1-44; Num. 28:1-29, 39 [c]Is. 66:23 [d]Ezek. 43:27; 1 Kin. 8:63

18 [a]Ex. 12:2 [b]Lev. 22:20; Heb. 9:14 [c]Ezek. 43:22, 26; Lev. 16:16, 33

19 [a]Ezek. 43:20; Lev. 16:18-20 [b]Ezek. 43:14, 17, 20

20 [1]Lit., *simple* [a]Lev. 4:27; Ps. 19:12 [b]Ezek. 45:15, 18; Lev. 16:20

21 [a]Ex. 12:1-24; Lev. 23:5-8

22 [a]Lev. 4:14

23 [a]Lev. 23:8 [b]Num. 28:16-25 [c]Num. 23:1, 2; Job 42:8

24 [1]Lit., *for* [a]Ezek. 46:5-7; Num. 28:12-15

25 [1]Lit., *according to* [a]Lev. 23:33-43; Num. 29:12-38; 2 Chr. 5:3; 7:8, 10

CHAPTER 46

'THUS says the Lord [1]GOD, "The gate of the [a]inner court
facing east shall be [b]shut the six [c]working days; but it shall be
opened on the [d]sabbath day, and opened on the day of the
[e]new moon.
2 "And the [a]prince shall enter by way of the [a]porch of the
gate from outside and stand by the [b]post of the gate. Then the
priests shall provide his burnt offering and his peace offerings,
and he shall worship at the threshold of the gate and then go
out; but the gate shall not be shut until the evening.
3 "The [a]people of the land shall also worship at the doorway of that gate before the LORD on the sabbaths and on the
new moons.
4 "And the [a]burnt offering which the prince shall offer to
the LORD on the sabbath day shall be [b]six lambs without blemish and a ram without blemish;
5 and the [a]grain offering shall be an ephah [1]with the ram,
and the grain offering [1]with the lambs [2]as much as he is [b]able
to give, and a hin of oil [1]with an ephah.
6 "And on the day of the new moon *he shall offer* a young
bull without blemish, also six lambs and a ram, *which* shall be
without blemish.
7 "And he shall provide a grain offering, an ephah [1]with
the bull, and an ephah [1]with the ram, and [1]with the lambs as
[2]much as he is [a]able, and a hin of oil [1]with an ephah.
8 "And when the prince enters, he shall go in by way of the
porch of the gate and go out [1]by the same way.
9 "But when the people of the land come [a]before the
LORD at the appointed feasts, he who enters by way of the
north gate to worship shall go out by way of the south gate.
And he who enters by way of the south gate shall go out by way
of the north gate. [1]No one shall return by way of the gate by
which he entered but shall go straight out.
10 "And when they go in, the prince shall go in [a]among
them; and when they go out, [1]he shall go out.
11 "And at the [a]festivals and the appointed feasts the grain
offering shall be an ephah [1]with a bull and an ephah [1]with a
ram, and [1]with the lambs as [2]much as one is able to give, and a
hin of oil [1]with an ephah.
12 "And when the prince provides a [a]freewill offering, a
burnt offering, or peace offerings *as* a freewill offering to the
LORD, the gate facing east shall be [b]opened for him. And he
shall provide his burnt offering and his peace offerings as he
does on the [c]sabbath day. Then he shall go out, and the gate
shall be shut after he goes out.
13 "And you shall provide a [a]lamb a year old without blemish for a burnt offering to the LORD daily; [b]morning by morning you shall provide it.
14 "Also you shall provide a grain offering with it morning
by morning, a [a]sixth of an ephah, and a third of a hin of oil to
moisten the fine flour, a grain offering to the LORD continually
by a perpetual [1]ordinance.
15 "Thus they shall provide the lamb, the grain offering,
and the oil, morning by morning, for a [a]continual burnt
offering."

1 [1]YHWH, usually rendered LORD, and so throughout the chap. [a]Ezek. 8:16; 10:3 [b]Ezek. 44:1, 2 [c]Ex. 20:9 [d]Ezek. 45:17; Is. 66:23 [e]Ezek. 46:3, 6; 45:18

2 [a]Ezek. 46:8; 44:3 [b]Ezek. 45:19

3 [a]Luke 1:10

4 [a]Ezek. 45:17 [b]Num. 28:9, 10

5 [1]Lit., *for* [2]Lit., *a gift of his hand* [a]Ezek. 46:7, 11; 45:24; Num. 28:12 [b]Ezek. 46:7

7 [1]Lit., *for* [2]Lit., *his hand can reach* [a]Ezek. 46:5; Lev. 14:21; Deut. 16:17

8 [1]Lit., *by its way*

9 [1]Lit., *He shall not* [a]Ex. 34:23; Ps. 84:7; Mic. 6:6

10 [1]So with many mss. and the ancient versions; M.T., *they* [a]2 Sam. 6:14, 15; 1 Chr. 29:20, 21; 2 Chr. 6:3; 7:4; Ps. 42:4

11 [1]Lit., *for* [2]Lit., *a gift of his hand* [a]Ezek. 45:17

12 [a]Lev. 23:38; 2 Chr. 29:31 [b]Ezek. 46:1, 2, 8; 44:3 [c]Ezek. 45:17

13 [a]Num. 28:3-5 [b]Is. 50:4

14 [1]Lit., *statutes* [a]Num. 28:5

15 [a]Ex. 29:42; Num. 28:6

16 [a]2 Chr. 21:3

16 "Thus says the Lord GOD, "If the prince gives a [a]gift *out of* his inheritance to any of his sons, it shall belong to his sons; it is their possession by inheritance.

17 [a]Lev. 25:10

17 "But if he gives a gift from his inheritance to one of his servants, it shall be his until the [a]year of liberty; then it shall return to the prince. His inheritance *shall be* only his sons'; it shall belong to them.

18 [1]Lit., *oppressing* [a]Ezek. 45:8; Is. 11:3, 4 [b]Ezek. 22:27; 1 Kin. 21:19; Mic. 2:1, 2

18 "And the prince shall [a]not take from the people's inheritance, [1b]thrusting them out of their possession; he shall give his sons inheritance from his own possession so that My people shall not be scattered, anyone from his possession." ' "

19 [a]Ezek. 42:9; 44:5

19 Then he brought me through the [a]entrance, which *was* at the side of the gate, into the holy chambers for the priests, which faced north; and behold, there *was* a place at the extreme rear toward the west.

20 [a]Ezek. 44:29; 2 Chr. 35:13 [b]Lev. 2:4-7

20 And he said to me, "This is the place where the priests shall boil the [a]guilt offering and the sin offering, *and* where they shall [b]bake the grain offering, in order that they may not bring *them* out into the outer court to transmit holiness to the people."

21 Then he brought me out into the outer court and led me across to the four corners of the court; and behold, in every corner of the court *there was* a *small* court.

22 [1]Lit., *one measure*

22 In the four corners of the court *there were* enclosed courts, forty *cubits* long and thirty wide; these four in the corners *were* [1]the same size.

23 And *there was* a row *of masonry* round about in them, around the four of them, and boiling places were made under the rows round about.

24 [1]Lit., *houses*

24 Then he said to me, "These are the boiling [1]places where the ministers of the house shall boil the sacrifices of the people."

CHAPTER 47

1 [a]Ezek. 41:2, 23-25 [b]Ps. 46:4; Is. 30:25; 55:1; Jer. 2:13; Joel 3:18; Zech. 13:1; 14:8; Rev. 22:1, 17

THEN he brought me back to the [a]door of the house; and behold, [b]water was flowing from under the threshold of the house toward the east, for the house faced east. And the water was flowing down from under, from the right side of the house, from south of the altar.

2 [1]Lit., *by way of*

2 And he brought me out by way of the north gate and led me around [1]on the outside to the outer gate by way of *the gate* that faces east. And behold, water was trickling from the south side.

3 When the man went out toward the east with a line in his hand, he measured a thousand cubits, and he led me through the water, water *reaching* the ankles.

4 Again he measured a thousand and led me through the water, water *reaching* the knees. Again he measured a thousand and led me through *the water,* water *reaching* the loins.

5 [a]Is. 11:9; Hab. 2:14

5 Again he measured a thousand; *and it was* a river that I could not ford, for the water had risen, *enough* water to swim in, a [a]river that could not be forded.

6 [1]Lit., *and caused me to return* [a]Ezek. 8:6; 40:4; 44:5

6 And he said to me, "Son of man, have you [a]seen *this?*" Then he brought me [1]back to the bank of the river.

7 Now when I had returned, behold, on the bank of the

river there *were* very many [a]trees on the one side and on the
other.
8 Then he said to me, "These waters go out toward the
eastern region and go down into the [a]Arabah; then they go
toward the sea, being made to flow into the [b]sea, and the
waters *of the sea* become [1]fresh.
9 "And it will come about that every living creature which
swarms in every place where the [1]river goes, will live. And there
will be very many fish, for these waters go there, and *the others*
[2]become fresh; so [a]everything will live where the river goes.
10 "And it will come about that [a]fishermen will stand [b]be-
side it; from [c]Engedi to Eneglaim there will be a place for the
[d]spreading of nets. Their fish will be according to their kinds,
like the fish of the [e]Great Sea, [f]very many.
11 "But its swamps and marshes will not become [1]fresh;
they will be [2]left for [a]salt.
12 "And [a]by the river on its bank, on one side and on the
other, will grow all *kinds of* [b]trees for food. Their [c]leaves will
not wither, and their fruit will not fail. They will bear every
month because their water flows from the sanctuary, and their
fruit will be for food and their [d]leaves for healing."
13 Thus says the Lord [1]GOD, "This *shall be* the [a]boundary
by which you shall divide the land for an inheritance among
the twelve tribes of Israel; Joseph *shall have two* [b]portions.
14 "And you shall divide it for an inheritance, each one
[1]equally with the other; for I [2a]swore to give it to your forefathers,
and this land shall fall to you [3]as an inheritance.
15 "And this *shall be* the boundary of the land: On the
[a]north side, from the Great Sea *by* the way of Hethlon, to the
entrance of [1b]Zedad;
16 [1a]Hamath, Berothah, Sibraim, which is between the
border of [b]Damascus and the border of Hamath; Hazer-hatti-
con, which is by the border of Hauran.
17 "And the boundary shall [1]extend from the sea *to* Hazar-
enan *at* the border of Damascus, and on the north toward the
north is the border of Hamath. This is the north side.
18 "And the [a]east side, from between Hauran, Damascus,
[b]Gilead, and the land of Israel, *shall be* the [c]Jordan; from the
north border to the Eastern Sea you shall measure. This is the
east side.
19 "And the [a]south side toward the south *shall extend* from
[b]Tamar as far as the waters of [c]Meribath-kadesh, to the [d]Brook
of Egypt, and to the [e]Great Sea. This is the south side toward
the south.
20 "And the [a]west side *shall be* the Great Sea, from the
south border to a point opposite [1b]Lebo-hamath. This is the
west side.
21 "So you shall divide this land among yourselves according to the tribes of Israel.
22 "And it will come about that you shall divide it by [a]lot
for an inheritance among yourselves and among the [b]aliens
who stay in your midst, who bring forth sons in your midst.
And they shall be to you as the native-born among the sons of
Israel; they shall be allotted an [c]inheritance with you among
the tribes of Israel.
23 "And it will come about that in the tribe with which the

7 [a]Ezek. 47:12; Is. 60:13, 21; 61:3

8 [1]Lit., *healed* [a]Deut. 3:17; Is. 35:6, 7; 41:17-19; 44:3 [b]Josh. 3:16

9 [1]Lit., *two rivers* [2]Lit., *are healed* [a]Is. 12:3; 55:1; John 4:14; 7:37, 38; Rev. 21:7

10 [a]Matt. 4:19; 13:47; Luke 5:10 [b]1 Sam. 23:24; 24:1 [c]Gen. 14:7; Josh. 15:62; 1 Sam. 23:29; 24:1; 2 Chr. 20:2 [d]Ezek. 26:5, 14 [e]Ezek. 47:15; 48:28; Num. 34:6; Ps. 104:25 [f]Luke 5:5-9; John 21:6

11 [1]Lit., *healed* [2]Lit., *given* [a]Deut. 29:23

12 [a]Ezek. 47:7; Rev. 22:2 [b]Gen. 2:9 [c]Ps. 1:3; Jer. 17:8 [d]Rev. 22:2

13 [1]YHWH, usually rendered LORD, and so throughout the chap. [a]Num. 34:2-12 [b]Ezek. 48:4, 5; Gen. 48:5; 49:26

14 [1]Lit., *like his brother* [2]Lit., *lifted up My hand* [3]Lit., *in* [a]Ezek. 20:6; Deut. 1:8

15 [1]Or, *Hamath* [a]Num. 34:7-9 [b]Num. 34:8

16 [1]Or, *Zedad* [a]Ezek. 47:17, 20; 48:1; Num. 13:21; Is. 10:9; Zech. 9:2 [b]Ezek. 47:17, 18; 48:1; Gen. 14:15

17 [1]Lit., *be*

18 [a]Num. 34:10-12 [b]Gen. 37:25; Jer. 50:19 [c]Gen. 13:10, 11

19 [a]Num. 34:3-5 [b]Ezek. 48:28 [c]Deut. 32:51 [d]Num. 34:5; 1 Kin. 8:65; Is. 27:12 [e]Ezek. 47:10, 15

20 [1]Or, *entrance of Hamath* [a]Num. 34:6 [b]Ezek. 48:1; Judg. 3:3; 2 Chr. 7:8; Amos 6:14

22 [a]Num. 26:55, 56 [b]Is. 14:1; 56:6, 7 [c]Acts 11:18; 15:9; Eph. 2:12-14; 3:6; Col. 3:11

alien stays, there you shall give *him* his inheritance," declares the Lord God.

Chapter 48

"Now [a]these are the names of the tribes: From the northern extremity, [1]beside the way of Hethlon to [2]Lebo-hamath, *as far as* Hazar-enan *at* the border of Damascus, toward the north [1]beside Hamath, [3]running from east to west, [b]Dan, one *portion.*

2 "And beside the border of Dan, from the east side to the west side, [a]Asher, one *portion.*

3 "And beside the border of Asher, from the east side to the west side, [a]Naphtali, one *portion.*

4 "And beside the border of Naphtali, from the east side to the west side, [a]Manasseh, one *portion.*

5 "And beside the border of Manasseh, from the east side to the west side, [a]Ephraim, one *portion.*

6 "And beside the border of Ephraim, from the east side to the west side, [a]Reuben, one *portion.*

7 "And beside the border of Reuben, from the east side to the west side, [a]Judah, one *portion.*

8 "And beside the border of Judah, from the east side to the west side, shall be the [1]allotment which you shall [2]set apart, 25,000 [3]*cubits* in width, and in length like one of the portions, from the east side to the west side; and the [a]sanctuary shall be in the middle of it.

9 "The allotment that you shall set apart to the Lord *shall be* 25,000 *cubits* in length, and 10,000 in width.

10 "And the holy allotment shall be for these, *namely* for the [a]priests, toward the north 25,000 *cubits in length,* toward the west 10,000 in width, toward the east 10,000 in width, and toward the south 25,000 in length; and the sanctuary of the Lord shall be in its midst.

11 "*It shall be* for the priests who are sanctified of the [a]sons of Zadok, who have kept My charge, who did not go astray when the sons of Israel went astray, as the [b]Levites went astray.

12 "And it shall be an allotment to them from the allotment of the land, a most holy place, by the border of the Levites.

13 "And alongside the border of the priests the Levites *shall have* 25,000 *cubits* in length and 10,000 in width. The whole length *shall be* 25,000 *cubits* and the width 10,000.

14 "Moreover, they shall not [a]sell or exchange any of it, or alienate this [1]choice *portion* of land; for it is holy to the Lord.

15 "And the remainder, 5,000 *cubits* in width and 25,000 [1]in length, shall be for [a]common use for the city, for dwellings and for [2]open spaces; and the city shall be in its midst.

16 "And these *shall be* its measurements: the north side 4,500 *cubits,* the south side [a]4,500 *cubits,* the east side 4,500 *cubits,* and the west side 4,500 *cubits.*

17 "And the city shall have [1]open spaces: on the north 250 *cubits,* on the south 250 *cubits,* on the east 250 *cubits,* and on the west 250 *cubits.*

18 "And the remainder of the length alongside the holy allotment shall be 10,000 *cubits* toward the east, and 10,000

1 [1]Lit., *at the hand of* [2]Or, *the entrance of Hamath* [3]Lit., *and there shall be to it an east and west side* [a]Ex. 1:1 [b]Josh. 19:40-48

2 [a]Josh. 19:24-31

3 [a]Josh. 19:32-39

4 [a]Josh. 13:29-31; 17:1-11

5 [a]Josh. 16:5-9; 17:8-10, 14-18

6 [a]Josh. 13:15-21

7 [a]Josh. 15:1-63; 19:9

8 [1]Or, *contribution,* and so throughout the chap. [2]Lit., *offer* [3]Or, possibly, *reeds,* and so throughout the chap. [a]Ezek. 45:3, 4; Is. 12:6; 33:20-22

10 [a]Ezek. 44:28; 45:4

11 [a]Ezek. 40:46; 44:15 [b]Ezek. 44:10, 12

14 [1]Lit., *first* or *first fruits* [a]Lev. 25:32-34

15 [1]Lit., *in front* [2]Or, *pasture land* [a]Ezek. 42:20; 45:6

16 [a]Rev. 21:16

17 [1]Or, *pasture land*

toward the west; and it shall be [1]alongside the holy allotment.
And its produce shall be food for the workers of the city.
19 "And the workers of the city, out of all the tribes of
Israel, shall cultivate it.
20 "The whole allotment *shall be* 25,000 by 25,000 *cubits;*
you shall [1]set apart the holy allotment, a [2]square, with the
[3]property of the city.
21 "And the [a]remainder *shall be* for the prince, on the one
side and on the other of the holy allotment and of the [1]prop-
erty of the city; in front of the 25,000 *cubits* of the allotment
toward the east border and westward in front of the 25,000
toward the west border, alongside the portions, *it shall be* for
the prince. And the holy allotment and the sanctuary of the
house shall be in the middle of it.
22 "And exclusive of the [1]property of the Levites and the
[1]property of the city, *which* are in the middle of that which
belongs to the prince, *everything* between the border of Judah
and the border of Benjamin shall be for the prince.
23 "As for the rest of the tribes: from the east side to the
west side, [a]Benjamin, one *portion.*
24 "And beside the border of Benjamin, from the east side
to the west side, [a]Simeon, one *portion.*
25 "And beside the border of Simeon, from the east side to
the west side, [a]Issachar, one *portion.*
26 "And beside the border of Issachar, from the east side to
the west side, [a]Zebulun, one *portion.*
27 "And beside the border of Zebulun, from the east side
to the west side, [a]Gad, one *portion.*
28 "And beside the border of Gad, at the south side toward
the south, the border shall be from [a]Tamar to the waters of
Meribath-kadesh, to the Brook *of Egypt,* to the [b]Great Sea.
29 "This is the [a]land which you shall divide by lot to the
tribes of Israel for an inheritance, and these are their *several*
portions," declares the Lord [1]GOD.
30 "And these are the exits of the city: On the [a]north side,
4,500 *cubits* by measurement,
31 [1]shall be the gates of the city, [2a]named for the tribes of
Israel, three gates toward the north: the gate of Reuben, one;
the gate of Judah, one: the gate of Levi, one.
32 "And on the east side, 4,500 *cubits,* [1]shall be three gates:
the gate of Joseph, one; the gate of Benjamin, one; the gate of
Dan, one.
33 "And on the south side, 4,500 *cubits* by measurement,
[1]shall be three gates: the gate of Simeon, one; the gate of
Issachar, one; the gate of Zebulun, one.
34 "On the west side, 4,500 *cubits, shall be* three gates: the
gate of Gad, one; the gate of Asher, one; the gate of Naphtali,
one.
35 "*The city shall be* 18,000 *cubits* round about; and the
[a]name of the city from *that* day *shall be,* '[1]The [b]LORD is
there.' "

18 [1]Or, *exactly as*

20 [1]Lit., *offer* [2]Lit., *fourth* [3]Or, *possession*

21 [1]Or, *possession* [a]Ezek. 48:22; 34:24; 45:7

22 [1]Or, *possession*

23 [a]Josh. 18:21-28

24 [a]Josh. 19:1-9

25 [a]Josh. 19:17-23

26 [a]Josh. 19:10-16

27 [a]Josh. 13:24-28

28 [a]Ezek. 47:19; Gen. 14:7; 2 Chr. 20:2 [b]Ezek. 47:10, 15, 19, 20

29 [1]YHWH, usually rendered LORD [a]Ezek. 47:13-20

30 [a]Ezek. 48:32, 33, 34

31 [1]Lit., *and* [2]Lit., *according to the names of* [a]Rev. 21:12, 13

32 [1]Lit., *and*

33 [1]Lit., *and*

35 [1]Heb., *YHWH-shammah* [a]Jer. 23:6; 33:16 [b]Ezek. 35:10; Is. 12:6; 14:32; 24:23; Jer. 3:17; 8:19; 14:9; Joel 3:21; Zech. 2:10; Rev. 21:3; 22:3

E 90-1

THE BOOK OF DANIEL

The Choice Young Men.

IN the third year of the reign of [a]Jehoiakim king of Judah, [b]Nebuchadnezzar king of Babylon came to Jerusalem and besieged it.

2 And the [a]Lord gave Jehoiakim king of Judah into his hand, along with some of the [b]vessels of the house of God; and he brought them to the land of [c]Shinar, to the house of his [1]god, and he brought the vessels into the treasury of his [1d]god.

3 Then the king [1]ordered Ashpenaz, the chief of his [2]officials, to bring in some of the sons of Israel, including some of the [3]royal [a]family and of the nobles,

4 youths in whom was [a]no defect, who were good looking, showing intelligence in every *branch of* wisdom, endowed with understanding, and discerning knowledge, and who had ability for [1]serving in the king's [2]court; and *he ordered him* to teach them the [3]literature and [b]language of the [c]Chaldeans.

5 And the king appointed for them a daily ration from the king's choice food and from the wine which he drank, and *appointed* that they should be [1]educated three years, at the end of which they were to [2a]enter the king's personal service.

6 Now among them from the sons of Judah were [a]Daniel, Hananiah, Mishael and Azariah.

7 Then the commander of the officials assigned *new* names to them; and to Daniel he assigned *the name* [a]Belteshazzar, to Hananiah [b]Shadrach, to Mishael [b]Meshach, and to Azariah [b]Abed-nego.

8 But Daniel [1]made up his mind that he would not [a]defile himself with the [b]king's choice food or with the [c]wine which he drank; so he sought *permission* from the commander of the officials that he might not defile himself.

9 Now God granted Daniel [1a]favor and compassion in the sight of the commander of the officials,

10 and the commander of the officials said to Daniel, "I am afraid of my lord the king, who has appointed your food and your drink; for why should he see your faces looking more haggard than the youths who are your own age? Then you would [1]make me forfeit my head to the king."

11 But Daniel said to the overseer whom the commander of the officials had appointed over Daniel, Hananiah, Mishael and Azariah,

12 "Please test your servants for ten days, and let us be given some vegetables to eat and water to drink.

13 "Then let our appearance be [1]observed in your presence, and the appearance of the youths who are eating the king's choice food; and deal with your servants according to what you see."

14 So he listened to them in this matter and tested them for ten days.

15 And at the end of ten days their appearance seemed

1 [a]2 Kin. 24:1; 2 Chr. 36:5, 6 [b]Jer. 25:1; 52:12, 28-30

2 [1]Or, *gods* [a]Dan. 2:37, 38; Is. 42:24 [b]Dan. 5:2; 2 Chr. 36:7; Jer. 27:19, 20 [c]Gen. 10:10; 11:2; Is. 11:11; Zech. 5:11 [d]Jer. 50:2; 51:44

3 [1]Or, *said to* [2]Or, *eunuchs,* and so throughout the chap. [3]Lit., *seed of the* [a]2 Kin. 24:14; Is. 39:7

4 [1]Lit., *standing* [2]Lit., *palace* [3]Or, *writing* [a]2 Sam. 14:25 [b]Dan. 2:4; Is. 36:11; Jer. 5:15 [c]Dan. 2:2, 4, 5, 10; 3:8; 4:7; 5:7, 11, 30; 9:1

5 [1]Or, *reared* [2]Lit., *stand before the king* [a]Dan. 1:19; 1 Sam. 16:22; Jer. 15:1

6 [a]Ezek. 14:14, 20; 28:3; Matt. 24:15

7 [a]Dan. 2:26; 4:8; 5:12 [b]Dan. 2:49; 3:12

8 [1]Lit., *set upon his heart* [a]Lev. 11:47; Ezek. 4:13, 14; Hos. 9:3, 4 [b]Dan. 1:5; Ps. 141:4 [c]Dan. 5:4; Deut. 32:38

9 [1]Lit., *lovingkindness* [a]Job 5:15, 16; Ps. 106:46; Prov. 16:7

10 [1]Lit., *make my head guilty*

13 [1]Lit., *seen*

[a]better and [1]they were fatter than all the youths who had been
eating the king's choice food.
16 So the overseer continued to [1]withhold their choice
food and the wine they were to drink, and kept giving them
vegetables.
17 And as for these four youths, [a]God gave them knowledge and intelligence in every *branch of* [1]literature and wisdom; Daniel even understood all *kinds of* [b]visions and dreams.
18 Then at the end of the days which the king had [1]speci-
fied [2]for presenting them, the commander of the officials [3]pre-
sented them before Nebuchadnezzar.
19 And the king talked with them, and out of them all not
one was found like Daniel, Hananiah, Mishael and Azariah; so
they [1a]entered the king's personal service.
20 And as for every matter of [a]wisdom [1]and understanding
about which the king consulted them, he found them [b]ten
times [c]better than all the [2d]magicians *and* conjurers who *were*
in all his realm.
21 And Daniel [1]continued until the [a]first year of Cyrus the
king.

Chapter 2

NOW in the second year of the reign of Nebuchadnezzar,
Nebuchadnezzar [1a]had dreams; and his spirit was troubled and
his [b]sleep [2]left him.
2 Then the king [1]gave orders to call in the [2a]magicians,
the conjurers, the sorcerers and the [3]Chaldeans, to tell the king
his dreams. So they came in and stood before the king.
3 And the king said to them, "I [1a]had a dream, and my
spirit [2]is anxious to [3]understand the dream."
4 Then the Chaldeans spoke to the king in [1a]Aramaic:
"O king, live forever! Tell the dream to your servants, and we
will declare the interpretation."
5 The king answered and said to the Chaldeans, "[1]The
command from me is firm: if you do not make known to me
the dream and its interpretation, you will be [2a]torn limb from
limb, and your houses will be made a rubbish heap.
6 "But if you declare the dream and its interpretation, you
will receive from me [a]gifts and a reward and great honor;
therefore declare to me the dream and its interpretation."
7 They answered a second time and said, "Let the king
tell the dream to his servants, and we will declare the
interpretation."
8 The king answered and said, "I know for certain that
you are [1]bargaining for time, inasmuch as you have seen that
[2]the command from me is firm,
9 that if you do not make the dream known to me, there
is only [a]one [1]decree for you. For you have agreed together to
speak lying and corrupt [2]words before me until the [3]situation is
changed; therefore tell me the dream, that I may [b]know that
you can declare to me its interpretation."
10 The Chaldeans answered [1]the king and said, "There is
not a man on earth who could declare the matter [2]for the king,
inasmuch as no great king or ruler has *ever* asked anything like
this of any [3]magician, conjurer or Chaldean.

15 [1]Lit., *fat of flesh* [a]Ex. 23:25; Prov. 10:22

16 [1]Lit., *take away*

17 [1]Or, *writing* [a]Dan. 1:20; 2:21, 23; 1 Kin. 3:12, 28; Job 32:8 [b]Dan. 2:19; 7:1; 8:1

18 [1]Lit., *said* [2]Lit., *to bring them in* [3]Lit., *brought in*

19 [1]Lit., *stood before the king* [a]Dan. 1:5; Gen. 41:46; 1 Kin. 17; Prov. 22:29; Jer. 15:1

20 [1]Lit., *of* [2]Or, *soothsayer priests* [a]Dan. 1:17; 1 Kin. 4:30, 31 [b]Gen. 31:7; Num. 14:22; Neh. 4:12; Job 19:3 [c]Dan. 2:27, 28, 46, 48 [d]Dan. 2:2; 4:18; 5:7; Is. 19:3

21 [1]Lit., *was until* [a]Dan. 6:28; 10:1

1 [1]Lit., *dreamed dreams* [2]Lit., *was gone upon him* [a]Dan. 2:3; 4:5; Gen. 40:5-8; 14:1; Job 33:15-17 [b]Dan. 6:18; Esth. 6:1

2 [1]Lit., *said to call* [2]Or, *soothsayer priests* [3]Or, *master astrologers,* and so throughout the chap. [a]Dan. 2:10, 27; 1:20; 4:6; 5:7; Gen. 41:8; Is. 47:12, 13

3 [1]Lit., *dreamed* [2]Lit., *was troubled* [3]Lit., *know* [a]Dan. 4:5; Gen. 40:8; 41:15

4 [1]The text is in Aramaic from here through 7:28 [a]Ezra 4:7; Is. 36:11

5 [1]Another reading is, *The word has gone from me* [2]Lit., *made into limbs* [a]Dan. 2:12; 3:29; Ezra 6:11

6 [a]Dan. 2:48; 5:7, 16, 29

8 [1]Lit., *buying* [2]See v. 5 nt. 1

9 [1]Or, *law* [2]Lit., *word* [3]Lit., *time* [a]Dan. 3:15; Esth. 4:11 [b]Is. 41:23

10 [1]Lit., *before the* [2]Lit., *of* [3]Or, *soothsayer priest*

11 [1]Or, *rare* [2]Lit., *before* [a]Dan. 5:11; Gen. 41:39 [b]Ex. 29:45; Is. 57:15

12 [a]Dan. 2:5; 3:13, 19; Ps. 76:10

13 [1]Or, *law* [2]Lit., *be killed*

14 [1]Or, *executioners*

15 [1]Or, *law* [2]Or, *harsh*

16 [1]Or, *appoint a time for him*

18 [a]Dan. 2:23; Esth. 4:15, 16; Is. 37:4; Jer. 33:3; Ezek. 36:37 [b]Gen. 18:28; Mal. 3:18

19 [a]Dan. 1:17; 7:2, 7, 13; Num. 12:6; Job 33:15, 16

20 [a]Ps. 103:1, 2; 113:1, 2 [b]Dan. 2:21-23; 1 Chr. 29:11, 12; Job 12:13, 16-22

21 [1]Or, *sets up* [2]Lit., *knowers* [a]Dan. 2:9; 7:25; Ps. 31:15 [b]Dan. 4:17, 32; Job 12:18; Ps. 75:6,7 [c]1 Kin. 3:9, 10; 4:29; James 1:5

22 [a]Dan. 2:19, 28; Job 12:22 [b]Job 26:6; Ps. 139:12; Is. 45:7; Jer. 23:24 [c]Dan. 5:11, 14; Ps. 36:9; 1 John 1:5

23 [a]Gen. 31:42; Ex. 3:15 [b]Dan. 2:21; 1:17 [c]Dan. 2:18, 29, 30; Ps. 21:2, 4

24 [1]Lit., *in before the king* [a]Dan. 2:12, 13; Acts27:24

25 [1]Lit., *in before the king* [2]Lit., *sons of the exile of* [a]Gen. 41:14 [b]Dan. 1:6; 5:13; 6:13

26 [a]Dan. 1:7; 4:8; 5:12

27 [a]Dan. 2:2, 10, 11; 5:7, 8

11 "Moreover, the thing which the king demands is [1]diffi-
cult, and there is no one else who could declare it [2]to the king
except [a]gods, whose [b]dwelling place is not with *mortal* flesh."
12 Because of this the king became [a]indignant and very
furious, and gave orders to destroy all the wise men of
Babylon.
13 So the [1]decree went forth that the wise men should be
slain; and they looked for Daniel and his friends to [2]kill *them.*
14 Then Daniel replied with discretion and discernment
to Arioch, the captain of the king's [1]bodyguard, who had gone
forth to slay the wise men of Babylon;
15 he answered and said to Arioch, the king's commander,
"For what reason is the [1]decree from the king *so* [2]urgent?"
Then Arioch informed Daniel about the matter.
16 So Daniel went in and requested of the king that he
would [1]give him time, in order that he might declare the interpretation to the king.
17 Then Daniel went to his house and informed his
friends, Hananiah, Mishael and Azariah, about the matter,
18 in order that they might [a]request compassion from the
God of heaven concerning this mystery, so that Daniel and his
friends might not be [b]destroyed with the rest of the wise men
of Babylon.
19 Then the mystery was revealed to Daniel in a night
[a]vision. Then Daniel blessed the God of heaven;
20 Daniel answered and said,

"Let the name of God be [a]blessed forever and ever,
For [b]wisdom and power belong to Him.

21 "And it is He who [a]changes the times and the epochs;
He [b]removes kings and [1]establishes kings;
He gives [c]wisdom to wise men,
And knowledge to [2]men of understanding.

22 "It is He who [a]reveals the profound and hidden things;
[b]He knows what is in the darkness,
And the [c]light dwells with him.

23 "To Thee, O [a]God of my fathers, I give thanks and praise,
For Thou hast given me [b]wisdom and power;
Even now Thou hast made known to me what we [c]requested of Thee,
For Thou hast made known to us the king's matter."

24 Therefore, Daniel went in to Arioch, whom the king
had appointed to destroy the wise men of Babylon; he went
and spoke to him as follows: "[a]Do not destroy the wise men of
Babylon! Take me [1]into the king's presence, and I will declare
the interpretation to the king."
25 Then Arioch hurriedly [a]brought Daniel [1]into the king's
presence and spoke to him as follows: "I have found a man
among the [2b]exiles from Judah who can make the interpretation known to the king!"
26 The king answered and said to Daniel, whose name was
[a]Belteshazzar, "Are you able to make known to me the dream
which I have seen and its interpretation?"
27 Daniel answered before the king and said, "As for the
mystery about which the king has inquired, neither [a]wise men,

conjurers, [1]magicians, *nor* diviners are able to declare *it* to the
king.
28 "However, there is a [a]God in heaven who reveals mysteries, and He has made known to King Nebuchadnezzar what
will take place in the [1b]latter days. This was your dream and
the visions [2]in your mind *while* on your bed.
29 "As for you, O king, *while* on your bed your thoughts
[1]turned to what would take place [2]in the future; and He who
reveals mysteries has made known to you what will take place.
30 "But as for me, this mystery has not been revealed to me
for any [a]wisdom [1]residing in me more than *in* any *other* living
man, but for the purpose of [b]making the interpretation known
to the king, and that you may [2]understand the [c]thoughts of
your [3]mind.
31 "You, O king, were looking and behold, there was a
single great statue; that statue, which was large and [1]of extraordinary splendor, was standing in front of you, and its appearance was [a]awesome.
32 "The head of that statue *was made* of fine gold, its
breast and its arms of silver, its belly and its thighs of bronze,
33 its legs of iron, its feet partly of iron and partly of clay.
34 "You [1]continued looking until a stone was cut out [a]with-
out hands, and it struck the statue on its feet of iron and clay,
and [b]crushed them.
35 "Then the iron, the clay, the bronze, the silver and the
gold were crushed [1]all at the same time, and became [a]like chaff
from the summer threshing floors; and the wind carried them
away so that [b]not a trace of them was found. But the stone
that struck the statue became a great [c]mountain and filled the
whole earth.
36 "This *was* the dream; now we shall tell its interpretation
before the king.
37 "You, O king, are the [a]king of kings, to whom the God
of heaven has given the [1]kingdom, the [b]power, the strength,
and the glory;
38 and wherever the sons of men dwell, *or* the [a]beasts of
the field, or the birds of the sky, He has given *them* into your
hand and has caused you to rule over them all. You are the
head of gold.
39 "And after you there will arise another kingdom inferior
to you, then another third kingdom of bronze, which will rule
over all the earth.
40 "Then there will be a fourth kingdom as strong as iron;
inasmuch as iron crushes and shatters all things, so, like iron
that breaks in pieces, it will crush and break all these in pieces.
41 "And in that you saw the feet and toes, partly of potter's
clay and partly of iron, it will be a divided kingdom; but it will
have in it the toughness of iron, inasmuch as you saw the iron
mixed with [1]common clay.
42 "And *as* the toes of the feet *were* partly of iron and
partly of pottery, *so* some of the kingdom will be strong and
part of it will be brittle.
43 "And in that you saw the iron mixed with [1]common
clay, they will combine with one another [2]in the seed of men;
but they will not adhere to one another, even as iron does not
combine with pottery.

27 [1]Or, *soothsayer priests*

28 [1]Lit., *end of the days* [2]Lit., *of your head* [a]Dan. 2:22, 45; Gen. 40:8; 41:16 [b]Dan. 10:14; Gen. 49:1; Is. 2:2; Mic. 4:1

29 [1]Lit., *came up* [2]Lit., *after this*

30 [1]Lit., *which is* [2]Lit., *know* [3]Lit., *heart* [a]Dan. 1:17; Gen. 41:16 [b]Is. 45:3 [c]Ps. 139:2; Amos 4:13

31 [1]Lit., *its splendor was surpassing* [a]Dan. 7:7; Is. 25: 3-5; Hab. 1:7

34 [1]Lit., *were* [a]Dan. 8:25; Zech. 4:6 [b]Ps. 2:9; Is. 60:12

35 [1]Lit., *like one* [a]Ps. 1:4; Is. 17:13; 41:15, 16; Hos. 13:3 [b]Ps. 37:10, 36 [c]Is. 2:2; Mic. 4:1

37 [1]Or, *sovereignty* [a]Is. 47:5; Jer. 27:6, 7; Ezek. 26:7 [b]Ps. 62:11

38 [a]Dan. 4:21, 22; Ps. 50:10, 11

41 [1]Lit., *clay of mud*

43 [1]Lit., *clay of mud* [2]Or, *with*

44 "And in the days of those kings the God of heaven will
[a]set up a [b]kingdom which will never be destroyed, and *that*
kingdom will not be [1]left for another people; it will [c]crush and
put an end to all these kingdoms, but it will itself endure
forever.
45 "Inasmuch as you saw that a stone was cut out of the
mountain without hands and that it crushed the iron, the
bronze, the clay, the silver, and the gold, the [a]great God has
made known to the king what [b]will take place [1]in the future; so
the dream is true, and its interpretation is trustworthy."
46 Then King Nebuchadnezzar fell on his face and did
[a]homage to Daniel, and gave orders to present to him an offering and [1b]fragrant incense.
47 The king answered Daniel and said, "Surely [a]your God
is a [b]God of gods and a Lord of kings and a [c]revealer of
mysteries, since you have been able to reveal this mystery."
48 Then the king [1a]promoted Daniel and gave him many
great gifts, and he made him ruler over the whole [b]province of
Babylon and chief [2]prefect over all the wise men of Babylon.
49 And Daniel made request of the king, and he appointed Shadrach, Meshach and Abed-nego over the administration of the province of Babylon, while Daniel *was* at the
king's [1a]court.

CHAPTER 3

NEBUCHADNEZZAR the king made an [a]image of gold,
the height of which *was* sixty [1]cubits *and* its width six [1]cubits;
he set it up on the plain of Dura in the [b]province of Babylon.
2 Then Nebuchadnezzar the king sent *word* to assemble
the [a]satraps, the prefects and the governors, the counselors, the
treasurers, the judges, the magistrates and all the rulers of the
provinces to come to the dedication of the image that Nebuchadnezzar the king had set up.
3 Then the satraps, the prefects and the governors, the
counselors, the treasurers, the judges, the magistrates and all
the rulers of the provinces were assembled for the dedication
of the image that Nebuchadnezzar the king had set up; and
they stood before the image that Nebuchadnezzar had set up.
4 Then the herald [a]loudly proclaimed: "To you [1]the
command is given, [b]O peoples, nations and *men of every*
[2]language,
5 that at the moment you [a]hear the sound of the horn,
flute, [1]lyre, [2]trigon, [3]psaltery, bagpipe, and all kinds of music,
you are to fall down and worship the golden image that Nebuchadnezzar the king has set up.
6 "But whoever does not fall down and worship shall [1]im-
mediately be [a]cast into the midst of a [b]furnace of blazing fire."
7 Therefore at that time, when all the peoples heard the
sound of the horn, flute, [1]lyre, trigon, psaltery, bagpipe, and all
kinds of music, all the peoples, nations and *men of every* [2]lan-
guage fell down *and* worshiped the golden image that Nebuchadnezzar the king had set up.
8 For this reason at that time certain [a]Chaldeans came
forward and [1b]brought charges against the Jews.

44 [1]Or, *passed on to* [a]Is. 9:6, 7 [b]Dan. 4:3, 34; 6:26; 7:14, 27; Ps. 145:13; Ezek. 37:25; Mic. 4:7 [c]Dan. 2:34, 35; Ps. 2:9; Is. 60:12

45 [1]Lit., *after this* [a]Dan. 2:29; Deut. 10:17; 2 Sam. 7:22; Ps. 48:1; Jer. 32:18, 19; Mal. 1:11 [b]Gen. 41:28, 32

46 [1]Lit., *sweet odors* [a]Dan. 3:5, 7; Acts 10:25; 14:13; Rev. 19:10; 22:8 [b]Lev. 26:31

47 [a]Dan. 3:15; 4:25 [b]Dan. 11:36; Deut. 10:17; Ps. 136:2, 3 [c]Dan. 2:22, 30; Amos 3:7

48 [1]Lit., *made great* [2]Lit., *of the prefects* [a]Dan. 2:6; 5:16, 29; Gen. 41:39-43 [b]Dan. 3:1, 12, 30

49 [1]Lit., *gate* [a]Esth. 2:19, 21; Amos 5:15

1 [1]A cubit equals approx. 18 inches [a]Dan. 2:31; Is. 46:6; Jer. 16:20; Hab. 2:19 [b]Dan. 3:30; 2:48

2 [a]Dan. 3:3, 27; 6:1-7

4 [1]Lit., *they command* [2]Lit., *tongue* [a]Dan. 4:14; Is. 40:9; 58:1; Rev. 18:2 [b]Dan. 3:7; 4:1; 6:25

5 [1]Or, *zither* [2]I.e., triangular lyre [3]Or, *a type of harp* [a]Dan. 3:7, 10, 15

6 [1]Or, *in the same hour* [a]Dan. 3:11, 15, 21; 6:7 [b]Jer. 29:22; Ezek. 22:18-22; Matt. 13:42, 50; Rev. 9:2; 14:11

7 [1]See notes at v. 5 [2]Lit., *tongues*

8 [1]Lit., *ate the pieces of* [a]Dan. 2:2, 10; 4:7 [b]Dan. 6:12, 13; Ezra 4:12-16; Esth. 3:8, 9

9 They responded and said to Nebuchadnezzar the king:
"[a]O king, live forever!
10 "You yourself, O king, have [a]made a decree that every
man who hears the sound of the horn, flute, [1]lyre, trigon,
psaltery, and bagpipe, and all kinds of music, is to fall down
and worship the golden image.
11 "But whoever does not fall down and worship shall be
cast into the midst of a furnace of blazing fire.
12 "There are certain Jews whom you have appointed over
the administration of the province of Babylon, *namely* Shadrach, Meshach, and Abed-nego. These men, O king, have disre-
garded you; they do not serve your gods or worship the golden
image which you have set up."
13 Then Nebuchadnezzar in [a]rage and anger gave orders
to bring Shadrach, Meshach, and Abed-nego; then these men
were brought before the king.
14 Nebuchadnezzar responded and said to them, "Is it
true, Shadrach, Meshach and Abed-nego, that you do not serve
[a]my gods or worship the golden image that I have set up?
15 "Now if you are ready, at the moment you hear the
sound of the horn, flute, [1]lyre, trigon, psaltery, and bagpipe,
and all kinds of music, to fall down and worship the image that
I have made, *very well*. But if you will not worship, you will
[2]immediately be cast into the midst of a furnace of blazing
fire; and [a]what god is there who can deliver you out of my
hands?"
16 [a]Shadrach, Meshach and Abed-nego answered and said
to the king, "O Nebuchadnezzar, we do not need to give you
an answer concerning this.
17 "[1]If it be *so*, our [a]God whom we serve is able to deliver
us from the furnace of blazing fire; [2]and He will deliver us out
of your hand, O king.
18 "[a]But *even* if *He does* not, let it be known to you, O
king, that we are not going to serve your gods or worship the
golden image that you have set up."
19 Then Nebuchadnezzar was filled with [a]wrath, and his
facial expression was altered toward Shadrach, Meshach and
Abed-nego. He answered [1]by giving orders to heat the furnace
[b]seven times more than it was usually heated.
20 And he commanded certain valiant warriors who *were*
in his army to tie up Shadrach, Meshach and Abed-nego, in
order to cast *them* into the furnace of blazing fire.
21 Then these men were tied up in their [1]trousers, their
[2]coats, their caps and their *other* clothes, and were cast into
the midst of the furnace of blazing fire.
22 For this reason, because the king's [1]command *was* [2a]ur-
gent and the furnace had been made extremely hot, the flame
of the fire slew those men who carried up Shadrach, Meshach
and Abed-nego.
23 But these three men, Shadrach, Meshach and Abed-
nego, fell into the midst of the furnace of blazing fire *still* tied
up.
24 Then Nebuchadnezzar the king was astounded and
stood up in haste; he responded and said to his high officials,
"Was it not three men we cast bound into the midst of the
fire?" They answered and said to the king, "Certainly, O king."

9 [a]Dan. 2:4; 5:10

10 [1]See notes at v. 5
[a]Dan. 3:4-6; 6:12; Esth. 3:12-14

13 [a]Dan. 2:12; 3:19

14 [a]Dan. 3:1; 4:8; Is. 46:1; Jer. 50:2

15 [1]See notes at v. 5 [2]Or, *in the same hour*
[a]Dan. 2:47; Ex. 5:2; Is. 36:18-20

16 [a]Dan. 1:7; 3:12

17 [1]Or, *If our God . . . is able* [2]Or, *then*
[a]Job 5:19; Ps. 27:1, 2; Is. 26:3, 4; Jer. 1:8; 15:20, 21

18 [a]Dan. 3:28; Josh. 24:15; 1 Kin. 19:14, 18; Is. 51:12, 13

19 [1]Lit., *and ordered to*
[a]Dan. 3:13; Esth. 7:7 [b]Lev. 26:18, 21, 24, 28

21 [1]Or, *cloaks* [2]Or, *leggings*

22 [1]Lit., *word* [2]Or, *harsh*
[a]Dan. 2:15; Ex. 12:33

25 [1]Lit., *there is no injury in them* [a]Ps. 91:3-9; Is. 43:2 [b]Jer. 1:8, 19; 15:21; Ezek. 34:10

26 [a]Dan. 3:17; 4:2 [b]Deut. 4:20; 1 Kin. 8:51; Jer. 11:4

27 [1]Lit., *power over* [2]Lit., *their* [3]Or, *cloaks* [4]Lit., *changed* [a]Is. 43:2; Heb.11:34 [b]Dan. 3:21

28 [1]Lit., *and changed the king's word* [a]Dan. 3:15; 2:47 [b]Dan. 3:25; 6:22; Ps. 34:7, 8; Is. 37:36; Acts 5:19; 12:7 [c]Ps. 22:4, 5; Is. 26:3, 4

29 [a]Dan. 3:12; 1:7, 19; 2:17, 49 [b]Dan. 2:5; Ezra 6:11 [c]Dan. 3:15; 2:47

30 [a]Dan. 3:12; 2:49

1 [1]Chap. 3:31 in Aram. [2]Lit., *tongue* [3]Or, *welfare* or *prosperity* [a]Dan. 6:25; Ezra 4:17

2 [a]Dan. 4:17, 24, 25, 32, 34; 3:26

3 [a]Dan. 6:27; Ps. 77:19; 105:27; Is. 25:1 [b]Dan. 4:34; 2:44; 6:26

4 [1]Chap. 4:1 in Aram. [a]Ps. 30:6; Is. 47:7, 8

5 [1]Lit., *of my head* [a]Dan. 4:10, 13; 2:28

6 [a]Dan. 2:2; Gen. 41:8

7 [1]Or, *soothsayer priests*, and so throughout the chap. [2]Or, *master astrologers* [3]Lit., *before* [a]Dan. 2:10, 27; 5:7 [b]Dan. 2:7; Is. 44:25; Jer. 27:9, 10

8 [1]Or, possibly, *the Spirit of the holy God*, and so throughout the chap. [2]Lit., *before* [a]Dan. 1:7; 2:26; 5:12 [b]Dan. 4:9, 18; 5:11, 14

9 [a]Dan. 1:20; 2:48; 5:11 [b]Dan. 4:8; Gen. 41:38 [c]Dan. 2:47; Ezek. 28:3

25 He answered and said, "Look! I see four men loosed
and [a]walking *about* in the midst of the fire [1]without harm, and
the appearance of the fourth is like a son of *the* [b]gods!"
26 Then Nebuchadnezzar came near to the door of the
furnace of blazing fire; he responded and said, "Shadrach,
Meshach and Abed-nego, come out, you servants of the [a]Most
High God, and come here!" Then Shadrach, Meshach and
Abed-nego [b]came out of the midst of the fire.
27 And the satraps, the prefects, the governors and the
king's high officials gathered around *and* saw in regard to these
men that the [a]fire had no [1]effect on [2]the bodies of these men
nor was the hair of their head singed, nor were their [3b]trousers
[4]damaged, nor had the smell of fire *even* come upon them.
28 Nebuchadnezzar responded and said, "Blessed be the
[a]God of Shadrach, Meshach, and Abed-nego, who has [b]sent
His angel and delivered His servants who put their [c]trust in
Him, [1]violating the king's command, and yielded up their
bodies so as not to serve or worship any god except their own
God.
29 "Therefore, I make a decree that any people, nation or
tongue that speaks anything offensive against the God of [a]Shad-
rach, Meshach and Abed-nego shall be torn limb from
limb and their [b]houses reduced to a rubbish heap, inasmuch as
there is [c]no other god who is able to deliver in this way."
30 Then the king [a]caused Shadrach, Meshach and Abed-
nego to prosper in the province of Babylon.

Chapter 4

1
NEBUCHADNEZZAR the king to all the peoples, nations,
and *men of every* [2]language that live in all the earth: "May
your [3a]peace abound!
2 "It has seemed good to me to declare the signs and
wonders which the [a]Most High God has done for me.
3 "How great are His [a]signs,
And how mighty are His wonders!
His [b]kingdom is an everlasting kingdom,
And His dominion is from generation to generation.
4 "[1]I, Nebuchadnezzar, was at ease in my house and [a]flour-
ishing in my palace.
5 "I saw a dream and it made me fearful; and *these* fanta-
sies *as I lay* on my bed and the [a]visions [1]in my mind kept
alarming me.
6 "So I gave orders to [a]bring into my presence all the wise
men of Babylon, that they might make known to me the interpretation of the dream.
7 "Then the [1a]magicians, the conjurers, the [2]Chaldeans,
and the diviners came in, and I related the dream [3]to them;
but they could not make its [b]interpretation known to me.
8 "But finally Daniel came in before me, whose name is
[a]Belteshazzar according to the name of my god, and in whom
is [1b]a spirit of the holy gods; and I related the dream [2]to him,
saying,
9 'O Belteshazzar, [a]chief of the magicians, since I know
that [b]a spirit of the holy gods is in you and [c]no mystery baffles

you, [d]tell *me* the visions of my dream which I have seen, along
with its interpretation.
10 'Now *these were* the visions [1]in my mind *as I lay* on my
bed: I was looking, and behold, *there was* a tree in the midst
of the [2]earth, and its height *was* great.

11 'The tree grew large and became strong,
And its height [a]reached to the sky,
And it *was* visible to the end of the whole earth.
12 'Its foliage *was* [a]beautiful and its fruit abundant,
And in it *was* food for all.
The [b]beasts of the field found [c]shade under it,
And the [d]birds of the sky dwelt in its branches,
And all [1]living creatures fed themselves from it.

13 'I was looking in the visions [1]in my mind *as I lay* on my
bed, and behold, an *angelic* watcher, a [a]holy one, descended
from heaven.

14 'He shouted out and spoke as follows:
"[a]Chop down the tree and cut off its branches,
Strip off its foliage and scatter its fruit;
Let the [b]beasts flee from under it,
And the birds from its branches.
15 "Yet [a]leave the stump [1]with its roots in the ground,
But with a band of iron and bronze *around it*
In the new grass of the field;
And let him be drenched with the dew of heaven,
And let [2]him share with the beasts in the grass of the
earth.
16 "Let his [1]mind be changed from *that of* a man,
And let a beast's [1]mind be given to him,
And let [a]seven [2]periods of time [b]pass over him.
17 "This sentence is by the decree of the *angelic* watchers,
And the decision is a command of the holy ones,
In order that the living may [a]know
That the Most High is ruler over the realm of mankind,
And [b]bestows it on whom He wishes,
And sets over it the [c]lowliest of men."

18 'This is the dream *which* I, King Nebuchadnezzar, have
seen. Now you, Belteshazzar, tell *me* its interpretation, inasmuch as none of the [a]wise men of my kingdom is able to make
known to me the interpretation; but you are able, for a spirit
of the holy gods is in you.'
19 "Then Daniel, whose name is Belteshazzar, was appalled
for a while as his [a]thoughts alarmed him. The king responded
and said, 'Belteshazzar, do not [b]let the dream or its interpretation alarm you.' Belteshazzar answered and said, '[c]My lord, *if
only* the dream applied to those who hate you, and its interpretation to [d]your adversaries!
20 'The tree that you saw, which became large and grew
strong, whose height reached to the sky and was visible to all
the earth,
21 and whose foliage *was* beautiful and its fruit abundant,
and in which *was* food for all, under which the beasts of the
field dwelt and in whose branches the birds of the sky lodged—
22 it is [a]you, O king; for you have become great and grown
strong, and your [1]majesty has become great and reached to the
sky and your [b]dominion to the end of the earth.

9 [d]Dan. 2:4, 5; Gen. 41:15

10 [1]Lit., *of my head* [2]Or, *land*, and so throughout the chap.

11 [a]Dan. 4:21, 22; Deut. 9:1

12 [1]Lit., *flesh*
[a]Ezek. 31:7 [b]Jer. 27:6; Ezek. 31:6 [c]Lam. 4:20 [d]Matt. 13:32; Luke 13:19

13 [1]Lit., *of my head*
[a]Dan. 8:13; Deut. 33:2; Ps. 89:7

14 [a]Dan. 4:23; Ezek. 31:10-14; Matt. 3:10; 7:19; Luke 13:7-9 [b]Dan. 4:12; Ezek. 31:12, 13

15 [1]Lit., *of* [2]Lit., *his portion be with*
[a]Job 14:7-9

16 [1]Lit., *heart* [2]I.e., years
[a]Dan. 4:23, 25, 32; 7:25; 11:13 [b]1 Chr. 29:30

17 [a]Ps. 9:16; 83:18 [b]Dan. 4:25; 5:18, 19; Jer. 27:5-7 [c]Dan. 11:21; 1 Sam. 2:8

18 [a]Dan. 4:7; 5:8, 15; Gen. 41:8

19 [a]Dan. 7:15, 28; 8:27; 10:16, 17; Jer. 4:19 [b]Dan. 4:4, 5; 1 Sam. 3:17 [c]Dan. 4:24; 10:16; 2 Sam. 18:31; 1 Kin. 18:7 [d]2 Sam. 18:32; Jer. 29:7

22 [1]Lit., *greatness*
[a]Dan. 2:37, 38; 2 Sam. 12:7 [b]Jer. 27:6, 7

23 [1]Lit., *of* [2]Lit., *his portion be with* [3]I.e., years

24 [a]Job 40:11, 12; Ps. 107:40

25 [1]I.e., years [a]Dan. 4:33; 5:21 [b]Dan. 4:2, 17; Ps. 83:18; Jer. 27:5 [c]Dan. 4:17; 2:37; 5:21

26 [1]Lit., *of* [2]Lit., *enduring* [a]Dan. 4:31; 2:18, 19, 28, 37, 44

27 [1]Or, *redeem now your sins* [a]Gen. 41:33-37 [b]Prov. 28:13; Is. 55:6, 7; Ezek. 18:21, 22 [c]Ps. 41:1-3; Is. 58:6, 7, 10 [d]1 Kin. 21:29; Jon. 3:9

28 [a]Num. 23:19; Zech. 1:6

29 [a]2 Pet. 3:9

30 [1]Lit., *answered* [2]Lit., *house* [a]Hab. 2:4

31 [1]Lit., *fell* [2]Or, *kingdom*

32 [1]I.e., years

33 [a]Dan. 4:25; 5:21

34 [1]Lit., *the days* [2]Lit., *knowledge* [a]Dan. 4:2; 5:18, 21 [b]Dan. 6:26; 12:7; Ps. 102:24 [c]Dan. 4:3; Ps. 145:13; Jer. 10:10

35 [1]Lit., *strike against* [a]Is. 40:17 [b]Dan. 6:27; Ps. 135:6 [c]Job 42:2; Is. 43:13 [d]Is. 45:9

23 'And in that the king saw an *angelic* watcher, a holy
one, descending from heaven and saying, "Chop down the tree
and destroy it; yet leave the stump [1]with its roots in the
ground, but with a band of iron and bronze *around it* in the
new grass of the field, and let him be drenched with the dew of
heaven, and let [2]him share with the beasts of the field until
seven [3]periods of time pass over him";
24 this is the interpretation, O king, and this is the decree
of the Most High, which has [a]come upon my lord the king:
25 that you be [a]driven away from mankind, and your dwelling place be with the beasts of the field, and you be given grass
to eat like cattle and be drenched with the dew of heaven; and
seven [1]periods of time will pass over you, until you recognize
that the [b]Most High is ruler over the realm of mankind, and
[c]bestows it on whomever He wishes.
26 'And in that it was commanded to leave the stump [1]with
the roots of the tree, your kingdom will be [2]assured to you
after you recognize that *it is* [a]Heaven *that* rules.
27 'Therefore, O king, may my [a]advice be pleasing to you:
[1b]break away now from your sins by *doing* righteousness, and
from your iniquities by [c]showing mercy to *the* poor, in case
there may be a [d]prolonging of your prosperity.'
28 "All *this* [a]happened to Nebuchadnezzar the king.
29 "[a]Twelve months later he was walking on the *roof of* the
royal palace of Babylon.
30 "The king [1]reflected and said, 'Is this not Babylon the
[a]great, which I myself have built as a royal [2]residence by the
might of my power and for the glory of my majesty?'
31 "While the word *was* in the king's mouth, a voice [1]came
from heaven, *saying*, 'King Nebuchadnezzar, to you it is declared: [2]sovereignty has been removed from you,
32 and you will be driven away from mankind, and your
dwelling place *will be* with the beasts of the field. You will be
given grass to eat like cattle, and seven [1]periods of time will
pass over you, until you recognize that the Most High is ruler
over the realm of mankind, and bestows it on whomever He
wishes.'
33 "Immediately the word concerning Nebuchadnezzar
was fulfilled; and he was [a]driven away from mankind and began eating grass like cattle, and his body was drenched with the
dew of heaven, until his hair had grown like eagles' *feathers*
and his nails like birds' *claws*.
34 "But at the end of [1]that period I, Nebuchadnezzar,
raised my eyes toward heaven, and my [2]reason returned to me,
and I blessed the [a]Most High and praised and honored Him
who [b]lives forever;

For His dominion is an [c]everlasting dominion,
And His kingdom *endures* from generation to generation.

35 "And [a]all the inhabitants of the earth are accounted as nothing,
But [b]He does according to His will in the host of heaven
And *among* the inhabitants of earth;
And [c]no one can [1]ward off His hand
Or say to Him, '[d]What hast Thou done?'

36 "At that time my [1a]reason returned to me. And my majesty and [b]splendor were [2]restored to me for the glory of my
kingdom, and my counselors and my nobles began seeking me
out; so I was re-established in my [3]sovereignty, and surpassing
[c]greatness was added to me.
37 "Now I Nebuchadnezzar praise, exalt, and honor the
King of [a]heaven, for [b]all His works are [1]true and His ways [2]just,
and He is able to humble those who [c]walk in pride."

CHAPTER 5

BELSHAZZAR the king [1]held a great [a]feast for a thousand
of his nobles, and he was drinking wine in the presence of the
thousand.
2 When Belshazzar tasted the wine, he gave orders to
bring the gold and silver [a]vessels which Nebuchadnezzar his
[1]father had taken out of the temple which *was* in Jerusalem, in
order that the king and his nobles, his wives, and his concubines might drink from them.
3 Then they brought the gold vessels that had been taken
out of the temple, the house of God which *was* in Jerusalem;
and the king and his nobles, his wives, and his concubines
drank from them.
4 They [a]drank the wine and praised the gods of [b]gold and
silver, of bronze, iron, wood, and stone.
5 Suddenly the fingers of a man's hand emerged and
began writing opposite the lampstand on the plaster of the
wall of the king's palace, and the king saw the [1]back of the
hand that did the writing.
6 Then the king's [1a]face grew pale, and his thoughts
alarmed him; and his [b]hip joints went slack, and his [c]knees
began knocking together.
7 The king called aloud to bring in the [a]conjurers, the
[1]Chaldeans and the diviners. The king spoke and said to the
wise men of Babylon, "Any man who can read this inscription
and explain its interpretation to me will be [b]clothed with
purple, and *have* a [c]necklace of gold around his neck, and have
authority as [2d]third *ruler* in the kingdom."
8 Then all the king's wise men came in, but they could
not read the inscription or make known its interpretation to
the king.
9 Then King Belshazzar was greatly [a]alarmed, his [1b]face
grew *even* paler, and his nobles were perplexed.
10 The queen entered the banquet [1]hall because of the
words of the king and his nobles; the queen spoke and said,
"[a]O king, live forever! Do not let your thoughts alarm you or
your [2]face be pale.
11 "There is a [a]man in your kingdom in whom is [1]a [b]spirit
of the holy gods; and in the days of your father, illumination,
insight, and wisdom like the wisdom of the gods were found in
him. And King Nebuchadnezzar, your father, your father [2]the
king, appointed him chief of the [3]magicians, conjurers, [4]Chal-
deans, *and* diviners.
12 "*This was* because an [a]extraordinary spirit, knowledge
and insight, interpretation of dreams, explanation of enigmas,

36 [1]Lit., *knowledge* [2]Lit., *returning* [3]Or, *kingdom* [a]Dan. 4:34; 2 Chr. 33:12, 13 [b]Dan. 2:31 [c]Dan. 4:22; Prov. 22:4

37 [1]Lit., *truth* [2]Lit., *justice* [a]Dan. 4:26; 5:23 [b]Deut. 32:4; Ps. 33:4, 5; Is. 5:16 [c]Dan. 5:20; Ex. 18:11; Job 40:11, 12

1 [1]Lit., *made* [a]Esth. 1:3; Is. 22:12-14

2 [1]Or, *forefather*, and so throughout the chap. [a]Dan. 1:2; 2 Kin. 24:13; 25:15; Ezra 1:7-11

4 [a]Dan. 5:23; Is. 42:8 [b]Dan. 3:1; Ps. 115:4; 135:15; Is. 40:19, 20; Hab. 2:19

5 [1]Or, *palm*

6 [1]Lit., *brightness changed for him* [a]Dan. 5:9, 10; 7:28 [b]Ps. 69:23; Nah. 2:10 [c]Ezek. 7:17; 21:7

7 [1]Or, *master astrologers* [2]Or, *a triumvir* [a]Dan. 5:11, 15; 4:6, 7; Is. 44:25; 47:13 [b]Dan. 5:16, 29; Gen. 41:42-44 [c]Ezek. 16:11 [d]Dan. 5:16, 29; 2:48; 6:2, 3

9 [1]Lit., *brightness was changing upon him* [a]Dan. 5:6; 2:1; Job 18:11; Is. 21:2-4; Jer 6:24 [b]Is. 13:6-8

10 [1]Lit., *house* [2]Lit., *brightness be changed* [a]Dan. 3:9; 6:6

11 [1]Or possibly, *the Spirit of the holy God* [2]Or, *O king* [3]Or, *soothsayer priests* [4]Or, *master astrologers* [a]Dan. 2:47; Gen. 41:11-15 [b]Dan. 5:14; 4:8, 9, 18

12 [a]Dan 5:14; 6:3

and solving of difficult problems were found in this Daniel,
whom the king named [b]Belteshazzar. Let Daniel now be summoned, and he will declare the interpretation."
13 Then Daniel was brought in before the king. The king
spoke and said to Daniel, "Are you that Daniel who is one of
the [1a]exiles from Judah, whom my father the king [b]brought
from Judah?
14 "Now I have heard about you that [1]a spirit of the gods is
in you, and that illumination, insight, and extraordinary wisdom have been found in you.
15 "Just now the wise men *and* the conjurers were brought
in before me that they might read this inscription and make its
interpretation known to me, but they [a]could not declare the
interpretation of the [1]message.
16 "But I personally have heard about you, that you are
able to give interpretations and solve difficult problems. Now
if you are able to read the inscription and make its [a]interpreta-
tion known to me, you will be clothed with purple and *wear* a
necklace of gold around your neck, and you will have authority
as the [1]third *ruler* in the kingdom."
17 Then Daniel answered and said before the king,
"[1]Keep your [a]gifts for yourself, or give your rewards to someone else; however, I will read the inscription to the king and
make the interpretation known to him.
18 "[1]O king, the [a]Most High God [b]granted [2]sovereignty,
[c]grandeur, glory, and majesty to Nebuchadnezzar your father.
19 "And because of the grandeur which He bestowed on
him, all the peoples, nations, and *men of every* [1]language
feared and trembled before him; [a]whomever he wished he
killed, and whomever he wished he spared alive; and whomever
he wished he elevated, and whomever he wished he humbled.
20 "But when his heart was [a]lifted up and his spirit became
so [1b]proud that he behaved arrogantly, he was [c]deposed from
his royal throne, and *his* glory was taken away from him.
21 "He was also [a]driven away from [1]mankind, and his heart
was made like *that of* beasts, and his dwelling place *was* with
the [b]wild donkeys. He was given grass to eat like cattle, and his
body was drenched with the dew of heaven, until he recognized that the [c]Most High God is ruler over the realm of
mankind, and *that* He sets over it whomever He wishes.
22 "Yet [a]you, his [1]son, Belshazzar, have [b]not humbled your
heart, [2]even though you knew all this,
23 but you have [a]exalted yourself against the [b]Lord of
heaven; and they have brought the vessels of His house before
you, and you and your nobles, your wives and your concubines
have been drinking wine from them; and you have praised the
gods of silver and gold, of bronze, iron, wood and stone, which
do not [c]see, hear or understand. But the God [d]in whose hand
are your life-breath and your [e]ways, you have not glorified.
24 "Then the [1]hand was sent from Him, and this inscription was written out.
25 "Now this is the inscription that was written out:
'[1]MENĒ, [1]MENĒ, [2]TEKĒL [3]UPHARSIN.'
26 "This is the interpretation of the [1]message: 'MENĒ'—
God has numbered your kingdom and [a]put an end to it.

12 [b]Dan. 1:7; 4:8

13 [1]Lit., *sons of the exile* [a]Dan. 2:25; 6:13; Ezra 4:1; 6:16, 19, 20 [b]Dan. 1:1, 2

14 [1]Or possibly, *the Spirit of God*

15 [1]Lit., *word* [a]Dan. 5:8; Is. 47:12

16 [1]Or, *triumvir* [a]Gen. 40:8

17 [1]Lit., *Let . . . be for* [a]2 Kin. 5:16

18 [1]Lit., *You, O king* [2]Or, *the kingdom* [a]Dan. 5:21; 4:2 [b]Dan. 2:37, 38; 4:17 [c]Jer. 25:9; 27:5-7

19 [1]Lit., *tongue* [a]Dan. 2:12, 13; 3:6; 11:3, 16, 36

20 [1]Lit., *strong* [a]Dan. 4:30, 31; Ex. 9:17; Job 15:25; Is. 14:13-15 [b]2 Kin. 17:14; 2 Chr. 36:13 [c]Job 40:11, 12; Jer. 13:18

21 [1]Lit., *the sons of man* [a]Dan. 4:33; Job 30:3-7 [b]Job 39:5-8 [c]Dan. 4:34, 35; Ex. 9:14-16; Ps. 83:17, 18; Ezek. 17:24

22 [1]Or, *descendant* [2]Lit., *inasmuch as you* [a]Ps. 119:46 [b]Ex. 10:3; 2 Chr. 33:23; 36:12

23 [a]Dan. 5:3, 4; 2 Kin. 14:10; Is. 2:12; 37:23; Jer. 50:29 [b]Dan. 4:37 [c]Ps. 115:4-8; Is. 37:19; Hab. 2:18, 19 [d]Job 12:10 [e]Job 31:4; Ps. 139:3; Prov. 20:24; Jer. 10:23

24 [1]Lit., *palm of the hand*

25 [1]Or, *a mina* (50 shekels)—from verb "to number" [2]Or, *a shekel*—from verb "to weigh" [3]Or, *and half-shekels* (sing.: *peres*—)from verb "to divide"

26 [1]Lit., *word* [a]Is. 13:6, 17; Jer. 27:7; 50:41-43

27 " 'TEKĒL'—you have been [a]weighed on the scales and
found deficient.
28 " 'PERĒS'—your kingdom has been divided and given
over to the [a]Medes and [1]Persians."
29 Then Belshazzar gave orders, and they clothed Daniel
with purple and *put* a necklace of gold around his neck, and
issued a proclamation concerning him that he *now* had authority as the [1]third *ruler* in the kingdom.
30 That same night Belshazzar the Chaldean king was
[a]slain.
31 [1]So [a]Darius the Mede received the kingdom at about
the age of sixty-two.

Chapter 6

1
It seemed good to Darius to appoint [a]120 satraps over the
kingdom, that they should be in charge of the whole kingdom,
2 and over them three commissioners (of whom [a]Daniel
was one), that these satraps might be accountable to them, and
that the king might not suffer [b]loss.
3 Then this Daniel began distinguishing himself [1]among
the commissioners and satraps because [2]he possessed an [a]ex-
traordinary spirit, and the king planned to appoint him over
the [b]entire kingdom.
4 Then the commissioners and satraps began [a]trying to
find a ground of accusation against Daniel in regard to [1]govern-
ment affairs; but they could find [b]no ground of accusation or
evidence of corruption, inasmuch as he was faithful, and no
negligence or corruption was *to be* found in him.
5 Then these men said, "We shall not find any ground of
accusation against this Daniel unless we find *it* against him
with regard to the [a]law of his God."
6 Then these commissioners and satraps came [1]by agreement to the king and spoke to him as follows: "King Darius,
[a]live forever!
7 "All the commissioners of the kingdom, the prefects and
the satraps, the high officials and the governors have [a]con-
sulted together that the king should establish a statute and
enforce an injunction that anyone who makes a petition to any
god or man besides you, O king, for thirty days, shall [b]be cast
into the lions' [1]den.
8 "Now, O king, [a]establish the injunction and sign the
document so that it may not be changed, according to the [b]law
of the Medes and Persians, which [1]may not be revoked."
9 Therefore King Darius [a]signed the document, that is,
the injunction.
10 Now when Daniel knew that the document was signed,
he entered his house (now in his roof chamber he had windows
open [a]toward Jerusalem); and he continued [b]kneeling on his
knees three times a day, [c]praying and [d]giving thanks before his
God, [1]as he had been doing previously.
11 Then these men came [1a]by agreement and found Daniel making petition and supplication before his God.
12 Then they approached and [a]spoke before the king
about the king's injunction, "Did you not sign an injunction

27 [a]Job 31:6; Ps. 62:9

28 [1]Aram.: *PĀRĀS* [a]Dan. 5:31; 6:8, 28; Is. 21:2; 45:1, 2

29 [1]Or, *triumvir*

30 [a]Is. 21:4-9; 47:9; Jer. 51:11, 31, 39, 57

31 [1]Chap. 6:1 in Aram. [a]Dan. 6:1; 9:1

1 [1]Chap. 6:2 in Aram. [a]Esth. 1:1

2 [a]Dan. 2:48, 49; 5:16, 29 [b]Ezra 4:22; Esth. 7:4

3 [1]Lit., *above* [2]Lit., *there was in him* [a]Dan. 5:12, 14; 9:23 [b]Gen. 41:40; Esth. 10:3

4 [1]Lit., *the kingdom* [a]Dan. 3:8; Gen. 43:18; Judg. 14:4; Jer. 20:10; Luke 20:20 [b]Luke 20:26; 23:14, 15

5 [a]Acts 24:13-16, 20, 21

6 [1]Or, *thronging* [a]Dan. 6:21; 5:10

7 [1]Or, *pit*, and so throughout the chap. [a]Ps. 59:3; 62:4; 64:2-6; 83:1-3 [b]Dan. 6:16; 3:6; Ps. 10:9

8 [1]Lit., *does not pass away* [a]Esth. 3:12; 8:10; Is. 10:1 [b]Dan. 6:12, 15: Esth. 1:19; 8:8

9 [a]Ps. 118:9; 146:3

10 [1]Or, *because* [a]1 Kin. 8:48, 49; Ps. 5:7; Jon. 2:4 [b]Ps. 95:6 [c]Dan. 9:4-19; Luke 14:26; Acts 4:17, 19 [d]Ps. 34:1; Phil. 4:6; 1 Thess. 5:17, 18

11 [1]Or, *thronging* [a]Dan. 6:6; Ps. 37:32, 33

12 [a]Dan. 3:8-12; Acts 16:19-21

that any man who makes a petition to any god or man besides
you, O king, for thirty days, is to be cast into the lions' den?"
The king answered and said, "The statement is true, according
to the [b]law of the Medes and Persians, which [1]may not be
revoked."
13 Then they answered and spoke before the king, "Daniel, who is one of the [1]exiles from Judah, pays [a]no attention
to you, O king, or to the injunction which you signed, but
keeps making his petition three times a day."
14 Then, as soon as the king heard this statement, he was
deeply [a]distressed and set *his* mind on delivering Daniel; and
even until sunset he kept exerting himself to rescue him.
15 Then these men came [1]by agreement to the king and
said to the king, "Recognize, O king, that it is a [a]law of the
Medes and Persians that no injunction or statute which the
king establishes may be changed."
16 Then the king gave orders, and Daniel was brought in
and [a]cast into the lions' den. The king spoke and said to Daniel, "[1b]Your God whom you constantly serve will Himself
deliver you."
17 And a [a]stone was brought and laid over the mouth of
the den; and the king sealed it with his own signet ring and
with the signet rings of his nobles, so that nothing might be
changed in regard to Daniel.
18 Then the king went off to his palace and spent the
night [a]fasting, and no entertainment was brought before him;
and his [b]sleep fled from him.
19 Then the king arose with the dawn, at the break of day,
and went in haste to the lions' den.
20 And when he had come near the den to Daniel, he
cried out with a troubled voice. The king spoke and said to
Daniel, "Daniel, servant of the living God, has your God,
whom you constantly serve, been [a]able to deliver you from the
lions?"
21 Then Daniel spoke [1]to the king, "O king, live forever!
22 "My God [a]sent His angel and [b]shut the lions' mouths,
and they have not harmed me, inasmuch as [1]I was found innocent before Him; and also [2]toward you, O king, I have committed no crime."
23 Then the king was very pleased and gave orders for
Daniel to be taken up out of the den. So Daniel was taken up
out of the den, and no injury whatever was found on him,
because he had [a]trusted in his God.
24 The king then gave orders, and they brought those men
who had [1]maliciously accused Daniel, and they [a]cast them,
their [b]children, and their wives into the lions' den; and they
had not reached the bottom of the den before the lions overpowered them and crushed all their bones.
25 Then Darius the king wrote to all the [a]peoples, nations,
and *men of every* [1]language who were living in all the land:
"[b]May your [2]peace abound!
26 "[1]I [a]make a decree that in all the dominion of my kingdom men are to fear and tremble before the God of Daniel;
For He is the [b]living God and [c]enduring forever,
And His kingdom is one which will not be destroyed,
And His dominion *will be* [2]forever.

12 [1]Lit., *does not pass away* [b]Dan. 6:8; Esth. 1:19

13 [1]Lit., *sons of the exile* [a]Dan. 3:12; Esth. 3:8; Acts 5:29

14 [a]Mark 6:26

15 [1]Or, *thronging* [a]Dan. 6:8, 12; Esth. 8:8; Ps. 94:20, 21

16 [1]Or, *May your God, . . . Himself deliver you* [a]Dan. 6:7; 2 Sam. 3:39; Jer. 38:5 [b]Dan. 6:20; 3:17, 28; Job 5:19; Ps. 37:39, 40

17 [a]Lam. 3:53; Matt. 27:66

18 [a]2 Sam. 12:16, 17 [b]Dan. 2:1; Esth. 6:1; Ps. 77:4

20 [a]Dan. 3:17; Gen. 18:14; Num. 11:23; Jer. 32:17

21 [1]Lit., *with*

22 [1]Lit., *innocence was found for me* [2]Lit., *before* [a]Dan. 3:28; Num. 20:16; Is. 63:9; Acts 12:11 [b]Ps. 91:11-13; 2 Tim. 4:17; Heb. 11:33

23 [a]Dan. 3:17, 28; 1 Chr. 5:20; 2 Chr. 20:20; Ps. 118:8, 9; Is. 26:3

24 [1]Lit., *eaten the pieces of Daniel* [a]Deut. 19:18, 19; Esth. 7:10 [b]Deut. 24:16; 2 Kin. 14:6; Esth. 9:10

25 [1]Lit., *tongues* [2]Or, *welfare* or *prosperity* [a]Dan. 4:1; Ezra 1:1, 2; Esth. 3:12; 8:9 [b]Ezra 4:17; 1 Pet. 1:2

26 [1]Lit., *from me a decree is made* [2]Lit., *to the end* [a]Dan. 3:29; Ezra 6:8-12; 7:13, 21 [b]Dan. 6:20; Hos. 1:10; Rom. 9:26 [c]Ps. 93:1, 2; Mal. 3:6

27 "He delivers and rescues and performs signs and wonders
In heaven and on earth,
Who has *also* delivered Daniel from the [1]power of the lions."

28 So this Daniel enjoyed success in the reign of Darius
and in the reign of Cyrus the Persian.

Chapter 7

In the first year of Belshazzar king of Babylon Daniel saw a
[a]dream and visions [1]in his mind *as he lay* on his bed; then he
[b]wrote the dream down *and* related the following [2]summary of
[3]it.
2 Daniel [1]said, "I was looking in my vision by night, and
behold, the [a]four winds of heaven were stirring up the great
sea.
3 "And four great [a]beasts were coming up from the sea,
different from one another.
4 "The first *was* like a lion and had *the* wings of an eagle. I
kept looking until its wings were plucked, and it was lifted up
from the ground and made to stand on two feet like a man; a
human [1]mind also was given to it.
5 "And behold, another beast, a second one, resembling a
bear. And it was raised up on one side, and three ribs *were* in
its mouth between its teeth; and thus they said to it, 'Arise,
devour much meat!'
6 "After this I kept looking, and behold, another one, like
a leopard, which had on its [1]back four wings of a bird; the beast
also had four heads, and dominion was given to it.
7 "After this I kept looking in the night visions, and behold, a fourth beast, dreadful and terrifying and extremely
strong; and it had large iron teeth. It devoured and crushed,
and trampled down the remainder with its feet; and it was
different from all the beasts that were before it, and it had [a]ten
horns.
8 "While I was contemplating the horns, behold, another
horn, a little one, came up among them, and three of the first
horns were pulled out by the roots before it; and behold, [1]this
horn possessed eyes like the eyes of a man, and a mouth uttering great *boasts*.

9 "I kept looking
Until thrones were set up,
And the Ancient of Days took *His* seat;
His [a]vesture *was* like white snow,
And the [b]hair of His head like pure wool.
His [c]throne *was* [1]ablaze with flames,
Its [d]wheels *were* a burning fire.
10 "A river of [a]fire was flowing
And coming out from before Him;
[b]Thousands upon thousands were attending Him,
And [c]myriads upon myriads were standing before Him;
The [d]court sat,
And [e]the books were opened.

11 "Then I kept looking because of the sound of the [1]boast-

27 [1]Lit., *hand*

1 [1]Lit., *of his head* [2]Or, *beginning* [3]Lit., *words* [a]Dan. 1:17; 2:1, 26-28; 4:5-9; Job 33:14-16; Joel 2:28 [b]Jer. 36:4, 32

2 [1]Lit., *spoke and said* [a]Rev. 7:1

3 [a]Rev. 13:1

4 [1]Lit., *heart*

6 [1]Or, *sides*

7 [a]Rev. 12:3; 13:1

8 [1]Lit., *in this horn* were *eyes*

9 [1]Lit., *flames of fire* [a]Mark 9:3 [b]Rev. 1:14 [c]Ezek. 1:13, 26 [d]Ezek. 10:2, 6

10 [a]Ps. 18:8; 50:3; 97:3; Is. 30:27, 33 [b]Rev. 5:11 [c]Deut. 33:2 [d]Dan. 7:22, 26; Ps. 96:11-13 [e]Dan. 12:1; Rev. 20:11-15

11 [1]Lit., *great*

11 [2]Lit., *of the fire* [a]Rev. 19:20; 20:10

13 [a]Matt. 26:64; Mark 14:62

14 [1]Or, *sovereignty* [2]Lit., *tongue* [a]Dan. 7:27; 1 Cor. 15:27; Eph. 1:20-22; Phil. 2:9-11; Rev. 1:6 [b]Dan. 2:37 [c]Ps. 72:11; 102:22 [d]Heb. 12:28

15 [1]Lit., *in the midst of* its *sheath* [2]Lit., *of my head* [a]Dan. 7:28; 4:19

16 [1]Lit., *truth concerning* [a]Zech. 1:9, 19; Rev. 5:5; 7:13, 14 [b]Dan. 8:16, 17; 9:22

18 [1]Lit., *holy ones* [2]Lit., *and unto the age of the ages* [a]Dan. 7:22, 25, 27 [b]Dan. 7:14; Ps. 149:5-9; Is. 60:12-14; Rev. 2:26, 27; 20:4

19 [1]Lit., *truth concerning* [2]Lit., *of them*

20 [1]Lit., *its appearance was larger*

21 [1]Lit., *holy ones* [a]Rev. 13:7

22 [1]Lit., *given for* [2]Lit., *holy ones* [a]Dan. 7:10; 1 Cor. 6:2, 3

25 [1]Lit., *words* [2]Lit., *holy ones* [3]I.e., the saints [4]I.e., year(s) [a]Dan. 11:36; Rev. 13:6 [b]Dan. 3:26; 4:2, 17, 34 [c]Rev. 13:7 [d]Dan. 12:7; Rev. 12:14

ful words which the horn was speaking; I kept looking until
the beast was slain, and its body was destroyed and given to the
[a]burning [2]fire.
12 "As for the rest of the beasts, their dominion was taken
away, but an extension of life was granted to them for an
appointed period of time.
13 "I kept looking in the night visions,
And behold, with the clouds of heaven
One like a [a]Son of Man was coming,
And He came up to the Ancient of Days
And was presented before Him.
14 "And to Him was given [a]dominion,
Glory and [1b]a kingdom,
[c]That all the peoples, nations, and *men of every* [2]language
Might serve him.
His dominion is an everlasting dominion
Which will not pass away;
And His kingdom is one
Which will [d]not be destroyed.
15 "As for me, Daniel, my spirit was distressed [1]within me,
and the visions [2]in my mind kept [a]alarming me.
16 "I approached one of those who were [a]standing by and
began asking him the [1]exact meaning of all this. So he [b]told me
and made known to me the interpretation of these things:
17 'These great beasts, which are four *in number*, are four
kings *who* will arise from the earth.
18 'But the [1a]saints of the Highest One will [b]receive the
kingdom and possess the kingdom forever, [2]for all ages to
come.'
19 "Then I desired to know the [1]exact meaning of the
fourth beast, which was different from all [2]the others, exceedingly dreadful, with its teeth of iron and its claws of bronze,
and which devoured, crushed, and trampled down the remainder with its feet,
20 and *the meaning* of the ten horns that *were* on its head,
and the other *horn* which came up, and before which three *of*
them fell, namely, that horn which had eyes and a mouth
uttering great *boasts*, and [1]which was larger in appearance than
its associates.
21 "I kept looking, and that horn was [a]waging war with the
[1]saints and overpowering them
22 until the Ancient of Days came, and [a]judgment was
[1]passed in favor of the [2]saints of the Highest One, and the time
arrived when the [2]saints took possession of the kingdom.
23 "Thus he said: 'The fourth beast will be a fourth kingdom on the earth, which will be different from all the *other*
kingdoms, and it will devour the whole earth and tread it down
and crush it.
24 'As for the ten horns, out of this kingdom ten kings will
arise; and another will arise after them, and he will be different
from the previous ones and will subdue three kings.
25 'And he will [a]speak [1]out against the [b]Most High and
[c]wear down the [2]saints of the Highest One, and he will intend
to make alterations in times and in law; and [3]they will be given
into his hand for a [4d]time, [4]times, and half a [4]time.

26 'But the court will sit *for judgment,* and his dominion
will be [a]taken away, [1]annihilated and destroyed [2]forever.
27 'Then the [1a]sovereignty, the dominion, and the greatness of *all* the kingdoms under the whole heaven will be given
to the people of the [2]saints of the Highest One; His kingdom
will be an [b]everlasting kingdom, and all the dominions will
[c]serve and obey Him.'
28 "[1]At this point the revelation ended. As for me, Daniel,
my thoughts were greatly alarming me and my [2]face grew pale,
but I [a]kept the matter [3]to myself."

Chapter 8

IN the third year of the reign of Belshazzar the king a vision
appeared to me, [1]Daniel, subsequent to the one which appeared to me [2]previously.
2 And I [a]looked in the vision, and it came about while I
was looking, that I was in the citadel of [b]Susa, which is in the
province of [c]Elam; and I looked in the vision, and I myself was
beside the Ulai [1]Canal.
3 Then I lifted my gaze and looked, and behold, a [a]ram
which had two horns was standing in front of the [1]canal. Now
the two horns *were* [2]long, but one *was* [2]longer than the other,
with the [2]longer one coming up last.
4 I saw the ram [a]butting westward, northward, and southward, and no *other* beasts could stand before him, nor was
there anyone to rescue from his [1]power; but he did as he
pleased and magnified *himself.*
5 While I was observing, behold, a male goat was coming
from the west over the surface of the whole earth without
touching the ground; and the [1]goat *had* a [a]conspicuous horn
between his eyes.
6 And he came up to the ram that had the two horns,
which I had seen standing in front of the [1]canal, and rushed at
him in his mighty wrath.
7 And I saw him come beside the ram, and he was enraged at him; and he struck the ram and shattered his two
horns, and the ram had no strength to withstand him. So he
hurled him to the ground and trampled on him, and there was
none to rescue the ram from his [1]power.
8 Then the male goat magnified *himself* exceedingly.
But as soon as [a]he was mighty, the large horn was broken; and
in its place there came up four conspicuous *horns* toward the
[b]four winds of heaven.
9 And out of one of them came forth a rather [a]small horn
which grew exceedingly great toward the south, toward the
east, and toward the [1b]Beautiful *Land.*
10 And it grew up to the host of heaven and caused some
of the host and some of the [a]stars to fall to the earth, and it
[b]trampled them down.
11 It even [a]magnified *itself* [1]to be equal with the [2]Com-
mander of the host; and it removed the [b]regular sacrifice from
Him, and the place of His sanctuary was thrown down.
12 And on account of transgression the host will be given

26 [1]Lit., *to annihilate and to destroy* [2]Lit., *to the end* [a]Rev. 17:14; 19:2

27 [1]Or, *kingdom* [2]Lit., *holy ones* [a]Dan. 7:14, 18, 22; Is. 54:3; Rev. 20:4 [b]Dan. 7:14; 2:44; 4:34; Ps. 145:13; Is. 9:7 [c]Ps. 2:6-12; 22:27; 72:11; 86:9; Is. 60:12; Rev. 11:1

28 [1]Lit., *To here the end of the word* [2]Lit., *brightness was changing upon me* [3]Lit., *in my heart* [a]Luke 2:19, 51

1 [1]Lit., *I, Daniel* [2]Lit., *at the beginning*

2 [1]Or, *river* [a]Dan. 8:3; 7:2, 15; Num. 12:6 [b]Neh. 1:1; Esth. 1:2; 2:8 [c]Gen. 10:22; 14:1; Is. 11:11; Jer. 25:25; Ezek. 32:24

3 [1]Or, *river* [2]Lit., *high(er)* [a]Dan. 8:20

4 [1]Lit., *hand* [a]Deut. 33:17; 1 Kin. 22:11; Ezek. 34:21

5 [1]Lit., *buck* [a]Dan. 8:8, 21; 11:3

6 [1]Or, *river*

7 [1]Lit., *hand*

8 [a]Dan. 5:20; 2 Chr. 26:16 [b]Dan. 7:2; Rev. 7:1

9 [1]I.e., Palestine [a]Dan. 8:23 [b]Dan. 11:16, 41

10 [a]Is. 14:13 [b]Dan. 8:7; 7:7

11 [1]Lit., *up to the* [2]Or, *Prince* [a]Dan. 8:25; 11:36, 37; 2 Kin. 19:22, 23; 2 Chr. 32:15-17; Is. 37:23 [b]Dan. 11:31; 12:11; Ezek. 46:14

over *to the horn* along with the regular sacrifice; and it will
[a]fling truth to the ground and perform *its will* and prosper.
13 Then I heard a [a]holy one speaking, and another holy
one said to that particular one who was speaking, "[b]How long
will the vision *about* the regular sacrifice apply, [1]while the
transgression causes horror, so as to allow both the holy place
and the host [2]to be [c]trampled?"
14 And he said to me, "For [a]2,300 evenings *and* mornings;
then the holy place will be [1]properly restored."
15 And it came about when I, Daniel, had seen the vision,
that I sought [1]to understand it; and behold, standing before
me was one [2]who looked like a [a]man.
16 And I heard the voice of a man between *the banks of*
Ulai, and he called out and said, "[a]Gabriel, give this *man* an
understanding of the vision."
17 So he came near to where I was standing, and when he
came I was frightened and [a]fell on my face; but he said to me,
"Son of man, understand that the vision pertains to the [b]time
of the end."
18 Now while he was talking with me, I [a]sank into a deep
sleep with my face to the ground; but he [b]touched me and
made me stand [1]upright.
19 And he said, "Behold, I am going to [a]let you know what
will occur at the final period of the indignation; for *it* pertains
to the appointed time of the end.
20 "The ram which you saw with the two horns represents
the kings of Media and Persia.
21 "And the shaggy [1]goat *represents* the [2]kingdom of
Greece, and the large horn that is between his eyes is the first
king.
22 "And the broken *horn* and the four *horns that* arose in
its place *represent* four kingdoms *which* will arise from *his*
nation, although not with his power.
23 "And in the latter period of their [1]rule,
When the transgressors have [2]run *their course,*
A king will arise
[3]Insolent and skilled in [4]intrigue.
24 "And his power will be mighty, but not by his *own*
power,
And he will [1a]destroy to an extraordinary degree
And prosper and perform *his will;*
He will [1]destroy mighty men and [2]the holy people.
25 "And through his shrewdness
He will cause deceit to succeed by his [1]influence;
And he will magnify *himself* in his heart,
And he will [2]destroy many while *they are* [3]at ease.
He will even [4]oppose the Prince of princes,
But he will be broken without [1a]human agency.
26 "And the vision of the evenings and mornings
Which has been told is true;
But keep the vision secret,
For *it* pertains to many days *in the future.*"
27 Then I, Daniel, was [1a]exhausted and sick for days.
Then I got up *again* and carried on the king's business; but I
was astounded at the vision, and there was none to [2]explain *it.*

12 [a]Is. 59:14

13 [1]Or possibly, *and the transgression that horrifies* [2]Lit., *as a trampling* [a]Dan. 4:13, 23 [b]Dan. 12:6, 8; Ps. 74:10; 79:5; Is. 6:11; Rev. 6:10 [c]Is. 63:18; Jer. 12:10; Luke 21:24; Heb. 10:29; Rev. 11:2

14 [1]Lit., *vindicate* [a]Dan. 7:25; 12:7, 11; Rev. 11:2, 3; 12:14; 13:5

15 [1]Lit., *understanding* [2]Lit., *like the appearance of a man* [a]Dan. 7:13; 10:16, 18

16 [a]Dan. 9:21; Luke 1:19, 26

17 [a]Dan. 2:46; Ezek. 1:28; 44:4 [b]Dan. 8:19; 11:35, 40

18 [1]Lit., *on my standing* [a]Dan. 10:9; Luke 9:32 [b]Dan. 10:10, 16, 18; Ezek. 2:2

19 [a]Dan. 8:15-17

21 [1]Lit., *buck* [2]Lit., *king*

23 [1]Or, *kingdom* [2]Lit., *finished* [3]Lit., *Strong of face* [4]Or, *ambiguous speech*

24 [1]Or, *corrupt* [2]Lit., *people of the saints* [a]Dan. 8:11-13; 12:7; Rev. 16:6

25 [1]Lit., *hand* [2]Or, *corrupt* [3]Or, *secure* [4]Lit., *stand against* [a]Dan. 2:34, 45; Job 34:20

27 [1]Or, *done in* [2]Lit., *make understand* [a]Dan. 7:28; 8:17; Hab. 3:16

Chapter 9

IN the first year of [a]Darius the son of Ahasuerus, of Median
descent, who was made king over the kingdom of the Chaldeans—
2 in the first year of his reign I, Daniel, observed in the
books the number of the years which was *revealed as* the word
of the LORD to [a]Jeremiah the prophet for the completion of
the desolations of Jerusalem, *namely,* [a]seventy years.
3 So I [1]gave my attention to the LORD God to seek *Him*
by prayer and supplications, with fasting, sackcloth, and ashes.
4 And I prayed to the LORD my God and confessed and
said, "Alas, O Lord, the [a]great and awesome God, who [b]keeps
His covenant and lovingkindness for those who love Him and
keep His commandments,
5 we have [a]sinned, committed iniquity, acted wickedly,
and [b]rebelled, even [c]turning aside from Thy commandments
and ordinances.
6 "Moreover, we have not [a]listened to Thy servants the
prophets, who spoke in Thy name to our kings, our princes,
our fathers, and all the people of the land.
7 "[a]Righteousness belongs to Thee, O Lord, but to us
[1b]open shame, as it is this day—to the men of Judah, the
inhabitants of Jerusalem, and all Israel, those who are near by
and those who are far away in all the countries to which Thou
hast driven them, because of their unfaithful deeds which they
have committed against Thee.
8 "[1]Open shame belongs to us, O LORD, to our kings, our
princes, and our fathers, because we have sinned against Thee.
9 "To the LORD our God belong [a]compassion and forgiveness, [1]for we have [b]rebelled against Him;
10 nor have we obeyed the voice of the LORD our God, to
walk in His [1]teachings which He [a]set before us through His
servants the prophets.
11 "Indeed all Israel has transgressed Thy law and turned
aside, not obeying Thy voice; so the curse has been poured out
on us, along with the oath which is written in the law of Moses
the servant of God, for we have sinned against Him.
12 "Thus He has [a]confirmed His words which he had spok-
en against us and against our [1b]rulers who ruled us, to bring
on us great calamity; for under the whole heaven there has
[c]not been done *anything* like what was done to Jerusalem.
13 "As it is written in the [a]law of Moses, all this calamity
has come on us; yet we have [b]not [1]sought the favor of the LORD
our God by [c]turning from our iniquity and [2]giving attention to
Thy truth.
14 "Therefore, the LORD has [1a]kept the calamity in store
and brought it on us; for the LORD our God is [b]righteous with
respect to all His deeds which He has done, but we have not
obeyed His voice.
15 "And now, O LORD our God, who hast [a]brought Thy
people out of the land of Egypt with a mighty hand and hast
[b]made a name for Thyself, as it is this day—we have sinned, we
have been wicked.
16 "O Lord, in accordance with all Thy [1]righteous acts, let
now Thine [a]anger and Thy wrath turn away from Thy city

1 [a]Dan. 5:31; 11:1

2 [a]2 Chr. 36:21; Ezra 1:1; Jer. 25:11, 12; 29:10; Zech. 7:5

3 [1]Lit., *set my face*

4 [a]Deut. 7:21; Neh. 9:32 [b]Deut. 7:9

5 [a]Ps. 106:6 [b]Lam. 1:18, 20 [c]Dan. 9:11; Ps. 119:176; Is. 53:6

6 [a]Jer. 44:4, 5, 21

7 [1]Lit., *the shame of face* [a]Dan. 9:18; Jer. 23:6; 33:16 [b]Ps. 44:15; Jer. 2:26, 27; 3:25

8 [1]Lit., *The shame of face*

9 [1]Or, *though* [a]Neh. 9:17; Ps. 130:4 [b]Dan. 9:5, 6; Ps. 106:43; Jer. 14:7

10 [1]Or, *laws* [a]2 Kin. 17:13-15; 18:12

12 [1]Lit., *judges who judged us* [a]Is. 44:26; Jer. 44:2-6; Lam. 2:17; Zech. 1:6 [b]Job 12:17; Ps. 82:2-7; 148:11 [c]Lam. 1:12; 2:13; Ezek. 5:9

13 [1]Lit., *softened the face of* [2]Or, *having insight into* [a]Dan. 9:11; Lev. 26:14-45; Deut. 28:15-68 [b]Job 36:13; Is.9:13; Jer. 2:30; 5:3 [c]Jer. 31:18

14 [1]Lit., *watched over the evil* [a]Jer. 31:28; 44:27 [b]Dan. 9:7; Ps. 51:14

15 [a]Deut. 5:15 [b]Neh. 9:10; Jer. 32:20

16 [1]Lit., *righteousnesses* [a]Jer. 32:31, 32

Jerusalem, Thy [b]holy mountain; for because of our sins and
the iniquities of our fathers, Jerusalem and Thy people *have
become* a [c]reproach to all those around us.
17 "So now, our God, listen to the prayer of Thy servant
and to his supplications, and for [1]Thy sake, O Lord, [a]let Thy
face shine on Thy [b]desolate sanctuary.
18 "O my God, [a]incline Thine ear and hear! Open Thine
eyes and [b]see our desolations and the city which is [c]called by
Thy name; for we are not [1d]presenting our supplications before Thee on account of [2]any merits of our own, but on
account of Thy great compassion.
19 "O Lord, hear! O Lord, forgive! O Lord, listen and take
action! For Thine own sake, O my God, do not [a]delay, because
Thy city and Thy people are called by Thy name."
20 Now while I was [a]speaking and praying, and confessing
my sin and the sin of [b]my people Israel, and [1]presenting my
supplication before the LORD my God in behalf of the holy
mountain of my God,
21 while I was still speaking in prayer, then the man [a]Gabriel,
whom I had seen in the vision [1]previously, [2]came to me [3]in
my extreme weariness about the time of the [b]evening offering.
22 And he gave *me* instruction and talked with me, and
said, "O Daniel, I have now come forth to give you insight
with [a]understanding.
23 "At the beginning of your supplications the [1]command
was issued, and I have come to tell *you*, for you are [2]highly
esteemed; so give heed to the message and gain [a]understanding
of the vision.
24 "Seventy [1a]weeks have been decreed for your people and
your holy city, to [2]finish the transgression, to [3]make an end of
sin, to [b]make atonement for iniquity, to bring in [c]everlasting
righteousness, to seal up vision and [4]prophecy, and to anoint
the most holy *place*.
25 "So you are to know and discern *that* from the issuing of
a [1a]decree to restore and rebuild Jerusalem until [2b]Messiah the
[c]Prince *there will be* seven weeks and sixty-two weeks; it will be
built again, with [3]plaza and moat, even in times of distress.
26 "Then after the sixty-two weeks the [1]Messiah will be
[a]cut off and have [2]nothing, and the people of the prince who is
to come will [b]destroy the city and the sanctuary. And [3]its end
will come with a [c]flood; even to the end [4]there will be war;
desolations are determined.
27 "And he will make a firm covenant with the many for
one week, but in the middle of the week he will put a stop to
sacrifice and grain offering; and on the wing of [1a]abominations
will come one who [2]makes desolate, even until a [b]complete
destruction, one that is decreed, is poured out on the one who
[2]makes desolate."

CHAPTER 10

IN the third year of [a]Cyrus king of Persia a [1]message was
revealed to Daniel, who was named Belteshazzar; and the
[1]message was true and *one of* great [2]conflict, but he understood the [1]message and had an [b]understanding of the vision.

16 [b]Dan. 9:20; Ps. 87:1-3; Joel 3:17; Zech. 8:3 [c]Ezek. 5:14

17 [1]Lit., *for the sake of the Lord* [a]Num. 6:24-26; Ps. 80:3, 7, 19 [b]Lam. 5:18

18 [1]Lit., *causing to fall* [2]Lit., *our righteousnesses* [a]Is. 37:17 [b]Ps. 80:14 [c]Jer. 7:10-12 [d]Jer. 36:7

19 [a]Ps. 44:23; 74:10, 11

20 [1]Lit., *causing to fall* [a]Dan. 9:3; 10:12; Ps. 145:18; Is. 58:9 [b]Is. 6:5

21 [1]Lit., *at the beginning* [2]Lit., *was reaching* or *touching* [3]Lit., *wearied with weariness* [a]Dan. 8:16; Luke 1:19, 26 [b]Ex. 29:39; 1 Kin. 18:36; Ezra 9:4

22 [a]Dan. 8:16; 10:21; Zech. 1:9, 14

23 [1]Lit., *word went out* [2]Lit., *desirable* or *precious* [a]Matt. 24:15

24 [1]Or, *units of seven*, and so throughout the chap. [2]Or, *restrain* [3]Another reading is: *seal up sins* [4]Lit., *prophet* [a]Lev. 25:8; Num. 14:34; Ezek. 4:6 [b]2 Chr. 29:24; Is. 53:10; Rom. 5:10 [c]Is. 51:6, 8; 56:1; Jer. 23:5, 6; Rom. 3:21, 22

25 [1]Lit., *word* [2]Or, *an anointed one* [3]Or, *streets* [a]Ezra 4:24; 6:1-15; Neh. 2:1-8; 3:1 [b]John 1:41; 4:25 [c]Dan. 8:11, 25; Is. 9:6

26 [1]Or, *anointed one* [2]Or, *no one* [3]Or, *his* [4]Or, *war will be decreed for desolations* [a]Is. 53:8; Mark 9:12; Luke 24:26 [b]Matt. 24:2; Mark 13:2; Luke 19:43, 44 [c]Nah. 1:8

27 [1]Or, *detestable things* [2]Or, *causes horror* [a]Dan. 11:31; Matt. 24:15; Mark 13:14; Luke 21:20 [b]Is. 10:23; 28:22

1 [1]Lit., *word* [2]Or, *warfare* [a]Dan. 1:21; 6:28 [b]Dan. 1:17; 2:21

2 In those days I, Daniel, had been [a]mourning for three
entire weeks.
3 I did not eat any [1]tasty food, nor did meat or wine
enter my mouth, nor did I use any ointment at all, until the
entire three weeks were completed.
4 And on the twenty-fourth day of the first month, while
I was by the bank of the great [a]river, that is, the [1]Tigris,
5 I lifted my eyes and looked, and behold, there was a
certain man [a]dressed in linen, whose waist was [b]girded with *a*
belt of pure [c]gold of Uphaz.
6 His body also was like [1]beryl, his face [2]had the appearance of lightning, his eyes were like flaming torches, his arms
and feet like the gleam of polished bronze, and the sound of
his words like the sound of a [3]tumult.
7 Now I, Daniel, [a]alone saw the vision, while the [b]men
who were with me did not see the vision; nevertheless, a great
[c]dread fell on them, and they ran away to hide themselves.
8 So I was [a]left alone and saw this great vision; yet no
strength was [b]left in me, for my [1]natural color turned to [2]a
deathly pallor, and I retained no strength.
9 But I heard the sound of his words; and as soon as I
heard the sound of his words, I [a]fell into a deep sleep on my
face, with my face to the ground.
10 Then behold, a hand touched me and set me trembling
on my [1]hands and knees.
11 And he said to me, "O Daniel, man of [1]high esteem,
[a]understand the words that I am about to tell you and [b]stand
[2]upright, for I have now been sent to you." And when he had
spoken this word to me, I stood up [c]trembling.
12 Then he said to me, "[a]Do not be afraid, Daniel, for
from the first day that you set your heart on understanding
this and on [b]humbling yourself before your God, your words
were heard, and I have come in response [c]to your words.
13 "But the prince of the kingdom of Persia was [1]withstand-
ing me for twenty-one days; then behold, [a]Michael, one of
the chief princes, came to help me, for I had been left there
with the kings of Persia.
14 "Now I have come to give you an understanding of what
will happen to your people in the [1a]latter days, for the vision
pertains to [b]the days yet *future*."
15 And when he had spoken to me according to these
words, I [1]turned my face toward the ground and became
[a]speechless.
16 And behold, [1]one who resembled a human being was
[a]touching my lips; then I opened my mouth and spoke, and
said to him who was standing before me, "O my lord, as a
result of the vision [2b]anguish has come upon me, and I have
retained no strength.
17 "For [a]how can such a servant of my lord talk with such
as my lord? As for me, there remains just now no strength in
me, nor has any breath been left in me."
18 Then *this* one with human appearance touched me
again and [a]strengthened me.
19 And he said, "O man of [1]high esteem, [a]do not be afraid.
Peace [2]be with you; take [b]courage and be courageous!"

2 [a]Ezra 9:4, 5; Neh. 1:4

3 [1]Lit., *bread of desirability*

4 [1]Heb., *Hiddeqel* [a]Dan. 8:2; Ezek. 1:3

5 [a]Dan. 12:6, 7; Ezek. 9:2 [b]Rev. 1:13; 15:6 [c]Jer. 10:9

6 [1]Or, *yellow serpentine* [2]Lit., *like* [3]Or, *roaring*

7 [a]2 Kin. 6:17 [b]Acts 9:7 [c]Ezek. 12:18

8 [1]Lit., *splendor* [2]Lit., *corruption* [a]Gen. 32:24 [b]Dan. 7:28; 8:27; Hab. 3:16

9 [a]Dan. 8:18; Gen. 15:12; Job 4:13

10 [1]Lit., *knees and the palms of my hands*

11 [1]Lit., *desirability*, or *preciousness* [2]Lit., *upon your standing* [a]Dan. 8:16, 17 [b]Ezek. 2:1 [c]Job 4:14, 15

12 [a]Dan. 10:19; Is. 41:10, 14 [b]Dan. 10:2, 3; 9:20-23 [c]Acts 10:30, 31

13 [1]Lit., *standing opposite* [a]Dan. 10:21; 12:1; Jude 9; Rev. 12:7

14 [1]Lit., *end of the days* [a]Dan. 2:28; Deut. 31:29 [b]Dan. 8:26; 12:4, 9

15 [1]Lit., *set* [a]Ezek. 24:27; Luke 1:20

16 [1]Lit., *as a likeness of sons of man* [2]Lit., *my pains have* [a]Is. 6:7; Jer. 1:9 [b]Dan. 10:8, 9; 7:15, 28; 8:17, 27

17 [a]Ex. 24:10, 11; Is. 6:1-5

18 [a]Is. 35:3, 4

19 [1]Lit., *desirability*, or *preciousness* [2]Lit., *to you* [a]Dan. 10:12; Judg. 6:23; Is. 43:1 [b]Josh. 1:6, 7, 9; Is. 35:4

Now as soon as he spoke to me, I received strength and said,
"May my lord speak, for you have [c]strengthened me."
20 Then he said, "Do you [1]understand why I came to you?
But I shall now return to fight against the [2]prince of Persia; so
I am going forth, and behold, the [2a]prince of [3]Greece is about
to come.
21 "However, I will tell you what is inscribed in the writing
of [a]truth. (Yet there is no one who [1]stands firmly with me
against these *forces* except Michael your prince.

CHAPTER 11

AND in the [a]first year of Darius the Mede I [1]arose to be [2]an
encouragement and a protection for him.)
2 "And now I will tell you the [a]truth. Behold, three more
kings are going to arise [1]in Persia. Then a fourth will gain far
more riches than all *of them;* as soon as he becomes strong
through his riches, [2]he will arouse the whole *empire* against the
realm of [3b]Greece.
3 "And a [a]mighty king will arise, and he will rule with great
authority and [b]do as he pleases.
4 "But as soon as he has arisen, his kingdom will be broken
up and parcelled out [a]toward the [b]four [1]points of the compass,
though not to his *own* descendants, nor according to his authority which he wielded; for his sovereignty will be [c]uprooted and
given to others besides [2]them.
5 "Then the [a]king of the South will grow strong, [1]along
with *one* of his princes [2]who will gain ascendancy over him and
obtain dominion; his domain *will be* a great dominion *indeed.*
6 "And after some years they will form an alliance, and
the daughter of the king of the South will come to the [a]king of
the North to carry out [1]a peaceful arrangement. But she will
not retain her [2]position of power, nor will he remain with his
[3]power, but she will be given up, along with those who brought
her in, and the one who sired her, as well as he who supported
her in *those* times.
7 "But one of the [1]descendants of her line will arise in his
place, and he will come against *their* army and enter the [a]for-
tress of the king of the North, and he will deal with them and
display *great* strength.
8 "And also their [a]gods with their [1]metal images *and* their
precious vessels of silver and gold he will take into captivity to
Egypt, and he on his part will [2]refrain from *attacking* the king
of the North for *some* years.
9 "Then [1]the latter will enter the realm of the king of the
South, but will return to his *own* land.
10 "And his sons will [1]mobilize and assemble a multitude of
great forces; and one of them will keep on coming and [a]over-
flow and pass through, that he may [2]again wage war up to his
very fortress.
11 "And the king of the South will be enraged and go forth
and fight [1]with the king of the North. Then the latter will raise
a great multitude, but *that* multitude will be given into [2]the
hand of the *former.*

19 [c]Ps. 138:3; 2 Cor. 12:9

20 [1]Lit., *know* [2]I.e., Satanic angel [3]Heb., *Javan* [a]Dan. 8:21; 11:2

21 [1]Lit., *shows himself strong* [a]Dan. 12:1, 4

1 [1]Lit., *my standing up* was [2]Lit., *for a strengthener* [a]Dan. 5:31; 9:1

2 [1]Lit., *for* [2]Or, they *all will stir up the realm of Greece* [3]Heb., *Javan* [a]Dan. 8:26; 10:1, 21 [b]Dan. 8:21; 10:20

3 [a]Dan. 8:5, 21 [b]Dan. 11:16, 36; 5:19; 8:4

4 [1]Lit., *winds of the heaven* [2]I.e., his descendants [a]Dan. 8:8, 22 [b]Dan. 7:2; 8:8; Jer. 49:36; Ezek. 37:9; Zech. 2:6; Rev. 7:1 [c]Jer. 12:15, 17; 18:7

5 [1]Lit., *and* [2]Lit., *and he* [a]Dan. 11:9, 11, 14, 25, 40

6 [1]Or, *an equitable agreement* [2]Lit., *strength of arm* [3]Lit., *arm* [a]Dan. 11:7, 13, 15, 40

7 [1]Lit., *branch of her roots* [a]Dan. 11:19, 38, 39

8 [1]Lit., *cast images* [2]Or, *stand against the king* [a]Is. 37:19; 46:1, 2; Jer. 43:12, 13

9 [1]Lit., *he will,* and so throughout the chap.

10 [1]Or, *wage war* [2]Or, *return and wage* [a]Dan. 11:26, 40; Is. 8:8; Jer. 46:7, 8; 51:42

11 [1]Lit., *with him, with* [2]Lit., *his hand*

12 "When the multitude is carried away, his heart will be
lifted up, and he will cause tens of thousands to fall; yet he will
not prevail.
13 "For the king of the North will again raise a greater
multitude than the former, and [1]after an [a]interval of some
years he will [2]press on with a great army and much equipment.
14 "Now in those times many will rise up against the king
of the South; the violent ones among your people will also lift
themselves up in order to fulfill the vision, but they will [1]fall
down.
15 "Then the king of the North will come, cast up a siege
[a]mound, and capture a well fortified city; and the forces of the
South will not stand *their ground*, not even [1]their choicest
troops, for there will be no strength to make a stand.
16 "But he who comes against him will [a]do as he pleases,
and [b]no one will *be able to* withstand him; he will also stay *for
a time* in the [1c]Beautiful Land, with destruction in his hand.
17 "And he will [a]set his face to come with the power of his
whole kingdom, [1]bringing with him [2]a proposal of peace which
he will put into effect; he will also give him the daughter of
women to ruin it. But she will not take a stand *for him* or be
[3]on his side.
18 "Then he will turn his face to the [a]coastlands and capture many. But a commander will put a stop to his scorn
against him; moreover, he will [b]repay him for his scorn.
19 "So he will turn his face toward the fortresses of his own
land, but he will [a]stumble and fall and be found [b]no more.
20 "Then in his place one will arise who will [a]send an [1]op-
pressor through the [2]Jewel of *his* kingdom; yet within a few
days he will be shattered, though neither in anger nor in battle.
21 "And in his place a despicable person will arise, on
whom the honor of kingship has not been conferred, but he
will come in a time of tranquility and seize the kingdom by
intrigue.
22 "And the overflowing [a]forces will be flooded away before him and shattered, and also the prince of the covenant.
23 "And after an alliance is made with him he will practice
deception, and he will go up and gain power with a small *force
of* people.
24 "[1]In a time of tranquility he will enter the [a]richest *parts*
of the [2]realm, and he will accomplish what his fathers never
did, nor his [3]ancestors; he will distribute plunder, booty, and
possessions among them, and he will devise his schemes against
strongholds, but *only* for a time.
25 "And he will stir up his strength and [1]courage against the
king of the South with a large army; so the king of the South
will mobilize an extremely large and mighty army for war; but
he will not stand, for schemes will be devised against him.
26 "And those who eat his choice food will [1]destroy him,
and his army will [2a]overflow, but many will fall down slain.
27 "As for both kings, their hearts will be *intent* on [a]evil,
and they will [b]speak lies *to each other* at the same table; but it
will not succeed, for the [c]end is still *to come* at the appointed
time.
28 "Then he will return to his land with much [1]plunder; but

13 [1]Lit., *at the end of the times, years* [2]Or, *keep on coming* [a]Dan. 4:16; 12:7

14 [1]Lit., *stumble*, and so throughout the chap.

15 [1]Lit., *the people of its choice ones* [a]Jer. 6:6; Ezek. 4:2; 17:17

16 [1]I.e., Palestine [a]Dan. 11:3, 36; 5:19 [b]Josh. 1:5 [c]Dan. 11:41; 8:9

17 [1]Lit., *and* [2]Lit., *equitable things* [3]Lit., *for him;* i.e., for her father [a]2 Kin. 12:17; Ezek. 4:3, 7

18 [a]Gen. 10:5; Is. 66:19; Jer. 2:10; 31:10; Zeph. 2:11 [b]Hos. 12:14

19 [a]Ps. 27:2; Jer. 46:6 [b]Job 20:8; Ps. 37:36; Ezek. 26:21

20 [1]Or, *exactor* of tribute [2]Lit., *adornment;* i.e., probably Jerusalem and its temple [a]Is. 60:17

22 [a]Dan. 11:10; 9:26

24 [1]Lit., *Into tranquility and the richest . . . he will enter* [2]Or, *province* [3]Lit., *fathers' fathers* [a]Num. 13:20; Neh. 9:25; Ezek. 34:14

25 [1]Lit., *heart*

26 [1]Lit., *break* [2]Or, *be swept away, and many* [a]Dan. 11:10, 40

27 [a]Ps. 52:1; 64:6 [b]Jer. 9:3-5; 41:1-3 [c]Dan. 11:35, 40; 8:19; Hab. 2:3

28 [1]Lit., *possessions*

his heart will be *set* against the holy covenant, and he will take
action and *then* return to his *own* land.
29 "At the appointed time he will return and come into the
South, but [1]this last time it will not turn out the way it did
before.
30 "For ships of [a]Kittim will come against him; therefore
he will be disheartened, and will return and become enraged at
the holy covenant and take action; so he will come back and
show regard for those who forsake the holy covenant.
31 "And forces from him will arise, [a]desecrate the sanctuary
fortress, and do away with the regular sacrifice. And they will
set up the [b]abomination [1]of desolation.
32 "And by [a]smooth *words* he will [1]turn to godlessness
those who act wickedly toward the covenant, but the people
who know their God will display [b]strength and take action.
33 "And [1]those who have insight among the people will
give understanding to the many; yet they will [a]fall by sword
and by flame, by captivity and by plunder, for *many* days.
34 "Now when they fall they will be granted a little help,
and many will [a]join with them in [b]hypocrisy.
35 "And some of [1]those who have insight will fall, in order
to [a]refine, [b]purge, and make them [2c]pure, until the end time;
because *it is* still *to come* at the appointed time.
36 "Then the king will [a]do as he pleases, and he will exalt
and [b]magnify himself above every god, and will speak [1c]mon-
strous things against the [d]God of gods; and he will prosper until
the [e]indignation is finished, for that which is [f]decreed will be
done.
37 "And he will show no regard for the [1]gods of his fathers
or for the desire of women, nor will he show regard for any
other god; for he will magnify himself above *them* all.
38 "But [1]instead he will honor a god of fortresses, a god
whom his fathers did not know; he will honor *him* with gold,
silver, costly stones, and treasures.
39 "And he will take action against the strongest of fortresses with *the help of* a foreign god; he will give great honor
to [1]those who acknowledge *him*, and he will cause them to rule
over the many, and will parcel out land for a price.
40 "And at the end [a]time the king of the South will collide
with him, and the king of the North will [b]storm against him
with chariots, with horsemen, and with many ships; and he will
enter countries, overflow *them*, and pass through.
41 "He will also enter the [1]Beautiful Land, and many
countries will fall; but these will be rescued out of his hand:
Edom, [a]Moab and the foremost of the sons of [b]Ammon.
42 "Then he will stretch out his hand against *other*
countries, and the land of Egypt will not escape.
43 "But he will [1]gain control over the hidden treasures of
gold and silver, and over all the precious things of Egypt; and
[a]Libyans and [b]Ethiopians *will follow* at his [2]heels.
44 "But rumors from the East and from the North will
disturb him, and he will go forth with great wrath to destroy
and [1]annihilate many.
45 "And he will pitch the tents of his royal pavilion between
the seas and the beautiful [a]Holy Mountain; yet he will
come to his end, and no one will help him.

29 [1]Lit., *it will not happen as the first and as the last*

30 [a]Gen. 10:4; Num. 24:24; Is. 23:1, 12; Jer. 2:10

31 [1]Lit., *that makes desolate*, or *that causes horror* [a]Dan. 8:11-13; 12:11 [b]Dan. 9:27; 12:11; Matt. 24:15; Mark 13:14

32 [1]Or, *pollute those* [a]Dan. 11:21, 34 [b]Mic. 5:7-9; Zech. 9:13-16; 10:3-6

33 [1]Or, *instructors of* the *people* [a]Matt. 24:9; John 16:2; Heb. 11:36-38

34 [a]Matt. 7:15; Acts 20:29, 30 [b]Dan. 11:21, 32; Rom. 16:18

35 [1]Or, *the instructors* [2]Lit., *white* [a]Dan. 12:10; Deut. 8:16; Prov. 17:3; Zech. 13:9; Mal. 3:2, 3 [b]John 15:2 [c]Rev. 7:14

36 [1]Lit., *extraordinary* [a]Dan. 11:3, 16; 5:19 [b]Dan. 5:20; 8:11, 25; Is. 14:13; 2 Thess. 2:4 [c]Dan. 7:8, 11; Rev. 13:5, 6 [d]Dan. 2:47; Deut. 10:17; Ps. 136:2 [e]Dan. 8:19; Is. 10:25; 26:20 [f]Dan. 9:27

37 [1]Or, *God*

38 [1]Lit., *in his place*

39 [1]Lit., *the one who acknowledges*

40 [a]Dan. 11:27, 35; 12:4, 9 [b]Is. 5:28; Jer. 4:13

41 [1]I.e., Palestine [a]Jer. 48:47 [b]Jer. 49:6

43 [1]Or, *rule over* [2]Lit., *footsteps* [a]2 Chr. 12:3; Nah. 3:9 [b]2 Chr. 12:3; Ezek. 30:4, 5; Nah. 3:9

44 [1]Lit., *devote to destruction*

45 [a]Dan. 9:16, 20; Is. 11:9; 27:13; 65:25; 66:20

CHAPTER 12

"NOW at that time Michael, the great prince who stands
guard over the sons of your people, will arise. And there will be
a time of distress [a]such as never occurred since there was a
nation until that time; and at that time your people, everyone
who is found written in the [b]book, will be rescued.
2 "And [a]many of those who sleep in the dust of the
ground will awake, [b]these to everlasting life, but the others to
disgrace *and* everlasting [1]contempt.
3 "And [1]those who have [a]insight will [b]shine brightly like
the brightness of the [2]expanse of heaven, and those who [c]lead
the many to righteousness, like the stars forever and ever.
4 "But as for you, Daniel, [a]conceal these words and [b]seal
up the book until the end of [c]time; [d]many will go back and
forth, and knowledge will increase."
5 Then I, Daniel, looked and behold, two others were
standing, one on this bank of the river, and the other on that
bank of the river.
6 And [a]one said to the man [b]dressed in linen, who was
above the waters of the river, "[c]How long *will it be* until the
end of *these* wonders?"
7 And I heard the man dressed in linen, who was above
the waters of the river, [1]as he [a]raised his right hand and his left
toward heaven, and swore by Him who lives forever that it
would be for a [2b]time, [2]times, and half *a [2]time;* and as soon as
[3]they finish [c]shattering the [4]power of the holy people, all these
events will be completed.
8 As for me, I heard but could not understand; so I said,
"My lord, what *will be* the [1]outcome of these *events?*"
9 And he said, "Go *your way*, Daniel, for *these* words are
concealed and sealed up until the end time.
10 "Many will be purged, [1]purified and refined; but the
[a]wicked will act wickedly, and none of the wicked will understand, but [2]those who [b]have insight will understand.
11 "And from the time that the regular sacrifice is abolished, and the [1a]abomination of desolation is set up, *there will
be* 1290 days.
12 "How [a]blessed is he who keeps waiting and attains to the
[b]1335 days!
13 "But as for you, go *your way* to the [1]end; then you will
enter into [a]rest and rise *again* for your [b]allotted portion at the
end of the [2]age."

1 [a]Dan. 9:12; Jer. 30:7; Ezek. 5:9; Matt. 24:21; Mark 13:19 [b]Dan. 12:4; 7:10; 10:21

2 [1]Lit., *abhorrence* [a]Is. 26:19; Ezek. 37:12-14 [b]John 5:28, 29

3 [1]Or, *the instructors will* [2]Or, *firmament* [a]Dan. 12:10; 11:33, 35 [b]John 5:35 [c]Dan. 11:33; Is. 53:11

4 [a]Dan. 12:9; 8:26 [b]Dan. 12:9; Is. 8:16 [c]Dan. 12:9, 13; 8:17 [d]Dan. 11:33; Is. 11:9; 29:18, 19

6 [a]Dan. 8:16; Zech. 1:12, 13 [b]Dan. 10:5; Ezek. 9:2 [c]Dan. 12:8; 8:13; Matt. 24:3; Mark 13:4

7 [1]Lit., *and* [2]I.e., year(s) [3]Lit., *to finish* [4]Lit., *hand* [a]Ezek. 20:5; Rev. 10:5, 6 [b]Dan. 7:25; Rev. 12:14 [c]Dan. 8:24; Luke 21:24

8 [1]Or, *final end*

10 [1]Lit., *made white* [2]Or, *the instructors will* [a]Is. 32:6, 7 [b]Dan. 12:3; Hos. 14:9

11 [1]Or, *horrible abomination* [a]Dan. 9:27; 11:31; Matt. 24:15; Mark 13:14

12 [a]Is. 30:18 [b]Dan. 8:14; Rev. 11:2; 12:6; 13:5

13 [1]I.e., end of your life [2]Lit., *days* [a]Rev. 14:13 [b]Ps. 16:5

THE BOOK OF HOSEA

Hosea's Wife and Children. Restoration of Israel.

THE word of the LORD which came to [a]Hosea the son of
Beeri, during the days of [b]Uzziah, [c]Jotham, [d]Ahaz, *and* [e]Heze-
kiah, kings of Judah, and during the days of Jeroboam the son
of Joash, king of Israel.
2 When the LORD first spoke through Hosea, the LORD
said to Hosea, "[a]Go, take to yourself a wife of harlotry, and
have children of harlotry; for the land commits flagrant harlotry, [1]forsaking the LORD."
3 So he went and took Gomer the daughter of Diblaim,
and she conceived and bore him a son.
4 And the LORD said to him, "Name him Jezreel; for yet
a little while, and I will [1]punish the house of Jehu for the
bloodshed of Jezreel, and I will put an end to the kingdom of
the house of Israel.
5 "And it will come about on that day, that I will [a]break
the bow of Israel in the [b]valley of Jezreel."
6 Then she conceived again and gave birth to a daughter.
And [1]the LORD said to him, "Name her [2]Lo-ruhamah, for I will
no longer have compassion on the house of Israel, that I
should ever forgive them.
7 "But I will have [a]compassion on the house of Judah and
[b]deliver them by the LORD their God, and will not deliver them
by [c]bow, sword, battle, horses, or horsemen."
8 When she had weaned Lo-ruhamah, she conceived and
gave birth to a son.
9 And [1]the LORD said, "Name him [2]Lo-ammi, for you are
not My people and I am not [3]your God."

10 [1]Yet the number of the sons of Israel
Will be like the [a]sand of the sea,
Which cannot be measured or numbered;
And it will come about that, in the place
Where it is said to them,
"You are [b]not My people,"
It will be said to them,
"*You are* the [c]sons of the living God."

11 And the sons of Judah and the sons of Israel will be
gathered together,
And they will appoint for themselves [a]one leader,
And they will go up from the land,
For great will be the day of Jezreel.

CHAPTER 2

1 SAY to your brothers, "[2]Ammi," and to your sisters,
"[3]Ruhamah."

2 "Contend with your mother, [a]contend,
For she is not my wife, and I am not her husband;
And let her put away her harlotry from her face,
And her adultery from between her breasts,
3 Lest I strip her [a]naked
And expose her as on the day when she was born.

1 [a]Rom. 9:25 [b]2 Chr: 26:1-23; Is. 1:1; Amos 1:1 [c]2 Kin. 15:5, 7, 32-38; 2 Chr. 27:1-9 [d]2 Kin. 16:1-20; 2 Chr. 28:1-27; Is. 1:1; 7:1-17; Mic. 1:1 [e]2 Kin. 18:1-20:21; 2 Chr. 29:1-32:33; Mic. 1:1

2 [1]Lit., *from not following after* [a]Hos. 3:1; Is. 20:2, 3

4 [1]Lit., *visit the bloodshed of Jezreel on the house of Jehu*

5 [a]Jer. 49:35; Ezek. 39:3 [b]Josh. 17:16; Judg. 6:33

6 [1]Lit., *He* [2]I.e., she has not obtained compassion

7 [a]Is. 30:18 [b]Jer. 25:5, 6; Zech. 9:9, 10 [c]Ps. 44:3-7

9 [1]Lit., *He* [2]I.e., not my people [3]Lit., *yours*

10 [1]Ch. 2:1 in Heb. [a]Gen. 22:17; Jer. 33:22 [b]Hos. 1:9; Is. 65:1 [c]Is. 63:16; 64:8

11 [a]Hos. 3:5; Jer. 30:21

1 [1]Ch. 2:3 in Heb. [2]I.e., my people [3]I.e., she has obtained compassion

2 [a]Hos. 2:5; 4:5; Ezek. 23:45

3 [a]Ezek. 16:7, 22, 39

I will also [b]make her like a wilderness,
Make her like desert land,
And slay her with [c]thirst.
4 "Also, I will have no compassion on her children,
Because they are children of harlotry.
5 "For their mother has played the harlot;
She who conceived them has acted shamefully.
For she said, '[a]I will go after my lovers,
Who [b]give *me* my bread and my water,
My wool and my flax, my oil and my drink.'
6 "Therefore, behold, I will [a]hedge up [1]her way with thorns,
And I will build [2]a wall against her so that she cannot find her [b]paths.
7 "And she will [a]pursue her lovers, but she will not overtake them;
And she will seek them, but will not find *them*.
Then she will say, 'I will go back to my [b]first husband,
For it was [c]better for me then than now!'

8 "For she does [a]not know that it was [b]I who gave her the grain, the new wine, and the oil,
And lavished on her silver and gold,
Which they [1]used for Baal.
9 "Therefore, I will take back My grain at [1]harvest time
And My new wine in its season.
I will also take away My wool and My flax
Given to cover her nakedness.
10 "And then I will [a]uncover her lewdness
In the sight of her lovers,
And no one will rescue her out of My hand.
11 "I will also [a]put an end to all her gaiety,
Her [b]feasts, her [c]new moons, her sabbaths,
And all her festal assemblies.
12 "And I will [a]destroy her vines and fig trees,
Of which she said, 'These are my wages
Which my lovers have given me.'
And I will [b]make them a forest,
And the [c]beasts of the field will devour them.
13 "And I will punish her for the [a]days of the Baals
When she used to [1b]offer sacrifices to them
And adorn herself with her [2]earrings and jewelry,
And follow her lovers, so that she forgot Me," declares the LORD.

14 "Therefore, behold, I will allure her,
[a]Bring her into the wilderness,
And speak [1]kindly to her.
15 "Then I will give her her [a]vineyards from there,
And the [b]valley of Achor as a door of hope.
And she will [1c]sing there as in the days of her youth,
As in the day when she came up from the land of Egypt.
16 "And it will come about in that day," declares the LORD,
"That you will call Me [1a]Ishi
And will no longer call Me [2]Baali.

3 [b]Hos. 13:15; Is. 32:13, 14 [c]Jer. 14:3; Amos 8: 11-13

5 [a]Jer. 2:25; 3:1, 2 [b]Hos. 2:12; Jer. 44:17, 18

6 [1]So with some ancient versions; Heb., *your* [2]Lit., *her wall so that* [a]Job 19:8 [b]Jer. 18:15

7 [a]Hos. 5:13; 2 Chr. 28:20-22 [b]Jer. 2:2; 3:1; Ezek. 16:8; 23:4 [c]Hos. 13:6; Jer.14: 22

8 [1]Or, *made into the* [a]Is. 1:3 [b]Ezek. 16:19

9 [1]Lit., *its time*

10 [a]Ezek. 16:37

11 [a]Jer. 7:34; 16:9 [b]Hos. 3:4; Amos 5:21; 8:10 [c]Is. 1:13, 14

12 [a]Jer. 5:17; 8:13 [b]Ps. 80:12; Is. 5:5; 7:23 [c]Hos. 13:8; Is. 32:13-15

13 [1]Or, *burn incense* [2]Or, *nose rings* [a]Hos. 4:13; 11:2 [b]Jer. 7:9

14 [1]Lit., *upon her heart* [a]Ezek. 20:33-38

15 [1]Or, *give answer* [a]Ezek. 28:25,26 [b]Josh. 7:26 [c]Jer. 2:1-3

16 [1]I.e., my Husband [2]I.e., my Master, or my Baal [a]Hos. 2:7; Is. 54:5

17 "For I will remove the names of the Baals from her mouth,
So that they will be [1]mentioned by their names no more.
18 "In that day I will also make a covenant for them
With the beasts of the field,
The birds of the sky,
And the creeping things of the ground.
And I will [1a]abolish the bow, the sword, and war from the land,
And will make them [b]lie down in safety.
19 "And I will [a]betroth you to Me forever;
Yes, I will betroth you to Me in [b]righteousness and in justice,
In lovingkindness and in compassion,
20 And I will betroth you to Me in faithfulness.
Then you will [a]know the LORD.

21 "And it will come about in that day that [a]I will respond," declares the LORD.
"I will respond to the heavens, and they will respond to the earth,
22 And the [a]earth will respond to the grain, to the new wine, and to the oil,
And they will respond to [1]Jezreel.
23 "And I will [a]sow her for Myself in the land.
I will also have compassion on [1]her who had not obtained compassion,
And [b]I will say to [2]those who were [c]not My people,
'You are My people!'
And [3]they will say, '*Thou art* my God!' "

CHAPTER 3

1 THEN the LORD said to me, "Go, again love a [1]woman *who*
is loved by *her* [2]husband, yet an adulteress, even as the LORD
loves the sons of Israel, though they turn to other gods and
love raisin [a]cakes."
2 So I [a]bought her for myself for fifteen *shekels* of silver
and a homer and a [1]half of barley.
3 Then I said to her, "You shall stay with me for many
days. You shall not play the harlot, nor shall you have a [1]man;
so I will also be toward you."
4 For the sons of Israel will remain for many days without king or prince, [a]without sacrifice or sacred [b]pillar, and
without [c]ephod or [1]household idols.
5 Afterward the sons of Israel will [a]return and seek the
LORD their God and [b]David their king; and they will come
trembling to the LORD and to His goodness in the last days.

CHAPTER 4

1 LISTEN to the word of the LORD, O sons of Israel,
For the LORD has a [a]case against the inhabitants of the land,

17 [1]Or, *remembered*

18 [1]Lit., *break* [a]Ezek. 39:1-10 [b]Ezek. 34:25

19 [a]Is. 62:4, 5; Jer. 3:14 [b]Is. 1:27; 54:6-8

20 [a]Hos. 6:6; 13:4

21 [a]Is. 55:10; Zech. 8:12; Mal. 3:10, 11

22 [1]I.e., God sows [a]Jer. 31:12; Joel 2:19

23 [1]Heb., *Lo-ruhamah* [2]Heb., *Lo-ammi* [3]Lit., *he* [a]Jer. 31:27 [b]Rom. 9:25 [c]Hos. 1:9

3:1 [1]I.e., Gomer [2]Lit., *companion* [a]2 Sam. 6:19; 1 Chr. 16:3; Song of Sol. 2:5

2 [1]Heb., *lethech* [a]Ruth 4:10

3 [1]Or, *husband*

4 [1]Heb., *teraphim* [a]Hos. 2:11; Dan. 9:27; 11:31; 12:11 [b]Hos. 10:1, 2 [c]Ex. 28:4-12; 1 Sam. 23:9-12

5 [a]Jer. 50:4, 5 [b]Ezek. 34:24

4:1 [a]Hos. 12:2; Mic. 6:2

Because there is [b]no [1]faithfulness or [2]kindness
Or knowledge of God in the land.
2 *There is* swearing, deception, murder, stealing, and adultery.
They employ violence, so that bloodshed [1]follows bloodshed.
3 Therefore the land [a]mourns,
And every one who lives in it languishes
Along with the beasts of the field and the birds of the sky;
And also the fish of the sea [1]disappear.

4 Yet let no one [1a]find fault, and let none offer reproof;
For your people are like those who [b]contend with the priest.
5 So you will [a]stumble by day,
And the prophet also will stumble with you by night;
And I will destroy your [b]mother.
6 My people are destroyed for lack of knowledge.
Because you have [a]rejected knowledge,
I also will reject you from being My priest.
Since you have forgotten the law of your God,
I also will forget your children.

7 The more they [a]multiplied, the more they sinned against Me;
I will [b]change their glory into shame.
8 They feed on the [1]sin of My people,
And [a]direct their desire toward their iniquity.
9 And it will be, like people, [a]like priest;
So I will punish them for their ways,
And repay them for their deeds.
10 And they will eat, but not have enough;
They will play the harlot, but not increase,
Because they have [1]stopped giving heed to the LORD.

11 Harlotry, wine, and new wine [a]take away the [1]understanding.
12 My people [a]consult their wooden idol, and their *diviner's* wand informs them;
For a spirit of harlotry has led *them* astray,
And they have played the harlot, *departing* [1]from their God.
13 They offer sacrifices on the [a]tops of the mountains
And [1b]burn incense on the hills,
[c]Under oak, poplar, and terebinth,
Because their shade is pleasant.
Therefore your daughters play the harlot,
And your [2]brides commit adultery.
14 I will not punish your daughters when they play the harlot
Or your [1]brides when they commit adultery,
For *the men* themselves go apart with harlots
And offer sacrifices with temple [a]prostitutes;
So the people without understanding are [2]ruined.

1 [1]Or, *truth* [2]Or, *loyalty* [b]Is. 50:4; Jer. 7:28
2 [1]Lit., *touches*
3 [1]Lit., *are taken away* [a]Is. 24:4; 33:9
4 [1]Lit., *contend* [a]Ezek. 3:26; Amos 5:10, 13 [b]Deut. 17:12
5 [a]Hos. 5:5; Ezek. 14:3, 7 [b]Hos. 2:2, 5
6 [a]Hos. 4:14; Zech. 11:8, 9, 15-17
7 [a]Hos. 10:1; 13:6 [b]Hab. 2:16
8 [1]Or, *sin offering* [a]Is. 56:11; Mic. 3:11
9 [a]Is. 24:2; Jer. 5:31
10 [1]Lit., *forsaken giving heed;* or, *forsaken the* LORD *to practice* (v. 11) *harlotry.*
11 [1]Lit., *heart* [a]Is. 5:12; 28:7
12 [1]Lit., *from under* [a]Is. 44:19; Jer. 2:27
13 [1]Or, *offer sacrifices* [2]Or, *daughters-in-law* [a]Jer. 3:6 [b]Hos. 2:13; 11:2 [c]Jer. 2:20
14 [1]Or, *daughters-in-law* [2]Lit., *thrust down* [a]Deut. 23:17

15 [a]Jer. 5:2; 44:26

16 [1]Or, *Now the LORD will pasture . . . field.* [a]Ps. 78:8 [b]Is. 5:17; 7:25

17 [a]Hos. 13:2 [b]Hos. 4:4; Ps. 81:12

18 [1]Lit., *shields*

19 [a]Hos. 12:1; 13:15

2 [1]Or, *waded deep in slaughter* [a]Hos. 4:2; 6:9

3 [a]Amos 3:2; 5:12

4 [a]Hos. 4:6, 14

5 [a]Ezek. 23:31-35

6 [a]Hos. 8:13; Mic. 6:6, 7 [b]Is. 1:15; Jer. 14:12 [c]Ezek. 8:6

7 [1]Lit., *strange* [2]Lit., *portions* [a]Hos. 6:7; Is. 48:8 [b]Hos. 2:4 [c]Hos. 2:11, 12; Is. 1:14

8 [a]Judg. 5:14

9 [a]Hos. 9:11-17; Is. 28:1-4 [b]Is. 37:3 [c]Is. 46:10; Zech. 1:6

10 [a]Deut. 27:17 [b]Ezek. 7:8 [c]Ps. 32:6; 93:3, 4

15 Though you, Israel, play the harlot,
Do not let Judah become guilty;
Also do not go to Gilgal,
Or go up to Beth-aven,
[a]And take the oath:
"As the LORD lives!"
16 Since Israel is [a]stubborn
Like a stubborn heifer,
[1]Can the LORD now [b]pasture them
Like a lamb in a large field?
17 Ephraim is joined to [a]idols;
[b]Let him alone.
18 Their liquor gone,
They play the harlot continually;
Their [1]rulers dearly love shame.
19 [a]The wind wraps them in its wings,
And they will be ashamed because of their sacrifices.

CHAPTER 5

HEAR this, O priests!
Give heed, O house of Israel!
Listen, O house of the king!
For the judgment applies to you,
For you have been a snare at Mizpah,
And a net spread out on Tabor.
2 And the revolters have [1a]gone deep in depravity,
But I will chastise all of them.
3 I [a]know Ephraim, and Israel is not hidden from Me;
For now, O Ephraim, you have played the harlot,
Israel has defiled itself.
4 Their deeds will not allow them
To return to their God.
For a spirit of harlotry is within them,
And they do not [a]know the LORD.
5 Moreover, the pride of Israel testifies against him,
And Israel and Ephraim stumble in their iniquity;
[a]Judah also has stumbled with them.
6 They will [a]go with their flocks and herds
To seek the LORD, but they will [b]not find *Him;*
He has [c]withdrawn from them.
7 They have [a]dealt treacherously against the LORD,
For they have borne [1b]illegitimate children.
Now the [c]new moon will devour them with their [2]land.

8 Blow the horn in Gibeah,
The trumpet in Ramah.
Sound an alarm at Beth-aven:
"[a]Behind you, Benjamin!"
9 Ephraim will become a [a]desolation in the [b]day of rebuke;
Among the tribes of Israel I declare what is [c]sure.
10 The princes of Judah have become like those who [a]move a boundary;
On them I will [b]pour out My wrath [c]like water.

11 Ephraim is oppressed, crushed in judgment,
Because he was determined to [1]follow *man's* command.
12 Therefore I am like a [a]moth to Ephraim,
And like rottenness to the house of Judah.
13 When Ephraim saw his sickness,
And Judah his [1]wound,
Then Ephraim went to Assyria
And sent to [2]King Jareb.
But he is unable to heal you,
Or to cure you of your [1]wound.
14 For I *will be* [a]like a lion to Ephraim,
And like a young lion to the house of Judah.
[b]I, even I, will tear to pieces and go away,
I will carry away, and there will be [c]none to deliver.
15 I will go away *and* return to My place
Until they [1a]acknowledge their guilt and seek My face;
In their affliction they will earnestly [b]seek Me.

Chapter 6

1 "[a]Come, let us return to the Lord.
For he has torn *us,* but He will heal us;
He has [1]wounded *us,* but He will [b]bandage us.
2 "He will [a]revive us after two days;
He will raise us up on the third day
That we may live before Him.
3 "So let us [a]know, let us press on to know the Lord.
His [b]going forth is as certain as the dawn;
And He will come to us like the [c]rain,
Like the spring rain watering the earth."

4 What shall I do with you, O Ephraim?
What shall I do with you, O Judah?
For your [1]loyalty is like a [a]morning cloud,
And like the dew which goes away early.
5 Therefore I have [a]hewn *them* in pieces by the prophets;
I have slain them by the words of My mouth;
And the judgments on you are *like* the light that goes forth.
6 For [a]I delight in loyalty rather than sacrifice,
And in the knowledge of God rather than burnt offerings.
7 But like [1]Adam they have transgressed the covenant;
There they have dealt treacherously against Me.
8 Gilead is a city of wrongdoers,
Tracked with bloody *footprints.*
9 And as raiders wait for a man,
So a band of priests [a]murder on the way to Shechem;
Surely they have committed [1b]crime.
10 In the house of Israel I have seen a [a]horrible thing;
Ephraim's harlotry is there, Israel has defiled itself.
11 Also, O Judah, there is a [a]harvest appointed for you,
When I [b]restore the fortunes of My people.

11 [1]Or, with some ancient versions, *follow nothingness*

12 [a]Ps. 39:11; Is. 51:8

13 [1]Or, *ulcer* [2]Or, *the avenging king;* or, *the great king*

14 [a]Hos. 13:7, 8; Ps. 7:2; Amos 3:4 [b]Ps. 50:22 [c]Mic. 5:8

15 [1]Or, *bear their punishment* [a]Is. 64:7-9; Jer. 3:13, 14 [b]Hos. 3:5; Ps. 50:15; 78:34; Jer. 2:27

1 [1]Lit., *struck* [a]Jer. 50:4, 5 [b]Is. 30:26

2 [a]Ps. 30:5

3 [a]Is. 2:3; Mic. 4:2 [b]Ps. 19:6; Mic. 5:2 [c]Joel 2:23

4 [1]Or, *lovingkindness* [a]Hos. 13:3; Ps. 78:34-37

5 [a]1 Sam. 15:32, 33; Jer. 1:10, 18; 5:14

6 [a]Matt. 9:13; 12:7

7 [1]Or, *men*

9 [1]Or, *lewdness* [a]Hos. 4:2; Jer. 7:9, 10 [b]Hos. 2:10; Ezek. 22:9; 23:27

10 [a]Jer. 5:30, 31; 23:14

11 [a]Jer. 51:33; Joel 3:13 [b]Zeph. 2:7

1 [a]Hos. 7:13; 6:4; 11:8; Ezek. 24:13

2 [1]Lit., *say to their heart* [a]Hos. 8:13; 9:9; Ps. 25:7; Jer. 14:10; Amos 8:7 [b]Hos. 4:9; Jer. 2:19; 4:18

3 [a]Hos. 7:5; Jer. 28:1-4; Mic. 7:3

4 [a]Jer. 9:2; 23:10

5 [1]I.e., a festive occasion [a]Is. 28:1, 7, 8 [b]Is. 28:14

6 [1]Lit., *ambush* [2]So with some ancient versions; M.T., *baker* [3]Lit., *sleeps* [a]Ps. 21:9

8 [1]Lit., *peoples*

9 [a]Is. 1:7

11 [1]Lit., *heart*

12 [1]Lit., *report* [a]Ezek. 12:13

13 [a]Hos. 9:17; Jer. 14:10; Ezek. 34:6 [b]Hos. 7:1; Jer. 51:9; Matt. 23:37

14 [1]Or, with Gk. and many ancient mss., *gash themselves* [a]Judg. 9:27; Amos 2:8; Mic. 2:11

15 [a]Nah. 1:9

Chapter 7

WHEN I [a]would heal Israel,
The iniquity of Ephraim is uncovered,
And the evil deeds of Samaria,
For they deal falsely;
The thief enters in,
Bandits raid outside,
2 And they do not [1]consider in their hearts
That I [a]remember all their wickedness.
Now their [b]deeds are all around them;
They are before My face.
3 With their wickedness they make the [a]king glad,
And the princes with their lies.
4 They are [a]all adulterers
Like an oven heated by the baker,
Who ceases to stir up *the fire*
From the kneading of the dough until it is leavened.
5 On the [1]day of our king the princes [a]became sick with the heat of wine;
He stretched out his hand with [b]scoffers,
6 For their hearts are like an [a]oven
As they approach their [1]plotting;
Their [2]anger [3]smolders all night,
In the morning it burns like a flaming fire.
All of them are hot like an oven,
And they consume their rulers;
7 All their kings have fallen.
None of them calls on Me.

8 Ephraim mixes himself with the [1]nations;
Ephraim has become a cake not turned.
9 [a]Strangers devour his strength,
Yet he does not know *it;*
Gray hairs also are sprinkled on him,
Yet he does not know *it.*
10 Though the pride of Israel testifies against him,
Yet they have neither returned to the LORD their God,
Nor have they sought Him, for all this.
11 So Ephraim has become like a silly dove, without [1]sense;
They call to Egypt, they go to Assyria.
12 When they go, I will [a]spread My net over them;
I will bring them down like the birds of the sky.
I will chastise them in accordance with the [1]proclamation to their assembly.
13 Woe to them, for they have [a]strayed from Me!
Destruction is theirs, for they have rebelled against Me!
I [b]would redeem them, but they speak lies against Me.
14 And they do not cry to Me from their heart
When they wail on their beds;
For the sake of grain and new wine they [1a]assemble themselves,
They turn away from Me.
15 Although I trained *and* strengthened their arms,
Yet they [a]devise evil against Me.

16 They turn, *but* not [1]upward,
They are like a [a]deceitful bow;
Their princes will fall by the sword
Because of the [2b]insolence of their tongue.
This *will be* their [c]derision in the land of Egypt.

CHAPTER 8

PUT the trumpet to your [1]lips!
[a]Like an eagle *the enemy comes* [b]against the house of the LORD,
Because they have transgressed My covenant,
And rebelled against My law.
2 They cry out to Me,
"My God, we of Israel know Thee!"
3 Israel has rejected the good;
The enemy will pursue him.
4 They have set up kings, but not by Me;
They have appointed princes, but I did not know *it*.
With their [a]silver and gold they have made idols for themselves,
That [1]they might be cut off.
5 [1]He has rejected your calf, O Samaria, saying,
"My anger burns against them!"
How long will they be incapable of [a]innocence?
6 For from Israel is even this!
A craftsman made it, so it is not God;
Surely the calf of Samaria will be broken to [1]pieces.
7 For they sow the wind,
And they reap the [a]whirlwind.
The standing grain has no [1]heads;
It yields no [2]grain.
Should it yield, strangers would swallow it up.

8 Israel is [a]swallowed up;
They are now among the nations
Like a [b]vessel in which no one delights.
9 For they have gone up to Assyria,
Like a wild donkey all alone;
Ephraim has [a]hired [1]lovers.
10 Even though they hire *allies* among the nations,
Now I will [a]gather them up;
And they will begin [1b]to diminish
Because of the burden of the [c]king of princes.

11 Since Ephraim has multiplied altars for sin,
They have become altars of sinning for him.
12 Though I wrote for him ten thousand *precepts* of My law,
They are regarded as a strange thing.
13 As for My sacrificial gifts,
They [a]sacrifice the flesh and eat *it*,
But the LORD has taken no delight in them.
Now He will [b]remember their iniquity,
And punish *them* for their sins;
They will return to Egypt.

16 [1]Or possibly, *to the Most High* [2]Lit., *indignation* or *cursing*
[a]Ps. 78:57 [b]Ps. 12:3, 4; 17:10; Dan. 7:25; Mal. 3:13, 14
[c]Ezek. 23:32

1 [1]Lit., *palate*
[a]Hab. 1:8 [b]Deut. 28:49

4 [1]Lit., *he*
[a]Hos. 2:8; 13:1, 2

5 [1]Or, *Your calf has rejected you*
[a]Ps. 19:13; Jer. 13:27

6 [1]Or, *splinters*

7 [1]Lit., *growth* [2]Or, *meal*
[a]Is. 66:15; Nah. 1:3

8 [a]Jer. 51:34 [b]Hos. 13:15; Jer. 25:34

9 [1]Lit., *loves*
[a]Ezek. 16:33

10 [1]Lit., Or, *suffer for awhile*
[a]Ezek. 22:20 [b]Jer. 42:2 [c]Is. 10:8

13 [a]Jer. 6:20; 7:21 [b]Hos. 7:2; Luke 12:2; 1 Cor. 4:5

14 For Israel has [a]forgotten his Maker and [b]built palaces;
And Judah has multiplied fortified cities,
But I will send a [c]fire on its cities that it may consume
its palatial dwellings.

[a]CHAPTER 9

DO not rejoice, O Israel, [1]with exultation like the [2]nations!
For you have played the harlot, [3]forsaking your God.
You have loved *harlots'* earnings on [4]every threshing
floor.
2 Threshing floor and wine press will not feed them,
And the new wine will fail [1]them.
3 They will not remain in the LORD's land,
But Ephraim will return to Egypt,
And in Assyria they will eat [a]unclean *food.*
4 They will not pour out libations of [a]wine to the LORD,
Their sacrifices will not please Him.
Their bread will [1]*be* like [2]mourners' bread;
All who eat of it will be [b]defiled,
For their bread will be for [3]themselves *alone;*
It will not enter the house of the LORD.
5 [a]What will you do on the day of the appointed festival
And on the day of the [b]feast of the LORD?
6 For behold, they will go because of destruction;
Egypt will gather them up, Memphis will bury them.
Weeds will take over their treasures of silver;
[a]Thorns *will be* in their tents.

7 The days of [a]punishment have come,
The days of [b]retribution have come;
[1]Let Israel know *this*!
The prophet is a [c]fool,
The [2]inspired man is [d]demented,
Because of the grossness of your [e]iniquity,
And *because* your hostility is *so* great.
8 Ephraim *was* a watchman with my God, a prophet;
Yet the snare of a bird catcher is in all his ways,
And there is *only* hostility in the house of his God.
9 They have gone [a]deep [1]in depravity
As in the days of Gibeah;
He will [b]remember their iniquity,
He will punish their sins.

10 I found Israel like [a]grapes in the wilderness;
I saw your forefathers as the [b]earliest fruit on the fig
tree in its first *season.*
But they came to Baal-peor and devoted themselves to
[1c]shame,
And they became as [d]detestable as that which they
loved.
11 As for Ephraim, their glory will [a]fly away like a bird—
No birth, no pregnancy, and no conception!
12 Though they bring up their children,
Yet I will bereave them [1]until not a man is left.
Yes, woe to them indeed when I depart from them!

14 [a]Hos. 2:13; 4:6; 13:6 [b]Is. 9:9, 10 [c]Jer. 17:27

1 [1]Lit., *to* [2]Lit., *peoples* [3]Lit., *away from your God* [4]Lit., *all threshing floors of grain* [a]Hos. 10:5; Is. 22:12, 13

2 [1]Lit., *her*

3 [a]Ezek. 4:13

4 [1]Lit., be *to them* [2]Or, *bread of misfortune* [3]Lit., *their appetite* [a]Ex. 29:40 [b]Hag. 2:14

5 [a]Is. 10:3; Jer. 5:31 [b]Hos. 2:11; Joel 1:13

6 [a]Hos. 10:8; Is. 5:6; 7:23

7 [1]Or, *Israel will know it* [2]Lit., *man of the spirit* [a]Is. 10:3; Jer. 10:15; Mic. 7:4 [b]Is. 34:8; Jer. 16:18; 25:14 [c]Lam. 2:14; Ezek. 13:3, 10 [d]Is. 44:25 [e]Ezek. 14:9, 10

9 [1]Lit., *they have corrupted* [a]Is. 31:6 [b]Hos. 7:2; 8:13

10 [1]I.e., Baal [a]Mic. 7:1 [b]Jer. 24:2 [c]Hos. 4:18; Jer. 11:13 [d]Ezek. 20:8

11 [a]Hos. 4:7; 10:5

12 [1]Lit., *without a man*

13 Ephraim, as I have seen,
Is planted in a pleasant meadow like Tyre;
But Ephraim will bring out his children for slaughter.
14 Give them, O LORD— what wilt Thou give?
Give them a [a]miscarrying womb and dry breasts.

15 All their evil is at Gilgal;
Indeed, I came to hate them there!
Because of the [a]wickedness of their deeds
I will drive them out of My house!
I will love them no more;
All their princes are [b]rebels.
16 Ephraim is stricken, their root is dried up,
They will bear no fruit.
Even though they bear children,
I will slay the [a]precious ones of their womb.
17 My God will cast them away
Because they have not listened to Him;
And they will be wanderers among the nations.

CHAPTER 10

ISRAEL is a [1]luxuriant [a]vine;
He produces fruit for himself.
The more his fruit,
The more altars he [b]made;
The [2]richer his land,
The better [3]he made the sacred [c]pillars.
2 Their heart is [1a]faithless;
Now they must bear their [b]guilt.
[2]The LORD will [c]break down their altars
And destroy their sacred pillars.

3 Surely now they will say, "We have [a]no king,
For we do not revere the LORD.
As for the king, what can he do for us?"
4 They speak *mere* words,
[1]With worthless [a]oaths they make covenants;
And [b]judgment sprouts like poisonous weeds in the furrows of the field.
5 The inhabitants of Samaria will fear
For the [1]calf of Beth-aven.
Indeed, its people will mourn for it,
And its idolatrous priests [2]will cry out over it,
Over its glory, since it has departed from it.
6 The thing itself will be carried to Assyria
As tribute to [1]King Jareb;
Ephraim will [2]be seized with shame,
And Israel will be ashamed of its [a]own counsel.
7 Samaria will be [a]cut off *with* her king,
Like a stick on the surface of the water.
8 Also the [a]high places of Aven, the [b]sin of Israel, will be destroyed;
[c]Thorn and thistle will grow on their altars,
Then they will [d]say to the mountains,
"Cover us!" And to the hills, "Fall on us!"

14 [a]Hos. 9:11

15 [a]Hos. 4:9; 7:2; 12:2 [b]Hos. 5:2

16 [a]Ezek. 24:21

1 [1]Or, *degenerate* [2]Or, *better* [3]Lit., *they* [a]Is. 5:1-7; Ezek. 15:1-5 [b]Hos. 8:11; 12:11; Jer. 2:28 [c]Hos. 3:4; 1 Kin. 14:23

2 [1]Lit., *smooth* [2]Lit., *He* [a]1 Kin. 18:21; Zeph. 1:5 [b]Hos. 13:16 [c]Hos. 10:8; Mic. 5:13

3 [a]Ps. 12:4; Is. 5:19

4 [1]Or, *Swearing falsely in making a covenant* [a]Hos. 4:2; Ezek. 17:13-19 [b]Deut. 31:16, 17; 2 Kin. 17:3, 4

5 [1]So with some ancient versions; Heb., *calves* [2]Or, who *used to rejoice over*

6 [1]Or, *the avenging king*; or, *the great king* [2]Lit., *receive shame* [a]Is. 30:3; Jer. 7:24

7 [a]Hos. 13:11

8 [a]Hos. 4:13 [b]1 Kin. 12:28-30; 13:34 [c]Hos. 10:2; 9:6; Is. 32:13 [d]Luke 23:30; Rev. 6:16

9 From the days of Gibeah you have sinned, O Israel;
There they stand!
Will not the battle against the sons of iniquity overtake
them in Gibeah?
10 When it is My [a]desire, I will [1]chastise them;
And the peoples will be gathered against them
When they are bound for their double guilt.

11 And Ephraim is a trained [a]heifer that loves to thresh,
But I will [b]come over her fair neck *with a yoke;*
I will [c]harness Ephraim,
Judah will plow, Jacob will harrow for himself.
12 [a]Sow with a view to righteousness,
Reap in accordance with [1]kindness;
[b]Break up your fallow ground,
For it is time to seek the LORD
Until He comes to [2c]rain righteousness on you.
13 You have [a]plowed wickedness, you have reaped
injustice,
You have eaten the fruit of [b]lies.
Because you have trusted in your way, in your [c]numerous
warriors,
14 Therefore, a tumult will arise among your people,
And all your [a]fortresses will be destroyed,
As Shalman destroyed Beth-arbel on the day of battle,
When [b]mothers were dashed in pieces with *their*
children.
15 Thus it will be done to you at Bethel because of your
great wickedness.
At dawn the king of Israel will be completely cut off.

CHAPTER 11

WHEN Israel *was* a youth I loved him,
And [a]out of Egypt I [b]called My son.
2 The more [1a]they called them,
The more they went from [1]them;
They kept sacrificing to the Baals
And [b]burning incense to idols.
3 Yet it is I who taught Ephraim to walk,
[1]I [a]took them in [1]My arms;
But they did not know that I [b]healed them.
4 I [a]led them with cords of a man, with bonds of love,
And I became to them as one who lifts the yoke from
their jaws;
And I bent down *and* [b]fed them.

5 [1]They will not return to the land of Egypt;
But Assyria—he will be [2]their king,
Because they refused to return *to Me.*
6 And the sword will whirl against [1]their cities,
And will demolish [1]their gate bars
And [a]consume *them* because of their [b]counsels.
7 So My people are bent on [a]turning from Me.
Though [1]they call [2]them to *the One* on high,
None at all exalts *Him.*

10 [1]Or, *bind* [a]Ezek. 5:13

11 [a]Hos. 4:16; Jer. 50:11 [b]Jer. 28:14 [c]Ps. 66:12

12 [1]Or, *loyalty* [2]Or, *teach* [a]Prov. 11:18 [b]Jer. 4:3 [c]Is. 44:3; 45:8

13 [a]Job 4:8; Gal. 6:7 [b]Hos. 4:2; 7:3; 11:12 [c]Ps. 33:16

14 [a]Is. 17:3 [b]Hos. 13:16

1 [a]Hos. 2:15; 12:9, 13; 13:4 [b]Matt. 2:15

2 [1]I.e., God's prophets [a]2 Kin. 17:13-15 [b]Is. 65:7; Jer. 18:15

3 [1]So ancient versions; Heb., *He . . . His* [a]Deut. 1:31; 32:10, 11 [b]Ps. 107:20; Jer. 30:17

4 [a]Jer. 31:2, 3 [b]Ex. 16:32

5 [1]Lit., *He* [2]Lit., *his*

6 [1]Lit., *his* [a]Lam. 2:9 [b]Hos. 4:16, 17

7 [1]I.e., God's prophets [2]Lit., *him;* i.e., Israel [a]Jer. 8:5

8 [a]How can I give you up, O Ephraim?
How can I surrender you, O Israel?
How can I [1]make you like [b]Admah?
How can I treat you like [b]Zeboiim?
My heart is turned over within Me,
[2]All my compassions are kindled.
9 I will [a]not execute My fierce anger;
I will not destroy Ephraim [b]again.
For I am God and not man, the [c]Holy One in your midst,
And I will not come in [1]wrath.
10 They will [a]walk after the LORD,
He will [b]roar like a lion;
Indeed He will roar,
And His sons will come [c]trembling from the west.
11 They will come trembling like birds from [a]Egypt,
And like [b]doves from the land of [a]Assyria;
And I will [c]settle them in their houses, declares the LORD.

12 [1]Ephraim surrounds Me with lies,
And the house of Israel with deceit;
Judah is also unruly against God,
Even against the Holy one who is faithful.

CHAPTER 12

1 EPHRAIM feeds on [a]wind,
And pursues the east [b]wind continually;
He multiplies lies and violence.
Moreover, [2]he makes a covenant with Assyria,
And oil is carried to Egypt.
2 The LORD also has a [a]dispute with Judah,
And will punish Jacob [b]according to his ways;
He will repay him according to his deeds.
3 In the womb he [a]took his brother by the heel,
And in his maturity he [b]contended with God.
4 Yes, he wrestled with the angel and prevailed;
He wept and [a]sought His favor.
He found Him at [b]Bethel,
And there He spoke with us,
5 Even the LORD, the God of hosts;
The LORD is His [1a]name.
6 Therefore, return to your God,
Observe [1]kindness and justice,
And [a]wait for your God continually.
7 A [1a]merchant, in whose hands are false [b]balances,
He loves to oppress.
8 And Ephraim said, "Surely I have become [a]rich,
I have found wealth for myself;
In all my labors they will find in me
[b]No iniquity, which *would be* sin."
9 But I *have been* the LORD your God since the land of Egypt;
I will make you [a]live in tents again,
As in the days of the appointed festival.

8 [1]Lit., *give* [2]Lit., *Together* [a]Hos. 6:4; 7:1 [b]Gen. 14:8; Deut. 29:23

9 [1]Lit., *excitement* [a]Deut. 13:17 [b]Jer. 26:3; 30:11 [c]Is. 5:24; 12:6; 41:14, 16

10 [a]Hos. 3:5; 6:1-3 [b]Is. 31:4; Joel 3:16; Amos 1:2 [c]Is. 66:2, 5

11 [a]Is. 11:11 [b]Hos. 7:11; Is. 60:8 [c]Ezek. 34:27, 28

12 [1]Chap. 12:1 in Heb.

1 [1]Chap. 12:2 in Heb. [2]Lit., *they make* [a]Jer. 22:22 [b]Gen. 41:6; Ezek. 17:10

2 [a]Hos. 4:1 [b]Hos. 4:9; 7:2

3 [a]Gen. 25:26 [b]Gen. 32:28

4 [a]Gen. 32:26 [b]Gen. 28:13-15; 35:10-15

5 [1]Lit., *memorial* [a]Ex. 3:15

6 [1]Or, *royalty* [a]Mic. 7:7

7 [1]Or, *Canaanite* [a]Hos. 7:14 [b]Prov. 11:1; Amos 8:5; Mic. 6:11

8 [a]Hos. 13:6; Ps. 62:10 [b]Hos. 4:8; 14:1

9 [a]Lev. 23:42

10 I have also spoken to the [a]prophets,
And I [1]gave numerous visions;
And through the prophets I gave [b]parables.
11 Is there iniquity *in* Gilead?
Surely they are worthless.
In Gilgal they sacrifice bulls,
Yes, their altars are like the stone heaps
Beside the furrows of the field.

12 Now [a]Jacob fled to the [1]land of Aram,
And [b]Israel worked for a wife,
And for a wife he kept *sheep*.
13 But by a [a]prophet the LORD brought Israel from Egypt,
And by a prophet he was kept.
14 [a]Ephraim has provoked to bitter anger;
So his Lord will leave his [b]blood guilt on him,
And bring back his [c]reproach to him.

CHAPTER 13

[a]WHEN Ephraim [1]spoke, *there was* trembling.
He [b]exalted himself in Israel,
But through [c]Baal he [2]did wrong and died.
2 And now they sin more and more,
And make for themselves [a]molten images,
Idols [1b]skillfully made from their silver,
All of them the [c]work of craftsmen.
They say of them, "Let the [2]men who sacrifice kiss the calves!"
3 Therefore, they will be like the morning cloud,
And like dew which [1]soon disappears,
Like [a]chaff which is blown away from the threshing floor,
And like [b]smoke from a [2]chimney.

4 Yet I *have been* the LORD your God
Since the land of Egypt;
And you were not to know [a]any god except Me,
For there is no savior [b]besides Me.
5 I [1a]cared for you in the wilderness,
In the land of drought.
6 As *they had* their pasture, they became [a]satisfied,
And being satisfied, their heart became proud;
Therefore, they [b]forgot Me.
7 So I will be like a lion to them;
Like a [a]leopard I will [1]lie in wait by the wayside.
8 I will encounter them like a bear robbed of her cubs,
And I will tear open [1]their chests;
There I will also [a]devour them like a lioness,
As a wild beast would tear them.

9 *It is* your destruction, O Israel,
[1]That *you are* [a]against Me, against your [b]help.
10 Where now is your [a]king
That he may save you in all your cities,

10 [1]Lit., *multiplied the vision*
[a]Jer. 7:25 [b]Ezek. 17:2; 20:49

12 [1]Lit., *field*
[a]Gen. 28:5 [b]Gen. 29:20

13 [a]Ex. 14:19-22; Is. 63:11-14

14 [a]2 Kin. 17:7-18 [b]Ezek. 18:10-13 [c]Dan. 11:18; Mic. 6:16

1 [1]Or, *spoke with trembling* [2]Or, *became guilty*
[a]Job 29:21, 22 [b]Judg. 8:1; 12:1 [c]Hos. 2:8-17; 11:2

2 [1]Or, *according to their own understanding* [2]Lit., *sacrificers of* (or, *among*) *mankind*
[a]Hos. 2:8; Is. 46:6; Jer. 10:4 [b]Is. 44:17-20 [c]Hos. 8:6

3 [1]Lit., *goes away early* [2]Lit., *window*
[a]Ps. 1:4; Is. 17:13; Dan. 2:35 [b]Ps. 68:2

4 [a]Ex. 20:3; 2 Kin. 18:35 [b]Is. 43:11; 45:21, 22

5 [1]Or, *knew*
[a]Deut. 32:10

6 [a]Deut. 8:12, 14; 32:13-15; Jer. 5:7 [b]Hos. 2:13; 4:6; 8:14

7 [1]Or, *watch*
[a]Jer. 5:6

8 [1]Lit., *the enclosure of their heart*
[a]Ps. 50:22

9 [1]Or, *But in Me is your help*
[a]Jer. 2:17, 19; Mal. 1:12, 13 [b]Deut. 33:26, 29

10 [a]Hos. 8:4; 2 Kin. 17:4

And your judges of whom you [1]requested,
"Give me a king and princes"?
11 I [a]gave you a king in My anger,
And [b]took him away in My wrath.

12 The iniquity of Ephraim is bound up;
His sin is [a]stored up.
13 The pains of [a]childbirth come upon him;
He is [b]not a wise son,
For [1]it is not the time that he should [c]delay at the
opening of the womb.
14 I will [a]ransom them from the [1]power of Sheol;
I will redeem them from death.
[b]O Death, where are your thorns?
O Sheol, where is your sting?
[c]Compassion will be hid from My sight.

15 Though he [a]flourishes among the [1]reeds,
An [b]east wind will come,
The wind of the LORD coming up from the wilderness;
And his fountain will [c]become dry,
And his spring will be dried up;
It will [d]plunder *his* treasury of every precious article.
16 [1]Samaria will be held guilty,
For she has rebelled against her God.
They will fall by the sword,
Their little ones will be dashed in pieces,
And their pregnant [a]women will be ripped open.

Chapter 14

1a RETURN, O Israel, to the LORD your God,
For you have stumbled [2]because of your [b]iniquity.
2 Take words with you and return to the LORD.
Say to Him, "[a]Take away all iniquity,
And [1]receive *us* graciously,
That we may [b]present [2]the fruit of our lips.
3 "Assyria will not save us,
We will [a]not ride on horses;
Nor will we say again, '[b]Our god,'
To the [c]work of our hands;
For in [d]Thee the [1]orphan finds mercy."

4 I will [a]heal their apostasy,
I will [b]love them freely,
For My anger has [c]turned away from them.
5 I will be like the [a]dew to Israel;
He will blossom like the [b]lily
And he will [1]take root like *the cedars of* Lebanon.
6 His shoots will [1]sprout,
And his [2]beauty will be like the [a]olive tree,
And his fragrance like *the cedars of* [b]Lebanon.
7 Those who [a]live in his shadow;
Will [1]again raise grain,
And they will blossom like the vine.
His renown *will be* like the wine of Lebanon.

10 [1]Lit., *said*

11 [a]1 Sam. 8:7 [b]Hos. 10:7; 1 Kin. 14:7-10

12 [a]Deut. 32:34, 35; Job 14:17; Rom. 2:5

13 [1]Lit., *it is the time that he should not tarry at the breaking forth of children* [a]Mic. 4:9, 10 [b]Hos. 5:4; Deut. 32:6 [c]Is. 37:3; 66:9

14 [1]Lit., *hand* [a]Ps. 49:15; Ezek. 37:12, 13 [b]1 Cor. 15:55 [c]Jer. 20:16; 31:35-37

15 [1]Or, *brothers* [a]Hos. 10:1; Gen. 49:22 [b]Gen. 41:6; Ezek. 17:10; 19:12 [c]Jer. 51:36 [d]Jer. 20:5

16 [1]Ch. 14:1 in Heb. [a]2 Kin. 15:16

1 [1]Ch. 14:2 in Heb. [2]Or, *in* [a]Hos. 6:1; 10:12; 12:6 [b]Hos. 4:8; 5:5; 9:7

2 [1]Or, *accept that which is good* [2]So with ancient versions; M.T., *our lips as bulls* [a]Mic. 7:18, 19 [b]Hos. 6:6; Ps. 51:16, 17

3 [1]Or, *fatherless* [a]Is. 31:1 [b]Hos. 8:6; 13:2 [c]Hos. 4:12 [d]Ps. 68:5

4 [a]Hos. 6:1; Is. 57:18 [b]Zeph. 3:17 [c]Is. 12:1

5 [1]Lit., *strike his roots* [a]Is. 26:19 [b]Song of Sol. 2:1; Matt. 6:28

6 [1]Lit., *go* [2]Or, *splendor* [a]Jer. 11:16 [b]Song of Sol. 4:11

7 [1]Or, *return, they will raise grain* [a]Ezek. 17:23

8 O Ephraim, what more have I to do with [a]idols?
It is I who answer and look after [1]you.
I am like a luxuriant [b]cypress;
From [c]Me comes your fruit.

9 [a]Whoever is wise, let him understand these things;
Whoever is discerning, let him know them.
For the [b]ways of the LORD are right,
And the [c]righteous will walk in them,
But [d]transgressors will stumble in them.

8 [1]Lit., *him* [a]Hos. 14:3; Job 34:32 [b]Is. 41:19 [c]Ezek. 17:23

9 [a]Ps. 107:43; Jer. 9:12 [b]Ps. 111:7, 8; Zeph. 3:5 [c]Is. 26:7 [d]Is. 1:28

THE BOOK OF JOEL

Devastation of Locusts.

THE [a]word of the LORD that came to [b]Joel, the son of
Pethuel.
2 [a]Hear this, O [b]elders,
And listen, all inhabitants of the land.
Has *anything like* this happened in [c]your days
Or in your fathers' days?
3 [a]Tell your sons about it,
And *let* your sons *tell* their sons,
And their sons the next generation.

4 What the [a]gnawing locust has left, the swarming locust has eaten;
And what the swarming locust has left, the [b]creeping locust has eaten;
And what the creeping locust has left, the [c]stripping locust has eaten.
5 Awake, drunkards, and weep;
And wail, all you wine drinkers,
On account of the sweet wine,
That is cut off from your mouth.
6 For a [a]nation has [1]invaded my land,
Mighty and without number;
Its teeth are the teeth of a lion,
And it has the fangs of a lioness.
7 It has [a]made my vine a waste,
And my fig tree [1]splinters.
It has stripped them bare and cast *them* away;
Their branches have become white.

8 Wail like a virgin [a]girded with sackcloth
For the bridegroom of her youth.
9 The [a]grain offering and the libation are cut off
From the house of the LORD.
The priests mourn,
The ministers of the LORD.
10 The field is [a]ruined,
The land mourns;

1 [a]Jer. 1:2; Ezek. 1:3; Hos. 1:1 [b]Acts 2:16

2 [a]Hos. 4:1; 5:1 [b]Joel 1:14; Job 8:8 [c]Joel 2:2; Jer. 30:7

3 [a]Ex. 10:2; Ps. 78:4

4 [a]Joel 2:25; Amos 4:9 [b]Nah. 3:15, 16 [c]Is. 33:4

6 [1]Lit., *come up against* [a]Joel 2:2, 11, 25

7 [1]Or, *a stump* [a]Amos 4:9

8 [a]Joel 1:13; Amos 8:10

9 [a]Joel 1:13; 2:14; Hos. 9:4

10 [a]Is. 24:4, 7

For the grain is ruined,
The new wine dries up,
Fresh oil [1]fails.
11 [1a]Be ashamed, O farmers,
Wail, O vinedressers,
For the wheat and the barley;
Because the [b]harvest of the field is destroyed.
12 The [a]vine dries up,
And the fig tree [1]fails;
The [b]pomegranate, the [c]palm also, and the [2d]apple tree,
All the trees of the field dry up.
Indeed, [e]rejoicing dries up
From the sons of men.

13 Gird yourselves *with sackcloth,*
And lament, O priests;
[a]Wail, O ministers of the altar!
Come, [b]spend the night in sackcloth,
O ministers of my God,
For the grain offering and the libation
Are withheld from the house of your God.
14 Consecrate a fast,
Proclaim a solemn assembly;
Gather the elders
And all the inhabitants of the land
To the house of the LORD your God,
And [a]cry out to the LORD.
15 [a]Alas for the day!
For the day of the LORD is near,
And it will come as [b]destruction from the [1]Almighty.
16 Has not [a]food been cut off before our eyes,
Gladness and [b]joy from the house of our God?
17 The [1a]seeds shrivel under their [2]clods;
The storehouses are desolate,
The barns are torn down,
For the grain is dried up.
18 How the beasts groan!
The herds of cattle wander aimlessly
Because there is no pasture for them;
Even the flocks of sheep [1]suffer.
19 [a]To Thee, O LORD, I cry;
For [b]fire has devoured the pastures of the wilderness,
And the flame has burned up all the trees of the field.
20 Even the beasts of the field [1a]pant for Thee;
For the [b]water brooks are dried up,
And fire has devoured the pastures of the wilderness.

CHAPTER 2

[a]BLOW a trumpet in Zion,
And sound an alarm on My holy mountain!
Let all the inhabitants of the land tremble,
For the [b]day of the LORD is coming;
Surely it is near,
2 A day of [a]darkness and gloom,

10 [1]Lit., *wastes away*

11 [1]Or, *The farmers are ashamed, The vinedressers wail*
[a]Jer. 14:4; Amos 5:16 [b]Is. 17:11; Jer. 9:12

12 [1]Lit., *wastes away* [2]Or, *apricot*
[a]Hab. 3:17, 18 [b]Hag. 2:19 [c]Song of Sol. 7:8 [d]Song of Sol. 2:3 [e]Is. 16:10; 24:11

13 [a]Jer. 9:10 [b]1 Kin. 21:27

14 [a]Jon. 3:8

15 [1]Heb., *Shaddai*
[a]Jer. 30:7; Amos 5:16 [b]Is. 13:6; Ezek. 7:2-12

16 [a]Is. 3:7; Amos 4:6, 7 [b]Deut. 12:6, 7; Ps. 43:4

17 [1]Or, *dried figs* [2]Or, *shovels*
[a]Is. 17: 10, 11

18 [1]Lit., *bear punishment*

19 [a]Ps. 50:15; Mic. 7:7 [b]Jer. 9:10; Amos 7:4

20 [1]Lit., *long for*
[a]Joel 1:18; Ps. 104:21; 147:9 [b]1 Kin. 17:7; 18:5

1 [a]Joel 2:15; Zeph. 1:16 [b]Joel 2:11, 31; 1:15; 3:14

2 [a]Joel 2:10, 31; Zeph. 1:15

A day of clouds and thick darkness.
As the dawn is spread over the mountains,
So there is a [b]great and mighty people;
There has [c]never been *anything* like it,
Nor will there be again after it
To the years of many generations.
3 A [a]fire consumes before them,
And behind them a flame burns.
The land is [b]like the garden of Eden before them,
But a [c]desolate wilderness behind them,
And nothing at all escapes them.
4 Their [a]appearance is like the appearance of horses;
And like war horses, so they run.
5 [1]With a [a]noise as of chariots
They leap on the tops of the mountains,
Like the [2]crackling of a [b]flame of fire consuming the stubble,
Like a mighty people arranged for battle.
6 Before them the peoples are in [a]anguish;
All [b]faces [1]turn pale.
7 They run like [a]mighty men;
They climb the wall like soldiers;
And they each march [1]in line,
Nor do they deviate from their paths.
8 They do not crowd each other;
They march every one in his path.
When they [1]burst through the [2]defenses,
They do not break ranks.
9 They rush on the city,
They run on the wall;
They climb into the [a]houses,
They [b]enter through the windows like a thief.
10 Before them the earth [a]quakes,
The heavens tremble,
The [b]sun and the moon grow dark,
And the stars lose their brightness.
11 And the LORD [a]utters His voice before His army;
Surely His camp is very great,
For [b]strong is He who carries out His word.
The [c]day of the LORD is indeed great and very awesome,
And [d]who can endure it?
12 "Yet even now," declares the LORD,
"[a]Return to Me with all your heart,
And with fasting, weeping, and mourning;
13 And rend your heart and not your garments."
Now return to the LORD your God,
For He is [a]gracious and compassionate,
Slow to anger, abounding in lovingkindness,
And [b]relenting of evil.
14 Who knows whether He will *not* turn and relent,
And leave a [a]blessing behind Him,
Even a grain offering and a libation
For the LORD your God?
15 Blow a trumpet in Zion,
Consecrate a fast, proclaim a solemn assembly,

2 [b]Joel 2:11, 25; 1:6 [c]Joel 1:2; Lam. 1:12; Dan. 9:12; 12:1
3 [a]Ps. 97:3; Is. 9:18, 19 [b]Is. 51:3; Ezek. 36:35 [c]Ex. 10:5, 15; Ps. 105:34, 35
4 [a]Rev. 9:7
5 [1]Lit., *Like the noise of chariots* [2]Lit., *noise* [a]Rev. 9:9 [b]Is. 5:24; 30:30
6 [1]Or, *become flushed* [a]Is. 13:8; Nah. 2:10 [b]Jer. 30:6
7 [1]Lit., *in his ways* [a]Is. 5:26, 27
8 [1]Lit., *fall* [2]Lit., *weapon*, probably *javelin*
9 [a]Ex. 10:6 [b]Jer. 9:21
10 [a]Joel 3:16, Ps. 18:7; Nah. 1:5 [b]Joel 2:31; 3:15; Is. 13:10; 34:4; Jer. 4:23; Ezek. 32:7
11 [a]Joel 3:16; Ps. 46:6; Is. 13:4 [b]Jer. 50:34; Rev. 18:8 [c]Joel 1:31; 1:15; 3:14 [d]Ezek. 22:14
12 [a]Deut. 4:29; Ezek. 33:11
13 [a]Ex. 34:6 [b]Jer. 18:8; 42:10; Amos 7:3, 6
14 [a]Hag. 2:19

16 Gather the people, sanctify the congregration,
Assemble the elders,
Gather the children and the nursing infants.
Let the [a]bridegroom come out of his room
And the bride out of her *bridal* chamber.
17 Let the priests, the LORD's ministers,
[a]Weep between the porch and the altar,
And let them say, "[b]Spare Thy people, O LORD,
And do not make Thine inheritance a [c]reproach,
A byword among the nations.
Why should they among the peoples say,
'[d]Where is their God?' "

18 Then the LORD [1]will be [a]zealous for His land,
And [2]will have [b]pity on His people.
19 And the LORD [1]will answer and say to His people,
"Behold, I am going to send you grain, new wine, and oil,
And you will be satisfied *in full* with [2]them;
And I will [a]never again make you a reproach among the nations.
20 "But I will remove the [a]northern *army* far from you,
And I will drive it into a parched and desolate land,
And its vanguard into the [b]eastern sea,
And its rear guard into the [c]western sea.
And its [d]stench will arise and its foul smell will come up,
For it has done great things."

21 Do not [a]fear, O land, rejoice and be glad,
For the LORD has done [b]great things.
22 Do not fear, beasts of the field,
For the pastures of the wilderness have turned green,
For the tree has borne its fruit,
The fig tree and the vine have yielded [1]in full.
23 So rejoice, O sons of Zion,
And [a]be glad in the LORD your God;
For He has [b]given you [1]the early rain for *your* vindication.
And He has poured down for you the rain,
The [2]early and [3c]latter rain [4]as before.
24 And the threshing [a]floors will be full of grain,
And the vats will overflow with the new wine and oil.
25 "Then I will make up to you for the years
That the swarming [a]locust has eaten,
The creeping locust, the stripping locust, and the gnawing locust,
My great army which I sent among you.
26 "And you shall have plenty to [a]eat and be satisfied,
And [b]praise the name of the LORD your God,
Who has [c]dealt wondrously with you;
Then My people will never be [d]put to shame.
27 "Thus you will [a]know that I am in the midst of Israel,
And that I am the LORD your God
And there is [b]no other;
And My people will never be put to shame.

16 [a]Ps. 19:5

17 [a]2 Chr. 8:12; Ezek. 8:16 [b]Is. 37:20; Amos 7:2, 5 [c]Ps. 44:13; 74:10 [d]Ps. 79:10; 115:2

18 [1]Or, *was zealous* [2]Or, *had pity* [a]Zech. 1:14; 8:2 [b]Is. 60:10; 63:9, 15

19 [1]Or, *answered and said* [2]Lit., *it* [a]Ezek. 34:29; 36:15

20 [a]Jer. 1:14, 15 [b]Zech. 14:8 [c]Deut. 11:24 [d]Is. 34:3; Amos 4:10

21 [a]Is. 54:4; Jer. 30:10; Zeph. 3:16, 17 [b]Joel 2:26; Ps. 126:3

22 [1]Lit., *their wealth*

23 [1]I.e., autumn; or possibly, *the teacher for righteousness* [2]I.e., autumn [3]I.e., spring [4]So with ancient versions; Heb., *in the first* [a]Is. 12:2-6 [b]Deut. 11:14; Jer. 5:24 [c]Hos. 6:3; Zech. 10:1

24 [a]Lev. 26:10; Amos 9:13; Mal. 3:10

25 [a]Joel 2:2-11; 1:4-7

26 [a]Deut. 11:15; Is. 62:9 [b]Deut. 12:7; Ps. 67:5-7 [c]Ps. 126:2, 3; Is. 25:1 [d]Is. 45:17

27 [a]Joel 3:17, 21 [b]Is. 45:5, 6

28 “[1]And it will come about after this
That I will pour out My [a]Spirit on all [2b]mankind;
And your sons and daughters will prophesy,
Your old men will dream dreams,
Your young men will see visions.
29 “And even on the [a]male and female servants
I will pour out My Spirit in those days.
30 “And I will [a]display wonders in the sky and on the earth,
Blood, fire, and columns of smoke.
31 “The [a]sun will be turned into darkness,
And the moon into blood,
Before the [b]great and awesome day of the LORD comes.
32 “And it will come about that [a]whoever calls on the name of the LORD
Will be delivered;
For on Mount Zion and in Jerusalem
There will be those who [b]escape,
As the LORD has said,
Even among the survivors whom the LORD calls.

CHAPTER 3

“[1]FOR behold, in those days and at that time,
When I restore the fortunes of Judah and Jerusalem,
2 I will [a]gather all the nations,
And bring them down to the [b]valley of [1]Jehoshaphat.
Then I will [c]enter into judgment with them there
On behalf of My people and My inheritance, Israel,
Whom they have [d]scattered among the nations;
And they have [e]divided up My land.
3 “They have also [a]cast lots for my people,
[1b]Traded a boy for a harlot,
And sold a girl for wine that they may drink.

4 “Moreover, what are you to Me, O Tyre, Sidon, and all
the regions of Philistia? Are you rendering Me a recompense?
But if you do recompense Me, swiftly and speedily I will return your recompense on your head.
5 “Since you have [a]taken My silver and My gold, brought
My precious [1]treasures to your temples,
6 and sold the sons of Judah and Jerusalem to the
[1]Greeks in order to remove them far from their territory,
7 behold, I am going to arouse them from the place
where you have sold them, and return your recompense on
your head.
8 “Also I will sell your sons and your daughters into the
hand of the sons of Judah, and they will sell them to the
Sabeans, to a distant nation,” for the LORD has spoken.

9 [a]Proclaim this among the nations:
[b]Prepare a war; [c]rouse the mighty men!
Let all the soldiers draw near, let them come up!
10 [a]Beat your plowshares into swords,
And your pruning hooks into spears;
Let the weak say, “I am a mighty man.”
11 [1]Hasten and come all you surrounding nations,
And gather yourselves there.
Bring down, O LORD, Thy [a]mighty ones.

28 [1]Chap. 3:1 in Heb. [2]Lit., *flesh* [a]Is. 32:15; 44:3; Ezek. 39:29 [b]Is. 40:5; 49:6

29 [a]1 Cor. 12:13

30 [a]Luke 21:11, 25, 26; Acts 2:19

31 [a]Joel 2:10; 3:15; Is. 13:9, 10; 34:4; Matt. 24:29; Mark 13:24; Acts 2:20 [b]Zeph. 1:14-16; Mal. 4:1, 5

32 [a]Jer. 33:3; Acts 2:21; Rom. 10:13 [b]Is. 4:2; Obad. 17

1 [1]Chap. 4:1 in Heb.

2 [1]I.e., YHWH judges [a]Is. 66:18; Mic. 4:12 [b]Joel 3:14 [c]Is. 66:16; Jer. 25:31 [d]Jer. 50:17; Ezek. 34:6 [e]Ezek. 35:10; 36:1-5

3 [1]Lit., *Given* [a]Obad. 11; Nah. 3:10 [b]Amos 2:6

5 [1]Lit., *goodly things* [a]2 Kin. 12:18; 2 Chr. 21:16, 17

6 [1]Lit., *sons of Javan*

9 [a]Jer. 51:27, 28 [b]Jer. 6:4; Mic. 3:5 [c]Is. 8:9, 10; Jer. 46:3, 4; Zech. 14:2, 3

10 [a]Is. 2:4; Mic. 4:3

11 [1]Or, *Lend aid* [a]Is. 13:3

12 Let the nations be aroused
And come up to the [a]valley of [1]Jehoshaphat,
For there I will sit to [b]judge
All the surrounding nations.
13 Put in the sickle, for the [a]harvest is ripe.
Come, tread, for the wine press is full;
The vats overflow, for their [b]wickedness is great.
14 [a]Multitudes, multitudes in the [b]valley of [1]decision!
For the [c]day of the LORD is near in the valley of [1]decision.
15 The [a]sun and moon grow dark,
And the stars lose their brightness.
16 And the LORD [a]roars from Zion
And utters His voice from Jerusalem,
And the [b]heavens and the earth tremble.
But the LORD is a [c]refuge for His people
And a [d]stronghold to the sons of Israel.
17 Then you will know that I am the LORD your God,
Dwelling in Zion My [a]holy mountain.
So Jerusalem will be [b]holy,
And [c]strangers will pass through it no more.

18 And it will come about in that day
That the [a]mountains will drip with [1]sweet wine,
And the hills will [b]flow with milk,
And all the [c]brooks of Judah will flow with water;
And a [d]spring will go out from the house of the LORD,
To water the valley of [2]Shittim.
19 Egypt will become a waste,
And Edom will become a desolate wilderness,
Because of the [a]violence done to the sons of Judah,
In whose land they have shed innocent blood.
20 But Judah will be [a]inhabited forever,
And Jerusalem for all generations.
21 And I will [a]avenge their blood which I have not avenged,
For the LORD dwells in Zion.

THE BOOK OF AMOS

Judgment on Neighbor Nations.

THE words of Amos, who was among the sheepherders from
[a]Tekoa, which he [1]envisioned in visions concerning Israel in
the days of Uzziah king of Judah, and in the days of Jeroboam
son of Joash king of Israel, two years before the [b]earthquake.
2 And he said,
"The [a]LORD roars from Zion,
And from Jerusalem He utters His voice;
And the shepherds' [b]pasture grounds mourn,
And the [1]summit of Carmel dries up."

3 Thus says the LORD,
"For three transgressions of Damascus and for four

12 [1]I.e., YHWH judges [a]Joel 3:2, 14 [b]Ps. 7:6; 98:9; Is. 3:13

13 [a]Jer. 51:33; Hos. 6:11 [b]Gen. 18:20

14 [1]I.e., God's verdict [a]Is. 34:2-8 [b]Joel 3:2, 12 [c]Joel 1:15; 2:1, 11, 31

15 [a]Joel 2:10, 31

16 [a]Hos. 11:10; Amos 1:2 [b]Joel 2:10; Ezek. 38:19; Hag. 2:6 [c]Ps. 61:3; Is. 33:16; Jer. 17:17 [d]Jer. 16:19; Nah. 1:7

17 [a]Is. 11:9; 56:7; Ezek. 20:40 [b]Is. 4:3; Obad. 17 [c]Is. 52:1; Nah. 1:15

18 [1]Lit., *freshly pressed out grape juice* [2]Or, *acacias* [a]Amos 9:13 [b]Ex. 3:8 [c]Is. 30:25; 35:6 [d]Ezek. 47:1-12

19 [a]Obad. 10

20 [a]Ezek. 37:25; Amos 9:15

21 [a]Is. 4:4; Ezek. 36:25

1 [1]Lit., *concerning saw* [a]2 Sam. 14:2; Jer. 6:1 [b]Zech. 14:5

2 [1]Lit., *head* [a]Is. 42:13; Jer. 25:30; Joel 3:16 [b]Jer. 12:4; Joel 1: 18, 19

I will [a]not [1]revoke its *punishment*,
Because they threshed Gilead with *implements* of sharp iron.
4 "So I will send fire upon the house of Hazael,
And it will consume the citadels of Behadad.
5 "I will also [a]break the *gate* bar of Damascus,
And cut off the inhabitant from the [1]Valley of Aven,
And him who holds the scepter, from Beth Eden;
So the people of Syria will go exiled to Kir,"
Says the LORD.

6 Thus says the LORD,
"For three transgressions of [a]Gaza and for four
I will not revoke its *punishment*,
Because they deported an entire population
To deliver *it* up to [b]Edom.
7 "So I will send fire upon the wall of Gaza,
And it will consume her citadels.
8 "I will also cut off the inhabitant from [a]Ashdod,
And him who holds the scepter, from [b]Ashkelon;
I will even [1]unleash My [2]power upon Ekron,
And the remnant of the [c]Philistines will perish,"
Says the Lord [3]GOD.

9 Thus says the LORD,
"For three transgressions of [a]Tyre and for four
I will not revoke its *punishment*,
Because they delivered up an entire population to Edom
And did not remember *the* covenant of [1b]brotherhood.
10 "So I will send fire upon the wall of Tyre,
And it will consume her citadels."

11 Thus says the LORD,
"For three transgressions of [a]Edom and for four
I will not revoke its *punishment*,
Because he [b]pursued his brother with the sword,
While he [1]stifled his compassion;
His anger also [c]tore continually,
And he maintained his fury forever.
12 "So I will send fire upon [a]Teman,
And it will consume the citadels of Bozrah."

13 Thus says the LORD,
"For three transgressions of the sons of [a]Ammon and for four
I will not revoke its *punishment*,
Because they [b]ripped open the pregnant women of Gilead
In order to [c]enlarge their borders.
14 "So I will kindle a fire on the wall of Rabbah,
And it will consume her citadels
Amid [1a]war cries on the day of battle
And a [b]storm on the day of tempest.
15 "Their [a]king will go into exile,
He and his princes together," says the LORD.

3 [1]Lit., *cause it to turn back*, and so throughout the chap. [a]Is. 8:4

5 [1]Possibly *Baalbek* [a]Jer. 51:30; Lam. 2:9

6 [a]1 Sam. 6:17; Jer. 47:1, 5; Zeph. 2:4 [b]Ezek. 35:5; Obad. 11

8 [1]Lit., *cause to return* [2]Lit., *hand* [3]YHWH, usually rendered LORD [a]Amos 3:9; 2 Chr. 26:6; Zech. 9:6 [b]Jer. 47:5; Zeph. 2:4 [c]Is. 14:29-31; Ezek. 25:16

9 [1]Lit., *brothers* [a]Is. 23:1-18; Jer. 25:22; Ezek. 26:2-4 [b]1 Kin. 5:1; 9:11-14

11 [1]Lit., *corrupted* [a]Is. 34:5, 6; 63:1-6; Jer. 49:7-22 [b]Num. 20:14-21; 2 Chr. 28:17; Obad. 10-12 [c]Is. 57:16; Mic. 7:18

12 [a]Jer. 49:7, 20

13 [a]Jer. 49:1-6; Ezek. 25:2-7; Zeph. 2:8, 9 [b]2 Kin. 15:16; Hos. 13:16 [c]Is. 5:8; Ezek. 35:10

14 [1]Or, *shouts* [a]Amos 2:2; Ezek. 21:22 [b]Is. 29:6; 30:30

15 [a]Jer. 49:3

CHAPTER 2

THUS says the LORD,
"For three transgressions of [a]Moab and for four
I will not [1]revoke its *punishment,*
Because he burned the bones of the king of Edom to lime.
2 "So I will send fire upon Moab,
And it will consume the citadels of [a]Kerioth;
And Moab will die amid [b]tumult,
With [1]war cries and the sound of a trumpet.
3 "I will also cut off the [1a]judge from her midst,
And slay all her princes with him," says the LORD.

4 Thus says the LORD,
"For three transgressions of [a]Judah and for four
I will not revoke its *punishment,*
Because they [b]rejected the law of the LORD
And have not kept His statutes;
Their [1c]lies also have led them astray,
Those after which their [d]fathers walked.
5 "So I will [a]send fire upon Judah,
And it will consume the citadels of Jerusalem."

6 Thus says the LORD,
"For three transgressions of Israel and for four
I will not revoke its *punishment,*
Because they [a]sell the righteous for money
And the needy for a pair of sandals.
7 "These who [1]pant after the *very* dust of the earth on the head of the [a]helpless
Also turn aside the way of the humble;
And a [b]man and his father [2]resort to the same [3]girl
In order to profane My holy name.
8 "And on garments [a]taken as pledges they stretch out beside every altar,
And in the house of their God they drink the wine of those who have been fined.

9 "Yet it was I who destroyed the Amorite before them,
[1]Though his height *was* like the height of cedars
And he *was* strong as the oaks;
I even destroyed his [a]fruit above and his root below.
10 "And it was I who brought you up from the land of Egypt,
And I led you in the wilderness [a]forty years
[1]That you might take possession of the land of the Amorite.
11 "Then I [a]raised up some of your sons to be prophets
And some of your young men to be [b]Nazirites.
Is this not so, O sons of Israel?" declares the LORD.
12 "But you made the Nazirites drink wine,
And you commanded the prophets saying, 'You shall not [a]prophesy!'

1 [1]Lit., *cause it to turn back,* and so throughout the chap. [a]Is. 15:1-16:14; Jer. 48:1-47; Zeph. 2:8, 9

2 [1]Or, *shouts* [a]Jer. 48:24, 41 [b]Jer. 48:45

3 [1]Or, *executive officer* [a]Amos 5:7, 12; 6:12; Ps. 2:10; 141:6

4 [1]Or, *false gods* [a]Amos 3:2; 2 Kin. 17:19; Hos. 12:2 [b]Judg. 2:17-20; 2 Kin. 22:11-17; Jer 6:19; 8:9 [c]Is. 9:15, 16; 28:15; Hab. 2:18 [d]Jer. 9:14; 16:11, 12; Ezek. 20:18, 24, 30

5 [a]Jer. 17:27; 21:10

6 [a]Amos 5:11, 12; 8:6; Joel 3:3

7 [1]Or, *trample the head of the helpless on the dust;* or, *snap at,* etc. [2]Lit., *go* [3]Possibly a harlot, or a temple prostitute [a]Amos 8:4; Mic. 2:2, 9 [b]Hos. 4:14

8 [a]Ex. 22:26

9 [1]Lit., *Whose height* [a]Ezek. 17:9; Mal. 4:1

10 [1]Lit., *To possess* [a]Deut. 2:7

11 [a]Deut. 18:17; Jer. 7:25 [b]Num. 6:2, 3

12 [a]Amos 7:13, 16; Jer. 11:21

13 "Behold, I am [1a]weighted down beneath you
As a wagon is [2]weighted down when filled with sheaves.
14 "[1a]Flight will perish from the swift,
And the stalwart will not strengthen his power,
Nor the [b]mighty man save his [2]life.
15 "He who grasps the bow will not stand *his ground,*
The swift of foot will not escape,
Nor will he who [a]rides the horse save his [1]life.
16 "Even the [1]bravest among the warriors will [a]flee naked
in that day," declares the LORD.

CHAPTER 3

HEAR this word which the LORD has spoken against you,
sons of Israel, against the entire [1a]family which [2]He brought up
from the land of Egypt,
2 "[a]You only have Me among all the families of the earth;
Therefore, I will [1]punish you for all your iniquities."
3 Do two men [a]walk together unless they have made an
[1]appointment?
4 Does a lion [a]roar in the forest when he has no prey?
Does a young lion [1]growl from his den unless he has
captured *something?*
5 Does a bird fall into a trap on the ground when there is
no [1]bait in it?
Does a trap spring up from the earth when it captures
nothing at all?
6 If a [a]trumpet is blown in a city will not the people
tremble?
If a [b]calamity occurs in a city has not the LORD done it?
7 [1]Surely the LORD God does nothing
Unless He [a]reveals His secret counsel
To His servants the prophets.
8 A lion has roared! Who will not fear?
The [a]Lord [1]GOD has spoken! [b]Who can but prophesy?
9 Proclaim on the citadels in Ashdod and on the citadels
in the land of Egypt and say, "Assemble yourselves on the
[a]mountains of Samaria and see *the* great tumults within her
and *the* [b]oppressions in her midst.
10 "But they do not [a]know how to do what is right," declares
the LORD, "these who [b]hoard up [1]violence and devastation in their citadels."
11 Therefore, thus says the Lord GOD,
"An enemy, even one surrounding the land,
Will pull down your [1]strength from you
And your citadels will be looted."
12 Thus says the LORD,
"Just as the shepherd [1a]snatches from the lion's mouth a
couple of legs or a piece of an ear,
So will the sons of Israel dwelling in Samaria be
[2]snatched away—
With *the* corner of a bed and *the* [3]cover of a couch!
13 "Hear and [a]testify against the house of Jacob,"
Declares the Lord GOD, the God of hosts.
14 "For on the day that I punish Israel's transgressions,
I will also punish the altars of [a]Bethel;

13 [1]Or, *tottering* [2]Or, *totters* [a]Joel 3:13

14 [1]Or, *A place of refuge* [2]Lit., *soul* [a]Is. 30:16, 17 [b]Jer. 9:23

15 [1]Lit., *soul* [a]Is. 31:3

16 [1]Lit., *stout of heart* [a]Judg. 4:17; Jer. 48:41

1 [1]I.e., nation [2]Lit., *I* [a]Jer. 8:3; 13:11

2 [1]Lit., *visit* [a]Ex. 19:5, 6; Deut. 4:32:37

3 [1]Or, *agreement* [a]Lev. 26:23, 24

4 [1]Lit., *give his voice* [a]Ps. 104:21; Hos. 5:14; 11:10

5 [1]Or, *striker-bar set*

6 [a]Jer. 4:5, 19, 21; 6:1; Hos. 5:8; Zeph. 1:16 [b]Is. 14:24-27; 45:7

7 [1]Or, *For* [a]Gen. 18:17; Jer. 23:22; Dan. 9:22

8 [1]YHWH, usually rendered LORD, and so throughout the chap. [a]Jon. 1:1-3; 3:1-3 [b]Jer. 20:9

9 [a]Amos 4:1; 6:1; Is. 28:1; Ezek. 37:22 [b]Amos 4:1; 5:11; 8:6

10 [1]I.e., the booty from violence, etc. [a]Amos 5:7; 6:12; Ps. 14:4; Jer. 4:22 [b]Hab. 2:8-11; Zeph. 1:9; Zech. 5:3, 4

11 [1]Or, *stronghold*

12 [1]Or, *delivers* [2]Or, *delivered* [3]Lit., *damask* [a]1 Sam. 17:34-37

13 [a]Ezek. 2:7

14 [a]Amos 4:4; 5:5, 6; 7:10, 13; Hos. 10:5-8, 14, 15

The horns of the altar will be cut off,
And they will fall to the ground.
15 "I will also smite the [1a]winter house together with the [b]summer house;
The houses of [2c]ivory will also perish
And the great houses will come to an end,"
Declares the LORD.

CHAPTER 4

HEAR this word, you cows of [a]Bashan who are on the mountain of Samaria,
Who oppress the poor, who crush the needy,
Who say to [1]your husbands, "Bring now, that we may drink!"
2 The Lord [1]GOD has sworn by His [a]holiness,
"Behold, the days are coming upon you
When [2]they will take you away with [b]meat hooks.
And the last of you with [c]fish hooks.
3 "You will [a]go out *through* breaches *in the walls*,
Each one straight before her,
And you [1]will be cast to Harmon," declares the LORD.

4 "Enter Bethel and transgress;
In Gilgal multiply transgression!
Bring your sacrifices every morning,
Your tithes every three days.
5 "[1]Offer a [a]thank offering also from that which is leavened,
And proclaim [b]freewill offerings, make them known.
For so you [c]love *to do*, you sons of Israel,"
Declares the Lord GOD.

6 "But I gave you also [a]cleanness of teeth in all your cities
And lack of bread in all your places,
Yet you have [b]not returned to Me," declares the LORD.
7 "And furthermore, I [a]withheld the rain from you
While there *were* still three months until harvest.
Then I would send rain on one city
And on [b]another city I would not send rain;
One part would be rained on,
While the part not rained on would dry up.
8 "So two or three cities would stagger to another city to drink [a]water,
But would [b]not be satisfied;
Yet you have [c]not returned to Me," declares the LORD.
9 "I [a]smote you with scorching *wind* and mildew;
And the [b]caterpillar was devouring
Your many gardens and vineyards, fig trees and olive trees;
Yet you have not returned to Me," declares the LORD.
10 "I sent a [a]plague among you after the manner of Egypt;
I slew your [b]young men by the sword along with your [c]captured horses,
And I made the [d]stench of your camp rise up in your nostrils;
Yet you have [e]not returned to Me," declares the LORD.

15 [1]Or, *autumn* [2]I.e., ivory inlay
[a]Jer. 36:22 [b]Judg. 3:20
[c]1 Kin. 22:39; Ps. 45:8

1 [1]Lit., *their lords*
[a]Ps. 22:12; Ezek. 39:18

2 [1]YHWH, usually rendered LORD, and so throughout the chap. [2]Lit., *he*
[a]Ps. 89:35 [b]Is. 37:29; Ezek. 38:4 [c]Ezek. 29:4

3 [1]So Gk.; M.T. reads, *will cast*
[a]Jer. 52:7

5 [1]Lit., *Offer up in smoke*
[a]Lev. 7:13 [b]Lev. 22:18-21
[c]Hos. 9:1, 10; Jer. 7:9, 10

6 [a]Is. 3:1; Jer. 14:18 [b]Is. 9:13; Jer. 5:3; Hag. 2:17

7 [a]Deut. 11:17; 2 Chr. 7:13; Is. 5:6 [b]Ex. 9:4, 26; 10:22, 23

8 [a]1 Kin. 18:5; Jer. 14:4
[b]Ezek. 4:16; Hag. 1:6 [c]Jer. 3:7

9 [a]Deut. 28:22; Hag. 2:17
[b]Amos 7:1, 2; Joel 1:4, 7

10 [a]Lev. 26:25; Deut. 28:27, 60 [b]Jer. 11:22; 18:21; 48:15
[c]2 Kin. 13:3, 7 [d]Joel 2:20 [e]Is. 9:13

11 "I overthrew you as [a]God overthrew Sodom and
Gomorrah,
And you were like a [b]firebrand snatched from a blaze;
Yet you have [c]not returned to Me," declares the LORD.
12 "Therefore, thus I will do to you, O Israel;
Because I shall do this to you,
Prepare to [a]meet your God, O Israel."
13 For behold, He who [a]forms mountains and [b]creates the
wind
And [c]declares to man what are His thoughts,
He who [d]makes dawn into darkness
And [e]treads on the high places of the earth,
The LORD God of hosts is His name.

CHAPTER 5

HEAR this word which I take up for you as a [a]dirge, O house
of Israel.
2 She has fallen, she will not rise again—
The [a]virgin Israel.
She *lies* neglected on her land;
There is [b]none to raise her up.
3 For thus says the Lord [1]GOD,
"The city which goes forth a thousand *strong*
Will have a [a]hundred left,
And the *one* which goes forth a hundred *strong*
Will have ten left to the house of Israel."

4 For thus says the LORD to the house of Israel,
"[a]Seek Me that you may live.
5 "But do not [1]resort to Bethel,
And do not come to Gilgal,
Nor cross over to Beersheba;
For Gilgal will certainly go into captivity,
And Bethel will [2]come to trouble.
6 "[a]Seek the LORD that you may live,
Lest He break forth like a [b]fire, [1]O house of Joseph,
And it consume with none to quench *it* for Bethel,
7 *For* those who turn [a]justice into wormwood
And [1]cast righteousness down to the earth."

8 He who made the [a]Pleiades and Orion
And [b]changes deep darkness into morning,
Who also [1]darkens day *into* night,
Who [c]calls for the waters of the sea
And pours them out on the surface of the earth,
The LORD is His name.
9 It is He who [a]flashes forth *with* destruction upon the
strong,
So that [b]destruction comes upon the fortress.

10 They hate him who [a]reproves in the [1]gate,
And they [b]abhor him who speaks *with* integrity.
11 Therefore, because you [1]impose heavy rent on the poor
And exact a tribute of grain from them,

11 [a]Gen. 19:25; Deut. 29:23 [b]Zech. 3:2 [c]Jer. 23:14

12 [a]Is. 32:11; 64:2; Jer. 5:22

13 [a]Job 38:4-7; Ps. 65:6; Is. 40:12 [b]Ps. 135:7; Jer. 10:13 [c]Ps. 139:2; Dan. 2:30 [d]Amos 5:8; Jer. 13:16; Joel 2:2 [e]Mic. 1:3

1 [a]Jer. 7:29; 9:10, 17; Ezek. 19:1

2 [a]Jer. 14:17 [b]Is. 51:18; Jer. 50:32

3 [1]YHWH, usually rendered LORD, and so throughout the chap. [a]Is. 6:13

4 [a]Deut. 4:29; 32:46, 47

5 [1]Lit., *seek* [2]Or, *become iniquity*

6 [1]Or, in *the house* [a]Amos 5:14; Is. 55:3, 6, 7 [b]Deut. 4:24

7 [1]Lit., *they have put down* [a]Amos 5:12; 2:3; 6:12

8 [1]Lit., *He darkened* [a]Job 9:9; 38:31 [b]Job 12:22; 38:12; Is. 42:16 [c]Amos 9:6; Ps. 104:6-9

9 [a]Amos 2:14; Job 5:3; Is. 29:5 [b]Mic. 5:11

10 [1]I.e., the place where court was held [a]Amos 5:15; Is. 29:21 [b]Is. 59:15; Jer. 17:16-18

11 [1]Another reading is: *trample upon*

Though you have built houses of well hewn stone,
Yet you will not live in them;
You have planted pleasant vineyards, yet you will [a]not drink their wine.
12 Because I know your transgressions are many and your sins are great,
You who [a]distress the righteous *and* accept bribes,
And [1]turn aside the poor in the [2]gate.
13 Therefore, at [1]such a time the prudent person [a]keeps silent, for it is an evil time.

14 Seek good and not evil, that you may live;
And thus may the LORD God of hosts be with you,
Just as you have said!
15 [a]Hate evil, love good,
And establish justice in the [1]gate!
Perhaps the LORD God of hosts
[b]May be gracious to the [c]remnant of Joseph.

16 Therefore, thus says the LORD God of hosts, the Lord,
"There is [a]wailing in all the plazas,
And in all the streets they say, 'Alas! Alas!'
They also call the [b]farmer to mourning
And [1c]professional mourners to lamentation.
17 "And in all the [a]vineyards *there is* wailing,
Because I shall pass through the midst of you," says the LORD.

18 Alas, you who are longing for the [a]day of the LORD,
For what purpose *will* the day of the LORD *be* to you?
It *will be* [b]darkness and not light;
19 As when a man [a]flees from a lion,
And a bear meets him,
[1]Or goes home, leans his hand against the wall,
And a snake bites him.
20 *Will* not the day of the LORD *be* [a]darkness instead of light,
Even gloom with no brightness in it?

21 "I hate, I [a]reject your festivals,
Nor do I [1b]delight in your solemn assemblies.
22 "Even though you [a]offer up to Me burnt offerings and your grain offerings,
I will not accept *them;*
And I will not *even* look at the [b]peace offering of your fatlings.
23 "Take away from Me the noise of your songs;
I will not even listen to the sound of your harps.
24 "But let [a]justice roll down like waters
And righteousness like an ever-flowing stream.
25 "[1]Did you present Me with sacrifices and grain offering
in the wilderness for forty years, O house of Israel?
26 "You also carried along [1]Sikkuth your [2]king and
[2]Kiyyun, your images, [3]the star of your gods which you made
for yourselves.

11 [a]Mic. 6:15

12 [1]Lit., *they turn* [2]I.e., the place where court was held [a]Is. 1:23; 5:23

13 [1]Lit., *that time* [a]Eccles. 3:7; Hos. 4:4

15 [1]I.e., the place where court was held [a]Ps. 97:10 [b]Joel 2:14 [c]Mic. 5:3, 7, 8

16 [1]Lit., *those who know lamentation* [a]Amos 8:3; Jer. 9:10, 18-20 [b]Joel 1:11 [c]2 Chr. 35:25

17 [a]Is. 16:10; Jer. 48:33

18 [a]Is. 5:19; Joel 1:15; 2:1, 11, 31 [b]Is. 5:30; 9:19; Jer. 30:7

19 [1]Or, *Then* [a]Job 20:24; Is. 24:17, 18; Jer. 15:2, 3

20 [a]Is. 13:10; Zeph. 1:15

21 [1]Lit., *like to smell* [a]Amos 4:4, 5; 8:10; Is. 1:11-16; 66:3 [b]Lev. 26:31; Jer. 14:12; Hos. 5:6

22 [a]Mic. 6:6, 7 [b]Amos 4:5; Lev. 7:11-15

24 [a]Jer. 22:3; Ezek. 45:9; Mic. 6:8

25 [1]Or, *You presented Me with the sacrifices and a grain offering*

26 [1]Or, *Sakkuth* or *(Saturn);* or else, *shrine of your Moloch* [2]Or, *Kaiwan (Saturn);* or else: *stands of* [3]Or, *your star gods*

27 "Therefore, I will make you go into exile beyond Damascus," says the LORD, whose name is the God of hosts.

CHAPTER 6

[a]WOE to those who are at ease in Zion,
And to those who *feel* secure in the mountain of Samaria,
The [b]distinguished men of the foremost of nations,
To whom the house of Israel comes.
2 Go over to [a]Calneh and look,
And go from there to [b]Hamath the great,
Then go down to [c]Gath of the Philistines.
Are [1]they better than these kingdoms,
Or is their territory greater than yours?
3 Do you [a]put off the day of calamity,
And would you [b]bring near the seat of violence?

4 Those who recline on beds of ivory
And sprawl on their couches,
And [a]eat lambs from the flock
And calves from the midst of the stall,
5 Who improvise to the sound of the harp,
And like David have [1a]composed songs for themselves,
6 Who drink wine from [1]sacrificial bowls
While they anoint themselves with the finest of oils,
Yet they have not [a]grieved over the ruin of Joseph.
7 Therefore, they will now go into exile at the head of the exiles,
And the [a]sprawlers' [1]banqueting will [2]pass away.

8 The Lord [1]GOD has sworn by Himself, the LORD God of hosts has declared:
"I [a]loathe the arrogance of Jacob,
And I [2]detest his citadels;
Therefore, I will [b]deliver up *the* city and [3]all it contains.
9 And it will be, if ten men are left in one house, they will
die.
10 Then one's [1]uncle, or his [2a]undertaker, will lift him up
to carry out *his* bones from the house, and he will say to the
one who is in the innermost part of the house, "Is anyone else
with you?" And that one will say, "No one." Then he will
[3]answer, "[b]Keep quiet. For [4]the name of the LORD is [c]not to be
mentioned."
11 For behold, the LORD is going to command that the
great house be smashed to pieces and the small house to
fragments.
12 Do horses run on rocks?
Or does one plow [1]them with oxen?
Yet you have turned [a]justice into poison,
And the fruit of righteousness into [2]wormwood,
13 You who rejoice in [1a]Lo-debar,
[2]And say, "Have we not by our *own* strength [b]taken [3]Karnaim for ourselves?"
14 "For behold, I am going to raise up a nation against you,

1 [a]Is. 32:9-11; Zeph. 1:12 [b]Amos 3:2; Ex. 19:5

2 [1]Or, *you* [a]Gen. 10:10; Is. 10:9 [b]1 Kin. 8:65; 2 Kin. 18:34; Is. 10:9 [c]1 Sam. 5:8; 2 Chr. 26:6

3 [a]Amos 9:10; Is. 56:12 [b]Ps. 94:20

4 [a]Ezek. 34:2, 3

5 [1]Or, *invented musical instruments* [a]1 Chr. 15:16

6 [1]Lit., *sprinkling basins* [a]Ezek. 9:4

7 [1]Or, *cultic feasts* [2]Lit., *turn aside* [a]1 Kin. 20:16-20; Dan. 5:4-6, 30

8 [1]YHWH, usually rendered LORD [2]Lit., *hate* [3]Lit., *its fulness* [a]Amos 5:21; Lev. 26:30; Deut. 32:19; Ps. 106:40 [b]Hos. 11:6

10 [1]Or, *beloved one* [2]Lit., *one who burns him* [3]Lit., *say* [4]Lit., *not to make mention of the name of* [a]1 Sam. 31:12 [b]Amos 5:13; 8:3 [c]Jer. 44:26; Ezek. 20:39

12 [1]Another reading is: *the sea with oxen* [2]I.e., bitterness [a]Amos 5:7, 11, 12; 1 Kin. 21:7-13; Is. 59:13, 14

13 [1]Lit., *a thing of nothing* [2]Lit., *who* [3]Lit., *a pair of horns* [a]Job 8:14, 15; Ps. 2:2-4; Luke 12:19, 20 [b]Ps. 75:4, 5; Is. 28:14, 15

O house of Israel," declares the LORD God of
hosts,
"And they will afflict you from the [a]entrance of Hamath
To the [a]brook of the Arabah.

CHAPTER 7

THUS the Lord [1]GOD showed me, and behold, He was forming a [a]locust-swarm [2]when the spring crop began to sprout.
And behold, the spring crop *was* after the king's [3]mowing.
2 And it came about, [1]when it had [a]finished eating the
vegetation of the land, that I said,
"[b]Lord GOD, please pardon!
[2]How can Jacob stand,
For he is [c]small?"
3 The LORD [1a]changed His mind about this.
"It shall not be," said the LORD.
4 Thus the Lord GOD showed me, and behold, the Lord
GOD was calling to contend *with them* by [a]fire, and it consumed the great deep and began to consume the [1]farm land.
5 Then I said,
"[a]Lord GOD, please stop!
How can Jacob stand, for he is small?"
6 The LORD [1a]changed His mind about this.
"This too shall not be," said the Lord GOD.
7 Thus He showed me, and behold, the Lord was standing [1]by a [2]vertical wall, with a plumb line in His hand.
8 And the LORD said to me, "What do you see, [a]Amos?"
And I said, "A plumb line." Then the LORD said,
"Behold I am about to put a [b]plumb line
In the midst of my people Israel.
I will [1]spare them [c]no longer.
9 "The [a]high places of Isaac will be desolated
And the [b]sanctuaries of Israel laid waste.
Then shall I [c]rise up against the house of Jeroboam
with the sword."
10 Then Amaziah, the [a]priest of Bethel, sent *word* to Jeroboam, king of Israel, saying, "Amos has [b]conspired against you
in the midst of the house of Israel; the land is unable to endure
all his words.
11 "For thus Amos says, 'Jeroboam will die by the sword
and Israel will certainly go from its land into exile.' "
12 Then Amaziah said to Amos, "[a]Go, you seer, flee away
to the land of Judah, and there eat bread and there do your
prophesying!
13 "But no longer [a]prophesy at Bethel, for it is a [b]sanctuary
of the king and a royal [1]residence."
14 Then Amos answered and said to Amaziah, "I am not a
prophet, nor am I the [a]son of a prophet; for I am a herdsman
and a [1]grower of sycamore figs.
15 "But the LORD took me from [1]following the flock and
the LORD said to me, 'Go [a]prophesy to My people Israel.'
16 "And now hear the word of the LORD: you are saying,
'You shall not [a]prophesy against Israel nor shall you [1b]preach
against the house of Isaac.'
17 "Therefore, thus says the LORD, 'Your [a]wife will become

14 [a]Num. 34:7, 8; 2 Kin. 14:25

1 [1]YHWH, usually rendered LORD, and so throughout the chap. [2]Lit., *at the beginning of the coming up of* [3]Or, *shearings* [a]Amos 4:9; Joel 1:4; Nah. 3:15

2 [1]Lit., *if* [2]Lit., as *who* [a]Ex. 10:15 [b]Jer. 14:7, 20, 21; Ezek. 9:8; 11:13 [c]Is. 37:4; Jer. 42:2

3 [1]Or, *relented* [a]Amos 5:15; Jer. 26:19; Hos. 11:8

4 [1]Lit., *portion* [a]Amos 2:5; Deut. 32:22; Is. 66:15, 16

5 [a]Ps. 85:4; Joel 2:17

6 [1]Or, *relented* [a]Amos 7:3; Ps. 106:45; Jon. 3:10

7 [1]Or, *upon* [2]Lit., *wall of a plumb line*

8 [1]Lit., *pass him by* [a]Amos 8:2; Jer. 1:11 [b]Is. 28:17; 34:11; Lam. 2:8 [c]Amos 8:2; Jer. 15:6; Ezek. 7:2-9

9 [a]Hos. 10:8; Mic. 1:5 [b]Amos 7:13; Lev. 26:31; Is. 63:18; Jer. 51:51 [c]Amos 7:11; 2 Kin. 15:8-10

10 [a]1 Kin. 12:31, 32; 13:33 [b]Jer. 26:8-11; 38:4

12 [a]Matt. 8:34

13 [1]Lit., *house* [a]Amos 2:12; Acts 4:18 [b]Amos 7:9; 1 Kin. 12:29, 32

14 [1]Or, *nipper* [a]2 Kin. 2:3; 4:38; 2 Chr. 19:2

15 [1]Lit., *behind* [a]Jer. 1:7; Ezek. 2:3, 4

16 [1]Lit., *drip* [a]Amos 7:13; 2:12 [b]Deut. 32:2; Ezek. 20:46; 21:2

17 [a]Hos. 4:13, 14

a harlot in the city, your [b]sons and your daughters will fall by
the sword, your land will be parceled up by a *measuring* line,
and you yourself will die [1]upon [c]unclean soil. Moreover, Israel
will certainly go from its land into exile.' "

CHAPTER 8

THUS the Lord [1]GOD showed me, and behold, *there was* a
basket of summer fruit.
2 And He said, "What do you see, Amos?" And [a]I said,
"A basket of summer fruit." Then the LORD said to me, "The
[b]end has come for My people Israel. I will [1]spare them no
longer.
3 "The [a]songs of the palace will [1]turn to wailing in that
day," declares the Lord GOD. "Many *will be* the corpses; in
every place [2]they will cast them forth [3]in silence."
4 Hear this, you who [1]trample the [a]needy, to do away
with the humble of the land,
5 saying,
"When will the [a]new moon [1]be over,
So that we may buy grain,
And the [b]sabbath, that we may open the wheat *market*,
To make the [2]bushel smaller and the shekel bigger,
And to [c]cheat with [3]dishonest scales,
6 So as to buy the helpless for [1]money
And the needy for a pair of sandals,
And *that* we may sell the refuse of the wheat."

7 The LORD has sworn by the [a]pride of Jacob,
"Indeed, I will [b]never forget any of their deeds.
8 "Because of this will not the land [a]quake
And everyone who dwells in it [b]mourn?
Indeed, all of it will [c]rise up like the Nile,
And it will be tossed about,
And subside like the Nile of Egypt.
9 "And it will come about in that day," declares the Lord
GOD,
"That I shall make the [a]sun go down at noon
And [b]make the earth dark in [1]broad daylight.
10 "Then I shall turn your [a]festivals into mourning
And all your songs into [1]lamentation;
And I will bring [b]sackcloth on everyone's loins
And baldness on every head.
And I will make it [c]like *a time of* mourning for an only
son,
And the end of it will be like a bitter day.

11 "Behold days are coming," declares the Lord GOD,
"When I will send a famine on the land,
Not a famine for bread or a thirst for water,
But rather for hearing the words of the LORD.
12 "And people will stagger from sea to sea,
And from the north even to the east;
They will go to and fro to [a]seek the word of the LORD,
But they will not find *it*.
13 "In that day the beautiful [a]virgins
And the young men will [b]faint from thirst.

17 [1]Or, *in an unclean land* [b]Jer. 14:16 [c]2 Kin. 17:6; Ezek. 4:13; Hos. 9:3

1 [1]YHWH, usually rendered LORD, and so throughout the chap.

2 [1]Lit., *pass him by* [a]Jer. 24:3 [b]Ezek. 7:2, 3, 6

3 [1]Or, *they will howl the palace songs* [2]Lit., *he has thrown* [3]Or, *hush!* [a]Amos 8:10; 5:23; 6:4, 5

4 [1]Or, *snap at* [a]Amos 2:7; 5:11, 12

5 [1]Lit., *pass by* [2]Lit., *ephah* [3]Lit., *balances of deception* [a]Num. 28:11; 2 Kin. 4:23 [b]Ex. 31:13-17 [c]Hos. 12:7

6 [1]Lit., *silver*

7 [a]Deut. 33:26, 29; Ps. 68:34 [b]Ps. 10:11; Jer. 17:1; Hos. 7:2

8 [a]Ps. 18:7; 60:2; Is. 5:25 [b]Hos. 4:3 [c]Amos 9:5; Jer. 46:7, 8

9 [1]Lit., *a day of light* [a]Is. 13:10; Jer. 15:9; Mic. 3:6 [b]Amos 4:13; 5:8; Is. 59:9, 10

10 [1]Or, *a dirge* [a]Amos 5:21; Job 20:23 [b]Ezek. 7:18 [c]Jer. 6:26; Zech. 12:10

12 [a]Ezek. 20:3, 31

13 [a]Lam. 1:18; 2:21 [b]Is. 41:17; Hos. 2:3

14 "*As for* those who swear by the [1a]guilt of Samaria,
Who say, 'As your god lives, O [b]Dan,'
And, 'As the way of Beersheba lives,'
They will fall and not rise again."

CHAPTER 9

I SAW the Lord standing beside the altar, and He said,
"Smite the [a]capitals so that the thresholds will shake,
And break them on the heads of them all!
Then I will slay the rest of them with the sword;
They will not have a [b]fugitive who will flee,
Or a refugee who will escape.
2 "Though they dig into [a]Sheol,
From there shall My hand take them;
And though they [b]ascend to heaven,
From there will I bring them down.
3 "And though they hide on the summit of Carmel,
I will [a]search them out and take them from there;
And though they [b]conceal themselves from My sight on the floor of the sea,
From there I will command the [c]serpent and it will bite them.
4 "And though they go into [a]captivity before their enemies,
From there I will command the sword that it slay them,
And I will [b]set My eyes against them for evil and not for good."

5 And the Lord [1]GOD of hosts,
The One who [a]touches the land so that it melts,
And all those who dwell in it mourn,
And all of it rises up like the Nile
And subsides like the Nile of Egypt;
6 The One who builds His [1]upper [a]chambers in the heavens,
And has founded His vaulted dome over the earth,
He who calls for the waters of the sea
And [b]pours them out on the face of the earth,
The LORD is His name.

7 "Are you not as the sons of [a]Ethiopia to Me,
O sons of Israel?" declares the LORD.
"Have I not brought up Israel from the land of Egypt,
And the Philistines from Caphtor and [1]the Syrians from Kir?
8 "Behold, the eyes of the Lord GOD are on the sinful kingdom,
And I will [a]destroy it from the face of the earth;
Nevertheless, I will [b]not totally destroy the house of Jacob,"
Declares the LORD.
9 "For behold, I am commanding,
And I will [a]shake the house of Jacob among all nations
As *grain* is shaken in a sieve,
But not a [1]kernel will fall to the ground.

14 [1]Or, *Ashimah* [a]Hos. 8:5 [b]1 Kin. 12:28, 29
1 [a]Zeph. 2:14 [b]Jer. 11:11
2 [a]Ps. 139:8 [b]Jer. 51:53; Obad. 4
3 [a]Jer. 16:16 [b]Job 34:22; Ps. 139:9-12; Jer. 16:16, 17 [c]Is. 27:1
4 [a]Lev. 26:33 [b]Jer. 21:10; 39:16; 44:11
5 [1]YHWH, usually rendered LORD, and so throughout the chap. [a]Ps. 104:32; 144:5; Is. 64:1
6 [1]Or, *stairs* [a]Ps. 104:3, 13 [b]Ps. 104:6
7 [1]Lit., *Aram* [a]2 Chr. 14:9, 12; Is. 20:4; 43:3
8 [a]Amos 9:10; 3:12; 7:17 [b]Jer. 5:10; 30:11; 31:35, 36; Joel 2:32
9 [1]Or, *pebble* [a]Is. 30:28; Luke 22:31

10 "All the [a]sinners of My people will die by the sword,
Those who say, 'The calamity will not overtake or confront us.'
11 "In that day I will [a]raise up the fallen [1b]booth of David,
And wall up its [c]breaches;
I will also raise up its ruins,
And rebuild it as in the [d]days of old;
12 That they may possess the remnant of Edom
And all the [1]nations who are [a]called by My name,"
Declares the LORD who does this.

13 "Behold, days are coming," declares the LORD,
"When the [a]plowman will overtake the reaper
And the treader of grapes him who sows seed;
When the [b]mountains will drip sweet wine,
And all the hills will be dissolved.
14 "Also I will [a]restore the [1]captivity of My people Israel,
And they will [b]rebuild the ruined cities and live *in them*,
They will also plant vineyards and drink their wine,
And make gardens and eat their fruit.
15 "I will also plant them on their land,
And they will not again be rooted out from their land
Which I have given them,"
Says the LORD your God.

10 [a]Is. 33:14; Zech. 13:8, 9

11 [1]Or, *shelter;* or, *tabernacle* [a]Acts 15:16-18 [b]Is. 16:5 [c]Ps. 80:12 [d]Is. 63:11; Jer. 46:26

12 [1]Or, *Gentiles* [a]Is. 43:7

13 [a]Lev. 26:5 [b]Joel 3:18

14 [1]Or, *fortunes* [a]Ps. 53:6; Is. 60:4; Jer. 30:18 [b]Is. 61:4; 65:21

THE BOOK OF OBADIAH

Edom Will Be Humbled.

THE vision of Obadiah.
Thus says the Lord [1]GOD concerning [a]Edom—
[b]We have heard a report from the LORD,
And an [c]envoy has been sent among the nations saying,
"[d]Arise and let us go against her for battle"—
2 "Behold, I will make you [a]small among the nations;
You are greatly despised.
3 "The [a]arrogance of your heart has deceived you,
You who live in the clefts of [1]the [b]rock,
In the loftiness of your dwelling place,
Who say in your heart,
'[c]Who will bring me down to earth?'
4 "Though you [a]build high like the eagle,
Though you set your nest among the [b]stars,
From there I will bring you down," declares the LORD.
5 "If [a]thieves came to you,
If [1]robbers by night—
O how you will be ruined!—
Would they not steal *only* [2]until they had enough?
If grape gatherers came to you,
Would they not leave *some* gleanings?

1 [1]YHWH, usually rendered LORD [a]Ps. 137:7; Is. 34:1-17; 63:1-6; Jer. 49:7-22; Ezek. 25:12-14 [b]Obad. 1-4; Jer. 49:14-16 [c]Is. 18:2; 30:4 [d]Jer. 6:4, 5

2 [a]Num. 24:18; Is. 23:9

3 [1]Or, *Sela* [a]Is. 16:6; Jer. 49:16 [b]2 Kin. 14:7; 2 Chr. 25:12 [c]Is. 14:13-15

4 [a]Job 20:6, 7; Hab. 2:9 [b]Is. 14:12-15

5 [1]Lit., *devastators of the night* [2]Lit., *their sufficiency* [a]Jer. 49:9

6 "O how Esau will be [a]ransacked,
And his hidden treasures searched out!
7 "All the [a]men [1]allied with you
Will send you forth to the border,
And the men at [b]peace with you
Will deceive you and overpower you.
They who eat your [c]bread
Will set an ambush for you.
(There is no [d]understanding [2]in him.)
8 "Will I not on that day," declares the LORD,
"[a]Destroy wise men from Edom
And understanding from the mountain of Esau?
9 "Then your [a]mighty men will be dismayed, O Teman,
In order that every one may be [b]cut off from the mountain of Esau by slaughter.

10 "Because of [a]violence to your brother Jacob,
[1]You will be covered *with* shame,
And you will be cut off forever.
11 "On the day that you [a]stood aloof,
On the day that strangers carried off his wealth,
And foreigners entered his gate
And [b]cast lots for Jerusalem—
[c]You too were as one of them.
12 "Do not [1a]gloat over your brother's day,
The day of his misfortune.
And do not [b]rejoice over the sons of Judah
In the day of their destruction;
Yes, do not [2c]boast
In the day of *their* distress.
13 "Do not enter the gate of My people
In the [a]day of their disaster.
Yes you, do not [1]gloat over their calamity
In the day of their disaster.
And do not [b]loot their wealth
In the day of their disaster.
14 "And do not [a]stand at the fork of the road
To cut down their fugitives;
And do not imprison their survivors
In the day of their distress.

15 "For the [a]day of the LORD draws near on all the nations.
[b]As you have done, it will be done to you.
Your [c]dealings will return on your own head.
16 "Because just as you drank on My holy mountain,
All the nations will drink continually.
They will drink and [1]swallow,
And become as if they had never existed.
17 "But on Mount [a]Zion there will be those who escape,
And it will be holy.
And the house of Jacob will [b]possess their possessions.
18 "Then the house of Jacob will be a [a]fire
And the house of Joseph a flame;
But the house of Esau *will be* as stubble.
And they will set [1]them on fire and consume [1]them,
So that there will be [b]no survivor of the house of Esau,"
For the LORD has spoken.

6 [a]Jer. 49:10

7 [1]Lit., *of your covenant* [2]I.e., in Esau; or, *of it* [a]Jer. 30:14 [b]Jer. 38:22 [c]Ps. 41:9 [d]Jer. 49:7

8 [a]Job 5:12-14

9 [a]Jer. 49:22 [b]Obad. 5; Is. 34:5-8; 63:1-3

10 [1]Lit., *Shame will cover you* [a]Ezek. 25:12; Joel 3:19; Amos 1:11

11 [a]Ps. 83:5, 6; 137:7; Amos 1:6, 9 [b]Joel 3:3; Nah. 3:10 [c]Ezek. 35:10

12 [1]Lit., *look on* [2]Lit., *make your mouth large* [a]Mic. 4:11; 7:10 [b]Ezek. 35:15; 36:5 [c]Ps. 31:18; Ezek. 35:12

13 [1]Lit., *look on* [a]Ezek. 35:5 [b]Ezek. 35:10; 36:2, 3

14 [a]Is. 16:3, 4

15 [a]Joel 1:15; 2:1, 11, 31; Amos 5:18, 20 [b]Jer. 50:29; 51:56 [c]Ezek. 35:11

16 [1]Or, *stagger*

17 [a]Is. 4:2, 3 [b]Is. 14:1, 2; Amos 9:11-15

18 [1]I.e., the people of Esau [a]Is. 5:24; 9:18, 19 [b]Jer. 11:23; Amos 1:8

19 [1]I.e., South country [2]I.e., the foothills [a]Is. 11:14; Amos 9:12 [b]Is. 11:14 [c]Jer. 31:5; 32:44

20 [a]Jer. 32:44; 33:13

21 [a]Neh. 9:27 [b]Ps. 22:28; 47:7-9; 67:4; Zech. 14:9

19 Then *those of* the [1]Negev will [a]possess the mountain of
Esau,
And *those of* the [2]Shephelah the [b]Philistine *plain;*
Also, they will [c]possess the territory of Ephraim and the
territory of Samaria,
And Benjamin *will possess* Gilead.
20 And the exiles of this host of the sons of Israel,
Who are *among* the Canaanites as far as Zarephath,
And the exiles of Jerusalem who are in Sephared
Will possess the [a]cities of the Negev.
21 The [a]deliverers will ascend Mount Zion
To judge the mountain of Esau,
And the [b]kingdom will be the LORD's.

THE BOOK OF JONAH

Jonah's Disobedience.

1 [a]2 Kin. 14:25; Matt. 12:39-41; 16:4; Luke 11:29, 30, 32

2 [a]Gen. 10:11; 2 Kin. 19:36; Is. 37:37; Nah. 1:1; Zeph. 2:13 [b]Is. 58:1 [c]Gen. 18:20; Hos. 7:2

3 [a]Ps. 139:7, 9, 10

4 [1]Lit., *be broken*

5 [1]Lit., *vessels* [2]Lit., *from upon them* [a]1 Kin. 18:26 [b]Acts 27:18, 19, 38

6 [a]Ps. 107:28 [b]Jon. 3:9; 2 Sam. 12:22; Amos 5:15

7 [1]Lit., *know* [a]Num. 32:23; Prov. 16:33

8 [a]Josh. 7:19; 1 Sam. 14:43 [b]Gen. 47:3; 1 Sam. 30:13

9 [a]Gen. 14:13; Ex. 1:15; 2:13 [b]2 Kin. 17:25, 28, 32, 33 [c]Ezra 1:2; Neh. 1:4; Ps. 136:26; Dan. 2:18 [d]Neh. 9:6; Ps. 95:5; 146:6

10 [1]Lit., *What is this you have done* [a]Jon. 1:3; Job 27:22

THE word of the LORD came to [a]Jonah the son of Amittai
saying,
2 "Arise, go to [a]Nineveh the great city, and [b]cry against it,
for their [c]wickedness has come up before Me."
3 But Jonah rose up to flee to Tarshish [a]from the presence of the LORD. So he went down to Joppa, found a ship
which was going to Tarshish, paid the fare, and went down into
it to go with them to Tarshish from the presence of the LORD.
4 And the LORD hurled a great wind on the sea and there
was a great storm on the sea so that the ship was about to
[1]break up.
5 Then the sailors became afraid, and every man cried to
[a]his god, and they [b]threw the [1]cargo which was in the ship into
the sea to lighten *it* [2]for them. But Jonah had gone below into
the hold of the ship, lain down, and fallen sound asleep.
6 So the captain approached him and said, "How is it
that you are sleeping? Get up, [a]call on your god. Perhaps *your*
[b]god will be concerned about us so that we will not perish."
7 And each man said to his mate, "Come, let us cast lots
so we may [1]learn on whose account this calamity *has struck*
us." So they cast lots and the [a]lot fell on Jonah.
8 Then they said to him, "[a]Tell us, now! On whose
account *has* this calamity *struck* us? What is your [b]occupa-
tion? And where do you come from? What is your country?
From what people are you?"
9 And he said to them, "I am a [a]Hebrew, and I [b]fear the
LORD [c]God of heaven who [d]made the sea and the dry land."
10 Then the men became extremely frightened and they
said to him, "[1]How could you do this?" For the men knew that
he was [a]fleeing from the presence of the LORD, because he had
told them.
11 So they said to him, "What should we do to you that

the sea may become calm [1]for us?"—for the sea was becoming
increasingly stormy.
12 And he said to them, "[a]Pick me up and throw me into
the sea. Then the sea will become calm [1]for you, for I know
that [b]on account of me this great storm *has come* upon you."
13 However, the men [1]rowed *desperately* to return to land
but they [a]could not, for the sea was becoming *even* stormier
against them.
14 Then they called on the [a]LORD and said, "We earnestly
pray, O LORD, do not let us perish on account of this man's life
and do not put innocent blood on us; for Thou, O LORD, hast
done as Thou hast pleased."
15 So they picked up Jonah, threw him into the sea, and
the sea [a]stopped its raging.
16 Then the men feared the LORD greatly, and they offered a sacrifice to the LORD and made [a]vows.
17 [1]And the LORD appointed a great fish to swallow Jonah,
and Jonah was in the stomach of the fish three days and three
nights.

CHAPTER 2

1 THEN Jonah prayed to the LORD his God [a]from the stomach
of the fish,
2 and he said,
"I [a]called out of my distress to the LORD,
And He answered me.
I cried for help from the [1]depth of Sheol;
Thou didst hear my voice.
3 "For Thou hadst [a]cast me into the deep,
Into the heart of the seas,
And the current [1]engulfed me.
All Thy [b]breakers and billows passed over me.
4 "So I said, 'I have been [a]expelled from [1]Thy sight.'
Nevertheless I will look again [b]toward Thy holy
temple.
5 "[a]Water encompassed me to the *very* soul,
The great [b]deep [1]engulfed me,
Weeds were wrapped around my head.
6 "I [a]descended to the roots of the mountains.
The earth with its [b]bars *was* around me forever,
But Thou hast [c]brought up my life from [1]the pit, O
LORD my God.
7 "While [1]I was [a]fainting away,
I [b]remembered the LORD;
And my [c]prayer came to Thee,
Into Thy holy temple.
8 "Those who regard [1]vain idols
Forsake their faithfulness,
9 But I will [a]sacrifice to Thee
With the voice of thanksgiving.
That which I have vowed I will [b]pay.
[c]Salvation is from the LORD."
10 Then the LORD commanded the fish, and it vomited
Jonah up onto the dry land.

11 [1]Lit., *from upon us*

12 [1]Lit., *from upon you* [a]2 Sam. 24:17 [b]1 Chr. 21:17

13 [1]Lit., *dug their oars into the water* [a]Prov. 21:30

14 [a]Jon. 1:16; Ps. 107:28

15 [a]Ps. 65:7; 93:3, 4; 107:29

16 [a]Ps. 50:14; 66:13, 14

17 [1]Chap. 2:1 in Heb.

1 [1]Chap. 2:2 in Heb. [a]Job 13:15; Ps. 130:1, 2; Lam. 3:53-56

2 [1]Lit., *belly* [a]1 Sam. 30:6; Ps. 18:4-6; 22:24; 120:1

3 [1]Lit., *surrounded* [a]Ps. 69:1, 2, 14, 15; Lam. 3:54 [b]Ps. 42:7

4 [1]Lit., *before Thine eyes* [a]Ps. 31:22; Jer. 7:15 [b]1 Kin. 8:38; 2 Chr. 6:38; Ps. 5:7

5 [1]Lit., *surrounded* [a]Lam. 3:54 [b]Ps. 69:1, 2

6 [1]Or, *corruption* [a]Ps. 18:5; 116:3 [b]Is. 38:10; Matt. 16:18 [c]Job 33:28; Ps. 16:10; 30:3; Is. 38:17

7 [1]Lit., *my soul . . . within me* [a]Ps. 142:3 [b]Ps. 77:10, 11; 143:5 [c]2 Chr. 30:27; Ps. 18:6

8 [1]Lit., *empty vanities*

9 [a]Ps. 50:14, 23; Jer. 33:11; Hos. 14:2 [b]Job 22:27; Eccles. 5:4, 5 [c]Ps. 3:8; Is. 45:17

Chapter 3

NOW the word of the LORD came to Jonah the second time,
saying,
2 "Arise, go to Nineveh the great city and [a]proclaim to it
the proclamation which I am going to tell you."
3 So Jonah arose and went to Nineveh according to the
word of the LORD. Now Nineveh was [1]an [a]exceedingly great
city, a three days' walk.
4 Then Jonah began to go through the city one day's
walk; and he [a]cried out and said, "Yet forty days and Nineveh
will be overthrown."
5 Then the people of Nineveh believed in God; and they
called a [a]fast and put on sackcloth from the greatest to the
least of them.
6 When the word reached the king of Nineveh, he arose
from his throne, laid aside his robe from him, covered *himself*
with sackcloth, and sat on the [1]ashes.
7 And he issued a [a]proclamation and it said, "In Nineveh
by the decree of the king and his nobles: Do not let man,
beast, herd, or flock taste a thing. Do not let them eat or drink
water.
8 "But both man and beast must be covered with sackcloth; and let [1]men [a]call on God earnestly that each may [b]turn
from his wicked way and from the violence which is in [2]his
hands.
9 "[a]Who knows, God may turn and relent, and withdraw
His burning anger so that we shall not perish?"
10 When God saw their deeds, that they [a]turned from
their wicked way, then [b]God relented concerning the calamity
which He had declared He would [1]bring upon them. And He
did not do *it*.

Chapter 4

BUT it greatly displeased Jonah, and he became angry.
2 And he [a]prayed to the LORD and said, "Please LORD,
was not this [1]what I said while I was still in my *own* country?
Therefore, [2]in order to forestall this I fled to Tarshish, for I
knew that Thou art a [b]gracious and compassionate God, slow
to anger and abundant in lovingkindness, and One who relents
concerning calamity.
3 "Therefore now, O LORD, please [a]take my [1]life from me,
for death is [b]better to me than life."
4 And the LORD said, "Do you have good reason to be
angry?"
5 Then Jonah went out from the city and sat east of [1]it.
There he made a shelter for himself and [a]sat under it in the
shade until he could see what would happen in the city.
6 So the LORD God appointed a [1]plant and it grew up
over Jonah to be a shade over his head to deliver him from his
discomfort. And Jonah was [2a]extremely happy about the
[1]plant.
7 But God appointed a worm when dawn came the next
day, and it attacked the plant and it [a]withered.
8 And it came about when the sun came up that God

2 [a]Jer. 1:17; Ezek. 2:7

3 [1]Lit., *a great city to God* [a]Jon. 1:2; 4:11

4 [a]Matt. 12:41; Luke 11:32

5 [a]Dan. 9:3; Joel 1:14

6 [1]Or, *dust*

7 [a]Jon. 3:5; 2 Chr. 20:3; Ezra 8:21

8 [1]Lit., *them* [2]Lit., *their* [a]Jon. 1:6, 14; Ps. 130:1 [b]Is. 1:16-19; 55:6, 7; Jer. 18:11

9 [a]2 Sam. 12:22; Joel 2:14

10 [1]Lit., *do* [a]1 Kin. 21:27-29; Jer. 31:18 [b]Ex. 32:14; Jer. 18:8; Amos 7:3, 6

2 [1]Lit., *my word* [2]Lit., *I was beforehand in fleeing* [a]Jer. 20:7 [b]Ex. 34:6; Num. 14:18; Ps. 86:5, 15; Joel 2:13; Mic. 7:8

3 [1]Lit., *soul* [a]Jon. 3:8; 1 Kin. 19:4; Job 6:8, 9 [b]Job 7:15, 16; Eccles. 7:1

5 Lit., *the city* [a]1 Kin. 19:9, 13

6 [1]Probably a castor oil plant, and so in v. 7, 9 and 10 [2]Lit., *greatly* [a]Amos 6:13

7 [a]Joel 1:12

appointed a scorching [a]east wind, and the [b]sun beat down on
Jonah's head so that he became faint and begged with *all* his
soul to die, saying, "Death is better to me than life."
9 Then God said to Jonah, "Do you have good reason to
be angry about the plant?" And he said, "I have good reason to
be angry, even to death."
10 Then the LORD said, "You had compassion on the
plant for which you did not work, and *which* you did not cause
to grow, which *came up* [1]overnight and perished [1]overnight.
11 "And should I not [a]have compassion on Nineveh, the
great city in which there are more than 120,000 persons who
do not [b]know *the difference* between their right and left hand,
as well as many [c]animals?"

8 [a]Ezek. 19:12; Hos. 13:15 [b]Ps. 121:6; Is. 49:10

10 [1]Lit., *a son of a night*

11 [a]Jon. 3:10 [b]Deut. 1:39; Is. 7:16 [c]Ps. 36:6

THE BOOK OF MICAH

Destruction in Israel and Judah.

THE word of the LORD which came *to* [a]Micah [1]the Morashtite in the days of Jotham, Ahaz, *and* Hezekiah, kings of
Judah, which he saw concerning Samaria and Jerusalem.

2 Hear, O peoples, all of [1]you;
[a]Listen, O earth and [2]all it contains,
And let the Lord [3]GOD be a [b]witness against you,
The Lord from His holy temple.
3 For behold, the LORD is [a]coming forth from His place.
He will come down and [b]tread on the high places of the
[1]earth.
4 [a]The mountains will melt under Him,
And the valleys will be split,
Like wax before the fire,
Like water poured down a steep place.
5 All this is for the rebellion of Jacob
And for the sins of the house of Israel.
What is the rebellion of Jacob?
Is it not [a]Samaria?
What is the [b]high [1]place of Judah?
Is it not Jerusalem?
6 For I will make Samaria a heap of ruins [1]in the open
country,
[a]Planting places for a vineyard.
I will [b]pour her stones down into the valley,
And will [c]lay bare her foundations.
7 All of her [a]idols will be smashed,
All of her [b]earnings will be burned with fire,
And all of her images I will make desolate.
For she collected *them* from a harlot's earnings,
And to the earnings of a harlot they will return.

8 Because of this I must lament and wail,
I must go [a]barefoot and naked;
I must make a lament like the [b]jackals
And a mourning like the ostriches.

1 [1]I.e., of Moresheth [a]Jer. 26:18

2 [1]Lit., *them* [2]Lit., *its fulness* [3]YHWH, usually rendered LORD [a]Jer. 6:19; 22:29 [b]Is. 50:7

3 [1]Or, *land* [a]Is. 26:21 [b]Amos 4:13

4 [a]Ps. 97:5; Is. 64:1, 2; Nah. 1:5

5 [1]Lit., *places* [a]Is. 7:9; 28:1; Amos 8:14 [b]2 Chr. 34:3, 4

6 [1]Lit., *of the field* [a]Jer. 31:5; Amos 5:11 [b]Lam. 4:1 [c]Ezek. 13:14

7 [a]Deut. 9:21; 2 Chr. 34:7 [b]Deut. 23:18; Is. 23:17

8 [a]Is. 32:11 [b]Is. 13:21, 22

9 For her [1a]wound is incurable,
For it has come to Judah;
It has reached the [b]gate of my people,
Even to Jerusalem.
10 [a]Tell it not in Gath,
Weep not at all.
At [1]Beth-le-aphrah roll yourself in the dust.
11 [1]Go on your way, inhabitant of [2]Shaphir, in [a]shameful nakedness.
The inhabitant of [3b]Zaanan does not [4]escape.
The lamentation of [5]Beth-ezel: "He will take from you its [6]support."
12 For the inhabitant of [1]Maroth
Becomes weak [a]waiting for good,
Because a calamity has come down from the LORD
To the gate of Jerusalem.
13 [a]Harness the chariot to the team of horses,
O inhabitant of [b]Lachish—
She was the beginning of sin
To the daughter of Zion—
Because in you were found
The rebellious acts of Israel.
14 Therefore, you will give parting [a]gifts
On behalf of Moresheth-gath;
The houses of [b]Achzib *will* become a [c]deception
To the kings of Israel.
15 Moreover, I will bring on you
The one who takes possession,
O inhabitant of [1a]Mareshah.
The glory of Israel will enter [b]Adullam.
16 Make yourself [a]bald and cut off your hair,
Because of the children of your delight;
Extend your baldness like the eagle,
For they will [b]go from you into exile.

CHAPTER 2

WOE to those who [a]scheme iniquity,
Who work out evil on their beds!
[1b]When morning comes, they do it,
For it is in the [c]power of their hands.
2 They [a]covet fields and then [b]seize *them*,
And houses, and take *them* away.
They [1c]rob a man and his house,
A man and his inheritance.
3 Therefore, thus says the LORD:
Behold, I am [a]planning against this [b]family a calamity
From which you [c]cannot remove your necks;
And you will not walk [d]haughtily,
For it will be an [e]evil time.
4 On that day they will [a]take up against you a [1]taunt
And [2b]utter a bitter lamentation *and* say,
"We are completely [c]destroyed!
He exchanges the portion of my people;
How He removes it from me!
To the apostate He [d]apportions our fields."

---

9 [1]Lit., *wounds* [a]Jer. 30:12, 15 [b]Mic. 1:12; Is. 3:26

10 [1]I.e., house of dust [a]2 Sam. 1:20

11 [1]I.e., Go into captivity [2]I.e., Pleasantness [3]I.e., Going Out [4]Lit., *go out* [5]I.e., House of Removal [6]Lit., *standing place* [a]Ezek. 23:29 [b]Josh. 15:37

12 [1]I.e., Bitterness [a]Is. 59:9-11; Jer. 14:19

13 [a]Amos 2:14 [b]Josh. 10:3; 2 Kin. 14:19; Is. 36:2

14 [a]2 Kin. 16:8 [b]Josh. 15:44 [c]Jer. 15:18

15 [1]I.e., Possession [a]Josh. 15:44 [b]Josh. 12:14; 15:35; 2 Sam. 23:13

16 [a]Is. 22:12 [b]Amos 7:11, 17

1 [1]Lit., *In the light of the morning* [a]Ps. 36:4; Is. 32:7; Nah. 1:11 [b]Hos. 7:6, 7 [c]Gen. 31:29; Deut. 28:32; Prov. 3:27

2 [1]Lit., *oppress* [a]Jer. 22:17; Amos 8:4 [b]Is. 5:8 [c]1 Kin. 21:1-15

3 [a]Deut. 28:48; Jer. 18:11 [b]Jer. 8:3; Amos 3:1, 2 [c]Lam. 1:14; 5:5 [d]Is. 2:11, 12 [e]Amos 5:13

4 [1]Or, *proverb* [2]Lit., *lament* [a]Hab. 2:6 [b]Mic. 1:8; Jer. 9:10, 17-21 [c]Is. 6:11; 24:3; Jer. 4:13 [d]Jer. 6:12; 8:10

5 Therefore, you will have no one [1a]stretching a measuring line
For you by lot in the assembly of the LORD.

6 "Do not [1a]speak out," *so* they [1]speak out.
But if [2]they do [b]not [1]speak out concerning these things,
Reproaches will not be turned back.
7 Is it being said, O house of Jacob:
"Is the Spirit of the LORD [a]impatient?
Are these His doings?"
Do not My words [b]do good
To the one [c]walking uprightly?
8 [1]Recently My people have arisen as an [a]enemy—
You [b]strip the [2]robe off a fellow-Israelite,
From [c]unsuspecting passers-by,
From those returned from war.
9 The women of My people you [a]evict,
Each *one* from her pleasant house.
From her children you take My [b]splendor forever.
10 Arise and go,
For this is no place [a]of rest
Because of the [b]uncleanness that brings on destruction,
A painful destruction.
11 If a man walking after wind and falsehood
Had told lies *and said,*
"I will [1]speak out to you concerning wine and liquor,"
He would be [2]spokesman to [a]this people.

12 I will surely assemble all of you, Jacob,
I will surely gather the [a]remnant of Israel.
I will put them together like sheep in the fold;
Like a flock in the midst of its pasture
They will be noisy with men.
13 The breaker goes up before them;
They break out, pass through the gate, and go out by it.
So their king goes on before them,
And the LORD at their head.

CHAPTER 3

AND I said,
"[a]Hear now, heads of Jacob
And rulers of the house of Israel.
Is it not for you to [b]know justice?
2 "You who hate good and love evil,
Who [a]tear off their skin from them
And their flesh from their bones,
3 "And who [a]eat the flesh of my people,
[b]Strip off their skin from them,
Break their bones,
And [c]chop *them* up as for the pot
And as meat in a kettle."
4 Then they will cry out to the LORD,
But He will not answer them.
Instead, He will [a]hide His face from them at that time,
Because they have [b]practiced evil deeds.

5 [1]Lit., *casting* [a]Num. 34:13, 16-29; Josh. 18:4, 10

6 [1]Lit., *drip* [2]I.e., God's prophets [a]Is. 30:10; Amos 2:12; 7:16 [b]Mic. 3:6; Is. 29:10

7 [a]Is. 50:2; 59:1 [b]Ps. 119:65, 68, 116; Jer. 15:16 [c]Ps. 15:2; 84:11

8 [1]Lit., *And yesterday* [2]Or, *ornaments* [a]Jer. 12:8 [b]Mic. 3:2, 3; 7:2, 3 [c]Ps. 120:6, 7

9 [a]Jer. 10:20 [b]Ezek. 39:21; Hab. 2:14

10 [a]Deut. 12:9 [b]Ps. 106:38

11 [1]Lit., *drip* [2]Lit., *one who drips* [a]Is. 30:10, 11

12 [a]Mic. 5:7, 8; 7:18

1 [a]Mic. 3:9; Is. 1:10 [b]Ps. 82:1-5; Jer. 5:5

2 [a]Mic. 2:8; 7:2, 3; Ps. 53:4; Ezek. 22:27

3 [a]Ps. 14:4; 27:2; Zeph. 3:3 [b]Ezek. 34:2, 3 [c]Ezek. 11:3, 6, 7

4 [a]Deut. 31:17; Is. 59:2 [b]Mic. 7:13; Is. 3:11

5 Thus says the LORD concerning the prophets
Who [a]lead my people astray;
When they have *something* to [b]bite with their teeth,
They [d]cry, "Peace,"
But against him who puts nothing in their mouths,
They declare holy war.
6 Therefore *it will be* [a]night for you—without vision,
And darkness for you—without divination.
The [b]sun will go down on the prophets,
And the day will become dark over them.
7 The seers will be [a]ashamed
And the [b]diviners will be embarrassed.
Indeed, they will all cover *their* [1]mouths
Because there is [c]no answer from God.
8 On the other hand [a]I am filled with power—
With the Spirit of the LORD—
And with justice and courage
To make [b]known to Jacob his rebellious act,
Even to Israel his sin.
9 Now hear this, heads of the house of Jacob
And rulers of the house of Israel,
Who [a]abhor justice
And twist everything that is straight,
10 Who [a]build Zion with bloodshed
And Jerusalem with violent injustice.
11 Her leaders pronounce [a]judgment for a bribe,
Her [b]priests instruct for a price,
And her prophets divine for money.
Yet they lean on the LORD saying,
"[c]Is not the LORD in our midst?
Calamity will not come upon us."
12 Therefore, on account of you,
[a]Zion will be plowed as a field,
[b]Jerusalem will become a heap of ruins,
And the mountain of the [1]temple *will become* high places of a forest.

CHAPTER 4

AND it will come about in the [a]last days
That the [b]mountain of the house of the LORD
Will be established [1]as the chief of the mountains.
It will be raised above the hills,
And the [c]peoples will stream to it.
2 And [a]many nations will come and say,
"[b]Come and let us go up to the mountain of the LORD
And to the house of the God of Jacob,
That [c]He may teach us about His ways
And that we may walk in His paths."
For [d]from Zion will go forth the law,
Even the word of the LORD from Jerusalem.
3 And He will [a]judge between many peoples
And render decisions for mighty, [1]distant nations.
Then they will hammer their swords into plowshares

5 [a]Is. 3:12; 9:15, 16; Jer. 14:14, 15 [b]Is. 56:9-11 [c]Jer. 6:14

6 [a]Is. 8:20-22; 29:10-12 [b]Is. 59:10

7 [1]Lit., *mustache* [a]Zech. 13:4 [b]Is. 44:25; 47:12-14 [c]Mic. 3:4; 1 Sam. 28:6

8 [a]Is. 61:1, 2; Jer. 1:18 [b]Is. 58:1

9 [a]Ps. 58:1, 2; Is. 1:23

10 [a]Jer. 22:13, 17; Hab. 2:12

11 [a]Mic. 7:3; Is. 1:23 [b]Jer. 6:13 [c]Is. 48:2

12 [1]Lit., *house* [a]Jer. 26:18 [b]Jer. 9:11

1 [1]Lit., *on* [a]Dan. 2:28; 10:14; Hos. 3:5 [b]Mic. 3:12; Ezek. 43:12; Zech. 8:3 [c]Ps. 22:27; 86:9; Jer. 3:17

2 [a]Zech. 2:11; 14:16 [b]Is. 2:3; Jer. 31:6 [c]Ps. 25:8, 9, 12; Is. 54:13 [d]Is. 42:1-4; Zech. 14:8, 9

3 [1]Lit., *at a distance* [a]Is. 2:4; 11:3-5

And their spears into pruning hooks;
Nation will not lift up sword against nation,
And never again will they [2]train for war.
4 And each of them will sit under his vine
And under his fig tree,
With [a]no one to make *them* afraid,
For the [b]mouth of the LORD of hosts has spoken.
5 Though all the peoples walk
Each in the [a]name of his god,
As for us, we will walk
In the name of the LORD our God forever and ever.

6 "In that day," declares the LORD,
"I will assemble the [a]lame,
And gather the outcasts,
Even those whom I have afflicted.
7 "I will make the lame a [a]remnant,
And the outcasts a strong nation,
And the [b]LORD will reign over them in Mount Zion
From now on and forever.
8 "And as for you, [1a]tower of the flock,
[2]Hill of the daughter of Zion,
To you it will come—
Even the [b]former dominion will come,
The kingdom of the daughter of Jerusalem.

9 "Now, why do you [a]cry out loudly?
Is there no king among you,
Or has your [b]counselor perished,
That agony has gripped you like a woman in childbirth?
10 "Writhe and labor to give birth,
Daugher of Zion,
Like a woman in childbirth,
For now you will [a]go out of the city,
Dwell in the field,
And go to Babylon.
[b]There you will be rescued;
[c]There the LORD will redeem you
From the hand of your enemies.
11 "And now [a]many nations have been assembled against you
Who say, 'Let her be polluted,
And let our eyes [1]gloat over Zion.'
12 "But they do not [a]know the thoughts of the LORD,
And they do not understand His purpose;
For He has gathered them like sheaves to the threshing floor.
13 "Arise and [a]thresh, daughter of Zion,
For your horn I will make iron
And your hoofs I will make bronze,
That you may [b]pulverize many peoples,
That you may [c]devote to the LORD their unjust gain
And their wealth to the Lord of all the earth.

3 [2]Lit., *learn*

4 [a]Lev. 26:6; Jer. 30:10 [b]Is. 1:20; 40:5

5 [a]2 Kin. 17:29

6 [a]Zeph. 3:19

7 [a]Mic. 5:7, 8; 7:18 [b]Is. 24:23

8 [1]Heb., *Migdal-eder* [2]Heb., *Ophel of* [a]Ps. 48:3, 12; 61:3 [b]Is. 1:26; Zech. 9:10

9 [a]Jer. 8:19 [b]Is. 3:1-3; 28:29

10 [a]2 Kin. 20:18; Hos. 2:14 [b]Mic. 7:8-12; Is. 43:14; 45:13 [c]Is. 48:20; 52:9-12

11 [1]Lit., *look on* [a]Is. 5:25-30; 17:12-14

12 [a]Ps. 147:19, 20

13 [a]Is. 41:15 [b]Jer. 51:20-23 [c]Is. 60:9

Chapter 5

“[1]Now [a]muster yourselves in troops, daughter of troops;
[2]They have laid siege against us;
With a rod they will [b]smite the judge of Israel on the cheek.
2 “[1]But as for [a]you, Bethlehem Ephrathah,
Too little to be among the clans of Judah,
From [b]you One will go forth for Me to be [c]ruler in Israel.
[2]His goings forth are [d]from long ago,
From the days of eternity.”
3 Therefore, He will [a]give them *up* until the time
When she who is in labor has borne a child.
Then the [b]remainder of His brethren
Will return to the sons of Israel.
4 And He will arise and [a]shepherd *His flock*
In the strength of the Lord,
In the majesty of the name of the Lord His God.
And they will [1]remain,
Because [2]at that time He will be great
To the [b]ends of the earth.
5 And this One will be *our* peace.

When the [a]Assyrian invades our land,
When he tramples on our [1]citadels,
Then we will raise against him
Seven shepherds and eight leaders of men.
6 And they will [a]shepherd the land of Assyria with the sword,
The land of [b]Nimrod at its entrances;
And He will [c]deliver *us* from the Assyrian
When he attacks our land
And when he tramples our territory.

7 Then the [a]remnant of Jacob
Will be among many peoples
Like [b]dew from the Lord,
Like [c]showers on vegetation
Which do not wait for man
Or delay for the sons of men.
8 And the remnant of Jacob
Will be among the nations,
Among many peoples
[a]Like a lion among the beasts of the forest,
Like a young lion among flocks of sheep,
Which, if he passes through,
[b]Tramples down and [c]tears,
And there is [d]none to rescue.
9 Your hand will be lifted up against your adversaries,
And all your enemies will be cut off.

10 “And it will be in that day,” declares the Lord,
“That I will cut off your horses from among you
And destroy your chariots.
11 “I will also cut off the [a]cities of your land
And tear down all your [b]fortifications.

1 [1]Chap. 4:14 in Heb. [2]Lit., *He has*
[a]Jer. 5:7 [b]1 Kin. 22:24; Job 16:10; Lam. 3:30

2 [1]Chap. 5:1 in Heb. [2]Or, *His appearances are from long ago, from days of old*
[a]Matt. 2:6 [b]Is. 11:1; Luke 2:4 [c]Jer. 30:21; Zech. 9:9 [d]Ps. 102:25; Prov. 8:22, 23

3 [a]Mic. 4:10; 7:13; Hos. 11:8 [b]Mic. 5:7, 8; Is. 10:20-22

4 [1]Or, *live* in safety [2]Lit., *now*
[a]Mic. 7:14; Is. 40:11; 49:9; Ezek. 34:13-15, 23, 24 [b]Is. 45:22; 52:10

5 [1]Or, *palaces*
[a]Is. 8:7, 8; 10:24-27

6 [a]Nah. 2:11-13; Zeph. 2:13 [b]Gen. 10:8-11 [c]Is. 14:25; 37:36, 37

7 [a]Mic. 5:3; 2:12; 4:7; 7:18 [b]Deut. 32:2; Ps. 110:3; Hos. 14:5 [c]Ps. 72:6; Is. 44:3

8 [a]Gen. 49:9; Num. 24:9 [b]Mic. 4:13; Ps. 44:5; Is. 41:15, 16; Zech. 10:5 [c]Hos. 5:14 [d]Ps. 50:22

11 [a]Is. 1:7; 6:11 [b]Is. 2:12-17; Hos. 10:14; Amos 5:9

12 "I will cut off [a]sorceries from your hand,
And you will have fortune tellers no more.
13 "[a]I will cut off your carved images
And your sacred pillars from among you,
So that you will no longer bow down
To the work of your hands.
14 "I will root out your [1a]Asherim from among you
And destroy your cities.
15 "And I will [a]execute vengeance in anger and wrath
On the nations which have not obeyed."

Chapter 6

HEAR now what the LORD is saying:
"Arise, plead your case [1]before the mountains,
And let the hills hear your voice.
2 "Listen, you mountains, to the indictment of the LORD,
And you enduring [a]foundations of the earth,
Because the [b]LORD has a case against His people;
Even with Israel He will dispute.
3 "[a]My people, [b]what have I done to you,
And [c]how have I wearied you? Answer Me.
4 "Indeed, I [a]brought you up from the land of Egypt
And [b]ransomed you from the house of slavery,
And I sent before you [c]Moses, Aaron, and [d]Miriam.
5 "My people, remember now
What [a]Balak king of Moab counselled
And what Balaam son of Beor answered him,
And from Shittim to Gilgal,
In order [1]that you might know the [b]righteous acts of
the LORD."

6 [a]With what shall I come to the LORD
And bow myself before the God on high?
Shall I come to Him with [b]burnt offerings,
With yearling calves?
7 Does the LORD take delight in [a]thousands of rams,
In ten thousand rivers of oil?
Shall I present my [b]first-born *for* my rebellious acts,
The fruit of my body for the sin of my soul?
8 He has [a]told you, O man, what is good;
And [b]what does the LORD require of you
But to [c]do justice, to [d]love [1]kindness,
And to walk [2e]humbly with your God?

9 The voice of the LORD will call to the city—
And it is sound wisdom to fear Thy name:
"Hear, O [a]tribe. Who has appointed [1]its time?
10 "Is there yet a man in the wicked house,
Along with treasures of [a]wickedness,
And a [1b]short measure *that is* cursed?
11 "Can I justify wicked [a]scales
And a bag of deceptive weights?
12 "For the rich men of *the* [1]city are full of violence,
Her residents speak lies,
And their [a]tongue is deceitful in their mouth.

12 [a]Deut. 18:10-12; Is. 2:6; 8:19

13 [a]Is. 2:18; 17:8; Ezek. 6:9

14 [1]I.e., wooden symbols of the goddess Asherah [a]Ex. 34:13; Is. 17:8; 27:9

15 [a]Is. 1:24; 65:12

1 [1]Lit., *with*

2 [a]2 Sam. 22:16; Ps. 104:5 [b]Is. 1:18; Hos. 4:1; 12:2

3 [a]Ps. 50:7 [b]Jer. 2:5 [c]Is. 43:22, 23

4 [a]Ex. 20:2 [b]Deut. 7:8 [c]Ps. 77:20 [d]Ex. 15:20

5 [1]Lit., *to know* [a]Num. 22:5, 6 [b]1 Sam. 12:7; Is. 1:27

6 [a]Ps. 40:6-8 [b]Ps. 51:16, 17

7 [a]Is. 40:16 [b]Lev. 18:21; 20:1-5; Jer. 7:31

8 [1]Or, *loyalty* [2]Or, *circumspectly* [a]Deut. 30:15 [b]Deut. 10:12 [c]Is. 56:1; Jer. 22:3 [d]Hos. 6:6 [e]Is. 57:15; 66:2

9 [1]Lit., *it* [a]Job 5:6-8, 17; Is. 11:4

10 [1]Lit., *shrunken ephah* [a]Jer. 5:26, 27; Amos 3:10 [b]Ezek. 45:9, 10; Amos 8:5

11 [a]Lev. 19:36; Hos. 12:7

12 [1]Lit., *her* [a]Is. 3:8

13 "So also I will make *you* sick, striking you down,
[a]Desolating *you* because of your sins.
14 "You will eat, but you will [a]not be satisfied,
And your [1]vileness will be in your midst.
You will *try to* remove *for safekeeping,*
But you will [b]not preserve *anything,*
And what you do preserve I will give to the sword.
15 "You will sow but you will [a]not reap.
You will tread the olive but will not anoint yourself with oil;
And the grapes, but you will [b]not drink wine.
16 "The statutes of [a]Omri
And all the works of the house of [b]Ahab are observed;
And in their devices you [c]walk.
Therefore, I will give you up for [d]destruction
And [1]your inhabitants for [e]derision,
And you will bear the [f]reproach of My people."

13 [a]Is. 1:7; 6:11

14 [1]Or possibly, *garbage* or *excreta*
[a]Is. 9:20 [b]Is. 30:6

15 [a]Deut. 28:38-40; Jer. 12:13 [b]Amos 5:11; Zeph. 1:13

16 [1]Lit., *her*
[a]1 Kin. 16:25, 26 [b]1 Kin. 16:29-33 [c]Jer. 7:24 [d]Mic. 6:13; Jer. 18:16 [e]Jer. 19:8; 25:9, 18; 29:18 [f]Ps. 44:13; Jer. 51:51; Hos. 12:14

CHAPTER 7

WOE is me! For I am
Like the fruit pickers and the [a]grape gatherers.
There is not a cluster of grapes to eat,
Or a [b]first-ripe fig *which* [1]I crave.
2 The [1]godly person has [a]perished from the land,
And there is no upright *person* among men.
All of them lie in wait for [b]bloodshed;
Each of them hunts the other with a [c]net.
3 Concerning evil, both hands do it [a]well.
The prince asks, also the judge, for a [b]bribe,
And a great man speaks the desire of his soul;
So they weave it together.
4 The best of them is like a [a]briar,
The most upright like a [b]thorn hedge.
The day when you post a watchman,
Your [c]punishment will come.
Then their [d]confusion will occur.
5 Do not [a]trust in a neighbor;
Do not have confidence in a friend.
From her who lies in your bosom
Guard [1]your lips.
6 For son treats father contemptuously,
Daughter rises up against her mother,
Daughter-in-law against her mother-in-law;
[a]A man's enemies are the men of his own household.

7 But as for me, I will [a]watch expectantly for the LORD;
I will [b]wait for the God of my salvation.
My [c]God will hear me.
8 Do not rejoice over me, O my enemy.
Though I fall I will [a]rise;
Though I dwell in darkness, the LORD is a [b]light for me.

9 I will bear the indignation of the LORD
Because I have sinned against Him,

1 [1]Lit., *my soul*
[a]Is. 24:13 [b]Is. 28:4; Hos. 9:10

2 [1]Or, *loyal*
[a]Is. 57:1 [b]Mic. 3:10; Is. 59:7 [c]Jer. 5:26; Hos. 5:1

3 [a]Prov. 4:16, 17 [b]Mic. 3:11; Amos 5:12

4 [a]Ezek. 2:6; 28:24 [b]Nah. 1:10 [c]Is. 10:3; Hos. 9:7 [d]Is. 22:5

5 [1]Lit., *openings of your mouth*
[a]Jer. 9:4

6 [a]Matt. 10:36

7 [a]Hab. 2:1 [b]Ps. 130:5; Is. 25:9 [c]Ps. 4:3

8 [a]Amos 9:11 [b]Is. 9:2

Until He [a]pleads my case and executes justice for me.
He will bring me out to the [b]light,
And I will see His [1c]righteousness.
10 Then my enemy will see,
And shame will cover her who [a]said to me,
"Where is the LORD your God?"
My eyes will look on her;
[1]At that time she will [2]be [b]trampled down,
Like mire of the streets.
11 *It will be* a day for [a]building your walls.
On that day will your [b]boundary be extended.
12 It *will be* a day when [1]they will [a]come to you
From Assyria and the cities of Egypt,
From Egypt even to [2]the Euphrates,
Even from sea to sea and mountain to mountain.
13 And the earth will become [a]desolate because of her inhabitants,
On account of the [b]fruit of their deeds.

14 Shepherd Thy people with Thy [a]scepter,
The flock of Thy [1]possession
Which dwells by itself in the woodland,
In the midst of a [b]fruitful field.
Let them feed in Bashan and Gilead
[b]As in the days of old.
15 "As in the days when you came out from the land of Egypt,
I will show [1a]you miracles."
16 Nations will see and be ashamed
Of all their might.
They will [a]put *their* hand on *their* mouth,
Their ears will be deaf.
17 They will [a]lick the dust like a serpent,
Like reptiles of the earth.
They will come trembling out of their [1]fortresses;
To the LORD our God they will come in [b]dread,
And they will be afraid before Thee.
18 Who is a God like Thee, who [a]pardons iniquity
And passes over the rebellious act of the [b]remnant of His [1]possession?
He does not [c]retain His anger forever,
Because He [d]delights in [2]unchanging love.
19 He will again have compassion on us;
[a]He will tread our iniquities underfoot.
Yes, Thou wilt [b]cast all their [1]sins
Into the depths of the sea.
20 Thou wilt give [1a]truth to Jacob
And [2]unchanging love to Abraham,
Which Thou didst [b]swear to our forefathers
From the days of old.

9 [1]I.e., right dealing [a]Jer. 50:34 [b]Ps. 37:6; Is. 42:7, 16 [c]Is. 46:13; 56:1

10 [1]Lit., *Now* [2]Lit., *become a trampled* place [a]Joel 2:17 [b]Is. 51:23; Zech. 10:5

11 [a]Is. 54:11; Amos 9:11 [b]Zeph. 2:2

12 [1]Lit., *he* [2]Lit., the *River* [a]Is. 19:23-25; 60:4, 9

13 [a]Mic. 6:13; Jer. 25:11 [b]Mic. 3:4; Is. 3:10, 11

14 [1]Or, *inheritance* [2]Or, *Carmel* [a]Lev. 27:32; Ps. 23:4 [b]Amos 9:11

15 [1]Lit., *him* [a]Ex. 3:20; 34:10; Ps. 78:12

16 [a]Mic. 3:7

17 [1]Lit., *fastnesses* [a]Ps. 72:9; Is. 49:23 [b]Is. 25:3; 59:19

18 [1]Or, *inheritance* [2]Or, *lovingkindness* [a]Ex. 34:7, 9; Is. 43:25 [b]Mic. 2:12; 4:7; 5:7, 8 [c]Ps. 103:8, 9, 13 [d]Jer. 32:41

19 [1]Several ancient versions read, *our* [a]Jer. 50:20 [b]Is. 38:17; 43:25; Jer. 31:34

20 [1]Or, *faithfulness* [2]Or, *lovingkindness* [a]Gen. 24:27; 32:10 [b]Deut. 7:8, 12

THE BOOK OF NAHUM

God Is Awesome.

THE [1a]oracle of Nineveh. The book of the vision of Nahum
the Elkoshite.

2 A jealous and avenging God is the LORD;
The LORD is [a]avenging and [1]wrathful.
The LORD takes [b]vengeance on His adversaries,
And He reserves wrath for His enemies.
3 The LORD is [a]slow to anger and great in power,
And the LORD will by no means leave *the guilty* unpunished.
In [b]whirlwind and storm is His way,
And [c]clouds are the dust beneath His feet.
4 He [a]rebukes the sea and makes it dry;
He dries up all the rivers.
[b]Bashan and Carmel wither;
The blossoms of Lebanon wither.
5 Mountains [a]quake because of Him,
And the hills [b]dissolve;
Indeed the earth is [c]upheaved by His presence,
The [d]world and all the inhabitants in it.
6 Who can stand before His [a]indignation?
Who can endure the [b]burning of His anger?
His [c]wrath is poured out like fire,
And the [d]rocks are broken up by Him.
7 The LORD is [a]good,
A stronghold in the day of trouble,
And He knows those who take refuge in Him.
8 But with an [a]overflowing flood
He will make a complete end of [1]its site,
And will pursue His enemies into [b]darkness.

9 Whatever you [a]devise against the LORD,
He will make a [b]complete end of it.
Distress will not rise up twice.
10 Like tangled [a]thorns,
And like those who are [b]drunken with their drink,
They are [c]consumed
As stubble completely withered.
11 From you has gone forth
One who [a]plotted evil against the LORD,
A [1]wicked [b]counselor.
12 Thus says the LORD,
"Though they are at full *strength* and likewise many,
Even so, they will be [a]cut off and pass away.
Though I have afflicted you,
I will afflict you no longer.
13 "So now, I will [a]break his yoke bar from upon you,
And I will tear off your shackles."

14 The LORD has issued a command concerning [1]you:
"[2]Your name will no longer be perpetuated.

1 [1]Or, *burden* [a]Is. 13:1; 19:1; Jer. 23:33, 34; Hab. 1:1; Zech. 9:1; Mal. 1:1

2 [1]Lit., *a possessor of wrath* [a]Deut. 32:35, 41 [b]Ps. 94:1

3 [a]Ex. 34:6, 7 [b]Is. 29:6; Amos 1:1 [c]Ps. 104:3; Is. 19:1

4 [a]Ps. 106:9; Is. 50:2 [b]Is. 33:9

5 [a]Ex. 19:18 [b]Mic. 1:4 [c]Is. 24:1, 20 [d]Ps. 98:7

6 [a]Jer. 10:10 [b]Is. 13:13 [c]Is. 66:15 [d]1 Kin. 19:11

7 [a]Ps. 25:8; 37:39, 40

8 [1]I.e., Nineveh's [a]Is. 28:2, 18 [b]Is. 13:9, 10

9 [a]Nah. 1:11 [b]Is. 28:22

10 [a]Mic. 7:4 [b]Is. 56:12 [c]Is. 5:24; 10:17

11 [1]Or, *worthless;* Heb., *Belial* [a]Nah. 1:9; Is. 10:7-11 [b]Ezek. 11:2

12 [a]Is. 10:16-19, 33, 34

13 [a]Is. 9:4; 10:27; Jer. 2:20

14 [1]I.e., the king of Nineveh [2]Lit., *No more of your name will be sown*

I will cut off [a]idol and [3]image
From the house of your gods.
I will prepare your [b]grave,
For you are contemptible."

15 [1]Behold, [a]on the mountains the feet of him who brings good news,
Who announces peace!
[b]Celebrate your feasts, O Judah;
Pay your vows.
For never again will the [2]wicked one [c]pass through you;
He is [d]cut off completely.

CHAPTER 2

1 THE one who [a]scatters has come up against [2]you.
Man the fortress, watch the road;
[3]Strengthen your back, [4]summon all *your* strength.
2 For the LORD will restore the [a]splendor of Jacob
[b]Like the splendor of Israel,
Even though devastators have [c]devastated them
And [d]destroyed their vine branches.

3 The shields of [1]his mighty men are *colored* red,
The warriors are dressed in scarlet,
The [a]chariots are *enveloped* in [2]flashing steel
[3]When he is prepared *to march*,
And the cypress *spears* are brandished.
4 The [a]chariots race madly in the streets,
They rush wildly in the [1]squares,
Their appearance is like torches,
They [b]dash to and fro like lightning flashes.
5 He remembers his nobles;
They stumble in their march,
They hurry to her wall,
And the [1]mantelet is set up.
6 The gates of the rivers are opened,
And the palace is dissolved.
7 And it is fixed:
She is stripped, she is carried away,
And her handmaids are moaning like the sound of doves,
Beating on their [1]breasts.

8 Though Nineveh *was* like a pool of water throughout her days,
Now they are fleeing;
"Stop, stop,"
But [a]no one turns back.
9 Plunder the silver!
Plunder the gold!
For there is no limit to the treasure—
Wealth from every kind of desirable object.
10 She is [a]emptied! Yes, she is desolate and waste!
[b]Hearts are melting and knees knocking!

14 [3]Lit., *cast* metal *image* [a]Is. 46:1, 2; Mic. 5:13, 14 [b]Ezek. 32:22, 23

15 [1]Chap. 2:1 in Heb. [2]Or, *worthless one;* Heb., *Belial* [a]Is. 40:9; 52:7; Rom. 10:15 [b]Lev. 23:2, 4 [c]Is. 52:1; Joel 3:17 [d]Is. 29:7, 8

1 [1]Chap. 2:2 in Heb. [2]Lit., *your face* [3]Lit., *Make strong your loins* [4]Lit., *strengthen power greatly* [a]Jer. 51:20-23

2 [a]Is. 60:15 [b]Ezek. 37:21-23 [c]Jer. 48:11 [d]Ps. 80:12, 13

3 [1]I.e., those attacking Nineveh [2]Lit., *fire of steel* [3]Lit., *On the day of his preparation*

4 [1]Lit., *broad places* [a]Nah. 3:2, 3; Is. 66:15; Ezek. 26:10 [b]Jer. 4:13

5 [1]Lit., *covering* used in a siege

7 [1]Lit., *hearts*

8 [a]Jer. 46:5; 47:3

10 [a]Nah. 2:2; Is. 24:1; 34:10-15 [b]Ps. 22:14; Is. 13:7, 8; Ezek. 21:7

Also anguish is in [1]the whole body,
And all their [c]faces are grown pale!
11 Where is the den of the lions
And the feeding place of the young lions,
Where the lion, lioness, and lion's cub prowled,
With nothing to disturb *them?*
12 The lion tore enough for his cubs,
[1]Killed *enough* for his lionesses,
And filled his lairs with prey
And his dens with torn flesh.
13 "Behold, [a]I am against you," declares the LORD of hosts.
"I will [b]burn up her chariots in smoke, a sword will devour your
young lions, I will cut off your prey from the land, and no
longer will the voice of your messengers be heard."

CHAPTER 3

[a]WOE to the bloody city, completely full of lies *and* pillage;
Her prey never departs.
2 The [a]noise of the whip,
The noise of the rattling of the wheel,
Galloping horses,
And [1]bounding chariots!
3 Horsemen charging,
Swords flashing, spears [a]gleaming,
[b]Many slain, a mass of corpses,
And [1c]countless dead bodies—
They stumble over [2]the dead bodies!
4 *All* because of the many harlotries of the harlot,
The charming one, the mistress of sorceries,
Who sells nations by her harlotries
And families by her sorceries.
5 "Behold, [a]I am against you," declares the LORD of hosts;
"And I will [1b]lift up your skirts over your face,
And [c]show to the nations your nakedness
And to the kingdoms your disgrace.
6 "I will [a]throw [1]filth on you
And [b]make you vile,
And set you up as a [c]spectacle.
7 "And it will come about that all who see you
Will [1]shrink from you and say,
'Nineveh is devastated!
[a]Who will grieve for her?'
Where will I seek comforters for you?"

8 Are you better than [1a]No-amon,
Which was situated by the [b]waters of the Nile,
With water surrounding her,
Whose rampart *was* [2]the sea,
Whose wall *consisted* of [2]the sea?
9 [a]Ethiopia was *her* might,
And Egypt too, without limits.
Put and Lubim were among [1]her helpers.
10 Yet she [a]became an exile,
She went into captivity;
Also her [b]small children were dashed to pieces

10 [1]Lit., *all the loin* [c]Joel 2:6

12 [1]Lit., *Strangled*

13 [a]Nah. 3:5; Jer. 21:13; Ezek. 5:8 [b]Josh. 11:6, 9; Ps. 46:9

1 [a]Ezek. 24:6, 9

2 [1]Lit., *skipping* [a]Nah. 2:3, 4; Job 39:22-25; Jer. 47:3

3 [1]Lit., *there is no end to* [2]Lit., *their* [a]Hab. 3:11 [b]Is. 34:3; 66:16 [c]Is. 37:36; Ezek. 39:4

5 [1]Lit., *uncover your* [a]Nah. 2:13; Jer. 50:31; Ezek. 26:3 [b]Jer. 13:26 [c]Ezek. 16:37

6 [1]Lit., *detestable things* [a]Job 9:31 [b]Job 30:8; Mal. 2:9 [c]Is. 14:16; Jer. 51:37

7 [1]Lit., *flee* [a]Is. 51:19; Jer. 15:5

8 [1]I.e., the city of Amon: Tuebes [2]I.e., the Nile [a]Jer. 46:25; Ezek. 30:14-16 [b]Is. 19:6-8

9 [1]Lit., *your* [a]Is. 20:5

10 [a]Is. 19:4; 20:4 [b]Hos. 1:16

At the head of every street;
They [c]cast lots for her honorable men,
And all her great men were bound with fetters.
11 You too will become [a]drunk,
You will be hidden.
You too will search for a refuge from the enemy.
12 All your fortifications are fig trees with [1a]ripe fruit—
When shaken, they fall into the eater's mouth.
13 Behold, your people are [a]women in your midst!
The gates of your land are [b]opened wide to your enemies;
Fire consumes your gate bars.
14 [a]Draw for yourself water for the siege!
[b]Strengthen your fortifications!
Go into the clay and tread the mortar!
Take hold of the brick mold!
15 There [a]fire will consume you,
The sword will cut you down;
It will consume you as the locust *does*.

Multiply yourself like the creeping locust,
Multiply yourself like the swarming locust.
16 You have increased your traders more than the stars of heaven—
The creeping locust [1]strips and flies away.
17 Your [1]guardsmen are like the swarming locust.
Your marshals are like hordes of grasshoppers
Settling in the stone walls on a cold day.
The sun rises and they flee,
And the place where they are is not known.
18 Your shepherds are [a]sleeping, O king of Assyria;
Your nobles are lying down.
Your people are [b]scattered on the mountains,
And there is no one to regather *them*.
19 There is no [a]relief for your breakdown,
Your [b]wound is incurable.
All who hear [1]about you
Will [c]clap *their* hands over you,
For on whom has not your evil passed continually?

10 [c]Joel 3:3; Obad. 11

11 [a]Is. 49:26; Jer. 25:27

12 [1]Lit., *first fruits* [a]Is. 28:4; Hab. 1:10

13 [a]Is. 19:16; Jer. 51:30 [b]Nah. 2:6; Is. 45:1, 2

14 [a]2 Chr. 32:3, 4, 11 [b]Nah. 2:1

15 [a]Nah. 3:13; 2:13; Is. 66:15, 16

16 [1]I.e., strips vegetation; or, *molts*

17 [1]Or, *officials*

18 [a]Ps. 76:5, 6; Is. 56:10; Jer. 51:57 [b]1 Kin. 22:17; Is. 13:14

19 [1]Lit., *your report* [a]Jer. 46:11; Mic. 1:9 [b]Jer. 30:12 [c]Job 27:23; Lam. 2:15

THE BOOK OF HABAKKUK

Chaldeans Raised Up to Punish Judah.

THE [1a]oracle which Habakkuk the prophet saw.
2 [a]How long, O LORD, will I call for help,
And Thou wilt not hear?
I cry out to Thee, "Violence!"
Yet Thou dost [b]not save.
3 Why dost Thou make me see iniquity,
And cause *me* to look on wickedness?
Yes, [a]destruction and violence are before me;
[b]Strife exists and contention arises.
4 Therefore, the [a]law is [1]ignored
And justice [2]is never upheld.
For the wicked [b]surround the righteous;
Therefore, justice comes out [c]perverted.

5 "Look among the nations! Observe!
Be astonished! [a]Wonder!
Because *I* am doing [b]something in your days—
You would not believe if [1]you were told.
6 "For behold, I am [a]raising up the Chaldeans,
That [1]fierce and impetuous people
Who march [2]throughout the earth
To [3b]seize dwelling places which are not theirs.
7 "They are dreaded and [a]feared.
Their [b]justice and [1]authority [2]originate with themselves.
8 "Their horses are swifter than leopards
And [1]keener than wolves in the evening.
Their [2]horsemen come galloping,
Their horsemen come from afar;
They fly like an [a]eagle swooping *down* to devour.
9 "All of them come for violence.
[1]Their [a]horde of faces *moves* forward.
They collect captives like sand.
10 "They [a]mock at kings,
And rulers are a laughing matter to them.
They [b]laugh at every fortress,
And [c]heap up rubble to capture it.
11 "Then they will sweep through *like* the wind and pass on.
But they will be held [a]guilty,
They whose [b]strength is their god."

12 Art Thou not from everlasting,
O LORD, my God, my Holy One?
We will not die.
Thou, O LORD, hast [a]appointed them to judge;
And Thou, O [b]Rock, has established them to correct.
13 *Thine* eyes are too [a]pure to [1]approve evil,
And Thou canst not look on wickedness *with favor.*
Why dost Thou [b]look with favor

1 [1]Or, *burden* [a]Is. 13:1; Nah. 1:1

2 [a]Ps. 13:1, 2; 22:1, 2 [b]Jer. 14:9

3 [a]Jer. 20:8 [b]Jer. 15:10

4 [1]Or, *ineffective;* lit., *numbed* [2]Lit., *never goes forth* [a]Ps. 119:126; Is. 59:12-14 [b]Ps. 22:12; Is. 1:21-23 [c]Is. 5:20; Ezek. 9:9

5 [1]Lit., *it* [a]Is. 29:9 [b]Is. 29:14; Ezek. 12:22-28

6 [1]Lit., *bitter* [2]Lit., *the breadth of* [3]Lit., *take possession of* [a]2 Kin. 24:2; Jer. 4:11-13 [b]Jer. 8:10

7 [1]Lit., *eminence* [2]Lit., *proceeds from* [a]Is. 18:2, 7 [b]Jer. 39:5-9

8 [1]Or, *more eager* to attack [2]Or, *steeds paw* the ground [a]Ezek. 17:3; Hos. 8:1

9 [1]Or, *The eagerness of their faces* [a]2 Kin. 12:17; Dan. 11:17

10 [a]2 Chr. 36:6, 10; Is. 37:13 [b]Is. 10:9; 14:16 [c]Jer. 32:24; Ezek. 26:8

11 [a]Jer. 2:3 [b]Hab. 1:16; Dan. 4:30

12 [a]Is. 10:5, 6; Mal. 3:5 [b]Deut. 32:4

13 [1]Lit., *look at* [a]Ps. 11:4-6; 34:16 [b]Jer. 12:1, 2

On those who deal [c]treacherously?
Why art Thou [d]silent when the wicked swallowed up
Those more righteous than they?
14 *Why* hast Thou made men like the fish of the sea,
Like creeping things without a ruler over them?
15 *The Chaldeans* [a]bring all of them up with a hook,
[b]Drag them away with their net,
And gather them together in their fishing net.
Therefore, they rejoice and are glad.
16 Therefore, they offer a sacrifice to their net.
And [1]burn incense to their fishing net;
Because through [a]these things their [2]catch is [3]large,
And their food is [4]plentiful.
17 Will they therefore empty their [a]net
And continually [b]slay nations without sparing?

CHAPTER 2

I WILL [a]stand on my guard post
And station myself on the rampart;
And I will [b]keep watch to see [c]what He will speak to me,
And how I may reply [1]when I am reproved.
2 Then the LORD answered me and said,
"[a]Record the vision
And inscribe *it* on tablets,
That [1]the one who [2]reads it may run.
3 "For the vision is yet for the [a]appointed time;
It [1]hastens toward the goal, and it will not [2]fail.
Though it tarries, [b]wait for it;
For it will certainly come, it will not delay.

4 "Behold, as for the [a]proud one,
His soul is not right within him;
But the [b]righteous will live by his [1]faith.
5 "Furthermore, wine betrays the haughty man,
So that he does not [a]stay at home.
He [b]enlarges his appetite like Sheol,
And he is like death, never satisfied.
He also gathers to himself all nations
And collects to himself all peoples.

6 "Will not all of these [a]take up a taunt-song against him,
Even mockery *and* insinuations against him,
And say, '[b]Woe to him who increases what is not his—
For how long—
And makes himself [1]rich with loans?'
7 "Will not [1]your creditors [a]rise up suddenly,
And those who [2]collect from you awaken?
Indeed, you will become plunder for them.
8 "Because you have [a]looted many nations,
All the remainder of the peoples will loot you—
Because of human bloodshed and violence done to the land,
To the town and all its inhabitants.

13 [c]Is. 24:16 [d]Ps. 50:21

15 [a]Jer. 16:16; Amos 4:2 [b]Ps. 10:9

16 [1]Or, *sacrifice* [2]Lit., *portion* [3]Lit., *fat* or *plentiful* [4]Lit., *the fat portion* [a]Jer. 44:17

17 [a]Is. 19:8 [b]Is. 14:5, 6

1 [1]Lit., *upon my reproof* [a]Is. 21:8 [b]Ps. 5:3 [c]Ps. 85:8

2 [1]Or, *one may read it fluently* [2]Or, *is to proclaim it* [a]Deut. 27:8; Rev. 1:19

3 [1]Lit., *pants* [2]Or, *lie* [a]Dan. 8:17, 19 [b]Ps. 27:14

4 [1]Or, *faithfulness* [a]Ps. 49:18; Ps. 13:11 [b]Rom. 1:17; Gal. 3:11

5 [a]2 Kin. 14:10 [b]Is. 5:11-15

6 [1]Lit., *heavy* [a]Is. 14:4-10; Jer. 50:13 [b]Hab. 2:12; Job 20:15-29

7 [1]Lit., *those who bite you* [2]Lit., *violently shake you* [a]Prov. 29:1

8 [a]Is. 33:1; Jer. 27:7; Zech. 2:8

9 "Woe to him who gets [a]evil gain for his house
To [b]put his nest on high
To be delivered from the hand of calamity!
10 "You have devised a [a]shameful thing for your house
By cutting off many peoples;
So you are sinning against yourself.
11 "Surely the [a]stone will cry out from the wall,
And the rafter will answer it from the [1]framework.

12 "Woe to him who [a]builds a city with bloodshed
And founds a town with [1]violence!
13 "Is it not indeed from the LORD of hosts
That peoples [a]toil for fire,
And nations grow weary for nothing?
14 "For the earth will be [a]filled
With the knowledge of the glory of the LORD,
As the waters cover the sea.

15 "Woe to you who make [1]your neighbors drink,
Who mix in your venom even to make *them* drunk
So as to look on their nakedness!
16 "You will be filled with disgrace rather than honor.
Now you yourself drink and [1]expose your *own* nakedness.
The [a]cup in the LORD's right hand will come around to you,
And [b]utter disgrace *will come* upon your glory.
17 "For the [a]violence done to Lebanon will [1]overwhelm you,
And the devastation of *its* beasts [2]by which you terrified them,
[b]Because of human bloodshed and [c]violence *done* to the land,
To the town and all its inhabitants.

18 "What [a]profit is the idol when its maker has carved it,
Or an [1]image, a [b]teacher of falsehood?
For *its* maker [c]trusts in his *own* handiwork
When he fashions speechless idols.
19 "Woe to him who says to a *piece of* wood, '[a]Awake!'
To a dumb stone, 'Arise!'
And that is *your* teacher?
Behold, it is overlaid with [b]gold and silver,
And there is [c]no breath at all inside it.
20 "But the LORD is in His holy temple.
[1]Let all the earth [a]be silent before Him."

CHAPTER 3

A PRAYER of Habakkuk the prophet, according to [1]Shigionoth.
2 LORD, I have [a]heard [1]the report about Thee [2]*and* I [b]fear.
O LORD, [c]revive [d]Thy work in the midst of the years,
In the midst of the years make it known;
In wrath remember [3][e]mercy.

9 [a]Jer. 22:13; Ezek. 22:27 [b]Is. 47:7; Jer. 49:16

10 [a]Hab. 2:16; 2 Kin. 9:26; Nah. 1:14

11 [1]Lit., *wood* [a]Josh. 24:27; Luke 19:40

12 [1]Or, *injustice* [a]Mic. 3:10; Nah. 3:1

13 [a]Is. 50:11; 55:2; Jer. 51:58

14 [a]Ps. 22:27; Is. 11:9; Zech. 14:8, 9

15 [1]Lit., *his neighbor*

16 [1]Lit., *show yourself uncircumcised;* or, *stagger;* so DSS and ancient versions [a]Jer. 25:15, 27 [b]Nah. 3:6

17 [1]Lit., *cover* [2]Lit., which *terrified them* [a]Joel 3:19; Zech. 11:1 [b]Hab. 2:8; Ps. 55:23 [c]Hab. 2:8; Jer. 51:35

18 [1]Lit., *cast* metal *image* [a]Is. 42:17; 44:9; Jer. 2:27, 28 [b]Jer. 10:8, 14; Zech. 10:2 [c]Ps. 115:4, 8

19 [a]1 Kin. 18:26-29 [b]Jer. 10:9, 14 [c]Ps. 135:17

20 [1]Lit., *Hush before Him, all the earth.* [a]Zeph. 1:7; Zech. 2:13

1 [1]I.e., a highly emotional poetic form

2 [1]Or, *Thy report* [2]Or, *I stand in awe of Thy work, O* LORD; *In the midst of the years revive it,* [3]Or, *compassion* [a]Job 42:5, 6 [b]Ps. 119:120; Jer. 10:7 [c]Ps. 71:20; 85:6 [d]Hab. 1:5; Ps. 44:1-8 [e]Num. 14:19; 2 Sam. 24:15-17; Is. 54:8

3 God comes from Teman,
And the Holy One from Mount Paran. [Selah.
His [a]splendor covers the heavens,
And the [b]earth is full of His praise.
4 *His* [a]radiance is like the sunlight;
He has rays *flashing* from His hand,
And there is the hiding of His [b]power.
5 Before Him goes [a]pestilence,
And [b]plague comes [1]after Him.
6 He stood and surveyed the earth;
He looked and [a]startled the nations.
Yes, the perpetual mountains were shattered,
The ancient hills [1]collapsed.
His ways are everlasting.
7 I saw the tents of Cushan under [a]distress,
The tent curtains of the land of Midian were trembling.

8 Did the LORD rage against the [a]rivers,
Or *was* Thy anger against the rivers,
Or *was* Thy wrath against the [b]sea,
That Thou didst [c]ride on Thy horses,
On Thy [d]chariots of salvation?
9 Thy [a]bow was made bare,
The rods of [1b]chastisement were sworn. [Selah.
Thou didst [c]cleave the earth with rivers.
10 The mountains saw Thee *and* quaked;
The downpour of waters swept by.
The deep [a]uttered forth its voice,
It lifted high its hands.
11 [a]Sun *and* moon stood in their places;
They went away at the [b]light of Thine arrows,
At the radiance of Thy gleaming spear.
12 In indignation Thou didst [a]march through the earth;
In anger Thou didst [1b]trample the nations.
13 Thou didst go forth for the [a]salvation of Thy people,
For the salvation of Thine [b]anointed.
Thou didst strike the [c]head of the house of the evil
To lay him open from [1d]thigh to neck. [Selah.
14 Thou didst pierce with his [a]own [1]spears
The head of his [2]throngs.
They [b]stormed in to scatter [3]us;
Their exultation *was* like those
Who [c]devour the oppressed in secret.
15 Thou didst tread on the sea with Thy horses,
On the [a]surge of many waters.

16 I heard and my [1]inward parts [a]trembled;
At the sound my lips quivered.
Decay enters my [b]bones,
And in my place I tremble.
Because I must [c]wait quietly for the day of distress,
[2]For the people to [d]arise *who* will invade us.
17 Though the fig tree should not blossom,
And there be no [1]fruit on the vines,
Though the yield of the [a]olive should fail,

3 [a]Ps. 113:4; 148:13 [b]Ps. 48:10

4 [a]Ps. 18:12 [b]Job 26:14

5 [1]Lit., *at His feet*
[a]Ex. 12:29, 30; Num. 16:46-49 [b]Num. 11:1-3; Ps. 18:12, 13

6 [1]Lit., *bowed* or *sank down*
[a]Job 21:18; Ps. 35:5

7 [a]Ex. 15:14-16

8 [a]Ex. 7:19, 20; Josh. 3:16; Is. 50:2 [b]Ex. 14:16, 21; Ps. 114:3, 5 [c]Deut. 33:26; Ps. 18:10 [d]Ps. 68:17

9 [1]Lit., *word*
[a]Hab. 3:11; Ps. 7:12, 13 [b]Gen. 26:3; Deut. 7:8 [c]Ps. 78:16; 105:41

10 [a]Ps. 93:3; 98:7, 8

11 [a]Josh 10:12-14; Ps. 18:9, 11 [b]Ps. 18:14

12 [1]Or, *thresh*
[a]Ps. 68:7 [b]Is. 41:15; Jer. 51:33; Mic. 4:13

13 [1]Lit., *foundation*
[a]Ex. 15:2; Ps. 68:19, 20 [b]Ps. 20:6; 28:8 [c]Ps. 68:21; 110:6 [d]Ezek. 13:14

14 [1]Lit., *shafts* [2]Or, *warriors* or, *villagers* [3]Lit., *me*
[a]Judg. 7:22 [b]Dan. 11:40; Zech. 9:14 [c]Ps. 10:8; 64:2-5

15 [a]Ex. 15:8

16 [1]Lit., *belly* [2]Or, *To come upon the people who will*
[a]Hab. 3:2; Dan. 10:8 [b]Job 30:17, 30; Jer. 23:9 [c]Luke 21:19 [d]Jer. 5:15

17 [1]Lit., *produce*
[a]Mic. 6:15

17 [b]Joel 1:18 [c]Jer. 5:17

18 [a]Ex. 15:1, 2; Is. 61:10; Rom. 5:2, 3; Phil. 4:4 [b]Ps. 46:1-5 [c]Ps. 25:5; 27:1; Is. 12:2

19 [1]YHWH, usually rendered LORD [a]Ps. 18:32, 33; Is. 45:24

And the fields produce no food,
Though the [b]flock should be cut off from the fold,
And there be [c]no cattle in the stalls,
18 Yet I will [a]exult in the LORD,
I will [b]rejoice in the [c]God of my salvation.
19 The Lord [1]GOD is my [a]strength,
And He has made my feet like hinds' *feet*,
And makes me walk on my high places.

For the choir director, on my stringed instruments.

THE BOOK OF ZEPHANIAH

Day of Wrath upon Judah.

2 [1]Lit., *ground* [a]Jer. 7:20; Ezek. 33:27, 28

3 [1]Or, *stumbling blocks* [2]Lit., *ground* [a]Is. 6:11, 12 [b]Jer. 4:25; 9:10 [c]Ezek. 7:19; 14:3, 4, 8

4 [a]Jer. 6:12; Ezek. 6:14 [b]Mic. 5:13

5 [1]Or, *their king;* M.T., *Malcam,* probably a variant spelling of Milcom [a]2 Kin. 23:12; Jer. 19:13 [b]Jer. 5:2, 7; 7:9, 10

6 [a]Is. 1:4 [b]Is. 9:13

7 [1]Lit., *Hush* [2]YHWH, usually rendered LORD [a]Hab. 2:20; Zech. 2:13 [b]Is. 34:6; Jer. 46:10 [c]1 Sam. 16:5; Is. 13:3

8 [a]Is. 24:21; Hab. 1:10 [b]Is. 2:6

9 [1]Or, *Lord* [a]Jer. 5:27; Amos 3:10

THE word of the LORD which came to Zephaniah son of
Cushi, son of Godaliah, son of Amariah, son of Hezekiah, in
the days of Josiah son of Amon, king of Judah:
2 "I will completely [a]remove all *things*
From the face of the [1]earth," declares the LORD.
3 "I will remove [a]man and beast;
I will remove the [b]birds of the sky
And the fish of the sea,
And the [1c]ruins along with the wicked;
And I will cut off man from the face of the [2]earth,"
declares the LORD.
4 "So I will [a]stretch out My hand against Judah
And against all the inhabitants of Jerusalem.
And I will [b]cut off the remnant of Baal from this place,
And the names of the idolatrous priests along with the
priests.
5 And those who bow down on the housetops to the
[a]host of heaven,
And those who bow down *and* [b]swear to the LORD and
yet swear by [1]Milcom,
6 And those who have [a]turned back from following the
LORD,
And those who have [b]not sought the LORD or inquired
of Him."

7 [1a]Be silent before the Lord [2]GOD!
For the day of the LORD is near,
For the LORD has prepared a [b]sacrifice,
He has [c]consecrated His guests.
8 "Then it will come about on the day of the LORD's
sacrifice,
That I will [a]punish the princes, the king's sons,
And all who clothe themselves with [b]foreign garments.
9 "And I will punish on that day all who leap on the
temple threshold,
Who fill the house of their [1]lord with [a]violence and
deceit.

10 "And on that day," declares the LORD,
"There will be the sound of a cry from the [a]Fish Gate,
A wail from the [1b]Second Quarter,
And a loud crash from the [c]hills.
11 "Wail, O inhabitants of the [1]Mortar,
For all the [2]people of Canaan will be silenced;
All who weigh out [a]silver will be cut off.
12 "And it will come about at that time
That I will [a]search Jerusalem with lamps,
And I will punish the men
Who are [1b]stagnant in spirit,
Who say in their hearts,
'The LORD will [c]not do good or evil!'
13 "Moreover, their wealth will become [a]plunder,
And their houses desolate;
Yes, [b]they will build houses but not inhabit *them*,
And plant vineyards but not drink their wine."

14 Near is the [a]great [b]day of the LORD,
Near and coming very quickly;
Listen, the day of the LORD!
[1]In it the warrior [c]cries out bitterly.
15 A day of wrath is that day,
A day of [a]trouble and distress,
A day of destruction and desolation,
A day of [b]darkness and gloom,
A day of clouds and thick darkness,
16 A day of [a]trumpet and battle cry,
Against the [b]fortified cities
And the high corner towers.
17 And I will bring [a]distress on men,
So that they will walk [b]like the blind,
Because they have sinned against the LORD;
And their [c]blood will be poured out like dust,
And their [d]flesh like dung.
18 Neither their silver nor their gold
Will be able to deliver them
On the day of the LORD's wrath;
And all the earth will be devoured
In the fire of His jealousy,
For He will [a]make a complete end,
Indeed a terrifying one,
Of all the inhabitants of the earth.

CHAPTER 2

GATHER yourselves together, yes, [a]gather,
O nation [b]without [1]shame,
2 Before the decree [1]takes effect—
The day passes [a]like the chaff—
Before the [b]burning anger of the LORD comes upon
you,
Before the day of the LORD's anger comes upon you.
3 [a]Seek the LORD,
All you [b]humble of the [1]earth
Who have carried out His [2]ordinances;

10 [1]I.e., a district of Jerusalem [a]2 Chr. 33:14 [b]2Chr. 34:22 [c]2 Sam. 5:7; Ezek. 6:13

11 [1]I.e., a district of Jerusalem [2]Or, *merchant people will* [a]Job 27:16, 17; Hos. 9:6

12 [1]Lit., *thickening on their lees* [a]Jer. 16:16, 17; Ezek. 9:4-11; Amos 9:1-3 [b]Jer. 48:11; Amos 6:1 [c]Ezek. 8:12; 9:9

13 [a]Jer. 15:13; 17:3 [b]Amos 5:11; Mic. 6:15

14 [1]Lit., *There* [a]Jer. 30:7; Joel 2:11; Mal. 4:5 [b]Zeph. 1:7; Ezek. 7:7, 12; 30:3; Joel 1:15; 3:14 [c]Ezek. 7:16-18

15 [a]Is. 22:5 [b]Joel 2:2, 31; Amos 5:18-20

16 [a]Jer. 4:19 [b]Is. 2:12-15

17 [a]Jer. 10:18 [b]Deut. 28:29 [c]Ezek. 24:7, 8 [d]Jer. 8:2; 9:22

18 [a]Ezek. 7:5-7

1 [1]Or, *longing* [a]2 Chr. 20:4; Joel 1:14 [b]Jer. 3:3; 6:15

2 [1]Lit., *is born* [a]Is. 17:13; Hos. 13:3 [b]Lam. 4:11; Nah. 1:6

3 [1]Or, *land* [2]Or, *justice* [a]Ps. 105:4; Amos 5:6 [b]Ps. 22:26; Is. 11:4

[c]Seek righteousness, seek humility.
Perhaps you will be [d]hidden
In the day of the LORD's anger.

4 For [a]Gaza will be abandoned,
And Ashkelon a desolation;
[a]Ashdod will be driven out at noon,
And [a]Ekron will be uprooted.
5 Woe to the inhabitants of the seacoast,
The nation of the [1]Cherethites!
The word of the LORD is [a]against you,
O Canaan, land of the Philistines;
And I will [b]destroy you,
So that there will be no inhabitant.
6 So the seacoast will be [a]pastures,
With [1]caves for shepherds and folds for flocks.
7 And the coast will be
For the [a]remnant of the house of Judah,
They will [b]pasture on it.
In the houses of Ashkelon they will lie down at evening;
For the LORD their God will [c]care for them
And [d]restore their fortune.

8 "I have heard the [1a]taunting of Moab
And the [b]revilings of the sons of Ammon,
With which they have [2]taunted My people
And [3c]become arrogant against their territory.
9 "Therefore, as I live," declares the LORD of hosts,
The God of Israel,
"Surely Moab will be like Sodom,
And the sons of Ammon like Gomorrah—
A place possessed by nettles and salt pits,
And a perpetual desolation.
The remnant of My people will [a]plunder them,
And the remainder of My nation will inherit them."
10 This they will have in return for their [a]pride, because
they have [1]taunted and [2]become arrogant against the people
of the LORD of hosts.
11 The LORD will be [a]terrifying to them, for He will
[1]starve all the gods of the earth; and all the [b]coastlands of the
nations will [c]bow down to Him, every one from his *own* place.
12 "You also, O [a]Ethiopians, will be slain by My sword."
13 And He will stretch out His hand against the north
And destroy Assyria,
And He will make [a]Nineveh a desolation,
Parched like the wilderness.
14 And flocks will lie down in her midst,
[1]All beasts which range in herds;
Both the [2a]pelican and the hedgehog
Will lodge in [3]the tops of her pillars;
[4]Birds will sing in the window,
Desolation *will be* on the threshold;
For He has laid bare the cedar work.
15 This is the [a]exultant city
Which [b]dwells securely,
Who says in her heart,

3 [c]Amos 5:14, 15 [d]Ps. 57:1; Is. 26:20

4 [a]Amos 1:7, 8; Zech. 9:5-7

5 [1]I.e., a segment of the Philistines with roots in Crete [a]Amos 3:1 [b]Is. 14:29, 30

6 [1]Or, *meadows;* or, *wells* [a]Is. 7:25

7 [a]Is. 11:14; Jer. 32:44 [b]Is. 32:14 [c]Ex. 4:31; Ps. 80:14 [d]Zeph. 3:20; Ps. 126:4

8 [1]Lit., *reproach* [2]Lit., *reproached* [3]Lit., *made* themselves *great* [a]Ezek. 25:8 [b]Ezek. 25:3 [c]Amos 1:13

9 [a]Is. 11:14

10 [1]Lit., *reproached* [2]Lit., *made* themselves *great* [a]Is. 16:6

11 [1]Lit., *make lean* [a]Joel 2:11 [b]Is. 24:15 [c]Zeph. 3:9; Ps. 72:8-11

12 [a]Is. 20:4, 5; Ezek. 30:4-9

13 [a]Nah. 3:7

14 [1]Or, *All* kinds of *beasts in crowds;* lit., *Every* kind of *beast of a nation* [2]Or, *owl;* or, *jackdaw* [3]Lit., *her capitals* [4]Lit., *A voice* [a]Is. 14:23; 34:11-15

15 [a]Is. 22:2 [b]Is. 32:9, 11; 47:8

"[c]I am, and there is no one besides me."
How she has become a [d]desolation,
A resting place for beasts!
[e]Every one who passes by her will hiss
And wave his hand *in contempt*.

CHAPTER 3

WOE to her who is [a]rebellious and [b]defiled,
The [c]tyrannical city!
2 She [a]heeded no voice;
She [b]accepted no instruction.
She did not [c]trust in the LORD;
She did not [d]draw near to her God.
3 Her [a]princes within her are roaring lions,
Her judges are [b]wolves at evening;
They leave nothing for the morning.
4 Her prophets are [a]reckless, treacherous men;
Her [b]priests have profaned the sanctuary.
They have done violence to the law.
5 The LORD is [a]righteous within her;
He will do no [b]injustice.
[c]Every morning He brings His justice to light;
He does not fail.
But the unjust knows no shame.
6 "I have cut off nations;
Their corner towers are in ruins.
I have made their streets [a]desolate,
With no one passing by;
Their [b]cities are laid waste,
Without a man, without an inhabitant.
7 "I said, 'Surely you will revere Me,
Accept instruction.'
So her dwelling will [a]not be cut off
According to all that I have appointed concerning her.
But they were eager to [b]corrupt all their deeds.

8 "Therefore, [a]wait for Me," declares the LORD,
"For the day when I rise up to the prey.
Indeed, My decision is to [b]gather nations,
To assemble kingdoms,
To pour out on them My indignation,
All My burning anger;
For all the earth will be devoured
By the fire of My zeal.
9 "For then I will [1]give to the peoples [a]purified lips,
That all of them may [b]call on the name of the LORD,
To serve Him [2]shoulder to shoulder.
10 "From beyond the rivers of Ethiopia
My [1]worshipers, [2]My dispersed ones,
Will [a]bring My offerings.
11 "In that day you will [a]feel no shame
Because of all your deeds
By which you have rebelled against Me;
For then I will remove from your midst
Your [b]proud, exulting ones,

15 [c]Is. 47:8; Ezek. 28:2, 9 [d]Is. 32:14 [e]Jer. 18:16; 19:8

1 [a]Jer. 5:23 [b]Ezek. 23:30 [c]Jer. 6:6

2 [a]Jer. 7:23-28 [b]Jer. 2:30; 5:3 [c]Ps. 78:22; Jer. 13:25 [d]Ps. 73:28

3 [a]Ezek. 22:27 [b]Jer. 5:6; Hab. 1:8

4 [a]Judg. 9:4 [b]Ezek. 22:26; Mal. 2:7, 8

5 [a]Deut. 32:4 [b]Ps. 92:15 [c]Job 7:18

6 [a]Jer. 9:12 [b]Is. 6:11

7 [a]Jer. 7:7 [b]Hos. 9:9

8 [a]Ps. 27:14; Is. 30:18; Hab. 2:3 [b]Ezek. 38:14-23; Joel 3:2

9 [1]Lit., *change* [2]Lit., *with one shoulder* [a]Is. 19:18; 57:19 [b]Zeph. 2:11; Ps. 22:27; 86:9; Hab. 2:14

10 [1]Or, *suppliants* [2]Lit., *the daughter of My dispersed ones* [a]Is. 60:6, 7

11 [a]Is. 45:17; 54:4; Joel 2:26, 27 [b]Is. 2:12; 5:15

And you will never again be haughty
On My [c]holy mountain.
12 "But I will leave among you
A [a]humble and lowly people,
And they will [b]take refuge in the name of the LORD.
13 "The [a]remnant of Israel will [b]do no wrong
And [c]tell no lies,
Nor will a deceitful tongue
Be found in their mouths;
For they shall feed and lie down
With no one to make them tremble."

14 Shout for joy, O daughter of Zion!
Shout *in triumph*, O Israel!
Rejoice and exult with all *your* heart,
O daughter of Jerusalem!
15 The LORD has taken away *His* judgments against you,
He has cleared away your enemies.
The King of Israel, the LORD, is [a]in your midst;
You will [b]fear disaster no more.
16 In that day it will be said to Jerusalem:
"[a]Do not be afraid, O Zion;
Do not let your hands fall limp.
17 "The LORD your God is in your midst,
A [1a]victorious warrior.
He will [b]exult over you with joy,
He will [2]be quiet in His love,
He will rejoice over you with shouts of joy.
18 "I will gather those who [a]grieve about the appointed feasts—
They [1]came from you, *O Zion;*
The reproach *of exile* is a burden on [2]them.
19 "Behold, I am going to deal at that time
With all your [a]oppressors,
I will save the lame
And gather the outcast,
And I will turn their [b]shame into [c]praise and renown
In all the earth.
20 "At that time I will [a]bring you in,
Even at the time when I gather you together;
Indeed, I will give you [b]renown and praise
Among all the peoples of the earth,
When I [c]restore your fortunes before your eyes,"
Says the LORD.

11 [c]Is. 11:9; 56:7; Ezek. 20:40

12 [a]Is. 14:30, 32; Zech. 13:8, 9 [b]Is. 50:10; Nah. 1:7

13 [a]Zeph. 2:7; Is. 10:20-22; Mic. 4:7 [b]Zeph. 3:5; Ps. 119:3; Jer. 31:33 [c]Zech. 8:3, 16

15 [a]Zeph. 3:5; Ezek. 37:26-28 [b]Is. 54:14

16 [a]Is. 35:3, 4

17 [1]Lit., *A warrior who saves* [2]Or, with some ancient versions, *renew* you *in* [a]Is. 63:1 [b]Is. 62:5

18 [1]Lit., *were* [2]Lit., *her* [a]Ps. 42:2-4; Ezek. 9:4, 6

19 [a]Is. 60:14; Zech. 8:23 [b]Ezek. 16:27, 57 [c]Is. 60:18; 62:7

20 [a]Ezek. 37:12, 21 [b]Deut. 26:18, 19; Is. 56:5; 66:22 [c]Zeph. 2:7; Jer. 29:14; Joel 3:1

THE BOOK OF HAGGAI

Haggai Begins Temple Building.

IN the second year of Darius the King, on the first day of the
sixth month, the word of the LORD came by the prophet [a]Hag-
gai to Zerubbabel the son of Shealtiel, [b]governor of Judah, and
to Joshua the son of Jehozadak, the high priest saying,
2 "Thus says the LORD of [1]hosts, 'This people says, "The
time has not come, *even* the time for the house of the LORD to
be rebuilt." ' "
3 Then the word of the LORD came by Haggai the prophet saying,
4 "Is it time for you yourselves to dwell in your paneled
houses while this house [a]*lies* desolate?"
5 Now therefore, thus says the LORD of hosts, "[1]Consider
your ways!
6 "You have [a]sown much, but [1]harvest little; *you* eat, but
there is not *enough* to be satisfied; *you* drink, but *there is* not
enough [2]to become drunk; *you* put on clothing, but no one is
warm *enough*; and he who earns, earns wages *to put* into a
purse with holes."
7 Thus says the LORD of hosts, "[1]Consider your ways!
8 "Go up to the [1]mountains, bring wood and rebuild the
[2]temple, that I may be [a]pleased with it and be glorified," says
the LORD.
9 "*You* look for much, but behold, *it comes* to little; when
you bring *it* home, I [a]blow it *away*. Why?" declares the LORD
of hosts, "Because of My house which *lies* desolate, while each
of you runs to his own house.
10 "Therefore, because of you the [a]sky has withheld [1]its
dew, and the earth has withheld its produce.
11 "And I called for a [a]drought on the land, on the mountains, on the grain, on the new wine, on the oil, on what the
ground produces, on [b]men, on cattle, and on all the labor of
[1]your hands."
12 Then Zerubbabel the son of Shealtiel, and Joshua the
son of Jehozadak, the high priest, with all the remnant of the
people, [a]obeyed the voice of the LORD their God and the
words of Haggai the prophet, as the LORD their God had sent
him. And the people [1b]showed reverence for the LORD.
13 Then Haggai, the [a]messenger of the LORD, spoke [1]by
the commission of the LORD to the people saying, " '[b]I am with
you,' declares the LORD."
14 So the LORD stirred up the spirit of [a]Zerubbabel the
son of Shealtiel, [a]governor of Judah, and the spirit of Joshua
the son of Jehozadak, the high priest, and the spirit of all the
[b]remnant of the people; and they came and [c]worked on the
house of the LORD of hosts, their God,
15 on the twenty-fourth day of the sixth month in the
second year of Darius the king.

1 [a]Hag. 1:3, 12, 13; 2:1, 10, 20; Ezra 5:1; 6:14 [b]1 Kin. 10:15; Ezra 5:3

2 [1]Lit., *hosts, saying*

4 [a]Hag. 1:9; Jer. 33:10, 12

5 [1]Lit., *set your heart on*

6 [1]Lit., *bring in* [2]Lit., *not becoming drunk* [a]Hag. 1:9, 10; 2:16, 17; Deut. 28:38-40; Hos. 8:7

7 [1]Lit., *set your heart on*

8 [1]Lit., *mountain* [2]Lit., *house* [a]Ps. 132:13, 14

9 [a]Is. 40:7

10 [1]Lit., *from dew* [a]Deut. 28:23-24; 1 Kin. 17:1; Joel 1:18-20

11 [1]Lit., *the palms* [a]Jer. 14:2-6; Mal. 3:9, 11 [b]Deut. 28:22

12 [1]Lit., *feared before* [a]Is. 1:19; 1 Thess. 2:13 [b]Deut. 31:12, 13; Ps. 112:1; Is. 50:10

13 [1]Or, *the message* [1]Is. 44:26; Ezek. 3:17; Mal. 2:7; 3:1 [b]Ps. 46:11; Is. 41:10; 43:2

14 [a]Hag. 1:1; 2:2, 21 [b]Hag. 1:12 [c]Ezra 5:2; Neh. 4:6

Chapter 2

ON the twenty-first of the seventh month, the word of the
Lord came by [a]Haggai the prophet saying,
2 "Speak now to [a]Zerubbabel the son of Shealtiel, [a]gover-
nor of Judah, and to [a]Joshua the son of Jehozadak, the high
priest, and to the [b]remnant of the people saying,
3 'Who is [a]left among you who saw this [1]temple in its
former glory? And how do you see it now? Does it not [2]seem to
you like nothing [3]in comparison?
4 'But now [1a]take courage, Zerubbabel,' declares the
Lord, 'take courage also, Joshua son of Jehozadak, the high
priest, and all you people of the land take courage,' declares
the Lord, 'and work; for [b]I am with you,' says the Lord of
hosts.
5 'As for the [1]promise which I [2a]made you when you came
out of Egypt, [3]My [b]Spirit is abiding in your midst; [c]do not
fear!'
6 "For thus says the Lord of hosts, '[a]Once more [1]in a
[b]little while, I am going to shake the heavens and the earth, the
sea also and the dry land.
7 'And I will shake [a]all the nations; and [1]they will come
with the [b]wealth of all nations; and I will [c]fill this house with
glory,' says the Lord of hosts.
8 'The [a]silver is Mine, and the gold is Mine,' declares the
Lord of hosts.
9 'The latter [a]glory of this house will be greater than the
former,' says the Lord of hosts, 'and in this place I shall give
[b]peace,' declares the Lord of hosts."
10 On the twenty-fourth of the ninth *month,* in the second year of Darius, the word of the Lord came to Haggai the
prophet saying,
11 "Thus says the Lord of hosts, '[a]Ask now the priests *for* a
[1]ruling:
12 'If a man carries [a]holy meat in the [1]fold of his garment,
and touches bread with [2]this fold, or cooked food, wine, oil, or
any *other* food, will it become holy?' " And the priests answered and said, "No."
13 Then Haggai said, "[a]If one who is unclean from a
[1]corpse touches any of these, will *the latter* become unclean?"
And the priests answered and said, "It will become unclean."
14 Then Haggai answered and said, " '[a]So is this people,
and so is this nation before Me,' declares the Lord, 'and so is
every work of their hands; and what they offer there is unclean.
15 'But now, do [1]consider from this day [2]onward: before
one [a]stone was placed on another in the temple of the Lord,
16 [1]from that time *when* one came to a *grain* heap of
twenty *measures,* there would be only ten; and *when* one came
to the wine vat to draw fifty [2]measures, there would be *only*
twenty.
17 'I smote you *and* every work of your hands with [a]blast-
ing wind, mildew, and hail; yet you did not [1]come *back* to
me,' declares the Lord.
18 'Do [1a]consider from this day [2]onward, from the twenty-
fourth day of the ninth *month;* from the day when the temple
of the Lord was [b]founded, [1]consider:

1 [a]Hag. 1:1

2 [a]Hag. 1:1 [b]Hag. 1:12

3 [1]Lit., *house* [2]Lit., *is in your eyes* [3]Lit., *like it* [a]Ezra 3:12

4 [1]Lit., *be strong* [a]Deut. 31:23; 1 Chr. 22:13; 28:20; Zech. 8:9; Eph. 6:10 [b]2 Sam. 5:10; Acts 7:9

5 [1]Lit., *word* [2]Lit., *cut with* [3]Or, *while . . . was standing* [a]Ex. 19:4-6; 33:12-14; 34:8-10 [b]Neh. 9:20; Is. 63:11, 14 [c]Is. 41:10, 13; Zech. 8:13

6 [1]Lit., *it is a little* [a]Heb. 12:26 [b]Is. 10:25; 29:17

7 [1]Or, *the Desire of all nations will come* [a]Dan. 2:44; Joel 3:9, 16 [b]Is. 60:4-9 [c]1 Kin. 8:11; Is. 60:7

8 [a]1 Chr. 29:14, 16; Is. 60:17

9 [a]Zech. 2:5 [b]Is. 9:6, 7; 66:12

11 [1]Lit., *law* [a]Deut. 17:8-11; Mal. 2:7

12 [1]Lit., *wing* [2]Lit., *his wing* [a]Ex. 29:37; Lev. 6:27, 29; 7:6; Ezek. 44:19; Matt. 23:19

13 [1]Lit., *soul* [a]Lev. 22:4-6; Num. 19:22

14 [a]Prov. 15:8; Is. 1:11-15

15 [1]Lit., *set your heart* [2]Or, *backward* [a]Ezra 3:10; 4:24

16 [1]Lit., *since they were* [2]Or, *troughs full*

17 [1]Heb. obscure; perhaps, *but what did we have in common?* [a]Deut. 28:22; 1 Kin. 8:37; Amos 4:9

18 [1]Lit., *set your heart* [2]Or, *backward* [a]Hag. 2:15; Deut. 32:29 [b]Ezra 5:1, 2; Zech. 8:9, 12

19 'Is the seed still in the barn? Even including the vine,
the fig tree, the pomegranate, and the olive tree, it has not
borne fruit. Yet from this day on I will [a]bless *you.*' "
20 Then the word of the LORD came a second time to
Haggai on the twenty-fourth *day* of the month saying,
21 "Speak to Zerubbabel governor of Judah saying, 'I am
going to shake the heavens and the earth.
22 'And I will overthrow the [a]thrones of kingdoms and
destroy the [b]power of the kingdoms of the [1]nations; and I will
overthrow the [c]chariots and their riders, and the horses and
their riders will go down, [d]every one by the sword of another.'
23 'On that day,' declares the LORD of hosts, 'I will take
you, Zerubbabel, son of Shealtiel, my servant,' declares the
LORD, 'and I will make you like a [1a]signet *ring,* for [b]I have
chosen you,' " declares the LORD of hosts.

19 [a]Ps. 128:1-6; Jer. 31:12, 14; Mal. 3:10

22 [1]Or, *Gentiles* [a]Ezek. 26:16; Zeph. 3:8 [b]Mic. 7:16 [c]Ps. 46:9; Ezek. 39:20; Mic. 5:10 [d]Judg. 7:22; 2 Chr. 20:23

23 [1]Or, *seal* [a]Song of Sol. 8:6; Jer. 22:24 [b]Is. 42:1; 43:10

THE BOOK OF ZECHARIAH

The Vision of Horses.

IN the eighth month of the second year of Darius, the word
of the LORD came to Zechariah the prophet, the son of Berechiah, the son of Iddo saying,
2 "The LORD was very [a]angry with your fathers.
3 "Therefore say to them, 'Thus says the LORD of hosts,
"[a]Return to Me," declares the LORD of hosts, "that I may
return to you," says the LORD of hosts.
4 "Do not be [a]like your fathers, to whom the [b]former
prophets proclaimed, saying, 'Thus says the LORD of hosts,
"[c]Return now from your evil ways and from your evil deeds." '
But they did not [d]listen or give heed to Me," declares the
LORD.
5 "Your fathers, where are they? And the [a]prophets, do
they live forever?
6 "But did not My words and My statutes, which I commanded My servants the prophets, [a]overtake your fathers?
Then they repented and said, '[b]As the LORD of hosts purposed
to do to us in accordance with our ways and our deeds, so He
has dealt with us.' " ' "
7 On the twenty-fourth day of the eleventh month,
which is the month Shebat, in the second year of Darius, the
word of the LORD came to Zechariah the prophet, the son of
Berechiah, the son of Iddo, as follows—
8 I saw at night, and behold, a man was riding on a red
horse, and he was standing among the [a]myrtle trees which were
in the ravine, with red, sorrel, and white horses behind him.
9 Then I said, "My [a]lord, what are these?" And the angel
who was speaking with me said to me, "I will show you what
these are."
10 And the man who was standing among the myrtle trees
answered and said, "These are those whom the LORD has sent
to [1a]patrol the earth."

2 [a]Zech. 1:15; 2 Chr. 36:16; Jer. 44:6

3 [a]Is. 31:6; Mal. 3:7

4 [a]Ps. 78:8; 106:6, 7 [b]2 Chr. 24:19; 36:15 [c]Is. 1:16-19; Jer. 4:1; Ezek. 33:11 [d]Jer. 6:17; 11:7, 8

5 [a]John 8:52

6 [a]Jer. 12:16, 17; 44:28, 29; Amos 9:10 [b]Lam. 2:17

8 [a]Zech. 1:10, 11; Neh. 8:15; Is. 41:19; 55:13

9 [a]Zech. 1:19; 4:4, 5, 13; 6:4

10 [1]Lit., *walk about through* [a]Zech. 1:11; 4:10; 6:5-8; Job 1:7

11 So they answered the angel of the LORD who was standing among the myrtle trees, and said, "We have [1]patrolled
the earth, and behold, [a]all the earth is [1]peaceful and quiet."
12 Then the angel of the LORD answered and said, "O
LORD of hosts, [a]how long wilt Thou [b]have no compassion for
Jerusalem and the cities of Judah, with which Thou hast been
[c]indignant these [d]seventy years?"
13 And the LORD answered the angel who was speaking
with me with [1]gracious words, [a]comforting words.
14 So the angel who was speaking with me said to me,
"[a]Proclaim, saying, 'Thus says the LORD of hosts, "I am exceedingly jealous for Jerusalem and Zion.
15 "But I am very angry with the nations who are [a]at ease;
for while I was only a little angry, they [1b]furthered the
disaster."
16 'Therefore, thus says the LORD, "I will [a]return to Jerusalem with compassion; My [b]house will be built in it," declares
the LORD of hosts, "and a measuring [c]line will be stretched
over Jerusalem."
17 "Again, proclaim, saying, 'Thus says the LORD of hosts,
"My [a]cities will again overflow with prosperity, and the LORD
will again [b]comfort Zion and again choose Jerusalem." ' "
18 [1]Then I lifted up my eyes and looked, and behold,
there were four horns.
19 So I said to the angel who was speaking with me,
"What are these?" And he answered me, "These are the
[a]horns which have scattered Judah, Israel, and Jerusalem."
20 Then the LORD showed me four [a]craftsmen.
21 And I said, "What are these coming to do?" And he
said, "These are the [a]horns which have scattered Judah, so that
no man lifts up his head; but these *craftsmen* have come to
terrify them, to [b]throw down the horns of the nations who
have lifted up *their* horns against the land of Judah in order to
scatter it."

CHAPTER 2

1
THEN I lifted up my eyes and looked, and behold, *there was*
a man with a [a]measuring line in his hand.
2 So I said, "Where are you going?" And he said to me,
"To [a]measure Jerusalem, to see how wide it is and how long it
is."
3 And behold, the angel who was speaking with me was
going out, and another angel was coming out to meet him,
4 and said to him, "Run, speak to that [a]young man,
saying, 'Jerusalem will be inhabited [1b]without walls, because of
the [c]multitude of men and cattle within it.
5 'For I,' declares the LORD, 'will be a [a]wall of fire [1]around
her, and I will be the [b]glory in her midst.' "
6 "[1]Ho there! [a]Flee from the land of the north," declares
the LORD, "for I have [b]dispersed you as the four winds of the
heavens," declares the LORD.
7 "Ho, Zion! [a]Escape, you who are living with the daughter of Babylon."
8 For thus says the LORD of hosts, "After [1a]glory He has

11 [1]Lit., *walked about through* [2]Lit., *sitting* [a]Zech. 1:15; Is. 14:7

12 [a]Ps. 74:10; Jer. 12:4; Hab. 1:2 [b]Ps. 102:13; Jer. 30:18 [c]Ps. 102:10; Jer. 15:17 [d]Jer. 25:11; 29:10; Dan. 9:2; Zech. 7:5

13 [1]Lit., *good* [a]Is. 40:1, 2; 57:18

14 [a]Zech. 1:17; Is. 40:2, 6

15 [1]Lit., *helped for evil* [a]Ps. 123:4; Jer. 48:11 [b]Amos 1:11

16 [a]Zech. 2:10, 11; Is. 54:8-10 [b]Zech. 4:9; Ezra 6:14, 15 [c]Zech. 2:2, 4; Jer. 31:39

17 [a]Is. 44:26; 61:4 [b]Is. 51:3

18 [1]Ch. 2:1 in Heb.

19 [a]1 Kin. 22:11; Ps. 75:4, 5; Amos 6:13

20 [a]Is. 44:12; 54:16

21 [a]Zech. 1:17 [b]Ps. 73:10

1 [1]Ch. 2:5 in Heb. [a]Zech. 1:16; Jer. 31:39; Ezek. 40:3; 47:3

2 [a]Jer. 31:39; Ezek. 40:3; Rev. 21:15-17

4 [1]Lit., like *unwalled villages*; or, like *open country* [a]Jer. 1:6; Dan. 1:4; 1 Tim. 4:12 [b]Ezek. 38:11 [c]Is. 49:20; Jer. 30:19; 33:22

5 [1]Lit., *to her* [a]Is. 4:5; 26:1; 60:18 [b]Zech. 2:10, 11; Hag. 2:9

6 [1]Lit., *Ho! ho!* [a]Jer. 3:18 [b]Jer. 31:10; Ezek. 11:16

7 [a]Is. 48:20; Jer. 51:6

8 [1]Or, *the glory* [a]Is. 60:7-9

sent Me against the nations which plunder you, for he who
touches you, touches the [2b]apple of His eye.
9 "For behold, I will [a]wave My hand over them, so that
they will be [b]plunder for their slaves. Then you will know that
the LORD of hosts has sent Me.
10 "[a]Sing for joy and be glad, O daughter of Zion; for
behold I am coming and I will dwell in your midst," declares
the LORD.
11 "And [a]many nations will join themselves to the LORD in
that day and will become My people. Then I will dwell in your
midst, and you will know that the LORD of hosts has sent Me to
you.
12 "And the LORD will [1a]possess Judah as His portion in the
holy land, and will again [b]choose Jerusalem.
13 "[1a]Be silent, all flesh, before the LORD; for He is [b]aroused
from His holy habitation."

CHAPTER 3

THEN he showed me [a]Joshua the high priest standing before
the angel of the LORD, and [1b]Satan standing at his right hand to
accuse him.
2 And the LORD said to Satan, "The LORD rebuke you,
Satan! Indeed, the LORD who has [a]chosen Jerusalem rebuke
you! Is this not a brand plucked from the fire?"
3 Now Joshua was clothed with [a]filthy garments and
standing before the angel.
4 And he spoke and said to those who were standing
before him saying, "[a]Remove the filthy garments from him."
Again he said to him, "See, I have [b]taken your iniquity away
from you and [1]will [c]clothe you with festal robes."
5 Then I said, "Let them put a clean [a]turban on his
head." So they put a clean turban on his head and clothed him
with garments, while the angel of the LORD was standing by.
6 And the angel of the LORD admonished Joshua saying,
7 "Thus says the LORD of hosts, 'If you will [a] walk in My
ways, and if you will perform My service, then you will also
[b]govern My house and also have charge of My [c]courts, and I
will grant you [1]free access among these who are standing *here*.
8 'Now listen, Joshua the high priest, you and your friends
who are sitting in front of you—indeed they are men who are a
[a]symbol, for behold, I am going to bring in My Servant the
[1b]Branch.
9 'For behold, the stone that I have set before Joshua; on
one stone are seven eyes. Behold, I will engrave an inscription
on it,' declares the LORD of hosts, 'and I will remove the iniquity of that land in one day.
10 'In that day,' declares the LORD of hosts, 'every one of
you will invite his neighbor to *sit* under *his* [a]vine and under *his*
fig tree.' "

CHAPTER 4

THEN the angel who was speaking with me returned, and
[a]roused me as a man who is awakened from his sleep.
2 And he said to me, "[a]What do you see?" And I said, "I

8 [2]Lit., *pupil* [b]Deut. 32:10; Ps. 19:8

9 [a]Is. 19:16 [b]Is. 14:2

10 [a]Zech. 9:9; Is. 65:18, 19

11 [a]Mic. 4:2

12 [1]Or, *inherit* [a]Deut. 32:9; Ps. 33:12; Jer. 10:16 [b]Zech. 1:17; 2 Chr. 6:6; Ps. 132:13, 14

13 [1]Lit., *Hush* [a]Hab. 2:20; Zeph. 1:7 [b]Ps. 78:65; Is. 51:9

1 [1]Or, the *Adversary* or, *Accuser* [a]Zech. 6:11; Ezra 5:2; Hag. 1:1 [b]1 Chr. 21:1; Job 1:6; Ps. 109:6

2 [a]Zech. 2:12

3 [a]Ezra 9:15; Is. 4:4; 64:6

4 [1]Lit., *to clothe* [a]Is. 43:25; Ezek. 36:25 [b]Zech. 3:9; Mic. 7:18, 19 [c]Is. 52:1; 61:10

5 [a]Job 29:14; Is. 3:23

7 [1]Lit., *goings* [a]1 Kin. 3:14 [b]Deut. 17:9, 12 [c]Is. 62:9

8 [1]Lit., *Sprout* [a]Is. 8:18; 20:3; Ezek. 12:11 [b]Zech. 6:12; Is. 11:1; 53:2; Jer. 33:15

10 [a]1 Kin. 4:25; Is. 36:16; Mic. 4:4

1 [a]1 Kin. 19:5-7; Jer. 31:26

2 [a]Zech. 5:2; Jer. 1:13

see, and behold, a [b]lampstand all of gold with its bowl on the
top of it, and its [c]seven lamps on it with seven spouts belonging
to each of the lamps which are on the top of it;
3 also [a]two olive trees by it, one on the right side of the
bowl and the other on its left side."
4 Then I answered and said to the angel who was speaking with me saying, "What are these, my lord?"
5 So the angel who was speaking with me answered and
said to me, "Do you not know what these are?" And I said,
"No, my lord."
6 Then he answered and [1]said to me, "This is the word of
the LORD to [a]Zerubbabel saying, '[b]Not by might nor by power,
but by My [c]Spirit,' says the LORD of hosts.
7 'What are you, O great mountain? Before Zerubbabel
you will become a plain; and he will bring forth the top stone
with [a]shouts of "Grace, grace to it!" ' "
8 Also the word of the LORD came to me saying,
9 "The hands of Zerubbabel have [a]laid the foundation of
this house, and his hands will [b]finish *it.* Then you will know
that the LORD of hosts has sent Me to [1]you.
10 "For who has despised the day of [a]small things? [1]But
these [b]seven will be glad when they see the [2c]plumb line in the
hand of Zerubbabel—*these are* the eyes of the LORD which
range to and fro throughout the earth."
11 Then I answered and said to him, "What are these two
olive trees on the right of the lampstand and on its left?"
12 And I answered the second time and said to him,
"What are the two olive [1]branches which are beside the two
golden pipes, which empty the golden *oil* from themselves?"
13 So he answered me saying, "Do you not know what
these are?" And I said, "No, my lord."
14 Then he said, "These are the two [1a]anointed ones, who
are [b]standing by the [c]Lord of the whole earth."

CHAPTER 5

THEN I lifted up my eyes again and looked, and behold,
there was a flying [a]scroll.
2 And he said to me, "What do you see?" And I answered, "I see a flying scroll; its length is twenty [1]cubits and its
width ten cubits."
3 Then he said to me, "This is the [a]curse that is going
forth over the face of the whole [1]land; surely everyone who
[b]steals will be purged away according to [2]the writing on one
side, and everyone who swears will be purged away according
to [2]the writing on the other side.
4 "I will [a]make it go forth," declares the LORD of hosts,
"and it will [b]enter the house of the [c]thief and the house of the
one who swears falsely by My name; and it will spend the night
within that house and [d]consume it with its timber and stones."
5 Then the angel who was speaking with me went out,
and said to me, "Lift up now your eyes, and see what this is,
going forth."
6 And I said, "What is it?" And he said, "This is the
[1a]ephah going forth." Again he said, "This is their [2]appearance
in all the [3]land

2 [b]Ex. 25:31, 37; Jer. 52:19 [c]Rev. 4:5

3 [a]Zech. 4:11; Rev. 11:4

6 [1]Lit., *said to me, saying* [a]Hag. 2:4, 5 [b]Is. 11:2-4; 30:1; Hos. 1:7 [c]2 Chr. 32:7, 8; Eph. 6:17

7 [a]Ezra 3:10, 11; Ps. 84:11

9 [1]Lit., *you* (plural) [a]Ezra 3:8-10; 5:16; Hag. 2:18 [b]Zech. 6:12, 13; Ezra 6:14, 15

10 [1]Or, *But they will rejoice when they see . . . Zerubbabel. These seven are the eyes of the LORD* [2]Lit., *plummet stone* [a]Neh. 4:2-4; Amos 7:2, 5; Hag. 2:3 [b]Zech. 3:9; Rev. 8:2 [c]Amos 7:7, 8

12 [1]Or, *clusters*

14 [1]Lit., *sons of fresh oil* [a]Ex. 29:7; 40:15; 1 Sam. 16:1, 12, 13; Is. 61:1-3; Dan. 9:24-26 [b]Zech. 3:1-7 [c]Mic. 4:13

1 [a]Jer. 36:2; Ezek. 2:9

2 [1]A cubit equals 18 in.

3 [1]Or, *earth* [2]Lit., *it* [a]Is. 24:6; 43:28; Jer. 26:6 [b]Ex. 20:15; Lev. 19:11; Mal. 3:8, 9

4 [a]Mal. 3:5 [b]Hos. 4:2, 3 [c]Jer. 2:26 [d]Lev. 14:34-35; Job 18:15

6 [1]I.e., a bushel measure [2]Lit., *eye;* some ancient versions read, *iniquity* [3]Or, *earth* [a]Lev. 19:36; Amos 8:5

7 (and behold, a lead cover was lifted up); and this is a
woman sitting inside the ephah."
8 Then he said, "This is [a]Wickedness!" And he threw her
down into the middle of the ephah and cast the lead weight on
its [1]opening.
9 Then I lifted up my eyes and looked, and there two
women were coming out with the wind in their wings; and they
had wings like the wings of a [a]stork, and they lifted up the
ephah between the earth and the heavens.
10 And I said to the angel who was speaking with me,
"Where are they taking the ephah?"
11 Then he said to me, "To build a [1]temple for her in the
land of [a]Shinar; and when it is prepared, she will be set there
on her own pedestal."

Chapter 6

Now I lifted up my eyes again and looked, and behold,
[a]four chariots were coming forth from between the two mountains; and the mountains *were* bronze mountains.
2 With the first chariot *were* red horses, with the second
chariot black horses,
3 with the third chariot white horses, and with the fourth
chariot strong dappled horses.
4 Then I spoke and said to the angel who was speaking
with me, "What are these, my lord?"
5 And the angel answered and said to me, "These are the
[a]four spirits of heaven, going forth after standing before the
Lord of all the earth,
6 with one of which the black horses are going forth to
the [a]north country; and the white ones go forth after them,
while the dappled ones go forth to the [b]south country.
7 "When the strong ones went out, they [1]were eager to go
to [2]patrol the earth." And he said, "Go, [2]patrol the earth." So
they [3]patrolled the earth.
8 Then he cried out to me and spoke to me saying, "See,
those who are going to the land of the north have [1a]appeased
My wrath in the land of the north."
9 The word of the LORD also came to me saying,
10 "[a]Take *an offering* from the exiles, from Heldai, Tobijah, and Jedaiah; and you go the same day and enter the house
of Josiah the son of Zephaniah, where they have arrived from
Babylon.
11 "And take silver and gold, make an *ornate* [a]crown, and
set *it* on the head of [b]Joshua the son of Jehozadak, the high
priest.
12 "Then say to him, 'Thus says the LORD of hosts, "Behold, a man whose name is [1a]Branch, for He will [2b]branch out
from where He is; and He will [c]build the temple of the LORD.
13 "Yes, it is He who will build the temple of the LORD, and
He who will [a]bear the honor and sit and [b]rule on His throne.
Thus, He will be a [c]priest on His throne, and the counsel of
peace will be between the two [1]offices." '
14 "Now the crown will become a reminder in the temple
of the LORD to Helem, Tobijah, [1]Jedaiah, and Hen the son of
Zephaniah.

8 [1]Lit., *mouth* [a]Hos. 12:7; Amos 8:5; Mic. 6:11

9 [a]Lev. 11:13, 19; Ps. 104:17; Jer. 8:7

11 [1]Lit., *house* [a]Gen. 10:10; 11:2; 14:1; Is. 11:11; Dan. 1:2

1 [a]Zech. 6:5; 1:18; Dan. 7:3; 8:22

5 [a]Jer. 49:36; Ezek. 37:9; Dan. 7:2; 11:4; Matt. 24:31; Rev. 7:1

6 [a]Jer. 1:14, 15; 4:6; 6:1; 25:9; 46:10; Ezek. 1:4 [b]Is. 43:6; Dan. 11:5

7 [1]Lit., *sought to go* [2]Lit., *walked about through* [3]Lit., *walked about through*

8 [1]Lit., *caused My spirit to rest in* [a]Zech. 1:15; Ezek. 5:13; 24:13

10 [a]Ezra 7:14-16; 8:26-30; Jer. 28:6

11 [a]2 Sam. 12:30; Ps. 21:3; Song of Sol. 3:11 [b]Zech. 3:1; Ezra 3:2; Hag. 1:1

12 [1]Lit., *Sprout* [2]Lit., *sprout up* [a]Zech. 3:8; Is. 4:2; 11:1; Jer. 23:5; 33:15 [b]Is. 53:2 [c]Zech. 4:6-9; Ezra 3:8, 10; Amos 9:11

13 [1]Lit., *of them* [a]Is. 9:6; 11:10; 22:24; 49:5, 6 [b]Is. 9:7 [c]Ps. 110:1, 4

14 [1]I.e., Josiah

15 "And [a]those who are far off will come and [1]build the
temple of the LORD." Then you will know that the LORD of
hosts has sent me to you. And it will take place, if you completely [b]obey the LORD your God.

CHAPTER 7

THEN it came about in the fourth year of King Darius, that
the word of the LORD came to Zechariah on the fourth *day* of
the ninth month, *which is* Chislev.
2 Now *the town of* Bethel had sent Sharezer and Regem-
melech and [1]their men to [2a]seek the favor of the LORD,
3 speaking to the [a]priests who belong to the house of the
LORD of hosts, and to the prophets saying, "Shall I weep in the
fifth month [1]and abstain, as I have done these many years?"
4 Then the word of the LORD of hosts came to me saying,
5 "Say to all the people of the land and to the priests,
'When you fasted and mourned in the fifth and seventh
months [1]these [a]seventy years, was it actually for [b]Me that you
fasted?
6 'And when you eat and drink, [1]do you not eat for yourselves and do you not drink for yourselves?
7 'Are not *these* the words which the LORD [a]proclaimed
by the former prophets, when Jerusalem was inhabited and
[1b]prosperous with its cities around it, and the [2c]Negev and the
[3]foothills were inhabited?' "
8 Then the word of the LORD came to Zechariah saying,
9 "Thus has the LORD of hosts said, '[a]Dispense true justice, and practice [b]kindness and compassion each to his
brother;
10 and do not [a]oppress the widow or the [1]orphan, the
[2]stranger or the poor; and do [b]not devise evil in your hearts
against one another.'
11 "But they [a]refused to pay attention, and [1b]turned a stubborn shoulder and [2c]stopped their ears from hearing.
12 "And they made their [a]hearts like [1b]flint [2]so that they
could not hear the law and the words which the LORD of hosts
had sent by His Spirit through the [c]former prophets; therefore
great [d]wrath came from the LORD of hosts.
13 "And it came about that just as [a]He called and they
would not listen, so [b]they called and I would not listen," says
the LORD of hosts;
14 "but I [1a]scattered them with a [b]storm wind among all
the nations whom they have not known. Thus the land is
[c]desolated behind them, [2]so that [d]no one went back and forth,
for they [e]made the pleasant land desolate."

CHAPTER 8

THEN the word of the LORD of hosts came saying,
2 "Thus says the LORD of hosts, 'I am exceedingly jealous
for Zion, yes, with great wrath I am jealous for her.'
3 "Thus says the LORD, 'I will return to Zion and will
dwell in the midst of Jerusalem. Then Jerusalem will be called
the City of Truth, and the mountain of the LORD of hosts *will
be called* the Holy Mountain.'

15 [1]Lit., *build in* [a]Is. 56:6-8; 60:10 [b]Zech. 3:7; Is. 58:10-14; Jer. 7:23

2 [1]Lit., *his* [2]Lit., *soften the face of* [a]Zech. 8:21; 1 Kin. 13:6; Jer. 26:19

3 [1]Lit., *abstaining;* or, *dedicating myself* [a]Ezra 3:10-12

5 [1]Lit., *and these* [a]Zech. 1:12 [b]Is. 1:11, 12; 58:5

6 [1]Lit., *is it not you who eat and you who drink*

7 [1]Or, *at ease* [2]I.e., South country [3]Heb., *Shephelah* [a]Zech. 1:4; Is. 1:16-20; Jer. 7:5, 23 [b]Jer. 22:21 [c]Jer. 13:19; 32:44

9 [a]Zech. 8:16; Ezek. 18:8; 45:9 [b]2 Sam. 9:7; Job 6:14; Mic. 6:8

10 [1]Or, *fatherless* [2]Or, *resident alien* [a]Ex. 22:22; Ps. 72:4; Jer. 7:6 [b]Zech. 8:17; Ps. 21:11; Mic. 2:1

11 [1]Lit., *gave* [2]Lit., *made heavy* [a]Jer. 5:3; 8:5; 11:10 [b]Jer. 7:26; 17:23 [c]Ps. 58:4; Jer. 5:21

12 [1]Lit., *corundum* [2]Lit., *from hearing* [a]2 Chr. 36:13; Ezek. 2:4; 3:7-9 [b]Jer. 17:1; Ezek. 3:9 [c]Neh. 9:30 [d]2 Chr. 36:16; Dan. 9:11, 12

13 [a]Jer. 11:10, 14; 14:12 [b]Prov. 1:24-28; Is. 1:15

14 [1]Lit., *stormed them away upon all* [2]Lit., *from passing and from returning* [a]Deut. 4:27; 28:64 [b]Jer. 23:19 [c]Jer. 44:6 [d]Is. 60:15 [e]Jer. 12:10

4 "Thus says the LORD of hosts, '[a]Old men and old women
will again sit in the [1]streets of Jerusalem, each man with his
staff in his hand because of [2]age.
5 'And the [1]streets of the city will be filled with [a]boys and
girls playing in its [1]streets.'
6 "Thus says the LORD of hosts, 'If it is [1a]too difficult in
the sight of the remnant of this people in those days, will it
also be [1]too difficult in [b]My sight?' declares the LORD of hosts.
7 "Thus says the LORD of hosts, 'Behold, I am going to
save My people from the land of the [1a]east and from the land
of the [2]west;
8 and I will [a]bring them *back*, and they will [b]live in the
midst of Jerusalem, and they will be [c]My people and I will be
their God in [1]truth and righteousness.'
9 "Thus says the LORD of hosts, 'Let your hands be [a]strong,
you who are listening in these days to these words from
the mouth of the [b]prophets, *those* who *spoke* in the day that
the foundation of the house of the LORD of hosts was laid, to
the end that the temple might be built.
10 'For before those days there was [a]no wage for man or
any wage for animal; and for him who went out or came in
there was no [1b]peace because of [2]his enemies, and I [c]set all
men one against another.
11 'But now I will [a]not [1]treat the remnant of this people as
in the former days,' declares the LORD of hosts.
12 'For *there will be* peace for the seed: the vine will yield
its fruit, the land will yield its produce, and the heavens will
give their [a]dew; and I will cause the remnant of this people to
inherit [b]all these *things*.
13 'And it will come about that just as you were a [a]curse
among the nations, O house of Judah and house of Israel, so I
will save you that you may become a [b]blessing. Do not fear; let
your hands be strong.'
14 "For thus says the LORD of hosts, 'Just as I [a]purposed to
do harm to you when your fathers provoked Me to wrath,' says
the LORD of hosts, 'and I have not [b]relented,
15 so I have again purposed in these days to [a]do good to
Jerusalem and to the house of Judah. Do not fear!
16 'These are the things which you should do: Speak the
[a]truth to one another; judge with truth and judgment for
peace in your [1]gates.
17 'Also let none of you [a]devise evil in your heart against
another, and do not love [1b]perjury; for all these are what I
[c]hate,' declares the LORD."
18 Then the word of the LORD of hosts came to me saying,
19 "Thus says the LORD of hosts, 'The fast of the [a]fourth,
the fast of the fifth, the fast of the [b]seventh, and the fast of the
[c]tenth *months* will become [d]joy, gladness, and [1]cheerful feasts
for the house of Judah; so [e]love truth and peace.'
20 "Thus says the LORD of hosts, '*It will* yet *be* that
[a]peoples will come, even the inhabitants of many cities;
21 and the inhabitants of one will go to another saying,
"Let us go at once to entreat the favor of the LORD, and to
seek the LORD of hosts; [1]I will also go."
22 'So [a]many peoples and mighty nations will come to seek

4 [1]Or, *squares* [2]Lit., *the multitude of days* [a]Is. 65:20

5 [1]Or, *squares* [a]Jer. 30:19, 20; 31:12, 13

6 [1]Or, *wonderful* [a]Ps. 118:23; 126:1-3 [b]Jer. 32:17, 27

7 [1]Lit., *rising* [2]Lit., *setting sun* [a]Ps. 107:3; Is. 11:11; 27:12, 13; 43:5

8 [1]Or, *faithfulness* [a]Zech. 10:10; Zeph. 3:20 [b]Jer. 3:17; Ezek. 37:25 [c]Zech. 2:11; Ezek. 11:20; 36:28

9 [a]1 Chr. 22:13; Is. 35:4; Hag. 2:4 [b]Ezra 5:1; 6:14

10 [1]Or, *safety* [2]Lit., *the adversary* [a]Hag. 2:15-19 [b]2 Chr. 15:5 [c]Is. 19:2; Amos 3:6; 9:4

11 [1]Lit., *be to the* [a]Ps. 103:9; Is. 12:1; Hag. 2:19

12 [a]Gen. 27:28; Deut. 33:13, 28; Hos. 13:3 [b]Is. 61:7; Obad. 17

13 [a]Jer. 29:18; Dan. 9:11 [b]Zech. 14:11; Ps. 72:17; Is. 19:24, 25; Ezek. 34:26

14 [a]Jer. 31:28 [b]Jer. 4:28; Ezek. 24:14

15 [a]Jer. 29:11; Mic. 7:18-20

16 [1]I.e., law courts [a]Zech. 8:3; Ps. 15:2; Prov. 12:17-19

17 [1]Lit., *false oath* [a]Zech. 7:10; Prov. 3:29; Jer. 4:14 [b]Zech. 5:4; Mal. 3:5 [c]Prov. 6:16-19; Hab. 1:13

19 [1]Or, *goodly* [a]2 Kin. 25:3, 4; Jer. 39:2 [b]Zech. 7:5; 2 Kin. 25:25 [c]Jer. 52:4 [d]Ps. 30:11; Is. 12:1 [e]Zech. 8:16; Luke 1:74, 75

20 [a]Zech. 2:11; 14:16; Ps. 117:1; Jer. 16:19; Mic. 4:2, 3

21 [1]Or, *Let me go too*

22 [a]Is. 2:2, 3; 25:7; 49:6, 22, 23; 60:3-12

the LORD of hosts in Jerusalem and to entreat the favor of the
LORD.'
23 "Thus says the LORD of hosts, 'In those days ten men
from the nations of every language will [1a]grasp the [2]garment of
a Jew saying, "Let us go with you, for we have heard that God
is with you." ' "

CHAPTER 9

THE [1]burden of the word of the LORD is against the land of
Hadrach, with [a]Damascus as its resting place (for the eyes of
men, especially of all the tribes of Israel, are toward the LORD),

2 And [a]Hamath also, which borders on it;
[b]Tyre and [c]Sidon, [1]though they are [b]very [2]wise.
3 For Tyre built herself a [a]fortress
And [b]piled up silver like dust,
And [c]gold like the mire of the streets.
4 Behold, the Lord will [a]dispossess her
And cast her wealth into the sea;
And she will be [b]consumed with fire.
5 Ashkelon will see *it* and be afraid.
Gaza too will writhe in great pain;
Also Ekron, for her expectation has been confounded.
Moreover, the king will perish from Gaza,
And Ashkelon will not be inhabited.
6 And a [1]mongrel race will dwell in Ashdod,
And I will cut off the pride of the Philistines.
7 And I will remove their blood from their mouth,
And their detestable things from between their teeth.
Then they also will be a remnant for our God,
And be like a [1]clan in Judah,
And Ekron like a Jebusite.
8 But I will camp around My house [1]because of an army,
Because of [a]him who passes by and returns;
And [b]no oppressor will pass over them any more,
For now I have seen with My eyes.
9 [a]Rejoice greatly, O daughter of Zion!
Shout *in triumph*, O daughter of Jerusalem!
Behold, your [b]king is coming to you;
He is [1c]just and [d]endowed with salvation,
[e]Humble, and mounted on a donkey,
Even on a [f]colt, the [2]foal of a donkey.
10 And I will cut off the chariot from Ephraim,
And the horse from Jerusalem;
And the bow of war will be cut off.
And He will speak [a]peace to the nations;
And His [b]dominion will be from sea to sea,
And from [1]the River to the ends of the earth.

11 As for you also, because of the [a]blood of *My* covenant
with you,
I have set your [b]prisoners free from the [1]waterless pit.
12 Return to the [1a]stronghold, O prisoners [2]who have the
hope;
This very day I am declaring that I will restore [b]double
to you.

8:23 [1]Lit., *grasp, and they will grasp* [2]Or, *corner of the garment* [a]Is. 45:14, 24; 60:14

9:1 [1]Or, *oracle* [a]Is. 17:1

2 [1]Or, *because* [2]I.e., they think they are (cf. Ezek. 28:2) [a]Jer. 49:23 [b]Ezek. 28:3-5, 12 [c]Ezek. 28:21

3 [a]Josh. 19:29; 2 Sam. 24:7 [b]Job 27:16; Ezek. 27:33; 28:4, 5 [c]1 Kin. 10:21, 27

4 [a]Ezek. 26:3-5 [b]Ezek. 28:18

6 [1]Lit., *bastard will*

7 [1]Or, *chief*

8 [1]Or, *as a guard, so that none will go back and forth* [a]Is. 52:1; Joel 3:1 [b]Is. 54:14; 60:18

9 [1]Or, *vindicated and victorious* [2]Lit., *son of a female donkey* [a]Zech. 2:10; Zeph. 3:14, 15 [b]Ps. 110:1; Is. 9:6, 7; Jer. 23:5, 6; Matt. 21:5; John 12:15 [c]Zeph. 3:5 [d]Is. 43:3, 11 [e]Is. 57:15 [f]Judg. 10:4; Is. 30:6

10 [1]I.e., the Euphrates [a]Is. 57:19; Mic. 4:2-4 [b]Ps. 72:8; Is. 60:12

11 [1]Lit., *cistern in which there is no water* [a]Ex. 24:8; Heb. 10:2 [b]Is. 24:22; 51:14

12 [1]Or, *Stronghold* [2]Lit., *of the hope* [a]Jer. 16:19; Joel 3:16 [b]Is. 61:7

13 For I will [a]bend Judah [1]as My bow,
I will fill the bow with Ephraim.
And I will stir up your sons, O Zion, against your sons,
O [b]Greece;
And I will make you like a warrior's sword.
14 Then the LORD will appear [a]over them,
And His [b]arrow will go forth like lightning;
And the Lord [1]GOD will blow the [c]trumpet,
And will march in the [d]storm winds of the south.
15 The LORD of hosts will defend them.
And they will devour, and [a]trample on the sling stones;
And they will drink, *and* be [b]boisterous as with wine;
And they will be filled like a *sacrificial* basin,
Drenched like the [c]corners of the altar.
16 And the LORD their God will [a]save them in that day
As the flock of His people;
For *they are as* the stones of a [b]crown,
[1]Sparkling in His land.
17 "For what [1a]comeliness and [b]beauty *will be* [2]theirs!
Grain will make the young men flourish, and new wine
the virgins.

13 [1]Lit., *for Me*
[a]Jer. 51:20 [b]Joel 3:6

14 [1]YHWH, usually rendered LORD
[a]Zech. 2:5; Is. 31:5 [b]Ps. 18:14; Hab. 3:11 [c]Is. 27:13 [d]Is. 21:1; 66:15

15 [a]Job 41:28 [b]Ps. 78:65 [c]Ex. 27:2

16 [1]Or, *Displayed over*
[a]Jer. 31:10, 11 [b]Is. 62:3

17 [1]Lit., *goodness* [2]Lit., *his*
[a]Jer. 31:12, 14 [b]Ps. 27:4; Is. 33:17

CHAPTER 10

"ASK [a]rain from the LORD at the time of the spring rain—
The LORD who [b]makes the [1]storm clouds;
And He will give them [c]showers of rain, vegetation in
the field to *each* man.
2 "For the [a]teraphim speak [1]iniquity,
And the [b]diviners see [2]lying visions,
And tell [c]false dreams;
They comfort in vain.
Therefore *the people* [3]wander like [d]sheep,
They are afflicted, because there is no shepherd.
3 "My [a]anger is kindled against the shepherds,
And I will punish the [1]male goats;
For the LORD of hosts has [b]visited His flock, the house
of Judah,
And will make them like His majestic horse in battle.
4 "From [1]them will come the cornerstone,
From [1]them the tent peg,
From [1]them the bow of [a]battle,
From [1]them every [2]ruler, *all* of them together.
5 "And they will be as mighty men,
[a]Treading down *the enemy* in the mire of the streets in
battle;
And they will fight, for the LORD *will be* with them;
And the [b]riders on horses will be put to shame.
6 "And I shall strengthen the house of Judah,
And I shall save the house of Joseph,
And I shall [1]bring them back,
Because I have had [a]compassion on them;
And they will be as though I had [b]not rejected them,
For I am the LORD their God, and I will answer them.
7 "And Ephraim will be like a mighty man,
And their heart will be glad as if *from* wine;

1 [1]Or, *thunderbolts*
[a]Joel 2:23 [b]Jer. 10:13 [c]Is. 30:23

2 [1]Or, *futility* [2]Lit., *lie* [3]Lit., *journey*
[a]Ezek. 21:21; Hos. 3:4 [b]Jer. 27:9 [c]Jer. 23:32 [d]Ezek. 34:5, 8

3 [1]I.e., leaders
[a]Jer. 25:34-36 [b]Ezek. 34:12

4 [1]Lit., *him* [2]Or, *oppressor*
[a]Zech. 9:10; Jer. 51:20

5 [a]2 Sam. 22:43 [b]Amos 2:15; Hag. 2:22

6 [1]Or, *make them dwell*
[a]Zech. 1:16; Is. 54:8 [b]Is. 54:4

Indeed, their [a]children will see *it* and be glad,
[1]Their heart will rejoice in the LORD.
8 "I will [a]whistle for them to gather them together,
For I have redeemed them;
And they will be as [b]numerous as they [1c]were before.
9 "When I [1]scatter them among the peoples,
They will [a]remember Me in far countries,
And they with their children will live and come back.
10 "I will [a]bring them back from the land of Egypt,
And gather them from Assyria;
And I will bring them into the land of [b]Gilead and Lebanon,
[1]Until [c]no *room* can be found for them.
11 "And He will pass through the [a]sea *of* distress,
And strike the waves in the sea,
So that all the depths of the [b]Nile will dry up;
And the pride of [c]Assyria will be brought down,
And the scepter of [d]Egypt will depart.
12 "And I shall strengthen them in the LORD,
And in His name [a]they will walk," declares the LORD.

CHAPTER 11

OPEN your doors, O Lebanon,
That a fire may feed on your [b]cedars.
2 Wail, O [1]cypress, for the cedar has fallen,
Because the glorious *trees* have been destroyed;
Wail, O oaks of Bashan,
For the [2]impenetrable forest has come down.
3 There is a sound of the shepherds' [a]wail,
For their glory is ruined;
There is a [b]sound of the young lions' roar,
For the [1]pride of the Jordan is ruined.

4 Thus says the LORD my God: "Pasture the flock
doomed to slaughter.
5 "Those who buy them slay them and [1]go [a]unpunished,
and *each of* those who sell them says, 'Blessed be the LORD, for
[b]I have become rich!' And their [c]own shepherds have no pity
on them.
6 "For I shall [a]no longer have pity on the inhabitants of
the land," declares the LORD; "but behold, I shall [b]cause the
men to [1]fall into one another's [2]power and into the [2]power of
his king; and they will strike the land, and I shall [c]not deliver
them from their [2]power."
7 So I pastured the flock *doomed* to slaughter, [1]hence
the [a]afflicted of the flock. And I took for myself two [b]staffs:
the one I called [2c]Favor, and the other I called [3d]Union; so I
pastured the flock.
8 Then I annihilated the three shepherds in [a]one month,
for my soul was impatient with them, and their soul also [1]was
weary of me.
9 Then I said, "I will not pasture you. What is to [a]die,
[1]let it die, and what is to be annihilated, [2]let it be annihilated;
and [3]let those who are left eat one another's flesh."
10 And I took my staff [1]Favor and cut it in pieces, to
[2a]break my covenant which I had made with all the peoples.

7 [1]Or, *Let their heart rejoice* [a]Is. 54:13; Ezek. 37:25

8 [1]Lit., *were numerous* [a]Is. 5:26; 7:18, 19 [b]Jer. 33:22 [c]Jer. 30:20; Ezek. 36:11

9 [1]Lit., *sow* [a]1 Kin. 8:47, 48; Ezek. 6:9

10 [1]Lit., *And* [a]Is. 11:11 [b]Jer. 50:19 [c]Is. 49:19, 20

11 [a]Is. 51:9, 10 [b]Is. 19:5-7 [c]Zeph. 2:13 [d]Ezek. 30:13

12 [a]Mic. 4:5

1 [a]Jer. 22:6, 7 [b]Ezek. 31:3

2 [1]Or, *juniper* [2]Another reading is: *forest of the vintage*

3 [1]Or, *jungle* [a]Jer. 25:34-36 [b]Jer. 2:15; 50:44

5 [1]Lit., *are not held guilty* [a]Jer. 50:7 [b]Hos. 12:8; 1 Tim. 6:9 [c]Ezek. 34:2, 3

6 [1]Lit., *find* [2]Lit., *hand* [a]Jer. 13:14 [b]Zech. 14:13; Is. 9:19-21; Mic. 7:2-6 [c]Ps. 50:22; Mic. 5:8

7 [1]Another reading is: *for the sheep dealers* [2]Or, *Pleasantness* [3]Or, *Cords* [a]Jer. 39:10; Zeph. 3:12 [b]Ezek. 37:16 [c]Zech. 11:10; Ps. 27:4; 90:17 [d]Zech. 11:14; Ps. 133:1; Ezek. 37:16-23

8 [1]Or, *detested* [a]Hos. 5:7

9 [1]Or, *will die* [2]Or, *will be annihilated* [3]Or, *those . . . will eat* [a]Jer. 15:2

10 [1]Or, *Pleasantness* [2]Or, *annul* [a]Ps. 89:39; Jer. 14:21

11 So it was [1]broken on that day; and [2]thus the [a]afflicted
of the flock who were watching me realized that it was the
word of the LORD.
12 And I said to them, "If it is good in your sight, give *me*
my [a]wages; but if not, [1]never mind!" So they weighed out
[b]thirty *shekels* of silver as my wages.
13 Then the LORD said to me, "Throw it to the [a]potter,
that magnificent price at which I was valued by them." So I
took the thirty *shekels* of silver and threw them to the potter in
the house of the LORD.
14 Then I cut my second staff, [1]Union, in pieces, to [a]break
the brotherhood between Judah and Israel.
15 And the LORD said to me, "Take again for yourself the
equipment of a [1a]foolish shepherd.
16 "For behold, I am going to raise up a shepherd in the
land who will not [a]care for the perishing, seek the scattered,
heal the broken, or sustain [2]the one standing, but will [b]devour
the flesh of the fat *sheep* and tear off their hoofs.
17 "[a]Woe to the worthless shepherd
Who leaves the flock!
A sword will be on his arm
And on his right eye!
His arm will be totally withered,
And his right eye will be [1]blind."

CHAPTER 12

THE [1]burden of the word of the LORD concerning Israel.
Thus declares the LORD who [a]stretches out the heavens,
[b]lays the foundation of the earth, and [c]forms the spirit of man
within him:
2 "Behold, I am going to make Jerusalem a [a]cup [1]that
causes reeling to all the peoples around; and when the siege is
against Jerusalem, it will also be against Judah.
3 "And it will come about in that day that I will make
Jerusalem a heavy [a]stone for all the peoples; all who lift it will
be [b]severely [1]injured. And all the nations of the earth will be
gathered against it.
4 "In that day," declares the LORD, "I will strike every
horse with bewilderment, and his rider with madness. But I will
[1]watch over the house of Judah, while I strike every horse of
the peoples with blindness.
5 "Then the clans of Judah will say in their hearts, '[1]A
strong support for us are the inhabitants of Jerusalem through
the LORD of hosts, their God.'
6 "In that day I will make the clans of Judah like a [a]firepot
among pieces of wood and a flaming torch among sheaves, so
they will consume on the right hand and on the left all the
surrounding peoples, while the inhabitants of Jerusalem again
dwell on their own sites in Jerusalem.
7 "The LORD also will [a]save the tents of Judah first in
order that the glory of the house of [b]David and the glory of the
inhabitants of Jerusalem may not be magnified above Judah.
8 "In that day the LORD will [a]defend the inhabitants of
Jerusalem, and the one who [1b]is feeble among them in that day

11 [1]Or, *annulled* [2]Another reading is: *the sheep dealers who*
[a]Zeph. 3:12

12 [1]Lit., *cease*
[a]1 Kin. 3:5 [b]Gen. 37:28; Ex. 21:32; Matt. 26:15; 27:9, 10

13 [a]Matt. 27:3-10; Acts 1:18, 19

14 [1]Or, *cords*
[a]Zech. 11:6; Is. 9:21

15 [1]Or, *useless*
[a]Zech. 11:17; Is. 6:10-12

16 [a]Jer. 23:2 [b]Ezek. 34:2-6

17 [1]Lit., *completely dimmed*
[a]Zech. 11:15, 10:2; Jer. 23:1

1 [1]Or, *oracle*
[a]Is. 42:5; 44:24; Jer. 51:15
[b]Job 26:7; Ps. 102:25, 26; Heb. 1:10-12 [c]Is. 57:16; Heb. 12:9

2 [1]Lit., *of reeling*
[a]Ps. 75:8; Is. 51:22, 23

3 [1]Lit., *scratched*
[a]Dan. 2:34, 35, 44, 45 [b]Matt. 21:44

4 [1]Lit., *open My eyes*

5 [1]Lit., *My strength is*

6 [a]Zech. 11:1; Is. 10:17, 18; Obad. 18

7 [a]Jer. 30:18 [b]Amos 9:11

8 [1]Or, *stumbles*
[a]Zech. 9:14, 15; Joel 3:16
[b]Lev. 26:8; Josh. 23:10; Mic. 7:8

8 [c]Ps. 8:5; 82:6 [d]Ex. 14:19; 33:2

9 [1]Lit., *seek to*

10 [1]Or, *a spirit* [a]Is. 44:3; Ezek. 39:29; Joel 2:28, 29 [b]John 19:37; Rev. 1:7 [c]Jer. 6:26; Amos 8:10

11 [1]I.e., broad valley [2]Heb., *Megiddon* [a]Matt. 24:30; Rev. 1:7

1 [a]Jer. 2:13; 17:13 [b]Ps. 51:2, 7; Is. 1:16-18; John 1:29 [c]Num. 19:17; Is. 4:4; Ezek. 36:25

2 [a]Ex. 23:13; Hos. 2:17 [b]Jer. 23:14, 15 [c]1 Kin. 22:22; Ezek. 36:25, 29

3 [a]Jer. 23:34 [b]Deut. 18:20; Ezek. 14:9 [c]Jer. 23:25 [d]Deut. 13:6-11; Matt. 10:37

4 [a]Jer. 6:15; 8:9; Mic. 3:7 [b]2 Kin. 1:8; Is. 20:2; Matt. 3:4

5 [1]Lit., *caused another to buy me* [a]Amos 7:14

6 [1]Lit., *hands* [2]Lit., *those who love me*

7 [1]Or, *upon* [a]Is. 40:11; Ezek. 34:23, 24; 37:24; Mic. 5:2, 4 [b]Ps. 2:2; Jer. 23:5, 6 [c]Is. 53:4, 5, 10; Matt. 26:31; Mark 14:27 [d]Is. 1:25

8 [a]Is. 6:13; Ezek. 5:2-4, 12

9 [a]Is. 48:10; Mal. 3:3

will be like David, and the house of David *will be* like [c]God,
like the [d]angel of the LORD before them.
9 "And it will come about in that day that I will [1]set about
to destroy all the nations that come against Jerusalem.
10 "And I will [a]pour out on the house of David and on the
inhabitants of Jerusalem [1]the Spirit of grace and of supplication, so that they will look on Me whom they have [b]pierced;
and they will mourn for Him, as one [c]mourns for an only son,
and they will weep bitterly over Him, like the bitter weeping
over a first-born.
11 "In that day there will be great [a]mourning in Jerusalem,
like the mourning of Hadadrimmon in the [1]plain of [2]Megiddo.
12 "And the land will mourn, every family by itself; the
family of the house of David by itself, and their wives by
themselves; the family of the house of Nathan by itself, and
their wives by themselves;
13 the family of the house of Levi by itself, and their wives
by themselves; the family of the Shimeites by itself, and their
wives by themselves;
14 all the families that remain, every family by itself, and
their wives by themselves.

CHAPTER 13

"IN that day a [a]fountain will be opened for the house of
David and for the inhabitants of Jerusalem, for [b]sin and for
[c]impurity.
2 "And it will come about in that day," declares the LORD
of hosts, "that I will [a]cut off the names of the idols from the
land, and they will no longer be remembered; and I will also
remove the [b]prophets and the [c]unclean spirit from the land.
3 "And it will come about that if anyone still [a]prophesies,
then his father and mother who gave birth to him will say to
him, 'You shall [b]not live, for you have spoken [c]falsely in the
name of the LORD'; and his [d]father and mother who gave birth
to him will pierce him through when he prophesies.
4 "Also it will come about in that day that the prophets
will each be [a]ashamed of his vision when he prophesies, and
they will not put on a [b]hairy robe in order to deceive;
5 but he will say, 'I am [a]not a prophet; I am a tiller of the
ground, for a man [1]sold me as a slave in my youth.'
6 "And one will say to him, 'What are these wounds between
your [1]arms?' Then he will say, '*Those* with which I was
wounded in the house of [2]my friends.'
7 "Awake, O sword, against My [a]Shepherd,
And against the man, My [b]Associate,"
Declares the LORD of hosts.
"[c]Strike the Shepherd that the sheep may be scattered;
And I will [d]turn My hand [1]against the little ones.
8 "And it will come about in all the land,"
Declares the LORD,
"That [a]two parts in it will be cut off *and* perish;
But the third will be left in it.
9 "And I will bring the third part through the [a]fire,
Refine them as silver is refined,
And test them as gold is tested.

They will [b]call on My name,
And I will [c]answer them;
I will say, 'They are [d]My people,'
And they will say, 'The LORD is my God.' "

CHAPTER 14

BEHOLD, a [a]day is coming for the LORD when the spoil
taken from you will be divided among you.
2 For I will gather all the nations against Jerusalem to
battle, and the city will be captured, the [a]houses plundered,
the women ravished, and half of the city exiled, but the rest of
the people will not be cut off from the city.
3 Then the LORD will go forth and fight against those
nations, as [1]when He fights on a day of battle.
4 And in that day His feet will [a]stand on the Mount of
Olives, which is in front of Jerusalem on the east; and the
Mount of Olives will be [b]split in its middle from east to west
by a very large valley, so that half of the mountain will move
toward the north and the other half toward the south.
5 And you will flee by the valley of My mountains, for
the valley of the mountains will reach to Azel; yes, you will flee
just as you fled before the [a]earthquake in the days of Uzziah
king of Judah. Then the LORD, O My God, will come, *and* all
the holy ones with [1]Him!
6 And it will come about in that day that there will be
[a]no light; the [1]luminaries will dwindle.
7 For it will be [a]a unique day which is [b]known to the
LORD, neither day nor night; but it will come about that at
[c]evening time there will be light.
8 And it will come about in that day that [a]living waters
will flow out of Jerusalem, half of them toward the eastern sea
and the other half toward the western sea; it will be in summer
as well as in winter.
9 And the LORD will be [a]king over all the earth; in that
day the LORD will be *the only* [b]one, and His name *the only*
one.
10 All the land will be changed into a plain from [a]Geba to
[b]Rimmon south of Jerusalem; but [1]Jerusalem will [c]rise and
[d]remain on its site from [e]Benjamin's gate as far as the place of
the First Gate to the [f]Corner Gate, and from the [g]Tower of
Hananel to the king's wine presses.
11 And [1]people will live in it, and there will be [a]no more
curse, for Jerusalem will [b]dwell in security.
12 "Now this will be the plague with which the LORD will
strike all the peoples who have gone to war against Jerusalem;
their flesh will [a]rot while they stand on their feet, and their
eyes will rot in their sockets, and their tongue will rot in their
mouth.
13 And it will come about in that day that a great panic
from the LORD will [1]fall on them; and they will seize one
another's hand, and the hand of one will [2]be lifted against the
hand of another.
14 And Judah also will fight at Jerusalem; and the [a]wealth
of all the surrounding nations will be gathered, gold and silver
and garments in great abundance.

9 [b]Zech. 12:10; Ps. 34:15-17; 50:15 [c]Zech. 10:6; Is. 58:9; 65:24; Jer. 29:11-13 [d]Hos. 2:23

1 [a]Is. 13:6, 9; Joel 2:1; Mal. 4:1

2 [a]Is. 13:16

3 [1]Lit., *His day of fighting*

4 [a]Ezek. 11:23 [b]Zech. 14:8; 4:7; Is. 64:1, 2; Ezek. 47:1-10; Mic. 1:3, 4; Hab. 3:6

5 [1]So the versions; Heb., *Thee* [a]Is. 29:6; Amos 1:1

6 [1]Lit., *glorious ones will congeal* [a]Is. 13:10; Jer. 4:23; Ezek. 32:7, 8; Joel 2:30, 31; Acts 2:16, 19

7 [a]Jer. 30:7; Amos 8:9 [b]Is. 45:21; Acts 15:18 [c]Is. 58:10; Rev. 22:5

8 [a]Ezek. 47:1-12; Joel 3:18; Rev. 22:1, 2

9 [a]Zech. 14:16, 17; 9:9; Is. 2:2-4; 45:23 [b]Deut. 6:4; Is. 45:21-24

10 [1]Lit., *it* [a]1 Kin. 15:22 [b]Josh. 15:32; Judg. 20:45, 47 [c]Is. 2:2; Amos 9:11 [d]Zech. 12:6; Jer. 30:18 [e]Jer. 37:13; 38:7 [f]2 Kin. 14:13 [g]Jer. 31:8

11 [1]Lit., *they* [a]Zech. 8:13; Rev. 22:3 [b]Jer. 23:5, 6; Ezek. 34:25-28

12 [a]Lev. 26:16; Deut. 28:21, 22

13 [1]Lit., *be among* [2]Lit., *rise up against*

14 [a]Zech. 14:1; Is. 23:18

15 So also like this plague, will be the plague on the horse, the mule, the camel, the donkey, and all the cattle that will be in those camps.

16 Then it will come about that any who are left of all the nations that went against Jerusalem will [a]go up from year to year to worship the King, the LORD of hosts, and to celebrate the [b]Feast of Booths.

17 And it will be that whichever of the families of the earth does not go up to Jerusalem to worship the King, the LORD of hosts, there will be [a]no rain on them.

18 And if the family of Egypt does not go up or enter, then no *rain will fall* on them; it will be the plague with which the LORD smites the nations who do not go up to celebrate the Feast of Booths.

19 This will be the [1]punishment of Egypt, and the [1]punishment of all the nations who do not go up to celebrate the Feast of Booths.

20 In that day there will *be inscribed* on the bells of the horses, "[a]HOLY TO THE LORD." And the [b]cooking pots in the LORD's house will be like the bowls before the altar.

21 And every cooking pot in Jerusalem and in Judah will be [a]holy to the LORD of hosts; and all who sacrifice will come and take of them and boil in them. And there will no longer be a [1]Canaanite in the house of the LORD of hosts in that day.

16 [a]Is. 60:6-9; 66:18-21, 23 [b]Lev. 23:34-44

17 [a]Jer. 14:3-6; Amos 4:7

19 [1]Lit., *sin*

20 [a]Ex. 28:36-38 [b]Ezek. 46:20

21 [1]Or, *merchant* [a]Neh. 8:10; Rom. 14:6, 7; 1 Cor. 10:31

THE BOOK OF MALACHI

God's Love for Jacob.

THE [1a]oracle of the word of the LORD to Israel through [2]Malachi.

2 "I have [a]loved you," says the LORD. But you say, "How hast Thou loved us?" "*Was* not Esau Jacob's brother?" declares the LORD. "Yet I [b]have loved Jacob;

3 but I have hated Esau, and I have made his mountains a desolation, and *appointed* his inheritance for the jackals of the wilderness."

4 Though Edom says, "We have been [a]beaten down, but we will [1b]return and build up the ruins"; thus says the LORD of hosts, "They may [c]build, but I will tear down; and *men* will call them the [2]wicked territory, and the people [3]toward whom the LORD is indignant forever."

5 And your eyes will see this and you will say, "The LORD [1a]be magnified beyond the [2]border of Israel!"

6 "A son [a]honors *his* father, and a servant his master. Then if I am a [b]father, where is My honor? And if I am a master, where is My [1]respect? says the LORD of hosts to you, O [c]priests who despise My name. But you say, 'How have we despised Thy name?'

7 "*You* are presenting defiled [1a]food upon My altar. But you say, 'How have we defiled Thee?' In that you say, 'The table of the LORD is to be despised.'

1 [1]Lit., *burden* [2]Or, *My messenger* [a]Is. 13:1; Nah. 1:1; Hab. 1:1; Zech. 9:1

2 [a]Rom. 9:13 [b]Jer. 49:16-18; Ezek. 35:8, 15

4 [1]Or, *rebuild the ruins* [2]Lit., *border of wickedness* [3]Or, *whom the LORD has cursed* [a]Jer. 5:17 [b]Is. 9:9, 10 [c]Amos 3:15; 5:11; 6:11

5 [1]Or, *will be great* [2]Or, *territory* [a]Ps. 35:27; Mic. 5:4

6 [1]Lit., *fear* [a]Ex. 20:12; Prov. 30:11, 17 [b]Mal. 2:10; Deut. 1:31; Is. 1:2; Jer. 3:4 [c]Mal. 2:1-9; Zeph. 3:4

7 [1]Lit., *bread* [a]Lev. 21:6, 8

8 "But when you present the [a]blind for sacrifice, is it not
evil? And when you present the lame and sick, is it not evil?
[1]Why not offer it to your governor? Would he be pleased with
you? Or would he receive you kindly?" says the LORD of hosts.
9 "But now [1]will you not [a]entreat God's favor, that He
may be gracious to us? [2]With such an offering on your part,
will He [b]receive any of you kindly?" says the LORD of hosts.
10 "Oh that there were one among you who would [a]shut
the [1]gates, that you might not uselessly kindle *fire on* My altar!
I am not pleased with you," says the LORD of hosts, "nor will I
[b]accept an offering from [2]you.
11 "For from the [a]rising of the sun, even to its setting, My
name *will be* great among the nations, and in every place
[b]incense is going to be offered to My name, and a grain offering *that is* pure; for My name *will be* [c]great among the nations," says the LORD of hosts.
12 "But you are profaning it, in that you say, 'The table of
the LORD is defiled, and as for its fruit, its food is to be
despised.'
13 "You also say, '[1]My, how [a]tiresome it is!' And you dis-
dainfully sniff at it," says the LORD of hosts, "and you bring
what was taken by [b]robbery, and *what is* lame or sick; so you
bring the offering! Should I receive that from your hand?" says
the LORD.
14 "But cursed be the swindler who has a male in his flock,
and vows it, but sacrifices a [a]blemished animal to the Lord, for
I am a great [b]King," says the LORD of hosts, "and My name is
[1c]feared among the [2]nations."

CHAPTER 2

"AND now, this commandment is for you, O priests.
2 "If you do [a]not listen, and if you do not take it to heart
to give honor to My name," says the LORD of hosts, "then I
will send the [b]curse upon you, and I will curse your blessings;
and indeed, I have cursed them *already*, because you are not
taking *it* to heart.
3 "Behold, I am going to [a]rebuke your [1]offspring, and I
will [b]spread [2]refuse on your faces, the [2]refuse of your [c]feasts;
and you will be taken away [3]with it.
4 "Then you will know that I have sent this commandment to you, [1]that My [a]covenant may [2]continue with Levi,"
says the LORD of hosts.
5 "My covenant with him was *one of* life and [a]peace, and I
gave them to him *as an object of* [1]reverence; so he [2b]revered
Me, and stood in awe of My name.
6 "[1a]True instruction was in his mouth, and unrighteousness was not found on his lips; he walked [b]with Me in peace
and uprightness, and he [c]turned many back from iniquity.
7 "For the lips of a priest should preserve [a]knowledge, and
[1]men should [b]seek [2]instruction from his mouth; for he is the
messenger of the LORD of hosts.
8 "But as for you, you have turned aside from the way;
you have caused many to [a]stumble [1]by the instruction; you
have [2b]corrupted the covenant of Levi," says the LORD of
hosts.

8 [1]Lit., *Offer, please* [a]Deut. 15:21

9 [1]Lit., *entreat please* [2]Lit., *This has been from your hand* [a]Jer. 27:18; Joel 2:12-14 [b]Amos 5:22

10 [1]Or, *doors* [2]Lit., *your hand* [a]Is. 1:13 [b]Jer. 14:10, 12; Hos. 5:6

11 [a]Is. 45:6 [b]Is. 60:6 [c]Is. 12:4, 5; 54:5; Jer. 10:6, 7

13 [1]Lit., *Behold it is weariness* [a]Is. 43:22 [b]Lev. 6:4; Is. 61:8

14 [1]Or, *revered* [2]Or, *Gentiles* [a]Lev. 22:18-20; Acts 5:1-4 [b]Zech. 14:9 [c]Zeph. 2:11

2 [a]Lev. 26:14, 15; Deut. 28:15 [b]Deut. 28:16-20

3 [1]Lit., *seed* [2]Or, *vomit* [3]Lit., *to* [a]Lev. 26:16; Deut. 28:38 [b]Nah. 3:6 [c]Ex. 29:14

4 [1]Or, *to be My covenant with* [2]Lit., *be* [a]Num. 3:45; 18:21

5 [1]Or, *fear* [2]Or, *feared* [a]Num. 25:12 [b]Num. 25:7, 8, 13

6 [1]Or, *Law of truth* [a]Ps. 119:142, 151, 160 [b]Deut. 33:8, 9; Ps. 37:37 [c]Jer. 23:22

7 [1]Lit., *they* [2]Or, *law* [a]Lev. 10:11; Neh. 8:7 [b]Num. 27:21; Deut. 17:8-11

8 [1]Or, *in the law* [2]Or, *violated* [a]Jer. 18:15 [b]Ezek. 44:10

9 "So I also have made you despised and abased [1]before
all the people, just as you are not keeping My ways, but are
showing [a]partiality in the [2]instruction.
10 "Do we not all have [a]one father? Has not one God
created us? Why do we deal [b]treacherously each against his
brother so as to profane the [c]covenant of our fathers?
11 "Judah has dealt [a]treacherously, and an abomination has
been committed in Israel and in Jerusalem; for Judah has [b]pro-
faned the sanctuary of the LORD [1]which He loves, and has
married the daughter of a foreign god.
12 "*As* for the man who does this, may the [a]LORD cut off
from the tents of Jacob *everyone* who awakes and answers, or
who presents an [1]offering to the LORD of hosts.
13 "And this is [1]another thing you do: you cover the altar of
the LORD with tears, with weeping and with groaning, because
He [a]no longer regards the [2]offering or accepts *it with* favor
from your hand.
14 "Yet you say, 'For what reason?' Because the LORD has
been a witness between you and the wife of your youth, against
whom you have dealt [a]treacherously, though she is your companion and your wife by covenant.
15 "[1]But not one has [a]done *so* who has a remnant of the
Spirit. And [2]what did *that* one *do* while he was seeking a [b]godly
[3]offspring? Take heed then, to your spirit, and let no one deal
[c]treacherously against the wife of your youth.
16 "For [1]I hate [2a]divorce," says the LORD, the God of Israel,
"and [3]him who covers his garment with [4b]wrong," says the
LORD of hosts. "So take heed to your spirit, that you do not
deal treacherously."
17 You have [a]wearied the LORD with your words. Yet you
say, "How have we wearied *Him?*" In that you say, "[b]Everyone
who does evil is good in the sight of the LORD, and He [c]delights
in them," or, "Where is the God of [d]justice?"

CHAPTER 3

"[a]BEHOLD, I am going to send My [1]messenger, and he will
[2]clear the way before Me. And the Lord, whom you seek, will
suddenly come to His temple; [3]and the [1b]messenger of the
covenant, in whom you delight, behold, he is coming," says the
LORD of hosts.
2 "But who can [a]endure the day of His coming? And who
can stand when He appears? For He is like a [b]refiner's fire and
like [1]fullers' soap.
3 "And He will sit as a smelter and purifier of silver, and
He will [a]purify the sons of Levi and refine them like gold and
silver, so that they may [b]present to the LORD [1]offerings in
righteousness.
4 "Then the [1]offering of Judah and Jerusalem will be [a]pleas-
ing to the LORD, as in the [b]days of old and as in former
years.
5 "Then I will draw near to you for judgment; and I will
be a swift witness against the [a]sorcerers and against the [b]adul-
terers and against those who [c]swear falsely, and against those
who oppress the [d]wage earner in his wages, the [e]widow and the

---

9 [1]Lit., *to* [2]Or, *law* [a]Deut. 1:17; Mic. 3:11

10 [a]Is. 63:16; 64:8; Jer 31:9 [b]Jer. 9:4, 5 [c]Ex. 19:4-6; 24:3, 7, 8

11 [1]Or, *in that he has loved and married* [a]Jer. 3:7-9 [b]Ezra 9:1, 2

12 [1]Or, *grain offering* [a]Ezek. 24:21; Hos. 9:12

13 [1]Lit., *second* [2]Or, *grain offering* [a]Jer. 11:14; 14:12

14 [a]Mal. 3:5; Jer. 9:2

15 [1]Or, *Did He not make one, although He had the remnant* [2]Or, *Why one? He sought a godly offspring* [3]Lit., *seed* [a]Gen. 2:24; Matt. 19:4, 5 [b]Ruth 4:12; 1 Sam. 2:20 [c]Ex. 20:14; Lev. 20:10

16 [1]Lit., *He hates* [2]Lit., *sending away* [3]Lit., *he covers* [4]Or, *violence* [a]Deut. 24:1; Matt. 5:31; 19:6-8 [b]Ps. 73:6; Is. 59:6

17 [a]Is. 43:22, 24 [b]Is. 5:20; Zeph. 1:12 [c]Job 9:24 [d]Is. 5:19; Jer. 17:15

1 [1]Or, *angel* [2]Or, *prepare* [3]Or, *even* [a]Matt. 11:10, 14; Mark 1:2; Luke 7:27 [b]Is. 63:9

2 [1]Lit., *laundrymen* [a]Is. 33:14; Ezek. 22:14 [b]Zech. 13:9; Matt. 3:10-12; 1 Cor. 3:13-15

3 [1]Or, *grain offerings* [a]Is. 1:25; Dan 12:10 [b]Ps. 4:5; 51:19

4 [1]Or, *grain offering* [a]Ps. 51:17-19 [b]2 Chr. 7:1-3, 12

5 [a]Deut. 18:10; Jer. 27:9, 10 [b]Ezek. 22:9-11 [c]Jer. 5:2; 7:9; Zech. 5:4 [d]Lev. 19:13 [e]Ex. 22:22-24

[1]orphan, and those who turn aside the [2f]alien, and do not [3]fear
Me," says the LORD of hosts.
6 "For [1]I, the LORD, do not change; therefore you, O sons
of Jacob, [2]are not consumed.
7 "From the days of your fathers you have turned aside
from My statutes, and have not kept *them.* [a]Return to Me,
and I will return to you," says the Lord of hosts. "But you say,
'How shall we return?'
8 "Will a man [1]rob God? Yet you are robbing Me! But
you say, 'How have we robbed Thee?' In [a]tithes and
[2]contributions.
9 "You are cursed with a curse, for you are [1]robbing Me,
the whole nation *of you*!
10 "Bring the whole tithe into the storehouse, so that there
may be [1]food in My house, and test Me now in this," says the
LORD of hosts, "if I will not [a]open for you the windows of
heaven, and [b]pour out for you a blessing until there is [2c]no
more need.
11 "Then I will rebuke the [a]devourer for you, so that it may
not [1]destroy the fruits of the ground; nor will your vine in the
field cast *its grapes*," says the LORD of hosts.
12 "And [a]all the nations will call you blessed, for you shall
be a [b]delightful land," says the LORD of hosts.
13 "Your words have been [1]arrogant against Me," says the
LORD. "Yet you say, 'What have we spoken against Thee?'
14 "You have said, 'It is [a]vain to serve God; and what [b]prof-
it is it that we have kept His charge, and that we have walked
in mourning before the LORD of hosts?
15 'So now we call the arrogant blessed; not only are the
doers of wickedness built up, but they also test God and
[a]escape.' "
16 Then those who [1]feared the LORD spoke to one another,
and the LORD [a]gave attention and heard *it*, and a [b]book of
remembrance was written before Him for those who [2]fear the
LORD and who esteem His name.
17 "And they will be [a]Mine," says the LORD of hosts, "on
the [b]day that I [1]prepare *My* [2c]own possession, and I will [3]spare
them as a man [3d]spares his own son who serves him."
18 So you will again [a]distinguish between the righteous
and the wicked, between one who serves God and one who
does not serve him.

CHAPTER 4

"[1]FOR behold, the day is coming, [a]burning like a furnace;
and all the arrogant and every evildoer will be [b]chaff; and the
day that is coming will [c]set them ablaze," says the LORD of
hosts, "so that it will leave them neither root nor branch."
2 "But for you who [1]fear My name the [a]sun of righteousness will rise with [b]healing in its wings; and you will go forth
and [c]skip about like calves from the stall.
3 "And you will [a]tread down the wicked, for they shall be
[b]ashes under the soles of your feet on the day [1]which I am
preparing," says the LORD of hosts.

5 [1]Or., *fatherless* [2]Or, *sojourner* [3]Or, *revere* [f]Deut. 27:19

6 [1]Or, *I am the Lord; I do not* [2]Or, *have not come to an end*

7 [a]Zech. 1:3

8 [1]Or, *defraud* [2]Or, *heave offerings* [a]Neh. 13:11

9 [1]Or, *defrauding*

10 [1]Lit., *prey* [2]Or, *not room enough* [a]Ps. 78:23-29 [b]Ezek. 34:26 [c]Lev. 26:3-5

11 [1]Lit., *ruin* [a]Joel 1:4; 2:25

12 [a]Is. 61:9 [b]Is. 62:4

13 [1]Lit., *strong*

14 [a]Jer. 2:25; 18:12 [b]Is. 58:3

15 [a]Jer. 7:10

16 [1]Or, *revered* [2]Or, *revere* [a]Ps. 34:15; Jer. 31:18-20 [b]Is. 4:3; Dan. 12:1

17 [1]Lit., *make* [2]Or, *special treasure* [3]Or, *have (has) compassion on* [a]Is. 43:1 [b]Is. 4:2 [c]Ex. 19:5; Deut. 7:6; Is. 43:21; 1 Pet. 2:9 [d]Neh. 13:22; Ps. 103:13; Is. 26:20

18 [a]Gen. 18:25; Amos 5:15

1 [1]In Heb. chap. 3, v. 19 [a]Mal. 3:2, 3; Ps. 21:9; Nah. 1:5, 6 [b]Is. 5:24; Obad. 18 [c]Is. 9:18, 19

2 [1]I, Or, *revere* [a]2 Sam. 23:4; Is. 30:26; 60:1 [b]Jer. 30:17; 33:6 [c]Is. 35:6

3 [1]Or, *when I act* [a]Job 40:12; Is. 26:6; Mic. 5:8 [b]Ezek. 28:18

4 [1]In. Heb., chap. 3, v. 22 [a]Deut. 4:23; 8:11, 19

5 [a]Matt. 11:14; Mark 9:11-13; Luke 1:17

6 [1]Or, *turn* [2]Or, *ban the destruction* [a]Luke 1:17 [b]Is. 11:4; Rev. 19:15

4 "[1a]Remember the law of Moses My servant, *even the*
statutes and ordinances which I commanded him in Horeb for
all Israel.
5 "Behold, I am going to send you [a]Elijah the prophet
before the coming of the great and terrible day of the LORD.
6 "And he will [1a]restore the hearts of the fathers to *their*
children, and the hearts of the children to their fathers, lest I
come and [b]smite the land with a [2]curse."

New

American Standard

Bible

New Testament

THE GOSPEL
ACCORDING TO
MATTHEW

Genealogy of Jesus. Birth of Jesus.

THE book of the genealogy of Jesus Christ, [a]the son of
David, [b]the son of Abraham.
2 To Abraham was born Isaac; and to Isaac, Jacob; and
to Jacob, [1]Judah and his brothers;
3 and to Judah were born Perez and Zerah by Tamar;
and to [a]Perez was born Hezron; and to Hezron, [1]Ram;
4 and to Ram was born Amminadab; and to Amminadab, Nahshon; and to Nahshon, Salmon;
5 and to Salmon was born Boaz by Rahab; and to Boaz
was born Obed by Ruth; and to Obed, Jesse;
6 and to Jesse was born David the king.
And to David [a]was born Solomon by her *who had been the*
wife of Uriah;
7 and to Solomon [a]was born Rehoboam; and to Rehoboam, Abijah; and to Abijah, [1]Asa;
8 and to Asa was born Jehoshaphat; and to Jehoshaphat,
[1]Joram; and to Joram, Uzziah;
9 and to Uzziah was born [1]Jotham; and to Jotham, Ahaz;
and to Ahaz, Hezekiah;
10 and to Hezekiah was born Manasseh; and to Manasseh,
[1]Amon; and to Amon, Josiah;
11 and to Josiah were born [1]Jeconiah and his brothers, at
the time of the [a]deportation to Babylon.
12 And after the [a]deportation to Babylon, to Jeconiah was
born [1]Shealtiel; and to Shealtiel, Zerubbabel;
13 and to Zerubbabel was born [1]Abiud; and to Abiud,
Eliakim; and to Eliakim, Azor;
14 and to Azor was born Zadok; and to Zadok, Achim;
and to Achim, Eliud;
15 and to Eliud was born Eleazar; and to Eleazar, Matthan; and to Matthan, Jacob;
16 and to Jacob was born Joseph the husband of Mary, by
whom was born Jesus, [a]who is called [1]Christ.
17 Therefore all the generations from Abraham to David
are fourteen generations; and from David to the [a]deportation
to Babylon fourteen generations; and from the [a]deportation to
Babylon to *the time of* [1]Christ fourteen generations.
18 Now the birth of Jesus Christ was as follows. When His
[a]mother Mary had been betrothed to Joseph, before they
came together she was [b]found to be with child by the Holy
Spirit.
19 And Joseph her husband, being a righteous man, and
not wanting to disgrace her, desired [1]to put her away secretly.
20 But when he had considered this, behold, an angel of
the Lord appeared to him in a dream, saying, "Joseph, son of
David, do not be afraid to take Mary as your wife; for that
which has been [1]conceived in her is of the Holy Spirit.

1 [a]2 Sam. 7:12-16; Ps. 89:3f.; 132:11; Is. 9:6f.; 11:1; Luke 1:32, 69; John 7:42; Acts 13:23; Rom. 1:3; Rev. 22:16; Matt. 9:27 [b]Gen. 22:18; Gal. 3:16; Matt. 1:1-6: *Luke* 3:32-34

2 [1]Gr., *Judas.* Names of Old Testament characters will be given in their Old Testament form throughout this version.

3 [1]Gr., *Aram* [a]Matt. 1:3-6; Ruth 4:18-22; 1 Chr. 2:1-15

6 [a]2 Sam. 11:27; 12:24

7 [1]Gr., *Asaph* [a]1 Chr. 3:10ff.

8 [1]Gr., *Jehoram*

9 [1]Gr., *Joatham*

10 [1]Gr., *Amos*

11 [1]Or, *Jehoiachin* [a]2 Kin. 24:14f.; Jer. 27:20; Matt. 1:17

12 [1]Gr., *Salathiel* [a]2 Kin. 24:14f.; Jer. 27:20; Matt. 1:17

13 [1]Gr., *Abihud*

16 [1]I.e., the Messiah [a]Matt. 27:17, 22; Luke 2:11; John 4:25

17 [1]I.e., the Messiah [a]2 Kin. 24:14f.; Jer. 27:20; Matt. 1:11, 12

18 [a]Luke 1:27; Matt. 12:46 [b]Luke 1:35

19 [1]Or, *to divorce her*

20 [1]Gr., *begotten*

21 "And she will bear a Son; and [a]you shall call His name
Jesus, for it is He who [b]will save His people from their sins."
22 Now all this [1]took place that what was spoken by the
Lord through the prophet might be fulfilled, saying,
23 "[a]BEHOLD, THE VIRGIN SHALL BE WITH CHILD, AND SHALL
BEAR A SON, AND THEY SHALL CALL HIS NAME [1]IMMANUEL,"
which translated means, "GOD WITH US."
24 And Joseph arose from his sleep, and did as the angel of
the Lord commanded him, and [1]took *her* as his wife;
25 and [1]kept her a virgin until she gave birth to a Son; and
[a]he called His name Jesus.

CHAPTER 2

NOW after Jesus was [a]born in Bethlehem of Judea in the
days of [b]Herod the king, behold, [1]magi from the East arrived
in Jerusalem, saying,
2 "Where is He who has been born [a]King of the Jews? For
we saw [b]His star in the East, and have come to worship Him."
3 And when Herod the king heard it, he was troubled,
and all Jerusalem with him.
4 And gathering together all the chief priests and scribes
of the people, he *began* to inquire of them where [1]the Christ
was to be born.
5 And they said to him, "[a]In Bethlehem of Judea; for so
it has been written [1]by the prophet,
6 '[a]AND YOU, BETHLEHEM, LAND OF JUDAH;
ARE BY NO MEANS LEAST AMONG THE LEADERS OF JUDAH;
FOR OUT OF YOU SHALL COME FORTH A RULER,
WHO WILL [b]SHEPHERD MY PEOPLE ISRAEL.' "
7 Then Herod secretly called the magi, and ascertained
from them [1]the time the star appeared.
8 And he sent them to Bethlehem, and said, "Go and
make careful search for the Child; and when you have found
Him, report to me, that I too may come and worship Him."
9 And having heard the king, they went their way; and lo,
the star, which they had seen in the East, went on before them,
until it came and stood over where the Child was.
10 And when they saw the star, they rejoiced exceedingly,
with great joy.
11 And they came into the house and saw the Child with
[a]Mary His mother; and they fell down and worshiped Him;
and opening their treasures they presented to Him gifts of gold
and frankincense and myrrh.
12 And having been [a]warned *by God* in a dream not to
return to Herod, they departed for their own country by another
way.
13 Now when they had departed, behold, an angel of the
Lord *[a]appeared to Joseph in a dream, saying, "Arise and take
the Child and His mother, and flee to Egypt, and remain there
until I tell you; for Herod is going to search for the Child to
destroy Him."
14 And he arose and took the Child and His mother by
night, and departed for Egypt;
15 and was there until the death of Herod; that what was

21 [a]Luke 1:31; 2:21 [b]Luke 2:11; Acts 13:23; John 1:29

22 [1]Or, *has taken place*

23 [1]Or, *Emmanuel* [a]Is. 7:14

24 [1]Or, *took his wife to himself*

25 [1]Lit., *was not knowing her* [a]Matt. 1:21

1 [1]Pronounced may-ji, a caste of wise-men specializing in astrology, medicine and natural science [a]Luke 2:4-7 [b]Luke 1:5

2 [a]Jer. 23:5; 30:9; Zech. 9:9; Matt. 27:11; Luke 19:38; 23:38; John 1:49 [b]Num. 24:17; Rev. 22:16

4 [1]I.e., the Messiah

5 [1]Lit., *through* [a]John 7:42

6 [a]Mic. 5:2 [b]John 21:16

7 [1]Lit., *the time of the appearing star*

11 [a]Matt. 1:18; 12:46

12 [a]Matt. 2:22; Acts 10:22; Heb. 8:5; 11:7; Matt. 2:13, 19; Luke 2:26

13 [a]Matt. 2:19; 2:12

spoken by the Lord through the prophet might be fulfilled,
saying, "[a]OUT OF EGYPT DID I CALL [b]MY SON."
16 Then when Herod saw that he had been tricked by the
magi, he became very enraged, and sent and slew all the male
children who were in Bethlehem and in all its environs, from
two years old and under, according to the time which he had
ascertained from the magi.
17 Then that which was spoken through Jeremiah the
prophet was fulfilled, saying,
18 "[a]A VOICE WAS HEARD IN RAMAH,
WEEPING AND GREAT MOURNING,
RACHEL WEEPING FOR HER CHILDREN;
AND SHE REFUSED TO BE COMFORTED,
BECAUSE THEY WERE NO MORE."
19 But when Herod was dead, behold, an angel of the
Lord *[a]appeared in a dream to Joseph in Egypt, saying,
20 "Arise and take the Child and His mother, and go into
the land of Israel; for those who sought the Child's life are
dead."
21 And he arose and took the Child and His mother, and
came into the land of Israel.
22 But when he heard that Archelaus was reigning over
Judea in place of his father Herod, he was afraid to go there;
and being [a]warned *by God* in a dream, he departed for the
regions of Galilee,
23 and came and resided in a city called [a]Nazareth; that
what was spoken through the prophets might be fulfilled, "[b]He
shall be called a [c]Nazarene."

CHAPTER 3

NOW [a]in those days John the Baptist *[1]came, [2]preaching in
the [b]wilderness of Judea, saying,
2 "[a]Repent, for [b]the kingdom of [1]heaven [2]is at hand."
3 For this is the one referred to [1]by Isaiah the prophet,
saying,
"[a]THE VOICE OF ONE CRYING IN THE WILDERNESS,
'[b]MAKE READY THE WAY OF THE LORD,
MAKE HIS PATHS STRAIGHT!' "
4 Now John himself had [1][a]a garment of camel's hair, and
a leather belt about his waist; and his food was [b]locusts and
wild honey.
5 Then Jerusalem was going out to him, and all Judea,
and all [a]the district around the Jordan;
6 and they were being baptized by him in the Jordan
River, as they confessed their sins.
7 But when he saw many of the [a]Pharisees and [b]Saddu-
cees coming for baptism, he said to them, "You [c]brood of
vipers, who warned you to flee from [d]the wrath to come?
8 "Therefore bring forth fruit [a]in keeping with *your*
repentance;
9 and do not suppose that you can say to yourselves,
'[a]We have Abraham for our father;' for I say to you, that God
is able from these stones to raise up children to Abraham.
10 "And the axe is already laid at the root of the trees;

15 [a]Hos. 11:1 [b]Ex. 4:22f.

18 [a]Jer. 31:15

19 [a]Matt. 2:13; 2:12, 22

22 [a]Matt. 2:12

23 [a]Luke 1:26 [b]Is. 11:1 [c]Mark 1:24

1 [1]Or, *arrived* [2]Or, *proclaiming as a herald* [a]Matt. 3:1-12: *Mark 1:3-8; Luke* 3:2-17; John 1:6-8, 19-28 [b]Judg. 1:16; Josh. 15:61

2 [1]Lit., *of the heavens* [2]Lit., *has come near* [a]Matt. 4:17 [b]Dan. 2:44; Matt. 4:17; 6:10; 10:7; Mark 1:15; Luke 10:9f.; 11:20; 21:31; Matt. 4:23

3 [1]Lit., *through* [a]Is. 40:3 [b]John 1:23

4 [1]Lit., *his garment* [a]2 Kin. 1:8; Zech. 13:4 [b]Lev. 11:22

5 [a]Luke 3:3

7 [a]Matt. 23:13, 15; 16:1ff. [b]Matt. 22:23; 16:1ff; Acts 4:1; 5:17; 23:6ff. [c]Matt. 12:34; 23:33 [d]1 Thess. 1:10

8 [a]Acts 26:20

9 [a]John 8:33, 39

[a]every tree therefore that does not bear good fruit is cut down,
and thrown into the fire.
11 "As for me, [a]I baptize you [1]in water for repentance; but
He who is coming after me is mightier than I, and I am not
even fit to remove His sandals; [b]He Himself will baptize you
[1]with the Holy Spirit and fire.
12 "And His [a]winnowing fork is in His hand, and He will
thoroughly clean His threshing floor; and He will [b]gather His
wheat into the barn, but He will burn up the chaff with [c]un-
quenchable fire."
13 [a]Then Jesus *arrived [b]from Galilee at the Jordan *coming* to John, to be baptized by him.
14 But John tried to prevent Him, saying, "I have need to
be baptized by You, and do You come to me?"
15 But Jesus answering said to him, "Permit *it* at this time;
for in this way it is fitting for us to fulfill all righteousness."
Then he *permitted Him.
16 And after being baptized, Jesus went up immediately
from the water; and behold, the heavens were opened, and
[1a]he saw the Spirit of God descending as a dove, *and* coming
upon Him;
17 and behold, a voice out of the heavens, saying, "[a]This is
[1]My beloved Son, in whom I am well pleased."

Chapter 4

[a]THEN Jesus was led up by the Spirit into the wilderness to
be tempted by the devil.
2 And after He had [a]fasted forty days and forty nights,
He [1]then became hungry.
3 And [a]the tempter came and said to Him, "If You are
the Son of God, command that these stones become [1]bread."
4 But He answered and said, "It is written, '[a]MAN SHALL
NOT LIVE ON BREAD ALONE, BUT ON EVERY WORD THAT PROCEEDS
OUT OF THE MOUTH OF GOD.' "
5 Then the devil *took Him into [a]the holy city; and he
stood Him on the pinnacle of the temple,
6 and *said to Him, "If You are the Son of God throw
Yourself down; for it is written,
'[a]HE WILL GIVE HIS ANGELS CHARGE CONCERNING YOU;
AND ON THEIR HANDS THEY WILL BEAR YOU UP,
LEST YOU STRIKE YOUR FOOT AGAINST A STONE.' "
7 Jesus said to him, "[1]On the other hand, it is written,
'[a]YOU SHALL NOT [2]TEMPT THE LORD YOUR GOD.' "
8 Again, the devil *took Him to a very high mountain,
and *showed Him all the kingdoms of the world, and their
glory;
9 and he said to Him, "All these things will I give You, if
You fall down and worship me."
10 Then Jesus *said to him, "Begone, Satan! For it is
written, '[a]YOU SHALL WORSHIP THE LORD YOUR GOD, AND [1]SERVE
HIM ONLY.' "
11 Then the devil *left Him; and behold, [a]angels came
and *began* to minister to Him.
12 Now when He heard that [a]John had [1]been taken into
custody, [b]He withdrew into Galilee;

10 [a]Matt. 7:19
11 [1]The Greek here can be translated *in, with* or *by* [a]John 1:26 [b]John 1:33
12 [a]Luke 3:17; Is. 30:24 [b]Matt. 13:30 [c]Mark 9:43, 48
13 [a]Matt. 3:13-17: *Mark 1:9-11; Luke 3:21, 22;* John 1:31-34 [b]Matt. 2:22
16 [1]Or, *He* [a]John 1:32
17 [1]Lit., *My son, the Beloved* [a]Matt. 12:18; 17:5; Mark 9:7; Luke 9:35; Is. 42:1
1 [a]Matt. 4:1-11: *Mark 1:12, 13; Luke 4:1-13*
2 [1]Lit., *later, afterward* [a]Ex. 34:28; 1 Kin. 19:8
3 [1]Lit., *loaves* [a]1 Thess. 3:5
4 [a]Deut. 8:3
5 [a]Matt. 27:53; Neh. 11:1, 18; Dan. 9:24
6 [a]Ps. 91:11-12
7 [1]Lit., *again* [2]Or, *put to the test* [a]Deut. 6:16
10 [1]Or, *fulfill religious duty to Him* [a]Deut. 6:13
11 [a]Matt. 26:53; Luke 22:43
12 [1]Lit., *been delivered up* [a]Matt. 14:3; Mark 1:14; Luke 3:20; John 3:24 [b]Mark 1:14; Luke 4:14; John 1:43; 2:11

13 and leaving Nazareth, He came and [a]settled in Capernaum, which is by the sea, in the region of Zebulun and
Naphtali.
14 *This was* to fulfill what was spoken through Isaiah the
prophet, saying,
15 "[a]THE LAND OF ZEBULUN AND THE LAND OF NAPHTALI,
[1]BY THE WAY OF THE SEA, BEYOND THE JORDAN, GALILEE
OF THE [2]GENTILES.
16 "[a]THE PEOPLE WHO WERE SITTING IN DARKNESS SAW A
GREAT LIGHT,
AND TO THOSE WHO WERE SITTING IN THE LAND AND
SHADOW OF DEATH,
UPON THEM A LIGHT DAWNED."
17 [a]From that time Jesus began to [1]preach and say, "[b]Re-
pent; for the kingdom of heaven is at hand."
18 [a]And walking by [b]the sea of Galilee, He saw two brothers, [c]Simon who was called Peter, and Andrew his brother,
casting a net into the sea; for they were fishermen.
19 And He *said to them, "[1]Follow Me, and I will make
you fishers of men."
20 And they immediately left the nets, and followed Him.
21 And going on from there He saw two other brothers,
[1a]James the *son* of Zebedee, and [2]John his brother, in the boat
with Zebedee their father, mending their nets; and He called
them.
22 And they immediately left the boat and their father,
and followed Him.
23 And *Jesus* was going about [a]in all Galilee, [b]teaching in
their synagogues, and [c]proclaiming the [1]gospel of the kingdom, and [d]healing every kind of disease and every kind of
sickness among the people.
24 And the news about Him went out [a]into all Syria; and
they brought to Him all who were ill, taken with various diseases and pains, [b]demoniacs, [1c]epileptics, [d]paralytics; and He
healed them.
25 And great multitudes [a]followed Him from Galilee and
[b]Decapolis and Jerusalem and Judea and *from* [c]beyond the
Jordan.

[a] CHAPTER 5

AND when He saw the multitudes, He went up on [b]the
[1]mountain; and after He sat down, His disciples came to Him.
2 And [a]opening His mouth He *began* to teach them,
saying,
3 "[a]Blessed are the poor in spirit, for [b]theirs is the kingdom of heaven.
4 "Blessed are [a]those who mourn, for they shall be
comforted.
5 "Blessed are [a]the [1]gentle, for they shall inherit the earth.
6 "Blessed are [a]those who hunger and thirst for righteousness, for they shall be satisfied.
7 "Blessed are the merciful, for they shall receive mercy.
8 "Blessed are [a]the pure in heart, for [b]they shall see God.
9 "Blessed are the peacemakers, for [a]they shall be called
sons of God.

13 [a]Mark 1:21; 2:1; Luke 4:23, 31; John 2:12; 4:46f.; Matt. 11:23

15 [1]Or, *toward the sea* [2]Or, *nations* [a]Is. 9:1

16 [a]Is. 9:2

17 [1]Or, *proclaim* [a]Mark 1:14, 15 [b]Matt. 3:2

18 [a]Matt. 4:18-22: *Mark 1:16-20;* Luke 5:2-11; John 1:40-42 [b]Matt. 15:29; Mark 7:31; John 6:1; Luke 5:1 [c]Matt. 10:2; 16:18; John 1:40, 42

19 [1]Lit., *come here after Me*

21 [1]Or, *Jacob* [2]Gr., *Joannes,* Heb., *Johanan* [a]Matt. 10:2; 20:20

23 [1]Or, *good news* [a]Mark 1:39; Luke 4:15, 44 [b]Matt. 9:35; 13:54; Mark 1:21; 6:2; Luke 4:15; 6:6; 13:10; John 6:59; 18:20; Mark 10:1 [c]Matt. 9:35; Mark 1:14; Matt. 24:14; Luke 4:43; 8:1; 16:16; Acts 20:25; 28:31; Matt. 3:2 [d]Matt. 8:16; 9:35; 14:14; 15:30; 19:2; 21:14; Mark 1:34; 3:10; Luke 4:40; 7:21; Acts 10:38

24 [1]Lit., *moon-smitten* [a]Luke 2:2; Acts 15:23; 18:18; 20:3; 21:3; Gal. 1:21; Mark 7:26 [b]Matt. 8:16, 28, 33; 9:32; 12:22; 15:22; Mark 1:32; 5:15, 16, 18; Luke 8:36; John 10:21 [c]Matt. 17:15 [d]Matt. 8:6; 9:2, 6; Mark 2:3, 4, 5, 9; Luke 5:24

25 [a]Mark 3:7, 8; Luke 6:17 [b]Mark 5:20; 7:31 [c]Matt. 4:15

1 [1]Or, *hill* [a]Matt. 5-7: Luke 6:20-49 [b]Mark 3:13; Luke 9:28; John 6:3, 15; Luke 6:17

2 [a]Acts 8:35; 10:34; 18:14; Matt. 13:35

3 [a]Matt. 5:3-12; Luke 6:20-23 [b]Matt. 5:10; 19:14; 25:34; Mark 10:14; Luke 6:20; 22:29f.

4 [a]Is. 61:2; John 16:20; Rev. 7:17

5 [1]Or, *humble, meek* [a]Ps. 37:11

6 [a]Is. 55:1, 2; John 4:14; 6:48ff.; 7:37

8 [a]Ps. 24:4 [b]Heb. 12:14; 1 John 3:2; Rev. 22:4

9 [a]Rom. 8:14; Matt. 5:45; Luke 6:35

10 "Blessed are those who have been [a]persecuted for the
sake of righteousness, for [b]theirs is the kingdom of heaven.
11 "Blessed are you when *men* [a]revile you, and persecute
you, and say all kinds of evil against you falsely, on account of
Me.
12 "Rejoice, and be glad, for your reward in heaven is great,
for [a]so they persecuted the prophets who were before you.
13 "You are the salt of the earth; but [a]if the salt has become tasteless, how will it be made salty *again*? It is good for
nothing any more, except to be thrown out and trampled
under foot by men.
14 "You are [a]the light of the world. A city set on a [1]hill
cannot be hidden.
15 "[a]Nor do *men* light a lamp, and put it under the peck-
measure, but on the lampstand; and it gives light to all who are
in the house.
16 "Let your light shine before men in such a way that they
may [a]see your good works, and [b]glorify your Father who is in
heaven.
17 "Do not think that I came to abolish the Law or the
Prophets; I did not come to abolish, but to fulfill.
18 "For truly I say to you, [a]until heaven and earth pass
away, not the [1]smallest letter or stroke shall pass away from the
Law, until all is accomplished.
19 "Whoever then annuls one of the least of these commandments, and so teaches [1]others, shall be called least in the
kingdom of heaven; but whoever [2]keeps and teaches *them*, he
shall be called great in the kingdom of heaven.
20 "For I say to you, that unless your righteousness surpasses *that* of the scribes and Pharisees, you shall not enter the
kingdom of heaven.
21 "[a]You have heard that [1]the ancients were told, '[b]You
shall not commit murder;' and 'Whoever commits murder
shall be [2]liable to [c]the court;'
22 but I say to you that every one who is angry with his
brother[1] shall be [2]guilty before [a]the court; and whoever shall
say to his brother, '[3]Raca,' shall be [2]guilty before [4b]the supreme
court; and whoever shall say, 'You fool,' shall be [2]guilty
enough to go into the [5c]hell of fire.
23 "If therefore you are presenting your [1]offering at the
altar, and there remember that your brother has something
against you,
24 leave your [1]offering there before the altar, and go your
way, first be reconciled to your brother, and then come and
present your [1]offering.
25 "[a]Make friends quickly with your opponent at law while
you are with him on the way; in order that your opponent may
not deliver you to the judge, and the judge to the officer, and
you be thrown into prison.
26 "Truly I say to you, you shall not come out of there,
until you have paid up the last [1]cent.
27 "[a]You have heard that it was said, '[b]YOU SHALL NOT COM-
MIT ADULTERY;'
28 but I say to you, that every one who looks on a woman
to lust for her has committed adultery with her already in his
heart.

10 [a]1 Pet. 3:14 [b]Matt. 5:3; 19:14; 25:34; Mark 10:14; Luke 6:20; 22:29f.

11 [a]1 Pet. 4:14

12 [a]2 Chr. 36:16; Matt. 23:37; Acts 7:52; 1 Thess. 2:15; James 5:10; Heb. 11:33ff.

13 [a]Mark 9:50; Luke 14:34f.

14 [1]Or, *mountain* [a]John 8:12

15 [a]Mark 4:21; Luke 8:16; 11:33

16 [a]1 Pet. 2:12 [b]Matt. 9:8

18 [1]Lit., *one iota* or (yodh) or *one projection of a letter* (serif) [a]Luke 16:17; Matt. 24:35

19 [1]Lit., *the men* [2]Lit., *does*

21 [1]Lit., *it was said to the ancients* [2]Or, *guilty before* [a]Matt. 5:27, 33, 38, 43 [b]Ex. 20:13; Deut. 5:17 [c]Deut. 16:18; 2 Chr. 19:5f.

22 [1]Some mss. insert here: *without cause* [2]Or, *liable to* [3]Aramaic for *empty-head* or, *good for nothing* [4]Lit., *the Sanhedrin* [5]Gr. *Gehenna* [a]Deut. 16:18; 2 Chr. 19:5f. [b]Matt. 10:17; 26:59; Mark 13:9; 14:55; 15:1; Luke 22:66; John 11:47; Acts 4:15; 5:21; 6:12; 22:30; 23:1; 24:20 [c]Matt. 5:29f.; 10:28; 18:9; 23:15, 33; Mark 9:43ff.; Luke 12:5; James 3:6

23 [1]Or, *gift*

24 [1]Or, *gift*

25 [a]Luke 12:58

26 [1]Lit., *quadrans* (equaling two lepta or mites), I.e., 1/64 of a denarius

27 [a]Matt. 5:21, 33, 38, 43 [b]Ex. 20:14; Deut. 5:18

29 "And [a]if your right eye makes you [1]stumble, tear it out,
and throw it from you; for it is better for you that one of the
parts of your body perish, [2]than for your whole body to be
thrown into [3b]hell.
30 "And [a]if your right hand makes you [1]stumble, cut it off,
and throw it from you; for it is better for you that one of the
parts of your body perish, [2]than for your whole body to go into
[3b]hell.
31 "And it was said, '[a]WHOEVER [1]DIVORCES HIS WIFE, LET
HIM GIVE HER A CERTIFICATE OF DISMISSAL;'
32 [a]but I say to you that every one who divorces his wife,
except for *the* cause of unchastity, makes her commit adultery;
and whoever marries a divorced woman commits adultery.
33 "Again, [a]you have heard that [1]the ancients were told,
'[2b]YOU SHALL NOT [3]MAKE FALSE VOWS, BUT SHALL FULFILL YOUR
[4]VOWS TO THE LORD.'
34 "But I say to you, [a]make no oath at all; either by heaven,
for it is [b]THE THRONE OF GOD;
35 or by the earth, for it is the [a]footstool of His feet; or [1]by
Jerusalem, for it is [b]THE CITY OF THE GREAT KING.
36 "Nor shall you make an oath by your head, for you
cannot make one hair white or black.
37 "But let your statement be, 'Yes, yes' *or* 'No, no;' and
anything beyond these is of [1a]evil.
38 "[a]You have heard that it was said, '[b]AN EYE FOR AN EYE,
AND A TOOTH FOR A TOOTH.'
39 "But I say to you, do not resist him who is evil; but
[a]whoever slaps you on your right cheek, turn to him the other
also.
40 "And if any one wants to sue you, and take your [1]shirt,
let him have your [2]coat also.
41 "And whoever shall force you to go one mile, go with
him two.
42 "[a]Give to him who asks of you, and do not turn away
from him who wants to borrow from you.
43 "[a]You have heard that it was said, '[b]YOU SHALL LOVE
YOUR NEIGHBOR, AND HATE YOUR ENEMY.'
44 "But I say to you, [a]love your enemies, and pray for those
who persecute you;
45 in order that you may [1]be [a]sons of your Father who is in
heaven; for He causes His sun to rise on *the* evil and *the* good,
and sends rain on *the* righteous and *the* unrighteous.
46 "For [a]if you love those who love you, what reward have
you? Do not even the [1]tax gatherers do the same?
47 "And if you greet your brothers only, what do you do
more *than others*? Do not even the Gentiles do the same?
48 "Therefore [a]you are to be perfect, as your heavenly Father
is perfect.

CHAPTER 6

"BEWARE of practicing your righteousness before men [a]to
be noticed by them; otherwise you have no reward with your
Father who is in heaven.
2 "When therefore you [1]give alms, do not sound a trumpet before you, as the hypocrites do in the synagogues and in

29 [1]I.e., cause to sin [2]Lit., *not your whole body* [3]Gr., *Gehenna* [a]Matt. 18:9; Mark 9:47; Matt. 17:27 [b]Matt. 5:22

30 [1]I.e., cause to sin [2]Lit., *not your whole body* [3]Gr., *Gehenna* [a]Matt. 18:8; Mark 9:43; Matt. 17:27 [b]Matt. 5:22

31 [1]Lit., *puts away* [a]Deut. 24:1, 3

32 [a]Matt. 19:9; Mark 10:11f.; Luke 16:18; 1 Cor. 7:11f.

33 [1]Lit., *it was said to the ancients* [2]*you* and *your* are singular here [3]Or, *break your vows* [4]Lit., *your oaths* [a]Matt. 5:21, 27, 38, 43; 23:16ff. [b]Lev. 19:12; Num. 30:2; Deut. 23:21

34 [a]James 5:12 [b]Matt. 23:22; Is. 66:1

35 [1]Or, *toward* [a]Is. 66:1; Acts 7:49 [b]Ps. 48:2

37 [1]Or, *from the evil one* [a]Matt. 6:13; 13:19, 38; John 17:15; 2 Thess. 3:3; 1 John 2:13f.; 3:12; 5:18f.

38 [a]Matt. 5:21, 27, 33, 43 [b]Ex. 21:24; Lev. 24:20; Deut. 19:21

39 [a]Matt. 5:39-42: *Luke 6:29, 30*; 1 Cor. 6:7

40 [1]*Tunic* or garment worn next to the body [2]*Cloak* or outer garment

42 [a]Luke 6:34f.

43 [a]Matt. 5:21, 27, 33, 38 [b]Lev. 19:18

44 [a]Luke 6:27f.; Luke 23:34; Acts 7:60

45 [1]Or, *show yourselves to be* [a]Matt. 5:9

46 [1]Publicans who collected Roman taxes on commission [a]Luke 6:32

48 [a]Lev. 19:2

1 [a]Matt. 6:5, 16; 23:5

2 [1]Or, *do an act of charity*

the streets, that they [a]may be honored by men. [b]Truly I say to
you, they have their reward in full.
3 "But when you give alms, do not let your left hand know
what your right hand is doing;
4 that your [1]alms may be in secret; and [a]your Father who
sees in secret will repay you.
5 "And when you pray, you are not to be as the hypocrites;
for they love to [a]stand and pray in the synagogues and on the
street corners, [1b]in order to be seen by men. [c]Truly I say to
you, they have their reward in full.
6 "But you, when you pray, [a]GO INTO YOUR INNER ROOM,
AND WHEN YOU HAVE SHUT YOUR DOOR, pray to your Father who
is in secret, and [b]your Father who sees in secret will repay you.
7 "And when you are praying, do not use meaningless
repetition, as the Gentiles do, for they suppose that they will
be heard for their [a]many words.
8 "Therefore do not be like them; for [a]your Father knows
what you need, before you ask Him.
9 "[a]Pray, then, in this way:
'Our Father who art in [1]heaven,
Hallowed be Thy name.
10 '[a]Thy kingdom come.
Thy will be done,
On earth as it is in heaven.
11 '[a]Give us this day [1]our daily bread.
12 'And forgive us our [1]debts, as we also have forgiven
our debtors.
13 'And do not lead us into temptation, but deliver us
from [1a]evil. [2][For Thine is the kingdom, and the
power, and the glory, forever. Amen].'
14 "[a]For if you forgive men for their transgressions, your
heavenly Father will also forgive you.
15 "But if you do not forgive men, then your Father will
not forgive your transgressions.
16 "And [a]whenever you fast, do not put on a gloomy face as
the hypocrites *do;* for they [1]neglect their appearance in order
to be seen fasting by men. [b]Truly I say to you, they have their
reward in full.
17 "But you, when you fast, anoint your head, and wash
your face;
18 so that you may not be seen fasting by men, but by
your Father who is in secret; and your [a]Father who sees in
secret will repay you.
19 "Do not lay up for yourselves treasures upon earth,
where moth and rust destroy, and where thieves break in and
steal;
20 but lay up for yourselves [a]treasures in heaven, where
neither moth nor rust destroys, and where thieves do not break
in or steal;
21 for [a]where your treasure is, there will your heart be also.
22 "[a]The lamp of the body is the eye; if therefore your eye
is [1]clear, your whole body will be full of light.
23 "But if [a]your eye is bad, your whole body will be full of
darkness. If therefore the light that is in you is darkness, how
great is the darkness!
24 "[a]No one can serve two masters; for either he will hate

2 [a]Matt. 6:5, 16; 23:5 [b]Matt. 6:5, 16; Luke 6:24
4 [1]Or, *deeds of charity* [a]Matt. 6:6, 18
5 [1]Lit., *to be apparent to men* [a]Mark 11:25; Luke 18:11, 13 [b]Matt. 6:1, 16 [c]Matt. 6:2, 16; Luke 6:24
6 [a]Is. 26:20 [b]Matt. 6:4, 18
7 [a]1 Kin. 18:26f.
8 [a]Matt. 6:32
9 [1]Lit., *the heavens* [a]Matt. 6:9-13; *Luke 11:2-4*
10 [a]Matt. 3:2
11 [1]Or, *our bread for the coming day* or, *our needful bread* [a]Prov. 30:8
12 [1]I.e., moral debts or sins
13 [1]Or, *the evil one* [2]This clause omitted in the earliest manuscripts [a]Matt. 5:37
14 [a]Mark 11:25f.; Matt. 18:35
16 [1]Lit., *render their faces unrecognizable* (sc., by neglect) [a]Is. 58:5 [b]Matt. 6:2
18 [a]Matt. 6:4, 6
20 [a]Matt. 19:21; Luke 12:33; 1 Tim. 6:19
21 [a]Luke 12:34
22 [1]Or, *healthy* [a]Matt. 6:22, 23: *Luke 11:34, 35*
23 [a]Matt. 20:15; Mark 7:22
24 [a]Luke 16:13

the one and love the other, or he will hold to one and despise
the other. You cannot serve God and [1b]Mammon.
25 "[a]For this reason I say to you, [1]do not be [b]anxious for
your life, *as to* what you shall eat, or what you shall drink; nor
for your body, *as to* what you shall put on. Is not life more
than food, and the body than clothing?
26 "[a]Look at the birds of the [1]air, that they do not sow,
neither do they reap, nor gather into barns; and *yet* your heavenly Father feeds them. Are you not worth much more than
they?
27 "And which of you by being [a]anxious can [b]add a *single*
[1]cubit to his [2]life's span?
28 "And why are you [a]anxious about clothing? Observe
how the lilies of the field grow; they do not toil nor do they
spin,
29 yet I say to you that even [a]Solomon in all his glory did
not clothe himself like one of these.
30 "But if God so arrays the grass of the field, which is *alive*
today and tomorrow is thrown into the furnace, *will He* not
much more *do so for* you, [a]O men of little faith?
31 "Do not be [a]anxious then, saying, 'What shall we eat?'
or, 'What shall we drink?' or, 'With what shall we clothe
ourselves?'
32 "For all these things the Gentiles eagerly seek; for [a]your
heavenly Father knows that you need all these things.
33 "But [1]seek first [2]His kingdom, and His righteousness;
and [a]all these things shall be [3]added to you.
34 "Therefore do not be [a]anxious for tomorrow; for tomorrow will [1]care for itself. *Each* day has enough trouble of its
own.

Chapter 7

"[1a]Do not judge lest you be judged *yourselves.*
2 "For in the way you judge, you will be judged; and [1a]by
your standard of measure, it shall be measured to you.
3 "And why do you look at the speck in your brother's eye,
but do not notice the log that is in your own eye?
4 "Or how [1]can you say to your brother, 'Let me take the
speck out of your eye,' and behold, the log is in your own eye?
5 "You hypocrite, first take the log out of your own eye;
and then you will see clearly *enough* to take the speck out of
your brother's eye.
6 "Do not give what is holy to dogs, and do not throw
your pearls before swine, lest they trample them under their
feet, and turn and tear you to pieces.
7 "[1a]Ask, and [b]it shall be given to you; [2]seek, and you shall
find; [3]knock, and it shall be opened to you.
8 "For every one who asks receives; and he who seeks
finds; and to him who knocks it shall be opened.
9 "Or what man is there among you, [1]when his son shall
ask him for a loaf, [2]will give him a stone?
10 "Or [1]if he shall ask for a fish, he will not give him a
snake, will he?
11 "If you then, being evil, know how to give good gifts to

24 [1]Or, *riches* [b]Luke 16:9, 11, 13

25 [1]Or, *stop being anxious* [a]Matt. 6:25-33: *Luke 12:22-31* [b]Matt. 6:27, 28, 31, 34; Luke 10:41; 12:11, 22; Phil. 4:6; 1 Pet. 5:7

26 [1]Lit., *heaven* [a]Matt. 10:29ff.

27 [1]I.e., approximately 18 inches [2]Or, *height* [a]Matt. 6:25, 28, 31, 34; Luke 10:41; 12:11, 22; Phil. 4:6; 1 Pet. 5:7 [b]Ps. 39:5

28 [a]Matt. 6:25, 27, 31, 34; Luke 10:41; 12:11, 22; Phil. 4:6; 1 Pet. 5:7

29 [a]1 Kin. 10:4-7

30 [a]Matt. 8:26; 14:31; 16:8

31 [a]Matt. 6:25, 27, 28, 34; Luke 10:41; 12:11, 22; Phil. 4:6; 1 Pet. 5:7

32 [a]Matt. 6:8

33 [1]Or, *continually seek* [2]Or, *the kingdom* [3]Or, *provided* [a]Matt. 19:28; Mark 10:29f.; Luke 18:29f.; 1 Tim. 4:8

34 [1]Or., *will worry about itself* [a]Matt. 6:25, 27, 28, 31; Luke 10:41; 12:11, 22; Phil. 4:6; 1 Pet. 5:7

1 [1]Or, *do not pass judgments* [a]Matt. 7:1-5: *Luke 6:37f., 41f.*

2 [1]Lit., *by what measure you measure* [a]Mark 4:24; Luke 6:38

4 [1]Lit., *will*

7 [1]Or, *Keep asking* [2]Or, *keep seeking* [3]Or, *keep knocking* [a]Matt. 7:7-11: *Luke 11:9-13* [b]Matt. 18:19; 21:22; John 14:13; 15:7, 16; 16:23f.; James 1:5f.; 1 John 3:22; 5:14f.; Mark 11:24

9 [1]Lit., *whom* [2]Lit., *he will not give him a stone, will he?*

10 [1]Lit., *also*

your children, how much more shall your Father who is in
heaven give what is good to those who ask Him!
12 "[a]Therefore whatever you want others to do for you, [1]do
so for them; for [b]this is the Law and the Prophets.
13 "[a]Enter by the narrow gate; for the gate is wide, and the
way is broad that leads to destruction, and many are those who
enter by it.
14 "For the gate is small, and the way is narrow that leads
to life, and few are those who find it.
15 "Beware of the [a]false prophets, who come to you in
sheep's clothing, but inwardly are [b]ravenous wolves.
16 "You will [1]know them [a]by their fruits. [2]Grapes are not
gathered from thornbushes, nor figs from thistles, are they?
17 "Even so every good tree bears good fruit; but the rotten
tree bears bad fruit.
18 "A good tree cannot produce bad fruit, nor can a rotten
tree produce good fruit.
19 "[a]Every tree that does not bear good fruit is cut down,
and thrown into the fire.
20 "So then, you will [1]know them [a]by their fruits.
21 "[a]Not every one who says to Me, 'Lord, Lord,' will enter
the kingdom of heaven; but he who does the will of My Father,
who is in heaven.
22 "[a]Many will say to Me on [b]that day, 'Lord, Lord, did we
not prophesy in Your name, and in Your name cast out demons, and in Your name perform many [1]miracles?'
23 "And then I will declare to them, 'I never knew you;
[a]DEPART FROM ME, YOU WHO PRACTICE LAWLESSNESS.'
24 "Therefore [a]every one who hears these words of Mine,
and [1]acts upon them, [2]may be compared to a wise man, who
built his house upon the rock;
25 and the rain descended, and the [1]floods came, and the
winds blew, and burst against that house; and *yet* it did not
fall; for it had been founded upon the rock.
26 "And every one who hears these words of Mine, and
does not [1]act upon them, will be like a foolish man, who built
his house upon the sand.
27 "And the rain descended, and the [1]floods came, and the
winds blew, and burst against that house; and it fell, and great
was its fall."
28 [1a]The result was that when Jesus had finished these
words, [b]the multitudes were amazed at His teaching;
29 for He was teaching them as *one* having authority, and
not as their scribes.

CHAPTER 8

AND when He had come down from the mountain, great
multitudes followed Him.
2 And behold, a leper [a]came to Him, and [1b]bowed down
to Him, saying, "Lord, if You are willing, You can make me
clean."
3 And stretching out His hand, He touched him, saying,
"I am willing; be cleansed." And immediately his leprosy was
cleansed.
4 And Jesus *said to him, "[a]See that you tell no one; but

12 [1]Or, *you too do so* [a]Luke 6:31; [b]Matt. 22:40; Gal. 5:14; Rom. 13:8ff.

13 [a]Luke 13:24

15 [a]Matt. 24:11, 24; Mark 13:22; Luke 6:26; Acts 13:6; 2 Pet. 2:1; 1 John 4:1; Rev. 16:13; 19:20; 20:10 [b]Ezek. 22:27; Acts 20:29; John 10:12

16 [1]Or, *recognize* [2]Lit., *they do not gather* [a]Matt. 7:20; 12:33; Luke 6:44; James 3:12

19 [a]Matt. 3:10; Luke 13:7

20 [1]Or, *recognize* [a]Matt. 7:16; 12:33; Luke 6:44; James 3:12

21 [a]Luke 6:46

22 [1]Or, *works of power* [a]Matt. 25:11f.; Luke 13:25ff. [b]Matt. 10:15

23 [a]Matt. 25:41; Luke 13:27; Ps. 6:8

24 [1]Lit., *does* [2]Lit., *will be compared to* [a]Matt. 7:24-27: *Luke 6:47-49*; James 1:22-25

25 [1]Lit., *rivers*

26 [1]Lit., *do*

27 [1]Lit., *rivers*

28 [1]Lit., *And it came to pass* [a]Matt. 11:1; 13:53; 19:1; 26:1 [b]Matt. 13:54; 22:33; Mark 1:22; 6:2; 11:18; Luke 4:32; John 7:46

2 [1]Or, *worshiped* [a]Matt. 8:2-4: *Mark 1:40-44; Luke 5:12-14* [b]Matt. 9:18; 15:25; 18:26; 20:20; John 9:38; Acts 10:25

4 [a]Matt. 9:30; 12:16; 17:9; Mark 1:44; 3:12; 5:43; 7:36; 8:30; 9:9; Luke 4:41; 8:56; 9:21

[b]go, [c]SHOW YOURSELF TO THE PRIEST, and present the [1]offering
that Moses prescribed, for a testimony to them."
5 And [a]when He had entered Capernaum, a centurion
came to Him, entreating Him,
6 and saying, "[1]Sir, my [2]servant is [3]lying [a]paralyzed at
home, [4]suffering great pain."
7 And He *said to him, "I will come and heal him."
8 But the centurion answered and said, "[1]Lord, I am not
qualified for You to come under my roof, but [2]just say the
word, and my [3]servant will be healed.
9 "For I too am a man under authority, with soldiers under
me; and I say to this one, 'Go!' and he goes, and to another,
'Come!' and he comes, and to my slave, 'Do this!' and he
does *it*."
10 Now when Jesus heard *this*, He marveled, and said to
those who were following, "Truly I say to you, I have not
found such great faith [1]with anyone in Israel.
11 "And I say to you, that many [a]shall come from east and
west, and [1]recline *at table* with Abraham, and Isaac, and Jacob,
in the kingdom of heaven;
12 but [a]the sons of the kingdom shall be cast out into [b]the
outer darkness; in that place [c]there shall be weeping and gnashing
of teeth."
13 And Jesus said to the centurion, "Go your way; let it be
done to you [a]as you have believed." And the [1]servant was
healed that *very* hour.
14 [a]And when Jesus had come to Peter's [1]home, He saw
his mother-in-law lying [2]sick in bed with a fever.
15 And He touched her hand, and the fever left her; and
she arose, and began to [1]wait on Him.
16 And when evening had come, they brought to Him
many [a]who were demon-possessed; and He cast out the spirits
with a word, and [b]healed all who were ill;
17 in order that what was spoken through Isaiah the
prophet might be fulfilled, saying, "[a]HE HIMSELF TOOK OUR
INFIRMITIES, AND [1]CARRIED AWAY OUR DISEASES."
18 Now when Jesus saw a crowd around Him, [a]He gave
orders to depart to the other side.
19 [a]And a certain scribe came and said to Him, "Teacher,
I will follow You wherever You go."
20 And Jesus *said to him, "The foxes have holes, and the
birds of the [1]air *have* [2]nests; but [a]the Son of Man has nowhere
to lay His head."
21 And another of the disciples said to Him, "Lord, permit
me first to go and bury my father."
22 But Jesus *said to him, "[a]Follow Me; and allow the
dead to bury their own dead."
23 [a]And when He got into the boat, His disciples followed
Him.
24 And behold, there arose [1]a great storm in the sea, so
that the boat was covered with the waves; but He Himself was
asleep.
25 And they came to *Him*, and awoke Him, saying, "Save
us, Lord; we are perishing!"
26 And He *said to them, "Why are you timid, [a]you men

4 [1]Or, *gift* [b]Mark 1:44; Luke 5:14; 17:14 [c]Lev. 13:49; 14:2ff.

5 [a]Matt. 8:5-13: *Luke 7:1-10*

6 [1]Or, *Lord* [2]Lit., *boy* [3]Lit., *throwing* [4]Lit., *fearfully tormented* [a]Matt. 4:24

8 [1]Or, *Sir* [2]Lit., *say with a word* [3]Lit., *boy*

10 [1]Some manuscripts read, *not even in Israel*

11 [1]Or, *dine* [a]Luke 13:29; Is. 49:12; 59:19; Mal. 1:11

12 [a]Matt. 13:38 [b]Matt. 22:13; 25:30 [c]Matt. 13:42, 50; 22:13; 24:51; 25:30; Luke 13:28

13 [1]Lit., *boy* [a]Matt. 9:29; 9:22

14 [1]Or, *house* [2]Lit., *thrown* [a]Matt. 8:14-16: *Mark 1:29-34; Luke 4:38-41*

15 [1]Or, *serve*

16 [a]Matt. 4:24 [b]Matt. 4:23; 8:33

17 [1]Or, *removed* [a]Is. 53:4

18 [a]Mark 4:35; Luke 8:22

19 [a]Matt. 8:19-22: *Luke 9:57-60*

20 [1]Or, *sky* [2]Gr., *roosting-places* [a]Often; for example, Matt. 9:6; 12:8, 32, 40; 13:41; 16:13, 27f.; 17:9; 19:28; 26:64; Mark 8:38; Luke 12:8; 18:8; 21:36; John 1:51; 3:13f.; 6:27; 12:34; Acts 7:56; Dan. 7:13

22 [a]Matt. 9:9; Mark 2:14; Luke 9:59; John 1:43; 21:19

23 [a]Matt. 8:23-27: *Mark 4:36-41; Luke 8:22-25*

24 [1]Lit., *a shaking*

26 [a]Matt. 6:30; 14:31; 16:8

of little faith?" Then He arose, and rebuked the winds and the
sea; and [1]it became perfectly calm.
27 And the men marveled, saying, "What kind of a man is
this, that even the winds and the sea obey Him?"
28 [a]And when He had come to the other side into the
country of the Gadarenes, two men who were [b]demon-
possessed met Him as they were coming out of the tombs;
they were so exceedingly violent that no one could pass by that
road.
29 And behold, they cried out, saying, "[a]What do we have
to do with You, Son of God? Have you come here to torment
us before [1]the time?"
30 Now there was at a distance from them a herd of many
swine feeding.
31 And the demons *began* to entreat Him, saying, "If You
are *going to* cast us out, send us into the herd of swine."
32 And He said to them, "Begone!" And they came out,
and went into the swine, and behold, the whole herd rushed
down the steep bank into the sea, and perished in the waters.
33 And the herdsmen fled, and went away to the city, and
reported everything, [1]including the *incident* of the demo-
niacs.
34 And behold, the whole city came out to meet Jesus;
and when they saw Him, they entreated *Him* to depart from
their region.

Chapter 9

AND getting into a boat, He crossed over, and came to [a]His
own city.
2 [a]And behold, they were bringing to Him a [b]paralytic,
[1]lying on a bed; and Jesus seeing their faith said to the paralytic, "[c]Take courage, *My* [2]son, [d]your sins [3]are forgiven."
3 And behold, some of the scribes said [1]to themselves,
"This *fellow* blasphemes."
4 And Jesus [a]knowing their thoughts said, "Why are you
thinking evil in your hearts?
5 "For which is easier, to say, '[a]Your sins are [1]forgiven,' or
to say, 'Rise, and walk'?
6 "But in order that you may know that [a]the Son of Man
has authority on earth to forgive sins"—then He *said to the
[b]paralytic, "Rise, take up your bed, and go home."
7 And he rose, and [1]went to his home.
8 But when the multitudes saw *this*, they [1]were filled
with awe, and [a]glorified God, who had given such authority to
men.
9 [a]And as Jesus passed on from there, He saw a man,
called [b]Matthew, sitting [1]in the tax office; and He *said to
him, "[c]Follow Me!" And he rose, and followed Him.
10 And it happened that as He was reclining *at table* in
the house, behold many [1]tax-gatherers and [2]sinners came and
[3]joined Jesus and His disciples *at the table*.
11 And when the Pharisees saw *this*, they said to His disciples, "[a]Why does your Teacher eat with the tax-gatherers
and sinners?"

26 [1]Lit., *a great calm occurred*

28 [a]Matt. 8:28-34: *Mark 5:1-17; Luke 8:26-37* [b]Matt. 4:24

29 [1]I.e., the appointed time of judgment [a]Judg. 11:12; 2 Sam. 16:10; 19:22; 1 Kin. 17:18; 2 Kin. 3:13; 2 Chr. 35:21; Mark 1:24; 5:7; Luke 4:34; 8:28; John 2:4

33 [1]Lit., *and* [a]Matt. 4:24

1 [a]Matt. 4:13; Mark 5:21

2 [1]Lit., *thrown* [2]Gr., *child* [3]Lit., *are being forgiven* [a]Matt. 9:2-8: *Mark 2:3-12; Luke 5:18-26* [b]Matt. 4:24; 9:6 [c]Matt. 9:22; 14:27; Mark 6:50; 10:49; John 16:33; Acts 23:11 [d]Mark 2:5, 9; Luke 5:20, 23; 7:48

3 [1]Lit., *within*

4 [a]Matt. 12:25; Luke 6:8; 9:47

5 [1]Lit., *are being forgiven* [a]Mark 2:5, 9; Luke 5:20, 23; 7:48

6 [a]Matt. 8:20 [b]Matt. 4:24; 9:2

7 [1]Or, *departed*

8 [1]Lit., *were afraid* [a]Matt. 5:16; 15:31; Mark 2:12; Luke 2:20; 5:25, 26; 7:16; 13:13; 17:15; 23:47; John 15:8; Acts 4:21; 11:18; 21:20; 2 Cor. 9:13; Gal. 1:24

9 [1]Lit., *at the tax booth* [a]Matt. 9:9-17: *Mark 2:14-22; Luke 5:27-38* [b]Matt. 10:3; Mark 3:18; Luke 6:15; Acts 1:13; Mark 2:14 [c]Matt. 8:22

10 [1]Publicans who collected Roman taxes for profit [2]I.e., irreligious or non-practicing Jews [3]Lit., *reclined with*

11 [a]Matt. 11:19; Mark 2:16; Luke 5:30; 15:2

12 But when He heard this, He said, "*It is* not [a]those who
are healthy who need a physician, but those who are ill.
13 "But go and learn [a]what *this* means, '[b]I DESIRE [1]COMPAS-
SION, [2]AND NOT SACRIFICE;' for [c]I did not come to call *the*
righteous, but sinners."
14 Then the disciples of John *came to Him, saying,
"Why do we and [a]the Pharisees fast, but Your disciples do not
fast?"
15 And Jesus said to them, "The [1]attendants of the bridegroom cannot mourn, as long as the bridegroom is with them,
can they? But the days will come when the bridegroom is taken
away from them, and then they will fast.
16 "But no one puts a [1]patch of unshrunk cloth on an old
garment; for the [2]patch pulls away from the garment, and a
worse tear results.
17 "Nor do *men* put new wine into old [1]wineskins; otherwise the wineskins burst, and the wine pours out, and the
wineskins are ruined; but they put new wine into fresh wineskins,
and both are preserved."
18 [a]While He was saying these things to them, behold,
there came [1]a [2]synagogue official, and [3b]bowed down before
Him, saying, "My daughter has just died; but come and lay
Your hand on her, and she will live."
19 And Jesus rose and *began* to follow him, and *so did* His
disciples.
20 And behold, a woman who had been suffering from a
hemorrhage for twelve years, came up behind Him and
touched [a]the fringe of His [1]cloak;
21 for she was saying [1]to herself, "If I only [a]touch His
garment, I shall [2]get well."
22 But Jesus turning and seeing her said, "Daughter, [a]take
courage; [b]your faith has [1]made you well." And [2]at once the
woman was [1]made well.
23 And when Jesus came into the [1]official's house, and saw
[a]the flute-players, and the crowd in noisy disorder,
24 He *began* to say, "Depart; for the girl [a]is not dead, but
is asleep." And they were laughing at Him.
25 But when the crowd had been put out, He entered and
took her by the hand; and the girl [1]arose.
26 And [a]this news went out into all that land.
27 And as Jesus passed on from there, two blind men followed Him, crying out, and saying, "Have mercy on us, [a]Son of
David!"
28 And after He had come into the house, the blind men
came up to Him, and Jesus *said to them, "Do you believe
that I am able to do this?" They *said to Him, "Yes, Lord."
29 Then He touched their eyes, saying, "Be it done to you
[a]according to your faith."
30 And their eyes were opened. And Jesus [a]sternly warned
them, saying, "See *here*, let no one know *about this!*"
31 But they went out, and [a]spread the news about Him in
all that land.
32 And as they were going out, behold, [a]a dumb man
[b]demon-possessed [1]was brought to Him.
33 And after the demon was cast out, the dumb man

12 [a]Mark 2:17; Luke 5:31

13 [1]Or, *mercy* [2]I.e., more than [a]Matt. 12:7 [b]Hos. 6:6 [c]Mark 2:17; Luke 5:32; 1 Tim. 1:15

14 [a]Luke 18:12

15 [1]Lit., *sons of the bridalchamber*

16 [1]Lit., *that which is put on* [2]Lit., *that which fills up*

17 [1]I.e., skins used as bottles

18 [1]Or, *one* [2]Lit., *ruler* [3]Or, *worshiped* [a]Matt. 9:18-26: *Mark 5:22-43; Luke 8:41-56* [b]Matt. 8:2

20 [1]Or, *outer garment* [a]Num. 15:38; Deut. 22:12; Matt. 14:36; 23:5

21 [1]Lit., *in herself* [2]Lit., *be saved* [a]Matt. 14:36; Mark 3:10; Luke 6:19

22 [1]Lit., *saved* [2]Lit., *from that hour* [a]Matt. 9:2 [b]Mark 5:34; 10:52; Luke 7:50; 8:48; 17:19; 18:42; Matt. 9:29; 15:28

23 [1]Lit., *ruler's* [a]2 Chr. 35:25; Jer. 9:17; 16:6; Ezek. 24:17

24 [a]John 11:13; Acts 20:10

25 [1]Or, *was raised up*

26 [a]Matt. 9:31; 4:24; 14:1; Mark 1:28, 45; Luke 4:14, 37; 5:15; 7:17

27 [a]Matt. 12:23; 15:22; 20:30, 31; 21:9, 15; 22:42; Mark 10:47, 48; 12:35; Luke 18:38, 39; 20:41f.; Matt. 1:1

29 [a]Matt 9:22; 8:13

30 [a]Matt. 8:4

31 [a]Matt. 9:26; 4:24; 14:1; Mark 1:28, 45; Luke 4:14, 37; 5:15; 7:17

32 [1]Lit., *they brought* [a]Matt. 12:22, 24 [b]Matt. 4:24

spoke; and the multitudes marveled, saying, "[a]Nothing like
this was [1]ever seen in Israel."
34 But the Pharisees were saying, "He casts out the demons [a]by the ruler of the demons."
35 And Jesus was going about all the cities and the villages,
[a]teaching in their synagogues, and proclaiming the gospel of
the kingdom, and [b]healing every kind of disease and every kind
of sickness.
36 And [a]seeing the multitudes, He felt compassion for
them, [b]because they were [1]distressed and [2]downcast like sheep
[3]without a shepherd.
37 Then He *said to His disciples, "[a]The harvest is plentiful, but the workers are few.
38 "[a]Therefore beseech the Lord of the harvest to send out
workers into His harvest."

Chapter 10

AND [a]having summoned His twelve disciples, He gave them
authority over unclean spirits, to cast them out, and to [b]heal
every kind of disease and every kind of sickness.
2 [a]Now the names of the twelve apostles are these: The
first, [b]Simon, who is called Peter, and [c]Andrew his brother; and
[1d]James the *son* of Zebedee, and [2]John his brother;
3 [a]Philip and [1]Bartholomew; [b]Thomas and [c]Matthew the
tax-gatherer; [2d]James the *son* of Alphaeus, and [e]Thaddaeus;
4 Simon the [1]Cananaean, and [a]Judas Iscariot, the one
who betrayed Him.
5 [a]These twelve Jesus sent out after instructing them,
saying, "Do not [1]go in *the* way of *the* Gentiles, and do not
enter *any* city of the [b]Samaritans;
6 but rather [1]go to [a]the lost sheep of the house of Israel.
7 "And as you [1]go, [2]preach, saying, '[a]The kingdom of heav-
en is [3]at hand.'
8 "Heal *the* sick, raise *the* dead, cleanse *the* lepers, cast
out demons; freely you received, freely give.
9 "[a]Do not acquire gold, or silver, or copper [1]for your
money belts;
10 or a [1]bag for *your* journey, or even two [2]tunics, or
sandals, or a staff; for [a]the worker is worthy of his [3]support.
11 "And into whatever city or village you enter, inquire
who is worthy in it; and abide there until you go away.
12 "And as you enter the [1]house, [a]give it your greeting.
13 "And if the house is worthy, let your *greeting of* peace
come upon it; but if it is not worthy, let your *greeting of* peace
return to you.
14 "And whoever does not receive you, nor heed your
words, as you go out of that house or that city, [a]shake off the
dust of your feet.
15 "Truly I say to you, [a]it will be more tolerable for *the*
land of [b]Sodom and Gomorrah in [c]the day of judgment, than
for that city.
16 "[a]Behold, I send you out as sheep in the midst of wolves;
therefore [1]be [b]shrewd as serpents, and [c]innocent as doves.
17 "But beware of men; for they will deliver you up to *the*
[1a]courts, and scourge you [b]in their synagogues;

33 [1]Lit., *ever appeared* [a]Mark 2:12

34 [a]Matt. 12:24; Mark 3:22; Luke 11:15; John 7:20f.

35 [a]Matt. 4:23 [b]Matt. 4:23; Mark 1:14

36 [1]Or, *harassed* [2]Lit., *thrown down* [3]Lit., *not having* [a]Matt. 14:14; 15:32; Mark 6:34; 8:2 [b]Mark 6:34; Num. 27:17; Ezek. 34:5; Zech. 10:2

37 [a]Luke 10:2

38 [a]Luke 10:2

1 [a]Mark 3:13-15; 6:7 [b]Matt. 9:35; Luke 9:1

2 [1]Or, *Jacob* [2]Gr., *Joannes* from Heb., *Johanan* [a]Matt. 10:2-4: *Mark 3:16-19; Luke 6:14-16; Acts 1:13* [b]Matt. 4:18 [c]Matt. 4:18 [d]Matt. 4:21

3 [1]I.e., son of Talmai (Aram) [2]Or, *Jacob* [a]John 1:45ff. [b]John 11:16; 14:5; 20:24ff.; 21:2 [c]Matt 9:9 [d]Mark 15:40 [e]Mark 3:18; Luke 6:16; Acts 1:13

4 [1]Or, *the Zealot* [a]Luke 22:3; John 6:71; 13:2, 26; Matt. 26:14

5 [1]Or, *go off to* [a]Mark 6:7; Luke 9:2 [b]2 Kin. 17:24ff.; Luke 9:52; 10:33; 17:16; John 4:9, 39f.; 8:48; Acts 8:25

6 [1]Or, *proceed* [a]Matt. 15:24

7 [1]Or, *proceed* [2]Or, *proclaim* [3]Lit., *has come near* [a]Matt. 3:2

9 [1]Lit., *into* [a]Matt. 10:9-15: *Mark 6:8-11; Luke 9:3-5; 10:4-12;* Luke 22:35

10 [1]Or, *knapsack* or, *beggars' bag* [2]Or, *inner garments* [3]Lit., *nourishment* [a]1 Cor. 9:14; 1 Tim. 5:18

12 [1]Or, *household* [a]1 Sam. 25:6; Ps. 122:7, 8

14 [a]Acts 13:51

15 [a]Matt. 11:22, 24 [b]Matt. 11:24; 2 Pet. 2:6; Jude 7 [c]Matt. 11:22, 24; 12:36; Acts 17:31; 2 Pet. 2:9; 3:7; 1 John 4:17; Jude 6; Matt. 7:22; 1 Thess. 5:4; Heb. 10:25

16 [1]Or, *show yourselves to be* [a]Luke 10:3 [b]Gen. 3:1; Rom. 16:19; Matt. 24:45 [c]Hos. 7:11

17 [1]Or, *Sanhedrins*, or *Councils* [a]Matt. 5:22 [b]Matt. 23:34; Mark 13:9; Acts 5:40; 22:19; 26:11; Luke 12:11

18 and you shall even be brought before governors and
kings for My sake, as a testimony to them and to the Gentiles.
19 "[a]But when they deliver you up, [b]do not become anxious
about how or what you will speak; for it shall be given you in
that hour what you are to speak.
20 "For [a]it is not you who speak, but *it is* the Spirit of your
Father who speaks in you.
21 "[a]And brother will deliver up brother to death, and a
father *his* child; and [b]CHILDREN WILL RISE UP AGAINST PARENTS,
and [1]cause them to be put to death.
22 "And [a]you will be hated by all on account of My name,
but [b]it is the one who has endured to the end who will be
saved.
23 "But whenever they [a]persecute you in this city, flee to
[1]the next; for truly I say to you, you shall not finish *going
through* the cities of Israel, [b]until the Son of Man comes.
24 "[a]A [1]disciple is not above his teacher, nor a slave above
his master.
25 "It is enough for the disciple that he become as his
teacher, and the slave as his master. [a]If they have called the
head of the house [1b]Beelzebul, how much more the members
of his household!
26 "Therefore do not [a]fear them, [b]for there is nothing covered that will not be revealed, and hidden that will not be
known.
27 "[a]What I tell you in the darkness, speak in the light; and
what you hear *whispered* in *your* ear, proclaim [b]upon the
housetops.
28 "And do not fear those who kill the body, but are unable
to kill the soul; but rather [a]fear Him who is able to destroy
both soul and body in [1b]hell.
29 "[a]Are not two sparrows sold for a [1]cent? And *yet* not one
of them will fall to the ground apart from your Father.
30 "But [a]the very hairs of your head are all numbered.
31 "Therefore do not fear; [a]you are of more value than
many sparrows.
32 "Every one therefore who shall confess [1]Me before men,
I will also confess [2a]him before My Father who is in heaven.
33 "But [a]whoever shall deny Me before men, I will also
deny him before My Father who is in heaven.
34 "[a]Do not think that I came to [1]bring peace on the earth;
I did not come to bring peace, but a sword.
35 "For I came to [a]SET A MAN AGAINST HIS FATHER, AND A
DAUGHTER AGAINST HER MOTHER, AND A DAUGHTER-IN-LAW
AGAINST HER MOTHER-IN-LAW;
36 and [a]A MAN'S ENEMIES WILL BE THE MEMBERS OF HIS
HOUSEHOLD.
37 "[a]He who loves father or mother more than Me is not
worthy of Me; and he who loves son or daughter more than
Me is not worthy of Me.
38 "And [a]he who does not take his cross and follow after
Me is not worthy of Me.
39 "[a]He who has found his [1]life shall lose it, and he who has
lost his [1]life for My sake shall find it.
40 "[a]He who receives you receives Me, and [b]he who receives Me receives Him who sent Me.

19 [a]Matt. 10:19-22: *Mark 13:11-13; Luke 21:12-17* [b]Matt. 6:25

20 [a]Luke 12:12; Acts 4:8; 13:9; 2 Cor. 13:3

21 [1]Or, *put them to death* [a]Matt. 10:35, 36 [b]Mic. 7:6

22 [a]Matt. 24:9; John 15:18ff. [b]Matt. 24:13

23 [1]Lit., *the other* [a]Matt. 23:34 [b]Matt. 16:27f.

24 [1]Or, *pupil* [a]Luke 6:40; John 13:16; 15:20

25 [1]Or, *Beezebul*; others read *Beelzebub* [a]Matt. 9:34 [b]2 Kin. 1:2; Matt. 12:24, 27; Mark 3:22; Luke 11:15, 18, 19

26 [a]Matt. 10:26-33: *Luke 12:2-9* [b]Mark 4:22; Luke 8:17; 12:2

27 [a]Luke 12:3 [b]Matt. 24:17

28 [1]Gr., *Gehenna* [a]Heb. 10:31 [b]Matt. 5:22

29 [1]Gr., *assarion*, the smallest copper coin [a]Luke 12:6

30 [a]Luke 21:18; 1 Sam. 14:45; 2 Sam. 14:11; 1 Kin. 1:52; Acts 27:34

31 [a]Matt. 12:12

32 [1]Gr., *in Me* [2]Gr., *in him* [a]Rev. 3:5; Luke 12:8

33 [a]2 Tim. 2:12; Mark 8:38; Luke 9:26

34 [1]Lit., *cast* [a]Matt. 10:34, 35: *Luke 12:51-53*

35 [a]Matt. 10:21; Mic. 7:6

36 [a]Matt. 10:21 Mic. 7:6

37 [a]Luke 14:26

38 [a]Matt. 16:24; Mark 8:34; Luke 9:23; 14:27

39 [1]Or, *soul-life* [a]Matt. 16:25; Mark 8:35; Luke 9:24; 17:33; John 12:25

40 [a]Luke 10:16; John 13:20; Matt. 18:5; Gal. 4:14 [b]Mark 9:37; Luke 9:48; John 12:44

41 "He who receives a prophet in *the* name of a prophet
shall receive a prophet's reward; and he who receives a righteous man in the name of a righteous man shall receive a
righteous man's reward.
42 "And [a]whoever in the name of a disciple gives to one of
these [1]little ones even a cup of cold water to drink, truly I say
to you he shall not lose his reward."

[a] Chapter 11

AND it came about that when Jesus had finished [1]giving
instructions to His twelve disciples, He departed from there
[b]to teach and [2]preach in their cities.
2 [a]Now when [b]John in prison heard of the works of
Christ, he sent *word* by his disciples,
3 and said to Him, "Are You [a]the Coming One, or shall
we look for someone else?"
4 And Jesus answered and said to them, "Go and report
to John the things which you hear and see:
5 [a]*the* BLIND RECEIVE SIGHT and *the* lame walk, *the* lepers
are cleansed and *the* deaf hear, and *the* dead are raised up, and
the POOR HAVE THE [1]GOSPEL PREACHED to them.
6 "And blessed is he [1]who [a]keeps from [2]stumbling over
Me."
7 And as these were going *away*, Jesus began to say to the
multitudes concerning John, "What did you go out into [a]the
wilderness to look at? A reed shaken by the wind?
8 "[1]But what did you go out to see? A man dressed in soft
clothing? Behold, those who wear soft *clothing* are in kings'
[2]palaces.
9 "[1]But why did you go out? To see [a]a prophet? Yes, I tell
you, and one who is more than a prophet.
10 "This is the one about whom it [1]was written,
'[a]BEHOLD, I SEND MY MESSENGER BEFORE YOUR FACE,
WHO WILL PREPARE YOUR WAY BEFORE YOU.'
11 "Truly, I say to you, among those born of women there
has not arisen *anyone* greater than John the Baptist; yet he
who is [1]least in the kingdom of heaven is greater than he.
12 "And [a]from the days of John the Baptist until now the
kingdom of heaven [1]suffers violence, and violent men [2]take it
by force.
13 "For [a]all the prophets and the Law prophesied until
John.
14 "And if you care to accept *it*, he himself is [a]Elijah, who
[1]was to come.
15 "[a]He who has ears to hear, let him hear.
16 "But to what shall I compare this generation? It is like
children sitting in the market places, who call out to the other
children,
17 and say, 'We played the flute for you, and you did not
dance; we sang a dirge, and you did not [1]mourn.'
18 "For John came neither [a]eating nor [b]drinking, and they
say, '[c]He has a demon!'
19 "The Son of Man came eating and drinking, and they
say, 'Behold, a gluttonous man and a [1]drunkard, [a]a friend of

42 [1]Or, *humble folk* [a]Mark 9:41; Matt. 25:40

1 [1]Or, *commanding* [2]Or, *proclaim* [a]Matt. 7:28 [b]Matt. 9:35

2 [a]Matt. 11:2-19: *Luke 7:18-35* [b]Matt. 14:3; Mark 6:17; Luke 9:7ff.

3 [a]John 6:14; 11:27; Heb. 10:37; Matt. 11:10; Ps. 118:26

5 [1]Or, *good news* [a]Is. 35:5f.; 61:1

6 [1]Lit., *whoever* [2]Or, *taking offense at* [a]Matt. 13:21, 57; 24:10; 26:31; Mark 6:3; John 6:61; 16:1; Matt. 5:29

7 [a]Matt. 3:1

8 [1]Or, *Well then,* [2]Lit., *houses*

9 [1]Or, *Well then,* [a]Matt. 14:5; 21:26; Luke 1:76; 20:6

10 [1]Lit., *has been written* [a]Mark 1:2; Mal. 3:1

11 [1]Lit., *less*

12 [1]Or, *is forcibly entered* [2]Or, *seize it for themselves* [a]Luke 16:16

13 [a]Luke 16:16

14 [1]Or, *is to come* [a]Mal. 4:5; Matt. 17:10-13; Mark 9:11-13; Luke 1:17; John 1:21

15 [a]Matt. 13:9, 43; Mark 4:9, 23; Luke 8:8; 14:35; Rev. 13:9; 2:7, 11, 17, 29; 3:6, 13, 22

17 [1]Lit., *beat the breast*

18 [a]Matt. 3:4 [b]Luke 1:15 [c]John 7:20; 8:48f., 52; 10:20; Matt. 9:34

19 [1]Or, *wine-drinker* [a]Matt. 9:11; Luke 15:2

[2]tax-gatherers and sinners!' [3]Yet wisdom is vindicated by her deeds."

20 Then He began to reproach the cities in which most of His [1]miracles were done, because they did not repent.

21 "[a]Woe to you, Chorazin! Woe to you, [b]Bethsaida! For if the [1]miracles had occurred in [c]Tyre and [c]Sidon which occurred in you, they would have repented long ago in [d]sackcloth and ashes.

22 "Nevertheless I say to you, [a]it shall be more tolerable for Tyre and Sidon in [b]*the* day of judgment, than for you.

23 "And you, [a]Capernaum, will not be exalted to heaven, will you? You shall [1b]DESCEND TO [c]HADES; for if the [2]miracles had occurred in [d]Sodom which occurred in you, it would have remained to this day.

24 "Nevertheless I say to you that [a]it shall be more tolerable for the land of [b]Sodom in [b]*the* day of judgment, than for you."

25 [a]At that [1]time Jesus [b]answered and said, "I [2]praise Thee, O [c]Father, Lord of heaven and earth, that [d]Thou didst hide these things from *the* wise and intelligent and didst reveal them to babes.

26 "Yes, [a]Father, for thus it was well-pleasing in Thy sight.

27 "[a]All things [1]have been handed over to Me by My Father; and no one [2]knows the Son, except the Father; nor does anyone [2]know the Father, [b]except the Son, and anyone to whom the Son wills to reveal *Him*.

28 "[a]Come to Me, all who are [1]weary and heavy laden, and I will give you rest.

29 "Take My yoke upon you, and [a]learn from Me, for I am gentle and humble in heart; and [b]YOU SHALL FIND REST FOR YOUR SOULS.

30 "For My yoke is [1]easy, and My load is light."

CHAPTER 12

[a]AT that [1]time Jesus went on the Sabbath through the grainfields, and His disciples became hungry and began to [b]pick the heads of *grain* and eat.

2 But when the Pharisees saw it, they said to Him, "Behold, Your disciples do what [a]is not lawful to do on a Sabbath."

3 But He said to them, "Have you not read what David did, when he became hungry, he and his companions;

4 how he entered the house of God, and [a]they ate the [1]consecrated bread, which was not lawful for him to eat, nor for those with him, but for the priests alone?

5 "Or have you not read in the Law, that on the Sabbath the priests in the temple [1]break the Sabbath, and are innocent?

6 "But I say to you, that something [a]greater than the temple is here.

7 "But if you had known what this [1]means, '[a]I DESIRE [2]COMPASSION, AND NOT A SACRIFICE,' you would not have condemned the innocent.

19 [2]Or, *publicans* who collected Roman taxes for profit [3]Lit., *and*

20 [1]Or, *works of power*

21 [1]Or, *works of power* [a]Matt. 11:21-23: *Luke 10:13-15* [b]Mark 6:45; 8:22; Luke 9:10; John 1:44; 12:21 [c]Matt. 11:22; 15:21; Mark 3:8; 7:24, 31; Luke 6:17; Acts 12:20; Luke 4:26; Acts 27:3 [d]Rev. 11:3

22 [a]Matt. 10:15; 11:24 [b]Matt. 10:15

23 [1]Some mss. read, *shall be brought down* [2]Or, *works of power* [a]Matt. 4:13 [b]Is. 14:13, 15; Ezek. 26:20; 31:14; 32:18, 24 [c]Matt. 16:18; Luke 10:15; 16:23; Acts 2:27, 31; Rev. 1:18; 6:8; 20:13f. [d]Matt. 10:15

24 [a]Matt. 10:15; 11:22 [b]Matt. 10:15

25 [1]Or, *occasion* [2]Or, *acknowledge to Thy praise* [a]Matt. 11:25-27: *Luke 10:21, 22* [b]Acts 3:12 [c]Luke 22:42; 23:34; John 11:41; 12:27, 28 [d]1 Cor. 1:26ff.

26 [a]Luke 22:42; 23:34; John 11:41; 12:27, 28

27 [1]Lit., *were given over* [2]Or, *perfectly know(s)* [a]Matt. 28:18; John 3:35; 13:3; 17:2 [b]John 7:29; 10:15; 17:25

28 [1]Or, *who work to exhaustion* [a]John 7:37; Jer. 31:25

29 [a]John 13:15; Eph. 4:20; Phil. 2:5; 1 Pet. 2:21; 1 John 2:6 [b]Jer. 6:16

30 [1]Or, *kindly*, or, *pleasant*

1 [1]Or, *occasion* [a]Matt. 12:1-8: *Mark 2:23-28; Luke 6:1-5* [b]Deut. 23:25

2 [a]Matt. 12:10; Luke 13:14; 14:3; John 5:10; 7:23; 9:16

4 [1]Or, *showbread*; lit., *loaves of presentation* [a]1 Sam. 21:6

5 [1]Or, *profane*

6 [a]Matt. 12:41, 42

7 [1]Lit., *is* [2]Or, *mercy* [a]Hos. 6:6

8 "For [a]the Son of Man is Lord of the Sabbath."
9 [a]And departing from there, He went into their
synagogue.
10 And behold, *there was* a man with a withered hand.
And they questioned Him, saying, "[a]Is it lawful to heal on the
Sabbath?"—in order that they might accuse Him.
11 And He said to them, "What man shall there be
[1]among you, who shall have one sheep, and if it falls into a pit
on the Sabbath, will he not take hold of it, and lift it out?
12 "Of [a]how much more value then is a man than a sheep!
So then, it is lawful to do [1]good on the Sabbath."
13 Then He *said to the man, "Stretch out your hand!"
And he stretched it out, and it was restored to [1]normal, like the
other.
14 But the Pharisees went out, and [a]counseled together
against Him, *as to* how they might destroy Him.
15 But Jesus, [1]aware of *this,* withdrew from there. And
many followed Him, and [a]He healed them all,
16 and [a]warned them not to make Him [1]known;
17 in order that what was spoken through Isaiah the prophet, might be fulfilled, saying,
18 "[a]BEHOLD, MY [1]SERVANT WHOM I [2]HAVE CHOSEN;
[b]MY BELOVED IN WHOM MY SOUL IS [3]WELL PLEASED;
[c]I WILL PUT MY SPIRIT UPON HIM,
[a]AND HE SHALL PROCLAIM [4]JUSTICE TO THE [5]GENTILES.
19 "[a]HE WILL NOT QUARREL, NOR CRY OUT;
NOR WILL ANY ONE HEAR HIS VOICE IN THE STREETS.
20 "[a]A BATTERED REED HE WILL NOT BREAK OFF,
AND A SMOLDERING WICK HE WILL NOT PUT OUT,
UNTIL HE [1]LEADS [2]JUSTICE TO VICTORY.
21 "[a]AND IN HIS NAME THE [1]GENTILES WILL HOPE."
22 [a]Then there was brought to Him a [b]demon-possessed
man *who was* blind and dumb, and He healed him, so that the
dumb man spoke and saw.
23 And all the multitudes were amazed, and *began* to say,
"This *man* cannot be the [a]Son of David, can he?"
24 But when the Pharisees heard it, they said, "This man
casts out demons only [a]by [1]Beelzebul the ruler of the
demons."
25 [a]And [b]knowing their thoughts He said to them, "[1]Any
kingdom divided against itself is laid waste; and [1]any city or
house divided against itself shall not stand.
26 "And if [a]Satan casts out [a]Satan, he [1]is divided against
himself; how then shall his kingdom stand?
27 "And if I [a]by [1]Beelzebul cast out demons, [b]by whom do
your sons cast them out? Consequently they shall be your
judges.
28 "But if I cast out demons by the Spirit of God, then the
kingdom of God has come upon you.
29 "Or how can anyone enter the strong man's house and
carry off his property, unless he first binds the strong *man*?
And then he will plunder his house.
30 "[a]He who is not with Me is against Me; and he who does
not gather with Me scatters.
31 "[a]Therefore I say to you, any sin and blasphemy shall be

8 [a]Matt. 8:20; 12:32, 40

9 [a]Matt. 12:9-14: *Mark 3:1-6; Luke 6:6-11*

10 [a]Matt. 12:2; Luke 13:14; 14:3; John 5:10; 7:23; 9:16

11 [1]Lit., *of*

12 [1]Lit., *well*
[a]Matt. 10:31

13 [1]Lit., *healthy, well*

14 [a]Matt. 26:4; Mark 14:1; Luke 22:2; John 7:30, 44; 8:59; 10:31, 39; 11:53

15 [1]Lit., *knowing*
[a]Matt. 4:23

16 [1]Lit., *evident*
[a]Matt. 8:4

18 [1]Lit., *child* [2]Lit., *chose* [3]Or, *took pleasure* [4]Or, *judgment* [5]Or, *nations*
[a]Is. 42:1 [b]Matt. 3:17; 17:5 [c]Luke 4:18; John 3:34

19 [a]Is. 42:2

20 [1]Or, *puts forth* [2]Or, *judgment*
[a]Is. 42:3

21 [1]Or, *nations*
[a]Is. 42:4; Rom. 15:12

22 [a]Matt. 12:22, 24: *Luke 11:14, 15;* Matt. 9:32, 34 [b]Matt. 4:24

23 [a]Matt. 9:27

24 [1]Or, *Beezebul*; others read *Beelzebub*
[a]Matt. 9:34

25 [1]Lit., *every*
[a]Matt. 12:25-29: *Mark 3:23-27; Luke 11:17-22* [b]Matt. 9:4

26 [1]Lit., *was*
[a]Matt. 4:10

27 [1]vs. 24
[a]Matt. 9:34 [b]Acts 19:13

30 [a]Luke 11:23; Mark 9:40; Luke 9:50

31 [a]Matt. 12:31, 32; Mark 3:28-30; Luke 12:10

forgiven men; but blasphemy against the Spirit shall not be
forgiven.
32 "And whoever shall speak a word against the Son of
Man, it shall be forgiven him; but whoever shall speak against
the Holy Spirit, it shall not be forgiven him, either in [a]this age,
or in the *age* to come.
33 "Either make the tree good, and its fruit good; or make
the tree rotten, and its fruit rotten; for [a]the tree is known by its
fruit.
34 "[a]You brood of vipers, how can you, being evil, speak
[1]what is good? [b]For the mouth speaks out of that which fills
the heart.
35 "The good man out of *his* good treasure brings forth
[1]what is good; and the evil man out of *his* evil treasure brings
forth [2]what is evil.
36 "And I say to you, that every [1]careless word that men
shall speak, they shall render account for it in [a]the day of
judgment.
37 "For [1]by your words you shall be justified, and [1]by your
words you shall be condemned."
38 Then some of the scribes and Pharisees answered Him,
saying, "Teacher, [a]we want to see a [1]sign from You."
39 But He answered and said to them, "[a]An evil and adulterous generation craves for a [1]sign; and *yet* no [1]sign shall be
given to it but the [1]sign of Jonah the prophet;
40 for just as [a]JONAH WAS THREE DAYS AND THREE NIGHTS IN
THE BELLY OF THE SEA-MONSTER; so shall [b]the Son of Man be
[c]three days and three nights in the heart of the earth.
41 "[a]The men of Nineveh shall stand up with this generation at the judgment, and shall condemn it because [b]they repented at the preaching of Jonah; and behold, [c]something
greater than Jonah is here.
42 "[a]*The* Queen of *the* South shall rise up with this generation at the judgment and shall condemn it; because she came
from the ends of the earth to hear the wisdom of Solomon;
and behold, [b]something greater than Solomon is here.
43 "[a]Now when the unclean spirit goes out of a man, it
passes through waterless places, seeking rest, and does not find
it.
44 "Then it says, 'I will return to my house from which I
came;' and when it comes, it finds it unoccupied, swept, and
put in order.
45 "Then it goes, and takes along with it seven other spirits
more wicked than itself, and they go in and live there; and [a]the
last state of that man becomes worse than the first. That is the
way it will also be with this evil generation."
46 [a]While He was still speaking to the multitudes, behold,
His [b]mother and His [c]brothers were standing outside, seeking
to speak to Him.
47 And someone said to Him, "Behold, Your mother and
Your brothers are standing outside seeking to speak to You."
48 But He answered the one who was telling Him and
said, "Who is My mother and who are My brothers?"
49 And stretching out His hand toward His disciples, He
said, "Behold, My mother and My brothers!

32 [a]Mark 10:30; Luke 16:8; 18:30; 20:34, 35; Eph. 1:21; 1 Tim. 6:17; 2 Tim. 4:10; Titus 2:12; Heb. 6:5; Matt. 13:22 and 13:39

33 [a]Matt. 7:16

34 [1]Lit., *good things* [a]Matt. 3:7; 23:33 [b]Matt. 12:34, 35; Luke 6:45; Matt. 15:18; Eph. 4:29; James 3:2-12; 1 Sam. 24:13

35 [1]Lit., *good things* [2]Lit., *evil things*

36 [1]Or, *useless* [a]Matt. 10:15

37 [1]Or, *in accordance with*

38 [1]Or, *attesting miracle* [a]Matt. 16:1; Mark 8:11, 12; Luke 11:16; John 2:18; 6:30; 1 Cor. 1:22

39 [1]Or, *attesting miracle* [a]Matt. 12:39-42: *Luke 11:29-32*; Matt. 16:4

40 [a]Jonah 1:17 [b]Matt. 8:20 [c]Matt. 16:21

41 [a]Jonah 1:2 [b]Jonah 3:5 [c]Matt. 12:6, 42

42 [a]1 Kin. 10:1; 2 Chr. 9:1 [b]Matt. 12:6, 41

43 [a]Matt. 12:43-45: *Luke 11:24-26*

45 [a]2 Pet. 2:20

46 [a]Matt. 12:46-50: *Mark 3:31-35; Luke 8:19-21* [b]Matt. 1:18; 2:11ff.; 13:55; Luke 1:43; 2:33f., 48, 51; John 2:1, 5, 12; 19:25f.; Acts 1:14 [c]Matt. 13:55; Mark 6:3; John 2:12; 7:3, 5, 10; Acts 1:14; 1 Cor. 9:5; Gal. 1:19

50 "For whoever shall do the will of My Father who is in
heaven, he is My brother and sister and mother."

Chapter 13

ON that day Jesus went out of [a]the house, and was sitting [b]by
the sea.
2 And great multitudes gathered about Him, so that [a]He
got into a boat and sat down, and the whole multitude was
standing on the beach.
3 And He spoke many things to them in [a]parables,
saying, "Behold, the sower went out to sow;
4 and as he sowed, some *seeds* fell beside the road, and
the birds came and devoured them.
5 "And others fell upon the rocky places, where they [1]did
not have much soil; and immediately they sprang up, because
they had no depth of soil.
6 "But when the sun had risen, they were scorched; and
because they had no root, they withered away.
7 "And others fell[1]among the thorns, and the thorns came
up and choked them out.
8 "And others fell on the good soil, and *yielded a crop,
some a [a]hundredfold, some sixty, and some thirty.
9 "[a]He who has ears, let him hear."
10 And the disciples came and said to Him, "Why do You
speak to them in parables?"
11 And He answered and said to them, "[a]To you it has
been granted to know the mysteries of the kingdom of heaven,
but to them it has not been granted.
12 "[a]For whoever has, to him shall *more* be given, and he
shall have an abundance; but whoever does not have, even
what he has shall be taken away from him.
13 "Therefore I speak to them in parables; because while
[a]seeing they do not see, and while hearing they do not hear,
nor do they understand.
14 "And [1]in their case the prophecy of Isaiah is being fulfilled, which says,

'[2][a]You will keep on hearing, [3]but will not understand;
And [4]you will keep on seeing, but will not perceive;
15 [a]For the heart of this people has become dull,
And with their ears they scarcely hear,
And they have closed their eyes;
Lest they should see with their eyes,
And hear with their ears,
And understand with their heart and turn again,
And I should heal them.'

16 "[a]But blessed are your eyes, because they see; and your
ears, because they hear.
17 "For truly I say to you, that [a]many prophets and righteous men desired to see what you see, and did not see *it*; and
to hear what you hear, and did not hear *it*.
18 "[a]Hear then the parable of the sower.
19 "When any one hears [a]the word of the kingdom, and
does not understand it, [b]the evil *one* comes and snatches away

1 [a]Matt. 13:36; 9:28; Mark 3:19 [b]Matt. 13:1-15: *Mark 4:1-12; Luke 8:4-10*
2 [a]Luke 5:3
3 [a]Matt. 13:10ff.; Mark 4:2ff.
5 [1]Lit., *were not having*
7 [1]Lit., *upon*
8 [a]Matt. 13:23; Gen. 26:12
9 [a]Matt. 11:15
11 [a]Matt. 19:11; 20:23; John 6:65; 1 Cor. 2:10; Col. 1:27; 1 John 2:20, 27
12 [a]Matt. 25:29; Mark 4:25; Luke 8:18; 19:26
13 [a]Jer. 5:21; Ezek. 12:2; Is. 42:19, 20; Deut. 29:4
14 [1]Lit., *for them* [2]Lit., *with a hearing* [3]Lit., *and* [4]Lit., *seeing you will see* [a]Is. 6:9; Mark 4:12; Luke 8:10; John 12:40; Acts 28:26, 27; Rom. 10:16; 11:8
15 [a]Is. 6:10
16 [a]Matt. 13:16, 17: *Luke 10:23, 24*
17 [a]John 8:56; Heb. 11:13; 1 Pet. 1:10-12
18 [a]Matt. 13:18-23: *Mark 4:13-20; Luke 8:11-15*
19 [a]Matt. 4:23 [b]Matt. 5:37

what has been sown in his heart. This is the one on whom seed
was sown beside the road.
20 "And the one on whom seed was sown on the rocky
places, this is the man who hears the word, and immediately
receives it with joy;
21 yet he has no *firm* root in himself, but is *only* temporary, and when affliction or persecution arises because of the
word, immediately he [1a]falls away.
22 "And the one on whom seed was sown among the
thorns, this is the man who hears the word, and the worry of
[a]the [1]world, and the [b]deceitfulness of riches choke the word,
and it becomes unfruitful.
23 "And the one on whom seed was sown on the good
ground, this is the man who hears the word and understands it;
who indeed bears fruit, and brings forth, some [a]a hundredfold,
some sixty, and some thirty."
24 He presented another parable to them, saying, "[a]The
kingdom of heaven [1]may be compared to [b]a man who sowed
good seed in his field.
25 "But while men were sleeping, his enemy came and
sowed [1]tares also among the wheat, and went away.
26 "But when the [1]wheat sprang up and bore grain, then
the tares became evident also.
27 "And the slaves of the landowner came and said to him,
'Sir, did you not sow good seed in your field? [1]How then does
it have tares?'
28 "And he said to them, 'An [1]enemy has done this!' And
the slaves *said to him, 'Do you want us, then, to go and gather
them up?'
29 "But he *said, 'No; lest while you are gathering up the
tares, you may root up the wheat with them.
30 'Allow both to grow together until the harvest; and in
the time of the harvest I will say to the reapers, "First gather
up the tares; and bind them in bundles to burn them up; but
[a]gather the wheat into my barn." ' "
31 He presented another parable to them, saying, "[a]The
kingdom of heaven is like [b]a mustard seed, which a man took
and sowed in his field;
32 and this is smaller than all *other* seeds; but when it is
full grown, it is larger than the garden plants, and becomes a
tree, so that [a]THE BIRDS OF THE [1]AIR come and NEST IN ITS
BRANCHES."
33 He spoke another parable to them; "[a]The kingdom of
heaven is like leaven, which a woman took, and hid in [b]three
[1]pecks of meal, until it was all leavened."
34 All these things Jesus spoke to the multitudes in parables, and He was not talking to them [a]without a parable,
35 so that what was spoken through the prophet might be
fulfilled, saying,

"[a]I WILL OPEN MY MOUTH IN PARABLES;
I WILL UTTER THINGS HIDDEN SINCE THE FOUNDATION OF
THE WORLD."

36 Then He left the multitudes, and went into [a]the house.
And His disciples came to Him, saying, "[b]Explain to us the
parable of the [1]tares of the field."

21 [1]Lit., *is caused to stumble* [a]Matt. 11:6

22 [1]Or, *age* [a]Mark 4:19; Rom. 12:2; 1 Cor. 1:20; 2:6, 8; 3:18; 2 Cor. 4:4; Gal. 1:4; Eph. 2:2; Matt. 12:32 and 13:39 [b]Matt. 19:23; 1 Tim. 6:9, 10, 17

23 [a]Matt 13:8

24 [1]Lit., *was compared to* [a]Matt. 13:31, 33, 45, 47; 18:23; 20:1; 22:2; 25:1; Mark 4:30; Luke 13:18, 20 [b]Mark 4:26-29

25 [1]Or, *darnel*, a weed resembling wheat.

26 [1]Lit., *grass*

27 [1]Lit., *from where*

28 [1]Lit., *an enemy man*

30 [a]Matt. 3:12

31 [a]Matt. 13:31, 32: *Mark 4:30-32; Luke 13:18, 19;* Matt. 13:24 [b]Matt. 17:20; Luke 17:6

32 [1]Or, *sky* [a]Ps. 104:12; Ezek. 17:23; 31:6; Dan. 4:12

33 [1]Gr., *sata* [a]Matt. 13:33: *Luke 13:21;* Matt. 13:24 [b]Gen. 18:6; Judg. 6:19; 1 Sam. 1:24

34 [a]Mark 4:34; John 10:6; 16:25

35 [a]Ps. 78:2

36 [1]Or, *darnel* cf. vs. 25 [a]Matt. 13:1 [b]Matt. 15:15

37 And He answered and said, "The one who sows the
good seed is [a]the Son of Man,
38 and the field is the world; and *as for* the good seed,
these are [a]the sons of the kingdom; and the tares are [b]the sons
of [c]the evil *one;*
39 and the enemy who sowed them is the devil, and the
harvest is [a]the [1]end of the age; and the reapers are angels.
40 "Therefore just as the tares are gathered up and burned
with fire, so shall it be at [a]the [1]end of the age.
41 "[a]The Son of Man [b]will send forth His angels, and they
will gather out of His kingdom all [1c]STUMBLING BLOCKS, AND
THOSE WHO COMMIT LAWLESSNESS,
42 and [a]will cast them into the furnace of fire; in that
place [b]there shall be weeping and gnashing of teeth.
43 "[a]Then THE RIGHTEOUS WILL SHINE FORTH AS THE SUN in
the kingdom of their Father. [b]He who has ears, let him hear.
44 "[a]The kingdom of heaven is like a treasure hidden in the
field; which a man found and hid; and from joy over it he goes
and [b]sells all that he has, and buys that field.
45 "Again, [a]the kingdom of heaven is like a merchant seeking fine pearls,
46 and upon finding one pearl of great value, he went and
sold all that he had, and bought it.
47 "Again, [a]the kingdom of heaven is like a drag-net cast
into the sea, and gathering *fish* of every kind;
48 and when it was filled, they drew it up on the beach;
and they sat down, and gathered the good *fish* into containers,
but the bad they threw away.
49 "So it will be at [a]the [1]end of the age; the angels shall
come forth, and [2]take out the wicked from among the
righteous,
50 and [a]will cast them into the furnace of fire; [b]there shall
be weeping and gnashing of teeth.
51 "Have you understood all these things?" They *said to
Him, "Yes."
52 And He said to them, "Therefore every scribe who has
become a disciple of the kingdom of heaven is like a head of a
household, who brings forth out of his treasure things new and
old."
53 [a]And it came about that when Jesus had finished these
parables, He departed from there.
54 [a]And coming to [1]His home town He [2b]*began* teaching
them in their synagogue, so that [c]they became astonished, and
said, "Where *did* this man *get* this wisdom, and *these* [3]miracu-
lous powers?
55 "Is not this the carpenter's son? Is not [a]His mother
called Mary, and His [a]brothers, James and Joseph and Simon
and Judas?
56 "And [a]His sisters, are they not all with us? Where then
did this man *get* all these things?"
57 And they [1]took [a]offense at Him. But Jesus said to
them, "[b]A prophet is not without honor except in his [2]home
town, and in his *own* household."
58 And He did not do many [1]miracles there because of
their unbelief.

37 [a]Matt. 8:20

38 [a]Matt. 8:12; [b]John 8:44; Acts 13:10; 1 John 3:10 [c]Matt. 5:37

39 [1]Or, *consummation* [a]Matt. 13:40, 49; 24:3; 28:20; 1 Cor. 10:11; Heb. 9:26; Matt. 12:32 and 13:22

40 [1]Or, *consummation* [a]Matt. 13:39, 49; 24:3; 28:20; 1 Cor. 10:11; Heb. 9:26; Matt. 12:32 and 13:22

41 [1]Or, *everything that is offensive* [a]Matt. 8:20 [b]Matt. 24:31 [c]Zeph. 1:3

42 [a]Matt. 13:50 [b]Matt. 8:12

43 [a]Dan. 12:3 [b]Matt. 11:15

44 [a]Matt. 13:24 [b]Matt. 13:46

45 [a]Matt. 13:24

47 [a]Matt. 13:44

49 [1]Or, *consummation* [2]Or, *separate* [a]Matt. 13:39, 40

50 [a]Matt. 13:42 [b]Matt. 8:12

53 [a]Matt. 7:28

54 [1]Or, *His own part of the country* [2]Or, *was teaching* [3]Or, *miracles* [a]Matt. 13:54-58: *Mark 6:1-6* [b]Matt. 4:23 [c]Matt. 7:28

55 [a]Matt. 12:46

56 [a]Mark 6:3

57 [1]Lit., *were being made to stumble* [2]Or, *his own part of the country* [a]Matt. 11:6 [b]Mark 6:4; Luke 4:24; John 4:44

58 [1]Or, *works of power*

[a] CHAPTER 14

AT that [1]time [b]Herod the tetrarch heard the news about
Jesus,
2 and said to his servants, "[a]This is John the Baptist; [1]he
has risen from the dead; and that is why miraculous powers are
at work in him."
3 For [a]Herod had seized John, and bound him, and put
him [b]in prison on account of [c]Herodias, the wife of his brother
Philip.
4 For John had been saying to him, "[a]It is not lawful for
you to have her."
5 And although he wanted to put him to death, he feared
the multitude, because [1]they regarded him as [a]a prophet.
6 But when Herod's birthday [1]came, the daughter of
[a]Herodias danced [2]before *them* and pleased [b]Herod.
7 Thereupon he promised with an oath to give her whatever she asked.
8 And having been prompted by her mother, she *said,
"Give me here on a platter the head of John the Baptist."
9 And although he was grieved, the king commanded *it*
to be given because of his oaths, and because of [1]his dinner-
guests.
10 And he sent and had John beheaded in the prison.
11 And his head was brought on a platter and given to the
girl; and she brought *it* to her mother.
12 And his disciples came and took away the body and
buried [1]it; and they went and reported to Jesus.
13 [a]Now when Jesus heard *it*, He withdrew from there in a
boat, to a lonely place by Himself; and when the multitudes
heard *of this*, they followed Him on foot from the cities.
14 And when He came out, He [a]saw a great multitude,
and felt compassion for them, and [b]healed their sick.
15 And when it was evening, the disciples came to Him,
saying, "The place is desolate, and the time is already past; so
send the multitudes away, that they may go into the villages,
and buy food for themselves."
16 But Jesus said to them, "They do not need to go away;
you give them *something* to eat!"
17 And they *said to Him, "We have here only [a]five
loaves, and two fish."
18 And He said, "Bring them here to Me."
19 And ordering the multitudes to recline on the grass, He
took the five loaves and the two fish, and looking up toward
heaven, He [a]blessed *the food*, and breaking the loaves He gave
them to the disciples, and the disciples *gave* to the multitudes,
20 and they all ate, and were satisfied. And they picked up
what was left over of the broken pieces, twelve full [1a]baskets.
21 And there were about five thousand men who ate, aside
from women and children.
22 [a]And immediately He [1]made the disciples get into the
boat, and go ahead of Him to the other side, while He sent the
multitudes away.
23 And after He had sent the multitudes away, [a]He went
up to the mountain by Himself to pray; and when it was
evening, He was there alone.

1 [1]Or, *occasion*
[a]Matt. 14:1-12: *Mark 6:14-29;* Matt. 14:1, 2: *Luke* 9:7-9
[b]Matt. 14:1-12: *Mark 6:14-29;* Matt. 14:1, 2: *Luke* 9:7-9, also Mark 8:15; Luke 3:1, 19; 8:3; 13:31; 23:7f., 11f., 15; Acts 4:27; 12:1

2 [1]Or, *he, himself*
[a]Matt. 16:14; Mark 6:14; Luke 9:7

3 [a]Matt. 14:1-12: *Mark 6:14-29; Matt. 14:1, 2; Luke* 9:7-9; also Mark 8:15; Luke 3:1, 19; 8:3; 13:31; 23:7f., 11f., 15; Acts 4:27; 12:1
[b]Matt. 4:12; 11:2 [c]Matt. 14:6; Mark 6:17, 19, 22; Luke 3:19

4 [a]Lev. 18:16; 20:21

5 [1]Lit., *they were holding*
[a]Matt. 11:9

6 [1]Lit., *occurred* [2]Lit., *in the midst*
[a]Matt. 14:3; Mark 6:17, 19, 22; Luke 3:19 [b]Matt. 14:1-12: *Mark 6:14-29;* Matt. 14:1, 2: *Luke 9:7-9;* also Mark 8:15; Luke 3:1, 19; 8:3; 13:31; 23:7f. 11f. 15; Acts 4:27; 12:1

9 [1]Lit., *those who reclined at table with him*

12 [1]Lit., *him*

13 [a]Matt. 14:13-21: *Mark 6:32-44; Luke 9:10-17; John 6:1-13;* Matt. 15:32-38

14 [a]Matt. 9:36 [b]Matt. 4:23

17 [a]Matt. 16:9

19 [a]1 Sam. 9:13; Matt. 15:36; 26:26; Mark 6:41; 8:7; 14:22; Luke 24:30; Acts 27:35; Rom. 14:6

20 [1]I.e., large-sized baskets
[a]Matt. 16:9; Mark 6:43; 8:19; Luke 9:17; John 6:13

22 [1]Lit., *compelled*
[a]Matt. 14:22-33: *Mark 6:45-51; John 6:15-21*

23 [a]Mark 6:46; Luke 6:12; 9:28; John 6:15

24 [1]A stadion was about 600 feet [2]Lit., *tormented*

25 [1]I.e., 3-6 a.m. [a]Mark 13:35; Matt. 24:43

26 [1]Or, *troubled* [a]Luke 24:37

27 [a]Matt. 9:2 [b]Matt. 17:7; 28:10; Mark 6:50; Luke 5:10; 12:32; John 6:20; Rev. 1:17; Matt. 28:5; Luke 1:13, 30; 2:10

31 [a]Matt. 6:30; 8:26; 16:8

33 [a]Matt. 4:3

34 [1]Lit., *the land* [a]Matt. 14:34-36: *Mark* 6:53-56; John 6:24, 25 [b]Mark 6:53; Luke 5:1

35 [1]Or, *knew*

36 [a]Matt. 9:20 [b]Matt. 9:21; Mark 3:10; 6:56; 8:22; Luke 6:19

1 [a]Matt. 15:1-20: *Mark* 7:*1-23* [b]Mark 3:22; 7:1; John 1:19; Acts 25:7

2 [a]Luke 11:38

3 [1]Or, *you also*

4 [1]Lit., *die the death* [a]Ex. 20:12; Deut. 5:16 [b]Ex. 21:17; Lev. 20:9

5 [1]Or, *a gift, an offering*

6 [1]Many mss. omit, *or his mother* [2]I.e., by supporting them with it [3]Some mss. read, *law*

8 [a]Is. 29:13

9 [a]Is. 29:13 [b]Col. 2:22

24 But the boat was already many [1]stadia away from the
land, [2]battered by the waves; for the wind was contrary.
25 And in [a]the [1]fourth watch of the night He came to
them, walking upon the sea.
26 And when the disciples saw Him walking on the sea,
they were [1]frightened, saying, "It is [a]a ghost!" And they cried
out for fear.
27 But immediately Jesus spoke to them, saying, "[a]Take
courage, it is I; [b]do not be afraid."
28 And Peter answered Him and said, "Lord, if it is You,
command me to come to You on the water."
29 And He said, "Come!" And Peter got out of the boat,
and walked on the water and came toward Jesus.
30 But seeing the wind, he became afraid, and beginning
to sink, he cried out, saying, "Lord, save me!"
31 And immediately Jesus stretched out His hand and
took hold of him, and *said to him, "[a]O you of little faith, why
did you doubt?"
32 And when they got into the boat, the wind stopped.
33 And those who were in the boat worshiped Him,
saying, "You are certainly [a]God's Son!"
34 [a]And when they had crossed over, they came to [1]land at
[b]Gennesaret.
35 And when the men of that place [1]recognized Him, they
sent into all that surrounding district and brought to Him all
who were ill;
36 and they *began* to entreat Him that they might just
touch [a]the fringe of His cloak; and as many as [b]touched *it* were
cured.

Chapter 15

[a]THEN some Pharisees and scribes *came to Jesus [b]from
Jerusalem, saying,
2 "Why do Your disciples transgress the tradition of the
elders? For they [a]do not wash their hands when they eat
bread."
3 And He answered and said to them, "And why do [1]you
yourselves transgress the commandment of God for the sake
of your tradition?
4 "For God said, '[a]HONOR YOUR FATHER AND MOTHER,'
and, '[b]HE WHO SPEAKS EVIL OF FATHER OR MOTHER, LET HIM [1]BE
PUT TO DEATH.'
5 "But you say, 'Whoever shall say to *his* father or mother,
"Anything of mine you might have been helped by has
been [1]given *to God*,"
6 he is not to honor his father [1]or his mother[2].' And *thus*
you invalidated the [3]word of God for the sake of your
tradition.
7 "You hypocrites, rightly did Isaiah prophesy of you,
saying,
8 '[a]THIS PEOPLE HONORS ME WITH THEIR LIPS,
BUT THEIR HEART IS FAR AWAY FROM ME.
9 [a]BUT IN VAIN DO THEY WORSHIP ME,
TEACHING AS THEIR [b]DOCTRINES THE PRECEPTS OF MEN.' "

10 And He called to Himself the multitude, and said to
them, "Hear, and understand.
11 "[a]Not what enters into the mouth defiles the man, but
what proceeds out of the mouth, this defiles the man."
12 Then the disciples *came and *said to Him, "Do You
know that the Pharisees were [1]offended when they heard this
statement?"
13 But He answered and said, "[a]Every plant which My
heavenly Father did not plant shall be rooted up.
14 "Let them alone; [a]they are blind guides [1]of the blind.
And [b]if a blind man guides a blind man, both will fall into a
pit."
15 And Peter answered and said to Him, "[a]Explain the
parable to us."
16 And He said, "Are you also still without understanding?
17 "Do you not understand that everything that goes into
the mouth passes into the [1]stomach, and is [2]eliminated?
18 "But [a]the things that proceed out of the mouth come
from the heart, and those defile the man.
19 "[a]For out of the heart come evil thoughts, murders,
adulteries, [1]fornications, thefts, false witness, slanders.
20 "These are the things which defile the man; but to eat
with unwashed hands does not defile the man."
21 [a]And Jesus went away from there, and withdrew into
the district of [b]Tyre and [b]Sidon.
22 And behold, a Canaanite woman came out from that
region, and *began* to cry out, saying, "Have mercy on me, O
Lord, [a]Son of David; my daughter is cruelly [b]demon-
possessed."
23 But He did not answer her a word. And His disciples
came to *Him* and kept asking Him, saying, "Send her away, for
she is shouting out after us."
24 But He answered and said, "I was sent only to [a]the lost
sheep of the house of Israel."
25 But she came and [a]*began* [1]to bow down before Him,
saying, "Lord, help me!"
26 And He answered and said, "It is not [1]good to take the
children's bread and throw *it* to the dogs."
27 But she said, "Yes, Lord; [1]but even the dogs feed on
the crumbs which fall from their master's table."
28 Then Jesus answered and said to her, "O woman, [a]your
faith is great; be it done for you as you wish." And her daughter was healed [1]at once.
29 [a]And departing from there, Jesus went along by [b]the
sea of Galilee, and having gone up to the mountain, He was
sitting there.
30 And great multitudes came to Him, bringing with them
those who were lame, crippled, blind, dumb, and many others,
and they laid them down at His feet; and [a]He healed them,
31 so that the multitude marveled as they saw the dumb
speaking, the crippled [1]restored, and the lame walking, and the
blind seeing; and they [a]glorified the God of Israel.
32 [a]And Jesus summoned to Himself His disciples, and
said, "[b]I feel compassion for the multitude, because they [1]have
remained with Me now for three days and have nothing to eat;

11 [a]Acts 10:14, 15; Matt. 15:18; 1 Tim. 4:3

12 [1]Lit., *caused to stumble*

13 [a]Is. 60:21; 61:3; John 15:2; 1 Cor. 3:9

14 [1]Some mss. omit *of the blind* [a]Matt. 23:16, 24 [b]Luke 6:39

15 [a]Matt. 13:36

17 [1]Lit., *belly* [2]Lit., *cast out into the latrine*

18 [a]Mark 7:20; Matt. 12:34

19 [1]I.e., sexual immorality [a]Gal. 5:19ff.

21 [a]Matt. 15:21-28: *Mark* 7:24-30 [b]Matt. 11:21

22 [a]Matt. 9:27 [b]Matt. 4:24

24 [a]Matt. 10:6

25 [1]Or, *to worship* [a]Matt. 8:2

26 [1]Or, *proper*

27 [1]Lit., *for*

28 [1]Lit., *from that hour* [a]Matt. 9:22

29 [a]Matt. 15:29-31; Mark 7:31-37 [b]Matt. 4:18

30 [a]Matt. 4:23

31 [1]Or, *healthy* [a]Matt. 9:8

32 [1]Lit., *are remaining* [a]Matt. 15:32-39: *Mark* 8:1-10; Matt. 14:13-21 [b]Matt. 9:36

E98-1

and I do not wish to send them away hungry, lest they faint on
the way."
33 And the disciples *said to Him, "Where would we get
so many loaves in a desert place to satisfy such a great
multitude?"
34 And Jesus *said to them, "How many loaves do you
have?" And they said, "Seven, and a few small fish."
35 And He directed the multitude to [1]sit down on the
ground;
36 and He took the seven loaves and the fish; and [a]giving
thanks, He broke *them* and started giving *them* to the disciples, and the disciples *in turn,* to the multitudes.
37 And they all ate, and were satisfied, and they picked up
what was left over of the broken pieces, seven [a]full baskets.
38 And those who ate were four thousand men, besides
women and children.
39 And dismissing the multitudes, He got into [a]the boat,
and came to the region of [b]Magadan.

[a] Chapter 16

AND the [b]Pharisees and Sadducees came up, and testing
Him [c]asked Him to show them a [1]sign from heaven.
2 [1]But He answered and said to them, "[a]When it is evening, you say, '*It will be* fair weather, for the sky is red.'
3 "And in the morning, '*There will be* a storm today, for
the sky is red and threatening.' Do you know how to discern
the [1]appearance of the sky, but cannot *discern* the signs of the
times?
4 "[a]An evil and adulterous generation seeks after a [1]sign;
and a [1]sign will not be given it, except the sign of Jonah." And
He left them, and went away.
5 And the disciples came to the other side and had forgotten to take bread.
6 And Jesus said to them, "Watch out and [a]beware of the
[1]leaven of the [b]Pharisees and Sadducees."
7 And they began to discuss among themselves, saying,
"*It is* because we took no bread."
8 But Jesus, aware of this, said, "[a]You men of little faith,
why do you discuss among yourselves because you have no
bread?
9 "Do you not yet understand or remember [a]the five
loaves of the five thousand, and how many large [b]baskets you
took up?
10 "Or [a]the seven loaves of the four thousand, and how
many [b]baskets you took up?
11 "How is it that you do not understand that I did not
speak to you concerning bread? But [a]beware of the [1]leaven of
the [b]Pharisees and Sadducees."
12 Then they understood that He did not say to beware of
the leaven of bread, but of the teaching of the [a]Pharisees and
Sadducees.
13 [a]Now when Jesus came into the district of [b]Caesarea
Philippi, He *began* asking His disciples, saying, "Who do
people say that [c]the Son of Man is?"

35 [1]Lit., *recline*

36 [a]Matt. 14:19

37 [a]Matt. 16:10; Mark 8:8, 20; Acts 9:25

39 [a]Mark 3:9 [b]Mark 8:10

1 [1]Or, *attesting miracle* [a]Matt. 16:1-12: *Mark 8:11-21* [b]Matt. 16:6, 11, 12; Matt. 3:7 [c]Matt. 12:38

2 [1]The earliest mss. omit verses 2 & 3 [a]Luke 12:54f.

3 [1]Lit., *face*

4 [1]Or, *attesting miracle* [a]Matt. 12:39

6 [1]Or, *yeast* [a]Matt. 16:11; Mark 8:15; Luke 12:1 [b]Matt. 16:1, 11, 12; 3:7

8 [a]Matt. 6:30; 8:26; 14:31

9 [a]Matt. 14:17-21 [b]Matt. 14:20

10 [a]Matt. 15:34-38 [b]Matt. 15:37

11 [1]Or, *yeast* [a]Matt. 16:6; Mark 8:15; Luke 12:1 [b]Matt. 16:6, 12; 3:7

12 [a]Matt. 16:6, 11; 3:7

13 [a]Matt. 16:13-16: *Mark 8:27-29; Luke 9:18-20* [b]Mark 8:27 [c]Matt. 8:20; 16:27, 28

14 And they said, "Some *say* [a]John the Baptist; some, [1b]Eli-
jah; and others, [2]Jeremiah, or one of the prophets."
15 He *said to them, "But who do you say that I am?"
16 And Simon Peter answered and said, "Thou art [1a]the
Christ, [b]the Son of [c]the living God."
17 And Jesus answered and said to him, "Blessed are you,
[1a]Simon Barjonas, because [b]flesh and blood did not reveal *this*
to you, but My Father who is in heaven.
18 "And I also say to you that you are [1a]Peter, and upon
this [2]rock I will build My church; and [3]the gates of [b]Hades
shall not overpower it.
19 "I will give you [a]the keys of the kingdom of heaven; and
[b]whatever you shall bind on earth shall have been bound in
heaven, and whatever you shall loose on earth shall have been
loosed in heaven."
20 [a]Then He [1]warned the disciples that they should tell no
one that He was [2b]the Christ.
21 [a]From that time Jesus Christ began to show His disciples that He must go to Jerusalem, and [b] suffer many things
from the elders and chief priests and scribes, and be killed, and
be raised up on the third day.
22 And Peter took Him aside and began to rebuke Him,
saying, "[1]God forbid *it*, Lord! This shall never [2]happen to
You."
23 But He turned and said to Peter, "Get behind Me,
[a]Satan! You are a stumbling-block to Me; for you are not
setting your mind on [1]God's interests, but man's."
24 Then Jesus said to His disciples, "If any one wishes to
come after Me, let him deny himself, and [a]take up his cross,
and follow Me.
25 "For [a]whoever wishes to save his [1]life shall lose it; but
whoever loses his [1]life for My sake shall find it.
26 "For what will a man be profited, if he gains the whole
world, and forfeits his [1]soul? Or what will a man give in exchange for his [1]soul?
27 "For the [a]Son of Man [b]is going to come in the glory of
His Father with His angels; and [c]WILL THEN RECOMPENSE EVERY
MAN ACCORDING TO HIS [1]DEEDS.
28 "Truly I say to you, there are some of those who are
standing here who shall not taste death until they see the [a]Son
of Man [b]coming in His kingdom."

CHAPTER 17

[a] AND six days later Jesus *took with him [b]Peter and [1]James
and John his brother, and *brought them up to a high mountain by themselves.
2 And He was transfigured before them; and His face
shone like the sun, and His garments became as white as light.
3 And behold, Moses and Elijah appeared to them, talking with Him.
4 And Peter [a]answered and said to Jesus, "Lord, it is good
for us to be here; if You wish, [b]I will make three [1]tabernacles
here, one for You, and one for Moses, and one for Elijah."
5 While he was still speaking, behold, a bright cloud
overshadowed them; and behold, [a]a voice out of the cloud,

14 [1]Gr., *Elias* [2]Gr. *Jeremias* [a]Matt. 14:2 [b]Mark 6:15; Luke 9:8; Matt. 17:10; John 1:21

16 [1]I.e., the Messiah [a]Matt. 16:20; John 11:27; Matt. 1:16 [b]Matt. 4:3 [c]Ps. 42:2; Matt. 26:63; Acts 14:15; Rom. 9:26; 2 Cor. 3:3; 6:16; 1 Thess. 1:9; 1 Tim. 3:15; 4:10; Heb. 3:12; 9:14; 10:31; 12:22; Rev. 7:2

17 [1]I.e., son of Jonas [a]John 1:42; 21:15-17 [b]1 Cor. 15:50; Gal. 1:16; Eph. 6:12; Heb. 2:14

18 [1]Gr., *Petros*, a stone [2]Gr., *petra*, large rock, bed-rock [3]I.e., the powers of death [a]Matt. 4:18 [b]Matt. 11:23

19 [a]Is. 22:22; Rev. 1:18; 3:7 [b]Matt. 18:18; John 20:23

20 [1]Or, *strictly admonished* [2]I.e., the Messiah [a]Mark 8:30; Luke 9:21; Matt. 8:4 [b]Matt. 16:16; John 11:27; Matt. 1:16

21 [a]Matt. 16:21-28: *Mark 8:31-9:1; Luke 9:22-27* [b]Matt. 17:9, 12, 22f.; 20:18f.; 27:63; Mark 9:12, 31; Luke 17:25; 18:32; 24:7; Matt. 12:40; John 2:19

22 [1]Lit., (God be) *merciful to You* [2]Lit., *be*

23 [1]Lit., *the things of God* [a]Matt. 4:10

24 [a]Matt. 10:38

25 [1]Or, *soul-life* [a]Matt. 10:39

26 [1]Or, *soul-life*

27 [1]Lit., *doing* [a]Matt. 8:20 [b]Matt. 10:23; 24:3, 27, 37, 39; 26:64; Mark 8:38f.; 13:26; Luke 21:27; Acts 1:11; 1 Cor. 15:23; 1 Thess. 1:10; 4:16; 2 Thess. 1:7, 10; 2:1, 8; James 5:7f.; 2 Pet. 1:16; 3:4, 12; 1 John 2:28; Rev. 1:7; John 21:22 [c]Ps. 62:12; Prov. 24:12; Rom. 2:6; 14:12; 2 Cor. 5:10; Eph. 6:8; Col. 3:25; Rev. 2:23; 20:12; 22:12; 1 Cor. 3:13

28 [a]Matt. 8:20 [b]Matt. 10:23; 24:3, 27, 37, 39; 26:64; Mark 8:38f.; 13:26; Luke 21:27: Acts 1:11; 1 Cor. 15:23; 1 Thess. 1:10; 4:16; 2 Thess. 1:7, 10; 2:1, 8; James 5:7f.; 2 Pet. 1:16; 3:4, 12; 1 John 2:28; Rev. 1:7; John 21:22

1 [1]Or, *Jacob* [a]Matt. 17:1-8: *Mark 9:2-8; Luke 9:28-36* [b]Matt. 26:37; Mark 5:37; Mark 13:3

4 [1]Or, *sacred tents* [a]Acts 3:12 [b]Mark 9:5; Luke 9:33

5 [a]2 Pet. 1:17f.

saying, "[b]This is My beloved Son, with whom I am well
pleased; hear Him!"
6 And when the disciples heard *this*, they fell on their
faces and were much afraid.
7 And Jesus came to *them* and touched them and said,
"Arise, and [a]do not be afraid."
8 And lifting up their eyes, they saw no one, except Jesus
Himself alone.
9 [a]And as they were coming down from the mountain,
Jesus commanded them, saying, "[b]Tell the vision to no one
until [c]the Son of Man has [d]risen from the dead."
10 And His disciples asked Him, saying, "Why then do
the scribes say that [a]Elijah must come first?"
11 And He answered and said, "Elijah is coming and will
restore all things;
12 but I say to you, that Elijah already came, and they did
not recognize him, but did [1]to him whatever they wished. So
also [a]the Son of Man is going to suffer [2]at their hands."
13 Then the disciples understood that He had spoken to
them about John the Baptist.
14 [a]And when they came to the multitude, a man came up
to Him, falling on his knees before Him, and saying,
15 "[1]Lord, have mercy on my son; for he is an [2a]epileptic,
and is very ill; for he often falls into the fire, and often into the
water.
16 "And I brought him to Your disciples, and they could
not cure him."
17 And Jesus answered and said, "O unbelieving and perverted generation, how long shall I be with you? How long
shall I put up with you? Bring him here to Me."
18 And Jesus rebuked him, and the demon came out of
him, and the boy was cured [1]at once.
19 Then the disciples came to Jesus privately and said,
"Why could we not cast it out?"
20 And He *said to them, "Because of the littleness of
your faith; for truly I say to you, [a]if you have faith as [b]a
mustard seed, you shall say to [c]this mountain, 'Move from
here to there,' and it shall move; and [d]nothing shall be impossible to you.
21 ([1a]See marginal note.)
22 [a]And while they were gathering together in Galilee,
Jesus said to them, "The Son of Man is going to be [1]delivered
into the hands of men;
23 and [a]they will kill Him, and He will be raised again on
the third day." And they were deeply grieved.
24 And when they had come to Capernaum, those who
collected [a]the [1]two-drachma *tax* came to Peter, and said,
"Does your teacher not pay [a]the [1]two-drachma *tax*?"
25 He *said, "Yes." And when he came into the house,
Jesus [1]spoke to him first, saying, "What do you think, Simon?
From whom do the kings of the earth collect [a]customs or [b]poll-
tax, from their sons or from strangers?"
26 And upon his saying, "From strangers," Jesus said to
him, "Consequently the sons are [1]exempt.
27 "But, lest we [1a]give them offense, go to the sea, and
throw in a hook, and take the first fish that comes up; and

5 [b]Matt. 3:17

7 [a]Matt. 14:27

9 [a]Matt. 17:9-13: *Mark 9:9-13* [b]Matt. 8:4 [c]Matt. 17:12, 22; 8:20 [d]Matt. 16:21

10 [a]Matt. 11:14; 16:14

12 [1]Lit., *in him* (or: *in his case*) [2]Lit., *by them* [a]Matt. 17:9, 22; 8:20

14 [a]Matt. 17:14-19: *Mark 9:14-28;* Matt. 17:14-18: *Luke* 9:37-42

15 [1]Or, *Sir* [2]Lit., *moon-smitten* [a]Matt. 4:24

18 [1]Lit., *from that hour*

20 [a]Matt. 21:21f.; Mark 11:23f.; Luke 17:6 [b]Matt. 13:31; Luke 17:6 [c]Matt. 17:9; 1 Cor. 13:2 [d]Mark 9:23; John 11:40

21 [1]Some late mss. add verse 21, "*But this kind does not go out except by prayer and fasting.*" [a]Mark 9:29

22 [1]Or, *betrayed* [a]Matt. 17:22, 23: *Mark 9:30-32; Luke 9:44, 45*

23 [a]Matt. 16:21; and 17:9

24 [1]Equivalent to two denarii or two days wages paid as a temple tax [a]Ex. 30:13; 38:26

25 [1]Or, *anticipated what he was going to say,* [a]Rom. 13:7 [b]Matt. 22:17, 19

26 [1]Or, *free*

27 [1]Lit., *cause them to stumble* [a]Matt. 5:29, 30; 18:6, 8, 9; Mark 9:42, 43, 45, 47; Luke 17:2; John 6:61; 1 Cor. 8:13

when you open its mouth, you will find a [2]stater; take that and
give it to them for you and Me."

CHAPTER 18

[a]AT that [1]time the disciples came to Jesus, saying, "Who then
is [2]greatest in the kingdom of heaven?"
2 And He called a child to Himself and stood him in
their midst,
3 and said, "Truly I say to you, unless you [1]are converted
and [a]become like children, you shall not enter the kingdom of
heaven.
4 "Whoever then humbles himself as this child, he is the
greatest in the kingdom of heaven.
5 "And whoever receives one such child in My name receives Me;
6 but [a]whoever [b]causes one of these little ones who believe in Me to stumble, it is better for him that a [1]heavy
millstone be hung around his neck, and that he be drowned in
the depth of the sea.
7 "Woe to the world because of *its* stumbling-blocks! For
[a]it is inevitable that stumbling-blocks come; but woe to that
man through whom the stumbling-block comes!
8 "And [a]if your hand or your foot [b]causes you to stumble,
cut it off and throw it from you; it is better for you to enter life
crippled or lame, than having two hands or two feet, to be cast
into the eternal fire.
9 "And [a]if your eye [b]causes you to stumble, pluck it out,
and throw it from you. It is better for you to enter life with one
eye, than having two eyes, to be cast into the [1c]hell of fire.
10 "See that you do not despise one of these little ones, for
I say to you, that [a]their angels in heaven continually behold
the face of My Father who is in heaven.
11 ["[1a]For the Son of Man has come to save that which
was lost.]
12 "What do you think? [a]If any man [1]has a hundred sheep,
and one of them has gone astray, does he not leave the ninety-
nine on the mountains and go and search for the one that is
straying?
13 "And if it turns out that he finds it, truly I say to you, he
rejoices over it more than over the ninety-nine which have not
gone astray.
14 "Thus it is not *the* will [1]of your Father who is in heaven
that one of these little ones perish.
15 "And [a]if your brother sins[1], go and reprove him [2]in private; if he listens to you, you have won your brother.
16 "But if he does not listen *to you,* take one or two more
with you, so that [a]BY THE MOUTH OF TWO OR THREE WITNESSES
EVERY [1]FACT MAY BE CONFIRMED.
17 "And if he refuses to listen to them, [a]tell it to the
church; and if he refuses to listen even to the church, [b]let him
be to you as [1]a Gentile and [1]a [2]tax-gatherer.
18 "Truly I say to you, [a]whatever you shall [1]bind on earth
shall have been bound in heaven; and whatever you [2]loose on
earth shall have been loosed in heaven.
19 "Again I say to you, that if two of you agree on earth

27 [2]Or, *shekel,* worth four drachmas

1 [1]Lit., *hour* [2]Lit., *greater* [a]Matt. 18:1-5; Mark 9:33-37; Luke 9:46-48

3 [1]Lit., *are turned* [a]Matt. 19:14; Mark 10:15; Luke 18:17; 1 Cor. 14:20; 1 Pet. 2:2

6 [1]Lit., *millstone turned by a donkey* [a]Mark 9:42; Luke 17:2; 1 Cor. 8:12 [b]Matt. 17:27

7 [a]Luke 17:1; 1 Cor. 11:19; 1 Tim. 4:1

8 [a]Matt. 5:30; Mark 9:43; Matt. 17:27 [b]Matt. 17:27

9 [1]Gr. *Gehenna of fire* [a]Matt. 5:29; Mark 9:47; Matt. 17:27 [b]Matt. 17:27 [c]Matt. 5:22

10 [a]Acts 12:15; Luke 1:19; Rev. 8:2; 2 Kin. 25:19; 1 Kin. 10:8

11 [1]Most ancient mss. omit this verse [a]Luke 19:10

12 [1]Or, *comes to have* [a]Matt. 18:12-14; Luke 15:4-7

14 [1]Lit., *before*

15 [1]Many mss. add here: *against you* [2]Lit., *between you and him alone* [a]Luke 17:3; Gal. 6:1; 2 Thess. 3:15; James 5:19; Lev. 19:17

16 [1]Lit., *word* [a]Deut. 19:15; John 8:17; 2 Cor. 13:1; 1 Tim. 5:19; Heb. 10:28

17 [1]Lit., *the* [2]A publican who collected Roman taxes [a]1 Cor. 6:1ff. [b]2 Thess. 3:6, 14f.

18 [1]Or, *forbid* [2]Or, *permit* [a]Matt. 16:19; John 20:23

about anything that they may ask, [a]it shall be done for them
[1]by My Father who is in heaven.
20 "For where two or three have gathered together in My
name, there I am in their midst."
21 Then Peter came and said to Him, "Lord, [a]how often
shall my brother sin against me and I forgive him? Up to
[b]seven times?"
22 Jesus *said to him, "I do not say to you, up to seven
times, but up to [a]seventy times seven.
23 "For this reason [a] the kingdom of heaven may be compared to a certain king who wished to [b]settle accounts with his
slaves.
24 "And when he had begun to settle *them,* there was
brought to him one who owed him [1]ten thousand talents.
25 "But since he [1a]did not have *the means* to repay, his lord
commanded him [b]to be sold, along with his wife and children
and all that he had, and repayment to be made.
26 "The slave therefore falling down, [a]prostrated himself
before him, saying, 'Have patience with me, and I will repay
you everything.'
27 "And the lord of that slave felt compassion and released
him and forgave him the [1]debt.
28 "But that slave went out and found one of his fellow-
slaves who owed him a hundred [1]denarii; and he seized him
and *began* to choke *him,* saying, 'Pay back what you owe.'
29 "So his fellow-slave fell down and *began* to entreat him,
saying, 'Have patience with me and I will repay you.'
30 "He was unwilling however, but went and threw him in
prison until he should pay back what was owed.
31 "So when his fellow-slaves saw what had happened, they
were deeply grieved and came and reported to their lord all
that had happened.
32 "Then summoning him, his lord *said to him, 'You
wicked slave, I forgave you all that debt because you entreated
me.
33 'Should you not also have had mercy on your fellow-
slave, even as I had mercy on you?'
34 "And his lord, moved with anger, handed him over to
the torturers until he should repay all that was owed him.
35 "[a]So shall My heavenly Father also do to you, if each of
you does not forgive his brother from [1]your heart."

[a]

Chapter 19

AND it came about that when Jesus had finished these
words, He departed from Galilee, and [b]came into the region of
Judea beyond the Jordan;
2 and great multitudes followed Him, and [a]He healed
them there.
3 And *some* Pharisees came to Him, testing Him, and
saying, "[a]Is it lawful *for a man* to divorce his wife for any cause
at all?"
4 And He answered and said, "Have you not read, [a]that
He who created *them* from the beginning MADE THEM MALE
AND FEMALE,
5 and said, '[a]FOR THIS CAUSE A MAN SHALL LEAVE HIS FATHER

18:19 [1]Lit., *from* [a]Matt. 7:7

21 [a]Matt. 18:15 [b]Luke 17:4

22 [a]Gen. 4:24

23 [a]Matt. 13:24 [b]Matt. 25:19

24 [1]About $10,000,000 in silver content but worth much more in buying power

25 [1]Or, *was unable to* [a]Luke 7:42 [b]Ex. 21:2; Lev. 25:39; 2 Kin. 4:1; Neh. 5:5

26 [a]Matt. 8:2

27 [1]Or, *loan*

28 [1]The denarius was worth 18 cents in silver, equivalent to a day's wage

35 [1]Lit., *your hearts* [a]Matt. 6:14

19:1 [a]Matt. 7:28 [b]Matt. 19:1-9: *Mark 10:1-12*

2 [a]Matt. 4:23

3 [a]Matt. 5:31

4 [a]Gen. 1:27; 5:2

5 [a]Eph. 5:31; Gen. 2:24

AND MOTHER, AND SHALL CLEAVE TO HIS WIFE; AND [b]THE TWO
SHALL BECOME ONE FLESH'?
6 "Consequently they are no more two, but one flesh.
What therefore God has joined together, let no man
separate."
7 They *said to Him, "[a]Why then did Moses command
to GIVE HER A CERTIFICATE AND DIVORCE HER?"
8 He *said to them, "[1]Because of your hardness of heart,
Moses permitted you to divorce your wives; but from the beginning it has not been this way.
9 "And I say to you, [a]whoever divorces his wife, except for
[1]immorality, and marries another [2]commits adultery."[3]
10 The disciples *said to Him, "If the relationship of the
man with his wife is like this, it is better not to marry."
11 But He said to them, "[a]Not all men *can* accept this
statement, but [b]*only* those to whom it has been given.
12 "For there are eunuchs who were born that way from
their mother's womb; and there are eunuchs who were made
eunuchs by men; and there are *also* eunuchs who made themselves eunuchs for the sake of the kingdom of heaven. He who
is able to accept *this* let him accept *it*."
13 [a]Then *some* children were brought to Him so that He
might lay His hands on them and pray; and the disciples rebuked them.
14 But Jesus said, "[1a]Let the children alone, and do not
hinder them from coming to Me; for [b]the kingdom of heaven
belongs to such as these."
15 And after laying His hands on them, He departed from
there.
16 [a]And behold, one came to Him and said, "Teacher,
what good thing shall I do that I may obtain [b]eternal life?"
17 And He said to him, "Why are you asking Me about
what is good? There is *only* One who is good; but [a]if you wish
to enter into life, keep the commandments."
18 He *said to Him, "Which ones?" And Jesus said,
"[a]YOU SHALL NOT COMMIT MURDER; YOU SHALL NOT COMMIT
ADULTERY; YOU SHALL NOT STEAL; YOU SHALL NOT BEAR FALSE
WITNESS;
19 [a]HONOR YOUR FATHER AND MOTHER; and [b]YOU SHALL
LOVE YOUR NEIGHBOR AS YOURSELF."
20 The young man *said to Him, "All these things I have
kept; what am I still lacking?"
21 Jesus said to him, "If you wish to be [1]complete, go *and*
[a]sell your possessions and give to *the* poor, and you shall have
[b]treasure in heaven; and come, follow Me."
22 But when the young man heard this statement, he went
away grieved; for he was one who owned much property.
23 And Jesus said to His disciples, "Truly I say to you, [a]it
is hard for a rich man to enter the kingdom of heaven.
24 "And again I say to you, [a]it is easier for a camel to go
through the eye of a needle, than for a rich man to enter the
kingdom of God."
25 And when the disciples heard *this*, they were very astonished and said, "Then who can be saved?"
26 And looking upon *them* Jesus said to them, "[a]With
men this is impossible, but with God all things are possible."

5 [b]1 Cor. 6:16

7 [a]Deut. 24:1-4

8 [1]Or, *with reference to*

9 [1]I.e., sexual immorality [2]Some early mss. read: *makes her commit adultery* [3]Some early mss. add: *and he who marries a divorced woman commits adultery* [a]Matt. 5:32

11 [a]1 Cor. 7:7ff. 17 [b]Matt. 13:11

13 [a]Matt. 19:13-15: *Mark 10:13-16; Luke 18:15-17*

14 [1]Or, *permit the children* [a]Matt. 18:3; Mark 10:15; Luke 18:17; 1 Cor. 14:20; 1 Pet. 2:2 [b]Matt. 5:3

16 [a]Matt. 19:16-29: *Mark 10:17-30; Luke 18:18-30;* Luke 10:25-28 [b]Matt. 25:46

17 [a]Lev. 18:5; Neh. 9:29; Ezek. 20:21

18 [a]Ex. 20:13-16; Deut. 5:17-20

19 [a]Ex. 20:12; Deut. 5:16 [b]Lev. 19:18

21 [1]Or, *perfect* [a]Luke 12:33; Luke 16:9; Acts 2:45; 4:34f. [b]Matt 6:20

23 [a]Matt. 13:22; Mark 10:23f; Luke 18:24

24 [a]Mark 10:25; Luke 18:25

26 [a]Gen. 18:14; Job 42:2; Jer. 32:17; Zech. 8:6; Mark 10:27; Luke 18:27; 1:37

27 Then Peter answered and said to Him, "Behold, we
have left everything and followed You; what then will there be
for us?"
28 And Jesus said to them, "Truly I say to you, that you
who have followed Me, in the regeneration when [a]the Son of
Man will sit on [1]His glorious throne, [b]you also shall sit upon
twelve thrones, judging the twelve tribes of Israel.
29 "And [a]everyone who has left houses or brothers or sisters
or father or mother[1] or children or farms for My name's sake,
shall receive [2]many times as much, and shall inherit eternal
life.
30 "[a]But many *who are* first will be last; and *the* last, first.

Chapter 20

"FOR [a]the kingdom of heaven is like [1]a landowner who
went out early in the morning to hire laborers [2]for his
[b]vineyard.
2 "And when he had agreed with the laborers for a [1]denar-
ius for the day, he sent them into his vineyard.
3 "And he went out about the [1]third hour and saw others
standing idle in the market place;
4 and to those he said, 'You too go into the vineyard, and
whatever is right I will give you.' And *so* they went.
5 "Again he went out about the [1]sixth and the ninth hour,
and did [2]the same thing.
6 "And about the [1]eleventh *hour* he went out, and found
others standing; and he *said to them, 'Why have you been
standing here idle all day long?'
7 "They *said to him, 'Because no one hired us.' He *said
to them, 'You too go into the vineyard.'
8 "And when [a]evening had come, the [1]owner of the vineyard *said to his [b]foreman, 'Call the laborers and pay them
their wages, beginning with the last *group* to the first.'
9 "And when those *hired* about the eleventh hour came,
each one received a [1]denarius.
10 "And when those *hired* first came, they thought that
they would receive more; and they also received each one a
denarius.
11 "And when they received it, they grumbled at the
landowner,
12 saying, 'These last men have worked *only* one hour,
and you have made them equal to us who have borne the
burden and the [a]scorching heat of the day.'
13 "But he answered and said to one of them, '[a]Friend, I
am doing you no wrong; did you not agree with me for a
denarius?
14 'Take what is yours and go your way, but I wish to give
to this last man the same as to you.
15 'Is it not lawful for me to do what I wish with what is my
own? Or is your [a]eye [1]envious because I am [2]generous?'
16 "Thus [a]the last shall be first, and the first last."
17 [a]And as Jesus was about to go up to Jerusalem, He took
the twelve *disciples* aside by themselves, and on the way He
said to them,
18 "Behold, we are going up to Jerusalem; and the Son of

28 [1]Lit., *the throne of His glory* [a]Matt. 25:31 [b]Luke 22:30; Rev. 3:21; 4:4; 11:16; 20:4

29 [1]Many mss. add here: *or wife* [2]Many mss. read: *a hundredfold* [a]Mark 10:29f.; Luke 18:29f.; Matt. 6:33

30 [a]Matt. 20:16; Mark 10:31; Luke 13:30

1 [1]Lit., *a man, a landowner* [2]Lit., *into* [a]Matt. 13:24 [b]Matt. 21:28, 33

2 [1]Cf. Matt. 18:28

3 [1]I.e., 9 a.m.

5 [1]I.e., Noon and 3 p.m. [2]Lit., *similarly*

6 [1]I.e., 5 p.m.

8 [1]Or, *lord* [a]Lev. 19:13 [b]Luke 8:3

9 [1]The denarius was worth 18 cents in silver, equivalent to one day's wage

12 [a]Jonah 4:8; Luke 12:55; James 1:11

13 [a]Matt. 22:12; 26:50

15 [1]Lit., *evil* [2]Lit., *good* [a]Matt. 6:23; Mark 7:22; Deut. 15:9

16 [a]Matt. 19:30

17 [a]Matt. 20:17-19: *Mark 10:32-34; Luke 18:31-33*

Man [a]will be [1]delivered up to the chief priests and scribes, and
they will condemn Him to death,
19 and [a]will deliver Him up to the Gentiles to mock and
scourge and crucify *Him,* and on [b]the third day He will be
raised up."
20 [a]Then the mother of [b]the sons of Zebedee came to
Him with her sons, [c]bowing down, and making a request of
Him.
21 And He said to her, "What do you wish?" She *said to
Him, "Command that in Your kingdom these two sons of
mine [a]may sit, one on Your right and one on Your left."
22 But Jesus answered and said, "You do not know what
you are asking for. Are you able [a]to drink the cup that I am
about to drink?" They *said to Him, "We are able."
23 He *said to them, "[a]My cup you shall drink; but to sit
on My right and on *My* left, this is not Mine to give, [b]but *it is*
for those for whom it has been [c]prepared by My Father."
24 And hearing *this,* the ten became indignant at the two
brothers.
25 [a]But Jesus called them to Himself, and said, "You
know that the rulers of the Gentiles lord it over them, and
their great men exercise authority over them.
26 "It is not so among you, [a]but whoever wishes to become
great among you shall be your servant,
27 and whoever wishes to be first among you shall be your
slave;
28 just as [a]the Son of Man [b]did not come to be served, but
to serve, and to give His [1]life a ransom for many."
29 [a]And as they were going out from Jericho, a great multitude followed Him.
30 And behold, two blind men sitting by the road, hearing
that Jesus was passing by, cried out, saying, "Lord, [a]have mercy
on us, [b]Son of David!"
31 And the multitude sternly told them to be quiet; but
they cried out all the more, saying, "Lord, have mercy on us,
[a]Son of David!"
32 And Jesus stopped and called them, and said, "What
do you wish Me to do for you?"
33 They *said to Him, "Lord, we want our eyes to be
opened."
34 And moved with compassion, Jesus touched their eyes;
and immediately they received their sight, and followed Him.

Chapter 21

[a]AND when they had approached Jerusalem and had come to
Bethphage, to [b]the Mount of Olives, then Jesus sent two
disciples,
2 saying to them, "Go into the village opposite you, and
immediately you will find a donkey tied *there* and a colt with
her; untie *them,* and bring *them* to Me.
3 "And if anyone says something to you, you shall say,
'The Lord has need of them;' and immediately he will send
them."
4 [a]Now this took place that what was spoken through the
prophet might be fulfilled, saying,

18 [1]Or, *betrayed* [a]Matt. 16:21

19 [a]Matt. 27:2; Acts 2:23; 3:13; 4:27; 21:11 [b]Matt. 16:21

20 [a]Matt. 20:20-28: *Mark 10:35-45* [b]Matt. 4:21; 10:2 [c]Matt. 8:2

21 [a]Matt. 19:28

22 [a]Matt. 26:39, 42; Luke 22:42; John 18:11; Is. 51:17, 22; Jer. 49:12

23 [a]Acts 12:2; Rev. 1:9 [b]Matt. 13:11 [c]Matt. 25:34

25 [a]Matt. 20:25-28; Luke 22:25-27

26 [a]Matt. 23:11; Mark 9:35; 10:43

28 [1]Or, *soul* [a]Matt. 8:20 [b]Matt. 26:28; John 13:13ff.; 2 Cor. 8:9; Phil. 2:7; 1 Tim. 2:6; Titus 2:14; Heb. 9:28; Rev. 1:5

29 [a]Matt. 20:29-34: *Mark 10:46-52; Luke 18:35-43;* Matt. 9:27-31

30 [a]Matt. 20:31 [b]Matt. 9:27

31 [a]Matt. 9:27

1 [a]Matt. 21:1-9: *Mark 11:1-10; Luke 19:29-38* [b]Matt. 24:3; 26:30; Mark 11:1; 13:3; 14:26; Luke 19:37; 22:39; John 8:1; Luke 19:29; 21:37; Acts 1:12

4 [a]Matt. 21:4-9: *John 12:12-15*

5 “[a]SAY TO THE DAUGHTER OF ZION,
‘BEHOLD YOUR KING IS COMING TO YOU,
GENTLE, AND MOUNTED UPON A DONKEY,
EVEN UPON A COLT, THE FOAL OF A BEAST OF BURDEN.’ ”
6 And the disciples went and did just as Jesus had directed them,
7 and brought the donkey and the colt, and laid on them
their garments; [1]on which He sat.
8 And most of the multitude [a]spread their garments in
the road, and others were cutting branches from the trees, and
spreading them in the road.
9 And the multitudes going before Him, and those who
followed after were crying out, saying,
“[a]HOSANNA to the [b]Son of David;
[a]BLESSED IS HE WHO COMES IN THE NAME OF THE LORD;
HOSANNA [c]in the highest!”
10 And when He had entered Jerusalem, all the city was
stirred, saying, “Who is this?”
11 And the multitudes were saying, “This is [a]the prophet
Jesus, from [b]Nazareth in Galilee.”
12 [a]And Jesus entered the temple and cast out all those
who were buying and selling in the temple, and overturned the
tables of the [b]money-changers and the seats of those who were
selling [1c]doves.
13 And He *said to them, “It is written, ‘[a]MY HOUSE SHALL
BE CALLED A HOUSE OF PRAYER;’ but you are making it a robbers’
[1]den.”
14 And *the* blind and *the* lame came to Him in the
temple, and [a]He healed them.
15 But when the chief priests and the scribes saw the wonderful things that He had done, and the children who were
crying out in the temple and saying, “Hosanna to the [a]Son of
David,” they became indignant,
16 and said to Him, “Do You hear what these are saying?”
And Jesus *said to them, “Yes; have you never read, ‘[a]OUT OF
THE MOUTH OF INFANTS AND NURSING BABES THOU HAST PRE-
PARED PRAISE FOR THYSELF’?”
17 And He left them and went out of the city to [a]Bethany,
and lodged there.
18 [a]Now in the morning, when He returned to the city,
He became hungry.
19 And seeing a lone fig tree by the road, He came to it,
and found nothing on it except leaves only; and He *said to it,
“No longer shall there ever be *any* fruit from you.” And at
once the fig tree withered.
20 And seeing *this,* the disciples marveled, saying, “How
did the fig tree wither at once?”
21 And Jesus answered and said to them, “Truly I say to
you, [a]if you have faith, and do not doubt, you shall not only do
what was done to the fig tree, but even if you say to this
mountain, ‘Be taken up and cast into the sea,’ it shall happen.
22 “And [a]everything you ask in prayer, believing, you shall
receive.”
23 [a]And when He had come into the temple, the chief
priests and the elders of the people came to Him as He was

5 [a]Is. 62:11; Zech. 9:9
7 [1]Lit., *on them*
8 [a]2 Kin. 9:13
9 [a]Ps. 118:26f. [b]Matt. 9:27 [c]Luke 2:14
11 [a]John 1:21, 25; 6:14; 7:40; Acts 3:22f.; 7:37; Matt. 21:26; Mark 6:15; Luke 7:16, 39; 13:33; 24:19; John 4:19; 9:17 [b]Matt. 2:23
12 [1]Lit. *the doves* [a]Matt. 21:12-16: *Mark 11:15-18; Luke 19:45-47;* Matt. 21:12, 13: *John 2:13-16* [b]Ex. 30:13 [c]Lev. 1:14; 5:7; 12:8
13 [1]Lit., *cave* [a]Is. 56:7; Jer. 7:11
14 [a]Matt. 4:23
15 [a]Matt. 9:27
16 [a]Ps. 8:2
17 [a]Matt. 26:6; Mark 11:1, 11, 12; 14:3; Luke 19:29; 24:50; John 11:1, 18; 12:1
18 [a]Matt. 21:18-22: *Mark 11:12-14, 20-24*
21 [a]Matt. 17:20; Mark 11:23; Luke 17:6; James 1:6
22 [a]Matt. 7:7
23 [a]Matt. 21:23-27: *Mark 11:27-33; Luke 20:1-8*

teaching, and said, "By what authority are You doing these
things, and who gave You this authority?"
24 But Jesus answered and said to them, "I will ask you
one [1]thing too, which if you tell Me, I will also tell you by what
authority I do these things.
25 "The baptism of John was from what *source*, from heav-
en or from men?" And they *began* reasoning among themselves, saying, "If we say, 'From heaven,' He will say to us,
'Then why did you not believe him?'
26 "But if we say, 'From men,' we fear the multitude; for
they all hold John to be [a]a prophet."
27 And they answered Jesus and said, "We do not know."
He also said to them, "Neither will I tell you by what authority
I do these things.
28 "But what do you think? A man had two [1]sons, and he
came to the first and said, '[2]Son, go work today in the
[a]vineyard.'
29 "And he answered and said, '[1]I will, sir'; and he did not
go.
30 "And he came to the second and said [1]the same thing.
But he answered and said, '[2]I will not'; *yet* he afterward regretted *it* and went.
31 "Which of the two did the will of his father?" They
*said, "The latter." Jesus *said to them, "Truly I say to you
that [a]the [1]tax-gatherers and harlots [2]will get into the kingdom
of God before you.
32 "For John came to you in the way of righteousness and
you did not believe him; but [a]the tax-gatherers and harlots did
believe him; and you, seeing this, did not even feel remorse
afterward so as to believe him.
33 "Listen to another parable. [a]There was a [1]landowner
who [b]PLANTED A [c]VINEYARD AND PUT A WALL AROUND IT AND DUG
A [d]WINE PRESS IN IT, AND [d]BUILT A TOWER, and rented it out to
[2]vine-growers, and [e]went on a journey.
34 "And when the [1]harvest time approached, he [a]sent his
slaves to the vine-growers to receive his produce.
35 "And the vine-growers took his slaves and beat one, and
killed another, and stoned a third.
36 "Again he [a]sent another group of slaves larger than the
first; and they did [1]the same thing to them.
37 "But afterward he sent his son to them, saying, 'They
will respect my son.'
38 "But when the vine-growers saw the son, they said
among themselves, 'This is the heir; come, let us kill him, and
seize his inheritance.'
39 "And they took him, and cast him out of the vineyard,
and killed *him*.
40 "Therefore when the [1]owner of the vineyard comes,
what will he do to those vine-growers?"
41 They *said to Him, "He will bring those wretches to a
wretched end, and [a]will rent out the vineyard to other vine-
growers, who will pay him the proceeds at the *proper* seasons."
42 Jesus *said to them, "Did you never read in the
Scriptures,

'[a]THE STONE WHICH THE BUILDERS REJECTED,
THIS BECAME THE CHIEF CORNER *STONE*;

24 [1]Lit., *word*

26 [a]Matt. 11:9; Mark 6:20

28 [1]Lit., *children* [2]Lit., *Child*
[a]Matt. 21:33; 20:1

29 [1]Some mss. read *'I will not'; yet he afterward regretted and went*

30 [1]Lit., *likewise* [2]Some mss. read *'I will'; and he did not go*

31 [1]A publican who collected Roman taxes [2]Or, *are getting into*
[a]Luke 7:29, 37-50

32 [a]Luke 3:12

33 [1]Lit., *a man, a householder* [2]Or, *tenant farmers* (Here and in vss. 34 35, 38, 40)
[a]Matt. 21:33-46: *Mark 12:1-12; Luke 20:9-19* [b]Ps. 80:8; Is. 5:1ff. [c]Matt. 21:28; 20:1 [d]Is. 5:2 [e]Matt. 25:14

34 [1]Lit., *the season of the fruits*
[a]Matt. 22:3

36 [1]Lit., *likewise*
[a]Matt. 22:4

40 [1]Lit., *lord*

41 [a]Matt. 8:11f.; Acts 13:46; 18:6; 28:28

42 [a]Ps. 118:22; Acts 4:11; 1 Pet. 2:7; Rom. 9:33

THIS CAME ABOUT FROM THE LORD,
AND IT IS MARVELOUS IN OUR EYES'?
43 "Therefore I say to you, the kingdom of God will be
taken away from you, and be given to a nation producing the
fruit of it.
44 "And he who falls on this stone will be broken to pieces;
but on whomever it falls, it will scatter him like dust."
45 And when the chief priests and the Pharisees heard His
parables, they understood that He was speaking about them.
46 And when they sought to seize Him, they [a]became afraid
of the multitudes, because they held Him to be a
[b]prophet.

CHAPTER 22

AND Jesus [a]answered and spoke to them again in parables,
saying,
2 "[a]The kingdom of heaven may be compared to [1]a king,
who [2]gave a wedding feast for his son.
3 "And he [a]sent out his slaves to call those who had been
invited to the wedding feast, and they were unwilling to come.
4 "Again he [a]sent out other slaves saying, 'Tell those who
have been invited, "Behold, I have prepared my dinner; my
oxen and my fattened livestock are *all* butchered and everything
is ready; come to the wedding feast."'
5 "But they paid no attention and went their way, one to
his own [1]farm, another to his business,
6 and the rest seized his slaves and mistreated them and
killed them.
7 "But the king was enraged and sent his armies, and
destroyed those murderers, and set their city on fire.
8 "Then he *said to his slaves, 'The wedding is ready, but
those who were invited were not worthy.
9 'Go therefore to [a]the main highways, and as many as
you find *there,* invite to the wedding feast.'
10 "And those slaves went out into the streets, and gathered
together all they found, both evil and good; and the wedding
hall was filled with [1]dinner guests.
11 "But when the king came in to look over the dinner
guests, he saw there [a]a man not dressed in wedding clothes,
12 and he *said to him, '[a]Friend, how did you come in
here [1]without wedding clothes?' And he was speechless.
13 "Then the king said to the servants, 'Bind him hand and
foot, and cast him into [a]the outer darkness; in that place [a]there
shall be weeping and gnashing of teeth.'
14 "For many are [1a]called, but few *are* [a]chosen."
15 [a]Then the Pharisees went and counseled together how
they might trap Him [1]in what He said.
16 And they *sent their disciples to Him, along with the
[a]Herodians, saying, "Teacher, we know that You are truthful
and teach the way of God in truth, and [1]defer to no one; for
You are not partial to any.
17 "Tell us therefore, what do You think? Is it [1]lawful to
give a [a]poll-tax to [b]Caesar, or not?"
18 But Jesus perceived their [1]malice, and said, "Why are
you testing Me, you hypocrites?

46 [a]Matt. 21:26 [b]Matt. 21:11

1 [a]Acts 3:12

2 [1]Lit., *a man, a king* [2]Lit., *made* [a]Matt. 22:2-14; Luke 14:16-24; Matt. 13:24

3 [a]Matt. 21:34

4 [a]Matt. 21:36

5 [1]Or, *field*

9 [a]Ezek. 21:21; Obad. 14

10 [1]Lit., *those reclining at table*

11 [a]2 Kin. 10:22

12 [1]Lit., *not having* [a]Matt. 20:13; 26:50

13 [a]Matt. 8:12

14 [1]Or, *invited* [a]Rev. 17:14; 2 Pet. 1:10; Matt. 24:22

15 [1]Lit., *in word* [a]Matt. 22:15-22: *Mark 12:13-17; Luke 20:20-26*

16 [1]I.e., you court no man's favor [a]Mark 3:6; 12:13; Mark 8:15

17 [1]Or, *permissible* [a]Matt. 17:25 [b]Luke 2:1; 3:1

18 [1]Or, *wickedness*

19 "Show Me the [a]coin *used* for the poll-tax." And they
brought Him a [1]denarius.
20 And He *said to them, "Whose likeness and inscription is this?"
21 They *said to Him, "Caesar's." Then He *said to
them, "[a]Then render to Caesar the things that are Caesar's;
and to God the things that are God's."
22 And hearing *this*, they marveled, and [a]leaving Him,
they went away.
23 [a]On that day *some* [b]Sadducees (who say [c]there is no
resurrection) came to Him and questioned Him,
24 saying, "Teacher, Moses said, '[a]IF A MAN DIES, HAVING
NO CHILDREN, HIS BROTHER AS NEXT OF KIN SHALL MARRY HIS
WIFE, AND RAISE UP AN OFFSPRING TO HIS BROTHER.'
25 "Now there were seven brothers with us; and the first
married and died, and having no offspring left his wife to his
brother;
26 so also the second, and the third, down to the seventh.
27 "And last of all, the woman died.
28 "In the resurrection therefore whose wife of the seven
shall she be? For they all had her."
29 But Jesus answered and said to them, "You are mistaken,
[a]not [1]understanding the Scriptures, or the power of God.
30 "For in the resurrection they neither [a]marry, nor are
given in marriage, but are like angels[1] in heaven.
31 "But regarding the resurrection of the dead, have you
not read that which was spoken to you by God, saying,
32 '[a]I AM THE GOD OF ABRAHAM, AND THE GOD OF ISAAC,
AND THE GOD OF JACOB'? God is not *the God* of *the* dead but of
the living."
33 And when the multitudes heard *this*, [a]they were astonished at His teaching.
34 [a]But when the Pharisees heard that He had put [b]the
Sadducees to silence, they gathered themselves together.
35 And one of them, [1a]a lawyer, asked Him a question,
testing Him,
36 "Teacher, which is the great commandment in the
Law?"
37 And He said to him, " '[a]YOU SHALL LOVE THE LORD
YOUR GOD WITH ALL YOUR HEART, AND WITH ALL YOUR SOUL,
AND WITH ALL YOUR MIND.'
38 "This is the great and [1]foremost commandment.
39 "And a second is like it, '[a]YOU SHALL LOVE YOUR NEIGH-
BOR AS YOURSELF.'
40 "[a]On these two commandments depend the whole Law
and the Prophets."
41 [a]Now while the Pharisees were gathered together, Jesus
asked them a question,
42 saying, "What do you think about [1]the Christ, whose
son is He?" They *said to Him, "[a]*The son* of David."
43 He *said to them, "Then how does David [1a]in the
Spirit call Him 'Lord,' saying,
44 '[a]THE LORD SAID TO MY LORD,
"SIT AT MY RIGHT HAND,
UNTIL I PUT THINE ENEMIES BENEATH THY FEET." '
45 "If David then calls Him 'Lord', how is He his son?"

19 [1]The denarius was worth 18 cents in silver, equivalent to one day's wage [a]Matt. 17:25
21 [a]Mark 12:17; Luke 20:25; Rom. 13:7
22 [a]Mark 12:12
23 [a]Matt. 22:23-33: *Mark 12:18-27; Luke 20:27-40* [b]Matt. 3:7 [c]Acts 23:8
24 [a]Deut. 25:5
29 [1]Or, *knowing* [a]John 20:9
30 [1]Other mss. add: *of God* [a]Matt. 24:38; Luke 17:27
32 [a]Ex. 3:6
33 [a]Matt. 7:28
34 [a]Matt. 22:34-40: *Mark 12:28-31;* Luke 10:25-37 [b]Matt. 3:7
35 [1]I.e., an expert in the Mosaic Law [a]Luke 7:30; 10:25; 11:45, 46, 52; 14:3; Titus 3:13
37 [a]Deut. 6:5
38 [1]Or, *first*
39 [a]Matt. 19:19; Gal. 5:14; Lev. 19:18
40 [a]Matt. 7:12
41 [a]Matt. 22:41-46: *Mark 12:35-37; Luke 20:41-44*
42 [1]I.e., the Messiah [a]Matt. 9:27
43 [1]Or, *by inspiration* [a]Rev. 1:10; 4:2; 2 Sam. 23:2
44 [a]Ps. 110:1; Acts 2:34f.; Heb. 1:13; 1 Cor. 15:25; Heb. 10:13; Matt. 26:64; Mark 16:19

46 And [a]no one was able to answer Him a word, nor did
anyone dare from that day on to ask Him another question.

[a] Chapter 23

THEN Jesus spoke to the multitudes and to His disciples,
2 saying, "[a]The scribes and the Pharisees have seated
themselves in the chair of Moses;
3 therefore all that they tell you, do and observe, but do
not do according to their deeds; for they say *things*, and do not
do *them*.
4 "And [a]they tie up heavy loads, and lay them on men's
shoulders; but they themselves are unwilling to move them
with *so much as* a finger.
5 "But they do all their deeds [a]to be noticed by men; for
they [b]broaden their [1]phylacteries, and lengthen [c]the tassels *of
their garments*.
6 "And they [a]love the place of honor at banquets, and the
chief seats in the synagogues,
7 and respectful greetings in the market places, and being
called by men, [a]Rabbi.
8 "But [a]do not be called [b]Rabbi; for One is your Teacher,
and you are all brothers.
9 "And do not call *anyone* on earth your father; for [a]One
is your Father, He who is in heaven.
10 "And do not be called [1]leaders; for One is your Leader,
that is, Christ.
11 "[a]But the greatest among you shall be your servant.
12 "And [a]whoever exalts himself shall be humbled; and
whoever humbles himself shall be exalted.
13 "[a]But woe to you, scribes and Pharisees, hypocrites, [b]be-
cause you shut off the kingdom of heaven [1]from men, for you
do not enter in yourselves; nor do you allow those who are
entering to go in.
14 [1]["Woe to you, scribes and Pharisees, hypocrites, because [a]you devour widows' houses, even while for a pretense
you make long prayers; therefore you shall receive greater
condemnation.]
15 "Woe to you, scribes and Pharisees, hypocrites, because
you travel about on sea and land to make one [1a]proselyte; and
when he becomes one, you make him twice as much a son of
[2b]hell as yourselves.
16 "Woe to you, [a]blind guides, who say, '[b]Whoever swears
by the [1]temple, that is nothing; but whoever swears by the gold
of the [1]temple, he is obligated.'
17 "You fools and blind men; [a]which is [1]more important,
the gold, or the [2]temple that sanctified the gold?
18 "And, 'Whoever swears by the altar, *that* is nothing, but
whoever swears by the [1]offering upon it, he is obligated.'
19 "You blind men, [a]which is [1]more important, the [2]offer-
ing or the altar that sanctifies the [2]offering?
20 "Therefore he who swears, swears *both* by the altar and
by everything on it.
21 "And he who swears by the [1]temple, swears *both* by the
[2]temple and by Him who [a]dwells within it.

46 [a]Mark 12:34; Luke 14:6; 20:40

1 [a]Matt. 23:1-7: *Mark 12:38, 39; Luke 20:45, 46*

2 [a]Ezra 7:6, 25; Neh. 8:4; Deut. 33:3f.

4 [a]Luke 11:46; Acts 15:10

5 [1]I.e., small boxes containing Scripture texts worn for religious purposes [a]Matt. 6:1, 5, 16 [b]Ex. 13:9; Deut. 6:8; 11:18 [c]Matt. 9:20

6 [a]Luke 11:43; Luke 14:7; 20:46

7 [a]Matt. 23:8; 26:25, 49; Mark 9:5; 11:21; John 1:38, 49; 3:2, 26; 4:31; 6:25; 9:2; 11:8; Mark 10:51; John 20:16

8 [a]James 3:1 [b]Matt. 23:7; 26:25, 49; Mark 9:5; 11:21; 14:45; John 1:38, 49; 3:2, 26; 4:31; 6:25; 9:2; 11:8; Mark 10:51; John 20:16

9 [a]Matt. 6:9; 7:11

10 [1]Or, *teachers* or *guides*

11 [a]Matt. 20:26

12 [a]Luke 14:11; 18:14

13 [1]Lit., *in front of* [a]Matt. 23:15, (16), 23, 25, 27, 29 [b]Luke 11:52

14 [1]This verse not found in the earliest mss. [a]Mark 12:40; Luke 20:47

15 [1]Or, *convert* [2]Lit., *Gehenna* [a]Acts 2:10; 6:5; 13:43 [b]Matt. 5:22

16 [1]Or, *sanctuary* [a]Matt. 23:24; 15:14 [b]Matt. 5:33-35

17 [1]Lit., *greater* [2]Or, *sanctuary* [a]Ex. 30:29

18 [1]Or, *gift*

19 [1]Lit., *greater* [2]Or, *gift* [a]Ex. 29:37

21 [1]Or, *sanctuary* [2]Lit., *it* [a]1 Kin. 8:13; Ps. 26:8; 132:14

22 "And he who swears by heaven, [a]swears *both* by the
throne of God and by Him who sits upon it.
23 "[a]Woe to you, scribes and Pharisees, hypocrites! For
you tithe mint and dill and [1]cummin, and have neglected the
weightier provisions of the law: justice and mercy and faithfulness; but these are the things you should have done without
neglecting the others.
24 "You [a]blind guides, who strain out a gnat and swallow a
camel!
25 "[a]Woe to you, scribes and Pharisees, hypocrites! For
[a]you clean the outside of the cup and of the dish, but inside
they are full [1]of robbery and self-indulgence.
26 "You blind Pharisee, first [a]clean the inside of the cup
and of the dish, so that the outside of it may become clean
also.
27 "[a]Woe to you, scribes and Pharisees, hypocrites! For
you are like whitewashed tombs which on the outside appear
beautiful, but inside they are full of dead men's bones and all
uncleanness.
28 "Even so you too outwardly appear righteous to men,
but inwardly you are full of hypocrisy and lawlessness.
29 "[a]Woe to you, scribes and Pharisees, hypocrites! For
you build the tombs of the prophets and adorn the monuments of the righteous,
30 and say, 'If we had been *living* in the days of our fathers,
we would not have been partners with them in *shedding*
the blood of the prophets.'
31 "Consequently you bear witness against yourselves, that
you [a]are [1]sons of those who murdered the prophets.
32 "[1]Fill up then the measure *of the guilt* of your fathers.
33 "You serpents, [a]you brood of vipers, how shall you escape the [1]sentence of [2b]hell?
34 "[a]Therefore, behold, [b]I am sending you prophets and
wise men and scribes; some of them you will kill and crucify,
and some of them you will [c]scourge in your synagogues, and
[d]persecute from city to city;
35 that upon you may fall *the guilt of* all the righteous
blood shed on earth, from the blood of righteous [a]Abel to the
blood of Zechariah, the [b]son of Berechiah, whom [c]you murdered between the [1]temple and the altar.
36 "Truly I say to you, all these things shall come upon
[a]this generation.
37 "[a]O Jerusalem, Jerusalem, who [b]kills the prophets and
stones those who are sent to her! How often I wanted to gather
your children together, [c]the way a hen gathers her chicks under
her wings, and you were unwilling.
38 "Behold, [a]your house is being left to you [1]desolate.
39 "For I say to you, from now on you shall not see Me
until you say, '[a]Blessed is He who comes in the name of the
Lord.' "

Chapter 24

[a]

AND Jesus [b]came out from the temple and was going away
[1]when His disciples came up to point out the temple buildings
to Him.

22 [a]Matt. 5:34

23 [1](Similar to caraway seeds) [a]Matt. 23:13; Luke 11:42

24 [a]Matt. 23:16

25 [1]Or, *as a result of* [a]Luke 11:39f.; Mark 7:4

26 [a]Luke 11:39f.; Mark 7:4

27 [a]Luke 11:44; Acts 23:3

29 [a]Luke 11:47f.

31 [1]Or, *descendants* [a]Acts 7:51f.; Matt. 23:34, 37

32 [1]Lit., *and fill up*

33 [1]Or, *judgment* [2]Gr. *Gehenna* [a]Matt. 3:7 [b]Matt. 5:22

34 [a]Matt. 23:34-36; Luke 11:49-51 [b]2 Chr. 36:15, 16 [c]Matt. 10:17 [d]Matt. 10:23

35 [1]Or, *sanctuary* [a]Gen. 4:8ff.; Heb. 11:4 [b]Zech. 1:1 [c]2 Chr. 24:21

36 [a]Matt. 10:23; 24:34

37 [a]Matt. 23:37-39: *Luke 13:34, 35* [b]Matt. 5:12 [c]Ruth 2:12

38 [1]Some mss. omit, *desolate* [a]1 Kin. 9:7f.; Jer. 22:5

39 [a]Ps. 118:26; Matt. 21:9

1 [1]Lit., *and* [a]Matt. 24:1-51: *Mark 13; Luke 21:5-36* [b]Matt. 21:23

2 And He answered and said to them, "Do you not see
all these things? Truly I say to you, [a]not one stone here shall be
left upon another, which will not be torn down."
3 And as He was sitting on [a]the Mount of Olives, the
disciples came to Him privately, saying, "Tell us, when will
these things be, and what *will be* the sign of [b]Your [1]coming,
and of the [2]end of the age?"
4 And Jesus answered and said to them, "[a]See to it that
no one misleads you.
5 "For [a]many will come in My name, saying, 'I am the
[1]Christ,' and will mislead many.
6 "And you will be hearing of wars and rumors of wars; see
that you are not frightened, for *those things* must take place,
but *that* is not yet the end.
7 "For [a]nation will rise against nation, and kingdom
against kingdom, and in various places there will be [b]famines
and earthquakes.
8 "But all these things are *merely* the beginning of birth-
pangs.
9 "[a]Then they will deliver you up to tribulation, and will
kill you, and [b]you will be hated by all nations on account of
My name.
10 "And at that time many will [1a]fall away and will [2]betray
one another and hate one another.
11 "And many [a]false prophets will arise, and will mislead
many.
12 "And because lawlessness is increased, [1]most people's
love will grow cold.
13 "[a]But the one who endures to the end, it is he who shall
be saved.
14 "And this [a]gospel of the kingdom [b]shall be preached in
the whole [1c]world for a witness to all the nations, and then the
end shall come.
15 "Therefore when you see the [a]ABOMINATION OF DESOLA-
TION which was spoken of through Daniel the prophet, standing IN [b]THE HOLY PLACE ([c]let the reader understand),
16 then let those who are in Judea flee to the mountains;
17 let him who is on [a]the housetop not go down to get the
things out that are in his house;
18 and let him who is in the field not turn back to get his
cloak.
19 "But [a]woe to those who are with child and to those who
nurse babes in those days!
20 "But pray that your flight may not be in the winter, or
on a Sabbath;
21 for then there will be a [a]great tribulation, such as has
not occurred since the beginning of the world until now, nor
ever shall.
22 "And unless those days had been cut short, no [1]life
would have been saved; but for [a]the sake of the [2]elect those
days shall be cut short.
23 "[a]Then if any one says to you, 'Behold, here is the
[1]Christ,' or '[2]There *He is,*' do not believe *him.*
24 "For false Christs and [a]false prophets will arise and will
show great [1b]signs and wonders, so as to mislead, if possible,
even [c]the [2]elect.

2 [a]Luke 19:44

3 [1]Or, *presence* [2]Or, *consummation* [a]Matt. 21:1 [b]Matt. 24:27, 37, 39; Matt. 16:27f.

4 [a]Jer. 29:8

5 [1]I.e., Messiah [a]Matt. 24:24; 1 John 2:18; Matt. 24:11; Acts 5:36f.; 1 John 4:3

7 [a]2 Chr. 15:6; Is. 19:2 [b]Acts 11:28

9 [a]Matt. 10:17; John 16:2 [b]Matt. 10:22; John 15:18ff.

10 [1]Lit., *be caused to stumble* [2]Or, *deliver up* [a]Matt. 11:6

11 [a]Matt. 24:24; Matt. 7:15

12 [1]Lit., *the love of many*

13 [a]Matt. 10:22

14 [1]Lit., *inhabited earth* [a]Matt. 4:23 [b]Rom. 10:18; Col. 1:6, 23 [c]Luke 2:1; 4:5; Acts 11:28; 17:6, 31; 19:27; Rom. 10:18; Heb. 1:6; 2:5; Rev. 3:10; 16:14

15 [a]Dan. 9:27; 11:31; 12:11 [b]Acts 6:13f.; 21:28; John 11:48; Luke 21:20; Mark 13:14 [c]Mark 13:14; Rev. 1:3

17 [a]Matt. 10:27; Luke 5:19; 12:3; Acts 10:9; 1 Sam. 9:25; 2 Sam. 11:2

19 [a]Luke 23:29

21 [a]Dan. 12:1; Joel 2:2; Matt. 24:29

22 [1]Lit., *flesh* [2]Or, *chosen ones* [a]Matt. 24:24, 31; 22:14; Luke 18:7

23 [1]Or, *the Messiah* [2]Lit., *here* [a]Luke 17:23f.

24 [1]Or, *attesting miracles* [2]Or, *chosen ones* [a]Matt. 24:11; 7:15 [b]John 4:48; 2 Thess. 2:9 [c]Matt. 24:22, 31; 22:14 [Gr.]; Luke 18:7

25 "Behold, I have told you in advance.
26 "If therefore they say to you, 'Behold, He is in the wilderness,' do not go forth, *or,* 'Behold, He is in the inner
rooms,' do not believe *them.*
27 "[a]For just as the lightning comes from the east, and
flashes even to the west, so shall the [1b]coming of the [c]Son of
Man be.
28 "[a]Wherever the corpse is, there the [1]vultures will gather.
29 "But immediately after the [a]tribulation of those days
[b]THE SUN WILL BE DARKENED, AND THE MOON WILL NOT GIVE ITS
LIGHT, AND [c]THE STARS WILL FALL from [1]the sky, and the POWERS
OF [1]THE HEAVENS WILL BE shaken,
30 and then [a]the sign of the Son of Man will appear in the
sky, and then all the tribes of the earth will mourn, and they
will see [b]the SON OF MAN COMING ON THE CLOUDS OF THE SKY
with power and great glory.
31 "And [a]He will send forth His angels WITH [b]A GREAT
TRUMPET and THEY WILL GATHER TOGETHER His [1c]elect FROM
[d]THE FOUR WINDS, [e]FROM ONE END OF THE SKY TO THE OTHER.
32 "Now learn the parable FROM THE FIG TREE: when its
branch has already become tender, and puts forth its leaves,
you know that summer is near;
33 even so you too, when you see all these things, [1]recog-
nize that [2]He is near, *right* [a]at the [3]door.
34 "Truly I say to you, [a]this [1]generation will not pass away
until all these things take place.
35 "[a]Heaven and earth will pass away, but My words shall
not pass away.
36 "But [a]of that day and hour no one knows, not even the
angels of heaven, nor the Son, but the Father alone.
37 "For [1]the [2a]coming of the Son of Man will be [b]just like
the days of Noah.
38 "For as in those days which were before the flood they
were eating and drinking, they were [a]marrying and giving in
marriage, until the day that [b]NOAH ENTERED THE ARK,
39 and they did not [1]understand until the flood came and
took them all away, so shall the [2a]coming of the Son of Man
be.
40 "Then there shall be two men in the field; one [1]will be
taken, and one [1]will be left.
41 "[a]Two women *will be* grinding at the [1b]mill; one [2]will be
taken, and one [2]will be left.
42 "Therefore [a]be on the alert, for you do not know which
day your Lord is coming.
43 "But [1]be sure of this, that [a]if the head of the house had
known [b]at what time of the night the thief was coming, he
would have been on the alert and would not have allowed his
house to be [2]broken into.
44 "For this reason [a]you be ready too; for [b]the Son of Man
is coming at an hour when you do not think *He will.*
45 "[a]Who then is the [b]faithful and [c]sensible slave whom his
[1]master [d]put in charge of his household to give them their food
at the proper time?
46 "Blessed is that slave whom his [1]master finds so doing
when he comes.

27 [1]Or, *presence* [a]Luke 17:23f. [b]Matt. 24:3, 37, 39 [c]Matt. 8:20

28 [1]Or, *eagles* [a]Luke 17:37; Job 39:30; Hab. 1:8; Ezek. 39:17

29 [1]Or, *heaven* [a]Matt. 24:21 [b]Is. 13:10; 24:23; Ezek. 32:7; Joel 2:10, 31; 3:15; Acts 2:20; Amos 5:20; 8:9; Zeph. 1:15; Rev. 6:12; 8:12 [c]Rev. 6:13; Is. 34:4

30 [a]Matt. 24:3; Dan. 7:13; Rev. 1:7 [b]Matt. 24:3, 37, 39; 16:27

31 [1]Or, *chosen ones* [a]Matt. 13:41 [b]Is. 27:13; 1 Cor. 15:52; 1 Thess. 4:16; Ex. 19:16; Zech. 9:14; Rev. 8:2; 11:15; Heb. 12:19 [c]Matt. 24:22 [d]Dan. 7:2; Zech. 2:6; Rev. 7:1 [e]Deut. 4:32

33 [1]Lit., *know* [2]Or, *it* [3]Lit., *doors* [a]James 5:9; Rev. 3:20

34 [1]Or, *race* [a]Matt. 16:28; Matt. 10:23; 23:36

35 [a]Mark 13:31; Luke 21:33; Matt. 5:18

36 [a]Mark 13:32; Acts 1:7

37 [1]Lit., *just as . . . were the days* [2]Or, *presence* [a]Matt. 24:3, 30, 39; 16:27 [b]Luke 17:26f.; Gen. 6:5; 7:6-23

38 [a]Matt. 22:30 [b]Gen. 7:7

39 [1]Lit., *know* [2]Or, *presence* [a]Matt. 24:3, 30, 37; 16:27

40 [1]Lit., *is*

41 [1]I.e., handmill [2]Lit., *is* [a]Luke 17:35 [b]Deut. 24:6; Ex. 11:5; Is. 47:2

42 [a]Matt. 24:43, 44; 25:10, 13; Luke 12:39f.; Luke 21:36

43 [1]Lit., *know this* [2]Lit., *dug through* [a]Matt. 24:42, 44; 25:10, 13; Luke 12:39f.; 21:36 [b]Luke 12:38; Matt. 14:25; Mark 6:48; 13:35

44 [a]Matt. 24:42, 43; 25:10, 13; Luke 12:39f.; 21:36 [b]Matt. 24:27

45 [1]Or, *lord* [a]Matt. 24:45-51: *Luke 1:42-46* [b]Matt. 25:21, 23; Luke 16:10 [c]Matt. 7:24; 10:16; 25:2ff. [d]Matt. 25:21, 23

46 [1]Or, *lord*

47 "Truly I say to you, that [a]he will put him in charge of all
his possessions.
48 "But if that evil slave says in his heart, 'My [1]master [2]is
not coming for a long time,'
49 and shall begin to beat his fellow-slaves and eat and
drink with [1]drunkards;
50 the [1]master of that slave will come on a day when he
does not expect *him* and at an hour which he does not know,
51 and shall [1]cut him in pieces and [2]assign him a place
with the hypocrites; [a]weeping shall be there and the gnashing
of teeth.

Chapter 25

"THEN [a]the kingdom of heaven will be comparable to ten
virgins, who took their [b]lamps, and went out to meet the
bridegroom.
2 "And five of them were foolish, and five were [a]prudent.
3 "For when the foolish took their lamps, they took no oil
with them,
4 but the [a]prudent took oil in flasks along with their
lamps.
5 "Now while the bridegroom was delaying, they all got
drowsy and *began* to sleep.
6 "But at midnight there was a shout, 'Behold, the bridegroom! Come out to meet *him.*'
7 "Then all those virgins arose, and trimmed their lamps.
8 "And the foolish said to the prudent, 'Give us some of
your oil, for our lamps are going out.'
9 "But the [a]prudent answered, saying, 'No, there will not
be enough for us and you *too;* go instead to the dealers and
buy *some* for yourselves.'
10 "And while they were going away to make the purchase,
the bridegroom came, and those who were [a]ready went in with
him to [b]the wedding feast; and [c]the door was shut.
11 "And later the other virgins also came, saying, '[a]Lord,
Lord, open up for us.'
12 "But he answered and said, 'Truly I say to you, I do not
know you.'
13 "[a] Be on the alert then, for you do not know the day nor
the hour.
14 "[a]For *it is* just like a man [b]*about* to go on a journey, who
called his own slaves, and entrusted his possessions to them.
15 "And to one he gave five [1a]talents, to another, two, and
to another, one, each according to his own ability; and he
[b]went on his journey.
16 "Immediately the one who had received the five [a]talents
went and traded with them, and gained five more talents.
17 "In the same manner the one who had *received* the two
talents gained two more.
18 "But he who received the one *talent* went away and dug
in the ground, and hid his [1]master's money.
19 "Now after a long time the master of those slaves *came
and *[a]settled accounts with them.
20 "And the one who had received the five [a]talents came up

47 [a]Matt. 25:21, 23
48 [1]Or, *lord* [2]Lit., *lingers*
49 [1]Lit., *those who get drunk*
50 [1]Or, *Lord*
51 [1]Or, *severely scourge him* [2]Lit., *appoint his portion* [a]Matt. 8:12
1 [a]Matt. 13:24 [b]John 18:3; Acts 20:8; Rev. 4:5; 8:10 [Gr.]
2 [a]Matt. 7:24; 10:16; 25:2ff.
4 [a]Matt. 7:24; 10:16; 25:2ff.
9 [a]Matt. 7:24; 10:16; 25:2ff.
10 [a]Matt. 24:42ff. [b]Luke 12:35f. [c]Luke 13:25; Matt. 7:21ff.
11 [a]Luke 13:25; Matt. 7:21ff.
13 [a]Matt. 24:42ff.
14 [a]Matt. 25:14-30; Luke 19:12-27 [b]Matt. 21:33
15 [1]A talent was $1,000 in silver content, much more in buying power. [a]Matt. 18:24; Luke 19:13 [b]Matt. 21:33
16 [a]Matt. 18:24; Luke 19:13
18 [1]Or, *lord's*
19 [a]Matt. 18:23
20 [a]Matt. 18:24; Luke 19:13

and brought five more talents, saying, 'Master, you entrusted
five talents to me; see, I have gained five more talents.'
21 "His master said to him, 'Well done, good and [a]faithful
slave; you were faithful with a few things, I will put you in
charge of many things, enter into the joy of your [1]master.'
22 "The one also who had *received* the two [a]talents came
up and said, 'Master, you entrusted to me two talents; see, I
have gained two more talents.'
23 "His master said to him, 'Well done, good and [a]faithful
slave; you were faithful with a few things, I will put you in
charge of many things; enter into the joy of your master.'
24 "And the one also who had received the one [a]talent
came up and said, 'Master, I knew you to be a hard man,
reaping where you did not sow, and gathering where you scattered no *seed*.
25 'And I was afraid, and went away and hid your talent in
the ground; see, you have what is yours.'
26 "But his master answered and said to him, 'You wicked,
lazy slave, you knew that I reap where I did not sow, and
gather where I scattered no *seed?*
27 'Then you ought to have put my money [1]in the bank,
and on my arrival I would have received my *money* back with
interest.
28 'Therefore take away the talent from him, and give it to
the one who has the ten talents.'
29 "[a]For to everyone who has shall *more* be given, and he
shall have an abundance; but from the one who does not have,
even what he does have shall be taken away.
30 "And cast out the worthless slave into [a]the outer darkness; in that place there shall be weeping and gnashing of
teeth.
31 "But when [a]the Son of Man comes in His glory, and all
the angels with Him, then [b]He will sit on His glorious throne.
32 "And all the nations will be gathered before Him; and
He will separate them from one another, [a]as the shepherd
separates the sheep from the goats;
33 and He will put the sheep [a]on His right, and the goats
[b]on the left.
34 "Then the King will say to those on His right, 'Come,
you who are blessed of My Father, [a]inherit the kingdom prepared for you [b]from the foundation of the world.
35 'For [a]I was hungry, and you gave Me *something* to eat; I
was thirsty, and you gave Me drink; [b]I was a stranger, and you
invited Me in;
36 [a]naked, and you clothed Me; I was sick, and you [b]vis-
ited Me; [c]I was in prison, and you came to Me.'
37 "Then the righteous will answer Him, saying, 'Lord,
when did we see You hungry, and feed You, or thirsty, and give
You drink?
38 'And when did we see You a stranger, and invite You in,
or naked, and clothe You?
39 'And when did we see You sick, or in prison, and come
to You?'
40 "And [a]the King will answer and say to them, 'Truly I say
to you, [b]to the extent that you did it to one of these brothers
of Mine, *even* the least *of them*, you did it to Me.'

21 [1]Or, *lord* [a]Matt. 25:23; Matt. 24:45, 47

22 [a]Matt. 18:24; Luke 19:13

23 [a]Matt. 25:21; Matt. 24:45, 47

24 [a]Matt. 18:24; Luke 19:13

27 [1]Lit., *to the bankers*

29 [a]Matt. 13:12

30 [a]Matt. 8:12

31 [a]Matt. 16:27f. [b]Matt. 19:28

32 [a]Ezek. 34:17, 20

33 [a]1 Kin. 2:19; Ps. 45:9 [b]Eccles. 10:2

34 [a]Luke 12:32; 1 Cor. 6:9; 15:50; Gal. 5:21; James 2:5; Matt. 5:3; 19:29 [b]Luke 11:50; Heb. 4:3; 9:26; Rev. 13:8; 17:8; John 17:24; Eph. 1:4; 1 Pet. 1:20; Matt. 13:35

35 [a]Is. 58:7; Ezek. 18:7, 16; James 2:15, 16; [b]Job 31:32; Heb. 13:2

36 [a]Is. 58:7; Ezek. 18:7, 16; James 2:15, 16; [b]James 1:27 [c]2 Tim. 1:16f.

40 [a]Matt. 25:34; Luke 19:38; Rev. 17:14; 19:16 [b]Matt. 10:42; Heb. 6:10; Prov. 19:17

41 "Then He will also say to those on His left, '[a]Depart
from Me, accursed ones, into the [b]eternal fire which has been
prepared for [c]the devil and his angels;
42 for I was hungry, and you gave Me *nothing* to eat; I was
thirsty, and you gave Me nothing to drink;
43 I was a stranger, and you did not invite Me in; naked,
and you did not clothe Me; sick, and in prison, and you did not
visit Me.'
44 "Then they themselves also will answer, saying, 'Lord,
when did we see You hungry, or thirsty, or a stranger, or naked,
or sick, or in prison, and did not [1]take care of You?'
45 "Then He will answer them, saying, 'Truly I say to you,
to the extent that you did not do it to one of the least of these,
you did not do it to Me.'
46 "And these will go away into [a]eternal punishment, but
the righteous into [b]eternal life."

Chapter 26

[a]AND it came about that when Jesus had finished all these
words, He said to His disciples,
2 "[a]You know that after two days [b]the Passover is coming,
and the Son of Man is *to be* [c]delivered up for crucifixion."
3 [a]Then the chief priests and the elders of the people
were gathered together in [b]the court of the high priest, named
[c]Caiaphas;
4 and they [a]plotted together to seize Jesus by stealth, and
kill *Him*.
5 But they were saying, "Not during the festival, [a]lest a
riot occur among the people."
6 [a]Now when Jesus was in [b]Bethany, at the home of Simon the leper,
7 a woman came to Him with an alabaster vial of very
costly perfume, and she poured it upon His head as He reclined
at table.
8 But the disciples were indignant when they saw *this*,
and said, "What is the point of this waste?
9 "For this *perfume* might have been sold for a high price
and *the money* given to the poor."
10 But Jesus, aware of this, said to them, "Why do you
bother the woman? For she has done a good deed to Me.
11 "For [a]the poor you have with you always; but you do not
always have Me.
12 "For when she poured this perfume upon My body, she
did it [a]to prepare Me for burial.
13 "Truly I say to you, [a]wherever this gospel is preached in
the whole world, what this woman has done shall also be spoken of in memory of her."
14 [a]Then one of the twelve, named [b]Judas Iscariot, went
to the chief priests,
15 and said, "What are you willing to give me [1]to [2a]deliver
Him up to you?" And [b]they weighed out to him thirty [3]pieces
of silver.
16 And from then on he *began* looking for a good opportunity to [1]betray Him.
17 [a]Now on the first *day* of [b]the *Feast* of Unleavened

41 [a]Matt. 7:23 [b]Mark 9:48; Luke 16:24; Jude 7 [c]Rev. 12:9; Matt. 4:10

44 [1]Or, *serve*

46 [a]Dan. 12:2; John 5:29; Acts 24:15 [b]Matt. 19:29; John 3:15f., 36; 5:24; 6:27, 40, 47, 54; 17:2f.; Acts 13:46, 48; Rom. 2:7; 5:21; 6:23; Gal. 6:8; 1 John 5:11

1 [a]Matt. 7:28

2 [a]Matt. 26:2-5: *Mark 14:1-2; Luke 22:1-2;* [b]John 11:55; 13:1 [c]Matt. 10:4

3 [a]John 11:47 [b]Matt. 26:58, 69; Mark 14:54, 66; 15:16; Luke 11:21; 22:55; John 18:15; Matt. 27:27 [c]Matt. 26:57; Luke 3:2; John 11:49; 18:13, 14, 24, 28; Acts 4:6

4 [a]Matt. 12:14

5 [a]Matt. 27:24

6 [a]Matt. 26:6-13: *Mark 14:3-9;* John 12:1-8; Luke 7:37-39 [b]Matt. 21:17

11 [a]Mark 14:7; John 12:8; Deut. 15:11

12 [a]John 19:40

13 [a]Mark 14:9

14 [a]Matt. 26:14-16: *Mark 14:10, 11; Luke 22:3-6* [b]Matt. 10:4; 26:25, 47; 27:3; John 6:71; 12:4; 13:26; Acts 1:16

15 [1]Lit., *and I will* [2]Or, *betray* [3]Or, *silver shekels* [a]Matt. 10:4 [b]Zech. 11:12; Ex. 21:32

16 [1]Or, *deliver Him up*

17 [a]Matt. 26:17-19: *Mark 14:12-16; Luke 22:7-13* [b]Ex. 12:18-20

Bread the disciples came to Jesus, saying, "Where do You
want us to prepare for You to eat the Passover?"
18 And He said, "Go into the city to [a]a certain man, and
say to him, 'The Teacher says, "[b]My time is at hand; I *am to*
keep the Passover at your house with My disciples." ' "
19 And the disciples did as Jesus had directed them; and
they prepared the Passover.
20 [a]Now when evening had come, He was reclining *at*
table with the twelve disciples.
21 And as they were eating, He said, "[a]Truly I say to you
that one of you will betray Me."
22 And being deeply grieved, they [1]each one began to say
to Him, "Surely not I, Lord?"
23 And He answered and said, "[a]He who dipped his hand
with Me in the bowl is the one who will betray Me.
24 "The Son of Man *is to* go, [a]just as it is written of Him;
but woe to that man through whom the Son of Man is
betrayed! [b]It would have been good [1]for that man if he had not
been born."
25 And [a]Judas, who was betraying Him, answered and
said, "Surely it is not I, [b]Rabbi?" He *said to him, "[c]You have
said *it* yourself."
26 [a]And while they were eating, Jesus took *some* bread,
and [1b]after a blessing, He broke it and gave *it* to the disciples,
and said, "Take, eat; this is My body."
27 And He took a cup and gave thanks, and gave *it* to
them, saying, "Drink from it, all of you;
28 for [a]this is My blood of the covenant, which is *to be*
shed on behalf of [b]many for forgiveness of sins.
29 "But I say to you, I will not drink of this fruit of the vine
from now on until that day when I drink it new with you in My
Father's kingdom."
30 [a]And after singing a hymn, they went out to [b]the
Mount of Olives.
31 Then Jesus *said to them, "You will all [1a]fall away
because of Me this night, for it is written, '[b]I WILL STRIKE DOWN
THE SHEPHERD, AND THE SHEEP OF THE FLOCK SHALL BE
[c]SCATTERED.'
32 "But after I have been raised, [a]I will go before you to
Galilee."
33 But Peter answered and said to Him, "*Even* though all
may [1]fall away because of You, I will never fall away."
34 Jesus said to him, "[a]Truly I say to you that [b]this *very*
night, before a cock crows, you shall deny Me three times."
35 Peter *said to Him, "[a]Even if I must die with You, I
will not deny You." All the disciples said the same thing too.
36 [a]Then Jesus *came with them to a place called [b]Geth-
semane, and *said to His disciples, "Sit here while I go over
there and pray."
37 And He took with Him [a]Peter and the two sons of
Zebedee, and began to be grieved and distressed.
38 Then He *said to them, "[a]My soul is deeply grieved, to
the point of death; remain here and [b]keep watch with Me."
39 And He went a little beyond *them*, and fell on His face
and prayed, saying, "My Father, if it is possible, let [a]this cup
pass from Me; [b]yet not as I will, but as Thou wilt."

18 [a]Mark 14:13; Luke 22:10 [b]John 7:6, 8

20 [a]Matt. 26:20-24: *Mark 14:17-21*

21 [a]Luke 22:21-23; John 13:21f.

22 [1]Or, *one after another*

23 [a]John 13:26; John 13:18

24 [1]Lit., *for him if that man had not been born* [a]Matt. 26:31, 54, 56; Mark 9:12; Luke 24:25-27, 46; Acts 17:2f.; 26:22f.; 1 Cor. 15:3; 1 Pet. 1:10f. [b]Mark 14:21; Matt. 18:7

25 [a]Matt. 26:14 [b]Matt. 23:7; 26:49 [c]Matt. 26:64; 27:11; Luke 22:70

26 [1]Lit., *having blessed* [a]Matt. 26:26-29: *Mark 14:22-25; Luke 22:17-20; 1 Cor. 11:23-25*; 1 Cor. 10:16 [b]Matt. 14:19

28 [a]Heb. 9:20 [b]Matt. 20:28

30 [a]Matt. 26:30-35: *Mark 14:26-31; Luke 22:31-34* [b]Matt. 21:1

31 [1]Or, *stumble* [a]Matt. 11:6 [b]Zech. 13:7 [c]John 16:32

32 [a]Matt. 28:7, 10, 16; Mark 16:7

33 [1]Or, *stumble*

34 [a]John 13:38; Matt. 26:75 [b]Mark 14:30

35 [a]John 13:37

36 [a]Matt. 26:36-46: *Mark 14:32-42; Luke 22:40-46* [b]Mark 14:32; Luke 22:39; John 18:1

37 [a]Matt. 17:1; Mark 5:37; Matt. 4:21

38 [a]John 12:27 [b]Matt. 26:40, 41

39 [a]Matt. 20:22 [b]Matt. 26:42; Mark 14:36; Luke 22:42; John 6:38

40 And He *came to the disciples and *found them sleeping, and *said to Peter, "So, you *men* could not [a]keep watch
with Me for one hour?
41 "[a]Keep watching and praying, that you may not enter
into temptation; [b]the spirit is willing, but the flesh is weak."
42 He went away again a second time and prayed, saying,
"My Father, if this [a]cannot pass away unless I drink it, [b]Thy
will be done."
43 And He came back and found them sleeping, for their
eyes were heavy.
44 And He left them again, and went away and prayed a
third time, saying the same thing once more.
45 Then He *came to the disciples, and *said to them,
"[1]Are you still sleeping and taking your rest? Behold, [a]the hour
is at hand and the Son of Man is being betrayed into the hands
of sinners.
46 "Arise, let us be going; behold, the one who betrays Me
is at hand!"
47 [a]And while He was still speaking, behold, [b]Judas, one of
the twelve, came up, [1]accompanied by a great multitude with
swords and clubs, from the chief priests and elders of the
people.
48 Now he who was betraying Him gave them a sign,
saying, "Whomever I shall kiss, He is the one; seize Him."
49 And immediately he came to Jesus and said, "Hail,
[a]Rabbi;" and kissed Him.
50 And Jesus said to him, "[a]Friend, *do* what you have
come for." Then they came and laid hands on Jesus and seized
Him.
51 And behold, [a]one of those who were with Jesus
[1]reached and drew out his [b]sword, and struck the [c]slave of the
high priest, and [2]cut off his ear.
52 Then Jesus *said to him, "Put your sword back into its
place; for [a]all those who take up the sword shall perish by the
sword.
53 "Or do you think that I cannot appeal to My Father,
and He will at once put at My disposal more than twelve
[1a]legions of [b]angels?
54 "How then shall [a]the Scriptures be fulfilled, that it must
happen this way?"
55 At that time Jesus said to the multitudes, "Have you
come out with swords and clubs to arrest Me [1]as though *I were*
a robber? [a]Every day I used to sit in the temple teaching and
you did not seize Me.
56 "But all this has taken place that [a]the Scriptures of the
prophets may be fulfilled." Then all the disciples left Him and
fled.
57 [a]And those who had seized Jesus led Him away to
[b]Caiaphas, the high priest, where the scribes and the elders
were gathered together.
58 But [a]Peter also followed Him at a distance as far as the
[b]courtyard of the high priest, and entered in, and sat down
with the [1c]officers to see the outcome.
59 Now the chief priests and the whole [1a]Council kept
trying to obtain false testimony against Jesus, in order that
they might put Him to death;

40 [a]Matt. 26:38

41 [a]Matt. 26:38 [b]Mark 14:38

42 [a]Matt. 20:22 [b]Matt. 26:39; Mark 14:36; Luke 22:42; John 6:38

45 [1]Or, *keep on sleeping therefore* [a]Mark 14:41; John 12:27; 13:1

47 [1]Lit., *and with him* [a]Matt. 26:47-56: *Mark 14:43-50; Luke 22:47-53; John 18:3-11* [b]Matt. 26:14

49 [a]Matt. 23:7; 26:25

50 [a]Matt. 20:13; 22:12

51 [1]Lit., *extending the hand* [2]Lit., *took off* [a]John 18:10; Mark 14:47; Luke 22:50 [b]Luke 22:38 [c]John 18:10; Mark 14:47; Luke 22:50

52 [a]Gen. 9:6; Rev. 13:10

53 [1]A legion equaled 6,000 troops [a]Mark 5:9, 15; Luke 8:30 [b]Matt. 4:11

54 [a]Matt. 26:24

55 [1]Lit., *as against a robber* [a]Mark 12:35; 14:49; Luke 4:20; 19:47; 20:1; 21:37; John 7:14, 28; 8:2, 20; 18:20

56 [a]Matt. 26:24

57 [a]Matt. 26:57-68: *Mark 14:53-65; John 18:12f., 19-24* [b]Matt. 26:3

58 [1]Or, *servants* [a]John 18:15 [b]Matt. 26:3 [c]Matt. 5:25; John 7:32, 45f.; 19:6; Acts 5:22, 26

59 [1]Or, *Sanhedrin* [a]Matt. 5:22

60 and they did not find it, even though many false witnesses came forward. But later on [a]two came forward,
61 and said, "This man stated, '[a]I am able to destroy the
[1]temple of God and to rebuild it [2]in three days.' "
62 And the high priest stood up and said to Him, "Do
You make no answer? What is it that these men are testifying
against You?"
63 But [a]Jesus kept silent. [b]And the high priest said to Him,
"I [1c]adjure You by [d]the living God, that You tell us whether
You are [2]the Christ, [e]the Son of God."
64 Jesus *said to him, "[a]You have said it *yourself*; nevertheless I tell you, [1]hereafter you shall see [b]THE SON OF MAN
SITTING AT THE RIGHT HAND OF POWER, *and* [c]COMING ON THE
CLOUDS OF HEAVEN."
65 Then the high priest [a]tore his [1]robes, saying, "He has
blasphemed! What further need do we have of witnesses? Behold, you have now heard the blasphemy;
66 what do you think?" They answered and said, "[a]He is
deserving of death!"
67 [a]Then they [b]spat in His face and beat Him with their
fists, and others [1]slapped Him,
68 and said, "[a]Prophesy to us, You [1]Christ; who is the one
who hit You?"
69 [a]Now Peter was sitting outside in the [b]courtyard, and a
certain servant-girl came to him and said, "You too were with
Jesus the Galilean."
70 But he denied *it* before them all, saying, "I do not
know what you are talking about."
71 And when he had gone out to the gateway, another
servant-girl saw him and *said to those who were there, "This
man was with Jesus of Nazareth."
72 And again he denied *it* with an oath, "I do not know
the man."
73 And a little later the bystanders came up and said to
Peter, "Surely you too are *one* of them; [a]for the way you talk
[1]gives you away."
74 Then he began to curse and swear, "I do not know the
man!" And immediately a cock crowed.
75 And Peter remembered the word which Jesus had said,
"[a]Before a cock crows, you will deny Me three times." And he
went out and wept bitterly.

CHAPTER 27

[a]NOW when morning had come, all the chief priests and the
elders of the people took counsel against Jesus to put Him to
death;
2 and they bound Him, and led Him away, and [a]deliv-
ered Him up to [b]Pilate the governor.
3 Then when [a]Judas, who had betrayed Him, saw that
He had been condemned, he felt remorse and returned [b]the
thirty [1]pieces of silver to the chief priests and elders,
4 saying, "I have sinned by betraying innocent blood."
But they said, "What is that to us? [a]See *to that* yourself!"
5 And he threw the pieces of silver into [a]the sanctuary
and departed; and [b]he went away and hanged himself.

60 [a]Deut. 19:15

61 [1]Or, *sanctuary* [2]Or, *after*
[a]Matt. 27:40; Mark 14:58; 15:29; John 2:19; Acts 6:14

63 [1]Or, *charge You under oath* [2]I.e., the Messiah
[a]Matt. 27:12, 14; John 19:9 [b]Matt. 26:63-66; Luke 22:67-71 [c]Lev. 5:1 [d]Matt. 16:16 [e]Matt. 4:3

64 [1]Or, *from now on*
[a]Matt. 26:25 [b]Ps. 110:1 [c]Dan. 7:13; Matt. 16:27f.

65 [1]Or, *outer garments*
[a]Mark 14:63; Num. 14:6; Acts 14:14

66 [a]Lev. 24:16; John 19:7

67 [1]Or, possibly, *beat Him with rods*
[a]Matt. 26:67, 68; Luke 22:63-65; John 18:22 [b]Matt. 27:30; Mark 10:34

68 [1]I.e., the Messiah
[a]Mark 14:65; Luke 22:64

69 [a]Matt. 26:69-75: *Mark 14:66-72; Luke 22:55-62; John 18:16-18, 25-27* [b]Matt. 26:3

73 [1]Lit., *makes you evident*
[a]Mark 14:70; Luke 22:59; John 18:26

75 [a]Matt. 26:34

1 [a]Mark 15:1; Luke 22:66; John 18:28

2 [a]Matt. 20:19 [b]Luke 3:1; 13:1; 23:12; Acts 3:13; 4:27; 1 Tim. 6:13

3 [1]Or, *silver shekels*
[a]Matt. 26:14 [b]Matt. 26:15

4 [a]Matt. 27:24

5 [a]Luke 1:9, 21; Matt. 26:61 marg. [b]Acts 1:18

6 And the chief priests took the pieces of silver and said,
"It is not lawful to put them into the temple treasury, since it
is the price of blood."
7 And they counseled together and with [1]the money
bought the Potter's Field as a burial place for strangers.
8 [a]For this reason that field has been called the Field of
Blood to this day.
9 Then that which was spoken through Jeremiah the
prophet was fulfilled, saying, "[a]AND [1]THEY TOOK THE THIRTY
PIECES OF SILVER, THE PRICE OF THE ONE WHOSE PRICE HAD BEEN
SET BY THE SONS OF ISRAEL;
10 AND [1]THEY GAVE THEM FOR THE POTTER'S FIELD, AS THE
LORD DIRECTED ME."
11 [a]Now Jesus stood before the governor, and the governor questioned Him, saying, "Are You the [b]King of the Jews?"
And Jesus said to him, "[c]*It is as* you say."
12 And while He was being accused by the chief priests
and elders, [a]He made no answer.
13 Then Pilate *said to Him, "Do You not hear how
many things they testify against You?"
14 And [a]He did not answer him with regard to even a
single [1]charge, so that the governor was quite amazed.
15 [a]Now at *the* feast the governor was accustomed to release for the multitude *any* one prisoner whom they wanted.
16 And they were holding at that time a notorious prisoner, called Barabbas.
17 When therefore they were gathered together, Pilate
said to them, "Whom do you want me to release for you?
Barabbas, or Jesus [a]who is called Christ?"
18 For he knew that because of envy they had delivered
Him up.
19 And [a]while he was sitting on the judgment-seat, his wife
sent to him, saying, "Have nothing to do with that [b]righteous
Man; for [1]last night I suffered greatly [c]in a dream because of
Him."
20 But the chief priests and the elders persuaded the multitudes to [a]ask for Barabbas, and to put Jesus to death.
21 But the governor answered and said to them, "Which
of the two do you want me to release for you?" And they said,
"Barabbas."
22 Pilate *said to them, "What then shall I do with Jesus
[a]who is called Christ?" They all *said, "Let Him be crucified!"
23 And he said, "Why, what evil has He done?" But they
kept shouting all the more, saying, "Let Him be crucified!"
24 And when Pilate saw that he was accomplishing nothing, but rather that [a]a riot was starting, he took water and
[b]washed his hands in front of the multitude, saying, "I am
innocent of [1c]this Man's blood; [d]see *to that* yourselves."
25 And all the people answered and said, "[a]His blood *be*
on us and on our children!"
26 Then he released Barabbas [1]for them; but Jesus he
[a]scourged and delivered over to be crucified.
27 [a]Then the soldiers of the governor took Jesus into [b]the
Praetorium and gathered the whole *Roman* [1c]cohort around
Him.

7 [1]Lit., *them*

8 [a]Acts 1:19

9 [1]Some mss. read, *I took* [a]Zech. 11:12, 13; cf., Jer. 18:2; 19:2, 11; 32:6-9

10 [1]Some mss. read, *I gave*

11 [a]Matt. 27:11-14: *Mark 15:2-5; Luke 23:2-3; John 18:29-38* [b]Matt. 2:2 [c]Matt. 26:25

12 [a]Matt. 26:63; John 19:9

14 [1]Lit., *word* [a]Matt. 27:12; Mark 15:5; John 19:9; Luke 23:9

15 [a]Matt. 27:15-26: *Mark 15:6-15; Luke 23:[17]-25;* John 18:39-19:16

17 [a]Matt. 1:16; 27:22

19 [1]Lit., *today* [a]John 19:13; Acts 12:21 marg.; 18:12, 16f.; 25:6, 10, 17 [b]Matt. 27:24 [c]Matt. 1:20; 2:12f., 19, 22; Gen. 20:6; 31:11; Num. 12:6; Job 33:15

20 [a]Acts 3:14

22 [a]Matt. 1:16

24 [1]Many mss. read, *the blood of this righteous Man* [a]Matt. 26:5 [b]Deut. 21:6-8 [c]Matt. 27:19 [d]Matt. 27:4

25 [a]Josh. 2:19; Acts 5:28

26 [1]Or, *to them* [a]Mark 15:15; John 19:1; Luke 23:16

27 [1]Or, *battalion* [a]Matt. 27:27-31: *Mark 15:16-20* [b]John 18:28, 33; 19:9; Matt. 26:3 [c]Acts 10:1

28 And they stripped Him, and [a]put a scarlet robe on
Him.
29 [a]And after weaving a crown of thorns, they put it on
His head, and a [1]reed in His right hand; and they kneeled
down before Him and mocked Him, saying, "[b]Hail, King of
the Jews!"
30 And [a]they spat on Him, and took the reed and *began*
to beat Him on the head.
31 [a]And after they had mocked Him, they took His robe
off and put His garments on Him, and led Him away to crucify
Him.
32 [a]And as they were coming out, they found a [1]certain
[b]Cyrenian named Simon; this man they pressed into service to
bear His cross.
33 [a]And when they had come to a place called [b]Golgotha,
which means Place of a Skull,
34 [a]THEY GAVE HIM [b]WINE TO DRINK MINGLED WITH GALL;
and after tasting *it*, He was unwilling to drink.
35 And when they had crucified Him, [a]THEY DIVIDED UP
HIS GARMENTS AMONG THEMSELVES, CASTING [1]LOTS;
36 and sitting down, they *began* to [a]keep watch over Him
there.
37 And they put up above His head the charge against
Him [1]which read, "[a]THIS IS JESUS THE KING OF THE
JEWS."
38 At that time two robbers *were crucified with Him,
one on the right and one on the left.
39 And those who were passing by were [1]hurling abuse at
Him, [a]WAGGING THEIR HEADS,
40 and saying, "[a]You who destroy the temple and rebuild
it in three days, save Yourself! [b]If You are the Son of God,
come down from the cross."
41 In the same way the chief priests, along with the scribes
and elders, were mocking *Him*, and saying,
42 "[a]He saved others; [1]He cannot save Himself. [b]He is the
King of Israel; let Him now come down from the cross, and we
shall believe in Him.
43 "[a]HE TRUSTS IN GOD; LET HIM DELIVER *Him* now, IF HE
TAKES PLEASURE IN HIM; for He said, 'I am the Son of God.' "
44 [a]And the robbers also who had been crucified with Him
were casting the same insult at Him.
45 [a]Now from the [1]sixth hour darkness [2]fell upon all the
land until the [3]ninth hour.
46 And about the ninth hour Jesus cried out with a loud
voice, saying, "ELI, ELI LAMA SABACHTHANI?" that is, "[a]MY
GOD, MY GOD, WHY HAST THOU FORSAKEN ME?"
47 And some of those who were standing there, when they
heard it, *began* saying, "This man is calling for Elijah."
48 And [a]immediately one of them ran, and taking a
sponge, he filled it with sour wine, and put it on a reed, and
gave Him a drink.
49 But the rest *of them* said, "[1]Let us see whether Elijah
will come to save Him."[2]
50 And Jesus [a]cried out again with a loud voice, and
yielded up *His* spirit.
51 [a]And behold, [b]the veil of the temple was torn in two

28 [a]Mark 15:17; John 19:2

29 [1]Or, *staff* (made of a reed) [a]Mark 15:17; John 19:2 [b]Mark 15:18; John 19:1

30 [a]Matt. 26:67; Mark 10:34; 14:65; 15:19

31 [a]Mark 15:20

32 [1]Lit., *a man, a Cyrenian* [a]Matt. 27:32: *Mark 15:21; Luke 23:26;* John 19:17 [b]Acts 2:10; 6:9; 11:20; 13:1

33 [a]Matt. 27:34-44: *Mark 15:22-32; Luke 23:33-43; John 19:17-24* [b]John 19:17; Luke 23:33 and marg.

34 [a]Ps. 69:21 [b]Mark 15:23

35 [1]Lit., *a lot* [a]Ps. 22:18

36 [a]Matt. 27:54

37 [1]Lit., *written* [a]Mark 15:26; Luke 23:38; John 19:19

39 [1]Or, *blaspheming* [a]Mark 15:29; Job 16:4; Ps. 22:7; 109:25; Lam. 2:15

40 [a]Matt. 26:61 [b]Matt. 27:42

42 [1]Or, *can He not save Himself* [a]Mark 15:31; Luke 23:35 [b]John 1:49; 12:13; Matt. 27:37; Luke 23:37

43 [a]Ps. 22:8

44 [a]Luke 23:39-43

45 [1]I.e., noon [2]Or, *occurred* [3]I.e., 3 p.m. [a]Matt. 27:45-56: *Mark 15:33-41; Luke 23:44-49*

46 [a]Ps. 22:1

48 [a]Mark 15:36; Luke 23:36; John 19:29

49 [1]Lit., *Permit that we see* [2]Some early mss. add: *And another took a spear and pierced His side, and there came out water and blood.* (cf. John 19:34)

50 [a]Mark 15:37; Luke 23:46; John 19:30

51 [a]Matt. 27:51-56: *Mark 15:38-41;* Luke 23:47-49 [b]Mark 15:38; Luke 23:45; Ex. 26:31ff.; Heb. 9:3

from top to bottom, and [c]the earth shook; and the rocks were
split,
52 and the tombs were opened; and many bodies of the
[1]saints who had [a]fallen asleep were raised;
53 and coming out of the tombs after His resurrection
they entered [a]the holy city and appeared to many.
54 [a]Now the centurion, and those who were with him
[b]keeping guard over Jesus, when they saw [c]the earthquake and
the things that were happening, became very frightened and
said, "Truly this was [1d]the Son of God!"
55 [a]And many women were there looking on from a distance, who had followed Jesus from Galilee, [1b]ministering to
Him;
56 among whom was [a]Mary Magdalene, *along with* Mary
the mother of James and Joseph, and [b] the mother of the sons
of Zebedee.
57 [a]And when it was evening, there came a rich man from
Arimathea, named Joseph, who himself had also become a
disciple of Jesus.
58 This man came to Pilate and asked for the body of
Jesus. Then Pilate ordered *it* to be given over *to him.*
59 And Joseph took the body and wrapped it in a clean
linen cloth,
60 and laid it in his own new tomb, which he had hewn out
in the rock; and he rolled [a]a large stone against the entrance of
the tomb and went away.
61 And [a]Mary Magdalene was there, and the other Mary,
sitting opposite the grave.
62 Now on the next day, which is *the one* after [1a]the preparation, the chief priests and the Pharisees gathered together
with Pilate,
63 and said, "Sir, we remember that when he was still alive
that deceiver said, '[a]After three days I *am to* rise again.'
64 "Therefore, give orders for the grave to be made secure
until the third day, lest the disciples come and steal Him away
and say to the people, 'He has risen from the dead,' and the
last deception will be worse than the first."
65 Pilate said to them, "You have a [a]guard; go, make it *as*
secure as you know how."
66 And they went and made the grave secure, and along
with [a]the guard they set a [b]seal on [c]the stone.

Chapter 28

[a]NOW late on the Sabbath, as it began to dawn toward the
first *day* of the week, [b]Mary Magdalene and the other Mary
came to look at the grave.
2 And behold, a severe earthquake had occurred, for [a]an
angel of the Lord descended from heaven and came and rolled
away [b]the stone and sat upon it.
3 And [a]his appearance was like lightning, and his garment
as white as snow;
4 and the guards shook for fear of him, and became like
dead men.
5 And the angel answered and said to the women, "[1a]Do

51 [c]Matt. 27:54

52 [1]I.e. true believers; lit., *holy ones* [a]Acts 7:60

53 [a]Matt. 4:5

54 [1]Or, possibly, *a son of God*, or, *a son of a god* [a]Mark 15:39; Luke 23:47 [b]Matt. 27:36 [c]Matt. 27:51 [d]Matt. 4:3; Matt. 27:43

55 [1]Or, *waiting on* [a]Mark 15:40f.; Luke 23:49; John 19:25 [b]Luke 8:2, 3; Mark 15:41

56 [a]Matt. 28:1; Mark 15:40, 47; 16:9; Luke 8:2; John 19:25; 20:1, 18 [b]Matt. 20:20

57 [a]Matt. 27:57-61: *Mark 15:42-47; Luke 23:50-56; John 19:38-42*

60 [a]Mark 16:4; Matt. 27:66; 28:2

61 [a]Matt. 27:56; 28:1

62 [1]Or, *Friday* [a]Mark 15:42; Luke 23:54; John 19:14, 31, 42

63 [a]Matt. 16:21

65 [a]Matt. 27:66; 28:11

66 [a]Matt. 27:65; 28:11 [b]Dan. 6:17 [c]Mark 16:4; Matt. 27:60; 28:2

1 [a]Matt. 28:1-8: *Mark 16:1-8; Luke 24:1-10;* John 20:1-8 [b]Matt. 27:56, 61

2 [a]Luke 24:4; John 20:12 [b]Mark 16:4; Matt. 27:66; 28:2

3 [a]Dan. 7:9; 10:6; Mark 9:3; John 20:12; Acts 1:10

5 [1]Or, *Stop being afraid* [a]Matt. 28:10; 14:27

not be afraid; for I know that you are looking for Jesus who has
been crucified.
6 "He is not here, for He has risen, [a]just as He said. Come,
see the place where He was lying.
7 "And go quickly and tell His disciples that He has risen
from the dead; and behold, He is going before you [a]into Galilee,
there you will see Him; behold, I have told you."
8 And they departed quickly from the tomb with fear
and great joy and ran to report it to His disciples.
9 And behold, Jesus met them [1]and greeted them. And
they came up and took hold of His feet and worshiped Him.
10 Then Jesus *said to them, "[1a]Do not be afraid; go and
take word to [b]My brethren to leave [c]for Galilee, and there they
shall see Me."
11 Now while they were on their way, behold, some of
[a]the guard came into the city and reported to the chief priests
all that had happened.
12 And when they had assembled with the elders and
counseled together, they gave a large sum of money to the
soldiers,
13 and said, "You are to say, 'His disciples came by night
and stole Him away while we were asleep.'
14 "And if this should come to [a]the governor's ears, we will
win him over and [1]keep you out of trouble."
15 And they took the money and did as they had been
instructed; and this story was widely [a]spread among the Jews,
and is [b]to this day.
16 But the eleven disciples proceeded [a]to Galilee, to the
mountain which Jesus had designated.
17 And when they saw Him, they worshiped *Him*; but
[a]some were doubtful.
18 And Jesus came up and spoke to them, saying, "[a]All
authority has been given to Me in heaven and on earth.
19 "[a]Go therefore and [b]make disciples of [c]all the nations,
[d]baptizing them [1]in the name of the Father and the Son and
the Holy Spirit,
20 teaching them to observe all that I commanded you;
and lo, [a]I am with you [1]always, even to [b]the end of the age."

6 [a]Matt. 27:63; 12:40; 16:21

7 [a]Matt. 26:32; 28:10, 16

9 [1]Lit., *saying hello*

10 [1]Or, *Stop being afraid* [a]Matt. 28:5; 14:27 [b]John 20:17; Rom. 8:29; Heb. 2:11f., 17 [c]Matt. 26:32; 28:7, 16

11 [a]Matt. 27:65, 66

14 [1]Lit., *make you free from care* [a]Matt. 27:2

15 [a]Matt. 9:31; Mark 1:45 [b]Matt. 27:8

16 [a]Matt. 26:32; 28:7, 10

17 [a]Mark 16:11

18 [a]Matt. 26:64; Dan. 7:13f.; Rom. 14:9; Eph. 1:20-22; Phil. 2:9f.; Col. 2:10; 1 Pet. 3:22; Matt. 11:27

19 [1]Lit., *into* [a]Mark 16:15f. [b]Matt. 13:52; Acts 14:21 [c]Luke 24:47; Matt. 25:32 [d]Acts 2:38; 8:16; Rom. 6:3; 1 Cor. 1:13, 15ff.; Gal. 3:27

20 [1]Lit., *all the days* [a]Matt. 18:20; Acts 18:10 [b]Matt. 13:39

THE GOSPEL
ACCORDING TO
MARK

Preaching of the Baptist. Baptism of Jesus. Temptation of Jesus.

THE beginning of the gospel of Jesus Christ, [1a]the Son of
God.
2 [a]As it is written in Isaiah the prophet,
"[b]BEHOLD, I SEND MY MESSENGER BEFORE YOUR FACE,
WHO WILL PREPARE YOUR WAY;
3 "[a]THE VOICE OF ONE CRYING IN THE WILDERNESS,
'MAKE READY THE WAY OF THE LORD,
MAKE HIS PATHS STRAIGHT.' "
4 John the Baptist appeared in the wilderness [1a]preaching
a baptism of repentance for the [b]forgiveness of sins.
5 And all the country of Judea was going out to him, and
all the people of Jerusalem; and they were being baptized by
him in the Jordan River, confessing their sins.
6 And John was clothed with camel's hair and *wore* a
leather belt around his waist, and [1]his diet was locusts and wild
honey.
7 And he was [1]preaching, and saying, "After me comes
One who is mightier than I, and I am not *even* fit to stoop
down and untie the thong of His sandals.
8 "I baptized you [1]with water; but He will baptize you
[1]with the Holy Spirit."
9 [a]And it came about in those days that Jesus [b]came from
Nazareth in Galilee, and was baptized by John in the Jordan.
10 And immediately coming up out of the water, he saw
the heavens [1]opening, and the Spirit like a dove descending
upon Him;
11 and a voice came out of the heavens: "[a]Thou art My
beloved Son, in Thee I am well pleased."
12 [a]And immediately the Spirit *impelled Him *to go* out
into the wilderness.
13 And He was in the wilderness forty days being tempted
by [a]Satan; and He was with the wild beasts, and the angels were
ministering to Him.
14 [a]And after John had been [1]taken into custody, Jesus
came into Galilee, [2b]preaching the gospel of God,
15 and saying, "[a]The time is fulfilled, and the kingdom of
God is at hand; [b]repent and [1]believe in the gospel."
16 [a]And as He was going along by the sea of Galilee, He
saw Simon and Andrew, the brother of Simon, casting a net in
the sea; for they were fishermen.
17 And Jesus said to them, "Follow Me, and I will make
you become fishers of men."
18 And they immediately left the nets and followed Him.
19 And going on a little farther, He saw [1]James the *son* of
Zebedee, and John his brother, who were also in the boat
mending the nets.

1 [1]Many mss. omit, *the Son of God* [a]Matt. 4:3

2 [a]Mark 1:2-8: *Matt. 3:1-11; Luke 3:2-16* [b]Mal. 3:1; Matt. 11:10; Luke 7:27

3 [a]Is. 40:3; Matt. 3:3; Luke 3:4; John 1:23

4 [1]Or, *proclaiming* [a]Acts 13:24; [b]Luke 1:77

6 [1]Lit., *he was eating*

7 [1]Or, *proclaiming*

8 [1]The Greek here can be translated *in, with* or *by*

9 [a]Mark 1:9-11: *Matt. 3:13-17; Luke 3:21, 22* [b]Matt. 2:23; Luke 2:51

10 [1]Or, *being parted*

11 [a]Luke 3:22; Matt. 3:17

12 [a]Mark 1:12, 13: *Matt. 4:1-11; Luke 4:1-13*

13 [a]Matt. 4:10

14 [1]Lit., *delivered up* [2]Or, *proclaiming* [a]Matt. 4:12 [b]Matt. 4:23

15 [1]Or, *put your trust in* [a]Gal. 4:4; Eph. 1:10; 1 Tim. 2:6; Titus 1:3 [b]Acts 20:21

16 [a]Mark 1:16-20: *Matt. 4:18-22;* Luke 5:2-11; John 1:40-42

19 [1]Or, *Jacob*

20 And immediately He called them; and they left their
father Zebedee in the boat with the hired servants, [1]and went
away to follow Him.
21 [a]And they *went into Capernaum; and immediately on
the Sabbath [b]He entered the synagogue and *began* to teach.
22 And [a]they were amazed at His teaching; for He was
teaching them as *one* having authority, and not as the scribes.
23 And just then there was in their synagogue a man with
an unclean spirit; and he cried out,
24 saying, "[a]What do we have to do with You, Jesus of
[1b]Nazareth? Have You come to destroy us? I know who You
are—[c]the Holy One of God!"
25 And Jesus rebuked him, saying, "Be quiet, and come
out of him!"
26 And throwing him into convulsions, the unclean spirit
cried out with a loud voice, and came out of him.
27 And they were all [a]amazed, so that they debated among
themselves, saying, "What is this? A new teaching with authority! He commands even the unclean spirits, and they obey
Him."
28 And immediately the news about Him went out everywhere into all the surrounding district of Galilee.
29 [a]And immediately [1]after they had come [b]out of the
synagogue, they came into the house of Simon and Andrew,
with [2]James and John.
30 Now Simon's mother-in-law was lying sick with a fever;
and immediately they *spoke to Him about her.
31 And He came to her and raised her up, taking her by
the hand, and the fever left her, and she began to [1]wait on
them.
32 [a]And [b]when evening had come, [b]after the sun had set,
they *began* bringing to Him all who were ill and those who
were [c]demon-possessed.
33 And the whole [a]city had gathered at the door.
34 And He [a]healed many who were ill with various diseases, and cast out many demons; and He was not permitting
the demons to speak, because they [1]knew who He was.
35 [a]And in the early morning, while it was still dark, He
arose and went out and departed to a lonely place, and [b]was
praying there.
36 And Simon and his companions hunted for Him;
37 and they found Him, and *said to Him, "Everyone is
looking for You."
38 And He *said to them, "Let us go somewhere else to
the towns nearby, in order that I may [1]preach there also; for
that is what I came out for."
39 [a]And He went into their synagogues throughout all Galilee, [1]preaching and casting out the demons.
40 [a]And a leper *came to Him, beseeching Him and [b]falling on his knees before Him, and saying to Him, "If You are
willing, You can make me clean."
41 And moved with compassion, He stretched out His
hand and touched him, and *said to him, "I am willing; be
cleansed."
42 And immediately the leprosy left him and he was
cleansed.

20 [1]Lit., *after Him*

21 [a]Mark 1:21-28; Luke 4:31-37 [b]Matt. 4:23; Mark 1:39; 10:1

22 [a]Matt. 7:28

24 [1]Lit., *Nazarene* [a]Matt. 8:29 [b]Mark 10:47; 14:67; 16:6; Luke 4:34; 24:19; Matt. 2:23; Acts 24:5 [c]Luke 4:34; John 6:69; Luke 1:35; Acts 3:14

27 [a]Mark 10:24, 32; Mark 14:33; 16:5, 6

29 [1]Some mss. read: *after He had come out, He came* [2]Or, *Jacob* [a]Mark 1:29-31: *Matt. 8:14, 15; Luke* 4:38, 39 [b]Mark 1:21, 23

31 [1]Or, *serve*

32 [a]Mark 1:32-34: *Matt. 8:16, 17; Luke 4:40, 41* [b]Matt. 8:16; Luke 4:40 [c]Matt. 4:24

33 [a]Mark 1:21

34 [1]Some mss. read: *knew Him to be Christ* [a]Matt. 4:23

35 [a]Mark 1:35-38: *Luke 4:42, 43* [b]Luke 5:16; Matt. 14:23

38 [1]Or, *proclaim*

39 [1]Or, *proclaiming* [a]Matt. 4:23; Mark 1:23; 3:1

40 [a]Mark 1:40-44: *Matt. 8:2-4; Luke 5:12-14* [b]Mark 10:17; Matt. 8:2; Luke 5:12

44 [a]Matt. 8:4 [b]Matt. 8:4

45 [1]Lit., *was*
[a]Luke 5:15; Matt. 28:15
[b]Mark 2:2, 13; 3:7; Luke 5:17; John 6:2

2 [a]Mark 2:13; Mark 1:45

3 [a]Mark 2:3-12: *Matt. 9:2-8; Luke 5:18-26* [b]Matt. 4:24

4 [1]Lit., *bring to* [2]Lit., *where He was*
[a]Luke 5:19 [b]Matt. 4:24

5 [1]Lit., *child*
[a]Matt. 9:2

7 [1]Lit., *if not one, God*
[a]Is. 43:25

8 [1]Lit., *by*

9 [a]Matt. 4:24

12 [a]Matt. 9:8 [b]Matt. 9:33

13 [a]Mark 1:45

14 [a]Mark 2:14-17: *Matt. 9:9-13; Luke 5:27-32* [b]Matt. 9:9 [c]Matt. 8:22

15 [1]Lit., *comes* [2]Publicans who collected Roman taxes for profit [3]Lit., *were reclining with*

16 [a]Acts 23:9; Luke 5:30
[b]Matt. 9:11

17 [a]Matt. 9:12, 13; Luke 5:31, 32

43 And He sternly warned him and immediately sent him
away,
44 and He *said to him, "[a]See that you say nothing to
anyone; but [b]go, show yourself to the priest and offer for your
cleansing what Moses commanded, for a testimony to them."
45 But he went out and began to [a]proclaim it freely and to
[a]spread the news about, to such an extent that Jesus could no
longer publicly enter a city, but [1]stayed out in unpopulated
areas; and [b]they were coming to Him from everywhere.

Chapter 2

AND when He had come back to Capernaum several days
afterward, it was heard that He was at home.
2 And [a]many were gathered together, so that there was
no longer room, even near the door; and He was speaking the
word to them.
3 [a]And they *came, bringing to Him a [b]paralytic, carried
by four men.
4 And being unable to [1]get to Him on account of the
crowd, they [a]removed the roof [2]above Him; and when they
had dug an opening, they let down the pallet on which the
[b]paralytic was lying.
5 And Jesus seeing their faith *said to the paralytic, "My
[1]son, [a]your sins are forgiven."
6 But there were some of the scribes sitting there and
reasoning in their hearts,
7 "Why does this man speak that way? He is blaspheming;
[a]who can forgive sins [1]but God alone?"
8 And immediately Jesus, perceiving [1]in His spirit that
they were reasoning that way within themselves, *said to them,
"Why are you reasoning about these things in your hearts?
9 "Which is easier, to say to the [a]paralytic, 'Your sins are
forgiven;' or to say, 'Arise, and take up your pallet and walk'?
10 "But in order that you may know that the Son of Man
has authority on earth to forgive sins"—He *said to the
paralytic,
11 "I say to you, rise, take up your pallet and go home."
12 And he rose and immediately took up the pallet and
went out in the sight of all; so that they were all amazed and
[a]were glorifying God, saying, "[b]We have never seen anything
like this."
13 And He went out again by the seashore; and [a]all the
multitude were coming to Him, and He was teaching them.
14 [a]And as He passed by, He saw [b]Levi the *son* of Alpheus
sitting in the tax office, and He *said to him, "[c]Follow Me!"
And he rose and followed Him.
15 And it [1]came about that He was reclining *at table* in his
house, and many [2]tax-gatherers and sinners [3]were dining with
Jesus and His disciples; for there were many of them, and they
were following Him.
16 And when [a]the scribes of the Pharisees saw that He was
eating with the sinners and tax-gatherers, they *began* saying
to His disciples, "[b]Why is He eating and drinking with tax-
gatherers and sinners?"
17 And hearing this, Jesus *said to them, "[a]*It is not* those

who are healthy who need a physician, but those who are sick;
I did not come to call *the* righteous, but sinners."
18 [a]And John's disciples and the Pharisees were fasting;
and they *came and *said to Him, "Why do John's disciples
and the disciples of the Pharisees fast, but Your disciples do
not fast?"
19 And Jesus said to them, "While the bridegroom is with
them, [1]the attendants of the bridegroom do not fast, do they?
So long as they have the bridegroom with them, they cannot
fast.
20 "But the [a]days will come when the bridegroom is taken
away from them, and then they will fast in that day.
21 "No one sews a [1]patch of unshrunk cloth on an old
garment; otherwise the [2]patch pulls away from it, the new
from the old, and a worse tear results.
22 "And no one puts new wine into old [1]wineskins; otherwise the wine will burst the skins, and the wine is lost, and the
skins *as well;* but *one puts* new wine into fresh wineskins."
23 [a]And it came about that He was passing through the
grainfields on the Sabbath, and His disciples began to make
their way along while [b]picking the heads *of grain.*
24 And the Pharisees were saying to Him, "See here, [a]why
are they doing what is not lawful on the Sabbath?"
25 And He *said to them, "Have you never read what
David did when he was in need and became hungry, he and his
companions:
26 "How he entered into the house of God in the time of
[a]Abiathar *the* high priest, and ate the [1]consecrated bread,
which is not lawful for *anyone* to eat except the priests, and he
gave *it* also to those who were with him?"
27 And He was saying to them, "[a]The Sabbath [1]was made
[2]for man, and [b]not man [2]for the Sabbath.
28 "Consequently, the Son of Man is Lord even of the
Sabbath."

CHAPTER 3

[a]
AND He [b]entered again into a synagogue; and a man was
there with a withered hand.
2 And [a]they were watching Him *to see* if He would heal
him on the Sabbath, [b]in order that they might accuse Him.
3 And He *said to the man with the withered hand,
"[1]Rise and *come* forward!"
4 And He *said to them, "Is it lawful on the Sabbath to
do good or to do harm, to save a life or to kill?" But they kept
silent.
5 And after [a]looking around at them with anger, grieved
at their hardness of heart, He *said to the man, "Stretch out
your hand." And he stretched it out, and his hand was restored.
6 And the Pharisees went out and immediately *began*
[1]taking counsel with the [a]Herodians against Him, *as to* how
they might destroy Him.
7 [a]And Jesus withdrew to the sea with His disciples; and
[b]a great multitude from Galilee followed; and *also* from Judea,
8 and from Jerusalem, and from [a]Idumea, and beyond

18 [a]Mark 2:18-22: *Matt. 9:14-17; Luke 5:33-38*

19 [1]Lit., *sons of the bridalchamber*

20 [a]Luke 17:22; Matt. 9:15

21 [1]Lit., *that which is put on* [2]Lit., *that which fills up*

22 [1]I.e., skins used as bottles

23 [a]Mark 2:23-28: *Matt. 12:1-8; Luke 6:1-5* [b]Deut. 23:25

24 [a]Matt. 12:2

26 [1]Or, *showbread;* lit., *loaves of presentation* [a]1 Chr. 24:6; 1 Sam. 21:1; 2 Sam. 8:17

27 [1]Or, *came into being* [2]Lit., *for the sake of* [a]Ex. 23:12; Deut. 5:14 [b]Col. 2:16

1 [a]Mark 3:1-6: *Matt. 12:9-14; Luke 6:6-11* [b]Mark 1:21, 39

2 [a]Luke 6:7; 14:1; 20:20 [b]Matt. 12:10; Luke 6:7; Luke 11:54

3 [1]Lit., *Arise into the midst*

5 [a]Luke 6:10

6 [1]Lit., *giving* [a]Matt. 22:16; Mark 12:13

7 [a]Mark 3:7-12: *Matt. 12:15, 16; Luke 6:17-19* [b]Matt. 4:25; Luke 6:17

8 [a]Josh. 15:1, 21; Ezek. 35:15; 36:5

the Jordan, and the vicinity of [b]Tyre and Sidon, a great multitude heard of all that He was doing and came to Him.
9 And He told His disciples that a boat should stand
ready for Him because of the multitude, in order that they
might not crowd Him;
10 for He had [a]healed many, with the result that all those
who had [b]afflictions pressed about Him in order to [c]touch
Him.
11 And whenever the unclean spirits beheld Him, they
would fall down before Him and cry out, saying, "You are [a]the
Son of God!"
12 And He [a]earnestly warned them not to [1]reveal His
identity.
13 And He *went up to [a]the mountain and *[b]summoned
those whom He Himself wanted, and they came to Him.
14 And He appointed twelve[1], that they might be with
Him, and that He might send them out to preach,
15 and to have authority to cast out the demons.
16 And He appointed the twelve: [a]Simon (to whom He
gave the name Peter),
17 and [1]James, the *son* of Zebedee, and John the brother
of [1]James (to them He gave the name Boanerges, which
means, "Sons of thunder");
18 and Andrew, and Philip, and Bartholomew, and Matthew, and Thomas, and [1]James the *son* of Alphaeus, and
Thaddaeus, and Simon [2]the Cananaean;
19 and Judas Iscariot, who also betrayed Him.
20 And He *came [1a]home, and the [b]multitude *gathered
again, [c]to such an extent that they could not even eat [2]a meal.
21 And when [a]His own [1]people heard *of this*, they went
out to take custody of Him; for they were saying, "[b]He has lost
His senses."
22 And the scribes who came down [a]from Jerusalem were
saying, "He is possessed by [1b]Beelzebul," and "[c]He casts out
the demons by the ruler of the demons."
23 [a]And He called them to Himself and began speaking to
them in [b]parables, "How can [c]Satan cast out Satan?
24 "And if a kingdom is divided against itself, that kingdom
cannot stand.
25 "And if a house is divided against itself, that house will
not be able to stand.
26 "And if [a]Satan has risen up against himself and is divided, he cannot stand, but [1]he is finished!
27 "[a]But no one can enter the strong man's house and plunder his property unless he first binds the strong man, and then
he will plunder his house.
28 "[a]Truly I say to you, all sins shall be forgiven the sons of
men, and whatever blasphemies they utter;
29 but whoever blasphemes against the Holy Spirit never
has forgiveness, but is guilty of an eternal sin;"—
30 because they were saying, "He has an unclean spirit."
31 [a]And His mother and His brothers *arrived, and standing outside they sent *word* to Him, and called Him.
32 And a multitude was sitting around Him, and they
*said to Him, "Behold, Your mother and Your brothers[1] are
outside looking for You."

8 [b]Matt. 11:21

10 [a]Matt. 4:23 [b]Mark 5:29, 34; Luke 7:21 [c]Mark 6:56; 8:22; Matt 9:21; 14:36

11 [a]Matt. 4:3

12 [1]Lit., *make Him manifest* [a]Matt. 8:4

13 [a]Luke 6:12; Matt 5:1 [b]Matt 10:1; Mark 6:7; Luke 9:1-6

14 [1]Some early mss. add: *whom He named apostles*

16 [a]Mark 3:16-19: *Matt. 10:2-4; Luke 6:14-16;* Acts 1:13; names in Matthew's list.

17 [1]Or, *Jacob*

18 [1]Or, *Jacob* [2]Or, *the Zealot*

20 [1]Lit., *into a house* [2]Lit., *bread* [a]Mark 2:1; 7:17; 9:28 [b]Mark 1:45; Mark 3:7 [c]Mark 6:31

21 [1]Or, *kinsmen* [a]Mark 3:31f. [b]John 10:20; Acts 26:24

22 [1]Or, *Beezebul;* others read: *Beelzebub* [a]Matt. 15:1 [b]Matt. 10:25; Matt. 11:18 [c]Matt. 9:34

23 [a]Mark 3:23-27: *Matt. 12:25-29; Luke 11:17-22* [b]Mark 4:2; Matt. 13:3ff.; Mark 4:2ff.; [c]Matt. 4:10

26 [1]Lit., *he has an end* [a]Matt. 4:10

27 [a]Is. 49:24, 25

28 [a]Mark 3:28-30; Matt. 12:31, 32; Luke 12:10

31 [a]Mark 3:31-35: *Matt. 12:46-50; Luke 8:19-21*

32 [1]Later mss. add: *and Your sisters*

33 And answering them, He *said, "Who are My mother
and My brothers?"
34 And looking about on those who were sitting around
Him, He *said, "Behold, My mother and My brothers!
35 "For whoever does the will of God, he is My brother and
sister and mother."

Chapter 4

[a]AND He began to teach again [b]by the seashore. And such a
very great multitude [1]gathered before Him that He got into a
boat in the sea and sat down; and all the multitude were by the
seashore on the land.
2 And He was teaching them many things in [a]parables,
and was saying to them in His teaching,
3 "Listen *to this*! Behold, the sower went out to sow;
4 and it came about that as he was sowing, some *seed* fell
beside the road, and the birds came and ate it up.
5 "And other *seed* fell on the rocky *ground* where it did
not have much soil; and immediately it sprang up because it
had no depth of soil.
6 "And after the sun had risen, it was scorched; and because it had no root, it withered away.
7 "And other *seed* fell among the thorns, and the thorns
grew up and choked it, and it yielded no crop.
8 "And other *seeds* fell into the good soil and as they grew
up and increased, they were yielding a crop and were producing thirty, sixty, and a hundredfold."
9 And He was saying, "[a]He who has ears to hear, let him
hear."
10 And as soon as He was alone, [1]His followers, along with
the twelve, *began* asking Him *about* the parables.
11 And He was saying to them, "To you has been given
the mystery of the kingdom of God; but [a]those who are outside get everything [b]in parables;
12 [a]in order that WHILE SEEING, THEY MAY SEE AND NOT
PERCEIVE; AND WHILE HEARING, THEY MAY HEAR AND NOT UNDER-
STAND; LEST THEY RETURN AGAIN AND BE FORGIVEN."
13 [a]And He *said to them, "Do you not understand this
parable? And how will you understand all the parables?
14 "The sower sows the word.
15 "And these are the ones who are beside the road where
the word is sown; and when they hear, immediately [a]Satan
comes and takes away the word which has been sown in them.
16 "And in a similar way these are the ones on whom seed
was sown on the rocky *places,* who, when they hear the word,
immediately receive it with joy;
17 and they have no *firm* root in themselves, but are *only*
temporary; then, when affliction or persecution arises because
of the word, immediately they [1]fall away.
18 "And others are the ones on whom seed was sown
among the thorns; these are the ones who have heard the word,
19 and the worries of [a]the [1]world, and the deceitfulness of
riches, and the desires for other things enter in and choke the
word, and it becomes unfruitful.

1 [1]Lit., *is gathered* [a]Mark 4:1-12: *Matt. 13:1-15; Luke 8:4-10* [b]Mark 2:13; 3:7

2 [a]Mark 3:23; Matt. 13:3ff.; Mark 4:2ff.

9 [a]Matt. 11:15; Mark 4:23

10 [1]Lit., *those about Him*

11 [a]1 Cor. 5:12f.; Col. 4:5; 1 Thess. 4:12; 1 Tim. 3:7 [b]Mark 4:2; Mark 3:23

12 [a]Is. 6:9; Matt. 13:14

13 [a]Mark 4:13-20: *Matt. 13:18-23; Luke 8:11-15*

15 [a]Matt. 4:10

17 [1]Lit., *are caused to stumble*

19 [1]Or, *age* [a]Matt. 13:22

20 "And those are the ones on whom seed was sown on the
good ground; and they hear the word and accept it, and bear
fruit, thirty, sixty, and a hundredfold."
21 And He was saying to them, "[a]A lamp is not brought to
be put under a peck-measure, is it, or under a bed? Is it not
brought to be put on the lampstand?
22 "[a]For nothing is hidden, except to be revealed; nor has
anything been secret, but that it should come to light.
23 "[a]If any man has ears to hear, let him hear."
24 And He was saying to them, "Take care what you listen
to; [1a]by your standard of measure it shall be measured to you;
and more shall be given you besides.
25 "[a]For whoever has, to him shall *more* be given; and
whoever does not have, even what he has shall be taken away
from him."
26 And He was saying, "[a]The kingdom of God is like a
man who casts seed upon the ground;
27 and goes to bed at night and gets up by day, and the
seed sprouts up and grows — how, he himself does not know.
28 "The earth produces crops by itself; first the blade, then
the head, then the mature grain in the head.
29 "But when the crop permits, he immediately [1]puts in the
sickle, because the harvest has come."
30 [a]And He said, "How shall we [1b]picture the kingdom of
God, or by what parable shall we present it?
31 "*It is* like a mustard seed, which, when sown upon the
ground, though it is smaller than all the seeds that are upon
the ground,
32 yet when it is sown, grows up and becomes larger than
all the garden plants and forms large branches; so that the
birds of the [1]air can nest under its shade."
33 And with many such parables He was speaking the
word to them as they were able to hear it;
34 and He was not speaking to them [a]without [1]parables;
but He was explaining everything privately to His own
disciples.
35 [a]And on that day, when evening had come, He *said to
them, "Let us go over to the other side."
36 And [1]leaving the multitude, they *took Him along with
them, just as He was, [a]in the boat; and other boats were with
Him.
37 And there *arose a fierce gale of wind, and the waves
were breaking over the boat so much that the boat was already
filling up.
38 And He Himself was in the stern, asleep on the cush-
ion; and they *awoke Him and *said to Him, "Teacher, do
You not care that we are perishing?"
39 And being aroused, He rebuked the wind and said to
the sea, "Hush, be still." And the wind died down and [1]it
became perfectly calm.
40 And He said to them, "Why are you so timid? How is
it that you have no faith?"
41 And they became very much afraid and said to one
another, "Who then is this, that even the wind and the sea
obey Him?"

21 [a]Matt. 5:15; Luke 8:16; 11:33

22 [a]Matt. 10:26; Luke 8:17; 12:2

23 [a]Mark 4:9; Matt. 11:15

24 [1]Lit., *by what measure you measure* [a]Matt. 7:2; Luke 6:38

25 [a]Matt. 13:12

26 [a]Mark 4:26-29; Matt. 13:24-30

29 [1]Lit., *sends forth*

30 [1]Lit., *compare* [a]Mark 4:30-32: *Matt. 13:31, 32; Luke 13:18, 19* [b]Matt. 13:24

32 [1]Or, *sky*

34 [1]Lit., *a parable* [a]Matt. 13:34; John 10:6; 16:25

35 [a]Mark 4:35-41: *Matt. 8:18, 23-27; Luke 8:22, 25*

36 [1]Or, *sending away* [a]Mark 4:1; 5:2, 21; Mark 3:9

39 [1]Lit., *a great calm occurred*

[a] CHAPTER 5

AND they came to the other side of the sea, into the country
of the Gerasenes.
2 And when He had come out of [a]the boat, immediately
a man from the tombs [b]with an unclean spirit met Him,
3 and he had his dwelling among the tombs; and no one
was able to bind him any more, even with a chain;
4 because he had often been bound with shackles and
chains, and the chains had been torn apart by him, and the
shackles broken in pieces, and no one was strong enough to
subdue him.
5 And constantly night and day, among the tombs and in
the mountains, he was crying out and gashing himself with
stones.
6 And seeing Jesus from a distance, he ran up and bowed
down before Him;
7 and crying out with a loud voice, he *said, "[a]What do I
have to do with You, Jesus, [b]Son of [c]the Most High God? I
implore You by God, do not torment me!"
8 For He had been saying to him, "Come out of the
man, you unclean spirit!"
9 And He was asking him, "What is your name?" And he
*said to Him, "My name is [a]Legion; for we are many."
10 And he *began* to entreat Him earnestly not to send
them out of the country.
11 Now there was a big herd of swine feeding there on the
mountain side.
12 And they entreated Him, saying, "Send us into the
swine so that we may enter them."
13 And He gave them permission. And coming out, the
unclean spirits entered the swine; and the herd rushed down
the steep bank into the sea, about two thousand *of them;* and
they [1]were drowned in the sea.
14 And those who tended them ran away and reported it
in the city and *out* in the country. And *the people* came to see
what it was that had happened.
15 And they *came to Jesus and *observed the man who
had been [a]demon-possessed sitting down, [b]clothed and [c]in his
right mind, the very man who had had the "[d]legion;" and they
became frightened.
16 And those who had seen it described to them how it
had happened to the [a]demon-possessed man, and *all* about the
swine.
17 And they began to entreat Him to depart from their
region.
18 [a]And as He was getting into the boat, the man who had
been [b]demon-possessed was entreating Him that he might [1]ac-
company Him.
19 And He did not let him, but He *said to him, "Go
home to your people and report to them [1]what great things the
Lord has done for you, and *how* He had mercy on you."
20 And he went off and began to proclaim in [a]Decapolis
[1]what great things Jesus had done for him; and everyone
marveled.
21 [a]And when Jesus had crossed over again in [b]the boat to

1 [a]Mark 5:1-17: *Matt. 8:28-34; Luke 8:26-37*

2 [a]Mark 4:1, 36; 5:21; Mark 3:9 [b]Mark 1:23

7 [a]Matt. 8:29 [b]Matt. 4:3 [c]Luke 8:28; Acts 16:17; Heb. 7:1

9 [a]Mark 5:15; Matt. 26:53; Luke 8:30

13 [1]Lit., *were drowning*

15 [a]Mark 5:16, 18; Matt. 4:24 [b]Luke 8:27 [c]Luke 8:35 [d]Mark 5:9

16 [a]Mark 5:15; Matt. 4:24

18 [1]Lit., *be with Him* [a]Mark 5:18-20: *Luke* 8:38, 39 [b]Mark 5:15, 16; Matt. 4:24

19 [1]Or, *everything that*

20 [1]Or, *everything that* [a]Mark 7:31; Matt. 4:25

21 [a]Matt. 9:1; Luke 8:40 [b]Mark 4:36

the other side, a great multitude gathered about Him; and He
[1]stayed [c]by the seashore.
22 [a]And one of [b]the synagogue [1]officials named Jairus
*came up, and upon seeing Him, *fell at His feet,
23 and *entreated Him earnestly, saying, "My little daughter is at the point of death; *please* come and [a]lay Your hands
on her, that she may [1]get well and live."
24 And He went off with him; and a great multitude was
following Him and pressing in on Him.
25 And a woman who had had a hemorrhage for twelve
years,
26 and had endured much at the hands of many physicians, and had spent all that she had and was not helped at all,
but rather had grown worse,
27 after hearing about Jesus, came up in the crowd behind
Him, and touched His [1]cloak.
28 For she [1]thought, "If I just touch His garments, I shall
[2]get well."
29 And immediately the flow of her blood was dried up;
and she felt in her body that she was healed of her [a]affliction.
30 And immediately Jesus, perceiving in Himself that [a]the
power *proceeding* from Him had gone forth, turned around in
the crowd and said, "Who touched My garments?"
31 And His disciples said to Him, "You see the multitude
pressing in on You, and You say, 'Who touched Me?' "
32 And He looked around to see the woman who had
done this.
33 But the woman fearing and trembling, aware of what
had happened to her, came and fell down before Him, and
told Him the whole truth.
34 And He said to her, "Daughter, [a]your faith has [1]made
you well; [b]go in peace, and be healed of your [c]affliction."
35 While He was still speaking, they *came from the
house of the [a]synagogue official, saying, "Your daughter has
died; why trouble the Teacher any more?"
36 But Jesus, overhearing what was being spoken, *said to
the [a]synagogue official, "[b]Do not be afraid *any longer,* only
[1]believe."
37 And He allowed no one to follow with Him, except
[a]Peter and [1]James and John the brother of [1]James.
38 And they *came to the house of the [a]synagogue official; and He *beheld a commotion, and *people* loudly weeping
and wailing.
39 And entering in, He *said to them, "Why make a commotion and weep? The child has not died, but is asleep."
40 And they were laughing at Him. But putting them all
out, He *took along the child's father and mother and His
own companions, and *entered the *room* where the child was.
41 And taking the child by the hand, He *said to her,
"Talitha kum!" (which translated means, "Little girl, [a]I say to
you, arise!")
42 And immediately the girl got up and *began* to walk; for
she was twelve years old. And immediately they were completely astounded.
43 And He [a]gave them strict orders that no one should

21 [1]Lit., *was* [c]Mark 4:1

22 [1]Or, *rulers* [a]Mark 5:22-43: *Matt. 9:18-26; Luke 8:41-56* [b]Mark 5:35, 36, 38; Luke 8:49; 13:14; Acts 13:15; 18:8, 17; Matt. 9:18

23 [1]Lit., *be saved* [a]Mark 6:5; 7:32; 8:23; 16:18; Luke 4:40; 13:13; Acts 9:17; 28:8; Acts 6:6

27 [1]Or, *outer garment*

28 [1]Lit., *was saying* [2]Lit., *be saved*

29 [a]Mark 5:34; Mark 3:10

30 [a]Luke 5:17

34 [1]Lit., *saved you* [a]Matt. 9:22 [b]Luke 7:50; 8:48; Acts 16:36; James 2:16 [c]Mark 5:29; Mark 3:10

35 [a]Mark 5:22

36 [1]Or, *keep on believing* [a]Mark 5:22 [b]Luke 8:50

37 [1]Or, *Jacob* [a]Matt. 17:1; 26:37

38 [a]Mark 5:22

41 [a]Luke 7:14; Acts 9:40

43 [a]Matt. 8:4

know about this; and He said that *something* should be given
her to eat.

CHAPTER 6

[a]AND He went out from there; and He *came into [1b]His
home town; and His disciples *followed Him.
2 And when the Sabbath had come, He began [a]to teach
in the synagogue; and the [b]many listeners were astonished,
saying, "Where did this man *get* these things, and what is *this*
wisdom given to Him, and such [1]miracles as these performed
by His hands?
3 "Is not this [a]the carpenter, [b]the son of Mary, and brother of [1]James, and Joses, and Judas, and Simon? Are not [c]His
sisters here with us?" And they [2]took [d]offense at Him.
4 And Jesus said to them, "[a]A prophet is not without
honor except in [1b]his home town and among his *own* relatives
and in his *own* household."
5 And He could do no [1]miracle there except that He
[a]laid His hands upon a few sick people and healed them.
6 And He wondered at their unbelief.
[a]And He was going around the villages teaching.
7 [a]And [b]He *[1]summoned the twelve and began to send
them out [c]in pairs; and He was giving them authority over the
unclean spirits;
8 [a]and He instructed them that they should take nothing
for *their* journey, except a mere staff; no bread, no [1]bag, no
money in their belt;
9 but [1]*to* wear sandals; and *He added*, "Do not put on
two [2]tunics."
10 And He said to them, "Wherever you enter a house,
stay there until you [1]leave town.
11 "And any place that does not receive you or listen to
you, as you go out from there, [a]shake off the dust [1]from the
soles of your feet for a testimony against them."
12 [a]And they went out and [1]preached that *men* should
repent.
13 And they were casting out many demons and [a]were
anointing with oil many sick people and healing them.
14 [a]And King Herod heard *of it;* for His name had become well known; and *people* were saying, "[b]John the Baptist
has risen from the dead, and therefore these miraculous powers are at work in him."
15 But others were saying, "*He is* [a]Elijah." And others
were saying, "*He is* [b]a prophet, like one of the prophets *of
old.*"
16 But when Herod heard *of it,* he kept saying, "John,
whom I beheaded, he has risen!"
17 For Herod himself had sent and had John arrested and
bound in prison on account of [a]Herodias, the wife of his brother Philip, because he had married her.
18 For John had been saying to Herod, "[a]It is not lawful
for you to have your brother's wife."
19 And [a]Herodias had a grudge against him and wanted to
kill him; and could not *do so;*
20 for [a]Herod was afraid of John, knowing that he was a

1 [1]Or, *His own part of the country* [a]Mark 6:1-6: *Matt. 13:54-58* [b]Luke 4:16, 23; Matt. 13:54, 57

2 [1]Or, *works of power* [a]Matt. 4:23; Mark 10:1 [b]Matt. 7:28

3 [1]Or, *Jacob* [2]Lit., *were being made to stumble* [a]Matt. 13:55 [b]Matt. 12:46 [c]Matt. 13:56 [d]Matt. 11:6

4 [1]Or, *his own part of the country* [a]Matt. 13:57 [b]Mark 6:1

5 [1]Or, *work of power* [a]Mark 5:23

6 [a]Matt. 9:35; Luke 13:22; Mark 1:39; 10:1

7 [1]Lit., *summons* [a]Mark 6:7-11: *Matt. 10:1, 9-14; Luke 9:1, 3-5;* Luke 10:4-11 [b]Mark 3:13; Matt. 10:1, 5; Luke 9:1 [c]Luke 10:1

8 [1]Or, *knapsack* or, *beggar's bag* [a]Matt. 10:10

9 [1]Lit., *being shod with* [2]Or, *inner garments*

10 [1]Lit., *go out from there*

11 [1]Lit., *under your feet* [a]Matt. 10:14

12 [1]Or, *proclaimed as a herald* [a]Matt. 11:1; Luke 9:6

13 [a]James 5:14

14 [a]Mark 6:14-29: *Matt. 14:1-12;* Mark 6:14-16: *Luke 9:7-9* [b]Matt. 14:2

15 [a]Matt. 16:14; Mark 8:28 [b]Matt. 21:11

17 [a]Matt. 14:3

18 [a]Matt. 14:4

19 [a]Matt. 14:3

20 [a]Matt. 21:26

righteous and holy man, and kept him safe. And when he heard him, he was very perplexed; [1]but he [2]used to enjoy listening to him.

21 And a strategic day came when Herod on his birthday [a]gave a banquet for his lords and [1]military commanders and the leading men [b]of Galilee;

22 and when the daughter of [a]Herodias herself came in and danced, she pleased Herod and his [1]dinner guests; and the king said to the girl, "Ask me for whatever you want and I will give it to you."

23 And he swore to her, "Whatever you ask of me, I will give it to you; up to [a]half of my kingdom."

24 And she went out and said to her mother, "What shall I ask for?" And she said, "The head of John the Baptist."

25 And immediately she came in haste before the king and asked, saying, "I want you to give me right away the head of John the Baptist on a platter."

26 And although the king was very sorry, *yet* because of his oaths and because of his [1]dinner guests, he was unwilling to refuse her.

27 And immediately the king sent an executioner and commanded *him* to bring *back* his head. And he went and beheaded him in the prison,

28 and brought his head on a platter, and gave it to the girl; and the girl gave it to her mother.

29 And when his disciples heard *about this*, they came and took away his body and laid it in a tomb.

30 [a]And the [b]apostles *gathered together with Jesus; and they reported to Him all that they had done and taught.

31 And He *said to them, "Come away by yourselves to a lonely place and rest a while." (For there were many *people* coming and going, and [a]they did not even have time to eat.)

32 [a]And they went away in [b]the boat to a lonely place by themselves.

33 And *the people* saw them going, and many recognized *them*, and they ran there together on foot from all the cities, and got there ahead of them.

34 And [1]disembarking, He [a]saw a great multitude, and He felt compassion for them because [a]they were like sheep without a shepherd; and He began to teach them many things.

35 And when it was already quite late, His disciples came up to Him and *began* saying, "The place is desolate and it is already quite late;

36 send them away so that they may go into the surrounding countryside and villages and buy themselves [1]something to eat."

37 But He answered and said to them, "You give them something to eat!" [a]And they *said to Him, "Shall we go and spend two hundred [1b]denarii on bread and give them something to eat?"

38 And He *said to them, "How many loaves do you have? Go look!" And when they found out, they *said, "Five and two fish."

39 And He commanded them all to recline by groups on the green grass.

20 [1]Lit., *and* [2]Lit., *was hearing him gladly*

21 [1]Lit., *chiliarchs in command of a thousand troops* [a]Esther 1:3; 2:18 [b]Luke 3:1

22 [1]Lit., *those who reclined at table with him* [a]Matt. 14:3

23 [a]Esther 5:3, 6; 7:2

26 [1]Lit., *those reclining at table*

30 [a]Luke 9:10 [b]Matt. 10:2 [Mark 3:14 in Gr.]; Luke 6:13; 9:10; 17:5; 22:14; 24:10; Acts 1:2, 26

31 [a]Mark 3:20

32 [a]Mark 6:32-44: *Matt. 14:13-21; Luke 9:10-17; John 6:5-13;* Mark 8:2-9 [b]Mark 6:45; 3:9; 4:36

34 [1]Lit., *having come forth* [a]Matt. 9:36

36 [1]Lit., *what they may eat*

37 [1]A denarius represented a day's wages for a common laborer [a]John 6:7 [b]Matt. 18:28; Luke 7:41

40 And they reclined in companies of hundreds, and of
fifties.
41 And He took the five loaves and the two fish, and
looking up toward heaven, He [a]blessed *the food* and broke the
loaves and He kept giving *them* to the disciples to set before
them; and He divided up the two fish among them all.
42 And they all ate and were satisfied.
43 And they picked up twelve full [1a]baskets of the broken
pieces, and also of the fish.
44 And there were [a]five thousand men who ate the loaves.
45 [a]And immediately He made His disciples get into [b]the
boat and go ahead of *Him* to the other side to [c]Bethsaida,
while He Himself was sending the multitude away.
46 And after [a]bidding them farewell, He departed [b]to the
mountain to pray.
47 And when it was evening, the boat was in the midst of
the sea, and He *was* alone on the land.
48 And seeing them [1]straining at the oars, for the wind was
against them, at about the [2a]fourth watch of the night, He
*came to them, walking on the sea; and He intended to pass by
them.
49 But when they saw Him walking on the sea, they supposed that it was a ghost, and cried out;
50 for they all saw Him and were [1]frightened. But immediately He spoke with them and *said to them, "[a]Take courage; it is I, [b]do not be afraid."
51 And He got into [a]the boat with them, and the wind
stopped; and they were greatly astonished,
52 for [a]they [1]had not gained any insight from the *incident*
of the loaves, but [2]their heart [b]was hardened.
53 [a]And when they had crossed over they came to land at
Gennesaret, and moored to the shore.
54 And when they had come out of the boat, immediately
the people recognized Him,
55 and ran about that whole country and began to carry
about on their pallets those who were sick, to [1]the place they
heard He was.
56 And wherever He entered villages, or cities, or countryside, they were laying the sick in the market places, and entreating Him that they might just [a]touch [b]the fringe of His cloak;
and as many as touched it were being cured.

Chapter 7

[a]AND the Pharisees and some of the scribes gathered together
around Him when they had come [b]from Jerusalem,
2 and had seen that some of His disciples were eating
their bread with [a]impure hands, that is, unwashed.
3 (For the Pharisees and all the Jews do not eat unless
they [1]carefully wash their hands, *thus* observing the [a]traditions
of the elders;
4 and *when they come* from the market place, they do
not eat unless they [1]cleanse themselves; and there are many
other things which they have received in order to observe, such
as the [2]washing of [a]cups and pitchers and copper pots.)
5 And the Pharisees and the scribes *asked Him, "Why

41 [a]Matt. 14:19
43 [1]I.e., large-sized baskets [a]Matt. 14:20
44 [a]Matt. 14:21
45 [a]Mark 6:45-51: *Matt. 14:22-32; John 6:15-21* [b]Mark 6:32 [c]Matt. 11:21; Mark 8:22
46 [a]Acts 18:18, 21; 2 Cor. 2:13 [b]Matt. 14:23
48 [1]Lit., *harassed in rowing* [2]I.e., 3-6 a.m. [a]Mark 13:35; Matt. 24:43
50 [1]Or, *troubled* [a]Matt. 9:2 [b]Matt. 14:27
51 [a]Mark 6:32
52 [1]Lit., *had not understood on the basis of* [2]Or, *their mind was closed, made dull, or insensible* [a]Mark 8:17ff. [b]Rom. 11:7
53 [a]Mark 6:53-56: *Matt. 14:34-36; John 6:24, 25*
55 [1]Or, *where they were hearing that He was*
56 [a]Mark 3:10 [b]Matt. 9:20
1 [a]Mark 7:1-23: *Matt. 15:1-20* [b]Matt. 15:1
2 [a]Mark 7:5; Acts 10:14, 28; 11:8; Rom. 14:14; Heb. 10:29; Rev. 21:27; Matt. 15:2; Luke 11:38
3 [1]Lit., *with the fist* [a]Mark 7:5, 8, 9, 13; Gal. 1:14
4 [1]Or, *sprinkle* [2]Lit., *baptizing* [a]Matt. 23:25

do Your disciples not walk according to the [a]tradition of the
elders, but eat their bread with [b]impure hands?"
6 And He said to them, "Rightly did Isaiah prophesy of
you hypocrites, as it is written,
'[a]THIS PEOPLE HONORS ME WITH THEIR LIPS,
BUT THEIR HEART IS FAR AWAY FROM ME.
7 '[a]BUT IN VAIN DO THEY WORSHIP ME,
TEACHING AS DOCTRINES THE PRECEPTS OF MEN.'
8 "Neglecting the commandment of God, you hold to the
[a]tradition of men."
9 He was also saying to them, "You nicely set aside the
commandment of God in order to keep your [a]tradition.
10 "For Moses said, '[a]HONOR YOUR FATHER AND YOUR MOTH-
ER;' and, '[b]HE WHO SPEAKS EVIL OF FATHER OR MOTHER, LET HIM
[1]BE PUT TO DEATH;'
11 but you say, 'If a man says to *his* father or *his* mother,
anything of mine you might have been helped by is [a]Corban
(that is to say, [1]given *to God*),'
12 you no longer permit him to do anything for *his* father
or *his* mother;
13 *thus* invalidating the word of God by your [a]tradition
which you have handed down; and you do many such things
like that."
14 And summoning the multitude again, He *began* saying
to them, "Listen to Me, all of you, and understand:
15 there is nothing outside the man which going into him
can defile him; but the things which proceed out of the man
are what defile the man."
16 (See marginal note.[1])
17 And when leaving the multitude, He had entered [a]the
house, [b]His disciples questioned Him about the parable.
18 And He *said to them, "Are you too so uncomprehend-
ing? Do you not see that whatever goes into the man from
outside cannot defile him;
19 because it does not go into his heart, but into his stomach, and [1]is eliminated?" (*Thus He* declared [a]all foods
[b]clean.)
20 And He was saying, "[a]That which proceeds out of the
man, that is what defiles the man.
21 "For from within, out of the heart of men, proceed the
evil thoughts and [1]fornications, thefts, murders, adulteries,
22 deeds of coveting *and* wickedness, *as well as* deceit,
sensuality, [1a]envy, slander, [2]pride *and* foolishness.
23 "All these evil things proceed from within and defile the
man."
24 [a]And from there He arose and went away to the region
of [b]Tyre[1]. And when He had entered a house, He wanted no
one to know *of it;* [2]yet He could not escape notice.
25 But after hearing of Him, a woman whose little daughter had an unclean spirit, immediately came and fell at His
feet.
26 Now the woman was a [1]Gentile, of the Syrophoenician
race. And she kept asking Him to cast the demon out of her
daughter.
27 And He was saying to her, "Let the children be satisfied

5 [a]Mark 7:3, 8, 9, 13; Gal. 1:14 [b]Mark 7:2

6 [a]Is. 29:13

7 [a]Is. 29:13

8 [a]Mark 7:3, 5, 9, 13; Gal. 1:14

9 [a]Mark 7:3, 5, 8, 13; Gal. 1:14

10 [1]Lit., *die the death* [a]Ex. 20:12; Deut. 5:16 [b]Ex. 21:17; Lev. 20:9

11 [1]Or, *a gift, an offering* [a]Lev. 1:2 [Heb.]; Matt. 27:6 marg.

13 [a]Mark 7:3, 5, 8, 9; Gal. 1:14

16 [1]Later mss. add verse 16: *"If any man has ears to hear, let him hear."*

17 [a]Mark 9:28; Mark 2:1; 3:19 [b]Matt. 15:15

19 [1]Lit., *goes out into the latrine* [a]Rom. 14:1-12; Col. 2:16 [b]Luke 11:41; Acts 10:15; 11:9

20 [a]Matt. 15:18; Mark 7:23

21 [1]I.e., acts of sexual immorality

22 [1]Lit., *an evil eye* [2]Or, *arrogance* [a]Matt. 6:23; 20:15

24 [1]Some early mss. add: *and Sidon* [2]Lit., *and* [a]Mark 7:24-30: *Matt. 15:21-28* [b]Matt. 11:21; Mark 7:31

26 [1]Lit., *Greek*

first, for it is not [1]good to take the children's bread and throw
it to the dogs."
28 But she answered and *said to Him, "Yes, Lord, *but*
even the dogs under the table feed on the children's crumbs."
29 And He said to her, "Because of this [1]answer go your
way; the demon has gone out of your daughter."
30 And going back to her home, she found the child [1]lying
on the bed, [2]the demon having departed.
31 [a]And again He went out from the region of [b]Tyre, and
came through Sidon to [c]the sea of Galilee, within the region of
[d]Decapolis.
32 And they *brought to Him one who was deaf and
spoke with difficulty, and they *entreated Him to [a]lay His
hand upon him.
33 And [a]He took him aside from the multitude by himself, and put His fingers into his ears, and after [a]spitting, He
touched his tongue *with the saliva;*
34 and looking up to heaven with a deep [a]sigh, He *said to
him, "Ephphatha!" that is, "Be opened!"
35 And his ears were opened, and the [1]impediment of his
tongue [2]was removed, and he *began* speaking plainly.
36 And [a]He gave them orders not to tell anyone; but the
more He ordered them, the more widely they [b]continued to
proclaim it.
37 And they were utterly astonished, saying, "He has done
all things well; He makes even the deaf to hear, and the dumb
to speak."

Chapter 8

In those days again, when there was a great multitude and
they had nothing to eat, [a]He summoned His disciples and
*said to them,
2 "[a]I feel compassion for the multitude because they have
remained with Me now three days, and have nothing to eat;
3 and if I send them away fasting to their home, they will
faint on the way; and some of them have come from a
distance."
4 And His disciples answered Him, "Where will anyone
be able to *find enough* to satisfy these men with [1]bread here in
the wilderness?"
5 And He was asking them, "How many loaves do you
have?" And they said, "Seven."
6 And He *directed the multitude to [1]sit down on the
ground; and taking the seven loaves, He gave thanks and broke
them, and *began* giving them to His disciples to [2]serve to
them, and they [2]served them to the multitude.
7 They also had a few small fish; and [a]after He had
blessed them, He ordered these to be [1]served as well.
8 And they ate and were satisfied; and they picked up
seven full [a]baskets of what was left over of the broken pieces.
9 And about four thousand were *there;* and He sent
them away.
10 And immediately He entered the boat with His disciples, and came to the district of [a]Dalmanutha.

27 [1]Or, *proper*

29 [1]Lit., *word*

30 [1]Lit., *thrown* [2]Lit., *and the*

31 [a]Mark 7:31-37: *Matt. 15:29-31* [b]Matt. 11:21; Mark 7:24 [c]Matt. 4:18 [d]Mark 5:20; Matt. 4:25

32 [a]Mark 5:23

33 [a]Mark 8:23

34 [a]Mark 8:12

35 [1]Or, *bond* [2]Lit., *was loosed*

36 [a]Matt. 8:4 [b]Mark 1:45

1 [a]Mark 8:1-9: [6:34-44] *Matt. 15:32-39*

2 [a]Matt. 9:36; Mark 6:34

4 [1]Lit., *loaves*

6 [1]Lit., *to recline* [2]Lit., *set before*

7 [1]Lit., *set before* [a]Matt. 14:19

8 [a]Mark 8:20; Matt. 15:37

10 [a]Matt. 15:39

11 [a]And the Pharisees came out and began to argue with
Him, [b]seeking from Him a [1]sign from heaven, [2]to test Him.
12 And [a]sighing deeply [1]in His spirit, He *said, "Why does
this generation seek for a [2]sign? Truly I say to you, [3]no [2]sign
shall be given to this generation."
13 And leaving them, He again embarked and went away
to the other side.
14 And they had forgotten to take bread; and [1]did not
have more than one loaf in the boat with them.
15 And He was giving orders to them, saying, "[a]Watch
out! Beware of the leaven of the Pharisees and the leaven of
[b]Herod."
16 And they *began* to discuss with one another *the fact*
that they had no bread.
17 And Jesus, aware of this, *said to them, "Why do you
discuss *the fact* that you have no bread? [a]Do you not yet see or
understand? Do you have a [1]hardened heart?
18 "[a]HAVING EYES, DO YOU NOT SEE? AND HAVING EARS, DO
YOU NOT HEAR? And do you not remember,
19 when I broke [a]the five loaves for the five thousand, how
many large [b]baskets full of broken pieces you picked up?"
They *said to Him, "Twelve."
20 "And when *I broke* [a]the seven for the four thousand,
how many [b]basketfuls of broken pieces did you pick up?" And
they *said to Him, "Seven."
21 And He was saying to them, "[a]Do you not yet
understand?"
22 And they *came to [a]Bethsaida. And they *brought a
blind man to Him, and *entreated Him to [b]touch him.
23 And taking the blind man by the hand, He [a]brought
him out of the village; and after [a]spitting on his eyes, and
[b]laying His hands upon him, He asked him, "Do you see
anything?"
24 And he [1]looked up and said, "I see men, for [2]I am
seeing *them* like trees, walking about."
25 Then again He laid His hands upon his eyes; and he
looked intently and was restored, and *began* to see everything
clearly.
26 And He sent him to his home, saying, "[a]Do not even
enter [b]the village."
27 [a]And Jesus went out, along with His disciples, to the
villages of [b]Caesarea Philippi; and on the way He questioned
His disciples, saying to them, "Who do people say that I am?"
28 [a]And they told Him, saying, "John the Baptist; and
others *say* Elijah; but still others, one of the prophets."
29 And He *continued* by questioning them, "But who do
you say that I am?" Peter *answered and *said to Him, "Thou
art [1]the Christ."
30 And [a]He [1]warned them to tell no one about Him.
31 [a]And He began to teach them that [b]the Son of Man
must suffer many things and be rejected by the elders and the
chief priests and the scribes, and be killed, and after three days
rise again.
32 And He was stating the matter [a]plainly. And Peter took
Him aside and began to rebuke Him.
33 But turning around and seeing His disciples, He

11 [1]Or, *attesting miracle* [2]Lit., *testing Him* [a]Mark 8:11-21: *Matt. 16:1-12* [b]Matt. 12:38

12 [1]Or, *to Himself* [2]Or, *attesting miracle* [3]Lit., *if a sign shall be given* [a]Mark 7:34

14 [1]Lit., *were not having*

15 [a]Matt. 16:6; Luke 12:1 [b]Matt. 14:1; 22:16

17 [1]Or, *dull, insensible* [a]Mark 6:52

18 [a]Ezek. 12:2

19 [a]Mark 6:41-44 [b]Matt. 14:20

20 [a]Mark 8:6-9 [b]Mark 8:8

21 [a]Mark 6:52

22 [a]Matt. 11:21; Mark 6:45 [b]Mark 3:10

23 [a]Mark 7:33 [b]Mark 5:23

24 [1]Or, *gained sight* [2]Or, *they look to me*

26 [a]Matt. 8:4 [b]Mark 8:23

27 [a]Mark 8:27-29: *Matt. 16:13-16; Luke 9:18-20* [b]Matt. 16:13

28 [a]Mark 6:14

29 [1]I.e., the Messiah

30 [1]Or, *strictly admonished* [a]Matt. 16:20; Luke 9:21; Matt. 8:4

31 [a]Mark 8:31-9:1: *Matt. 16:21-28; Luke 9:22-27* [b]Matt. 16:21

32 [a]John 18:20; John 10:24; 11:14; 16:25, 29 [in Gr.]

rebuked Peter, and *said, "Get behind Me, [a]Satan; for you are
not setting your mind on [1]God's interests, but man's."
34 And He summoned the multitude with His disciples,
and said to them, "If anyone wishes to come after Me, let him
deny himself, and [a]take up his cross, and follow Me.
35 "For [a]whoever wishes to save his [1]life shall lose it; and
whoever loses his [1]life for My sake and the gospel's shall save
it.
36 "For what does it profit a man to gain the whole world,
and forfeit his [1]soul?
37 "For what shall a man give in exchange for his [1]soul?
38 "For [a]whoever is ashamed of Me and My words in this
adulterous and sinful generation, [b]the Son of Man will also be
ashamed of him when He [c]comes in the glory of His Father
with the holy angels."

Chapter 9

AND He was saying to them, "[a]Truly I say to you, there are
some of those who are standing here who shall not taste of
death until they see the kingdom of God after it has come with
power."
2 [a]And six days later, Jesus *took with Him [b]Peter and
[1]James and John, and *brought them up to a high mountain
by themselves. And He was transfigured before them;
3 and [a]His garments became radiant and exceedingly
white, as no launderer on earth can whiten them.
4 And Elijah appeared to them along with Moses; and
they were conversing with Jesus.
5 And Peter *answered and *said to Jesus, "[a]Rabbi, it is
good for us to be here; and [b]let us make three [1]tabernacles, one
for You, and one for Moses, and one for Elijah."
6 For he did not know what to answer; for they became
terrified.
7 Then a cloud [1]formed, overshadowing them, and [a]a
voice [1]came out of the cloud, "[b]This is My beloved Son, [2]listen
to Him!"
8 And all at once they looked around and saw no one
with them any more, except Jesus only.
9 [a]And as they were coming down from the mountain,
He [b]gave them orders not to relate to anyone what they had
seen, [1]until the Son of Man should rise from the dead.
10 And they [1]seized upon [2]that statement, discussing with
one another [3]what rising from the dead might mean.
11 And they *began* questioning Him, saying, "*Why is it*
that the scribes say that first [a]Elijah must come?"
12 And He said to them, "Elijah does first come and restore
everything. And *yet* how is it written of [a]the Son of Man
that [b]He should suffer many things and be treated with
contempt?
13 "But I say to you, that Elijah has [1]indeed come, and
they did to him whatever they wished, just as it is written of
him."
14 [a]And when they came *back* to the disciples, they saw a
large crowd around them, and *some* scribes arguing with them.

33 [1]Lit., *the things of God* [a]Matt. 4:10
34 [a]Matt. 10:38
35 [1]Gr., *soul-life* [a]Matt. 10:39
36 [1]Gr., *soul-life*
37 [1]Gr., *soul-life*
38 [a]Luke 9:26; Matt. 10:33; Heb. 11:16 [b]Matt. 8:20 [c]Matt. 16:27; Mark 13:26; Luke 9:27
1 [a]Matt. 16:27; Mark 13:26; Luke 9:27
2 [1]Or, *Jacob* [a]Mark 9:2-8: *Matt. 17:1-8; Luke 9:28-36* [b]Mark 5:37
3 [a]Matt. 28:3
5 [1]Or, *sacred tents* [a]Matt. 23:7 [b]Matt. 17:4; Luke 9:33
7 [1]Or, *occurred* [2]Or, *give constant heed* [a]2 Pet. 1:17f. [b]Mark 1:11; Matt. 3:17
9 [1]Lit., *except when* [a]Mark 9:9-13: *Matt. 17:9-13* [b]Mark 5:43; 7:36; Mark 8:30; Matt. 8:4
10 [1]Or, *kept to themselves* [2]Lit., *the statement* [3]Lit., *what was the rising from the dead*
11 [a]Matt. 11:14
12 [a]Mark 9:31 [b]Matt. 16:21; 26:24
13 [1]Lit., *also*
14 [a]Mark 9:14-28: *Matt. 17:14-19; Luke 9:37-42*

15 And immediately, when the entire crowd saw Him,
they were [a]amazed, and *began* running up to greet Him.
16 And He asked them, "What are you discussing with
them?"
17 And one of the crowd answered Him, "Teacher, I
brought You my son, possessed with a spirit which makes him
mute;
18 and [1]whenever it seizes him, it [2]dashes him *to the*
ground and he foams *at the mouth*, and grinds his teeth, and
[3]stiffens out. And I told Your disciples to cast it out, and they
could not *do it*."
19 And He *answered them and *said, "O unbelieving
generation, how long shall I be with you? How long shall I put
up with you? Bring him to Me!"
20 And they brought [1]the boy to Him. And when he saw
Him, immediately the spirit threw him into a convulsion, and
falling to the ground, he *began* rolling about and foaming *at*
the mouth.
21 And He asked his father, "How long has this been
happening to him?" And he said, "From childhood.
22 "And it has often thrown him both into the fire and into
the water to destroy him. But if You can do anything, take pity
on us and help us!"
23 And Jesus said to him, " 'If You can!' [a]All things are
possible to him who believes."
24 Immediately the boy's father cried out and *began*
saying, "I do believe; help *me in* my unbelief."
25 And when Jesus saw that [a]a crowd was [1]rapidly gathering, He rebuked the unclean spirit, saying to it, "You deaf and
dumb spirit, I [2]command you, come out of him and do not
enter him [3]again."
26 And after crying out and throwing him into terrible
convulsions, it came out; and *the boy* became so much like a
corpse that most *of them* said, "He is dead!"
27 But Jesus took him by the hand and raised him; and he
got up.
28 And when He had come [a]into *the* house, His disciples
began questioning Him privately, "Why is it that we could not
cast it out?"
29 And He said to them, "This kind cannot come out by
anything but prayer."[1]
30 [a]And from there they went out and *began* to go
through Galilee, and He was unwilling for anyone to know
about it.
31 For He was teaching His disciples and telling them,
"[a]The Son of Man is to be [1]delivered up into the hands of
men, and they will kill Him; and when He has been killed, He
will rise again three days later."
32 But [a]they [1]did not understand *this* statement, and they
were afraid to ask him.
33 [a]And they came to Capernaum; and when He [1]was in
[b]the house, He *began* to question them, "What were you
discussing on the way?"
34 But they kept silent, for on the way [a]they had discussed
with one another which *of them was* the greatest.
35 And sitting down, He called the twelve and *said to

15 [a]Mark 14:33; 16:5, 6

18 [1]Or, *wherever* [2]Or, *tears him* [3]Or, *withers away*

20 [1]Lit., *him*

23 [a]Matt. 17:20; John 11:40

25 [1]Or, *running together* [2]Or, *I Myself command* [3]Or, *from now on* [a]Mark 9:15

28 [a]Mark 7:17; 2:1

29 [1]Many mss. add: *and fasting*

30 [a]Mark 9:30-32: *Matt. 17:22-23; Luke 9:43-45*

31 [1]Or, *betrayed* [a]Mark 9:12; 8:31; Matt. 16:21

32 [1]Lit., *were not knowing* [a]Luke 2:50; 9:45; 18:34; John 12:16

33 [1]Lit., *had become* [a]Mark 9:33-37: *Matt. [17:24] 18:1-5; Luke 9:46-48* [b]Mark 3:19

34 [a]Luke 22:24; Mark 9:50

them, "[a]If any one wants to be first, [1]he shall be last of all, and
servant of all."
36 And taking a child, He stood him in the midst of them;
and taking him in His arms, He said to them,
37 "[a]Whoever receives [1]one child like this in My name is
receiving Me; and whoever receives Me is not receiving Me,
but Him who sent Me."
38 [a]John said to Him, "Teacher, we saw someone casting
out demons in Your name, and [b]we tried to hinder him because he was not following us."
39 But Jesus said, "Do not hinder him, for there is no one
who shall perform a miracle in My name, and be able soon
afterward to speak evil of Me.
40 "[a]For he who is not against us is [1]for us.
41 "For [a]whoever gives you a cup of water to drink [1]because
of your name as *followers* of Christ, truly I say to you, he shall
not lose his reward.
42 And [a]whoever causes one of these little ones who believe to stumble, it [1]would be better for him if with a heavy
millstone hung around his neck, he [2]had been cast into the sea.
43 "And [a]if your hand causes you to stumble, cut it off; it is
better for you to enter life crippled, than having your two
hands, to go into [1b]hell, into the [c]unquenchable fire.[2]
44 (See marginal note[2], vs. 43.)
45 "And if your foot causes you to stumble, cut it off; it is
better for you to enter life lame, than having your two feet, to
be cast into [1a]hell[2].
46 (See marginal note [2], vs. 43.)
47 "And [a]if your eye causes you to stumble, cast it out; it is
better for you to enter the kingdom of God with one eye, than
having two eyes, to be cast into [1b]hell;
48 [a]where THEIR WORM DOES NOT DIE, AND [b]THE FIRE IS NOT
QUENCHED.
49 "For everyone will be salted with fire.
50 "Salt is good, but [a]if the salt becomes unsalty, with what
will you [1]make it salty *again?* [b]Have salt in yourselves, and [c]be
at peace with one another."

Chapter 10

[a]

AND rising up, He *went from there to the region of Judea,
and beyond the Jordan; and crowds *gathered around Him
again, and, [b]according to His custom, He once more *began* to
teach them.
2 And *some* Pharisees came up to Him, testing Him, and
began to question Him whether it was lawful for a man to
divorce a wife.
3 And He answered and said to them, "What did Moses
command you?"
4 And they said, "[a]Moses permitted *a man* to write a
certificate of divorce and [1]send *her* away."
5 But Jesus said to them, "[1a]Because of your hardness of
heart he wrote you this commandment.
6 "But [a]from the beginning of creation, *God* [b]MADE THEM
MALE AND FEMALE.

35 [1]Or, *let him be* [a]Matt. 20:26

37 [1]Lit., *one of such children* [a]Matt. 10:40

38 [a]Mark 9:38-40: *Luke 9:49-50* [b]Num. 11:27-29

40 [1]Or, *on our side* [a]Matt. 12:30

41 [1]Lit., *in a name that you are Christ's* [a]Matt. 10:42

42 [1]Lit., *is better for him if a millstone turned by a donkey is hung* [2]Lit., *has been cast* [a]Matt. 18:6; Luke 17:2; 1 Cor. 8:12

43 [1]Lit., *Gehenna* [2]Verses 44 and 46, which are identical with verse 48, are omitted by the best ancient mss. [a]Matt. 5:30; 18:8; 17:27 [b]Matt. 5:22 [c]Matt. 3:12; 25:41

45 [1]Lit., *Gehenna* [2]cf. vs. 43, note 2 [a]Matt. 5:22

47 [1]Lit., *Gehenna* [a]Matt. 5:29; 18:9; Matt. 17:27 [b]Matt. 5:22

48 [a]Is. 66:24 [b]Matt. 3:12; Matt. 25:41

50 [1]Lit., *season it* [a]Matt. 5:13; Luke 14:34f. [b]Col. 4:6 [c]Mark 9:34; Rom. 12:18; 2 Cor. 13:11; 1 Thess. 5:13

1 [a]Mark 10:1-12: *Matt. 19:1-9* [b]Mark 1:21; 2:13; 4:2; 6:2, 6, 34; 12:35; 14:49; Matt. 4:23; 26:55

4 [1]Or, *divorce her* [a]Deut. 24:1, 3

5 [1]Or, *with reference to* [a]Matt. 19:8

6 [a]Mark 13:19; 2 Pet. 3:4 [b]Gen. 1:27; 5:2

7 "[a]FOR THIS CAUSE A MAN SHALL LEAVE HIS FATHER AND
MOTHER,[1]
8 [a]AND THE TWO SHALL BECOME ONE FLESH; consequently
they are no longer two, but one flesh.
9 "What therefore God has joined together, let no man
separate."
10 And in the house the disciples *began* questioning Him
about this again.
11 And He *said to them, "[a]Whoever divorces his wife
and marries another woman commits adultery against her;
12 and [a]if she herself divorces her husband and marries
another man, she is committing adultery."
13 [a]And they *began* bringing children to Him, so that He
might touch them; and the disciples rebuked them.
14 But when Jesus saw this, He was indignant and said to
them, "Permit the children to come to Me; do not hinder
them; [a]for the kingdom of God belongs to such as these.
15 "Truly I say to you, [a]whoever does not receive the kingdom of God like a child shall not enter it *at all*."
16 And He [a]took them in His arms and *began* blessing
them, laying His hands upon them.
17 [a]And as He was setting out on a journey, a man ran up
to Him and [b]knelt before Him, and *began* asking Him, "Good
Teacher, what shall I do to [c]inherit eternal life?"
18 And Jesus said to him, "Why do you call Me good? No
one is good except God alone.
19 "You know the commandments, '[a]DO NOT MURDER, DO
NOT COMMIT ADULTERY, DO NOT STEAL, DO NOT BEAR FALSE
WITNESS, Do not defraud, HONOR YOUR FATHER AND MOTHER.' "
20 And he said to Him, "Teacher, I have kept [a]all these
things from my youth up."
21 And looking at him, Jesus felt a love for him, and said
to him, "One thing you lack: go and sell all you possess, and
give *it* to the poor, and you shall have [a]treasure in heaven; and
come, follow Me."
22 But at these words [1]his face fell, and he went away
grieved, for he was one who owned much property.
23 And Jesus, looking around, *said to His disciples,
"[a]How hard it will be for those who are wealthy to enter the
kingdom of God!"
24 And the disciples [a]were amazed at His words. But Jesus
*answered again and *said to them, "Children, how hard it is
[1]to enter the kingdom of God!
25 "[a]It is easier for a camel to go through the eye of [1]a
needle than for a rich man to enter the kingdom of God."
26 And they were even more astonished and said [1]to Him,
"[2]Then who can be saved?"
27 Looking upon them, Jesus *said, "[a]With men it is impossible, but not with God; for all things are possible with
God."
28 [a]Peter began to say to Him, "Behold, we have left
everything and followed You."
29 Jesus said, "Truly I say to you, [a]there is no one who has
left house or brothers or sisters or mother or father or children
or farms, for My sake and for the gospel's sake,
30 but that he shall receive a hundred times as much now

7 [1]Some mss. add: *and shall cleave to his wife* [a]Gen. 2:24
8 [a]Gen. 2:24
11 [a]Matt. 5:32
12 [a]1 Cor. 7:11, 13
13 [a]Mark 10:13-16: *Matt. 19:13-15; Luke 18:15-17*
14 [a]Matt. 5:3
15 [a]Matt. 18:3; 19:14; Luke 18:17; 1 Cor. 14:20; 1 Pet. 2:2
16 [a]Mark 9:36
17 [a]Mark 10:17-31: *Matt. 19:16-30; Luke 18:18-30* [b]Mark 1:40 [c]Luke 10:25; 18:18; Acts 20:32; Eph. 1:18; 1 Pet. 1:4; Matt. 25:34
19 [a]Ex. 20:12-16; Deut. 5:16-20
20 [a]Matt. 19:20
21 [a]Matt. 6:20
22 [1]Or, *he became gloomy*
23 [a]Matt. 19:23
24 [1]Later mss. insert: *for those who trust in wealth* [a]Mark 1:27
25 [1]Lit., *the* [a]Matt. 19:24
26 [1]Later mss. read: *to one another* [2]Lit., *and*
27 [a]Matt. 19:26
28 [a]Matt. 4:20-22
29 [a]Matt. 19:29; Luke 18:29f.; Matt. 6:33

in the [1]present age, houses and brothers and sisters and mothers and children and farms, along with persecutions; and in
[a]the [2]world to come, eternal life.
31 "But [a]many *who are* first, will be last; and the last, first."
32 [a]And they were on the road, going up to Jerusalem, and
Jesus was walking on ahead of them; and they [b]were amazed,
and those who followed were fearful. And again He took the
twelve aside and began to tell them what was going to happen
to Him,
33 *saying,* "Behold, we are going up to Jerusalem, and [a]the
Son of Man will be [1]delivered up to the chief priests and the
scribes; and they will condemn Him to death, and will [2]deliver
Him up to the Gentiles.
34 "And they will mock Him and [a]spit upon Him, and
scourge Him, and kill *Him,* and three days later He will rise
again."
35 [a]And [1]James and John, the two sons of Zebedee, *came
up to Him, saying to Him, "Teacher, we want You to do for us
whatever we ask of You."
36 And He said to them, "What do you want Me to do
for you?"
37 And they said to Him, "[1]Grant that we [a]may sit in Your
glory, one on Your right, and one on *Your* left."
38 But Jesus said to them, "You do not know what you are
asking for. Are you able [a]to drink the cup that I drink, or [b]to be
baptized with the baptism with which I am baptized?"
39 And they said to Him, "We are able." And Jesus said
to them, "The cup that I drink [a]you shall drink; and you shall
be baptized with the baptism with which I am baptized.
40 "But to sit on My right or on *My* left, this is not Mine to
give; [a]but *it is for those* for whom it has been prepared."
41 [a]And hearing this, the ten began to feel indignant toward [1]James and John.
42 And calling them to Himself, Jesus *said to them,
"You know that those who are recognized as rulers of the
Gentiles lord it over them; and their great men exercise authority over them.
43 "But it is not so among you, [a]but whoever wishes to
become great among you shall be your servant;
44 and whoever wishes to be first among you shall be slave
of all.
45 "For even the Son of Man [a]did not come to be served,
but to serve, and to give His [1]life a ransom for many."
46 [a]And they *came to Jericho. And [b]as He was going out
from Jericho with His disciples and a great multitude, a blind
beggar *named* Bartimaeus, the son of Timaeus, was sitting by
the road.
47 And when he heard that it was Jesus the [a]Nazarene, he
began to cry out and say, "Jesus, [b]Son of David, have mercy on
me!"
48 And many were sternly telling him to be quiet, but he
began crying out all the more, "[a]Son of David, have mercy on
me!"
49 And Jesus stopped and said, "Call him *here.*" And they
*called the blind man, saying to him, "[a]Take courage, arise!
He is calling for you."

30 [1]Lit., *this time* [2]Or, *age* [a]Matt. 12:32

31 [a]Matt. 19:30

32 [a]Mark 10:32-34: *Matt. 20:17-19; Luke 18:31-33* [b]Mark 1:27

33 [1]Or, *betrayed* [2]Or, *betray* [a]Mark 8:31; 9:12

34 [a]Matt. 26:67; 27:30; Mark 14:65; Matt. 16:21; Mark 9:31

35 [1]Or, *Jacob* [a]Mark 10:35-45: *Matt. 20:20-28*

37 [1]Lit., *give to us* [a]Matt. 19:28

38 [a]Matt. 20:22 [b]Luke 12:50

39 [a]Acts 12:2; Rev. 1:9

40 [a]Matt. 13:11

41 [1]Or, *Jacob* [a]Mark 10:42-45; Luke 22:25-27

43 [a]Matt. 20:26; Mark 9:35

45 [1]Or, *soul* [a]Matt. 20:28

46 [a]Mark 10:46-52: *Matt. 20:29-34; Luke 18:35-43* [b]Luke 18:35; 19:1

47 [a]Mark 1:24 [b]Matt. 9:27

48 [a]Matt. 9:27

49 [a]Matt. 9:2

51 [1]I.e., My Master [a]John 20:16; Matt. 23:7
52 [1]Lit., *saved you* [a]Matt. 9:22
1 [a]Mark 11:1-10: *Matt. 21:1-9; Luke 19:29-38* [b]Matt. 21:17 [c]Matt. 21:1
3 [1]Lit., *sends*
7 [a]Mark 11:7-10: *John 12:12-15*
9 [a]Matt. 21:9; Ps. 118:25
10 [a]Matt. 21:9
11 [a]Matt. 21:12 [b]Matt. 21:17
12 [a]Mark 11:12-14 [20-24]: *Matt. 21:18-22*
15 [1]Lit., *the doves* [a]Mark 11:15-18: *Matt. 21:12-16; Luke 19:45-47;* John 2:13-16
16 [1]Lit., *a vessel,* I.e., a receptacle or implement of any kind
17 [1]Lit., *cave* [a]Is. 56:7 [b]Jer. 7:11

50 And casting aside his cloak, he jumped up, and came to
Jesus.
51 And answering him, Jesus said, "What do you want Me
to do for you?" And the blind man said to Him, "[1a]Rabboni, *I*
want to regain my sight!"
52 And Jesus said to him, "Go your way; [a]your faith has
[1]made you well." And immediately he received his sight and
began following Him on the road.

[a] Chapter 11

And as they *approached Jerusalem, at Bethphage and
[b]Bethany, near [c]the Mount of Olives, He *sent two of His
disciples,
2 and *said to them, "Go into the village opposite you,
and immediately as you enter it, you will find a colt tied *there,*
on which no one yet has ever sat; untie it and bring it *here.*
3 "And if anyone says to you, 'Why are you doing this?'
you say, 'The Lord has need of it;' and immediately he [1]will
send it back here."
4 And they went away and found a colt tied at the door
outside in the street; and they *untied it.
5 And some of the bystanders were saying to them,
"What are you doing, untying the colt?"
6 And they spoke to them just as Jesus had told *them,*
and they gave them permission.
7 [a]And they *brought the colt to Jesus and put their
garments on it; and He sat upon it.
8 And many spread their garments in the road, and others *spread* leafy branches which they had cut from the fields.
9 And those who went before, and those who followed
after, were crying out,
"[a]Hosanna!
Blessed is He who comes in the name of the Lord;
10 Blessed *is* the coming kingdom of our father David;
Hosanna [a]in the highest."
11 And [a]He entered Jerusalem *and came* into the temple;
and after looking all around, [b]He departed for Bethany with
the twelve, since it was already late.
12 [a]And on the next day, when they had departed from
Bethany, He became hungry.
13 And seeing at a distance a fig tree in leaf, He went *to*
see if perhaps He would find anything on it; and when He
came to it, He found nothing but leaves, for it was not the
season for figs.
14 And He answered and said to it, "May no one ever eat
fruit from you again!" And His disciples were listening.
15 [a]And they *came to Jerusalem. And He entered the
temple and began to cast out those who were buying and
selling in the temple, and overturned the tables of the money-
changers and the seats of those who were selling [1]doves;
16 and He would not permit anyone to carry [1]goods
through the temple.
17 And He *began* to teach and say to them, "Is it not
written, '[a]My house shall be called a house of prayer for
all the nations'? [b]But you have made it a robbers' [1]den."

18 And the chief priests and the scribes heard *this,* and
[a]*began* seeking how to destroy Him; for they were afraid of
Him, for [b]all the multitude was astonished at His teaching.
19 And [a]whenever evening came, [1]they would go out of
the city.
20 [a]And as they were passing by in the morning, they saw
the fig tree withered from the roots *up.*
21 And being reminded, Peter *said to Him, "[a]Rabbi, behold, the fig tree which You cursed has withered."
22 And Jesus *answered saying to them, "[a]Have faith in
God.
23 "Truly I say to you, whoever says to this mountain, 'Be
taken up and cast into the sea,' and does not doubt in his
heart, but believes that what he says is going to happen; it shall
be *granted* him.
24 "Therefore I say to you, [a]all things for which you pray
and ask, believe that you have received them, and they shall be
granted you.
25 "And whenever you [a]stand praying, [b]forgive, if you have
anything against anyone; so that your Father also who is in
heaven may forgive you your transgressions."
26 (See marginal note.[1])
27 And they *came again to Jerusalem. [a]And as He was
walking in the temple, the chief priests, and scribes, and elders
*came to Him,
28 and *began* saying to Him, "By what authority are You
doing these things, or who gave You this authority to do these
things?"
29 And Jesus said to them, "I will ask you one question,
and you answer Me, and *then* I will tell you by what authority
I do these things.
30 "Was the baptism of John from heaven, or from men?
Answer Me."
31 And they *began* reasoning with one another, saying, "If
we say, 'From heaven,' He will say, 'Then why did you not
believe him?'
32 "But [1]shall we say, 'From men'?" —they were afraid of
the multitude, for all considered John to have been a prophet
indeed.
33 And answering Jesus, they *said, "We do not know."
And Jesus *said to them, "Neither [1]will I tell you by what
authority I do these things."

Chapter 12

[a]AND He began to speak to them in parables: "[b]A man
[c]PLANTED A VINEYARD, AND PUT A [1]WALL AROUND IT, AND DUG A
VAT UNDER THE WINE PRESS, AND BUILT A TOWER, and rented
it out to [2]vine-growers and went on a journey.
2 "And at the *harvest* time he sent a slave to the vine-
growers, in order to receive *some* of the produce of the vineyard from the vine-growers.
3 "And they took him, and beat him, and sent him away
empty-handed.

18 [a]Mark 12:12; Matt. 21:46; Luke 20:19; John 7:1 [b]Matt. 7:28

19 [1]I.e., Jesus and His disciples [a]Luke 21:37; Matt. 21:17; Mark 11:11

20 [a]Mark 11:20-24 [Mark 11:12-14]: *Matt. 21:19-22*

21 [a]Matt. 23:7

22 [a]Matt. 17:20; 21:21f.

24 [a]Matt. 7:7f.

25 [a]Matt. 6:5 [b]Matt. 6:14

26 [1]Later mss. add vs. 26: *"But if you do not forgive, neither will your Father who is in heaven forgive your transgressions."* Matt. 6:15; 18:35

27 [a]Mark 11:27-33: *Matt. 21:23-27; Luke 20:1-8*

32 [1]Or, *if we say*

33 [1]Lit., *do I tell*

1 [1]Or, *fence* [2]Here and in verses 2, 7, and 9: or, *tenant farmers* [a]Mark 3:23; 4:2ff. [b]Mark 12:1-12: *Matt. 21:33-46; Luke 20:9-19* [c]Is. 5:2

4 "And again he sent them another slave, and they
wounded him in the head, and treated him shamefully.
5 "And he sent another, and that one they killed; and *so*
with many others, beating some, and killing others.
6 "He had one more *to send*, a beloved son; he sent him
last *of all* to them, saying, 'They will respect my son.'
7 "But those vine-growers said to one another, 'This is the
heir; come, let us kill him, and the inheritance will be ours!'
8 "And they took him, and killed him, and threw him out
of the vineyard.
9 "What will the [1]owner of the vineyard do? He will come
and destroy the vine-growers, and will give the vineyard to
others.
10 "Have you not even read this scripture:
'[a]THE STONE WHICH THE BUILDERS REJECTED,
THIS BECAME THE CHIEF CORNER *STONE*;
11 '[a]THIS CAME ABOUT FROM THE LORD,
AND IT IS MARVELOUS IN OUR EYES'?"
12 And [a]they were seeking to seize Him; and *yet* they
feared the multitude; for they understood that He had spoken
the parable against them. And *so* [b]they left Him, and went
away.
13 [a]And they *sent some of the Pharisees and [b]Herodians
to Him, in order to [c]trap Him in a statement.
14 And they *came and *said to Him, "Teacher, we know
that You are truthful, and [1]defer to no one; for You are not
partial to any, but teach the way of God in truth. Is it [2]lawful
to pay a poll-tax to Caesar, or not?
15 "Shall we pay, or shall we not pay?" But He, knowing
their hypocrisy, said to them, "Why are you testing Me? Bring
Me a [1]denarius to look at."
16 And they brought *one*. And He *said to them, "Whose
likeness and inscription is this?" And they said to Him,
"Caesar's."
17 And Jesus said to them, "[a]Render to Caesar the things
that are Caesar's, and to God the things that are God's." And
they [1]were amazed at Him.
18 [a]And *some* Sadducees (who say that there is no resurrection) *came to Him, and *began* questioning Him, saying,
19 "Teacher, Moses wrote for us *a law* that [a]IF A MAN'S
BROTHER DIES, and leaves behind a wife, AND LEAVES NO CHILD,
HIS BROTHER SHOULD TAKE THE WIFE, AND RAISE UP OFFSPRING TO
HIS BROTHER.
20 "There were seven brothers; and the first one took a
wife, and died, leaving no offspring.
21 "And the second one took her, and died, leaving behind
no offspring; and the third likewise;
22 and *so* [1]all seven left no offspring. Last of all the woman died too.
23 "In the resurrection, [1]when they rise again, which one's
wife will she be? For [2]all seven had her as wife."
24 Jesus said to them, "Is this not the reason you are
mistaken, that you do not [1]understand the Scriptures, or the
power of God?
25 "For when they rise from the dead, they neither marry,
nor are given in marriage, but are like angels in heaven.

9 [1]Lit., *lord*

10 [a]Ps. 118:22

11 [a]Ps. 118:23

12 [a]Mark 11:18 [b]Matt. 22:22

13 [a]Mark 12:13-17: *Matt. 22:15-22; Luke 20:20-26* [b]Matt. 22:16 [c]Luke 11:54

14 [1]Lit., *it is not a concern to You about anyone*, i.e., You court no man's favor [2]Or, *permissible*

15 [1]The denarius was worth 18 cents in silver, equivalent to a day's wage

17 [1]Or, *were greatly marveling* [a]Matt. 22:21

18 [a]Mark 12:18-27: *Matt. 22:23-33; Luke 20:27-38*

19 [a]Deut. 25:5

22 [1]Lit., *the seven*

23 [1]Most ancient mss. omit: *when they rise again* [2]Lit., *the seven*

24 [1]Or, *know*

26 "But [1]regarding the fact that the dead rise again, have
you not read in the book of Moses, [a]in the *passage about the*
burning bush, how God spoke to him, saying, '[b]I AM THE GOD
OF ABRAHAM, AND THE GOD OF ISAAC, AND THE GOD OF JACOB'?
27 "[a]He is not *the* God [1]of *the* dead, but of *the* living; you
are greatly mistaken."
28 [a]And one of the scribes came and heard them arguing,
and [b]recognizing that He had answered them well, asked Him,
"What commandment is the [1]foremost of all?"
29 Jesus answered, "The foremost is, '[a]HEAR, O ISRAEL;
THE LORD OUR GOD IS ONE LORD;
30 [a]AND YOU SHALL LOVE THE LORD YOUR GOD WITH ALL
YOUR HEART, AND WITH ALL YOUR SOUL, AND WITH ALL YOUR
MIND, AND WITH ALL YOUR STRENGTH.'
31 "The second is this, '[a]YOU SHALL LOVE YOUR NEIGHBOR AS
YOURSELF.' There is no other commandment greater than
these."
32 And the scribe said to Him, "Right, Teacher, You have
truly stated that [a]HE IS ONE; AND THERE IS NO ONE ELSE BESIDES
HIM;
33 [a]AND TO LOVE HIM WITH ALL THE HEART AND WITH ALL
THE UNDERSTANDING AND WITH ALL THE STRENGTH, AND TO LOVE
ONE'S NEIGHBOR AS HIMSELF, [b]is much more than all burnt offerings and sacrifices."
34 And when Jesus saw that he had answered intelligently,
He said to him, "You are not far from the kingdom of God."
[a]And after that, no one would venture to ask Him any more
questions.
35 [a]And Jesus answering *began* to say, as He [b]taught in the
temple, "How *is it that* the scribes say that [1]the Christ is the
[c]son of David?
36 "David himself said [1]in the Holy Spirit,
'[a]THE LORD SAID TO MY LORD,
"SIT AT MY RIGHT HAND,
UNTIL I PUT THINE ENEMIES BENEATH THY FEET." '
37 "David himself calls Him 'Lord;' and *so* in what sense is
He his son?" And [a]the great crowd [1]enjoyed listening to Him.
38 [a]And in His teaching He was saying: "Beware of the
scribes who like to walk around in long robes, and *like* [b]respect-
ful greetings in the market places,
39 and chief seats in the synagogues, and places of honor
at banquets.
40 "[a]They *are* the ones who devour widows' houses, and for
appearance's sake offer long prayers; these will receive greater
condemnation."
41 [a]And He sat down opposite [b]the treasury, and *began*
observing how the multitude were [c]putting [1]money into the
treasury; and many rich people were putting in large sums.
42 And a poor widow came and put in two [1]small copper
coins, which amount to a [2]cent.
43 And calling His disciples to Him, He said to them,
"Truly I say to you, this poor widow put in more than all [1]the
contributors to the treasury;
44 for they all put in out of their [1]surplus, but she, out of
her poverty, put in all she owned, [2]all she had [a]to live on."

26 [1]Lit., *concerning the dead, that they rise* [a]Luke 20:37; Rom. 11:2 [b]Ex. 3:6

27 [1]Or, *of corpses* [a]Matt. 22:32; Luke 20:38

28 [1]Or, *first* [a]Mark 12:28-34: *Matt. 22:34-40;* Luke 10:25-28; 20:39f. [b]Luke 20:39; Matt. 22:34

29 [a]Deut. 6:4

30 [a]Deut. 6:5

31 [a]Lev. 19:18

32 [a]Deut. 4:35

33 [a]Deut. 6:5 [b]1 Sam. 15:22; Hos. 6:6; Mic. 6:6-8; Matt. 9:13; 12:7

34 [a]Matt. 22:46

35 [1]I.e., the Messiah [a]Mark 12:35-37: *Matt. 22:41-46; Luke 20:41-44* [b]Matt. 26:55; Mark 10:1 [c]Matt. 9:27

36 [1]Or, *by* [a]Ps. 110:1

37 [1]Lit., *was gladly hearing Him* [a]John 12:9

38 [a]Mark 12:38-40: *Matt. 23:1-7; Luke 20:45-47* [b]Luke 11:43; Matt. 23:6

40 [a]Luke 20:47

41 [1]I.e., copper coins [a]Mark 12:41-44: *Luke 21:1-4* [b]John 8:20 [c]2 Kin. 12:9

42 [1]Lit., *lepta* [2]Lit., *quadrans*, i.e., 1/64 of a denarius

43 [1]Lit., *those who were putting in*

44 [1]Or, *abundance* [2]Lit., *her whole livelihood* [a]Luke 8:43; 15:12, 30; 21:4

Chapter 13

[a]AND as He was going out of the temple, one of His disciples
*said to Him, "Teacher, behold [1]what wonderful stones and
[1]what wonderful buildings!"
2 And Jesus said to him, "Do you see these great buildings? [a]Not one stone shall be left upon another which will not
be torn down."
3 And as He was sitting on [a]the Mount of Olives opposite the temple, [b]Peter and [1]James and John and Andrew were
questioning Him privately,
4 "Tell us, when will these things be, and what *will be* the
[1]sign when all these things are going to be fulfilled?"
5 And Jesus began to say to them, "See to it that no one
misleads you.
6 "Many will come in My name, saying, '[a]I am *He!*' and
will mislead many.
7 "And when you hear of wars and rumors of wars, do not
be frightened; *those things* must take place; but *that is* not yet
the end.
8 "For nation will arise against nation, and kingdom
against kingdom; there will be earthquakes in various places;
there will *also* be famines. These things are *merely* the beginning of birth pangs.
9 "But [1]be on your guard; for they will [a]deliver you up to
the [2]courts, and you will be flogged [b]in *the* synagogues, and
you will stand before governors and kings for My sake, as a
testimony to them.
10 "[a]And the gospel must first be preached to all the
nations.
11 "[a]And when they [1]arrest you and deliver you up, do not
be anxious beforehand about what you are to say, but say
whatever is given you in that hour; for it is not you who speak,
but *it is* the Holy Spirit.
12 "And brother will deliver up brother to death, and a
father *his* child; and children will rise up against parents and
[1]cause them to be put to death.
13 "And [a]you will be hated by all on account of My name,
but it is the one who has endured to the end who will be saved.
14 "But [a]when you see the [b]ABOMINATION OF DESOLATION
standing where it should not be (let the reader understand),
then let those who are in Judea flee to the mountains.
15 "And let him who is on the housetop not go down, or
enter in, to get anything out of his house;
16 and let him who is in the field not turn back to get his
cloak.
17 "But woe to those who are with child and to those who
nurse babes in those days!
18 "But pray that it may not happen in the winter.
19 "For those days will be a *time of* tribulation such as has
not occurred [a]since the beginning of the creation which God
created, until now, and never shall.
20 "And unless the Lord had shortened *those* days, no [1]life
would have been saved; but for the sake of the [2]elect whom He
chose, He shortened the days.

1 [1]Lit., *how great* [a]Mark 13:1-37: *Matt. 24; Luke 21:5-36*
2 [a]Luke 19:44
3 [1]Or, *Jacob* [a]Matt. 21:1 [b]Matt. 17:1
4 [1]Or, *attesting miracle*
6 [a]John 8:24
9 [1]Lit., *look to yourselves* [2]Or, *Sanhedrins*, or *councils* [a]Matt. 10:17 [b]Matt. 10:17
10 [a]Matt. 24:14
11 [1]Lit., *lead* [a]Mark 13:11-13: *Matt. 10:19-22; Luke 21:12-17*
12 [1]Lit., *put them to death*
13 [a]John 15:21
14 [a]Matt. 24:15 [b]Dan. 9:27; 11:31; 12:11
19 [a]Mark 10:6
20 [1]Lit., *flesh* [2]Or, *chosen ones*

21 "And then if anyone says to you, 'Behold, here is [1]the
Christ;' or, 'Behold, *He is* there;' do not believe *him;*
22 for false Christs and [a]false prophets will arise, and will
show [1b]signs and [b]wonders, in order, if possible, to lead the
elect astray.
23 "But take heed; behold, I have told you everything in
advance.
24 "But in those days, after that tribulation, [a]THE SUN WILL
BE DARKENED, AND THE MOON WILL NOT GIVE ITS LIGHT,
25 [a]AND THE STARS WILL BE FALLING from heaven, and the
POWERS THAT ARE IN [1]THE HEAVENS WILL BE shaken.
26 "[a]AND THEN THEY SHALL SEE THE SON OF MAN [b]COMING IN
CLOUDS with great power and glory.
27 "And then He will send forth the angels, and [a]WILL GATH-
ER TOGETHER His [1]elect FROM THE FOUR WINDS, [b]FROM THE
FARTHEST END of the earth, TO THE FARTHEST END OF HEAVEN.
28 "Now learn the parable from the fig tree: when its
branch has already become tender, and puts forth its leaves,
you know that the summer is near.
29 "Even so you too, when you see these things happening,
[1]recognize that [2]He is near, *right* at the [3]door.
30 "Truly I say to you, this [1]generation will not pass away
until all these things take place.
31 "Heaven and earth will pass away, but My words will not
pass away.
32 "[a]But of that day or hour no one knows, not even the
angels in heaven, nor the Son, but the Father *alone.*
33 "Take heed, [a]keep on the alert; for you do not know
when the *appointed* time is.
34 "*It is* like a man, away on a journey, *who* upon leaving
his house and [1]putting his slaves in charge, *assigning* to each
one his task, also commanded the doorkeeper to stay on the
alert.
35 "Therefore, [a]be on the alert — for you do not know
when the [1]master of the house is coming, whether in the evening, at midnight, at [b]cockcrowing, or [c]in the morning;—
36 lest he come suddenly and find you [a]asleep.
37 "And what I say to you I say to all, '[a]Be on the alert!' "

CHAPTER 14

[a]NOW *the feast of* [b]the Passover and Unleavened Bread was
two days off; and the chief priests and the scribes [c]were seeking
how to seize Him by stealth, and kill *Him;*
2 for they were saying, "Not during the festival, lest there
be a riot of the people."
3 [a]And while He was in [b]Bethany at the home of Simon
the leper, and reclining *at table,* there came a woman with an
alabaster vial of [c]costly perfume of pure nard; *and* she broke
the vial and poured it over His head.
4 But some were indignantly *remarking* to one another,
"For what purpose has this perfume been wasted?
5 "For this perfume might have been sold for over three

21 [1]I.e., the Messiah

22 [1]Or, *attesting miracles* [a]Matt. 7:15 [b]Matt. 24:24; John 4:48

24 [a]Is. 13:10

25 [1]Or, *heaven* [a]Is. 34:4

26 [a]Dan. 7:13 [b]Matt. 16:27; Mark 8:38

27 [1]Or, *chosen ones* [a]Deut. 30:4 [b]Zech. 2:6

29 [1]Lit., *know* [2]Or, *it* [3]Lit., *doors*

30 [1]Or, *race*

32 [a]Matt. 24:36; Acts 1:7

33 [a]Eph. 6:18; Col. 4:2

34 [1]Lit., *giving the authority to*

35 [1]Lit., *lord* [a]Mark 13:37; Matt. 24:42 [b]Mark 14:30 [c]Mark 6:48; Matt. 14:25

36 [a]Rom. 13:11

37 [a]Mark 13:35; Matt. 24:42

1 [a]Mark 14:1, 2: *Matt. 26:2-5; Luke 22:1, 2* [b]John 11:55; 13:1; Mark 14:12 [c]Matt. 12:14

3 [a]Mark 14:3-9: *Matt. 26:6-13;* Luke 7:37-39; John 12:1-8 [b]Matt. 21:17 [c]Matt. 26:6f.; John 12:3

hundred [1]denarii, and *the money* given to the poor." And they
were scolding her.
6 But Jesus said, "Let her alone; why do you bother her?
She has done a good deed to Me.
7 "For [a]the poor you always have with you, and whenever
you wish, you can do them good; but you do not always have
Me.
8 "She has done what she could; [a]she has anointed My
body beforehand for the burial.
9 "And truly I say to you, [a]wherever the gospel is preached
in the whole world, that also which this woman has done shall
be spoken of in memory of her."
10 [a]And Judas Iscariot, [b]who was one of the twelve, went
off to the chief priests, in order to [1]betray Him to them.
11 And they were glad when they heard *this,* and promised
to give him money. And he *began* seeking how to betray Him
at an opportune time.
12 [a]And on the first day of *the Feast of* [b]Unleavened
Bread, when the Passover *lamb* was being [1c]sacrificed, His
disciples *said to Him, "Where do You want us to go and
prepare for You to eat the Passover?"
13 And He *sent two of His disciples, and *said to them,
"Go into the city, and a man will meet you carrying a pitcher
of water; follow him;
14 and wherever he enters, say to the owner of the house,
'The Teacher says, "Where is My [a]guest room in which I may
eat the Passover with My disciples?" '
15 "And he himself will show you a large upper room furnished *and* ready; and prepare for us there."
16 And the disciples went out, and came to the city, and
found *it* just as He had told them; and they prepared the
Passover.
17 [a]And when it was evening He *came with the twelve.
18 And as they were reclining *at table* and eating, Jesus
said, "Truly I say to you that one of you will [1]betray Me,—
[2]one who is eating with Me."
19 They began to be grieved and to say to Him one by
one, "Surely not I?"
20 And He said to them, "*It is* one of the twelve, [1]one who
dips with Me in the bowl.
21 "For the Son of Man *is to* go, just as it is written of Him;
but woe to that man [1]by whom the Son of Man is betrayed! *It
would have been* good [2]for that man if he had not been born."
22 [a]And while they were eating, He took *some* bread, and
[1]after a [b]blessing He broke *it;* and gave *it* to them, and said,
"Take *it;* this is My body."
23 And He took a cup, and when He had given thanks, He
gave *it* to them; and they all drank from it.
24 And He said to them, "This is My blood of the covenant,
which is *to be* shed on behalf of many.
25 "Truly I say to you, I shall never again drink of the fruit
of the vine until that day when I drink it new in the kingdom
of God."
26 [a]And after singing a hymn, they went out to [b]the
Mount of Olives.
27 [a]And Jesus *said to them, "You will all [1]fall away,

5 [1]The denarius was worth 18 cents in silver, equivalent to a day's wage

7 [a]Matt. 26:11; John 12:8; Deut. 15:11

8 [a]John 19:40

9 [a]Matt. 26:13

10 [1]Or, *deliver Him up* [a]Mark 14:10, 11: *Matt. 26:14-16; Luke 22:3-6* [b]John 6:71

12 [1]Lit., *they were sacrificing* [a]Mark 14:12-16: *Matt. 26:17-19; Luke 22:7-13* [b]Matt. 26:17 [c]Luke 22:7; 1 Cor. 5:7; Deut. 16:5; Mark 14:1

14 [a]Luke 22:11; Luke 2:7 Gr.

17 [a]Mark 14:17-21: *Matt. 26:20-24; Luke 22:14, 21-23;* John 13:18ff.

18 [1]Or, *deliver Me up* [2]Or, *the one*

20 [1]Or, *the one*

21 [1]Or, *through* [2]Lit., *for him if that man had not been born*

22 [1]Lit., *having blessed* [a]Mark 14:22-25: *Matt. 26:26-29; Luke 22:17-20; 1 Cor. 11:23-25;* Mark 10:16 [b]Matt. 14:19

26 [a]Matt. 26:30 [b]Matt 21:1

27 [1]Or, *stumble* [a]Mark 14:27-31: *Matt. 26:31-35*

because it is written, '[b]I WILL STRIKE DOWN THE SHEPHERD, AND THE SHEEP SHALL BE SCATTERED.'

28 "But after I have been raised, I will go before you to Galilee."

29 But Peter said to Him, "*Even* though all may [1]fall away, yet I will not."

30 And Jesus *said to him, "Truly I say to you, that you yourself [1][a]this very night, before [b]a cock crows twice, shall three times deny Me."

31 But *Peter* kept saying insistently, "*Even* if I have to die with You, I will not deny You!" And they all were saying the same thing, too.

32 [a]And they *came to a place named Gethsemane; and He *said to His disciples, "Sit here until I have prayed."

33 And He *took with him Peter and [1]James and John, and began to be very [a]distressed and troubled.

34 And He *said to them, "[a]My soul is deeply grieved to the point of death; remain here and keep watch."

35 And He went a little beyond *them,* and [1]fell to the ground, and *began* praying that if it were possible, [a]the hour might [2]pass Him by.

36 And He was saying, "[a]Abba (Father), all things are possible for Thee; remove this cup from Me; [b]yet not what I will, but what Thou wilt."

37 And He *came and *found them sleeping, and *said to Peter, "Simon, are you asleep? Could you not keep watch for one hour?

38 "[a]Keep watching and praying, that you may not come into temptation; the spirit is willing, but the flesh is weak."

39 And again He went away and prayed, saying the same [1]words.

40 And again He came and found them sleeping, for their eyes were very heavy; and they did not know what to answer Him.

41 And He *came the third time, and *said to them, "[1]Are you still sleeping and taking your rest? It is enough; [a]the hour has come; behold, the Son of Man is being [2]betrayed into the hands of sinners.

42 "Arise, let us be going; behold, the one who betrays Me is at hand!"

43 [a]And immediately while He was still speaking, Judas, one of the twelve, *came up, [1]accompanied by a multitude with swords and clubs, from the chief priests and the scribes and the elders.

44 Now he who was betraying Him had given them a signal, saying, "Whomever I shall kiss, He is the one; seize Him, and lead Him away [1]under guard."

45 And after coming, he immediately went up to Him, saying, "[a]Rabbi!" and kissed Him.

46 And they laid hands on Him, and seized Him.

47 But a certain one of those who stood by drew his sword, and struck the slave of the high priest, and [1]cut off his ear.

48 And Jesus answered and said to them, "Have you come out with swords and clubs to arrest Me, as though I were a robber?

49 "Every day I was with you [a]in the temple teaching, and

27 [b]Zech. 13:7

29 [1]Or, *stumble*

30 [1]Lit., *today, on this night* [a]Matt. 26:34 [b]Mark 14:68, 72; John 13:38

32 [a]Mark 14:32-42: *Matt. 26:36-46; Luke 22:40-46*

33 [1]Or, *Jacob* [a]Mark 9:15; 16:5, 6

34 [a]Matt. 26:38; John 12:27

35 [1]Lit., *was falling* [2]Lit., *pass from Him* [a]Mark 14:41; Matt. 26:45

36 [a]Rom. 8:15; Gal. 4:6 [b]Matt. 26:39

38 [a]Matt. 26:41

39 [1]Lit., *word*

41 [1]Or, *keep on sleeping therefore* [2]Or, *delivered up* [a]Mark 14:35

43 [1]Lit., *and with him* [a]Mark 14:43-50: *Matt. 26:47-56; Luke 22:47-53; John 18:3-11*

44 [1]Lit., *safely*

45 [a]Matt. 23:7

47 [1]Lit., *took off*

49 [a]Mark 12:35

you did not seize Me; but [1]*this has happened* that the Scriptures might be fulfilled."
50 And they all left Him and fled.
51 And a certain young man was following Him, wearing
nothing but a linen sheet over *his* naked *body;* and they
*seized him.
52 But he left the linen sheet behind, and escaped naked.
53 [a]And they led Jesus away to the high priest; and all the
chief priests and the elders and the scribes *gathered together.
54 And Peter had followed Him at a distance, [a]right into
[b]the courtyard of the high priest; and he was sitting with the
[1]officers, and [c]warming himself at the [2]fire.
55 Now the chief priests and the whole [1a]Council kept
trying to obtain testimony against Jesus to put Him to death;
and they were finding none.
56 For many were giving false testimony against Him, and
yet their testimony was not consistent.
57 And some stood up and *began* to give false testimony
against Him, saying,
58 "We heard Him say, '[a]I will destroy this [1]temple made
with hands, and in three days I will build another made without hands.' "
59 And not even in this respect was their testimony
consistent.
60 And the high priest arose *and came* forward and questioned Jesus, saying, "Do You make no answer [1]to what these
men are testifying against You?"
61 [a]But He kept silent, and made no answer. [b]Again the
high priest was questioning Him, and [1]saying to Him, "Are
You [2]the Christ, the Son of the Blessed *One?"*
62 And Jesus said, "I am; and you shall see the [a]SON OF
MAN SITTING AT THE RIGHT HAND OF POWER, and [b]COMING WITH
THE CLOUDS OF HEAVEN."
63 And [a]tearing his clothes, the high priest *said, "What
further need do we have of witnesses?
64 "You have heard the blasphemy; how does it seem to
you?" And they all condemned Him to be deserving of death.
65 And some began to [a]spit at Him, and [1b]to blindfold
Him, and to beat Him with their fists, and to say to Him,
"[c]Prophesy!" And the officers [2]received Him with [3]slaps *in the
face.*
66 [a]And as Peter was below in [b]the courtyard, one of the
servant-girls of the high priest *came,
67 and seeing Peter [a]warming himself, she looked at him,
and *said, "You, too, were with Jesus the [b]Nazarene."
68 But he denied *it,* saying, "I neither know nor understand what you are talking about." And he [a]went out onto the
[1]porch.[2]
69 And the maid saw him, and began once more to say to
the bystanders, "This is *one* of them!"
70 But again [a]he was denying it. And after a little while the
bystanders were again saying to Peter, "Surely you are *one* of
them, [b]for you are a Galilean too."
71 But he began to [1]curse and swear, "I do not know this
fellow you are talking about!"
72 And immediately a cock crowed a second time. And

49 [1]Or possibly: *let the Scriptures be fulfilled*

53 [a]Mark 14:53-65: *Matt. 26:57-68; John 18:12f.; 19-24*

54 [1]Or, *servants* [2]Lit., *light* [a]Mark 14:68 [b]Matt. 26:3 [c]Mark 14:67; John 18:18

55 [1]Or, *Sanhedrin* [a]Matt. 5:22

58 [1]Or, *sanctuary* [a]Mark 15:29; Matt. 26:61

60 [1]Or, *what do these testify?*

61 [1]Lit., *says* [2]I.e., the Messiah [a]Matt. 26:63 [b]Mark 14:61-63: *Matt. 26:63ff.; Luke 22:67-71*

62 [a]Ps. 110:1; Mark 13:26 [b]Dan. 7:13

63 [a]Matt. 26:65; Acts 14:14; Num. 14:6

65 [1]Or, *cover over His face* [2]Or, *treated* [3]Or possibly: *blows with rods* [a]Mark 10:34; Matt. 26:67 [b]Esther 7:8 [c]Matt. 26:68; Luke 22:64

66 [a]Mark 14:66-72: *Matt. 26:69-75; Luke 22:56-62; John 18:16-18, 25-27* [b]Mark 14:54

67 [a]Mark 14:54 [b]Mark 1:24

68 [1]Or, *forecourt, gateway* [2]Later mss. add: *and a cock crowed* [a]Mark 14:54

70 [a]Mark 14:68 [b]Matt. 26:73; Luke 22:59

71 [1]Or, *put himself under a curse*

Peter remembered how Jesus had made the remark to him,
"Before [a]a cock crows twice, you will deny Me three times."
[1]And he *began* to weep.

CHAPTER 15

a AND early in the morning the chief priests with the elders
and scribes, and the whole [1b]Council, immediately held a consultation, and binding Jesus, they led Him away, and delivered
Him up to Pilate.
2 [a]And Pilate questioned Him, "Are You the King of the
Jews?" And answering He *said to him, "*It is as* you say."
3 And the chief priests *began* to accuse Him [1]harshly.
4 And Pilate was questioning Him again, saying, "Do
You make no answer? See how many charges they bring
against You!"
5 But Jesus [a]made no further answer; so that Pilate was
astonished.
6 [a]Now at *the* feast he used to release for them *any* one
prisoner whom they requested.
7 And the man named Barabbas had been imprisoned
with the insurrectionists who had committed murder in the
insurrection.
8 And the multitude went up and began asking him *to do*
as he had been accustomed to do for them.
9 And Pilate answered them, saying, "Do you want me to
release for you the King of the Jews?"
10 For he was aware that the chief priests had delivered
Him up because of envy.
11 But the chief priests stirred up the multitude [a]*to ask*
him to release Barabbas for them instead.
12 And answering again, Pilate was saying to them, "Then
what shall I do to Him whom you call the King of the Jews?"
13 And they shouted [1]back, "Crucify Him!"
14 But Pilate was saying to them, "Why, what evil has He
done?" But they shouted all the more, "Crucify Him!"
15 And wishing to satisfy the multitude, Pilate released
Barabbas for them, and after having Jesus [a]scourged, he delivered Him over to be crucified.
16 [a]And the soldiers took Him away into [b]the [1]palace
(that is, the Praetorium), and they *called together the whole
Roman [2c]cohort.
17 And they *dressed Him up in [1]purple, and after weaving a crown of thorns, they put it on Him;
18 and they began to acclaim Him, "Hail, King of the
Jews!"
19 And they kept beating His head with a [1]reed, and spitting at Him, and kneeling and bowing before Him.
20 And after they had mocked Him, they took the purple
off Him, and put His garments on Him. And they *led Him
out to crucify Him.
21 [a]And they *pressed into service a passerby coming from
the country, Simon of Cyrene (the father of Alexander and
Rufus), that he might bear His cross.
22 [a]And they *brought Him to the place [b]Golgotha, which
is translated, Place of a Skull.

72 [1]Or, *thinking of this, he* began *weeping;* or, *rushing out, he* began *weeping* [a]Mark 14:30, 68

1 [1]Or, *Sanhedrin* [a]Matt. 27:1 [b]Matt. 5:22

2 [a]Mark 15:2-5: *Matt. 27:11-14; Luke 23:2, 3; John 18:29-38*

3 [1]Or, *of many things*

5 [a]Matt. 27:12

6 [a]Mark 15:6-15: *Matt. 27:15-26; Luke 23:18-25; John 18:39-19:16*

11 [a]Acts 3:14

13 [1]Or, *again*

15 [a]Matt. 27:26

16 [1]Or, *court* [2]Or, *battalion* [a]Mark 15:16-20: *Matt. 27:27-31* [b]Matt. 27:27; Mark 26:3 [c]Acts 10:1

17 [1]A term for shades varying from rose to purple

19 [1]Or, *staff* (made of a reed)

21 [a]Mark 15:21: *Matt. 27:32; Luke 23:26*

22 [a]Mark 15:22-32: *Matt. 27:33-44; Luke 23:33-43; John 19:17-24* [b]John 19:17; Luke 23:33 and marg.

23 And they tried to give Him [a]wine mixed with myrrh;
but He did not take it.
24 And they *crucified Him, and *[a]DIVIDED UP HIS GAR-
MENTS AMONG THEMSELVES, CASTING [1]LOTS FOR THEM, *to decide*
[2]what each should take.
25 And it was the [1a]third hour [2]when they crucified Him.
26 And the inscription of the charge against Him [1]read,
"[a]THE KING OF THE JEWS."
27 And they *crucified two robbers with Him; one on the
right and one on the left.
28 (See marginal note.[1])
29 And those passing by were [1]hurling abuse at Him,
[a]WAGGING THEIR HEADS, and saying, "Ha! You who *were going*
to [b]destroy the temple and rebuild it in three days,
30 save Yourself, and come down from the cross!"
31 In the same way the chief priests along with the scribes
were also mocking *Him* among themselves and saying, "[a]He
saved others; [1]He cannot save Himself.
32 "Let *this* Christ, [a]the King of Israel, now come down
from the cross, so that we may see and believe!" And [b]those
who were crucified with Him were casting the same insult at
Him.
33 [a]And when the [1b]sixth hour had come, darkness [2]fell
over the whole land until the [3b]ninth hour.
34 And at the [a]ninth hour Jesus cried out with a loud
voice, "[b]ELOI, ELOI, LAMA SABACHTHANI?" which is translated,
"MY GOD, MY GOD, WHY HAST THOU FORSAKEN ME?"
35 And when some of the bystanders heard it, they *began*
saying, "Behold, He is calling for Elijah."
36 And someone ran and filled a sponge with sour wine,
put it on a reed, and gave Him a drink, saying, "[1]Let us see
whether Elijah will come to take Him down."
37 [a]And Jesus uttered a loud cry, and breathed His last.
38 [a]And the veil of the temple was torn in two from top to
bottom.
39 [a]And when the centurion, who was standing [1]right in
front of Him, saw [2]the way He breathed His last, he said,
"Truly this man was [3]the Son of God!"
40 [a]And there were also *some* women looking on from
afar, among whom *were* Mary Magdalene, and Mary the mother of [1]James [b]the [2]Less and Joses, and [c]Salome.
41 And when He was in Galilee, they used to follow Him
and [1a]minister to Him; and *there were* many other women who
had come up with Him to Jerusalem.
42 [a]And when evening had already come, because it was
[b]the Preparation Day, that is, the day before the Sabbath,
43 Joseph of Arimathea came, a [a]prominent member of
the Council, a man who was himself [b]waiting for the kingdom
of God; and he [c]gathered up courage and went in before
Pilate, and asked for the body of Jesus.
44 And Pilate wondered if He was dead by this time, and
summoning the centurion, he questioned him as to whether
He was already dead.
45 And ascertaining this from [a]the centurion, he granted
the body to Joseph.

23 [a]Matt. 27:34

24 [1]Lit., *a lot upon* [2]Lit., *who should take what* [a]Ps. 22:18; John 19:24

25 [1]I.e., 9 a.m. [2]Lit., *and* [a]John 19:14; Mark 15:33

26 [1]Lit., *had been inscribed* [a]Matt. 27:37

28 [1]Later mss. add verse 28: *And the Scripture was fulfilled which says, "And He was reckoned with transgressors."*

29 [1]Or, *blaspheming* [a]Ps. 22:8; Matt. 27:39 [b]Mark 14:58

31 [1]Or, *can He not save Himself?* [a]Matt. 27:42; Luke 23:35

32 [a]Matt. 27:42; Mark 15:26 [b]Mark 15:27; Matt. 27:44; Luke 23:39-43

33 [1]I.e., noon [2]Or, *occurred* [3]I.e., 3 p.m. [a]Mark 15:33-41: *Matt. 27:45-56; Luke 23:44-49* [b]Matt. 27:45f.; Luke 23:44; Mark 15:25

34 [a]Matt. 27:45f.; Luke 23:44; Mark 15:25 [b]Ps. 22:1; Matt. 27:46

36 [1]Lit., *permit that we see;* or: *hold off, let us see*

37 [a]Matt. 27:50; Luke 23:46; John 19:30

38 [a]Matt. 27:51; Luke 23:45

39 [1]Or, *opposite Him* [2]Lit., *that He thus* [3]Or, possibly: *a son of God,* or, *son of a god* [a]Matt. 27:54; Luke 23:47; Mark 15:45

40 [1]Or, *Jacob* [2]Lit., *little* (either in stature or age) [a]Mark 15:40, 41: *Matt. 27:55f.;* Luke 23:49; John 19:25 [b]Luke 19:3 [c]Mark 16:1

41 [1]Or, *wait on* [a]Matt. 27:55f.

42 [a]Mark 15:42-47: *Matt. 27:57-61; Luke 23:50-56; John 19:38-42* [b]Matt. 27:62

43 [a]Luke 23:51; Acts 13:50; 17:12; Matt. 27:57 [b]Luke 23:51; 2:25, 38; Matt. 27:57; John 19:38 [c]John 19:38

45 [a]Mark 15:39

46 And *Joseph* bought a linen sheet, took Him down,
wrapped Him in the linen sheet, and laid Him in a tomb which
had been hewn out in the rock; and he rolled a stone against
the entrance of the tomb.
47 And [a]Mary Magdalene and Mary the *mother* of Joses
were looking on *to see* where He was laid.

Chapter 16

a
AND when the Sabbath was over, [b]Mary Magdalene, and
Mary the *mother* of [1]James, and Salome, [c]bought spices, that
they might come and anoint Him.
2 And very early on the first day of the week, they *came
to the tomb when the sun had risen.
3 And they were saying to one another, "Who will roll
away [a]the stone for us from the entrance of the tomb?"
4 And looking up, they *saw that the stone had been
rolled away, [1]although it was extremely large.
5 And [a]entering the tomb, they saw a young man sitting
at the right, wearing a white robe; and they [b]were amazed.
6 And he *said to them, "[a]Do not be amazed; you are
looking for Jesus the [b]Nazarene, who has been crucified. [c]He
has risen; He is not here; behold, *here is* the place where they
laid Him.
7 "But go, tell His disciples and Peter, '[a]He is going before
you into Galilee; there you will see Him, just as He said to
you.' "
8 And they went out and fled from the tomb, for trembling and astonishment had gripped them; and they said nothing to anyone, for they were afraid.[1]
9 [[1]Now after He had risen early on the first day of the
week, He first appeared to [a]Mary Magdalene, from whom He
had cast out seven demons.
10 [a]She went and reported to those who had been with
Him, while they were mourning and weeping.
11 And when they heard that He was alive, and had been
seen by her, [a]they refused to believe it.
12 And after that, [a]He appeared in a different form [b]to
two of them, while they were walking along on their way to the
country.
13 And they went away and reported it to the others, but
they [a]did not believe them either.
14 And afterward [a]He appeared [b]to the eleven themselves
as they were reclining *at table;* and He reproached them for
their [c]unbelief and hardness of heart, because they had not
believed those who had seen Him after He had risen.
15 And He said to them, "[a]Go into all the world and
preach the gospel to all creation.
16 "[a]He who has believed and has been baptized shall be
saved; but he who has disbelieved shall be condemned.
17 "And these [1]signs will accompany those who have believed: [a]in My name they will cast out demons, they will [b]speak
with new tongues;
18 they will [a]pick up serpents, and if they drink any deadly

47 [a]Mark 15:40; 16:1; Matt. 27:56

1 [1]Or, *Jacob* [a]Mark 16:1-8: *Matt. 28:1-8; Luke 24:1-10;* John 20:1-8 [b]Mark 15:47 [c]Luke 23:56; John 19:39f.

3 [a]Mark 16:3, 4; 15:46; Matt. 27:60

4 [1]Lit., *for*

5 [a]John 20:11, 12 [b]Mark 9:15

6 [a]Mark 9:15 [b]Mark 1:24 [c]Matt. 28:6; Luke 24:6

7 [a]Matt. 26:32; Mark 14:28

8 [1]See addition at end of chapter.

9 [1]Some of the oldest mss. omit from verse 9 through 20. [a]John 20:14; Matt. 27:56

10 [a]John 20:18

11 [a]Mark 16:13, 14; Luke 24:11, 41; John 20:25; Matt. 28:17

12 [a]Mark 16:14; John 21:1, 14 [b]Luke 24:13-35

13 [a]Mark 16:11, 14; Luke 24:11, 41; John 20:25; Matt. 28:17

14 [a]Mark 16:12; John 21:1, 14 [b]Luke 24:36; John 20:19, 26; 1 Cor. 15:5 [c]Mark 16:11, 13; Luke 24:11, 41; John 20:25; Matt. 28:17

15 [a]Matt. 28:19

16 [a]John 3:18, 36; Acts 16:31

17 [1]Or, *attesting miracles* [a]Mark 9:38; Luke 10:17; Acts 5:16; 8:7; 16:18; 19:12 [b]Acts 2:4; 10:46; 19:6; 1 Cor. 12:10, 28, 30; 13:1; 14:2

18 [a]Luke 10:19; Acts 28:3-5

18 [b]Mark 5:23

19 [a]Acts 1:3 [b]Luke 9:51; 24:51; John 6:62; 20:17; Acts 1:2; 1 Tim 3:16 [c]Ps. 110:1; Luke 22:69; Acts 7:55f.; Rom. 8:34; Eph. 1:20; Col. 3:1; Heb. 1:3; 8:1; 10:12; 12:2; 1 Pet. 3:22

20 [1]Or, *attesting miracles* [2]Many mss. add: *Amen*

Addition: [1]A few later mss. and versions contain this paragraph, usually after verse 8; a few have it at the end of chapter.

poison, it shall not hurt them; they will [b]lay hands on the sick, and they will recover."
19 So then, when the Lord Jesus had [a]spoken to them, He [b]was received up into heaven, and [c]SAT DOWN AT THE RIGHT HAND OF GOD.
20 And they went out and preached everywhere, while the Lord worked with them, and confirmed the word by the [1]signs that followed.[2]]

ADDITION [1]

And they promptly reported all these instructions to Peter and his companions. And after that, Jesus Himself sent out through them from east to west the sacred and imperishable proclamation of eternal salvation.

THE GOSPEL
ACCORDING TO
LUKE

Preface. Zacharias Visited.

1 [1]Or, *on which there is full conviction* [a][Gr. in] Rom. 4:21; 14:5; Col. 4:12; 2 Tim. 4:5, 17; Col. 2:2; 1 Thess. 1:5; Heb. 6:11; 10:22

2 [1]Lit., *became* [2]Or, *ministers* [3]I.e., Gospel [a]John 15:27; Acts 1:21f. [b]2 Pet. 1:16; 1 John 1:1 [c]Acts 26:16; 1 Cor. 4:1; Heb. 2:3 [d]Mark 4:14; 16:20; Acts 8:4; 14:25; 16:6; 17:11

3 [1]Or, *followed* [a]1 Tim. 4:6; 2 Tim. 3:10 [in Gr.] [b]Acts 11:4; 18:23 [c]Acts 23:26; 24:3; 26:25 [d]Acts 1:1

4 [1]Or, *orally instructed in* [a]Acts 18:25; Rom. 2:18; 1 Cor. 14:19; Gal. 6:6 [Gr.]

5 [1]Lit., *came into being* [2]I.e., Zechariah [3]Gr., Abia [4]I.e., of priestly descent [a]Matt. 2:1 [b]1 Chr. 24:10

6 [a]Gen. 7:1; Acts 2:25; 8:21 [b]Phil. 2:15; 3:6; 1 Thess. 3:13 [Gr.]

7 [1]Lit., *days*

8 [a]1 Chr. 24:19; 2 Chr. 8:14; 31:2

9 [a]Ex. 30:7f.

10 [a]Lev. 16:17

11 [a]Luke 2:9; Acts 5:19

INASMUCH as many have undertaken to compile an account of the things [1a]accomplished among us,
2 just as those who [a]from the beginning [1]were [b]eyewitnesses and [2c]servants of [d]the [3]Word have handed them down to us,
3 it seemed fitting for me as well, [a]having [1]investigated everything carefully from the beginning, to write *it* out for you [b]in consecutive order, [c]most excellent [d]Theophilus;
4 so that you might know the exact truth about the things you have been [1a]taught.
5 [a]In the days of Herod, King of Judea, there [1]was a certain priest named [2]Zacharias, of the [b]division of [3]Abijah; and he had a wife [4]from the daughters of Aaron, and her name was Elizabeth.
6 And they were both [a]righteous in the sight of God, walking [b]blamelessly in all the commandments and requirements of the Lord.
7 And they had no child, because Elizabeth was barren, and they were both advanced in [1]years.
8 Now it came about, while [a]he was performing his priestly service before God in the *appointed* order of his division,
9 according to the custom of the priestly office, he was chosen by lot [a]to enter the temple of the Lord and burn incense.
10 And the whole multitude of the people were in prayer [a]outside at the hour of the incense offering.
11 And [a]an angel of the Lord appeared to him, standing to the right of the altar of incense.

12 And Zacharias was troubled when he saw *him,* and fear
[1]gripped him.
13 But the angel said to him, "[a]Do not be afraid, Zacharias, for your petition has been heard, and your wife Elizabeth
will bear you a son, and [b]you will [1]give him the name John.
14 "And you will have joy and gladness, and many will
rejoice at his birth.
15 "For he will be great in the sight of the Lord, and he will
[a]drink no wine or liquor; and he will be filled with the Holy
Spirit, [1]while yet in his mother's womb.
16 "And he will turn back many of the sons of Israel to the
Lord their God.
17 "And it is he who will [a]go *as a forerunner* before Him in
the spirit and power of [b]Elijah, [c]TO TURN THE HEARTS OF THE
FATHERS BACK TO THE CHILDREN, and the disobedient to the
attitude of the righteous; so as to [a]make ready a people prepared for the Lord."
18 And Zacharias said to the angel, "How shall I know this
for certain? For I am an old man, and my wife is advanced in
[1]years."
19 And the angel answered and said to him, "I am [a]Gabriel, who [1b]stands in the presence of God; and I have been sent
to speak to you, and to bring you this good news.
20 "And behold, you shall be silent and unable to speak
until the day when these things take place, because you did not
believe my words, which shall be fulfilled in their proper
time."
21 And the people were waiting for Zacharias, and were
wondering at his delay in the temple.
22 But when he came out, he was unable to speak to them;
and they realized that he had seen a vision in the temple; and
he [a]kept [1]making signs to them, and remained mute.
23 And it came about, when the days of his priestly service
were ended, that he went back home.
24 And after these days Elizabeth his wife became pregnant; and she [1]kept herself in seclusion for five months, saying,
25 "This is the way the Lord has dealt with me in the days
when He looked *with favor* upon *me,* to [a]take away my disgrace among men."
26 Now in the sixth month the angel [a]Gabriel was sent
from God to a city in Galilee, called [b]Nazareth,
27 to [a]a virgin engaged to a man whose name was Joseph,
[b]of the [1]descendants of David; and the virgin's name was
Mary.
28 And coming in, he said to her, "Hail, [1]favored one! The
Lord [2]*is* with you."[3]
29 But she [a]was greatly troubled at *this* statement, and
kept pondering what kind of salutation this might be.
30 And the angel said to her, "[a]Do not be afraid, Mary; for
you have found favor with God.
31 "And behold, you will conceive in your womb, and bear
a son, and you [a]shall name Him Jesus.
32 "He will be great, and will be called the Son of [a]the
Most High; and the Lord God will give Him the throne of His
father David;

12 [1]Or, *fell upon*

13 [1]Lit., *call his name* [a]Luke 1:30; Matt. 14:27 [b]Luke 1:60, 63

15 [1]Lit., *even from* [a]Num. 6:3; Judg. 13:4; Matt. 11:18; Luke 7:33

17 [a]Luke 1:76 [b]Matt. 11:14 [c]Mal. 4:6

18 [1]Lit., *days*

19 [1]Lit., *stand beside* [a]Luke 1:26; Dan. 8:16; 9:21 [b]Matt. 18:10

22 [1]Or, *beckoning to,* or, *nodding to* [a]Luke 1:62

24 [1]Lit., *was hidden*

25 [a]Gen. 30:23; Is. 4:1

26 [a]Luke 1:19 [b]Matt. 2:23

27 [1]Lit., *house* [a]Matt. 1:18 [b]Matt. 1:16, 20; Luke 2:4

28 [1]Or, *O woman richly blessed* [2]Or, *be* [3]Later mss. add: *you are blessed among women*

29 [a]Luke 1:12

30 [a]Luke 1:13; Matt. 14:27

31 [a]Matt. 1:21, 25; Luke 2:21

32 [a]Luke 1:35, 76; 6:35; Acts 7:48; Mark 5:7

33 [a]and He will reign over the house of Jacob forever; [b]and
His kingdom will have no end."
34 And Mary said to the angel, "How [1]can this be, since I
[2]am a virgin?"
35 And the angel answered and said to her, "[a]The Holy
Spirit will come upon you, and the power of [b]the Most High
will overshadow you; and for that reason [c]the [1]holy offspring
shall be called [d]the Son of God.
36 "And behold, even your relative Elizabeth has also conceived a son in her old age; and [1]she who was called barren is
now in her sixth month.
37 "For [1a]nothing will be impossible with God."
38 And [1]Mary said, "Behold, the [2]bondslave of the Lord;
be it done to me according to your word." And the angel
departed from her.
39 Now [1]at this time Mary arose and went with haste to
[a]the hill country, to a city of Judah,
40 and entered the house of Zacharias and greeted
Elizabeth.
41 And it came about that when Elizabeth heard Mary's
greeting, the baby leaped in her womb; and Elizabeth was
[a]filled with the Holy Spirit.
42 And she cried out with a loud voice, and said, "Blessed
among women *are* you, and blessed *is* the fruit of your womb!
43 "And [1]how has it *happened* to me, that the mother of
[a]my Lord should come to me?
44 "For behold, when the sound of your greeting reached
my ears, the baby leaped in my womb for joy.
45 "And [a]blessed *is* she who believed [1]that there would be a
fulfillment of what had been spoken to her [2]by the Lord."
46 And Mary said:

"[a]My soul [1b]exalts the Lord,
47 And [a]my spirit has rejoiced in [b]God my Savior.
48 For He has had regard for the humble state of His [1]bondslave;
For behold, from this time on all generations will count me [a]blessed.
49 For the Mighty One has done great things for me;
And holy is His name.
50 [a]AND HIS MERCY IS [1]UPON GENERATION AFTER GENERATION
TOWARDS THOSE WHO FEAR HIM.
51 [a]He has done [1]mighty deeds with His arm;
He has scattered *those who were* proud in the [2]thoughts of their heart.
52 He has brought down rulers from *their* thrones,
And has exalted those who were humble.
53 [a]HE HAS FILLED THE HUNGRY WITH GOOD THINGS;
And sent away the rich empty-handed.
54 He has given help to Israel His servant,
[1]In remembrance of His mercy,
55 [a]As He spoke to our fathers,
To Abraham and his [1]offspring forever."

56 And Mary stayed with her about three months, and
then returned to her home.

33 [a]Matt. 1:1 [b]Matt. 28:18; Dan. 2:44; 7:14, 18, 27

34 [1]Lit., *shall* [2]Lit., *know no man*

35 [1]Lit., *the holy thing begotten* [a]Matt. 1:18 [b]Luke 1:32 [c]Mark 1:24 [d]Matt. 4:3

36 [1]Lit., *this is the sixth month to her who*

37 [1]Lit., *not any word* [a]Matt. 19:26

38 [1]Gr. *Mariam*, i.e., Miriam; so throughout Luke [2]I.e., female slave

39 [1]Lit., *in these days* [a]Luke 1:65; Josh. 20:7; 21:11

41 [a]Luke 1:67

43 [1]Lit., *whence this to me* [a]Luke 2:11

45 [1]Or, possibly: *because there will be* [2]Lit., *from* [a]Luke 1:48; Luke 1:20

46 [1]Lit., *makes great* [a]Luke 1:46-53: *1 Sam. 2:1-10* [b]Ps. 34:2f.

47 [a]Ps. 35:9 [b]1 Tim. 1:1; 2:3; Titus 1:3; 2:10; 3:4; Jude 25

48 [1]I.e., female slave [a]Luke 1:45

50 [1]Lit., *unto generations and generations* [a]Ps. 103:17

51 [1]Lit., *might* [2]Lit., *thought, attitude* [a]Ps. 98:1; 118:15

53 [a]Ps. 107:9

54 [1]Lit., *so as to remember*

55 [1]Lit., *seed* [a]Gen. 17:19; Ps. 132:11; Gal. 3:16

57 Now the time [1]had come for Elizabeth to give birth,
and she brought forth a son.
58 And her neighbors and her relatives heard that the
Lord had [1a]displayed His great mercy toward her; and they
were rejoicing with her.
59 And it came about that on [a]the eighth day they came
to circumcise the child, and they were going to call him Zacharias, [1]after his father.
60 And his mother answered and said, "No indeed; but
[a]he shall be called John."
61 And they said to her, "There is no one among your
relatives who is called by that name."
62 And they [a]made signs to his father, as to what he
wanted him called.
63 And he asked for a tablet, and wrote as follows, "[a]His
name is John." And they were all astonished.
64 [a]And at once his mouth was opened and his tongue
loosed, and he *began* to speak in praise of God.
65 And fear came on all those living around them; and all
these matters were being talked about in all [a]the hill country of
Judea.
66 And all who heard them kept them in mind, saying,
"What then will this child *turn out to* be?" For [a]the hand of
the Lord was certainly with him.
67 And his father Zacharias [a]was filled with the Holy
Spirit, and [b]prophesied, saying;
68 "Blessed *be* the Lord God of Israel,
For He has visited us and accomplished [a]redemption
for His people,
69 And has raised up a [a]horn of salvation for us
In the house of David [b]His servant—
70 [a]As He spoke by the mouth of His holy prophets [b]from
of old—
71 [1a]Salvation [b]FROM OUR ENEMIES,
And FROM THE HAND OF ALL WHO HATE US;
72 [a]To show mercy toward our fathers,
[b]And to remember His holy covenant,
73 [a]The oath which He swore to Abraham our father,
74 To grant us that we being delivered from the hand of
our enemies,
Might serve Him without fear,
75 In holiness and righteousness before Him all our days.
76 And you, child, will be called the [a]prophet of [b]the Most
High;
For you will go on [c]BEFORE THE LORD TO [d]PREPARE HIS
WAYS;
77 To give to His people *the* knowledge of salvation
[1]By [a]the forgiveness of their sins,
78 Because of the tender mercy of our God,
With which [a]the Sunrise from on high shall visit us,
79 [a]TO SHINE UPON THOSE WHO SIT IN DARKNESS AND THE
SHADOW OF DEATH,
To guide our feet into the way of peace."
80 [a]And the child continued to grow, and to become
strong in spirit, and he lived in the deserts until the day of his
public appearance to Israel.

57 [1]Lit., *was fulfilled*
58 [1]Lit., *magnified* [a]Gen. 19:19
59 [1]Lit., *after the name of* [a]Gen. 17:12; Lev. 12:3; Luke 2:21; Phil. 3:5
60 [a]Luke 1:13, 63
62 [a]Luke 1:22
63 [a]Luke 1:13, 60
64 [a]Luke 1:20
65 [a]Luke 1:39
66 [a]Acts 11:21
67 [a]Luke 1:41 [b]Joel 2:28
68 [a]Luke 2:38; Heb. 9:12; Luke 1:71; Acts 1:6
69 [a]1 Sam. 2:1, 10; Ps. 18:2; 89:17; 132:17; Ezek. 29:21; [b]Matt. 1:1
70 [a]Rom. 1:2 [b]Acts 3:21
71 [1]Or, *Deliverance* [a]Luke 1:68 [b]Ps. 106:10
72 [a]Mic. 7:20 [b]Ps. 105:8f.; 106:45
73 [a]Gen. 22:16ff.
76 [a]Matt. 11:9 [b]Luke 1:32 [c]Mal. 3:1 [d]Luke 1:17
77 [1]Or, *consisting in* [a]Mark 1:4; Jer. 31:34
78 [a]Mal. 4:2; Eph. 5:14; 2 Pet. 1:19
79 [a]Is. 9:1, 2; 59:8; Matt. 4:16
80 [a]Luke 2:40

Chapter 2

NOW it came about in those days that a decree went out
from [a]Caesar Augustus, that a census be taken of [b]all [1]the
inhabited earth.
2 [1]This was the first census taken while [2]Quirinius was
governor of [a]Syria.
3 And all were proceeding to register for the census,
everyone to his own city.
4 And Joseph also went up from Galilee, from the city of
Nazareth, to Judea, to the city of David, which is called Bethlehem, because [a]he was of the house and family of David;
5 in order to register, along with Mary, who was engaged
to him, and was with child.
6 And it came about that while they were there, the days
were completed for her to give birth.
7 And she gave birth to her first-born son; and she
wrapped Him in cloths, and laid Him in a [1]manger, because
there was no room for them in the inn.
8 And in the same region there were *some* shepherds
staying out in the fields, and keeping watch over their flock by
night.
9 And [a]an angel of the Lord suddenly [b]stood before
them, and the glory of the Lord shone around them; and they
were terribly frightened.
10 And the angel said to them, "[a]Do not be afraid; for
behold, I bring you good news of a great joy which shall be for
all the people;
11 for today in the city of David there has been born for
you a [a]Savior, who is [1b]Christ [c]the Lord.
12 "And [a]this *will be* a sign for you: you will find a baby
wrapped in cloths, and lying in a [1]manger."
13 And suddenly there appeared with the angel a multitude of the heavenly host praising God, and saying,
14 "[a]Glory to God in the highest,
And on earth peace among men [1b]with whom He is
pleased."
15 And it came about that when the angels had gone away
from them into heaven, the shepherds *began* saying to one
another, "Let us go straight to Bethlehem then, and see this
thing that has happened which the Lord has made known to
us."
16 And they came in haste and found their way to Mary
and Joseph, and the baby as He lay in the [1]manger.
17 And when they had seen this, they made known the
statement which had been told them about this Child.
18 And all who heard it wondered at the things which
were told them by the shepherds.
19 But Mary [a]treasured up all these things, pondering
them in her heart.
20 And the shepherds went back, [a]glorifying and praising
God for all that they had heard and seen, just as had been told
them.
21 And when [a]eight days were completed [1]before His circumcision, [b]His name was *then* called Jesus, the name given
by the angel before He was conceived in the womb.

1 [1]I.e., the Roman empire [a]Luke 3:1; Matt. 22:17 [b]Matt. 24:14

2 [1]Or, *this took place as a first census* [2]Gr., *Kyrenios* [a]Matt. 4:24

4 [a]Luke 1:27

7 [1]Or, *feeding trough*

9 [a]Luke 1:11; Acts 5:19 [b]Luke 24:4; Acts 12:7

10 [a]Matt. 14:27

11 [1]I.e., Messiah [a]John 4:42; Acts 5:31; Matt. 1:21 [b]Matt. 16:16, 20; John 11:27; Matt. 1:16 [c]Acts 2:36; 10:36; Luke 1:43

12 [1]Or, *feeding trough* [a]1 Sam. 2:34; 2 Kin. 19:29; 20:8f.; Is. 7:11, 14

14 [1]Lit., *of His good pleasure;* or possibly, *of good will* [a]Luke 19:38; Matt. 21:9 [b]Luke 3:22; Eph. 1:9; Phil. 2:13

16 [1]Or, *feeding trough*

19 [a]Luke 2:51

20 [a]Matt. 9:8

21 [1]Lit., *so as to circumcise Him* [a]Luke 1:59 [b]Luke 1:31

22 And when the days for their purification according to
the law of Moses were completed, they brought Him up to
Jerusalem to present Him to the Lord
23 (as it is written in the Law of the Lord, "[a]EVERY *first-*
born MALE THAT OPENS THE WOMB SHALL BE CALLED HOLY TO
THE LORD"),
24 and to offer a sacrifice according to what was said in
the Law of the Lord, "[a]A PAIR OF TURTLEDOVES, OR TWO YOUNG
PIGEONS."
25 And behold, there was a man in Jerusalem whose name
was Simeon; and this man was [a]righteous and devout, [b]looking
for the consolation of Israel; and the Holy Spirit was upon
him.
26 And [a]it had been revealed to him by the Holy Spirit
that he would not [b]see death before he had seen the Lord's
[1]Christ.
27 And he came in the Spirit into the temple; and when
the parents brought in the child Jesus, [1a]to carry out for Him
the custom of the Law,
28 then he took Him into his arms, and blessed God, and
said,
29 "Now Lord, Thou dost let Thy bond-servant depart,
In peace, [a]according to Thy word;
30 For mine eyes have [a]seen Thy salvation,
31 Which Thou hast prepared in the presence of all
peoples,
32 [a]A LIGHT [1]OF REVELATION TO THE GENTILES,
And the glory of Thy people Israel."
33 And His father and [a]mother were amazed at the things
which were being said about Him.
34 And Simeon blessed them, and said to Mary [a]His mother, "Behold, this *Child* is appointed for [b]the fall and [1]rise of
many in Israel, and for a sign to be opposed —
35 and a sword will pierce even your own soul — to the
end that thoughts from many hearts may be revealed."
36 And there was a [a]prophetess, [1]Anna the daughter of
Phanuel, of [b]the tribe of Asher. She was advanced in [2]years,
[c]having lived with a husband seven years after her [3]marriage,
37 and then as a widow to the age of eighty-four. And she
never left the temple, serving night and day with [a]fastings and
prayers.
38 And at that very [1]moment she came up and *began*
giving thanks to God, and continued to speak of Him to all
those who were [a]looking for the redemption of Jerusalem.
39 And when they had performed everything according to
the Law of the Lord, they returned to Galilee, to [a]their own
city of Nazareth.
40 [a]And the Child continued to grow and become strong,
[1]increasing in wisdom; and the grace of God was upon Him.
41 And His parents used to go to Jerusalem every year at
[a]the Feast of the Passover.
42 And when He became twelve, they went up *there* according to the custom of the Feast;
43 and as they were returning, after spending the [a]full
number of days, the boy Jesus stayed behind in Jerusalem. And
His parents were unaware of it,

23 [a]Ex. 13:2, 12

24 [a]Lev. 12:8; 5:11

25 [a]Luke 1:6 [b]Luke 2:38; 23:51; Mark 15:43

26 [1]Or, *Messiah* [a]Matt. 2:12 [b]Ps. 89:48; Heb. 11:5; John 8:51

27 [1]Lit., *to do for Him according to* [a]Luke 2:22

29 [a]Luke 2:26

30 [a]Is. 52:10; Luke 3:6

32 [1]Or, *for* [a]Is. 42:6; 49:6; Acts 13:47; 26:23

33 [a]Matt. 12:46

34 [1]Or, *resurrection* [a]Matt. 12:46 [b]Matt. 21:44; 1 Cor. 1:23; 2 Cor. 2:16; 1 Pet. 2:8

36 [1]Or, *Hannah* [2]Lit., *days* [3]Lit., *virginity* [a]Acts 21:9; Luke 2:38 [b]Josh. 19:24 [c]1 Tim. 5:9

37 [a]Luke 5:33; Acts 13:3; 14:23; 1 Tim. 5:5

38 [1]Lit., *hour* [a]Luke 2:25; Luke 1:68

39 [a]Luke 2:51; 4:16; Luke 1:26; Matt. 2:23

40 [1]Lit., *becoming full of* [a]Luke 1:80; Luke 2:52

41 [a]Ex. 23:15; Deut. 16:1-6

43 [a]Ex. 12:15

44 but supposed Him to be in the caravan, and went a
day's journey; and they *began* looking for Him among their
relatives and acquaintances.
45 And when they did not find Him, they returned to
Jerusalem, looking for Him.
46 And it came about that after three days they found
Him in the temple, sitting in the midst of the teachers, both
listening to them, and asking them questions.
47 And all who heard Him were amazed at His understanding and His answers.
48 And when they saw Him, they were astonished; and
[a]His mother said to Him, "[1]Son, why have You treated us this
way? Behold, [b]Your father and I [2]have been anxiously looking
for You."
49 And He said to them, "Why is it that you were looking
for Me? Did you not know that I had to be in My Father's
[1]*house?*"
50 And [a]they did not understand the statement which He
[1]had made to them.
51 And He went down with them, and came to [a]Nazareth;
and He continued in subjection to them; and [b]His mother
[1c]treasured all *these* [2]things in her heart.
52 And Jesus kept increasing in wisdom and [1]stature, and
in [a]favor with God and men.

Chapter 3

NOW in the fifteenth year of the reign of Tiberius Caesar,
when [a]Pontius Pilate was governor of Judea, and [b]Herod was
tetrarch of Galilee, and his brother Phillip was tetrarch of the
region of Ituraea and Trachonitis, and Lysanias was tetrarch of
Abilene,
2 in the high priesthood of [a]Annas and [b]Caiaphas, [c]the
word of God came to John, the son of Zacharias, in the
wilderness.
3 And he came into all [a]the district around the Jordan,
preaching a baptism of repentance for forgiveness of sins;
4 as it is written in the book of the words of Isaiah the
prophet, "The voice of one crying in the wilderness,
'[a]MAKE READY THE WAY OF THE LORD,
MAKE HIS PATHS STRAIGHT.
5 [a]EVERY RAVINE SHALL BE FILLED UP,
AND EVERY MOUNTAIN AND HILL SHALL BE [1]BROUGHT LOW;
AND THE CROOKED SHALL BECOME STRAIGHT,
AND THE ROUGH ROADS SMOOTH;
6 [a]AND ALL [1]FLESH SHALL [b]SEE THE SALVATION OF GOD.' "
7 He therefore *began* saying to the multitudes who were
going out to be baptized by him, "You brood of vipers, who
warned you to flee from the wrath to come?
8 "Therefore bring forth fruits in keeping with your repentance, and [a]do not begin to say [1]to yourselves, 'We have Abraham for our father,' for I say to you that God is able from
these stones to raise up children to Abraham.
9 "And also the axe is already laid at the root of the trees;
every tree therefore that does not bear good fruit is cut down
and thrown into the fire."

48 [1]Lit., *Child* [2]Lit., *are looking* [a]Matt. 12:46 [b]Luke 3:23; 4:22; Luke 2:49

49 [1]Or, *affairs;* lit., *in the things of My Father*

50 [1]Lit., *had spoken* [a]Mark 9:32

51 [1]Lit., *was treasuring* [2]Lit., *words* [a]Luke 2:39 [b]Matt. 12:46 [c]Luke 2:19

52 [1]Or, *age* [a]Luke 2:40

1 [a]Matt. 27:2 [b]Matt. 14:1

2 [a]John 18:13, 24; Acts 4:6 [b]Matt. 26:3 [c]Luke 3:3-10: *Matt. 3:1-10; Mark 1:3-5*

3 [a]Matt. 3:5

4 [a]Is. 40:3

5 [1]Or, *leveled* [a]Is. 40:4

6 [1]Or, *mankind* [a]Is. 40:5 [b]Luke 2:30

8 [1]Or, *in* [a]Luke 5:21; 13:25, 26; 14:9

10 And the multitudes were questioning him, saying,
"Then what shall we do?"
11 And he would answer and say to them, "Let the man
who has two tunics share with him who has none; and let him
who has food do likewise."
12 And *some* [1]tax-gatherers also came to be baptized, and
they said to him, "Teacher, what shall we do?"
13 And he said to them, "[1]Collect no more than what you
have been ordered to."
14 And *some* [1]soldiers were questioning him, saying, "And
what about us, what shall we do?" And he said to them, "Do
not take money from anyone by force, or accuse *anyone* falsely, and be content with your wages."
15 Now while the people were in a state of expectation
and all were [1]wondering in their hearts about John, [a]as to
whether he might be [2]the Christ;
16 [a]John answered and said to them all, "As for me, I
baptize you with water; but He who is mightier than I is coming, and I am not fit to untie the thong of His sandals; He
Himself will baptize you [1]in the Holy Spirit and fire.
17 "And His [a]winnowing fork is in His hand to clean out
His threshing floor, and to gather the wheat into His barn;
but He will burn up the chaff with [b]unquenchable fire."
18 So with many other exhortations also he preached the
gospel to the people.
19 But when [a]Herod the tetrarch was reproved by him on
account of [a]Herodias, his brother's wife, and on account of all
the wicked things which [b]Herod had done,
20 he added this also to them all, that [a]he locked John up
in prison.
21 [a]Now it came about that when all the people were
baptized, that Jesus also was baptized, and while He was
[b]praying, heaven was opened,
22 and the Holy Spirit descended upon Him in bodily
form like a dove, and a voice came out of heaven, "[a]Thou art
My beloved Son, in Thee I am well pleased."
23 And [a]when He began His ministry, Jesus Himself was
about thirty years of age, being [1]supposedly *the* son of [b]Joseph,
the *son* of [2]Eli,
24 the *son* of Matthat, the *son* of Levi, the *son* of Melchi,
the *son* of Jannai, the *son* of Joseph,
25 the *son* of Mattathias, the *son* of Amos, the *son* of
Nahum, the *son* of [1]Hesli, the *son* of Naggai,
26 the *son* of Maath, the *son* of Mattathias, the *son* of
Semein, the *son* of Josech the *son* of Joda,
27 the *son* of Johanan, the *son* of Resa, [a]the *son* of Zerubbabel, the *son* of [1]Shealtiel, the *son* of Neri,
28 the *son* of Melchi, the *son* of Addi, the *son* of Cosam,
the *son* of Elmadam, the *son* of Er,
29 the *son* of [1]Joshua, the *son* of Eliezer, the *son* of Jorim,
the *son* of Matthat, the *son of Levi*,
30 the *son* of Simeon, the *son* of [1]Judah, the *son* of Joseph, the *son* of Jonam, the *son* of Eliakim,
31 the *son* of Melea, the *son* of Menna, the *son* of Mat-
tatha, the *son* of Nathan, the *son* of David,

12 [1]Publicans who collected Roman taxes on commission

13 [1]Or, *Extort*

14 [1]I.e., men in active military service

15 [1]Or, *reasoning*, or *debating* [2]I.e., the Messiah [a]John 1:19f.

16 [1]Or, *with* [a]Luke 3:16, 17: *Matt. 3:11, 12; Mark 1:7, 8*

17 [a]Is. 30:24 [b]Mark 9:43, 48

19 [a]Matt. 14:3; Mark 6:17 [b]Luke 3:1; Matt. 14:1

20 [a]John 3:24

21 [a]Luke 3:21, 22: *Matt. 3:13-17; Mark 1:9-11* [b]Luke 5:16; 9:18, 28f.; Matt. 14:23

22 [a]Matt. 3:17

23 [1]Lit., *as it was being thought* [2]Also spelled *Heli* [a]Matt. 4:17; Acts 1:1 [b]Luke 3:23-27; Matt. 1:16

25 [1]Also spelled *Esli*

27 [1]Gr., *Salathiel* [a]Matt. 1:12

29 [1]Gr., *Jesus*

30 [1]Gr., *Judas*

32 [a]the *son* of Jesse, the *son* of Obed, the *son* of Boaz, the
son of [1]Salmon, the *son* of [2]Nahshon,
33 the *son* of Amminadab, the *son* of Admin, the *son* of
[1]Ram, the *son* of Hezron, the *son* of Perez, the *son* of Judah,
34 the *son* of Jacob, the *son* of Isaac, [a]the *son* of Abraham,
the *son* of Terah, the *son* of Nahor,
35 the *son* of Serug, the *son* of [1]Reu, the *son* of Peleg, the
son of [2]Heber, the *son* of Shelah,
36 the *son* of Cainan, the *son* of Arphaxad, the *son* of
Shem, [a]the *son* of Noah, the *son* of Lamech,
37 the *son* of Methuselah, the *son* of Enoch, the *son* of
Jared, the *son* of Mahalaleel, the *son* of Cainan,
38 the *son* of Enosh, the *son* of Seth, the *son* of Adam, the
son of God.

[a] CHAPTER 4

AND Jesus, full of the Holy Spirit, [b]returned from the Jordan
and was led about [1]by the Spirit in the wilderness
2 for forty days, while tempted by the devil. And He ate
nothing during those days; and when they had ended, He became hungry.
3 And the devil said to Him, "If You are the Son of God,
tell this stone to become bread."
4 And Jesus answered him, "It is written, '[a]MAN SHALL
NOT LIVE ON BREAD ALONE.' "
5 [a]And he led Him up and showed Him all the kingdoms
of [1b]the world in a moment of time.
6 And the devil said to Him, "I will give You all this
domain and [1]its glory; [a]for it has been handed over to me, and
I give it to whomever I wish.
7 "Therefore if You [1]worship before me, it shall all be
Yours."
8 And Jesus answered and said to him, "It is written,
'[a]YOU SHALL WORSHIP THE LORD YOUR GOD AND SERVE HIM
ONLY.' "
9 [a]And he led Him to Jerusalem and set Him on the
pinnacle of the temple, and said to Him, "If You are the Son
of God, cast Yourself down from here;
10 for it is written,
'[a]HE WILL GIVE HIS ANGELS CHARGE CONCERNING YOU
TO GUARD YOU.'
11 and,
'[a]ON THEIR HANDS THEY WILL BEAR YOU UP,
LEST YOU STRIKE YOUR FOOT AGAINST A STONE.' "
12 And Jesus answered and said to him, "It is said, '[a]YOU
SHALL NOT [1]FORCE A TEST ON THE LORD YOUR GOD.' "
13 And when the devil had finished every temptation, he
departed from Him until an opportune time.
14 And [a]Jesus returned to Galilee in the power of the
Spirit; and [b]news about Him spread through all the surrounding district.
15 And He *began* [a]teaching in their synagogues and was
praised by all.
16 And He came to [a]Nazareth, where He had been
brought up; and as was His custom, [b]He entered the synagogue
on the Sabbath, and [c]stood up to read.

32 [1]Gr., *Sala* [2]Gr., *Naasson* [a]Luke 3:32-34: *Matt. 1:1-6*

33 [1]Gr., *Arni*

34 [a]Luke 3:34-36: *Gen. 11:26-30; 1 Chr. 1:24-27*

35 [1]Gr., *Ragau* [2]Gr., *Eber*

36 [a]Luke 3:36-38: *Gen. 5:3-32; 1 Chr. 1:1-4*

1 [1]Or, *under the influence of*, lit., *in* [a]Luke 4:1-13: *Matt. 4:1-11; Mark 1:12, 13* [b]Luke 3:3, 21

4 [a]Deut. 8:3

5 [1]Lit., *the inhabited earth* [a]Matt. 4:8-10 [b]Matt. 24:14

6 [1]Lit., *their* (referring to the kingdom) [a]1 John 5:19

7 [1]Or, *bow down*

8 [a]Deut. 6:13

9 [a]Matt. 4:5-7

10 [a]Ps. 91:11

11 [a]Ps. 91:12

12 [1]Or, *tempt* [a]Deut. 6:16

14 [a]Matt. 4:12 [b]Luke 4:37; Matt. 9:26

15 [a]Matt. 4:23

16 [a]Luke 2:39, 51 [b]Matt. 13:54; Mark 6:1f. [c]Acts 13:14-16

17 And the [1]book of the prophet Isaiah was handed to
Him. And He opened the [1]book, and found the place where it
was written,
18 "[a]The Spirit of the Lord is upon Me,
Because He anointed Me to preach the gospel to
the poor.
He has sent Me to proclaim release to the captives,
And recovery of sight to the blind,
To set free those who are downtrodden,
19 [a]To proclaim the favorable year of the Lord."
20 And He [a]closed the [1]book, and gave it back to the
attendant, and [b]sat down; and the eyes of all in the synagogue
were fixed upon Him.
21 And He began to say to them, "Today this Scripture
has been fulfilled in your [1]hearing."
22 And all [1]were speaking well of Him, and wondering at
the gracious words which [2]were falling from His lips; and they
were saying, "[a]Is this not Joseph's son?"
23 And He said to them, "No doubt you will quote this
proverb to Me, 'Physician, heal yourself; whatever we heard
was done [a]at Capernaum, do here in [b]your home town as
well.' "
24 And He said, "Truly I say to you, [a]no prophet is welcome in his home town.
25 "But I say to you in truth, there were many widows in
Israel [a]in the days of Elijah, when the sky was shut up for three
years and six months, when a great famine came over all the
land;
26 and yet Elijah was sent to none of them, but [a]only to
[1]Zarephath, in the land of [b]Sidon, to a woman who was a
widow.
27 "And there were many lepers in Israel in the time of
Elisha the prophet; and none of them was cleansed, but [a]only
Naaman the Syrian."
28 And all in the synagogue were filled with rage as they
heard these things;
29 and they rose up and [a]cast Him out of the city, and led
Him to the brow of the hill on which their city had been built,
in order to throw Him down the cliff.
30 But [a]passing through their midst, He went His way.
31 And [a]He came down to [b]Capernaum, a city of Galilee.
And He was teaching them on Sabbath days;
32 and [a]they were *continually* amazed at His teaching; for
[b]His [1]message was with authority.
33 And there was a man in the synagogue [1]possessed by
the spirit of an unclean demon, and he cried out with a loud
voice,
34 "[1]Ha! [a]What do we have to do with You, Jesus of [2][b]Naz-
areth? Have You come to destroy us? I know who You are—
[b]the Holy One of God!"
35 And Jesus [a]rebuked him, saying, "Be quiet and come
out of him!" And when the demon had thrown him down in
their midst, he went out of him without doing him any harm.
36 And amazement came upon them all, and they *began*
discussing with one another, and saying, "What is [1]this mes-

17 [1]Or, *scroll*

18 [a]Is. 61:1; Matt. 12:18; Matt. 11:5; John 3:34

19 [a]Is. 61:2; Lev. 25:10

20 [1]Or, *scroll* [a]Luke 4:17 [b]Matt. 26:55

21 [1]Lit., *ears*

22 [1]Or, *testifying* [2]Lit., *were proceeding out of His mouth* [a]Matt. 13:55; Mark 6:3; John 6:42

23 [a]Matt. 4:13; Mark 1:21ff.; 2:1ff.; John 4:46ff.; Luke 4:35ff. [b]Luke 4:16; 2:39, 51; Mark 6:1

24 [a]Matt. 13:57; Mark 6:4; John 4:44

25 [a]1 Kin. 17:1; 18:1; James 5:17

26 [1]Gr., *Serepta* [a]1 Kin. 17:9 [b]Matt. 11:21

27 [a]2 Kin. 5:1-14

29 [a]Acts 7:58; Num. 15:35, Heb. 13:12

30 [a]John 10:39

31 [a]Luke 4:31-37: *Mark 1:21-28* [b]Matt. 4:13; Luke 4:23

32 [1]Lit., *word* [a]Matt. 7:28 [b]Luke 4:36; John 7:46

33 [1]Lit., *having a spirit*

34 [1]Or possibly, *Let us alone* [2]Lit., *Nazarene* [a]Matt. 8:29 [b]Mark 1:24

35 [a]Luke 4:39, 41; Matt. 8:26; Mark 4:39; Luke 8:24

36 [1]Or, *this word, that with authority . . . come out?*

sage? For [a]with authority and power He commands the unclean spirits, and they come out."
37 And [a]the report about Him was getting out into every
locality in the surrounding district.
38 [a]And He arose and *left* the synagogue, and entered
Simon's home. Now Simon's mother-in-law was [b]suffering
from a high fever; and they made request of Him on her
behalf.
39 And standing over her, He [a]rebuked the fever, and it
left her; and she immediately arose and *began* to [1]wait on
them.
40 [a]And while [b]the sun was setting, all who had any sick
with various diseases brought them to Him; and [c]laying His
hands on every one of them, He was [d]healing them.
41 And demons also were coming out of many, crying out
and saying, "You are [a]the Son of God!" And [b]rebuking them,
He would [c]not allow them to speak, because they knew Him to
be [1]the Christ.
42 [a]And when day came, He departed and went to a lonely place; and the multitudes were searching for Him, and
came to Him, and tried to keep Him from going away from
them.
43 But He said to them, "I must preach the kingdom of
God to the other cities also, [a]for I was sent for this purpose."
44 And He kept on preaching in the synagogues [a]of
[1]Judea.

[a]Chapter 5

NOW it came about that while the multitude were pressing
around Him and listening to the word of God, He was standing by [b]the lake of Gennesaret;
2 and He saw two boats lying at the edge of the lake; but
the fishermen had gotten out of them, and were washing their
nets.
3 And [a]He got into one of the boats, which was Simon's,
and asked him to put out a little way from the land. And He
sat down and *began* teaching the multitudes from the boat.
4 And when He had finished speaking, He said to Simon,
"Put out into the deep water and [a]let down your nets for a
catch."
5 And Simon answered and said, "[a]Master, we worked
hard all night and caught nothing, but at Your [1]bidding I will
let down the nets."
6 And when they had done this, they enclosed a great
quantity of fish; and their nets *began* to break;
7 and they signaled to their partners in the other boat,
for them to come and help them. And they came, and filled
both of the boats, so that they began to sink.
8 But when Simon Peter saw *that,* he fell down at Jesus'
[1]feet, saying, "Depart from me, for I am a sinful man, O
Lord!"
9 For amazement had seized him and all his companions
because of the catch of fish which they had taken;
10 and so also [1]James and John, sons of Zebedee, who

36 [a]Luke 4:32

37 [a]Luke 4:14

38 [a]Luke 4:38, 39: *Matt. 8:14-15; Mark 1:29-31* [b]Matt. 4:24

39 [1]Or, *serve* [a]Luke 4:35, 41

40 [a]Luke 4:40, 41: *Matt. 8:16-17; Mark 1:32-34* [b]Mark 1:32 [c]Mark 5:23 [d]Matt. 4:23

41 [1]I.e., the Messiah [a]Matt. 4:3 [b]Luke 4:35 [c]Mark 1:34; Matt. 8:4

42 [a]Luke 4:42, 43: *Mark 1:35-38*

43 [a]Mark 1:38

44 [1]I.e., the country of the Jews (including Galilee); some mss. read, *of Galilee* [a]Matt. 4:23

1 [a]Luke 5:1-11; Matt. 4:18-22; Mark 1:16-20; John 1:40-42 [b]Num. 34:11; Deut. 3:17; Josh. 12:3; 13:27; Matt. 4:18

3 [a]Matt. 13:2; Mark 4:1

4 [a]John 21:6

5 [1]Or, *word* [a]Gr. as in Luke 8:24; 9:33, 49; 17:13

8 [1]Lit., *knees*

10 [1]Or, *Jacob*

were partners with Simon. And Jesus said to Simon, "[a]Do not
fear, from now on you will be [b]catching men."
11 And when they had brought their boats to land, [a]they
left everything and followed Him.
12 [a]And it came about that while He was in one of the
cities, behold, *there was* a man full of leprosy; and when he
saw Jesus, he fell on his face and implored Him, saying, "Lord,
if You are willing, You can make me clean."
13 And He stretched out His hand, and touched him,
saying, "I am willing; be cleansed." And immediately the leprosy left him.
14 And He ordered him to tell no one, "But go and show
yourself to the priest, and make an offering for your cleansing,
just as Moses commanded, for a testimony to them."
15 But [a]the news about Him was spreading even farther,
and great multitudes were gathering to hear *Him* and to be
healed of their sicknesses.
16 But He Himself would *often* slip away [1]to the [2]wilder-
ness and [a]pray.
17 And it came about [1]one day that He was teaching; and
[a]there were *some* Pharisees and [b]teachers of the law sitting
there, who had [c]come from every village of Galilee and Judea
and *from* Jerusalem; and [d]the power of the Lord was *present*
for Him to perform healing.
18 [a]And behold, *some* men *were* carrying on a [1]bed a man
who was paralyzed; and they were trying to bring him in, and
to set him down in front of Him.
19 And not finding any *way* to bring him in because of the
crowd, they went up on [a]the roof and let him down [b]through
the tiles with his stretcher, right in the center, in front of Jesus.
20 And seeing their faith, He said, "[1]Friend, [a]your sins are
forgiven you."
21 And the scribes and the Pharisees [a]began to reason,
saying, "Who is this *man* who speaks blasphemies? [b]Who can
forgive sins, but God alone?"
22 But Jesus, [1]aware of their reasonings, answered and said
to them, "Why are you reasoning in your hearts?
23 "Which is easier, to say, 'Your sins have been forgiven
you,' or to say, 'Rise and walk'?
24 "But in order that you may know that the Son of Man
has authority on earth to forgive sins"—He said to the [a]paralyt-
ic, "I say to you, rise, and take up your stretcher and go
home."
25 And at once he rose up before them, and took up what
he had been lying on, and went home, [a]glorifying God.
26 And they were all seized with astonishment and *began*
[a]glorifying God; and they were filled [b]with fear, saying, "We
have seen remarkable things today."
27 [a]And after that He went out, and noticed a [1]tax-
gatherer named [b]Levi, sitting in the tax office, and He said to
him, "Follow Me."
28 And he [a]left everything behind, and rose up and *began*
to follow Him.
29 And [a]Levi gave a big [1]reception for Him in his house;
and there was a great crowd of [b]tax-gatherers and other *people*
who were reclining *at table* with them.

10 [a]Matt. 14:27 [b]2 Tim. 2:26

11 [a]Matt. 4:20, 22; Mark 1:18, 20; Luke 5:28; Matt. 19:29

12 [a]Luke 5:12-14: *Matt. 8:2-4; Mark 1:40-44*

15 [a]Matt. 9:26

16 [1]Lit., *in* [2]Or, *lonely places*
[a]Matt. 14:23; Mark 1:35; Luke 6:12

17 [1]Lit., *on one of the days*
[a]Matt. 15:1 [b]Luke 2:46 [c]Mark 1:45 [d]Mark 5:30; Luke 6:19; 8:46

18 [1]Here, *stretcher*
[a]Luke 5:18-26: *Matt. 9:2-8; Mark 2:3-12*

19 [a]Matt. 24:17 [b]Mark 2:4

20 [1]Lit., *man*
[a]Matt. 9:2

21 [a]Luke 3:8 [b]Is. 43:25

22 [1]Or, *perceiving*

24 [a]Matt. 4:24

25 [a]Matt. 9:8

26 [a]Matt. 9:8 [b]Luke 7:16; 1:65

27 [1]Publicans who collected Roman taxes for profit
[a]Luke 5:27-39: *Matt. 9:9-17; Mark 2:14-22* [b]Matt. 9:9

28 [a]Luke 5:11

29 [1]Or, *banquet*
[a]Matt. 9:9 [b]Luke 15:1

30 And the Pharisees and [a]their scribes *began* grumbling
at His disciples, saying, "Why do you eat and drink with the
tax-gatherers and sinners?"
31 And Jesus answered and said to them, "[a]*It is* not those
who are well who need a physician, but those who are sick.
32 "I have not come to call righteous men but sinners to
repentance."
33 And they said to Him, "[a]The disciples of John often
fast and offer prayers; the *disciples* of the Pharisees also do
[1]the same; but Yours eat and drink."
34 And Jesus said to them, "You cannot make the [1]attend-
ants of the bridegroom fast while the bridegroom is with
them, can you?
35 "[a]But *the* days will come; and when the bridegroom is
taken away from them, then they will fast in those days."
36 And He was also telling them a parable: "No one tears
a piece from a new [1]garment and puts it on an old [1]garment;
otherwise he will both tear the new, and the piece from the
new will not match the old.
37 "And no one puts new wine into old [1]wineskins; otherwise the new wine will burst the [1]skins, and it will be spilled
out, and the [1]skins will be ruined.
38 "But new wine must be put into fresh wineskins.
39 "And no one, after drinking old *wine* wishes for new; for
he says, 'The old is good *enough.*' "

Chapter 6

[a]NOW it came about that on a *certain* [1]Sabbath He was
passing through *some* grainfields; and His disciples [b]were picking and eating the heads *of wheat,* rubbing them in their
hands.
2 But some of the Pharisees said, "Why do you do what
[a]is not lawful on the Sabbath?"
3 And Jesus answering them said, "Have you not even
read [a]what David did when he was hungry, he and those who
were with him,
4 how he entered the house of God, and took and ate the
[1]consecrated bread which is not lawful for any to eat except
the priests alone, and gave it to his companions?"
5 And He was saying to them, "The Son of Man is lord
of the Sabbath."
6 [a]And it came about [b]on another Sabbath, that He entered [c]the synagogue and was teaching; and there was a man
there [1]whose right hand was withered.
7 And the scribes and the Pharisees [a]were watching Him
closely, *to see* if He healed on the Sabbath; in order that they
might find *reason* to accuse Him.
8 But He [a]knew [1]what they were thinking, and He said to
the man with the withered hand, "Arise and [2]come forward!"
And he arose and [3]came forward.
9 And Jesus said to them, "I ask you, is it lawful on the
Sabbath to do good, or [1]to do evil, to save a life, or to destroy
it?"

30 [a]Mark 2:16; Acts 23:9

31 [a]Matt. 9:12, 13; Mark 2:17

33 [1]Or, *likewise* [a]Matt. 9:14; Mark 2:18

34 [1]Lit., *sons of the bridalchamber*

35 [a]Matt. 9:15; Mark 2:20; Luke 17:22

36 [1]Or, *cloak*

37 [1]I.e., skins used as bottles

1 [1]Many mss. read, *the second-first Sabbath;* i.e., the second Sabbath after the first [a]Luke 5:1-5: *Matt. 12:1-8; Mark 2:23-28* [b]Deut. 23:25

2 [a]Matt. 12:2

3 [a]1 Sam. 21:6

4 [1]Or, *showbread,* lit., *loaves of presentation*

6 [1]Lit., *and his* [a]Luke 5:6-11: *Matt. 12:9-14; Mark 3:1-6* [b]Luke 6:1 [c]Matt. 4:23

7 [a]Mark 3:2

8 [1]Lit., *their thoughts* [2]Lit., *stand* or *stood into the midst* [3]Lit., *stood* [a]Matt. 9:4

9 [1]Or, *to harm*

10 And after [a]looking around at them all, He said to him,
"Stretch out your hand!" And he did *so;* and his hand was
completely restored.
11 But they themselves were filled with [1]rage, and discussed together what they might do to Jesus.
12 And it was [1]at this time that He went off to [a]the mountain to [b]pray, and He spent the whole night in prayer to God.
13 And when day came, [a]He called His disciples to Him;
and chose twelve of them, whom He also named as [b]apostles:
14 Simon, whom He also named Peter, and Andrew his
brother; [1]James and John; Philip and Bartholomew;
15 [a]Matthew and Thomas; James *the son* of Alphaeus,
and Simon who was called the Zealot;
16 Judas *the son* of James, and Judas Iscariot, who became
a traitor.
17 And He [a]descended with them, and stood on a level
place; and *there was* [b]a great multitude of His disciples, and a
great throng of people from all Judea and Jerusalem and the
coastal region of [c]Tyre and Sidon,
18 [1]who had come to hear Him, and to be healed of their
diseases; and those who were troubled with unclean spirits
were being cured.
19 And all the multitude were trying to [a]touch Him, for
[b]power was coming from Him and healing *them* all.
20 And turning His gaze on His disciples, He *began* to say,
"[a]Blessed *are* you *who are* poor, for [b]yours is the kingdom of
God.
21 "Blessed *are* you who hunger now, for you shall be satisfied. Blessed *are* you who weep now, for you shall laugh.
22 "Blessed are you when men hate you, and [a]ostracize you,
and heap insults upon you, and spurn your name as evil, for
the sake of the Son of Man.
23 "Be glad in that day, and [a]leap *for joy,* for behold, your
reward is great in heaven; for in the same way their fathers
used to [1]treat the prophets.
24 "But woe to [a]you who are rich, for [b]you are receiving
your comfort in full.
25 "Woe to you who are [1]well-fed now, for you shall be
hungry. Woe *to you* who laugh now, for you shall mourn and
weep.
26 "Woe *to you* when all men speak well of you, for in the
same way their fathers used to [1]treat the [a]false prophets.
27 "But I say to you who hear, [a]love your enemies, do good
to those who hate you,
28 bless those who curse you, [a]pray for those who [1]mis-
treat you.
29 "[a]Whoever hits you on the cheek, offer him the other
also; and whoever takes away your [1]coat, do not withhold your
[2]shirt from him either.
30 "Give to everyone who asks of you, and whoever takes
away what is yours, do not demand it back.
31 "[a]And just as you want men to [1]treat you, [1]treat them in
the same way.
32 "And [a]if you love those who love you, what credit is *that*
to you? For even sinners love those who love them.

10 [a]Mark 3:5

11 [1]Lit., *folly*

12 [1]Lit., *in these days* [a]Matt. 5:1 [b]Matt. 14:23; Luke 9:28; 9:18; 5:16

13 [a]Luke 6:13-16: *Matt. 10:2-4; Mark 3:16-19; Acts 1:13* [b]Mark 6:30

14 [1]Here and in verses 15 and 16, Gr., *Jacob*

15 [a]Matt. 9:9

17 [a]Luke 6:12 [b]Matt 4:25; Mark 3:7, 8 [c]Matt. 11:21

18 [1]Most English versions begin verse 18 with, *and those who*

19 [a]Mark 3:10; Matt. 9:21; 14:36 [b]Luke 5:17

20 [a]Luke 6:20-23; Matt. 5:3-12 [b]Matt. 5:3

22 [a]John 9:22; 16:2

23 [1]Lit., *do to* [a]Mal. 4

24 [a]James 5:1; Luke 16:25 [b]Matt. 6:2

25 [1]Lit., *having been filled*

26 [1]Lit., *do to* [a]Matt. 7:15

27 [a]Matt. 5:44; Luke 6:35

28 [1]Or, *revile* [a]Matt. 5:44; Luke 6:35

29 [1]Or, *cloak,* or, outer garment [2]Or, *tunic,* or, garment worn next to body [a]Luke 6:29, 30: *Matt. 5:39-42*

31 [1]Or, *do to* [a]Matt. 7:12

32 [a]Matt. 5:46

33 "And if you do good to those who do good to you, what
credit is *that* to you? For even sinners do the same thing.
34 "[a]And if you lend to those from whom you expect to
receive, what credit is *that* to you? Even sinners lend to sinners, in order to receive back the same *amount*.
35 "But [a]love your enemies, and do good, and lend, [1]expect-
ing nothing in return; and your reward will be great, and you
will be [b]sons of [c]the Most High; for He Himself is kind to
ungrateful and evil *men*.
36 "[1]Be merciful, just as your Father is merciful.
37 "[a]And [1]do not pass judgment and you will not be
judged; and do not condemn, and you shall not be condemned; [2b]pardon, and you will be pardoned.
38 "Give, and it will be given to you; [a]good measure,
pressed down, shaken together, running over, they will pour
[b]into your lap. For whatever measure you deal out *to others*, it
will be dealt to you in return."
39 And He also spoke a parable to them: "[a]A blind man
cannot guide a blind man, can he? Will they not both fall into
a pit?
40 "[a]A [1]pupil is not above his teacher; but everyone, after
he has been fully trained, will [2]be like his teacher.
41 "And why do you look at the speck that is in your brother's eye, but do not notice the log that is in your own eye?
42 "Or how can you say to your brother, 'Brother, let me
take out the speck that is in your eye,' when you yourself do
not see the log that is in your own eye? You hypocrite, first
take the log out of your own eye, and then you will see clearly
to take out the speck that is in your brother's eye.
43 "[a]For there is no good tree which produces bad fruit; nor
[1]on the other hand, a bad tree which produces good fruit.
44 "[a]For each tree is known by its own fruit. For men do
not gather figs from thorns, nor do they pick grapes from a
briar bush.
45 "[a]The good man out of the good [1]treasure of his heart
brings forth what is good; and the evil *man* out of the evil
[1]*treasure* brings forth what is evil; [b]for his mouth speaks from
[2]that which fills his heart.
46 "And [a]why do you call Me, 'Lord, Lord,' and do not do
what I say?
47 "[a]Everyone who comes to Me, and hears My words, and
[1]acts upon them, I will show you whom he is like:
48 he is like a man building a house, who [1]dug deep and
laid a foundation upon the rock; and when a flood arose, the
river burst against that house and could not shake it, because it
had been well built.
49 "But the one who has heard, and has not acted *accordingly*, is like a man who built a house upon the ground without
any foundation; and the river burst against it and immediately
it collapsed, and the ruin of that house was great."

CHAPTER 7

[a]WHEN He had completed all His discourse in the hearing
of the people, [b]He went to Capernaum.

34 [a]Matt. 5:42

35 [1]Or, *not despairing at all* [a]Luke 6:27 [b]Matt. 5:9 [c]Luke 1:32

36 [1]Or, *become*

37 [1]Lit., *do not judge* [2]Lit., *release* [a]Luke 6:37-42: *Matt. 7:1-5* [b]Luke 23:16; Acts 3:13; Matt. 6:14

38 [a]Mark 4:24 [b]Ps. 79:12; Is. 65:6, 7; Jer. 32:18

39 [a]Matt. 15:14

40 [1]Or, *disciple* [2]Or, *reach his teacher's level* [a]Matt. 10:24

43 [1]Lit., *again* [a]Luke 6:43, 44: *Matt. 7:16, 18, 20*

44 [a]Matt. 7:16

45 [1]Or, *treasury, storehouse* [2]Lit., *the abundance of* [a]Matt. 12:35 [b]Matt. 12:34

46 [a]Matt. 7:21; Mal. 1:6

47 [1]Lit., *does* [a]Luke 6:47-49; *Matt. 7:24-27*

48 [1]Lit., *dug and went deep*

1 [a]Matt. 7:28 [b]Luke 7:1-10: *Matt. 8:5-13*

2 And a certain centurion's slave, [1]who was highly regarded by him, was sick and about to die.
3 And when he heard about Jesus, [a]he sent some [1]Jewish
elders asking Him to come and [2]save the life of his slave.
4 And when they had come to Jesus, they earnestly entreated Him, saying, "He is worthy for You to grant this to
him;
5 for he loves our nation, and it was he who built us our
synagogue."
6 Now Jesus *started* on His way with them; and when He
was already not far from the house, the centurion sent friends,
saying to Him, "[1]Lord, do not trouble Yourself further, for I
am not fit for You to come under my roof;
7 for this reason I did not even consider myself worthy to
come to You, but just [1]say the word, and my [2]servant will be
healed.
8 "For indeed, I am a man under authority, with soldiers
under me; and I say to this one, 'Go!' and he goes; and to
another, 'Come!' and he comes; and to my slave, 'Do this!' and
he does it."
9 And when Jesus heard this, He marveled at him, and
turned and said to the multitude that was following Him, "I
say to you, [a]not even in Israel have I found such great faith."
10 And when those who had been sent returned to the
house, they found the slave in good health.
11 And it came about [1]soon afterwards, that He went to a
city called Nain; and His disciples were going along with Him,
[2]accompanied by a large multitude.
12 Now as He approached the gate of the city, behold, [1]a
dead man was being carried out, the [2]only son of his mother,
and she was a widow; and a sizeable crowd from the city was
with her.
13 And when [a]the Lord saw her, He felt compassion for
her, and said to her, "[1]Do not weep."
14 And He came up and touched the coffin; and the bearers came to a halt. And He said, "Young man, I say to you,
arise!"
15 And the [1]dead man sat up, and began to speak. And
Jesus gave him back to his mother.
16 And [a]fear gripped them all, and they *began* [b]glorifying
God, saying, "A great [c]prophet has arisen among us!" and,
"God has [1]visited His people!"
17 [a]And this report concerning Him went out all over Judea, and in all the surrounding district.
18 [a]And the disciples of John reported to him about all
these things.
19 And summoning [1]two of his disciples, John sent them
to [a]the Lord, saying, "Are You the One who is coming, or do
we look for someone [2]else?"
20 And when the men had come to Him, they said, "John
the Baptist has sent us to You, saying, 'Are You the One who is
coming, or do we look for someone else?' "
21 At that [1]very time He [a]cured many *people* of diseases
and [b]afflictions and evil spirits; and He granted sight to many
who were blind.
22 And He answered and said to them, "Go and report to

2 [1]Lit., *to whom he was honorable*

3 [1]Lit., *elders of the Jews* [2]Lit., *bring safely through, rescue* [a]Matt. 8:5

6 [1]Or, *Sir*

7 [1]Lit., *speak with a word* [2]Or, *boy*

9 [a]Matt. 8:10; Luke 7:50

11 [1]Some mss read, *on the next day* [2]Lit., *and*

12 [1]Lit., *one who had died* [2]Or, *only begotten*

13 [1]Or, *stop weeping* [a]Luke 7:19; 10:1; 11:1, 39; 12:42; 13:15; 17:5, 6; 18:6; 19:8; 22:61; 24:34; John 4:1; 6:23; 11:2

15 [1]Or, *corpse*

16 [1]Or, *cared for* [a]Luke 5:26 [b]Matt. 9:8 [c]Matt. 21:11; Luke 7:39

17 [a]Matt. 9:26

18 [a]Luke 7:18-35: *Matt. 11:2-19*

19 [1]Lit., *a certain two* [2]Some early mss. read, *one who is different* [a]Luke 7:13; 10:1; 11:1, 39; 12:42; 13:15; 17:5, 6; 18:6; 19:8; 22:61; 24:34; John 4:1; 6:23; 11:2

21 [1]Lit., *hour* [a]Matt. 4:23 [b]Mark 3:10

John what you have seen and heard: *the* [a]BLIND RECEIVE SIGHT,
the lame walk, *the* lepers are cleansed, and *the* deaf hear, *the*
dead are raised up, *the* [a]POOR HAVE THE GOSPEL PREACHED TO
THEM.
23 "And blessed is he [1]who keeps from stumbling over
Me."
24 And when the messengers of John had left, He began
to speak to the multitudes about John, "What did you go out
into the wilderness to look at? A reed shaken by the wind?
25 "[1]But what did you go out to see? A man dressed in soft
[2]clothing? Behold, those who are splendidly clothed and live in
luxury are *found* in royal palaces.
26 "But what did you go out to see? A prophet? Yes, I say
to you, and one who is more than a prophet.
27 "This is the one about whom it [1]is written,
'[a]BEHOLD, I SEND MY MESSENGER BEFORE YOUR FACE,
WHO WILL PREPARE YOUR WAY BEFORE YOU.'
28 "I say to you, among those born of women, there is no
one greater than John; yet he who is [1]least in the kingdom of
God is greater than he."
29 And when all the people and the [1]tax-gatherers heard
this, they [2]acknowledged [a]God's justice, [b]having been baptized
with [c]the baptism of John.
30 But the Pharisees and the [1a]lawyers rejected God's purpose for themselves, not having been baptized by [2]John.
31 "To what then shall I compare the men of this generation, and what are they like?
32 "They are like children who sit in the market place and
call to one another; and they say, 'We played the flute for you,
and you did not dance; we sang a dirge, and you did not weep.'
33 "For John the Baptist has come [a]eating no bread and
drinking no wine; and you say, 'He has a demon!'
34 "The Son of Man has come eating and drinking; and
you say, 'Behold, a gluttonous man, and a [1]drunkard, a friend
of [2]tax-gatherers and sinners!'
35 "[1]Yet wisdom [a]is vindicated by all her children."
36 Now one of the Pharisees was requesting Him to [1]dine
with him. And He entered the Pharisee's house, and reclined
at table.
37 [a]And behold, there was a woman in the city who was a
[1]sinner; and when she learned that He was reclining *at table* in
the Pharisee's house, she brought an alabaster vial of perfume,
38 and standing behind *Him* at His feet, weeping, she
began to wet His feet with her tears, and kept wiping them
with the hair of her head, and kissing His feet, and anointing
them with the perfume.
39 Now when the Pharisee who had invited Him saw this,
he said [1]to himself, "If this man were [2a]a prophet He would
know who and what sort of person this woman is who is touching Him, that she is a [3]sinner."
40 And Jesus answered and said to him, "Simon, I have
something to say to you." And he [1]replied, "Say it, Teacher."
41 "A certain money-lender had two debtors: one owed five
hundred [1a]denarii, and the other fifty.
42 "When they [a]were unable to repay, he graciously for-

22 [a]Is. 61:1

23 [1]Lit., *whoever*

25 [1]Or, *Well then, what* [2]Or, *garments*

27 [1]Lit., *has been written* [a]Mal. 3:1; Matt. 11:10; Mark 1:2

28 [1]Lit., *less*

29 [1]Publicans who collected Roman taxes on commission [2]Or, *justified God* [a]Luke 7:35 [b]Luke 3:12; Matt. 21:32 [c]Acts 18:25; 19:3

30 [1]I.e., experts on the Mosaic Law [2]Lit., *him* [a]Matt. 22:35

33 [a]Luke 1:15

34 [1]Or, *wine-drinker* [2]Publicans who collected Roman taxes on commission

35 [1]Lit., *And* [a]Luke 7:29

36 [1]Lit., *eat*

37 [1]I.e., an immoral woman [a]Luke 7:37-39: Matt 26:6-13; Mark 14:3-9; John 12:1-8

39 [1]Lit., *to himself, saying* [2]Some mss. read, *the prophet* [3]I.e., an immoral woman [a]Luke 7:16; John 4:19

40 [1]Lit., *says*

41 [1]The denarius was worth 18 cents in silver, equivalent to a day's wage [a]Matt. 18:28; Mark 6:37

42 [a]Matt. 18:25

gave them both. Which of them therefore will love him
more?"
43 Simon answered and said, "I suppose the one whom he
forgave more." And He said to him, "You have judged
correctly."
44 And turning toward the woman, He said to Simon,
"Do you see this woman? I entered your house; you [a]gave Me
no water for My feet, but she has wet My feet with her tears,
and wiped them with her hair.
45 "You [a]gave Me no kiss; but she, since the time I came in,
[1]has not ceased to kiss My feet.
46 "[a]You did not anoint My head with oil, but she anointed
My feet with perfume.
47 "For this reason I say to you, her sins, which are many,
have been forgiven, for she loved much, but he who is forgiven
little, loves little."
48 And He said to her, "[a]Your sins have been forgiven."
49 And those who were reclining *at table* with Him began
to say [1]to themselves, "Who is this *man* who even forgives
sins?"
50 And He said to the woman, "[a]Your faith has saved you;
[b]go in peace."

Chapter 8

AND it came about soon afterwards, that He *began* going
about from one city and village to another, [a]proclaiming and
preaching the kingdom of God; and the twelve were with Him,
2 and *also* [a]some women who had been healed of evil
spirits and sicknesses: [a]Mary who was called Magdalene, from
whom seven demons had gone out,
3 and Joanna the wife of Chuza, [a]Herod's [b]steward, and
Susanna, and many others who were contributing to their support out of their private means.
4 [a]And when a great multitude were coming together,
and those from the various cities were journeying to Him, He
spoke by way of a parable:
5 "The sower went out to sow his seed; and as he sowed,
some fell beside the road; and it was trampled under foot, and
the birds of the [1]air devoured it.
6 "And other *seed* fell on rocky *soil*, and as soon as it grew
up, it withered away, because it had no moisture.
7 "And other *seed* fell among the thorns; and the thorns
grew up with it, and choked it out.
8 "And other *seed* fell into the good ground, and grew up,
and produced a crop a hundred times as great." As He said
these things, He would call out, "[a]He who has ears to hear, let
him hear."
9 [a]And His disciples *began* questioning Him as to what
this parable might be.
10 And He said, "[a]To you it is granted to know the mysteries of the kingdom of God, but to the rest in parables; in order
that [b]SEEING THEY MAY NOT SEE, AND HEARING THEY MAY NOT
UNDERSTAND.
11 "Now the parable is this: [a]the seed is the word of God.
12 "And those beside the road are those who have heard;

44 [a]Gen. 18:4; 19:2; 43:24; Judg. 19:21; 1 Tim. 5:10

45 [1]Lit., *was not ceasing* [a]2 Sam. 15:5

46 [a]Ps. 23:5; Eccles. 9:8; 2 Sam. 12:20; Dan. 10:3

48 [a]Matt. 9:2

49 [1]Or, *among*

50 [a]Matt. 9:22 [b]Luke 8:48; Mark 5:34

1 [a]Matt. 4:23

2 [a]Matt. 27:55f.; Luke 23:49

3 [a]Matt. 14:1 [b]Matt. 20:8

4 [a]Luke 8:4-8: *Matt. 13:2-9; Mark 4:1-9*

5 [1]Lit., *heaven*

8 [a]Matt. 11:15

9 [a]Luke 8:9-15: *Matt. 13:10-23; Mark 4:10-20*

10 [a]Matt. 13:11 [b]Is. 6:9; Matt. 13:14

11 [a]1 Pet. 1:23

then the devil comes and takes away the word from their heart,
so that they may not believe and be saved.
13 "And those on the rocky *soil are* those who, when they
hear, receive the word with joy; and these have no *firm* root;
[1]they believe for a while, and in time of temptation fall away.
14 "And the *seed* which fell among the thorns, these are the
ones who have heard, and as they go on their way they are
choked with worries and riches and pleasures of *this* life, and
bring no fruit to maturity.
15 "And the *seed* in the good ground, these are the ones
who have heard the word in an honest and good heart, and
hold it fast, and bear fruit with [1]perseverance.
16 "Now [a]no one after lighting a lamp covers it over with a
container, or puts it under a bed; but he puts it on a lampstand, in order that those who come in may see the light.
17 "[a]For nothing is hidden that shall not become evident,
nor *anything* secret that shall not be known and come to light.
18 "Therefore take care how you listen; [a]for whoever has,
to him shall *more* be given; and whoever does not have, even
what he [1]thinks he has shall be taken away from him."
19 [a]And His mother came to Him and *His* brothers *also,*
and they were unable to get to Him because of the crowd.
20 And it was reported to Him, "Your mother and Your
brothers are standing outside, wishing to see You."
21 But He answered and said to them, "My mother and
My brothers are these [a]who hear the word of God and do it."
22 [a]Now it came about on one of *those* days, that He and
His disciples got into a boat, and He said to them, "Let us go
over to the other side of [b]the lake." And they launched out.
23 But as they were sailing along He fell asleep; and a
fierce gale of wind descended upon [a]the lake, and they *began*
to be swamped and to be in danger.
24 And they came to Him, and woke Him up, saying,
"[a]Master, Master, we are perishing!" And being aroused, He
[b]rebuked the wind and the surging waves, and they stopped,
and [1]it became calm.
25 And He said to them, "Where is your faith?" And they
were fearful and amazed, saying to one another, "Who then is
this, that He commands even the winds and the water, and
they obey Him?"
26 [a]And they sailed to the country of the [1]Gerasenes,
which is opposite Galilee.
27 And when He had come out onto the land, a certain
man from the city met Him who was possessed with demons;
and who had not put on any clothing for a long time, and was
not living in a house, but in the tombs.
28 And seeing Jesus, he cried out and fell before Him, and
said in a loud voice, "[a]What do I have to do with You, Jesus,
Son of [b]the Most High God? I beg You, do not torment me."
29 For He [1]had been commanding the unclean spirit to
come out of the man. For it had seized him many times; and
he was bound with chains and shackles and kept under guard;
and *yet* he would burst his fetters and be driven by the demon
into the deserts.
30 And Jesus asked him, "What is your name?" And he
said, "[a]Legion"; for many demons had entered him.

13 [1]Lit., *who believe*

15 [1]Or, *steadfastness*

16 [a]Matt. 5:15; Mark 4:21; Luke 11:33

17 [a]Luke 12:2; Matt. 10:26; Mark 4:22

18 [1]Or, *seems to have* [a]Matt. 13:12; Luke 19:26

19 [a]Luke 8:19-21: *Matt. 12:46-50; Mark 3:31-35*

21 [a]Luke 11:28

22 [a]Luke 8:22-25: *Matt. 8:23-27; Mark 4:36-41* [b]Luke 8:23; 5:1f.

23 [a]Luke 8:22; 5:1f.

24 [1]Lit., *a calm occurred* [a]Luke 5:5 [b]Luke 4:39

26 [1]Other mss. read, *Gergesenes*, or *Gadarenes* [a]Luke 8:26-37: *Matt. 8:28-34; Mark 5:1-17*

28 [a]Matt. 8:29 [b]Mark 5:7

29 [1]Or, *was commanding*

30 [a]Matt. 26:53

31 And they were entreating Him not to command them
to depart into [a]the abyss.
32 Now there was a herd of many swine feeding there on
the mountain; and *the demons* entreated Him to permit them
to enter [1]the swine. And He gave them permission.
33 And the demons came out from the man and entered
the swine; and the herd rushed down the steep bank into [a]the
lake, and were drowned.
34 And when those who tended them saw what had happened, they ran away and reported it in the city and *out* in the
country.
35 And *the people* went out to see what had happened;
and they came to Jesus, and found the man from whom the
demons had gone out, sitting down [a]at the feet of Jesus,
clothed and in his right mind; and they became frightened.
36 And those who had seen it reported to them how the
man who was [a]demon-possessed had been [1]made well.
37 And all the people of the country of the [1]Gerasenes
and the surrounding district asked Him to depart from them;
for they were gripped with great fear; and He got into a boat,
and returned.
38 [a]But the man from whom the demons had gone out
was begging Him that he might [1]accompany Him; but He sent
him away, saying,
39 "Return to your house and describe what great things
God has done for you." And he departed, proclaiming throughout the whole city what great things Jesus had done for him.
40 [a]And as Jesus returned, the multitude welcomed Him,
for they had all been waiting for Him.
41 [a]And behold, there came a man named Jairus, and he
was an [1b]official of the synagogue; and he fell at Jesus' feet,
and *began* to entreat Him to come to his house;
42 for he had an [1]only daughter, about twelve years old,
and she was dying. But as He went, the multitudes were pressing against Him.
43 And a woman who had a hemorrhage for twelve years,
[1]and could not be healed by anyone,
44 came up behind Him, and touched the fringe of His
[1]cloak; and immediately her hemorrhage stopped.
45 And Jesus said, "Who is the one who touched Me?"
And while they were all denying it, Peter said,[1] "[a]Master, the
multitudes are crowding and pressing upon You."
46 But Jesus said, "Someone did touch Me, for I was
aware that [a]power had gone out of Me."
47 And when the woman saw that she had not escaped
notice, she came trembling and fell down before Him, and
declared in the presence of all the people the reason why she
had touched Him, and how she had been immediately healed.
48 And He said to her, "Daughter, [a]your faith has [1]made
you well; [b]go in peace."
49 While He was still speaking, someone *came from *the
house of* [a]the synagogue official, saying, "Your daughter has
died; do not trouble the Teacher any more."
50 But when Jesus heard *this*, He answered him, "[a]Do not
be afraid *any longer;* only believe, and she shall be [1]made
well."

31 [a]Rom. 10:7; Rev. 9:1f., 11; 11:7; 17:8; 20:1, 3

32 [1]Lit., *them*

33 [a]Luke 8:22; 5:1f.

35 [a]Luke 10:39

36 [1]Or, *saved* [a]Matt. 4:24

37 [1]Other mss. read, *Gergesenes* or *Gadarenes*

38 [1]Lit., *be with* [a]Luke 8:38, 39: *Mark 5:18-20*

40 [a]Matt. 9:1; Mark 5:21

41 [1]Lit., *ruler* [a]Luke 8:41-56: *Matt. 9:18-26; Mark 5:22-43* [b]Luke 8:49; Mark 5:22

42 [1]Or, *only begotten*

43 [1]Some mss. add, *who had spent all her living upon physicians*

44 [1]Or, *outer garment*

45 [1]Some early mss. add, *and those with him* [a]Luke 5:5

46 [a]Luke 5:17

48 [1]Lit., *saved you* [a]Matt. 9:22 [b]Luke 7:50; Mark 5:34

49 [a]Luke 8:41

50 [1]Or, *saved* [a]Mark 5:36

51 And when He had come to the house, He did not allow
anyone to enter with Him, except Peter, John and James, and
the girl's father and mother.
52 Now they were all weeping and [a]lamenting for her; but
He said, "Stop weeping, for she has not died, but [b]is asleep."
53 And they *began* laughing at Him, knowing that she had
died.
54 He, however, took her by the hand and called, saying,
"Child, arise!"
55 And her spirit returned, and she rose up immediately;
and He gave orders for *something* to be given her to eat.
56 And her parents were amazed; but He [a]instructed them
to tell no one what had happened.

[a] Chapter 9

AND He called the twelve together, and gave them power
and authority over all the demons, and to heal diseases.
2 And He sent them out to [a]proclaim the kingdom of
God, and [1]to perform healing.
3 And He said to them, "[a]Take nothing for *your* journey,
[b]neither a staff, nor a [1]bag, nor bread, nor money; and do not
even have [2]two tunics apiece.
4 "And whatever house you enter, stay there, and take
your leave from there.
5 "And as for those who do not receive you, when you
depart from that city, [a]shake off the dust from your feet as a
testimony against them."
6 And departing, they *began* going about [1]among the
villages, [a]preaching the gospel, and healing everywhere.
7 [a]Now [b]Herod the tetrarch heard of all that was happening; and he was greatly perplexed, because it was said by some
that [c]John had risen from the dead,
8 and by some that [a]Elijah had appeared, and by others,
that one of the prophets of old had risen again.
9 And Herod said, "I myself had John beheaded; but
who is this man about whom I hear such things?" And [a]he kept
trying to see Him.
10 [a]And when the [b]apostles returned, they gave an account to Him of all that they had done. [c]And taking them with
Him, He withdrew privately to a city called [d]Bethsaida.
11 But the multitudes were aware of this and followed
Him; and welcoming them, He *began* speaking to them about
the kingdom of God and curing those who had need of
healing.
12 And the day began to decline, and the twelve came and
said to Him, "Send the multitude away, that they may go into
the surrounding villages and countryside and find lodging and
get [1]something to eat; for here we are in a desolate place."
13 But He said to them, "You give them something to
eat!" And they said, "We have no more than five loaves and
two fish, unless perhaps we go and buy food for all these
people."
14 (For there were about five thousand men). And He said
to His disciples, "Have them recline *to eat* [a]in groups of about
fifty each."

52 [a]Luke 23:27; Matt. 11:17 [b]John 11:13

56 [a]Matt. 8:4

1 [a]Matt. 10:5; Mark 6:7

2 [1]Some mss. read, *to heal the sick* [a]Matt. 10:7

3 [1]Or, *knapsack*, or *beggar's bag* [2]Or, *inner garment* [a]Luke 9:3-5: *Matt. 10:9-15; Mark 6:8-11;* Luke 10:4-12; 22:35 [b]Matt. 10:10; Mark 6:8; Luke 22:35f.

5 [a]Acts 13:51; Luke 10:11

6 [1]Or, *from village to village* [a]Luke 8:1; Mark 6:12

7 [a]Luke 9:7-9: *Matt. 14:1, 2;* Mark 6:14f. [b]Matt. 14:1; Luke 3:1; 13:31; 23:7 [c]Matt. 14:2

8 [a]Matt. 16:14

9 [a]Luke 23:8

10 [a]Mark 6:30 [b]Mark 6:30 [c]Luke 9:10-17: *Matt. 14:13-21; Mark 6:32-44; John 6:5-13* [d]Matt. 11:21

12 [1]Lit., *provisions*

14 [a]Mark 6:39

15 And they did so, and had them all recline.
16 And He took the five loaves and the two fish, and
looking up to heaven, He blessed them, and broke *them*, and
kept giving *them* to the disciples to set before the multitude.
17 And they all ate and were satisfied; and that which was
left over to them of the broken pieces was picked up, twelve
[1a]baskets *full*.
18 [a]And it came about that while He was [b]praying alone,
the disciples were with Him, and He questioned them, saying,
"Who do the multitudes say that I am?"
19 And they answered and said, "John the Baptist; but
others *say*, Elijah; and others, that one of the prophets of old
has risen again."
20 And He said to them, "But who do you say that I am?"
And Peter answered and said, "[a]The [1]Christ of God."
21 But He [1a]warned them, and instructed *them* not to tell
this to anyone,
22 [a]saying, "[b]The Son of Man must suffer many things,
and be rejected by the elders and chief priests and scribes, and
be killed, and be raised up on the third day."
23 And He was saying to *them* all, "If anyone wishes to
come after Me, let him deny himself, and [a]take up his cross
daily, and follow Me.
24 "For [a]whoever wishes to save his [1]life shall lose it, but
whoever loses his [1]life for My sake, he is the one who will save
it.
25 "For what is a man profited if he gains the whole world,
and [a]loses or forfeits himself?
26 "[a]For whoever is ashamed of Me and My words, of him
will the Son of Man be ashamed when He comes in His glory,
and *the glory* of the Father and of the holy angels.
27 "But I tell you truly, [a]there are some of those standing
here who shall not taste death until they see the kingdom of
God."
28 [a]And some eight days after these sayings, it came about
that He took along [b]Peter and John and James, and [c]went up
to the mountain [d]to pray.
29 And while He was [a]praying, the appearance of His face
[b]became different, and His clothing *became* white *and*
[1]gleaming.
30 And behold, two men were talking with Him; and they
were Moses and Elijah,
31 who, appearing in [1]glory, were speaking of His [a]depar-
ture which He was about to accomplish at Jerusalem.
32 Now Peter and his companions [a]had been overcome
with sleep; but when they were fully awake, they saw His glory
and the two men standing with Him.
33 And it came about, as [1]these were parting from Him,
Peter said to Jesus, "[a]Master, it is good for us to be here; and
[b]let us make three [2]tabernacles: one for You, and one for
Moses, and one for Elijah"—[c]not realizing what he was saying.
34 And while he was saying this, a cloud [1]formed and
began to overshadow them; and they were afraid as they
entered the cloud.
35 And [a]a voice came out of the cloud, saying, "[b]This is
My Son, *My* Chosen One; listen to Him!"

17 [1]I.e., large-sized baskets [a]Matt. 14:20

18 [a]Luke 9:18-20: *Matt. 16:13-16; Mark 8:27-29* [b]Matt. 14:23; Luke 6:12; 9:28

20 [1]I.e., Messiah [a]John 6:68f.

21 [1]Or, *strictly admonished* [a]Matt. 16:20; Mark 8:30; Matt. 8:4

22 [a]Luke 9:22-27: *Matt. 16:21-28; Mark 8:31-9:1* [b]Matt. 16:21; Luke 9:44

23 [a]Matt. 10:38

24 [1]Gr., *soul-life* [a]Matt. 10:39

25 [a]Heb. 10:34 marg.

26 [a]Luke 12:9; Matt. 10:33

27 [a]Matt. 16:28

28 [a]Luke 9:28-36: *Matt. 17:1-8; Mark 9:2-8* [b]Matt. 17:1 [c]Matt. 5:1 [d]Luke 3:21; 5:16; 6:12; 9:18

29 [1]Lit., *flashing like lightning* [a]Luke 3:21; 5:16; 6:12; 9:18 [b]Mark 16:12

31 [1]Or, *splendor* [a]2 Pet. 1:15

32 [a]Matt. 26:43; Mark 14:40

33 [1]Lit., *they* [2]Or, *sacred tents* [a]Luke 5:5; 9:49 [b]Matt. 17:4; Mark 9:5 [c]Mark 9:6

34 [1]Or, *occurred*

35 [a]2 Pet. 1:17f. [b]Matt. 3:17; Luke 3:22

36 And when the voice [1]had spoken, Jesus was found
alone. And [a]they kept silent, and reported to no one in those
days any of the things which they had seen.
37 [a]And it came about on the next day, that when they
had come down from the mountain, a great multitude met
Him.
38 And behold, a man from the multitude shouted out,
saying, "Teacher, I beg You to look at my son, for he is my
[1]only *boy,*
39 and behold, a spirit seizes him, and he suddenly
screams, and it throws him into a convulsion with foaming *at*
the mouth, and as it mauls him, it scarcely leaves him.
40 "And I begged Your disciples to cast it out, and they
could not."
41 And Jesus answered and said, "O unbelieving and perverted generation, how long shall I be with you, and put up
with you? Bring your son here."
42 And while he was still approaching, the demon [1]dashed
him *to the ground,* and threw him into a violent convulsion.
But Jesus rebuked the unclean spirit, and healed the boy, and
gave him back to his father.
43 And they were all amazed at the [1a]greatness of God.
[b]**B**ut while everyone was marveling at all that He was doing,
He said to His disciples,
44 "Let these words sink into your ears; [a]for the Son of
Man is going to be [1]delivered into the hands of men."
45 But [a]they [1]did not understand this statement, and it
was concealed from them so that they might not perceive it;
and they were afraid to ask Him about this statement.
46 [a]And an argument [1]arose among them as to which of
them might be the greatest.
47 But Jesus, [a]knowing [1]what they were thinking in their
heart, took a child and stood him by His side,
48 and said to them, "[a]Whoever receives this child in My
name receives Me; and whoever receives Me receives Him who
sent Me; [b]for he who is [1]least among you, this is the one who is
great."
49 [a]And John answered and said, "[b]Master, we saw someone casting out demons in Your name; and we tried to
hinder him because he does not follow along with us."
50 But Jesus said to him, "Do not hinder *him;* [a]for he who
is not against you is [1]for you."
51 And it came about, when the days were approaching
for [a]His [1]ascension, that He resolutely set His face [b]to go to
Jerusalem;
52 and He sent messengers on ahead of Him. And they
went, and entered a village of the [a]Samaritans, to [1]make
arrangements for Him.
53 And they did not receive Him, [a]because [1]He was journeying with His face toward Jerusalem.
54 And when His disciples [a]James and John saw *this,* they
said, "Lord, do You want us to command fire to come down
from heaven and consume them[1]?"
55 But He turned and rebuked them.[1]
56 And they went on to another village.

36 [1]Lit., *occurred* [a]Matt. 17:9; Mark 9:9f.

37 [a]Luke 9:37-42: *Matt. 17:14-18; Mark 9:14-27*

38 [1]Or, *only begotten*

42 [1]Or, *tore him*

43 [1]Or, *majesty* [a]2 Pet. 1:16 [b]Luke 9:43-45: *Matt. 17:22f.; Mark 9:30-32*

44 [1]Or, *betrayed* [a]Luke 9:22

45 [1]Lit., *were not knowing* [a]Mark 9:32

46 [1]Lit., *entered in* [a]Luke 9:46-48: *Matt. 18:1-5; Mark 9:33-37*

47 [1]Lit., *the reasoning or argument* [a]Matt. 9:4

48 [1]Or, *lowliest* [a]Matt. 10:40 [b]Luke 22:26

49 [a]Luke 9:49, 50: *Mark 9:38-40* [b]Luke 5:5; 9:33

50 [1]Or, *on your side* [a]Matt. 12:30; Luke 11:23

51 [1]Lit., *taking up* [a]Mark 16:19 [b]Luke 13:22; 17:11; 18:31; 19:11, 28

52 [1]Or, *prepare* [a]Matt. 10:5; Luke 10:33; 17:16; John 4:4

53 [1]Lit., *His face was proceeding toward* [a]John 4:9

54 [1]Some mss. add, *as Elijah did* [a]Mark 3:17

55 [1]Later mss. add, *and said, "You do not know what kind of spirit you are of.*

56 *For the Son of Man did not come to destroy men's lives, but to save them."*

57 And [a]as they were going along the road, [b]someone said
to Him, "I will follow You wherever You go."
58 And Jesus said to him, "The foxes have holes, and the
birds of the [1]air *have* [2]nests, but [a]the Son of Man has nowhere
to lay His head."
59 And He said to another, "[a]Follow Me." But he said,
"[1]Permit me first to go and bury my father."
60 But He said to him, "Allow the dead to bury their own
dead; but as for you, go and [a]proclaim everywhere the kingdom of God."
61 And another also said, "I will follow You, Lord; but
[a]first permit me to say good-bye to those at home."
62 But Jesus said to him, "[a]No one, after putting his hand
to the plow and looking back, is fit for the kingdom of God."

Chapter 10

NOW after this [a]the Lord appointed [1]seventy [b]others, and
sent them [c]two and two ahead of Him to every city and place
where He Himself was going to come.
2 And He was saying to them, "[a]The harvest is plentiful,
but the laborers are few; therefore beseech the Lord of the
harvest to send out laborers into His harvest.
3 "Go your ways; [a]behold, I send you out as lambs in the
midst of wolves.
4 "[a]Carry no purse, no [1]bag, no shoes; and greet no one on
the way.
5 "And whatever house you enter, first say, 'Peace *be* to
this house.'
6 "And if a [1]man of peace is there, your peace will rest
upon him; but if not, it will return to you.
7 "And stay in [1]that house, eating and drinking [2]what they
give you; for [a]the laborer is worthy of his wages. Do not keep
moving from house to house.
8 "And whatever city you enter, and they receive you, [a]eat
what is set before you;
9 and heal those in it who are sick, and say to them, '[a]The
kingdom of God has come near to you.'
10 "But whatever city you enter and they do not receive
you, go out into its streets and say,
11 '[a]Even the dust of your city which clings to our feet, we
wipe off *in protest* against you; yet [1]be sure of this, that [b]the
kingdom of God has come near.'
12 "I say to you, [a]it will be more tolerable in that day for
[b]Sodom, than for that city.
13 "[a]Woe to you, [b]Chorazin! Woe to you, [b]Bethsaida! For
if the [1]miracles had been performed in [b]Tyre and Sidon which
occurred in you, they would have repented long ago, sitting in
[c]sackcloth and ashes.
14 "But it will be more tolerable for [a]Tyre and Sidon in the
judgment, than for you.
15 "And you, [a]Capernaum, will not be exalted to heaven,
will you? You will be brought down to [b]Hades!
16 "[a]The one who listens to you listens to Me, and [b]the one

57 [a]Luke 9:51 [b]Luke 9:57-60: *Matt. 8:19-22*

58 [1]Or, *sky* [2]Gr., *roosting-places* [a]Matt. 8:20

59 [1]Some mss. add, *Lord* [a]Matt. 8:22

60 [a]Matt. 4:23

61 [a]1 Kin. 19:20

62 [a]Phil. 3:13

1 [1]Some mss. read, *seventy-two* [a]Luke 7:13 [b]Luke 9:1f., 52 [c]Mark 6:7

2 [a]Matt. 9:37, 38; John 4:35

3 [a]Matt. 10:16

4 [1]Gr., *knapsack*, or *beggar's bag* [a]Luke 10:4-12; Matt. 10:9-14; Mark 6:8-11; Luke 9:3-5

6 [1]Lit., *son*

7 [1]Or, *the house itself* [2]Lit., *the things from them* [a]Matt. 10:10; 1 Cor. 9:14; 1 Tim. 5:18

8 [a]1 Cor. 10:27

9 [a]Matt. 3:2; 10:7; Luke 10:11

11 [1]Lit., *know* [a]Matt. 10:14; Mark 6:11; Luke 9:5 [b]Matt. 3:2; 10:7; Luke 10:9

12 [a]Matt. 10:15; 11:24 [b]Matt. 10:15

13 [1]Or, *works of power* [a]Luke 10:13-15: *Matt. 11:21-23* [b]Matt. 11:21 [c]Rev. 11:3

14 [a]Matt. 11:21

15 [a]Matt. 4:13 [b]Matt. 11:23

16 [a]Matt. 10:40; John 13:20; Gal. 4:14 [b]John 12:48; 1 Thess. 4:8

who rejects you rejects Me; and he who rejects Me rejects the
One who sent Me."
17 And the [1]seventy returned with joy, saying, "Lord, even
[a]the demons are subject to us in Your name."
18 And He said to them, "I was watching [a]Satan fall from
heaven like lightning.
19 "Behold, I have given you authority to [a]tread upon serpents and scorpions, and over all the power of the enemy, and
nothing shall injure you.
20 "Nevertheless do not rejoice in this, that the spirits are
subject to you, but rejoice that [a]your names are recorded in
heaven."
21 [a]At that very [1]time He rejoiced greatly in the Holy
Spirit, and said, "I [2]praise Thee, O Father, Lord of heaven and
earth, that Thou didst hide these things from *the* wise and
intelligent and didst reveal them to babes. Yes, Father, for
thus it was well-pleasing in Thy sight.
22 "All things have been handed over to Me by My Father,
and no one knows who the Son is except the Father, and who
the Father is except the Son, and anyone to whom the Son
wills to reveal *Him*."
23 [a]And turning to the disciples, He said privately,
"Blessed *are* the eyes which see the things you see,
24 for I say to you, that many prophets and kings wished
to see the things which you see, and did not see *them*, and to
hear the things which you hear, and did not hear *them*."
25 [a]And behold, a certain [1b]lawyer stood up and put Him
to the test, saying, "Teacher, what shall I do to inherit eternal
life?"
26 And He said to him, "What is written in the Law? How
[1]does it read to you?"
27 And he answered and said, "[a]YOU SHALL LOVE THE LORD
YOUR GOD WITH ALL YOUR HEART, AND WITH ALL YOUR SOUL,
AND WITH ALL YOUR STRENGTH, AND WITH ALL YOUR MIND; AND
YOUR NEIGHBOR AS YOURSELF."
28 And He said to him, "You have answered correctly; [a]DO
THIS, AND YOU WILL LIVE."
29 But wishing [a]to justify himself, he said to Jesus, "And
who is my neighbor?"
30 Jesus replied and said, "A certain man was [a]going down
from Jerusalem to Jericho; and he fell among robbers, and
they stripped him and [1]beat him, and went off leaving him half
dead.
31 "And by chance a certain priest was going down on that
road, and when he saw him, he passed by on the other side.
32 "And likewise a Levite also, when he came to the place
and saw him, passed by on the other side.
33 "But a certain [a]Samaritan, who was on a journey, came
upon him; and when he saw him, he felt compassion,
34 and came to him, and bandaged up his wounds, pouring oil and wine on *them*; and he put him on his own beast,
and brought him to an inn, and took care of him.
35 "And on the next day he took out two [1]denarii and gave
them to the innkeeper and said, 'Take care of him; and whatever
more you spend, when I return, I will repay you.'

17 [1]Some mss. read, *seventy-two* [a]Mark 16:17

18 [a]Matt. 4:10

19 [a]Mark 16:18

20 [a]Ex. 32:32; Ps. 69:28; Is. 4:3; Ezek. 13:9; Dan. 12:1; Phil. 4:3; Heb. 12:23; Rev. 3:5; 13:8; 17:8; 20:12, 15; 21:27

21 [1]Lit., *hour* [2]Or, *acknowledge to Thy praise* [a]Luke 10:21, 22: *Matt. 11:25-27*

23 [a]Luke 10:23, 24: *Matt. 13:16, 17*

25 [1]I.e., an expert in the Mosaic law [a]Luke 10:25-28: *Matt. 22:34-40; Mark 12:28-31;* Matt. 19:16-19 [b]Matt. 22:35

26 [1]Lit., *do you read*

27 [a]Deut. 6:5; Lev. 19:18

28 [a]Matt. 19:17; Lev. 18:5

29 [a]Luke 16:15

30 [1]Lit., *laid blows upon* [a]Luke 18:31; 19:28

33 [a]Matt. 10:5; Luke 9:52

35 [1]The denarius was worth 18 cents in silver, equivalent to a day's wage

36 "Which of these three do you think proved to be a
neighbor to the man who fell into the robbers' *hands?*"
37 And he said, "The one who showed mercy toward
him." And Jesus said to him, "Go and do [1]the same."
38 Now as they were traveling along, He entered a certain
village; and a [1]woman named [a]Martha welcomed Him into her
home.
39 And she had a sister called [a]Mary, who moreover was
listening to the Lord's word, [b]seated at His feet.
40 But [a]Martha was distracted with [1]all her preparations;
and she came up *to Him,* and said, "Lord, do You not care
that my sister has left me to do all the serving alone? Then tell
her to help me."
41 But the Lord answered and said to her, "[a]Martha, Martha, you are [b]worried and bothered about so many things;
42 [1a]but *only* a few things are necessary, [2]really *only* one:
for [b]Mary has chosen the good part, which shall not be taken
away from her."

CHAPTER 11

AND it came about that while He was praying in a certain
place, after He had finished, one of His disciples said to Him,
"[a]Lord, teach us to pray just as John also taught his disciples."
2 And He said to them, "[a]When you pray, say:
'[1]Father, hallowed be Thy name.
Thy kingdom come.
3 Give us [a]each day our [1]daily bread.
4 And forgive us our sins,
For we ourselves also forgive everyone who [a]is indebted to us.
And lead us not into temptation.' "
5 And He said to them, "[1]Suppose one of you shall have
a friend, and shall go to him at midnight, and say to him,
'Friend, lend me three loaves;
6 for a friend of mine has come to me from a journey,
and I have nothing to set before him';
7 and from inside he shall answer and say, 'Do not bother
me; the door has already been shut and my children [1]and I are
in bed; I cannot get up and give you *anything.*'
8 "I tell you, even though he will not get up and give him
anything because he is his friend, yet [a]because of his [1]persis-
tence he will get up and give him as much as he needs.
9 "And I say to you, [1a]ask, and it shall be given to you;
[2]seek, and you shall find; [3]knock, and it shall be opened to you.
10 "For everyone who asks receives; and he who seeks finds;
and to him who knocks it shall be opened.
11 "Now [1]suppose one of you fathers is asked by his son for
a [2]fish; he will not give him a snake instead of a fish, will he?
12 "Or *if* he is asked for an egg, he will not give him a
scorpion, will he?
13 "[a]If you then, being evil, know how to give good gifts to
your children, how much more shall *your* [1]Heavenly Father
give the [b]Holy Spirit to those who ask Him?"

37 [1]Or, *likewise*

38 [1]Lit., *certain woman* [a]Luke 10:40f.; John 11:1, 5, 19ff., 30, 39; 12:2

39 [a]Luke 10:42; John 11:1f., 19f., 28, 31f., 45; 12:3 [b]Luke 8:35; Acts 22:3

40 [1]Lit., *much service* [a]Luke 10:38, 41; John 11:1, 5, 19ff., 30, 39; 12:2

41 [a]Luke 10:38, 40; John 11:1, 5, 19ff., 30, 39; 12:2 [b]Matt. 6:25

42 [1]Some mss. read, *but one thing is necessary* [2]Lit., *or* [a]John 6:27; Ps. 27:4 [b]Luke 10:39; John 11:1f., 19f., 28, 31f., 45; 12:3

1 [a]Luke 7:13

2 [1]Some mss. insert phrases from Matt. 6:9-13 to make the two passages closely similar [a]Luke 11:2-4: *Matt.* 6:9-13

3 [1]Or, *bread for the coming day,* or *needful bread* [a]Acts 17:11

4 [a]Luke 13:4 marg.

5 [1]Lit., *which one of you*

7 [1]Lit., *with me*

8 [1]Or, *shamelessness* [a]Luke 18:1-6

9 [1]Or, *keep asking* [2]Or, *keep seeking* [3]Or, *keep knocking* [a]Luke 11:9-13: *Matt.* 7:7-11

11 [1]Lit., *which of you shall a son ask the father* [2]Some early mss. insert: *loaf, he will not give him a stone, will he, or for a . . .*

13 [1]Lit., *Father from heaven* [a]Luke 18:7f. [b]Matt. 7:11

14 [a]And He was casting out a demon, *and it was* dumb;
and it came about that when the demon had gone out, the
dumb man spoke; and the multitudes marveled.
15 But some of them said, "He casts out demons [a]by
[1b]Beelzebul, the ruler of the demons."
16 And others, [1]to test *Him,* [a]were demanding of Him a
[2]sign from heaven.
17 [a]But He knew their thoughts, and said to them, "[1]Any
kingdom divided against itself is laid waste; and [2]a house divided against itself falls.
18 "And if [a]Satan also is divided against himself, how shall
his kingdom stand? For you say that I cast out demons by
[b]Beelzebul.
19 "And if I by [a]Beelzebul cast out demons, by whom do
your sons cast them out? Consequently they shall be your
judges.
20 "But if I cast out demons by the [a]finger of God, then
[b]the kingdom of God has come upon you.
21 "When [1]a strong *man* fully armed guards his own
[a]homestead, his possessions are [2]undisturbed;
22 but when someone stronger than he attacks him and
overpowers him, he takes away from him all his armor on
which he had relied, and distributes his plunder.
23 "[a]He who is not with Me is against Me; and he who does
not gather with Me, scatters.
24 "[a]When the unclean spirit goes out of [1]a man, it passes
through waterless places seeking rest, and not finding any, it
says, 'I will return to my house from which I came.'
25 "And when it comes, it finds it swept and put in order.
26 "Then it goes and takes *along* seven other spirits more
evil than itself, and they go in and live there; and the last state
of that man becomes worse than the first."
27 And it came about while He said these things, one of
the women in the crowd raised her voice, and said to Him,
"[a]Blessed is the womb that bore You, and the breasts at which
You nursed."
28 But He said, "On the contrary, blessed are [a]those who
hear the word of God, and observe it."
29 And as the crowds were increasing, He began to say,
"[a]This generation is a wicked generation; it [b]seeks for a [1]sign,
and *yet* no [1]sign shall be given to it but the [1]sign of Jonah.
30 "For just as Jonah became a [1]sign to the Ninevites, so
shall the Son of Man be to this generation.
31 "The Queen of the South shall rise up with the men of
this generation at the judgment and condemn them, because
she came from the ends of the earth to hear the wisdom of
Solomon; and behold, something greater than Solomon is
here.
32 "The men of Nineveh shall stand up with this generation at the judgment and condemn it, because they repented
at the preaching of Jonah; and behold, something greater than
Jonah is here.
33 "No [a]one, after lighting a lamp, puts it away in a cellar,
nor under a peck-measure, but on the lampstand, in order that
those who enter may see the light.

14 [a]Luke 11:14, 15: *Matt. 12:22, 24;* Matt. 9:32-34

15 [1]Here and in verses 18 and 19 some mss. read, *Beezebul* [a]Matt. 9:34 [b]Matt. 10:25

16 [1]Lit., *were testing* [2]Or, *attesting miracle* [a]Matt. 12:38

17 [1]Lit., *every* [2]Lit., *a house against a house falls* [a]Luke 11:17-22: *Matt. 12:25-29; Mark 3:23-27*

18 [a]Matt. 4:10 [b]Matt. 10:25

19 [a]Matt. 10:25

20 [a]Ex. 8:19 [b]Matt. 3:2

21 [1]Lit., *the* [2]Lit., *in peace* [a]Matt. 26:3

23 [a]Matt. 12:30

24 [1]Lit., *the* [a]Luke 11:24-26: *Matt. 12:43-45*

27 [a]Luke 23:29

28 [a]Luke 8:21

29 [1]Or, *attesting miracle* [a]Luke 11:29-32: *Matt. 12:39-42* [b]Luke 11:16; Matt. 12:38

30 [1]Or, *attesting miracle*

33 [a]Luke 8:16; Matt. 5:15; Mark 4:21

34 "[a]The lamp of your body is your eye; when your eye is
[1]clear, your whole body also is full of light; but when it is bad,
your body also is full of darkness.
35 "Then watch out that the light in you may not be
darkness.
36 "If therefore your whole body is full of light, with no
dark part in it, it shall be wholly illumined, as when the lamp
illumines you with its rays."
37 Now when He had spoken, a Pharisee *asked Him to
have lunch with him; and He went in, and reclined *at table*.
38 And when the Pharisee saw it, he was surprised that He
had not first [1a]ceremonially washed before the [2]meal.
39 But [a]the Lord said to him, "Now [b]you Pharisees clean
the outside of the cup and of the platter; but [1]inside of you,
you are full of robbery and wickedness.
40 "[a]You foolish ones, did not He who made the outside
make the inside also?
41 "But [a]give that which is within as charity, and [1]then all
things are [b]clean for you.
42 "[a]But woe to you Pharisees! For you [b]pay tithe of mint
and rue and every *kind of* garden herb, and *yet* disregard justice and the love of God; but these are the things you should
have done without neglecting the others.
43 "Woe to you Pharisees! For you [a]love the front seats in
the synagogues, and the respectful greetings in the market
places.
44 "[a]Woe to you! For you are like [1]concealed tombs, and
the people who walk over *them* are unaware *of it*."
45 And one of the [1a]lawyers *said to Him in reply, "Teacher, when You say this, You insult us too."
46 But He said, "Woe to you [a]lawyers as well! For [b]you
weigh men down with burdens hard to bear, [1]while you yourselves will not even touch the burdens with one of your fingers.
47 "[a]Woe to you! For you build the [1]tombs of the prophets, and *it was* your fathers *who* killed them.
48 "Consequently, you are witnesses and approve the deeds
of your fathers; because it was they who killed them, and you
build *their tombs*.
49 "For this reason also [a]the Wisdom of God said, '[b]I will
send to them prophets and apostles, and *some* of them they
will kill and *some* they will [1]persecute,
50 in order that the blood of all the prophets, shed [a]since
the foundation of the world, may be [1]charged against this
generation,
51 from the blood of Abel to the blood of Zechariah, who
perished between the altar and the House *of God*, yes, I tell
you, it shall be [1]charged against this generation.'
52 "Woe to you [1a]lawyers! For you have taken away the key
of knowledge; [b]you did not enter in yourselves, and those who
were entering in you hindered."
53 And when He left there, the scribes and the Pharisees
began to be very hostile and to question Him closely on many
subjects,
54 [a]plotting against Him, [b]to catch *Him* [1]in something He
might say.

34 [1]Or, *healthy* [a]Luke 11:34, 35: *Matt. 6:22, 23*

38 [1]Gr., *baptized* [2]Or, *lunch* [a]Matt. 15:2; Mark 7:3f.

39 [1]Lit., *your inside is full* [a]Luke 7:13 [b]Matt. 23:25f.

40 [a]Luke 12:20; 1 Cor. 15:36

41 [1]Lit., *behold* [a]Luke 12:33; 16:9 [b]Mark 7:19; Titus 1:15

42 [a]Matt. 23:23 [b]Luke 18:12

43 [a]Matt. 23:6f.; Mark 12:38f.; Luke 20:46; 14:7

44 [1]Or, *indistinct, unseen* [a]Matt. 23:27

45 [1]I.e., experts in the Mosaic law [a]Luke 11:46, 52; Matt. 22:35

46 [1]Lit., *and* [a]Luke 11:45, 52; Matt. 22:35 [b]Matt. 23:4

47 [1]Or, *monuments to* [a]Matt. 23:29ff.

49 [1]Or, *drive out* [a]1 Cor. 1:24, 30; Col. 2:3 [b]Luke 11:49-51; Matt. 23:34-36

50 [1]Or, *required of* [a]Matt. 25:34

51 [1]Or, *required of*

52 [1]I.e., experts in the Mosaic law [a]Luke 11:45, 46; Matt. 22:35 [b]Matt. 23:13

54 [1]Lit., *something out of His mouth* [a]Acts 23:21; Luke 20:20; Mark 3:2 [b]Mark 12:13

CHAPTER 12

UNDER these circumstances, after [1]so many thousands of
the multitude had gathered together that they were stepping
on one another, He began saying to His disciples first *of all,*
"[a]Beware of the leaven of the Pharisees, which is hypocrisy.
2 "[a]But there is nothing covered up that will not be revealed, and hidden that will not be known.
3 "Accordingly whatever you have said in the dark shall be
heard in the light, and what you have [1]whispered in the inner
rooms shall be proclaimed upon [a]the housetops.
4 "And I say to you [a]my friends, do not be afraid of those
who kill the body, and after that have no more that they can
do.
5 "But I will [1]warn you whom to fear: [a]Fear the One who
after He has killed has authority to cast into [2b]hell; yes, I tell
you, fear Him!
6 "Are not [a]five sparrows sold for two [1]cents? And *yet* not
one of them is forgotten before God.
7 "[a]Indeed the very hairs of your head are all numbered.
Do not fear; you are of more value than many sparrows.
8 "And I say to you, everyone who confesses Me before
men, the Son of Man shall confess him also [a]before the angels
of God;
9 but [a]he who denies Me before men shall be denied
[b]before the angels of God.
10 "[a]And everyone who will speak a word against the Son of
Man, it shall be forgiven him; but he who blasphemes against
the Holy Spirit, it shall not be forgiven him.
11 "And when they bring you before [a]the synagogues and
the rulers and the authorities, do not become [b]anxious about
how or what you should speak in your defense, or what you
should say;
12 for [a]the Holy Spirit will teach you in that very hour
what you ought to say."
13 And someone [1]in the crowd said to Him, "Teacher, tell
my brother to divide the *family* inheritance with me."
14 But He said to him, "[a]Man, who appointed Me a judge
or arbiter over you?"
15 And He said to them, "[a]Beware, and be on your guard
against every form of greed; for not *even* when one has an
abundance does his life consist of his possessions."
16 And He told them a parable, saying, "The land of a
certain rich man was very productive.
17 "And he began reasoning to himself, saying, 'What shall
I do, since I have no place to store my crops?'
18 "And he said, 'This is what I will do: I will tear down my
barns and build larger ones, and there I will store all my grain
and my goods.
19 'And I will say to my soul, "Soul, [a]you have many goods
laid up for many years *to come;* take your ease, eat, drink *and*
be merry." '
20 "But God said to him, '[a]You fool! This *very* night [1b]your
soul is required of you; and [c]*now* who will own what you have
prepared?'

1 [1]Gr., *myriads* [a]Matt. 16:6, 11ff.; Mark 8:15

2 [a]Luke 12:2-9: *Matt. 10:26-33;* Luke 8:17; Matt. 10:26; Mark 4:22

3 [1]Lit., *spoken in the ear* [a]Matt. 10:27; Matt. 24:17

4 [a]John 15:13-15

5 [1]Or, *show* [2]Gr. *Gehenna* [a]Heb. 10:31 [b]Matt. 5:22

6 [1]Gr., *assaria,* the smallest of copper coins [a]Matt. 10:29

7 [a]Matt. 10:30

8 [a]Matt. 10:32; Luke 15:10; Rom. 10:9

9 [a]Luke 9:26; Matt. 10:33 [b]Matt. 10:32; Luke 15:10; Rom. 10:9

10 [a]Matt. 12:31, 32; Mark 3:28-30

11 [a]Matt. 10:17 [b]Luke 12:22; Matt. 6:25; 10:19; Mark 13:11; Luke 21:14

12 [a]Matt. 10:20; Luke 21:15

13 [1]Lit., *out of*

14 [a]Mic. 6:8; Rom. 2:1, 3; 9:20

15 [a]1 Tim. 6:6-10

19 [a]Eccles. 11:9

20 [1]Lit., *they are demanding your soul from you* [a]Jer. 17:11; Luke 11:40 [b]Job 27:8 [c]Ps. 39:6

21 "So is the man who [a]lays up treasure for himself, and is
not rich toward God."
22 And He said to His disciples, "[a]For this reason I say to
you, do not be anxious for *your* [1]life, *as to* what you shall eat;
nor for your body, *as to* what you shall put on.
23 "For life is more than food, and the body than clothing.
24 "Consider the [a]ravens, for they neither sow nor reap; and
they have no storeroom nor [b]barn; and *yet* God feeds them;
how much more valuable you are than the birds!
25 "And which of you by being anxious can add a *single*
[1a]cubit to his [2]life's span?
26 "If then you cannot do even a very little thing, why are
you anxious about other matters?
27 "Consider the lilies, how [1]they grow; they neither toil
nor spin; but I tell you, even [a]Solomon in all his glory did not
clothe himself like one of these.
28 "But if God so *arrays* the grass in the field, which is *alive*
today and tomorrow is thrown into the furnace, how much
more *will He clothe* you, [a]O men of little faith!
29 "And do not seek what you shall eat, and what you shall
drink, and do not [a]keep worrying.
30 "For [1]all these things the nations of the world eagerly
seek; but your Father knows that you need these things.
31 "But seek for His kingdom, and [a]these things shall be
added to you.
32 "[a]Do not be afraid, [b]little flock, for [c]your Father has
chosen gladly to give you the kingdom.
33 "[a]Sell your possessions and give to charity; make yourselves purses which do not wear out, [b]an unfailing treasure in
heaven, where no thief comes near, nor moth destroys.
34 "For [a]where your treasure is, there will your heart be
also.
35 "[1a]Be dressed in [b]readiness, and *keep* your lamps alight.
36 "And be like men who are waiting for their master when
he returns from the wedding feast, so that they may immediately open *the door* to him when he comes and knocks.
37 "Blessed are those slaves whom the master shall find [a]on
the alert when he comes; truly I say to you, that [b]he will gird
himself *to serve,* and have them recline *at table,* and will come
up and wait on them.
38 "Whether he comes in the [1a]second watch, or even in
the [2a]third, and finds *them* so, blessed are those *slaves.*
39 "[a]And [1]be sure of this, that if the head of the house had
known at what hour the thief was coming, he would not have
allowed his house to be [2b]broken into.
40 "[a]You too, be ready; for the Son of Man is coming at an
hour that you do not [1]expect."
41 And Peter said, "Lord, are You addressing this parable
to us, or [a]to everyone *else* as well?"
42 And [a]the Lord said, "[b]Who then is the faithful and
sensible [c]steward, whom his master will put in charge of his
[1]servants, to give them their rations at the proper time?
43 "Blessed is that [a]slave whom his [1]master finds so doing
when he comes.
44 "Truly I say to you, that he will put him in charge of all
his possessions.

21 [a]Luke 12:33

22 [1]Gr., *soul-life*
[a]Luke 12:22-31: *Matt.* 6:25-33

24 [a]Job 38:41 [b]Luke 12:18

25 [1]I.e., 18 inches [2]Or, *height*
[a]Ps. 39:5

27 [1]Some mss. omit, *they grow*
[a]1 Kin. 10:4-7

28 [a]Matt. 6:30

29 [a]Matt. 6:31

30 [1]Or, *these things all the nations of the world*

31 [a]Matt. 6:33

32 [a]Matt. 14:27 [b]John 21:15-17 [c]Eph. 1:5, 9

33 [a]Matt. 19:21; Luke 18:22; 11:41 [b]Matt. 6:20; Luke 12:21

34 [a]Matt. 6:21

35 [1]Lit., *Let your loins be girded*
[a]Luke 12:35, 36; Matt. 25:1ff. [b]Eph. 6:14; 1 Pet. 1:13

37 [a]Matt. 24:42 [b]Luke 17:8; John 13:4

38 [1]I.e., 9 p.m. to midnight [2]I.e., Midnight to 3 a.m.
[a]Matt. 24:43

39 [1]Lit., *know* [2]Lit., *dug through*
[a]Luke 12:39, 40: *Matt.* 24:43, 44 [b]Matt. 6:19

40 [1]Lit., *think, suppose*
[a]Luke 21:36; Mark 13:33

41 [a]Luke 12:47, 48

42 [1]Lit., *service*
[a]Luke 7:13 [b]Luke 12:42-46: *Matt.* 24:45-51 [c]Matt. 24:45; Luke 16:1ff.

43 [1]Or, *lord*
[a]Luke 12:42

45 "But if that slave says in his heart, 'My master [1]will be a
long time in coming,' and begins to beat the slaves, *both* men
and women, and to eat and drink and get drunk;
46 the master of that slave will come on a day when he
does not expect *him,* and at an hour he does not know, and will
cut him in pieces, and assign him a place with the unbelievers.
47 "And that slave who knew his master's will and did not
get ready or act in accord with his will, shall [a]receive many
lashes,
48 but the one who did not [a]know *it,* and committed
deeds worthy of [1]a flogging, will receive but few. [b]And from
everyone who has been given much shall much be required;
and to whom they entrusted much, of him they will ask all the
more.
49 "I [1]have come to cast fire upon the earth; and [2]how I
wish it were already kindled!
50 "But I have a [a]baptism to [1]undergo, and how distressed I
am until it is accomplished!
51 "[a]Do you suppose that I came to grant peace on earth? I
tell you, no, but rather division;
52 for from now on five *members* in one household will be
divided, three against two, and two against three.
53 "They will be divided, [a]father against son, and son
against father; mother against daughter, and daughter against
mother; mother-in-law against daughter-in-law, and daughter-
in-law against mother-in-law."
54 And He was also saying to the multitudes, "[a]When you
see a cloud rising in the west, immediately you say, 'A shower is
coming,' and so it turns out.
55 "And when *you see* a south wind blowing, you say, 'It
will be a [a]hot day,' and it turns out *that way.*
56 "You hypocrites! [a]You know how to analyze the appearance of the earth and the sky, but [1]why do you not analyze
this present time?
57 "And [a]why do you not even on your own initiative judge
what is right?
58 "For [a]while you are going with your opponent to appear
before the magistrate, on *your* way *there* make an effort to
[1]settle with him, in order that he may not drag you before the
judge, and the judge turn you over to the constable, and the
constable throw you into prison.
59 "I say to you, you shall not get out of there until you
have paid the very last [1a]cent."

Chapter 13

NOW on the same occasion there were some present who
reported to Him about the Galileans, whose blood [a]Pilate had
[1]mingled with their sacrifices.
2 And He answered and said to them, "[a]Do you suppose
that these Galileans were *greater* sinners than all *other* Galileans, because they suffered this *fate?*
3 "I tell you, no, but, unless you [1]repent, you will all likewise perish.
4 "Or do you suppose that those eighteen on whom the

45 [1]Lit., *is délaying to come*
47 [a]Deut. 25:2
48 [1]Lit., *blows* [a]Lev. 5:17; Num. 15:29f. [b]Matt. 13:12
49 [1]Or, *came* [2]Lit., *what do I wish if . . . ?*
50 [1]Lit., *be baptized with* [a]Mark 10:38
51 [a]Luke 12:51-53: *Matt. 10:34-36*
53 [a]Mic. 7:6; Matt. 10:21
54 [a]Matt. 16:2f.
55 [a]Matt. 20:12
56 [1]Lit., *how* [a]Matt. 16:3
57 [a]Luke 21:30
58 [1]Lit., *be released from him* [a]Luke 12:58, 59: *Matt. 5:25, 26*
59 [1]Lit., *lepton,* i.e., 1/128 of a denarius [a]Mark 12:42
1 [1]Or, *shed along with* [a]Matt. 27
2 [a]John 9:2f.
3 [1]Or, *are repentant*

tower in [a]Siloam fell and killed them, were *worse* [1b]culprits
than all the men who live in Jerusalem?
5 "I tell you, no, but, unless you repent, you will all likewise perish."
6 And He *began* telling this parable: "A certain man had
[a]a fig tree which had been planted in his vineyard; and he came
looking for fruit on it, and did not find any.
7 "And he said to the vineyard-keeper, 'Behold, for three
years I have come looking for fruit on this fig tree [1]without
finding any. [a]Cut it down! Why does it even use up the
ground?'
8 "And he answered and said to him, 'Let it alone, sir, for
this year too, until I dig around it and put in fertilizer;
9 and if it bears fruit next year, *fine;* but if not, cut it
down.' "
10 And He was [a]teaching in one of the synagogues on the
Sabbath.
11 And behold, there was a woman who for eighteen years
had had [a]a sickness caused by a spirit; and she was bent double,
and could not straighten up at all.
12 And when Jesus saw her, He called her over and said to
her, "Woman, you are freed from your sickness."
13 And He [a]laid His hands upon her; and immediately she
was made erect again, and *began* [b]glorifying God.
14 And [a]the synagogue official, indignant because Jesus
[b]had healed on the Sabbath, *began* saying to the multitude in
response, "[c]There are six days in which work should be done;
therefore come during them and get healed, and not on the
Sabbath day."
15 But [a]the Lord answered him and said, "You hypocrites,
[b]does not each of you on the Sabbath untie his ox or his
donkey from the stall, and lead him away to water *him?*
16 "And this woman, [a]a daughter of Abraham as she is,
whom [b]Satan has bound for eighteen long years, should she
not have been released from this bond on the Sabbath day?"
17 And as He said this, all his opponents were being humiliated; and [a]the entire multitude was rejoicing over all
the glorious things being done by Him.
18 Therefore [a]He was saying, "[b]What is the kingdom of
God like, and to what shall I compare it?
19 "It is like a mustard seed, which a man took and threw
into his own garden; and it grew and became a tree; and the
birds of the [1]air nested in its branches."
20 And again He said, "[a]To what shall I compare the
kingdom of God?
21 "[a]It is like leaven, which a woman took and hid in [b]three
[1]pecks of meal, until it was all leavened."
22 And He was passing through from one city and village
to another, teaching, and [a]proceeding on His way to
Jerusalem.
23 And someone said to Him, "Lord, are there *just* a few
who are being saved?" And He said to them,
24 "[a]Strive to enter by the narrow door; for many, I tell
you, will seek to enter and will not be able.[1]
25 "Once the head of the house gets up and [a]shuts the
door, and you [b]begin to stand outside and knock on the door,

4 [1]Lit., *debtors*
[a]Is. 8:6 [Neh. 3:15]; John 9:7, 11 [b]Matt. 6:12; Luke 11:4

6 [a]Matt. 21:19

7 [1]Lit., *and I do not find* [a]Matt. 3:10; 7:19; Luke 3:9

10 [a]Matt. 4:23

11 [a]Luke 13:16

13 [a]Mark 5:23 [b]Matt. 9:8

14 [a]Mark 5:22 [b]Matt. 12:2; Luke 14:3 [c]Ex. 20:9; Deut. 5:13

15 [a]Luke 7:13 [b]Luke 14:5

16 [a]Luke 19:9 [b]Matt. 4:10; Luke 13:11

17 [a]Luke 18:43

18 [a]Luke 13:18, 19: *Matt. 13:31, 32; Mark 4:30-32* [b]Matt. 13:24; Luke 13:20

19 [1]Or, *sky*

20 [a]Matt. 13:24; Luke 13:18

21 [1]Gr., *sata*
[a]Luke 13:20, 21: *Matt. 13:33* [b]Matt. 13:33

22 [a]Luke 9:51

24 [1]Or, *able, once . . .*
[a]Matt. 7:13

25 [a]Matt. 25:10 [b]Luke 3:8

saying, '[c]Lord, open up to us!' [1]then He will answer and say to
you, '[d]I do not know where you are from.'
26 "Then you will [a]begin to say, 'We ate and drank in Your
presence, and You taught in our streets';
27 and He will say, 'I tell you, [a]I do not know where you
are from; [b]DEPART FROM ME, ALL YOU EVILDOERS.'
28 "[a]There will be weeping and gnashing of teeth there
when you see Abraham and Isaac and Jacob and all the prophets in the kingdom of God, and yourselves being cast out.
29 "And they [a]will come from east and west, and from
north and south, and will recline *at table* in the kingdom of
God.
30 "And behold, [a]*some* are last who will be first and *some*
are first who will be last."
31 Just at that time some Pharisees came up, saying to
Him, "Go away and depart from here, for [a]Herod wants to kill
You."
32 And He said to them, "Go and tell that fox, 'Behold, I
cast out demons and perform cures today and tomorrow, and
the third *day* I [1a]reach My goal.'
33 "Nevertheless [a]I must journey on today and tomorrow
and the next *day;* for it cannot be that a [b]prophet should
perish outside of Jerusalem.
34 "[a]O Jerusalem, Jerusalem, *the city* that kills the prophets and stones those sent to her! How often I wanted to
gather your children together, [b]just as a hen *gathers* her brood
under her wings, and you would not *have it!*
35 "Behold, your house is left to you [1]*desolate;* and I say to
you, you shall not see Me until *the time* comes when you say,
'[a]Blessed *is* He who comes in the name of the Lord!' "

CHAPTER 14

AND it came about that when He went into the house of one
of the [1]leaders of the Pharisees on *the* Sabbath to eat bread,
[a]they were watching Him closely.
2 And [1]there, in front of Him was a certain man suffering
from dropsy.
3 And Jesus [a]answered and spoke to the [1b]lawyers and
Pharisees, saying, "[c]Is it lawful to heal on the Sabbath, or
not?"
4 But they kept silent. And He took hold of him, and
healed him, and sent him away.
5 And He said to them, "[a]Which one of you shall have a
[1]son or an ox fall into a well, and will not immediately pull him
out on a Sabbath day?"
6 [a]And they could make no reply to this.
7 And He *began* speaking a parable to the invited guests
when He noticed how [a]they had been picking out the places of
honor *at the table;* saying to them,
8 "When you are invited by someone to a wedding feast,
[a]do not [1]take the place of honor, lest someone more distinguished than you may have been invited by him,
9 and he who invited you both shall come and say to you,
'Give place to this man', and then [a]in disgrace you [1]proceed to
occupy the last place.

25 [1]Lit., *and* [c]Matt. 25:11; 7:22 [d]Luke 13:27; Matt. 7:23; 25:12

26 [a]Luke 3:8

27 [a]Luke 13:25 [b]Ps. 6:8; Matt. 25:41

28 [a]Matt. 8:12

29 [a]Matt. 8:11

30 [a]Matt. 19:30

31 [a]Matt. 14:1; Luke 3:1; 9:7; 23:7

32 [1]Or possibly, *am perfected* [a]Heb. 2:10; 5:9; 7:28

33 [a]John 11:9 [b]Matt. 21:11

34 [a]Luke 13:34, 35: *Matt.* 23:37-39; Luke 19:41 [b]Matt. 23:37

35 [1]Later mss. add, *desolate* [a]Ps. 118:26; Matt. 21:9; Luke 19:38

1 [1]I.e., members of the Sanhedrin [a]Mark 3:2

2 [1]Lit., *behold*

3 [1]I.e., experts in Mosaic Law [a]Acts 3:12 [b]Matt. 22:35 [c]Matt. 12:2; Luke 13:14

5 [1]Some ancient mss. read, *donkey* [a]Luke 13:15

6 [a]Matt. 22:46; Luke 20:40

7 [a]Matt. 23:6

8 [1]Lit., *recline at* [a]Prov. 25:6, 7

9 [1]Lit., *begin* [a]Luke 3:8

10 "But when you are invited, go and recline at the last
place, so that when the one who has invited you comes, he may
say to you, 'Friend, [a]move up higher'; then you will have honor
in the sight of all who [1]are at the table with you.
11 "[a]For everyone who exalts himself shall be humbled,
and he who humbles himself shall be exalted."
12 And He also went on to say to the one who had invited
Him, "When you give a luncheon or a dinner, do not invite
your friends or your brothers or your relatives or rich neighbors, lest they also invite you in return, and repayment come
to you.
13 "But when you give a [1]reception, invite *the* poor, *the*
crippled, *the* lame, *the* blind,
14 and you will be [1]blessed, since they [2]do not have *the*
means to repay you; for you will be repaid at [a]the resurrection
of the righteous."
15 And when one of those who were reclining *at table*
with Him heard this, he said to Him, "[a]Blessed is everyone
who shall eat bread in the kingdom of God!"
16 But He said to him, "[a]A certain man was giving a big
dinner, and he invited many;
17 and at the dinner hour he sent his slave to say to those
who had been invited, 'Come; for everything is ready now.'
18 "But they all alike began to make excuses. The first one
said to him, 'I have bought a [1]piece of land and I need to go
out and look at it; [2]please consider me excused.'
19 "And another one said, 'I have bought five yoke of oxen,
and I am going to try them out; [1]please consider me excused.'
20 "And another one said, '[a]I have married a wife, and for
that reason I cannot come.'
21 "And the slave came *back* and reported this to his master. Then the head of the household became angry and said to
his slave, 'Go out at once into the streets and lanes of the city
and bring in here the poor and crippled and blind and lame.'
22 "And the slave said, 'Master, what you commanded has
been done, and still there is room.'
23 "And the master said to the slave, 'Go out into the
highways along the hedges, and compel *them* to come in, that
my house may be filled.
24 'For I tell you, none of those men who were invited
shall taste of my dinner.'"
25 Now great multitudes were going along with Him; and
He turned and said to them,
26 "[a]If anyone comes to Me, and does not [1]hate his own
father and mother and wife and children and brothers and
sisters, yes, and even his own life, he cannot be My disciple.
27 "Whoever does not [a]carry his own cross and come after
Me cannot be My disciple.
28 "For which one of you, when he wants to build a tower,
does not first sit down and calculate the cost, to see if he has
enough to complete it?
29 "Otherwise, when he has laid a foundation, and is not
able to finish, all who observe it begin to ridicule him,
30 saying, 'This man began to build and was not able to
finish.'
31 "Or what king, when he sets out to meet another king in

10 [1]Lit., *recline at table* [a]Prov. 25:6, 7

11 [a]Luke 18:14; Matt. 23:12

13 [1]Or, *banquet*

14 [1]Or, *happy* [2]Or, *are unable to* [a]John 5:29; Acts 24:15; Rev. 20:4, 5[?]

15 [a]Rev. 19:9

16 [a]Luke 14:16-24; Matt. 22:2-14

18 [1]Or, *field* [2]Lit., *I request you*

19 [1]Lit., *I request you*

20 [a]Deut. 24:5; 1 Cor. 7:33

26 [1]I.e., by comparison of his love for Me [a]Matt. 10:37f.

27 [a]Matt. 10:38

battle, will not first sit down and take counsel whether he is
strong enough with ten thousand *men* to encounter the one
coming against him with twenty thousand?
32 "Or else, while the other is still far away, he sends a
[1]delegation and asks terms of peace.
33 "So therefore, no one of you can be My disciple who
[a]does not give up all his own possessions.
34 "Therefore, salt is good; but [a]if even salt has become
tasteless, with what will it be seasoned?
35 "It is useless either for the soil or for the manure pile; [1]it
is thrown out. [a]He who has ears to hear, let him hear."

Chapter 15

NOW all the [1a]tax-gatherers and the [2]sinners were coming
near Him to listen to Him.
2 And both the Pharisees and the scribes [1]*began* to
grumble, saying, "This man receives sinners and [a]eats with
them."
3 And He told them this parable, saying,
4 "[a]What man among you, if he has a hundred sheep and
has lost one of them, does not leave the ninety-nine in the
[1]open pasture, and go after the one which is lost, until he finds
it?
5 "And when he has found it, he lays it on his shoulders,
rejoicing.
6 "And when he comes home, he calls together his friends
and his neighbors, saying to them, 'Rejoice with me, for I have
found my sheep which was lost!'
7 "I tell you that in the same way, there will be *more* joy in
heaven over one sinner who repents, than over ninety-nine
righteous persons who need no repentance.
8 "Or what woman, if she has ten [1]silver coins and loses
one coin, does not light a lamp and sweep the house and
search carefully until she finds it?
9 "And when she has found it, she calls together her
[1]friends and neighbors, saying, 'Rejoice with me, for I have
found the coin which I had lost!'
10 "In the same way, I tell you, there is joy [a]in the presence
of the angels of God over one sinner who repents."
11 And He said, "A certain man had two sons;
12 and the younger of them said to his father, 'Father, give
me [a]the share of the estate that falls to me.' And he divided his
[1b]wealth between them.
13 "And not many days later, the younger son gathered
everything together and went on a journey into a distant country, and there he squandered his estate with loose living.
14 "Now when he had spent everything, a severe famine
occurred in that country, and he began to be in need.
15 "And he went and [1]attached himself to one of the citizens of that country, and he sent him into his fields to feed
swine.
16 "And he was longing [1]to fill his [2]stomach with the [3]pods
that the swine were eating, and no one was giving *anything* to
him.
17 "But when he came to [1]his senses, he said, 'How many of

32 [1]Or, *embassy*

33 [a]Phil. 3:7; Heb. 11:26

34 [a]Matt. 5:13; Mark 9:50

35 [1]Lit., *they throw it out* [a]Matt. 11:15

1 [1]Publicans who collected Roman taxes for profit [2]I.e., irreligious or non-practicing Jews [a]Luke 5:29

2 [1]Lit., *grumble among themselves* [a]Matt. 9:11

4 [1]Lit., *wilderness* [a]Luke 15:4-7; Matt. 18:12-14

8 [1]Gr., *drachmas,* one drachma was equivalent to a day's wages

9 [1]Lit., *women friends and neighbors*

10 [a]Luke 15:7; Matt. 10:32

12 [1]Lit., *living* [a]Deut. 21:17 [b]Mark 12:44; Luke 15:30

15 [1]Lit., *was joined to*

16 [1]Some mss. read *to be satisfied with* [2]Lit., *belly* [3]I.e., of the carob tree

17 [1]Lit., *himself*

my father's hired men have more than enough bread, but I am
dying here with hunger!
18 'I will get up and go to my father, and will say to him,
"Father, I have sinned against heaven, and [1]in your sight;
19 "I am no longer worthy to be called your son; make me
as one of your hired men."'
20 "And he got up and came to [1]his father. But while he
was still a long way off, his father saw him, and felt compassion
for him, and ran and [2a]embraced him, and [3]kissed him.
21 "And the son said to him, 'Father, I have sinned against
heaven and in your sight; I am no longer worthy to be called
your son.'[1]
22 "But the father said to his slaves, 'Quickly bring out [a]the
best robe and put it on him, and [b]put a ring on his hand and
sandals on his feet;
23 and bring the fattened calf, kill it, and let us eat and be
merry;
24 for this son of mine was [a]dead, and has come to life
again; he was lost, and has been found.' And they began to be
merry.
25 "Now his older son was in the field, and when he came
and approached the house, he heard music and dancing.
26 "And he summoned one of the servants and *began* inquiring what these things might be.
27 "And he said to him, 'Your brother has come, and your
father has killed the fattened calf, because he has received him
back safe and sound.'
28 "But he became angry, and was not willing to go in; and
his father came out and *began* entreating him.
29 "But he answered and said to his father, 'Look! For so
many years I have been serving you, and I have never [1]neglect-
ed a command of yours; and *yet* you have never given me a
[2]kid, that I might be merry with my friends;
30 but when this son of yours came, who has devoured
your [1a]wealth with harlots, you killed the fattened calf for
him.'
31 "And he said to him, '*My* child, you [1]have always been
with me, and all that is mine is yours.
32 'But [1]we had to be merry and rejoice, for this brother of
yours was [a]dead and *has begun* to live, and *was* lost and has
been found.'"

Chapter 16

NOW He was also saying to the disciples, "There was a
certain rich man who had a steward, and this *steward* was
[1]reported to him as [a]squandering his possessions.
2 "And he called him and said to him, 'What is this I hear
about you? Give an account of your stewardship, for you can
no longer be steward.'
3 "And the steward said to himself, 'What shall I do, since
my [1]master is taking the stewardship away from me? I am not
strong enough to dig; I am ashamed to beg.
4 'I [1]know what I shall do, so that when I am removed
from the stewardship, they will receive me into their homes.'

18 [1]Lit., *before you*

20 [1]Lit., *his own* [2]Lit., *fell on his neck* [3]Lit., *kissed him again and again* [a]Gen. 45:14; 46:29; Acts 20:37

21 [1]Some ancient mss. add: *make me as one of your hired men*

22 [a]Zech. 3:4; Rev. 6:11 [b]Gen. 41:42

24 [a]Luke 15:32; Matt. 8:22; Luke 9:60; 1 Tim. 5:6; Eph. 2:1, 5; 5:14; Col. 2:13; Rom. 11:15

29 [1]Or, *disobeyed* [2]Or, *young goat*

30 [1]Lit., *living* [a]Luke 15:12; Prov. 29:3

31 [1]Lit., *are always with me*

32 [1]Lit., *it was necessary* [a]Luke 15:24

1 [1]Or, *accused* [a]Luke 15:13

3 [1]Or, *lord*

4 [1]Lit., *have come to the knowledge of*

God and Mammon. Self-righteous Pharisees. Divorce. The Rich Man and Lazarus.

5 "And he summoned each one of his [1]master's debtors,
and he *began* saying to the first, 'How much do you owe my
master?'
6 "And he said, 'A hundred [1]measures of oil.' And he said
to him, 'Take your bill, and sit down quickly and write fifty.'
7 "Then he said to another, 'And how much do you owe?'
And he said, 'A hundred [1]measures of wheat.' He *said to him,
'Take your bill, and write eighty.'
8 "And his [1]master praised the unrighteous steward because he had acted shrewdly; for the sons of [a]this age are more
shrewd in relation to their own [2]kind than the [b]sons of light.
9 "And I say to you, [a]make friends for yourselves by means
of the [1b]Mammon of unrighteousness; that when it fails, [c]they
may receive you into the eternal dwellings.
10 "[a]He who is faithful in a very little thing is faithful also
in much; and he who is unrighteous in a very little thing is
unrighteous also in much.
11 "If therefore you have not been faithful in the *use of*
unrighteous [1a]Mammon, who will entrust the true *riches* to
you?
12 "And if you have not been faithful in *the use of* that
which is another's, who will give you that which is [1]your own?
13 "[a]No [1]servant can serve two masters; for either he will
hate the one, and love the other, or else he will hold to one,
and despise the other. You cannot serve God and
[2b]Mammon."
14 Now the Pharisees, who were [a]lovers of money, were
listening to all these things, and they [b]were scoffing at Him.
15 And He said to them, "You are those who [a]justify yourselves [1]in the sight of men, but [b]God knows your hearts; for
that which is [2]highly esteemed among men is detestable [3]in the
sight of God.
16 "[a]The Law and the Prophets *were* proclaimed until
John; since then [b]the gospel of the kingdom of God is
preached, and every one is forcing his way into it.
17 "[a]But it is easier for heaven and earth to pass away than
for one [1]stroke of a letter of the Law to fail.
18 "[a]Every one who divorces his wife and marries another
commits adultery; and he who marries one who is divorced
from a husband commits adultery.
19 "Now there was a certain rich man, and he habitually
dressed in purple and fine linen, gaily living in splendor every
day.
20 "And a certain poor man named Lazarus [a]was laid at his
gate, covered with sores,
21 and longing to be fed with the *crumbs* which were
falling from the rich man's table; besides, even the dogs were
coming and licking his sores.
22 "Now it came about that the poor man died and he was
carried away by the angels to [a]Abraham's bosom; and the rich
man also died and was buried.
23 "And in [a]Hades [1]he lifted up his eyes, being in torment,
and *saw Abraham far away, and Lazarus in his bosom.
24 "And he cried out and said, '[a]Father Abraham, have
mercy on me, and send Lazarus, that he may dip the tip of his

5 [1]Or, *lord's*

6 [1]Gr., *baths,* one bath equals between 8 and 9 gallons

7 [1]Gr., *cors,* one cor equals between 10 and 12 bushels.

8 [1]Or, *lord* [2]Lit., *generation* [a]Matt. 12:32; Luke 20:34 [b]John 12:36; Eph. 5:8; 1 Thess. 5:5

9 [1]Or, *riches* [a]Matt. 19:21; Luke 11:41; 12:33 [b]Luke 16:11, 13; Matt. 6:24 [c]Luke 16:4

10 [a]Matt. 25:21, 23

11 [1]Or, *riches* [a]Luke 16:9

12 [1]Some mss. read, *our own*

13 [1]Or, *house-servant* [2]Or, *riches* [a]Matt. 6:24 [b]Luke 16:9

14 [a]2 Tim. 3:2 [b]Luke 23:35

15 [1]Lit., *before men* [2]Lit., *high* [3]Lit., *before God* [a]Luke 10:29; 18:9, 14 [b]1 Sam. 16:7; Prov. 21:2; Rom. 8:27; Acts 1:24

16 [a]Matt. 11:12f. [b]Matt. 4:23

17 [1]I.e., projection of a letter (serif) [a]Matt. 5:18

18 [a]Matt. 5:32

20 [a]Acts 3:2

22 [a]John 13:23; 1:18

23 [1]Lit., *having lifted up* [a]Matt. 11:23

24 [a]Luke 16:30; Luke 3:8; 19:9

finger in water and cool off my tongue; for I am in agony in
[b]this flame.'
25 "But Abraham said, 'Child, remember that [a]during your
life you received your good things, and likewise Lazarus bad
things; but now he is being comforted here, and you are in
agony.
26 'And [1]besides all this, between us and you there is a
great chasm fixed, in order that those who wish to come over
from here to you may not be able, and *that* none may cross
over from there to us.'
27 "And he said, 'Then I beg you, Father, that you send
him to my father's house —
28 for I have five brothers — that he may [a]warn them, lest
they also come to this place of torment.'
29 "But Abraham *said, 'They have [a]Moses and the Prophets; let them hear them.'
30 "But he said, 'No, [a]Father Abraham, but if someone
goes to them from the dead, they will repent!'
31 "But he said to him, 'If they do not listen to Moses and
the Prophets, neither will they be persuaded if someone rises
from the dead.' "

Chapter 17

And He said to His disciples, "[a]It is inevitable that
[1]stumbling blocks should come, but woe to him through
whom they come!
2 "[a]It would be better for him if a millstone were hung
around his neck and he were thrown into the sea, than that he
should cause one of these little ones to stumble.
3 "[1]Be on your guard! [a]If your brother sins, rebuke him;
and if he repents, forgive him.
4 "And if he sins against you [a]seven times a day, and returns to you seven times, saying, 'I repent,' [1]forgive him."
5 And [a]the apostles said to [b]the Lord, "Increase our
faith!"
6 And [a]the Lord said, "If you had faith like [b]a mustard
seed, you would say to this [c]mulberry tree, 'Be uprooted and
be planted in the sea'; and it would [1]obey you.
7 "But which of you, having a slave plowing or tending
sheep, will say to him when he has come in from the field,
'Come immediately and [1]sit down to eat'?
8 "But will he not say to him, '[a]Prepare something for me
to eat, and *properly* [1]clothe yourself and serve me until I have
eaten and drunk; and [2]afterward you will eat and drink'?
9 "He does not thank the slave because he did the things
which were commanded, does he?
10 "So you too, when you do all the things which are commanded you, say, 'We are unworthy slaves; we have done *only*
that which we ought to have done.' "
11 And it came about while He was [a]on the way to Jerusalem, that [b]He was passing [1]between Samaria and Galilee.
12 And as He entered a certain village, there met Him ten
leprous men, who [a]stood at a distance;

24 [b]Matt. 25:41
25 [a]Luke 6:24
26 [1]Lit., *in all these things*
28 [a]Acts 2:40; 8:25; 10:42; 18:5; 20:21ff.; 23:11; 28:23; Gal. 5:3; Eph. 4:17; 1 Thess. 2:11; 4:6
29 [a]Luke 4:17; Acts 15:21; John 5:45-47
30 [a]Luke 16:24; 3:8; 19:9
1 [1]Or, *temptations to sin* [a]Matt. 18:7; 1 Cor. 11:19; 1 Tim. 4:1
2 [a]Matt. 18:6; Mark 9:42; 1 Cor. 8:12
3 [1]Lit., *Take heed to yourselves* [a]Matt. 18:15
4 [1]Lit., *you shall forgive* [a]Matt. 18:21f.
5 [a]Mark 6:30 [b]Luke 7:13
6 [1]Gr., *have obeyed* [a]Luke 7:13 [b]Matt. 13:31; 17:20; Mark 4:31; Luke 13:19 [c]Luke 19:4
7 [1]Lit., *recline*
8 [1]Lit., *gird* [2]Lit., *after these things* [a]Luke 12:37
11 [1]Lit., *through the midst of*, or, *along the borders of* [a]Luke 9:51 [b]Luke 9:52ff.; John 4:3f.
12 [a]Lev. 13:45f.

13 [a]Luke 5:5

14 [a]Luke 5:14; Matt. 8:4

15 [a]Matt. 9:8

16 [a]Matt. 10:5

18 [1]Lit., *were there not found those who* [a]Matt. 9:8

19 [1]Lit., *has saved you* [a]Matt. 9:22; Luke 18:42

20 [1]Or, *observation* [a]Luke 19:11; Acts 1:6 [b]Luke 14:1 [Gr.]

21 [1]Or, *within you* [a]Luke 17:23

22 [a]Matt. 9:15; Mark 2:20; Luke 5:35

23 [a]Matt. 24:23; Mark 13:21; Luke 21:8

24 [1]Lit., *under heaven* [a]Matt. 24:27

25 [a]Matt. 16:21; Luke 9:22

26 [a]Luke 17:26, 27: *Matt.* 24:37-39 [b]Gen. 7

28 [1]Lit., *in the same way as* [a]Gen. 19

29 [1]Or, *sulphur*

30 [1]Lit., *according to the same things* [a]1 Cor. 1:7; 2 Thess. 1:7; 1 Pet. 1:7; Col. 3:4; 1 John 2:28; 1 Pet. 4:13; Matt. 16:27

31 [a]Matt. 24:17, 18; Mark 13:15f.; Luke 21:21

32 [a]Gen. 19:26

33 [1]Or, *soul-life* [a]Matt. 10:39

35 [a]Matt. 24:41

36 [1]Some mss. add verse 36, *Two men will be in the field; one will be taken and the other will be left.* cf. Matt. 24:40

13 and they raised their voices, saying, "Jesus, [a]Master,
have mercy on us!"
14 And when He saw them, He said to them, "[a]Go and
show yourselves to the priests." And it came about that as they
were going, they were cleansed.
15 Now one of them, when he saw that he had been
healed, turned back, [a]glorifying God with a loud voice,
16 and he fell on his face at His feet, giving thanks to Him.
And he was a [a]Samaritan.
17 And Jesus answered and said, "Were there not ten
cleansed? But the nine — where are they?
18 "[1]Were none found who turned back to [a]give glory to
God, except this foreigner?"
19 And He said to him, "Rise, and go your way; [a]your
faith [1]has made you well."
20 Now having been questioned by the Pharisees [a]as to
when the kingdom of God was coming, He answered them
and said, "The kingdom of God is not coming with [1b]signs to
be observed;
21 nor will [a]they say, 'Look, here *it is!*' or, 'There *it is!*' For
behold, the kingdom of God is [1]in your midst."
22 And He said to the disciples, "[a]The days shall come
when you will long to see one of the days of the Son of Man,
and you will not see it.
23 "[a]And they will say to you, 'Look there! Look here!' Do
not go away, and do not run after *them.*
24 "[a]For just as the lightning, when it flashes out of one
part [1]of the sky, shines to the other part [1]of the sky, so will the
Son of Man be in His day.
25 "[a]But first He must suffer many things and be rejected
by this generation.
26 "[a]And just as it happened [b]in the days of Noah, so it
shall be also in the days of the Son of Man:
27 they were eating, they were drinking, they were marrying, they were being given in marriage, until the day that
Noah entered the ark, and the flood came and destroyed them
all.
28 "[1]It was the same as happened in [a]the days of Lot: they
were eating, they were drinking, they were buying, they were
selling, they were planting, they were building;
29 but on the day that Lot went out from Sodom it rained
fire and [1]brimstone from heaven and destroyed them all.
30 "It will be [1]just the same on the day that the Son of Man
[a]is revealed.
31 "On that day, let not the one who is [a]on the housetop
and whose goods are in the house go down to take them away;
and likewise let not the one who is in the field turn back.
32 "[a]Remember Lot's wife.
33 "[a]Whoever seeks to keep his [1]life shall lose it, and
whoever loses *his life* shall preserve it alive.
34 "I tell you, on that night there will be two men in one
bed; one will be taken, and the other will be left.
35 "[a]There will be two women grinding at the same place;
one will be taken, and the other will be left."
36 (See marginal note.[1])

37 And answering they *said to Him, "Where, Lord?"
And He said to them, "[a]Where the body *is*, there also will the
[1]vultures be gathered."

Chapter 18

NOW He was telling them a parable to show that at all
times they [a]ought to pray and not to [b]lose heart,
2 saying, "There was in a certain city a judge who did not
fear God, and did not [a]respect man.
3 "And there was a widow in that city, and she kept coming to him, saying, '[1]Give me legal protection from my
opponent.'
4 "And for a while he was unwilling; but afterward he said
to himself, 'Even though I do not fear God nor [a]respect man,
5 yet [a]because this widow bothers me, I will [1]give her
legal protection, lest by continually coming she [2b]wear me
out.' "
6 And [a]the Lord said, "Hear what the unrighteous judge
*said;
7 now shall not God [a]bring about justice for His [b]elect,
who cry to Him day and night, [1]and will He [c]delay long over
them?
8 "I tell you that He will bring about justice for them
speedily. However, when the Son of Man comes, [a]will He find
[1]faith on the earth?"
9 And He also told this parable to certain ones who
[a]trusted in themselves that they were righteous, and [b]viewed
others with contempt:
10 "Two men [a]went up into the temple to pray, one a
Pharisee, and the other a [1]tax-gatherer.
11 "The Pharisee [a]stood and was praying thus to himself,
'God, I thank Thee that I am not like other people, swindlers,
unjust, adulterers, or even like this [1]tax-gatherer.
12 'I [a]fast twice a week; I [b]pay tithes of all that I get.'
13 "But the [1]tax-gatherer, [a]standing some distance away,
[b]was even unwilling to lift up his eyes to heaven, but [c]was
beating his breast, saying, 'God, be [2]merciful to me, the
sinner!'
14 "I tell you, this man went down to his house justified
rather than the other; [a]for every one who exalts himself shall
be humbled, but he who humbles himself shall be exalted."
15 [a]And they were bringing even their babies to Him, in
order that He might touch them, but when the disciples saw it,
they *began* rebuking them.
16 But Jesus called for them, saying, "Permit the children
to come to Me, and stop hindering them, for the kingdom of
God belongs to such as these.
17 "Truly I say to you, [a]whoever does not receive the kingdom of God like a child shall not enter it *at all.*"
18 [a]And a certain ruler questioned Him, saying, "Good
Teacher, what shall I do to obtain eternal life?"
19 And Jesus said to him, "Why do you call Me good? No
one is good except God alone.
20 "You know the commandments, '[a]DO NOT COMMIT

37 [1]Or, *eagles* [a]Matt. 24:28

1 [a]Luke 11:5-10 [b]2 Cor. 4:1

2 [a]Luke 18:4; 20:13; Heb. 12:9

3 [1]Lit., *do me justice*

4 [a]Luke 18:2; 20:13; Heb. 12:9

5 [1]Lit., *do her justice* [2]Lit., *hit me under the eye* [a]Luke 11:8 [b]1 Cor. 9:27 [Gr.]

6 [a]Luke 7:13

7 [1]Or, *and yet He is long-suffering over them* [a]Rev. 6:10 [b]Matt. 24:22; Rom. 8:33; Col. 3:12; 2 Tim. 2:10; Titus 1:1 [c]2 Pet. 3:9

8 [1]Lit., *the faith* [a]Luke 17:26ff.

9 [a]Luke 16:15 [b]Rom. 14:3, 10

10 [1]A publican who collected Roman taxes for profit [a]Acts 3:1; 2 Kin. 20:5, 8; 1 Kin. 10:5

11 [1]Note, verse 10 [a]Matt. 6:5; Mark 11:25; Luke 22:41

12 [a]Matt. 9:14 [b]Luke 11:42

13 [1]Note, verse 10 [2]Or, *propitious* [a]Matt. 6:5; Mark 11:25; Luke 22:41 [b]Ezra 9:6 [c]Luke 23:48

14 [a]Luke 14:11; Matt. 23:12

15 [a]Luke 18:15-17: *Matt. 19:13-15; Mark 10:13-16*

17 [a]Matt. 18:3; 19:14; Mark 10:15; 1 Cor. 14:20; 1 Pet. 2:2

18 [a]Luke 18:18-30: *Matt. 19:16-29; Mark 10:17-30;* Luke 10:25-28

20 [a]Ex. 20:12-16; Deut. 5:16-20

22 [a]Luke 12:33; Matt. 19:21 [b]Matt. 6:20

24 [a]Matt. 19:23; Mark 10:23f.

25 [1]Lit., *enter* [a]Matt. 19:24; Mark 10:25

26 [1]Lit., *and*

27 [a]Matt. 19:26

28 [1]Lit., *our own things* [a]Luke 5:11

29 [a]Matt. 19:29; Mark 10:29f.; Matt. 6:33

30 [a]Matt. 12:32

31 [a]Luke 18:31-33: *Matt. 20:17-19; Mark 10:32-34* [b]Luke 9:51 [c]Ps. 22; Is. 53

32 [1]Or, *betrayed* [a]Matt. 16:21

34 [a]Mark 9:32; Luke 9:45

35 [a]Luke 18:35-43: *Matt. 20:29-34; Mark 10:46-52* [b]Matt. 20:29; Mark 10:46; Luke 19:1

38 [a]Luke 18:39; Matt. 9:27

39 [a]Luke 18:38

40 [1]Lit., *stood*

42 [1]Or, *saved you* [a]Matt. 9:22

43 [a]Matt. 9:8 [b]Luke 13:17; Luke 9:43; 19:37

ADULTERY, DO NOT MURDER, DO NOT STEAL, DO NOT BEAR FALSE
WITNESS, HONOR YOUR FATHER AND MOTHER.' "
21 And he said, "All these things I have kept from *my*
youth."
22 And when Jesus heard *this,* He said to him, "One thing
you still lack; [a]sell all that you possess, and distribute it to the
poor, and you shall have [b]treasure in heaven; and come, follow
Me."
23 But when he had heard these things, he became very
sad; for he was extremely rich.
24 And Jesus looked at him and said, "[a]How hard it is for
those who are wealthy to enter the kingdom of God!
25 "For [a]it is easier for a camel to [1]go through the eye of a
needle, than for a rich man to enter the kingdom of God."
26 And they who heard it said, "[1]Then who can be saved?"
27 But He said, "[a]The things impossible with men are
possible with God."
28 And Peter said, "Behold, [a]we have left [1]our own *homes,*
and followed You."
29 And He said to them, "Truly I say to you, [a]there is no
one who has left house or wife or brothers or parents or children, for the sake of the kingdom of God,
30 who shall not receive many times as much at this time
and in [a]the age to come, eternal life."
31 [a]And He took the twelve aside and said to them, "Behold, [b]we are going up to Jerusalem, and [c]all things which are
written through the prophets about the Son of Man will be
accomplished.
32 "[a]For He will be [1]delivered up to the Gentiles, and will
be mocked and mistreated and spit upon,
33 and after they have scourged Him, they will kill Him;
and the third day He will rise again."
34 And [a]they understood none of these things, and this
saying was hidden from them, and they did not comprehend
the things that were said.
35 [a]And it came about that [b]as He was approaching Jericho, a certain blind man was sitting by the road, begging.
36 Now hearing a multitude going by, he *began* to inquire
what this might be.
37 And they told him that Jesus of Nazareth was passing
by.
38 And he called out, saying, "Jesus, [a]Son of David, have
mercy on me!"
39 And those who led the way were sternly telling him to
be quiet; but he kept crying out all the more, "[a]Son of David,
have mercy on me!"
40 And Jesus [1]stopped and commanded that he be
brought to Him; and when he had come near, He questioned
him,
41 "What do you want Me to do for you?" And he said,
"Lord, *I want* to receive my sight!"
42 And Jesus said to him, "Receive your sight; [a]your faith
has [1]made you well."
43 And immediately he received his sight, and *began* following Him, [a]glorifying God; and when [b]all the people saw
it, they gave praise to God.

CHAPTER 19

AND He [a]entered and was passing through Jericho.
2 And behold, there was a man called by the name of
Zaccheus; and he was a chief [1]tax-gatherer, and he was rich.
3 And he was trying to see who Jesus was, and he was
unable because of the crowd, for he was small in stature.
4 And he ran on ahead and climbed up into a [1a]sycamore
tree in order to see Him, for He was about to pass through that
way.
5 And when Jesus came to the place, He looked up and
said to him, "Zaccheus, hurry and come down, for today I
must stay at your house."
6 And he hurried and came down, and received Him
[1]gladly.
7 And when they saw it, they all *began* to [1]grumble,
saying, "He has gone [2]to be the guest of a man who is a
sinner."
8 And Zaccheus [1]stopped and said to [a]the Lord, "Behold, Lord, half of my possessions I will give to the poor, and if
I have [b]defrauded anyone of anything, I will give back [c]four
times as much."
9 And Jesus said to him, "Today salvation has come to
this house, because he, too, is [a]a son of Abraham.
10 "For [a]the Son of Man has come to seek and to save that
which was lost."
11 And while they were listening to these things, He went
on to tell a parable, because [a]He was near Jerusalem, and they
supposed that [b]the kingdom of God was going to appear
immediately.
12 He said therefore, "[a]A certain nobleman went to a distant country to receive a kingdom for himself, and *then* return.
13 "And he called ten of his slaves, and gave them ten
[1]minas, and said to them, 'Do business *with this* [2]until I come
back.'
14 "But his citizens hated him, and sent [1]a delegation after
him, saying, 'We do not want this man to reign over us.'
15 "And it came about that when he returned, after receiving the kingdom, he ordered that these slaves, to whom he
had given the money, be called to him in order that he might
know what business they had done.
16 "And the first appeared, saying, '[1]Master, your [2]mina has
made ten minas more.'
17 "And he said to him, 'Well done, good slave, because
you have been [a]faithful in a very little thing, be in authority
over ten cities.'
18 "And the second came, saying, 'Your [1]mina, [2]master, has
made five minas.'
19 "And he said to him also, 'And you are to be over five
cities.'
20 "And another came, saying, 'Master, behold your mina,
which I kept put away in a handkerchief;
21 for I was afraid of you, because you are an exacting
man; you take up what you did not lay down, and reap what
you did not sow.'
22 "He *said to him, '[1]By your own words I will judge you,

1 [a]Luke 18:35

2 [1]A publican who collected Roman taxes for profit

4 [1]I.e., a fig-mulberry [a]1 Kin. 10:27; 1 Chr. 27:28; 2 Chr. 1:15; 9:27; Ps. 78:47; Is. 9:10; Luke 17:6 [?]

6 [1]Lit., *rejoicing*

7 [1]Lit., *grumble among themselves* [2]Or, *to find lodging*

8 [1]Lit., *stood* [a]Luke 7:13 [b]Luke 3:14 [Gr.] [c]Ex. 22:1; Lev. 6:5; Num. 5:7; 2 Sam. 12:6

9 [a]Luke 3:8; 13:16; Rom. 4:16; Gal. 3:7

10 [a]Matt. 18:11 marg.

11 [a]Luke 9:51 [b]Luke 17:20

12 [a]Luke 19:12-27; Matt. 25:14-30

13 [1]A mina is equal to about 100 days' wages or nearly $20 [2]Lit., *while I am coming*

14 [1]Or, *an embassy*

16 [1]Lit., *Lord* [2]Note, verse 13

17 [a]Luke 16:10

18 [1]Note, verse 13 [2]Lit., *lord*

22 [1]Lit., *out of your own mouth*

you worthless slave. Did you know that I am an exacting man,
taking up what I did not lay down, and reaping what I did not
sow?
23 '[1]Then why did you not put the money in the bank, and
having come, I would have collected it with interest?'
24 "And he said to the bystanders, 'Take the mina away
from him, and give it to the one who has the ten minas.'
25 "And they said to him, 'Master, he has ten minas
already.'
26 "[a]I tell you, that to everyone who has shall *more* be
given, but from the one who does not have, even what he does
have shall be taken away.
27 'But [a]these enemies of mine, who did not want me to
reign over them, bring them here, and [b]slay them in my
presence.' "
28 And after He had said these things, He [a]was going on
ahead, [b]ascending to Jerusalem.
29 And it came about that [a]when He approached Bethphage and [b]Bethany, near the [1]mount that is called [2c]Olivet,
He sent two of the disciples,
30 saying, "Go into the village opposite *you*, in which as
you enter you will find a colt tied, on which no one yet has
ever sat; untie it, and bring it *here*.
31 "And if anyone asks you, 'Why are you untying it?' thus
shall you speak, 'The Lord has need of it.' "
32 And those who were sent went away and found it just as
He had told them.
33 And as they were untying the colt, its [1]owners said to
them, "Why are you untying the colt?"
34 And they said, "The Lord has need of it."
35 And they brought it to Jesus, [a]and they threw their
garments on the colt, and put Jesus *on it*.
36 And as He was going, they were spreading their garments in the road.
37 And as He was now approaching, near the descent of
[a]the Mount of Olives, the whole multitude of the disciples
began to [b]praise God [1]joyfully with a loud voice for all the
[2]miracles which they had seen,
38 saying,

"[a]BLESSED IS THE [b]KING WHO COMES IN THE NAME OF
THE LORD;
Peace in heaven and [c]glory in the highest!"

39 [a]And some of the Pharisees [1]in the multitude said to
Him, "Teacher, rebuke Your disciples."
40 And He answered and said, "I tell you, if these become
silent, [a]the stones will cry out!"
41 And when He approached, He saw the city and [a]wept
over it,
42 saying, "If you had known in this day, even you, the
things which make for peace! But now they have been hidden
from your eyes.
43 "For the days shall come upon you [1]when your enemies
will [a]throw up a [2]bank before you, and [b]surround you, and hem
you in on every side,
44 and will level you to the ground and your children

23 [1]Lit., *and*

26 [a]Matt. 13:12; Luke 8:18

27 [a]Luke 19:14 [b]Matt. 22:7; Luke 20:16

28 [a]Mark 10:32 [b]Luke 9:51

29 [1]Or, *hill* [2]Or, *Olive Grove* [a]Luke 19:29-38: *Matt. 21:1-9; Mark 11:1-10* [b]Matt. 21:17 [c]Luke 21:37; Acts 1:12

33 [1]Lit., *lords*

35 [a]Luke 19:35-38: *John 12:12-15*

37 [1]Lit., *as they were rejoicing* [2]Or, *works of power* [a]Matt. 21:1; Luke 19:29 [b]Luke 18:43

38 [a]Ps. 118:26 [b]Matt. 2:2; Matt. 25:34 [c]Luke 2:14; Matt. 21:9

39 [1]Lit., *from* [a]Matt. 21:15f.

40 [a]Hab. 2:11

41 [a]Luke 13:34, 35

43 [1]Lit., *and* [2]I.e., a dirt wall or mound for siege purposes [a]Eccles. 9:14; Is. 29:3; 37:33; Jer. 6:6; Ezek. 4:2; 26:8 [b]Luke 21:20

within you, and [a]they will not leave in you one stone upon
another, because you did not recognize [b]the time of your
visitation."
45 [a]And He entered the temple and began to cast out
those who were selling,
46 saying to them, "It is written, '[a]AND MY HOUSE SHALL BE
A HOUSE OF PRAYER,' but you have made it a robbers' [1]den."
47 And [a]He was teaching daily in the temple; but the chief
priests and the scribes and the leading men among the people
[b]were trying to destroy Him,
48 and they could not find [1]anything that they might do,
for all the people were hanging upon [2]His words.

CHAPTER 20

[a]
AND it came about on one of the days while [b]He was teaching the people in the temple and [c]preaching the gospel, that
the chief priests and the scribes with the elders [d]confronted
Him,
2 and they spoke, saying to Him, "Tell us by what authority You are doing these things, or who is the one who gave
You this authority?"
3 And He answered and said to them, "I shall also ask
you a [1]question, and you tell Me:
4 "Was the baptism of John from heaven or from men?"
5 And they reasoned among themselves, saying, "If we
say, 'From heaven,' He will say, 'Why did you not believe
him?'
6 "But if we say, 'From men,' all the people will stone us
to death, for they are convinced that John was a [a]prophet."
7 And they answered that they did not know where *it*
came from.
8 And Jesus said to them, "Neither [1]will I tell you by
what authority I am doing these things."
9 [a]And He began to tell the people this parable: "A man
planted a vineyard and rented it out to [1]vine-growers, and went
on a journey for a long time.
10 "And at the *harvest* time he sent a slave to the vine-
growers, in order that they might give him *some* of the produce
of the vineyard; but the vine-growers beat him and sent him
away empty-handed.
11 "And he proceeded to send another slave; and they beat
him also and treated him shamefully, and sent him away
empty-handed.
12 "And he proceeded to send a third; and this one also
they wounded and cast out.
13 "And the [1]owner of the vineyard said, 'What shall I do?
I will send my beloved son; perhaps they will [a]respect him.'
14 "But when the vine-growers saw him, they reasoned with
one another, saying, 'This is the heir; let us kill him that the
inheritance may be ours.'
15 "And they cast him out of the vineyard and killed him.
What, therefore, will the [1]owner of the vineyard do to them?
16 "He will come and [a]destroy these vine-growers and will

44 [a]Matt. 24:2; Mark 13:2; Luke 21:6 [b]1 Pet. 2:12

45 [a]Luke 19:45, 46: *Matt. 21:12-16; Mark 11:15-18;* John 2:13-16

46 [1]Lit., *cave*
[a]Is. 56:7; Jer. 7:11; Matt. 21:13; Mark 11:17

47 [a]Matt. 26:55 [b]Luke 20:19

48 [1]Lit., *what they might do* [2]Lit., *Him, listening*

1 [a]Luke 20:1-8: *Matt. 21:23-27; Mark 11:27-33* [b]Matt. 26:55 [c]Luke 8:1 [d]Acts 4:1; 6:12

3 [1]Lit., *word*

6 [a]Matt. 11:9; Luke 7:29, 30

8 [1]Lit., *do I tell*

9 [1]Here and in verses 10, 14 and 16, or, *tenant farmers*
[a]Luke 20:9-19: *Matt. 21:33-46; Mark 12:1-12*

13 [1]Lit., *lord*
[a]Luke 18:2 [Gr.]

15 [1]Lit., *lord*

16 [a]Luke 19:27; Matt. 21:41; Mark 12:9

give the vineyard to others." And when they heard it, they said,
"[b]May it never be!"
17 But He looked at them and said, "What then is this
that is written,
'[a]*The* STONE WHICH THE BUILDERS REJECTED,
THIS BECAME [b]THE CHIEF CORNER *STONE*'?
18 "[a]Every one who falls on that stone will be broken to
pieces; but on whomever it falls, it will scatter him like dust."
19 And the scribes and the chief priests [a]tried to lay hands
on Him that very hour, and they feared the people; for they
understood that He spoke this parable against them.
20 [a]And they watched Him, and sent spies who [1]pretended
to be righteous, in order [b]that they might [2]catch Him in some
statement, so as to deliver Him up to the rule and the authority of [c]the governor.
21 And they questioned Him, saying, "Teacher, we know
that You speak and teach correctly, and You [1]are not partial to
any, but teach the way of God in truth.
22 "Is it [1]lawful for us [a]to pay taxes to Caesar, or not?"
23 But He detected their trickery and said to them,
24 "Show Me a [1]denarius. Whose [2]head and inscription
does it have?" And they said, "Caesar's."
25 And He said to them, "Then [a]render to Caesar the
things that are Caesar's, and to God the things that are God's."
26 And they were unable to [1a]catch Him in a saying in the
presence of the people; and marveling at His answer, they
became silent.
27 [a]Now there came to Him some of the Sadducees (who
say that there is no resurrection),
28 and they questioned Him, saying, "Teacher, Moses
wrote us that [a]IF A MAN'S BROTHER DIES, having a wife, AND HE IS
CHILDLESS, HIS BROTHER SHOULD TAKE THE WIFE AND RAISE UP
OFFSPRING TO HIS BROTHER.
29 "Now there were seven brothers; and the first took a
wife, and died childless;
30 and the second
31 and the third took her; and in the same way the seven
also [1]died, leaving no children.
32 "Finally the woman died also.
33 "In the resurrection therefore, which one's wife will the
woman be? For the seven had her as wife."
34 And Jesus said to them, "The sons of [a]this age marry
and are given in marriage,
35 but those who are considered worthy to attain to [a]that
age and the resurrection from the dead, neither marry, nor are
given in marriage;
36 for neither can they die any more, for they are like
angels, and are [a]sons of God, being sons of the resurrection.
37 "But that the dead are raised, even Moses showed, in
[a]the *passage about the burning* bush, where he calls the Lord
[b]THE GOD OF ABRAHAM, AND THE GOD OF ISAAC, AND THE GOD
OF JACOB.
38 "[a]Now He is not the God of the dead, but of the living;
for [b]all live to Him."
39 And some of the scribes answered and said, "Teacher,
You have spoken well."

16 [b]Rom. 3:4, 6, 31; 6:2, 15; 7:7, 13; 9:14; 11:1, 11; 1 Cor. 6:15; Gal. 2:17; 3:21; 6:14, [Gr.]

17 [a]Ps. 118:22 [b]Eph. 2:20; 1 Pet 2:6

18 [a]Matt. 21:44

19 [a]Luke 19:47

20 [1]Lit., *feigned themselves* [2]Lit., *take hold of His word* [a]Luke 20:20-26: *Matt. 22:15-22; Mark 12:13-17;* Mark 3:2 [b]Luke 11:54; 20:26 [c]Matt. 27:2

21 [1]Lit., *do not receive a face*

22 [1]Or, *permissible* [a]Luke 23:2; Matt. 17:25

24 [1]The denarius was worth 18 cents in silver, equivalent to one day's wages [2]Lit., *image*

25 [a]Matt. 22:21; Mark 12:17

26 [1]Lit., *take hold of His saying* [a]Luke 11:54; 20:26

27 [a]Luke 20:27-40: *Matt. 22:23-33; Mark 12:18-27*

28 [a]Deut. 25:5

31 [1]Lit., *left no children, and died*

34 [a]Matt. 12:32; Luke 16:8

35 [a]Matt. 12:32; Luke 16:8

36 [a]Rom. 8:16f.; 1 John 3:1, 2

37 [a]Mark 12:26 [b]Ex. 3:6

38 [a]Matt. 22:32; Mark 12:27 [b]Rom. 14:8

40 For [a]they did not have courage to question Him any
longer about anything.
41 [a]And He said to them, "How *is it that* they say [1]the
Christ is [b]David's son?
42 "For David himself says in the book of Psalms,
'[a]THE LORD SAID TO MY LORD,
"SIT AT MY RIGHT HAND,
43 [a]UNTIL I MAKE THINE ENEMIES A FOOTSTOOL FOR THY
FEET."'
44 "David therefore calls Him 'Lord,' and how is He his
son?"
45 [a]And while all the people were listening, He said to the
disciples,
46 "Beware of the scribes, [a]who like to walk around in long
robes, and love respectful greetings in the market places, and
chief seats in the synagogues, and places of honor at banquets,
47 who devour widows' houses, and for appearance's sake
offer long prayers; these will receive greater condemnation."

[a] CHAPTER 21

AND He looked up and saw the rich putting their gifts into
the treasury.
2 And He saw a certain poor widow putting [1]in [a]two
[2]small copper coins.
3 And He said, "Truly I say to you, this poor widow put
in more than all *of them;*
4 for they all out of their [1]surplus put into the [2]offering;
but she out of her poverty put in all [3]that she had [a]to live on."
5 [a]And while some were talking about the temple, that it
was adorned with beautiful stones and votive gifts, He said,
6 "*As for* these things which you are looking at, the days
will come in which [a]there will not be left one stone upon
another which will not be torn down."
7 And they questioned Him, saying, "Teacher, when therefore will these things be? And what *will be* the [1]sign when
these things are about to take place?"
8 And He said, "Take heed that you be not misled; for
many will come in My name, saying, '[a]I am *He,*' and, 'The
time is at hand'; [b]do not go after them.
9 "And when you hear of wars and disturbances, do not be
terrified; for these things must take place first, but the end
does not *follow* immediately."
10 Then He continued by saying to them, "Nation will
rise against nation, and kingdom against kingdom,
11 and there will be great earthquakes, and in various
places plagues and famines; and there will be terrors and great
[1]signs from heaven.
12 "But before all these things, [a]they will lay their hands on
you and will persecute you, delivering you to the synagogues
and prisons, [1]bringing you before kings and governors for My
name's sake.
13 "[a]It will lead to an [1]opportunity for your testimony.
14 "[a]So make up your minds not to prepare beforehand to
defend yourselves;

40 [a]Matt. 22:46; Luke 14:6

41 [1]I.e., the Messiah [a]Luke 20:41-44: *Matt. 22:41-46; Mark 12:35-37* [b]Matt. 9:27

42 [a]Ps. 110:1

43 [a]Ps. 110:1

45 [a]Luke 20:45-47: *Matt. 23:1-7; Mark 12:38-40*

46 [a]Luke 11:43; Luke 14:7

1 [a]Luke 21:1-4: *Mark 12:41-44*

2 [1]Or, *therein* [2]Lit., *lepta* [a]Mark 12:42

4 [1]Or, *abundance* [2]Lit., *gifts* [3]Lit., *the living that she had* [a]Mark 12:44

5 [a]Luke 21:5-36: *Matt. 24; Mark 13*

6 [a]Luke 19:44

7 [1]Or, *attesting miracle*

8 [a]John 8:24 [b]Luke 17:23

11 [1]Or, *attesting miracles*

12 [1]Lit., *being brought* [a]Luke 21:12-17: *Matt. 10:19-22; Mark 13:11-13*

13 [1]Lit., *a testimony for you* [a]Phil. 1:12

14 [a]Luke 12:11

15 for [a]I will give you [1]utterance and wisdom which none
of your opponents will be able to resist or refute.
16 "But you will be betrayed even by parents and brothers
and relatives and friends, and they will put *some* of you to
death,
17 and you will be hated by all on account of My name.
18 "Yet [a]not a hair of your head will perish.
19 "[a]By your perseverance you will win your souls.
20 "But when you see Jerusalem [a]surrounded by armies,
then [1]recognize that her desolation is at hand.
21 "Then let those who are in Judea flee to the mountains,
and let those who are in the midst of [1]the city depart, and [a]let
not those who are in the country enter [1]the city;
22 because these are [a]days of vengeance, in order that all
things which are written may be fulfilled.
23 "Woe to those who are with child and to those who
nurse babes in those days; for [a]there will be great distress upon
the [1]land, and wrath to this people,
24 and they will fall by [a]the edge of the sword, and will be
led captive into all the nations; and [b]Jerusalem will be
[c]trampled underfoot by the Gentiles until [d]the times of the
Gentiles be fulfilled.
25 "And there will be [1]signs in sun and moon and stars, and
upon the earth dismay among nations, in perplexity at the
roaring of the sea and the waves,
26 men fainting from fear and the expectation of the
things which are coming upon the [1]world; for the powers of
[2]the heavens will be shaken.
27 "And [a]then will they see [b]THE SON OF MAN COMING IN A
CLOUD with power and great glory.
28 "But when these things begin to take place, straighten
up and lift up your heads, because [a]your redemption is drawing
near."
29 And He told them a parable: "Behold the fig tree, and
all the trees;
30 as soon as they put forth *leaves*, you see it and [a]know
for yourselves that the summer is now near.
31 "Even so you too, when you see these things happening,
[1]recognize that [a]the kingdom of God is near.
32 "Truly I say to you, this [1]generation will not pass away
until all things take place.
33 "[a]Heaven and earth will pass away, but My words will
not pass away.
34 "[a]Be on guard, that your hearts may not be weighted
down with dissipation and drunkenness and the worries of life,
and that day come on you suddenly like a trap;
35 for it will come upon all those who dwell on the face of
all the earth.
36 "But [a]keep on the alert at all times, praying in order that
you may have strength to escape all these things that are about
to take place, and to [b]stand before the Son of Man."
37 Now [1]during the day He was [a]teaching in the temple,
but [2b]at evening He would go out and spend the night on [3c]the
mount that is called [4]Olivet.
38 And all the people would get up [a]early in the morning
to come to Him in the temple to listen to Him.

15 [1]Lit., *a mouth* [a]Luke 12:12
18 [a]Matt. 10:30; Luke 12:7
19 [a]Matt. 10:22; 24:13; Rom. 2:7; 5:3f.; James 1:3; Heb. 10:36; 2 Pet. 1:6
20 [1]Lit., *know* [a]Luke 19:43
21 [1]Lit., *her* [a]Luke 17:31
22 [a]Is. 63:4; Hos. 9:7; Dan. 9:24-27
23 [1]Or, *earth* [a]Dan. 8:19; 1 Cor. 7:26
24 [a]Gen. 34:26; Ex. 17:13; Heb. 11:34 [b]Is. 63:18; Dan. 8:13; Rev. 11:2 [c]Rev. 11:2 [d]Rom. 11:25
25 [1]Or, *attesting miracles*
26 [1]Lit., *inhabited earth* [2]Or, *heaven*
27 [a]Matt. 24:30; Mark 13:26; Matt. 16:27; 26:64 [b]Dan. 7:13
28 [a]Luke 18:7
30 [a]Luke 12:57
31 [1]Lit., *know* [a]Matt. 3:2
32 [1]Or, *race*
33 [a]Matt. 5:18; Luke 16:17
34 [a]Matt. 24:42-44; Luke 12:40, 45; Mark 4:19; 1 Thess. 5:2ff.
36 [a]Mark 13:33; Luke 12:40 [b]Luke 1:19; Rev. 7:9; 8:2; 11:4
37 [1]Lit., *days* [2]Lit., *nights* [3]Or, *the hill* [4]Or, *Olive Grove* [a]Matt. 26:55 [b]Mark 11:19 [c]Matt. 21:1
38 [a]John 8:2

Chapter 22

[a]NOW the Feast of Unleavened Bread, which is called the
[b]Passover, was approaching.
2 And the chief priests and the scribes [a]were seeking how
they might put Him to death; for they were afraid of the
people.
3 [a]And [b]Satan entered into Judas who was called Iscariot,
[1]belonging to the number of the twelve.
4 And he went away and discussed with the chief priests
and [a]officers how he might betray Him to them.
5 And they were delighted, and agreed to give him
money.
6 And he consented, and *began* seeking a good opportunity to betray Him to them [1]apart from the multitude.
7 [a]Then came the day of Unleavened Bread on which
[b]the Passover *lamb* had to be sacrificed.
8 And He sent [a]Peter and John, saying, "Go and prepare
the Passover for us, that we may eat it."
9 And they said to Him, "Where do You want us to
prepare it?"
10 And He said to them, "Behold, when you have entered
the city, a man will meet you carrying a pitcher of water;
follow him into the house that he enters.
11 "And you shall say to the owner of the house, 'The
Teacher says to you, "Where is the guest room in which I may
eat the Passover with My disciples?"'
12 "And he will show you a large, furnished, upper room;
prepare it there."
13 And they departed and found *everything* just as He
had told them; and they prepared the Passover.
14 [a]And when the hour had come He reclined *at table*,
and [b]the apostles with Him.
15 And He said to them, "I have earnestly desired to eat
this Passover with you before I suffer;
16 for I say to you, I shall never again eat it [a]until it is
fulfilled in the kingdom of God."
17 [a]And having taken a cup, [b]when He had given thanks,
He said, "Take this and share it among yourselves;
18 for [a]I say to you, I will not drink of the fruit of the vine
from now on until the kingdom of God comes."
19 And having taken *some* bread, [a]when He had given
thanks, He broke *it*, and gave *it* to them, saying, "This is My
body [1]which is given for you; do this in remembrance of Me."
20 And in the same way *He took* the cup after they had
eaten, saying, "This cup which is [a]poured out for you is the
[b]new covenant in My blood.
21 "[a]But behold, the hand of the one betraying Me is with
Me on the table.
22 "For indeed, the Son of Man is going [a]as it has been
determined; but woe to that man through whom He is
betrayed!"
23 And they began to discuss among themselves which
one of them it might be who was going to do this thing.
24 And there arose also [a]a dispute among them *as to*
which one of them was regarded to be greatest.

1 [a]Luke 22:1, 2: *Matt. 26:2-5; Mark 14:1, 2* [b]John 11:55; 13:1
2 [a]Matt. 12:14
3 [1]Lit., *being of* [a]Luke 22:3-6: *Matt. 26:14-16; Mark 14:10-11* [b]Matt. 4:10; John 13:2, 27
4 [a]Luke 22:52; Acts 4:1; 5:24, 26; 1 Chr. 9:11; Neh. 11:11
6 [1]Or, *without a disturbance*
7 [a]Luke 22:7-13: *Matt. 26:17-19; Mark 14:12-16* [b]Mark 14:12
8 [a]Acts 3:1, 11; 4:13, 19; 8:14; Gal. 2:9
14 [a]Matt. 26:20; Mark 14:17 [b]Mark 6:30
16 [a]Luke 22:18, 30; 14:15; Rev. 19:9
17 [a]Luke 22:17-20: *Matt. 26:26-29; Mark 14:22-25; 1 Cor. 11:23-25*; 10:16 [b]Matt. 14:19
18 [a]Matt. 26:29; Mark 14:25
19 [1]Some ancient mss. omit the remainder of verse 19 and all of verse 20 [a]Matt. 14:19
20 [a]Matt. 26:28; Mark 14:24 [b]1 Cor. 11:25; 2 Cor. 3:6; Heb. 9:15; 8:8; Jer. 31:31; Ex. 24:8 [Heb. 8:13]
21 [a]Luke 22:21-23: *Matt. 26:21-24; Mark 14:18-21*; John 13:18, 21, 22, 26
22 [a]Acts 2:23; 4:28; 10:42; 17:31
24 [a]Mark 9:34; Luke 9:46

25 [a]And He said to them, "The kings of the Gentiles lord
it over them; and those who have authority over them are
called 'Benefactors.'
26 "But not so with you, [a]but let him who is the greatest
among you become as [b]the youngest, and the leader as the
servant.
27 "For [a]who is greater, the one who reclines *at table*, or
the one who serves? Is it not the one who reclines *at table?* But
[b]I am among you as the one who serves.
28 "And you are those who have stood by Me in My [a]trials;
29 and just as My Father has granted Me a [a]kingdom, I
grant you
30 that you may [a]eat and drink at My table in My [b]king-
dom, and [c]you will sit on thrones judging the twelve tribes of
Israel.
31 "Simon, Simon, behold, [a]Satan has [1]demanded *permission* to [b]sift you like wheat;
32 but I [a]have prayed for you, that your faith may not fail;
and you, when once you have turned again, [b]strengthen your
brothers."
33 [a]And he said to Him, "Lord, with You I am ready to go
both to prison and to death!"
34 And He said, "I tell you, Peter, the cock will not crow
today until you have denied three times that you know Me."
35 And He said to them, "[a]When I sent you out without
purse and bag and sandals, you did not lack anything, did
you?" And they said, "*No,* nothing."
36 And He said to them, "But now, let him who has a
purse take it along, likewise also a bag, and let him who has no
sword sell his [1]robe and buy one.
37 "For I tell you, that this which is written must be fulfilled in Me, '[a]AND HE WAS [1]CLASSED AMONG CRIMINALS'; for
[b]that which refers to Me has *its* fulfillment."
38 And they said, "Lord, look, here are two [a]swords." And
He said to them, "It is enough."
39 [a]And He came out and proceeded [b]as was His custom
to [c]the Mount of Olives; and the disciples also followed Him.
40 [a]And when He arrived at the place, He said to them,
"[b]Pray that you may not enter into temptation."
41 And He withdrew from them about a stone's throw,
and He [a]knelt down and *began* to pray,
42 saying, "Father, if Thou art willing, remove this [a]cup
from Me; [b]yet not My will, but Thine be done."
43 [1]Now an [a]angel from heaven appeared to Him, strengthening Him.
44 And [a]being in agony He was praying very fervently; and
His sweat became like drops of blood, falling down upon the
ground.
45 And when He rose from prayer, He came to His disciples and found them sleeping from sorrow,
46 and said to them, "Why are you sleeping? Rise and
[a]pray that you may not enter into temptation."
47 [a]While He was still speaking, behold, a multitude
came, and the one called Judas, one of the twelve, was preced-
ing them; and he approached Jesus to kiss Him.

25 [a]Luke 22:25-27: *Matt. 20:25-28; Mark 10:42-45*

26 [a]Luke 9:48 [b]1 Pet. 5:5

27 [a]Luke 12:37 [b]Matt. 20:28

28 [a]Heb. 2:18; 4:15

29 [a]Matt. 5:3; 2 Tim. 2:12

30 [a]Luke 22:16 [b]Matt. 5:3; 2 Tim. 2:12 [c]Matt. 19:28

31 [1]Or, *obtained by asking* [a]Matt. 4:10; Job 1:6-12; 2:1-6 [b]Amos 9:9

32 [a]John 17:9, 15 [b]John 21:15-17

33 [a]Luke 22:33, 34: *Matt. 26:33-35; Mark 14:29-31; John 13:37, 38*

35 [a]Luke 9:3ff.; 10:4; Matt. 10:9f.; Mark 6:8

36 [1]Or, *outer garment*

37 [1]Or, *reckoned with transgressors* [a]Is. 53:12 [b]John 17:4; 19:30

38 [a]Luke 22:36, 49

39 [a]Matt. 26:30; Mark 14:26; John 18:1 [b]Luke 21:37 [c]Matt. 21:1

40 [a]Luke 22:40-46: *Matt. 26:36-46; Mark 14:32-42* [b]Luke 22:46; Matt. 6:13

41 [a]Matt. 26:39; Mark 14:35; Luke 18:11

42 [a]Matt. 20:22 [b]Matt. 26:39

43 [1]Some ancient mss. omit verses 43 and 44 [a]Matt. 4:11

44 [a]Heb. 5:7

46 [a]Luke 22:40

47 [a]Luke 22:47-53: *Matt. 26:47-56; Mark 14:43-50; John 18:3-11*

48 But Jesus said to him, "Judas, are you betraying the
Son of Man with a kiss?"
49 And when those who were around Him saw what was
going to happen, they said, "Lord, shall we strike with the
[a]sword?"
50 And a certain one of them struck the slave of the high
priest and cut off his right ear.
51 But Jesus answered and said, "[1]Stop! No more of this."
And He touched his ear and healed him.
52 And Jesus said to the chief priests and [a]officers of the
temple and elders who had come against Him, "Have you
come out with swords and clubs [b]as against a robber?
53 "While I was with you daily in the temple, you did not
lay hands on Me; but [1]this hour and the power of darkness are
yours."
54 [a]And having arrested Him, they led Him *away*, and
brought Him to the house of the high priest; but [b]Peter was
following at a distance.
55 [a]And after they had kindled a fire in the middle of [b]the
courtyard and had sat down together, Peter was sitting among
them.
56 And a certain servant-girl, seeing him as he sat in the
firelight, and looking intently at him, said, "This man was with
Him too."
57 But he denied *it*, saying, "Woman, I do not know
Him."
58 And a little later, [a]another saw him and said, "You are
one of them too!" But Peter said, "Man, I am not!"
59 And after about an hour had passed, another man *began* to insist, saying, "Certainly this man also was with Him,
[a]for he is a Galilean too."
60 But Peter said, "Man, I do not know what you are
talking about." And immediately, while he was still speaking, a
cock crowed.
61 And [a]the Lord turned and looked at Peter. And Peter
remembered the word of the Lord, how He had told him,
"[b]Before a cock crows today, you will deny Me three times."
62 And he went outside and wept bitterly.
63 [a]And the men who were holding [1]Jesus in custody were
mocking Him, and beating Him,
64 and they blindfolded Him and were asking Him,
saying, "[a]Prophesy, who is the one who hit You?"
65 And they were saying many other things against Him,
[a]blaspheming.
66 [a]And when it was day, [b]the [1]Council of Elders of the
people assembled, both chief priests and scribes, and they led
Him away to their [c]council *chamber*, saying,
67 "[a]If You are the [1]Christ, tell us." But He said to them,
"If I tell you, you will not believe;
68 and if I ask a question, you will not answer.
69 "[a]But from now on [b]THE SON OF MAN WILL BE SEATED AT
THE RIGHT HAND of the power OF GOD."
70 And they all said, "Are You [a]the Son of God, then?"
And He said to them, "[1b]Yes, I am."
71 And they said, "What further need do we have of testimony? For we have heard it ourselves from His own mouth."

49 [a]Luke 22:38

51 [1]Or, *"Let Me at least do this," and He touched . . .*

52 [a]Luke 22:4 [b]Luke 22:37

53 [1]Lit., *this is your hour and power of darkness*

54 [a]Matt. 26:57; Mark 14:53 [b]Matt. 26:58; Mark 14:54; John 18:15

55 [a]Luke 22:55-62: *Matt. 26:69-75; Mark 14:66-72; John 18:16-18, 25-27* [b]Matt. 26:3

58 [a]John 18:26

59 [a]Matt. 26:73; Mark 14:70

61 [a]Luke 7:13 [b]Luke 22:34

63 [1]Lit., *Him* [a]Luke 22:63-65: Matt. 26:67f.; Mark 14:65; John 18:22f.

64 [a]Matt. 26:68; Mark 14:65

65 [a]Matt. 27:39 Gr.

66 [1]Or, *Sanhedrin* [a]Matt. 27:1f.; Mark 15:1; John 18:28 [b]Acts 22:5 Gr. [c]Matt. 5:22

67 [1]I.e., Messiah [a]Luke 22:67-71: Matt. 26:63-66; Mark 14:61-63; John 18:19-21

69 [a]Matt. 26:64; Mark 14:62; Mark 16:19 [b]Ps. 110:1

70 [1]Lit., *you say that I am* [a]Matt. 4:3 [b]Matt. 27:11; Luke 23:3; Matt. 26:64

Chapter 23

THEN the whole body of them arose and [a]brought Him
before Pilate.
2 [a]And they began to accuse Him, saying, "We found
this man [b]misleading our nation and [c]forbidding to pay taxes
to Caesar, and saying that He Himself is [1]Christ, a King."
3 And Pilate asked Him, saying, "Are You the King of
the Jews?" And He answered him and said, "[a]*It is as* you say."
4 And Pilate said to the chief priests and the multitudes,
"[a]I find no guilt in this man."
5 But they kept on insisting, saying, "He stirs up the
people, teaching all over Judea, [a]starting from Galilee, even as
far as this place."
6 But when Pilate heard it, he asked whether the man
were a Galilean.
7 And when he learned that He belonged to Herod's
jurisdiction, he sent Him to [a]Herod, who himself also was in
Jerusalem [1]at that time.
8 Now Herod was very glad when he saw Jesus; for [a]he
had wanted to see Him for a long time, because he had been
hearing about Him and was hoping to see some [1]sign performed by Him.
9 And he questioned Him [1]at some length; but [a]He answered him nothing.
10 And the chief priests and the scribes were standing
there, accusing Him vehemently.
11 And Herod with his soldiers, after treating Him with
contempt and mocking Him, [a]dressed Him in a gorgeous robe
and sent Him back to Pilate.
12 Now [a]Herod and Pilate became friends with one another that very day; for before they had been at enmity with
each other.
13 And Pilate summoned the chief priests and the [a]rulers
and the people,
14 and said to them, "You brought this man to me as one
who [a]incites the people to rebellion, and behold, having examined Him before you, I [b]have found no guilt in this man
regarding the charges which you make against Him.
15 "No, nor has [a]Herod, for he sent Him back to us; and
behold, nothing deserving death has been done by Him.
16 "I will therefore [a]punish Him and release Him."
17 (See marginal note.[1])
18 But they cried out all together, saying, "[a]Away with this
man, and release for us Barabbas!"
19 (He was one who had been thrown in prison for a
certain insurrection made in the city, and for murder.)
20 And Pilate, wanting to release Jesus, addressed them
again,
21 but they kept on calling out, saying, "Crucify, crucify
Him!"
22 And he said to them the third time, "Why, what evil
has this man done? I have found in Him no guilt *demanding*
death; I will therefore [a]punish Him and release Him."
23 But they were insistent, with loud voices asking that He
be crucified. And their voices *began* to prevail.

1 [a]Matt. 27:2; Mark 15:1; John 18:28

2 [1]I.e., Messiah [a]Luke 23:2, 3: *Matt. 27:11-14; Mark 15:2-5; John 18:29-37* [b]Luke 23:14 [c]Luke 20:22; John 18:33ff.; 19:12; Acts 17:7

3 [a]Luke 22:70

4 [a]Luke 23:14, 22; Matt. 27:23; Mark 15:14; John 18:38; 19:4, 6

5 [a]Matt. 4:12

7 [1]Lit., *in these days* [a]Matt. 14:1; Mark 6:14; Luke 3:1; 9:7; 13:31

8 [1]Or, *attesting miracle* [a]Luke 9:9

9 [1]Lit., *in many words* [a]Matt. 27:12, 14; Mark 15:5; John 19:9

11 [a]Matt. 27:28

12 [a]Acts 4:27

13 [a]Luke 23:35; John 7:26, 48; 12:42; Acts 3:17; 4:5, 8; 13:27

14 [a]Luke 23:2 [b]Luke 23:4

15 [a]Luke 9:9

16 [a]Matt. 27:26; Mark 15:15; John 19:1; Acts 16:37; Luke 23:22

17 [1]Some mss. insert verse 17, *Now he was obliged to release to them at the feast one* prisoner

18 [a]Luke 23:18-25: *Matt. 27:15-26; Mark 15:6-15;* John 18:39-19:16

22 [a]Luke 23:16

24 And Pilate pronounced sentence that their demand
should be granted.
25 And he released the man they were asking for who had
been thrown into prison for insurrection and murder, but he
turned Jesus over to their will.
26 [a]And when they led Him away, they laid hold of one
Simon, a [b]Cyrenian, coming in from the country, and placed
on him the cross to carry behind Jesus.
27 And there were following Him a great multitude of the
people, and of women who were [1a]mourning and lamenting
Him.
28 But Jesus turning to them said, "Daughters of Jerusalem, stop weeping for Me, but weep for yourselves and for
your children.
29 "For behold, the days are coming when they will say,
'[a]Blessed are the barren, and the wombs that never bore, and
the breasts that never nursed.'
30 "Then they will begin TO [a]SAY TO THE MOUNTAINS, 'FALL
ON US,' AND TO THE HILLS, 'COVER US.'
31 "For if they do these things in the green tree, what will
happen in the dry?"
32 [a]And two others also, who were criminals, were being
led away to be put to death with Him.
33 [a]And when they came to the place called [1]The Skull,
there they crucified Him and the criminals, one on the right
and the other on the left.
34 [1]But Jesus was saying, "[a]Father forgive them; for they
do not know what they are doing." [b]AND THEY CAST LOTS,
DIVIDING UP HIS GARMENTS AMONG THEMSELVES.
35 And the people stood by, looking on. And even the
[a]rulers were sneering at Him, saying, "He saved others; [b]let
Him save Himself if this is the [1]Christ of God, His Chosen
One."
36 And the soldiers also mocked Him, coming up to Him,
[a]offering Him sour wine,
37 and saying, "[a]If You are the King of the Jews, save
Yourself!"
38 Now there was also an inscription above Him, "[a]THIS
IS THE KING OF THE JEWS."
39 [a]And one of the criminals who were hanged *there* was
[1]hurling abuse at Him, saying, "Are You not the [2]Christ? [b]Save
Yourself and us!"
40 But the other answered, and rebuking him said, "Do
you not even fear God, since you are under the same sentence
of condemnation?
41 "And we indeed justly, for we are receiving [1]what we
deserve for our deeds; but this man has done nothing wrong."
42 And he was saying, "Jesus, remember me when You
come [1]in Your kingdom!"
43 And He said to him, "Truly I say to you, today you
shall be with Me in [a]Paradise."
44 [a]And it was now about [1b]the sixth hour, and darkness
[2]fell over the whole land until [3]the ninth hour,
45 the sun [1]being obscured; and [a]the veil of the temple
was torn [2]in two.
46 And Jesus, [a]crying out with a loud voice, said, "Father,

26 [a]Luke 23:26: *Matt. 27:32; Mark 15:21;* John 19:17 [b]Matt. 27:32

27 [1]Lit., *beating the breast* [a]Luke 8:52

29 [a]Matt. 24:19; Luke 21:23; 11:27

30 [a]Hos. 10:8; Rev. 6:16; Is. 2:19, 20

32 [a]Matt. 27:38; Mark 15:27; John 19:18

33 [1]In Latin, *Calvarius,* or *Calvary* [a]Luke 23:33-43: *Matt. 27:33-44; Mark 15:22-32; John 19:17-24*

34 [1]Some mss. omit, *"But Jesus was saying. . . doing."* [a]Matt. 11:25; Luke 22:42 [b]Ps. 22:18; John 19:24

35 [1]I.e., Messiah [a]Luke 23:13 [b]Matt. 27:43

36 [a]Matt. 27:48

37 [a]Matt. 27:43

38 [a]Matt. 27:37; Mark 15:26; John 19:19

39 [1]Or, *blaspheming* [2]I.e., Messiah [a]Luke 23:39-43: Matt. 27:44; Mark 15:32 [b]Luke 23:35, 37

41 [1]Lit., *things worthy of what we have done*

42 [1]Or, *into*

43 [a]2 Cor. 12:4; Rev. 2:7; Gen. 2:8 [Sept.]

44 [1]I.e., 12 noon [2]Or, *occurred* [3]I.e., 3 p.m. [a]Luke 23:44-49: *Matt. 27:45-56; Mark 15:33-41* [b]John 19:14

45 [1]Lit., *failing* [2]Lit., *in the middle* [a]Matt. 27:51

46 [a]Matt. 27:50; Mark 15:37; John 19:30

46 [b]Ps. 31:5

47 [1]Lit., *righteous* [a]Matt. 27:54; Mark 15:39 [b]Matt. 9:8

48 [a]Luke 18:13; Luke 8:52

49 [a]Matt. 27: 55f.; Mark 15:40f.; Luke 8:2; John 19:25

50 [a]Luke 23:50-56: *Matt. 27:57-61; Mark 15:42-47; John 19:38-42* [b]Mark 15:43

51 [a]Mark 15:43; Luke 2:25

54 [1]Lit., *dawn* [a]Mark 15:42; Matt. 27:62

55 [a]Luke 23:49

56 [a]Mark 16:1; Luke 24:1 [b]Ex. 20:10

1 [a]Luke 24:1-10: *Matt. 28:1-8; Mark 16:1-8;* John 20:1-8

3 [a]Acts 1:21; Luke 7:13

4 [a]John 20:12 [b]Luke 2:9; Acts 12:7

6 [1]Some ancient mss. omit: *He is not here, but He has risen* [2]Or, *been raised* [a]Mark 16:6 [b]Matt. 17:22f.; Mark 9:30f.; Luke 9:44; Luke 24:44

7 [a]Matt. 16:21; Luke 24:46

8 [a]John 2:22

10 [a]Matt. 27:56 [b]Mark 6:30

11 [1]Lit., *in their sight* [a]Mark 16:11

12 [1]Some ancient mss. omit verse 12 [a]John 20:3-6

[b]INTO THY HANDS I COMMIT MY SPIRIT." And having said this,
He breathed His last.
47 [a]Now when the centurion saw what had happened, he
began [b]praising God, saying, "Certainly this man was
[1]innocent."
48 And all the multitudes who came together for this spectacle, when they observed what had happened, *began* to return, [a]beating their breasts.
49 [a]And all His acquaintances and [a]the women who accompanied Him from Galilee, were standing at a distance,
seeing these things.
50 [a]And behold, a man named Joseph, who was a [b]mem-
ber of the Council, a good and righteous man,
51 (he had not consented to their plan and action) *a man*
from Arimathea, a city of the Jews, who was [a]waiting for the
kingdom of God,
52 this man went to Pilate and asked for the body of Jesus.
53 And he took it down and wrapped it in a linen cloth,
and laid Him in a tomb cut into the rock, where no one had
ever lain.
54 And it was [a]the Preparation Day, and the Sabbath was
about to [1]begin.
55 Now [a]the women who had come with Him out of Galilee followed after, and saw the tomb and how His body was
laid.
56 And they returned and [a]prepared spices and perfumes.
And on the Sabbath they rested according to [b]the commandment.

[a] CHAPTER 24

BUT on the first day of the week, at early dawn, they came to
the tomb, bringing the spices which they had prepared.
2 And they found the stone rolled away from the tomb,
3 but when they entered, they did not find the body of
[a]the Lord Jesus.
4 And it happened that while they were perplexed about
this, behold, [a]two men suddenly [b]stood near them in dazzling
apparel;
5 and as *the women* were terrified and bowed their faces
to the ground, *the men* said to them, "Why do you seek the
living One among the dead?
6 "[1]He is not here, but He [a]has [2]risen. Remember how
He spoke to you [b]while He was still in Galilee,
7 saying that [a]the Son of Man must be delivered into the
hands of sinful men, and be crucified, and the third day rise
again."
8 And [a]they remembered His words,
9 and returned from the tomb and reported all these
things to the eleven and to all the rest.
10 Now they were [a]Mary Magdalene and Joanna and
Mary the *mother* of James; also the other women with them
were telling these things to [b]the apostles.
11 And these words appeared [1]to them as nonsense, and
they [a]would not believe them.
12 [[1]But Peter arose and [a]ran to the tomb; [a]stooping and

looking in, he *saw the linen wrappings [2]only; and he went
away [b]to his home, marveling at that which had happened.]
13 And behold, [a]two of them were going that very day to a
village named Emmaus, which was [1]about seven miles from
Jerusalem.
14 And they were conversing with each other about all
these things which had taken place.
15 And it came about that while they were conversing and
discussing, Jesus Himself approached, and *began* traveling
with them.
16 But [a]their eyes [1]were prevented from recognizing Him.
17 And He said to them, "What are these words that you
are exchanging with one another as you are walking?" And
they stood still, looking sad.
18 And one of them, named Cleopas, answered and said
to Him, "[1]Are You the only one visiting Jerusalem and unaware
of the things which have happened here in these days?"
19 And He said to them, "What things?" And they said to
Him, "The things about [a]Jesus the Nazarene, who was a [b]proph-
et mighty in deed and word in the sight of God and all the
people,
20 and how the chief priests and our [a]rulers delivered Him
up to the sentence of death, and crucified Him.
21 "But we were hoping that it was He who was going to
[a]redeem Israel. Indeed, besides all this, it is the third day since
these things happened.
22 "But also some women among us amazed us. [a]When
they were at the tomb early in the morning,
23 and did not find His body, they came, saying that they
had also seen a vision of angels, who said that He was alive.
24 "And some of those who were with us went to the tomb
and found it just exactly as the women also had said; but Him
they did not see."
25 And He said to them, "O foolish men and slow of heart
to believe in all that [a]the prophets have spoken!
26 "[a]Was it not necessary for the [1]Christ to suffer these
things and to enter into His glory?"
27 And beginning [1]with [a]Moses and [1]with all the [b]proph-
ets, He explained to them the things concerning Himself in
all the Scriptures.
28 And they approached the village where they were
going, and [a]He acted as though He would go farther.
29 And they urged Him, saying, "Stay with us, for it is
getting toward evening, and the day [1]is now nearly over." And
He went in to stay with them.
30 And it came about that when He had reclined *at table*
with them, He took the bread and [a]blessed *it*, and breaking *it*,
He *began* giving *it* to them.
31 And their [a]eyes were opened and they recognized Him;
and He vanished from [1]their sight.
32 And they said to one another, "[1]Were not our hearts
burning within us while He was speaking to us on the road,
while He [a]was [2]explaining the Scriptures to us?"
33 And they arose that very hour and returned to Jerusalem, and [a]found gathered together the eleven and [b]those who
were with them,

12 [2]Or, *by themselves* [b]John 20:10

13 [1]I.e., 60 stadia, one stadion equals 600 feet [a]Mark 16:12

16 [1]Lit., *were being prevented* [a]John 20:14; 21:4; Luke 24:31

18 [1]Or, *Are You visiting Jerusalem alone . . .*

19 [a]Mark 1:24 [b]Matt. 21:11

20 [a]Luke 23:13

21 [a]Luke 1:68

22 [a]Luke 24:1ff.

25 [a]Matt. 26:24

26 [1]I.e., Messiah [a]Luke 24:7, 44ff.; Heb. 2:10; 1 Pet. 1:11

27 [1]Lit., *from* [a]Gen. 3:15; 12:3; Num. 21:9 [John 3:14]; Deut. 18:15 [John 1:45]; John 5:46 [b]2 Sam. 7:12-16; Is. 7:14 [Matt. 1:23]; 9:1f. [Matt. 4:15f.]; 42: [Matt. 12:18ff.]; 53: [Matt. 8:17; Luke 22:37]; Dan. 7:13 [Matt. 24:30]; Mic. 5:2 [Matt. 2:6]; Zech. 9:9 [Matt. 21:5]; Acts 13:27

28 [a]Mark 6:48

29 [1]Lit., *has now declined*

30 [a]Matt. 14:19

31 [1]Lit., *them* [a]Luke 24:16

32 [1]Lit., *was not our heart* [2]Lit., *opening* [a]Luke 24:45

33 [a]Mark 16:13 [b]Acts 1:14

34 saying, "[a]The Lord has really risen, and [b]has appeared
to Simon."
35 And they *began* to relate [1]their experiences on the road
and how [a]He was recognized by them in the breaking of the
bread.
36 And while they were telling these things, [a]He Himself
stood in their midst.[1]
37 But they were startled and frightened and thought that
they were seeing [a]a spirit.
38 And He said to them, "Why are you troubled, and why
do doubts arise in your [1]hearts?
39 "[a]See My hands and My feet, that it is I Myself; [b]touch
Me and see, for a spirit does not have flesh and bones as you
see that I have."
40 (See marginal note.[1])
41 And while they still [1a]could not believe *it* for joy and
were marveling, He said to them, "[b]Have you anything here to
eat?"
42 And they gave Him a piece of a broiled fish;
43 and He took it and [a]ate *it* [1]in their sight.
44 Now He said to them, "[a]These are My words which I
spoke to you while I was still with you, that all things which are
written about Me in the [b]Law of Moses and [b]the Prophets and
[c]the Psalms must be fulfilled."
45 Then He [a]opened their [1]minds to understand the
Scriptures,
46 and He said to them, "[a]Thus it is written, that the
[1]Christ should suffer and [b]rise again from the dead the third
day;
47 and that [a]repentance [1]for forgiveness of sins should be
proclaimed [2]in His name to [b]all the nations—beginning from
Jerusalem.
48 "You are [a]witnesses of these things.
49 "And behold, [a]I am sending forth the promise of My
Father upon you; but [b]you are to stay in the city until you are
clothed with power from on high."
50 And He led them out as far as [a]Bethany, and He lifted
up His hands and blessed them.
51 And it came about that while He was blessing them, He
parted from them.[1]
52 And they[1] returned to Jerusalem with great joy,
53 and were continually in the temple, [1]praising God.

34 [a]Luke 24:6 [b]1 Cor. 15:5

35 [1]Lit., *the things* [a]Luke 24:30f.

36 [1]Some ancient mss. insert, *And He says to them, "Peace be to you."* [a]Mark 16:14

37 [a]Matt. 14:26; Mark 6:49

38 [1]Lit., *heart*

39 [a]John 20:20, 27 [b]1 John 1:1; John 20:27

40 [1]Some mss. add verse 40, *And when He had said this, He showed them His hands and His feet.*

41 [1]Lit., *were disbelieving* [a]Luke 24:11 [b]John 21:5

43 [1]Lit., *before them* [a]Acts 10:41

44 [a]Luke 9:22, 44f.; 18:31-34; 22:37 [b]Luke 24:27 [c]Ps. 2 [Acts 13:33]; Ps. 16 [Acts 2:27]; Ps. 22 [Matt. 27:34-46]; Ps. 69 [John 19:28ff.]; Ps. 72; 110 [Matt. 22:43f.]; Ps. 118 [Matt. 21:42]

45 [1]Lit., *mind* [a]Luke 24:32; Acts 16:14; 1 John 5:20

46 [1]I.e., Messiah [a]Luke 24:26, 44 [b]Luke 24:7

47 [1]Some mss. read, *and forgiveness* [2]Or, *on the basis of* [a]Acts 5:31; 10:43; 13:38; 26:18 [b]Matt. 28:19

48 [a]Acts 1:8, 22; 2:32; 3:15; 4:33; 5:32; 10:39, 41; 13:31; 1 Pet. 5:1

49 [a]John 14:26 [b]Acts 1:4

50 [a]Matt. 21:17; Acts 1:12

51 [1]Some mss. add, *and was carried up into heaven*

52 [1]Some mss. insert, *worshiped Him, and . . .*

53 [1]Lit., *blessing*

THE GOSPEL
ACCORDING TO
JOHN

The Prologue. The Word Made Flesh Announced by John.

[a]IN the beginning was [b]the Word, and the Word was [c]with
God, and [d]the Word was God.
2 [1]He was in the beginning with God.
3 [a]All things came into being through Him; and apart
from Him nothing came into being that has come into being.
4 [a]In Him was life; and the life was [b]the light of men.
5 And [a]the light shines in the darkness; and the darkness
did not [1]comprehend it.
6 There [1]came a man, sent from God, whose name was
[a]John.
7 [1]He came [a]for a witness, that he might bear witness of
the light, [b]that all might believe through him.
8 [1][a]He was not the light, but *came* that he might bear
witness of the light.
9 There was [a]the true light [1]which, coming into the
world, enlightens every man.
10 He was in the world, and [a]the world was made through
Him, and the world did not know Him.
11 He came to His [1]own, and those who were His own did
not receive Him.
12 But as many as received Him, to them He gave the
right to become [a]children of God, *even* [b]to those who believe
in His name:
13 [a]who were [1]born not of [2]blood, nor of the will of the
flesh, nor of the will of man, but of God.
14 And [a]the Word [b]became flesh, and [1][c]dwelt among us,
and [d]we beheld His glory, glory as of [2]the only begotten from
the Father, full of [e]grace and [f]truth.
15 John *[a]bore witness of Him, and cried out, saying,
"This was He of whom I said, '[b]He who comes after me [1]has a
higher rank than I, [c]for He existed before me.' "
16 For of His [a]fulness [1]we have all received, and [2]grace
upon grace.
17 For [a]the law was given through Moses; [b]grace and
[c]truth were realized through Jesus Christ.
18 [a]No man has seen God at any time; [b]the only begotten
[1]God, who is [c]in the bosom of the Father, [d]He has explained
Him.
19 And this is [a]the witness of John, when [b]the Jews sent to
him priests and Levites [c]from Jerusalem to ask him, "Who are
you?"
20 And he confessed, and did not deny, and he confessed,
"[a]I am not [1]the Christ."
21 And they asked him, "What then? Are you [a]Elijah?"
And he *said, "I am not." "Are you [b]the Prophet?" And he
answered, "No."

1 [a]Gen. 1:1; Col. 1:17; 1 John 1:1 [b]John 1:14; Rev. 19:13 [c]1 John 1:2; John 17:5 [d]Phil. 2:6
2 [1]Lit., *This One*
3 [a]John 1:10; 1 Cor. 8:6; Col. 1:16; Heb. 1:2
4 [a]John 5:26; John 11:25; 14:6 [b]John 8:12; 9:5; 12:46
5 [1]Or, *overpower* [a]John 3:19
6 [1]Or, *came into being* [a]Matt. 3:1
7 [1]Lit., *This One* [a]John 1:15, 19, 32; 3:26; 5:33 [b]John 1:12; Acts 19:4; Gal. 3:26
8 [1]Lit., *That One* [a]John 1:20
9 [1]Or, *which enlightens every man coming into the world* [a]1 John 2:8
10 [a]1 Cor. 8:6; Col. 1:16; Heb. 1:2
11 [1]Gr., *His own things, possessions, domain*
12 [a]John 11:52; Gal. 3:26 [b]John 1:7; 3:18; 1 John 5:13; 1 John 3:23
13 [1]Or, *begotten* [2]Or, Gr., *bloods* [a]John 3:5f.; 1 Pet. 1:23; James 1:18; 1 John 2:29; 3:9
14 [1]Or, Gr., *tabernacled* [2]Lit., *an only or unique one* or, *an only begotten from a father* [a]Rev. 19:13 [b]Rom. 1:3; Gal. 4:4; Phil. 2:7f.; 1 Tim. 3:16; Heb. 2:14; 1 John 1:1f.; 4:2; 2 John 7 [c]Rev. 21:3 [d]Luke 9:32; John 2:11; 17:22, 24; 2 Pet. 1:16f.; 1 John 1:1 [e]John 1:17; Rom. 5:21; 6:14 [f]John 8:32; 14:6; 18:37
15 [1]Lit., *is become before me* [a]John 1:7 [b]John 1:27, 30; Matt. 3:11 [c]John 1:30
16 [1]Lit., *we all received* [2]Lit., *grace for grace* [a]Eph. 1:23; 3:19; 4:13; Col. 1:19; 2:9
17 [a]John 7:19 [b]John 1:14; Rom. 5:21; 6:14 [c]John 8:32; 14:6; 18:37
18 [1]Some later mss. read, *Son* [a]Ex. 33:20; John 6:46; Col. 1:15; 1 Tim. 6:16; 1 John 4:12 [b]John 3:16, 18; 1 John 4:9 [c]John 13:23; Luke 16:22 [d]John 3:11
19 [a]John 1:7 [b]John 2:18, 20; 5:10, 15f., 18; 6:41, 52; 7:1, 11, 13, 15, 35; 8:22, 48, 52, 57; 9:18, 22; 10:24, 31, 33 [c]Matt. 15:1
20 [1]I.e., the Messiah [a]John 3:28; cf. Luke 3:15f.
21 [a]Matt. 11:14; 16:14 [b]Deut. 18:15, 18; John 1:25; Matt. 21:11

22 They said then to him, "Who are you, so that we may
give an answer to those who sent us? What do you say about
yourself?"
23 He said, "[a]I am a voice of one crying in the wilderness,
'[b]MAKE STRAIGHT THE WAY OF THE LORD,' as Isaiah the prophet
said."
24 Now they had been sent from the Pharisees.
25 And they asked him, and said to him, "Why then are
you baptizing, if you are not the [1]Christ, nor Elijah, nor [a]the
Prophet?"
26 John answered them saying, "[a]I baptize [1]in water, *but*
among you stands One whom you do not know.
27 "*It is* [a]He who comes after me, the [b]thong of whose
sandal I am not worthy to untie."
28 These things took place in Bethany [a]beyond the Jordan, where John was baptizing.
29 The next day he *saw Jesus coming to him, and *said,
"Behold, [a]the Lamb of God who [b]takes away the sin of the
world!
30 "This is He on behalf of whom I said, '[a]After me comes
a Man who [1]has a higher rank than I, [b]for He existed before
me.'
31 "And I did not recognize [1]Him, but in order that He
might be manifested to Israel, I came baptizing [2]in water."
32 And John [a]bore witness saying, "[b]I have beheld the
Spirit descending as a dove out of heaven; and He remained
upon Him.
33 "And I did not recognize [1]Him, but He who sent me to
baptize [2]in water said to me, 'He upon whom you see the Spirit
descending and remaining upon Him, [a]this is the one who
baptizes [2]in the Holy Spirit.'
34 "And I have seen, and have borne witness that this is
[a]the Son of God."
35 Again [a]the next day John was standing, and two of his
disciples;
36 and he looked upon Jesus as He walked, and *said,
"Behold, [a]the Lamb of God!"
37 And the two disciples heard him speak, and they followed Jesus.
38 And Jesus turned, and beheld them following, and
*said to them, "What do you seek?" And they said to Him,
"[a]Rabbi (which translated means Teacher), where are You
staying?"
39 He *said to them, "Come, and you will see." They
came therefore and saw where He was staying; and they stayed
with Him that day, for it was about the [1]tenth hour.
40 [a]One of the two who heard John *speak*, and followed
Him, was Andrew, Simon Peter's brother.
41 He *found first his own brother Simon, and *said to
him, "We have found the [a]Messiah" (which translated means
[1]Christ).
42 He brought him to Jesus. Jesus looked at him, and said,
"You are Simon the son of [1a]John; you shall be called [b]Cephas"
(which translated means [2c]Peter).
43 [a]The next day *He* purposed to go forth into [b]Galilee,
and He *found [c]Philip, and Jesus *said to him, "[d]Follow Me."

23 [a]Matt. 3:3; Mark 1:3; Luke 3:4 [b]Is. 40:3

25 [1]I.e., Messiah [a]Deut. 18:15, 18; John 1:21; Matt. 21:11

26 [1]The Gr. here can be translated *in, with,* or *by* [a]Matt. 3:11; Mark 1:8; Luke 3:16; Acts 1:5

27 [a]John 1:30; Matt. 3:11 [b]Mark 1:7; Luke 3:16; Matt. 3:11

28 [a]John 3:26; 10:40

29 [a]Is. 53:7; John 1:36; Acts 8:32; 1 Pet. 1:19; Rev. 5:6, 8, 12f.; 6:1 [b]1 John 3:5; Matt. 1:21

30 [1]Lit., *has become before me* [a]John 1:27; Matt. 3:11 [b]John 1:15

31 [1]I.e., as the Messiah [2]The Gr. here can be translated *in, with,* or *by*

32 [a]John 1:7 [b]Matt. 3:16; Mark 1:10; Luke 3:22

33 [1]I.e., as the Messiah [2]The Gr. here can be translated *in, with,* or *by* [a]Matt. 3:11; Mark 1:8; Luke 3:16; Acts 1:5

34 [a]John 1:49; Matt. 4:3

35 [a]John 1:29

36 [a]John 1:29

38 [a]Matt. 23:7f.; John 1:49

39 [1]I.e., 4 p.m.

40 [a]John 1:40-42; Matt. 4:18-22; Mark 1:16-20; Luke 5:2-11

41 [1]Greek for *Anointed One* [a]Dan. 9:25 marg.; John 4:25

42 [1]Gr. *Joannes*, called in Matt. 16:17, Jonas [2]I.e., Rock or Stone [a]John 21:15-17 [b]1 Cor. 1:12; 3:22; 9:5; 15:5; Gal. 1:18; 2:9, 11, 14 [c]Matt. 16:18

43 [a]John 1:35; John 1:29 [b]John 1:28; Matt. 4:12; John 2:11 [c]Matt. 10:3; John 1:44-48; John 6:5, 7; 12:21f.; 14:8f. [d]Matt. 8:22

44 Now [a]Philip was from [b]Bethsaida, of the city of Andrew and Peter.
45 [a]Philip *found [b]Nathanael, and *said to him, "We
have found Him, of whom [c]Moses in the Law and also [c]the
Prophets wrote, Jesus of [d]Nazareth, [e]the son of Joseph."
46 And Nathanael *said to him, "[a]Can any good thing
come out of Nazareth?" [b]Philip *said to him, "Come and
see."
47 Jesus saw Nathanael coming to Him, and *said of him,
"Behold, an [a]Israelite indeed, in whom is no guile!"
48 Nathanael *said to Him, "How do You know me?"
Jesus answered and said to him, "Before [a]Philip called you,
when you were under the fig tree, I saw you."
49 Nathanael answered Him, "[a]Rabbi, You are [b]the Son
of God; You are the [c]King of Israel."
50 Jesus answered and said to him, "Because I said to you
that I saw you under the fig tree, do you believe? You shall see
greater things than these."
51 And He *said to him, "Truly, truly, I say to you,
you shall see [a]the heavens opened, and [b]the angels of God
ascending and descending upon [c]the Son of Man."

CHAPTER 2

AND on [a]the third day there was a wedding in [b]Cana of
Galilee; and the [c]mother of Jesus was there;
2 and Jesus also was invited, and His [a]disciples, to the
wedding.
3 And when the wine gave out, the mother of Jesus *said
to Him, "They have no wine."
4 And Jesus *said to her, "[a]Woman, [1b]what do I have to
do with you? [c]My hour has not yet come."
5 His [a]mother *said to the servants, "Whatever He says
to you, do it."
6 Now there were six stone waterpots set there [a]for the
Jewish custom of purification, containing [1]twenty or thirty
gallons each.
7 Jesus *said to them, "Fill the waterpots with water."
And they filled them up to the brim.
8 And He *said to them, "Draw *some* out now, and take
it to the [1]headwaiter." And they took it *to him.*
9 And when the headwaiter tasted the water [a]which had
become wine, and did not know where it came from (but the
servants who had drawn the water knew), the headwaiter
*called the bridegroom,
10 and *said to him, "Every man serves the good wine
first, and when *men* [a]have [1]drunk freely, *then* that which is
poorer; you have kept the good wine until now."
11 This beginning of *His* [1a]signs Jesus did in Cana of [b]Gal-
ilee, and manifested His [c]glory, and His disciples believed in
Him.
12 After this He went down to [a]Capernaum, He and His
[b]mother, and *His* [b]brothers, and His [c]disciples; and there they
stayed a few days.
13 And [a]the Passover of the Jews was at hand, and Jesus
[b]went up to Jerusalem.

44 [a]Matt. 10:3; John 1:44-48: John 6:5, 7; 12:21f.; 14:8f. [b]Matt. 11:21

45 [a]Matt. 10:3; John 1:44-48; John 6:5, 7; 12:21f.; 14:8f. [b]John 1:46-49; 21:2 [c]Luke 24:27 [d]Matt. 2:23 [e]Luke 3:23; 2:48; 4:22; John 6:42

46 [a]John 7:41, 52 [b]Matt. 10:3; John 1:44-48: John 6:5, 7; 12:21f.; 14:8f.

47 [a]Rom. 9:4

48 [a]Matt. 10:3; John 1:44-48: John 6:5, 7; 12:21f.; 14:8f.

49 [a]John 1:38 [b]John 1:34 [c]Matt. 2:2; 27:42; Mark 15:32; John 12:13

51 [a]Ezek. 1:1; Matt. 3:16; Luke 3:21; Acts 7:56; 10:11; Rev. 19:11 [b]Gen. 28:12 [c]Matt. 8:20

1 [a]John 1:29, 35, 43 [b]John 2:11; 4:46; 21:2 [c]Matt. 12:46

2 [a]John 1:40-49; 2:12, 17, 22; 3:22; 4:2, 8, 27ff.; 6:8, 12, 16:22, 24; John 6:60f., 66; 7:3; 8:31

4 [1]Lit., *what to Me and to you (a Hebrew idiom)* [a]John 19:26 [b]Matt. 8:29 [c]John 7:6, 8, 30; 8:20

5 [a]Matt. 12:46

6 [1]Two or three metretai [a]Mark 7:3f.; John 3:25

8 [1]Or, *steward*

9 [a]John 4:46

10 [1]Lit., *have become drunk* [a]Matt. 24:49; Luke 12:45; Acts 2:15; 1 Cor. 11:21; Eph. 5:18; 1 Thess. 5:7; Rev. 17:2, 6

11 [1]Or, *attesting miracles,* I.e., one which points to the supernatural power of God in redeeming grace [a]John 2:23; 3:2; 4:54; 6:2, 14, 26, 30; 7:31; 9:16; 10:41; 11:47; 12:18, 37; 20:30 [b]John 1:43 [c]John 1:14

12 [a]Matt. 4:13 [b]Matt. 12:46 [c]John 2:2

13 [a]John 6:4; 11:55; John 5:1 marg. [?] [b]Deut. 16:1-6; Luke 2:41; John 2:23

14 [a]And He found in the temple those who were selling
oxen and sheep and doves, and the money-changers seated.
15 And He made a scourge of cords, and drove *them* all
out of the temple, with the sheep and the oxen; and He
poured out the coins of the money-changers, and overturned
their tables;
16 and to those who were selling [a]the doves He said,
"Take these things away; stop making [b]My Father's house a
house of merchandise."
17 His [a]disciples remembered that it was written, "[b]ZEAL
FOR THY HOUSE WILL CONSUME ME."
18 [a]The Jews therefore answered and said to Him,
"[b]What sign do You show to us, seeing that You do these
things?"
19 Jesus answered and said to them, "[a]Destroy this
[1]temple, and in three days I will raise it up."
20 [a]The Jews therefore said, "It took [b]forty-six years to
build this [1]temple, and will You raise it up in three days?"
21 But He was speaking of [1a] the temple of His body.
22 When therefore He was raised from the dead, His [a]dis-
ciples [b]remembered that He said this; and they believed [c]the
Scripture, and the word which Jesus had spoken.
23 Now when He was in Jerusalem at [a]the Passover, during the feast, many believed in His name, [b]beholding His signs
which He was doing.
24 But Jesus, on His part, was not entrusting Himself to
them, for He knew all men,
25 and because He did not need any one to bear witness
concerning man [a]for He Himself knew what was in man.

CHAPTER 3

NOW there was a man of the Pharisees, named [a]Nicodemus,
a [b]ruler of the Jews;
2 this man came to Him by night, and said to Him,
"[a]Rabbi, we know that You have come from God *as* a teacher;
for no one can do these [1b]signs that You do unless [c]God is with
him."
3 Jesus answered and said to him, "Truly, truly, I say to
you, unless one [a]is born [1]again, he cannot see [b]the kingdom of
God."
4 Nicodemus *said to Him, "How can a man be born
when he is old? He cannot enter a second time into his mother's womb and be born, can he?"
5 Jesus answered, "Truly, truly, I say to you, unless one is
born of [a]water and the Spirit, he cannot enter into [b]the kingdom of God.
6 "[a]That which is born of the flesh is flesh; and that which
is born of the Spirit is spirit.
7 "Do not marvel that I said to you, 'You must be born
[1]again.'
8 "[a]The wind blows where it wishes and you hear the
sound of it, but do not know where it comes from and where it
is going; so is every one who is born of the Spirit."
9 Nicodemus answered and said to Him, "How can these
things be?"

14 [a]John 2:14-16; *Matt. 21:12ff.; Mark 11:15, 17; Luke 19:45f.;* Mal. 3:1ff.
16 [a]Matt. 21:12 [b]Luke 2:49
17 [a]John 2:2 [b]Ps. 69:9
18 [a]John 1:19 [b]Matt. 12:38
19 [1]Or, *sanctuary* [a]Matt. 26:61; 27:40; Mark 14:58; 15:29; Acts 6:14
20 [1]Or, *sanctuary* [a]John 1:19 [b]Ezra 5:16
21 [1]Or, *sanctuary* [a]1 Cor. 6:19
22 [a]John 2:2 [b]Luke 24:8; John 12:16; 2:17; 14:26 [c]Ps. 16:10; John 20:9; Luke 24:26f.; Acts 13:33
23 [a]John 2:13 [b]John 2:11
25 [a]John 6:61, 64; 13:11; Matt. 9:4; John 1:42, 47
1 [a]John 7:50; 19:39 [b]Luke 23:13; John 7:26, 48
2 [1]Or, *attesting miracles* [a]Matt. 23:7; John 3:26 [b]John 2:11 [c]Acts 10:38; John 9:33; 10:38; 14:10f.; Acts 2:22
3 [1]Or, *from above* [a]1 Pet. 1:23; 2 Cor. 5:17 [b]John 3:5; Matt. 19:24; 21:31; Mark 9:47; 10:14f.
5 [a]Ezek. 36:25-27; Eph. 5:26; Titus 3:5 [b]John 3:3; Matt. 19:24; 21:31; Mark 9:47; 10:14f.
6 [a]John 1:13; 1 Cor. 15:50
7 [1]Or, *from above*
8 [a]Eccles. 11:5; Ezek. 37:9; Ps. 135:7

10 Jesus answered and said to him, "Are you [a]the teacher
of Israel, and do not understand these things?
11 "Truly, truly, I say to you, [a]we speak that which we
know, and [b]bear witness of that which we have seen; and [b]you
do not receive our witness.
12 "If I told you earthly things and you do not believe, how
shall you believe if I tell you heavenly things?
13 "And [a]no one has ascended into heaven, but [b]He who
descended from heaven, *even* [c]the Son of Man.[1]
14 "And as [a]Moses lifted up the serpent in the wilderness,
even so must [b]the Son of Man [c]be lifted up;
15 that whoever [1]believes may [a]in Him have eternal life.
16 "For God so [a]loved the world, that He [b]gave His [1c]only
begotten Son, that whoever [d]believes in Him should not perish, but have eternal life.
17 "For God [a]did not send the Son into the world [b]to judge
the world; but that the world should be saved through Him.
18 "[a]He who believes in Him is not judged; he who does
not believe has been judged already, because he has not believed in the name of [b]the [1]only begotten Son of God.
19 "And this is the judgment, that [a]the light is come into
the world, and men loved the darkness rather than the light;
for [b]their deeds were evil.
20 "[a]For everyone who does evil hates the light, and does
not come to the light, lest his deeds should be exposed.
21 "But he who [a]practices the truth comes to the light, that
his deeds may be manifested as having been wrought in God."
22 After these things Jesus and His [a]disciples came into
the land of Judea; and there He was spending time with them,
and [b]baptizing.
23 And John also was baptizing in Aenon near Salim, because there was much [1]water there; and they were coming, and
were being baptized.
24 For [a]John had not yet been thrown into prison.
25 There arose therefore a discussion on the part of John's
disciples with a Jew about [a]purification.
26 And they came to John, and said to him, "[a]Rabbi, He
who was with you [b]beyond the Jordan, to whom you [c]have
borne witness, behold, He is baptizing, and all are coming to
Him."
27 John answered and said, "[a]A man can receive nothing,
unless it has been given him from heaven.
28 "You yourselves bear me witness, that I said, '[a]I am not
the [1]Christ', but, 'I have been sent before Him.'
29 "He who has the bride is [a]the bridegroom; but the friend
of the bridegroom, who stands and hears him, rejoices greatly
because of the bridegroom's voice. And so this [b]joy of mine
has been made full.
30 "He must increase, but I must decrease.
31 "[a]He who comes from above is above all, he who is of
the earth is from the earth and speaks [b]of the earth. [a]He who
comes from heaven is above all.
32 "What He has seen and heard, of that He [a]bears witness;
and [a]no man receives His witness.
33 "He who has received His witness [a]has set his seal to *this*,
that God is true.

10 [a]Luke 2:46; 5:17; Acts 5:34

11 [a]John 7:16f.; 8:26, 28; 12:49; 14:24; John 1:18 [b]John 3:32

13 [1]Later manuscripts add, *who is in heaven*
[a]Prov. 30:4; Deut. 30:12; Acts 2:34; Rom. 10:6; Eph. 4:9 [b]John 3:31; 6:38, 42 [c]Matt. 8:20

14 [a]Num. 21:9 [b]Matt. 8:20 [c]John 8:28; 12:34

15 [1]Some mss. read, *believes in Him may have eternal life*
[a]John 20:31; 1 John 5:11-13

16 [1]Or, *unique*, only one of His kind
[a]Rom. 5:8; Eph. 2:4; 2 Thess. 2:16; 1 John 4:10; Rev. 1:5 [b]Rom. 8:32; 1 John 4:9 [c]John 1:18; 3:18; 1 John 4:9 [d]John 3:36; 6:40; 11:25f.

17 [a]John 3:34; 5:36, 38; 6:29, 38, 57; 7:29; 8:42; 10:36; 11:42; 17:3, 8, 18, 21, 23, 25; 20:21 [b]John 8:15; 12:47; Luke 19:10; 1 John 4:14

18 [1]Or, *unique*, only one of His kind
[a]Mark 16:16; John 5:24 [b]John 1:18; 1 John 4:9

19 [a]John 1:4; 8:12; 9:5; 12:46 [b]John 7:7

20 [a]John 3:20, 21; Eph. 5:11, 13

21 [a]1 John 1:6

22 [a]John 2:2 [b]John 4:1, 2

23 [1]Lit., *many waters*

24 [a]Matt. 4:12

25 [a]John 2:6

26 [a]John 3:2; Matt. 23:7 [b]John 1:28 [c]John 1:7

27 [a]1 Cor. 4:7; Heb. 5:4

28 [1]I.e., Messiah
[a]John 1:20, 23

29 [a]Matt. 25:1; 9:15 [b]John 15:11; 16:24; 17:13; Phil. 2:2; 1 John 1:4; 2 John 12

31 [a]John 3:13; 8:23 [b]1 John 4:5

32 [a]John 3:11

33 [a]John 6:27; Rom. 4:11; 15:28; 1 Cor. 9:2; 2 Cor. 1:22; Eph. 1:13; 4:30; 2 Tim. 2:19; Rev. 7:3-8

34 "For He whom God has [a]sent speaks the words of God;
[1b]for He gives the Spirit without measure.
35 "[a]The Father loves the Son, and has given all things into
His hand.
36 "He who [a]believes in the Son has eternal life; but he who
[b]does not [1]obey the Son shall not see life, but the wrath of
God abides on him."

Chapter 4

WHEN therefore [a]the Lord knew that the Pharisees had
heard that Jesus was making and [b]baptizing more disciples
than John
2 (although [a]Jesus Himself was not baptizing, but His
[b]disciples were),
3 He left [a]Judea, and departed [b]again into Galilee.
4 And He had to pass through [a]Samaria.
5 So He *came to a city of [a]Samaria, called Sychar, near
the parcel of ground that [b]Jacob gave to his son Joseph;
6 and Jacob's well was there. Jesus therefore, being
wearied from His journey, was sitting thus by the well. It was
about the [1]sixth hour.
7 There *came a woman of Samaria to draw water. Jesus
*said to her, "Give Me a drink."
8 For His [a]disciples had gone away into [b]the city to buy
food.
9 The [a]Samaritan woman therefore *said to Him, "How
is it that You, being a Jew, ask me for a drink since I am a
Samaritan woman?" (For [b]Jews have no dealings with Samaritans.)
10 Jesus answered and said to her, "If you knew the gift of
God, and who it is who says to you, 'Give Me a drink,' you
would have asked Him, and He would have given you [a]living
water."
11 She *said to Him, "[1]Sir, You have nothing to draw with
and the well is deep; where then do You get that [a]living water?
12 "You are not greater than our father Jacob, are You,
who [a]gave us the well, and drank of it himself, and his sons, and
his cattle?"
13 Jesus answered and said to her, "Everyone who drinks
of this water shall thirst again;
14 but whoever drinks of the water that I shall give him
[a]shall never thirst; but the water that I shall give him shall
become in him a well of water springing up to [b]eternal life."
15 The woman *said to Him, "[1]Sir, [a]give me this water, so
I will not be thirsty, nor come all the way here to draw."
16 He *said to her, "Go, call your husband, and come
here."
17 The woman answered and said, "I have no husband."
Jesus *said to her, "You have well said, 'I have no husband';
18 for you have had five husbands; and the one whom you
now have is not your husband; this you have said truly."
19 The woman *said to Him, "[1]Sir, I perceive that You
are [a]a prophet.
20 "[a]Our fathers worshiped in [b]this mountain; and you

34 [1]Lit., *for He does not give the Spirit by measure* [a]John 3:17 [b]Matt. 12:18; Luke 4:18; Acts 1:2; 10:38

35 [a]John 5:20; 17:2; Matt. 28:18

36 [1]Or, *believe* [a]John 3:16 [b]Acts 14:2; Heb. 3:18

1 [a]Luke 7:13 [b]John 3:22, 26; 1 Cor. 1:17

2 [a]John 3:22, 26; 1 Cor. 1:17 [b]John 2:2

3 [a]John 3:22 [b]John 2:11f.

4 [a]Luke 9:52

5 [a]Luke 9:52 [b]Gen. 33:19; 48:22; Josh. 24:32; John 4:12

6 [1]I.e., noon

8 [a]John 2:2 [b]John 4:5, 39

9 [a]Luke 9:52 [b]Matt. 10:5; John 8:48; Ezra 4:3-6, 11ff.

10 [a]John 7:37f.; Rev. 21:6; 22:17

11 [1]Or, *Lord* [a]John 7:37f.; Rev. 21:6; 22:17

12 [a]John 4:6

14 [a]John 6:35; 7:38 [b]Matt. 25:46; John 6:27

15 [1]Or, *Lord* [a]John 6:34

19 [1]Or, *Lord* [a]Matt. 21:11; Luke 7:39

20 [a]Gen. 33:20? [John 4:12] [b]Deut. 11:29; Josh. 8:33

people say that [c]in Jerusalem is the place where men ought to
worship."
21 Jesus *said to her, "Woman, believe Me, [a]an hour is
coming when [b]neither in this mountain, nor in Jerusalem, shall
you worship the Father.
22 "[a]You worship that which you do not know; we worship
that which we know; for [b]salvation is from the Jews.
23 "But [a]an hour is coming, and now is, when the true
worshipers shall worship the Father [b]in spirit and truth; for
such people the Father seeks to be His worshipers.
24 "God is [1]spirit; and those who worship Him must worship [a]in spirit and truth."
25 The woman *said to Him, "I know that [a]Messiah is
coming ([b]He who is called Christ); when that One comes, He
will declare all things to us."
26 Jesus *said to her, "[a]I who speak to you am *He*."
27 And at this point His [a]disciples [b]came, and they marveled that He had been speaking with a woman; yet no one
said, "What do You seek?" or, "Why do You speak with her?"
28 So the woman left her waterpot, and went into the city,
and *said to the men,
29 "Come, see a man [a]who told me all the things that I
have done; [b]this is not [1]the Christ, is it?"
30 They went out of the city, and were coming to Him.
31 In the meanwhile the disciples were requesting Him,
saying, "[a]Rabbi, eat."
32 But He said to them, "I have food to eat that you do
not know about."
33 The [a]disciples therefore were saying to one another,
"No one brought Him *anything* to eat, did he?"
34 Jesus *said to them, "My food is to [a]do the will of Him
who sent Me, and to [b]accomplish His work.
35 "Do you not say, 'There are yet four months, and *then*
comes the harvest'? Behold, I say to you, lift up your eyes, and
look on the fields, that they are white [a]for harvest.
36 "Already he who reaps is receiving [a]wages, and is gathering [b]fruit for [c]life eternal; that he who sows and he who reaps
may rejoice together.
37 "For in this *case* the saying is true, '[a]One sows, and
another reaps.'
38 "I sent you to reap that for which you have not labored;
others have labored, and you have entered into their labor."
39 And from [a]that city many of the Samaritans believed in
Him because of the word of the woman who testified, "[b]He
told me all the things that I *have* done."
40 So when the Samaritans came to Him, they were asking
Him to stay with them; and He stayed there two days.
41 And many more believed because of His word;
42 and they were saying to the woman, "It is no longer
because of what you said that we believe, for we have heard for
ourselves and know that this One is indeed [a]the Savior of the
world."
43 And after [a]the two days He went forth from there into
Galilee.
44 For Jesus Himself testified that [a]a prophet has no hon-
or in his own country.

20 [c]Luke 9:53

21 [a]John 5:28; 16:2; John 4:23; 5:25; 16:32 [b]Mal. 1:11; 1 Tim. 2:8

22 [a]2 Kin. 17:28-41 [b]Is. 2:3; Rom. 3:1f.; 9:4f.

23 [a]John 5:25; 16:32; John 4:21; 5:28; 16:2 [b]Phil. 3:3

24 [1]Or, *God is a Spirit* [a]Phil. 3:3

25 [a]John 1:41 [b]Matt. 1:16

26 [a]John 8:24; John 9:35-37

27 [a]John 4:8 [b]John 2:2

29 [1]I.e., The Messiah [a]John 4:17f. [b]John 7:26, 31; Matt. 12:23

31 [a]Matt. 23:7

33 [a]John 2:2

34 [a]John 5:30; 6:38 [b]John 5:36; 17:4; 19:28, 30

35 [a]Luke 10:2

36 [a]1 Cor. 9:17f. [b]Rom. 1:13 [c]John 4:14

37 [a]Job 31:8; Mic. 6:15

39 [a]John 4:5, 30 [b]John 4:29

42 [a]1 John 4:14; 1 Tim. 4:10; Luke 2:11; Acts 5:31; 13:23

43 [a]John 4:40

44 [a]Matt. 13:57

45 So when He came to Galilee, the Galileans received
Him, [a]having seen all the things that He did in Jerusalem at
the feast; for they themselves also went to the feast.
46 He came therefore again to [a]Cana of Galilee [b]where
He had made the water wine. And there was a certain royal
official, whose son was sick at [c]Capernaum.
47 When he heard that Jesus had come [a]out of Judea into
Galilee, he went to Him, and was requesting *Him* to come
down and heal his son; for he was at the point of death.
48 Jesus therefore said to him, "Unless you *people* see
[1a]signs and [a]wonders, you *simply* will not believe."
49 The royal official *said to Him, "[1]Sir, come down before my child dies."
50 Jesus *said to him, "Go your way; your son lives." The
man believed the word that Jesus spoke to him, and he started
off.
51 And as he was now going down, *his* slaves met him,
saying that his [1]son was living.
52 So he inquired of them the hour when he began to get
better. They said therefore to him, "Yesterday at the [1]seventh
hour the fever left him."
53 So the father knew that *it was* at that hour in which
Jesus said to him, "Your son lives;" and he himself believed,
and [a]his whole household.
54 This is again a [a]second [1]sign that Jesus performed,
when He had [b]come out of Judea into Galilee.

Chapter 5

After these things there was [1]a feast of the Jews; and Jesus
went up to Jerusalem.
2 Now there is in Jerusalem by [a]the sheep *gate* a pool,
which is called [b]in [1]Hebrew [2]Bethesda, having five porticoes.
3 In these lay a multitude of those who were sick, blind,
lame, withered.
4 (See marginal note.)
5 And a certain man was there, who had been thirty-eight
years in his sickness.
6 When Jesus saw him lying there, and knew that he had
already been a long time *in that condition,* He *said to him,
"Do you wish to get well?"
7 The sick man answered Him, "Sir, I have no man to
put me into the pool when [a]the water is stirred up, but while I
am coming, another steps down before me."
8 Jesus *said to him, "[a]Arise, take up your pallet, and
walk."
9 And immediately the man became well, and took up
his pallet and *began* to walk.
[a]Now it was the Sabbath on that day.
10 Therefore [a]the Jews were saying to him who was cured,
"It is the Sabbath, and [b]it is not permissible for you to carry
your pallet."
11 But he answered them, "He who made me well was the
one who said to me, 'Take up your pallet and walk.'"
12 They asked him, "Who is the man who said to you,
'Take up *your* pallet, and walk'?"

45 [a]John 2:23

46 [a]John 2:1 [b]John 2:9 [c]John 2:12; Luke 4:23

47 [a]John 4:3, 54

48 [1]Or, *attesting miracles* [a]Dan. 4:2f.; 6:27; Matt. 24:24; Mark 13:22; Acts 2:19, 22, 43; 4:30; 5:12; 6:8; 7:36; 14:3; 15:12; Rom. 15:19; 2 Cor. 12:12; 2 Thess. 2:9; Heb. 2:4; 1 Cor. 1:22

49 [1]Or, *Lord*

51 [1]Or, *boy*

52 [1]I.e., 1 p.m.

53 [a]Acts 11:14

54 [1]Or, *attesting miracle* [a]John 2:11 [b]John 4:45f.

1 [1]Many good mss. read, *the feast,* i.e., the Passover

2 [1]I.e., Jewish Aramaic [2]Many good mss. read, *Bethsaida* or *Bethzatha* [a]Neh. 3:1, 32; 12:39 [b]John 19:13, 17, 20; 20:16; Rev. 9:11; 16:16; Acts 21:40

4 Many authorities insert, wholly or in part, *waiting for the moving of the waters;* V. 4 *for an angel of the Lord went down at certain seasons into the pool, and stirred up the water: whoever then first after the stirring up of the water stepped in was made well from whatever disease with which he was afflicted.*

7 [a]John 5:4 in marg.

8 [a]Matt. 9:6; Mark 2:11; Luke 5:24

9 [a]John 9:14

10 [a]John 5:15, 16, 18; 1:19 [b]Neh. 13:19; Jer. 17:21f.; John 7:23; 9:16; Matt. 12:2

13 But he who was healed did not know who it was; for
Jesus had slipped away while there was a crowd in *that* place.
14 Afterward Jesus *found him in the temple, and said to
him, "Behold, you have become well; do not [a]sin any more, [b]so
that nothing worse may befall you."
15 The man went away, and told [a]the Jews that it was
Jesus who had made him well.
16 And for this reason [a]the Jews were persecuting Jesus,
because He was doing these things on the Sabbath.
17 But He answered them, "My Father is working until
now, and I Myself am working."
18 For this cause therefore [a]the Jews [b]were seeking all the
more to kill Him, because He not only was breaking the Sabbath, but also was calling God His own Father, [c]making Himself equal with God.
19 Jesus therefore answered and was saying to them,
"Truly, truly, I say to you, [a]the Son can do nothing of Himself,
unless *it is* something He sees the Father doing; for whatever
the Father does, these things the Son also does in like manner.
20 "[a]For the Father loves the Son, and shows Him all things
that He Himself is doing; and [b]greater works than these will
He show Him, that you may marvel.
21 "For just as the Father raises the dead and [a]gives them
life, even so [b]the Son also gives life to whom He wishes.
22 "For not even the Father judges any one, but [a]He has
given all judgment to the Son,
23 in order that all may honor the Son, even as they honor
the Father. [a]He who does not honor the Son does not honor
the Father who sent Him.
24 "Truly, truly, I say to you, he who hears My word, and
[a]believes Him who sent Me, has eternal life, and [b]does not
come into judgment, but has [c]passed out of death into life.
25 "Truly, truly, I say to you, [a]an hour is coming and now
is, when [b]the dead shall hear the voice of the Son of God; and
those who [c]hear shall live.
26 "For just as the Father has life in Himself, even so He
[a]gave to the Son also to have life in Himself;
27 and He gave Him authority to [a]execute judgment, because He is [1]*the* Son of Man.
28 "Do not marvel at this; for [a]an hour is coming, in which
[b]all who are in the tombs shall hear His voice,
29 and shall come forth; [a]those who did the good *deeds*, to
a resurrection of life, those who committed the evil *deeds* to a
resurrection of judgment.
30 "[a]I can do nothing on My own initiative, as I hear, I
judge; and [b]My judgment is just; because I do not seek My
own will but [c]the will of Him who sent Me.
31 "[a]If I *alone* bear witness of Myself, My testimony is not
[1]true.
32 "There is [a]another who bears witness of Me; and I know
that the testimony which He bears of Me is true.
33 "You have sent to John, and he [a]has borne witness to the
truth.
34 "But [a]the witness which I receive is not from man; but I
say these things, that you may be saved.

14 [a]John 8:11; Mark 2:5 [b]Ezra 9:14
15 [a]John 5:16, 18; 1:19
16 [a]John 5:10, 15, 18; 1:19
18 [a]John 5:15, 16; 1:19 [b]John 5:16; 7:1 [c]John 10:33; 19:7
19 [a]John 5:30; 8:28; 12:49; 14:10
20 [a]John 3:35 [b]John 14:12
21 [a]Rom. 4:17; 8:11 [b]John 11:25
22 [a]John 5:27; 9:39; Acts 10:42; 17:31
23 [a]Luke 10:16; 1 John 2:23
24 [a]John 3:18; 12:44; 20:31; 1 John 5:13 [b]John 3:18 [c]1 John 3:14
25 [a]John 4:23; 5:28; 4:21 [b]Luke 15:24 [c]John 6:60; 8:43, 47; 9:27
26 [a]John 1:4; 6:57
27 [1]Or, *a son of man* [a]John 9:39; Acts 10:42; 17:31
28 [a]John 4:21 [b]John 11:24; 1 Cor. 15:52
29 [a]Dan. 12:2; Acts 24:15; Matt. 25:46
30 [a]John 5:19 [b]John 8:16 [c]John 4:34; 6:38
31 [1]I.e., admissible as legal evidence [a]John 8:14
32 [a]John 5:37
33 [a]John 1:7
34 [a]1 John 5:9; John 5:32

35 "He was [a]the lamp that was burning and was shining and you [b]were willing to rejoice for a while in his light.

36 "But the witness which I have is greater than *that of* John; for [a]the works which the Father has given Me [b]to accomplish, the very works that I do, bear witness of Me, that the Father [c]has sent Me.

37 "And the Father who sent Me, [a]He has borne witness of Me. You have neither heard His voice at any time, nor seen His form.

38 "And you do not have [a]His word abiding in you, for you do not believe Him whom He [b]sent.

39 "[1a]You search the Scriptures, because you think that in them you have eternal life; and it is [b]these that bear witness of Me;

40 and you are unwilling to come to Me, that you may have life.

41 "[a]I do not receive glory from men;

42 but I know you, that you do not have the love of God in yourselves.

43 "I have come in My Father's name, and you do not receive Me; [a]if another shall come in his own name, you will receive him.

44 "How can you believe, when you [a]receive [1]glory from one another, and you do not seek [b]the [1]glory that is from [c]the *one and* only God?

45 "Do not think that I will accuse you before the Father; the one who accuses you is [a]Moses, in whom you have set your hope.

46 "For if you believed Moses, you would believe Me; for [a]he wrote of Me.

47 "But [a]if you do not believe his writings, how will you believe My words?"

Chapter 6

AFTER these things [a]Jesus went away to the other side of [b]the sea of Galilee (or [c]Tiberias).

2 And a great multitude was following Him, because they were seeing the [1a]signs which He was performing on those who were sick.

3 And Jesus went up on [a]the mountain, and there He sat with His disciples.

4 Now [a]the Passover, the feast of the Jews, was at hand.

5 Jesus therefore lifting up His eyes, and seeing that a great multitude was coming to Him, *said to [a]Philip, "Where are we to buy bread, that these may eat?"

6 And this He was saying to [a]test him; for He Himself knew what He was intending to do.

7 [a]Philip answered Him, "[b]Two hundred [1]denarii worth of bread is not sufficient for them, for every one to receive a little."

8 One of His [a]disciples, [b]Andrew, Simon Peter's brother, *said to Him,

9 "There is a lad here, who has five barley loaves, and two [a]fish; but what are these for so many people?"

10 Jesus said, "Have the people [1]sit down." Now there was

35 [a]2 Sam. 21:17; 2 Pet. 1:19 [b]Mark 1:5

36 [a]John 10:25, 38; 14:11; 15:24; 2:23; Matt. 11:4 [b]John 4:34 [c]John 3:17

37 [a]John 8:18; Luke 24:27

38 [a]1 John 2:14 [b]John 3:17

39 [1]Or, (a command) *Search the Scriptures!* [a]John 7:52; Rom. 2:17ff. [b]Luke 24:25, 27; Acts 13:27

41 [a]John 5:44; 7:18

43 [a]Matt. 24:5

44 [1]Or, *honor or fame* [a]John 5:41 [b]Rom. 2:29 [c]John 17:3; 1 Tim. 1:17

45 [a]John 9:28; Rom. 2:17ff.

46 [a]Luke 24:27

47 [a]Luke 16:29, 31

1 [a]John 6:1-13: *Matt. 14:13-21; Mark 6:32-44; Luke 9:10-17* [b]Matt. 4:18; Luke 5:1 [c]John 21:1; 6:23

2 [1]Or, *attesting miracles* [a]John 2:11

3 [a]John 6:15; Matt. 5:1

4 [a]John 2:13

5 [a]John 1:43

6 [a]2 Cor. 13:5 and Rev. 2:2 in Gr.

7 [1]A denarius represented a days wages for a common laborer [a]John 1:43 [b]Mark 6:37

8 [a]John 2:2 [b]John 1:40

9 [a]John 21:9, 10, 13; John 6:11

10 [1]Lit., *recline(d)*

[a]much grass in the place. So the men [1]sat down, in number
about [b]five thousand.
11 Jesus therefore took the loaves; and [a]having given
thanks, He distributed to those who were seated; likewise also
of the [b]fish as much as they wanted.
12 And when they were filled, He *said to His [a]disciples,
"Gather up the left-over fragments that nothing may be lost."
13 And so they gathered them up, and filled twelve [a]bas-
kets with fragments from the five barley loaves, which were left
over by those who had eaten.
14 When therefore the people saw the [1]sign which He had
performed, they said, "This is of a truth the [a]Prophet who is to
come into the world."
15 Jesus therefore perceiving that they were [1]intending to
come and take Him by force, [a]to make Him king, [b]withdrew
again to [c]the mountain by Himself alone.
16 Now when evening came, His [a]disciples went down to
the sea,
17 and after getting into a boat, they *started to* cross the
sea [a]to Capernaum. And it had already become dark, and Jesus
had not yet come to them.
18 And the sea *began* to be stirred up because a strong
wind was blowing.
19 When therefore they had rowed about [1]three or four
miles, they *beheld Jesus walking on the sea, and drawing near
to the boat; and they were frightened.
20 But He *said to them, "It is I; [1a]do not be afraid."
21 They were willing therefore to receive Him into the
boat; and immediately the boat was at the land to which they
were going.
22 The next day [a]the multitude that stood on the other
side of the sea saw that there was no other small boat there,
except one, and that Jesus [b]had not entered with His disciples
into the boat, but *that* His disciples had gone away alone.
23 There came other small boats from [a]Tiberias near to
the place where they ate the bread after the [b]Lord [c]had given
thanks.
24 When the multitude therefore saw that Jesus was not
there, nor His disciples, they themselves got into the small
boats, and [a]came to Capernaum, seeking Jesus.
25 And when they found Him on the other side of the sea,
they said to Him, "[a]Rabbi, when did You get here?"
26 Jesus answered them and said, "Truly, truly, I say to
you, you [a]seek Me, not because you saw [b]signs, but because
you ate of the loaves, and were filled.
27 "Do not [a]work for the food which perishes, but for the
food which endures to [b]eternal life, which [c]the Son of Man
shall give to you, for on Him the Father, *even* God, [d]has set
His seal."
28 They said therefore to Him, "What shall we do, that
we may work the works of God?"
29 Jesus answered and said to them, "This is [a]the work of
God, that you believe in Him whom He [b]has sent."
30 They said therefore to Him, "[a]What then do You do
for a [b]sign, that we may see, and believe You? What work do
You perform?

10 [a]John 6:4; Mark 6:39 [b]Matt. 14:21

11 [a]John 6:23; Matt. 15:36 [b]John 21:9, 10, 13; John 6:9

12 [a]John 2:2

13 [a]Matt. 14:20

14 [1]Or, *attesting miracle* [a]John 1:21; Matt. 11:3; 21:11

15 [1]Or, *about* [a]John 18:36f. [b]John 6:15-21: *Matt. 14:22-33; Mark 6:45-51* [c]John 6:3

16 [a]John 2:2

17 [a]Mark 6:45; John 6:24, 59

19 [1]Lit., 25 or 30 stadia

20 [1]Or, *stop fearing* [a]Matt. 14:27

22 [a]John 6:2 [b]John 6:15ff.

23 [a]John 6:1 [b]Luke 7:13 [c]John 6:11

24 [a]John 6:17, 59; Matt. 14:34; Mark 6:53

25 [a]Matt. 23:7

26 [a]John 6:24 [b]John 6:2, 14, 30

27 [a]Is. 55:2 [b]John 6:40, 47, 54; 3:15f.; 4:14; 10:28; 17:2f. [c]Matt. 8:20; John 6:53, 62 [d]John 3:33

29 [a]1 Thess. 1:3; James 2:22; 1 John 3:23; Rev. 2:26 [b]John 3:17

30 [a]Matt. 12:38 [b]John 6:2, 14, 26

31 “[a]Our fathers ate the manna in the wilderness; as it is
written, ‘[b]HE GAVE THEM BREAD OUT OF HEAVEN TO EAT.’ ”
32 Jesus therefore said to them, “Truly, truly, I say to you,
it is not Moses who has given you the bread out of heaven, but
it is My Father who gives you the true bread out of heaven.
33 “For the bread of God is [1]that which [a]comes down out
of heaven, and gives life to the world.”
34 They said therefore to Him, “Lord, evermore [a]give us
this bread.”
35 Jesus said to them, “[a]I am the bread of life; he who
comes to Me shall not hunger, and he who believes in Me
[b]shall never thirst.
36 “But [a]I said to you, that you have seen Me, and yet do
not believe.
37 “[a]All that the Father gives Me shall come to Me; and
the one who comes to Me I will certainly not cast out.
38 “For [a]I have come down from heaven, [b]not to do My
own will, but [c]the will of Him who [d]sent Me.
39 “And this is the will of Him who sent Me, that of [a]all
that He has given Me I [b]lose nothing, but [c]raise it up on the
last day.
40 “For this is the will of My Father, that every one who
[a]beholds the Son, and [b]believes in Him, may have eternal life;
and I Myself will [c]raise him up on the last day.”
41 [a]The Jews therefore were grumbling about Him, because He said, “I am the bread that [b]came down out of
heaven.”
42 And they were saying, “[a]Is not this Jesus, the son of
Joseph, whose father and mother [b]we know? How does He
now say, ‘[c]I have come down out of heaven’?”
43 Jesus answered and said to them, “Do not grumble
among yourselves.
44 “No one can come to Me, unless the Father who sent
Me [a]draws him; and I will [b]raise him up on the last day.
45 “It is written [a]in the prophets, ‘[b]AND THEY SHALL ALL BE
[c]TAUGHT OF GOD.’ Every one who has heard and learned from
the Father, comes to Me.
46 “[a]Not that any man has seen the Father, except the One
who is from God, He has seen the Father.
47 “Truly, truly, I say to you, he who believes [a]has eternal
life.
48 “[a]I am the bread of life.
49 “[a]Your fathers ate the manna in the wilderness, and they
died.
50 “This is the bread which [a]comes down out of heaven, so
that one may eat of it and [b]not die.
51 “[a]I am the living bread that [b]came down out of heaven;
if any one eats of this bread, [c]he shall live forever; and the
bread also which I shall give [d]for the life of the world is [e]My
flesh.”
52 [a]The Jews therefore [b]*began* to argue with one another,
saying, “How can this man give us *His* flesh to eat?”
53 Jesus therefore said to them, “Truly, truly, I say to you,
unless you eat the flesh of [a]the Son of Man and drink His
blood, you have no life in yourselves.

31 [a]Ex. 16:21; Num. 11:8; John 6:49, 58 [b]Neh. 9:15; Ex. 16:4, 15; Ps. 78:24; 105:40

33 [1]Or, *He who comes* [a]John 6:50; 6:41

34 [a]John 4:15

35 [a]John 6:48, 51 [b]John 4:14

36 [a]John 6:26

37 [a]John 6:39; 17:2, 24

38 [a]John 3:13 [b]Matt. 26:39 [c]John 4:34; 5:30 [d]John 6:29

39 [a]John 6:37; 17:2, 24 [b]John 17:12; 18:9 [c]John 6:40, 44, 54; 11:24; Matt. 10:15

40 [a]John 12:45; 14:17, 19 [b]John 3:16 [c]John 6:39, 44, 54; 11:24; Matt. 10:15

41 [a]John 1:19; 6:52 [b]John 6:51, 58; 6:33

42 [a]Luke 4:22 [b]John 7:27f. [c]John 6:38, 62

44 [a]Jer. 31:3; Hos. 11:4; John 12:32; 6:65 [b]John 6:39

45 [a]Acts 7:42; 13:40; Heb. 8:11 [b]Is. 54:13; Jer. 31:34 [c]1 Thess. 4:9; Phil. 3:15; 1 John 2:27

46 [a]John 1:18

47 [a]John 6:51, 58; 3:36; 5:24; 11:26

48 [a]John 6:35, 51

49 [a]John 6:31, 58

50 [a]John 6:33 [b]John 6:47, 51, 58; 3:36; 5:24; 11:26

51 [a]John 6:35, 48 [b]John 6:41, 58 [c]John 6:47, 58; 3:36; 5:24; 11:26 [d]John 1:29; 3:14f.; Heb. 10:10; 1 John 4:10 [e]John 6:53-56

52 [a]John 1:19; 6:41 [b]John 9:16; 10:19

53 [a]John 6:27, 62; Matt. 8:20

54 "He who eats My flesh and drinks My blood has eternal
life; and I will [a]raise him up on the last day.
55 "For My flesh is true food, and My blood is true drink.
56 "He who eats My flesh and drinks My blood [a]abides in
Me, and I in him.
57 "As the [a]living Father [b]sent Me, and I live because of the
Father; so he who eats Me, he also shall live because of Me.
58 "This is the bread which [a]came down out of heaven; not
as [b]the fathers ate, and died; he who eats this bread [c]shall live
forever."
59 These things He said [a]in the synagogue, as He taught
[b]in Capernaum.
60 Many therefore of His [a]disciples, when they heard *this*
said, "[b]This is a difficult statement; who can listen to it?"
61 But Jesus, [a]conscious that His disciples grumbled at
this, said to them, "Does this [b]cause you to stumble?
62 "*What* then if you should behold [a]the Son of Man
[b]ascending where He was before?
63 "[a]It is the Spirit who gives life; the flesh profits nothing;
[b]the words that I have spoken to you are spirit and are life.
64 "But there are [a]some of you who do not believe." For
Jesus [b]knew from the beginning who they were who did not
believe, and [c]who it was that would [1]betray Him.
65 And He was saying, "For this reason I have [a]said to
you, that no one can come to Me, unless [b]it has been granted
him from the Father."
66 As a result of this many of His [a]disciples [b]withdrew, and
were not walking with Him any more.
67 Jesus said therefore to [a]the twelve, "You do not want
to go away also, do you?"
68 [a]Simon Peter answered Him, "Lord, to whom shall we
go? You have [b]words of eternal life.
69 "And we have believed and have come to know that You
are [a]the Holy One of God."
70 Jesus answered them, "[a]Did I Myself not choose you,
[b]the twelve, and *yet* one of you is [c]a devil?"
71 Now He meant Judas [a]*the son* of Simon Iscariot, for
he, [b]one of [c]the twelve, [1]was going to betray Him.

Chapter 7

AND after these things Jesus [a]was walking in Galilee; for He
was unwilling to walk in Judea, because [b]the Jews [c]were seeking
to kill Him.
2 Now the feast of the Jews, [a]the Feast of Tabernacles,
was at hand.
3 His [a]brothers therefore said to Him, "Depart from
here, and go into Judea, that Your [b]disciples also may behold
Your works which You are doing.
4 "For no one does anything in secret, [1]when he himself
seeks to be *known* publicly. If You do these things, show
Yourself to the world."
5 For not even His [a]brothers were believing in Him.
6 Jesus therefore *said to them, "[a]My time is not yet at
hand; but your time is always opportune.

54 [a]John 6:39

56 [a]John 15:4f.; 1 John 2:24; 3:24; 4:15f.; John 17:23

57 [a]Matt. 16:16; John 5:26 [b]John 6:29, 38; 3:17

58 [a]John 6:41, 51; 6:33 [b]John 6:31, 49 [c]John 6:47, 51; 3:36; 5:24; 11:26

59 [a]Matt. 4:23 [b]John 6:24

60 [a]John 2:2; 6:66; 7:3 [b]John 6:52

61 [a]John 6:64 [b]Matt. 11:6

62 [a]John 6:27, 53; Matt. 8:20 [b]Mark 16:19; John 3:13

63 [a]2 Cor. 3:6 [b]John 6:68

64 [1]Or, *deliver Him up* [a]John 6:60, 66 [b]John 2:25 [c]John 6:71; 13:11; Matt. 10:4

65 [a]John 6:37, 44 [b]Matt. 13:11; John 3:27

66 [a]John 2:2; 7:3 [b]John 6:60, 64

67 [a]John 6:70f.; 20:24; Matt. 10:2; John 2:2

68 [a]Matt. 16:16 [b]John 6:63; 12:49f.; 17:8

69 [a]Mark 1:24

70 [a]John 15:16, 19 [b]John 6:71; 20:24; Matt. 10:2; John 2:2 [c]John 13:2, 27; 8:44; 17:12

71 [1]Or, *was intending to* [a]John 13:26; 12:4; 13:2 [b]Mark 14:10 [c]John 6:70f.; 20:24; Matt. 10:2; John 2:2

1 [a]John 4:3; 6:1; 11:54 [b]John 1:19; 7:11, 13, 15, 35 [c]John 7:19; 5:18; 8:37, 40; 11:53

2 [a]Lev. 23:34; Zech. 14:16-19; Deut. 16:16

3 [a]Matt. 12:46; John 7:5, 10; Mark 3:21 [b]John 6:60

4 [1]Lit., *and*

5 [a]Matt. 12:46; John 7:3, 10; Mark 3:21

6 [a]Matt. 26:18; John 7:8, 30; 2:4

7 "[a]The world cannot hate you; but it hates Me, because I
testify of it, that [b]its deeds are evil.
8 "Go up to the feast yourselves; I do not go up to this
feast because [a]My time has not yet fully come."
9 And having said these things to them, He stayed in
Galilee.
10 But when His [a]brothers had gone up to the feast, then
He Himself also went up, not publicly, but as it were, in secret.
11 [a]The Jews therefore [b]were seeking Him at the feast,
and were saying, "Where is He?"
12 And there was much grumbling among the multitudes
concerning Him; [a]some were saying, "He is a good man;"
others were saying, "No, on the contrary, He leads the multitude astray."
13 Yet no one was speaking openly of Him for [a]fear of the
Jews.
14 But when it was now the midst of the feast Jesus went
up into the temple, and *began to* [a]teach.
15 [a]The Jews therefore were marveling, saying, "How has
this man [b]become learned, having never been educated?"
16 Jesus therefore answered them, and said, "[a]My teaching is not Mine, but His who sent Me.
17 "[a]If any man is willing to do His will, he shall know of
the teaching, whether it is of God, or *whether* I speak from
Myself.
18 "He who speaks from himself [a]seeks his own glory; but
He who is seeking the glory of the one who sent Him, He is
true, and there is no unrighteousness in Him.
19 "[a]Did not Moses give you the law, and *yet* none of you
carries out the law? Why do you [b]seek to kill Me?"
20 The multitude answered, "[a]You have a [1]demon! Who
seeks to kill You?"
21 Jesus answered and said to them, "I did [a]one [1]deed, and
you all marvel.
22 "On this account [a]Moses has given you circumcision
(not because it is from Moses, but from [b]the fathers); and on
the Sabbath you circumcise a man.
23 "[a]If a man receives circumcision on *the* Sabbath that the
Law of Moses may not be broken, are you angry with Me
because I made an entire man well on *the* Sabbath?
24 "Do not [a]judge according to appearance, but [1]judge
with righteous judgment."
25 Therefore some of the people of Jerusalem were
saying, "Is this not the man whom they are seeking to kill?
26 "And look, He is speaking publicly, and they are saying
nothing to Him. [a]The rulers do not really know that this is [1]the
Christ, do they?
27 "However [a]we know where this man is from; but whenever the Christ may come, no one knows where He is from."
28 Jesus therefore cried out in the temple, [a]teaching and
saying, "[b]You both know Me, and know where I am from; and
[c]I have not come of Myself, but He who sent Me is true, whom
you do not know.
29 "[a]I know Him; because [b]I am from Him, and [c]He sent
Me."

7 [a]John 15:18f. [b]John 3:19f.
8 [a]John 7:6
10 [a]Matt. 12:46; John 7:3, 5; Mark 3:21
11 [a]John 7:13, 15, 35 [b]John 11:56
12 [a]John 7:40-43
13 [a]John 19:38; 20:19; 9:22; 12:42
14 [a]John 7:28; Matt. 26:55
15 [a]John 1:19; John 7:11, 13, 35 [b]Acts 26:24 [Gr.]
16 [a]John 3:11
17 [a]John 3:21; 8:43f.; Ps. 25:9, 14; Prov. 3:32; Dan. 12:10
18 [a]John 5:41; 8:50, 54; 12:43
19 [a]John 1:17 [b]John 7:1; Mark 11:18
20 [1]Or, *you are demented* [a]John 8:48f., 52; 10:20; Matt. 11:18
21 [1]Or, *work* [a]John 7:23; 5:2-9, 16
22 [a]Lev. 12:3 [b]Gen. 17:10ff.; 21:4; Acts 7:8
23 [a]Matt. 12:2; John 5:10
24 [1]Lit., *judge the righteous judgment* [a]Lev. 19:15; Is. 11:3; Zech. 7:9; John 8:15
26 [1]I.e., the Messiah [a]Luke 23:13; John 3:1
27 [a]John 6:42; 7:41f.; 9:29
28 [a]John 7:14 [b]John 6:42; 7:14f.; 9:29 [c]John 8:42
29 [a]John 8:55; 17:25; Matt. 11:27 [b]John 6:46 [c]John 3:17

30 They [a]were seeking therefore to seize Him; and no man
laid his hand on Him, because His [b]hour had not yet come.
31 But [a]many of the multitude believed in Him; and they
were saying, "[b]When [1]the Christ shall come, He will not perform more [2c]signs than those which this man has, will He?"
32 The Pharisees heard the multitude muttering these
things about Him; and the chief priests and the Pharisees sent
[a]officers to [b]seize Him.
33 Jesus therefore said, "[a]For a little while longer I am
with you, then [b]I go to Him who sent Me.
34 "[a]You shall seek Me, and shall not find Me; and where I
am, you cannot come."
35 [a]The Jews therefore said to one another, "[b]Where does
this man intend to go that we shall not find Him? He is not
intending to go to [c]the Dispersion among [d]the Greeks, and
teach the Greeks, is He?
36 "What is this statement that He said, '[a]You will seek
Me, and will not find Me; and where I am, you cannot
come'?"
37 Now on [a]the last day, the great *day* of the feast, Jesus
stood and cried out, saying, "[b]If any man is thirsty, let him
[1]come to Me and drink.
38 "He who believes in Me, [a]as the Scripture said, 'From
[1]his innermost being shall flow rivers of [b]living water.' "
39 But this He spoke [a]of the Spirit, whom those who believed in Him were to receive; [1]for [b]the Spirit was not yet
given, because Jesus was not yet [c]glorified.
40 *Some* of the multitude therefore, when they heard
these words, were saying, "This certainly is [a]the Prophet."
41 Others were saying, "This is [1]the Christ." Still others
were saying, "[a]Surely [1]the Christ is not going to come from
Galilee, is He?
42 "Has not the Scripture said that THE CHRIST COMES FROM
[a]THE OFFSPRING OF DAVID, AND FROM BETHLEHEM, the village
where David was?"
43 So [a]there arose a division in the multitude because of
Him.
44 And [a]some of them wanted to seize Him, but no one
laid hands on Him.
45 The [a]officers therefore came to the chief priests and
Pharisees, and they said to them, "Why did you not bring
Him?"
46 The [a]officers answered, "[b]Never did a man speak the
way this man speaks."
47 The Pharisees therefore answered them, "[a]You have
not also been led astray, have you?
48 "[a]No one of [b]the rulers or Pharisees has believed in
Him, has he?
49 "But this multitude which does not know the Law is
accursed."
50 [a]Nicodemus *said to them (he who came to Him before, being one of them),
51 "[a]Our Law does not judge a man, unless it first hears
from him and knows what he is doing, does it?"
52 They answered and said to him, "[a]You are not also

30 [a]John 7:32, 44; 10:39; Matt. 21:46 [b]John 8:20; John 7:6

31 [1]I.e., the Messiah [2]Or, *attesting miracles* [a]John 8:30; 10:42; 11:45; 12:11, 42; 2:23 [b]John 7:26 [c]John 2:11

32 [a]John 7:45f., Matt. 26:58 [b]Matt. 12:14

33 [a]John 12:35; 13:33; 14:19; 16:16-19 [b]John 16:5, 10, 17, 28; John 14:12, 28; 20:17

34 [a]John 7:36; 8:21; 13:33

35 [a]John 7:1 [b]John 8:22 [c]James 1:1; 1 Pet. 1:1; in the Gr. Ps. 147:2; Is. 11:12; 56:8; Zeph. 3:10 [d]John 12:20; Acts 14:1; 17:4; 18:4; Rom. 1:16

36 [a]John 7:34; 8:21; 13:33

37 [1]I.e., let him keep coming to Me and let him keep drinking [a]Lev. 23:36; Num. 29:35; Neh. 8:18 [b]John 4:10, 14; 6:35

38 [1]Lit., *out of his belly* [a]Is. 44:3; 55:1; 58:11 [b]John 4:10

39 [1]Other mss. read, *for the Holy Spirit was not yet given* [a]Joel 2:28; John 1:33 [b]Acts 1:4f.; 2:4, 33; 19:2; John 20:22 [c]John 12:16, 23; 13:31f.; 16:14; 17:1

40 [a]Matt. 21:11; John 1:21

41 [1]I.e., The Messiah [a]John 7:52; 1:46

42 [a]Matt. 1:1; 2:5f.; Luke 2:4ff.; Ps. 89:4; Micah 5:2

43 [a]John 10:19; 9:16

44 [a]John 7:30

45 [a]John 7:32

46 [a]John 7:32 [b]Matt. 7:28

47 [a]John 7:12

48 [a]John 12:42 [b]Luke 23:13; John 7:26

50 [a]John 3:1; 19:39

51 [a]Ex. 23:1; Deut. 17:6; 19:15; Prov. 18:13; Acts 23:3

52 [a]John 7:41; 1:46

E106-1

from Galilee, are you? Search, and see that no prophet arises
out of Galilee."
53 [[1]And everyone went to his home;

CHAPTER 8

BUT Jesus went to [a]the Mount of Olives.
2 And early in the morning He came again into the
temple, and all the people were coming to Him; and [a]He sat
down and *began* to teach them.
3 And the scribes and the Pharisees *brought a woman
caught in adultery, and having set her in the midst,
4 they *said to Him, "Teacher, this woman has been
caught in adultery, in the very act.
5 "Now in the Law [a]Moses commanded us to stone such
women; what then do You say?"
6 And they were saying this, [a]testing Him, [b]in order that
they might have grounds for accusing Him. But Jesus stooped
down, and with His finger wrote on the ground.
7 But when they persisted in asking Him, [a]He straightened up, and said to them, "[b]He who is without sin among
you, let him *be the* [c]first to throw a stone at her."
8 And again He stooped down, and wrote on the ground.
9 And when they heard it, they *began* to go out one by
one, beginning with the older ones, and He was left alone, and
the woman, *where she had been*, in the midst.
10 And [a]straightening up, Jesus said to her, "Woman,
where are they? Did no one condemn you?"
11 And she said, "No one, [1]Lord." And Jesus said, "[a]Nei-
ther do I condemn you; go your way; from now on [b]sin no
more."]
12 Again therefore Jesus spoke to them, saying, "[a]I am the
light of the world; [b]he who follows Me shall not walk in the
darkness, but shall have the light of life."
13 The Pharisees therefore said to Him, "[a]You are bearing
witness of Yourself; Your witness is not [1]true."
14 Jesus answered and said to them, "[a]Even if I bear witness of Myself, My witness is true; for I know [b]where I came
from, and where I am going; but [c]you do not know where I
come from, or where I am going.
15 "[a]You people judge [1]according to the flesh; [b]I am not
judging any one.
16 "But even [a]if I do judge, My judgment is true; for I am
not alone *in it*, but I and [1]He who sent Me.
17 "Even in [a]your law it has been written, that the testimony of [b]two men is [1]true.
18 "I am He who bears witness of Myself, and [a]the Father
who sent Me bears witness of Me."
19 And so they were saying to Him, "Where is Your
Father?" Jesus answered, "You know neither Me, nor My
Father; [a]if you knew Me, you would know My Father also."
20 These words He spoke in [a]the treasury, as [b]He taught
in the temple; and no one seized Him, because [c]His hour had
not yet come.
21 He said therefore again to them, "I go away, and [a]you

53 [1]John 7:53-8:11 is not found in most of the old mss.

1 [a]Matt. 21:1

2 [a]Matt. 26:55; John 8:20

5 [a]Lev. 20:10; Deut. 22:22f.

6 [a]Matt. 16:1; 19:3; 22:18, 35; Mark 8:11; 10:2; 12:15; Luke 10:25; 11:16 [b]Mark 3:2

7 [a]John 8:10 [b]Matt. 7:1; Rom. 2:1 [c]Deut. 17:7

10 [a]John 8:7

11 [1]Or, *Sir*
[a]John 3:17 [b]John 5:14

12 [a]John 1:4; 12:35 [b]Matt. 5:14

13 [1]Or, *valid*
[a]John 5:31

14 [a]John 18:37; Rev. 1:5; 3:14 [b]John 13:3; 16:28; 8:42 [c]John 7:28; 9:29

15 [1]I.e., a carnal standard
[a]1 Sam. 16:7; John 7:24 [b]John 3:17

16 [1]Many ancient mss. read, *the Father who sent Me*
[a]John 5:30

17 [1]I.e., valid or admissible
[a]Deut. 19:15; 17:6 [b]Matt. 18:16

18 [a]John 5:37; 1 John 5:9

19 [a]John 14:7; 16:3; 7:28; 14:9; 8:55

20 [a]Mark 12:41, 43; Luke 21:1 [b]John 7:14; John 8:2 [c]John 7:30

21 [a]John 7:34

shall seek Me, and [b]shall die in your sin; where I am going, you
cannot come."
22 Therefore [a]the Jews were saying, "Surely He will not
kill Himself, will He, since He says, '[b]Where I am going, you
cannot come'?"
23 And He was saying to them, "[a]You are from below, I
am from above; [b]you are of this world; [c]I am not of this world.
24 "I said therefore to you, that you [a]shall die in your sins;
for unless you believe that [1b]I am *He,* [a]you shall die in your
sins."
25 And so they were saying to Him, "Who are You?"
Jesus said to them, "[1]What have I been saying to you *from* the
beginning?
26 "I have many things to speak and to judge concerning
you, but [a]He who sent Me is true; and [b]the things which I
heard from Him, these I speak to the world."
27 They did not realize that He had been speaking to
them about the Father.
28 Jesus therefore said, "When you [a]lift up the Son of
Man, then you will know that [1b]I am *He,* and [c]I do nothing on
My own initiative, but I speak these things as the Father
taught Me.
29 "And He who sent Me is with Me; [a]He [1]has not left Me
alone, for [b]I always do the things that are pleasing to Him."
30 As He spoke these things, [a]many came to believe in
Him.
31 Jesus therefore was saying to those Jews who had believed Him, "[a]If you abide in My word, *then* you are truly
[b]disciples of Mine;
32 and [a]you shall know the truth, and [b]the truth shall
make you free."
33 They answered Him, "[a]We are Abraham's offspring,
and have never yet been enslaved to any one; how is it that
You say, 'You shall become free'?"
34 Jesus answered them, "Truly, truly, I say to you, [a]every
one who commits sin is the slave of sin.
35 "And [a]the slave does not remain in the house forever;
[b]the son does remain forever.
36 "If therefore the Son [a]shall make you free, you shall be
free indeed.
37 "I know that you are [a]Abraham's offspring; yet [b]you seek
to kill Me, because My word [1]has no place in you.
38 "I speak the things which I have seen [1]with *My* Father;
therefore you also do the things which you heard from [a]*your*
father."
39 They answered and said to Him, "Abraham is [a]our
father." Jesus *said to them, "[b]If you are Abraham's children,
do the deeds of Abraham.
40 "But as it is, [a]you are seeking to kill Me, a man who has
[b]told you the truth, which I heard from God; this Abraham did
not do.
41 "You are doing the deeds of [a]your father." They said to
Him, "We were not born of fornication; [b]we have one Father,
even God."
42 Jesus said to them, "If God were your Father, [a]you
would love Me; [b]for I proceeded forth and have come from

21 [b]John 8:24

22 [a]John 1:19; John 8:48, 52, 57 [b]John 7:35

23 [a]John 3:31 [b]1 John 4:5 [c]John 17:14, 16

24 [1]Most auth. connect this with Ex. 3:14 *I AM THAT I AM*
[a]John 8:21 [b]John 8:28; Mark 13:6; Luke 21:8 [Matt. 24:5]; John 4:26; 13:19

25 [1]Or, *that which I have been saying to you from the beginning.*

26 [a]John 7:28; 3:33 [b]John 12:49; 15:15; 8:40

28 [1]Lit., *I am* (vs. 24 note)
[a]John 3:14; 12:32 [b]John 8:24; Mark 13:6; Luke 21:8 [Matt. 24:5]; John 4:26; 13:19 [c]John 5:19; 3:11

29 [1]Or, *did not leave*
[a]John 8:16; 16:32 [b]John 4:34

30 [a]John 7:31

31 [a]John 15:7; 2 John 9
[b]John 2:2

32 [a]John 1:14, 17 [b]John 8:36; Rom. 8:2; 2 Cor. 3:17; Gal. 5:1, 13; James 2:12; 1 Pet. 2:16

33 [a]John 8:37, 39; Matt. 3:9

34 [a]Rom. 6:16; 2 Pet. 2:19

35 [a]Gen. 21:10; Gal. 4:30
[b]Luke 15:31

36 [a]John 8:32

37 [1]Or, *makes no progress*
[a]John 8:39; Matt. 3:9 [b]John 8:40; 7:1

38 [1]Or, *in the presence of*
[a]John 8:41, 44

39 [a]John 8:37; Matt. 3:9
[b]Rom. 9:7; Gal. 3:7

40 [a]John 8:37; 7:1 [b]John 8:26

41 [a]John 8:38, 44 [b]Deut. 32:6; Is. 63:16; 64:8

42 [a]1 John 5:1 [b]John 13:3; 16:28, 30; 17:8

God, for I have [c]not even come on My own initiative, but [1d]He
sent Me.
43 "Why do you not understand [1a]what I am saying? *It is*
because you cannot [b]hear My word.
44 "[a]You are of [b]*your* father the devil, and [c]you want to do
the desires of your father. [d]He was a murderer from the beginning, and does not stand in the truth, because [e]there is no truth
in him. Whenever he speaks a [1]lie, he [f]speaks from his own
nature; for he is a liar, and the father of [2]lies.
45 "But because [a]I speak the truth, you do not believe Me.
46 "Which one of you convicts Me of sin? If [a]I speak truth,
why do you not believe Me?
47 "[a]He who is of God hears the words of God; for this
reason you do not hear *them,* because you are not of God."
48 [a]The Jews answered and said to Him, "Do we not say
rightly that You are a [b]Samaritan and [c]have a demon?"
49 Jesus answered, "I do not [a]have a demon; but I honor
My Father, and you dishonor Me.
50 "But [a]I do not seek My glory; there is One who seeks
and judges.
51 "Truly, truly, I say to you, if anyone [a]keeps My word he
shall never [b]see death."
52 [a]The Jews said to Him, "Now we know that You [b]have
a demon. Abraham died, and the prophets *also;* and You say,
'If anyone [c]keeps My word, he shall never [d]taste of death.'
53 "Surely You [a]are not greater than our father Abraham,
who died? The prophets died too; whom do You make Yourself out *to be?*"
54 Jesus answered, "[a]If I glorify Myself, My glory is nothing; [b]it is My Father who glorifies Me, of whom you say, 'He
is our God;'
55 and [a]you have not come to know Him, [b]but I know
Him; and if I say that I do not know Him, I shall be [c]a liar like
you, [b]but I do know Him, and [d]keep His word.
56 "[a]Your father Abraham [b]rejoiced [1]to see My day; and he
saw *it,* and was glad."
57 [a]The Jews therefore said to Him, "You are not yet fifty
years old, and have You seen Abraham?"
58 Jesus said to them, "Truly, truly, I say to you, before
Abraham [1]was born, [2a]I AM."
59 Therefore they [a]picked up stones to throw at Him; but
Jesus [1b]hid Himself, [2]and went out of the temple.

Chapter 9

AND as He passed by, He saw a man blind from birth.
2 And His disciples asked Him, saying, "[a]Rabbi, who
sinned, [b]this man, or his [c]parents, that he should be born
blind?"
3 Jesus answered, "*It was* neither *that* this man sinned,
nor his parents; but *it was* in order [a]that the works of God
might be displayed in him.
4 "We must work the works of Him who sent Me, [a]as long
as it is day; night is coming, when no man can work.
5 "While I am in the world, I am [a]the light of the world."

42 [1]Lit., *that One* [c]John 7:28 [d]John 3:17

43 [1]Or, *My mode of speaking* [a]John 8:33, 39, 41 [b]John 5:25

44 [1]Lit., *the lie* [2]Lit., *the father of it* [a]1 John 3:8 [b]John 8:38, 41 [c]John 7:17 [d]Gen. 3:4; 1 John 3:8, 15 [e]1 John 2:4 [f]Matt. 12:34

45 [a]John 18:37

46 [a]John 18:37

47 [a]1 John 4:6

48 [a]John 1:19 [b]Matt. 10:5; John 4:9 [c]John 7:20

49 [a]John 7:20

50 [a]John 5:41; 8:54

51 [a]John 14:23; 15:20; 17:6; John 8:55 [b]Luke 2:26; Heb. 11:5; Matt. 16:28; Heb. 2:9; John 8:52

52 [a]John 1:19 [b]John 7:20 [c]John 14:23; 15:20; 17:6; 8:55 [d]John 8:51

53 [a]John 4:12

54 [a]John 8:50 [b]John 7:39

55 [a]John 8:19; 15:21 [b]John 7:29 [c]John 8:44 [d]John 15:10; 8:51

56 [1]Lit., *in order that he might see* [a]John 8:37, 39 [b]Matt. 13:17; Heb. 11:13

57 [a]John 1:19

58 [1]Lit., *came into being* [2]Or, *I have been* [a]John 17:5, 24; 1:1

59 [1]Lit., *was hidden* [2]Some mss. add, *and going through the midst of them went His way and so passed by* [a]John 10:31; 11:8; Matt. 12:14 [b]John 12:36

2 [a]Matt. 23:7 [b]John 9:34; Luke 13:2; Acts 28:4 [c]Ex. 20:5

3 [a]John 11:4

4 [a]John 11:9; 12:35; 7:33; Gal. 6:10

5 [a]John 1:4; 8:12; 12:46

6 When He had said this, He [a]spat on the ground, and
made clay of the spittle, and applied the clay to his eyes,
7 and said to him, "Go, wash in [a]the pool of Siloam"
(which is translated, Sent). And so he went away and washed,
and [b]came *back* seeing.
8 The neighbors therefore, and those who previously saw
him as a beggar, were saying, "Is not this the one who used to
[a]sit and beg?"
9 Others were saying, "This is he," *still* others were
saying, "No, but he is like him." He kept saying, "I am the
one."
10 Therefore they were saying to him, "How then were
your eyes opened?"
11 He answered, "The man who is called Jesus made clay,
and anointed my eyes, and said to me, 'Go to [a]Siloam, and
wash'; so I went away and washed, and I received sight."
12 And they said to him, "Where is He?" He *said, "I do
not know."
13 They *brought to the Pharisees him who was formerly
blind.
14 [a]Now it was a Sabbath on the day when Jesus made the
clay, and opened his eyes.
15 [a]Again therefore the Pharisees also were asking him
how he received his sight. And he said to them, "He applied
clay to my eyes, and I washed, and I see."
16 Therefore some of the Pharisees were saying, "[a]This
man is not from God, because he does not keep the Sabbath."
But others were saying, "How can a man who is a sinner perform such [1b]signs?" And [c]there was a division among them.
17 They *said therefore to the blind man [a]again, "What
do you say about Him, since He opened your eyes?" And he
said, "He is a [b]prophet."
18 [a]The Jews therefore did not believe *it* of him, that he
had been blind, and had received sight, until they called the
parents of the very one who had received his sight,
19 and questioned them, saying, "Is this your son, who
you say was born blind? Then how does he now see?"
20 His parents answered then, and said, "We know that
this is our son, and that he was born blind;
21 but how he now sees, we do not know; or who opened
his eyes, we do not know. Ask him; he is of age, he shall speak
for himself."
22 His parents said this because they [a]were afraid of the
Jews; for the Jews [b]had already agreed, that if any one should
confess Him to be [1]Christ, [c]he should be put out of the
synagogue.
23 For this reason his parents said, "[a]He is of age; ask
him."
24 So a second time they called the man who had been
blind, and said to him, "[a]Give glory to God; we know that [b]this
man is a sinner."
25 He therefore answered, "Whether He is a sinner, I do
not know; one thing I do know, that, whereas I was blind, now
I see."
26 They said therefore to him, "What did He do to you?
How did He open your eyes?"

6 [a]Mark 7:33; 8:23
7 [a]John 9:11; Luke 13:4 [b]John 11:37
8 [a]Acts 3:2, 10
11 [a]John 9:7
14 [a]John 5:9
15 [a]John 9:10
16 [1]Or, *attesting miracles* [a]Matt. 12:2 [b]John 2:11 [c]John 6:52; 7:43; 10:19
17 [a]John 9:15 [b]Matt. 21:11
18 [a]John 1:19; 9:22
22 [1]I.e., the Messiah [a]John 7:13 [b]John 7:45-52 [c]John 12:42; 16:2; Luke 6:22
23 [a]John 9:21
24 [a]Josh 7:19; Ezra 10:11; Rev. 11:13 [b]John 9:16

27 [a]John 9:15 [b]John 5:25

28 [a]John 5:45; Rom. 2:17

29 [a]John 8:14

31 [a]Job 27:8f.; 35:13; Ps. 34:15f.; 66:18; 145:19; Prov. 15:29; 28:9; Is. 1:15; James 5:16ff.

32 [1]Lit., *from antiquity it was not heard*

33 [a]John 9:16; 3:2

34 [a]John 9:2 [b]John 9:22, 35; 3 John 10

35 [a]John 9:22, 34; 3 John 10 [b]Matt. 4:3

36 [1]Or, *Sir* [a]Rom. 10:14

37 [a]John 4:26

38 [a]Matt. 8:2

39 [a]John 5:22, 27; 3:19 [b]Luke 4:18 [c]Matt. 13:13; 15:14

40 [a]Rom. 2:19

41 [a]John 15:22, 24 [b]Prov. 26:12

1 [a]John 10:8

2 [a]John 10:11f.

3 [a]John 10:4f., 16, 27 [b]John 10:9

4 [a]John 10:5, 16, 27

5 [a]John 10:4f., 16, 27

6 [a]John 16:25, 29; 2 Pet. 2:22

7 [a]John 10:1f., 9

8 [a]John 10:1; Jer. 23:1f.; Ezek. 34:2ff.

9 [a]John 10:1f., 9

27 He answered them, "[a]I told you already, and you did
not [b]listen; why do you want to hear *it* again? You do not want
to become His disciples too, do you?"
28 And they reviled him, and said, "You are His disciple;
but [a]we are disciples of Moses.
29 "We know that God has spoken to Moses; but as for this
man, [a]we do not know where He is from."
30 The man answered and said to them, "Well, here is an
amazing thing, that you do not know where He is from, and
yet He opened my eyes.
31 "We know that [a]God does not hear sinners; but if any
one is God-fearing, and does His will, He hears him.
32 "[1]Since the beginning of time it has never been heard
that any one opened the eyes of a person born blind.
33 "[a]If this man were not from God, He could do nothing."
34 They answered and said to him, "[a]You were born entirely in sins, and are you teaching us?" And they [b]put him out.
35 Jesus heard that they had [a]put him out; and finding
him, He said, "Do you believe in the [b]Son of Man?"
36 He answered and said, "And [a]who is He, [1]Lord, that I
may believe in Him?"
37 Jesus said to him, "You have both seen Him, and [a]He is
the one who is talking with you."
38 And he said, "Lord, I believe." And he [a]worshiped
Him.
39 And Jesus said, "[a]For judgment I came into this world,
that [b]those who do not see may see; and that [c]those who see
may become blind."
40 Those of the Pharisees who were with Him heard these
things, and said to Him, "[a]We are not blind too, are we?"
41 Jesus said to them, "[a]If you were blind, you would have
no sin; but now you say, '[b]We see;' your sin remains.

Chapter 10

"TRULY, truly, I say to you, he who does not enter by the
door into the fold of the sheep, but climbs up some other way,
he is [a]a thief and a robber.
2 "But he who enters by the door is [a]a shepherd of the
sheep.
3 "To him the doorkeeper opens; and the sheep hear [a]his
voice; and he calls his own sheep by name, and [b]leads them
out.
4 "When he puts forth all his own, he goes before them,
and the sheep follow him because they know [a]his voice.
5 "And a stranger they simply will not follow, but will flee
from him, because they do not know [a]the voice of strangers."
6 This [a]figure of speech Jesus spoke to them, but they
did not understand what those things were which He had been
saying to them.
7 Jesus therefore said to them again, "Truly, truly, I say
to you, I am [a]the door of the sheep.
8 "All who came before Me are [a]thieves and robbers; but
the sheep did not hear them.
9 "[a]I am the door; if anyone enters through Me, he shall
be saved, and shall go in and out, and find pasture.

10 "The thief comes only to steal, and kill, and destroy; I
came that they [a]might have life, and might [1]have *it*
abundantly.
11 "[a]I am the good shepherd; the good shepherd [b]lays down
His life for the sheep.
12 "He who is a hireling, and not a [a]shepherd, who is not
the owner of the sheep, beholds the wolf coming, and leaves
the sheep, and flees, and the wolf snatches them, and scatters
them.
13 "*He flees* because he is a hireling, and is not concerned
about the sheep.
14 "[a]I am the good shepherd; and [b]I know My own, and My
own know Me,
15 even as [a]the Father knows Me and I know the Father;
and [b]I lay down My life for the sheep.
16 "And I have [a]other sheep, which are not of this fold; I
must bring them also, and they shall hear My voice; and they
shall become [b]one flock *with* [c]one Shepherd.
17 "For this reason the Father loves Me, because I [a]lay
down My life that I may take it again.
18 "[a]No one [1]has taken it away from Me, but I [b]lay it down
on My own initiative. I have authority to lay it down, and I
have authority to take it up again. [c]This commandment I
received from My Father."
19 [a]There arose a division again among the Jews because
of these words.
20 And many of them were saying, "He [a]has a demon, and
[b]is insane; why do you listen to Him?"
21 Others were saying, "These are not the sayings of one
[a]demon-possessed. [b]A demon cannot open the eyes of the
blind, can he?"
22 At that time the Feast of the Dedication took place at
Jerusalem;
23 it was winter, and Jesus was walking in the temple in
the portico of [a]Solomon.
24 [a]The Jews therefore gathered around Him, and were
saying to Him, "How long will You keep us in suspense? If
You are [1]the Christ, tell us [b]plainly."
25 Jesus answered them, "[a]I told you, and you do not
believe; [b]the works that I do in My Father's name, these bear
witness of Me.
26 "But you do not believe, because [a]you are not of My
sheep.
27 "My sheep [a]hear My voice, and [b]I know them, and they
follow Me;
28 and I give [a]eternal life to them; and they shall never
perish, and [b]no one shall snatch them out of My hand.
29 "[1]My Father, who has given *them* to Me, is greater than
all; and no one is able to snatch *them* out of the Father's hand.
30 "[a]I and the Father are [1]one."
31 The Jews [a]took up stones again to stone Him.
32 Jesus answered them, "I showed you many good works
from the Father; for which of them are you stoning Me?"
33 The Jews answered Him, "For a good work we do not
stone You, but for [a]blasphemy; and because You, being a man,
[b]make Yourself out *to be* God."

10 [1]Or, *have abundance* [a]John 5:40

11 [a]John 10:14; Is. 40:11; Ezek. 34:11-16, 23; Heb. 13:20; 1 Pet. 5:4; Rev. 7:17 [b]John 10:15, 17, 18; 1 John 3:16; John 15:13

12 [a]John 10:2

14 [a]John 10:11 [b]John 10:27

15 [a]Matt. 11:27 [b]John 10:11, 17, 18

16 [a]Is. 56:8 [b]John 11:52; 17:20f.; Eph. 2:13-18; 1 Pet. 2:25 [c]Ezek. 34:23; 37:24

17 [a]John 10:11, 15, 18

18 [1]Many Greek mss. read, *takes* [a]Matt. 26:53; John 2:19; 5:26 [b]John 10:11, 15, 17 [c]John 14:31; 15:10; Phil. 2:8; Heb. 5:8

19 [a]John 7:43; 9:16

20 [a]John 7:20 [b]Mark 3:21

21 [a]Matt. 4:24 [b]John 9:32f.; Ex. 4:11

23 [a]Acts 3:11; 5:12

24 [1]I.e., the Messiah [a]John 1:19; 10:31, 33 [b]John 16:25; Luke 22:67

25 [a]John 8:56, 58 [b]John 5:36; 10:38

26 [a]John 8:47

27 [a]John 10:16; John 10:4 [b]John 10:14

28 [a]John 17:2f.; 1 John 2:25; 5:11 [b]John 6:37, 39

29 [1]Some early mss. read, *What My Father has given Me is greater than all*

30 [1](Lit. neuter) *a unity,* or, *one essence.* [a]John 17:21ff.

31 [a]John 8:59

33 [a]Lev. 24:16 [b]John 5:18

34 [a]John 8:17 [b]John 12:34; 15:25; Rom. 3:19; 1 Cor. 14:21 [c]Ps. 82:6

36 [a]John 6:69; Jer. 1:5 [b]John 3:17 [c]John 10:30; 5:17f.

37 [a]John 15:24; 10:25

38 [1]Lit., *know and continue knowing* [a]John 10:25; 14:11 [b]John 14:10f., 20; 17:21, 23

39 [a]John 7:30 [b]John 8:59; Luke 4:30

40 [a]John 1:28

41 [a]John 2:11 [b]John 1:27, 30, 34; 3:27-30

42 [a]John 7:31

1 [a]Matt. 21:17; John 11:18 [b]John 11:5, 19ff.; Luke 10:38

2 [a]John 12:3; Luke 7:38 [b]Luke 7:13; John 11:3, 21, 32; 13:13f.

3 [a]Luke 7:13; John 11:2, 21, 32; 13:13f. [b]John 11:5, 11, 36

4 [a]John 11:40; 9:3; 10:38

5 [a]John 11:1

7 [a]John 10:40

8 [a]Matt. 23:7 [b]John 10:31; 8:59

9 [a]Luke 13:33; John 9:4; 12:35

11 [a]John 11:3 [b]Matt. 27:52; Mark 5:39; John 11:13; Acts 7:60

12 [1]Lit., *he will be saved*

13 [1]Lit., *the slumber of sleep* [a]Matt. 9:24; Luke 8:52

34 Jesus answered them, "Has it not been written in [a]your
[b]Law, 'I said, [c]you are gods'?
35 "If he called them gods, to whom the word of God came
(and the Scripture cannot be broken),
36 do you say of Him, whom the Father [a]sanctified and
[b]sent into the world, 'You are blaspheming'; because I said, '[c]I
am the Son of God'?
37 "[a]If I do not do the works of My Father, do not believe
Me;
38 but if I do them, though you do not believe Me, believe [a]the works; that you may [1]know and understand that [b]the
Father is in Me, and I in the Father."
39 Therefore [a]they were seeking again to seize Him; and
[b]He eluded their grasp.
40 And He went away [a]again beyond the Jordan to the
place where John was first baptizing; and He was staying there.
41 And many came to Him; and they were saying, "While
John performed no [a]sign, yet [b]everything John said about this
man was true."
42 And [a]many believed in Him there.

Chapter 11

NOW a certain man was sick, Lazarus of [a]Bethany, of the
village of Mary and her sister [b]Martha.
2 And it was the Mary who [a]anointed [b]the Lord with
ointment, and wiped His feet with her hair, whose brother
Lazarus was sick.
3 The sisters therefore sent to Him, saying, "[a]Lord, behold, [b]he whom You love is sick."
4 But when Jesus heard it, He said, "This sickness is not
unto death, but for [a]the glory of God, that the Son of God
may be glorified by it."
5 Now Jesus loved [a]Martha, and her sister, and Lazarus.
6 When therefore He heard that he was sick, He stayed
then two days *longer* in the place where He was.
7 Then after this He *said to the disciples, "[a]Let us go to
Judea again."
8 The disciples *said to Him, "[a]Rabbi, the Jews were just
now seeking [b]to stone You; and are You going there again?"
9 Jesus answered, "[a]Are there not twelve hours in the
day? If anyone walks in the day, he does not stumble, because
he sees the light of this world.
10 "But if anyone walks in the night, he stumbles, because
the light is not in him."
11 This He said, and after that He *said to them, "Our
[a]friend Lazarus [b]has fallen asleep; but I go, that I may awaken
him out of sleep."
12 The disciples therefore said to Him, "Lord, if he has
fallen asleep, he will [1]recover."
13 Now [a]Jesus had spoken of his death; but they thought
that He was speaking of [1]literal sleep.
14 Then Jesus therefore said to them plainly, "Lazarus is
dead,
15 and I am glad for your sakes that I was not there, so
that you may believe; but let us go to him."

16 [a]Thomas therefore, who is called [1b]Didymus, said to *his*
fellow disciples, "Let us also go, that we may die with Him."
17 So when Jesus came, He found that he had already
been in the tomb [a]four days.
18 Now [a]Bethany was near Jerusalem, about [1]two miles
off;
19 and many of [a]the Jews had come to [b]Martha and Mary,
[c]to console them concerning *their* brother.
20 [a]Martha therefore, when she heard that Jesus was coming, went to meet Him; but [a]Mary still sat in the house.
21 Martha therefore said to Jesus, "[a]Lord, [b]if You had
been here, my brother would not have died.
22 "Even now I know that [a]whatever You ask of God, God
will give You."
23 Jesus *said to her, "Your brother shall rise again."
24 Martha *said to Him, "[a]I know that he will rise again in
the resurrection on the last day."
25 Jesus said to her, "[a]I am the resurrection, and the life;
he who believes in Me shall live even if he dies,
26 and everyone who lives and believes in Me [a]shall never
die. Do you believe this?"
27 She *said to Him, "Yes, Lord; I have believed that You
are [1a]the Christ, the Son of God, *even* [2b]He who comes into
the world."
28 And when she had said this, she [a]went away, and called
Mary her sister, saying secretly, "[b]The Teacher is here, and is
calling for you."
29 And when she heard it, she *arose quickly, and was
coming to Him.
30 Now Jesus had not yet come into the village, but [a]was
still in the place where Martha met Him.
31 [a]The Jews then who were with her in the house, and
[b]consoling her, when they saw that Mary rose up quickly and
went out, followed her, supposing that she was going to the
tomb to [1]weep there.
32 Therefore, when Mary came where Jesus was, she saw
Him, and fell at His feet, saying to Him, "[a]Lord, [b]if You had
been here, my brother would not have died."
33 When Jesus therefore saw her [1]weeping, and [a]the Jews
who came with her, *also* [1]weeping, He [b]was deeply moved in
spirit, and [2c]was troubled,
34 and said, "Where have you laid him?" They *said to
Him, "Lord, come and see."
35 Jesus [a]wept.
36 And so [a]the Jews were saying, "Behold how He [1b]loved
him!"
37 But some of them said, "Could not this man, who
[a]opened the eyes of him who was blind, [1]have kept this man
also from dying?"
38 Jesus therefore again being deeply moved within,
*came to the tomb. Now it was a [a]cave, and a stone was lying
against it.
39 Jesus *said, "Remove the stone." Martha, the sister of
the deceased, *said to Him, "Lord, by this time [1]there will be a
stench; for he *has been dead* [a]four days."

16 [1]I.e., the Twin [a]Matt. 10:3; Mark 3:18; Luke 6:15; John 14:5; 20:26-28; Acts 1:13 [b]John 20:24; 21:2

17 [a]John 11:39

18 [1]Lit., 15 stadia (9090 ft.) [a]John 11:1

19 [a]John 1:19; 11:8 [b]John 11:1 [c]John 11:31; Job 2:11; 1 Sam. 31:13; 1 Chr. 10:12

20 [a]Luke 10:38-42

21 [a]John 11:2 [b]John 11:32, 37

22 [a]John 11:41f.; 9:31

24 [a]Dan. 12:2; Acts 24:15; John 5:28f.

25 [a]John 1:4; 5:26; 6:39f.; Rev. 1:18

26 [a]John 6:47, 50, 51; 8:51

27 [1]I.e., the Messiah [2]The Coming One was the Messianic title [a]Matt. 16:16; Luke 2:11 [b]John 6:14

28 [a]John 11:30 [b]Matt. 26:18; Mark 14:14; Luke 22:11; John 13:13

30 [a]John 11:20

31 [1]Lit., *wail* [a]John 11:19, 33 [b]John 11:19

32 [a]John 11:2 [b]John 11:21

33 [1]Lit., *wailing* [2]Lit., *troubled Himself* [a]John 11:19 [b]John 11:38 [c]John 12:27; 13:21

35 [a]Luke 19:41 [where Gr. as in John 11:33 marg.]

36 [1]Lit., *was loving* [a]John 11:19 [b]John 11:3

37 [1]Lit., *have caused that this man also not die* [a]John 9:7

38 [a]Matt. 27:60; Mark 15:46; Luke 24:2; John 20:1

39 [1]Lit., *he stinks* [a]John 11:17

40 [a]John 11:4, 23ff.

41 [a]Matt. 27:60; Mark 15:46; Luke 24:2; John 20:1 [b]John 17:1; Acts 7:55 [c]Matt. 11:25

42 [a]John 12:30; 17:21 [b]John 3:17

44 [a]John 19:40 [b]John 20:7

45 [a]John 7:31 [b]John 11:19; John 12:17f. [c]John 2:23

46 [a]John 11:57; John 7:32, 45

47 [1]Or, *attesting miracles* [a]John 11:57; John 7:32, 45 [b]Matt. 26:3 [c]Matt. 5:22 [d]John 2:11

48 [a]Matt. 24:15

49 [a]Matt. 26:3 [b]John 11:51; 18:13

50 [a]John 18:14

51 [1]Lit., *from himself* [a]John 11:51; 18:13 [b]Ex. 28:30; Num. 27:21; 1 Sam. 23:9; 30:7; Ezra 2:63

52 [a]John 10:16

53 [a]Matt. 26:4

54 [a]John 7:1 [b]2 Chr. 13:19 marg.

55 [a]Matt. 26:1f.; Mark 14:1; Luke 22:1; John 12:1; 13:1; John 2:13 [b]Num. 9:10; 2 Chr. 30:17f.; John 18:28

56 [a]John 7:11

57 [a]John 11:47

1 [a]John 12:1-8: *Matt. 26:6-13; Mark 14:3-9;* also *Luke* 7:37-39 [b]John 11:55; John 12:20 [c]Matt. 21:17; John 11:43f.

2 [a]Luke 10:38

40 Jesus *said to her, "[a]Did I not say to you, if you believe,
you will see the glory of God?"
41 And so they removed the [a]stone. And Jesus [b]raised His
eyes, and said, "[c]Father, I thank Thee that Thou heardest Me.
42 "And I knew that Thou hearest Me always; but [a]because
of the people standing around I said it, that they may believe
that [b]Thou didst send Me."
43 And when He had said these things, He cried out with a
loud voice, "Lazarus, come forth."
44 He who had died came forth, [a]bound hand and foot
with wrappings; and [b]his face was wrapped around with a cloth.
Jesus *said to them, "Unbind him, and let him go."
45 [a]Many therefore of the Jews, [b]who had come to Mary
and [c]beheld what He had done, believed in Him.
46 But some of them went away to the [a]Pharisees, and
told them the things which Jesus had done.
47 Therefore [a]the chief priests and the Pharisees [b]con-
vened a [c]council, and were saying, "What are we doing? For
this man is performing many [1d]signs.
48 "If we let Him *go on* like this, all men will believe in
Him, and the Romans will come and take away both our
[a]place and our nation."
49 But a certain one of them, [a]Caiaphas, [b]who was high
priest that year, said to them, "You know nothing at all,
50 nor do you take into account that [a]it is expedient for
you that one man should die for the people, and that the
whole nation should not perish."
51 Now this he did not say [1]on his own initiative; but
[a]being high priest that year, he [b]prophesied that Jesus was
going to die for the nation;
52 and not for the nation only, but that He might also
[a]gather together into one the children of God who are scattered abroad.
53 So from that day on they [a]planned together to kill
Him.
54 Jesus therefore [a]no longer continued to walk publicly
among the Jews, but went away from there to the country near
the wilderness, into a city called [b]Ephraim; and there He
stayed with the disciples.
55 Now [a]the Passover of the Jews was at hand, and many
went up to Jerusalem out of the country before the Passover,
[b]to purify themselves.
56 Therefore they [a]were seeking for Jesus, and were saying
to one another, as they stood in the temple, "What do you
think; that He will not come to the feast at all?"
57 Now [a]the chief priests and the Pharisees had given orders that if any one knew where He was, he should report it,
that they might seize Him.

Chapter 12

[a]JESUS therefore six days before [b]the Passover, came to [c]Beth-
any where Lazarus was, whom Jesus had raised from the
dead.
2 So they made Him a supper there; and [a]Martha was

serving; but Lazarus was one of those reclining *at the table*
with Him.
3 [a]Mary therefore took a pound of very costly, [b]genuine
spikenard-ointment, and anointed the feet of Jesus, and wiped
His feet with her hair; and the house was filled with the fragrance
of the ointment.
4 But [a]Judas Iscariot, one of His disciples, who was intending to [1]betray Him, *said,
5 "Why was this ointment not sold for [1]three hundred
denarii, and given to poor *people?*"
6 Now he said this, not because he was concerned about
the poor, but because he was a thief, and as he [a]had the money
box, he used to pilfer [b]what was put into it.
7 Jesus therefore said, "Let her alone, in order that she
may keep [1]it for [a]the day of My burial.
8 "[a]For the poor you always have with you; but you do not
always have Me."
9 The [a]great multitude therefore of the Jews learned that
He was there; and they came, not for Jesus' sake only, but that
they might also see Lazarus, [b]whom He raised from the dead.
10 But the chief priests took counsel that they might put
Lazarus to death also;
11 because [a]on account of him [b]many of the Jews were
going away, and were believing in Jesus.
12 On the next day [1a]the great multitude who had come
to [b]the feast, when they heard that Jesus was coming to
Jerusalem,
13 took the branches of the palm trees, and went out to
meet Him, and *began* to cry out, "[a]Hosanna! Blessed *is* He
who comes in the name of the Lord, even the [b]King of
Israel."
14 And Jesus, finding a young donkey, sat on it; as it is
written,
15 "[a]Fear not, daughter of Zion; behold, your King
comes sitting on a donkey's colt."
16 [a]These things His disciples did not understand at the
first; but when Jesus [b]was glorified, then they remembered that
these things were written of Him, and that they had done these
things to Him.
17 And so [a]the multitude who were with Him when He
called Lazarus out of the tomb, and raised him from the dead,
were bearing Him witness.
18 [a]For this cause also the multitude went and met Him,
[b]because they heard that He had performed this [1]sign.
19 The Pharisees therefore said to one another, "You see
that you are not doing any good; look, the world has gone after
Him."
20 Now there were certain [a]Greeks among those who were
going up to worship at [b]the feast;
21 these therefore came to [a]Philip, who was from [b]Beth-
saida of Galilee, and *began to* ask him, saying, "Sir, we wish
to see Jesus."
22 Philip *came and *told [a]Andrew; Andrew and Philip
*came, and they *told Jesus.
23 And Jesus *answered them, saying, "[a]The hour has
come for the Son of Man to [b]be glorified.

3 [a]John 11:2 [b]Mark 14:3

4 [1]Or, *deliver Him up* [a]John 6:71

5 [1]Monetary value $50, but equal to 11 months' wages

6 [a]John 13:29 [b]Luke 8:3

7 [1]I.e., The custom of anointing for burial [a]John 19:40

8 [a]Matt. 26:11; Mark 14:7; Deut. 15:11

9 [a]Mark 12:37; John 12:12 marg. [b]John 11:43f.; 12:1, 17f.

11 [a]John 12:18; 11:45f. [b]John 7:31; 11:42

12 [1]Or, *the common people* [a]John 12:12-15: *Matt. 21:4-9: Mark 11:7-10; Luke 19:35-38* [b]John 12:1

13 [a]Ps. 118:25f. [b]John 1:49

15 [a]Zech. 9:9

16 [a]Mark 9:32; John 2:22; 14:26 [b]John 7:39; 12:23

17 [a]John 11:42

18 [1]Or, *attesting miracle* [a]Luke 19:37; John 12:12 [b]John 12:11

20 [a]John 7:35 [b]John 12:1

21 [a]John 1:44 [b]Matt. 11:21

22 [a]John 1:44

23 [a]John 13:1, 32; 17:1; Matt. 26:45; Mark 14:35, 41 [b]John 7:39; 12:16

24 "Truly, truly, I say to you, [a]unless a grain of wheat falls
into the earth and dies, it remains by itself alone; but if it dies,
it bears much fruit.
25 "[a]He who loves his [1]life loses it; and he who [b]hates his
[1]life in this world shall keep it to life eternal.
26 "If any one serves Me, let him follow Me; and [a]where I
am, there shall My servant also be; if any one serves Me, the
Father will [b]honor him.
27 "[a]Now My soul has become troubled; and what shall I
say, '[b]Father, save Me from [c]this hour'? But for this purpose I
came to this hour.
28 "[a]Father, glorify Thy name." There came therefore a
[b]voice out of heaven: "I have both glorified it, and will glorify
it again."
29 The multitude therefore, who stood by and heard it,
were saying that it had thundered; others were saying, "[a]An
angel has spoken to Him."
30 Jesus answered and said, "[a]This voice has not come for
My sake, but for your sakes.
31 "[a]Now judgment is upon this world; now [b]the ruler of
this world shall be cast out.
32 "And I, if I [a]be lifted up from the earth, will [b]draw all
men to Myself."
33 But He was saying this [a]to indicate the kind of death by
which He was to die.
34 The multitude therefore answered Him, "We have
heard out of [a]the Law that [1b]the Christ is to remain forever;
and how can You say, 'The [c]Son of Man must be [d]lifted up'?
Who is this [c]Son of Man?"
35 Jesus therefore said to them, "[a]For a little while longer
[b]the light is among you. [c]Walk while you have the light, that
darkness may not overtake you; he who [d]walks in the darkness
does not know where he goes.
36 "While you have the light, [a]believe in the light, in order
that you may become [b]sons of light."
These things Jesus spoke, and He departed and [1c]hid Himself from them.
37 But though He had performed so many [1]signs before
them, *yet* they were not believing in Him;
38 that the word of Isaiah the prophet might be fulfilled,
which he spoke, "[a]LORD, WHO HAS BELIEVED OUR REPORT? AND
TO WHOM HAS THE ARM OF THE LORD BEEN REVEALED?"
39 For this cause they could not believe, for Isaiah said
again,
40 "[a]HE HAS BLINDED THEIR EYES, AND HE [b]HARDENED THEIR
HEART; LEST THEY SEE WITH THEIR EYES, AND PERCEIVE WITH
THEIR HEART, AND [1]BE CONVERTED, AND I HEAL THEM."
41 These things Isaiah said, because [a]he saw His glory, and
[b]he spoke of Him.
42 Nevertheless [a]many even of [b]the rulers believed in
Him, but [c]because of the Pharisees they were not confessing
Him, lest they should be [1d]put out of the synagogue;
43 [a]for they loved the approval of men rather than the
approval of God.
44 And Jesus cried out and said, "[a]He who believes in Me
does not believe in Me, but in Him who sent Me.

24 [a]1 Cor. 15:36; Rom. 14:9

25 [1]Or, *soul*
[a]Matt. 10:39 [b]Luke 14:26

26 [a]John 14:3; 17:24; 2 Cor. 5:8; Phil. 1:23; 1 Thess. 4:17 [b]1 Sam. 2:30; Ps. 91:15; Luke 12:37

27 [a]Matt. 26:38; Mark 14:34; John 11:33 [b]Matt. 11:25 [c]John 12:23

28 [a]Matt. 11:25 [b]Matt. 3:17; 17:5; Mark 1:11; 9:7; Luke 3:22; 9:35

29 [a]Acts 23:9

30 [a]John 11:42

31 [a]John 16:11; 3:19; 9:39 [b]John 14:30; 16:11; 2 Cor. 4:4; Eph. 2:2; Eph. 6:12; 1 John 4:4; 5:19

32 [a]John 3:14; 8:28; 12:34 [b]John 6:44

33 [a]John 18:32; 21:19

34 [1]I.e., The Messiah
[a]John 10:34 [b]Ps. 110:4; Is. 9:7; Ezek. 37:25; Dan. 7:14 [c]Matt. 8:20 [d]John 3:14; 8:28; 12:32

35 [a]John 7:33; 9:4; 1 John 2:10 [b]John 12:46 [c]Eph. 5:8; Gal. 6:10 [d]1 John 1:6; 2:11

36 [1]Lit., *was hidden*
[a]John 12:46 [b]Luke 16:8; John 8:12 [c]John 8:59

37 [1]Or, *attesting miracles*

38 [a]Is. 53:1; Rom. 10:16

40 [1]Lit., *should be turned*, i.e., turn about
[a]Is. 6:10; Matt. 13:14f. [b]Mark 6:52

41 [a]Is. 6:1ff. [b]Luke 24:27

42 [1]I.e., excommunicated
[a]John 7:48; 12:11 [b]Luke 23:13 [c]John 7:13 [d]John 9:22

43 [a]John 5:41, 44

44 [a]Matt. 10:40; John 5:24

45 "And [a]he who beholds Me beholds the One who sent
Me.
46 "[a]I have come *as* light into the world, that everyone who
believes in Me may not remain in darkness.
47 "And if any one hears My sayings, and does not keep
them, I do not judge him; for [a]I did not come to judge the
world, but to save the world.
48 "[a]He who rejects Me, and does not receive My sayings,
has one who judges him; [b]the word I spoke is what will judge
him at [c]the last day.
49 "[a]For I did not speak [1]on My own initiative, but the
Father Himself who sent Me [b]has given Me commandment,
what to say, and what to speak.
50 "And I know that [a]His commandment is eternal life;
therefore the things I speak, I speak [b]just as the Father has told
Me."

Chapter 13

NOW before the feast of [a]the Passover, Jesus knowing that
[b]His hour had come that He should depart out of this world
[c]to the Father, having loved His own who were in the world,
He loved them [1]to the end.
2 And during supper, [a]the devil having already put into
the heart of [b]Judas Iscariot, *the son* of Simon, to betray Him,
3 *Jesus*, [a]knowing that the Father had given all things
into His hands, and that [b]He had come forth from God, and
was going back to God,
4 *rose from supper, and *laid aside His garments; and
taking a towel, [a]girded Himself about.
5 Then He *poured water into the basin, and began to
[a]wash the disciples' feet, and to wipe them with the towel with
which He was girded.
6 And so He *came to Simon Peter. He *said to Him,
"Lord, do You wash my feet?"
7 Jesus answered and said to him, "What I do you do not
realize now; but you shall understand [a]hereafter."
8 Peter *said to Him, "Never shall You wash my feet!"
Jesus answered him, "If I do not wash you, [a]you have no part
with Me."
9 Simon Peter *said to Him, "Lord, not my feet only,
but also my hands and my head."
10 Jesus *said to him, "He who has bathed needs only to
wash his feet, but is completely clean; and [a]you are clean, but
not all *of you*."
11 For [a]He knew the one who was betraying Him; for this
reason He said, "Not all of you are clean."
12 And so when He had washed their feet, and [a]taken His
garments, and reclined *at table* again, He said to them, "Do
you know what I have done to you?
13 "You call me [a]Teacher, and [b]Lord; and [1]you are right;
for *so* I am.
14 "If I then, [a]the Lord and the Teacher, washed your feet,
you also ought to wash one another's feet.
15 "For I gave you [a]an example that you also should do as I
did to you.

45 [a]John 14:9
46 [a]John 1:4; 3:19; 8:12; 9:5; 12:35f.
47 [a]John 3:17; 8:15f.
48 [a]Luke 10:16 [b]Deut. 18:18f.; John 5:45ff.; 8:47 [c]Matt. 10:15
49 [1]Lit., *of Myself* [a]John 3:11 [b]John 14:31; 17:8
50 [a]John 6:68 [b]John 8:28
1 [1]Lit., *to the uttermost* or, *eternally* [a]John 11:55; 2:13 [b]John 12:23 [c]John 16:28; 13:3
2 [a]John 6:70; 13:27 [b]John 6:71
3 [a]John 3:35 [b]John 8:42
4 [a]Luke 12:37
5 [a]Luke 7:44
7 [a]John 13:12ff.
8 [a]Deut. 12:12; 2 Sam. 20:1; 1 Kin. 12:16
10 [a]John 15:3
11 [a]John 6:64; 13:2
12 [a]John 13:4
13 [1]Lit., *you say well* [a]John 11:28 [b]John 11:2; 1 Cor. 12:3; Phil. 2:11
14 [a]John 11:2; 1 Cor. 12:3; Phil. 2:11
15 [a]1 Pet. 5:3

16 "Truly, truly, I say to you, [a]a slave is not greater than his
master; neither [b]one who is sent greater than the one who sent
him.
17 "If you know these things, you are [a]blessed if you do
them.
18 "[a]I do not speak of all of you. I know the ones I have
[b]chosen; but *it is* [c]that the Scripture may be fulfilled, '[d]HE WHO
EATS MY BREAD HAS LIFTED UP HIS HEEL AGAINST ME.'
19 "From now on [a]I am telling you before *it* comes to pass,
so that when it does occur, you may believe that [b]I am *He*.
20 "Truly, truly, I say to you, [a]he who receives whomever I
send receives Me; and he who receives Me receives Him who
sent Me."
21 When Jesus had said this, He [a]became troubled in spirit, and testified, and said, "Truly, truly, I say to you, that [b]one
of you will [1]betray Me."
22 The disciples *began* looking at one another, [a]at a loss
to know of which one He was speaking.
23 There was reclining on [a]Jesus' breast one of His disciples, [b]whom Jesus loved.
24 Simon Peter therefore *gestured to him, and *said to
him, "Tell *us* who it is of whom He is speaking."
25 He, [a]leaning back thus on Jesus' breast, *said to Him,
"Lord, who is it?"
26 Jesus therefore *answered, "That is the one for whom I
shall dip the morsel, and give it to him." So when He had
dipped the morsel, He *took and *gave it to Judas, [a]*the son* of
Simon Iscariot.
27 And after the morsel, [a]Satan then [b]entered into him.
Jesus therefore *said to him, "What you do, do quickly."
28 Now no one of those reclining *at table* knew for what
purpose He had said this to him.
29 For some were supposing, because Judas [a]had the money box, that Jesus was saying to him, "Buy the things we have
need of [b]for the feast"; or else, that he should [c]give something
to the poor.
30 And so after receiving the morsel he went out immediately; and [a]it was night.
31 When therefore he had gone out, Jesus *said, "Now [1]is
[a]the Son of Man [b]glorified, and [c]God [1]is glorified in Him;
32 [1]if God is glorified in Him, [a]God will also glorify Him
in Himself, and will glorify Him immediately.
33 "[a]Little children, I am with you [b]a little while longer.
[c]You shall seek Me; and as I said to the Jews, 'Where I am
going, you cannot come', now I say to you also.
34 "A [a]new commandment I give to you, [b]that you love one
another, [c]even as I have loved you, that you also love one
another.
35 "[a]By this all men will know that you are My disciples, if
you have love for one another."
36 Simon Peter *said to Him, "Lord, where are You
going?" Jesus answered, "[a]Where I go, you cannot follow Me
now; but [b]you shall follow later."
37 Peter *said to Him, "Lord, why can I not follow You
right now? [a]I will lay down my life for You."
38 Jesus *answered, "Will you lay down your life for Me?

16 [a]Matt. 10:24 [b]2 Cor. 8:23; Phil. 2:25

17 [a]Luke 11:28; James 1:25; Matt. 7:24ff.

18 [a]John 13:10f. [b]John 6:70; 15:16, 19 [c]John 17:12; 19:24, 36; 15:25; 18:32 [d]Ps. 41:9; John 13:18, 21, 22, 26; Matt. 26:21ff. Mark 14:18f.; Luke 22:21ff.

19 [a]John 14:29; 16:4 [b]John 8:24

20 [a]Matt. 10:40; Luke 10:16; Gal. 4:14

21 [1]Or, *deliver Me up* [a]John 11:33 [b]John 13:18, 21, 22, 26: Matt. 26:21f.; Mark 14:18ff. Luke 22:21ff.

22 [a]John 13:18, 21, 22, 26: Matt. 26:21ff.; Mark 14:18ff.; Luke 22:21ff.

23 [a]John 1:18 [b]John 19:26; 20:2; 21:7, 20

25 [a]John 21:20

26 [a]John 6:71

27 [a]Matt. 4:10 [b]Luke 22:3; John 13:2

29 [a]John 12:6 [b]John 13:1 [c]John 12:5

30 [a]Luke 22:53

31 [1]Or, *was* [a]Matt. 8:20 [b]John 7:39 [c]John 14:13; 17:4; 1 Pet. 4:11

32 [1]Some ancient mss. omit this phrase [a]John 17:1

33 [a]1 John 2:1 [b]John 7:33 [c]John 7:34

34 [a]1 John 2:7f.; 3:11, 23; 2 John 5; John 15:12, 17 [b]Lev. 19:18; 1 Thess. 4:9; 1 Pet. 1:22; 1 John 4:7; Heb. 13:1; Gal. 5:14; Matt. 5:44 [c]Eph. 5:2; 1 John 4:10f.

35 [a]1 John 3:14; 4:20

36 [a]John 13:33; John 14:2; 16:5 [b]John 21:18f.; 2 Pet. 1:14

37 [a]John 13:37, 38: *Matt. 26:33-35; Mark 14:29-31; Luke 22:33-34*

Truly, truly, I say to you, [a]a cock shall not crow, until you deny
Me three times.

CHAPTER 14

"[a]LET not your heart be troubled; [1]believe in God, believe
also in Me.
2 "In My Father's house are many dwelling places; if it
were not so, I would have told you; for [a]I go to prepare a place
for you.
3 "And if I go and prepare a place for you, [a]I will come
again, and receive you to Myself; that [b]where I am, *there* you
may be also.
4 "[1]And you know the way where I am going."
5 [a]Thomas *said to Him, "Lord, we do not know where
You are going; how do we know the way?"
6 Jesus *said to him, "I am [a]the way, and [b]the truth, and
[c]the life; no one comes to the Father, but through Me.
7 "[a]If you had known Me, you would have known My
Father also; from now on you [b]know Him, and have [c]seen
Him."
8 [a]Philip *said to Him, "Lord, show us the Father, and it
is enough for us."
9 Jesus *said to him, "Have I been so long with you, and
yet you have not come to know Me, Philip? [a]He who has seen
Me has seen the Father; how do you say, 'Show us the Father'?
10 "Do you not believe that [a]I am in the Father, and the
Father is in Me? [b]The words that I say to you I do not speak
on My own initiative, but the Father abiding in Me does His
works.
11 "Believe Me that [a]I am in the Father, and the Father in
Me; otherwise [b]believe on account of the works themselves.
12 "Truly, truly, I say to you, he who believes in Me, the
works that I do shall he do also; and [a]greater *works* than these
shall he do; because [b]I go to the Father.
13 "And [a]whatever you ask in My name, that will I do, that
[b]the Father may be glorified in the Son.
14 "If you ask Me anything [a]in My name, I will do *it*.
15 "[a]If you love Me, you will keep My commandments.
16 "And I will ask the Father, and He will give you another
[1a]Helper, that He may be with you forever;
17 *that is* [a]the Spirit of truth, [b]whom the world cannot
receive, because it does not behold Him or know Him, *but* you
know Him because He abides with you, and will be in you.
18 "I will not leave you as orphans; [a]I will come to you.
19 "[1a]After a little while [b]the world will behold Me no
more; but you *will* behold Me; [c]because I live, you shall live
also.
20 "[a]In that day you shall know that [b]I am in My Father,
and you in Me, and I in you.
21 "[a]He who has My commandments, and keeps them, he
it is who loves Me; and [b]he who loves Me shall be loved by My
Father, and I will love him, and will [c]disclose Myself to him."
22 [a]Judas (not Iscariot) *said to Him, "Lord, what then
has happened [b]that You are going to disclose Yourself to us,
and not to the world?"

38 [a]John 18:27; Mark 14:30

1 [1]Or, *you believe in God* [a]John 14:27; 16:22, 24

2 [a]John 13:33, 36

3 [a]John 14:18, 28 [b]John 12:26

4 [1]Many ancient authorities read, *And where I go you know, and the way you know*

5 [a]John 11:16

6 [a]John 10:9; Rom. 5:2; Heb. 10:20; Eph. 2:18 [b]John 1:14 [c]John 1:4; 11:25; 1 John 5:20

7 [a]John 8:19 [b]1 John 2:13 [c]John 6:46

8 [a]John 1:43

9 [a]John 12:45; 1:14; Col. 1:15; Heb. 1:3

10 [a]John 10:38; 14:11, 20 [b]John 14:24; 5:19

11 [a]John 10:38; 14:10, 20 [b]John 5:36

12 [a]John 5:20; 4:37f. [b]John 7:33; 14:28

13 [a]Matt. 7:7 [b]John 13:31

14 [a]John 15:16; 16:23f.

15 [a]John 14:21, 23; John 15:10; 1 John 5:3; 2 John 6

16 [1]Gr., *Paracletos*, equals one called alongside to help, or *Intercessor* [a]John 14:26; 15:26; 16:7; 1 John 2:1 marg.; John 7:39; Rom. 8:26

17 [a]John 15:26; 16:13; 1 John 4:6; 5:7 [b]1 Cor. 2:14

18 [a]John 14:3, 28

19 [1]Lit., *yet a little and the world* [a]John 7:33 [b]John 16:16, 22 [c]John 6:57

20 [a]John 16:23, 26 [b]John 10:38; 14:11

21 [a]John 14:15, 23; 15:10; 1 John 5:3; 2 John 6 [b]John 16:27; 14:23 [c]Ex. 33:18f.; Prov. 8:17

22 [a]Luke 6:16; Acts 1:13; Matt. 10:3 [b]Acts 10:40, 41

23 Jesus answered and said to him, "[a]If anyone loves Me, he will [b]keep My word; and [c]My Father will love him, and We [d]will come to him, and make Our abode with him.

24 "He who does not love Me [a]does not keep My words; and [b]the word which you hear is not Mine, but the Father's who sent Me.

25 "These things I have spoken to you, while abiding with you.

26 "But the [a]Helper, the Holy Spirit, [b]whom the Father will send in My name, [c]He will teach you all things, and [d]bring to your remembrance all that I said to you.

27 "[a]Peace I leave with you; My peace I give to you; not as the world gives, do I give to you. [b]Let not your heart be troubled, nor let it be fearful.

28 "[a]You heard that I said to you, 'I go away, and [b]I will come to you.' If you loved Me, you would have rejoiced, because [c]I go to the Father; for [d]the Father is greater than I.

29 "And now [a]I have told you before it comes to pass, that when it comes to pass, you may believe.

30 "I will not speak much more with you, for [a]the ruler of the world is coming, and [b]he has nothing in Me;

31 but that the world may know that I love the Father, and as [a]the Father gave Me commandment, even so I do. Arise, [b]let us go from here.

Chapter 15

"[a]I AM the true vine, and My Father is the [b]vinedresser.

2 "Every branch in Me that does not bear fruit, He takes away; and every *branch* that bears fruit, He [1]prunes it, that it may bear more fruit.

3 "[a]You are already clean because of the word which I have spoken to you.

4 "[a]Abide in Me, and I in you. As the branch cannot bear fruit of itself, unless it abides in the vine, so neither *can* you, unless you abide in Me.

5 "I am the vine, you are the branches; he who abides in Me, and I in him, he [a]bears much fruit; for apart from Me you can do nothing.

6 "If anyone does not abide in Me, he is [a]thrown away as a branch, and dries up; and they gather them, and cast them into the fire, and they are burned.

7 "If you abide in Me, and My words abide in you, [a]ask whatever you wish, and it shall be done for you.

8 "[a]By this is My Father glorified, [1]that you bear much fruit, and *so* [b]prove to be My disciples.

9 "Just as [a]the Father has loved Me, I have also loved you; abide in My love.

10 "[a]If you keep My commandments, you will abide in My love; just as [b]I have kept My Father's commandments, and abide in His love.

11 "[a]These things I have spoken to you, that My joy may be in you, and *that* your [b]joy may be made full.

12 "This is [a]My commandment, that you love one another, just as I have loved you.

23 [a]John 14:15, 21; 15:10; 1 John 5:3; 2 John 6 [b]John 8:51; 1 John 2:5 [c]John 14:21 [d]Rev. 3:20; Eph. 3:17; 1 John 2:24; Rev. 21:3; 2 Cor. 6:16 for O.T.

24 [a]John 14:23 [b]John 14:10; 7:16

26 [a]John 14:16 [b]John 1:33; 15:26; 16:7; Luke 24:49; and esp. Acts 2:33 [c]John 16:13f.; 1 John 2:20, 27 [d]John 2:22

27 [a]John 16:33; Col. 3:15; Phil. 4:7; John 20:19 [b]John 14:1

28 [a]John 14:2-4 [b]John 14:3, 18 [c]John 14:12 [d]John 10:29; Phil. 2:6

29 [a]John 13:19

30 [a]John 12:31 [b]Heb. 4:15

31 [a]John 10:18; 12:49 [b]John 13:1; 18:1

1 [a]Is. 5:1ff.; Ezek. 19:10ff.; Ps. 80:8ff.; Matt. 21:33ff. [b]Matt. 15:13; Rom. 11:17; 1 Cor. 3:9

2 [1]Lit., *cleanses*

3 [a]John 13:10; 17:17; Eph. 5:26

4 [a]John 15:4-7; 1 John 2:6; John 6:56

5 [a]John 15:16

6 [a]John 15:2

7 [a]Matt. 7:7; John 15:16

8 [1]Another reading, *that you bear much fruit, and become My disciples* [a]Matt. 5:16 [b]John 8:31

9 [a]John 17:23, 24, 26; 3:35

10 [a]John 14:15 [b]John 8:29

11 [a]John 17:13 [b]John 3:29

12 [a]John 13:34; 15:17

13 "[a]Greater love has no one than this, that one [b]lay down
his life for his friends.
14 "You are My [a]friends, if [b]you do what I command you.
15 "No longer do I call you slaves; for the slave does not
know what his master is doing; but I have called you friends,
for [a]all things that I have heard from My Father I have made
known to you.
16 "[a]You did not choose Me, but I chose you, and appointed you, that you should go and [b]bear fruit, and *that* your
fruit should remain; that [c]whatever you ask of the Father in
My name, He may give to you.
17 "This [a]I command you, that you love one another.
18 "[a]If the world hates you, [1]you know that it has hated Me
before *it hated* you.
19 "[a]If you were of the world, the world would love its own;
but because you are not of the world, but [b]I chose you out of
the world, [c]therefore the world hates you.
20 "Remember the word that I said to you, '[a]A slave is not
greater than his master.' If they persecuted Me, [b]they will also
persecute you; if they [c]kept My word, they will keep yours also.
21 "But all these things they will do to you [a]for My name's
sake, [b]because they do not know the One who sent Me.
22 "[a]If I had not come and spoken to them, they would not
have [1]sin, but now they have no excuse for their sin.
23 "He who hates Me hates My Father also.
24 "[a]If I had not done among them [b]the works which no
one else did, they would not have [1]sin; but now they have both
seen and hated Me and My Father as well.
25 "But *they have done this* in order that the word may be
fulfilled that is written in their [a]Law, '[b]THEY HATED ME WITH-
OUT A CAUSE.'
26 "When the [1a]Helper comes, [b]whom I will send to you
from the Father, *that is* [c]the Spirit of truth, who proceeds
from the Father, [d]He will bear witness of Me,
27 [1]and [a]you *will* bear witness also, because you have been
with Me [b]from the beginning.

CHAPTER 16

"[a]THESE things I have spoken to you, that you may be
kept from [b]stumbling.
2 "[1]They will [a]make you outcasts from the synagogue; but
[b]an hour is coming for everyone [c]who kills you to think that he
is offering service to God.
3 "And these things they will do, [a]because they have not
known the Father, or Me.
4 "But these things I have spoken to you, [a]that when their
hour comes, you [1]may remember that I told you of them. And
these things I did not say to you [b]at the beginning, because I
was with you.
5 "But now [a]I am going to Him who sent Me; and none of
you asks Me, '[b]Where are You going?'
6 "But because I have said these things to you, [a]sorrow has
filled your heart.
7 "But I tell you the truth, it is to your advantage that I go

13 [a]Rom. 5:7f. [b]John 10:11
14 [a]Luke 12:4 [b]Matt. 12:50
15 [a]John 8:26; 16:12
16 [a]John 15:19; 6:70; 13:18 [b]John 15:5 [c]John 14:13; 16:23; 15:7
17 [a]John 15:12
18 [1]Or, (imperative) *know that* [a]John 7:7; 1 John 3:13
19 [a]Matt. 10:22; 24:9 [b]John 15:16 [c]John 17:14
20 [a]John 13:16 [b]1 Cor. 4:12; 2 Cor. 4:9; 2 Tim. 3:12 [c]John 8:51
21 [a]Matt. 10:22; 24:9; Mark 13:13; Luke 21:12, 17; Acts 4:17; 5:41; 9:14; 26:9; 1 Pet. 4:14; Rev. 2:3 [b]John 16:3; John 8:19, 55; 17:25; Acts 3:17; 1 John 3:1
22 [1]I.e., guilt [a]John 9:41; John 15:24
24 [1]I.e., guilt [a]John 9:41; 15:21 [b]John 5:36; 10:37
25 [a]John 10:34 [b]Ps. 35:19; 69:4
26 [1]Gr. *Paracletos*, equals one called alongside to help, or, *Intercessor* [a]John 14:16 [b]John 14:26 [c]John 14:17 [d]1 John 5:7
27 [1]Or (imperative), *and bear witness* [a]John 19:35; 21:24; 1 John 1:2; 4:14; Luke 24:48 [b]Luke 1:2
1 [a]John 15:18-27 [b]Matt. 11:6
2 [1]Or, *they will make you excommunicated* [a]John 9:22 [b]John 4:21; 16:25 [c]Acts 26:9-11; Is. 66:5; Rev. 6:9
3 [a]John 15:21; 8:19, 55; 17:25; Acts 3:17; 1 John 3:1
4 [1]Lit., *may remember them, that I told you* [a]John 13:19 [b]Luke 1:2
5 [a]John 7:33; 16:10, 17, 28 [b]John 13:36; 14:5
6 [a]John 16:22; 14:1

away; for if I do not go away, the [1a]Helper shall not come to
you; but if I go, [b]I will send Him to you.
8 "And He, when He comes, will convict the world concerning sin, and righteousness, and judgment;
9 concerning sin, [a]because they do not believe in Me;
10 and concerning [a]righteousness, because [b]I go to the
Father, and you no longer behold Me;
11 [a]and concerning judgment, because the ruler of this
world has been judged.
12 "I have many more things to say to you, but you cannot
bear *them* now.
13 "But when He, [a]the Spirit of truth, comes, He will
[b]guide you into all the truth; for He will not speak on His own
initiative, but whatever He hears, He will speak; and He will
disclose to you what is to come.
14 "He shall [a]glorify Me; for He shall take of Mine, and
shall disclose *it* to you.
15 "[a]All things that the Father has are Mine; therefore I
said, that He takes of Mine, and will disclose *it* to you.
16 "[a]A little while, and [b]you *will* no longer behold Me; and
again a little while, and [c]you will see Me."
17 *Some* of His disciples therefore said to one another,
"What is this thing He is telling us, '[a]A little while, and you
will not behold Me; and again a little while, and you will see
Me'; and, 'Because [b]I go to the Father'?"
18 And so they were saying, "What is this that He says,
'A little while'? We do not know what He is talking about."
19 [a]Jesus knew that they wished to question Him, and He
said to them, "Are you deliberating together about this, that I
said, 'A little while, and you *will* not behold Me, and again a
little while, and you *will* see Me'?
20 "Truly, truly, I say to you, that [a]you will weep and lament, but the world will rejoice; you will be sorrowful, but
[b]your sorrow will be turned to joy.
21 "[a]Whenever a woman is in travail she has sorrow, because her hour has come; but when she gives birth to the child,
she remembers the anguish no more, for joy that a [1]child has
been born into the world.
22 "Therefore [a]you, too, now have sorrow; but [b]I will see
you again, and your heart will rejoice, and no one takes your
joy away from you.
23 "And [a]in that day [b]you will [1]ask Me no question. Truly,
truly, I say to you, [c]if you shall ask the Father for anything, He
will give it to you in My name.
24 "[a]Until now you have asked for nothing in My name;
ask, and you will receive, that your [b]joy may be made full.
25 "These things I have spoken to you in [1a]figurative language; [b]an hour is coming, when I will speak no more to you in
[1]figurative language, but will tell you plainly of the Father.
26 "[a]In that day [b]you will ask in My name; and I do not say
to you that I will request the Father on your behalf;
27 for [a]the Father Himself loves you, because you have
loved Me, and [b]have believed that [c]I came forth from the
Father.
28 "[a]I came forth from the Father, and have come into the
world; I am leaving the world again, and [b]going to the Father."

7 [1]Gr. *Paracletos*, equals one called alongside to help, or, *Intercessor* [a]John 14:16 [b]John 14:26

9 [a]John 15:22, 24

10 [a]Acts 3:14; 7:52; 17:31; 1 Pet. 3:18 [b]John 16:5

11 [a]John 12:31

13 [a]John 14:17 [b]John 14:26

14 [a]John 7:39

15 [a]John 17:10

16 [a]John 7:33 [b]John 16:16-24: 14:18-24 [c]John 16:22

17 [a]John 16:16 [b]John 16:5

19 [a]John 6:61; Mark 9:32

20 [a]Mark 16:10; Luke 23:27 [b]John 20:20

21 [1]Lit., *a human being* [a]Is. 13:8; 21:3; 26:17; 66:7; Hos. 13:13; Mic. 4:9; 1 Thess. 5:3

22 [a]John 16:6 [b]John 16:16

23 [1]Lit., *will question Me nothing* [a]John 16:26; 14:20 [b]John 16:19, 30 [c]John 15:16

24 [a]John 14:14 [b]John 3:29; 15:11

25 [1]Lit., *in proverbs* or, *in figures of speech* [a]John 16:29; 10:6; Matt. 13:34 [b]John 16:2

26 [a]John 16:23; 14:20 [b]John 16:19, 30

27 [a]John 14:21, 23 [b]John 16:30; 2:11 [c]John 8:42; 16:30

28 [a]John 8:42; 16:30 [b]John 16:5, 10, 17; 13:1, 3

29 His disciples *said, "Lo, now You are speaking plainly,
and are not using [a]a [1]figure of speech.
30 "Now we know that You know all things, and have no
need for anyone to question You; by this we [a]believe that You
[b]came from God."
31 Jesus answered them, "Do you now believe?
32 "Behold, [a]an hour is coming, and has *already* come, for
[b]you to be scattered, each to [c]his own *home*, and to leave Me
alone; and *yet* [d]I am not alone, because the Father is with Me.
33 "These things I have spoken to you, that [a]in Me you
may have peace. [b]In the world you have tribulation, but [c]take
courage; [d]I have overcome the world."

Chapter 17

THESE things Jesus spoke; and [a]lifting up His eyes to heav-
en, He said, "Father, the hour has come; [b]glorify Thy Son,
that the Son may glorify Thee,
2 even as [a]Thou gavest Him authority over all [1]mankind,
that [b]to [2]all whom Thou hast given Him, [c]He may give eternal
life.
3 "And this is eternal life, that they may know Thee [a]the
only true God, and Jesus Christ whom [b]Thou hast sent.
4 "[a]I glorified Thee on the earth, [b]having accomplished
the work which Thou hast given Me to do.
5 "And now, [a]glorify Thou Me together with Thyself, Father, with the glory which I ever had [b]with Thee before the
world was.
6 "[a]I manifested Thy name to the men whom [b]Thou gavest Me out of the world; [c]Thine they were, and Thou gavest
them to Me, and they have [d]kept Thy word.
7 "Now they have come to know that everything Thou
hast given Me is from Thee;
8 for [a]the words which [a]Thou gavest Me [b]I have given to
them; and they received *them*, and truly understood that [c]I
came forth from Thee, and they believed that [d]Thou didst
send Me.
9 "[a]I ask on their behalf; [b]I do not ask on behalf of the
world, but of those whom [c]Thou hast given Me; for [d]they are
Thine;
10 and [a]all things that are Mine are Thine, and Thine are
Mine; and I have been glorified in them.
11 "And I am no more in the world; and *yet* [a]they themselves are in the world, and [b]I come to Thee. [c]Holy Father,
keep them in Thy name, *the name* [d]which Thou hast given
Me, that [e]they may be one, even as We *are*.
12 "While I was with them, I was keeping them in Thy
name [a]which Thou hast given Me; and I guarded them, and
[b]not one of them perished but [c]the son of perdition, that the
[d]Scripture might be fulfilled.
13 "But now [a]I come to Thee; and [b]these things I speak in
the world, that they may have My [c]joy made full in themselves.
14 "I have given them Thy word; and [a]the world has hated
them, because [b]they are not of the world, even as I am not of
the world.

29 [1]Lit., *a proverb* [a]John 16:25; 10:6; Matt. 13:34

30 [a]John 16:27; 2:11 [b]John 8:42; 16:28

32 [a]John 4:23; 16:2, 25 [b]Matt. 26:31; Zech. 13:7 [c]John 19:27 [d]John 8:29

33 [a]John 14:27 [b]John 15:18ff. [c]Matt. 9:2 [d]Rom. 8:37; 2 Cor. 2:14; 4:7ff.; 6:4ff.; Rev. 3:21; 12:11

1 [a]John 11;41 [b]John 7:39; 13:31f.

2 [1]Lit., *flesh* [2]Lit., *all that which Thou hast given Him, to them He* [a]John 3:35 [b]John 17:6, 9, 24; 6:37, 39 [c]John 10:28

3 [a]John 5:44 [b]John 3:17; 17:8, 21, 23, 25

4 [a]John 13:31 [b]John 4:34; Luke 22:37

5 [a]John 17:1 [b]John 1:1; 8:58; Phil. 2:6; John 17:24

6 [a]John 17:26 [b]John 17:2, 9, 24; John 6:37, 39 [c]John 17:9 [d]John 8:51

8 [a]John 6:68; 12:49 [b]John 17:14, 26; 15:15 [c]John 8:42; 16:27, 30 [d]John 3:17; 17:18, 21, 23, 25

9 [a]Luke 22:32; John 14:16 [b]John 17:20f.; Luke 23:34 [c]John 17:2, 6, 24; 6:37, 39 [d]John 17:6

10 [a]John 16:15

11 [a]John 13:1 [b]John 17:13; 7:33 [c]John 17:25 [d]Phil. 2:9; Rev. 19:12; John 17:6 [e]John 17:21f.; Rom. 12:5; Gal. 3:28

12 [a]Phil. 2:9; Rev. 19:12; John 17:6 [b]John 6:39; 18:9 [c]John 6:70 [d]Ps. 41:9

13 [a]John 17:11; 7:33 [b]John 15:11 [c]John 3:29

14 [a]John 15:19 [b]John 17:16; 8:23

15 "I do not ask Thee to take them out of the world, but to
keep them [1]from [2a]the evil *one*.
16 "[a]They are not of the world, even as I am not of the
world.
17 "[a]Sanctify them in the truth; Thy word is truth.
18 "As [a]Thou didst send Me into the world, [b]I also have
sent them into the world.
19 "And for their sakes I [a]sanctify Myself, that they themselves also may be [b]sanctified [c]in truth.
20 "I do not ask in behalf of these alone, but for those also
who believe in Me through their word;
21 that they may all be one; [a]even as Thou, Father, *art* in
Me, and I in Thee, that they also may be in Us; [b]that the world
may [1]believe that [c]Thou didst send Me.
22 "And the [a]glory which Thou hast given Me I have given
to them; that they may be one, just as We are one;
23 [a]I in them, and Thou in Me, that they may be perfected [1]in unity, that the world may [2]know that [b]Thou didst
send Me, and didst [c]love them, even as Thou didst love Me.
24 "Father, [1]I desire that [a]they also whom Thou hast given
Me [b]be with Me where I am, in order that they may behold
My [c]glory, which Thou hast given Me; for Thou didst love Me
before [d]the foundation of the world.
25 "O [a]righteous Father, [1]although [b]the world has not
known Thee, [1]yet I have known Thee; and these have known
that [c]Thou didst send Me;
26 and [a]I have made Thy name known to them, and will
make it known; that [b]the love wherewith Thou didst love Me
may be in them, and I in them."

CHAPTER 18

WHEN Jesus had spoken these words, [a]He went forth with
His disciples over [b]the [1]ravine of the Kidron, where there was
[c]a garden, into which He Himself entered, and His disciples.
2 Now Judas also, who was [1]betraying Him, knew the
place; for Jesus had [a]often met there with His disciples.
3 [a]Judas then, having received [b]the [1]*Roman* cohort, and
[c]officers from the chief priests and the Pharisees, *came there
with lanterns and [d]torches and weapons.
4 Jesus therefore, [a]knowing all the things that were coming upon Him, went forth, and *said to them, "[b]Whom do
you seek?"
5 They answered Him, "Jesus the Nazarene." He *said
to them, "I am *He*." And Judas also who was betraying Him,
was standing with them.
6 When therefore He said to them, "I am *He*", they
drew back, and fell to the ground.
7 Again therefore He asked them, "[a]Whom do you
seek?" And they said, "Jesus the Nazarene."
8 Jesus answered, "I told you that I am *He;* if therefore
you seek Me, let these go their way,"
9 that the word might be fulfilled which He spoke, "[a]Of
those whom Thou hast given Me I lost not one."
10 Simon Peter therefore [a]having a sword, drew it, and

15 [1]Or, *out of* the power of [2]Or, *evil* [a]Matt. 5:37

16 [a]John 17:14

17 [a]John 15:3

18 [a]John 17:3, 8, 21, 23, 25; 3:17 [b]John 20:21; Matt. 10:5; John 4:38

19 [a]John 15:13 [b]John 15:3 [c]2 Cor. 7:14; Col. 1:6; 1 John 3:18

21 [1]Gr. tense indicates *continually believe* [a]John 10:38; 17:23; 17:11 [b]John 17:8 [c]John 17:3, 8, 18, 23, 25; 3:17

22 [a]John 17:24; 1:14

23 [1]Lit., *into a unit* [2]Gr. tense indicates *continually know* [a]John 10:38; 17:21; John 17:11 [b]John 17:3, 8, 18, 21, 25; John 3:17 [c]John 16:27

24 [1]Gr., *that which Thou hast given Me, I desire that where I am, they also may be with Me, that* [a]John 17:2 [b]John 12:26 [c]John 17:22; 1:14 [d]Matt. 25:34; John 17:5

25 [1]Lit., *and* [a]John 17:11; 1 John 1:9 [b]John 7:29; 15:21 [c]John 17:3, 8, 18, 21, 23; 3:17

26 [a]John 17:6 [b]John 15:9

1 [1]Gr., *winter-torrent* [a]Matt. 26:30, 36; Mark 14:26, 32; Luke 22:39 [b]2 Sam. 15:23; 1 Kin. 2:37; 15:13; 2 Kin. 23:4, 6, 12; 2 Chr. 15:16; 29:16; 30:14; Jer. 31:40 [c]Matt. 26:36; Mark 14:32; John 18:26

2 [1]Or, *delivering Him up* [a]Luke 21:37; 22:39

3 [1]Normally 600 men; *a battalion* [a]John 18:3-11; *Matt. 26:47-56; Mark 14:43-50; Luke 22:47-53* [b]John 18:12; Acts 10:1 [c]John 7:32; 18:12, 18 [d]Matt. 25:1 and marg.

4 [a]John 6:64; 13:1, 11 [b]John 18:7

7 [a]John 18:4

9 [a]John 17:12

10 [a]Matt. 26:51; Mark 14:47

struck the high priest's slave, and cut off his right ear; and the
slave's name was Malchus.
11 Jesus therefore said to Peter, "Put the sword into the
sheath; [a]the cup which the Father has given Me, shall I not
drink it?"
12 [a]So [b]the *Roman* [1]cohort and the [2]commander, and the
[b]officers of the Jews, arrested Jesus and bound Him,
13 and led Him to [a]Annas first; for he was father-in-law of
[b]Caiaphas, who was high priest that year.
14 Now Caiaphas was the one who had advised the Jews
that [a]it was expedient for one man to die on behalf of the
people.
15 And [a]Simon Peter was following Jesus, and *so was* another disciple. Now that disciple was known to the high priest,
and entered with Jesus into [b]the court of the high priest,
16 [a]but Peter was standing at the door outside. So the
other disciple, who was known to the high priest, went out and
spoke to the doorkeeper, and brought in Peter.
17 [a]The slave-girl therefore who kept the door *said to
Peter, "[b]You are not also *one* of this man's disciples, are you?"
He *said, "I am not."
18 Now the slaves and the [a]officers were standing *there*,
[b]having made [c]a charcoal fire, for it was cold and they were
warming themselves; and Peter also was with them, standing
and warming himself.
19 [a]The high priest therefore questioned Jesus about His
disciples, and about His teaching.
20 Jesus answered him, "I [a]have spoken openly to the
world; I always [b]taught in [1]synagogues, and [c]in the temple,
where all the Jews come together; and I spoke nothing in
secret.
21 "Why do you question Me? Question those who have
heard what I spoke to them; behold, these know what I said."
22 And when He had said this, one of the [a]officers standing by [b]gave Jesus a blow, saying, "Is that the way You answer
the high priest?"
23 [a]Jesus answered him, "If I have spoken wrongly, bear
witness of the wrong; but if rightly, why do you strike Me?"
24 [a]Annas therefore sent Him bound to [a]Caiaphas the
high priest.
25 [a]Now [b]Simon Peter was standing and warming himself.
They said therefore to him, "[c]You are not also *one* of His
disciples, are you?" He denied *it*, and said, "I am not."
26 One of the slaves of the high priest, being a relative of
the one [a]whose ear Peter cut off, *said, "Did I not see you in
[b]the garden with Him?"
27 Peter therefore denied *it* again; and immediately [a]a
cock crowed.
28 [a]They *led Jesus therefore from [b]Caiaphas into [c]the
[1]Praetorium; and it was early; and they themselves did not
enter into [c]the [1]Praetorium in order that [d]they might not be
defiled, but might eat the Passover.
29 [a]Pilate therefore went out to them, and *said, "What
accusation do you bring against this Man?"
30 They answered and said to him, "If this Man were not
an evildoer, we would not have delivered Him up to you."

11 [a]Matt. 20:22

12 [1]Or, *battalion* [2]Lit., *chiliarch*, in command of a thousand troops [a]John 18:12f.: Matt. 26:57ff. [b]John 18:3

13 [a]John 18:24; Luke 3:2 [b]Matt. 26:3; John 11:49, 51

14 [a]John 11:50

15 [a]Matt. 26:58; Mark 14:54; Luke 22:54 [b]Matt. 26:3; John 18:24, 28

16 [a]John 18:16-18: *Matt. 26:69f.; Mark 14:66-68; Luke 22:55-57*

17 [a]Acts 12:13 [b]John 18:25

18 [a]John 18:3 [b]Mark 14:54, 67 [c]John 21:9

19 [a]John 18:19-24: Matt. 26:59-68; Mark 14:55-65; Luke 22:63-71

20 [1]Lit., *synagogue* [a]John 7:26; 8:26 [b]Matt. 4:23; John 6:59 [c]Matt. 26:55

22 [a]John 18:3 [b]John 19:3

23 [a]Matt. 5:39; Acts 23:2-5

24 [a]John 18:13

25 [a]John 18:25-27; *Matt. 26:71-75; Mark 14:69-72; Luke 22:58-62* [b]John 18:18 [c]John 18:17

26 [a]John 18:10 [b]John 18:1

27 [a]John 13:38

28 [1]Or, *governor's official residence* [a]Matt. 27:2; Mark 15:1; Luke 23:1 [b]John 18:13 [c]John 18:33; 19:9; Matt. 27:27 [d]John 11:55; Acts 11:3

29 [a]John 18:29-38; *Matt. 27:11-14; Mark 15:2-5; Luke 23:2, 3*

31 Pilate therefore said to them, "Take Him yourselves,
and judge Him according to your law." The Jews said to him,
"We are not permitted to put any one to death,"
32 that [a]the word of Jesus might be fulfilled, which He
spoke, signifying by what kind of death He was about to die.
33 Pilate therefore [a]entered again into the Praetorium,
and summoned Jesus, and said to Him, "[b]You are the King of
the Jews?"
34 Jesus answered, "Are you saying this [1]on your own initiative, or did others tell you about Me?"
35 Pilate answered, "I am not a Jew, am I? Your own
nation and the chief priests delivered You up to me; what have
You done?"
36 Jesus answered, "[a]My kingdom [1]is not of this world. If
My kingdom were of this world, then My servants would be
fighting, that I might not be delivered up to the Jews; but as it
is, My kingdom is not [2]of this realm."
37 Pilate therefore said to Him, "So You are a king?"
Jesus answered, "[a]You say *correctly* that I am a king. For this I
have been born, and for this I have come into the world, [b]to
bear witness to the truth. [c]Every one who is of the truth hears
My voice."
38 Pilate *said to Him, "What is truth?"
And when he had said this, he [a]went out again to the Jews,
and *said to them, "[b]I find no guilt in Him.
39 "[a]But you have a custom, that I should release someone
[1]for you at the Passover; do you wish then that I release [1]for
you the King of the Jews?"
40 Therefore they cried out again, saying, "[a]Not this Man,
but Barabbas." Now Barabbas was a robber.

Chapter 19

THEN Pilate therefore took Jesus, and [1a]scourged Him.
2 [a]And the soldiers wove a crown of thorns and put it on
His head, and arrayed Him in a purple robe;
3 and they *began* to come up to Him, and say, "[a]Hail,
King of the Jews!" and to [b]give Him blows in the face.
4 And Pilate [a]came out again, and *said to them, "Behold, I am bringing Him out to you, that you may know that [b]I
find no guilt in Him."
5 Jesus therefore came out, [a]wearing the crown of thorns
and the purple robe. And *Pilate* *said to them, "Behold, the
Man!"
6 When therefore the chief priests and the [a]officers saw
Him, they cried out, saying, "Crucify, crucify!" Pilate *said to
them, "Take Him yourselves, and crucify Him, for [b]I find no
guilt in Him."
7 The Jews answered him, "[a]We have a law, and by that
law He ought to die because He [b]made Himself out *to be* the
Son of God."
8 When Pilate therefore heard this statement, he was the
more afraid;
9 and he [a]entered into the [1]Praetorium again, and *said
to Jesus, "Where are You from?" But [b]Jesus gave him no
answer.

32 [a]John 12:32f.; 3:14; 8:28; Matt. 20:19; 26:2; Mark 10:33f.; Luke 18:32f.

33 [a]John 18:28, 29; 19:9 [b]Luke 23:3; John 19:12

34 [1]Lit., *from yourself*

36 [1]Or, *is not derived from* [2]Lit., *from here* [a]John 6:15; Matt. 26:53; Luke 17:21

37 [a]Matt. 27:11; Mark 15:2; Luke 22:70; 23:3 [b]John 3:32; 8:14; 1:14 [c]John 8:47; 1 John 4:6

38 [a]John 19:4; 18:33 [b]Luke 23:4; John 19:4

39 [1]Or, *to you* [a]John 18:39-19:16: *Matt. 27:15-18, 20-23; Mark 15:6-15; Luke 23:18-25*

40 [a]Acts 3:14

1 [1]Or, *had Him scourged* [a]Matt. 27:26

2 [a]Matt. 27:27-30: Mark 15:16-19

3 [a]Matt. 27:29; Mark 15:18 [b]John 18:22

4 [a]John 18:38; 18:33 [b]John 18:38; 19:6; Luke 23:4

5 [a]John 19:2

6 [a]John 18:3; Matt. 26:58 [b]John 18:38; 19:4; Luke 23:4

7 [a]Lev. 24:16; Matt. 26:63-66 [b]John 5:18; 10:33

9 [1]Or, *governor's official residence* [a]John 18:33 [b]Matt. 26:63; 27:12, 14; John 18:34-37

10 Pilate therefore *said to Him, "You do not speak to
me? Do You not know that I have authority to release You,
and I have authority to crucify You?"
11 Jesus answered, "[a]You would have no authority [1]over
Me, unless it had been given you from above; for this reason
[b]he who delivered Me up to you has *the* greater sin."
12 As a result of this Pilate [1]made efforts to release Him,
but the Jews cried out, saying, "[a]If you release this Man, you
are no friend of Caesar; every one who makes himself out *to be*
a king [2]opposes Caesar."
13 When Pilate therefore heard these words, he brought
Jesus out, and [a]sat down on the judgment-seat at a place called
[1]The Pavement, but [b]in [2]Hebrew, Gabbatha.
14 Now it was [a]the day of preparation for the Passover; it
was about the [1b]sixth hour. And he *said to the Jews, "Behold,
[c]your King!"
15 They therefore cried out, "[a]Away with *Him,* away with
Him, crucify Him!" Pilate *said to them, "Shall I crucify your
King?" The chief priests answered, "We have no king but
Caesar."
16 And so he then [a]delivered Him up to them to be
crucified.
17 [a]They took Jesus therefore; and He went out, [1b]bearing
His own cross, to the place called [c]the Place of a Skull, which is
called [d]in [2]Hebrew Golgotha;
18 where they crucified Him, and with Him [a]two other
men, one on either side, and Jesus in between.
19 And Pilate wrote an inscription also, and put it on the
cross. And it was written, "[a]JESUS THE NAZARENE, [b]THE
KING OF THE JEWS."
20 Therefore this inscription many of the Jews read, for
the place where Jesus was crucified was near the city; and it was
written [a]in [1]Hebrew, Latin, *and* in Greek.
21 And so the chief priests of the Jews were saying to
Pilate, "Do not write, '[a]The King of the Jews'; but that He
said, 'I am [a]King of the Jews.'"
22 Pilate answered, "[a]What I have written I have written."
23 [a]The soldiers therefore, when they had crucified Jesus,
took His outer garments and made [b]four parts, a part to every
soldier and *also* the [1]tunic; now the tunic was seamless, woven
[2]in one piece.
24 They said therefore to one another, "[a]Let us not tear it,
but cast [1]lots for it, *to decide* whose it shall be;" [b]that the
Scripture might be fulfilled, "THEY [c]DIVIDED MY OUTER GAR-
MENTS AMONG THEM, AND FOR MY CLOTHING THEY CAST [1]LOTS."
25 Therefore the soldiers did these things. [a]But there were
standing by the cross of Jesus [b]His mother, and His mother's
sister, Mary the *wife* of [c]Clopas, and [d]Mary Magdalene.
26 When Jesus therefore saw His mother, and [a]the disciple whom He loved standing nearby, He *said to His mother, "[b]Woman, behold, your son!"
27 Then He *said to the disciple, "Behold, your mother!"
And from that hour the disciple took her into [a]his own
household.
28 After this, Jesus, [a]knowing that all things had already

11 [1]Lit., *against*
[a]Rom. 13:1 [b]John 18:13f., 28ff.; Acts 3:13

12 [1]Lit., *was seeking to* [2]Or, *speaks against*
[a]Luke 23:2; John 18:33ff.

13 [1]Gr., *The Lithostrotos* [2]I.e., Jewish Aramaic
[a]Matt. 27:19 [b]John 5:2; 19:17, 20

14 [1]I.e., noon
[a]Matt. 27:62; John 19:31, 42 [b]Mark 15:25; Matt. 27:45 [c]John 19:19, 21

15 [a]Luke 23:18

16 [a]Matt. 27:26; Mark 15:15; Luke 23:25

17 [1]Lit., *bearing the cross for Himself* [2]I.e., Jewish Aramaic
[a]John 19:17-24: *Matt. 27:33-44; Mark 15:22-32; Luke 23:33-43* [b]Luke 14:27; Matt. 27:32; Mark 15:21; Luke 23:26 [c]Luke 23:33 and marg. [d]John 19:13

18 [a]Luke 23:32

19 [a]Matt. 27:37; Mark 15:26; Luke 23:38 [b]John 19:14, 21

20 [1]I.e., Jewish Aramaic
[a]John 19:13

21 [a]John 19:14, 19

22 [a]Gen. 43:14; Esther 4:16

23 [1]Gr., *khiton*, the garment worn next to the skin [2]Lit., *woven from the upper part through the whole*
[a]Matt. 27:35; Mark 15:24; Luke 23:34 [b]Acts 12:4

24 [1]Lit., *a lot*
[a]Matt. 27:35; Mark 15:24; Luke 23:34; Ex. 28:32 [b]John 19:28, 36f. [c]Ps. 22:18

25 [a]Matt. 27:55f.; Mark 15:40f.; Luke 23:49 [b]Matt. 12:46 [c]Luke 24:18 [d]John 20:1, 18; Luke 8:2

26 [a]John 13:23 [b]John 2:4

27 [a]Luke 18:28 marg.; John 1:11; 16:32; Acts 21:6 [Gr.]

28 [a]John 13:1; 17:4

been accomplished, [b]in order that the Scripture might be fulfilled, *said, "[c]I am thirsty."
29 A jar full of sour wine was standing there; so [a]they put a
sponge full of the sour wine upon *a branch of* hyssop, and
brought it up to His mouth.
30 When Jesus therefore had received the sour wine, He
said, "[a]It is finished!" And He bowed His head, and [b]gave up
His spirit.
31 The Jews therefore, because it was [a]the day of preparation, so that [b]the bodies should not remain on the cross on the
Sabbath ([1]for that Sabbath was a [c]high *day*), asked Pilate that
their legs might be broken, and *that* they might be taken away.
32 The soldiers therefore came, and broke the legs of the
first man, and of the other man who was [a]crucified with Him;
33 but coming to Jesus, when they saw that He was already dead, they did not break His legs;
34 but one of the soldiers pierced His side with a spear,
and immediately there came out [a]blood and water.
35 And he who has seen has [a]borne witness, and his witness
is true; and he knows that he is telling the truth, so that you
also may believe.
36 For these things came to pass, [a]that the Scripture might
be fulfilled, "[b]NOT A BONE OF HIM SHALL BE [1]BROKEN."
37 And again another Scripture says, "[a]THEY SHALL LOOK
ON HIM WHOM THEY PIERCED."
38 [a]And after these things Joseph of Arimathea, being a
disciple of Jesus, but a [b]secret *one*, for [c]fear of the Jews, asked
Pilate that he might take away the body of Jesus; and Pilate
granted permission. He came therefore, and took away His
body.
39 And [a]Nicodemus came also, who had first come to
Him by night; [b]bringing a [1]mixture of [c]myrrh and aloes, about
a [d]hundred [2]pounds *weight*.
40 And so they took the body of Jesus, and [a]bound it in
[b]linen wrappings with the spices, as is the burial custom of the
Jews.
41 Now in the place where He was crucified there was a
garden; and in the garden a [a]new tomb, [b]in which no one had
yet been laid.
42 Therefore on account of the Jewish day of [a]preparation,
because the tomb was [b]nearby, they laid Jesus there.

CHAPTER 20

[a]NOW on the first *day* of the week [b]Mary Magdalene *came
early to the tomb, while it *was still dark, and *saw [c]the stone
already taken away from the tomb.
2 And so she *ran and *came to Simon Peter, and to the
other [a]disciple whom Jesus [1]loved, and *said to them, "[b]They
have taken away the Lord out of the tomb, and we do not
know where they have laid Him."
3 [a]Peter therefore went forth, and the other disciple, and
they were going to the tomb.
4 And the two were running together; and the other disciple ran ahead faster than Peter, and came to the tomb first;

28 [b]John 19:24, 36f. [c]Ps. 69:21

29 [a]John 19:29, 30; Matt. 27:48, 50; Mark 15:36f.; Luke 23:36

30 [a]John 17:4 [b]Matt. 27:50; Mark 15:37; Luke 23:46

31 [1]Lit., *for the day of that Sabbath was great* [a]John 19:14, 42 [b]Deut. 21:23; Josh. 8:29; 10:26f. [c]Ex. 12:16

32 [a]John 19:18

34 [a]1 John 5:6, 8

35 [a]John 15:27; 21:24

36 [1]Or, *crushed* or *shattered* [a]John 19:24, 28 [b]Ex. 12:46; Num. 9:12; Ps. 34:20

37 [a]Zech. 12:10

38 [a]John 19:38-42: *Matt. 27:57-61; Mark 15:42-47; Luke 23:50-56* [b]Mark 15:43 [c]John 7:13

39 [1]Another reading, *package of* [2]Lit., 100 litras (12 oz. each) [a]John 3:1 [b]Mark 16:1 [c]Ps. 45:8; Prov. 7:17; Song 4:14; Matt. 2:11 [d]John 12:3

40 [a]John 11:44; Matt. 26:12; Mark 14:8 [b]John 20:5, 7; Luke 24:12

41 [a]Matt. 27:60 [b]Luke 23:53

42 [a]John 19:14, 31 [b]John 19:20, 41

1 [a]John 20:1-8: Matt. 28:1-8; Mark 16:1-8; Luke 24:1-10 [b]John 19:25; John 20:18 [c]Matt. 27:60, 66; 28:2; Mark 15:46; 16:3f.; Luke 24:2; John 11:38

2 [1]Lit., *was loving* [a]John 13:23 [b]John 20:13

3 [a]John 20:3-10; Luke 24:12

5 and [a]stooping and looking in, he *saw the [b]linen wrappings lying *there;* but he did not go in.
6 Simon Peter therefore also *came, following him, and
entered the tomb; and he *beheld the linen wrappings lying
there,
7 and [a]the face-cloth, which had been on His head, not
lying with the [b]linen wrappings, but rolled up in a place by
itself.
8 Then entered in therefore the other disciple also, who
[a]had first come to the tomb, and he saw, and believed.
9 For as yet [a]they did not understand the Scripture, [b]that
He must rise again from the dead.
10 So the disciples went away again [a]to their own homes.
11 [a]But Mary was standing outside the tomb weeping; and
so, as she wept, she [b]stooped and looked into the tomb;
12 and she *beheld [a]two angels in white sitting, one at the
head, and one at the feet, where the body of Jesus had been
lying.
13 And they *said to her, "[a]Woman, why are you weeping?" She *said to them, "Because [b]they have taken away my
Lord, and I do not know where they have laid Him."
14 When she had said this, she turned around, and *[a]be-
held Jesus standing *there,* and [b]did not know that it was Jesus.
15 Jesus *said to her, "[a]Woman, why are you weeping?
Whom are you seeking?" Supposing Him to be the gardener,
she *said to Him, "Sir, if you have carried Him away, tell me
where you have laid Him, and I will take Him away."
16 Jesus *said to her, "Mary!" She *turned and *said to
Him [a]in [1]Hebrew, "[b]Rabboni," (which means, Teacher).
17 Jesus *said to her, "Stop clinging to Me; for I have not
yet ascended to the Father; but go to [a]My brethren, and say to
them, 'I [b]ascend to My Father and your Father, and My God
and your God.' "
18 [a]Mary Magdalene *came, [b]announcing to the disciples,
"I have seen the Lord;" and *that* He had said these things to
her.
19 When therefore it was evening, on that day, the first
day of the week, and when the doors were shut where the
disciples were, for [a]fear of the Jews, Jesus came and stood in
their midst, and *said to them, "[1b]Peace *be* with you."
20 And when He had said this, [a]He showed them both His
hands and His side. The disciples therefore [b]rejoiced when
they saw the Lord.
21 Jesus therefore said to them again, "[1a]Peace *be* with
you; [b]as the Father has sent Me, I also send you."
22 And when He had said this, He breathed on them, and
*said to them, "Receive the Holy Spirit.
23 "[a]If you forgive the sins of any, *their sins* [1]have been
forgiven them; if you retain the *sins* of any, they have been
retained."
24 But [a]Thomas, one of [b]the twelve, called [1a]Didymus,
was not with them when Jesus came.
25 The other disciples therefore were saying to him, "We
have seen the Lord!" But he said to them, "Unless I shall see in
[a]His hands the imprint of the nails, and put my finger into the

5 [a]John 20:11 [b]John 19:40
7 [a]John 11:44 [b]John 19:40
8 [a]John 20:4
9 [a]Matt. 22:29; John 2:22 [b]Luke 24:26ff., 46
10 [a]Luke 24:12
11 [a]Mark 16:5 [b]John 20:5
12 [a]Luke 24:4; Matt. 28:2f.; Mark 16:5
13 [a]John 20:15 [b]John 20:2
14 [a]Mark 16:9; Matt. 28:9 [b]John 21:4
15 [a]John 20:13
16 [1]I.e., Jewish Aramaic [a]John 5:2 [b]Mark 10:51; Matt. 23:7
17 [a]Matt. 28:10 [b]John 7:33; Mark 16:19; 12:26
18 [a]John 20:1 [b]Mark 16:10; Luke 24:10, 23
19 [1]Lit., *Peace to you* [a]John 7:13 [b]John 20:21, 26; Luke 24:36; John 14:27
20 [a]Luke 24:39, 40; John 19:34 [b]John 16:20, 22
21 [1]Here as in verse 19 and 26 [a]John 20:19, 26; Luke 24:36; John 14:27 [b]John 17:18
23 [1]I.e., have previously been forgiven [a]Matt. 18:18; Matt. 16:19
24 [1]I.e., the Twin [a]John 11:16 [b]John 6:67
25 [a]John 20:20

place of the nails, and put my hand into His side, [b]I will not
believe."
26 And [1]after eight days again His disciples were inside,
and Thomas with them. Jesus *came, the doors having been
[2]shut, and stood in their midst, and said, "[a]Peace *be* with you."
27 Then He *said to Thomas, "[a]Reach here your finger,
and see My hands; and reach here your hand, and put it into
My side; and be not unbelieving, but believing."
28 Thomas answered and said to Him, "My Lord and my
God!"
29 Jesus *said to him, "Because you have seen Me, have
you believed? [a]Blessed *are* they who did not see, and *yet*
believed."
30 [a]Many other [1b]signs therefore Jesus also performed in
the presence of the disciples, which are not written in this
book;
31 but these have been written [a]that you may believe that
Jesus is [1]the Christ, [b]the Son of God; and that [c]believing you
may have life in His name.

CHAPTER 21

AFTER these things Jesus [1a]manifested Himself [b]again to
the disciples at the [c]sea of Tiberias; and He manifested *Himself* in this way.
2 There were together Simon Peter, and [a]Thomas called
[1]Didymus, and [b]Nathanael of [c]Cana in Galilee, and [d]the *sons*
of Zebedee, and two others of His disciples.
3 Simon Peter *said to them, "I am going fishing." They
*said to him, "We will also come with you." They went out,
and got into the boat; and [a]that night they caught nothing.
4 But when the day was now breaking, Jesus stood on the
beach; yet the disciples did not [a]know that it was Jesus.
5 Jesus therefore *said to them, "Children, [a]you do not
have any [1]fish, do you?" They answered Him, "No."
6 And He said to them, "[a]Cast the net on the right-hand
side of the boat, and you will find *a catch.*" They cast therefore, and then they were not able to haul it in because of the
great number of fish.
7 [a]That disciple therefore whom Jesus [1]loved *said to
Peter, "It is the Lord." And so when Simon Peter heard that it
was the Lord, he put his outer garment on (for he was stripped
for work), and threw himself into the sea.
8 But the other disciples came in the little boat, for they
were not far from the land, but about [1]one hundred yards
away, dragging the net *full* of fish.
9 And so when they got out upon the land, they *saw a
charcoal [a]fire *already* laid, and [b]fish placed on it, and bread.
10 Jesus *said to them, "Bring some of the [a]fish which you
have now caught."
11 Simon Peter went up, and drew the net to land, full of
large fish, a hundred and fifty-three; and although there were
so many, the net was not torn.
12 Jesus *said to them, "Come *and* have [a]breakfast."
None of the disciples ventured to question Him, "Who are
You?" knowing that it was the Lord.

25 [b]Mark 16:11

26 [1]Or, *a week later* [2]Or, *locked*
[a]John 20:19, 21; Luke 24:36; John 14:27

27 [a]John 20:25; Luke 24:40

29 [a]1 Pet. 1:8

30 [1]Or, *attesting miracles*
[a]John 21:25 [b]John 2:11

31 [1]I.e., The Messiah
[a]John 19:35 [b]Matt. 4:3 [c]John 3:15

1 [1]Or, *made Himself visible*
[a]John 21:14; Mark 16:12
[b]John 20:19, 26 [c]John 6:1

2 [1]I.e., the Twin
[a]John 11:16 [b]John 1:45ff.
[c]John 2:1 [d]Matt. 4:21; Mark 1:19; Luke 5:10

3 [a]Luke 5:5

4 [a]John 20:14; Luke 24:16

5 [1]Lit., *something eaten with bread*
[a]Luke 24:41

6 [a]Luke 5:4ff.

7 [1]Lit., *was loving*
[a]John 13:23; John 21:20

8 [1]Lit., *200 cubits*

9 [a]John 18:18 [b]John 21, 10, 13; John 6:9, 11

10 [a]John 21:10, 13; John 6:9, 11

12 [a]John 21:15

13 Jesus *came and *took [a]the bread, and *gave them, and
the [b]fish likewise.
14 This is now the [a]third time that Jesus [1]was manifested
to the disciples, after He was raised from the dead.
15 So when they had [a]finished breakfast, Jesus *said to
Simon Peter, "Simon, [1]*son* of John, do you [2b]love Me more
than these?" He *said to Him, "Yes, Lord; You know that I
[3]love You." He *said to him, "Tend [c]My lambs."
16 He *said to him again a second time, "Simon, *son* of
John, do you [1]love Me?" He *said to Him, "Yes, Lord; You
know that I [2]love You." He *said to him, "[a]Shepherd My
sheep."
17 He *said to him the third time, "Simon, *son* of John,
do you [1]love Me?" Peter was grieved because He said to him
[a]the third time, "Do you [1]love Me?" And he said to Him,
"Lord, [b]You know all things; You know that I [1]love You."
Jesus *said to him, "[c]Tend My sheep.
18 "Truly, truly, I say to you, when you were younger, you
used to gird yourself, and walk wherever you wished; but when
you grow old, you will stretch out your hands, and someone
else will gird you, and bring you where you do not wish to *go*."
19 Now this He said, [a]signifying by [b]what kind of death he
would glorify God. And when He had spoken this, He *said to
him, "[c]Follow Me!"
20 Peter, turning around, *saw the [a]disciple whom Jesus
loved following *them;* the one who also had [b]leaned back on
His breast at the supper, and said, "Lord, who is the one who
betrays You?"
21 Peter therefore seeing him *said to Jesus, "Lord, and
what about this man?"
22 Jesus *said to him, "If I want him to remain [a]until I
come, what *is that* to you? You [b]follow Me!"
23 This saying therefore went out among [a]the brethren
that that disciple would not die; yet Jesus did not say to him
that he would not die; but *only*, "If I want him to remain
[b]until I come, what *is that* to you?"
24 This is the disciple who [a]bears witness of these things,
and wrote these things; and we know that his witness is true.
25 And there are also [a]many other things which Jesus did,
which if they *were written in detail, I suppose that even the
world itself *would not contain the books which *were written.

13 [a]John 21:9 [b]John 21:9, 10; 6:9, 11

14 [1]Or, *made Himself visible*
[a]John 20:19, 26

15 [1]Here and in verses 16 and 17 some mss. read, *son of Jonas* [2]Gr., agapao [3]Gr., phileo
[a]John 21:12 [b]John 13:37; Matt. 26:33; Mark 14:29
[c]Luke 12:32

16 [1]Gr., agapao [2]Gr., phileo
[a]Matt. 2:6; Acts 20:28; 1 Pet. 5:2; Rev. 7:17

17 [1]Gr., phileo
[a]John 13:38 [b]John 16:30
[c]John 21:16

19 [a]John 12:33; 18:32
[b]2 Pet. 1:14 [c]Matt. 8:22; 16:24; John 21:22

20 [a]John 21:7 [b]John 13:25

22 [a]1 Cor. 4:5; 11:26; James 5:7; Rev. 2:25; Matt. 16:27f.
[b]Matt. 8:22; 16:24; John 21:19

23 [a]Acts 1:15 [b]1 Cor. 4:5; 11:26; James 5:7; Rev. 2:25; Matt. 16:27f.

24 [a]John 15:27

25 [a]John 20:30

THE ACTS OF THE APOSTLES

The Introduction. The Ascension. The Upper Room.

THE first account I [1]composed, [a]Theophilus, about all that
Jesus [b]began to do and teach,
2 until the day when He [a]was taken up, after He [b]had [1]by
the Holy Spirit given orders to [c]the apostles whom He had
[d]chosen.
3 To [1]these [a]He also presented Himself alive, after His
suffering, by many convincing proofs, appearing to them over
a period of forty days, and speaking of [b]the things concerning
the kingdom of God.
4 And [1]gathering them together, He commanded them
[a]not to leave Jerusalem, but to wait for [2b]what the Father had
promised, "Which," *He said,* "you heard of from Me;
5 for [a]John baptized with water, but you shall be baptized [1]with the Holy Spirit [2b]not many days from now."
6 And so when they had come together, they were asking
Him, saying, "Lord, [a]is it at this time You are restoring the
kingdom to Israel?"
7 He said to them, "It is not for you to know times or
epochs which [a]the Father has fixed by His own authority;
8 but you shall receive power [a]when the Holy Spirit has
come upon you; and you shall be [b]My witnesses both in Jerusalem, and in all Judea and [c]Samaria, and even to [d]the remotest
part of the earth."
9 And after He had said these things, [a]He was lifted up
while they were looking on, and a cloud received Him out of
their sight.
10 And as they were gazing intently into [1]the sky while He
was departing, [2]behold, [a]two men in white clothing stood beside them;
11 and they also said, "[a]Men of Galilee, why do you stand
looking into [1]the sky? This Jesus, who [b]has been taken up from
you into heaven, will [c]come in just the same way as you have
watched Him go into heaven."
12 Then they [a]returned to Jerusalem from the [1b]mount
called [2]Olivet, which is near Jerusalem, a Sabbath day's journey away.
13 And when they had entered, they went up to [a]the upper
room, where they were staying; [b]that is, Peter and John and
[1]James and Andrew, Philip and Thomas, Bartholomew and
Matthew, [1]James *the son* of Alphaeus, and Simon the Zealot,
and [c]Judas *the* [2]*son* of [1]James.
14 These all with one mind [a]were continually devoting
themselves to prayer, along with [1b]*the* women, and Mary the
[c]mother of Jesus, and with His [c]brothers.
15 And [1]at this time Peter stood up in the midst of [a]the
brethren (a gathering of about one hundred and twenty [2]per-
sons was there together), and said,
16 "Brethren, [a]the Scripture had to be fulfilled, which the

1 [1]Lit., *made*
[a]Luke 1:3 [b]Luke 3:23

2 [1]Or, *through*
[a]Mark 16:19; Acts 1:9, 11, 22 [b]Matt. 28:19f.; Mark 16:15; John 20:21f.; Acts 10:42 [c]Mark 6:30 [and so elsewhere] [d]John 13:18; Acts 10:41

3 [1]Lit., *whom*
[a]Matt. 28:17; Mark 16:12, 14; Luke 24:34, 36; John 20:19, 26; 21:1, 14; 1 Cor. 15:5-7 [b]Acts 8:12; 19:8; 28:23, 31

4 [1]Or, *eating with;* or possibly, *lodging with* [2]Lit., *the promise of the Father*
[a]Luke 24:49 [b]Acts 2:33; John 14:16, 26; 15:26

5 [1]Or, *in* [2]Lit., *after these many days*
[a]Acts 11:16; Matt. 3:11 [b]Acts 2:1-4

6 [a]Matt. 17:11; Mark 9:12; Luke 17:20; 19:11

7 [a]Matt. 24:36; Mark 13:32

8 [a]Acts 2:1-4 [b]Luke 24:48; John 15:27 [c]Acts 8:1, 5, 14 [d]Matt. 28:19; Mark 16:15; Col. 1:23; Rom. 10:18

9 [a]Acts 1:2

10 [1]Or, *heaven* [2]Lit., *and behold*
[a]Luke 24:4; John 20:12

11 [1]Or, *heaven*
[a]Acts 2:7; 13:31 [b]Mark 16:19; Acts 1:9, 22 [c]Matt. 16:27f., Acts 3:21

12 [1]Or, *hill* [2]Or, *Olive Grove*
[a]Luke 24:50, 52 [b]Matt. 21:1

13 [1]Or, *Jacob* [2]Or possibly, *brother*
[a]Acts 9:37, 39; 20:8; Mark 14:15; Luke 22:12 [b]Acts 1:13: *Matt. 1:2-4; Mark 3:16-19; Luke 6:14-16* [c]John 14:22

14 [1]Or, *certain women*
[a]Acts 2:42; 6:4; Rom. 12:12; Col. 4:2; Eph. 6:18 [b]Luke 8:2f. [c]Matt. 12:46

15 [1]Lit., *in these days* [2]Lit., *names*
[a]John 21:23; Acts 6:3; 9:30; 10:23; 11:1, 12, 29; 12:17; 14:2; 15:1, 3, 22, 23, 32f., 40; 16:2, 40; 17:6, 10, 14; 18:18, 27; 21:7, 17; 22:5; 28:14f.; Rom. 1:13; Acts 11:26

16 [a]Acts 1:20; John 13:18; 17:12

Holy Spirit foretold by the mouth of David concerning Judas,
[b]who became a guide to those who arrested Jesus.
17 "For he was [a]counted among us, and received his portion in [b]this ministry."
18 (Now this man [a]acquired a field with [b]the price of his
wickedness; and falling headlong, he burst open in the middle
and all his bowels gushed out.
19 And it became known to all who were living in Jerusalem; so that in [a]their own language that field was called [1]Hak-
eldama, that is, Field of Blood).
20 "For it is written in the book of Psalms,

'[a]LET HIS HOMESTEAD BE MADE DESOLATE,
AND LET NO MAN DWELL IN IT;'

and,

'[b]HIS [1]OFFICE LET ANOTHER MAN TAKE.'

21 "It is therefore necessary that of the men who have
accompanied us all the time that [a]the Lord Jesus went in and
out [1]among us—
22 [a]beginning [1]with the baptism of John, until the day that
He [b]was taken up from us—one of these should become a
[c]witness with us of His resurrection."
23 And they put forward two men, Joseph called Barsab-
bas (who was also called Justus), and [a]Matthias.
24 And they [a]prayed, and said, "Thou, Lord, [b]who knowest the hearts of all men, show which one of these two Thou
hast chosen
25 to [1]occupy [a]this ministry and [b]apostleship from which
Judas turned aside to go to his own place."
26 And they [1a]drew lots for them, and the lot fell [2]to
[b]Matthias; and he was [3]numbered with [c]the eleven apostles.

CHAPTER 2

AND when [a]the day of Pentecost [1]had come, they were all
together in one place.
2 And suddenly there came from heaven a noise like a
violent, rushing wind, and it filled [a]the whole house where they
were sitting.
3 And there appeared to them tongues as of fire [1]distrib-
uting themselves, and [2]they [3]rested on each one of them.
4 And they were all [a]filled with the Holy Spirit and began
to [b]speak with other tongues, as the Spirit was giving them
[1]utterance.
5 Now there were Jews living in Jerusalem, [a]devout men,
from every nation under heaven.
6 And when [a]this sound occurred, the multitude came
together, and were bewildered, because they were each one
hearing them speak in his own [1]language.
7 And [a]they were amazed and marveled, saying, "[1]Why,
are not all these who are speaking [b]Galileans?
8 "And how is it that we each hear *them* in our own [1]lan-
guage [2]to which we were born?
9 "Parthians and Medes and Elamites, and residents of
Mesopotamia, Judea and [a]Cappadocia, [b]Pontus and [1c]Asia,
10 [a]Phrygia and [b]Pamphylia, Egypt and the districts of
Libya around [c]Cyrene, and [1d]visitors from Rome, both Jews
and [2e]proselytes,

16 [b]Matt. 26:47; Mark 14:43; Luke 22:47; John 18:3

17 [a]John 6:70f. [b]Acts 1:25; 20:24; 21:19

18 [a]Matt. 27:3-10 [b]Matt. 26:14f.

19 [1]Some early mss. read, *Hakeldamach* [a]Acts 21:40; Matt. 27:8

20 [1]Lit., *position as overseer* [a]Ps. 69:25 [b]Ps. 109:8

21 [1]Lit., *to us* [a]Luke 24:3

22 [1]Lit., *from* [a]Mark 1:1-4 [b]Acts 1:2 [c]Acts 1:8; 2:32

23 [a]Acts 1:26

24 [a]Acts 6:6; 13:3; 14:23 [b]Acts 15:8; Rom. 8:27; 1 Sam. 16:7; Jer. 17:10

25 [1]Lit., *take the place of* [a]Acts 1:17 [b]Rom. 1:5; 1 Cor. 9:2; Gal. 2:8

26 [1]Lit., *gave* [2]Or, *upon* [3]Lit., *chosen* [a]Lev. 16:8; Josh. 14:2; 1 Sam. 14:41f.; Neh. 10:34; 11:1; Prov. 16:33 [b]Acts 1:23 [c]Acts 2:14

1 [1]Lit., *was being fulfilled* [a]Acts 20:16; 1 Cor. 16:8; Lev. 23:15f.

2 [a]Acts 4:31

3 [1]Or, *being distributed* [2]Lit., *it* [3]Or, *sat*

4 [1]Or, *ability to speak out* [a]Acts 4:8, 31; 9:17; 13:9, 52; 1:5, 8; 6:3, 5; 7:55; 8:17; 11:15; Matt. 10:20 [b]Mark 16:17; 1 Cor. 12:10f.; 14:21

5 [a]Acts 8:2; Luke 2:25

6 [1]Or, *dialect* [a]Acts 2:2

7 [1]Lit., *behold* [a]Acts 2:12 [b]Acts 1:11; Matt. 26:73

8 [1]Or, *dialect* [2]Lit., *in*

9 [1]I.e., west coast province of Asia Minor [a]1 Pet. 1:1 [b]1 Pet. 1:1; Acts 18:2 [c]Acts 6:9; 16:6; 19:10, 20:4; 21:27; 24:18; 27:2; Rom. 16:5; 1 Cor. 16:19; 2 Cor. 1:8; 2 Tim. 1:15; Rev. 1:4

10 [1]Lit., *the sojourning Romans* [2]I.e., Gentile converts to Judaism [a]Acts 16:6; 18:23 [b]Acts 13:13; 14:24; 15:38; 27:5 [c]Matt. 27:32 [d]Acts 17:21 [e]Matt. 23:15

11 Cretans and Arabs—we hear them in our *own* tongues
speaking of the mighty deeds of God."
12 And [a]they continued in amazement and great perplexity, saying to one another, "What does this mean?"
13 But others were mocking and saying, "[a]They are full of
[1]sweet wine."
14 But Peter, [1]taking his stand with [a]the eleven, raised his
voice and declared to them: "Men of Judea, and all you who
live in Jerusalem, let this be known to you, and give heed to my
words.
15 "For these men are not drunk, as you suppose, [a]for it is
only the [1]third hour of the day;
16 but this is what was spoken of through the prophet
Joel:
17 '[a]AND IT SHALL BE IN THE LAST DAYS, GOD SAYS,
THAT I WILL POUR FORTH OF MY SPIRIT UPON ALL
[1]MANKIND;
AND YOUR SONS AND YOUR DAUGHTERS SHALL PROPHESY,
AND YOUR YOUNG MEN SHALL SEE VISIONS,
AND YOUR OLD MEN SHALL DREAM DREAMS;
18 EVEN UPON MY BONDSLAVES, BOTH MEN AND WOMEN,
I WILL IN THOSE DAYS POUR FORTH OF MY SPIRIT
And they shall prophesy.
19 'AND I WILL GRANT WONDERS IN THE SKY ABOVE,
AND SIGNS ON THE EARTH BENEATH,
BLOOD, AND FIRE, AND VAPOR OF SMOKE.
20 'THE SUN SHALL BE TURNED INTO DARKNESS,
AND THE MOON INTO BLOOD,
BEFORE THE GREAT AND GLORIOUS DAY OF THE LORD
SHALL COME.
21 'AND IT SHALL BE, THAT [a]EVERY ONE WHO CALLS ON THE
NAME OF THE LORD SHALL BE SAVED.'
22 "Men of Israel, listen to these words: [a]Jesus the Nazarene, [b]a man [1]attested to you by God with [2]miracles and [c]won-
ders and [3]signs which God performed through Him in your
midst, just as you yourselves know—
23 this *Man*, delivered up by the [a]predetermined plan and
foreknowledge of God, [b]you nailed to a cross by the hands of
[1]godless men and put *Him* to death.
24 "[1]And [a]God raised Him up again, putting an end to the
[2]agony of death, since it [b]was impossible for Him to be held in
its power.
25 "For David says of Him,
'[a]I WAS ALWAYS BEHOLDING THE LORD IN MY PRESENCE;
FOR HE IS AT MY RIGHT HAND, THAT I MAY NOT BE
SHAKEN.
26 'THEREFORE MY HEART WAS GLAD AND MY TONGUE
EXULTED;
MOREOVER MY FLESH ALSO WILL ABIDE IN HOPE;
27 BECAUSE THOU WILT NOT ABANDON MY SOUL TO
[a]HADES,
[b]NOR [1]ALLOW THY [2]HOLY ONE TO [3]UNDERGO DECAY.
28 'THOU HAST MADE KNOWN TO ME THE WAYS OF LIFE;
THOU WILT MAKE ME FULL OF GLADNESS WITH THY
PRESENCE.'

12 [a]Acts 2:7

13 [1]Or, *new wine* [a]1 Cor. 14:23

14 [1]Or, *being put forward* as spokesman [a]Acts 1:26

15 [1]I.e., 9 a.m. [a]1 Thess. 5:7

17 [1]Lit., *flesh* [a]Joel 2:28-32

21 [a]Rom. 10:13

22 [1]Or, *exhibited;* or *accredited* [2]Or, *works of power* [3]Or, *attesting miracles* [a]Acts 10:38; 3:6; 4:10 [b]John 3:2 [c]Acts 2:19, 43; John 4:48

23 [1]Or, *men without the Law*, i.e., heathen [a]Acts 3:18; 4:28; Luke 22:22; 1 Pet. 1:20 [b]Acts 3:13; Luke 24:20

24 [1]Lit., *Whom God raised up* [2]Lit., *birth pangs* [a]Acts 2:32; 3:15, 26; 4:10; 5:30; 10:40; 13:30, 33, 34, 37; 17:31; Rom. 4:24; 6:4; 8:11; 10:9; 1 Cor. 6:14; 15:15; 2 Cor. 4:14; Gal. 1:1; Eph. 1:20; Col. 2:12; 1 Thess. 1:10; Heb. 13:20; 1 Pet. 1:21 [b]John 20:9

25 [a]Ps. 16:8-11

27 [1]Lit., *give* [2]Or, *devout* or *pious* [3]Lit., *see corruption* [a]Matt. 11:23; Acts 2:31 [b]Acts 13:35

29 "[1]Brethren, I may confidently say to you regarding the [a]patriarch David that he both [b]died and [c]was buried, and [d]his tomb is [2]with us to this day.

30 "And so, because he was [a]a prophet, and knew that [b]God had sworn to him with an oath to seat [1]*one* of his descendants upon his throne,

31 he looked ahead and spoke of the resurrection of [1]the Christ, that He was neither abandoned to [a]Hades, nor did His flesh [2]suffer decay.

32 "This Jesus [a]God raised up again, to which we are all [b]witnesses.

33 "Therefore having been exalted [1a]to the right hand of God, and [b]having received from the Father [c]the promise of the Holy Spirit, He has [d]poured forth this which you both see and hear.

34 "For it was not David who ascended into [1]heaven, but he himself says:

'[a]The Lord said to my Lord,
"Sit at My right hand,
35 Until I make Thine enemies a footstool for Thy feet." '

36 "Therefore let all the [a]house of Israel know for certain that God has made Him both [b]Lord and [1]Christ—this Jesus [c]whom you crucified."

37 Now when they heard *this*, they were [1]pierced to the heart, and said to Peter and the rest of the apostles, "[2]Brethren, [a]what shall we do?"

38 And Peter *said* to them, "[a]Repent, and let each of you be [b]baptized in the name of Jesus Christ for the forgiveness of your sins; and you shall receive the gift of the Holy Spirit.

39 "For [a]the promise is for you and your children, and for all who are [b]far off, as many as the Lord our God shall call to Himself."

40 And with many other words he solemnly [a]testified and kept on exhorting them, saying, "[1]Be saved from this [b]perverse generation!"

41 So then, those who had received his word were baptized; and there were added that day about three thousand [1a]souls.

42 And they were [a]continually devoting themselves to the apostles' teaching and to fellowship, to [b]the breaking of bread and [1a]to prayer.

43 And [1]everyone kept feeling a sense of awe; and many [a]wonders and [2]signs were taking place through the apostles[3].

44 And all those who had believed [1]were together, and [a]had all things in common;

45 and they [a]*began* selling their property and possessions, and were sharing them with all, as anyone might have need.

46 [a]And day by day continuing with one mind in the temple, and [b]breaking bread [1]from house to house, they were taking their [2]meals together with gladness and [3]sincerity of heart,

47 praising God, and [a]having favor with all the people. And the Lord [b]was adding [1]to their number day by day [c]those who were being saved.

29 [1]Lit., *men brothers* [2]Lit., *among* [a]Acts 7:8f.; Heb. 7:4 [b]Acts 13:36 [c]1 Kin. 2:10 [d]Neh. 3:16

30 [1]Lit., *of the fruit of his loins* [a]Matt. 22:43 [b]2 Sam. 7:12f.; Ps. 89:3f.; 132:11

31 [1]I.e., the Messiah [2]Lit., *see corruption* [a]Matt. 11:23; Acts 2:27

32 [a]Acts 2:24; 3:15, 26; 4:10; 5:30; 10:40; 13:30, 33, 34, 37; 17:31; Rom. 4:24; 6:4; 8:11; 10:9; 1 Cor. 6:14; 15:15; 2 Cor. 4:14; Gal. 1:1; Eph. 1:20; Col. 2:12; 1 Thess. 1:10; Heb. 13:20; 1 Pet. 1:21 [b]Acts 1:8

33 [1]Or, *by* [a]Acts 5:31; Mark 16:19 [b]Acts 1:4 [c]Gal. 3:14; John 7:39 [d]Acts 2:17; 10:45

34 [1]Lit., *the heavens* [a]Ps. 110:1; Matt. 22:44f.

36 [1]I.e., Messiah [a]Ezek. 36:22, 32, 37; 45:6 [b]Luke 2:11 [c]Acts 2:23

37 [1]Or, *smitten in conscience* [2]Lit., *men brothers* [a]Luke 3:10, 12, 14

38 [a]Acts 3:19; 5:31; 20:21; Luke 24:47; Mark 1:15 [b]Acts 8:12, 16; 22:16; Mark 16:16

39 [a]Rom. 9:4; Is. 44:3; 54:13; 57:19; Joel 2:32; Eph. 2:12 [b]Eph. 2:13, 17

40 [1]Or, *Escape* [a]Luke 16:28 [b]Deut. 32:5; Phil. 2:15; Matt. 17:17

41 [1]I.e., persons [a]Acts 3:23; 7:14; 27:37; Rom. 13:1; 1 Pet. 3:20; Rev. 16:3

42 [1]Lit., *the prayers* [a]Acts 1:14 [b]Luke 24:30; Acts 20:7; 1 Cor. 10:16; Acts 2:46

43 [1]Lit., *fear was occurring to every soul* [2]Or, *attesting miracles* [3]Some ancient mss. add, *in Jerusalem; and great fear was upon all* [a]Acts 2:22

44 [1]Some ancient mss. omit, *were* [a]Acts 4:32; Acts 4:37; 5:2

45 [a]Matt. 19:21; Acts 4:34

46 [1]Or, *in the various private homes* [2]Lit., *food* [3]Or, simplicity [a]Acts 5:42 [b]Luke 24:30; Acts 20:7; 1 Cor. 10:16; Acts 2:42

47 [1]Lit., *together* [a]Acts 5:13 [b]Acts 2:41; 5:14; 6:1, 7; 11:24; Acts 4:4; 9:31, 35, 42; 11:21; 14:1, 21; 16:5; 17:12 [c]1 Cor. 1:18

CHAPTER 3

NOW [a]Peter and John were going up to the temple at the
[1]ninth *hour*, [b]the hour of prayer.
2 And [a]a certain man who had been lame from his mother's womb was being carried along, whom they [b]used to set
down every day at the gate of the temple which is called Beautiful, [c]in order to beg [1]alms of those who were entering the
temple.
3 And when he saw [a]Peter and John about to go into the
temple, he *began* asking to receive alms.
4 And Peter, along with John, [a]fixed his gaze upon him
and said, "Look at us!"
5 And he *began* to give them his attention, expecting to
receive something from them.
6 But Peter said, "I do not possess silver and gold, but
what I do have I give to you: [a]In the name of Jesus Christ the
Nazarene—walk!"
7 And seizing him by the right hand, he raised him up;
and immediately his feet and his ankles were strengthened.
8 [a]And [1]with a leap, he stood upright and *began* to walk;
and he entered the temple with them, walking and leaping and
praising God.
9 And [a]all the people saw him walking and praising God;
10 and they were taking note of him as being the one who
used to [a]sit at the Beautiful Gate of the temple to *beg* alms,
and they were filled with wonder and amazement at what had
happened to him.
11 And while he was clinging to [a]Peter and John, all the
people ran together to them at the so-called [1b]portico of Solomon, full of amazement.
12 But when Peter saw *this*, he [a]replied to the people,
"Men of Israel, why do you marvel at this, or why do you gaze
at us, as if by our own power or piety we had made him walk?
13 "[a]The God of Abraham, Isaac, and Jacob, [b]the God of
our fathers, has glorified His [1c]Servant Jesus, *the one* whom
[d]you delivered up, and disowned in the presence of [e]Pilate,
when he had [f]decided to release Him.
14 "But you disowned [a]the Holy and Righteous One, and
[b]asked for a murderer to be granted to you,
15 but put to death the [1a]Prince of life, *the one* whom
[b]God raised from the dead,—*a fact* to which we are [c]witnesses.
16 "And on the basis of faith [a]in His name, *it is* the name of
[1]Jesus which has strengthened this man whom you see and
know; and the faith which *comes* through Him has given him
this perfect health in the presence of you all.
17 "And now, brethren, I know that you acted [a]in ignorance, just as your [b]rulers did also.
18 "But the things which [a]God announced beforehand by
the mouth of all the prophets, [b]that His [1]Christ should suffer,
He has thus fulfilled.
19 "[a]Repent therefore and return, that your sins may be
wiped away, in order that [b]times of refreshing may come from
the presence of the Lord;
20 and that he may send Jesus, the [1]Christ appointed for
you,

1 [1]I.e., 3 p.m. [a]Luke 22:8; Acts 3:3, 4, 11 [b]Ps. 55:17; Acts 10:30; Matt. 27:45

2 [1]Or, *a gift of charity* [a]Acts 14:8 [b]Luke 16:20 [c]Acts 3:10; John 9:8

3 [a]Luke 22:8; Acts 3:1, 4, 11

4 [a]Acts 10:4

6 [a]Acts 4:10; 3:16; 2:22

8 [1]Lit., *leaping up* [a]Acts 14:10

9 [a]Acts 4:16, 21

10 [a]Acts 3:2; John 9:8

11 [1]Or, *colonnade* [a]Luke 22:8; Acts 3:3, 4 [b]Acts 5:12; John 10:23

12 [a]Matt. 11:25; 17:4; 22:1; Luke 14:3; Acts 5:8, 10:46

13 [1]Or, *Child* [a]Matt. 22:32 [b]Acts 5:30; 7:32; 22:14; Ex. 3:13, 15 [c]Acts 3:26; 4:27, 30 [d]Acts 2:23; Matt. 20:19; John 19:11 [e]Matt. 27:2 [f]Luke 23:4

14 [a]Mark 1:24; Acts 4:27; 7:52; 2 Cor. 5:21 [b]Matt. 27:20; Mark 15:11; Luke 23:18-25

15 [1]Or, *Author* [a]Acts 5:31; Heb. 2:10; 12:2 [b]Acts 2:24 [c]Luke 24:48

16 [1]Lit., *His* [a]Acts 3:6

17 [a]Luke 23:34; Acts 13:27; 26:9; John 15:21; Eph. 4:18 [b]Luke 23:13

18 [1]Or, *Anointed One, Messiah* [a]Acts 2:23 [b]Luke 24:27; Acts 17:3; 26:23

19 [a]Acts 2:38; 26:20 [b]2 Thess. 1:7; Heb. 4:1ff.

20 [1]I.e., Messiah

21 [a]whom heaven must receive until *the* [1]period of [b]resto-
ration of all things, about which [c]God spoke by the mouth of
His holy prophets from ancient time.
22 "Moses said, '[a]THE LORD GOD SHALL RAISE UP FOR YOU A
PROPHET [1]LIKE ME FROM YOUR BRETHREN; TO HIM YOU SHALL
GIVE HEED IN EVERYTHING HE SAYS TO YOU.
23 '[a]AND IT SHALL BE THAT EVERY [b]SOUL THAT DOES NOT HEED
THAT PROPHET SHALL BE UTTERLY DESTROYED FROM AMONG THE
PEOPLE.'
24 "And likewise, [a]all the prophets who have spoken, from
Samuel and *his* successors onward, also announced these days.
25 "It is you who are [a]the sons of the prophets, and of the
[b]covenant which God [1]made with your fathers, saying to Abraham, '[c]AND IN YOUR SEED ALL THE FAMILIES OF THE EARTH SHALL
BE BLESSED.'
26 "For you [a]first, God [b]raised up His [1]Servant, and sent
Him to bless you by turning every one *of you* from your
wicked ways."

CHAPTER 4

AND as they were speaking to the people, the priests and
[a]the captain of the temple *guard*, and [b]the Sadducees, [c]came
upon them,
2 being greatly disturbed because they were teaching the
people and proclaiming [1a]in Jesus the resurrection from the
dead.
3 And they laid hands on them, and [a]put them in jail
until the next day, for it was already evening.
4 But many of those who had heard the [1]message believed; and [a]the number of the men came to be about five
thousand.
5 And it came about on the next day, that their [a]rulers
and elders and scribes were gathered together in Jerusalem;
6 and [a]Annas the high priest *was there*, and [b]Caiaphas
and John and Alexander, and all who were of high-priestly
descent.
7 And when they had placed them in the center, they
began to inquire, "By what power, or in what name, have you
done this?"
8 Then Peter, [1a]filled with the Holy Spirit, said to them,
"[2b]Rulers and elders of the people,
9 if we are on trial today for [a]a benefit done to a sick
man, [1]as to how this man has been made well,
10 let it be known to all of you, and to all the people of
Israel, that [1a]by the name of Jesus Christ the Nazarene, whom
you crucified, whom [b]God raised from the dead,—[1]by [2]this
name this man stands here before you in good health.
11 "[1a]He is the [b]STONE WHICH WAS [c]REJECTED by you, THE
BUILDERS, *but* WHICH BECAME THE VERY CORNER *STONE*.
12 "And there is salvation in [a]no one else; for there is no
other name under heaven that has been given among men, by
which we must be saved."
13 Now as they observed the [a]confidence of [b]Peter and
John, and understood that they were uneducated and un-

21 [1]Lit., *periods, times* [a]Acts 1:11 [b]Matt. 17:11; Rom. 8:21 [c]Luke 1:70

22 [1]Or, *as* He raised up *me* [a]Deut. 18:15; Acts 7:37

23 [a]Deut. 18:19 [b]Acts 2:41

24 [a]Luke 24:27; Acts 17:3; 26:23

25 [1]Lit., *covenanted* [a]Acts 2:39 [b]Rom. 9:4f. [c]Gen. 22:18

26 [1]Or, *Child* [a]Acts 13:46; Rom. 1:16; 2:9f.; Matt. 15:24; John 4:22 [b]Acts 2:24

1 [a]Luke 22:4 [b]Matt. 3:7 [c]Luke 20:1; Acts 6:12

2 [1]Or, *in the case of* [a]Acts 17:18; 3:15

3 [a]Acts 5:18

4 [1]Or, *word* [a]Acts 2:41

5 [a]Luke 23:13; Acts 4:8

6 [a]Luke 3:2 [b]Matt. 26:3

8 [1]Or, *having* just *been filled* [2]Or, *rulers of the people and elders* [a]Acts 13:9; 2:4 [b]Luke 23:13; Acts 4:5

9 [1]Or, *by whom* [a]Acts 3:7f.

10 [1]Or, *in* [2]Or, *him* [a]Acts 3:6; 2:22 [b]Acts 2:24

11 [1]Lit., *This One* [a]Matt. 21:42 [b]Ps. 118:22 [c]Mark 9:12

12 [a]1 Tim. 2:5; Matt. 1:21; Acts 10:43

13 [a]Acts 4:31 [b]Luke 22:8; Acts 4:19

trained men, they were marveling, and [c]*began* to recognize
them [1]as having been with Jesus.
14 And seeing the man who had been healed standing with
them, they had nothing to say in reply.
15 But when they had ordered them to go aside out of the
[1a]Council, they *began* to confer with one another,
16 saying, "[a]What shall we do with these men? For the
fact that a [b]noteworthy [1]miracle has taken place through them
is apparent to all who live in Jerusalem, and we cannot deny it.
17 "But in order that it may not spread any further among
the people, let us warn them to speak no more to any man [a]in
this name."
18 And when they had summoned them, they [a]com-
manded them not to speak or teach at all [1]in the name of
Jesus.
19 But [a]Peter and John answered and said to them,
"[b]Whether it is right in the sight of God to give heed to you
rather than to God, you be the judge;
20 for [a]we cannot stop speaking what we have seen and
heard."
21 And when they had threatened them further, they let
them go (finding no basis on which they might punish them)
[a]on account of the people, because they were all [b]glorifying
God for what had happened;
22 for the man was more than forty years old on whom
this [1]miracle of healing had been performed.
23 And when they had been released, they went to their
own *companions,* and reported all that the chief priests and
the elders had said to them.
24 And when they heard *this,* they lifted their voice to
God with one accord and said, "O [1]Lord, it is Thou who [a]DIDST
MAKE THE HEAVEN AND THE EARTH AND THE SEA, AND ALL THAT IS
IN THEM,
25 who [a]by the Holy Spirit, [1]*through* the mouth of our
father David Thy servant, didst say,
'[b]WHY DID THE [2]GENTILES RAGE,
AND THE PEOPLES DEVISE FUTILE THINGS?
26 '[a]THE KINGS OF THE EARTH [1]TOOK THEIR STAND,
AND THE RULERS WERE GATHERED TOGETHER,
AGAINST THE LORD, AND AGAINST HIS [2b]CHRIST.'
27 "For truly in this city there were gathered together
against Thy holy [1a]Servant Jesus, whom Thou didst anoint,
both [b]Herod and [c]Pontius Pilate, along with [d]the [2]Gentiles
and the peoples of Israel,
28 to do whatever Thy hand and [a]Thy purpose predestined to occur.
29 "And [1]now, Lord, take note of their threats, and grant
that Thy bond-servants may [a]speak Thy word with all
[b]confidence,
30 while Thou dost extend Thy hand to heal, and [1a]signs
and wonders take place through the name of Thy holy [2b]Ser-
vant Jesus."
31 And when they had prayed, the [a]place where they had
gathered together was shaken, and they were all [b]filled with the
Holy Spirit, and *began* to [c]speak the word of God with
[d]boldness.

13 [1]Lit., *that they had been* [c]John 7:15

15 [1]Or, *Sanhedrin* [a]Matt. 5:22

16 [1]Or, *sign* [a]John 11:47 [b]Acts 3:7-10

17 [a]John 15:21

18 [1]Or, *on the basis of* [a]Acts 5:28f.

19 [a]Acts 4:13 [b]Acts 5:28f.

20 [a]1 Cor. 9:16

21 [a]Acts 5:26 [b]Matt. 9:8

22 [1]Or, *sign*

24 [1]Or, *Master* [a]Ex. 20:11; Ps. 146:6

25 [1]This word is missing in the Greek [2]Or, *Nations* [a]Acts 1:16 [b]Ps. 2:1

26 [1]Or, *approached* [2]I.e., Messiah, Anointed One [a]Ps. 2:2 [b]Dan. 9:24f.; Luke 4:18; Acts 10:38; Heb. 1:9

27 [1]Or, *Child* [2]Or, *nations* [a]Acts 4:30; 3:13 [b]Matt. 14:1 [c]Luke 23:12; Matt. 27:2 [d]Matt. 20:19

28 [a]Acts 2:23

29 [1]Or, *as for the present situation* [a]Phil. 1:14 [b]Acts 4:13, 31; 14:3

30 [1]Or, *attesting miracles* [2]Or, *Child* [a]John 4:48 [b]Acts 4:27; 3:13

31 [a]Acts 2:1 [b]Acts 2:4 [c]Phil. 1:14 [d]Acts 4:13; 14:3

32 And the [1]congregation of those who believed were of
one heart and soul; and not one *of them* [2]claimed that anything
belonging to him was his own; but [a]all things were common property to them.
33 And [a]with great power the apostles were giving [b]witness
to the resurrection of the Lord Jesus[1], and abundant grace was
upon them all.
34 For there was not a needy person among them, for all
who were owners of lands or houses [a]would sell them and bring
the [1]proceeds of the sales,
35 and [a]lay them at the apostles' feet; and they would be
[b]distributed to each, as any had need.
36 And Joseph, a Levite of [a]Cyprian birth, who was also
called [b]Barnabas by the apostles (which translated means, Son
of [1c]Encouragement),
37 and who owned a tract of land, sold it and brought the
money and [a]laid it at the apostles' feet.

Chapter 5

BUT a certain man named Ananias, with his wife Sapphira,
sold a piece of property,
2 and [a]kept back *some* of the price for himself, with his
wife's [1]full knowledge, and bringing a portion of it, he [b]laid it
at the apostles' feet.
3 But Peter said, "Ananias, why has [a]Satan filled your
heart to lie [b]to the Holy Spirit, and to [c]keep back *some* of the
price of the land?
4 "While it remained *unsold,* did it not remain your own?
And after it was sold, was it not [1]under your control? Why is it
that you have [2]conceived this deed in your heart? You have
not lied to men, but [a]to God."
5 And as he heard these words, Ananias [a]fell down and
breathed his last; and [b]great fear came upon all who heard of
it.
6 And the [1]young men arose and [a]covered him up, and
after carrying him out, they buried him.
7 Now there elapsed an interval of about three hours,
and his wife came in, not knowing what had happened.
8 And Peter [a]responded to her, "Tell me whether you
sold the land [1b]for such and such a price?" And she said, "Yes,
[1]that was the price."
9 Then Peter *said* to her, "Why is it that you have agreed
together to [a]put [b]the Spirit of the Lord to the test? Behold, the
feet of those who have buried your husband are at the door,
and they shall carry you out *as well.*"
10 And she [a]fell immediately at his feet, and breathed her
last; and the young men came in and found her dead, and they
carried her out and buried her beside her husband.
11 And [a]great fear came upon the whole church, and upon
all who heard of these things.
12 And [1]at the hands of the apostles many [a]signs and wonders were taking place among the people; and they were all
with one accord in [b]Solomon's portico.
13 But none of the rest dared to associate with them;
however, [a]the people [1]held them in high esteem.

32 [1]Or, *multitude* [2]Lit., *was saying* [a]Acts 2:44

33 [1]Some mss. add, *Christ* [a]Acts 1:8 [b]Luke 24:48

34 [1]Lit., *the prices of the things being sold* [a]Matt. 19:21; Acts 2:45

35 [a]Acts 4:37; 5:2 [b]Acts 6:1; 2:45

36 [1]Or, *Exhortation,* or, *Consolation* [a]Acts 11:19f.; 13:4; 15:39; 21:3, 16; 27:4 [b]Acts 9:27; 11:22, 30; 12:25; 13:15; 1 Cor. 9:6; Gal. 2:1, 9, 13; Col. 4:10 [c]Acts 13:15; 1 Cor. 14:3; 1 Thess. 2:3; Acts 2:40; 11:23

37 [a]Acts 4:35; 5:2

2 [1]Or, *collusion* [a]Acts 5:3 [b]Acts 4:35, 37

3 [a]Matt. 4:10; Luke 22:3; John 13:2, 27 [b]Acts 5:4, 9 [c]Acts 5:2

4 [1]Or, *in your authority* [2]Or, *placed* [a]Acts 5:3, 9

5 [a]Acts 5:10; Ezek. 11:13 [b]Acts 5:11; 2:43

6 [1]Lit., *younger* [a]John 19:40

8 [1]Lit., *for so much* [a]Acts 3:12 [b]Acts 5:2

9 [a]Acts 15:10 [b]Acts 5:3, 4

10 [a]Acts 5:5; Ezek. 11:13

11 [a]Acts 5:5; 2:43

12 [1]Lit., *through* [a]John 4:48 [b]Acts 3:11; John 10:23

13 [1]Lit., *were holding* [a]Acts 2:47; 4:21

14 And all the more [a]believers in the Lord, multitudes of
men and women, were constantly [b]added to *their number*;
15 to such an extent that they even carried the sick out
into the streets, and laid them on cots and pallets, so that when
Peter came by, [a]at least his shadow might fall on any one of
them.
16 And also the [1]people from the cities in the vicinity of
Jerusalem were coming together, bringing people who were
sick [2]or afflicted with unclean spirits; and they were all being
healed.
17 But the high priest rose up, along with all his associates
(that is [a]the sect of [b]the Sadducees), and they were filled with
jealousy;
18 and they laid hands on the apostles, and [a]put them in a
public jail.
19 But [a]an angel of the Lord during the night opened the
gates of the prison, and taking them out he said,
20 "Go your way, stand and [1]speak to the people in the
temple [2a]the whole message of this Life."
21 And upon hearing *this*, they entered into the temple
[a]about daybreak, and *began* to teach. Now when [b]the high
priest and his associates had come, they called [c]the [1]Council
together, and all the Senate of the sons of Israel, and sent
orders to the prison-house for them to be brought.
22 But [a]the officers who came did not find them in the
prison; and they returned, and reported back,
23 saying, "We found the prison-house locked quite securely and the guards standing at the doors; but when we had
opened up, we found no one inside."
24 Now when [a]the captain of the temple *guard* and the
chief priests heard these words, they were greatly perplexed
about them as to what [1]would come of this.
25 But someone came and reported to them, "Behold, the
men whom you put in prison are standing in the temple and
teaching the people!"
26 Then [a]the captain went along with [b]the officers and
proceeded to bring them *back* without violence; (for [c]they
were afraid of the people, lest they should be stoned).
27 And when they had brought them, they stood them
[1]before [a]the Council. And the high priest questioned them,
28 saying, "We gave you [a]strict orders not to continue
teaching in this name, and behold, you have filled Jerusalem
with your teaching, and [b]intend to bring this man's blood upon
us."
29 But Peter and the apostles answered and said, "[a]We
must obey God rather than men.
30 "[a]The God of our fathers [b]raised up Jesus, [1]whom you
had [c]put to death by hanging Him on a [2]cross.
31 "[a]He is the one whom God exalted [1]to His right hand as
a [2b]Prince and a [c]Savior, to grant [d]repentance to Israel, and
forgiveness of sins.
32 "And we are [a]witnesses[1] of these things; and [b]*so is* the
Holy Spirit, whom God has given to those who obey Him."
33 But when they heard this, they were [1a]cut to the quick
and were intending to slay them.
34 But a certain Pharisee named [a]Gamaliel, a [b]teacher of

14 [a]2 Cor. 6:15 [b]Acts 2:47; 11:24

15 [a]Acts 19:12

16 [1]Lit., *multitude* [2]Lit., *and*

17 [a]Acts 15:5 [b]Matt. 3:7; Acts 4:1

18 [a]Acts 4:3

19 [a]Matt. 1:20, 24; 2:13, 19; 28:2; Luke 1:11; 2:9; Acts 8:26; 12:7, 23; 10:3; 27:23

20 [1]Or, *continue to speak* [2]Lit., *all the words* [a]John 6:63, 68

21 [1]Or, *Sanhedrin* [a]John 8:2 [b]Acts 4:6 [c]Matt. 5:22; Acts 5:27, 34, 41

22 [a]Matt. 26:58; Acts 5:26

24 [1]Lit., *this would become* [a]Acts 4:1; 5:26

26 [a]Acts 5:24 [b]Acts 5:22 [c]Acts 4:21; 5:13

27 [1]Lit., *in* [a]Matt. 5:22; Acts 5:21, 34, 41

28 [a]Acts 4:18 [b]Acts 2:23, 36; 3:14f.; 7:52; Matt. 23:35; 27:25

29 [a]Acts 4:19

30 [1]Or, *on whom you had laid violent hands* [2]Lit., *wood* [a]Acts 3:13 [b]Acts 2:24 [c]Acts 10:39; 13:29; Gal. 3:13; 1 Pet. 2:24

31 [1]Or, *by* [2]Or, *Leader* [a]Acts 2:33 [b]Acts 3:15 [c]Luke 2:11 [d]Luke 24:47; Acts 2:38

32 [1]Some mss. add, *in Him* or, *of Him* [a]Luke 24:48 [b]John 15:26; Acts 15:28; Rom. 8:16; Heb. 2:4

33 [1]Lit., *being sawed through* [a]Acts 7:54; 2:37

34 [a]Acts 22:3 [b]Luke 2:46; 5:17

the Law, respected by all the people, stood up in [c]the Council
and gave orders to put the men outside for a short time.
35 And he said to them, "Men of Israel, take care what
you propose to do with these men.
36 "For sometime ago Theudas rose up, [a]claiming to be
somebody; and a group of about four hundred men joined up
with him. [1]And he was slain; and all who [2]followed him were
dispersed and came to nothing.
37 "After this man Judas of Galilee rose up in the days of
[a]the census, and drew away *some* people after him, he too
perished, and all those who [1]followed him were scattered.
38 "And so in the present case, I say to you, stay away from
these men and let them alone, for if this plan or [1]action should
[a]be of men, it will be overthrown;
39 but if it is of God, you will not be able to overthrow
them; or else you may even be found [a]fighting against God."
40 And they [1]took his advice; and after calling the apostles
in, they [a]flogged them and ordered them to [2]speak no more in
the name of Jesus, and *then* released them.
41 So they went on their way from the presence of the
[1a]Council, [b]rejoicing that they had been considered worthy to
suffer shame [c]for [2]*His* name.
42 [a]And every day, in the temple and [1]from house to
house, they [2]kept right on teaching and [3b]preaching Jesus *as*
the [4]Christ.

CHAPTER 6

NOW [1]at this time while the [a]disciples were increasing [b]*in
number*, a complaint arose on the part of the [2c]Hellenistic
Jews against the *native* [d]Hebrews, because their [e]widows were
being overlooked in [f]the daily serving *of food*.
2 And the Twelve summoned the [1]congregation of the
disciples and said, "It is not desirable for us to neglect the
word of God in order to serve tables.
3 "But select from among you, [a]brethren, seven men of
good reputation, [b]full of the Spirit and of wisdom, whom we
may put in charge of this task.
4 "But we will [a]devote ourselves to prayer, and to the
[1]ministry of the word."
5 And the statement found approval with the whole
[1]congregation; and they chose [a]Stephen, a man [b]full of faith
and of the Holy Spirit, and [c]Philip, Prochorus, Nicanor, Ti-
mon, Parmenas and [2]Nicolas, a [3d]proselyte from [e]Antioch.
6 And these they brought before the apostles; and after
[a]praying, they [b]laid their hands on them.
7 And [a]the word of God kept on spreading; and [b]the
number of the disciples continued to increase greatly in Jerusalem, and a great many of the priests were becoming obedient
to [c]the faith.
8 And Stephen, full of grace and power, was performing
great [a]wonders and [1]signs among the people.
9 But some men from what was called the Synagogue of
the Freedmen, *including* both [a]Cyrenians and [b]Alexandrians,
and some from [c]Cilicia and [1d]Asia, rose up and argued with
Stephen.

34 [c]Acts 5:21

36 [1]Lit., *who was slain* [2]Lit., *were obeying* [a]Acts 8:9; Gal. 2:6; 6:3

37 [1]Lit., *were obeying* [a]Luke 2:2

38 [1]Or, *work* [a]Mark 11:30

39 [a]Acts 11:17; Prov. 21:30

40 [1]Lit., *were persuaded by him* [2]Lit., *not be speaking* [a]Matt. 10:17

41 [1]Or, *Sanhedrin* [2]Lit., the *name* (par excellence) [a]Acts 5:21 [b]1 Pet. 4:14, 16 [c]John 15:21

42 [1]Or, *in the various private homes* [2]Lit., *were not ceasing to* [3]Or, *telling the good news of* [4]I.e., Messiah [a]Acts 2:46 [b]Acts 8:35; 11:20; 17:18; Gal. 1:16

1 [1]Lit., *in these days* [2]I.e., non-Palestinian Jews who normally spoke Greek [a]Acts 11:26 [b]Acts 6:7; 2:47 [c]Acts 9:29; 11:20 marg. [d]2 Cor. 11:22; Phil. 3:5 [e]Acts 9:39, 41; 1 Tim. 5:3 [f]Acts 4:35; 11:29

2 [1]Or, *multitude*

3 [a]Acts 1:15; John 21:23 [b]Acts 2:4

4 [1]Or, *service* [a]Acts 1:14

5 [1]Lit., *multitude* [2]Gr, *Nikolaos* [3]I.e., a former convert to Judaism [a]Acts 6:8ff.; 11:19; 22:20 [b]Acts 6:3; Acts 11:24 [c]Acts 8:5ff.; 21:8 [d]Matt. 23:15 [e]Acts 11:19

6 [a]Acts 1:24 [b]Acts 13:3; 1 Tim. 4:14; 2 Tim. 1:6; Num. 8:10; 27:18; Deut. 34:9; Acts 8:17ff.; 9:17; 19:6; Heb. 6:2; Mark 5:23

7 [a]Acts 12:24; 19:20 [b]Acts 6:1 [c]Acts 13:8; 14:22; Gal. 1:23; 6:10; Jude 3, 20

8 [1]Or, *attesting miracles* [a]John 4:48

9 [1]I.e., west coast province of Asia Minor [a]Acts 2:10; Matt. 27:32 [b]Acts 18:24, [c]Acts 15:23, 41; 21:39; 22:3; 23:34, 27:5; Gal. 1:21 [d]Acts 16:6; 19:10; 21:27; 24:18

10 And *yet* they were unable to cope with the wisdom and
the Spirit with which he was speaking.
11 Then they secretly induced men [1]to say, "We have
heard him speak blasphemous words against Moses and
against God."
12 And they stirred up the people, the elders and the
scribes, and they [a]came upon him and dragged him away, and
brought him [1]before [b]the [2]Council.
13 And they put forward [a]false witnesses who said, "This
man incessantly speaks against this [b]holy place, and the Law;
14 for we have heard him say that [a]this Nazarene, Jesus,
will destroy this place and alter [b]the customs which Moses
handed down to us."
15 And fixing their gaze on him, all who were sitting in the
[1a]Council saw his face like the face of an angel.

CHAPTER 7

AND the high priest said, "Are these things so?"
2 And he said, "Hear me, [a]brethren and fathers! [b]The
God of glory [c]appeared to our father Abraham when he was in
Mesopotamia, before he lived in [1]Haran,
3 AND SAID TO HIM, '[a]DEPART FROM YOUR COUNTRY AND
YOUR RELATIVES, AND COME INTO THE LAND THAT I WILL SHOW
YOU.'
4 "[a]Then he departed from the land of the Chaldeans,
and settled in [1]Haran. And [b]from there, after his father died,
God removed him into this country in which you are now
living.
5 "And He gave him no inheritance in it, not even a foot
of ground; and *yet*, even when he had no child, [a]He promised
that HE WOULD GIVE IT TO HIM AS A POSSESSION, AND TO HIS
OFFSPRING AFTER HIM.
6 "But [a]God spoke to this effect, that HIS OFFSPRING
WOULD BE ALIENS IN A FOREIGN LAND, AND THAT THEY WOULD [1]BE
ENSLAVED AND MISTREATED FOR FOUR HUNDRED YEARS.
7 " 'AND WHATEVER NATION TO WHICH THEY SHALL BE IN
BONDAGE I MYSELF WILL JUDGE,' said God, 'AND [a]AFTER THAT
THEY WILL COME OUT AND [1]SERVE ME IN THIS PLACE.'
8 "And He [a]gave him [1]the covenant of circumcision; and
so [b]*Abraham* became the father of Isaac, and circumcised him
on the eighth day; and [c]Isaac *became the father of* Jacob, and
[d]Jacob *of* the twelve [e]patriarchs.
9 "And the patriarchs [a]BECAME JEALOUS OF JOSEPH AND SOLD
HIM INTO EGYPT. And *yet* God WAS WITH HIM,
10 and rescued him from all his afflictions, and [a]GRANTED
HIM FAVOR and wisdom IN THE SIGHT OF PHARAOH, KING OF
EGYPT; AND HE MADE HIM GOVERNOR OVER EGYPT AND ALL HIS
HOUSEHOLD.
11 "Now [a]A FAMINE CAME OVER ALL EGYPT AND CANAAN, and
great affliction *with it;* and our fathers [1]could find no [2]food.
12 "But [a]WHEN JACOB HEARD THAT THERE WAS GRAIN IN
EGYPT, he sent our fathers *there* the first time.
13 "And on the second *visit* [a]Joseph [1]made himself known
to his brothers, and Joseph's family was disclosed to Pharaoh.

11 [1]Lit., *saying*

12 [1]Lit., *into* [2]Or, *Sanhedrin*
[a]Acts 4:1; Luke 20:1 [b]Matt. 5:22

13 [a]Matt. 26:59-61; Acts 7:58 [b]Matt. 24:15; Acts 21:28; Acts 25:8

14 [a]Matt. 26:61 [b]Acts 15:1; 21:21; 26:3; 28:17

15 [1]Or, *Sanhedrin*
[a]Matt. 5:22

2 [1]Gr., *Kharran*
[a]Acts 22:1 [b]Ps. 29:3; 1 Cor. 2:8 [c]Gen. 11:31; 15:7

3 [a]Gen. 12:1

4 [1]Gr., *Kharran*
[a]Gen. 11:31; 15:7; [b]Gen. 12:5

5 [a]Gen. 12:7; 17:8

6 [1]Lit., *enslave them and mistreat them*
[a]Gen. 15:13f.

7 [1]Or, *worship*
[a]Ex. 3:12

8 [1]Or, *a*
[a]Gen. 17:10ff. [b]Gen. 21:2-4 [c]Gen. 25:26 [d]Gen. 29:31ff.; 30:5ff.; 35:23ff. [e]Acts 2:29

9 [a]Gen. 37:11, 28; 45:4; 39:2, 21f.

10 [a]Gen. 39:21; 41:40-46; Ps. 105:21

11 [1]Lit., *were not finding* [2]Or, *fodder*
[a]Gen. 41:54f.; 42:5

12 [a]Gen. 42:2

13 [1]Or, *was made known*
[a]Gen. 45:1-4

14 "And [a]Joseph sent *word* and invited Jacob his father and all his relatives to come to him, [b]seventy-five [c]persons *in all.*

15 "And [a]Jacob WENT DOWN TO EGYPT AND *there* PASSED AWAY, he and our fathers.

16 "And *from there* they were removed to [1a]Shechem, and laid in the tomb which Abraham had purchased for a sum of money from the sons of [2]Hamor in [1]Shechem.

17 "But as the time of the promise was approaching which God had assured to Abraham, [a]the people increased and multiplied in Egypt,

18 until [a]THERE AROSE ANOTHER KING OVER EGYPT WHO KNEW NOTHING ABOUT JOSEPH.

19 "It was he who took [a]shrewd advantage of our race, and mistreated our fathers so that they would [1]expose their infants and they would not survive.

20 "And it was at this time that [a]Moses was born; and he was lovely [1]in the sight of God; and he was nurtured three months in his father's home.

21 "And after he had been [1]exposed, [a]Pharaoh's daughter [2]took him away, and nurtured him as her own son.

22 "And Moses was educated in all [a]the learning of the Egyptians, and he was a man of power in words and deeds.

23 "But when he was approaching the age of forty, [a]it entered his [1]mind to visit his brethren, the sons of Israel.

24 "And when he saw one *of them* being treated unjustly, he defended him and took vengeance for the oppressed by striking down the Egyptian.

25 "And he [1]supposed that his brethren understood that God was granting them [2]deliverance [3]through him; but they did not understand.

26 "[a]And on the following day he appeared to them as they were fighting together, and he tried to reconcile them in peace, saying, 'Men, you are brethren, why do you injure one another?'

27 "[a]BUT THE ONE WHO WAS INJURING HIS NEIGHBOR pushed him away, saying, 'WHO MADE YOU A RULER AND JUDGE OVER US?

28 '[a]YOU DO NOT MEAN TO KILL ME AS YOU KILLED THE EGYPTIAN YESTERDAY, DO YOU?'

29 "AND AT THIS REMARK [a]MOSES FLED, AND BECAME AN ALIEN IN THE LAND OF [1]MIDIAN, where he became the father of two sons.

30 "And after forty years had passed, [a]AN ANGEL APPEARED TO HIM IN THE WILDERNESS OF MOUNT Sinai, IN THE FLAME OF A BURNING THORN-BUSH.

31 "And when Moses saw it, he *began* to marvel at the sight; and as he approached to look *more* closely, there came the voice of the Lord:

32 '[a]I AM THE GOD OF YOUR FATHERS, THE GOD OF ABRAHAM AND ISAAC AND JACOB.' And Moses shook *with fear* and would not venture to look.

33 "BUT THE LORD SAID TO HIM, '[a]TAKE OFF THE SANDALS FROM YOUR FEET, FOR THE PLACE ON WHICH YOU ARE STANDING IS HOLY GROUND.

34 '[a]I HAVE CERTAINLY SEEN THE OPPRESSION OF MY PEOPLE IN EGYPT, AND HAVE HEARD THEIR GROANS, AND I HAVE COME

14 [a]Gen. 45:9f. [b]Gen. 46:26f.; Ex. 1:5; Deut. 10:22 [c]Acts 2:41

15 [a]Gen. 46:5; 49:33; Ex. 1:6

16 [1]Gr., *Sychem* [2]Gr., *Emmor* [a]Gen. 23:16; 50:13; 33:19; Josh. 24:32

17 [a]Ex. 1:7f.

18 [a]Ex. 1:8

19 [1]Or, *put out to die* [a]Ex. 1:10f., 16ff.

20 [1]Lit., *to God* [a]Ex. 2:2

21 [1]Or, *put out to die* [2]Or, *adopted him* [a]Ex. 2:5f., 10

22 [a]1 Kin. 4:30; Is. 19:11

23 [1]Lit., *heart* [a]Ex. 2:11f.

25 [1]Lit., *was thinking* [2]Or, *salvation* [3]Lit., *through his hand*

26 [a]Ex. 2:13f.

27 [a]Ex. 2:14; Acts 7:35

28 [a]Ex. 2:14

29 [1]Gr., *Madiam* [a]Ex. 2:15, 22

30 [a]Ex. 3:1f.

32 [a]Ex. 3:6

33 [a]Ex. 3:5

34 [a]Ex. 3:7

DOWN TO DELIVER THEM; [1b]COME NOW, AND I WILL SEND YOU TO EGYPT.'

35 "This Moses whom they [a]disowned, saying, 'WHO MADE YOU A RULER AND A JUDGE?' is the one whom God [1]sent *to be* both a ruler and a deliverer with the [2]help of the angel who appeared to him in the thorn-bush.

36 "[a]This man led them out, performing [b]wonders and [1]signs in the land of Egypt and in the Red Sea and in the [c]wilderness for forty years.

37 "This is the Moses who said to the sons of Israel, 'GOD SHALL RAISE UP FOR YOU [a]A PROPHET [1]LIKE ME FROM YOUR BRETHREN.'

38 "This is the one who was in [a]the [1]congregation in the wilderness together with [b]the angel who was speaking to him in Mount Sinai, and *who was* with our fathers; and he received [c]living [d]oracles to pass on to you.

39 "And our fathers were unwilling to be obedient to him, but [a]repudiated him and in their hearts turned back to Egypt,

40 SAYING TO AARON, '[a]MAKE FOR US GODS WHO WILL GO BEFORE US; FOR THIS MOSES WHO LED US OUT OF THE LAND OF EGYPT—WE DO NOT KNOW WHAT HAPPENED TO HIM.'

41 "And [1]at that time [a]they made a [2]calf and brought a sacrifice to the idol, and were rejoicing in [b]the works of their hands.

42 "But God [a]turned away and delivered them up to [1]serve the [2]host of heaven; as it is written in the book of the prophets, '[b]IT WAS NOT TO ME THAT YOU OFFERED VICTIMS AND SACRIFICES [c]FORTY YEARS IN THE WILDERNESS, WAS IT, O HOUSE OF ISRAEL?

43 '[a]YOU ALSO TOOK ALONG THE TABERNACLE OF MOLOCH AND THE STAR OF THE GOD [1]ROMPHA, THE IMAGES WHICH YOU MADE TO WORSHIP THEM. I ALSO WILL REMOVE YOU BEYOND BABYLON.'

44 "Our fathers had [a]the tabernacle of testimony in the wilderness, just as He who spoke to Moses directed *him* to make it according to the pattern which he had seen.

45 "And having received it in their turn, our fathers [a]brought it in with [1]Joshua upon dispossessing the [2]nations whom God drove out before our fathers, until the time of David.

46 "And [a]*David* found favor in God's sight, and asked that he might find a dwelling place for the [1]God of Jacob.

47 "But it was [a]Solomon who built a house for Him.

48 "However, [a]the Most High does not dwell in *houses* made by *human* hands; as the prophet says:

49 '[a]HEAVEN IS MY THRONE,
AND EARTH IS THE FOOTSTOOL OF MY FEET;
WHAT KIND OF HOUSE WILL YOU BUILD FOR ME? says the Lord;
OR WHAT PLACE IS THERE FOR MY REPOSE?

50 '[a]WAS IT NOT MY HAND WHICH MADE ALL THESE THINGS?'

51 "You men who are [a]stiffnecked and uncircumcised in heart and ears are always resisting the Holy Spirit; you are doing just as your fathers did.

52 "[a]Which one of the prophets did your fathers not persecute? And they killed those who had previously announced the

34 [1]Lit., *and now hither!* [b]Ex. 3:10

35 [1]Lit., *has sent* [2]Lit., *hand* [a]Acts 7:27

36 [1]Or, *attesting miracles* [a]Ex. 12:41; 33:1; Heb. 8:9 [b]Ex. 7:3; John 4:48 [c]Ex. 16:35; Num. 14:33; Ps. 95:8-10; Heb. 3:8f.; Acts 7:42; 13:18

37 [1]Or, *as* He raised up *me* [a]Deut. 18:15; Acts 3:22

38 [1]Or, *church* (Gr. ekklesia) [a]Ex. 19:17 [b]Acts 7:53 [c]Deut. 32:47; Heb. 4:12 [d]Rom. 3:2; Heb. 5:12; 1 Pet. 4:11

39 [a]Num. 14:3f.

40 [a]Ex. 32:1, 23

41 [1]Lit., *in those days* [2]Or, *young bull* [a]Ex. 32:4, 6 [b]Rev. 9:20

42 [1]Or, *worship* [2]I.e., heavenly bodies [a]Josh. 24:20; Is. 63:10; Jer. 19:13; Ezek. 20:39 [b]Amos 5:25 [c]Acts 7:36

43 [1]Other mss. spell it: *Romphan*, or *Rempham*, or *Raiphan*, or *Rephan* [a]Amos 5:26, 27

44 [a]Ex. 25:8, 9; 38:21

45 [1]Gr., *Jesus* [2]Or, *Gentiles* [a]Josh. 3:14ff.; 18:1; 23:9; 24:18; Deut. 32:49; Ps. 44:2f.

46 [1]The earliest mss. read *house* instead of *God;* the Septuagint reads, *God* [a]2 Sam. 7:8ff.; Ps. 132:1-5; Acts 13:22

47 [a]1 Kin. 8:20

48 [a]Luke 1:32

49 [a]Is. 66:1; Matt. 5:34f.

50 [a]Is. 66:2

51 [a]Ex. 32:9; 33:3, 5; Lev. 26:41; Num. 27:14; Is. 63:10; Jer. 6:10; 9:26

52 [a]2 Chr. 36:15f.; Matt. 23:31, 37; 5:12

coming of [b]the Righteous One, whose betrayers and murderers
[c]you have now become;
53 you who received the law as [a]ordained by angels, and
yet did not keep it."
54 Now when they heard this, they were [a]cut [1]to the quick,
and they *began* gnashing their teeth at him.
55 But being [a]full of the Holy Spirit, he [b]gazed intently
into heaven and saw the glory of God, and Jesus standing [c]at
the right hand of God;
56 and he said, "Behold, I see the [a]heavens opened up and
[b]the Son of Man standing at the right hand of God."
57 But they cried out with a loud voice, and covered their
ears, and they rushed upon him with one impulse.
58 And when they had [a]driven him out of the city, they
began stoning *him*, and [b]the witnesses [c]laid aside their robes at
the feet of [d]a young man named Saul.
59 And they went on stoning Stephen as he [a]called upon
the Lord and said, "Lord Jesus, receive my spirit!"
60 And [a]falling on his knees, he cried out with a loud
voice, "Lord, [b]do not hold this sin against them!" And having
said this, he [1c]fell asleep.

Chapter 8

And [a]Saul was in hearty agreement with putting him to
death.
And on that day a great persecution arose against [b]the
church in Jerusalem; and they were all [c]scattered throughout
the regions of Judea and [d]Samaria, except the apostles.
2 And *some* devout men buried Stephen, and made loud
lamentation over him.
3 But [a]Saul *began* ravaging the church, entering house
after house; and [b]dragging off men and women, he would put
them in prison.
4 Therefore, those [a]who had been scattered went about
[1b]preaching the word.
5 And [a]Philip went down to the city of Samaria and *be-*
gan proclaiming [1]Christ to them.
6 And the multitudes with one accord were giving attention to what was said by Philip, as they heard and saw the
[1]signs which he was performing.
7 For *in the case of* many who had [a]unclean spirits, they
were coming out *of them* shouting with a loud voice; and many
who had been [b]paralyzed and lame were healed.
8 And there was [a]much rejoicing in that city.
9 Now there was a certain man named Simon, who formerly was practicing [a]magic in the city, and astonishing the
people of Samaria, [b]claiming to be someone great;
10 and they all, from smallest to greatest, were giving attention to him, saying, "[a]This man is what is called the Great
Power of God."
11 And they were giving him attention because he had for
a long time astonished them with his [a]magic arts.
12 But when they believed Philip [a]preaching the good
news about the kingdom of God and the name of Jesus Christ,
they were being [b]baptized, men and women alike.

52 [b]Acts 22:14; 3:14; 1 John 2:1 [c]Acts 3:14; 5:28

53 [a]Acts 7:38; Gal. 3:19; Heb. 2:2; Deut. 33:2 [Sept.]

54 [1]Lit., *in their hearts* [a]Acts 5:33

55 [a]Acts 2:4 [b]John 11:41 [c]Mark 16:19

56 [a]John 1:51 [b]Matt. 8:20

58 [a]Lev. 24:14, 16; Luke 4:29 [b]Acts 6:13; Deut. 13:9f.; 17:7 [c]Acts 22:20 [d]Acts 8:1; 22:20; 26:10

59 [a]Acts 9:14, 21; 22:16; Rom. 10:12, 13f.; 1 Cor. 1:2; 2 Tim. 2:22

60 [1]Or, *expired* [a]Luke 22:41 [b]Matt. 5:44; Luke 23:34 [c]Dan. 12:2; Matt. 27:52; John 11:11f.; Acts 13:36; 1 Cor. 15:6, 18, 20; 1 Thess. 4:13ff.; 2 Pet. 3:4

1 [a]Acts 7:58; 22:20; 26:10 [b]Acts 9:31 [c]Acts 8:4; 11:19 [d]Acts 1:8; 8:5, 14; 9:31

3 [a]Acts 9:1, 13, 21; 22:4, 19; 26:10f.; 1 Cor. 15:9; Gal. 1:13; Phil. 3:6; 1 Tim. 1:13 [b]James 2:6

4 [1]Or, *bringing the good tidings of* [a]Acts 8:1 [b]Acts 8:12; 15:35

5 [1]I.e., the Messiah [a]Acts 6:5; 8:26, 30

6 [1]Or, *attesting miracles*

7 [a]Mark 16:17 [b]Matt. 4:24

8 [a]Acts 8:39; John 4:40-42

9 [a]Acts 8:11; 13:6 [b]Acts 5:36

10 [a]Acts 14:11; 28:6

11 [a]Acts 8:9; 13:6

12 [a]Acts 8:4; 1:3 [b]Acts 2:38

13 And even Simon himself believed; and after being baptized, he continued on with Philip; and as he observed [a]signs
and [b]great miracles taking place, he was constantly amazed.
14 Now when [a]the apostles in Jerusalem heard that Samaria had received the word of God, they sent them [b]Peter and
John,
15 who came down and prayed for them, [a]that they might
receive the Holy Spirit.
16 For He had not yet fallen upon any of them; they had
simply been [a]baptized [1]in the name of the Lord Jesus.
17 Then they [a]*began* laying their hands on them, and they
were [b]receiving the Holy Spirit.
18 Now when Simon saw that the Spirit was bestowed
through the laying on of the apostles' hands, he offered them
money,
19 saying, "Give this authority to me as well, so that everyone on whom I lay my hands may receive the Holy Spirit."
20 But Peter said to him, "May your silver perish with
you, because you thought you could [a]obtain the gift of God
with money!
21 "You have [a]no part or portion in this [1]matter, for your
heart is not [b]right before God.
22 "Therefore repent of this wickedness of yours, and pray
the Lord that if possible, the intention of your heart may be
forgiven you.
23 "For I see that you are in the gall of bitterness and in
[a]the [1]bondage of iniquity."
24 But Simon answered and said, "Pray to the Lord for
me yourselves, so that nothing of what you have said may
come upon me."
25 And so, when they had solemnly [a]testified and spoken
[b]the word of the Lord, they started back to Jerusalem, and
were [c]preaching the gospel to many villages of the [d]Samaritans.
26 But [a]an angel of the Lord spoke to [b]Philip saying,
"Arise and go south to the road that descends from Jerusalem
to [c]Gaza." ([1]This is a desert *road*.)
27 And he arose and went; and behold, [a]there was an Ethiopian eunuch, a court official of Candace, queen of the
Ethiopians, who was in charge of all her treasure; and he [b]had
come to Jerusalem to worship.
28 And he was returning and sitting in his [1]chariot, and
was reading the prophet Isaiah.
29 And [a]the Spirit said to Philip, "Go up and join this
[1]chariot."
30 And when Philip had run up, he heard him reading
Isaiah the prophet, and said, "Do you understand what you are
reading?"
31 And he said, "Well, how could I, unless someone
guides me?" And he invited Philip to come up and sit with
him.
32 Now the passage of Scripture which he was reading was
this:

"[a]HE WAS LED AS A SHEEP TO SLAUGHTER;
AND AS A LAMB BEFORE ITS SHEARER IS SILENT,
SO HE DOES NOT OPEN HIS MOUTH.
33 "[a]IN HUMILIATION HIS JUDGMENT WAS TAKEN AWAY;

13 [a]Acts 8:6 [b]Acts 19:11
14 [a]Acts 8:1 [b]Luke 22:8
15 [a]Acts 2:38; 19:2
16 [1]Lit., *into* [a]Matt. 28:19
17 [a]Acts 6:6; Mark 5:23 [b]Acts 2:4
20 [a]Acts 2:38; Matt. 10:8; Is. 55:1; 2 Kin. 5:16; Dan. 5:17
21 [1]Or, *teaching*; lit., *word* [a]Deut. 10:9; 12:12; Eph. 5:5 [b]Ps. 78:37
23 [1]Or, *fetter* [a]Is. 58:6
25 [a]Luke 16:28 [b]Acts 13:12 [c]Acts 8:40 [d]Matt. 10:5
26 [1]Or, *this city is deserted* [a]Acts 5:19; 8:29 [b]Acts 8:5 [c]Gen. 10:19
27 [a]Ps. 68:31; 87:4; Is. 56:3ff. [b]1 Kin. 8:41f.; John 12:20
28 [1]Or, *carriage*
29 [1]Or, *carriage* [a]Acts 10:19; 11:12; 13:2; 20:23; 21:11; 16:6, 7; 28:25; Heb. 3:7; Acts 8:39
32 [a]Is. 53:7
33 [a]Is. 53:8f.

WHO SHALL [1]RELATE HIS [2]GENERATION?
FOR HIS LIFE IS REMOVED FROM THE EARTH."

34 And the eunuch answered Philip and said, "Please *tell me*, of whom does the prophet say this? Of himself, or of someone else?"

35 And Philip [a]opened his mouth, and [b]beginning from this Scripture he [c]preached Jesus to him.

36 And as they went along the road they came to some water; and the eunuch *said, "Look! Water! [a]What prevents me from being baptized?"

37 (See marginal note.)

38 And he ordered the [1]chariot to stop; and they both went down into the water, Philip as well as the eunuch; and he baptized him.

39 And when they came up out of the water, [a] the Spirit of the Lord snatched Philip away; and the eunuch saw him no more, but went on his way rejoicing.

40 But Philip [1]found himself at [2a]Azotus; and as he passed through he [b]kept preaching the gospel to all the cities, until he came to [c]Caesarea.

[a] CHAPTER 9

NOW Saul, still [b]breathing [1]threats and murder against the disciples of the Lord, went to the high priest,

2 and asked for [a]letters from him to [b]the synagogues at [c]Damascus, so that if he found any belonging to [d]the Way, both men and women, he might bring them bound to Jerusalem.

3 And it came about that as he journeyed, he was approaching Damascus, and [a]suddenly a light from heaven flashed around him;

4 and [a]he fell to the ground, and heard a voice saying to him, "Saul, Saul, why are you persecuting Me?"

5 And he said, "Who art Thou, Lord?" And He *said*, "I am Jesus whom you are persecuting,

6 but rise, and enter the city, and [a]it shall be told you what you must do."

7 And the men who traveled with him [a]stood speechless, [b]hearing the [1]voice, but seeing no one.

8 And Saul got up from the ground, and [a]though his eyes were open, he [1]could see nothing; and leading him by the hand, they brought him into [b]Damascus.

9 And he was three days without sight, and neither ate nor drank.

10 Now there was a certain disciple at [a]Damascus, named [b]Ananias; and the Lord said to him in [c]a vision, "Ananias." And he said, "Behold, *here am* I, Lord."

11 And the Lord *said* to him, "Arise and go to the street called Straight, and inquire at the house of Judas for a man from [a]Tarsus named Saul, for behold, he is praying,

12 and he has seen [1]in a vision a man named Ananias come in and [a]lay his hands on him, so that he might regain his sight."

13 But Ananias answered, "Lord, I have heard from many

33 [1]Or, *describe* [2]Or, *family*, or, *origin*

35 [a]Matt. 5:2 [b]Luke 24:27; Acts 17:2; 18:28; 28:23 [c]Acts 5:42

36 [a]Acts 10:47

37 Late mss. insert verse 37: *And Philip said, "If you believe with all your heart, you may." And he answered and said "I believe that Jesus Christ is the Son of God."*

38 [1]Or, *carriage*

39 [a]1 Kin. 18:12; 2 Kin. 2:16; Ezek. 3:12, 14; 8:3; 11:1, 24; 43:5; 2 Cor. 12:2

40 [1]Or, *was found* [2]O.T.: Ashdod
[a]Josh. 11:22; 1 Sam. 5:1
[b]Acts 8:25 [c]Acts 9:30; 10:1, 24; 11:11; 12:19; 18:22; 21:8, 16; 23:23, 33; 25:1, 4, 6, 13

1 [1]Lit., *threat*
[a]Acts 9:1-22; 22:3-16; 26:9-18
[b]Acts 8:3; Acts 9:13-21

2 [a]Acts 22:5; 26:10; 9:14, 21 [b]Matt. 10:17 [c]Gen. 14:15; 2 Cor. 11:32; Gal. 1:17 [d]Acts 19:9, 23; 22:4; 24:14, 22; 18:25f.; John 14:6

3 [a]1 Cor. 15:8

4 [a]Acts 22:7; 26:14

6 [a]Acts 9:16

7 [1]Or, *sound*
[a]Acts 26:14 [b]Acts 22:9 [John 12:29f.]

8 [1]Lit., *was seeing*
[a]Acts 22:11; 9:18 [b]Gen. 14:15 2 Cor. 11:32; Gal. 1:17

10 [a]Gen. 14:15; 2 Cor. 11:32; Gal. 1:17 [b]Acts 22:12 [c]Acts 10:3, 17, 19; 11:5; 12:9; 16:9f.; 18:9

11 [a]Acts 9:30; 11:25; 21:39; 22:3

12 [1]Some mss. omit, *in a vision*
[a]Acts 9:17; Mark 5:23; Acts 6:6

about this man, [a]how much harm he did to [b]Thy [1]saints at
Jerusalem;
14 and here he [a]has authority from the chief priests to
bind all who [b]call upon Thy name."
15 But the Lord said to him, "Go, for [a]he is a chosen
[1]instrument of Mine, to bear My name before [b]the Gentiles
and [c]kings and the sons of Israel;
16 for [a]I will show him how much he must suffer for My
name's sake."
17 And Ananias departed and entered the house, and after
[a]laying his hands on him said, "[b]Brother Saul, the Lord Jesus,
who appeared to you on the road by which you were coming,
has sent me so that you may regain your sight, and be [c]filled
with the Holy Spirit."
18 And immediately there fell from his eyes something
like scales, and he regained his sight, and he arose and was
baptized;
19 and he took food and was strengthened.
Now [a]for several days he was with [b]the disciples who were
at Damascus,
20 and immediately he *began* to proclaim Jesus [a]in the
synagogues, [1]saying, "He is [b]the Son of God."
21 And all those hearing him continued to be amazed, and
were saying, "Is this not he who in Jerusalem [a]destroyed those
who [b]called on this name, and *who* had come here for the
purpose of bringing them bound before the chief priests?"
22 But Saul kept increasing in strength and confounding
the Jews who lived at Damascus by proving that this *Jesus* is
the [1]Christ.
23 And when [a]many days had elapsed, [b]the Jews plotted
together to do away with him,
24 but [a]their plot became known to Saul. And [b]they were
also watching the gates day and night so that they might put
him to death;
25 but his disciples took him by night, and let him down
through *an opening in* the wall, lowering him in a [a]basket.
26 And [a]when he had come to Jerusalem, he was trying to
associate with the disciples; and they were all afraid of him,
not believing that he was a disciple.
27 But [a]Barnabas took hold of him and brought him to
the apostles and described to them how he had [b]seen the Lord
on the road, and that He had talked to him, and how [c]at
Damascus he had [d]spoken out boldly in the name of Jesus.
28 And he was with them [1]moving about freely in Jerusalem, [a]speaking out boldly in the name of the Lord.
29 And he was talking and arguing with the [a]Hellenistic
Jews; but they were attempting to put him to death.
30 But when [a]the brethren learned *of it,* they brought him
down to [b]Caesarea and [c]sent him away to [d]Tarsus.
31 So [a]the church throughout all Judea and Galilee and
Samaria [1]enjoyed peace, being built up; and, going on in the
fear of the Lord and in the comfort of the Holy Spirit, it
continued to increase.
32 Now it came about that as Peter was traveling through
all *those parts,* he came down also to [a]the [1]saints who lived at
[b]Lydda.

13 [1]I.e., true believers; lit., *holy ones*
[a]Acts 8:3 [b]Acts 9:32, 41; 26:10; Rom 1:7; 15:25f., 31; 16:2, 15; 1 Cor. 1:2

14 [a]Acts 9:2, 21 [b]Acts 7:59

15 [1]Or, *vessel*
[a]Acts 13:2; Rom. 1:1; Gal. 1:15; Eph. 3:7; Rom. 9:23 [b]Rom. 1:5 marg.; 11:13; 15:16; Gal. 1:16; 2:7ff.; Eph. 3:2, 8; 1 Tim. 2:7; 2 Tim. 4:17; Acts 22:21; 26:17 [c]Acts 25:22f.; 26:1, 32; 2 Tim. 4:16

16 [a]Acts 20:23; 21:11 [4 and 13]; 1 Thess. 3:3; 2 Cor. 6:4f.; 11:23-27

17 [a]Acts 9:12; Mark 5:23; Acts 6:6 [b]Acts 22:13 [c]Acts 2:4

19 [a]Acts 26:20 [b]Acts 11:26; 9:26, 38

20 [1]Lit., *that*
[a]Acts 13:5, 14; 14:1; 17:2, 10; 18:4, 19; 19:8; 16:13; 28:17 [b]Matt. 4:3; Acts 13:33; 9:22

21 [a]Acts 8:3; 9:13; Gal. 1:13, 23 [b]Acts 9:14

22 [1]I.e., Messiah

23 [a]Gal. 1:17, 18 [b]1 Thess. 2:16

24 [a]Acts 20:3, 19; 23:12, 30; 25:3 [b]2 Cor. 11:32f.

25 [a]Matt. 15:37

26 [a]Acts 22:17-20; 26:20

27 [a]Acts 4:36 [b]Acts 9:3-6 [c]Acts 9:20, 22 [d]Acts 9:29; 4:13, 29

28 [1]Lit., *going in and going out*
[a]Acts 9:29; 4:13, 29

29 [a]Acts 6:1

30 [a]Acts 1:15 [b]Acts 8:40 [c]Gal. 1:21 [d]Acts 9:11

31 [1]Lit., *was having*
[a]Acts 5:11; 8:1; 16:5

32 [1]I.e., true believers; lit., *holy ones*
[a]Acts 9:13 [b]1 Chr. 8:12; Ezra 2:33; Neh. 7:37; 11:35

33 And there he found a certain man named Aeneas, who had been bedridden eight years, for he was paralyzed.

34 And Peter said to him, "Aeneas, Jesus Christ heals you; arise, and make your bed." And immediately he arose.

35 And all who lived at [a]Lydda and [b]Sharon saw him, and they [c]turned to the Lord.

36 Now in [a]Joppa there was a certain disciple named Tabitha (which translated *in Greek* is called [1]Dorcas); this woman was abounding with deeds of kindness and charity, which she continually did.

37 And it came about [1]at that time that she fell sick and died; and when they had washed her body, they laid it in an [a]upper room.

38 And since Lydda was near [a]Joppa, [b]the disciples, having heard that Peter was there, sent two men to him, entreating him, "Do not delay to come to us."

39 And Peter arose and went with them. And when he had come, they brought him into the [a]upper room; and all the [b]widows stood beside him weeping, and showing all the [1]tunics and garments that Dorcas used to make while she was with them.

40 But Peter [a]sent them all out and [b]knelt down and prayed, and turning to the body, he said, "[c]Tabitha, arise." And she opened her eyes, and when she saw Peter, she sat up.

41 And he gave her his hand and raised her up; and calling [a]the [1]saints and [b]widows, he presented her alive.

42 And it became known all over [a]Joppa, and [b]many believed in the Lord.

43 And it came about that he stayed many days in [a]Joppa with [b] a certain tanner, Simon.

CHAPTER 10

NOW *there was* a certain man at [a]Caesarea named Cornelius, a centurion of what was [b]called the Italian [1]cohort,

2 a devout man, and [a]one who feared God with all his household, and [b]gave many [1]alms to the *Jewish* people, and prayed to God continually.

3 About [a]the [1]ninth hour of the day he clearly saw [b]in a vision [c]an angel of God who had *just* come in to him, and said to him, "Cornelius!"

4 And [a]fixing his gaze upon him and being much alarmed, he said, "What is it, Lord?" And he said to him, "Your prayers and [1]alms [b]have ascended [c]as a memorial before God.

5 "And now dispatch *some* men to [a]Joppa, and send for a man *named* Simon, who is also called Peter;

6 he [1]is staying with a certain tanner *named* [a]Simon, whose house is by the sea."

7 And when the angel who was speaking to him had departed, he summoned two of his [1]servants and a devout soldier of those who were in constant attendance upon him,

8 and after he had explained everything to them, he sent them to [a]Joppa.

9 And on the next day, as they were on their way, and

35 [a]1 Chr. 8:12; Ezra 2:33; Neh. 7:37; 11:35 [b]1 Chr. 5:16; 27:29; Is. 33:9; 35:2; 65:10 [c]Acts 11:21; 2:47; 9:42

36 [1]Or, *Gazelle* [a]Josh. 19:46; 2 Chr. 2:16; Ezra 3:7; Jonah 1:3; Acts 9:38, 42f.; 10:5, 8, 23, 32; 11:5, 13

37 [1]Lit., *in those days* [a]Acts 9:39; 1:13

38 [a]Josh. 19:46; 2 Chr. 2:16; Ezra 3:7; Jonah 1:3; Acts 9:36, 42f.; 10:5, 8, 23, 32; 11:5, 13 [b]Acts 11:26

39 [1]Or, *inner garments* [a]Acts 9:37; 1:13 [b]Acts 6:1

40 [a]Matt. 9:25 [b]Acts 7:60; Luke 22:41 [c]Mark 5:41

41 [1]Note vs. 32 [a]Acts 9:13 [b]Acts 6:1

42 [a]Josh. 19:46; 2 Chr. 2:16; Jonah 1:3; Acts 9:38, 42f.; 10:5, 8, 23, 32; 11:5, 13 [b]Acts 9:35

43 [a]Josh. 19:46; 2 Chr. 2:16; Ezra 3:7; Jonah 1:3; Acts 9:38, 42f.; 10:5, 8, 23, 32; 11:15, 13 [b]Acts 10:6

1 [1]Or, *battalion* [a]Acts 8:40; 10:24 [b]Matt. 27:27; Mark 15:16; John 18:3, 12; Acts 21:31; 27:1

2 [1]Or, *gifts of charity* [a]Acts 10:22, 35; 13:16, 26 [b]Luke 7:4f.

3 [1]I.e., 3 p.m. [a]Acts 3:1 [b]Acts 9:10; 10:17, 19 [c]Acts 5:19

4 [1]Or, *deeds of charity* [a]Acts 3:4 [b]Rev. 8:4 [c]Matt. 26:13; Phil. 4:18; Heb. 6:10

5 [a]Acts 9:36

6 [1]Or, *is lodging* [a]Acts 9:43

7 [1]Or, *household slaves*

8 [a]Acts 9:36

approaching the city, [a]Peter went up on [b]the housetop about
[c]the [1]sixth hour to pray.
10 And he became hungry, and was desiring to eat; but
while they were making preparations, he [a]fell into a trance;
11 and he *beheld [a]the [1]sky opened up, and a certain
[2]object like a great sheet coming down, lowered by four corners to the ground,
12 and there were in it all *kinds of* four-footed animals and
[1]crawling creatures of the earth and birds of the [2]air.
13 And a voice came to him, "Arise, Peter, [1]kill and eat!"
14 But Peter said, "By no means, [a]Lord, for [b]I have never
eaten anything [1]unholy and unclean."
15 And again a voice *came* to him a second time, "[a]What
God has cleansed, no *longer* consider [1]unholy."
16 And this happened three times; and immediately the
[1]object was taken up into the [2]sky.
17 Now while Peter was greatly perplexed [1]in mind as to
what [a]the vision which he had seen might be, behold, [b]the men
who had been sent by Cornelius, having asked directions for
Simon's house, appeared at the gate;
18 and calling out, they were asking whether Simon, who
was also called Peter, was [1]staying there.
19 And while Peter was reflecting on [a]the vision, [b]the
Spirit said to him, "Behold, [1]three men are looking for you.
20 "But arise, go downstairs, and [a]accompany them [1]with-
out misgivings; for I have sent them Myself."
21 And Peter went down to the men and said, "Behold, I
am the one you are looking for; what is the reason for which
you have come?"
22 And they said, "Cornelius a centurion, a righteous and
[a]God-fearing man well spoken of by the entire nation of the
Jews, [b]was *divinely* directed by a [c]holy angel to send for you *to
come* to his house and hear [d]a [1]message from you."
23 And so he invited them in and gave them lodging.
And on the next day he arose and went away with them,
and [a]some of [b]the brethren from [c]Joppa accompanied him.
24 And on the following day he entered [a]Caesarea. Now
Cornelius was waiting for them, and had called together his
relatives and close friends.
25 And when it came about that Peter entered, Cornelius
met him, and fell at his feet and [1a]worshiped *him.*
26 But Peter raised him up, saying, "[a]Stand up; I too am
just a man."
27 And as he talked with him, he entered, and [1]found
[a]many people assembled.
28 And he said to them, "You yourselves know how [a]un-
lawful it is for a man who is a Jew to associate with a foreigner
or to visit him; and *yet* [b]God has shown me that I should not
call any man [1]unholy or unclean.
29 "That is why I came without even raising any objection
when I was sent for. And so I ask for what reason you have sent
for me."
30 And Cornelius said, "[a]Four days ago to this hour, I was
praying in my house during [b]the [1]ninth hour; and behold, [c]a
man stood before me in shining garments,

9 [1]I.e., noon [a]Acts 10:9-32; 11:5-14 [b]Matt. 24:17; Jer. 19:13; 32:29; Zeph. 1:5 [c]Acts 10:3; Ps. 55:17

10 [a]Acts 22:17; 11:5

11 [1]Or, *heaven* [2]Or, *vessel* [a]John 1:51

12 [1]Or possibly, *reptiles* [2]Or, *heaven*

13 [1]Or, *sacrifice*

14 [1]Or, *profane;* lit., *common* [a]Matt. 8:2ff.; John 4:11ff.; Acts 9:5; 22:8; [b]Acts 10:28; Ezek. 4:14; Dan. 1:8; Lev. 11:20-25; Deut. 14:4-20

15 [1]Lit., *make common* [a]Mark 7:19; Rom. 14:14; 1 Cor. 10:25ff.; 1 Tim. 4:4f.; Titus 1:15; Matt. 15:11

16 [1]Or, *vessel* [2]Or, *heaven*

17 [1]Lit., *himself* [a]Acts 10:3 [b]Acts 10:8

18 [1]Or, *lodging*

19 [1]One early ms. reads, *two* [a]Acts 10:3 [b]Acts 8:29

20 [1]Lit., *doubting nothing* [a]Acts 15:7-9

22 [1]Lit., *words* [a]Acts 10:2 [b]Matt. 2:12 [c]Mark 8:38; Luke 9:26; Rev. 14:10 [d]Acts 11:14

23 [a]Acts 10:45; 11:12 [b]Acts 1:15 [c]Acts 9:36

24 [a]Acts 10:1; 8:40

25 [1]Or, *prostrated himself in reverence* [a]Matt. 8:2

26 [a]Rev. 19:10; 22:8f.; Acts 14:15

27 [1]Lit., *finds* [a]Acts 10:24

28 [1]Or, *profane;* lit., *common* [a]Acts 11:3; John 4:9; 18:28 [b]Acts 10:14f.; 10:35; 15:9

30 [1]I.e., 3 to 4 p.m. [a]Acts 10:9, 22f. [b]Acts 10:3; 3:1 [c]Acts 10:30-32; 10:3-6

31 and he *said, 'Cornelius, your prayer has been heard
and your [1]alms have been remembered before God.
32 'Send therefore to [a]Joppa and invite Simon, who is also
called Peter, to come to you; he is [1]staying at the house of
Simon *the* tanner by the sea.'
33 "And so I sent to you immediately, and you have [1]been
kind enough to come. Now then, we are all here present before
God to hear all that you have been commanded by the Lord."
34 And [a]opening his mouth, Peter said:
"I most certainly understand *now* that [b]God is not one to
show partiality,
35 but [a]in every nation the man who [1b]fears Him and
[2]does what is right, is welcome to Him.
36 "[1]The word which He sent to the sons of Israel, [a]preach-
ing [2b]peace through Jesus Christ (He is [c]Lord of all)—
37 you yourselves know the thing which took place
throughout all Judea, starting from Galilee, after the baptism
which John proclaimed.
38 "[1]*You know of* [a]Jesus of Nazareth, how God [b]anointed
Him with the Holy Spirit and with power, [2c]and *how* He went
about doing good, and healing all who were oppressed by the
devil; for [d]God was with Him.
39 "And we are [a]witnesses of all the things He did both in
the [1]land of the Jews and in Jerusalem. And they also [b]put Him
to death by hanging Him on a [2]cross.
40 "[a]God raised Him up on the third day, and granted that
He should become visible,
41 [a]not to all the people, but to [b]witnesses who were chosen beforehand by God, *that is,* to us, [c]who ate and drank with
Him after He arose from the dead.
42 "And He [a]ordered us to [1]preach to the people, and solemnly to [b]testify that this is the One who has been [c]appointed
by God as [d]Judge of the living and the dead.
43 "Of Him [a]all the prophets bear witness that through
[b]His name every one who believes in Him has received forgiveness of sins."
44 While Peter was still speaking these words, [a]the Holy
Spirit fell upon all those who were listening to the [1]message.
45 And [a]all the [1]circumcised believers who had come with
Peter were amazed, because the gift of the Holy Spirit had
been [b]poured out upon the Gentiles also.
46 For they were hearing them [a]speaking with tongues and
exalting God. Then Peter [b]answered,
47 "[a]Surely no one can refuse the water for these to be
baptized who [b]have received the Holy Spirit just as we *did,* can
he?"
48 And he [a]ordered them to be baptized [b]in the name of
Jesus Christ. Then they asked him to stay on for a few days.

Chapter 11

NOW the apostles and [a]the brethren who were throughout
Judea heard that the Gentiles also had received the word of
God.
2 And when Peter came up to Jerusalem, [1a]those who
were circumcised took issue with him,

31 [1]Or, *deeds of charity*

32 [1]Or, *lodging*
[a]Acts 11:3; John 4:9; 18:28

33 [1]Lit., *done well in coming*

34 [a]Matt. 5:2 [b]Deut. 10:17; 2 Chr. 19:7; Rom. 2:11; Gal. 2:6; Eph. 6:9; Col. 3:25; 1 Pet. 1:17

35 [1]Or, *reverences* [2]Lit., *works righteousness*
[a]Acts 10:28 [b]Acts 10:2

36 [1]Some mss. read, *He sent the word to* [2]Or, *preaching the gospel of peace*
[a]Acts 13:32 [b]Luke 1:79; 2:14; Rom. 5:1; Eph. 2:17 [c]Rom. 10:12; Acts 2:36; Matt. 28:18

38 [1]Or, possibly, *how God anointed Jesus of Nazareth* [2]Lit., *who went*
[a]Acts 2:22 [b]Acts 4:26 [c]Matt. 4:23 [d]John 3:2

39 [1]Or, *countryside* [2]Lit., *wood*
[a]Luke 24:48; Acts 10:41
[b]Acts 5:30

40 [a]Acts 2:24

41 [a]John 14:19, 22; 15:27
[b]Luke 24:48; Acts 10:39
[c]Luke 24:43; Acts 1:4 marg.

42 [1]Or, *proclaim*
[a]Acts 1:2 [b]Luke 16:28 [c]Luke 22:22 [d]2 Tim. 4:1; 1 Pet. 4:5; John 5:22, 27; Acts 17:31

43 [a]Acts 3:18 [b]Luke 24:47; Acts 2:38; 4:12

44 [1]Lit., *word*
[a]Acts 11:15; 15:8

45 [1]Lit., *believers from among the circumcision;* i.e., Jewish Christians
[a]Acts 10:23 [b]Acts 2:33, 38

46 [a]Acts 2:4; 19:6; Mark 16:17 [b]Acts 3:12

47 [a]Acts 8:36 [b]Acts 10:44f.; 11:17; 15:8; 2:4

48 [a]1 Cor. 1:14-17 [b]Acts 2:38; 8:16; 19:5

1 [a]Acts 1:15

2 [1]Lit., *those of the circumcision; i.e.,* Jewish Christians
[a]Acts 10:45

3 saying, "[a]You [1]went to uncircumcised men and ate
with them."
4 But Peter began *speaking* and *proceeded* to explain to
them [a]in orderly sequence, saying,
5 "[a]I was in the city of Joppa praying; and in a trance I saw
[b]a vision, a certain [1]object coming down like a great sheet
lowered by four corners from [2]the sky; and it came right down
to me,
6 and when I had fixed my gaze upon it and was observing it [1]I saw the four-footed animals of the earth and the wild
beasts and the [2]crawling creatures and the birds of the [3]air.
7 "And I also heard a voice saying to me, 'Arise, Peter;
[1]kill and eat.'
8 "But I said, 'By no means, Lord, for nothing [1]unholy or
unclean has ever entered my mouth.'
9 "But a voice from heaven answered a second time, '[a]What
God has cleansed, no longer [1]consider unholy.'
10 "And this happened three times, and everything was
drawn back up into [1]the sky.
11 "And behold, at that moment three men appeared before the house in which we were *staying*, having been sent to
me from [a]Caesarea.
12 "And [a]the Spirit told me to go with them [1b]without
misgivings. And [c]these six brethren also went with me, and we
entered the man's house.
13 "And he reported to us how he had seen the angel [1]stand-
ing in his house, and saying, 'Send to Joppa, and have Simon,
who is also called Peter, brought here;
14 and he shall speak [a]words to you by which you will be
saved, you and [b]all your household.'
15 "And as I began to speak, [a]the Holy Spirit fell upon
them, just [b]as *He did* upon us at the beginning.
16 "And I remembered the word of the Lord, how He used
to say, '[a]John baptized with water, but you shall be baptized
[1]with the Holy Spirit.'
17 "If [a]God therefore gave to them the same gift as *He
gave* to us also after believing in the Lord Jesus Christ, [b]who
was I that I could [1]stand in God's way?"
18 And when they heard this, they [1]quieted down, and
[a]glorified God, saying, "Well then, God has granted to the
Gentiles also the [b]repentance *that leads* to life."
19 [a]So then those who were scattered because of the [1]per-
secution that arose in connection with Stephen made their way
[2]to [b]Phoenicia and [c]Cyprus and [d]Antioch, speaking the word
to no one except to Jews alone.
20 But there were some of them, men of [a]Cyprus and
[b]Cyrene, who came to [c]Antioch and *began* speaking to the
[1d]Greeks also, [2e]preaching the Lord Jesus.
21 And [a]the hand of the Lord was with them, and [b]a large
number who believed turned to the Lord.
22 And the [1]news about them [2]reached the ears of the
church at Jerusalem, and they sent [a]Barnabas off [3]to [b]Antioch.
23 Then when he had come and [1]witnessed [a]the grace of
God, he rejoiced and *began* to encourage them all with [2]reso-
lute heart to remain *true* to the Lord;
24 for he was a good man, and [a]full of the Holy Spirit and

3 [1]Or, *entered the house of* [a]Matt. 9:11; Gal 2:12; Acts 10:28

4 [a]Luke 1:3

5 [1]Or, *vessel* [2]Or, *heaven* [a]Acts 11:5-14; Acts 10:9-32 [b]Acts 9:10

6 [1]Lit., *and I saw* [2]Or possibly, *reptiles* [3]Or, *heaven*

7 [1]Or, *sacrifice*

8 [1]Or, *profane;* lit., *common*

9 [1]Lit., *make common* [a]Acts 10:15

10 [1]Or, *heaven*

11 [a]Acts 8:40

12 [1]Or, *without making any distinction* [a]Acts 8:29 [b]Acts 15:9; Rom. 3:22 [c]Acts 10:23

13 [1]Or, *after he had stood in his house and said*

14 [a]Acts 10:22 [b]Acts 10:2; 16:15, 31-34; 18:8; John 4:53; 1 Cor. 1:16

15 [a]Acts 10:44 [b]Acts 2:4

16 [1]Or, *in* [a]Acts 1:5

17 [1]Or, *prevent God* [a]Acts 10:45, 47 [b]Acts 5:39

18 [1]Lit., *became silent* [a]Matt. 9:8 [b]2 Cor. 7:10

19 [1]Or, *tribulation* [2]Lit., *as far as* [a]Acts 8:1, 4 [b]Acts 15:3; 21:2 [c]Acts 4:36 [d]Acts 11:20, 22, 27; 6:5; 13:1; 14:26; 15:22f. 30, 35; 18:22; Gal. 2:11

20 [1]Some mss. read, *Greek-speaking Jews* [2]Or, *bringing the good news of* [a]Acts 4:36 [b]Acts 2:10; 6:9; 13:1; Matt. 27:32 [c]Acts 11:19, 22, 27; 6:5; 13:1; 14:26; 15:22f. 30, 35; 18:22; Gal. 2:11 [d]John 7:35 [e]Acts 5:42

21 [a]Luke 1:66 [b]Acts 2:47

22 [1]Lit., *word* [2]Lit., *was heard in* [3]Lit., *as far as* [a]Acts 4:36 [b]Acts 11:19, 20, 27; 6:5; 13:1; 14:26; 15:22f. 30, 35; 18:22; Gal. 2:11

23 [1]Lit., *seen* [2]Lit., *purpose of heart* [a]Acts 13:43; 14:26; 15:40; 20:24, 32

24 [a]Acts 2:4

of faith. And [b]considerable [1]numbers were [2]brought to the
Lord.
25 And he left for [a]Tarsus to look for Saul;
26 and when he had found him, he brought him to
[a]Antioch. And it came about that for an entire year they [1]met
with the church, and taught considerable [2]numbers; and [b]the
disciples were first called [c]Christians in [a]Antioch.
27 Now [1]at this time [a]some prophets [b]came down from
Jerusalem to [c]Antioch.
28 And one of them named [a]Agabus stood up and *began*
to indicate [1]by the Spirit that there would certainly be a great
famine [b]all over the [2]world. And this took place in the *reign* of
[c]Claudius.
29 And in the proportion that any of [a]the disciples had
means, each of them determined to send *a contribution* for
the [1]relief of [b]the brethren living in Judea.
30 [a]And this they did, sending it [1]in charge of [b]Barnabas
and Saul to the [c]elders.

Chapter 12

NOW about that time [1]Herod the king laid hands on some
who belonged to the church, in order to mistreat them.
2 And he [a]had James the brother of John [b]put to death
with a sword.
3 And when he saw that it [a]pleased the Jews, he proceeded to arrest Peter also. Now [1]it was during [b]the days of *the
Feast of* Unleavened Bread.
4 And when he had seized him, he put him in prison,
delivering him to four [1a]squads of soldiers to guard him, intending after [b]the Passover to bring him out before the people.
5 So Peter was kept in the prison, but prayer for him was
being made fervently by the church to God.
6 And on the very night when Herod was about to bring
him forward, Peter was sleeping between two soldiers, [a]bound
with two chains; and guards in front of the door were watching
over the prison.
7 And behold, [a]an angel of the Lord suddenly [b]appeared,
and a light shone in the cell; and he struck Peter's side and
roused him, saying, "Get up quickly." And [c]his chains fell off
his hands.
8 And the angel said to him, "Gird yourself and [1]put on
your sandals." And he did so. And he *said to him, "Wrap
your cloak around you and follow me."
9 And he went out and continued to follow, and he did
not know that what was being done by the angel was real, but
thought he was seeing [a]a vision.
10 And when they had passed the first and second guard,
they came to the iron gate that leads into the city, which
[a]opened for them by itself; and they went out and went along
one street; and immediately the angel departed from him.
11 And when Peter [a]came to himself, he said, "Now I
know for sure that [b]the Lord has sent forth His angel and
rescued me from the hand of Herod and from all [1]that the
Jewish people were expecting."
12 And when he realized *this*, he went to the house of

24 [1]Lit., *multitudes* [2]Lit., *added* [b]Acts 5:14; 2:47; 11:21

25 [a]Acts 9:11

26 [1]Or, *were gathered together* [2]Lit., *multitude* [a]Acts 11:20, 22, 27; 6:5; 13:1; 14:26; 15:22f., 30, 35; 18:22; Gal. 2:11 [b]Acts 6:1f.; 9:19, 26, 38; 11:29; 13:52; 14:20, 22, 28; John 2:2; Acts 9:25; 1:15 [c]Acts 26:28; 1 Pet. 4:16

27 [1]Lit., *in these days* [a]Acts 13:1; 2:17; Luke 11:49; 1 Cor. 12:10, 28f. [b]Acts 18:22 [c]Acts 11:20, 22, 26; 6:5; 13:1; 14:26; 15:22f., 30, 35; 18:22; Gal. 2:11

28 [1]Or, *through* [2]Lit., *inhabited earth* [a]Acts 21:10 [b]Matt. 24:14 [c]Acts 18:2

29 [1]Lit., *service* [a]Acts 6:1f.; 9:19, 26, 38; Acts 11:26; 13:52; 14:20, 22, 28; John 2:2; Acts 9:25; 1:15 [b]Acts 11:1

30 [1]Lit., *through the hand of* [a]Acts 12:25 [b]Acts 4:36 [c]Acts 14:23; 15:2, 4, 6, 22f.; 16:4; 20:17; 21:18; 1 Tim. 5:17, 19; Titus 1:5; James 5:14; 1 Pet. 5:1; 2 John 1; 3 John 1

1 [1]I.e., Herod Agrippa I

2 [a]Matt. 4:21; 20:23 [b]Mark 10:39

3 [1]Lit., *they were the days* [a]Acts 24:27; 25:9 [b]Ex. 12:15; 23:15; Acts 20:6

4 [1]Lit., *quaternions*; one quaternion is composed of four soldiers [a]John 19:23 [b]Mark 14:1; Acts 12:3

6 [a]Acts 21:33

7 [a]Acts 5:19 [b]Luke 2:9; 24:4 [c]Acts 16:26

8 [1]Lit., *bind*

9 [a]Acts 9:10

10 [a]Acts 5:19; 16:26

11 [1]Lit., *the expectation of the people of the Jews* [a]Luke 15:17 [b]Dan. 3:28; 6:22

12 [a]Acts 12:25; 13:5, 13; 15:37, 39; Col. 4:10; 2 Tim. 4:11; Philem. 24; 1 Pet. 5:13 [b]Acts 12:5

13 [a]John 18:16f.

14 [a]Luke 24:41

15 [a]Matt. 18:10

17 [1]Or, *Jacob* [a]Acts 13:16; 19:33; 21:40 [b]Acts 15:13; 21:18; 1 Cor. 15:7; Gal. 1:19; 2:9, 12; Mark 6:3 [c]Acts 1:15

18 [1]Lit., *what therefore had become*

19 [a]Acts 16:27; 27:42 [b]Acts 8:40

20 [a]Matt. 11:21 [b]1 Kin. 5:11; Ezra 3:7; Ezek. 27:17

21 [1]Or, *judgment-seat*

23 [1]Lit., *breathed his last* [a]Acts 5:19; 2 Sam. 24:16; 2 Kin. 19:35

24 [a]Acts 6:7; 19:20

25 [1]Some ancient mss. read, *to Jerusalem* [2]Lit., *ministry* [a]Acts 13:1ff.; 4:36 [b]Acts 11:30 [c]Acts 12:12

1 [a]Acts 11:19 [b]Acts 11:26 [c]Acts 11:27; 15:32; 1 Cor. 14:29, 32, 37; Acts 19:6; 21:9; 1 Cor. 11:4f.; 13:2, 8f. [d]1 Cor. 12:28f.; Eph. 4:11; Rom. 12:6f.; James 3:1 [e]Acts 13:1ff.; 4:36 [f]Matt. 27:32; Acts 11:20 [g]Matt. 14:1

2 [a]Acts 8:29; 13:4 [b]Acts 13:1ff.; 4:36 [c]Acts 9:15

3 [a]Acts 1:24 [b]Acts 6:6 [c]Acts 14:26; 13:4

4 [a]Acts 13:2f. [b]Acts 4:36

5 [a]Acts 9:20; 13:14 [b]Acts 12:12

Mary, the mother of [a]John who was also called Mark, where
many were gathered together and [b]were praying.
13 And when he knocked at the door of the gate, [a]a
servant-girl named Rhoda came to answer.
14 And when she recognized Peter's voice, [a]because of her
joy she did not open the gate, but ran in and announced that
Peter was standing in front of the gate.
15 And they said to her, "You are out of your mind!" But
she kept insisting that it was so. And they kept saying, "It is [a]his
angel."
16 But Peter continued knocking; and when they had
opened, they saw him and were amazed.
17 But [a]motioning to them with his hand to be silent, he
described to them how the Lord had led him out of the prison.
And he said, "Report these things to [1b]James and [c]the brethren."
And he departed and went to another place.
18 Now when day came, there was no small disturbance
among the soldiers *as to* [1]what could have become of Peter.
19 And when Herod had searched for him and had not
found him, he examined the guards and ordered that they [a]be
led away *to execution.* And he went down from Judea to
[b]Caesarea and was spending time there.
20 Now he was very angry with the people of [a]Tyre and
Sidon; and with one accord they came to him, and having won
over Blastus the king's chamberlain, they were asking for
peace, because [b]their country was fed by the king's country.
21 And on an appointed day Herod, having put on his
royal apparel, took his seat on the [1]rostrum and *began* delivering
an address to them.
22 And the people kept crying out, "The voice of a god
and not of a man!"
23 And immediately [a]an angel of the Lord struck him
because he did not give God the glory, and he was eaten by
worms and [1]died.
24 But [a]the word of the Lord continued to grow and to be
multiplied.
25 And [a]Barnabas and [a]Saul returned [1]from Jerusalem
[b]when they had fulfilled their [2]mission, taking along with *them*
[c]John, who was also called Mark.

Chapter 13

NOW there were at [a]Antioch, in the [b]church that was *there,*
[c]prophets and [d]teachers: [e]Barnabas, and Simeon who was
called Niger, and Lucius of [f]Cyrene, and Manaen who had
been brought up with [g]Herod the tetrarch, and [e]Saul.
2 And while they were ministering to the Lord and fasting,
[a]the Holy Spirit said, "Set apart for Me [b]Barnabas and
Saul for [c]the work to which I have called them."
3 Then, when they had fasted and [a]prayed and [b]laid their
hands on them, [c]they sent them away.
4 So, being [a]sent out by the Holy Spirit, they went down
to Seleucia and from there they sailed to [b]Cyprus.
5 And when they reached Salamis, they *began* to proclaim
the word of God in [a]the synagogues of the Jews; and they
also had [b]John as their helper.

6 And when they had gone through the whole island as
far as Paphos, they found a certain [a]magician, a Jewish [b]false
prophet whose name was Bar-Jesus,
7 who was with the [a]proconsul, Sergius Paulus, a man of
intelligence. This man summoned Barnabas and Saul and
sought to hear the word of God.
8 But Elymas the [a]magician (for thus his name is translated) was opposing them, seeking to turn the [b]proconsul
away from [c]the faith.
9 But Saul, who was also *known as* Paul, [1a]filled with the
Holy Spirit, fixed his gaze upon him,
10 and said, "You who are full of all deceit and fraud, you
[a]son of the devil, you enemy of all righteousness, will you not
cease to make crooked [b]the straight ways of the Lord?
11 "And now, behold, [a]the hand of the Lord is upon you,
and you will be blind and not see the sun for a time." And
immediately a mist and a darkness fell upon him, and he went
about seeking those who would lead him by the hand.
12 Then the [a]proconsul believed when he saw what had
happened, being amazed at [b]the teaching of the Lord.
13 Now Paul and his companions put out to sea from
[a]Paphos and came to [b]Perga in [c]Pamphylia; and [d]John left
them and returned to Jerusalem.
14 But going on from Perga, they arrived at [a]Pisidian [b]An-
tioch, and on [c]the Sabbath day they went into [d]the synagogue
and sat down.
15 And after [a]the reading of the Law and [b]the Prophets
[c]the synagogue officials sent to them, saying, "Brethren, if you
have any word of exhortation for the people, say it."
16 And Paul stood up, and [a]motioning with his hand, he
said,
"**M**en of Israel, and [b]you who fear God, listen:
17 "The God of this people Israel [a]chose our fathers, and
[1]made the people great during their stay in the land of Egypt,
and with an uplifted arm He led them out from it.
18 "And for about [a]a period of forty years [b]He [1]put up with
them in the wilderness.
19 "And [a]when He had destroyed [b]seven nations in the land
of Canaan, He [c]distributed their land as an inheritance—*all of
which took* [d]about four hundred and fifty years.
20 "And after these things He [a]gave *them* judges until [b]Sam-
uel the prophet.
21 "And then they [a]asked for a king, and God gave them
[b]Saul the son of Kish, a man of the tribe of Benjamin, for forty
years.
22 "And after He had [a]removed him, He raised up David to
be their king, concerning whom He also testified and said, 'I
have found [b]David the son of Jesse, a man after My heart, who
will do all My [1]will.'
23 "[a]From the offspring of this man [b]according to promise
God has brought to Israel [c]a Savior, Jesus,
24 after [a]John had proclaimed before [1]His coming a baptism of repentance to all the people of Israel.
25 "And while John [a]was completing his course, [b]he kept
saying, 'What do you suppose that I am? I am not *He.* But

6 [a]Acts 8:9 [b]Matt. 7:15

7 [a]Acts 13:8, 12; 18:12; 19:38

8 [a]Acts 8:9 [b]Acts 13:7, 12; Acts 18:12; 19:38 [c]Acts 6:7

9 [1]Or, *having just been filled* [a]Acts 4:8; 2:4

10 [a]Matt. 13:38; John 8:44 [b]Hos. 14:9; 2 Pet. 2:15

11 [a]Ex. 9:3; 1 Sam. 5:6f.; Ps. 32:4; Job 19:21; Heb. 10:31

12 [a]Acts 13:7, 8; 18:12; 19:38 [b]Acts 13:49; 8:25; 15:35f.; 19:10, 20

13 [a]Acts 13:6 [b]Acts 14:25 [c]Acts 2:10; 14:24; 15:38; 27:5 [d]Acts 12:12

14 [a]Acts 14:24 [b]Acts 14:19, 21; 2 Tim. 3:11 [c]Acts 13:42, 44; 16:13; 18:4; 17:2 [d]Acts 9:20; 13:5

15 [a]Acts 15:21; 2 Cor. 3:14f. [b]Acts 13:27 [c]Mark 5:22

16 [a]Acts 12:17 [b]Acts 10:2; 13:26

17 [1]Or, *exalted* [a]Deut. 7:6-8; Ex. 6:1, 6; 13:14, 16; Acts 7:17ff.

18 [1]Some ancient mss. read, *bore them up in His arms as a nurse in the wilderness* [a]Acts 7:36 [b]Deut. 1:31

19 [a]Acts 7:45 [b]Deut. 7:1 [c]Josh. 19:51; Ps. 78:55 [d]Judg. 11:26; 1 Kin. 6:1

20 [a]Judg. 2:16 [b]Acts 3:24

21 [a]1 Sam. 8:5 [b]1 Sam. 10:1; 9:1f.

22 [1]Lit., *wills* [a]1 Sam. 15:23, 26, 28; 16:1, 13 [b]1 Sam. 13:14; Ps. 89:20; Acts 7:46

23 [a]Matt. 1:1 [b]Acts 13:32f. [c]Luke 2:11; John 4:42

24 [1]Lit., *the face of His entering* [a]Mark 1:1-4; Acts 1:22; 19:4

25 [a]Acts 20:24 [b]John 1:20, 27; Matt. 3:11; Mark 1:7; Luke 3:16

behold, one is coming after me the sandals of whose feet I am
not worthy to untie.'
26 "Brethren, sons of Abraham's family, and those among
you who fear God, to us the word of [a]this salvation is sent out.
27 "For those who live in Jerusalem, and their [a]rulers, [b]rec-
ognizing neither Him nor the [1]utterances of [c]the prophets
which are [d]read every Sabbath, fulfilled *these* by condemning
Him.
28 "And though they found no ground for *putting Him to*
death, they [a]asked Pilate that He be [1]executed.
29 "And when they had [a]carried out all that was written
concerning Him, [b]they took Him down from [c]the [1]cross and
laid Him in a tomb.
30 "But God [a]raised Him from the dead;
31 and for many days He appeared to those who came up
with Him [a]from Galilee to Jerusalem, the very ones who are
now [b]His witnesses to the people.
32 "And we [a]preach to you the good news of [b]the promise
made to the fathers,
33 that God has fulfilled this *promise* [1]to our children in
that He [a]raised up Jesus, as it is also written in the second
Psalm, '[b]THOU ART MY SON; TODAY I HAVE BEGOTTEN THEE.'
34 "*And as for the fact* that He [a]raised Him up from the
dead, no more to return to decay, He has spoken in this way:
'[b]I WILL GIVE YOU THE HOLY *and* SURE *blessings* OF DAVID.'
35 "Therefore He also says in another *Psalm,* '[a]THOU WILT
NOT [1]ALLOW THY [2]HOLY ONE TO [3]UNDERGO DECAY.'
36 "For [a]David, after he had [1]served [b]the purpose of God
in his own generation, [c]fell asleep, and was laid among his
fathers, and [2]underwent decay;
37 but He whom God [a]raised did not [1]undergo decay.
38 "Therefore let it be known to you, brethren, that
[a]through [1]Him forgiveness of sins is proclaimed to you,
39 and through Him [a]everyone who believes is [1]freed[2]
from all things, from which you could not be [1]freed through
the Law of Moses.
40 "Take heed therefore, so that the thing spoken of [a]in the
Prophets may not come upon *you:*
41 '[a]BEHOLD, YOU SCOFFERS, AND MARVEL, AND [1]PERISH;
FOR I AM ACCOMPLISHING A WORK IN YOUR DAYS,
A WORK WHICH YOU WILL NEVER BELIEVE, THOUGH SOME-
ONE SHOULD DESCRIBE IT TO YOU.' "
42 And as [1]Paul and Barnabas were going out, [2]the people
kept begging that these [3]things might be spoken to them the
next [a]Sabbath.
43 Now when *the meeting of* the synagogue had broken
up, many of the Jews and of the [a]God-fearing [1b]proselytes
followed Paul and Barnabas, who, speaking to them, were
urging them to continue in [c]the grace of God.
44 And the next [a]Sabbath nearly the whole city assembled
to hear the word of [1]God.
45 But when [a]the Jews saw the crowds, they were filled
with jealousy, and *began* contradicting the things spoken by
Paul, and were [1]blaspheming.
46 And Paul and Barnabas spoke out boldly and said, "It
was necessary that the word of God should be spoken to you

26 [a]Acts 28:28; Acts 5:20; 4:12; 13:46; John 6:68

27 [1]Lit., *voices* [a]Luke 23:13 [b]Acts 3:17 [c]Luke 24:27 [d]Acts 13:15

28 [1]Lit., *destroyed* [a]Acts 3:14

29 [1]Lit., *wood* [a]Acts 26:22 [b]Luke 23:53 [c]Acts 5:30

30 [a]Acts 13:33, 34, 37; 2:24

31 [a]Acts 1:11 [b]Luke 24:48

32 [a]Acts 5:42; 14:15 [b]Acts 26:6; Rom. 1:2; 4:13; 9:4; Acts 13:23

33 [1]Some mss. read, *to us their children* [a]Acts 13:30, 34, 37; 2:24 [b]Ps. 2:7

34 [a]Acts 13:30, 33, 37; 2:24 [b]Is. 55:3

35 [1]Lit., *give* [2]Or, *Devout,* or, *Pious* [3]Lit., *see corruption* [a]Ps. 16:10; Acts 2:27

36 [1]Or, *served his own generation by the purpose of God* [2]Lit., *saw corruption* [a]Acts 2:29 [b]Acts 13:22; 20:27 [c]Acts 8:1; 1 Kin. 2:10

37 [1]Lit., *see corruption* [a]Acts 13:30, 33, 34; 2:24

38 [1]Lit., *this One* [a]Luke 24:47; Acts 2:38

39 [1]Lit., *justified* [2]In the Greek text the remainder of this vs. is part of vs. 38 [a]Rom. 3:28; 10:4; Acts 10:43

40 [a]John 6:45; Acts 7:42; Luke 24:44

41 [1]Lit., *disappear* [a]Hab. 1:5

42 [1]Lit., *they were* [2]Lit., *they* [3]Lit., *words* [a]Acts 13:14

43 [1]I.e., Gentile converts to Judaism [a]Acts 13:50; 17:4, 17; Acts 16:14; 18:7 [b]Matt. 23:15 [c]Acts 11:23

44 [1]Some ancient mss. read, *the Lord* [a]Acts 13:14

45 [1]Or, *reviling* [a]Acts 13:50; 14:2, 4, 5, 19; 1 Thess. 2:16

[a]first; since you repudiate it, and judge yourselves unworthy of
eternal life, behold, [b]we are turning to the Gentiles.
47 "For thus the Lord has commanded us,
'[a]I HAVE PLACED YOU AS A [b]LIGHT FOR THE GENTILES,
THAT YOU SHOULD [1]BRING SALVATION TO THE END OF
THE EARTH.'"
48 And when the Gentiles heard this, they *began* rejoicing
and glorifying [a]the word of [1]the Lord; and as many as [b]had
been appointed to eternal life believed.
49 And [a]the word of the Lord was being spread through
the whole region.
50 But [a]the Jews aroused the [1b]devout women [c]of promi-
nence and the leading men of the city, and instigated a persecution against Paul and Barnabas, and drove them out of their
[2]district.
51 But [a]they shook off the dust of their feet *in protest*
against them and went to [b]Iconium.
52 And the disciples were continually [a]filled with joy and
with the Holy Spirit.

CHAPTER 14

AND it came about that in [a]Iconium [b]they entered the synagogue of the Jews together, and spoke in such a manner [c]that a
great multitude believed, both of Jews and of [d]Greeks.
2 But [a]the Jews who [1b]disbelieved stirred up the [2]minds
of the Gentiles, and embittered them against [c]the brethren.
3 Therefore they spent a long time *there* [a]speaking boldly
with reliance upon the Lord, who was bearing witness to
the word of His grace, granting that [1b]signs and wonders be
done by their hands.
4 [a]But the multitude of the city was divided; and some
[1]sided with [b]the Jews, and some with [c]the apostles.
5 And when an attempt was made by both the Gentiles
and [a]the Jews with their rulers, to mistreat and to [b]stone them,
6 they became aware of it and fled to the cities of [a]Ly-
caonia, [b]Lystra and [c]Derbe, and the surrounding region;
7 and there they continued to [a]preach the gospel.
8 And at [a]Lystra there was sitting [b]a certain man, without
strength in his feet, lame from his mother's womb, who had
never walked.
9 This man was listening to Paul as he spoke, who, [a]when
he had fixed his gaze upon him, and had seen that he had
[b]faith to be [1]made well,
10 said with a loud voice, "Stand upright on your feet."
[a]And he leaped up and *began* to walk.
11 And when the multitudes saw what Paul had done, they
raised their voice, saying in the [a]Lycaonian language, "[b]The
gods have become like men and have come down to us."
12 And they *began* calling Barnabas, [1]Zeus, and Paul,
[2]Hermes, because he was [3]the chief speaker.
13 And the priest of Zeus, whose *temple* was [1]just outside
the city, brought oxen and garlands to the gates, and [a]wanted
to offer sacrifice with the crowds.
14 But when [a]the apostles, Barnabas and Paul, heard of it,
they [b]tore their [1]robes and rushed out into the crowd, crying
out

46 [a]Acts 3:26; 13:5, 14; 9:20 [b]Acts 18:6; 22:21; 26:20; 28:28; 19:9, 15

47 [1]Lit., *be for salvation* [a]Is. 49:6 [b]Luke 2:32

48 [1]Some ancient mss. read, *God* [a]Acts 13:12 [b]Rom. 8:28ff.; Eph. 1:4f., 11

49 [a]Acts 13:12

50 [1]Or, *worshipping* [2]Lit., *boundaries* [a]Acts 13:45; 14:2, 4, 5, 19; 1 Thess. 2:16 [b]Acts 13:43; 17:4, 17; 16:14; 18:7 [c]Mark 15:43

51 [a]Matt. 10:14; Acts 18:6 [b]Acts 14:1, 19, 21; 16:2; 2 Tim. 3:11

52 [a]Acts 2:4

1 [a]Acts 13:51; 14:19, 21; 16:2; 2 Tim. 3:11 [b]Acts 13:5 [c]Acts 2:47 [d]John 7:35; Acts 18:4

2 [1]Or, *disobeyed* [2]Lit., *souls* [a]Acts 13:45, 50; 14:4, 5, 19; 1 Thess. 2:16 [b]John 3:36 [c]Acts 1:15

3 [1]Or, *attesting miracles* [a]Acts 4:29f.; 20:32; Heb. 2:4 [b]John 4:48

4 [1]Lit., *were* [a]Acts 17:4f.; 19:9; 28:24 [b]Acts 13:45, 50; 14:2, 5, 19; 1 Thess. 2:16 [c]Acts 14:14

5 [a]Acts 13:45, 50; 14:2, 4, 19; 1 Thess. 2:16 [b]Acts 14:19

6 [a]Acts 14:11 [b]Acts 14:8, 21; 16:1f.; 2 Tim. 3:11 [c]Acts 14:20; 16:1; 20:4

7 [a]Acts 14:21; 16:10; 14:15

8 [a]Acts 14:6, 21; Acts 16:1f.; 2 Tim. 3:11 [b]Acts 3:2

9 [1]Lit., *saved* [a]Acts 3:4; 10:4 [b]Matt. 9:28

10 [a]Acts 3:8

11 [a]Acts 14:6 [b]Acts 8:10; 28:6

12 [1]Lat., Jupiter [2]Lat., Mercurius [3]Lit., *the leader of the speaking*

13 [1]Lit., *in front of* [a]Dan. 2:46

14 [1]Or, *outer garments* [a]Acts 14:4 [b]Num. 14:6; Matt. 26:65; Mark 14:63

15 and saying, "Men, why are you doing these things? We are also [a]men of the same nature as you, and [b]preach the gospel to you in order that you should turn from these [1c]vain things to a [d]living God, [e]WHO MADE THE HEAVEN AND THE EARTH AND THE SEA, AND ALL THAT IS IN THEM.

16 "[1]And in the generations gone by He [a]permitted all the [2]nations to [b]go their own ways;

17 and yet [a]He did not leave Himself without witness, in that He did good and [b]gave you rains from heaven and fruitful seasons, [1]satisfying your hearts with food and gladness."

18 And *even* saying these things, they with difficulty restrained the crowds from offering sacrifice to them.

19 But [a]Jews came from [b]Antioch and [c]Iconium, and having won over the multitudes, they [d]stoned Paul and [1]dragged him out of the city, supposing him to be dead.

20 But while [a]the disciples stood around him, he arose and entered the city. And the next day he went away with Barnabas to [b]Derbe.

21 And after they had [a]preached the gospel to that city and had [b]made many disciples, they returned to [c]Lystra and to [d]Iconium and to [e]Antioch,

22 strengthening the souls of [a]the disciples, encouraging them to continue in [b]the faith, and *saying*, "[c]Through many tribulations we must enter the kingdom of God."

23 And when [a]they had appointed [b]elders for them in every church, having [c]prayed with fasting, they [d]commended them to the Lord in whom they had believed.

24 And they passed through [a]Pisidia and came into [b]Pamphylia.

25 And when they had spoken the word in [a]Perga, they went down to Attalia;

26 and from there they sailed to [a]Antioch, from [b]which they had been [c]commended to the grace of God for the work that they had [1]accomplished.

27 And when they had arrived and gathered the church together, they *began* to [a]report all things that God had done with them and [1]how He had opened a [b]door of faith to the Gentiles.

28 And they spent [1]a long time with [a]the disciples.

Chapter 15

AND [a]some men came down from Judea and *began* teaching [b]the brethren, "Unless you are [c]circumcised according to [d]the custom of Moses, you cannot be saved."

2 And when Paul and Barnabas had [1]great dissension and [a]debate with them, [2b]*the brethren* determined that Paul and Barnabas and certain others of them, should go up to Jerusalem to the [c]apostles and elders concerning this issue.

3 Therefore, being [a]sent on their way by the church, they were passing through both [b]Phoenicia and Samaria, [c]describing in detail the conversion of the Gentiles, and were bringing great joy to all [d]the brethren.

4 And when they arrived at Jerusalem, they were received by the church and [a]the apostles and the elders, and they [b]reported all that God had done with them.

15 [1]I.e., idols [a]James 5:17; Acts 10:26 [b]Acts 13:32; Acts 14:7, 21 [c]Deut. 32:21; 1 Sam. 12:21; Jer. 8:19; 14:22; 1 Cor. 8:4 [d]Matt. 16:16 [e]Ex. 20:11; Ps. 146:6; Rev. 14:7; Acts 4:24; 17:24

16 [1]Lit., *who in the generations gone by permitted* [2]Or, *Gentiles* [a]Acts 17:30 [b]Mic. 4:5; Ps. 81:12

17 [1]Lit., *filling* [a]Acts 17:26f.; Rom. 1:19f. [b]Deut. 11:14; Job 5:10; Ps. 65:10f.; Ezek. 34:26f.; Joel 2:23

19 [1]Lit., *were dragging* [a]Acts 13:45, 50; 14:2, 4, 5; 1 Thess. 2:16 [b]Acts 13:14; 14:21, 26 [c]Acts 13:51; 14:1, 21 [d]Acts 14:5; 2 Cor. 11:25; 2 Tim. 3:11

20 [a]Acts 11:26; 14:22, 28 [b]Acts 14:6

21 [a]Acts 14:7 [b]Acts 2:47 [c]Acts 14:6 [d]Acts 13:51; 14:1, 19 [e]Acts 13:14; Acts 14:19, 26

22 [a]Acts 11:26; Acts 14:28 [b]Acts 6:7 [c]John 16:33; 1 Thess. 3:3; 2 Tim. 3:12; Mark 10:30; John 15:18, 20; 1 Pet. 2:21; Rev. 1:9; Acts 9:16

23 [a]Titus 1:5; 2 Cor. 8:19 [b]Acts 11:30 [c]Acts 13:3; 1:24 [d]Acts 20:32

24 [a]Acts 13:14 [b]Acts 13:13

25 [a]Acts 13:13

26 [1]Lit., *fulfilled* [a]Acts 11:19 [b]Acts 13:3 [c]Acts 15:40; 11:23

27 [1]Lit., *that* [a]Acts 15:4; 15:3, 12; 21:19 [b]1 Cor. 16:9; 2 Cor. 2:12; Col. 4:3; Rev. 3:8

28 [1]Lit., *not a little* [a]Acts 11:26; 14:22

1 [a]Acts 15:24 [b]Acts 1:15; 15:3, 22, 32 [c]Acts 15:5; Gal. 5:2f.; 1 Cor. 7:18; Gal. 2:11, 14 [d]Acts 6:14

2 [1]Lit., *not a little* [2]Or, *it was determined* [a]Acts 15:7 [b]Gal. 2:2 [c]Acts 15:4, 6, 22, 23; 16:4; 11:30

3 [a]Acts 20:38; 21:5; Rom. 15:24; 1 Cor. 16:6, 11; 2 Cor. 1:16; Titus 3:13; 3 John 6 [b]Acts 11:19 [c]Acts 14:27; 15:4, 12 [d]Acts 1:15; 15:22, 32

4 [a]Acts 15:6, 22, 23; 16:4; 11:30 [b]Acts 14:27; Acts 15:12

5 But certain ones of [a]the sect of the [b]Pharisees who had
believed, stood up, saying, "It is necessary to [c]circumcise them,
and to direct them to observe the Law of Moses."
6 And [a]the apostles and the elders came together to [1]look
into this [2]matter.
7 And after there had been much [a]debate, Peter stood up
and said to them, "Brethren, you know that [1]in the early days
[b]God made a choice among you, that by my mouth the Gentiles should hear the word of [c]the gospel and believe.
8 "And God, [a]who knows the heart, bore witness to them,
[b]giving them the Holy Spirit, just as He also did to us;
9 and [a]He made no distinction between us and them,
[b]cleansing their hearts by faith.
10 "Now therefore why do you [a]put God to the test by
placing upon the neck of the disciples a yoke which [b]neither
our fathers nor we have been able to bear?
11 "But we believe that we are saved through [a]the grace of
the Lord Jesus, in the same way as they also are."
12 And all the multitude kept silent, and they were listening to Barnabas and Paul as they were [a]relating what [b]signs
and wonders God had done through them among the
Gentiles.
13 And after they had stopped speaking, [1a]James answered, saying, "Brethren, listen to me.
14 "[a]Simeon has related how God first concerned Himself
about taking from among the Gentiles a people for His name.
15 "And with this the words of [a]the Prophets agree, just as
it is written,
16 '[a]AFTER THESE THINGS [b]I WILL RETURN,
AND I WILL REBUILD THE [1]TABERNACLE OF DAVID WHICH
HAS FALLEN,
AND I WILL REBUILD ITS RUINS,
AND I WILL RESTORE IT,
17 [a]IN ORDER THAT THE REST OF [1]MANKIND MAY SEEK THE
LORD,
AND ALL THE GENTILES [2b]WHO ARE CALLED BY MY NAME,
18 [a]SAYS THE LORD, WHO [1b]MAKES THESE THINGS KNOWN
FROM OF OLD.'
19 "Therefore it is [a]my judgment that we do not trouble
those who are turning to God from among the Gentiles,
20 but that we write to them that they abstain from [1a]things
contaminated by idols and from fornication and from
[b]what is strangled and from blood.
21 "For [a]Moses from ancient generations has in every city
those who preach him, since he is read in the synagogues every
Sabbath."
22 Then it seemed good to [a]the apostles and the elders,
with the whole church, to choose men from among them to
send to [b]Antioch with Paul and Barnabas—Judas called Bar-
sabbas, and [c]Silas, leading men among [d]the brethren,
23 and they [1]sent this letter by them,
"[a]The apostles and the brethren who are elders, to
[b]the brethren in [c]Antioch and [d]Syria and [e]Cilicia who
are from the Gentiles, [f]greetings.
24 "Since we have heard that [a]some [1]of our number to

5 [a]Acts 5:17; 24:5, 14; 26:5; 28:22 [b]Matt. 3:7; Acts 26:5 [c]Gal. 5:2f.; 1 Cor. 7:18; Gal. 2:11, 14

6 [1]Lit., *see about* [2]Lit., *word* [a]Acts 15:4, 22, 23; 16:4; 11:30

7 [1]Lit., *from days of old* [a]Acts 15:2 [b]Acts 10:19f. [c]Acts 20:24

8 [a]Acts 1:24 [b]Acts 10:47

9 [a]Acts 10:28, 34; 11:12 [b]Acts 10:43

10 [a]Acts 5:9 [b]Matt. 23:4; Gal. 5:1

11 [a]Rom. 5:15; 3:24; 2 Cor. 13:14; Eph. 2:5-8

12 [a]Acts 14:27; 15:3, 4 [b]John 4:48

13 [1]Or, *Jacob* [a]Acts 12:17

14 [a]2 Pet. 1:1 marg.; Acts 15:7

15 [a]Acts 13:40

16 [1]Or, *tent* [a]Amos 9:11 [b]Jer. 12:15

17 [1]Lit., *men* [2]Lit., *upon whom My name is called* [a]Amos 9:12 [b]James 2:7 marg.; Sept. of Deut. 28:10; Is. 63:19; Jer. 14:9; Dan. 9:19.

18 [1]Or, *does these things* which were *known* [a]Amos 9:12 [b]Is. 45:21

19 [a]Acts 15:28; 21:25

20 [1]Lit., *the pollutions of* [a]Acts 15:29; Dan. 1:8; 1 Cor. 8:7-13; 10:7f., 14-28; Rev. 2:14, 20 [b]Gen. 9:4; Lev. 3:17; 7:26; 17:10, 14; 19:26; Deut. 12:16, 23; 15:23; 1 Sam. 14:33

21 [a]Acts 13:15; 2 Cor. 3:14f.

22 [a]Acts 15:2 [b]Acts 11:20 [not 13:14] [c]Acts 15:27, 32, 40; 16:19, 25, 29; 17:4, 10, 14f.; 18:5; 2 Cor. 1:19; 1 Thess. 1:1; 2 Thess. 1:1; 1 Pet. 5:12 [d]Acts 15:1

23 [1]Lit., *wrote by their hand* [a]Acts 15:2 [b]Acts 15:1 [c]Acts 11:20 [d]Matt. 4:24; Acts 15:41; Gal. 1:21 [e]Acts 6:9 [f]Acts 23:26; James 1:1; 2 John 10f.

24 [1]Lit., *from us* [a]Acts 15:1

whom we gave no instruction have [b]disturbed you
with *their* words, unsettling your souls,
25 [a]it seemed good to us, having [1]become of one mind,
to select men to send to you with our beloved Barnabas and Paul,
26 men who have [1a]risked their lives for the name of our
Lord Jesus Christ.
27 "Therefore we have sent [a]Judas and [b]Silas, who themselves will also report the same things by word *of*
mouth.
28 "For [a]it seemed good to [b]the Holy Spirit and to [c]us to
lay upon you no greater burden than these essentials:
29 that you abstain from [a]things sacrificed to idols and
from [a]blood and from [a]things strangled and from
[a]fornication; [1]if you keep yourselves free from such
things, you will do well. Farewell."

30 So, when they were sent away, [a]they went down to
Antioch; and having gathered the [1]congregation together, they
delivered the letter.
31 And when they had read it, they rejoiced because of its
[1]encouragement.
32 And [a]Judas and [b]Silas, also being [c]prophets themselves,
[1]encouraged and strengthened [d]the brethren with a lengthy
message.
33 And after they had spent time *there,* they were sent
away from the brethren [a]in peace to those who had [b]sent them
out.
34 (See marginal note.[1])
35 But [a]Paul and Barnabas stayed in Antioch, teaching
and [b]preaching with many others also [c]the word of the Lord.
36 And after some days Paul said to Barnabas, "Let us
return and visit the brethren in [a]every city in which we proclaimed
[b]the word of the Lord, *and see* how they are."
37 And Barnabas was desirous of taking [a]John, called
Mark, along with them also.
38 But Paul kept insisting that they should not take him
along who had [a]deserted them [1]in Pamphylia and had not
gone with them to the work.
39 And there arose such a sharp disagreement that they
separated from one another, and Barnabas took [a]Mark with
him and sailed away to [b]Cyprus.
40 But Paul chose [a]Silas and departed, being [b]committed
by the brethren to the grace of the Lord.
41 And he was traveling through [a]Syria and [b]Cilicia,
strengthening the churches.

Chapter 16

AND he came also to [a]Derbe and to [a]Lystra. And behold, a
certain disciple was there, named [b]Timothy, the son of a [c]Jew-
ish woman who was a believer, but his father was a Greek,
2 and he was well spoken of by [a]the brethren who were in
[b]Lystra and [c]Iconium.
3 Paul wanted this man to [1]go with him; and he [a]took
him and circumcised him because of the Jews who were in
those parts, for they all knew that his father was a Greek.
4 Now while they were passing through the cities, they

24 [b]Gal. 1:7; 5:10

25 [1]Or, *met together* [a]Acts 15:28

26 [1]Lit., *given over* [a]Acts 9:23ff.; 14:19

27 [a]Acts 15:22, 32 [b]Acts 15:22

28 [a]Acts 15:25 [b]Acts 15:8; 5:32 [c]Acts 15:19, 25

29 [1]Lit., *from which keeping yourselves free* [a]Acts 15:20

30 [1]Or, *multitude* [a]Acts 15:22f.

31 [1]Or, *exhortation*

32 [1]Or, *exhorted* [a]Acts 15:22, 27 [b]Acts 15:22 [c]Acts 13:1 [d]Acts 15:1

33 [a]Mark 5:34; Acts 16:36; 1 Cor. 16:11; Heb. 11:31 [b]Acts 15:22

34 [1]Some mss. add verse 34, *But it seemed good to Silas to remain there.*

35 [a]Acts 12:25 [b]Acts 8:4 [c]Acts 13:12

36 [a]Acts 13:4, 13, 14, 51; 14:6, 24f. [b]Acts 13:12

37 [a]Acts 12:12

38 [1]Lit., *from* [a]Acts 13:13

39 [a]Col. 4:10; Acts 12:12; 15:37 [b]Acts 4:36

40 [a]Acts 15:22 [b]Acts 14:26; 11:23

41 [a]Matt. 4:24; Acts 15:23 [b]Acts 6:9

1 [a]Acts 14:6 [b]Acts 17:14f.; 18:5; 19:22; 20:4; Rom. 16:21; 1 Cor. 4:17; 16:10; 2 Cor. 1:1, 19; Phil. 1:1; 2:19; Col. 1:1; 1 Thess. 1:1; 3:2, 6; 2 Thess. 1:1; 1 Tim. 1:2, 18; 6:20; 2 Tim. 1:2; Philem. 1; Heb. 13:23 [c]2 Tim. 1:5; 3:15

2 [a]Acts 16:40 [b]Acts 14:6 [c]Acts 13:51

3 [1]Lit., *go out* [a]Gal. 2:3

were delivering [a]the decrees, which had been decided upon by
[b]the apostles and [c]elders who were in Jerusalem, for them to
observe.
5 So [a]the churches were being strengthened [1]in the faith,
and were [b]increasing in number daily.
6 And they passed through the [1a]Phrygian and [b]Galatian
region, having been forbidden by the Holy Spirit to speak the
word in [2c]Asia;
7 and when they had come to [a]Mysia, they were trying to
go into [b]Bithynia, and the [c]Spirit of Jesus did not permit them;
8 and passing [1]by [a]Mysia, they came down to [b]Troas.
9 And [a]a vision appeared to Paul in the night: [1]A certain
man of [b]Macedonia was standing and appealing to him, and
saying, "Come over to Macedonia and help us."
10 And when he had seen [a]the vision, immediately [b]we
sought to [1]go into Macedonia, concluding that God had called
us to [c]preach the gospel to them.
11 [1]Therefore putting out to sea from [a]Troas, we ran [b]a
straight course to Samothrace, and on the day following to
Neapolis;
12 and from there to [a]Philippi, which is a leading city of
the district of [b]Macedonia, [c]a *Roman* colony; and we were
staying in this city for some days.
13 And on [a]the Sabbath day we went outside the gate to a
river side, where we were supposing that there would be a place
of prayer; and we sat down and began speaking to the women
who had assembled.
14 And a certain woman named Lydia, from the city of
[a]Thyatira, a seller of purple fabrics, [b]a worshiper of God, was
listening; [1]and the Lord [c]opened her heart to respond to the
things spoken by Paul.
15 And when she and [a]her household had been baptized,
she urged us, saying, "If you have judged me to be faithful to
the Lord, come into my house and stay." And she prevailed
upon us.
16 And it happened that as we were going to [a]the place of
prayer, a certain slave-girl having [b]a spirit of divination met us,
who was bringing her masters much profit by fortune-telling.
17 Following after Paul and us, she kept crying out,
saying, "These men are bond-servants of [a]the Most High
God, who are proclaiming to you [1]the way of salvation."
18 And she continued doing this for many days. But Paul
was greatly annoyed, and turned and said to the spirit, "I
command you [a]in the name of Jesus Christ to come out of
her!" And it came out at that very [1]moment.
19 But when her masters saw that their hope of [a]profit was
[1]gone, they seized [b]Paul and Silas and [c]dragged them into the
market place before the authorities,
20 and when they had brought them to the chief magistrates, they said, "These men are throwing our city into confusion, being Jews,
21 and [a]are proclaiming customs which it is not lawful for
us to accept or to observe, being [b]Romans."
22 And the crowd rose up together against them, and the
chief magistrates tore their [1]robes off them, and proceeded to
order [2]*them* to be [a]beaten with rods.

4 [a]Acts 15:28f. [b]Acts 15:2 [c]Acts 11:30

5 [1]Or, *in faith* [a]Acts 9:31 [b]Acts 2:47

6 [1]Or, *Phrygia and the Galatian region* [2]I.e., west coast province of Asia Minor [a]Acts 2:10; 18:23 [b]Acts 18:23; 1 Cor. 16:1; Gal. 1:2; 3:1; 2 Tim. 4:10; 1 Pet. 1:1 [c]Acts 2:9

7 [a]Acts 16:8 [b]1 Pet. 1:1 [c]Luke 24:49; Rom. 8:9; Gal. 4:6; Phil. 1:19; 1 Pet. 1:11; Acts 8:29

8 [1]Or, *through* [a]Acts 16:7 [b]Acts 16:11; 20:5f.; 2 Cor. 2:12; 2 Tim. 4:13

9 [1]Or, *A man* [a]Acts 9:10 [b]Acts 16:10, 12; 18:5; 19:21f., 29; 20:1, 3; 27:2; Rom. 15:26

10 [1]Lit., *go out* [a]Acts 9:10 [b][we] Acts 16:10-17; 20:5-15; 21:1-18; 27:1-28:16 [c]Acts 14:7

11 [1]Some ancient mss. read, *and* [a]Acts 16:8; 20:5f.; 2 Cor. 2:12; 2 Tim. 4:13 [b]Acts 21:1

12 [a]Acts 20:6; Phil. 1:1; 1 Thess. 2:2 [b]Acts 16:9, 10; 18:5; 19:21f., 29; 20:1, 3; 27:2; Rom. 15:26 [c]Acts 16:21

13 [a]Acts 13:14

14 [1]Lit., *whose heart the Lord opened* [a]Rev. 1:11; 2:18, 24 [b]Acts 18:7; 13:43 [c]Luke 24:45

15 [a]Acts 11:14

16 [a]Acts 16:13 [b]Lev. 19:31; 20:6, 27; Deut. 18:11; 1 Sam. 28:3, 7; 2 Kin. 21:6; 1 Chr. 10:13; Is. 8:19

17 [1]Lit., *a way* [a]Mark 5:7

18 [1]Lit., *hour* [a]Mark 16:17

19 [1]Lit., *gone out* [a]Acts 16:16; 19:25f. [b]Acts 15:40; 16:25, 29; Acts 15:22 [c]Acts 17:6f.; 21:30; James 2:6; Acts 8:3

21 [a]Esther 3:8 [b]Acts 16:12

22 [1]Or, *outer garments* [2]Lit., *to beat with rods* [a]2 Cor. 11:25; 1 Thess. 2:2

23 And when they had inflicted many blows upon them,
they threw them into prison, commanding [a]the jailer to guard
them securely;
24 [1]and he, having received such a command, threw them
into the inner prison, and fastened their feet in [a]the stocks.
25 But about midnight [a]Paul and Silas were praying and
[b]singing hymns of praise to God, and the prisoners were listening to them;
26 and suddenly [a]there came a great earthquake, so that
the foundations of the prison-house were shaken; and immediately [b]all the doors were opened, and everyone's [c]chains were
unfastened.
27 And when [a]the jailer had been roused out of sleep and
had seen the prison doors opened, he drew his sword and was
about [b]to kill himself, supposing that the prisoners had
escaped.
28 But Paul cried out with a loud voice, saying, "Do yourself no harm, for we are all here!"
29 And he called for lights and rushed in and trembling
with fear, he fell down before [a]Paul and Silas,
30 and after he brought them out, he said, "Sirs, [a]what
must I do to be saved?"
31 And they said, "[a]Believe in the Lord Jesus, and you
shall be saved, you and [b]your household."
32 And they spoke the word of [1]the Lord to him together
with all who were in his house.
33 And he took them [a]that *very* hour of the night and
washed their wounds, and immediately he was baptized, he
and all his *household.*
34 And he brought them into his house and set [1]food
before them, and rejoiced [2]greatly, having believed in God
with [a]his whole household.
35 Now when day came, the chief magistrates sent their
policemen, saying, "Release those men."
36 And [a]the jailer reported these words to Paul, *saying,*
"The chief magistrates have sent to release you. Now therefore come out and go [b]in peace."
37 But Paul said to them, "They have beaten us in public
without trial, [a]men who are Romans, and have thrown us into
prison; and now are they sending us away secretly? No indeed!
But let them come themselves and bring us out."
38 And the policemen reported these words to the chief
magistrates. And [a]they were afraid when they heard that they
were Romans,
39 and they came and appealed to them, and when they
had brought them out, they kept begging them [a]to leave the
city.
40 And they went out of the prison and entered *the house
of* [a]Lydia, and when they saw [b]the brethren, they [1]encouraged
them and departed.

Chapter 17

NOW when they had traveled through Amphipolis and
Apollonia, they came to [a]Thessalonica, where there was a synagogue of the Jews.

23 [a]Acts 16:27, 36

24 [1]Lit., *who, having received* [a]Job 13:27; 33:11; Jer. 20:2f.; 29:26

25 [a]Acts 16:19 [b]Eph. 5:19

26 [a]Acts 4:31 [b]Acts 12:10 [c]Acts 12:7

27 [a]Acts 16:23, 36 [b]Acts 12:19

29 [a]Acts 16:19

30 [a]Acts 2:37; 22:10

31 [a]Mark 16:16 [b]Acts 11:14; 16:15

32 [1]Some ancient mss. read, *God*

33 [a]Acts 16:25

34 [1]Lit., *a table* [2]Or, *greatly with his whole household, having believed in God* [a]Acts 11:14; 16:15

36 [a]Acts 16:27 [b]Acts 15:33

37 [a]Acts 22:25-29

38 [a]Acts 22:29

39 [a]Matt. 8:34

40 [1]Or, *exhorted* [a]Acts 16:14 [b]Acts 16:2; 1:15

1 [a]Acts 17:11, 13; 27:2; Phil. 4:16; 2 Tim. 4:10; Acts 20:4; 1 Thess. 1:1; 2 Thess. 1:1

2 And [a]according to Paul's custom, he went to them, and
for three [b]Sabbaths reasoned with them from [c]the Scriptures,
3 [1]explaining and [2]giving evidence that the [3]Christ [a]had
to suffer and [b]rise again from the dead, and *saying,* "[c]This
Jesus whom I am proclaiming to you is the [3]Christ."
4 [a]And some of them were persuaded and joined [b]Paul
and Silas, [1]along with a great multitude of the [c]God-fearing
[d]Greeks and [2]a number of the [e]leading women.
5 But [a]the Jews, becoming jealous and taking along some
wicked men from the market place, formed a mob and set the
city in an uproar; and coming upon the house of [b]Jason, they
were seeking to bring them out to the people.
6 And when they did not find them, they *began* [a]drag-
ging Jason and some brethren before the city authorities, shouting, "These men who have upset [1b]the world have come here
also;
7 [1]and Jason [a]has welcomed them, and they all act [b]con-
trary to the decrees of Caesar, saying that there is another king,
Jesus."
8 And they stirred up the crowd and the city authorities
who heard these things.
9 And when they had received a [1]pledge from [a]Jason and
the others, they released them.
10 And [a]the brethren immediately sent [b]Paul and Silas
away by night to [c]Berea; [1]and when they arrived, they went
into [d]the synagogue of the Jews.
11 Now these were more noble-minded than those in
[a]Thessalonica, [1]for they received the word with [2]great eagerness, examining the Scriptures daily, *to see* whether these
things were so.
12 [a]Many of them therefore believed, [1]along with a number of [b]prominent Greek [c]women and men.
13 But when the Jews of [a]Thessalonica found out that the
word of God had been proclaimed by Paul in [b]Berea also, they
came there likewise, agitating and stirring up the crowds.
14 And then immediately [a]the brethren sent Paul out to
go as far as the sea; and [b]Silas and [c]Timothy remained there.
15 Now [a]those who conducted Paul brought him as far as
[b]Athens; and receiving a command for [c]Silas and Timothy to
[d]come to him as soon as possible, they departed.
16 Now while Paul was waiting for them at [a]Athens, his
spirit was being provoked within him as he was beholding the
city full of idols.
17 So he was reasoning [a]in the synagogue with the Jews
and [b]the God-fearing *Gentiles,* and in the market place every
day with those who happened to be present.
18 And also some of the Epicurean and Stoic philosophers
were [1]conversing with him. And some were saying, "What
would [a]this [2]idle babbler wish to say?" Others, "He seems to
be a proclaimer of strange [3]deities,"—because he was preaching [b]Jesus and the resurrection.
19 And they [a]took him and brought him [1]to the [2b]Areopa-
gus, saying, "May we know what [c]this new teaching is [3]which
you are proclaiming?
20 "For you are bringing some strange things to our ears;
we want to know therefore what these things mean."

2 [a]Acts 9:20; 17:10, 17 [b]Acts 13:14 [c]Acts 8:35

3 [1]Lit., *opening* [2]Lit., *placing before* [3]I.e., Messiah [a]Acts 3:18 [b]John 20:9 [c]Acts 9:22; 18:5, 28

4 [1]Lit., *and a great* [2]Lit., *not a few* [a]Acts 14:4 [b]Acts 17:10; 15:40; 15:22; 17:14f. [c]Acts 17:17; 13:43 [d]John 7:35 [e]Acts 13:50

5 [a]Acts 17:13; 1 Thess. 2:16 [b]Acts 17:6, 7, 9; Rom. 16:21

6 [1]Lit., *the inhabited earth* [a]Acts 16:19f. [b]Acts 17:31; Matt. 24:14

7 [1]Lit., *whom Jason has welcomed* [a]Luke 10:38; James 2:25 [b]Luke 23:2

9 [1]Or, *bond* [a]Acts 17:5

10 [1]Lit., *who when . . . arrived went* [a]Acts 17:6, 14f.; 1:15 [b]Acts 17:4 [c]Acts 17:13; 20:4 [d]Acts 17:2

11 [1]Lit., *who received* [2]Lit., *all* [a]Acts 17:1

12 [1]Lit., *and not a few* [a]Acts 2:47 [b]Mark 15:43 [c]Acts 13:50

13 [a]Acts 17:1 [b]Acts 17:10; 20:4

14 [a]Acts 17:6, 10; 1:15 [b]Acts 17:4, 10; 15:22 [c]Acts 16:1

15 [a]Acts 15:3 [b]Acts 17:16, 21f.; 18:1; 1 Thess. 3:1 [c]Acts 17:14 [d]Acts 18:5

16 [a]Acts 17:15, 21f.; 18:1; 1 Thess. 3:1

17 [a]Acts 9:20; 17:2 [b]Acts 17:4

18 [1]Or, *disputing* [2]I.e., one who makes his living by picking up scraps [3]Lit., *demons* [a]1 Cor. 4:10; 1:20 [b]Acts 4:2; 17:31f.

19 [1]Or, *before* [2]Or, *Hill of Ares,* god of war [3]Lit., *which is being spoken by you* [a]Acts 23:19 [b]Acts 17:22 [c]Mark 1:27

21 (Now all the Athenians and the strangers [a]visiting there
used to spend their time in nothing other than telling or hearing something new.)
22 And Paul stood in the midst of the [1]Areopagus and
said, "Men of [a]Athens, I observe that you are very [b]religious in
all respects.
23 "For while I was passing through and examining the
[a]objects of your worship, I also found an altar with this inscription, 'TO AN UNKNOWN GOD.' What therefore [b]you
worship in ignorance, this I proclaim to you.
24 "[a]The God who made the world and all things in it,
since He is [b]Lord of heaven and earth, does not [c]dwell in
temples made with hands;
25 neither is He served by human hands, [a]as though He
needed anything, since He Himself gives to all life and breath
and all things;
26 and [a]He made from [1]one every nation of mankind to
live on all the face of the earth, having [b]determined *their*
appointed times, and the boundaries of their habitation,
27 that they should seek God, if perhaps they might grope
for Him and find Him, [a]though He is not far from each one of
us;
28 for [a]in Him we live and move and [1]exist, as even some
of your own poets have said, 'For we also are His offspring.'
29 "Being then the offspring of God, we [a]ought not to
think that the Divine Nature is like gold or silver or stone, an
image formed by the art and thought of man.
30 "Therefore having [a]overlooked [b]the times of ignorance,
God is [c]now declaring to men that all everywhere should
repent,
31 because He has fixed [a]a day in which [b]He will judge
[1c]the world in righteousness through a Man whom He has
[d]appointed, having furnished proof to all men [2]by [e]raising Him
from the dead."
32 Now when they heard of [a]the resurrection of the dead,
some *began* to sneer, but others said, "We shall hear you
[1]again concerning this."
33 So Paul went out of their midst.
34 But some men joined him and believed, among whom
also was Dionysius the [a]Areopagite and a woman named Dama-
ris and others with them.

Chapter 18

AFTER these things he left [a]Athens and went to [b]Corinth.
2 And he found a certain Jew named [a]Aquila, a native of
[b]Pontus, having recently come from [c]Italy with his wife [a]Pris-
cilla, because [d]Claudius had commanded all the Jews to leave
Rome. He came to them,
3 and because he was of the same trade, he stayed with
them and [a]they were working; for by trade they were tent-
makers.
4 And he was reasoning [a]in the synagogue every [b]Sabbath
and trying to persuade [c]Jews and Greeks.
5 But when [a]Silas and Timothy [b]came down from [c]Mace-

21 [a]Acts 2:10

22 [1]Or possibly, the Council of the Areopagus [a]Acts 17:15 [b]Acts 25:19

23 [a]2 Thess. 2:4 marg. [b]John 4:22

24 [a]Is. 42:5; Acts 14:15 [b]Matt. 11:25; Deut. 10:14; Ps. 115:16 [c]Acts 7:48

25 [a]Ps. 50:10-12; Job 22:2

26 [1]Some later mss. read, *one blood* [a]Mal. 2:10 [b]Deut. 32:8; Job 12:23

27 [a]Deut. 4:7; Jer. 23:23f.; Acts 14:17

28 [1]Lit., *are* [a]Job 12:10; Dan. 5:23

29 [a]Is. 40:18ff.; Rom. 1:23

30 [a]Acts 14:16; Rom. 3:25 [b]Acts 17:23 [c]Luke 24:47; Acts 26:20; Titus 2:11f.

31 [1]Lit., *the inhabited earth* [2]Or, *when He raised* [a]Matt. 10:15 [b]John 5:22, 27; Acts 10:42; Ps. 9:8; 96:13; 98:9 [c]Matt. 24:14; Acts 17:6 [d]Luke 22:22 [e]Acts 2:24

32 [1]Lit., *also again* [a]Acts 17:18, 31

34 [a]Acts 17:19, 22

1 [a]Acts 17:15 [b]Acts 19:1; 1 Cor. 1:2; 2 Cor. 1:1, 23; 2 Tim. 4:20; Acts 18:8; 2 Cor. 6:11

2 [a]Acts 18:18, 26; Rom. 16:3; 1 Cor. 16:19; 2 Tim. 4:19 [b]Acts 2:9 [c]Acts 27:1, 6; Heb. 13:24 [d]Acts 11:28

3 [a]Acts 20:34; 1 Cor. 4:12; 1 Thess. 2:9; 2 Thess. 3:8; 1 Cor. 9:15; 2 Cor. 11:7; 12:13; 1 Thess. 4:11

4 [a]Acts 9:20; 18:19 [b]Acts 13:14 [c]Acts 14:1

5 [a]Acts 17:14; 15:22; 16:1 [b]Acts 17:15 [c]Acts 16:9

donia, Paul *began* devoting himself completely to the word,
solemnly [d]testifying to the Jews that [e]Jesus was the [1]Christ.
6 And when they resisted and blasphemed, he [a]shook out
his garments and said to them, "[b]Your blood *be* upon your
own heads, I am clean; from now on I shall go [c]to the
Gentiles."
7 And he departed from there and went to the house of a
certain man named [1]Titius Justus, [a]a worshiper of God, whose
house was next to the synagogue.
8 And [a]Crispus, [b]the leader of the synagogue, believed in
the Lord [c]with all his household, and many of the [d]Corinthians
when they heard were believing and being baptized.
9 And the Lord said to Paul in the night by [a]a vision, "Do
not be afraid *any longer*, but go on speaking and do not be
silent;
10 for I am with you, and no man will attack you in order
to harm you, for I have many people in this city."
11 And he settled *there* a year and six months, teaching
the word of God among them.
12 But while Gallio was [a]proconsul of [b]Achaia, [c]the Jews
with one accord rose up against Paul and brought him before
[d]the judgment-seat,
13 saying, "This man persuades men to worship God contrary to [a]the law."
14 But when Paul was about to [a]open his mouth, Gallio
said to the Jews, "If it were a matter of wrong or of vicious
crime, O Jews, it would be reasonable for me to put up with
you;
15 but if there are [a]questions about words and names and
your own Law, look after it yourselves; I am unwilling to be a
judge of these matters."
16 And he drove them away from [a]the judgment-seat.
17 And they all took hold of [a]Sosthenes, [b]the leader of the
synagogue, and *began* beating him in front of [c]the judgment-
seat. And Gallio was not concerned about any of these things.
18 And Paul, having remained many days longer, [a]took
leave of [b]the brethren and put out to sea for [c]Syria, and with
him were [d]Priscilla and [d]Aquila. In [e]Cenchrea [1]he [f]had his hair
cut, for he was keeping a vow.
19 And they came to [a]Ephesus, and he left them there.
Now he himself entered [b]the synagogue and reasoned with the
Jews.
20 And when they asked him to stay for a longer time, he
did not consent,
21 but [a]taking leave of them and saying, "I will return to
you again [b]if God wills," he set sail from [c]Ephesus.
22 And when he had landed at [a]Caesarea, he went up and
greeted the church, and went down to [b]Antioch.
23 And having spent some time *there*, he departed and
passed successively through the [a]Galatian region and Phrygia,
strengthening all the disciples.
24 Now a certain Jew named [a]Apollos, an [b]Alexandrian by
birth, [1]an eloquent man, came to [c]Ephesus; and he was mighty
in the Scriptures.
25 This man had been instructed in [a]the way of the Lord;
and being fervent in spirit, he was speaking and teaching accu-

5 [1]I.e., Messiah [d]Acts 20:21; Luke 16:28 [e]Acts 17:3; 18:28

6 [a]Neh. 5:13; Acts 13:51 [b]2 Sam. 1:16; 1 Kin. 2:33; Ezek. 18:13; 33:4, 6, 8; Matt. 27:25; Acts 20:26 [c]Acts 13:46

7 [1]Some ancient mss. read, *Titus*, others omit it altogether [a]Acts 16:14; Acts 13:43

8 [a]1 Cor. 1:14 [b]Mark 5:22 [c]Acts 11:14 [d]Acts 19:1; 1 Cor. 1:2; 2 Cor. 1:1, 23; 2 Tim. 4:20; Acts 18:1; 2 Cor. 6:11

9 [a]Acts 9:10

12 [a]Acts 13:7 [b]Acts 18:27; 19:21; Rom. 15:26; 1 Cor. 16:15; 2 Cor. 1:1; 9:2; 11:10; 1 Thess. 1:7f. [c]1 Thess. 2:16 [d]Matt. 27:19

13 [a]Acts 18:15; John 19:7

14 [a]Matt. 5:2

15 [a]Acts 23:29; 25:19

16 [a]Matt. 27:19

17 [a]1 Cor. 1:1 [b]Acts 18:8 [c]Matt. 27:19

18 [1]Lit., *having his hair cut* [a]Mark 6:46 [b]Acts 1:15; 18:27 [c]Matt. 4:24 [d]Acts 18:2, 26 [e]Rom. 16:1 [f]Num. 6:2, 5, 9, 18; Acts 21:24

19 [a]Acts 18:21, 24; 19:1, 17, 26 [28, 34f.]; 20:16f.; [21:29]; 1 Cor. 15:32; 16:8; Eph. 1:1; 1 Tim. 1:3; 2 Tim. 1:18; 4:12; Rev. 1:11; 2:1 [b]Acts 18:4

21 [a]Mark 6:46 [b]1 Cor. 4:19; 16:7; Heb. 6:3; James 4:15; Rom. 1:10; 15:32; 1 Pet. 3:17 [c]Acts 18:19, 24; 19:1, 17, 26 [28, 34f.]; 20:16f.; [21:29]; 1 Cor. 15:32; 16:8; Eph. 1:1; 1 Tim. 1:3; 2 Tim. 1:18; 4:12; Rev. 1:11; 2:1

22 [a]Acts 8:40 [b]Acts 11:19

23 [a]Acts 16:6

24 [1]Or, *a learned man* [a]Acts 19:1; 1 Cor. 1:12; 3:5, 6, 22; 4:6; 16:12; Titus 3:13 [b]Acts 6:9 [c]Acts 18:19

25 [a]Acts 9:2; 18:26

rately the things concerning Jesus, being acquainted only with
[b]the baptism of John;
26 and he began to speak out boldly in the synagogue. But
when [a]Priscilla and Aquila heard him, they took him aside and
explained to him [b]the way of God more accurately.
27 And when he wanted to go across to [a]Achaia, [b]the brethren encouraged him and wrote to [c]the disciples to welcome
him; and when he had arrived, he [1]helped greatly those who
had believed through grace;
28 for he powerfully refuted the Jews in public, demonstrat-
ing [a]by the Scriptures that [b]Jesus was the [1]Christ.

Chapter 19

AND it came about that while [a]Apollos was at [b]Corinth, Paul
having passed through the [c]upper country came to [d]Ephesus,
and found some disciples,
2 and he said to them, "[a]Did you receive the Holy Spirit
when you believed?" And they *said* to him, "No, [b]we have not
even heard whether [1]there is a Holy Spirit."
3 And he said, "Into what then were you baptized?" And
they said, "[a]Into John's baptism."
4 And Paul said, "[a]John baptized with the baptism of
repentance, telling the people [b]to believe in Him who was
coming after him, that is, in Jesus."
5 And when they heard this, they were [a]baptized [1]in the
name of the Lord Jesus.
6 And when Paul had [a]laid his hands upon them, the
Holy Spirit came on them, and they *began* [b]speaking with
tongues and [c]prophesying.
7 And there were in all about twelve men.
8 And he entered [a]the synagogue and continued speaking
out boldly for three months, reasoning and [1]persuading *them*
[b]about the kingdom of God.
9 But when [a]some were becoming hardened and disobedient, speaking evil of [b]the Way before the multitude, he
withdrew from them and took away [c]the disciples, reasoning
daily in the school of Tyrannus.
10 And this took place for [a]two years, so that all who lived
in [1b]Asia heard [c]the word of the Lord, both Jews and Greeks.
11 And God was performing [a]extraordinary [1]miracles by
the hands of Paul,
12 [a]so that handkerchiefs or aprons were even carried
from his body to the sick, and the diseases left them and [b]the
evil spirits went out.
13 But also some of the Jewish [a]exorcists, who went from
place to place, attempted to name over those who had the evil
spirits the name of the Lord Jesus, saying, "I adjure you by
Jesus whom Paul preaches."
14 And seven sons of one Sceva, a Jewish chief priest, were
doing this.
15 And the evil spirit answered and said to them, "I recognize Jesus, and I know about Paul, but who are you?"
16 And the man in whom was the evil spirit leaped on
them and subdued both of them and overpowered them, so
that they fled out of that house naked and wounded.

25 [b]Luke 7:29; Acts 19:3

26 [a]Acts 18:2, 18 [b]Acts 18:25

27 [1]Or, *helped greatly through grace those who had believed*
[a]Acts 18:12; 19:1 [b]Acts 18:18 [c]Acts 11:26

28 [1]I.e., Messiah
[a]Acts 8:35 [b]Acts 18:5

1 [a]Acts 18:24; 1 Cor. 1:12; 3:5, 6, 22; 4:6; 16:12; Titus 3:13 [b]Acts 18:1 [c]Acts 18:23 [d]Acts 18:21, 24; 19:1, 17, 26 [28, 34f.]; 20:16f.; [21:29]; 1 Cor. 15:32; 16:8; Eph. 1:1; 1 Tim. 1:3; 2 Tim. 1:18; 4:12; Rev. 1:11; 2:1

2 [1]Or, *the Holy Spirit has been* given
[a]Acts 8:15f.; 11:16f. [b]John 7:39

3 [a]Luke 7:29; Acts 18:25

4 [a]Acts 13:24 [b]John 1:7

5 [1]Lit., *into*
[a]Acts 8:12, 16; 10:48

6 [a]Acts 6:6; 8:17 [b]Acts 2:4; 10:46; Mark 16:17 [c]Acts 13:1

8 [1]Some ancient mss. read, *persuading* as to *the things about*
[a]Acts 9:20; 18:26 [b]Acts 1:3

9 [a]Acts 14:4 [b]Acts 9:2; 19:23 [c]Acts 11:26; 19:30

10 [1]I.e., west coast province of Asia Minor
[a]Acts 19:8; 20:31 [b]Acts 16:6; 19:22, 26, 27 [c]Acts 13:12; 19:20

11 [1]Or, *works of power*
[a]Acts 8:13

12 [a]Acts 5:15 [b]Mark 16:17

13 [a]Matt. 12:27; Luke 11:19

17 And this became known to all, both Jews and Greeks,
who lived in [a]Ephesus; and fear fell upon them all and the
name of the Lord Jesus was being magnified.
18 Many also of those who had believed kept coming,
confessing and disclosing their practices.
19 And many of those who practiced magic brought their
books together and *began* burning them in the sight of all; and
they counted up the price of them and found it [1]fifty thousand
[a]pieces of silver.
20 So [1a]the word of the Lord [b]was growing mightily and
prevailing.
21 Now after these things were finished, Paul purposed in
the [1]spirit to [a]go to Jerusalem [b]after he had passed through
[c]Macedonia and [d]Achaia, saying, "After I have been there, [e]I
must also see Rome."
22 And having sent into [a]Macedonia two of [b]those who
ministered to him, [c]Timothy and [d]Erastus, he himself stayed
in [1e]Asia for a while.
23 And about that time there arose no small disturbance
concerning [a]the Way.
24 For a certain man named Demetrius, a silversmith,
who made silver shrines of [1]Artemis, [a]was bringing no little
[2]business to the craftsmen;
25 these he gathered together with the workmen of similar
trades, and said, "Men, you know that our prosperity [1]depends
upon this business.
26 "And you see and hear that not only in [a]Ephesus, but in
almost all of [1b]Asia, this Paul has persuaded and turned away a
considerable number of people, saying that [c]gods made with
hands are no gods *at all*.
27 "And not only is there danger that this trade of ours fall
into disrepute, but also that the temple of the great goddess
[1]Artemis be regarded as worthless and that she whom all of
[2a]Asia and [b]the [3]world worship should even be dethroned from
her magnificence."
28 And when they heard *this* and were filled with rage,
they *began* crying out, saying, "Great is [1]Artemis of the
[a]Ephesians!"
29 And the city was filled with the confusion, and they
rushed with one accord into the theater, [1]dragging along
[a]Gaius and [b]Aristarchus, Paul's traveling [c]companions from
[d]Macedonia.
30 And when Paul wanted to go in to the [1]assembly, [a]the
disciples would not let him.
31 And also some of the [1]Asiarchs who were friends of his
sent to him and repeatedly urged him not to [2]venture into the
theater.
32 [a]So then, some were shouting one thing and some another, for the [1]assembly was in confusion, and the majority did
not know [2]for what cause they had come together.
33 And some of the crowd [1]concluded *it was* Alexander,
since the Jews had put him forward; and having [a]motioned
with his hand, Alexander was intending to make a defense to
the [2]assembly.
34 But when they recognized that he was a Jew, a single

17 [a]Acts 18:19

19 [1]Or probably, fifty thousand Greek drachmas. A drachma approximated a day's wage. [a]Luke 15:8 and marg.

20 [1]Or, *according to the power of the Lord the word was growing* [a]Acts 19:10 [b]Acts 6:7; 12:24

21 [1]Or, *Spirit* [a]Acts 20:16, 22; 21:15; Rom. 15:25; 2 Cor. 1:16 [b]1 Cor. 16:5; Acts 20:1 [c]Rom. 15:26; 1 Thess. 1:7f.; Acts 16:9; 19:22, 29 [d]Acts 18:12 [e]Rom. 15:24, 28; Acts 23:11

22 [1]I.e., west coast province of Asia Minor [a]Acts 16:9; 19:21, 29 [b]Acts 19:29; 13:5; 20:34; 2 Cor. 8:19 [c]Acts 16:1 [d]Rom. 16:23; 2 Tim. 4:20 [e]Acts 19:10

23 [a]Acts 19:9

24 [1]Latin, *Diana* [2]Or, *profit* [a]Acts 16:16, 19f.

25 [1]Lit., *is from*

26 [1]Note vs. 22 [a]Acts 18:19 [b]Acts 19:10 [c]Acts 17:29; 1 Cor. 8:4; 10:19; Deut. 4:28; Ps. 115:4; Is. 44:10-20; Jer. 10:3ff.; Rev. 9:20

27 [1]Latin, *Diana* [2]Note vs. 22 [3]Lit., *the inhabited earth* [a]Acts 19:10 [b]Matt. 24:14

28 [1]Latin, *Diana* [a]Acts 18:19

29 [1]Lit., *having dragged* [a]Acts 20:4 [b]Acts 20:4; 27:2; Col. 4:10; Philem. 24 [c]Acts 19:22; 13:5; 20:34; 2 Cor. 8:19 [d]Acts 16:9; 19:22

30 [1]Lit., *people* [a]Acts 19:9

31 [1]I.e., political or religious officials of the province of Asia [2]Lit., *give himself*

32 [1]Gr., ekklesia [2]Or, *on whose account* [a]Acts 21:34

33 [1]Or, *instructed Alexander* [2]Lit., *people* [a]Acts 12:17

outcry arose from them all as they shouted for about two
hours, "Great is [1]Artemis of the Ephesians!"
35 And after quieting the multitude the townclerk *said,
"Men of [a]Ephesus, what man is there after all who does not
know that the city of the Ephesians is guardian of the temple
of the great [1]Artemis, and of the *image* which fell down from
[2]heaven?
36 "Since then these are undeniable facts, you ought to
keep calm and to do nothing rash.
37 "For you have brought these men *here* who are neither
[a]robbers of temples nor blasphemers of our goddess.
38 "So then, if Demetrius and the craftsmen who are with
him have a complaint against any man, the courts are in ses-
sion and [1a]proconsuls are *available;* let them bring charges
against one another.
39 "But if you want anything beyond this, it shall be settled
in the [1]lawful [2]assembly.
40 "For indeed we are in danger of being accused of a riot
in connection with today's affair, since there is no *real* cause
for it; and in this connection we shall be unable to account for
this disorderly gathering."
41 And after saying this he dismissed the [1]assembly.

Chapter 20

AND after the uproar had ceased, Paul sent for [a]the disciples
and when he had exhorted them and taken his leave of them,
he departed [b]to go to [c]Macedonia.
2 And when he had gone through those districts and had
given them much exhortation, he came to Greece.
3 And *there* he spent three months, and when [a]a plot was
formed against him by the Jews as he was about to set sail for
[b]Syria, he determined to return through [c]Macedonia.
4 And [1]he was accompanied by Sopater of [a]Berea, *the
son* of Pyrrhus; and by [b]Aristarchus and Secundus of the [c]Thes-
salonians; and [d]Gaius of [e]Derbe, and [f]Timothy; and [g]Tychicus
and [h]Trophimus of [2i]Asia.
5 But these had gone on ahead and were waiting for [a]us
at [b]Troas.
6 And [a]we sailed from [b]Philippi after [c]the days of Unleavened Bread, and came to them at [d]Troas within five days; and
there we stayed seven days.
7 And on [a]the first day of the week, when [b]we were gathered together to [c]break bread, Paul *began* talking to them,
intending to depart the next day, and he prolonged his [1]mes-
sage until midnight.
8 And there were many [a]lamps in the [b]upper room where
we were gathered together.
9 And there was a certain young man named Eutychus
sitting [1]on the window-sill, sinking into a deep sleep; and as
Paul kept on talking, he was overcome by sleep and fell down
from the third floor, and was picked up dead.
10 But Paul went down and [a]fell upon him and after embracing him, he [b]said, "[1]Do not be troubled, for his life is in
him."
11 And when he had gone *back* up, and had [a]broken the

34 [1]Latin, *Diana*

35 [1]Latin, *Diana* [2]Lit., *Zeus* or, *Jupiter* [a]Acts 18:19

37 [a]Rom. 2:22

38 [1]Or, *provincial governors* [a]Acts 13:7

39 [1]Or, *regular* [2]Gr., ekklesia

41 [1]Gr., ekklesia

1 [a]Acts 11:26 [b]Acts 19:21 [c]Acts 16:9; 20:3

3 [a]Acts 9:24; Acts 20:19 [b]Matt. 4:24 [c]Acts 16:9; 20:1

4 [1]Lit., *there accompanied him* [2]I.e., west coast province of Asia Minor [a]Acts 17:10 [b]Acts 19:29 [c]Acts 17:1 [d]Acts 19:29 [e]Acts 14:6 [f]Acts 16:1 [g]Eph. 6:21; Col. 4:7; 2 Tim. 4:12; Titus 3:12 [h]Acts 21:29; 2 Tim. 4:20 [i]Acts 16:6; 20:16, 18

5 [a]Acts 20:5-15; 16:10 [b]Acts 16:8

6 [a]Acts 20:5-15; 16:10 [b]Acts 16:12 [c]Acts 12:3 [d]Acts 16:8

7 [1]Lit., *word, speech* [a]1 Cor. 16:2; Rev. 1:10 [b]Acts 20:5-15; 16:10 [c]Acts 2:42; 20:11

8 [a]Matt. 25:1 [b]Acts 1:13

9 [1]Or, *at the window*

10 [1]Or, *Stop being troubled* [a]1 Kin. 17:21; 2 Kin. 4:34 [b]Matt. 9:23f.; Mark 5:39

11 [a]Acts 2:42; 20:7

bread and [1]eaten, he talked with them a long while, until
daybreak, and so departed.
12 And they took away the boy alive, and were [1]greatly
comforted.
13 But [a]we, going ahead to the ship, set sail for Assos,
intending from there to take Paul on board; for thus he had
arranged it, intending himself to go [1]by land.
14 And when he met us at Assos, we took him on board
and came to Mitylene.
15 And sailing from there, we arrived the following day
opposite Chios; and the next day we crossed over to Samos;
and [1]the day following we came to [a]Miletus.
16 For Paul had decided to sail past [a]Ephesus in order that
he might not have to spend time in [1b]Asia; for he was hurrying
[c]to be in Jerusalem, if possible, [d]on the day of Pentecost.
17 And from Miletus he sent to [a]Ephesus and called to
him [b]the elders of the church.
18 And when they had come to him, he said to them,
"**Y**ou yourselves know, [a]from the first day that I set foot in
[1a]Asia, how I was with you the whole time,
19 serving the Lord with all humility and with tears and
with trials which came upon me through [a]the plots of the Jews;
20 how I [a]did not shrink from declaring to you anything
that was profitable, and teaching you publicly and [1]from house
to house,
21 solemnly [a]testifying to both Jews and Greeks of [b]repent-
ance toward God and [c]faith in our Lord Jesus Christ.
22 "And now, behold, bound in [1]spirit, [a]I am on my way to
Jerusalem, not knowing what will happen to me there,
23 except that [a]the Holy Spirit solemnly [b]testifies to me in
every city, saying that [c]bonds and afflictions await me.
24 "But [a]I do not consider my life of any account as dear to
myself, in order that I may [b]finish my course, and [c]the ministry
which I received from the Lord Jesus, to [d]testify solemnly of
the gospel of [e]the grace of God.
25 "And now, behold, I know that you all, among whom I
went about [a]preaching the kingdom, will see my face no more.
26 "Therefore I [1]testify to you this day, that [a]I am [2]inno-
cent of the blood of all men.
27 "For I [a]did not shrink from declaring to you the whole
[b]purpose of God.
28 "Be on guard for yourselves and for all [a]the flock, among
which the Holy Spirit has made you [1]overseers, to shepherd
[b]the church of [2]God which [c]He [3]purchased with His own
blood.
29 "I know that after my departure [a]savage wolves will
come in among you, not sparing [b]the flock;
30 and from among your own selves men will arise, speaking perverse things, to draw away [a]the disciples after them.
31 "Therefore be on the alert, remembering that night and
day for a period of [a]three years I did not cease to admonish
each one [b]with tears.
32 "And now I [a]commend you to [1]God and to [b]the word of
His grace, which is able to [c]build *you* up and to give *you* [d]the
inheritance among all those who are sanctified.
33 "[a]I have coveted no one's silver or gold or clothes.

11 [1]Lit., *tasted*

12 [1]Lit., *not moderately*

13 [1]Or, *on foot*
[a]Acts 20:5-15; 16:10

15 [1]Later mss. add, *after staying at Trogyllium, the day following . . .*
[a]Acts 20:17; 2 Tim. 4:20

16 [1]I.e., west coast province of Asia Minor
[a]Acts 18:19 [b]Acts 16:6; 20:4, 18 [c]Acts 19:21; 20:22; 20:6; 1 Cor. 16:8 [d]Acts 2:1

17 [a]Acts 18:19 [b]Acts 11:30

18 [1]Note vs. 16
[a]Acts 18:19; 19:1, 10; 20:4, 16

19 [a]Acts 20:3

20 [1]Or, *in the various private homes*
[a]Acts 20:27

21 [a]Acts 18:5; Luke 16:28; Acts 20:23, 24 [b]Acts 2:38; 11:18; 26:20 [c]Acts 24:24; 26:18; Eph. 1:15; Col. 2:5; Philem. 5

22 [1]Or, *the Spirit*
[a]Acts 20:16; 17:16

23 [a]Acts 8:29 [b]Acts 18:5; Luke 16:28; Acts 20:21, 24 [c]Acts 9:16; 21:33

24 [a]Acts 21:13 [b]Acts 13:25 [c]Acts 1:17 [d]Acts 18:5; Luke 16:28; Acts 20:21 [e]Acts 11:23; 20:32

25 [a]Acts 28:31; Matt. 4:23

26 [1]Or, *call you to witness* [2]Lit., *pure from*
[a]Acts 18:6

27 [a]Acts 20:20 [b]Acts 13:36

28 [1]Or, *bishops* [2]Some ancient mss. read, *the Lord* [3]Lit., *acquired*
[a]Acts 20:29; Luke 12:32; 1 Pet. 5:2f.; John 21:15-17 [b]Matt. 16:18; Rom. 16:16; 1 Cor. 10:32 [c]Eph. 1:7, 14; Titus 2:14; 1 Pet. 1:19; 2:9; Rev. 5:9

29 [a]Ezek. 22:27; Matt. 7:15 [b]Acts 20:28; Luke 12:32; 1 Pet. 5:2f.; John 21:15-17

30 [a]Acts 11:26

31 [a]Acts 19:1, 8, 10; 24:17 [b]Acts 20:19

32 [1]One ancient mss. reads, *the Lord*
[a]Acts 14:23 [b]Acts 14:3; 20:24 [c]Acts 9:31 [d]Acts 26:18; Eph. 1:14; 5:5; Col. 1:12; 3:24; Heb. 9:15; 1 Pet. 1:4

33 [a]1 Cor. 9:4-18; 2 Cor. 11:7-12; 12:14-18; 1 Thess. 2:5f.

34 "You yourselves know that [a]these hands ministered to
my *own* needs and to the [b]men who were with me.
35 "In every thing I showed you that by working hard in
this manner you must help the weak and remember the words
of the Lord Jesus, that He Himself said, 'It is more blessed to
give than to receive.' "
36 And when he had said these things, he [a]knelt down and
prayed with them all.
37 And [1]they *began* to weep aloud and [2a]embraced Paul,
and repeatedly kissed him,
38 grieving especially over [a]the word which he had spoken, that they should see his face no more. And they were
[b]accompanying him to the ship.

Chapter 21

AND when it came about that [a]we had parted from them
and had set sail, we ran [b]a straight course to Cos and the next
day to Rhodes and from there to Patara;
2 and having found a ship crossing over to [a]Phoenicia, we
went aboard and set sail.
3 And when we had come in sight of [a]Cyprus, leaving it
on the left, we kept sailing to [b]Syria and landed at [c]Tyre; for
[d]there the ship was to unload its cargo.
4 And after looking up [a]the disciples, we stayed there
seven days; and they kept telling Paul [1b]through the Spirit not
to set foot in Jerusalem.
5 And when it came about that [1]our days there were
ended, we departed and started on our journey, while they all,
with wives and children, [a]escorted us until *we were* out of the
city. And after [b]kneeling down on the beach and praying, we
said farewell to one another.
6 Then we went on board the ship, and they returned
[a]home again.
7 And when we had finished the voyage from [a]Tyre, we
arrived at Ptolemais; and after greeting [b]the brethren, we
stayed with them for a day.
8 And on the next day we departed and came to [a]Caesar-
ea; and entering the house of [b]Philip the [c]evangelist, who was
[b]one of the seven, we stayed with him.
9 Now this man had four virgin daughters who were
[a]prophetesses.
10 And as we were staying there for some days, a certain
prophet named [a]Agabus came down from Judea.
11 And coming to us, he [a]took Paul's belt and bound his
own feet and hands, and said, "This [b]is what the Holy Spirit
says: 'In this way the Jews at Jerusalem will [c]bind the man who
owns this belt and [d]deliver him into the hands of the
Gentiles.' "
12 And when we had heard this, we as well as the local
residents *began* begging him [a]not to go up to Jerusalem.
13 Then Paul answered, "What are you doing, weeping
and breaking my heart? For [a]I am ready not only to be bound,
but even to die at Jerusalem for [b]the name of the Lord Jesus."
14 And since he would not be persuaded, we fell silent,
remarking, "[a]The will of the Lord be done!"

34 [a]Acts 18:3 [b]Acts 19:22

36 [a]Acts 9:40; 21:5; Luke 22:41

37 [1]Lit., *a considerable weeping of all occurred* [2]Lit., *fell on Paul's neck* [a]Luke 15:20

38 [1]Lit., *suffering pain* [a]Acts 20:25 [b]Acts 15:3

1 [a]["we"] Acts 21:1-18; 16:10 [b]Acts 16:11

2 [a]Acts 11:19; 21:3

3 [a]Acts 4:36; 21:16 [b]Matt. 4:24 [c]Acts 12:20; 21:7 [d]Acts 21:2

4 [1]I.e., because of impressions made by the Spirit [a]Acts 21:16; 11:26 [b]Acts 21:11; 20:23

5 [1]Lit., *we had completed the days* [a]Acts 15:3 [b]Acts 9:40; 20:36; Luke 22:41

6 [a]John 19:27

7 [a]Acts 12:20; 21:3 [b]Acts 1:15; 21:17

8 [a]Acts 8:40; 21:16 [b]Acts 6:5 [c]Eph. 4:11; 2 Tim. 4:5

9 [a]Acts 13:1; Luke 2:36; 1 Cor. 11:5

10 [a]Acts 11:28

11 [a]1 Kin. 22:11; Is. 20:2; Jer. 13:1-11; 19:1, 11; John 18, [b]Acts 8:29 [c]Acts 9:16; 21:33 [d]Matt. 20:19

12 [a]Acts 21:15

13 [a]Acts 20:24 [b]Acts 5:41; 9:16

14 [a]Luke 22:42

15 And after these days we got ready and [a]started on our
way up to Jerusalem.
16 And *some* of [a]the disciples from [b]Caesarea also came
with us, taking us to Mnason of [c]Cyprus, a [d]disciple of long
standing with whom we were to lodge.
17 And when we had come to Jerusalem, [a]the brethren
received us gladly.
18 And now the following day Paul went in with us to
[1a]James, and all [b]the elders were present.
19 And after he had greeted them, he [a]*began* to relate one
by one the things which God had done among the Gentiles
through his [b]ministry.
20 And when they heard it they *began* [a]glorifying God;
and they said to him, "You see, brother, how many [1]thousands
there are among the Jews of those who have believed, and they
are all [b]zealous for the Law;
21 and they have been told about you, that you are [a]teach-
ing all the Jews who are among the Gentiles to forsake
Moses, telling them [b]not to circumcise their children nor to
walk according to [c]the customs.
22 "What, then, is *to be done?* They will certainly hear that
you have come.
23 "Therefore do this that we tell you: We have four men
who [1a]are under a vow;
24 take them and [a]purify yourself along with them, and
[1]pay their expenses in order that they may [b]shave their [2]heads;
and all will know that there is nothing to the things which they
have been told about you, but that you yourself also walk
orderly, keeping the Law.
25 "But concerning the Gentiles who have believed, we
wrote, [a]having decided that they should abstain from [1]meat
sacrificed to idols and from blood and from what is strangled
and from fornication."
26 Then Paul [1]took the men, and the next day [a]purifying
himself along with them [b]went into the temple, giving notice
of the completion of the days of purification, until the sacrifice was offered for each one of them.
27 And when [a]the seven days were almost over, [b]the Jews
from [1c]Asia, upon seeing him in the temple, *began* to stir up all
the multitude and laid hands on him,
28 crying out, "Men of Israel, come to our aid! [a]This is the
man who preaches to all men everywhere against our people,
and the Law, and this place; and besides he has even brought
Greeks into the temple and has [b]defiled this [a]holy place."
29 For they had previously seen [a]Trophimus the [b]Ephe-
sian in the city with him, and they supposed that Paul had
brought him into the temple.
30 And all the city was aroused, and [1]the people rushed
together; and taking hold of Paul, they [a]dragged him out of
the temple; and immediately the doors were shut.
31 And while they were seeking to kill him, a report came
up to the [1]commander of the [a]*Roman* [2]Cohort that all Jerusalem was in confusion.
32 And at once he [a]took along *some* soldiers and centurions, and ran down to them; and then they saw the [1]command-
er and the soldiers, they stopped beating Paul.

15 [a]Acts 21:12

16 [a]Acts 21:4 [b]Acts 8:40 [c]Acts 4:36; 21:3 [d]Acts 15:7 marg.

17 [a]Acts 1:15; 21:7

18 [1]Or, *Jacob* [a]Acts 12:17 [b]Acts 11:30

19 [a]Acts 14:27 [b]Acts 1:17

20 [1]Lit., *ten thousands* [a]Matt. 9:8 [b]Acts 15:1; 22:3; Rom. 10:2; Gal. 1:14

21 [a]Acts 21:28 [b]Acts 15:19ff.; 1 Cor. 7:18f. [c]Acts 6:14

23 [1]Lit., *have a vow on them* [a]Acts 18:18

24 [1]Lit., *spend on them* [2]Lit., *head* [a]Acts 21:26; 24:18; John 11:55 [b]Acts 18:18

25 [1]Lit., *the thing* [a]Acts 15:19f., 29

26 [1]Or, *took the men the next day, and purifying himself* [a]Acts 21:24; 24:18; John 11:55 [b]Num. 6:13; Acts 24:18

27 [1]I.e., west coast province of Asia Minor [a]Num. 6:9, 13-20 [b]Acts 24:18; 20:19 [c]Acts 16:6

28 [a]Acts 6:13 [b]Acts 24:6; Matt. 24:15; Acts 6:13f.

29 [a]Acts 20:4 [b]Acts 18:19

30 [1]Lit., *a running together of the people occurred* [a]Acts 26:21; 2 Kin. 11:15; Acts 16:19

31 [1]Lit., *chiliarch*, in command of one thousand troops [2]Or, *Battalion* [a]Acts 10:1

32 [1]Vs. 31 note [a]Acts 23:27

33 Then the [1]commander came up and took hold of him,
and ordered him to be [a]bound with [b]two chains; and he *began*
asking who he was and what he had done.
34 But among the crowd [a]some were shouting one thing
and some another, and when he could not find out the [1]facts
on account of the uproar, he ordered him to be brought into
[b]the barracks.
35 And when he got to [a]the stairs, it so happened that he
was carried by the soldiers because of the violence of the [1]mob;
36 for the multitude of the people kept following behind,
crying out, "[a]Away with him!"
37 And as Paul was about to be brought into [a]the barracks,
he said to the [1]commander, "May I say something to you?"
And he *said, "Do you know Greek?
38 "Then you are not [a]the Egyptian who some [1]time ago
stirred up a revolt and led the four thousand men of the Assas-
sins out [b]into the wilderness?"
39 But Paul said, "[a]I am a Jew of Tarsus in [b]Cilicia, a
citizen of no insignificant city; and I beg you, allow me to
speak to the people."
40 And when he had given him permission, Paul, standing
on [a]the stairs, [b]motioned to the people with his hand; and
when there [1]was a great hush, he spoke to them in the [2c]Hebrew
dialect, saying,

Chapter 22

"[a]BRETHREN and fathers, hear my defense which I now
offer to you."
2 And when they heard that he was addressing them in
the [1a]Hebrew dialect, they became even more quiet; and he
*said,
3 "[a]I am [b]a Jew, born in [c]Tarsus of [d]Cilicia, but brought
up in this city, [e]educated [1]under [f]Gamaliel, [2g]strictly according
to the law of our fathers, being zealous for God, just as [h]you all
are today.
4 "And [a]I persecuted this [b]Way to the death, binding and
putting both men and women into prisons,
5 as also [a]the high priest and all [b]the Council of the
elders [1]can testify. From them I also [c]received letters to [d]the
brethren, and started off for [e]Damascus in order to bring even
those who were there to Jerusalem [2]as prisoners to be
punished.
6 "[a]And it came about that as I was on my way, approaching Damascus about noontime, a very bright light suddenly
flashed from heaven all around me,
7 and I fell to the ground and heard a voice saying to me,
'Saul, Saul, why are you persecuting Me?'
8 "And I answered, 'Who art Thou, Lord?' And He said
to me, 'I am [a]Jesus the Nazarene, whom you are persecuting.'
9 "And those who were with me [a]beheld the light, to be
sure, but [b]did not [1]understand the voice of the One who was
speaking to me.
10 "And I said, '[a]What shall I do, Lord?' And the Lord said
to me, 'Arise and go on into Damascus; and there you will be
told of all that has been appointed for you to do.'

33 [1]Vs. 31 note [a]Acts 20:23; 21:11; 22:29; 26:29; 28:20; 2 Tim. 1:16; 2:9; Eph. 6:20 [b]Acts 12:6

34 [1]Lit., *certainty* [a]Acts 19:32 [b]Acts 21:37; 22:24; 23:10, 16, 32

35 [1]Or, *multitude* [a]Acts 21:40

36 [a]Acts 22:22; Luke 23:18; John 19:15

37 [1]Vs. 31 note [a]Acts 21:34; 22:24; 23:10, 16, 32

38 [1]Lit., *days* [a]Acts 5:36 [b]Matt. 24:26

39 [a]Acts 22:3; 9:11 [b]Acts 6:9

40 [1]Lit., *occurred* [2]I.e., Jewish Aramaic [a]Acts 21:35 [b]Acts 12:17 [c]Acts 22:2; 26:14; 1:19; John 5:2

1 [a]Acts 7:2

2 [1]I.e., Jewish Aramaic [a]Acts 21:40

3 [1]Lit., *at the feet of* [2]Lit., *according to the strictness of the ancestral law* [a]Acts 22:3-16; 9:1-22; 26:9-18 [b]Acts 21:39 [c]Acts 9:11 [d]Acts 6:9 [e]Deut. 33:3; 2 Kin. 4:38; Luke 10:39 [f]Acts 5:34 [g]Acts 26:5; Phil. 3:6; Acts 23:6 [h]Acts 21:20

4 [a]Acts 8:3; 22:19f. [b]Acts 9:2

5 [1]Lit., *testifies for me* [2]Lit., *having been bound* [a]Acts 9:1 [b]Luke 22:66 [Gr.]; 1 Tim. 4:14 [Gr.]; Acts 5:21 [Gr.] [c]Acts 9:2 [d]Acts 2:29; 3:17; 13:26; 23:1; 28:17, 21; Rom. 9:3 [e]Acts 9:2

6 [a]Acts 22:6-11: *Acts 9:3-8; 26:12-18*

8 [a]Acts 26:9

9 [1]Or, *hear* (with comprehension) [a]Acts 26:13 [b]Acts 9:7

10 [a]Acts 16:30

11 "But since I [a]could not see because of the [1]brightness of
that light, I was led by the hand by those who were with me,
and came into Damascus.
12 "And a certain [a]Ananias, a man who was devout by the
standard of the Law, *and* [b]well spoken of by all the Jews who
lived there,
13 came to me, and standing near said to me, '[a]Brother
Saul, receive your sight!' And [1b]at that very time I looked up at
him.
14 "And he said, '[a]The God of our fathers has [b]appointed
you to know His will, and to [c]see the [d]Righteous One, and to
hear an [1]utterance from His mouth.
15 'For you will be [a]a witness for Him to all men of [b]what
you have seen and heard.
16 'And now why do you delay? [a]Arise, and be baptized,
and [b]wash away your sins, [c]calling on His name.'
17 "And it came about that when I [a]returned to Jerusalem
and was praying in the temple, I [b]fell into a trance,
18 and I saw Him saying to me, '[a]Make haste, and get out
of Jerusalem quickly, because they will not accept your testimony about Me.'
19 "And I said, 'Lord, they themselves understand that in
one synagogue after another [a]I used to imprison and [b]beat
those who believed in Thee.
20 'And [a]when the blood of Thy witness Stephen was being
shed, I also was standing by approving, and watching out for
the cloaks of those who were slaying him.'
21 "And He said to me, 'Go! For I will send you far away
[a]to the Gentiles.' "
22 And they listened to him up to this statement, and
then they raised their voices and said, "[a]Away with such a
fellow from the earth, for [b]he should not be allowed to live!"
23 And as they were crying out and [a]throwing off their
cloaks and [b]tossing dust into the air,
24 the [1]commander ordered him to be brought into [a]the
barracks, stating that he should be [b]examined by scourging so
that he might find out the reason why they were shouting
against him that way.
25 And when they stretched him out [1]with thongs, Paul
said to the centurion who was standing by, "Is it lawful for you
to scourge [a]a man who is a Roman and uncondemned?"
26 And when the centurion heard *this,* he went to the
[1]commander and told him, saying, "What are you about to
do? For this man is a Roman."
27 And the [1]commander came and said to him, "Tell me,
are you a Roman?" And he said, "Yes."
28 And the [1]commander answered, "I acquired this citi-
zenship with a large sum of money." And Paul said, "But I was
actually born *a citizen.*"
29 Therefore those who were about to [a]examine him immediately [1]let go of him; and the [2]commander also [b]was afraid
when he found out that he was a Roman, and because he had
[3c]put him in chains.
30 But on the next day, [a]wishing to know for certain why
he had been accused by the Jews, he [b]released him and ordered

11 [1]Or, *glory* [a]Acts 9:8
12 [a]Acts 9:10 [b]Acts 6:3; 10:22
13 [1]Or, *instantly;* lit., *at that very hour* [a]Acts 9:17 [b]Acts 9:18
14 [1]Or, *message;* lit., *voice* [a]Acts 3:13 [b]Acts 9:15; 26:16 [c]Acts 9:17; 26:16; 1 Cor. 9:1; 15:8 [d]Acts 7:52
15 [a]Acts 23:11; 26:16 [b]Acts 22:14
16 [a]Acts 9:18 [b]1 Cor. 6:11; Heb. 10:22; Acts 2:38; Eph. 5:26 [c]Acts 7:59
17 [a]Acts 9:26; 26:20 [b]Acts 10:10
18 [a]Acts 9:29
19 [a]Acts 8:3; 22:4 [b]Acts 26:11; Matt. 10:17
20 [a]Acts 7:58f.; 8:1; 26:10
21 [a]Acts 9:15
22 [a]Acts 21:36; 1 Thess. 2:16 [b]Acts 25:24
23 [a]Acts 7:58 [b]2 Sam. 16:13
24 [1]Lit., *chiliarch,* in command of one thousand troops [a]Acts 21:34 [b]Acts 22:29
25 [1]Lit., *for the thongs* [a]Acts 16:37
26 [1]Vs. 24 note
27 [1]Vs. 24 note
28 [1]Vs. 24 note
29 [1]Or, *withdrew from* [2]Vs. 24 note [3]Lit., *bound him* [a]Acts 22:24 [b]Acts 16:38 [c]Acts 22:24f.
30 [a]Acts 23:28 [b]Acts 21:33

the chief priests and all [c]the [1]Council to assemble, and brought
Paul down and set him before them.

CHAPTER 23

AND Paul, looking intently at [a]the [1]Council, said, "[b]Brethren, [c]I have [2]lived my life with a perfectly good conscience
before God up to this day."
2 And the high priest [a]Ananias commanded those standing beside him [b]to strike him on the mouth.
3 Then Paul said to him, "God is going to strike you,
[a]you white-washed wall! And do you [b]sit to try me according to
the Law, and in violation of the Law order me to be struck?"
4 But the bystanders said, "Do you revile God's high
priest?"
5 And Paul said, "I was not aware, brethren, that he was
high priest; for it is written, '[a]YOU SHALL NOT SPEAK EVIL OF A
RULER OF YOUR PEOPLE.' "
6 But perceiving that one party were [a]Sadducees and the
other Pharisees, Paul *began* crying out in [b]the [1]Council,
"[c]Brethren, [d]I am a Pharisee, a son of Pharisees; I am on trial
for [e]the hope and resurrection of the dead!"
7 And as he said this, there arose a dissension between
the Pharisees and Sadducees; and the assembly was divided.
8 For [a]the Sadducees say that there is no resurrection,
nor an angel, nor a spirit; but the Pharisees acknowledge them
[1]all.
9 And there arose a great uproar; and some of [a]the
scribes of the Pharisaic party stood up and *began* to argue
heatedly, saying, "[b]We find nothing wrong with this man; [c]suppose a spirit or an angel has spoken to him?"
10 And as a great dissension was developing, the [1]commander was afraid Paul would be torn to pieces by them and
ordered the troops to go down and take him away from them
by force, and bring him into [a]the barracks.
11 But on [a]the night *immediately* following, the Lord
stood at his side and said, "[b]Take courage; for [c]as you have
[d]solemnly witnessed to My cause at Jerusalem, so you must
witness at Rome also."
12 And when it was day, [a]the Jews formed a [1]conspiracy
and [b]bound themselves under an oath, saying that they would
neither eat nor drink until they had killed Paul.
13 And there were more than forty who formed this plot.
14 And they came to the chief priests and the elders, and
said, "We have [a]bound ourselves under a solemn oath to taste
nothing until we have killed Paul.
15 "Now, therefore, you [1]and [a]the [2]Council notify the
[3]commander to bring him down to you, as though you were
going to determine his case by a more thorough investigation;
and we for our part are ready to slay him before he comes near
the place."
16 But the son of Paul's sister heard of their ambush, [1]and
he came and entered [a]the barracks and told Paul.
17 And Paul called one of the centurions to him and said,
"Lead this young man to the [1]commander, for he has something
to report to him."

30 [1]Or, *Sanhedrin* [c]Matt. 5:22

1 [1]Or, *Sanhedrin* [2]Or, *conducted myself as a citizen* [a]Acts 22:30; 23:6, 15, 20, 28 [b]Acts 22:5 [c]Acts 24:16; 2 Cor. 1:12; 2 Tim. 1:3

2 [a]Acts 24:1 [b]John 18:22

3 [a]Matt. 23:27 [b]Lev. 19:15; Deut. 25:2; John 7:51

5 [a]Ex. 22:28

6 [1]Or, *Sanhedrin* [a]Matt. 22:23; 3:7 [b]Acts 22:30; 23:1, 15, 20, 28 [c]Acts 22:5 [d]Acts 26:5; Phil. 3:5 [e]Acts 24:15, 21; 26:8

8 [1]Lit., *both* [a]Matt. 22:23; Acts 3:7

9 [a]Mark 2:16; Luke 5:30 [b]Acts 23:29 [c]Acts 22:6ff.; John 12:29

10 [1]Lit., *chiliarch,* in command of one thousand troops [a]Acts 21:34; 23:16, 32

11 [a]Acts 18:9 [b]Matt. 9:2 [c]Acts 19:21 [d]Acts 28:23; Luke 16:28

12 [1]Or, *mob* [a]Acts 23:30; Acts 9:23; 1 Thess. 2:16 [b]Acts 23:14, 21

14 [a]Acts 23:12, 21

15 [1]Lit., *with* [2]Or, *Sanhedrin* [3]Vs. 10 note [a]Acts 22:30; 23:1, 6, 20, 28

16 [1]Or, *having been present* with them, *and he entered* [a]Acts 21:34; 23:10, 32

17 [1]Vs. 10 note

18 So he took him and led him to the [1]commander and
*said, "Paul [a]the prisoner called me to him and asked me to
lead this young man to you since he has something to tell
you."
19 And the [1]commander took him by the hand and stepping aside, *began* to inquire of him privately, "What is it that
you have to report to me?"
20 And he said, "[a]The Jews have agreed to ask you to
bring Paul down tomorrow to [b]the [1]Council, as though you
were going to inquire somewhat more thoroughly about him.
21 "So do not [1]listen to them, for more than forty of them
are [a]lying in wait for him who have [b]bound themselves under a
curse not to eat or drink until they slay him; and now they are
ready and waiting for the promise from you."
22 Therefore the [1]commander let the young man go, instructing him, "Tell no one that you have notified me of these
things."
23 And he called to him two of the centurions, and said,
"Get two hundred soldiers ready by [1]the third hour of the
night to proceed to [a]Caesarea, [2]with seventy horsemen and
two hundred [3]spearmen."
24 *They were* also to provide mounts to put Paul on and
bring him safely to [a]Felix the governor.
25 And he wrote a letter having this form:
26 "Claudius Lysias, to the [a]most excellent governor Felix, [b]greetings.
27 "When this man was arrested by the Jews and [a]was
about to be slain by them, [a]I came upon them with
the troops and rescued him, [b]having learned that he
was a Roman.
28 "And [a]wanting to ascertain the charge for which they
were accusing him, I [b]brought him down to their
[1c]Council;
29 and I found him to be accused over [a]questions about
their Law, but [1]under [b]no accusation deserving death
or [2]imprisonment.
30 "And when I was [a]informed that there would be [b]a
plot against the man, I sent him to you at once, also
instructing [c]his accusers to [1]bring charges against him
before you.[2]"
31 So the soldiers, in accordance with their orders, took
Paul and brought him by night to Antipatris.
32 But the next day, leaving [a]the horsemen to go on with
him, they returned to [b]the barracks.
33 And when these had come to [a]Caesarea and delivered
the letter to [b]the governor, they also presented Paul to him.
34 And when he had read it, he asked from what [a]province
he was; and when he learned that [b]he was from Cilicia,
35 he said, "I will give you a hearing after your [a]accusers
arrive also," giving orders for him to be [b]kept in Herod's
[1]Praetorium.

Chapter 24

AND after [a]five days the high priest [b]Ananias came down
with some elders, [1]with a certain [2]attorney *named* Tertullus;
and they [3]brought charges to [c]the governor against Paul.

18 [1]Vs. 10 note [a]Eph. 3:1

19 [1]Vs. 10 note

20 [1]Or, *Sanhedrin* [a]Acts 23:14f. [b]Acts 22:30; 23:1, 6, 15, 28

21 [1]Lit., *be persuaded by them* [a]Luke 11:54 [b]Acts 23:12, 14

22 [1]Vs. 10 note

23 [1]I.e., 9 p.m. [2]Lit., *and* [3]Or, *slingers* or *bowmen* [a]Acts 8:40; 23:33

24 [a]Acts 23:26, 33; 24:1, 3, 10; 25:14

26 [a]Acts 24:3; 26:25; Luke 1:3 [b]Acts 15:23

27 [a]Acts 21:32f. [b]Acts 22:25-29

28 [1]Or, *Sanhedrin* [a]Acts 22:30 [b]Acts 23:10 [c]Acts 23:1

29 [1]Lit., *having* [2]Lit., *bonds* [a]Acts 18:15; Acts 25:19 [b]Acts 25:25; 26:31; 28:18; 23:9

30 [1]Lit., *speak against him* [2]Some mss. add, *Farewell* [a]Acts 23:20f. [b]Acts 23:12; 9:24 [c]Acts 23:35; 24:19; 25:16

32 [a]Acts 23:23 [b]Acts 23:10

33 [a]Acts 8:40; 23:23 [b]Acts 23:24, 26; 24:1, 3, 10; 25:14

34 [a]Acts 25:1 [b]Acts 21:39; 6:9

35 [1]Or, *governor's official residence* [a]Acts 23:30; 24:19; 25:16 [b]Acts 24:27

1 [1]Lit., *and* [2]Lit., *orator* [3]Or, *presented their evidence*, or *case* [a]Acts 24:11 [b]Acts 23:2 [c]Acts 23:24

2 And after *Paul* had been summoned, Tertullus began to accuse him, saying *to the governor*,

"**S**ince we have through you attained much peace, and since by your providence reforms are being carried out for this nation,

3 we acknowledge *this* in every way and everywhere, [a]most excellent Felix, with all thankfulness.

4 "But, that I may not weary you any further, I beg you [1]to grant us, by your kindness, a brief hearing.

5 "For we have found this man a real pest and a fellow who stirs up dissension among all the Jews throughout [1]the world, and a ringleader of the [a]sect of the Nazarenes.

6 "And he even tried to [a]desecrate the temple; and [1]then we arrested him.[2]

7 (See marginal note[2], vs. 6.)

8 "And by examining him yourself concerning all these matters, you will be able to ascertain the things of which we accuse him."

9 And [a]the Jews also joined in the attack, asserting that these things were so.

10 And when [a]the governor had nodded for him to speak, Paul responded:

"**K**nowing that for many years you have been a judge to this nation, I cheerfully make my defense,

11 since you can take note of the fact that no more than [a]twelve days ago I went up to Jerusalem to worship.

12 "And [a]neither in the temple, nor in the synagogues, nor in the city *itself* did they find me carrying on a discussion with anyone or [b]causing [1]a riot.

13 "[a]Nor can they prove to you the charges of which they now accuse me.

14 "But this I admit to you, that according to [a]the Way which they call a [b]sect I do serve [1c]the God of our fathers, [d]believing everything that is in accordance with the Law, and that is written in the Prophets;

15 having a hope in God, which [a]these men cherish themselves, that there shall certainly be a resurrection of both the righteous and the wicked.

16 "In view of this, [a]I also [1]do my best to maintain always a blameless conscience *both* before God and before men.

17 "Now [a]after several years I [b]came to bring [1]alms to my nation and to present offerings;

18 in which they found me *occupied* in the temple, having been [a]purified, without *any* [b]crowd or uproar. But *there were* certain [c]Jews from [1]Asia—

19 who ought to have been present before you, and to [a]make accusation, if they should have anything against me.

20 "Or else let these men themselves tell what misdeed they found when I stood before [a]the [1]Council,

21 other than for this one statement which [a]I shouted out while standing among them, 'For the resurrection of the dead I am on trial before you today.' "

22 But Felix, having a more exact knowledge about [a]the Way, put them off, saying, "When Lysias the [1]commander comes down, I will decide your case."

23 And he gave orders to the centurion for him to be [a]kept

3 [a]Acts 23:26; 26:25

4 [1]Lit., *to hear. . . . briefly*

5 [1]Lit., *the inhabited earth* [a]Acts 15:5; 24:14

6 [1]Lit., *also* [2]Some later mss. add, *[And we wanted to judge him according to our own Law. 7 "But Lysias the commander came along, and with much violence took him out of our hands, 8 ordering his accusers to come before you.]* [a]Acts 21:28

9 [a]1 Thess. 2:16

10 [a]Acts 23:24

11 [a]Acts 21:18, 27; 24:1

12 [1]Lit., *an attack of a mob* [a]Acts 25:8 [b]Acts 24:18

13 [a]Acts 25:7

14 [1]Lit., *the ancestral god* [a]Acts 24:22; 9:2 [b]Acts 15:5; 24:5 [c]Acts 3:13 [d]Acts 25:8; 26:4ff., 22f.; 28:23

15 [a]Dan. 12:2; John 5:28f.; 11:24; Acts 23:6

16 [1]Lit., *practice myself* [a]Acts 23:1

17 [1]Or, *gifts to charity* [a]Acts 20:31 [b]Rom. 15:25-28; 1 Cor. 16:1-4; 2 Cor. 8:1-4; 9:1, 2, 12; Acts 11:29f.; Gal. 2:10

18 [1]I.e., west coast province of Asia Minor [a]Acts 21:26 [b]Acts 24:12 [c]Acts 21:27

19 [a]Acts 23:30

20 [1]Or, *Sanhedrin* [a]Matt. 5:22

21 [a]Acts 23:6; 24:15

22 [1]Lit., *chiliarch,* in command of one thousand troops [a]Acts 24:14

23 [a]Acts 23:35

in custody and *yet* [b]have *some* freedom, and not to prevent
any of [c]his friends from ministering to him.
24 But some days later, Felix arrived with Drusilla, his
[1]wife who was a Jewess, and sent for Paul, and heard him *speak*
about [a]faith in Christ Jesus.
25 And as he was discussing [a]righteousness, [b]self-control
and [c]the judgment to come, Felix became frightened and said,
"Go away for the present, and when I find time, I will summon
you."
26 At the same time too, he was hoping that [a]money
would be given him by Paul; therefore he also used to send for
him quite often and converse with him.
27 But after two years had passed, Felix [1]was succeeded by
Porcius [a]Festus; and [b]wishing to do the Jews a favor, Felix left
Paul [c]imprisoned.

CHAPTER 25

FESTUS therefore, having arrived in [a]the province, three
days later went up to Jerusalem from [b]Caesarea.
2 And the chief priests and the leading men of the Jews
[a]brought charges against Paul; and they were urging him,
3 requesting a [1]concession against [2]Paul, that he might
[3]have him brought to Jerusalem, (*at the same time*, [a]setting an
ambush to kill him on the way).
4 Festus then [a]answered that Paul [b]was being kept in
custody at [c]Caesarea and that he himself was about to leave
shortly.
5 "Therefore," he *said, "let the influential men among
you [1]go there with me, and if there is anything wrong [2]about
the man, let them [3]prosecute him."
6 And after he had spent not more than eight or ten days
among them, he went down to [a]Caesarea; and on the next day
he took his seat on [b]the tribunal and ordered Paul to be
brought.
7 And after he had arrived, the Jews who had come down
from Jerusalem stood around him, bringing [a]many and serious
charges against him [b]which they could not prove;
8 while Paul said in his own defense, "[a]I have committed
no offense either against the Law of the Jews or against the
temple or against Caesar."
9 But Festus, [a]wishing to do the Jews a favor, answered
Paul and said, "[b]Are you willing to go up to Jerusalem and
[1]stand trial before me on these charges?"
10 But Paul said, "I am standing before Caesar's [a]tribunal,
where I ought to be tried. I have done no wrong to *the* Jews, as
you also very well know.
11 "If then I am a wrongdoer, and have committed anything
worthy of death, I do not refuse to die; but if none of
those things is *true* of which these men accuse me, no one can
hand me over to them. I [a]appeal to Caesar."
12 Then when Festus had conferred with [a]his council, he
answered, "You have appealed to Caesar, to Caesar you shall
go."
13 Now when several days had elapsed, King Agrippa and
Bernice arrived at [a]Caesarea, [1]and paid their respects to
Festus.

[b]Acts 28:16 [c]Acts 23:16; 27:3

24 [1]Lit., *own wife* [a]Acts 20:21

25 [a]Titus 2:12 [b]Gal. 5:23; 2 Pet. 1:6; Titus 1:8 [c]Acts 10:42

26 [a]Acts 24:17

27 [1]Lit., *received a successor, Porcius Festus* [a]Acts 25:1, 4, 9, 12; 26:24f., 32 [b]Acts 25:9; 12:3 [c]Acts 23:35; 25:14

1 [a]Acts 23:34 [b]Acts 8:40; 25:4, 6, 13

2 [a]Acts 24:1; 25:15

3 [1]Or, *favor* [2]Lit., *him* [3]Lit., *send for him to Jerusalem* [a]Acts 9:24

4 [a]Acts 25:16 [b]Acts 24:23 [c]Acts 8:40; 25:1, 6, 13

5 [1]Lit., *go down* [2]Lit., *in* [3]Or, *accuse*

6 [a]Acts 8:40; 25:1, 4, 13 [b]Matt. 27:19; Acts 25:10, 17

7 [a]Acts 24:5f. [b]Acts 24:13

8 [a]Acts 24:12; 28:17; 6:13

9 [1]Lit., *be judged* [a]Acts 24:27; 12:3 [b]Acts 25:20

10 [a]Matt. 27:19; Acts 25:10, 17

11 [a]Acts 25:21, 25; 26:32; 28:19

12 [a]A different body from that mentioned Acts 4:15 and subsequently [e.g. Acts 24:20]

13 [1]Lit., *greeting Festus* [a]Acts 8:40; 25:1, 4, 6

14 And while they were spending many days there, Festus
laid Paul's case before the king, saying, "There is a certain man
[a]left a prisoner by Felix;
15 and when I was at Jerusalem, the chief priests and the
elders of the Jews [a]brought charges against him, asking for a
sentence of condemnation upon him.
16 "And I [a]answered them that it is not the custom of the
Romans to hand over any man before [b]the accused meets his
accusers face to face, and has an opportunity to make his
defense against the charges.
17 "And so after they had assembled here, I made no delay,
but on the next day took my seat on [a]the tribunal, and ordered
the man to be brought.
18 "And when the accusers stood up, they *began* bringing
charges against him not of such crimes as I was expecting;
19 but they *simply* had some [a]points of disagreement with
him about their own [1b]religion and about a certain dead man,
Jesus, whom Paul asserted to be alive.
20 "And [a]being at a loss how to investigate [1]such matters, I
asked whether he was willing to go to Jerusalem and there
stand trial on these matters.
21 "But when Paul [a]appealed to be held in custody for [1]the
Emperor's decision, I ordered him to be kept in custody until I
send him to Caesar."
22 And [a]Agrippa *said* to Festus, "I also would like to hear
the man myself." "Tomorrow," he *said, "you shall hear him."
23 And so, on the next day when [a]Agrippa had come [1]to-
gether with [a]Bernice, amid great pomp, and had entered the
auditorium [2]accompained by the [3]commanders and the promi-
nent men of the city, at the command of Festus, Paul was
brought in.
24 And Festus *said, "King Agrippa, and all you gentle-
men here present with us, you behold this man about whom
[a]all the people of the Jews appealed to me, both at Jerusalem
and here, loudly declaring that [b]he ought not to live any
longer.
25 "But I found that he had committed [a]nothing worthy of
death; and since he himself [b]appealed to [1]the Emperor, I decided to send him.
26 "[1]Yet I have nothing definite about him to write to my
lord. Therefore I have brought him before you *all* and especially before you, King Agrippa, so that after the investigation
has taken place, I may have something to write.
27 "For it seems absurd to me in sending a prisoner, not to
indicate also the charges against him."

Chapter 26

AND [a]Agrippa said to Paul, "You are permitted to speak for
yourself." Then Paul stretched out his hand and *proceeded* to
make his defense:
2 "In regard to all the things of which I am accused by the
Jews, I consider myself fortunate, King Agrippa, that I am
about to make my defense before you today;
3 [1]especially because you are an expert in all [a]customs
and [2]questions among *the* Jews; therefore I beg you to listen to
me patiently.

14 [a]Acts 24:27
15 [a]Acts 24:1; 25:2
16 [a]Acts 25:4f. [b]Acts 23:30
17 [a]Matt. 27:19; Acts 25:6, 10
19 [1]Or, *superstition* [a]Acts 18:15; 23:29 [b]Acts 17:22
20 [1]Lit., *these* [a]Acts 25:9
21 [1]Lit., *the Augustus* (in this case Nero) [a]Acts 25:11f.
22 [a]Acts 9:15
23 [1]Lit., *and Bernice* [2]Lit., *and with* [3]Lit., *chiliarchs*, in command of one thousand troops [a]Acts 25:13; 26:30
24 [a]Acts 25:2, 7 [b]Acts 22:22
25 [1]Note vs. 21 [a]Acts 23:29 [b]Acts 25:11f.
26 [1]Lit., *About whom I have nothing definite*
1 [a]Acts 9:15
3 [1]Or, *because you are especially expert* [2]Or, *controversial issues* [a]Acts 6:14; 25:19; 26:7

4 "So then, all Jews know [a]my manner of life from my
youth up, which from the beginning was spent among my *own*
nation and at Jerusalem;
5 since they have known about me for a long time previously, if they are willing to testify, that I lived *as* a [a]Pharisee
[b]according to the strictest [c]sect of our religion.
6 "And now I am [1]standing trial [a]for the hope of [b]the
promise made by God to our fathers;
7 *the promise* [a]to which our twelve tribes hope to attain,
as they earnestly serve *God* night and day. And for this [b]hope,
O King, I am being [c]accused by Jews.
8 "Why is it considered incredible among you *people* [a]if
God does raise the dead?
9 "So then, [a]I thought to myself that I had to do many
things hostile to [b]the name of Jesus of Nazareth.
10 "And this is [1]just what I [a]did in Jerusalem; not only did I
lock up many of the [2]saints in prisons, having [b]received authority from the chief priests, but also when they were being put
to death I [c]cast my vote against them.
11 "And [a]as I punished them often in all the synagogues, I
tried to force them to blaspheme; and being [b]furiously enraged
at them, I kept pursuing them [c]even to [1]foreign cities.
12 "[1]While thus engaged [a]as I was journeying to Damascus
with the authority and commission of the chief priests,
13 at midday, O King, I saw on the way a light from
heaven, [1]brighter than the sun, shining all around me and
those who were journeying with me.
14 "And when we had [a]all fallen to the ground, I heard a
voice saying to me in the [1b]Hebrew dialect, 'Saul, Saul, why are
you persecuting me? It is hard for you to kick against the
goads.'
15 "And I said, 'Who art Thou, Lord?' And the Lord said,
'I am Jesus whom you are persecuting.
16 'But arise, and [a]stand on your feet; for this purpose I
have appeared to you, to [b]appoint you a [c]minister and [d]a
witness not only to the things which you have [1]seen, but also to
the things in which I will appear to you;
17 [a]delivering you [b]from the *Jewish* people and from the
Gentiles, to whom I am sending you,
18 to [a]open their eyes so that they may turn from [b]dark-
ness to light and from the dominion of [c]Satan to God, in
order that they may receive [d]forgiveness of sins and an [e]inheri-
tance among those who have been sanctified by [f]faith in Me.'
19 "Consequently, King Agrippa, I did not prove disobedient to the heavenly vision,
20 but *kept* declaring both [a]to those of Damascus first,
and *also* [b]at Jerusalem and *then* throughout all the region of
Judea, and *even* [c]to the Gentiles, that they should [d]repent and
turn to God, performing deeds [e]appropriate to repentance.
21 "For this reason *some* Jews [a]seized me in the temple and
tried [b]to put me to death.
22 "And so, having obtained help from God, I stand to this
day [a]testifying both to small and great, stating nothing but
what [b]the Prophets and Moses said was going to take place;
23 [1a]that [2]the Christ was [3]to suffer, *and* [1]that [b]by reason of

4 [a]Gal. 1:13f.; Phil. 3:5

5 [a]Acts 23:6 [b]Acts 22:3 [c]Acts 15:5

6 [1]Lit., *being tried* [a]Acts 28:20; 24:15 [b]Acts 13:32

7 [a]James 1:1 [b]Acts 28:20; 24:15 [c]Acts 26:2

8 [a]Acts 23:6

9 [a]1 Tim. 1:13; John 16:2 [b]John 15:21

10 [1]Lit., *also* [2]I.e., true believers; lit., *holy ones* [a]Acts 8:3; 9:13 [b]Acts 9:1f. [c]Acts 22:20

11 [1]Or, *outlying* [a]Acts 22:19; Matt. 10:17 [b]Acts 9:1 [c]Acts 22:5

12 [1]Lit., *In which things* [a]Acts 26:12-18; 9:3-8; *22:6-11*

13 [1]Lit., *above the brightness of*

14 [1]I.e., Jewish Aramaic [a]Acts 9:7 [b]Acts 21:40

16 [1]Some early mss. read, *seen Me* [a]Ezek. 2:1; Dan. 10:11 [b]Acts 22:14 [c]Luke 1:2 [d]Acts 22:15

17 [a]Jer. 1:8, 19 [b]1 Chr. 16:35; Acts 9:15

18 [a]Is. 35:5; 42:7, 16; Eph. 5:8; Col. 1:13; 1 Pet. 2:9 [b]John 1:5; Eph. 5:8; Col. 1:12f.; 1 Thess. 5:5; 1 Pet. 2:9 [c]Matt. 4:10 [d]Luke 24:47; Acts 2:38 [e]Acts 20:32 [f]Acts 20:21

20 [a]Acts 9:19ff. [b]Acts 9:26-29; 22:17-20 [c]Acts 13:46; 9:15 [d]Acts 3:19 [e]Matt. 3:8; Luke 3:8

21 [a]Acts 21:27, 30 [b]Acts 21:31

22 [a]Luke 16:28 [b]Acts 10:43; 24:14

23 [1]Lit., *whether* [2]I.e., the Messiah [3]Lit., *subject to suffering* [a]Matt. 26:24; Acts 3:18 [b]1 Cor. 15:20, 23; Col. 1:18; Rev. 1:5

His resurrection from the dead He should be the first to proclaim
[c]light both to the *Jewish* people and to the Gentiles."
24 And while *Paul* was saying this in his defense, Festus
*said in a loud voice, "Paul, you are out of your mind! [1]*Your*
great [a]learning is [2]driving you mad."
25 But Paul *said, "I am not out of my mind, [a]most excellent Festus, but I utter words [1]of sober truth.
26 "For the king [1a]knows about these matters, and I speak
to him also with confidence, [2]since I am persuaded that none
of these things escape his notice; for this has not been done in
a corner.
27 "King Agrippa, do you believe the Prophets? I know
that you do."
28 And Agrippa *replied* to Paul, "[1]In a short time you [2]will
persuade me to [3]become a [a]Christian."
29 And Paul *said*, "[1]I would to God, that whether [2]in a
short or long time, not only you, but also all who hear me this
day, might become such as I am, except for these [a]chains."
30 And [a]the king arose and the governor and Bernice, and
those who were sitting with them,
31 and when they had drawn aside, they *began* talking to
one another, saying, "[a]This man is not doing anything worthy
of death or [1]imprisonment."
32 And Agrippa said to Festus, "This man might have
been [a]set free if he had not [b]appealed to Caesar."

Chapter 27

AND when it was decided that [a]we [b]should sail for [c]Italy,
they proceeded to deliver Paul and some other prisoners to a
centurion of the Augustan [1d]cohort named Julius.
2 And embarking in an Adramyttian ship, which was
about to sail to the regions along the coast of [1a]Asia, we put
out to sea, accompanied by [b]Aristarchus, a [c]Macedonian of
[d]Thessalonica.
3 And the next day we put in at [a]Sidon; and Julius
[b]treated Paul with consideration and [c]allowed him to go to his
friends and receive care.
4 And from there we put out to sea and sailed under the
shelter of [a]Cyprus because [b]the winds were contrary.
5 And when we had sailed through the sea along the
coast of [a]Cilicia and [b]Pamphylia, we landed at Myra in Lycia.
6 And there the centurion found an [a]Alexandrian ship
sailing for [b]Italy, and he put us aboard it.
7 And when we had sailed slowly for a good many days,
and with difficulty had arrived off Cnidus, [a]since the wind did
not permit us *to go* farther, we sailed under the shelter of
[b]Crete, off Salmone;
8 and with difficulty [a]sailing past it we came to a certain
place called Fair Havens, near which was the city of Lasea.
9 And when considerable time had passed and the voyage
was now dangerous, since even [a]the [1]Fast was already over,
Paul *began* to admonish them,
10 and said to them, "Men, I perceive that the voyage will
certainly be *attended* with [a]damage and great loss, not only of
the cargo and the ship, but also of our lives."

23 [c]Luke 2:32; 2 Cor. 4:4

24 [1]Lit., *The many letters* [2]Lit., *turning you to madness* [a]John 7:15; 2 Tim. 3:15

25 [1]Lit., *of truth and rationality* [a]Acts 23:26; 24:3

26 [1]Or, *understands* [2]Or, *for* [a]Acts 26:3

28 [1]Or, *with a little* [2]Or, *try to convince* [3]Lit., *make* [a]Acts 11:26

29 [1]Lit., *I would pray to* [2]Or, *with a little or with much* [a]Acts 21:33

30 [a]Acts 25:23

31 [1]Lit., *bonds* [a]Acts 23:29

32 [a]Acts 28:18 [b]Acts 25:11

1 [1]Or, *battalion* [a][we] Acts 27:1-28; 16:10 [b]Acts 25:12, 25 [c]Acts 18:2; 27:6 [d]Acts 10:1

2 [1]I.e., west coast province of Asia Minor [a]Acts 2:9 [b]Acts 19:29 [c]Acts 16:9 [d]Acts 17:1

3 [a]Matt. 11:21 [b]Acts 27:43 [c]Acts 24:23

4 [a]Acts 4:36 [b]Acts 27:7

5 [a]Acts 6:9 [b]Acts 13:13

6 [a]Acts 28:11 [b]Acts 18:2; 27:1

7 [a]Acts 27:4 [b]Acts 27:12f., 21; Titus 1:5; Acts 2:11; Titus 1:12

8 [a]Acts 27:13 [Gr.]

9 [1]I.e., the Day of Atonement in October [a]Lev. 16:29-31; 23:27-29; Num. 29:7

10 [a]Acts 27:21

11 But the centurion was more persuaded by the [a]pilot
and the [1]captain of the ship, than by what was being said by
Paul.
12 And because the harbor was not suitable for wintering,
the majority reached a decision to put out to sea from there, if
somehow they could reach Phoenix, a harbor of [a]Crete, facing
[1]northeast and southeast, and spend the winter *there*.
13 And [1]when a moderate south wind came up, supposing
that they had gained their purpose, they weighed anchor and
began [a]sailing along [b]Crete, close *inshore*.
14 But before very long there [a]rushed down from [1]the land
a violent wind, called [2]Euraquilo;
15 and when the ship was caught *in it*, and could not face
the wind, we gave way *to it*, and let ourselves be driven along.
16 And running under the shelter of a small island called
[1]Clauda, we were scarcely able to get the *ship's* boat under
control.
17 And after they had hoisted it up, they used [1]supporting
cables in undergirding the ship; and fearing that they might
[a]run aground on *the shallows* of Syrtis, they let down the [2]sea
anchor, and so let themselves be driven along.
18 The next day as we were being violently storm-tossed,
[1]they began to [a]jettison the cargo;
19 and on the third day they threw the ship's tackle overboard with their own hands.
20 And since neither sun nor stars appeared for many
days, and no small storm was assailing *us*, from then on all
hope of our being saved was gradually abandoned.
21 And [1]when they had gone a long time without food,
then Paul stood up in their midst and said, "[a]Men, you ought
to have [2]followed my advice and not to have set sail from
[b]Crete, and [3]incurred this [a]damage and loss.
22 "And *yet* now I urge you to [a]keep up your courage, for
there shall be no loss of life among you, but *only* of the ship.
23 "For this very night [a]an angel of the God to whom I
belong and [b]whom I serve [c]stood before me,
24 saying, 'Do not be afraid, Paul; [a]you must stand before
Caesar; and behold, God has granted you [b]all those who are
sailing with you.'
25 "Therefore, [a]keep up your courage, men, for I believe
God, that [1]it will turn out exactly as I have been told.
26 "But we must [a]run aground on a certain [b]island."
27 But when the fourteenth night had come, as we were
being driven about in the Adriatic Sea, about midnight the
sailors *began* to surmise that [1]they were approaching some
land.
28 And they took soundings, and found *it to be* twenty
fathoms; and a little farther on they took another sounding
and found *it to be* fifteen fathoms.
29 And fearing that we might [a]run aground somewhere on
the [1]rocks, they cast four anchors from the stern and [2]wished
for daybreak.
30 And as the sailors were trying to escape from the ship,
and had let down [a]the *ship's* boat into the sea, on the pretense
of intending to lay out anchors from the bow,

11 [1]Or, *owner* [a]Rev. 18:17

12 [1]Or possibly, *southwest and northwest* [a]Acts 27:13, 21; Titus 1:5; Acts 2:11; Titus 1:12

13 [1]Lit., *a south wind having gently blown* [a]Acts 27:8 [Gr.] [b]Acts 27:12f., 21; Titus 1:5; Acts 2:11; Titus 1:12

14 [1]Lit., *it* [2]I.e., a northeaster [a]Mark 4:37

16 [1]Some ancient mss. read, *Cauda*

17 [1]Lit., *helps* [2]Or possibly, *sail* [a]Acts 27:26, 29

18 [1]Lit., *they were doing a throwing out* [a]Acts 27:38; Jonah 1:5

21 [1]Lit., *there being much abstinence from food* [2]Lit., *obeyed me* [3]Lit., *gained* [a]Acts 27:10 [b]Acts 27:7

22 [a]Acts 27:25, 36

23 [a]Acts 5:19 [b]Rom. 1:9 [c]Acts 23:11; 18:9; 2 Tim. 4:17

24 [a]Acts 23:11 [b]Acts 27:44; Acts 27:31, 42

25 [1]Lit., *it will be* [a]Acts 27:22, 36

26 [a]Acts 27:17, 29 [b]Acts 28:1

27 [1]Lit., *some land was approaching them*

29 [1]Lit., *rough places* [2]Lit., *they were praying for it to become day* [a]Acts 27:17, 26

30 [a]Acts 27:16

31 Paul said to the centurion and to the soldiers, "Unless
these men remain in the ship, you yourselves cannot be saved."
32 Then the soldiers cut away the [a]ropes of the *ship's*
boat, and let it fall away.
33 And until the day was about to dawn, Paul was encouraging them all to take some food, saying, "Today is the fourteenth day that you have been constantly watching and going
without eating, having taken nothing.
34 "Therefore I encourage you to take some food, for this
is for your preservation; for [a]not a hair from the head of any of
you shall perish."
35 And having said this, he took bread and [a]gave thanks to
God in the presence of all; and he broke it and began to eat.
36 And all [a]of them [1]were encouraged, and they themselves also took food.
37 And all of us in the ship were two hundred and seventy-
six [1a]persons.
38 And when they had eaten enough, they *began* to light-
en the ship by [a]throwing out the wheat into the sea.
39 And when day came, [a]they [1]could not recognize the
land; but they [2]did observe a certain bay with a beach, and
they [3]resolved to [4]drive the ship onto it if they could.
40 And casting off [a]the anchors, they [1]left them in the sea
while at the same time they were loosening the ropes of the
rudders, and hoisting the foresail to the wind, they were head-
ing for the beach.
41 But striking a [1]reef where two seas met, they ran the
vessel aground; and the prow stuck fast and remained immovable, but the stern *began* to be broken up by the force *of the
waves.*
42 And the soldiers' plan was to [a]kill the prisoners, that
none *of them* should swim away and escape;
43 but the centurion, [a]wanting to bring Paul safely
through, kept them from their intention, and commanded that
those who could swim should [1]jump overboard first and get to
land,
44 and the rest *should follow,* some on planks, and others
on various things from the ship. And thus it happened that
[a]they all were brought safely to land.

Chapter 28

AND when [a]they had been brought safely through, [b]then we
found out that [c]the island was called [1]Malta.
2 And [a]the [1]natives showed us extraordinary kindness; for
because of the rain that had set in and because of the cold,
they kindled a fire and [b]received us all.
3 But when Paul had gathered a bundle of sticks and laid
them on the fire, a viper came out [1]because of the heat, and
fastened on his hand.
4 And when [a]the [1]natives saw the creature hanging from
his hand, they *began* saying to one another, "[b]Undoubtedly
this man is a murderer, and though he has been saved from the
sea, [2]Justice has not allowed him to live."
5 However [a]he shook the creature off into the fire and
suffered no harm.

32 [a]John 2:15 [Gr.]

34 [a]Matt. 10:30

35 [a]Matt. 14:19

36 [1]Lit., *became cheerful* [a]Acts 27:22, 25

37 [1]Lit., *souls* [a]Acts 2:41

38 [a]Acts 27:18; Jonah 1:5

39 [1]Or, *were not recognizing* [2]Or, *were observing* [3]Or, *were resolving* [4]Some ancient mss. read, *bring the ship safely ashore* [a]Acts 28:1

40 [1]Or, *were leaving* [a]Acts 27:29

41 [1]Lit., *place*

42 [a]Acts 12:19

43 [1]Lit., *cast themselves* [a]Acts 27:3

44 [a]Acts 27:22, 31

1 [1]Or, *Melita.* Some mss. read, *Melitene* [a]"we": Acts 27:1 [16:10] [b]Acts 27:39 [c]Acts 27:26

2 [1]Lit., *barbarians* [a]Rom. 1:14; 1 Cor. 14:11; Col. 3:11; Acts 28:4 [b]Rom. 14:1

3 [1]Or, *from the heat*

4 [1]Lit., *barbarians* [2]I.e., personification of a goddess [a]Acts 28:2 [b]Luke 13:2, 4

5 [a]Mark 16:18

6 But they were expecting that he was about to swell up
or suddenly fall down dead. But after they had waited a long
time and had seen nothing unusual happen to him, they
changed their minds and [a]*began* to say that he was a god.
7 Now in the neighborhood of that place were lands belonging to the leading man of the island, named Publius, who
welcomed us and entertained us courteously three days.
8 And it came about that the father of Publius was lying
in bed afflicted with *recurrent* fever and dysentery; and Paul
went in *to see* him and after he had [a]prayed, he [b]laid his hands
on him and healed him.
9 And after this had happened, the rest of the people on
the island who had diseases were coming to him and getting
cured.
10 And they also honored us with many [1]marks of respect;
and when we were setting sail, they [2]supplied *us* with [3]all we
needed.
11 And at the end of three months we set sail on [a]an
Alexandrian ship which had wintered at the island, and which
had [1]the Twin Brothers for its figurehead.
12 And after we put in at Syracuse, we stayed there for
three days.
13 And from there we [1]sailed around and arrived at Rhe-
gium, and a day later a south wind sprang up, and on the
second day we came to Puteoli.
14 [1]There we found *some* [a]brethren, and were invited to
stay with them for seven days; and thus we came to Rome.
15 And the [a]brethren, when they heard about us, came
from there as far as the [1]Market of Appius and [2]Three Inns to
meet us; and when Paul saw them, he thanked God and took
courage.
16 And when we entered Rome, Paul was [a]allowed to stay
by himself, with the soldier who was guarding him.
17 And it happened that after three days he called together those who were [a]the leading men of the Jews, and when
they had come together, he *began* saying to them, "[b]Brethren,
[c]though I had done nothing against our people, or [d]the customs of our [1]fathers, yet I was delivered prisoner from Jerusalem into the hands of the Romans.
18 "And when they had examined me, they [a]were willing to
release me because there was [b]no ground [1]for putting me to
death.
19 "But when the Jews [1]objected, I was forced to [a]appeal to
Caesar; not that I had any accusation against my nation.
20 "For this reason therefore, I [1]requested to see you and
to speak with you, for I am wearing [a]this chain for [b]the sake of
the hope of Israel."
21 And they said to him, "We have neither received letters from Judea concerning you, nor have any of [a]the brethren
come here and reported or spoken anything bad about you.
22 "But we desire to hear from you what [1]your views are;
for concerning this [a]sect, it is known to us that [b]it is spoken
against everywhere."
23 And when they had set a day for him, they came to him
at [a]his lodging in large numbers; and he was explaining to them
by solemnly [b]testifying about the kingdom of God, and trying

6 [a]Acts 14:11

8 [a]Acts 9:40; James 5:14f. [b]Mark 5:23

10 [1]Lit., *honors* [2]Or, *put on board* [3]Lit., *the things pertaining to the needs*

11 [1]Gr., *the Dioscuri*, i.e., the twin sons of Zeus, Castor and Pollux [a]Acts 27:6

13 [1]Some early mss. read, *weighed anchor*

14 [1]Lit., *where* [a]Acts 1:15

15 [1]Lat., Appii Forum, a station about 43 miles from Rome [2]Lat., Tres Tabernae, a station about 33 miles from Rome [a]Acts 1:15

16 [a]Acts 24:23

17 [1]Or, *forefathers* [a]Acts 13:50; 25:2 [b]Acts 22:5 [c]Acts 25:8 [d]Acts 6:14

18 [1]Lit., *of death in me* [a]Acts 26:32 [b]Acts 23:29

19 [1]Lit., *spoke against it* [a]Acts 25:11

20 [1]Or, *invited you to see me and speak with me* [a]Acts 21:33 [b]Acts 26:6f.

21 [a]Acts 22:5

22 [1]Lit., *you think* [a]Acts 24:14 [b]1 Pet. 2:12; 3:16; 4:14, 16

23 [a]Philem. 22 [b]Luke 16:28; Acts 1:3; 23:11

to persuade them concerning Jesus, [c]from both the Law of
Moses and from the Prophets, from morning until evening.
24 And [a]some were being persuaded by the things spoken,
but others would not believe.
25 And when they did not agree with one another, they
began leaving after Paul had spoken one parting word, "The
Holy Spirit rightly spoke through Isaiah the prophet to your
fathers,
26 saying,

'[a]GO TO THIS PEOPLE AND SAY,
"[1b]YOU WILL KEEP ON HEARING, [2]BUT WILL NOT UNDERSTAND;
AND [3]YOU WILL KEEP ON SEEING, BUT WILL NOT PERCEIVE;
27 [a]FOR THE HEART OF THIS PEOPLE HAS BECOME DULL,
AND WITH THEIR EARS THEY SCARCELY HEAR,
AND THEY HAVE CLOSED THEIR EYES;
LEST THEY SHOULD SEE WITH THEIR EYES,
AND HEAR WITH THEIR EARS,
AND UNDERSTAND WITH THEIR HEART AND TURN AGAIN,
AND I SHOULD HEAL THEM." '

28 "Let it be known to you therefore, that [a]this salvation of
God has been sent [b]to the Gentiles; they will also listen."
29 (See marginal note.[1])
30 And he stayed two full years [1]in his own rented quar-
ters, and was welcoming all who came to him,
31 [1a]preaching the kingdom of God, and teaching concerning the Lord Jesus Christ [b]with all openness, unhindered.

23 [c]Acts 8:35

24 [a]Acts 14:4

26 [1]Lit., *with a hearing* [2]Lit., *and* [3]Lit., *seeing you will see* [a]Is. 6:9 [b]Acts 28:26, 27; Matt. 13:14f.

27 [a]Is. 6:10

28 [a]Acts 13:26; Ps. 98:3; Luke 2:30 [b]Acts 13:46; 9:15

29 [1]Some mss. add vs. 29, *And when he had spoken these words, the Jews departed, having a great dispute among themselves.*

30 [1]Or, *at his own expense*

31 [1]Or, *proclaiming* [a]Matt. 4:23; Acts 20:25; 28:23 [b]2 Tim. 2:9

THE EPISTLE OF PAUL TO THE ROMANS

Salutation. Personal Explanations. The Gospel.

PAUL, a bond-servant of Christ Jesus, [1a]called *as* an apostle,
[b]set apart for [c]the gospel of God,
2 which He [a]promised beforehand through His [b]prophets
in the holy Scriptures,
3 concerning His Son, who was born [a]of the seed of
David [b]according to the flesh,
4 who was declared [1]with power *to be* [a]the Son of God
[2]by the resurrection from the dead, according to the [3]Spirit of
holiness, Jesus Christ our Lord,
5 through whom we have received grace and [a]apostleship
[1]to bring about *the* [b]obedience of faith among [c]all the Gentiles, for His name's sake,
6 among whom you also are the [a]called of Jesus Christ;
7 to all who are [a]beloved of God in Rome, called *as*
[1b]saints: [c]Grace to you and peace from God our Father and
the Lord Jesus Christ.
8 First, [a]I thank my God through Jesus Christ for you all,

1 [1]Lit., *a called apostle* [a]1 Cor. 1:1; 9:1; 2 Cor. 1:1 [b]Acts 9:15; 13:2; Gal. 1:15 [c]Mark 1:14; Rom. 15:16; 2 Cor. 11:7; 1 Thess. 2:2, 8, 9; 1 Pet. 4:17; 2 Cor. 2:12

2 [a]Titus 1:2; [b]Luke 1:70; Rom. 3:21; 16:26

3 [a]Matt. 1:1 [b]Rom. 4:1; 9:3, 5; 1 Cor. 10:18; John 1:14

4 [1]Or, *in an act of power* [2]Or, *as a result of* [3]Or, *spirit* [a]Matt. 4:3

5 [1]Lit., *for obedience* [a]Acts 1:25; Gal. 1:16 [b]Rom. 16:26; Acts 6:7 [c]Acts 9:15

6 [a]Jude 1; Rev. 17:14

7 [1]I.e., true believers; lit., *holy ones* [a]1 Thess. 1:4; Rom. 5:5ff.; 8:39 [b]1 Cor. 1:2, 24; Rom. 8:28ff.; Acts 9:13 [c]1 Cor. 1:3; 2 Cor. 1:2; Gal. 1:3; Eph. 1:2; Phil. 1:2; Col. 1:2; 1 Thess. 1:1; 2 Thess. 1:2; 1 Tim. 1:2; 2 Tim. 1:2; Titus 1:4; Philem. 3; 2 John 3; 2 Pet. 1:2; Num. 6:25f.

8 [a]1 Cor. 1:4; Eph. 1:15f.; Phil. 1:3f.; Col. 1:3f.; 1 Thess. 1:2; 2:13; 2 Thess. 1:3; 2:13; 2 Tim. 1:3; Philem. 4

because [b]your faith is being proclaimed throughout the whole
world.
9 For [a]God, whom I [b]serve in my spirit in the *preaching*
of the gospel of His Son, is my witness *as to* how unceasingly [c]I
make mention of you,
10 always in my prayers making request, if perhaps now at
last by [a]the will of God I may succeed in coming to you.
11 For [a]I long to see you in order that I may impart some
spiritual gift to you, that you may be established;
12 that is, that I may be encouraged together with you
while among you, each of us by the other's faith, both yours
and mine.
13 And [a]I do not want you to be unaware, [b]brethren, that
often I [c]have planned to come to you (and have been prevented thus far) in order that I might obtain some [d]fruit
among you also, even as among the rest of the Gentiles.
14 [a]I am [1]under obligation both to Greeks and to [b]barbar-
ians, both to the wise and to the foolish.
15 Thus, [a]for my part, I am eager to [b]preach the gospel to
you also who are in Rome.
16 For I am not [a]ashamed of the gospel, for [b]it is the
power of God for salvation to every one who believes, to the
[c]Jew first and also to [d]the Greek.
17 For in it [a]*the* righteousness of God is revealed [1]from
faith to faith; as it is written, "[2b]BUT THE RIGHTEOUS *man* SHALL
LIVE BY FAITH."
18 For [a]the wrath of God is revealed from heaven against
all ungodliness and unrighteousness of men, who [b]suppress the
truth [1]in unrighteousness,
19 because [a]that which is known about God is evident
[1]within them; for God made it evident to them.
20 For [a]since the creation of the world His invisible attri-
butes, His eternal power and divine nature, have been clearly
seen, [b]being understood through what has been made, so that
they are without excuse.
21 For even though they knew God, they did not [1]honor
Him as God, or give thanks; but they became [a]futile in their
speculations, and their foolish heart was darkened.
22 [a]Professing to be wise, they became fools,
23 and [a]exchanged the glory of the incorruptible God for
an image in the form of corruptible man and of birds and four-
footed animals and [1]crawling creatures.
24 Therefore [a]God gave them over in the lusts of their
hearts to impurity, that their bodies might be [b]dishonored
among them.
25 For they exchanged the truth of God for [1]a [a]lie, and
worshiped and served the creature rather than the Creator,
[b]who is blessed [2]forever. Amen.
26 For this reason [a]God gave them over to [b]degrading
passions; for their women exchanged the natural function for
that which is [1]unnatural,
27 and in the same way also the men abandoned the natural function of the woman and burned in their desire towards
one another, [a]men with men committing [1]indecent acts and
receiving in [2]their own persons the due penalty of their error.

8 [b]Rom. 16:19; Acts 28:22

9 [a]Rom. 9:1; 2 Cor. 1:23; 11:31; Phil. 1:8; 1 Thess. 2:5, 10 [b]Acts 24:14; 2 Tim. 1:3 [c]Eph. 1:16; Phil. 1:3f.; 1 Thess. 1:2f.; 2 Tim. 1:3; Philem. 4

10 [a]Rom. 15:32; Acts 18:21

11 [a]Rom. 15:23; Acts 19:21

13 [a]Rom. 11:25; 1 Cor. 10:1; 12:1; 2 Cor. 1:8; 1 Thess. 4:13 [b]Rom. 7:1; 1 Cor. 1:10; 14:20, 26; Gal. 3:15; Acts 1:15 [c]Rom. 15:22f.; Acts 19:21 [d]John 4:36; 15:16; Phil. 1:22; Col. 1:6

14 [1]Lit., *debtor* [a]1 Cor. 9:16 [b]Acts 28:2

15 [a]Rom. 12:18 [b]Rom. 15:20

16 [a]2 Tim. 1:8, 12, 16 [b]1 Cor. 1:18, 24 [c]Acts 3:26; Rom. 2:9 [d]John 7:35

17 [1]Or, *by* [2]Or, *"But he who is righteous by faith shall live."* [a]Rom. 3:21; Phil. 3:9; Rom. 9:30 [b]Hab. 2:4; Gal. 3:11; Heb. 10:38

18 [1]Or, *by* [a]Eph. 5:6; Col. 3:6; Rom. 5:9 [b]2 Thess. 2:6f. [Gr.]

19 [1]Or, *among* [a]Acts 14:17; 17:24ff.

20 [a]Mark 10:6 [b]Ps. 19:1-6; Job 12:7-9; Jer. 5:21f.

21 [1]Lit., *glorify* [a]2 Kin. 17:15; Jer. 2:5; Eph. 4:17f.

22 [a]Jer. 10:14; 1 Cor. 1:20

23 [1]Or possibly, *reptiles* [a]Ps. 106:20; Jer. 2:11; Acts 17:29

24 [a]Rom. 1:26, 28; Eph. 4:19 [b]Eph. 2:3

25 [1]Lit., *the lie* [2]Lit., *unto the ages* [a]Is. 44:20; Jer. 10:14; 13:25; 16:19 [b]Rom. 9:5; 2 Cor. 11:31

26 [1]Lit., *against nature* [a]Rom. 1:24 [b]1 Thess. 4:5

27 [1]Lit., *the shameless deed* [2]Lit., *themselves* [a]Lev. 18:22; 20:13; 1 Cor. 6:9

28 And just as they did not see fit [1]to acknowledge God
any longer, [a]God gave them over to a depraved mind, to do
those things which are not proper,
29 being filled with all unrighteousness, wickedness, greed,
malice; full of envy, murder, strife, deceit, malice; *they are*
[a]gossips,
30 slanderers, [1a]haters of God, insolent, arrogant, boastful,
inventors of evil, [b]disobedient to parents,
31 without understanding, untrustworthy, [a]unloving, un-
merciful;
32 and, although they know the ordinance of God, that
those who practice such things are worthy of [a]death, they not
only do the same, but also [b]give hearty approval to those who
practice them.

CHAPTER 2

THEREFORE you are [a]without excuse, [b]every man *of you*
who passes judgment, for in that [c]you judge another, you condemn yourself; for you who judge practice the same things.
2 And we know that the judgment of God [1]rightly falls
upon those who practice such things.
3 And do you suppose this, [a]O man, [1]when you pass judgment upon those who practice such things and do the same
yourself, that you will escape the judgment of God?
4 Or do you think lightly of [a]the riches of His [b]kindness
and [c]forbearance and [d]patience, not knowing that [e]the kindness of God leads you to repentance?
5 But [1]because of your stubbornness and unrepentant
heart [a]you are storing up wrath for yourself [b]in the day of
wrath and revelation of the righteous judgment of God;
6 [a]who WILL RENDER TO EVERY MAN ACCORDING TO HIS
DEEDS:
7 to those who by [a]perseverance in doing good seek for
[b]glory and honor and [c]immortality, [d]eternal life;
8 but to those who are [a]selfishly ambitious and [b]do not
obey the truth, but obey unrighteousness, wrath and
indignation.
9 *There will be* [a]tribulation and distress [1]for every soul of
man who does evil, of the Jew [b]first and also of the Greek,
10 but [a]glory and honor and peace to every man who does
good, to the Jew [b]first and also to the Greek.
11 For [a]there is no partiality with God.
12 For all who have sinned [1a]without the Law will also
perish [1]without the Law; and all who have sinned [2]under the
Law will be judged [3]by the Law;
13 for [a]not the hearers [1]of the Law are [2]just before God,
but the doers [1]of the Law will be justified.
14 For when Gentiles who do not have [1]the Law do [2a]in-
stinctively the things of the Law, these, not having [1]the Law,
are a law to themselves,
15 in that they show [a]the work of the Law written in their
hearts, their conscience bearing witness, and their thoughts
alternately accusing or else defending themselves,

28 [1]Lit., *to have God in knowledge*
[a]Rom. 1:24

29 [a]2 Cor. 12:20

30 [1]Or, *hateful to God*
[a]Ps. 5:5 [b]2 Tim. 3:2

31 [a]2 Tim. 3:3

32 [a]Rom. 6:21 [b]Luke 11:48; Acts 8:1; 22:20

1 [a]Rom. 1:20 [b]Rom. 2:3; 9:20; Luke 12:14 [c]2 Sam. 12:5-7; Matt. 7:1; Rom. 14:22

2 [1]Lit., *is according to truth against . . .*

3 [1]Lit., *who pass judgment*
[a]Rom. 2:1; 9:20; Luke 12:14

4 [a]Rom. 9:23; 11:33; 2 Cor. 8:2; Eph. 1:7, 18; 2:7; Phil. 4:19; Col. 1:27; 2:2; Titus 3:6 [b]Rom. 11:22 [c]Rom. 3:25 [d]Rom. 9:22; 1 Tim. 1:16; 1 Pet. 3:20; 2 Pet. 3:15; Ex. 34:6 [e]2 Pet. 3:9

5 [1]Or, *in accordance with*
[a]Deut. 32:34f.; Prov. 1:18 [b]Ps. 110:5; Jude 6; 2 Cor. 5:10; 2 Thess. 1:5

6 [a]Ps. 62:12; Matt. 16:27

7 [a]Luke 8:15; Heb. 10:36 [b]Rom. 2:10; Heb. 2:7; 1 Pet. 1:7 [c]1 Cor. 15:42, 50, 53f.; Eph. 6:24 marg.; 2 Tim. 1:10 marg. [d]Matt. 25:46

8 [a]Phil. 1:17 marg.; 2 Cor. 12:20; Gal. 5:20; Phil. 2:3; James 3:14, 16 [b]2 Thess. 2:12

9 [1]Lit., *upon*
[a]Rom. 8:35 [b]1 Pet. 4:17; Acts 3:26; Rom. 1:16

10 [a]Rom. 2:7; Heb. 2:7; 1 Pet. 1:7 [b]Rom. 2:9

11 [a]Acts 10:34

12 [1]Or, *without law* [2]Or, *under law* [3]Or, *by law*
[a]1 Cor. 9:21; Acts 2:23

13 [1]Or, *of law* [2]Or, *righteous*
[a]James 1:22f., 25; Matt. 7:21, 24ff.; John 13:17

14 [1]Or, *law* [2]Lit., *by nature*
[a]Rom. 2:15; Rom. 1:19; Acts 10:35

15 [a]Rom. 2:14, 27

16 on the day when, [a]according to my gospel, [b]God will
judge the secrets of men through Christ Jesus.
17 But if you bear the name 'Jew,' and [a]rely [1]upon the
Law, and boast in God,
18 and know *His* will, and [1a]approve the things that are
essential, being instructed out of the Law,
19 and are confident that you yourself are a guide to the
blind, a light to those who are in darkness,
20 a [1]corrector of the foolish, a teacher of [2]the immature,
having in the Law [a]the embodiment of knowledge and of the
truth;
21 you therefore [a]who teach another, do you not teach
yourself? You who [1]preach that one should not steal, do you
steal?
22 You who say that one should not commit adultery, do
you commit adultery? You who abhor idols, do you [a]rob
temples?
23 You who [a]boast [1]in the Law, through your breaking the
Law, do you dishonor God?
24 For "[a]THE NAME OF GOD IS BLASPHEMED AMONG THE
GENTILES [b]BECAUSE OF YOU," just as it is written.
25 For indeed circumcision is of value, if you [a]practice
[1]the Law; but if you are a transgressor [2]of the Law, [b]your
circumcision has become uncircumcision.
26 [a]If therefore [b]the [1]uncircumcised man [c]keep the requirements of the Law, will not his uncircumcision be regarded as
circumcision?
27 And will not [a]he who is physically uncircumcised, if he
keeps the Law, will he not [b]judge you who [1]though having the
letter *of the Law* and circumcision are a transgressor [2]of the
Law?
28 For [a]he is not a Jew who is one outwardly; neither is
circumcision that which is outward in the flesh;
29 but [a]he is a Jew who is one inwardly; and circumcision
is that which is of the heart, by the [b]Spirit, not by the letter;
[c]and his praise is not from men, but from God.

CHAPTER 3

THEN what [1]advantage has the Jew? Or what is the benefit
of circumcision?
2 Great in every respect. First of all, that [a]they were entrusted with the [b]oracles of God.
3 What then? If [a]some [1]did not believe, their [2]unbelief
will not nullify the faithfulness of God, will it?
4 [a]May it never be! Rather, let God be found true,
though every man *be found* [b]a liar, as it is written,

"[c]THAT THOU MIGHTEST BE JUSTIFIED IN THY WORDS,
AND MIGHTEST PREVAIL WHEN THOU [1]ART JUDGED."

5 But if our unrighteousness [1a]demonstrates the righteousness of God, [b]what shall we say? The God who inflicts
wrath is not unrighteous, is He? ([c]I am speaking in human
terms.)
6 [a]May it never be! For otherwise how will [b]God judge
the world?

16 [a]Rom. 16:25; 2 Tim. 2:8; 1 Cor. 15:1; Gal. 1:11; 1 Tim. 1:11 [b]Acts 10:42; 17:31; Rom. 3:6; 14:10

17 [1]Or, *upon law* [a]Rom. 2:23; 9:4; Mic. 3:11; John 5:45

18 [1]Or, *distinguish between the things which differ* [a]Phil. 1:10

20 [1]Or, *instructor* [2]Lit., *infants* [a]2 Tim. 1:13; Rom. 3:31

21 [1]Or, *proclaim* [a]Matt. 23:3ff.

22 [a]Acts 19:37

23 [1]Or, *in law* [a]Rom. 2:17; 9:4; Mic. 3:11; John 5:45

24 [a]Is. 52:5 [b]Ezek. 36:20ff.; 2 Pet. 2:2

25 [1]Or, *law* [2]Or, *of law* [a]Rom. 2:13f., 27 [b]Jer. 4:4; 9:25f.

26 [1]Lit., *uncircumcision* [a]1 Cor. 7:19 [b]Eph. 2:11; Rom. 3:30 [c]Rom. 8:4; 2:25, 27

27 [1]Lit., *through the letter* [2]Or, *of law* [a]Eph. 2:11; Rom. 3:30 [b]Matt. 12:41

28 [a]Rom. 9:6; John 8:39; Gal. 6:15; Rom. 2:17

29 [a]Phil. 3:3; Col. 2:11 [b]Rom. 7:6; 2 Cor. 3:6; Rom. 2:27 [c]1 Cor. 4:5; 2 Cor. 10:18; John 5:44, 12:43

1 [1]Lit., *is the advantage of the Jew*

2 [a]Deut. 4:8; Ps. 147:19; Rom. 9:4 [b]Acts 7:38

3 [1]Or, *were unfaithful* [2]Or, *unfaithfulness* [a]Rom. 10:16; Heb. 4:2

4 [1]Or, *dost enter into judgment* [a]Luke 20:16; Rom. 3:6, 31 [b]Rom. 3:7; Ps. 116:11 [c]Ps. 51:4

5 [1]Or, *commends* [a]Rom. 5:8; 2 Cor. 6:4; 7:11 [Gr.]; Gal. 2:18 [Gr.] [b]Rom. 7:7; 8:31; 9:14, 30; 4:1 [c]Rom. 6:19; 1 Cor. 9:8; Gal. 3:15; 1 Cor. 15:32

6 [a]Luke 20:16; Rom. 3:4, 31 [b]Rom. 2:16

7 But if through my lie [a]the truth of God abounded to
His glory, [b]why am I also still being judged as a sinner?
8 And why not *say* (as we are slanderously reported and
as some affirm that we say), "[a]Let us do evil that good may
come"? [1]Their condemnation is just.
9 What then? [1a]Are we better than they? Not at all; for
we have already charged that both [b]Jews and [c]Greeks are [d]all
under sin;
10 as it is written,
"[a]THERE IS NONE RIGHTEOUS, NOT EVEN ONE;
11 THERE IS NONE WHO UNDERSTANDS,
THERE IS NONE WHO SEEKS FOR GOD;
12 ALL HAVE TURNED ASIDE, TOGETHER THEY HAVE BE-
COME USELESS;
THERE IS NONE WHO DOES GOOD,
THERE IS NOT EVEN ONE."
13 "[a]THEIR THROAT IS AN OPEN GRAVE,
WITH THEIR TONGUES THEY KEEP DECEIVING,"
"THE POISON OF ASPS IS UNDER THEIR LIPS;"
14 "[a]WHOSE MOUTH IS FULL OF CURSING AND BITTERNESS;"
15 "[a]THEIR FEET ARE SWIFT TO SHED BLOOD,
16 DESTRUCTION AND MISERY ARE IN THEIR PATHS,
17 AND THE PATH OF PEACE HAVE THEY NOT KNOWN."
18 "[a]THERE IS NO FEAR OF GOD BEFORE THEIR EYES."
19 Now we know that whatever the [a]Law says, it speaks to
[b]those who are [1]under the Law, that every mouth may be
closed, and [c]all the world may become accountable to God;
20 because [a]by the works [1]of the Law no flesh will be
justified in His sight; for [2b]through the Law *comes* the knowledge of sin.
21 But now apart [1]from the Law [a]*the* righteousness of
God has been manifested, being [b]witnessed by the Law and
the Prophets;
22 even *the* [a]righteousness of God through [b]faith [c]in Jesus
Christ for [d]all those who believe; for [e]there is no distinction;
23 for [1]all [a]have sinned and fall short of the glory of God,
24 being justified as a gift [a]by His grace through [b]the redemption which is in Christ Jesus;
25 whom God displayed publicly as [a]a [1]propitiation [2b]in
His blood through faith. *This was* to demonstrate His righteousness, [3]because in the [c]forbearance of God He [d]passed
over the sins previously committed;
26 for the demonstration, *I say,* of His righteousness at
the present time, that He might be just and the justifier of the
one who [1]has faith in Jesus.
27 Where then is [a]boasting? It is excluded. By [b]what kind
of law? Of works? No, but by a law of faith.
28 [1]For [a]we maintain that a man is justified by faith apart
from works [2]of the Law.
29 Or [a]is God *the God* of Jews only? Is He not *the God* of
Gentiles also? Yes, of Gentiles also—
30 if indeed [a]God is one—and [b]He will justify the [1]circum-
cised [2]by faith and the [3]uncircumcised through faith.
31 Do we then nullify [1]the Law through faith? [a]May it
never be! On the contrary, we [b]establish the Law.

7 [a]Rom. 3:4 [b]Rom. 9:19

8 [1]Lit., *Whose* [a]Rom. 6:1

9 [1]Or possibly, *Are we worse* [a]Rom. 3:1 [b]Rom. 2:1-29 [c]Rom. 1:18-32 [d]Rom. 3:19, 23; 11:32; Gal. 3:22

10 [a]Ps. 14:1-3; 53:1-4

13 [a]Ps. 5:9; Ps. 140:3

14 [a]Ps. 10:7

15 [a]Is. 59:7f.

18 [a]Ps. 36:1

19 [1]Lit., *in* [a]John 10:34 [b]Rom. 2:12 [c]Rom. 3:9

20 [1]Or, *of law* [2]Or, *through law* [a]Acts 13:39; Gal. 2:16; Ps. 143:2 [b]Rom. 7:7; 4:15; 5:13, 20

21 [1]Or, *from law* [a]Rom. 1:17; 9:30 [b]Rom. 1:2; Acts 10:43

22 [a]Rom. 1:17; 9:30 [b]Rom. 4:5 [c]Acts 3:16; Gal. 2:16, 20; 3:22; Eph. 3:12 [d]Rom. 4:11, 16; 10:4 [e]Rom. 10:12; Gal. 3:28; Col. 3:11

23 [1]Or, *all sinned* [a]Rom. 3:9

24 [a]Rom. 4:4f. 16; Eph. 2:8 [b]Eph. 1:7; Col. 1:14; Heb. 9:15; 1 Cor. 1:30

25 [1]Or, *a propitiatory sacrifice* [2]Or, *by* [3]Lit., *because of the passing over of the sins previously committed in the forbearance of God* [a]1 John 2:2; 4:10 [b]1 Cor. 5:7; Heb. 9:14, 28; 1 Pet. 1:19; Rev. 1:5 [c]Rom. 2:4 [d]Acts 17:30; 14:16

26 [1]Lit., *is of the faith of Jesus.*

27 [a]Rom. 2:17, 23; 4:2; 1 Cor. 1:29 ff. [b]Rom. 9:31

28 [1]Some ancient mss. read, *Therefore* [2]Or, *of law* [a]Rom. 3:20, 21; Acts 13:39; Eph. 2:9; James 2:20, 24, 26

29 [a]Rom. 9:24; 10:12; 15:9; Gal. 3:28; Acts 10:34f.

30 [1]Lit., *circumcision* [2]Lit., *out of* [3]Lit., *uncircumcision* [a]Rom. 10:12 [b]Rom. 4:11f., 16; Gal. 3:8; Rom. 3:22

31 [1]Or, *law* [a]Luke 20:16; Rom. 3:4 [b]Rom. 4:3; 8:4; Matt. 5:17

CHAPTER 4

WHAT then shall we say that Abraham, [1]our forefather
[a]according to the flesh, has found?
2 For if Abraham was justified by works, he has something
to boast about; but [a]not [1]before God.
3 For what does the Scripture say? "[a]AND ABRAHAM BE-
LIEVED GOD, AND IT WAS RECKONED TO HIM AS RIGHTEOUSNESS."
4 Now to the one who [a]works, his wage is not reckoned as
a favor but as what is due.
5 But to the one who does not work, but [a]believes in Him
who justifies the ungodly, his faith is reckoned as righteousness.
6 Just as David also speaks of the blessing upon the man
to whom God reckons righteousness apart from works:
7 "[a]BLESSED ARE THOSE WHOSE LAWLESS DEEDS HAVE BEEN
FORGIVEN,
AND WHOSE SINS HAVE BEEN COVERED.
8 "[a]BLESSED IS THE MAN WHOSE SIN THE LORD WILL NOT
[1b]TAKE INTO ACCOUNT."
9 Is this blessing then upon [1a]the circumcised, or upon
the [2]uncircumcised also? For [b]we say, "[c]FAITH WAS RECKONED
TO ABRAHAM AS RIGHTEOUSNESS."
10 How then was it reckoned? While he was [1]circumcised,
or [2]uncircumcised? Not while [1]circumcised, but while
[2]uncircumcised;
11 and he [a]received the sign of circumcision, [b]a seal of the
righteousness of the faith which he had while uncircumcised,
that he might be [c]the father of [d]all who believe without being
circumcised, that righteousness might be reckoned to them,
12 and the father of circumcision to those who not only
are of the circumcision, but who also follow in the steps of
the faith of our father Abraham which he had while
uncircumcised.
13 For [a]the promise to Abraham or to his [1]descendants
[b]that he would be heir of the world was not [2]through the Law,
but through the righteousness of faith.
14 For [a]if those who are [1]of the Law are heirs, faith is
made void and the promise is nullified;
15 for [a]the Law brings about wrath, but [b]where there is no
law, neither is there violation.
16 For this reason *it is* [1]by faith, that *it might be* in accordance with [a]grace, in order that the promise may be certain to
[b]all the [2]descendants, not only to [3]those who are of the Law,
but also to [3]those who are of the faith of Abraham, who is [c]the
father of us all,
17 (as it is written, "[a]A FATHER OF MANY NATIONS HAVE I
MADE YOU") in the sight of Him whom he believed, *even* God,
[b]who gives life to the dead and [1c]calls into being [d]that which
does not exist.
18 In hope against hope he believed, in order that he
might become [a]a father of many nations, according to that
which had been spoken, "[b]SO SHALL YOUR [1]DESCENDANTS BE."
19 And without becoming weak in faith he contemplated
his own body, now [a]as good as dead since [b]he was about a
hundred years old, and [c]the deadness of Sarah's womb;

1 [1]Or, *our forefather, has found according to the flesh* [a]Rom. 1:3

2 [1]Lit., *toward* [a]1 Cor. 1:31

3 [a]Gen. 15:6; Rom. 4:9, 22; Gal. 3:6; James 2:23

4 [a]Rom. 11:6

5 [a]Rom. 3:22; John 6:29

7 [a]Ps. 32:1

8 [1]Or, *reckon* [a]Ps. 32:2 [b]2 Cor. 5:19

9 [1]Lit., *circumcision* [2]Lit., *uncircumcision* [a]Rom. 3:30 [b]Rom. 4:3 [c]Gen. 15:6

10 [1]Lit., *in circumcision* [2]Lit., *in uncircumcision*

11 [a]Gen. 17:10f. [b]John 3:33 [c]Rom. 4:16f.; Luke 19:9 [d]Rom. 3:22; 4:16

13 [1]Lit., *seed* [2]Or, *through law* [a]Rom. 9:8; Gal. 3:16 [b]Gen. 17:4-6; 22:17f.

14 [1]Or, *of law* [a]Gal. 3:18

15 [a]Rom. 7:7, 10-25; 1 Cor. 15:56; Gal. 3:10 [b]Rom. 3:20

16 [1]Or, *of* [2]Lit., *seed* [3]Lit., *that which is* [a]Rom. 3:24 [b]Rom. 4:11; 9:8; 15:8 [c]Rom. 4:11; Luke 19:9

17 [1]Lit., *calls the things which do not exist as existing* [a]Gen. 17:5 [b]John 5:21 [c]Is. 48:13; 51:2 [d]1 Cor. 1:28

18 [1]Lit., *seed* [a]Rom. 4:17 [b]Gen. 15:5

19 [a]Heb. 11:12 [b]Gen. 17:17 [c]Gen. 18:11

20 yet, with respect to the promise of God, he did not
waver in unbelief, but grew strong in faith, [a]giving glory to
God,
21 and [a]being fully assured that [b]what He had promised,
He was able also to perform.
22 Therefore also [a]IT WAS RECKONED TO HIM AS
RIGHTEOUSNESS.
23 Now [a]not for his sake only was it written, that "IT WAS
RECKONED TO HIM,"
24 but for our sake also, to whom it will be reckoned, as
those [a]who believe in Him who [b]raised Jesus our Lord from the
dead,
25 *Him* who was [a]delivered up because of our transgressions, and was [b]raised because of our justification.

CHAPTER 5

[a]THEREFORE having been justified by faith, [1b]we have
peace with God through our Lord Jesus Christ,
2 through whom also we have [a]obtained our introduction
by faith into this grace [b]in which we stand; and [1]we exult in
hope of the glory of God.
3 [a]And not only this, but [1]we also [b]exult in our tribulations; knowing that tribulation brings about [c]perseverance;
4 and [a]perseverance, [b]proven character; and proven character, hope;
5 and hope [a]does not disappoint; because the love of
God has been [b]poured out within our hearts through the Holy
Spirit who was given to us.
6 For while we were still [a]helpless, [b]at the right time
[c]Christ died for the ungodly.
7 For one will hardly die for a righteous man; though
perhaps for the good man someone would dare even to die.
8 But God [a]demonstrates [b]His own love toward us, in
that while we were yet sinners, [c]Christ died for us.
9 Much more then, having now been justified [1a]by His
blood, we shall be saved [b]from the wrath *of God* through Him.
10 For if while we were [a]enemies, we were reconciled to
God through the death of His Son, much more, having been
reconciled, we shall be saved [1b]by His life.
11 [a]And not only this, [1]but we also exult in God through
our Lord Jesus Christ, through whom we have now received
[b]the reconciliation.
12 Therefore, just as through [a]one man sin entered into
the world, and [b]death through sin, and [c]so death spread to all
men, because all sinned—
13 for [1]until the Law sin was in the world; but [a]sin is not
imputed when there is no law.
14 Nevertheless death reigned from Adam until Moses,
even over those who had not sinned [a]in the likeness of Adam's
offense, who is a [1b]type of Him who was to come.
15 But [1]the free gift is not like the transgression. For if by
the transgression of [a]the one [b]the many died, much more did
the grace of God and the gift by [c]the grace of the one Man,
Jesus Christ, abound to [b]the many.
16 And the gift is not like *that which came* through the

20 [a]Matt. 9:8

21 [a]Rom. 14:5 [b]Gen. 18:14; Heb. 11:19

22 [a]Rom. 4:3

23 [a]Rom. 15:4; 1 Cor. 9:9f.; 10:11; 2 Tim. 3:16f.

24 [a]Rom. 10:9; 1 Pet. 1:21 [b]Acts 2:24

25 [a]Rom. 5:6, 8; 8:32; Gal. 2:20; Eph. 5:2 [b]1 Cor. 15:17; 2 Cor. 5:15; Rom. 5:18

1 [1]Some ancient mss. read, *let us have* [a]Rom. 3:28 [b]Rom. 5:11

2 [1]Or, *let us exult* [a]Eph. 2:18; 3:12; Heb. 10:19f.; 1 Pet. 3:18 [b]1 Cor. 15:1

3 [1]Or, *let us also exult* [a]Rom. 5:11; 8:23; 9:10; 2 Cor. 8:19 [b]Matt. 5:12; James 1:2f. [c]Luke 21:19

4 [a]Luke 21:19 [b]Phil. 2:22; James 1:12

5 [a]Ps. 119:116; Rom. 9:33; Heb. 6:18f. [b]Acts 2:33; 10:45; Titus 3:6; Gal. 4:6

6 [a]Rom. 5:8, 10 [b]Gal. 4:4 [c]Rom. 4:25; 5:8; 8:32; Gal. 2:20; Eph. 5:2

8 [a]Rom. 3:5 [b]Rom. 8:39; John 3:16; 15:13 [c]Rom. 4:25; 5:6; 8:32; Gal. 2:20; Eph. 5:2

9 [1]Or, *in* [a]Rom. 3:25 [b]1 Thess. 1:10; Rom. 1:18

10 [1]Or, *in* [a]Rom. 11:28; Eph. 2:3; Col. 1:21f.; 2 Cor. 5:18f. [b]Rom. 8:34; Heb. 7:25; 1 John 2:1

11 [1]Lit., *but also exulting* [a]Rom. 5:3; 8:23; 9:10; 2 Cor. 8:19 [b]Rom. 5:10; 11:15; 2 Cor. 5:18f.

12 [a]Gen. 2:17; 3:6, 19; 1 Cor. 15:21f.; Rom. 5:15, 16, 17 [b]Rom. 6:23; 1 Cor. 15:56; James 1:15 [c]Rom. 5:14, 19, 21; 1 Cor. 15:22

13 [1]Or, *until law* [a]Rom. 4:15

14 [1]Or, *foreshadowing* [a]Hos. 6:7 [b]1 Cor. 15:45

15 [1]Lit., *not as the trespass, so also is the free gift* [a]Rom. 5:12, 18 [b]Rom. 5:19; Rom. 5:18 [c]Acts 15:11

one who sinned; for on the one hand [a]the judgment *arose* from
one *transgression* [1]resulting in condemnation, but on the other
hand the free gift *arose* from many transgressions [2]resulting in
justification.
17 For if by the transgression of the one, death reigned
[a]through the one, much more those who receive the abundance of grace and of the gift of righteousness will [b]reign in life
through the One, Jesus Christ.
18 So then as through [a]one transgression [1]there resulted
condemnation to all men; even so through one [b]act of righteousness [2]there resulted [c]justification of life to all men.
19 For as through the one man's disobedience [a]the many
[b]were made sinners, even so through [c]the obedience of the
One [a]the many will be made righteous.
20 And [1a]the Law came in that the transgression might
increase; but where sin increased, [b]grace abounded all the
more,
21 that, as [a]sin reigned in death, even so [b]grace might reign
through righteousness to eternal life through Jesus Christ our
Lord.

Chapter 6

[a]WHAT shall we say then? Are we to [b]continue in sin that
grace might increase?
2 [a]May it never be! How shall we who [b]died to sin still
live in it?
3 Or do you not know that all of us who have been
[a]baptized into [b]Christ Jesus have been baptized into His
death?
4 Therefore we have been [a]buried with Him through
baptism into death, in order that as Christ was [b]raised from the
dead through the [c]glory of the Father, so we too might walk in
[d]newness of life.
5 For [a]if we have become [1]united with *Him* in the likeness of His death, certainly we shall be also [2]*in the likeness* of
His resurrection,
6 knowing this, that our [a]old [1]self was [b]crucified with
Him, that our [c]body of sin might be [2]done away with, that we
should no longer be slaves to sin;
7 for [a]he who has died is [1]freed from sin.
8 Now [a]if we have died with Christ, we believe that we
shall also live with Him,
9 knowing that Christ, having been [a]raised from the
dead, is never to die again; [b]death no longer is master over
Him.
10 For the death that He died, He died to sin, once for all;
but the life that He lives, He lives to God.
11 Even so consider yourselves to be [a]dead to sin, but alive
to God in Christ Jesus.
12 Therefore do not let sin [a]reign in your mortal body that
you should obey its lusts,
13 and do not go on [a]presenting [1]the members of your
body to sin *as* [2]instruments of unrighteousness; but [b]present
yourselves to God as those alive from the dead, and your
members *as* [2]instruments of righteousness to God.

16 [1]Lit., *to condemnation* [2]Lit., *to an act of righteousness* [a]1 Cor. 11:32 [Gr.]

17 [a]Gen. 2:17; 3:6, 19; 1 Cor. 15:21f.; Rom. 5:12, 15, 16 [b]2 Tim. 2:12; Rev. 22:5

18 [1]Lit., *to condemnation* [2]Lit., *to justification* [a]Rom. 5:12, 15 [b]Rom. 3:25 [c]Rom. 4:25

19 [a]Rom. 5:15, 18 [b]Rom. 5:12; 11:32 [c]Phil. 2:8

20 [1]Or, *law* [a]Gal. 3:19; Rom. 3:20; 7:7f. [b]Rom. 6:1; 1 Tim. 1:14

21 [a]Rom. 5:12, 14 [b]John 1:17; Rom. 6:23

1 [a]Rom. 3:5 [b]Rom. 6:15; 3:8

2 [a]Luke 20:16; Rom. 6:15 [b]Rom. 6:11; 7:4, 6; Gal. 2:19; Col. 2:20; 3:3; 1 Pet. 2:24

3 [a]Matt. 28:19 [b]Acts 2:38; 8:16; 19:5; Gal. 3:27

4 [a]Col. 2:12 [b]Acts 2:24; Rom. 6:9 [c]John 11:40; 2 Cor. 13:4 [d]Rom. 7:6; 2 Cor. 5:17; Gal. 6:15; Eph. 4:23f.; Col. 3:10

5 [1]Or, *united with the likeness* [2]Or, *with* [a]2 Cor. 4:10; Phil. 3:10f.; Col. 2:12; 3:1

6 [1]Lit., *man* [2]Or, *made powerless* [a]Eph. 4:22; Col. 3:9 [b]Gal. 2:20; 5:24; 6:14 [c]Rom. 7:24

7 [1]Or, *acquitted* [a]1 Pet. 4:1

8 [a]2 Tim. 2:11; 2 Cor. 4:10; Rom. 6:4

9 [a]Acts 2:24; Rom. 6:4 [b]Rev. 1:18

11 [a]Rom. 6:2; 7:4, 6; Gal. 2:19; Col. 2:20; 3:3; 1 Pet. 2:24

12 [a]Rom. 6:14

13 [1]Lit., *your members to sin* [2]Or, *weapons* [a]Rom. 7:5; Col. 3:5; Rom. 6:16, 19 [b]Rom. 12:1; 2 Cor. 5:14f.; 1 Pet. 2:24

14 For [a]sin shall not [b]be master over you, for [c]you are not under law, but [d]under grace.

15 What then? [a]Shall we sin because we are not under law but under grace? [b]May it never be!

16 Do you not [a]know that when you present yourselves to someone *as* [b]slaves for obedience, you are slaves of the one whom you obey, either of [c]sin [1]resulting in death, or of obedience [2]resulting in righteousness?

17 But [a]thanks be to God that [1]though you were slaves of sin, you became obedient from the heart to that [b]form of teaching to which you were committed,

18 and having been [a]freed from sin, you became slaves of righteousness.

19 [a]I am speaking in human terms because of the weakness of your flesh. For just [b]as you presented your members *as* slaves to impurity and to lawlessness, [1]resulting in *further* lawlessness, so now present your members *as* slaves to righteousness, [2]resulting in sanctification.

20 For [a]when you were slaves of sin, you were free in regard to righteousness.

21 Therefore what [1a]benefit were you then [2]deriving [3]from the things of which you are now ashamed? For the outcome of those things is [b]death.

22 But now having been [a]freed from sin and [b]enslaved to God, you [1]derive your [2c]benefit, [3]resulting in sanctification, and [d]the outcome, eternal life.

23 For the wages of [a]sin is death, but the free gift of God is [b]eternal life in Christ Jesus our Lord.

Chapter 7

Or do you not know, [a]brethren (for I am speaking to those who know the law), that the law has jurisdiction over a person as long as he lives?

2 For [a]the married woman is bound by law to her husband while he is living; but if her husband dies, she is released from the law concerning the husband.

3 So then if, while her husband is living, she is joined to another man, she shall be called an adulteress; but if her husband dies, she is free from the law, so that she is not an adulteress, though she is joined to another man.

4 Therefore, my brethren, you also were [a]made to die [b]to the Law [c]through the body of Christ, that you might be joined to another, to Him who was raised from the dead, that we might bear fruit for God.

5 For while we were [a]in the flesh, the sinful passions, which were [b]*aroused* by the Law, were at work [c]in [1]the members of our body to bear fruit for death.

6 But now we have been [a]released from the Law, having [b]died to that by which we were bound, so that we serve in [c]newness of [d]the [1]Spirit and not in oldness of the letter.

7 [a]What shall we say then? Is the Law sin? [b]May it never be! On the contrary, [c]I would not have come to know sin except [1]through the Law; for I would not have known about [2]coveting if the Law had not said, "[d]YOU SHALL NOT [3]COVET."

8 But sin, [a]taking opportunity [b]through the command-

14 [a]Rom. 8:2, 12 [b]Rom. 6:12 [c]Rom. 7:4, 6; Gal. 4:21; Rom. 5:18 [d]Rom. 5:17, 21

15 [a]Rom. 6:1 [b]Luke 20:16; Rom. 6:2

16 [1]Lit., *to death* [2]Lit., *to righteousness* [a]Rom. 11:2; 1 Cor. 3:16; 5:6; 6:2, 3, 9, 15, 16, 19; 9:13, 24 [b]John 8:34; 2 Pet. 2:19 [c]Rom. 6:21, 23

17 [1]Lit., *you were slaves . . . but you became* [a]Rom. 1:8; 2 Cor. 2:14 [b]2 Tim. 1:13

18 [a]Rom. 8:2; John 8:32; Rom. 6:22

19 [1]Lit., *to lawlessness* [2]Lit., *to sanctification* [a]Rom. 3:5 [b]Rom. 6:13

20 [a]Rom. 6:16; Matt. 6:24

21 [1]Lit., *fruit* [2]Lit., *having* [3]Lit., *in* [a]Rom. 7:5; Jer. 12:13; Ezek. 16:63 [b]Rom. 6:16, 23; 1:32; 8:6, 13; Gal. 6:8; Rom. 5:12

22 [1]Lit., *have* [2]Lit., *fruit* [3]Lit., *to sanctification* [a]Rom. 8:2; John 8:32; Rom. 6:18 [b]1 Cor. 7:22; 1 Pet. 2:16 [c]Rom. 7:4 [d]1 Pet. 1:9

23 [a]Rom. 6:16, 21; 1:32; 8:6, 13; Gal. 6:8; Rom. 5:12 [b]Rom. 5:21; 8:39; Matt. 25:46

1 [a]Rom. 1:13

2 [a]1 Cor. 7:39

4 [a]Rom. 7:6; 6:2 [b]Gal. 2:19; 5:18; Rom. 8:2 [c]Col. 1:22

5 [1]Lit., *our members to bear* [a]Rom. 8:8f.; 2 Cor. 10:3 [b]Rom. 7:7f. [c]Rom. 6:13, 21, 23

6 [1]Or, *spirit* [a]Rom. 7:2 [b]Rom. 6:2 [c]Rom. 6:4 [d]Rom. 2:29

7 [1]Or, *through law* [2]Or, *lust* [3]Or, *LUST* [a]Rom. 3:5 [b]Luke 20:16 [c]Rom. 3:20; 4:15; 5:20 [d]Ex. 20:17; Deut. 5:21

8 [a]Rom. 7:11 [b]Rom. 3:20; 7:11

ment, produced in me [1]coveting of every kind; for [c]apart
[2]from the Law sin *is* dead.
9 And I was once alive apart [1]from the Law; but when the
commandment came, sin became alive, and I died;
10 and this commandment, which was [1a]to result in life,
proved [2]to result in death for me;
11 for sin, [a]taking opportunity [b]through the commandment, [c]deceived me, and through it killed me.
12 [a]So then, the Law is holy, and the commandment is
holy and righteous and good.
13 Therefore did that which is good become *a cause of*
death for me? [a]May it never be! Rather it was sin, in order that
it might be shown to be sin by effecting my death through that
which is good, that through the commandment sin might become utterly sinful.
14 For we know that the Law is [a]spiritual; but I am [a]of
flesh, [b]sold [1c]into bondage to sin.
15 For that which I am doing, [a]I do not understand; for I
am not practicing [b]what I *would* like to *do,* but I am doing the
very thing I hate.
16 But if I do the very thing I do not wish *to do,* I agree
with [a]the Law, *confessing* that it is good.
17 So now, [a]no longer am I the one doing it, but sin which
indwells me.
18 For I know that nothing good dwells in me, that is, in
my [a]flesh; for the wishing is present in me, but the doing of the
good *is* not.
19 For [a]the good that I wish, I do not do; but I practice
the very evil that I do not wish.
20 But if I am doing the very thing I do not wish, [a]I am no
longer the one doing it, but sin which dwells in me.
21 I find then [a]the [1]principle that evil is present in me, the
one who wishes to do good.
22 For I joyfully concur with the law of God [1]in [a]the inner
man,
23 but I see [a]a different law in [1]the members of my body,
waging war against the [b]law of my mind, and making me a
prisoner [2]of [c]the law of sin which is in my members.
24 Wretched man that I am! Who will set me free from
[1a]the body of this [b]death?
25 [a]Thanks be to God through Jesus Christ our Lord! So
then, on the one hand I myself with my mind am serving the
law of God, but on the other, with my flesh [b]the law of sin.

Chapter 8

THERE is therefore now no [a]condemnation for those who
are [b]in [c]Christ Jesus.
2 For [a]the law of the Spirit of life [1]in [b]Christ Jesus [c]has
set [2]you free from the law of sin and of death.
3 For [a]what the Law could not do, [1b]weak as it was
through the flesh, God *did:* sending His own Son in [c]the likeness of [2]sinful flesh and *as an offering* for sin, He condemned
sin in the flesh,
4 in order that the [a]requirement of the Law might be

8 [1]Or, *lust* [2]Or, *from law*
[c]1 Cor. 15:56

9 [1]Or, *from law*

10 [1]Lit., *to life* [2]Lit., *to death*
[a]Lev. 18:5; Rom. 10:5; Gal. 3:12; Luke 10:28

11 [a]Rom. 7:8 [b]Rom. 3:20; 7:8 [c]Gen. 3:13

12 [a]Rom. 7:16; 1 Tim. 1:8

13 [a]Luke 20:16

14 [1]Lit., *under sin*
[a]1 Cor. 3:1 [b]1 Kin. 21:20, 25; 2 Kin. 17:17; Rom. 6:6; Gal. 4:3 [c]Rom. 3:9

15 [a]John 15:15 [b]Gal. 5:17; Rom. 7:19

16 [a]Rom. 7:12; 1 Tim. 1:8

17 [a]Rom. 7:20

18 [a]Rom. 7:25; 8:3; John 3:6

19 [a]Rom. 7:15

20 [a]Rom. 7:17

21 [1]Lit., *law*
[a]Rom. 7:23, 25; 8:2

22 [1]Or, *concerning*
[a]2 Cor. 4:16; Eph. 3:16; 1 Pet. 3:4

23 [1]Lit., *my members* [2]Lit., *in*
[a]Gal. 5:17; James 4:1; 1 Pet. 2:11; Rom. 6:19 [b]Rom. 7:25 [c]Rom. 7:21, 25; 8:2

24 [1]Or, *this body of death*
[a]Rom. 6:6; Col. 2:11 [b]Rom. 8:2

25 [a]1 Cor. 15:57 [b]Rom. 7:21, 23; 8:2

1 [a]Rom. 8:34; 5:16 [b]Rom. 8:9f. [c]Rom. 8:2, 11, 39; 16:3

2 [1]Or, *has set you free in Christ Jesus* [2]Some ancient mss. read, *me*
[a]1 Cor. 15:45 [b]Rom. 8:1, 11, 39; 16:3 [c]Rom 6:14, 18; 7:4; John 8:32, 36

3 [1]Lit., *wherein it was weak* [2]Lit., *flesh of sin*
[a]Heb. 10:1ff.; Acts 13:39 [b]Heb. 7:18; Rom. 7:18f. [c]Phil. 2:7; Heb. 2:14, 17; 4:15

4 [a]Luke 1:6; Rom. 2:26

fulfilled in us, who [b]do not walk according to the flesh, but
according to the Spirit.
5 For those who are according to the flesh set their minds
on [a]the things of the flesh, but those who are according to the
Spirit, [b]the things of the Spirit.
6 [a]For the mind set on the flesh is [b]death, but the mind
set on the Spirit is life and peace;
7 because the mind set on the flesh is [a]hostile toward
God; for it does not subject itself to the Law of God, for it is
not even able *to do so;*
8 and those who are [a]in the flesh cannot please God.
9 However you are not [a]in the flesh but in the Spirit, if
indeed the Spirit of God [b]dwells in you. But [c]if anyone does
not have the Spirit of Christ, he does not belong to Him.
10 And [a]if Christ is in you, though the body is dead because of sin, yet the spirit is [1]alive because of righteousness.
11 But if the Spirit of Him who [a]raised Jesus from the
dead dwells in you, [b]He who raised [c]Christ Jesus from the dead
will also give life to your mortal bodies [1]through His Spirit who
indwells you.
12 So then, brethren, we are under obligation, not to the
flesh, to live according to the flesh—
13 for [a]if you are living according to the flesh, you [1]must
die; but if by the Spirit you are [b]putting to death the deeds of
the body, you will live.
14 For all who are [a]being led by the Spirit of God, these
are [b]sons of God.
15 For you [a]have not received a spirit of slavery [1]leading to
fear again, but you [b]have received [2]a spirit of adoption as sons
by which we cry out, "[c]Abba! Father!"
16 The Spirit Himself [a]bears witness with our spirit that
we are [b]children of God,
17 and if children, [a]heirs also, heirs of God and fellow-
heirs with Christ, [b]if indeed we suffer with *Him* in order that
we may also be glorified with *Him.*
18 For I consider that the sufferings of this present time
[a]are not worthy to be compared with the [b]glory that is to be
revealed to us.
19 For the [a]anxious longing of the creation waits eagerly
for [b]the revealing of the [c]sons of God.
20 For the creation [a]was subjected to [b]futility, not of its
own will, but [c]because of Him who subjected it, [1]in hope
21 that [a]the creation itself also will be set free from its
slavery to corruption into the freedom of the glory of the
children of God.
22 For we know that the whole creation [a]groans and suffers the pains of childbirth together until now.
23 [a]And not only this, but also we ourselves, having [b]the
first fruits of the Spirit, even we ourselves [c]groan within ourselves, [d]waiting eagerly for *our* adoption as sons, [e]the redemption of our body.
24 For [a]in hope we have been saved, but [b]hope that is seen
is not hope; for [1]why does one also hope for what he sees?
25 But [a]if we hope for what we do not see, with perseverance we wait eagerly for it.
26 And in the same way the Spirit also helps our weakness;

4 [b]Gal. 5:16, 25

5 [a]Gal. 5:19-21 [b]Gal. 5:22-25

6 [a]Gal. 6:8 [b]Rom. 6:21; 8:13

7 [a]James 4:4

8 [a]Rom. 7:5

9 [a]Rom. 7:5 [b]Rom. 8:11; 1 Cor. 3:16; 6:19; 2 Cor. 6:16; 2 Tim. 1:14; John 14:23 [c]John 14:17; Gal. 4:6; Phil. 1:19; 1 John 4:13

10 [1]Lit., *life*
[a]Gal. 2:20; Eph. 3:17; Col. 1:27; John 17:23

11 [1]Some ancient mss. read, *because of*
[a]Acts 2:24; Rom. 6:4 [b]John 5:21 [c]Rom. 8:1, 2, 39; 16:3

13 [1]Or, *are about to*
[a]Rom. 8:6 [b]Col. 3:5

14 [a]Gal. 5:18 [b]Hos. 1:10; [Rom. 9:26]; Matt. 5:9; John 1:12; 2 Cor. 6:18; Gal. 3:26; 1 John 3:1; Rev. 21:7; Rom. 8:16, 19; 9:8

15 [1]Lit., *for fear again* [2]Or, *the Spirit*
[a]2 Tim. 1:7; Heb. 2:15 [b]Gal. 4:5f.; Rom. 8:23 [c]Mark 14:36; Gal. 4:6

16 [a]Acts 5:32 [b]Hos. 1:10; [Rom. 9:26]; Matt. 5:9; John 1:12; 2 Cor. 6:18; Gal. 3:26; 1 John 3:1; Rev. 21:7; Rom. 8:14, 19; 9:8

17 [a]Gal. 4:7; Acts. 20:32; Gal. 3:29; Eph. 3:6; Titus 3:7; Heb. 1:14; Rev. 21:7 [b]2 Cor. 1:5, 7; Phil. 3:10; 2 Tim. 2:12; 1 Pet. 4:13; Col. 1:24

18 [a]2 Cor. 4:17; 1 Pet. 4:13 [b]Col. 3:4; Titus 2:13; 1 Pet. 5:1; 1:5

19 [a]Phil. 1:20 [b]1 Cor. 1:7f.; Col. 3:4; 1 Pet. 1:7, 13; 1 John 3:2; Rom. 8:18 [c]Hos. 1:10; [Rom. 9:26]; Matt. 5:9; John 1:12; 2 Cor. 6:18; Gal. 3:26; 1 John 3:1; Rev. 21:7; Rom. 8:14, 16; 9:8

20 [1]Some ancient mss. read, *in hope; because the creation . . .*
[a]Gen. 3:17-19 [b]Ps. 39:5f.; Eccl. 1:2 [c]Gen. 3:17; 5:29

21 [a]Acts. 3:21; 2 Pet. 3:13; Rev. 21:1

22 [a]Jer. 12:4, 11

23 [a]Rom. 5:3 [b]2 Cor. 1:22; Rom. 8:16 [c]2 Cor. 5:2, 4 [d]Rom. 8:19, 25; 8:15; Gal. 5:5 [e]Rom. 7:24

24 [1]Some ancient mss. read, *who hopes for what he sees?*
[a]Rom. 8:20; 1 Thess. 5:8; Titus 3:7 [b]2 Cor. 5:7 [cf. Rom. 4:18]; Heb. 11:1

25 [a]1 Thess. 1:3

for [a]we do not know how to pray as we should, but [b]the Spirit
Himself intercedes for *us* with groanings too deep for words;
27 and [a]He who searches the hearts knows what [b]the mind
of the Spirit is, because He [c]intercedes for the [1]saints according
to *the will of* God.
28 And we know that [1]God causes [a]all things to work together
for good to those who love God, to those who are
[b]called according to *His* purpose.
29 For whom He [a]foreknew, He also [b]predestined *to become*
[c]conformed to the image of His Son, that He might be
the [d]first-born among many brethren;
30 and whom He [a]predestined, these He also [b]called; and
whom He called, these He also [c]justified; and whom He justified,
these He also [d]glorified.
31 [a]What then shall we say to these things? [b]If God *is* for
us, who *is* against us?
32 He who [a]did not spare His own Son, but [b]delivered
Him up for us all, how will He not also with Him freely give us
all things?
33 Who will bring a charge against [a]God's elect? [b]God is
the one who justifies;
34 who is the one who [a]condemns? Christ Jesus is He who
[b]died, yes, rather who was [1c]raised, who is [d]at the right hand of
God, who also [e]intercedes for us.
35 Who shall separate us from [a]the love of [1]Christ? Shall
[b]tribulation, or distress, or [c]persecution, or [c]famine, or [c]nakedness,
or [c]peril, or sword?
36 Just as it is written,

> "[a]FOR THY SAKE WE ARE BEING PUT TO DEATH ALL DAY LONG;
> WE WERE CONSIDERED AS SHEEP TO BE SLAUGHTERED."

37 But in all these things we overwhelmingly [a]conquer
through [b]Him who loved us.
38 For I am convinced that neither [a]death, nor life, nor
[b]angels, nor principalities, nor [c]things present, nor things to
come, nor powers,
39 nor height, nor depth, nor any other created thing, shall
be able to separate us from [a]the love of God, which is [b]in
Christ Jesus our Lord.

CHAPTER 9

[a]I AM telling the truth in Christ, I am not lying, my conscience
bearing me witness in the Holy Spirit,
2 that I have great sorrow and unceasing grief in my
heart.
3 For [a]I could [1]wish that I myself were [b]accursed, *separated*
from Christ for the sake of my brethren, my kinsmen
[c]according to the flesh,
4 who are [a]Israelites, to whom belongs [b]the adoption as
sons and [c]the glory and [d]the covenants and [e]the giving of the
Law and [f]the *temple* service and [g]the promises,
5 whose are [a]the fathers, and [b]from whom is [1]the Christ
according to the flesh, [c]who is over all, [d]God [e]blessed [2]forever.
Amen.

26 [a]Matt. 20:22; 2 Cor. 12:8 [b]John 14:16; Eph. 6:18; Rom. 8:15f.

27 [1]I.e., true believers; lit., *holy ones* [a]Ps. 139:1f.; Luke 16:15; Rev. 2:23; Acts 1:24 [b]Rom. 8:6 [c]Rom. 8:34

28 [1]Some ancient mss. read, *all things work together for good* [a]Rom. 8:32 [b]Rom. 8:30; 9:24; 1 Cor. 1:9; Gal. 1:6, 15; 5:8; Eph. 1:11; 3:11; 2 Thess. 2:14; Heb. 9:15; 1 Pet. 2:9; 3:9; Rom. 11:29

29 [a]Rom. 11:2; 1 Pet. 1:2, 20; 2 Tim. 1:9; 1 Cor. 8:3 [b]1 Cor. 2:7; Eph. 1:5, 11; Rom. 9:23 [c]1 Cor. 15:49; Phil. 3:21; Col. 3:10; 1 John 3:2 [d]Col. 1:18; Heb. 1:6

30 [a]1 Cor. 2:7; Eph. 1:5, 11; Rom. 9:23 [b]Rom. 8:28; 9:24; 1 Cor. 1:9; Gal. 1:6, 15; 5:8; Eph. 1:11; 3:11; 2 Thess. 2:14; Heb. 9:15; 1 Pet. 2:9; 3:9; Rom. 11:29 [c]1 Cor. 6:11 [d]John 17:22; 1 Cor. 2:7; Rom. 8:21; 9:23

31 [a]Rom. 3:5; 4:1 [b]Ps. 118:6; Matt. 1:23

32 [a]John 3:16; Rom. 5:8 [b]Rom. 4:25

33 [a]Luke 18:7 [b]Is. 50:8f.

34 [1]Some ancient mss. read, *raised from the dead* [a]Rom. 8:1 [b]Rom. 5:6f. [c]Acts 2:24 [d]Mark 16:19 [e]Heb. 7:25; Rom. 8:27; Heb. 9:24; 1 John 2:1

35 [1]Some ancient mss. read, *God* [a]Rom. 8:37f. [b]Rom. 2:9; 2 Cor. 4:8 [c]1 Cor. 4:11; 2 Cor. 11:26f.

36 [a]Ps. 44:22; 1 Cor. 4:9; 15:30f.; 2 Cor. 1:9; 4:10f.; 6:9; 11:23; Acts 20:24

37 [a]1 Cor. 15:57; John 16:33 [b]Gal. 2:20; Eph. 5:2; Rev. 1:5

38 [a]1 Cor. 3:22 [b]1 Cor. 15:24; Eph. 1:21; 1 Pet. 3:22 [c]1 Cor. 3:22

39 [a]Rom. 5:8 [b]Rom. 8:1

1 [a]2 Cor. 11:10; Gal. 1:20; 1 Tim. 2:7; Rom. 1:9

3 [1]Lit., *pray* [a]Ex. 32:32 [b]1 Cor. 12:3; 16:22; Gal. 1:8f. [c]Rom. 11:14; Eph. 6:5; Rom. 1:3

4 [a]Rom. 9:6 [b]Ex. 4:22; Rom. 8:15 [c]Ex. 40:34; 1 Kin. 8:11; Ezek. 1:28; Heb. 9:5 [d]Gen. 17:2; Deut. 29:14; Eph. 2:12; Luke 1:72; Acts 3:25 [e]Deut. 4:13f.; Ps. 147:19 [f]Heb. 9:1, 6; Deut. 7:6; 14:1f. [g]Acts 2:39; 13:32; Eph. 2:12

5 [1]I.e., the Messiah [2]Lit., *unto the ages* [a]Rom. 11:28; Acts 3:13 [b]Matt. 1:1-16; Rom. 1:3 [c]Col. 1:16-19 [d]John 1:1; Col. 2:9 [e]Rom. 1:25

6 But *it is* not as though [a]the word of God has failed.
[b]For they are not all Israel who are *descended* from Israel;
7 neither are they all children [a]because they are Abraham's [1]descendants, but: "[b]THROUGH ISAAC YOUR [1]DESCENDANTS
WILL BE NAMED."
8 That is, it is not the children of the flesh who are
[a]children of God, but the [b]children of the promise are regarded as [1]descendants.
9 For this is a word of promise: "[a]AT THIS TIME I WILL
COME, AND SARAH SHALL HAVE A SON."
10 [a]And not only this, but there was [b]Rebekah also, when
she had conceived *twins* by one man, our father Isaac;
11 for though *the twins* were not yet born, and had not
done anything good or bad, in order that [a]God's purpose according to *His* choice might stand, not because of works, but
because of Him who calls,
12 it was said to her, "[a]THE OLDER WILL SERVE THE
YOUNGER."
13 Just as it is written, "[a]JACOB I LOVED, BUT ESAU I
HATED."
14 [a]What shall we say then? [b]There is no injustice with
God, is there? [c]May it never be!
15 For He says to Moses, "[a]I WILL HAVE MERCY ON WHOM I
HAVE MERCY, AND I WILL HAVE COMPASSION ON WHOM I HAVE
COMPASSION."
16 So then it *does* not *depend* on the man who wills or the
man who [a]runs, but on [b]God who has mercy.
17 For the Scripture says to Pharaoh, "[a]FOR THIS VERY
PURPOSE I RAISED YOU UP, TO DEMONSTRATE MY POWER IN YOU,
AND THAT MY NAME MIGHT BE PROCLAIMED [1]THROUGHOUT THE
WHOLE EARTH."
18 So then He has mercy on whom He desires, and He
[a]hardens whom He desires.
19 [a]You will say to me then, "[b]Why does He still find
fault? For [c]who resists His will?"
20 On the contrary, who are you, [a]O man, who [b]answers
back to God? [c]The thing molded will not say to the molder,
"Why did you make me like this," will it?
21 Or does not the potter have a right over the clay, to
make from the same lump one vessel [1]for honorable use, and
another [2]for common use?
22 What if God, although willing to demonstrate His
wrath and to make His power known, endured with much
[a]patience vessels of wrath [b]prepared for destruction?
23 And *He did so* in order that He might make known
[a]the riches of His glory upon [b]vessels of mercy, which He
[c]prepared beforehand for glory,
24 *even* us, whom He also [a]called, [b]not from among Jews
only, but also from among Gentiles.
25 As He says also in Hosea,
"[a]I WILL CALL THOSE WHO WERE NOT MY PEOPLE, 'MY
PEOPLE,'
AND HER WHO WAS NOT BELOVED, 'BELOVED.'"
26 "[a]AND IT SHALL BE THAT IN THE PLACE WHERE IT WAS
SAID TO THEM, 'YOU ARE NOT MY PEOPLE.'

6 [a]Num. 23:19 [b]Rom. 2:28f.; Gal. 6:16; John 1:47

7 [1]Lit., *seed* [a]Gal. 4:23; John 8:33, 39 [b]Gen. 21:12; Heb. 11:18

8 [1]Lit., *seed* [a]Rom. 8:14 [b]Rom. 4:13, 16; Gal. 3:29; 4:28; Heb. 11:11

9 [a]Gen. 18:10

10 [a]Rom. 5:3 [b]Gen. 25:21

11 [a]Rom. 8:28; 4:17

12 [a]Gen. 25:23

13 [a]Mal. 1:2f.

14 [a]Rom. 3:5 [b]2 Chr. 19:7; Rom. 2:11 [c]Luke 20:16

15 [a]Ex. 33:19

16 [a]Gal. 2:2 [b]Eph. 2:8

17 [1]Lit., *in* [a]Ex. 9:16

18 [a]Ex. 4:21; 7:3; 9:12; 10:20, 27; 11:10; 14:4, 17; Deut. 2:30; Josh. 11:20; John 12:40; Rom. 11:7, 25

19 [a]Rom. 11:19; 1 Cor. 15:35; James 2:18 [b]Rom. 3:7 [c]2 Chr. 20:6; Job 9:12; Dan. 4:35

20 [a]Rom. 2:1 [b]Job. 33:13 [c]Is. 29:16; 45:9; 64:8; Jer. 18:6; 2 Tim. 2:20; Rom. 9:22f.

21 [1]Lit., *for honor* [2]Lit., *for dishonor*

22 [a]Rom. 2:4 [b]Prov. 16:4; 1 Pet. 2:8

23 [a]Rom. 2:4; Eph. 3:16 [b]Acts 9:15 [c]Rom. 8:29f.

24 [a]Rom. 8:28 [b]Rom. 3:29

25 [a]Hos. 2:23; 1 Pet. 2:10

26 [a]Hos. 1:10

THERE THEY SHALL BE CALLED SONS OF [b]THE LIVING
GOD."
27 And Isaiah cries out concerning Israel, "[a]THOUGH THE
NUMBER OF THE SONS OF ISRAEL BE [b]AS THE SAND OF THE SEA, IT IS
[c]THE REMNANT THAT WILL BE SAVED;
28 [a]FOR THE LORD WILL EXECUTE HIS WORD UPON THE
EARTH, [1]THOROUGHLY AND [2]QUICKLY."
29 And just as Isaiah foretold,
"[a]EXCEPT [b]THE LORD OF [1]SABAOTH HAD LEFT TO US A
[2]POSTERITY,
[c]WE WOULD HAVE BECOME AS SODOM, AND WOULD
HAVE [3]RESEMBLED GOMORRAH."
30 [a]What shall we say then? That Gentiles, who did not
pursue righteousness, attained righteousness, even [b]the righteousness which is [1]by faith;
31 but Israel, [a]pursuing a law of righteousness, did not
[b]arrive at *that* law.
32 Why? Because *they did* not *pursue it* [1]by faith, but
as though *it were* [1]by works. They stumbled over [a]THE
STUMBLING-STONE,
33 just as it is written,
"[a]BEHOLD, I LAY IN ZION A STONE OF STUMBLING AND A
ROCK OF OFFENSE,
[b]AND HE WHO BELIEVES IN HIM [c]WILL NOT BE
[1]DISAPPOINTED."

CHAPTER 10

BRETHREN, my heart's desire and my prayer to God for
them is for *their* salvation.
2 For I bear them witness that they have [a]a zeal for God,
but not in accordance with knowledge.
3 For not knowing about [a]God's righteousness, and [b]seek-
ing to establish their own, they did not subject themselves to
the righteousness of God.
4 For [a]Christ is the [1]end of the law for righteousness to
[b]everyone who believes.
5 For Moses writes that the man who practices the righteousness which is [1]based on law [a]shall live [2]by that
righteousness.
6 But [a]the righteousness [1]based on faith speaks thus,
"[b]DO NOT SAY IN YOUR HEART, 'WHO WILL ASCEND INTO HEAV-
EN?' (that is, to bring Christ down),
7 or 'WHO WILL DESCEND INTO THE [a]ABYSS?' (that is, to
[b]bring Christ up from the dead)."
8 But what does it say? "[a]THE WORD IS NEAR YOU, IN YOUR
MOUTH AND IN YOUR HEART"—that is, the word of faith which
we are preaching,
9 [1]that [a]if you confess with your mouth Jesus *as* Lord,
and [b]believe in your heart that [c]God raised Him from the
dead, you shall be saved;
10 for with the heart man believes, [1]resulting in righteousness, and with the mouth he confesses, [2]resulting in salvation.
11 For the Scripture says, "[a]WHOEVER BELIEVES IN HIM
WILL NOT BE [1]DISAPPOINTED."
12 For [a]there is no distinction between Jew and Greek; for

26 [b]Matt. 16:16

27 [a]Is. 10:22 [b]Gen. 22:17; Hos. 1:10 [c]Rom. 11:5

28 [1]Lit., *finishing it* [2]Lit., *cutting it short*
[a]Is. 10:23

29 [1]I.e., *Hosts* [2]Lit., *seed* [3]Lit., *been made like*
[a]Is. 1:9 [b]James 5:4 [c]Deut. 29:23; Is. 13:19; Jer. 49:18; 50:40; Amos 4:11

30 [1]Lit., *out of*
[a]Rom. 9:14 [b]Rom. 10:6; Gal. 2:16; 3:24; Phil. 3:9; Heb. 11:7; Rom. 1:17; 3:21f.

31 [a]Is. 51:1; Rom. 10:2f.; 11:7; 9:30; 10:20 [b]Gal. 5:4

32 [1]Lit., *out of*
[a]Is. 8:14; 1 Pet. 2:6, 8

33 [1]Lit., *put to shame*
[a]Is. 28:16 [b]Rom. 10:11 [c]Rom. 5:5

2 [a]Acts 21:20

3 [a]Rom. 1:17 [b]Is. 51:1; Rom. 10:2f.; 11:7; 8:30; 10:20

4 [1]Or, *goal*
[a]Gal. 3:24; 4:5; Rom. 7:1-4 [b]Rom. 3:22

5 [1]Lit., *out of, from* [2]Lit., *by it*
[a]Lev. 18:5; Neh. 9:29; Ezek. 20:11, 13, 21; Rom. 7:10

6 [1]Lit., *out of, from*
[a]Rom. 9:30 [b]Deut. 30:12f.

7 [a]Luke 8:31 [b]Heb. 13:20

8 [a]Deut. 30:14

9 [1]Or, *because*
[a]Matt. 10:32; Luke 12:8; Rom. 14:9; 1 Cor. 12:3; Phil. 2:11 [b]Rom. 4:24; Acts 16:31 [c]Acts 2:24

10 [1]Lit., *to righteousness* [2]Lit., *to salvation*

11 [1]Lit., *put to shame*
[a]Is. 28:16; Rom. 9:33

12 [a]Rom. 3:22, 29

12 [b]Acts 10:36 [c]Rom. 3:29
13 [a]Joel 2:32; Acts 2:21
14 [a]Eph. 2:17; 4:21 [b]Acts 8:31; Titus 1:3
15 [1]Or, *preach the gospel* [a]Is. 52:7 [b]Rom. 1:15; 15:20
16 [1]Lit., *gospel* [a]Rom. 3:3 [b]Is. 53:1; John 12:38
17 [1]Or, *concerning Christ* [a]Gal. 3:2, 5 [b]Col. 3:16
18 [1]Or, *inhabited earth* [a]Ps. 19:4; Col. 1:6, 23; 1 Thess. 1:8; Rom. 1:8
19 [a]Deut. 32:21 [b]Rom. 11:11, 14
20 [a]Is. 65:1; Rom. 9:30
21 [a]Is. 65:2
1 [1]Lit., *of the seed of Abraham* [a]1 Sam. 12:22; Jer. 31:37; 33:24-26 [b]Luke 20:16 [c]2 Cor. 11:22; Phil. 3:5
2 [a]Ps. 94:14 [b]Rom. 8:29 [c]Rom. 6:16
3 [1]Gr., *soul-life* [a]1 Kin. 19:10
4 [1]Lit., *says* [a]1 Kin. 19:18
5 [1]Lit., *choice of grace* [a]Rom. 9:27; 2 Kin. 19:4
6 [a]Rom. 4:4
7 [1]Lit., *the election* [a]Rom. 9:31 [b]Mark 6:52; 2 Cor. 3:14; Rom. 11:25; 9:18
8 [a]Is. 29:10; Deut. 29:4; Matt. 13:13f.

the same *Lord* is [b]Lord of [c]all, abounding in riches for all who
call upon Him;
13 for "[a]WHOEVER WILL CALL UPON THE NAME OF THE LORD
WILL BE SAVED."
14 How then shall they call upon Him in whom they have
not believed? And how shall they believe in Him [a]whom they
have not heard? And how shall they hear without [b]a preacher?
15 And how shall they preach unless they are sent? Just as
it is written, "[a]HOW BEAUTIFUL ARE THE FEET OF THOSE WHO
[1b]BRING GLAD TIDINGS OF GOOD THINGS!"
16 However, they [a]did not all heed the [1]glad tidings; for
Isaiah says, "[b]LORD, WHO HAS BELIEVED OUR REPORT?"
17 So faith *comes* from [a]hearing, and hearing by [b]the word
[1]of Christ.
18 But I say, surely they have never heard, have they?
Indeed they have:

> "[a]THEIR VOICE HAS GONE OUT INTO ALL THE EARTH,
> AND THEIR WORDS TO THE ENDS OF THE [1]WORLD."

19 But I say, surely Israel did not know, did they? At the
first Moses says,

> "[a]I WILL [b]MAKE YOU JEALOUS BY THAT WHICH IS NOT A NATION,
> BY A NATION WITHOUT UNDERSTANDING WILL I ANGER YOU."

20 And Isaiah is very bold and says,

> "[a]I WAS FOUND BY THOSE WHO SOUGHT ME NOT,
> I BECAME MANIFEST TO THOSE WHO DID NOT ASK FOR ME."

21 But as for Israel he says, "[a]ALL THE DAY LONG I HAVE
STRETCHED OUT MY HANDS TO A DISOBEDIENT AND OBSTINATE
PEOPLE."

CHAPTER 11

I SAY then, God has not [a]rejected His people, has He? [b]May
it never be! For [c]I too am an Israelite, [1]a descendant of Abraham, of the tribe of Benjamin.
2 God [a]has not rejected His people whom He [b]foreknew.
[c]Or do you not know what the Scripture says in *the passage*
about Elijah, how he pleads with God against Israel?
3 "Lord, [a]THEY HAVE KILLED THY PROPHETS, THEY HAVE
TORN DOWN THINE ALTARS, AND I ALONE AM LEFT, AND THEY ARE
SEEKING MY [1]LIFE."
4 But what [1]is the divine response to him? "[a]I HAVE KEPT
for Myself SEVEN THOUSAND MEN WHO HAVE NOT BOWED THE
KNEE TO BAAL."
5 In the same way then, there has also come to be at the
present time [a]a remnant according to *God's* [1]gracious choice.
6 But [a]if it is by grace, it is no longer on the basis of
works, otherwise grace is no longer grace.
7 What then? That which [a]Israel is seeking for, it has not
obtained, but [1]those who were chosen obtained it, and the rest
were [b]hardened;
8 just as it is written,

> "[a]GOD GAVE THEM A SPIRIT OF STUPOR,
> EYES TO SEE NOT AND EARS TO HEAR NOT,
> DOWN TO THIS VERY DAY."

9 And David says,

"[a]LET THEIR TABLE BECOME A SNARE and a trap,
AND A STUMBLING BLOCK AND A RETRIBUTION TO
THEM.
10 [a]LET THEIR EYES BE DARKENED TO SEE NOT,
AND BEND THEIR BACKS FOREVER."
11 [a]I say then, they did not stumble so as to fall, did they?
[b]May it never be! But by their transgression [c]salvation *has*
come to the Gentiles, to [d]make them jealous.
12 Now if their transgression be riches for the world and
their failure be riches for the Gentiles, how much more will
their [1a]fulfillment be!
13 But I am speaking to you who are Gentiles. Inasmuch
then as [a]I am an apostle of Gentiles, I magnify my ministry,
14 if somehow I might [a]move to jealousy [b]my [1]fellow-
countrymen and [c]save some of them.
15 For if their rejection be the [a]reconciliation of the
world, what will *their* acceptance be but [b]life from the dead?
16 And if the [a]first piece *of dough* be holy, the lump is
also; and if the root be holy, the branches are too.
17 But if some of the [a]branches were broken off, and [b]you,
being a wild olive, were grafted in among them and became
partaker with them of the [1]rich root of the olive tree,
18 do not be arrogant toward the branches; but if you are
arrogant, *remember that* [a]it is not you who supports the root,
but the root *supports* you.
19 [a]You will say then, "Branches were broken off so that I
might be grafted in."
20 Quite right, they were broken off for their unbelief,
and you [a]stand *only* by your faith. [b]Do not be conceited, but
fear;
21 for if God did not spare the natural branches, neither
will He spare you.
22 Behold then the kindness and severity of God; to those
who fell, severity, but to you, God's [a]kindness, [b]if you continue
in His kindness; otherwise you also [c]will be cut off.
23 And they also, [a]if they do not continue in their unbelief, will be grafted in; for God is able to graft them in again.
24 For if you were cut off from what is by nature a wild
olive tree, and were grafted contrary to nature into a cultivated
olive tree, how much more shall these who are the natural
branches be grafted into their own olive tree?
25 For [a]I do not want you, brethren, to be uninformed of
this [b]mystery, lest you be [c]wise in your own estimation, that a
partial [d]hardening has happened to Israel until the [e]fulness of
the Gentiles has come in;
26 and thus all Israel will be saved; just as it is written,
"[a]THE DELIVERER WILL COME FROM ZION,
HE WILL REMOVE UNGODLINESS FROM JACOB."
27 "[a]AND THIS IS [1]MY COVENANT WITH THEM,
WHEN I TAKE AWAY THEIR SINS."
28 [1]From the standpoint of the gospel they are [a]enemies
for your sake, but [2]from the standpoint of *God's* choice they
are beloved for [b]the sake of the fathers;
29 for the gifts and the [a]calling of God [b]are irrevocable.
30 For just as you once were disobedient to God but now
have been shown mercy because of their disobedience,

9 [a]Ps. 69:22f.

10 [a]Ps. 69:23

11 [a]Rom. 11:1 [b]Luke 20:16 [c]Acts 28:28 [d]Rom. 11:14

12 [1]Or, *fulness* [a]Rom. 11:25

13 [a]Acts 9:15

14 [1]Lit., *flesh* [a]Rom. 11:11 [b]Rom. 9:3; Gen. 29:14; 2 Sam. 19:12f. [c]1 Cor. 7:16; 9:22; 1 Tim. 1:15; 2:4; 2 Tim. 1:9; Titus 3:5; 1 Cor. 1:21

15 [a]Rom. 5:11 [b]Luke 15:24, 32

16 [a]Num. 15:18ff.; Neh. 10:37; Ezek. 44:30

17 [1]Lit., *root of the fatness* [a]Jer. 11:16; John 15:2 [b]Eph. 2:11ff.

18 [a]John 4:22

19 [a]Rom. 9:19

20 [a]2 Cor. 1:24; 1 Cor. 10:12; Rom. 5:2 [b]Rom. 12:16; 1 Tim. 6:17; 1 Pet. 1:17

22 [a]Rom. 2:4 [b]1 Cor. 15:2; Heb. 3:6, 14 [c]John 15:2

23 [a]2 Cor. 3:16

25 [a]Rom. 1:13 [b]Rom. 16:25; 1 Cor. 2:7-10; Eph. 3:3-5, 9; Matt. 13:11 [c]Rom. 12:16 [d]Rom. 11:7 [e]Rom. 11:12; Luke 21:24; John 10:16

26 [a]Is. 59:20, 21

27 [1]Lit., *the covenant from Me* [a]Is. 27:9; Heb. 8:10, 12

28 [1]Lit., *according to the gospel* [2]Lit., *according to the election* [a]Rom. 5:10 [b]Rom. 9:5; Deut. 7:8; 10:15

29 [a]1 Cor. 1:26; Eph. 1:18; 4:1, 4; Phil. 3:14; 2 Thess. 1:11; 2 Tim. 1:9; Heb. 3:1; 2 Pet. 1:10; Rom. 8:28 [b]Heb. 7:21

32 [a]Gal. 3:22f.; Rom. 3:9

33 [1]Or, *and the wisdom* [a]Eph. 3:8; Rom. 2:4 [b]Col. 2:3; Eph. 3:10 [c]Job 5:9; 11:7; 15:8

34 [a]Is. 40:13f.; 1 Cor. 2:16

35 [1]Lit., *and it will be paid back* [a]Job 35:7; 41:11

36 [1]Lit., *to the ages* [a]1 Cor. 8:6; 11:12; Col. 1:16; Heb. 2:10 [b]Rom. 16:27; Eph. 3:21; Phil. 4:20; 1 Tim. 1:17; 2 Tim. 4:18; 1 Pet. 4:11; 5:11; 2 Pet. 3:18; Jude 25; Rev. 1:6; 5:13; 7:12

1 [1]Or, *well-pleasing* [2]Or, *rational* [a]1 Cor. 1:10; 2 Cor. 10:2; Eph. 4:1; 1 Pet. 2:11 [b]Rom. 6:13, 16, 19; 1 Cor. 6:20; Heb. 13:15; 1 Pet. 2:5

2 [1]Or, *age* [2]Or, *well-pleasing* [a]1 Pet. 1:14 [b]Matt. 13:22; Gal. 1:4; 1 John 2:15 [c]Titus 3:5; Eph. 4:23 [d]Eph. 5:10, 17; Col. 1:9

3 [a]Rom. 15:15; 1 Cor. 3:10; 15:10; Gal. 2:9; Eph. 3:7f.; Rom. 1:5 [b]Rom. 11:20; 12:16; [c]1 Cor. 7:17; 2 Cor. 10:13; Eph. 4:7; 1 Pet. 4:11

4 [a]1 Cor. 12:12-14; Eph. 4:4, 16

5 [a]1 Cor. 10:17, 33 [b]1 Cor. 12:20, 27; Eph. 4:12, 25

6 [a]1 Cor. 7:7; 12:4; 1 Pet. 4:10f.; Rom. 12:3 [b]1 Cor. 12:10; Acts 13:1

7 [1]Or, *office of service* [a]1 Cor. 12:5, 28; Acts 6:1 [b]1 Cor. 12:28; 14:26; Acts 13:1

8 [1]Or, *simplicity* [2]Or, *gives aid* [a]Acts 4:36; 11:23; 13:15 [b]2 Cor. 8:2; 9:11, 13 [c]1 Tim. 5:17; 1 Cor. 12:28 [d]2 Cor. 9:7

9 [a]2 Cor. 6:6; 1 Tim. 1:5 [b]1 Thess. 5:21f.

10 [1]Or, *outdo one another in showing honor* [a]1 Thess. 4:9; Heb. 13:1; 2 Pet. 1:7; John 13:34 [b]Phil. 2:3; Rom. 13:7; 1 Pet. 2:17

11 [a]Acts 18:25 [b]Acts 20:19

12 [a]Rom. 5:2 [b]Heb. 10:32, 36 [c]Acts 1:14

13 [1]I.e., true believers; lit., *holy ones* [2]Lit., *pursuing* [a]Rom. 15:25; 1 Cor. 16:15; 2 Cor. 9:1; Heb. 6:10 [b]1 Tim. 3:2; Matt. 25:35

14 [1]Some ancient mss. omit, *you* [a]Matt. 5:44; Luke 6:28; 1 Cor. 4:12

15 [a]Job 30:25; Heb. 13:3

16 [1]Or, *accommodate yourself to lowly things* [a]Rom. 15:5; 2 Cor. 13:11; Phil. 2:2; 4:2; 1 Pet. 3:8 [b]Rom. 12:3; Rom. 11:20 [c]Rom. 11:25; Prov. 3:7

31 so these also now have been disobedient, in order that
because of the mercy shown to you they also may now be
shown mercy.
32 For [a]God has shut up all in disobedience that He might
show mercy to all.
33 Oh the depth of [a]the riches [1]both of the [b]wisdom and
knowledge of God! [c]How unsearchable are His judgments and
unfathomable His ways!
34 For [a]WHO HAS KNOWN THE MIND OF THE LORD, OR WHO
BECAME HIS COUNSELOR?
35 Or [a]WHO HAS FIRST GIVEN TO HIM [1]THAT IT MIGHT BE
PAID BACK TO HIM AGAIN?
36 For [a]from Him and through Him and to Him are all
things. [b]To Him *be* the glory [1]forever. Amen.

Chapter 12

[a]I URGE you therefore, brethren, by the mercies of God, to
[b]present your bodies a living and holy sacrifice, [1]acceptable to
God, *which is* your [2]spiritual service of worship.
2 And do not [a]be conformed to [b]this [1]world, but be transformed by the [c]renewing of your mind, that you may [d]prove
what the will of God is, that which is good and [2]acceptable and
perfect.
3 For through [a]the grace given to me I say to every man
among you [b]not to think more highly of himself than he ought
to think; but to think so as to have sound judgment, as God
has allotted to [c]each a measure of faith.
4 For [a]just as we have many members in one body and all
the members do not have the same function,
5 so we, [a]who are many, are [b]one body in Christ, and
individually members one of another.
6 And since we have gifts that [a]differ according to the
grace given to us, *let each exercise them accordingly:* if [b]proph-
ecy, according to the proportion of his faith;
7 if [1a]service, in his serving; or he who [b]teaches, in his
teaching;
8 or he who [a]exhorts, in his exhortation; he who gives,
with [1b]liberality; [c]he who [2]leads, with diligence; he who shows
mercy, with [d]cheerfulness.
9 Let [a]love be without hypocrisy. [b]Abhor what is evil;
cleave to what is good.
10 Be [a]devoted to one another in brotherly love; [1]give
preference to one another [b]in honor;
11 not lagging behind in diligence, [a]fervent in spirit, [b]serv-
ing the Lord;
12 [a]rejoicing in hope, [b]persevering in tribulation, [c]devoted
to prayer,
13 [a]contributing to the needs of the [1]saints, [2b]practicing
hospitality.
14 [a]Bless those who persecute [1]you; bless and curse not.
15 [a]Rejoice with those who rejoice, and weep with those
who weep.
16 [a]Be of the same mind toward one another; do not be
haughty in mind, [b]but [1]associate with the lowly. [c]Do not be
wise in your own estimation.

17 [a]Never pay back evil for evil to anyone. [1b]Respect what
is right in the sight of all men.
18 If possible, [a]so far as it depends on you, [b]be at peace
with all men.
19 [a]Never take your own revenge, beloved, but [1]leave
room for the wrath *of God,* for it is written, "[b]VENGEANCE IS
MINE, I WILL REPAY, SAYS THE LORD."
20 "[a]BUT IF YOUR ENEMY IS HUNGRY, FEED HIM, AND IF HE IS
THIRSTY, GIVE HIM A DRINK; FOR [b]IN SO DOING YOU WILL HEAP
BURNING COALS UPON HIS HEAD."
21 Do not be overcome by evil, but overcome evil with
good.

CHAPTER 13

LET every [1a]person be in [b]subjection to the governing authorities. For [c]there is no authority except [2]from God, and those
which exist are established by God.
2 Therefore he who resists authority has opposed the
ordinance of God; and they who have opposed will receive
condemnation upon themselves.
3 For [a]rulers are not a cause of fear for [1]good behavior,
but for evil. Do you want to have no fear of authority? Do
what is good, and you will have praise from the same;
4 for it is a minister of God to you for good. But if you
do what is evil, be afraid; for it does not bear the sword for
nothing; for it is a minister of God, an [a]avenger who brings
wrath upon the one who practices evil.
5 Wherefore it is necessary to be in subjection, not only
because of wrath, but also [a]for conscience' sake.
6 For because of this you also pay taxes, for *rulers* are
servants of God, devoting themselves to this very thing.
7 [a]Render to all what is due them: [b]tax to whom tax *is
due;* [c]custom to whom custom; fear to whom fear; honor to
whom honor.
8 Owe nothing to anyone except to love one another; for
[a]he who loves [1]his neighbor has fulfilled *the* law.
9 For this, "[a]YOU SHALL NOT COMMIT ADULTERY, YOU
SHALL NOT MURDER, YOU SHALL NOT STEAL, YOU SHALL NOT
COVET," and if there is any other commandment, it is summed
up in this saying, "[b]YOU SHALL LOVE YOUR NEIGHBOR AS
YOURSELF."
10 Love [1]does no wrong to a neighbor; [a]love therefore is
the fulfillment of *the* law.
11 And this *do,* knowing the time, that it is [a]already the
hour for you to [b]awaken from sleep; for now [1]salvation is
nearer to us than when we believed.
12 [a]The night is almost gone, and [b]the day is at hand. Let
us therefore lay aside [c]the deeds of darkness and put on [d]the
armor of light.
13 Let us [1a]behave properly as in the day, [b]not in carousing
and drunkenness, not in sexual promiscuity and sensuality, not
in strife and jealousy.
14 But [a]put on the Lord Jesus Christ, and make no provision for the flesh [b]in regard to *its* lusts.

17 [1]Lit., *take thought for* [a]Prov. 20:22; 24:29; Rom. 12:19 [b]2 Cor. 8:21

18 [a]Rom. 1:15 [b]Mark 9:50; Rom. 14:19

19 [1]Lit., *give a place* [a]Prov. 20:22; 24:29; Rom. 12:17 [b]Deut. 32:35; Heb. 10:30; 1 Thess. 4:6; Ps. 94:1

20 [a]Prov. 25:21f.; Matt. 5:44; Luke 6:27 [b]2 Kin, 6:22

1 [1]Lit., *soul* [2]Lit., *by* [a]Acts 2:41 [b]Titus 3:1; 1 Pet. 2:13f. [c]John 19:11; Dan. 2:21; 4:17

3 [1]Lit., *the good work* [a]1 Pet. 2:14

4 [a]1 Thess. 4:6

5 [a]1 Pet. 2:19; 1 Pet. 2:13; Eccl. 8

7 [a]Matt. 22:21 [b]Luke 20:22; 23:2 [c]Matt. 17:25

8 [1]Lit., *the other* [a]Matt. 22:39f.; Gal. 5:14; Rom. 13:10; Matt. 7:12; John 13:34; James 2:8

9 [a]Ex. 20:13ff.; Deut. 5:17ff. [b]Lev. 19:18; Matt. 19:19

10 [1]Lit., *works no evil* [a]Matt. 22:39f.; Gal. 5:14; Rom. 13:8; Matt. 7:12; John 13:34; James 2:8

11 [1]Or, *our salvation is nearer than when . . .* [a]1 Cor. 7:29f.; 10:11; James 5:8; 1 Pet. 4:7; 2 Pet. 3:9, 11; 1 John 2:18; Rev. 1:3; 22:10 [b]1 Cor. 15:34; Eph. 5:14; 1 Thess. 5:6; Mark 13:37

12 [a]1 Cor. 7:29f.; 10:11; James 5:8; 1 Pet. 4:7; 2 Pet. 3:9, 11; 1 John 2:18; Rev. 1:3; 22:10 [b]Heb. 10:25; 1 John 2:8; Rev. 1:3; 22:10 [c]Eph. 5:11 [d]2 Cor. 6:7; 10:4; Eph. 6:11, 13; 1 Thess. 5:8

13 [1]Lit., *walk* [a]1 Thess. 4:12 [b]Luke 21:34; Gal. 5:21; Eph. 5:18; 1 Pet. 4:3

14 [a]Gal. 3:27; Job 29:14; Eph. 4:24; Col. 3:10, 12 [b]Gal. 5:16; 1 Pet. 2:11

Chapter 14

NOW [a]accept the one who is [b]weak in faith, *but* not for *the*
purpose of passing judgment on his opinions.
2 [a]One man has faith that he may eat all things, but he
who is [b]weak eats vegetables *only*.
3 Let not him who eats [a]regard with contempt him who
does not eat, and let not him who does not eat [b]judge him who
eats, for God has [c]accepted him.
4 [a]Who are you to judge the [1]servant of another? To his
own [2]master he stands or falls; and stand he will, for the Lord is
able to make him stand.
5 [a]One man [1]regards one day above another, another
regards every day *alike*. Let each man be [b]fully convinced in
his own mind.
6 He who observes the day, observes it for the Lord, and
he who eats, [1]does so for the Lord, for he [a]gives thanks to God;
and he who eats not, for the Lord he does not eat, and gives
thanks to God.
7 For not one of us [a]lives for himself, and not one dies
for himself;
8 for if we live, we live for the Lord, or if we die, we die
for the Lord; therefore [a]whether we live or die, we are the
Lord's.
9 For to this end [a]Christ died and lived *again*, that He
might be [b]Lord both of the dead and of the living.
10 But you, why do you judge your brother? Or you again,
why do you [a]regard your brother with contempt? For [b]we shall
all stand before the judgment-seat of God.
11 For it is written,
"[a]AS I LIVE, SAYS THE LORD, [b]EVERY KNEE SHALL BOW TO
ME,
AND EVERY TONGUE SHALL [1]GIVE PRAISE TO GOD."
12 So then [a]each one of us shall give account of himself to
God.
13 Therefore let us not [a]judge one another any more,
but rather determine this — [b]not to put an obstacle or a
stumbling block in a brother's way.
14 I know and am convinced in the Lord Jesus that [a]noth-
ing is unclean in itself; but to him who [b]thinks anything to be
unclean, to him it is unclean.
15 For if because of food your brother is hurt, you are no
longer [a]walking according to love. [b]Do not destroy with your
food him for whom Christ died.
16 Therefore [a]do not let what is for you a good thing be
[1]spoken of as evil;
17 for the kingdom of God [a]is not eating and drinking, but
righteousness and [b]peace and [b]joy in the Holy Spirit.
18 For he who in this *way* [a]serves Christ is [b]acceptable to
God and approved by men.
19 So then [1]let us [a]pursue the things which make for peace
and the [b]building up of one another.
20 [a]Do not tear down the work of God for the sake of
food. [b]All things indeed are clean, but [c]they are evil for the
man who eats [1]and gives offense.

1 [a]Rom. 14:3; 15:7; Acts 28:2; Rom. 11:15 [b]Rom. 14:2; Rom. 15:1; 1 Cor. 8:9ff.; 9:22

2 [a]Rom. 14:14 [b]Rom. 14:1; 15:1; 1 Cor. 8:9ff.; 9:22

3 [a]Rom. 14:10; Luke 18:9 [b]Col. 2:16; Rom. 14:10, 13 [c]Rom. 14:1; 15:7; Acts 28:2; Rom. 11:15

4 [1]Or, *house-servant* [2]Lit., *lord* [a]James 4:12; Rom. 9:20

5 [1]Lit., *judges* [a]Gal. 4:10 [b]Rom. 4:21; Luke 1:1; Rom. 14:23

6 [1]Lit., *eats* [a]1 Cor. 10:30; 1 Tim. 4:3f.; Matt. 14:19

7 [a]2 Cor. 5:15; Gal. 2:20; Phil. 1:20f.; Rom. 8:38

8 [a]Phil. 1:20; 1 Thess. 5:10; Rev. 14:13; Luke 20:38

9 [a]Rev. 1:18; 2:8 [b]Phil. 2:11; Matt. 28:18; John 12:24; 1 Thess. 5:10

10 [a]Rom. 14:3; Luke 18:9 [b]Rom. 2:16; 2 Cor. 5:10

11 [1]Or, *confess* [a]Is. 45:23 [b]Phil. 2:10f.

12 [a]Matt. 12:36; 1 Pet. 4:5; Matt. 16:27

13 [a]Rom. 14:3; Matt. 7:1 [b]1 Cor. 8:13

14 [a]Rom. 14:2, 20; Acts 10:15 [b]1 Cor. 8:7

15 [a]Eph. 5:2 [b]1 Cor. 8:11; Rom. 14:20

16 [1]Lit., *blasphemed* [a]1 Cor. 10:30; Titus 2:5

17 [a]1 Cor. 8:8 [b]Gal. 5:22; Rom. 15:13

18 [a]Rom. 16:18 [b]2 Cor. 8:21; Phil. 4:8; 1 Pet. 2:12

19 [1]Many ancient mss. read, *we pursue* [a]Ps. 34:14; 1 Cor. 7:15; 2 Tim. 2:22; Heb. 12:14; Rom. 12:18 [b]Rom. 15:2; 1 Cor. 10:23; 14:3f., 26; 2 Cor. 12:19; Eph. 4:12, 29

20 [1]Lit., *with offense* [a]Rom. 14:15 [b]Rom. 14:2, 14; Acts 10:15 [c]1 Cor. 8:9-12

21 [a]It is good not to eat meat or to drink wine, or *to do*
anything by which your brother stumbles.
22 The faith which you have, have [1]as your own conviction before God. Happy is he who [a]does not condemn himself
in what he approves.
23 But [a]he who doubts is condemned if he eats, because
his eating is not from faith; and whatever is not from faith is
sin.

Chapter 15

NOW we who are strong ought to bear the weaknesses of
[a]those without strength and not *just* please ourselves.
2 Let each of us [a]please his neighbor [1]for his good, to his
[b]edification.
3 For even [a]Christ did not please Himself; but as it is
written, "[b]THE REPROACHES OF THOSE WHO REPROACHED THEE
FELL UPON ME."
4 For [a]whatever was written in earlier times was written
for our instruction, that through perseverance and the encouragement of the Scriptures we might have hope.
5 Now may the [a]God [1]who gives perseverance and encouragement grant you [b]to be of the same mind with one another
according to Christ Jesus;
6 that with one accord you may with one [1]voice glorify
[a]the God and Father of our Lord Jesus Christ.
7 Wherefore, [a]accept one another, just as Christ also accepted [1]us to the glory of God.
8 For I say that Christ has become a servant to [a]the
circumcision on behalf of the truth of God to confirm [b]the
promises *given* to the fathers,
9 and for [a]the Gentiles to [b]glorify God for His mercy; as
it is written,

"[c]THEREFORE I WILL [1]GIVE PRAISE TO THEE AMONG THE
GENTILES,
AND I WILL SING TO THY NAME."

10 And again he says,
"[a]REJOICE, O GENTILES, WITH HIS PEOPLE."
11 And again,
"[a]PRAISE THE LORD ALL YOU GENTILES,
AND LET ALL THE PEOPLES PRAISE HIM."
12 And again Isaiah says,
"[a]THERE SHALL COME [b]THE ROOT OF JESSE,
AND HE WHO ARISES TO RULE OVER THE GENTILES;
[c]IN HIM SHALL THE GENTILES HOPE."
13 Now may the God of hope fill you with all [a]joy and
peace in believing, that you may abound in hope [b]by the power of the Holy Spirit.
14 And concerning you, my brethren, I myself also am
convinced that you yourselves are full of [a]goodness, filled with
[b]all knowledge, and able also to admonish one another,
15 But I have written very boldly to you on some points,
so as to remind you again, because of [a]the grace that was given
me [1]from God,
16 to be [a]a minister of Christ Jesus to the Gentiles, ministering as a priest the [b]gospel of God, that *my* [c]offering of the

21 [a]1 Cor. 8:13

22 [1]Lit., *according to yourself* [a]1 John 3:21

23 [a]Rom. 14:5

1 [a]Rom. 14:1; Gal. 6:2; 1 Thess. 5:14

2 [1]Lit., *for what is good to edification* [a]1 Cor. 10:33; 1 Cor. 9:22; 10:24; 2 Cor. 13:9 [b]Rom. 14:19; 1 Cor. 10:23; 14:3f., 26; 2 Cor. 12:19; Eph. 4:12, 29

3 [a]2 Cor. 8:9 [b]Ps. 69:9

4 [a]Rom. 4:23f.; 2 Tim. 3:16

5 [1]Lit., *of perseverance* [a]2 Cor. 1:3 [b]Rom. 12:16

6 [1]Lit., *mouth* [a]Rev. 1:6

7 [1]Some mss. read, *you* [a]Rom. 14:1

8 [a]Matt. 15:24; Acts 3:26 [b]Rom. 4:16; 2 Cor. 1:20

9 [1]Or, *confess* [a]Rom. 3:29; 11:30 [b]Matt. 9:8 [c]Ps. 18:49 [or 2 Sam. 22:50]

10 [a]Deut. 32:43

11 [a]Ps. 117:1

12 [a]Is. 11:10 [b]Rev. 5:5; 22:16 [c]Matt. 12:21

13 [a]Rom. 14:17 [b]Rom. 15:19; 1 Cor. 2:4; 1 Thess. 1:5

14 [a]Eph. 5:9; 2 Thess. 1:11 [b]1 Cor. 1:5; 13:2; 1 Cor. 8:1, 7, 10; 12:8

15 [1]Some mss. read, *by God* [a]Rom. 12:3

16 [a]Rom. 11:13; Acts 9:15 [b]Rom. 15:19, 20; 1:1 [c]Eph. 5:2; Phil. 2:17; Rom. 12:1

Gentiles might become acceptable, sanctified by the Holy
Spirit.
17 Therefore in Christ Jesus I have found [a]reason for
boasting in [b]things pertaining to God.
18 For I will not presume to speak of anything [1]except
what [a]Christ has accomplished through me, [2]resulting in the
obedience of the Gentiles by word and deed,
19 in the power of [1a]signs and [a]wonders, [b]in the power of
the Spirit; so that [c]from Jerusalem and round about as [d]far as
Illyricum I have [2]fully preached the gospel of Christ.
20 And thus I aspired to [a]preach the gospel, not where
Christ was *already* named, [b]that I might not build upon another
man's foundation;
21 but as it is written,

"[a]THEY WHO HAD NO NEWS OF HIM SHALL SEE,
AND THEY WHO HAVE NOT HEARD SHALL UNDERSTAND."

22 For this reason [a]I have often been hindered from coming to you;
23 but now, with no further place for me in these regions,
and since I [a]have had for many years a longing to come to you
24 whenever I [a]go to Spain — for I hope to see you in
passing, and to be [b]helped on my way there by you, when I
have first [c]enjoyed your company [1]for awhile —
25 but now, [a]I am going to Jerusalem [b]serving the [1]saints.
26 For [a]Macedonia and [b]Achaia have been pleased to
make a contribution for the poor among the [1]saints in
Jerusalem.
27 Yes, they were pleased *to do so,* and they are indebted
to them. For [a]if the Gentiles have shared in their spiritual
things, they are indebted to minister to them also in material
things.
28 Therefore, when I have finished this, and [a]have [1]put
my seal on this fruit of theirs, I will [b]go on by way of you to
Spain.
29 And I know that when [a]I come to you, I will come in
the fulness of the blessing of Christ.
30 Now I urge you, brethren, by our Lord Jesus Christ and
by [a]the love of the Spirit to [b]strive together with me in your
prayers to God for me,
31 that I may be [a]delivered from those who are disobedient in Judea, and *that* my [b]service for Jerusalem may prove
acceptable to the [1c]saints;
32 so that [a]I may come to you in joy by [b]the will of God
and find *refreshing* rest in your company.
33 Now [a]the God of peace be with you all. Amen.

CHAPTER 16

I [a]COMMEND to you our sister Phoebe, who is a [1]servant of
the church which is at [b]Cenchrea;
2 that you [a]receive her in the Lord in a manner worthy of
the [1b]saints, and that you help her in whatever matter she may
have need of you; for she herself has also been a helper of
many, [2]and of myself as well.
3 Greet [a]Prisca and [a]Aquila my fellow-workers [b]in [c]Christ
Jesus,

17 [a]Phil. 3:3 [b]Heb. 2:17; 5:1

18 [1]Or, *which Christ has not accomplished* [2]Lit., *to the obedience* [a]Acts 15:12; 21:19; Rom. 1:5; 2 Cor. 3:5

19 [1]Or, *attesting miracles* [2]Lit., *fulfilled* [a]John 4:48 [b]Rom. 15:13; 1 Cor. 2:4; 1 Thess. 1:5 [c]Acts 22:17-21 [d]Acts 20:1f.

20 [a]Rom. 1:15; 10:15; 15:16 [b]2 Cor. 10:15f.; 1 Cor. 3:10

21 [a]Is. 52:15

22 [a]Rom. 1:13; 1 Thess. 2:18

23 [a]Acts 19:21; Rom. 1:10f.; 15:29, 32

24 [1]Lit., *in part* [a]Rom. 15:28 [b]Acts 15:3 [c]Rom. 1:12

25 [1]I.e., true believers; lit., *holy ones* [a]Acts 19:21 [b]Acts 24:17

26 [1]Note vs. 25 [a]1 Cor. 16:5; 2 Cor. 1:16; 2:13; 7:5; 8:1; 9:2, 4; 11:9; Phil. 4:15; 1 Thess. 1:7f.; 4:10; 1 Tim. 1:3; Acts 16:9 [b]Acts 18:12; 19:21

27 [a]1 Cor. 9:11

28 [1]Lit., *sealed to them this fruit* [a]John 3:33 [b]Rom. 15:24

29 [a]Acts 19:21; Rom. 1:10f.; Rom. 15:23, 32

30 [a]Gal. 5:22; Col. 1:8 [b]Col. 4:12; 2 Cor. 1:11

31 [1]Note vs. 25 [a]2 Cor. 1:10; 2 Thess. 3:2; 2 Tim. 3:11; 4:17 [b]Rom. 15:25f.; 2 Cor. 8:4; 9:1 [c]Acts 9:13, 15

32 [a]Rom. 15:23 [b]Rom. 1:10; Acts 18:21

33 [a]Rom. 16:20; 2 Cor. 13:11; Phil. 4:9; 1 Thess. 5:23; Heb. 13:20; 2 Thess. 3:16

1 [1]Or, *deaconess* [a]2 Cor. 3:1 [b]Acts 18:18

2 [1]I.e., true believers; lit., *holy ones* [2]Lit., *and of me, myself* [a]Phil. 2:29 [b]Acts 9:13, 15

3 [a]Acts 18:2 [b]2 Cor. 5:17; 12:2; Gal. 1:22; Rom. 16:7, 9, 10; 8:11ff. [c]Rom. 8:1

4 who for my life risked their own necks, to whom not
only do I give thanks, but also all the churches of the Gentiles;
5 also *greet* [a]the church that is in their house. Greet
Epaenetus my beloved, who is the [b]first convert to Christ from
[1c]Asia.
6 Greet Mary, who has worked hard for you.
7 Greet Andronicus and [1]Junias, my [a]kinsmen, and my
[b]fellow-prisoners, who are outstanding among the apostles,
who also were [c]in Christ before me.
8 Greet Ampliatus my beloved in the Lord.
9 Greet Urbanus our fellow-worker [a]in Christ, and Stachys
my beloved.
10 Greet Apelles the approved [a]in Christ. Greet [b]those
who are of the *household* of Aristobulus.
11 Greet Herodion my [a]kinsman. [b]Greet those of the *house-hold* of Narcissus, who are in the Lord.
12 Greet Tryphaena and Tryphosa, workers in the Lord.
Greet Persis the beloved, who has worked hard in the Lord.
13 Greet [a]Rufus, a choice man in the Lord, also his moth-er and mine.
14 Greet Asyncritus, Phlegon, Hermes, Patrobas, Hermas
and the brethren with them.
15 Greet Philologus and Julia, Nereus and his sister, and
Olympas, and all [a]the [1]saints who are with them.
16 [a]Greet one another with a holy kiss. All the churches of
Christ greet you.
17 Now I urge you, brethren, keep your eye on those who
cause dissensions and [1]hindrances [a]contrary to the teaching
which you learned, and [b]turn away from them.
18 For such men are [a]slaves not of our Lord Christ but of
[b]their own [1]appetites; and by their [c]smooth and flattering
speech they deceive the hearts of the unsuspecting.
19 For the report of your obedience [a]has reached to all;
therefore I am rejoicing over you, but [b]I want you to be wise in
what is good, and innocent in what is evil.
20 And [a]the God of peace will soon crush [b]Satan under
your feet.
[c]The grace of our Lord Jesus be with you.
21 [a]Timothy my fellow-worker greets you; and *so do*
[b]Lucius and [c]Jason and [d]Sosipater, my [e]kinsmen.
22 I Tertius, who [a]write this letter, greet you in the Lord.
23 [a]Gaius, host to me and to the whole church, greets you.
[b]Erastus, the city treasurer greets you, and Quartus, the
brother.
24 (See marginal note.[1])
25 [a]Now to Him who is able to establish you [b]according to
my gospel and the preaching of Jesus Christ, according to the
revelation of [c]the mystery which has been kept secret for [d]long
ages past,
26 but now is manifested, and by [a]the Scriptures of the
prophets, according to the commandment of the eternal God,
has been made known to all the nations, *leading* to [b]obedience
of faith;
27 to the only wise God, through Jesus Christ, [a]to whom
be the glory forever. Amen.

5 [1]I.e., west coast province of Asia Minor
[a]1 Cor. 16:19; Col. 4:15; Philem. 2 [b]1 Cor. 16:15 [c]Acts 16:6

7 [1]Or, *Junia* (fem.)
[a]Rom. 16:11, 21; 9:3 [b]Col. 4:10; Philem. 23 [c]2 Cor. 5:17; 12:2; Gal. 1:22; Rom. 16:3, 9, 10; 8:11ff.

9 [a]2 Cor. 5:17; 12:2; Gal. 1:22; Rom. 16:3, 7, 10; 8:11ff.

10 [a]2 Cor. 5:17; 12:2; Gal. 1:22; Rom. 16:3, 7, 9; 8:11ff. [b]1 Cor. 1:11

11 [a]Rom. 16:7, 21; 9:3 [b]1 Cor. 1:11

13 [a]Mark 15:21

15 [1]Note 1, vs. 2
[a]Rom. 16:2, 14

16 [a]1 Cor. 16:20; 2 Cor. 13:12; 1 Thess. 5:26; 1 Pet. 5:14

17 [1]Lit., *occasions of stumbling*
[a]1 Tim. 1:3; 6:3 [b]Gal. 1:8f.; 2 Thess. 3:6, 14; Titus 3:10; 2 John 10; Matt. 7:15

18 [1]Lit., *belly*
[a]Rom. 14:18 [b]Phil. 3:19 [c]Col. 2:4; 2 Pet. 2:3

19 [a]Rom. 1:8 [b]1 Cor. 14:20; Matt. 10:16; Jer. 4:22

20 [a]Rom. 15:33 [b]Matt. 4:10 [c]1 Cor. 16:23; 2 Cor. 13:14; Gal. 6:18; Phil. 4:23; 1 Thess. 5:28; 2 Thess. 3:18; Rev. 22:21

21 [a]Acts 16:1 [b]Acts 13:1 [?] [c]Acts 17:5 [?] [d]Acts 20:4 [?] [e]Rom. 16:7, 11; 9:3

22 [a]1 Cor. 16:21; Gal. 6:11; Col. 4:18; 2 Thess. 3:17; Philem. 19

23 [a]1 Cor. 1:14; Acts 20:4 [?] [b]Acts 19:22

24 [1]Some ancient mss. add vs. 24, *The grace of our Lord Jesus Christ be with you all. Amen.*

25 [a]Eph. 3:20; Jude 24 [b]Rom. 2:16 [c]1 Cor. 2:1, 7; 4:1; Eph. 1:9; 3:3, 9; 6:19; Col. 1:26f.; 2:2; 4:3; 1 Tim. 3:16; Rom. 11:25; Matt. 13:35 [d]2 Tim. 1:9; Titus 1:2

26 [a]Rom. 1:2 [b]Rom. 1:5

27 [a]Rom. 11:36

THE FIRST EPISTLE OF PAUL TO THE

CORINTHIANS

Salutation. Thanksgiving. Exhortation to Unity.

PAUL, [a]called *as* an apostle of Jesus Christ [1]by [b]the will of
God, and [c]Sosthenes our [d]brother,
2 to [a]the church of God which is at [b]Corinth, to those
who have been sanctified in Christ Jesus, [1]saints [c]by calling,
with all who in every place [d]call upon the name of our Lord
Jesus Christ, their *Lord* and ours:
3 [a]Grace to you and peace from God our Father and the
Lord Jesus Christ.
4 [a]I thank [1]my God always concerning you, for the grace
of God which was given you in Christ Jesus,
5 that in everything you were [a]enriched in Him, in all
[b]speech and [b]all knowledge,
6 even as [a]the testimony concerning Christ was confirmed [1]in you,
7 so that you are not lacking in any gift, [a]awaiting eagerly
the revelation of our Lord Jesus Christ,
8 [a]who shall also confirm you to the end, blameless in
[b]the day of our Lord Jesus Christ.
9 [a]God is faithful, through whom you were [b]called into
[c]fellowship with His Son, Jesus Christ our Lord.
10 Now [a]I exhort you, [b]brethren, by the name of our Lord
Jesus Christ, that you all [1]agree, and there be no [2c]divisions
among you, but you be [3]made complete in [d]the same mind
and in the same judgment.
11 For I have been informed concerning you, my brethren, by [a]Chloe's *people,* that there are quarrels among you.
12 Now I mean this, that [a]each one of you is saying, "I am
of Paul," and "I of [b]Apollos," and "I of [c]Cephas," and "I of
Christ."
13 [1]Has Christ been divided? Paul was not crucified for
you, was he? Or were you [a]baptized [2]in the name of Paul?
14 [1]I thank God that I [a]baptized none of you, except
[a]Crispus and [b]Gaius,
15 that no man should say you were baptized [1]in my name.
16 Now I did baptize also the [a]household of Stephanas;
beyond that, I do not know whether I baptized any other.
17 [a]For Christ did not send me to baptize, but to preach
the gospel, [b]not in [1]cleverness of speech, that the cross of
Christ should not be made void.
18 For the word of the cross is to [a]those who [1]are perishing
[b]foolishness, but to us who [2]are being saved it is [c]the power of
God.
19 For it is written,

"[a]I WILL DESTROY THE WISDOM OF THE WISE,
AND THE CLEVERNESS OF THE CLEVER I WILL SET ASIDE."

20 [a]Where is the wise man? Where is the scribe? Where is
the debater of [b]this age? Has not God [c]made foolish the wisdom of [d]the world?
21 For since in the wisdom of God [a]the world through its

1 [1]Lit., *through*
[a]Rom. 1:1 [b]Rom. 15:32; 2 Cor. 1:1; Eph. 1:1; Col. 1:1; 2 Tim. 1:1; Rom. 1:10; 2 Cor. 8:5 [c]Acts 18:17 [d]Acts 1:15

2 [1]I.e., *true believers;* lit., *holy ones*
[a]1 Cor. 10:32 [b]Acts 18:1 [c]Rom. 1:7; 8:28 [d]Acts 7:59

3 [a]Rom. 1:7

4 [1]Some ancient mss. omit *my*
[a]Rom. 1:8

5 [a]2 Cor. 9:11 [b]2 Cor. 8:7; Rom. 15:14

6 [1]Or, *among*
[a]2 Tim. 1:8; 2 Thess. 1:10; 1 Tim. 2:6; Rev. 1:2

7 [a]Rom. 8:19, 23; Phil. 3:20; Luke 17:30; 2 Pet. 3:12

8 [a]Phil. 1:6; Col. 2:7; 1 Thess. 3:13; 5:23; Rom. 8:19 [b]1 Cor. 5:5; 2 Cor. 1:14; Phil. 1:6, 10; 2:16; 1 Thess. 5:2; 2 Thess. 2:2; Luke 17:24, 30

9 [a]Deut. 7:9; Is. 49:7; 1 Cor. 10:13; 2 Cor. 1:18; 1 Thess. 5:24; 2 Thess. 3:3 [b]Rom. 8:28 [c]1 John 1:3

10 [1]Lit., *speak the same thing* [2]Lit., *schisms* [3]Or, *united*
[a]Rom. 12:1 [b]Rom. 1:13 [c]1 Cor. 11:18 [d]Rom. 12:16; Phil. 1:27

11 [a]Rom. 16:10f.

12 [a]1 Cor. 3:4; Matt. 23:8-10 [b]Acts 18:24; 1 Cor. 3:22 [c]John 1:42; 1 Cor. 3:22; 9:5; 15:5

13 [1]Or, *Christ has been divided!* or, *Christ is divided!* [2]Lit., *into*
[a]Matt. 28:19; Acts 2:38

14 [1]Some ancient mss. read, *I give thanks that*
[a]Acts 18:8 [b]Rom. 16:23

15 [1]Lit., *into*

16 [a]1 Cor. 16:15 [17]

17 [1]Lit., *wisdom*
[a]John 4:2; Acts 10:48 [b]1 Cor. 2:1, 4, 13; 2 Cor. 10:10; 11:6

18 [1]Or, *perish* [2]Or, *are saved*
[a]2 Cor. 2:15; 4:3; 2 Thess. 2:10; Acts 2:47 [b]1 Cor. 1:21, 23, 25; 2:14; 4:10 [c]1 Cor. 1:24; Rom. 1:16

19 [a]Is. 29:14

20 [a]Job 12:17; Is. 19:11f.; 33:18 marg. [b]Matt. 13:22; 1 Cor. 2:6, 8; 3:18, 19 [c]Rom. 1:20ff. [d]1 Cor. 1:27f.; 6:2; 11:32; John 12:31; James 4:4

21 [a]1 Cor. 1:27f.; 6:2; 11:32; John 12:31; James 4:4

wisdom did not *come to* know God, [b]God was well pleased
through the [c]foolishness of the [1]message preached to [d]save
those who believe.
22 For indeed [a]Jews ask for [1]signs, and Greeks search for
wisdom;
23 but we preach [1a]Christ crucified, [b]to Jews a stumbling
block, and to Gentiles [c]foolishness,
24 but to those who are [a]the called, both Jews and Greeks,
Christ [b]the power of God and [c]the wisdom of God.
25 Because the [a]foolishness of God is wiser than men, and
[b]the weakness of God is stronger than men.
26 For [1]consider your [a]call, brethren, that there were [b]not
many wise according to [2]the flesh, not many mighty, not many
noble;
27 but [a]God has chosen the foolish things of [b]the world to
shame the wise, and God has chosen the weak things of [b]the
world to shame the things which are strong,
28 and the base things of [a]the world and the despised, God
has chosen, [b]the things that are not, that He might [c]nullify the
things that are,
29 that [a]no [1]man should boast before God.
30 But [1]by His doing you are in [a]Christ Jesus, who became
to us [b]wisdom from God, [2]and [c]righteousness and [d]sanctifica-
tion, and [e]redemption,
31 that, just as it is written, "[a]LET HIM WHO BOASTS, BOAST
IN THE LORD."

CHAPTER 2

AND when I came to you, brethren, I [a]did not come with
superiority of speech or of wisdom, proclaiming to you [b]the
[1]testimony of God.
2 For I determined to know nothing among you except
[a]Jesus Christ, and Him crucified.
3 And I [a]was with you in [b]weakness and in [c]fear and in
much trembling.
4 And my [1]message and my preaching were [a]not in per-
suasive words of wisdom, but in demonstration of [b]the Spirit
and of power,
5 that your faith should not [1]rest on the wisdom of men,
but on [a]the power of God.
6 Yet we do speak wisdom among those who are [a]mature;
a wisdom, however, not of [b]this age, nor of the rulers of [b]this
age, who are [c]passing away;
7 but we speak God's wisdom in a [a]mystery, the hidden
wisdom, which God [b]predestined before the [c]ages to our glory;
8 *the wisdom* [a]which none of the rulers of [b]this age has
understood; for if they had understood it, they would not have
crucified [c]the Lord of glory;
9 but just as it is written,

"[a]THINGS WHICH EYE HAS NOT SEEN AND EAR HAS NOT HEARD,
AND *which* HAVE NOT ENTERED THE HEART OF MAN,
ALL THAT GOD HAS PREPARED FOR THOSE WHO LOVE HIM."

21 [1]Lit., *preaching* [b]Gal. 1:15; Col. 1:19; Luke 12:32 [c]1 Cor. 1:18, 23, 25; 2:14; 4:10 [d]1 Tim. 4:16; 2 Tim. 2:10; 3:15; 4:18; Heb. 7:25; James 5:20; Rom. 11:14

22 [1]Or, *attesting miracles* [a]Matt. 12:38

23 [1]I.e., Messiah [a]1 Cor. 2:2; Gal. 3:1; 5:11 [b]Luke 2:34; 1 Pet. 2:8 [c]1 Cor. 1:18, 21, 25; 2:14; 4:10

24 [a]Rom. 8:28 [b]1 Cor. 1:18; Rom. 1:16 [c]Luke 11:49; 1 Cor. 1:30

25 [a]1 Cor. 1:18, 21, 23; 2:14; 1 Cor. 4:10 [b]2 Cor. 13:4

26 [1]Lit., *see* [2]Or, *human standards* [a]Rom. 11:29 [b]1 Cor. 2:8; 1:20; Matt. 11:25

27 [a]James 2:5 [b]1 Cor. 1:20

28 [a]1 Cor. 1:20 [b]Rom. 4:17 [c]1 Cor. 2:6; Job 34:19; 2 Thess. 2:8; Heb. 2:14

29 [1]Lit., *flesh* [a]Eph. 2:9

30 [1]Lit., *of Him* [2]Or, *both* [a]1 Cor. 4:15; Rom. 8:1 [b]1 Cor. 1:24 [c]2 Cor. 5:21; Phil. 3:9; Jer. 23:5f.; 33:16 [d]1 Cor. 1:2; 6:11; 1 Thess. 5:23 [e]Eph. 1:7, 14; Col. 1:4; Rom. 3:24

31 [a]Jer. 9:23f.; 2 Cor. 10:17

1 [1]Some ancient mss. read, *mystery* [a]1 Cor. 2:4, 13; 1:17 [b]1 Cor. 2:7

2 [a]Gal. 6:14; 1 Cor. 1:23

3 [a]Acts 18:1, 6, 12 [b]1 Cor. 4:10; 2 Cor. 11:30; 12:5, 9f.; 13:9 [c]Is. 19:16; Eph. 6:5; 2 Cor. 7:15

4 [1]Lit., *word* [a]1 Cor. 2:1, 13; 1:17 [b]Rom. 15:19; 1 Cor. 4:20

5 [1]Lit., *be* [a]2 Cor. 4:7; 6:7; 2 Cor. 12:9

6 [a]Eph. 4:13; Phil. 3:15 marg.; Heb. 5:14; 6:1 [b]1 Cor. 1:20; Matt. 13:22 [c]1 Cor. 1:28

7 [a]1 Cor. 2:1; Rom. 11:25; 16:25f. [b]Rom. 8:29f. [c]Heb. 1:2; 11:3

8 [a]1 Cor. 2:6; 1:26 [b]1 Cor. 1:20; Matt. 13:22 [c]Acts 7:2; James 2:1

9 [a]Is. 64:4; 65:17

10 [1a]For to us God revealed *them* [b]through the Spirit; for
the Spirit searches all things, even the [c]depths of God.
11 For who among men knows the *thoughts* of a man
except the [a]spirit of the man, which is in him? Even so the
thoughts of God no one knows except the Spirit of God.
12 Now we [a]have received, not the spirit of [b]the world, but
the Spirit who is from God, that we might know the things
freely given to us by God,
13 which things we also speak, [a]not in words taught by
human wisdom, but in those taught by the Spirit, [1]combining
spiritual *thoughts* with spiritual *words.*
14 But a [1a]natural man [b]does not accept the things of the
Spirit of God; for they are [c]foolishness to him, and he cannot
understand them, because they are spiritually [2]appraised.
15 But he who is [a]spiritual appraises all things, yet he himself is appraised by no man.
16 For [a]WHO HAS KNOWN THE MIND OF THE LORD, THAT HE
SHOULD INSTRUCT HIM? But [b]we have the mind of Christ.

10 [1]Some ancient mss. use, *But* [a]Matt. 11:25; 13:11; 16:17; Gal. 1:12; Eph. 3:3, 5 [b]John 14:26 [c]Rom. 11:33ff.

11 [a]Prov. 20:27

12 [a]Rom. 8:15 [b]1 Cor. 1:27

13 [1]Or, *interpreting spiritual things to spiritual* men [a]1 Cor. 1:17; 1 Cor. 2:1, 4

14 [1]Or, *unspiritual* [2]Or, *examined* [a]1 Cor. 15:44, 46; James 3:15 marg.; Jude 19 marg. [b]John 14:17 [c]1 Cor. 1:18

15 [a]1 Cor. 3:1; 14:37; Gal. 6:1

16 [a]Is. 40:13; Rom. 11:34 [b]John 15:15

Chapter 3

AND I, brethren, could not speak to you as to [a]spiritual men,
but as to [b]men of flesh, as to [c]babes in Christ.
2 I gave you [a]milk to drink, not solid food; for you [b]were
not yet able *to receive it.* Indeed, even now you are not yet
able,
3 for you are still fleshly. For since there is [a]jealousy and
strife among you, are you not fleshly, and are you not walking
[1b]like mere men?
4 For when [a]one says, "I am of Paul," and another, "I am
of Apollos," are you not *mere* [b]men?
5 What then is Apollos? And what is Paul? [a]Servants
through whom you believed, even [b]as the Lord gave *opportunity* to each one.
6 [a]I planted, [b]Apollos watered, but [c]God was causing the
growth.
7 So then neither the one who plants nor the one who
waters is anything, but God who causes the growth.
8 Now he who plants and he who waters are one; but
each will [a]receive his own [1]reward according to his own labor.
9 For we are God's [a]fellow-workers; you are God's [1b]field,
God's [c]building.
10 According to [a]the grace of God which was given to me,
as a wise masterbuilder [b]I laid a foundation, and [c]another is
building upon it. But let each man be careful how he builds
upon it.
11 For no man can lay a [a]foundation other than the one
which is laid, which is Jesus Christ.
12 Now if any man builds upon the foundation with gold,
silver, [1]precious stones, wood, hay, straw,
13 [a]each man's work will become evident; for [b]the day will
show it, because it is *to be* revealed with fire; and the fire itself
will test [1]the quality of each man's work.
14 If any man's work which he has built upon it remains,
he shall [a]receive a reward.

1 [a]1 Cor. 2:15; 14:37; Gal. 6:1 [b]Rom. 7:14; 1 Cor. 2:14 [c]Heb. 5:13; 1 Cor. 2:6; Eph. 4:14

2 [a]Heb. 5:12f.; 1 Pet. 2:2 [b]John 16:12

3 [1]Lit., *according to man* [a]Rom. 13:13; 1 Cor. 1:10f.; 11:18 [b]1 Cor. 3:4

4 [a]1 Cor. 1:12 [b]1 Cor. 3:3

5 [a]2 Cor. 6:4; Eph. 3:7; Col. 1:25; Rom. 15:16; 2 Cor. 3:3, 6; 4:1; 5:18; 1 Tim. 1:12 [b]Rom. 12:6; 1 Cor. 3:10

6 [a]Acts 18:4-11, 18; 1 Cor. 4:15; 9:1; 15:1; 2 Cor. 10:14f. [b]Acts 18:27; 1 Cor. 1:12 [c]1 Cor. 15:10

8 [1]Or, *wages* [a]1 Cor. 3:14; 1 Cor. 4:5; 9:17; Gal. 6:4

9 [1]Or, *cultivated land* [a]Mark 16:20; 2 Cor. 6:1 [b]Is. 61:3; Matt. 15:13 [c]Eph. 2:20-22; Col. 2:7; 1 Pet. 2:5; 1 Cor. 3:16

10 [a]Rom. 12:3; 1 Cor. 15:10 [b]Rom. 15:20; 1 Cor. 3:11f. [c]1 Thess. 3:2

11 [a]Is. 28:16; 1 Pet. 2:4ff.; Eph. 2:20

12 [1]Or, *costly*

13 [1]Lit., *of what sort each man's work is* [a]1 Cor. 4:5 [b]2 Thess. 1:7-10; 2 Tim. 1:12, 18; 4:8; 1 Cor. 1:8; Matt. 10:15; 1 Cor. 4:3 marg.

14 [a]1 Cor. 3:8; 4:5; 9:17; Gal. 6:4

15 If any man's work is burned up, he shall suffer loss; but
he himself shall be saved, yet [a]so as through fire.
16 [a]Do you not know that [b]you are a [1]temple of God, and
that the Spirit of God dwells in you?
17 If any man destroys the [1]temple of God, God will destroy
him, for the [1]temple of God is holy, and [2]that is what you
are.
18 [a]Let no man deceive himself. [b]If any man among you
thinks that he is wise in [c]this age, let him become foolish that
he may become wise.
19 For [a]the wisdom of this world is foolishness before
God. For it is written, "*He is* [b]THE ONE WHO CATCHES THE WISE
IN THEIR CRAFTINESS";
20 and again, "[a]THE LORD KNOWS THE REASONINGS of the
wise, THAT THEY ARE USELESS."
21 So then [a]let no one boast in men. For [b]all things belong
to you,
22 [a]whether Paul or Apollos or Cephas or the world or
[b]life or death or things present or things to come; all things
belong to you,
23 and [a]you belong to Christ; and [b]Christ belongs to God.

CHAPTER 4

LET a man regard us in this manner, as [a]servants of Christ,
and [b]stewards of [c]the mysteries of God.
2 In this case, moreover, it is required [1]of stewards that
one be found trustworthy.
3 But to me it is a very small thing that I should be
examined by you, or by *any* human [1]court; in fact, I do not
even examine myself.
4 I [a]am conscious of nothing against myself, yet I am not
by this [b]acquitted; but the one who examines me is the Lord.
5 Therefore [a]do not go on [1]passing judgment before [2]the
time, *but wait* [b]until the Lord comes who will both [c]bring to
light the things hidden in the darkness and disclose the motives
of *men's* hearts; and then each man's [d]praise will come to him
from God.
6 Now these things, brethren, I have figuratively applied
to myself and Apollos for your sakes, that in us you might
learn not to exceed [a]what is written, in order that no one of
you might [b]become [1]arrogant [c]in behalf of one against the
other.
7 For who regards you as superior? And [a]what do you
have that you did not receive? But if you did receive it, why do
you boast as if you had not received it?
8 You are [a]already filled, you have already become rich,
you have become kings without us; and would indeed that you
had become kings so that we also might reign with you.
9 For, I think, God has exhibited us apostles last of all, as
men [a]condemned to death; because we [b]have become a spectacle to the world, [1]both to angels and to men.
10 We are [a]fools for Christ's sake, but [b]you are prudent in
Christ; [c]we are weak, but you are strong; you are distinguished,
but we are without honor.
11 To this present hour we are both [a]hungry and thirsty,

15 [a]Job 23:10; Ps. 66:10, 12; Jude 23

16 [1]Or, *sanctuary* [a]Rom. 6:16 [b]1 Cor. 6:19; 2 Cor. 6:16; Eph. 2:21f.; Rom. 8:9

17 [1]Or, *sanctuary* [2]Lit., *which you are*

18 [a]Is. 5:21 [b]1 Cor. 8:2; Gal. 6:3 [c]1 Cor. 1:20

19 [a]1 Cor. 1:20 [b]Job 5:13

20 [a]Ps. 94:11

21 [a]1 Cor. 4:6 [b]Rom. 8:32

22 [a]1 Cor. 1:12; 3:5, 6 [b]Rom. 8:38

23 [a]1 Cor. 15:23; 2 Cor. 10:7; Gal. 3:29 [b]1 Cor. 11:3; 15:28

1 [a]Luke 1:2 [b]1 Cor. 9:17; Titus 1:7; 1 Pet. 4:10 [c]Rom. 11:25; 16:25

2 [1]Lit., *in*

3 [1]Lit., *day*

4 [a]2 Cor. 1:12; Acts 23:1 [b]Ps. 143:2; Rom. 2:13

5 [1]Lit., *judging anything* [2]I.e., the appointed time of judgment [a]Matt. 7:1; Rom. 2:1 [b]Rom. 2:16; John 21:22 [c]1 Cor. 3:13 [d]2 Cor. 10:18; Rom. 2:29; 1 Cor. 3:8

6 [1]Lit., *puffed up* [a]1 Cor. 1:19, 31; 3:19f. [b]1 Cor. 4:18f.; 1 Cor. 8:1; 13:4 [c]1 Cor. 1:12; 3:4

7 [a]John 3:27; Rom. 12:3, 6; 1 Pet. 4:10

8 [a]Rev. 3:17f.

9 [1]Or, *and to angels and to men* [a]1 Cor. 15:31; 2 Cor. 11:23; Rom. 8:36 [b]Heb. 10:33

10 [a]1 Cor. 1:18; Acts 17:18; 26:24 [b]2 Cor. 11:19; 1 Cor. 1:19f.; 3:18 [c]2 Cor. 13:9; 1 Cor. 2:3

11 [a]Rom. 8:35; 2 Cor. 11:23-27

and are poorly clothed, and are roughly treated, and are
homeless;
12 and we toil, [a]working with our own hands; when we are
[b]reviled, we bless; when we are [c]persecuted, we endure;
13 when we are slandered, we try to [1]conciliate; we have
[a]become as the scum of the world, the dregs of all things, *even*
until now.
14 I do not write these things to [a]shame you, but to admonish you as my beloved [b]children.
15 For if you were to have countless [a]tutors in Christ, yet
you would not *have* many fathers; for in [b]Christ Jesus I [c]be-
came your father through the [d]gospel.
16 I exhort you therefore, be [a]imitators of me.
17 For this reason I [a]have sent to you [b]Timothy, who is
my [c]beloved and faithful child in the Lord, and he will remind
you of my ways which are in Christ, [d]just as I teach everywhere
in every church.
18 Now some have become [1a]arrogant, as though I were
not [b]coming to you.
19 But I [a]will come to you soon, [b]if the Lord wills, and I
shall find out, not the [1]words of those who are [c]arrogant, but
their power.
20 For the kingdom of God does [a]not consist in [1]words,
but in power.
21 What do you desire? [a]Shall I come to you with a rod or
with love and a spirit of gentleness?

Chapter 5

IT is actually reported that there is immorality among you,
and immorality of such a kind as does not exist even among
the Gentiles, that someone has [a]his father's wife.
2 And [1]you [a]have become [2]arrogant, and [3]have not
[b]mourned instead, in order that the one who had done this
deed might be [c]removed from your midst.
3 For I, on my part, though [a]absent in body but present
in spirit, have already judged him who has so committed this,
as though I were present.
4 [a]In the name of our Lord Jesus, when you are assembled, and [1]I with you in spirit, [b]with the power of our Lord
Jesus,
5 *I have decided* to [a]deliver such a one to [b]Satan for the
destruction of his flesh, that his spirit may be saved in [c]the day
of the Lord [1]Jesus.
6 [a]Your boasting is not good. [b]Do you not know that [c]a
little leaven leavens the whole lump *of dough?*
7 Clean out the old leaven, that you may be a new lump,
just as you are *in fact* unleavened. For Christ our [a]Passover
also has been sacrificed.
8 Let us therefore celebrate the feast, [a]not with old leav-
en, nor with the leaven of malice and wickedness, but with
the unleavened bread of sincerity and truth.
9 I wrote you in my letter [a]not to associate with immoral
people;
10 I *did* not at all *mean* with the immoral people of this

12 [a]Acts 18:3 [b]1 Pet. 3:9 [c]John 15:20; Rom. 8:35

13 [1]Or, *console* [a]Lam. 3:45

14 [a]1 Cor. 6:5; 15:34 [b]2 Cor. 6:13; 12:14; 1 Thess. 2:11; 1 John 2:1; 3 John 4

15 [a]Gal. 3:24f. [b]1 Cor. 1:30; [c]Philem. 10; Gal. 4:19; 1 Cor. 3:8; Num. 11:12 [d]1 Cor. 9:12, 14, 18, 23; 15:1

16 [a]1 Cor. 11:1; Phil. 3:17; 4:9; 1 Thess. 1:6; 2 Thess. 3:9

17 [a]1 Cor. 16:10 [b]Acts 16:1 [c]1 Tim. 1:2, 18; 2 Tim. 1:2; 1 Cor. 4:14 [d]1 Cor. 7:17; 11:34; 14:33; 16:1; Titus 1:5

18 [1]Lit., *puffed up* [a]1 Cor. 4:6 [b]1 Cor. 4:21

19 [1]Lit., *word* [a]1 Cor. 11:34; 16:5f.; 1 Cor. 16:8; 2 Cor. 1:15f.; Acts 19:21; 20:2 [b]Acts 18:21 [c]1 Cor. 4:6

20 [1]Lit., *word* [a]1 Cor. 2:4

21 [a]2 Cor. 1:23; 2:1, 3; 12:20; 13:2, 10

1 [a]Lev. 18:8; Deut. 22:30; 27:20

2 [1]Or, *have you . . . ?* [2]Lit., *puffed up* [3]Or, *have you . . . ?* [a]1 Cor. 4:6 [b]2 Cor. 7:7-10 [c]1 Cor. 5:13

3 [a]Col. 2:5; 1 Thess. 2:17

4 [1]Lit., *my spirit, with the power* [a]2 Thess. 3:6 [b]John 20:23; 2 Cor. 2:6, 10; 13:3, 10; 1 Tim. 5:20

5 [1]Some ancient mss. omit, *Jesus* [a]Luke 22:31; 1 Tim. 1:20; Prov. 23:14 [b]Matt. 4:10 [c]1 Cor. 1:8

6 [a]James 4:16; 1 Cor. 5:2 [b]Rom. 6:16 [c]Gal. 5:9; Matt. 16:6, 12; Hos. 7:4

7 [a]Mark 14:12; 1 Pet. 1:19

8 [a]Ex. 12:19; 13:7; Deut. 16:3

9 [a]2 Cor. 6:14; Eph. 5:11; 2 Thess. 3:6

world, or with the covetous and swindlers, or with [a]idolaters;
for then you would have to go out of the world.
11 But [1]actually, I wrote to you not to associate [2]with any
so-called [a]brother if he should be an immoral person, or covetous, or [b]an idolater, or a reviler, or a drunkard, or a swindler—
not even to eat with such a one.
12 For what have I to do with judging [a]outsiders? [b]Do you
not judge those who are within *the church?*
13 But those who are outside, God [1]judges. [a]Remove the
wicked man from among yourselves.

CHAPTER 6

DOES any one of you, when he has a [1]case against his neighbor, dare to go to law before the unrighteous, and [a]not before
the [2]saints?
2 Or [a]do you not know that [b]the [1]saints will judge [c]the
world? And if the world is judged by you, are you not compe-
tent *to* [2]*constitute* the smallest law courts?
3 [a]Do you not know that we shall judge angels? How
much more, matters of this life?
4 If then you have law courts dealing with matters of this
life, [1]do you appoint them as judges who are of no account in
the church?
5 [a]I say *this* to your shame. *Is it* so, *that* there is not
among you one wise man who will be able to decide between
his [b]brethren,
6 but brother goes to law with brother, and that before
[a]unbelievers?
7 Actually, then, it is already a defeat for you, that you
have lawsuits with one another. [a]Why not rather be wronged?
Why not rather be defrauded?
8 On the contrary, you yourselves wrong and defraud,
and that *your* [a]brethren.
9 Or [a]do you not know that the unrighteous shall not
[b]inherit the kingdom of God? [c]Do not be deceived; [d]neither
fornicators, nor idolaters, nor adulterers, nor [1]effeminate, nor
homosexuals,
10 nor thieves, nor covetous, nor drunkards, nor revilers,
nor swindlers, shall [a]inherit the kingdom of God.
11 And [a]such were some of you; but you were [b]washed,
but you were [c]sanctified, but you were [d]justified in the name
of the Lord Jesus Christ, and in the Spirit of our God.
12 [a]All things are lawful for me, but not all things are
profitable. All things are lawful for me, but I will not be mas-
tered by anything.
13 [a]Food is for the [1]stomach, and the [1]stomach is for food;
but God will [b]do away with both [2]of them. Yet the body is not
for immorality, but [c]for the Lord; and [d]the Lord is for the
body.
14 Now God has not only [a]raised the Lord, but [b]will also
raise us up through His power.
15 [a]Do you not know that [b]your bodies are members of
Christ? Shall I then take away the members of Christ and
make them members of a harlot? [c]May it never be!
16 Or [a]do you not know that the one who joins himself to

10 [a]1 Cor. 10:27

11 [1]Or, *now I write* [2]Lit., *together if any man called a brother should be* [a]2 Thess. 3:6; Acts 1:15 [b]1 Cor. 10:7, 14, 20f.

12 [a]Mark 4:11 [b] Cor. 5:3-5; 6: 1-4

13 [1]Or. *will judge* [a]1 Cor. 5:2; Deut. 13:5; 17:7, 12; 21:21; 22:21

1 [1]Lit., *matter* [2]I.e., true believers; lit., *holy ones* [a]Matt. 18:17

2 [1]Note 2, vs. 1 [2]Or, try *the trivial cases?* [a]Rom. 6:16 [b]Matt. 19:28; Dan. 7:18, 22, 27 [c]1 Cor. 1:20

3 [a]Rom. 6:16

4 [1]Or, *appoint them . . . . church.*

5 [a]1 Cor. 15:34; 4:14 [b]Acts 1:15; 1 Cor. 6:1 and Acts 9:13

6 [a]2 Cor. 6:14f.; 1 Tim. 5:8

7 [a]Matt. 5:39f.

8 [a]1 Thess. 4:6

9 [1]I.e., effeminate, by perversion [a]Rom. 6:16 [b]1 Cor. 15:50; Gal. 5:21; Eph. 5:5; Acts 20:32 [c]1 Cor. 15:33; Gal. 6:7; James 1:16; Luke 21:8; 1 John 3:7 [d]Rom. 13:13; 1 Cor. 5:11; Gal. 5:19-21; Eph. 5:5; 1 Tim. 1:10; Rev. 21:8; 22:15

10 [a]1 Cor. 15:50; Gal. 5:21; Eph. 5:5; Acts 20:32

11 [a]1 Cor. 12:2; Eph. 2:2f.; Col. 3:5-7; Titus 3:3-7 [b]Acts 22:16; Eph. 5:26 [c]1 Cor. 1:2, 30 [d]Rom. 8:30

12 [a]1 Cor. 10:23

13 [1]Lit., *belly* [2]Lit., *it and them* [a]Matt. 15:17 [b]Col. 2:22 [c]1 Cor. 6:15, 19 [d]Gal. 5:24; Eph. 5:23

14 [a]Acts 2:24 [b]1 Cor. 15:23; John 6:39f.

15 [a]1 Cor. 6:3 [b]1 Cor. 6:13; Rom. 12:5; 12:27; Eph. 5:30 [c]Luke 20:16

16 [a]1 Cor. 6:3

a harlot is one body *with her?* For He says, "[b]THE TWO WILL
BECOME ONE FLESH."
17 But the one who joins himself to the Lord is [a]one spirit
with Him.
18 [a]Flee immorality. Every *other* sin that a man commits
is outside the body, but the [1]immoral man sins against his own
body.
19 Or [a]do you not know that [b]your body is a [1]temple of
the Holy Spirit who is in you, whom you have from [2]God, and
that [c]you are not your own?
20 For [a]you have been bought with a price: therefore glorify God in [b]your body.

Chapter 7

NOW concerning the things about which you wrote, it is
[a]good for a man not to touch a woman.
2 But because of immoralities, let each man have his own
wife, and let each woman have her own husband.
3 Let the husband [1]fulfill his duty to his wife, and likewise also the wife to her husband.
4 The wife does not have authority over her own body,
but the husband *does;* and likewise also the husband does not
have authority over his own body, but the wife *does.*
5 [a]Stop depriving one another, except by agreement for a
time that you may devote yourselves to prayer, and [1]come
together again lest [b]Satan tempt you because of your lack of
self-control.
6 But this I say by way of concession, [a]not of command.
7 [1]Yet I wish that all men were [a]even as I myself am.
However, [b]each man has his own gift from God, one in this
manner, and another in that.
8 But I say to the unmarried and to widows that it is
[a]good for them if they remain [b]even as I.
9 But if they do not have self-control, [a]let them marry;
for it is better to marry than to [1]burn.
10 But to the married I give instructions, [a]not I, but the
Lord, that the wife should not [1]leave her husband
11 (but if she does leave, let her remain unmarried, or else
be reconciled to her husband), and that the husband should
not [1]send his wife away.
12 But to the rest [a]I say, not the Lord, that if any brother
has a wife who is an unbeliever, and she consents to live with
him, let him not [1]send her away.
13 And a woman who has an unbelieving husband, and he
consents to live with her, let her not [1]send her husband away.
14 For the unbelieving husband is sanctified through his
wife, and the unbelieving wife is sanctified through [1]her believing husband; for otherwise your children are unclean, but now
they are [a]holy.
15 Yet if the unbelieving one leaves, let him leave; the
brother or the sister is not under bondage in such *cases,* but
God has called [1]us [2a]to peace.
16 For how do you know, O wife, whether you will [a]save
your husband? Or how do you know, O husband, whether you
will save your wife?

16 [b]Gen. 2:24; Matt. 19:5; Mark 10:8; Eph. 5:31

17 [a]John 17:21-23; Rom. 8:9-11; Gal. 2:20; 1 Cor. 6:15

18 [1]Or, *one who practices immorality* [a]2 Cor. 12:21; Eph. 5:3; Col. 3:5; Heb. 13:4; 1 Cor. 6:9

19 [1]Or, *sanctuary* [2]Or, *God? And you . . . own* [a]1 Cor. 6:3 [b]John 2:21 [c]Rom. 14:7f.

20 [a]1 Cor. 7:23; Acts 20:28; 1 Pet. 1:18f.; 2 Pet. 2:1; Rev. 5:9 [b]Rom. 12:1; Phil. 1:20

1 [a]1 Cor. 7:8, 26

3 [1]Lit., *render*

5 [1]Lit., *be* [a]Ex. 19:15; 1 Sam. 21:5 [b]Matt. 4:10

6 [a]2 Cor. 8:8

7 [1]Some ancient mss. read, *For* [a]1 Cor. 7:8; 9:5 [b]1 Cor. 12:4, 11; Rom. 12:6; Matt. 19:11f.

8 [a]1 Cor. 7:1, 26 [b]1 Cor. 7:7; 9:5

9 [1]I.e., burn with passion [a]1 Tim. 5:14

10 [1]Lit., *depart from* [a]1 Cor. 7:6; Mal. 2:16; Matt. 5:32; 19:3-9; Mark 10:2-12; Luke 16:18

11 [1]Or, *leave his wife*

12 [1]Or, *leave her* [a]1 Cor. 7:6; 2 Cor. 11:17

13 [1]Or, *leave her husband*

14 [1]Lit., *the brother* [a]Ezra 9:2; Mal. 2:15

15 [1]Some ancient mss. read, *you* [2]Lit., *in* [a]Rom. 14:19

16 [a]1 Pet. 3:1; Rom. 11:14

17 Only, [a]as the Lord has assigned to each one, as God has
called each, in this manner let him walk. And [b]thus I direct in
[c]all the churches.
18 Was any man called *already* circumcised? Let him not
become uncircumcised. Has anyone been called in uncircumcision? [a]Let him not be circumcised.
19 [a]Circumcision is nothing, and uncircumcision is nothing, but *what matters is* [b]the keeping of the commandments
of God.
20 [a]Let each man remain in that [1]condition in which he
was called.
21 Were you called while a slave? [1]Do not worry about it;
but if you are able also to become free, rather [2]do that.
22 For he who was called in the Lord while a slave, is [a]the
Lord's freedman; likewise he who was called while free, is
[b]Christ's slave.
23 [a]You were bought with a price; do not become slaves of
men.
24 Brethren, [a]let each man remain with God in that *condition* in which he was called.
25 Now concerning virgins I have [a]no command of the
Lord, but I give an opinion as one who [1b]by the mercy of the
Lord is trustworthy.
26 I think then that this is good in view of the [1]present
[a]distress, that [b]it is good for a man [2]to remain as he is.
27 Are you bound to a wife? Do not seek to be released.
Are you released from a wife? Do not seek a wife.
28 But if you should marry, you have not sinned; and if a
virgin should marry, she has not sinned. Yet such will have
[1]trouble in this life, and I am trying to spare you.
29 But this I say, brethren, [a]the time has been shortened,
so that from now on both those who have wives should be as
though they had none;
30 and those who weep, as though they did not weep; and
those who rejoice, as though they did not rejoice; and those
who buy, as though they did not possess;
31 and those who use the world, as though they did not
[a]make full use of it; for [b]the form of this world is passing away.
32 But I want you to be free from concern. One who is
[a]unmarried is concerned about the things of the Lord, how he
may please the Lord;
33 but one who is married is concerned about the things
of the world, how he may please his [1]wife,
34 and *his interests* are divided. And the woman who is
unmarried, and the virgin, is concerned about the things of the
Lord, that she may be holy both in body and spirit; but one
who is married is concerned about the things of the world, how
she may please her husband.
35 And this I say for your own benefit; not to put a restraint
upon you, but [1]to promote what is seemly, and *to secure*
undistracted devotion to the Lord.
36 But if any man thinks that he is acting unbecomingly
toward his virgin *daughter,* if she should be of full age, and if it
must be so, let him do what he wishes, he does not sin; let
[1]her marry.
37 But he who stands firm in his heart, [1]being under no

17 [a]Rom. 12:3 [b]1 Cor. 4:17 [c]1 Cor. 14:33; 11:16; 2 Cor. 8:18; 11:28; Gal. 1:22; 1 Thess. 2:14; 2 Thess. 1:4

18 [a]Acts 15:1ff.

19 [a]Gal. 5:6; 6:15; Col. 3:11; Rom. 2:27, 29; Gal. 3:28 [b]Rom. 2:25

20 [1]Lit., *calling* [a]1 Cor. 7:24

21 [1]Lit., *Let it not be a care to you* [2]Lit., *use*

22 [a]John 8:32, 36; Philem. 16 [b]Eph. 6:6; Col. 3:24; 1 Pet. 2:16

23 [a]1 Cor. 6:20

24 [a]1 Cor. 7:20

25 [1]Lit., *has had mercy shown on him by the Lord to be trustworthy* [a]1 Cor. 7:6 [b]2 Cor. 4:1; 1 Tim. 1:13, 16

26 [1]Or, *impending* [2]Lit., *so to be* [a]Luke 21:23; 2 Thess. 2:2 [b]1 Cor. 7:1, 8

28 [1]Lit., *tribulation in the flesh*

29 [a]Rom. 13:11f.; 1 Cor. 7:31

31 [a]1 Cor. 9:18 [b]1 Cor. 7:29; 1 John 2:17

32 [a]1 Tim. 5:5

33 [1]Some mss. read, *wife. And there is a difference also between the wife and the virgin. One who is unmarried is concerned . . . .*

35 [1]Lit., *for what is seemly*

36 [1]Lit., *them*

37 [1]Lit., *having no necessity*

constraint, but has authority [2]over his own will, and has decided this in his own heart, to keep his own [3]virgin *daughter*,
he will do well.
38 So then both he who gives his own virgin *daughter* in
marriage does well, and he who does not give her in marriage
will do better.
39 [a]A wife is bound as long as her husband lives; but if her
husband [1]is dead, she is free to be married to whom she wishes,
only [b]in the Lord.
40 But [a]in my opinion she is happier if she remains as she
is; and I think that I also have the Spirit of God.

Chapter 8

NOW concerning [a]things sacrificed to idols, we know that
we all have [b]knowledge. Knowledge [1c]makes arrogant, but love
[d]edifies.
2 [a]If any one supposes that he knows anything, he has not
yet [b]known as he ought to know;
3 but if any one loves God, he [a]is known by Him.
4 Therefore concerning the eating of [a]things sacrificed to
idols, we know that [1]there is [b]no such thing as an idol in the
world, and that [c]there is no God but one.
5 For even if [a]there are so-called gods whether in heaven
or on earth, as indeed there are many gods and many lords,
6 yet for us [a]there is *but* one God, [b]the Father, [c]from
whom are all things, and we *exist* for Him; and [d]one Lord,
Jesus Christ, [e]through whom are all things, and we *exist*
through Him.
7 However not all men [a]have this knowledge; but [b]some,
being accustomed to the idol until now, eat food as if it were
sacrificed to an idol; and their conscience being weak is
defiled.
8 But [a]food will not [1]commend us to God; we are neither
[2]the worse if we do not eat, nor [3]the better if we do eat.
9 But [a]take care lest this [1]liberty of yours somehow become a stumbling block to the [b]weak.
10 For if someone sees you who have [a]knowledge dining in
an idol's temple, will not his conscience, if he is weak, be
strengthened to eat [b]things sacrificed to idols?
11 For through [a]your knowledge he who is weak [b]is ruined,
the brother for whose sake Christ died.
12 [a]And thus, by sinning against the brethren and wounding their conscience when it is weak, you sin [b]against Christ.
13 Therefore, [a]if food causes my brother to stumble, I will
never eat meat again, that I might not cause my brother to
stumble.

Chapter 9

AM I not [a]free? Am I not an [b]apostle? Have I not [c]seen Jesus
our Lord? Are you not [d]my work in the Lord?
2 If to others I am not an apostle, at least I am to you;
for you are the [a]seal of my [b]apostleship in the Lord.
3 My defense to those who examine me is this:
4 [1a]Do we not have a right to eat and drink?

37 [2]Lit., *pertaining to* [3]Or, *virgin*

39 [1]Lit., *has fallen asleep* [a]Rom. 7:2 [b]2 Cor. 6:14

40 [a]1 Cor. 7:6, 25

1 [1]Lit., *puffs up* [a]1 Cor. 8:4, 7, 10; Acts 15:20 [b]1 Cor. 8:7, 10; 10:15; Rom. 15:14 [c]1 Cor. 4:6 [d]Rom. 14:19

2 [a]1 Cor. 3:18 [b]1 Cor. 13:8, 9, 12; 1 Tim. 6:4

3 [a]Gal. 4:9; Rom. 8:29; 11:2; Ps. 1:6; Jer. 1:5; Amos 3:2

4 [1]I.e., has no real existence [a]1 Cor. 8:1, 7, 10; Acts 15:20 [b]1 Cor. 10:19; Acts 14:15; Gal. 4:8 [c]1 Cor. 8:6; Deut. 4:35, 39; 6:4

5 [a]2 Thess. 2:4

6 [a]1 Cor. 8:4; Deut. 4:35, 39; 6:4 [b]Mal. 2:10; Eph. 4:6 [c]Rom. 11:36 [d]1 Cor. 1:2; Eph. 4:5; John 13:13; 1 Tim. 2:5 [e]John 1:3; Col. 1:16

7 [a]1 Cor. 8:4ff. [b]Rom. 14:14, 22f.

8 [1]Or, *present* [2]Lit., *lacking* [3]Lit., *abounding* [a]Rom. 14:17

9 [1]Lit., *right* [a]Rom. 14:13, 21; 1 Cor. 10:28; Gal. 5:13 [b]1 Cor. 8:10f.; Rom. 14:1

10 [a]1 Cor. 8:4ff. [b]1 Cor. 8:1, 4, 7; Acts 15:20

11 [a]1 Cor. 8:4ff. [b]Rom. 14:15, 20

12 [a]Matt. 18:6; Rom. 14:20 [b]Matt. 25:45

13 [a]Rom. 14:21; 1 Cor. 10:32; 2 Cor. 6:3; 11:29

1 [a]1 Cor. 9:19; 10:29 [b]Acts 14:14; 2 Cor. 12:12; 1 Thess. 2:6; 1 Tim. 2:7; 2 Tim. 1:11; Rom. 1:1 [c]Acts 9:3, 17; 18:9; 22:14, 18; 23:11; 1 Cor. 15:8 [d]1 Cor. 3:6; 4:15

2 [a]John 3:33; 2 Cor. 3:2f. [b]Acts 1:25

4 [1]Lit., *It is not that we have no right to eat and drink, is it?* [a]1 Cor. 9:14; 1 Thess. 2:6, 9; 2 Thess. 3:8f.

5 [1a]Do we not have a right to take along a [2]believing wife,
even as the rest of the apostles, and the [b]brothers of the Lord,
and [c]Cephas?
6 Or do only [1a]Barnabas and I not have a right to refrain
from working?
7 Who at any time serves [a]as a soldier at his own expense? Who [b]plants a vineyard, and does not eat the fruit of
it? Or who tends a flock and does not [1]use the milk of the
flock?
8 I am not speaking these things [a]according to [1]human
judgment, am I? Or does not the Law also say these things?
9 For it is written in the Law of Moses, "[a]YOU SHALL NOT
MUZZLE THE OX WHILE HE IS THRESHING." God is not concerned
about [b]oxen, is He?
10 Or is He speaking altogether for our sake? Yes, [a]for our
sake it was written, because [b]the plowman ought to plow in
hope, and the thresher *to thresh* in hope of sharing *the crops*.
11 [a]If we sowed spiritual things in you, is it too much if we
should reap material things from you?
12 If others share the right over you, do we not more?
Nevertheless, we [a]did not use this right, but we endure all
things, [b]that we may cause no hindrance to the [c]gospel of
Christ.
13 [a]Do you not know that those who [b]perform sacred services eat the *food* of the temple, *and* those who attend regularly to the altar have their share with the altar?
14 So also [a]the Lord directed those who proclaim the [b]gos-
pel to [c]get their living from the gospel.
15 But I have [a]used none of these things. And I am not
writing these things that it may be done so in my case; for it
would be better for me to die than have any man make [b]my
boast an empty one.
16 For if I preach the gospel, I have nothing to boast of,
for [a]I am under compulsion; for woe is me if I do not preach
[b]the gospel.
17 For if I do this voluntarily, I have a [a]reward; but if
against my will, I have a [b]stewardship entrusted to me.
18 What then is my [a]reward? That, when I preach the
gospel, I may offer the gospel [b]without charge, so as [c]not to
make full use of my right in the gospel.
19 For though I am [a]free from all *men*, I have made myself [b]a slave to all, that I might [c]win the more.
20 And [a]to the Jews I became as a Jew, that I might win
Jews; to those who are under [1]the Law, as under [1]the Law,
though [b]not being myself under [1]the Law, that I might win
those who are under [1]the Law;
21 to those who are [a]without law, [b]as without law, though
not being without the law of God but [c]under the law of Christ,
that I might win those who are without law.
22 To the [a]weak I became weak, that I might win the
weak; I have become [b]all things to all men, [c]that I may by all
means save some.
23 And I do all things for the sake of the gospel, that I
may become a fellow-partaker of it.
24 [a]Do you not know that those who run in a race all run,

5 [1]Lit., *It is not that we have no right to take along . . . Cephas, is it?* [2]Lit., *sister, as wife*
[a]1 Cor. 7:7f. [b]Matt. 12:46 [c]Matt. 8:14; John 1:42

6 [1]Lit., *I and Barnabas* [a]Acts 4:36

7 [1]Lit., *eat of* [a]2 Cor. 10:4; 1 Tim. 1:18; 2 Tim. 2:3f. [b]1 Cor. 3:6, 8; Deut. 20:6; Prov. 27:18

8 [1]Lit., *man* [a]Rom. 3:5

9 [a]Deut. 25:4; 1 Tim. 5:18 [b][Deut. 22:1-4; Prov. 12:10]

10 [a]Rom. 4:23f. [b]2 Tim. 2:6

11 [a]Rom. 15:27; 1 Cor. 9:14

12 [a]1 Cor. 9:15, 18; Acts 18:3; Acts 20:33 [b]2 Cor. 6:3; 11:12 [c]1 Cor. 4:15; 9:14; 16, 18, 23; 2 Cor. 2:12

13 [a]Rom. 6:16 [b]Lev. 6:16, 26; 7:6, 31ff.; Num. 5:9f.; 18:8-20, 31; Deut. 18:1

14 [a]Matt. 10:10; Luke 10:7; 1 Tim. 5:18 [b]1 Cor. 4:15; 9:12, 16, 18, 23; 2 Cor. 2:12 [c]1 Cor. 9:4; Luke 10:8

15 [a]1 Cor. 9:12, 18; Acts 18:3; Acts 20:33 [b]2 Cor. 11:10

16 [a]Rom. 1:14; Acts 9:15 [b]1 Cor. 4:15; 9:12, 14, 18, 23; 2 Cor. 2:12

17 [a]1 Cor. 9:18; John 4:36 [Gr.]; 1 Cor. 3:8 [b]1 Cor. 4:1; Gal. 2:7; Eph. 3:2 marg.; Phil. 1:16; Col. 1:25 marg.

18 [a]1 Cor. 9:17; John 4:36 [Gr.]; 1 Cor. 3:8 [b]2 Cor. 11:7; 12:13; Acts 18:3 [c]1 Cor. 7:31; 9:12

19 [a]1 Cor. 9:1 [b]2 Cor. 4:5 marg.; Gal. 5:13 [c]Matt. 18:15; 1 Pet. 3:1

20 [1]Or, *law* [a]Acts 16:3; 21:23-26; Rom. 11:14 [b]Gal. 2:19

21 [a]Rom. 2:12, 14 [b]Gal. 2:3; 3:2 [c]Gal. 6:2; 1 Cor. 7:22

22 [a]2 Cor. 11:29; Rom. 14:1; 15:1 [b]1 Cor. 10:33 [c]Rom. 11:14

24 [a]1 Cor. 9:13

but *only* one receives [b]the prize? [c]Run in such a way that you
may win.
25 And everyone who [a]competes in the games exercises
self-control in all things. They then *do it* to receive a perishable [b]wreath, but we an imperishable.
26 Therefore I [a]run in such a way, as not without aim; I
box in such a way, as not [b]beating the air;
27 but I [1]buffet [a]my body and make it my slave, lest possibly, after I have preached to others, I myself should be
disqualified.

Chapter 10

FOR [a]I do not want you to be unaware, brethren, that our
fathers were all [b]under the cloud, and all [c]passed through the
sea;
2 and all [1]were [a]baptized into Moses in the cloud and in
the sea;
3 and all [a]ate the same spiritual food;
4 and all [a]drank the same spiritual drink, for they were
drinking from a spiritual rock which followed them; and the
rock was [1]Christ.
5 Nevertheless, with most of them God was not well
pleased; for [a]they were laid low in the wilderness.
6 Now these things happened as [a]examples for us, that
we should not crave evil things, as [b]they also craved.
7 And do not be [a]idolaters, as some of them were; as it is
written, "[b]THE PEOPLE SAT DOWN TO EAT AND DRINK, AND STOOD
UP TO [c]PLAY."
8 Nor let us act immorally, as [a]some of them [1]did, and
[b]twenty-three thousand fell in one day.
9 Nor let us try the Lord, as [a]some of them [1]did, and
were destroyed by the serpents.
10 Nor grumble, [a]as some of them [1]did, and [b]were [2]de-
stroyed by the [c]destroyer.
11 Now these things happened to them as an [a]example,
and [b]they were written for our instruction, upon whom [c]the
ends of the ages have come.
12 Therefore let him who [a]thinks he stands take heed lest
he fall.
13 No temptation has overtaken you but such as is common to man; and [a]God is faithful, who will not allow you to be
[b]tempted beyond what you are able; but with the temptation
will provide the way of escape also, that you may be able to
endure it.
14 Therefore, my [a]beloved, flee from [b]idolatry.
15 I speak as to wise men; you judge what I say.
16 Is not the [a]cup of blessing which we bless a sharing in
the blood of Christ? Is not the [1b]bread which we break a
sharing in the body of Christ?
17 Since there is one [1]bread, we [a]who are many are one
body; for we all partake of the one [1]bread.
18 Look at [1]the nation [a]Israel; are not those who [b]eat the
sacrifices sharers in the altar?
19 What do I mean then? That a thing sacrificed to idols
is anything, or [a]that an idol is anything?

24 [b]Phil. 3:14; Col. 2:18 [c]Heb. 12:1; 2 Tim. 4:7; Gal. 2:2

25 [a]1 Tim. 6:12; 2 Tim. 2:5; 4:7; Eph. 6:12 [b]2 Tim. 4:8; James 1:12; 1 Pet. 5:4; Rev. 2:10; 3:11

26 [a]Heb. 12:1; 2 Tim. 4:7; Gal. 2:2 [b]1 Cor. 14:9

27 [1]Lit., *bruise* [a]Rom. 8:13

1 [a]Rom. 1:13 [b]Ex. 13:21; Ps. 105:39 [c]Ex. 14:22, 29; Ps. 66:6

2 [1]Some ancient mss. read, *received baptism* [a]Rom. 6:3; Gal. 3:27; 1 Cor. 1:13

3 [a]Ex. 16:4, 35; Deut. 8:3; Neh. 9:15, 20; Ps. 78:24f.; John 6:31

4 [1]I.e., the Messiah [a]Ex. 17:6; Num. 20:11; Ps. 78:15

5 [a]Num. 14:29ff., 37; 26:65; Heb. 3:17; Jude 5

6 [a]1 Cor. 10:11 [b]Num. 11:4, 34; Ps. 106:14

7 [a]Ex. 32:4; 1 Cor. 10:14; 5:11 [b]Ex. 32:6 [c]Ex. 32:19

8 [1]Lit., *acted immorally* [a]Num. 25:1ff. [b]Num. 25:9

9 [1]Lit., *made trial* [a]Num. 21:5f.

10 [1]Lit., *grumbled* [2]Lit., *being destroyed* [a]Num. 16:41; 17:5, 10 [b]Num. 16:49 [c]Ex. 12:23; 2 Sam. 24:16; 1 Chr. 21:15; Heb. 11:28

11 [a]1 Cor. 10:6 [b]Rom. 4:23 [c]Rom. 13:11

12 [a]Rom. 11:20; 2 Pet. 3:17

13 [a]1 Cor. 1:9 [b]2 Pet. 2:9

14 [a]Heb. 6:9 [b]1 Cor. 10:7; 1 Cor. 10:19f.; 1 John 5:21

16 [1]Lit., *loaf* [a]Matt. 26:27f.; 1 Cor. 11:25 [b]Matt. 26:26; 1 Cor. 11:32f.; Acts 2:42

17 [1]Lit., *loaf* [a]Rom. 12:5; 1 Cor. 12:12f., 27; Eph. 4:4, 16; Col. 3:15

18 [1]Lit., *Israel according to the flesh* [a]Rom. 1:3 [b]Lev. 7:6, 14f.; Deut. 12:17f.

19 [a]1 Cor. 8:4

20 No; but *I say* that the things which the Gentiles sacrifice, they [a]sacrifice to demons, and not to God; and I do not
want you to become sharers in demons.
21 [a]You cannot drink the cup of the Lord and the cup of
demons; you cannot partake of the table of the Lord and [b]the
table of demons.
22 Or do we [a]provoke the Lord to jealousy? We are not
[b]stronger than He, are we?
23 [a]All things are lawful, but not all things are profitable.
All things are lawful, but not all things [b]edify.
24 Let no one [a]seek his own *good*, but that of his
[1]neighbor.
25 [a]Eat anything that is sold in the meat market, without
asking questions for conscience' sake;
26 [a]FOR THE EARTH IS THE LORD'S, AND EVERYTHING THAT IS
IN IT.
27 If [a]one of the unbelievers invites you, and you wish to
go, [b]eat anything that is set before you, without asking questions for conscience' sake.
28 But [a]if anyone should say to you, "This is meat sacrificed to idols," do not eat *it*, for the sake of the one who
informed *you*, and for conscience' sake;
29 I mean not your own conscience, but the other *man's*;
for [a]why is my freedom judged by another's conscience?
30 If I partake with thankfulness, [a]why am I slandered
concerning that for which I [b]give thanks?
31 Whether, then, you eat or drink or [a]whatever you do,
do all to the glory of God.
32 [a]Give no offense either to Jews or to Greeks or to [b]the
church of God;
33 just as I also [a]please all men in all things, [b]not seeking
my own profit, but the *profit* of the many, [c]that they may be
saved.

Chapter 11

[a]BE imitators of me, just as I also am of Christ.
2 Now [a]I praise you because you [b]remember me in everything, and [c]hold firmly to the traditions, just as I delivered
them to you.
3 But I want you to understand that [1]Christ is the [a]head
of every man, and [b]the man is the head of a woman, and God
is the [c]head of [1]Christ.
4 Every man who has *something* on his head while
praying or [a]prophesying, disgraces his head.
5 But every [a]woman who has her head uncovered while
praying or prophesying, disgraces her head; for she is one and
the same with her [1]whose head is [b]shaved.
6 For if a woman does not cover [1]her head, let her also
[2]have her hair cut off; but if it is disgraceful for a woman to
[2]have her hair cut off or [1]her head shaved, let her cover [1]her
head.
7 For a man ought not to have his head covered, since he
is the [a]image and glory of God; but the woman is the glory of
man.

20 [a]Deut. 32:17; Ps. 106:37; Rev. 9:20; Gal. 4:8

21 [a]2 Cor. 6:16 [b]Is. 65:11

22 [a]Deut. 32:21 [b]Eccl. 6:10; Is. 45:9

23 [a]1 Cor. 6:12 [b]Rom. 14:19

24 [1]Or, *the other* [a]1 Cor. 10:33; 13:5; Phil. 2:21; 2 Cor. 12:14; Rom. 15:2

25 [a]Acts 10:15; 1 Cor. 8:7

26 [a]Ps. 24:1; Ps. 50:12; 1 Tim. 4:4

27 [a]1 Cor. 5:10 [b]Luke 10:8

28 [a]1 Cor. 8:7, 10-12

29 [a]1 Cor. 9:19; Rom. 14:16

30 [a]1 Cor. 9:1 [b]Rom. 14:6

31 [a]Col. 3:17; 1 Pet. 4:11

32 [a]1 Cor. 8:13; Acts 24:16 [b]Acts 20:28 marg.; 1 Cor. 1:2; 11:22; 15:9; 2 Cor. 1:1; Gal. 1:13; 1 Tim. 3:5, 15; 1 Cor. 7:17; Phil. 3:6

33 [a]1 Cor. 9:22; Rom. 15:2; Gal. 1:10 [b]1 Cor. 13:5; Phil. 2:21; 2 Cor. 12:14; Rom. 15:2 [c]1 Thess. 2:16; Rom. 11:14

1 [a]1 Cor. 4:16

2 [a]1 Cor. 11:17, 22 [b]1 Cor. 4:17; 15:2; 1 Thess. 1:6; 3:6 [c]2 Thess. 2:15; 3:6

3 [1]I.e., the Messiah [a]Eph. 1:22; 4:15; 5:23; Col. 1:18; 2:19 [b]Eph. 5:23; Gen. 3:16 [c]1 Cor. 3:23

4 [a]Acts 13:1; 1 Thess. 5:20

5 [1]Lit., *who is shaved* [a]Luke 2:36; Acts 21:9; 1 Cor. 14:34 [b]Deut. 21:12

6 [1]Lit., *herself* [2]Lit., *shear herself*

7 [a]James 3:9; Gen. 1:26; 5:1; 9:6

8 For [a]man [1]does not originate from woman, but woman
from man;
9 for indeed man was not created for the woman's sake,
but [a]woman for the man's sake.
10 Therefore the woman ought to have *a symbol of* authority on her head, because of the angels.
11 However, in the Lord, neither is woman [1]independent
of man, nor is man [1]independent of woman.
12 For as the woman [1]originates from the man, so also the
man has his birth through the woman; and [a]all things [2]origi-
nate [b]from God.
13 [a]Judge [1]for yourselves: is it proper for a woman to pray
to God *with head* uncovered?
14 Does not even nature itself teach you that if a man has
long hair, it is a dishonor to him,
15 but if a woman has long hair, it is a glory to her? For
her hair is given to her for a covering.
16 But if one is inclined to be contentious, [a]we have no
[1]other practice, nor have [b]the churches of God.
17 But in giving this instruction, [a]I do not praise you,
because you come together not for the better but for the
worse.
18 For, in the first place, when you come together [1]as a
church, I hear that [2a]divisions exist among you; and in part, I
believe it.
19 For there [a]must also be factions among you, [b]in order
that those who are approved may have become [1]evident
among you.
20 Therefore when you meet together, it is not to eat the
Lord's Supper,
21 for in your eating each one takes his own supper first;
and one is hungry and [a]another is drunk.
22 What! Do you not have houses in which to eat and
drink? Or do you despise the [a]church of God, and [b]shame
those who have nothing? What shall I say to you? Shall [c]I
praise you? In this I will not praise you.
23 For [a]I received from the Lord that which I also delivered to you, that [b]the Lord Jesus in the night in which He was
betrayed took bread;
24 and when He had given thanks, He broke it, and said,
"This is My body, which [1]is for you; do this in remembrance of
Me."
25 In the same way [a]the cup also, after supper, saying,
"This cup is the [b]new covenant in My blood; do this, as often
as you drink *it*, in remembrance of Me."
26 For as often as you eat this bread and drink the cup,
you proclaim the Lord's death [a]until He comes.
27 Therefore whoever eats the bread or drinks the cup of
the Lord in an unworthy manner, shall be [a]guilty of the body
and the blood of the Lord.
28 But let a man [a]examine himself, and so let him eat of
the bread and drink of the cup.
29 For he who eats and drinks, eats and drinks judgment
to himself, if he does not judge the body rightly.
30 For this reason many among you are weak and sick, and
a number [a]sleep.

8 [1]Lit., *is not from* [a]Gen. 2:21-23; 1 Tim. 2:13

9 [a]Gen. 2:18

11 [1]Lit., *without*

12 [1]Lit., *is* [2]Lit., *are* [a]2 Cor. 5:18 [b]Rom. 11:36

13 [1]Lit., *in* [a]Luke 12:57

16 [1]Lit., *such* [a]1 Cor. 9:1-3, 6; 4:5 [b]1 Cor. 7:17

17 [a]1 Cor. 11:2, 22

18 [1]Lit., *in church* [2]Lit., *schisms* [a]1 Cor. 1:10; 3:3

19 [1]Or, *manifest* [a]Matt. 18:7; Luke 17:1; 1 Tim. 4:1; 2 Pet. 2:1 [b]1 John 2:19; Deut. 13:3

21 [a]Jude 12

22 [a]1 Cor. 10:32 [b]James 2:6 [c]1 Cor. 11:2, 17

23 [a]1 Cor. 15:3; Gal. 1:12; Col. 3:24 [b]1 Cor. 11:23-25: *Matt. 26:26-28; Mark 14:22-24; Luke 22:17-20;* 1 Cor. 10:16

24 [1]Some ancient mss. read, *is broken*

25 [a]1 Cor. 10:16 [b]2 Cor. 3:6; Luke 22:20

26 [a]1 Cor. 4:5; John 21:22

27 [a]Heb. 10:29

28 [a]2 Cor. 13:5; Gal. 6:4; Matt. 26:22

30 [a]Acts 7:60

31 But if we judged ourselves rightly, we should not be
judged.
32 But when we are judged, we are [a]disciplined by the
Lord in order that we may not be condemned along with [b]the
world.
33 So then, my brethren, when you come together to eat,
wait for one another.
34 If anyone is [a]hungry, let him eat [b]at home, so that you
may not come together for judgment. And the remaining matters I shall [c]arrange [d]when I come.

Chapter 12

NOW concerning [a]spiritual *gifts*, brethren, [b]I do not want
you to be unaware.
2 [a]You know that when you were pagans, *you were* [b]led
astray to the [c]dumb idols, however you were led.
3 Therefore I make known to you, that no one speaking
[1a]by the Spirit of God says, "Jesus is [2b]accursed"; and no one
can say, "Jesus is [c]Lord," except [1a]by the Holy Spirit.
4 Now there are [a]varieties of gifts, but the same Spirit.
5 And there are varieties of ministries, and the same
Lord.
6 And there are varieties of effects, but the same [a]God
who works all things in all *persons.*
7 But to each one is given the manifestation of the Spirit
[a]for the common good.
8 For to one is given the word of [a]wisdom through the
Spirit, and to another the word of [b]knowledge according to the
same Spirit;
9 to another [a]faith [1]by the same Spirit, and to another
[b]gifts of [2]healing [1]by the one Spirit,
10 and to another the [1]effecting of [2a]miracles, and to another [b]prophecy, and to another the [3c]distinguishing of spirits, to
another *various* [d]kinds of tongues, and to another the [e]inter-
pretation of tongues.
11 But one and the same Spirit works all these things,
[a]distributing to each one individually just as He wills.
12 For even [a]as the body is one and *yet* has many members, and all the members of the body, though they are many,
are one body, [b]so also is Christ.
13 For [1a]by one Spirit we were all baptized into one body,
whether [b]Jews or Greeks, whether slaves or free, and we were
all made to [c]drink of one Spirit.
14 For [a]the body is not one member, but many.
15 If the foot should say, "Because I am not a hand, I am
not *a part* of the body," it is not for this reason [1]any the less *a
part* of the body.
16 And if the ear should say, "Because I am not an eye, I
am not *a part* of the body," it is not for this reason [1]any the
less *a part* of the body.
17 If the whole body were an eye, where would the hearing be? If the whole were hearing, where would the sense of
smell be?
18 But now God has [a]placed the members, each one of
them, in the body, [b]just as He desired.

32 [a]2 Sam. 7:14; Ps. 94:12; Heb. 12:7-10; Rev. 3:19 [b]1 Cor. 1:20

34 [a]1 Cor. 11:21 [b]1 Cor. 11:22 [c]1 Cor. 7:17; 16:1; 4:17 [d]1 Cor. 4:19

1 [a]1 Cor. 14:1; 12:4 [b]Rom. 1:13

2 [a]Eph. 2:11f.; 1 Pet. 4:3; 1 Cor. 6:11 [b]1 Thess. 1:9 [c]Hab. 2:18f.; Ps. 115:5; Is. 46:7; Jer. 10:5

3 [1]Or, *in* [2]Gr. *anathema* [a]1 John 4:2f.; Matt. 22:43; Rev. 1:10, [b]Rom. 9:3 [c]John 13:13; Rom. 10:9

4 [a]Rom. 12:6f.; 1 Cor. 12:11; Eph. 4:4ff., 11; Heb. 2:4

6 [a]1 Cor. 15:28; Eph. 1:23; 4:6

7 [a]Eph. 4:12; 1 Cor. 12:12-30; 14:26

8 [a]1 Cor. 2:6; 2 Cor. 1:12 [b]Rom. 15:14; 1 Cor. 2:11, 16; 2 Cor. 2:14; 4:6; 8:7; 11:6

9 [1]Or, *in* [2]Lit., *healings* [a]1 Cor. 13:2; 2 Cor. 4:13 [b]1 Cor. 12:28, 30

10 [1]Lit., *effects* [2]Or, *works of power* [3]Lit., *distinguishings* [a]1 Cor. 12:28f.; Gal. 3:5 [b]1 Cor. 11:4; 13:2, 8 [c]1 Cor. 14:29; 1 John 4:1 [d]1 Cor. 12:28, 30; 13:1; 14:2ff.; Mark 16:17 [e]1 Cor. 12:30; 14:26

11 [a]1 Cor. 12:4 and ref.

12 [a]Rom. 12:4; 1 Cor. 10:17 [b]1 Cor. 12:27

13 [1]Or, *in* [a]Eph. 2:18 [b]Gal. 3:28; Col. 3:11; Eph. 2:13-18; Rom. 3:22 [c]John 7:37-39

14 [a]1 Cor. 12:20

15 [1]Lit., *not* a part

16 [1]Lit., *not* a part

18 [a]1 Cor. 12:28 [b]1 Cor. 12:11; Rom. 12:6

19 And if they were all one member, where would the
body be?
20 But now [a]there are many members, but one body.
21 And the eye cannot say to the hand, "I have no need of
you"; or again the head to the feet, "I have no need of you."
22 On the contrary, [1]it is much truer that the members of
the body which seem to be weaker are necessary;
23 and those *members* of the body, which we [1]deem less
honorable, [2]on these we bestow more abundant honor, and
our unseemly *members come to* have more abundant
seemliness,
24 whereas our seemly *members* have no need *of it.* But
God has *so* composed the body, giving more abundant honor
to that *member* which lacked,
25 that there should be no [1]division in the body, but *that*
the members should have the same care for one another.
26 And if one member suffers, all the members suffer with
it; if *one* member is [1]honored, all the members rejoice with it.
27 Now you are [a]Christ's body, and [b]individually members
of it.
28 And God has [1a]appointed in [b]the church, first [c]apostles,
second [d]prophets, third [e]teachers, then [2f]miracles, then [g]gifts
of healings, helps, [h]administrations, *various* [i]kinds of tongues.
29 All are not apostles, are they? All are not prophets, are
they? All are not teachers, are they? All are not *workers of*
[1]miracles, are they?
30 All do not have gifts of healings, do they? All do not
speak with tongues, do they? All do not [a]interpret, do they?
31 But [a]earnestly desire the greater gifts.
And I show you a still more excellent way.

CHAPTER 13

1 IF I speak with the [a]tongues of men and of [b]angels, but do not
have love, I have become a noisy gong or a [c]clanging cymbal.
2 And if I have *the gift of* [a]prophecy, and know all [b]mys-
teries and all [c]knowledge; and if I have [d]all faith, so as to
[e]remove mountains, but do not have love, I am nothing.
3 And if I [a]give all my possessions to feed *the poor,* and if
I [b]deliver my body [1]to be burned, but do not have love, it
profits me nothing.
4 Love [a]is patient, love is kind, *and* [b]is not jealous; love
does not brag *and* is not [c]arrogant,
5 does not act unbecomingly; it [a]does not seek its own, is
not provoked, [b]does not take into account a wrong *suffered,*
6 [a]does not rejoice in unrighteousness, but [b]rejoices with
the truth;
7 [1a]bears all things, believes all things, hopes all things,
endures all things.
8 Love never fails; but if *there are gifts of* [1a]prophecy,
they will be done away; if *there are* [b]tongues, they will cease; if
there is knowledge, it will be done away.
9 For we [a]know in part, and we prophesy in part;
10 but when the perfect comes, the partial will be done
away.
11 When I was a child, I used to speak as a child, think as

20 [a]1 Cor. 12:14; 12:12

22 [1]Lit., *to a much greater degree the members*

23 [1]Or, *think to be* [2]Or, *these we clothe with*

25 [1]Lit., *schism*

26 [1]Lit., *glorified*

27 [a]1 Cor. 12:12; 1:2; Eph. 1:23; 4:12; Col. 1:18, 24; 2:19 [b]Eph. 5:30; Rom. 12:5

28 [1]Lit., *set some in* [2]Or, *works of power* [a]1 Cor. 12:18 [b]1 Cor. 10:32 [c]Eph. 4:11 [d]Eph. 2:20; 3:5; Acts 13:1 [e]Acts 13:1 [f]1 Cor. 12:10, 29 [g]1 Cor. 12:9, 30 [h]Rom. 12:8 [i]1 Cor. 12:10

29 [1]Or, *works of power*

30 [a]1 Cor. 12:10

31 [a]1 Cor. 14:1, 39

1 [a]1 Cor. 12:10 [b]2 Cor. 12:4; Rev. 14:2 [c]Ps. 150:5 Sept.

2 [a]Acts 13:1; 1 Cor. 11:4; 13:8; 14:1, 39; Matt. 7:22 [b]1 Cor. 14:2; 15:51 [c]Rom. 15:14 [d]1 Cor. 12:9 [e]Matt. 17:20; 21:21

3 [1]Some ancient mss. read, *that I may boast* [a]Matt. 6:2 [b]Dan. 3:28

4 [a]Prov. 10:12; 17:9; 1 Thess. 5:14; 1 Pet. 4:8 [b]Acts 7:9 [c]1 Cor. 4:6

5 [a]1 Cor. 10:24; Phil. 2:21 [b]2 Cor. 5:19

6 [a]2 Thess. 2:12 [b]2 John 4; 3 John 3f.

7 [1]Or, *covers* [a]1 Cor. 9:12

8 [1]Lit., *prophecies* [a]1 Cor. 13:2 [b]1 Cor. 13:1

9 [a]1 Cor. 13:12; 8:2

a child, reason as a child; when I became a man, I did away
with childish things.
12 For now we [a]see in a mirror [1]dimly, but then [b]face to
face; now I know in part, but then I shall know fully just as I
also [c]have been fully known.
13 But now abide faith, hope, love, these three; but the
[1]greatest of these is [a]love.

CHAPTER 14

[a]PURSUE love, yet [b]desire earnestly [c]spiritual *gifts*, but especially that you may [d]prophesy.
2 For one who [a]speaks in a tongue does not speak to
men, but to God; for no one [1]understands, but [2]in *his* spirit he
speaks [b]mysteries.
3 But one who prophesies speaks to men for [a]edification
and [b]exhortation and consolation.
4 One who [a]speaks in a tongue [b]edifies himself; but one
who [c]prophesies [b]edifies the church.
5 Now I wish that you all [a]spoke in tongues, but [b]*even*
more that you would prophesy; and greater is one who prophesies
than one who [a]speaks in tongues, unless he interprets, so
that the church may receive [c]edifying.
6 But now, brethren, if I come to you speaking in
tongues, what shall I profit you, unless I speak to you either by
way of [a]revelation or of [b]knowledge or of [c]prophecy or of
[d]teaching?
7 Yet *even* lifeless things, either flute or harp, in producing a sound, if they do not produce a distinction in the tones,
how will it be known what is played on the flute or on the
harp?
8 For if [a]the [1]bugle produces an indistinct sound, who
will prepare himself for battle?
9 So also you, unless you utter by the tongue speech that
is clear, how will it be known what is spoken? For you will be
[a]speaking into the air.
10 There are, perhaps, a great many kinds of [1]languages in
the world, and no *kind* is without meaning.
11 If then I do not know the meaning of the language, I
shall be to the one who speaks a [1a]barbarian, and the one who
speaks will be a [1]barbarian [2]to me.
12 So also you, since you are zealous of [1]spiritual *gifts*,
seek to abound for the [a]edification of the church.
13 Therefore let one who speaks in a tongue pray that he
may interpret.
14 For if I pray in a tongue, my spirit prays, but my mind
is unfruitful.
15 [a]What is *the outcome* then? I shall pray with the spirit
and I shall pray with the mind also; I shall [b]sing with the spirit
and I shall sing with the mind also.
16 Otherwise if you bless [1]in the spirit *only*, how will the
one who fills the place of the [2]ungifted say [a]the "Amen" at
your [b]giving of thanks, since he does not know what you are
saying?
17 For you are giving thanks well enough, but the other
man is not [a]edified.

12 [1]Lit., *in a riddle* [a]2 Cor. 5:7; Phil. 3:12; James 1:23 [b]Gen. 32:30; Num. 12:8; 1 John 3:2 [c]1 Cor. 8:3

13 [1]Lit., *greater* [a]Gal. 5:6

1 [a]1 Cor. 16:14 [b]1 Cor. 12:31; 14:39 [c]1 Cor. 12:1 [d]1 Cor. 13:2

2 [1]Lit., *hears* [2]Or, *by the Spirit* [a]1 Cor. 12:10, 28, 30; 13:1; 14:18ff.; Mark 16:17 [b]1 Cor. 13:2

3 [a]1 Cor. 14:5, 12, 17, 26; Rom. 14:19 [b]Acts 4:36

4 [a]1 Cor. 12:10, 28, 30; 13:1; 14:18ff., 26f.; Mark 16:17 [b]1 Cor. 14:5, 12, 17, 26; Rom. 14:19 [c]1 Cor. 13:2

5 [a]1 Cor. 12:10, 28, 30; 13:1; 14:18ff., 26f.; Mark 16:17 [b]Num. 11:29 [c]1 Cor. 14:4, 12, 17, 26; Rom. 14:19

6 [a]1 Cor. 14:26; Eph. 1:17 [b]1 Cor. 12:8 [c]1 Cor. 13:2 [d]1 Cor. 14:26; Acts 2:42; Rom. 6:17

8 [1]Lit., *trumpet* [a]Num. 10:9; Jer. 4:19; Ezek. 33:3-6; Joel 2:1

9 [a]1 Cor. 9:26

10 [1]Lit., *voices*

11 [1]Or, *foreigner* [2]Or, *in my estimation* [a]Acts 28:2

12 [1]Lit., *spirits* [a]1 Cor. 14:4, 5, 17, 26; Rom. 14:19

15 [a]1 Cor. 14:26; Acts 21:22 [b]Eph. 5:19; Col. 3:16

16 [1]Or, *with the* [2]I.e., unversed in spiritual gifts [a]Deut. 27:15-26; 1 Chr. 16:36 [Ps. 106:48]; Neh. 5:13; 8:6; Jer. 11:5; 28:6; Rev. 5:14; 7:12 [b]Matt. 15:36

17 [a]1 Cor. 14:4, 5, 12, 26; Rom. 14:19

18 I thank God, I speak in tongues more than you all;
19 however, in the church I desire to speak five words with
my mind, that I may instruct others also, rather than ten thousand words in a tongue.
20 [a]Brethren, [b]do not be children in your thinking; yet in
evil [c]be babes, but in your thinking be mature.
21 In [a]the Law it is written, "[b]BY MEN OF STRANGE TONGUES
AND BY THE LIPS OF STRANGERS I WILL SPEAK TO THIS PEOPLE, AND
EVEN SO THEY WILL NOT LISTEN TO ME," says the Lord.
22 So then tongues are for a sign, not to those who believe, but to unbelievers; but [a]prophecy *is for a sign,* not to
unbelievers, but to those who believe.
23 If therefore the whole church should assemble together
and all speak in tongues, and [1]ungifted men or unbelievers
enter, will they not say that [a]you are mad?
24 But if all [a]prophesy, and an unbeliever or an [1]ungifted
man enters, he is [b]convicted by all, he is called to account by
all;
25 [a]the secrets of his heart are disclosed; and so he will
[b]fall on his face and worship God, [c]declaring that God is certainly among you.
26 [a]What is *the outcome* then, [b]brethren? When you
assemble, [c]each one has a [d]psalm, has a [e]teaching, has a [e]revela-
tion, has a [f]tongue, has an [g]interpretation. Let [h]all things be
done for edification.
27 If any one speaks in a [a]tongue, *it should be* by two or at
the most three, and *each* in turn, and let one [b]interpret;
28 but if there is no interpreter, let him keep silent in the
church; and let him speak to himself and to God.
29 And let two or three [a]prophets speak, and let the others
[b]pass judgment.
30 But if a revelation is made to another who is seated, let
the first keep silent.
31 For you can all prophesy one by one, so that all may
learn and all may be exhorted;
32 and the spirits of prophets are subject to prophets;
33 for God is not *a God* of [a]confusion but of [1]peace, as in
[b]all the churches of the [c]saints.
34 Let the women [a]keep silent in the churches; for they
are not permitted to speak, but [b]let them subject themselves,
just as [c]the Law also says.
35 And if they desire to learn anything, let them ask their
own husbands at home; for it is [1]improper for a woman to
speak in church.
36 [1]Was it from you that the word of God *first* went
forth? Or has it come to you only?
37 [a]If any one thinks he is a prophet or [b]spiritual, let him
recognize that the things which I write to you [c]are the Lord's
commandment.
38 But if any one [1]does not recognize *this,* he is not
recognized.
39 Therefore, my brethren, [a]desire earnestly to [b]prophesy,
and do not forbid to speak in tongues.
40 But [a]let all things be done properly and in an orderly
manner.

20 [a]Rom. 1:13 [b]Eph. 4:14; Heb. 5:12f. [c]Ps. 131:2; Rom. 16:19; 1 Pet. 2:2; Matt. 18:3

21 [a]John 10:34; 1 Cor. 14:34 [b]Is. 28:11f.

22 [a]1 Cor. 14:1

23 [1]Note 2, vs. 16 [a]Acts 2:13

24 [1]Note 2, vs. 16 [a]1 Cor. 14:1 [b]John 16:8

25 [a]John 4:19 [b]Luke 17:16 [c]Is. 45:14; Zech. 8:23; Dan. 2:47; Acts 4:13

26 [a]1 Cor. 14:15 [b]Rom. 1:13 [c]1 Cor. 12:8-10 [d]Eph. 5:19 [e]1 Cor. 14:6 [f]1 Cor. 14:2 [g]1 Cor. 14:5, 13, 27f.; 12:10 [h]Rom. 14:19

27 [a]1 Cor. 14:2 [b]1 Cor. 14:5, 13, 26ff.; 12:10

29 [a]1 Cor. 14:32, 37; 13:2 [b]1 Cor. 12:10

33 [1]Or, *peace. As in all . . . saints, let . . .* [a]1 Cor. 14:40 [b]1 Cor. 4:17; 7:17 [c]Acts 9:13

34 [a]1 Cor. 11:5, 13 [b]1 Tim. 2:11f.; 1 Pet. 3:1 [c]1 Cor. 14:21

35 [1]Or, *disgraceful*

36 [1]Lit., *Or was*

37 [a]2 Cor. 10:7 [b]1 Cor. 2:15 [c]1 Cor. 7:40; 1 John 4:6

38 [1]Some ancient mss. read, *is ignorant, let him be ignorant*

39 [a]1 Cor. 12:31 [b]1 Cor. 14:1; 13:2

40 [a]1 Cor. 14:33

CHAPTER 15

NOW [a]I make known to you, brethren, the [b]gospel which I
preached to you, which also you received, [c]in which also you
stand,
2 by which also you are saved, [a]if you hold fast [1]the word
which I preached to you, [b]unless you believed in vain.
3 For [a]I delivered to you [1]as of first importance what I
also received, that Christ died [b]for our sins [c]according to the
Scriptures,
4 and that He was buried, and that He was [a]raised on the
third day [b]according to the Scriptures,
5 and that [a]He appeared to [b]Cephas, then [c]to the twelve.
6 After that He appeared to more than five hundred
brethren at one time, most of whom remain until now, but
some [a]have fallen asleep;
7 then He appeared to [1a]James, then to [b]all the apostles;
8 and last of all, as it were [1]to one untimely born, [a]He
appeared to me also.
9 For I am [a]the least of the apostles, who am not fit to be
called an apostle, because I [b]persecuted the church of God.
10 But by [a]the grace of God I am what I am, and His grace
toward me did not prove vain; but I [b]labored even more than
all of them, yet [c]not I, but the grace of God with me.
11 Whether then *it was* I or they, so we preach and so you
believed.
12 Now if Christ is preached, that He has been raised
from the dead, how do some among you say that there [a]is no
resurrection of the dead?
13 But if there is no resurrection of the dead, not even
Christ has been raised;
14 and [a]if Christ has not been raised, then our preaching is
vain, your faith also is vain.
15 Moreover we are even found *to be* false witnesses of
God, because we witnessed [1]against God that He [a]raised
[2]Christ, whom He did not raise, if in fact the dead are not
raised.
16 For if the dead are not raised, not even Christ has been
raised;
17 and if Christ has not been raised, your faith is worthless; [a]you are still in your sins.
18 Then those also who [a]have fallen asleep in Christ have
perished.
19 If we have only hoped in Christ in this life, we are [a]of
all men most to be pitied.
20 But now Christ [a]has been raised from the dead, the
[b]first fruits of those who [c]are asleep.
21 For since [a]by a man *came* death, by a man also *came*
the resurrection of the dead.
22 For [a]as in Adam all die, so also in [1]Christ all shall be
made alive.
23 But each in his own order: Christ [a]the first fruits, after
that [b]those who are Christ's at [c]His coming,
24 then *comes* the end, when He delivers up [a]the kingdom
to the [b]God and Father, when He has abolished [c]all rule and
all authority and power.

1 [a]Gal. 1:11; Rom. 2:16 [b]1 Cor. 3:6; 4:15; Rom. 2:16 [c]Rom. 5:2; 11:20; 2 Cor. 1:24

2 [1]Lit., *to what word I* [a]Rom. 11:22 [b]Gal. 3:4

3 [1]Lit., *among the first* [a]1 Cor. 11:23 [b]John 1:29; Gal. 1:4; Heb. 5:1, 3; 1 Pet. 2:24 [c]Is. 53:5-12; Matt. 26:24; Luke 24:25-27; Acts 8:32f.; 17:2f.; 26:22

4 [a]Matt. 16:21; John 2:21f.; Acts 2:24 [b]Ps. 16:8ff.; Acts 2:31; 26:22f.

5 [a]Luke 24:34 [b]1 Cor. 1:12 [c]Mark 16:14

6 [a]Acts 7:60; 1 Cor. 15:18, 20

7 [1]Lit., *Jacob* [a]Acts 12:17 [b]Luke 24:33, 36f.; Acts 1:3f.

8 [1]Lit., *to an untimely birth* [a]1 Cor. 9:1; Acts 9:3-8; 22:6-11; 26:12-18

9 [a]Eph. 3:8; 2 Cor. 12:11; 1 Tim. 1:15 [b]Acts 8:3

10 [a]Rom. 12:3 [b]2 Cor. 11:23; Col. 1:29; 1 Tim. 4:10 [c]1 Cor. 3:6; 2 Cor. 3:5; Phil. 2:13

12 [a]Acts 17:32; 23:8; 2 Tim. 2:18

14 [a]1 Thess. 4:14

15 [1]Or, *concerning* [2]I.e., the Messiah [a]Acts 2:24

17 [a]Rom. 4:25

18 [a]1 Thess. 4:16; Rev. 14:13; 1 Cor. 15:6

19 [a]1 Cor. 4:9; 2 Tim. 3:12

20 [a]1 Pet. 1:3; Acts 2:24 [b]1 Cor. 15:23; Acts 26:23; Rev. 1:5 [c]1 Thess. 4:16; Rev. 14:13; 1 Cor. 15:6

21 [a]Rom. 5:12

22 [1]I.e., the Messiah [a]Rom. 5:14-18

23 [a]1 Cor. 15:20; Acts 26:23; Rev. 1:5 [b]1 Cor. 15:52; 6:14; 1 Thess. 4:16 [c]1 Thess. 2:19

24 [a]Dan. 2:44; 7:14, 27; 2 Pet. 1:11 [b]Eph. 5:20 [c]Rom. 8:38

25 For He must reign [a]until He has put all His enemies
under His feet.
26 The last enemy that will be [a]abolished is death.
27 For [a]HE HAS PUT ALL THINGS IN SUBJECTION UNDER HIS
FEET. But when He says, "[b]All things are put in subjection," it
is evident that He is excepted who put all things in subjection
to Him.
28 And when [a]all things are subjected to Him, then the
Son Himself also will be subjected to the one who subjected all
things to Him, that God may be all in all.
29 Otherwise, what will those do who are baptized for the
dead? If the dead are not raised at all, why then are they
baptized for them?
30 Why are we also [a]in danger every hour?
31 I protest, brethren, by the boasting in you, which I have
in Christ Jesus our Lord, [a]I die daily.
32 If [1]from human motives I [a]fought with wild beasts at
[b]Ephesus, what does it profit me? If the dead are not raised,
[c]LET US EAT AND DRINK, FOR TOMORROW WE DIE.
33 [a]Do not be deceived: "Bad company corrupts good
morals."
34 [a]Become sober-minded [1]as you ought, and stop sinning;
for some have [b]no knowledge of God. [c]I speak *this* to your
shame.
35 But [a]some one will say, "How are [b]the dead raised?
And with what kind of body do they come?"
36 [a]You fool! That which you [b]sow does not come to life
unless it dies;
37 and that which you sow, you do not sow the body
which is to be, but a bare grain, perhaps of wheat or of [1]something
else.
38 But God gives it a body just as He wished, and [a]to each
of the seeds a body of its own.
39 All flesh is not the same flesh, but there is *one flesh* of
men, and another flesh of beasts, and another flesh of birds,
and another of fish.
40 There are also heavenly bodies and earthly bodies, but
the glory of the heavenly is one, and the *glory* of the earthly is
another.
41 There is one glory of the sun, and another glory of the
moon, and another glory of the stars; for star differs from star
in glory.
42 [a]So also is the resurrection of the dead. It is sown [1b]a
perishable *body*, it is raised [2c]an imperishable *body;*
43 it is sown in dishonor, it is raised in [a]glory; it is sown in
weakness, it is raised in power;
44 it is sown a [a]natural body, it is raised a [b]spiritual body.
If there is a natural body, there is also a spiritual *body*.
45 So also it is written, "The first [a]MAN, Adam, BECAME A
LIVING SOUL." The [b]last Adam *became* a [c]life-giving spirit.
46 However, the spiritual is not first, but the natural; then
the spiritual.
47 The first man is [a]from the earth, [1b]earthy; the second
man is from heaven.
48 As is the earthy, so also are those who are earthy; and as
is the heavenly, [a]so also are those who are heavenly.

25 [a]Ps. 110:1; Matt. 22:44

26 [a]2 Tim. 1:10; Rev. 20:14; 21:4

27 [a]Ps. 8:7 [b]Eph. 1:22; Heb. 2:8; Matt. 11:27; 28:18

28 [a]Phil. 3:21 [b]1 Cor. 12:6; 3:23

30 [a]2 Cor. 11:26

31 [a]Rom. 8:36

32 [1]Lit., *according to man* [a]2 Cor. 1:8? [b]1 Cor. 16:8f.; Acts 18:19 [c]Is. 22:13; 56:12; Luke 12:19

33 [a]1 Cor. 6:9

34 [1]Lit., *righteously* [a]Rom. 13:11 [b]Matt. 22:29; Acts 26:8 [c]1 Cor. 6:5

35 [a]Rom. 9:19 [b]Ezek. 37:3

36 [a]Luke 11:40 [b]John 12:24

37 [1]Lit., *some of the rest*

38 [a]Gen. 1:11

42 [1]Lit., *in corruption* [2]Lit., *in incorruption* [a]Dan. 12:3; Matt. 13:43 [b]1 Cor. 15:50; Rom. 8:21; Gal. 6:8 [c]Rom. 2:7

43 [a]Phil. 3:21; Col. 3:4

44 [a]1 Cor. 2:14 [b]1 Cor. 15:50

45 [a]Gen. 2:7 [b]Rom. 5:14 [c]John 5:21; 6:57f.; Rom. 8:2

47 [1]Lit., *made of dust* [a]John 3:31 [b]Gen. 2:7; 3:19

48 [a]Phil. 3:20f.

49 And just as we have [a]borne the image of the earthy, [1]we
[b]shall also bear the image of the heavenly.
50 Now I say this, brethren, that [a]flesh and blood cannot
[b]inherit the kingdom of God; nor does [1]the perishable inherit
[2c]the imperishable.
51 Behold, I tell you a [a]mystery; we shall not all sleep, but
we shall all be [b]changed,
52 in a moment, in the twinkling of an eye, at the last
trumpet; for [a]the trumpet will sound, and [b]the dead will be
raised [1]imperishable, and [c]we shall be changed.
53 For this [1]perishable must put on [2a]the imperishable,
and this [b]mortal must put on immortality.
54 But when this [1]perishable will have put on [1]the imperishable, and this mortal will have put on immortality, then will
come about the saying that is written, "[a]DEATH IS SWALLOWED
UP IN VICTORY.
55 "[a]O DEATH, WHERE IS YOUR VICTORY? O DEATH, WHERE IS
YOUR STING?"
56 The sting of [a]death is sin, and [b]the power of sin is the
law;
57 but [a]thanks be to God, who gives us the [b]victory
through our Lord Jesus Christ.
58 [a]Therefore, my beloved brethren, be steadfast, immovable, always abounding in [b]the work of the Lord, knowing
that your toil is not *in* vain in the Lord.

CHAPTER 16

NOW concerning [a]the collection for [b]the saints, as [c]I directed the churches of [d]Galatia, so do you also.
2 On [a]the first day of every week let each one of you [1]put
aside and save, as he may prosper, that [b]no collections be made
when I come.
3 And when I arrive, [a]whomever you may approve, I shall
send them with letters to carry your gift to Jerusalem;
4 and if it is fitting for me to go also, they will go with
me.
5 But I [a]shall come to you after I go through [b]Macedo-
nia, for I [c]am going through Macedonia;
6 and perhaps I shall stay with you, or even spend the
winter, that you may [a]send me on my way wherever I may go.
7 For I do not wish to see you now [a]*just* in passing; for I
hope to remain with you for some time, [b]if the Lord permits.
8 But I shall remain in [a]Ephesus until [b]Pentecost;
9 for a [a]wide door [1]for effective *service* has opened to
me, and [b]there are many adversaries.
10 Now if [a]Timothy comes, see that he is with you without [1]cause to be afraid; for he is doing [b]the Lord's work, as I
also am.
11 [a]Let no one therefore despise him. But [b]send him on
his way [c]in peace, so that he may come to me; for I expect him
with the brethren.
12 But concerning [a]Apollos our brother, I encouraged him
greatly to come to you with the brethren; and it was not at all
his desire to come now, but he will come when he has
opportunity.

49 [1]Some ancient mss. read, *let us also* [a]Gen. 5:3 [b]Rom. 8:29

50 [1]Lit., *corruption* [2]Lit., *incorruption* [a]Matt. 16:17; John 3:5f. [b]1 Cor. 6:9 [c]Rom. 2:7

51 [a]1 Cor. 13:2 [b]2 Cor. 5:2, 4

52 [1]Lit., *incorruptible* [a]Matt. 24:31 [b]John 5:28 [c]1 Thess. 4:15, 17

53 [1]Lit., *corruptible* [2]Lit., *incorruption* [a]Rom. 2:7 [b]2 Cor. 5:4

54 [1]Note vs. 53 [a]Is. 25:8

55 [a]Hos. 13:14

56 [a]Rom. 5:12 [b]Rom. 3:20; 4:15; 7:8

57 [a]2 Cor. 2:14; Rom. 7:25 marg. [b]Rom. 8:37; Heb. 2:14f.; 1 John 5:4; Rev. 21:4

58 [a]2 Pet. 3:14 [b]1 Cor. 16:10

1 [a]Acts 24:17 [b]Acts 9:13 [c]1 Cor. 4:17 [d]Acts 16:6

2 [1]Lit., *put by himself* [a]Acts 20:7 [b]2 Cor. 9:4f.

3 [a]2 Cor. 8:18f.; 3:1

5 [a]1 Cor. 4:19 [b]Rom. 15:26 [c]Acts 19:21

6 [a]1 Cor. 16:11; Acts 15:3

7 [a]2 Cor. 1:15f. [b]Acts 18:21

8 [a]Acts 18:19 [b]Acts 2:1

9 [1]Lit., *and* [a]Acts 14:27 [b]Acts 19:9

10 [1]Lit., *fear; for* [a]Acts 16:1; 1 Cor. 4:17; 2 Cor. 1:1 [b]1 Cor. 15:58

11 [a]1 Tim. 4:12; Titus 2:15 [b]1 Cor. 16:6; Acts 15:3 [c]Acts 15:33

12 [a]Acts 18:24 [1 Cor. 1:12; 3:5f.]

13 [a]Be on the alert, [b]stand firm in the faith, [c]act like men,
[d]be strong.
14 Let all that you do be done [a]in love.
15 Now I urge you, brethren (you know the [a]household of
Stephanas, that [1]they were the [b]firstfruits of [c]Achaia, and that
they have devoted themselves for [d]ministry to [e]the saints),
16 that [a]you also be in subjection to such men and to
everyone who helps in the work and labors.
17 And I rejoice over the [1a]coming of Stephanas and For-
tunatus and Achaicus; because they have [2]supplied [b]what was
lacking on your part.
18 For they [a]have refreshed my spirit and yours. Therefore
[b]acknowledge such men.
19 The churches of [a]Asia greet you. [b]Aquila and Prisca
greet you heartily in the Lord, with [c]the church that is in their
house.
20 All the brethren greet you. [a]Greet one another with a
holy kiss.
21 The greeting is in [a]my own hand—[1]Paul.
22 If any one does not love the Lord, let him be [1a]ac-
cursed. [2b]Maranatha.
23 [a]The grace of the Lord Jesus be with you.
24 My love be with you all in Christ Jesus. Amen.

13 [a]Matt. 24:42 [b]Gal. 5:1; Phil. 1:27; 4:1; 1 Thess. 3:8; 2 Thess. 2:15; 1 Cor. 15:1 [c]1 Sam. 4:9; 2 Sam. 10:12; Is. 46:8 [d]Ps. 31:24; Eph. 6:10; 3:16; Col. 1:11

14 [a]1 Cor. 14:1

15 [1]Lit., *it was* [a]1 Cor. 1:16 [b]Rom. 16:5 [c]Acts 18:12 [d]Rom. 15:31 [e]1 Cor. 16:1

16 [a]1 Thess. 5:12; Heb. 13:17

17 [1]Or, *presence* [2]Or, *made up for your absence* [a]2 Cor. 7:6f. [b]Phil. 2:30; 2 Cor. 11:9

18 [a]2 Cor. 7:13; Philem. 7, 20 [b]Phil. 2:29; 1 Thess. 5:12

19 [a]Acts 16:6 [b]Acts 18:2 [c]Rom. 16:5

20 [a]Rom. 16:16

21 [1]Lit., *Paul's* [a]Col. 4:18; 2 Thess. 3:17; Rom. 16:22; Gal. 6:11; Philem. 19

22 [1]Gr., anathema [2]I.e., O [our] Lord come! [a]Rom. 9:3 [b]Rev. 22:20; Phil. 4:5

23 [a]Rom. 16:20

THE SECOND EPISTLE OF PAUL TO THE

CORINTHIANS

Salutation. The Divine Comfort.

PAUL, [a]an apostle of [b]Christ Jesus [c]by the will of God, and
[d]Timothy *our* brother, to [e]the church of God which is at [f]Cor-
inth with all the [1]saints who are throughout [g]Achaia:
2 [a]Grace to you and peace from God our Father and the
Lord Jesus Christ.
3 [a]Blessed *be* the God and Father of our Lord Jesus
Christ, the Father of mercies and [b]God of all comfort;
4 who [a]comforts us in all our affliction so that we may be
able to comfort those who are in any affliction with the comfort with which we ourselves are comforted by God.
5 For just [a]as the sufferings of Christ are [1]ours in abundance, so also our comfort is abundant through Christ.
6 But if we are afflicted, it is [a]for your comfort and salvation; or if we are comforted, it is for your comfort, which is
effective in the patient enduring of the same sufferings which
we also suffer;
7 and our hope for you is firmly grounded, knowing that
[a]as you are sharers of our sufferings, so also you are *sharers* of
our comfort.
8 For [a]we do not want you to be unaware, brethren, of
our [b]affliction which came *to us* in [1c]Asia, that we were burdened excessively, beyond our strength, so that we despaired
even of life;

1 [1]I.e., true believers; lit., *holy ones* [a]Eph. 1:1; Col. 1:1; 2 Tim. 1:1; Titus 1:1; Rom. 1:1; Gal. 1:1 [b]Gal. 3:26 [c]1 Cor. 1:1 [d]2 Cor. 1:19; 1 Cor. 16:10; Acts 16:1 [e]1 Cor. 10:32 [f]Acts 18:1 [g]Acts 18:12

2 [a]Rom. 1:7

3 [a]Eph. 1:3; 1 Pet. 1:3 [b]Rom. 15:5

4 [a]2 Cor. 7:6, 7, 13; Is. 51:12; 66:13

5 [1]Lit., *to us* [a]2 Cor. 4:10; Phil. 3:10; Col. 1:24

6 [a]2 Tim. 2:10; 2 Cor. 4:15; 12:15; Eph. 3:1, 13

7 [a]Rom. 8:17

8 [1]I.e., west coast province of Asia Minor [a]Rom. 1:13 [b]Acts 19:23; 1 Cor. 15:32 [c]Acts 16:6

9 [1]indeed, we had the sentence of death within ourselves in order that we should not trust in ourselves, but in God who raises the dead;

10 who [a]delivered us from so great a *peril of* death, and will deliver *us,* [1]He [b]on whom we have set our hope. And He will yet deliver us,

11 you also joining in [a]helping us through your prayers, that thanks may be given by [b]many persons on our behalf for the favor bestowed upon us through *the prayers of* many.

12 For our [1]proud confidence is this, the testimony of [a]our conscience that in holiness and [b]godly sincerity, [c]not in fleshly wisdom but in the grace of God, we have conducted ourselves in the world, and especially toward you.

13 For we write nothing else to you than what you read and understand, and I hope you will understand [a]until the end;

14 just as you also partially did understand us, that we are your reason to be proud as you also are ours, in [a]the day of our Lord Jesus.

15 And in this confidence I intended at first to [a]come to you, that you might [1]twice receive a [2b]blessing;

16 [1]that is, to [a]pass [2]your way into [b]Macedonia, and again from Macedonia to come to you, and by you to be [c]helped on my journey [d]to Judea.

17 Therefore, I was not vacillating when I intended to do this, was I? Or that which I purpose, do I purpose [a]according to the flesh, that with me there should be yes, yes and no, no *at the same time?*

18 But as [a]God is faithful, [b]our word to you is not yes and no.

19 For [a]the Son of God, Christ Jesus, who was preached among you by us,—by me and [b]Silvanus and [c]Timothy—was not yes and no, but is yes [d]in Him.

20 For [a]as many as may be the promises of God, [b]in Him they are yes; wherefore also by Him is [c]our Amen to the glory of God through us.

21 Now He who [a]establishes us with you in Christ and [b]anointed us is God,

22 who also [a]sealed us and [b]gave *us* the Spirit in our hearts as a [1]pledge.

23 But [a]I call God as witness [1]to my soul, that [b]to spare you I came no more to [c]Corinth.

24 Not that we [a]lord it over your faith, but are workers with you for your joy; for in your faith you are [b]standing firm.

Chapter 2

BUT I determined this [1]for my own sake, that I [a]would not come to you in sorrow again.

2 For if I [a]cause you sorrow, who then makes me glad but the one whom I made sorrowful?

3 And this is the very thing I [a]wrote you, lest, [b]when I came, I should have sorrow from those who ought to make me rejoice; having [c]confidence in you all, that my joy would be *the joy* of you all.

4 For out of much affliction and anguish of heart I [a]wrote to you with many tears; not that you should be made

9 [1]Lit., *but we ourselves*

10 [1]Or, *on whom we have set our hope that He will also . . .*
[a]Rom. 15:31 [b]1 Tim. 4:10

11 [a]Rom. 15:30; Phil. 1:19; Philem. 22 [b]2 Cor. 4:15; 9:11f.

12 [1]Lit., *boasting*
[a]Acts 23:1; 1 Thess. 2:10; Heb. 13:18 [b]2 Cor. 2:17
[c]1 Cor. 1:17; James 3:15

13 [a]1 Cor. 1:8

14 [a]1 Cor. 1:8

15 [1]Lit., *have a second grace* [2]Some ancient mss. read, *joy*
[a]1 Cor. 4:19 [b]Rom. 1:11; 15:29

16 [1]Lit., *and* [2]Lit., *through you into*
[a]Acts 19:21; 1 Cor. 16:5-7
[b]Rom. 15:26 [c]Acts 15:3; 1 Cor. 16:6, 11 [d]Acts 19:21

17 [a]2 Cor. 10:2f.; 11:18

18 [a]1 Cor. 1:9 [b]2 Cor. 2:17

19 [a]Matt. 16:16; 26:63, 4:3
[b]1 Thess. 1:1; 2 Thess. 1:1; 1 Pet. 5:12; Acts 15:22
[c]2 Cor. 1:1 [d]Heb. 13:8

20 [a]Rom. 15:8 [b]Heb. 13:8
[c]1 Cor. 14:16; Rev. 3:14

21 [a]1 Cor. 1:8 [b]1 John 2:20, 27

22 [1]Or, *down payment*
[a]John 3:33 [b]2 Cor. 5:5; Eph. 1:14; Rom. 8:16

23 [1]Lit., *upon*
[a]Rom. 1:9; Gal. 1:20 [b]1 Cor. 4:21; 2 Cor. 2:1, 3 [c]2 Cor. 1:1

24 [a]1 Pet. 5:3; 2 Cor. 4:5; 11:20 [b]Rom 11:20; 1 Cor. 15:1

1 [1]Or, *as far as I am concerned*
[a]1 Cor. 4:21; 2 Cor. 12:21

2 [a]2 Cor. 7:8

3 [a]2 Cor. 2:9; 7:8, 12
[b]1 Cor. 4:21; 2 Cor. 12:21
[c]Gal. 5:10; 2 Thess. 3:4; Philem. 21

4 [a]2 Cor. 2:9; 7:8, 12

sorrowful, but that you might know the love which I have
especially for you.
5 But [a]if any has caused sorrow, he has caused sorrow not
to me, but in some degree—[1]in order not to say too much—to
all of you.
6 Sufficient for such a one is [a]this punishment which was
inflicted by the majority,
7 so that on the contrary you should rather [a]forgive and
comfort *him*, lest somehow such a one be overwhelmed by
excessive sorrow.
8 Wherefore I urge you to reaffirm *your* love for him.
9 For to this end also [a]I wrote that I might [1b]put you to
the test, whether you are [c]obedient in all things.
10 But whom you forgive anything, I *forgive* also; for
indeed what I have forgiven, if I have forgiven anything, *I did
it* for your sakes [a]in the presence of Christ,
11 in order that no advantage be taken of us by [a]Satan; for
[b]we are not ignorant of his schemes.
12 Now when I came to [a]Troas for the [b]gospel of Christ
and when a [c]door was opened for me in the Lord,
13 I [a]had no rest for my spirit, not finding [b]Titus my
brother; but [c]taking my leave of them, I went on to
[d]Macedonia.
14 [a]But thanks be to God, who always [b]leads us in His
triumph in Christ, and manifests through us the [c]sweet aroma
of the [d]knowledge of Him in every place.
15 For we are a [a]fragrance of Christ to God among [b]those
who are being saved and among those who are perishing;
16 [a]to the one an aroma from death to death, to the other
an aroma from life to life. And who is [b]adequate for these
things?
17 For we are not like many, [1a]peddling the word of God,
but [b]as from sincerity, but as from God, we speak in Christ [c]in
the sight of God.

Chapter 3

ARE we beginning to [a]commend ourselves again? Or do we
need, as some, [b]letters of commendation to you or from you?
2 [a]You are our letter, written in our hearts, known and
read by all men;
3 being manifested that you are a letter of Christ, [1a]cared
for by us, written not with ink, but with the Spirit of [b]the living
God, not on [c]tablets of stone, but on [d]tablets of [2e]human
hearts.
4 And such [a]confidence we have through Christ toward
God.
5 Not that we are adequate in ourselves to consider anything as *coming* from ourselves, but [a]our adequacy is from God,
6 who also made us adequate *as* [a]servants of a [b]new covenant, not of [c]the letter, but of the Spirit; for the letter kills, but
[d]the Spirit gives life.
7 But if the [a]ministry of death, [b]in letters engraved on
stones, came [1]with glory, [c]so that the sons of Israel could not
look intently at the face of Moses because of the glory of his
face, fading *as* it was,

5 [1]Lit., *that I be not burdensome* [a]1 Cor. 5:1f.

6 [a]1 Cor. 5:4f.; 2 Cor. 7:11

7 [a]Gal. 6:1; Eph. 4:32

9 [1]Lit., *know the proof of you* [a]2 Cor. 2:3f. [b]Phil. 2:22; 2 Cor. 8:2 [c]2 Cor. 7:15; 10:6

10 [a]1 Cor. 5:4; 2 Cor. 4:6

11 [a]Matt. 4:10 [b]Luke 22:31; 2 Cor. 4:4; 1 Pet. 5:8

12 [a]Acts 16:8 [b]2 Cor. 4:3, 4; 8:18; 9:13; 10:14; 11:4, 7; 1 Thess. 3:2; Rom. 1:1 [c]Acts 14:27

13 [a]2 Cor. 7:5 [b]2 Cor. 7:6, 13f.; 8:6, 16, 23; 12:18; Gal. 2:1, 3; 2 Tim. 4:10; Titus 1:4 [c]Mark 6:46 [d]Rom. 15:26

14 [a]Rom. 1:8; 6:17; 1 Cor. 15:57; 2 Cor. 8:16; 9:15 [b]Col. 2:15 [Gr.] [c]Eph. 5:2; Phil. 4:18; Song of Sol. 1:3; Ezek. 20:41 [d]1 Cor. 12:8

15 [a]Eph. 5:2; Phil. 4:18; Song of Sol. 1:3; Ezek. 20:41 [b]1 Cor. 1:18

16 [a]Luke 2:34; John 9:39; 1 Pet. 2:7f. [b]2 Cor. 3:5f.

17 [1]Or, *corrupting* [a]2 Cor. 4:2; Gal. 1:6-9 [b]2 Cor. 1:12; 1 Cor. 5:8; 1 Thess. 2:4; 1 Pet. 4:11 [c]2 Cor. 12:19

1 [a]2 Cor. 5:12; 10:12, 18; 12:11 [b]Acts 18:27; Rom. 16:1; 1 Cor. 16:3

2 [a]1 Cor. 9:2

3 [1]Lit., *served* [2]Lit., *hearts of flesh* [a]2 Cor. 3:6 [b]Matt. 16:16 [c]2 Cor. 3:7; Ex. 24:12; 31:18; 32:15f. [d]Prov. 3:3; 7:3; Jer. 17:1 [e]Jer. 31:33; Ezek. 11:19

4 [a]Eph. 3:12

5 [a]1 Cor. 15:10

6 [a]1 Cor. 3:5 [b]Luke 22:20 [c]Rom. 2:29 [d]John 6:63; Rom. 7:6

7 [1]Or, *in glory* [a]2 Cor. 3:9; Rom. 7:5f.; Gal. 3:10, 21f.; Rom. 4:15; 5:20 [b]2 Cor. 3:3; Ex. 24:12; 31:18; 32:15f. [c]2 Cor. 3:13; Ex. 34:29-35

8 how shall the ministry of the Spirit fail to be even more
with glory?
9 For if [a]the ministry of condemnation has glory, much
more does the [b]ministry of righteousness abound in glory.
10 For indeed what had glory, in this case has no glory on
account of the glory that surpasses *it*.
11 For if that which fades away *was* [1]with glory, much
more that which remains *is* in glory.
12 [a]Having therefore such a hope, [b]we use great boldness
in *our* speech,
13 and *are* not as Moses, [a]*who* used to put a veil over his
face that the sons of Israel might not look intently at the end
of what was fading away.
14 But their minds were [a]hardened; for until this very day
at the [b]reading of [c]the old covenant the same veil [1]remains
unlifted, because it is removed in Christ.
15 But to this day whenever Moses is read, a veil lies over
their heart;
16 [a]BUT WHENEVER A MAN TURNS TO THE LORD, THE VEIL IS
TAKEN AWAY.
17 Now the Lord is the Spirit; and where [a]the Spirit of the
Lord is, [b]*there* is liberty.
18 But we all, with unveiled face [a]beholding as in a mirror
the [b]glory of the Lord, are being [c]transformed into the same
image from glory to glory, just as from [d]the Lord, the Spirit.

CHAPTER 4

1 THEREFORE since we have this [a]ministry, as we [b]received
mercy, we [c]do not lose heart,
2 but we have renounced the [a]things hidden because of
shame, not walking in craftiness or [b]adulterating the word of
God, but by the manifestation of truth [c]commending ourselves to every man's conscience in the sight of God.
3 And even if our [a]gospel is [b]veiled, it is veiled [1]to [c]those
who are perishing,
4 in whose case [a]the god of [b]this [1]world has [c]blinded the
minds of the unbelieving, [2]that they might not see the [d]light of
the gospel of the [e]glory of Christ, who is the [f]image of God.
5 For we [a]do not preach ourselves but Christ Jesus as
Lord, and ourselves as your bond-servants [1]for Jesus' sake.
6 For God, who said, "[a]Light shall shine out of darkness," is the One who has [b]shone in our hearts to give the
[c]light of the knowledge of the glory of God in the face of
Christ.
7 But we have this treasure in [a]earthen vessels, that the
surpassing greatness of [b]the power may be of God and not
from ourselves;
8 *we are* [a]afflicted in every way, but not [b]crushed; [c]per-
plexed, but not despairing;
9 [a]persecuted, but not [b]forsaken; [c]struck down, but not
destroyed;
10 [a]always carrying about in the body the dying of Jesus,
that [b]the life of Jesus also may be manifested in our body.
11 For we who live are constantly being delivered over to

9 [a]2 Cor. 3:7; Deut. 27:26; Heb. 12:18-21 [b]Rom. 1:17; 3:21f.

11 [1]Lit., *through*

12 [a]2 Cor. 7:4 [b]2 Cor. 7:4; Eph. 6:19; Acts 4:13, 29; 1 Thess. 2:2

13 [a]2 Cor. 3:7

14 [1]Or, *remains, it not being revealed that it is done away in Christ.* [a]Rom. 11:7; 2 Cor. 4:4 [b]Acts 13:15 [c]2 Cor. 3:6

16 [a]Ex. 34:34; Rom. 11:23

17 [a]Gal. 4:6; Is. 61:1f. [b]John 8:32; Gal. 5:1, 13

18 [a]1 Cor. 13:12 [b]2 Cor. 4:4, 6; John 17:22, 24 [c]Rom. 8:29 [d]2 Cor. 3:17

1 [a]1 Cor. 3:5 [b]1 Cor. 7:25 [c]2 Cor. 4:16; Luke 18:1; Gal. 6:9; Eph. 3:13; 2 Thess. 3:13

2 [a]Rom. 6:21; 1 Cor. 4:5 [b]2 Cor. 2:17 [c]2 Cor. 5:11f.

3 [1]Lit., *in* [a]2 Cor. 2:12 [b]2 Cor. 3:14; 1 Cor. 2:6ff. [c]1 Cor. 1:18; 2 Cor. 2:15

4 [1]Lit., *age* [2]Or, *that the light . . . image of God, should not dawn* upon them [a]John 12:31 [b]Matt. 13:22 [c]2 Cor. 3:14 [d]2 Cor. 4:6; Acts 26:18 [e]2 Cor. 3:18; 4:6 [f]Col. 1:15; Phil. 2:6; Heb. 1:3; John 1:18

5 [1]Or, *through Jesus* [a]1 Thess. 2:6f. [1 Cor. 4:15f.]

6 [a]Gen. 1:3 [b]2 Pet. 1:19 [c]2 Cor. 4:4; Acts 26:18

7 [a]2 Cor. 5:1; 2 Tim. 2:20; Job 4:19; 10:9; 33:6; Lam. 4:2 [b]1 Cor. 2:5; Judg. 7:2

8 [a]2 Cor. 7:5; 1:8 [b]2 Cor. 6:12 [c]Gal. 4:20

9 [a]John 15:20; Rom. 8:35f. [b]Heb. 13:5; Ps. 129:2 [c]Ps. 37:24; Prov. 24:16; Mic. 7:8

10 [a]Rom. 6:5; 8:36; Gal. 6:17 [b]Rom. 6:8

death for Jesus' sake, that the life of Jesus also may be manifested in our mortal flesh.

12 So death works in us, but life in you.

13 But having the same [a]spirit of faith, according to what is written, "[b]I BELIEVED, THEREFORE I SPOKE," we also believe, therefore also we speak;

14 knowing that He who [a]raised the Lord Jesus [b]will raise us also with Jesus and will [c]present us with you.

15 For all things *are* [a]for your sakes, that the grace which is [1b]spreading to more and more people may cause the giving of thanks to abound to the glory of God.

16 Therefore we [a]do not lose heart, but though our outer man is decaying, yet our [b]inner man is [c]being renewed day by day.

17 For momentary, [a]light affliction is producing for us an eternal weight of glory far beyond all comparison,

18 while we [a]look not at the things which are seen, but at the things which are not seen; for the things which are seen are temporal, but the things which are not seen are eternal.

CHAPTER 5

FOR we know that if [1]the [a]earthly [b]tent which is our house is torn down, we have a building from God, a house [c]not made with hands, eternal in the heavens.

2 For indeed in this *house* we [a]groan, longing to be [b]clothed with our dwelling from heaven;

3 inasmuch as we, having put it on, shall not be found naked.

4 For indeed while we are in this tent, we [a]groan, being burdened, because we do not want to be unclothed, but to be [b]clothed, in order that what is [c]mortal may be swallowed up by life.

5 Now He who prepared us for this very purpose is God, who [a]gave to us the Spirit as a [1]pledge.

6 Therefore, being always of good courage, and knowing that [a]while we are at home in the body we are absent from the Lord—

7 for [a]we walk by faith, not by [1]sight—

8 we are of good courage, I say, and [a]prefer rather to be absent from the body and [b]to be at home with the Lord.

9 Therefore also we have as our ambition, whether at home or absent, to be [a]pleasing to Him.

10 For we must all appear before [a]the judgment-seat of Christ, that each one may be recompensed for [1]his deeds in the body, according to what he has done, whether good or bad.

11 Therefore knowing the [a]fear of the Lord, we persuade men, but we are made manifest to God; and I hope that we are [b]made manifest also in your consciences.

12 We are not [a]again commending ourselves to you but *are* giving you an [b]occasion to be proud of us, that you may have *an answer* for those who take pride in appearance, and not in heart.

13 For if we [1]are [a]beside ourselves, it is for God; if we are of sound mind, it is for you.

13 [a]1 Cor. 12:9 [b]Ps. 116:10

14 [a]Acts 2:24 [b]1 Thess. 4:14 [c]Eph. 5:27; Col. 1:22; Jude 24; Luke 21:36

15 [1]Lit., *being multiplied through the many*
[a]2 Cor. 1:6; Rom. 8:28
[b]2 Cor. 1:11; 1 Cor. 9:19

16 [a]2 Cor. 4:1 [b]Rom. 7:22 [c]Col. 3:10; Is. 40:29, 31

17 [a]Rom. 8:18

18 [a]2 Cor. 5:7; Rom. 8:24; Heb. 11:1, 13

1 [1]Lit., *our earthly house of the tent*
[a]1 Cor. 15:47; 2 Cor. 4:7; Job 4:19 [b]2 Pet. 1:13f. [c]Mark 14:58; Acts 7:48; Heb. 9:11, 24

2 [a]Rom. 8:23; 2 Cor. 5:4 [b]1 Cor. 15:53f.; 2 Cor. 5:4

4 [a]2 Cor. 5:2 [b]1 Cor. 15:53f.; 2 Cor. 5:2 [c]1 Cor. 15:54

5 [1]Or, *down payment*
[a]2 Cor. 1:22; Rom. 8:23

6 [a]Heb. 11:13f.

7 [1]Or, *appearance*
[a]2 Cor. 4:18; 1 Cor. 13:12

8 [a]Phil. 1:23 [b]John 12:26; Phil. 1:23

9 [a]Rom. 14:18; Col. 1:10; 1 Thess. 4:1

10 [1]Lit., *the things through the body*
[a]Matt. 16:27; Acts 10:42; Rom. 2:16; 14:10, 12; Eph. 6:8

11 [a]Heb. 10:31; 12:29; Jude 23 [b]2 Cor. 4:2

12 [a]2 Cor. 3:1 [b]2 Cor. 1:14; Phil. 1:26

13 [1]Lit., *were*
[a]2 Cor. 11:1, 16ff.; 12:11; Mark 3:21

14 For the love of Christ [a]controls us, having concluded
this, that [b]one died for all, therefore all died;
15 and He died for all, that they who live should no longer
[a]live for themselves, but for Him who died and rose again on
their behalf.
16 Therefore from now on we recognize no man [1a]accord-
ing to the flesh; even though we have known Christ [1]accord-
ing to the flesh, yet now we know *Him thus* no longer.
17 Therefore if any man is [a]in Christ, [1]*he is* [b]a new creature; [c]the old things passed away; behold, new things have
come.
18 Now [a]all *these* things are from God, [b]who reconciled us
to Himself through Christ, and gave us the [c]ministry of
reconciliation,
19 namely, that [a]God was in Christ reconciling the world
to Himself, [b]not counting their trespasses against them, and
[1]He has [2]committed to us the word of reconciliation.
20 Therefore, we are [a]ambassadors for Christ, [b]as though
God were entreating through us; we beg you on behalf of
Christ, be [c]reconciled to God.
21 He made Him who [a]knew no sin *to be* [b]sin on our
behalf, that we might become the [c]righteousness of God in
Him.

Chapter 6

AND [a]working together *with Him*, [b]we also urge you not to
receive [c]the grace of God in vain;—
2 for He says,
"[a]At the acceptable time I listened to you,
And on the day of salvation I helped you";
behold, now is "the acceptable time," behold, now is "the
day of salvation";—
3 [a]giving no cause for offense in anything, in order that
the ministry be not discredited,
4 but in everything [a]commending ourselves as [1b]servants
of God, [c]in much endurance, in afflictions, in hardships, in
distresses,
5 in [a]beatings, in [a]imprisonments, in [b]tumults, in labors,
in sleeplessness, in [c]hunger,
6 in purity, in [a]knowledge, in [b]patience, in kindness, in
the [c]Holy Spirit, in [d]genuine love,
7 in [a]the word of truth, in [b]the power of God; by [c]the
weapons of righteousness for the right hand and the left,
8 by glory and [a]dishonor, by [b]evil report and good report;
regarded as [c]deceivers and yet [d]true;
9 as unknown yet well-known, as [a]dying yet behold, [b]we
live; as [1]punished yet not put to death,
10 as [a]sorrowful yet always [a]rejoicing, as [b]poor yet making
many rich, as [c]having nothing yet possessing [d]all things.
11 [a]Our mouth [1]has spoken freely to you, O Corinthians,
our [b]heart is opened wide.
12 You are not restrained [1]by us, but [a]you are restrained in
your own [2]affections.
13 Now in a like [a]exchange—I speak as to [b]children,—
open wide *to us* also.

14 [a]Acts 18:5 [b]Rom. 5:15; 6:6f.; Gal. 2:20; Col. 3:3

15 [a]Rom. 14:7-9

16 [1]I.e., by what he is in the flesh [a]2 Cor. 11:18; Phil. 3:4; John 8:15

17 [1]Or, *there is* a new creation [a]Rom. 16:7 [b]Gal. 6:15; John 3:3; Rom. 6:4 [c]Is. 43:18f.; 65:17; Eph. 4:24; Rev. 21:4f.

18 [a]1 Cor. 11:12 [b]Col. 1:20; Rom. 5:10 [c]1 Cor. 3:5

19 [1]Lit., *having committed* [2]Lit., *placed in us* [a]Col. 2:9 [b]Rom. 4:8; 1 Cor. 13:5

20 [a]Eph. 6:20; Mal. 2:7 [b]2 Cor. 6:1 [c]Col. 1:20; Rom. 5:10

21 [a]Heb. 4:15; 7:26; 1 Pet. 2:22; 1 John 3:5; Acts 3:14, [b]Rom. 8:3; Gal. 3:13; Rom. 3:25; 4:25 [c]Rom. 1:17; 3:21f.; 1 Cor. 1:30

1 [a]1 Cor. 3:9 [b]2 Cor. 5:20 [c]Acts 11:23

2 [a]Is. 49:8

3 [a]1 Cor. 8:9, 13; 9:12

4 [1]Or, *ministers* [a]Rom. 3:5 [b]1 Cor. 3:5; 2 Tim. 2:24f. [c]2 Cor. 6:4ff.; 4:8-11; 11:23-27; 12:10; Acts 9:16

5 [a]Acts 16:23 [b]Acts 19:23ff. [c]1 Cor. 4:11

6 [a]2 Cor. 11:6; 1 Cor. 12:8 [b]2 Cor. 1:23; 2:10; 13:10 [c]1 Thess. 1:5; 1 Cor. 2:4 [d]Rom. 12:9

7 [a]2 Cor. 2:17; 4:2 [b]1 Cor. 2:5 [c]2 Cor. 10:4; Rom. 13:12; Eph. 6:11ff.

8 [a]1 Cor. 4:10 [b]1 Cor. 4:13; Rom. 3:8; 2 Cor. 12:16 [c]Matt. 27:63 [d]2 Cor. 1:18; 4:2; 1 Thess. 2:3f.

9 [1]Or, *disciplined* [a]Rom. 8:36 [b]2 Cor. 1:8, 10; 4:11

10 [a]2 Cor. 7:4; 1 Thess. 1:6; Phil. 2:17; 4:4; Col. 1:24; John 16:22 [b]2 Cor. 8:9; 1 Cor. 1:5 [c]Acts 3:6 [d]Rom. 8:32; 1 Cor. 3:21

11 [1]Lit., *is open to you* [a]Ezek. 33:22; Eph. 6:19 [b]2 Cor. 7:3; Is. 60:5

12 [1]Or, *in us* [2]Lit., *inward parts* [a]2 Cor. 7:2

13 [a]Gal. 4:12 [b]1 Cor. 4:14

14 [1]Lit., *unequally yoked* [a]Deut. 22:10; 1 Cor. 5:9f. [b]1 Cor. 6:6 [c]Eph. 5:7, 11; 1 John 1:6

15 [1]Gr., *Beliar* [2]Lit., *what part has a believer with an unbeliever* [a]1 Cor. 10:21 [b]Acts 5:14; 1 Pet. 1:21 [c]1 Cor. 6:6

16 [a]1 Cor. 10:21 [b]1 Cor. 3:16 [c]Matt. 16:16 [d]Lev. 26:12; Ex. 29:45; Ezek. 37:27; Jer. 31:1 [e]Ex. 25:8; John 14:23 [f]Rev. 2:1

17 [a]Is. 52:11 [b]Rev. 18:4

18 [a]Hos. 1:10; Is. 43:6 [b]Rom. 8:14

1 [a]Heb. 6:9 [b]1 Pet. 1:15f.

2 [a]2 Cor. 6:12f.; 12:15

3 [a]2 Cor. 6:11f. [b]Phil. 1:7

4 [1]Lit., *to* [a]2 Cor. 3:12 [b]2 Cor. 7:14; 8:24; 9:2f.; 10:8; 2 Thess. 1:4; Phil. 1:26 [c]2 Cor. 1:4 [d]2 Cor. 6:10

5 [a]2 Cor. 2:13; Rom. 15:26 [b]2 Cor. 4:8 [c]Deut. 32:25

6 [1]Or, *humble* [a]2 Cor. 1:3f. [b]2 Cor. 7:13 [c]2 Cor. 2:13; 7:13f.

8 [a]2 Cor. 2:2

10 [1]Or, leading *to a salvation without regret* [a]Acts 11:18

11 [1]Lit., *sorrow according to God* [a]2 Cor. 7:7 [b]2 Cor. 2:6 [c]Rom. 3:5

12 [a]2 Cor. 7:8; 2:3, 9 [b]1 Cor. 5:1f.

14 [a]Do not be [1]bound together with [b]unbelievers; for what
[c]partnership have righteousness and lawlessness, or what fellowship has light with darkness?
15 Or what [a]harmony has Christ with [1]Belial, or [2]what has
a [b]believer in common with an [c]unbeliever?
16 Or [a]what agreement has the temple of God with idols?
For we are [b]the temple of [c]the living God; just as God said,

"[d]I WILL [e]DWELL IN THEM AND [f]WALK AMONG THEM;
AND I WILL BE THEIR GOD, AND THEY SHALL BE MY PEOPLE.
17 "[a]Therefore, [b]COME OUT FROM THEIR MIDST AND BE SEPARATE, says the Lord.
AND DO NOT TOUCH WHAT IS UNCLEAN;
AND I WILL WELCOME YOU.
18 [a]AND I WILL BE A FATHER TO YOU,
AND YOU SHALL BE [b]SONS and daughters TO ME,
SAYS THE LORD ALMIGHTY."

CHAPTER 7

THEREFORE, having these promises, [a]beloved, [b]let us
cleanse ourselves from all defilement of flesh and spirit, per-
fecting holiness in the fear of God.
2 [a]Make room for us *in your hearts;* we wronged no one,
we corrupted no one, we took advantage of no one.
3 I do not speak to condemn you; for I have said [a]before
that you are [b]in our hearts to die together and to live together.
4 Great is my [a]confidence [1]in you, great is my [b]boasting
on your behalf; I am filled with [c]comfort. I am overflowing
with [d]joy in all our affliction.
5 For even when we came into [a]Macedonia our flesh had
no rest, but we were [b]afflicted on every side: [c]conflicts without,
fears within.
6 But [a]God, who comforts the [1]depressed, [b]comforted us
by the coming of [c]Titus;
7 and not only by his coming, but also by the comfort
with which he was comforted in you, as he reported to us your
longing, your mourning, your zeal for me; so that I rejoiced
even more.
8 For though I [a]caused you sorrow by my letter, I do not
regret it; though I did regret it,—*for* I see that that letter
caused you sorrow, though only for a while—
9 I now rejoice, not that you were made sorrowful, but
that you were made sorrowful to *the point of* repentance; for
you were made sorrowful according to *the will of* God, in
order that you might not suffer loss in anything through us.
10 For the sorrow that is according to *the will of* God
produces a [a]repentance [1]without regret, *leading* to salvation;
but the sorrow of the world produces death.
11 For behold what earnestness this very thing, this [1]godly
sorrow, has produced in you, what vindication of yourselves,
what indignation, what fear, what [a]longing, what zeal, what
[b]avenging of wrong! In everything you [c]demonstrated yourselves to be innocent in the matter.
12 So although [a]I wrote to you *it was* not for the sake of
[b]the offender, nor for the sake of the one offended, but that

your earnestness on our behalf might be made known to you in
the sight of God.
13 For this reason we have been [a]comforted.
And besides our comfort, we rejoiced even much more for
the joy of [b]Titus, because his [c]spirit has been refreshed by you
all.
14 For if in anything I have [a]boasted to him about you, I
was not put to shame; but as we spoke all things to you in
truth, so also our boasting before [b]Titus proved to be *the*
truth.
15 And his [1]affection abounds all the more toward you, as
he remembers the [a]obedience of you all, how you received him
with [b]fear and trembling.
16 I rejoice that in everything [a]I have confidence in you.

Chapter 8

NOW, brethren, we *wish to* make known to you the grace of
God which has been [a]given in the churches of [b]Macedonia,
2 that in a great ordeal of affliction their abundance of
joy and their deep poverty overflowed in the [a]wealth of their
liberality.
3 For I testify that [a]according to their ability, and
beyond their ability *they gave* of their own accord,
4 begging us with much entreaty for the [a]favor of participation in the [1b]support of the [2]saints,
5 and *this,* not as we had [1]expected, but they first [a]gave
themselves to the Lord and to us by [b]the will of God.
6 Consequently we [a]urged [b]Titus that as he had previously [c]made a beginning, so he would also complete in you
[d]this gracious work as well.
7 But just as you [a]abound [b]in everything, in faith and
utterance and knowledge and in all earnestness and in the
[1]love we inspired in you, *see* that you [a]abound in this gracious
work also.
8 I [a]am not speaking *this* as a command, but as proving
through the earnestness of others the sincerity of your love
also.
9 For you know [a]the grace of our Lord Jesus Christ, that
[b]though He was rich, yet for your sake He became poor, that
you through His poverty might become rich.
10 And I [a]give *my* opinion in this matter, for this is to your
advantage, who were the first to begin [b]a year ago not only to
do *this,* but also to desire *to do it.*
11 But now finish [1]doing it also; that just as *there was* the
[a]readiness to desire it, so *there may be* also the completion of
it by your ability.
12 For if the readiness is present, it is acceptable [a]accord-
ing to what *a man* has, not according to what he does not
have.
13 For *this* is not for the ease of others *and* for your
affliction, but by way of equality—
14 at this present time your abundance *being a supply* for
[a]their want, that their abundance also may become *a supply*
for [a]your want, that there may be equality;

13 [a]2 Cor. 7:6 [b]2 Cor. 2:13; 7:6, 14 [c]1 Cor. 16:18

14 [a]2 Cor. 7:4; 8:24; 9:2f.; 10:8; 2 Thess. 1:4; Phil. 1:26 [b]2 Cor. 2:13; 7:6, 13

15 [1]Lit., *inward parts* [a]2 Cor. 2:9 [b]Phil. 2:12; 1 Cor. 2:3

16 [a]2 Cor. 2:3

1 [a]2 Cor. 8:5 [b]Acts 16:9

2 [a]Rom. 2:4

3 [a]2 Cor. 8:11; 1 Cor. 16:2

4 [1]Lit., *service to the saints* [2]I.e., true believers; lit., *holy ones* [a]Rom. 15:25f.; Acts 24:17 [b]2 Cor. 8:19f.; 9:1, 12f.; Rom. 15:31

5 [1]Lit., *hoped* [a]2 Cor. 8:1 [b]1 Cor. 1:1

6 [a]2 Cor. 8:17; 12:18 [b]2 Cor. 8:16, 23; 2:13 [c]2 Cor. 8:10 [d]Rom. 15:25f.; Acts 24:17

7 [1]Lit., *love from us in you;* some ancient mss. read, *your love for us* [a]2 Cor. 9:8 [b]1 Cor. 1:5; 12:8; Rom. 15:14

8 [a]1 Cor. 7:6

9 [a]2 Cor. 13:14 [b]Phil. 2:6f.; Matt. 20:28; 2 Cor. 6:10

10 [a]1 Cor. 7:25, 40 [b]2 Cor. 9:2; 1 Cor. 16:2f.

11 [1]Lit., *the doing* [a]2 Cor. 8:12, 19; 9:2

12 [a]Mark 12:43f.; Luke 21:3; 2 Cor. 9:7

14 [a]2 Cor. 9:12; Acts 4:34

15 as it is written, "[a]HE WHO *gathered* MUCH DID NOT HAVE
TOO MUCH, AND HE WHO *gathered* LITTLE HAD NO LACK."
16 But [a]thanks be to God, who [b]puts the same earnestness
on your behalf in the heart of [c]Titus.
17 For he not only accepted our [a]appeal, but being himself very earnest, he has gone to you of his own accord.
18 And we have sent along with him [a]the brother whose
fame in *the things of* the [b]gospel *has spread* through [c]all the
churches;
19 [a]and not only *this,* but he has also been [b]appointed by
the churches to travel with us in [c]this gracious work, which is
being administered by us for the glory of the Lord Himself,
and *to show* our [d]readiness,
20 [1]taking precaution that no one should discredit us in
our administration of this generous gift;
21 for we [a]have regard for what is honorable, not only in
[b]the sight of the Lord, but also in the sight of men.
22 And we have sent with them our brother, whom we
have often tested and found diligent in many things, but now
even more diligent, because of *his* great confidence in you.
23 As for [a]Titus, *he is* my [b]partner and fellow-worker
[1]among you; as for our [c]brethren, *they are* [2d]messengers of the
churches, [e]a glory to Christ.
24 Therefore [1]openly before the churches [2]show them the
proof of your love and of our [a]reason for boasting about you.

CHAPTER 9

FOR [a]it is superfluous for me to write to you about this
[b]ministry to the [1]saints;
2 for I know your readiness, of which I [a]boast about you
to the [b]Macedonians, *namely,* that [c]Achaia has been prepared
since [d]last year, and your zeal has stirred up most of them.
3 But I have sent the brethren, that our [a]boasting about
you may not be made empty in this case, that, [b]as I was saying,
you may be prepared;
4 lest if any [a]Macedonians come with me and find you
unprepared, we (not to speak of you) should be put to shame
by this confidence.
5 So I thought it necessary to urge the [a]brethren that
they would go on ahead to you and arrange beforehand your
previously promised [1b]bountiful gift, that the same might be
ready as a [1c]bountiful gift, and not [2d]affected by covetousness.
6 Now this *I say,* [a]he who sows sparingly shall also reap
sparingly; and he who sows [1]bountifully shall also reap
[1]bountifully.
7 Let each one *do* just as he has purposed in his heart;
not [a]grudgingly or under compulsion; for [b]God loves a cheerful giver.
8 And [a]God is able to make all grace abound to you, that
always having all sufficiency in everything, you may have an
abundance for every good deed;
9 as it is written,
"[a]HE SCATTERED ABROAD, HE GAVE TO THE POOR,
HIS RIGHTEOUSNESS ABIDES FOREVER."
10 Now He who supplies [a]seed to the sower and bread for

15 [a]Ex. 16:18

16 [a]2 Cor. 2:14 [b]Rev. 17:17 [c]2 Cor. 8:6, 23; 2:13

17 [a]2 Cor. 8:6; 12:18

18 [a]2 Cor. 12:18; 1 Cor. 16:3 [b]2 Cor. 2:12 [c]1 Cor. 7:17; 4:17

19 [a]Rom. 5:3 [b]1 Cor. 16:3f.; Acts 14:23 [c]2 Cor. 8:4, 6 [d]2 Cor. 8:11, 12; 9:2

20 [1]Lit., *avoiding this*

21 [a]Rom. 12:17 [b]Rom. 14:18

23 [1]Lit., *for you* [2]Lit., *apostles* [a]2 Cor. 8:6 [b]Philem. 17 [c]2 Cor. 8:18, 22 [d]Phil. 2:25; John 13:16 [e]1 Cor. 11:7

24 [1]Lit., *in the face of the churches* [2]Or, *show the proof . . . for boasting to them about you* [a]2 Cor. 7:4

1 [1]I.e., true believers; lit., *holy ones* [a]1 Thess. 4:9 [b]2 Cor. 8:4

2 [a]2 Cor. 7:4 [b]Rom. 15:26 [c]Acts 18:12 [d]2 Cor. 8:10

3 [a]2 Cor. 7:4 [b]1 Cor. 16:2

4 [a]Rom. 15:26

5 [1]Gr., *blessing* [2]Lit., *as covetousness* [a]2 Cor. 9:3 [b]Gen. 33:11; Judg. 1:15; 2 Cor. 9:6 [c]Phil. 4:17 [d]2 Cor. 12:17f.

6 [1]Lit., *with blessings* [a]Prov. 11:24f.; 22:9; Gal. 6:7, 9

7 [a]Deut. 15:10; 1 Chr. 29:17; Rom. 12:8; 2 Cor. 8:12 [b]Prov. 22:8 [Sept.]; Ex. 25:2; 2 Cor. 8:12

8 [a]Eph. 3:20

9 [a]Ps. 112:9

10 [a]Is. 55:10

food, will supply and multiply your seed for sowing and [b]in-
crease the harvest of your righteousness;
11 you will be [a]enriched in everything for all liberality,
which through us is producing [b]thanksgiving to God.
12 For the ministry of this service is not only fully sup-
plying [a]the needs of the [1]saints, but is also overflowing
[b]through many thanksgivings to God.
13 Because of the proof given by this [a]ministry they will
[b]glorify God for *your* obedience to your [c]confession of the
[d]gospel of Christ, and for the liberality of your [1]contribution
to them and to all,
14 while they also, by prayer on your behalf, yearn for you
because of the surpassing grace of God in you.
15 [a]Thanks be to God for His indescribable [b]gift!

Chapter 10

NOW [a]I Paul myself [b]urge you by the [c]meekness and gentleness of Christ,—I who [d]am [1]meek when face to face with you,
but bold toward you when absent!—
2 I ask that [a]when I am present I may not be bold with
the confidence with which I propose to be courageous against
[b]some, who regard us as if we walked [c]according to the flesh.
3 For though we walk in the flesh, we do not war [a]accord-
ing to the flesh,
4 for the [a]weapons of our warfare are not of the flesh, but
[1b]divinely powerful [c]for the destruction of fortresses.
5 We *are* destroying speculations and every [a]lofty thing
raised up against the knowledge of God, and *we are* taking
every thought captive to the [b]obedience of Christ,
6 and we are ready to punish all disobedience, whenever
[a]your obedience is complete.
7 [1a]You are looking at [2]things as they are outwardly. [b]If
any one is confident in himself that he is Christ's, let him
consider this again within himself, that just as he is Christ's, [c]so
also are we.
8 For even if [a]I should boast somewhat [1]further about
our [b]authority, which the Lord gave for building you up and
not for destroying you, I shall not be put to shame,
9 [1]for I do not wish to seem as if I would terrify you by
my letters.
10 For they say, "His letters are weighty and strong, but
his [1]personal presence is [a]unimpressive, and [b]his speech
contemptible."
11 Let such a person consider this, that what we are in
word by letters when absent, such persons *we are* also in deed
when present.
12 For we are not bold to class or compare ourselves with
[1]some of those who [a]commend themselves; but when they
measure themselves by themselves, and compare themselves
with themselves, they are without understanding.
13 But we will not boast [a]beyond *our* measure, but [1b]with-
in the measure of the sphere which God apportioned to us as
a measure, to reach even as far as you.
14 For we are not overextending ourselves, as if we did not

10 [b]Hos. 10:12

11 [a]1 Cor. 1:5 [b]2 Cor. 1:11

12 [1]I.e., true believers; lit., *holy ones* [a]2 Cor. 8:14 [b]2 Cor. 1:11

13 [1]Or, *sharing with them* [a]2 Cor. 8:4; Rom. 15:31 [b]Matt. 9:8 [c]1 Tim. 6:12f.; Heb. 3:1; 4:14; 10:23 [d]2 Cor. 2:12

15 [a]2 Cor. 2:14 [b]Rom. 5:15f.

1 [1]Lit., *lowly* [a]Gal. 5:2; Eph. 3:1; Col. 1:23 [b]Rom. 12:1 [c]Matt. 11:29; 1 Cor. 4:21; Phil. 4:5 [d]2 Cor. 10:10; 1 Cor. 2:3f.

2 [a]2 Cor. 13:2, 10; 1 Cor. 4:21 [b]1 Cor. 4:18f. [c]2 Cor. 1:17; Rom. 8:4

3 [a]2 Cor. 1:17; Rom. 8:4

4 [1]Or, *mighty before God* [a]2 Cor. 6:7; 1 Cor. 9:7; 1 Tim. 1:18 [b]Acts 7:20 marg. [c]Jer. 1:10; 2 Cor. 10:8; 13:10

5 [a]Is. 2:11f. [b]2 Cor. 9:13

6 [a]2 Cor. 2:9

7 [1]Or, *Look at . . .*, or, *Do you look at . . . ?* [2]Lit., *what is before your face* [a]John 7:24; 2 Cor. 5:12 [b]1 Cor. 1:12; 14:37 [c]2 Cor. 11:23; 1 Cor. 9:1; Gal. 1:12

8 [1]Or, *more abundantly* [a]2 Cor. 7:4 [b]2 Cor. 13:10

9 [1]Lit., *that I may not seem . . .*

10 [1]Lit., *bodily presence is weak* [a]1 Cor. 2:3; 2 Cor. 12:7; Gal. 4:13f. [b]1 Cor. 1:17; 2 Cor. 11:6

12 [1]Or, *any* [a]2 Cor. 10:18; 3:1

13 [1]Lit., *according to the measure* [a]2 Cor. 10:15 [b]Rom. 12:3; 2 Cor. 10:15f.

reach to you, for [a]we were the first to come even as far as you
in the [b]gospel of Christ;
15 not boasting [a]beyond *our* measure, *that is,* in [b]other
men's labors, but with the hope that as [c]your faith grows, we
shall be, [1]within our sphere, [d]enlarged even more by you,
16 so as to [a]preach the gospel even to [b]the regions beyond
you, *and* not to boast [1c]in what has been accomplished in the
sphere of another.
17 But [a]HE WHO BOASTS, LET HIM BOAST IN THE LORD.
18 For not he who [a]commends himself is approved, but
[b]whom the Lord commends.

CHAPTER 11

I WISH that you would [a]bear with me in a little [b]foolishness;
but [1]indeed you are bearing with me.
2 For I am jealous for you with a godly jealousy; for I
[a]betrothed you to one husband, that to Christ I might [b]present
you *as* a pure virgin.
3 But I am afraid, lest as the [a]serpent deceived Eve by his
craftiness, your minds should be led astray from the simplicity
and purity *of devotion* to Christ.
4 For if one comes and preaches [a]another Jesus whom we
have not preached, or you receive a [b]different spirit which you
have not received, or a [c]different gospel which you have not
accepted, you [d]bear *this* [e]beautifully.
5 For I consider myself [a]not in the least inferior to the
[1]most eminent apostles.
6 But even if I am [a]unskilled in speech, yet I am not *so* in
[b]knowledge; in fact, in every way we have [c]made *this* evident to
you in all things.
7 Or [a]did I commit a sin in humbling myself that you
might be exalted, because I preached the [b]gospel of God to
you [c]without charge?
8 I robbed other churches, [a]taking wages *from them* to
serve you;
9 and when I was present with you and was in need, I was
[a]not a burden to anyone; for when [b]the brethren came from
[c]Macedonia, they fully supplied my need, and in everything I
kept myself from [a]being a burden to you, [1]and will continue to
do so.
10 [a]As the truth of Christ is in me, [b]this boasting of mine
will not be stopped in the regions of [c]Achaia.
11 Why? [a]Because I do not love you? [b]God knows *I do!*
12 But what I am doing, I will continue to do, [a]that I may
cut off opportunity from those who desire an opportunity to
be [1]regarded just as we are in the matter about which they are
boasting.
13 For such men are [a]false apostles, [b]deceitful workers,
disguising themselves as apostles of Christ.
14 And no wonder, for even [a]Satan disguises himself as an
[b]angel of light.
15 Therefore it is not surprising if his servants also disguise
themselves as servants of righteousness; [a]whose end shall be
according to their deeds.

14 [a]1 Cor. 3:6 [b]2 Cor. 2:12

15 [1]Lit., *according to our sphere* [a]2 Cor. 10:13 [b]Rom. 15:20 [c]2 Thess. 1:3 [d]Acts 5:13

16 [1]Lit., *to the things prepared in the . . .* [a]2 Cor. 11:7 [b]Acts 19:21 [c]Rom. 15:20

17 [a]Jer. 9:24; 1 Cor. 1:31

18 [a]2 Cor. 10:12 [b]Rom. 2:29; 1 Cor. 4:5

1 [1]Or, *do indeed bear with me* [a]2 Cor. 11:4, 19f.; Matt. 17:17; 2 Cor. 11:16 [b]2 Cor. 11:17, 21; 5:13

2 [a]Hos. 2:19f.; Eph. 5:26f. [b]2 Cor. 4:14

3 [a]Gen. 3:4, 13; 1 Tim. 2:14; Rev. 12:9, 15; John 8:44; 1 Thess. 3:5

4 [a]1 Cor. 3:11 [b]Rom. 8:15 [c]Gal. 1:6 [d]2 Cor. 11:1 [e]Mark 7:9

5 [1]Or, *super-apostles* [a]2 Cor. 12:11; Gal. 2:6

6 [a]1 Cor. 1:17 [b]1 Cor. 12:8; Eph. 3:4 [c]2 Cor. 4:2

7 [a]2 Cor. 12:13 [b]Rom. 1:1; 2 Cor. 2:12 [c]1 Cor. 9:18; Acts 18:3

8 [a]Phil. 4:15, 18; 1 Cor. 4:12; 9:6

9 [1]Lit., *and I will keep* [a]2 Cor. 12:13f., 16 [b]Acts 18:5 [c]Rom. 15:26

10 [a]Rom. 9:1; 1:9; 2 Cor. 1:23; Gal. 2:20 [b]1 Cor. 9:15 [c]Acts 18:12

11 [a]2 Cor. 12:15 [b]2 Cor. 11:31; 2 Cor. 12:2f.; Rom. 1:9; 2 Cor. 2:17

12 [1]Lit., *found* [a]1 Cor. 9:12

13 [a]Rev. 2:2; Acts 20:30; Gal. 1:7; 2:4; Phil. 1:15; Titus 1:10f.; 2 Pet. 2:1 [b]Phil. 3:2

14 [a]Matt. 4:10; Eph. 6:12; Col. 1:13 [b]Col. 1:12

15 [a]Rom. 2:6; 3:8

16 [a]Again I say, let no one think me foolish; but if *you do,*
receive me even as foolish, that I also may boast a little.
17 That which I am speaking, I am not speaking [1a]as the
Lord would, but as [b]in foolishness, in this confidence of
boasting.
18 Since [a]many boast [b]according to the flesh, I will boast
also.
19 For you, [a]being *so* wise, bear with the foolish gladly.
20 For you bear with anyone if he [a]enslaves you, if he
[b]devours you, if he [c]takes advantage of you, if he [d]exalts himself, if he [e]hits you in the face.
21 To *my* [a]shame I *must* say that we have been [b]weak *by*
comparison. But in whatever respect anyone *else* [c]is bold (I
[d]speak in foolishness), I am just as bold myself.
22 Are they [a]Hebrews? [b]So am I. Are they [c]Israelites? [c]So
am I. Are they [1d]descendants of Abraham? [e]So am I.
23 Are they [a]servants of Christ? (I speak as if insane) I
more so; in [1b]far more labors, in [1c]far more imprisonments,
[2d]beaten times without number, often in [e]danger of death.
24 Five times I received from the Jews [a]thirty-nine *lashes.*
25 Three times I was [a]beaten with rods, once I was
[b]stoned, three times I was shipwrecked, a night and a day I
have spent in the deep.
26 *I have been* on frequent journeys, in dangers from rivers, dangers from robbers, dangers from *my* [a]countrymen,
dangers from the [b]Gentiles, dangers in the [c]city, dangers in the
wilderness, dangers on the sea, dangers among [d]false brethren;
27 *I have been* in [a]labor and hardship, [1]through many
sleepless nights, in [b]hunger and thirst, often [c]without food, in
cold and [2d]exposure.
28 Apart from *such* [1]external things, there is the daily pressure upon me *of* concern for [a]all the churches.
29 Who is [a]weak without my being weak? Who is [1]led into
sin [2]without my intense concern?
30 If I have to boast, I will boast of what pertains to my
[a]weakness.
31 The God and Father of the Lord Jesus, [a]He who is
blessed forever, [b]knows that I am not lying.
32 In [a]Damascus the ethnarch under Aretas the king was
[b]guarding the city of the Damascenes in order to seize me,
33 and I was let down in a basket [a]through a window [1]in
the wall, and *so* escaped his hands.

Chapter 12

[a]BOASTING is necessary, though it is not profitable; but I
will go on to visions and [b]revelations [1]of the Lord.
2 I know a man [a]in Christ who fourteen years ago—whether in the body I do not know, or out of the body I do not
know, [b]God knows—such a man was [c]caught up to the [d]third
heaven.
3 And I know how such a man—whether in the body or
apart from the body I do not know, [a]God knows—
4 was [a]caught up into [b]Paradise, and heard inexpressible
words, which a man is not permitted to speak.

16 [a]2 Cor. 11:1

17 [1]Lit., *in accordance with the Lord* [a]1 Cor. 7:12, 25 [b]2 Cor. 11:21

18 [a]Phil. 3:3f. [b]2 Cor. 5:16

19 [a]1 Cor. 4:10

20 [a]Gal. 2:4; 2 Cor. 1:24; Gal. 4:3, 9; 5:1 [b]Mark 12:40 [c]Luke 5:5; 2 Cor. 11:3; 12:16 [d]2 Cor. 10:5 [e]1 Cor. 4:11

21 [a]2 Cor. 6:8 [b]2 Cor. 10:10 [c]2 Cor. 10:2 [d]2 Cor. 11:17

22 [1]Lit., *seed* [a]Acts 6:1 [b]Phil. 3:5 [c]Rom. 9:4 [d]Gal. 3:16 [e]Rom. 11:1

23 [1]Lit., *more abundantly* [2]Lit., *exceedingly in stripes* [a]2 Cor. 3:6; 1 Cor. 3:5; 2 Cor. 10:7 [b]1 Cor. 15:10 [c]2 Cor 6:5 [d]Acts 16:23; 2 Cor. 6:5 [e]Rom. 8:36

24 [a]Deut. 25:3

25 [a]Acts 16:22 [b]Acts 14:19

26 [a]Acts 9:23; 13:45, 50; 14:5; 17:5, 13; 18:12; 20:3, 19; 21:27; 23:10, 12; 25:3; 1 Thess. 2:15 [b]Acts 14:5, 19; 19:23ff.; 27:42 [c]Acts 21:31 [d]Gal. 2:4

27 [1]Lit., *often in wakefulness* [2]Lit., *nakedness,* lack of clothing [a]1 Thess. 2:9; 2 Thess. 3:8 [b]1 Cor. 4:11; Phil. 4:12 [c]2 Cor. 6:5 [d]1 Cor. 4:11

28 [1]Or, *the things unmentioned* [a]1 Cor. 7:17

29 [1]Lit., *made to stumble* [2]Lit., *and I do not burn* [a]1 Cor. 9:22; 1 Cor. 8:9, 13

30 [a]1 Cor. 2:3

31 [a]Rom. 1:25 [b]2 Cor. 11:11

32 [a]Acts 9:2 [b]Acts 9:24

33 [1]Lit., *through* [a]Acts 9:25

1 [1]Or possibly, *from* [a]2 Cor. 11:30; 11:16, 18; 12:5, 9 [b]2 Cor. 12:7; Gal. 1:12; 2:2; Eph. 3:3; 1 Cor. 14:6

2 [a]Rom. 16:7 [b]2 Cor. 11:11 [c]2 Cor. 12:4; 1 Thess. 4:17; Rev. 12:5; Acts 8:39; Ezek. 8:3 [d]Deut. 10:14; Ps. 148:4; Eph. 4:10; Heb. 4:14

3 [a]2 Cor. 11:11

4 [a]2 Cor. 12:2; 1 Thess. 4:17; Rev. 12:5; Acts 8:39; Ezek. 8:3 [b]Luke 23:43

5 [a]On behalf of such a man will I boast; but on my own
behalf I will not boast, except in regard to *my* [b]weaknesses.
6 For if I do wish to boast I shall not be [a]foolish, [b]for I
shall be speaking the truth; but I refrain *from this,* so that no
one may credit me with more than he sees *in* me or hears from
me.
7 And because of the surpassing greatness of the [a]revela-
tions, for this reason, to keep me from exalting myself, there
was given me a [b]thorn in the flesh, a [c]messenger of Satan to
buffet me—to keep me from exalting myself!
8 Concerning this I entreated the Lord [a]three times that
it might depart from me.
9 And He has said to me, "My grace is sufficient for you,
for [1a]power is perfected in weakness." Most gladly, therefore, I
will rather [b]boast about my weaknesses, that the power of
Christ may dwell in me.
10 Therefore [a]I am well content with weaknesses, with
[1]insults, with [b]distresses, with [c]persecutions, with [b]difficulties,
[d]for Christ's sake; for [e]when I am weak, then I am strong.
11 I have become [a]foolish; you yourselves compelled me.
Actually I should have been commended by you, for [b]in no
respect was I inferior to the [1]most eminent apostles, even
though [c]I am a nobody.
12 The [1a]signs [2]of a true apostle were performed among
you with all perseverance, by [1]signs and wonders and [3]miracles.
13 For in what respect were you treated as inferior to the
rest of the churches, except that [a]I myself did not become a
burden to you? Forgive me [b]this wrong!
14 Here [a]for this third time I am ready to come to you,
and I [b]will not be a burden to you; for I [c]do not seek what is
yours, but [d]you; for [e]children are not responsible to save up for
their parents, but [f]parents for *their* children.
15 And I will [a]most gladly spend and be expended for your
souls. If [b]I love you the more, am I to be loved the less?
16 But be that as it may, I [a]did not burden you myself;
nevertheless, crafty fellow that I am, I [b]took you in by deceit.
17 [a]Certainly I have not taken advantage of you through
any of those whom I have sent to you, have I?
18 I [a]urged [b]Titus *to go,* and sent [c]the brother with him.
Titus did not take any advantage of you, did he? Did we not
[1]conduct ourselves [2]in the same [d]spirit *and walk* [e]in the same
steps?
19 All this time [1]you have been thinking that we are defending ourselves to you. *Actually,* [a]it is in the sight of God that
we have been speaking in Christ; and [b]all for your upbuilding,
[c]beloved.
20 For I am afraid that perhaps [a]when I come I may find
you to be not what I wish and may be found by you to be not
what you wish; that perhaps *there may be* [b]strife, jealousy,
[c]angry tempers, [d]disputes, [e]slanders, [f]gossip, [g]arrogance,
[h]disturbances;
21 I am afraid that when I come again my God may humil-
iate me before you, and I may mourn over many of those who
have [a]sinned in the past and not repented of the [b]impurity,
[1]immorality and sensuality which they have practiced.

5 [a]2 Cor. 12:1 [b]1 Cor. 2:3; 2 Cor. 12:9f.

6 [a]2 Cor. 11:16f.; 2 Cor. 12:11; 2 Cor. 5:13 [b]2 Cor. 7:14

7 [a]2 Cor. 12:1 [b]Num. 33:55; Ezek. 28:24; Hos. 2:6 [c]Job 2:6; 1 Cor. 5:5; Matt. 4:10

8 [a]Matt. 26:44

9 [1]Later mss. read, *My power* [a]Phil. 4:13; 1 Cor. 2:5; Eph. 3:16 [b]1 Cor. 2:3; 2 Cor. 12:5

10 [1]Or, *mistreatment* [a]Rom. 5:3; 8:35 [b]2 Cor. 6:4 [c]2 Thess. 1:4; 2 Tim. 3:11 [d]2 Cor. 5:15, 20 [e]2 Cor. 13:4

11 [1]Or, *super-apostles* [a]2 Cor. 11:16f.; 12:6; 5:13 [b]2 Cor. 11:5; 1 Cor. 15:10 [c]1 Cor. 3:7; 13:2; 15:9

12 [1]Or, *attesting miracles* [2]Lit., *of the apostle* [3]Or, *works of power* [a]1 Cor. 9:1; Rom. 15:19; esp. John 4:48

13 [a]1 Cor. 9:12, 18; 2 Cor. 11:9; 12:14 [b]2 Cor. 11:7

14 [a]2 Cor. 13:1; 1:15; 13:2 [b]1 Cor. 9:12, 18; 2 Cor. 11:9; 12:13 [c]1 Cor. 10:24, 33 [d]1 Cor. 9:19 [e]1 Cor. 4:14f.; Gal. 4:19 [f]Prov. 19:14; Ezek. 34:2

15 [a]2 Cor. 1:6; Rom. 9:3; Phil. 2:17; Col. 1:24; 1 Thess. 2:8; 2 Tim. 2:10 [b]2 Cor. 11:11

16 [a]2 Cor. 11:9 [b]2 Cor. 11:20

17 [a]2 Cor. 9:5

18 [1]Lit., *walk* [2]Or, *by the same Spirit* [a]2 Cor. 8:6 [b]2 Cor. 2:13 [c]2 Cor. 8:18 [d]1 Cor. 4:21 [e]Rom. 4:12

19 [1]Or, *have you been thinking . . . ?* [a]2 Cor. 2:17; Rom. 9:1 [b]2 Cor. 10:8; Rom. 14:19; 1 Thess. 5:11 [c]Heb. 6:9

20 [a]2 Cor. 2:1-4; 1 Cor. 4:21 [b]1 Cor. 1:11; 3:3 [c]Gal. 5:20 [d]Rom. 2:8; 1 Cor. 11:19 [e]Rom. 1:30; James 4:11; 1 Pet. 2:1 [f]Rom. 1:29 [g]1 Cor. 4:6, 18; 5:2 [h]1 Cor. 14:33

21 [1]I.e., sexual immorality [a]2 Cor. 13:2 [b]Gal. 5:19; 1 Cor. 6:9, 18; Col. 3:5

Chapter 13

[a]THIS is the third time I am coming to you. [b]EVERY [1]FACT [2]IS
TO BE CONFIRMED BY THE [3]TESTIMONY OF TWO OR THREE
WITNESSES.
2 I have previously said when present the second time,
and though now absent I say in advance to those who have
[a]sinned in the past and to all the rest as well, that [b]if I come
again, I will not [c]spare *anyone,*—
3 since you are [a]seeking for proof of the [b]Christ who
speaks in me, and who is not weak toward you, but [c]mighty in
you.
4 For indeed He was [a]crucified because of weakness, yet
He lives [b]because of the power of God. For we also are [c]weak
[1]in Him, yet [d]we shall live with Him because of the power of
God *directed* toward you.
5 [a]Test yourselves *to see* if you are in the faith; [b]examine
yourselves! Or do you not recognize this about yourselves, that
Jesus Christ is in you—unless indeed you [1c]fail the test?
6 But I trust that you will realize that we ourselves [1]do
not fail the test.
7 Now we pray to God that you do no wrong; not that we
ourselves may appear approved, but that you may do what is
right, even though we should [1]appear unapproved.
8 For we can do nothing against the truth, but *only* for
the truth.
9 For we rejoice when we ourselves are [a]weak but you are
strong; this we also pray for, [1]that you be [b]made complete.
10 For this reason I am writing these things while absent,
in order that when present [a]I may not use [b]severity in accordance with the [c]authority which the Lord gave me for building
up and not for tearing down.
11 [a]Finally, brethren, [1]rejoice, [2b]be made complete, be
comforted, [c]be like-minded, [d]live in peace; and [e]the God of
love and peace shall be with you.
12 [a]Greet one another with a holy kiss.
13 [a]All the [1]saints greet you.
14 [a]The grace of the Lord Jesus Christ, and the [b]love of
God, and the [c]fellowship of the Holy Spirit, be with you all.

1 [1]Lit., *word* [2]Lit., *will be* [3]Lit., *mouth*
[a]2 Cor. 12:14 [b]Deut. 19:15; Matt. 18:16

2 [a]2 Cor. 12:21 [b]2 Cor. 13:10; 1 Cor. 4:21 [c]2 Cor. 1:23; 10:11

3 [a]2 Cor. 10:1, 10 [b]1 Cor. 5:4; 7:40; Matt. 10:20 [c]2 Cor. 9:8; 10:4

4 [1]Some early mss. read, *with Him*
[a]Phil. 2:7f.; 1 Pet. 3:18 [b]Rom. 1:4; 6:4; 1 Cor. 6:14 [c]1 Cor. 2:3; 2 Cor. 13:19 [d]Rom. 6:8

5 [1]Lit., *are unapproved*
[a]John 6:6 [b]1 Cor. 11:28 [c]1 Cor. 9:27

6 [1]Lit., *are not unapproved*

7 [1]Lit., *be as*

9 [1]Lit., *your completion*
[a]2 Cor. 13:4; 12:10 [b]1 Cor. 1:10; 2 Cor. 13:11; Eph. 4:12; 1 Thess. 3:10

10 [a]2 Cor. 2:3 [b]Titus 1:13 [c]2 Cor. 10:8; 1 Cor. 5:4

11 [1]Or possibly, *farewell* [2]Or, *put yourselves in order*
[a]1 Thess. 4:1; 2 Thess. 3:1, [b]1 Cor. 1:10; 2 Cor. 13:9; Eph. 4:12; 1 Thess. 3:10 [c]Rom. 12:16 [d]Mark 9:50 [e]Rom. 15:33; Eph. 6:23

12 [a]Rom. 16:16

13 [1]I.e., true believers; lit., *holy ones*
[a]Phil. 4:22

14 [a]Rom. 16:20; 2 Cor. 8:9 [b]Rom. 5:5; Jude 21 [c]Phil. 2:1

THE EPISTLE OF PAUL TO THE

GALATIANS

Salutation. The Galatians' Falling Away. The Gospel I Preach Came from Christ. Visit to Jerusalem.

PAUL, [a]an apostle ([b]not *sent* from men, nor through the
agency of man, but [c]through Jesus Christ, and God the Father,
who [d]raised Him from the dead),
2 and all [a]the brethren who are with me, to [b]the churches
of Galatia:
3 [a]Grace to you and peace from [1]God our Father, and
the Lord Jesus Christ,
4 who [a]gave Himself for our sins, that He might deliver
us out of [b]this present evil [1]age, according to the will of [c]our
God and Father,
5 [a]to whom *be* the glory forevermore. Amen.
6 I am amazed that you are [a]so quickly deserting [b]Him
who called you [1]by the grace of Christ, for a [c]different gospel;
7 which is *really* not another; only there are some who
are [a]disturbing you, and want to distort the gospel of Christ.
8 But even though we, or [a]an angel from heaven, should
preach to you a gospel [1]contrary to that which we have
preached to you, let him be [2b]accursed.
9 As we [a]have said before, so I say again now, [b]if any man
is preaching to you a gospel [1]contrary to that which you received, let him be [2c]accursed.
10 For am I now [a]seeking the favor of men, or of God? Or
am I striving to please men? If I were still trying to please men,
I would not be a [b]bond-servant of Christ.
11 For [a]I would have you know, brethren, that the gospel
which was preached by me is [b]not according to man.
12 For [a]I neither received it from man, nor was I taught it,
but *I received it* through a [b]revelation of Jesus Christ.
13 For you have heard of [a]my former manner of life in
Judaism, how I [b]used to persecute [c]the church of God beyond
measure, and [d]tried to destroy it;
14 and I [a]was advancing in Judaism beyond many of my
contemporaries among my [1]countrymen, being more extremely zealous for my [b]ancestral traditions.
15 But when He who had set me apart, *even* from my
mother's womb, and [a]called me through His grace, was
[b]pleased
16 to reveal His Son in me, that I might [a]preach Him
among the Gentiles, [b]I did not immediately consult with
[1c]flesh and blood,
17 [a]nor did I go up to Jerusalem to those who were
apostles before me; but I went away to Arabia, and returned
once more to [b]Damascus.
18 Then [a]three years later I went up [b]to Jerusalem to
[1]become acquainted with [c]Cephas, and stayed with him fifteen
days.

1 [a]2 Cor. 1:1 [b]Gal. 1:11f. [c]Acts 20:24; 9:15; Gal. 1:15f. [d]Acts 2:24

2 [a]Phil. 4:21 [b]1 Cor. 16:1; Acts 16:6

3 [1]Some early mss. read, *God the Father, and our Lord Jesus Christ* [a]Rom. 1:7

4 [1]Or, *world* [a]Matt. 20:28; Rom. 4:25; 1 Cor. 15:3; Gal. 2:20 [b]Matt. 13:22; Rom. 12:2; 2 Cor. 4:4 [c]Phil. 4:20; 1 Thess. 1:3; 3:11, 13

5 [a]Rom. 11:36

6 [1]Lit., *in* [a]Acts 16:6; 18:23; Gal. 4:13 [b]Gal. 5:8; 1:15; Rom. 8:28 [c]2 Cor. 11:4; 1 Tim. 1:3; Gal. 1:7, 11; 2:2, 7; Gal. 5:14

7 [a]Acts 15:24; Gal. 5:10

8 [1]Or, *other than, more than* [2]Gr., *anathema* [a]2 Cor. 11:14 [b]Rom. 9:3

9 [1]Or, *other than, more than* [2]Gr., *anathema* [a]Acts 18:23 [b]Rom. 16:17 [c]Rom. 9:3

10 [a]1 Thess. 2:4; 1 Cor. 10:33 [b]Rom. 1:1; Phil. 1:1

11 [a]1 Cor. 15:1; Rom. 2:16 [b]1 Cor. 9:8; 3:4

12 [a]Gal. 1:1; 1 Cor. 11:23 [b]Gal. 1:16; 1 Cor. 2:10; 2 Cor. 12:1; Gal. 2:2

13 [a]Acts 26:4f. [b]Acts 8:3 [c]1 Cor. 10:32 [d]Acts 9:21

14 [1]Lit., *race* [a]Acts 22:3 [b]Matt. 15:2; Mark 7:3; Col. 2:8; Jer. 9:14

15 [a]Gal. 1:6 [b]Acts 9:15; Rom. 1:1; Is. 49:1, 5; Jer. 1:5

16 [1]I.e., human beings [a]Gal. 2:9; Acts 9:15 [b]Acts 9:20 [c]Matt. 16:17

17 [a]Acts 9:19-22 [b]Acts 9:2

18 [1]Or, *visit Cephas* [a]Acts 9:22f. [b]Acts 9:26f. [c]John 1:42; Gal. 2:9, 11, 14

19 But I did not see any other of the apostles except
[1a]James the Lord's brother.
20 (Now in what I am writing to you, [1]I assure you [a]before
God *that* I am not lying.)
21 Then [a]I went into the regions of [b]Syria and [c]Cilicia.
22 And I was *still* unknown by [1]sight to [a]the churches of
Judea which were [b]in Christ;
23 but only, they kept hearing, "He who once persecuted
us is now preaching [a]the faith which he once [b]*tried to* destroy."
24 And they [a]were glorifying God [1]because of me.

Chapter 2

THEN after an interval of fourteen years I [a]went up again to
Jerusalem with [b]Barnabas, taking [c]Titus along also.
2 And [1]it was because of a [a]revelation that I went up; and
I submitted to them the [b]gospel which I preach among the
Gentiles, but I did so in private to those who were of reputation, for fear that I might be [c]running, or had run, in vain.
3 But not even [a]Titus who was with me, though he was a
Greek, was [b]compelled to be circumcised.
4 But *it was* because of the [a]false brethren who [b]had
sneaked in to spy out our [c]liberty which we have in Christ
Jesus, in order to [d]bring us into bondage.
5 But we did not yield in subjection to them for even an
hour, so that [a]the truth of the gospel might remain with you.
6 But from those who [1]were of high [a]reputation (what
they were makes no difference to me; [b]God [2]shows no partiality)—well, those who were of reputation contributed nothing
to me.
7 But on the contrary, seeing that I had been [a]entrusted
with the [b]gospel [1]to the uncircumcised, just as [c]Peter with *the
gospel* [2]to the circumcised
8 (for He who effectually worked for Peter in *his* [a]apos-
tleship [1]to the circumcised effectually worked for me also to
the Gentiles),
9 and recognizing [a]the grace that had been given to me,
[1b]James and [c]Cephas and John, who were [d]reputed to be [e]pil-
lars, gave to me and [f]Barnabas the [g]right [2]hand of fellowship,
that we might [h]go to the Gentiles, and they to the circumcised.
10 *They* only *asked* us to remember the poor—[a]the very
thing I also was eager to do.
11 But when [a]Cephas came to [b]Antioch, I opposed him to
his face, because he [1]stood condemned.
12 For prior to the coming of certain men from [1a]James,
he used to [b]eat with the Gentiles; but when they came, he
began to withdraw and hold himself aloof, [c]fearing the [2]party
of the circumcision.
13 And the rest of the Jews joined him in hypocrisy, with
the result that even [a]Barnabas was carried away by their
hypocrisy.
14 But when I saw that they [a]were not [1]straightforward
about [b]the truth of the gospel, I said to [c]Cephas in the presence of all, "If you, being a Jew, [d]live like the Gentiles and
not like the Jews, how *is it that* you compel the Gentiles to live
like Jews?[2]

19 [1]Or, *Jacob* [a]Matt. 12:46; Acts 12:17

20 [1]Lit., *behold before God* [a]Rom. 9:1; 2 Cor. 1:23; 11:31

21 [a]Acts 9:30 [b]Acts 15:23, 41 [c]Acts 6:9

22 [1]Lit., *face* [a]1 Thess. 2:14; 1 Cor. 7:17 [b]Rom. 16:7

23 [a]Acts 6:7; Gal. 6:10 [b]Acts 9:21

24 [1]Lit., *in me* [a]Matt. 9:8

1 [a]Acts 15:2 [b]Acts 4:36; Gal. 2:9, 13 [c]2 Cor. 2:13; Gal. 2:3

2 [1]Lit., *according to revelation I went up* [a]Acts 15:2; Gal. 1:12 [b]Gal. 1:6 [c]Gal. 5:7; Phil. 2:16; Rom. 9:16; 1 Cor. 9:24ff.; Heb. 12:1; 2 Tim. 4:7

3 [a]2 Cor. 2:13; Gal. 2:1 [b]Acts 16:3; 1 Cor. 9:21

4 [a]Gal. 1:7; Acts 15:1, 24; 2 Cor. 11:13, 26 [b]2 Pet. 2:1; Jude 4 [c]Gal. 5:1, 13; James 1:25 [d]2 Cor. 11:20; Rom. 8:15

5 [a]Gal. 2:14; Col. 1:5; Gal. 1:6

6 [1]Lit., *seemed to be something* [2]Lit., *does not receive a face.* [a]Gal. 2:9; Gal. 6:3; 2 Cor. 11:5; 12:11 [b]Acts 10:34

7 [1]Lit., *of the uncircumcision* [2]Lit., *of the circumcision* [a]1 Thess. 2:4; 1 Tim. 1:11; 1 Cor. 9:17 [b]Gal. 1:16; Acts 9:15 [c]Gal. 2:9, 11, 14; Gal. 1:18

8 [1]Lit., *of the circumcision* [a]Acts 1:25

9 [1]Or, *Jacob* [2]Lit., *hands* [a]Rom. 12:3 [b]Acts 12:17; Gal. 2:12 [c]Gal. 2:7, 11, 14; 1:18; Luke 22:8 [d]Gal. 2:2, 6; 6:3; 2 Cor. 11:5; 12:11 [e]Rev. 3:12; 1 Tim. 3:15 [f]Acts 4:36; Gal. 2:1, 13 [g]2 Kin. 10:15; Ezra 10:19 [h]Gal. 1:16

10 [a]Acts 24:17

11 [1]Or, *was to be condemned;* lit., *was one who was condemned,* or, was self condemned [a]Gal. 2:6, 9, 14; Gal. 1:18 [b]Acts 11:19; Acts 15:1

12 [1]Or, *Jacob* [2]Or, converts *from the circumcised;* lit., *those from the circumcision* [a]Acts 12:17; Gal. 2:9 [b]Acts 11:3 [c]Acts 11:2

13 [a]Acts 4:36; Gal. 2:1, 9

14 [1]Or, *progressing toward;* lit., *walking straightly* [2]Some close the direct quotation here, others extend it through vs. 21. [a]Heb. 12:13 [b]Gal. 2:5; Col. 1:5; Gal. 1:6 [c]Gal. 2:7, 9, 11; 1:18 [d]Gal. 2:12; Acts 10:28

15 "We *are* [a]Jews by nature, and not [b]sinners from among
the Gentiles;
16 nevertheless knowing that [a]a man is not justified by the
works of [1]the Law but through faith in Christ Jesus, even we
have believed in Christ Jesus, that we may be justified by [b]faith
in Christ, and not by the works of [1]the Law; since [c]by the works
of [1]the Law shall no [2]flesh be justified.
17 "But if, while seeking to be justified in Christ, we
ourselves have also been found [a]sinners, is Christ then a minister of sin? [b]May it never be!
18 "For if I rebuild what I have *once* destroyed, I [a]prove
myself to be a transgressor.
19 "For through [1]the Law I [a]died to [1]the Law, that I might
live to God.
20 "I have been [a]crucified with Christ; and it is no longer I
who live, but [b]Christ lives in me; and [1]the *life* which I now live
in the flesh I live by faith in [c]the Son of God, who [d]loved me,
and [e]delivered Himself up for me.
21 "I do not nullify the grace of God; for [a]if righteousness
comes through [1]the Law, then Christ died needlessly."

Chapter 3

1 YOU foolish [a]Galatians, who has bewitched you, before
whose eyes Jesus Christ [b]was publicly portrayed *as* crucified?
2 This is the only thing I want to find out from you: Did
you receive the Spirit by the works of [1]the Law, or by [2a]hearing
with faith?
3 Are you so foolish? Having begun [1]by the Spirit, are
you now [2]being perfected by the flesh?
4 Did you suffer so many things in vain—[a]if indeed it was
in vain?
5 Does He then who [a]provides you with the Spirit and
[b]works [1]miracles among you, do it by the works of [2]the Law, or
by [3c]hearing with faith?
6 [1]Even so [a]Abraham [b]BELIEVED GOD, AND IT WAS RECK-
ONED TO HIM AS RIGHTEOUSNESS.
7 Therefore, [1]be sure that [a]it is those who are of faith
that are [b]sons of Abraham.
8 And the Scripture, foreseeing that God [1]would justify
the [2]Gentiles by faith, preached the gospel beforehand to Abraham, *saying*, "[a]ALL THE NATIONS SHALL BE BLESSED IN YOU."
9 So then [a]those who are of faith are blessed with [1]Abra-
ham, the believer.
10 For as many as are of the works of [1]the Law are under a
curse; for it is written, "[a]CURSED IS EVERY ONE WHO DOES NOT
ABIDE BY ALL THINGS WRITTEN IN THE BOOK OF THE LAW, TO
PERFORM THEM."
11 Now that [a]no one is justified [1]by [2]the Law before God
is evident; for, "[3b]THE RIGHTEOUS MAN SHALL LIVE BY FAITH."
12 [1]However, the Law is not [2]of faith; on the contrary,
"[a]HE WHO PRACTICES THEM SHALL LIVE [3]BY THEM."
13 Christ [a]redeemed us from the curse of the Law, having
become a curse for us—for it is written, "[b]CURSED IS EVERY ONE
WHO HANGS ON [c]A [1]TREE"—
14 in order that [a]in Christ Jesus the blessing of Abraham

15 [a]Phil. 3:4f. [b]1 Sam. 15:18; Luke 24:7; 1 Cor. 6:1

16 [1]Or, *law* [2]Or, *mortal man* [a]Gal. 3:11; Acts 13:39 [b]Rom. 9:30 [c]Rom. 3:20; Ps. 143:2

17 [a]Gal. 2:15 [b]Gal. 3:21; Luke 20:16

18 [a]Rom. 3:5 [Gr.]

19 [1]Or, *law* [a]Rom. 7:4; 6:2; 1 Cor. 9:20

20 [1]Or, *insofar as I* [a]Rom. 6:6; Gal. 5:24; 6:14 [b]Rom. 8:10 [c]Matt. 4:3 [d]Rom. 8:37 [e]Gal. 1:4

21 [1]Or, *law* [a]Gal. 3:21

1 [1]Lit., O [a]Gal. 1:2 [b]1 Cor. 1:23; Gal. 5:11

2 [1]Or, *law* [2]Lit., *the hearing of faith* [a]Rom. 10:17

3 [1]Or, *with* [2]Or, *ending with*

4 [a]1 Cor. 15:2

5 [1]Or, *works of power* [2]Or, *law* [3]Lit., *the hearing of faith* [a]Phil. 1:19; 2 Cor. 9:10 [b]1 Cor. 12:10 [c]Rom. 10:17

6 [1]Lit., *Just as* [a]Rom. 4:3 [b]Gen. 15:6

7 [1]Lit., *know* [a]Gal. 3:9 [b]Luke 19:9; Gal. 6:16

8 [1]Lit., *justifies* [2]Lit., *nations* [a]Gen. 12:3

9 [1]Lit., *the believing Abraham* [a]Gal. 3:7

10 [1]Or, *law* [a]Deut. 27:26

11 [1]Or, *in* [2]Or, *law* [3]Or, *"But he who is righteous by faith shall live."* [a]Gal. 2:16 [b]Hab. 2:4; Rom. 1:17; Heb. 10:38

12 [1]Or, *and* [2]Or, *based on* [3]Or, *in* [a]Lev. 18:5; Rom. 10:5

13 [1]Or, *cross;* lit., *wood* [a]Gal. 4:5 [b]Deut. 21:23 [c]Acts 5:30

14 [a]Rom. 4:9, 16; Gal. 3:28

might [1]come to the Gentiles, so that we [b]might receive [c]the
promise of the Spirit through faith.
15 [a]Brethren, [b]I speak [1]in terms of human relations: [c]even
though it is *only* a man's [2]covenant, yet when it has been
ratified, no one sets it aside or adds [3]conditions to it.
16 Now the promises were spoken [a]to Abraham and to his
seed. He does not say, "[b]AND TO SEEDS," as *referring* to many,
but *rather* to one, "[c]AND TO YOUR SEED," that is, Christ.
17 What I am saying is this: the Law, which came [a]four
hundred and thirty years later, does not invalidate a covenant
previously ratified by God, so as to nullify the promise.
18 For [a]if the inheritance is [1]based on law, it is no longer
[1]based on a promise; but [b]God has granted it to Abraham by
means of a promise.
19 [a]Why the Law then? It was added [1]because of transgressions, having been [b]ordained through angels [c]by the
[2]agency of a mediator, until [d]the seed should come to whom
the promise had been made.
20 Now [a]a mediator is not [1]for one *party only;* whereas
God is *only* one.
21 Is the Law then contrary to the promises of God? [a]May
it never be! For [b]if a law had been given which was able to
impart life, then righteousness [1]would indeed have been
[2]based on law.
22 But the Scripture has [a]shut up all [1b]men under sin, that
the promise by faith in Jesus Christ might be given to those
who believe.
23 But before faith came, we were kept in custody under
the law, [a]being shut up to the faith which was later to be
revealed.
24 Therefore the Law has become our [1a]tutor *to lead us* to
Christ, that [b]we may be justified by faith.
25 But now that faith has come, we are no longer under a
[1a]tutor.
26 For you are all [a]sons of God through faith in [b]Christ
Jesus.
27 For all of you who were [a]baptized into Christ have
[b]clothed yourselves with Christ.
28 [a]There is neither Jew nor Greek, there is neither slave
nor free man, there is [1]neither male nor female; for [b]you are all
one in [c]Christ Jesus.
29 And if [a]you [1]belong to Christ, then you are Abraham's
[2]offspring, heirs according to [b]promise.

CHAPTER 4

NOW I say, as long as the heir is a [1]child, he does not differ
at all from a slave although he is [2]owner of everything,
2 but he is under guardians and [1]managers until the date
set by the father.
3 So also we, while we were children, were held [a]in bondage under the [1b]elemental things of the world.
4 But when [a]the fulness of the time came, God sent forth
His Son, [b]born of a woman, born [c]under [1]the Law,
5 in order that He might redeem those who were under
[1]the Law, that we might receive the adoption as [a]sons.

14 [1]Or, *occur*
[b]Gal. 3:2 [c]Acts 2:33; Eph. 1:13

15 [1]Lit., *according to man* [2]Or, *will,* or, *testament* [3]Or, *a codicil*
[a]Gal. 6:18; Rom. 1:13; Acts 1:15 [b]Rom. 3:5 [c]Heb. 6:16

16 [a]Luke 1:55; Rom. 4:13, 16; 9:4 [b]Gen. 13:15 [c]Gen. 17:8; Acts 3:25

17 [a]Ex. 12:40; Gen. 15:13f.; Acts 7:6

18 [1]Lit., *out of, from*
[a]Rom. 4:14 [b]Heb. 6:14

19 [1]Or, *for the sake of defining* [2]Lit., *hand*
[a]Rom. 5:20 [b]Acts 7:53 [c]Ex. 20:19; Deut. 5:5 [d]Gal. 3:16

20 [1]Lit., *of one*
[a]1 Tim. 2:5; Heb. 8:6; 9:15; 12:24

21 [1]Or, *would indeed be* [2]Lit., *out of, from*
[a]Luke 20:16; Gal. 2:17 [b]Gal. 2:21

22 [1]Lit., *things*
[a]Rom. 11:32 [b]1 Cor. 1:27

23 [a]Rom. 11:32

24 [1]Lit., *a child-conductor*
[a]1 Cor. 4:15 [b]Gal. 2:16

25 [1]Lit., *a child-conductor*
[a]1 Cor. 4:15

26 [a]Gal. 4:5 Rom. 8:14
[b]Gal. 3:28; 4:14; 5:6, 24; Rom. 8:1; Eph. 1:1; Col. 1:4; Phil. 1:1; 1 Tim. 1:12; 2 Tim. 1:1; Titus 1:4

27 [a]Matt. 28:19; Rom. 6:3; 1 Cor. 10:2 [b]Rom. 13:14

28 [1]Lit., *not male and female*
[a]1 Cor. 12:13; Col. 3:11; Rom. 3:22 [b]John 17:11; Eph. 2:15 [c]Gal. 3:26; 4:14; 5:6, 24; Rom. 8:1; Eph. 1:1; Col. 1:4; Phil. 1:1; 1 Tim. 1:12; 2 Tim. 1:1; Titus 1:4

29 [1]Lit., *are Christ's* [2]Lit., *seed*
[a]1 Cor. 3:23 [b]Gal. 3:18; 4:28; Rom. 9:8

1 [1]Or, *minor* [2]Lit., *lord*

2 [1]Or, *stewards*

3 [1]Or, *rudimentary teachings,* or, *principles*
[a]Gal. 4:8f.; 4:24f.; 2:4 [b]Col. 2:8, 20; Heb. 5:12; Gal. 4:9

4 [1]Or, *law*
[a]Mark 1:15 [b]John 1:14; Rom. 1:3; 8:3; Phil. 2:7 [c]Luke 2:21f., 27

5 [1]Or, *law*
[a]Gal. 3:26; Rom. 8:14

6 And because you are sons, [a]God has sent forth the
Spirit of His Son into our hearts, crying, "[b]Abba! Father!"
7 Therefore you are no longer a slave, but a son; and [a]if a
son, then an heir [1]through God.
8 However at that time, [a]when you did not know God,
you were [b]slaves to [c]those which by nature are no gods.
9 But now that you have come to know God, or rather to
be [a]known by God, [b]how is it that you turn back again to the
weak and worthless [1c]elemental things, to which you desire to
be enslaved all over again?
10 You [a]observe days and months and seasons and years.
11 I fear for you, that perhaps I have labored [1]over you in
vain.
12 I beg of you, [a]brethren, [b]become as *I am,* for I also
have become as you *are.* You have done me no wrong;
13 but you know that it was because of a [1]bodily illness
that I preached the gospel to you the [2]first time;
14 and that which was a [1]trial to you in my [2]bodily condition you did not despise or [3]loathe, but [a]you received me as an
angel of God, as [b]Christ Jesus *Himself.*
15 Where then is [1]that sense of blessing you had? For I
bear you witness, that if possible, you would have plucked out
your eyes and given them to me.
16 Have I therefore become your enemy [a]by [1]telling you
the truth?
17 They eagerly seek you, not commendably, but they
wish to shut you out, in order that you may seek them.
18 But it is good always to be eagerly sought in a commend-
able manner, and [a]not only when I am present with you.
19 [a]My children, with whom [b]I am again in labor until
[c]Christ is formed in you—
20 but I could wish to be present with you now and to
change my tone, for [a]I am perplexed about you.
21 Tell me, you who want to be under law, do you not
[a]listen to the law?
22 For it is written that Abraham had two sons, one by the
bondwoman and one by the free woman.
23 But [a]the son by the bondwoman was born according to
the flesh, and [b]the son by the free woman through the
promise.
24 [1a]This contains an allegory: for these *women* are two
covenants, one *proceeding* from [b]Mount Sinai bearing children [2]who are to be [c]slaves; [3]she is Hagar.
25 Now this Hagar is Mount Sinai in Arabia, and corre-
sponds to the present Jerusalem, for she is in slavery with her
children.
26 But [a]the Jerusalem above is free; [1]she is our mother.
27 For it is written,

"[a]REJOICE, BARREN WOMAN WHO DOES NOT BEAR;
BREAK FORTH AND SHOUT, YOU WHO ARE NOT IN LABOR;
FOR MORE ARE THE CHILDREN OF THE DESOLATE
THAN OF THE ONE WHO HAS A HUSBAND."

28 And you brethren, [a]like Isaac, are [b]children of promise.
29 But as at that time [a]he who was born according to the
flesh [b]persecuted him *who was born* according to the Spirit,
[c]so it is now also.

6 [a]Rom. 5:5; 8:9, 16; 2 Cor. 3:17; Acts 16:7 [b]Mark 14:36; Rom. 8:15

7 [1]I.e., through the gracious act of [a]Rom. 8:17

8 [a]1 Cor. 1:21; 1 Thess. 4:5; 2 Thess. 1:8; Eph. 2:12 [b]Gal. 4:3 [c]2 Chr. 13:9; Is. 37:19; Jer. 2:11; 1 Cor. 8:4f.; 1 Cor. 10:20

9 [1]Or, *rudimentary teachings,* or *principles* [a]1 Cor. 8:3 [b]Col. 2:20 [c]Gal. 4:3 and marg.

10 [a]Rom. 14:5; Col. 2:16

11 [1]Or, *for*

12 [a]Gal. 6:18 [b]2 Cor. 6:11, 13

13 [1]Lit., *weakness of the flesh* [2]Or, *former*

14 [1]Or, *temptation* [2]Lit., *flesh* [3]Lit., *spit out at* [a]Matt. 10:40; 1 Thess. 2:13 [b]Gal. 3:26

15 [1]Lit., *the congratulation of yourselves*

16 [1]Or, *dealing truthfully with you* [a]Amos 5:10

18 [a]Gal. 4:13f.

19 [a]1 John 2:1 [b]1 Cor. 4:15 [c]Eph. 4:13

20 [a]2 Cor. 4:8

21 [a]Luke 16:29

23 [a]Gal. 4:29; Rom. 9:7 [b]Gal. 4:28; Gen. 17:16ff.; 18:10ff.; 21:1; Heb. 11:11

24 [1]Lit., *which things are allegorical utterances* [2]Lit., *into slavery* [3]Lit., *which* [a]1 Cor. 10:11 [b]Deut. 33:2 [c]Gal. 4:3

26 [1]Lit., *which* [a]Heb. 12:22; Rev. 3:12; 21:2, 10

27 [a]Is. 54:1

28 [a]Gal. 4:23 [b]Gal. 3:29; Rom. 9:7ff.

29 [a]Gal. 4:23 [b]Gen. 21:9 [c]Gal. 5:11

30 But what does the Scripture say?
"[a]CAST OUT THE BONDWOMAN AND HER SON,
FOR [b]THE SON OF THE BONDWOMAN SHALL NOT BE AN
HEIR WITH THE SON OF THE FREE WOMAN."
31 So then, brethren, we are not children of a bondwoman,
[1]but of the free woman.

CHAPTER 5

1[a]
IT was for freedom that Christ set us free; therefore [b]keep
standing firm and do not be subject again to a [c]yoke of slavery.
2 Behold I, [a]Paul, say to you that if you receive [b]circum-
cision, Christ will be of no benefit to you.
3 And I [a]testify again to every man who receives [b]circum-
cision, that he is under obligation to [c]keep the whole Law.
4 You have been severed from Christ, you who [1]are seeking to be justified by law; you have [a]fallen from grace.
5 For we through the Spirit, by faith, are [a]waiting for the
hope of righteousness.
6 For in [a]Christ Jesus [b]neither circumcision nor uncircumcision means anything, but [c]faith working through love.
7 You were [a]running well; who hindered you from
obeying the truth?
8 This persuasion *did* not *come* from [a]Him who calls
you.
9 [a]A little leaven leavens the whole lump *of dough*.
10 [a]I have confidence [1]in you in the Lord, that you [b]will
adopt no other view; but the one who is [c]disturbing you shall
bear his judgment, whoever he is.
11 But I, brethren, if I still preach circumcision, why am I
still [a]persecuted? Then [b]the stumbling block of the cross has
been abolished.
12 Would that [a]those who are troubling you would even
[1b]mutilate themselves.
13 For you were called to [a]freedom, brethren; [b]only *do*
not *turn* your freedom into an opportunity for the flesh, but
through love [c]serve one another.
14 For [a]the whole Law is fulfilled in one word, in the
statement, "[b]YOU SHALL LOVE YOUR NEIGHBOR AS YOURSELF."
15 But if you [a]bite and devour one another, take care lest
you be consumed by one another.
16 But I say, [a]walk by the Spirit, and you will not carry out
[b]the desire of the flesh.
17 For [a]the flesh [1]sets its desire against the Spirit, and the
Spirit against the flesh; for these are in opposition to one
another, [b]so that you may not do the things that you [2]please.
18 But if you are [a]led by the Spirit, [b]you are not under the
Law.
19 Now the deeds of the flesh are evident, which are:
[1a]immorality, impurity, sensuality,
20 idolatry, [a]sorcery, enmities, [b]strife, jealousy, outbursts
of anger, [c]disputes, dissensions, [1d]factions,
21 envyings, [a]drunkenness, carousings, and things like
these, of which I forewarn you just as I have forewarned you
that those who practice such things shall not [b]inherit the kingdom of God.

30 [a]Gen. 21:10, 12 [b]John 8:35

31 [1]Note next vs., 5:1

1 [1]Some authorities prefer to join with 4:31 and render, *but with the freedom of the free woman Christ set us free*
[a]Gal. 2:4; 5:13; John 8:32, 36; Rom. 8:15; 2 Cor. 3:17
[b]1 Cor. 16:13 [c]Acts 15:10; Gal. 2:4

2 [a]2 Cor. 10:1 [b]Acts 15:1; Gal. 5:3, 6, 11

3 [a]Luke 16:28 [b]Acts 15:1; Gal. 5:2, 6, 11 [c]Rom. 2:25

4 [1]Or, *would be*
[a]2 Pet. 3:17; Heb. 12:15 marg.

5 [a]Rom. 8:23; 1 Cor. 1:7

6 [a]Gal. 3:26 [b]1 Cor. 7:19; Gal. 6:15 [c]Col. 1:4f.; 1 Thess. 1:3; James 2:18, 20, 22

7 [a]Gal. 2:2

8 [a]Rom. 8:28; Gal. 1:6

9 [a]1 Cor. 5:6

10 [1]Lit., *toward*
[a]2 Cor. 2:3 [b]Phil. 3:15; Gal. 5:7 [c]Gal. 1:7; 5:12

11 [a]Gal. 4:29; 6:12 [b]1 Cor. 1:23; Rom. 9:33

12 [1]Or, *cut themselves off*
[a]Gal. 5:10; 2:4 [b]Deut. 23:1

13 [a]Gal. 5:1 [b]1 Cor. 8:9; 1 Pet. 2:16 [c]1 Cor. 9:19; Eph. 5:21

14 [a]Matt. 7:12; 22:40; Rom. 13:8, 10; Gal. 6:2 [b]Lev. 19:18; Matt. 19:19; John 13:34

15 [a]Phil. 3:2; Gal. 5:20

16 [a]Rom. 8:4; 13:14; Gal. 5:24f. [b]Eph. 2:3; Rom. 13:14

17 [1]Lit., *lusts against* [2]Lit., *wish*
[a]Rom. 7:18, 23; 8:5ff. [b]Rom. 7:15ff.

18 [a]Rom. 8:14 [b]Rom. 6:14; 7:4; 1 Tim. 1:9

19 [1]I.e., sexual immorality
[a]1 Cor. 6:9, 18; 2 Cor. 12:21

20 [1]Or, *heresies*
[a]Rev. 21:8 [b]2 Cor. 12:20
[c]Rom. 2:8; James 3:14ff.
[d]1 Cor. 11:19

21 [a]Rom. 13:13 [b]1 Cor. 6:9

22 But [a]the fruit of the Spirit is [b]love, joy, peace, patience,
kindness, goodness, faithfulness,
23 gentleness, [a]self-control; against such things [b]there is no
law.
24 Now those who [1]belong to [a]Christ Jesus have [b]crucified
the flesh with its passions and [c]desires.
25 If we live by the Spirit, let us also [1]walk [a]by the Spirit.
26 Let us not become [a]boastful, challenging one another,
envying one another.

Chapter 6

[a]BRETHREN, even if a man is caught in any trespass, you
who are [b]spiritual, [c]restore such a one [d]in a spirit of gentleness;
looking to yourself, lest you too be tempted.
2 [a]Bear one another's burdens, and thus fulfil [b]the law of
Christ.
3 For [a]if anyone thinks he is something when he is nothing, he deceives himself.
4 But let each one [a]examine his own work, and then he
will have *reason for* [b]boasting in regard to himself alone, and
not in regard to another.
5 For [a]each one shall bear his own load.
6 And [a]let the one who is taught [b]the word share all good
things with him who teaches.
7 [a]Do not be deceived, [b]God is not mocked; for [c]whatever
a man sows, this he will also reap.
8 [a]For the one who sows to his own flesh shall from the
flesh reap [b]corruption, but [c]the one who sows to the Spirit
shall from the Spirit reap eternal life.
9 And [a]let us not lose heart in doing good, for in due
time we shall reap if we [b]do not grow weary.
10 So then, [1a]while we have opportunity, let us do good to
all men, and especially to those who are of the [b]household of
[c]the faith.
11 See with what large letters I [1]am writing to you [a]with
my own hand.
12 Those who desire [a]to make a good showing in the flesh
try to [b]compel you to be circumcised, simply that they [c]may
not be persecuted [1]for the cross of Christ.
13 For those who [1]are circumcised do not even [a]keep [2]the
Law themselves, but they desire to have you circumcised, that
they may [b]boast in your flesh.
14 But [a]may it never be that I should boast, [b]except in the
cross of our Lord Jesus Christ, [c]through [1]which the world has
been crucified to me, and [d]I to the world.
15 For [a]neither is circumcision anything, nor uncircumcision, but a [b]new [1]creation.
16 And those who will [1]walk by this rule, peace and mercy
be upon them, and upon the [a]Israel of God.
17 From now on let no one cause trouble for me, for I
bear on my body the [a]brand-marks of Jesus.
18 [a]The grace of our Lord Jesus Christ be [b]with your spirit, [c]brethren. Amen.

22 [a]Matt. 7:16ff.; Rom. 6:21; Eph. 5:9 [b]1 Cor. 13:4; Rom. 5:1-5; Col. 3:12-15

23 [a]Acts 24:25 [b]Gal. 5:18

24 [1]Lit., *are of Christ Jesus* [a]Gal. 3:26 [b]Rom. 6:6; Gal. 2:20; 6:14 [c]Gal. 5:16f.

25 [1]Or, *follow the Spirit* [a]Gal. 5:16

26 [a]Phil. 2:3

1 [a]Gal. 6:18; 1 Thess. 4:1 [b]1 Cor. 2:15 [c]2 Cor. 2:7; 2 Thess. 3:15; Heb. 12:13; James 5:19f. [d]1 Cor. 4:21

2 [a]Rom. 15:1 [b]1 Cor. 9:21; James 1:25; 2:12; Rom. 8:2; 2 Pet. 3:2

3 [a]1 Cor. 3:18; 2 Cor. 12:11; Acts 5:36

4 [a]1 Cor. 11:28 [b]Phil. 1:26

5 [a]Prov. 9:12; Rom. 14:12; 1 Cor. 3:8

6 [a]1 Cor. 9:11, 14 [b]2 Tim. 4:2

7 [a]1 Cor. 6:9 [b]Job 13:9 [c]2 Cor. 9:6

8 [a]Job 4:8; Hos. 8:7; Rom. 6:21 [b]1 Cor. 15:42 [c]James 3:18; Rom. 8:11

9 [a]2 Cor. 4:1; 1 Cor. 15:58 [b]Heb. 12:3, 5; James 5:7f.; Matt. 10:22

10 [1]Or, *as* [a]Prov. 3:27; John 12:35 [b]Eph. 2:19; Heb. 3:6; 1 Pet. 2:5; 4:17 [c]Acts 6:7; Gal. 1:23

11 [1]Or, *have written* [a]1 Cor. 16:21

12 [1]Or, *because of* [a]Matt. 23:27f. [b]Acts 15:1 [c]Gal. 5:11

13 [1]Some ancient mss. read, *have been* [2]Or, *law* [a]Rom. 2:25 [b]Phil. 3:3

14 [1]Or, *whom* [a]Gal. 2:17; 3:21; Luke 20:16 [in the Gr.] [b]1 Cor. 2:2 [c]Gal. 2:20; Col. 2:20 [d]Rom. 6:2, 6; Gal. 2:19f.; 5:24

15 [1]Or, *creature* [a]Gal. 5:6; 1 Cor. 7:19; Rom. 2:26, 28 [b]2 Cor. 5:17; Eph. 2:10, 15; 4:24; Col. 3:10

16 [1]Or, *follow this rule* [a]Rom. 9:6; Gal. 3:7, 29; Phil. 3:3

17 [a]Is. 44:5 marg.; Ezek. 9:4; Rev. 13:16; 2 Cor. 4:10; 11:23

18 [a]Rom. 16:20 [b]2 Tim. 4:22 [c]Gal. 3:15; 4:12, 28, 31; Rom. 1:13; Acts 1:15

THE EPISTLE OF PAUL TO THE

EPHESIANS

Salutation. The Blessings of Redemption. Prayer.

PAUL, [a]an apostle of [b]Christ Jesus [1c]by the will of God, to
the [2d]saints who are [3]at [e]Ephesus, and [f]*who are* faithful in
[b]Christ Jesus:
2 [a]Grace to you and peace from God our Father and the
Lord Jesus Christ.
3 [a]Blessed *be* the God and Father of our Lord Jesus
Christ, who has blessed us with every spiritual blessing in [b]the
heavenly *places* in Christ,
4 just as [a]He chose us in Him before [b]the foundation of
the world, that we should be [c]holy and blameless before [1]Him.
[d]In love
5 [1]He [a]predestined us to [b]adoption as sons through Jesus
Christ to Himself, [c]according to the [2]kind intention of His
will,
6 [a]to the praise of the glory of His grace, which He freely
bestowed on us in [b]the Beloved.
7 [a]In [1]Him we have [b]redemption [c]through His blood, the
[d]forgiveness of our trespasses, according to [e]the riches of His
grace,
8 which He [1]lavished upon [2]us. In all wisdom and insight
9 He [1a]made known to us the mystery of His will, [b]accord-
ing to His [2]kind intention which He [c]purposed in Him
10 with a view to an administration [1]suitable to [a]the fulness of the times, *that is*, [b]the summing up of all things in
Christ, things [2]in the heavens and things upon the earth. In
Him
11 [1]also we [2a]have obtained an inheritance, having been
[b]predestined [c]according to His purpose who works all things
[d]after the counsel of His will,
12 to the end that we who were the first to hope in [1]Christ
should be [a]to the praise of His glory.
13 In [1]Him, you also, after listening to [a]the message of
truth, the gospel of your salvation—having also [2]believed, you
were [b]sealed in [1]Him with [c]the Holy Spirit of promise,
14 who is [1a]given as a pledge of [b]our inheritance, with a
view to the [c]redemption of [d]*God's own* possession, [e]to the
praise of His glory.
15 For this reason I too, [a]having heard of the faith in the
Lord Jesus which *exists* among you, and [1]your love for [b]all the
[2]saints,
16 [a]do not cease giving thanks for you, [b]while making
mention *of you* in my prayers;
17 that the [a]God of our Lord Jesus Christ, [b]the Father of
glory, may give to you a spirit of [c]wisdom and of [d]revelation in
the [1]knowledge of Him.
18 *I pray that* [a]the eyes of your heart [1]may be enlightened,
so that you may know what is the [b]hope of His [c]calling, what
are [d]the riches of the glory of [e]His inheritance in [f]the [2]saints,
19 and what is the surpassing greatness of His power

1 [1]Lit., *through* [2]I.e., true believers; lit., *holy ones* [3]Some ancient mss. omit, *at Ephesus* [a]2 Cor. 1:1 [b]Eph. 2:6, 7, 10, 13, 20; 3:1, 6, 11, 21; Col. 1:4; 2:6; 4:12; Rom. 8:1; Gal. 3:26 [c]1 Cor. 1:1 [d]Acts 9:13; Phil. 1:1; Col. 1:1 [e]Acts 18:19 [f]Col. 1:2
2 [a]Rom. 1:7
3 [a]2 Cor. 1:3 [b]Eph. 1:20; 2:6; 3:10; 6:12; Phil. 3:20
4 [1]Or, *Him, in love* [a]2 Thess. 2:13f.; Eph. 2:10 [b]Matt. 25:34 [c]Eph. 5:27; Col. 1:22; 2 Tim. 1:9 [d]Eph. 4:2, 15, 16; 5:2
5 [1]Lit., *having predestined* [2]Lit., *good pleasure* [a]Eph. 1:11; Rom. 8:29f.; Acts 13:48 [b]Rom. 8:14ff.; Gal. 4:5 [c]Luke 12:32; 1 Cor. 1:21; Gal. 1:15; Phil. 2:13; Col. 1:19
6 [a]Eph. 1:12, 14 [b]Matt. 3:17
7 [1]Lit., *whom* [a]Col. 1:14 [b]Eph. 1:14; 1 Cor. 1:30; Rom. 3:24 [c]Acts 20:28; Rom. 3:25 [d]Acts 2:38 [e]Rom. 2:4; Eph. 1:18; 2:7; 3:8, 16; Col. 1:27
8 [1]Lit., *made abundant toward* [2]Or, *us, in all wisdom and insight*
9 [1]Lit., *making known* [2]Lit., *good pleasure* [a]Rom. 11:25; 16:25; Eph. 3:3 [b]Luke 12:32; 1 Cor. 1:21; Gal. 1:15; Phil. 2:13; Col. 1:19 [c]Eph. 1:11; Rom. 8:28
10 [1]Lit., *of* [2]Lit., *upon* [a]Mark 1:15 [b]Col. 1:16, 20; Eph. 3:15; Phil. 2:9f.
11 [1]Lit., *in whom also* [2]Or, *were made a heritage* [a]Eph. 1:14, 18; Titus 2:14; Deut. 4:20; 9:26, 29; 32:9 [b]Eph. 1:5 [c]Eph. 3:11; Rom. 8:28f. [d]Rom. 9:11; Heb. 6:17
12 [1]I.e., the Messiah [a]Eph. 1:6, 14
13 [1]Lit., *whom* [2]Or, *believed in Him, you were sealed* [a]Col. 1:5; Acts 13:26; Eph. 4:21 [b]Eph. 4:30; John 3:33 [c]Acts 1:4f.; 2:33
14 [1]Or, *down payment* [a]2 Cor. 1:22 [b]Acts 20:32 [c]Eph. 1:7 [d]Eph. 1:11 [e]Eph. 1:6, 12
15 [1]Many ancient mss. omit, *your love* [2]Note 2, vs. 1 [a]Col. 1:4; Philem. 5; Rom. 1:8 [b]Eph. 3:18; Eph. 1:1
16 [a]Col. 1:9; Rom. 1:8f. [b]Rom. 1:9
17 [1]Or, *true knowledge* [a]John 20:17; Rom. 15:6 [b]Acts 7:2; 1 Cor. 2:8 [c]Col. 1:9 [d]1 Cor. 14:6
18 [1]Lit., *being* [2]I.e., true believers; lit., *holy ones* [a]Acts 26:18; 2 Cor. 4:6; Heb. 6:4 [b]Eph. 4:4 [c]Rom. 11:29 [d]Eph. 1:7 [e]Eph. 1:11 [f]Col. 1:12; Acts 9:13

toward us who believe. [a]*These are* in accordance with the
working of the [b]strength of His might
20 which He brought about in Christ, when He [a]raised
Him from the dead, and [b]seated Him at His right hand in [c]the
heavenly *places*,
21 far above [a]all rule and authority and power and dominion, and every [b]name that is named, not only in [c]this age, but
also in the one to come.
22 And He [a]put all things in subjection under His feet,
and gave Him as [b]head over all things to the church,
23 which is His [a]body, the [b]fulness of Him who [c]fills [d]all in
all.

Chapter 2

AND you [1]were [a]dead [2]in your trespasses and sins,
2 in which you [a]formerly walked according to the [1]course
of [b]this world, according to [c]the prince of the power of the air,
of the spirit that is now working in [d]the sons of disobedience.
3 Among them we too all [a]formerly lived in [b]the lusts of
our flesh, [1]indulging the desires of the flesh and of the [2]mind,
and were [c]by nature [d]children of wrath, [e]even as the rest.
4 But God, being [a]rich in mercy, because of [b]His great
love with which He loved us,
5 even when we were [a]dead [1]in our transgressions, [a]made
us alive together [2]with Christ ([b]by grace you have been saved),
6 and [a]raised us up with Him, and [b]seated us with Him in
[c]the heavenly *places*, in [d]Christ Jesus,
7 in order that in the ages to come He might show the
surpassing [a]riches of His grace in [b]kindness toward us in Christ
Jesus.
8 For [a]by grace you have been saved [b]through faith; and
[1]that not of yourselves, *it is* [c]the gift of God;
9 [a]not as a result of works, that [b]no one should boast.
10 For we are His workmanship, [a]created in [b]Christ Jesus
for [c]good works, which God [d]prepared beforehand, that we
should [e]walk in them.
11 Therefore remember, that [a]formerly [b]you, the Gentiles
in the flesh, who are called "[c]Uncircumcision" by the so-called
"[c]Circumcision," *which is* performed in the flesh by human
hands—
12 *remember* that you were at that time separate from
Christ, [1a]excluded from the commonwealth of Israel, and
strangers to [b]the covenants of promise, having [c]no hope and
[d]without God in the world.
13 But now in [a]Christ Jesus you who [b]formerly were [c]far
off [1]have [c]been brought near [2d]by the blood of Christ.
14 For He Himself is [a]our peace, [b]who made both *groups*
into one, and broke down the [1]barrier of the dividing wall,
15 [1]by [a]abolishing in His flesh the enmity, *which is* [b]the
Law of commandments *contained* in ordinances, that in
Himself He might [2c]make the two into [d]one new man, *thus*
establishing [e]peace,
16 and might [a]reconcile them both in [b]one body to God
through the cross, [1]by it having [c]put to death the enmity.

19 [a]Eph. 3:7; Phil. 3:21; Col. 1:29 [b]Eph. 6:10
20 [a]Acts 2:24 [b]Mark 16:19 [c]Eph. 1:3
21 [a]Col. 1:16; Eph. 3:10; Rom. 8:38; Matt. 28:18 [b]Phil. 2:9; Heb. 1:4; Rev. 19:12; John 17:11 [c]Eph. 2:2; Matt. 12:32
22 [a]1 Cor. 15:27 [fr. Ps. 8:6] [b]Eph. 4:15; 5:23; Col. 1:18; 2:19; 1 Cor. 11:3
23 [a]Eph. 4:12; 5:30; Col. 1:18, 24; 2:19; 1 Cor. 12:27 [b]John 1:16; Eph. 3:19 [c]Eph. 4:10 [d]Col. 3:11
1 [1]Lit., *being* [2]Or, *by reason of* [a]Eph. 2:5; Col. 2:13; Luke 15:24, 32
2 [1]Lit., *age* [a]Eph. 2:3, 11, 13; 5:8; Col. 3:7; Rom. 13:13; 1 Cor. 6:11; 1 Pet. 4:3 [b]Eph. 1:21 [c]Eph. 6:12; John 12:31 [d]Eph. 5:6
3 [1]Lit., *doing* [2]Lit., *thoughts* [a]Eph. 2:2 [b]Gal. 5:16f. [c]Rom. 2:14; Gal. 2:15 [d]Rom. 5:10; Col. 1:21; 2 Pet. 2:14 [e]Rom. 5:12, 19; 1 Thess. 4:13; 5:6
4 [a]Eph. 1:7 [b]John 3:16
5 [1]Or, *by reason of* [2]Some ancient mss. read, *in Christ* [a]Eph. 2:1 [b]Eph. 2:8; Acts 15:11
6 [a]Col. 2:12 [b]Eph. 1:20 [c]Eph. 1:3 [d]Eph. 1:1; 2:10, 13
7 [a]Rom. 2:4; Eph. 1:7 [b]Titus 3:4
8 [1]I.e., that salvation [a]Eph. 2:5; Acts 15:11 [b]1 Pet. 1:5 [c]John 4:10; Heb. 6:4
9 [a]2 Tim. 1:9; Titus 3:5; Rom. 3:28 [b]1 Cor. 1:29
10 [a]Eph. 2:15; 4:24; Col. 3:10 [b]Eph. 1:1; 2:6, 13 [c]Titus 2:14 [d]Eph. 1:4 [e]Eph. 4:1
11 [a]Eph. 2:2, 3, 13; 5:8; Col. 3:7; Rom. 13:13; 1 Cor. 6:11; 1 Pet. 4:3 [b]1 Cor. 12:2; Eph. 5:8 [c]Col. 2:11, 13; Rom. 2:28f.
12 [1]Or, *alienated* [a]Rom. 9:4; Col. 1:21 [b]Gal. 3:17; Heb. 8:6 [c]1 Thess. 4:13 [d]Gal. 4:8; 1 Thess. 4:5; Eph. 4:18
13 [1]Lit., *became*, or, *were made* [2]Or, *in* [a]Eph. 1:1; 2:6, 10 [b]Eph. 2:2, 3, 11; 5:8; Col. 3:7; Rom. 13:13; 1 Cor. 6:11; 1 Pet. 4:3 [c]Eph. 2:17; Acts 2:39; Is. 57:19 [d]Col. 1:20; Rom. 3:25
14 [1]Lit., *the dividing wall of the barrier* [a]Eph. 2:15; Col. 3:15; Gal. 3:28; Col. 3:11; Is. 9:6 [b]1 Cor. 12:13
15 [1]Or, *the enmity, by abolishing in His flesh the Law* [2]Lit., *create* [a]Eph. 2:16; Col. 1:21f. [b]Col. 2:14; 2:20 [c]Eph. 2:10; 4:24; Col. 3:10 [d]Gal. 3:28; Col. 3:10f. [e]Eph. 2:14; Col. 3:15; Gal. 3:28; Col. 3:11; Is. 9:6
16 [1]Or, *in Himself* [a]Col. 1:20, 22; 2 Cor. 5:18 [b]Eph. 4:4; 1 Cor. 10:17 [c]Eph. 2:15

17 AND [a]HE CAME AND PREACHED [b]PEACE TO YOU WHO WERE
[c]FAR AWAY, AND PEACE TO THOSE WHO WERE [c]NEAR;
18 for through Him we both have [a]our access in [b]one
Spirit to [c]the Father.
19 So then you are no longer [a]strangers and aliens, but you
are [b]fellow-citizens with the [1]saints, and are of [c]God's
household,
20 having been [a]built upon [b]the foundation of [c]the
apostles and prophets, [d]Christ Jesus Himself being the
[e]cornerstone,
21 [a]in whom the whole building, being fitted together is
growing into [b]a holy [1]temple in the Lord;
22 in whom you also are being [a]built together into a [b]dwell-
ing of God in the Spirit.

CHAPTER 3

FOR this reason I Paul, [a]the prisoner of [b]Christ Jesus [c]for the
sake of you [d]Gentiles—
2 if indeed you have heard of the [a]stewardship of God's
grace which was given to me for you;
3 [a]that [b]by revelation there was [c]made known to me [d]the
mystery, [e]as I wrote before in brief.
4 [1]And by referring to this, when you read you can understand [a]my insight [2]into the [b]mystery of Christ,
5 which in other generations was not made known to the
sons of men, as it has now been revealed to His holy [a]apostles
and prophets [1]in the Spirit;
6 *to be specific,* that the Gentiles are [a]fellow-heirs and
[b]fellow-members of the body, and [c]fellow-partakers of the promise in [d]Christ Jesus through the gospel,
7 [a]of which I was made a [b]minister, according to the gift
of [c]God's grace which was given to me [d]according to the working of His power.
8 To me, [a]the very least of all [1]saints, this grace was
given, to [b]preach to the Gentiles the unfathomable [c]riches of
Christ,
9 and to bring to light what is the administration of the
[a]mystery which for ages has been [b]hidden in God, [c]who created
all things;
10 in order that the manifold [a]wisdom of God might now
be [b]made known through the church to the [c]rulers and the
authorities in [d]the heavenly *places.*
11 *This was* in [a]accordance with the [1]eternal purpose
which He [2]carried out in [b]Christ Jesus our Lord,
12 in whom we have [a]boldness and [1b]confident [c]access
through faith [2]in Him.
13 Therefore I ask [1]you not [a]to lose heart at my tribulations [b]on your behalf, [2]for they are your glory.
14 For this reason, I [a]bow my knees before the Father,
15 from whom [1]every family in heaven and on earth de-
rives its name,
16 that He would grant you, according to [a]the riches of
His glory, to be [b]strengthened with power through His Spirit in
[c]the inner man;

17 [a]Is. 57:19; Rom. 10:14; Eph. 4:21 [b]Acts 10:36; Eph. 2:14 [c]Eph. 2:13; Acts 2:39; Is. 57:19

18 [a]Eph. 3:12; Rom. 5:2 [b]Eph. 4:4; 1 Cor. 12:13 [c]Col. 1:12

19 [1]I.e., true believers; lit., *holy ones* [a]Eph. 2:12; Heb. 11:13; 1 Pet. 2:11 [b]Phil. 3:20; Heb. 12:22f. [c]Gal. 6:10

20 [a]1 Cor. 3:9 [b]Matt. 16:18; Rev. 21:14; 1 Cor. 3:10 [c]1 Cor. 12:28; Eph. 3:5 [d]1 Cor. 3:11 [e]Luke 20:17 [Ps. 118:22]; 1 Pet. 2:6 [Is. 28:16]

21 [1]Or, *sanctuary* [a]Eph. 4:15f.; Col. 2:19 [b]1 Cor. 3:16f.

22 [a]1 Cor. 3:9, 16; 2 Cor. 6:16 [b]Eph. 3:17

1 [a]Acts 23:18; Eph. 4:1; 2 Tim. 1:8; Philem. 1, 9; 23 [b]Gal. 5:24 [c]Eph. 3:13; 2 Cor. 1:6 [d]Eph. 3:8

2 [a]Col. 1:25; 1 Tim. 1:4; Eph. 1:10; 3:9

3 [a]Acts 22:17, 21; 26:16ff. [b]Gal. 1:12 [c]Eph. 1:9; 3:4, 9 [d]Eph. 3:4, 9; 6:19; Col. 1:26f.; 4:3; Rom. 11:25; 16:25 [e]Eph. 1:9f. [Heb. 13:22; 1 Pet. 5:12]

4 [1]Lit., *to which, when you read* [2]Lit., *in* [a]2 Cor. 11:6 [b]Eph. 3:3, 9; 6:19; Col. 1:26f.; 4:3; Rom. 11:25; 16:25

5 [1]Or, *by* [a]1 Cor. 12:28; Eph. 2:20

6 [a]Gal. 3:29 [b]Eph. 2:16 [c]Eph. 5:7 [d]Gal. 5:24

7 [a]Col. 1:23, 25 [b]1 Cor. 3:5 [c]Eph. 3:2; Rom. 12:3; Acts 9:15 [d]Eph. 1:19; 3:20

8 [1]I.e., true believers; lit., *holy ones* [a]1 Cor. 15:9 [b]Eph. 3:1f.; Acts 9:15 [c]Eph. 3:16; 1:7; Rom. 2:4

9 [a]Eph. 3:3, 4; 6:19; Col. 1:26f.; 4:3; Rom. 11:25; 16:25 [b]Col. 3:3 [c]Rev. 4:11

10 [a]Rom. 11:33; 1 Cor. 2:7 [b]1 Pet. 1:12; Eph. 1:23 [c]Eph. 1:21; 6:12; Col. 2:10, 15 [d]Eph. 1:3

11 [1]Lit., *purpose of the ages* [2]Or, *formed* [a]Eph. 1:11 [b]Gal. 5:24; Eph. 3:1

12 [1]Lit., *access in confidence* [2]Lit., *of Him* [a]Heb. 4:16; 10:19, 35; 1 John 2:28; 3:21 [b]2 Cor. 3:4 [c]Eph. 2:18

13 [1]Or, *that I may not lose* [2]Lit., *which are* [a]2 Cor. 4:1 [b]Eph. 3:1

14 [a]Phil. 2:10

15 [1]Or, *the whole*

16 [a]Eph. 3:8; 1:18 [b]Phil. 4:13; Col. 1:11; 1 Cor. 16:13 [c]Rom. 7:22

17 so that [a]Christ may dwell in your hearts through faith;
and that you, being [b]rooted and [c]grounded in love,
18 may be able to comprehend with [a]all the [1]saints what is
[b]the breadth and length and height and depth,
19 and to know [a]the love of Christ which [b]surpasses knowledge, that you may be [c]filled up to all the [d]fulness of God.
20 [a]Now to Him who is [b]able to do exceeding abundantly
beyond all that we ask or think, [c]according to the power that
works within us,
21 [a]to Him *be* the glory in the church and in Christ Jesus
to all generations [1]forever and ever. Amen.

Chapter 4

I, THEREFORE, [a]the prisoner of the Lord, [b]entreat you to
[c]walk in a manner worthy of the [d]calling with which you have
been [e]called,
2 with all [a]humility and gentleness, with patience, showing forbearance to one another [b]in love,
3 being diligent to preserve the unity of the Spirit in the
[a]bond of peace.
4 *There is* [a]one body and one Spirit, just as also you were
called in one [b]hope of your calling;
5 [a]one Lord, one faith, one baptism,
6 one God and Father of all [a]who is over all and through
all and in all.
7 But [a]to each one of us [b]grace was given [c]according to
the measure of Christ's gift.
8 Therefore [1]it says,
"[a]WHEN HE ASCENDED ON HIGH,
HE [b]LED CAPTIVE A HOST OF CAPTIVES,
AND HE GAVE GIFTS TO MEN."
9 (Now this *expression,* "He [a]ascended," what [1]does it
mean except that He also [2]had descended into [b]the lower parts
of the earth?
10 He who descended is Himself also He who ascended
[a]far above all the heavens, that He might [b]fill all things.)
11 And He [a]gave [b]some *as* apostles, and some *as* prophets,
and some *as* [c]evangelists, and some *as* pastors and [d]teachers,
12 [a]for the equipping of the [1]saints for the work of service,
to the building up of [b]the body of Christ;
13 until we all attain to [a]the unity of the faith, and of the
[1b]knowledge of the Son of God, to a [c]mature man, to the
measure of the stature [2]which belongs to the [d]fulness of Christ.
14 [1]As a result, we are [a]no longer to be children, [b]tossed
here and there by waves, and carried about by every wind of
doctrine, by the trickery of men, by [c]craftiness [2]in [d]deceitful
scheming;
15 but [1]speaking the truth [a]in love, we [2]are to [b]grow up in
all *aspects* into Him, who is the [c]head, *even* Christ,
16 from whom [a]the whole body, being fitted and held
together [1]by that which every joint supplies, according to the
[2]proper working of each individual part, causes the growth of
the body for the building up of itself [b]in love.
17 [a]This I say therefore, and [b]affirm together with the

17 [a]John 14:23; Rom. 8:9f.; 2 Cor. 13:5; Eph. 2:22 [b]Col. 2:7; 1 Cor. 3:6 [c]Col. 1:23

18 [1]Note vs. 8 [a]Eph. 1:15 [b]Job 11:8f.

19 [a]Rom. 8:39; 8:35 [b]Phil. 4:7 [c]Col. 2:10 [d]Eph. 1:23

20 [a]Rom. 16:25 [b]2 Cor. 9:8 [c]Eph. 3:7

21 [1]Lit., *of the age of the ages* [a]Rom. 11:36

1 [a]Eph. 3:1 [b]Rom. 12:1 [c]Col. 1:10; 1 Thess. 2:12; Eph. 2:10; Col. 2:6 [d]Rom. 11:29 [e]Rom. 8:28f.

2 [a]Col. 3:12f. [b]Eph. 1:4

3 [a]Col. 3:14f.

4 [a]Eph. 2:16, 18; 1 Cor. 12:4ff. [b]Eph. 1:18

5 [a]1 Cor. 8:6

6 [a]Rom. 11:36; Col. 1:16

7 [a]1 Cor. 12:7, 11 [b]Eph. 3:2 [c]Rom. 12:3

8 [1]Or, *He* [a]Ps. 68:18 [b]Judg. 5:12; Col. 2:15

9 [1]Lit., *is it except* [2]Some ancient mss. read, *had first descended* [a]John 3:13 [b]Is. 44:23; Ps. 63:9

10 [a]Heb. 4:14; 7:26; 9:24; Eph. 1:20f. [b]Eph. 1:23

11 [a]Eph. 4:8 [b]1 Cor. 12:28; Acts 13:1 [c]Acts 21:8 [d]Acts 13:1

12 [1]I.e., true believers; lit., *holy ones* [a]2 Cor. 13:9 [b]Eph. 1:23; 1 Cor. 12:27

13 [1]Or, *true knowledge* [2]Lit., *of the fulness* [a]Eph. 4:3, 5 [b]Eph. 1:17; Phil. 3:10; John 6:69 [c]Heb. 5:14; 1 Cor. 14:20; Col. 1:28 [d]John 1:16; Gal. 4:19; Eph. 1:23

14 [1]Lit., *that we may no longer be* [2]Lit., *with regard to the scheming of deceit* [a]1 Cor. 14:20 [b]James 1:6; Jude 12 [c]1 Cor. 3:19; 2 Cor. 4:2; 11:3 [d]Eph. 6:11

15 [1]Or, *holding to,* or, *walking in* [2]Lit., *may grow up* [a]Eph. 1:4 [b]Eph. 2:21 [c]Eph. 1:22

16 [1]Lit., *through every joint of the supply* [2]Lit., *working in measure* [a]Col. 2:19; Rom. 12:4f.; 1 Cor. 10:17 [b]Eph. 1:4

17 [a]Col. 2:4 [b]Luke 16:28

Lord, [c]that you walk no longer just as the Gentiles also walk, in
the [d]futility of their mind,
18 being [a]darkened in their understanding, [1]excluded from
[b]the life of God, because of the [c]ignorance that is in them,
because of the [d]hardness of their heart;
19 and they, having [a]become callous, [b]have given themselves over to [c]sensuality, [1]for the practice of every kind of
impurity with greediness.
20 But you did not [a]learn [1]Christ in this way,
21 if indeed you [a]have heard Him and have [b]been taught
in Him, just as truth is in Jesus,
22 that, in reference to your former manner of life, you
[a]lay aside the [b]old [1]self, which is being corrupted in accordance
with the [c]lusts of deceit,
23 and that you be [a]renewed in the spirit of your mind,
24 and [a]put on the [b]new [1]self, which [2c]in *the likeness of*
God has been created in righteousness and holiness of the
truth.
25 Therefore, [a]laying aside falsehood, [b]SPEAK TRUTH, EACH
ONE *of you*, WITH HIS NEIGHBOR, for we are [c]members of one
another.
26 [a]BE ANGRY, AND *yet* DO NOT SIN; do not let [b]the sun go
down on your anger,
27 and do not [a]give the devil an [1]opportunity.
28 Let him who steals steal no longer; but rather [a]let him
labor, [b]performing with his own hands what is good, [c]in order
that he may have *something* to share with him who has need.
29 Let no [1a]unwholesome word proceed from your
mouth, but only such *a word* as is good for [b]edification [2]accord-
ing to the need *of the moment*, that it may give grace to
those who hear.
30 And [a]do not grieve the Holy Spirit of God, [1]by whom
you were [b]sealed for the day of redemption.
31 [a]Let all bitterness and wrath and anger and clamor and
slander be [b]put away from you, along with all [c]malice.
32 And [a]be kind to one another, tender-hearted, forgiving
each other, [b]just as God in Christ also has forgiven [1]you.

CHAPTER 5

[a]THEREFORE be imitators of God, as beloved children;
2 and [a]walk in love, just as Christ also [b]loved [1]you, and
[c]gave Himself up for us, an [d]offering and a sacrifice to God [2]as
a [e]fragrant aroma.
3 But do not let [a]immorality [1]or any impurity or greed
even be named among you, as is proper among [2]saints;
4 and *there must be no* [a]filthiness and silly talk, or coarse
jesting, which [b]are not fitting, but rather [c]giving of thanks.
5 For this you know with certainty, that [a]no [1]immoral or
impure person or covetous man, who is an idolater, has an
inheritance in the kingdom [b]of Christ and God.
6 [a]Let no one deceive you with empty words, for because
of these things [b]the wrath of God comes upon [c]the sons of
disobedience.
7 Therefore do not be [a]partakers with them;

17 [c]Eph. 2:2; 4:22 [d]Rom. 1:21; Col. 2:18; 1 Pet. 1:18; 2 Pet. 2:18

18 [1]Or, *alienated* [a]Rom. 1:21 [b]Eph. 2:1, 12 [c]Acts 17:30; Heb. 5:2; 9:7; 1 Pet. 1:14; Acts 3:17; 1 Cor. 2:8 [d]Mark 3:5; Rom. 11:7, 25; 2 Cor. 3:14

19 [1]Or, *greedy for the practice of every kind of impurity* [a]1 Tim. 4:2 [b]Rom. 1:24 [c]Col. 3:5

20 [1]I.e., the Messiah [a]Matt. 11:29

21 [a]Rom. 10:14; Eph. 1:13; 2:17; Col. 1:5 [b]Col. 2:7

22 [1]Lit., *man* [a]Eph. 4:25, 31; Col. 3:8; Heb. 12:1 [Gr.]; James 1:21; 1 Pet. 2:1 [b]Rom. 6:6 [c]2 Cor. 11:3; Heb. 3:13

23 [a]Rom. 12:2

24 [1]Lit., *man* [2]Lit., *according to God* [a]Rom. 13:14 [b]Col. 3:10; Rom. 6:4; 7:6; 12:2; 2 Cor. 5:17 [c]Eph. 2:10

25 [a]Eph. 4:22, 31; Col. 3:8; Heb. 12:1 [Gr.]; James 1:21; 1 Pet. 2:1 [b]Zech. 8:16; Col. 3:9; Eph. 4:15 [c]Rom. 12:5

26 [a]Ps. 4:4 [b]Deut. 24:15

27 [1]Lit., *place* [a]James 4:7; Rom. 12:19

28 [a]Acts 20:35; 1 Cor. 4:12; Gal. 6:10 [b]1 Thess. 4:11; 2 Thess. 3:8, 11f.; Titus 3:8, 14 [c]Luke 3:11; 1 Thess. 4:12

29 [1]Lit., *rotten* [2]Lit., *of the need* [a]Eph. 5:4; Col. 3:8; Matt. 12:34 [b]Rom. 14:19; Col. 4:6; Eccl. 10:12

30 [1]Lit., *in* [a]Is. 63:10; 1 Thess. 5:19 [b]Eph. 1:13; John 3:33

31 [a]Col. 3:8, 19; Rom. 3:14 [b]Eph. 4:22 [c]1 Pet. 2:1

32 [1]Some ancient mss. read, *us* [a]Col. 3:12f.; 1 Cor. 13:4; 1 Pet. 3:8 [b]Matt. 6:14f.; 2 Cor. 2:10

1 [a]Eph. 4:32; Luke 6:36; Matt. 5:48

2 [1]Some ancient mss. read, *us* [2]Lit., *for an odor of fragrance* [a]Rom. 14:15; Col. 3:14 [b]John 13:34; Rom. 8:37 [c]Eph. 5:25; Gal. 2:20; Rom. 4:25; John 6:51 [d]Heb. 7:27; 9:14; 10:10, 12 [e]2 Cor. 2:14; Ex. 29:18, 25

3 [1]Lit., *and all* [2]I.e., true believers; lit., *holy ones* [a]Col. 3:5

4 [a]Eph. 4:29; Col. 3:8; Matt. 12:34 [b]Rom. 1:28 [c]Eph. 5:20

5 [1]I.e., one who commits sexual immorality [a]1 Cor. 6:9; Col. 3:5 [b]Col. 1:13

6 [a]Col. 2:8 [b]Rom. 1:18; Col. 3:6 [c]Eph. 2:2; Col. 3:6

7 [a]Eph. 3:6

8 for [a]you were formerly [b]darkness, but now you are light
in the Lord; walk as [c]children of light
9 (for [a]the fruit of the light *consists* in all [b]goodness and
righteousness and truth),
10 [1a]trying to learn what is pleasing to the Lord.
11 And [a]do not participate in the unfruitful [b]deeds of [c]dark-
ness, but instead even [1d]expose them;
12 for it is disgraceful even to speak of the things which
are done by them in secret.
13 But all things become visible [a]when they are [1]exposed
by the light, for everything that becomes visible is light.
14 For this reason [1a]it says,

"[b]AWAKE, SLEEPER,
AND ARISE FROM [c]THE DEAD,
AND CHRIST [d]WILL SHINE ON YOU."

15 Therefore [1]be careful how you [a]walk, not [b]as unwise
men, but as wise,
16 [1a]making the most of your time, because [b]the days are
evil.
17 So then do not be foolish, but [a]understand what the
will of the Lord is.
18 And [a]do not get drunk with wine, [1]for that is [b]dissipa-
tion, but be [c]filled with the Spirit,
19 [a]speaking to [1]one another in [b]psalms and [c]hymns and
spiritual [d]songs, [e]singing and making melody with your heart to
the Lord;
20 [a]always giving thanks for all things in the name of our
Lord Jesus Christ to [1b]God, even the Father;
21 [1a]and be subject to one another in the [2b]fear of Christ.
22 [a]Wives, [b]*be subject* to your own husbands, [c]as to the
Lord.
23 For [a]the husband is the head of the wife, as Christ also
is the [b]head of the church, He Himself [c]*being* the Savior of the
body.
24 But as the church is subject to Christ, so also the wives
ought to be to their husbands in everything.
25 [a]Husbands, love your wives, just as Christ also loved the
church and [b]gave Himself up for her;
26 [a]that He might sanctify her, having [b]cleansed her by
the [c]washing of water with [d]the word,
27 that He might [a]present to Himself the church [1]in all
her glory, having no spot or wrinkle or any such thing; but that
she should be [b]holy and blameless.
28 So husbands ought also to [a]love their own wives as their
own bodies. He who loves his own wife loves himself;
29 for no one ever hated his own flesh, but nourishes and
cherishes it, just as Christ also *does* the church,
30 because we are [a]members of His [b]body.
31 [a]FOR THIS CAUSE A MAN SHALL LEAVE HIS FATHER AND
MOTHER, AND SHALL CLEAVE TO HIS WIFE; AND THE TWO SHALL
BECOME ONE FLESH.
32 This mystery is great; but I am speaking with reference
to Christ and the church.
33 Nevertheless let each individual among you also [a]love
his own wife even as himself; and *let* the wife *see to it* that she
[1b]respect her husband.

8 [a]Eph. 2:2 [b]Acts 26:18; Col. 1:12f. [c]Luke 16:8; John 12:36; Rom. 13:12

9 [a]Gal. 5:22 [b]Rom. 15:14

10 [1]Lit., *proving what* [a]Rom. 12:2

11 [1]Or, *reprove* [a]1 Cor. 5:9; 2 Cor. 6:14 [b]Rom. 13:12 [c]Acts 26:18; Col. 1:12f. [d]1 Tim. 5:20

13 [1]Or, *reproved* [a]John 3:20f.

14 [1]Or, *He* [a]Is. 26:19; Is. 51:17; 52:1; 60:1 [b]Rom. 13:11 [c]Eph. 2:1 [d]Luke 1:78f.

15 [1]Lit., *look carefully* [a]Eph. 5:2 [b]Col. 4:5

16 [1]Lit., *redeeming the time* [a]Col. 4:5 [b]Eph. 6:13; Gal. 1:4

17 [a]Rom. 12:2; Col. 1:9; 1 Thess. 4:3

18 [1]Lit., *in which is* [a]Prov. 20:1; 23:31f.; Rom. 13:13; 1 Cor. 5:11; 1 Thess. 5:7 [b]Titus 1:6; 1 Pet. 4:4 [c]Luke 1:15

19 [1]Or, *yourselves* [a]Col. 3:16; James 5:13 [b]1 Cor. 14:26 [c]Acts 16:25 [d]Rev. 5:9 [e]1 Cor. 14:15

20 [1]Lit., *the God and Father* [a]Eph. 5:4; Col. 3:17; Rom. 1:8 [b]1 Cor. 15:24

21 [1]Lit., *being subject* [2]Or, *reverence* [a]Gal. 5:13; 1 Pet. 5:5; Phil. 2:3 [b]2 Cor. 5:11

22 [a]Eph. 5:22 to Eph. 6:9; *Col. 3:18 to 4:1* [b]1 Cor. 14:34f.; Titus 2:5; 1 Pet. 3:1 [c]Eph. 6:5

23 [a]1 Cor. 11:3 [b]Eph. 1:22 [c]1 Cor. 6:13

25 [a]Eph. 5:28, 33; 1 Pet. 3:7 [b]Eph. 5:2

26 [a]Heb. 10:10, 14, 29; 13:12; Titus 2:14 [b]2 Pet. 1:9 [c]Titus 3:5; Acts 22:16; 1 Cor. 6:11 [d]John 15:3; 17:17; Eph. 6:17; Rom. 10:8f.

27 [1]Lit., *glorious* [a]2 Cor. 11:2; Col. 1:22; 2 Cor. 4:14 [b]Eph. 1:4

28 [a]Eph. 5:25, 33; 1 Pet. 3:7

30 [a]1 Cor. 6:15; 12:27 [b]Eph. 1:23

31 [a]Gen. 2:24; Matt. 19:5; Mark 10:7f.

33 [1]Lit., *fear* [a]Eph. 5:25, 28; 1 Pet. 3:7 [b]1 Pet. 3:2, 5f.

Chapter 6

[a]CHILDREN, obey your parents in the Lord, for this is right.
2 [a]HONOR YOUR FATHER AND MOTHER (which is the first
commandment with a promise),
3 [a]THAT IT MAY BE WELL WITH YOU, AND THAT YOU MAY
LIVE LONG ON THE EARTH.
4 And, [a]fathers, do not provoke your children to anger;
but [b]bring them up in the discipline and instruction of the
Lord.
5 [a]Slaves, be obedient to those who are your [1]masters
according to the flesh, with [b]fear and trembling, in the sincerity of your heart, [c]as to Christ;
6 [a]not [1]by way of eyeservice, as [b]men-pleasers, but as
[c]slaves of Christ, doing the will of God from the [2]heart.
7 With good will [1]render service, [a]as to the Lord, and not
to men,
8 [a]knowing that [b]whatever good thing each one does, this
he will receive back from the Lord, [c]whether slave or free.
9 And, masters, do the same things to them, and [a]give up
threatening, knowing that [b]both their Master and yours is in
heaven, and there is [c]no partiality with Him.
10 Finally, [a]be strong in the Lord, and in [b]the strength of
His might.
11 [a]Put on the full armor of God, that you may be able to
stand firm against the [b]schemes of the devil.
12 For our [a]struggle is not against [1b]flesh and blood, but
[c]against the rulers, against the powers, against the [d]world-
forces of this [e]darkness, against the [f]spiritual *forces* of wickedness in [g]the heavenly *places*.
13 Therefore take up [a]the full armor of God, that you
may be able to [b]resist in [c]the evil day, and having done everything, to stand firm.
14 Stand firm therefore, [a]HAVING GIRDED YOUR LOINS WITH
TRUTH, and HAVING [b]PUT ON THE [c]BREASTPLATE OF RIGH-
TEOUSNESS,
15 and having [a]shod YOUR FEET WITH THE PREPARATION OF
THE GOSPEL OF PEACE;
16 [1]in addition to all, taking up the [a]shield of faith with
which you will be able to extinguish all the [b]flaming missiles of
[c]the evil *one*.
17 And take the [a]helmet of salvation, and the [b]sword of
the Spirit, which is [c]the word of God.
18 With all [a]prayer and petition [1b]pray at all times [c]in the
Spirit, and with this in view, [2d]be on the alert with all [e]persever-
ance and [f]petition for all the saints,
19 and [a]*pray* on my behalf, that utterance may be given to
me [b]in the opening of my mouth, to make known with [c]bold-
ness [d]the mystery of the gospel,
20 for which I am an [a]ambassador [b]in [1]chains; that [2]in
proclaiming it I may speak [c]boldly, [d]as I ought to speak.
21 [a]But that you also may know about my circumstances,
how I am doing, [b]Tychicus, [c]the beloved brother and faithful
minister in the Lord, will make everything known to you.
22 [1]And [a]I have sent him to you for this very purpose, so

1 [a]Col. 3:20; Prov. 6:20; 23:22

2 [a]Ex. 20:12; Deut. 5:16

3 [a]Ex. 20:12; Deut. 5:16

4 [a]Col. 3:21 [b]Gen. 18:19; Deut. 6:7; 11:19; Ps. 78:4; Prov. 22:6; 2 Tim. 3:15

5 [1]I.e., earthly masters, with fear
[a]Col. 3:22; 1 Tim. 6:1; Titus 2:9 [b]1 Cor. 2:3 [c]Eph. 5:22

6 [1]Lit., *according to* [2]Lit., *soul*
[a]Col. 3:22 [b]Gal. 1:10 [c]1 Cor. 7:22

7 [1]Lit., *rendering*
[a]Col. 3:23

8 [a]Col. 3:24 [b]Matt. 16:27; 2 Cor. 5:10; Col. 3:24f. [c]1 Cor. 12:13; Col. 3:11

9 [a]Lev. 25:43 [b]Job 31:13ff.; John 13:13 [c]Acts 10:34; Col. 3:25

10 [a]1 Cor. 16:13; 2 Tim. 2:1 [b]Eph. 1:19

11 [a]Eph. 6:13; Rom. 13:12 [b]Eph. 4:14

12 [1]Lit., *blood and flesh*
[a]1 Cor. 9:25 [b]Matt. 16:17 [c]Eph. 1:21; 2:2; 3:10 [d]John 12:31 [e]Acts 26:18; Col. 1:13 [f]Eph. 3:10 [g]Eph. 1:3

13 [a]Eph. 6:11 [b]James 4:7 [c]Eph. 5:16

14 [a]Is. 11:5; Luke 12:35; 1 Pet. 1:13 [b]Eph. 6:13; Rom. 13:12 [c]Is. 59:17; 1 Thess. 5:8

15 [a]Is. 52:7; Rom. 10:15

16 [1]Lit., *in all*
[a]1 Thess. 5:8 [b]Ps. 7:13; 120:4 [c]Matt. 5:37

17 [a]Is. 59:17 [b]Heb. 4:12; Is. 49:2; Hos. 6:5 [c]Heb. 6:5; Eph. 5:26

18 [1]Lit., *praying* [2]Lit., *being*
[a]Phil. 4:6 [b]Luke 18:1; Col. 1:3; 4:2; 1 Thess. 5:17 [c]Rom. 8:26f. [d]Mark 13:33 [e]Acts 1:14 [Gr.] [f]1 Tim. 2:1

19 [a]Col. 4:3; 1 Thess. 5:25 [b]2 Cor. 6:11 [c]2 Cor. 3:12 [d]Eph. 3:3

20 [1]Lit., *a chain* [2]Some ancient mss. read, *I may speak it boldly*
[a]2 Cor. 5:20; Philem. 9 marg. [b]Acts 21:33; 28:20; Col. 4:3; Eph. 3:1; Phil. 1:7 [c]2 Cor. 3:12 [d]Col 4:4

21 [a]Eph. 6:21, 22: Col. 4:7-9 [b]Acts 20:4 [c]Col. 4:7

22 [1]Lit., *whom I have sent to you*
[a]Col. 4:8

that you may know [2]about us, and that he may [b]comfort your hearts.

23 [a]Peace be to the brethren, and [b]love with faith, from God the Father and the Lord Jesus Christ.

24 Grace be with all those who love our Lord Jesus Christ [1]with *a love* incorruptible.

22 [2]Lit., *the things about us* [b]Col. 2:2; 4:8
23 [a]Gal. 6:16; 2 Thess. 3:16; 1 Pet. 5:14; Rom. 15:33 [b]Gal. 5:6; 1 Thess. 5:8
24 [1]Lit., *in incorruption*

THE EPISTLE OF PAUL TO THE

PHILIPPIANS

Salutation. Thanksgiving and Supplication.

[a]Paul and [b]Timothy, [c]bond-servants of [d]Christ Jesus, to [e]all the [1f]saints in Christ Jesus who are in [g]Philippi, including the [h]overseers and [i]deacons:

2 [a]Grace to you and peace from God our Father and the Lord Jesus Christ.

3 [a]I thank my God in all my remembrance of you,

4 always offering prayer with joy in [a]my every prayer for you all,

5 in view of your [1a]participation in the [b]gospel [c]from the first day until now.

6 *For I am* confident of this very thing, that He who began a good work in you will perfect it until [a]the day of Christ Jesus.

7 [1]For [a]it is only right for me to feel this way about you all, because I [b]have you in my heart, since both in my [2c]imprisonment and in the [d]defense and confirmation of the [e]gospel, you all are partakers of grace with me.

8 For [a]God is my witness, how I long for you all with the [1]affection of [b]Christ Jesus.

9 And this I pray, that [a]your love may abound still more and more in [b]real knowledge and all discernment,

10 so that you may [1a]approve the things that are excellent, in order to be sincere and blameless [2]until [b]the day of Christ;

11 having been filled with the [a]fruit of righteousness which *comes* through Jesus Christ, to the glory and praise of God.

12 Now I want you to know, brethren, that my circumstances [a]have turned out for the greater progress of the [b]gospel,

13 so that my [1a]imprisonment in *the cause of* Christ has become well-known throughout the whole [2]praetorian guard and to [b]everyone else,

14 and that most of the [1]brethren, trusting in the Lord because of my [2a]imprisonment, have [b]far more courage to speak the word of God without fear.

15 [a]Some, to be sure, are preaching Christ even from envy and strife, but some also from good will;

16 [1]the latter *do it* out of love, knowing that I am [a]appointed for the defense of the [b]gospel;

17 the former proclaim Christ [a]out of selfish ambition, [1]rather than from pure motives, thinking to cause me distress in my [2b]imprisonment.

1 [1]I.e., true believers; lit., *holy ones* [a]2 Cor. 1:1; Col. 1:1; Philem. 1; 1 Thess. 1:1; 2 Thess. 1:1 [b]Acts 16:1 [c]Rom. 1:1; Gal. 1:10 [d]Phil. 1:8; 2:5; 3:3, 8, 12, 14; 4:7, 19, 21; Gal. 3:26 [e]2 Cor. 1:1; Col. 1:2 [f]Acts 9:13 [g]Acts 16:12 [h]Acts 20:28; 1 Tim. 3:1f.; Titus 1:7 [i]1 Tim. 3:8ff.
2 [a]Rom. 1:7
3 [a]Rom. 1:8
4 [a]Rom. 1:9
5 [1]Or, *sharing in the preaching of the gospel* [a]Acts 2:42; Phil. 4:15 [b]Phil. 1:7, 12, 16, 27; 2:22; 4:3, 15 [c]Phil. 2:12; 4:15; Acts 16:12-40
6 [a]1 Cor. 1:8; Phil. 1:10; 2:16
7 [1]Lit., *Just as it is right* [2]Lit., *bonds* [a]2 Pet. 1:13 [b]2 Cor. 7:3 [c]Phil. 1:13f., 17; Acts 21:33; Eph. 6:20 [d]Phil. 1:16 [e]Phil. 1:5, 12, 16, 27; 2:22; 4:3, 15
8 [1]Lit., *inward parts* [a]Rom. 1:9 [b]Phil. 1:1; 2:5; 3:3, 8, 12, 14; 4:7, 19, 21; Gal. 3:26
9 [a]1 Thess. 3:12 [b]Col. 1:9
10 [1]Or, *distinguish between the things which differ* [2]Lit., *for* [a]Rom. 2:18 [b]1 Cor. 1:8; Phil. 1:6; 2:16
11 [a]James 3:18
12 [a]Luke 21:13 [b]Phil. 1:5, 7, 16, 27; 2:22; 4:3, 15
13 [1]Lit., *bonds* [2]Or, *governor's palace* [a]Phil. 1:7; 2 Tim. 2:9 [b]Acts 28:30
14 [1]Or, *brethren in the Lord, trusting because of my bonds* [2]Lit., *bonds* [a]Phil. 1:7; 2 Tim. 2:9 [b]Phil. 1:20; 2 Cor. 3:12; 7:4; Acts 4:31
15 [a]2 Cor. 11:13
16 [1]Some later mss. reverse the order of vss. 16 and 17 [a]1 Cor. 9:17 [b]Phil. 1:5, 7, 12, 27; 2:22; 4:3, 15
17 [1]Lit., *not sincerely* [2]Lit., *bonds* [a]Phil. 2:3; Rom. 2:8 [b]Phil. 1:7; 2 Tim. 2:9

18 What then? Only that in every way, whether in pretense or in truth, Christ is proclaimed; and in this I rejoice, yes,
and I will rejoice.
19 For I know that this shall turn out for my [1]deliverance
[a]through your [2]prayers and the provision of [b]the Spirit of Jesus
Christ,
20 according to my [a]earnest expectation and [b]hope, that I
shall not be [b]put to shame in anything, but *that* with [c]all
boldness, Christ shall even now, as always, be [d]exalted in my
body, [e]whether by life or by death.
21 For to me, [a]to live is Christ, and to die is gain.
22 [1]But if *I am* to live *on* in the flesh, this *will mean*
[a]fruitful labor for me; and I do not know [2]which to choose.
23 But I am hard pressed from both *directions,* having the
[a]desire to depart and [b]be with Christ, for *that* is very much
better;
24 yet to remain on in the flesh is more necessary for your
sake.
25 And [a]convinced of this, I know that I shall remain and
continue with you all for your progress and joy in the faith,
26 so that your [a]proud confidence in me may abound in
Christ Jesus through my coming to you again.
27 Only conduct yourselves in a manner [a]worthy of the
[b]gospel of Christ; so that whether I come and see you or
remain absent, I may hear of you that you are [c]standing firm
in [d]one spirit, with one [1]mind [e]striving together for the faith
of the gospel;
28 in no way alarmed by *your* opponents—which is a [a]sign
of destruction for them, but of salvation for you, and that *too,*
from God.
29 For to you [a]it has been granted for Christ's sake, not
only to believe in Him, but also to [b]suffer for His sake,
30 experiencing the same [a]conflict which [b]you saw in me,
and now hear *to be* in me.

Chapter 2

IF therefore there is any encouragement in Christ, if there is
any consolation of love, if there is any [a]fellowship of the Spirit,
if any [1b]affection and compassion,
2 [a]make my joy complete [1]by [b]being of the same mind,
maintaining the same love, united in spirit, intent on one
purpose.
3 Do nothing from [1a]selfishness or [b]empty conceit, but
with humility of mind let [c]each of you regard one another as
more important than himself;
4 [a]do not *merely* look out for your own personal interests, but also for the interests of others.
5 [a]Have this attitude [1]in yourselves which was also in
[b]Christ Jesus,
6 who, although He [a]existed in the [b]form of God, [c]did
not regard equality with God a thing to be grasped,
7 but [1a]emptied Himself, taking the form of a [b]bond-
servant, *and* [c]being made in the likeness of men.
8 And being found in appearance as a man, [a]He humbled

19 [1]Or, *salvation* [2]Lit., *supplication* [a]2 Cor. 1:11 [b]Acts 16:7

20 [a]Rom. 8:19 [b]Rom. 5:5; 1 Pet. 4:16 [c]Phil. 1:14; 2 Cor. 3:12; 7:4; Acts 4:31 [d]1 Cor. 6:20 [e]Rom. 14:8

21 [a]Gal. 2:20

22 [1]Or, *But if to live in the flesh, this will be fruitful labor for me, then I . . .* [2]Lit., *what I shall choose* [a]Rom. 1:13

23 [a]2 Cor. 5:8; 2 Tim. 4:6 [b]John 12:26

25 [a]Phil. 2:24

26 [a]2 Cor. 5:12; 7:4; Phil. 2:16

27 [1]Lit., *soul* [a]Eph. 4:1 [b]Phil. 1:5 [c]Phil. 4:1; 1 Cor. 16:13 [d]Acts 4:32 [e]Jude 3

28 [a]2 Thess. 1:5

29 [a]Matt. 5:12 [b]Acts 14:22

30 [a]1 Thess. 2:2; Heb. 10:32; also Col. 1:29; 2:1; 1 Tim. 6:12; 2 Tim. 4:7; Heb. 12:1, [Gr.] [b]Acts 16:19-40; Phil. 1:13

1 [1]Lit., *inward parts* [a]2 Cor. 13:14 [Gr.] [b]Col. 3:12

2 [1]Lit., *that you be* [a]John 3:29 [b]Rom. 12:16; Phil. 4:2

3 [1]Or, *contentiousness* [a]Phil. 1:17 marg.; Rom. 2:8 [b]Gal. 5:26 [c]Rom. 12:10; Eph. 5:21

4 [a]Rom. 15:1f.

5 [1]Or, *among* [a]Matt. 11:29; Rom. 15:3 [b]Phil. 1:1

6 [a]John 1:1 [b]2 Cor. 4:4 [c]John 5:18; 10:33; 14:28

7 [1]I.e., laid aside His privileges [a]2 Cor. 8:9 [b]Matt. 20:28 [c]John 1:14; Rom. 8:3; Gal. 4:4; Heb. 2:17

8 [a]2 Cor. 8:9

Himself by becoming [b]obedient to the point of death, even
[c]death [1]on a cross.
9 [a]Therefore also God [b]highly exalted Him, and bestowed
on Him [c]the name which is above every name,
10 that at the name of Jesus [a]every knee should bow, of
[b]those who are in heaven, and on earth, and under the earth,
11 and that every tongue should confess that Jesus Christ
is [a]Lord, to the glory of God the Father.
12 So then, my beloved, [a]just as you have always obeyed,
not as in my presence only, but now much more in my absence, work out your [b]salvation with [c]fear and trembling;
13 for it is [a]God who is at work in you, both to will and to
work [b]for *His* good pleasure.
14 Do all things without [a]grumbling or disputing;
15 that you may [1]prove yourselves to be [a]blameless and
innocent, [b]children of God above reproach in the midst of a
[c]crooked and perverse generation, among whom you [2d]appear
as [3e]lights in the world,
16 holding [1]fast the word of life, so that in [a]the day of
Christ I may have cause to glory because I did not [b]run in vain
nor [c]toil in vain.
17 But even if I am being [a]poured out as a drink offering
upon [b]the sacrifice and service of your faith, I rejoice and share
my joy with you all.
18 And you too, *I urge you*, rejoice in the same way and
share your joy with me.
19 But I hope [1]in the Lord Jesus to [a]send [b]Timothy to
you shortly, so that I also may be encouraged when I learn of
your condition.
20 For I have no one *else* [a]of kindred spirit who will genu-
inely be concerned for your welfare.
21 For they all [a]seek after their own interests, not those of
Christ Jesus.
22 But you know [a]of his proven worth that [b]he served with
me in the furtherance of the gospel [c]like a child *serving* his
father.
23 [a]Therefore I hope to send him immediately, as soon as
I see how things *go* with me;
24 and [a]I trust in the Lord that I myself also shall be
coming shortly.
25 But I thought it necessary to send to you [a]Epaphrodi-
tus, my brother and [b]fellow-worker and [c]fellow-soldier, who is
also your [1d]messenger and [e]minister to my need;
26 because he was longing [1]for you all and was distressed
because you had heard that he was sick.
27 For indeed he was sick to the point of death, but God
had mercy on him, and not on him only but also on me, lest I
should have sorrow upon sorrow.
28 Therefore I have sent him all the more eagerly in order
that when you see him again you may rejoice and I may be less
concerned *about you*.
29 Therefore [a]receive him in the Lord with all joy, and
[b]hold men like him in high regard;
30 because he came close to death [a]for the work of Christ,
risking his life to [b]complete [1]what was deficient in your service
to me.

8 [1]Lit., *of* [b]Heb. 5:8; Matt. 26:39; John 10:18; Rom. 5:19 [c]Heb. 12:2

9 [a]Heb. 1:9 [b]Matt. 28:18; Acts 2:33; Heb. 2:9 [c]Eph. 1:21

10 [a]Rom. 14:11 [b]Eph. 1:10

11 [a]John 13:13; Rom. 10:9; 14:9

12 [a]Phil. 1:5, 6; 4:15 [b]Heb. 5:9 [c]2 Cor. 7:15

13 [a]1 Cor. 12:6; 15:10; Rom. 12:3; Heb. 13:21 [b]Eph. 1:5

14 [a]1 Cor. 10:10; 1 Pet. 4:9

15 [1]Or, *become* [2]Or, *shine* [3]Or, *luminaries, stars* [a]Luke 1:6; Phil. 3:6 [b]Matt. 5:45; Eph. 5:1 [c]Acts 2:40 [d]Matt. 24:27 [e]Gen. 1:16

16 [1]Or, *forth* [a]Phil. 1:6 [b]Gal. 2:2 [c]Gal. 4:11; 1 Thess. 3:5; Is. 49:4

17 [a]2 Tim. 4:6; 2 Cor. 12:15 [b]Rom. 15:16; Num. 28:6, 7

19 [1]Or, *trusting in* [a]Phil. 2:23 [b]Phil. 1:1

20 [a]1 Cor. 16:10; 2 Tim. 3:10

21 [a]1 Cor. 10:24; 13:5; Phil. 2:4

22 [a]Rom. 5:4 [Gr.] [b]1 Cor. 16:10; 2 Tim. 3:10 [c]1 Cor. 4:17

23 [a]Phil. 2:19

24 [a]Phil. 1:25

25 [1]Lit., *apostle* [a]Phil. 4:18 [b]Rom. 16:3, 9, 21; Phil. 4:3; Philem. 1, 24 [c]Philem. 2 [d]2 Cor. 8:23; John 13:16 [e]Phil. 4:18

26 [1]Some ancient mss. read, *to see you all*

29 [a]Rom. 16:2 [b]1 Cor. 16:18

30 [1]Lit., *your deficiency of service* [a]Acts 20:24 [b]1 Cor. 16:17; Phil. 4:10

Chapter 3

FINALLY, my brethren, [a]rejoice in the Lord. To write the
same things *again* is no trouble to me, and it is a safeguard for
you.
2 Beware of the [a]dogs, beware of the [b]evil workers, beware of the [1]false circumcision;
3 for [a]we are the *true* [1]circumcision, who [b]worship in the
Spirit of God and [c]glory in [d]Christ Jesus and put no confidence
in the flesh,
4 although [a]I myself might have confidence even in the
flesh. If anyone else has a mind to put confidence in the flesh,
I far more:
5 [a]circumcised the eighth day, of the [b]nation of Israel, of
the [c]tribe of Benjamin, a [b]Hebrew of Hebrews; as to the Law,
[d]a Pharisee;
6 as to zeal, [a]a persecutor of the church; as to the [b]righ-
teousness which is in the Law, found [c]blameless.
7 But [a]whatever things were gain to me, those things I
have counted as loss for the sake of Christ.
8 More than that, I count all things to be loss in view of
the surpassing value of [1a]knowing [b]Christ Jesus my Lord, for
whom I have suffered the loss of all things, and count them
but rubbish in order that I may gain Christ,
9 and may be found in Him, not having [a]a righteousness
of my own derived from *the* Law, but that which is through
faith in Christ, [b]the righteousness which *comes* from God on
the basis of faith,
10 that I may [a]know Him, and [b]the power of His resurrection and [1c]the fellowship of His sufferings, being [d]conformed
to His death;
11 [1]in order that I may [a]attain to the resurrection from
the dead.
12 Not that I have already [a]obtained *it*, or have already
[b]become perfect, but I press on [1]in order that I may [c]lay hold
of that [2]for which also I [d]was laid hold of by [e]Christ Jesus.
13 Brethren, I do not regard myself as having laid hold of
it yet; but one thing *I do:* [a]forgetting what *lies* behind and
reaching forward to what *lies* ahead.
14 I [a]press on toward the goal for the prize of the [b]upward
call of God in [c]Christ Jesus.
15 Let us therefore, as many as are [1a]perfect, have this
attitude; and if in anything you have a [b]different attitude,
[c]God will reveal that also to you;
16 however, let us keep [1a]living by that same *standard* to
which we have attained.
17 Brethren, [a]join in following my example, and observe
those who walk according to the [b]pattern you have in us.
18 For [a]many walk, of whom I often told you, and now
tell you even [b]weeping, *that they are* enemies of [c]the cross of
Christ,
19 whose end is destruction, whose god is *their* [1a]appetite,
and *whose* [b]glory is in their shame, who [c]set their minds on
earthly things.
20 For [a]our [1]citizenship is in heaven, from which also we
eagerly [b]wait for a Savior, the Lord Jesus Christ;

1 [a]Phil. 4:4; Phil. 2:18

2 [1]Lit., *mutilation* (Gr., katatomé) [a]Ps. 22:16, 20; Rev. 22:15; Gal. 5:15 [b]2 Cor. 11:13

3 [1]Gr., peritomé [a]Rom. 2:29; 9:6; Gal. 6:15 [b]Gal. 5:25 [c]Rom. 15:17; Gal. 6:14 [d]Phil. 3:12; Phil. 1:1; Rom. 8:39

4 [a]2 Cor. 11:18; 5:16

5 [a]Luke 1:59 [b]2 Cor. 11:22; Rom. 11:1 [c]Rom. 11:1 [d]Acts 22:3; 23:6; 26:5

6 [a]Acts 8:3 [b]Phil. 3:9 [c]Phil. 2:15

7 [a]Luke 14:33

8 [1]Lit., *the knowledge of* [a]John 17:3; Eph. 4:13; 2 Pet. 1:3; Phil. 3:10; Jer. 9:23f. [b]Phil. 3:12; 1:1; Rom. 8:39

9 [a]Rom. 10:5; Phil. 3:6 [b]Rom. 9:30; 1 Cor. 1:30

10 [1]Or, *participation in* [a]John 17:3; Eph. 4:13; 2 Pet. 1:13; Phil. 3:8; Jer. 9:23f. [b]Rom. 6:5 [c]Rom. 8:17 [d]Rom. 6:5; 8:36; Gal. 6:17

11 [1]Lit., *if somehow* [a]1 Cor. 15:23; Rev. 20:5f.; Acts 26:7

12 [1]Lit., *if I may even* [2]Or, *because also* [a]1 Cor. 9:24f.; 1 Tim. 6:12, 19 [b]1 Cor. 13:10 [c]1 Tim. 6:12, 19 [d]Acts 9:5f. [e]Phil. 3:3, 8, Phil. 1:1; Rom. 8:39

13 [a]Luke 9:62

14 [a]1 Cor. 9:24; Heb. 6:1 [b]Rom. 11:29; 8:28; 2 Tim. 1:9 [c]Phil. 3:3

15 [1]Or, *mature* [a]1 Cor. 2:6 Matt. 5:48 [b]Gal. 5:10 [c]Eph. 1:17; 1 Thess. 4:9; John 6:45

16 [1]Lit., *following in line* [a]Gal. 6:16

17 [a]1 Cor. 4:16; Phil. 4:9 [b]1 Pet. 5:3

18 [a]2 Cor. 11:13 [b]Acts 20:31 [c]Gal. 6:14

19 [1]Lit., *belly* [a]Rom. 16:18; Titus 1:12 marg. [b]Rom. 6:21; Jude 13 [c]Rom. 8:5f.; Col. 3:2

20 [1]Lit., *commonwealth* [a]Eph. 2:19; Phil. 1:27 marg.; Col. 3:1; Heb. 12:22 [b]1 Cor. 1:7

21 who will [a]transform [1]the body of our humble state into
[b]conformity with [2]the [c]body of His glory, [d]by the exertion of
the power that He has even to [e]subject all things to Himself.

CHAPTER 4

THEREFORE, my beloved brethren [1]whom I [a]long *to see,*
my joy and crown, so [b]stand firm in the Lord, my beloved.
2 I urge Euodia and I urge Syntyche to [1a]live in harmony
in the Lord.
3 Indeed, true comrade, I ask you also to help these
women who have shared my struggle in *the cause of* the gospel, together with Clement also, and the rest of my [a]fellow-
workers, whose [b]names are in the book of life.
4 [a]Rejoice in the Lord always; again I will say, rejoice!
5 Let your forbearing *spirit* be known to all men. [a]The
Lord is [1]near.
6 [a]Be anxious for nothing, but in everthing by [b]prayer
and supplication with thanksgiving let your requests be made
known to God.
7 And [a]the peace of God, which [b]surpasses all [1]compre-
hension, shall [c]guard your hearts and your [d]minds in [e]Christ
Jesus.
8 Finally, brethren, [a]whatever is true, whatever is honorable, whatever is right, whatever is pure, whatever is lovely,
whatever is [1]of good repute, if there is any excellence and if
anything worthy of praise, [2]let your mind dwell on these
things.
9 The things you have learned and received and heard
and seen [a]in me, practice these things; and [b]the God of peace
shall be with you.
10 But I rejoiced in the Lord greatly, that now at last [a]you
have revived your concern for me; indeed, you were concerned
before, but you lacked opportunity.
11 Not that I speak [1]from want; for I have learned to be
[2a]content in whatever circumstances I am.
12 I know how to get along with humble means, and I also
know how to live in prosperity; in any and every circumstance I
have learned the secret of being filled and going [a]hungry, both
of having abundance and [b]suffering need.
13 I can do all things [1]through Him who [a]strengthens me.
14 Nevertheless, you have done well to [a]share *with me* in
my affliction.
15 And you yourselves also know, Philippians, that at the
[1a]first preaching of the gospel, after I departed from [b]Macedo-
nia, no church [c]shared with me in the matter of giving and
receiving but you alone;
16 for even in [a]Thessalonica you sent *a gift* more than
once for my needs.
17 [a]Not that I seek the gift itself, but I seek for the [1]profit
which increases to your account.
18 But I have received everything in full, and have an
abundance; I am [1]amply supplied, having received from [a]Epa-

21 [1]Or, *our lowly body* [2]Or, *His glorious body* [a]1 Cor. 15:43-53 [b]Rom. 8:29; Col. 3:4 [c]1 Cor. 15:43, 49 [d]Eph. 1:19 [e]1 Cor. 15:28

1 [1]Lit., *and longed for* [a]Phil. 1:8 [b]1 Cor. 16:13; Phil. 1:27

2 [1]Or, *be of the same mind* [a]Phil. 2:2

3 [a]Phil. 2:25 [b]Luke 10:20

4 [a]Phil. 3:1

5 [1]Or, *at hand* [a]1 Cor. 16:22 marg.; Heb. 10:37; James 5:8f.

6 [a]Matt. 6:25 [b]Eph. 6:18; 1 Tim. 2:1; 5:5

7 [1]Lit., *mind* [a]Is. 26:3; Phil. 4:9; John 14:27; Col. 3:15 [b]Phil. 3:19 [c]1 Pet. 1:5 [d]2 Cor. 10:5 [e]Phil. 1:1; 4:19, 21

8 [1]Or, *attractive* [2]Lit., *ponder these things* [a]Rom. 14:18; 1 Pet. 2:12

9 [a]Phil. 3:17 [b]Rom. 15:33

10 [a]2 Cor. 11:9; Phil. 2:30

11 [1]Lit., *according to* [2]Or, *self-sufficient* [a]1 Tim. 6:6, 8; 2 Cor. 9:8; Heb. 13:5

12 [a]1 Cor. 4:11 [b]2 Cor. 11:9

13 [1]Lit., *in* [a]2 Cor. 12:9; Eph. 3:16; Col. 1:11

14 [a]Heb. 10:33; Rev. 1:9, [in Gr.]

15 [1]Lit., *beginning of* [a]Phil. 1:5 [b]Rom. 15:26 [c]2 Cor. 11:9

16 [a]Acts 17:1; 1 Thess. 2:9

17 [1]Lit., *fruit* [a]2 Cor. 9:5; 1 Cor. 9:11f.

18 [1]Lit., *made full* [a]Phil. 2:25

phroditus [2]what you have sent, [3b]a fragrant aroma, an acceptable sacrifice, well pleasing to God.
19 And [a]my God shall supply [1]all your needs according to
His [b]riches in glory in Christ Jesus.
20 Now to [a]our God and Father [b]*be* the glory [1]forever and
ever. Amen.
21 Greet every [1]saint in Christ Jesus. [a]The brethren who
are with me greet you.
22 [a]All the [1b]saints greet you, especially those of Caesar's
household.
23 [a]The grace of the Lord Jesus Christ [b]be with your spirit.

18 [2]Lit., *the things from you* [3]Lit., *an odor of fragrance*
[b]2 Cor. 2:14; Eph. 5:2
19 [1]Or, *every need of yours*
[a]2 Cor. 9:8 [b]Rom. 2:4
20 [1]Lit., *to the ages of the ages*
[a]Gal. 1:4 [b]Rom. 11:36
21 [1]I.e., true believer; lit., *holy one*
[a]Gal. 1:2
22 [1]Note vs. 21
[a]2 Cor. 13:13 [b]Acts 9:13
23 [a]Rom. 16:20 [b]2 Tim. 4:22

THE EPISTLE OF PAUL TO THE
COLOSSIANS

Salutation. Thanksgiving for their Attainments.

[a]
PAUL, [b]an apostle of Jesus Christ [1c]by the will of God, and
[d]Timothy [2]our brother,
2 to the [1a]saints and faithful brethren in Christ *who are*
at Colossae: [b]Grace to you and peace from God our Father.
3 [a]We give thanks to God, [b]the Father of our Lord Jesus
Christ, praying always for you,
4 [a]since we heard of your faith in Christ Jesus and the
[b]love which you have [1]for [c]all the [2]saints;
5 because of the [a]hope [b]laid up for you in [1]heaven, of
which you previously [c]heard in the word of truth, [2]the gospel,
6 which has come to you, just as [1a]in all the world also it
is constantly bearing [b]fruit and [2]increasing, even as *it has been*
doing in you also since the day you [c]heard *of it* and [3]under-
stood the grace of God in truth;
7 just as you learned *it* from [a]Epaphras, our [b]beloved
fellow bond-servant, who is a faithful servant of Christ on [1]our
behalf,
8 and he also informed us of your [a]love in the Spirit.
9 For this reason also, [a]since the day we heard *of it,* [b]we
have not ceased to pray for you and to ask that you may be
filled with the [1c]knowledge of His will in all spiritual [d]wisdom
and understanding,
10 so that you may [a]walk in a manner worthy of the Lord,
[1b]to please *Him* in all respects, [c]bearing fruit in every good
work and [2]increasing in the [3]knowledge of God;
11 [a]strengthened with all power, according to [1]His glorious might, [2]for the attaining of all steadfastness and [3]pa-
tience, [b]joyously
12 giving thanks to [a]the Father, who has qualified us [1]to
share in [b]the inheritance of the [2]saints in [c]light.
13 For He delivered us from the [1a]domain of darkness,
and transferred us to the kingdom of [2b]His beloved Son,
14 [a]in whom we have redemption, the forgiveness of sins.

1 [1]Lit., *through* [2]Lit., *the*
[a]Phil. 1:1 [b]2 Cor. 1:1 [c]1 Cor. 1:1 [d]2 Cor. 1:1; 1 Thess. 3:2; Philem. 1; Heb. 13:23
2 [1]I.e., true believers; lit., *holy ones*
[a]Acts 9:13; Eph. 1:1; Phil. 1:1 [b]Rom. 1:7; Col. 4:18
3 [a]Rom. 1:8 [b]Rom. 15:6; 2 Cor. 1:3
4 [1]Or, *toward* [2]I.e., true believers; lit., *holy ones*
[a]Eph. 1:15 [b]Gal. 5:6 [c]Eph. 6:18
5 [1]Lit., *the heavens* [2]Or, *of the gospel*
[a]Col. 1:23; Rom. 5:2; 1 Thess. 5:8; Titus 1:2; Acts 23:6 [b]2 Tim. 4:8; 1 Pet. 1:4 [c]Eph. 1:13; Col. 1:6, 23
6 [1]Or, *it is in the world* [2]Or, *spreading abroad* [3]Or, *came really to know*
[a]Rom. 10:18; 1 Tim. 3:16; Col. 1:23 [b]Rom. 1:13 [c]Eph. 4:21; Col. 1:5
7 [1]Some later mss. read, *your*
[a]Col. 4:12; Philem. 23 [b]Col. 4:7
8 [a]Rom. 15:30
9 [1]Or, *real knowledge*
[a]Col. 1:4 [b]Eph. 1:16 [c]Eph. 5:17; Phil. 1:9 [d]Eph. 1:17
10 [1]Lit., *unto all pleasing* [2]Or, *growing by the knowledge* [3]Or, *real knowledge*
[a]Eph. 4:1; Col. 2:6 [b]2 Cor. 5:9; Eph. 5:10 [c]Rom. 1:13
11 [1]Lit., *the might of His glory* [2]Lit., *unto all* [3]Or, *patience with joy*
[a]Eph. 3:16; 1 Cor. 16:13 [b]Eph. 4:2
12 [1]Lit., *unto the portion of* [2]I.e., true believers; lit., *holy ones*
[a]Eph. 2:18 [b]Acts 20:32 [c]Acts 26:18; Eph. 6:12
13 [1]Lit., *authority* [2]Lit., *the Son of His love*
[a]Acts 26:18; Eph. 6:12 [b]Matt. 3:17; Eph. 1:6
14 [a]Eph. 1:7; Rom. 3:24

15 And He is the [a]image of the [b]invisible God, the [c]first-
born of all creation.
16 For [a]in Him all things were created, [a]*both* in the heavens and on earth, visible and invisible, whether [b]thrones or
dominions or rulers or authorities—[c]all things have been
created through Him and for Him.
17 And He [1a]is before all things, and in Him all things
[2]hold together.
18 He is also [a]head of [b]the body, the church; and He is
[c]the beginning, [d]the first-born from the dead; so that He
Himself might come to have first place in everything.
19 For [1]it was [a]the *Father's* good pleasure for all [b]the
[2]fulness to dwell in Him,
20 and through Him to [a]reconcile all things to Himself,
having made [b]peace through [c]the blood of His cross; through
Him, *I say*, [d]whether things on earth or things in [1]heaven.
21 And although you were [a]formerly alienated and hostile
in mind, *engaged* in evil deeds,
22 yet He has now [a]reconciled you in His fleshly [b]body
through death, in order to [c]present you before Him [d]holy and
blameless and beyond reproach—
23 if indeed you continue in [1]the faith firmly [a]established
and steadfast, and not moved away from the [b]hope of the
gospel that you have heard, which was proclaimed [c]in all creation under heaven, [d]and of which I Paul [2]was made a
[3e]minister.
24 [a]Now I rejoice in my sufferings for your sake, and in my
flesh [b]I [1]do my share on behalf of [c]His body (which is the
church) in filling up that which is lacking [2]in Christ's
afflictions.
25 [a]Of *this church* I [1]was made a minister according to the
[b]stewardship from God bestowed on me for your benefit, that
I might [2]fully carry out the *preaching of* the word of God,
26 *that is*, [a]the mystery which has been hidden from the
past ages and generations; but has now been manifested to His
[1]saints,
27 to whom [a]God willed to make known what is [b]the
riches of the glory of this mystery among the Gentiles, which is
[c]Christ in you, the [d]hope of glory.
28 And we proclaim Him, [a]admonishing every man and
teaching every man [1]with all [b]wisdom, that we may [c]present
every man [2d]complete in Christ.
29 And for this purpose also I [a]labor, [b]striving [c]according
to His [1]power, which [2]mightily works within me.

Chapter 2

FOR I want you to know how great a [a]struggle I have on your
behalf, and for those who are at [b]Laodicea, and for all those
who have not [1]personally seen my face,
2 that their [a]hearts may be encouraged, having been [b]knit
together in love, and *attaining* to all [c]the wealth [1]that comes
from the [d]full assurance of understanding, *resulting* in a [e]true
knowledge of [f]God's mystery, *that is*, Christ *Himself*,

15 [a]2 Cor. 4:4 [b]1 Tim. 1:17; Heb. 11:27; John 1:18 [c]Col. 1:17f.; Rom. 8:29

16 [a]Eph. 1:10 [b]Eph. 1:20f.; Col. 2:15 [c]John 1:3; Rom. 11:36; 1 Cor. 8:6

17 [1]Or, *has existed prior to* [2]Or, *endure* [a]John 1:1; 8:58

18 [a]Eph. 1:22 [b]Eph. 1:23; Col. 1:24; Col. 2:19 [c]Rev. 3:14 [d]Acts 26:23

19 [1]Or, *all the fulness was pleased to dwell* [2]I.e., fulness of diety [a]Eph. 1:5 [b]John 1:16

20 [1]Lit., *the heavens* [a]2 Cor. 5:18; Eph. 2:16 [b]Rom. 5:1; Eph. 2:14 [c]Eph. 2:13 [d]Col. 1:16

21 [a]Rom. 5:10; Eph. 2:3; 2:12

22 [a]2 Cor. 5:18; Eph. 2:16 [b]Rom. 7:4 [c]Eph. 5:27; Col. 1:28 [d]Eph. 1:4

23 [1]Or omit, *the* [2]Lit., *became* [3]Or, *servant* [a]Eph. 3:17; Col. 2:7 [b]Col. 1:5 [c]Col. 1:6; Mark 16:15; Acts 2:5 [d]Col. 1:25; Eph. 3:7 [e]1 Cor. 3:5

24 [1]Or, *representatively . . . fill up* [2]Lit., *of* [a]Phil. 2:17; Rom. 8:17; 2 Cor. 1:5; 12:15 [b]2 Tim. 1:8; 2:10 [c]Col. 1:18

25 [1]Lit., *became* [2]Lit., *make full the word of God* [a]Col. 1:23 [b]Eph. 3:2

26 [1]I.e., true believers; lit., *holy ones* [a]Eph. 3:3f.; Rom. 16:25f.; Col. 2:2; 4:3

27 [a]Matt. 13:11 [b]Eph. 1:18; 3:16; Eph. 1:7 [c]Rom. 8:10 [d]1 Tim. 1:1

28 [1]Lit., *in* [2]Or, *perfect* [a]Acts 20:31; Col. 3:16 [b]1 Cor. 2:6f.; Col. 2:3 [c]Col. 1:22 [d]Matt. 5:48; Eph. 4:13

29 [1]Lit., *working* [2]Lit., *in power* [a]1 Cor. 15:10 [b]Col. 4:12; 2:1 [c]Eph. 1:19; Col. 2:12

1 [1]Lit., *in the flesh* [a]Col. 4:12; 1:29 [b]Col. 4:13, 15f.; Rev. 1:11

2 [1]Lit., *of the full assurance* [a]Eph. 6:22; Col. 4:8; 1 Cor. 14:31 [b]Col. 2:19 [c]Eph. 1:18; 3:16; 1:7 [d]Luke 1:1 [Gr.] [e]Matt. 13:11 [f]Eph. 3:3f.; Rom. 16:25f.; Col. 1:26; 4:3

3 in whom are hidden all [a]the treasures of wisdom and
knowledge.
4 [a]I say this in order that no one may delude you with
[b]persuasive argument.
5 For even though I am [a]absent in body, nevertheless I
am with you in spirit, rejoicing [1]to see [2]your [b]good discipline
and the [c]stability of your faith in Christ.
6 As you therefore have received [a]Christ Jesus the Lord,
so [1b]walk in Him,
7 having been firmly [a]rooted *and now* being [b]built up in
Him and [c]established [1]in your faith, just as you [d]were instructed, *and* overflowing [2]with gratitude.
8 [a]See to it that no one takes you captive through [b]philos-
ophy and empty deception, according to the tradition of men,
according to the [c]elementary principles of the world, [1]rather
than according to Christ.
9 For in Him all the [a]fulness of Deity dwells in bodily
form,
10 and in Him you have been [a]made [1]complete, and [b]He
is the head [2]over all [c]rule and authority;
11 and in Him [a]you were also circumcised with a circumcision made without hands, in the removal of [b]the body of the
flesh by the circumcision of Christ;
12 having been [a]buried with Him in baptism, in which you
were also [b]raised up with Him through faith in the working of
God, who [c]raised Him from the dead.
13 And when you were [a]dead [1]in your transgressions and
the uncircumcision of your flesh, He [b]made you alive together
with Him, having forgiven us all our transgressions,
14 having cancelled out [a]the certificate of debt consisting
of decrees against us *and* which was hostile to us; and [b]He has
taken it out of the way, having nailed it to the cross.
15 When He had [1a]disarmed the [b]rulers and authorities,
He [c]made a public display of them, having [d]triumphed over
them through [2]Him.
16 Therefore let no one [1a]act as your judge in regard to
[b]food or [b]drink or in respect to a [c]festival or a [d]new moon or a
[e]Sabbath [2]day—
17 things which are [a]a *mere* shadow of what is to come;
but the [1]substance [2]belongs to Christ.
18 Let no one keep [1a]defrauding you of your prize by
[b]delighting in [2]self-abasement and the worship of the angels,
taking his stand on *visions* he has seen, [c]inflated without cause
by his [d]fleshly mind,
19 and not holding fast to [a]the Head, from whom [b]the
entire body, being supplied and held together by the joints and
[1]ligaments, grows with a growth [2]which is from God.
20 [a]If you have died with Christ [1]to the [b]elementary principles of the world, [c]why, as if you were living in the world, do
you submit yourself to [d]decrees, such as,
21 "Do not handle, do not taste, do not touch!"
22 (which all *refer* [a]*to* things destined to perish [1]with the
using)—in accordance with the [b]commandments and teachings of men?
23 These are matters which have, to be sure, the appearance of wisdom in [1a]self-made religion and self-abasement

3 [a]Is. 11:2; Rom. 11:33

4 [a]Eph. 4:17 [b]Rom. 16:18

5 [1]Lit., *and seeing* [2]Or, *your ordered array*
[a]1 Cor. 5:3 [b]1 Cor. 14:40
[c]1 Pet. 5:9

6 [1]Or, *lead your life*
[a]Gal. 3:26 [b]Col. 1:10

7 [1]Or, *by* [2]Some mss. read, *in it with*
[a]Eph. 3:17 [b]Eph. 2:20; 1 Cor. 3:9 [c]1 Cor. 1:8 [d]Eph. 4:21

8 [1]Lit., *and not*
[a]1 Cor. 8:9; 10:12; Gal. 5:15; Heb. 3:12 [b]Col. 2:23; 1 Tim. 6:20; Eph. 5:6 [c]Col. 2:20; Gal. 4:3

9 [a]Col. 1:19; 2 Cor. 5:19

10 [1]Or, *full* [2]Lit., *of*
[a]Eph. 3:19 [b]Eph. 1:21f. [c]Col. 2:15; Eph. 3:10; 1 Cor. 15:24

11 [a]Rom. 2:29; Eph. 2:11
[b]Rom. 6:6; 7:24; Gal. 5:24; Col. 3:5

12 [a]Rom. 6:4f. [b]Rom. 6:5; Eph. 2:6; Col. 2:13; 3:1 [c]Acts 2:24

13 [1]Or, *by reason of*
[a]Eph. 2:1 [b]Eph. 2:1, 5; Col. 2:12

14 [a]Eph. 2:15; Col. 2:20
[b]1 Pet. 2:24

15 [1]Or, *divested Himself of* [2]Or, *it;* i.e., the cross.
[a]Eph. 4:8 [b]Col. 2:10; Eph. 3:10; 1 Cor. 15:24 [c]Is. 53:12; Matt. 12:29; Luke 10:18; John 12:31; Eph. 4:8 [d]2 Cor. 2:14 [Gr.]

16 [1]Lit., *judge you* [2]Or, *days*
[a]Rom. 14:3 [b]Mark 7:19; Rom. 14:17; Heb. 9:10 [c]Lev. 23:2; Rom. 14:5 [d]1 Chr. 23:31; 2 Chr. 31:3; Neh. 10:33; [e]Mark 2:27f.; Gal. 4:10f.

17 [1]Lit., *body* [2]Lit., *of Christ*
[a]Heb. 8:5; 10:1

18 [1]Or, *giving judgment against you* [2]Or, *humility*
[a]1 Cor. 9:24; Phil. 3:14 [b]Col. 2:23 [c]1 Cor. 4:6 [d]Rom. 8:7

19 [1]Lit., *bonds* [2]Lit., *of God*
[a]Eph. 1:22 [b]Eph. 1:23; 4:16

20 [1]Lit., *from*
[a]Rom. 6:2 [b]Col. 2:8 [c]Gal. 4:9
[d]Col. 2:14, 16

22 [1]Or, *by being consumed*
[a]1 Cor. 6:13 [b]Is. 29:13; Matt. 15:9; Titus 1:14

23 [1]Or, *delight in religiousness*
[a]Col. 2:18

and [b]severe treatment of the body, *but are* of no value against
[c]fleshly indulgence.

Chapter 3

IF then you have been [a]raised up with Christ, keep seeking
the things above, where Christ is, [b]seated at the right hand of
God.
2 [1a]Set your mind on the things above, not on the things
that are on earth.
3 For you have [a]died and your life is hidden with Christ
in God.
4 When Christ, [a]who is our life, is revealed, [b]then you
also will be revealed with Him in glory.
5 [a]Therefore [1]consider [b]the members of your earthly
body as dead to [2c]immorality, impurity, passion, evil desire,
and greed, which [3]amounts to idolatry.
6 For it is on account of these things that [a]the wrath of
God will come[1],
7 and [a]in them you also once walked, when you were
living in them.
8 But now you also, [a]put them all aside: [b]anger, wrath,
malice, slander, *and* [c]abusive speech from your mouth.
9 [1a]Do not lie to one another, since you [b]laid aside the
old [2]self with its *evil* practices,
10 and have [a]put on the new [1]self who is being [2b]renewed
to a true knowledge [c]according to the image of the One who
[d]created him,
11 —*a renewal* in which [a]there is no *distinction between*
Greek and Jew, [b]circumcised and uncircumcised, [c]barbarian,
Scythian, [d]slave and freeman, but [e]Christ is all, and in all.
12 And so, as those who have been [a]chosen of God, holy
and beloved, [b]put on a [c]heart of compassion, kindness, [d]humil-
ity, gentleness and [1e]patience;
13 [a]bearing with one another, and [b]forgiving each other,
whoever has a complaint against any one; [b]just as the Lord
forgave you, so also should you.
14 And beyond all these things *put on* love, which is [1a]the
perfect bond of [b]unity.
15 And let [a]the peace of Christ [1]rule in your hearts, to
which [2]indeed you were called in [b]one body; and [3]be thankful.
16 Let [a]the word of [1]Christ richly dwell within you; [2]with
all wisdom [b]teaching and admonishing one another [c]with
psalms *and* hymns *and* spiritual songs, [d]singing [3]with thankfulness in your hearts to God.
17 And [a]whatever you do in word or deed, *do* all in the
name of the Lord Jesus, [b]giving thanks through Him to God
the Father.
18 [a]Wives, [b]be subject to your husbands, as is fitting in the
Lord.
19 [a]Husbands, love your wives, and do not be embittered
against them.
20 [a]Children, be obedient to your parents in all things, for
this is well pleasing [1]to the Lord.

---

23 [b]1 Tim. 4:3 [c]Rom. 13:14; 1 Tim. 4:8

1 [a]Col. 2:12 [b]Mark 16:19

2 [1]Or, *Be intent on* [a]Phil. 3:19, 20; Matt. 16:23

3 [a]Rom. 6:2; 2 Cor. 5:14; Col. 2:20

4 [a]Gal. 2:20; John 11:25 [b]1 Cor. 1:7; 1 Pet. 1:13; 1 John 2:28; 3:2; Phil. 3:21

5 [1]Lit., *put to death the members which are upon the earth* [2]Lit., *fornication* [3]Lit., *is* [a]Rom. 8:13 [b]Col. 2:11 [c]Mark 7:21f.; Gal. 5:19; 1 Cor. 6:9f., 18; 2 Cor. 12:21; Eph. 4:19; 5:3, 5

6 [1]Some early mss. add, *upon the sons of disobedience* [a]Rom. 1:18; Eph. 5:6

7 [a]Eph. 2:2

8 [a]Eph. 4:22 [b]Eph. 4:31 [c]Eph. 4:29

9 [1]Or, *Stop lying* [2]Lit., *man* [a]Eph. 4:25 [b]Eph. 4:22

10 [1]Lit., *man* [2]Lit., *renovated* [a]Eph. 4:24 [b]Rom. 12:2; 2 Cor. 4:16; Eph. 4:23 [c]Rom. 8:29 [d]Eph. 2:10

11 [a]Rom. 10:12; 1 Cor. 12:13; Gal. 3:28 [b]1 Cor. 7:19; Gal. 5:6 [c]Acts 28:2 [d]Eph. 6:8 [e]Eph. 1:23

12 [1]I.e., forbearance toward others [a]Luke 18:7 [b]Eph. 4:24 [c]Gal. 5:22f.; Phil. 2:1; Luke 1:78 marg. [d]Eph. 4:2; Phil. 2:3 [e]2 Cor. 6:6; 1 Cor. 13:4

13 [a]Eph. 4:2 [b]Eph. 4:32; Rom. 15:7

14 [1]Lit., *the uniting bond of perfectness* [a]Eph. 4:3 [b]Heb. 6:1; John 17:23

15 [1]Or, *act as arbiter* [2]Lit., *also* [3]Or, *show yourselves thankful* [a]John 14:27 [b]Eph. 2:16

16 [1]Some mss. read, *the Lord;* others read, *God* [2]Or, *in* [3]Or, *by;* lit., *in His grace* [a]Rom. 10:17; Eph. 5:26; 1 Thess. 1:8 [b]Eph. 5:19; Col. 1:28 [c]Eph. 5:19 [d]1 Cor. 14:15

17 [a]1 Cor. 10:31 [b]Eph. 5:20; Col. 3:15

18 [a]Col. 3:18 to 4:1: *Eph. 5:22 to 6:9* [b]Eph. 5:22

19 [a]Eph. 5:25

20 [1]Lit., *in* [a]Eph. 6:1

21 [a]Fathers, do not [1]exasperate your children, that they
may not lose heart.
22 [a]Slaves, in all things obey those who are your masters
[1]on earth, [b]not with [2]external service, as those who *merely*
please men, but with sincerity of heart, fearing the Lord.
23 Whatever you do, do your work [1]heartily, [a]as for the
Lord [2]rather than for men;
24 [a]knowing that from the Lord you will receive the reward [1]of [b]the inheritance. It is the Lord Christ whom you
[c]serve.
25 For [a]he who does wrong will receive the consequences
of the wrong which he has done, and [1b]that without partiality.

Chapter 4

MASTERS, grant to your slaves justice and fairness, knowing that you too have a Master in heaven.
2 [a]Devote yourselves to prayer, keeping alert in it with *an*
attitude of thanksgiving;
3 praying at the same time [a]for us as well, that God may
open up to us a [b]door for [c]the word, so that we may speak
forth [d]the mystery of Christ, for which I have also [e]been
imprisoned;
4 in order that I may make it clear [a]in the way I ought to
speak.
5 [1a]Conduct yourselves with wisdom toward [b]outsiders,
[2c]making the most of the opportunity.
6 [a]Let your speech always be [1]with grace, seasoned, *as it*
were, with [b]salt, so that you may know how you should [c]respond
to each person.
7 [a]As to all my affairs, [b]Tychicus, *our* [c]beloved brother
and faithful servant and fellow-bondslave in the Lord, will
bring you information.
8 [a]For I have sent him to you for this very purpose, that
you may know *about* our circumstances and that he may [b]en-
courage your hearts;
9 [1]and with him [a]Onesimus, *our* faithful and [b]beloved
brother, [c]who is one of your *number.* They will inform you
about the whole situation here.
10 [a]Aristarchus, my [b]fellow prisoner, sends you his greetings; and *also* [c]Barnabas' cousin Mark (about whom you received [1]instructions: [d]if he comes to you, welcome him);
11 and *also* Jesus who is called Justus; these are the only
[a]fellow-workers for the kingdom of God [b]who are from the
circumcision; and they have proved to be an encouragement to
me.
12 [a]Epaphras, [b]who is one of your number, a bondslave of
Jesus Christ, sends you his greetings, always [c]laboring earnestly
for you in his prayers, that you may [1]stand [2d]perfect and [3e]fully
assured in all the will of God.
13 For I bear him witness that he has [1]a deep concern for
you and for those who are in [a]Laodicea and Hierapolis.
14 [a]Luke, the beloved physician, sends you his greetings,
and *also* [b]Demas.
15 Greet the brethren who are in [a]Laodicea and also
[1]Nympha and [b]the church that is in [2]her house.

21 [1]Some early mss. read, *provoke to anger* [a]Eph. 6:4

22 [1]Lit., *according to the flesh* [2]Lit., *eye-service* [a]Eph. 6:5 [b]Eph. 6:6

23 [1]Lit., *from the soul* [2]Lit., *and not* [a]Eph. 6:7

24 [1]I.e., consisting of [a]Eph. 6:8 [b]Acts 20:32; 1 Pet. 1:4 [c]1 Cor. 7:22

25 [1]Lit., *there is no partiality* [a]Eph. 6:8 [b]Acts 10:34; Eph. 6:9

2 [a]Acts 1:14; Eph. 6:18

3 [a]Eph. 6:19 [b]Acts 14:27 [c]2 Tim. 4:2 [d]Eph. 3:3, 4; 6:19 [e]Eph. 6:20

4 [a]Eph. 6:20

5 [1]Lit., *Walk* [2]Lit., *redeeming the time* [a]Eph. 5:15 [b]Mark 4:11 [c]Eph. 5:16

6 [1]Or, *gracious* [a]Eph. 4:29 [b]Mark 9:50 [c]1 Pet. 3:15

7 [a]Col. 4:7-9: *Eph. 6:21, 22* [b]Acts 20:4 [c]Eph. 6:21; Col. 1:7

8 [a]Eph. 6:22 [b]Col. 2:2

9 [1]Lit., *along with Onesimus* [a]Philem. 10 [b]Col. 1:7 [c]Col. 4:12

10 [1]Or, *orders* [a]Acts 19:29 [b]Rom. 16:7 [c]Acts 12:12; 15:37, 39; 4:36 [d]2 Tim. 4:11

11 [a]Rom. 16:3 [b]Acts 11:2

12 [1]Or, *stand firm* [2]Or, *complete;* or, *mature* [3]Or, *made complete* [a]Col. 1:7 [b]Col. 4:9 [c]Rom. 15:30 [d]Col. 1:28 [e]Luke 1:1 and marg.

13 [1]Or, *much toil;* or, *great pain* [a]Col. 2:1; 4:15f.

14 [a]2 Tim. 4:11; Philem. 24 [b]2 Tim. 4:10; Philem. 24

15 [1]Or, *Nymphas* (masc.) [2]Some ancient mss. read, *their* [a]Col. 2:1; 4:13, 16 [b]Rom. 16:5

16 And [a]when [1]this letter is read among you, have it also
read in the church of the Laodiceans; and you, for your part
[a]read [1]my letter *that is coming* from [b]Laodicea.
17 And say to [a]Archippus, "Take heed to the [b]ministry
which you have received in the Lord, that you may [1]fulfill it."
18 [1]I, Paul, [a]write this greeting with my own hand. [b]Re-
member my [2c]imprisonment. [d]Grace be with you.

16 [1]Lit., *the*
[a]1 Thess. 5:27; 2 Thess. 3:14 [b]Col. 2:1; 4:13, 15

17 [1]Or, *continually fulfill*
[a]Philem. 2 [b]2 Tim. 4:5

18 [1]Lit., *the greeting by my hand of Paul* [2]Lit., *bonds*
[a]1 Cor. 16:21 [b]Heb. 13:3 [c]Phil. 1:7; Col. 4:3 [d]1 Tim. 6:21; 2 Tim. 4:22; Titus 3:15; Heb. 13:25

THE FIRST EPISTLE OF PAUL TO THE
THESSALONIANS

Salutation. Thanksgiving for their Reception of the Gospel.

[a]PAUL and [b]Silvanus and [c]Timothy to the [d]church of the
Thessalonians in God the Father and the Lord Jesus Christ:
[e]Grace to you and peace.
2 [a]We give thanks to God always for all of you, [b]making
mention *of you* in our prayers;
3 constantly bearing in mind your [a]work of faith and
labor of [b]love and [1c]steadfastness of hope [2]in our Lord Jesus
Christ in the presence of [d]our God and Father;
4 knowing, [a]brethren beloved by God, [b]*His* choice of
you,
5 for our [a]gospel did not come to you in word only, but
also [b]in power and in the Holy Spirit and with [c]full conviction;
just as you know [d]what kind of men we [1]proved to be among
you for your sake.
6 You also became [a]imitators of us and of the Lord,
[b]having received [c]the word in much tribulation with the [d]joy
[1]of the Holy Spirit,
7 so that you became an example to all the believers in
[a]Macedonia and in [b]Achaia.
8 For [a]the word of the Lord has [b]sounded forth from
you, not only in [c]Macedonia and [d]Achaia, but also [e]in every
place your faith toward God has gone forth, so that we have no
need to say anything.
9 For they themselves report about us what kind of a
[1a]reception we had [2]with you, and how you [b]turned to God
[c]from [3]idols to serve [4d]a living and true God,
10 and to [a]wait for His Son from [1]heaven, whom He
[b]raised from the dead, *that is* Jesus, who [c]delivers us from [d]the
wrath to come.

1 [a]2 Thess. 1:1 [b]2 Cor. 1:19 [c]Acts 16:1 [2 Thess. 1:1] [d]2 Thess. 1:1; Acts 17:1 [e]Rom. 1:7

2 [a]2 Thess. 1:3; Rom. 1:8; Eph. 5:20; 1 Thess. 2:13 [b]Rom. 1:9

3 [1]Or, *perseverance* [2]Lit., *of*
[a]2 Thess. 1:11; John 6:29; Gal. 5:6 [b]1 Thess. 3:6; 2 Thess. 1:3f.; 1 Cor. 13:13 [c]Rom. 8:25; 15:4 [d]Gal. 1:4

4 [a]2 Thess. 2:13; Rom. 1:7 [b]2 Pet. 1:10; Rom. 9:11

5 [1]Lit., *became*
[a]2 Cor. 2:12; 1 Cor. 9:14; 1 Thess. 2:2, 4, 8f.; 3:2; 2 Thess. 2:14 [b]Rom. 15:19; 1 Cor. 2:4; 2 Cor. 6:6 [c]Col. 2:2; Luke 1:1 [Gr.] [d]1 Thess. 2:10

6 [1]Lit., *inspired by*
[a]1 Cor. 4:16; 11:1f. [b]Acts 17:5-10 [c]2 Tim. 4:2 [d]Acts 13:52; 2 Cor. 6:10; Gal. 5:22

7 [a]Rom. 15:26 [b]Acts 18:12

8 [a]2 Thess. 3:1; Col. 3:16 [b]Rom. 10:18 [c]Rom. 15:26 [d]Acts 18:12 [e]Rom. 1:8; 2 Cor. 2:14; Rom. 16:19

9 [1]Lit., *entrance* [2]Lit., *to* [3]Or, *the idols* [4]Or, *the*
[a]1 Thess. 2:1 [b]Acts 14:15 [c]1 Cor. 12:2 [d]Matt. 16:16

10 [1]Lit., *the heavens*
[a]Matt. 16:27f.; 1 Cor. 1:7 [b]Acts 2:24 [c]Rom. 5:9 [d]Matt. 3:7; 1 Thess. 2:16; 5:9

CHAPTER 2

FOR you yourselves know, brethren, that our [1a]coming to
you [b]was not in vain,
2 but after we had already suffered and been [a]mistreated
in [b]Philippi, as you know, we had the boldness in our God [c]to
speak to you the [d]gospel of God amid much [1e]opposition.
3 For our [a]exhortation does not *come* from [b]error or
[c]impurity or [1]by way of [d]deceit;

1 [1]Lit., *entrance*
[a]1 Thess. 1:9 [b]2 Thess. 1:10

2 [1]Or, *struggle, conflict*
[a]Phil. 1:30; Acts 14:5 [b]Acts 16:22-24 [c]Acts 17:1-9 [d]Rom. 1:1 [e]Phil. 1:30

3 [1]Lit., *in deceit*
[a]Acts 13:15 [b]2 Thess. 2:11 [c]1 Thess. 4:7 [d]2 Cor. 4:2

4 [a]but just as we have been approved by God to be [b]en-
trusted with the gospel, so we speak, [c]not as pleasing men but
God, who [1d]examines our hearts.
5 For we never came [1]with flattering speech, as you
know, nor with [a]a pretext for greed—[b]God is witness —
6 nor did we [a]seek glory from men, either from you or
from others, even though as [b]apostles of Christ we might have
[1]asserted our authority.
7 But we [1]proved to be [2a]gentle [3]among you, [b]as a nursing
mother [4]tenderly cares for her own children.
8 Having thus a fond affection for you, we were well
pleased to [a]impart to you not only the [b]gospel but also our
own [1]lives, because you had become [2]very dear to us.
9 For you recall, brethren, our [a]labor and hardship, *how*
[b]working night and day so as not to be a [c]burden to any of you,
we proclaimed to you the [d]gospel of God.
10 You are witnesses, and *so is* [a]God, [b]how devoutly and
uprightly and blamelessly we [1]behaved toward you [2]believers;
11 just as you know how we *were* [a]exhorting and encouraging and [1b]imploring each one of you as [c]a father *would*
his own children,
12 so that you may [a]walk in a manner worthy of the God
who [b]calls you into His own kingdom and [c]glory.
13 And for this reason we also constantly [a]thank God that
when you received from us the [b]word of God's message, you
accepted *it* [c]not *as* the word of men, but *for* what it really is,
the word of God, [d]which also performs its work in you who
believe.
14 For you, brethren, became [a]imitators of [b]the churches
of God in Christ Jesus that are [c]in Judea, for [d]you also endured
the same sufferings at the hands of your own countrymen,
[e]even as they *did* from the Jews,
15 [a]who both killed the Lord Jesus and [b]the prophets, and
[1]drove us out; [2]they are not pleasing to God, [3]but hostile to all
men,
16 [a]hindering us from speaking to the Gentiles [b]that they
might be saved; with the result that they always [c]fill up the
measure of their sins. But [d]wrath has come upon them [1]to the
utmost.
17 But we, brethren, having been bereft of you for a [1]short
while—[a]in [2]person, not in [3]spirit—were all the more eager with
great desire [b]to see your face.
18 [1]For [a]we wanted to come to you—I, Paul, [2b]more than
once—and *yet* [c]Satan [d]thwarted us.
19 For who is our hope or [a]joy or crown of exultation? Is it
not even you, in the presence of our Lord Jesus at His
[1b]coming?
20 For you are [a]our glory and joy.

Chapter 3

THEREFORE [a]when we could endure *it* no longer, we
thought it best to be left behind at [b]Athens alone;
2 and we sent [a]Timothy, our brother and God's fellow-
worker in the gospel of Christ, to strengthen and encourage
you as to your faith;

4 [1]Or, *approves*
[a]2 Cor. 2:17 [b]Gal. 2:7 [c]Gal. 1:10 [d]Rom. 8:27

5 [1]Lit., *in a word of flattery*
[a]Acts 20:33; 2 Pet. 2:3 [b]1 Thess. 2:10; Rom. 1:9

6 [1]Or, *been burdensome*
[a]John 5:41, 44; 2 Cor. 4:5 [b]1 Cor. 9:1f.

7 [1]Lit., *became gentle* [2]Some ancient mss. read, *babes* [3]Lit., *in the midst of you* [4]Or, *cherishes*
[a]2 Tim. 2:24 [b]1 Thess. 2:11; Gal. 4:19

8 [1]Or, *selves*, lit., *souls* [2]Lit., *beloved*
[a]2 Cor. 12:5; 1 John 3:16 [b]Rom. 1:1

9 [a]2 Thess. 3:8; Phil. 4:16 [b]Acts 18:3 [c]2 Cor. 11:9; 1 Cor. 9:4f. [d]Rom. 1:1

10 [1]Lit., *became* [2]Or, who *believe*
[a]1 Thess. 2:5 [b]1 Thess. 1:5; 2 Cor. 1:12

11 [1]Or, *testifying*
[a]1 Thess. 5:14 [b]Luke 16:28; 1 Thess. 4:6 [c]1 Cor. 4:14; 1 Thess. 2:7

12 [a]Eph. 4:1 [b]1 Thess. 5:24; 2 Thess. 2:14; Rom. 8:28 [c]1 Pet. 5:10; 2 Cor. 4:6

13 [a]Rom. 1:8; 1 Thess. 1:2 [b]Heb. 4:2; Rom. 10:17 [c]Gal. 4:14; Matt. 10:20 [d]Heb. 4:12

14 [a]1 Thess. 1:6 [b]1 Cor. 7:17; 10:32 [c]Gal. 1:22 [d]Acts 17:5; 1 Thess. 3:4; 2 Thess. 1:4f. [e]Heb. 10:33f.

15 [1]Or, *persecuted us* [2]Lit., *and* [3]Lit., *and*
[a]Luke 24:20; Acts 2:23 [b]Acts 7:52; Matt. 5:12

16 [1]Or, *forever*; or, *altogether*
[a]Acts 9:23; 13:45, 50; 14:2, 5, 19; 17:5, 13; 18:12; 21:21f., 27; 25:2, 7 [b]1 Cor. 10:33 [c]Gen. 15:16; Dan. 8:23; Matt. 23:32 [d]1 Thess. 1:10

17 [1]Lit., *occasion of an hour* [2]Lit., *face* [3]Lit., *heart*
[a]1 Cor. 5:3 [b]1 Thess. 3:10

18 [1]Or, *because* [2]Lit., *both once and twice*
[a]Rom. 15:22 [b]Phil. 4:16 [c]Matt. 4:10 [d]Rom. 15:22; 1:13

19 [1]Or, *presence*
[a]Phil. 4:1 [b]1 Thess. 3:13; 4:15; 5:23; Matt. 16:27; Mark 8:38; John 21:22

20 [a]2 Cor. 1:14

1 [a]1 Thess. 3:5; Phil. 2:19 [b]Acts 17:15f.

2 [a]2 Cor. 1:1; Col. 1:1

3 so that no man may be [1]disturbed by these afflictions;
for you yourselves know that [a]we have been destined for this.
4 For indeed when we were with you, we *kept* telling you
in advance that we were going to suffer affliction; [1a]and so it
came to pass, [2]as you know.
5 For this reason, [a]when I could endure *it* no longer, I
also [b]sent to [1]find out about your faith, for fear that [c]the
tempter might have tempted you, and [d]our labor should be in
vain.
6 But now that [a]Timothy has come to us from you, and
has brought us good news of [b]your faith and love, and that you
always [c]think kindly of us, longing to see us just as we also long
to see you,
7 for this reason, brethren, in all our distress and affliction we were comforted about you through your faith;
8 for now we *really* live, if you [a]stand firm in the Lord.
9 For [a]what thanks can we render to God for you in
return for all the joy with which we rejoice before our God on
your account,
10 as we [a]night and day keep praying most earnestly that
we may [b]see your face, and may [c]complete what is lacking in
your faith?
11 [a]Now may [b]our God and Father [c]Himself and Jesus our
Lord [d]direct our way to you;
12 and may the Lord cause you to increase and [a]abound in
love for one another, and for all men, just as we also *do* for
you;
13 so that He may [a]establish your hearts [b]unblamable in
holiness before [c]our God and Father at the [1d]coming of our
Lord Jesus [e]with all His [2]saints.

Chapter 4

[a]FINALLY then, [b]brethren, we request and exhort you in the
Lord Jesus that, as you received from us *instruction* as to
how you ought to [1c]walk and [d]please God (just as you actually
do [1]walk), that you may [e]excel still more.
2 For you know what commandments we gave you [1]by
the authority of the Lord Jesus.
3 For this is the will of God, your sanctification; *that is,*
that you [a]abstain from [1]sexual immorality;
4 that [a]each of you know how to [1]possess his own [2b]vessel
in sanctification and [c]honor,
5 not in [1a]lustful passion, like the Gentiles who [b]do not
know God;
6 *and* that no man transgress and [a]defraud his brother [b]in
the matter because [c]the Lord is *the* avenger in all these things,
just as we also [d]told you before and solemnly warned *you.*
7 For [a]God has not called us for [b]the purpose of impurity, but [1]in sanctification.
8 Consequently, he who rejects *this* is not rejecting man
but the God who [a]gives His Holy Spirit to you.
9 Now as to the [a]love of the brethren, you [b]have no need
for *any one* to write to you, for you yourselves are [c]taught by
God to love one another;
10 for indeed [a]you do practice it toward all the brethren

3 [1]Or, *deceived* [a]Acts 9:16; 14:22

4 [1]Lit., *just as* [2]Lit., *and* [a]1 Thess. 2:14

5 [1]Or, *to know, to ascertain* [a]1 Thess. 3:1; Phil. 2:19 [b]1 Thess. 3:2 [c]Matt. 4:3 [d]Phil. 2:16; 2 Cor. 6:1

6 [a]Acts 18:5 [b]1 Thess. 1:3 [c]1 Cor. 11:2

8 [a]1 Cor. 6:13

9 [a]1 Thess. 1:2

10 [a]2 Tim. 1:3 [b]1 Thess. 2:17 [c]2 Cor. 13:9

11 [a]2 Thess. 2:16 [b]Gal. 1:4; 1 Thess. 3:13 [c]1 Thess. 4:16; 5:23; 2 Thess. 2:16; 3:16; Rev. 21:3 [d]2 Thess. 3:5

12 [a]Phil. 1:9; 1 Thess. 4:1, 10; 2 Thess. 1:3

13 [1]Or, *presence* [2]I.e., true believers; lit., *holy ones* [a]1 Cor. 1:8; 1 Thess. 3:2 [b]Luke 1:6 [c]Gal. 1:4; 1 Thess. 3:11 [d]1 Thess. 2:19 [e]Matt. 25:31; Mark 8:38; 2 Thess. 1:7; 1 Thess. 4:17

1 [1]Or, *conduct yourselves* [a]2 Thess. 3:1; 2 Cor. 13:11 [b]1 Thess. 5:12; 2 Thess. 1:3; 2:1; 3:1, 13; Gal. 6:1 [c]Eph. 4:1 [d]2 Cor. 5:9 [e]Phil. 1:9; 1 Thess. 3:12; 4:10; 2 Thess. 1:3

2 [1]Lit., *through the Lord*

3 [1]Or, *fornication* [a]1 Cor. 6:18

4 [1]Or, *acquire* [2]I.e., body, or possibly, *wife* [a]1 Cor. 7:2, 9 [b]1 Pet. 3:7; 2 Cor. 4:7 [c]Rom. 1:24

5 [1]Lit., *passion of lust* [a]Rom. 1:26 [b]Gal. 4:8

6 [a]1 Cor. 6:8 [b]2 Cor. 7:11 [c]Heb. 13:4; Rom. 12:19; 13:4 [d]Luke 16:28; 1 Thess. 2:11; Heb. 2:6

7 [1]I.e., in the state or sphere of [a]1 Pet. 1:15 [b]1 Thess. 2:3

8 [a]Rom. 5:5; 2 Cor. 1:22; Gal. 4:6; 1 John 3:24

9 [a]John 13:34; Rom. 12:10 [b]1 Thess. 5:1; 2 Cor. 9:1 [c]John 6:45; 1 John 2:27; Jer. 31:33f.

10 [a]1 Thess. 1:7

who are in all Macedonia. But we urge you, brethren, to [b]excel
still more,
11 and to make it your ambition [a]to lead a quiet life and
[b]attend to your own business and [c]work with your hands, just
as we commanded you;
12 so that you may [1a]behave properly toward [b]outsiders
and [2c]not be in any need.
13 But [a]we do not want you to be uninformed, brethren,
about those who [b]are asleep, that you may not grieve, as do
[c]the rest who have [d]no hope.
14 For if we believe that Jesus died and rose again, [a]even
so God will bring with Him [b]those who have fallen asleep [1]in
Jesus.
15 For this we say to you [a]by the word of the Lord, that
[b]we who are alive, [1]and remain until [c]the coming of the Lord,
shall not precede [d]those who have fallen asleep.
16 For the Lord [a]Himself [b]will descend from heaven with
a [1c]shout, with the voice of [d]*the* archangel, and with the [e]trum-
pet of God; and [f]the dead in Christ shall rise first.
17 Then [a]we who are alive [1]and remain shall be [b]caught up
together with them [c]in the clouds to meet the Lord in the air,
and thus we shall always [d]be with the Lord.
18 Therefore comfort one another with these words.

Chapter 5

NOW as to the [a]times and the epochs, brethren, you [b]have
no need of anything to be written to you.
2 For you yourselves know full well that [a]the day of the
Lord [1]will come [b]just like a thief in the night.
3 While they are saying, "[a]Peace and safety!" then [1b]de-
struction [2]will come upon them suddenly like [c]birth pangs upon
a woman with child; and they shall not escape.
4 But you, brethren, are not in [a]darkness, that the day
should overtake you [1b]like a thief;
5 for you are all [a]sons of light and sons of day. We are
not of night nor of [b]darkness;
6 so then let us not [a]sleep as [1b]others do, but let us be
alert and [2c]sober.
7 For those who sleep do their sleeping at night, and
those who get drunk get [a]drunk at night.
8 But since [a]we are of *the* day, let us [b]be [1]sober, having put on the [c]breastplate of [d]faith and love, and as a [e]helmet,
the [f]hope of salvation.
9 For God has not destined us for [a]wrath, but for [b]obtain-
ing salvation through our Lord Jesus Christ,
10 [a]who died for us, that whether we are awake or asleep,
we may live together with Him.
11 Therefore [1]encourage one another, and [a]build up one
another, just as you also are doing.
12 But we request of you, brethren, that you [1a]appreciate
those [b]who diligently labor among you, and [c]have charge over
you in the Lord and give you [2]instruction,
13 and that you esteem them very highly in love because
of their work. [a]Live in peace with one another.
14 And we urge you, brethren, admonish [a]the [1]unruly, en-

10 [b]1 Thess. 3:12

11 [a]2 Thess. 3:12 [b]1 Pet. 4:15 [c]Eph. 4:28; 2 Thess. 3:10-12; Acts 18:3

12 [1]Lit., *walk* [2]Lit., *have need of nothing* [a]Rom. 13:13; Col 4:5 [b]Mark 4:11 [c]Eph. 4:28

13 [a]Rom. 1:13 [b]Acts 7:60 [c]1 Thess. 5:6; Eph. 2:3 [d]Eph. 2:12

14 [1]Lit., *through* [a]Rom. 14:9; 2 Cor. 4:14 [b]1 Cor. 15:18; 1 Thess. 4:13

15 [1]Lit., *who* [a]1 Kin. 13:17f.; 20:35; Gal. 1:12; 2 Cor. 12:1 [b]1 Cor. 15:52; 1 Thess. 5:10 [c]1 Thess. 2:19 [d]1 Cor. 15:18; 1 Thess. 4:13

16 [1]Or, *cry of command* [a]1 Thess. 3:11 [b]2 Thess. 1:7; 1 Thess. 1:10 [c]Joel 2:11 [d]Jude 9 [e]Matt. 24:31 [f]1 Cor. 15:23; 2 Thess. 2:1; Rev. 14:13

17 [1]Lit., *who* [a]1 Cor. 15:52; 1 Thess. 5:10 [b]2 Cor. 12:2 [c]Dan. 7:13; Acts 1:9; Rev. 11:12 [d]John 12:26

1 [a]Acts 1:7 [b]1 Thess. 4:9

2 [1]Lit., *is coming* [a]1 Cor. 1:8 [b]Luke 21:34; 1 Thess. 5:4; 2 Pet. 3:10; Rev. 3:3; 16:15

3 [1]Or, *sudden destruction* [2]Lit., *is at hand* [a]Jer. 6:14; 8:11; Ezek. 13:10 [b]2 Thess. 1:9 [c]John 16:21

4 [1]Some early mss. read, *like thieves* [a]1 John 2:8; Acts 26:18 [b]Luke 21:34; 1 Thess. 5:2; 2 Pet. 3:10; Rev. 3:3; 16:15

5 [a]Luke 16:8 [b]1 John 2:8; Acts 26:18

6 [1]Lit., *the remaining ones* [2]Or, *self-controlled* [a]Rom. 13:11; 1 Thess. 5:10 [b]Eph. 2:3; 1 Thess. 4:13 [c]1 Pet. 1:13

7 [a]Acts 2:15; 2 Pet. 2:13

8 [1]Or, *self-controlled* [a]1 Thess. 5:5 [b]1 Pet. 1:13 [c]Eph. 6:14 [d]Eph. 6:23 [e]Eph. 6:17 [f]Rom. 8:24

9 [a]1 Thess. 1:10 [b]2 Thess. 2:13f.

10 [a]Rom. 14:9

11 [1]Or, *comfort* [a]Eph. 4:29

12 [1]Lit., *know* [2]Or, *admonition* [a]1 Cor. 16:18; 1 Tim. 5:17; Ps. 144:3 [b]1 Cor. 16:16; Rom. 16:6, 12; 1 Cor. 15:10 [c]Heb. 13:17

13 [a]Mark 9:50

14 [1]Or, *undisciplined* [a]2 Thess. 3:6, 7, 11

courage [b]the fainthearted, help [c]the weak, be [d]patient with all
men.
15 See that [a]no one repays another with evil for evil, but
always [b]seek after that which is good for one another and for
all men.
16 [a]Rejoice always;
17 [a]pray without ceasing;
18 in everything [a]give thanks; for this is God's will for you
in Christ Jesus.
19 [a]Do not quench the Spirit;
20 do not despise [a]prophetic [1]utterances.
21 But [a]examine everything *carefully;* [b]hold fast to that
which is good;
22 abstain from every [1]form of evil.
23 Now [a]may the God of peace [b]Himself sanctify you
entirely; and may your [c]spirit and soul and body be preserved
complete, [d]without blame at [e]the coming of our Lord Jesus
Christ.
24 [a]Faithful is He who [b]calls you, and He also will bring it
to pass.
25 Brethren, [a]pray for us[1].
26 [a]Greet all the brethren with a holy kiss.
27 I adjure you by the Lord to [a]have this letter read to all
the [b]brethren.
28 [a]The grace of our Lord Jesus Christ be with you.

14 [b]Is. 35:4 [Sept.] [c]Rom. 14:1f.; 1 Cor. 8:7ff. [Rom. 15:1] [d]1 Cor. 13:4
15 [a]Rom. 12:17; 1 Pet. 3:9; Matt. 5:44 [b]Rom. 12:9; 1 Thess. 5:21; Gal. 6:10
16 [a]Phil. 4:4
17 [a]Eph. 6:18
18 [a]Eph. 5:20
19 [a]Eph. 4:30
20 [1]Or, *gifts* [a]Acts 13:1; 1 Cor. 14:31
21 [a]1 Cor. 14:29; 1 John 4:1 [b]Rom. 12:9; 1 Thess. 5:15; Gal. 6:10
22 [1]Or, *appearance*
23 [a]Rom. 15:33 [b]1 Thess. 3:11 [c]Luke 1:46f.; Heb. 4:12 [d]2 Pet. 3:14; James 1:4 [e]1 Thess. 2:19
24 [a]1 Cor. 1:9; 2 Thess. 3:3 [b]1 Thess. 2:12
25 [1]Some mss. add, *also* [a]Eph. 6:19; 2 Thess. 3:1; Heb. 13:18
26 [a]Rom. 16:16
27 [a]Col. 4:16 [b]Acts 1:15
28 [a]Rom. 16:20; 2 Thess. 3:18

THE SECOND EPISTLE OF PAUL TO THE
THESSALONIANS

Salutation. Thanksgiving for their Faith and Perseverance.

[a]PAUL and [b]Silvanus and [c]Timothy to the [d]church of the
Thessalonians in God our Father and the Lord Jesus Christ:
2 [a]Grace to you and peace from God the Father and the
Lord Jesus Christ.
3 We ought always [a]to give thanks to God for you, [b]breth-
ren, as is *only* fitting, because your faith is greatly enlarged,
and the [c]love of each one of you all toward one another grows
ever greater;
4 therefore, we ourselves [a]speak proudly of you among
[b]the churches of God for your [1]perseverance and faith [b]in the
midst of all your persecutions and afflictions which you
endure.
5 *This is* a [a]plain indication of God's righteous judgment
so that you may be [b]considered worthy of the kingdom of
God, for which indeed you are suffering.
6 [1]For after all [a]it is *only* just [2]for God to repay with
affliction those who afflict you,
7 and *to give* relief to you who are afflicted [1]and to us as
well [2a]when the Lord Jesus shall be revealed [b]from heaven
[c]with [3]His mighty angels [d]in flaming fire,

1 [a]1 Thess. 1:1 [b]2 Cor. 1:19 [c]Acts 16:1 [1 Thess. 1:1] [d]1 Thess. 1:1; Acts 17:1
2 [a]Rom. 1:7
3 [a]1 Thess. 1:2; 2 Thess. 2:13; Rom. 1:8; Eph. 5:20 [b]1 Thess. 4:1; 2 Thess. 2:1 [c]1 Thess. 3:12
4 [1]Or, *steadfastness* [a]2 Cor. 7:4; 1 Thess. 2:19 [b]1 Thess. 2:14; 1 Cor. 7:17
5 [a]Phil. 1:28 [b]Luke 20:35; 2 Thess. 1:11
6 [1]Lit., *If indeed* [2]Or, *in the sight of* [a]Ex. 23:22; Col. 3:25; Heb. 6:10
7 [1]Lit., *along with us* [2]Lit., *at the revelation of the Lord Jesus* [3]Lit., *the angels of His power* [a]Luke 17:30 [b]1 Thess. 4:16 [c]Jude 14 [d]1 Cor. 3:13; Heb. 10:27; 12:29; 2 Pet. 3:7; Jude 7; Rev. 14:10; Ex. 3:2; 19:18; Is. 66:15; Ezek. 1:13f.; Dan. 7:9; Matt. 25:41

8 dealing out retribution to those who [a]do not know God
and to those who [b]do not obey the gospel of our Lord Jesus.
9 And these will pay the penalty of [a]eternal destruction,
[b]away from the presence of the Lord and from the glory of His
power,
10 when He comes to be [a]glorified [1]in His [2]saints on that
[b]day, and to be marveled at among all who have believed—for
our [c]testimony to you was believed.
11 To this end also we [a]pray for you always that our God
may [1b]count you worthy of your [c]calling, and fulfill every desire for [d]goodness and the [e]work of faith with power;
12 in order that the [a]name of our Lord Jesus may be glorified in you, and you in Him, according to the grace of our God
and [1]the Lord Jesus Christ.

Chapter 2

NOW we request you, [a]brethren, with regard to the [1b]com-
ing of our Lord Jesus Christ, and our [c]gathering together to
Him,
2 that you may not be quickly shaken from your [1]compo-
sure or be disturbed either by a [a]spirit or a [2b]message or a
[c]letter as if from us, to the effect that [d]the day of the Lord [e]has
come.
3 [a]Let no one in any way deceive you, for *it will not come*
unless the [1b]apostasy comes first, and the [c]man of [2]lawlessness
is revealed, the [d]son of destruction,
4 who opposes and exalts himself above [1a]every so-called
god or object of worship, so that he takes his seat in the temple
of God, [b]displaying himself as being God.
5 Do you not remember that [a]while I was still with you, I
was telling you these things?
6 And you know [a]what restrains him now, so that in his
time he may be revealed.
7 For [a]the mystery of lawlessness is already at work; only
[b]he who now restrains *will do so* until he is taken out of the
way.
8 And then that lawless one [a]will be revealed whom the
Lord will slay [b]with the breath of His mouth and bring to an
end by the [c]appearance of His [1]coming;
9 *that is,* the one whose [1]coming is in accord with the
activity of [a]Satan, with all power and [2b]signs and false wonders,
10 and with [1]all the deception of wickedness for [a]those
who perish, because they did not receive the love of [b]the truth
so as to be saved.
11 And for this reason [a]God [1]will send upon them [2]a [b]de-
luding influence so that they might believe [3]what is false,
12 in order that they all may be [1]judged who [a]did not
believe the truth, but [2b]took pleasure in wickedness.
13 [a]But we should always give thanks to God for you,
[b]brethren beloved by the Lord, because [c]God has chosen you
[1]from the beginning [d]for salvation [2e]through sanctification [3]by
the Spirit and faith in the truth.
14 And it was for this He [a]called you through [b]our gospel,
[1]that you may gain the glory of our Lord Jesus Christ.
15 So then, brethren, [a]stand firm and [b]hold to the tradi-

8 [a]Gal. 4:8 [b]Rom 2:8

9 [a]1 Thess. 5:3; Phil. 3:19 [b]Is. 2:10, 19, 21; 2 Thess. 2:8

10 [1]Or, *in the persons of* [2]I.e., true believers; lit., *holy ones* [a]John 17:10; 1 Thess. 2:12; Is. 49:3 [b]1 Cor. 3:13; Is. 2:11ff. [c]1 Thess. 2:1; 1 Cor. 1:6

11 [1]Or, *make* [a]Col. 1:9 [b]2 Thess. 1:5 [c]Rom. 11:29 [d]Rom. 15:14 [e]1 Thess. 1:3

12 [1]Or omit, *the* [a]Phil. 2:9ff.; Is. 24:15; 66:5; Mal. 1:11

1 [1]Or, *presence* [a]2 Thess. 1:3 [b]1 Thess. 2:19 [c]Mark 13:27; 1 Thess. 4:15-17

2 [1]Lit., *mind* [2]Lit., *word* [a]1 Cor. 14:32; 1 John 4:1 [b]2 Thess. 2:15; 1 Thess. 5:2 [c]2 Thess. 3:17 [d]1 Cor. 1:8 [e]1 Cor. 7:26

3 [1]Or, *falling away* from the faith [2]Some early mss. read, *sin* [a]Eph. 5:6 [b]1 Tim. 4:1 [c]2 Thess. 2:8; Dan. 7:25; 8:25; 11:36; Rev. 13:5ff. [d]John 17:12

4 [1]Or, *all that is called God* [a]1 Cor. 8:5 [b]Is. 14:14; Ezek. 28:2

5 [a]1 Thess. 3:4

6 [a]2 Thess. 2:7

7 [a]Rev. 17:5, 7 [b]2 Thess. 2:6

8 [1]Or, *presence* [a]2 Thess. 2:3; Dan. 7:25; 8:25; 11:36; Rev. 13:5ff. [b]Is. 11:4; Rev. 2:16; 19:15 [c]1 Tim. 6:14; 2 Tim. 1:10; 4:1, 8; Titus 2:13

9 [1]Or, *presence* [2]Or, *attesting miracles* [a]Matt. 4:10 [b]Matt. 24:24; John 4:48

10 [1]Or, *every deception* [a]1 Cor. 1:18 [b]2 Thess. 2:12; 2:13

11 [1]Lit., *sends* [2]Lit., *an activity of error* [3]Or, *the lie* [a]Rom. 1:28; 1 Kin. 22:22 [b]1 Thess. 2:3; 2 Tim. 4:4

12 [1]Or, *condemned* [2]Or, *approved* [a]Rom. 2:8 [b]Rom. 1:32; 1 Cor. 13:6

13 [1]Some ancient mss. read, *first fruits* [2]Lit., *in* [3]Lit., *of* [a]2 Thess. 1:3 [b]1 Thess. 1:4 [c]Eph. 1:4ff. [d]1 Thess. 5:9; 2:12; 1 Pet. 1:5; 1 Cor. 1:21 [e]1 Pet. 1:2; 1 Thess. 4:7

14 [1]Lit., *to the gaining of* [a]1 Thess. 2:12 [b]1 Thess. 1:5

15 [a]1 Cor. 16:13 [b]1 Cor. 11:2; 2 Thess. 3:6

tions which you were taught, whether [c]by word *of mouth* or
[c]by letter [1]from us.
16 [a]Now may our Lord Jesus Christ [b]Himself and God our
Father, who has [c]loved us and given us eternal comfort and
[d]good hope by grace,
17 [a]comfort and [b]strengthen your hearts in every good
work and word.

Chapter 3

[a]FINALLY, brethren, [b]pray for us that [c]the word of the Lord
may [1]spread rapidly and be glorified, just as *it did* also with
you;
2 and that we may be [a]delivered from [1]perverse and evil
men; for not all have [2]faith.
3 But [a]the Lord is faithful, and [1]He will strengthen and
protect you [2]from [b]the evil *one.*
4 And we have [a]confidence in the Lord concerning you,
that you [b]are doing and will continue to do what we command.
5 And may the Lord [a]direct your hearts into the love of
God and into the steadfastness of Christ.
6 Now we command you, brethren, [a]in the name of our
Lord Jesus Christ, that you [1b]keep aloof from every brother
who [2]leads an [3c]unruly life and not according to [d]the tradition
which [4]you received from us.
7 For you yourselves know how you ought to [1a]follow our
example; because we did not act in an undisciplined manner
among you,
8 nor did we [a]eat [1]anyone's bread [2]without paying for it,
but with [b]labor and hardship we *kept* [c]working night and day
so that we might not be a burden to any of you;
9 not because we do not have [a]the right *to this,* but in
order to offer ourselves [b]as a model for you, that you might
[1]follow our example.
10 For even [a]when we were with you, we used to give you
this order: [b]If anyone will not work, neither let him eat.
11 For we hear that some among you are [a]leading an undisciplined life, doing no work at all, but acting like
[b]busybodies.
12 Now such persons we command and [a]exhort in the
Lord Jesus Christ to [b]work in quiet fashion and eat their own
bread.
13 But as for you, [a]brethren, [b]do not grow weary of doing
good.
14 And if anyone does not obey our [1]instruction [2a]in this
letter, take special note of that man [3b]and do not associate
with him, so that he may be [c]put to shame.
15 And *yet* [a]do not regard him as an enemy, but [1b]admon-
ish him as a [c]brother.
16 Now [a]may the Lord of peace [b]Himself continually
grant you peace in every [1]circumstance. [c]The Lord be with you
all!
17 [1]I, Paul, write this greeting [a]with my own hand, and this
is a distinguishing mark in every letter: this is the way I write.
18 [a]The grace of our Lord Jesus Christ be with you all.

15 [1]Lit., *of* [c]2 Thess. 2:2

16 [a]1 Thess. 3:11 [b]1 Thess. 3:11 [c]John 3:16 [d]Titus 3:7; 1 Pet. 1:3

17 [a]1 Thess. 3:2, 13 [b]2 Thess. 3:3

1 [1]Lit., *run* [a]1 Thess. 4:1 [b]1 Thess. 5:25 [c]1 Thess. 1:8

2 [1]Lit., *improper* [2]Or, *the faith* [a]Rom. 15:31

3 [1]Lit., *will* [2]Or, *from evil* [a]1 Cor. 1:9; 1 Thess. 5:24 [b]Matt. 5:37

4 [a]2 Cor. 2:3 [b]1 Thess. 4:10

5 [a]1 Thess. 3:11

6 [1]Or, *avoid* [2]Lit., *walks disorderly* [3]Or, *undisciplined* [4]Many ancient mss. read, *they* [a]1 Cor. 5:4 [b]Rom. 16:17; 1 Cor. 5:11; 2 Thess. 3:14 [c]1 Thess. 5:14; 2 Thess. 3:7, 11 [d]1 Cor. 11:2; 2 Thess. 2:15

7 [1]Lit., *imitate us* [a]1 Thess. 1:6; 2 Thess. 3:9

8 [1]Lit., *from any one* [2]Lit., *freely* [a]1 Cor. 9:4 [b]1 Thess. 2:9 [c]Acts 18:3; Eph. 4:28

9 [1]Lit., *imitate us* [a]1 Cor. 9:4ff. [b]2 Thess. 3:7

10 [a]1 Thess. 3:4 [b]1 Thess. 4:11

11 [a]2 Thess. 3:6 [b]1 Tim. 5:13; 1 Pet. 4:15

12 [a]1 Thess. 4:1 [b]1 Thess. 4:11

13 [a]1 Thess. 4:1 [b]Gal. 6:9; 2 Cor. 4:1

14 [1]Lit., *word* [2]Lit., *through* [3]Lit., *not to associate* [a]Col. 4:16 [b]2 Thess. 3:6 [c]1 Cor. 4:14

15 [1]Or, *keep admonishing* [a]Gal. 6:1 [b]1 Thess. 5:14 [c]2 Thess. 3:6, 13

16 [1]Lit., *way* [a]Rom. 15:33 [b]1 Thess. 3:11 [c]Ruth 2:4

17 [1]Lit., *the greeting by my hand of Paul* [a]1 Cor. 16:21

18 [a]Rom. 16:20; 1 Thess. 5:28

THE FIRST EPISTLE OF PAUL TO

TIMOTHY

Salutation. Charge Respecting Misuse of the Law. Personal Thanksgiving.

PAUL, [a]an apostle of [b]Christ Jesus [c]according to the commandment of [d]God our Savior, and of [b]Christ Jesus, *who is* our
[e]hope;
2 to [a]Timothy, [b]*my* true child in *the* faith: [c]Grace, mercy
and peace from God the Father and [d]Christ Jesus our Lord.
3 As I urged you [1]upon my departure for [a]Macedonia,
[2]remain on at [b]Ephesus, in order that you may instruct certain
men not to [c]teach strange doctrines,
4 nor to [1]pay attention to [a]myths and endless [b]genealo-
gies, which give rise to mere [c]speculation rather than [d]*further-
ing* [2]God's provision which is by faith.
5 But the goal of our [1a]instruction is love [b]from a pure
heart and a [c]good conscience and a sincere [d]faith.
6 For some men, straying from these things, have turned
aside to [a]fruitless discussion,
7 [a]wanting to be [b]teachers of the Law, even though they
do not understand either what they are saying or the matters
about which they make confident assertions.
8 But we know that [a]the Law is good, if one uses it
lawfully,
9 realizing the fact that [a]law is not made for a righteous
man, but for those who are lawless and [b]rebellious, for the
[c]ungodly and sinners, for the unholy and [d]profane, for those
who kill their fathers or mothers, for murderers
10 [1]and [2a]immoral men [1]and [b]homosexuals [1]and [c]kidnap-
pers [1]and [d]liars [1]and [e]perjurers, and whatever else is contrary to
[f]sound teaching,
11 according to [a]the glorious gospel of [b]the blessed God,
with which I have been [c]entrusted.
12 I thank [a]Christ Jesus our Lord, who has [b]strengthened
me, because He considered me faithful, [c]putting me into
service;
13 even though I was formerly a blasphemer and a [a]perse-
cutor and a violent aggressor. And yet I was [b]shown mercy,
because [c]I acted ignorantly in unbelief;
14 and the [a]grace of our Lord was more than abundant,
with the [b]faith and love which are *found* in Christ Jesus.
15 [a]It is a trustworthy statement, deserving full acceptance, that [b]Christ Jesus came into the world to [c]save sinners,
among whom [d]I am foremost *of all*.
16 And yet for this reason I [a]found mercy, in order that in
me as the foremost, Jesus Christ might [b]demonstrate His perfect patience, as an example for those [1]who would believe in
Him for eternal life.
17 Now to the [a]King [1]eternal, [b]immortal, [c]invisible, the
[d]only God, [e]*be* honor and glory [2]forever and ever. Amen.
18 This [a]command I entrust to you, Timothy, [b]my [1]son, in

1 [a]2 Cor. 1:1; 2 Tim. 1:1 [b]1 Tim. 1:12 [c]Titus 1:3 [d]Luke 1:47; Titus 1:3 [e]Col. 1:27

2 [a]Acts 16:1; 2 Tim. 1:2 [b]2 Tim. 1:2; Titus 1:4 [c]2 Tim. 1:2; Titus 1:4; Rom. 1:7 [d]1 Tim. 1:12

3 [1]Lit., *while departing* [2]Lit., *to remain* [a]Rom. 15:26 [b]Acts 18:19 [c]1 Tim. 6:3; Rom. 16:17; 2 Cor. 11:4; Gal. 1:6f.

4 [1]Or, *occupy themselves with* [2]Lit., *the administration of God which* [a]1 Tim. 4:7; 2 Tim. 4:4; Titus 1:14; 2 Pet. 1:16 [b]Titus 3:9 [c]1 Tim. 6:4; 2 Tim. 2:23; Titus 3:9 [d]Eph. 3:2

5 [1]Lit., *commandment* [a]1 Tim. 1:18 [b]2 Tim. 2:22 [c]1 Pet. 3:16, 21; 1 Tim. 1:19; 3:9; 2 Tim. 1:3 [d]2 Tim. 1:5

6 [a]Titus 1:10

7 [a]James 3:1 [b]Luke 2:46

8 [a]Rom. 7:12, 16

9 [a]Gal. 5:23 [b]Titus 1:6, 10 [c]1 Pet. 4:18; Jude 15 [d]1 Tim. 4:7; 6:20; 2 Tim. 2:16; Heb. 12:16

10 [1]Lit., *for* [2]Or, *fornicators* [a]1 Cor. 6:9 [b]Lev. 18:22 [c]Ex. 21:16; Rev. 18:13 [d]Rev. 21:8, 27; 22:15 [e]Matt. 5:33; 23:16 [f]2 Tim. 4:3; Titus 1:9; 2:1; 1 Tim. 4:6; 6:3; 2 Tim. 1:13; Titus 1:13; 2:2

11 [a]2 Cor. 4:4 [b]1 Tim. 6:15 [c]Gal. 2:7

12 [a]1 Tim. 1:1, 2, 15; 2:5; 6:13; Titus 1:4; Gal. 3:26 [b]Phil. 4:13; 2 Tim. 4:17; Acts 9:22 [c]Acts 9:15

13 [a]Acts 8:3; Phil. 3:6 [b]1 Tim. 1:16; 1 Cor. 7:25 [c]Acts 26:9

14 [a]Rom. 5:20; 2 Cor. 4:15; 1 Cor. 3:10; 1:13-16 [b]2 Tim. 1:13; 1 Thess. 1:3; 1 Tim. 2:15; 4:12; 6:11; 2 Tim. 2:22; Titus 2:2

15 [a]1 Tim. 3:1; 4:9; 2 Tim. 2:11; Titus 3:8 [b]Mark 2:17; Luke 15:2ff.; 19:10 [c]Rom. 11:14 [d]1 Cor. 15:9; Eph. 3:8

16 [1]Or, *destined to* [a]1 Tim. 1:13; 1 Cor. 7:25 [b]Eph. 2:7

17 [1]Lit., *of the ages* [2]Lit., *the ages of the ages* [a]Rev. 15:3 [Gr.] [b]1 Tim. 6:16 [c]Col. 1:15 [d]1 Tim. 6:15; Jude 25; John 5:44 [e]Rom. 11:36; 2:7, 10; Heb. 2:7

18 [1]Lit., *child* [a]1 Tim. 1:5 [b]1 Tim. 1:2

accordance with the [c]prophecies previously made concerning you, that by them you may [d]fight the good fight,

19 keeping [a]faith and a good conscience, which some have rejected and suffered shipwreck in regard to [1b]their faith.

20 [1]Among these are [a]Hymenaeus and [b]Alexander, whom I have [c]delivered over to Satan, so that they may be [d]taught not to blaspheme.

Chapter 2

FIRST of all, then, I urge that [a]entreaties *and* prayers, petitions *and* thanksgivings, be made on behalf of all men,

2 [a]for kings and all who are in [1]authority, in order that we may lead a tranquil and quiet life in all godliness and [2]dignity.

3 This is good and acceptable in the sight of [a]God our Savior,

4 [a]who desires all men to be [b]saved and to [c]come to the [1]knowledge of the truth.

5 For there is [a]one God, *and* [b]one mediator also between God and men, *the* [c]man Christ Jesus,

6 who [a]gave Himself as a ransom for all, the [b]testimony [1]*borne* at [2c]the proper time.

7 [a]And for this I was appointed a [1]preacher and [b]an apostle ([c]I am telling the truth, I am not lying) as a teacher of [d]the Gentiles in faith and truth.

8 Therefore [a]I want the men [b]in every place to pray, [c]lifting up [d]holy hands, without wrath and dissension.

9 Likewise, *I want* [a]women to adorn themselves with proper clothing, [1]modestly and discreetly, not with braided hair and gold or pearls or costly garments;

10 but rather by means of good works, as befits women making a claim to godliness.

11 [a]Let a woman quietly receive instruction with entire submissiveness.

12 [a]But I do not allow a woman to teach or exercise authority over a man, but to remain quiet.

13 [a]For it was Adam who was first [1]created, *and* then Eve.

14 And *it was* not Adam *who* was deceived, but [a]the woman being quite deceived, fell into transgression.

15 But women shall be [1]preserved through the bearing of children if *they* continue in [a]faith and love and sanctity with [2]self restraint.

[a] Chapter 3

IT is a trustworthy statement; if any man aspires to the [b]office of [1]overseer, it is a fine work he desires *to do.*

2 [1a]An overseer, then, must be above reproach, [b]the husband of one wife, [c]temperate, prudent, respectable, [d]hospitable, [e]able to teach,

3 [a]not addicted to wine [1]or pugnacious, but gentle, uncontentious, [b]free from the love of money.

4 *He must be* one who [a]manages his own household well, keeping his children under control with all dignity

5 (but if a man does not know how to manage his own household, how will he take care of [a]the church of God?);

18 [c]1 Tim. 4:14 [d]2 Cor. 10:4; 2 Tim. 2:3f.; 4:7; 1 Tim. 6:12

19 [1]Lit., *the* [a]1 Tim. 1:5 [b]1 Tim. 6:12, 21; 2 Tim. 2:18

20 [1]Lit., *of* [a]2 Tim. 2:17 [b]2 Tim. 4:14 [c]1 Cor. 5:5 [d]1 Cor. 11:32; Heb. 12:5ff.

1 [a]Eph. 6:18

2 [1]Or, *a high position* [2]Or, *seriousness* [a]Ezra 6:10; Rom. 13:1

3 [a]1 Tim. 1:1; Luke 1:47; 1 Tim. 4:10

4 [1]Or, *recognition* [a]Ezek. 18:23, 32; 1 Tim. 4:10; Titus 2:11; 2 Pet. 3:9; John 3:17 [b]Rom. 11:14 [c]2 Tim. 2:25; 3:7; Titus 1:1; Heb. 10:26

5 [a]Rom. 3:30; 10:12; 1 Cor. 8:4 [b]Gal. 3:20; 1 Cor. 8:6 [c]Matt. 1:1; Rom. 1:3

6 [1]Or, to be borne [2]Lit., *its own times* [a]Matt. 20:28; Gal. 1:4 [b]1 Cor. 1:6 [c]1 Tim. 6:15; Titus 1:3; Gal. 4:4; Mark 1:15

7 [1]Or, *herald* [a]2 Tim. 1:11; 1 Tim. 1:11; Eph. 3:8 [b]1 Cor. 9:1 [c]Rom. 9:1 [d]Acts 9:15

8 [a]1 Tim. 5:14; Phil. 1:12; Titus 3:8, [in Gr.] [b]John 4:21; 1 Cor. 1:2; 2 Cor. 2:14; 1 Thess. 1:8 [c]Ps. 63:4; Luke 24:50 [d]Ps. 24:4; James 4:8

9 [1]Lit., *with modesty* [a]1 Pet. 3:3

11 [a]1 Cor. 14:34; Titus 2:5

12 [a]1 Cor. 14:34; Titus 2:5

13 [1]Or, *formed* [a]Gen. 2:7, 22; 3:16; 1 Cor. 11:8ff.

14 [a]Gen. 3:6, 13; 2 Cor. 11:3

15 [1]Lit., *saved* [2]Or, *discretion* [a]1 Tim. 1:14

1 [1]Or, *bishop* [a]1 Tim. 1:15 [b]Acts 20:28; Phil. 1:1

2 [1]Lit., *the* [a]1 Tim. 3:2-4; Titus 1:6-8 [b]Titus 1:6; Luke 2:36f.; 1 Tim. 5:9 [c]1 Tim. 3:11; Titus 2:2; 1 Tim. 3:8 [d]Titus 1:8; Rom. 12:13; Heb. 13:2; 1 Pet. 4:9 [e]2 Tim. 2:24

3 [1]Lit., *not* [a]Titus 1:7 [b]Heb. 13:5; 1 Tim. 6:10; Titus 1:7; 1 Tim. 3:8

4 [a]1 Tim. 3:12

5 [a]1 Cor. 10:32; 1 Tim. 3:15

6 *and* not a new convert, lest he become [a]conceited and
fall into the [b]condemnation [1]incurred by the devil.
7 And he must [a]have a good reputation with [b]those
outside *the church,* so that he may not fall into reproach and
[c]the snare of the devil.
8 [a]Deacons likewise *must be* men of dignity, not [1]double-
tongued, [2b]or addicted to much wine [2c]or fond of sordid gain,
9 [a]*but* holding to the mystery of the faith with a clear
conscience.
10 And [a]let these also first be tested; then let them serve as
deacons if they are beyond reproach.
11 [1]Women *must* likewise *be* dignified, [a]not malicious
gossips, but [b]temperate, faithful in all things.
12 Let [a]deacons be [b]husbands of *only* one wife, *and*
[1c]good managers of *their* children and their own households.
13 For those who have served well as deacons [a]obtain for
themselves a [1]high standing and great confidence in the faith
that is in Christ Jesus.
14 I am writing these things to you, hoping to come to you
before long;
15 but [1]in case I am delayed, *I write* so that you may know
how [2]one ought to conduct himself in [a]the household of God,
which is the [b]church of [c]the living God, the [d]pillar and support
of the truth.
16 And by common confession great is [a]the mystery of
godliness:

[1]He who was [b]revealed in the flesh,
Was [2c]vindicated [3]in the Spirit,
[d]Beheld by angels,
[e]Proclaimed among the nations,
[f]Believed on in the world,
[g]Taken up in glory.

6 [1]Lit., *of the devil* [a]1 Tim. 6:4; 2 Tim. 3:4 [b]1 Tim. 3:7

7 [a]2 Cor. 8:21 [b]Mark 4:11 [c]2 Tim. 2:26; 1 Tim. 6:9

8 [1]Or, *given to double-talk* [2]Lit., *not* [a]Phil. 1:1; 1 Tim. 3:12 [b]Titus 2:3; 1 Tim. 5:23 [c]Titus 1:7; 1 Tim. 3:3; 1 Pet. 5:2

9 [a]1 Tim. 1:19; 1 Tim. 1:5

10 [a]1 Tim. 5:22

11 [1]I.e., either deacons' wives or deaconesses [a]2 Tim. 3:3; Titus 2:3 [b]1 Tim. 3:2

12 [1]Lit., *managing well* [a]Phil. 1:1; 1 Tim. 3:8 [b]1 Tim. 3:2 [c]1 Tim. 3:4

13 [1]Lit., *good* [a]Matt. 25:21

15 [1]Lit., *if I delay* [2]Or, *you ought to conduct yourself* [a]Eph. 2:21f.; 1 Cor. 3:16; 2 Cor. 6:16; 1 Pet. 2:5; 4:17 [b]1 Tim. 3:5 [c]Matt. 16:16; 1 Tim. 4:10 [d]Gal. 2:9; 2 Tim. 2:19

16 [1]Some later mss. read, *God* [2]Or, *justified* [3]Or, *by* [a]Rom. 16:25 [b]John 1:14; 1 Pet. 1:20; 1 John 3:5, 8 [c]Rom. 3:4 [d]Luke 2:13; 24:4; 1 Pet. 1:12 [e]Rom. 16:26; 2 Cor. 1:19; Col. 1:23 [f]2 Thess. 1:10 [g]Mark 16:19; Acts 1:9

Chapter 4

BUT [a]the Spirit explicitly says that [b]in later times some will
fall away from the faith, paying attention to [c]deceitful spirits
and [d]doctrines of demons,
2 by means of the hypocrisy of liars [a]seared in their own
conscience as with a branding iron,
3 *men* who [a]forbid marriage *and advocate* [b]abstaining
from foods, which [c]God has created to be [d]gratefully shared in
by those who believe and know the truth.
4 For [a]everything created by God is good, and nothing is
to be rejected, if it is [b]received with gratitude:
5 for it is sanctified by means of [a]the word of God and
prayer.
6 In pointing out these things to [a]the brethren, you will
be a good [b]servant of Christ Jesus, *constantly* nourished on the
words of the faith and of the [1c]sound doctrine which you [d]have
been following.
7 But have nothing to do with [a]worldly [b]fables fit only
for old women. On the other hand, discipline yourself for the
purpose of [c]godliness;
8 for [a]bodily discipline is only little profit, but [b]godliness

1 [a]John 16:13; Acts 20:23; 21:11; 1 Cor. 2:10f. [b]2 Thess. 2:3ff.; 2 Tim. 3:1; 2 Pet. 3:3; Jude 18 [c]1 John 4:6 [d]James 3:15

2 [a]Eph. 4:19

3 [a]Heb. 13:4 [b]Col. 2:16; 2:23 [c]Gen. 1:29; 9:3 [d]1 Tim. 4:4; Rom. 14:6; 1 Cor. 10:30f.

4 [a]1 Cor. 10:26 [b]1 Tim. 4:3; Rom. 14:6; 1 Cor. 10:30f.

5 [a]Gen. 1:25, 31; Heb. 11:3

6 [1]Lit., *good* [a]Acts 1:15 [b]2 Cor. 11:23 [c]1 Tim. 1:10 [d]Luke 1:3 [Gr.]; 2 Tim. 3:10; Phil. 2:20, 22

7 [a]1 Tim. 1:9 [b]1 Tim. 1:4 [c]1 Tim. 4:8; 6:3, 5f.; 2 Tim. 3:5

8 [a]Col. 2:23 [b]1 Tim. 4:7; 6:3, 5f.; 2 Tim. 3:5

is profitable for all things, since it [c]holds promise for the [d]present life and *also* for the *life* to come.

9 [a]It is a trustworthy statement deserving full acceptance.

10 For it is for this we labor and strive, because we have fixed [a]our hope on [b]the living God, who is [c]the Savior of all men, especially of believers.

11 [1a]Prescribe and teach these things.

12 [a]Let no one look down on your youthfulness, but *rather* in speech, conduct, [b]love, faith *and* purity, show yourself [c]an example [1]of those who believe.

13 [a]Until I come, give attention to the *public* [b]reading of *Scripture*, to exhortation and teaching.

14 Do not neglect the spiritual gift within you, which was bestowed upon you through [a]prophetic utterance with [b]the laying on of hands by the [1c]presbytery.

15 Take pains with these things; be *absorbed* in them, so that your progress may be evident to all.

16 [a]Pay close attention to yourself and to your teaching; persevere in these things; for as you do this you will [1b]insure salvation both for yourself and for those who hear you.

[a] Chapter 5

Do not sharply rebuke an [b]older man, *but rather* appeal to him as a father; [c]the younger men as brothers,

2 the older women as mothers, *and* the younger women as sisters, in all purity.

3 Honor widows who are [a]widows indeed;

4 but if any widow has children or grandchildren, [a]let them first learn to practice piety in regard to their own family, and to [1]make some return to their parents; for this is [b]acceptable in the sight of God.

5 Now she who is a [a]widow indeed and who has been left alone [b]has fixed her hope on God, and continues in [c]entreaties and prayers night and day.

6 But she who [a]gives herself to wanton pleasure is [b]dead even while she lives.

7 [1a]Prescribe these things as well, so that they may be above reproach.

8 But if any one does not provide for his own, and especially for those of his household, he has [a]denied the faith, and is worse than an unbeliever.

9 Let a widow be [a]put on the list only if she is not less than sixty years old, *having been* [b]the wife of one man,

10 having a reputation for [a]good works; *and* if she has brought up children, if she has [b]shown hospitality to strangers, if she [c]has washed the [1]saints' feet, if she has [d]assisted those in distress, *and* if she has devoted herself to every good work.

11 But refuse *to put* younger widows *on the list*, for when they feel [a]sensual desires in disregard of Christ, they want to get married,

12 *thus* incurring condemnation, because they have set aside their previous [1]pledge.

13 And at the same time they also learn *to be* idle, as they go around from house to house; and not merely idle, but also

8 [c]Ps. 37:9, 11; Prov. 19:23; 22:4; Matt. 6:33 [d]Matt. 12:32; 6:33; Mark 10:30

9 [a]1 Tim. 1:15

10 [a]2 Cor. 1:10; 1 Tim. 6:17 [b]1 Tim. 3:15 [c]1 Tim. 2:4; John 4:42

11 [1]Or, *Keep commanding and teaching* [a]1 Tim. 5:7; 6:2

12 [1]Or, *to* [a]1 Cor. 16:11; Titus 2:15 [b]1 Tim. 1:14 [c]Titus 2:7; 1 Pet. 5:3

13 [a]1 Tim. 3:14 [b]2 Tim. 3:15ff.

14 [1]Or else, *board of elders* [a]1 Tim. 1:18 [b]1 Tim. 5:22; 2 Tim. 1:6; Acts 6:6 [c][in Gr.] Acts 11:30

16 [1]Lit., *save both yourself and those . . .* [a]Acts 20:28 [b]1 Cor. 1:21

1 [a]Lev. 19:32 [b]Titus 2:2 [c]Titus 2:6

3 [a]1 Tim. 5:5, 16; Acts 6:1; 9:39, 41

4 [1]Lit., *give back recompenses* [a]Eph. 6:2 [b]1 Tim. 2:3

5 [a]1 Tim. 5:3, 16; Acts 6:1; 9:39, 41 [b]1 Pet. 3:5; 1 Cor. 7:34 [c]Luke 2:37; 1 Tim. 2:1; 2 Tim. 1:3

6 [a]James 5:5 [b]Rev. 3:1; Luke 15:24; 2 Tim. 3:6

7 [1]Or, *Keep commanding* [a]1 Tim. 4:11

8 [a]2 Tim. 2:12; Titus 1:16; 2 Pet. 2:1; Jude 4

9 [a]1 Tim. 5:16 [b]1 Tim. 3:2

10 [1]I.e., true believers; lit., *holy ones* [a]Acts 9:36; 1 Tim. 6:18; 1 Pet. 2:12; Titus 2:7; 3:8 [b]1 Tim. 3:2 [c]Luke 7:44; John 13:14 [d]1 Tim. 5:16

11 [a]Rev. 18:7

12 [1]Lit., *faith*

[a]gossips and [b]busybodies, talking about [c]things not proper *to*
mention.
14 Therefore, [a]I want younger *widows* to get [b]married,
bear children, [c]keep house, *and* [d]give the enemy no occasion
for reproach;
15 for some [a]have already turned aside to follow [b]Satan.
16 If any woman who is a believer [a]has *dependent* widows,
let her [b]assist them, and let not the church be burdened, so
that it may assist those who are [c]widows indeed.
17 Let [a]the elders who [b]rule well be considered worthy of
double honor, especially those who [c]work hard [1]at preaching
and teaching.
18 For the Scripture says, "[a]YOU SHALL NOT MUZZLE THE OX
WHILE HE IS THRESHING," and "[b]The laborer is worthy of his
wages."
19 Do not receive an accusation against an [a]elder except
on the basis of [b]two or three witnesses.
20 Those who continue in sin, [a]rebuke in the presence of
all, [b]so that the rest also may be fearful *of sinning.*
21 [a]I solemnly charge you in the presence of God and of
Christ Jesus and of *His* chosen angels, to maintain these *prin-*
ciples without bias, doing nothing in a *spirit of* partiality.
22 [a]Do not lay hands upon any one *too* hastily and [1]thus
share [b]*responsibility for* the sins of others; keep yourself [2]free
from sin.
23 No longer drink water *exclusively,* but [a]use a little wine
for the sake of your stomach and your frequent ailments.
24 The sins of some men are quite evident, going before
them to judgment; for others, their *sins* [a]follow after.
25 Likewise also, deeds that are good are quite evident,
and [a]those which are otherwise cannot be concealed.

CHAPTER 6

1 [a]LET all who are under the yoke as slaves regard their own
masters as worthy of all honor so [b]that the name of God and
our doctrine may not be spoken against.
2 And let those who have believers as their masters not
be disrespectful to them because they are [a]brethren, but let
them serve them all the more, because those who [1]partake of
the benefit are believers and beloved. [b]Teach and [2]preach
these *principles.*
3 If any one [a]advocates a different doctrine, and does not
[1]agree with [b]sound words, those of our Lord Jesus Christ, and
with the doctrine [c]conforming to godliness,
4 he is [a]conceited *and* understands nothing; but he [1]has a
morbid interest in [b]controversial questions and [c]disputes about
words, out of which arise envy, strife, abusive language, evil
suspicions,
5 and constant friction between [a]men of depraved mind
and deprived of the truth, who [b]suppose that [1]godliness is a
means of gain.
6 [a]But godliness *actually* is a means of [b]great gain, when
accompanied by [c]contentment.
7 For [a]we have brought nothing into the world, [1]so we
cannot take anything out of it either.

13 [a]3 John 10 [Gr.] [b]2 Thess. 3:11 [c]Titus 1:11

14 [a]1 Tim. 2:8 [b]1 Cor. 7:9; 1 Tim. 4:3 [c]Titus 2:5 [d]1 Tim. 6:1

15 [a]1 Tim. 1:20 [b]Matt. 4:10

16 [a]1 Tim. 5:4 [b]1 Tim. 5:10 [c]1 Tim. 5:3

17 [1]Lit., *in word* [a]Acts 11:30; 1 Tim. 5:19; 4:14 [Gr.] [b]Rom. 12:8 [c]1 Thess. 5:12

18 [a]Deut. 25:4; 1 Cor. 9:9 [b]Matt. 10:10; Luke 10:7; 1 Cor. 9:14; Lev. 19:13; Deut. 24:15

19 [a]Acts 11:30; 1 Tim. 5:17; 4:14 [Gr.] [b]Matt. 18:16

20 [a]Eph. 5:11; Gal. 2:14; 2 Tim. 4:2 [b]2 Cor. 7:11

21 [a]1 Tim. 6:13; 2 Tim. 4:1; 2:14; Luke 9:26

22 [1]Lit., *do not share* [2]Lit., *pure* [a]1 Tim. 4:14; 3:10 [b]Eph. 5:11; 1 Tim. 3:2-7

23 [a]1 Tim. 3:8

24 [a]Rev. 14:13

25 [a]Prov. 10:9

1 [a]Titus 2:9; 1 Pet. 2:18; Eph. 6:5 [b]Titus 2:5

2 [1]Or, *benefit by their service* [2]Lit., *exhort, urge* [a]Acts 1:15; Gal. 3:28; Philem. 16 [b]1 Tim. 4:11

3 [1]Lit., *come to,* or, *come with* [a]1 Tim. 1:3 [b]1 Tim. 1:10 [c]Titus 1:1

4 [1]Lit., *is sick about* [a]1 Tim. 3:6 [b]1 Tim. 1:4 [c]2 Tim. 2:14; Acts 18:15

5 [1]Or, *religion* [a]2 Tim. 3:8; Titus 1:15 [b]Titus 1:11; 2 Pet. 2:3

6 [a]1 Tim. 6:6-10; Luke 12:15-21 [b]1 Tim. 4:8 [c]Phil. 4:11; Heb. 13:5

7 [1]Later mss. read, *it is clear that* [a]Job 1:21; Eccl. 5:15

8 And if we [a]have food and covering, with these we shall
be content.
9 [a]But those who want to get rich fall into temptation
and [b]a snare and many foolish and harmful desires which
plunge men into ruin and destruction.
10 For [a]the love of money is a [b]root of all [1]sorts of evil,
and some by longing for it have [c]wandered away from the
faith, and pierced themselves with many a pang.
11 But [a]flee from these things, you [b]man of God; and
pursue after righteousness, godliness, [c]faith, [d]love, [1]persever-
ance *and* gentleness.
12 [a]Fight the good fight of [b]faith; [c]take hold of the eternal
life [d]to which you were called, and you made the good [e]confes-
sion in the presence of [f]many witnesses.
13 [a]I charge you in the presence of God, who [1]gives life to
all things, and of [b]Christ Jesus, who testified the [c]good confession [d]before Pontius Pilate;
14 that you keep the commandment without stain or reproach, until the [a]appearing of our Lord Jesus Christ,
15 which He will [1]bring about at [a]the proper time—He
who is [b]the blessed and [c]only Sovereign, [d]the King of [2]kings
and [e]Lord of [3]lords;
16 [a]who alone possesses immortality and [b]dwells in unap-
proachable light; [c]whom no man has seen or can see. [d]To Him
be honor and eternal dominion! Amen.
17 Instruct those who are rich in [a]this present world [b]not
to be conceited or to [c]fix their hope on the uncertainty of
riches, but on God, [d]who richly supplies us with all things to
enjoy.
18 *Instruct them* to do good, to be rich in [a]good [1]works,
[b]to be generous and ready to share,
19 [a]storing up for themselves the treasure of a good foundation for the future, so that they may [b]take hold of that
which is life indeed.
20 O [a]Timothy, guard [b]what has been entrusted to you,
avoiding [c]worldly *and* empty chatter *and* the opposing arguments of what is falsely called 'knowledge'—
21 which some have professed and thus [a]gone astray [1]from
[b]the faith.
[c]Grace be with you.

8 [a]Prov. 30:8

9 [a]Prov. 15:27; 23:4; 28:20; 1 Tim. 6:17; Luke 12:21 [b]1 Tim. 3:7

10 [1]Lit., *the evils* [a]1 Tim. 6:9; 3:3; Col. 3:5 [b]Rom. 11:16ff. [c]James 5:19

11 [1]Or, *steadfastness* [a]2 Tim. 2:22 [b]2 Tim. 3:17 [c]1 Tim. 1:14 [d]2 Tim. 3:10

12 [a]1 Cor. 9:25f.; Phil. 1:30; 1 Tim. 1:18 [b]1 Tim. 1:19 [c]Phil. 3:12; 1 Tim. 6:19 [d]Col. 3:15 [e]2 Cor. 9:13; 1 Tim. 6:13 [f]2 Tim. 2:2; 1 Tim. 4:14

13 [1]Or, *preserves alive* [a]1 Tim. 5:21 [b]1 Tim. 1:12, 15; 2:5; Gal. 3:26 [c]2 Cor. 9:13; 1 Tim. 6:12 [d]John 18:37; Matt. 27:2

14 [a]2 Thess. 2:8

15 [1]Lit., *show* [2]Lit., *those who reign as kings* [3]Lit., *those who rule as lords* [a]1 Tim. 2:6 [b]1 Tim. 1:11 [c]1 Tim. 1:17 [d]Rev. 19:16; 17:14; Deut. 10:17 [e]Ps. 136:3

16 [a]1 Tim. 1:17 [b]Ps. 104:2; 1 John 1:5; James 1:17 [c]John 1:18 [d]1 Tim. 1:17

17 [a]2 Tim. 4:10; Titus 2:12; Matt. 12:32 [b]Ps. 62:10; Luke 12:20; 1 Tim. 6:9; Rom. 11:20 [c]1 Tim. 4:10 [d]Acts 14:17

18 [1]Or, *deeds* [a]1 Tim. 5:10 [b]Rom. 12:8; Eph. 4:28

19 [a]Matt. 6:20 [b]1 Tim. 6:12

20 [a]1 Tim. 1:2 [b]2 Tim. 1:12, 14 [c]2 Tim. 2:16; 1 Tim. 1:9

21 [1]Lit., *concerning* [a]2 Tim. 2:18 [b]1 Tim. 1:19 [c]Col. 4:18

THE SECOND EPISTLE OF PAUL TO
TIMOTHY

Salutation. Timothy Charged to Guard His Trust.

PAUL, [a]an apostle of [b]Christ Jesus [1c]by the will of God,
according to the promise of [d]life in Christ Jesus,
2 to [a]Timothy, my beloved [1b]son: [c]Grace, mercy *and*
peace from God the Father and Christ Jesus our Lord.
3 [a]I thank God, whom I [b]serve with a [c]clear conscience
[1]the way my forefathers did, [d]as I constantly remember you in
my [2]prayers night and day,
4 [a]longing to see you, [b]even as I recall your tears, so that I
may be filled with joy.
5 [1]For I am mindful of the [a]sincere faith within you,
which first dwelt in your grandmother Lois, and [b]your mother
Eunice, and I am sure that *it is* in you as well.
6 And for this reason I remind you to kindle afresh [a]the
gift of God which is in you through [a]the laying on of my hands.
7 For God has not given us a [a]spirit of timidity, but of
power and love and [1]discipline.
8 Therefore [a]do not be ashamed of the [b]testimony of our
Lord, or of me [c]His prisoner; but join with *me* in [d]suffering for
the [e]gospel according to the power of God;
9 who has [a]saved us, and [b]called us with a holy [c]calling,
[d]not according to our works, but according to His own [b]purpose
and grace which was granted us in [e]Christ Jesus from [f]all
eternity,
10 but [a]now has been revealed by the [b]appearing of our
Savior [c]Christ Jesus, who [d]abolished death, and brought life
and immortality to light through the gospel,
11 [a]for which I was appointed a preacher and an apostle
and a teacher.
12 For this reason I also suffer these things, but [a]I am not
ashamed; for I know [b]whom I have believed and I am convinced that He is able to [c]guard what I have entrusted to Him
[1]until [d]that day.
13 [1a]Retain the [b]standard of [c]sound words [d]which you
have heard from me, in the [e]faith and love which are in [f]Christ
Jesus.
14 Guard through the Holy Spirit who [a]dwells in us, the
[1b]treasure which has been entrusted to *you.*
15 You are aware of the fact that all who are in [1a]Asia
[b]turned away from me, among whom are Phygelus and
Hermogenes.
16 The Lord grant mercy to [a]the house of Onesiphorus for
he often refreshed me, and [b]was not ashamed of my [1c]chains;
17 but when he was in Rome, he eagerly searched for me,
and found me—
18 the Lord grant to him to find mercy from the Lord on
[a]that day—and you know very well what services he rendered
at [b]Ephesus.

1 [1]Lit., *through* [a]2 Cor. 1:1 [b]2 Tim. 1:2, 9, 13; 2:1, 3, 10; 3:12, 15; 1 Tim. 1:12; Gal. 3:26 [c]1 Cor. 1:1 [d]1 Tim. 6:19

2 [1]Lit., *child* [a]Acts 16:1; 1 Tim. 1:2 [b]1 Tim. 1:2; 2 Tim. 2:1; Titus 1:4 [c]1 Tim. 1:2

3 [1]Lit., *from my forefathers* [2]Or, *petitions* [a]Rom. 1:8 [b]Acts 24:14 [c]Acts 23:1; 24:16; 1 Tim. 1:5 [d]Rom. 1:9

4 [a]2 Tim. 4:9, 21 [b]Acts 20:37

5 [1]Lit., *Receiving remembrance of* [a]1 Tim. 1:5 [b]Acts 16:1; 2 Tim. 3:15

6 [a]1 Tim. 4:14

7 [1]Or, *sound judgment* [a]Rom. 8:15; John 14:27

8 [a]2 Tim. 1:12, 16; Mark 8:38; Rom. 1:16 [b]1 Cor. 1:6 [c]Eph. 3:1; 2 Tim. 1:16 [d]2 Tim. 2:3, 9; 4:5 [e]2 Tim. 1:10; 2:8

9 [a]Rom. 11:14 [b]Rom. 8:28f. [c]Rom. 11:29 [d]Eph. 2:9 [e]2 Tim. 1:1 [f]Titus 1:2; Rom. 16:25; Eph. 1:4

10 [a]Rom. 16:26 [b]Titus 2:11; 2 Thess. 2:8; 2 Tim. 4:1, 8 [c]2 Tim. 1:1 [d]1 Cor. 15:26; Heb. 2:14f.

11 [a]1 Tim. 2:7

12 [1]Or, *for* [a]2 Tim. 1:8; 1:16 [b]Titus 3:8 [c]2 Tim. 1:14; 1 Tim. 6:20 [d]2 Tim. 1:18; 4:8; 1 Cor. 3:13; 1:8

13 [1]Or, *Hold the example* [a]2 Tim. 3:14; Titus 1:9 [b]Rom. 2:20; 6:17 [c]1 Tim. 1:10 [d]2 Tim. 2:2 [e]1 Tim. 1:14 [f]2 Tim. 1:1

14 [1]Lit., *good deposit* [a]Rom. 8:9 [b]2 Tim. 1:12; 1 Tim. 6:20

15 [1]I.e., the province of Asia [a]Acts 2:9 [b]2 Tim. 4:10, 11, 16

16 [1]Lit., *chain* [a]2 Tim. 4:19 [b]2 Tim. 1:8 [c]Eph. 6:20

18 [a]2 Tim. 1:12; 4:8; 1 Cor. 3:13; 1:8 [b]Acts 18:19; 1 Tim. 1:3

Chapter 2

YOU therefore, my [1a]son, [b]be strong in the grace that is in
[c]Christ Jesus.
2 And the things [a]which you have heard from me in the
presence of [b]many witnesses, these [c]entrust to [d]faithful men,
who will be [e]able to teach others also.
3 [a]Suffer hardship with *me*, as a good [b]soldier of [c]Christ
Jesus.
4 No soldier in active service [a]entangles himself in the
affairs of everyday life, so that he may please the one who
enlisted him as a soldier.
5 And also if any one [a]competes as an athlete, he [1]does
not win the prize unless he competes according to the rules.
6 [a]The hard-working farmer ought to be the first to receive his share of the crops.
7 Consider what I say, for the Lord will give you understanding in everything.
8 Remember Jesus Christ, [a]risen from the dead, [b]descend-
ant of David, [c]according to my gospel;
9 [1]for which I [a]suffer hardship even to [b]imprisonment as
a [c]criminal, but [d]the word of God [e]is not imprisoned.
10 For this reason [a]I endure all things for [b]the sake of
those who are chosen, [c]that they also may obtain the [d]salvation
which is in [e]Christ Jesus *and* with *it* [f]eternal glory.
11 [a]It is a trustworthy statement:

For [b]if we died with Him, we shall also live with
Him;
12 If we endure, [a]we shall also reign with Him;
If we [1b]deny Him, He also will deny us;
13 If we are faithless, [a]He remains faithful; for [b]He cannot deny Himself.

14 Remind *them* of these things, and solemnly [a]charge
them in the presence of God not to [b]wrangle about words,
which is useless, *and leads* to the ruin of the hearers.
15 Be diligent to [a]present yourself approved to God as a
workman who does not need to be ashamed, handling accurately [b]the word of truth.
16 But [a]avoid [b]worldly *and* empty chatter, for [1]it will lead
to further ungodliness,
17 and their [1]talk will spread like [2]gangrene. Among them
are [a]Hymenaeus and Philetus,
18 *men* who have gone astray from the truth saying that
[a]the resurrection has already taken place, and thus they upset
[b]the faith of some.
19 Nevertheless, the [a]firm foundation of God stands, having this [b]seal, "[c]The Lord knows those who are His," and,
"[d]Let every one who names the name of the Lord abstain from
wickedness."
20 Now in a large house there are not only gold and silver
vessels, but also vessels of wood and of earthenware, and [a]some
to honor and some to dishonor.
21 Therefore, if a man cleanses himself from [a]these
things, he will be a vessel for honor, sanctified, useful to the
Master, [b]prepared for every good work.
22 Now [a]flee from youthful lusts, and [a]pursue after

1 [1]Lit., *child* [a]2 Tim. 1:2 [b]Eph. 6:10 [c]2 Tim. 1:1

2 [a]2 Tim. 1:13 [b]1 Tim. 6:12 [c]1 Tim. 1:18 [d]1 Tim. 1:12 [e][in Gr.] 2 Cor. 2:16; 3:5

3 [a]2 Tim. 1:8 [b]1 Cor. 9:7; 1 Tim. 1:18 [c]2 Tim. 1:1

4 [a]2 Pet. 2:20

5 [1]Lit., *not crowned* [a]1 Cor. 9:25

6 [a]1 Cor. 9:10

8 [a]Acts 2:24 [b]Matt. 1:1 [c]Rom. 2:16

9 [1]Lit., *in which* [a]2 Tim. 1:8; 2:3 [b]Phil. 1:7 [c]Luke 23:32 [d]1 Thess. 1:8 [e]Acts 28:31; 2 Tim. 4:17

10 [a]Col. 1:24 [b]Luke 18:7; Titus 1:1 [c]2 Cor. 1:6; 1 Thess. 5:9 [d]1 Cor. 1:21 [e]2 Tim. 2:1, 3; 2 Tim. 1:1 [f]2 Cor. 4:17; 1 Pet. 5:10

11 [a]1 Tim. 1:15 [b]Rom. 6:8; 1 Thess. 5:10

12 [1]Lit., *shall deny* [a]Luke 22:29; Matt. 19:28; Rom. 5:17; 8:17 [b]Matt. 10:33; 1 Tim. 5:8

13 [a]1 Cor. 1:9; Rom. 3:3 [b]Num. 23:19; Titus 1:2

14 [a]1 Tim. 5:21; 2 Tim. 4:1 [b]1 Tim. 6:4; 2 Tim. 2:23; Titus 3:9

15 [a]Rom. 6:13; James 1:12 [b]Eph. 1:13; James 1:18

16 [1]Lit., *they will make further progress in ungodliness* [a]Titus 3:9 [b]1 Tim. 6:20; 1:9

17 [1]Lit., *word* [2]Or, *cancer* [a]1 Tim. 1:20

18 [a]1 Cor. 15:12 [b]1 Tim. 1:19; Titus 1:11

19 [a]1 Tim. 3:15; Is. 28:16f. [b]John 3:33 [c]John 10:14; 1 Cor. 8:3 [d]Luke 13:27; 1 Cor. 1:2

20 [a]Rom. 9:21

21 [a]2 Tim. 2:16-18; 1 Tim. 6:11 [b]2 Tim. 3:17; 2 Cor. 9:8; Eph. 2:10

22 [a]1 Tim. 6:11

righteousness, [b]faith, love *and* peace, with those who [c]call on
the Lord [d]from a pure heart.
23 But refuse foolish and ignorant [a]speculations, knowing
that they [b]produce [1]quarrels.
24 And [a]the Lord's bond-servant must not be quarrelsome,
but be kind to all, [b]able to teach, patient when wronged,
25 [a]with gentleness correcting those who are in opposition; [b]if perhaps God may grant them repentance leading to
[c]the knowledge of the truth,
26 and they may come to their senses *and escape* from
[a]the snare of the devil, having been [b]held captive [1]by him to do
his will.

Chapter 3

BUT realize this, that [a]in the last days difficult times will
come.
2 For men will be [a]lovers of self, [b]lovers of money, [c]boast-
ful, [c]arrogant, [d]revilers, [c]disobedient to parents, [e]ungrateful,
[f]unholy,
3 [a]unloving, irreconcilable, [b]malicious gossips, without
self-control, brutal, [1c]haters of good,
4 [a]treacherous, [b]reckless, [c]conceited, [d]lovers of pleasure
rather than lovers of God;
5 holding to a [a]form of [1b]godliness, although they have
[c]denied its power; and [d]avoid such men as these.
6 For among them are those who [1a]enter into households
and captivate [b]weak women weighed down with sins, led on by
[c]various impulses,
7 always learning and never able to [a]come to the [1]knowl-
edge of the truth.
8 And just as [a]Jannes and Jambres [b]opposed Moses, so
these *men* also oppose the truth, [c]men of depraved mind,
rejected as regards the faith.
9 But they will not make further progress; for their [a]folly
will be obvious to all, [b]as also that of those *two* came to be.
10 But you [a]followed my teaching, conduct, purpose,
faith, patience, [b]love, [1]perseverance,
11 [a]persecutions, [b]sufferings, such as happened to me at
[c]Antioch, at [d]Iconium *and* at [e]Lystra; what [f]persecutions I
endured, and out of them all [g]the Lord delivered me!
12 And indeed, all who desire to live godly in Christ Jesus
[a]will be persecuted.
13 But evil men and impostors [a]will proceed *from bad* to
worse, [b]deceiving and being deceived.
14 You, however, [a]continue in the things you have learned
and become convinced of, knowing from whom you have
learned *them;*
15 and that [a]from childhood you have known [b]the sacred
writings which are able to [c]give you the wisdom that leads to
[d]salvation through faith which is in [e]Christ Jesus.
16 [1a]All Scripture is [2]inspired by God and profitable for
teaching, for reproof, for correction, for [3]training in
righteousness;
17 that [a]the man of God may be adequate, [b]equipped for
every good work.

22 [b]1 Tim. 1:14 [c]Acts 7:59 [d]1 Tim. 1:5

23 [1]Lit., *fightings* [a]1 Tim. 6:4; Titus 3:9; 2 Tim. 2:14 [b]Titus 3:9; James 4:1

24 [a]1 Tim. 3:3; Titus 1:7 [b]1 Tim. 3:2

25 [a]Titus 3:2; Gal. 6:1; 1 Pet. 3:15 [b]Acts 8:22 [c]1 Tim. 2:4

26 [1]Or possibly, *by him, to do His will* [a]1 Tim. 3:7 [b]Luke 5:10

1 [a]1 Tim. 4:1

2 [a]Phil. 2:21 [b]Luke 16:14; 1 Tim. 3:3; 6:10 [c]Rom. 1:30 [d]2 Pet. 2:10-12 [e]Luke 6:35 [f]1 Tim. 1:9

3 [1]Lit., *not loving good* [a]Rom. 1:31 [b]1 Tim. 3:11 [c]Titus 1:8

4 [a]Acts 7:52 [Gr.] [b]Acts 19:36 [Gr.] [c]1 Tim. 3:6 [d]Phil. 3:19

5 [1]Or, *religion* [a]Rom. 2:20 [b]1 Tim. 4:7 [c]1 Tim. 5:8 [d]2 Thess. 3:6; Matt. 7:15

6 [1]Or, *creep into* [a]Jude 4 [b]1 Tim. 5:6; Titus 3:3 [c]Titus 3:3

7 [1]Or, *recognition* [a]2 Tim. 2:25

8 [a]Ex. 7:11 [b]Acts 13:8 [c]1 Tim. 6:5

9 [a]Luke 6:11 [Gr.] [b]Ex. 7:12; 8:18; 9:11

10 [1]Or, *steadfastness* [a]1 Tim. 4:6; Luke 1:3 [Gr.]; Phil. 2:20, 22 [b]1 Tim 6:11

11 [a]2 Cor. 12:10 [b]2 Cor. 1:5, 7 [c]Acts 13:14, 45, 50 [d]Acts 14:5 [e]Acts 14:19 [f]2 Cor. 11:23-27 [g]Rom. 15:31

12 [a]John 15:20; Acts 14:22; 2 Cor. 4:9f.

13 [a]2 Tim. 2:16 [b]Titus 3:3

14 [a] Tim. 1:13; Titus 1:9

15 [a]2 Tim. 1:5 [b]John 5:47; Rom. 2:27 [c]Ps. 119:98f. [d]1 Cor. 1:21 [e]2 Tim. 1:1

16 [1]Or, possibly, *Every Scripture inspired by God is also . . .* [2]Lit., *God-breathed* [3]Lit., *training which is in* [a]Rom. 4:23f.; 15:4; 2 Pet. 1:20f.

17 [a]1 Tim. 6:11 [b]2 Tim. 2:21; Heb. 13:21

Chapter 4

[a]I SOLEMNLY charge *you* in the presence of God and of
Christ Jesus, who is to [b]judge the living and the dead, and by
His [c]appearing and His kingdom:
2 preach [a]the word; be ready in season *and* out of season;
[b]reprove, rebuke, exhort, with [1]great [c]patience and instruction.
3 For [a]the time will come when they will not endure
[b]sound doctrine; but *wanting* to have their ears tickled, they
will accumulate for themselves teachers in accordance to their
own desires;
4 and [a]will turn away their ears from the truth, and [b]will
turn aside to myths.
5 But you, [a]be sober in all things, [b]endure hardship, do
the work of an [c]evangelist, [d]fulfill your [e]ministry.
6 For I am already being [a]poured out as a drink offering,
and the time of [b]my departure has come.
7 [a]I have fought the good fight, I have finished [b]the
course, I have kept [c]the faith;
8 in the future there [a]is laid up for me [b]the crown of
righteousness, which the Lord, the righteous Judge, will award
to me on [c]that day; and not only to me, but also to [d]all who
have loved His [e]appearing.
9 [a]Make every effort to come to me soon;
10 for [a]Demas, having loved [b]this present [1]world, has deserted me and gone to [c]Thessalonica; Crescens *has gone* to
[2d]Galatia, [e]Titus to Dalmatia.
11 [a]Only [b]Luke is with me. Pick up [c]Mark and bring him
with you, [d]for he is useful to me for service.
12 But [a]Tychicus I have sent to [b]Ephesus.
13 When you come bring the cloak which I left at [a]Troas
with Carpus, and the books, especially the parchments.
14 [a]Alexander the coppersmith did me much harm; [b]the
Lord will repay him according to his deeds.
15 Be on guard against him yourself, for he vigorously
opposed our [1]teaching.
16 At my first defense no one supported me, but all deserted me; [a]may it not be counted against them.
17 But the Lord stood with me, and [a]strengthened me, in
order that through me [b]the proclamation might [1]be [c]fully accomplished, and that all [d]the Gentiles might hear; and I was
[e]delivered out of [f]the lion's mouth.
18 The Lord will deliver me from every evil deed, and will
[1a]bring me safely to His [b]heavenly kingdom; [c]to [2]Him *be* the
glory forever and ever. Amen.
19 Greet Prisca and [a]Aquila, and [b]the household of
Onesiphorus.
20 [a]Erastus remained at [b]Corinth; but Trophimus I left
sick at [c]Miletus.
21 [a]Make every effort to come before [b]winter. Eubulus
greets you, also Pudens and Linus and Claudia and all the
brethren.
22 [a]The Lord be with your spirit. [b]Grace be with you.

1 [a]2 Tim. 2:14; 1 Tim. 5:21 [b]Acts 10:42 [c]2 Thess. 2:8; 2 Tim. 4:8; 1:10

2 [1]Lit., *all* [a]Gal. 6:6; Col. 4:3; 1 Thess. 1:6 [b]1 Tim. 5:20; Titus 1:13; 2:15 [c]2 Tim. 3:10

3 [a]2 Tim. 3:1 [b]1 Tim. 1:10; 2 Tim. 1:13

4 [a]2 Thess. 2:11; Titus 1:14 [b]1 Tim. 1:4

5 [a]1 Pet. 1:13 [b]2 Tim. 1:8 [c]Acts 21:8 [d]Luke 1:1 [e]Col. 4:17; Eph. 4:12

6 [a]Phil. 2:17 [b]Phil. 1:23; 2 Pet. 1:14

7 [a]1 Tim. 6:12; 1 Cor. 9:25f.; Phil. 1:30; 1 Tim. 1:18 [b]1 Cor. 9:24; Acts 20:24 [c]2 Tim. 3:10

8 [a]Col. 1:5; 1 Pet. 1:4 [b]1 Cor. 9:25; 2 Tim. 2:5 [c]2 Tim. 1:12 [d]Phil. 3:11 [e]2 Tim. 4:1

9 [a]2 Tim. 1:4; 4:21; Titus 3:12

10 [1]Or, *age* [2]Some ancient mss. read, *Gaul* [a]Col. 4:14 [b]1 Tim. 6:17 [c]Acts 17:1 [d]Acts 16:6 [e]2 Cor. 2:13

11 [a]2 Tim. 1:15 [b]Col. 4:14 [c]Acts 12:12 [d]Col. 4:10; 2 Tim. 2:21

12 [a]Acts 20:4 [b]Acts 18:19

13 [a]Acts 16:8

14 [a]1 Tim. 1:20; Acts 19:33 [b]Rom. 12:19; 2:6

15 [1]Lit., *words*

16 [a]Acts 7:60; 1 Cor. 13:5

17 [1]Or, *be fulfilled* [a]2 Tim. 2:1; 1 Tim. 1:12 [b]Titus 1:3 [c]2 Tim. 4:5 [d]Acts 9:15; Phil. 1:12ff. [e]2 Tim. 3:11; Rom. 15:31 [f]Ps. 22:21; 1 Sam. 17:37

18 [1]Or, *save me for* [2]Lit., *whom* [a]1 Cor. 1:21 [b]2 Tim. 4:1; 1 Cor. 15:50; Heb. 11:16; 12:22 [c]Rom. 11:36; 2 Pet. 3:18

19 [a]Acts 18:2 [b]2 Tim. 1:16

20 [a]Acts 19:22 [b]Acts 18:1 [c]Acts 20:15

21 [a]2 Tim. 4:9 [b]Titus 3:12

22 [a]Gal. 6:18; Phil. 4:23; Philem. 25 [b]Col. 4:18

THE EPISTLE OF PAUL TO

TITUS

Salutation. Qualifications of an Elder. Disorderly Teachers to be Reproved.

PAUL, [a]a bond-servant of God, and an [b]apostle of Jesus
Christ, [1]for the faith of those [c]chosen of God and [d]the knowledge of the truth which is [e]according to godliness,
2 in [a]the hope of eternal life, which God, [b]who cannot
lie, [c]promised [1d]long ages ago,
3 but [a]at the proper time manifested, *even* His word, in
[b]the proclamation [c]with which I was entrusted [d]according to
the commandment of [e]God our Savior;
4 to [a]Titus, [b]my true child [1]in a [c]common faith: [d]Grace
and peace from God the Father and [e]Christ Jesus our Savior.
5 For this reason I left you in [a]Crete, that you might set
in order what remains, and [b]appoint [c]elders in every city as I
directed you,
6 namely, [a]if any man be above reproach, the [b]husband
of one wife, having children who believe, not accused of [c]dissi-
pation or [d]rebellion.
7 For the [1a]overseer must be above reproach as [b]God's
steward, not [c]self-willed, not quick-tempered, not [d]addicted to
wine, not pugnacious, [e]not fond of sordid gain,
8 but [a]hospitable, [b]loving what is good, sensible, just, devout, self-controlled,
9 [a]holding fast the faithful word which is in accordance
with the teaching, that he may be able both to exhort in
[b]sound doctrine and to refute those who contradict.
10 [a]For there are many [b]rebellious men, [c]empty talkers
and deceivers, especially [d]those of the circumcision,
11 who must be silenced because they are upsetting [a]whole
families, teaching [b]things they should not *teach,* [c]for the
sake of sordid gain.
12 [a]One of themselves, a prophet of their own, said,
“[b]Cretans are always liars, evil beasts, lazy gluttons.”
13 This testimony is true. For this cause [a]reprove them
[b]severely that they may be [c]sound in the faith,
14 not paying attention to Jewish [a]myths and [b]command-
ments of men who [c]turn away from the truth.
15 [a]To the pure, all things are pure; but [b]to those who are
defiled and unbelieving, nothing is pure, but both their [c]mind
and their conscience are defiled.
16 [a]They profess to know God, but by *their* deeds they
[b]deny *Him,* being [c]detestable and [d]disobedient, and [e]worthless
[f]for any good deed.

CHAPTER 2

BUT as for you, speak the things which are fitting for [a]sound
doctrine.
2 [a]Older men are to be [b]temperate, dignified, [b]sensible,
[c]sound [d]in faith, in love, in [1]perseverance.

1 [1]Or, *according to* [a]James 1:1; Rev. 1:1; Rom. 1:1 [b]2 Cor. 1:1 [c]Luke 18:7 [d]1 Tim. 2:4 [e]1 Tim. 6:3

2 [1]Lit., *before times eternal* [a]Titus 3:7; 2 Tim. 1:1 [b]2 Tim. 2:13 [c]Rom. 1:2 [d]2 Tim. 1:9

3 [a]1 Tim. 2:6 [b]2 Tim. 4:17; Rom. 16:25 [c]1 Tim. 1:11 [d]1 Tim. 1:1 [e]1 Tim. 1:1; Titus 2:10; 3:4; Luke 1:47

4 [1]Lit., *according to* [a]2 Cor. 2:13 [b]2 Tim. 1:2 [c]2 Pet. 1:1 [d]Rom. 1:7 [e]1 Tim. 1:12; 2 Tim. 1:1

5 [a]Acts 27:7; Titus 1:12 [b]Acts 14:23 [c]Acts 11:30

6 [a]Titus 1:6-8; 1 Tim. 3:2-4 [b]1 Tim. 3:2 [c]Eph. 5:18 [d]Titus 1:10

7 [1]Or, *bishop* [a]1 Tim. 3:2 [b]1 Cor. 4:1 [c]2 Pet. 2:10 [d]1 Tim. 3:3 [e]1 Tim. 3:3, 8

8 [a]1 Tim. 3:2 [b]2 Tim. 3:3

9 [a]1 Tim. 1:19; 2 Tim. 1:13; 2 Thess. 2:15 [b]1 Tim. 1:10; Titus 2:1

10 [a]2 Cor. 11:13 [b]Titus 1:6 [c]1 Tim. 1:6 [d]Acts 11:2

11 [a]1 Tim. 5:4 [in Gr.]; 2 Tim. 3:6 [b]1 Tim. 5:13 [c]1 Tim. 6:5

12 [a]Acts 17:28. The Gr. hexameter is said to be taken from a work by the Cretan poet Epimenides [b]Acts 2:11; 27:7

13 [a]1 Tim. 5:20; 2 Tim. 4:2; Titus 2:15 [b]2 Cor. 13:10 [c]Titus 2:2

14 [a]1 Tim. 1:4 [b]Col. 2:22 [c]2 Tim. 4:4

15 [a]Luke 11:41; Rom. 14:20 [b]Rom. 14:14, 23 [c]1 Tim. 6:5

16 [a]1 John 2:4 [b]1 Tim. 5:8 [c]Rev. 21:8 [d]Titus 3:3 [e]2 Tim. 3:8 [f]2 Tim. 3:17; Titus 3:1

1 [a]Titus 1:9

2 [1]Or, *steadfastness* [a]Philem. 9 [b]1 Tim. 3:2 [c]Titus 1:13 [d]1 Tim. 1:2, 14

3 [a]1 Tim. 3:11 [b]1 Tim. 3:8

4 [1]Or, *train*

5 [a]1 Tim. 5:14 [b]Eph. 5:22 [c]1 Tim. 6:1

6 [1]Or, *sensible in all things; show . . .* [a]1 Tim. 5:1 [b]1 Tim. 3:2

7 [1]Or, *soundness*, lit., *uncorruptness* [a]1 Tim. 4:12

8 [a]1 Pet. 2:12; 2 Thess. 3:14

9 [1]Lit., *contradicting* [a]Eph. 6:5; 1 Tim. 6:1

10 [a]Titus 1:3

11 [1]Or, *to all men, bringing* [a]2 Tim. 1:10; Titus 3:4 [b]1 Tim. 2:4

12 [1]Or, *disciplining* [a]1 Tim. 6:9; Titus 3:3 [b]2 Tim. 3:12 [c]1 Tim. 6:17

13 [1]Or, *the great God and our Savior* [a]2 Thess. 2:8 [b]2 Pet. 1:1; 1 Tim. 1:1; 2 Tim. 1:2; Titus 1:4

14 [a]1 Tim. 2:6 [b]Ps. 130:8; 1 Pet. 1:18f. [c]Heb. 1:3; 9:14; 1 John 1:7 [d]Ex. 19:5; Deut. 14:2; 1 Pet. 2:9; Eph. 1:11 [e]Eph. 2:10; Titus 3:8; 1 Pet. 3:13

15 [1]Lit., *command* [a]1 Tim. 4:13; 5:20; 2 Tim. 4:2 [b]1 Tim. 4:12

1 [a]2 Tim. 2:14 [b]Rom. 13:1 [c]2 Tim. 2:21

2 [a]1 Tim. 3:3; 1 Pet. 2:18 [b]2 Tim. 2:25

3 [a]Rom. 11:30; 1 Cor. 6:11; Col. 3:7 [b]Titus 1:16 [c]2 Tim. 3:13 [d]Rom. 6:6, 12 [e]2 Tim. 3:6; Titus 2:12 [f]Rom. 1:29

4 [a]Eph. 2:7; Rom. 2:4; 1 Pet. 2:3 [b]Titus 2:10 [c]Titus 2:11

5 [a]2 Tim. 1:9; Rom. 11:14 [b]Eph. 2:9 [c]1 Pet. 1:3; Eph. 2:4 [d]Eph. 5:26; John 3:5; 1 Pet. 3:21 [e]Rom. 12:2

6 [a]Rom. 5:5 [b]Rom. 2:4; 1 Tim. 6:17

7 [1]Or, *of eternal life according to hope* [a]Rom. 8:17, 24; Titus 1:2; Matt. 25:34; Mark 10:17

8 [a]1 Tim. 1:15 [b]1 Tim. 2:8 [c]2 Tim. 1:12 [d]Titus 3:14; 2:7, 14

9 [a]2 Tim. 2:16 [b]2 Tim. 2:23; 1 Tim. 1:4 [c]1 Tim. 1:4 [d]James 4:1 [e]2 Tim. 2:14

3 Older women likewise are to be reverent in their behavior, [a]not malicious gossips, nor [b]enslaved to much wine,
teaching what is good,
4 that they may [1]encourage the young women to love
their husbands, to love their children,
5 *to be* sensible, pure, [a]workers at home, kind, being [b]sub-
ject to their own husbands, [c]that the word of God may not be
dishonored.
6 Likewise urge [a]the young men to be [1b]sensible;
7 in all things show yourself to be [a]an example of good
deeds, *with* [1]purity in doctrine, dignified,
8 sound *in* speech which is beyond reproach, in order
[a]that the opponent may be put to shame, having nothing bad
to say about us.
9 Urge [a]bondslaves to be subject to their own masters in
everything, to be well pleasing, not [1]argumentative,
10 not pilfering, but showing all good faith that they may
adorn the doctrine of [a]God our Savior in every respect.
11 For the grace of God has [a]appeared, [1b]bringing salvation to all men,
12 [1]instructing us to deny ungodliness and [a]worldly desires
and [b]to live sensibly, righteously and godly [c]in the present age,
13 looking for the blessed hope and the [a]appearing of the
glory of [1b]our great God and Savior, Christ Jesus;
14 who [a]gave Himself for us, [b]that HE MIGHT REDEEM US
FROM EVERY LAWLESS DEED AND [c]PURIFY FOR HIMSELF A [d]PEOPLE
FOR HIS OWN POSSESSION, [e]zealous for good deeds.
15 These things speak and [a]exhort and [a]reprove with all
[1]authority. [b]Let no one disregard you.

[a] CHAPTER 3

REMIND them [b]to be subject to rulers, to authorities, to be
obedient, to be [c]ready for every good deed,
2 to malign no one, [a]to be uncontentious, [a]gentle, [b]show-
ing every consideration for all men.
3 [a]For we also once were foolish ourselves, [b]disobedient,
[c]deceived, [d]enslaved to [e]various lusts and pleasures, spending
our life in [f]malice and [f]envy, hateful, hating one another.
4 But when the [a]kindness of [b]God our Savior and *His*
love for mankind [c]appeared,
5 [a]He saved us, [b]not on the basis of deeds which we have
done in righteousness, but [c]according to His mercy, by the
[d]washing of regeneration and [e]renewing by the Holy Spirit,
6 [a]whom He poured out upon us [b]richly through Jesus
Christ our Savior,
7 that being justified by His grace we might be made
[a]heirs [1]according to *the* hope of eternal life.
8 [a]This is a trustworthy statement, and concerning these
things I [b]want you to speak confidently, so that those who have
[c]believed God may be careful to [d]engage in good deeds. These
things are good and profitable for men.
9 But [a]shun [b]foolish controversies and [c]genealogies and
strife and [d]disputes about the Law; for they are [e]unprofitable
and worthless.

10 [a]Reject a [b]factious man [c]after a first and second
warning,
11 knowing that such a man is [a]perverted and is sinning,
being self-condemned.
12 When I send Artemas or [a]Tychicus to you, [b]make
every effort to come to me at [c]Nicopolis, for I have decided to
[d]spend the winter there.
13 [a]Diligently help Zenas the [b]lawyer and [c]Apollos on
their way so that nothing is lacking for them.
14 And let [a]our *people* also learn to [b]engage in good
[1]deeds to meet [c]pressing needs, that they may not be
[d]unfruitful.
15 [a]All who are with me greet you. Greet those who love
us [b]in *the* faith.
[c]Grace be with you all.

10 [a]2 John 10 [b]Rom. 16:17 [c]Matt. 18:15f.

11 [a]Titus 1:14

12 [a]Acts 20:4; 2 Tim. 4:12 [b]2 Tim. 4:9 [c]2 Tim. 4:10 [d]2 Tim. 4:21

13 [a]Acts 15:3 [b]Matt. 22:35 [c]Acts 18:24

14 [1]Or, *occupations* [a]Titus 2:8 [b]Titus 3:8 [c]Rom. 12:13; Phil. 4:16 [d]Matt. 7:19; Phil. 1:11; Col. 1:10

15 [a]Acts 20:34 [b]1 Tim. 1:2 [c]Col. 4:18

THE EPISTLE OF PAUL TO
PHILEMON

Salutation. Thanksgiving for Philemon's Love and Fellowship.

[a]PAUL, [b]a prisoner of [c]Christ Jesus, and [d]Timothy [1]our brother, to Philemon our beloved *brother* and [e]fellow-worker,
2 and to Apphia [1a]our sister, and to [b]Archippus our
[c]fellow-soldier, and to [d]the church in your house:
3 [a]Grace to you and peace from God our Father and the
Lord Jesus Christ.
4 [a]I thank my God always, [b]making mention of you in
my prayers,
5 because I [a]hear of your love, and of the faith which you
have toward the Lord Jesus, and toward all the [1]saints;
6 *and I pray* that the fellowship of your faith may become effective [1]through the [a]knowledge of every good thing
which is in [2]you [3]for Christ's sake.
7 For I have come to have much [a]joy and comfort in
your love, because the [1]hearts of the [2]saints have been [2b]refreshed
through you, brother.
8 Therefore, [a]though I have [1]enough confidence in
Christ to order you *to do* that which is [b]proper,
9 yet for love's sake I rather [a]appeal *to you*—since I am
such a person as Paul [1]the [b]aged, and now also [c]a prisoner of
[d]Christ Jesus—
10 I [a]appeal to you for my [b]child, whom I have begotten
in my [1]imprisonment, [2c]Onesimus,
11 who formerly was useless to you, but now is useful both
to you and to me.
12 And I have sent him back to you in person, that is,
sending my very heart;
13 whom I wished to keep with me, that in your behalf he
might minister to me in my [1a]imprisonment for the gospel;
14 but without your consent I did not want to do anything,

1 [1]Lit., *the* [a]Phil. 1:1 [b]Philem. 9, 23; Eph. 3:1 [c]Philem. 9, 23; Gal. 3:26; 1 Tim. 1:12 [d]2 Cor. 1:1; Col. 1:1 [e]Philem. 24; Phil. 2:25

2 [1]Lit., *the* [a]Rom. 16:1 [b]Col. 4:17 [c]Phil. 2:25; 2 Tim. 2:3 [d]Rom. 16:5

3 [a]Rom. 1:7

4 [a]Rom. 1:8 [b]Rom. 1:9

5 [1]I.e., true believers; lit., *holy ones* [a]Eph. 1:15; Col. 1:4; 1 Thess. 3:6

6 [1]Or, *in* [2]Some ancient mss. read, *us* [3]Lit., *toward Christ* [a]Phil. 1:9; Col. 1:9; 3:10

7 [1]Lit., *inward parts* [2]I.e., true believers; lit., *holy ones* [a]2 Cor. 7:4, 13 [b]Philem. 20; 1 Cor. 16:18; 2 Cor. 7:13

8 [1]Lit., *much* [a]2 Cor. 3:12; 1 Thess. 2:6 [b]Eph. 5:4

9 [1]Or, *an ambassador* [a]Rom. 12:1 [b]Titus 2:2 [c]Philem. 1 [d]Philem. 9, 23; Gal. 3:26; 1 Tim. 1:12

10 [1]Lit., *bonds* [2]I.e., Useful [a]Rom. 12:1 [b]1 Cor. 4:14f. [c]Col. 4:9

13 [1]Lit., *bonds* [a]Philem. 10; Phil. 1:7

that your goodness should [a]not be as it were by compulsion, but of your own free will.

15 For perhaps [a]he was for this reason parted *from you* for a while, that you should have him back forever,

16 [a]no longer as a slave, but more than a slave, [b]a beloved brother, especially to me, but how much more to you, both [c]in the flesh and in the Lord.

17 If then you regard me a [a]partner, accept him as *you would* me.

18 But if he has wronged you in any way, or owes you anything, charge that to my account;

19 [a]I, Paul, am writing this with my own hand, I will repay it ([b]lest I should [1]mention to you that you owe to me even your own self as well).

20 Yes, brother, let me benefit from you in the Lord; [a]refresh my heart in Christ.

21 [a]Having confidence in your obedience, I write to you, since I know that you will do even more than what I say.

22 And at the same time also prepare me a [a]lodging; for [b]I hope that through [c]your prayers [d]I shall be given to you.

23 [a]Epaphras, my [b]fellow-prisoner in [c]Christ Jesus, greets you;

24 *as do* [a]Mark, [b]Aristarchus, [c]Demas, [c]Luke, my [d]fellow-workers.

25 [a]The grace of the Lord Jesus Christ be [b]with your spirit.[1]

14 [a]1 Pet. 5:2; 2 Cor. 9:7

15 [a]Gen. 45:5, 8

16 [a]1 Cor. 7:22 [b]Matt. 23:8; 1 Tim. 6:2 [c]Eph. 6:5; Col. 3:22

17 [a]2 Cor. 8:23; Philem. 6

19 [1]Lit., *say* [a]1 Cor. 16:21; 2 Cor. 10:1; Gal. 5:2 [b]2 Cor. 9:4

20 [a]Philem. 7

21 [a]2 Cor. 2:3

22 [a]Acts 28:23 [b]Phil. 1:25; 2:24 [c]2 Cor. 1:11 [d]Acts 27:24; Heb. 13:19

23 [a]Col. 1:7 [b]Rom. 16:7; Philem. 1 [c]Philem. 1

24 [a]Acts 12:12 [b]Acts 19:29; Col. 4:10 [c]Col. 4:14; 2 Tim. 4:10f. [d]Philem. 1

25 [1]Some ancient mss. add, *Amen* [a]Gal. 6:18 [b]2 Tim. 4:22

THE EPISTLE TO THE
HEBREWS

God's Final Word spoken through His Son.

GOD, after He [a]spoke long ago to the fathers in [b]the prophets in many portions and [c]in many ways,

2 [1a]in these last days [b]has spoken to us in [c]*His* Son, whom He appointed [d]heir of all things, [e]through whom also He made the [2f]world.

3 [1]And He is the radiance of His glory and the exact [a]representation of His nature, and [2b]upholds all things by the word of His power. When He had made [c]purification of sins, He [d]sat down at the right hand of the [e]Majesty on high;

4 having become as much better than the angels, as He has inherited a more excellent [a]name than they.

5 For to which of the angels did He ever say,

"[a]Thou art My Son,
Today I have begotten Thee"?

And again,

"[b]I will be a Father to Him,
And He shall be a Son to Me"?

6 And [1]when He again [a]brings the first-born into [2b]the world, He says,

1 [a]Heb. 2:2f.; 3:5; 4:8; 5:5; 11:18; 12:25; John 9:29; 16:13 [b]Acts 2:30; 3:21 [c]Num. 12:6, 8; Joel 2:28

2 [1]Or, *at the end of these days* [2]Lit., *ages* [a]Heb. 9:26; 1 Pet. 1:20; Matt. 13:39 [b]Heb. 2:2f.; 3:5; 4:8; 5:5; 11:18; 12:25; John 9:29; John 16:13 [c]Heb. 3:6; 5:8; 7:28; John 5:26, 27 [d]Ps. 2:8; Matt. 28:18; Mark 12:7; Rom. 8:17; Heb. 2:8 [e]John 1:3; Col. 1:16; 1 Cor. 8:6 [f]Heb. 11:3; 1 Cor. 2:7

3 [1]Lit., *who being* [2]Lit., *upholding* [a]2 Cor. 4:4 [b]Col. 1:17 [c]Titus 2:14; Heb. 9:14 [d]Heb. 8:1; 10:12; 12:2; Mark 16:19 [e]2 Pet. 1:17

4 [a]Eph. 1:21; Phil. 2:9

5 [a]Ps. 2:7; Acts 13:13; Heb. 5:5 [b]2 Sam. 7:14

6 [1]Or, *again when He brings* [2]Lit., *the inhabited earth* [a]Heb. 10:5 [b]Matt. 24:14

"[c]And let all the angels of God worship Him."
7 And of the angels He says,
"[a]Who makes His angels winds,
And His ministers a flame of fire."
8 But of the Son *He says,*
"[a]Thy [b]throne, O God, is forever and ever,
And the righteous scepter is the scepter of [1]His kingdom.
9 "[a]Thou hast loved righteousness and hated lawlessness;
[b]Therefore God, Thy God, hath [c]anointed Thee
With the oil of gladness above Thy companions."
10 And,
"[a]Thou, Lord, in the beginning didst lay the foundation of the earth,
And the heavens are the works of Thy hands;
11 [a]They will perish, but Thou remainest;
[b]And they all will become old as a garment,
12 [a]And as a mantle Thou wilt roll them up;
As a garment they will also be changed.
But Thou art [b]the same,
And Thy years will not come to an end."
13 But to which of the angels has He ever said,
"[a]Sit at My right hand,
[b]Until I make Thine enemies
A footstool for Thy feet"?
14 Are they not all [a]ministering spirits, sent out to render
service for the sake of those who will [b]inherit [c]salvation?

Chapter 2

For this reason we must pay much closer attention to [1]what
we have heard, lest [a]we drift away *from it.*
2 For if the word [a]spoken through [b]angels proved [1]unal-
terable, and [c]every transgression and disobedience received a
just [d]recompense,
3 [a]how shall we escape if we neglect so great a [b]salvation?
[1]After it was at the first [c]spoken through the Lord, it was
[d]confirmed to us by those who heard,
4 God also bearing witness with them, both by [a]signs and
[a]wonders and by [b]various [1]miracles and by [2c]gifts of the Holy
Spirit [d]according to His own will.
5 For He did not subject to angels [1a]the world to come,
concerning which we are speaking.
6 But one has [a]testified [b]somewhere, saying,
"[c]What is man, that Thou rememberest him?
Or the son of man, that Thou art concerned about him?
7 "[a]Thou hast made him [1]for a little while lower than the angels;
Thou hast crowned him with glory and honor,
[2]And hast appointed him over the works of Thy hands;
8 [a]Thou hast put all things in subjection under his feet."
For in subjecting all things to him, He left nothing that is not

6 [c]Deut. 32:43 Sept.; Ps. 97:7

7 [a]Ps. 104:4

8 [1]Some mss. read, *Thy* [a]Ps. 45:6 [b]Deut. 33:27; Ps. 71:3; 90:1; 91:2, 9

9 [a]Ps. 45:7 [b]Phil. 2:9; John 10:17; Heb. 2:9 [c]Is. 61:1, 3

10 [a]Ps. 102:25

11 [a]Ps. 102:26 [b]Is. 51:6; Heb. 8:13

12 [a]Ps. 102:26, 27 [b]Heb. 13:8

13 [a]Ps. 110:1; Matt. 22:44; Heb. 1:3 [b]Heb. 10:13; Josh. 10:24

14 [a]Dan. 7:10; Ps. 103:20f. [b]Matt. 25:34; Mark 10:17; Titus 3:7; Heb. 6:12 [c]Heb. 2:3; 5:9; 9:28; Rom. 11:14; 1 Cor. 1:21

1 [1]Lit., *the things that have been heard* [a]Prov. 3:21 [Sept.]

2 [1]Or, *steadfast* [a]Heb. 1:1 [b]Acts 7:53 [c]Heb. 10:28 [d]Heb. 10:35; 11:26

3 [1]Lit. *which was* [a]Heb. 10:29; 12:25 [b]Heb. 1:14; 5:9; 9:28; Rom. 11:14; 1 Cor. 1:21 [c]Heb. 1:1 [d]Mark 16:20; Luke 1:2; 1 John 1:1

4 [1]Or, *works of power* [2]Lit., *distributions* [a]John 4:48 [b]Mark 6:14 [c]1 Cor. 12:4, 11; Eph. 4:7 [d]Eph. 1:5

5 [1]Lit., *the inhabited earth* [a]Heb. 6:5; Matt. 24:14; Heb. 1:6

6 [a]1 Thess. 4:6 [b]Heb. 4:4 [c]Ps. 8:4

7 [1]Or, *a little lower* [2]Some ancient mss. omit, *And .... hands* [a]Ps. 8:5, 6

8 [a]Ps. 8:6; 1 Cor. 15:27

subject to him. But now [b]we do not yet see all things subjected
to him.
9 But we do see Him who has been [a]made [1]for a little
while lower than the angels, *namely,* Jesus, [b]because of the
suffering of death [c]crowned with glory and honor, that [d]by the
grace of God He might [e]taste death [f]for every one.
10 For [a]it was fitting for Him, [b]for whom are all things,
and [b]through whom are all things, in bringing many sons to
glory, to [c]perfect the [1d]author of their salvation through
sufferings.
11 For both He who [a]sanctifies and those who [b]are [1]sancti-
fied are all [c]from one *Father;* for which reason He is not
ashamed to call them [d]brethren,
12 saying,
"[a]I WILL PROCLAIM THY NAME TO MY BRETHREN,
IN THE MIDST OF THE [1]CONGREGATION I WILL SING THY
PRAISE."
13 And again,
"[a]I WILL PUT MY TRUST IN HIM."
And again,
"[b]BEHOLD, I AND THE CHILDREN WHOM GOD HAS GIVEN
ME."
14 Since then the children share in [1a]flesh and blood, [b]He
Himself likewise also partook of the same, that [c]through death
He might render powerless [d]him who had the power of death,
that is, the devil;
15 and might deliver those who through [a]fear of death
were subject to slavery all their lives.
16 For assuredly He does not [1]give help to angels, but He
gives help to the [2]seed of Abraham.
17 Therefore, He [1]had [a]to be made like His brethren in all
things, that He might [b]become a merciful and faithful [c]high
priest in [d]things pertaining to God, to [e]make propitiation for
the sins of the people.
18 For since He Himself was [a]tempted in that which He
has suffered, He is able to come to the aid of those who are
tempted.

CHAPTER 3

THEREFORE, [a]holy brethren, partakers of a [b]heavenly calling, consider Jesus, [c]the Apostle and [d]High Priest of our
[e]confession.
2 [1]He was faithful to Him who [2]appointed Him, as
[a]Moses also was in all His house.
3 [a]For He has been counted worthy of more glory than
Moses, by just so much as the builder of the house has more
honor than the house.
4 For every house is built by someone, but the builder of
all things is God.
5 Now [a]Moses was faithful in all His house as [b]a servant,
[c]for a testimony of those things [d]which were to be spoken later;
6 but Christ *was faithful* as [a]a Son over His house [b]whose
house we are, [c]if we hold fast our [d]confidence and the [e]boast of
our [f]hope firm until the end.
7 Therefore, just as [a]the Holy Spirit says,

8 [b]1 Cor. 15:25

9 [1]Or, *a little lower* [a]Heb. 2:7 [b]Phil. 2:9; Heb. 1:9 [c]Acts 2:33; 3:13; 1 Pet. 1:21 [d]John 3:16 [e]Matt. 16:28; John 8:52 [f]Heb. 6:20; 7:25

10 [1]Or, *leader* [a]Luke 24:26 [b]Rom. 11:36 [c]Heb. 5:9; 7:28; Luke 13:32 [d]Acts 3:15; 5:31

11 [1]Or, *being sanctified* [a]Heb. 13:12 [b]Heb. 10:10 [c]Acts 17:28 [d]Matt. 25:40; Mark 3:34f.; John 20:17

12 [1]Lit., *church* [a]Ps. 22:22

13 [a]Is. 8:17 [b]Is. 8:18

14 [1]Lit., *blood and flesh* [a]Matt. 16:17 [b]John 1:14; Heb. 7:13 marg. [c]1 Cor. 15:54-57; 2 Tim. 1:10 [d]1 John 3:8; John 12:31

15 [a]Rom. 8:15

16 [1]Lit., *take hold of angels, but He takes hold of* [2]I.e., offspring

17 [1]Lit., *was obligated to be* [a]Heb. 2:14; Phil. 2:7 [b]Heb. 4:15f.; 5:2 [c]Heb. 3:1; 4:14f; 5:5, 10; 6:20; 7:26, 28; 8:1, 3; 9:11; Heb. 10:21 [d]Heb. 5:1; Rom. 15:17 [e]1 John 2:2; 4:10; Dan. 9:24

18 [a]Heb. 4:15

1 [a]Heb. 2:11; 3:12; 10:19; 13:22; Acts 1:15 [b]Phil. 3:14 [c]John 17:3 [d]Heb. 2:17; 4:14f.; 5:5, 10; 6:20; 7:26, 28; 8:1, 3; 9:11; Heb. 10:21 [e]Heb. 4:14; 10:23; 2 Cor. 9:13

2 [1]Lit., *being faithful* [2]Or, *made* [a]Heb. 3:5; Num. 12:7; Ex. 40:16

3 [a]2 Cor. 3:7-11

5 [a]Heb. 3:2; Num. 12:7; Ex. 40:16 [b]Ex. 14:31; Num. 12:7 [c]Deut. 18:18f. [d]Heb. 1:1

6 [a]Heb. 1:2 [b]1 Tim. 3:15; 1 Cor. 3:16 [c]Rom. 11:22; Heb. 3:14; 4:14 [d]Heb. 4:16; 10:19, 35; Eph. 3:12 [e]Rom. 5:2 marg. [f]Heb. 6:11; 7:19; 10:23; Heb. 11:1; 1 Pet. 1:3

7 [a]Heb. 9:8; 10:15; Acts 28:25

"[b]TODAY IF YOU HEAR HIS VOICE,
8 [a]DO NOT HARDEN YOUR HEARTS AS [1]WHEN THEY PROVOKED ME,
AS IN THE DAY OF TRIAL IN THE WILDERNESS,
9 [a]WHERE YOUR FATHERS TRIED *Me* BY TESTING *Me*,
AND SAW MY WORKS FOR [b]FORTY YEARS.
10 "[a]THEREFORE I WAS ANGRY WITH THIS GENERATION,
AND SAID, 'THEY ALWAYS GO ASTRAY IN THEIR HEART;
AND THEY DID NOT KNOW MY WAYS';
11 [a]AS I SWORE IN MY WRATH,
'THEY SHALL NOT ENTER MY REST.' "
12 [a]Take care, brethren, lest there should be in any one of
you an evil, unbelieving heart, in falling away from [b]the living
God.
13 But [a]encourage one another day after day, as long as it
is *still* called "Today," lest any one of you be hardened by
the [b]deceitfulness of sin.
14 For we have become partakers of Christ, [a]if we hold
fast the beginning of our [b]assurance firm until the end;
15 while it is said,
"[a]TODAY IF YOU HEAR HIS VOICE,
DO NOT HARDEN YOUR HEARTS, AS [1]WHEN THEY PROVOKED ME."
16 For who [a]provoked *Him* when they had heard? Indeed,
[b]did not all those who came out of Egypt *led* by Moses?
17 And with whom was He angry for forty years? Was it
not with those who sinned, [a]whose bodies fell in the
wilderness?
18 And to whom did He swear [a]that they should not enter
His rest, but to those who were [b]disobedient?
19 And *so* we see that they were not able to enter because
of [a]unbelief.

CHAPTER 4

THEREFORE, let us fear lest, while a promise remains of
entering His rest, any one of you should seem to have [a]come
short of it.
2 For indeed we have had good news preached to us, just
as they also; but [a]the word [1]they heard did not profit them,
because [2]it was not united by faith in those who heard.
3 [1]For we who have believed enter that rest; just as He
has said,
"[a]AS I SWORE IN MY WRATH,
THEY SHALL NOT ENTER MY REST,"
although His works were finished [b]from the foundation of the
world.
4 For He has thus said [a]somewhere concerning the seventh *day*, "[b]AND GOD [c]RESTED ON THE SEVENTH DAY FROM ALL
HIS WORKS";
5 and again in this *passage*, "[a]THEY SHALL NOT ENTER MY
REST."
6 Since therefore it remains for some to enter it, and
those who formerly had good news preached to them failed to
enter because of [a]disobedience,

7 [b]Ps. 95:7; Heb. 3:15; 4:7
8 [1]Lit., *in the provocation* [a]Ps. 95:8
9 [a]Ps. 95:9, 10 [b]Acts 7:36
10 [a]Ps. 95:10
11 [a]Ps. 95:11; Heb. 4:3, 5
12 [a]Heb. 12:25; Col. 2:8 [b]Heb. 9:14; 10:31; 12:22; Matt. 16:16
13 [a]Heb. 10:24f. [b]Eph. 4:22
14 [a]Heb. 3:6 [b]Heb. 11:1 [Gr.]
15 [1]Lit., *in the provocation* [a]Ps. 95:7f.
16 [a]Jer. 32:29; 44:3, 8 [b]Num. 14:2, 11; Deut. 1:35; Num. 14:30; Deut. 1:36, 38
17 [a]Num. 14:29; 1 Cor. 10:5
18 [a]Num. 14:23; Deut. 1:34f.; Heb. 4:2 [b]Heb. 4:6, 11; Rom. 11:30-32
19 [a]John 3:36
1 [a]Heb. 12:15
2 [1]Lit., *of hearing* [2]Or, *they were. . .faith with those who heard* [a]1 Thess. 2:13
3 [1]Some ancient mss. read, *Therefore* [a]Ps. 95:11; Heb. 3:11 [b]Matt. 25:34
4 [a]Heb. 2:6 [b]Gen. 2:2 [c]Ex. 20:11; 31:17
5 [a]Ps. 95:11; Heb. 3:11
6 [a]Heb. 3:18; 4:11

7 [1]Or, *in* [a]Ps. 95 title in Sept. [b]Heb. 3:7f. [c]Ps. 95:7f.

8 [a]Josh. 22:4 [b]Heb. 1:1

10 [a]Rev. 14:13 [b]Heb. 4:4

11 [a]2 Pet. 2:6 [b]Heb. 3:18; 4:6

12 [a]1 Pet. 1:23; Jer. 23:29; Heb. 6:5; Eph. 5:26 [b]Acts 7:38 [c]1 Thess. 2:13 [d]Eph. 6:17 [e]1 Thess. 5:23 [f]John 12:48; 1 Cor. 14:24f.

13 [a]2 Chr. 16:9; Ps. 33:13-15 [b]Job 26:6

14 [a]Heb. 2:17 [b]Eph. 4:10; Heb. 6:20; 8:1; 9:24 [c]Heb. 6:6; 7:3; 10:29; Matt. 4:3; Heb. 1:2 [d]Heb. 3:1

15 [a]Heb. 2:17 [b]Heb. 2:18 [c]2 Cor. 5:21; Heb. 7:26

16 [a]Heb. 7:19 [b]Heb. 3:6

1 [a]Ex. 28:1 [b]Heb. 2:17 [c]Heb. 8:3f.; 9:9; 7:27; 10:11 [d]Heb. 7:27; 10:12; 1 Cor. 15:3

2 [1]Lit., *being able to* [2]Or, *subject to weakness* [a]Heb. 2:18; 4:15 [b]Heb. 9:7 marg.; Eph. 4:18 [c]James 5:19; 1 Pet. 2:25 [d]Heb. 7:28

3 [a]Heb. 7:27; 10:12; 1 Cor. 15:3 [b]Heb. 7:27; 9:7; Lev. 9:7; 16:6

4 [a]Num. 16:40; 18:7; 2 Chr. 26:18 [b]Ex. 28:1; 1 Chr. 23:13

5 [a]John 8:54 [b]Heb. 2:17; 5:10 [c]Heb. 1:1, 5 [d]Ps. 2:7

6 [a]Ps. 110:4; Heb. 7:17 [b]Heb. 5:10; 6:20; 7:11, 17

7 [1]Or, *out of* [a]Matt. 26:39, 42, 44; Mark 14:36, 39; Luke 22:41, 44 [b]Matt. 27:46, 50; Mark 15:34, 37; Luke 23:46 [c]Mark 14:36 [d]Heb. 12:28 marg.; Heb. 11:7

8 [a]Heb. 1:2 [b]Phil. 2:8

9 [a]Heb. 2:10

7 He again fixes a certain day, "Today," saying [1a]through David after so long a time just [b]as has been said before.

"[c]TODAY IF YOU HEAR HIS VOICE,
DO NOT HARDEN YOUR HEARTS."

8 For [a]if Joshua had given them rest, He would not have [b]spoken of another day after that.

9 There remains therefore a Sabbath rest for the people of God.

10 For the one who has entered His rest has himself also [a]rested from his works, as [b]God did from His.

11 Let us therefore be diligent to enter that rest, lest anyone fall through *following* the same [a]example of [b]disobedience.

12 For [a]the word of God is [b]living and [c]active and sharper than any two-edged [d]sword, and piercing as far as the division of [e]soul and [e]spirit, of both joints and marrow, and [f]able to judge the thoughts and intentions of the heart.

13 And [a]there is no creature hidden from His sight, but all things are [b]open and laid bare to the eyes of Him with whom we have to do.

14 Since then we have a great [a]high priest who has [b]passed through the heavens, Jesus [c]the Son of God, let us hold fast our [d]confession.

15 For we do not have [a]a high priest who cannot sympathize with our weaknesses, but one who has been [b]tempted in all things as *we are, yet* [c]without sin.

16 Let us therefore [a]draw near with [b]confidence to the throne of grace, that we may receive mercy and may find grace to help in time of need.

CHAPTER 5

FOR every high priest [a]taken from among men is appointed on behalf of men in [b]things pertaining to God in order to [c]offer both gifts and sacrifices [d]for sins;

2 [1a]he can deal gently with the [b]ignorant and [c]misguided, since he himself also is [2d]beset with weakness;

3 and because of it he is obligated to offer *sacrifices* [a]for sins, [b]as for the people, so also for himself.

4 And [a]no one takes the honor to himself, but *receives it* when he is called by God, even [b]as Aaron was.

5 So also Christ [a]did not glorify Himself so as to become a [b]high priest, but He who [c]said to Him,

"[d]THOU ART MY SON,
TODAY I HAVE BEGOTTEN THEE";

6 just as He says also in another *passage,*

"[a]THOU ART A PRIEST FOREVER
ACCORDING TO [b]THE ORDER OF MELCHIZEDEK."

7 In the days of His flesh, [a]when He offered up both prayers and supplications with [b]loud crying and tears to Him who was [c]able to save Him [1]from death, and who was heard because of His [d]piety,

8 although He was [a]a Son, He learned [b]obedience from the things which He suffered;

9 and having been made [a]perfect, He became to all those who obey Him the source of eternal salvation;

10 being designated by God as [a]a high priest according to
[b]the order of Melchizedek.
11 Concerning [1]him we have much to say, and *it is* hard to
explain, since you have become dull of hearing.
12 For though [1]by this time you ought to be teachers, you
have need again for some one to teach you [a]the [2b]elementary
principles of the [c]oracles of God, and you have come to need
[d]milk and not solid food.
13 For every one who partakes *only* of milk is not accustomed to the word of righteousness, for he is a [a]babe.
14 But solid food is for [a]the mature, who because of practice have their senses [b]trained to [c]discern good and evil.

Chapter 6

THEREFORE [a]leaving [b]the [1]elementary teaching about the
[2]Christ, let us press on to [3c]maturity, not laying again a foundation of repentance from [d]dead works and of faith toward God,
2 of [a]instruction about washings, and [b]laying on of hands,
and the [c]resurrection of the dead, and [c]eternal judgment.
3 And this we shall do, [a]if God permits.
4 For in the case of those who have once been [a]enlight-
ened and have tasted of [b]the heavenly gift and have been
made [c]partakers of the Holy Spirit,
5 and [a]have tasted the good [b]word of God and the powers of [c]the age to come,
6 and *then* have fallen away, it is [a]impossible to renew
them again to repentance, [1b]since they again crucify to themselves the Son of God, and put Him to open shame.
7 For ground that drinks the rain which often [1]falls upon
it and brings forth vegetation useful to those [a]for whose sake it
is also tilled, receives a blessing from God;
8 but if it yields thorns and thistles, it is worthless and
[a]close [1]to being cursed, and [2]it ends up being burned.
9 But, [a]beloved, we are convinced of better things concerning you, and things that [1]accompany salvation, though we
are speaking in this way.
10 For [a]God is not unjust so as to forget [b]your work and
the love which you have shown toward His name, in having
[c]ministered and in still ministering to the [1]saints.
11 And we desire that each one of you show the same
diligence [1]so as to realize the [a]full assurance of [b]hope until the
end,
12 that you may not be sluggish, but [a]imitators of those
who through [b]faith and patience [c]inherit the promises.
13 For [a]when God made the promise to Abraham, since
He could swear by no one greater, He [b]swore by Himself,
14 saying, "[a]I WILL SURELY BLESS YOU, AND I WILL SURELY
MULTIPLY YOU."
15 And thus, [a]having patiently waited, he obtained the
promise.
16 [a]For men swear by one greater *than themselves,* and
with them [b]an oath *given* as confirmation is an end of every
dispute.
17 [1]In the same way God, desiring even more to show to

10 [a]Heb. 2:17; 5:5 [b]Heb. 5:6

11 [1]Or, *Him;* or, *this*

12 [1]Lit., *because of the time* [2]Lit., *elements of the beginning*
[a]Gal. 4:3 [b]Heb. 6:1 [c]Acts 7:38 [d]1 Cor. 3:2; 1 Pet. 2:2

13 [a]1 Cor. 3:1; 1 Cor. 14:20; 1 Pet. 2:2

14 [a]1 Cor. 2:6; Eph. 4:13; Heb. 6:1 marg. [b]1 Tim. 4:7 [c]Rom. 14:1

1 [1]Lit., *word of the beginning* [2]I.e., Messiah [3]Or, *perfection*
[a]Phil. 3:13f. [b]Heb. 5:12 [c]Heb. 5:14 and marg. [d]Heb. 9:14; John 8:21

2 [a]Acts 19:3f.; John 3:25 [b]Acts 6:6 [c]Acts 17:31f.

3 [a]Acts 18:21

4 [a]Heb. 10:32; 2 Cor. 4:4, 6 [b]Eph. 2:8; John 4:10 [c]Heb. 2:4; Gal. 3:2

5 [a]1 Pet. 2:3 [b]Eph. 6:17 [c]Heb. 2:5

6 [1]Or, *while*
[a]Heb. 10:26f.; 1 John 5:16; 2 Pet. 2:21; Matt. 19:26 [b]Heb. 10:29

7 [1]Lit., *comes*
[a]2 Tim. 2:6

8 [1]Lit., *to a curse* [2]Lit., *its end is for burning*
[a]Deut. 29:22ff.

9 [1]Or, *belong to*
[a]1 Cor. 10:14; 2 Cor. 7:1; 12:19; 1 Pet. 2:11; 2 Pet. 3:1; 1 John 2:7; Jude 3

10 [1]I.e., true believers; lit., *holy ones*
[a]Prov. 19:17; Matt. 10:42; 25:40; Acts 10:4 [b]1 Thess. 1:3 [c]Heb. 10:32-34; Rom. 15:25

11 [1]Lit., *to the full*
[a]Heb. 10:22; Luke 1:1 [b]Heb. 3:6

12 [a]Heb. 13:7 [b]2 Thess. 1:4; James 1:3; Rev. 13:10 [c]Heb. 1:14

13 [a]Gal. 3:15, 18 [b]Gen. 22:16; Luke 1:73

14 [a]Gen. 22:16f.

15 [a]Gen. 12:4; 21:5

16 [a]Gal. 3:15 [b]Ex. 22:11

17 [1]Or, *Therefore God*

[a]the heirs of the promise [b]the unchangeableness of His purpose, [2]interposed with an oath,
18 in order that by two unchangeable things, in which [a]it is
impossible for God to lie, we may have strong encouragement,
we who have fled for refuge in laying hold of [b]the hope set
before us.
19 [1]This hope we have as an anchor of the soul, a *hope*
both sure and steadfast and one which [a]enters [2]within the veil,
20 [a]where Jesus has entered as a forerunner for us, having
become a [b]high priest forever according to the order of
Melchizedek.

Chapter 7

FOR this [a]Melchizedek, king of Salem, priest of the [b]Most
High God, who met Abraham as he was returning from the
slaughter of the kings and blessed him,
2 to whom also Abraham apportioned a tenth part of all
the spoils, was first of all, by the translation *of his name,* king
of righteousness, and then also king of Salem, which is king of
peace.
3 Without father, without mother, [a]without genealogy,
having neither beginning of days nor end of life, but made like
[b]the Son of God, he abides a priest perpetually.
4 Now observe how great this man was to whom Abraham, the [a]patriarch, gave a tenth of the choicest spoils.
5 And those indeed of [a]the sons of Levi who receive the
priest's office have commandment [1]in the Law to collect [2]a
tenth from the people, that is, from their brethren, although
these [3]are descended from Abraham.
6 But the one [a]whose genealogy is not traced from them
[b]collected [1]a tenth from Abraham, and [b]blessed the one who
[c]had the promises.
7 But without any dispute the lesser is blessed by the
greater.
8 And in this case mortal men receive tithes, but in that
case one *receives them,* [a]of whom it is witnessed that he lives
on.
9 And, so to speak, through Abraham even Levi, who
received tithes, paid tithes,
10 for he was still in the loins of his father when Melchizedek
met him.
11 [a]Now if perfection was through the Levitical priesthood (for on the basis of it [b]the people received the Law),
what further need *was there* for another priest to arise [c]accord-
ing to the order of Melchizedek, and not be designated according to the order of Aaron?
12 For when the priesthood is changed, of necessity there
takes place a change of law also.
13 For [a]the one concerning whom [b]these things are spoken belongs to another tribe, from which no one has officiated
at the altar.
14 For it is evident that our Lord [1]was [a]descended from
Judah, a tribe with reference to which Moses spoke nothing
concerning priests.

17 [2]Or, *guaranteed* [a]Heb. 11:9 [b]Ps. 110:4; Prov. 19:21; Heb. 6:18

18 [a]Titus 1:2; Num. 23:19 [b]Heb. 3:6; 7:19

19 [1]Lit., *which we have* [2]Or, *inside* [a]Lev. 16:2; Heb. 9:2f.

20 [a]Heb. 4:14; John 14:2 [b]Heb. 5:6; 2:17

1 [a]Gen. 14:18-20; Heb. 7:6 [b]Mark 5:7

3 [a]Heb. 7:6 [b]Heb. 7:28; 7:1; Matt. 4:3

4 [a]Acts 2:29

5 [1]Lit., *according to* [2]Or, *tithes* [3]Lit., *have come out of the loins of* [a]Num. 18:21, 26; 2 Chr. 31:4f.

6 [1]Or, *tithes* [a]Heb. 7:3 [b]Heb. 7:1f. [c]Rom. 4:13

8 [a]Heb. 5:6; 6:20

11 [a]Heb. 7:18f.; 8:7 [b]Heb. 9:6; 10:1 [c]Heb. 7:17; 5:6

13 [a]Heb. 7:14 [b]Heb. 7:11

14 [1]Lit., *rose from* [a]Rev. 5:5; Matt. 2:6 [Mic. 5:2]; Is. 11:1; Num. 24:17

15 And this is clearer still, if another priest arises according
to the likeness of Melchizedek,
16 who has become *such* not on the basis of a law of
[a]physical requirement, but according to the power of [b]an in-
destructible life.
17 For it is witnessed *of Him*,

"[a]THOU ART A PRIEST FOREVER
ACCORDING TO THE ORDER OF MELCHIZEDEK."

18 For, on the one hand, there is a setting aside of a
former commandment [a]because of its weakness and
uselessness
19 (for [a]the Law made nothing perfect), and on the other
hand there is a bringing in of a better [b]hope, through which we
[c]draw near to God.
20 And inasmuch as *it was* not without an oath
21 (for they indeed became priests without an oath, but
He with an oath through the One who said to Him,

"[a]THE LORD HAS SWORN
AND [b]WILL NOT CHANGE HIS MIND,
'THOU ART A PRIEST [c]FOREVER' ");

22 so much the more also Jesus has become the [a]guarantee
of [b]a better covenant.
23 And the *former* priests, on the one hand, existed in
greater numbers, because they were prevented by death from
continuing,
24 but He, on the other hand, because He abides [a]forever,
holds His priesthood permanently.
25 Hence also He is able to [a]save [1]forever those who [b]draw
near to God through Him, since He always lives to [c]make
intercession for them.
26 For it was fitting that we should have such a [a]high
priest, [b]holy, [c]innocent, undefiled, separated from sinners and
[d]exalted above the heavens;
27 who does not need daily, like those high priests, to
[a]offer up sacrifices, [b]first for His own sins, and then for the *sins*
of the people, because this He did [c]once for all when He
[d]offered up Himself.
28 For the Law appoints men as high priests [a]who are
weak, but the word of the oath, which came after the Law,
appoints [b]a Son, [c]made perfect forever.

CHAPTER 8

NOW the main point in what has been said *is this:* we have
such a [a]high priest, who has taken His seat at [b]the right hand of
the throne of the [b]Majesty in the heavens,
2 a [a]minister [1]in the sanctuary, and [1]in the [b]true [2]taber-
nacle, which the Lord [c]pitched, not man.
3 For every [a]high priest is appointed [b]to offer both gifts
and sacrifices; hence it is necessary that this *high priest* also
have something to offer.
4 Now if He were on earth, He would not be a priest at
all, since there are those who [a]offer the gifts according to the
Law;
5 who serve [a]a copy and [b]shadow of the heavenly things,
just as Moses is [c]warned *by God* when he was about to erect

16 [a]Heb. 9:10 [b]Heb. 9:14

17 [a]Ps. 110:4; Heb. 7:21; 5:6

18 [a]Heb. 7:11; Rom. 8:3; Gal. 3:21

19 [a]Heb. 9:9; 10:1; Acts 13:39; Rom. 3:20; 7:7f.; Gal. 2:16; 3:21 [b]Heb. 3:6 [c]Heb. 7:25; 4:16; 10:1, 22; Lam. 3:57; James 4:8

21 [a]Ps. 110:4; Heb. 7:17; Heb. 5:6 [b]Num. 23:19; 1 Sam. 15:29; Rom. 11:29 [c]Heb. 7:23f., 28

22 [a]Ps. 119:122; Is. 38:14 [b]Heb. 8:6

24 [a]Heb. 7:23f.

25 [1]Or, *completely* [a]1 Cor. 1:21 [b]Heb. 7:19 [c]Rom. 8:34; Heb. 9:24

26 [a]Heb. 2:17 [b]2 Cor. 5:21; Heb. 4:15 [c]1 Pet. 2:22 [d]Heb. 4:14

27 [a]Heb. 5:1 [b]Heb. 5:3 [c]Heb. 9:12; 10:10; 9:28 [d]Eph. 5:2; Heb. 9:14, 28; 10:10, 12

28 [a]Heb. 5:2 [b]Heb. 1:2 [c]Heb. 2:10

1 [a]Heb. 2:17 [b]Heb. 1:3

2 [1]Or, *of* [2]Or, *sacred tent* [a]Heb. 10:11 [b]Heb. 9:11, 24 [c]Ex. 33:7

3 [a]Heb. 2:17 [b]Heb. 5:1; 8:4

4 [a]Heb. 5:1; 8:3

5 [a]Heb. 9:23 [b]Col. 2:17; Heb. 10:1 [c]Heb. 11:7; 12:25; Matt. 2:12;

the [1]tabernacle; for, "[d]SEE," He says, "THAT YOU MAKE ALL
THINGS ACCORDING TO THE PATTERN WHICH WAS SHOWN YOU ON
THE MOUNTAIN."
6 But now He has obtained a more excellent ministry, by
as much as He is also the [a]mediator of [b]a better covenant,
which has been enacted on better promises.
7 For [a]if that first *covenant* had been faultless, there
would have been no occasion sought for a second.
8 For finding fault with them, He says,

"[a]BEHOLD, DAYS ARE COMING, SAYS THE LORD,
[1]WHEN I WILL EFFECT [b]A NEW COVENANT
WITH THE HOUSE OF ISRAEL AND WITH THE HOUSE OF JUDAH;
9 [a]NOT LIKE THE COVENANT WHICH I MADE WITH THEIR FATHERS
ON THE DAY WHEN I [b]TOOK THEM BY THE HAND
TO LEAD THEM OUT OF THE LAND OF EGYPT;
FOR THEY DID NOT CONTINUE IN MY COVENANT,
AND I DID NOT CARE FOR THEM, SAYS THE LORD.
10 "[a]FOR [b]THIS IS THE COVENANT THAT I WILL MAKE WITH THE HOUSE OF ISRAEL
AFTER THOSE DAYS, SAYS THE LORD:
I WILL PUT MY LAWS INTO THEIR MINDS,
AND I WILL WRITE THEM [c]UPON THEIR HEARTS.
AND I WILL BE THEIR GOD,
AND THEY SHALL BE MY PEOPLE.
11 "[a]AND THEY SHALL NOT TEACH EVERY ONE HIS FELLOW-CITIZEN,
AND EVERY ONE HIS BROTHER, SAYING, 'KNOW THE LORD,'
FOR [b]ALL SHALL KNOW ME,
FROM THE LEAST TO THE GREATEST OF THEM.
12 "[a]FOR I WILL BE MERCIFUL TO THEIR INIQUITIES,
[b]AND I WILL REMEMBER THEIR SINS NO MORE."

13 [1]When He said, "[a]A new *covenant*," He has made the
first obsolete. [b]But whatever is becoming obsolete and growing
old is [2]ready to disappear.

CHAPTER 9

NOW even the first *covenant* had [a]regulations of divine
worship and [b]the earthly sanctuary.
2 For there was [a]a [1]tabernacle prepared, the [2]outer one,
in which *were* [b]the lampstand and [c]the table and [d]the [3]sacred
bread; this is called the holy place.
3 And behind [a]the second veil, there was a [1]tabernacle
which is called the [b]Holy of Holies,
4 having a golden [1a]altar of incense and [b]the ark of the
covenant covered on all sides with gold, in which *was* [c]a golden
jar holding the manna, and [d]Aaron's rod which budded, and
[e]the tables of the covenant.
5 And above it *were* the [a]cherubim of glory [b]overshadow-
ing the mercy seat; but of these things we cannot now speak in
detail.
6 Now when these things have been thus prepared, the
priests [a]are continually entering [b]the [1]outer [2]tabernacle, performing the divine worship,

5 [1]Or, *sacred tent* [d]Ex. 25:40
6 [a]1 Tim. 2:5 [b]Heb. 7:22; 8:8; 9:15; 12:24; Luke 22:20
7 [a]Heb. 7:11
8 [1]Lit., *and* [a]Jer. 31:31 [b]Heb. 8:13; 9:15; 12:24; 2 Cor. 3:6; Luke 22:20; Heb. 7:22; 8:6
9 [a]Jer. 31:32 [b]Heb. 2:16 marg.; Ex. 19:5f.
10 [a]Jer. 31:33 [b]Heb. 10:16; Rom. 11:27 [c]2 Cor. 3:3
11 [a]Jer. 31:34 [b]Is. 54:13; John 6:45; 1 John 2:27
12 [a]Jer. 31:34 [b]Heb. 10:17
13 [1]Or, *In His saying* [2]Or, *near* [a]Heb. 8:8; 9:15; 12:24; 2 Cor. 3:6; Luke 22:20; Heb. 7:22; 8:6 [b]Heb. 1:11; 2 Cor. 5:17
1 [a]Heb. 9:10 [b]Ex. 25:8; Heb. 9:11, 24; 8:2
2 [1]Or, *sacred tent* [2]Lit., *first* [3]Lit., *loaves of presentation* [a]Ex. 25:8, 9 [b]Ex. 25:31-39 [c]Ex. 25:23-29 [d]Ex. 25:30; Lev. 24:5ff.[Matt. 12:4]
3 [1]Or, *sacred tent* [a]Ex. 26:31-33 [b]Ex. 26:33
4 [1]Or, *censer* [a]Ex. 30:1-5; 37:25f. [b]Ex. 25:10ff.; 37:1ff. [c]Ex. 16:32f. [d]Num. 17:10 [e]Ex. 31:18; 32:15; Deut. 9:9, 11, 15
5 [a]Ex. 25:18ff. [b]Ex. 25:17, 20
6 [1]Lit., *first* [2]Or, *sacred tent* [a]Num. 28:3 [b]Ex. 25:8, 9

7 but into [a]the second only [b]the high priest *enters,* [c]once
a year, [d]not without *taking* blood, which he [e]offers for himself
and for the [1f]sins of the people committed in ignorance.
8 [a]The Holy Spirit *is* signifying this, [b]that the way into
the holy place has not yet been disclosed, while the [1]outer
tabernacle is still standing;
9 which *is* [a]a symbol for the time *then* present, according
to which both gifts and sacrifices are [b]offered which cannot
[c]make the worshiper perfect in conscience,
10 since they *relate* only to [a]food and [b]drink and various
[c]washings, [d]regulations for the [1]body imposed until [e]a time of
reformation.
11 But when Christ appeared *as* a [a]high priest of the [b]good
things [1]to come, *He entered* through [c]the greater and more
perfect [2]tabernacle, [d]not made with hands, that is to say, [e]not
of this creation;
12 and not through [a]the blood of goats and calves, but
[b]through His own blood, He [c]entered the holy place [d]once for
all, [1]having obtained [e]eternal redemption.
13 For if [a]the blood of goats and bulls and [b]the ashes of a
heifer sprinkling those who have been defiled, sanctify for the
[1]cleansing of the flesh,
14 how much more will [a]the blood of Christ, who through
[1b]the eternal Spirit [c]offered Himself without blemish to God,
[d]cleanse [2]your conscience from [e]dead works to serve [f]the living
God?
15 And for this reason [a]He is the [b]mediator of a [c]new
covenant, in order that since a death has taken place for the
redemption of the transgressions that were *committed* under
the first covenant, those who have been [d]called may [e]receive
the promise of [f]the eternal inheritance.
16 For where a [1]covenant is, there must of necessity [2]be
the death of the one who made it.
17 For a [1]covenant is valid *only* when [2]men are dead, [3]for
it is never in force while the one who made it lives.
18 Therefore even the first *covenant* was not inaugurated
without blood.
19 For when every commandment had been [a]spoken by
Moses to all the people according to the Law, [b]he took the
[c]blood of the calves and the goats, with [d]water and scarlet wool
and hyssop, and sprinkled both [e]the book itself and all the
people,
20 saying, "[a]THIS IS THE BLOOD OF THE COVENANT WHICH
GOD COMMANDED YOU."
21 And in the same way he sprinkled both the [1a]tabernacle
and all the vessels of the ministry with the blood.
22 And according to the [1]Law, *one may* [a]almost *say,* all
things are cleansed with blood, and [b]without shedding of
blood there is no forgiveness.
23 Therefore it was necessary for the [a]copies of the things
in the heavens to be cleansed with these, but [a]the heavenly
things themselves with better sacrifices than these.
24 For Christ [a]did not enter a holy place made with hands,
a *mere* copy of [b]the true one, but into [c]heaven itself, now [d]to
appear in the presence of God for us;
25 nor was it that He should offer Himself often, as [a]the

7 [1]Lit., *ignorance of the people*
[a]Heb. 9:3 [b]Lev. 16:12ff. [c]Ex. 30:10; Lev. 16:34; Heb. 10:3 [d]Lev. 16:11, 14 [e]Heb. 5:3 [f]Num. 15:25; Heb. 5:2

8 [1]Lit., *first*
[a]Heb. 3:7 [b]Heb. 10:20; John 14:6

9 [a]Heb. 11:19; 10:1 [b]Heb. 5:1 [c]Heb. 7:19

10 [1]Lit., *flesh*
[a]Lev. 11:2ff.; Col. 2:16 [b]Num. 6:3 [c]Lev. 11:25; Num. 19:13; Mark 7:4 [d]Heb. 7:16 [e]Heb. 7:12

11 [1]Some ancient mss. read, *that have come* [2]Or, *sacred tent*
[a]Heb. 2:17 [b]Heb. 10:1 [c]Heb. 9:24; 8:2 [d]Mark 14:58; 2 Cor. 5:1 [e]2 Cor. 4:18; Heb. 12:27; 13:14

12 [1]Or, *obtaining*
[a]Lev. 4:3; 16:6, 15; Heb. 9:19 [b]Heb. 9:14; 13:12 [c]Heb. 9:24 [d]Heb. 7:27 [e]Heb. 9:15; 5:9

13 [1]Lit., *purity*
[a]Heb. 9:19; 10:4 [b]Num. 19:9, 17f.

14 [1]Or, His *eternal spirit* [2]Some ancient mss. read, *our*
[a]Heb. 9:12; 13:12 [b]1 Cor. 15:45; 1 Pet. 3:18 [c]Eph. 5:2; Heb. 7:27; 10:10, 12 [d]Acts 15:9; Titus 2:14; Heb. 10:2, 22; 1:3 [e]Heb. 6:1 [f]Matt. 16:16; Heb. 3:12

15 [a]Rom. 3:24 [b]1 Tim. 2:5; Heb. 8:6; 12:24 [c]Heb. 8:8 [d]Rom. 8:28f.; Heb. 3:1; Matt. 22:3ff. [e]Heb. 6:15; 10:36; Heb. 11:39 [f]Acts 20:32

16 [1]Or, *testament* [2]Lit., *be brought*

17 [1]Note vs. 16 [2]Lit., *over the dead* [3]Some ancient mss. read, *for is it then . . . lives?*

19 [a]Heb. 1:1 [b]Ex. 24:6ff. [c]Heb. 9:12 [d]Lev. 14:4, 7; Num. 19:6, 18 [e]Ex. 24:7

20 [a]Ex. 24:8; Matt. 26:28

21 [1]Or, *sacred tent*
[a]Ex. 40:9; 24:6; Lev. 8:15, 19; 16:14-16

22 [1]Or, *Law, almost all things*
[a]Lev. 5:11f. [b]Lev. 17:11

23 [a]Heb. 8:5

24 [a]Heb. 9:12; 4:14 [b]Heb. 8:2 [c]Heb. 9:12 [d]Heb. 7:25; Matt. 18:10

25 [a]Heb. 9:7

high priest enters [b]the holy place [a]year by year with blood not
his own.
26 Otherwise, He would have needed to suffer often since
[a]the foundation of the world; but now [b]once at [c]the consummation He has been [d]manifested to put away sin [1e]by the
sacrifice of Himself.
27 And inasmuch as [a]it is [1]appointed for men to die once,
and after this [b]*comes* judgment;
28 so Christ also, having been [a]offered once to [b]bear the
sins of many, shall appear [c]a second time, [1d]not to bear sin, to
those who [e]eagerly await Him, for [f]salvation.

Chapter 10

FOR the Law, since it has *only* [a]a shadow of [b]the good things
to come *and* not the very [1]form of things, [2]can [c]never by the
same sacrifices year by year, which they offer continually,
[d]make perfect those who draw near.
2 Otherwise, would they not have ceased to be offered,
because the worshipers, having once been cleansed, would no
longer have had [a]consciousness of sins?
3 But [a]in [1]those *sacrifices* there is a reminder of sins year
by year.
4 For it is [a]impossible for the [b]blood of bulls and goats to
take away sins.
5 Therefore, [a]when He comes into the world, He says,
"[b]Sacrifice and offering Thou hast not desired,
But [c]a body Thou hast prepared for Me;
6 [a]In whole burnt offerings and *sacrifices* for sin
Thou hast taken no pleasure.
7 "[a]Then I said, 'Behold, I have come
(In [b]the roll of the book it is written of Me)
To do Thy will, O God.' "
8 After saying above, "[a]Sacrifices and offerings and
[b]whole burnt offerings and *sacrifices* [c]for sin Thou hast
not desired, nor hast Thou taken pleasure *in them*" (which
are offered according to the Law),
9 then He said, "[a]Behold, I have come to do Thy
will." He takes away the first in order to establish the second.
10 By [1]this will we have been [a]sanctified through [b]the offering of [c]the body of Jesus Christ [d]once for all.
11 And every priest stands daily ministering and [a]offering
time after time the same sacrifices, which [b]can never take away
sins;
12 but He, having offered one sacrifice [a]for [1]sins [b]for all
time, [c]sat down at the right hand of God,
13 waiting from that time onward [a]until His enemies be
made a footstool for His feet.
14 For by one offering He has [a]perfected [b]for all time
those who are [1]sanctified.
15 And [a]the Holy Spirit also bears witness to us; for after
saying,
16 "[a]This is the covenant that I will make with them
After those days, says the Lord:
I will put My laws upon their heart,
And upon their mind I will write them,"

25 [a]Heb. 9:7 [b]Heb. 9:2; 10:19

26 [1]Or, *by His sacrifice* [a]Matt. 25:34; Heb. 4:3 [b]Heb. 9:12; 7:27 [c]Matt. 13:39; Heb. 1:2 [d]1 John 3:5, 8 [e]Heb. 9:12, 14

27 [1]Lit., *laid up* [a]Gen. 3:19 [b]2 Cor. 5:10; 1 John 4:17

28 [1]Lit., *without sin* [a]Heb. 7:27 [b]1 Pet. 2:24 [c]Acts 1:11 [d]Heb. 4:15 [e]1 Cor. 1:7; Titus 2:13 [f]Heb. 5:9

1 [1]Lit., *image* [2]Some ancient mss. read, *they can* [a]Heb. 8:5 [b]Heb. 9:11 [c]Heb. 10:4, 11; 9:9; Rom. 8:3 [d]Heb. 7:19

2 [a]1 Pet. 2:19 marg.

3 [1]Lit., *them there is* [a]Heb. 9:7

4 [a]Heb. 10:1, 11 [b]Heb. 9:12f.

5 [a]Heb. 1:6 [b]Ps. 40:6 [c]1 Pet. 2:24; Heb. 2:14; 5:7

6 [a]Ps. 40:6

7 [a]Ps. 40:7, 8 [b]Jer. 36:2; Ezek. 2:9; 3:1f.; Ezra 6:2 [Sept.]

8 [a]Ps. 40:6; Heb. 10:5f. [b]Mark 12:33 [c]Rom. 8:3 marg.

9 [a]Ps. 40:7, 8; Heb. 10:7

10 [1]Lit., *which* [a]Eph. 5:26; Heb. 10:14, 29; 2:11; 13:12; John 17:19 [b]Heb. 7:27; 9:14, 28; 10:12; Eph. 5:2; John 6:51 [c]1 Pet. 2:24; Heb. 2:14; 5:7 [d]Heb. 7:27

11 [a]Heb. 5:1 [b]Heb. 10:1, 4; Mic. 6:6-8

12 [1]Or, *sins, forever sat down* [a]Heb. 5:1 [b]Heb. 10:14 [c]Heb. 1:3

13 [a]Ps. 110:1; Heb. 1:13

14 [1]Or, *being sanctified* [a]Heb. 10:1 [b]Heb. 10:12

15 [a]Heb. 3:7

16 [a]Jer. 31:33; Heb. 8:10

He then says,
17 "[a]AND THEIR SINS AND THEIR LAWLESS DEEDS
I WILL REMEMBER NO MORE."
18 Now where there is forgiveness of these things, there is
no longer *any* offering for sin.
19 Since therefore, brethren, we [a]have confidence to [b]en-
ter the holy place by the blood of Jesus,
20 by [a]a new and living way which He inaugurated for us
through [b]the veil, that is, His flesh,
21 and since *we have* [a]a great priest [b]over the house of
God,
22 let us [a]draw near with a [1]sincere heart in [b]full assurance
of faith, having our hearts [c]sprinkled *clean* from an evil conscience and our body [d]washed with pure water.
23 Let us hold fast the [a]confession of our [b]hope without
wavering, for [c]He who promised is faithful;
24 and let us consider how [a]to stimulate one another to
love and [b]good deeds,
25 not forsaking our own [a]assembling together, as is the
habit of some, but [b]encouraging *one another;* and all the
more, as you see [c]the day drawing near.
26 For if we go on [a]sinning willfully after receiving [b]the
knowledge of the truth, there no longer remains a sacrifice for
sins,
27 but a certain terrifying expectation of [a]judgment, and
THE [b]FURY OF A FIRE WHICH WILL CONSUME THE ADVERSARIES.
28 [a]Anyone who has set aside the Law of Moses dies without mercy on *the testimony of* two or three witnesses.
29 [a]How much severer punishment do you think he will
deserve [b]who has trampled under foot the Son of God, and has
regarded as unclean [c]the blood of the covenant [d]by which he
was sanctified, and has [e]insulted the Spirit of grace?
30 For we know Him who said, "[a]VENGEANCE IS MINE, I
WILL REPAY." And again, "[b]THE LORD WILL JUDGE HIS PEOPLE."
31 It is a [a]terrifying thing to fall into the hands of the
[b]living God.
32 But remember [a]the former days, [1]when, after being
[b]enlightened, you endured a great [c]conflict of sufferings,
33 partly, by being [a]made a public spectacle through reproaches and tribulations, and partly by becoming [b]sharers with
those who were so treated.
34 For you [a]showed sympathy to the prisoners, and accepted [b]joyfully the seizure of your property, knowing that you
have for yourselves [c]a better possession and an abiding one.
35 Therefore, do not throw away your [a]confidence, which
has a great [b]reward.
36 For you have need of [a]endurance, so that when you
have done the will of God, you may [b]receive [1]what was
promised.
37 [a]FOR YET IN A VERY LITTLE WHILE,
[b]HE WHO IS COMING WILL COME, AND WILL NOT DELAY.
38 [a]BUT MY RIGHTEOUS ONE SHALL LIVE BY FAITH;
AND IF HE SHRINKS BACK, MY SOUL HAS NO PLEASURE IN
HIM.
39 But [1]we are not of those who shrink back to destruction, but of those who have faith to the [2]preserving of the soul.

17 [a]Jer. 31:34; Heb. 8:12

19 [a]Heb. 10:35; 3:6 [b]Heb. 9:25

20 [a]Heb. 9:8 [b]Heb. 6:19; 9:3

21 [a]Heb. 2:17 [b]Heb. 3:6; 1 Tim. 3:15

22 [1]Lit., *true* [a]Heb. 10:1; 7:19 [b]Heb. 6:11 [c]Heb. 12:24; 1 Pet. 1:2; Heb. 9:19; Ezek. 36:25 [d]Acts 22:16; 1 Cor. 6:11; Eph. 5:26; Titus 3:5; 1 Pet. 3:21

23 [a]Heb. 3:1 [b]Heb. 3:6 [c]Heb. 11:11; 1 Cor. 1:9; 10:13

24 [a]Heb. 13:1 [b]Titus 3:8

25 [a]Acts 2:42 [b]Heb. 3:13 [c]1 Cor. 3:13

26 [a]Heb. 5:2; 6:4-8; 2 Pet. 2:20f.; Num. 15:30 [b]1 Tim. 2:4

27 [a]John 5:29; Heb. 9:27 [b]Is. 26:11; 2 Thess. 1:7

28 [a]Deut. 17:2-6; Matt. 18:16; Heb. 2:2

29 [a]Heb. 2:3 [b]Heb. 6:6 [c]Heb. 13:20; Matt. 26:28, [d]Eph. 5:26; Rev. 1:5; Heb. 9:13f. [e]Heb. 6:4; Eph. 4:30; 1 Cor. 6:11

30 [a]Deut. 32:35; Rom. 12:19 [b]Deut. 32:36

31 [a]2 Cor. 5:11 [b]Matt. 16:16; Heb. 3:12

32 [1]Lit., *in which* [a]Heb. 5:12 [b]Heb. 6:4 [c]Phil. 1:30

33 [a]1 Cor. 4:9; Heb. 12:4 [b]Phil. 4:14 [Gr.]; 1 Thess. 2:14

34 [a]Heb. 13:3 [b]Matt. 5:12 [c]Heb. 9:15; 11:16; 13:14; 1 Pet. 1:4f.

35 [a]Heb. 10:19 [b]Heb. 2:2

36 [1]Lit., *the promise* [a]Heb. 12:1; Luke 21:19 [b]Heb. 9:15

37 [a]Hab. 2:3; Heb. 10:25; Rev. 22:20 [b]Matt. 11:3

38 [a]Hab. 2:4; Rom. 1:17; Gal. 3:11

39 [1]Lit., *we are not of shrinking back . . . but of faith* [2]Or, *possessing*

Chapter 11

NOW faith is the [1a]assurance of *things* [b]hoped for, the [2]con-
viction of [c]things not seen.
2 For by it the [a]men of old [1b]gained approval.
3 By faith we understand that the [1a]worlds were prepared
[b]by the [c]word of God, so that what is seen [d]was not made out
of things which are visible.
4 By faith [a]Abel offered to God a better sacrifice than
Cain, through which he [b]obtained the testimony that he was
righteous, God testifying [1]about his [c]gifts, and through [2]faith,
though [d]he is dead, he still speaks.
5 By faith [a]Enoch was taken up so that he should not [b]see
death; and he was not found because God took him up; for he
obtained the witness that before his being taken up he was
pleasing to God.
6 And without faith it is impossible to please *Him,* for he
who [a]comes to God must believe that He is, and *that* He is a
rewarder of those who seek Him.
7 By faith [a]Noah, being [b]warned *by God* about [c]things
not yet seen, [1d]in reverence [e]prepared an ark for the salvation
of his household, by which he condemned the world, and became an heir of [f]the righteousness which is according to faith.
8 By faith [a]Abraham, when he was called, obeyed by
going out to a place which he was to [b]receive for an inheritance; and he went out, not knowing where he was going.
9 By faith he lived as an alien in [a]the land of promise, as
in a foreign *land,* [b]dwelling in tents with Isaac and Jacob,
[c]fellow-heirs of the same promise;
10 for he was looking for [a]the city which has [b]foundations,
[c]whose architect and builder is God.
11 By faith even [a]Sarah herself received [1]ability to conceive, even beyond the proper time of life, since she considered Him [b]faithful who had promised;
12 therefore also there was born of one man, and [a]him as
good as dead [1]at that, *as many descendants* [b]AS THE STARS OF
HEAVEN IN NUMBER, AND INNUMERABLE AS THE SAND WHICH IS BY
THE SEASHORE.
13 [a]All these died in faith, [b]without receiving the promises, but [c]having seen them and having welcomed them from
a distance, and [d]having confessed that they were strangers and
exiles on the earth.
14 For those who say such things make it clear that they
are seeking a country of their own.
15 And indeed if they had been [1]thinking of that *country*
from which they went out, [a]they would have had opportunity
to return.
16 But as it is, they desire a better *country,* that is a [a]heav-
enly one. Therefore [b]God is not [1]ashamed to be [c]called their
God; for [d]He has prepared a city for them.
17 By faith [a]Abraham, when he was tested, offered up
Isaac; and he who had [b]received the promises was offering up
his only begotten *son;*
18 *it was he* to whom it was said, "[a]IN ISAAC YOUR SEED
SHALL BE CALLED."

1 [1]Or, *substance* [2]Or, *evidence* [a]Heb. 3:14 [Gr.] [b]Heb. 3:6 [c]Rom. 8:24; 2 Cor. 4:18; 5:7; Heb. 11:7, 27

2 [1]Lit., *obtained a testimony* [a]Heb. 1:1 [b]Heb. 11:4, 39

3 [1]Lit., *ages* [a]Heb. 1:2 [b]Gen. 1; Heb. 1:2 [c]Heb. 6:5; 2 Pet. 3:5 [d]Rom. 4:17

4 [1]I.e., by receiving his gifts [2]Lit., *it* [a]Gen. 4:4; Matt. 23:35; 1 John 3:12 [b]Heb. 11:2 [c]Heb. 5:1 [d]Gen. 4:8-10; Heb. 12:24

5 [a]Gen. 5:21-24 [b]Luke 2:26; John 8:51; Heb. 2:9

6 [a]Heb. 7:19

7 [1]Lit., *having become reverent* [a]Gen. 6:13-22 [b]Heb. 8:5 [c]Heb. 11:1 [d]Heb. 5:7 [e]1 Pet. 3:20 [f]Gen. 6:9; Ezek. 14:14, 20; Rom. 4:13; 9:30

8 [a]Gen. 12:1-4; Acts 7:2-4 [b]Gen. 12:7

9 [a]Acts 7:5 [b]Gen. 12:8; 13:3, 18; 18:1, 9 [c]Heb. 6:17

10 [a]Heb. 12:22; 13:14 [b]Rev. 21:14ff. [c]Heb. 11:16

11 [1]Lit., *power for the laying down of seed* [a]Gen. 17:19; 18:11-14; 21:2 [b]Heb. 10:23

12 [1]Lit., *in these things* [a]Rom. 4:19 [b]Gen. 15:5; 22:17; 32:12

13 [a]Matt. 13:17 [b]Heb. 11:39 [c]John 8:56; Heb. 11:27 [d]Gen. 23:4; 47:9; Ps. 39:12; Eph. 2:19; 1 Pet. 1:1; 2:11

15 [1]Or, *remembering* [a]Gen. 24:6-8

16 [1]Lit., *ashamed of them, to be* [a]2 Tim. 4:18 [b]Mark 8:38; Heb. 2:11 [c]Gen. 26:24; 28:13; Ex. 3:6, 15; 4:5 [d]Heb. 11:10; Rev. 21:2

17 [a]Gen. 22:1-10; James 2:21 [b]Heb. 11:13

18 [a]Gen. 21:12; Rom. 9:7

19 [1]He considered that [a]God is able to raise *men* even
from the dead; from which he also received him back [2]as a
[b]type.
20 By faith [a]Isaac blessed Jacob and Esau, even regarding
things to come.
21 By faith [a]Jacob, as he was dying, blessed each of the
sons of Joseph, and [b]worshiped, *leaning* on the top of his staff.
22 By faith [a]Joseph, when he was dying, made mention of
the exodus of the sons of Israel, and gave orders concerning his
bones.
23 By faith [a]Moses, when he was born, was hidden for
three months by his parents, because they saw he was a beautiful child; and they were not afraid of the [b]king's edict.
24 By faith Moses, [a]when he had grown up, refused to be
called the son of Pharaoh's daughter;
25 choosing rather to [a]endure ill-treatment with the
people of God, than to enjoy the passing pleasures of sin;
26 [a]considering the reproach of [1]Christ greater riches than
the treasures of Egypt; for he was looking to the [b]reward.
27 By faith he [a]left Egypt, not [b]fearing the wrath of the
king; for he endured, as [c]seeing Him who is unseen.
28 By faith he [a]kept the Passover and the sprinkling of the
blood, so that [d]he who destroyed the first-born might not
touch them.
29 By faith they [a]passed through the Red Sea as though
they were passing through dry land; and the Egyptians, when
they attempted it, were [1]drowned.
30 By faith [a]the walls of Jericho fell down, [b]after they had
been encircled for seven days.
31 By faith [a]Rahab the harlot did not perish along with
those who were disobedient, after she had welcomed the spies
[1]in peace.
32 And what more shall I say? For time will fail me if I tell
of [a]Gideon, [b]Barak, [c]Samson, [d]Jephthah; of [e]David and [f]Sam-
uel and the prophets;
33 who by faith [a]conquered kingdoms, [b]performed *acts of*
righteousness, [c]obtained promises, [d]shut the mouths of lions,
34 [a]quenched the power of fire, [b]escaped the edge of the
sword, from weakness were made strong, [c]became mighty in
war, [c]put foreign armies to flight.
35 [a]Women received *back* their dead by resurrection; and
others were tortured, not accepting their [1]release, in order that
they might obtain a better resurrection;
36 and others [1]experienced mockings and scourgings, yes,
also [a]chains and imprisonment.
37 They were [a]stoned, they were [b]sawn in two, [1]they were
tempted, they were [c]put to death with the sword; they went
about [d]in sheepskins, in goatskins; being destitute, afflicted,
[e]ill-treated
38 (*men* of whom the world was not worthy), [a]wandering
in deserts and mountains and caves and holes [1]in the ground.
39 And all these, having [1a]gained approval through their
faith, [b]did not receive [2]what was promised,
40 because God had [1]provided [a]something better for us,
so that [b]apart from us they should not be made perfect.

19 [1]Lit., *Considering* [2]Or, *figuratively speaking;* lit., *in a parable* [a]Rom. 4:21 [b]Heb. 9:9

20 [a]Gen. 27:27-29, 39f.

21 [a]Gen. 48:1, 5, 16, 20 [b]Gen. 47:31 [Sept.]; 1 Kin. 1:47

22 [a]Gen. 50:24f.; Ex. 13:19

23 [a]Ex. 2:2 [Sept.] [b]Ex. 1:16, 22

24 [a]Ex. 2:10, 11ff.

25 [a]Heb. 11:37

26 [1]I.e., the Messiah [a]Luke 14:33; Phil. 3:7f. [b]Heb. 2:2

27 [a]Ex. 12:50f.; 13:17f.; Ex. 2:15 [b]Ex. 10:28f.; Ex. 2:14 [c]Heb. 11:1, 13; Col. 1:15

28 [a]Ex. 12:21ff. [b]Ex. 12:23, 29f.; 1 Cor. 10:10

29 [1]Lit., *swallowed up* [a]Ex. 14:22-29

30 [a]Josh. 6:20 [b]Josh. 6:15f.

31 [1]Lit., *with* [a]Josh. 2:9ff.; 6:23; James 2:25

32 [a]Judg. 6-8 [b]Judg. 4-5 [c]Judg. 13-16 [d]Judg. 11-12 [e]1 Sam. 16:1, 13 [f]1 Sam. 1:20

33 [a]Judg. 4, 7, 11, 14; 2 Sam. 5:17; 8:2; 10:12 [b]1 Sam. 12:4; 2 Sam. 8:15 [c]2 Sam. 7:11f. [d]Dan. 6:22; Judg. 14:6; 1 Sam. 17:34

34 [a]Dan. 3:23ff. [b]Ex. 18:4; 1 Sam. 18:11; 19:10; Ps. 144:10; 1 Kin. 19; 2 Kin. 6 [c]Judg. 7:21; 15:8, 15f.; 1 Sam. 17:51f.; 2 Sam. 8:1-6; 10:15ff.

35 [1]Lit., *redemption* [a]1 Kin. 17:23; 2 Kin. 4:36f.

36 [1]Lit., *received the trial of* [a]Gen. 39:20; Jer. 20:2; 37:15

37 [1]Some mss. omit, *they were tempted* [a]2 Chr. 24:21; 1 Kin. 21:13 [b]2 Sam. 12:31; 1 Chr. 20:3 [c]1 Kin. 19:10; Jer. 26:23 [d]1 Kin. 19:13, 19; 2 Kin. 2:8, 13f.; Zech. 13:4 [e]Heb. 11:25; 13:3

38 [1]Lit., *of* [a]1 Kin. 18:4, 13; 19:9

39 [1]Lit., *obtained a testimony* [2]Lit., *the promise* [a]Heb. 11:2 [b]Heb. 11:13; 10:36

40 [1]Or, *foreseen* [a]Heb. 11:16 [b]Rev. 6:11

Chapter 12

THEREFORE, since we have so great a cloud of witnesses
surrounding us, let [a]us also [b]lay aside every encumbrance, and
the sin which so easily entangles us, and let us [c]run with [d]endur-
ance the race that is set before us,
2 [1]fixing our eyes on Jesus the [2a]author and perfecter of
faith, who for the joy set before Him [b]endured the cross, [c]despis-
ing the shame, and has [d]sat down at the right hand of the
throne of God.
3 For [a]consider Him who has endured such hostility by
sinners against Himself, so that you may not grow weary [1b]and
lose heart.
4 [a]You have not yet resisted [1b]to the point of shedding
blood, in your striving against sin;
5 and you have forgotten the exhortation which is addressed to you as sons,
"[a]MY SON, DO NOT REGARD LIGHTLY THE DISCIPLINE OF
THE LORD,
NOR [b]FAINT WHEN YOU ARE REPROVED BY HIM;
6 [a]FOR THOSE [b]WHOM THE LORD LOVES HE DISCIPLINES,
AND HE SCOURGES EVERY SON WHOM HE RECEIVES."
7 It is for discipline that you endure; [a]God deals with you
as with sons; for what son is there whom *his* father does not
discipline?
8 But if you are without discipline, [a]of which all have
become partakers, then you are illegitimate children and not
sons.
9 Furthermore, we had [1]earthly fathers to discipline us,
and we [a]respected them; shall we not much rather be subject
to [b]the Father of [2]spirits, and [c]live?
10 For they [1]disciplined us for a short time as seemed best
to them, but He disciplines us for *our* good, [a]that we may share
His holiness.
11 All discipline [a]for the moment seems not to be joyful,
but sorrowful; yet to those who have been trained by it, afterwards it yields the [b]peaceful fruit of righteousness.
12 Therefore, [1a]strengthen the hands that are weak and
the knees that are feeble,
13 and [a]make straight paths for your feet, so that *the limb*
which is lame may not be put out of joint, but rather [b]be
healed.
14 [a]Pursue after peace with all men, and after the [b]sancti-
fication without which no one will [c]see the Lord.
15 See to it that no one [a]comes short of the grace of God;
that no [b]root of bitterness springing up cause trouble, and by it
many be [c]defiled;
16 that *there be* no [a]immoral or [b]godless person like Esau,
[c]who sold his own birthright for a single meal.
17 For you know that even afterwards, [a]when he desired to
inherit the blessing, he was rejected, for he found no place for
repentance, though he sought for it with tears.
18 [a]For you have not come to [b]*a mountain* that may be
touched and to a blazing fire, and to darkness and gloom and
whirlwind,
19 and to the [a]blast of a trumpet and the [b]sound of words

1 [a]Heb. 10:39 [b]Eph. 4:22 [Gr.]; Rom. 13:12 [c]1 Cor. 9:24; Gal. 2:2 [d]Heb. 10:36

2 [1]Lit., *looking to* [2]Or, *leader* [a]Heb. 2:10 [b]Heb. 2:9; Phil. 2:8f. [c]1 Cor. 1:18, 23; Heb. 13:13 [d]Heb. 1:3

3 [1]Lit., *fainting in your souls* [a]Matt. 10:24; Rev. 2:3 [b]Gal. 6:9; Heb. 12:5

4 [1]Lit., *as far as blood* [a]Heb. 10:32ff.; 13:13 [b]Phil. 2:8

5 [a]Prov. 3:11 [b]Heb. 12:3

6 [a]Prov. 3:12 [b]Ps. 119:75; Rev. 3:19

7 [a]Deut. 8:5; 2 Sam. 7:14; Prov. 13:24; 19:18; 23:13f.

8 [a]1 Pet. 5:9

9 [1]Lit., *fathers of our flesh* [2]Or, *our spirits* [a]Luke 18:2 [b]Num. 16:22; 27:16; Rev. 22:6 [c]Is. 38:16

10 [1]Lit., *were disciplining* [a]2 Pet. 1:4

11 [a]1 Pet. 1:6 [b]James 3:17f.; Is. 32:17; 2 Tim. 4:8

12 [1]Lit., *make straight* [a]Is. 35:3

13 [a]Prov. 4:26; Gal. 2:14 [b]James 5:16; Gal. 6:1

14 [a]Rom. 14:19 [b]Rom. 6:22; Heb. 12:10 [c]Matt. 5:8; Heb. 9:28

15 [a]Heb. 4:1; 2 Cor. 6:1; Gal. 5:4 [b]Deut. 29:18 [c]Titus 1:15

16 [a]Heb. 13:4 [b]1 Tim. 1:9 [c]Gen. 25:33f.

17 [a]Gen. 27:30-40

18 [a]Heb. 12:18ff.; 2 Cor. 3:7-13 [b]Ex. 19:12, 16ff.; 20:18; Deut. 4:11, 5:22

19 [a]Ex. 19:16, 19; 20:18; Matt. 24:31 [b]Deut. 4:12; Ex. 19:19

which *sound was such that* those who heard [c]begged that no
further word should be spoken to them.
20 For they could not bear the command, "[a]IF EVEN A
BEAST TOUCHES THE MOUNTAIN, IT WILL BE STONED."
21 And so terrible was the sight, *that* Moses said, "[a]I AM
FULL OF FEAR AND TREMBLING."
22 But [a]you have come to Mount Zion and to [b]the city of
[c]the living God, [d]the heavenly Jerusalem, and to [e]myriads of
[1]angels,
23 to the general assembly and [a]church of the first-born
who [b]are enrolled in heaven, and to God [c]the Judge of all, and
to the [d]spirits of righteous men made perfect,
24 and to Jesus the [a]mediator of a new covenant and to
the [b]sprinkled blood, which speaks better than [c]*the blood* of
Abel.
25 [a]See to it that you do not refuse him who is [b]speaking.
For [c]if those [1]did not escape when they [d]refused him who
[e]warned *them* on earth, much [2]less *shall* we *escape* who turn
away from Him who [e]*warns* from heaven.
26 And [a]His voice shook the earth then, but now He has
promised, saying, "[b]YET ONCE MORE I WILL SHAKE NOT ONLY
THE EARTH, BUT ALSO THE HEAVEN."
27 And this *expression*, "Yet once more," denotes [a]the
removing of those things which can be shaken, as of created
things, in order that those things which cannot be shaken may
remain.
28 Therefore, since we receive a [a]kingdom which cannot
be shaken, let us [1]show gratitude, by which we may [b]offer to
God an acceptable service with reverence and awe;
29 for [a]our God is a consuming fire.

CHAPTER 13

LET [a]love of the brethren continue.
2 Do not neglect to [a]show hospitality to strangers, for by
this some have [b]entertained angels without knowing it.
3 [a]Remember [b]the prisoners, as though in prison with
them; and those who are ill-treated, since you yourselves also
are in the body.
4 [a]*Let* marriage *be held* in honor among all, and let the
marriage bed *be* undefiled; [b]for fornicators and adulterers
God will judge.
5 Let your way of life be [a]free from the love of money,
[b]being content with what you have; for He Himself has said,
"[c]I WILL NEVER DESERT YOU, NOR WILL I EVER FORSAKE YOU,"
6 so that we confidently say,
"[a]THE LORD IS MY HELPER, I WILL NOT BE AFRAID.
WHAT SHALL MAN DO TO ME?"
7 Remember [a]those who led you, who spoke [b]the word of
God to you; and considering the [1]outcome of their way of life,
[c]imitate their faith.
8 [a]Jesus Christ *is* the same yesterday and today, *yes* and
forever.
9 [a]Do not be carried away by varied and strange teachings; for it is good for the heart to [b]be strengthened by grace,

19 [c]Ex. 20:19; Deut. 5:25; 18:16

20 [a]Ex. 19:12f.

21 [a]Deut. 9:19

22 [1]Or, *angels in festal assembly, and to the church . . .* [a]Rev. 14:1 [b]Heb. 11:10; Eph. 2:19; Phil. 3:20; Rev. 21:2 [c]Heb. 3:12 [d]Gal. 4:26; Heb. 11:16 [e]Rev. 5:11

23 [a]Heb. 2:12 marg.; Ex. 4:22 [b]Luke 10:20 [c]Gen. 18:25; Ps. 50:6; 94:2 [d]Rev. 6:9, 11; Heb. 11:40

24 [a]1 Tim. 2:5; Heb. 8:6; 9:15 [b]Heb. 9:19; 10:22; 1 Pet. 1:2 [c]Heb. 11:4

25 [1]Lit., *were not escaping* [2]Lit., *more* [a]Heb. 3:12 [b]Heb. 1:1 [c]Heb. 2:2f.; 10:28f. [d]Heb. 12:19 [Gr.] [e]Heb. 8:5; 11:7

26 [a]Ex. 19:18; Judg. 5:4f. [b]Hag. 2:6

27 [a]1 Cor. 7:31; Rom. 8:19, 21; Heb. 1:10ff.; Is. 34:4; 54:10; 65:17

28 [1]Lit., *have* [a]Dan. 2:44 [b]Heb. 13:15, 21

29 [a]Deut. 4:24; 9:3; Is. 33:14; 2 Thess. 1:7; Heb. 10:27, 31

1 [a]Rom. 12:10; 1 Thess. 4:9; 1 Pet. 1:22

2 [a]Matt. 25:35; Rom. 12:13; 1 Pet. 4:9 [b]Gen. 18:3; 19:2

3 [a]Col. 4:18 [b]Heb. 10:34; Matt. 25:36

4 [a]1 Cor. 7:38; 1 Tim. 4:3 [b]1 Cor. 6:9; Gal. 5:19, 21; 1 Thess. 4:6

5 [a]1 Tim. 3:3; Eph. 5:3; Col 3:5 [b]Phil. 4:11 [c]Deut. 31:6; Josh. 1:5

6 [a]Ps. 118:6

7 [1]Or, *end of their life* [a]Heb. 13:17, 24 [b]Luke 5:1; [c]Heb. 6:12

8 [a]2 Cor. 1:19; Heb. 1:12

9 [a]Eph. 4:14; Jude 12 [b]2 Cor. 1:21; Col. 2:7

not by [c]foods, [d]through which those who [1]were thus occupied
were not benefited.
10 We have an altar, [a]from which those [b]who serve the
[1]tabernacle have no right to eat.
11 For [a]the bodies of those animals whose blood is
brought into the holy place by the high priest *as an offering* for
sin, are burned outside the camp.
12 Therefore Jesus also, [a]that He might sanctify the
people [b]through His own blood, suffered [c]outside the gate.
13 Hence, let us go out to Him outside the camp, [a]bearing
His reproach.
14 For here [a]we do not have a lasting city, but we are
seeking [b]*the city* which is to come.
15 [a]Through Him then let us continually offer up a [b]sacri-
fice of praise to God, that is, [c]the fruit of lips that [1]give thanks
to His name.
16 And do not neglect doing good and [a]sharing; for [b]with
such sacrifices God is pleased.
17 [a]Obey your leaders, and submit *to them;* for [b]they keep
watch over your souls, as those who will give an account. [1]Let
them do this with joy and not [2]with grief, for this would be
unprofitable for you.
18 [a]Pray for us, for we are sure that we have a [b]good
conscience, desiring to conduct ourselves honorably in all
things.
19 And I urge *you* all the more to do this, [a]that I may be
restored to you the sooner.
20 Now [a]the God of peace, who [b]brought up from the
dead the [c]great Shepherd of the sheep [1]through [d]the blood of
the [e]eternal covenant, *even* Jesus our Lord,
21 [a]equip you in every good thing to do His will, [b]working
in us that [c]which is pleasing in His sight, through Jesus Christ;
[d]to whom *be* the glory forever and ever. Amen.
22 But [a]I urge you, [b]brethren, [1]bear with [2]this [b]word of
exhortation, for [c]I have written to you briefly.
23 Take notice that [a]our brother Timothy has been released; with whom, if he comes soon, I shall see you.
24 Greet [a]all of your leaders and all the [1][b]saints. Those
from [c]Italy greet you.
25 [a]Grace be with you all.

9 [1]Lit., *walked* [c]Col. 2:16 [d]Heb. 9:10

10 [1]Or, *sacred tent* [a]1 Cor. 10:18 [b]Heb. 8:5

11 [a]Ex. 29:14; Lev. 4:12, 21; 9:11; 16:27; Num. 19:3, 7

12 [a]Eph. 5:26; Heb. 2:11 [b]Heb. 9:12 [c]John 19:17

13 [a]Heb. 11:26; 12:2; Luke 9:23

14 [a]Heb. 10:34; 12:27 [b]Heb. 11:10, 16; 12:22; 2:5; Eph. 2:19

15 [1]Lit., *confess* [a]1 Pet. 2:5 [b]Lev. 7:12 [c]Is. 57:19; Hos. 14:2 marg.

16 [a]Rom. 12:13 [b]Phil. 4:18

17 [1]Lit., *in order that they may do this* [2]Lit., *groaning* [a]Heb. 13:7, 24; 1 Cor. 16:16 [b]Is. 62:6; Ezek. 3:17; Acts 20:28

18 [a]1 Thess. 5:25 [b]Acts 24:16; 1 Tim. 1:5

19 [a]Philem. 22

20 [1]Or, *in* [a]Rom. 15:33 [b]Acts 2:24; Rom. 10:7 [c]Is. 63:11 marg.; John 10:11; 1 Pet. 2:25 [d]Zech. 9:11; Heb. 10:29 [e]Is. 55:3; Jer. 32:40; Ezek. 37:26

21 [a]1 Pet. 5:10 [b]Phil. 2:13 [c]1 John 3:22; Heb. 12:28 [d]Rom. 11:36

22 [1]Or, *listen to* [2]Lit., *the* [a]Heb. 13:19; 3:13; 10:25; 12:5; Acts 13:15 [b]Heb. 3:1 [c]1 Pet. 5:12

23 [a]Acts 16:1; Col. 1:1

24 [1]I.e., true believers; lit., *holy ones* [a]Heb. 13:7, 17; 1 Cor. 16:16 [b]Acts 9:13 [c]Acts 18:2

25 [a]Col. 4:18

THE EPISTLE OF
JAMES

Address and Greeting. Pray in Faith. Rejoice in Lowliness. Temptation not from God.

[1a]
JAMES, a [b]bond-servant of God and [c]of the Lord Jesus
Christ, to [d]the twelve tribes who are [2e]dispersed abroad,
[f]greetings.
2 [a]Consider it all joy, my brethren, when you encounter
[b]various [1]trials;
3 knowing that [a]the testing of your [b]faith produces
[1c]endurance.
4 And let [1a]endurance have *its* perfect [2]result, that you
may be [3b]perfect and complete, lacking in nothing.
5 But if any of you [a]lacks wisdom, let him ask of God,
who gives to all men generously and [1]without reproach, and [b]it
will be given to him.
6 But let him [a]ask in faith [b]without any doubting, for the
one who doubts is like the surf of the sea [c]driven and tossed by
the wind.
7 For let not that man expect that he will receive anything
from the Lord,
8 *being* a [1a]double-minded man, [b]unstable in all his ways.
9 [a]But let the [1]brother of humble circumstances glory in
his high position;
10 and *let* the rich man *glory* in his humiliation, because
[a]like [1]flowering grass he will pass away.
11 For the sun rises with [1a]a scorching wind, and [b]withers
the grass; and its flower falls off, and the beauty of its appearance is destroyed; so too the rich man in the midst of his
pursuits will fade away.
12 [a]Blessed is a man who perseveres under trial; for once
he has [1]been approved, he will receive [b]the crown of life, which
the Lord [c]has promised to those who [d]love Him.
13 Let no one say when he is tempted, "[a]I am being
tempted [1]by God"; for God cannot be tempted [2]by evil, and
He Himself does not tempt any one.
14 But each one is tempted when he is carried away and
enticed by his own lust.
15 Then [a]when lust has conceived, it gives birth to sin; and
when [b]sin is accomplished, it brings forth death.
16 [a]Do not be deceived, [b]my beloved brethren.
17 Every good thing bestowed and every perfect gift is
[a]from above, coming down from [b]the Father of lights, [c]with
whom there is no variation, or [1]shifting shadow.
18 In the exercise of [a]His will He [b]brought us forth by [c]the
word of truth, so that we might be [1]as it were the [d]first fruits
[2]among His creatures.
19 [1]*This* [a]you know, [b]my beloved brethren. But let every
one be quick to hear, [c]slow to speak *and* [d]slow to anger;
20 for [a]the anger of man does not achieve the righteousness of God.

1 [1]Or, *Jacob* [2]Lit., *in the Dispersion* [a]Acts 12:17, 2 [b]Titus 1:1 [c]Rom. 1:1; 2 Pet. 1:1; Jude 1 [d]Luke 22:30; Acts 26:7 [e]1 Pet. 1:1; Phil. 3:20; Heb. 13:14; John 7:35 [f]Acts 15:23

2 [1]Or, *temptations* [a]Matt. 5:12; James 1:12; 5:11 [b]1 Pet. 1:6

3 [1]Or, *steadfastness* [a]1 Pet. 1:7 [b]Heb. 6:12 [c]Luke 21:19

4 [1]Note vs. 3 [2]Lit., *work* [3]Or, *mature* [a]Luke 21:19 [b]James 3:2; Matt. 5:48; Col. 4:12; 1 Thess. 5:23

5 [1]Lit., *does not reproach* [a]1 Kin. 3:9ff.; Prov. 2:3-6; James 3:17 [b]Matt. 7:7

6 [a]Matt. 21:21 [b]Mark 11:23; Acts 10:20 [c]Eph. 4:14 [Matt. 14:28-31]

8 [1]Or, *doubting, hesitating* [a]James 4:8 [b]2 Pet. 2:14

9 [1]I.e., church member [a]Luke 14:11

10 [1]Lit., *the flower of the grass* [a]1 Pet. 1:24; 1 Cor. 7:31

11 [1]Lit., *the* [a]Matt. 20:12 [b]Is. 40:7f.; Ps. 102:4, 11

12 [1]Or, *passed the test* [a]James 5:11; Luke 6:22; 1 Pet. 3:14; 4:14 [b]1 Cor. 9:25 [c]James 2:5; Ex. 20:6 [d]1 Cor. 2:9; 8:3

13 [1]Lit., *from* [2]Lit., *of evil things* [a]Gen. 22:1

15 [a]Job 15:35; Ps. 7:14; Is. 59:4 [b]Rom. 5:12; 6:23

16 [a]1 Cor. 6:9 [b]James 1:2, 19; 2:1, 5, 14; 3:1, 10; 4:11; 5:12, 19; Acts 1:15

17 [1]Lit., *shadow of turning* [a]James 3:15, 17; John 3:3 [b]Ps. 136:7; 1 John 1:5 [c]Mal. 3:6

18 [1]Lit., *a certain first fruits* [2]Lit., *of* [a]John 1:13 [b]James 1:15; 1 Pet. 1:3, 23 [c]2 Cor. 6:7; Eph. 1:13; 2 Tim. 2:15 [d]Jer. 2:3; Rev. 14:4

19 [1]Or, *Know* this [a]1 John 2:21 [b]James 1:2, 16; 2:1, 5, 14; 3:1, 10; 4:11; 5:12, 19; Acts 1:15 [c]Prov. 10:19; 17:27 [d]Prov. 16:32; Eccles. 7:9

20 [a]Matt. 5:22; Eph. 4:26

21 Therefore [a]putting aside all filthiness and *all* [1]that remains of wickedness, in [2]humility receive [b]the word implanted,
which is able to save your souls.
22 [a]But prove yourselves doers of the word, and not merely hearers who delude themselves.
23 For if any one is a hearer of the word and not a doer, he
is like a man who looks at his [1]natural face [a]in a mirror;
24 for *once* he has looked at himself and gone away, [1]he
has immediately forgotten what kind of person he was.
25 But one who looks intently at the perfect law, [a]the *law*
of liberty and abides by it, not having become a forgetful
hearer but [1]an effectual doer, this man shall be [b]blessed in
[2]what he does.
26 If any one thinks himself to be religious, and yet does
not [a]bridle his tongue but deceives his *own* heart, this man's
religion is worthless.
27 This is pure and undefiled religion [a]in the sight of *our*
God and Father, to [b]visit [c]orphans and widows in their distress,
and to keep oneself unstained [1]by [d]the world.

Chapter 2

[a]MY brethren, [b]do not hold your faith in our [c]glorious Lord
Jesus Christ with *an attitude of* [d]personal favoritism.
2 For if a man comes into your [1]assembly with a gold ring
and dressed in [2a]fine clothes, and there also comes in a poor
man in [b]dirty clothes,
3 and you [1]pay special attention to the one who is wearing the [a]fine clothes, and say, "You sit here in a good place,"
and you say to the poor man, "You stand over there, or sit
down by my footstool";
4 have you not made distinctions among yourselves, and
become judges [a]with evil [1]motives?
5 Listen, [a]my beloved brethren: did not [b]God choose the
poor [1]of this world *to be* [c]rich in faith and [d]heirs of the kingdom which He [e]promised to those who love Him?
6 But you have dishonored the poor man. Is it not the
rich who oppress you and [1]personally [a]drag you into [2]court?
7 [a]Do they not blaspheme the fair name [1]by which you
have been called?
8 If, however, you [a]are fulfilling the [1]royal law, according
to the Scripture, "[b]YOU SHALL LOVE YOUR NEIGHBOR AS YOUR-
SELF," you are doing well.
9 But if you [a]show partiality, you are committing sin *and*
are [b]convicted by the [1]law as transgressors.
10 For whoever keeps the whole [1]law and yet [a]stumbles in
one *point*, he has become [b]guilty of all.
11 For He who said, "[a]DO NOT COMMIT ADULTERY," also
said, "[b]DO NOT COMMIT MURDER." Now if you do not commit
adultery, but do commit murder, you have become a transgressor of the [1]law.
12 So speak and so act, as those who are to be judged by
[a]*the* law of liberty.
13 For [a]judgment *will be* merciless to one who has shown
no mercy; mercy [1]triumphs over judgment.

21 [1]Lit., *abundance of malice* [2]Or, *gentleness* [a]Eph. 4:22; 1 Pet. 2:1 [b]1 Pet. 1:22f.; Eph. 1:13

22 [a]James 1:22-25; Matt. 7:24-27 [Luke 6:46-49]; Rom. 2:13; James 2:14-20

23 [1]Lit., *the face of his birth;* or, *nature* [a]1 Cor. 13:12

24 [1]Lit., *and he*

25 [1]Lit., *a doer of a work* [2]Lit., *his doing* [a]James 2:12; Gal. 2:4; John 8:32; Rom. 8:2; Gal. 6:2; 1 Pet. 2:16 [b]John 13:17

26 [a]James 3:2-12; Ps. 39:1; 141:3

27 [1]Lit., *from* [a]Rom. 2:13; Gal 3:11 [b]Matt. 25:36 [c]Deut. 14:29; Job 31:16, 17, 21; Ps. 146:9; Is. 1:17, 23 [d]James 4:4; Titus 2:12; 2 Pet. 1:4; 2:20; Eph. 2:2; Matt. 12:32; 1 John 2:15-17

1 [a]James 1:16 [b]Heb. 12:2 [c]1 Cor. 2:8; Acts 7:2 [d]James 2:9; Acts 10:34

2 [1]Or, *synagogue* [2]Or, *bright* [a]Luke 23:11; James 2:3 [b]Zech. 3:3f.

3 [1]Lit., *look upon* [a]Luke 23:11; James 2:3

4 [1]Lit., *reasonings* [a]Luke 18:6 marg.; John 7:24

5 [1]Lit., *to the* [a]James 1:16 [b]1 Cor. 1:27f.; Job 34:19 [c]Luke 12:21; Rev. 2:9 [d]Matt. 5:3; 25:34 [e]James 1:12

6 [1]Lit., *they themselves* [2]Lit., *courts* [a]Acts 8:3; 16:19

7 [1]Lit., *which has been called upon you* [a]1 Pet. 4:16; Acts 11:26

8 [1]Or, *of our King* [a]Matt. 7:12 [b]Lev. 19:18

9 [1]Or, *Law* [a]James 2:1; Acts 10:34 [b]Deut. 1:17

10 [1]Or, *Law* [a]James 3:2; 2 Pet. 1:10; Jude 24 [b]Gal. 5:3; Matt. 5:19

11 [1]Or, *Law* [a]Ex. 20:14; Deut. 5:18 [b]Ex. 20:13; Deut. 5:17

12 [a]James 1:25

13 [1]Lit., *boasts against* [a]Matt. 5:7; 18:32-35; Luke 6:37f.; Prov. 21:13

14 [a]What use is it, [b]my brethren, if a man says he has faith,
but he has no works? Can [1]that faith save him?
15 [a]If a brother or sister is without clothing and in need of
daily food,
16 and one of you says to them, "[a]Go in peace, be warmed
and be filled"; and yet you do not give them what is necessary
for *their* body; what use is that?
17 Even so [a]faith, if it has no works, is dead, *being* by
itself.
18 [a]But someone [1]may *well* say, "You have faith, and I
have works; show me your [b]faith without the works, and I will
[c]show you my faith [d]by my works."
19 You believe that [1a]God is one. [b]You do well; [c]the demons also believe, and shudder.
20 But are you willing to recognize, [a]you foolish fellow,
that [b]faith without works is useless?
21 [a]Was not Abraham our father justified by works, when
he offered up Isaac his son on the altar?
22 You see that [a]faith was working with his works, and [1]as
a result of the [b]works, faith was [2]perfected;
23 and the Scripture was fulfilled which says, "[a]AND ABRA-
HAM BELIEVED GOD, AND IT WAS RECKONED TO HIM AS RIGH-
TEOUSNESS," and he was called [b]the friend of God.
24 You see that a man is justified by works, and not by
faith alone.
25 And in the same way was not [a]Rahab the harlot also
justified by works, [b]when she received the messengers and sent
them out by another way?
26 For just as the body without *the* spirit is dead, so also
[a]faith without works is dead.

CHAPTER 3

[a]LET not many *of you* become teachers, [b]my brethren, knowing that as such we shall incur a [1]stricter judgment.
2 For we all [a]stumble in many *ways*. [b]If any one does not
stumble in [1]what he says, he is a [c]perfect man, able to [d]bridle
the whole body as well.
3 Now [a]if we put the bits into the horses' mouths so that
they may obey us, we direct their entire body as well.
4 Behold, the ships also, though they are so great and are
driven by strong winds, are still directed by a very small rudder,
wherever the inclination of the pilot desires.
5 So also the tongue is a small part of the body, and *yet* it
[a]boasts of great things. [b]Behold, how great a forest is set aflame
by such a small fire!
6 And [a]the tongue is a fire, the *very* world of iniquity; the
tongue is set among our members as that which [b]defiles the
entire body, and sets on fire the course of *our* [1]life, and is set
on fire by [2c]hell.
7 For every [1]species of beasts and birds, of reptiles and
creatures of the sea, is tamed, and has been tamed by the
human [1]race.
8 But no one can tame the tongue; *it is* a restless evil *and*
full of [a]deadly poison.

14 [1]Lit., *the* [a]James 1:22ff. [b]James 1:16

15 [a]Matt. 25:35f.; Luke 3:11

16 [a]1 John 3:17f.

17 [a]Gal. 5:6; James 2:20, 26

18 [1]Lit., *will* [a]Rom. 9:19 [b]Rom. 3:28; 4:6; Heb. 11:33 [c]James 3:13 [d]Matt. 7:16f.; Gal. 5:6

19 [1]Or, *there is one God* [a]Deut. 6:4; Mark 12:29 [b]James 2:8 [c]Matt. 8:29; Mark 1:24; 5:7; Luke 4:34; Acts 19:15

20 [a]Rom. 9:20; 1 Cor. 15:36 [b]Gal. 4:6; James 2:17, 26

21 [a]Gen. 22:9, 10, 12, 16-18

22 [1]Or, *by the deeds* [2]Or, *completed* [a]Heb. 11:17; John 6:29 [b]1 Thess. 1:3

23 [a]Gen. 15:6; Rom. 4:3 [b]Is. 41:8; 2 Chr. 20:7

25 [a]Heb. 11:31 [b]Josh. 2:4, 6, 15

26 [a]Gal. 5:6; James 2:17, 20

1 [1]Or, *greater condemnation* [a]Matt. 23:8; Rom. 2:20f.; 1 Tim. 1:7 [b]James 1:16; 3:10

2 [1]Lit., *word* [a]James 2:10 [b]James 3:2-12; Matt. 12:34-37 [c]James 1:4 [d]James 1:26

3 [a]Ps. 32:9

5 [a]Ps. 12:3f.; 73:8f. [b]Prov. 26:20f.

6 [1]Or, *existence, origin* [2]Gr., *Gehenna* [a]Ps. 120:3, 4; Prov. 16:27 [b]Matt. 15:11, 18f.; 12:36f. [c]Matt. 5:22

7 [1]Lit., *nature;* Gr., genos

8 [a]Ps. 140:3; Rom. 3:13; Eccles. 10:11 marg.

9 With it we bless [a]*our* Lord and Father; and with it we
curse men, [b]who have been made in the likeness of God;
10 from the same mouth come *both* blessing and cursing.
My brethren, these things ought not to be this way.
11 Does a fountain send out from the same opening *both*
[1]fresh and bitter *water?*
12 [a]Can a fig tree, my brethren, produce olives, or a vine
produce figs? Neither *can* salt water produce [1]fresh.
13 Who among you is wise and understanding? [a]Let him
show by his [b]good behavior his deeds in the gentleness of
wisdom.
14 But if you have bitter [a]jealousy and [1]selfish ambition in
your heart, do not be arrogant and *so* lie against [b]the truth.
15 This wisdom is not that which comes down [a]from
above, but is [b]earthly, [1c]natural, [d]demonic.
16 For where [a]jealousy and [1]selfish ambition exist, there is
disorder and every evil thing.
17 But the wisdom [a]from above is first [b]pure, then [c]peace-
able, [d]gentle, [1]reasonable, [e]full of mercy and good fruits,
[f]unwavering, without [g]hypocrisy.
18 And the [1a]seed whose fruit is righteousness is sown in
peace [2]by those who make peace.

Chapter 4

1
WHAT is the source of quarrels and [a]conflicts among you?
[2]Is not the source your pleasures that wage [b]war in your
members?
2 You lust and do not have; *so* you [a]commit murder. And
you are envious and cannot obtain; *so* you fight and quarrel.
You do not have because you do not ask.
3 You ask and [a]do not receive, because you ask [1]with
wrong motives, so that you may spend *it* [2]on your pleasures.
4 You [a]adulteresses, do you not know that friendship
with [b]the world is [c]hostility toward God? [d]Therefore whoever
wishes to be a friend of the world makes himself an enemy of
God.
5 Or do you think that the Scripture [a]speaks to no purpose: "[1]He [2]jealously desires [b]the spirit which He has made to
dwell in us"?
6 But [a]He gives a greater grace. Therefore *it* says, "[b]GOD
IS OPPOSED TO THE PROUD, BUT GIVES GRACE TO THE HUMBLE."
7 [a]Submit therefore to God. [b]Resist the devil and he will
flee from you.
8 [a]Draw near to God and He will draw near to you.
[b]Cleanse your hands, you sinners; and [c]purify your hearts, you
[d]double-minded.
9 [a]Be miserable and mourn and weep: let your laughter
be turned into mourning, and your joy to gloom.
10 [a]Humble yourselves in the presence of the Lord, and
He will exalt you.
11 [a]Do not speak against one another, [b]brethren. He who
speaks against a brother, or [c]judges his brother, speaks against
[d]the law, and judges the law; but if you judge the law, you are
not [e]a doer of the law, but a judge *of it.*
12 There is *only* one [a]Lawgiver and Judge, the One who is

9 [a]James 1:27 [b]1 Cor. 11:7

11 [1]Lit., *sweet*

12 [1]Note vs. 11 [a]Matt. 7:16

13 [a]James 2:18 [b]1 Pet. 2:12

14 [1]Or, *strife* [a]James 3:16; Rom. 2:8; 2 Cor. 12:20 [b]James 5:19; 1:18; 1 Tim. 2:4

15 [1]Or, *unspiritual* [a]James 1:17 [b]1 Cor. 2:6; 3:19 [c]2 Cor. 1:12; Jude 19 [d]2 Thess. 2:9f.; 1 Tim. 4:1; Rev. 2:24

16 [1]Note vs. 14 [a]James 3:14; Rom 2:8; 2 Cor. 12:20

17 [1]Or, *willing to yield* [a]James 1:17 [b]James 4:8; 2 Cor. 7:11 [c]Matt. 5:9; Heb. 12:11 [d]Titus 3:2; Phil. 4:5 marg. [e]Luke 6:36; James 2:13 [f]James 2:4 [Gr.] [g]Rom. 12:9; 2 Cor. 6:6

18 [1]Lit., *fruit of righteousness* [2]Or, *for* [a]Prov. 11:18; Is. 32:17; Hos. 10:12; Amos 6:12; Phil. 1:11; Gal. 6:8

1 [1]Lit., *Whence wars and whence fightings* [2]Lit., Are they *not hence,* from your . . . [a]Titus 3:9 [b]Rom. 7:23

2 [a]1 John 3:15; James 5:6

3 [1]Lit., *wickedly* [2]Lit., *in* [a]1 John 3:22; 5:14

4 [a]Is. 54:5; Jer. 2:2; Ezek. 16:32; Matt. 12:39 [b]James 1:27 [c]Rom. 8:7; 1 John 2:15 [d]John 15:19; Matt. 6:24

5 [1]Or, *The Spirit which He has made to dwell in us jealously desires us* [2]Lit., *desires to jealousy* [a]Num. 23:19 [b]1 Cor. 6:19; 2 Cor. 6:16

6 [a]Is. 54:7f.; Matt. 13:12 [b]Prov. 3:34; 1 Pet. 5:5; Ps. 138:6; Matt. 23:12

7 [a]1 Pet. 5:6 [b]1 Pet. 5:8f.; Eph. 4:27; 6:11f.

8 [a]2 Chr. 15:2; Zech. 1:3; Mal. 3:7; Heb. 7:19 [b]Is. 1:16; Job 17:9; 1 Tim. 2:8 [c]Jer. 4:14; 1 Pet. 1:22; 1 John 3:3; James 3:17 [d]James 1:8

9 [a]Luke 6:25; Prov. 14:13; Neh. 8:9

10 [a]James 4:6; Job 5:11; Ezek. 21:26; Luke 1:52

11 [a]2 Cor. 12:20; 1 Pet. 2:1; James 5:9 [b]James 5:7, 9, 10; 1:16 [c]Matt. 7:1; Rom. 14:4 [d]James 2:8 [e]James 1:22

12 [a]Is. 33:22; James 5:9

[b]able to save and to destroy; but [c]who are you who judge your
neighbor?
13 [a]Come now, you who say, "[b]Today or tomorrow, we
shall go to such and such a city, and spend a year there and
engage in business and make a profit."
14 [1]Yet you do not know [2]what your life will be like tomorrow. [a]You are *just* a vapor that appears for a little while
and then vanishes away.
15 [1]Instead, *you ought* to say, "[a]If the Lord wills, we shall
live and also do this or that."
16 But as it is, you boast in your [1]arrogance; [a]all such
boasting is evil.
17 Therefore, [a]to one who knows *the* [1]right thing to do,
and does not do it, to him it is sin.

Chapter 5

[a]COME now, [b]you rich, [c]weep and howl for your miseries
which are coming upon you.
2 [a]Your riches have rotted and your garments have become moth-eaten.
3 Your gold and your silver have rusted; and their rust
will be a witness against you and will consume your flesh like
fire. It is [a]in the Last Days that you have stored up your
treasure!
4 Behold, [a]the pay of the laborers who mowed your
fields, *and* which has been withheld by you, cries out *against
you;* and [b]the outcry of those who did the harvesting has
reached the ears of [c]the Lord of [1]Sabaoth.
5 You have [a]lived luxuriously on the earth and led a life
of wanton pleasure; you have [1]fattened your hearts in [b]a day of
slaughter.
6 You have condemned and [1a]put to death [b]the righteous
man; he does not resist you.
7 Be patient, therefore, [a]brethren, [b]until the coming of
the Lord. [c]Behold, the farmer waits for the precious produce
of the soil, being patient about it, until [1]it gets [d]the early and
late rains.
8 [a]You too be patient; [b]strengthen your hearts, for [c]the
coming of the Lord is [d]at hand.
9 [a]Do not [1]complain, [b]brethren, against one another,
that you yourselves may not be judged; behold, [c]the Judge is
standing [2d]right at the [3]door.
10 As an example, [a]brethren, of suffering and patience,
take [b]the prophets who spoke in the name of the Lord.
11 Behold, we count those [a]blessed who endured. You
have heard of [b]the [1]endurance of Job and have seen [c]the [2]out-
come of the Lord's dealings, that [d]the Lord is full of compassion and *is* merciful.
12 But above all, [a]my brethren, [b]do not swear, either by
heaven or by earth or with any other oath; but [1]let your yes be
yes, and your no, no; so that you may not fall under judgment.
13 Is anyone among you [a]suffering? [b]Let him pray. Is
anyone cheerful? Let him [c]sing praises.
14 Is anyone among you sick? Let him call for [a]the elders

12 [b]Matt. 10:28 [c]Rom. 14:4

13 [a]James 5:1 [b]Prov. 27:1; Luke 12:18-20

14 [1]Lit., *who do not . . .* [2]Some mss. read, *the morrow; for what kind of life is yours* [a]Ps. 102:3; Job 7:7; Ps. 39:5; 144:4

15 [1]Lit., *instead of your saying* [a]Acts 18:21

16 [1]Or, *pretensions* [a]1 Cor. 5:6

17 [1]Or, *good* [a]Luke 12:47; 2 Pet. 2:21; John 9:41

1 [a]James 4:13 [b]Luke 6:24; 1 Tim. 6:9 [c]Is. 13:6; 15:3; Ezek. 30:2

2 [a]Job 13:28; Is. 50:9; Matt. 6:19f.

3 [a]James 5:7, 8

4 [1]I.e., Hosts [a]Lev. 19:13; Job 24:10f.; Jer. 22:13; Mal. 3:5 [b]Deut. 24:15; Job 31:38f.; Ex. 2:23 [c]Rom. 9:29

5 [1]Lit., *nourished* [a]Luke 16:19; 2 Pet. 2:13; Ezek. 16:49; 1 Tim. 5:6 [b]Jer. 12:3; 25:34

6 [1]Or, *murdered* [a]James 4:2 [b]Heb. 10:38; 1 Pet. 4:18

7 [1]Or, *he* [a]James 4:11; 5:9, 10 [b]John 21:22; 1 Thess. 2:19 [c]Gal. 6:9 [d]Deut. 11:14; Jer. 5:24; Joel 2:23

8 [a]Luke 21:19 [b]1 Thess. 3:13 [c]John 21:22; 1 Thess. 2:19 [d]Rom. 13:11, 12; 1 Pet. 4:7

9 [1]Lit., *groan* [2]Lit., *before* [3]Lit., *doors* [a]James 4:11 [b]James 4:11; 5:7, 10 [c]James 4:12; 1 Cor. 4:5; Heb. 10:25; 1 Pet. 4:5 [d]Matt. 24:33; Mark 13:29

10 [a]James 4:11; 5:7, 9 [b]Matt. 5:12

11 [1]Or, *steadfastness* [2]Lit., *end of the Lord* [a]Matt. 5:10; 1 Pet. 3:14 [b]Job 1:21f.; 2:10 [c]Job 42:10, 12 [d]Ex. 34:6; Ps. 103:8

12 [1]Lit., *let yours be the yes, yes, and the no, no* [a]James 1:16 [b]Matt. 5:34-37

13 [a]James 5:10 [b]Ps. 50:15 [c]Col. 3:16; 1 Cor. 14:15

14 [a]Acts 11:30

of the church, and let them pray over him, [1b]anointing him
with oil in the name of the Lord;
15 and the [a]prayer [1]offered in faith will [2b]restore the one
who is sick, and the Lord will [c]raise him up, and if he has
committed sins, [3]they will be forgiven him.
16 Therefore, [a]confess your sins to one another, and pray
for one another, so that you may be [b]healed. [c]The effective
[1]prayer of a righteous man can accomplish much.
17 Elijah was [a]a man with a nature like ours, and [b]he
prayed [1]earnestly that it might not rain; and it did not rain on
the earth for [c]three years and six months.
18 And he [a]prayed again, and [b]the [1]sky [2]poured rain, and
the earth produced its fruit.
19 My brethren, [a]if any among you strays from [b]the truth,
and one turns him back;
20 let him know that he who turns a sinner from the error
of his way will [a]save his soul from death, and will [b]cover a
multitude of sins.

14 [1]Lit., *having anointed* [b]Mark 6:13; 16:18

15 [1]Lit., *of* [2]Or, *save* [3]Lit., *it* [a]James 1:6 [b]1 Cor. 1:21; James 5:20 [c]John 6:39; 2 Cor. 4:14

16 [1]Lit., *supplication* [a]Matt. 3:6; Mark 1:5; Acts 19:18 [b]Heb. 12:13; 1 Pet. 2:24 [c]Gen. 18:23-32, John 9:31

17 [1]Lit., *with prayer* [a]Acts 14:15 [b]1 Kin. 17:1; 18:1 [c]Luke 4:25

18 [1]Lit., *heaven* [2]Lit., *gave* [a]1 Kin. 18:42 [b]1 Kin. 18:45

19 [a]Matt. 18:15; Gal. 6:1 [b]James 3:14

20 [a]Rom. 11:14; 1 Cor. 1:21; James 1:21 [b]1 Pet. 4:8

THE FIRST EPISTLE OF
PETER

Salutation. Our Living Hope through Christ's Resurrection.

[a]PETER, an apostle of Jesus Christ, to those who reside as
[b]aliens, [c]scattered throughout [d]Pontus, [e]Galatia, [d]Cappadocia,
[d]Asia, and [f]Bithynia, [g]who are chosen
2 according to the [a]foreknowledge of God the Father,
[b]by the sanctifying work of the Spirit, [1]that you may [c]obey
Jesus Christ and be [d]sprinkled with His blood: [e]May grace and
peace [2]be yours in fullest measure.
3 [a]Blessed be the God and Father of our Lord Jesus
Christ, who [b]according to His great mercy [c]has caused us to be
born again to [d]a living hope through the [e]resurrection of Jesus
Christ from the dead,
4 to *obtain* an [a]inheritance *which is* imperishable and
undefiled and [b]will not fade away, [c]reserved in heaven for you,
5 who are [a]protected by the power of God [b]through faith
for [c]a salvation ready [d]to be revealed in the last time.
6 [a]In this you greatly rejoice, even though now [b]for a
little while, [c]if necessary, you have been distressed by [d]various
[1]trials,
7 that the [1a]proof of your faith, *being* more precious than
gold which [2]is perishable, [b]even though tested by fire, [c]may be
found to result in praise and glory and honor at [d]the revelation
of Jesus Christ;
8 and [a]though you have not seen Him, you [b]love Him,
and though you do not see Him now, but believe in Him, you
greatly rejoice with joy inexpressible and [1]full of glory,
9 obtaining as [a]the outcome of your faith the salvation of
[1]your souls.

1 [a]2 Pet. 1:1 [b]1 Pet. 2:11 [c]James 1:1 [d]Acts 2:9 [e]Acts 16:6 [f]Acts 16:7 [g]Matt. 24:22; Luke 18:7

2 [1]Lit., *unto obedience and sprinkling* [2]Lit., *be multiplied for you* [a]Rom. 8:29; 1 Pet. 1:20 [b]2 Thess. 2:13 [c]1 Pet. 1:14, 22; Rom. 1:5; 6:16; 16:19 [d]Heb. 10:22; 12:24 [e]2 Pet. 1:2

3 [a]2 Cor. 1:3 [b]Titus 3:5; Gal. 6:16 [c]1 Pet. 1:23; James 1:18 [d]1 Pet. 1:13, 21; 3:5, 15; Heb. 3:6; 2 Thess. 2:16; 1 John 3:3 [e]1 Pet. 3:21; 1 Cor. 15:20

4 [a]Acts 20:32; Rom. 8:17; Col. 3:24 [b]1 Pet. 5:4 [c]2 Tim. 4:8; Heb. 11:16

5 [a]Phil. 4:7; John 10:28 [b]Eph. 2:8 [c]1 Cor. 1:21; 2 Thess. 2:13 [d]1 Pet. 4:13; 5:1; Rom. 8:18

6 [1]Or, *temptations* [a]Rom. 5:2 [b]1 Pet. 5:10 [c]1 Pet. 3:17 [d]James 1:2; 1 Pet. 4:12

7 [1]Or, *genuineness* [2]Lit., *perishes* [a]James 1:3 [b]Job 23:10; Ps. 66:10; Prov. 17:3; Is. 48:10; Zech. 13:9; Mal. 3:3; 1 Cor. 3:13 [c]Rom. 2:7, 10; 2 Cor. 4:17; Heb. 12:11 [d]1 Pet. 1:13; 4:13; Luke 17:30

8 [1]Lit., *glorified* [a]John 20:29 [b]Eph. 3:19

9 [1]Some ancient mss. omit *your* [a]Rom. 6:22

10 [a]As to this salvation, the prophets who [b]prophesied of the [c]grace that *would come* to you made careful search and inquiry,

11 [1]seeking to know what person or time [a]the Spirit of Christ within them was indicating as He [b]predicted the sufferings of Christ and the glories [2]to follow.

12 It was revealed to them that they were not serving themselves but you in these things which now have been announced to you through those who [a]preached the gospel to you by [b]the Holy Spirit sent from heaven,—things into which [c]angels long to [1]look.

13 Therefore, [a]gird [1]your minds for action, [2b]keep sober *in spirit,* fix your [c]hope completely on the [d]grace [3]to be brought to you at [e]the revelation of Jesus Christ.

14 As [1a]obedient children, do not [2b]be conformed to the former lusts *which were yours* in your [c]ignorance,

15 but [1a]like the Holy One who called you, [2b]be holy yourselves also [c]in all *your* behavior;

16 because it is written, "[a]YOU SHALL BE HOLY, FOR I AM HOLY."

17 And if you [a]address as Father the One who [b]impartially [c]judges according to each man's work, conduct yourselves [d]in fear during the time of your [e]stay *upon earth;*

18 knowing that you were not [1a]redeemed with perishable things like silver or gold from your [b]futile way of life inherited from your forefathers,

19 but with precious [a]blood, as of a [b]lamb unblemished and spotless, *the blood* of Christ.

20 For He was [a]foreknown before [b]the foundation of the world, but has [c]appeared [1]in these last times [d]for the sake of you

21 who through Him are [a]believers in God, who raised Him from the dead and [b]gave Him glory, so that your faith and [c]hope are in God.

22 Since you have [a]in obedience to the truth [b]purified your souls for a [1c]sincere love of the brethren, fervently love one another from [2]the heart,

23 for you have been [a]born again [b]not of seed which is perishable but imperishable, *that is,* through the living and abiding [c]word of God.

24 For,

"[a]ALL FLESH IS LIKE GRASS,
AND ALL ITS GLORY LIKE THE FLOWER OF GRASS.
THE GRASS WITHERS,
AND THE FLOWER FALLS OFF,

25 [a]BUT THE WORD OF THE LORD ABIDES FOREVER."
And this is [b]the word which was [1]preached to you.

CHAPTER 2

THEREFORE, [a]putting aside all [1]malice and all guile and [2]hypocrisy and [2]envy and all [2b]slander,

2 [a]like newborn babes, long for the [1b]pure milk [2]of the word, that by it you may [c]grow [3]in respect to salvation,

3 if you have [a]tasted [1b]the kindness of the Lord.

10 [a]1 Pet. 1:10-12; Matt. 13:17; Luke 10:24 [b]Matt. 26:24; Luke 24:27, 44 [c]1 Pet. 1:13; Col. 3:4

11 [1]Lit., *inquiring* [2]Lit., *after these* [a]Rom. 8:9; 2 Pet. 1:21 [b]Matt. 26:24; Luke 24:27, 44

12 [1]Or, *gain a clear glimpse* [a]1 Pet. 1:25; 4:6 [b]Acts 2:2-4 [c]Luke 2:13; Eph. 3:10; 1 Tim. 3:16

13 [1]Lit., *the loins of your mind* [2]Lit., *be sober* [3]Or, *which is announced* [a]Eph. 6:14 [b]1 Pet. 4:7; 5:8; 1 Thess. 5:6, 8; 2 Tim. 4:5; Rom. 12:3; Titus 2:6 [c]1 Pet. 1:3 [d]1 Pet. 1:10; Col. 3:4 [e]1 Pet. 1:7; 4:13; Luke 17:30

14 [1]Lit., *children of obedience* [2]Or, *conform yourselves* [a]1 Pet. 1:2 [b]Rom. 12:2; 1 Pet. 4:2f. [c]Eph. 4:18

15 [1]Lit., *according to* [2]Or, *become* [a]1 Thess. 4:7; 1 John 3:3 [b]2 Cor. 7:1 [c]James 3:13

16 [a]Lev. 11:44f.; 19:2; 20:7

17 [a]Ps. 89:26; Jer. 3:19; Mal. 1:6; Matt. 6:9 [b]Acts 10:34 [c]Matt. 16:27 [d]1 Pet. 3:15; 2 Cor. 7:1; Heb. 12:28 [e]1 Pet. 2:11; Eph. 2:19

18 [1]Or, *ransomed* [a]Is. 52:3; 1 Cor. 6:20; Titus 2:14; Heb. 9:12; 2 Pet. 2:1; Matt. 20:28 [b]Eph. 4:17

19 [a]Acts 20:28; 1 Pet. 1:2 [b]John 1:29; Heb. 9:14

20 [1]Lit., *at the end of the times* [a]Acts 2:23; 1 Pet. 1:2; Eph. 1:4; Rev. 13:8 [b]Matt. 25:34 [c]Heb. 9:26 [d]Heb. 2:14

21 [a]Rom. 4:24; 10:9 [b]Heb. 2:9; 1 Tim. 3:16; John 17:5, 24 [c]1 Pet. 1:3

22 [1]Lit., *unhypocritical* [2]Some mss. read, *a clean heart* [a]1 Pet. 1:2 [b]James 4:8 [c]John 13:34; Rom. 12:10; Heb. 13:1; 1 Pet. 2:17; 3:8

23 [a]1 Pet. 1:3; John 3:3 [b]John 1:13 [c]Heb. 4:12

24 [a]Is. 40:6ff.; James 1:10f.

25 [1]Lit., *preached as good news to you* [a]Is. 40:8 [b]Heb. 6:5

1 [1]Or, *wickedness* [2]plural nouns [a]Eph. 4:22, 25, 31; James 1:21 [b]James 4:11

2 [1]Or, *unadulterated* [2]Or, *spiritual* (Gr., logikos) *milk* [3]Or, *up to salvation* [a]Matt. 18:3; 19:14; Mark 10:15; Luke 18:17; 1 Cor. 14:20 [b]1 Cor. 3:2 [c]Eph. 4:15f.

3 [1]Lit., *that the Lord is kind* [a]Heb. 6:5 [b]Ps. 34:8; Titus 3:4

4 And coming to Him as to a living stone, [a]rejected by
men, but [1]choice and precious in the sight of God,
5 [a]you also, as living stones, [1]are being built up as a [b]spiri-
tual house for a holy [c]priesthood, to [d]offer up spiritual sacrifices acceptable to God through Jesus Christ.
6 For *this* is contained in [1]Scripture:
"[a]BEHOLD I LAY IN ZION A CHOICE STONE, A [b]PRECIOUS
CORNER *STONE*,
AND HE WHO BELIEVES IN [2]HIM SHALL NOT BE
[3]DISAPPOINTED."
7 [a]This precious value, then, is for you who believe, but
for those who disbelieve,
"[b]THE STONE WHICH THE BUILDERS [c]REJECTED,
THIS BECAME THE VERY CORNER *STONE*,"
8 and,
"[a]A STONE OF STUMBLING AND A ROCK OF OFFENSE";
[b]for they stumble because they are disobedient to the word,
[c]and to this *doom* they were also appointed.
9 But you are [a]A CHOSEN RACE, A ROYAL [b]PRIESTHOOD, A
[c]HOLY NATION, [d]A PEOPLE FOR *God's* OWN POSSESSION, that you
may proclaim the excellencies of Him who has called you [e]out
of darkness into His marvelous light;
10 [a]for you once were NOT A PEOPLE, but now you are THE
PEOPLE OF GOD; you had NOT RECEIVED MERCY, but now you
have RECEIVED MERCY.
11 [a]Beloved, [b]I urge you as [c]aliens and strangers to abstain
from [d]fleshly lusts, which wage [e]war against the soul.
12 [a]Keep your behavior excellent among the Gentiles, so
that in the thing in which they [b]slander you as evildoers, they
may [1]on account of your good deeds, as they observe *them*,
[c]glorify God [d]in the day of [2]visitation.
13 [a]Submit yourselves for the Lord's sake to every human
institution: whether to a king as the one in authority;
14 or to governors as sent [1]by him [a]for the punishment of
evildoers and the [b]praise of those who do right.
15 For [a]such is the will of God that by doing right you
may [b]silence the ignorance of foolish men.
16 *Act* as [a]free men, and do not use your freedom as a
covering for evil, but *use it* as [b]bondslaves of God.
17 [a]Honor all men; [b]love the brotherhood, [c]fear God, [d]hon-
or the [1]king.
18 [a]Servants, be submissive to your masters with all respect,
not only to those who are good and [b]gentle, but also to
those who are [1]unreasonable.
19 For this *finds* [1]favor, if for the sake of [a]conscience toward God a man bears up under sorrows when suffering
unjustly.
20 For what credit is there if, when you sin and are harshly
treated, you endure it with patience? But if [a]when you do what
is right and suffer *for it* you patiently endure it, this *finds*
[1]favor with God.
21 For [a]you have been called for this purpose, [b]since
Christ also suffered for you, leaving you [c]an example for you
to follow in His steps,
22 WHO [a]COMMITTED NO SIN, NOR WAS ANY DEECEIT FOUND IN
HIS MOUTH;

4 [1]Lit., *chosen;* or, *elect* [a]1 Pet. 2:7

5 [1]Or, *allow yourselves to be built up;* or, *build yourselves up* [a]1 Cor. 3:9 [b]1 Tim. 3:15; Gal. 6:10 [c]1 Pet. 2:9; Is. 61:6; 66:21; Rev. 1:6 [d]Heb. 13:15; Rom. 15:16

6 [1]Or, *a scripture* [2]Or, *it* [3]Or, *put to shame* [a]Is. 28:16; 1 Pet. 2:6, 8; Rom. 9:32, 33; 10:11 [b]Eph. 2:20

7 [a]1 Pet. 2:7, 8; 2 Cor. 2:16 [b]Ps. 118:22; Matt. 21:42; Luke 2:34 [c]1 Pet. 2:4

8 [a]Is. 8:14 [b]1 Cor. 1:23; Gal. 5:11 [c]Rom. 9:22

9 [a]Deut. 10:15; Is. 43:20f. [b]1 Pet. 2:5; Is. 61:6; 66:21; Rev. 1:6 [c]Ex. 19:6; Deut. 7:6 [d]Titus 2:14 [e]Acts 26:18; Is. 42:16; 2 Cor. 4:6

10 [a]Hos. 1:10; 2:23; Rom. 9:25; Rom. 10:19

11 [a]Heb. 6:9; 1 Pet. 4:12 [b]Rom. 12:1 [c]Lev. 25:23; Ps. 39:12; 1 Pet. 1:17; Heb. 11:13; Eph. 2:19 [d]Rom. 13:14; Gal. 5:16, 24 [e]James 4:1

12 [1]Or, *as a result of* [2]I.e., Christ's coming again in judgment [a]1 Pet. 2:15; 3:16; 2 Cor. 8:21; Phil. 2:15; Titus 2:8 [b]Acts 28:22 [c]1 Pet. 4:11, 16; Matt. 5:16; Matt. 9:8; John 13:31 [d]Is. 10:3; Luke 19:44

13 [a]Rom. 13:1

14 [1]Lit., *through* [a]Rom. 13:4 [b]Rom. 13:3

15 [a]1 Pet. 3:17 [b]1 Pet. 2:12

16 [a]John 8:32; James 1:25 [b]1 Cor. 7:22; Rom. 6:22

17 [1]Or, *emperor* [a]Rom. 12:10; 13:7 [b]1 Pet. 1:22 [c]Prov. 24:21 [d]Prov. 24:21; Matt. 22:21; 1 Pet. 2:13

18 [1]Or, *perverse* [a]Eph. 6:5 [b]James 3:17

19 [1]Or, *grace* [a]1 Pet. 3:14, 17; Rom. 13:5

20 [1]Note vs. 19 [a]1 Pet. 3:17

21 [a]1 Pet. 3:9; Acts 14:22 [b]1 Pet. 3:18; 4:1, 13 [c]Matt. 11:29; 16:24

22 [a]Is. 53:9; 2 Cor. 5:21

23 [1]and while being [a]reviled, He [2]did not revile in return;
while suffering, He uttered no threats, but kept entrusting
Himself to Him who judges righteously;
24 and He Himself [1a]bore our sins in His body on the
[2b]cross, that we [c]might die to [3]sin and live to righteousness; for
[d]by His [4]wounds you were [e]healed.
25 For you were [a]continually straying like sheep, but now
you have returned to the [b]Shepherd and [1]Guardian of your
souls.

Chapter 3

[a]IN the same way, you wives, [b]be submissive to your own
husbands so that even if any *of them* are disobedient to the
word they may be [c]won without a word by the behavior of
their wives,
2 as they observe your chaste and [1]respectful behavior.
3 [a]And let not your adornment be external *only*—braid-
ing the hair, and wearing gold jewelry, and putting on dresses;
4 but *let it be* [a]the hidden person of the heart, with the
imperishable quality of a gentle and quiet spirit, which is precious in the sight of God.
5 For in this way in former times the holy women also,
[a]who hoped in God, used to adorn themselves, being submissive to their own husbands.
6 Thus Sarah obeyed Abraham, [a]calling him lord, and
you have become her children if you do what is right [1b]without
being frightened by any fear.
7 [a]You husbands likewise, live with your wives in an understanding way, as with a weaker [b]vessel, since she is a woman;
and grant her honor as a fellow-heir of the grace of life, so that
your prayers may not be hindered.
8 [1]To sum up, [a]let all be harmonious, sympathetic, [b]broth-
erly, [c]kind-hearted, and [d]humble in spirit;
9 [a]not returning evil for evil, or [b]insult for insult, but
[1]giving a [c]blessing instead; for [d]you were called for the very
purpose that you might [e]inherit a blessing.
10 For

"[a]LET HIM WHO MEANS TO LOVE LIFE AND SEE GOOD DAYS
REFRAIN HIS TONGUE FROM EVIL AND HIS LIPS FROM
SPEAKING GUILE.

11 "[a]AND LET HIM TURN AWAY FROM EVIL AND DO GOOD;
LET HIM SEEK PEACE AND PURSUE IT.

12 "[a]FOR THE EYES OF THE LORD ARE UPON THE RIGHTEOUS,
AND HIS EARS ATTEND TO THEIR PRAYER,
BUT THE FACE OF THE LORD IS AGAINST THOSE WHO DO
EVIL."

13 And [a]who is there to harm you if you prove zealous for
what is good?
14 But even if you should [a]suffer for the sake of righteousness, [b]*you are* blessed. [c]AND DO NOT FEAR THEIR [1]INTIMIDATION,
AND DO NOT BE TROUBLED,
15 but [1]SANCTIFY [a]Christ as Lord in your hearts, always
being ready [b]to make a defense to every one who asks you to
give an account for the [c]hope that is in you, yet [d]with gentleness and [2e]reverence;

23 [1]Lit., *who* [2]Lit., *was not reviling* [a]1 Pet. 3:9; Is. 53:7; Heb. 12:3

24 [1]Or, *carried . . . up to the cross* [2]Lit., *wood* [3]Lit., *sins* [4]Lit., *wound,* or *welt* [a]Is. 53:4, 11; 1 Cor. 15:3; Heb. 9:28 [b]Acts 5:30 [c]Rom. 6:2, 13 [d]Is. 53:5 [e]Heb. 12:13; James 5:16

25 [1]Or, *Bishop, Overseer* [a]Is. 53:6 [b]John 10:11; 1 Pet. 5:4

1 [a]1 Pet. 2:18; 3:7 [b]Eph. 5:22 [c]1 Cor. 9:19

2 [1]Lit., *with fear*

3 [a]1 Tim. 2:9; Is. 3:18ff.

4 [a]Rom. 7:22

5 [a]1 Tim. 5:5; 1 Pet. 1:3

6 [1]Lit., *and are not* [a]Gen. 18:12 [b]1 Pet. 3:14

7 [a]Eph. 5:25; Col. 3:19 [b]1 Thess. 4:4

8 [1]Or, *Finally* [a]Rom. 12:16 [b]1 Pet. 1:22 [c]Eph. 4:32 [d]Eph. 4:2; Phil. 2:3; 1 Pet. 5:5

9 [1]Lit., *blessing instead* [a]Rom. 12:17; 1 Thess. 5:15 [b]1 Pet. 2:23; 1 Cor. 4:12 [c]Luke 6:28; Rom. 12:14; 1 Cor. 4:12 [d]1 Pet. 2:21 [e]Gal. 3:14; Heb. 6:14; 12:17

10 [a]Ps. 34:12, 13

11 [a]Ps. 34:14

12 [a]Ps. 34:15, 16

13 [a]Prov. 16:7

14 [1]Lit., *fear* [a]1 Pet. 2:19ff.; 4:15f. [b]James 5:11 [c]Is. 8:12f.; 1 Pet. 3:6

15 [1]I.e., set apart [2]Or, *fear* [a]1 Pet. 1:3 [b]Col. 4:6 [c]1 Pet. 1:3 [d]2 Tim. 2:25 [e]1 Pet. 1:17

16 [1]and keep a [a]good conscience so that in the thing in which [b]you are slandered, those who revile your good behavior in Christ may be put to shame.

17 For [a]it is better, [b]if [1]God should will it so, that you suffer for doing what is right rather than for doing what is wrong.

18 For [a]Christ also died for sins [b]once for all, *the* just for *the* unjust, in order that He might [c]bring us to God, having been put to death [d]in the flesh, but made alive [e]in the [1]spirit;

19 in [1]which also He went and [a]made proclamation to the spirits *now* in prison,

20 who once were disobedient, when the [a]patience of God [b]kept waiting in the days of Noah, during the construction of [c]the ark, in which a few, that is, [d]eight [e]persons, were brought safely through *the* water.

21 [a]And corresponding to that, baptism now saves you—[b]not the removal of dirt from the flesh, but an appeal to God for a [c]good conscience—through [d]the resurrection of Jesus Christ,

22 [a]who is at the right hand of God, [b]having gone into heaven, [c]after angels and authorities and powers had been subjected to Him.

Chapter 4

1 THEREFORE, since [a]Christ has [1]suffered in the flesh, [b]arm yourselves also with the same purpose, because [c]he who has [1]suffered in the flesh has ceased from sin,

2 [a]so as to live [b]the rest of the time in the flesh no longer for the lusts of men, but for the will of God.

3 For [a]the time already past is sufficient *for you* to have carried out the desire of the Gentiles, [b]having pursued a course of sensuality, lusts, drunkenness, carousals, drinking parties and [1]abominable idolatries.

4 And in *all* this, they are surprised that you do not run with *them* into the same excess of [a]dissipation, and they [b]malign *you;*

5 but they shall give account to Him who is ready to judge [a]the living and the dead.

6 For [a]the gospel has for this purpose been preached even to those who are dead, that though they are judged in the flesh as men, they may live in the spirit according to *the will of* God.

7 [a]The end of all things [1]is at hand; therefore, [b]be of sound judgment and sober *spirit* for the purpose of [2]prayer.

8 Above all, [a]keep fervent in your love for one another, because [b]love covers a multitude of sins.

9 [a]Be hospitable to one another without [b]complaint.

10 [a]As each one has received a *special* gift, employ it in serving one another, as good [b]stewards of the manifold grace of God.

11 [a]Whoever speaks, *let him speak,* as it were, the [b]utterances of God; whoever serves, *let him do so* as [1][c]by the strength which God supplies; so that [d]in all things God may be

16 [1]Lit., *having a good* . . . [a]1 Pet. 3:21; 1 Tim. 1:5; Heb. 13:18 [b]1 Pet. 2:12, 15

17 [1]Lit., *the will of God* [a]1 Pet. 2:20; 4:15f. [b]1 Pet. 1:6; 2:15; 4:19; Acts 18:21

18 [1]Or, *Spirit* [a]1 Pet. 2:21 [b]Heb. 9:26, 28; 10:10 [c]Rom. 5:2; Eph. 3:12 [d]1 Pet. 4:1; Col. 1:22 [e]1 Pet. 4:6

19 [1]Or, *whom* [a]1 Pet. 4:6

20 [a]Rom. 2:4 [b]Gen. 6:3, 5, 13f. [c]Heb. 11:7 [d]2 Pet. 2:5; Gen. 8:18 [e]Acts 2:41; 1 Pet. 1:9, 22; 2:25; 4:19

21 [a]Titus 3:5; Acts 16:33 [b]Heb. 9:14; 10:22 [c]1 Pet. 3:16; 1 Tim. 1:5; Heb. 13:18 [d]1 Pet. 1:3

22 [a]Mark 16:19 [b]Heb. 4:14; 6:20 [c]Rom. 8:38f.; Heb. 1:6

1 [1]I.e., suffered death [a]1 Pet. 2:21 [b]Eph. 6:13 [c]Rom. 6:7

2 [a]Rom. 6:2; Col. 3:3 [b]1 Pet. 1:14

3 [1]Lit., *lawless* [a]1 Cor. 12:2 [b]Rom. 13:13; Eph. 2:2; 4:17ff.

4 [a]Eph. 5:18 [b]1 Pet. 3:16

5 [a]Acts 10:42; 2 Tim. 4:1; Rom. 14:9

6 [a]1 Pet. 1:12; 3:19

7 [1]Lit., *has come near* [2]Lit., *prayers* [a]Rom. 13:11; James 5:8; Heb. 9:26; 1 John 2:18 [b]1 Pet. 1:13

8 [a]1 Pet. 1:22 [b]Prov. 10:12; James 5:20; 1 Cor. 13:4ff.

9 [a]1 Tim. 3:2; Heb. 13:2 [b]Phil. 2:14

10 [a]Rom. 12:6f. [b]1 Cor. 4:1

11 [1]Lit., *from* [a]1 Thess. 2:4; Titus 2:1, 15; Heb. 13:7 [b]Acts 7:38 [c]Eph. 6:10; 1:19 [d]1 Cor. 10:31; 1 Pet. 2:12

glorified through Jesus Christ, [e]to whom belongs the glory and
dominion forever and ever. Amen.
12 [a]Beloved, do not be surprised at the [b]fiery ordeal
among you, which comes upon you for your testing, as though
some strange thing were happening to you;
13 but to the degree that you [a]share the sufferings of
Christ, keep on rejoicing; so that also at the [b]revelation of His
glory, [c]you may rejoice with exultation.
14 If you are reviled [1a]for the name of Christ, [b]you are
blessed, [c]because the Spirit of glory and of God rests upon
you.
15 By no means [a]let any of you suffer as a murderer, or
thief, or evil-doer, or a [1b]troublesome meddler;
16 but if *anyone suffers* as a [a]Christian, let him not feel
ashamed, but in that name let him [b]glorify God.
17 For *it is* time for judgment [a]to begin [1]with [b]the household of God; and if *it* [c]*begins* with us first, what *will be* the
outcome for those [d]who do not obey the [e]gospel of God?
18 [a]AND IF IT IS WITH DIFFICULTY THAT THE RIGHTEOUS IS
SAVED, [1]WHAT WILL BECOME OF THE [b]GODLESS MAN AND THE
SINNER?
19 Therefore, let those also who suffer according to [a]the
will of God entrust their souls to a faithful Creator in doing
what is right.

CHAPTER 5

[a]THEREFORE, I exhort the elders among you, as *your* [b]fel-
low-elder and [c]witness of the sufferings of Christ, and a [d]partak-
er also of the glory that is to be revealed,
2 shepherd [a]the flock of God among you, [b]not under
compulsion, but voluntarily, according to *the will of* God; and
[c]not for sordid gain, but with eagerness;
3 nor yet as [a]lording it over [1]those allotted to your
charge, but [2]proving to be [b]examples to the flock.
4 And when the Chief [a]Shepherd appears, you will receive the [b]unfading [1c]crown of glory.
5 [a]You younger men, likewise, [b]be subject to your elders;
and all of you, clothe yourselves with [c]humility toward one
another, for [d]GOD IS OPPOSED TO THE PROUD, BUT GIVES GRACE
TO THE HUMBLE.
6 [a]Humble yourselves, therefore, under the mighty hand
of God, that He may exalt you at the proper time,
7 casting all your [a]anxiety upon Him, because He cares
for you.
8 [a]Be of sober *spirit,* [b]be on the alert. Your adversary,
[c]the devil, prowls about like a roaring [d]lion, seeking someone
to devour.
9 [1a]But resist him, [b]firm in *your* faith, knowing that [c]the
same experiences of suffering are being accomplished by your
[2]brethren who are in the world.
10 And after you have suffered [a]for a little, the [b]God of all
grace, who [c]called you to His [d]eternal glory in Christ, will
Himself [e]perfect, [f]confirm, strengthen *and* [1]establish you.
11 [a]To Him *be* dominion forever and ever. Amen.

11 [e]Rev. 1:6; 5:13; 1 Pet. 5:11; Rom. 11:36

12 [a]1 Pet. 2:11 [b]1 Pet. 1:6f.

13 [a]Phil. 3:10; 2 Cor. 1:5; 4:10; Rom. 8:17 [b]1 Pet. 1:7; 5:1 [c]2 Tim. 2:12

14 [1]Lit., *in* [a]John 15:21; 1 Pet. 4:16; Heb. 11:26 [b]Matt. 5:11; Luke 6:22; Acts 5:41 [c]2 Cor. 4:10f., 16

15 [1]Lit., *one who oversees others' affairs* [a]1 Pet. 2:19f.; 3:17 [b]1 Thess. 4:11; 2 Thess. 3:11; 1 Tim. 5:13

16 [a]Acts 5:41; 28:22; James 2:7 [b]1 Pet. 4:11

17 [1]Lit., *from* [a]Jer. 25:29; Ezek. 9:6; Amos 3:2 [b]1 Tim. 3:15; Heb. 3:6; 1 Pet. 2:5 [c]Rom. 2:9 [d]2 Thess. 1:8 [e]Rom. 1:1

18 [1]Lit., *where will appear* [a]Prov. 11:31; Luke 23:31 [b]1 Tim. 1:9

19 [a]1 Pet. 3:17

1 [a]Acts 11:30 [b]2 John 1; 3 John 1 [c]Luke 24:48; Heb. 12:1 [d]1 Pet. 1:5, 7; 4:13; Rev. 1:9

2 [a]John 21:16; Acts 20:28 [Gr.] [b]Philem. 14 [c]1 Tim. 3:8

3 [1]Lit., *the allotments* [2]Or, *becoming* [a]Ezek. 34:4; Matt. 20:25f. [b]Phil. 3:17; 1 Thess. 1:7; 2 Thess. 3:9; 1 Tim. 4:12; Titus 2:7; John 13:15

4 [1]Lit., *wreath* [a]1 Pet. 2:25 [b]1 Pet. 1:4 [c]1 Cor. 9:25

5 [a]Luke 22:26; 1 Tim. 5:1 [b]Eph. 5:21 [c]1 Pet. 3:8 [d]Prov. 3:34; James 4:6

6 [a]James 4:10

7 [a]Matt. 6:25

8 [a]1 Pet. 1:13 [b]Matt. 24:42 [c]James 4:7 [d]2 Tim. 4:17

9 [1]Lit., *whom resist* [2]Lit., *brotherhood* [a]James 4:7 [b]Col. 2:5 [c]Acts 14:22; Heb. 12:8

10 [1]Omitted by some ancient mss. [a]1 Pet. 1:6 [b]1 Pet. 4:10 [c]1 Cor. 1:9; 1 Thess. 2:12 [d]2 Cor. 4:17; 2 Tim. 2:10 [e]1 Cor. 1:10; Heb. 13:21 [f]Rom. 16:25; 2 Thess. 2:17; 3:3

11 [a]Rom. 11:36; 1 Pet. 4:11

12 Through [a]Silvanus, our faithful brother ([1]for so I regard *him*), [b]I have written to you briefly, exhorting and testifying that this is [c]the true grace of God. [d]Stand firm in it!
13 [1]She who is in Babylon, chosen together with you,
sends you greetings, and *so does* my son, [a]Mark.
14 [a]Greet one another with a kiss of love.
[b]**P**eace be to you all who are in Christ.

THE SECOND EPISTLE OF
PETER

Salutation. Growth in Christian Virtue.

1
SIMON PETER, a [a]bond-servant and [b]apostle of Jesus
Christ, to those who have received [c]a faith of the same [2]kind as
ours, [3]by [d]the righteousness of [e]our God and Savior, Jesus
Christ:
2 [a]Grace and peace be multiplied to you in [b]the knowledge of God and of Jesus our Lord;
3 seeing that His [a]divine power has granted to us everything pertaining to life and godliness, through the true [b]knowl-
edge of Him who [c]called us [1]by His own glory and [2]excellence.
4 [1]For by these He has granted to us His precious and
magnificent [a]promises, in order that by them you might become [b]partakers of *the* divine nature, having [c]escaped the [d]cor-
ruption that is in [e]the world by lust.
5 Now for this very reason also, applying all diligence, in
your faith [a]supply [b]moral [1]excellence, and in *your* moral excellence, [c]knowledge;
6 and in *your* knowledge, [a]self-control, and in *your* self-
control, [b]perseverance, and in *your* perseverance, [c]godliness;
7 and in *your* godliness, [a]brotherly kindness, and in *your*
brotherly kindness, *Christian* love.
8 For if these *qualities* are yours and are increasing, they
render you neither useless nor [a]unfruitful in the true [b]knowl-
edge of our Lord Jesus Christ.
9 For he who lacks these *qualities* is [a]blind *or* short-
sighted, having forgotten *his* [b]purification from his former sins.
10 Therefore, brethren, be all the more diligent to make
certain about His [a]calling and [b]choosing you; for as long as you
practice these things, you will never [c]stumble;
11 for in this way the entrance into [a]the eternal kingdom
of our [b]Lord and Savior Jesus Christ will be [c]abundantly
[d]supplied to you.
12 Therefore, [a]I shall always be ready to remind you of
these things, even though you *already* know *them*, and have
been established in [b]the truth which is present with *you*.
13 And I consider it [a]right, as long as I am in [b]this *earthly*
dwelling, to [c]stir you up by way of reminder,
14 knowing that [a]the laying aside of my *earthly* dwelling is
imminent, [b]as also our Lord Jesus Christ has made clear to me.

12 [1]Lit., *(as I consider)* [a]2 Cor. 1:19 [b]Heb. 13:22 [c]1 Pet. 1:13; 4:10; Acts 11:23 [d]1 Cor. 15:1

13 [1]Some mss. read, *The church which* [a]Acts 12:12

14 [a]Rom. 16:16 [b]Eph. 6:23

1 [1]Most early mss. read, *Simeon* [2]Or, *value* [3]Or, *in* [a]Rom. 1:1; Phil. 1:1; Jude 1; James 1:1 [b]1 Pet. 1:1 [c]Rom. 1:12; 2 Cor. 4:13; Titus 1:4 [d]Rom. 3:21-26 [e]Titus 2:13

2 [a]1 Pet. 1:2; Rom. 1:7 [b]2 Pet. 1:3, 8; 2:20; 3:18; John 17:3; Phil. 3:8

3 [1]Or possibly, *to* [2]Or, *virtue* [a]1 Pet. 1:5 [b]2 Pet. 1:2, 8; 2:20; 3:18; John 17:3; Phil. 3:8 [c]1 Thess. 2:12; 2 Thess. 2:14; 1 Pet. 5:10

4 [1]Lit., *through which* (things) [a]2 Pet. 3:9, 13 [b]Eph. 4:13, 24; Heb. 12:10; 1 John 3:2 [c]2 Pet. 2:18, 20 [d]2 Pet. 2:19 [e]James 1:27

5 [1]Or, *virtue* [a]2 Pet. 1:11 [b]2 Pet. 1:3 [c]Col. 2:3; 2 Pet. 1:2

6 [a]Acts 24:25 [b]Luke 21:19 [c]2 Pet. 1:3

7 [a]Rom. 12:10; 1 Pet. 1:22

8 [a]Col. 1:10 [b]2 Pet. 1:2, 3; 2:20; 3:18; John 17:3; Phil. 3:8

9 [a]1 John 2:11 [b]Eph. 5:26; Titus 2:14

10 [a]Rom. 11:29; 2 Pet. 1:3; Matt. 22:14 [b]1 Thess. 1:4 [c]Jude 24; 2 Pet. 3:17; James 2:10

11 [a]2 Tim. 4:18 [b]2 Pet. 2:20; 3:18 [c]Rom. 2:4; 1 Tim. 6:17 [d]2 Pet. 1:5

12 [a]Jude 5; Phil. 3:1; 1 John 2:21 [b]Col. 1:5f.; 2 John 2

13 [a]Phil. 1:7 [b]2 Cor. 5:1, 4; 2 Pet. 1:14 [c]2 Pet. 3:1

14 [a]2 Tim. 4:6; 2 Cor. 5:1 [b]John 13:36; 21:19

15 And I will also be diligent that at any time after my
[a]departure you may be able to call these things to mind.
16 For we did not follow cleverly devised [a]tales when we
made known to you the [b]power and coming of our Lord Jesus
Christ, but we were [c]eyewitnesses of His majesty.
17 For when He received honor and glory from God the
Father, such an [1a]utterance as this was [2]made to Him by the
[b]Majestic Glory, "This is My beloved Son with whom I am
well pleased,"—
18 and we ourselves heard this [1]utterance made from heav-
en when we were with Him on the [a]holy mountain.
19 [1]And *so* we have [a]the prophetic word *made* more [b]sure,
to which you do well to pay attention as to [c]a lamp shining in a
dark place, until the [d]day dawns and the [e]morning star arises
[f]in your hearts.
20 But [a]know this first of all, that [b]no prophecy of Scripture is *a matter* of one's own interpretation,
21 for [a]no prophecy was ever made by an act of human
will, but men [b]moved by the Holy Spirit spoke from God.

Chapter 2

But [a]false prophets also arose among the people, just as
there will also be [b]false teachers [c]among you, who will [d]secretly
introduce [e]destructive heresies, even [f]denying the [g]Master who
[h]bought them, bringing swift destruction upon themselves.
2 And many will follow their [a]sensuality, and because of
them [b]the way of the truth will be [c]maligned;
3 and in *their* [a]greed they will [b]exploit you with [c]false
words; [d]their judgment from long ago is not idle, and their
destruction is not asleep.
4 For [a]if God did not spare angels when they sinned, but
cast them into hell and [b]committed them to pits of darkness,
reserved for judgment;
5 and did not spare [a]the ancient world, but preserved
[b]Noah, a [1]preacher of righteousness, with seven others, when
He brought a [c]flood upon the world of the ungodly;
6 and *if* He [a]condemned the cities of Sodom and Gomorrah to destruction by reducing *them* to ashes, having made
them an [b]example to those who would [c]live ungodly
thereafter;
7 and if He [a]rescued righteous Lot, oppressed by the
[b]sensual conduct of [c]unprincipled men
8 (for by what he saw and heard *that* [a]righteous man,
while living among them, felt *his* righteous soul tormented day
after day with *their* lawless deeds),
9 [a]*then* the Lord knows how to rescue the godly from
[1]temptation, and to keep the unrighteous under punishment
for the [b]day of judgment,
10 and especially those who [1a]indulge the flesh in *its* corrupt desires and [b]despise authority. Daring, [c]self-willed, they
do not tremble when they [b]revile [2]angelic majesties,
11 [a]whereas angels who are greater in might and power do
not bring a reviling judgment against them before the Lord.
12 But [a]these, like unreasoning animals, [b]born as creatures
of instinct to be captured and killed, reviling where they have

15 [a]Luke 9:31

16 [a]1 Tim. 1:4; 2 Pet. 2:3 [b]Mark 13:26; 14:62; 1 Thess. 2:19 [c]Matt. 17:1ff.; Mark 9:2ff.; Luke 9:28ff.

17 [1]Lit., *voice* [2]Lit., *borne* [a]Matt. 17:5; Mark 9:7; Luke 9:35 [b]Heb. 1:3

18 [1]Lit., *voice borne* [a]Ex. 3:5; Josh. 5:15

19 [1]Or, *And we have the even surer prophetic word* [a]1 Pet. 1:10f. [b]Heb. 2:2 [c]Ps. 119:105 [d]Luke 1:78 [e]Rev. 22:16 [f]2 Cor. 4:6

20 [a]2 Pet. 3:3 [b]Rom. 12:6

21 [a]Jer. 23:26; 2 Tim. 3:16 [b]1 Pet. 1:11; 2 Sam. 23:2; Luke 1:70; Acts 1:16; 3:18

1 [a]Deut. 13:1ff.; Jer. 6:13 [b]2 Cor. 11:13 [c]1 Tim. 4:1; Matt. 7:15 [d]Gal. 2:4; Jude 4 [e]1 Cor. 11:19; Gal. 5:20 [f]Jude 4 [g]Rev. 6:10 [h]1 Cor. 6:20

2 [a]Gen. 19:5ff.; Jude 4; 2 Pet. 2:7, 18 [b]Acts 16:17; 22:4; 24:14 [c][Gr.] Rom. 2:24; 1 Tim. 6:1

3 [a]2 Pet. 2:14; 1 Tim. 6:5; Jude 16 [b]2 Cor. 2:17 marg.; 1 Thess. 2:5 [c]Rom. 16:18; 2 Pet. 1:16 [d]Deut. 32:35

4 [a]Gen. 6; Jude 6 [b]Rev. 20:1f.

5 [1]Or, *herald* [a]2 Pet. 3:6; Ezek. 26:20 [b]1 Pet. 3:20 [c]2 Pet. 3:6

6 [a]Gen. 19:24; Jude 7 [b]Jude 7; Matt. 10:15; 11:23; Rom. 9:29 [Is. 1:9] [c]Jude 15

7 [a]Gen. 19:16, 29 [b]Gen. 19:5ff.; Jude 4; 2 Pet. 2:2, 18 [c]2 Pet. 3:17

8 [a]Heb. 11:4

9 [1]Or, *trial* [a]1 Cor. 10:13; Rev. 3:10 [b]Matt. 10:15; Jude 6

10 [1]Lit., *go after* [2]Lit., *glories* [a]2 Pet. 3:3; Jude 16, 18 [b]Jude 8; Ex. 22:28 [c]Titus 1:7

11 [a]Jude 9

12 [a]Jude 10 [b]Jer. 12:3; Col. 2:22

no knowledge, will in [1]the destruction of those creatures also be destroyed,

13 suffering wrong as [a]the wages of doing wrong. They count it a pleasure to [b]revel in the [c]daytime. They are stains and blemishes, [b]reveling in their [1]deceptions, as they [d]carouse with you;

14 having eyes full of adultery and that never cease from sin; [a]enticing [b]unstable souls, having a heart trained in [c]greed, [d]accursed children;

15 forsaking [a]the right way they have gone astray, having followed [b]the way of Balaam, the *son* of Beor, who loved [c]the wages of unrighteousness,

16 but he received a rebuke for his own transgression; [a]*for* a dumb donkey, speaking with a voice of a man, restrained the madness of the prophet.

17 These are [a]springs without water, and mists driven by a storm, [b]for whom the [1]black darkness has been reserved.

18 For speaking out [a]arrogant *words* of [b]vanity they [c]entice by fleshly desires, by [d]sensuality, those who barely [e]escape from the ones who live in error,

19 promising them freedom while they themselves are slaves of corruption; for [a]by what a man is overcome, by this he is enslaved.

20 For if after they have [a]escaped the defilements of the world by [b]the knowledge of the [c]Lord and Savior Jesus Christ, they are again [d]entangled in them and are overcome, [e]the last state has become worse for them than the first.

21 [a]For it would be better for them not to have known the way of righteousness, than having known it, to turn away from [b]the holy commandment [c]delivered to them.

22 It has happened to them according to the true proverb, "[a]A DOG RETURNS TO ITS OWN VOMIT," and, "A sow, after washing, *returns* to wallowing in the mire."

CHAPTER 3

THIS is now, [a]beloved, the second letter I am writing to you in which I am [b]stirring up your sincere mind by way of reminder,

2 that you should [a]remember the words spoken beforehand by [b]the holy prophets and [c]the commandment of the Lord and Savior *spoken* by your apostles.

3 [a]Know this first of all, that [b]in the last days [c]mockers will come with *their* mocking, [d]following after their own lusts,

4 and saying, "[a]Where is the promise of His [b]coming? For *ever* since the fathers [c]fell asleep, all continues just as it was [d]from the beginning of creation."

5 For [1]when they maintain this, it escapes their notice that [a]by the word of God *the* heavens existed long ago and *the* earth was [b]formed out of water and by water,

6 through which [a]the world at that time was [b]destroyed, being flooded with water.

7 But [a]the present heavens and earth by His word are being reserved for [b]fire, kept for [c]the day of judgment and destruction of ungodly men.

8 But do not let this one *fact* escape your notice,

12 [1]Lit., *their destruction also*

13 [1]Some ancient mss. read, *love-feasts*, cf. Jude 12 [a]2 Pet. 2:15 [b]Rom. 13:13 [c]1 Thess. 5:7 [d]Jude 12; 1 Cor. 11:21

14 [a]2 Pet. 2:18 [b]James 1:8; 2 Pet. 3:16 [c]2 Pet. 2:3 [d]Eph. 2:3

15 [a]Acts 13:10 [b]Num. 22:5, 7; Deut. 23:4; Neh. 13:2; Jude 11; Rev. 2:14 [c]2 Pet. 2:13

16 [a]Num. 22:21, 23, 28, 30f.

17 [1]Lit., *blackness of darkness* [a]Jude 12 [b]Jude 13

18 [a]Jude 16 [b]Eph. 4:17 [c]2 Pet. 2:14 [d]2 Pet. 2:2 [e]2 Pet. 2:20; 1:4

19 [a]Rom. 6:16; John 8:34

20 [a]2 Pet. 2:18 [b]2 Pet. 1:2 [c]2 Pet. 1:11; 3:18 [d]2 Tim. 2:4 [e]Matt. 12:45; Luke 11:26

21 [a]Ezek. 18:24; Heb. 6:4ff.; 10:26f.; James 4:17 [b]2 Pet. 3:2; Gal. 6:2; 1 Tim. 6:14 [c]Jude 3

22 [a]Prov. 26:11

1 [a]2 Pet. 3:8, 14, 17; 1 Pet. 2:11 [b]2 Pet. 1:13

2 [a]Jude 17 [b]Luke 1:70; Acts 3:21; Eph. 3:5 [c]2 Pet. 2:21; Gal. 6:2; 1 Tim. 6:14

3 [a]2 Pet. 1:20 [b]1 Tim. 4:1; Heb. 1:2 [c]Jude 18 [d]2 Pet. 2:10

4 [a]Is. 5:19; Jer. 17:15; Ezek. 11:3; 12:22, 27; Mal. 2:17; Matt. 24:48 [b]2 Pet. 3:12; 1 Thess. 2:19 [c]Acts 7:60 [d]Mark 10:6

5 [1]Or, *they are willfully ignorant of this fact*, that [a]Gen. 1:6, 9; Heb. 11:3 [b]Col. 1:17 [Gr.]; Ps. 24:2; 136:6

6 [a]2 Pet. 2:5 [b]Gen. 7:21f.

7 [a]2 Pet. 3:10, 12 [b]Is. 66:15; Dan. 7:9f.; 2 Thess. 1:7; Heb. 12:29 [c]Matt. 10:15; 1 Cor. 3:13; Jude 7

[a]beloved, that with the Lord one day is as a thousand years,
and [b]a thousand years as one day.
9 [a]The Lord is not slow about His promise, as some
count slowness, but [b]is patient toward you, [c]not wishing for
any to perish but for all to come to repentance.
10 But [a]the day of the Lord [b]will come like a thief, in
which [c]the heavens [d]will pass away with a roar and the [e]ele-
ments will be destroyed with intense heat, and [f]the earth and
[1]its works will be [2]burned up.
11 Since all these things are to be destroyed in this way,
what sort of people ought you to be in holy conduct and
godliness,
12 [a]looking for and hastening the coming of the day of
God, on account of which [b]the heavens will be destroyed by
burning, and the [c]elements will melt with intense heat.
13 But according to His [a]promise we are looking for [b]new
heavens and a new earth, [c]in which righteousness dwells.
14 [a]Therefore, [b]beloved, since you look for these things,
be diligent to be [c]found by Him in peace, [d]spotless and
blameless,
15 and regard the [a]patience of our Lord *to be* salvation;
just as also [b]our beloved brother Paul, [c]according to the wisdom given him, wrote to you,
16 as also in all *his* letters, speaking in them of [a]these
things, [b]in which are some things hard to understand, which
the untaught and [c]unstable distort, as *they do* also [d]the rest of
the Scriptures, to their own destruction.
17 You therefore, [a]beloved, knowing this beforehand, [b]be
on your guard lest, being carried away by [c]the error of [d]unprin-
cipled men, you [e]fall from your own steadfastness,
18 but grow in the grace and [a]knowledge of our [b]Lord and
Savior Jesus Christ. [c]To Him *be* the glory, both now and to the
day of eternity. Amen.

8 [a]2 Pet. 3:1 [b]Ps. 90:4

9 [a]Hab. 2:3; Heb. 10:37; Rom. 13:11 [b]Rom. 2:4; Rev. 2:21 [c]1 Tim. 2:4; Rev. 2:21

10 [1]Lit., *the works in it* [2]Some ancient mss. read, *discovered* [a]1 Cor. 1:8 [b]1 Thess. 5:2; Matt. 24:43; Rev. 3:3; 16:15 [c]2 Pet. 3:7, 12 [d]Matt. 24:35; Rev. 21:1 [e]Is. 34:4; 24:19; Mic. 1:4; Gal. 4:3 marg. [f]2 Pet. 3:7

12 [a]1 Cor. 1:7 [b]2 Pet. 3:7, 10 [c]Is. 34:4; 24:19; Mic. 1:4; Gal. 4:3 marg.

13 [a]Is. 65:17; 66:22 [b]Rev. 21:1; Rom. 8:21 [c]Is. 60:21; 65:25; Rev. 21:27

14 [a]2 Pet. 1:10; 1 Cor. 15:58 [b]2 Pet. 3:1 [c]1 Pet. 1:7 [d]Phil. 2:15; 1 Tim. 6:14; James 1:27; 1 Thess. 5:23

15 [a]2 Pet. 3:9 [b]Acts 9:17; 15:25; 2 Pet. 3:2 [c]1 Cor. 3:10; Eph. 3:3

16 [a]2 Pet. 3:14 [b]Heb. 5:11 [c]2 Pet. 2:14 [d]Is. 28:13; 2 Pet. 3:2

17 [a]2 Pet. 3:1 [b]1 Cor. 10:12 [c]2 Pet. 2:18 [d]2 Pet. 2:7 [e]Rev. 2:5

18 [a]2 Pet. 1:2 [b]2 Pet. 1:11; 2:20 [c]Rom. 11:36; 2 Tim. 4:18; Rev. 1:6

THE FIRST EPISTLE OF JOHN

Introduction. Our Joy Complete.

WHAT was [a]from the beginning, what we have [b]heard, what
we have [c]seen with our eyes, what we [d]beheld and our hands
[e]handled, concerning the [f]Word of life—
2 and [a]the life was manifested, and we have [b]seen and
[c]bear witness and proclaim to you [d]the eternal life, which was
[e]with the Father and was [a]manifested to us—
3 what we have [a]seen and [b]heard we proclaim to you also,
that you also may have fellowship with us; and indeed our
[c]fellowship is with the Father, and with His Son Jesus Christ.
4 And [a]these things we write, so that our [b]joy may be
made complete.

1 [a]John 1:1f.; 1 John 2:13, 14 [b]1 John 1:3; Acts 4:20 [c]1 John 1:2; John 19:35; 2 Pet. 1:16 [d]John 1:14; 1 John 4:14 [e]Luke 24:39; John 20:27 [f]John 1:1, 4

2 [a]John 1:4; Rom. 16:26; 1 Tim. 3:16; 1 Pet. 1:20; 1 John 3:5, 8; 5:20 [b]1 John 1:1; John 19:35 [c]1 John 4:14; John 15:27 [d]1 John 2:25; 5:11, 13, 20; John 10:28; 17:3 [e]John 1:1

3 [a]1 John 1:1; John 19:35; 2 Pet. 1:16 [b]1 John 1:1; Acts 4:20 [c]John 17:3, 21; 1 Cor. 1:9

4 [a]1 John 2:1 [b]John 3:29

5 And [a]this is the message we have heard from Him and
announce to you, that [b]God is light, and in Him there is no
darkness at all.
6 [a]If we say that we have fellowship with Him and *yet*
walk in the darkness, we [b]lie and [c]do not practice the truth;
7 but if we [a]walk in the light as [b]He Himself is in the
light, we have fellowship with one another, and [c]the blood of
Jesus His Son cleanses us from all sin.
8 [a]If we say that we have no sin, we are deceiving ourselves, and the [b]truth is not in us.
9 [a]If we confess our sins, He is faithful and righteous to
forgive us our sins and [b]to cleanse us from all unrighteousness.
10 [a]If we say that we have not sinned, we [b]make Him a
liar, and [c]His word is not in us.

Chapter 2

[a]My little children, I am writing [b]these things to you that you
may not sin. And if anyone sins, [c]we have an [1d]Advocate with
the Father, Jesus Christ the righteous;
2 and He Himself is [a]the [1]propitiation for our sins; and
not for ours only, but also [b]for *those of* the whole world.
3 And [a]by this we know that we have come to [b]know
Him, if we [c]keep His commandments.
4 The one who says, "[a]I have come to [b]know Him," and
does not keep His commandments, is a [c]liar, and [d]the truth is
not in him;
5 but whoever [a]keeps His word, in him the [b]love of God
has truly been perfected. [c]By this we know that we are in Him:
6 the one who says he [a]abides in Him [b]ought himself to
walk in the same manner as He walked.
7 [a]Beloved, I am [b]not writing a new commandment to
you, but an old commandment which you [1]have had [c]from the
beginning; the old commandment is the word which you have
heard.
8 [1]On the other hand, I am writing [a]a new commandment to you, which is true in Him and in you, because [b]the
darkness is passing away, and [c]the true light is already shining.
9 The one who says he is in the light and *yet* [a]hates his
[b]brother is in the darkness until now.
10 [a]The one who loves his brother abides in the light and
there is no cause for stumbling in him.
11 But the one who [a]hates his brother is in the darkness
and [b]walks in the darkness, and does not know where he is
going because the darkness has [c]blinded his eyes.
12 I am writing to you, [a]little children, because [b]your sins
are forgiven you for His name's sake.
13 I am writing to you, fathers, because you know Him
[a]who has been from the beginning. I am writing to you, young
men, because [b]you have overcome [c]the evil one. I have written
to you, children, because [d]you know the Father.
14 I have written to you, fathers, because you know Him
[a]who has been from the beginning. I have written to you,
young men, because you are [b]strong, and the [c]word of God
abides in you, and [d]you have overcome the evil one.

5 [a]1 John 3:11; John 1:19 [b]1 Tim. 6:16; James 1:17

6 [a]John 8:12; 2 Cor. 6:14; Eph. 5:8; 1 John 2:11 [b]John 8:55; 1 John 2:4; 4:20 [c]John 3:21

7 [a]Is. 2:5 [b]1 Tim. 6:16 [c]Heb. 9:14; Rev. 7:14; Titus 2:14

8 [a]Job 15:14; Prov. 20:9; Rom. 3:10ff.; James 3:2 [b]1 John 2:4; John 8:44

9 [a]Ps. 32:5; Prov. 28:13 [b]Heb. 9:14; Rev. 7:14; Titus 2:14

10 [a]Job 15:14; Prov. 20:9; Rom. 3:10ff.; James 3:2 [b]1 John 5:10; John 3:33 [c]1 John 2:14

1 [1]Gr., *Paracletos*, one called alongside to help [a]1 John 2:12, 28; 3:7, 18; 4:4; 5:21; John 13:33; Gal. 4:19 [b]1 John 1:4 [c]Rom. 8:34; 1 Tim. 2:5; Heb. 7:25; 9:24 [d]John 14:16

2 [1]Or, *satisfaction* [a]1 John 4:10; Rom. 3:25; Heb. 2:17 [b]1 John 4:14; John 4:42; 11:51f.

3 [a]1 John 2:5; 3:24; 4:13; 5:2 [b]1 John 2:4; 3:6; 4:7f. [c]1 John 3:22, 24; 5:3; John 14:15; 15:10; Rev. 12:17; 14:12

4 [a]Titus 1:10 [b]1 John 3:6; 4:7f. [c]1 John 1:6 [d]1 John 1:8

5 [a]John 14:23 [b]1 John 4:12 [c]1 John 2:3; 3:24; 4:13; 5:2

6 [a]John 15:4 [b]John 13:15; 15:10; 1 Pet. 2:21

7 [1]Lit., *were having* [a]1 John 3:2, 21; 4:1, 7, 11; Heb. 6:9 [b]1 John 3:11, 23; 4:21; 2 John 5 [c]1 John 2:24; 3:11; 2 John 5, 6

8 [1]Lit., *Again* [a]John 13:34 [b]Eph. 5:8; 1 Thess. 5:4f.; Rom. 13:12 [c]John 1:9

9 [a]1 John 2:11; 3:15; 4:20 [b]1 John 3:10, 16; 4:20f.; Acts 1:15

10 [a]1 John 2:10, 11; John 11:9 and ref.

11 [a]1 John 2:9; 3:15; 4:20 [b]John 12:35; 1 John 1:6 [c]2 Cor. 4:4; 2 Pet. 1:9

12 [a]1 John 2:1 [b]1 Cor. 6:11; Acts 13:38

13 [a]1 John 1:1 [b]1 John 2:14; 1 John 4:4; 5:4f.; Rev. 2:7; John 16:33 [c]Matt. 5:37; 1 John 2:14; 3:12; 5:18f. [d]1 John 2:3; John 14:7

14 [a]1 John 1:1 [b]Eph. 6:10 [c]1 John 1:10; John 5:38; 8:37 [d]1 John 2:13

15 Do not love [a]the world, nor the things in the world. [b]If any one loves the world, the love of the Father is not in him.

16 For all that is in the world, [a]the lust of the flesh and [b]the lust of the eyes and [c]the boastful pride of life, is not from the Father, but is from the world.

17 And [a]the world is passing away, and *also* its lusts; but the one who does the will of God abides forever.

18 Children, [a]it is the last hour; and just as you heard that [b]antichrist is coming, [c]even now many antichrists have arisen; from this we know that it is the last hour.

19 [a]They went out from us, but they were not *really* of us; for if they had been of us, they would have remained with us; but *they went out,* [b]in order that [1]it might be shown that they all are not of us.

20 [1]But you have an [a]anointing from [b]the Holy One, and [2c]you all know.

21 I have not written to you because you do not know the truth, but [a]because you do know it, and [1]because no lie is [b]of the truth.

22 Who is the liar but [a]the one who denies that Jesus is the [1]Christ? This is [b]the antichrist, the one who denies the Father and the Son.

23 [a]Whoever denies the Son does not have the Father; the one who confesses the Son has the Father also.

24 As for you, let that abide in you which you heard [a]from the beginning. If what you heard from the beginning abides in you, you also [b]will abide in the Son and in the Father.

25 And [a]this is the promise which He Himself [1]made to us: eternal life.

26 These things I have written to you concerning those who are trying to [a]deceive you.

27 And as for you, the [a]anointing which you received from Him abides in you, and you have no need for any one to teach you; but as His anointing [b]teaches you about all things, and is [c]true and is not a lie, and just as it has taught you, [1]you abide in Him.

28 And now, [a]little children, abide in Him, so that if He [b]should appear, we may have [c]confidence and [d]not [1]shrink away from Him in shame [2]at His [e]coming.

29 If you know that [a]He is righteous, you know that every one also who practices righteousness [b]is [1]born of Him.

Chapter 3

SEE [1a]how great a love the Father has bestowed upon us, that we should be called [b]children of God; and *such* we are. For this reason the world does not know us, because [c]it did not know Him.

2 [a]Beloved, now we are [b]children of God, and [c]it has not appeared as yet that we shall be. We know that, if He [d]should appear, we shall be [e]like Him, because we shall [f]see Him just as He is.

3 And every one who has this [a]hope *fixed* on Him [b]purifies himself, just as He is pure.

4 Every one who practices sin also practices lawlessness; and [a]sin is lawlessness.

15 [a]James 1:27; Rom. 12:2 [b]James 4:4

16 [a]Rom. 13:14; Eph. 2:3; 1 Pet. 2:11 [b]Prov. 27:20 [c]James 4:16

17 [a]1 Cor. 7:31

18 [a]Rom. 13:11; 1 Tim. 4:1; 1 Pet. 4:7 [b]1 John 2:22; 4:3; 2 John 7; Matt. 24:5, 24 [c]1 John 4:1, 3; Mark 13:22

19 [1]Lit., *they might be made manifest* [a]Acts 20:30 [b]1 Cor. 11:19

20 [1]Lit., *And* [2]Some ancient mss. read, *you know all things* [a]1 John 2:27; 2 Cor. 1:21 [b]Mark 1:24; Acts 10:38 [c]1 John 2:27; Prov. 28:5; Matt. 13:11; John 14:26; 1 Cor. 2:15f.

21 [1]Or, know *that* [a]James 1:19; 2 Pet. 1:12; Jude 5 [b]1 John 3:19; John 8:44; 18:37

22 [1]I.e., Messiah [a]1 John 4:3; 2 John 7 [b]1 John 2:18; 4:3; 2 John 7; Matt. 24:5, 24

23 [a]1 John 4:15; 5:1; 2 John 9; John 8:19; 16:3; 17:3

24 [a]1 John 2:7 [b]1 John 1:3; John 14:23; 2 John 9

25 [1]Lit., *promised us* [a]John 3:15; 6:40; 1 John 1:2

26 [a]1 John 3:7; 2 John 7

27 [1]Or, *abide in Him* [a]1 John 2:20; John 14:16 [b]John 14:26; 1 Cor. 2:12; 1 Thess. 4:9 [c]John 14:17

28 [1]Lit., *be put to shame from Him* [2]Or, *in His presence* [a]1 John 2:1 [b]1 John 3:2; Col. 3:4; Luke 17:30 [c]1 John 3:21; 4:17; 5:14; Eph. 3:12 [d]Mark 8:38 [e]1 Thess. 2:19

29 [1]Or, *begotten* [a]1 John 3:7; John 7:18 [b]1 John 3:9; 4:7; 5:1, 4, 18 [3 John 11]; John 1:13; 3:3

1 [1]Lit., *what kind of love* [a]1 John 4:10; John 3:16 [b]1 John 3:2, 10; John 1:12; 11:52; Rom. 8:16 [c]John 15:21; 16:3; 15:18

2 [a]1 John 2:7 [b]1 John 3:1, 10; John 1:12; 11:52; Rom. 8:16 [c]Rom. 8:19, 23f. [d]1 John 2:28; Col. 3:4; Luke 17:30 [e]Rom. 8:29; 2 Pet. 1:4 [f]John 17:24; 2 Cor. 3:18

3 [a]Rom. 15:12; 1 Pet. 1:3 [b]2 Cor. 7:1; 2 Pet. 3:13f.; 1 John 2:6; John 17:19

4 [a]1 John 5:17; Rom. 4:15

5 And you know that He [a]appeared in order to [b]take
away sins; and [c]in Him there is no sin.
6 No one who abides in Him [a]sins; no one who sins has
seen Him or [1b]knows Him.
7 [a]Little children, let no one [b]deceive you; [c]the one who
practices righteousness is righteous, just as He is righteous;
8 the one who practices sin is [a]of the devil; for the devil
[1]has sinned from the beginning. [b]The Son of God [c]appeared
for this purpose, [d]that He might destroy the works of the devil.
9 No one who is [1a]born of God [b]practices sin, because
His seed abides in him; and he cannot sin, because he is [1]born
of God.
10 By this the [a]children of God and the [b]children of the
devil are obvious; any one who does not practice righteousness
is not of God, nor the one who [c]does not love his [d]brother.
11 [a]For this is the message [b]which you have heard from
the beginning, [c]that we should love one another;
12 not as [a]Cain *who* was of [b]the evil one, and slew his
brother. And for what reason did he slay him? Because [c]his
deeds were evil, and his brother's were righteous.
13 Do not marvel, brethren, if [a]the world hates you.
14 We know that we have [a]passed out of death into life,
[b]because we love the brethren. He who does not love abides in
death.
15 Every one who [a]hates his brother is a murderer; and
you know that [b]no murderer has eternal life abiding in him.
16 We know love by this, that [a]He laid down His life for
us; and [b]we ought to lay down our lives for the [c]brethren.
17 But [a]whoever has the world's goods, and beholds his
brother in need and [b]closes his [1]heart [2]against him, [c]how does
the love of God abide in him?
18 [a]Little children, let us not love with word or with
tongue, but in deed and [b]truth.
19 We shall know by this that we are [a]of the truth, and
shall [1]assure our heart [2]before Him,
20 in whatever our heart condemns us; for God is greater
than our heart, and knows all things.
21 [a]Beloved, if our heart does not condemn us, we have
[b]confidence [1]before God;
22 and [a]whatever we ask we receive from Him, because we
[b]keep His commandments and do [c]the things that are pleasing
in His sight.
23 And this is His commandment, that we [1a]believe in [b]the
name of His Son Jesus Christ, and love one another, just as
[c]He [2]commanded us.
24 And the one who [a]keeps His commandments [b]abides in
Him, and He in him. And [c]we know by this that [d]He abides in
us, by the Spirit which He has given us.

Chapter 4

[a]BELOVED, do not believe every [b]spirit, but test the spirits
to see whether they are from God; because [c]many false prophets have gone out into the world.
2 By this you know the Spirit of God: [a]every spirit that
[b]confesses that [c]Jesus Christ has come in the flesh is from God;

5 [a]1 John 1:2; 3:8 [b]John 1:29; 1 Pet. 1:18-20; 1 John 2:2 [c]2 Cor. 5:21; 1 John 2:29

6 [1]Or, *has known*
[a]1 John 3:9 [b]1 John 2:3; 3 John 11

7 [a]1 John 2:1 [b]1 John 2:26 [c]1 John 2:29

8 [1]Lit., *sins*
[a]1 John 3:10; Matt. 13:38; John 8:44 [b]Matt. 4:3 [c]1 John 3:5 [d]John 16:11; John 12:31

9 [1]Or, *begotten*
[a]1 John 2:29; 4:7; 5:1, 4, 18 [3 John 11]; John 1:13; 3:3 [b]1 John 3:6; 5:18; James 1:18; 1 Pet. 1:23

10 [a]1 John 3:1, 2; John 1:12; 11:52; Rom. 8:16 [b]1 John 3:8; Matt. 13:38; John 8:44 [c]1 John 4:8; Rom. 13:8ff.; Col. 3:14; 1 Tim. 1:5 [d]1 John 2:9

11 [a]1 John 1:5 [b]1 John 2:7 [c]John 13:34f.; 15:12; 1 John 4:7, 11f., 21; 2 John 5

12 [a]Gen. 4:8 [b]1 John 2:13f.; Matt. 5:37 [c]Ps. 38:20; Prov. 29:10; John 8:40, 41

13 [a]John 15:18; 17:14

14 [a]John 5:24 [b]1 John 2:10; John 13:35

15 [a]Matt. 5:21f.; John 8:44 [b]Gal. 5:20f.; Rev. 21:8

16 [a]John 15:13; John 10:11 [b]Phil. 2:17; 1 Thess. 2:8 [c]1 John 2:9

17 [1]Lit., *inward parts* [2]Lit., *from*
[a]James 2:15f. [b]Deut. 15:7 [c]1 John 4:20

18 [a]1 John 3:7; 1 John 2:1 [b]2 John 1; 3 John 1

19 [1]Or, *persuade* [2]Or, *before Him; because if our heart . . .*
[a]1 John 2:21

21 [1]Lit., *toward*
[a]1 John 2:7 [b]1 John 5:14; 2:28

22 [a]Job 22:26f.; Matt. 21:22; 7:7; John 9:31 [b]1 John 2:3 [c]John 8:29; Heb. 13:21

23 [1]Or, *believe the name* [2]Or, *gave us a commandment*
[a]John 6:29 [b]John 1:12; 2:23; 3:18 [c]John 13:34; 15:12; 1 John 2:8

24 [a]1 John 2:3 [b]1 John 2:6, 24; 4:15; John 6:56; 10:38 [c]1 John 4:13; John 14:17; Rom. 8:9, 14, 16; 1 Thess. 4:8 [d]1 John 2:5

1 [a]1 John 2:7 [b]Jer. 29:8; 1 Cor. 12:10; 2 Thess. 2:2; 1 Thess. 5:20f. [c]1 John 2:18; Jer. 14:14; 2 Pet. 2:1

2 [a]1 Cor. 12:3 [b]1 John 2:23 [c]1 John 1:2; John 1:14

3 and every spirit that [a]does not confess Jesus is not from
God; and this is the *spirit* of the [b]antichrist, of which you have
heard that it is coming, and [c]now it is already in the world.
4 You are from God, [a]little children, and [b]have overcome
them; because [c]greater is He who is in you than [d]he who is in
the world.
5 [a]They are from the world; therefore they speak *as* from
the world, and the world listens to them.
6 [a]We are from God; [b]he who knows God listens to us;
[c]he who is not from God does not listen to us. By this we know
[d]the spirit of truth and [e]the spirit of error.
7 [a]Beloved, let us [b]love one another, for love is from
God; and [c]every one who loves is [1d]born of God and [e]knows
God.
8 The one who does not love does not know God, for
[a]God is love.
9 By this the love of God was manifested [1a]in us, that
[b]God has sent His [2]only begotten Son into the world so that
we might live through Him.
10 In this is love, [a]not that we [1]loved God, but that [b]He
loved us and sent His Son *to be* [c]the propitiation for our sins.
11 [a]Beloved, if God so loved us, [b]we also ought to love one
another.
12 [a]No one has beheld God at any time; if we love one
another, God abides in us, and His [b]love is perfected in us.
13 [a]By this we know that we abide in Him and He in us,
because He has given us of His Spirit.
14 And we have beheld and [a]bear witness that the Father
has [b]sent the Son *to be* the Savior of the world.
15 [a]Whoever confesses that [b]Jesus is the Son of God, God
[c]abides in him, and he in God.
16 And [a]we have come to know and have believed the love
which God has [1b]for us. [c]God is love, and the one who [d]abides
in love abides in God, and God abides in him.
17 By this, [a]love is perfected with us, that we may have
[b]confidence in [c]the day of judgment; because [d]as He is, so also
are we in this world.
18 There is no fear in love; but [a]perfect love casts out fear,
because fear [1]involves punishment, and the one who fears is
not [b]perfected in love.
19 [a]We love, because He first loved us.
20 [a]If some one says, "I love God," and [b]hates his brother,
he is a [c]liar; for [d]the one who does not love his brother whom
he has seen, [1e]cannot love God whom he has not seen.
21 And [a]this commandment we have from Him, that the
one who loves God [b]should love his brother also.

CHAPTER 5

[a]WHOEVER believes that Jesus is the [1]Christ is [2b]born of
God; and whoever loves the [3]Father [c]loves the *child* [2]born of
Him.
2 [a]By this we know that [b]we love the children of God,
when we love God and [1]observe His commandments.

3 [a]2 John 7; 1 John 2:22 [b]1 John 2:22; 2:18 [c]1 John 2:18; 2 Thess. 2:3-7

4 [a]1 John 2:1 [b]1 John 2:13 [c]1 John 3:20; 2 Kin. 2:16; Rom. 8:31 [d]John 12:31

5 [a]John 15:19; 17:14, 16

6 [a]1 John 4:4; John 8:23 [b]John 8:47; 10:3ff.; 18:37 [c]1 Cor. 14:37 [d]John 14:17 [e]1 Tim. 4:1

7 [1]Or, *begotten* [a]1 John 2:7 [b]1 John 3:11 [c]1 John 5:1 [d]1 John 2:29 [e]1 John 2:3; 1 Cor. 8:3

8 [a]1 John 4:16; 1 John 4:7

9 [1]Or, *in our case* [2]Or, *unique*, only one of His kind [a]1 John 4:16; John 9:3 [b]John 3:16f.; 1 John 4:10; 5:11

10 [1]Some mss. read, *had loved* [a]Rom. 5:8, 10; 1 John 4:19 [b]John 3:16f.; 1 John 4:9; 5:11 [c]1 John 2:2

11 [a]1 John 2:7 [b]1 John 4:7

12 [a]John 1:18; 1 Tim. 6:16; 1 John 4:20 [b]1 John 2:5; 4:17f.

13 [a]1 John 3:24; Rom. 8:9

14 [a]1 John 1:2; John 15:27 [b]John 3:17; 4:42; 1 John 2:2

15 [a]1 John 2:23 [b]1 John 5:5; 3:23; 4:2; 5:1; Rom. 10:9 [c]1 John 2:24; 3:24

16 [1]Lit., *in* [a]John 6:69 [b]1 John 4:9; John 9:3 [c]1 John 4:8; 4:7 [d]1 John 4:12f.

17 [a]1 John 2:5; 4:12 [b]1 John 2:28 [c]Matt. 10:15 [d]1 John 2:6; 3:1, 7, 16; John 17:22

18 [1]Lit., *has* [a]Rom. 8:15; Gal. 4:30f. [b]1 John 4:12

19 [a]1 John 4:10

20 [1]Some mss. read, *how can he love God . . . seen?* [a]1 John 1:6, 8, 10; 2:4 [b]1 John 2:9, 11 [c]1 John 1:6 [d]1 John 3:17 [e]1 John 4:12; 1 Pet. 1:8

21 [a]Matt. 5:43f.; 22:37ff.; John 13:34; Lev. 19:18 [b]1 John 3:11

1 [1]I.e., Messiah [2]Or, *begotten* [3]Lit., *one who begets* [a]1 John 4:2; 4:15; 2:22f. [b]1 John 5:4, 18; 2:29; John 1:13; 3:3 marg. [c]John 8:42

2 [1]Lit., *do* [a]1 John 2:5 [b]1 John 3:14

3 For [a]this is the love of God, that we [b]keep His commandments; and [c]His commandments are not burdensome.
4 For whatever is [1a]born of God [b]overcomes the world;
and this is the victory that has overcome the world—our faith.
5 And who is the one who overcomes the world, but he
who [a]believes that Jesus is the Son of God?
6 This is the one who came [a]by water and blood, Jesus
Christ; not [1]with the water only, but [1]with the water and [1]with
the blood.
7 And it is [a]the Spirit who bears witness, because the
Spirit is the truth.
8 For there are [a]three that bear witness, [1]the Spirit and
the water and the blood; and the three are [2]in agreement.
9 [a]If we receive the witness of men, the witness of God is
greater; for the witness of God is this, that [b]He has borne
witness concerning His Son.
10 The one who believes in the Son of God [a]has the witness in himself; the one who does not believe God has [b]made
Him a liar, because he has not believed in the witness that God
has borne concerning His Son.
11 And the witness is this, that God has given us [a]eternal
life, and [b]this life is in His Son.
12 [a]He who has the Son has the life; he who does not have
the Son of God does not have the life.
13 [a]These things I have written to you who [b]believe in the
name of the Son of God, in order that you may know that you
have [c]eternal life.
14 And this is [a]the confidence which we have [1]before Him,
that, [b]if we ask anything according to His will, He hears us.
15 And if we know that He hears us *in* whatever we ask,
[a]we know that we have the requests which we have asked from
Him.
16 If any one sees his brother [1]committing a sin not *lead-*
ing to death, [a]he shall ask and *God* will for him give life to
those who commit sin not *leading* to death. [b]There is a sin
leading to death; [c]I do not say that he should make request for
this.
17 [a]All unrighteousness is sin, and [b]there is a sin not *lead-*
ing to death.
18 [a]We know that [b]no one who is [1]born of God sins; but
He who was [1]born of God [c]keeps him and [d]the evil one does
not [e]touch him.
19 [a]We know that [b]we are of God, and [c]the whole world
lies in *the power of* the evil one.
20 And [a]we know that [b]the Son of God has come, and has
[c]given us understanding, in order that we might know [d]Him
who is true, and we [e]are in Him who is true, in His Son Jesus
Christ. [f]This is the true God and [g]eternal life.
21 [a]Little children, guard yourselves from [b]idols.

3 [a]John 14:15; 2 John 6 [b]1 John 2:3 [c]Matt. 11:30; 23:4

4 [1]Or, *begotten* [a]1 John 5:1, 18; 2:29; John 1:13; 3:3 marg. [b]1 John 2:13; 4:4

5 [a]1 John 4:15; 1 John 5:1

6 [1]Lit., *in* [a]John 19:34

7 [a]John 15:26; 16:13-15 [Matt. 3:16f.]

8 [1]A few late mss. read *in heaven, the Father, the Word, and the Holy Spirit, and these three are one. And there are three that bear witness on earth, the Spirit . . .* [2]Lit., *for the one thing* [a]Matt. 18:16

9 [a]John 5:34, 37; 8:18 [b]Matt. 3:17; John 5:32, 37

10 [a]Rom. 8:16; Gal. 4:6; Rev. 12:17 [b]1 John 1:10; John 3:18, 33

11 [a]1 John 5:13, 20; 1:2; 2:25; 4:9 [b]John 1:4

12 [a]John 3:15f., 36

13 [a]John 20:31 [b]1 John 3:23 [c]1 John 5:11, 20; 1:2; 2:25; 4:9

14 [1]Lit., *toward* [a]1 John 3:21f.; 2:28 [b]1 John 3:22; Matt. 7:7; John 14:13

15 [a]1 John 5:18, 19, 20

16 [1]Lit., *sinning* [a]James 5:15 [b]Heb. 6:4-6; 10:26; Num. 15:30 [c]Jer. 7:16; 14:11

17 [a]1 John 3:4 [b]1 John 2:1f.; 5:16

18 [1]Or, *begotten* [a]1 John 5:15, 19, 20 [b]1 John 3:9 [c]James 1:27; Jude 21 [d]1 John 2:13 [e]John 14:30

19 [a]1 John 5:15, 18, 20 [b]1 John 4:6 [c]John 12:31; 17:15; Gal. 1:4

20 [a]1 John 5:15, 18, 19 [b]1 John 5:5; John 8:42 [c]Luke 24:45 [d]John 17:3; Rev. 3:7 [e]John 1:18; 14:9; 1 John 2:23; Rev. 3:7 [f]1 John 1:2 [g]1 John 5:11

21 [a]1 John 2:1 [b]1 Cor. 10:7, 14; 1 Thess. 1:9

THE SECOND EPISTLE OF

JOHN

Salutation. "Walk According to His Commandments." "Abide in the Teachings of Christ." Farewell.

[a]
THE elder to the [b]chosen [c]lady and her children, whom I
[d]love in truth; and not only I, but also all who [e]know the truth,
2 for [a]the sake of the truth which abides [b]in us and will be
[c]with us forever:
3 [a]Grace, mercy *and* peace will be with us, from God the
Father and from Jesus Christ, the Son of the Father, in truth
and love.
4 [a]I was very glad to find *some* of your children walking
in truth, just as we have received commandment *to do* from
the Father.
5 And now I ask you, lady, [a]not as writing to you a new
commandment, but the one which we have had [a]from the
beginning, that we [b]love one another.
6 And [a]this is love, that we walk according to His commandments. This is the commandment, [b]just as you have
heard [c]from the beginning, that you should walk in it.
7 For [a]many deceivers have [b]gone out into the world,
those who [c]do not acknowledge Jesus Christ *as* coming in the
flesh. This is [a]the deceiver and the [d]antichrist.
8 [a]Watch yourselves, [b]that you might not lose what [1]we
have accomplished, but that you may receive a full reward.
9 Any one who [1]goes too far and [a]does not abide in the
teaching of Christ, does not have God; the one who abides in
the teaching, he has both the Father and the Son.
10 If any one comes to you and does not bring this teaching, [a]do not receive him into *your* house, and do not give him
a greeting;
11 for the one who gives him a greeting [a]participates in his
evil deeds.
12 [a]Having many things to write to you, I do not want to
do so with paper and ink; but I hope to come to you and speak
face to face, that [1]your [b]joy may be made full.
13 The children of your [a]chosen sister greet you.

1 [a]3 John 1; 1 Pet. 5:1; Acts 11:30 [b]2 John 13; Rom. 16:13 [Gr.]; 1 Pet. 5:13 [c]2 John 5 [d]1 John 3:18; 3 John 1; 2 John 3 [e]John 8:32; 1 Tim. 2:4

2 [a]2 Pet. 1:12 [b]1 John 1:8 [c]John 14:16

3 [a]1 Tim. 1:2; Rom. 1:7

4 [a]3 John 3f.

5 [a]1 John 2:7 [b]1 John 3:11

6 [a]1 John 5:3; 2:5 [b]1 John 2:24 [c]1 John 2:7

7 [a]1 John 2:26 [b]1 John 4:1; 2:19 [c]1 John 4:2f. [d]1 John 2:18

8 [1]Some ancient mss. read, *you*
[a]Mark 13:9 [b]Heb. 10:35; 1 Cor. 3:8

9 [1]Lit., *goes on ahead*
[a]John 8:31; 7:16; 1 John 2:23

10 [a]Rom. 16:17; 1 Kin. 13:16f.

11 [a]1 Tim. 5:22; Jude 23

12 [1]Some ancient mss. read, *our*
[a]3 John 13, 14 [b]1 John 1:4; John 3:29

13 [a]2 John 1

THE THIRD EPISTLE OF

JOHN

Address to Gaius. Prayer for His Prosperity. "The One Who Does Good is of God." "Peace be to You."

[a]THE elder to the beloved Gaius, whom I [b]love in truth.
2 Beloved, I pray that in all respects you may prosper and
be in good health, just as your soul prospers.
3 For I [1a]was very glad when [b]brethren came and bore
witness to your truth, *that is,* how you [a]are walking in truth.
4 I have no greater joy than [1]this, to hear of [a]my children
[b]walking in the truth.
5 Beloved, you are acting faithfully in whatever you accomplish for the [a]brethren, and especially *when they are*
[b]strangers;
6 and they bear witness to your love before the church;
and you will do well to [a]send them on their way in a manner
[b]worthy of God.
7 For they went out for the sake of [a]the Name, [b]accept-
ing nothing from the Gentiles.
8 Therefore we ought to [1]support such men, that we may
be fellow-workers [2]with the truth.
9 I wrote something to the church; but Diotrephes, who
loves to [a]be first among them, does not accept [1]what we say.
10 For this reason, [a]if I come, I will call attention to his
deeds which he does, unjustly accusing us with wicked words;
and not satisfied with this, neither does he himself [b]receive the
[c]brethren, and he forbids those who desire *to do so,* and [d]puts
them out of the church.
11 Beloved, [a]do not imitate what is evil, but what is good.
[b]The one who does good is of God; [c]the one who does evil has
not seen God.
12 Demetrius [a]has received a good testimony from every
one, and from the truth itself; and we also bear witness, and
[b]you know that our witness is true.
13 [a]I had many things to write to you, but I am not willing
to write *them* to you with pen and ink;
14 but I hope to see you shortly, and we shall speak face to
face. [a]Peace *be* to you. The friends greet you. Greet the
friends [b]by name.

1 [a]2 John 1 [b]1 John 3:18; 2 John 1

3 [1]Or, *am very glad when brethren come and bear witness*
[a]2 John 4 [b]3 John 5, 10; Acts 1:15; Gal. 6:10

4 [1]Lit., *these things, that I hear*
[a]1 John 2:1; 1 Cor. 4:14f.; 2 Cor. 6:13; Gal. 4:19; 1 Thess. 2:11; 1 Tim. 1:2; 2 Tim. 1:2; Philem. 10
[b]2 John 3

5 [a]3 John 3, 10; Acts 1:15; Gal. 6:10 [b]Rom. 12:13; Heb. 13:2

6 [a]Acts 15:3; Titus 3:13 [b]1 Thess. 2:12; Col. 1:10

7 [a]Acts 5:41; John 15:21; Phil. 2:9 [b]Acts 20:33, 35

8 [1]Or, *receive such men as guests* [2]Or, *for*

9 [1]Lit., *us*
[a]2 John 9 marg.

10 [a]2 John 12 [b]3 John 5; 2 John 10 [c]3 John 3, 5; Acts 1:15; Gal. 6:10 [d]John 9:34

11 [a]Ps. 34:14; 37:27; [b]1 John 2:29; 3:10 [c]1 John 3:6

12 [a]Acts 6:3; 1 Tim. 3:7 [b]John 21:24; John 19:35

13 [a]2 John 12

14 [a]1 Pet. 5:14; Eph. 6:23; John 20:19, 21, 26 [b]John 10:3

THE EPISTLE OF
JUDE

General Salutation. "Contend Earnestly for the Faith." The Warnings of History to the Ungodly.

[1a]JUDE, a [b]bond-servant of Jesus Christ, and brother of [2]James,
to [c]those who are the called, beloved in God the Father, and
[d]kept for Jesus Christ:
2 [a]May mercy and peace and love [b]be multiplied to you.
3 [a]Beloved, while I was making every effort to write you
about our [b]common salvation, I felt the necessity to write to
you appealing that you [c]contend earnestly for [d]the faith which
was once for all [e]delivered to [f]the [1]saints.
4 For certain persons have [a]crept in unnoticed, those
who were long beforehand [1b]marked out for this condemnation, ungodly persons who turn [c]the grace of our God into
[d]licentiousness and [e]deny our only Master and Lord, Jesus
Christ.
5 Now I desire to [a]remind you, though [b]you know all
things once for all, that [1]the Lord, [c]after saving a people out of
the land of Egypt, [2]subsequently destroyed those who did not
believe.
6 And [a]angels who did not keep their own domain, but
abandoned their proper abode, He has [b]kept in eternal bonds
under darkness for the judgment of the great day.
7 Just as [a]Sodom and Gomorrah and the [b]cities around
them, since they in the same way as these indulged in gross
immorality and [c]went after strange flesh, are exhibited as an
[1d]example, in undergoing the [e]punishment of eternal fire.
8 Yet in the same manner these men also by dreaming
[a]defile the flesh, and [a]reject authority, and [a]revile [1]angelic
majesties.
9 But [a]Michael [b]the archangel, when he disputed with
the devil and argued about [c]the body of Moses did not dare
pronounce against him a railing judgment, but said, "[d]THE
LORD REBUKE YOU."
10 But [a]these men revile the things which they do not
understand; and [b]the things which they know by instinct, [a]like
unreasoning animals, by these things they are [1]destroyed.
11 Woe to them! For they have gone [a]the way of Cain,
and for pay [1]they have rushed headlong into [b]the error of
Balaam, and [c]perished in the rebellion of Korah.
12 These men are those who are [1]hidden reefs [a]in your
love-feasts when they feast with you [b]without fear, caring for
themselves; [c]clouds without water, [d]carried along by winds;
autumn trees without fruit, [2]doubly dead, [e]uprooted;
13 [a]wild waves of the sea, casting up [b]their own [1]shame
like foam; wandering stars, [c]for whom the [2]black darkness has
been reserved forever.
14 And about these also [a]Enoch, *in* the seventh *genera-*
tion from Adam, prophesied, saying, "[b]Behold, the Lord came
with [1]many thousands of His holy ones,
15 [a]to execute judgment upon all, and to convict all the

1 [1]Gr. *Judas* [2]Lit., *Jacob* [a]Matt. 13:55; Mark 6:3; [Luke 6:16; John 14:22; Acts 1:13?] [b]Rom. 1:1 [c]Rom. 1:6f. [d]John 17:11f.; Jude 21; 1 Pet. 1:5

2 [a]Gal. 6:16; 1 Tim. 1:2 [b]1 Pet. 1:2; 2 Pet. 1:2

3 [1]I.e., true believers; lit., *holy ones* [a]Heb. 6:9; Jude 1, 17, 20 [b]Titus 1:4 [c]1 Tim. 6:12 [d]Jude 20; Acts 6:7 [e]2 Pet. 2:21 [f]Acts 9:13

4 [1]Or, *written about* [a]2 Tim. 3:6; Gal. 2:4 [b]1 Pet. 2:8 [c]Acts 11:23 [d]2 Pet. 2:7 [e]2 Pet. 2:1; 2 Tim. 2:12; Titus 1:16; 1 John 2:22

5 [1]Some ancient mss. read, *Jesus* [2]Lit., *the second time* [a]2 Pet. 1:12f.; 3:1f. [b]1 John 2:20 [c]1 Cor. 10:5-10; Heb. 3:16f.

6 [a]2 Pet. 2:4 [b]2 Pet. 2:9

7 [1]Or, *example of eternal fire, in undergoing punishment* [a]2 Pet. 2:6 [b]Deut. 29:23; Hos. 11:8 [c]2 Pet. 2:2 [d]2 Pet. 2:6 [e]Matt. 25:41; 2 Thess. 1:8f.; 2 Pet. 3:7

8 [1]Lit., *glories* [a]2 Pet. 2:10

9 [a]Dan. 10:13, 21; 12:1; Rev. 12:7 [b]1 Thess. 4:16; 2 Pet. 2:11 [c]Deut. 34:6 [d]Zech. 3:2

10 [1]Lit., *corrupted* [a]2 Pet. 2:12 [b]Phil. 3:19

11 [1]Lit., *they have poured themselves out* [a]Gen. 4:3-8; Heb. 11:4; 1 John 3:12 [b]2 Pet. 2:15; Num. 31:16; Rev. 2:14 [c]Num. 16:1-3, 31-35

12 [1]Or, *stains* [2]Lit., *twice* [a]2 Pet. 2:13 and marg.; 1 Cor. 11:20ff. [b]Ezek. 34:2, 8, 10 [c]Prov. 25:14; 2 Pet. 2:17 [d]Eph. 4:14 [e]Matt. 15:13

13 [1]Or, *shameless deeds* [2]Lit., *blackness of darkness;* or, *nether gloom* [a]Is. 57:20 [b]Phil. 3:19 [c]2 Pet. 2:17; Jude 6

14 [1]Lit., *His holy ten thousands* [a]Gen. 5:18, 21ff. [b]Deut. 33:2; Matt. 16:27; Dan. 7:10; Heb. 12:22

15 [a]2 Pet. 2:6ff.

ungodly of all their ungodly deeds which they have done in an
ungodly way, and of all the harsh things which [b]ungodly sinners have spoken against Him."
16 These are [a]grumblers, finding fault, [b]following after
their *own* lusts, [1]they speak [c]arrogantly, flattering people [d]for
the sake of *gaining an* advantage.
17 But you, [a]beloved, [b]ought to remember the words that
were spoken beforehand by [c]the apostles of our Lord Jesus
Christ;
18 that they were saying to you, "[a]In the last time there
shall be mockers, [b]following after their own ungodly lusts."
19 These are the ones who cause divisions, [1a]worldly-
minded, [2]devoid of the Spirit.
20 But you, [a]beloved, [b]building yourselves up on your
most holy [a]faith; [c]praying in the Holy Spirit;
21 keep yourselves in the love of God, [a]waiting anxiously
for the mercy of our Lord Jesus Christ to eternal life.
22 And [1]have mercy on some, who are doubting;
23 save others, [a]snatching them out of the fire; and on
some have mercy with fear, [b]hating even the garment polluted
by the flesh.
24 [a]Now to Him who is able to keep you from stumbling,
and to [b]make you stand in the presence of His glory blameless
with [c]great joy,
25 to the [a]only [b]God our Savior, through Jesus Christ our
Lord, [c]*be* glory, majesty, dominion and authority, [d]before all
time and now and [1]forever. Amen.

15 [b]1 Tim. 1:9

16 [1]Lit., *their mouth speaks* [a]Num. 16:11, 41; 1 Cor. 10:10 [b]2 Pet. 2:10; Jude 18 [c]2 Pet. 2:18 [d]2 Pet. 2:3

17 [a]Jude 3 [b]2 Pet. 3:2 [c]Heb. 2:3

18 [a]2 Pet. 3:3; Acts 20:29; 1 Tim. 4:1; 2 Tim. 3:1f.; 4:3 [b]Jude 4, 16

19 [1]Or, *merely natural* [2]Lit., *not having* [a]1 Cor. 2:14f.; James 3:15

20 [a]Jude 3 [b]Col. 2:7; 1 Thess. 5:11 [c]Eph. 6:18

21 [a]Titus 2:13; Heb. 9:28; 2 Pet. 3:12

22 [1]Some ancient mss. read, *convince*

23 [a]Amos 4:11; Zech. 3:2; 1 Cor. 3:15 [b]Rev. 3:4; Zech. 3:3f.

24 [a]Rom. 16:25 [b]2 Cor. 4:14 [c]1 Pet. 4:13

25 [1]Lit., *to all the ages* [a]John 5:44; 1 Tim. 1:17 [b]Luke 1:47 [c]Rom. 11:36 [d]Heb. 13:8

THE REVELATION OF JOHN

The Revelation of Jesus Christ.

THE Revelation of Jesus Christ, which [a]God gave Him to
[b]show to His bond-servants, [c]the things which must shortly
take place; and He sent and [1]communicated *it* [d]by His angel to
His bond-servant [e]John;
2 who bore witness to [a]the word of God and to [b]the
testimony of Jesus Christ, *even* to all that he saw.
3 [a]Blessed is he who reads and those who hear the words
of the prophecy, and [1]heed the things which are written in it;
[b]for the time is near.
4 [a]John to [b]the seven churches that are in [c]Asia: [d]Grace
to you and peace, from [e]Him who is and who was and who is to
come; and from [f]the seven Spirits who are before His throne;
5 and from Jesus Christ, [a]the faithful witness, the [b]first-
born of the dead, and the [c]ruler of the kings of the earth. To
Him who [d]loves us, and released us from our sins [1]by His
blood,
6 and He has made us *to be* a [a]kingdom, [a]priests to [1b]His
God and Father; [c]to Him *be* the glory and the dominion
forever and ever. Amen.

1 [1]Or, *signified* [a]Rev. 5:7; John 17:8 [b]Rev. 22:6 [c]Rev. 1:19; Dan. 2:28f. [d]Rev. 17:1; 19:9f.; 21:9; 22:16 [e]Rev. 1:4, 9; 22:8

2 [a]Rev. 1:9; 6:9; 20:4; 12:17; 1 Cor. 1:6 [b]Rev. 12:17

3 [1]Or, *keep* [a]Rev. 22:7; Luke 11:28 [b]Rev. 22:10; 3:11; 22:7, 12; Rom. 13:11

4 [a]Rev. 1:1, 9; 22:8 [b]Rev. 1:20; 1:11 [c]Acts 2:9 [d]Rom. 1:7 [e]Rev. 1:8; 4:8; Ex. 3:14; Rev. 16:5; 1:17; Heb. 13:8; Is. 41:4 [f]Rev. 3:1; 4:5; 5:6; Is. 11:2; Rev. 8:2

5 [1]Or, *in* [a]Rev. 3:14; John 8:14; 18:37; 1 Tim. 6:13; Rev. 19:11 [b]1 Cor. 15:20; Col. 1:18 [c]Rev. 17:14; 19:16; 1 Tim. 6:15; Dan. 2:47 [d]Rom. 8:37

6 [1]Or, *God and His Father* [a]Rev. 20:6; 1 Pet. 2:5, 9; Ex. 19:6; Is. 61:6 [b]Rom. 15:6 [c]Rom. 11:36

7 [a]BEHOLD, HE IS COMING WITH THE CLOUDS, and [b]every
eye will see Him, even those who pierced Him; AND ALL THE
TRIBES OF THE EARTH WILL [c]MOURN OVER HIM. Even so. Amen.
8 "I am [a]the Alpha and the Omega," says the [b]Lord God,
"[c]who is and who was and who is to come, the Almighty."
9 [a]I, John, your [b]brother and [c]fellow-partaker in the tribulation and [d]kingdom and [1][e]perseverance *which are* in Jesus,
was on the island called Patmos, [f]because of the word of God
and the testimony of Jesus.
10 I was [1][a]in the Spirit on [b]the Lord's day, and I heard
behind me a loud voice [c]like *the sound* of a trumpet,
11 saying, "[a]Write in a [1]book what you see, and send *it* to
the [b]seven churches: to [c]Ephesus and to [d]Smyrna and to [e]Per-
gamum and to [f]Thyatira and to [g]Sardis and to [h]Philadelphia
and to [i]Laodicea."
12 And I turned to see the voice that was speaking with
me. And having turned I saw [a]seven golden lampstands;
13 and [a]in the middle of the lampstands one [b]like [1]a son of
man, [c]clothed in a robe reaching to the feet, and [d]girded across
His breasts with a golden girdle.
14 And His head and His [a]hair were white like white wool,
like snow; and [b]His eyes were like a flame of fire;
15 and His [a]feet *were* like burnished bronze, when it has
been caused to glow in a furnace, and His [b]voice *was* like the
sound of many waters.
16 And in His right hand He held [a]seven stars; and out of
His mouth came a [b]sharp two-edged sword; and His [c]face was
like [d]the sun [1]shining in its strength.
17 And when I saw Him, I [a]fell at His feet as a dead man.
And He [b]laid His right hand upon me, saying, "[c]Do not be
afraid; [d]I am the first and the last,
18 and the [a]living One; and I [1][b]was dead, and behold, I am
alive forevermore, and I have [c]the keys of death and of Hades.
19 "[a]Write therefore [b]the things which you have seen, and
the things which are, and the things which shall take place
[c]after these things.
20 "As for the [a]mystery of the [b]seven stars which you saw in
My right hand, and the [c]seven golden lampstands, the [b]seven
stars are the angels of [d]the seven churches, and the seven
[e]lampstands are the seven churches.

CHAPTER 2

"TO the angel of the church in [a]Ephesus write:
'The One who holds [b]the seven stars in His right hand, the
One who walks [1][c]among the seven golden lampstands, says
this:
2 '[a]I know your deeds and your toil and [1]perseverance,
and that you cannot endure evil men, and you [b]put to the test
those who call themselves [c]apostles, and they are not, and you
found them *to be* false;
3 and you have [1]perseverance and have endured [a]for My
name's sake, and have not grown weary.
4 'But I have *this* against you, that you have [a]left your
first love.
5 'Remember therefore from where you have fallen, and

7 [a]Matt. 16:27f.; 24:30; Dan. 7:13 [b]Zech. 12:10; John 19:37 [c]Luke 23:28

8 [a]Rev. 21:6; 22:13; Is. 41:4 [b]Rev. 4:8; 11:17; 15:3; 16:7; 21:22; 19:6 [c]Rev. 1:4

9 [1]Or, *steadfastness* [a]Rev. 1:1 [b]Acts 1:15 [c]2 Cor. 1:7; Phil. 4:14; Matt. 20:23; Acts 14:22 [d]Rev. 1:6; 2 Tim. 2:12 [e]Rev. 3:10; 2 Thess. 3:5 [f]Rev. 1:2

10 [1]Or, *in spirit* [a]Rev. 4:2; 17:3; 21:10; Matt. 22:43 [b]Acts 20:7 [c]Rev. 4:1

11 [1]Or, *scroll* [a]Rev. 1:19; 1:2 [b]Rev. 1:4, 20 [c]Rev. 2:1 [d]Rev. 2:8 [e]Rev. 2:12 [f]Rev. 2:18, 24; Acts 16:14 [g]Rev. 3:1, 4 [h]Rev. 3:7 [i]Rev. 3:14; Col. 2:1

12 [a]Rev. 1:20; 2:1; Ex. 25:37; 37:23; Zech. 4:2

13 [1]Or, *the Son of Man* [a]Rev. 2:1 [b]Rev. 14:14; Ezek. 1:26; Dan. 7:13; 10:16 [c]Dan. 10:5 [d]Rev. 15:6

14 [a]Dan. 7:9 [b]Rev. 2:18; 19:12; Dan. 7:9; 10:6

15 [a]Rev. 2:18; Ezek. 1:7; Dan. 10:6 [b]Rev. 14:2; 19:6; Ezek. 43:2

16 [1]Lit., *shines* [a]Rev. 1:20; 2:1; 3:1 [b]Rev. 2:12, 16; 19:15; Is. 49:2; Heb. 4:12 [c]Matt. 17:2; Rev. 10:1 [d]Judg. 5:31

17 [a]Dan. 8:17; 10:9, 10, 15 [b]Dan. 8:18; 10:10, 12 [c]Matt. 14:27; 17:7 [d]Rev. 2:8; 22:13; Is. 41:4; 44:6; 48:12

18 [1]Lit., *became* [a]Luke 24:5; Rev. 4:9f. [b]Rev. 2:8; Rom. 6:9; Rev. 10:6; 15:7 [c]Rev. 9:1; 20:1; Job 38:17; Matt. 16:19; 11:23

19 [a]Rev. 1:11 [b]Rev. 1:12-16 [c]Rev. 4:1

20 [a]Rom. 11:25 [b]Rev. 1:16; 2:1; 3:1 [c]Rev. 1:12; 2:1; Ex. 25:37; 37:23; Zech. 4:2 [d]Rev. 1:4, 11 [e]Matt. 5:14f.

1 [1]Lit., *in the middle of* [a]Rev. 1:11 [b]Rev. 1:16 [c]Rev. 1:12f.

2 [1]Or, *steadfastness* [a]Rev. 2:19; 3:1, 8, 15 [b]1 John 4:1; John 6:6 [c]2 Cor. 11:13

3 [1]Note vs. 2 [a]John 15:21

4 [a]Matt. 24:12; Jer. 2:2

[a]repent and [b]do the [1]deeds you did at first; or else I am coming
to you, and will remove your [c]lampstand out of its place —
unless you repent.
6 'Yet this you do have, that you hate the deeds of the
[a]Nicolaitans, which I also hate.
7 '[a]He who has an ear, let him hear what the Spirit says to
the churches. [b]To him who overcomes, I will grant to eat of
[c]the tree of life, which is in the [d]Paradise of God.'
8 "And to the angel of the church in [a]Smyrna write:
'[b]The first and the last, who [1][c]was dead, and has come to life,
says this:
9 'I know your [a]tribulation and your [b]poverty (but you are
[b]rich), and the blasphemy by those who [c]say they are Jews and
are not, but are a synagogue of [d]Satan.
10 'Do not fear what you are about to suffer. Behold, the
devil is about to cast some of you into prison, that you may be
[a]tested, and you will have tribulation [b]ten days. Be [c]faithful
until death, and I will give you [d]the crown of life.
11 '[a]He who has an ear, let him hear what the Spirit says to
the churches. [b]He who overcomes shall not be hurt by the
[c]second death.'
12 "And to the angel of the church in [a]Pergamum write:
'The One who has [b]the sharp two-edged sword says this:
13 'I know where you dwell, where [a]Satan's throne is; and
you hold fast My name, and did not deny [b]My faith, even in
the days of Antipas My [c]witness, My [d]faithful one, who was
killed among you, [e]where Satan dwells.
14 'But [a]I have a few things against you, because you have
there some who hold the [b]teaching of Balaam, who kept teaching Balak to put a stumbling block before the sons of Israel,
[c]to eat things sacrificed to idols, and to commit *acts of*
immorality.
15 'Thus you also have some who in the same way hold the
teaching of the [a]Nicolaitans.
16 '[a]Repent therefore; or else [b]I am coming to you quickly,
and I will make war against them with [c]the sword of My
mouth.
17 '[a]He who has an ear, let him hear what the Spirit says to
the churches. [a]To him who overcomes, to him I will give *some*
of the hidden [b]manna, and I will give him a white stone, and a
[c]new name written on the stone [d]which no one knows but he
who receives it.'
18 "And to the angel of the church in [a]Thyatira write:
'[b]The Son of God, [c]who has [1]eyes like a flame of fire, and
His feet are like burnished bronze, says this:
19 '[a]I know your deeds, and your love and faith and service
and [1]perseverance, and that your [2]deeds of late are greater
than [3]at first.
20 'But [a]I have *this* against you, that you tolerate the woman [b]Jezebel, who calls herself a prophetess, and she teaches
and leads my bond-servants astray, so that they [c]commit *acts*
of immorality and eat things sacrificed to idols.
21 'And [a]I gave her time to repent; and she [b]does not want
to repent of her immorality.
22 'Behold, [1]I will cast her [2]upon a bed *of sickness*, and

5 [1]Lit., *first deeds* [a]Rev. 2:16, 22; 3:3, 19 [b]Rev. 2:2; Heb. 10:32 [c]Rev. 1:20; Matt. 5:14ff.; Phil. 2:15

6 [a]Rev. 2:15

7 [a]Rev. 2:17; 3:6, 13, 22; 13:9; Matt. 11:15 [b]Rev. 2:11, 17, 26; 3:5, 12, 21; 21:7 [c]Rev. 22:2, 14; Gen. 2:9 [3:22]; Prov. 3:18; 11:30; 13:12; 15:4 [d]Ezek. 31:8 [Sept.]; Luke 23:43

8 [1]Lit., *became* [a]Rev. 1:11 [b]Rev. 1:17 [c]Rev. 1:18

9 [a]Rev. 1:9 [b]2 Cor. 6:10; 8:9; James 2:5 [c]Rev. 3:9 [d]Rev. 2:13, 24; Matt. 4:10

10 [a]Rev. 3:10; 13:14ff. [b]Dan. 1:12, 14 [c]Rev. 2:13; 17:14; 12:11 [d]1 Cor. 9:25; Rev. 3:11

11 [a]Rev. 2:7, 17, 29; 3:6, 13, 22; 13:9; Matt. 11:15 [b]Rev. 2:7, 17, 26; 3:5, 12, 21; 21:7 [c]Rev. 20:6, 14; 21:8

12 [a]Rev. 1:11 [b]Rev. 2:16; 1:16

13 [a]Rev. 2:13, 24; Matt. 4:10 [b]Rev. 14:12; 1 Tim. 5:8 [c]Rev. 1:5; 11:3; 17:6 marg.; Acts 22:20 [d]Rev. 2:10; 17:14; 12:11 [e]Rev. 2:9

14 [a]Rev. 2:20 [b]2 Pet. 2:15 [c]Rev. 2:20; Acts 15:29; 1 Cor. 10:20

15 [a]Rev. 2:6

16 [a]Rev. 2:5 [b]Rev. 22:7, 20 [c]Rev. 1:16; 2 Thess. 2:8

17 [a]Rev. 2:7 [b]John 6:49f. [c]Is. 56:5; 62:2; 65:15 [d]Rev. 19:12; Rev. 14:3

18 [1]Lit., *His eyes* [a]Rev. 2:24; 1:11 [b]Matt. 4:3 [c]Rev. 1:14f.

19 [1]Or, *steadfastness* [2]Lit., *last deeds* [3]Lit., *the first* [a]Rev. 2:2

20 [a]Rev. 2:14 [b]1 Kin. 16:31; 21:25; 2 Kin. 9:7 [c]Rev. 2:14; Acts 15:29; 1 Cor. 10:20

21 [a]Rom. 2:4; 2 Pet. 3:9 [b]Rev. 9:20f.; 16:9, 11; Rom. 2:5

22 [1]Lit., *I cast* [2]Lit., *into*

those who [a]commit adultery with her into great tribulation,
unless they repent of [3]her deeds.
23 'And I will kill her children with [1]pestilence; and all the
churches will know that I am He who [a]searches the [2]minds and
hearts; and I will give to each one of you according to your
deeds.
24 'But I say to you, the rest who are in [a]Thyatira, who do
not hold this teaching, who have not known the [b]deep things
of Satan, as they call them — I [c]place no other burden on you.
25 'Nevertheless [a]what you have, hold fast [b]until I come.
26 'And [a]he who overcomes, and he who keeps My deeds
[b]until the end, [c]TO HIM I WILL GIVE AUTHORITY OVER THE
[1]NATIONS;
27 AND HE SHALL [1a]RULE THEM WITH A ROD OF IRON, [b]AS THE
VESSELS OF THE POTTER ARE BROKEN TO PIECES, as I also have
received *authority* from My Father;
28 and I will give him [a]the morning star.
29 '[a]He who has an ear, let him hear what the Spirit says to
the churches.'

Chapter 3

"AND to the angel of the church in [a]Sardis write:
'He who has [b]the seven Spirits of God, and [c]the seven stars,
says this: [d]I know your deeds, that you have a name that you
are alive, and you are [e]dead.
2 'Wake up, and strengthen the things that remain, which
were about to die; for I have not found your deeds completed
in the sight of My God.
3 '[a]Remember therefore [1]what you have received and
heard; and keep *it,* and [a]repent. If therefore you will not wake
up, [b]I will come [c]like a thief, and you will not know at [d]what
hour I will come upon you.
4 'But you have a few [1a]people in [b]Sardis who have not
[c]soiled their garments; and they will walk with Me [d]in white;
for they are worthy.
5 '[a]He who overcomes shall thus be clothed in [b]white
garments; and I will not [c]erase his name from the book of life,
and [d]I will confess his name before My Father, and before His
angels.
6 '[a]He who has an ear, let him hear what the Spirit says to
the churches.'
7 "And to the angel of the church in [a]Philadelphia write:
'[b]He who is holy, [c]who is true, who has [d]the key of David,
who opens and no one will shut, and who shuts and no one
opens, says this:
8 '[a]I know your [1]deeds. Behold, I have put before you [b]an
open door which no one can shut, because you have a little
power, and have kept My word, and [c]have not denied My
name.
9 'Behold, I [1]will cause *those* of [a]the synagogue of Satan,
who say that they are Jews, and are not, but lie — behold, I will
make them to [b]come and bow down [2]at your feet, and to know
that [c]I have loved you.
10 'Because you have [a]kept the word of [b]My [1]perseverance,
[c]I also will keep you from the hour of [2d]testing, that *hour*

22 [3]Some mss. read, *their* [a]Rev. 17:2; 18:9

23 [1]Or, *death* [2]Lit., *kidneys,* figurative for inner man [a]Ps. 7:9; 26:2; 139:1; Jer. 11:20; 17:10; Luke 16:15; Acts 1:24; Rom. 8:27; Matt. 16:27

24 [a]Rev. 2:18 [b]1 Cor. 2:10 [c]Acts 15:28

25 [a]Rev. 3:11 [b]John 21:22

26 [1]Or, *Gentiles* [a]Rev. 2:7 [b]Matt. 10:22; Heb. 3:6 [c]Ps. 2:8; Rev. 3:21; 20:4

27 [1]Or, *shepherd* [a]Rev. 12:5; 19:15 [b]Is. 30:14; Jer. 19:11

28 [a]Rev. 22:16; 1 John 3:2

29 [a]Rev. 2:7

1 [a]Rev. 1:11 [b]Rev. 1:4 [c]Rev. 1:16 [d]Rev. 3:8, 15; 2:2 [e]1 Tim. 5:6

3 [1]Lit., *how* [a]Rev. 2:5 [b]Rev. 2:5 [c]Rev. 16:15; 1 Thess. 5:2; 2 Pet. 3:10 [d]Matt. 24:43

4 [1]Lit., *names* [a]Rev. 11:13 marg.; Acts 1:15 marg. [b]Rev. 1:11 [c]Jude 23 [d]Rev. 3:5, 18; 4:4; 6:11; 7:9, 13f.; 19:14; 19:8; Eccles. 9:8

5 [a]Rev. 2:7 [b]Rev. 3:4 [c]Rev. 13:8; 17:8; 20:12, 15; 21:27; Luke 10:20 [d]Matt. 10:32; Luke 12:8

6 [a]Rev. 2:7

7 [a]Rev. 1:11 [b]Rev. 6:10 [c]Rev. 3:14; 19:11; 1 John 5:20 [d]Is. 22:22; Matt. 16:19; Rev. 1:18; Job 12:14

8 [1]Or, *deeds (behold . . . shut), that you* [a]Rev. 3:1 [b]Acts 14:27 [c]Rev. 2:13

9 [1]Lit., *give* [2]Lit., *before* [a]Rev. 2:9 [b]Is. 45:14; 49:23; 60:14 [c]Is. 43:4; John 17:23

10 [1]Or, *steadfastness* [2]Or, *temptation* [a]Rev. 3:8; John 17:6 [b]Rev. 1:9 [c]2 Pet. 2:9; 2 Tim. 2:12 [d]Rev. 2:10

which is about to come upon the whole [3e]world, to [4]test [f]those
who dwell upon the earth.
11 '[a]I am coming quickly; [b]hold fast what you have, in
order that no one take your [c]crown.
12 '[a]He who overcomes, I will make him a [b]pillar in the
temple of My God, and he will not go out from it any more;
and I will write upon him the [c]name of My God, and [d]the
name of the city of My God, [e]the new Jerusalem, which comes
down out of heaven from My God, and My [f]new name.
13 '[a]He who has an ear, let him hear what the Spirit says to
the churches.'
14 "And to the angel of the church in [a]Laodicea write:
'[b]The Amen, [c]the faithful and true Witness, [d]the [1]Beginning
of the creation of God, says this:
15 '[a]I know your deeds, that you are neither cold nor hot;
[b]I would that you were cold or hot.
16 'So because you are lukewarm, and neither hot nor cold,
I will [1]spit you out of My mouth.
17 'Because you say, "[a]I am rich, and have become wealthy,
and have need of nothing," and you do not know that you
are wretched and miserable and poor and blind and naked.
18 'I advise you to [a]buy from Me [b]gold refined by fire, that
you may become rich, and [c]white garments, that you may
clothe yourself, and *that* [d]the shame of your nakedness may
not be revealed, and eyesalve to anoint your eyes, that you
may see.
19 '[a]Those whom I love, I reprove and discipline; be zealous therefore, and [b]repent.
20 'Behold, I stand [a]at the door and [b]knock; if any one
hears My voice and opens the door, [c]I will come in to him, and
will dine with him, and he with Me.
21 '[a]He who overcomes, I will grant to him [b]to sit down
with Me on My throne, as [c]I also overcame and sat down with
My Father on His throne.
22 '[a]He who has an ear, let him hear what the Spirit says to
the churches.' "

Chapter 4

AFTER [a]these things I looked, and behold, [b]a door *standing*
open in heaven, and the first voice which I had heard, [c]like *the*
sound of a trumpet speaking with me, [1]said, "[d]Come up here,
and I will [e]show you what must take place after these things."
2 Immediately I was [1a]in the spirit; and behold, [b]a throne
was standing in heaven, and [c]One sitting on the throne.
3 And He who was sitting *was* like a [a]jasper stone and a
[b]sardius in appearance; and *there was* a [1c]rainbow around the
throne, like an [d]emerald in appearance.
4 And [a]around the throne *were* [b]twenty-four thrones; and
upon the thrones *I saw* [c]twenty-four elders [d]sitting, clothed in
[e]white garments, and [f]golden crowns on their heads.
5 And from the throne proceed [a]flashes of lightning and
sounds and peals of thunder. And *there were* [b]seven lamps of
fire burning before the throne, which are [c]the seven Spirits of
God;
6 and before the throne *there was*, as it were, a [a]sea of

10 [3]Lit., *inhabited earth* [4]Or, *tempt* [e]Rev. 16:14; Matt. 24:14 [f]Rev. 6:10; 8:13; 11:10; 13:8, 14; 17:8

11 [a]Rev. 22:7, 12, 20; 1:3 [b]Rev. 2:25 [c]Rev. 2:10

12 [a]Rev. 3:5 [b]1 Kin. 7:21; Jer. 1:18; Gal. 2:9 [c]Rev. 14:1; 22:4 [d]Rev. 21:2; Ezek. 48:35 [e]Rev. 21:2, 10; Gal. 4:26; Heb. 13:14 [f]Rev. 2:17

13 [a]Rev. 3:6

14 [1]I.e., origin or source [a]Rev. 1:11 [b]Is. 65:16 marg.; 2 Cor. 1:20 [c]Rev. 1:5; 3:7 [d]John 1:3; Col. 1:18; Rev. 21:6; 22:13; Gen. 49:3; Deut. 21:17; Prov. 8:22 marg.

15 [a]Rev. 3:1 [b]Rom. 12:11

16 [1]Lit., *vomit*

17 [a]Hos. 12:8; Zech. 11:5; 1 Cor. 4:8; Matt. 5:3

18 [a]Is. 55:1; Matt. 13:44 [b]1 Pet. 1:7 [c]Rev. 3:4 [d]Rev. 16:15

19 [a]Heb. 12:6; 1 Cor. 11:32 [b]Rev. 2:5

20 [a]Matt. 24:33; James 5:9 [b]Luke 12:36; John 10:3 [c]John 14:23

21 [a]Rev. 2:7 [b]Rev. 20:4; 2:26; Matt. 19:28; 2 Tim. 2:12 [c]Rev. 5:5; 6:2; 17:14; John 16:33

22 [a]Rev. 2:7

1 [1]Lit., *saying* [a]Rev. 1:12ff., 19 [b]Rev. 19:11; Ezek. 1:1 [c]Rev. 1:10 [d]Rev. 11:12 [e]Rev. 1:19; 22:6

2 [1]Or, *in spirit* [a]Rev. 1:10 [b]Rev. 4:9f.; 1 Kin. 22:19; Is. 6:1; Ezek. 1:26; Dan. 7:9 [c]Rev. 4:9

3 [1]Or, *halo* [a]Rev. 21:11 [b]Rev. 21:20 [c]Ezek. 1:28; Rev. 10:1 [d]Rev. 21:19

4 [a]Rev. 4:6; 5:11; 7:11 [b]Rev. 11:16 [c]Rev. 4:10; 5:6, 8, 14; 19:4 [d]Rev. 20:4; 2:26; Matt. 19:28; 2 Tim. 2:12 [e]Rev. 3:18 [f]Rev. 4:10

5 [a]Rev. 8:5; 11:19; 16:18; Ex. 19:16 [b]Zech. 4:2; Ex. 25:37 [c]Rev. 1:4

6 [a]Rev. 15:2; 21:18, 21; Ezek. 1:22

glass like crystal; and in the [1]center and [b]around the throne,
[c]four living creatures [d]full of eyes in front and behind.
7 [a]And the first creature *was* like a lion, and the second
creature like a calf, and the third creature had a face like that
of a man, and the fourth creature *was* like a flying eagle.
8 And the [a]four living creatures, each one of them having
[b]six wings, are [c]full of eyes around and within; and [d]day and
night [1]they do not cease to say,
"[e]HOLY, HOLY, HOLY, *is* THE [f]LORD GOD, THE ALMIGHTY,
[g]who was and who is and who is to come."
9 And when the living creatures give glory and honor and
thanks to Him who [a]sits on the throne, to [b]Him who lives
forever and ever,
10 the [a]twenty-four elders will [b]fall down before Him who
[c]sits on the throne, and will worship [d]Him who lives forever
and ever, and will cast their [e]crowns before the throne, saying,
11 "[a]Worthy art Thou, our Lord and our God, to receive
glory and honor and power; for Thou [b]didst create
all things, and because of Thy will they [1]existed, and
were created."

6 [1]Lit., *middle of the throne and around . . .* [b]Rev. 4:4 [c]Ezek. 1:5; Rev. 4:8f.; 5:6; 6:1, 6; 7:11; 14:3; 15:7; 19:4 [d]Ezek. 1:18; 10:12

7 [a]Ezek. 1:10; 10:14

8 [1]Lit., *they have no rest, saying,* [a]Ezek. 1:5; Rev. 4:6, 9; 5:6; 6:1, 6; 7:11; 14:3; 15:7; 19:4 [b]Is. 6:2 [c]Ezek. 1:18; 10:12 [d]Rev. 14:11 [e]Is. 6:3 [f]Rev. 1:8 [g]Rev. 1:4

9 [a]Rev. 4:2; Is. 6:1; Ps. 47:8 [b]Rev. 10:6; 15:7; Deut. 32:40; Dan. 4:34; 12:7

10 [a]Rev. 4:4 [b]Rev. 5:8, 14; 7:11; 11:16; 19:4 [c]Rev. 4:2; Is. 6:1; Ps. 47:8 [d]Rev. 10:6; 15:7; Deut. 32:40; Dan. 4:34; 12:7 [e]Rev. 4:4

11 [1]Lit., *were* [a]Rev. 5:12; 1:6 [b]Rev. 10:6; 14:7; Acts 14:15

CHAPTER 5

AND I saw [1]in the right hand of Him who [a]sat on the throne
a [2b]book written inside and on the back, [c]sealed up with seven
seals.
2 And I saw a [a]strong angel proclaiming with a loud
voice, "Who is worthy to open the [1]book and to break its
seals?"
3 And no one [a]in heaven, or on the earth, or under the
earth, was able to open the [1]book, or to look into it.
4 And I *began* to weep greatly, because no one was found
worthy to open the [1]book, or to look into it;
5 and one of the elders *said to me, "Stop weeping; behold, the [a]Lion that is [b]from the tribe of Judah, the [c]Root of
David, has overcome so as to open the [1]book and its seven
seals."
6 And I saw [1]between the throne (with the four living
creatures) and [a]the elders a [b]Lamb standing, as if [c]slain, having
seven [d]horns and [e]seven eyes, which are [f]the seven Spirits of
God, sent out into all the earth.
7 And He came, and He took [a]*it* out of the right hand of
Him who [a]sat on the throne.
8 And when He had taken the [1]book, the [a]four living
creatures and the [b]twenty-four elders [c]fell down before the
[d]Lamb, having each one a [e]harp, and [f]golden bowls full of
incense, which are the [g]prayers of the [2]saints.
9 And they *sang a [a]new song, saying,
"[b]Worthy art Thou to take the [1]book, and to break its
seals; for Thou wast [c]slain, and didst [d]purchase for
God with Thy blood *men* from [e]every tribe and
tongue and people and nation.
10 "And Thou hast made them *to be* a [a]kingdom and
[a]priests to our God; and they will [b]reign upon the
earth."
11 And I looked, and I heard the voice of many angels

1 [1]Lit., *upon* [2]Or, *scroll* [a]Rev. 5:7, 13; 4:9 [b]Ezek. 2:9, 10 [c]Is. 29:11; Dan. 12:4

2 [1]Or, *scroll* [a]Rev. 10:1; 18:21

3 [1]Or, *scroll* [a]Rev. 5:13; Phil. 2:10

4 [1]Or, *scroll*

5 [1]Or, *scroll* [a]Gen. 49:9 [b]Heb. 7:14 [c]Rev. 22:16; Is. 11:1, 10; Rom. 15:12

6 [1]Lit., *in the middle of the throne and of the four living creatures, and in the middle of the elders* [a]Rev. 5:8, 14; 4:4 [b]Rev. 5:8, 12f.; 13:8; John 1:29 [c]Rev. 5:9, 12; 13:8 [d]Dan. 8:3f. [e]Zech. 3:9; 4:10 [f]Rev. 1:4

7 [a]Rev. 5:1

8 [1]Or, *scroll* [2]I.e., true believers; lit., *holy ones* [a]Rev. 5:6, 11, 14; 4:6 [b]Rev. 5:6, 14; 4:4 [c]Rev. 4:10 [d]Rev. 5:6, 12f.; 13:8; John 1:29 [e]Rev. 14:2; 15:2 [f]Rev. 15:7 [g]Rev. 8:3f.; Ps. 141:2

9 [1]Or, *scroll* [a]Rev. 14:3; 15:3; Ps. 40:3; 98:1; 149:1; Is. 42:10 [b]Rev. 4:11 [c]Rev. 5:6, 12; 13:8 [d]Rev. 14:3f.; 1 Cor. 6:20 [e]Rev. 7:9; 11:9; 13:7; 14:6; 10:11; 17:15; Dan. 3:4; 5:19

10 [a]Rev. 1:6 [b]Rev. 20:4; 3:21

[a]around the throne and the [b]living creatures and the [c]elders;
and the number of them was [d]myriads of myriads, and thousands of thousands;
12 saying with a loud voice,
"[a]Worthy is the [b]Lamb that was [b]slain to receive power and riches and wisdom and might and honor and
glory and blessing."
13 And [a]every created thing which is in heaven and on the
earth and under the earth and on the sea, and all things in
them, I heard saying,
"To Him who [b]sits on the throne, and to the [c]Lamb,
[d]*be* blessing and honor and glory and dominion forever
and ever."
14 And the [a]four living creatures kept saying, "[b]Amen."
And the [c]elders [d]fell down and worshiped.

Chapter 6

1 AND I saw when the [a]Lamb broke one of the [b]seven seals,
and I heard one of the [c]four living creatures saying as with a
[d]voice of thunder, "Come.[1]"
2 And I looked, and behold, a [a]white horse, and he who
sat on it had a bow; and [b]a crown was given to him; and he
went out [c]conquering, and to conquer.
3 And when He broke the second seal, I heard the [a]sec-
ond living creature saying, "Come.[1]"
4 And another, [a]a red horse, went out; and to him who
sat on it, it was granted to [b]take peace from the earth, and that
men should slay one another; and a great sword was given to
him.
5 And when He broke the third seal, I heard the [a]third
living creature saying, "Come.[1]" And I looked, and behold, a
[b]black horse; and he who sat on it had a [c]pair of scales in his
hand.
6 And I heard as it were a voice in the center of the [a]four
living creatures saying, "A [1]quart of wheat for a [2]denarius, and
three [1]quarts of barley for a [2]denarius; and [b]do not harm the
oil and the wine."
7 And when He broke the fourth seal, I heard the voice
of the [a]fourth living creature saying, "Come.[1]"
8 And I looked, and behold, an [1a]ashen horse; and he
who sat on it had the name "[b]Death"; and [b]Hades was following with him. And authority was given to them over a fourth
of the earth, [c]TO KILL WITH SWORD AND WITH FAMINE AND WITH
[2]PESTILENCE AND BY THE WILD BEASTS OF THE EARTH.
9 And when He broke the fifth seal, I saw [a]underneath
the [b]altar the [c]souls of those who had been slain [d]because of
the word of God, and because of the [e]testimony which they
had maintained;
10 and they cried out with a loud voice, saying, "[a]How
long, O [1b]Lord, [c]holy and true, [2]wilt Thou refrain from [d]judg-
ing and avenging our blood on [e]those who dwell on the
earth?"
11 And [a]there was given to each of them a white robe; and
they were told that they should [b]rest for a little while longer,
[c]until *the number of* their fellow-servants and their brethren

11 [a]Rev. 4:4 [b]Rev. 5:6, 8, 14; 4:6 [c]Rev. 5:6, 14; 4:4 [d]Dan. 7:10; Rev. 9:16; Heb. 12:22; Jude 14

12 [a]Rev. 1:6; 4:11; 5:9 [b]Rev. 5:6, 13; 13:8; John 1:29

13 [a]Phil. 2:10; Rev. 5:3 [b]Rev. 5:1 [c]Rev. 5:6, 12f. 13:8; John 1:29 [d]Rom. 11:36; Rev. 1:6

14 [a]Rev. 5:6, 8, 11; 4:6 [b]1 Cor. 14:16; Rev. 7:12; 19:4 [c]Rev. 5:6, 8; 4:4 [d]Rev. 4:10

1 [1]Some mss. add, *and see* [a]Rev. 5:6, 12f.; 13:8; John 1:29 [b]Rev. 5:1 [c]Rev. 5:6, 8, 11, 14; 4:6 [d]Rev. 14:2; 19:6

2 [a]Rev. 19:11; Zech. 1:8; 6:3f. [b]Rev. 14:14; 9:7; 19:12; Zech. 6:11 [c]Rev. 3:21

3 [1]Some mss. add, *and see* [a]Rev. 4:7

4 [a]Zech. 1:8; 6:2 [b]Matt. 10:34

5 [1]Some mss. add, *and see* [a]Rev. 4:7 [b]Zech. 6:2 [c]Ezek. 4:16

6 [1]Lit., *choenix;* a dry measure almost equal to a quart [2]A denarius was worth about 18 cents in silver, equal to a day's wage [a]Rev. 4:6f. [b]Rev. 7:3; 9:4

7 [1]Some mss. add, *and see* [a]Rev. 4:7

8 [1]Or, *sickly pale* [2]Or, *death* [a]Zech. 6:3 [b]Rev. 1:18; 20:13f.; Prov. 5:5; Hos. 13:14; Matt. 11:23 [c]Jer. 15:2f.; 24:10; 29:17f. Ezek. 5:12, 17; 14:21

9 [a]Ex. 29:12; Lev. 4:7; John 16:2 [b]Rev. 14:18; 16:7 [c]Rev. 20:4 [d]Rev. 1:2, 9 [e]Rev. 12:17

10 [1]Or, *Master* [2]Lit., *dost Thou not judge and avenge* [a]Zech. 1:12 [b]2 Pet. 2:1; Luke 2:29 [c]Rev. 3:7 [d]Rev. 19:2; Deut. 32:43; Ps. 79:10; Luke 18:7 [e]Rev. 3:10

11 [a]Rev. 3:5; 7:9; 3:4 [b]Rev. 14:13; 2 Thess. 1:7; Heb. 4:10 [c]Heb. 11:40

who were to be killed even as they had been, should be [d]com-
pleted also.
12 And I looked when He broke the sixth seal, and there
was a great [a]earthquake; and the [b]sun became black as [c]sack-
cloth *made* of hair, and the whole moon became like blood;
13 and [a]the stars of the sky fell to the earth, [b]as a fig tree
casts its unripe figs when shaken by a great wind.
14 And [a]the sky was split apart like a scroll when it is rolled
up; and [b]every mountain and island were moved out of their
places.
15 And [a]the kings of the earth and the great men and the
[1]commanders and the rich and the strong and every slave and
free man, hid themselves in the caves and among the rocks of
the mountains;
16 and they *[a]said to the mountains and to the rocks,
"Fall on us and hide us from the [1]presence of Him [b]who sits on
the throne, and from the [c]wrath of the Lamb;
17 for [a]the great day of their wrath has come; and [b]who is
able to stand?"

Chapter 7

AFTER this I saw [a]four angels standing at the [b]four corners
of the earth, holding back [c]the four winds of the earth, [d]so that
no wind should blow on the earth or on the sea or on any tree.
2 And I saw another angel ascending [a]from the rising of
the sun, having the [b]seal of [c]the living God; and he cried out
with a loud voice to the [d]four angels to whom it was granted to
harm the earth and the sea,
3 saying, "[a]Do not harm the earth or the sea or the trees,
until we have [b]sealed the bond-servants of our God on their
[c]foreheads."
4 And I heard the [a]number of those who were sealed,
[b]one hundred and forty-four thousand sealed from every tribe
of the sons of Israel:
5 from the tribe of Judah, twelve thousand *were* sealed,
from the tribe of Reuben twelve thousand, from the tribe of
Gad twelve thousand,
6 from the tribe of Asher twelve thousand, from the tribe
of Naphtali twelve thousand, from the tribe of Manasseh
twelve thousand,
7 from the tribe of Simeon twelve thousand, from the
tribe of Levi twelve thousand, from the tribe of Issachar twelve
thousand,
8 from the tribe of Zebulun twelve thousand, from the
tribe of Joseph twelve thousand, from the tribe of Benjamin,
twelve thousand *were* sealed.
9 After these things I looked, and behold, a great multitude, which no one could count, from [a]every nation and *all*
tribes and peoples and tongues, standing [b]before the throne
and [c]before the Lamb, clothed in [d]white robes, and [e]palm
branches *were* in their hands;
10 and they cry out with a loud voice, saying,
"[a]**S**alvation to our God [b]who sits on the throne, and to the
Lamb."
11 And all the angels were standing [a]around the throne

11 [d]Acts 20:24; 2 Tim. 4:7

12 [a]Rev. 8:5; 11:13; 16:18; Matt. 24:7 [b]Matt. 24:29 [c]Is. 50:3; Matt. 11:21

13 [a]Rev. 8:10; 9:1; Matt. 24:29 [b]Is. 34:4

14 [a]Is. 34:4; Rev. 20:11; 21:1; 2 Pet. 3:10 [b]Rev. 16:20; Is. 54:10; Jer. 4:24; Ezek. 38:20; Nah. 1:5

15 [1]Lit., *chiliarch*, in command of one thousand troops
[a]Is. 2:10f., 19, 21; 24:21; Rev. 19:18

16 [1]Lit., *face*
[a]Luke 23:30; Rev. 9:6 [b]Rev. 4:9; 5:1 [c]Mark 3:5

17 [a]Is. 63:4; Jer. 30:7; Joel 1:15; 2:1f., 11, 31; Zeph. 1:14f.; Rev. 16:14 [b]Ps. 76:7; Nah. 1:6; Mal. 3:2; Luke 21:36

1 [a]Rev. 9:14 [b]Rev. 20:8; Is. 11:12; Ezek. 7:2 [c]Jer. 49:36; Zech. 6:5; Matt. 24:31; [d]Rev. 7:3; 8:7; 9:4

2 [a]Rev. 16:12; Is. 41:2 [b]Rev. 9:4; 7:3 [c]Matt. 16:16 [d]Rev. 9:14

3 [a]Rev. 6:6 [b]Rev. 7:3-8; John 3:33 [c]Rev. 14:1; 22:4; Ezek. 9:4, 6; Rev. 13:16; 14:9; 20:4

4 [a]Rev. 9:16 [b]Rev. 14:1, 3

9 [a]Rev. 5:9 [b]Rev. 7:15 [c]Rev. 22:3 [d]Rev. 6:11; 7:14 [e]Lev. 23:40

10 [a]Rev. 12:10; 19:1; Ps. 3:8 [b]Rev. 22:3

11 [a]Rev. 4:4

and *around* [a]the elders and the [b]four living creatures; and they [c]fell on their faces before the throne and worshiped God,

12 saying,

"[a]**A**men, [b]blessing and glory and wisdom and thanksgiving and honor and power and might, *be* to our God forever and ever. [a]Amen."

13 And one of the elders [a]answered, saying to me, "These who are clothed in the [b]white robes, who are they, and from where have they come?"

14 And I [1]said to him, "My lord, you know." And he said to me, "These are the ones who come out of the [a]great tribulation, and they have [b]washed their robes and made them [c]white in the [d]blood of the Lamb.

15 "For this reason, they are [a]before the throne of God; and they [b]serve Him day and night in His [1c]temple; and [d]He who sits on the throne shall spread His [e]tabernacle over them.

16 "[a]They shall hunger no more, neither thirst any more; neither shall the sun [1]beat down on them, nor any heat;

17 for the Lamb in the center of the throne shall be their [a]shepherd, and shall guide them to springs of the [1b]water of life; and [c]God shall wipe every tear from their eyes."

Chapter 8

AND when He broke the [a]seventh seal, there was [b]silence in heaven for about half an hour.

2 And I saw [a]the seven angels who stand before God; and seven [b]trumpets were given to them.

3 And [a]another angel came and stood at the [b]altar, holding a [c]golden censer; and much [d]incense was given to him, that he might [1]add it to the [d]prayers of all the [2]saints upon the [e]golden altar which was before the throne.

4 And [a]the smoke of the incense, [1]with the prayers of the [2]saints, went up before God out of the angel's hand.

5 And the angel took the censer; and he [a]filled it with the fire of the altar and [b]threw it to the earth; and there followed [c]peals of thunder and sounds and flashes of lightning and an [d]earthquake.

6 [a]And the seven angels who had the seven trumpets prepared themselves to sound them.

7 And the first sounded, and there came [a]hail and fire, mixed with blood, and they were thrown to the earth; and [b]a third of the earth was burnt up, and [b]a third of the [c]trees were burnt up, and all the green [c]grass was burnt up.

8 And the second angel sounded, and *something* like a great [a]mountain burning with fire was thrown into the sea; and [b]a third of the [c]sea became blood;

9 and [a]a third of the creatures, which were in the sea [1]and had life, died; and a third of the [b]ships were destroyed.

10 And the third angel sounded, and a great star [a]fell from heaven, burning like a torch, and it fell on a [b]third of the rivers and on the [c]springs of waters;

11 and the name of the star is called Wormwood; and a [a]third of the waters became [b]wormwood; and many men died from the waters, because they were made bitter.

12 And the fourth angel sounded, and a [a]third of the [b]sun

11 [a]Rev. 4:4 [b]Rev. 4:6 [c]Rev. 4:10

12 [a]Rev. 5:14 [b]Rev. 5:12

13 [a]Acts 3:12 [b]Rev. 7:9

14 [1]Lit., *have said* [a]Matt. 24:21 [b]Rev. 22:14; Zech. 3:3-5 [c]Rev. 6:11; 7:9 [d]Heb. 9:14; 1 John 1:7

15 [1]Or, *sanctuary* [a]Rev. 7:9 [b]Rev. 22:3; 4:8 [c]Rev. 11:19; 21:22 [d]Rev. 4:9 [e]Rev. 21:3; Lev. 26:11; Ezek. 37:27; John 1:14

16 [1]Lit., *fall* [a]Is. 49:10; Ps. 121:5f.

17 [1]Lit., *waters* [a]Ps. 23:1f.; Matt. 2:6; John 10:11 [b]Rev. 21:6; 22:1; John 4:14 [c]Rev. 21:4; Is. 25:8; Matt. 5:4

1 [a]Rev. 5:1; 6:1, 3, 5, 7, 9, 12 [b]Rev. 5:9

2 [a]Rev. 8:6-13; 9:1, 13; 11:15; 1:4; Matt. 18:10 [b]1 Cor. 15:52; 1 Thess. 4:16

3 [1]Lit., *give* [2]I.e., true believers; lit., *holy ones* [a]Rev. 7:2 [b]Rev. 6:9; Amos 9:1 [c]Heb. 9:4 [d]Rev. 5:8 [e]Ex. 30:1, 3; Num. 4:11; Rev. 8:5; 9:13

4 [1]Or, *for* [2]Note 2, v. 3 [a]Ps. 141:2

5 [a]Lev. 16:12 [b]Ezek. 10:2 [c]Rev. 4:5 [d]Rev. 6:12

6 [a]Rev. 8:2

7 [a]Ezek. 38:22; Is. 28:2; Joel 2:30 [b]Rev. 8:7-12; 9:15, 18; 12:4; Zech. 13:8, 9 [c]Rev. 9:4

8 [a]Jer. 51:25 [b]Rev. 8:7-12; 9:15, 18; 12:4; Zech. 13:8, 9 [c]Rev. 16:3; 11:6; Ex. 7:17ff.

9 [1]Lit., *those which had* [a]Rev. 8:7-12; 9:15, 18; 12:4; Zech. 13:8, 9 [b]Is. 2:16

10 [a]Rev. 9:1; 6:13; Is. 14:12; [b]Rev. 8:7-12; 9:15, 18; 12:4; Zech. 13:8, 9 [c]Rev. 14:7; 16:4

11 [a]Rev. 8:7-12; 9:15, 18; 12:4; Zech. 13:8, 9 [b]Jer. 9:15; 23:15

12 [a]Rev. 8:7-12; 9:15, 18; 12:4; Zech. 13:8, 9 [b]Rev. 6:12f.; Ex. 10:21ff.

and a third of the [b]moon and a [a]third of the [b]stars were smitten, so that a [a]third of them might be darkened and the day
might not shine for a [a]third of it, and the night in the same
way.
13 And I looked, and I heard [1]an eagle flying in [a]mid-
heaven, saying with a loud voice, "[b]Woe, woe, woe, to [c]those
who dwell on the earth; because of the remaining blasts of the
trumpet of the [d]three angels who are about to sound!"

CHAPTER 9

AND the [a]fifth angel sounded, and I saw a [b]star from heaven
which had fallen to the earth; and the [c]key of the [1d]bottomless
pit was given to him.
2 And he opened the [1]bottomless pit; and [a]smoke went
up out of the pit, like the smoke of a great furnace; and [b]the
sun and the air were darkened by the smoke of the pit.
3 And out of the smoke came forth [a]locusts [1]upon the
earth; and power was given them, as the [b]scorpions of the earth
have power.
4 And they were told that they should not [a]hurt the
[b]grass of the earth, nor any green thing, nor any tree, but only
the men who do not have the [c]seal of God on their foreheads.
5 And [1]they were not permitted to kill [2]anyone, but to
torment for [a]five months; and their torment was like the torment of a [b]scorpion when it [3]stings a man.
6 And in those days [a]men will seek death and will not
find it; and they will long to die and death flees from them.
7 And the [1a]appearance of the locusts was like horses
prepared for battle; and on their heads, as it were, crowns like
gold, and their faces were like the faces of men.
8 And they had hair like the hair of women, and their
[a]teeth were like *the teeth* of lions.
9 And they had breastplates like breastplates of iron; and
the [a]sound of their wings was like the sound of chariots, of
many horses rushing to battle.
10 And they have tails like [a]scorpions, and stings; and in
their [b]tails is their power to hurt men for [c]five months.
11 They have as king over them, the angel of the [a]abyss;
his name in [b]Hebrew is [1c]Abaddon, and in the Greek he has
the name [2]Apollyon.
12 [a]The first Woe is past; behold, two Woes are still coming after these things.
13 And the sixth angel sounded, and I heard [1]a voice from
the [2]four [a]horns of the [b]golden altar which is before God,
14 one saying to the sixth angel who had the trumpet,
"Release the [a]four angels who are bound at the [b]great river
Euphrates."
15 And the four angels, who had been prepared for the
hour and day and month and year, were [a]released, so that they
might kill a [b]third of [1]mankind.
16 And the number of the armies of the horsemen was
[a]two hundred million; [b]I heard the number of them.
17 And [1]this is how I saw [a]in the vision the horses and
those who sat on them: *the riders* had breastplates *the color* of
fire and of hyacinth and of [2b]brimstone; and the heads of the

12 [a]Rev. 8:7-12; 9:15, 18; 12:4; Zech. 13:8, 9 [b]Rev. 6:12f.; Ex. 10:21ff.

13 [1]Lit., *one eagle* [a]Rev. 14:6; 19:17 [b]Rev. 9:12; 11:14; 12:12 [c]Rev. 3:10 [d]Rev. 8:2

1 [1]Lit., *shaft of the abyss* [a]Rev. 8:2 [b]Rev. 8:10 [c]Rev. 1:18 [d]Luke 8:31; Rev. 9:2, 11

2 [1]Note v. 1 [a]Gen. 19:28; Ex. 19:18 [b]Joel 2:2, 10

3 [1]Lit., *into* [a]Rev. 9:7; Ex. 10:12-15 [b]Rev. 9:5, 10; 2 Chr. 10:11, 14; Ezek. 2:6

4 [a]Rev. 6:6 [b]Rev. 8:7 [c]Rev. 7:2, 3

5 [1]Lit., *it was given to them* [2]Lit., *them* [3]Lit., *strikes* [a]Rev. 9:10 [b]Rev. 9:3, 10; 2 Chr. 10:11, 14; Ezek. 2:6

6 [a]Job 3:21; 7:15; Jer. 8:3; Rev. 6:16

7 [1]Lit., *appearances* [a]Joel 2:4

8 [a]Joel 1:6

9 [a]Joel 2:5; Jer. 47:3

10 [a]Rev. 8:3, 5; 2 Chr. 10:11, 14; Ezek. 2:6 [b]Rev. 9:19 [c]Rev. 9:5

11 [1]Or, *Destruction* [2]Or, *Destroyer* [a]Luke 8:31; Rev. 9:1, 2 [b]Rev. 16:16; John 5:2 [c]Job 26:6; 28:22 marg.; 31:12 marg.; Ps. 88:11 marg.; Prov. 15:11

12 [a]Rev. 8:13; 11:14

13 [1]Lit., *one voice* [2]Some ancient mss. omit, *four* [a]Ex. 30:2f., 10 [b]Rev. 8:3

14 [a]Rev. 7:1 [b]Gen. 15:18; Deut. 1:7; Josh. 1:4; Rev. 16:12

15 [1]Lit., *men* [a]Rev. 20:7 [b]Rev. 9:18; 8:7

16 [a]Rev. 5:11 [b]Rev. 7:4

17 [1]Lit., *thus I saw* [2]Or, *sulphur* [a]Dan. 8:2; 9:21 [b]Rev. 9:18; 14:10; 19:20; 20:10; 21:8

horses are like the heads of lions; and [c]out of their mouths
proceed fire and smoke and [2b]brimstone.
18 A [a]third of [1]mankind was killed by these three plagues,
by the [b]fire and the smoke and the [2]brimstone, which proceeded out of their mouths.
19 For the power of the horses is in their mouth and in
their tails; for their tails are like serpents and have heads; and
with them they do harm.
20 And the rest of [1]mankind, who were not killed by these
plagues, [a]did not repent of [b]THE WORKS OF THEIR HANDS, SO as
not to [c]worship DEMONS, AND [d]THE IDOLS OF GOLD AND OF SILVER
AND OF BRASS AND OF STONE AND OF WOOD, WHICH CAN NEITHER
SEE NOR HEAR NOR WALK;
21 and they [a]did not repent of their murders nor of their
[b]sorceries nor of their [c]immorality nor of their thefts.

CHAPTER 10

AND I saw another [a]strong angel [b]coming down out of heav-
en, clothed with a cloud; and the [c]rainbow was upon his head,
and [d]his face was like the sun, and his [e]feet like pillars of fire;
2 and he had in his hand a [a]little book which was open.
And he placed [b]his right foot on the sea and his left on the
land;
3 and he cried out with a loud voice, [a]as when a lion
roars; and when he had cried out, the [b]seven peals of thunder
[1]uttered their voices.
4 And when the seven peals of thunder had spoken, [a]I
was about to write; and I [b]heard a voice from heaven saying,
"[c]Seal up the things which the seven peals of thunder have
spoken, and do not write them."
5 And the angel whom I saw standing on the sea and on
the land [a]LIFTED UP HIS RIGHT HAND TO HEAVEN,
6 AND SWORE BY [a]HIM WHO LIVES FOREVER AND EVER, WHO
[b]CREATED HEAVEN AND THE THINGS IN IT, AND THE EARTH AND
THE THINGS IN IT, AND THE SEA AND THE THINGS IN IT, that [c]there
shall be delay no longer,
7 but in the days of the voice of the [a]seventh angel, when
he is about to sound, then [b]the mystery of God is finished, as
He [1]preached to His servants the prophets.
8 And [a]the voice which I heard from heaven, *I heard*
again speaking with me, and saying, "Go, take [b]the [1]book
which is open in the hand of the angel who [b]stands on the sea
and on the land."
9 And I went to the angel, telling him to give me the
little book. And he *said to me, "[a]Take it, and eat it; and it will
make your stomach bitter, but in your mouth it will be sweet
as honey."
10 And I took the little book out of the angel's hand and
ate it, and it was in my mouth sweet as honey; and when I had
eaten it, my stomach was made bitter.
11 And [a]they *said to me, "You must [b]prophesy again
concerning [c]many peoples and nations and tongues and
[d]kings."

17 [2]Or, *sulphur* [b]Rev. 9:18; 14:10; 19:20; 20:10; 21:8 [c]Rev. 11:5

18 [1]Lit., *men* [2]Or, *sulphur* [a]Rev. 9:15; 8:7 [b]Rev. 9:17

20 [1]Lit., *men* [a]Rev. 2:21 [b]Deut. 4:28; Jer. 1:16; Mic. 5:13; Acts 7:41 [c]1 Cor. 10:20 [d]Ps. 115:4-7; 135:15-17; Dan. 5:23

21 [a]Rev. 9:20 [b]Is. 47:9, 12; Rev. 18:23 [c]Rev. 17:2, 5

1 [a]Rev. 5:2 [b]Rev. 18:1; 20:1 [c]Rev. 4:3 [d]Rev. 1:16; Matt. 17:2 [e]Rev. 1:15

2 [a]Rev. 10:8-10; Rev. 5:1 [b]Rev. 10:5, 8

3 [1]Or, *spoke* [a]Is. 31:4; Hos. 11:10 [b]Rev. 4:5; Ps. 29:3-9

4 [a]Rev. 1:11, 19 [b]Rev. 10:8 [c]Dan. 8:26; 12:4, 9; Rev. 22:10

5 [a]Gen. 14:22; Ex. 6:8; Num. 14:30; Deut. 32:40; Ezek. 20:5; Dan 12:7

6 [a]Rev. 4:9 [b]Rev. 4:11 [c]Rev. 6:11; 12:12; 16:17; 21:6

7 [1]Lit., *preached the gospel* [a]Rev. 11:15 [b]Amos 3:7; Rom. 16:25

8 [1]Or, *scroll* [a]Rev. 10:4 [b]Rev. 10:2

9 [a]Ezek. 2:8; 3:1-3; Jer. 15:16

11 [a]Rev. 11:1 [b]Ezek. 37:4, 9 [c]Rev. 5:9 [d]Rev. 17:10, 12

CHAPTER 11

AND there was given me a [1a]measuring rod like a staff; [2]and
[b]someone said, "Rise and measure the [3]temple of God, and
the altar, and those who worship in it.
2 "And [1]leave out the [a]court which is outside the [2]temple,
and do not measure it, for [b]it has been given to the nations;
and they will [b]tread under foot [c]the holy city for [d]forty-two
months.
3 "And I will grant *authority* to my two [a]witnesses, and
they will prophesy for [b]twelve hundred and sixty days, clothed
in [c]sackcloth."
4 These are the [a]two olive trees and the two lampstands
that stand before the Lord of the earth.
5 And if any one desires to harm them, [a]fire proceeds out
of their mouth and devours their enemies; and if any one
would desire to harm them, [b]in this manner he must be killed.
6 These have the power to [a]shut up the sky, in order that
rain may not fall during [b]the days of their prophesying; and
they have power over the waters to [c]turn them into blood, and
to smite the earth with every plague, as often as they desire.
7 And when they have finished their testimony, [a]the
beast [b]that comes up out of the [c]abyss will [d]make war with
them, and overcome them and kill them.
8 And their dead [1]bodies *will lie* in the street of the [a]great
city which [2]mystically is called [b]Sodom and [c]Egypt, where also
their Lord was crucified.
9 And those from [a]the peoples and tribes and tongues
and nations *will* look at their dead [1]bodies for three days and a
half, and [2b]will not permit their dead bodies to be laid in a
tomb.
10 And [a]those who dwell on the earth *will* rejoice over
them and make merry; and they will [b]send gifts to one another,
because these two prophets tormented [a]those who dwell on
the earth.
11 And after the three days and a half [a]the breath of life
from God came into them, and they stood on their feet; and
great fear fell upon those who were beholding them.
12 And they heard a loud voice from heaven saying to
them, "[a]Come up here." And they [b]went up into heaven in the
cloud, and their enemies beheld them.
13 And in that hour there was a great [a]earthquake, and a
tenth of the city fell; and [1]seven thousand people were killed in
the earthquake, and the rest were terrified and [b]gave glory to
the [c]God of heaven.
14 The second [a]Woe is past; behold, the third Woe is
coming quickly.
15 And the [a]seventh angel sounded; and there arose [b]loud
voices in heaven, saying,
"[c]The kingdom of the world has become *the kingdom* of our
Lord, and of [d]His [1]Christ; and [e]He will reign forever and ever."
16 And the twenty-four elders, who [a]sit on their thrones
before God, [b]fell on their faces and worshiped God,
17 saying,
"We give Thee thanks, [a]O Lord God, the Almighty, who art

1 [1]Lit., *reed* [2]Lit., *saying* [3]Or, *sanctuary* [a]Rev. 21:15f.; Ezek. 40:3-42:20; Zech. 2:1 [b]Rev. 10:11

2 [1]Lit., *throw out* [2]Or, *sanctuary* [a]Ezek. 40:17, 20 [b]Luke 21:24 [c]Is. 52:1; Matt. 27:53; 4:5; Rev. 21:2, 10; 22:19 [d]Rev. 12:6; 13:5; Dan. 7:25; 12:7

3 [a]Rev. 2:13; 1:5 [b]Rev. 12:6; 13:5; Dan. 7:25; 12:7 [c]Gen. 37:34; 2 Sam. 3:31; 1 Kin. 21:27; 2 Kin. 19:1f.; Neh. 9:1; Esther 4:1; Ps. 69:11; Joel 1:13; Jonah 3:5f, 8

4 [a]Zech. 4:3, 11, 14; Ps. 52:8; Jer. 11:16

5 [a]Rev. 9:17f.; 2 Kin. 1:10-12; Jer. 5:14 [b]Num. 16:29, 35

6 [a]Luke 4:25 [b]Rev. 11:3 [c]Rev. 8:8

7 [a]Rev. 13:1ff. [b]Rev. 13:1 [c]Rev. 9:1 [d]Rev. 13:7; Dan. 7:21

8 [1]Some ancient mss. read, *body* [2]Lit., *spiritually* [a]Rev. 14:8; 16:19; 17:18; 18:2, 10, 16, 18, 19, 21 [b]Is. 1:9, 10; 3:9; Jer. 23:14; Ezek. 16:46, 49 [c]Ezek. 23:3, 8, 19, 27

9 [1]Lit., *body* [2]Lit., *do not permit* [a]Rev. 10:11; 5:9 [b]Ps. 79:2f.; 1 Kin. 13:22

10 [a]Rev. 3:10 [b]Neh. 8:10, 12; Esther 9:19, 22

11 [a]Ezek. 37:5, 9, 10, 14

12 [a]Rev. 4:1 [b]2 Kin. 2:11; Acts 1:9

13 [1]Lit., *names of men, seven thousand* [a]Rev. 6:12; 8:5; 16:18; 11:19 [b]Rev. 14:7; 16:9; 19:7; John 9:24 [c]Rev. 16:11

14 [a]Rev. 9:12; 8:13

15 [1]I.e., Messiah [a]Rev. 10:7; 8:2 [b]Rev. 16:17; 19:1 [c]Rev. 12:10 [d]Acts 4:26 marg. [Ps. 2:2] [e]Dan. 2:44; 7:14, 27; Luke 1:33

16 [a]Rev. 4:4; Matt. 19:28 [b]Rev. 4:10

17 [a]Rev. 1:8

and who wast, because Thou hast taken Thy great power and
[1]hast begun to [b]reign.
18 "And [a]the nations were enraged, and Thy wrath came,
and [b]the time *came* for the dead to be judged, and *the time* to
give their reward to Thy [c]bond-servants the prophets and to
the [1]saints and to those who fear Thy name, [d]the small and the
great, and to destroy those who destroy the earth."
19 And [a]the [1]temple of God which is in heaven was
opened; and [b]the ark of His covenant appeared in His [1]temple,
and there were flashes of [c]lightning and sounds and peals of
thunder and an earthquake and a [d]great [2]hailstorm.

Chapter 12

1 And a great [a]sign appeared [b]in heaven: [c]a woman [d]clothed
with the sun, and the moon under her feet, and on her head a
crown of twelve stars;
2 and she was with child; and she *[a]cried out, being in
labor and in pain to give birth.
3 And [a]another sign appeared in heaven: and behold, a
great red [b]dragon having [c]seven heads and [d]ten horns, and on
his heads *were* [e]seven diadems.
4 And his tail *swept away a [a]third of the stars of heaven,
and [b]threw them to the earth. And the [c]dragon stood before
the woman who was about to give birth, so that when she gave
birth [d]he might devour her child.
5 And she gave birth to a son, a male *child*, who is to
[1a]rule all the [2]nations with a rod of iron; and her child was
[b]caught up to God and to His throne.
6 And the woman fled into the wilderness where she
*had a place prepared by God, so that there [1]she might be
nourished for [a]one thousand two hundred and sixty days.
7 And there was war in heaven, [a]Michael and his angels
waging war with the [b]dragon. And the dragon and [c]his angels
waged war,
8 and they were not strong enough, and there was no
longer a place found for them in heaven.
9 And the great [a]dragon was thrown down, the [b]serpent
of old who is called the Devil and [c]Satan, who [d]deceives the
whole [1]world; he was [e]thrown down to the earth, and his angels
were thrown down with him.
10 And I heard [a]a loud voice in heaven, saying,
"**N**ow the [b]salvation, and the power, and the [a]kingdom of
our God and the authority of His Christ have come, for the
[c]accuser of our brethren has been thrown down, who accuses
them before our God day and night.
11 "And they [a]overcame him because of [b]the blood of the
Lamb and because of [c]the word of their testimony, and they
[d]did not love their life even to death.
12 "For this reason, [a]rejoice, O heavens and [b]you who
[1]dwell in them. [c]Woe to the earth and the sea; because [d]the
devil has come down to you, having great wrath, knowing that
he has *only* [e]a short time."
13 And when the [a]dragon saw that he was thrown down to
the earth, he persecuted [b]the woman who gave birth to the
male *child*.

17 [1]Lit., *didst reign* [b]Rev. 19:6

18 [1]I.e., true believers; lit., *holy ones* [a]Ps. 2:1 [b]Rev. 20:12; Dan. 7:10 [c]Rev. 10:7; 16:6 [d]Rev. 13:16; 19:5; Ps. 115:13

19 [1]Or, *sanctuary* [2]Lit., *hail* [a]Rev. 15:5; 4:1 [b]Heb. 9:4 [c]Rev. 4:5 [d]Rev. 16:21

1 [a]Rev. 12:3; Matt. 24:30 [b]Rev. 11:19 [c]Gal. 4:26 [d]Ps. 104:2; Song of Sol. 6:10

2 [a]Is. 26:17; 66:6-9; Mic. 4:9, 10

3 [a]Rev. 12:1; 15:1 [b]Rev. 12:4, 7; 12:9, 13, 16f.; 13:2, 4, 11; 16:13; 20:2; Is. 27:1 [c]Rev. 13:1; 17:3, 7, 9ff. [d]Rev. 13:1; 17:12, 16; Dan 7:7, 20, 24 [e]Rev. 13:1; 19:12

4 [a]Rev. 8:7, 12 [b]Dan. 8:10 [c]Rev. 12:3, 7; 12:9, 13, 16f.; 13:2, 4, 11; 16:13; 20:2; Is. 27:1 [d]Matt. 2:16

5 [1]Or, *shepherd* [2]Or, *Gentiles* [a]Rev. 2:27 [b]2 Cor. 12:2

6 [1]Lit., *they may nourish her for* [a]Rev. 11:3; Rev. 13:5

7 [a]Jude 9 [b]Rev. 12:3 [c]Matt. 25:41

9 [1]Lit., *inhabited earth* [a]Rev. 12:3 [b]Rev. 12:15; 20:2; Gen. 3:1; 2 Cor. 11:3 [c]Matt. 4:10; 25:41 [d]Rev. 20:3, 8, 10; 13:14 [e]Luke 10:18; John 12:31

10 [a]Rev. 11:15 [b]Rev. 7:10 [c]Job 1:11; 2:5; Zech. 3:1; Luke 22:31; 1 Pet. 5:8

11 [a]Rev. 15:2; John 16:33; 1 John 2:13 [b]Rev. 7:14 [c]Rev. 6:9 [d]Rev. 2:10; Luke 14:26

12 [1]Or, *tabernacle* [a]Rev. 18:20; Ps. 96:11; Is. 44:23 [b]Rev. 13:6 [c]Rev. 8:13 [d]Rev. 12:9 [e]Rev. 10:6

13 [a]Rev. 12:3 [b]Rev. 12:5

14 And the [a]two wings of the great eagle were given to the
woman, in order that she might fly [b]into the wilderness to her
place, where she *was nourished for [c]a time and times and half
a time, from the [1]presence of the serpent.
15 And the [a]serpent [1]poured water [b]like a river out of his
mouth after the woman, so that he might cause her to be
swept away with the flood.
16 And the earth helped the woman, and the earth opened
its mouth and drank up the river which the dragon [1]poured out
of his mouth.
17 And the dragon was enraged with the woman, and went
off to [a]make war with the rest of her [b]offspring, who [c]keep the
commandments of God and [d]hold to the testimony of Jesus.

Chapter 13

AND [1]he stood on the sand of the [2]seashore.
And I saw a [a]beast coming up out of the sea, having [b]ten
horns and [b]seven heads, and on his horns *were* [c]ten diadems,
and on his heads *were* [d]blasphemous names.
2 And the beast which I saw was [a]like a leopard, and his
feet were *like those* of [b]a bear, and his mouth like the mouth
of [c]a lion. And the [d]dragon gave him his power and his [e]throne
and great authority.
3 And *I saw* one of his heads as if it had been [1]slain, and
his [a]fatal wound was healed. And the whole earth [b]was amazed
and followed after the beast;
4 and they worshiped the [a]dragon, because he [a]gave his
authority to the beast; and they worshiped the beast, saying,
"[b]Who is like the beast, and who is able to wage war with
him?"
5 And there was given to him a mouth [a]speaking [1]arro-
gant words and blasphemies; and authority to [2]act for [b]forty-
two months was given to him.
6 And he opened his mouth in blasphemies against God,
to blaspheme His name and His tabernacle, *that is,* [a]those who
[1]dwell in heaven.
7 And it was given to him to [a]make war with the [1]saints
and to overcome them; and authority over [b]every tribe and
people and tongue and nation was given to him.
8 And all who [a]dwell on the earth will worship him, *every
one* [b]whose name has not been [1]written [c]from the foundation
of the world in the book of life of [d]the Lamb who has been
slain.
9 [a]If any one has an ear, let him hear.
10 [a]If any one [1]*is destined* for captivity, to captivity he
goes; [b]if any one kills with the sword, with the sword he must
be killed. Here is [c]the [2]perseverance and the faith of the
[3]saints.
11 And [a]I saw another beast coming up out of the earth;
and he [1]had [b]two horns like a lamb, and he [2]spoke as a [c]dragon.
12 And he [a]exercises all the authority of the first beast [1][b]in
his presence. And he makes [c]the earth and those who dwell in
it to [d]worship the first beast, whose [e]fatal wound was healed.
13 And he [a]performs great signs, so that he even makes

14 [1]Lit., *face*
[a]Ex. 19:4; Deut. 32:11; Is. 40:31 [b]Rev. 12:6 [c]Dan. 7:25; 12:7

15 [1]Lit., *threw*
[a]Rev. 12:9; 20:2; Gen. 3:1; 2 Cor. 11:3 [b]Hos. 5:10; Is. 59:19

16 [1]Lit., *threw*

17 [a]Rev. 11:7; 13:7 [b]Gen. 3:15 [c]Rev. 14:12; 1 John 2:3 [d]Rev. 1:2; 6:9; [14:12]; 19:10

1 [1]Some mss. read, *I stood* [2]Lit., *sea*
[a]Rev. 13:14, 15; 15:2; 16:13; Rev. 11:7; 17:8; Dan. 7:3 [b]Rev. 12:3 [c]Rev. 12:3; 17:12 [d]Rev. 17:3; Dan. 7:8; 11:36

2 [a]Dan 7:6; Hos. 13:7f. [b]Dan. 7:5 [c]Dan. 7:4 [d]Rev. 13:4, 12; 12:3 [e]Rev. 2:13; 16:10

3 [1]Lit., *smitten to death*
[a]Rev. 13:21; Rev. 13:14 [b]Rev. 17:8

4 [a]Rev. 13:2, 12; 12:3 [b]Rev. 18:18; Ex. 15:11; Is. 46:5

5 [1]Lit., *great things* [2]Lit., *do*
[a]Dan. 7:8, 11, 20, 25; 11:36; 2 Thess. 2:3f. [b]Rev. 11:2

6 [1]Or, *tabernacle*
[a]Rev. 12:12; 7:15

7 [1]I.e., true believers; lit., *holy ones*
[a]Rev. 11:7 [b]Rev. 5:9

8 [1]Or, *written in the book . . . slain from the foundation of the world*
[a]Rev. 13:12, 14; 3:10 [b]Rev. 3:5 [c]Rev. 17:8; Matt. 25:34 [d]Rev. 5:6

9 [a]Rev. 2:7

10 [1]Or, *leads into captivity* [2]Or, *steadfastness* [3]I.e., true believers; lit., *holy ones*
[a]Is. 33:1; Jer. 15:2; 43:11 [b]Gen. 9:6; Matt. 26:52; Rev. 11:18 [c]Heb. 6:12; Rev. 14:12

11 [1]Lit., *was having* [2]Lit., *was speaking*
[a]Rev. 13:1. 14; 16:13 [b]Dan. 8:3 [c]Rev. 13:4

12 [1]Or, *by his authority*
[a]Rev. 13:4 [b]Rev. 13:14; 19:20 [c]Rev. 13:8 [d]Rev. 13:15; 14:9, 11; 16:2; 19:20; 20:4 [e]Rev. 13:3

13 [a]Rev. 19:20; 16:14; Matt. 24:24

[b]fire come down out of heaven to the earth in the presence of
men.
14 And he [a]deceives [b]those who dwell on the earth because of [c]the signs which it was given him to perform [1d]in the
presence of the beast, telling those who dwell on the earth to
make an image to the beast who *had the [e]wound of the sword
and has come to life.
15 And there was given to him to give breath to the image
of the beast, that the image of the beast might even [1]speak and
cause [a]as many as do not [b]worship the image of the beast to be
killed.
16 And he causes all, [a]the small and the great, and the rich
and the poor, and the free men and the slaves, [1]to be given a
[b]mark on their right hand, or on their forehead,
17 and *he provides* that no one should be able to buy or to
sell, except the one who has the [a]mark, *either* [b]the name of the
beast or [c]the number of his name.
18 [a]Here is wisdom. Let him who has understanding calculate the number of the beast, for the number is that [b]of a man;
and his number is [1]six hundred and sixty-six.

CHAPTER 14

AND I looked, and behold, [a]the Lamb *was* standing on
[b]Mount Zion, and with Him [c]one hundred and forty-four
thousand, having [d]His name and the [d]name of His Father
written [e]on their foreheads.
2 And I heard a voice from heaven, like [a]the sound of
many waters and like the [b]sound of loud thunder, and the
voice which I heard *was* like *the sound* of [c]harpists playing on
their harps.
3 And they [1]*sang [a]a new song before the throne and
before the [b]four living creatures and the [c]elders; and [d]no one
could learn the song except the [e]one hundred and forty-four
thousand who had been [a]purchased from the earth.
4 [a]These are the ones who have not been defiled with
women, for they are [1]celibates. These *are* the ones who [b]follow
the Lamb wherever He goes. These have been [c]purchased
from among men [d]as first fruits to God and to the Lamb.
5 And no lie was found [a]in their mouth; they are
[b]blameless.
6 And I saw another angel flying in [a]midheaven, having
[b]an eternal gospel to preach to [c]those who [1]live on the earth,
and to [d]every nation and tribe and tongue and people;
7 and He said with a loud voice, "[a]Fear God, and [b]give
Him glory, because the hour of His judgment has come; and
worship Him who [c]made the heaven and the earth and sea and
[d]springs of waters."
8 And another angel, a second one, followed, saying,
"[a]Fallen, fallen is [b]Babylon the great, she who has [c]made all
the nations drink of the [d]wine of the [1]passion of her
immorality."
9 And another angel, a third one, followed them, saying
with a loud voice, "If any one [a]worships the beast and his
[b]image, and receives a [c]mark on his forehead or upon his hand,
10 he also will drink of the [a]wine of the wrath of God,

13 [b]Rev. 20:9; 1 Kin. 18:38; Luke 9:54; Rev. 11:5

14 [1]Lit., *by the authority of* [a]Rev. 12:9 [b]Rev. 13:8 [c]2 Thess. 2:9f. [d]Rev. 13:12; 19:20 [e]Rev. 13:3

15 [1]Some ancient mss. read, *speak, and he will cause* [a]Dan. 3:3ff. [b]Rev. 13:12; 14:9, 11; 16:2; 19:20; 20:4

16 [1]Lit., *that they give to them a mark* [a]Rev. 11:18; 19:5, 18 [b]Rev. 14:9; 20:4; Gal. 6:17; Rev. 7:3

17 [a]Rev. 14:9; 20:4; Gal. 6:17; Rev. 7:3 [b]Rev. 14:11 [c]Rev. 15:2

18 [1]Some mss. read, 616 [a]Rev. 17:9 [b]Rev. 21:17

1 [a]Rev. 5:6 [b]Ps. 2:6; Heb. 12:22 [c]Rev. 14:3; 7:4 [d]Rev. 3:12 [e]Rev. 7:3

2 [a]Rev. 1:15 [b]Rev. 6:1 [c]Rev. 5:8

3 [1]Some ancient mss. read, *sing, as it were, a new song* [a]Rev. 5:9 [b]Rev. 4:6 [c]Rev. 4:4 [d]Rev. 2:17 [e]Rev. 14:1; 7:4

4 [1]Or, *chaste men*, lit., *virgins* [a]Matt. 19:12; Rev. 3:4; 2 Cor. 11:2; Eph. 5:27 [b]Rev. 7:17; Rev. 3:4; 17:14 [c]Rev. 5:9 [d]James 1:18; Heb. 12:23

5 [a]Zeph. 3:13; Ps. 32:2; Mal. 2:6; John 1:47; 1 Pet. 2:22 [b]Jude 24; Heb. 9:14; 1 Pet. 1:19

6 [1]Lit., *sit* [a]Rev. 8:13 [b]Rev. 10:7; 1 Pet. 1:25 [c]Rev. 3:10 [d]Rev. 5:9

7 [a]Rev. 15:4 [b]Rev. 11:13 [c]Rev. 4:11 [d]Rev. 8:10

8 [1]Or, *wrath* [a]Rev. 18:2; Is. 21:9; Jer. 51:8 [b]Rev. 16:19; 17:5; 18:10; Dan. 4:30 [c]Jer. 51:7 [d]Rev. 18:3; 17:2, 4

9 [a]Rev. 14:11; Rev. 13:12 [b]Rev. 14:11; 13:14f. [c]Rev. 13:16

10 [a]Rev. 16:19; 19:15; Is. 51:17; Jer. 25:15f., 27

which is mixed [1]in full strength [b]in the cup of His anger; and
he will be tormented with [c]fire and brimstone in the presence
of the [d]holy angels and in the presence of the Lamb.
11 "And the [a]smoke of their torment goes up forever and
ever; and [b]they have no rest day and night, those who [c]worship
the beast and his [c]image, and whoever receives the [d]mark of his
name."
12 Here is [a]the [1]perseverance of the [2]saints who [b]keep the
commandments of God and [3c]their faith in Jesus.
13 And I heard a voice from heaven, saying, "Write,
'[a]Blessed are the dead who [b]die in the Lord [c]from now on!' "
"Yes," [d]says the Spirit, "that they may [e]rest from their labors,
for their [f]deeds follow with them."
14 And I looked, and behold, a [a]white cloud, and sitting
on the cloud *was* one [b]like [1]a son of man, having a golden
[c]crown on His head, and a sharp sickle in His hand.
15 And another angel [a]came out of the [1]temple, crying out
with a loud voice to Him who sat on the cloud, "[2b]Put in your
sickle and reap, because the hour to reap has come, because
the [c]harvest of the earth [3]is ripe."
16 And He who sat on the cloud [1]swung His sickle over
the earth; and the earth was reaped.
17 And another angel [a]came out of the [1]temple which is in
heaven, [2]and he also had a sharp sickle.
18 And another angel, [a]the one who has power over fire,
came out from [b]the altar; and he called with a loud voice to
him who had the sharp sickle, saying, "[1c]Put in your sharp
sickle, and gather the clusters [2]from the vine of the earth,
[d]because her grapes are ripe."
19 And the angel [1]swung his sickle to the earth, and gathered *the clusters from* the vine of the earth, and threw them
into [a]the great wine press of the wrath of God.
20 And the wine press was trodden [a]outside the city, and
[b]blood came out from the wine press, up to the horses' bridles,
[1]for a distance of [2]two hundred miles.

Chapter 15

AND I saw [a]another sign in heaven, great and marvelous,
[b]seven angels who had [c]seven plagues, *which are* [d]the last,
because in them the wrath of God is finished.
2 And I saw, as it were, a [a]sea of glass mixed with fire, and
those who had [b]come off victorious from the [c]beast and from
[d]his image and from the [e]number of his name, standing on the
[a]sea of glass, holding [f]harps of God.
3 And they *sang the [a]song of Moses [b]the bond-servant
of God and the [c]song of the Lamb, saying,

"[d]GREAT AND MARVELOUS ARE THY WORKS,
[e]O LORD GOD, THE ALMIGHTY;
RIGHTEOUS AND TRUE ARE THY WAYS,
THOU [f]KING OF THE [1]NATIONS.
4 "[a]WHO WILL NOT FEAR, O LORD, AND GLORIFY THY NAME?
FOR THOU ALONE ART HOLY;
FOR [b]ALL THE NATIONS WILL COME AND WORSHIP BEFORE
THEE,
For Thy [1c]righteous acts have been revealed."

10 [1]Lit., *unmixed* [b]Rev. 18:6; Ps. 75:8 [c]Rev. 19:20; 20:10, 14f.; 21:8; Ezek. 38:22; 2 Thess. 1:7 [d]Mark 8:38

11 [a]Rev. 18:9, 18; 19:3; Is. 34:8-10 [b]Rev. 4:8 [c]Rev. 14:9; 13:12 [d]Rev. 13:17

12 [1]Or, *steadfastness* [2]I.e., true believers; lit., *holy ones* [3]Lit., *the faith of* [a]Rev. 13:10 [b]Rev. 12:17 [c]Rev. 2:13

13 [a]Rev. 20:6 [b]1 Cor. 15:18; 1 Thess. 4:16 [c]Rev. 11:18 [d]Rev. 2:7; 22:17 [e]Rev. 6:11; Heb. 4:9f. [f]1 Tim. 5:25

14 [1]Or, *the Son of Man* [a]Matt. 17:5 [b]Rev. 1:13 [c]Rev. 6:2; Ps. 21:3

15 [1]Or, *sanctuary* [2]Lit., *Send forth* [3]Lit., *has become dry* [a]Rev. 14:17; 15:6; 16:17; 11:19 [b]Rev. 14:18; Mark 4:29; Joel 3:13 [c]Matt. 13:39-41; Jer. 51:33

16 [1]Lit., *cast*

17 [1]Or, *sanctuary* [2]Lit., *having himself also* [a]Rev. 14:15; 15:6; 16:17; 11:19

18 [1]Lit., *Send forth* [2]Lit., *of* [a]Rev. 16:8 [b]Rev. 6:9; 8:3 [c]Rev. 14:15; Mark 4:29; Joel 3:13 [d]Joel 3:13

19 [1]Lit., *cast* [a]Rev. 19:15; Is. 63:2f.

20 [1]Lit., *from two hundred miles* [2]Lit., *sixteen hundred stadia.* A stadion was about six hundred feet. [a]Heb. 13:12; Rev. 11:8 [b]Gen. 49:11; Deut. 32:14

1 [a]Rev. 12:1, 3 [b]Rev. 15:6-8; 16:1; 17:1; 21:9 [c]Lev. 26:21, [d]Rev. 9:20

2 [a]Rev. 4:6 [b]Rev. 12:11 [c]Rev. 13:1 [d]Rev. 13:14f. [e]Rev. 13:17 [f]Rev. 5:8

3 [1]Some ancient mss. read, *ages* [a]Ex. 15:1ff. [b]Josh. 22:5; Heb. 3:5 [c]Rev. 5:9f., 12f. [d]Deut. 32:3f.; Ps. 111:2; 139:14; Hos. 14:9 [e]Rev. 1:8 [f]1 Tim. 1:17 marg.

4 [1]Or, *judgments* [a]Rev. 14:7; Jer. 10:7 [b]Ps. 86:9; Is. 66:23 [c]Rev. 19:8

5 After these things I looked, and [a]the [1]temple of the
[b]tabernacle of testimony in heaven was opened,
6 and the [a]seven angels who had the seven plagues [b]came
out of the [1]temple, clothed [c]in [2]linen, clean *and* bright, and
[d]girded around their breasts with golden girdles.
7 And one of the [a]four living creatures gave to the [b]seven
angels seven [c]golden bowls full of the [d]wrath of God, who
[e]lives forever and ever.
8 And the [1]temple was filled with [a]smoke from the glory
of God and from His power; and no one was able to enter the
[1]temple until the seven plagues of the seven angels were
finished.

Chapter 16

AND I heard a loud voice from [a]the [1]temple, saying to the
[b]seven angels, "Go and [c]pour out the [d]seven bowls of the wrath
of God into the earth."
2 And the first *angel* went and poured out his bowl [a]into
the earth; and it became a loathsome and malignant [b]sore
upon the men [c]who had the mark of the beast and who worshiped his image.
3 And the second *angel* poured out his bowl [a]into the
sea, and it became blood like *that* of a dead man; and every
living [1]thing in the sea died.
4 And the third *angel* poured out his bowl into the [a]rivers
and the springs of waters; and [1]they [b]became blood.
5 And I heard the angel of the waters saying, "[a]Righteous
art Thou, [b]who art and who wast, O [c]Holy One, because Thou
didst [d]judge these things;
6 for they poured out [a]the blood of saints and prophets,
and Thou hast given them [b]blood to drink. They [1]deserve it."
7 And I heard [a]the altar saying, "Yes, O [b]Lord God, the
Almighty, [c]true and righteous are Thy judgments."
8 And the fourth *angel* poured out his bowl upon [a]the
sun; [b]and it was given to it to scorch men with fire.
9 And men were scorched with [1]fierce heat; and they
[a]blasphemed the name of God who has the power over these
plagues; and they [b]did not repent, so as to [c]give Him glory.
10 And the fifth *angel* poured out his bowl upon the [a]throne
of the beast; and his kingdom became [b]darkened; and
they gnawed their tongues because of pain,
11 and they [a]blasphemed the [b]God of heaven because of
their pains and their [c]sores; and they [d]did not repent of their
deeds.
12 And the sixth *angel* poured out his bowl upon the
[a]great river, the Euphrates; and [b]its water was dried up, that
[c]the way might be prepared for the kings [d]from the [1]east.
13 And I saw *coming* out of the mouth of the [a]dragon and
out of the mouth of the [b]beast and out of the mouth of the
[c]false prophet, three [d]unclean spirits like [e]frogs;
14 for they are [a]spirits of demons, [b]performing signs,
which go out to the kings of the [c]whole [1]world, to [d]gather them
together for the war of the [e]great day of God, the Almighty.
15 (Behold, [a]I am coming like a thief. [b]Blessed is the one

---

5 [1]Or, *sanctuary* [a]Rev. 11:19 [b]Ex. 38:21; Num. 1:50; Heb. 8:5; Rev. 13:6

6 [1]Or, *sanctuary* [2]Some mss. read, *stone* [a]Rev. 15:1 [b]Rev. 14:15 [c]Ezek. 28:13 [d]Rev. 1:13

7 [a]Rev. 4:6 [b]Rev. 15:1 [c]Rev. 5:8 [d]Rev. 15:1; 14:10 [e]Rev. 4:9

8 [1]Or, *sanctuary* [a]Ex. 19:18; Is. 6:4; Ex. 40:34f.; Lev. 16:2; 1 Kin. 8:10f.; 2 Chr. 5:13f.

1 [1]Or, *sanctuary* [a]Rev. 11:19 [b]Rev. 15:1 [c]Rev. 16:2ff.; Ps. 79:6; Jer. 10:25; Ezek. 22:31; Zeph. 3:8 [d]Rev. 5:8

2 [a]Rev. 8:7 [b]Rev. 16:11; Ex. 9:9-11; Deut. 28:35 [c]Rev. 13:15-17; 14:9

3 [1]Lit., *soul.* Some ancient mss. read, *thing, the things in the sea.* [a]Rev. 8:8f.; Ex. 7:17-21; Rev. 11:6

4 [1]Some ancient mss. read, *it became* [a]Rev. 8:10 [b]Ex. 7:17-20; Rev. 11:6

5 [a]John 17:25 [b]Rev. 11:17 [c]Rev. 15:4 [d]Rev. 6:10

6 [1]Lit., *are worthy* [a]Rev. 18:24; Rev. 17:6 [b]Is. 49:26; Luke 11:49-51

7 [a]Rev. 6:9; 14:18 [b]Rev. 1:8 [c]Rev. 19:2; 15:3

8 [a]Rev. 6:12 [b]Rev. 14:18

9 [1]Lit., *great* [a]Rev. 16:11, 21 [b]Rev. 2:21 [c]Rev. 11:13

10 [a]Rev. 13:2 [b]Rev. 8:12; 9:2; Ex. 10:21f.; Is. 8:22

11 [a]Rev. 16:9, 21 [b]Rev. 11:13 [c]Rev. 16:2 [d]Rev. 2:21

12 [1]Lit., *rising of the sun* [a]Rev. 9:14 [b]Is. 11:15f.; 44:27; Jer. 51:32, 36 [c]Is. 41:2, 25; 46:11 [d]Rev. 7:2

13 [a]Rev. 12:3 [b]Rev. 13:1 [c]Rev. 19:20; 20:10; Rev. 13:11, 14 [d]Rev. 18:2 [e]Ex. 8:6

14 [1]Lit., *inhabited earth* [a]1 Tim. 4:1 [b]Rev. 13:13 [c]Rev. 3:10 [d]Rev. 20:8; 17:14; 19:19; 1 Kin. 22:21-23 [e]Rev. 6:17

15 [a]Rev. 3:3, 11 [b]Luke 12:37

who stays awake and keeps his garments, [c]lest he walk about
naked and [1]men see his shame.)
16 And they [a]gathered them together to the place which
[b]in Hebrew is called [1]Har-[c]Magedon.
17 And the seventh *angel* poured out his bowl upon [a]the
air; and a [b]loud voice came out of the [1c]temple from the
throne, saying, "[d]It is done."
18 And there were flashes of [a]lightning and sounds and
peals of thunder; and there was [b]a great earthquake, [c]such as
there had not been since man came to be upon the earth, so
great an earthquake *was it, and* so mighty.
19 And [a]the great city was split into three parts, and the
cities of the [1]nations fell. And [b]Babylon the great was [c]remem-
bered before God, to give her [d]the cup of the wine of His
fierce wrath.
20 And [a]every island fled away, and the mountains were
not found.
21 And [a]huge [1]hailstones, about [2]one hundred pounds
each, *came down from heaven upon men; and men [b]blas-
phemed God because of the [c]plague of the hail, because its
plague *was extremely [3]severe.

Chapter 17

[a]AND one of the [b]seven angels who had the [c]seven bowls
came and spoke with me, saying, "Come here, I shall show you
[d]the judgment of the [e]great harlot who [f]sits on many waters,
2 with whom [a]the kings of the earth committed *acts of*
immorality, and [b]those who dwell on the earth were [c]made
drunk with the wine of her immorality."
3 And [a]he carried me away [1b]in the Spirit [c]into a wilderness; and I saw a woman sitting on a [d]scarlet beast, full of
[e]blasphemous names, having [f]seven heads and ten horns.
4 And the woman [a]was clothed in purple and scarlet, and
[1]adorned with gold and precious [2]stones and pearls, having in
her hand [b]a gold cup full of abominations and of the unclean
things of her immorality,
5 and upon her forehead a name *was* written, a [a]mystery,
"[b]BABYLON THE GREAT, THE MOTHER OF HAR-
LOTS AND OF [c]THE ABOMINATIONS OF THE
EARTH."
6 And I saw the woman drunk with the [a]blood of the
[1]saints, and with the blood of the witnesses of Jesus. And when
I saw her, I wondered [2]greatly.
7 And the angel said to me, "Why [1]do you wonder? I
shall tell you the [a]mystery of the woman and of the beast that
carries her, which has the [b]seven heads and the ten horns.
8 "The beast that you saw [a]was and is not, and is about to
[b]come up out of the [c]abyss and [1]to [d]go to destruction. And
[e]those who dwell on the earth will [f]wonder, [g]whose name has
not been written in the book of life [h]from the foundation of
the world, when they see the beast, that [a]he was and is not and
will come.
9 "[a]Here is the mind which has wisdom. The [b]seven heads
are seven mountains on which the woman sits,
10 and they are seven [a]kings; five have fallen, one is, the

15 [1]Lit., *they* [c]Rev. 3:18

16 [1]Some authorities read, *Armageddon* [a]Rev. 19:19 [b]Rev. 9:11 [c]Judg. 5:19; 2 Kin. 23:29f.; 2 Chr. 35:22; Zech. 12:11

17 [1]Or, *sanctuary* [a]Eph. 2:2 [b]Rev. 11:15 [c]Rev. 14:15 [d]Rev. 21:6; Rev. 10:6

18 [a]Rev. 4:5 [b]Rev. 6:12 [c]Dan. 12:1; Matt. 24:21

19 [1]Or, *Gentiles* [a]Rev. 17:18; 18:10, 18f., 21; 11:8 [b]Rev. 14:8 [c]Rev. 18:5 [d]Rev. 14:10

20 [a]Rev. 6:14; 20:11

21 [1]Lit., *hail* [2]Lit., *the weight of a talent* [3]Lit., *great* [a]Rev. 11:19; 8:7 [b]Rev. 16:9, 11 [c]Ex. 9:18-25

1 [a]Rev. 21:9; 1:1 [b]Rev. 15:1 [c]Rev. 15:7 [d]Rev. 16:19 [e]Rev. 17:5, 15f.; 19:2; Nah. 3:4; Is. 1:21; Jer. 2:20 [f]Rev. 17:15; Jer. 51:13

2 [a]Rev. 18:3, 9; 2:22 [b]Rev. 17:8; 3:10 [c]Rev. 14:8

3 [1]Or, *in spirit* [a]Rev. 21:10 [b]Rev. 1:10 [c]Rev. 12:6, 14; 21:10 [d]Rev. 18:12, 16; Matt. 27:28 [e]Rev. 13:1 [f]Rev. 17:7, 9, 12, 16; 12:3

4 [1]Lit., *gilded* [2]Lit., *stone* [a]Rev. 18:16; 18:12; Ezek. 28:13 [b]Jer. 51:7; Rev. 18:6

5 [a]Rev. 17:7; 2 Thess. 2:7; Rev. 1:20 [b]Rev. 14:8; 16:19 [c]Rev. 17:2

6 [1]I.e., true believers; lit., *holy ones* [2]Lit., *with great wonder* [a]Rev. 16:6

7 [1]Lit., *have you wondered* [a]Rev. 17:5; 2 Thess. 2:7; Rev. 1:20 [b]Rev. 17:3

8 [1]Some ancient mss. read, *he goes* [a]Rev. 17:11; 13:3, 12, 14 [b]Rev. 11:7; 13:1 [c]Rev. 9:1; 13:1 [d]Rev. 17:11; 13:10 [e]Rev. 3:10 [f]Rev. 13:3 [g]Rev. 3:5 [h]Rev. 13:8; Matt. 25:34

9 [a]Rev. 13:18 [b]Rev. 17:3

10 [a]Rev. 10:11

other has not yet come; and when he comes, he must remain a
little while.
11 "And the beast which [a]was and is not, is himself also an
eighth, and is *one* of the seven, and he [b]goes to destruction.
12 "And the [a]ten horns which you saw are ten kings, who
have not yet received a kingdom, but they receive authority as
kings with the beast [b]for one hour.
13 "These have [a]one [1]purpose and they give their power
and authority to the beast.
14 "These will wage [a]war against the Lamb, and the Lamb
will [b]overcome them, because He is [c]Lord of lords and [c]King
of kings, and [d]those who are with Him *are the* [e]called and
chosen and faithful."
15 And he *said to me, "The [a]waters which you saw where
the harlot sits, are [b]peoples and multitudes and nations and
tongues.
16 "And the [a]ten horns which you saw, and the beast, these
will hate the harlot and will make her [b]desolate and [c]naked,
and will [d]eat her flesh and will [e]burn her up with fire.
17 "For [a]God has put it in their hearts to execute His [1]pur-
pose [2]by [b]having a common purpose, and by giving their kingdom to the beast, until the [c]words of God should be fulfilled.
18 "And the woman whom you saw is [a]the great city, which
[1]reigns over the kings of the earth."

Chapter 18

After these things I saw [a]another angel [b]coming down
from heaven, having great authority, and the earth was [c]illu-
mined with his glory.
2 And he cried out with a mighty voice, saying, "[a]Fallen,
fallen is Babylon the great! And she [b]has become a dwelling
place of demons and a [1]prison of every [c]unclean spirit, and a
[1]prison of every unclean and hateful bird.
3 "For all the nations [1]have drunk of the [a]wine of the
[2]passion of her immorality, and [b]the kings of the earth have
committed *acts of* immorality with her, and the [c]merchants of
the earth have become rich by the [3]wealth of her [4d]sensuality."
4 And I heard another voice from heaven, saying,
"[a]Come out of her, my people, that you may not participate in
her sins and that you may not receive of her plagues;
5 for her sins have [1a]piled up as high as heaven, and God
has [b]remembered her iniquities.
6 "[a]Pay her back even as she has paid, and [1]give back *to
her* double according to her deeds; in the [b]cup which she has
mixed, mix twice as much for her.
7 "[a]To the degree that she glorified herself and [b]lived [1]sen-
suously, to the same degree give her torment and mourning;
for she says in her heart, '[c]I sit *as* a queen and I am not a
widow, and will never see mourning.'
8 "For this reason [a]in one day her plagues will come, [1]pes-
tilence and mourning and famine, and she will be [b]burned up
with fire; for the Lord God who judges her [c]is strong.
9 "And [a]the kings of the earth, who committed *acts of*
immorality and [b]lived [1]sensuously with her, will [c]weep and
lament over her when they [d]see the smoke of her burning,

11 [a]Rev. 17:8; 13:3, 12, 14 [b]Rev. 17:8; 13:10

12 [a]Rev. 17:16; 12:3; 13:1 [b]Rev. 18:10, 17, 19

13 [1]Or, *mind* [a]Rev. 17:17

14 [a]Rev. 16:14 [b]Rev. 3:21 [c]Rev. 19:16; 1 Tim. 6:15 [d]Rev. 2:10f. [e]Matt. 22:14

15 [a]Rev. 17:1; Is. 8:7; Jer. 47:2 [b]Rev. 5:9

16 [a]Rev. 17:12 [b]Rev. 18:17, 19 [c]Ezek. 16:37, 39 [d]Rev. 19:18 [e]Rev. 18:8

17 [1]Or, *mind* [2]Lit., *even to do one mind and to give* [a]2 Cor. 8:16 [b]Rev. 17:13 [c]Rev. 10:7

18 [1]Lit., *has a kingdom* [a]Rev. 16:19; 11:8

1 [a]Rev. 17:1, 7 [b]Rev. 10:1 [c]Ezek. 43:2

2 [1]Or, *haunt* [a]Rev. 14:8 [b]Is. 13:21f.; 34:11, 13-15; Jer. 50:39; 51:37; Zeph. 2:14f. [c]Rev. 16:13

3 [1]Many ancient mss. read, *have fallen by* [2]Lit., *wrath* [3]Lit., *power* [4]Or, *luxury* [a]Rev. 14:8 [b]Rev. 18:9; 17:2 [c]Rev. 18:11, 15; 18:19, 23; Ezek. 27:9-25 [d]Rev. 18:7, 9; 1 Tim. 5:11

4 [a]Is. 52:11; Jer 50:8; 51:6, 9, 45; 2 Cor. 6:17

5 [1]Lit., *joined together* [a]Jer. 51:9 [b]Rev. 16:19

6 [1]Lit., *double to her* [a]Ps. 137:8; Jer. 50:15, 29 [b]Rev. 17:4

7 [1]Or, *luxuriously* [a]Ezek. 28:2-8 [b]Rev. 18:3, 9; 1 Tim. 5:11 [c]Is. 47:7f.; Zeph. 2:15

8 [1]Or, *death* [a]Is. 47:9; Jer. 50:31f.; Rev. 18:10 [b]Rev. 17:16 [c]Jer. 50:34; Rev. 11:17f.

9 [1]Or, *luxuriously* [a]Rev. 18:3; 17:2 [b]Rev. 18:3, 7; 1 Tim. 5:11 [c]Ezek. 26:16f.; 27:35 [d]Rev. 18:18; 14:11; 19:3

10 [a]standing at a distance because of the fear of her torment, saying, '[b]Woe, woe, [c]the great city, Babylon, the strong
city! For in [d]one hour your judgment has come.'
11 "And the [a]merchants of the earth [b]weep and mourn over
her, because no one buys their cargoes any more;
12 cargoes of [a]gold and silver and precious [1]stones and
pearls and fine linen and purple and silk and scarlet, and every
kind of citron wood and every article of ivory and every article
made from very costly wood and [2]bronze and iron and marble,
13 and cinnamon and [1]spice and incense and perfume and
frankincense and wine and olive oil and fine flour and wheat
and cattle and sheep, and *cargoes* of horses and chariots and
[2]slaves, and [3][a]human lives.
14 "And the fruit [1]you long for has gone from you, and all
things that were luxurious and splendid have passed away from
you and *men* will no longer find them.
15 "The [a]merchants of [b]these things, who became rich
from her, will [c]stand at a distance because of the fear of her
torment, weeping and mourning,
16 saying, '[a]Woe, woe, [b]the great city, she who [c]was
clothed in fine linen and purple and scarlet, and [1]adorned with
gold and precious [2]stones and pearls;
17 for in [a]one hour such great wealth has been laid [b]waste.'
And [c]every shipmaster and every [1]passenger and sailor, and as
many as make their living by the sea, [a]stood at a distance,
18 and were [a]crying out as they [b]saw the smoke of her
burning, saying, '[c]What *city* is like [d]the great city?'
19 "And they threw [a]dust on their heads and were crying
out, weeping and mourning, saying, '[b]Woe, woe, the great city,
in which all who had ships at sea [c]became rich by her [1]wealth,
for in [b]one hour she has been laid [d]waste.'
20 "[a]Rejoice over her, O heaven, and you [1]saints and [b]apos-
tles and prophets, because [c]God has [2]pronounced judgment for you against her."
21 And [1]a [a]strong angel [b]took up a stone like a great millstone and threw it into the sea, saying, "Thus will Babylon,
[c]the great city, be thrown down with violence, and will not be
found any longer.
22 "And [a]the sound of harpists and musicians and flute-
players and trumpeters will not be heard in you any longer;
and no craftsman of any craft will be found in you any longer;
and the [b]sound of a mill will not be heard in you any longer;
23 and the light of a lamp will not shine in you any longer;
and the [a]voice of the bridegroom and bride will not be heard in
you any longer; for your [b]merchants were the great men of the
earth, because all the nations were deceived [c]by your sorcery.
24 "And in her was found the [a]blood of prophets and of
[1]saints and of [b]all who have been slain on the earth."

Chapter 19

1 AFTER these things I heard, as it were, a [a]loud voice of a
great multitude in heaven, saying,
"[b]Hallelujah! [c]Salvation and [d]glory and power belong to our
God;
2 [a]BECAUSE HIS [b]JUDGMENTS ARE [c]TRUE AND RIGHTEOUS; for

10 [a]Rev. 18:15, 17 [b]Rev. 18:16, 19 [c]Rev. 18:16, 18, 19, 21; 11:8; 16:19 [d]Rev. 18:17, 19; 17:12; 18:8

11 [a]Rev. 18:3, 15; 18:19, 23; Ezek. 27:9-25 [b]Ezek. 27:27-34

12 [1]Lit., *stone* [2]Or, *brass* [a]Rev. 17:4; Ezek. 27:12-22

13 [1]Lit., *amomum* [2]Lit., *bodies* [3]Lit., *souls of men* [a]Ezek. 27:13; 1 Chr. 5:21 marg.; 1 Tim. 1:10

14 [1]Lit., *of your soul's desire*

15 [a]Rev. 18:3 [b]Rev. 18:12, 13 [c]Rev. 18:10

16 [1]Lit., *gilded* [2]Lit., *stone and pearl* [a]Rev. 18:10, 19 [b]Rev. 18:10, 18, 19, 21 [c]Rev. 17:4

17 [1]Lit., *one who sails anywhere* [a]Rev. 18:10 [b]Rev. 18:19; 17:16 [c]Ezek. 27:28f.

18 [a]Ezek. 27:30 [b]Rev. 18:9 [c]Ezek. 27:32; Rev. 13:4 [d]Rev. 18:10

19 [1]Lit., *costliness* [a]Josh. 7:6; Job 2:12; Lam. 2:10 [b]Rev. 18:10 [c]Rev. 18:3, 15 [d]Rev. 18:17; 17:16

20 [1]I.e., true believers; lit., *holy ones* [2]Lit., *judged your judgment of her* [a]Jer. 51:48; Rev. 12:12 [b]Luke 11:49f. [c]Rev. 19:2; 18:6ff.; 6:10

21 [1]Lit., *one* [a]Rev. 5:2; 10:1 [b]Jer. 51:63f. [c]Rev. 18:10

22 [a]Is. 24:8; Ezek. 26:13; Matt. 9:23 [b]Eccles. 12:4; Jer. 25:10

23 [a]Jer. 7:34; 16:9 [b]Is. 23:8; Rev. 18:3; 6:15 [c]Nah. 3:4; Rev. 9:21

24 [1]I.e., true believers, lit., *holy ones* [a]Rev. 16:6; 17:6 [b]Matt. 23:35

1 [a]Rev. 19:6; 11:15; Jer. 51:48 [b]Rev. 19:3, 4, 6; Ps. 104:35 marg. [c]Rev. 7:10 [d]Rev. 4:11

2 [a]Ps. 19:9 [b]Rev. 6:10 [c]Rev. 16:7

He has judged the [d]great harlot who was corrupting the earth
with her immorality, and HE HAS [e]AVENGED THE BLOOD OF HIS
BOND-SERVANTS [1]ON HER."
3 And a second time they said, "[a]HALLELUJAH! HER
[b]SMOKE RISES UP FOREVER AND EVER."
4 And the [a]twenty-four elders and the [b]four living creatures [c]fell down and worshiped God who sits on the throne
saying, "[d]Amen. [e]Hallelujah!"
5 And a voice came from the throne, saying,
"[a]GIVE PRAISE TO OUR GOD, ALL YOU HIS BOND-SERVANTS,
[b]YOU WHO FEAR HIM, THE SMALL AND THE GREAT."
6 And I heard, as it were, [a]the voice of a great multitude
and as [b]the sound of many waters and as the [c]sound of mighty
peals of thunder, saying,
"[a]Hallelujah! For the [d]Lord our God, the Almighty, reigns.
7 "Let us rejoice and be glad and [a]give the glory to Him,
for [b]the marriage of the Lamb has come and His [1c]bride has
made herself ready."
8 And it was given to her to clothe herself in [a]fine linen,
bright *and* clean; for the fine linen is the [b]righteous acts of the
[1]saints.
9 And [a]he *said to me, "[b]Write, '[c]Blessed are those who
are invited to the marriage supper of the Lamb.' " And he
*said to me, "[d]These are true words of God."
10 And [a]I fell at his feet to worship him. [b]And he *said to
me, "Do not do that; I am a [c]fellow-servant of yours and your
brethren who [d]hold the testimony of Jesus; worship God. For
the testimony of Jesus is the spirit of prophecy."
11 And I saw [a]heaven opened; and behold, a [b]white horse,
and He who sat upon it *is* called [c]Faithful and True; and in
[d]righteousness He judges and wages war.
12 And His [a]eyes *are* a flame of fire, and upon His head
are many [b]diadems; and He has a [c]name written *upon Him*
which no one knows except Himself.
13 And *He is* clothed with a [a]robe dipped in blood; and
His name is called [b]The Word of God.
14 And the armies which are in heaven, clothed in [a]fine
linen, [b]white *and* clean, were following Him on white horses.
15 And [a]from His mouth comes a sharp sword, so that
[b]with it He may smite the nations; and He will [1c]rule them
with a rod of iron; and [d]He treads the [2]wine press of the fierce
wrath of God, the Almighty.
16 And on His robe and on His thigh He has [a]a name
written, "[b]KING OF KINGS, AND LORD OF LORDS."
17 And I saw [1]an angel standing in the sun; and he cried
out with a loud voice, saying to [a]all the birds which fly in
[b]midheaven, "[c]Come, assemble for the [d]great supper of God;
18 in order that you may [a]eat the flesh of kings and the
flesh of [1]commanders and the flesh of mighty men and the
flesh of horses and of those who sit on them and the flesh of all
men, [b]both free men and slaves, and [c]small and great."
19 And I saw [a]the beast and [b]the kings of the earth and
their armies, assembled to make war against Him who [c]sat
upon the horse, and against His army.
20 And the beast was seized, and with him the [a]false prophet who [b]performed the signs [1c]in his presence, by which he

2 [1]Lit., *from her hand* [d]Rev. 17:1 [e]Deut. 32:43; Rev. 18:20; 16:6; 2 Kin. 9:7

3 [a]Is. 34:10; Rev. 19:1, 4, 6; Ps. 104:35 [b]Rev. 14:11

4 [a]Rev. 4:4, 10 [b]Rev. 4:6 [c]Rev. 4:10 [d]Rev. 5:14; Ps. 106:48 and marg. [e]Rev. 19:3, 6; Ps. 104:35

5 [a]Ps. 115:13; 134:1; 135:1 [b]Rev. 11:18

6 [a]Rev. 19:1; 11:15; Jer. 51:48 [b]Rev. 1:15 [c]Rev. 6:1 [d]Rev. 1:8

7 [1]Lit., *wife* [a]Rev. 11:13 [b]Rev. 19:9; Matt. 22:2; 25:10; Luke 12:36; John 3:29; Eph. 5:23, 32 [c]Rev. 21:2; Matt. 1:20; Rev. 21:9

8 [1]I.e., true believers; lit., *holy ones* [a]Rev. 19:14; Rev. 15:6 marg. [b]Rev. 15:4

9 [a]Rev. 19:10; 17:1 [b]Rev. 1:19 [c]Luke 14:15; 22:16 [d]Rev. 21:5; 22:6; 17:17

10 [a]Rev. 22:8 [b]Rev. 22:9; Acts 10:26 [c]Rev. 1:1f. [d]Rev. 12:17

11 [a]Rev. 4:1; John 1:51 [b]Rev. 19:19, 21; 6:2 [c]Rev. 3:14 [d]Is. 11:4

12 [a]Rev. 1:14 [b]Rev. 6:2; 12:3 [c]Rev. 19:16; 2:17

13 [a]Is. 63:3 [b]John 1:1

14 [a]Rev. 19:8 [b]Rev. 3:4; 19:8

15 [1]Or, *shepherd* [2]Lit., *wine press of the wine of His fierce wrath* [a]Rev. 1:16; 19:21 [b]Is. 11:4; 2 Thess. 2:8 [c]Rev. 2:27 [d]Rev. 14:19, 20

16 [a]Rev. 19:12; 2:17 [b]Rev. 17:14

17 [1]Lit., *one* [a]Rev. 19:21 [b]Rev. 8:13 [c]Jer. 12:9; Ezek. 39:17; 1 Sam. 17:44 [d]Is. 34:6; Jer. 46:10

18 [1]Lit., *chiliarchs,* in command of one thousand troops [a]Ezek. 39:18-20 [b]Rev. 6:15 [c]Rev. 11:18; 13:16; 19:5

19 [a]Rev. 11:7; 13:1 [b]Rev. 16:14, 16 [c]Rev. 19:11, 21

20 [1]Or, *by his authority* [a]Rev. 16:13 [b]Rev. 13:13 [c]Rev. 13:12

[d]deceived those who had received the [e]mark of the beast and
those who [f]worshiped his image; these two were thrown alive
into the [g]lake of [h]fire which burns with brimstone.
21 And the rest were killed with the sword which [a]came
from the mouth of him who [b]sat upon the horse, and [c]all the
birds were filled with their flesh.

Chapter 20

AND I saw [a]an angel coming down from heaven, having the
[b]key of the abyss and a great chain [1]in his hand.
2 And he laid hold of the [a]dragon, the serpent of old,
who is the Devil and Satan, and [b]bound him for a thousand
years,
3 and threw him into the [a]abyss, and shut *it* and [b]sealed *it*
over him, so that he should [c]not deceive the nations any longer, until the thousand years were completed; after these things
he must be released for a short time.
4 And I saw [a]thrones, and [b]they sat upon them, and [c]judg-
ment was given to them. And I *saw* [d]the souls of those who
had been [d]beheaded because of the [e]testimony of Jesus and
because of the word of God, and those who had not [f]wor-
shiped the beast or his image, and had not received the [g]mark
upon their forehead and upon their hand; and they [h]came to
life and [i]reigned with Christ for a thousand years.
5 The rest of the dead did not come to life until the
thousand years were completed. [a]This is the first resurrection.
6 [a]Blessed and holy is the one who has a part in the first
resurrection; over these the [b]second death has no power, but
they will be [c]priests of God and of Christ and will [d]reign with
Him for a thousand years.
7 And when the thousand years are completed, Satan will
be [a]released from his prison,
8 and will come out to [a]deceive the nations which are in
the [b]four corners of the earth, [c]Gog and Magog, to [d]gather
them together for the war; the number of them is like the
[e]sand of the [1]seashore.
9 And they [a]came up on the [1]broad plain of the earth and
surrounded the [b]camp of the [2]saints and the [c]beloved city, and
[d]fire came down from heaven and devoured them.
10 And [a]the devil who [a]deceived them was thrown into the
[b]lake of fire and brimstone, where the [c]beast and the [c]false
prophet are also; and they will be [d]tormented day and night
forever and ever.
11 And I saw a great white [a]throne and Him who sat upon
it, from whose [1]presence [b]earth and heaven fled away, and [c]no
place was found for them.
12 And I saw the dead, the [a]great and the small, standing
before the throne, and [1b]books were opened; and another
[2]book was opened, which is [c]*the book* of life; and the dead
[d]were judged from the things which were written in the [1]books,
[e]according to their deeds.
13 And the sea gave up the dead which were in it, and
[a]death and Hades [b]gave up the dead which were in them; and
they were judged, every one *of them* [c]according to their deeds.

20 [d]Rev. 13:14 [e]Rev. 13:16f. [f]Rev. 13:15 [12] [g]Rev. 20:10, 14f.; 21:8 [h]Rev. 14:10; Is. 30:33; Dan. 7:11

21 [a]Rev. 19:15 [b]Rev. 19:11, 19 [c]Rev. 19:17

1 [1]Lit., *upon* [a]Rev. 10:1 [b]Rev. 1:18; 9:1

2 [a]Rev. 12:9 [b]Is. 24:22; 2 Pet. 2:4; Jude 6

3 [a]Rev. 20:1 [b]Dan. 6:17; Matt 27:66 [c]Rev. 20:8, 10; 12:9

4 [a]Dan. 7:9 [b]Rev. 3:21; Matt. 19:28 [c]Dan. 7:22; 1 Cor. 6:2 [d]Rev. 6:9 [e]Rev. 1:9 [f]Rev. 13:15 [12] [g]Rev. 13:16f. [h]John 14:19; Is. 26:14 [i]Rev. 20:6; 22:5; 3:21; 5:10

5 [a]Luke 14:14; Phil. 3:11; 1 Thess. 4:16

6 [a]Rev. 14:13 [b]Rev. 20:14; 2:11 [c]Rev. 1:6 [d]Rev. 20:4; 22:5; 3:21; 5:10

7 [a]Rev. 20:2

8 [1]Lit., *sea* [a]Rev. 20:3, 10; 12:9 [b]Rev. 7:1 [c]Ezek. 38:2; 39:1, 6 [d]Rev. 16:14 [e]Heb. 11:12

9 [1]Lit., *breadth of the earth* [2]I.e., true believers; lit., *holy ones* [a]Ezek. 38:9, 16; Hab. 1:6 [b]Deut. 23:14 [c]Ps. 87:2 [d]Ezek. 38:22; 39:6; Rev. 13:13

10 [a]Rev. 20:2f. [b]Rev. 20:14, 15; 19:20 [c]Rev. 16:13 [d]Rev. 14:10f.

11 [1]Lit., *face* [a]Rev. 4:2 [b]Rev. 6:14; 21:1 [c]Dan. 2:35; Rev. 12:8

12 [1]Or, *scrolls* [2]Or, *scroll* [a]Rev. 11:18 [b]Dan. 7:10; Jer. 17:1, 10 [c]Rev. 20:15; 3:5 [d]Rev. 11:18 [e]Rev. 20:13; 2:23; Matt. 16:27

13 [a]Rev. 6:8; Rev. 1:18; 21:4; 1 Cor. 15:26 [b]Is. 26:19 [c]Rev. 20:12; 2:23; Matt. 16:27

14 And [a]death and Hades were thrown into [b]the lake of
fire. This is the [c]second death, the lake of fire.
15 And if [1]anyone's name was not found written in [a]the
book of life, he was thrown into the lake of fire.

Chapter 21

AND I saw [a]a new heaven and a new earth; for [b]the first
heaven and the first earth passed away, and there is no longer
any sea.
2 And I saw [a]the holy city, [b]new Jerusalem, [c]coming
down out of heaven from God, [d]made ready as a bride
adorned for her husband.
3 And I heard a loud voice from the throne, saying, "Behold, [a]the tabernacle of God is among men, and He shall
[1b]dwell among them, and they shall be His peoples, and God
Himself shall be among them,[2]
4 and He shall [a]wipe away every tear from their eyes; and
[b]there shall no longer be *any* death; [c]there shall no longer be
any mourning, or crying, or pain: [d]the first things have passed
away."
5 And [a]He who sits on the throne said, "Behold, I am
[b]making all things new." And He *said, "Write, for [c]these
words are faithful and true."
6 And He said to me, "[1a]It is done. I am the [b]Alpha and
the Omega, the beginning and the end. [c]I will give to the one
who thirsts from the spring of the [d]water of life without cost.
7 "[a]He who overcomes shall inherit these things, and [b]I
will be his God and he will be My son.
8 "[a]But for the cowardly and [1]unbelieving and abominable and murderers and immoral persons and sorcerers and
idolaters and all liars, their part *will be* in [b]the lake that burns
with fire and brimstone, which is the [c]second death."
9 [a]And one of the seven angels who had the [b]seven bowls
[1]full of the [c]seven last plagues, came and spoke with me,
saying, "[d]Come here, I shall show you the [e]bride, the wife of
the Lamb."
10 And [a]he carried me away [1b]in the Spirit to a great and
high mountain, and showed me [c]the holy city, Jerusalem, coming down out of heaven from God,
11 having [a]the glory of God. Her [1]brilliance was like a very
costly stone, as a [b]stone of [c]crystal-clear jasper.
12 [1]It had a great and high wall, [1a]with twelve [b]gates, and
at the gates twelve angels; and names *were* written on them,
which are *those* of the twelve tribes of the sons of Israel.
13 *There were* three gates on the east and three gates on
the north and three gates on the south and three gates on the
west.
14 And the wall of the city had [a]twelve foundation stones,
and on them *were* the twelve names of the [b]twelve apostles of
the Lamb.
15 And the one who spoke with me had a [1]gold measuring
[a]rod to measure the city, and its [b]gates and its wall.
16 And the city is laid out as a square, and its length is as
great as the width; and he measured the city with the [1]rod,

14 [a]Rev. 6:8; 1:18; 21:4; 1 Cor. 15:26 [b]Rev. 20:10, 15; 19:20 [c]Rev. 20:6

15 [1]Lit., *anyone was* [a]Rev. 20:12; 3:5

1 [a]Is. 65:17; 66:22; 2 Pet. 3:13 [b]Rev. 20:11; 2 Pet. 3:10

2 [a]Rev. 21:10; 22:19; 11:2 [b]Rev. 3:12; 21:10 [c]Rev. 21:10; Heb. 11:10, 16 [d]Rev. 21:9; 22:17; 19:7; Is. 61:10

3 [1]Or, *tabernacle* [2]Some ancient mss. add, and be *their God* [a]Lev. 26:11f.; Ezek. 37:27; 48:35; Rev. 7:15; Heb. 8:2 [b]John 14:23; 2 Cor. 6:16

4 [a]Rev. 7:17 [b]Rev. 20:14; 1 Cor. 15:26 [c]Is. 25:8; 35:10; 51:11; 65:19 [d]2 Cor. 5:17; Heb. 12:27

5 [a]Rev. 20:11; 4:9 [b]2 Cor. 5:17; Heb. 12:27 [c]Rev. 22:6; 19:9

6 [1]Lit., *They are* [a]Rev. 16:17; 10:6 [b]Rev. 1:8; 22:13 [c]Rev. 22:17; Is. 55:1; John 4:10; Rev. 7:17 [d]Rev. 7:17

7 [a]Rev. 2:7 [b]Rev. 21:3; 2 Sam. 7:14; 2 Cor. 6:16, 18

8 [1]Or, *untrustworthy* [a]Rev. 21:27; 22:15; 1 Cor. 6:9; Gal. 5:19-21; Rev. 9:21 [b]Rev. 19:20 [c]Rev. 2:11

9 [1]Lit., *who were full* [a]Rev. 17:1 [b]Rev. 15:7 [c]Rev. 15:1 [d]Rev. 17:1 [e]Rev. 21:2; 19:7

10 [1]Or, *in spirit* [a]Rev. 17:3; Ezek. 40:2 [b]Rev. 1:10 [c]Rev. 21:2

11 [1]Lit. *luminary* [a]Rev. 15:8; 21:23; Is. 60:1f.; Ezek. 43:2; Rev. 22:5 [b]Rev. 21:18, 19; 4:3 [c]Rev. 4:6

12 [1]Lit., *having* [a]Ezek. 48:31-34 [b]Rev. 21:15, 21, 25; 22:14

14 [a]Eph. 2:20; Heb. 11:10 [b]Acts 1:26

15 [1]Lit., *measure, a gold reed* [a]Rev. 11:1 [b]Rev. 21:21, 25; 21:12

16 [1]Lit., *reed*

[2]fifteen hundred miles; its length and width and height are
equal.
17 And he measured its wall, [1]seventy-two yards, *according to* [a]human [2]measurements, which are *also* [b]angelic
measurements.
18 And the material of the wall was [a]jasper; and the city
was [b]pure gold, like [1]clear [c]glass.
19 [a]The foundation stones of the city wall were adorned
with every kind of precious stone. The first foundation stone
was [b]jasper; the second, sapphire; the third, chalcedony; the
fourth, [c]emerald;
20 the fifth, sardonyx; the sixth, [a]sardius; the seventh,
chrysolite; the eighth, beryl; the ninth, topaz; the tenth, chrys-
oprase; the eleventh, jacinth; the twelfth, amethyst.
21 And the twelve [a]gates were twelve [b]pearls; each one of
the gates was a single pearl. And the street of the city was [c]pure
gold, like transparent [d]glass.
22 And I saw [a]no [1]temple in it, for the [b]Lord God, the
Almighty, and the [c]Lamb, are its [1]temple.
23 And the city [a]has no need of the sun or of the moon to
shine upon it, for [b]the glory of God has illumined it, and its
lamp *is* the [c]Lamb.
24 And [a]the nations shall walk by its light, and the [b]kings
of the earth [1]shall bring their glory into it.
25 And in the daytime (for [a]there shall be no night there)
[b]its gates [c]shall never be closed;
26 and [a]they shall bring the glory and the honor of the
nations into it;
27 and nothing unclean and no one who practices abomination and lying, [a]shall ever come into it, but only those
[1]whose names are [b]written in the Lamb's book of life.

Chapter 22

AND [a]he showed me a [b]river of the [c]water of life, [1]clear [d]as
crystal, coming from the throne of God and of [2]the Lamb,
2 in the middle of [a]its street. And [b]on either side of the
river was [c]the tree of life, bearing twelve [1]*kinds of* fruit,
yielding its fruit every month; and the [b]leaves of the tree were
for the healing of the nations.
3 And [a]there shall no longer be any curse; and [b]the
throne of God and of the Lamb shall be in it, and His bond-
servants shall [c]serve Him;
4 and they shall [a]see His face, and His [b]name *shall be* on
their [c]foreheads.
5 And [a]there shall no longer be *any* night; and they [1]shall
not have need [b]of the light of a lamp nor the light of the sun,
because the Lord God shall illumine them; and they shall
[c]reign forever and ever.
6 And [a]he said to me, "[b]These words are faithful and
true"; and the Lord, the [c]God of the spirits of the prophets,
[d]sent His angel to show to His bond-servants the things which
must shortly take place.
7 "And behold, [a]I am coming quickly. [b]Blessed is he who
[1]heeds [c]the words of the prophecy of this book."
8 And [a]I, John, am the one who heard and saw these

16 [2]Lit., *twelve thousand stadia,* a stadion was about 600 ft.

17 [1]Lit., *one hundred forty-four cubits* [2]Lit., *measure* [a]Deut. 3:11; Rev. 13:18 [b]Rev. 21:9

18 [1]Lit., *pure* [a]Rev. 21:11 [b]Rev. 21:21 [c]Rev. 4:6

19 [a]Is. 54:11f.; Rev. 21:19, 20; Ex. 28:17-20; Ezek. 28:13 [b]Rev. 21:11 [c]Rev. 4:3

20 [a]Rev. 4:3

21 [a]Rev. 21:15, 25; 21:12 [b]Rev. 17:4; Is. 54:12 [c]Rev. 21:18 [d]Rev. 4:6

22 [1]Or, *sanctuary* [a]John 4:21; Matt. 24:2 [b]Rev. 1:8 [c]Rev. 5:6; 7:17; 14:4

23 [a]Is. 60:19, 20; 24:23; Rev. 21:25; 22:5 [b]Rev. 21:11 [c]Rev. 5:6; 7:17; 14:4

24 [1]Lit., *bring* [a]Is. 60:3, 5; Rev. 22:2 [b]Ps. 72:10f.; Is. 49:23; 60:16; Rev. 21:26

25 [a]Rev. 22:5; 21:23; Zech. 14:7 [b]Rev. 21:15; 21:12 [c]Is. 60:11

26 [a]Ps. 72:10f.; Is. 49:23; 60:16

27 [1]Lit., *who are* [a]Rev. 22:14f.; Is. 52:1; Ezek. 44:9; Zech. 14:21 [b]Rev. 3:5

1 [1]Lit., *bright* [2]Or, *the Lamb. In the middle of its street, and on either side of the river, was* [a]Rev. 21:9; 22:6; 1:1 [b]Ps. 46:4; Ezek. 47:1 [c]Rev. 22:17; 7:17 [d]Rev. 4:6

2 [1]Or, *crops of fruit* [a]Rev. 21:21 [b]Ezek. 47:12 [c]Rev. 22:14, 19; 2:7

3 [a]Zech. 14:11 [b]Rev. 21:3, 23 [c]Rev. 7:15

4 [a]Matt. 5:8; Ps. 17:15; 42:2 [b]Rev. 14:1 [c]Rev. 7:3

5 [1]Lit., *do not have* [a]Rev. 21:25; Zech. 14:7 [b]Rev. 21:23 [c]Dan. 7:18, 27; Rev. 20:4; Matt. 19:28; Rom. 5:17

6 [a]Rev. 21:9; 1:1 [b]Rev. 21:5; 19:9 [c]1 Cor. 14:32; Heb. 12:9 [d]Rev. 22:16; 1:1

7 [1]Or, *keeps* [a]Rev. 22:12, 20; 3:11; 1:3; 3:3; 16:15 [b]Rev. 1:3; 16:15 [c]Rev. 22:10, 18f.; 22:9; 1:11

8 [a]Rev. 1:1

things. And when I heard and saw, [b]I fell down to worship at
the feet of the angel who showed me these things.
9 And [a]he *said to me, "Do not do that; I am a [b]fellow-
servant of yours and of your brethren the prophets and of
those who [1]heed the words of [c]this book: worship God."
10 And he *said to me, "[a]Do not seal up [b]the words of the
prophecy of this book, [c]for the time is near.
11 "[a]Let the one who does wrong, still do wrong; and let the
one who is filthy, still be filthy; and let the one who is righteous, still practice righteousness; and let the one who is holy,
still keep himself holy.
12 "Behold, [a]I am coming quickly, and My [b]reward is with
Me, [c]to render to every man [1]according to what he has done.
13 "I am the [a]Alpha and the Omega, [b]the first and the last,
[c]the beginning and the end."
14 Blessed are those who [a]wash their robes, that they may
have the right to [b]the tree of life, and may [c]enter by the [d]gates
into the city.
15 [a]Outside are the [b]dogs and the sorcerers and the immoral persons and the murderers and the idolaters, and everyone
who loves and practices lying.
16 "[a]I, Jesus, have sent [b]My angel to testify to you these
things [1c]for the churches. I am [d]the root and the [e]offspring of
David, the bright [f]morning star."
17 And the [a]Spirit and the [b]bride say, "Come." And let the
one who hears say, "Come." And [c]let the one who is thirsty
come; let the one who wishes take the [d]water of life without
cost.
18 I testify to everyone who hears [a]the words of the prophecy of this book: if anyone [b]adds to them, God shall add to
him [c]the plagues which are written in [d]this book;
19 and if anyone [a]takes away from the [b]words of the book
of this prophecy, God shall take away his part from [c]the tree of
life and [1]from the holy city, [d]which are written in this book.
20 He who [a]testifies to these things says, "Yes, [b]I am coming quickly." Amen. [c]Come, Lord Jesus.
21 [a]The grace of the Lord Jesus be with [1]all. Amen.

8 [b]Rev. 19:10

9 [1]Or, *keep*
[a]Rev. 19:10 [b]Rev. 1:1 [c]Rev. 22:10, 18f.; Rev. 1:11

10 [a]Rev. 10:4; Dan. 8:26
[b]Rev. 22:18f.; 22:9; 1:11
[c]Rev. 1:3

11 [a]Ezek. 3:27; Dan. 12:10

12 [1]Lit., *as his work is*
[a]Rev. 22:7 [b]Is. 40:10; 62:11
[c]Rev. 2:23; Jer. 17:10; Matt. 16:27

13 [a]Rev. 1:8 [b]Rev. 1:17
[c]Rev. 21:6

14 [a]Rev. 7:14 [b]Rev. 22:2
[c]Rev. 21:27 [d]Rev. 21:12

15 [a]Rev. 21:8; 1 Cor. 6:9f.; Gal. 5:19ff.; Matt. 8:12
[b]Deut. 23:18; Matt. 7:6; Phil. 3:2

16 [1]Or, *concerning*
[a]Rev. 1:1 [b]Rev. 22:6; 1:1
[c]Rev. 1:4, 11; 3:22 [d]Rev. 5:5
[e]Matt. 1:1 [f]Rev. 2:28; Matt. 2:2

17 [a]Rev. 2:7; 14:13 [b]Rev. 21:9; 21:2 [c]Rev. 21:6 [d]Rev. 7:17; 22:1

18 [a]Rev. 22:7 [b]Deut. 4:2; 12:32; Prov. 30:6 [c]Rev. 15:6-16, 21 [d]Rev. 22:7

19 [1]Lit., *out of*
[a]Deut. 4:2; 12:32; Prov. 30:6
[b]Rev. 22:7 [c]Rev. 22:2 [d]Rev. 21:10-22:5

20 [a]Rev. 1:2 [b]Rev. 22:7
[c]1 Cor. 16:22 marg.

21 [1]Some ancient mss. read, *the saints*
[a]Rom. 16:20

The last days

17 yrs! The last days of the church—
the days before Christ comes
again / will raise up his
church

Satan will reign
Anti Christ comes

3½ years and Jesus will
raise the believers leaving
the non believers will
exist for 3½ years